THE NEW
STRONG'S®
EXHAUSTIVE
CONCORDANCE
OF THE BIBLE

THE NEW
STRONG'S®
EXHAUSTIVE
CONCORDANCE
OF THE BIBLE

- *Easy-to-Read Print*
- *Words of Christ Emphasized*
- *Fan-Tab™ Thumb-Index Reference System*
- *Greek and Hebrew Dictionaries*
- *Strong's Numbering System*

JAMES STRONG, LL.D., S.T.D.

THOMAS NELSON PUBLISHERS
Nashville • Atlanta • London • Vancouver

Published in Nashville, Tennessee, by Thomas Nelson, Inc. Distributed in Canada by Nelson/Word Inc.

Library of Congress Cataloging-in-Publication Data

Strong, James, 1822–1894.
   [New exhaustive concordance of the Bible]
   The new Strong's exhaustive concordance of the Bible : with main concordance, appendix to the main concordance, Hebrew and Aramaic dictionary of the Old Testament, Greek dictionary of the New Testament / James Strong.
    p. cm.
   ISBN 0-7852-1195-0 (hardcover)
   1. Bible—Concordances, English. 2. Hebrew language—Dictionaries—English. 3. Aramaic language—Dictionaries—English.
4. Greek language, Biblical—Dictionaries—English. 5. Bible—Indexes. I. Title. II. Title: Exhaustive concordance of the Bible.
BS425.S76 1997
220.5'2033—DC20   96–36198
                                  CIP
                                    r96

Printed in the United States of America
4 5 6 7 8 9 10 — 01 00 99 98 97

PUBLISHER'S PREFACE

For over 100 years, Dr. James Strong's monumental work, *Strong's Exhaustive Concordance of the Bible,* has been the most widely used Bible concordance ever compiled. Assembled without the aid of computers or other electronic devices and based on the King James Version of the Bible, *Strong's* has stood the test of time. It has confirmed Dr. Strong's vision for a complete, simple, and accurate concordance that would become "a permanent standard for purposes of reference."

With the publication of *The New Strong's™ Exhaustive Concordance of the Bible* in 1984, Thomas Nelson Publishers sought to extend the vision and influence of the original with new typesetting and enhanced features. These included placing Strong's Hebrew & Greek numbers next to the Scripture location for easy reference, adding a more complete numbering system, and cross-referencing proper names so the book could be used with translations other than the King James Version.

It's hard to make a good thing better, but *The New Strong's™ Exhaustive Concordance of the Bible* continues the tradition of success. Many of the features from the best-selling 1984 edition are included in this edition:

- Proper names are defined, and those referring to more than one person have their occurrences grouped accordingly.
- Proper names also include variant spellings so Strong's can be used with other Bible translations, including the NASB, RSV, NIV, TEV, and NKJV.
- It is truly exhaustive—every word and every reference in the King James Version is indexed.
- The computer-generated Appendix of non-essential words includes references previously omitted in other editions.
- The exclusive Fan-Tab™ thumb-index system provides quick access.
- Scripture references are listed next to Strong's reference numbers for accurate identification.

In addition to these features, this new edition offers a number of unique improvements:

- A completely new typesetting—including the Hebrew and Greek Dictionaries—provides an easy-to-read text set in clear type.
- A corrected and enhanced Main Concordance, including the numbering system, offers greater accuracy and dependability.
- Strong's entries with multiple numbers referencing multiple Hebrew and Greek words are cited in full.
- An expanded Appendix of non-essential words unclutters the Main Concordance, allowing faster word searches.
- Comprehensive Hebrew and Greek Dictionary improvements include: new enlarged type; hundreds of corrections and updated entries, including corrections of outright errors, inconsistencies, variant readings, and syllabification of pronunciations; consistent abbreviations throughout; clarification of obscure terminology; and updated, reader-friendly introductions.
- All words of Christ in the context lines appear in boldface type, enabling quick identification.

With the publication of this edition of *The New Strong's™ Exhaustive Con-

cordance of the Bible, this classic reference tool is now much easier to read and use. The clear type will allow users to study more thoroughly than before without straining or tiring their eyes.

This edition of *The New Strong's™ Exhaustive Concordance of the Bible* retains the best of the original version, while adding new strengths and enhanced accuracy for all who seek to discover the full riches of God's Word. The Publisher sends out this timeless, practical Bible reference work with the sincere desire that it will continue to serve generations of Bible students for the 21st century and beyond.

INSTRUCTIONS TO THE READER

The New Strong's™ Exhaustive Concordance of the Bible enables the reader to locate any Scripture passage in the King James Version, as well as every Hebrew or Greek word behind the English words. The most direct way of using these features is as follows:

1. Beginning with the word you are researching, find that word in the Main Concordance, which lists every occurrence of every word in the Bible. If you are looking for a specific occurrence of that word, you should read the context lines until you find the reference.

2. Each context line has three segments. From left to right, they are: The text of the Scripture in which the reference word appears; the reference to the book, chapter and verse where it may be found; and a reference number to the Hebrew and Greek dictionaries at the back of the concordance. If the reference number is set in Italic type (such as this: *2614*) you should look for it in the Greek Dictionary. Otherwise, it appears in the Hebrew/Aramaic Dictionary. If no number appears, the word may have been supplied by the translators to clarify the meaning, even though no specific Hebrew or Greek word was used to express it.

ABBREVIATIONS

Old Testament

Gen . . . . Genesis	2Chr . . . 2 Chronicles	Dan . . . . Daniel
Ex . . . . . Exodus	Ezr . . . . . Ezra	Hos . . . . Hosea
Lev . . . . . Leviticus	Neh . . . . Nehemiah	Joel . . . . Joel
Num . . . Numbers	Est . . . . . Esther	Amos . . . Amos
Deut . . . Deuteronomy	Job . . . . . Job	Obad . . . Obadiah
Josh . . . . Joshua	Ps . . . . . . Psalms	Jonah . . . Jonah
Judg . . . Judges	Prov . . . . Proverbs	Mic . . . . Micah
Ruth . . . Ruth	Eccl . . . . Ecclesiastes	Nah . . . . Nahum
1Sa . . . . 1 Samuel	Song . . . Song of Solomon	Hab . . . . Habakkuk
2Sa . . . . 2 Samuel	Is . . . . . . Isaiah	Zeph . . . Zephaniah
1Kin . . . . 1 Kings	Jer . . . . . Jeremiah	Hag . . . . Haggai
2Kin . . . . 2 Kings	Lam . . . Lamentations	Zec . . . . Zechariah
1Chr . . . 1 Chronicles	Eze . . . . Ezekiel	Mal . . . . Malachi

New Testament

Mt . . . . . Matthew	Eph . . . . Ephesians	Heb . . . . Hebrews
Mk . . . . . Mark	Phil . . . . Philippians	Jas . . . . . James
Lk . . . . . Luke	Col . . . . . Colossians	1Pet . . . . 1 Peter
Jn . . . . . . John	1Th . . . . 1 Thessalonians	2Pet . . . . 2 Peter
Acts . . . . Acts	2Th . . . . 2 Thessalonians	1Jn . . . . . 1 John
Rom . . . . Romans	1Ti . . . . . 1 Timothy	2Jn . . . . . 2 John
1Cor . . . 1 Corinthians	2Ti . . . . . 2 Timothy	3Jn . . . . . 3 John
2Cor . . . 2 Corinthians	Titus . . . Titus	Jude . . . . Jude
Gal . . . . Galatians	Philem . . Philemon	Rev . . . . . Revelation

MAIN CONCORDANCE

A See APPENDIX.

AARON (a'-ur-un) See AARON'S, AARONITES. *First High Priest of Israel; brother of Moses.*

Is not *A* the Levite thy brother	Ex 4:14	175
And the LORD said to *A*, Go into	Ex 4:27	175
Moses told *A* all the words of the	Ex 4:28	175
A went and gathered together all	Ex 4:29	175
A spake all the words which the	Ex 4:30	175
A went in, and told Pharaoh, Thus	Ex 5:1	175
them, Wherefore do ye, Moses and *A*	Ex 5:4	175
And they met Moses and *A*, who stood	Ex 5:20	175
LORD spake unto Moses and unto *A*	Ex 6:13	175
and she bare him *A* and Moses	Ex 6:20	175
A took him Elisheba, daughter of	Ex 6:23	175
These are that *A* and Moses, to	Ex 6:26	175
these are that Moses and *A*	Ex 6:27	175
A thy brother shall be thy	Ex 7:1	175
A thy brother shall speak unto	Ex 7:2	175
A did as the LORD commanded them,	Ex 7:6	175
A fourscore and three years old,	Ex 7:7	175
LORD spake unto Moses and unto *A*	Ex 7:8	175
then thou shalt say unto *A*	Ex 7:9	175
A went in unto Pharaoh, and they	Ex 7:10	175
A cast down his rod before	Ex 7:10	175
LORD spake unto Moses, Say unto *A*	Ex 7:19	175
A did so, as the LORD commanded	Ex 7:20	175
LORD spake unto Moses, Say unto *A*	Ex 8:5	175
A stretched out his hand over the	Ex 8:6	175
Pharaoh called for Moses and *A*	Ex 8:8	175
Moses and *A* went out from Pharaoh	Ex 8:12	175
LORD said unto Moses, Say unto *A*	Ex 8:16	175
for *A* stretched out his hand with	Ex 8:17	175
Pharaoh called for Moses and for *A*	Ex 8:25	175
LORD said unto Moses and unto *A*	Ex 9:8	175
sent, and called for Moses and *A*	Ex 9:27	175
A came in unto Pharaoh, and said	Ex 10:3	175
A were brought again unto Pharaoh	Ex 10:8	175
called for Moses and *A* in haste	Ex 10:16	175
A did all these wonders before	Ex 11:10	175
A in the land of Egypt, saying,	Ex 12:1	175
LORD had commanded Moses and *A*	Ex 12:28	175
A by night, and said, Rise up, and	Ex 12:31	175
And the LORD said unto Moses and *A*	Ex 12:43	175
the LORD commanded Moses and *A*	Ex 12:50	175
the prophetess, the sister of *A*	Ex 15:20	175
Moses and *A* in the wilderness	Ex 16:2	175
A said unto all the children of	Ex 16:6	175
And Moses spake unto *A*, Say unto	Ex 16:9	175
as *A* spake unto the whole	Ex 16:10	175
And Moses said unto *A*, Take a pot,	Ex 16:33	175
so *A* laid it up before the	Ex 16:34	175
and Moses, *A*, and Hur went up to	Ex 17:10	175
and *A* and Hur stayed up his hands,	Ex 17:12	175
A came, and all the elders of	Ex 18:12	175
come up, thou, and *A* with thee	Ex 19:24	175
Come up unto the LORD, thou, and *A*	Ex 24:1	175
Then went up Moses, and *A*, Nadab,	Ex 24:9	175
and, behold, *A* and Hur are with you	Ex 24:14	175
which is before the testimony, *A*	Ex 27:21	175
take thou unto thee *A* thy brother	Ex 28:1	175
me in the priest's office, even *A*	Ex 28:1	175
for *A* thy brother for glory	Ex 28:2	175
holy garments for *A* thy brother	Ex 28:4	175
A shall bear their names before	Ex 28:12	175
A shall bear the names of the	Ex 28:29	175
A shall bear the judgment of the	Ex 28:30	175
And it shall be upon *A* to minister	Ex 28:35	175
that *A* may bear the iniquity of	Ex 28:38	175
shalt put them upon *A* thy brother	Ex 28:41	175
And they shall be upon *A*, and upon	Ex 28:43	175
And *A* and his sons thou shalt bring	Ex 29:4	175
garments, and put upon *A* the coat	Ex 29:5	175
shalt gird them with girdles, *A*	Ex 29:9	175
and thou shalt consecrate *A*	Ex 29:9	175
and *A* and his sons shall put their	Ex 29:10	175
and *A* and his sons shall put their	Ex 29:15	175
and *A* and his sons shall put their	Ex 29:19	175
the tip of the right ear of *A*	Ex 29:20	175
oil, and sprinkle it upon *A*	Ex 29:21	175
shalt put all in the hands of *A*	Ex 29:24	175
even of that which is for *A*	Ex 29:27	175
the holy garments of *A* shall be	Ex 29:29	175
And *A* and his sons shall eat the	Ex 29:32	175
And thus shalt thou do unto *A*	Ex 29:35	175
I will sanctify also both *A*	Ex 29:44	175
A shall burn thereon sweet	Ex 30:7	175
when *A* lighteth the lamps at even	Ex 30:8	175
A shall make an atonement upon	Ex 30:10	175
For *A* and his sons shall wash	Ex 30:19	175
And thou shalt anoint *A* and his	Ex 30:30	175
holy garments for *A* the priest	Ex 31:10	175
themselves together unto *A*	Ex 32:1	175
A said unto them, Break off the	Ex 32:2	175
ears, and brought them unto *A*	Ex 32:3	175
when *A* saw it, he built an altar	Ex 32:5	175
A made proclamation, and said, To	Ex 32:5	175
And Moses said unto *A*, What did	Ex 32:21	175
A said, Let not the anger of my	Ex 32:22	175
(for *A* had made them naked unto	Ex 32:25	175
they made the calf, which *A* made	Ex 32:35	175
And when *A* and all the children of	Ex 34:30	175
and *A* and all the rulers of the	Ex 34:31	175
holy garments for *A* the priest	Ex 35:19	175
of Ithamar, son to *A* the priest	Ex 38:21	175
and made the holy garments for *A*	Ex 39:1	175
of fine linen of woven work for *A*	Ex 39:27	175
holy garments for *A* the priest	Ex 39:41	175
And thou shalt bring *A* and his sons	Ex 40:12	175
put upon *A* the holy garments	Ex 40:13	175
And Moses and *A* and his sons	Ex 40:31	175
the sons of *A* the priest shall	Lev 1:7	175
the sons of *A* shall sprinkle the	Lev 3:13	175
Command *A* and his sons, saying,	Lev 6:9	175
the sons of *A* shall offer it	Lev 6:14	175
And the remainder thereof shall *A*	Lev 6:16	175
the children of *A* shall eat of it	Lev 6:18	175
This is the offering of *A*	Lev 6:20	175
Speak unto *A* and to his sons,	Lev 6:25	175
dry, shall all the sons of *A* have	Lev 7:10	175
He among the sons of *A*, that	Lev 7:33	175
have given them unto *A* the priest	Lev 7:34	175
the portion of the anointing of *A*	Lev 7:35	175
Take *A* and his sons with him, and	Lev 8:2	175
And Moses brought *A* and his sons,	Lev 8:6	175
and *A* and his sons laid their hands	Lev 8:14	175
and *A* and his sons laid their hands	Lev 8:18	175
and *A* and his sons laid their hands	Lev 8:22	175
the altar, and sprinkled it upon *A*	Lev 8:30	175
and sanctified *A*, and his garments,	Lev 8:30	175
And Moses said unto *A* and to his	Lev 8:31	175
as I commanded, saying, *A*	Lev 8:31	175
So *A* and his sons did all things	Lev 8:36	175
eighth day, that Moses called *A*	Lev 9:1	175
And he said unto *A*, Take thee a	Lev 9:2	175
And Moses said unto *A*, Go unto the	Lev 9:7	175
A therefore went unto the altar,	Lev 9:8	175
the sons of *A* brought the blood	Lev 9:9	175
the right shoulder *A* waved for a	Lev 9:21	175
A lifted up his hand toward the	Lev 9:22	175
A went into the tabernacle of the	Lev 9:23	175
And Nadab and Abihu, the sons of *A*	Lev 10:1	175
Then Moses said unto *A*, This is	Lev 10:3	175
And *A* held his peace	Lev 10:3	175
the sons of Uzziel the uncle of *A*	Lev 10:4	175
And Moses said unto *A*, and unto	Lev 10:6	175
And the LORD spake unto *A*, saying,	Lev 10:8	175
And Moses spake unto *A*, and unto	Lev 10:12	175
the sons of *A* which were left	Lev 10:16	175
A said unto Moses, Behold, this	Lev 10:19	175
the LORD spake unto Moses and to *A*	Lev 11:1	175
the LORD spake unto Moses and *A*	Lev 13:1	175
be brought unto *A* the priest	Lev 13:2	175
LORD spake unto Moses and unto *A*	Lev 14:33	175
the LORD spake unto Moses and to *A*	Lev 15:1	175
the death of the two sons of *A*	Lev 16:1	175
Speak unto *A* thy brother, that he	Lev 16:2	175
Thus shall *A* come into the holy	Lev 16:3	175
A shall offer his bullock of the	Lev 16:6	175
A shall cast lots upon the two	Lev 16:8	175
A shall bring the goat upon which	Lev 16:9	175
A shall bring the bullock of the	Lev 16:11	175
A shall lay both his hands upon	Lev 16:21	175
A shall come into the tabernacle	Lev 16:23	175
Speak unto *A*, and unto his sons,	Lev 17:2	175
unto the priests the sons of *A*	Lev 21:1	175
Speak unto *A*, saying, Whosoever	Lev 21:17	175
A the priest shall come nigh to	Lev 21:21	175
And Moses told it unto *A*, and to	Lev 21:24	175
Speak unto *A* and to his sons, that	Lev 22:2	175
of the seed of *A* is a leper	Lev 22:4	175

Speak unto *A*, and to his sons, and	Lev 22:18	175
shall *A* order it from the evening	Lev 24:3	175
A shall number them by their	Num 1:3	175
A took these men which are	Num 1:17	175
A numbered, and the princes of	Num 1:44	175
LORD spake unto Moses and unto *A*	Num 2:1	175
also are the generations of *A*	Num 3:1	175
are the names of the sons of *A*	Num 3:2	175
are the names of the sons of *A*	Num 3:3	175
in the sight of *A* their father	Num 3:4	175
present them before the priest	Num 3:6	175
shalt give the Levites unto *A*	Num 3:9	175
And thou shalt appoint *A* and his	Num 3:10	175
Eleazar the son of *A* the priest	Num 3:32	175
eastward, shall be Moses, and *A*	Num 3:38	175
A numbered at the commandment of	Num 3:39	175
of them is to be redeemed, unto *A*	Num 3:48	175
of them that were redeemed unto *A*	Num 3:51	175
LORD spake unto Moses and unto *A*	Num 4:1	175
A shall come, and his sons, and	Num 4:5	175
And when *A* and his sons have made	Num 4:15	175
office of Eleazar the son of *A*	Num 4:16	175
LORD spake unto Moses and unto *A*	Num 4:17	175
A and his sons shall go in, and	Num 4:19	175
At the appointment of *A* and his	Num 4:27	175
Ithamar the son of *A* the priest	Num 4:28	175
Ithamar the son of *A* the priest	Num 4:33	175
And Moses and *A* and the chief of the	Num 4:34	175
A did number according to the	Num 4:37	175
A did number according to the	Num 4:41	175
A numbered according to the word	Num 4:45	175
of the Levites, whom Moses and *A*	Num 4:46	175
Speak unto *A* and unto his sons,	Num 6:23	175
Ithamar the son of *A* the priest	Num 7:8	175
Speak unto *A*, and say unto him,	Num 8:2	175
And *A* did so	Num 8:3	175
A shall offer the Levites before	Num 8:11	175
shalt set the Levites before *A*	Num 8:13	175
given the Levites as a gift to *A*	Num 8:19	175
And Moses, and *A*, and all the	Num 8:20	175
A offered them as an offering	Num 8:21	175
A made an atonement for them to	Num 8:21	175
of the congregation before *A*	Num 8:22	175
Moses and before *A* on that day	Num 9:6	175
And the sons of *A*, the priests,	Num 10:8	175
A spake against Moses because of	Num 12:1	175
suddenly unto Moses, and unto *A*	Num 12:4	175
of the tabernacle, and called *A*	Num 12:5	175
A looked upon Miriam, and, behold,	Num 12:10	175
A said unto Moses, Alas, my lord,	Num 12:11	175
went and came to Moses, and to *A*	Num 13:26	175
against Moses and against *A*	Num 14:2	175
A fell on their faces before all	Num 14:5	175
LORD spake unto Moses and unto *A*	Num 14:26	175
brought him unto Moses and *A*	Num 15:33	175
against Moses and against *A*	Num 16:3	175
and what is *A*, that ye murmur	Num 16:11	175
the LORD, thou, and they, and *A*	Num 16:16	175
thou also, and, *A*, each of you his	Num 16:17	175
the congregation with Moses and *A*	Num 16:18	175
LORD spake unto Moses and unto *A*	Num 16:20	175
Eleazar the son of *A* the priest	Num 16:37	175
which is not of the seed of *A*	Num 16:40	175
against Moses and against *A*	Num 16:41	175
against Moses and against *A*	Num 16:42	175
A came before the tabernacle of	Num 16:43	175
And Moses said unto *A*, Take a	Num 16:46	175
A took as Moses commanded, and ran	Num 16:47	175
A returned unto Moses unto the	Num 16:50	175
the rod of *A* was among their rods	Num 17:6	175
the rod of *A* for the house of	Num 17:8	175
And the LORD said unto *A*, Thou and	Num 18:1	175
And the LORD spake unto *A*, Behold,	Num 18:8	175
And the LORD spake unto *A*, Thou	Num 18:20	175
heave offering to *A* the priest	Num 18:28	175
LORD spake unto Moses and unto *A*	Num 19:1	175
against Moses and against *A*	Num 20:2	175
A went from the presence of the	Num 20:6	175
A thy brother, and speak ye unto	Num 20:8	175
A gathered the congregation	Num 20:10	175
the LORD spake unto Moses and *A*	Num 20:12	175
A in mount Hor, by the coast of	Num 20:23	175
A shall be gathered unto his	Num 20:24	175
Take *A* and Eleazar his son, and	Num 20:25	175
strip *A* of his garments, and put	Num 20:26	175
A shall be gathered unto his	Num 20:26	175
Moses stripped *A* of his garments,	Num 20:28	175
A died there in the top of the	Num 20:28	175
congregation saw that *A* was dead	Num 20:29	175
they mourned for *A* thirty days	Num 20:29	175
Eleazar, the son of *A* the priest	Num 25:7	175

Eleazar, the son of *A* the priest	Num 25:11	175
Eleazar the son of *A* the priest	Num 26:1	175
against *A* in the company of Korah	Num 26:9	175
bare unto Amram *A* and Moses	Num 26:59	175
unto *A* was born Nadab, and Abihu,	Num 26:60	175
A the priest numbered, when they	Num 26:64	175
as *A* thy brother was gathered	Num 27:13	175
under the hand of Moses and *A*	Num 33:1	175
A the priest went up into mount	Num 33:38	175
A was an hundred and twenty and	Num 33:39	175
with *A* to have destroyed him	Deut 9:20	175
I prayed for *A* also the same time	Deut 9:20	175
there *A* died, and there he was	Deut 10:6	175
as *A* thy brother died in mount	Deut 32:50	175
and the children of *A* the priest	Josh 21:4	175
Which the children of *A*, being of	Josh 21:10	175
of *A* the priest Hebron with her	Josh 21:13	175
the cities of the children of *A*	Josh 21:19	175
I sent Moses also and *A*, and I	Josh 24:5	175
And Eleazar the son of *A* died	Josh 24:33	175
the son of Eleazar, the son of *A*	Judg 20:28	175
the LORD that advanced Moses and *A*	1Sa 12:6	175
then the LORD sent Moses and *A*	1Sa 12:8	175
A, and Moses, and Miriam	1Chr 6:3	175
The sons also of *A*	1Chr 6:3	175
But *A* and his sons offered upon	1Chr 6:49	175
And these are the sons of *A*	1Chr 6:50	175
in their coasts, of the sons of *A*	1Chr 6:54	175
to the sons of *A* they gave the	1Chr 6:57	175
David assembled the children of *A*	1Chr 15:4	175
sons of Amram; *A* and Moses	1Chr 23:13	175
A was separated, that he should	1Chr 23:13	175
was to wait on the sons of *A* for	1Chr 23:28	175
of the sons of *A* their brethren	1Chr 23:32	175
the divisions of the sons of *A*	1Chr 24:1	175
The sons of *A*; Nadab, and Abihu	1Chr 24:1	175
under *A* their father, as the LORD	1Chr 24:19	175
their brethren the sons of *A* in	1Chr 24:31	175
of the LORD, the sons of *A*	2Chr 13:9	175
unto the LORD, are the sons of *A*	2Chr 13:10	175
but to the priests the sons of *A*	2Chr 26:18	175
the priests the sons of *A* to	2Chr 29:21	175
Also of the sons of *A* the priests	2Chr 31:19	175
of *A* were busied in offering of	2Chr 35:14	175
and for the priests the sons of *A*	2Chr 35:14	175
the son of *A* the chief priest	Ezr 7:5	175
the priest the son of *A* shall be	Neh 10:38	175
them unto the children of *A*	Neh 12:47	175
a flock by the hand of Moses and *A*	Ps 77:20	175
A among his priests, and Samuel	Ps 99:6	175
and *A* whom he had chosen	Ps 105:26	175
camp, and *A* the saint of the LORD	Ps 106:16	175
O house of *A*, trust in the LORD	Ps 115:10	175
he will bless the house of *A*	Ps 115:12	175
Let the house of *A* now say	Ps 118:3	175
bless the LORD, O house of *A*	Ps 135:19	175
and I sent before thee Moses, *A*	Mic 6:4	175
wife was of the daughters of *A*	Lk 1:5	2
Saying unto *A*, Make us gods to go	Acts 7:40	2
that is called of God, as was *A*	Heb 5:4	2
be called after the order of *A*	Heb 7:11	2

AARONITES (*a'-ur-un-ites*) Priests; Aaron's descendants.

Jehoiada was the leader of the *A*	1Chr 12:27	175
of the *A*, Zadok	1Chr 27:17	175

AARON'S (*a'-ur-uns*)

Eleazar *A* son took him one of the	Ex 6:25	175
but *A* rod swallowed up their rods	Ex 7:12	175
Abihu, Eleazar and Ithamar, *A* sons	Ex 28:1	175
that they may make *A* garments to	Ex 28:3	175
and they shall be upon *A* heart	Ex 28:30	175
And it shall be upon *A* forehead	Ex 28:38	175
for *A* sons thou shalt make coats,	Ex 28:40	175
of the ram of *A* consecration	Ex 29:26	175
And it shall be *A* and his sons' by	Ex 29:28	175
A sons, shall bring the blood, and	Lev 1:5	175
A sons, shall lay the parts, the	Lev 1:8	175
A sons, shall sprinkle his blood	Lev 1:11	175
bring it to *A* sons the priests	Lev 2:2	175
of the meat offerings shall be *A*	Lev 2:3	175
of the meat offering shall be *A*	Lev 2:10	175
A sons the priests shall sprinkle	Lev 3:2	175
A sons shall burn it on the altar	Lev 3:5	175
A sons shall sprinkle the blood	Lev 3:8	175
but the breast shall be *A*	Lev 7:31	175
of the anointing oil upon *A* head	Lev 8:12	175
And Moses brought *A* sons, and put	Lev 8:13	175
it upon the tip of *A* right ear	Lev 8:23	175
And he brought *A* sons, and Moses	Lev 8:24	175
And he put all upon *A* hands	Lev 8:27	175

A sons presented unto him the	Lev 9:12	175
A sons presented unto him the	Lev 9:18	175
And it shall be A and his sons'	Lev 24:9	175
thou shalt write A name upon the	Num 17:3	175
Bring A rod again before the	Num 17:10	175
down upon the beard, even A beard	Ps 133:2	175
A rod that budded, and the tables	Heb 9:4	2

ABADDON (ab-ad'-dun) *Angel of the Abyss.*

name in the Hebrew tongue is A	Rev 9:11	3

ABAGTHA (ab-ag'-thah) *Servant of King Ahasuerus.*

Biztha, Harbona, Bigtha, and A	Est 1:10	5

ABANA (ab-ay'-nah) *A river in Syria.*

Are not A and Pharpar, rivers of	2Kin 5:12	71

ABANAH See ABANA.

ABARIM (ab'-ar-im) See IJE-ABARIM. *A mountain range in Moab.*

Get thee up into this mount A	Num 27:12	5682
and pitched in the mountains of A	Num 33:47	5682
departed from the mountains of A	Num 33:48	5682
Get thee up into this mountain A	Deut 32:49	5682

ABASE

every one that is proud, and a him	Job 40:11	8213
nor a himself for the noise of	Is 31:4	6031
is low, and a him that is high	Eze 21:26	8213
walk in pride he is able to a	Dan 4:37	8214

ABASED

shall exalt himself shall be a	Mt 23:12	5013
exalteth himself shall be a	Lk 14:11	5013
that exalteth himself shall be a	Lk 18:14	5013
I know both how to be a, and I	Phil 4:12	5013

ABASING

Have I committed an offence in a	2Cor 11:7	5013

ABATED

and fifty days the waters were a	Gen 8:3	2637
to see if the waters were a from	Gen 8:8	7043
waters were a from off the earth	Gen 8:11	7043
it shall be a from thy estimation	Lev 27:18	1639
not dim, nor his natural force a	Deut 34:7	5127
Then their anger was a toward him	Judg 8:3	7503

ABBA (ab'-bah) *Aramaic for "Father."*

And he said, A, Father, all things	Mk 14:36	5
of adoption, whereby we cry, A	Rom 8:15	5
Son into your hearts, crying, A	Gal 4:6	5

ABDA (ab'-dah)
  1. Father of Adoniram.

Adoniram the son of A was over	1Kin 4:6	5653

  2. A chief Levite after the exile.

A the son of Shammua, the son of	Neh 11:17	5653

ABDEEL (ab'-de-el) *Father of Shelemiah.*

Azriel, and Shelemiah the son of A	Jer 36:26	5655

ABDI (ab'-di)
  1. Levite grandfather of Ethan.

the son of Kishi, the son of A	1Chr 6:44	5660
sons of Merari, Kish the son of A	2Chr 29:12	5660

  2. Married a foreigner while in exile.

Zechariah, and Jehiel, and A	Ezr 10:26	5660

ABDIEL (ab'-de-el) *Son of Guni.*

Ahi the son of A, the son of Guni	1Chr 5:15	5661

ABDON (ab'-dun)
  1. Levitical city in Asher.

her suburbs, A with her suburbs,	Josh 21:30	5658
suburbs, and A with her suburbs,	1Chr 6:74	5658

  2. A judge of Israel.

after him A the son of Hillel, a	Judg 12:13	5658
And A the son of Hillel the	Judg 12:15	5658

  3. A Benjamite in Jerusalem.

And A, and Zichri, and Hanan,	1Chr 8:23	5658

  4. Son of Jehiel.

And his firstborn son A, and Zur,	1Chr 8:30	5658
And his firstborn son A, then Zur,	1Chr 9:36	5658

  5. Son of Micah.

A the son of Micah, and Shaphan	2Chr 34:20	5658

ABED-NEGO (ab-ed'-ne-go) *A companion of Daniel in captivity.*

and to Azariah, of A	Dan 1:7	5664
and he set Shadrach, Meshach, and A	Dan 2:49	5665
Babylon, Shadrach, Meshach, and A	Dan 3:12	5665
to bring Shadrach, Meshach, and A	Dan 3:13	5665
true, O Shadrach, Meshach, and A	Dan 3:14	5665
Shadrach, Meshach, and A, answered	Dan 3:16	5665
against Shadrach, Meshach, and A	Dan 3:19	5665
to bind Shadrach, Meshach, and A	Dan 3:20	5665
took up Shadrach, Meshach, and A	Dan 3:22	5665

men, Shadrach, Meshach, and A	Dan 3:23	5665
and said, Shadrach, Meshach, and A	Dan 3:26	5665
Then Shadrach, Meshach, and A	Dan 3:26	5665
God of Shadrach, Meshach, and A	Dan 3:28	5665
God of Shadrach, Meshach, and A	Dan 3:29	5665
promoted Shadrach, Meshach, and A	Dan 3:30	5665

ABEL (a'-bel)
  1. Second son of Adam.

And she again bare his brother A	Gen 4:2	1893
A was a keeper of sheep, but Cain	Gen 4:2	1893
And A, he also brought of the	Gen 4:4	1893
And the LORD had respect unto A	Gen 4:4	1893
And Cain talked with A his brother	Gen 4:8	1893
rose up against A his brother	Gen 4:8	1893
unto Cain, Where is A thy brother	Gen 4:9	1893
me another seed instead of A	Gen 4:25	1893
from the blood of righteous A	Mt 23:35	6
From the blood of A unto the	Lk 11:51	6
By faith A offered unto God a	Heb 11:4	6
better things than that of A	Heb 12:24	6

  2. Great stone near Beth-shemesh.

even unto the great stone of A	1Sa 6:18	59

  3. A city in Naphtali.

all the tribes of Israel unto A	2Sa 20:14	62
besieged him in A of Beth-maachah	2Sa 20:15	62
shall surely ask counsel at A	2Sa 20:18	59

ABEL ACACIA GROVE See ABEL-SHITTIM.

ABEL BETH MAACAH See BETH-MAACHAH.

ABEL-BETH-MAACHAH (a'-bel-beth-ma'-a-kah) *A city in northern Israel.*

and smote Ijon, and Dan, and A	1Kin 15:20	62
of Assyria, and took Ijon, and A	2Kin 15:29	62

ABEL-MAIM (a'-bel-ma'-im) *Another name for Abel-beth-maachah.*

and they smote Ijon, and Dan, and A	2Chr 16:4	66

ABEL-MEHOLAH (a'-bel-me-ho'-lah) *A city in Issachar.*

Zererath, and to the border of A	Judg 7:22	65
Jezreel, from Beth-shean to A	1Kin 4:12	65
Elisha the son of Shaphat of A	1Kin 19:16	65

ABEL-MIZRAIM (a'-bel-miz'-ra-im) *A place east of the Jordan River.*

the name of it was called A	Gen 50:11	67

ABEL-SHITTIM (a'-bel-shit'-tim) *A place in Moab.*

even unto A in the plains of Moab	Num 33:49	63

ABEZ (a'-bez) *A place in Issachar.*

And Rabbith, and Kishion, and A	Josh 19:20	77

ABHOR

and my soul shall not a you	Lev 26:11	1602
or if your soul a my judgments	Lev 26:15	1602
idols, and my soul shall a you	Lev 26:30	1602
them away, neither will I a them	Lev 26:44	1602
it, and thou shalt utterly a it	Deut 7:26	8581
Thou shalt not a an Edomite	Deut 23:7	8581
thou shalt not a an Egyptian	Deut 23:7	8581
people Israel utterly to a him	1Sa 27:12	887
and mine own clothes shall a me	Job 9:31	8581
They a me, they flee far from me,	Job 30:10	8581
Wherefore I a myself, and repent	Job 42:6	3988
the LORD will a the bloody	Ps 5:6	8581
I hate and a lying	Ps 119:163	8581
people curse, nations shall a him	Prov 24:24	2194
Do not a us, for thy name's sake,	Jer 14:21	5006
gate, and they a him that speaketh	Amos 5:10	8581
I a the excellency of Jacob, and	Amos 6:8	8374
that a judgment, and pervert all	Mic 3:9	8581
A that which is evil	Rom 12:9	655

ABHORRED

to be a in the eyes of Pharaoh	Ex 5:21	887
things, and therefore I a them	Lev 20:23	6973
because their soul a my statutes	Lev 26:43	1602
he a them, because of the	Deut 32:19	5006
for men a the offering of the	1Sa 2:17	5006
that thou art a of thy father	2Sa 16:21	887
he a Israel, and reigned over	1Kin 11:25	6973
All my inward friends a me	Job 19:19	8581
For he hath not despised nor a	Ps 22:24	8262
he was wroth, and greatly a Israel	Ps 78:59	3988
But thou hast cast off and a	Ps 89:38	3988
insomuch that he a his own	Ps 106:40	8581
he that is a of the LORD shall	Prov 22:14	2194
he hath a his sanctuary, he hath	Lam 2:7	5010
and hast made thy beauty to be a	Eze 16:25	8581
them, and their soul also a me	Zec 11:8	973

ABHORREST
the land that thou *a* shall be..................Is 7:16 — 6973
thou that *a* idols, dost thou......................Rom 2:22 — *948*

ABHORRETH
So that his life *a* bread, and his ....Job 33:20 — 2092
the covetous, whom the LORD *a* ....Ps 10:3 — 5006
he *a* not evil..Ps 36:4 — 3988
Their soul *a* all manner of meat ....Ps 107:18 — 8581
to him whom the nation *a*........................Is 49:7 — 8581

ABHORRING
they shall be an *a* unto all flesh ....Is 66:24 — 1860

ABI (*a'-bi*) See ABI-ABLON, ABI-EZER. *Mother of King Hezekiah.*
His mother's name also was *A* ....2Kin 18:2 — 21

ABIA (*ab-i'-ah*) See ABIAH, ABIJAH, ABIJAM.
1. *A son of Rehoboam.*
Rehoboam, *A* his son, Asa his son,........1Chr 3:10 — 29
and Roboam begat *A* ....Mt 1:7 — 7
and *A* begat Asa ....Mt 1:7 — 7
2. *A priest.*
Zacharias, of the course of *A* ....Lk 1:5 — 7

ABIAH (*ab-i'-ah*) See ABIA.
1. *A son of Samuel.*
and the name of his second, *A* ....1Sa 8:2 — 29
the firstborn Vashni, and *A*....................1Chr 6:28 — 29
2. *Mother of Ashur.*
then *A* Hezron's wife bare him ....1Chr 2:24 — 29
3. *Son of Becher.*
and Omri, and Jerimoth, and *A* ....1Chr 7:8 — 29

ABI-ALBON (*ab'-i-al'-bun*) *A "mighty man" of David.*
A the Arbathite, Azmaveth the ....2Sa 23:31 — 45

ABIASAPH (*ab-i'-as-af*) See EBIASAPH. *A son of Korah.*
Assir, and Elkanah, and *A*........................Ex 6:24 — 23

ABIATHAR (*ab-i'-uth-ur*) See ABITHAR'S. *High Priest during David's reign.*
the son of Ahitub, named *A* ....1Sa 22:20 — 54
A shewed David that Saul had ....1Sa 22:21 — 54
And David said unto *A*, I knew it............1Sa 22:22 — 54
when *A* the son of Ahimelech fled ....1Sa 23:6 — 54
and he said to *A* the priest ....1Sa 23:9 — 54
And David said to *A* the priest ....1Sa 30:7 — 54
A brought thither the ephod to ....1Sa 30:7 — 54
Ahitub, and Ahimelech the son of *A*.....2Sa 8:17 — 54
A went up, until all the people ....2Sa 15:24 — 54
thy son, and Jonathan the son of *A* ......2Sa 15:27 — 54
A carried the ark of God again to.........2Sa 15:29 — 54
with these Zadok and *A* the priests ....2Sa 15:35 — 54
tell it to Zadok and *A* the priests...........2Sa 15:35 — 54
to *A* the priests, Thus and thus..............2Sa 17:15 — 54
to *A* the priests, saying, Speak ....2Sa 19:11 — 54
and Zadok and *A* were the priests.........2Sa 20:25 — 54
of Zeruiah, with with *A* the priest ....1Kin 1:7 — 54
A the priest, and Joab the captain ....1Kin 1:19 — 54
of the host, and *A* the priest...................1Kin 1:25 — 54
the son of *A* the priest came ....1Kin 1:42 — 54
for *A* the priest, and for Joab the...........1Kin 2:22 — 54
unto *A* the priest said the king, ...1Kin 2:26 — 54
So Solomon thrust out *A* from ....1Kin 2:27 — 54
did the king put in the room of *A* ....1Kin 2:35 — 54
and Zadok and *A* were the priests.........1Kin 4:4 — 54
A the priests, and for the Levites............1Chr 15:11 — 54
Ahitub, and Abimelech the son of *A* .....1Chr 18:16 — 54
priest, and Ahimelech the son of *A* ....1Chr 24:6 — 54
Jehoiada the son of Benaiah, and *A*.......1Chr 27:34 — 54
in the days of *A* the high priest.............Mk 2:26 — 8

ABIATHAR'S (*ab-i'-uth-urs*)
Zadok's son, and Jonathan *A* son ....2Sa 15:36 — 54

ABIB (*a'-bib*) See TEL-ABIB. *First month of the Hebrew year.*
day came ye out in the month *A* ....Ex 13:4 — 24
the time appointed of the month *A* ....Ex 23:15 — 24
thee, in the time of the month *A* ....Ex 34:18 — 24
for in the month *A* thou camest ....Ex 34:18 — 24
Observe the month of *A*, and keep ....Deut 16:1 — 24
for in the month of *A* the LORD...............Deut 16:1 — 24

ABIDA (*ab'-id-ah*) See ABIDAH. *A son of Midian.*
Ephah, and Epher, and Henoch, and *A* ...1Chr 1:33 — 28

ABIDAH (*ab'-id-ah*) See ABIDA. *Same as Abida.*
Ephah, and Epher, and Hanoch, and *A* ..Gen 25:4 — 28

ABIDAN (*ab'-id-an*) *Son of Gideoni.*
A the son of Gideoni ....Num 1:11 — 27
shall be *A* the son of Gideoni ....Num 2:22 — 27
On the ninth day *A* the son of ....Num 7:60 — 27
offering of *A* the son of Gideoni ....Num 7:65 — 27
Benjamin was *A* the son of Gideoni ....Num 10:24 — 27

ABIDE
but we will *a* in the street all ....Gen 19:2 — 3885
young men, *A* ye here with the ass........Gen 22:5 — 3427
Let the damsel *a* with us a few ....Gen 24:55 — 3427
a with me ....Gen 29:19 — 3427
let thy servant *a* instead of the..............Gen 44:33 — 3427
a ye every man in his place, in................Ex 16:29 — 3427
Therefore shall ye *a* at the door ....Lev 8:35 — 3427
a with thee all night until the ....Lev 19:13 — 3427
earth, and they *a* over against me ....Num 22:5 — 3427
do ye *a* without the camp seven ....Num 31:19 — 2583
Every thing that may *a* the fire ....Num 31:23 — 935
he shall *a* in it unto the death.................Num 35:25 — 3427
a in your cities which I............................Deut 3:19 — 3427
Judah shall *a* in their coast on ....Josh 18:5 — 5975
the house of Joseph shall *a* in ....Josh 18:5 — 5975
but *a* here fast by my maidens ....Ruth 2:8 — 1692
the LORD, and there *a* for ever ....1Sa 1:22 — 3427
God of Israel shall not *a* with us ....1Sa 5:7 — 3427
a in a secret place, and hide ....1Sa 19:2 — 3427
unto David, *A* not in the hold ....1Sa 22:5 — 3427
A thou with me, fear not.........................1Sa 22:23 — 3427
made also to *a* at the brook Besor ....1Sa 30:21 — 3427
and Israel, and Judah, *a* in tents ....2Sa 11:11 — 3427
to thy place, and *a* with the king ....2Sa 15:19 — 3427
will I be, and with him will I *a*................2Sa 16:18 — 3427
place for thee to *a* in for ever ....1Kin 8:13 — 3427
a now at home ....2Chr 25:19 — 3427
that ye *a* in the siege in ....2Chr 32:10 — 3427
nor *a* in the paths thereof.......................Job 24:13 — 3427
a in the covert to lie in wait ....Job 38:40 — 3427
to serve thee, or *a* by thy crib ....Job 39:9 — 3885
who shall *a* in thy tabernacle ....Ps 15:1 — 1481
I will *a* in thy tabernacle for ....Ps 61:4 — 1481
He shall *a* before God for ever ....Ps 61:7 — 3427
shall *a* under the shadow of the ....Ps 91:1 — 3885
her feet *a* not in her house ....Prov 7:11 — 7937
he that hath it shall *a* satisfied..............Prov 19:23 — 3885
for that shall *a* with him of his ....Eccl 8:15 — 3867
not be able to *a* his indignation ....Jer 10:10 — 3557
If ye will still *a* in this land ....Jer 42:10 — 3427
the LORD, no man shall *a* there...............Jer 49:18 — 3427
there shall no man *a* there ....Jer 49:33 — 3427
so shall no man *a* there, neither ....Jer 50:40 — 3427
Thou shalt *a* for me many days ....Hos 3:3 — 3427
shall *a* many days without a king ....Hos 3:4 — 3427
the sword shall *a* on his cities ....Hos 11:6 — 2342
and who can *a* it ....Joel 2:11 — 3557
and they shall *a* ....Mic 5:4 — 3427
who can *a* in the fierceness of................Nah 1:6 — 6965
But who may *a* the day of his ....Mal 3:2 — 3557
there *a* till ye go thence ....Mt 10:11 — *3306*
there *a* till ye depart from that..............Mk 6:10 — *3306*
house ye enter into, there *a* ....Lk 9:4 — *3306*
for to day I must *a* at thy house ....Lk 19:5 — *3306*
him, saying, *A* with us ....Lk 24:29 — *3306*
on me should not *a* in darkness ....Jn 12:46 — *3306*
that he may *a* with you for ever ....Jn 14:16 — *3306*
A in me, and I in you ....Jn 15:4 — *3306*
itself, except it *a* in the vine ....Jn 15:4 — *3306*
no more can ye, except ye *a* in me ......Jn 15:4 — *3306*
If a man *a* not in me, he is cast ....Jn 15:6 — *3306*
If ye *a* in me, and my words *a* ....Jn 15:7 — *3306*
a in me, and my words *a* in you ....Jn 15:7 — *3306*
ye shall *a* in my love ....Jn 15:10 — *3306*
commandments, and *a* in his love ....Jn 15:10 — *3306*
it pleased Silas to *a* there still ....Acts 15:34 — *1961*
come into my house, and *a* there ....Acts 16:15 — *3306*
that bonds and afflictions *a* me ....Acts 20:23 — *3306*
Except these *a* in the ship ....Acts 27:31 — *3306*
if they *a* not still in unbelief, ...Rom 11:23 — *1961*
If any man's work *a* which he hath ....1Cor 3:14 — *3306*
good for them if they *a* even as I ....1Cor 7:8 — *3306*
Let every man *a* in the same ....1Cor 7:20 — *3306*
he is called, therein *a* with God ....1Cor 7:24 — *3306*
But she is happier if she so *a* ....1Cor 7:40 — *3306*
And it may be that I will *a* ....1Cor 16:6 — *3887*
Nevertheless to *a* in the flesh is..............Phil 1:24 — *1961*
confidence, I know that I shall *a*.............Phil 1:25 — *3306*
thee to *a* still at Ephesus.........................1Ti 1:3 — *4357*
Let that therefore *a* in you.......................1Jn 2:24 — *3306*
taught you, ye shall *a* in him ....1Jn 2:27 — *3306*
And now, little children, *a* in him ....1Jn 2:28 — *3306*

ABIDETH
all that *a* not the fire ye shall ....Num 31:23 — 935
king, Behold, he *a* at Jerusalem ....2Sa 16:3 — 3427
a on the rock, upon the crag of..............Job 39:28 — 3885
man being in honour *a* not ....Ps 49:12 — 3885
them, even he that *a* of old ....Ps 55:19 — 3427
established the earth, and it *a*.................Ps 119:90 — 5975

cannot be removed, but *a* for ever .... Ps 125:1   3427
reproof of life *a* among the wise .... Prov 15:31   3885
but the earth *a* for ever .... Eccl 1:4   5975
He that *a* in this city shall die .... Jer 21:9   3427
but the wrath of God *a* on him .... Jn 3:36   3306
the servant *a* not in the house .... Jn 8:35   *3306*
but the Son *a* ever. .... Jn 8:35   *3306*
the ground and die, it *a* alone .... Jn 12:24   *3306*
of the law that Christ *a* for ever .... Jn 12:34   *3306*
He that *a* in me, and I in him, the .... Jn 15:5   *3306*
now *a* faith, hope, charity, these 1Cor 13:13   *3306*
we believe not, yet he *a* faithful 2Ti 2:13   *3306*
a a priest continually .... Heb 7:3   *3306*
God, which liveth and *a* for ever 1Pet 1:23   *3306*
He that saith he *a* in him ought.............. 1Jn 2:6   *3306*
loveth his brother *a* in the light 1Jn 2:10   *3306*
and the word of God *a* in you 1Jn 2:14   *3306*
doeth the will of God *a* for ever 1Jn 2:17   *3306*
ye have received of him *a* in you 1Jn 2:27   *3306*
Whosoever *a* in him sinneth not 1Jn 3:6   *3306*
loveth not his brother *a* in death 1Jn 3:14   *3306*
And hereby we know that he *a* in us 1Jn 3:24   *3306*
a not in the doctrine of Christ,.............. 2Jn 9   *3306*
He that *a* in the doctrine of.................... 2Jn 9   *3306*

ABIDING

he saw Israel *a* in his tents .... Num 24:2   7931
a with her in the chamber .... Judg 16:9   3427
liers in wait *a* in the chamber .... Judg 16:12   3427
driven me out this day from *a* in 1Sa 26:19   5596
as a shadow, and there is none *a*............. 1Chr 29:15   4723
country shepherds *a* in the field............. Lk 2:8   63
And ye have not his word *a* in you .... Jn 5:38   *3306*
were in that city *a* certain days .... Acts 16:12   1304
hath eternal life *a* in him 1Jn 3:15   *3306*

ABIEL (a'-be-el)
1. Grandfather of King Saul.
whose name was Kish, the son of *A* 1Sa 9:1   22
father of Abner was the son of *A* 1Sa 14:51   22
2. A "mighty man" of David.
brooks of Gaash, *A* the Arbathite,.......... 1Chr 11:32   22

ABI-EZER (ab-i-e'-zur) See ABIEZRITE, JEEZER.
1. A descendant of Manasseh.
and *A* was gathered after him .... Judg 6:34   44
better than the vintage of *A* .... Judg 8:2   44

ABIEZER
for the children of *A*, and for the .... Josh 17:2   44
A the Anethothite, Mebunnai the 2Sa 23:27   44
Hammoleketh bare Ishod, and *A* 1Chr 7:18   44
the Tekoite, *A* the Antothite, ... 1Chr 11:28   44
ninth month was *A* the Anetothite 1Chr 27:12   44

ABI-EZRITE (ab-i-ez'-rite) See ABI-EZRITES. *A descendant of Abiezer.*
that pertained unto Joash the *A* .... Judg 6:11   33

ABI-EZRITES (ab-i-ez'-rites)
day it is yet in Ophrah of the *A* .... Judg 6:24   33
his father, in Ophrah of the *A* .... Judg 8:32   33

ABIGAIL (ab'-e-gul)
1. A wife of David.
and the name of his wife *A* 1Sa 25:3   26
But one of the young men told *A* 1Sa 25:14   26
Then *A* made haste, and took two 1Sa 25:18   26
when *A* saw David, she hasted, and....... 1Sa 25:23   26
And David said to *A*, Blessed be 1Sa 25:32   26
And *A* came to Nabal 1Sa 25:36   26
And David sent and communed with *A* . 1Sa 25:39   26
of David were come to *A* to Carmel........ 1Sa 25:40   26
A hasted, and arose, and rode upon 1Sa 25:42   26
A the Carmelitess, Nabal's wife............. 1Sa 27:3   26
A the wife of Nabal the Carmelite 1Sa 30:5   26
A Nabal's wife the Carmelite 2Sa 2:2   26
of *A* the wife of Nabal the 2Sa 3:3   26
Daniel, of *A* the Carmelitess 1Chr 3:1   26
2. Mother of Amosa.
that went in to *A* the daughter of............ 2Sa 17:25   26
Whose sisters were Zeruiah, and *A*........ 1Chr 2:16   26
And *A* bare Amasa 1Chr 2:17   26

ABIHAIL (ab-e-ha'-il)
1. Head of Levital family of Merari.
of Merari was Zuriel the son of *A* .... Num 3:35   32
2. Wife of Abishur.
name of the wife of Abishur was *A* 1Chr 2:29   32
3. Chief of a family of Gad.
the children of *A* the son of Huri 1Chr 5:14   32
4. Descendant of Eliab.
A the daughter of Eliab the son 2Chr 11:18   32

5. Father of Esther.
the daughter of *A* the uncle of................ Est 2:15   32
the queen, the daughter of *A* .... Est 9:29   32

ABIHU (a-bi'-hew) A son of Aaron.
and she bare him Nadab, and *A*............. Ex 6:23   30
LORD, thou, and Aaron, Nadab, and *A* ... Ex 24:1   30
up Moses, and Aaron, Nadab, and *A* ...... Ex 24:9   30
office, even Aaron, Nadab and *A* .... Ex 28:1   30
And Nadab and *A*, the sons of Aaron, ... Lev 10:1   30
Nadab the firstborn, and *A* .... Num 3:2   30
A died before the LORD, when they .... Num 3:4   30
unto Aaron was born Nadab, and *A* .... Num 26:60   30
A died, when they offered strange .... Num 26:61   30
Nadab, and *A*, Eleazar, and Ithamar 1Chr 6:3   30
Nadab, and *A*, Eleazar, and Ithamar. 1Chr 24:1   30
A died before their father, and 1Chr 24:2   30

ABIHUD (a-bi'-hud) A son of Bela.
Bela were, Addar, and Gera, and *A* 1Chr 8:3   31

ABIJAH (a-bi'-jah) See ABIA, ABIJAM.
1. A son of Jeroboam I.
At that time *A* the son of......................... 1Kin 14:1   29
2. A priest during David's reign.
to Hakkoz, the eighth to *A* 1Chr 24:10   29
3. A son of Rehoboam.
which bare him *A*, and Attai, and 2Chr 11:20   29
Rehoboam made *A* the son of................ 2Chr 11:22   29
A his son reigned in his stead 2Chr 12:16   29
began *A* to reign over Judah................... 2Chr 13:1   29
And there was war between *A* 2Chr 13:2   29
A set the battle in array with an............ 2Chr 13:3   29
A stood up upon mount Zemaraim, ... 2Chr 13:4   29
Jeroboam and all Israel before *A* 2Chr 13:15   29
And *A* and his people slew them with ... 2Chr 13:17   29
A pursued after Jeroboam, and took..... 2Chr 13:19   29
strength again in the days of *A* 2Chr 13:20   29
But *A* waxed mighty, and married 2Chr 13:21   29
And the rest of the acts of *A* 2Chr 13:22   29
So *A* slept with his fathers, and 2Chr 14:1   29
4. Mother of King Hezekiah.
And his mother's name was *A* 2Chr 29:1   29
5. A priest in Nehemiah's time.
Meshullam, *A*, Mijamin, ... Neh 10:7   29
6. A priest who returned from Exile under Zerubbabel.
Iddo, Ginnetho, *A*.................................. Neh 12:4   29
Of *A*, Zichri.. Neh 12:17   29

ABIJAM (a-bi'-jum) Son and successor of King Rehoboam.
A his son reigned in his stead 1Kin 14:31   38
son of Nebat reigned *A* over Judah 1Kin 15:1   38
Now the rest of the acts of *A* 1Kin 15:7   38
And there was war between *A* 1Kin 15:7   38
And *A* slept with his fathers.................... 1Kin 15:8   38

ABILENE (ab-i-le'-ne) A Roman tetrarchy in northern Palestine.
and Lysanias the tetrarch of *A* .... Lk 3:1   9

ABILITY
according to his *a* that vowed................ Lev 27:8   5381
They gave after their *a* unto the .... Ezr 2:69   3581
We after our *a* have redeemed our......... Neh 5:8   1767
such as had *a* in them to stand in .... Dan 1:4   3581
man according to his several *a* .... Mt 25:15   *1411*
every man according to his *a* .... Acts 11:29   2141
it as of the *a* which God giveth............... 1Pet 4:11   2479

ABIMAEL (a-bim'-ah-el) A son of Joktan in Arabia.
And Obal, and *A*, and Sheba, ... Gen 10:28   39
And Ebal, and *A*, and Sheba, ... 1Chr 1:22   39

ABIMELECH (a-bim'-e-lek) See ABIMELECH'S.
1. Philistine king in Abraham's time.
A king of Gerar sent, and took .... Gen 20:2   40
But God came to *A* in a dream by .... Gen 20:3   40
But *A* had not come near her.................. Gen 20:4   40
Therefore *A* rose early in the .... Gen 20:8   40
Then *A* called Abraham, and said .... Gen 20:9   40
A said unto Abraham, What sawest ...... Gen 20:10   40
A took sheep, and oxen, and .... Gen 20:14   40
A said, Behold, my land is before .... Gen 20:15   40
and God healed *A*, and his wife, and .... Gen 20:17   40
all the wombs of the house of *A* .... Gen 20:18   40
came to pass at that time, that *A* .... Gen 21:22   40
Abraham reproved *A* because of a......... Gen 21:25   40
A said, I wot not who hath done .... Gen 21:26   40
and oxen, and gave them unto *A* .... Gen 21:27   40
A said unto Abraham, What mean .... Gen 21:29   40
then *A* rose up, and Phichol the .... Gen 21:32   40
Isaac went unto *A* king of the .... Gen 26:1   40
that *A* king of the Philistines .... Gen 26:8   40
A called Isaac, and said, Behold,.......... Gen 26:9   40

ABIMELECH'S (continued)

A said, What is this thou hast	Gen 26:10	40
A charged all his people, saying,	Gen 26:11	40
A said unto Isaac, Go from us	Gen 26:16	40
Then *A* went to him from Gerar, and	Gen 26:26	40

2. Son of Gideon.

him a son, whose name he called *A*	Judg 8:31	40
A the son of Jerubbaal went to	Judg 9:1	40
their hearts inclined to follow *A*	Judg 9:3	40
wherewith *A* hired vain and light	Judg 9:4	40
of Millo, and went, and made *A* a king	Judg 9:6	40
in that ye have made *A* a king	Judg 9:16	40
upon one stone, and have made *A*	Judg 9:18	40
this day, then rejoice ye in *A*	Judg 9:19	40
if not, let fire come out from *A*	Judg 9:20	40
the house of Millo, and devour *A*	Judg 9:20	40
there, for fear of *A* his brother	Judg 9:21	40
When *A* had reigned three years	Judg 9:22	40
God sent an evil spirit between *A*	Judg 9:23	40
dealt treacherously with *A*	Judg 9:23	40
be laid upon *A* their brother	Judg 9:24	40
and it was told *A*	Judg 9:25	40
and did eat and drink, and cursed *A*	Judg 9:27	40
the son of Ebed said, Who is *A*	Judg 9:28	40
then would I remove *A*	Judg 9:29	40
And he said to *A*, Increase thine	Judg 9:29	40
he sent messengers unto *A* privily	Judg 9:31	40
A rose up, and all the people that	Judg 9:34	40
A rose up, and the people that	Judg 9:35	40
wherewith thou saidst, Who is *A*	Judg 9:38	40
men of Shechem, and fought with *A*	Judg 9:39	40
A chased him, and he fled before	Judg 9:40	40
And *A* dwelt at Arumah	Judg 9:41	40
and they told *A*	Judg 9:42	40
And *A*, and the company that was	Judg 9:44	40
A fought against the city all	Judg 9:45	40
And it was told *A*, that all the	Judg 9:47	40
A gat him up to mount Zalmon, he	Judg 9:48	40
A took an axe in his hand, and cut	Judg 9:48	40
man his bough, and followed *A*	Judg 9:49	40
Then went *A* to Thebez, and	Judg 9:50	40
A came unto the tower, and fought	Judg 9:52	40
men of Israel saw that *A* was dead	Judg 9:55	40
God rendered the wickedness of *A*	Judg 9:56	40
after *A* there arose to defend	Judg 10:1	40
Who smote *A* the son of	2Sa 11:21	40

3. Son of Abiathar the High Priest.

A the son of Abiathar, were the	1Chr 18:16	40

4. Used in title of Psalm 34.

he changed his behaviour before *A*	Ps 34:t	40

ABIMELECH'S *(a-bim'-e-leks)*

which *A* servants had violently	Gen 21:25	40
piece of a millstone upon *A* head	Judg 9:53	40

ABINADAB *(a-bin'-ah-dab)*
1. A Levite of Kirjath-jearim.

into the house of *A* in the hill	1Sa 7:1	41
the house of *A* that was in Gibeah	2Sa 6:3	41
and Uzzah and Ahio, the sons of *A*	2Sa 6:3	41
house of *A* which was at Gibeah	2Sa 6:4	41
a new cart out of the house of *A*	1Chr 13:7	41

2. A brother of David.

Then Jesse called *A*, and made him	1Sa 16:8	41
first born, and next unto him *A*	1Sa 17:13	41
A the second, and Shimma the third	1Chr 2:13	41

3. A son of King Saul.

Philistines slew Jonathan, and *A*	1Sa 31:2	41
Jonathan, and Malchi-shua, and *A*	1Chr 8:33	41
Jonathan, and Malchi-shua, and *A*	1Chr 9:39	41
Philistines slew Jonathan, and *A*	1Chr 10:2	41

4. Father of an officer of Solomon.

The son of *A*, in all the region	1Kin 4:11	41

ABINOAM *(a-bin'-o-am)* Father of Barak.

son of *A* out of Kedesh-naphtali	Judg 4:6	42
of *A* was gone up to mount Tabor	Judg 4:12	42
and Barak the son of *A* on that day	Judg 5:1	42
captivity captive, thou son of *A*	Judg 5:12	42

ABIRAM *(a-bi'-rum)*
1. A conspirator against Moses.

the son of Levi, and Dathan and *A*	Num 16:1	48
And Moses sent to call Dathan and *A*	Num 16:12	48
tabernacle of Korah, Dathan, and *A*	Num 16:24	48
rose up and went unto Dathan and *A*	Num 16:25	48
tabernacle of Korah, Dathan, and *A*	Num 16:27	48
A came out, and stood in the door	Num 16:27	48
Nemuel, and Dathan, and *A*	Num 26:9	48
This is that Dathan and *A*, which	Num 26:9	48
And what he did unto Dathan and *A*	Deut 11:6	48
and covered the company of *A*	Ps 106:17	48

2. Son of Hiel the Bethelite.

thereof in *A* his firstborn	1Kin 16:34	48

ABISHAG *(ab'-e-shag)* An attendant of David.

found *A* a Shunammite, and brought	1Kin 1:3	49
A the Shunammite ministered unto	1Kin 1:15	49
that he give me *A* the Shunammite	1Kin 2:17	49
Let *A* the Shunammite be given to	1Kin 2:21	49
And why dost thou ask *A* the	1Kin 2:22	49

ABISHAI *(ab'-e-shahee)* David's nephew.

to *A* the son of Zeruiah, brother	1Sa 26:6	52
A said, I will go down with thee	1Sa 26:6	52
A came to the people by night	1Sa 26:7	52
Then said *A* to David, God hath	1Sa 26:8	52
And David said to *A*, Destroy him	1Sa 26:9	52
sons of Zeruiah there, Joab, and *A*	2Sa 2:18	52
also and *A* pursued after Abner	2Sa 2:24	52
A his brother slew Abner, because	2Sa 3:30	52
into the hand of *A* his brother	2Sa 10:10	52
then fled they also before *A*	2Sa 10:14	52
Then said *A* the son of Zeruiah	2Sa 16:9	52
And David said to *A*, and to all his	2Sa 16:11	52
the hand of *A* the son of Zeruiah	2Sa 18:2	52
And the king commanded Joab and *A*	2Sa 18:5	52
the king charged thee and *A*	2Sa 18:12	52
But *A* the son of Zeruiah answered	2Sa 19:21	52
And David said to *A*, Now shall	2Sa 20:6	52
A his brother pursued after Sheba	2Sa 20:10	52
But *A* the son of Zeruiah	2Sa 21:17	52
And *A*, the brother of Joab, the	2Sa 23:18	52
A, and Joab, and Asahel, three	1Chr 2:16	52
A the brother of Joab, he was	1Chr 11:20	52
A the son Zeruiah slew of the	1Chr 18:12	52
unto the hand of *A* his brother	1Chr 19:11	52
fled before *A* his brother	1Chr 19:15	52

ABISHALOM *(a-bish'-ah-lum)* See ABSALOM. *Father of Maachah.*

was Maachah, the daughter of *A*	1Kin 15:2	53
was Maachah, the daughter of *A*	1Kin 15:10	53

ABISHUA *(a-bish'-u-ah)*
1. Son of Phinehas.

begat Phinehas, Phinehas begat *A*	1Chr 6:4	50
A begat Bukki, and Bukki begat	1Chr 6:5	50
son, Phinehas his son, *A* his son,	1Chr 6:50	50
The son of *A*, the son of Phinehas	Ezr 7:5	50
And *A*, and Naaman, and Ahoah,	1Chr 8:4	50

ABISHUR *(ab'-e-shur)* A son of Shammai.

Nadab, and *A*	1Chr 2:28	51
name of the wife of *A* was Abihail	1Chr 2:29	51

ABITAL *(ab'-e-tal)* A wife of David.

fifth, Shephatiah the son of *A*	2Sa 3:4	37
The fifth, Shephatiah of *A*	1Chr 3:3	37

ABITUB *(ab'-e-tub)* Son of Shahareim.

And of Hushim he begat *A*, and	1Chr 8:11	36

ABIUD *(a-bi'-ud)* A descendant of Zerubbabel; ancestor of Jesus.

And Zorobabel begat *A*	Mt 1:13	10
and *A* begat Eliakim	Mt 1:13	10

ABJECTS

the *a* gathered themselves	Ps 35:15	5222

ABLE

the land was not *a* to bear them	Gen 13:6	5375
if thou be *a* to number them	Gen 15:5	3201
me and the children be *a* to endure	Gen 33:14	7272
one cannot be *a* to see the earth	Ex 10:5	3201
thou art not *a* to perform it	Ex 18:18	3201
out of all the people *a* men	Ex 18:21	2428
then thou shalt be *a* to endure	Ex 18:23	3201
Moses chose *a* men out of all	Ex 18:25	2428
Moses was not *a* to enter into the	Ex 40:35	3201
if he be not *a* to bring a lamb,	Lev 5:7	5060,1767
But if he be not *a* to bring two	Lev 5:11	5381
if she be not *a* to bring a lamb,	Lev 12:8	4672,1767
pigeons, such as he is *a* to get	Lev 14:30	5381
Even such as he is *a* to get	Lev 14:31	5381
whose hand is not *a* to get that	Lev 14:32	5381
himself be *a* to redeem it	Lev 25:26	5381
But if he be not *a* to restore it	Lev 25:28	4672,1767
or if he be *a*, he may redeem	Lev 25:49	5381
all that are *a* to go forth to war	Num 1:3	3318
all that were *a* to go forth to	Num 1:20	3318
all that were *a* to go forth to	Num 1:22	3318
all that were *a* to go forth to	Num 1:24	3318
all that were *a* to go forth to	Num 1:26	3318
all that were *a* to go forth to	Num 1:28	3318
all that were *a* to go forth to	Num 1:30	3318
all that were *a* to go forth to	Num 1:32	3318
all that were *a* to go forth to	Num 1:34	3318
all that were *a* to go forth to	Num 1:36	3318

all that were *a* to go forth to	Num 1:38	3318
all that were *a* to go forth to	Num 1:40	3318
all that were *a* to go forth to	Num 1:42	3318
all that were *a* to go forth to	Num 1:45	3318
I am not *a* to bear all this	Num 11:14	3201
for we are well *a* to overcome it	Num 13:30	3201
We be not *a* to go up against the	Num 13:31	3201
Because the LORD was not *a* to	Num 14:16	3201
I shall be *a* to overcome them	Num 22:11	3201
am I not *a* indeed to promote thee	Num 22:37	3201
all that are *a* to go to war in	Num 26:2	3318
I am not *a* to bear you myself	Deut 1:9	3201
no man be *a* to stand before thee	Deut 7:24	3320
Because the LORD was not *a* to	Deut 9:28	3201
no man be *a* to stand before you	Deut 11:25	3320
that thou art not *a* to carry it	Deut 14:24	3201
Every man shall give as he is *a*	Deut 16:17	4979,3027
There shall not any man be *a* to	Josh 1:5	3320
then I shall be *a* to drive them	Josh 14:12	
no man hath been *a* to stand	Josh 23:9	5975
what was I *a* to do in comparison	Judg 8:3	
Who is *a* to stand before this	1Sa 6:20	3201
If he be *a* to fight with me, and	1Sa 17:9	3201
Thou art not *a* to go against this	1Sa 17:33	3201
for who is *a* to judge this thy so	1Kin 3:9	3201
were not *a* utterly to destroy	1Kin 9:21	3201
all that were *a* to put on armour	2Kin 3:21	2296
if thou be *a* on thy part to set	2Kin 18:23	3201
for he shall not be *a* to deliver	2Kin 18:29	3201
men *a* to bear buckler and sword,	1Chr 5:18	5375
very *a* men for the work of the	1Chr 9:13	2428
a men for strength for the	1Chr 26:8	2428
that we should be *a* to offer so	1Chr 29:14	6113,3581
But who is *a* to build him an	2Chr 2:6	6113,3581
a to receive the burnt offerings	2Chr 7:7	3201
so that none is *a* to withstand	2Chr 20:6	
they were not *a* to go to Tarshish	2Chr 20:37	6113
a to go forth to war, that could	2Chr 25:5	
The LORD is *a* to give thee much	2Chr 25:9	
a to deliver their lands out of	2Chr 32:13	3201
that your God should be *a* to	2Chr 32:14	3201
a to deliver his people out of	2Chr 32:15	3201
we are not *a* to stand without,	Ezr 10:13	3581
we are not *a* to build the wall	Neh 4:10	3201
who then is *a* to stand before me	Job 41:10	
them that they were not *a* to rise	Ps 18:38	3201
which they are not *a* to perform	Ps 21:11	3201
down, and shall not be *a* to rise	Ps 36:12	3201
me, so that I am not *a* to look up	Ps 40:12	3201
but who is *a* to stand before envy	Prov 27:4	
yet shall he not be *a* to find it	Eccl 8:17	3201
if thou be *a* on thy part to set	Is 36:8	3201
he shall not be *a* to deliver you	Is 36:14	3201
thou shalt not be *a* to put it off	Is 47:11	3201
so be thou shalt be *a* to profit	Is 47:12	3201
not be *a* to abide his indignation	Jer 10:10	3201
they shall not be *a* to escape	Jer 11:11	3201
he shall not be *a* to hide himself	Jer 49:10	3201
from whom I am not *a* to rise up	Lam 1:14	3201
their gold shall not be *a* to	Eze 7:19	3201
a to live for his righteousness	Eze 33:12	
lambs as he shall be *a* to give	Eze 46:5	4991,3027
to the lambs as he is *a* to give	Eze 46:11	4991,3027
Art thou *a* to make known unto me	Dan 2:26	3546
our God whom we serve is *a* to	Dan 3:17	3202
not *a* to make known unto me the	Dan 4:18	3202
but thou art *a*	Dan 4:18	3546
walk in pride he is *a* to abase	Dan 4:37	3202
a to deliver thee from the lions	Dan 6:20	3202
the land is not *a* to bear all his	Amos 7:10	3201
a to deliver them in the day of	Zeph 1:18	3201
that God is *a* of these stones to	Mt 3:9	1410
Believe ye that I am *a* to do this	Mt 9:28	1410
but are not *a* to kill the soul	Mt 10:28	1410
which is *a* to destroy both soul	Mt 10:28	1410
He that is *a* to receive it, let	Mt 19:12	1410
Are ye *a* to drink of the cup that	Mt 20:22	1410
They say unto him, We are *a*	Mt 20:22	1410
no man was *a* to answer him a word	Mt 22:46	1410
I am *a* to destroy the temple of	Mt 26:61	1410
them, as they were *a* to hear it	Mk 4:33	1410
not *a* to speak, until the day	Lk 1:20	1410
That God is *a* of these stones to	Lk 3:8	1410
If ye then be not *a* to do that	Lk 12:26	1410
to enter in, and shall not be *a*	Lk 13:24	2480
is not *a* to finish it, all that	Lk 14:29	2480
to build, and was not *a* to finish	Lk 14:30	2480
consulteth whether he be *a* with	Lk 14:31	1415
not be *a* to gainsay nor resist	Lk 21:15	1410
no man is *a* to pluck them out of	Jn 10:29	1410
now they were not *a* to draw it	Jn 21:6	2480

they were not *a* to resist the	Acts 6:10	2480
our fathers nor we were *a* to bear	Acts 15:10	2480
which is *a* to build you up, and to	Acts 20:32	1410
said he, which among you are *a*	Acts 25:5	1415
he was *a* also to perform	Rom 4:21	1415
shall be *a* to separate us from	Rom 8:39	1410
for God is *a* to graff them in	Rom 11:23	1415
for God is *a* to make him stand	Rom 14:4	1415
a also to admonish one another	Rom 15:14	1410
hitherto ye were not *a* to bear it	1Cor 3:2	1410
neither yet now are ye *a*.	1Cor 3:2	1410
not one that shall be *a* to judge	1Cor 6:5	1410
to be tempted above that ye are *a*	1Cor 10:13	1415
that ye may be *a* to bear it	1Cor 10:13	1410
that we may be *a* to comfort them	2Cor 1:4	1410
Who also hath made us *a* ministers	2Cor 3:6	2427
God is *a* to make all grace abound	2Cor 9:8	1415
May be *a* to comprehend with all	Eph 3:18	1840
Now unto him that is *a* to do	Eph 3:20	1410
that ye may be *a* to stand against	Eph 6:11	1410
that ye may be *a* to withstand in	Eph 6:13	1410
wherewith ye shall be *a* to quench	Eph 6:16	1410
to the working whereby he is *a* to	Phil 3:21	1410
am persuaded that he is *a* to keep	2Ti 1:12	1415
who shall be *a* to teach others	2Ti 2:2	2425
never *a* to come to the knowledge	2Ti 3:7	1410
which are *a* to make thee wise	2Ti 3:15	1410
that he may be *a* by sound	Titus 1:9	1415
he is *a* to succour them that are	Heb 2:18	1410
that was *a* to save him from death	Heb 5:7	1410
Wherefore he is *a* also to save	Heb 7:25	1410
that God was *a* to raise him up	Heb 11:19	1415
which is *a* to save your souls	Jas 1:21	1410
a also to bridle the whole body	Jas 3:2	1415
who is *a* to save and to destroy	Jas 4:12	1410
a after my decease to have these	2Pet 1:15	2192
Now unto him that is *a* to keep	Jude 24	1410
was *a* to open the book, neither	Rev 5:3	1410
and who shall be *a* to stand	Rev 6:17	1410
who is *a* to make war with him	Rev 13:4	1410
no man was *a* to enter into the	Rev 15:8	1410

ABNER (ab'-nur) See ABNER'S. *King Saul's military commander.*

of the captain of his host was *A*	1Sa 14:50	74
Ner the father of *A* was the son	1Sa 14:51	74
the Philistine, he said unto *A*	1Sa 17:55	74
the captain of the host, *A*,	1Sa 17:55	74
A said, As thy soul liveth, O	1Sa 17:55	74
A took him, and brought him before	1Sa 17:57	74
A sat by Saul's side, and David's	1Sa 20:25	74
A the son of Ner, the captain of	1Sa 26:5	74
but *A* and the people lay round	1Sa 26:7	74
to *A* the son of Ner, saying,	1Sa 26:14	74
Answerest thou not, *A*	1Sa 26:14	74
Then *A* answered and said, Who art	1Sa 26:14	74
And David said to *A*, Art not thou	1Sa 26:15	74
But *A* the son of Ner, captain of	2Sa 2:8	74
A the son of Ner, and the servants	2Sa 2:12	74
A said to Joab, Let the young men	2Sa 2:14	74
A was beaten, and the men of	2Sa 2:17	74
And Asahel pursued after *A*	2Sa 2:19	74
nor to the left from following *A*	2Sa 2:19	74
Then *A* looked behind him, and said	2Sa 2:20	74
A said to him, Turn thee aside to	2Sa 2:21	74
A said again to Asahel, Turn thee	2Sa 2:22	74
wherefore *A* with the hinder end	2Sa 2:23	74
also and Abishai pursued after *A*	2Sa 2:24	74
themselves together after *A*	2Sa 2:25	74
Then *A* called to Joab, and said,	2Sa 2:26	74
And *A* and his men walked all that	2Sa 2:29	74
And Joab returned from following *A*	2Sa 2:30	74
that *A* made himself strong for	2Sa 3:6	74
and Ish-bosheth said to *A*,	2Sa 3:7	74
Then was *A* very wroth for the	2Sa 3:8	74
So do God to *A*, and more also,	2Sa 3:9	74
could not answer *A* a word again	2Sa 3:11	74
A sent messengers to David on his	2Sa 3:12	74
Then said *A* unto him, Go, return	2Sa 3:16	74
A had communication with the	2Sa 3:17	74
A also spake in the ears of	2Sa 3:19	74
A went also to speak in the ears	2Sa 3:19	74
So *A* came to David to Hebron, and	2Sa 3:20	74
And David made *A* and the men that	2Sa 3:20	74
A said unto David, I will arise	2Sa 3:21	74
And David sent *A* away	2Sa 3:21	74
but *A* was not with David in	2Sa 3:22	74
A the son of Ner came to the king	2Sa 3:23	74
behold, *A* came unto thee	2Sa 3:24	74
Thou knowest *A* the son of Ner,	2Sa 3:25	74
David, he sent messengers after *A*	2Sa 3:26	74

when *A* was returned to Hebron,	2Sa 3:27	74
the blood of *A* the son of Ner	2Sa 3:28	74
and Abishai his brother slew *A*	2Sa 3:30	74
with sackcloth, and mourn before *A*	2Sa 3:31	74
And they buried *A* in Hebron	2Sa 3:32	74
voice, and wept at the grave of *A*	2Sa 3:32	74
And the king lamented over *A*	2Sa 3:33	74
and said, Died *A* as a fool dieth	2Sa 3:33	74
the king to slay *A* the son of Ner	2Sa 3:37	74
heard that *A* was dead in Hebron	2Sa 4:1	74
in the sepulchre of *A* in Hebron	2Sa 4:12	74
unto *A* the son of Ner, and unto	1Kin 2:5	74
A the son of Ner, captain of the	1Kin 2:32	74
A the son of Ner, and Joab the son	1Chr 26:28	74
of Benjamin, Jaasiel the son of *A*	1Chr 27:21	74

ABNER'S (ab'-nurs)

of *A* men, so that three hundred	2Sa 2:31	74

ABOARD

over unto Phenicia, we went *a*	Acts 21:2	1910

ABODE

he *a* with him the space of a	Gen 29:14	3427
But his bow *a* in strength	Gen 49:24	3427
of the LORD *a* upon mount Sinai	Ex 24:16	7931
because the cloud *a* thereon	Ex 40:35	7931
and in the place where the cloud *a*	Num 9:17	7931
as long as the cloud *a* upon the	Num 9:18	7931
of the LORD *a* in their tents	Num 9:20	2583
when the cloud *a* from even unto	Num 9:21	1961
of Israel *a* in their tents	Num 9:22	2583
and *a* at Hazeroth	Num 11:35	1961
and the people *a* in Kadesh	Num 20:1	3427
the princes of Moab *a* with Balaam	Num 22:8	3427
Israel *a* in Shittim, and the	Num 25:1	3427
So ye *a* in Kadesh many days,	Deut 1:46	3427
unto the days that ye *a* there	Deut 1:46	3427
So we *a* in the valley over	Deut 3:29	3427
then I *a* in the mount forty days	Deut 9:9	3427
a there three days, until the	Josh 2:22	3427
that they *a* in their places in	Josh 5:8	3427
a between Beth-el and Ai, on the	Josh 8:9	3427
Gilead *a* beyond Jordan	Judg 5:17	7931
sea shore, and *a* in his breaches	Judg 5:17	7931
and Israel *a* in Kadesh	Judg 11:17	3427
and he *a* with him three days	Judg 19:4	3427
a in the rock Rimmon four months	Judg 20:47	3427
a there till even before God, and	Judg 21:2	3427
So the woman *a*, and gave her son	1Sa 1:23	3427
while the ark *a* in Kirjath-jearim	1Sa 7:2	3427
them, *a* in Gibeah of Benjamin	1Sa 13:16	3427
(now Saul *a* in Gibeah under a	1Sa 22:6	3427
David *a* in the wilderness in	1Sa 23:14	3427
David *a* in the wood, and Jonathan	1Sa 23:18	3427
a in the wilderness of Maon	1Sa 23:25	3427
two hundred *a* by the stuff	1Sa 25:13	3427
But David *a* in the wilderness, and	1Sa 26:3	3427
for two hundred *a* behind, which	1Sa 30:10	5975
David had *a* two days in Ziklag	2Sa 1:1	3427
So Uriah *a* in Jerusalem that day,	2Sa 11:12	3427
vow while I *a* at Geshur in Syria	2Sa 15:8	3427
him up into a loft, where he *a*	1Kin 17:19	3427
But I know thy *a*, and thy going	2Kin 19:27	3427
there *a* we in tents three days	Ezr 8:15	2583
Jerusalem, and *a* there three days	Ezr 8:32	3427
But I know thy *a*, and thy going	Is 37:28	3427
So Jeremiah *a* in the court of the	Jer 38:28	3427
And while they *a* in Galilee	Mt 17:22	390
Mary *a* with her about three	Lk 1:56	3306
neither *a* in any house, but in	Lk 8:27	3306
a in the mount that is called the	Lk 21:37	835
like a dove, and it *a* upon him	Jn 1:32	3306
he dwelt, and *a* with him that day	Jn 1:39	3306
and he *a* there two days	Jn 4:40	3306
unto them, he *a* still in Galilee	Jn 7:9	3306
a not in the truth, because there	Jn 8:44	2476
and there he *a*	Jn 10:40	3306
he *a* two days still in the same	Jn 11:6	3306
unto him, and make our *a* with him	Jn 14:23	3438
where *a* both Peter, and James, and	Acts 1:13	2650
Judaea to Caesarea, and there *a*	Acts 12:19	1304
Long time therefore *a* they	Acts 14:3	1304
there they *a* long time with the	Acts 14:28	1304
Silas and Timotheus *a* there still	Acts 17:14	5278
he *a* with them, and wrought	Acts 18:3	3306
And there *a* three months	Acts 20:3	4160
where we *a* seven days	Acts 20:6	1304
brethren, and *a* with them one day	Acts 21:7	3306
of the seven; and *a* with him	Acts 21:8	3306
Peter, and *a* with him fifteen days	Gal 1:18	1961
Erastus *a* at Corinth	2Ti 4:20	3306

ABODEST

Why *a* thou among the sheepfolds,	Judg 5:16	3427

ABOLISH

And the idols he shall utterly *a*	Is 2:18	2498

ABOLISHED

my righteousness shall not be *a*	Is 51:6	2865
cut down, and your works may be *a*	Eze 6:6	4229
to the end of that which is *a*	2Cor 3:13	2673
Having *a* in his flesh the enmity,	Eph 2:15	2673
Jesus Christ, who hath *a* death	2Ti 1:10	2673

ABOMINABLE

or any *a* unclean thing, and eat of	Lev 7:21	8263
a with any creeping thing that	Lev 11:43	8262
not any one of these *a* customs	Lev 18:30	8441
at all on the third day, it is *a*	Lev 19:7	6292
not make your souls *a* by beast	Lev 20:25	8262
Thou shalt not eat any *a* thing	Deut 14:3	8441
for the king's word was *a* to Joab	1Chr 21:6	8581
put away the *a* idols out of all	2Chr 15:8	8251
How much more *a* and filthy is man,	Job 15:16	8581
corrupt, they have done *a* works	Ps 14:1	8581
are they, and have done *a* iniquity	Ps 53:1	8581
out of thy grave like an *a* branch	Is 14:19	8581
broth of *a* things is in their	Is 65:4	6292
of their detestable and *a* things	Jer 16:18	8441
do not this *a* thing that I hate	Jer 44:4	8441
neither came there *a* flesh into	Eze 4:14	6292
a beasts, and all the idols of the	Eze 8:10	8263
hast committed more *a* than they	Eze 16:52	8581
and the scant measure that is *a*	Mic 6:10	2194
I will cast *a* filth upon thee, and	Nah 3:6	8251
in works they deny him, being *a*	Titus 1:16	947
banquetings, and *a* idolatries	1Pet 4:3	111
fearful, and unbelieving, and the *a*	Rev 21:8	948

ABOMINABLY

he did very *a* in following idols,	1Kin 21:26	8581

ABOMINATION

for that is an *a* unto the	Gen 43:32	8441
is an *a* unto the Egyptians	Gen 46:34	8441
for we shall sacrifice the *a* of	Ex 8:26	8441
shall we sacrifice the *a* of the	Ex 8:26	8441
it shall be an *a*, and the soul	Lev 7:18	6292
they shall be an *a* unto you	Lev 11:10	8263
They shall be even an *a* unto you	Lev 11:11	8263
ye shall have their carcases in *a*	Lev 11:11	8262
that shall be an *a* unto you	Lev 11:12	8263
shall have in *a* among the fowls	Lev 11:13	8262
shall not be eaten, they are an *a*	Lev 11:13	8263
all four, shall be an *a* unto you	Lev 11:20	8263
four feet, shall be an *a* unto you	Lev 11:23	8263
upon the earth shall be an *a*.	Lev 11:41	8263
for they are an *a*	Lev 11:42	8263
with womankind: it is an *a*	Lev 18:22	8441
both of them have committed an *a*	Lev 20:13	8441
for it is an *a* to the LORD thy	Deut 7:25	8441
thou bring an *a* into thine house	Deut 7:26	8441
for every *a* to the LORD, which he	Deut 12:31	8441
that such is wrought among you	Deut 13:14	8441
for that is an *a* unto the LORD	Deut 17:1	8441
that such *a* is wrought in Israel	Deut 17:4	8441
things are an *a* unto the LORD	Deut 18:12	8441
do so are *a* unto the LORD thy God	Deut 22:5	8441
these are an *a* unto the LORD thy God	Deut 23:18	8441
for that is *a* before the LORD	Deut 24:4	8441
are an *a* unto the LORD thy God	Deut 25:16	8441
an *a* unto the LORD, the work of	Deut 27:15	8441
was had in *a* with the Philistines	1Sa 13:4	887
Milcom the *a* of the Ammonites	1Kin 11:5	8251
the *a* of Moab, in the hill that	1Kin 11:7	8251
the *a* of the children of Ammon	1Kin 11:7	8251
Ashtoreth the *a* of the Zidonians	2Kin 23:13	8251
for Chemosh the *a* of the Moabites	2Kin 23:13	8251
for Milcom the *a* of the children	2Kin 23:13	8441
thou hast made me an *a* unto them	Ps 88:8	8441
For the froward is *a* to the LORD	Prov 3:32	8441
yea, seven are an *a* unto him	Prov 6:16	8441
and wickedness is an *a* to my lips	Prov 8:7	8441
A false balance is *a* to the LORD	Prov 11:1	8441
a froward heart are *a* to the LORD	Prov 11:20	8441
Lying lips are *a* to the LORD	Prov 12:22	8441
but it is *a* to fools to depart	Prov 13:19	8441
of the wicked is an *a* to the LORD	Prov 15:8	8441
the wicked is an *a* unto the LORD	Prov 15:9	8441
the wicked are an *a* to the LORD	Prov 15:26	8441
in heart is an *a* to the LORD	Prov 16:5	8441
It is an *a* to kings to commit	Prov 16:12	8441
even they both are *a* to the LORD	Prov 17:15	8441
of them are alike *a* to the LORD	Prov 20:10	8441

weights are an *a* unto the LORD	Prov 20:23	8441
The sacrifice of the wicked is *a*	Prov 21:27	8441
and the scorner is an *a* to men	Prov 24:9	8441
law, even his prayer shall be *a*	Prov 28:9	8441
An unjust man is an *a* to the just	Prov 29:27	8441
in the way is *a* to the wicked	Prov 29:27	8441
incense is an *a* unto me	Is 1:13	8441
an *a* is he that chooseth you	Is 41:24	8441
I make the residue thereof an *a*	Is 44:19	8441
eating swine's flesh, and the *a*	Is 66:17	8263
land, and made mine heritage an *a*	Jer 2:7	8441
ashamed when they had committed *a*	Jer 6:15	8441
ashamed when they had committed *a*	Jer 8:12	8441
mind, that they should do this *a*	Jer 32:35	8441
haughty, and committed *a* before me	Eze 16:50	8441
to the idols, hath committed *a*	Eze 18:12	8441
one hath committed *a* with his	Eze 22:11	8441
stand upon your sword, ye work *a*	Eze 33:26	8441
place the *a* that maketh desolate	Dan 11:31	8251
the *a* that maketh desolate set up	Dan 12:11	8251
an *a* is committed in Israel and in	Mal 2:11	8441
shall see the *a* of desolation	Mt 24:15	*946*
ye shall see the *a* of desolation	Mk 13:14	*946*
men is *a* in the sight of God	Lk 16:15	*946*
neither whatsoever worketh *a*	Rev 21:27	*946*

ABOMINATIONS

shall not commit any of these *a*	Lev 18:26	8441
(For all these *a* have the men of	Lev 18:27	8441
shall commit any of these *a*	Lev 18:29	8441
do after the *a* of those nations	Deut 18:9	8441
because of these *a* the LORD thy	Deut 18:12	8441
you not to do after all their *a*	Deut 20:18	8441
And ye have seen their *a*, and their	Deut 29:17	8251
with *a* provoked they him to anger	Deut 32:16	8441
a of the nations which the LORD	1Kin 14:24	8441
according to the *a* of the heathen	2Kin 16:3	8441
after the *a* of the heathen, whom	2Kin 21:2	8441
king of Judah hath done these *a*	2Kin 21:11	8441
all the *a* that were spied in the	2Kin 23:24	8441
after all the *a* of the heathen whom	2Chr 28:3	8441
like unto the *a* of the heathen,	2Chr 33:2	8441
Josiah took away all the *a* out of	2Chr 34:33	8441
his *a* which he did, and that which	2Chr 36:8	8441
after all the *a* of the heathen	2Chr 36:14	8441
lands, doing according to their *a*	Ezr 9:1	8441
people of the lands, with their *a*	Ezr 9:11	8441
with the people of these *a*	Ezr 9:14	8441
there are seven *a* in his heart	Prov 26:25	8441
their soul delighteth in their *a*	Is 66:3	8251
put away thine *a* out of my sight	Jer 4:1	8251
are delivered to do all these *a*	Jer 7:10	8441
they have set their *a* in the	Jer 7:30	8251
thine *a* on the hills in the	Jer 13:27	8251
But they set their *a* in the house	Jer 32:34	8251
because of the *a* which ye have	Jer 44:22	8441
the like, because of all thine *a*	Eze 5:9	8441
things, and with all thine *a*	Eze 5:11	8441
have committed in all their *a*	Eze 6:9	8441
Alas for all the evil *a* of the	Eze 6:11	8441
recompense upon thee all thine *a*	Eze 7:3	8441
thine *a* shall be in the midst of	Eze 7:4	8441
recompense thee for all thine *a*	Eze 7:8	8441
thine *a* that are in the midst of	Eze 7:9	8441
they made the images of their *a*	Eze 7:20	8441
even the great *a* that the house	Eze 8:6	8441
and thou shalt see greater *a*	Eze 8:6	8441
the wicked *a* that they do here	Eze 8:9	8441
shalt see greater *a* that they do	Eze 8:13	8441
shalt see greater *a* than these	Eze 8:15	8441
the *a* which they commit here	Eze 8:17	8441
that cry for all the *a* that be	Eze 9:4	8441
all the *a* thereof from thence	Eze 11:18	8441
detestable things and their *a*	Eze 11:21	8441
a among the heathen whither they	Eze 12:16	8251
away your faces with all your *a*	Eze 14:6	8441
cause Jerusalem to know her *a*	Eze 16:2	8441
And in all thine *a* and thy	Eze 16:22	8441
and with all the idols of thy *a*	Eze 16:36	8441
this lewdness above all thine *a*	Eze 16:43	8441
ways, nor done after thy *a*	Eze 16:47	8441
multiplied thine *a* more than they	Eze 16:51	8441
all thine *a* which thou hast done	Eze 16:51	8441
borne thy lewdness and thine *a*	Eze 16:58	8441
he hath done all these *a*	Eze 18:13	8441
the *a* that the wicked man doeth	Eze 18:24	8441
to know the *a* of their fathers	Eze 20:4	8441
away every man the *a* of his eyes	Eze 20:7	8251
man cast away the *a* of their eyes	Eze 20:8	8251
commit ye whoredom after their *a*	Eze 20:30	8251
thou shalt shew her all her *a*	Eze 22:2	8441

yea, declare unto them their *a*	Eze 23:36	8441
their *a* which they have committed	Eze 33:29	8441
for your iniquities and for your *a*	Eze 36:31	8441
their *a* that they have committed	Eze 43:8	8441
let it suffice you of all your *a*	Eze 44:6	8441
my covenant because of all your *a*	Eze 44:7	8441
their *a* which they have committed	Eze 44:13	8441
for the overspreading of *a* he	Dan 9:27	8251
their *a* were according as they	Hos 9:10	8251
his *a* from between his teeth	Zec 9:7	8251
golden cup in her hand full of *a*	Rev 17:4	*946*
AND *A* OF THE EARTH	Rev 17:5	*946*

ABOUND

man shall *a* with blessings	Prov 28:20	7227
And because iniquity shall *a*	Mt 24:12	*4129*
entered, that the offence might *a*	Rom 5:20	*4121*
abounded, grace did much more *a*	Rom 5:20	*5248*
continue in sin, that grace may *a*	Rom 6:1	*4121*
believing, that ye may *a* in hope	Rom 15:13	*4052*
the sufferings of Christ *a* in us	2Cor 1:5	*4052*
as ye *a* in every thing, in faith,	2Cor 8:7	*4052*
see that ye *a* in this grace also	2Cor 8:7	*4052*
to make all grace *a* toward you	2Cor 9:8	*4052*
things, may *a* to every good work	2Cor 9:8	*4052*
that your love may *a* yet more	Phil 1:9	*4052*
to be abased, and I know how to *a*	Phil 4:12	*4052*
full and to be hungry, both to *a*	Phil 4:12	*4052*
fruit that may *a* to your account	Phil 4:17	*4121*
But I have all, and *a*	Phil 4:18	*4052*
a in love one toward another, and	1Th 3:12	*4052*
to please God, so ye would *a* more	1Th 4:1	*4052*
if these things be in you, and *a*	2Pet 1:8	*4121*

ABOUNDED

a through my lie unto his glory	Rom 3:7	*4052*
Jesus Christ, hath *a* unto many	Rom 5:15	*4052*
But where sin *a*, grace did much	Rom 5:20	*4121*
their deep poverty *a* unto the	2Cor 8:2	*4052*
Wherein he hath *a* toward us in	Eph 1:8	*4052*

ABOUNDETH

a furious man *a* in transgression	Prov 29:22	7227
our consolation also *a* by Christ	2Cor 1:5	*4052*
of you all toward each other *a*	2Th 1:3	*4121*

ABOUNDING

were no fountains *a* with water	Prov 8:24	3513
always *a* in the work of the Lord,	1Cor 15:58	*4052*
a therein with thanksgiving	Col 2:7	*4052*

ABOUT See APPENDIX.

ABOVE See APPENDIX.

ABRAHAM (a'-bra-ham) See ABRAHAM'S, ABRAM. *Father of the nation of Israel.*

Abram, but thy name shall be *A*	Gen 17:5	85
And God said unto *A*, Thou shalt	Gen 17:9	85
And God said unto *A*, As for Sarai	Gen 17:15	85
Then *A* fell upon his face, and	Gen 17:17	85
A said unto God, O that Ishmael	Gen 17:18	85
with him, and God went up from *A*	Gen 17:22	85
A took Ishmael his son, and all	Gen 17:23	85
A was ninety years old and nine,	Gen 17:24	85
selfsame day was *A* circumcised	Gen 17:26	85
A hastened into the tent unto	Gen 18:6	85
A ran unto the herd, and fetcht a	Gen 18:7	85
Now *A* and Sarah were old and well	Gen 18:11	85
And the LORD said unto *A*,	Gen 18:13	85
A went with them to bring them on	Gen 18:16	85
Shall I hide from *A* that thing	Gen 18:17	85
Seeing that *A* shall surely become	Gen 18:18	85
A that which he hath spoken of	Gen 18:19	85
but *A* stood yet before the LORD	Gen 18:22	85
A drew near, and said, Wilt thou	Gen 18:23	85
A answered and said, Behold now, I	Gen 18:27	85
as he had left communing with *A*	Gen 18:33	85
A returned unto his place	Gen 18:33	85
A gat up early in the morning to	Gen 19:27	85
the plain, that God remembered *A*	Gen 19:29	85
A journeyed from thence toward	Gen 20:1	85
A said of Sarah his wife, She is	Gen 20:2	85
Then Abimelech called *A*, and said	Gen 20:9	85
And Abimelech said unto *A*, What	Gen 20:10	85
A said, Because I thought, Surely,	Gen 20:11	85
and gave them unto *A*, and restored	Gen 20:14	85
So *A* prayed unto God	Gen 20:17	85
bare a son in his old age, at	Gen 21:2	85
A called the name of his son that	Gen 21:3	85
A circumcised his son Isaac being	Gen 21:4	85
A was an hundred years old, when	Gen 21:5	85
said, Who would have said unto *A*	Gen 21:7	85
A made a great feast the same day	Gen 21:8	85

which she had born unto *A*	Gen 21:9	85
Wherefore she said unto *A*	Gen 21:10	85
And God said unto *A*, Let it not be	Gen 21:12	85
A rose up early in the morning,	Gen 21:14	85
captain of his host spake unto *A*	Gen 21:22	85
And *A* said, I will swear	Gen 21:24	85
A reproved Abimelech because of a	Gen 21:25	85
A took sheep and oxen, and gave	Gen 21:27	85
A set seven ewe lambs of the	Gen 21:28	85
And Abimelech said unto *A*, What	Gen 21:29	85
A planted a grove in Beer-sheba,	Gen 21:33	85
A sojourned in the Philistines'	Gen 21:34	85
things, that God did tempt *A*	Gen 22:1	85
and said unto him, *A*	Gen 22:1	85
A rose up early in the morning,	Gen 22:3	85
third day *A* lifted up his eyes	Gen 22:4	85
A said unto his young men, Abide	Gen 22:5	85
A took the wood of the burnt	Gen 22:6	85
And Isaac spake unto *A* his father	Gen 22:7	85
A said, My son, God will provide	Gen 22:8	85
A built an altar there, and laid	Gen 22:9	85
A stretched forth his hand, and	Gen 22:10	85
of heaven, and said, *A*, *A*	Gen 22:11	85
A lifted up his eyes, and looked,	Gen 22:13	85
A went and took the ram, and	Gen 22:13	85
A called the name of that place	Gen 22:14	85
A out of heaven the second time	Gen 22:15	85
So *A* returned unto his young men,	Gen 22:19	85
and *A* dwelt at Beer-sheba	Gen 22:19	85
these things, that it was told *A*	Gen 22:20	85
A came to mourn for Sarah, and to	Gen 23:2	85
A stood up from before his dead,	Gen 23:3	85
the children of Heth answered *A*	Gen 23:5	85
A stood up, and bowed himself to	Gen 23:7	85
Ephron the Hittite answered *A* in	Gen 23:10	85
A bowed down himself before the	Gen 23:12	85
And Ephron answered *A*, saying unto	Gen 23:14	85
And *A* hearkened unto Ephron	Gen 23:16	85
A weighed to Ephron the silver,	Gen 23:16	85
Unto *A* for a possession in the	Gen 23:18	85
A buried Sarah his wife in the	Gen 23:19	85
were made sure unto *A* for a	Gen 23:20	85
A was old, and well stricken in	Gen 24:1	85
LORD had blessed *A* in all things	Gen 24:1	85
A said unto his eldest servant of	Gen 24:2	85
A said unto him, Beware thou that	Gen 24:6	85
under the thigh of *A* his master	Gen 24:9	85
said, O LORD God of my master *A*	Gen 24:12	85
and shew kindness unto my master *A*	Gen 24:12	85
be the LORD God of my master *A*	Gen 24:27	85
said, O LORD God of my master *A*	Gen 24:42	85
the LORD God of my master *A*	Gen 24:48	85
Then again *A* took a wife, and her	Gen 25:1	85
A gave all that he had unto Isaac	Gen 25:5	85
of the concubines, which *A* had	Gen 25:6	85
A gave gifts, and sent them away	Gen 25:6	85
Then *A* gave up the ghost, and died	Gen 25:8	85
The field which *A* purchased of	Gen 25:10	85
there was *A* buried, and Sarah his	Gen 25:10	85
came to pass after the death of *A*	Gen 25:11	85
Sarah's handmaid, bare unto *A*	Gen 25:12	85
A begat Isaac	Gen 25:19	85
famine that was in the days of *A*	Gen 26:1	85
which I sware unto *A* thy father	Gen 26:3	85
Because that *A* obeyed my voice,	Gen 26:5	85
in the days of *A* his father	Gen 26:15	85
in the days of *A* his father	Gen 26:18	85
stopped them after the death of *A*	Gen 26:18	85
I am the God of *A* thy father	Gen 26:24	85
And give thee the blessing of *A*	Gen 28:4	85
a stranger, which God gave unto *A*	Gen 28:4	85
I am the LORD God of *A* thy father	Gen 28:13	85
God of my father, the God of *A*	Gen 31:42	85
The God of *A*, and the God of Nahor	Gen 31:53	85
Jacob said, O God of my father *A*	Gen 32:9	85
And the land which I gave *A*	Gen 35:12	85
Arbah, which is Hebron, where *A*	Gen 35:27	85
God, before whom my fathers *A*	Gen 48:15	85
them, and the name of my fathers *A*	Gen 48:16	85
which *A* bought with the field of	Gen 49:30	85
There they buried *A* and Sarah his	Gen 49:31	85
which *A* bought with the field for	Gen 50:13	85
unto the land which he sware to *A*	Gen 50:24	85
remembered his covenant with *A*	Ex 2:24	85
God of thy father, the God of *A*	Ex 3:6	85
God of your fathers, the God of *A*	Ex 3:15	85
God of your fathers, the God of *A*	Ex 3:16	85
of their fathers, the God of *A*	Ex 4:5	85
And I appeared unto *A*, unto Isaac,	Ex 6:3	85
which I did swear to give it to *A*	Ex 6:8	85
Remember *A*, Isaac, and Israel, thy	Ex 32:13	85

the land which I sware unto *A*	Ex 33:1	85
covenant with *A* will I remember	Lev 26:42	85
see the land which I sware unto *A*	Num 32:11	85
LORD sware unto your fathers, *A*	Deut 1:8	85
he sware unto thy fathers, to *A*	Deut 6:10	85
LORD sware unto thy fathers, *A*	Deut 9:5	85
Remember thy servants, *A*, Isaac,	Deut 9:27	85
hath sworn unto thy fathers, to *A*	Deut 29:13	85
LORD sware unto thy fathers, to *A*	Deut 30:20	85
is the land which I sware unto *A*	Deut 34:4	85
time, even Terah, the father of *A*	Josh 24:2	85
I took your father *A* from the	Josh 24:3	85
came near, and said, LORD God of *A*	1Kin 18:36	85
because of his covenant with *A*	2Kin 13:23	85
Abram; the same is *A*	1Chr 1:27	85
The sons of *A*; Isaac, and	1Chr 1:28	85
And *A* begat Isaac	1Chr 1:34	85
the covenant which he made with *A*	1Chr 16:16	85
O LORD God of *A*, Isaac, and of	1Chr 29:18	85
the seed of *A* thy friend for ever	2Chr 20:7	85
turn again unto the LORD God of *A*	2Chr 30:6	85
and gavest him the name of *A*	Neh 9:7	85
even the people of the God of *A*	Ps 47:9	85
O ye seed of *A* his servant	Ps 105:6	85
Which covenant he made with *A*	Ps 105:9	85
holy promise, and *A* his servant	Ps 105:42	85
saith the LORD, who redeemed *A*	Is 29:22	85
chosen, the seed of *A* my friend	Is 41:8	85
Look unto *A* your father, and unto	Is 51:2	85
though *A* be ignorant of us, and	Is 63:16	85
to be rulers over the seed of *A*	Jer 33:26	85
A was one, and he inherited the	Eze 33:24	85
truth to Jacob, and the mercy to *A*	Mic 7:20	85
the son of David, the son of *A*	Mt 1:1	11
A begat Isaac	Mt 1:2	11
from *A* to David are fourteen	Mt 1:17	11
We have *A* to our father	Mt 3:9	11
to raise up children unto *A*	Mt 3:9	11
and west, and shall sit down with *A*	Mt 8:11	11
I am the God of *A*, and the God of	Mt 22:32	11
him, saying, I am the God of *A*	Mk 12:26	11
As he spake to our fathers, to *A*	Lk 1:55	11
which he sware to our father *A*	Lk 1:73	11
We have *A* to our father	Lk 3:8	11
to raise up children unto *A*	Lk 3:8	11
of Isaac, which was the son of *A*	Lk 3:34	11
this woman, being a daughter of *A*	Lk 13:16	11
of teeth, when ye shall see *A*	Lk 13:28	11
seeth *A* afar off, and Lazarus in	Lk 16:23	11
And he cried and said, Father *A*	Lk 16:24	11
But *A* said, Son, remember that	Lk 16:25	11
_A_ saith unto him, They have Moses	Lk 16:29	11
And he said, Nay, father *A*	Lk 16:30	11
as he also is a son of *A*	Lk 19:9	11
he calleth the Lord the God of *A*	Lk 20:37	11
and said unto him, *A* is our father	Jn 8:39	11
ye would do the works of *A*	Jn 8:39	11
of God: this did not *A*	Jn 8:40	11
A is dead, and the prophets	Jn 8:52	11
thou greater than our father *A*	Jn 8:53	11
Your father *A* rejoiced to see my	Jn 8:56	11
years old, and hast thou seen *A*	Jn 8:57	11
I say unto you, Before *A* was	Jn 8:58	11
The God of *A*, and of Isaac, and of	Acts 3:13	11
with our fathers, saying unto *A*	Acts 3:25	11
glory appeared unto our father *A*	Acts 7:2	11
so *A* begat Isaac, and circumcised	Acts 7:8	11
laid in the sepulchre that *A*	Acts 7:16	11
nigh, which God had sworn to *A*	Acts 7:17	11
God of thy fathers, the God of *A*	Acts 7:32	11
children of the stock of *A*	Acts 13:26	11
we say then that *A* our father	Rom 4:1	11
For if *A* were justified by works,	Rom 4:2	11
A believed God, and it was counted	Rom 4:3	11
reckoned to *A* for righteousness	Rom 4:9	11
of that faith of our father *A*	Rom 4:12	11
heir of the world, was not to *A*	Rom 4:13	11
also which is of the faith of *A*	Rom 4:16	11
because they are the seed of *A*	Rom 9:7	11
am an Israelite, of the seed of *A*	Rom 11:1	11
Are they the seed of *A*	2Cor 11:22	11
Even as *A* believed God, and it was	Gal 3:6	11
the same are the children of *A*	Gal 3:7	11
preached before the gospel unto *A*	Gal 3:8	11
faith are blessed with faithful *A*	Gal 3:9	11
That the blessing of *A* might come	Gal 3:14	11
Now to *A* and his seed were the	Gal 3:16	11
but God gave it to *A* by promise	Gal 3:18	11
that *A* had two sons, the one by a	Gal 4:22	11
but he took on him the seed of *A*	Heb 2:16	11
For when God made promise to *A*	Heb 6:13	11

who met *A* returning from the	Heb 7:1	*11*
To whom also *A* gave a tenth part	Heb 7:2	*11*
A gave the tenth of the spoils	Heb 7:4	*11*
they come out of the loins of *A*	Heb 7:5	*11*
from them received tithes of *A*	Heb 7:6	*11*
tithes, payed tithes in *A*	Heb 7:9	*11*
By faith *A*, when he was called to	Heb 11:8	*11*
By faith *A*, when he was tried,	Heb 11:17	*11*
Was not *A* our father justified by	Jas 2:21	*11*
A believed God, and it was imputed	Jas 2:23	*11*
Even as Sarah obeyed *A*, calling	1Pet 3:6	*11*

ABRAHAMS *(a'-bra-hams)*

male among the men of *A* house	Gen 17:23	*85*
because of Sarah *A* wife	Gen 20:18	*85*
in *A* sight because of his son	Gen 21:11	*85*
did bear to Nahor, *A* brother	Gen 22:23	*85*
A brother, with her pitcher upon	Gen 24:15	*85*
And he said, I am *A* servant	Gen 24:34	*85*
when *A* servant heard their words,	Gen 24:52	*85*
nurse, and *A* servant, and his men	Gen 24:59	*85*
years of *A* life which he lived	Gen 25:7	*85*
A son, whom Hagar the Egyptian,	Gen 25:12	*85*
the generations of Isaac, *A* son	Gen 25:19	*85*
thy seed for my servant *A* sake	Gen 26:24	*85*
the daughter of Ishmael *A* son	Gen 28:9	*85*
the sons of Keturah, *A* concubine	1Chr 1:32	*85*
by the angels into *A* bosom	Lk 16:22	*11*
They answered him, We be *A* seed	Jn 8:33	*11*
I know that ye are *A* seed	Jn 8:37	*11*
unto them, If ye were *A* children	Jn 8:39	*11*
be Christ's, then are ye *A* seed	Gal 3:29	*11*

ABRAM *(a'-brum)* See ABRAHAM, ABRAM'S. *Abraham's original name.*

lived seventy years, and begat *A*	Gen 11:26	*87*
Terah begat *A*, Nahor, and Haran	Gen 11:27	*87*
And *A* and Nahor took them wives	Gen 11:29	*87*
And Terah took *A* his son, and Lot	Gen 11:31	*87*
Now the LORD had said unto *A*	Gen 12:1	*87*
So *A* departed, as the LORD had	Gen 12:4	*87*
A was seventy and five years old	Gen 12:4	*87*
A took Sarai his wife, and Lot his	Gen 12:5	*87*
A passed through the land unto	Gen 12:6	*87*
And the LORD appeared unto *A*	Gen 12:7	*87*
A journeyed, going on still	Gen 12:9	*87*
A went down into Egypt to sojourn	Gen 12:10	*87*
when *A* was come into Egypt, the	Gen 12:14	*87*
he entreated *A* well for her sake	Gen 12:16	*87*
And Pharaoh called *A*, and said,	Gen 12:18	*87*
A went up out of Egypt, he, and	Gen 13:1	*87*
A was very rich in cattle, in	Gen 13:2	*87*
there *A* called on the name of the	Gen 13:4	*87*
And Lot also, which went with *A*	Gen 13:5	*87*
A said to Lot, Let there be no	Gen 13:8	*87*
A dwelled in the land of Canaan,	Gen 13:12	*87*
And the LORD said unto *A*, after	Gen 13:14	*87*
Then *A* removed his tent, and came	Gen 13:18	*87*
had escaped, and told *A* the Hebrew	Gen 14:13	*87*
and these were confederate with *A*	Gen 14:13	*87*
when *A* heard that his brother was	Gen 14:14	*87*
Blessed be *A* of the most high God	Gen 14:19	*87*
And the king of Sodom said unto *A*	Gen 14:21	*87*
A said to the king of Sodom, I	Gen 14:22	*87*
shouldest say, I have made *A* rich	Gen 14:23	*87*
the LORD came unto *A* in a vision	Gen 15:1	*87*
in a vision, saying, Fear not, *A*	Gen 15:1	*87*
A said, Lord GOD, what wilt thou	Gen 15:2	*87*
A said, Behold, to me thou hast	Gen 15:3	*87*
the carcases, *A* drove them away	Gen 15:11	*87*
down, a deep sleep fell upon *A*	Gen 15:12	*87*
And he said unto *A*, Know of a	Gen 15:13	*87*
the LORD made a covenant with *A*	Gen 15:18	*87*
And Sarai said unto *A*, Behold now,	Gen 16:2	*87*
A hearkened to the voice of Sarai	Gen 16:2	*87*
after *A* had dwelt ten years in	Gen 16:3	*87*
to her husband *A* to be his wife	Gen 16:3	*87*
And Sarai said unto *A*, My wrong be	Gen 16:5	*87*
But *A* said unto Sarai, Behold,	Gen 16:6	*87*
And Hagar bare *A* a son	Gen 16:15	*87*
A called his son's name, which	Gen 16:15	*87*
A was fourscore and six years old,	Gen 16:16	*87*
old, when Hagar bare Ishmael to *A*	Gen 16:16	*87*
when *A* was ninety years old and	Gen 17:1	*87*
and nine, the LORD appeared unto *A*	Gen 17:1	*87*
And *A* fell on his face	Gen 17:3	*87*
thy name any more be called *A*	Gen 17:5	*87*
A; the same is Abraham	1Chr 1:27	*87*
LORD the God, who didst choose *A*	Neh 9:7	*87*

ABRAM'S *(a'-brums)*

the name of *A* wife was Sarai	Gen 11:29	*87*
daughter in law, his son *A* wife	Gen 11:31	*87*
plagues because of Sarai *A* wife	Gen 12:17	*87*
between the herdmen of *A* cattle	Gen 13:7	*87*
A brother's son, who dwelt in	Gen 14:12	*87*
Now Sarai *A* wife bare him no	Gen 16:1	*87*
Sarai *A* wife took Hagar her maid	Gen 16:3	*87*

ABROAD

of the Canaanites spread *a*	Gen 10:18	*5310*
lest we be scattered *a* upon the	Gen 11:4	*6527*
So the LORD scattered them *a* from	Gen 11:8	*6527*
did the LORD scatter them *a* upon	Gen 11:9	*6527*
And he brought him forth *a*	Gen 15:5	*2351*
they had brought them forth *a*	Gen 19:17	*2351*
thou shalt spread *a* to the west	Gen 28:14	*6555*
a throughout all the land of	Ex 5:12	*6527*
I will spread *a* my hands unto the	Ex 9:29	*6566*
spread *a* his hands unto the LORD	Ex 9:33	*6566*
of the flesh *a* out of the house	Ex 12:46	*2351*
walk *a* upon his staff, then shall	Ex 21:19	*2351*
he spread *a* the tent over the	Ex 40:19	*6566*
scab spread much *a* in the skin	Lev 13:5	*6581*
a leprosy break out *a* in the skin	Lev 13:12	*6524*
if it spread much *a* in the skin	Lev 13:22	*6581*
it be spread much *a* in the skin	Lev 13:27	*6581*
shall tarry *a* out of his tent	Lev 14:8	*2351*
she be born at home, or born *a*	Lev 18:9	*2351*
they spread them all *a* for	Num 11:32	*7849*
shall he go *a* out of the camp	Deut 23:10	*2351*
whither thou shalt go forth *a*	Deut 23:12	*2351*
be, when thou wilt ease thyself *a*	Deut 23:13	*2351*
Thou shalt stand *a*, and the man to	Deut 24:11	*2351*
bring out the pledge *a* unto thee	Deut 24:11	*2351*
her young, spreadeth *a* her wings	Deut 32:11	*6566*
thirty daughters, whom he sent *a*	Judg 12:9	*2351*
daughters from *a* for his sons	Judg 12:9	*2351*
out both of them, he and Samuel, *a*	1Sa 9:26	*2351*
they were spread *a* upon all the	1Sa 30:16	*5203*
the street, and did spread them *a*	2Sa 22:43	*7554*
walkest *a* any whither, that thou	1Kin 2:42	
borrow thee vessels *a* of all thy	2Kin 4:3	*2351*
let us send *a* unto our brethren	1Chr 13:2	*2351*
spread themselves *a* in the valley	1Chr 14:13	*6584*
his name spread *a* even to the	2Chr 26:8	
And his name spread far *a*	2Chr 26:15	*7350*
to carry it out *a* into the brook	2Chr 29:16	*2351*
as soon as the commandment came *a*	2Chr 31:5	*6555*
scatter you *a* among the nations	Neh 1:8	*6327*
queen shall come *a* unto all women	Est 1:17	*3318*
is a certain people scattered *a*	Est 3:8	*6340*
lion's whelps are scattered *a*	Job 4:11	*6504*
He wandereth *a* for bread, saying,	Job 15:23	*5074*
Cast *a* the rage of thy wrath	Job 40:11	*6327*
when he goeth *a*, he telleth it	Ps 41:6	*2351*
thine arrows also went *a*	Ps 77:17	*1980*
Let thy fountains be dispersed *a*	Prov 5:16	*2351*
scattereth the inhabitants	Is 24:1	*6327*
doth he not cast *a* the fitches	Is 28:25	*6327*
that spreadeth *a* the earth by	Is 44:24	*7554*
pour it out upon the children *a*	Jer 6:11	*2351*
a the sword bereaveth, at home	Lam 1:20	*2351*
till ye have scattered them *a*	Eze 34:21	*2351*
prosperity shall yet be spread *a*	Zec 1:17	*6527*
for I have spread you *a* as the	Zec 2:6	*6566*
hereof went *a* into all that land	Mt 9:26	*1831*
spread *a* his fame in all that	Mt 9:31	*1310*
they fainted, and were scattered *a*	Mt 9:36	*4496*
not with me scattereth *a*	Mt 12:30	*4650*
of the flock shall be scattered *a*	Mt 26:31	*1287*
immediately his fame spread *a*	Mk 1:28	*1831*
to blaze *a* the matter, insomuch	Mk 1:45	*1310*
secret, but that it should come *a*	Mk 4:22	*1519,5318*
(for his name was spread *a*	Mk 6:14	*1519,1096*
all these sayings were noised *a*	Lk 1:65	*1255*
they made known *a* the saying	Lk 2:17	*1232*
more went there a fame *a* of him	Lk 5:15	*1330*
shall not be known and come *a*	Lk 8:17	*1519,5318*
of God that were scattered *a*	Jn 11:52	*1287*
this saying *a* among the brethren	Jn 21:23	*1831*
Now when this was noised *a*	Acts 2:6	*1096,5456*
they were all scattered *a*	Acts 8:1	*1289*
they that were scattered *a* went	Acts 8:4	*1289*
Now they which were scattered *a*	Acts 11:19	*1289*
a in our hearts by the Holy Ghost	Rom 5:5	*1632*
obedience is come *a* unto all men	Rom 16:19	*864*
is written, He hath dispersed *a*	2Cor 9:9	*4650*
faith to God-ward is spread *a*	1Th 1:8	*1831*
tribes which are scattered *a*	Jas 1:1	*1290*

ABRONAH See EBRONAH.

ABSALOM (ab'-sal-um) *A son of David.*
A the son of Maachah the daughter	2Sa 3:3	53
that *A* the son of David had a	2Sa 13:1	53
A her brother said unto her, Hath	2Sa 13:20	53
A spake unto his brother Amnon	2Sa 13:22	53
for *A* hated Amnon, because he had	2Sa 13:22	53
that *A* had sheepshearers in	2Sa 13:23	53
A invited all the king's sons	2Sa 13:23	53
A came to the king, and said,	2Sa 13:24	53
And the king said to *A*, Nay, my	2Sa 13:25	53
Then said *A*, If not, I pray thee	2Sa 13:26	53
But *A* pressed him, that he let	2Sa 13:27	53
Now *A* had commanded his servants,	2Sa 13:28	53
the servants of *A* did unto Amnon	2Sa 13:29	53
did unto Amnon as *A* had commanded	2Sa 13:29	53
A hath slain all the king's sons,	2Sa 13:30	53
for by the appointment of *A* this	2Sa 13:32	53
But *A* fled	2Sa 13:34	53
But *A* fled, and went to Talmai,	2Sa 13:37	53
So *A* fled, and went to Geshur, and	2Sa 13:38	53
David longed to go forth unto *A*	2Sa 13:39	53
the king's heart was toward *A*	2Sa 14:1	53
bring the young man *A* again	2Sa 14:21	53
Geshur, and brought *A* to Jerusalem	2Sa 14:23	53
So *A* returned to his own house,	2Sa 14:24	53
much praised as *A* for his beauty	2Sa 14:25	53
unto *A* there were born three sons	2Sa 14:27	53
So *A* dwelt two full years in	2Sa 14:28	53
Therefore *A* sent for Joab, to	2Sa 14:29	53
came to *A* unto his house, and said	2Sa 14:31	53
A answered Joab, Behold, I sent	2Sa 14:32	53
and when he had called for *A*	2Sa 14:33	53
and the king kissed *A*	2Sa 14:33	53
that *A* prepared him chariots and	2Sa 15:1	53
A rose up early, and stood beside	2Sa 15:2	53
then *A* called unto him, and said,	2Sa 15:2	53
A said unto him, See, thy matters	2Sa 15:3	53
A said moreover, Oh that I were	2Sa 15:4	53
on this manner did *A* to all	2Sa 15:6	53
so *A* stole the hearts of the men	2Sa 15:6	53
that *A* said unto the king, I pray	2Sa 15:7	53
But *A* sent spies throughout all	2Sa 15:10	53
shall say, *A* reigneth in Hebron	2Sa 15:10	53
with *A* went two hundred men out	2Sa 15:11	53
A sent for Ahithophel the	2Sa 15:12	53
increased continually with *A*	2Sa 15:12	53
of the men of Israel are after *A*	2Sa 15:13	53
we shall not else escape from *A*	2Sa 15:14	53
is among the conspirators with *A*	2Sa 15:31	53
return to the city, and say unto *A*	2Sa 15:34	53
city, and *A* came into Jerusalem	2Sa 15:37	53
into the hand of *A* thy son	2Sa 16:8	53
And *A*, and all the people the men	2Sa 16:15	53
David's friend, was come unto *A*	2Sa 16:16	53
A, that Hushai said unto *A*	2Sa 16:16	53
A said to Hushai, Is this thy	2Sa 16:17	53
And Hushai said unto *A*, Nay	2Sa 16:18	53
Then said *A* to Ahithophel, Give	2Sa 16:20	53
And Ahithophel said unto *A*	2Sa 16:21	53
So they spread *A* a tent upon the	2Sa 16:22	53
A went in unto his father's	2Sa 16:22	53
both with David and with *A*	2Sa 16:23	53
Moreover Ahithophel said unto *A*	2Sa 17:1	53
And the saying pleased *A* well	2Sa 17:4	53
Then said *A*, Call now Hushai the	2Sa 17:5	53
And when Hushai was come to *A*	2Sa 17:6	53
A spake unto him, saying,	2Sa 17:6	53
And Hushai said unto *A*, The	2Sa 17:7	53
among the people that follow *A*	2Sa 17:9	53
And *A* and all the men of Israel	2Sa 17:14	53
the LORD might bring evil upon *A*	2Sa 17:14	53
and thus did Ahithophel counsel *A*	2Sa 17:15	53
a lad saw them, and told *A*	2Sa 17:18	53
A passed over Jordan, he and all	2Sa 17:24	53
A made Amasa captain of the host	2Sa 17:25	53
A pitched in the land of Gilead	2Sa 17:26	53
with the young man, even with *A*	2Sa 18:5	53
the captains charge concerning *A*	2Sa 18:5	53
A met the servants of David	2Sa 18:9	53
A rode upon a mule, and the mule	2Sa 18:9	53
Behold, I saw *A* hanged in an oak	2Sa 18:10	53
that none touch the young man *A*	2Sa 18:12	53
them through the heart of *A*	2Sa 18:14	53
armour compassed about and smote *A*	2Sa 18:15	53
And they took *A*, and cast him into	2Sa 18:17	53
Now *A* in his lifetime had taken	2Sa 18:18	53
said, Is the young man *A* safe	2Sa 18:29	53
Cushi, Is the young man *A* safe	2Sa 18:32	53
my son *A*, my son, my son *A*	2Sa 18:33	53
God I had died for thee, O *A*	2Sa 18:33	53
king weepeth and mourneth for *A*	2Sa 19:1	53

loud voice, O my son *A*, O *A*	2Sa 19:4	53
that if *A* had lived, and all we	2Sa 19:6	53
he is fled out of the land for *A*	2Sa 19:9	53
And *A*, whom we anointed over us,	2Sa 19:10	53
Bichri Do us more harm than did *A*	2Sa 20:6	53
and his mother bare him after *A*	1Kin 1:6	53
I fled because of *A* thy brother	1Kin 2:7	53
though he turned not after *A*	1Kin 2:28	53
A the son of Maachah the daughter	1Chr 3:2	53
he took Maachah the daughter of *A*	2Chr 11:20	53
daughter of *A* above all his wives	2Chr 11:21	53
when he fled from *A* his son	Ps 3:*t*	53

ABSALOM'S (ab'-sal-ums)
I love Tamar, my brother *A* sister	2Sa 13:4	53
desolate in her brother *A* house	2Sa 13:20	53
A servants set the field on fire	2Sa 14:30	53
when *A* servants came to the woman	2Sa 17:20	53
is called unto this day, *A* place	2Sa 18:18	53

ABSENCE
them in the *a* of the multitude	Lk 22:6	817
only, but now much more in my *a*	Phil 2:12	666

ABSENT
when we are *a* one from another	Gen 31:49	5641
as *a* in body, but present in	1Cor 5:3	548
the body, we are *a* from the Lord	2Cor 5:6	553
rather to be *a* from the body	2Cor 5:8	553
that, whether present or *a*	2Cor 5:9	553
but being *a* am bold toward you	2Cor 10:1	548
in word by letters when we are *a*	2Cor 10:11	548
being *a* now I write to them which	2Cor 13:2	548
I write these things being *a*	2Cor 13:10	548
I come and see you, or else be *a*	Phil 1:27	548
For though I be *a* in the flesh	Col 2:5	548

ABSTAIN
that they *a* from pollutions of	Acts 15:20	567
That ye *a* from meats offered to	Acts 15:29	567
that ye should *a* from fornication	1Th 4:3	567
A from all appearance of evil	1Th 5:22	567
and commanding to *a* from meats	1Ti 4:3	567
a from fleshly lusts, which war	1Pet 2:11	567

ABSTINENCE
But after long *a* Paul stood forth	Acts 27:21	776

ABUNDANCE
of heart, for the *a* of all things	Deut 28:47	7230
shall suck of the *a* of the seas	Deut 33:19	8228
for out of the *a* of my complaint	1Sa 1:16	7230
the spoil of the city in great *a*	2Sa 12:30	7235
oxen and fat cattle and sheep in *a*	1Kin 1:19	7230
oxen and fat cattle and sheep in *a*	1Kin 1:25	7230
there came no more such *a* of	1Kin 10:10	7230
trees that are in the vale, for *a*	1Kin 10:27	7230
for there is a sound of *a* of rain	1Kin 18:41	1995
David prepared iron in *a* for the	1Chr 22:3	7230
brass in *a* without weight	1Chr 22:3	7230
Also cedar trees in *a*	1Chr 22:4	369,4557
for it is in *a*	1Chr 22:14	7230
there are workmen with thee in *a*	1Chr 22:15	7230
stones, and marble stones in *a*	1Chr 29:2	7230
sacrifices in *a* for all Israel	1Chr 29:21	7230
trees that are in the vale for *a*	2Chr 1:15	7230
Even to prepare me timber in *a*	2Chr 2:9	7230
made all these vessels in great *a*	2Chr 4:18	7230
that bare spices, and gold in *a*	2Chr 9:1	7230
of gold, and of spices great *a*	2Chr 9:9	7230
that are in the low plains in *a*	2Chr 9:27	7230
and he gave them victual in *a*	2Chr 11:23	7230
carried away sheep and camels in *a*	2Chr 14:15	7230
fell to him out of Israel in *a*	2Chr 15:9	7230
and he had riches and honour in *a*	2Chr 17:5	7230
had riches and honour in *a*	2Chr 18:1	7230
killed sheep and oxen for him in *a*	2Chr 18:2	7230
they found among them in *a* both	2Chr 20:25	7230
by day, and gathered money in *a*	2Chr 24:11	7230
the burnt offerings were in *a*	2Chr 29:35	7230
in *a* the firstfruits of corn	2Chr 31:5	7235
and made darts and shields in *a*	2Chr 32:5	7230
of flocks and herds in *a*	2Chr 32:29	7230
oliveyards, and fruit trees in *a*	Neh 9:25	7230
from another,) and royal wine in *a*	Est 1:7	7227
and *a* of waters cover thee	Job 22:11	8229
he giveth meat in *a*	Job 36:31	4342
that *a* of waters may cover thee	Job 38:34	8229
themselves in the *a* of peace	Ps 37:11	7230
trusted in the *a* of his riches	Ps 52:7	7230
a of peace so long as the moon	Ps 72:7	7230
land brought forth frogs in *a*	Ps 105:30	8317
he that loveth *a* with increase	Eccl 5:10	1995
but the *a* of the rich will not	Eccl 5:12	7647

for the *a* of milk that they shall .... Is 7:22   7230
Therefore the *a* they have gotten, ... Is 15:7   3502
and for the great *a* of thine .... Is 47:9   6109
because the *a* of the sea shall be .... Is 60:5   1995
delighted with the *a* of her glory .... Is 66:11   2123
reveal unto them the *a* of peace .... Jer 33:6   6283
a of idleness was in her and in.............. Eze 16:49   7962
By reason of the *a* of his horses........... Eze 26:10   8229
and silver, and apparel, in great *a*........ Zec 14:14   7230
for out of the *a* of the heart the .... Mt 12:34   4051
be given, and he shall have more *a* ...... Mt 13:12   4052
be given, and he shall have .... Mt 25:29   4052
all they did cast in of their *a* .... Mk 12:44   4052
for of the *a* of the heart his.................. Lk 6:45   4051
in the *a* of the things which he .... Lk 12:15   4052
For all these have of their *a* .... Lk 21:4   4052
they which receive of grace .... Rom 5:17   4050
of affliction the *a* of their joy 2Cor 8:2   4050
that now at this time your *a* may 2Cor 8:14   4051
that their *a* also may be a supply........ 2Cor 8:14   4051
a which is administered by us 2Cor 8:20   100
through the *a* of the revelations 2Cor 12:7   5236
through the *a* of her delicacies .... Rev 18:3   1411

ABUNDANT
and *a* in goodness and truth, ... Ex 34:6   7227
be as this day, and much more *a* .... Is 56:12   1419
a in treasures, thine end is come........... Jer 51:13   7227
these we bestow more *a* honour........... 1Cor 12:23   4055
parts have more *a* comeliness................ 1Cor 12:23   4055
having given more *a* honour to 1Cor 12:24   4055
that the *a* grace might through 2Cor 4:15   4121
affection is more *a* toward you............. 2Cor 7:15   4056
the saints, but is *a* also by many 2Cor 9:12   4052
in labours more *a*, in stripes 2Cor 11:23   4056
a in Jesus Christ for me by my .... Phil 1:26   4052
Lord was exceeding *a* with faith............ 1Ti 1:14   5250
which according to his *a* mercy............. 1Pet 1:3   4183

ABUNDANTLY
Let the waters bring forth *a* the.............. Gen 1:20   8317
which the waters brought forth *a* .... Gen 1:21   8317
they may breed *a* in the earth .... Gen 8:17   8317
bring forth *a* in the earth, and.............. Gen 9:7   8317
were fruitful, and increased *a* .... Ex 1:7   8317
river shall bring forth frogs *a* .... Ex 8:3   8317
and the water came out *a*, and the .... Num 20:11   7227
wine, and oil, and oxen, and sheep *a* 1Chr 12:40   7230
David prepared *a* before his death 1Chr 22:5   7230
saying, Thou hast shed blood *a* 1Chr 22:8   7230
of all things brought they in *a* 2Chr 31:5   7230
into whose hand God bringeth *a* .... Job 12:6
do drop and distil upon man *a* .... Job 36:28   7227
They shall be *a* satisfied with .... Ps 36:8   7301
waterest the ridges thereof *a*.................. Ps 65:10   7301
I will *a* bless her provision .... Ps 132:15   1288
They shall *a* utter the memory of .... Ps 145:7   5042
drink, yea, drink *a*, O beloved .... Song 5:1   7937
every one shall howl, weeping *a*............ Is 15:3   3381
It shall blossom *a*, and rejoice .... Is 35:2   6524
to our God, for he will *a* pardon .... Is 55:7   7235
and that they might have it more *a* .... Jn 10:10   4053
I laboured more *a* than they all.............. 1Cor 15:10   4054
the world, and more *a* to you-ward 2Cor 1:12   4056
love which I have more *a* unto you........ 2Cor 2:4   4056
by you according to our rule 2Cor 10:15   1519,4050
though the more *a* I love you 2Cor 12:15   4056
that is able to do exceeding *a* .... Eph 3:20   1537,4053
endeavoured the more *a* to see 1Th 2:17   4056
Which he shed on us *a* through .... Titus 3:6   4146
willing that *a* to shew unto the.............. Heb 6:17   4054
shall be ministered unto you *a* 2Pet 1:11   4146

ABUSE
and thrust me through, and *a* me 1Sa 31:4   5953
these uncircumcised come and *a* me 1Chr 10:4   5953
that I *a* not my power in the 1Cor 9:18   2710

ABUSED
a her all the night until the .... Judg 19:25   5953

ABUSERS
nor *a* of themselves with mankind, ... 1Cor 6:9   733

ABUSING
that use this world, as not *a* it 1Cor 7:31   2710

ACBOR See ACHBOR.

ACCAD (ak´·kad) A city of Shinar.
kingdom was Babel, and Erech, and *A* .. Gen 10:10   390

ACCEPT
peradventure he will *a* of me .... Gen 32:20   5375
the owner of it shall *a* thereof .... Ex 22:11   3947

they then *a* of the punishment of .... Lev 26:41   7521
they shall *a* of the punishment of .... Lev 26:43   7521
and *a* the work of his hands.................... Deut 33:11   7521
against me, let him *a* an offering 1Sa 26:19   7306
the king, The LORD thy God *a* thee........ 2Sa 24:23   7521
Will ye *a* his person................................. Job 13:8   5375
you, if ye do secretly *a* persons............. Job 13:10   5375
a any man's person, neither let .... Job 32:21   5375
for him will I *a* .... Job 42:8   5375
and *a* thy burnt sacrifice .... Ps 20:3   1878
a the persons of the wicked .... Ps 82:2   5375
A, I beseech thee, the freewill .... Ps 119:108   7521
It is not good to *a* the person of .... Prov 18:5   5375
the LORD doth not *a* them...................... Jer 14:10   7521
and an oblation, I will not *a* them .... Jer 14:12   7521
there will I *a* them, and there.................. Eze 20:40   7521
I will *a* you with your sweet .... Eze 20:41   7521
and I will *a* you, saith the Lord.............. Eze 43:27   7521
meat offerings, I will not *a* them .... Amos 5:22   7521
with thee, or *a* thy person .... Mal 1:8   5375
neither will I *a* an offering at .... Mal 1:10   7521
should I *a* this of your hand .... Mal 1:13   7521
We *a* it always, and in all places, ... Acts 24:3   588

ACCEPTABLE
for it shall not be *a* for you .... Lev 22:20   7522
let him be *a* to his brethren, and........... Deut 33:24   7522
be *a* in thy sight, O LORD, my .... Ps 19:14   7522
unto thee, O LORD, in an *a* time............. Ps 69:13   7522
of the righteous know what is *a* .... Prov 10:32   7522
judgment is more *a* to the LORD............ Prov 21:3   977
sought to find out *a* words...................... Eccl 12:10   2656
In an *a* time have I heard thee, ... Is 49:8   7522
a fast, and an *a* day to the LORD............ Is 58:5   7522
To proclaim the *a* year of the .... Is 61:2   7522
your burnt offerings are not *a* .... Jer 6:20   7522
let my counsel be *a* unto thee .... Dan 4:27   8232
To preach the *a* year of the Lord .... Lk 4:19   1184
a unto God, which is your .... Rom 12:1   2101
may prove what is that good, and *a*....... Rom 12:2   2101
things serveth Christ is *a* to God .... Rom 14:18   2101
up of the Gentiles might be *a*................. Rom 15:16   2144
Proving what is *a* unto the Lord .... Eph 5:10   2101
of a sweet smell, a sacrifice *a* .... Phil 4:18   1184
a in the sight of God our Saviour 1Ti 2:3   587
for that is good and *a* before God.......... 1Ti 5:4   587
a to God by Jesus Christ......................... 1Pet 2:5   2144
it patiently, this is *a* with God 1Pet 2:20   5285

ACCEPTABLY
we may serve God *a* with reverence ...... Heb 12:28   2102

ACCEPTANCE
come up with *a* on mine altar .... Is 60:7   7522

ACCEPTATION
saying, and worthy of all *a* 1Ti 1:15   594
saying and worthy of all *a*...................... 1Ti 4:9   594

ACCEPTED
doest well, shalt thou not be *a* .... Gen 4:7   7613
I have *a* thee concerning this .... Gen 19:21   5375
they may be *a* before the LORD............... Ex 28:38   7522
it shall be *a* for him to make.................. Lev 1:4   7521
the third day, it shall not be *a* .... Lev 7:18   7521
should it have been *a* in the .... Lev 10:19   3190
it shall not be *a* .... Lev 19:7   7521
it shall be perfect to be *a* .... Lev 22:21   7522
but for a vow it shall not be *a* .... Lev 22:23   7521
they shall not be *a* for you..................... Lev 22:25   7521
thenceforth it shall be *a* for an .... Lev 22:27   7521
before the LORD, to be *a* for you .... Lev 23:11   7522
he was *a* in the sight of all the.............. 1Sa 18:5   3190
thy voice, and have *a* thy person........... 1Sa 25:35   5375
a of the multitude of his.......................... Est 10:3   7521
the LORD also *a* Job .... Job 42:9   5375
shall be *a* upon mine altar .... Is 56:7   7522
I pray thee, be *a* before thee .... Jer 37:20   5307
our supplication be *a* before thee .... Jer 42:2   5307
No prophet is *a* in his own.................... Lk 4:24   1184
righteousness, is *a* with him .... Acts 10:35   1184
Jerusalem may be *a* of the saints .... Rom 15:31   2144
or absent, we may be *a* of him................ 2Cor 5:9   2101
I have heard thee in a time *a* 2Cor 6:2   1184
behold, now is the time *a* 2Cor 6:2   2144
it is *a* according to that a man 2Cor 8:12   2144
For indeed he *a* the exhortation 2Cor 8:17   1209
gospel, which ye have not *a* 2Cor 11:4   1209
he hath made us *a* in the beloved .... Eph 1:6   5487

ACCEPTEST
neither *a* thou the person of any, ... Lk 20:21   2983

ACCEPTETH

How much less to him that *a* not	Job 34:19	5375
for God now *a* thy works	Eccl 9:7	7521
but the LORD *a* them not	Hos 8:13	7521
God *a* no man's person	Gal 2:6	2983

ACCEPTING

were tortured, not a deliverance	Heb 11:35	4327

ACCESS

By whom also we have *a* by faith	Rom 5:2	4318
For through him we both have *a* by	Eph 2:18	4318
a with confidence by the faith of	Eph 3:12	4318

ACCHO *(ak'-ko) A coastal city in Asher.*

drive out the inhabitants of *A*	Judg 1:31	5910

ACCO See ACCHO.

ACCOMPANIED

certain brethren from Joppa *a* him	Acts 10:23	4905
these six brethren *a* me	Acts 11:12	2064,4862
there *a* him into Asia Sopater of	Acts 20:4	4902
And they *a* him unto the ship	Acts 20:38	4311

ACCOMPANY

you, and things that *a* salvation	Heb 6:9	2192

ACCOMPANYING

was at Gibeah, *a* the ark of God	2Sa 6:4	5973

ACCOMPLISH

unto the LORD to *a* his vow	Lev 22:21	6381
and thou shalt *a* my desire	1Kin 5:9	6213
that he may rest, till he shall *a*	Job 14:6	7521
they *a* a diligent search	Ps 64:6	8552
but it shall *a* that which I	Is 55:11	6213
ye will surely *a* your vows	Jer 44:25	6965
thus will I *a* my fury upon them	Eze 6:12	3615
thee, and *a* mine anger upon thee	Eze 7:8	3615
Thus will I *a* my wrath upon the	Eze 13:15	3615
to *a* my anger against them in the	Eze 20:8	3615
to *a* my anger against them in the	Eze 20:21	3615
that he would *a* seventy years in	Dan 9:2	4390
which he should *a* at Jerusalem	Lk 9:31	4137

ACCOMPLISHED

the mouth of Jeremiah might be *a*	2Chr 36:22	3615
the days of their purifications *a*	Est 2:12	4390
It shall be before his time, and	Job 15:32	4390
The desire *a* is sweet to the soul	Prov 13:19	1961
unto her, that her warfare is *a*	Is 40:2	4390
to pass, when seventy years are *a*	Jer 25:12	4390
and of your dispersions are *a*	Jer 25:34	4390
be *a* at Babylon I will visit you	Jer 29:10	4390
they shall be *a* in that day	Jer 39:16	
The LORD hath *a* his fury	Lam 4:11	3615
punishment of thine iniquity is *a*	Lam 4:22	8552
And when thou hast *a* them, lie	Eze 4:6	3615
Thus shall mine anger be *a*	Eze 5:13	3615
when I have *a* my fury in them	Eze 5:13	3615
prosper till the indignation be *a*	Dan 11:36	3615
when he shall have *a* to scatter	Dan 12:7	3615
days of his ministration were *a*	Lk 1:23	4130
the days were *a* that she should	Lk 2:6	4130
when eight days were *a* for the	Lk 2:21	4130
to the law of Moses were *a*	Lk 2:22	4130
how am I straitened till it be *a*	Lk 12:50	5055
the Son of man shall be *a*	Lk 18:31	5055
is written must yet be *a* in me	Lk 22:37	5055
that all things were now *a*	Jn 19:28	5055
And when we had *a* those days	Acts 21:5	1822
a in your brethren that are in	1Pet 5:9	2005

ACCOMPLISHING

tabernacle, *a* the service of God	Heb 9:6	2005

ACCOMPLISHMENT

to signify the *a* of the days of	Acts 21:26	1604

ACCORD

a of thy harvest thou shalt not	Lev 25:5	5599
Joshua and with Israel, with one *a*	Josh 9:2	6310
continued with one *a* in prayer	Acts 1:14	3661
were all with one *a* in one place	Acts 2:1	3661
daily with one *a* in the temple	Acts 2:46	3661
up their voice to God with one *a*	Acts 4:24	3661
all with one *a* in Solomon's porch	Acts 5:12	3661
ears, and ran upon him with one *a*	Acts 7:57	3661
the people with one *a* gave heed	Acts 8:6	3661
which opened to them of his own *a*	Acts 12:10	844
but they came with one *a* to him	Acts 12:20	3661
us, being assembled with one *a*	Acts 15:25	3661
with one *a* against Paul, and	Acts 18:12	3661
with one *a* into the theatre	Acts 19:29	3661
of his own *a* he went unto you	2Cor 8:17	830
the same love, being of one *a*	Phil 2:2	4861

ACCORDING See APPENDIX.

ACCORDINGLY

a he will repay, fury to his	Is 59:18	5922

ACCOUNT

of every one that passeth the *a*	2Kin 12:4	
was the number put in the *a* of	1Chr 27:24	4557
to the number of their *a* by the	2Chr 26:11	6486
for he giveth not *a* of any of his	Job 33:13	6030
of man, that thou makest *a* of him	Ps 144:3	2803
one by one, to find out the *a*	Eccl 7:27	2808
they shall give *a* thereof in the	Mt 12:36	3056
would take *a* of his servants	Mt 18:23	3056
give an *a* of thy stewardship	Lk 16:2	3056
may give an *a* of this concourse	Acts 19:40	3056
us shall give *a* of himself to God	Rom 14:12	3056
Let a man so *a* of us, as of the	1Cor 4:1	3049
fruit that may abound to your *a*	Phil 4:17	3056
thee ought, put that on mine *a*	Philem 1:18	1677
souls, as they that must give *a*	Heb 13:17	3056
Who shall give *a* to him that is	1Pet 4:5	3056
a that the longsuffering of our	2Pet 3:15	2233

ACCOUNTED

Which also were *a* giants, as the	Deut 2:11	2803
(That also was *a* a land of giants	Deut 2:20	2803
it was nothing *a* of in the days	1Kin 10:21	2803
it was not any thing *a* of in the	2Chr 9:20	2803
it shall be *a* to the Lord for a	Ps 22:30	5608
for wherein is he to be *a* of	Is 2:22	2803
are *a* to rule over the Gentiles	Mk 10:42	1380
But they which shall be *a* worthy	Lk 20:35	2661
that ye may be *a* worthy to escape	Lk 21:36	2661
of them should be *a* the greatest	Lk 22:24	1380
we are *a* as sheep for the	Rom 8:36	3049
it was *a* to him for righteousness	Gal 3:6	3049

ACCOUNTING

A that God was able to raise him	Heb 11:19	3049

ACCOUNTS

princes might give *a* unto them	Dan 6:2	2941

ACCURSED

for he that is hanged is *a* of God	Deut 21:23	7045
And the city shall be *a*, even it,	Josh 6:17	2764
keep yourselves from the *a* thing	Josh 6:18	2764
lest ye make yourselves *a*	Josh 6:18	2763
when ye take of the *a* thing	Josh 6:18	2764
a trespass in the *a* thing	Josh 7:1	2764
of Judah, took of the *a* thing	Josh 7:1	2764
have even taken of the *a* thing	Josh 7:11	2764
enemies, because they were *a*	Josh 7:12	2764
ye destroy the *a* from among you	Josh 7:12	2764
There is an *a* thing in the midst	Josh 7:13	2764
away the *a* thing from among you	Josh 7:13	2764
a thing shall be burnt with fire	Josh 7:15	2764
commit a trespass in the *a* thing	Josh 22:20	2764
who transgressed in the thing *a*	1Chr 2:7	2764
an hundred years old shall be *a*	Is 65:20	7043
a from Christ for my brethren	Rom 9:3	331
the Spirit of God calleth Jesus *a*	1Cor 12:3	331
preached unto you, let him be *a*	Gal 1:8	331
ye have received, let him be *a*	Gal 1:9	331

ACCUSATION

wrote they unto him an *a* against	Ezr 4:6	7855
up over his head his *a* written	Mt 27:37	156
of his *a* was written over	Mk 15:26	156
they might find an *a* against him	Lk 6:7	2724
any thing from any man by false *a*	Lk 19:8	4811
What *a* bring ye against this man	Jn 18:29	2724
they brought none *a* of such	Acts 25:18	156
Against an elder receive not an *a*	1Ti 5:19	2724
bring not railing *a* against them	2Pet 2:11	2920
not bring against him a railing *a*	Jude 9	2920

ACCUSE

A not a servant unto his master,	Prov 30:10	3960
that they might *a* him	Mt 12:10	2723
that they might *a* him	Mk 3:2	2723
to no man, neither *a* any falsely	Lk 3:14	4811
his mouth, that they might *a* him	Lk 11:54	2722
And they began to *a* him, saying,	Lk 23:2	2722
those things whereof ye *a* him	Lk 23:14	2722
that I will *a* you to the Father	Jn 5:45	2722
that they might have to *a* him	Jn 8:6	2722
forth, Tertullus began to *a* him	Acts 24:2	2722
these things, whereof we *a* him	Acts 24:8	2722
the things whereof they now *a* me	Acts 24:13	2722
a this man, if there be any	Acts 25:5	2722
these things whereof these *a* me	Acts 25:11	2722
I had ought to *a* my nation of	Acts 28:19	2722
a your good conversation in	1Pet 3:16	1908

ACCUSED
came near, and *a* the Jews .... Dan 3:8 399,7170
those men which had *a* Daniel .... Dan 6:24 399,7170
when he was *a* of the chief .... Mt 27:12 2723
the chief priests *a* him of many .... Mk 15:3 2723
the same was *a* unto him that he .... Lk 16:1 1225
scribes stood and vehemently *a* him ... Lk 23:10 2722
wherefore he was *a* of the Jews .... Acts 22:30 2722
the cause wherefore they *a* him .... Acts 23:28 1458
Whom I perceived to be *a* of .... Acts 23:29 1458
before that he which is a have .... Acts 25:16 2722
things whereof I am *a* of the Jews ..... Acts 26:2 1458
king Agrippa, I am *a* of the Jews .... Acts 26:7 1458
children not *a* of riot or unruly .... Titus 1:6 1722,2724
which *a* them before our God day .... Rev 12:10 2722

ACCUSER
for the *a* of our brethren is cast .... Rev 12:10 2723

ACCUSERS
Woman, where are those thine *a* .... Jn 8:10 2723
gave commandment to his *a* also to ...... Acts 23:30 2723
when thine *a* are also come .... Acts 23:35 2723
Commanding his *a* to come unto .... Acts 24:8 2723
accused have the *a* face to face .... Acts 25:16 2723
Against whom when the *a* stood up ...... Acts 25:18 2723
affection, trucebreakers, false *a* 2Ti 3:3 1228
as becometh holiness, not false *a* .... Titus 2:3 1228

ACCUSETH
there is one that *a* you, even .... Jn 5:45 2723

ACCUSING
a or else excusing one another .... Rom 2:15 2722

ACCUSTOMED
do good, that are *a* to do evil .... Jer 13:23 3928

ACELDAMA (as-el'-dam-ah) *A burial ground bought with Judas' betrayal money.*
called in their proper tongue, A .... Acts 1:19 184

ACHAIA (ak-ah'-yah) *Roman province in Greece.*
when Gallio was the deputy of A .... Acts 18:12 882
he was disposed to pass into A .... Acts 18:27 882
had passed through Macedonia and A ..... Acts 19:21 882
A to make a certain contribution .... Rom 15:26 882
the firstfruits of A unto Christ .... Rom 16:5 882
that it is the firstfruits of A 1Cor 16:15 882
all the saints which are in all A 2Cor 1:1 882
that A was ready a year ago 2Cor 9:2 882
this boasting in the regions of A 2Cor 11:10 882
that believe in Macedonia and A 1Th 1:7 882
Lord not only in Macedonia and A 1Th 1:8 882

ACHAICUS (ak-ah'-yah-cus) *A Corinthian who visited Paul in Philippi.*
of Stephanas and Fortunatus and A 1Cor 16:17 883
by Stephanus, and Fortunatus, and A .... 1Cor s

ACHAN (a'-kan) See ACHAR. *Soldier under Joshua executed for disobedience.*
for A, the son of Carmi, the son .... Josh 7:1 5912
and A, the son of Carmi, the son .... Josh 7:18 5912
And Joshua said unto A, My son, ... Josh 7:19 5912
A answered Joshua, and said, ... Josh 7:20 5912
took A the son of Zerah, and the .... Josh 7:24 5912
Did not A the son of Zerah commit .... Josh 22:20 5912

ACHAR (a'-kar) See ACHAN. *A form of Achan.*
A, the troubler of Israel, who 1Chr 2:7 5917

ACHAZ (a'-kaz) See AHAZ. *The Greek form of Ahaz.*
and Joatham begat A .... Mt 1:9 881
and A begat Ezekias .... Mt 1:9 881

ACHBOR (ak'-bor)
1. Father of an Edomite king.
the son of A reigned in his stead .... Gen 36:38 5907
And Baal-hanan the son of A died .... Gen 36:39 5907
the son of A reigned in his stead 1Chr 1:49 5907
2. A messenger of Josiah to Huldah.
A the son of Michaiah, and Shaphan 2Kin 22:12 5907
the priest, and Ahikam, and A 2Kin 22:14 5907
3. Father of Elnathan.
namely, Elnathan the son of A .... Jer 26:22 5907
and Elnathan the son of A .... Jer 36:12 5907

ACHIM (a'-kim) *Son of Sadoc; ancestor of Jesus.*
and Sadoc begat A .... Mt 1:14 885
and A begat Eliud .... Mt 1:14 885

ACHISH (a'-kish)
1. A king of Gath who aided David.
went to A the king of Gath 1Sa 21:10 397
the servants of A said unto him 1Sa 21:11 397
sore afraid of A the king of Gath 1Sa 21:12 397
Then said A unto his servants, Lo 1Sa 21:14 397

men that were with him unto A 1Sa 27:2 397
And David dwelt with A at Gath 1Sa 27:3 397
And David said unto A, If I have 1Sa 27:5 397
Then A gave him Ziklag that day 1Sa 27:6 397
and returned, and came to A 1Sa 27:9 397
A said, Whither have ye made a 1Sa 27:10 397
A believed David, saying, He hath 1Sa 27:12 397
A said unto David, Know thou 1Sa 28:1 397
And David said to A, Surely thou 1Sa 28:2 397
A said to David, Therefore will I 1Sa 28:2 397
passed on in the rereward with A 1Sa 29:2 397
A said unto the princes of the 1Sa 29:3 397
Then A called David, and said unto 1Sa 29:6 397
And David said unto A, But what 1Sa 29:8 397
A answered and said to David, I 1Sa 29:9 397
2. A king of Gath during Solomon's reign.
of Shimei ran away unto A son of 1Kin 2:39 397
went to Gath to A to seek his 1Kin 2:40 397

ACHMETHA (ak'-meth-ah) *A city in Media.*
And there was found at A, in the .... Ezr 6:2 307

ACHOR (a'-kor) *A valley near Jericho.*
brought them unto the valley of A .... Josh 7:24 5911
place was called, The valley of A .... Josh 7:26 5911
toward Debir from the valley of A .... Josh 15:7 5911
the valley of A a place for the .... Is 65:10 5911
the valley of A for a door of .... Hos 2:15 5911

ACHSA (ak'-sah) See ACHSAH. *Daughter of Caleb.*
and the daughter of Caleb was A 1Chr 2:49 5915

ACHSAH (ak'-sah) See ACHSA. *A form of Achsa.*
to him will I give A my daughter .... Josh 15:16 5915
he gave him A his daughter to .... Josh 15:17 5915
to him will I give A my daughter .... Judg 1:12 5919
he gave him A his daughter to .... Judg 1:13 5919

ACHSHAPH (ak'-shaf) *A Phoenician city in Asher.*
of Shimron, and to the king of A .... Josh 11:1 407
the king of A, one .... Josh 12:20 407
Helkath, and Hali, and Beten, and A ..... Josh 19:25 407

ACHZIB (ak'-zib) See CHEZIB.
1. A town in western Judah.
And Keilah, and A, and Mareshah .... Josh 15:44 392
the houses of A shall be a lie .... Mic 1:14 392
2. A coastal city in Asher.
at the sea from the coast to A .... Josh 19:29 392
of Zidon, nor of Ahlab, nor of A .... Judg 1:31 392

ACKNOWLEDGE
But he shall *a* the son of the .... Deut 21:17 5234
neither did he *a* his brethren .... Deut 33:9 5234
For I *a* my transgressions .... Ps 51:3 3045
In all thy ways *a* him, and he .... Prov 3:6 3045
and, ye that are near, *a* my might .... Is 33:13 3045
all that see them shall *a* them .... Is 61:9 5234
of us, and Israel *a* us not .... Is 63:16 5234
Only *a* thine iniquity, that thou .... Jer 3:13 3045
We *a*, O LORD, our wickedness, and ..... Jer 14:20 3045
so will I *a* them that are carried .... Jer 24:5 5234
a strange god, whom he shall *a* .... Dan 11:39 5234
till they *a* their offence, and .... Hos 5:15
let him *a* that the things that I 1Cor 14:37 1921
therefore *a* ye them that are such 1Cor 16:18 1921
unto you, than what ye read or *a* 2Cor 1:13 1921
trust ye shall *a* even to the end 2Cor 1:13 1921

ACKNOWLEDGED
And Judah *a* them, and said, She .... Gen 38:26 5234
I *a* my sin unto thee, and mine .... Ps 32:5 3045
As also ye have *a* us in part 2Cor 1:14 1922

ACKNOWLEDGEMENT
to the *a* of the mystery of God, ... Col 2:2 1922

ACKNOWLEDGETH
{ but } he that *a* the Son hath 1Jn 2:23

ACKNOWLEDGING
repentance to the *a* of the truth 2Ti 2:25 1922
the *a* of the truth which is after .... Titus 1:1 1922
may become effectual by the *a* of .... Philem 6 1922

ACQUAINT
A now thyself with him, and be at .... Job 22:21 5532

ACQUAINTANCE
it to them, every man of his *a* 2Kin 12:5 4378
receive no more money of your *a* 2Kin 12:7 4378
mine *a* are verily estranged from .... Job 19:13 3045
that had been of his *a* before .... Job 42:11 3045
neighbours, and a fear to mine *a* .... Ps 31:11 3045
mine equal, my guide, and mine *a* .... Ps 55:13 3045
hast put away mine *a* far from me .... Ps 88:8 3045
from me, and mine *a* into darkness ...... Ps 88:18 3045
him among their kinsfolk and *a* .... Lk 2:44 1110

And all his *a*, and the women that..........	Lk 23:49	*1110*
a to minister or come unto him	Acts 24:23	*2398*

ACQUAINTED

down, and art *a* with all my ways	Ps 139:3	5532
a man of sorrows, and *a* with grief	Is 53:3	3045

ACQUAINTING

yet *a* mine heart with wisdom	Eccl 2:3	5090

ACQUIT

thou wilt not *a* me from mine..................	Job 10:14	5352
and will not at all *a* the wicked	Nah 1:3	5352

ACRE

as it were an half *a* of land	1Sa 14:14	4618

ACRES

ten *a* of vineyard shall yield one	Is 5:10	6776

ACSAH See ACHSA.

ACSHAPH See ACHSHAPH.

ACT

to pass his *a*, his strange *a*	Is 28:21	5556
the *a* of violence is in their	Is 59:6	6467
taken in adultery, in the very *a*	Jn 8:4	*1888*

ACTIONS

and by him *a* are weighed......................	1Sa 2:3	5949

ACTIVITY

knowest any men of *a* among them	Gen 47:6	2428

ACTS

And his miracles, and his *a*....................	Deut 11:3	4640
great *a* of the LORD which he did	Deut 11:7	4640
the righteous *a* of the LORD	Judg 5:11	
even the righteous *a* toward the	Judg 5:11	
all the righteous *a* of the LORD................	1Sa 12:7	
of Kabzeel, who had done many *a*...........	2Sa 23:20	6467
I heard in mine own land of thy *a*	1Kin 10:6	1697
And the rest of the *a* of Solomon	1Kin 11:41	1697
in the book of the *a* of Solomon	1Kin 11:41	1697
And the rest of the *a* of Jeroboam	1Kin 14:19	1697
Now the rest of the *a* of Rehoboam	1Kin 14:29	1697
The rest of all the *a* of Asa......................	1Kin 15:7	1697
Now the rest of the *a* of Nadab................	1Kin 15:23	1697
Now the rest of the *a* of Baasha..............	1Kin 15:31	1697
Now the rest of the *a* of Elah	1Kin 16:5	1697
Now the rest of the *a* of Zimri.................	1Kin 16:14	1697
Now the rest of the *a* of Omri.................	1Kin 16:20	1697
Now the rest of the *a* of Ahab	1Kin 16:27	1697
the rest of the *a* of Jehoshaphat	1Kin 22:39	1697
Now the rest of the *a* of Ahaziah.............	1Kin 22:45	1697
And the rest of the *a* of Joram	2Kin 1:18	1697
Now the rest of the *a* of Jehu	2Kin 8:23	1697
And the rest of the *a* of Joash	2Kin 10:34	1697
Now the rest of the *a* of Jehoahaz	2Kin 12:19	1697
And the rest of the *a* of Joash	2Kin 13:8	1697
And the rest of the *a* of Jehoash	2Kin 13:12	1697
And the rest of the *a* of Amaziah	2Kin 14:15	1697
Now the rest of the *a* of Jeroboam...........	2Kin 14:18	1697
And the rest of the *a* of Azariah	2Kin 14:28	1697
And the rest of the *a* of Zachariah	2Kin 15:6	1697
And the rest of the *a* of Shallum	2Kin 15:11	1697
And the rest of the *a* of Menahem	2Kin 15:15	1697
And the rest of the *a* of Pekahiah...........	2Kin 15:21	1697
And the rest of the *a* of Pekah	2Kin 15:26	1697
Now the rest of the *a* of Jotham	2Kin 15:31	1697
And the rest of the *a* of Ahaz	2Kin 15:36	1697
And the rest of the *a* of Hezekiah...........	2Kin 16:19	1697
Now the rest of the *a* of Manasseh	2Kin 20:20	1697
Now the rest of the *a* of Amon	2Kin 21:17	1697
the *a* that he had done in Beth-el	2Kin 21:25	1697
Now the rest of the *a* of Josiah	2Kin 23:19	4640
the rest of the *a* of Jehoiakim	2Kin 23:28	1697
of Kabzeel, who had done many *a*..........	2Kin 24:5	1697
Now the *a* of David the king..................	1Chr 11:22	6467
heard in mine own land of thine *a*	1Chr 29:29	1697
Now the *a* of Solomon	2Chr 9:5	1697
Now the *a* of Rehoboam, first and	2Chr 9:29	1697
And the rest of the *a* of Abijah	2Chr 12:15	1697
the *a* of Asa, first and last, lo, ...	2Chr 13:22	1697
the rest of the *a* of Jehoshaphat	2Chr 16:11	1697
Now the rest of the *a* of Amaziah	2Chr 20:34	1697
Now the rest of the *a* of Uzziah.............	2Chr 25:26	1697
Now the rest of the *a* of Jotham	2Chr 26:22	1697
Now the rest of his *a* and of all.............	2Chr 27:7	1697
Now the rest of the *a* of Hezekiah..........	2Chr 28:26	1697
Now the rest of the *a* of Manasseh	2Chr 32:32	1697
Now the rest of the *a* of Josiah	2Chr 33:18	1697
the rest of the *a* of Jehoiakim	2Chr 35:26	1697
all the *a* of his power and his	2Chr 36:8	1697
	Est 10:2	4640

his *a* unto the children of Israel..............	Ps 103:7	5949
utter the mighty *a* of the LORD...............	Ps 106:2	
and shall declare thy mighty *a*	Ps 145:4	
of the might of thy terrible *a*	Ps 145:6	
to the sons of men his mighty *a*	Ps 145:12	
Praise him for his mighty *a*	Ps 150:2	

ACZIB See ACHZIB.

ADADAH (*ad'-ad-ah*) *A city in southern Judah.*

And Kinah, and Dimonah, and *A*	Josh 15:22	5735

ADAH (*a'-dah*)
  1. A wife of Lemech.

the name of the one was *A*	Gen 4:19	5711
And *A* bare Jabal...................................	Gen 4:20	5711
And Lamech said unto his wives, *A*	Gen 4:23	5711

  2. A wife of Esau.

A the daughter of Elon the	Gen 36:2	5711
And *A* bare to Esau Eliphaz	Gen 36:4	5711
the son of *A* the wife of Esau	Gen 36:10	5711
were the sons of *A* Esau's wife	Gen 36:12	5711
these were the sons of *A*	Gen 36:16	5711

ADAIAH (*ad-a-i'-yah*)
  1. Grandfather of King Josiah.

the daughter of *A* of Boscath	2Kin 22:1	5718

  2. A Levite descendant of Gershon.

the son of Zerah, the son of *A*	1Chr 6:41	5718

  3. A son of Shimhi.

And *A*, and Beraiah, and Shimrath, ...	1Chr 8:21	5718

  4. A Levite of Jerusalem.

A the son of Jeroham, the son of.............	1Chr 9:12	5718

  5. Father of Maaseiah.

of Obed, and Maaseiah the son of *A*	2Chr 23:1	5718

  6. Married a foreign wife in Exile.

Meshullam, Malluch, and *A*, ...	Ezr 10:29	5718

  7. Married a foreign wife in Exile.

And Shelemiah, and Nathan, and *A*	Ezr 10:39	5718

  8. A descendant of Pharez.

the son of Hazaiah, the son of *A*.............	Neh 11:5	5718

  9. An Aaronite Levite.

A the son of Jeroham, the son of.............	Neh 11:12	5718

ADALIA (*ad-al-i'-yah*) *A son of Haman.*

And Poratha, and *A*, and Aridatha, ...	Est 9:8	118

ADAM (*ad'-um*) See ADAM'S.
  1. First man created by God.

brought them unto *A* to see what	Gen 2:19	120
whatsoever *A* called every living............	Gen 2:19	120
A gave names to all cattle, and to	Gen 2:20	120
but for *A* there was not found an............	Gen 2:20	120
a deep sleep to fall upon *A*	Gen 2:21	121
A said, This is now bone of my	Gen 2:23	120
and *A* and his wife hid themselves.........	Gen 3:8	120
And the LORD God called unto *A*	Gen 3:9	120
unto *A* he said, Because thou hast	Gen 3:17	121
A called his wife's name Eve	Gen 3:20	120
Unto *A* also and to his wife did..............	Gen 3:21	120
And *A* knew Eve his wife........................	Gen 4:1	120
And *A* knew his wife again	Gen 4:25	120
the book of the generations of *A*	Gen 5:1	120
them, and called their name *A*	Gen 5:2	120
A lived an hundred and thirty	Gen 5:3	121
the days of *A* after he had	Gen 5:4	121
all the days that *A* lived were	Gen 5:5	121
when he separated the sons of *A*	Deut 32:8	120
A, Sheth, Enosh,...................................	1Chr 1:1	121
I covered my transgressions as *A*	Job 31:33	121
of Seth, which was the son of *A*	Lk 3:38	76
death reigned from *A* to Moses	Rom 5:14	76
For as in *A* all die, even so in.................	1Cor 15:22	76
The first man *A* was made a living	1Cor 15:45	76
the last *A* was made a quickening	1Cor 15:45	76
For *A* was first formed, then Eve	1Ti 2:13	76
A was not deceived, but the woman	1Ti 2:14	76
And Enoch also, the seventh from *A*	Jude 14	76

  2. A town in Manasseh.

an heap very far from the city *A*	Josh 3:16	121

ADAMAH (*ad'-am-ah*) *A walled city in Naphtali.*

And *A*, and Ramah, and Hazor,..............	Josh 19:36	128

ADAMANT

As an *a* harder than flint have I	Eze 3:9	8068
made their hearts as an *a* stone	Zec 7:12	8068

ADAMI (*ad'-am-i*) *A variant of Adamah.*

from Allon to Zaanannim, and *A*.............	Josh 19:33	129

ADAMI NEKEB See NEKEB.

ADAM'S (*ad'-ums*)

the similitude of *A* transgression...........	Rom 5:14	76

ADAR (a'-dar) See ADDAR, ATABOTH-ADAR.

1. A city in southern Judah.
along to Hezron, and went up to A ....Josh 15:3   146
2. Twelfth month of the Hebrew year.
on the third day of the month A ....Ezr 6:15   144
month, that is, the month A ....Est 3:7   143
month, which is the month A ....Est 3:13   143
month, which is the month A ....Est 8:12   143
month, that is, the month A ....Est 9:1   143
day also of the month A, and slew ....Est 9:15   143
the thirteenth day of the month A ....Est 9:17   143
of the month A a day of gladness ....Est 9:19   143
the fourteenth day of the month A ....Est 9:21   143

ADBEEL (ad'-be-el) Son of Ishmael.
and Kedar, and A, and Mibsam, ...Gen 25:13   110
then Kedar, and A, and Mibsam, ...1Chr 1:29   110

ADD
The LORD shall a to me another ....Gen 30:24   3254
shall a the fifth part thereto,.................Lev 5:16   3254
shall a the fifth part more.....................Lev 6:5   3254
then he shall a a fifth part ....Lev 27:13   3254
then he shall a the fifth part of.............Lev 27:15   3254
then he shall a the fifth part of ....Lev 27:19   3254
shall a a fifth part of it ....Lev 27:27   3254
he shall a thereto the fifth part ....Lev 27:31   3254
a unto it the fifth part thereof, ...Num 5:7   3254
and to them ye shall a forty ....Num 35:6   5414
Ye shall not a unto the word ....Deut 4:2   3254
thou shalt not a thereto, nor ....Deut 12:32   3254
then shalt thou a three cities ....Deut 19:9   3254
to a drunkenness to thirst ....Deut 29:19   5595
LORD thy God a unto the people 2Sa 24:3   3254
heavy yoke, I will a to your yoke 1Kin 12:11   3254
heavy, and I will a to your yoke 1Kin 12:14   3254
I will a unto thy days fifteen 2Kin 20:6   3254
and thou mayest a thereto 1Chr 22:14   3254
yoke heavy, but I will a thereto 2Chr 10:14   3254
ye intend to a more to our sins 2Chr 28:13   3254
A iniquity unto their iniquity ....Ps 69:27   5414
and peace, shall they a to thee ....Prov 3:2   3254
A thou not unto his words, lest ....Prov 30:6   3254
a ye year to year ....Is 29:1   5595
that they may a sin to sin ....Is 30:1   5595
I will a unto thy days fifteen ....Is 38:5   3254
can a one cubit unto his stature............Mt 6:27   4369
can a to his stature one cubit ....Lk 12:25   4369
supposing to a affliction to my ....Phil 1:16   2018
diligence, a to your faith virtue 2Pet 1:5   2023
If any man shall a unto these ....Rev 22:18   2007
God shall a unto him the plagues ....Rev 22:18   2007

ADDAN (ad'-dan) Home of some Exiles in Babylon.
Tel-melah, Tel-harsa, Cherub, A ....Ezr 2:59   135

ADDAR (ad'-dar) See ADAR, ATAROTH-ADDAR. Son of Bela.
And the sons of Bela were, A 1Chr 8:3   146

ADDED
and he a no more ....Deut 5:22   3254
for we have a unto all our sins...............1Sa 12:19   3254
there were a besides unto them ....Jer 36:32   3254
for the LORD hath a grief to my ....Jer 45:3   3254
excellent majesty was a unto me ....Dan 4:36   3255
these things shall be a unto you ....Mt 6:33   4369
A yet this above all, that he ....Lk 3:20   4369
these things shall be a unto you ....Lk 12:31   4369
as they heard these things, he a ....Lk 19:11   4369
the same day there were a unto...............Acts 2:41   4369
the Lord a to the church daily ....Acts 2:47   4369
were the more a to the Lord....................Acts 5:14   4369
much people was a unto the Lord...........Acts 11:24   4369
in conference a nothing to me ....Gal 2:6   4323
It was a because of ....Gal 3:19   4369

ADDER
an a in the path, that biteth the ....Gen 49:17   8207
the deaf a that stoppeth her ear ....Ps 58:4   6620
shalt tread upon the lion and a ....Ps 91:13   6620
a serpent, and stingeth like an a ....Prov 23:32   6848

ADDERS'
a poison is under their lips.....................Ps 140:3   5919

ADDETH
For he a rebellion unto his sin, ...Job 34:37   3254
rich, and he a no sorrow with it ....Prov 10:22   3254
mouth, and a learning to his lips...........Prov 16:23   3254
no man disannulleth, or a thereto ....Gal 3:15   1928

ADDI (ad'-di) Son of Cozam; ancestor of Jesus.
of Melchi, which was the son of A ....Lk 3:28   78

ADDICTED
that they have a themselves to 1Cor 16:15   5021

ADDITION
molten, at the side of every a 1Kin 7:30   3914

ADDITIONS
were certain a made of thin work...........1Kin 7:29   3914
of every one, and a round about 1Kin 7:36   3914

ADDON (ad'-don) A form of Addan.
Tel-melah, Tel-haresha, Cherub, A ....Neh 7:61   114

ADER (a'-dur) A son of Beriah.
And Zebadiah, and Arad, and A.............1Chr 8:15   5738

ADIEL (a'-de-el)
1. A descendant of Simeon.
and Jeshohaiah, and Asaiah, and A.......1Chr 4:36   5717
2. Father of Massiai.
and Maasiai the son of A, the son 1Chr 9:12   5717
3. Father of Azmaveth.
was Azmaveth the son of A 1Chr 27:25   5717

ADIN (a'-din)
1. Family who returned from exile.
The children of A, four hundred............Ezr 2:15   5720
The children of A, six hundred...............Neh 7:20   5720
2. Family who sealed the covenant with Nehemiah.
Adonijah, Bigvai, A,.............................Neh 10:16   5720
3. An exilic family with Ezra.
Of the sons also of A ....Ezr 8:6   5720

ADINA (ad'-in-ah) A "mighty man" of David.
A the son of Shiza the Reubenite,...........1Chr 11:42   5721

ADINO (ad'-in-o) A "mighty man" of David.
the same was A the Eznite 2Sa 23:8   5722

ADITHAIM (ad-ith-a'-im) A city in the plain of Judah.
Sharaim, and A, and Gederah, and.........Josh 15:36   5723

ADJURE
How many times shall I a thee 1Kin 22:16   7650
How many times shall I a thee 2Chr 18:15   7650
I a thee by the living God, that...............Mt 26:63   1844
I a thee by God, that thou ....Mk 5:7   3726
We a you by Jesus whom Paul ....Acts 19:13   3726

ADJURED
Joshua a them at that time, ...Josh 6:26   7650
for Saul had a the people 1Sa 14:24   422

ADLAI (ad'-la-i) Father of Shapat.
valleys was Shaphat the son of A 1Chr 27:29   5724

ADMAH (ad'-mah) A city destroyed with Sodom and Gomorrah.
unto Sodom, and Gomorrah, and A.........Gen 10:19   126
of Gomorrah, Shinab king of A ....Gen 14:2   126
of Gomorrah, and the king of A ....Gen 14:8   126
of Sodom, and Gomorrah, A, and ....Deut 29:23   126
how shall I make thee as A ....Hos 11:8   126

ADMATHA (ad'-math-ah) A prince of Persia.
unto him was Carshena, Shethar, A ....Est 1:14   133

ADMINISTERED
which is a by us to the glory of...............2Cor 8:19   1247
this abundance which is a by us 2Cor 8:20   1247

ADMINISTRATION
For the a of this service not....................2Cor 9:12   1248

ADMINISTRATIONS
And there are differences of a 1Cor 12:5   1248

ADMIRATION
persons in a because of advantage ....Jude 16   2296
saw her, I wondered with great a ....Rev 17:6   2295

ADMIRED
to be a in all them that believe 2Th 1:10   2296

ADMONISH
able also to a one another.....................Rom 15:14   3560
over you in the Lord, and a you 1Th 5:12   3560
an enemy, but a him as a brother 2Th 3:15   3560

ADMONISHED
king, who will no more be a ....Eccl 4:13   2094
further, by these, my son, be a ....Eccl 12:12   2094
that I have a you this day ....Jer 42:19   5749
was now already past, Paul a them........Acts 27:9   3867
as Moses was a of God when he ..... Heb 8:5   5537

ADMONISHING
a one another in psalms and hymns ......Col 3:16   3560

ADMONITION
and they are written for our a 1Cor 10:11   3559
in the nurture and a of the Lord.............Eph 6:4   3559
the first and second a reject ....Titus 3:10   3559

ADNA (ad'-nah) See ADNAH.
1. Married a foreigner while in exile.
A, and Chelal, Benaiah, Maaseiah, ... Ezr 10:30   5733
2. A priest during Joiakim's reign.
Of Harim, A................................... Neh 12:15   5733

ADNAH (ad'-nah) See ADNA.
1. A captain in David's army.
there fell to him of Manasseh, A 1Chr 12:20   5734
2. A commander in Jehoshaphat's army.
A the chief, and with him mighty 2Chr 17:14   5734

ADO
unto them, Why make ye this *a* .... Mk 5:39   2350

ADONI-BEZEK (ad'-on-i-be'-zek) A lord of a Canaanite
city.
And they found A in Bezek .... Judg 1:5   137
But A fled .... Judg 1:6   137
A said, Threescore and ten kings, ... Judg 1:7   137

ADONIJAH (ad-on-i'-jah) See TOB-ADONIJAH.
1. A son of David.
the fourth, A the son of Haggith 2Sa 3:4   138
Then A the son of Haggith exalted 1Kin 1:5   138
and they following A helped him 1Kin 1:7   138
to David, were not with A 1Kin 1:8   138
A slew sheep and oxen and fat 1Kin 1:9   138
Hast thou not heard that A the 1Kin 1:11   138
why then doth A reign 1Kin 1:13   138
And now, behold, A reigneth 1Kin 1:18   138
A shall reign after me, and he 1Kin 1:24   138
him, and say, God save king A 1Kin 1:25   138
And A and all the guests that were 1Kin 1:41   138
and A said unto him, Come in 1Kin 1:42   138
And Jonathan answered and said to A .. 1Kin 1:43   138
that were with A were afraid 1Kin 1:49   138
A feared because of Solomon, and... 1Kin 1:50   138
Behold, A feareth king Solomon............. 1Kin 1:51   138
A the son of Haggith came to 1Kin 2:13   138
Solomon, to speak unto him for A 1Kin 2:19   138
be given to A thy brother to wife 1Kin 2:21   138
ask Abishag the Shunammite for A 1Kin 2:22   138
if A have not spoken this word 1Kin 2:23   138
A shall be put to death this day 1Kin 2:24   138
for Joab had turned after A 1Kin 2:28   138
the fourth, A the son of Haggith 1Chr 3:2   138
2. A Levite under King Jehoshaphat.
Shemiramoth, and Jehonathan, and A...2Chr 17:8   138
*3. A clan leader who sealed the covenant with
Nehemiah.*
A, Bigvai, Adin, ... Neh 10:16   138

ADONIKAM (ad-on-i'-kam) A family in exile.
The children of A, six hundred................ Ezr 2:13   140
And of the last sons of A, whose............. Ezr 8:13   140
The children of A, six hundred............... Neh 7:18   140

ADONIRAM (ad-on-i'-ram) See ADORAM. A tribute officer under Solomon.
A the son of Abda was over the 1Kin 4:6   141
and A was over the levy 1Kin 5:14   141

ADONI-ZEDEK (ad'-on-i-ze'-dek) Canaanite king slain
by Joshua.
when A king of Jerusalem had .... Josh 10:1   139
Wherefore A king of Jerusalem .... Josh 10:3   139

ADOPTION
ye have received the Spirit of *a* .... Rom 8:15   5206
ourselves, waiting for the *a* .... Rom 8:23   5206
to whom pertaineth the *a*, and the .... Rom 9:4   5206
we might receive the *a* of sons .... Gal 4:5   5206
predestinated us unto the *a* of............... Eph 1:5   5206

ADORAIM (ad-o-ra'-im) A city built by Rehoboam.
And A, and Lachish, and Azekah, ... 2Chr 11:9   115

ADORAM (ad-o'-ram) See ADONIRAM.
1. A tribute officer under David.
And A was over the tribute 2Sa 20:24   151
2. A tribute officer under Solomon.
Then king Rehoboam sent A................. 1Kin 12:18   151

ADORN
that women *a* themselves in modest 1Ti 2:9   2885
that they may *a* the doctrine of .... Titus 2:10   2885

ADORNED
shalt again be *a* with thy tabrets .... Jer 31:4   5710
how it was *a* with goodly stones .... Lk 21:5   2885
a themselves, being in subjection 1Pet 3:5   2885
as a bride *a* for her husband.................. Rev 21:2   2885

ADORNETH
as a bride *a* herself with her .... Is 61:10   5710

ADORNING
Whose *a* let it not be that 1Pet 3:3   2889
outward *a* of plaiting the hair 1Pet 3:3   2889

ADRAMMELECH (a-dram'-mel-ek)
1. A god of the Avites.
burnt their children in fire to A 2Kin 17:31   152
2. A son of Sennacherib.
house of Nisroch his god, that A 2Kin 19:37   152
house of Nisroch his god, that A .... Is 37:38   152

ADRAMYTTIAN See ADRAMYTTIUM.

ADRAMYTTIUM (a-dram-mit'-te-um) A seaport of
Mysia in Asia Minor.
And entering into a ship of A .... Acts 27:2   98

ADRIA (a'-dre-ah) The Adriatic Sea.
as we were driven up and down in A ..... Acts 27:27   99

ADRIATIC See ADRIA.

ADRIEL (a'-dre-el) Husband of Merab, Saul's daughter.
unto A the Meholathite to wife 1Sa 18:19   5741
whom she brought up for A the son 2Sa 21:8   5741

ADULLAM (a-dul'-lam) See ADULLAMITE.
1. A city south of Jerusalem.
the king of A, one............................... Josh 12:15   5725
Jarmuth, and A, Socoh, and Azekah, ... Josh 15:35   5725
And Beth-zur, and Shoco, and A............ 2Chr 11:7   5725
Zanoah, A, and in their villages, ... Neh 11:30   5725
he shall come unto A the glory of .... Mic 1:15   5725
2. A large cave near the city of Adullam.
thence, and escaped to the cave A 1Sa 22:1   5725
harvest time unto the cave of A 2Sa 23:13   5725
rock to David, into the cave of A 1Chr 11:15   5725

ADULLAMITE (a-dul'-lam-ite) A native of Adullam.
and turned in to a certain A .... Gen 38:1   5726
he and his friend Hirah the A .... Gen 38:12   5726
by the hand of his friend the A .... Gen 38:20   5726

ADULTERER
with his neighbour's wife, the *a* .... Lev 20:10   5003
The eye also of the *a* waiteth for .... Job 24:15   5003
the sorceress, the seed of the *a*............. Is 57:3   5003

ADULTERERS
him, and hast been partaker with *a*........ Ps 50:18   5003
for they be all *a*, an assembly of............ Jer 9:2   5003
For the land is full of *a* .... Jer 23:10   5003
They are all *a*, as an oven heated .... Hos 7:4   5003
the sorcerers, and against the *a* .... Mal 3:5   5003
men are, extortioners, unjust, *a* .... Lk 18:11   3432
fornicators, nor idolaters, nor *a* 1Cor 6:9   3432
whoremongers and *a* God will judge...... Heb 13:4   3432
Ye *a* and adulteresses, know ye not....... Jas 4:4   3432

ADULTERESS
the *a* shall surely be put to .... Lev 20:10   5003
the *a* will hunt for the precious .... Prov 6:26   802,376
beloved of her friend, yet an *a* .... Hos 3:1   5003
man, she shall be called an *a* .... Rom 7:3   3428
so that she is no *a*, though she .... Rom 7:3   3428

ADULTERESSES
judge them after the manner of *a* .... Eze 23:45   5003
because they are *a*, and blood is .... Eze 23:45   5003
Ye adulterers and *a*, know ye not........... Jas 4:4   3428

ADULTERIES
I have seen thine *a*, and thy.................. Jer 13:27   5004
said I unto her that was old in *a* .... Eze 23:43   5004
her *a* from between her breasts .... Hos 2:2   5005
proceed evil thoughts, murders, *a* .... Mt 15:19   3430
of men, proceed evil thoughts, *a* .... Mk 7:21   3430

ADULTEROUS
Such is the way of an *a* woman .... Prov 30:20   5003
a generation seeketh after a sign .... Mt 12:39   3428
a generation seeketh after a sign .... Mt 16:4   3428
of me and of my words in this *a* .... Mk 8:38   3428

ADULTERY
Thou shalt not commit *a* .... Ex 20:14   5003
a with another man's wife .... Lev 20:10   5003
even he that committeth *a* with .... Lev 20:10   5003
Neither shalt thou commit *a* .... Deut 5:18   5003
committeth *a* with a woman lacketh...... Prov 6:32   5003
committed *a* I had put her away .... Jer 3:8   5003
committed *a* with stones and with .... Jer 3:9   5003
the full, they then committed *a* .... Jer 5:7   5003
ye steal, murder, and commit *a* .... Jer 7:9   5003
they commit *a*, and walk in lies .... Jer 23:14   5003
have committed *a* with their .... Jer 29:23   5003
But as a wife that committeth *a* .... Eze 16:32   5003
That they have committed *a* .... Eze 23:37   5003
their idols have they committed *a* .... Eze 23:37   5003

and stealing, and committing *a*	Hos 4:2	5003
and your spouses shall commit *a*	Hos 4:13	5003
your spouses when they commit *a*	Hos 4:14	5003
old time, Thou shalt not commit *a*	Mt 5:27	3431
***a* with her already in his heart**	Mt 5:28	3431
causeth her to commit *a*	Mt 5:32	3429
her that is divorced committeth *a*	Mt 5:32	3429
shall marry another, committeth *a*	Mt 19:9	3429
which is put away doth commit *a*	Mt 19:9	3429
murder, Thou shalt not commit *a*	Mt 19:18	3431
another, committeth *a* against her	Mk 10:11	3429
to another, she committeth *a*	Mk 10:12	3429
the commandments, Do not commit *a*	Mk 10:19	3431
and marrieth another, committeth *a*	Lk 16:18	3431
from her husband committeth *a*	Lk 16:18	3431
the commandments, Do not commit *a*	Lk 18:20	3431
unto him a woman taken in *a*	Jn 8:3	3430
Master, this woman was taken in *a*	Jn 8:4	3431
sayest a man should not commit *a*	Rom 2:22	3431
dost thou commit *a*?	Rom 2:22	3431
For this, Thou shalt not commit *a*	Rom 13:9	3431
A, fornication, uncleanness,	Gal 5:19	3430
For he that said, Do not commit *a*	Jas 2:11	3431
Now if thou commit no *a*, yet if	Jas 2:11	3431
Having eyes full of *a*, and that	2Pet 2:14	3428
them that commit *a* with her into	Rev 2:22	3431

ADUMMIM (*a-dum'-mim*)
that is before the going up to *A*	Josh 15:7	131
is over against the going up of *A*	Josh 18:17	131

ADVANCED
It is the LORD that *a* Moses	1Sa 12:6	6213
a him, and set his seat above all	Est 3:1	5375
how he had *a* him above the	Est 5:11	5375
whereunto the king *a* him	Est 10:2	1431

ADVANTAGE
What *a* will it be unto thee	Job 35:3	5532
What *a* then hath the Jew	Rom 3:1	4053
Lest Satan should get an *a* of us	2Cor 2:11	4122
in admiration because of *a*	Jude 16	5622

ADVANTAGED
For what is a man *a*, if he gain	Lk 9:25	5623

ADVANTAGETH
what *a* it me, if the dead rise	1Cor 15:32	3786

ADVENTURE
which would not *a* to set the sole	Deut 28:56	5254
not *a* himself into the theatre	Acts 19:31	1325

ADVENTURED
a his life far, and delivered you	Judg 9:17	7993

ADVERSARIES
and an adversary unto thine *a*	Ex 23:22	6696
lest their *a* should behave	Deut 32:27	6862
and will render vengeance to his *a*	Deut 32:43	6862
Art thou for us, or for our *a*	Josh 5:13	6862
The *a* of the LORD shall be broken	1Sa 2:10	7378
ye should this day be *a* unto me	2Sa 19:22	7854
Now when the *a* of Judah and	Ezr 4:1	6862
our *a* said, They shall not know,	Neh 4:11	6862
render evil for good are mine *a*	Ps 38:20	7853
mine *a* are all before thee	Ps 69:19	6887
and consumed that are *a* to my soul	Ps 71:13	7853
and turned my hand against their *a*	Ps 81:14	6862
set up the right hand of his *a*	Ps 89:42	6862
For my love they are my *a*	Ps 109:4	7853
reward of mine *a* from the LORD	Ps 109:20	7853
Let mine *a* be clothed with shame,	Ps 109:29	7853
Ah, I will ease me of mine *a*	Is 1:24	6862
set up the *a* of Rezin against him	Is 9:11	6862
the *a* of Judah shall be cut off	Is 11:13	6887
he will repay, fury to his *a*	Is 59:18	6862
our *a* have trodden down thy	Is 63:18	6862
to make thy name known to thine *a*	Is 64:2	6862
and all thine *a*, every one of them	Jer 30:16	6862
that he may avenge him of his *a*	Jer 46:10	6862
and their *a* said, We offend not,	Jer 50:7	6862
Her *a* are the chief, her enemies	Lam 1:5	6862
the *a* saw her, and did mock at her	Lam 1:7	6862
that his *a* should be round about	Lam 1:17	6862
hath set up the horn of thine *a*	Lam 2:17	6862
shall be lifted up upon thine *a*	Mic 5:9	6862
LORD will take vengeance on his *a*	Nah 1:2	6862
things, all his *a* were ashamed	Lk 13:17	480
which all your *a* shall not be	Lk 21:15	480
unto me, and there are many *a*	1Cor 16:9	480
And in nothing terrified by your *a*	Phil 1:28	480
which shall devour the *a*	Heb 10:27	5227

ADVERSARY
an *a* unto thine adversaries	Ex 23:22	6887
in the way for an *a* against him	Num 22:22	7854
her *a* also provoked her sore, for	1Sa 1:6	6869
in the battle he be an *a* to us	1Sa 29:4	7854
is neither *a* nor evil occurrent	1Kin 5:4	7854
LORD stirred up an *a* unto Solomon	1Kin 11:14	7854
And God stirred him up another *a*	1Kin 11:23	7854
he was an *a* to Israel all the	1Kin 11:25	7854
And Esther said, The *a* and enemy is	Est 7:6	6862
that mine *a* had written a book	Job 31:35	376,7379
how long shall the *a* reproach	Ps 74:10	6862
who is mine *a*?	Is 50:8	1166,4941
The *a* hath spread out his hand	Lam 1:10	6862
stood with his right hand as an *a*	Lam 2:4	6862
not have believed that the *a*	Lam 4:12	6862
An *a* there shall be even round	Amos 3:11	6862
Agree with thine *a* quickly	Mt 5:25	476
lest at any time the *a* deliver	Mt 5:25	476
with thine *a* to the magistrate	Lk 12:58	476
him, saying, Avenge me of mine *a*	Lk 18:3	476
to the *a* to speak reproachfully	1Ti 5:14	480
because your *a* the devil, as a	1Pet 5:8	476

ADVERSITIES
saved you out of all your *a*	1Sa 10:19	7451
thou hast known my soul in *a*	Ps 31:7	6869

ADVERSITY
redeemed my soul out of all *a*	2Sa 4:9	6869
for God did vex them with all *a*	2Chr 15:6	6869
for I shall never be in *a*	Ps 10:6	7451
But in mine *a* they rejoiced, and	Ps 35:15	6761
give him rest from the days of *a*	Ps 94:13	7451
times, and a brother is born for *a*	Prov 17:17	6869
If thou faint in the day of *a*	Prov 24:10	6869
but in the day of *a* consider	Eccl 7:14	7451
the Lord give you the bread of *a*	Is 30:20	6862
and them which suffer *a*, as being	Heb 13:3	2558

ADVERTISE
I will *a* thee what this people	Num 24:14	3289
And I thought to *a* thee, saying,	Ruth 4:4	1540,241

ADVICE
consider of it, take *a*, and speak	Judg 19:30	5779
give here your *a* and counsel	Judg 20:7	1697
And blessed be thy *a*, and blessed	1Sa 25:33	2940
that our *a* should not be first	2Sa 19:43	1697
What *a* give ye that we may return	2Chr 10:9	3289
them after the *a* of the young men	2Chr 10:14	6098
Then Amaziah king of Judah took *a*	2Chr 25:17	3289
and with good *a* make war	Prov 20:18	8458
And herein I give my *a*	2Cor 8:10	1106

ADVISE
now *a*, and see what answer I shall	2Sa 24:13	3045
How do ye *a* that I may answer	1Kin 12:6	3289
Now therefore *a* thyself what word	1Chr 21:12	7200

ADVISED
but with the well *a* is wisdom	Prov 13:10	3289
the more part *a* to depart thence	Acts 27:12	1012,5087

ADVISEMENT
Philistines upon *a* sent him away	1Chr 12:19	6098

ADVOCATE
we have an *a* with the Father,	1Jn 2:1	3875

AENEAS (*e'-ne-as*) *A paralytic healed by Peter.*
he found a certain man named *A*	Acts 9:33	132
And Peter said unto him, *A*	Acts 9:34	132

AENON (*e'-non*) *A place in the valley of Shechem.*
was baptizing in *A* near to Salim	Jn 3:23	137

AFAR See APPENDIX.

AFFAIRS
to God, and *a* of the king	1Chr 26:32	1697
will guide his *a* with discretion	Ps 112:5	1697
over the *a* of the province of	Dan 2:49	5673
the *a* of the province of Babylon	Dan 3:12	5673
But that ye also may know my *a*	Eph 6:21	2596
purpose, that ye might know our *a*	Eph 6:22	4012
be absent, I may hear of your *a*	Phil 1:27	4012
himself with the *a* of this life	2Ti 2:4	4230

AFFECT
They zealously *a* you, but not	Gal 4:17	2206
exclude you, that ye might *a* them	Gal 4:17	2206

AFFECTED
minds evil *a* against the brethren	Acts 14:2	2559
a always in a good thing, and not	Gal 4:18	2206

AFFECTETH
Mine eye *a* mine heart because of	Lam 3:51	5953

AFFECTION

because I have set my *a* to the	1Chr 29:3	7521
without natural *a*, implacable,	Rom 1:31	794
his inward *a* is more abundant	2Cor 7:15	4698
Set your *a* on things above, not	Col 3:2	5426
uncleanness, inordinate *a*	Col 3:5	3806
Without natural *a*, trucebreakers,	2Ti 3:3	794

AFFECTIONATELY

So being *a* desirous of you, we	1Th 2:8	2442

AFFECTIONED

Be kindly *a* one to another with	Rom 12:10	5387

AFFECTIONS

God gave them up unto vile *a*	Rom 1:26	3806
crucified the flesh with the *a*	Gal 5:24	3804

AFFINITY

Solomon made *a* with Pharaoh king	1Kin 3:1	2859
abundance, and joined *a* with Ahab	2Chr 18:1	2859
join in *a* with the people of	Ezr 9:14	2859

AFFIRM

as some *a* that we say,) Let us do	Rom 3:8	5346
what they say, nor whereof they *a*	1Ti 1:7	1226
I will that thou *a* constantly	Titus 3:8	1226

AFFIRMED

hour after another confidently *a*	Lk 22:59	1340
But she constantly *a* that it was	Acts 12:15	1340
was dead, whom Paul *a* to be alive	Acts 25:19	5335

AFFLICT

they shall *a* them four hundred	Gen 15:13	6031
If thou shalt *a* my daughters	Gen 31:50	6031
to *a* them with their burdens	Ex 1:11	6031
Ye shall not *a* any widow, or	Ex 22:22	6031
If thou *a* them in any wise, and	Ex 22:23	6031
ye shall *a* your souls, and do no	Lev 16:29	6031
ye shall *a* your souls, by a	Lev 16:31	6031
ye shall *a* your souls, and offer	Lev 23:27	6031
of rest, and ye shall *a* your souls	Lev 23:32	6031
a Asshur, and shall *a* Eber	Num 24:24	6031
and ye shall *a* your souls.	Num 29:7	6031
every binding oath to *a* the soul	Num 30:13	6031
that we may bind him to *a* him	Judg 16:5	6031
thou mightest be bound to *a* thee	Judg 16:6	6031
and she began to *a* him, and his	Judg 16:19	6031
of wickedness to *a* them any more	2Sa 7:10	6031
I will for this *a* the seed of	1Kin 11:39	6031
their sin, when thou dost *a* them	2Chr 6:26	6031
that we might *a* ourselves before	Ezr 8:21	6031
he will not *a*	Job 37:23	6031
how thou didst *a* the people	Ps 44:2	7489
a them, even he that abideth of	Ps 55:19	6031
nor the son of wickedness *a* him	Ps 89:22	6031
O Lord, and *a* thine heritage	Ps 94:5	6031
destroy all them that *a* my soul	Ps 143:12	6887
a her by the way of the sea	Is 9:1	3513
into the hand of them that *a* thee	Is 51:23	3013
a day for a man to *a* his soul	Is 58:5	6031
hold thy peace, and *a* us very sore	Is 64:12	6031
down, and to destroy, and to *a*	Jer 31:28	7489
For he doth not *a* willingly nor	Lam 3:33	6031
they *a* the just, they take a	Amos 5:12	6887
they shall *a* you from the	Amos 6:14	3905
thee, I will *a* thee no more	Nah 1:12	6031
time I will undo all that *a* thee	Zeph 3:19	6031

AFFLICTED

But the more they *a* them, the	Ex 1:12	6031
shall not be *a* in that same day	Lev 23:29	6031
Wherefore hast thou *a* thy servant	Num 11:11	7489
a us, and laid upon us hard	Deut 26:6	6031
me, and the Almighty hath *a* me	Ruth 1:21	7489
the *a* people thou wilt save	2Sa 22:28	6041
because thou hast been *a* in all	1Kin 2:26	6031
in all wherein my father was *a*	1Kin 2:26	6031
a them, and delivered them into	2Kin 17:20	6031
To him that is *a* pity should be	Job 6:14	4523
a me, they have also let loose	Job 30:11	6031
and he heareth the cry of the *a*	Job 34:28	6041
For thou wilt save the *a* people	Ps 18:27	6041
abhorred the affliction of the *a*	Ps 22:24	6041
for I am desolate and *a*	Ps 25:16	6041
do justice to the *a* and needy	Ps 82:3	6041
thou hast *a* me with all thy waves	Ps 88:7	6031
I am and ready to die from my	Ps 88:15	6041
the days wherein thou hast *a* us	Ps 90:15	6031
A Prayer of the *a*, when he is	Ps 102:*t*	6041
of their iniquities, are *a*	Ps 107:17	6031
I was greatly *a*	Ps 116:10	6031
Before I was *a* I went astray	Ps 119:67	6031
is good for me that I have been *a*	Ps 119:71	6031

thou in faithfulness hast *a* me	Ps 119:75	6031
I am *a* very much	Ps 119:107	6031
time have they *a* me from my youth	Ps 129:1	6887
time have they *a* me from my youth	Ps 129:2	6887
will maintain the cause of the *a*	Ps 140:12	6041
All the days of the *a* are evil	Prov 15:15	6041
neither oppress the *a* in the gate	Prov 22:22	6041
hateth those that are *a* by it	Prov 26:28	1790
the judgment of any of the *a*	Prov 31:5	6040
he lightly *a* the land of Zebulun	Is 9:1	7043
and will have mercy upon his *a*	Is 49:13	6041
Therefore hear now this, thou *a*	Is 51:21	6041
stricken, smitten of God, and *a*	Is 53:4	6031
He was oppressed, and he was *a*	Is 53:7	6031
O thou *a*, tossed with tempest, and	Is 54:11	6041
wherefore have we *a* our soul	Is 58:3	6031
the hungry, and satisfy the *a* soul	Is 58:10	6031
The sons also of them that *a* thee	Is 60:14	6031
In all their affliction he was *a*	Is 63:9	6862
priests sigh, her virgins are *a*	Lam 1:4	3013
for the Lord hath *a* her for the	Lam 1:5	3013
wherewith the Lord hath *a* me in	Lam 1:12	3013
driven out, and her that I have *a*	Mic 4:6	7489
Though I have *a* thee, I will	Nah 1:12	6031
leave in the midst of thee an *a*	Zeph 3:12	6041
shall they deliver you up to be *a*	Mt 24:9	2347
And whether we be *a*, it is for	2Cor 1:6	2346
feet, if she have relieved the *a*	1Ti 5:10	2346
being destitute, *a*, tormented	Heb 11:37	2346
Be *a*, and mourn, and weep	Jas 4:9	5003
Is any among you *a*	Jas 5:13	2553

AFFLICTEST

from their sin, when thou *a* them	1Kin 8:35	6031

AFFLICTION

because the Lord hath heard thy *a*	Gen 16:11	6040
the Lord hath looked upon my *a*	Gen 29:32	6040
God hath seen mine *a* and the	Gen 31:42	6040
be fruitful in the land of my *a*	Gen 41:52	6040
I have surely seen the *a* of my	Ex 3:7	6040
a of Egypt unto the land of the	Ex 3:17	6040
that he had looked upon their *a*	Ex 4:31	6040
therewith, even the bread of *a*	Deut 16:3	6040
our voice, and looked on our *a*	Deut 26:7	6040
look on the *a* of thine handmaid	1Sa 1:11	6040
that the Lord will look on mine *a*	1Sa 16:12	6040
bread of *a* and with water of *a*	1Kin 22:27	3905
For the Lord saw the *a* of Israel	2Kin 14:26	6040
bread of *a* and with water of *a*	2Chr 18:26	3905
house,) and cry unto thee in our *a*	2Chr 20:9	6869
And when he was in *a*, he besought	2Chr 33:12	6887
in the province are in great *a*	Neh 1:3	7451
didst see the *a* of our fathers in	Neh 9:9	6040
Although *a* cometh not forth of	Job 5:6	205
therefore see thou mine *a*	Job 10:15	6040
the days of *a* have taken hold	Job 30:16	6040
the days of *a* prevented me	Job 30:27	6040
and be holden in cords of *a*	Job 36:8	6040
He delivereth the poor in his *a*	Job 36:15	6040
hast thou chosen rather than *a*	Job 36:21	6040
abhorred the *a* of the afflicted	Ps 22:24	6039
Look upon mine *a* and my pain	Ps 25:18	6040
thy face, and forgettest our *a*	Ps 44:24	6040
thou laidst *a* upon our loins	Ps 66:11	4157
Mine eye mourneth by reason of *a*	Ps 88:9	6040
Nevertheless he regarded their *a*	Ps 106:44	6862
shadow of death, being bound in *a*	Ps 107:10	6040
brought low through oppression, *a*	Ps 107:39	7451
he the poor on high from *a*	Ps 107:41	6040
This is my comfort in my *a*	Ps 119:50	6040
then have perished in mine *a*	Ps 119:92	6040
Consider mine *a*, and deliver me	Ps 119:153	6040
of adversity, and the water of *a*	Is 30:20	3905
chosen thee in the furnace of *a*	Is 48:10	6040
In all their *a* he was afflicted,	Is 63:9	6869
publisheth *a* from mount Ephraim	Jer 4:15	205
time of evil and in the time of *a*	Jer 15:11	6040
and my refuge in the day of *a*	Jer 16:19	6869
Why criest thou for thine *a*	Jer 30:15	7667
to come, and his *a* hasteth fast	Jer 48:16	7451
gone into captivity because of *a*	Lam 1:3	6040
remembered in the days of her *a*	Lam 1:7	6040
O Lord, behold my *a*	Lam 1:9	6040
seen by the rod of his wrath	Lam 3:1	6040
Remembering mine *a* and my misery,	Lam 3:19	6040
in their *a* they will seek me	Hos 5:15	6862
not grieved for the *a* of Joseph	Amos 6:6	7667
not have looked on their *a* in the	Obad 13	7451
by reason of mine *a* unto the Lord	Jonah 2:2	6869
a shall not rise up the second	Nah 1:9	6869
I saw the tents of Cushan in *a*	Hab 3:7	205

and they helped forward the *a* .... Zec 1:15   7451
out or came in because of the *a* .... Zec 8:10   6862
shall pass through the sea with *a* .... Zec 10:11   6869
when *a* or persecution ariseth for .... Mk 4:17   2347
For in those days shall be *a* .... Mk 13:19   2347
of Egypt and Chanaan, and great *a* ..... Acts 7:11   2347
I have seen the *a* of my people .... Acts 7:34   2561
For out of much *a* and anguish of 2Cor 2:4   2347
For our light *a*, which is but for 2Cor 4:17   2347
of *a* the abundance of their joy 2Cor 8:2   2347
supposing to add *a* to my bonds .... Phil 1:16   2347
that ye did communicate with my *a* ..... Phil 4:14   2347
received the word in much *a* 1Th 1:6   2347
comforted over you in all our *a* 1Th 3:7   2347
suffer *a* with the people of God .... Heb 11:25   4797
fatherless and widows in their *a* .... Jas 1:27   2347
for an example of suffering *a* .... Jas 5:10   2552

AFFLICTIONS

Many are the *a* of the righteous .... Ps 34:19   7451
remember David, and all his *a* .... Ps 132:1   6031
And delivered him out of all his *a* .... Acts 7:10   2347
saying that bonds and *a* abide me .... Acts 20:23   2347
of God, in much patience, in *a* 2Cor 6:4   2347
a of Christ in my flesh for his .... Col 1:24   2347
no man should be moved by these *a* 1Th 3:3   2347
but be thou partaker of the *a* of 2Ti 1:8   4777
Persecutions, *a*, which came unto 2Ti 3:11   3804
thou in all things, endure *a* 2Ti 4:5   2553
ye endured a great fight of *a* .... Heb 10:32   3804
both by reproaches and *a* .... Heb 10:33   2347
knowing that the same *a* are 1Pet 5:9   3804

AFFORDING

be full, *a* all manner of store .... Ps 144:13   6329

AFFRIGHT

to *a* them, and to trouble them 2Chr 32:18   3372

AFFRIGHTED

Thou shalt not be *a* at them .... Deut 7:21   6206
as they that went before were *a* ...... Job 18:20   270,8178
He mocketh at fear, and is not *a* .... Job 39:22   2865
My heart panted, fearfulness *a* me .... Is 21:4   1204
fire, and the men of war are *a* .... Jer 51:32   926
and they were *a* .... Mk 16:5   1568
And he saith unto them, Be not *a* .... Mk 16:6   1568
But they were terrified and *a* .... Lk 24:37   1719
and the remnant were *a*, and gave .... Rev 11:13   1719

AFOOT

ran *a* thither out of all cities, ... Mk 6:33   3979
minding himself to go *a* .... Acts 20:13   3978

AFORE

a Isaiah was gone out into the 2Kin 20:4   3808
which withereth *a* it groweth up .... Ps 129:6   6924
For *a* the harvest, when the bud .... Is 18:5   6440
a he that was escaped came .... Eze 33:22   6440
(Which he had promised *a* by his .... Rom 1:2   4279
which he had *a* prepared unto .... Rom 9:23   4282
(as I wrote *a* in few words, ... Eph 3:3   4270

AFOREHAND

she is come *a* to anoint my body .... Mk 14:8   4301

AFORETIME

where *a* they laid the meat .... Neh 13:5   6440
and *a* I was as a tabret .... Job 17:6   6440
My people went down *a* into Egypt .... Is 52:4   7223
Their children also shall be as *a* .... Jer 30:20   6924
before his God, as he did *a* ...... Dan 6:10   4481,6928,1836
Pharisees him that *a* was blind .... Jn 9:13   4218
a were written for our learning .... Rom 15:4   4270

AFRAID

voice in the garden, and I was *a* .... Gen 3:10   3372
for she was *a* .... Gen 18:15   3372
and the men were sore *a* .... Gen 20:8   3372
And he was *a*, and said, How .... Gen 28:17   3372
and said to Laban, Because I was *a* ..... Gen 31:31   3372
Then Jacob was greatly *a* and .... Gen 32:7   3372
heart failed them, and they were *a* .... Gen 42:28   2729
the bundles of money, they were *a* .... Gen 42:35   3372
And the men were *a*, because they .... Gen 43:18   3372
for he was *a* to look upon God .... Ex 3:6   3372
and they were sore *a* .... Ex 14:10   3372
The people shall hear, and be *a* .... Ex 15:14   7264
they were *a* to come nigh him .... Ex 34:30   3372
down, and none shall make you *a* .... Lev 26:6   2729
wherefore then were ye not *a* to .... Num 12:8   3372
And Moab was sore *a* of the people ...... Num 22:3   1481
ye shall not be *a* of the face of .... Deut 1:17   1481
Dread not, neither be *a* of them .... Deut 1:29   3372
and they shall be *a* of you .... Deut 2:4   3372

for ye were *a* by reason of the .... Deut 5:5   3372
Thou shalt not be *a* of them .... Deut 7:18   3372
all the people of whom thou art *a* .... Deut 7:19   3373
For I was *a* of the anger and hot .... Deut 9:19   3025
thou shalt not be *a* of him .... Deut 18:22   1481
more than thou, be not *a* of them .... Deut 20:1   3372
and they shall be *a* of thee .... Deut 28:10   3372
of Egypt, which thou wast *a* of .... Deut 28:60   3025
fear not, nor be *a* of them .... Deut 31:6   6206
be not *a*, neither be thou .... Josh 1:9   6206
therefore we were sore *a* of our .... Josh 9:24   3372
Joshua, Be not *a* because of them .... Josh 11:6   3372
saying, Whosoever is fearful and *a* ...... Judg 7:3   2730
at midnight, that the man was *a* .... Ruth 3:8   2729
And the Philistines were *a* 1Sa 4:7   3372
they were *a* of the Philistines 1Sa 7:7   3372
they were dismayed, and greatly *a* 1Sa 17:11   3372
fled from him, and were sore *a* 1Sa 17:24   3372
And Saul was *a* of David, because 1Sa 18:12   3372
very wisely, he was *a* of him 1Sa 18:15   3372
Saul was yet the more *a* of David 1Sa 18:29   3372
Ahimelech was *a* at the meeting of 1Sa 21:1   2729
was sore *a* of Achish the king of 1Sa 21:12   3372
Behold, we be here in Judah 1Sa 23:3   3373
host of the Philistines, he was *a* 1Sa 28:5   3372
the king said unto her, Be not *a* 1Sa 28:13   3372
along on the earth, and was sore *a* 1Sa 28:20   3372
for he was sore *a* 1Sa 31:4   3372
How wast thou not *a* to stretch 2Sa 1:14   3372
David was *a* of the LORD that day, ... 2Sa 6:9   3372
because the people have made me *a* 2Sa 14:15   3372
weak handed, and will make him *a* 2Sa 17:2   2729
floods of ungodly men made me *a* 2Sa 22:5   1204
they shall be *a* out of their 2Sa 22:46   2296
that were with Adonijah were *a* 1Kin 1:49   2729
be not *a* of him 1Kin 1:15   3372
But they were exceedingly *a* 2Kin 10:4   3372
Be not *a* of the words which thou 2Kin 19:6   3372
for they were *a* of the Chaldees 2Kin 25:26   3372
for he was sore *a* 1Chr 10:4   3372
David was *a* of God that day, ... 1Chr 13:12   3372
for he was *a* because of the sword 1Chr 21:30   1204
Be not *a* nor dismayed by reason 2Chr 20:15   3372
be not *a* nor dismayed for the 2Chr 32:7   3372
Then I was very sore *a*, ... Neh 2:2   3372
the people, Be not ye *a* of them .... Neh 4:14   3372
For they all made us *a*, saying, ... Neh 6:9   3372
was he hired, that I should be *a* .... Neh 6:13   3372
Then Haman was *a* before the king ...... Est 7:6   1204
that which I was *a* of is come .... Job 3:25   3025
neither shalt thou be *a* of .... Job 5:21   3372
neither shalt thou be *a* of the .... Job 5:22   3372
ye see my casting down, and are *a* ...... Job 6:21   3372
I am *a* of all my sorrows, I know .... Job 9:28   3025
down, and none shall make thee *a* .... Job 11:19   2729
not his excellency make you *a* .... Job 13:11   1204
and let not thy dread make me *a* .... Job 13:21   1204
and anguish shall make him *a* .... Job 15:24   1204
shall make him *a* on every side .... Job 18:11   1204
Be ye *a* of the sword .... Job 19:29   1481
Even when I remember I am *a* .... Job 21:6   926
when I consider, I am *a* of him .... Job 23:15   6342
wherefore I was *a*, and durst not .... Job 32:6   2119
my terror shall not make thee *a* .... Job 33:7   1204
thou make him *a* as a grasshopper ...... Job 39:20   7493
up himself, the mighty are *a* .... Job 41:25   1481
I will not be *a* of ten thousands .... Ps 3:6   3372
floods of ungodly men made me *a* .... Ps 18:4   1204
be *a* out of their close places .... Ps 18:45   2727
of whom shall I be *a* .... Ps 27:1   6342
Be not thou *a* when one is made .... Ps 49:16   3372
What time I am *a*, I will trust in .... Ps 56:3   3372
I will not be *a* what man can do .... Ps 56:11   3372
parts are *a* at thy tokens .... Ps 65:8   3372
they were *a* .... Ps 77:16   2342
make them *a* with thy storm .... Ps 83:15   926
Thou shalt not be *a* for the .... Ps 91:5   3372
He shall not be *a* of evil tidings .... Ps 112:7   3372
is established, he shall not be *a* .... Ps 112:8   3372
and I am *a* of thy judgments .... Ps 119:120   3372
liest down, thou shalt not be *a* .... Prov 3:24   6342
Be not *a* of sudden fear, neither .... Prov 3:25   3372
She is not *a* of the snow for her .... Prov 31:21   3372
shall be *a* of that which is high .... Eccl 12:5   3372
fear ye their fear, nor be *a* .... Is 8:12   6206
in Zion, be not *a* of the Assyrian .... Is 10:24   3372
Ramah is *a* .... Is 10:29   2729
I will trust, and not be *a* .... Is 12:2   6342
And they shall be *a* .... Is 13:8   926
down, and none shall make them *a* ...... Is 17:2   2729
and it shall be *a* and fear because .... Is 19:16   2729

thereof shall be *a* in himself	Is 19:17	6342
And they shall be *a* and ashamed of	Is 20:5	2865
he will not be *a* of their voice	Is 31:4	2865
princes shall be *a* of the ensign	Is 31:9	2865
The sinners in Zion are *a*	Is 33:14	6342
Be not *a* of the words that thou	Is 37:6	3372
lift it up, be not *a*	Is 40:9	3372
the ends of the earth were *a*	Is 41:5	2729
Fear ye not, neither be *a*	Is 44:8	7297
of men, neither be ye *a* of their	Is 51:7	2865
that thou shouldest be *a* of a man	Is 51:12	3372
whom hast thou been *a* or feared	Is 57:11	1672
Be not *a* of their faces	Jer 1:8	3372
at this, and be horribly *a*	Jer 2:12	8175
Be not *a* of them	Jer 10:5	3372
when Urijah heard it, he was *a*	Jer 26:21	3372
quiet, and none shall make him *a*	Jer 30:10	2729
the words, they were *a* both one	Jer 36:16	6342
Yet they were not *a*, nor rent	Jer 36:24	6342
I am *a* of the Jews that are	Jer 38:19	1672
of the men of whom thou art *a*	Jer 39:17	3025
for they were *a* of them, because	Jer 41:18	3372
Be not *a* of the king of Babylon,	Jer 42:11	3372
of whom ye are *a*	Jer 42:11	3373
be not *a* of him, saith the LORD	Jer 42:11	3372
and the famine, whereof ye were *a*	Jer 42:16	1672
at ease, and none shall make him *a*	Jer 46:27	2729
be not *a* of them	Eze 2:6	3372
neither be *a* of their words,	Eze 2:6	3372
be not *a* of their words, nor be	Eze 2:6	3372
and their kings shall be sore *a*	Eze 27:35	8175
to make the careless Ethiopians *a*	Eze 30:9	2729
shall be horribly *a* for thee	Eze 32:10	8175
safely, and none shall make them *a*	Eze 34:28	2729
their land, and none made them *a*	Eze 39:26	2729
I saw a dream which made me *a*	Dan 4:5	1763
and when he came, I was *a*, and fell	Dan 8:17	1204
Be not *a*, ye beasts of the field	Joel 2:22	3372
the city, and the people not be *a*	Amos 3:6	2729
Then the mariners were *a*, and	Jonah 1:5	3372
Then were the men exceedingly *a*	Jonah 1:10	3372
and none shall make them *a*	Mic 4:4	2729
they shall be *a* of the LORD our	Mic 7:17	6342
lion's whelp, and none made them *a*	Nah 2:11	2729
of beasts, which made them *a*	Hab 2:17	2865
I have heard thy speech, and was *a*	Hab 3:2	3372
down, and none shall make them *a*	Zeph 3:13	2729
me, and was *a* before my name	Mal 2:5	2865
Herod, he was *a* to go thither	Mt 2:22	5399
be not *a*	Mt 14:27	5399
saw the wind boisterous, he was *a*	Mt 14:30	5399
on their face, and were sore *a*	Mt 17:6	5399
them, and said, Arise, and be not *a*	Mt 17:7	5399
And I was *a*, and went and hid thy	Mt 25:25	5399
said Jesus unto them, Be not *a*	Mt 28:10	5399
and they were *a*	Mk 5:15	5399
ruler of the synagogue, Be not *a*	Mk 5:36	5399
be not *a*	Mk 6:50	5399
for they were sore *a*	Mk 9:6	1630
that saying, and were *a* to ask him	Mk 9:32	5399
and as they followed, they were *a*	Mk 10:32	5399
thing to any man for they were *a*	Mk 16:8	5399
and they were sore *a*	Lk 2:9	5399
And they being *a* wondered, saying	Lk 8:25	5399
and they were *a*	Lk 8:35	5399
Be not *a* of them that kill the	Lk 12:4	5399
And as they were *a*, and bowed down	Lk 24:5	1719
and they were *a*	Jn 6:19	5399
be not *a*	Jn 6:20	5399
be troubled, neither let it be *a*	Jn 14:27	1168
that saying, he was the more *a*	Jn 19:8	5399
but they were all *a* of him	Acts 9:26	5399
when he looked on him, he was *a*	Acts 10:4	1719
the night by a vision, Be not *a*	Acts 18:9	5399
saw indeed the light, and were *a*	Acts 22:9	1719
and the chief captain also was *a*	Acts 22:29	5399
thou then not be *a* of the power	Rom 13:3	5399
thou do that which is evil, be *a*	Rom 13:4	5399
I am *a* of you, lest I have	Gal 4:11	5399
they were not *a* of the king's	Heb 11:23	5399
are not *a* with any amazement	1Pet 3:6	5399
be not *a* of their terror, neither	1Pet 3:14	5399
they are not *a* to speak evil of	2Pet 2:10	5141

AFRESH

to themselves the Son of God *a*	Heb 6:6	388

AFTER See APPENDIX.

AFTERNOON

And they tarried until *a*, and they	Judg 19:8	5186,3117

AFTERWARD See APPENDIX.

AFTERWARDS

a she bare a daughter, and called	Gen 30:21	310
a he will let you go hence	Ex 11:1	310,3651
a the hand of all the people	Deut 13:9	314
a they eat that be bidden	1Sa 9:13	310,3651
mark, and we will speak	Job 18:2	310
but *a* his mouth shall be filled	Prov 20:17	310
and *a* build thine house	Prov 24:27	310
He that rebuketh a man *a* shall	Prov 28:23	310
a wise man keepeth it in till *a*	Prov 29:11	268
A the spirit took me up, and	Eze 11:24	
but thou shalt follow me *a*	Jn 13:36	5305
A I came into the regions of	Gal 1:21	1899
faith which should *a* be revealed	Gal 3:23	

AGABUS (*ag'-ab-us*) *A Christian prophet.*

stood up one of them named *A*	Acts 11:28	13
Judaea a certain prophet, named *A*	Acts 21:10	13

AGAG (*a'-gag*) See AGAGITE. *A king of Amalek during Exodus.*

his king shall be higher than *A*	Num 24:7	90
he took *A* the king of the	1Sa 15:8	90
But Saul and the people spared *A*	1Sa 15:9	90
have brought *A* the king of Amalek	1Sa 15:20	90
Bring ye hither to me *A* the king	1Sa 15:32	90
A came unto him delicately	1Sa 15:32	90
A said, Surely the bitterness of	1Sa 15:32	90
Samuel hewed *A* in pieces before	1Sa 15:33	90

AGAGITE (*ag'-ag-ite*) *A member of an Amalekite tribe.*

Haman the son of Hammedatha the *A*	Est 3:1	91
Haman the son of Hammedatha the *A*	Est 3:10	91
away the mischief of Haman the *A*	Est 8:3	91
Haman the son of Hammedatha the *A*	Est 8:5	91
the son of Hammedatha, the *A*	Est 9:24	91

AGAIN See APPENDIX.

AGAINST See APPENDIX.

AGAR (*a'-gar*) See HAGAR. *Greek form of Hagar.*

gendereth to bondage, which is *A*	Gal 4:24	28
For this *A* is mount Sinai in	Gal 4:25	28

AGATE

And the third row a ligure, an *a*	Ex 28:19	7618
And the third row, a ligure, an *a*	Ex 39:12	7618
and fine linen, and coral, and *a*	Eze 27:16	3539

AGATES

And I will make thy windows of *a*	Is 54:12	3539

AGE

shalt be buried in a good old *a*	Gen 15:15	7872
were old and well stricken in *a*	Gen 18:11	3117
bare Abraham a son in his old *a*	Gen 21:2	
have born him a son in his old *a*	Gen 21:7	
was old, and well stricken in *a*	Gen 24:1	3117
ghost, and died in a good old *a*	Gen 25:8	7872
he was the son of his old *a*	Gen 37:3	
old man, and a child of his old *a*	Gen 44:20	
so the whole of Jacob was an	Gen 47:28	3117
the eyes of Israel were dim for *a*	Gen 48:10	2207
from the *a* of fifty years they	Num 8:25	1121
Joshua waxed old and stricken in *a*	Josh 23:1	3117
them, I am old and stricken in *a*	Josh 23:2	3117
son of Joash died in a good old *a*	Judg 8:32	7872
and a nourisher of thine old *a*	Ruth 4:15	7872
die in the flower of their *a*	1Sa 2:33	582
eyes were set by reason of his *a*	1Kin 14:4	7869
in the time of his old *a* he was	1Kin 15:23	
from the *a* of thirty years	1Chr 23:3	1121
from the *a* of twenty years and	1Chr 23:24	1121
And he died in a good old *a*	1Chr 29:28	7872
man, or him that stooped for *a*	2Chr 36:17	3485
come to thy grave in a full *a*	Job 5:26	3624
I pray thee, of the former *a*	Job 8:8	1755
thine *a* shall be clearer than the	Job 11:17	2465
in whom old *a* was perished	Job 30:2	3624
mine *a* is as nothing before thee	Ps 39:5	2465
me not off in the time of old *a*	Ps 71:9	
still bring forth fruit in old *a*	Ps 92:14	7872
Mine *a* is departed, and is removed	Is 38:12	1755
And even to your old *a* I am he	Is 46:4	2209
his staff in his hand for very *a*	Zec 8:4	3117
she was the *a* of twelve years	Mk 5:42	
also conceived a son in her old *a*	Lk 1:36	
she was of a great *a*, and had	Lk 2:36	2250
to be about thirty years of *a*	Lk 3:23	
daughter, about twelve years of *a*	Lk 8:42	2244
he is of *a*	Jn 9:21	2244
said his parents, He is of *a*	Jn 9:23	2244
if she pass the flower of her *a*	1Cor 7:36	5230

to them that are of full *a* .... Heb 5:14   5046
of a child when she was past *a* .... Heb 11:11   2244

AGED
Now Barzillai was a very *a* man 2Sa 19:32   2204
away the understanding of the *a* ....Job 12:20   2205
both the grayheaded and very *a* men ... Job 15:10   3453
and the *a* arose, and stood up ....Job 29:8   2205
neither do the *a* understand ....Job 32:9   2205
the *a* with him that is full of ....Jer 6:11   2205
That the *a* men be sober, grave, ...Titus 2:2   4246
The *a* women likewise, that they ....Titus 2:3   4247
being such an one as Paul the *a* ....Philem 9   4246

AGEE (ag'-ee) Father of a "mighty man" of David.
Shammah the son of *A* the Hararite 2Sa 23:11   89

AGES
That in the *a* to come he might............... Eph 2:7   165
Which in other *a* was not made .... Eph 3:5   1074
by Christ Jesus throughout all *a* .... Eph 3:21   1074
which hath been hid from *a* ....Col 1:26   165

AGO See APPENDIX.

AGONE
because three days *a* I fell sick...............1Sa 30:13

AGONY
being in an *a* he prayed more ....Lk 22:44   74

AGREE
A with thine adversary quickly, ...Mt 5:25   2132
That if two of you shall *a* on ....Mt 18:19   4856
didst not thou *a* with me for a ....Mt 20:13   4856
so did their witness *a* together ....Mk 14:59   2470
to this *a* the words of the......................Acts 15:15   4856
and these three *a* in one 1Jn 5:8   1526
to fulfil his will, and to *a* ....Rev 17:17   4160,3391,1106

AGREED
walk together, except they be *a* ....Amos 3:3   3259
when he had *a* with the labourers ....Mt 20:2   4856
but their witness *a* not together ....Mk 14:56   2470
for the Jews had *a* already......................Jn 9:22   4934
How is it that ye have *a* together ....Acts 5:9   4856
And to him they *a* ....Acts 5:40   3982
The Jews have *a* to desire thee ....Acts 23:20   4934
when they *a* not among themselves, ... Acts 28:25   800

AGREEMENT
Make an *a* with me by a present, ...2Kin 18:31
death, and with hell are we at *a* ....Is 28:15   2374
your *a* with hell shall not stand ....Is 28:18   2380
Make an *a* with me by a present, ...Is 36:16
king of the north to make an *a* ....Dan 11:6   4339
what *a* hath the temple of God 2Cor 6:16   4783

AGREETH
and thy speech *a* thereto........................Mk 14:70   3662
out of the new *a* not with the old ....Lk 5:36   4856

AGRIPPA (ag-rip'-pah) Great-grandson of Herod the Great.
And after certain days king *A* ....Acts 25:13   67
Then *A* said unto Festus, I would............Acts 25:22   67
when *A* was come, and Bernice, with ..... Acts 25:23   67
And Festus said, King *A*, and all ....Acts 25:24   67
specially before thee, O king *A* ....Acts 25:26   67
Then *A* said unto Paul, Thou art ....Acts 26:1   67
I think myself happy, king *A* ....Acts 26:2   67
For which hope's sake, king *A* ....Acts 26:7   67
Whereupon, O king *A*, I was not ....Acts 26:19   67
King *A*, believest thou the ....Acts 26:27   67
Then *A* said unto Paul, Almost ....Acts 26:28   67
Then said *A* unto Festus, This man ....Acts 26:32   67

AGROUND
two seas met, they ran the ship *a* ....Acts 27:41   2027

AGUE
consumption, and the burning *a* ....Lev 26:16   6920

AGUR (a'-gur) Son of Jakeh.
The words of *A* the son of Jakeh, ...Prov 30:1   94

AH See APPENDIX.

AHA See APPENDIX.

AHAB (a'-hab) See AHAB'S.
1. A king of Israel.
A his son reigned in his stead 1Kin 16:28   256
A the son of Omri to reign over 1Kin 16:29   256
A the son of Omri reigned over 1Kin 16:29   256
A the son of Omri did evil in the 1Kin 16:30   256
And *A* made a grove 1Kin 16:33   256
A did more to provoke the LORD 1Kin 16:33   256
of Gilead, said unto *A*, As the 1Kin 17:1   256
saying, Go, shew thyself unto *A* 1Kin 18:1   256

went to shew himself unto *A* 1Kin 18:2   256
A called Obadiah, which was the 1Kin 18:3   256
A said unto Obadiah, Go into the..........1Kin 18:5   256
A went one way by himself, and 1Kin 18:6   256
thy servant into the hand of *A* 1Kin 18:9   256
and so when I come and tell *A* 1Kin 18:12   256
So Obadiah went to meet *A* 1Kin 18:16   256
and *A* went to meet Elijah......................1Kin 18:16   256
when *A* saw Elijah, that *A* said............1Kin 18:17   256
So *A* sent unto all the children 1Kin 18:20   256
And Elijah said unto *A*, Get thee 1Kin 18:41   256
So *A* went up to eat and to drink 1Kin 18:42   256
And he said, Go up, say unto *A* 1Kin 18:44   256
A rode, and went to Jezreel 1Kin 18:45   256
ran before *A* to the entrance of............1Kin 18:46   256
A told Jezebel all that Elijah 1Kin 19:1   256
he sent messengers to *A* king of 1Kin 20:2   256
a prophet unto *A* king of Israel............1Kin 20:13   256
And *A* said, By whom 1Kin 20:14   256
Then said *A*, I will send thee 1Kin 20:34   256
the palace of *A* king of Samaria............1Kin 21:1   256
A spake unto Naboth, saying, Give 1Kin 21:2   256
And Naboth said to *A*, The LORD 1Kin 21:3   256
A came into his house heavy and 1Kin 21:4   256
was dead, that Jezebel said to *A* 1Kin 21:15   256
when *A* heard that Naboth was dead 1Kin 21:16   256
that *A* rose up to go down to the 1Kin 21:16   256
go down to meet *A* king of Israel 1Kin 21:18   256
A said to Elijah, Hast thou found 1Kin 21:20   256
will cut off from *A* him that 1Kin 21:21   256
Him that dieth of *A* in the city 1Kin 21:24   256
But there was none like unto *A* 1Kin 21:25   256
when *A* heard those words, that he 1Kin 21:27   256
Seest thou how *A* humbleth himself.......1Kin 21:29   256
LORD said, Who shall persuade *A* 1Kin 22:20   256
Now the rest of the acts of *A* 1Kin 22:39   256
So *A* slept with his fathers 1Kin 22:40   256
fourth year of *A* king of Israel 1Kin 22:41   256
the son of *A* unto Jehoshaphat 1Kin 22:49   256
Ahaziah the son of *A* began to 1Kin 22:51   256
Israel after the death of *A* 2Kin 1:1   256
Now Jehoram the son of *A* began to 2Kin 3:1   256
when *A* was dead, that the king of........2Kin 3:5   256
Joram the son of *A* king of Israel 2Kin 8:16   256
of Israel, as did the house of *A* 2Kin 8:18   256
the daughter of *A* was his wife............2Kin 8:18   256
year of Joram the son of *A* king............2Kin 8:25   256
in the way of the house of *A* 2Kin 8:27   256
the LORD, as did the house of *A* 2Kin 8:27   256
the son in law of the house of *A* 2Kin 8:27   256
he went with Joram the son of *A* 2Kin 8:28   256
see Joram the son of *A* in Jezreel 2Kin 8:29   256
smite the house of *A* thy master 2Kin 9:7   256
the whole house of *A* shall perish 2Kin 9:8   256
I will cut off from *A* him that 2Kin 9:8   256
I will make the house of *A* like 2Kin 9:9   256
rode together after *A* his father 2Kin 9:25   256
year of Joram the son of *A* began 2Kin 9:29   256
A had seventy sons in Samaria 2Kin 10:1   256
spake concerning the house of *A* 2Kin 10:10   256
of the house of *A* in Jezreel 2Kin 10:11   256
that remained unto *A* in Samaria 2Kin 10:17   256
unto them, *A* served Baal a little............2Kin 10:18   256
hast done unto the house of *A* 2Kin 10:30   256
a grove, as did *A* king of Israel..............2Kin 21:3   256
and the plummet of the house of *A* 2Kin 21:13   256
and joined affinity with *A* 2Chr 18:1   256
he went down to *A* to Samaria 2Chr 18:2   256
A killed sheep and oxen for him in........2Chr 18:2   256
A king of Israel said unto 2Chr 18:3   256
Who shall entice *A* king of Israel 2Chr 18:19   256
like as did the house of *A* 2Chr 21:6   256
he had the daughter of *A* to wife 2Chr 21:6   256
the whoredoms of the house of *A* 2Chr 21:13   256
in the ways of the house of *A* 2Chr 22:3   256
of the LORD like the house of *A* 2Chr 22:4   256
went with Jehoram the son of *A* 2Chr 22:5   256
Jehoram the son of *A* at Jezreel 2Chr 22:6   256
to cut off the house of *A* 2Chr 22:7   256
judgment upon the house of *A* 2Chr 22:8   256
all the works of the house of *A* ....Mic 6:16   256
2. A false prophet during the Exile.
of *A* the son of Kolaiah, and of................Jer 29:21   256
make like Zedekiah and like *A* ....Jer 29:22   256

AHAB'S (a'-habs)
So she wrote letters in *A* name...............1Kin 21:8   256
them that brought up *A* children............2Kin 10:6   256

AHARAH (a-har'-ah) See AHER, AHIRAM, EHI. Third son of Benjamin.
the second, and *A* the third, ...1Chr 8:1   315

AHARHEL *(a-har'-hel) A descendant of Judah.*
the families of *A* the son of 1Chr 4:8 316

AHASAI *(a-ha'-sa-i) Family of returned exiles.*
the son of Azareel, the son of *A* ....Neh 11:13 273

AHASBAI *(a-has'-ba-i) Father of a "mighty man" of David.*
Eliphelet the son of *A*, the son 2Sa 23:34 308

AHASUERUS *(a-has-u-e'-rus) See* AHASUERUS'.
 1. A Persian king, Cambyses.
And in the reign of *A*, in the ....Ezr 4:6 325
 2. Father of Darius the Mede.
first year of Darius the son of *A* ....Dan 9:1 325
 3. A king of Persia, Xerxes.
it came to pass in the days of *A* ....Est 1:1 325
(this is *A* which reigned from ....Est 1:1 325
when the king *A* sat on the throne ....Est 1:2 325
house which belonged to king *A* ....Est 1:9 325
in the presence of *A* the king ....Est 1:10 325
of the king *A* by the chamberlains ....Est 1:15 325
all the provinces of the king *A* ....Est 1:16 325
The king *A* commanded Vashti the ....Est 1:17 325
Vashti come no more before king *A*........Est 1:19 325
the wrath of king *A* was appeased.........Est 2:1 325
turn was come to go in to king *A* ....Est 2:12 325
A into his house royal in the ....Est 2:16 325
sought to lay hand on the king *A* ....Est 2:21 325
king *A* promote Haman the son of ....Est 3:1 325
throughout the whole kingdom of *A* ......Est 3:6 325
in the twelfth year of king *A* ....Est 3:7 325
And Haman said unto king *A* ....Est 3:8 325
the name of king *A* was it written ....Est 3:12 325
sought to lay hand on the king *A* ....Est 6:2 325
Then the king *A* answered and said ......Est 7:5 325
On that day did the king *A* give ....Est 8:1 325
Then the king *A* said unto Esther ....Est 8:7 325
in all the provinces of king *A* ....Est 8:12 325
all the provinces of the king *A* ....Est 9:2 325
all the provinces of the king *A* ....Est 9:20 325
provinces of the kingdom of *A* ....Est 9:30 325
the king *A* laid a tribute upon ....Est 10:1 325
the Jew was next unto king *A* ....Est 10:3 325

AHASUERUS' *(a-has-u-e'-rus) Refers to Ahasuerus 3.*
And he wrote in the king *A* name ....Est 8:10 325

AHAVA *(a-ha'-vah) See* IVA. *A river of Babylon.*
to the river than runneth to *A* ....Ezr 8:15 163
a fast there, at the river of *A*..................Ezr 8:21 163
we departed from the river of *A*.............Ezr 8:31 163

AHAZ *(a'-haz) See* ACHAZ.
 1. A king of Judah.
A his son reigned in his stead 2Kin 15:38 271
of Pekah the son of Remaliah *A* 2Kin 16:1 271
Twenty years old was *A* when he 2Kin 16:2 271
and they besieged *A*, but could not 2Kin 16:5 271
So *A* sent messengers to 2Kin 16:7 271
A took the silver and gold that 2Kin 16:8 271
king *A* went to Damascus to meet 2Kin 16:10 271
king *A* sent to Urijah the priest 2Kin 16:10 271
king *A* had sent from Damascus 2Kin 16:11 271
against king *A* came from Damascus....2Kin 16:11 271
king *A* commanded Urijah the 2Kin 16:15 271
to all that king *A* commanded 2Kin 16:16 271
king *A* cut off the borders of the 2Kin 16:17 271
of the acts of *A* which he did 2Kin 16:19 271
A slept with his fathers, and was 2Kin 16:20 271
In the twelfth year of *A* king of..............2Kin 17:1 271
that Hezekiah the son of *A* king 2Kin 18:1 271
it had gone down in the dial of *A*...........2Kin 20:11 271
the top of the upper chamber of *A* 2Kin 23:12 271
A his son, Hezekiah his son, ...1Chr 3:13 271
A his son reigned in his stead 2Chr 27:9 271
A was twenty years old when he 2Chr 28:1 271
At that time did king *A* send unto 2Chr 28:16 271
low because of *A* king of Israel 2Chr 28:19 271
For *A* took away a portion out of 2Chr 28:21 271
this is that king *A* 2Chr 28:22 271
A gathered together the vessels 2Chr 28:24 271
A slept with his fathers, and they 2Chr 28:27 271
which king *A* in his reign did 2Chr 29:19 271
in the days of Uzziah, Jotham, *A* ....Is 1:1 271
the days of *A* the son of Jotham ....Is 7:1 271
Isaiah, Go forth now to meet *A* ....Is 7:3 271
the LORD spake again unto *A* ....Is 7:10 271
But *A* said, I will not ask, ...Is 7:12 271
that king *A* died was this burden ....Is 14:28 271
is gone down in the sun dial of *A* ....Is 38:8 271
in the days of Uzziah, Jotham, *A* ....Hos 1:1 271
in the days of Jotham, *A*, and ....Mic 1:1 271

 2. A Benjaminite and relative of Saul.
Pithon, and Melech, and Tarea, and *A* ...1Chr 8:35 271
And *A* begat Jehoadah 1Chr 8:36 271
and Melech, and Tahrea, and *A*..............1Chr 9:41 271
And *A* begat Jarah 1Chr 9:42 271

AHAZIAH *(a-haz-i'-ah) See* AZARIAH, JEHOAHAZ.
 1. A king of Israel.
A his son reigned in his stead 1Kin 22:40 274
Then said *A* the son of Ahab unto 1Kin 22:49 274
A the son of Ahab began to reign 1Kin 22:51 274
A fell down through a lattice in.............2Kin 1:2 274
of the acts of *A* which he did.................2Kin 1:18 274
A his son, Joash his son, ...1Chr 3:11 274
himself with *A* king of Israel 2Chr 20:35 274
thou hast joined thyself with *A* 2Chr 20:37 274
 2. Son and successor of King Jehoram of Judah.
A his son reigned in his stead 2Kin 8:24 274
did *A* the son of Jehoram king of 2Kin 8:25 274
twenty years old was *A* when he 2Kin 8:26 274
A the son of Jehoram king of 2Kin 8:29 274
A king of Judah was come down to 2Kin 9:16 274
A king of Judah went out, each in 2Kin 9:21 274
his hands, and fled, and said to 2Kin 9:23 274
There is treachery, O *A*.........................2Kin 9:23 274
But when *A* the king of Judah saw 2Kin 9:27 274
Ahab began *A* to reign over Judah 2Kin 9:29 274
the brethren of *A* king of Judah............2Kin 10:13 274
We are the brethren of *A*.......................2Kin 10:13 274
of *A* saw that her son was dead.............2Kin 11:1 274
of king Joram, sister of *A*.....................2Kin 11:2 274
took Joash the son of *A* 2Kin 11:2 274
Jehoshaphat, and Jehoram, and *A* 2Kin 12:18 274
year of Joash the son of *A* king 2Kin 13:1 274
the son of Jehoash the son of *A* 2Kin 14:13 274
A his youngest son king in his 2Chr 22:1 274
So *A* the son of Jehoram king of...........2Chr 22:1 274
two years old was *A* when he began 2Chr 22:2 274
the destruction of *A* was of God 2Chr 22:7 274
and the sons of the brethren of *A* 2Chr 22:8 274
that ministered to *A*...............................2Chr 22:8 274
And he sought *A* 2Chr 22:9 274
So the house of *A* had no power to 2Chr 22:9 274
of *A* saw that her son was dead 2Chr 22:10 274
the king, took Joash the son of *A* 2Chr 22:11 274
(for she was the sister of *A* 2Chr 22:11 274

AHBAN *(ah'-ban) A descendant of Pharez.*
was Abihail, and she bare him *A*............1Chr 2:29 257

AHER *(a'-hur) See* AHARAH. *A descendant of Benjamin.*
of Ir, and Hushim, the sons of *A* 1Chr 7:12 313

AHI *(a'-hi)*
 1. A son of Abdiel.
A the son of Abdiel, the son of 1Chr 5:15 277
 2. A chief of the Asherites.
A, and Rohgah, Jehubbah, and Aram 1Chr 7:34 277

AHIAH *(a-hi'-ah) See* AHIJAH.
 1. Grandson of Phinehas.
And *A*, the son of Ahitub, ...1Sa 14:3 281
And Saul said unto *A*, Bring hither 1Sa 14:18 281
 2. A scribe of Solomon.
Elihoreph and *A*, the sons of 1Kin 4:3 281
 3. A descendant of Benjamin.
And Naaman, and *A*, and Gera, he 1Chr 8:7 281

AHIAM *(a-hi'-am) Son of Shahar.*
A the son of Sharar the Hararite, ...2Sa 23:33 279
A the son of Sacar the Hararite,.............1Chr 11:35 279

AHIAN *(a-hi'-an)*
And the sons of Shemidah were, *A* 1Chr 7:19 291

AHIEZER *(a-hi-e'-zer)*
 1. One who numbered the people.
A the son of Ammishaddai ....Num 1:12 295
shall be *A* the son of Ammishaddai ....Num 2:25 295
On the tenth day *A* the son of ....Num 7:66 295
of *A* the son of Ammishaddai ....Num 7:71 295
over his host was *A* the son of ....Num 10:25 295
 2. A chief of the Benjamites.
The chief was *A*, then Joash, the 1Chr 12:3 295

AHIHUD *(a-hi'-hud)*
 1. A prince of Asher.
of Asher, *A* the son of Shelomi ....Num 34:27 282
 2. A Benjamite of the Ehud family.
removed them, and begat Uzza, and *A*..1Chr 8:7 284

AHIJAH *(a-hi'-jah) See* AHIAH, AHIMELECH.
 1. A prophet during the reigns of Solomon and Rehoboam.
that the prophet *A* the Shilonite 1Kin 11:29 281
A caught the new garment that was 1Kin 11:30 281

which the LORD spake by *A* the 1Kin 12:15   281
there is *A* the prophet, which 1Kin 14:2   281
Shiloh, and came to the house of *A* 1Kin 14:4   281
But *A* could not see.............................1Kin 14:4   281
And the LORD said unto *A*, Behold, ...1Kin 14:5   281
when *A* heard the sound of her.............1Kin 14:6   281
hand of his servant *A* the prophet 1Kin 14:18   281
by his servant *A* the Shilonite 1Kin 15:29   281
the prophecy of *A* the Shilonite 2Chr 9:29   281
A the Shilonite to Jeroboam the 2Chr 10:15   281
  2. Father of Baasha.
And Baasha the son of *A*, of the 1Kin 15:27   281
of *A* to reign over all Israel in 1Kin 15:33   281
the house of Baasha the son of *A* 1Kin 21:22   281
the house of Baasha the son of *A* 2Kin 9:9   281
  3. Son of Jerahmeel.
Bunah, and Oren, and Ozem, and *A* 1Chr 2:25   281
  4. A "mighty man" of David.
the Mecherathite, *A* the Pelonite,............1Chr 11:36   281
  5. A treasury official under David.
A was over the treasures of the 1Chr 26:20   281
  6. A Levite who renewed the covenant.
And *A*, Hanan, Anan, ...Neh 10:26   281

AHIKAM *(a-hi'·kam) An officer in Josiah's court.*
A the son of Shaphan, and Achbor 2Kin 22:12   296
So Hilkiah the priest, and *A* 2Kin 22:14   296
he made Gedaliah the son of *A* 2Kin 25:22   296
A the son of Shaphan, and Abdon 2Chr 34:20   296
Nevertheless the hand of *A* the ....Jer 26:24   296
the son of *A* the son of Shaphan ....Jer 39:14   296
the son of *A* the son of Shaphan ....Jer 40:5   296
Gedaliah the son of *A* to Mizpah ....Jer 40:6   296
the son of *A* governor in the land ....Jer 40:7   296
Gedaliah the son of *A* the son of ....Jer 40:9   296
the son of *A* the son of Shaphan ....Jer 40:11   296
the son of *A* believed them not ....Jer 40:14   296
But Gedaliah the son of *A* said ....Jer 40:16   296
Gedaliah the son of *A* to Mizpah ....Jer 41:1   296
smote Gedaliah the son of *A* the ....Jer 41:2   296
Come to Gedaliah the son of *A* ....Jer 41:6   296
to Gedaliah the son of *A* ....Jer 41:10   296
had slain Gedaliah the son of *A* ....Jer 41:16   296
had slain Gedaliah the son of *A* ....Jer 41:18   296
the son of *A* the son of Shaphan ....Jer 43:6   296

AHILUD *(a-hi'·lud) Father of a recorder under David and Solomon.*
the son of *A* was recorder....................2Sa 8:16   286
the son of *A* was recorder....................2Sa 20:24   286
Jehoshaphat the son of *A*, the 1Kin 4:3   286
Baana the son of *A* 1Kin 4:12   286
and Jehoshaphat the son of *A* 1Chr 18:15   286

AHIMAAZ *(a-him'·a-az)*
  1. Father of Ahinoam.
was Ahinoam, the daughter of *A* 1Sa 14:50   290
  2. Son of Zadok.
A thy son, and Jonathan the son of 2Sa 15:27   290
A Zadok's son, and Jonathan 2Sa 15:36   290
Jonathan and *A* stayed by En-rogel 2Sa 17:17   290
the house, they said, Where is *A* 2Sa 17:20   290
Then said *A* the son of Zadok, Let 2Sa 18:19   290
Then said *A* the son of Zadok yet 2Sa 18:22   290
Then *A* ran by the way of the...............2Sa 18:23   290
the running of *A* the son of Zadok........2Sa 18:27   290
A called, and said unto the king, ...2Sa 18:28   290
A answered, When Joab sent the 2Sa 18:29   290
begat Zadok, and Zadok begat *A* 1Chr 6:8   290
A begat Azariah, and Azariah begat......1Chr 6:9   290
Zadok his son, *A* his son......................1Chr 6:53   290
  3. An officer of Solomon.
A was in Naphtali 1Kin 4:15   290

AHIMAN *(a-hi'·man)*
  1. A giant of Anak.
where *A*, Sheshai, and Talmai, the ....Num 13:22   289
three sons of Anak, Sheshai, and *A* ....Josh 15:14   289
and they slew Sheshai, and *A* ....Judg 1:10   289
  2. A Temple servant.
and Akkub, and Talmon, and *A* 1Chr 9:17   289

AHIMELECH *(a-him'·el-ek)*
  1. A priest.
came David to Nob to *A* the priest 1Sa 21:1   288
A was afraid at the meeting of 1Sa 21:1   288
And David said unto *A* the priest 1Sa 21:2   288
And David said unto *A*, And is there 1Sa 21:8   288
to Nob, to *A* the son of Ahitub 1Sa 22:9   288
king sent to call *A* the priest...............1Sa 22:11   288
Then *A* answered the king, and said 1Sa 22:14   288
said, Thou shalt surely die, *A* 1Sa 22:16   288
the sons of *A* the son of Ahitub............1Sa 22:20   288

son of *A* fled to David to Keilah............1Sa 23:6   288
A the son of Abiathar, were the..............2Sa 8:17   288
A of the sons of Ithamar, ...1Chr 24:3   288
A the son of Abiathar, and before 1Chr 24:6   288
of David the king, and Zadok, and *A*....1Chr 24:31   288
David is come to the house of *A* ....Ps 52:t   288
  2. A Hittite officer.
said to *A* the Hittite, and to..................1Sa 26:6   288

AHIMELECH'S *(a-him'·el-eks) Refers to Ahimelech 1.*
A son, I pray thee, bring me..................1Sa 30:7   288

AHIMOTH
Amasai, and *A*.....................................1Chr 6:25   287

AHINADAB *(a-hin'·ad-ab) A son of Iddo.*
A the son of Iddo had Mahanaim..........1Kin 4:14   292

AHINOAM *(a-hin'·o-am)*
  1. A wife of King Saul.
And the name of Saul's wife was *A* 1Sa 14:50   293
  2. A wife of David.
David also took *A* of Jezreel 1Sa 25:43   293
A the Jezreelitess, and Abigail..............1Sa 27:3   293
A the Jezreelitess, and Abigail..............1Sa 30:5   293
A the Jezreelitess, and Abigail..............2Sa 2:2   293
was Amnon, of *A* the Jezreelitess 2Sa 3:2   293
Amnon, of *A* the Jezreelitess.................1Chr 3:1   293

AHIO *(a-hi'·o)*
  1. A son of Abinadab.
and Uzzah and *A*, the sons of...............2Sa 6:3   283
and *A* went before the ark 2Sa 6:4   283
and Uzza and *A* drave the cart 1Chr 13:7   283
  2. A son of Beriah the Benjamite.
And *A*, Shashak, and Jeremoth, ...1Chr 8:14   283
  3. A son of Jehiel.
And Gedor, and *A*, and Zacher 1Chr 8:31   283
And Gedor, and *A*, and Zechariah, and..1Chr 9:37   283

AHIRA *(a-hi'·rah) A chief of Naphtali.*
A the son of Enan ....Num 1:15   299
shall be *A* the son of Enan ....Num 2:29   299
the twelfth day *A* the son of Enan ....Num 7:78   299
the offering of *A* the son of Enan ....Num 7:83   299
of Naphtali was *A* the son of Enan ....Num 10:27   299

AHIRAM *(a-hi'·rum) See AHARAH, AHIRAMITES. A descendant of Benjamin.*
of *A*, the family of the ....Num 26:38   297

AHIRAMITES *(a-hi'·rum-ites) Descendants of Ahiram.*
of Ahiram, the family of the *A* ....Num 26:38   298

AHISAMACH *(a-his'·am-ak) Father of Aholiab.*
with him Aholiab, the son of *A* ....Ex 31:6   294
both he, and Aholiab, the son of *A* ....Ex 35:34   294
And with him was Aholiab, son of *A* .....Ex 38:23   294

AHISHAHAR *(a-hish'·a-har) A son of Bilhan.*
and Zethan, and Tharshish, and *A* 1Chr 7:10   300

AHISHAR *(a-hi'·shar) Governor of the palace under Solomon.*
And *A* was over the household 1Kin 4:6   301

AHITHOPHEL *(a-hith'·o-fel) A counsellor of David.*
Absalom sent for *A* the Gilonite 2Sa 15:12   302
A is among the conspirators with...........2Sa 15:31   302
the counsel of *A* into foolishness...........2Sa 15:31   302
for me defeat the counsel of *A* 2Sa 15:34   302
came to Jerusalem, and *A* with him 2Sa 16:15   302
Then said Absalom to *A*, Give...............2Sa 16:20   302
A said unto Absalom, Go in unto...........2Sa 16:21   302
And the counsel of *A*, which he 2Sa 16:23   302
the counsel of *A* both with David 2Sa 16:23   302
Moreover *A* said unto Absalom, Let 2Sa 17:1   302
A hath spoken after this manner...........2Sa 17:6   302
The counsel that *A* hath given is 2Sa 17:7   302
is better than the counsel of *A* 2Sa 17:14   302
to defeat the good counsel of *A* 2Sa 17:14   302
thus did *A* counsel Absalom and the 2Sa 17:15   302
for thus hath *A* counselled 2Sa 17:21   302
when *A* saw that his counsel was 2Sa 17:23   302
Eliam the son of *A* the Gilonite 2Sa 23:34   302
A was the king's counsellor...................1Chr 27:33   302
after *A* was Jehoiada the son of.............1Chr 27:34   302

AHITUB *(a-hi'·tub)*
  1. The son of Phinehas.
And Ahiah, the son of *A*, ...1Sa 14:3   285
to Nob, to Ahimelech the son of *A* 1Sa 22:9   285
the priest, the son of *A*, and all 1Sa 22:11   285
said, Hear now, thou son of *A* 1Sa 22:12   285
sons of Ahimelech the son of *A* 1Sa 22:20   285
  2. Father of the high priest during David's reign.
And Zadok the son of *A*, and 2Sa 8:17   285
begat Amariah, and Amariah begat *A* ..1Chr 6:7   285

A begat Zadok, and Zadok begat	1Chr 6:8	285
son, Amariah his son, *A* his son,	1Chr 6:52	285
And Zadok the son of *A*, and	1Chr 18:16	285
the son of Zadok, the son of *A*	Ezr 7:2	285

3. *A priest seven generations later than Ahitub 2.*

begat Amariah, and Amariah begat *A*	1Chr 6:11	285
A begat Zadok, and Zadok begat	1Chr 6:12	285

4. *A priest in Nehemiah's time.*

the son of Meraioth, the son of *A*	1Chr 9:11	285
the son of Meraioth, the son of *A*	Neh 11:11	285

AHLAB (ah'-lab) *A city of Asher.*

inhabitants of Zidon, nor of *A*	Judg 1:31	303

AHLAI (ah'-lahee)
1. *A daughter of Sheshan.*

And the children of Sheshan; *A*	1Chr 2:31	304

2. *Father of a "mighty man" of David.*

the Hittite, Zabad the son of *A*	1Chr 11:41	304

AHOAH (a-ho'-ah) See AHOHITE. *The son of Bela.*

And Abishua, and Naaman, and *A*	1Chr 8:4	265

AHOHITE (a-ho'-hite)
1. *A descendant of Ahoah.*

Zalmon the *A*, Maharai the	2Sa 23:28	266
Eleazar the son of Dodo, the *A*	1Chr 11:12	266
the Hushathite, Ilai the *A*	1Chr 11:29	266
the second month was Dodai an *A*	1Chr 27:4	266

2. *A rendering of "son of Ahohi."*

Eleazar the son of Dodo the *A*	2Sa 23:9	1121,266

AHOLAH (a-ho'-lah) *A name for Samaria and the Ten Tribes.*

names of them were *A* the elder	Eze 23:4	170
Samaria is *A*, and Jerusalem	Eze 23:4	170
A played the harlot when she was	Eze 23:5	170
Son of man, wilt thou judge *A*	Eze 23:36	170
so went they in unto *A* and unto	Eze 23:44	170

AHOLIAB (a-ho'-lee-ab) *A Danite craftsman.*

behold, I have given with him *A*	Ex 31:6	171
that he may teach, both he, and *A*	Ex 35:34	171
Then wrought Bezaleel and *A*	Ex 36:1	171
And Moses called Bezaleel and *A*	Ex 36:2	171
And with him was *A*, son of	Ex 38:23	171

AHOLIBAH (a-hol'-ib-ah) *A name for Jerusalem and Judah.*

Aholah the elder, and *A* her sister	Eze 23:4	172
Samaria is Aholah, and Jerusalem *A*	Eze 23:4	172
And when her sister *A* saw this	Eze 23:11	172
Therefore, O *A*, thus saith the	Eze 23:22	172
man, wilt thou judge Aholah and *A*	Eze 23:36	172
they in unto Aholah and unto *A*	Eze 23:44	172

AHOLIBAMAH (a-hol'-ib-a'-mah)
l. *A wife of Esau.*

A the daughter of Anah the	Gen 36:2	173
A bare Jeush, and Jaalam, and Korah	Gen 36:5	173
And these were the sons of *A*	Gen 36:14	173
are the sons of *A* Esau's wife	Gen 36:18	173
came of *A* the daughter of Anah	Gen 36:18	173
Dishon, and *A* the daughter of Anah	Gen 36:25	173

2. *A chief from Esau.*

Duke *A*, duke Elah, duke Pinon,	Gen 36:41	173
Duke *A*, duke Elah, duke Pinon,	1Chr 1:52	173

AHUMAI (a-hoo'-mahee) *Grandson of Shobal.*

and Jahath begat *A*, and Lahad	1Chr 4:2	267

AHUZAM (a-hoo'-zam) *A son of Ashur.*

And Naarah bare him *A*, and Hepher,	1Chr 4:6	275

AHUZZAM See AHUZAM.

AHUZZATH (a-huz'-zath) *A friend of Ahimilech the Philistine king.*

A one of his friends, and Phichol	Gen 26:26	276

AHZAI See AHASAI.

AI (a'-i) See AIATH, AIJA, HAI. *A city near Bethel in Benjamin.*

Joshua sent men from Jericho to *A*	Josh 7:2	5857
And the men went up and viewed *A*	Josh 7:2	5857
thousand men go up and smite *A*	Josh 7:3	5857
and they fled before the men of *A*	Josh 7:4	5857
the men of *A* smote of them about	Josh 7:5	5857
with thee, and arise, go up to *A*	Josh 8:1	5857
given into thy hand the king of *A*	Josh 8:1	5857
And thou shalt do to *A* and her king	Josh 8:2	5857
people of war, to go up against *A*	Josh 8:3	5857
and *A*, on the west side of	Josh 8:9	5857
of Israel, before the people to *A*	Josh 8:10	5857
and pitched on the north side of *A*	Josh 8:11	5857
was a valley between them and *A*	Josh 8:11	5857
in ambush between Beth-el and *A*	Josh 8:12	5857

pass, when the king of *A* saw it	Josh 8:14	5857
all the people that were in *A*	Josh 8:17	5892
not a man left in *A* or Beth-el	Josh 8:17	5857
that is in thy hand toward *A*	Josh 8:18	5857
when the men of *A* looked behind	Josh 8:20	5857
again, and slew the men of *A*	Josh 8:21	5857
the king of *A* they took alive, and	Josh 8:23	5857
the inhabitants of *A* in the field	Josh 8:24	5857
the Israelites returned unto *A*	Josh 8:24	5857
thousand, even all the men of *A*	Josh 8:25	5857
all the inhabitants of *A*	Josh 8:26	5857
And Joshua burnt it an	Josh 8:28	5857
the king of *A* he hanged on a tree	Josh 8:29	5857
had done unto Jericho and her	Josh 9:3	5857
had heard how Joshua had taken *A*	Josh 10:1	5857
and her king, so he had done to *A*	Josh 10:1	5857
and because it was greater than *A*	Josh 10:2	5857
the king of *A*, which is beside	Josh 12:9	5857
The men of Beth-el and *A*, two	Ezr 2:28	5857
The men of Beth-el and *A*, an	Neh 7:32	5857
Howl, O Heshbon, for *A* is spoiled	Jer 49:3	5857

AIAH (a-i'-ah) See AJAH.
1. *A son of Zibeon the Horite.*

A, and Anah	1Chr 1:40	345

2. *The father of Saul's concubine.*

was Rizpah, the daughter of *A*	2Sa 3:7	345
sons of Rizpah the daughter of *A*	2Sa 21:8	345
the daughter of *A* took sackcloth	2Sa 21:10	345
what Rizpah the daughter of *A*	2Sa 21:11	345

AIATH (a-i'-ath) See AI. *A form of Ai.*

He is come to *A*, he is passed to	Is 10:28	5857

AIDED

which *a* him in the killing of his	Judg 9:24	2388,3027

AIJA (a-i'-jah) See AI. *A form of Ai.*

from Geba dwelt at Michmash, and *A*	Neh 11:31	5857

AIJALON (a-ij'-el-on) See AJALON.
1. *A Levitical city in Dan.*

With her suburbs, Gath-rimmon	Josh 21:24	357
would dwell in mount Heres in *A*	Judg 1:35	357

2. *A place in Zebulun.*

was buried in *A* in the country of	Judg 12:12	357

3. *A town between Benjamin and Judah.*

that day from Michmash to *A*	1Sa 14:31	357
fathers of the inhabitants of *A*	1Chr 8:13	357
And Zorah, and *A*, and Hebron, which	2Chr 11:10	357

4. *A Levitical city in Ephraim.*

And *A* with her suburbs, and	1Chr 6:69	357

AIJELETH (a-ij'-el-eth) *A musical notation.*

the chief Musician upon *A* Shahar	Ps 22:t	365

AILED

What *a* thee, O thou sea, that	Ps 114:5	

AILETH

and said unto her, What *a* thee	Gen 21:17	
and said unto Micah, What *a* thee	Judg 18:23	
that ye say unto me, What *a* thee	Judg 18:24	
What *a* the people that they weep	1Sa 11:5	
king said unto her, What *a* thee	2Sa 14:5	
king said unto her, What *a* thee	2Kin 6:28	
What *a* thee now, that thou art	Is 22:1	

AIN (ah'-yin) See EN.
1. *A place between Riblah and the Sea of Chinnereth.*

to Riblah, on the east side of *A*	Num 34:11	5871

2. *A Levitical city in Simeon.*

And Lebaoth, and Shilhim, and *A*	Josh 15:32	5871
A, Remmon, and Ether, and Ashan	Josh 19:7	5871
A with her suburbs, and Juttah	Josh 21:16	5871
their villages were, Etam, and *A*	1Chr 4:32	5871

AIR

sea, and over the fowl of the *a*	Gen 1:26	8064
sea, and over the fowl of the *a*	Gen 1:28	8064
earth, and to every fowl of the *a*	Gen 1:30	8064
the field, and every fowl of the *a*	Gen 2:19	8064
cattle, and to the fowl of the *a*	Gen 2:20	8064
thing, and the fowls of the *a*	Gen 6:7	8064
Of fowls also of the *a* by sevens	Gen 7:3	8064
and upon every fowl of the *a*	Gen 9:2	8064
winged fowl that flieth in the *a*	Deut 4:17	8064
be meat unto all fowls of the *a*	Deut 28:26	8064
thy field unto the fowls of the *a*	1Sa 17:44	8064
this day unto the fowls of the *a*	1Sa 17:46	8064
of the *a* to rest on them by day	2Sa 21:10	8064
shall the fowls of the *a* eat	1Kin 14:11	8064
shall the fowls of the *a* eat	1Kin 16:4	8064
shall the fowls of the *a* eat	1Kin 21:24	8064
and the fowls of the *a*, and they	Job 12:7	8064
close from the fowls of the *a*	Job 28:21	8064

ti:at no *a* can come between them	Job 41:16	7307
The fowl of the *a*, and the fish of	Ps 8:8	8064
The way of an eagle in the *a*	Prov 30:19	8064
for a bird of the *a* shall carry	Eccl 10:20	8064
Behold the fowls of the *a*	Mt 6:26	3772
and the birds of the *a* have nests	Mt 8:20	3772
so that the birds of the *a* come	Mt 13:32	3772
side, and the fowls of the *a* came	Mk 4:4	3772
so that the fowls of the *a* may	Mk 4:32	3772
and the fowls of the *a* devoured it	Lk 8:5	3772
and birds of the *a* have nests	Lk 9:58	3772
the fowls of the *a* lodged in the	Lk 13:19	3772
things, and fowls of the *a*	Acts 10:12	3772
things, and fowls of the *a*	Acts 11:6	3772
clothes, and threw dust into the *a*	Acts 22:23	109
I, so as one that beateth the *a*	1Cor 9:26	109
for ye shall speak into the *a*	1Cor 14:9	109
the prince of the power of the *a*	Eph 2:2	109
clouds, to meet the Lord in the *a*	1Th 4:17	109
the *a* were darkened by reason of	Rev 9:2	109
poured out his vial into the *a*	Rev 16:17	109

AJAH (*a'-jah*) See AIAH. *A son of Zibeon the Horite.*
both *A*, and Anah	Gen 36:24	345

AJALON (*aj'-a-lon*) See AIJALON.
1. A valley of Dan.
and thou, Moon, in the valley of *A*	Josh 10:12	357

2. A Levitical city in Dan.
And Shaalabbin, and *A*, and Jethlah,	Josh 19:42	357

3. A town between Benjamin and Judah.
and had taken Beth-shemesh, and *A*	2Chr 28:18	357

AKAN (*a'-kan*) See JAAKAN, JAKAN. *A son of Ezer.*
Bilhan, and Zaavan, and *A*	Gen 36:27	6130

AKEL DAMA See ACELDAMA.

AKKAD See ACCAD.

AKKUB (*ak'-kub*)
1. A descendant of David.
and Eliashib, and Pelaiah, and *A*	1Chr 3:24	6126

2. A Levitical gatekeeper.
the porters were, Shallum, and *A*	1Chr 9:17	6126
Moreover the porters, *A*, Talmon,	Neh 11:19	6126
Obadiah, Meshullam, Talmon, *A*	Neh 12:25	6126

3. A family of Levitical porters.
of Talmon, the children of *A*	Ezr 2:42	6126
of Talmon, the children of *A*	Neh 7:45	6126

4. A family of returned exiles.
of Hagabah, the children of *A*	Ezr 2:45	6126

5. A priest in Ezra's time.
and Bani, and Sherebiah, Jamin, *A*	Neh 8:7	6126

AKRABBIM (*ac-rab'-bim*) See MAALE-ACRABBIM. *An ascent south of the Dead Sea.*
from the south to the ascent of *A*	Num 34:4	6137
was from the going up to *A*	Judg 1:36	6137

ALABASTER
a box of very precious ointment	Mt 26:7	211
an *a* box of ointment of spikenard	Mk 14:3	211
brought an *a* box of ointment,	Lk 7:37	211

ALAMETH (*al'-am-eth*) *A son of Becher.*
and Abiah, and Anathoth, and *A*	1Chr 7:8	5964

ALAMMELECH (*a-lam'-mel-ek*) *A town in Asher.*
And *A*, and Amad, and Misheal	Josh 19:26	487

ALAMOTH (*al'-am-oth*) *A musical notation.*
and Benaiah, with psalteries on *A*	1Chr 15:20	5961
the sons of Korah, A Song upon *A*	Ps 46:t	5961

ALARM
When ye blow an *a*, then the camps	Num 10:5	8643
When ye blow an *a* the second time	Num 10:6	8643
blow an *a* for their journeys	Num 10:6	8643
blow, but ye shall not sound an *a*	Num 10:7	7321
shall blow an *a* with the trumpets	Num 10:9	7321
trumpets to cry *a* against you	2Chr 13:12	7321
of the trumpet, the *a* of war	Jer 4:19	8643
that I will cause an *a* of war to	Jer 49:2	8643
sound an *a* in my holy mountain	Joel 2:1	7321
a against the fenced cities, and	Zeph 1:16	8643

ALAS See APPENDIX.

ALBEIT
a I have not spoken	Eze 13:7	
a I do not say to thee how thou	Philem 19	2443

ALEMETH (*al-e'-meth*)
1. A Levitical city in Benjamin.
A with her suburbs, and Anathoth	1Chr 6:60	5964

2. A descendant of Jonathan.
and Jehoadah begat *A*, and Azmaveth,	1Chr 8:36	5964
Jarah begat *A*, and Azmaveth, and	1Chr 9:42	5964

ALEXANDER (*al-ex-an'-dur*)
1. Son of Simeon who bore Jesus' cross.
of the country, the father of *A*	Mk 15:21	223

2. A Christian leader in Jerusalem.
and Caiaphas, and John, and *A*	Acts 4:6	223

3. A participant in the Ephesian riot.
they drew *A* out of the multitude,	Acts 19:33	223
A beckoned with the hand, and	Acts 19:33	223

4. An opponent of Paul.
Of whom is Hymenaeus and *A*	1Ti 1:20	
A the coppersmith did me much	2Ti 4:14	223

ALEXANDRIA (*al-ex-an'-dree-ah*) See ALEXANDRIANS.
A city in Egypt.
Jew named Apollos, born at *A*	Acts 18:24	221
a ship of *A* sailing into Italy	Acts 27:6	221
months we departed in a ship of *A*	Acts 28:11	221

ALEXANDRIAN See ALEXANDRIA.

ALEXANDRIANS (*al-ex-an'-dree-uns*) *Residents of Alexandria.*
Libertines, and Cyrenians, and *A*	Acts 6:9	221

ALGUM
trees, and *a* trees, out of Lebanon	2Chr 2:8	418
gold from Ophir, brought *a* trees	2Chr 9:10	418
the king made of the *a* trees	2Chr 9:11	418

ALIAH (*a-li'-ah*) See ALVAH. *A chief of Edom.*
duke Timnah, duke *A*, duke Jetheth	1Chr 1:51	5933

ALIAN (*a-li'-un*) See ALVAN. *A son of Shobal.*
A, and Manahath, and Ebal, Shephi,	1Chr 1:40	5935

ALIEN
I have been an *a* in a strange	Ex 18:3	1616
or thou mayest sell it unto an *a*	Deut 14:21	5237
I am an *a* in their sight	Job 19:15	5237
an *a* unto my mother's children	Ps 69:8	5237
the sons of the *a* shall be your	Is 61:5	5236

ALIENATE
nor *a* the firstfruits of the land	Eze 48:14	5674

ALIENATED
them, and her mind was *a* from them	Eze 23:17	3363
then my mind was *a* from her	Eze 23:18	3363
as my mind was *a* from her sister	Eze 23:18	5361
thee, from whom thy mind is *a*	Eze 23:22	5361
of them from whom thy mind is *a*	Eze 23:28	5361
being *a* from the life of God	Eph 4:18	526
And you, that were sometime *a*	Col 1:21	526

ALIENS
to strangers, our houses to *a*	Lam 5:2	5237
being *a* from the commonwealth of	Eph 2:12	526
to flight the armies of the *a*	Heb 11:34	245

ALIKE See APPENDIX.

ALIVE
the ark, to keep them *a* with thee	Gen 6:19	2421
come unto thee, to keep them *a*	Gen 6:20	2421
to keep seed *a* upon the face of	Gen 7:3	2421
and Noah only remained *a*, and they	Gen 7:23	
me, but they will save me *a*	Gen 12:12	2421
saying, Is your father yet *a*	Gen 43:7	2416
Is he yet *a*	Gen 43:27	2416
is in good health, he is yet *a*	Gen 43:28	2416
told him, saying, Joseph is yet *a*	Gen 45:26	2416
Joseph my son is yet *a*	Gen 45:28	2416
thy face, because thou art yet *a*	Gen 46:30	2416
this day, to save much people *a*	Gen 50:20	2421
but saved the men children *a*	Ex 1:17	2421
and have saved the men children *a*	Ex 1:18	2421
and every daughter ye shall save *a*	Ex 1:22	2421
and see whether they be yet *a*	Ex 4:18	2416
be certainly found in his hand *a*	Ex 22:4	2421
sons of Aaron which were left *a*	Lev 10:16	
is to be cleansed two birds *a*	Lev 14:4	2416
be presented *a* before the LORD	Lev 16:10	2416
upon them that are left *a* of you	Lev 26:36	
went down *a* into the pit, and the	Num 16:33	2416
until there was none left him *a*	Num 21:35	8300
I had slain thee, and saved her *a*	Num 22:33	2421
Have ye saved all the women *a*	Num 31:15	2421
with him, keep *a* for yourselves	Num 31:18	2421
are *a* every one of you this day	Deut 4:4	2416
who are all of us here a this day	Deut 5:3	2416
that he might preserve us *a*	Deut 6:24	2421
thou shalt save *a* nothing that	Deut 20:16	2421
while I am yet *a* with you this	Deut 31:27	2416
I kill, and I make *a*	Deut 32:39	2421
And that ye will save *a* my father	Josh 2:13	2421
Joshua saved Rahab the harlot *a*	Josh 6:25	2421
And the king of Ai they took *a*	Josh 8:23	2416

behold, the LORD hath kept me *a*	Josh 14:10	2421
liveth, if ye had saved them *a*	Judg 8:19	2421
a of the women of Jabesh-gilead	Judg 21:14	2421
The LORD killeth, and maketh *a*	1Sa 2:6	2421
Agag the king of the Amalekites *a*	1Sa 15:8	2416
and left neither man nor woman *a*	1Sa 27:9	2421
saved neither man nor woman *a*	1Sa 27:11	2421
and with one full line to keep *a*	2Sa 8:2	2421
Behold, while the child was yet *a*	2Sa 12:18	2416
for the child, while it was *a*	2Sa 12:21	2416
said, While the child was yet *a*	2Sa 12:22	2416
while he was yet *a* in the midst	2Sa 18:14	2416
to save the horses and mules *a*	1Kin 18:5	2421
come out for peace, take them *a*	1Kin 20:18	2416
be come out for war, take them *a*	1Kin 20:18	2416
And he said, Is he yet *a*	1Kin 20:32	2416
for Naboth is not *a*, but dead	1Kin 21:15	2416
Am I God, to kill and to make *a*	2Kin 5:7	2421
if they save us *a*, we shall live	2Kin 7:4	2421
the city, we shall catch them *a*	2Kin 7:12	2416
And he said, Take them *a*	2Kin 10:14	2421
And they took them *a*, and slew them	2Kin 10:14	2416
other ten thousand left *a* did the	2Chr 25:12	2416
and none can keep *a* his own soul	Ps 22:29	2421
thou hast kept me *a*, that I	Ps 30:3	2421
and to keep them *a* in famine	Ps 33:19	2421
will preserve him, and keep him *a*	Ps 41:2	2421
us swallow them up *a* as the grave	Prov 1:12	2416
than the living which are yet *a*	Eccl 4:2	2416
children, I will preserve them *a*	Jer 49:11	2421
is sold, although they were yet *a*	Eze 7:13	2416
the souls *a* that come unto you	Eze 13:18	2421
to save the souls *a* that should	Eze 13:19	2421
right, he shall save his soul *a*	Eze 18:27	2421
and whom he would he kept *a*	Dan 5:19	2418
deceiver said, while he was yet *a*	Mt 27:63	2198
when they had heard that he was *a*	Mk 16:11	2198
my son was dead, and is *a* again	Lk 15:24	*326*
brother was dead, and is *a* again	Lk 15:32	*326*
angels, which said that he was *a*	Lk 24:23	2198
a after his passion by many	Acts 1:3	2198
saints and widows, presented her *a*	Acts 9:41	2198
And they brought the young man *a*	Acts 20:12	2198
dead, whom Paul affirmed to be *a*	Acts 25:19	2198
but *a* unto God through Jesus	Rom 6:11	2198
as those that are *a* from the dead	Rom 6:13	2198
For I was *a* without the law once	Rom 7:9	2198
so in Christ shall all be made *a*	1Cor 15:22	2227
of the Lord, that we which are *a*	1Th 4:15	2198
Then we which are *a* and remain	1Th 4:17	2198
I am *a* for evermore, Amen	Rev 1:18	2198
the last, which was dead, and is *a*	Rev 2:8	2198
These both were cast *a* into a	Rev 19:20	2198

ALL See APPENDIX.

ALLAMMELECH See ALAMMELECH.

ALLEGING

Opening and *a*, that Christ must	Acts 17:3	*3908*

ALLEGORY

Which things are an *a*	Gal 4:24	*238*

ALLELUIA (al-le-loo'-yah) *Greek form of Hallelujah.*

much people in heaven, saying, *A*	Rev 19:1	*239*
And again they said, *A*	Rev 19:3	*239*
saying, Amen; *A*.	Rev 19:4	*239*
of mighty thunderings, saying, *A*	Rev 19:6	*239*

ALLIED

of our God, was *a* unto Tobiah	Neh 13:4	*7138*

ALLON (al'-lon) See ALLON-BACHUTH, ELON.
1. A city in Naphtali.

from *A* to Zaanannim, and Adami,	Josh 19:33	*438*

2. A chief of a Simeonite family.

the son of Shiphi, the son of *A*	1Chr 4:37	*438*

ALLON-BACHUTH (al'-lon-bak'-ooth) *A place near Bethel.*

and the name of it was called *A*	Gen 35:8	*439*

ALLOW

ye *a* the deeds of your fathers	Lk 11:48	*4909*
God, which they themselves also *a*	Acts 24:15	*4327*
For that which I do I *a* not	Rom 7:15	*1097*

ALLOWANCE

his *a* was a continual *a*	2Kin 25:30	*737*

ALLOWED

But as we were *a* of God to be put	1Th 2:4	*1381*

ALLOWETH

himself in that thing which he *a*	Rom 14:22	*1381*

ALLURE

Therefore, behold, I will *a* her	Hos 2:14	*6601*
they *a* through the lusts of the	2Pet 2:18	*1185*

ALMIGHTY *A term for God meaning sufficient or all-powerful.*

and said unto him, I am the *A* God	Gen 17:1	7706
God *A* bless thee, and make thee	Gen 28:3	7706
And God said unto him, I am God *A*	Gen 35:11	7706
God *A* give you mercy before the	Gen 43:14	7706
God *A* appeared unto me at Luz in	Gen 48:3	7706
and by the *A*, who shall bless thee	Gen 49:25	7706
unto Jacob, by the name of God *A*	Ex 6:3	7706
which saw the vision of the *A*	Num 24:4	7706
which saw the vision of the *A*	Num 24:16	7706
for the *A* hath dealt very	Ruth 1:20	7706
me, and the *A* hath afflicted me	Ruth 1:21	7706
not thou the chastening of the *A*	Job 5:17	7706
the arrows of the *A* are within me	Job 6:4	7706
he forsaketh the fear of the *A*	Job 6:14	7706
or doth the *A* pervert justice	Job 8:3	7706
and make thy supplication to the *A*	Job 8:5	7706
find out the *A* unto perfection	Job 11:7	7706
Surely I would speak to the *A*	Job 13:3	7706
himself against the *A*	Job 15:25	7706
What is the *A*, that we should	Job 21:15	7706
shall drink of the wrath of the *A*	Job 21:20	7706
Is it any pleasure to the *A*	Job 22:3	7706
and what can the *A* do for them	Job 22:17	7706
If thou return to the *A*, thou	Job 22:23	7706
the *A* shall be thy defence, and	Job 22:25	7706
thou have thy delight in the *A*	Job 22:26	7706
heart soft, and the *A* troubleth me	Job 23:16	7706
times are not hidden from the *A*	Job 24:1	7706
and the *A*, who hath vexed my soul	Job 27:2	7706
Will he delight himself in the *A*	Job 27:10	7706
is with the *A* will I not conceal	Job 27:11	7706
which they shall receive of the *A*	Job 27:13	7706
When the *A* was yet with me, when	Job 29:5	7706
inheritance of the *A* from on high	Job 31:2	7706
that the *A* would answer me, and	Job 31:35	7706
the inspiration of the *A* giveth	Job 32:8	7706
the breath of the *A* hath given me	Job 33:4	7706
and from the *A*, that he should	Job 34:10	7706
will the *A* pervert judgment	Job 34:12	7706
neither will the *A* regard it	Job 35:13	7706
Touching the *A*, we cannot find	Job 37:23	7706
with the *A* instruct him	Job 40:2	7706
When the *A* scattered kings in it,	Ps 68:14	7706
abide under the shadow of the *A*	Ps 91:1	7706
come as a destruction from the *A*	Is 13:6	7706
waters, as the voice of the *A*	Eze 1:24	7706
as the voice of the *A* God when he	Eze 10:5	7706
from the *A* shall it come	Joel 1:15	7706
and daughters, saith the Lord *A*	2Cor 6:18	*3841*
was, and which is to come, the *A*	Rev 1:8	*3841*
Holy, holy, holy, Lord God *A*	Rev 4:8	*3841*
We give thee thanks, O Lord God *A*	Rev 11:17	*3841*
are thy works, Lord God *A*	Rev 15:3	*3841*
altar say, Even so, Lord God *A*	Rev 16:7	*3841*
battle of that great day of God *A*	Rev 16:14	*3841*
the fierceness and wrath of *A* God	Rev 19:15	*3841*
for the Lord God *A* and the Lamb	Rev 21:22	*3841*

ALMODAD (al-mo'-dad) *A descendant of Shem.*

And Joktan begat *A*, and Sheleph, and	Gen 10:26	486
And Joktan begat *A*, and Sheleph, and	1Chr 1:20	486

ALMON (al'-mon) *A Levitical town in Benjamin.*

suburbs, and *A* with her suburbs	Josh 21:18	5960

ALMOND

the *a* tree shall flourish, and the	Eccl 12:5	8247
I said, I see a rod of an *a* tree	Jer 1:11	8247

ALMON-DIBLATHAIM (al'-mon-dib-lath-a'-im) *An encampment of Israel in the Wilderness.*

from Dibon-gad, and encamped in *A*	Num 33:46	5963
And they removed from *A*, and	Num 33:47	5963

ALMONDS

spices, and myrrh, nuts, and *a*	Gen 43:11	8247
Three bowls made like unto *a*	Ex 25:33	8246
made like *a* in the other branch	Ex 25:33	8246
be four bowls made like unto *a*	Ex 25:34	8246
the fashion of *a* in one branch	Ex 37:19	8246
made like *a* in another branch	Ex 37:19	8246
were four bowls made like *a*	Ex 37:20	8246
and bloomed blossoms, and yielded *a*	Num 17:8	8247

ALMOST See APPENDIX.

ALMS

that ye do not your *a* before men	Mt 6:1	*1654*
Therefore when thou doest thine *a*	Mt 6:2	*1654*

But when thou doest *a*, let not .... Mt 6:3   *1654*
That thine *a* may be in secret .... Mt 6:4   *1654*
But rather give *a* of such things .... Lk 11:41   *1654*
Sell that ye have, and give *a* .... Lk 12:33   *1654*
to ask *a* of them that entered .... Acts 3:2   *1654*
to go into the temple asked an *a* .... Acts 3:3   *1654*
a at the Beautiful gate of the .... Acts 3:10   *1654*
which gave much *a* to the people .... Acts 10:2   *1654*
thine *a* are come up for a .... Acts 10:4   *1654*
thine *a* are had in remembrance in .... Acts 10:31   *1654*
I came to bring *a* to my nation .... Acts 24:17   *1654*

ALMSDEEDS
of good works and *a* which she did .... Acts 9:36   *1654*

ALMUG
Ophir great plenty of *a* trees 1Kin 10:11   *484*
the king made of the *a* trees 1Kin 10:12   *484*
there came no such *a* trees 1Kin 10:12   *484*

ALOES
as the trees of lign *a* which the .... Num 24:6   *174*
thy garments smell of myrrh, and *a* .... Ps 45:8   *174*
perfumed my bed with myrrh, *a* .... Prov 7:17   *174*
myrrh and *a*, with all the chief .... Song 4:14   *174*
brought a mixture of myrrh and *a* .... Jn 19:39   *250*

ALONE See APPENDIX.

ALONG See APPENDIX.

ALOOF
my friends stand *a* from my sore .... Ps 38:11   *5048*

ALOTH (a'-loth) See BEALOTH. *A region near Asher.*
of Hushai was in Asher and in A 1Kin 4:16   *1175*

ALOUD
And he wept *a* .... Gen 45:2   *5414,854,6963*
mocked them, and said, Cry *a* 1Kin 18:27   *6963,1419*
And they cried *a*, and cut 1Kin 18:28   *1419,3605*
and many shouted *a* for joy .... Ezr 3:12   *7311,1419*
I cry *a*, but there is no judgment .... Job 19:7   *7768*
shall sing *a* of thy righteousness .... Ps 51:14   *7442*
and at noon, will I pray, and cry *a* ...... Ps 55:17   *1993*
I will sing *a* of thy mercy in the .... Ps 59:16   *7442*
Sing *a* unto God our strength .... Ps 81:1   *7442*
her saints shall shout *a* for joy .... Ps 132:16   *7442*
let them sing *a* upon their beds .... Ps 149:5   *7442*
they shall cry *a* from the sea .... Is 24:14   *6670*
forth into singing, and cry *a* .... Is 54:1   *6670*
Cry *a*, spare not, lift up thy .... Is 58:1   *1627*
Then an herald cried *a*, To you it .... Dan 3:4   *2429*
He cried *a*, and said thus, Hew .... Dan 4:14   *2429*
The king cried *a* to bring in the .... Dan 5:7   *2429*
cry *a* at Beth-aven, after thee, O .... Hos 5:8   *7321*
Now why dost thou cry out *a* .... Mic 4:9   *7452*
the multitude crying *a* began to .... Mk 15:8   *310*

ALPHA (al'-fah) *First letter of Greek alphabet.*
I am A and Omega, the beginning .... Rev 1:8   *1*
Saying, I am A and Omega, the .... Rev 1:11   *1*
I am A and Omega, the beginning .... Rev 21:6   *1*
I am A and Omega, the beginning .... Rev 22:13   *1*

ALPHAEUS (al-fe'-us) See CLEOPAS.
1. Father of the apostle James.
James the son of A, and Lebbaeus ...... Mt 10:3   *256*
and Thomas, and James the son of A .... Mk 3:18   *256*
and Thomas, James the son of A .... Lk 6:15   *256*
and Matthew, James the son of A .... Acts 1:13   *256*
2. Father of the apostle Levi.
he saw Levi the son of A sitting .... Mk 2:14   *256*

ALREADY See APPENDIX.

ALSO See APPENDIX.

ALTAR
Noah builded an *a* unto the LORD .... Gen 8:20   *4196*
offered burnt offerings on the *a* .... Gen 8:20   *4196*
builded he an *a* unto the LORD .... Gen 12:7   *4196*
he builded an *a* unto the LORD .... Gen 12:8   *4196*
Unto the place of the *a*, which he .... Gen 13:4   *4196*
and built there an *a* unto the LORD .... Gen 13:18   *4196*
and Abraham built an *a* there .... Gen 22:9   *4196*
laid him on the *a* upon the wood .... Gen 22:9   *4196*
And he builded an *a* there, and .... Gen 26:25   *4196*
And he erected there an *a*, and .... Gen 33:20   *4196*
and make there an *a* unto God .... Gen 35:1   *4196*
I will make there an *a* unto God .... Gen 35:3   *4196*
And he built there an *a*, and called .... Gen 35:7   *4196*
And Moses built an *a*, and called .... Ex 17:15   *4196*
An *a* of earth thou shalt make .... Ex 20:24   *4196*
thou wilt make me an *a* of stone .... Ex 20:25   *4196*
thou go up by steps unto mine *a* .... Ex 20:26   *4196*
thou shalt take him from mine *a* .... Ex 21:14   *4196*
builded an *a* under the hill, and .... Ex 24:4   *4196*

the blood he sprinkled on the *a* .... Ex 24:6   *4196*
shalt make an *a* of shittim wood .... Ex 27:1   *4196*
the *a* shall be foursquare .... Ex 27:1   *4196*
the compass of the *a* beneath .... Ex 27:5   *4196*
may be even to the midst of the *a* .... Ex 27:5   *4196*
thou shalt make staves for the *a* .... Ex 27:6   *4196*
be upon the two sides of the *a* .... Ex 27:7   *4196*
a to minister in the holy place .... Ex 28:43   *4196*
horns of the *a* with thy finger .... Ex 29:12   *4196*
blood beside the bottom of the *a* .... Ex 29:12   *4196*
them, and burn them upon the *a* .... Ex 29:13   *4196*
it round about upon the *a* .... Ex 29:16   *4196*
burn the whole ram upon the *a* .... Ex 29:18   *4196*
the blood upon the *a* round about .... Ex 29:20   *4196*
of the blood that is upon the *a* .... Ex 29:21   *4196*
burn them upon the *a* for a burnt .... Ex 29:25   *4196*
and thou shalt cleanse the *a* .... Ex 29:36   *4196*
shalt make an atonement for the *a* .... Ex 29:37   *4196*
and it shall be an *a* most holy .... Ex 29:37   *4196*
toucheth the *a* shall be holy .... Ex 29:37   *4196*
which thou shalt offer upon the *a* .... Ex 29:38   *4196*
of the congregation, and the *a* .... Ex 29:44   *4196*
thou shalt make an *a* to burn .... Ex 30:1   *4196*
of the congregation and the *a* .... Ex 30:18   *4196*
come near to the *a* to minister .... Ex 30:20   *4196*
his vessels, and the *a* of incense, ... Ex 30:27   *4196*
the *a* of burnt offering with all .... Ex 30:28   *4196*
furniture, and the *a* of incense, ... Ex 31:8   *4196*
the *a* of burnt offering with all .... Ex 31:9   *4196*
saw it, he built an *a* before it .... Ex 32:5   *4196*
And the incense *a*, and his staves, ... Ex 35:15   *4196*
The *a* of burnt offering, with his .... Ex 35:16   *4196*
the incense *a* of shittim wood .... Ex 37:25   *4196*
he made the *a* of burnt offering .... Ex 38:1   *4196*
he made all the vessels of the *a* .... Ex 38:3   *4196*
he made for the *a* a brasen grate .... Ex 38:4   *4196*
the rings on the sides of the *a* .... Ex 38:7   *4196*
he made the *a* hollow with boards .... Ex 38:7
the congregation, and the brasen *a* .... Ex 38:30   *4196*
it, and all the vessels of the *a* .... Ex 38:30   *4196*
And the golden *a*, and the anointing ..... Ex 39:38   *4196*
The brasen *a*, and his grate of .... Ex 39:39   *4196*
thou shalt set the *a* of gold for .... Ex 40:5   *4196*
thou shalt set the *a* of the burnt .... Ex 40:6   *4196*
tent of the congregation and the *a* .... Ex 40:7   *4196*
the *a* of the burnt offering .... Ex 40:10   *4196*
his vessels, and sanctify the *a* .... Ex 40:10   *4196*
and it shall be an *a* most holy .... Ex 40:10   *4196*
he put the golden *a* in the tent .... Ex 40:26   *4196*
he put the *a* of burnt offering by .... Ex 40:29   *4196*
tent of the congregation and the *a* .... Ex 40:30   *4196*
and when they came near unto the *a* ..... Ex 40:32   *4196*
about the tabernacle and the *a* .... Ex 40:33   *4196*
the *a* that is by the door of the .... Lev 1:5   *4196*
priest shall put fire upon the *a* .... Lev 1:7   *4196*
on the fire which is upon the *a* .... Lev 1:8   *4196*
priest shall burn all on the *a* .... Lev 1:9   *4196*
the *a* northward before the LORD .... Lev 1:11   *4196*
his blood round about upon the *a* .... Lev 1:11   *4196*
on the fire which is upon the *a* .... Lev 1:12   *4196*
it all, and burn it upon the *a* .... Lev 1:13   *4196*
priest shall bring it unto the *a* .... Lev 1:15   *4196*
off his head, and burn it on the *a* .... Lev 1:15   *4196*
be wrung out at the side of the *a* .... Lev 1:15   *4196*
it beside the *a* on the east part .... Lev 1:16   *4196*
priest shall burn it upon the *a* .... Lev 1:17   *4196*
the memorial of it upon the *a* .... Lev 2:2   *4196*
he shall bring it unto the *a* .... Lev 2:8   *4196*
and shall burn it upon the *a* .... Lev 2:9   *4196*
burnt on the *a* for a sweet savour .... Lev 2:12   *4196*
the blood upon the *a* round about .... Lev 3:2   *4196*
on the *a* upon the burnt sacrifice .... Lev 3:5   *4196*
thereof round about upon the *a* .... Lev 3:8   *4196*
priest shall burn it upon the *a* .... Lev 3:11   *4196*
thereof upon the *a* round about .... Lev 3:13   *4196*
priest shall burn them upon the *a* .... Lev 3:16   *4196*
the *a* of sweet incense before the .... Lev 4:7   *4196*
of the *a* of the burnt offering .... Lev 4:7   *4196*
upon the *a* of the burnt offering .... Lev 4:10   *4196*
of the *a* which is before the LORD .... Lev 4:18   *4196*
of the *a* of the burnt offering .... Lev 4:18   *4196*
from him, and burn it upon the *a* .... Lev 4:19   *4196*
horns of the *a* of burnt offering .... Lev 4:25   *4196*
bottom of the *a* of burnt offering .... Lev 4:25   *4196*
shall burn all his fat upon the *a* .... Lev 4:26   *4196*
horns of the *a* of burnt offering .... Lev 4:30   *4196*
thereof at the bottom of the *a* .... Lev 4:30   *4196*
the *a* for a sweet savour unto the .... Lev 4:31   *4196*
horns of the *a* of burnt offering .... Lev 4:34   *4196*
thereof at the bottom of the *a* .... Lev 4:34   *4196*
priest shall burn them upon the *a* .... Lev 4:35   *4196*

offering upon the side of the *a*	Lev 5:9	4196
wrung out at the bottom of the *a*	Lev 5:9	4196
thereof, and burn it on the *a*	Lev 5:12	4196
the *a* all night unto the morning	Lev 6:9	4196
the fire of the *a* shall be	Lev 6:9	4196
with the burnt offering on the *a*	Lev 6:10	4196
and he shall put them beside the *a*	Lev 6:10	4196
the fire upon the *a* shall be	Lev 6:12	4196
shall ever be burning upon the *a*	Lev 6:13	4196
it before the LORD, before the *a*	Lev 6:14	4196
it upon the *a* for a sweet savour	Lev 6:15	4196
sprinkle round about upon the *a*	Lev 7:2	4196
a for an offering made by fire	Lev 7:5	4196
shall burn the fat upon the *a*	Lev 7:31	4196
thereof upon the *a* seven times	Lev 8:11	4196
seven times, and anointed the *a*	Lev 8:11	4196
the *a* round about with his finger	Lev 8:15	4196
his finger, and purified the *a*	Lev 8:15	4196
the blood at the bottom of the *a*	Lev 8:15	4196
and Moses burned it upon the *a*	Lev 8:16	4196
the blood upon the *a* round about	Lev 8:19	4196
burnt the whole ram upon the *a*	Lev 8:21	4196
the blood upon the *a* round about	Lev 8:24	4196
burnt them on the *a* upon the	Lev 8:28	4196
of the blood which was upon the *a*	Lev 8:30	4196
said unto Aaron, Go unto the *a*	Lev 9:7	4196
Aaron therefore went unto the *a*	Lev 9:8	4196
and put it upon the horns of the *a*	Lev 9:9	4196
the blood at the bottom of the *a*	Lev 9:9	4196
sin offering, he burnt upon the *a*	Lev 9:10	4196
sprinkled round about upon the *a*	Lev 9:12	4196
and he burnt them upon the *a*	Lev 9:13	4196
upon the burnt offering on the *a*	Lev 9:14	4196
thereof, and burnt it upon the *a*	Lev 9:17	4196
sprinkled upon the *a* round about	Lev 9:18	4196
and he burnt the fat upon the *a*	Lev 9:20	4196
consumed upon the *a* the burnt	Lev 9:24	4196
it without leaven beside the *a*	Lev 10:12	4196
and the meat offering upon the *a*	Lev 14:20	4196
from off the *a* before the LORD	Lev 16:12	4196
the *a* that is before the LORD	Lev 16:18	4196
the horns of the *a* round about	Lev 16:18	4196
of the congregation, and the *a*	Lev 16:20	4196
offering shall he burn upon the *a*	Lev 16:25	4196
of the congregation, and for the *a*	Lev 16:33	4196
sprinkle the blood upon the *a* of	Lev 17:6	4196
a to make an atonement for your	Lev 17:11	4196
vail, nor come nigh unto the *a*	Lev 21:23	4196
of them upon the *a* unto the LORD	Lev 22:22	4196
by the *a* round about, and the	Num 3:26	4196
upon the golden *a* they shall	Num 4:11	4196
take away the ashes from the *a*	Num 4:13	4196
basons, all the vessels of the *a*	Num 4:14	4196
by the *a* round about, and their	Num 4:26	4196
the LORD, and offer it upon the *a*	Num 5:25	4196
thereof, and burn it upon the *a*	Num 5:26	4196
instruments thereof, both the *a*	Num 7:1	4196
offered for dedicating of the *a*	Num 7:10	4196
their offering before the *a*	Num 7:10	4196
day, for the dedicating of the *a*	Num 7:11	4196
This was the dedication of the *a*	Num 7:84	4196
This was the dedication of the *a*	Num 7:88	4196
plates for a covering of the *a*	Num 16:38	4196
plates for a covering of the *a*	Num 16:39	4196
put fire therein from off the *a*	Num 16:46	4196
vessels of the sanctuary and the *a*	Num 18:3	4196
sanctuary, and the charge of the *a*	Num 18:5	4196
office for every thing of the *a*	Num 18:7	4196
sprinkle their blood upon the *a*	Num 18:17	4196
offered on every *a* a bullock	Num 23:2	4196
offered upon every *a* a bullock	Num 23:4	4196
a bullock and a ram on every *a*	Num 23:14	4196
a bullock and a ram on every *a*	Num 23:30	4196
upon the *a* of the LORD thy God	Deut 12:27	4196
upon the *a* of the LORD thy God	Deut 12:27	4196
unto the *a* of the LORD thy God	Deut 16:21	4196
before the *a* of the LORD thy God	Deut 26:4	4196
there shalt thou build an *a*	Deut 27:5	4196
the LORD thy God, an *a* of stones	Deut 27:5	4196
Thou shalt build the *a* of the	Deut 27:6	4196
burnt sacrifice upon thine *a*	Deut 33:10	4196
Then Joshua built an *a* unto the	Josh 8:30	4196
an *a* of whole stones, over which	Josh 8:31	4196
for the *a* of the LORD, even unto	Josh 9:27	4196
a by Jordan, a great *a*	Josh 22:10	4196
a over against the land of Canaan	Josh 22:11	4196
in that ye have builded you an *a*	Josh 22:16	4196
an *a* beside the *a* of the LORD	Josh 22:19	4196
That we have built us an *a* to	Josh 22:23	4196
us now prepare to build us an *a*	Josh 22:26	4196
the pattern of the *a* of the LORD	Josh 22:28	4196
to build an *a* for burnt offerings	Josh 22:29	4196
beside the *a* of the LORD our God	Josh 22:29	4196
children of Gad called the *a* Ed	Josh 22:34	4196
built an *a* there unto the LORD	Judg 6:24	4196
throw down the *a* of Baal that thy	Judg 6:25	4196
build an *a* unto the LORD thy God	Judg 6:26	4196
the *a* of Baal was cast down, and	Judg 6:28	4196
offered upon the *a* that was built	Judg 6:28	4196
he hath cast down the *a* of Baal	Judg 6:30	4196
because one hath cast down his *a*	Judg 6:31	4196
because he hath thrown down his *a*	Judg 6:32	4196
up toward heaven from off the *a*	Judg 13:20	4196
ascended in the flame of the *a*	Judg 13:20	4196
rose early, and built there an *a*	Judg 21:4	4196
my priest, to offer upon mine *a*	1Sa 2:28	4196
I shall not cut off from mine *a*	1Sa 2:33	4196
there he built an *a* unto the LORD	1Sa 7:17	4196
And Saul built an *a* unto the LORD	1Sa 14:35	4196
the same was the first *a* that he	1Sa 14:35	4196
rear an *a* unto the LORD in the	2Sa 24:18	4196
to build an *a* unto the LORD, that	2Sa 24:21	4196
built there an *a* unto the LORD	2Sa 24:25	4196
caught hold on the horns of the *a*	1Kin 1:50	4196
caught hold on the horns of the *a*	1Kin 1:51	4196
they brought him down from the *a*	1Kin 1:53	4196
caught hold on the horns of the *a*	1Kin 2:28	4196
and, behold, he is by the *a*	1Kin 2:29	4196
did Solomon offer upon that *a*	1Kin 3:4	4196
so covered the *a* which was of	1Kin 6:20	4196
also the whole *a* that was by the	1Kin 6:22	4196
the *a* of gold, and the table of	1Kin 7:48	4196
Solomon stood before the *a* of the	1Kin 8:22	4196
come before thine *a* in this house	1Kin 8:31	4196
from before the *a* of the LORD	1Kin 8:54	4196
because the brasen *a* that was	1Kin 8:64	4196
peace offerings upon the *a* which	1Kin 9:25	4196
the *a* that was before the LORD	1Kin 9:25	4196
Judah, and he offered upon the *a*	1Kin 12:32	4196
So he offered upon the *a* which he	1Kin 12:33	4196
and he offered upon the *a*, and	1Kin 12:33	4196
stood by the *a* to burn incense	1Kin 13:1	4196
he cried against the *a* in the	1Kin 13:2	4196
of the LORD, and said, O *a*, *a*	1Kin 13:2	4196
the *a* shall be rent, and the ashes	1Kin 13:3	4196
cried against the *a* in Beth-el	1Kin 13:4	4196
he put forth his hand from the *a*	1Kin 13:4	4196
The *a* also was rent	1Kin 13:5	4196
the ashes poured out from the *a*	1Kin 13:5	4196
the LORD against the *a* in Beth-el	1Kin 13:32	4196
he reared up an *a* for Baal in the	1Kin 16:32	4196
leaped upon the *a* which was made	1Kin 18:26	4196
he repaired the *a* of the LORD	1Kin 18:30	4196
an *a* in the name of the LORD	1Kin 18:32	4196
and he made a trench about the *a*	1Kin 18:32	4196
the water ran round about the *a*	1Kin 18:35	4196
of the temple, along by the *a*	2Kin 11:11	4196
lid of it, and set it beside the *a*	2Kin 12:9	4196
saw an *a* that was at Damascus	2Kin 16:10	4196
the priest the fashion of the *a*	2Kin 16:10	4196
Urijah the priest built an *a*	2Kin 16:11	4196
from Damascus, the king saw the *a*	2Kin 16:12	4196
and the king approached to the *a*	2Kin 16:12	4196
his peace offerings, upon the *a*	2Kin 16:13	4196
And he brought also the brasen *a*	2Kin 16:14	4196
of the house, from between the *a*	2Kin 16:14	4196
put it on the north side of the *a*	2Kin 16:14	4196
Upon the great *a* burn the morning	2Kin 16:15	4196
the brasen *a* shall be for me to	2Kin 16:15	4196
before this *a* in Jerusalem	2Kin 18:22	4196
to the *a* of the LORD in Jerusalem	2Kin 23:9	4196
Moreover the *a* that was at	2Kin 23:15	4196
to sin, had made, both that *a*	2Kin 23:15	4196
and burned them upon the *a*	2Kin 23:16	4196
done against the *a* of Beth-el	2Kin 23:17	4196
upon the *a* of the burnt offering	1Chr 6:49	4196
on the *a* of incense, and were	1Chr 6:49	4196
upon the *a* of the burnt offering	1Chr 16:40	4196
set up an *a* unto the LORD in the	1Chr 21:18	4196
that I may build an *a* therein	1Chr 21:22	4196
built there an *a* unto the LORD	1Chr 21:26	4196
fire upon the *a* of burnt offering	1Chr 21:26	4196
the *a* of the burnt offering, were	1Chr 21:29	4196
this is the *a* of the burnt	1Chr 22:1	4196
for the *a* of incense refined gold	1Chr 28:18	4196
Moreover the brasen *a*, that	2Chr 1:5	4196
to the brasen *a* before the LORD	2Chr 1:6	4196
Moreover he made an *a* of brass	2Chr 4:1	4196
house of God, the golden *a* also	2Chr 4:19	4196
stood at the east end of the *a*	2Chr 5:12	4196
he stood before the *a* of the LORD	2Chr 6:12	4196
come before thine *a* in this house	2Chr 6:22	4196

because the brasen *a* which	2Chr 7:7	4196
dedication of the *a* seven days	2Chr 7:9	4196
the LORD on the *a* of the LORD	2Chr 8:12	4196
and renewed the *a* of the LORD	2Chr 15:8	4196
of the temple, along by the *a*	2Chr 23:10	4196
incense upon the *a* of incense	2Chr 26:16	4196
LORD, from beside the incense *a*	2Chr 26:19	4196
the *a* of burnt offering, with all	2Chr 29:18	4196
they are before the *a* of the LORD	2Chr 29:19	4196
offer them on the *a* of the LORD	2Chr 29:21	4196
blood, and sprinkled it on the *a*	2Chr 29:22	4196
sprinkled the blood upon the *a*	2Chr 29:22	4196
sprinkled the blood upon the *a*	2Chr 29:22	4196
with their blood upon the *a*	2Chr 29:24	4196
the burnt offering upon the *a*	2Chr 29:27	4196
Ye shall worship before one *a*	2Chr 32:12	4196
And he repaired the *a* of the LORD	2Chr 33:16	4196
offerings upon the *a* of the LORD	2Chr 35:16	4196
builded the *a* of the God of	Ezr 3:2	4196
they set the *a* upon his bases	Ezr 3:3	4196
offer them upon the *a* of the	Ezr 7:17	4056
to burn upon the *a* of the LORD	Neh 10:34	4196
so will I compass thine *a*	Ps 26:6	4196
Then will I go unto the *a* of God	Ps 43:4	4196
they offer bullocks upon thine *a*	Ps 51:19	4196
even unto the horns of the *a*	Ps 118:27	4196
with the tongs from off the *a*	Is 6:6	4196
In that day shall there be an *a*	Is 19:19	4196
a as chalkstones that are beaten	Is 27:9	4196
Ye shall worship before this *a*	Is 36:7	4196
shall be accepted upon mine *a*	Is 56:7	4196
come up with acceptance on mine *a*	Is 60:7	4196
The Lord hath cast off his *a*	Lam 2:7	4196
northward at the gate of the *a*	Eze 8:5	4196
LORD, between the porch and the *a*	Eze 8:16	4196
in, and stood beside the brasen *a*	Eze 9:2	4196
keepers of the charge of the *a*	Eze 40:46	4196
the *a* that was before the house	Eze 40:47	4196
The *a* of wood was three cubits	Eze 41:22	4196
of the *a* after the cubits	Eze 43:13	4196
be the higher place of the *a*	Eze 43:13	4196
So the *a* shall be four cubits	Eze 43:15	741
and from the *a* and upward shall be	Eze 43:15	741
the *a* shall be twelve cubits long	Eze 43:16	741
a in the day when they shall make	Eze 43:18	4196
and they shall cleanse the *a*	Eze 43:20	4196
Seven days shall they purge the *a*	Eze 43:26	4196
your burnt offerings upon the *a*	Eze 43:27	4196
corners of the settle of the *a*	Eze 45:19	4196
house, at the south side of the *a*	Eze 47:1	4196
howl, ye ministers of the *a*	Joel 1:13	4196
weep between the porch and the *a*	Joel 2:17	4196
clothes laid to pledge by every *a*	Amos 2:8	4196
horns of the *a* shall be cut off	Amos 3:14	4196
saw the Lord standing upon the *a*	Amos 9:1	4196
bowls, and as the corners of the *a*	Zec 9:15	4196
be like the bowls before the *a*	Zec 14:20	4196
offer polluted bread upon mine *a*	Mal 1:7	4196
kindle fire on mine *a* for nought	Mal 1:10	4196
covering the *a* of the LORD with	Mal 2:13	4196
if thou bring thy gift to the *a*	Mt 5:23	2379
Leave there thy gift before the *a*	Mt 5:24	2379
Whosoever shall swear by the *a*	Mt 23:18	2379
or the *a* that sanctifieth the	Mt 23:19	2379
therefore shall swear by the *a*	Mt 23:20	2379
slew between the temple and the *a*	Mt 23:35	2379
right side of the *a* of incense	Lk 1:11	2379
which perished between the *a*	Lk 11:51	2379
devotions, I found an *a* with this	Acts 17:23	1041
a are partakers with the *a*	1Cor 9:13	2379
the sacrifices partakers of the *a*	1Cor 10:18	2379
no man gave attendance at the *a*	Heb 7:13	2379
We have an *a*, whereof they have	Heb 13:10	2379
offered Isaac his son upon the *a*	Jas 2:21	2379
I saw under the the souls of	Rev 6:9	2379
angel came and stood at the *a*	Rev 8:3	2379
a which was before the throne	Rev 8:3	2379
and filled it with fire of the *a*	Rev 8:5	2379
the golden *a* which is before God	Rev 9:13	2379
the temple of God, and the *a*	Rev 11:1	2379
another angel came out from the *a*	Rev 14:18	2379
I heard another out of the *a* say	Rev 16:7	2379

ALTARS

But ye shall destroy their *a*	Ex 34:13	4196
and the candlestick, and the *a*	Num 3:31	4196
unto Balak, Build me here seven *a*	Num 23:1	4196
unto him, I have prepared seven *a*	Num 23:4	4196
top of Pisgah, and built seven *a*	Num 23:14	4196
unto Balak, Build me here seven *a*	Num 23:29	4196
ye shall destroy their *a*, and	Deut 7:5	4196

And ye shall overthrow their *a*	Deut 12:3	4196
ye shall throw down their *a*	Judg 2:2	4196
thy covenant, thrown down thine *a*	1Kin 19:10	4196
thy covenant, thrown down thine *a*	1Kin 19:14	4196
his *a* and his images brake they in	2Kin 11:18	4196
the priest of Baal before the *a*	2Kin 11:18	4196
whose *a* Hezekiah hath taken away,	2Kin 18:22	4196
and he reared up *a* for Baal	2Kin 21:3	4196
he built *a* in the house of the	2Kin 21:4	4196
he built *a* for all the host of	2Kin 21:5	4196
the *a* that were on the top of the	2Kin 23:12	4196
the *a* which Manasseh had made in	2Kin 23:12	4196
places that were there upon the *a*	2Kin 23:20	4196
away the *a* of the strange gods	2Chr 14:3	4196
and brake it down, and brake his *a*	2Chr 23:17	4196
the priest of Baal before the *a*	2Chr 23:17	4196
he made him *a* in every corner of	2Chr 28:24	4196
took away the *a* that were in	2Chr 30:14	4196
all the *a* for incense took they	2Chr 30:14	4196
the *a* out of all Judah and	2Chr 31:1	4196
away his high places and his *a*	2Chr 32:12	4196
and he reared up *a* for Baalim	2Chr 33:3	4196
Also he built *a* in the house of	2Chr 33:4	4196
he built *a* for all the host of	2Chr 33:5	4196
all the *a* that he had built in	2Chr 33:15	4196
they brake down the *a* of Baalim	2Chr 34:4	4196
bones of the priests upon their *a*	2Chr 34:5	4196
And when he had broken down the *a*	2Chr 34:7	4196
may lay her young, even thine *a*	Ps 84:3	4196
And he shall not look to the *a*	Is 17:8	4196
whose *a* Hezekiah hath taken away,	Is 36:7	4196
burneth incense upon *a* of brick	Is 65:3	4196
set up *a* to that shameful thing	Jer 11:13	4196
even *a* to burn incense unto Baal	Jer 11:13	4196
and upon the horns of your *a*	Jer 17:1	4196
their children remember their *a*	Jer 17:2	4196
your *a* shall be desolate, and your	Eze 6:4	4196
your bones round about your *a*	Eze 6:5	4196
that your *a* may be laid waste and	Eze 6:6	4196
their idols round about their *a*	Eze 6:13	4196
Ephraim hath made many *a* to sin	Hos 8:11	4196
a shall be unto him to sin	Hos 8:11	4196
his fruit he hath increased the *a*	Hos 10:1	4196
he shall break down their *a*	Hos 10:2	4196
thistle shall come up on their *a*	Hos 10:8	4196
their *a* are as heaps in the	Hos 12:11	4196
will also visit the *a* of Beth-el	Amos 3:14	4196
prophets, and digged down thine *a*	Rom 11:3	2379

ALTASCHITH

To the chief Musician, A, Michtam	Ps 57:t	516
To the chief Musician, A, Michtam	Ps 58:t	516
To the chief Musician, A, Michtam	Ps 59:t	516
To the chief Musician, A, A Psalm	Ps 75:t	516

AL-TASHHETH See ALTASCHITH.

ALTER

He shall not *a* it, nor change it,	Lev 27:10	2498
that whosoever shall *a* this word	Ezr 6:11	8133
that shall put to their hand to *a*	Ezr 6:12	8133
nor *a* the thing that is gone out	Ps 89:34	8138

ALTERED

and the Medes, that it be not *a*	Est 1:19	5674
fashion of his countenance was *a*	Lk 9:29	1096,2087

ALTERETH

Medes and Persians, which *a* not	Dan 6:8	5709
Medes and Persians, which *a* not	Dan 6:12	5709

ALTHOUGH See APPENDIX.

ALTOGETHER See APPENDIX.

ALUSH (a'-lush) An Israelite encampment during the Exodus.

from Dophkah, and encamped in A	Num 33:13	442
And they removed from A, and	Num 33:14	442

ALVAH (al'-vah) See ALIAH. An Edomite chief.

duke Timnah, duke A, duke Jetheth	Gen 36:40	5933

ALVAN (al'-van) See ALIAN. A son of Shobal the Horite.

A, and Manahath, and Ebal, Shepho,	Gen 36:23	5935

ALWAY

the table shewbread before me *a*	Ex 25:30	8548
So it was *a*	Num 9:16	8548
and his commandments, *a*	Deut 11:1	3605,3117
be only oppressed and crushed *a*	Deut 28:33	3605,3117
son shall eat bread *a* at my table	2Sa 9:10	8548
a light *a* before me in Jerusalem	1Kin 11:36	3605,3117
him to give him *a* a light	2Kin 8:19	3605,3117
I would not live *a*	Job 7:16	5769
needy shall not *a* be forgotten	Ps 9:18	5331

heart to perform thy statutes *a* ....Ps 119:112   5769
Happy is the man that feareth *a* ....Prov 28:14   8548
and, lo, I am with you *a*, **even** ....Mt 28:20   *3956,2250*
but your time is *a* **ready** ....Jn 7:6   *3842*
to the people, and prayed to God *a* ....Acts 10:2   *1275*
not see, and bow down their back *a* ......Rom 11:10   *1275*
For we which live are *a* delivered 2Cor 4:11   *104*
As sorrowful, yet *a* rejoicing 2Cor 6:10   *104*
Rejoice in the Lord *a* ....Phil 4:4   *104*
Let your speech be *a* with grace ....Col 4:6   *104*
be saved, to fill up their sins *a* 1Th 2:16   *104*
to give thanks *a* to God for you 2Th 2:13   *104*
said, The Cretians are *a* liars ....Titus 1:12   *104*
They do *a* err in their heart ....Heb 3:10   *104*

ALWAYS
shall not *a* strive with man ....Gen 6:3   5769
to cause the lamp to burn *a* ....Ex 27:20   8548
it shall be *a* upon his forehead, ...Ex 28:38   8548
keep all my commandments *a* ....Deut 5:29   3605,3117
the LORD our God, for our good *a* ...Deut 6:24   3605,3117
of the LORD thy God are *a* upon it ....Deut 11:12   8548
learn to fear the LORD thy God *a* ....Deut 14:23   3605,3117
Be ye mindful *a* of his covenant............1Chr 16:15   5769
good unto me, but *a* evil 2Chr 18:7   3605,3117
will he *a* call upon God...........................Job 27:10   3605,6256
Great men are not *a* wise........................Job 32:9
His ways are *a* grievous ....Ps 10:5   3605,6256
I have set the LORD *a* before me ....Ps 16:8   8548
He will not *a* chide ....Ps 103:9   5331
be thou ravished *a* with her love............Prov 5:19   8548
delight, rejoicing *a* before him ....Prov 8:30   3605,6256
Let thy garments be *a* white ....Eccl 9:8   3605,6256
ever, neither will I be *a* wroth ....Is 57:16   5331
and her womb to be *a* great with me .....Jer 20:17   5769
Israel, which have been *a* waste............Eze 38:8   8548
a **behold the face of my Father** ....Mt 18:10   1223,3956
For ye have the poor *a* **with you** .....Mt 26:11   *3842*
but me ye have not *a* ....Mt 26:11   *3842*
And *a*, night and day, he was in the ......Mk 5:5   *1275*
For ye have the poor with you *a* ....Mk 14:7   *3842*
but me ye have not *a* ....Mk 14:7   *3842*
end, that men ought *a* to pray ....Lk 18:1   *3842*
ye therefore, and pray *a* ....Lk 21:36   *1722,3956,2540*
for I do *a* those things that ....Jn 8:29   *3842*
And I knew that thou hearest me *a* ......Jn 11:42   *3842*
For the poor *a* **ye have with you** ....Jn 12:8   *3842*
but me ye have not *a* ....Jn 12:8   *3842*
temple, whither the Jews *a* **resort**..........Jn 18:20   *3842*
the Lord *a* before my face ....Acts 2:25   1223,3956
ye do *a* resist the Holy Ghost ....Acts 7:51   *104*
We accept it *a*, and in all places,...........Acts 24:3   *3839*
to have *a* a conscience void of ....Acts 24:16   *1275*
mention of you *a* in my prayers ....Rom 1:9   *3842*
I thank my God *a* on your behalf...........1Cor 1:4   *3842*
a abounding in the work of the..............1Cor 15:58   *3842*
which *a* causeth us to triumph in 2Cor 2:14   *3842*
A bearing about in the body the 2Cor 4:10   *3842*
Therefore we are *a* confident..................2Cor 5:6   *3842*
a having all sufficiency in all 2Cor 9:8   *3842*
affected *a* in a good thing......................Gal 4:18   *3842*
Giving thanks *a* for all things................Eph 5:20   *3842*
Praying *a* with all prayer and ..Eph 6:18   *1722,3956,2540*
A in every prayer of mine for you ....Phil 1:4   *3842*
but that with all boldness, as *a*..............Phil 1:20   *3842*
my beloved, as ye have *a* obeyed...........Phil 2:12   *3842*
Jesus Christ, praying *a* for you ....Col 1:3   *3842*
a labouring fervently for you in ....Col 4:12   *3842*
give thanks to God *a* for you all 1Th 1:2   *3842*
ye have good remembrance of us *a* 1Th 3:6   *3842*
are bound to thank God *a* for you 2Th 1:3   *3842*
Wherefore also we pray *a* for you 2Th 1:11   *3842*
give you peace *a* by all means........2Th 3:16   1223,3956
mention of thee *a* in my prayers ....Philem 4   *3842*
the priests went *a* into the first..............Heb 9:6   *1275*
be ready *a* to give an answer to 1Pet 3:15   *104*
not be negligent to put you *a* in 2Pet 1:12   *104*
these things *a* in remembrance 2Pet 1:15   *1539*

AM See APPENDIX.

AMAD (*a'-mad*) *A town on the border of Asher.*
And Alammelech, and *A*, and Misheal...Josh 19:26   6008

AMAL (*a'-mal*) *A descendant of Asher.*
and Imna, and Shelesh, and *A*................1Chr 7:35   6000

AMALEK (*am'-al-ek*) See AMALEKITE.
  1. The son of Eliphaz.
and she bare to Eliphaz *A*......................Gen 36:12   6002
Duke Korah, duke Gatam, and duke *A* ..Gen 36:16   6002
and Gatam, Kenaz, and Timna, and *A* ..1Chr 1:36   6002

  2. Descendants of Amalek.
Then came *A*, and fought with ....Ex 17:8   6002
out men, and go out, fight with *A* ....Ex 17:9   6002
had said to him, and fought with *A* ....Ex 17:10   6002
he let down his hand, *A* prevailed ....Ex 17:11   6002
And Joshua discomfited *A* and his ....Ex 17:13   6002
of *A* from under heaven ....Ex 17:14   6002
the LORD will have war with *A* ....Ex 17:16   6002
And when he looked on *A*, he took ....Num 24:20   6002
A was the first of the nations ....Num 24:20   6002
Remember what *A* did unto thee by ....Deut 25:17   6002
of *A* from under heaven ....Deut 25:19   6002
him the children of Ammon and *A* ....Judg 3:13   6002
there a root of them against *A* ....Judg 5:14   6002
that which *A* did to Israel 1Sa 15:2   6002
Now go and smite *A*, and utterly 1Sa 15:3   6002
And Saul came to a city of *A* 1Sa 15:5   6002
have brought Agag the king of *A* 1Sa 15:20   6002
his fierce wrath upon *A*, ...1Sa 28:18   6002
and of the Philistines, and of *A* 2Sa 8:12   6002
from the Philistinesand, from *A* 1Chr 18:11   6002
Gebal, and Ammon, and *A* ....Ps 83:7   6002

AMALEKITE (*am'-al-ek-ite*) See AMALEKITES. *A descendant of Amalek.*
man of Egypt, servant to an *A* 1Sa 30:13   6003
And I answered him, I am an *A* 2Sa 1:8   6003
I am the son of a stranger, an *A* 2Sa 1:13   6003

AMALEKITES (*am'-al-ek-ites*)
and smote all the country of the *A* ....Gen 14:7   6003
The *A* dwell in the land of the ....Num 13:29   6003
(Now the *A* and the Canaanites...............Num 14:25   6003
For the *A* and the Canaanites are ....Num 14:43   6003
Then the *A* came down, and the ....Num 14:45   6003
the Midianites came up, and the *A* ....Judg 6:3   6003
Then all the Midianites and the *A* ....Judg 6:33   6003
And the Midianites and the *A*.................Judg 7:12   6003
The Zidonians also, and the *A* ....Judg 10:12   6003
of Ephraim, in the mount of the *A* ....Judg 12:15   6003
gathered an host, and smote the *A* 1Sa 14:48   6003
get you down from among the *A* 1Sa 15:6   6003
Kenites departed from among the *A* 1Sa 15:6   6003
Saul smote the *A* from Havilah 1Sa 15:7   6003
took Agag the king of the *A* alive 1Sa 15:8   6003
They have brought them from the *A* 1Sa 15:15   6003
utterly destroy the sinners the *A* 1Sa 15:18   6003
and have utterly destroyed the *A* 1Sa 15:20   6003
to me Agag the king of the *A* 1Sa 15:32   6003
and the Gezrites, and the *A* 1Sa 27:8   6003
that the *A* had invaded the south, ...1Sa 30:1   6003
all that the *A* had carried away..............1Sa 30:18   6003
from the slaughter of the *A* 2Sa 1:1   6003
rest of the *A* that were escaped 1Chr 4:43   6003

AMAM (*a'-mam*) *A city near Shema and Moladah.*
A, and Shema, and Moladah,.................Josh 15:26   538

AMANA (*am-a-'nah*) *A city in southern Judah.*
look from the top of *A*, from the...............Song 4:8   549

AMARIAH (*am-a-ri'-ah*)
  1. A descendant of Aaron.
begat *A*, and *A* begat Ahitub, ...1Chr 6:7   568
A his son, Ahitub his son,.......................1Chr 6:52   568
The son of *A*, the son of Azariah, ...Ezr 7:3   568
  2. A High Priest during Solomon's reign.
begat Amariah, and *A* begat Ahitub, ...1Chr 6:11   568
  3. A descendant of Kohath.
A the second, Jahaziel the third, ...1Chr 23:19   568
A the second, Jahaziel the third, ...1Chr 24:23   568
  4. Chief priest during Jehoshaphat's reign.
A the chief priest is over you in 2Chr 19:11   568
  5. A Levite in Hezekiah's time.
and Jeshua, and Shemaiah, *A* 2Chr 31:15   568
  6. Married a foreign wife in exile.
Shallum, *A*, and Joseph ....Ezr 10:42   568
  7. A priest who sealed the covenant with Nehemiah.
Pashur, *A*, Malchijah,.............................Neh 10:3   568
A, Malluch, Hattush,..............................Neh 12:2   568
of *A*, Jehohanan ....Neh 12:13   568
  8. A descendant of Judah.
son of Zechariah, the son of *A* ....Neh 11:4   568
  9. An ancestor of Zephaniah the prophet.
the son of Gedaliah, the son of *A* ....Zeph 1:1   568

AMASA (*am'-a-sah*)
  1. David's nephew.
Absalom made *A* captain of the 2Sa 17:25   6021
which *A* was a man's son, whose............2Sa 17:25   6021
And say ye to *A*, Art thou not of 2Sa 19:13   6021
Then said the king to *A*, Assemble 2Sa 20:4   6021
So *A* went to assemble the men of.........2Sa 20:5   6021
is in Gibeon, *A* went before them............2Sa 20:8   6021

And Joab said to A, Art thou in 2Sa 20:9   6021
And Joab took A, by the beard with 2Sa 20:9   6021
But A took no heed to the sword 2Sa 20:10   6021
A wallowed in blood in the midst 2Sa 20:12   6021
he removed A out of the highway 2Sa 20:12   6021
unto A the son of Jether, whom he 1Kin 2:5   6021
A the son of Jether, captain of 1Kin 2:32   6021
And Abigail bare A 1Chr 2:17   6021
the father of A was Jether the 1Chr 2:17   6021
   2. An Ephraimite who opposed the slavery of the Jews.
A the son of Hadlai, stood up 2Chr 28:12   6021

AMASAI (am'-as-ahee)
   l. A descendant of Kohath.
A, and Ahimoth 1Chr 6:25   6022
the son of Mahath, the son of A 1Chr 6:35   6022
arose, Mahath the son of A 2Chr 29:12   6022
   2. A captain in David's army.
Then the spirit came upon A 1Chr 12:18   6022
   3. A Levite who helped relocate the Ark.
Jehoshaphat, and Nethaneel, and A 1Chr 15:24   6022

AMASHAI (am-ash-ahee) A priest of the Emmer
   family.
A the son of Azareel, the son of .... Neh 11:13   6023

AMASHSAI See AMASHI.

AMASIAH (am-a-si'-ah) Chief captain of Jehoshaphat's
   army.
next him was A the son of Zichri, ... 2Chr 17:16   6007

AMAZED
Then the dukes of Edom shall be a .... Ex 15:15   926
again, the men of Benjamin were a .... Judg 20:41   926
They were a, they answered no .... Job 32:15   2865
they shall be a one at another .... Is 13:8   8539
I will make many people a at thee .... Eze 32:10   8074
And all the people were a, and said .... Mt 12:23   1839
heard it, they were exceedingly a .... Mt 19:25   1605
And they were all a, insomuch that .... Mk 1:27   2284
insomuch that they were all a .... Mk 2:12   1839
they were sore a in themselves .... Mk 6:51   1839
they beheld him, were greatly a .... Mk 9:15   1568
and they were a .... Mk 10:32   2284
and John, and began to be a .... Mk 14:33   1568
for they trembled and were a .... Mk 16:8   1611
And when they saw him, they were a ..... Lk 2:48   1605
And they were all a, and spake .... Lk 4:36   1096,2285
And they were all a, and they .... Lk 5:26   1611,2983
they were all a at the mighty .... Lk 9:43   1605
And they were all a and marvelled, ... Acts 2:7   1839
And they were all a, and were in .... Acts 2:12   1839
But all that heard him were a .... Acts 9:21   1839

AMAZEMENT
a at that which had happened unto .... Acts 3:10   1611
and are not afraid with any a 1Pet 3:6   4423

AMAZIAH (am-a-zi'-ah)
   1. Son and successor of King Joash of Judah.
A his son reigned in his stead 2Kin 12:21   558
he fought against A king of Judah 2Kin 13:12   558
A the son of Joash king of Judah 2Kin 14:1   558
Then A sent messengers to Jehoash 2Kin 14:8   558
of Israel sent to A king of Judah 2Kin 14:9   558
But A would not hear 2Kin 14:11   558
A king of Judah looked one 2Kin 14:11   558
of Israel took A king of Judah 2Kin 14:13   558
he fought with A king of Judah 2Kin 14:15   558
A the son of Joash king of Judah 2Kin 14:17   558
And the rest of the acts of A 2Kin 14:18   558
him king instead of his father A 2Kin 14:21   558
In the fifteenth year of A the 2Kin 14:23   558
son of A king of Judah to reign 2Kin 15:1   558
to all that his father A had done 2Kin 15:3   558
A his son, Azariah his son, ... 1Chr 3:12   558
A his son reigned in his stead 2Chr 24:27   558
A was twenty and five years old 2Chr 25:1   558
Moreover A gathered Judah................... 2Chr 25:5   558
A said to the man of God, But 2Chr 25:9   558
Then A separated them, to wit, ... 2Chr 25:10   558
A strengthened himself, and led 2Chr 25:11   558
of the army which A sent back 2Chr 25:13   558
after that A was come from the 2Chr 25:14   558
of the LORD was kindled against A 2Chr 25:15   558
Then A king of Judah took advice, ... 2Chr 25:17   558
of Israel sent to A king of Judah 2Chr 25:18   558
But A would not hear 2Chr 25:20   558
A king of Judah, at Beth-shemesh, ... 2Chr 25:21   558
of Israel took A king of Judah 2Chr 25:23   558
A the son of Joash king of Judah 2Chr 25:25   558
Now the rest of the acts of A 2Chr 25:26   558
Now after the time that A did 2Chr 25:27   558

king in the room of his father A 2Chr 26:1   558
to all that his father A did 2Chr 26:4   558
   2. A Simeonite.
Jamlech, and Joshah the son of A 1Chr 4:34   558
   3. A Levite from the Merari family.
son of Hashabiah, the son of A 1Chr 6:45   558
   4. Priest of the idols at Bethel.
Then A the priest of Beth-el sent .... Amos 7:10   558
Also A said unto Amos, O thou .... Amos 7:12   558
Then answered Amos, and said to A ...... Amos 7:14   558

AMBASSADOR
but a faithful a is health .... Prov 13:17   6735
an a is sent unto the heathen, ... Jer 49:14   6735
an a is sent among the heathen, ... Obad 1   6735
For which I am an a in bonds .... Eph 6:20   4243

AMBASSADORS
and made as if they had been a .... Josh 9:4   6735
the a of the princes of Babylon 2Chr 32:31   3887
But he sent a to him, saying, ... 2Chr 35:21   4397
That sendeth a by the sea..................... Is 18:2   6735
at Zoan, and his a came to Hanes .... Is 30:4   4397
the a of peace shall weep .... Is 33:7   4397
him in sending his a into Egypt............. Eze 17:15   4397
Now then we are a for Christ................. 2Cor 5:20   4243

AMBASSAGE
a great way off, he sendeth an a .... Lk 14:32   4242

AMBER
midst thereof as the colour of a .... Eze 1:4   2830
And I saw as the colour of a .... Eze 1:27   2830
of brightness, as the colour of a............. Eze 8:2   2830

AMBUSH
lay thee an a for the city behind............ Josh 8:2   693
Then ye shall rise up from the a .... Josh 8:7   693
and they went to lie in a, and, ... Josh 8:9   693
them to lie in a between Beth-el .... Josh 8:12   693
in a against him behind the city .... Josh 8:14   693
the a arose quickly out of their .... Josh 8:19   693
saw that the a had taken the city .... Josh 8:21   693

AMBUSHES
up the watchmen, prepare the a .... Jer 51:12   693

AMBUSHMENT
But Jeroboam caused an a to come 2Chr 13:13   3993
Judah, and the a was behind them........ 2Chr 13:13   3993

AMBUSHMENTS
the LORD set a against the 2Chr 20:22   693

AMEN
   1. A term meaning "so be it."
And the woman shall say, A, a .... Num 5:22   543
the people shall answer and say, A......... Deut 27:15   543
and all the people shall say, A............... Deut 27:16   543
And all the people shall say, A............... Deut 27:17   543
And all the people shall say, A............... Deut 27:18   543
And all the people shall say, A............... Deut 27:19   543
And all the people shall say, A............... Deut 27:20   543
And all the people shall say, A............... Deut 27:21   543
And all the people shall say, A............... Deut 27:22   543
And all the people shall say, A............... Deut 27:23   543
And all the people shall say, A............... Deut 27:24   543
And all the people shall say, A............... Deut 27:25   543
And all the people shall say, A............... Deut 27:26   543
answered the king, and said, A............... 1Kin 1:36   543
And all the people said, A 1Chr 16:36   543
And all the congregation said, A............ Neh 5:13   543
all the people answered, A, A................. Neh 8:6   543
A, and A... Ps 41:13   543
A, and A... Ps 72:19   543
A, and A... Ps 89:52   543
and let all the people say, A................... Ps 106:48   543
Even the prophet Jeremiah said, A......... Jer 28:6   543
and the glory, for ever. A. .... Mt 6:13   281
the end of the world. A. .... Mt 28:20   281
with signs following. A........................... Mk 16:20   281
praising and blessing God. A................. Lk 24:53   281
that should be written. A...................... Jn 21:25   281
who is blessed for ever. A...................... Rom 1:25   281
God blessed for ever. A......................... Rom 9:5   281
to whom be glory for ever. A................. Rom 11:36   281
peace be with you all. A........................ Rom 15:33   281
Jesus Christ be with you. A................... Rom 16:20   281
Jesus Christ be with you. A................... Rom 16:24   281
through Jesus Christ for ever. A. .... Rom 16:27   281
say A at thy giving of thanks................. 1Cor 14:16   281
with you all in Christ Jesus. A. 1Cor 16:24   281
God in him are yea, and in him A 2Cor 1:20   281
Holy Ghost, be with you all. A. 2Cor 13:14   281
be glory for ever and ever. A. .... Gal 1:5   281

Christ be with your spirit. *A*.	Gal 6:18	281
all ages, world without end. *A*.	Eph 3:21	281
Lord Jesus Christ in sincerity. *A*.	Eph 6:24	281
be glory for ever and ever. *A*.	Phil 4:20	281
Jesus Christ be with you all. *A*.	Phil 4:23	281
Grace be with you. *A*.	Col 4:18	281
Jesus Christ be with you. *A*.	1Th 5:28	281
Jesus Christ be with you all. *A*.	2Th 3:18	281
glory for ever and ever. *A*.	1Ti 1:17	281
honour and power everlasting. *A*.	1Ti 6:16	281
Grace be with thee. *A*.	1Ti 6:21	281
be glory for ever and ever. *A*.	2Ti 4:18	281
Grace be with you all. *A*.	2Ti 4:22	281
Grace be with you all. *A*.	Titus 3:15	281
Christ be with your spirit. *A*.	Philem 25	281
be glory for ever and ever. *A*.	Heb 13:21	281
Grace be with you all. *A*.	Heb 13:25	281
dominion for ever and ever. *A*.	1Pet 4:11	281
dominion for ever and ever. *A*.	1Pet 5:11	281
all that are in Christ Jesus. *A*.	1Pet 5:14	281
glory both now and for ever. *A*.	2Pet 3:18	281
keep yourselves from idols. *A*.	1Jn 5:21	281
thy elect sister greet thee. *A*.	2Jn 13	281
power, both now and ever. *A*.	Jude 25	281
dominion for ever and ever. *A*.	Rev 1:6	281
Even so, *A*.	Rev 1:7	281
I am alive for evermore, *A*	Rev 1:18	281
And the four beasts said, *A*.	Rev 5:14	281
Saying, *A*: Blessing, and glory	Rev 7:12	281
our God for ever and ever. *A*.	Rev 7:12	281
sat on the throne, saying, *A*;	Rev 19:4	281
Surely I come quickly. *A*.	Rev 22:20	281
Jesus Christ be with you all. *A*.	Rev 22:21	281

2. A title of Christ.

These things saith the *A*, the	Rev 3:14	281

AMEND
LORD, to repair and *a* the house	2Chr 34:10	2388
A your ways and your doings, and I	Jer 7:3	3190
For if ye throughly *a* your ways	Jer 7:5	3190
Therefore now *a* your ways	Jer 26:13	3190
a your doings, and go not after	Jer 35:15	3190
the hour when he began to *a*	Jn 4:52	2192,2866

AMENDS
he shall make *a* for the harm that	Lev 5:16	7999

AMERCE
they shall *a* him in an hundred	Deut 22:19	6064

AMETHYST
row a ligure, an agate, and an *a*	Ex 28:19	306
row, a ligure, an agate, and an *a*	Ex 39:12	306
the twelfth, an *a*	Rev 21:20	271

AMI (*a'-mi*) *A family of returned exiles.*
of Zebaim, the children of *A*	Ezr 2:57	532

AMIABLE
How *a* are thy tabernacles, O LORD	Ps 84:1	3039

AMINADAB (*a-min'-a-dab*) See AMMINADAB. *Son of Aram; ancestor of Jesus.*
And Aram begat *A*	Mt 1:4	284
and *A* begat Naasson	Mt 1:4	284
Which was the son of *A*, which was	Lk 3:33	284

AMISS
We have sinned, we have done *a*	2Chr 6:37	5753
which speak any thing *a* against	Dan 3:29	7955
but this man hath done nothing *a*	Lk 23:41	824
and receive not, because ye ask *a*	Jas 4:3	2560

AMITTAI (*a-mit'-tahee*) *Father of Jonah.*
his servant Jonah, the son of *A*	2Kin 14:25	573
LORD came unto Jonah the son of *A*	Jonah 1:1	573

AMMAH (*am'-mah*) See METHEG-AMMAH. *A hill near Gibeon.*
they were come to the hill of *A*	2Sa 2:24	522

AMMI (*am'-mi*) See AMMI-NADIB, BEN-AMMI, LO-AMMI. *A name given to Israel by Hosea meaning "my people."*
Say ye unto your brethren, *A*	Hos 2:1	5971

AMMIEL (*am'-me-el*) See ELIAM.
1. A spy for Moses.
of Dan, *A* the son of Gemalli	Num 13:12	5988

2. A Manassehite of Lodebar.
the house of Machir, the son of *A*	2Sa 9:4	5988
the house of Machir, the son of *A*	2Sa 9:5	5988
Machir the son of *A* of Lo-debar	2Sa 17:27	5988

3. Father of a wife of David.
of Bath-shua the daughter of *A*	1Chr 3:5	5988

4. A Levite Tabernacle servant.
A the sixth, Issachar the seventh	1Chr 26:5	5988

AMMIHUD (*am-mi'-hud*)
1. Father of Elishama.
Elishama the son of *A*	Num 1:10	5989
shall be Elishama the son of *A*	Num 2:18	5989
seventh day Elishama the son of *A*	Num 7:48	5989
offering of Elishama the son of *A*	Num 7:53	5989
host was Elishama the son of *A*	Num 10:22	5989
A his son, Elishama his son,	1Chr 7:26	5989

2. A Simeonite.
of Simeon, Shemuel the son of *A*	Num 34:20	5989

3. A Naphtalite.
of Naphtali, Pedahel the son of *A*	Num 34:28	5989

4. Father of the king of Geshur.
and went to Talmai, the son of *A*	2Sa 13:37	5989

5. A son of Omri.
Uthai the son of *A*, the son of	1Chr 9:4	5989

AMMINADAB (*am-min'-a-dab*) See AMINADAB, AMMI-NADIB.
1. Aaron's father-in-law.
took him Elisheba, daughter of *A*	Ex 6:23	5992

2. A prince of Judah.
Nahshon the son of *A*	Num 1:7	5992
Nahshon the son of *A* shall be	Num 2:3	5992
day was Nahshon the son of *A*	Num 7:12	5992
offering of Nahshon the son of *A*	Num 7:17	5992
his host was Nahshon the son of *A*	Num 10:14	5992
Hezron begat Ram, and Ram begat *A*	Ruth 4:19	5992
A begat Nahshon, and Nahshon begat	Ruth 4:20	5992
And Ram begat *A*	1Chr 2:10	5992
A begat Nahshon, prince of the	1Chr 2:10	5992

3. A son of Kohath.
A his son, Korah his son, Assir	1Chr 6:22	5992

4. A Levite who relocated the Ark.
A the chief, and his brethren	1Chr 15:10	5992
and Joel, Shemaiah, and Eliel, and *A*	1Chr 15:11	5992

AMMI-NADIB
made me like the chariots of *A*	Song 6:12	5993

AMMISHADDAI (*am-mi-shad'-dahee*) *Father of the chief of the tribe of Dan.*
Ahiezer the son of *A*	Num 1:12	5996
Dan shall be Ahiezer the son of *A*	Num 2:25	5996
tenth day Ahiezer the son of *A*	Num 7:66	5996
offering of Ahiezer the son of *A*	Num 7:71	5996
his host was Ahiezer the son of *A*	Num 10:25	5996

AMMIZABAD (*am-miz'-a-bad*) *Son of a captain of David.*
and in his course was *A* his son	1Chr 27:6	5990

AMMON (*am'-mon*) *Territory in Jordan.*
the children of *A* unto this day	Gen 19:38	5983
even unto the children of *A*	Num 21:24	5983
of the children of *A* was strong	Num 21:24	5983
over against the children of *A*	Deut 2:19	5983
the children of *A* any possession	Deut 2:19	5983
the children of *A* thou camest not	Deut 2:37	5983
in Rabbath of the children of *A*	Deut 3:11	5983
the border of the children of *A*	Deut 3:16	5983
the border of the children of *A*	Josh 12:2	5983
the border of the children of *A*	Josh 13:10	5983
the land of the children of *A*	Josh 13:25	5983
unto him the children of *A*	Judg 3:13	5983
and the gods of the children of *A*	Judg 10:6	5983
the hands of the children of *A*	Judg 10:7	5983
Moreover the children of *A* passed	Judg 10:9	5983
Amorites, from the children of *A*	Judg 10:11	5983
Then the children of *A* were	Judg 10:17	5983
fight against the children of *A*	Judg 10:18	5983
that the children of *A* made war	Judg 11:4	5983
of *A* made war against Israel	Judg 11:5	5983
may fight with the children of *A*	Judg 11:6	5983
fight against the children of *A*	Judg 11:8	5983
fight against the children of *A*	Judg 11:9	5983
the king of the children of *A*	Judg 11:12	5983
the king of the children of *A*	Judg 11:13	5983
the king of the children of *A*	Judg 11:14	5983
nor the land of the children of *A*	Judg 11:15	5983
of Israel and the children of *A*	Judg 11:27	5983
the king of the children of *A*	Judg 11:28	5983
over unto the children of *A*	Judg 11:29	5983
the children of *A* into mine hands	Judg 11:30	5983
in peace from the children of *A*	Judg 11:31	5983
of *A* to fight against them	Judg 11:32	5983
Thus the children of *A* were	Judg 11:33	5983
even of the children of *A*	Judg 11:36	5983
fight against the children of *A*	Judg 12:1	5983
strife with the children of *A*	Judg 12:2	5983
over against the children of *A*	Judg 12:3	5983
children of *A* came against you	1Sa 12:12	5983
and against the children of *A*	1Sa 14:47	5983

of Moab, and of the children of *A* 2Sa 8:12 5983
king of the children of *A* died 2Sa 10:1 5983
the land of the children of *A* 2Sa 10:2 5983
of *A* said unto Hanun their lord 2Sa 10:3 5983
when the children of *A* saw that 2Sa 10:6 5983
David, the children of *A* sent 2Sa 10:6 5983
And the children of *A* came out 2Sa 10:8 5983
array against the children of *A* 2Sa 10:10 5983
of *A* be too strong for thee 2Sa 10:11 5983
when the children of *A* saw that 2Sa 10:14 5983
returned from the children of *A* 2Sa 10:14 5983
help the children of *A* any more 2Sa 10:19 5983
they destroyed the children of *A* 2Sa 11:1 5983
the sword of the children of *A* 2Sa 12:9 5983
Rabbah of the children of *A* 2Sa 12:26 5983
the cities of the children of *A* 2Sa 12:31 5983
of Rabbah of the children of *A* 2Sa 17:27 5983
abomination of the children of *A* 1Kin 11:7 5983
the god of the children of *A* 1Kin 11:33 5983
abomination of the children of *A* 2Kin 23:13 5983
and bands of the children of *A* 2Kin 24:2 5983
Moab, and from the children of *A* 1Chr 18:11 5983
king of the children of *A* died 1Chr 19:1 5983
of the children of *A* to Hanun 1Chr 19:2 5983
the children of *A* said to Hanun 1Chr 19:3 5983
when the children of *A* saw that 1Chr 19:6 5983
the children of *A* sent a thousand 1Chr 19:6 5983
the children of *A* gathered 1Chr 19:7 5983
And the children of *A* came out 1Chr 19:9 5983
array against the children of *A* 1Chr 19:11 5983
of *A* be too strong for thee 1Chr 19:12 5983
when the children of *A* saw that 1Chr 19:15 5983
help the children of *A* any more 1Chr 19:19 5983
the country of the children of *A* 1Chr 20:1 5983
the cities of the children of *A* 1Chr 20:3 5983
of Moab, and the children of *A* 2Chr 20:1 5983
And now, behold, the children of *A* 2Chr 20:10 5983
against the children of *A* 2Chr 20:22 5983
For the children of *A* and Moab 2Chr 20:23 5983
the children of *A* gave him the 2Chr 27:5 5983
the children of *A* pay unto him 2Chr 27:5 5983
had married wives of Ashdod, of *A* .... Neh 13:23 5983
Gebal, and *A*, and Amalek .... Ps 83:7 5983
the children of *A* shall obey them .... Is 11:14 5983
and Edom, and the children of *A* .... Jer 9:26 5983
and Moab, and the children of *A* .... Jer 25:21 5983
captivity of the children of *A* .... Jer 49:6 5983
and the chief of the children of *A* .... Dan 11:41 5983
of the children of *A*, and for four .... Amos 1:13 5983
revilings of the children of *A* .... Zeph 2:8 5983
and the children of *A* as Gomorrah .... Zeph 2:9 5983

AMMONITE *(am'-mon-ite)* See AMMONITES, AMMONIT-
ESS. *A descendant of Ammon.*
An *A* or Moabite shall not enter .... Deut 23:3 5984
Then Nahash the *A* came up 1Sa 11:1 5984
Nahash the *A* answered them, On 1Sa 11:2 5984
Zelek the *A*, Nahari the 2Sa 23:37 5984
Zelek the *A*, Naharai the 1Chr 11:39 5984
and Tobiah the servant, the *A* .... Neh 2:10 5984
and Tobiah the servant, the *A* .... Neh 2:19 5984
Now Tobiah the *A* was by him .... Neh 4:3 5984
was found written, that the *A* .... Neh 13:1 5984

AMMONITES *(am'-mon-ites)*
the *A* call them Zamzummims .... Deut 2:20 5984
slew the *A* until the heat of the 1Sa 11:11 5984
Pharaoh, women of the Moabites, *A* 1Kin 11:1 5984
Milcom the abomination of the *A* 1Kin 11:5 5984
and with them other beside the *A* 2Chr 20:1 5984
the *A* gave gifts to Uzziah 2Chr 26:8 5984
also with the king of the *A* 2Chr 27:5 5984
Perizzites, the Jebusites, the *A* .... Ezr 9:1 5984
Tobiah, and the Arabians, and the *A* ...... Neh 4:7 5984
of Moab, and to the king of the *A* .... Jer 27:3 5984
that were in Moab, and among the *A* ..... Jer 40:11 5984
that Baalis the king of the *A* .... Jer 40:14 5984
and departed to go over to the *A* .... Jer 41:10 5984
with eight men, and went to the *A* .... Jer 41:15 5984
Concerning The *A*, thus saith the .... Jer 49:1 5984
to be heard in Rabbah of the *A* .... Jer 49:2 5984
may come to Rabbath of the *A* .... Eze 21:20 1121,5984
the Lord GOD concerning the *A* ...... Eze 21:28 1121,5984
man, set thy face against the *A* .... Eze 25:2 1121,5984
say unto the *A*, Hear the word .... Eze 25:3 1121,5984
the *A* a couchingplace for flocks..... Eze 25:5 1121,5984
the men of the east with the *A* .... Eze 25:10 1121,5984
the *A* may not be remembered .... Eze 25:10 1121,5984

AMMONITESS *(am'-mon-i-tess)*
his mother's name was Naamah an *A* ... 1Kin 14:21 5984
his mother's name was Naamah an *A* ... 1Kin 14:31 5984

his mother's name was Naamah an *A* ... 2Chr 12:13 5984
Zabad the son of Shimeath an *A* 2Chr 24:26 5984

AMNON *(am'-non)* See AMNON'S.
  1. A son of David.
and his firstborn was *A*, of 2Sa 3:2 550
A the son of David loved her 2Sa 13:1 550
A was so vexed, that he fell sick 2Sa 13:2 550
A thought it hard for him to do 2Sa 13:2 550
But *A* had a friend, whose name 2Sa 13:3 550
A said unto him, I love Tamar, my 2Sa 13:4 550
So *A* lay down, and made himself 2Sa 13:6 550
A said unto the king, I pray thee 2Sa 13:6 550
A said, Have out all men from me 2Sa 13:9 550
A said unto Tamar, Bring the meat 2Sa 13:10 550
into the chamber to *A* her brother 2Sa 13:10 550
Then *A* hated her exceedingly 2Sa 13:15 550
A said unto her, Arise, be gone 2Sa 13:15 550
Hath *A* thy brother been with thee 2Sa 13:20 550
brother *A* neither good nor bad 2Sa 13:22 550
for Absalom hated *A*, because he 2Sa 13:22 550
thee, let my brother *A* go with us 2Sa 13:26 550
pressed him, that he let *A* 2Sa 13:27 550
and when I say unto you, Smite *A* 2Sa 13:28 550
unto *A* as Absalom had commanded 2Sa 13:29 550
for *A* only is dead 2Sa 13:32 550
for *A* only is dead 2Sa 13:33 550
for he was comforted concerning *A* 2Sa 13:39 550
the firstborn *A*, of Ahinoam the 1Chr 3:1 550
  2. A son of Shimon.
And the sons of Shimon were, *A* 1Chr 4:20 550

AMNON'S *(am'-nons)* Refers to Amnon 1.
Go now to thy brother *A* house 2Sa 13:7 550
Tamar went to her brother *A* house........ 2Sa 13:8 550
Mark ye now when *A* heart is merry 2Sa 13:28 550

AMOK *(a'-mok)* *A priest who returned from exile under*
  Zerubbabel.
Sallu, *A*, Hilkiah, Jedaiah........................ Neh 12:7 5987
of *A*, Eber... Neh 12:20 5987

AMON *(a'-mon)*
  1. A governor of Samaria.
carry him back unto *A* the...................... 1Kin 22:26 526
carry him back to *A* the governor 2Chr 18:25 526
  2. Son and successor of King Manasseh of Judah.
A his son reigned in his stead 2Kin 21:18 526
A was twenty and two years old 2Kin 21:19 526
the servants of *A* conspired 2Kin 21:23 526
that had conspired against king *A* 2Kin 21:24 526
of the acts of *A* which he did 2Kin 21:25 526
A his son, Josiah his son 1Chr 3:14 526
A his son reigned in his stead 2Chr 33:20 526
A was two and twenty years old 2Chr 33:21 526
for *A* sacrificed unto all the 2Chr 33:22 526
but *A* trespassed more and more 2Chr 33:23 526
that had conspired against king *A*.......... 2Chr 33:25 526
Josiah the son of *A* king of Judah.......... Jer 1:2 526
Josiah the son of *A* king of Judah........... Jer 25:3 526
the days of Josiah the son of *A* .... Zeph 1:1 526
and Manasses begat *A* .... Mt 1:10 300
and *A* begat Josias .... Mt 1:10 300
  3. A descendant of Solomon who returned from the
   Exile under Zerubbabel.
of Zebaim, the children of *A* .... Neh 7:59 526

AMONG See APPENDIX.

AMONGST
God *a* the trees of the garden .... Gen 3:8 8432
of a buryingplace *a* you .... Gen 23:9 8432

AMORITE *(am'-o-rite)* *A descendant of Canaan, Ham's*
  son.
And the Jebusite, and the *A* .... Gen 10:16 567
dwelt in the plain of Mamre the *A* .... Gen 14:13 567
the hand of the *A* with my sword........... Gen 48:22 567
drive out the Canaanite, the *A* .... Ex 33:2 567
I drive out before thee the *A* .... Ex 34:11 567
the *A* which was in it .... Num 32:39 567
given into thine hand Sihon the *A* .... Deut 2:24 567
Lebanon, the Hittite, and the *A*............. Josh 9:1 567
east and on the west, and to the *A* .... Josh 11:3 567
The Jebusite also, and the *A* 1Chr 1:14 567
thy father was an *A*, and thy.................. Eze 16:3 567
an Hittite, and your father an *A* .... Eze 16:45 567
Yet destroyed I the *A* before them .... Amos 2:9 567
to possess the land of the *A* .... Amos 2:10 567

AMORITES *(am'-o-rites)*
of the Amalekites, and also the *A* .... Gen 14:7 567
iniquity of the *A* is not yet full .... Gen 15:16 567
And the *A*, and the Canaanites, and ...... Gen 15:21 567
and the Hittites, and the *A* .... Ex 3:8 567

and the Hittites, and the *A* .... Ex 3:17   567
and the Hittites, and the *A* .... Ex 13:5   567
thee, and bring thee in unto the *A* .... Ex 23:23   567
and the Jebusites, and the *A* .... Num 13:29   567
cometh out of the coasts of the *A* .... Num 21:13   567
of Moab, between Moab and the *A* ..... Num 21:13   567
unto Sihon king of the *A*, saying, ... Num 21:21   567
dwelt in all the cities of the *A* .... Num 21:25   567
city of Sihon the king of the *A* .... Num 21:26   567
unto Sihon king of the *A* .... Num 21:29   567
Israel dwelt in the land of the *A* .... Num 21:31   567
drove out the *A* that were there .... Num 21:32   567
didst unto Sihon king of the *A* .... Num 21:34   567
all that Israel had done to the *A*.......... Num 22:2   567
kingdom of Sihon king of the *A* .... Num 32:33   567
had slain Sihon the king of the *A* .... Deut 1:4   567
and go to the mount of the *A* .... Deut 1:7   567
the way of the mountain of the *A*........... Deut 1:19   567
come unto the mountain of the *A* .... Deut 1:20   567
deliver us into the hand of the *A* .... Deut 1:27   567
And the *A*, which dwelt in that .... Deut 1:44   567
didst unto Sihon king of the *A* .... Deut 3:2   567
hand of the two kings of the *A* .... Deut 3:8   567
and the *A* call it Shenir .... Deut 3:9   567
the land of Sihon king of the *A* .... Deut 4:46   567
of Bashan, two kings of the *A* .... Deut 4:47   567
and the Girgashites, and the *A* .... Deut 7:1   567
namely, the Hittites, and the *A* .... Deut 20:17   567
to Sihon and to Og, kings of the *A* .... Deut 31:4   567
did unto the two kings of the *A* .... Josh 2:10   567
and the Girgashites, and the *A* .... Josh 3:10   567
pass, when all the kings of the *A* .... Josh 5:1   567
deliver us into the hand of the *A* .... Josh 7:7   567
he did to the two kings of the *A* .... Josh 9:10   567
Therefore the five kings of the *A* .... Josh 10:5   567
for all the kings of the *A* that .... Josh 10:6   567
A before the children of Israel .... Josh 10:12   567
Sihon king of the *A*, who dwelt in .... Josh 12:2   567
the Hittites, the *A*, and the .... Josh 12:8   567
Aphek, to the borders of the *A* .... Josh 13:4   567
the cities of Sihon king of the *A* .... Josh 13:10   567
kingdom of Sihon king of the *A* .... Josh 13:21   567
you into the land of the *A* .... Josh 24:8   567
Jericho fought against you, the *A* .... Josh 24:11   567
you, even the two kings of the *A* .... Josh 24:12   567
the flood, or the gods of the *A* .... Josh 24:15   567
even the *A* which dwelt in .... Josh 24:18   567
the *A* forced the children of Dan .... Judg 1:34   567
But the *A* would dwell in mount .... Judg 1:35   567
the coast of the *A* was from the .... Judg 1:36   567
the Canaanites, Hittites, and *A* .... Judg 3:5   567
fear not the gods of the *A* .... Judg 6:10   567
side Jordan in the land of the *A* .... Judg 10:8   567
from the Egyptians, and from the *A* .... Judg 10:11   567
unto Sihon king of the *A*, the .... Judg 11:19   567
possessed all the land of the *A* .... Judg 11:21   567
possessed all the coasts of the *A* .... Judg 11:22   567
A from before his people Israel .... Judg 11:23   567
was peace between Israel and the *A*...... 1Sa 7:14   567
but of the remnant of the *A* 2Sa 21:2   567
country of Sihon king of the *A* 1Kin 4:19   567
people that were left of the *A* 1Kin 9:20   567
to all things as did the *A* 1Kin 21:26   567
wickedly above all that the *A* did 2Kin 21:11   567
left of the Hittites, and the *A*............... 2Chr 8:7   567
Moabites, the Egyptians, and the *A* .... Ezr 9:1   567
Canaanites, the Hittites, the *A* .... Neh 9:8   567
Sihon king of the *A*, and Og king .... Ps 135:11   567
Sihon king of the *A* .... Ps 136:19   567

AMOS (*a'-mos*)
1. A prophet during the reign of Uzziah.
The words of *A*, who was among the ...... Amos 1:1   5986
And the LORD said unto me, ... Amos 7:8   5986
A hath conspired against thee in .... Amos 7:10   5986
For thus *A* saith, Jeroboam shall .... Amos 7:11   5986
Also Amaziah said unto *A*, O thou .... Amos 7:12   5986
Then answered *A*, and said to .... Amos 7:14   5986
And he said, *A*, what seest thou .... Amos 8:2   5986
2. Son of Naum; an ancestor of Jesus.
which was the son of *A*, which .... Lk 3:25   *301*

AMOUNTING
gold, *a* to six hundred talents 2Chr 3:8

AMOZ (*a'-moz*) *Father of Isaiah.*
Isaiah the prophet the son of *A* 2Kin 19:2   531
the son of *A* sent to Hezekiah 2Kin 19:20   531
Isaiah the son of *A* came to him 2Kin 20:1   531
Isaiah the prophet, the son of *A* 2Chr 26:22   531
the prophet Isaiah the son of *A* 2Chr 32:20   531
Isaiah the prophet, the son of *A* 2Chr 32:32   531

The vision of Isaiah the son of *A* .... Is 1:1   531
the son of *A* saw concerning Judah .... Is 2:1   531
which Isaiah the son of *A* did see............ Is 13:1   531
the LORD by Isaiah the son of *A* .... Is 20:2   531
Isaiah the prophet the son of *A* .... Is 37:2   531
the son of *A* sent unto Hezekiah .... Is 37:21   531
the son of *A* came unto him .... Is 38:1   531

AMPHIPOLIS (*am-fip'-o-lis*) *A city in Macedonia.*
when they had passed through *A*........... Acts 17:1   *295*

AMPLIAS (*am'-ple-as*) *A Christian acquaintance of Paul's.*
Greet *A* my beloved in the Lord .... Rom 16:8   *291*

AMRAM (*am'-ram*) See AMRAMITES, AMRAM'S, HEMDAN.
1. Father of Moses and Aaron.
A, and Izhar, and Hebron, and Uzziel.... Ex 6:18   6019
A took him Jochebed his father's .... Ex 6:20   6019
of the life of *A* were an hundred .... Ex 6:20   6019
A, and Izehar, Hebron, and Uzziel.......... Num 3:19   6019
And Kohath begat *A* .... Num 26:58   6019
and she bare unto *A* Aaron and Moses . Num 26:59   6019
A, Izhar, and Hebron, and Uzziel............ 1Chr 6:2   6019
And the children of *A* 1Chr 6:3   6019
And the sons of Kohath were, *A*............. 1Chr 6:18   6019
A, Izhar, Hebron, and Uzziel, four 1Chr 23:12   6019
The sons of *A* 1Chr 23:13   6019
Of the sons of *A*..................................... 1Chr 24:20   6019
2. Married a foreign wife in Exile.
Maadai, *A*, and Uel, ... Ezr 10:34   6019
3. A son of Dishon.
A, and Eshban, and Ithran, and 1Chr 1:41   2566

AMRAMITES (*am'-ram-ites*) *Descendants of Amram 1.*
of Kohath was the family of the *A* .... Num 3:27   6020
Of the *A*, and the Izharites, the 1Chr 26:23   6020

AMRAM'S (*am'-rams*)
the name of *A* wife was Jochebed, ... Num 26:59   6019

AMRAPHEL (*am'-raf-el*) *King of Shinar in Abraham's time.*
in the days of *A* king of Shinar .... Gen 14:1   569
A king of Shinar, and Arioch king .... Gen 14:9   569

AMZI (*am'-zi*)
1. A son of Merari.
The son of *A*, the son of Bani, ... 1Chr 6:46   557
2. Ancestor of Adaiah.
the son of Pelaliah, the son of *A* .... Neh 11:12   557

AN See APPENDIX.

ANAB (*a'-nab*) *A Canaanite city.*
from Hebron, from Debir, from *A* .... Josh 11:21   6024
And *A*, and Eshtemoh, and Anim, ... Josh 15:50   6024

ANAH (*a'-nah*)
1. A daughter of Zibeon.
of *A* the daughter of Zibeon the .... Gen 36:2   6034
the daughter of *A* the daughter of.......... Gen 36:14   6034
of Aholibamah the daughter of *A* .... Gen 36:18   6034
And the children of *A* were these............ Gen 36:25   6034
and Aholibamah the daughter of *A* .... Gen 36:25   6034
2. A son of Seir.
Lotan, and Shobal, and Zibeon, and *A*... Gen 36:20   6034
duke Shobal, duke Zibeon, duke *A* .... Gen 36:29   6034
Lotan, and Shobal, and Zibeon, and *A*... 1Chr 1:38   6034
3. A son of Zibeon.
both Ajah, and *A* .... Gen 36:24   6034
this was that *A* that found the .... Gen 36:24   6034
Aiah, and *A* 1Chr 1:40   6034
The sons of *A* 1Chr 1:41   6034

ANAHARATH (*an-a-ha'-rath*) *A town in Issachar.*
And Haphraim, and Shihon, and *A* .... Josh 19:19   588

ANAIAH (*an-a-i'-ah*)
1. A priest who assisted Ezra.
stood Mattithiah, and Shema, and *A* ..... Neh 8:4   6043
2. A Jew who sealed the covenant.
Pelatiah, Hanan, *A*,............................... Neh 10:22   6043

ANAK (*a'-nak*) See ANAKIMS. *The son of Arba.*
and Talmai, the children of *A* .... Num 13:22   6061
we saw the children of *A* there.............. Num 13:28   6061
we saw the giants, the sons of *A* .... Num 13:33   6061
stand before the children of *A*............... Deut 9:2   6061
the city of Arba the father of *A* .... Josh 15:13   6061
drove thence the three sons of *A* .... Josh 15:14   6061
and Talmai, the children of *A* .... Josh 15:14   6061
the city of Arba the father of *A* .... Josh 21:11   6061
thence the three sons of *A*..................... Judg 1:20   6061

ANAKIM See ANAKIMS.

ANAKIMS *(an'-ak-ims) Descendants of Anak.*
have seen the sons of the *A* there	Deut 1:28	6062
great, and many, and tall, as the *A*	Deut 2:10	6062
were accounted giants, as the *A*	Deut 2:11	6062
great, and many, and tall, as the *A*	Deut 2:21	6062
and tall, the children of the *A*	Deut 9:2	6062
cut off the *A* from the mountains,	Josh 11:21	6062
There was none of the *A* left in	Josh 11:22	6062
in that day how the *A* were there	Josh 14:12	6062
Arba was a great man among the *A*	Josh 14:15	6062

ANAKITES See ANAKIMS.

ANAMIM *(an'-am-im) A people of northern Egypt.*
And Mizraim begat Ludim, and *A*	Gen 10:13	6047
And Mizraim begat Ludim, and *A*	1Chr 1:11	6047

ANAMITES See ANAMIM.

ANAMMELECH *(a-nam'-mel-ek) A god of the Babylonians.*
in fire to Adrammelech and *A*	2Kin 17:31	6048

ANAN *(a'-nan) An Israelite who sealed the covenant under Nehemiah.*
And Ahijah, Hanan, *A*,	Neh 10:26	6052

ANANI *(an-a'-ni) A son of Elioneai.*
and Johanan, and Dalaiah, and *A*	1Chr 3:24	6054

ANANIAH *(an-an-i'-ah)* See ANANIAS.
1. Grandfather of Azariah.
the son of *A* by his house	Neh 3:23	6055

2. A town in Benjamin.
And at Anathoth, Nob, *A*	Neh 11:32	6055

ANANIAS *(an-an-i'-as)* See ANANIAH.
1. A Christian who tried to deceive the apostles.
But a certain man named *A*	Acts 5:1	367
But Peter said, *A*, why hath Satan	Acts 5:3	367
A hearing these words fell down,	Acts 5:5	367
2. A Christian who aided Paul.
disciple at Damascus, named *A*	Acts 9:10	367
him said the Lord in a vision, *A*	Acts 9:10	367
a vision a man named *A* coming in	Acts 9:12	367
Then *A* answered, Lord, I have	Acts 9:13	367
A went his way, and entered into	Acts 9:17	367
And one *A*, a devout man according	Acts 22:12	367
3. The High Priest who interrogated Paul.
the high priest *A* commanded them	Acts 23:2	367
after five days *A* the high priest	Acts 24:1	367

ANATH *(a'-nath)* See BETH-ANATH. *Father of Shamgar the judge.*
him was Shamgar the son of *A*	Judg 3:31	6067
the days of Shamgar the son of *A*	Judg 5:6	6067

ANATHEMA *(a-nath'-em-ah) Greek word for "accursed."*
Christ, let him be *A* Maranatha	1Cor 16:22	331

ANATHOTH *(an'-a-thoth)* See ANETOTITHE.
1. A Levitical city in Benjamin.
A with her suburbs, and Almon with	Josh 21:18	6068
said the king, Get thee to *A*	1Kin 2:26	6068
suburbs, and *A* with her suburbs	1Chr 6:60	6068
The men of *A*, an hundred twenty	Ezr 2:23	6068
The men of *A*, an hundred twenty	Neh 7:27	6068
And at Nob, Ananiah,	Neh 11:32	6068
to be heard unto Laish, O poor *A*	Is 10:30	6068
were in *A* in the land of Benjamin	Jer 1:1	6068
saith the LORD of the men of *A*	Jer 11:21	6068
will bring evil upon the men of *A*	Jer 11:23	6068
thou not reproved Jeremiah of *A*	Jer 29:27	6068
Buy thee my field that is in *A*	Jer 32:7	6068
field, I pray thee, that is in *A*	Jer 32:8	6068
my uncle's son, that was in *A*	Jer 32:9	6068
2. A son of Becher.
Omri, and Jerimoth, and Abiah, and *A*	1Chr 7:8	6068
3. An Israelite who sealed the covenant under Nehemiah.
Hariph, Nebai,	Neh 10:19	6068

ANATHOTHITE See ANTOTHITE.

ANCESTORS
remember the covenant of their *a*	Lev 26:45	7223

ANCHOR
hope we have as an *a* of the soul	Heb 6:19	45

ANCHORS
they cast four *a* out of the stern	Acts 27:29	45
have cast *a* out of the foreship	Acts 27:30	
And when they had taken up the *a*	Acts 27:40	45

ANCIENT
chief things of the *a* mountains	Deut 33:15	6924
that *a* river, the river Kishon	Judg 5:21	6917

of *a* times that I have formed it	2Kin 19:25	6924
And these are *a* things	1Chr 4:22	6267
of the fathers, who were *a* men	Ezr 3:12	2204
With the *a* is wisdom	Job 12:12	3453
days of old, the years of *a* times	Ps 77:5	5769
Remove not the *a* landmark	Prov 22:28	5769
prophet, and the prudent, and the *a*	Is 3:2	2204
himself proudly against the *a*	Is 3:5	2204
The *a* and honourable, he is the	Is 9:15	2204
of the wise, the son of *a* kings	Is 19:11	6924
whose antiquity is of *a* days	Is 23:7	6924
of *a* times, that I have formed it	Is 37:26	6924
since I appointed the *a* people	Is 44:7	5769
hath declared this from *a* time	Is 45:21	6924
from *a* times the things that are	Is 46:10	6924
upon the *a* hast thou very heavily	Is 47:6	2204
awake, as in the *a* days, in the	Is 51:9	6924
mighty nation, it is an *a* nation	Jer 5:15	5769
in their ways from the *a* paths	Jer 18:15	5769
Then they began at the *a* men	Eze 9:6	2204
even the *a* high places are ours	Eze 36:2	5769
the *A* of days did sit, whose	Dan 7:9	6268
heaven, and came to the *A* of days	Dan 7:13	6268
Until the *A* of days came, and	Dan 7:22	6268

ANCIENTS
As saith the proverb of the *a*	1Sa 24:13	6931
I understand more than the *a*	Ps 119:100	2204
judgment with the *a* of his people	Is 3:14	2204
and before his *a* gloriously	Is 24:23	2204
take of the *a* of the people	Jer 19:1	2204
and of the *a* of the priests	Jer 19:1	2204
the priest, and counsel from the *a*	Eze 7:26	2204
of the *a* of the house of Israel	Eze 8:11	2204
hast thou seen what the *a* of the	Eze 8:12	2204
The *a* of Gebal and the wise men	Eze 27:9	2204

ANCLE
a bones received strength	Acts 3:7	4974

ANCLES
the waters were to the *a*	Eze 47:3	657

AND See APPENDIX.

ANDREW *(an'-drew) One of the twelve disciples.*
A his brother, casting a net into	Mt 4:18	406
is called Peter, and *A* his brother	Mt 10:2	406
A his brother casting a net into	Mk 1:16	406
into the house of Simon and *A*	Mk 1:29	406
And *A*, and Philip, and Bartholomew,	Mk 3:18	406
and John and *A* asked him privately,	Mk 13:3	406
A his brother, James and John,	Lk 6:14	406
speak, and followed him, was *A*	Jn 1:40	406
was of Bethsaida, the city of *A*	Jn 1:44	406
One of his disciples, *A*, Simon	Jn 6:8	406
Philip cometh and telleth *A*	Jn 12:22	406
and again *A* and Philip tell Jesus	Jn 12:22	406
Peter, and James, and John, and *A*	Acts 1:13	406

ANDRONICUS *(an-dro-ni'-cus) A relative of Paul.*
Salute *A* and Junia, my kinsmen, and	Rom 16:7	408

ANEM *(a'-nem)* See EN-GANNIM. *A Levitical city in Issachar.*
suburbs, and *A* with her suburbs	1Chr 6:73	6046

ANER *(a'-nur)*
1. An ally of Abraham.
of Eshcol, and brother of *A*	Gen 14:13	6063
of the men which went with me, *A*	Gen 14:24	6063
2. A Levitical city in Manasseh.
A with her suburbs, and Bileam	1Chr 6:70	6063

ANETHOTHITE *(an'-e-thoth-ite)* See ANETOTHITE. *A native of Anathoth.*
Abiezer the *A*, Mebunnai the	2Sa 23:27	6069

ANETOTHITE *(an'-e-toth-ite)* See ANETHOTHITE, ANTOTHITE. *Same as Anethothite.*
the ninth month was Abiezer the *A*	1Chr 27:12	6069

ANGEL
the *a* of the LORD found her by a	Gen 16:7	4397
the *a* of the LORD said unto her,	Gen 16:9	4397
the *a* of the LORD said unto her,	Gen 16:10	4397
the *a* of the LORD said unto her,	Gen 16:11	4397
the *a* of God called to Hagar out	Gen 21:17	4397
the *a* of the LORD called unto him	Gen 22:11	4397
the *a* of the LORD called unto	Gen 22:15	4397
he shall send his *a* before thee	Gen 24:7	4397
I walk, will send his *a* with thee	Gen 24:40	4397
the *a* of God spake unto me in a	Gen 31:11	4397
The *a* which redeemed me from all	Gen 48:16	4397
the *a* of the LORD appeared unto	Ex 3:2	4397
the *a* of God, which went before	Ex 14:19	4397

I send an *A* before thee, to keep	Ex 23:20	4397
For mine *A* shall go before thee,	Ex 23:23	4397
mine *A* shall go before thee	Ex 32:34	4397
And I will send an *a* before thee	Ex 33:2	4397
he heard our voice, and sent an *a*	Num 20:16	4397
the *a* of the LORD stood in the	Num 22:22	4397
the ass saw the *a* of the LORD	Num 22:23	4397
But the *a* of the LORD stood in a	Num 22:24	4397
the ass saw the *a* of the LORD	Num 22:25	4397
the *a* of the LORD went further,	Num 22:26	4397
the ass saw the *a* of the LORD	Num 22:27	4397
he saw the *a* of the LORD standing	Num 22:31	4397
the *a* of the LORD said unto him,	Num 22:32	4397
said unto the *a* of the LORD	Num 22:34	4397
the *a* of the LORD said unto	Num 22:35	4397
an *a* of the LORD came up from	Judg 2:1	4397
when the *a* of the LORD spake	Judg 2:4	4397
said the *a* of the LORD, curse ye	Judg 5:23	4397
And there came an *a* of the LORD	Judg 6:11	4397
the *a* of the LORD appeared unto	Judg 6:12	4397
the *a* of God said unto him, Take	Judg 6:20	4397
Then the *a* of the LORD put forth	Judg 6:21	4397
Then the *a* of the LORD departed	Judg 6:21	4397
that he was an *a* of the LORD	Judg 6:22	4397
an *a* of the LORD face to face	Judg 6:22	4397
the *a* of the LORD appeared unto	Judg 13:3	4397
the countenance of an *a* of God	Judg 13:6	4397
the *a* of God came again unto the	Judg 13:9	4397
the *a* of the LORD said unto	Judg 13:13	4397
said unto the *a* of the LORD	Judg 13:15	4397
the *a* of the LORD said unto	Judg 13:16	4397
not that he was an *a* of the LORD	Judg 13:16	4397
said unto the *a* of the LORD	Judg 13:17	4397
the *a* of the LORD said unto him,	Judg 13:18	4397
and the *a* did wonderously	Judg 13:19	
that the *a* of the LORD ascended	Judg 13:20	4397
But the *a* of the LORD did no more	Judg 13:21	4397
knew that he was an *a* of the LORD	Judg 13:21	4397
good in my sight, as an *a* of God	1Sa 29:9	
for as an *a* of God, so is my lord	2Sa 14:17	4397
to the wisdom of an *a* of God	2Sa 14:20	4397
lord the king is as an *a* of God	2Sa 19:27	4397
when the *a* stretched out his hand	2Sa 24:16	4397
said to the *a* that destroyed the	2Sa 24:16	4397
the *a* of the LORD was by the	2Sa 24:16	4397
saw the *a* that smote the people	2Sa 24:17	4397
an *a* spake unto me by the word of	1Kin 13:18	4397
then an *a* touched him, and said	1Kin 19:5	4397
the *a* of the LORD came again the	1Kin 19:7	4397
But the *a* of the LORD said to	2Kin 1:3	4397
the *a* of the LORD said unto	2Kin 1:15	4397
that the *a* of the LORD went out,	2Kin 19:35	4397
the *a* of the LORD destroying	1Chr 21:12	4397
God sent an *a* unto Jerusalem to	1Chr 21:15	4397
said to the *a* that destroyed, It	1Chr 21:15	4397
the *a* of the LORD stood by the	1Chr 21:15	4397
saw the *a* of the LORD stand	1Chr 21:16	4397
Then the *a* of the LORD commanded	1Chr 21:18	4397
Ornan turned back, and saw the *a*	1Chr 21:20	4397
And the LORD commanded the *a*	1Chr 21:27	4397
of the sword of the *a* of the LORD	1Chr 21:30	4397
And the LORD sent an *a*, which cut	2Chr 32:21	4397
The *a* of the LORD encampeth round	Ps 34:7	4397
let the *a* of the LORD chase them	Ps 35:5	4397
let the *a* of the LORD persecute	Ps 35:6	4397
neither say thou before the *a*	Eccl 5:6	4397
Then the *a* of the LORD went forth	Is 37:36	4397
the *a* of his presence saved them	Is 63:9	4397
and Abed-nego, who hath sent his *a*	Dan 3:28	4398
My God hath sent his *a*, and hath	Dan 6:22	4398
Yea, he had power over the *a*	Hos 12:4	4397
the *a* that talked with me said	Zec 1:9	4397
they answered the *a* of the LORD	Zec 1:11	4397
Then the *a* of the LORD answered	Zec 1:12	4397
the LORD answered the *a* that	Zec 1:13	4397
So the *a* that communed with me	Zec 1:14	4397
I said unto the *a* that talked	Zec 1:19	4397
the *a* that talked with me went	Zec 2:3	4397
another *a* went out to meet him,	Zec 2:3	4397
standing before the *a* of the LORD	Zec 3:1	4397
garments, and stood before the *a*	Zec 3:3	4397
the *a* of the LORD stood by	Zec 3:5	4397
the *a* of the LORD protested unto	Zec 3:6	4397
the *a* that talked with me came	Zec 4:1	4397
spake to the *a* that talked with	Zec 4:4	4397
Then the *a* that talked with me	Zec 4:5	4397
Then the *a* that talked with me	Zec 5:5	4397
Then said I to the *a* that talked	Zec 5:10	4397
said unto the *a* that talked with	Zec 6:4	4397
the *a* answered and said unto me,	Zec 6:5	4397
as the *a* of the LORD before them	Zec 12:8	4397
the *a* of the Lord appeared unto	Mt 1:20	32
the *a* of the Lord had bidden him	Mt 1:24	32
the *a* of the Lord appeareth to	Mt 2:13	32
an *a* of the Lord appeareth in a	Mt 2:19	32
for the *a* of the Lord descended	Mt 28:2	32
the *a* answered and said unto the	Mt 28:5	32
there appeared unto him an *a* of	Lk 1:11	32
But the *a* said unto him, Fear not	Lk 1:13	32
And Zacharias said unto the *a*	Lk 1:18	32
the *a* answering said unto him, I	Lk 1:19	32
in the sixth month the *a* Gabriel	Lk 1:26	32
the *a* came in unto her, and said,	Lk 1:28	32
the *a* said unto her, Fear not,	Lk 1:30	32
Then said Mary unto the *a*	Lk 1:34	32
the *a* answered and said unto her,	Lk 1:35	32
And the *a* departed from her	Lk 1:38	32
the *a* of the Lord came upon them,	Lk 2:9	32
the *a* said unto them, Fear not	Lk 2:10	32
the *a* a multitude of the heavenly	Lk 2:13	32
which was so named of the *a*	Lk 2:21	32
there appeared an *a* unto him from	Lk 22:43	32
For an *a* went down at a certain	Jn 5:4	32
others said, An *a* spake to him	Jn 12:29	32
But the *a* of the Lord by night	Acts 5:19	32
as it had been the face of an *a*	Acts 6:15	32
a of the Lord in a flame of fire	Acts 7:30	32
a which appeared to him in the	Acts 7:35	32
in the wilderness with the *a*	Acts 7:38	32
the *a* of the Lord spake unto	Acts 8:26	32
day an *a* of God coming in to him	Acts 10:3	32
when the *a* which spake unto	Acts 10:7	32
was warned from God by an holy *a*	Acts 10:22	32
how he had seen an *a* in his house	Acts 11:13	32
the *a* of the Lord came upon him,	Acts 12:7	32
the *a* said unto him, Gird thyself	Acts 12:8	32
was true which was done by the *a*	Acts 12:9	32
forthwith the *a* departed from him	Acts 12:10	32
that the Lord hath sent his *a*	Acts 12:11	32
Then said they, It is his *a*	Acts 12:15	32
immediately the *a* of the Lord	Acts 12:23	32
is no resurrection, neither *a*	Acts 23:8	32
spirit or an *a* hath spoken to him	Acts 23:9	32
by me this night the *a* of God	Acts 27:23	32
is transformed into an *a* of light	2Cor 11:14	32
or an *a* from heaven, preach any	Gal 1:8	32
but received me as an *a* of God	Gal 4:14	32
signified it by his *a* unto his	Rev 1:1	32
Unto the *a* of the church of	Rev 2:1	32
unto the *a* of the church in	Rev 2:8	32
to the *a* of the church in	Rev 2:12	32
unto the *a* of the church in	Rev 2:18	32
unto the *a* of the church in	Rev 3:1	32
to the *a* of the church in	Rev 3:7	32
unto the *a* of the church of the	Rev 3:14	32
I saw a strong *a* proclaiming with	Rev 5:2	32
I saw another *a* ascending from	Rev 7:2	32
And another *a* came and stood at the	Rev 8:3	32
the *a* took the censer, and filled	Rev 8:5	32
The first *a* sounded, and there	Rev 8:7	32
And the second *a* sounded, and as it	Rev 8:8	32
And the third *a* sounded, and there	Rev 8:10	32
And the fourth *a* sounded, and the	Rev 8:12	32
heard an *a* flying through the	Rev 8:13	32
And the fifth *a* sounded, and I saw	Rev 9:1	32
which is the *a* of the bottomless	Rev 9:11	32
And the sixth *a* sounded, and I	Rev 9:13	32
Saying to the sixth *a* which had	Rev 9:14	32
I saw another mighty *a* come down	Rev 10:1	32
the *a* which I saw stand upon the	Rev 10:5	32
of the voice of the seventh *a*	Rev 10:7	32
is open in the hand of the *a*	Rev 10:8	32
And I went unto the *a*, and said	Rev 10:9	32
the *a* stood, saying, Rise, and	Rev 11:1	32
And the seventh *a* sounded	Rev 11:15	32
I saw another *a* fly in the midst	Rev 14:6	32
And there followed another *a*	Rev 14:8	32
the third *a* followed them, saying	Rev 14:9	32
another *a* came out of the temple,	Rev 14:15	32
another *a* came out of the temple	Rev 14:17	32
another *a* came out from the altar	Rev 14:18	32
the *a* thrust in his sickle into	Rev 14:19	32
the second *a* poured out his vial	Rev 16:3	32
the third *a* poured out his vial	Rev 16:4	32
I heard the *a* of the waters say,	Rev 16:5	32
the fourth *a* poured out his vial	Rev 16:8	32
the fifth *a* poured out his vial	Rev 16:10	32
the sixth *a* poured out his vial	Rev 16:12	32
the seventh *a* poured out his vial	Rev 16:17	32
the *a* said unto me, Wherefore	Rev 17:7	32
another *a* come down from heaven	Rev 18:1	32
a mighty *a* took up a stone like a	Rev 18:21	32

I saw an *a* standing in the sun .... Rev 19:17   32
I saw an *a* come down from heaven, ... Rev 20:1   32
of a man, that is, of the *a* .... Rev 21:17   32
a to shew unto his servants the .... Rev 22:6   32
a which shewed me these things .... Rev 22:8   32
I Jesus have sent mine *a* to .... Rev 22:16   32

ANGEL'S

up before God out of the *a* hand .... Rev 8:4   32
the little book out of the *a* hand .... Rev 10:10   32

ANGELS

there came two *a* to Sodom at even .... Gen 19:1   4397
then the *a* hastened Lot, saying, ... Gen 19:15   4397
behold the *a* of God ascending and .... Gen 28:12   4397
his way, and the *a* of God met him .... Gen 32:1   4397
his *a* he charged with folly .... Job 4:18   4397
him a little lower than the *a* .... Ps 8:5   430
thousand, even thousands of *a* .... Ps 68:17   8136
by sending evil *a* among them .... Ps 78:49   4397
shall give his *a* charge over thee .... Ps 91:11   4397
Bless the LORD, ye his *a*, that .... Ps 103:20   4397
Who maketh his *a* spirits .... Ps 104:4   4397
Praise ye him, all his *a* .... Ps 148:2   4397
He shall give his *a* charge .... Mt 4:6   32
a came and ministered unto him .... Mt 4:11   32
and the reapers are the *a* .... Mt 13:39   32
Son of man shall send forth his *a* .... Mt 13:41   32
the *a* shall come forth, and sever .... Mt 13:49   32
glory of his Father with his *a* .... Mt 16:27   32
That in heaven their *a* do always .... Mt 18:10   32
but are as the *a* of God in heaven .... Mt 22:30   32
he shall send his *a* with a great .... Mt 24:31   32
not the *a* of heaven, but my .... Mt 24:36   32
glory, and all the holy *a* with him ...... Mt 25:31   32
prepared for the devil and his *a* .... Mt 25:41   32
me more than twelve legions of *a* .... Mt 26:53   32
the *a* ministered unto him .... Mk 1:13   32
of his Father with the holy *a* .... Mk 8:38   32
but are as the *a* which are in .... Mk 12:25   32
And then shall he send his *a* .... Mk 13:27   32
not the *a* which are in heaven, ... Mk 13:32   32
as the *a* were gone away from them ...... Lk 2:15   32
shall give his *a* charge over thee .... Lk 4:10   32
in his Father's, and of the holy *a* .... Lk 9:26   32
also confess before the *a* of God .... Lk 12:8   32
be denied before the *a* of God .... Lk 12:9   32
the *a* of God over one sinner that .... Lk 15:10   32
was carried by the *a* into .... Lk 16:22   32
for they are equal unto the *a* .... Lk 20:36   2465
they had also seen a vision of *a* .... Lk 24:23   32
the *a* of God ascending and .... Jn 1:51   32
seeth two *a* in white sitting, ... Jn 20:12   32
the law by the disposition of *a* .... Acts 7:53   32
neither death, nor life, nor *a* .... Rom 8:38   32
spectacle unto the world, and to *a* 1Cor 4:9   32
Know ye not that we shall judge *a* 1Cor 6:3   32
on her head because of the *a* 1Cor 11:10   32
with the tongues of men and of *a* 1Cor 13:1   32
it was ordained by *a* in the hand .... Gal 3:19   32
humility and worshipping of *a* .... Col 2:18   32
from heaven with his mighty *a* 2Th 1:7   32
in the Spirit, seen of *a* 1Ti 3:16   32
Lord Jesus Christ, and the elect *a* 1Ti 5:21   32
made so much better than the *a* .... Heb 1:4   32
of the *a* said he at any time .... Heb 1:5   32
let all the *a* of God worship him .... Heb 1:6   32
of the *a* he saith .... Heb 1:7   32
Who maketh his *a* spirits .... Heb 1:7   32
But to which of the *a* said he at .... Heb 1:13   32
the word spoken by *a* was stedfast .... Heb 2:2   32
For unto the *a* hath he not put in .... Heb 2:5   32
him a little lower than the *a* .... Heb 2:7   32
the *a* for the suffering of death .... Heb 2:9   32
took not on him the nature of *a* .... Heb 2:16   32
and to an innumerable company of *a*..... Heb 12:22   32
some have entertained *a* unawares .... Heb 13:2   32
which things the *a* desire to look 1Pet 1:12   32
a and authorities and powers being 1Pet 3:22   32
God spared not the *a* that sinned 2Pet 2:4   32
Whereas *a*, which are greater in 2Pet 2:11   32
the *a* which kept not their first .... Jude 6   32
are the *a* of the seven churches .... Rev 1:20   32
before my Father, and before his *a* .... Rev 3:5   32
of many *a* round about the throne .... Rev 5:11   32
after these things I saw four *a* .... Rev 7:1   32
with a loud voice to the four *a* .... Rev 7:2   32
all the *a* stood round about them .... Rev 7:11   32
I saw the seven *a* which stood .... Rev 8:2   32
the seven *a* which had the seven .... Rev 8:6   32
of the trumpet of the three *a* .... Rev 8:13   32
Loose the four *a* which are bound .... Rev 9:14   32

the four *a* were loosed, which .... Rev 9:15   32
his *a* fought against the dragon .... Rev 12:7   32
and the dragon fought and his *a* .... Rev 12:7   32
his *a* were cast out with him .... Rev 12:9   32
in the presence of the holy *a* .... Rev 14:10   32
seven *a* having the seven last .... Rev 15:1   32
the seven *a* came out of the .... Rev 15:6   32
a seven golden vials full of the .... Rev 15:7   32
of the seven *a* were fulfilled .... Rev 15:8   32
the temple saying to the seven *a* .... Rev 16:1   32
seven *a* which had the seven vials .... Rev 17:1   32
came unto me one of the seven *a*........... Rev 21:9   32
gates, and at the gates twelve *a* .... Rev 21:12   32

ANGELS'

Man did eat *a* food .... Ps 78:25   47

ANGER

brother's *a* turn away from thee .... Gen 27:45   639
Jacob's *a* was kindled against .... Gen 30:2   639
let not thine *a* burn against thy .... Gen 44:18   639
for in their *a* they slew a man, ... Gen 49:6   639
Cursed be their *a*, for it was .... Gen 49:7   639
the *a* of the LORD was kindled.............. Ex 4:14   639
out from Pharaoh in a great *a* .... Ex 11:8   639
Moses' *a* waxed hot, and he cast .... Ex 32:19   639
Let not the *a* of my lord wax hot .... Ex 32:22   639
and his *a* was kindled .... Num 11:1   639
the *a* of the LORD was kindled .... Num 11:10   639
the *a* of the LORD was kindled .... Num 12:9   639
God's *a* was kindled because he .... Num 22:22   639
Balaam's *a* was kindled, and he .... Num 22:27   639
Balak's *a* was kindled against .... Num 24:10   639
the *a* of the LORD was kindled .... Num 25:3   639
that the fierce *a* of the LORD may .... Num 25:4   639
the LORD's *a* was kindled the same .... Num 32:10   639
the LORD's *a* was kindled against .... Num 32:13   639
a of the LORD toward Israel .... Num 32:14   639
LORD thy God, to provoke him to *a*....... Deut 4:25   3707
a of the LORD thy God be kindled .... Deut 6:15   639
so will the *a* of the LORD be .... Deut 7:4   639
of the LORD, to provoke him to *a* .... Deut 9:18   3707
For I was afraid of the *a* .... Deut 9:19   639
turn from the fierceness of his *a* .... Deut 13:17   639
him, but then the *a* of the LORD .... Deut 29:20   639
which the LORD overthrew in his *a* .... Deut 29:23   639
meaneth the heat of this great *a* .... Deut 29:24   639
the *a* of the LORD was kindled .... Deut 29:27   639
them out of their land in *a* .... Deut 29:28   639
Then my *a* shall be kindled................... Deut 31:17   639
to provoke him to *a* through the .... Deut 31:29   3707
provoked they him to *a* .... Deut 32:16   3707
me to *a* with their vanities .... Deut 32:21   3707
them to *a* with a foolish nation .... Deut 32:21
For a fire is kindled in mine *a* .... Deut 32:22   639
the *a* of the LORD was kindled .... Josh 7:1   639
from the fierceness of his *a* .... Josh 7:26   639
then shall the *a* of the LORD be .... Josh 23:16   639
them, and provoked the LORD to *a*......... Judg 2:12   3707
the *a* of the LORD was hot against .... Judg 2:14   639
the *a* of the LORD was hot against .... Judg 2:20   639
Therefore the *a* of the LORD was .... Judg 3:8   639
Let not thine *a* be hot against me .... Judg 6:39   639
Then their *a* was abated toward............ Judg 8:3   7307
son of Ebed, his *a* was kindled .... Judg 9:30   639
the *a* of the LORD was hot against .... Judg 10:7   639
his *a* was kindled, and he went up .... Judg 14:19   639
his *a* was kindled greatly 1Sa 11:6   639
Eliab's *a* was kindled against 1Sa 17:28   639
Then Saul's *a* was kindled against 1Sa 20:30   639
arose from the table in fierce *a* 1Sa 20:34   639
the *a* of the LORD was kindled.............. 2Sa 6:7   639
David's *a* was greatly kindled 2Sa 12:5   639
again the *a* of the LORD was 2Sa 24:1   639
molten images, to provoke me to *a* 1Kin 14:9   3707
groves, provoking the LORD to *a* 1Kin 14:15   3707
the LORD God of Israel to *a* 1Kin 15:30   3707
provoke me to *a* with their sins 1Kin 16:2   3707
in provoking him to *a* with the 1Kin 16:7   3707
Israel to *a* with their vanities 1Kin 16:13   3707
Israel to *a* with their vanities 1Kin 16:26   3707
the LORD God of Israel to *a* than 1Kin 16:33   3707
thou hast provoked me to *a* 1Kin 21:22   3707
provoked to *a* the LORD God of 1Kin 22:53   3707
the *a* of the LORD was kindled.............. 2Kin 13:3   639
things to provoke the LORD to *a*........... 2Kin 17:11   3707
of the LORD, to provoke him to *a* 2Kin 17:17   3707
of the LORD, to provoke him to *a* 2Kin 21:6   3707
sight, and have provoked me to *a* 2Kin 21:15   3707
to *a* with all the works of their 2Kin 22:17   3707
had made to provoke the LORD to *a* 2Kin 23:19   3707
wherewith his *a* was kindled................. 2Kin 23:26   639

For through the *a* of the LORD it	2Kin 24:20	639
the *a* of the LORD was kindled	1Chr 13:10	639
wherefore their *a* was greatly	2Chr 25:10	639
and they returned home in great *a*	2Chr 25:10	639
Wherefore the *a* of the LORD was	2Chr 25:15	639
provoked to *a* the LORD God of his	2Chr 28:25	3707
of the LORD, to provoke him to *a*	2Chr 33:6	3707
to *a* with all the works of their	2Chr 34:25	3707
thee to *a* before the builders	Neh 4:5	3707
gracious and merciful, slow to *a*	Neh 9:17	639
wroth, and his *a* burned in him	Est 1:12	2534
which overturneth them in his *a*	Job 9:5	639
If God will not withdraw his *a*	Job 9:13	639
He teareth himself in his *a*	Job 18:4	639
God distributeth sorrows in his *a*	Job 21:17	639
not so, he hath visited in his *a*	Job 35:15	639
O lord, rebuke me not in thine *a*	Ps 6:1	639
Arise, O LORD, in thine *a*	Ps 7:6	639
fiery oven in the time of thine *a*	Ps 21:9	6440
put not thy servant away in *a*	Ps 27:9	639
For his *a* endureth but a moment	Ps 30:5	639
Cease from *a*, and forsake wrath	Ps 37:8	639
in my flesh because of thine *a*	Ps 38:3	2195
in thine *a* cast down the people,	Ps 56:7	639
let thy wrathful *a* take hold of	Ps 69:24	639
why doth thine *a* smoke against	Ps 74:1	639
hath he in *a* shut up his tender	Ps 77:9	639
a also came up against Israel	Ps 78:21	639
many a time turned he his *a* away	Ps 78:38	639
upon them the fierceness of his *a*	Ps 78:49	639
He made a way to his *a*	Ps 78:50	639
him to *a* with their high places	Ps 78:58	3707
from the fierceness of thine *a*	Ps 85:3	639
cause thine *a* toward us to cease	Ps 85:4	3708
out thine *a* to all generations	Ps 85:5	639
For we are consumed by thine *a*	Ps 90:7	639
Who knoweth the power of thine *a*	Ps 90:11	639
merciful and gracious, slow to *a*	Ps 103:8	639
will he keep his *a* for ever	Ps 103:9	639
him to *a* with their inventions	Ps 106:29	3707
slow to *a*, and of great mercy	Ps 145:8	639
but grievous words stir up *a*	Prov 15:1	639
is slow to *a* appeaseth strife	Prov 15:18	639
He that is slow to *a* is better	Prov 16:32	639
of a man deferreth his *a*	Prov 19:11	639
whoso provoketh him to *a* sinneth	Prov 20:2	5674
A gift in secret pacifieth *a*	Prov 21:14	639
and the rod of his *a* shall fail	Prov 22:8	5678
is cruel, and *a* is outrageous	Prov 27:4	639
for *a* resteth in the bosom of	Eccl 7:9	3708
the Holy One of Israel unto *a*	Is 1:4	5006
Therefore is the *a* of the LORD	Is 5:25	639
For all this his *a* is not turned	Is 5:25	639
for the fierce *a* of Rezin with	Is 7:4	639
For all this his *a* is not turned	Is 9:12	639
For all this his *a* is not turned	Is 9:17	639
For all this his *a* is not turned	Is 9:21	639
For all this his *a* is not turned	Is 10:4	639
O Assyrian, the rod of mine *a*	Is 10:5	639
mine *a* in their destruction	Is 10:25	639
thine *a* is turned away, and thou	Is 12:1	639
called my mighty ones for mine *a*	Is 13:3	639
cruel both with wrath and fierce *a*	Is 13:9	639
and in the day of his fierce *a*	Is 13:13	639
he that ruled the nations in *a*	Is 14:6	639
from far, burning with his *a*	Is 30:27	639
with the indignation of his *a*	Is 30:30	639
poured upon him the fury of his *a*	Is 42:25	639
name's sake will I defer mine *a*	Is 48:9	639
for I will tread them in mine *a*	Is 63:3	639
tread down the people in mine *a*	Is 63:6	639
me to *a* continually to my face	Is 65:3	3707
to render his *a* with fury	Is 66:15	639
surely his *a* shall turn from me	Jer 2:35	639
Will he reserve his *a* for ever	Jer 3:5	
not cause mine *a* to fall upon you	Jer 3:12	6440
and I will not keep *a* for ever	Jer 3:12	
for the fierce *a* of the LORD is	Jer 4:8	639
of the LORD, and by his fierce *a*	Jer 4:26	639
that they may provoke me to *a*	Jer 7:18	3707
Do they provoke me to *a*	Jer 7:19	3707
Behold, mine *a* and my fury shall	Jer 7:20	639
me to *a* with their graven images	Jer 8:19	3707
not in thine *a*, lest thou bring	Jer 10:24	639
themselves to provoke me to *a* in	Jer 11:17	3707
of the fierce *a* of the LORD	Jer 12:13	639
for a fire is kindled in mine *a*	Jer 15:14	639
ye have kindled a fire in mine *a*	Jer 17:4	639
with them in the time of thine *a*	Jer 18:23	639
and with a strong arm, even in *a*	Jer 21:5	639
The *a* of the LORD shall not	Jer 23:20	639

provoke me not to *a* with the	Jer 25:6	3707
that ye might provoke me to *a*	Jer 25:7	3707
of the fierce *a* of the LORD	Jer 25:37	639
and because of his fierce *a*	Jer 25:38	639
The fierce *a* of the LORD shall	Jer 30:24	639
other gods, to provoke me to *a*	Jer 32:29	3707
to *a* with the work of their hands	Jer 32:30	3707
to me as a provocation of mine *a*	Jer 32:31	639
they have done to provoke me to *a*	Jer 32:32	3707
I have driven them in mine *a*	Jer 32:37	639
men, whom I have slain in mine *a*	Jer 33:5	639
for great is the *a* and the fury	Jer 36:7	639
As mine *a* and my fury hath been	Jer 42:18	639
have committed to provoke me to *a*	Jer 44:3	3707
mine *a* was poured forth, and was	Jer 44:6	639
evil upon them, even my fierce *a*	Jer 49:37	639
from the fierce *a* of the LORD	Jer 51:45	639
For through the *a* of the LORD it	Jer 52:3	639
me in the day of his fierce *a*	Lam 1:12	639
of Zion with a cloud in his *a*	Lam 2:1	639
his footstool in the day of his *a*	Lam 2:1	639
fierce *a* all the horn of Israel	Lam 2:3	639
the indignation of his *a* the king	Lam 2:6	639
slain them in the day of thine *a*	Lam 2:21	639
a none escaped nor remained	Lam 2:22	639
Thou hast covered with *a*, and	Lam 3:43	639
destroy them in *a* from under the	Lam 3:66	639
he hath poured out his fierce *a*	Lam 4:11	639
The *a* of the LORD hath divided	Lam 4:16	6440
Thus shall mine *a* be accomplished	Eze 5:13	639
execute judgments in thee in *a*	Eze 5:15	639
and I will send mine *a* upon thee	Eze 7:3	639
and accomplish mine *a* upon thee	Eze 7:8	639
have returned to provoke me to *a*	Eze 8:17	3707
an overflowing shower in mine *a*	Eze 13:13	639
thy whoredoms, to provoke me to *a*	Eze 16:26	3707
to accomplish my *a* against them	Eze 20:8	639
to accomplish mine *a* against them	Eze 20:21	639
so will I gather you in mine *a*	Eze 22:20	639
do in Edom according to mine *a*	Eze 25:14	639
will even do according to thine *a*	Eze 35:11	639
I have consumed them in mine *a*	Eze 43:8	639
I beseech thee, let thine *a*	Dan 9:16	639
shall be destroyed, neither in *a*	Dan 11:20	639
mine *a* is kindled against them	Hos 8:5	639
execute the fierceness of mine *a*	Hos 11:9	639
provoked him to *a* most bitterly	Hos 12:14	3707
I gave thee a king in mine *a*	Hos 13:11	639
for mine *a* is turned away from	Hos 14:4	639
gracious and merciful, slow to *a*	Joel 2:13	639
his *a* did tear perpetually, and he	Amos 1:11	639
and turn away from his fierce *a*	Jonah 3:9	639
God, and merciful, slow to *a*	Jonah 4:2	639
And I will execute vengeance in *a*	Mic 5:15	639
he retaineth not his *a* for ever	Mic 7:18	639
The LORD is slow to *a*, and great	Nah 1:3	639
abide in the fierceness of his *a*	Nah 1:6	639
was thine *a* against the rivers	Hab 3:8	639
didst thresh the heathen in *a*	Hab 3:12	639
before the fierce *a* of the LORD	Zeph 2:2	639
day of the LORD's *a* come upon you	Zeph 2:2	639
be hid in the day of the LORD's *a*	Zeph 2:3	639
indignation, even all my fierce *a*	Zeph 3:8	639
Mine *a* was kindled against the	Zec 10:3	639
looked round about on them with *a*	Mk 3:5	3709
by a foolish nation I will *a* you	Rom 10:19	3949
all bitterness, and wrath, and *a*	Eph 4:31	3709
a, wrath, malice, blasphemy,	Col 3:8	3709
provoke not your children to *a*	Col 3:21	

ANGERED

They *a* him also at the waters of	Ps 106:32	7107

ANGLE

all they that cast *a* into the	Is 19:8	2443
take up all of them with the *a*	Hab 1:15	2443

ANGRY

him, Oh let not the LORD be *a*	Gen 18:30	2734
he said, Oh let not the Lord be *a*	Gen 18:32	2734
nor *a* with yourselves, that ye	Gen 45:5	2734
he was *a* with Eleazar and Ithamar,	Lev 10:16	7107
Also the LORD was *a* with me for	Deut 1:37	599
LORD was *a* with me for your sakes	Deut 4:21	599
so that the LORD was *a* with you	Deut 9:8	599
the LORD was very *a* with Aaron to	Deut 9:20	599
lest *a* fellows run upon thee,	Judg 18:25	4751,5315
then be ye *a* for this matter	2Sa 19:42	2734
thou be *a* with them, and deliver	1Kin 8:46	599
And the LORD was *a* with Solomon	1Kin 11:9	599
the LORD was very *a* with Israel	2Kin 17:18	599
thou be *a* with them, and deliver	2Chr 6:36	599

wouldest not thou be *a* with us	Ezr 9:14	599
I was very *a* when I heard their	Neh 5:6	2734
Kiss the Son, lest he be *a*	Ps 2:12	599
God is *a* with the wicked every	Ps 7:11	2194
in thy sight when once thou art *a*	Ps 76:7	639
wilt thou be *a* for ever	Ps 79:5	599
how long wilt thou be *a* against	Ps 80:4	6225
Wilt thou be *a* with us for ever	Ps 85:5	599
He that is soon *a* dealeth	Prov 14:17	639
with a contentious and an *a* woman	Prov 21:19	3708
Make no friendship with an *a* man	Prov 22:24	639
so doth an *a* countenance a	Prov 25:23	2194
An *a* man stirreth up strife, and a	Prov 29:22	639
should God be *a* at thy voice	Eccl 5:6	7107
not hasty in thy spirit to be *a*	Eccl 7:9	3707
mother's children were *a* with me	Song 1:6	2734
though thou wast *a* with me	Is 12:1	599
be quiet, and will be no more *a*	Eze 16:42	3707
For this cause the king was *a*	Dan 2:12	1149
exceedingly, and he was very *a*	Jonah 4:1	2734
the LORD, Doest thou well to be *a*	Jonah 4:4	2734
thou well to be *a* for the gourd	Jonah 4:9	2734
And he said, I do well to be *a*	Jonah 4:9	2734
That whosoever is *a* with his	Mt 5:22	3710
house being *a* said to his servant	Lk 14:21	3710
And he was *a*, and would not go in	Lk 15:28	3710
are ye *a* at me, because I have	Jn 7:23	5520
Be ye *a*, and sin not	Eph 4:26	3710
not selfwilled, not soon *a*	Titus 1:7	3711
And the nations were *a*, and thy	Rev 11:18	3710

ANGUISH

in that we saw the *a* of his soul	Gen 42:21	6869
not unto Moses for *a* of spirit	Ex 6:9	7115
and be in *a* because of thee	Deut 2:25	2342
for *a* is come upon me, because my	2Sa 1:9	7661
will speak in the *a* of my spirit	Job 7:11	6862
and *a* shall make him afraid	Job 15:24	4691
and *a* have taken hold on me	Ps 119:143	4689
distress and *a* cometh upon you	Prov 1:27	6695
trouble and darkness, dimness of *a*	Is 8:22	6695
into the land of trouble and *a*	Is 30:6	6695
the *a* as of her that bringeth	Jer 4:31	6869
a hath taken hold of us, and pain	Jer 6:24	6869
and sorrows have taken her, as *a*	Jer 49:24	6869
a took hold of him, and pangs as	Jer 50:43	6869
she remembereth no more the *a*	Jn 16:21	2347
Tribulation and *a*, upon every soul	Rom 2:9	4730
a of heart I wrote unto you with	2Cor 2:4	4928

ANIAM (a'-ne-am) A son of Shemida.

Ahian, and Shechem, and Likhi, and A .	1Chr 7:19	593

ANIM (a'-nim) A city in Judah.

And Anab, and Eshtemoh, and A	Josh 15:50	6044

ANISE

for ye pay tithe of mint and *a*	Mt 23:23	432

ANNA (an'-nah) A prophetess.

And there was one A, a prophetess,	Lk 2:36	451

ANNAS (an'-nas) A High Priest during Jesus' ministry.

A and Caiaphas being the high	Lk 3:2	452
And led him away to A first	Jn 18:13	452
Now A had sent him bound unto	Jn 18:24	452
A the high priest, and Caiaphas,	Acts 4:6	452

ANOINT

and shalt *a* them, and consecrate	Ex 28:41	4886
pour it upon his head, and *a* him	Ex 29:7	4886
for it, and thou shalt *a* it	Ex 29:36	4886
thou shalt *a* the tabernacle of	Ex 30:26	4886
And thou shalt *a* Aaron and his sons	Ex 30:30	4886
a the tabernacle, and all that is	Ex 40:9	4886
thou shalt *a* the altar of the	Ex 40:10	4886
And thou shalt *a* the laver	Ex 40:11	4886
and *a* him, and sanctify him	Ex 40:13	4886
And thou shalt *a* them	Ex 40:15	4886
as thou didst *a* their father	Ex 40:15	4886
And the priest, whom he shall *a*	Lev 16:32	4886
but thou shalt not *a* thyself with	Deut 28:40	5480
on a time to *a* a king over them	Judg 9:8	4886
If in truth ye *a* me king over you	Judg 9:15	4886
a thee, and put thy raiment upon	Ruth 3:3	5480
thou shalt *a* him to be captain	1Sa 9:16	4886
The LORD sent me to *a* thee to be	1Sa 15:1	4886
thou shalt *a* unto me him whom I	1Sa 16:3	4886
And the LORD said, Arise, *a* him	1Sa 16:12	4886
a not thyself with oil, but be as	2Sa 14:2	5480
Nathan the prophet *a* him there	1Kin 1:34	4886
a Hazael to be king over Syria	1Kin 19:16	4886
thou *a* to be king over Israel	1Kin 19:16	4886
thou *a* to be prophet in thy room	1Kin 19:16	4886

ye princes, and *a* the shield	Is 21:5	4886
prophecy, and to *a* the most Holy	Dan 9:24	4886
neither did I *a* myself at all	Dan 10:3	5480
a themselves with the chief	Amos 6:6	4886
thou shalt not *a* thee with oil	Mic 6:15	5480
***a* thine head, and wash thy face**	Mt 6:17	*218*
to *a* my body to the burying	Mk 14:8	*3462*
that they might come and *a* him	Mk 16:1	*218*
My head with oil thou didst not *a*	Lk 7:46	*218*
a thine eyes with eyesalve, that	Rev 3:18	*1472*

ANOINTED

and wafers unleavened *a* with oil	Ex 29:2	4886
to be *a* therein, and to be	Ex 29:29	4888
or unleavened wafers *a* with oil	Lev 2:4	4886
If the priest that is *a* do sin	Lev 4:3	4899
the priest that is *a* shall take	Lev 4:5	4899
the priest that is *a* shall bring	Lev 4:16	4899
the LORD in the day when he is *a*	Lev 6:20	4886
is *a* in his stead shall offer it	Lev 6:22	4899
and unleavened wafers *a* with oil	Lev 7:12	4886
Israel, in the day that he *a* them	Lev 7:36	4886
a the tabernacle and all that was	Lev 8:10	4886
a the altar and all his vessels,	Lev 8:11	4886
head, and *a* him, to sanctify him	Lev 8:12	4886
Aaron, the priests which were *a*	Num 3:3	4886
of unleavened bread *a* with oil	Num 6:15	4886
up the tabernacle, and had *a* it	Num 7:1	4886
had *a* them, and sanctified them	Num 7:1	4886
altar in the day that it was *a*	Num 7:10	4886
altar, in the day when it was *a*	Num 7:84	4886
of the altar, after that it was *a*	Num 7:88	4886
which was *a* with the holy oil	Num 35:25	4886
king, and exalt the horn of his *a*	1Sa 2:10	4899
shall walk before mine *a* for ever	1Sa 2:35	4899
a thee to be captain over his	1Sa 10:1	4886
before the LORD, and before his *a*	1Sa 12:3	4899
his *a* is witness this day, that	1Sa 12:5	4899
the LORD *a* thee king over Israel	1Sa 15:17	4886
Surely the LORD's *a* is before him	1Sa 16:6	4899
a him in the midst of his	1Sa 16:13	4886
unto my master, the LORD's *a*	1Sa 24:6	4899
seeing he is the *a* of the LORD	1Sa 24:6	4899
for he is the LORD's *a*	1Sa 24:10	4899
his hand against the LORD's *a*	1Sa 26:9	4899
mine hand against the LORD's *a*	1Sa 26:11	4899
kept your master, the LORD's *a*	1Sa 26:16	4899
mine hand against the LORD's *a*	1Sa 26:23	4899
hand to destroy the LORD's *a*	2Sa 1:14	4899
saying, I have slain the LORD's *a*	2Sa 1:16	4899
though he had not been *a* with oil	2Sa 1:21	4899
there they *a* David king over the	2Sa 2:4	4886
of Judah have *a* me king over them	2Sa 2:7	4886
I am this day weak, though *a* king	2Sa 3:39	4886
they *a* David king over Israel	2Sa 5:3	4886
they had *a* David king over Israel	2Sa 5:17	4886
I *a* thee king over Israel, and I	2Sa 12:7	4886
a himself, and changed his apparel	2Sa 12:20	5480
And Absalom, whom we *a* over us	2Sa 19:10	4886
because he cursed the LORD's *a*	2Sa 19:21	4899
and sheweth mercy to his *a*	2Sa 22:51	4899
the *a* of the God of Jacob, and the	2Sa 23:1	4899
of the tabernacle, and *a* Solomon	1Kin 1:39	4886
prophet have *a* him king in Gihon	1Kin 1:45	4886
had *a* him king in the room of his	1Kin 5:1	4886
I have *a* thee king over Israel	2Kin 9:3	4886
I have *a* thee king over the	2Kin 9:6	4886
I have *a* thee king over Israel	2Kin 9:12	4886
and they made him king, and *a* him	2Kin 11:12	4886
a him, and made him king in his	2Kin 23:30	4886
they *a* David king over Israel,	1Chr 11:3	4886
David was *a* king over all Israel	1Chr 14:8	4886
Saying, Touch not mine *a*, and do	1Chr 16:22	4899
a him unto the LORD to be the	1Chr 29:22	4886
turn not away the face of thine *a*	2Chr 6:42	4899
whom the LORD had *a* to cut off	2Chr 22:7	4886
And Jehoiada and his sons *a* him	2Chr 23:11	4886
a them, and carried all the feeble	2Chr 28:15	4886
the LORD, and against his *a*	Ps 2:2	4899
and sheweth mercy to his *a*	Ps 18:50	4899
know I that the LORD saveth his *a*	Ps 20:6	4899
is the saving strength of his *a*	Ps 28:8	4899
hath *a* thee with the oil of	Ps 45:7	4886
and look upon the face of thine *a*	Ps 84:9	4899
with my holy oil have I *a* him	Ps 89:20	4886
thou hast been wroth with thine *a*	Ps 89:38	4899
the footsteps of thine *a*	Ps 89:51	4899
I shall be *a* with fresh oil	Ps 92:10	1101
Saying, Touch not mine *a*, and do	Ps 105:15	4899
turn not away the face of thine *a*	Ps 132:10	4899
I have ordained a lamp for mine *a*	Ps 132:17	4899

Thus saith the LORD to his *a*	Is 45:1	4899
because the LORD hath *a* me to	Is 61:1	4886
the *a* of the LORD, was taken in	Lam 4:20	4899
from thee, and I *a* thee with oil	Eze 16:9	5480
Thou art the *a* cherub that	Eze 28:14	4473
even for salvation with thine *a*	Hab 3:13	4899
These are the two *a* ones	Zec 4:14	1121,3323
a with oil many that were sick,	Mk 6:13	218
because he hath *a* me to preach	Lk 4:18	5548
feet, and *a* them with the ointment	Lk 7:38	218
but this woman hath *a* my feet	Lk 7:46	218
he *a* the eyes of the blind man	Jn 9:6	2025,3323
a mine eyes, and said unto me, Go	Jn 9:11	2025
which *a* the Lord with ointment	Jn 11:2	218
a the feet of Jesus, and wiped his	Jn 12:3	218
child Jesus, whom thou hast *a*	Acts 4:27	5548
How God *a* Jesus of Nazareth with	Acts 10:38	5548
with you in Christ, and hath *a* us	2Cor 1:21	5548
hath *a* thee with the oil of	Heb 1:9	5548

ANOINTEDST

Beth-el, where thou *a* the pillar	Gen 31:13	4886

ANOINTEST

thou *a* my head with oil	Ps 23:5	1878

ANOINTING

for the light, spices for *a* oil	Ex 25:6	4888
Then shalt thou take the *a* oil	Ex 29:7	4888
upon the altar, and of the *a* oil	Ex 29:21	4888
it shall be an holy *a* oil	Ex 30:25	4888
This shall be an holy *a* oil unto	Ex 30:31	4888
And the *a* oil, and sweet incense	Ex 31:11	4888
the light, and spices for *a* oil	Ex 35:8	4888
and his staves, and the *a* oil	Ex 35:15	4888
for the light, and for the *a* oil	Ex 35:28	4888
And he made the holy *a* oil	Ex 37:29	4888
And the golden altar, and the *a* oil	Ex 39:38	4888
And thou shalt take the *a* oil	Ex 40:9	4888
for their *a* shall surely be an	Ex 40:15	4888
is the portion of the *a* of Aaron	Lev 7:35	4888
of the *a* of his sons, out of the	Lev 7:35	4888
and the garments, and the *a* oil	Lev 8:2	4888
And Moses took the *a* oil, and	Lev 8:10	4888
he poured of the *a* oil upon	Lev 8:12	4888
And Moses took of the *a* oil	Lev 8:30	4888
for the *a* oil of the LORD is upon	Lev 10:7	4888
whose head the *a* oil was poured	Lev 21:10	4888
for the crown of the *a* oil of his	Lev 21:12	4888
daily meat offering, and the *a* oil	Num 4:16	4888
I given them by reason of the *a*	Num 18:8	4888
be destroyed because of the *a*	Is 10:27	8081
a him with oil in the name of the	Jas 5:14	218
But the *a* which ye have received	1Jn 2:27	5545
but as the same *a* teacheth you of	1Jn 2:27	5545

ANON

word, and *a* with joy receiveth it	Mt 13:20	2117
fever, and *a* they tell him of her	Mk 1:30	2112

ANOTHER See APPENDIX.

ANOTHER'S See APPENDIX.

ANSWER See APPENDIX.

ANSWERABLE

a to the hangings of the court	Ex 38:18	5980

ANSWERED See APPENDIX.

ANSWEREDST

Thou *a* them, O LORD our God	Ps 99:8	6030
In the day when I cried thou *a* me	Ps 138:3	6030

ANSWEREST

of Ner, saying, A thou not, Abner	1Sa 26:14	6030
what emboldeneth thee that thou *a*	Job 16:3	6030
and said unto him, A thou nothing	Mt 26:62	611
Jesus, saying, A thou nothing	Mk 14:60	611
him again, saying, A thou nothing	Mk 15:4	611
A thou the high priest so	Jn 18:22	611

ANSWERETH

a me no more, neither by prophets	1Sa 28:15	6030
and the God that *a* by fire	1Kin 18:24	6030
who calleth upon God, and he *a* him	Job 12:4	6030
He that *a* a matter before he	Prov 18:13	7725
but the rich *a* roughly	Prov 18:23	6030
As in water face *a* to face	Prov 27:19	
because God *a* him in the joy of	Eccl 5:20	6030
but money *a* all things	Eccl 10:19	6030
And Peter *a* and saith unto him,	Mk 8:29	611
He *a* him, and saith, O faithless	Mk 9:19	611
But Jesus *a* again, and saith unto	Mk 10:24	611
He *a* and saith unto them, He that	Lk 3:11	611
a to Jerusalem which now is, and	Gal 4:25	4960

ANSWERING See APPENDIX.

ANSWERS See APPENDIX.

ANT

Go to the *a*, thou sluggard	Prov 6:6	5244

ANTHOTHIJAH See ANTOTHIJAH.

ANTICHRIST

ye have heard that *a* shall come	1Jn 2:18	500
He is *a*, that denieth the Father	1Jn 2:22	500
and this is that spirit of *a*	1Jn 4:3	500
This is a deceiver and an *a*	2Jn 7	500

ANTICHRISTS

come, even now are there many *a*	1Jn 2:18	500

ANTIOCH (an'-te-ok)
1. A city in Syria.

and Nicolas a proselyte of A	Acts 6:5	491
far as Phenice, and Cyprus, and A	Acts 11:19	490
which, when they were come to A	Acts 11:20	490
that he should go as far as A	Acts 11:22	490
found him, he brought him unto A	Acts 11:26	490
were called Christians first in A	Acts 11:26	490
prophets from Jerusalem unto A	Acts 11:27	490
that was at A certain prophets	Acts 13:1	490
And thence sailed to A, from	Acts 14:26	490
their own company to A with Paul	Acts 15:22	490
which are of the Gentiles in A	Acts 15:23	490
were dismissed, they came to A	Acts 15:30	490
also and Barnabas continued in A	Acts 15:35	490
the church, he went down to A	Acts 18:22	490
But when Peter was come to A	Gal 2:11	490

2. A city in Pisidia.

Perga, they came to A in Pisidia	Acts 13:14	490
came thither certain Jews from A	Acts 14:19	490
to Lystra, and to Iconium, and A	Acts 14:21	490
which came unto me at A, at	2Ti 3:11	490

ANTIPAS (an'-tip-as) A Christian martyr.

wherein A was my faithful martyr	Rev 2:13	493

ANTIPATRIS (an-tip'-at-ris) A city in northern Palestine.

and brought him by night to A	Acts 23:31	494

ANTIQUITY

whose *a* is of ancient days	Is 23:7	6927

ANTOTHIJAH (an-to-thi'-jah) Son of Shashak.

And Hananiah, and Elam, and A	1Chr 8:24	6070

ANTOTHITE (an'-to-thite) See ANETOTHITE. A native of Anathoth.

Ikkesh the Tekoite, Abiezer the A	1Chr 11:28	6069
and Berachah, and Jehu the A	1Chr 12:3	6069

ANTS

The *a* are a people not strong,	Prov 30:25	5244

ANUB (a'-nub) A descendant of Judah.

And Coz begat A, and Zobebah, and	1Chr 4:8	6036

ANVIL

the hammer him that smote the *a*	Is 41:7	6471

ANY See APPENDIX.

APACE

And he came *a*, and drew near	2Sa 18:25	
Kings of armies did flee *a*	Ps 68:12	
are beaten down, and are fled *a*	Jer 46:5	

APART See APPENDIX.

APELLES (a-pel'-leze) A Christian acquaintance of Paul.

Salute A approved in Christ	Rom 16:10	559

APES

gold, and silver, ivory, and *a*	1Kin 10:22	6971
gold, and silver, ivory, and *a*	2Chr 9:21	6971

APHARSACHITES (a-far'-sak-ites) See APHARSATH-CHITES. An Assyrian tribe.

and his companions the A, which	Ezr 5:6	671
and your companions the A	Ezr 6:6	671

APHARSATHCHITES (a-far'-sath-kites) See APHAR-SACHITES, APHARSITES. Same as Apharsachites.

the Dinaites, the A, the	Ezr 4:9	671

APHARSITES (a-far'-sites) See APHARSATHCHITES. Same as Apharsachites

the Tarpelites, the A, the	Ezr 4:9	670

APHEK (a'-fek) See APHIK.
1. A Canaanite city.

The king of A, one	Josh 12:18	663
and the Philistines pitched in A	1Sa 4:1	663
together all their armies to A	1Sa 29:1	663

2. *A city in Asher.*
is beside the Sidonians, unto *A* .... Josh 13:4   663
Ummah also, and, *A*, and Rehob .... Josh 19:30   663
    3. *Place where Ahab defeated Benhadad.*
the Syrians, and went up to *A* 1Kin 20:26   663
But the rest fled to *A*, into the 1Kin 20:30   663
thou shalt smite the Syrians in *A* 2Kin 13:17   663

APHEKAH (*afe'-kah*) *A city in Judah.*
And Janum, and Beth-tappuah, and *A*...Josh 15:53   664

APHIAH (*af-i'-ah*) *An ancestor of Saul.*
son of Bechorath, the son of *A* 1Sa 9:1   647

APHIK (*a'-fik*) See APHEK. *Same as Aphek 2.*
Achzib, nor of Helbah, nor of *A* .... Judg 1:31   663

APHRAH (*af-rah*) See BETH-LEAPHRAH, OPHRAH. *A city in Benjamin.*
in the house of *A* roll thyself in .... Mic 1:10   1036

APHSES (*af'-seze*) *A Levite chief.*
to Hezir, the eighteenth to *A* 1Chr 24:15   6483

APIECE
take five shekels *a* by the poll....(............. Num 3:47
incense, weighing ten shekels *a* .... Num 7:86
of their princes gave him a rod *a* .... Num 17:6
brass, of eighteen cubits high *a* 1Kin 7:15   5982,259
Every one had four faces *a* .... Eze 10:21   259
And the doors had two leaves *a* .... Eze 41:24
neither have two coats *a* .... Lk 9:3   303
containing two or three firkins *a* .... Jn 2:6   303

APOLLONIA (*ap-ol-lo'-ne-ah*) *A city in Macedonia.*
passed through Amphipolis and *A* .... Acts 17:1   624

APOLLOS (*ap-ol'-los*) *A Christian Jew from Alexandria.*
And a certain Jew named *A*, born at ..... Acts 18:24   625
while *A* was at Corinth, Paul .... Acts 19:1   625
and I of *A* 1Cor 1:12   625
and another, I am of *A* 1Cor 3:4   625
Who then is Paul, and who is *A* 1Cor 3:5   625
I have planted, *A* watered 1Cor 3:6   625
Whether Paul, or *A*, or Cephas, or......... 1Cor 3:22   625
to myself and to *A* for your sakes........... 1Cor 4:6   625
As touching our brother *A* 1Cor 16:12   625
A on their journey diligently, ... Titus 3:13   625

APOLLYON (*ap-ol'-le-on*) *The angel of the Abyss.*
the Greek tongue hath his name *A* .... Rev 9:11   623

APOSTLE
Jesus Christ, called to be an *a* .... Rom 1:1   652
as I am the *a* of the Gentiles.................. Rom 11:13   652
called to be an *a* of Jesus Christ 1Cor 1:1   652
Am I not an *a* 1Cor 9:1   652
If I be not an *a* unto others.................... 1Cor 9:2   652
am not meet to be called an *a* 1Cor 15:9   652
an *a* of Jesus Christ by the will 2Cor 1:1   652
Truly the signs of an *a* were 2Cor 12:12   652
Paul, an *a*, (not of men, neither .... Gal 1:1   652
an *a* of Jesus Christ by the will .... Eph 1:1   652
an *a* of Jesus Christ by the will .... Col 1:1   652
an *a* of Jesus Christ by the 1Ti 1:1   652
I am ordained a preacher, and an *a* 1Ti 2:7   652
an *a* of Jesus Christ by the will 2Ti 1:1   652
am appointed a preacher, and an *a* 2Ti 1:11   652
an *a* of Jesus Christ, according .... Titus 1:1   652
heavenly calling, consider the *A* .... Heb 3:1   652
an *a* of Jesus Christ, to the 1Pet 1:1   652
an *a* of Jesus Christ, to them 2Pet 1:1   652

APOSTLES
names of the twelve *a* are these .... Mt 10:2   652
the *a* gathered themselves .... Mk 6:30   652
twelve, whom also he named *a*............... Lk 6:13   652
And the *a*, when they were returned ...... Lk 9:10   652
I will send them prophets and *a* .... Lk 11:49   652
the *a* said unto the Lord, ... Lk 17:5   652
down, and the twelve *a* with him .... Lk 22:14   652
told these things unto the *a* .... Lk 24:10   652
unto the *a* whom he had chosen .... Acts 1:2   652
he was numbered with the eleven *a* ...... Acts 1:26   652
Peter and to the rest of the *a* .... Acts 2:37   652
and signs were done by the *a* .... Acts 2:43   652
with great power gave the *a* .... Acts 4:33   652
who by the *a* was surnamed .... Acts 4:36   652
hands of the *a* were many signs .... Acts 5:12   652
And laid their hands on the *a* .... Acts 5:18   652
Peter and the other *a* answered .... Acts 5:29   652
to put the *a* forth a little space.............. Acts 5:34   652
and when they had called the *a* .... Acts 5:40   652
Whom they set before the *a* .... Acts 6:6   652
Judaea and Samaria, except the *a* .... Acts 8:1   652
Now when the *a* which were at.............. Acts 8:14   652

took him, and brought him to the *a* .... Acts 9:27   652
And the *a* and brethren that were in...... Acts 11:1   652
with the Jews, and part with the *a* .... Acts 14:4   652
Which when the *a*, Barnabas and.......... Acts 14:14   652
go up to Jerusalem unto the *a* .... Acts 15:2   652
of the church, and of the *a* .... Acts 15:4   652
And the *a* and elders came together ...... Acts 15:6   652
Then pleased it the *a* and elders,........... Acts 15:22   652
The *a* and elders and brethren send ...... Acts 15:23   652
from the brethren unto the *a* .... Acts 15:33
keep, that were ordained of the *a* .... Acts 16:4   652
who are of note among the *a* .... Rom 16:7   652
God hath set forth us the *a* last 1Cor 4:9   652
a wife, as well as other *a* 1Cor 9:5   652
set some in the church, first *a* 1Cor 12:28   652
Are all *a*? 1Cor 12:29   652
then of all the *a* 1Cor 15:7   652
For I am the least of the *a* 1Cor 15:9   652
a whit behind the very chiefest *a* 2Cor 11:5   652
For such are false *a*, deceitful 2Cor 11:13   652
themselves into the *a* of Christ 2Cor 11:13   5570
am I behind the very chiefest *a* 2Cor 12:11   652
to them which were *a* before me .... Gal 1:17   652
But other of the *a* saw I none .... Gal 1:19   652
upon the foundation of the *a* .... Eph 2:20   652
is now revealed unto his holy *a* .... Eph 3:5   652
And he gave some, *a*, ... Eph 4:11   652
burdensome, as the *a* of Christ 1Th 2:6   652
of us the *a* of the Lord and 2Pet 3:2   652
of the *a* of our Lord Jesus Christ .... Jude 17   652
tried them **which say they are** *a* ...... Rev 2:2   652
her, thou heaven, and ye holy *a* .... Rev 18:20   652
names of the twelve *a* of the Lamb........ Rev 21:14   652

APOSTLES'
stedfastly in the *a* doctrine .... Acts 2:42   652
And laid them down at the *a* feet .... Acts 4:35   652
money, and laid it at the *a* feet............. Acts 4:37   652
part, and laid it at the *a* feet................. Acts 5:2   652
that through laying on of the *a* .... Acts 8:18   652

APOSTLESHIP
take part of this ministry and *a* .... Acts 1:25   *651*
whom we have received grace and *a* ..... Rom 1:5   *651*
seal of mine *a* are ye in the Lord 1Cor 9:2   *651*
to the *a* of the circumcision................... Gal 2:8   *651*

APOTHECARIES
Hananiah the son of one of the *a* .... Neh 3:8   7543

APOTHECARIES'
of spices prepared by the *a* art.............. 2Chr 16:14   4842

APOTHECARY
compound after the art of the *a* .... Ex 30:25   7543
confection after the art of the *a* .... Ex 30:35   7543
according to the work of the *a* .... Ex 37:29   7543
a to send forth a stinking savour........... Eccl 10:1   7543

APPAIM (*ap'-pa-im*) *A son of Nadab.*
Seled, and *A* 1Chr 2:30   649
And the sons of *A*.................................. 1Chr 2:31   649

APPAREL
by the year, and a suit of *a* .... Judg 17:10   899
asses, and the camels, and the *a* 1Sa 27:9   899
on ornaments of gold upon your *a* 2Sa 1:24   3830
himself, and changed his *a* 2Sa 12:20   8071
mourner, and put on now mourning *a* 2Sa 14:2   899
of his ministers, and their *a* 1Kin 10:5   4403
of his ministers, and their *a* 2Chr 9:4   4403
his cupbearers also, and their *a* 2Chr 9:4   4403
priests in their *a* with trumpets .... Ezr 3:10   3847
that Esther put on her royal *a* .... Est 5:1
Let the royal *a* be brought which .... Est 6:8   3830
And let this *a* and horse be .... Est 6:9   3830
Haman, Make haste, and take the *a* ...... Est 6:10   3830
Then took Haman the *a* and the............. Est 6:11   3830
of the king in royal *a* of blue .... Est 8:15   3830
The changeable suits of *a* .... Is 3:22   4254
our own bread, and wear our own *a* ...... Is 4:1   8071
this that is glorious in his *a* .... Is 63:1   3830
Wherefore art thou red in thine *a* .... Is 63:2   3830
work, and in chests of rich *a* .... Eze 27:24   1264
as are clothed with strange *a* .... Zeph 1:8   4403
together, gold, and silver, and *a* .... Zec 14:14   899
two men stood by them in white *a* .... Acts 1:10   2066
set day Herod, arrayed in royal *a* .... Acts 12:21   2066
no man's silver, or gold, or *a* .... Acts 20:33   2441
adorn themselves in modest *a* 1Ti 2:9   2689
man with a gold ring, in goodly *a*.......... Jas 2:2   2066
of gold, or of putting on of *a* 1Pet 3:3   2440

APPARELLED

daughters that were virgins a	2Sa 13:18	3847
they which are gorgeously a	Lk 7:25	2441

APPARENTLY

I speak mouth to mouth, even a	Num 12:8	4758

APPEAL

I a unto Caesar	Acts 25:11	1941
was constrained to a unto Caesar	Acts 28:19	1941

APPEALED

answered, Hast thou a unto Caesar	Acts 25:12	1941
But when Paul had a to be	Acts 25:21	1941
he himself hath a to Augustus	Acts 25:25	1941
if he had not a unto Caesar	Acts 26:32	1941

APPEAR

one place, and let the dry land a	Gen 1:9	7200
made the white a which was in the	Gen 30:37	4286
none shall a before me empty	Ex 23:15	7200
males shall a before the Lord GOD	Ex 23:17	7200
none shall a before me empty	Ex 34:20	7200
children a before the Lord GOD	Ex 34:23	7200
when thou shalt go up to a before	Ex 34:24	7200
to day the LORD will a unto you	Lev 9:4	7200
of the LORD shall a unto you	Lev 9:6	7200
if it a still in the garment,	Lev 13:57	7200
for I will a in the cloud upon	Lev 16:2	7200
in a year shall all thy males a	Deut 16:16	7200
they shall not a before the LORD	Deut 16:16	7200
When all Israel is come to a	Deut 31:11	7200
the LORD did no more a to Manoah	Judg 13:21	7200
that he may a before the LORD, and	1Sa 1:22	7200
Did I plainly a unto the house of	1Sa 2:27	1540
that night did God a unto Solomon	2Chr 1:7	7200
when shall I come and a before God	Ps 42:2	7200
Let thy work a unto thy servants,	Ps 90:16	7200
up Zion, he shall a in his glory	Ps 102:16	7200
The flowers a on the earth	Song 2:12	7200
goats, that a from mount Gilead	Song 4:1	1570
flock of goats that a from Gilead	Song 6:5	1570
whether the tender grape a	Song 7:12	6524
When ye come to a before me	Is 1:12	7200
but he shall a to your joy	Is 66:5	7200
thy face, that thy shame may a	Jer 13:26	7200
in all your doings your sins do a	Eze 21:24	7200
that they may a unto men to fast	Mt 6:16	5316
That thou a not unto men to fast,	Mt 6:18	5316
which indeed a beautiful outward,	Mt 23:27	5316
outwardly a righteous unto men	Mt 23:28	5316
then shall a the sign of the Son	Mt 24:30	5316
for ye are as graves which a not	Lk 11:44	82
of God should immediately a	Lk 19:11	398
priests and all their council to a	Acts 22:30	2064
in the which I will a unto thee	Acts 26:16	3700
But sin, that it might a sin	Rom 7:13	5316
For we must all a before the	2Cor 5:10	5319
the sight of God might a unto you	2Cor 7:12	5319
not that we should a approved	2Cor 13:7	5316
Christ, who is our life, shall a	Col 3:4	5319
shall ye also a with him in glory	Col 3:4	5319
that thy profiting may a to all	1Ti 4:15	5318,5600
now to a in the presence of God	Heb 9:24	1718
he a the second time without sin	Heb 9:28	3700
not made of things which do a	Heb 11:3	5316
shall the ungodly and the sinner a	1Pet 4:18	5316
when the chief Shepherd shall a	1Pet 5:4	5319
that, when he shall a, we may	1Jn 2:28	5319
it doth not yet a what we shall	1Jn 3:2	5319
but we know that, when he shall a	1Jn 3:2	5319
shame of thy nakedness do not a	Rev 3:18	5319

APPEARANCE

as it were the a of fire, until	Num 9:15	4758
by day, and the a of fire by night	Num 9:16	4758
for man looketh on the outward a	1Sa 16:7	5869
And this was their a	Eze 1:5	4758
their a was like burning coals of	Eze 1:13	4758
and like the a of lamps	Eze 1:13	4758
returned as the a of a flash of	Eze 1:14	4758
The a of the wheels and their work	Eze 1:16	4758
and their a and their work was as	Eze 1:16	4758
as the a of a sapphire stone	Eze 1:26	4758
as the a of a man above upon it	Eze 1:26	4758
as the a of fire round about	Eze 1:27	4758
from the a of his loins even	Eze 1:27	4758
from the a of his loins even	Eze 1:27	4758
I saw as it were the a of fire	Eze 1:27	4758
As the a of the bow that is in	Eze 1:28	4758
so was the a of the brightness	Eze 1:28	4758
This was the a of the likeness of	Eze 1:28	4758
and lo a likeness as the a of fire	Eze 8:2	4758

from the a of his loins even	Eze 8:2	4758
as the a of brightness, as the	Eze 8:2	4758
as the a of the likeness of a	Eze 10:1	4758
the a of the wheels was as the	Eze 10:9	4758
whose a was like the a	Eze 40:3	4758
the a of the one as the a	Eze 41:21	4758
the a of the chambers which were	Eze 42:11	4758
it was according to the a of the	Eze 43:3	4758
stood before me as the a of a man	Dan 8:15	4758
and his face as the a of lightning	Dan 10:6	4758
me one like the a of a man	Dan 10:18	4758
a of them is as the a of horses	Joel 2:4	4758
Judge not according to the a	Jn 7:24	3799
to answer them which glory in a	2Cor 5:12	4383
on things after the outward a	2Cor 10:7	4383
Abstain from all a of evil	1Th 5:22	1491

APPEARANCES

And as for their a, they four had	Eze 10:10	4758
by the river of Chebar, their a	Eze 10:22	4758

APPEARED

the LORD a unto Abram, and said,	Gen 12:7	7200
unto the LORD, who a unto him	Gen 12:7	7200
old and nine, the LORD a to Abram	Gen 17:1	7200
the LORD a unto him in the plains	Gen 18:1	7200
And the LORD a unto him, and said,	Gen 26:2	7200
the LORD a unto him the same	Gen 26:24	7200
that a unto thee when thou	Gen 35:1	7200
because there God a unto him,	Gen 35:7	1540
God unto Jacob again, when he	Gen 35:9	7200
God Almighty a unto me at Luz in	Gen 48:3	7200
the angel of the LORD a unto him	Ex 3:2	7200
a unto me, saying, I have surely	Ex 3:16	7200
The LORD hath not a unto thee	Ex 4:1	7200
God of Jacob, hath a unto thee	Ex 4:5	7200
I a unto Abraham, unto Isaac, and	Ex 6:3	7200
his strength when the morning a	Ex 14:27	6437
glory of the LORD a in the cloud	Ex 16:10	7200
of the LORD a unto all the people	Lev 9:23	7200
the glory of the LORD a in the	Num 14:10	7200
the glory of the LORD a unto all	Num 16:19	7200
it, and the glory of the LORD a	Num 16:42	7200
the glory of the LORD a unto them	Num 20:6	7200
the LORD a in the tabernacle in a	Deut 31:15	7200
the angel of the LORD a unto him	Judg 6:12	7200
of the LORD a unto the woman	Judg 13:3	7200
Behold, the man hath a unto me	Judg 13:10	7200
the LORD a again in Shiloh	1Sa 3:21	7200
And the channels of the sea a	2Sa 22:16	7200
In Gibeon the LORD a to Solomon	1Kin 3:5	7200
That the LORD a to Solomon the	1Kin 9:2	7200
as he had a unto him at Gibeon	1Kin 9:2	7200
which had a unto him twice	1Kin 11:9	7200
there a a chariot of fire, and	2Kin 2:11	
where the LORD a unto David his	2Chr 3:1	7200
the LORD a to Solomon by night,	2Chr 7:12	7200
of the morning till the stars a	Neh 4:21	3318
The LORD hath a of old unto me,	Jer 31:3	7200
a over them as it were a sapphire	Eze 10:1	7200
there a in the cherubims the form	Eze 10:8	7200
she a in her height with the	Eze 19:11	7200
days their countenances a fairer	Dan 1:15	7200
Belshazzar a vision a unto me	Dan 8:1	7200
after that which a unto me at the	Dan 8:1	7200
of the Lord a unto him in a dream	Mt 1:20	5316
diligently what time the star a	Mt 2:7	5316
fruit, then a the tares also	Mt 13:26	5316
there a unto them Moses and Elias	Mt 17:3	3700
the holy city, and a unto many	Mt 27:53	1718
there a unto them Elias with	Mk 9:4	3700
he a first to Mary Magdalene, out	Mk 16:9	5316
After that he a in another form	Mk 16:12	5319
Afterward he a unto the eleven as	Mk 16:14	5319
there a unto him an angel of the	Lk 1:11	3700
And of some, that Elias had a	Lk 9:8	5316
Who a in glory, and spake of his	Lk 9:31	3700
there a an angel unto him from	Lk 22:43	3700
risen indeed, and hath a to Simon	Lk 24:34	3700
there a unto them cloven tongues	Acts 2:3	3700
The God of glory a unto our	Acts 7:2	3700
there a to him in the wilderness	Acts 7:30	3700
angel which a to him in the bush	Acts 7:35	3700
that a unto thee in the way as	Acts 9:17	3700
a vision a to Paul in the night	Acts 16:9	3700
for I have a unto thee for this	Acts 26:16	3700
sun nor stars in many days a	Acts 27:20	2014
salvation hath a to all men	Titus 2:11	2014
of God our Saviour toward man a	Titus 3:4	2014
hath he a to put away sin by the	Heb 9:26	5319
there a a great wonder in heaven	Rev 12:1	3700
there a another wonder in heaven	Rev 12:3	3700

APPEARETH

But when raw flesh *a* in him	Lev 13:14	7200
as the leprosy *a* in the skin of	Lev 13:43	4758
him into thy hand, as *a* this day	Deut 2:30	
one of them in Zion *a* before God	Ps 84:7	7200
The way *a*, and the tender grass	Prov 27:25	1540
for evil *a* out of the north, and	Jer 6:1	8259
and who shall stand when he *a*	Mal 3:2	7200
the Lord *a* to Joseph in a dream	Mt 2:13	5316
an angel of the Lord *a* in a dream	Mt 2:19	5316
that *a* for a little time, and then	Jas 4:14	5316

APPEARING

until the *a* of our Lord Jesus	1Ti 6:14	2015
the *a* of our Saviour Jesus Christ	2Ti 1:10	2015
the quick and the dead at his *a*	2Ti 4:1	2015
all them also that love his *a*	2Ti 4:8	2015
the glorious *a* of the great God	Titus 2:13	2015
glory at the *a* of Jesus Christ	1Pet 1:7	602

APPEASE

I will *a* him with the present	Gen 32:20	3722,6440

APPEASED

the wrath of king Ahasuerus was *a*	Est 2:1	7918
the townclerk had *a* the people	Acts 19:35	2687

APPEASETH

he that is slow to anger *a* strife	Prov 15:18	8252

APPERTAIN

up, with all that *a* unto them	Num 16:30	
for to thee doth it *a*	Jer 10:7	2969

APPERTAINED

and all the men that *a* unto Korah	Num 16:32	
They, and all that *a* to them	Num 16:33	
the palace which *a* to the house	Neh 2:8	

APPERTAINETH

and give it unto him to whom it *a*	Lev 6:5	
It *a* not unto thee, Uzziah, to	2Chr 26:18	

APPETITE

or fill the *a* of the young lions,	Job 38:39	2416
if thou be a man given to *a*	Prov 23:2	5315
mouth, and yet the *a* is not filled	Eccl 6:7	5315
he is faint, and his soul hath *a*	Is 29:8	8264

APPHIA (af´-fee-ah) A Christian acquaintance of Paul.

And to our beloved *A*, and Archippus	Philem 2	682

APPII (ap´-pe-i) A place south of Rome.

came to meet us as far as *A* forum	Acts 28:15	675

APPIUS See APPII.

APPLE

he kept him as the *a* of his eye	Deut 32:10	380
Keep me as the *a* of the eye	Ps 17:8	380,1323
and my law as the *a* of thine eye	Prov 7:2	380
As the *a* tree among the trees of	Song 2:3	8598
I raised thee up under the *a* tree	Song 8:5	8598
let not the *a* of thine eye cease	Lam 2:18	1323
the *a* tree, even all the trees of	Joel 1:12	8598
you toucheth the *a* of his eye	Zec 2:8	892

APPLES

A word fitly spoken is like *a* of	Prov 25:11	8598
with flagons, comfort me with *a*	Song 2:5	8598
and the smell of thy nose like *a*	Song 7:8	8598

APPLIED

I *a* mine heart to know, and to	Eccl 7:25	5437
a my heart unto every work that	Eccl 8:9	5414
When I *a* mine heart to know	Eccl 8:16	5414

APPLY

that we may *a* our hearts unto	Ps 90:12	935
a thine heart to understanding	Prov 2:2	5186
a thine heart unto my knowledge	Prov 22:17	7896
A thine heart unto instruction,	Prov 23:12	935

APPOINT

A me thy wages, and I will give it	Gen 30:28	5344
let him *a* officers over the land,	Gen 41:34	6485
then I will *a* thee a place	Ex 21:13	7760
shalt *a* it for the service of the	Ex 30:16	5414
I will even *a* over you terror,	Lev 26:16	6485
But thou shalt *a* the Levites over	Num 1:50	6485
And thou shalt *a* Aaron and his sons	Num 3:10	6485
a them every one to his service	Num 4:19	7760
ye shall *a* unto them in charge	Num 4:27	6485
refuge, which ye shall *a* for the	Num 35:6	5414
Then ye shall *a* you cities to be	Num 35:11	7136
A out for you cities of refuge,	Josh 20:2	5414
a them for himself, for his	1Sa 8:11	7760
he will *a* him captains over	1Sa 8:12	7760
to *a* me ruler over the people of	2Sa 6:21	6680

Moreover I will *a* a place for my	2Sa 7:10	7760
my lord the king shall *a*	2Sa 15:15	977
to all that thou shalt *a*	1Kin 5:6	559
the place that thou shalt *a* me	1Kin 5:9	7971
to *a* their brethren to be the	1Chr 15:16	5975
a watches of the inhabitants of	Neh 7:3	5975
let the king *a* officers in all	Est 2:3	6485
thou wouldest *a* me a set time	Job 14:13	7896
salvation will God *a* for walls	Is 26:1	7896
To *a* unto them that mourn in Zion	Is 61:3	7760
I will *a* over them four kinds,	Jer 15:3	6485
chosen man, that I may *a* over her	Jer 49:19	6485
and who will *a* me the time	Jer 49:19	3259
chosen man, that I may *a* over her	Jer 50:44	6485
and who will *a* me the time	Jer 50:44	3259
a a captain against her	Jer 51:27	6485
a thee two ways, that the sword	Eze 21:19	7760
A a way, that the sword may come	Eze 21:20	7760
to *a* captains, to open the mouth	Eze 21:22	7760
to *a* battering rams against the	Eze 21:22	7760
ye shall *a* the possession of the	Eze 45:6	5414
a themselves one head, and they	Hos 1:11	7760
a him his portion with the	Mt 24:51	5087
will *a* him his portion with the	Lk 12:46	5087
I *a* unto you a kingdom, as my	Lk 22:29	1303
whom we may *a* over this business	Acts 6:3	2525

APPOINTED

hath *a* me another seed instead of	Gen 4:25	7896
At the time *a* I will return unto	Gen 18:14	4150
thou hast *a* for thy servant Isaac	Gen 24:14	3198
hath *a* out for my master's son	Gen 24:44	3198
the LORD *a* a set time, saying, To	Ex 9:5	7760
in the time *a* of the month Abib	Ex 23:15	4150
keep the passover at his *a* season	Num 9:2	4150
ye shall keep it in his *a* season	Num 9:3	4150
a season among the children of	Num 9:7	4150
of the LORD in his *a* season	Num 9:13	4150
he and all his people, at a time *a*	Josh 8:14	4150
they *a* Kedesh in Galilee in mount	Josh 20:7	6942
These were the cities *a* for all	Josh 20:9	4152
six hundred men *a* with weapons of	Judg 18:11	2296
the six hundred men *a* with their	Judg 18:16	2296
that were *a* with weapons of war	Judg 18:17	2296
Now there was an *a* sign between	Judg 20:38	4150
to the set time that Samuel had *a*	1Sa 13:8	
thou camest not within the days *a*	1Sa 13:11	4150
and Samuel standing as *a* over them	1Sa 19:20	5324
field at the time *a* with David	1Sa 20:35	4150
I have *a* my servants there and	1Sa 21:2	3045
shall have *a* thee ruler over	1Sa 25:30	6680
his place which thou hast *a* him	1Sa 29:4	6485
For the LORD had *a* to defeat the	2Sa 17:14	6680
the set time which he had *a* him	2Sa 20:5	3259
the morning even to the time *a*	2Sa 24:15	4150
I have *a* him to be ruler over	1Kin 1:35	6680
a him victuals, and gave him land	1Kin 11:18	559
the third day, as the king had *a*	1Kin 12:12	1696
man whom I *a* to utter destruction	1Kin 20:42	2764
the king *a* the lord on whose hand	2Kin 7:17	6485
So the king *a* unto her a certain	2Kin 8:6	5414
Jehu *a* fourscore men without, and	2Kin 10:24	7760
the priest *a* officers over the	2Kin 11:18	7760
the king of Assyria unto *a*	2Kin 18:14	7760
a unto all manner of service of	1Chr 6:48	5414
were *a* for all the work of the	1Chr 6:49	
were *a* to oversee the vessels	1Chr 9:29	4487
So the Levites *a* Heman the son of	1Chr 15:17	5975
were *a* to sound with cymbals of	1Chr 15:19	
he *a* certain of the Levites to	1Chr 16:4	5414
And he *a*, according to the order	2Chr 8:14	5975
he *a* singers unto the LORD, and	2Chr 20:21	5975
Also Jehoiada *a* the offices of	2Chr 23:18	7760
Hezekiah *a* the courses of the	2Chr 31:2	5975
He *a* also the king's portion of	2Chr 31:3	
which I have *a* for your fathers	2Chr 33:8	5975
and they that the king had *a*	2Chr 34:22	
a the Levites, from twenty years	Ezr 3:8	5975
the princes had *a* for the service	Ezr 8:20	5414
in our cities come at a times	Ezr 10:14	2163
from the time that I was *a* to be	Neh 5:14	6680
thou hast also *a* prophets to	Neh 6:7	5975
the singers and the Levites were *a*	Neh 7:1	6485
in their rebellion *a* a captain to	Neh 9:17	5414
at times a year by year, to burn	Neh 10:34	2163
a two great companies of them	Neh 12:31	5975
at that time were some *a* over the	Neh 12:44	6485
a the wards of the priests and the	Neh 13:30	5975
for the wood offering, at times *a*	Neh 13:31	2163
for so the king had *a* to all the	Est 1:8	3245
the keeper of the women, *a*	Est 2:15	559

whom he had *a* to attend upon her,	Est 4:5	5975
to their *a* time every year	Est 9:27	
days of Purim in their times *a*	Est 9:31	
Is there not an *a* time to man	Job 7:1	6635
and wearisome nights are *a* to me	Job 7:3	4487
thou hast *a* his bounds that he	Job 14:5	6213
the days of my *a* time will I wait	Job 14:14	6635
the heritage *a* him by God	Job 20:29	561
the thing that is *a* for me	Job 23:14	2706
to the house *a* for all living	Job 30:23	4150
given us like sheep *a* for meat	Ps 44:11	
a a law in Israel, which he	Ps 78:5	7760
thou those that are *a* to die	Ps 79:11	1121
in the new moon, in the time *a*	Ps 81:3	3677
loose those that are *a* to death	Ps 102:20	1121
He *a* the moon for seasons	Ps 104:19	6213
and will come home at the day *a*	Prov 7:20	3677
when he *a* the foundations of the	Prov 8:29	2710
all such as are *a* to destruction	Prov 31:8	1121
your *a* feasts my soul hateth	Is 1:14	4150
shall be alone in his *a* times	Is 14:31	4151
the *a* barley and the rie in their	Is 28:25	5567
since I *a* the ancient people	Is 44:7	7760
us the *a* weeks of the harvest	Jer 5:24	2708
in the heaven knoweth her *a* times	Jer 8:7	4150
if I have not *a* the ordinances of	Jer 33:25	7760
he hath passed the time *a*	Jer 46:17	4150
there hath he *a* it	Jer 47:7	3259
I have *a* thee each day for a year	Eze 4:6	5414
which have *a* my land into their	Eze 36:5	5414
it in the *a* place of the house	Eze 43:21	4662
the king *a* them *a* daily provision	Dan 1:5	4487
who hath *a* your meat and your	Dan 1:10	4487
for at the time *a* the end shall	Dan 8:19	4150
was true, but the time *a* was long	Dan 10:1	6635
the end shall be at the time *a*	Dan 11:27	4150
At the time *a* he shall return, and	Dan 11:29	4150
because it is yet for a time *a*	Dan 11:35	4150
hear ye the rod, and who hath *a* it	Mic 6:9	3259
the vision is yet for an *a* time	Hab 2:3	4150
disciples did as Jesus had *a* them	Mt 26:19	4929
potter's field, as the Lord *a* me	Mt 27:10	4929
a mountain where Jesus had *a* them	Mt 28:16	5021
no more than that which is *a* you	Lk 3:13	1299
the Lord *a* other seventy also	Lk 10:1	322
as my Father hath *a* unto me	Lk 22:29	1303
And they *a* two, Joseph called	Acts 1:23	1476
in the wilderness, as he had *a*	Acts 7:44	1299
determined the times before *a*	Acts 17:26	4384
Because he hath *a* a day, in the	Acts 17:31	2476
for so had he *a*, minding himself	Acts 20:13	1299
things which are *a* for thee to do	Acts 22:10	5021
And when they had *a* him a day	Acts 28:23	5021
last, as it were *a* to death	1Cor 4:9	1935
until the time *a* of the father	Gal 4:2	4287
know that we are *a* thereunto	1Th 3:3	2749
For God hath not *a* us to wrath	1Th 5:9	5087
Whereunto I am *a* a preacher	2Ti 1:11	5087
in every city, as I had *a* thee	Titus 1:5	1299
whom he hath *a* heir of all things	Heb 1:2	5081
was faithful to him that *a* him	Heb 3:2	4160
as it is *a* unto men once to die,	Heb 9:27	606
whereunto also they were *a*	1Pet 2:8	5087

APPOINTETH

that he *a* over it whomsoever he	Dan 5:21	6966

APPOINTMENT

At the *a* of Aaron and his sons	Num 4:27	6310
for by the *a* of Absalom this hath	2Sa 13:32	6310
according to the *a* of the priests	Ezr 6:9	3883
for they had made an *a* together	Job 2:11	3259

APPREHEND

with a garrison, desirous to *a* me	2Cor 11:32	4084
if that I may *a* that for which	Phil 3:12	2638

APPREHENDED

And when he had *a* him, he put him	Acts 12:4	4084
which also I am *a* of Christ Jesus	Phil 3:12	2638
I count not myself to have *a*	Phil 3:13	2638

APPROACH

None of you shall *a* to any that	Lev 18:6	7126
thou shalt not *a* to his wife	Lev 18:14	7126
Also thou shalt not *a* unto a	Lev 18:19	7126
if a woman *a* unto any beast, and	Lev 20:16	7126
let him not *a* to offer the bread	Lev 21:17	7126
hath a blemish, he shall not *a*	Lev 21:18	7126
when they *a* unto the most holy	Num 4:19	5066
battle, that the priest shall *a*	Deut 20:2	5066
ye *a* this day unto battle against	Deut 20:3	7126
thy days *a* that thou must die	Deut 31:14	7126

are with me, will *a* unto the city	Josh 8:5	7126
can make his sword to *a* unto him	Job 40:19	5066
and causest to *a* unto thee	Ps 65:4	7126
draw near, and he shall *a* unto me	Jer 30:21	5066
engaged his heart to *a* unto me	Jer 30:21	5066
where the priests that *a* unto the	Eze 42:13	7138
shall *a* to those things which are	Eze 42:14	7126
which *a* unto me, to minister unto	Eze 43:19	7126
the light which no man can *a* unto	1Ti 6:16	676

APPROACHED

Wherefore ye so nigh unto the	2Sa 11:20	5066
the king *a* to the altar, and	2Kin 16:12	7126

APPROACHETH

faileth not, where no thief *a*	Lk 12:33	1448

APPROACHING

they take delight in *a* to God	Is 58:2	7132
the more, as ye see the day *a*	Heb 10:25	1448

APPROVE

their posterity *a* their sayings	Ps 49:13	7520
ye shall *a* by your letters	1Cor 16:3	1381
That ye may *a* things that are	Phil 1:10	1381

APPROVED

a man *a* of God among you by	Acts 2:22	584
is acceptable to God, and *a* of men	Rom 14:18	1384
Salute Apelles *a* in Christ	Rom 16:10	1384
that they which are *a* may be made	1Cor 11:19	1384
In all things ye have *a*	2Cor 7:11	4921
he that commendeth himself is *a*	2Cor 10:18	1384
not that we should appear *a*	2Cor 13:7	1384
Study to shew thyself *a* unto God	2Ti 2:15	1384

APPROVEST

a the things that are more	Rom 2:18	1381

APPROVETH

man in his cause, the Lord *a* not	Lam 3:36	7200

APPROVING

But in all things *a* ourselves as	2Cor 6:4	4921

APRONS

together, and made themselves *a*	Gen 3:7	2290
unto the sick handkerchiefs or *a*	Acts 19:12	4612

APT

a for war, even them the king of	2Kin 24:16	6213
of them that were *a* to the war	1Chr 7:40	
given to hospitality, *a* to teach	1Ti 3:2	1317
all men, *a* to teach, patient,	2Ti 2:24	1317

AQUILA (*ac'-quil-ah*) *A Christian acquaintance of Paul.*

And found a certain Jew named *A*	Acts 18:2	207
Syria, and with him Priscilla and *A*	Acts 18:18	207
whom when *A* and Priscilla had	Acts 18:26	207
A my helpers in Christ Jesus	Rom 16:3	207
A and Priscilla salute you much in	1Cor 16:19	207
Salute Prisca and *A*, and the	2Ti 4:19	207

AR (*ar*) *The capital of Moab.*

goeth down to the dwelling of *A*	Num 21:15	6144
it hath consumed *A* of Moab	Num 21:28	6144
because I have given *A* unto the	Deut 2:9	6144
Thou art to pass over through *A*	Deut 2:18	6144
and the Moabites which dwell in *A*	Deut 2:29	6144
Because in the night *A* of Moab is	Is 15:1	6144

ARA (*a'-rah*) *A son of Jether.*

Jephunneh, and Pispah, and *A*	1Chr 7:38	690

ARAB (*a'-rab*) See ARBITE. *A city in Judah.*

A, and Dumah, and Eshean,	Josh 15:52	694

ARABAH (*ar'-ab-ah*) See BETH-ARABAH. *The Jordan Valley.*

the side over against *A* northward	Josh 18:18	6160
and went down unto *A*	Josh 18:18	6160

ARABIA (*a-ra'-be-ah*) *The northern part of the Arabian peninsula.*

and of all the kings of *A*	1Kin 10:15	6152
And all the kings of *A* and	2Chr 9:14	6152
The burden upon *A*	Is 21:13	6152
In the forest in *A* shall ye lodge	Is 21:13	6152
And all the kings of *A*, and all the	Jer 25:24	6152
A, and all the princes of Kedar,	Eze 27:21	6152
but I went into *A*, and returned	Gal 1:17	688
For this Agar is mount Sinai in *A*	Gal 4:25	688

ARABIAN (*a-ra'-be-un*) See ARABIANS. *An inhabitant of Arabia.*

the Ammonite, and Geshem the *A*	Neh 2:19	6163
and Tobiah, and Geshem the *A*	Neh 6:1	6163
shall the *A* pitch tent there	Is 13:20	6153
as the *A* in the wilderness	Jer 3:2	6163

ARABIANS (a-ra'-be-uns)
the *A* brought him flocks, seven 2Chr 17:11   6163
of the Philistines, and of the *A* 2Chr 21:16   6163
A to the camp had slain all the 2Chr 22:1   6163
against the *A* that dwelt in.......................2Chr 26:7   6163
Sanballat, and Tobiah, and the *A* ....Neh 4:7   6163
Cretes and *A*, we do hear them ....Acts 2:11   690

ARABS See ARABIANS.

ARAD (a'-rad)
   1. A Canaanite king.
when king *A* the Canaanite, which ....Num 21:1   6166
king *A* the Canaanite, which dwelt ....Num 33:40   6166
   2. A district in Judah.
the king of *A*, one ....Josh 12:14   6166
which lieth in the south of *A* ....Judg 1:16   6166
   3. A son of Beriah.
And Zebadiah, and *A*, and Ader,............1Chr 8:15   6166

ARAH (a'-rah)
   1. A son of Ulla.
A, and Haniel, and Rezia 1Chr 7:39   733
   2. A family of exiles who returned under Zerubbabel.
The children of *A*, seven hundred ....Ezr 2:5   733
The children of *A*, six hundred ....Neh 7:10   733
   3. Grandfather of Tobiah's wife.
in law of Shechaniah the son of *A* ....Neh 6:18   733

ARAM (a'-ram) See ARAMITESS, ARAM-NAHARAIM,
   ARAM-ZOBAH, BETH-ARAM, PADAN-ARAM, SYRIA.
   1. The son of Shem.
and Arphaxad, and Lud, and *A* ....Gen 10:22   758
And the children of *A*.............................Gen 10:23   758
and Arphaxad, and Lud, and *A* 1Chr 1:17   758
   2. The son of Kemuel.
and Kemuel the father of *A* ....Gen 22:21   758
   3. Another name for Syria.
of Moab hath brought me from *A* ....Num 23:7   758
   4. A district of Canaan.
And he took Geshur, and *A*, with the 1Chr 2:23   758
   5. The son of Shamer.
Ahi, and Rohgah, Jehubbah, and *A* 1Chr 7:34   758
and Esrom begat *A* ....Mt 1:3   689
And *A* begat Aminadab ....Mt 1:4   689
Aminadab, which was the son of *A* ....Lk 3:33   689

ARAMEAN See ARAMITESS.

ARAMITESS (a'-ram-i-tes) See SYRIAN. *Manasseh's con-*
   cubine.
(but his concubine the *A* bare 1Chr 7:14   761

ARAM-NAHARAIM (a'-ram-na-ha-ra'-im) See MESOPO-
   TAMIA. *The area between the Tigris and Euphrates*
   rivers.
when he strove with *A* and with ....Ps 60:t   763

ARAM-ZOBAH (a'-ram-zo'-bah) *The area between the*
   Orontes and Euphrates rivers.
with Aram-naharaim and with *A* ....Ps 60:t   760

ARAN (a'-ran) See BETH-ARAN. *The son of Seir the Ho-*
   rite.
of Dishan are these; Uz, and *A* ....Gen 36:28   765
sons of Dishan; Uz, and *A* 1Chr 1:42   765

ARARAT (ar'-ar-at) See ARMENIA. *A district in Ar-*
   menia.
month, upon the mountains of *A* ....Gen 8:4   780
against her the kingdoms of *A* ....Jer 51:27   780

ARAUNAH (a-raw'-nah) See ORNAN. *A Jebusite.*
threshingplace of *A* the Jebusite 2Sa 24:16   728
threshingfloor of *A* the Jebusite 2Sa 24:18   728
A looked, and saw the king and his........2Sa 24:20   728
A went out, and bowed himself...............2Sa 24:20   728
A said, Wherefore is my lord the 2Sa 24:21   728
A said unto David, Let my lord 2Sa 24:22   728
All these things did *A*, as a king 2Sa 24:23   728
A said unto the king, The LORD 2Sa 24:23   728
And the king said unto *A*, Nay................2Sa 24:24   728

ARBA (ar'-bah) See ARBAH, ARBATHITE, ARBITE,
   KIRJATH-ABBA. *Father of Anakim.*
even the city of *A* the father of ....Josh 15:13   704
the city of *A* father of Anak ....Josh 21:11   704

ARBAH (ar'-bah) See ARBA. *Another name for Hebron.*
unto Mamre, unto the city of *A*...............Gen 35:27   704

ARBATHITE (ar'-bath-ite) *A native of Arbah.*
Abi-albon the *A*, Azmaveth the 2Sa 23:31   6164
the brooks of Gaash, Abiel the *A*............1Chr 11:32   6164

ARBITE (ar'-bite) *A native of Arab.*
the Carmelite, Paarai the *A* 2Sa 23:35   701

ARCHANGEL
a shout, with the voice of the *a* 1Th 4:16   743
Yet Michael the *a*, when ....Jude 9   743

ARCHELAUS (ar-ke-la'-us) *A son of Herod the Great.*
But when he heard that *A* did.................Mt 2:22   745

ARCHER
in the wilderness, and became an *a* ....Gen 21:20   7198
bendeth let the *a* bend his bow...............Jer 51:3   1869

ARCHERS
The *a* have sorely grieved him........Gen 49:23   1167,2671
a in the places of drawing water ....Judg 5:11   2686
Saul, and the *a* hit him.............1Sa 31:3   3384,376,7198
and he was sore wounded of the *a* 1Sa 31:3   3384
were mighty men of valour, *a* 1Chr 8:40   1869,7198
the *a* hit him...........................1Chr 10:3   3384,7198
and he was wounded of the *a* 1Chr 10:3   3384
the *a* shot at king Josiah 2Chr 35:23   3384
His *a* compass me round about, he ....Job 16:13   7228
And the residue of the number of *a* ....Is 21:17   7198
together, they are bound by the *a* ....Is 22:3   7198
together the *a* against Babylon ....Jer 50:29   7228

ARCHES
round about, and likewise to the *a* ....Eze 40:16   361
the *a* thereof were after the ....Eze 40:21   361
And their windows, and their *a* ....Eze 40:22   361
the *a* thereof were before them ....Eze 40:22   361
the *a* thereof according to these ....Eze 40:24   361
in the *a* thereof round about, ...Eze 40:25   361
the *a* thereof were before them ....Eze 40:29   361
the *a* thereof, according to these ....Eze 40:29   361
in the *a* thereof round about ....Eze 40:30   361
the *a* round about were five and.............Eze 40:30   361
the *a* thereof were toward the ....Eze 40:31   361
the *a* thereof, were according to ....Eze 40:33   361
in the *a* thereof round about ....Eze 40:33   361
the *a* thereof were toward the ....Eze 40:34   361
the *a* thereof, and the windows to..........Eze 40:36   361

ARCHEVITES (ar'-ke-vites) *Chaldean settlers in Sa-*
   maria.
Tarpelites, the Apharsites, the *A* ....Ezr 4:9   756

ARCHI (ar'-kee) See ARCHITE. *A border city of Ephraim.*
unto the borders of *A* to Ataroth ....Josh 16:2   757

ARCHIPPUS (ar-kip'-pus) *A Christian acquaintance of*
   Paul.
And say to *A*, Take heed to the ....Col 4:17   751
A our fellowsoldier, and to the ....Philem 2   751

ARCHITE (ar'-kite) See ARCHI. *A friend of David.*
Hushai the *A* came to meet him 2Sa 15:32   757
came to pass, when Hushai the *A* 2Sa 16:16   757
Call now Hushai the *A* also 2Sa 17:5   757
The counsel of Hushai the *A* is 2Sa 17:14   757
Hushai the *A* was the king's 1Chr 27:33   757

ARCHITES See ARCHI.

ARCTURUS (ark-tu'-rus) *Another name for "the Great*
   Bear."
Which maketh *A*, Orion, and.................Job 9:9   5906
canst thou guide *A* with his sons............Job 38:32   5906

ARD (ard) See ARDITES.
   1. A son of Benjamin.
Rosh, Muppim, and Huppim, and *A*.......Gen 46:21   714
   2. A son of Bela.
And the sons of Bela were *A* ....Num 26:40   714
of *A*, the family of the Ardites ....Num 26:40   714

ARDITES (ar'-dites) *Descendants of Bela.*
of Ard, the family of the *A* ....Num 26:40   716

ARDON (ar'-don) *A son of Caleb.*
Jesher, and Shobab, and *A* 1Chr 2:18   715

ARE See APPENDIX.

ARELI (a-re'-li) See ARELITES. *A son of Gad.*
and Ezbon, Eri, and Arodi, and *A* ....Gen 46:16   692
of *A*, the family of the Arelites ....Num 26:17   692

ARELITES (a-re'-lites) See ARELI. *Descendants of Areli.*
of Areli, the family of the *A* ....Num 26:17   692

AREOPAGITE (a-re-op'-a-jite) *A title of Dionysius.*
the which was Dionysius the *A* ....Acts 17:34   698

AREOPAGUS (a-re-op'-a-gus) See AREOPAGITE, MARS'. *A*
   plaza in Athens.
took him, and brought him unto *A* ....Acts 17:19   697

ARETAS (ar'-e-tas) *A north Arabian ruler.*
A the king kept the city of the 2Cor 11:32   702

ARGOB (ar'-gob)
 1. A district of Og in Bashan.
 cities, all the region of A......................... Deut 3:4 709
 all the region of A, with all..................... Deut 3:13 709
 took all the country of A unto .... Deut 3:14 709
 also pertained the region of A 1Kin 4:13 709
 2. An official of King Pekah of Israel.
 of the king's house, with A 2Kin 15:25 709

ARGUING
 but what doth your a reprove .... Job 6:25 3198

ARGUMENTS
 him, and fill my mouth with a .... Job 23:4 8433

ARIDAI (a-rid'-a-i) *A son of Haman.*
 And Parmashta, and Arisai, and A .... Est 9:9 742

ARIDATHA (a-rid'-a-thah) *A son of Haman.*
 And Poratha, and Adalia, and A .... Est 9:8 743

ARIEH (a-ri'-eh) *A companion of Argob.*
 the king's house, with Argob and A 2Kin 15:25 745

ARIEL (a'-re-el) See JERUSALEM.
 1. An emissary of Ezra.
 Then sent I for Eliezer, for A .... Ezr 8:16 740
 2. A name for Jerusalem.
 Woe to Ariel, to A, the city .... Is 29:1 740
 Yet I will distress A, and there............... Is 29:2 740
 and it shall be unto me as A .... Is 29:2 740
 the nations that fight against A .... Is 29:7 740

ARIGHT
 a will I shew the salvation of .... Ps 50:23
 that set not their heart a .... Ps 78:8 3559
 of the wise useth knowledge a .... Prov 15:2 3190
 the cup, when it moveth itself a .... Prov 23:31 4339
 and heard, but they spake not a .... Jer 8:6 3651

ARIMATHAEA (ar-im-ath-e'-ah) *Another name for Ramah.*
 come, there came a rich man of A .... Mt 27:57 707
 Joseph of A, an honourable .... Mk 15:43 707
 he was of A, a city of the Jews .... Lk 23:51 707
 And after this Joseph of A..................... Jn 19:38 707

ARIMATHEA See ARIMATHAEA.

ARIOCH (a'-re-ok)
 1. King of Ellasar in Assyria.
 A king of Ellasar, Chedorlaomer............ Gen 14:1 746
 of Shinar, and A king of Ellasar .... Gen 14:9 746
 2. Captain of Nebuchadnezzar's guard.
 wisdom to A the captain of the .... Dan 2:14 746
 said to A the king's captain, Why .... Dan 2:15 746
 Then A made the thing known to .... Dan 2:15 746
 Therefore Daniel went in unto A........... Dan 2:24 746
 Then A brought in Daniel before .... Dan 2:25 746

ARISAI (a-ris'-a-i) *A son of Haman.*
 Parmashta, and A, and Aridai, and .... Est 9:9 747

ARISE
 A, walk through the land in the............. Gen 13:17 6965
 angels hastened Lot, saying, A .... Gen 19:15 6965
 A, lift up the lad, and hold him .... Gen 21:18 6965
 a, I pray thee, sit and eat of my .... Gen 27:19 6965
 unto his father, Let my father a .... Gen 27:31 6965
 and a, flee thou to Laban my .... Gen 27:43 6965
 A, go to Padan-aram, to the house .... Gen 28:2 6965
 now a, get thee out from this .... Gen 31:13 6965
 And God said unto Jacob, A .... Gen 35:1 6965
 And let us a, and go up to Beth-el......... Gen 35:3 6965
 there shall a after them seven .... Gen 41:30 6965
 the lad with me, and we will a .... Gen 43:8 6965
 Take also your brother, and a .... Gen 43:13 6965
 And the LORD said unto me, A................ Deut 9:12 6965
 And the LORD said unto me, A................ Deut 10:11 6965
 If there a among you a prophet, ... Deut 13:1 6965
 If there a a matter too hard for .... Deut 17:8 6965
 then shalt thou a, and get thee up........ Deut 17:8 6965
 now therefore a, go over this .... Josh 1:2 6965
 the people of war with thee, and a .... Josh 8:1 6965
 a, Barak, and lead thy captivity .... Judg 5:12 6965
 that the LORD said unto him, A .... Judg 7:9 6965
 the host of Israel, and said, A .... Judg 7:15 6965
 And they said, A, that we may go .... Judg 18:9 6965
 to a up out of the city with a .... Judg 20:40 5927
 of the servants with thee, and a 1Sa 9:3 6965
 And the LORD said, A, anoint him.......... 1Sa 16:12 6965
 the LORD answered him and said, A 1Sa 23:4 6965
 to Joab, Let the young men now a 2Sa 2:14 6965
 And Joab said, Let them a 2Sa 2:14 6965
 Abner said unto David, I will a 2Sa 3:21 6965
 if so be that the king's wrath a 2Sa 11:20 5927
 And Amnon said unto her, A 2Sa 13:15 6965

 were with him at Jerusalem, A 2Sa 15:14 6965
 twelve thousand men, and I will a 2Sa 17:1 6965
 king David, and said unto David, A....... 2Sa 17:21 6965
 Now therefore a, go forth, and 2Sa 19:7 6965
 them, that they could not a 2Sa 22:39 6965
 thee shall any a like unto thee.............. 1Kin 3:12 6965
 And Jeroboam said to his wife, A 1Kin 14:2 6965
 A thou therefore, get thee to 1Kin 14:12 6965
 A, get thee to Zarephath, which 1Kin 17:9 6965
 touched him, and said unto him, A........ 1Kin 19:5 6965
 time, and touched him, and said, A 1Kin 19:7 6965
 a, and eat bread, and let thine 1Kin 21:7 6965
 that Jezebel said to Ahab, A................. 1Kin 21:15 6965
 A, go down to meet Ahab king of 1Kin 21:18 6965
 said to Elijah the Tishbite, A 2Kin 1:3 6965
 had restored to life, saying, A............... 2Kin 8:1 6965
 make him a up from among his.............. 2Kin 9:2 6965
 A therefore, and be doing, and the 1Chr 22:16 6965
 a therefore, and build ye the 1Chr 22:19 6965
 Now therefore a, O LORD God, into........ 2Chr 6:41 6965
 A; for this matter belongeth .... Ezr 10:4 6965
 therefore we his servants will a .... Neh 2:20 6965
 Thus shall there a too much.................. Est 1:18
 deliverance a to the Jews from .... Est 4:14 5975
 I lie down, I say, When shall I a .... Job 7:4 6965
 and upon whom doth not his light a ...... Job 25:3 6965
 A, O LORD .... Ps 3:7 6965
 A, O LORD, in thine anger, lift.............. Ps 7:6 6965
 A, O LORD .... Ps 9:19 6965
 A, O LORD .... Ps 10:12 6965
 of the needy, now will I a...................... Ps 12:5 6965
 A, O LORD, disappoint him, cast .... Ps 17:13 6965
 a, cast us not off for ever...................... Ps 44:23 6974
 A for our help, and redeem us for.......... Ps 44:26 6965
 Let God a, let his enemies be................ Ps 68:1 6965
 A, O God, plead thine own cause .... Ps 74:22 6965
 who should a and declare them to .... Ps 78:6 6965
 A, O God, judge the earth .... Ps 82:8 6965
 shall the dead a and praise thee .... Ps 88:10 6965
 when the waves thereof a, thou............. Ps 89:9 7721
 Thou shalt a, and have mercy upon .... Ps 102:13 6965
 when they a, let them be ashamed .... Ps 109:28 6965
 A, O LORD, into thy rest .... Ps 132:8 6965
 when wilt thou a out of thy sleep .... Prov 6:9 6965
 Her children a up, and call her .... Prov 31:28 6965
 A, my love, my fair one, and come .... Song 2:13 6965
 a, ye princes, and anoint the .... Is 21:5 6965
 a, pass over to Chittim .... Is 23:12 6965
 with my dead body shall they a .... Is 26:19 6965
 but will a against the house of .... Is 31:2 6965
 of rulers, Kings shall see and a .... Is 49:7 6965
 a, and sit down, O Jerusalem .... Is 52:2 6965
 A, shine; .... Is 60:1 6965
 but the LORD shall a upon thee............. Is 60:2 2224
 therefore gird up thy loins, and a .... Jer 1:17 6965
 of their trouble they will say, A .... Jer 2:27 6965
 let them a, if they can save thee .... Jer 2:28 6965
 a, and let us go up at noon .... Jer 6:4 6965
 A, and let us go by night, and let.......... Jer 6:5 6965
 Shall they fall, and not a .... Jer 8:4 6965
 which is upon thy loins, and a .... Jer 13:4 6965
 that the LORD said unto me, A .... Jer 13:6 6965
 A, and go down to the potter's .... Jer 18:2 6965
 A ye, and let us go up to Zion .... Jer 31:6 6965
 and they said, A, and let us go.............. Jer 46:16 6965
 A ye, go up to Kedar, and spoil .... Jer 49:28 6965
 A, get you up unto the wealthy .... Jer 49:31 6965
 A, cry out in the night .... Lam 2:19 6965
 and he said unto me, A, go forth........... Eze 3:22 6965
 after thee shall a another...................... Dan 2:39 6965
 and they said thus unto it, A................ Dan 7:5 6966
 which shall a out of the earth .... Dan 7:17 6966
 are ten kings that shall a .... Dan 7:24 6966
 shall a tumult a among thy people .... Hos 10:14 6965
 by whom shall Jacob a .... Amos 7:2 6965
 by whom shall Jacob a .... Amos 7:5 6965
 A ye, and let us rise up against............. Obad 1 6965
 A, go to Nineveh, that great city .... Jonah 1:2 6965
 a, call upon thy God, if so be .... Jonah 1:6 6965
 A, go unto Nineveh, that great .... Jonah 3:2 6965
 came to pass, when the sun did a .... Jonah 4:8 2224
 A ye, and depart.................................. Mic 2:10 6965
 A and thresh, O daughter of Zion .... Mic 4:13 6965
 A, contend thou before the .... Mic 6:1 6965
 when I fall, I shall a .... Mic 7:8 6965
 to the dumb stone, A, it shall .... Hab 2:19 5782
 a with healing in his wings .... Mal 4:2 2224
 to Joseph in a dream, saying, A............. Mt 2:13 1453
 Saying, A, and take the young .... Mt 2:20 1453
 or to say, A, and walk .... Mt 9:5 1453
 he to the sick of the palsy,) A............... Mt 9:6 1453

came and touched them, and said, A ..... Mt 17:7   1453
For there shall a false Christs .... Mt 24:24   1453
or to say, A, and take up thy bed, ... Mk 2:9   1453
I say unto thee, A, and take up .... Mk 2:11   1453
Damsel, I say unto thee, A .... Mk 5:41   1453
of the palsy,) I say unto thee, A .... Lk 5:24   1453
Young man, I say unto thee, A .... Lk 7:14   1453
hand, and called, saying, Maid, a .... Lk 8:54   1453
I will a and go to my father, and .... Lk 15:18   450
And he said unto him, A, go thy .... Lk 17:19   450
why do thoughts a in your hearts .... Lk 24:38   305
A, let us go hence .... Jn 14:31   1453
Lord spake unto Philip, saying, A .... Acts 8:26   450
And the Lord said unto him, A .... Acts 9:6   450
And the Lord said unto him, A .... Acts 9:11   450
a, and make thy bed .... Acts 9:34   450
him to the body said, Tabitha, A .... Acts 9:40   450
A therefore, and get thee down, and ...... Acts 10:20   450
I heard a voice saying unto me, A .... Acts 11:7   450
him up, saying, A up quickly .... Acts 12:7   450
of your own selves shall men a .... Acts 20:30   450
And the Lord said unto me, A .... Acts 22:10   450
a, and be baptized, and wash away ...... Acts 22:16   450
a from the dead, and Christ shall .... Eph 5:14   450
the day star a in your hearts 2Pet 1:19   393

ARISETH
there a a little cloud out of the 1Kin 18:44   5927
The sun a, they gather themselves .... Ps 104:22   2224
there a light in the darkness .... Ps 112:4   2224
The sun also a, and the sun goeth .... Eccl 1:5   2224
when he a to shake terribly the .... Is 2:19   6965
when he a to shake terribly the .... Is 2:21   6965
but when the sun a they flee away .... Nah 3:17   2224
persecution a because of the word .... Mt 13:21   1096
persecution a for the word's sake .... Mk 4:17   1096
for out of Galilee a no prophet .... Jn 7:52   1453
there a another priest, ... Heb 7:15   450

ARISING
the king a from the banquet of .... Est 7:7   6965

ARISTARCHUS (ar-is-tar'-cus) A companion of Paul.
and having caught Gaius and A .... Acts 19:29   708
and of the Thessalonians, A .... Acts 20:4   708
one A, a Macedonian of .... Acts 27:2   708
A my fellowprisoner saluteth you, ... Col 4:10   708
Marcus, A, Demas, Lucas, my .... Philem 24   708

ARISTOBULUS See ARISTOBULUS'.

ARISTOBULUS' (a-rus-to-bu'-luz) A Christian acquaintance of Paul.
them which are of A household .... Rom 16:10   711

ARK
Make thee an a of gopher wood .... Gen 6:14   8392
rooms shalt thou make in the a .... Gen 6:14   8392
The length of the a shall be .... Gen 6:15   8392
A window shalt thou make to the a .... Gen 6:16   8392
the door of the a shalt thou set .... Gen 6:16   8392
and thou shalt come into the a .... Gen 6:18   8392
sort shalt thou bring into the a .... Gen 6:19   8392
thou and all thy house into the a .... Gen 7:1   8392
sons' wives with him, into the a .... Gen 7:7   8392
two and two unto Noah into the a .... Gen 7:9   8392
of his sons with them, into the a .... Gen 7:13   8392
they went in unto Noah into the a .... Gen 7:15   8392
increased, and bare up the a .... Gen 7:17   8392
the a went upon the face of the .... Gen 7:18   8392
they that were with him in the a .... Gen 7:23   8392
cattle that was with him in the a .... Gen 8:1   8392
the a rested in the seventh month .... Gen 8:4   8392
window of the a which he had made ...... Gen 8:6   8392
she returned unto him into the a .... Gen 8:9   8392
pulled her in unto him into the a .... Gen 8:9   8392
sent forth the dove out of the a .... Gen 8:10   8392
removed the covering of the a .... Gen 8:13   8392
Go forth of the a, thou, and thy .... Gen 8:16   8392
kinds, went forth out of the a .... Gen 8:19   8392
from all that go out of the a .... Gen 9:10   8392
of Noah, that went forth of the a .... Gen 9:18   8392
took for him an a of bulrushes .... Ex 2:3   8392
she saw the a among the flags .... Ex 2:5   8392
shall make an a of shittim wood .... Ex 25:10   727
the rings by the sides of the a .... Ex 25:14   727
that the a may be borne with them .... Ex 25:14   727
shall be in the rings of the a .... Ex 25:15   727
thou shalt put into the a the .... Ex 25:16   727
the mercy seat above upon the a .... Ex 25:21   727
in the a thou shalt put the .... Ex 25:21   727
are upon the a of the testimony .... Ex 25:22   727
the vail the a of the testimony .... Ex 26:33   727
put the mercy seat upon the a of .... Ex 26:34   727

that is by the a of the testimony .... Ex 30:6   727
and the a of the testimony, ... Ex 30:26   727
the a of the testimony, and the .... Ex 31:7   727
The a, and the staves thereof, ... Ex 35:12   727
made the a of shittim wood .... Ex 37:1   727
sides of the a, to bear the .... Ex 37:5   727
The a of the testimony, and the .... Ex 39:35   727
therein to put the a of the testimony .... Ex 40:3   727
cover the a with the vail .... Ex 40:3   727
before the a of the testimony, ... Ex 40:5   727
and put the testimony into the a .... Ex 40:20   727
and set the staves on the a .... Ex 40:20   727
the mercy seat above upon the a .... Ex 40:20   727
he brought the a into the .... Ex 40:21   727
covered the a of the testimony .... Ex 40:21   727
mercy seat, which is upon the a .... Lev 16:2   727
And their charge shall be the a .... Num 3:31   727
cover of testimony with it .... Num 4:5   727
that was upon the a of testimony .... Num 7:89   727
the a of the covenant of the LORD .... Num 10:33   727
when the a set forward, that .... Num 10:35   727
nevertheless the a of the .... Num 14:44   727
mount, and make thee an a of wood ..... Deut 10:1   727
and thou shalt put them in the a .... Deut 10:2   727
I made an a of shittim wood, and .... Deut 10:3   727
tables in the a which I had made .... Deut 10:5   727
to bear the a of the covenant of .... Deut 10:8   727
which bare the a of the covenant .... Deut 31:9   727
which bare the a of the covenant .... Deut 31:25   727
put it in the side of the a of .... Deut 31:26   727
When ye see the a of the covenant .... Josh 3:3   727
Take up the a of the covenant, and ...... Josh 3:6   727
took up the a of the covenant .... Josh 3:6   727
that bear the a of the covenant .... Josh 3:8   727
the a of the covenant of the Lord .... Josh 3:11   727
that bear the a of the LORD .... Josh 3:13   727
the priests bearing the a of the .... Josh 3:14   727
bare the a were come unto Jordan .... Josh 3:15   727
of the priests that bare the a .... Josh 3:15   727
the priests that bare the a .... Josh 3:17   727
Pass over before the a of the .... Josh 4:5   727
the a of the covenant of the LORD .... Josh 4:7   727
bare the a of the covenant stood .... Josh 4:9   727
a stood in the midst of Jordan .... Josh 4:10   727
that the a of the LORD passed .... Josh 4:11   727
that bear the a of the testimony .... Josh 4:16   727
the a of the covenant of the LORD .... Josh 4:18   727
a seven trumpets of rams' horns .... Josh 6:4   727
Take up the a of the covenant, and ...... Josh 6:6   727
horns before the a of the LORD .... Josh 6:6   727
pass on before the a of the LORD .... Josh 6:7   727
the a of the covenant of the LORD .... Josh 6:8   727
and the rereward came after the a .... Josh 6:9   727
So the a of the LORD compassed .... Josh 6:11   727
priests took up the a of the LORD .... Josh 6:12   727
of rams' horns before the a of .... Josh 6:13   727
came after the a of the LORD .... Josh 6:13   727
a of the LORD until the eventide .... Josh 7:6   727
judges, stood on this side the a .... Josh 8:33   727
which bare the a of the covenant .... Josh 8:33   727
(for the a of the covenant of God .... Judg 20:27   727
where the a of God was, and Samuel 1Sa 3:3   727
Let us fetch the a of the 1Sa 4:3   727
might bring from thence the a of 1Sa 4:4   727
were there with the a of the 1Sa 4:4   727
when the a of the covenant of the 1Sa 4:5   727
they understood that the a of the 1Sa 4:6   727
And the a of God was taken 1Sa 4:11   727
heart trembled for the a of God 1Sa 4:13   727
dead, and the a of God is taken 1Sa 4:17   727
he made mention of the a of God 1Sa 4:18   727
that the a of God was taken 1Sa 4:19   727
because the a of God was taken, ... 1Sa 4:21   727
for the a of God is taken 1Sa 4:22   727
the Philistines took the a of God 1Sa 5:1   727
the Philistines took the a of God 1Sa 5:2   727
earth before the a of the LORD 1Sa 5:3   727
ground before the a of the LORD 1Sa 5:4   727
The a of the God of Israel shall 1Sa 5:7   727
with the a of the God of Israel 1Sa 5:8   727
Let the a of the God of Israel be 1Sa 5:8   727
they carried the a of the God of 1Sa 5:8   727
they sent the a of God to Ekron 1Sa 5:10   727
as the a of God came to Ekron, ... 1Sa 5:10   727
the a of the God of Israel to us 1Sa 5:10   727
Send away the a of the God of 1Sa 5:11   727
the a of the LORD was in the 1Sa 6:1   727
shall we do to the a of the LORD 1Sa 6:2   727
If ye send away the a of the God 1Sa 6:3   727
take the a of the LORD, and lay it 1Sa 6:8   727
they laid the a of the LORD upon 1Sa 6:11   727

up their eyes, and saw the *a*	1Sa 6:13	727
took down the *a* of the Lord	1Sa 6:15	727
they set down the *a* of the Lord	1Sa 6:18	727
had looked into the *a* of the Lord	1Sa 6:19	727
brought again the *a* of the Lord	1Sa 6:21	727
and brought up the *a* of the Lord	1Sa 7:1	727
his son to keep the *a* of the Lord	1Sa 7:1	727
to pass, while the *a* abode in	1Sa 7:2	727
Ahiah, Bring hither the *a* of God	1Sa 14:18	727
For the *a* of God was at that time	1Sa 14:18	727
bring up from thence the *a* of God	2Sa 6:2	727
they set the *a* of God upon a new	2Sa 6:3	727
Gibeah, accompanying the *a* of God	2Sa 6:4	727
and Ahio went before the *a*	2Sa 6:4	727
forth his hand to the *a* of God	2Sa 6:6	727
and there he died by the *a* of God	2Sa 6:7	727
How shall the *a* of the Lord come	2Sa 6:9	727
a of the Lord unto him into the	2Sa 6:10	727
the *a* of the Lord continued in	2Sa 6:11	727
unto him, because of the *a* of God	2Sa 6:12	727
brought up the *a* of God from the	2Sa 6:12	727
that when they they that bare the *a* of	2Sa 6:13	727
the *a* of the Lord with shouting	2Sa 6:15	727
as the *a* of the Lord came into	2Sa 6:16	727
they brought in the *a* of the Lord	2Sa 6:17	727
but the *a* of God dwelleth within	2Sa 7:2	727
And Uriah said unto David, The *a*	2Sa 11:11	727
bearing the *a* of the covenant	2Sa 15:24	727
and they set down the *a* of God	2Sa 15:24	727
Carry back the *a* of God into the	2Sa 15:25	727
Abiathar carried the *a* of God	2Sa 15:29	727
because thou barest the *a* of the	1Kin 2:26	727
stood before the *a* of the	1Kin 3:15	727
to set there the *a* of the	1Kin 6:19	727
that they might bring up the *a* of	1Kin 8:1	727
and the priests took up the *a*	1Kin 8:3	727
they brought up the *a* of the Lord	1Kin 8:4	727
him, were with him before the *a*	1Kin 8:5	727
the priests brought in the *a* of	1Kin 8:6	727
two wings over the place of the *a*	1Kin 8:7	727
and the cherubims covered the *a*	1Kin 8:7	727
There was nothing in the *a* save	1Kin 8:9	727
have set there a place for the *a*	1Kin 8:21	727
Lord, after that the *a* had rest	1Chr 6:31	727
again the *a* of our God to us	1Chr 13:3	727
to bring the *a* of God from	1Chr 13:5	727
up thence the *a* of God the Lord	1Chr 13:6	727
they carried the *a* of God in a	1Chr 13:7	727
put forth his hand to hold the *a*	1Chr 13:9	727
because he put his hand to the *a*	1Chr 13:10	727
I bring the *a* of God home to me	1Chr 13:12	727
So David brought not the *a* home	1Chr 13:13	727
the *a* of God remained with the	1Chr 13:14	727
prepared a place for the *a* of God	1Chr 15:1	727
the *a* of God but the Levites	1Chr 15:2	727
Lord chosen to carry the *a* of God	1Chr 15:2	727
to bring up the *a* of the Lord	1Chr 15:3	727
that ye may bring up the *a* of the	1Chr 15:12	727
the *a* of the Lord God of Israel	1Chr 15:14	727
of the Levites bare the *a* of God	1Chr 15:15	727
were doorkeepers for the *a*	1Chr 15:23	727
the trumpets before the *a* of God	1Chr 15:24	727
Jehiah were doorkeepers for the *a*	1Chr 15:24	727
went to bring up the *a* of the	1Chr 15:25	727
the Levites that bare the *a* of	1Chr 15:26	727
all the Levites that bare the *a*	1Chr 15:27	727
the *a* of the covenant of the Lord	1Chr 15:28	727
as the *a* of the covenant of the	1Chr 15:29	727
So they brought the *a* of God	1Chr 16:1	727
minister before the *a* of the Lord	1Chr 16:4	727
the *a* of the covenant of God	1Chr 16:6	727
the *a* of the covenant of the Lord	1Chr 16:37	727
minister before the *a* continually	1Chr 16:37	727
but the *a* of the covenant of the	1Chr 17:1	727
to bring the *a* of the covenant of	1Chr 22:19	727
the *a* of the covenant of the Lord	1Chr 28:2	727
covered the *a* of the covenant of	1Chr 28:18	727
But the *a* of God had David	2Chr 1:4	727
to bring up the *a* of the covenant	2Chr 5:2	727
and the Levites took up the *a*	2Chr 5:4	727
And they brought up the *a*, and the	2Chr 5:5	727
assembled unto him before the *a*	2Chr 5:6	727
the priests brought in the *a* of	2Chr 5:7	727
wings over the place of the *a*	2Chr 5:8	727
and the cherubims covered the *a*	2Chr 5:8	727
they drew out the staves of the *a*	2Chr 5:9	727
seen from the *a* before the oracle	2Chr 5:9	727
There was nothing in the *a* save	2Chr 5:10	727
And in it have I put the *a*	2Chr 6:11	727
thou, and the *a* of thy strength	2Chr 6:41	727
whereunto the *a* of the Lord hath	2Chr 8:11	727

Put the holy *a* in the house which	2Chr 35:3	727
thou, and the *a* of thy strength	Ps 132:8	727
The *a* of the covenant of the Lord	Jer 3:16	727
day that Noe entered into the *a*	Mt 24:38	*2787*
day that Noe entered into the *a*	Lk 17:27	*2787*
the *a* of the covenant overlaid	Heb 9:4	*2787*
prepared an *a* to the saving of	Heb 11:7	*2787*
while the *a* was a preparing,	1Pet 3:20	*2787*
his temple the *a* of his testament	Rev 11:19	*2787*

ARKITE (*ar'-kite*) *A tribe descended from Canaan.*

And the Hivite, and the *A*, and the	Gen 10:17	6208
And the Hivite, and the *A*, and the	1Chr 1:15	6208

ARKITES See Archi.

ARM

redeem you with a stretched out *a*	Ex 6:6	2220
by the greatness of thine *a* they	Ex 15:16	2220
A some of yourselves unto the war	Num 31:3	2502
hand, and by a stretched out *a*	Deut 4:34	2220
hand and by a stretched out *a*	Deut 5:15	2220
hand, and the stretched out *a*	Deut 7:19	2220
power and by thy stretched out *a*	Deut 9:29	2220
hand, and his stretched out *a*	Deut 11:2	2220
hand, and with an outstretched *a*	Deut 26:8	2220
teareth the *a* with the crown of	Deut 33:20	2220
come, that I will cut off thine *a*	1Sa 2:31	2220
the *a* of thy father's house, that	1Sa 2:31	2220
and the bracelet that was on his *a*	2Sa 1:10	2220
hand, and of thy stretched out *a*	1Kin 8:42	2220
great power and a stretched out *a*	2Kin 17:36	2220
hand, and thy stretched out *a*	2Chr 6:32	2220
With his is an *a* of flesh	2Chr 32:8	2220
how savest thou the *a* that hath	Job 26:2	2220
Then let mine *a* fall from my	Job 31:22	3802
mine *a* be broken from the bone	Job 31:22	248
by reason of the *a* of the mighty	Job 35:9	2220
the high *a* shall be broken	Job 38:15	2220
Hast thou an *a* like God	Job 40:9	2220
Break thou the *a* of the wicked	Ps 10:15	2220
neither did their own *a* save them	Ps 44:3	2220
but thy right hand, and thine *a*	Ps 44:3	2220
with thine *a* redeemed thy people	Ps 77:15	2220
thine enemies with thy strong *a*	Ps 89:10	2220
Thou hast a mighty *a*	Ps 89:13	2220
mine *a* also shall strengthen him	Ps 89:21	2220
his right hand, and his holy *a*	Ps 98:1	2220
hand, and with a stretched out *a*	Ps 136:12	2220
heart, as a seal upon thine *a*	Song 8:6	2220
every man the flesh of his own *a*	Is 9:20	2220
and reapeth the ears with his *a*	Is 17:5	2220
shew the lighting down of his *a*	Is 30:30	2220
be thou their *a* every morning	Is 33:2	2220
hand, and his *a* shall rule for him	Is 40:10	2220
shall gather the lambs with his *a*	Is 40:11	2220
his *a* shall be on the Chaldeans	Is 48:14	2220
on mine *a* shall they trust	Is 51:5	2220
put on strength, O *a* of the Lord	Is 51:9	2220
Lord hath made bare his holy *a* in	Is 52:10	2220
to whom is the *a* of the Lord	Is 53:1	2220
therefore his *a* brought salvation	Is 59:16	2220
by the *a* of his strength, Surely	Is 62:8	2220
therefore mine own *a* brought	Is 63:5	2220
hand of Moses with his glorious *a*	Is 63:12	2220
in man, and maketh flesh his *a*	Jer 17:5	2220
hand and with a strong *a*, even in	Jer 21:5	2220
power and by my outstretched *a*	Jer 27:5	2220
great power and stretched out *a*	Jer 32:17	2220
hand, and with a stretched out *a*	Jer 32:21	248
his *a* is broken, saith the Lord	Jer 48:25	2220
thine *a* shall be uncovered, and	Eze 4:7	2220
hand, and with a stretched out *a*	Eze 20:33	2220
hand, and with a stretched out *a*	Eze 20:34	2220
I have broken the *a* of Pharaoh	Eze 30:21	2220
and they that were his *a*, that	Eze 31:17	2220
not retain the power of the *a*	Dan 11:6	2220
neither shall he stand, nor his *a*	Dan 11:6	2220
the sword shall be upon his *a*	Zec 11:17	2220
his *a* shall be clean dried up, and	Zec 11:17	2220
hath shewed strength with his *a*	Lk 1:51	*1023*
to whom hath the *a* of the Lord	Jn 12:38	*1023*
with an high *a* brought he them	Acts 13:17	*1023*
a yourselves likewise with the	1Pet 4:1	*3695*

ARMAGEDDON (*ar-mag-ed'-don*) *Scene of the last great battle of time.*

called in the Hebrew tongue *A*	Rev 16:16	*717*

ARMED

he *a* his trained servants, born	Gen 14:14	7324
tribe, twelve thousand *a* for war	Num 31:5	2502
a before the children of Israel	Num 32:17	2502

if ye will go *a* before the Lord	Num 32:20	2502
will go all of you *a* over Jordan	Num 32:21	2502
pass over, every man *a* for war	Num 32:27	2502
Jordan, every man *a* to battle	Num 32:29	2502
will not pass over with you *a*	Num 32:30	2502
We will pass over *a* before the	Num 32:32	2502
ye shall pass over *a* before your	Deut 3:18	2502
shall pass before your brethren *a*	Josh 1:14	2571
passed over *a* before the children	Josh 4:12	2571
let him that is *a* pass on before	Josh 6:7	2502
the *a* men went before the priests	Josh 6:9	2502
the *a* men went before them	Josh 6:13	2502
the *a* men that were in the host	Judg 7:11	2571
he was *a* with a coat of mail	1Sa 17:5	3847
Saul *a* David with his armour, and	1Sa 17:38	3847
also he *a* him with a coat of mail	1Sa 17:38	3847
They were *a* with bows, and could	1Chr 12:2	5401
that were ready *a* to the war	1Chr 12:23	2502
eight hundred, ready *a* to the war	1Chr 12:24	2502
with him *a* men with bow and shield	2Chr 17:17	5401
So the *a* men left the captives and	2Chr 28:14	2502
he goeth on to meet the *a* men	Job 39:21	5402
The children of Ephraim, being *a*	Ps 78:9	5401
and thy want as an *a* man	Prov 6:11	4043
and thy want as an *a* man	Prov 24:34	4043
therefore the *a* soldiers of Moab	Is 15:4	2502
When a strong man *a* keepeth his	Lk 11:21	*2528*

ARMENIA (ar·me'-ne-ah) A region between the lower ends of the Black and Caspian seas.

they escaped into the land of *A*	2Kin 19:37	780
they escaped into the land of *A*	Is 37:38	780

ARMHOLES

under thine *a* under the cords	Jer 38:12	679,3027
women that sew pillows to all *a*	Eze 13:18	679,3027

ARMIES

of Egypt according to their *a*	Ex 6:26	6635
upon Egypt, and bring forth mine *a*	Ex 7:4	6635
day have I brought your *a* out of	Ex 12:17	6635
of the land of Egypt by their *a*	Ex 12:51	6635
shall number them by their *a*	Num 1:3	6635
of Judah pitch throughout their *a*	Num 2:3	6635
four hundred, throughout their *a*	Num 2:9	6635
of Reuben according to their *a*	Num 2:10	6635
and fifty, throughout their *a*	Num 2:16	6635
of Ephraim according to their *a*	Num 2:18	6635
and an hundred, throughout their *a*	Num 2:24	6635
be on the north side by their *a*	Num 2:25	6635
of Judah according to their *a*	Num 10:14	6635
set forward according to their *a*	Num 10:18	6635
set forward according to their *a*	Num 10:22	6635
of Israel according to their *a*	Num 10:28	6635
their *a* under the hand of Moses	Num 33:1	6635
of the *a* to lead the people	Deut 20:9	6635
together their *a* to battle	1Sa 17:1	4264
and cried unto the *a* of Israel	1Sa 17:8	4634
I defy the *a* of Israel this day	1Sa 17:10	4634
out of the *a* of the Philistines,	1Sa 17:23	4630
defy the *a* of the living God	1Sa 17:26	4634
defied the *a* of the living God	1Sa 17:36	4634
hosts, the God of the *a* of Israel	1Sa 17:45	4634
against the *a* of the Philistines	1Sa 23:3	4634
their *a* together for warfare	1Sa 28:1	4264
together all their *a* to Aphek	1Sa 29:1	4264
And when all the captains of the *a*	2Kin 25:23	2428
great, and the captains of the *a*	2Kin 25:26	2428
the valiant men of the *a* were	1Chr 11:26	2428
sent the captains of his *a*	2Chr 16:4	2428
Is there any number of his *a*	Job 25:3	1416
and goest not forth with our *a*	Ps 44:9	6635
which didst not go out with our *a*	Ps 60:10	6635
Kings of *a* did flee apace	Ps 68:12	6635
As it were the company of two *a*	Song 6:13	4264
and his fury upon all their *a*	Is 34:2	6635
and he sent forth his *a*, and	Mt 22:7	*4753*
see Jerusalem compassed with *a*	Lk 21:20	*4760*
to flight the *a* of the aliens	Heb 11:34	*3925*
the *a* which were in heaven	Rev 19:14	*4753*
kings of the earth, and their *a*	Rev 19:19	*4753*

ARMONI (ar-mo'-ni) A son of King Saul.

Aiah, whom she bare unto Saul, *A*	2Sa 21:8	764

ARMOUR

the young man that bare his *a*	1Sa 14:1	3627
to the young man that bare his *a*	1Sa 14:6	3627
And Saul armed David with his *a*	1Sa 17:38	4055
David girded his sword upon his *a*	1Sa 17:39	4055
but he put his *a* in his tent	1Sa 17:54	3627
his head, and stripped off his *a*	1Sa 31:9	3627
they put his *a* in the house of	1Sa 31:10	3627

the young men, and take thee his *a*	2Sa 2:21	2488
bare Joab's *a* compassed about	2Sa 18:15	3627
of gold, and garments, and *a*	1Kin 10:25	5402
and they washed his *a*	1Kin 22:38	2185
all that were able to put on *a*	2Kin 3:21	2290
horses, a fenced city also, and *a*	2Kin 10:2	5402
and all the house of his *a*	2Kin 20:13	3627
him, they took his head, and his *a*	1Chr 10:9	3627
they put his *a* in the house of	1Chr 10:10	3627
the *a* of the house of the forest	Is 22:8	5402
and all the house of his *a*	Is 39:2	3627
them clothed with all sorts of *a*	Eze 38:4	3627
him all his *a* wherein he trusted	Lk 11:22	*3833*
and let us put on the *a* of light	Rom 13:12	*3696*
by the *a* of righteousness on the	2Cor 6:7	*3696*
Put on the whole *a* of God	Eph 6:11	*3833*
take unto you the whole *a* of God	Eph 6:13	*3833*

ARMOURBEARER

unto the young man his *a*	Judg 9:54	5375,3627
his *a* said unto him, Do all that	1Sa 14:7	5375,3627
answered Jonathan and his *a*	1Sa 14:12	5375,3627
And Jonathan said unto his *a*	1Sa 14:12	5375,3627
upon his feet, and his *a* after him	1Sa 14:13	5375,3627
and his *a* slew after him	1Sa 14:13	5375,3627
a made, was about twenty men,	1Sa 14:14	5375,3627
Jonathan and his *a* were not there	1Sa 14:17	5375,3627
and he became his *a*	1Sa 16:21	5375,3627
Then said Saul unto his *a*	1Sa 31:4	5375,3627
But his *a* would not	1Sa 31:4	5375,3627
his *a* saw that Saul was dead	1Sa 31:5	5375,3627
and his three sons, and his *a*	1Sa 31:6	5375,3627
a to Joab the son of Zeruiah,	2Sa 23:37	5375,3627
said Saul to his *a*, Draw thy	1Chr 10:4	5375,3627
But his *a* would not	1Chr 10:4	5375,3627
his *a* saw that Saul was dead	1Chr 10:5	5375,3627
the *a* of Joab the son of Zeruiah,	1Chr 11:39	5375,3627

ARMOURY

the *a* at the turning of the wall	Neh 3:19	5402
tower of David builded for an *a*	Song 4:4	8530
The Lord hath opened his *a*	Jer 50:25	214

ARMS

the *a* of his hands were made	Gen 49:24	2220
underneath are the everlasting *a*	Deut 33:27	2220
the cords that were upon his *a*	Judg 15:14	2220
them from off his *a* like a thread	Judg 16:12	2220
bow of steel is broken by mine *a*	2Sa 22:35	2220
and smote Jehoram between his *a*	2Kin 9:24	2220
the *a* of the fatherless have been	Job 22:9	2220
bow of steel is broken by mine *a*	Ps 18:34	2220
For the *a* of the wicked shall be	Ps 37:17	2220
strength, and strengtheneth her *a*	Prov 31:17	2220
it with the strength of his *a*	Is 44:12	2220
shall bring thy sons in their *a*	Is 49:22	2684
mine *a* shall judge the people	Is 51:5	2220
and I will tear them from your *a*	Eze 13:20	2220
of Egypt, and will break his *a*	Eze 30:22	2220
I will strengthen the *a* of the	Eze 30:24	2220
but I will break Pharaoh's *a*	Eze 30:24	2220
the *a* of the king of Babylon	Eze 30:25	2220
the *a* of Pharaoh shall fall down	Eze 30:25	2220
his *a* of silver, his belly and his	Dan 2:32	1672
eyes as lamps of fire, and his *a*	Dan 10:6	2220
the *a* of the south shall not	Dan 11:15	2220
with the *a* of a flood shall they	Dan 11:22	2220
a shall stand on his part, and	Dan 11:31	2220
bound and strengthened their *a*	Hos 7:15	2220
to go, taking them by their *a*	Hos 11:3	2220
and when he had taken him in his *a*	Mk 9:36	*1723*
And he took them up in his *a*	Mk 10:16	*1723*
Then took he him up in his *a*	Lk 2:28	*43*

ARMY

the chief captain of his *a*	Gen 26:26	6635
and his horsemen, and his *a*	Ex 14:9	2428
what he did unto the *a* of Egypt	Deut 11:4	2428
Sisera, the captain of Jabin's *a*	Judg 4:7	6635
we should give bread unto thine *a*	Judg 8:6	6635
to Abimelech, Increase thine *a*	Judg 9:29	6635
they slew of the *a* in the field	1Sa 4:2	4634
a man of Benjamin out of the *a*	1Sa 4:12	4634
I am he that came out of the *a*	1Sa 4:16	4634
and I fled to day out of the *a*	1Sa 4:16	4634
battle in array, *a* against *a*	1Sa 17:21	4634
battle in array, *a* against *a*	1Sa 17:21	2428
the carriage, and ran into the *a*	1Sa 17:22	4634
ran toward the *a* to meet the	1Sa 17:48	4634
the *a* which followed them	1Kin 20:19	2428
And number thee an *a*	1Kin 20:25	2428
like the *a* that thou hast lost,	1Kin 20:25	2428
the *a* of the Chaldees pursued	2Kin 25:5	2428

all his *a* were scattered from him	2Kin 25:5	2428
all the *a* of the Chaldees, that	2Kin 25:10	2428
Joab led forth the power of the *a*	1Chr 20:1	6635
general of the king's *a* was Joab	1Chr 27:34	6635
with an *a* of valiant men of war	2Chr 13:3	2428
Asa had an *a* of men that bare	2Chr 14:8	2428
as they went out before the *a*	2Chr 20:21	2502
For the *a* of the Syrians came	2Chr 24:24	2428
let not the *a* of Israel go with	2Chr 25:7	6635
I have given to the *a* of Israel	2Chr 25:9	1416
the *a* that was come to him out of	2Chr 25:10	1416
of the *a* which Amaziah sent back	2Chr 25:13	1416
And under their hand was an *a*	2Chr 26:13	2426,6635
king had sent captains of the *a*	Neh 2:9	2428
the *a* of Samaria, and said, What	Neh 4:2	2428
and dwelt as a king in the *a*	Job 29:25	1416
terrible as an *a* with banners	Song 6:4	
and terrible as an *a* with banners	Song 6:10	
unto king Hezekiah with a great *a*	Is 36:2	2426
forth the chariot and horse, the *a*	Is 43:17	2428
of Babylon's *a* besieged Jerusalem	Jer 32:2	2428
king of Babylon, and all his *a*	Jer 34:1	2428
a fought against Jerusalem	Jer 34:7	2428
hand of the king of Babylon's *a*	Jer 34:21	2428
fear of the *a* of the Chaldeans	Jer 35:11	2428
for fear of the *a* of the Syrians	Jer 35:11	2428
Then Pharaoh's *a* was come forth	Jer 37:5	2428
Behold, Pharaoh's *a*, which is	Jer 37:7	2428
a of the Chaldeans that fight	Jer 37:10	2428
that when the *a* of the Chaldeans	Jer 37:11	2428
Jerusalem for fear of Pharaoh's *a*	Jer 37:11	2428
hand of the king of Babylon's *a*	Jer 38:3	2428
all his *a* against Jerusalem, and	Jer 39:1	2428
Chaldeans' *a* pursued after them	Jer 39:5	2428
against the *a* of Pharaoh-necho	Jer 46:2	2428
for they shall march with an *a*	Jer 46:22	2428
of Babylon came, he and all his *a*	Jer 52:4	2428
But the *a* of the Chaldeans	Jer 52:8	2428
all his *a* was scattered from him	Jer 52:8	2428
all the *a* of the Chaldeans, that	Jer 52:14	2428
shall Pharaoh with his mighty *a*	Eze 17:17	2428
of Lud and of Phut were in thine *a*	Eze 27:10	2428
The men of Arvad with thine *a*	Eze 27:11	2428
his *a* to serve a great service	Eze 29:18	2428
yet had he no wages, nor his *a*	Eze 29:18	2428
it shall be the wages for his *a*	Eze 29:19	2428
all his *a* slain by the sword,	Eze 32:31	2428
their feet, an exceeding great *a*	Eze 37:10	2428
bring thee forth, and all thine *a*	Eze 38:4	2428
a great company, and a mighty *a*	Eze 38:15	2428
were in his *a* to bind Shadrach	Dan 3:20	2429
to his will in the *a* of heaven	Dan 4:35	2429
which shall come with an *a*	Dan 11:7	2428
certain years with a great *a*	Dan 11:13	2428
king of the south with a great *a*	Dan 11:25	2428
with a very great and mighty *a*	Dan 11:25	2428
him, and his *a* shall overflow	Dan 11:26	2428
utter his voice before his *a*	Joel 2:11	2428
far off from you the northern *a*	Joel 2:20	
my great *a* which I sent among you	Joel 2:25	2428
about mine house because of the *a*	Zec 9:8	4675
then came I with an *a*, and rescued	Acts 23:27	4753
the number of the *a* of the	Rev 9:16	4753
on the horse, and against his *a*	Rev 19:19	4753

ARNAN *(ar'-nan) Descendants of David.*

sons of Rephaiah, the sons of *A*	1Chr 3:21	770

ARNON *(ar'-non) A river in southern Canaan.*

and pitched on the other side of *A*	Num 21:13	769
for *A* is the border of Moab,	Num 21:13	769
Red sea, and in the brooks of *A*	Num 21:14	769
his land from *A* unto Jabbok	Num 21:24	769
land out of his hand, even unto *A*	Num 21:26	769
the lords of the high places of *A*	Num 21:28	769
Moab, which is in the border of *A*	Num 22:36	769
journey, and pass over the river *A*	Deut 2:24	769
is by the brink of the river of *A*	Deut 2:36	769
the river of *A* unto mount Hermon	Deut 3:8	769
Aroer, which is by the river *A*	Deut 3:12	769
unto the river *A* half the valley	Deut 3:16	769
is by the bank of the river *A*	Deut 4:48	769
from the river *A* unto mount	Josh 12:1	769
is upon the bank of the river *A*	Josh 12:2	769
is upon the bank of the river *A*	Josh 13:9	769
is on the bank of the river *A*	Josh 13:16	769
from *A* even unto Jabbok, and unto	Judg 11:13	769
and pitched on the other side of *A*	Judg 11:18	769
for *A* was the border of Moab	Judg 11:18	769
from *A* even unto Jabbok, and from	Judg 11:22	769
that be along by the coasts of *A*	Judg 11:26	769
Aroer, which is by the river *A*	2Kin 10:33	769

Moab shall be at the fords of *A*	Is 16:2	769
tell ye it in *A*, that Moab is	Jer 48:20	769

AROD *(a'-rod)* See ARODITES. *A son of Gad.*

Of *A*, the family of the Arodites	Num 26:17	720

ARODI *(ar'-o-di)* See ARODITES. *Descendants of Arod.*

Haggi, Shuni, and Ezbon, Eri, and *A*	Gen 46:16	722

ARODITES *(a'-ro-dites) Same as Arodi.*

Of Arod, the family of the *A*	Num 26:17	722

AROER *(ar'-o-ur)*

1. A city in the valley of Jabbok.

Gad built Dibon, and Ataroth, and *A*	Num 32:34	6177
unto *A* that is before Rabbah	Josh 13:25	6177
over Jordan, and pitched in *A*	2Sa 24:5	6177
The cities of *A* are forsaken	Is 17:2	6177

2. An Amorite city.

From *A*, which is by the brink of	Deut 2:36	6177
we possessed at that time, from *A*	Deut 3:12	6177
From *A*, which is by the bank of	Deut 4:48	6177
dwelt in Heshbon, and ruled from *A*	Josh 12:2	6177
From *A*, that is upon the bank of	Josh 13:9	6177
And their coast was from *A*	Josh 13:16	6177
in Heshbon and her towns, and in *A*	Judg 11:26	6177
And he smote them from *A*, even	Judg 11:33	6177
and the Manassites, from *A*	2Kin 10:33	6177
the son of Joel, who dwelt in *A*	1Chr 5:8	6177
O inhabitant of *A*, stand by the	Jer 48:19	6177

3. A city in southern Judah.

And to them which were in *A*	1Sa 30:28	6177

AROERITE *(ar'-o-ur-ite) A native of Aroer.*

Jehiel the sons of Hothan the *A*	1Chr 11:44	6200

AROSE

And when the morning *a*, then the	Gen 19:15	5927
when she lay down, nor when she *a*	Gen 19:33	6965
and the younger *a*, and lay with him	Gen 19:35	6965
when she lay down, nor when she *a*	Gen 19:35	6965
and he *a*, and went to Mesopotamia,	Gen 24:10	6965
And Rebekah *a*, and her damsels, and	Gen 24:61	6965
in the field, and, lo, my sheaf *a*	Gen 37:7	6965
And she *a*, and went away, and laid	Gen 38:19	6965
Now there *a* up a new king over	Ex 1:8	6965
there *a* not a prophet since in	Deut 34:10	6965
So Joshua *a*, and all the people of	Josh 8:3	6965
the ambush *a* quickly out of their	Josh 8:19	6965
And the men *a*, and went away	Josh 18:8	6965
son of Zippor, king of Moab, *a*	Josh 24:9	6965
there *a* another generation after	Judg 2:10	6965
And he *a* out of his seat	Judg 3:20	6965
And Deborah *a*, and went with Barak	Judg 4:9	6965
in Israel, until that I Deborah *a*	Judg 5:7	6965
that I *a* a mother in Israel	Judg 5:7	6965
the city *a* early in the morning	Judg 6:28	7925
And Gideon *a*, and slew Zebah and	Judg 8:21	6965
after Abimelech there *a* to defend	Judg 10:1	6965
And after him *a* Jair, a Gileadite,	Judg 10:3	6965
And Manoah *a*, and went after his	Judg 13:11	6965
a at midnight, and took the doors	Judg 16:3	6965
And her husband *a*, and went after	Judg 19:3	6965
when they *a* early in the morning,	Judg 19:5	6965
he *a* early in the morning on the	Judg 19:8	7925
And all the people *a* as one man	Judg 20:8	6965
And the children of Israel *a*	Judg 20:18	6965
Then she *a* with her daughters in	Ruth 1:6	6965
And Samuel *a* and went to Eli, and	1Sa 3:6	6965
And he *a* and went to Eli, and said,	1Sa 3:8	6965
of Ashdod *a* early on the morrow	1Sa 5:3	7925
when they *a* early on the morrow	1Sa 5:4	7925
And they *a* early	1Sa 9:26	7925
And Saul *a*, and they went out both	1Sa 9:26	6965
And Samuel *a*, and gat him up from	1Sa 13:15	6965
when he *a* against me, I caught	1Sa 17:35	6965
to pass, when the Philistine *a*	1Sa 17:48	6965
the men of Israel and of Judah *a*	1Sa 17:52	6965
Wherefore David *a* and went, he and	1Sa 18:27	6965
and Jonathan *a*, and Abner sat by	1Sa 20:25	6965
So Jonathan *a* from the table in	1Sa 20:34	6965
David *a* out of a place toward the	1Sa 20:41	6965
And he *a* and departed	1Sa 20:42	6965
And David *a*, and fled that day for	1Sa 21:10	6965
which were about six hundred, *a*	1Sa 23:13	6965
And Jonathan Saul's son *a*, and went	1Sa 23:16	6965
And they *a*, and went to Ziph before	1Sa 23:24	6965
Then David *a*, and cut off the	1Sa 24:4	6965
David also *a* afterward, and went	1Sa 24:8	6965
And David *a*, and went down to the	1Sa 25:1	6965
And she *a*, and bowed herself on her	1Sa 25:41	6965
And Abigail hasted, and *a*, and rode	1Sa 25:42	6965
Then Saul *a*, and went down to the	1Sa 26:2	6965
And David *a*, and came to the place	1Sa 26:5	6965

And David *a*, and he passed over	1Sa 27:2	6965
So he *a* from the earth, and sat	1Sa 28:23	6965
All the valiant men *a*, and went	1Sa 31:12	6965
Then there *a* and went over by	2Sa 2:15	6965
And David *a*, and went with all the	2Sa 6:2	6965
that David *a* from off his bed, and	2Sa 11:2	6965
And the elders of his house *a*	2Sa 12:17	6965
Then David *a* from the earth, and	2Sa 12:20	6965
Then all the king's sons *a*	2Sa 13:29	6965
Then the king *a*, and tare his	2Sa 13:31	6965
So Joab *a* and went to Geshur, and	2Sa 14:23	6965
Then Joab *a*, and came to Absalom	2Sa 14:31	6965
So he *a*, and went to Hebron	2Sa 15:9	6965
Then David *a*, and all the people	2Sa 17:22	6965
he saddled his ass, and *a*	2Sa 17:23	6965
Then the king *a*, and sat in the	2Sa 19:8	6965
He *a*, and smote the Philistines	2Sa 23:10	6965
feared because of Solomon, and *a*	1Kin 1:50	6965
And Shimei *a*, and saddled his ass,	1Kin 2:40	6965
she *a* at midnight, and took my son	1Kin 3:20	6965
he *a* from before the altar of the	1Kin 8:54	6965
they *a* out of Midian, and came to	1Kin 11:18	6965
And Jeroboam *a*, and fled into Egypt	1Kin 11:40	6965
And Jeroboam's wife did so, and	1Kin 14:4	6965
And Jeroboam's wife *a*, and departed	1Kin 14:17	6965
So he *a* and went to Zarephath	1Kin 17:10	6965
And when he saw that, he *a*	1Kin 19:3	6965
And he *a*, and did eat and drink, and	1Kin 19:8	6965
Then he *a*, and went after Elijah,	1Kin 19:21	6965
And he *a*, and went down with him	2Kin 1:15	6965
And he *a*, and followed her	2Kin 4:30	6965
Wherefore they *a* and fled in the	2Kin 7:7	6965
the king *a* in the night, and said	2Kin 7:12	6965
And the woman *a*, and did after the	2Kin 8:2	6965
And he *a*, and went into the house	2Kin 9:6	6965
And he *a* and departed, and came to	2Kin 10:12	6965
saw that her son was dead, she *a*	2Kin 11:1	6965
And his servants *a*, and made a	2Kin 12:20	6965
when they *a* early in the morning,	2Kin 19:35	7925
neither after him *a* there any	2Kin 23:25	6965
and the captains of the armies, *a*	2Kin 25:26	6965
They *a*, all the valiant men, and	1Chr 10:12	6965
that there *a* war at Gezer with	1Chr 20:4	5975
saw that her son was dead, she *a*	2Chr 22:10	6965
Then the Levites *a*, Mahath the	2Chr 29:12	6965
And they *a* took away the altars	2Chr 30:14	6965
Then the priests the Levites *a*	2Chr 30:27	6965
of the LORD *a* against his people	2Chr 36:16	5927
I *a* up from my heaviness	Ezr 9:5	6965
Then *a* Ezra, and made the chief	Ezr 10:5	6965
I *a* in the night, I and some few	Neh 2:12	6965
So Esther *a*, and stood before the	Est 8:4	6965
Then Job *a*, and rent his mantle,	Job 1:20	6965
I *a*, and they spake against me	Job 19:18	6965
and the aged *a*, and stood up	Job 29:8	6965
When God *a* to judgment, to save	Ps 76:9	6965
hasteth to his place where he *a*	Eccl 1:5	2224
when they *a* early in the morning,	Is 37:36	2224
Then *a* Ishmael the son of	Jer 41:2	6965
Then I *a*, and went forth into the	Eze 3:23	6965
Then the king *a* very early in the	Dan 6:19	6966
So Jonah *a*, and went unto Nineveh,	Jonah 3:3	6965
he *a* from his throne, and he laid	Jonah 3:6	6965
When he *a*, he took the young	Mt 2:14	1453
And he *a*, and took the young child	Mt 2:21	1453
and she *a*, and ministered unto them	Mt 8:15	1453
there *a* a great tempest in the	Mt 8:24	1096
Then he *a*, and rebuked the winds	Mt 8:26	1453
And he *a*, and departed to his house	Mt 9:7	1453
And he *a*, and followed him	Mt 9:9	450
And Jesus *a*, and followed him, and	Mt 9:19	1453
her by the hand, and the maid *a*	Mt 9:25	1453
Then all those virgins *a*, and	Mt 25:7	1453
And the high priest *a*, and said	Mt 26:62	450
of the saints which slept *a*	Mt 27:52	1453
And immediately he *a*, took up the	Mk 2:12	1453
And he *a* and followed him	Mk 2:14	450
there *a* a great storm of wind, and	Mk 4:37	1096
And he *a*, and rebuked the wind, and	Mk 4:39	1326
And straightway the damsel *a*	Mk 5:42	450
And from thence he *a*, and went into	Mk 7:24	450
and he *a*	Mk 9:27	450
he *a* from thence, and cometh into	Mk 10:1	450
there *a* a certain, and bare false	Mk 14:57	450
Mary *a* in those days, and went	Lk 1:39	450
he *a* out of the synagogue, and	Lk 4:38	450
and immediately she *a* and	Lk 4:39	450
And he *a* and stood forth	Lk 6:8	450
and when the flood *a*, the stream	Lk 6:48	1096
Then he *a*, and rebuked the wind and	Lk 8:24	1453
came again, and she *a* straightway	Lk 8:55	450

Then there *a* a reasoning among	Lk 9:46	1525
there *a* a mighty famine in that	Lk 15:14	1096
And he *a*, and came to his father	Lk 15:20	450
And the whole multitude of them *a*	Lk 23:1	450
Then a Peter, and ran unto the	Lk 24:12	450
Then there *a* a question between	Jn 3:25	1096
the sea *a* by reason of a great	Jn 6:18	1326
she *a* quickly, and came unto him	Jn 11:29	1453
And the young men *a*, wound him up,	Acts 5:6	450
there *a* a murmuring of the	Acts 6:1	1096
Then there *a* a certain of the	Acts 6:9	450
Till another king *a*, which knew	Acts 7:18	450
And he *a* and went	Acts 8:27	450
And Saul *a* from the earth	Acts 9:8	1453
he received sight forthwith, and *a*	Acts 9:18	450
And he *a* immediately	Acts 9:34	450
Then Peter *a* and went with them	Acts 9:39	450
upon the persecution that *a* about	Acts 11:19	1096
the same time there *a* no small	Acts 19:23	1096
there *a* a dissension between the	Acts 23:7	1096
And there *a* a great cry	Acts 23:9	1096
were of the Pharisees' part *a*	Acts 23:9	450
when there *a* a great dissension,	Acts 23:10	1096
But not long after there *a*	Acts 27:14	906
there *a* a smoke out of the pit,	Rev 9:2	305

ARPAD (ar'-pad) *A city near Hamath.*

are the gods of Hamath, and of *A*	2Kin 18:34	774
king of Hamath, and the king of *A*	2Kin 19:13	774
is not Hamath as *A*	Is 10:9	774
Hamath is confounded, and *A*	Jer 49:23	774

ARPHAD (ar'-fad) *See* ARPAD. *Same as Arpad.*

Where are the gods of Hamath and *A*	Is 36:19	774
king of Hamath, and the king of *A*	Is 37:13	774

ARPHAXAD

Elam, and Asshur, and *A*, and Lud,	Gen 10:22	775
And *A* begat Salah	Gen 10:24	775
begat *A* two years after the flood	Gen 11:10	775
he begat *A* five hundred years,	Gen 11:11	775
A lived five and thirty years, and	Gen 11:12	775
A lived after he begat Salah four	Gen 11:13	775
Elam, and Asshur, and *A*, and Lud,	1Chr 1:17	775
A begat Shelah, and Shelah begat	1Chr 1:18	775
Shem, *A*, Shelah,	1Chr 1:24	775
of Cainan, which was the son of *A*	Lk 3:36	742

ARRAY

a to fight against them at Gibeah	Judg 20:20	6186
set their battle again in *a* in	Judg 20:22	6186
put themselves in *a* the first day	Judg 20:22	6186
themselves in *a* against Gibeah	Judg 20:30	6186
put themselves in *a* at Baal-tamar	Judg 20:33	6186
themselves in *a* against Israel	1Sa 4:2	6186
set the battle in *a* against the	1Sa 17:2	6186
come out to set your battle in *a*	1Sa 17:8	6186
had put the battle in *a*, army	1Sa 17:21	6186
put the battle in *a* at the	2Sa 10:8	6186
put them in *a* against the Syrians	2Sa 10:9	6186
that he might put them in *a*	2Sa 10:10	6186
set themselves in *a* against David	2Sa 10:17	6186
his servants, Set yourselves in *a*	1Kin 20:12	
themselves in *a* against the city	1Kin 20:12	
put the battle in *a* before the	1Chr 19:9	6186
put them in *a* against the Syrians	1Chr 19:10	6186
they set themselves in *a* against	1Chr 19:11	6186
set the battle in *a* against them	1Chr 19:17	6186
battle in *a* against the Syrians	1Chr 19:17	6186
Abijah set the battle in *a* with	2Chr 13:3	631
a against him with eight hundred	2Chr 13:3	6186
they set the battle in *a* in the	2Chr 14:10	6186
that they may *a* the man withal	Est 6:9	3847
do set themselves in *a* against me	Job 6:4	6186
a thyself with glory and beauty	Job 40:10	3847
set themselves in *a* at the gate	Is 22:7	7896
set in *a* as men for war against	Jer 6:23	6186
he shall *a* himself with the land	Jer 43:12	5844
set themselves in *a* against her	Jer 50:9	6186
Put yourselves in *a* against	Jer 50:14	6186
upon horses, every one put in *a*	Jer 50:42	6186
a strong people set in battle *a*	Joel 2:5	6186
or gold, or pearls, or costly *a*	1Ti 2:9	2441

ARRAYED

a him in vestures of fine linen,	Gen 41:42	3847
being *a* in white linen, having	2Chr 5:12	3847
a them, and shod them, and gave	2Chr 28:15	3847
a Mordecai, and brought him on	Est 6:11	3847
glory was not *a* like one of these	Mt 6:29	4016
glory was not *a* like one of these	Lk 12:27	4016
a him in a gorgeous robe, and sent	Lk 23:11	4016
a in royal apparel, sat upon his	Acts 12:21	1746

these which are *a* in white robes .... Rev 7:13   4016
And the woman was *a* in purple .... Rev 17:4   4016
she should be *a* in fine linen .... Rev 19:8   4016

ARRIVED
they *a* at the country of the .... Lk 8:26   2668
and the next day we *a* at Samos .... Acts 20:15   3846

ARROGANCY
let not *a* come out of your mouth 1Sa 2:3   6277
pride, and *a*, and the evil way, and .... Prov 8:13   1347
I will cause the *a* of the proud .... Is 13:11   1347
proud) his loftiness, and his *a* .... Jer 48:29   1347

ARROW
lad ran, he shot an *a* beyond him 1Sa 20:36   2678
of the *a* which Jonathan had shot 1Sa 20:37   2678
and said, Is not the *a* beyond thee 1Sa 20:37   2678
the *a* went out at his heart, and 2Kin 9:24   2678
The *a* of the LORD's deliverance, ... 2Kin 13:17   2671
the *a* of deliverance from Syria 2Kin 13:17   2671
this city, nor shoot an *a* there 2Kin 19:32   2671
The *a* cannot make him flee .... Job 41:28   1121,7198
ready their *a* upon the string .... Ps 11:2   2671
God shall shoot at them with an *a* .... Ps 64:7   2671
nor for the *a* that flieth by day .... Ps 91:5   2671
a maul, and a sword, and a sharp *a* ...... Prov 25:18   2671
this city, nor shoot an *a* there .... Is 37:33   2671
Their tongue is as an *a* shot out .... Jer 9:8   2671
and set me as a mark for the *a* .... Lam 3:12   2671
his *a* shall go forth as the .... Zec 9:14   2671

ARROWS
and pierce them through with his *a* .... Num 24:8   2671
I will spend mine *a* upon them .... Deut 32:23   2671
will make mine *a* drunk with blood .... Deut 32:42   2671
I will shoot three *a* on the side 1Sa 20:20   2671
a lad, saying, Go, find out the *a* 1Sa 20:21   2671
the *a* are on this side of thee, ... 1Sa 20:21   2671
Behold, the *a* are beyond thee 1Sa 20:22   2671
find out now the *a* which I shoot 1Sa 20:36   2671
Jonathan's lad gathered up the *a* 1Sa 20:38   2671
And he sent out *a*, and scattered 2Sa 22:15   2671
said unto him, Take bow and *a* 2Kin 13:15   2671
And he took unto him bow and *a* 2Kin 13:15   2671
And he said, Take the *a* 2Kin 13:18   2671
shooting *a* out of a bow, even of 1Chr 12:2   2671
and upon the bulwarks, to shoot *a* 2Chr 26:15   2671
For the *a* of the Almighty are .... Job 6:4   2671
he ordaineth his *a* against the .... Ps 7:13   2671
Yea, he sent out his *a*, and .... Ps 18:14   2671
thou shalt make ready thine *a* .... Ps 21:12
For thine *a* stick fast in me, and .... Ps 38:2   2671
Thine *a* are sharp in the heart of .... Ps 45:5   2671
men, whose teeth are spears and *a* .... Ps 57:4   2671
he bendeth his bow to shoot his *a* .... Ps 58:7   2671
bend their bow to shoot their *a* .... Ps 64:3   2671
There brake he the *a* of the bow .... Ps 76:3   7565
thine *a* also went abroad .... Ps 77:17   2687
Sharp *a* of the mighty, with coals .... Ps 120:4   2671
As *a* are in the hand of a mighty .... Ps 127:4   2671
shoot out thine *a*, and destroy .... Ps 144:6   2671
mad man who casteth firebrands, *a* ...... Prov 26:18   2671
Whose *a* are sharp, and all their .... Is 5:28   2671
With a *a* and with bows shall men .... Is 7:24   2671
their *a* shall be as of a mighty .... Jer 50:9   2671
the bow, shoot at her, spare no *a* .... Jer 50:14   2671
Make bright the *a* .... Jer 51:11   1121
He hath caused the *a* of his .... Lam 3:13   2671
upon them the evil *a* of famine .... Eze 5:16   2671
he made his *a* bright, he .... Eze 21:21   2671
will cause thine *a* to fall out of .... Eze 39:3   2671
the bucklers, the bows and the *a* .... Eze 39:9   2671
at the light of thine *a* they went .... Hab 3:11   2671

ART See APPENDIX.

ARTAXERXES (ar-tax-erx'-ees) See ARTAXERXES'.
   1. A Persian king known as Longimanus.
And in the days of *A* wrote Bishlam ...... Ezr 4:7   783
companions, unto *A* king of Persia .... Ezr 4:7   783
to *A* the king in this sort .... Ezr 4:8   783
unto him, even unto *A* the king .... Ezr 4:11   783
   2. A Persian king known as Cambyses.
and Darius, and *A* king of Persia .... Ezr 6:14   783
   3. A Persian king known as Darius.
in the reign of *A* king of Persia .... Ezr 7:1   783
in the seventh year of *A* the king .... Ezr 7:7   783
king *A* gave unto Ezra the priest .... Ezr 7:11   783
A, king of kings, unto Ezra .... Ezr 7:12   783
even I *A* the king, do make a .... Ezr 7:21   783
in the reign of *A* the king .... Ezr 8:1   783
the twentieth year of *A* the king .... Neh 2:1   783

and thirtieth year of *A* the king .... Neh 5:14   783
thirtieth year of *A* king of .... Neh 13:6   783

ARTAXERXES' (ar-tax-erx'-eez) Refers to Artaxerxes 1.
Now when the copy of king *A* .... Ezr 4:23   783

ARTEMAS (ar'-te-mas) A companion of Paul.
When I shall send *A* unto thee .... Titus 3:12   734

ARTEMIS See DIANA.

ARTIFICER
an instructer of every *a* in brass .... Gen 4:22   2794
the counsellor, and the cunning *a* .... Is 3:3   2796

ARTIFICERS
work to be made by the hands of *a* 1Chr 29:5   2796
Even to the *a* and builders gave 2Chr 34:11   2796

ARTILLERY
Jonathan gave his *a* unto his lad 1Sa 20:40   3627

ARTS
a brought their books together .... Acts 19:19   4021

ARUBBOTH See ARUBOTH.

ARUBOTH (ar'-u-both) A district of Solomon's rule.
The son of Hesed, in *A* 1Kin 4:10   700

ARUMAH (a-ru'-mah) A place in Ephraim.
And Abimelech dwelt at *A* .... Judg 9:41   725

ARVAD (ar'-vad) See ARVADITE. An island near Zidon.
of Zidon and *A* were thy mariners .... Eze 27:8   719
The men of *A* with thine army were ...... Eze 27:11   719

ARVADITE (ar'-vad-ite) Descendants of Canaan.
And the *A*, and the Zemarite, and the .... Gen 10:18   721
And the *A*, and the Zemarite, and the.... 1Chr 1:16   721

ARVADITES See ARVADITE.

ARZA (ar'-zah) A steward of King Elah of Israel.
himself drunk in the house of *A* 1Kin 16:9   777

AS See APPENDIX.

ASA (a'-sah) See ASA'S.
   1. A king of Judah.
A his son reigned in his stead 1Kin 15:8   609
of Israel reigned *A* over Judah 1Kin 15:9   609
A did that which was right in the 1Kin 15:11   609
A destroyed her idol, and burnt it 1Kin 15:13   609
And there was war between *A* 1Kin 15:16   609
out or come in to *A* king of Judah 1Kin 15:17   609
Then *A* took all the silver and the 1Kin 15:18   609
king *A* sent them to Ben-hadad, ... 1Kin 15:18   609
Ben-hadad hearkened unto king *A* 1Kin 15:20   609
Then king *A* made a proclamation 1Kin 15:22   609
king *A* built with them Geba of 1Kin 15:22   609
The rest of all the acts of *A* 1Kin 15:23   609
A slept with his fathers, and was 1Kin 15:24   609
second year of *A* king of Judah 1Kin 15:25   609
Even in the third year of *A* king 1Kin 15:28   609
And there was war between *A* 1Kin 15:32   609
In the third year of *A* king of 1Kin 15:33   609
sixth year of *A* king of Judah 1Kin 16:8   609
seventh year of *A* king of Judah 1Kin 16:10   609
seventh year of *A* king of Judah 1Kin 16:15   609
first year of *A* king of Judah 1Kin 16:23   609
eighth year of *A* king of Judah 1Kin 16:29   609
Jehoshaphat the son of *A* began to 1Kin 22:41   609
in all the ways of *A* his father 1Kin 22:43   609
in the days of his father *A* 1Kin 22:46   609
A his son, Jehoshaphat his son, ... 1Chr 3:10   609
A his son reigned in his stead 2Chr 14:1   609
A did that which was good and 2Chr 14:2   609
A had an army of men that bare 2Chr 14:8   609
Then *A* went out against him, and 2Chr 14:10   609
A cried unto the LORD his God, and 2Chr 14:11   609
smote the Ethiopians before *A* 2Chr 14:12   609
And *A* and the people that were with 2Chr 14:13   609
And he went out to meet *A*, and said 2Chr 15:2   609
and said unto him, Hear ye me, *A* 2Chr 15:2   609
when *A* heard these words, and the 2Chr 15:8   609
fifteenth year of the reign of *A* 2Chr 15:10   609
Maachah the mother of the king 2Chr 15:16   609
A cut down her idol, and stamped 2Chr 15:16   609
of *A* was perfect all his days 2Chr 15:17   609
thirtieth year of the reign of *A* 2Chr 15:19   609
A Baasha king of Israel came up 2Chr 16:1   609
out or come in to *A* king of Judah 2Chr 16:1   609
Then *A* brought out silver and gold 2Chr 16:2   609
Ben-hadad hearkened unto king *A* 2Chr 16:4   609
Then *A* the king took all Judah 2Chr 16:6   609
the seer came to *A* king of Judah 2Chr 16:7   609
Then *A* was wroth with the seer, ... 2Chr 16:10   609
A oppressed some of the people 2Chr 16:10   609

And, behold, the acts of *A* 2Chr 16:11 609
A in the thirty and ninth year of 2Chr 16:12 609
A slept with his fathers, and died 2Chr 16:13 609
which *A* his father had taken................2Chr 17:2 609
walked in the way of *A* his father 2Chr 20:32 609
in the ways of *A* king of Judah...............2Chr 21:12 609
was it which *A* the king had made ....Jer 41:9 609
and Abia begat *A* ....Mt 1:7 760
And *A* begat Josaphat ....Mt 1:8 760
   2. Chief of a Levite family.
and Berechiah the son of *A* 1Chr 9:16 609

ASAHEL (*as'-a-hel*)
   1. The son of Zeruiah, David's sister.
there, Joab, and Abishai, and *A* 2Sa 2:18 760
A was as light of foot as a wild 2Sa 2:18 6214
And *A* pursued after Abner 2Sa 2:19 6214
behind him, and said, Art thou *A* 2Sa 2:20 6214
But *A* would not turn aside from 2Sa 2:21 6214
And Abner said again to *A*, Turn 2Sa 2:22 6214
to the place where *A* fell down 2Sa 2:23 6214
servants nineteen men and *A* 2Sa 2:30 6214
And they took up *A*, and buried him 2Sa 2:32 6214
for the blood of *A* his brother 2Sa 3:27 6214
brother *A* at Gibeon in the battle 2Sa 3:30 6214
A the brother of Joab was one of 2Sa 23:24 6214
Abishai, and Joab, and, *A*, three............1Chr 2:16 6214
A the brother of Joab, Elhanan 1Chr 11:26 6214
month was *A* the brother of Joab 1Chr 27:7 6214
   2. A Levite teacher.
and Nethaniah, and Zebadiah, and *A*....2Chr 17:8 6214
   3. A Levite officer.
and Azaziah, and Nahath, and *A*..........2Chr 31:13 6214
   4. Father of Jonathan.
Only Jonathan the son of *A*....................Ezr 10:15 6214

ASAHIAH (*as-a-hi'-ah*) See ASAIAH. *An officer of King Josiah.*
A a servant of the king's, saying 2Kin 22:12 6222
and Achbor, and Shaphan, and *A* 2Kin 22:14 6222

ASAIAH (*as-a'-yah*)
   1. A descendant of Simeon.
and Jaakobah, and Jeshohaiah, and *A* .. 1Chr 4:36 6222
   2. A descendant of Libni.
son, Haggiah his son, *A* his son............1Chr 6:30 6222
   3. A Shilonite of Jerusalem.
A the firstborn, and his sons..................1Chr 9:5 6222
   4. A descendant of Merari.
A the chief, and his brethren two 1Chr 15:6 6222
and for the Levites, for Uriel, *A*..............1Chr 15:11 6222
   5. Same as Asahiah.
A a servant of the king's, saying............2Chr 34:20 6222

ASAPH (*a'-saf*) See ASAPH'S.
   1. Father of Joah.
and Joah the son of *A* the recorder 2Kin 18:18 623
and Joah the son of *A* the recorder 2Kin 18:37 623
the scribe, and Joah, the son of *A* ....Is 36:22 623
   2. A musician of David and Solomon.
And his brother *A*, who stood in 1Chr 6:39 623
even *A* the son of Berachiah, the 1Chr 6:39 623
brethren, the son of Berechiah 1Chr 15:17 623
So the singers, Heman, *A*, and 1Chr 15:19 623
A the chief, and next to him 1Chr 16:5 623
but *A* made a sound with cymbals 1Chr 16:5 623
thank the LORD into the hand of *A* 1Chr 16:7 623
ark of the covenant of the LORD 1Chr 16:37 623
to the service of the sons of *A* 1Chr 25:1 623
Of the sons of *A*..................................1Chr 25:2 623
of Asaph under the hands of *A* 1Chr 25:2 623
to the king's order to *A*,........................1Chr 25:6 623
lot came forth for *A* to Joseph 1Chr 25:9 623
the singers, all of them of *A* 2Chr 5:12 623
a Levite of the sons of *A* 2Chr 20:14 623
and of the sons of *A* 2Chr 29:13 623
words of David, and of *A* the seer 2Chr 29:30 623
the sons of *A* were in their place 2Chr 35:15 623
to the commandment of David, and *A*....2Chr 35:15 623
the children of *A*, an hundred ....Ezr 2:41 623
the sons of *A* with cymbals ....Ezr 3:10 623
the children of *A*, an hundred ....Neh 7:44 623
the son of Zabdi, the son of *A* ....Neh 11:17 623
Of the sons of *A*, the singers ....Neh 11:22 623
the son of Zaccur, the son of *A*..............Neh 12:35 623
A of old there were chief of the ....Neh 12:46 623
A Psalm of *A* ....Ps 50:*t* 623
A Psalm of *A* ....Ps 73:*t* 623
Maschil of *A* ....Ps 74:*t* 623
Altaschith, A Psalm or Song of *A* ....Ps 75:*t* 623
on Neginoth, A Psalm or Song of *A* ....Ps 76:*t* 623
to Jeduthun, A Psalm of *A* ....Ps 77:*t* 623
Maschil of *A* ....Ps 78:*t* 623

A Psalm of *A* ....Ps 79:*t* 623
Shoshannim-Eduth, A Psalm of *A* ....Ps 80:*t* 623
upon Gittith, A Psalm of *A*.....................Ps 81:*t* 623
A Psalm of *A* ....Ps 82:*t* 623
A Song or Psalm of *A* ....Ps 83:*t* 623
   3. A Levite family in post-exilic Jerusalem.
the son of Zichri, the son of *A* 1Chr 9:15 623
   4. Descendants of Merari.
the son of Kore, of the sons of *A* 1Chr 26:1 623
   5. A Persian official.
a letter unto *A* the keeper of the ....Neh 2:8 623

ASAPH'S (*a'-safs*) Refers to Asaph 1.
and Joah, *A* son, the recorder ....Is 36:3 623

ASAREEL (*a-sar'-e-el*) *A son of Jehaleleel.*
Ziph, and Ziphah, Tiria, and *A* 1Chr 4:16 840

ASARELAH (*as-a-re'-lah*) See JESHABELAH. *A son of a musician of David.*
and Joseph, and Nethaniah, and *A* 1Chr 25:2 841

ASA'S (*a'-sahz*) Refers to Asa 1.
nevertheless *A* heart was perfect............1Kin 15:14 609

ASCEND
the people shall *a* up every man............Josh 6:5 5927
Who shall *a* into the hill of the ....Ps 24:3 5927
He causeth the vapours to *a* from ....Ps 135:7 5927
If I *a* up into heaven, thou art ....Ps 139:8 5927
I will *a* into heaven, I will.......................Is 14:13 5927
I will *a* above the heights of the ....Is 14:14 5927
he causeth the vapors to *a* from ....Jer 10:13 5927
he causeth the vapors to *a* from ....Jer 51:16 5927
Thou shalt *a* and come like a storm ....Eze 38:9 5927
of man *a* up where he was before ....Jn 6:62 305
I *a* unto my Father, and your ....Jn 20:17 305
heart, Who shall *a* into heaven. ....Rom 10:6 305
shall *a* out of the bottomless pit ....Rev 17:8 305

ASCENDED
the smoke thereof *a* as the smoke ....Ex 19:18 5927
they *a* by the south, and came unto ....Num 13:22 5927
smoke of the city *a* up to heaven ....Josh 8:20 5927
and that the smoke of the city *a* ....Josh 8:21 5927
So Joshua *a* from Gilgal, he, and..........Josh 10:7 5927
a up on the south side unto ....Josh 15:3 5927
LORD *a* in the flame of the altar ....Judg 13:20 5927
flame of the city *a* up to heaven ....Judg 20:40 5927
Thou hast *a* on high, thou hast............Ps 68:18 5927
Who hath *a* up into heaven, or ....Prov 30:4 5927
no man hath *a* up to heaven, but ....Jn 3:13 305
for I am not yet *a* to my Father ....Jn 20:17 305
David is not *a* into the heavens.............Acts 2:34 305
after three days he *a* from.....................Acts 25:1 305
When he *a* up on high, he led..............Eph 4:8 305
(Now that he *a*, what is it but ....Eph 4:9 305
that *a* up far above all heavens ....Eph 4:10 305
a up before God out of the ....Rev 8:4 305
they *a* up to heaven in a cloud ....Rev 11:12 305

ASCENDETH
the beast that *a* out of the.....................Rev 11:7 305
of their torment *a* up for ever ....Rev 14:11 305

ASCENDING
and behold the angels of God *a* ....Gen 28:12 5927
I saw gods *a* out of the earth.................1Sa 28:13 5927
he went before, *a* up to Jerusalem.........Lk 19:28 305
open, and the angels of God *a* ....Jn 1:51 305
saw another angel *a* from the east ....Rev 7:2 305

ASCENT
the south to the *a* of Akrabbim ....Num 34:4 4608
went up by the *a* of mount Olivet 2Sa 15:30 4608
his *a* by which he went up unto 1Kin 10:5 5930
his *a* by which he went up into 2Chr 9:4 5944

ASCRIBE
a ye greatness unto our God..................Deut 32:3 3051
will *a* righteousness to my Maker ....Job 36:3 5414
A ye strength unto God ....Ps 68:34 5414

ASCRIBED
They have *a* unto David ten 1Sa 18:8 5414
to me they have *a* but thousands...........1Sa 18:8 5414

ASENATH (*as'-e-nath*) *A great-grandson of Solomon.*
he gave him to wife *A* the......................Gen 41:45 621
came, which *A* the daughter of ....Gen 41:50 621
Ephraim, which *A* the daughter of ....Gen 46:20 621

ASER (*a'-sur*) See ASHER. *Greek form of Asher.*
of Phanuel, of the tribe of *A* ....Lk 2:36 768
Of the tribe of *A* were sealed ....Rev 7:6 768

ASH
he planteth an *a*, and the rain ....Is 44:14 766

ASHAMED

man and his wife, and were not *a*	Gen 2:25	954
should she not be *a* seven days	Num 12:14	3637
And they tarried till they were *a*	Judg 3:25	954
because the men were greatly *a*	2Sa 10:5	3637
as people being *a* steal away when	2Sa 19:3	3637
when they urged him till he was *a*	2Kin 2:17	954
stedfastly, until he was *a*	2Kin 8:11	954
for the men were greatly *a*	1Chr 19:5	3637
the priests and the Levites were *a*	2Chr 30:15	3637
For I was *a* to require of the	Ezr 8:22	954
And said, O my God, I am *a*	Ezr 9:6	954
they came thither, and were *a*	Job 6:20	2659
mockest, shall no man make thee *a*	Job 11:3	3637
ye are not *a* that ye make	Job 19:3	954
Let all mine enemies be *a*	Ps 6:10	954
let them return and be *a* suddenly	Ps 6:10	954
let me not be *a*, let not mine	Ps 25:2	954
let none that wait on thee be *a*	Ps 25:3	954
let them be *a* which transgress	Ps 25:3	954
let me not be *a*	Ps 25:20	954
let me never be *a*	Ps 31:1	954
Let me not be *a*, O LORD	Ps 31:17	954
let the wicked be *a*, and let them	Ps 31:17	954
and their faces were not *a*	Ps 34:5	2659
Let them be *a* and brought to	Ps 35:26	954
shall not be *a* in the evil time	Ps 37:19	954
Let them be *a* and confounded	Ps 40:14	954
GOD of hosts, be *a* for my sake	Ps 69:6	954
Let them be *a* and confounded that	Ps 70:2	954
O let not the oppressed return *a*	Ps 74:21	3637
which hate me may see it, and be *a*	Ps 86:17	954
when they arise, let them be *a*	Ps 109:28	954
Then shall I not be *a*, when I	Ps 119:6	954
before kings, and will not be *a*	Ps 119:46	954
Let the proud be *a*	Ps 119:78	954
that I be not *a*	Ps 119:80	954
and let me not be *a* of my hope	Ps 119:116	954
they shall not be *a*, but they	Ps 127:5	954
but she that maketh *a* is as	Prov 12:4	954
For they shall be *a* of the oaks	Is 1:29	954
a of Ethiopia their expectation,	Is 20:5	954
Be thou *a*, O Zidon	Is 23:4	954
shall be confounded, and the sun *a*	Is 24:23	954
be *a* for their envy at the people	Is 26:11	954
Jacob, Jacob shall not now be *a*	Is 29:22	954
They were all *a* of a people that	Is 30:5	954
Lebanon is *a* and hewn down	Is 33:9	2659
incensed against thee shall be *a*	Is 41:11	954
back, they shall be greatly *a*	Is 42:17	954
that they may be *a*	Is 44:9	954
all his fellows shall be *a*	Is 44:11	954
fear, and they shall be *a* together	Is 44:11	954
They shall be *a*, and also	Is 45:16	954
ye shall not be *a* nor confounded	Is 45:17	954
incensed against him shall be *a*	Is 45:24	954
shall not be *a* that wait for me	Is 49:23	954
and I know that I shall not be *a*	Is 50:7	954
for thou shalt not be *a*	Is 54:4	954
shall rejoice, but ye shall be *a*	Is 65:13	954
to your joy, and they shall be *a*	Is 66:5	954
As the thief is *a* when he is	Jer 2:26	1322
so is the house of Israel *a*	Jer 2:26	954
thou also shalt be *a* of Egypt	Jer 2:36	954
as thou wast *a* of Assyria	Jer 2:36	954
forehead, thou refusedst to be *a*	Jer 3:3	3637
Were they *a* when they had	Jer 6:15	954
nay, they were not at all *a*	Jer 6:15	954
The wise men are *a*, they are	Jer 8:9	954
Were they *a* when they had	Jer 8:12	954
nay, they were not at all *a*	Jer 8:12	954
they shall be *a* of your revenues	Jer 12:13	954
they were *a* and confounded, and	Jer 14:3	954
in the earth, the plowmen were *a*	Jer 14:4	954
she hath been *a* and confounded	Jer 15:9	954
all that forsake thee shall be *a*	Jer 17:13	954
they shall be greatly *a*	Jer 20:11	954
surely then shalt thou be *a*	Jer 22:22	954
I was *a*, yea, even confounded,	Jer 31:19	954
And Moab shall be *a* of Chemosh	Jer 48:13	954
as the house of Israel was *a* of	Jer 48:13	954
she that bare you shall be *a*	Jer 50:12	2659
which are *a* of thy lewd way	Eze 16:27	3637
shalt remember thy ways, and be *a*	Eze 16:61	3637
terror they are *a* of their might	Eze 32:30	954
be *a* and confounded for your own	Eze 36:32	954
that they may be *a* of their	Eze 43:10	3637
if they be *a* of all that they	Eze 43:11	3637
they shall be *a* because of their	Hos 4:19	954
Israel shall be *a* of his own	Hos 10:6	954
Be ye *a*, O ye husbandmen	Joel 1:11	954

and my people shall never be *a*	Joel 2:26	954
and my people shall never be *a*	Joel 2:27	954
Then shall the seers be *a*	Mic 3:7	954
thou not be *a* for all thy doings	Zeph 3:11	954
for her expectation shall be *a*	Zec 9:5	954
be *a* every one of his vision	Zec 13:4	954
therefore shall be *a* of me	Mk 8:38	1870
also shall the Son of man be *a*	Mk 8:38	1870
For whosoever shall be *a* of me	Lk 9:26	1870
of him shall the Son of man be *a*	Lk 9:26	1870
all his adversaries were *a*	Lk 13:17	2617
to beg I am *a*	Lk 16:3	153
For I am not *a* of the gospel of	Rom 1:16	1870
And hope maketh not *a*	Rom 5:5	2617
those things whereof ye are now *a*	Rom 6:21	1870
believeth on him shall not be *a*	Rom 9:33	2617
believeth on him shall not be *a*	Rom 10:11	2617
thing to him of you, I am not *a*	2Cor 7:14	2617
ye) should be *a* in this same	2Cor 9:4	2617
destruction, I should not be *a*	2Cor 10:8	153
that in nothing I shall be *a*	Phil 1:20	153
with him, that he may be *a*	2Th 3:14	1788
Be not thou therefore *a* of the	2Ti 1:8	1870
nevertheless I am not *a*	2Ti 1:12	1870
me, and was not *a* of my chain	2Ti 1:16	1870
workman that needeth not to be *a*	2Ti 2:15	422
is of the contrary part may be *a*	Titus 2:8	1788
he is not *a* to call them brethren	Heb 2:11	1870
wherefore God is not *a* to be	Heb 11:16	1870
they may be *a* that falsely accuse	1Pet 3:16	2617
as a Christian, let him not be *a*	1Pet 4:16	153
not be *a* before him at his coming	1Jn 2:28	153

ASHAN (a'-shan) See CHOR-ASHAN. *A Levitical city in Judah.*

Libnah, and Ether, and A,	Josh 15:42	6228
Ain, Remmon, and Ether, and A	Josh 19:7	6228
and Ain, Rimmon, and Tochen, and A	1Chr 4:32	6228
And A with her suburbs, and	1Chr 6:59	6228

ASHARELAH See ASARELAH.

ASHBEA (ash'-be-ah) *Descendants of Shelah.*

fine linen, of the house of A	1Chr 4:21	791

ASHBEL (ash'-bel) See ASHBELITES. *A son of Benjamin.*

were Belah, and Becher, and A	Gen 46:21	788
of A, the family of the	Num 26:38	788
A the second, and Aharah the third	1Chr 8:1	788

ASHBELITES (ash'-bel-ites) *Descendants of Ashbel.*

of Ashbel, the family of the A	Num 26:38	789

ASHCHENAZ (ash'-ke-naz) See ASHKENAZ.
  1. *A son of Gomer.*

A, and Riphath, and Togarmah	1Chr 1:6	813

  2. *A tribe near Armenia.*

kingdoms of Ararat, Minni, and A	Jer 51:27	813

ASHDOD (ash'-dod) See ASHDODITES, AZOTUS. *A Philistine city.*

only in Gaza, in Gath, and in A	Josh 11:22	795
unto the sea, all that lay near A	Josh 15:46	795
A with her towns and her villages,	Josh 15:47	795
brought it from Eben-ezer unto A	1Sa 5:1	795
when they of A arose early on the	1Sa 5:3	795
of Dagon in A unto this day	1Sa 5:5	795
the LORD was heavy upon them of A	1Sa 5:6	795
smote them with emerods, even A	1Sa 5:6	795
when the men of A saw that it was	1Sa 5:7	795
for A one, for Gaza one, for	1Sa 6:17	795
wall of Jabneh, and the wall of A	2Chr 26:6	795
and built cities about A	2Chr 26:6	795
Jews that had married wives of A	Neh 13:23	795
spake half in the speech of A	Neh 13:24	795
the year that Tartan came unto A	Is 20:1	795
sent him,) and fought against A	Is 20:1	795
and Ekron, and the remnant of A	Jer 25:20	795
cut off the inhabitant from A	Amos 1:8	795
Publish in the palaces at A	Amos 3:9	795
shall drive out A at the noonday	Zeph 2:4	795
And a bastard shall dwell in A	Zec 9:6	795

ASHDODITES (ash'-dod-ites) See ASHDOTHITES. *Inhabitants of Ashdod.*

and the Ammonites, and the A	Neh 4:7	796

ASHDOTHITES (ash'-doth-ites) See ASHDODITES. *Same as Ashdodites.*

the Gazathites, and the A, the	Josh 13:3	796

ASHDOTH-PISGAH (ash'-doth-piz'-gah) *The eastern slope of Mt. Pisgah.*

the salt sea, under A eastward	Deut 3:17	798,6449
and from the south, under A	Josh 12:3	798,6449
And Beth-peor, and A, and	Josh 13:20	798,6449

ASHER (ash'-ur) See Aser, Asherites.
  1. A son of Jacob by Zilpah.

and she called his name A	Gen 30:13	836
Gad, and A: these are the sons	Gen 35:26	836
And the sons of A	Gen 46:17	836
Out of A his bread shall be fat,	Gen 49:20	836
Dan, and Naphtali, Gad, and A	Ex 1:4	836
of the daughter of A was Sarah	Num 26:46	836
and Benjamin, Naphtali, Gad, and A	1Chr 2:2	836
The sons of A; Imnah, and Isuah	1Chr 7:30	836
All these were the children of A	1Chr 7:40	836

  2. A tribe descended from Asher 1.

Of A	Num 1:13	836
Of the children of A, by their	Num 1:40	836
of them, even of the tribe of A	Num 1:41	836
by him shall be the tribe of A	Num 2:27	836
of A shall be Pagiel the son of	Num 2:27	836
prince of the children of A	Num 7:72	836
of A was Pagiel the son of Ocran	Num 10:26	836
Of the tribe of A, Sethur the son	Num 13:13	836
Of the children of A after their	Num 26:44	836
of A according to those that were	Num 26:47	836
of the tribe of the children of A	Num 34:27	836
Reuben, Gad, and A, and Zebulun,	Deut 27:13	836
of A he said, Let Asher be	Deut 33:24	836
of A according to their families	Josh 19:24	836
of A according to their families	Josh 19:31	836
reacheth to A on the west side,	Josh 19:34	836
and out of the tribe of A	Josh 21:6	836
And out of the tribe of A, Mishal	Josh 21:30	836
Neither did A drive out the	Judg 1:31	836
A continued on the sea shore, and	Judg 5:17	836
and he sent messengers unto A	Judg 6:35	836
out of Naphtali, and out of A	Judg 7:23	836
and out of the tribe of A	1Chr 6:62	836
And out of the tribe of A	1Chr 6:74	836
And of A, such as went forth to	1Chr 12:36	836
Nevertheless divers of A and	2Chr 30:11	836
the west side, a portion for A	Eze 48:2	836
And by the border of A, from the	Eze 48:3	836
one gate of Gad, one gate of A	Eze 48:34	836

  3. A town in Manasseh.

Manasseh was from A to Michmethah	Josh 17:7	836
met together in A on the north	Josh 17:10	836
in A Beth-shean and her towns	Josh 17:11	836
Baanah the son of Hushai was in A	1Kin 4:16	836

ASHERITES (ash'-ur-ites) Same as Asher 2.

But the A dwelt among the	Judg 1:32	843

ASHES

the Lord, which am but dust and a	Gen 18:27	665
you handfuls of a of the furnace	Ex 9:8	6368
they took a of the furnace, and	Ex 9:10	6368
make his pans to receive his a	Ex 27:3	1878
east part, by the place of the a	Lev 1:16	1880
where the a are poured out, and	Lev 4:12	1880
where the a are poured out shall	Lev 4:12	1880
take up the a which the fire hath	Lev 6:10	1880
carry forth the a without the	Lev 6:11	1880
take away the a from the altar	Num 4:13	1878
gather up the a of the heifer	Num 19:9	665
he that gathereth the a of the	Num 19:10	665
of the a of the burnt heifer of	Num 19:17	6083
Tamar put a on her head, and rent	2Sa 13:19	665
the a that are upon it shall be	1Kin 13:3	1880
the a poured out from the altar,	1Kin 13:5	1880
himself with a upon his face	1Kin 20:38	665
took the a away from his face	1Kin 20:41	665
carried the a of them unto	2Kin 23:4	6083
and put on sackcloth with a	Est 4:1	665
and many lay in sackcloth and a	Est 4:3	665
and he sat down among the a	Job 2:8	665
Your remembrances are like unto a	Job 13:12	665
and I am become like dust and a	Job 30:19	665
myself, and repent in dust and a	Job 42:6	665
For I have eaten a like bread	Ps 102:9	665
scattereth the hoar frost like a	Ps 147:16	665
He feedeth on a	Is 44:20	665
spread sackcloth and a under him	Is 58:5	665
to give unto them beauty for a	Is 61:3	665
sackcloth, and wallow thyself in a	Jer 6:26	665
and wallow yourselves in the a	Jer 25:34	
of the dead bodies, and of the a	Jer 31:40	1880
stones, he hath covered me with a	Lam 3:16	665
shall wallow themselves in the a	Eze 27:30	665
I will bring thee to a upon the	Eze 28:18	665
with fasting, and sackcloth, and a	Dan 9:3	665
him with sackcloth, and sat in a	Jonah 3:6	665
for they shall be a under the	Mal 4:3	665
long ago in sackcloth and a	Mt 11:21	4700
sitting in sackcloth and a	Lk 10:13	4700

the a of an heifer sprinkling the	Heb 9:13	4700
Gomorrah into a condemned them	2Pet 2:6	5077

ASHHUR See Ashur.

ASHIMA (ash'-im-ah) An idol of Hamath.

and the men of Hamath made A	2Kin 17:30	807

ASHKELON (ash'-ke-lon) See Askelon, Eshkalonites.
  A Philistine city.

upon him, and he went down to A	Judg 14:19	831
the land of the Philistines, and A	Jer 25:20	831
A is cut off with the remnant of	Jer 47:5	831
hath given it a charge against A	Jer 47:7	831
that holdeth the sceptre from A	Amos 1:8	831
be forsaken, and A a desolation	Zeph 2:4	831
in the houses of A shall they lie	Zeph 2:7	831
A shall see it, and fear	Zec 9:5	831
Gaza, and A shall not be inhabited	Zec 9:5	831

ASHKENAZ (ash'-ke-naz) See Ashchenaz. A son of
  Gomer.

A, and Riphath, and Togarmah	Gen 10:3	813

ASHNAH (ash'-nah)
  1. A town in Judah near Dan.

valley, Eshtaol, and Zoreah, and A	Josh 15:33	823

  2. A town in Judah on the plains.

And Jiphtah, and A, and Nezib,	Josh 15:43	823

ASHPENAZ (ash'-pe-naz) A prince of the eunuchs under Nebuchadnezzar.

the king spake unto A the master	Dan 1:3	828

ASHRIEL (ash'-re-el) See Asriel. A grandson of Manasseh.

A, whom she bare	1Chr 7:14	845

ASHTAROTH (ash'-ta-roth) See Ashterathite, Ashteroth, Astoreth, Astaroth, Beeshterah.
  *1. A god of the Philistines, Phoenicians, and
  Zidonians.*

the Lord, and served Baal and A	Judg 2:13	6252
the Lord, and served Baalim, and A	Judg 10:6	6252
A from among you, and prepare your	1Sa 7:3	6252
Israel did put away Baalim and A	1Sa 7:4	6252
Lord, and have served Baalim and A	1Sa 12:10	6252
put his armour in the house of A	1Sa 31:10	6252

  2. A city in Bashan.

Og king of Bashan, which was at A	Josh 9:10	6252
of the giants, that dwelt at A	Josh 12:4	6252
Og in Bashan, which reigned in A	Josh 13:12	6252
And half Gilead, and A, and Edrei,	Josh 13:31	6252

  3. A Levitical city in Manasseh.

suburbs, and A with her suburbs	1Chr 6:71	6252

ASHTERATHITE (ash'-ter-a-thite) Family name of Uzziah.

Uzzia the A, Shama and Jehiel the	1Chr 11:44	6254

ASHTEROTH (ash'-te-roth) A city in Og.

smote the Rephaims in A Karnaim	Gen 14:5	6255

ASHTEROTH-KARNAIM See Ashteroth.

ASHTORETH (ash'-to-reth) See Ashtaroth. Same as
  Ashtaroth 1.

For Solomon went after A the	1Kin 11:5	6252
have worshipped A the goddess of	1Kin 11:33	6252
for A the abomination of the	2Kin 23:13	6252

ASHUR (ash'-ur) See Ashurites, Asshur, Assur, Assyria. A son of Hezron.

bare him A the father of Tekoa	1Chr 2:24	804
A the father of Tekoa had two	1Chr 4:5	804

ASHURBANIPAL See Asnapper.

ASHURITES (ash'-ur-ites) See Asshurim. A tribe in the
  plain of Esdraelon.

king over Gilead, and over the A	2Sa 2:9	843
the company of the A have made	Eze 27:6	843

ASHVATH (ash'-vath) A descendant of Asher.

Pasach, and Bimhal, and A	1Chr 7:33	6220

ASIA (a'-she-ah)
  1. A Roman province.

and Cappadocia, in Pontus, and A	Acts 2:9	773
and of them of Cilicia and of A	Acts 6:9	773
Ghost to preach the word in A	Acts 16:6	773
in A heard the word of the Lord	Acts 19:10	773
himself stayed in A for a season	Acts 19:22	773
And certain of the chief of A	Acts 19:31	775
him into A Sopater of Berea	Acts 20:4	773
and of A, Tychicus and Trophimus	Acts 20:4	773
he would not spend the time in A	Acts 20:16	773
the first day that I came into A	Acts 20:18	773
The churches of A salute you	1Cor 16:19	773
our trouble which came to us in A	2Cor 1:8	773

are in *A* be turned away from me...........2Ti 1:15   773
Pontus, Galatia, Cappadocia, *A*..............1Pet 1:1   773
the seven churches which are in *A*......Rev 1:4   773
the seven churches which are in *A*.......Rev 1:11   773
  2. *Another name for Asia Minor.*
but almost throughout all *A*...................Acts 19:26   773
should be destroyed, whom all *A*............Acts 19:27   773
ended, the Jews which were of *A*............Acts 21:27   773
Whereupon certain Jews from *A*...........Acts 24:18   773
to sail by the coasts of *A*......................Acts 27:2   773

ASIDE See APPENDIX.

ASIEL (*a'-se'-el*) *Grandfather of Jeha.*
the son of Seraiah, the son of *A*..............1Chr 4:35   6221

ASK See APPENDIX.

ASKED See APPENDIX.

ASKELON (*as'-ke-lon*) See ASHKELON. *A Philistine city.*
A with the coast thereof, and...................Judg 1:18   831
one, for Gaza one, for *A* one....................1Sa 6:17   831
it not in the streets of *A*.........................2Sa 1:20   831

ASKEST
Why *a* thou thus after my name,.............Judg 13:18   7592
a drink of me, which am a woman........Jn 4:9   154
Why *a* thou me? ....Jn 18:21   1905

ASKETH
a thee, saying, Whose art thou..............Gen 32:17   7592
thy son *a* thee in time to come............Ex 13:14   7592
when thy son *a* thee in time to ....Deut 6:20   7592
hands earnestly, the prince *a*................Mic 7:3   7592
and the judge *a* for a reward..................Mic 7:3   7592
Give to him that *a* thee, and from ....Mt 5:42   154
For every one that *a* receiveth ....Mt 7:8   154
Give to every man that *a* of thee ....Lk 6:30   154
For every one that *a* receiveth ....Lk 11:10   154
and none of you *a* me, Whither..............Jn 16:5   2065
an answer to every man that *a* you........1Pet 3:15   154

ASKING See APPENDIX.

ASLEEP
.for he was fast *a* and weary ....Judg 4:21   7290
for they were all *a* 1Sa 26:12   3463
lips of those that are *a* to speak ....Song 7:9   3463
and he lay, and was fast *a*......................Jonah 1:5   7290
but he was *a* ....Mt 8:24   2518
the disciples, and findeth them *a*............Mt 26:40   2518
And he came and found them *a* again ......Mt 26:43   2518
part of the ship, *a* on a pillow ....Mk 4:38   2518
returned, he found them *a* again ....Mk 14:40   2518
But as they sailed he fell *a* ....Lk 8:23   879
when he had said this, he fell *a* ....Acts 7:60   2837
present, but some are fallen *a*...............1Cor 15:6   2837
fallen *a* in Christ are perished...............1Cor 15:18   2837
concerning them which are *a*...................1Th 4:13   2837
not prevent them which are *a*.................1Th 4:15   2837
for since the fathers fell *a*......................2Pet 3:4   2837

ASNAH (*as'-nah*) *A family of exiles.*
The children of *A*, the children...............Ezr 2:50   619

ASNAPPER (*as-nap'-pur*) *An Assyrian king.*
noble *A* brought over, and set in ....Ezr 4:10   620

ASP
shall play on the hole of the *a*.................Is 11:8   6620

ASPATHA (*as'-pa-thah*) *A son of Haman.*
and Dalphon, and *A* ....Est 9:7   630

ASPS
dragons, and the cruel venom of *a* ....Deut 32:33   6620
it is the gall of *a* within him...................Job 20:14   6620
He shall suck the poison of *a*.................Job 20:16   6620
the poison of *a* is under their ....Rom 3:13   785

ASRIEL (*as'-re-el*) See ASHRIEL, ASRIELITES. *A grandson of Manasseh.*
And of *A*, the family of the ....Num 26:31   844
Helek, and for the children of *A*..............Josh 17:2   844

ASRIELITES (*as'-re-el-ites*) *Descendants of Asriel.*
And of Asriel, the family of the *A* ....Num 26:31   845

ASS
in the morning, and saddled his *a*..........Gen 22:3   2543
men, Abide ye here with the *a*................Gen 22:5   2543
give his *a* provender in the inn ....Gen 42:27   2543
clothes, and laded every man his *a*.........Gen 44:13   2543
Issachar is a strong *a* couching..............Gen 49:14   2543
his sons, and set them upon an *a*..........Ex 4:20   2543
every firstling of an *a* thou ....Ex 13:13   2543
nor his ox, nor his *a*, nor any ....Ex 20:17   2543
an ox or an *a* fall therein........................Ex 21:33   2543
alive, whether it be ox, or *a*...................Ex 22:4   2543

whether it be for ox, for *a* ....Ex 22:9   2543
deliver unto his neighbour an *a*..............Ex 22:10   2543
enemy's ox or his *a* going astray ....Ex 23:4   2543
If thou see the *a* of him that ....Ex 23:5   2543
thine *a* may rest, and the son of ....Ex 23:12   2543
But the firstling of an *a* thou ....Ex 34:20   2543
I have not taken one *a* from them ....Num 16:15   2543
in the morning, and saddled his *a*...........Num 22:21   860
Now he was riding upon his *a* ....Num 22:22   860
the *a* saw the angel of the LORD ....Num 22:23   860
the *a* turned aside out of the way ....Num 22:23   860
and Balaam smote the *a*, to turn...........Num 22:23   860
when the *a* saw the angel of the ....Num 22:25   860
when the *a* saw the angel of the ....Num 22:27   860
and he smote the *a* with a staff ....Num 22:27   860
LORD opened the mouth of the *a* ....Num 22:28   860
And Balaam said unto the *a* ....Num 22:29   860
the *a* said unto Balaam ....Num 22:30   860
Am not I thine *a*,....................................Num 22:30   860
smitten thine *a* these three times ....Num 22:32   860
the *a* saw me, and turned from me.........Num 22:33   860
nor thine ox, nor thine *a* ....Deut 5:14   2543
his maidservant, his ox, or his *a*............Deut 5:21   2543
manner shalt thou do with his *a* ....Deut 22:3   2543
shalt not see thy brother's *a* or ....Deut 22:4   2543
plow with an ox and an *a* together........Deut 22:10   2543
thine *a* shall be violently taken..............Deut 28:31   2543
and old, and ox, and sheep, and *a* ....Josh 6:21   2543
and she lighted off her *a* ....Josh 15:18   2543
and she lighted from off her *a*................Judg 1:14   2543
neither sheep, nor ox, nor *a* ....Judg 6:4   2543
sons that rode on thirty *a* colts..............Judg 10:4   5895
rode on threescore and ten *a* colts ....Judg 12:14   5895
And he found a new jawbone of an *a* ....Judg 15:15   2543
said, With the jawbone of an *a*..............Judg 15:16   2543
with the jaw of an *a* have I slain ....Judg 15:16   2543
the man took her up upon an *a* ....Judg 19:28   2543
or whose *a* have I taken 1Sa 12:3   2543
suckling, ox and sheep, camel and *a*.......1Sa 15:3   2543
Jesse took an *a* laden with bread,..........1Sa 16:20   2543
it was so, as she rode on the *a* 1Sa 25:20   2543
she hasted, and lighted off the *a* 1Sa 25:23   2543
and arose, and rode upon an *a* 1Sa 25:42   2543
not followed, he saddled his *a* 2Sa 17:23   2543
said, I will saddle me an *a* 2Sa 19:26   2543
And Shimei arose, and saddled his *a*......1Kin 2:40   2543
unto his sons, Saddle me the *a* 1Kin 13:13   2543
So they saddled him the *a* 1Kin 13:13   2543
that he saddled for him the *a* 1Kin 13:23   2543
the *a* stood by it, the lion also................1Kin 13:24   2543
his sons, saying, Saddle me the *a*...........1Kin 13:27   2543
carcase cast in the way, and the *a* 1Kin 13:28   2543
eaten the carcase, nor torn the *a* 1Kin 13:28   2543
man of God, and laid it upon the *a* 1Kin 13:29   2543
Then she saddled an *a*, and said to........2Kin 4:24   2543
Doth the wild *a* bray when he hath.......Job 6:5   6501
away the *a* of the fatherless ....Job 24:3   2543
Who hath sent out the wild *a* free..........Job 39:5   5601
loosed the bands of the wild *a* ....Job 39:5   6171
for the horse, a bridle for the *a* ....Prov 26:3   2543
owner, and a his master's crib ....Is 1:3   2543
the feet of the ox and the *a* ....Is 32:20   2543
A wild *a* used to the wilderness,..............Jer 2:24   6501
be buried with the burial of an *a*.............Jer 22:19   2543
a wild *a* alone by himself........................Hos 8:9   6501
lowly, and riding upon an *a* ....Zec 9:9   2543
and upon a colt the foal of an *a* ....Zec 9:9   860
mule, of the camel, and of the *a*.............Zec 14:15   860
ye shall find an *a* tied, and a ....Mt 21:2   3688
thee, meek, and sitting upon an *a* ....Mt 21:5   3688
and a colt the foal of an *a* ....Mt 21:5   5268
And brought the *a*, and the colt, and.....Mt 21:7   3688
his ox or his *a* from the stall ....Lk 13:15   3688
an *a* or an ox fallen into a pit ....Lk 14:5   3688
when he had found a young *a*.................Jn 12:14   3678
the dumb *a* speaking with man's...........2Pet 2:16   5268

ASSAULT
and province that would *a* them ....Est 8:11   6696
when there was an *a* made both of ....Acts 14:5   3730

ASSAULTED
a the house of Jason, and sought...........Acts 17:5   2186

ASSAY
If we *a* to commune with thee,...............Job 4:2   5254

ASSAYED
Or hath God *a* to go and take him *a*......Deut 4:34   5254
upon his armour, and he *a* to go............1Sa 17:39   2974
he *a* to join himself to the ....Acts 9:26   3987
they *a* to go into Bithynia......................Acts 16:7   3985

ASSAYING
Egyptians *a* to do were drowned .... Heb 11:29   3984,2983

ASSEMBLE
them, all the assembly shall *a*	Num 10:3	3259
A me the men of Judah within	2Sa 20:4	2199
Amasa went to *a* the men of Judah	2Sa 20:5	2199
shall *a* the outcasts of Israel,	Is 11:12	622
A yourselves and come	Is 45:20	6908
All ye, *a* yourselves, and hear	Is 48:14	6908
A yourselves, and let us go into	Jer 4:5	622
a yourselves, and let us enter	Jer 8:14	622
a all the beasts of the field,	Jer 12:9	622
I will *a* them into the midst of	Jer 21:4	622
a you out of the countries where	Eze 11:17	622
the field, *A* yourselves, and come	Eze 39:17	6908
shall *a* a multitude of great	Dan 11:10	622
they *a* themselves for corn and	Hos 7:14	1481
a the elders, gather the children	Joel 2:16	6908
A yourselves, and come, all ye	Joel 3:11	5789
A yourselves upon the mountains	Amos 3:9	622
I will surely *a*, O Jacob, all of	Mic 2:12	622
will I *a* her that halteth, and I	Mic 4:6	622
that I may *a* the kingdoms, to	Zeph 3:8	6908

ASSEMBLED
which *a* at the door of the	Ex 38:8	6638
they *a* all the congregation	Num 1:18	6950
of Israel *a* together at Shiloh	Josh 18:1	6950
of Israel *a* themselves together	Judg 10:17	622
they lay with the women that *a* at	1Sa 2:22	6633
that were with him *a* themselves	1Sa 14:20	2199
Then Solomon *a* the elders of	1Kin 8:1	6950
And all the men of Israel *a*	1Kin 8:2	6950
of Israel, that were *a* unto him	1Kin 8:5	3259
he *a* the house of Judah, with	1Kin 12:21	6950
David *a* the children of Aaron, and	1Chr 15:4	662
David *a* all the princes of Israel	1Chr 28:1	6950
Then Solomon *a* the elders of	2Chr 5:2	6950
a themselves unto the king in the	2Chr 5:3	6950
of Israel that were *a* unto him	2Chr 5:6	3259
And on the fourth day they *a*	2Chr 20:26	6950
there *a* at Jerusalem much people	2Chr 30:13	622
Then were *a* unto me every one	Ezr 9:4	622
there *a* unto him out of Israel a	Ezr 10:1	6908
of Israel were *a* with fasting	Neh 9:1	622
the Jews that were at Shushan *a*	Est 9:18	6950
For, lo, the kings were *a*	Ps 48:4	3259
together, and let the people be *a*	Is 43:9	
a themselves by troops in the	Jer 5:7	1413
thy company that are *a* unto thee	Eze 38:7	6950
princes *a* together to the king,	Dan 6:6	7284
Then these men *a*, and found Daniel	Dan 6:11	7284
Then these men *a* unto the king	Dan 6:15	7284
Then *a* together the chief priests	Mt 26:3	4863
the scribes and the elders were *a*	Mt 26:57	4863
when they were *a* with the elders,	Mt 28:12	4863
with him were *a* all the chief	Mk 14:53	4905
were *a* for fear of the Jews	Jn 20:19	4863
being *a* together with them,	Acts 1:4	4871
shaken where they were *a* together	Acts 4:31	4863
to pass, that a whole year they *a*	Acts 11:26	4863
being *a* with one accord, to send	Acts 15:25	1096

ASSEMBLIES
the *a* of violent men have sought	Ps 86:14	5712
fastened by the masters of *a*	Eccl 12:11	627
and sabbaths, the calling of *a*	Is 1:13	4744
of mount Zion, and upon her *a*	Is 4:5	4744
laws and my statutes in all mine *a*	Eze 44:24	4150
I will not smell in your solemn *a*	Amos 5:21	6116

ASSEMBLING
the lookingglasses of the women *a*	Ex 38:8	6633
Not forsaking the *a* of ourselves	Heb 10:25	1997

ASSEMBLY
unto their *a*, mine honour, be not	Gen 49:6	6951
the whole *a* of the congregation	Ex 12:6	6951
to kill this whole *a* with hunger	Ex 16:3	6951
be hid from the eyes of the *a*	Lev 4:13	6951
the *a* was gathered together unto	Lev 8:4	5712
it is a solemn *a*	Lev 23:36	6116
whole *a* of the children of Israel	Num 5:12	5712
use them for the calling of the *a*	Num 10:2	5712
them, all the *a* shall assemble	Num 10:3	5712
the *a* of the congregation the	Num 14:5	6951
hundred and fifty princes of the *a*	Num 16:2	5712
went from the presence of the *a*	Num 20:6	6951
and gather thou the *a* together	Num 20:8	5712
day ye shall have a solemn *a*	Num 29:35	6116
the LORD spake unto all your *a* in	Deut 5:22	6951
of the fire in the day of the *a*	Deut 9:10	6951

of the fire in the day of the *a*	Deut 10:4	6951
be a solemn *a* to the LORD thy God	Deut 16:8	6116
God in Horeb in the day of the *a*	Deut 18:16	6951
in the *a* of the people of God	Judg 20:2	6951
camp from Jabesh-gilead to the *a*	Judg 21:8	6951
all this *a* shall know that the	1Sa 17:47	6951
Proclaim a solemn *a* for Baal	2Kin 10:20	6116
eighth day they made a solemn *a*	2Chr 7:9	6116
the whole *a* took counsel to keep	2Chr 30:23	6951
And I set a great *a* against them	Neh 5:7	6952
on the eighth day was a solemn *a*	Neh 8:18	6116
the *a* of the wicked have inclosed	Ps 22:16	5712
be feared in the *a* of the saints	Ps 89:7	5475
praise him in the *a* of the elders	Ps 107:32	4186
in the *a* of the upright, and in	Ps 111:1	5475
midst of the congregation and *a*	Prov 5:14	5712
upon the *a* of young men together	Jer 6:11	5475
an *a* of treacherous men	Jer 9:2	6116
I sat not in the *a* of the mockers	Jer 15:17	5475
spake to all the *a* of the people	Jer 26:17	6951
to come up against Babylon an *a*	Jer 50:9	6951
he hath called an *a* against me to	Lam 1:15	4150
destroyed his places of the *a*	Lam 2:6	4150
not be in the *a* of my people	Eze 13:9	5475
with an *a* of people, which shall	Eze 23:24	6951
ye a fast, call a solemn *a*	Joel 1:14	6116
sanctify a fast, call a solemn *a*	Joel 2:15	6116
are sorrowful for the solemn *a*	Zeph 3:18	4150
for the *a* was confused	Acts 19:32	1577
shall be determined in a lawful *a*	Acts 19:39	1577
thus spoken, he dismissed the *a*	Acts 19:41	1577
To the general *a* and church of the	Heb 12:23	3831
your *a* a man with a gold ring	Jas 2:2	4864

ASSENT
good to the king with one *a* 2Chr 18:12   6310

ASSENTED
And the Jews also *a*, saying that .... Acts 24:9   4934

ASSES
and he had sheep, and oxen, and he *a*	Gen 12:16	2543
and maidservants, and she *a*	Gen 12:16	860
and maidservants, and camels, and *a*	Gen 24:35	2543
and menservants, and camels, and *a*	Gen 30:43	2543
And I have oxen, and *a*, flocks, and	Gen 32:5	2543
kine, and ten bulls, twenty she *a*	Gen 32:15	860
sheep, and their oxen, and their *a*	Gen 34:28	2543
as he fed the *a* of Zibeon his	Gen 36:24	2543
they laded their *a* with the corn	Gen 42:26	2543
and take us for bondmen, and our *a*	Gen 43:18	2543
and he gave their *a* provender	Gen 43:24	2543
were sent away, they and their *a*	Gen 44:3	2543
ten *a* laden with the good things	Gen 45:23	860
ten she *a* laden with corn and	Gen 45:23	2543
cattle of the herds, and for the *a*	Gen 47:17	2543
upon the horses, upon the *a*	Ex 9:3	2543
and of the beeves, and of the *a*	Num 31:28	2543
persons, of the beeves, of the *a*	Num 31:30	2543
And threescore and one thousand *a*	Num 31:34	2543
the *a* were thirty thousand and	Num 31:39	2543
And thirty thousand and five	Num 31:45	2543
daughters, and his oxen, and his *a*	Josh 7:24	2543
and took old sacks upon their *a*	Josh 9:4	2543
Speak, ye that ride on white *a*	Judg 5:10	860
with him, and a couple of *a*	Judg 19:3	2543
there were with him two *a* saddled	Judg 19:10	2543
both straw and provender for our *a*	Judg 19:19	2543
and gave provender unto the *a*	Judg 19:21	2543
goodliest young men, and your *a*	1Sa 8:16	2543
the *a* of Kish Saul's father were	1Sa 9:3	860
thee, and arise, go seek the *a*	1Sa 9:3	860
my father leave caring for the *a*	1Sa 9:5	860
as for thine *a* that were lost	1Sa 9:20	860
The *a* which thou wentest to seek	1Sa 10:2	860
hath left the care of the *a*	1Sa 10:2	860
And he said, To seek the *a*	1Sa 10:14	860
us plainly that the *a* were found	1Sa 10:16	860
and sucklings, and oxen, and *a*	1Sa 22:19	2543
cakes of figs, and laid them on *a*	1Sa 25:18	2543
the sheep, and the oxen, and the *a*	1Sa 27:9	2543
him, with a couple of *a* saddled	2Sa 16:1	2543
The *a* be for the king's household	2Sa 16:2	2543
of the young men, and one of the *a*	2Kin 4:22	860
and their horses, and their *a*	2Kin 7:7	2543
a tied, and the tents as they were	2Kin 7:10	2543
of a two thousand, and of men an	1Chr 5:21	2543
and Naphtali, brought bread on *a*	1Chr 12:40	2543
over the *a* was Jehdeiah the	1Chr 27:30	860
all the feeble of them upon *a*	2Chr 28:15	2543
their *a*, six thousand seven	Ezr 2:67	2543
seven hundred and twenty *a*	Neh 7:69	2543

bringing in sheaves, and lading *a* .... Neh 13:15 2543
of oxen, and five hundred she *a* .... Job 1:3 860
the *a* feeding beside them .... Job 1:14 860
as wild *a* in the desert, go they .... Job 24:5 6501
yoke of oxen, and a thousand she *a* .... Job 42:12 860
the wild *a* quench their thirst .... Ps 104:11 6501
of horsemen, a chariot of *a* .... Is 21:7 2543
upon the shoulders of young *a* .... Is 30:6 5895
the young *a* that ear the ground .... Is 30:24 5895
dens for ever, a joy of wild *a* .... Is 32:14 6501
the wild *a* did stand in the high .... Jer 14:6 6501
whose flesh is as the flesh of *a* .... Eze 23:20 2543
his dwelling was with the wild *a* .... Dan 5:21 6167

ASSHUR (ash'-ur) See ASHUR, ASSUR, ASSYRIA.
1. The builder of Nineveh.
Out of that land went forth *A* .... Gen 10:11 804
2. A son of Shem.
Elam, and *A*, and Arphaxad, and Lud, ... Gen 10:22 804
Elam, and *A*, and Arphaxad, and Lud, ... 1Chr 1:17 804
3. Another name for Assyria.
until *A* shall carry thee away .... Num 24:22 804
of Chittim, and shall afflict *A* .... Num 24:24 804
Eden, the merchants of Sheba, *A* .... Eze 27:23 804
A is there and all her company .... Eze 32:22 804
A shall not save us .... Hos 14:3 804

ASSHURIM (ash'-u-rim) See ASHURITES. Descendants of Dedan.
And the sons of Dedan were *A* .... Gen 25:3 805

ASSHURITES See ASSHURIM.

ASSIGNED
had a portion *a* them of Pharaoh .... Gen 47:22
they *a* Bezer in the wilderness .... Josh 20:8 5414
that he *a* Uriah unto a place 2Sa 11:16 5414

ASSIR (as'-sur)
1. A son of Korah.
A, and Elkanah, and Abiasaph .... Ex 6:24 617
son, Korah his son, *A* his son, ... 1Chr 6:22 617
2. A son of Ebiasaph.
Ebiasaph his son, and *A* his son, ... 1Chr 6:23 617
The son of Tahath, the son of *A* 1Chr 6:37 617
3. A son of Jeconiah.
A, Salathiel his son, ... 1Chr 3:17 617

ASSIST
that ye *a* her in whatsoever .... Rom 16:2 3936

ASSOCIATE
A yourselves, O ye people, and ye ... Is 8:9 7489

ASSOS (as'-sos) A seaport of Mysia in Asia Minor.
before to ship, and sailed unto *A* .... Acts 20:13 789
And when he met with us at *A* .... Acts 20:14 789

ASS'S
his *a* colt unto the choice vine .... Gen 49:11 860
until an *a* head was sold for 2Kin 6:25 2543
man be born like a wild *a* colt .... Job 11:12 6501
King cometh, sitting on an *a* colt .... Jn 12:15 3688

ASSUR (As'-sur) See ASSHUR. Same as Asshur 3.
the days of Esar-haddon king of *A* .... Ezr 4:2 804
A also is joined with them .... Ps 83:8 804

ASSURANCE
and shalt have none *a* of thy life .... Deut 28:66 539
quietness and *a* for ever .... Is 32:17 983
he hath given *a* unto all men .... Acts 17:31 4102
of the full *a* of understanding .... Col 2:2 4136
in the Holy Ghost, and in much *a* 1Th 1:5 4136
the full *a* of hope unto the end .... Heb 6:11 4136
a true heart in full *a* of faith .... Heb 10:22 4136

ASSURE
shall *a* our hearts before him 1Jn 3:19 3983

ASSURED
unto it, and it shall be *a* to him .... Lev 27:19 6966
give you *a* peace in this place .... Jer 14:13 571
hast learned and hast been *a* of 2Ti 3:14 4104

ASSUREDLY
said unto David, Know thou *a* 1Sa 28:1 3045
A Solomon thy son shall reign 1Kin 1:13 3588
A Solomon thy son shall reign 1Kin 1:17 3588
A Solomon thy son shall reign 1Kin 1:30 3588
this land *a* with my whole heart .... Jer 32:41 571
If thou wilt *a* go forth unto the .... Jer 38:17 3318
drink of the cup whom *a* drunken .... Jer 49:12 8354
all the house of Israel know *a* .... Acts 2:36 806
a gathering that the Lord had .... Acts 16:10 4822

ASSWAGE
of my lips should *a* your grief .... Job 16:5 2820

ASSWAGED
over the earth, and the waters *a* .... Gen 8:1 7918
Though I speak, my grief is not *a* .... Job 16:6 2820

ASSYRIA (as-sir'-e-ah) See ASSHUR, ASSYRIAN. A Mesopotamian empire.
which goeth toward the east of *A* .... Gen 2:14 804
Egypt, as thou goest toward *A* .... Gen 25:18 804
Pul the king of *A* came against 2Kin 15:19 804
silver, to give to the king of *A* 2Kin 15:20 804
So the king of *A* turned back 2Kin 15:20 804
came Tiglath-pileser king of *A* 2Kin 15:29 804
and carried them captive to *A* 2Kin 15:29 804
to Tiglath-pileser king of *A* 2Kin 16:7 804
it for a present to the king of *A* 2Kin 16:8 804
the king of *A* hearkened unto him 2Kin 16:9 804
for the king of *A* went up against 2Kin 16:9 804
to meet Tiglath-pileser king of *A* 2Kin 16:10 804
of the LORD for the king of *A* 2Kin 16:18 804
him came up Shalmaneser king of *A* 2Kin 17:3 804
the king of *A* found conspiracy in.......... 2Kin 17:4 804
no present to the king of *A* 2Kin 17:4 804
the king of *A* shut him up 2Kin 17:4 804
Then the king of *A* came up 2Kin 17:5 804
Hoshea the king of *A* took Samaria 2Kin 17:6 804
and carried Israel away into *A* 2Kin 17:6 804
their own land to *A* unto this day 2Kin 17:23 804
the king of *A* brought men from 2Kin 17:24 804
they spake to the king of *A* 2Kin 17:26 804
Then the king of *A* commanded.............. 2Kin 17:27 804
he rebelled against the king of *A* 2Kin 18:7 804
king of *A* came up against Samaria 2Kin 18:9 804
the king of *A* did carry away 2Kin 18:11 804
did carry away Israel unto *A* 2Kin 18:11 804
did Sennacherib king of *A* come up 2Kin 18:13 804
sent to the king of *A* to Lachish 2Kin 18:14 804
the king of *A* appointed unto 2Kin 18:14 804
and gave it to the king of *A* 2Kin 18:16 804
And the king of *A* sent Tartan 2Kin 18:17 804
the great king, the king of *A* 2Kin 18:19 804
pledges to my lord the king of *A* 2Kin 18:23 804
of the great king, the king of *A* 2Kin 18:28 804
into the hand of the king of *A* 2Kin 18:30 804
for thus saith the king of *A* 2Kin 18:31 804
out of the hand of the king of *A* 2Kin 18:33 804
whom the king of *A* his master 2Kin 19:4 804
the king of *A* have blasphemed me 2Kin 19:6 804
found the king of *A* warring 2Kin 19:8 804
into the hand of the king of *A* 2Kin 19:10 804
kings of *A* have done to all lands............ 2Kin 19:11 804
the kings of *A* have destroyed the 2Kin 19:17 804
king of *A* I have heard 2Kin 19:20 804
the LORD concerning the king of *A* 2Kin 19:32 804
So Sennacherib king of *A* departed 2Kin 19:36 804
out of the hand of the king of *A* 2Kin 20:6 804
king of *A* to the river Euphrates 2Kin 23:29 804
king of *A* carried away captive 1Chr 5:6 804
up the spirit of Pul king of *A* 1Chr 5:26 804
of Tilgath-pilneser king of *A* 1Chr 5:26 804
unto the kings of *A* to help him 2Chr 28:16 804
king of *A* came unto him, and................. 2Chr 28:20 804
and gave it unto the king of *A* 2Chr 28:21 804
out of the hand of the kings of *A* 2Chr 30:6 804
Sennacherib king of *A* came 2Chr 32:1 804
Why should the kings of *A* come 2Chr 32:4 804
nor dismayed for the king of *A* 2Chr 32:7 804
this did Sennacherib king of *A* 2Chr 32:9 804
Thus saith Sennacherib king of *A* 2Chr 32:10 804
out of the hand of the king of *A* 2Chr 32:11 804
in the camp of the king of *A*.................. 2Chr 32:21 804
hand of Sennacherib the king of *A* 2Chr 32:22 804
of the host of the king of *A* 2Chr 33:11 804
heart of the king of *A* unto them .... Ezr 6:22 804
of the kings of *A* unto this day .... Neh 9:32 804
even the king of *A* .... Is 7:17 804
the bee that is in the land of *A* .... Is 7:18 804
the river, by the king of *A* .... Is 7:20 804
taken away before the king of *A* .... Is 8:4 804
and many, even the king of *A* .... Is 8:7 804
the stout heart of the king of *A* .... Is 10:12 804
which shall be left, from *A* .... Is 11:11 804
which shall be left, from *A* .... Is 11:16 804
be a highway out of Egypt to *A* .... Is 19:23 804
Egypt, and the Egyptian into *A* .... Is 19:23 804
be the third with Egypt and with *A* ...... Is 19:24 804
A the work of my hands, and Israel .... Is 19:25 804
Sargon the king of *A* sent him .... Is 20:1 804
So shall the king of *A* lead away .... Is 20:4 804
be delivered from the king of *A* .... Is 20:6 804
ready to perish in the land of *A* .... Is 27:13 804
king of *A* came up against all the .... Is 36:1 804

the king of *A* sent Rabshakeh from .... Is 36:2   804
the great king, the king of *A* .... Is 36:4   804
thee, to my master the king of *A* .... Is 36:8   804
of the great king, the king of *A* .... Is 36:13   804
into the hand of the king of *A* .... Is 36:15   804
for thus saith the king of *A* .... Is 36:16   804
out of the hand of the king of *A* .... Is 36:18   804
whom the king of *A* his master .... Is 37:4   804
the king of *A* have blasphemed me .... Is 37:6   804
found the king of *A* warring .... Is 37:8   804
into the hand of the king of *A* .... Is 37:10   804
of *A* have done to all lands by .... Is 37:11   804
the kings of *A* have laid waste .... Is 37:18   804
me against Sennacherib king of *A* .... Is 37:21   804
the LORD concerning the king of *A* .... Is 37:33   804
So Sennacherib king of *A* departed .... Is 37:37   804
out of the hand of the king of *A* .... Is 38:6   804
hast thou to do in the way of *A* .... Jer 2:18   804
Egypt, as thou wast ashamed of *A* .... Jer 2:36   804
the king of *A* hath devoured him .... Jer 50:17   804
as I have punished the king of *A* .... Jer 50:18   804
that were the chosen men of *A* .... Eze 23:7   804
they call to Egypt, they go to *A* .... Hos 7:11   804
For they are gone up to *A* .... Hos 8:9   804
shall eat unclean things in *A* .... Hos 9:3   804
A for a present to king Jareb .... Hos 10:6   804
and as a dove out of the land of *A* .... Hos 11:11   804
the land of *A* with the sword .... Mic 5:6   804
he shall come even to thee from *A* .... Mic 7:12   804
shepherds slumber, O king of *A* .... Nah 3:18   804
against the north, and destroy *A* .... Zeph 2:13   804
of Egypt, and gather them out of *A* .... Zec 10:10   804
the pride of *A* shall be brought .... Zec 10:11   804

ASSYRIAN (*as-sir'-e-un*) See ASSYRIANS. *An inhab-itant of Assyria.*
O *A*, the rod of mine anger, and .... Is 10:5   804
in Zion, be not afraid of the *A* .... Is 10:24   804
I will break the *A* in my land .... Is 14:25   804
the *A* shall come into Egypt, and .... Is 19:23   804
til the *A* founded it for them .... Is 23:13   804
LORD shall the *A* be beaten down .... Is 30:31   804
Then shall the *A* fall with the .... Is 31:8   804
the *A* oppressed them without .... Is 52:4   804
the *A* was a cedar in Lebanon with .... Eze 31:3   804
wound, then went Ephraim to the *A* ...... Hos 5:13   804
but the *A* shall be his king, ... Hos 11:5   804
when the *A* shall come into our .... Mic 5:5   804
shall he deliver us from the *A* .... Mic 5:6   804

ASSYRIANS (*as-sir'-e-uns*)
of the *A* an hundred fourscore 2Kin 19:35   804
Egyptians shall serve with the *A* .... Is 19:23   804
in the camp of the *A* an hundred .... Is 37:36   804
to the Egyptians, and to the *A* .... Lam 5:6   804
played the whore also with the *A* .... Eze 16:28   804
lovers, on the *A* her neighbours, ... Eze 23:5   804
lovers, into the hand of the *A* .... Eze 23:9   804
doted upon the *A* her neighbours .... Eze 23:12   804
and Koa, and all the *A* with them .... Eze 23:23   804
do make a covenant with the *A* .... Hos 12:1   804

ASTAROTH (*as'-ta-roth*) See ASHTAROTH. *A city in Ba-shan.*
Bashan, which dwelt at *A* in Edrei .... Deut 1:4   6252

ASTONIED
and of my beard, and sat down *a* .... Ezr 9:3   8074
I sat *a* until the evening .... Ezr 9:4   8074
Upright men shall be *a* at this .... Job 17:8   8074
after him shall be *a* at his day .... Job 18:20   8074
As many were *a* at thee .... Is 52:14   8074
Why shouldest thou be as a man *a* .... Jer 14:9   1724
be *a* one with another, and consume ..... Eze 4:17   8074
Nebuchadnezzar the king was *a* .... Dan 3:24   8429
was *a* for one hour, and his .... Dan 4:19   8075
in him, and his lords were *a* .... Dan 5:9   7672

ASTONISHED
dwell therein shall be *a* at it .... Lev 26:32   8074
one that passeth by it shall be *a* 1Kin 9:8   8074
Mark me, and be *a*, and lay your .... Job 21:5   8074
tremble, and are *a* at his reproof .... Job 26:11   8539
Be *a*, O ye heavens, at this, and .... Jer 2:12   8074
and the priests shall be *a* .... Jer 4:9   8074
that passeth thereby shall be *a* .... Jer 18:16   8074
that passeth thereby shall be *a* .... Jer 19:8   8074
one that goeth by it shall be *a* .... Jer 49:17   8074
that goeth by Babylon shall be *a* .... Jer 50:13   8074
remained there *a* among them seven ..... Eze 3:15   8074
at every moment, and be *a* at thee .... Eze 26:16   8074
of the isles shall be *a* at thee .... Eze 27:35   8074
the people shall be *a* at thee .... Eze 28:19   8074

I was *a* at the vision, but none .... Dan 8:27   8074
the people were *a* at his doctrine .... Mt 7:28   1605
insomuch that they were *a* .... Mt 13:54   1605
they were *a* at his doctrine .... Mt 22:33   1605
they were *a* at his doctrine .... Mk 1:22   1605
And they were *a* with a great .... Mk 5:42   1839
and many hearing him were *a* .... Mk 6:2   1605
And were beyond measure *a*, saying, ... Mk 7:37   1605
the disciples were *a* at his words .... Mk 10:24   2284
they were *a* out of measure, ... Mk 10:26   1605
the people was *a* at his doctrine .... Mk 11:18   1605
him were *a* at his understanding .... Lk 2:47   1839
they were *a* at his doctrine .... Lk 4:32   1605
For he was *a*, and all that were .... Lk 5:9   4023,2285
And her parents were *a* .... Lk 8:56   1839
also of our company made us *a* .... Lk 24:22   1839
a said, Lord, what wilt thou have .... Acts 9:6   2284
which believed were *a*, as many as .... Acts 10:45   1839
the door, and saw him, they were *a* .... Acts 12:16   1839
being *a* at the doctrine of the .... Acts 13:12   1605

ASTONISHMENT
and blindness, and *a* of heart .... Deut 28:28   8541
And thou shalt become an *a* .... Deut 28:37   8047
shall be an *a* to every one that 2Chr 7:21   8074
delivered them to trouble, to *a* 2Chr 29:8   8047
made us to drink the wine of *a* .... Ps 60:3   8653
a hath taken hold on me .... Jer 8:21   8047
destroy them, and make them an *a* .... Jer 25:9   8047
shall be a desolation, and an *a* .... Jer 25:11   8047
to make them a desolation, an *a* .... Jer 25:18   8047
the earth, to be a curse, and an *a* .... Jer 29:18   8047
shall be an execration, and an *a* .... Jer 42:18   8047
shall be an execration, and an *a* .... Jer 44:12   8047
your land a desolation, and an *a* .... Jer 44:22   8047
dwelling place for dragons, an *a* .... Jer 51:37   8047
become an *a* among the nations .... Jer 51:41   8047
drink water by measure, and with *a* ...... Eze 4:16   8078
an *a* unto the nations that are .... Eze 5:15   8047
and drink their water with *a* .... Eze 12:19   8078
and sorrow, with the cup of *a* .... Eze 23:33   8047
I will smite every horse with *a* .... Zec 12:4   8541
were astonished with a great *a* .... Mk 5:42   1611

ASTRAY
enemy's ox or his ass going *a* .... Ex 23:4   8582
brother's ox or his sheep go *a* .... Deut 22:1   5080
they go *a* as soon as they be born .... Ps 58:3   8582
Before I was afflicted I went *a* .... Ps 119:67   7683
I have gone *a* like a lost sheep .... Ps 119:176   8582
of his folly he shall go *a* .... Prov 5:23   7686
her ways, go not *a* in her paths .... Prov 7:25   8582
righteous to go *a* in an evil way .... Prov 28:10   7686
All we like sheep have gone *a* .... Is 53:6   8582
have caused them to go *a*, they .... Jer 50:6   8582
Israel may go no more *a* from me .... Eze 14:11   8582
far from me, when Israel went *a* .... Eze 44:10   8582
which went *a* away from me after .... Eze 44:10   8582
children of Israel went *a* from me .... Eze 44:15   8582
which went not *a* when the .... Eze 48:11   8582
the children of Israel went *a* .... Eze 48:11   8582
as the Levites went *a* .... Eze 48:11   8582
sheep, and one of them be gone *a* .... Mt 18:12   4105
and seeketh that which is gone *a* .... Mt 18:12   4105
ninety and nine which went not *a* .... Mt 18:13   4105
For ye were as sheep going *a* 1Pet 2:25   4105
the right way, and are gone *a* 2Pet 2:15   4105

ASTROLOGER
such things at any magician, or *a* .... Dan 2:10   826

ASTROLOGERS
Let now the *a*, the stargazers, ... Is 47:13   1895,8064
a that were in all his realm .... Dan 1:20   825
to call the magicians, and the *a* .... Dan 2:2   825
cannot the wise men, the *a* .... Dan 2:27   826
Then came in the magicians, the *a* .... Dan 4:7   826
cried aloud to bring in the *a* .... Dan 5:7   826
made master of the magicians, *a* .... Dan 5:11   826
And now the wise men, the *a* .... Dan 5:15   826

ASUNDER
but shall not divide it *a* .... Lev 1:17
neck, but shall not divide it *a* .... Lev 5:8
clave *a* that was under them .... Num 16:31
of fire, and parted them both *a* 2Kin 2:11   996
at ease, but he hath broken me *a* .... Job 16:12
about, he cleaveth my reins *a* .... Job 16:13
Let us break their bands *a* .... Ps 2:3
he hath cut the cords of the .... Ps 129:4
of the whole earth cut in *a* .... Jer 50:23
great pain, and No shall be rent *a* .... Eze 30:16
he beheld, and drove *a* the nations ...... Hab 3:6

staff, even Beauty, and cut it *a* .... Zec 11:10
Then I cut *a* mine other staff, ... Zec 11:14
together, let not man put *a* .... Mt 19:6   5563
And shall cut him *a*, and appoint .... Mt 24:51   1371
chains had been plucked *a* by him .... Mk 5:4   1288
together, let not man put *a* .... Mk 10:9   5563
he burst *a* in the midst, and all............. Acts 1:18   2997
departed in *a* one from the other .... Acts 15:39   673
even to the dividing *a* of soul .... Heb 4:12
were stoned, they were sawn *a* .... Heb 11:37   4249

ASUPPIM *Storage for temple gods.*
and to his sons the house of *A* .... 1Cʰ r 26:15   624
four a day, and toward *A* two 1Chr 26:17   624

ASYNCRITUS *(a-sin'-cri-tus) A Christian acquaintance of Paul.*
Salute *A*, Phlegon, Hermas, ... Rom 16:14   799

AT See APPENDIX.

ATAD *(a'-tad) See* ABEL-MIZRAIM. *A place east of the Jordan.*
came to the threshingfloor of *A* .... Gen 50:10   329
the mourning in the floor of *A* .... Gen 50:11   329

ATARAH *(at'-a-rah) A wife of Jerahmeel.*
another wife, whose name was *A* 1Chr 2:26   5851

ATAROTH *(at'-a-roth) See* ATAROTH-ADAR, ATROTH.
  1. A city east of the Jordan.
A, and Dibon, and Jazer, and Nimrah, ... Num 32:3   5852
children of Gad built Dibon, and *A* .... Num 32:34   5852
  2. A city in Ephraim.
unto the borders of Archi to *A* .... Josh 16:2   5852
And it went down from Janohah to *A* ..... Josh 16:7   5852
  3. A city in Judah.
and the Netophathites, *A*, the 1Chr 2:54   5852

ATAROTH-ADAR *(at'-a-roth-a'-dar) See* ATAROTH-ADDAR. *A city on the border of Benjamin.*
and the border descended to *A* .... Josh 18:13   5853

ATAROTH-ADDAR *(at'-a-roth-ad'-dar) See* ATAROTH-ADAR. *Same as Ataroth-adar.*
on the east side was *A*, unto .... Josh 16:5   5853

ATE
a the sacrifices of the dead .... Ps 106:28   398
I *a* no pleasant bread, neither .... Dan 10:3   398
of the angel's hand, and *a* it up .... Rev 10:10   2719

ATER *(a'-tur)*
  1. An ancestor of an exiled family.
The children of *A* of Hezekiah .... Ezr 2:16   333
The children of *A* of Hezekiah .... Neh 7:21   333
  2. An exiled family who returned under Zerubbabel.
of Shallum, the children of *A* .... Ezr 2:42   333
of Shallum, the children of *A* .... Neh 7:45   333
  3. An Israelite who sealed the covenant with Nehemiah.
A, Hizkijah, Azzur, ... Neh 10:17   333

ATHACH *(a'-thak) A city in Judah.*
and to them which were in *A* 1Sa 30:30   6269

ATHAIAH *(ath-a-i'-ah) A son of Uzziah*
A the son of Uzziah, the son of .... Neh 11:4   6265

ATHALIAH *(ath-a-li'-ah)*
  1. Daughter of Jezebel.
And his mother's name was *A* 2Kin 8:26   6271
when *A* the mother of Ahaziah saw 2Kin 11:1   6271
nurse, in the bedchamber from *A* 2Kin 11:2   6271
A did reign over the land 2Kin 11:3   6271
when *A* heard the noise of the 2Kin 11:13   6271
A rent her clothes, and cried, ... 2Kin 11:14   6271
they slew *A* with the sword beside 2Kin 11:20   6271
also was *A* the daughter of Omri 2Chr 22:2   6271
But when *A* the mother of Ahaziah 2Chr 22:10   6271
of Ahaziah,) hid him from *A* 2Chr 22:11   6271
and *A* reigned over the land................... 2Chr 22:12   6271
Now when *A* heard the noise of the 2Chr 23:12   6271
Then *A* rent her clothes, and said, ... 2Chr 23:13   6271
they had slain *A* with the sword 2Chr 23:21   6271
For the sons of *A*, that wicked 2Chr 24:7   6271
  2. A son of Jeroham.
and Shehariah, and *A*............................ 1Chr 8:26   6271
  3. Father of Jeshiah.
Jeshaiah the son of *A*, and with............. Ezr 8:7   6271

ATHENIANS *(a-the'-ne-uns) Citizens of Athens*
(For all the *A* and strangers which .... Acts 17:21   117

ATHENS *(ath'-ens) See* ATHENIANS. *A city in Greece.*
conducted Paul brought him unto *A* .... Acts 17:15   116
while Paul waited for them at *A* .... Acts 17:16   116
Mars' hill, and said, Ye men of *A* .... Acts 17:22   117
these things Paul departed from *A* .... Acts 18:1   116

it good to be left at *A* alone 1Th 3:1   116
Thessalonians was written from *A* .... 1Th s   116
Thessalonians was written from *A* .... 2Th s   116

ATHIRST
And he was sore *a*, and called on .... Judg 15:18   6770
and when thou art *a*, go unto the .... Ruth 2:9   6770
when saw we thee an hungred, or *a* .. Mt 25:44   1372
I will give unto him that is *a* of.............. Rev 21:6   1372
And let him that is *a* come .... Rev 22:17   1372

ATHLAI *(ath'-lahee) Married a foreign wife in exile.*
Jehohanan, Hananiah, Zabbai, and *A* .... Ezr 10:28   6270

ATONEMENT
things wherewith the *a* was made .... Ex 29:33   3722
bullock for a sin offering for *a* .... Ex 29:36   3725
when thou hast made an *a* for it .... Ex 29:36   3722
shalt make an *a* for the altar .... Ex 29:37   3722
Aaron shall make an *a* upon the .... Ex 30:10   3722
he make a upon it throughout your .... Ex 30:10   3722
to make an *a* for your souls .... Ex 30:15   3722
thou shalt take the *a* money of.............. Ex 30:16   3725
to make an *a* for your souls .... Ex 30:16   3722
I shall make an *a* for your sin................ Ex 32:30   3722
for him to make *a* for him .... Lev 4:20   3722
priest shall make an *a* for them .... Lev 4:20   3722
the priest shall make an *a* for .... Lev 4:26   3722
priest shall make an *a* for him .... Lev 4:31   3722
an *a* for his sin that he hath .... Lev 4:35   3722
the priest shall make an *a* for................ Lev 5:6   3722
the priest shall make an *a* for................ Lev 5:10   3722
the priest shall make an *a* for................ Lev 5:13   3722
the priest shall make an *a* for................ Lev 5:16   3722
make an *a* for him concerning his.......... Lev 5:18   3722
make an *a* for him before the LORD .... Lev 6:7   3722
the priest that maketh *a* .... Lev 7:7   3722
to do, to make an *a* for you .... Lev 8:34   3722
make an *a* for thyself, and for the .... Lev 9:7   3722
the people, and make an *a* for them....... Lev 9:7   3722
to make *a* for them before the .... Lev 10:17   3722
the LORD, and make an *a* for her .... Lev 12:7   3722
priest shall make an *a* for her .... Lev 12:8   3722
make an *a* for him before the LORD .... Lev 14:18   3722
make an *a* for him that is to be .... Lev 14:19   3722
priest shall make an *a* for him .... Lev 14:20   3722
to be waved, to make an *a* for him .... Lev 14:21   3722
to make an *a* for him before the .... Lev 14:29   3722
the priest shall make an *a* for .... Lev 14:31   3722
and make an *a* for the house .... Lev 14:53   3722
the priest shall make an *a* for .... Lev 15:15   3722
the priest shall make an *a* for .... Lev 15:30   3722
make an *a* for himself, and for his .... Lev 16:6   3722
the LORD, to make an *a* with him .... Lev 16:10   3722
and shall make an *a* for himself............. Lev 16:11   3722
he shall make an *a* for the holy .... Lev 16:16   3722
in to make an *a* in the holy place .... Lev 16:17   3722
and have made an *a* for himself .... Lev 16:17   3722
the LORD, and make an *a* for it .... Lev 16:18   3722
make an *a* for himself, and for the .... Lev 16:24   3722
in to make *a* in the holy place................ Lev 16:27   3722
the priest make an *a* for you .... Lev 16:30   3722
father's stead, shall make the *a* .... Lev 16:32   3722
he shall make an *a* for the holy .... Lev 16:33   3722
he shall make an *a* for the .... Lev 16:33   3722
shall make an *a* for the priests .... Lev 16:33   3722
to make an *a* for the children of .... Lev 16:34   3722
altar to make an *a* for your souls .... Lev 17:11   3722
that maketh an *a* for the soul .... Lev 17:11   3722
the priest shall make an *a* for................ Lev 19:22   3722
month there shall be a day of *a* .... Lev 23:27   3725
for it is a day of *a* .... Lev 23:28   3725
to make an *a* for you before the .... Lev 23:28   3725
in the day of *a* shall ye make the .... Lev 25:9   3725
beside the ram of the *a* .... Num 5:8   3725
whereby an *a* shall be made for .... Num 5:8   3722
offering, and make an *a* for him .... Num 6:11   3722
to make an *a* for the Levites .... Num 8:12   3722
to make an *a* for the children of .... Num 8:19   3722
Aaron made an *a* for them to .... Num 8:21   3722
the priest shall make an *a* for .... Num 15:25   3722
the priest shall make an *a* for .... Num 15:28   3722
the LORD, to make an *a* for him .... Num 15:28   3722
and make an *a* for them .... Num 16:46   3722
and made an *a* for the people .... Num 16:47   3722
made an *a* for the children of.................. Num 25:13   3722
offering, to make an *a* for you .... Num 28:22   3722
the goats, to make an *a* for you .... Num 28:30   3722
offering, to make an *a* for you .... Num 29:5   3722
beside the sin offering of *a* .... Num 29:11   3725
to make an *a* for our souls before.......... Num 31:50   3722
and wherewith shall I make the *a* 2Sa 21:3   3722

holy, and to make an *a* for Israel .... 1Chr 6:49 — 3722
to make an *a* for all Israel .... 2Chr 29:24 — 3722
offerings to make an *a* for Israel .... Neh 10:33 — 3722
whom we have now received the *a* .... Rom 5:11 — 2643

ATONEMENTS
blood of the sin offering of *a* .... Ex 30:10 — 3725

ATROTH (*a'-troth*) See ATAROTH. *A city in Gad.*
And A, Shophan, and Jaazer, and .... Num 32:35 — 5855

ATROTH BETH JOAB See ATROTH.

ATTAI (*at'-tahee*)
1. A grandson of Sheshan.
and she bare him A .... 1Chr 2:35 — 6262
A begat Nathan, and Nathan begat .... 1Chr 2:36 — 6262
2. A Gadite in David's army.
A the sixth, Eliel the seventh, ... 1Chr 12:11 — 6262
3. A son of Rehoboam.
which bare him Abijah, and A .... 2Chr 11:20 — 6262

ATTAIN
it is high, I cannot *a* unto it .... Ps 139:6
shall *a* unto wise counsels .... Prov 1:5 — 7069
as his hand shall *a* unto, and an .... Eze 46:7 — 5381
it be ere they *a* to innocency .... Hos 8:5 — 3201
any means they might *a* to Phenice ...... Acts 27:12 — 2658
If by any means I might *a* unto .... Phil 3:11 — 2658

ATTAINED
have not *a* unto the days of the .... Gen 47:9 — 5381
howbeit he *a* not unto the first .... 2Sa 23:19 — 935
but he *a* not to the first three .... 2Sa 23:23 — 935
howbeit he *a* not to the first .... 1Chr 11:21 — 935
but *a* not to the first three .... 1Chr 11:25 — 935
have *a* to righteousness, even the .... Rom 9:30 — 2638
hath not *a* to the law of .... Rom 9:31 — 5348
Not as though I had already *a* .... Phil 3:12 — 2983
whereto we have already *a* .... Phil 3:16 — 5348
doctrine, whereunto thou hast *a* .... 1Ti 4:6 — 3877

ATTALIA (*at-ta-li'-ah*) *A seaport near Perga.*
in Perga, they went down into A .... Acts 14:25 — 825

ATTEND
he had appointed to *a* upon her .... Est 4:5 — 6440
a unto my cry, give ear unto my .... Ps 17:1 — 7181
A unto me, and hear me .... Ps 55:2 — 7181
a unto my prayer .... Ps 61:1 — 7181
and *a* to the voice of my .... Ps 86:6 — 7181
A unto my cry .... Ps 142:6 — 7181
and *a* to know understanding .... Prov 4:1 — 7181
My son, *a* to my words .... Prov 4:20 — 7181
a unto my wisdom, and bow thine .... Prov 5:1 — 7181
a to the words of my mouth .... Prov 7:24 — 7181
that ye may *a* upon the Lord .... 1Cor 7:35 — 2145

ATTENDANCE
the *a* of his ministers, and their .... 1Kin 10:5 — 4612
the *a* of his ministers, and their .... 2Chr 9:4 — 4612
give *a* to reading, to exhortation .... 1Ti 4:13 — 4337
which no man gave *a* at the altar .... Heb 7:13 — 4337

ATTENDED
I *a* unto you, and, behold, there .... Job 32:12 — 995
he hath *a* to the voice of my .... Ps 66:19 — 7181
that she *a* unto the things which .... Acts 16:14 — 4337

ATTENDING
a continually upon this very .... Rom 13:6 — 4343

ATTENT
let thine ears be *a* unto the .... 2Chr 6:40 — 7183
mine ears *a* unto the prayer that .... 2Chr 7:15 — 7183

ATTENTIVE
Let thine ear now be *a*, and thine .... Neh 1:6 — 7183
let now thine ear be *a* to the .... Neh 1:11 — 7183
were *a* unto the book of the law .... Neh 8:3 — 7183
let thine ears be *a* to the voice .... Ps 130:2 — 7183
people were very *a* to hear him .... Lk 19:48 — 1582

ATTENTIVELY
Hear *a* the noise of his voice, and .... Job 37:2 — 8085

ATTIRE
a woman with the *a* of an harlot .... Prov 7:10 — 7897
her ornaments, or a bride her *a* .... Jer 2:32 — 7196
in dyed *a* upon their heads .... Eze 23:15 — 2871

ATTIRED
the linen mitre shall he be *a* .... Lev 16:4 — 6801

AUDIENCE
in the *a* of the children of Heth .... Gen 23:10 — 241
the *a* of the people of the land .... Gen 23:13 — 241
in the *a* of the sons of Heth .... Gen 23:16 — 241
read in the *a* of the people .... Ex 24:7 — 241
I pray thee, speak in thine *a* .... 1Sa 25:24 — 241

in the *a* of our God, keep and seek ...... 1Chr 28:8 — 241
of Moses in the *a* of the people .... Neh 13:1 — 241
sayings in the *a* of the people .... Lk 7:1 — 189
Then in the *a* of all the people .... Lk 20:45 — 191
and ye that fear God, give *a* .... Acts 13:16 — 191
gave *a* to Barnabas and Paul, ... Acts 15:12 — 191
they gave him *a* unto this word, ... Acts 22:22 — 191

AUGMENT
to *a* yet the fierce anger of the .... Num 32:14 — 5595

AUGUSTAN See AUGUSTUS.

AUGUSTUS (*aw-gus'-tus*) See AUGUSTUS', CAESAR. *An emperor of Rome.*
went out a decree from Caesar A .... Lk 2:1 — 828
be reserved unto the hearing of A .... Acts 25:21 — 828
he himself hath appealed to A .... Acts 25:25 — 828

AUGUSTUS' (*aw-gus'-tus*)
Julius, a centurion of A band .... Acts 27:1 — 828

AUL
bore his ear through with an *a* .... Ex 21:6 — 4836
Then thou shalt take an *a* .... Deut 15:17 — 4836

AUNT
she is thine *a* .... Lev 18:14 — 1733

AUSTERE
thee, because thou art an *a* man .... Lk 19:21 — 840
Thou knewest that I was an *a* man ...... Lk 19:22 — 840

AUTHOR
For God is not the *a* of confusion 1Cor 14:33
he became the *a* of eternal .... Heb 5:9 — 159
Looking unto Jesus the *a* and .... Heb 12:2 — 747

AUTHORITIES
angels and *a* and powers being made .... 1Pet 3:22 — 1849

AUTHORITY
the Jew, wrote with all *a* .... Est 9:29 — 8633
When the righteous are in *a* .... Prov 29:2 — 7235
he taught them as one having *a* .... Mt 7:29 — 1849
For I am a man under *a*, having .... Mt 8:9 — 1849
are great exercise *a* upon them .... Mt 20:25 — 2715
By what *a* doest thou these things ...... Mt 21:23 — 1849
and who gave thee this *a* .... Mt 21:23 — 1849
you by what *a* I do these things .... Mt 21:24 — 1849
I you by what *a* I do these things .... Mt 21:27 — 1849
he taught them as one that had *a* .... Mk 1:22 — 1849
for with a commandeth he even the ...... Mk 1:27 — 1849
great ones exercise *a* upon them .... Mk 10:42 — 2715
By what *a* doest thou these things ...... Mk 11:28 — 1849
thee this *a* to do these things .... Mk 11:28 — 1849
you by what *a* I do these things .... Mk 11:29 — 1849
you by what *a* I do these things .... Mk 11:33 — 1849
gave *a* to his servants, and to .... Mk 13:34 — 1849
for with a and power he commandeth .... Lk 4:36 — 1849
For I also am a man set under *a* .... Lk 7:8 — 1849
a over all devils, and to cure .... Lk 9:1 — 1849
have thou *a* over ten cities .... Lk 19:17 — 1849
by what *a* doest thou these things ...... Lk 20:2 — 1849
who is he that gave thee this *a* .... Lk 20:2 — 1849
I you by what *a* I do these things .... Lk 20:8 — 1849
the power and of the governor .... Lk 20:20 — 1849
they that exercise *a* upon them .... Lk 22:25 — 1850
hath given him *a* to execute .... Jn 5:27 — 1849
an eunuch of great *a* under .... Acts 8:27 — 1413
here he hath *a* from the chief .... Acts 9:14 — 1849
having received *a* from the chief .... Acts 26:10 — 1849
as I went to Damascus with *a* .... Acts 26:12 — 1849
have put down all rule and all *a* .... 1Cor 15:24 — 1849
boast somewhat more of our *a* .... 2Cor 10:8 — 1849
kings, and for all that are in *a* .... 1Ti 2:2 — 5247
nor to usurp *a* over the man .... 1Ti 2:12 — 831
and exhort, and rebuke with all *a* .... Titus 2:15 — 2003
power, and his seat, and great *a* .... Rev 13:2 — 1849

AVA (*a'-vah*) See IVAH. *An area near Babylon.*
and from Cuthah, and from A .... 2Kin 17:24 — 5755

AVAILETH
Yet all this *a* me nothing .... Est 5:13 — 7737
neither circumcision *a* any thing .... Gal 5:6 — 2480
neither circumcision *a* any thing .... Gal 6:15 — 2480
prayer of a righteous man *a* much .... Jas 5:16 — 2480

AVEN See BETH-AVEN. *Another name for Heliopolis, in Egypt.*
The young men of A and of .... Eze 30:17 — 206
The high places also of A .... Hos 10:8 — 206
inhabitant from the plain of A .... Amos 1:5 — 206

AVENGE
Thou shalt not *a*, nor bear any .... Lev 19:18 — 5358
that shall *a* the quarrel of my .... Lev 26:25 — 5358

A the children of Israel of the ....Num 31:2 5358,5360
and a the LORD of Midian.................Num 31:3 5414,5360
for he will a the blood of his.................Deut 32:43 5358
and thee, and the LORD a me of thee......1Sa 24:12 5358
that I may a the blood of my 2Kin 9:7 5358
to a themselves on their enemies ....Est 8:13 5358
and a me of mine enemies ....Is 1:24 5358
that he may a him of his ....Jer 46:10 5358
I will a the blood of Jezreel....................Hos 1:4 6485
saying, A me of mine adversary ....Lk 18:3 *1556*
widow troubleth me, I will a her ....Lk 18:5 *1556*
shall not God a his own elect..Lk 18:7 *4160,3588,1557*
that he will a them speedily ...Lk 18:8 *4160,3588,1557*
a not yourselves, but rather give ....Rom 12:19 *1556*
a our blood on them that dwell on.........Rev 6:10 *1556*

AVENGED
If Cain shall be a sevenfold....................Gen 4:24 5358
until the people had a themselves ....Josh 10:13 5358
done this, yet will I be a of you ....Judg 15:7 5358
that I may be at once a of the ....Judg 16:28 5358
that I may be a on mine enemies 1Sa 14:24 5358
to be a of the king's enemies 1Sa 18:25 5358
or that my lord hath a himself...............1Sa 25:31 3467
LORD hath a my lord the king 2Sa 4:8 5414,5360
LORD hath a him of his enemies 2Sa 18:19 8199
for the LORD hath a thee this day 2Sa 18:31 8199
shall not my soul be a on such a ....Jer 5:9 5358
shall not my soul be a on such a ....Jer 5:29 5358
shall not my soul be a on such a ....Jer 9:9 5358
a him that was oppressed, and.............Acts 7:24
for God hath a you on her........Rev 18:20 2919,3588,2917
hath the blood of his servants ....Rev 19:2 *1556*

AVENGER
you cities for refuge from the a ....Num 35:12 1350
Lest the a of the blood pursue ....Deut 19:6 1350
into the hand of the a of blood ....Deut 19:12 1350
your refuge from the a of blood ....Josh 20:3 1350
if the a of blood pursue after ....Josh 20:5 1350
die by the hand of the a of blood ....Josh 20:9 1350
mightest still the enemy and the a ....Ps 8:2 5358
by reason of the enemy and a ....Ps 44:16 5358
the Lord is the a of all such....................1Th 4:6 *1558*

AVENGETH
It is God that a me, and that 2Sa 22:48 5414,5360
It is God that a me, and subdueth ..Ps 18:47 5414,5360

AVENGING
ye the LORD for the a of Israel.........Judg 5:2 6544,6546
from a thyself with thine own 1Sa 25:26 3467
from a myself with mine own hand........1Sa 25:33 3467

AVERSE
by securely as men a from war...............Mic 2:8 7725

AVIM *(a'-vim)* See AVIMS, AVITES. *A city near Bethel.*
And A, and Parah, and Ophrah, ...Josh 18:23 5761

AVIMS *(a'-vims)* See AVIMS. *A Canaanite tribe.*
the A which dwelt in Hazerim,.................Deut 2:23 5757

AVITES *(a'-vites)* See AVIM.
 1. Same as Avims.
and the Ekronites; also the A.........Josh 13:3 5757
 2. A tribe moved to Samaria.
the A made Nibhaz and Tartak, and......2Kin 17:31 5757

AVITH *(a'-vith) Capital of Edom.*
and the name of his city was A.......Gen 36:35 5762
and the name of his city was A..............1Chr 1:46 5762

AVOID
A it, pass not by it, turn from..................Prov 4:15 6544
and a them ....Rom 16:17 *1578*
to a fornication, let every man...............1Cor 7:2 1223
foolish and unlearned questions a..........2Ti 2:23 3868
But a foolish questions, and....................Titus 3:9 4026

AVOIDED
David a out of his presence twice 1Sa 18:11 5437

AVOIDING
A this, that no man should blame 2Cor 8:20 4724
a profane and vain babblings, and 1Ti 6:20 *1624*

AVOUCHED
Thou hast a the LORD this day to ....Deut 26:17 559
the LORD hath a thee this day to ....Deut 26:18 559

AVVA See AVA.

AVVIM See AVITES.

AWAIT
But their laying a was known of ....Acts 9:24 *1917*

AWAKE
A, a, Deborah ....Judg 5:12 5782
a, a, utter a song ....Judg 5:12 5782
surely now he would a for thee ....Job 8:6 5782
be no more, they shall not a...................Job 14:12 6974
a for me to the judgment that ....Ps 7:6 5782
I shall be satisfied, when I a ....Ps 17:15 6974
a to my judgment, even unto my ....Ps 35:23 6974
A, why sleepest thou, O Lord ....Ps 44:23 5782
A up, my glory..Ps 57:8 5782
a, psaltery and harp ....Ps 57:8 5782
I myself will a early ....Ps 57:8 5782
a to help me, and behold ....Ps 59:4 5782
a to visit all the heathen ....Ps 59:5 6974
A, psaltery and harp ....Ps 108:2 5782
I myself will a early ....Ps 108:2 5782
when I a, I am still with thee ....Ps 139:18 6974
when shall I a ....Prov 23:35 6974
nor a my love, till he please ....Song 2:7 5782
nor a my love, till he please ....Song 3:5 5782
A, O north wind..Song 4:16 5782
nor a my love, until he please ....Song 8:4 5782
A and sing, ye that dwell in dust ....Is 26:19 6974
A, a, put on strength, O arm ....Is 51:9 5782
a, as in the ancient days, in the ....Is 51:9 5782
A, a, stand up, O Jerusalem ....Is 51:17 5782
A, a; put on thy strength ....Is 52:1 5782
in the dust of the earth shall a ....Dan 12:2 6974
A, ye drunkards, and weep......................Joel 1:5 6974
a that shall vex thee, and thou ....Hab 2:7 6974
him that saith to the wood, A ....Hab 2:19 6974
A, O sword, against my shepherd, ...Zec 13:7 5782
and they a him, and say unto him,.........Mk 4:38 1326
and when they were a, they saw his ....Lk 9:32 1235
that I may a him out of sleep ....Jn 11:11 *1852*
it is high time to a out of sleep ....Rom 13:11 *1453*
A to righteousness, and sin not 1Cor 15:34 *1594*
A thou that sleepest, and arise ....Eph 5:14 *1453*

AWAKED
Jacob a out of his sleep, and he ....Gen 28:16 3364
he a out of his sleep, and went................Judg 16:14 3364
saw it, nor knew it, neither a 1Sa 26:12 6974
he sleepeth, and must be a 1Kin 18:27 3364
him, saying, The child is not a 2Kin 4:31 6974
I a; for the LORD sustained me ....Ps 3:5 6974
Then the Lord a as one out of ....Ps 78:65 3364
Upon this I a, and beheld ....Jer 31:26 6974

AWAKEST
so, O Lord, when thou a, thou.................Ps 73:20 5782
and when thou a, it shall talk ....Prov 6:22 6974

AWAKETH
As a dream when one a............................Ps 73:20 6974
but he a, and his soul is empty ....Is 29:8 6974
but he a, and, behold, he is faint ....Is 29:8 6974

AWAKING
of the prison a out of his sleep ....Acts 16:27 *1096,1853*

AWARE
Or ever I was a, my soul made me ....Song 6:12 3045
O Babylon, and thou wast not a ....Jer 50:24 3045
and in an hour that he is not a of ....Mt 24:50 *1097*
walk over them are not a of them ....Lk 11:44 *1492*
and at an hour when he is not a ....Lk 12:46 *1097*

AWAY See APPENDIX.

AWE
Stand in a, and sin not ....Ps 4:4 7264
of the world stand in a of him ....Ps 33:8 1481
heart standeth in a of thy word ....Ps 119:161 6342

AWOKE
Noah a from his wine, and knew ....Gen 9:24 3364
So Pharaoh a...Gen 41:4 3364
And Pharaoh a, and, behold, it was ......Gen 41:7 3364
So I a, and, behold, it was ....Gen 41:21 3364
he a out of his sleep, and said, I ....Judg 16:20 3364
And Solomon a...1Kin 3:15 3364
a him, saying, Lord, save us...................Mt 8:25 *1453*
a him, saying, Master, master, we ....Lk 8:24 *1326*

AX
by forcing an a against them..................Deut 20:19 1631
share, and his coulter, and his a 1Sa 13:20 7134
the a head fell into the water 2Kin 6:5 1270
Shall the a boast itself against................Is 10:15 1631
hands of the workman, with the a ....Jer 10:3 4621
Thou art my battle a and weapons ....Jer 51:20 4601
now also the a is laid unto the................Mt 3:10 *513*

AXE

with the *a* to cut down the tree	Deut 19:5	1631
Abimelech took an *a* in his hand	Judg 9:48	7134
there was neither hammer nor *a*	1Kin 6:7	1631
now also the *a* is laid unto the	Lk 3:9	*513*

AXES

and for the forks, and for the *a*	1Sa 13:21	7134
under *a* of iron, and made them	2Sa 12:31	4037
with harrows of iron, and with *a*	1Chr 20:3	4050
lifted up *a* upon the thick trees	Ps 74:5	7134
work thereof at once with *a*	Ps 74:6	3781
army, and come against her with *a*	Jer 46:22	7134
with his *a* he shall break down	Eze 26:9	2719

AXLETREES

the *a* of the wheels were joined	1Kin 7:32	3027
their *a*, and their naves, and their	1Kin 7:33	3027

AZAL (*a'-zal*) *A place near Jerusalem.*

the mountains shall reach unto *A*	Zec 14:5	682

AZALIAH (*az-a-li'-ah*) *Father of Shaphan.*

king sent Shaphan the son of *A*	2Kin 22:3	683
he sent Shaphan the son of *A*	2Chr 34:8	683

AZANIAH (*az-a-ni'-ah*) *Father of Jeshua.*

both Jeshua the son of *A*, Binnui	Neh 10:9	245

AZARAEL (*a-zar'-a-el*) See AZAREEL. *A priest from the Immer family.*

And his brethren, Shemaiah, and *A*	Neh 12:36	5832

AZAREEL (*a-zar'-e-el*) See AZARAEL.
1. *A Korahite in David's army.*

Elkanah, and Jesiah, and *A*, and	1Chr 12:6	5832

2. *A priest during David's time.*

The eleventh to *A*, he, his sons,	1Chr 25:18	5832

3. *A Danite prince during David's time.*

Of Dan, *A* the son of Jeroham	1Chr 27:22	5832

4. *Married a foreign wife in exile.*

A, and Shelemiah, Shemariah,	Ezr 10:41	5832

5. *Same as Azarael.*

and Amashai the son of *A*, the son	Neh 11:13	5832

AZAREL See AZAREEL.

AZARIAH (*az-a-ri'-ah*) See AHAZIAH.
1. *A descendant of Zadok.*

A the son of Zadok the priest,	1Kin 4:2	5838

2. *Captain of Solomon's guard.*

A the son of Nathan was over the	1Kin 4:5	5838

3. *A king of Judah.*

And all the people of Judah took *A*	2Kin 14:21	5838
Jeroboam king of Israel began *A*	2Kin 15:1	5838
And the rest of the acts of *A*	2Kin 15:6	5838
So *A* slept with his fathers	2Kin 15:7	5838
eighth year of *A* king of Judah	2Kin 15:8	5838
thirtieth year of *A* king of Judah	2Kin 15:17	5838
In the fiftieth year of *A* king of	2Kin 15:23	5838
fiftieth year of *A* king of Judah	2Kin 15:27	5838
A his son, Jotham his son,	1Chr 3:12	5838

4. *A descendant of Judah.*

the sons of Ethan; *A*	1Chr 2:8	5838

5. *A descendant of Jerahmeel.*

Obed begat Jehu, and Jehu begat *A*	1Chr 2:38	5838
A begat Helez, and Helez begat	1Chr 2:39	5838

6. *A son of Ahimaaz.*

And Ahimaaz begat *A*, and Azariah	1Chr 6:9	5838

7. *Grandson of Ahimaah.*

And Johanan begat *A*, (he it is	1Chr 6:10	5838
A begat Amariah, and Amariah begat	1Chr 6:11	5838

8. *Son of Hilkiah.*

begat Hilkiah, and Hilkiah begat *A*	1Chr 6:13	5838
A begat Seraiah, and Seraiah begat	1Chr 6:14	5838
A the son of Hilkiah, the son of	1Chr 9:11	5838
the son of Seraiah, the son of *A*	Ezr 7:1	5838

9. *A descendant of Kohath.*

the son of Joel, the son of *A*	1Chr 6:36	5838

10. *A prophet sent to King Asa.*

God came upon *A* the son of Oded	2Chr 15:1	5838

11. *A son of King Jehoshaphat.*

the sons of Jehoshaphat, *A*	2Chr 21:2	5838

12. *A brother of King Jehoram.*

and Jehiel, and Zechariah, and *A*	2Chr 21:2	5838

13. *A son of King Jehoram.*

A the son of Jehoram king of	2Chr 22:6	5838

14. *A conspirator with Joash.*

A the son of Jeroham, and Ishmael	2Chr 23:1	5838

15. *Another conspirator with Joash.*

A the son of Obed, and Maaseiah	2Chr 23:1	5838

16. *A High Priest.*

A the priest went in after him,	2Chr 26:17	5838
A the chief priest, and all the	2Chr 26:20	5838

17. *A chief of Ephraim.*

A the son of Johanan, Berechiah	2Chr 28:12	5838

18. *Father of Joel.*

of Amasai, and Joel the son of *A*	2Chr 29:12	5838

19. *Helped cleanse the Temple.*

Abdi, and *A* the son of Jehalelel	2Chr 29:12	5838

20. *A chief priest.*

A the chief priest of the house	2Chr 31:10	5838
A the ruler of the house of God	2Chr 31:13	5838

21. *Great-grandfather of Zadok.*

The son of Amariah, the son of *A*	Ezr 7:3	5838

22. *A repairer of the Jerusalem walls.*

After him repaired *A* the son of	Neh 3:23	5838
from the house of *A* unto the	Neh 3:24	5838

23. *An exile with Zerubbabel.*

Zerubbabel, Jeshua, Nehemiah, *A*	Neh 7:7	5838

24. *A priest with Ezra.*

Hodijah, Maaseiah, Kelita, *A*	Neh 8:7	5838

25. *A priest who renewed the covenant.*

Seraiah, *A*, Jeremiah,	Neh 10:2	5838

26. *A prince of Judah.*

And *A*, Ezra, and Meshullam,	Neh 12:33	5838

27. *The son of Hoshaiah.*

Then spake *A* the son of Hoshaiah,	Jer 43:2	5838

28. *A companion of Daniel.*

Daniel, Hananiah, Mishael, and *A*	Dan 1:6	5838
and to *A*, of Abed-nego	Dan 1:7	5838
Daniel, Hananiah, Mishael, and *A*	Dan 1:11	5838
Daniel, Hananiah, Mishael, and *A*	Dan 1:19	5838
known to Hananiah, Mishael, and *A*	Dan 2:17	5839

AZARYAHU See AZARIAH.

AZAZ (*a'-zaz*) *Father of Bela.*

And Bela the son of *A*, the son of	1Chr 5:8	5811

AZAZIAH (*az-a-zi'-ah*)
1. *A Levite who relocated the Ark.*

and Obed-edom, and Jeiel, and *A*	1Chr 15:21	5812

2. *Father of Hoshea.*

of Ephraim, Hoshea the son of *A*	1Chr 27:20	5812

3. *A Levite during Hezekiah's reign.*

And Jehiel, and *A*, and Nahath, and	2Chr 31:13	5812

AZBUK (*az'-buk*) *Father of Nehemiah.*

repaired Nehemiah the son of *A*	Neh 3:16	5802

AZEKAH (*a-ze'-kah*) *A town in Judah.*

to Beth-horon, and smote them to *A*	Josh 10:10	5825
from heaven upon them unto *A*	Josh 10:11	5825
Jarmuth, and Adullam, Socoh, and *A*	Josh 15:35	5825
and pitched between Shochoh and *A*	1Sa 17:1	5825
And Adoraim, and Lachish, and *A*	2Chr 11:9	5825
and the fields thereof, at *A*	Neh 11:30	5825
against Lachish, and against *A*	Jer 34:7	5825

AZEL (*a'-zel*) See JAAZIEL. *A descendant of King Saul.*

son, Eleasah his son, *A* his son	1Chr 8:37	682
A had six sons, whose names are	1Chr 8:38	682
All these were the sons of *A*	1Chr 8:38	682
son, Eleasah his son, *A* his son	1Chr 9:43	682
A had six sons, whose names are	1Chr 9:44	682
these were the sons of *A*	1Chr 9:44	682

AZEM (*a'-zem*) See EZEM. *A city in Judah.*

Baalah, and Iim, and *A*,	Josh 15:29	6107
And Hazar-shual, and Balah, and *A*	Josh 19:3	6107

AZGAD (*az'-gad*)
1. *A family of exiles.*

The children of *A*, a thousand two	Ezr 2:12	5803
The children of *A*, two thousand	Neh 7:17	5803

2. *An exile with Ezra.*

And of the sons of *A*	Ezr 8:12	5803

3. *A family who sealed the covenant.*

Bunni, *A*, Bebai,	Neh 10:15	5803

AZIEL (*a'-ze-el*) *A Levite who relocated the Ark.*

And Zechariah, and *A*, and	1Chr 15:20	5815

AZIZA (*a-zi'-zah*) *Married a foreigner in exile.*

and Jeremoth, and Zabad, and *A*	Ezr 10:27	5819

AZMAVETH (*az-ma'-veth*) See BETH-AZMAVETH.
1. *A "mighty man" of David.*

the Arbathite, *A* the Barhumite,	2Sa 23:31	5820
A the Baharumite, Eliahba the	1Chr 11:33	5820

2. *A descendant of Jonathan.*

and Jehoadah begat Alemeth, and *A*	1Chr 8:36	5820
and Jarah begat Alemeth, and *A*	1Chr 9:42	5820

3. *Father of Jeziel and Pelet.*

Jeziel, and Pelet, the sons of *A*	1Chr 12:3	5820

4. *A village on the border of Judah.*

The children of *A*, forty and two	Ezr 2:24	5820
and out of the fields of Geba and *A*	Neh 12:29	5820

5. *A treasurer of David.*
treasures was *A* the son of Adiel 1Chr 27:25   5820

AZMON (*az'-mon*) See HESHMON. *A place in southern Canaan.*
to Hazar-addar, and pass on to *A* .... Num 34:4   6111
from *A* unto the river of Egypt................. Num 34:5   6111
From thence it passed toward *A* .... Josh 15:4   6111

AZNOTH-TABOR (*az'-noth-ta'-bor*) *Hills on the border of Naphtali.*
the coast turneth westward to *A* .... Josh 19:34   243

AZOR (*a'-zor*) *Great-grandson of Zorobabel.*
and Eliakim begat *A*................................. Mt 1:13   107
And *A* begat Sadoc.................................. Mt 1:14   107

AZOTUS (*a-zo'-tus*) See ASHDOD. *Greek form of Ashdod.*
But Philip was found at *A* .... Acts 8:40   108

AZRIEL (*az'-re-el*)
1. *Chief of a family of Manasseh.*
Epher, and Ishi, and Eliel, and *A* 1Chr 5:24   5837
2. *Father of Jerimoth*
Naphtali, Jerimoth the son of *A* 1Chr 27:19   5837
3. *Father of Seraiah.*
and Seraiah the son of *A*, and .... Jer 36:26   5837

AZRIKAM (*az'-ri-kam*)
1. *A son of Neariah.*
Elioenai, and Hezekiah, and *A* 1Chr 3:23   5840

2. *A son of Azel.*
sons, whose names are these, *A* 1Chr 8:38   5840
sons, whose names are these, *A* 1Chr 9:44   5840
3. *A descendant of Merari.*
the son of Hasshub, the son of *A* 1Chr 9:14   5840
the son of Hashub, the son of *A* .... Neh 11:15   5840
4. *Governor of the house of King Ahaz.*
A the governor of the house, and 2Chr 28:7   5840

AZUBAH (*a-zu'-bah*)
1. *Mother of King Jehoshaphat.*
his mother's name was *A* the 1Kin 22:42   5806
his mother's name was *A* the 2Chr 20:31   5806
2. *Wife of Caleb.*
begat children of *A* his wife 1Chr 2:18   5806
when *A* was dead, Caleb took unto 1Chr 2:19   5806

AZUR (*a'-zur*) See AZZUR.
1. *Father of Hananiah.*
Hananiah the son of *A* the prophet .... Jer 28:1   5809
2. *Father of Jaazaniah.*
whom I saw Jaazaniah the son of *A* ...... Eze 11:1   5809

AZZAH (*az'-zah*) See GAZA. *A Philistine city.*
dwelt in Hazerim, even unto *A* .... Deut 2:23   5804
the river, from Tiphsah even to *A* 1Kin 4:24   5804
Philistines, and Ashkelon, and *A* .... Jer 25:20   5804

AZZAN (*az'-zan*) *A prince of Issachar.*
of Issachar, Paltiel the son of *A*............. Num 34:26   5821

AZZUR (*az'-zur*) *An Israelite who sealed the covenant under Nehemiah.*
Ater, Hizkijah, *A*,................................... Neh 10:17   5809

B

BAAL (*ba'-al*) See BAAL-BERITH, BAALE, BAAL-GAD, BAAL-HAMON, BAAL-HANAN, BAAL-HAZOR, BAAL-HERMON, BAALIM, BAAL-MEON, BAAL-PEOR, BAAL-PERAZIM, BAAL-SHALISHA, BAAL-TAMAR.
1. *Chief god of the Canaanites.*
him up into the high places of *B*............. Num 22:41   1168
forsook the LORD, and served *B* .... Judg 2:13   1168
altar of *B* that thy father hath................ Judg 6:25   1168
the altar of *B* was cast down, and .... Judg 6:28   1168
he hath cast down the altar of *B* .... Judg 6:30   1168
against him, Will ye plead for *B* .... Judg 6:31   1168
Let *B* plead against him, because .... Judg 6:32   1168
Zidonians, and went and served *B* 1Kin 16:31   1168
altar for *B* in the house of *B* 1Kin 16:32   1168
and the prophets of *B* four hundred 1Kin 18:19   1168
but if *B*, then follow him 1Kin 18:21   1168
said unto the prophets of *B* 1Kin 18:25   1168
called on the name of *B* from 1Kin 18:26   1168
even until noon, saying, O *B* 1Kin 18:26   1168
unto them, Take the prophets of *B* 1Kin 18:40   1168
knees which have not bowed unto *B* 1Kin 19:18   1168
For he served *B*, and worshipped........... 1Kin 22:53   1168
of *B* that his father had made 2Kin 3:2   1168
unto them, Ahab served *B* a little........... 2Kin 10:18   1168
unto me all the prophets of *B* 2Kin 10:19   1168
have a great sacrifice to do to *B* 2Kin 10:19   1168
destroy the worshippers of *B* 2Kin 10:19   1168
Proclaim a solemn assembly for *B* 2Kin 10:20   1168
and all the worshippers of *B* came 2Kin 10:21   1168
And they came into the house of *B* 2Kin 10:21   1168
the house of *B* was full from one............ 2Kin 10:21   1168
for all the worshippers of *B* 2Kin 10:22   1168
of Rechab, into the house of *B* 2Kin 10:23   1168
and said unto the worshippers of *B* 2Kin 10:23   1168
but the worshippers of *B* only 2Kin 10:23   1168
to the city of the house of *B* 2Kin 10:25   1168
the images out of the house of *B* 2Kin 10:26   1168
And they brake down the image of *B* 2Kin 10:27   1168
and brake down the house of *B* 2Kin 10:27   1168
Jehu destroyed *B* out of Israel 2Kin 10:28   1168
the land went into the house of *B* 2Kin 11:18   1168
the priest of *B* before the altars 2Kin 11:18   1168
the host of heaven, and served *B* 2Kin 17:16   1168
and he reared up altars for *B* 2Kin 21:3   1168
the vessels that were made for *B* 2Kin 23:4   1168
also that burned incense unto *B*............. 2Kin 23:5   1168
the people went to the house of *B* 2Chr 23:17   1168
the priest of *B* before the altars 2Chr 23:17   1168
and the prophets prophesied by *B* .... Jer 2:8   1168
falsely, and burn incense unto *B*............ Jer 7:9   1168
altars to burn incense unto *B*................. Jer 11:13   1168
anger in offering incense unto *B* .... Jer 11:17   1168
taught my people to swear by *B* .... Jer 12:16   1168
built also the high places of *B*................ Jer 19:5   1168

fire for burnt offerings unto *B* .... Jer 19:5   1168
they prophesied in *B*, and caused .... Jer 23:13   1168
have forgotten my name for *B* .... Jer 23:27   1168
they have offered incense unto *B* .... Jer 32:29   1168
they built the high places of *B* .... Jer 32:35   1168
gold, which they prepared for *B* .... Hos 2:8   1168
but when he offended in *B* .... Hos 13:1   1168
the remnant of *B* from this place........... Zeph 1:4   1168
bowed the knee to the image of *B* .... Rom 11:4   896
2. *A city in Simeon.*
about the same cities, unto *B*................. 1Chr 4:33   1168
3. *A descendant of Reuben.*
son, Reaia his son, *B* his son, ... 1Chr 5:5   1168
4. *A descendant of Benjamin.*
son Abdon, and Zur, and Kish, and *B* 1Chr 8:30   1168
Abdon, then Zur, and Kish, and *B*........... 1Chr 9:36   1168

BAALAH (*ba'-al-ah*) See BAALE, BALEH, BILHAH, KIRJATH-BAAL.
1. *A city in Judah.*
and the border was drawn to *B* .... Josh 15:9   1173
from *B* westward unto mount Seir .... Josh 15:10   1173
B, and Iim, and Azem .... Josh 15:29   1173
went up, and all Israel, to *B* 1Chr 13:6   1173
2. *A hill in Judah.*
and passed along to mount *B* .... Josh 15:11   1173

BAALATH (*ba'-al-ath*) See BAALATH-BEER. *A town in Dan.*
And Eltekeh, and Gibbethon, and *B* ...... Josh 19:44   1191
And *B*, and Tadmor in the wilderness 1Kin 9:18   1191
And *B*, and all the store cities................. 2Chr 8:6   1191

BAALATH-BEER (*ba'-al-ath-be'-ur*) *A city in Simeon.*
round about these cities to *B* .... Josh 19:8   1192

BAAL-BERITH (*ba'-al-be'-rith*) *An idol.*
after Baalim, and made *B* their god....... Judg 8:33   1170
of silver out of the house of *B*................ Judg 9:4   1170

BAALE (*ba'-al-eh*) *A form of Baalah.*
were with him from *B* of Judah.............. 2Sa 6:2   1184

BAALE-JUDAH See BAALE.

BAAL-GAD (*ba'-al-gad'*) *A Canaanite city.*
even unto *B* in the valley of.................... Josh 11:17   1171
from *B* in the valley of Lebanon............. Josh 12:7   1171
from *B* under mount Hermon unto .... Josh 13:5   1171

BAAL-HAMON (*ba'-al-ha'-mon*) *A place near Samaria.*
Solomon had a vineyard at *B*................. Song 8:11   1174

BAAL-HANAN (*ba'-al-ha'-nan*)
1. *A king of Edom.*
B the son of Achbor reigned in .... Gen 36:38   1177
B the son of Achbor died, and................ Gen 36:39   1177
B the son of Achbor reigned in 1Chr 1:49   1177
when *B* was dead, Hadad reigned in...... 1Chr 1:50   1177

2. *A superintendent for David.*
the low plains was B the Gederite 1Chr 27:28 1177

BAAL-HAZOR (ba'-al-ha'-zor) See HAZOR. *A place near Ephraim.*
Absalom had sheepshearers in B 2Sa 13:23 1178

BAAL-HERMON (ba'-al-her'-mon) *A city near Mt. Hermon.*
from mount B unto the entering in .... Judg 3:3 1179
they increased from Bashan unto B 1Chr 5:23 1179

BAALI (ba'-al-i) *A rejected title of God.*
and shalt call me no more B .... Hos 2:16 1180

BAALIM (ba'-al-im) See BAAL. *Plural of Baal.*
sight of the LORD, and served B .... Judg 2:11 1168
the LORD their God, and served B .... Judg 3:7 1168
again, and went a whoring after B .... Judg 8:33 1168
sight of the LORD, and served B .... Judg 10:6 1168
our God, and also served B .... Judg 10:10 1168
children of Israel did put away B 1Sa 7:4 1168
the LORD, and have served B................... 1Sa 12:10 1168
the LORD, and thou hast followed B 1Kin 18:18 1168
David, and sought not unto B 2Chr 17:3 1168
the LORD did they bestow upon B 2Chr 24:7 1168
and made also molten images for B 2Chr 28:2 1168
and he reared up altars for B 2Chr 33:3 1168
the altars of B in his presence 2Chr 34:4 1168
polluted, I have not gone after B .... Jer 2:23 1168
of their own heart, and after B .... Jer 9:14 1168
will visit upon her the days of B .... Hos 2:13 1168
the names of B out of her mouth .... Hos 2:17 1168
they sacrificed unto B, and burned .... Hos 11:2 1168

BAALIS (ba'-al-is) *A king of the Ammonites.*
Dost thou certainly know that B .... Jer 40:14 1185

BAAL-MEON (ba'-al-me'-on) See BETH-BAAL-MEON. *A Reubenite town.*
And Nebo, and B, (their names being..... Num 32:38 1186
in Aroer, even unto Nebo and B 1Chr 5:8 1186
of the country, Beth-jeshimoth, B .... Eze 25:9 1186

BAAL-PEOR (ba'-al-pe'-or) See PEOR. *A Moabite idol.*
And Israel joined himself unto B .... Num 25:3 1187
his men that were joined unto B .... Num 25:5 1187
what the LORD did because of B .... Deut 4:3 1187
for all the men that followed B .... Deut 4:3 1187
joined themselves also unto B .... Ps 106:28 1187
but they went to B, and separated......... Hos 9:10 1187

BAAL-PERAZIM (ba'-al-per'-a-zim) *A place near the valley of Rephaim.*
And David came to B, and David 2Sa 5:20 1188
called the name of that place B 2Sa 5:20 1188
So they came up to B................................ 1Chr 14:11 1188
called the name of that place B 1Chr 14:11 1188

BAAL'S (ba'-als)
but B prophets are four hundred 1Kin 18:22 1168

BAAL-SHALISHA (ba'-al-shal'-i-shah) *A place in Ephraim.*
And there came a man from B................ 2Kin 4:42 1190

BAAL-TAMAR (ba'-al-ta'-mar) *A place in Benjamin.*
and put themselves in array at B .... Judg 20:33 1193

BAAL-ZEBUB (ba'-al-ze'-bub) See BEELZEBUB. *A Philistine idol.*
enquire of B the god of Ekron 2Kin 1:2 1176
to enquire of B the god of Ekron........... 2Kin 1:3 1176
to enquire of B the god of Ekron........... 2Kin 1:6 1176
to enquire of B the god of Ekron........... 2Kin 1:16 1176

BAAL-ZEPHON (ba'-al-ze'-fon) *A place near the Red Sea crossing.*
Migdol and the sea, over against B .... Ex 14:2 1189
sea, beside Pi-hahiroth, before B .... Ex 14:9 1189
Pi-hahiroth, which is before B .... Num 33:7 1189

BAANA (ba'-an-ah) See BAANAH.
1. *An officer in Solomon's army.*
B the son of Ahilud.................................... 1Kin 4:12 1195
2. *Father of Zadok.*
them repaired Zadok the son of B .... Neh 3:4 1195

BAANAH (ba'-an-ah) See BAANA.
1. *A captain in Ishbosheth's army.*
the name of the one was B 2Sa 4:2 1195
the Beerothite, Rechab and B 2Sa 4:5 1195
Rechab and B his brother escaped 2Sa 4:6 1195
B his brother, the sons of Rimmon.......... 2Sa 4:9 1195
2. *Father of Heleb.*
Heleb the son of B, a................................ 2Sa 23:29 1195
the son of B the Netophathite 1Chr 11:30 1195
3. *An officer in Solomon's army.*
B the son of Hushai was in Asher 1Kin 4:16 1195

4. *An exile who returned with Zerubbabel.*
Bilshan, Mizpar, Bigvai, Rehum, B .... Ezr 2:2 1195
Mispereth, Bigvai, Nehum, B .... Neh 7:7 1195
Malluch, Harim, B................................... Neh 10:27 1195

BAARA (ba'-ar-ah) *A wife of Shaharaim.*
Hushim and B were his wives................. 1Chr 8:8 1199

BAASEIAH (ba-as-i'-ah) *A Gershonite Levite.*
The son of Michael, the son of B............ 1Chr 6:40 1202

BAASHA (ba'-ash-ah) *A king of Israel.*
B king of Israel all their days 1Kin 15:16 1201
B king of Israel went up against 1Kin 15:17 1201
thy league with B king of Israel 1Kin 15:19 1201
when B heard thereof, that he................ 1Kin 15:21 1201
thereof, wherewith B had builded 1Kin 15:22 1201
B the son of Ahijah, of the house 1Kin 15:27 1201
B smote him at Gibbethon, which 1Kin 15:27 1201
Asa king of Judah did B slay him 1Kin 15:28 1201
B king of Israel all their days 1Kin 15:32 1201
B the son of Ahijah to reign over 1Kin 15:33 1201
Jehu the son of Hanani against B 1Kin 16:1 1201
will take away the posterity of B 1Kin 16:3 1201
Him that dieth of B in the city 1Kin 16:4 1201
Now the rest of the acts of B................. 1Kin 16:5 1201
So B slept with his fathers, and 1Kin 16:6 1201
the word of the LORD against B 1Kin 16:7 1201
B to reign over Israel in Tirzah 1Kin 16:8 1201
that he slew all the house of B 1Kin 16:11 1201
Zimri destroy all the house of B 1Kin 16:12 1201
against B by Jehu the prophet 1Kin 16:12 1201
For all the sins of B, and the 1Kin 16:13 1201
the house of B the son of Ahijah 1Kin 21:22 1201
the house of B the son of Ahijah 2Kin 9:9 1201
year of the reign of Asa B king 2Chr 16:1 1201
thy league with B king of Israel 2Chr 16:3 1201
when B heard it, that he left off 2Chr 16:5 1201
thereof, wherewith B was building 2Chr 16:6 1201
made for fear of B king of Israel............ Jer 41:9 1201

BABBLER
and a b is no better.......................... Eccl 10:11 1167,3956
some said, What will this b say .... Acts 17:18 4691

BABBLING
who hath b.. Prov 23:29 7879

BABBLINGS
trust, avoiding profane and vain b 1Ti 6:20 2757
But shun profane and vain b 2Ti 2:16 2757

BABE
and, behold, the b wept .... Ex 2:6 5288
of Mary, the b in her womb .... Lk 1:41 1025
the b leaped in my womb for joy .... Lk 1:44 1025
Ye shall find the b wrapped in .... Lk 2:12 1025
and the b lying in a manger .... Lk 2:16 1025
for he is a b... Heb 5:13 3516

BABEL (ba'-bel) See BABYLON. *A city in the plain of Shinar.*
beginning of his kingdom was B............. Gen 10:10 894
is the name of it called B........................ Gen 11:9 894

BABES
Out of the mouth of b and .... Ps 8:2 5768
of their substance to their b .... Ps 17:14 5768
and b shall rule over them .... Is 3:4 8586
and hast revealed them unto b.............. Mt 11:25 3516
never read, Out of the mouth of b......... Mt 21:16 3516
and hast revealed them unto b.............. Lk 10:21 3516
of the foolish, a teacher of b .... Rom 2:20 3516
carnal, even as unto b in Christ 1Cor 3:1 3516
As newborn b, desire the sincere 1Pet 2:2 1025

BABYLON (bab'-il-un) See BABEL, BABYLONIANS, BABYLONISH, BABYLON'S, CHALDEA, SHESHACH. *Capital of the Babylonian Empire; located on the Euphrates River.*
of Assyria brought men from B 2Kin 17:24 894
the men of B made Succoth-benoth,....... 2Kin 17:30 894
the son of Baladan, king of B 2Kin 20:12 894
from a far country, even from B............. 2Kin 20:14 894
this day, shall be carried into B 2Kin 20:17 894
in the palace of the king of B 2Kin 20:18 894
Nebuchadnezzar king of B came up 2Kin 24:1 894
for the king of B had taken from 2Kin 24:7 894
of B came up against Jerusalem 2Kin 24:10 894
king of B came against the city 2Kin 24:11 894
Judah went out to the king of B 2Kin 24:12 894
the king of B took him in the 2Kin 24:12 894
he carried away Jehoiachin to B 2Kin 24:15 894
captivity from Jerusalem to B 2Kin 24:15 894
of B brought captive to B 2Kin 24:16 894
the king of B made Mattaniah his........ 2Kin 24:17 894

B

The daughter of *B* is like a ....Jer 51:33	894
the king of *B* hath devoured me..........Jer 51:34	894
to me and to my flesh be upon *B*..........Jer 51:35	894
B shall become heaps, a dwelling..........Jer 51:37	894
how is *B* become an astonishment..........Jer 51:41	894
The sea is come up upon *B*.......................Jer 51:42	894
And I will punish Bel in *B*......................Jer 51:44	894
yea, the wall of *B* shall fall....................Jer 51:44	894
upon the graven images of *B*...................Jer 51:47	894
that is therein, shall sing for *B*..............Jer 51:48	894
As *B* hath caused the slain of..................Jer 51:49	894
so at *B* shall fall the slain of.................Jer 51:49	894
Though *B* should mount up to..................Jer 51:53	894
A sound of a cry cometh from *B*..............Jer 51:54	894
Because the LORD hath spoiled *B*............Jer 51:55	894
is come upon her, even upon *B*................Jer 51:56	894
The broad walls of *B* shall be................Jer 51:58	894
B in the fourth year of his reign............Jer 51:59	894
the evil that should come upon *B*............Jer 51:60	894
words that are written against *B*............Jer 51:60	894
to Seraiah, When thou comest to *B*........Jer 51:61	894
thou shalt say, Thus shall *B* sink...........Jer 51:64	894
rebelled against the king of *B*.................Jer 52:3	894
Nebuchadrezzar king of *B* came.............Jer 52:4	894
B to Riblah in the land of Hamath.........Jer 52:9	894
the king of *B* slew the sons of...............Jer 52:10	894
the king of *B* bound him in chains..........Jer 52:11	894
and carried him to *B*.............................Jer 52:11	894
year of Nebuchadrezzar king of *B*..........Jer 52:12	894
guard, which served the king of *B*..........Jer 52:12	894
away, that fell to the king of *B*..............Jer 52:15	894
all the brass of them to *B*......................Jer 52:17	894
them to the king of *B* to Riblah.............Jer 52:26	894
And the king of *B* smote them................Jer 52:27	894
that Evil-merodach king of *B* in.............Jer 52:31	894
the kings that were with him in *B*..........Jer 52:32	894
diet given him of the king of *B*..............Jer 52:34	894
I will bring him to *B* to the land.............Eze 12:13	894
Behold, the king of *B* is come to............Eze 17:12	894
and led them with him to *B*....................Eze 17:12	894
in the midst of *B* he shall die................Eze 17:16	894
snare, and I will bring him to *B*.............Eze 17:20	894
and brought him to the king of *B*...........Eze 19:9	894
sword of the king of *B* may come...........Eze 21:19	894
For the king of *B* stood at the...............Eze 21:21	894
the king of *B* set himself against...........Eze 24:2	894
Tyrus Nebuchadrezzar king of *B*............Eze 26:7	894
Nebuchadrezzar king of *B* caused..........Eze 29:18	894
unto Nebuchadrezzar king of *B*..............Eze 29:19	894
hand of Nebuchadrezzar king of *B*..........Eze 30:10	894
the arms of the king of *B*......................Eze 30:24	894
the arms of the king of *B*......................Eze 30:25	894
into the hand of the king of *B*................Eze 30:25	894
king of *B* shall come upon thee.............Eze 32:11	894
king of *B* unto Jerusalem, and...............Dan 1:1	894
to destroy all the wise men of *B*............Dan 2:12	895
forth to slay the wise men of *B*..............Dan 2:14	895
the rest of the wise men of *B*.................Dan 2:18	895
to destroy the wise men of *B*.................Dan 2:24	895
Destroy not the wise men of *B*...............Dan 2:24	895
over the whole province of *B*.................Dan 2:48	895
over all the wise men of *B*.....................Dan 2:48	895
the affairs of the province of *B*.............Dan 2:49	895
of Dura, in the province of *B*.................Dan 3:1	895
the affairs of the province of *B*.............Dan 3:12	895
Abed-nego, in the province of *B*............Dan 3:30	895
all the wise men of *B* before me............Dan 4:6	895
in the palace of the kingdom of *B*.........Dan 4:29	895
and said, Is not this great *B*.................Dan 4:30	895
and said to the wise men of *B*...............Dan 5:7	895
king of *B* Daniel had a dream...............Dan 7:1	895
field, and thou shalt go even to *B*.........Mic 4:10	894
dwellest with the daughter of *B*............Zec 2:7	894
of Jedaiah, which are come from *B*........Zec 6:10	894
time they were carried away to *B*..........Mt 1:11	897
And after they were brought to *B*..........Mt 1:12	897
into *B* are fourteen generations.............Mt 1:17	897
into *B* unto Christ are fourteen.............Mt 1:17	897
and I will carry you away beyond *B*.......Acts 7:43	897
The church that is at *B*, elected............1Pet 5:13	897
B is fallen, is fallen, that....................Rev 14:8	897
great *B* came in remembrance..............Rev 16:19	897
B THE GREAT, THE MOTHER OF........Rev 17:5	897
B the great is fallen, is fallen,..............Rev 18:2	897
Alas, alas that great city *B*..................Rev 18:10	897
that great city *B* be thrown down..........Rev 18:21	897

BABYLONIA See BABYLONISH.

BABYLONIAN See CHALDEANS'.

BABYLONIANS *(bab-il-o'-ne-ans)* See CHALDEANS.
Inhabitants of Babylonia.

Apharsites, the Archevites, the *B*..........Ezr 4:9	896
the manner of the *B* of Chaldea......Eze 23:15	1121,894
the *B* came to her into the bed of ...Eze 23:17	1121,894
The *B*, and all the Chaldeans, ...Eze 23:23	1121,894

BABYLONISH *(bab-il-o'-nish)* See BABYLONIANS.

the spoils a goodly *B* garment.............Josh 7:21	8152

BABYLON'S *(bab'-il-ons)*

For then the king of *B* army..................Jer 32:2	894
When the king of *B* army fought...........Jer 34:7	894
the hand of the king of *B* army.............Jer 34:21	894
the hand of the king of *B* army.............Jer 38:3	894
forth unto the king of *B* princes............Jer 38:17	894
go forth to the king of *B* princes...........Jer 38:18	894
forth to the king of *B* princes................Jer 38:22	894
and all the king of *B* princes.................Jer 39:13	894

BACA *(ba'-cah) A valley near Jerusalem.*

the valley of *B* make it a well...............Ps 84:6	1056

BACHRITES *(bak'-rites) Descendants of Becher.*

of Becher, the family of the *B*...............Num 26:35	1076

BACK See APPENDIX.

BACKBITERS

B, haters of God, despiteful, ...Rom 1:30	2637

BACKBITETH

He that *b* not with his tongue..................Ps 15:3	7270

BACKBITING

an angry countenance a *b* tongue..........Prov 25:23	5643

BACKBITINGS

envyings, wraths, strifes, *b*....................2Cor 12:20	2636

BACKBONE

shall he take off hard by the *b*..............Lev 3:9	6096

BACKS

enemies turn their *b* unto thee..............Ex 23:27	6203
their *b* before their enemies..................Josh 7:8	6203
but turned their *b* before their...............Josh 7:12	6203
Therefore they turned their *b*................Judg 20:42	
of the LORD, and turned their *b*.............2Chr 29:6	6203
and cast thy law behind their *b*............Neh 9:26	1458
with their *b* toward the temple of..........Eze 8:16	268
And their whole body, and their *b*.........Eze 10:12	1354

BACKSIDE

the flock to the *b* of the desert...............Ex 3:1	310
hang over the *b* of the tabernacle..........Ex 26:12	268
a book written within and on the *b*........Rev 5:1	3693

BACKSLIDER

The *b* in heart shall be filled..................Prov 14:14	5472

BACKSLIDING

that which *b* Israel hath done.................Jer 3:6	4878
b Israel committed adultery I had..........Jer 3:8	4878
The *b* Israel hath justified.....................Jer 3:11	4878
thou *b* Israel, saith the LORD................Jer 3:12	4878
O *b* children, saith the LORD.................Jer 3:14	7726
ye *b* children, and I will heal.................Jer 3:22	7726
slidden back by a perpetual *b*................Jer 8:5	4878
thou go about, O thou *b* daughter..........Jer 31:22	7728
thy flowing valley, O *b* daughter............Jer 49:4	7728
Israel slideth back as a *b* heifer............Hos 4:16	5637
my people are bent to *b* from me...........Hos 11:7	4878
I will heal their *b*, I will love................Hos 14:4	4878

BACKSLIDINGS

thee, and thy *b* shall reprove thee.........Jer 2:19	4878
children, and I will heal your *b*.............Jer 3:22	4878
many, and their *b* are increased............Jer 5:6	4878
for our *b* are many................................Jer 14:7	4878

BACKWARD

both their shoulders, and went *b*...........Gen 9:23	322
and their faces were *b*, and they............Gen 9:23	322
so that his rider shall fall *b*..................Gen 49:17	268
seat by the side of the gate.....................1Sa 4:18	322
the shadow return *b* ten degrees...........2Kin 20:10	322
brought the shadow ten degrees *b*.........2Kin 20:11	322
and *b*, but I cannot perceive him...........Job 23:8	268
let them be driven *b* and put to.............Ps 40:14	268
let them be turned *b*, and put to...........Ps 70:2	268
unto anger, they are gone away *b*..........Is 1:4	268
that they might go, and fall *b*...............Is 28:13	268
sun dial of Ahaz, ten degrees *b*............Is 38:8	322
that turneth wise men *b*, and...............Is 44:25	268
And judgment is turned away *b*.............Is 59:14	268
of their evil heart, and went *b*..............Jer 7:24	268
saith the LORD, thou art gone *b*............Jer 15:6	268

yea, she sigheth, and turneth *b* .... Lam 1:8   268
I am he, they went *b* .... Jn 18:6   *1519,3588,3694*

BAD
cannot speak unto thee *b* or good .... Gen 24:50   7451
not to Jacob either good or *b* .... Gen 31:24   7451
not to Jacob either good or *b* .... Gen 31:29   7451
good for a *b*, or a *b* for a good .... Lev 27:10   7451
value it, whether it be good or *b* .... Lev 27:12   7451
it, whether it be good or *b* .... Lev 27:14   7451
search whether it be good or *b* .... Lev 27:33   7451
dwell in, whether it be good or *b* .... Num 13:19   7451
either good or *b* of mine own mind .... Num 24:13   7451
brother Amnon neither good nor *b* 2Sa 13:22   7451
the king to discern good and *b* 2Sa 14:17   7451
I may discern between good and *b* 1Kin 3:9   7451
the *b* city, and have set up the .... Ezr 4:12   873
not be eaten, they were so *b* .... Jer 24:2   7451
into vessels, but cast the *b* away .... Mt 13:48   *4550*
all as many as they found, both *b* .... Mt 22:10   *4190*
done, whether it be good or *b* 2Cor 5:10   2556

BADE
And the man did as Joseph *b* .... Gen 43:17   559
up till the morning, as Moses *b* .... Ex 16:24   6680
b stone them with stones .... Num 14:10   559
did unto them as the LORD *b* him .... Josh 11:9   559
all that her mother in law *b* her .... Ruth 3:6   6680
and some *b* me kill thee 1Sa 24:10   559
(Also he *b* them teach the 2Sa 1:18   559
for thy servant Joab, he *b* me 2Sa 14:19   6680
on the third day, as the king *b* 2Chr 10:12   1696
Then Esther *b* them return .... Est 4:15   559
understood they how that he *b* .... Mt 16:12   2036
And he that *b* thee and him come and .. Lk 14:9   *2564*
that when he that *b* thee cometh .... Lk 14:10   *2564*
said he also to him that *b* him .... Lk 14:12   *2564*
made a great supper, and *b* many .... Lk 14:16   *2564*
the Spirit *b* me go with them, ... Acts 11:12   2036
But *b* them farewell, saying, I .... Acts 18:21   *657*
b that he should be examined by .... Acts 22:24   2036

BADEST
have done according as thou *b* me .... Gen 27:19   1696

BADGERS'
b skins, and shittim wood, ... Ex 25:5   8476
and a covering above of *b* skins .... Ex 26:14   8476
b skins, and shittim wood, ... Ex 35:7   8476
of rams, and *b* skins, brought them ...... Ex 35:23   8476
a covering of *b* skins above that .... Ex 36:19   8476
red, and the covering of *b* skins........... Ex 39:34   8476
thereon the covering of *b* skins .... Num 4:6   8476
same with a covering of *b* skins .... Num 4:8   8476
within a covering of *b* skins .... Num 4:10   8476
it with a covering of *b* skins .... Num 4:11   8476
them with a covering of *b* skins.............. Num 4:12   8476
upon it a covering of *b* skins .... Num 4:14   8476
the covering of *b* skins that .... Num 4:25   8476
work, and shod thee with *b* skin............. Eze 16:10   8476

BADNESS
in all the land of Egypt for *b* .... Gen 41:19   7455

BAG
not have in thy *b* divers weights .... Deut 25:13   3599
in a shepherd's *b* which he had 1Sa 17:40   3627
And David put his hand in his *b* 1Sa 17:49   3627
transgression is sealed up in a *b* .... Job 14:17   6872
He hath taken a *b* of money with .... Prov 7:20   6872
the weights of the *b* are his work .... Prov 16:11   3599
They lavish gold out of the *b* .... Is 46:6   3599
with the *b* of deceitful weights .... Mic 6:11   3599
to put it into a *b* with holes .... Hag 1:6   6872
he was a thief, and had the *b* .... Jn 12:6   *1101*
thought, because Judas had the *b* .... Jn 13:29   *1101*

BAGS
two talents of silver in two *b* 2Kin 5:23   2754
came up, and they put up in *b* 2Kin 12:10   6696
yourselves *b* which wax not old .... Lk 12:33   *905*

BAHARUMITE (ba-ha'-rum-ite) See BARHUMITE. *Inhabitants of Bahurim.*
Azmaveth the *B*, Eliahba the 1Chr 11:33   978

BAHURIM (ba-hu'-rim) See BAHARUMITE. *A village near Jerusalem.*
her along weeping behind her to *B* 2Sa 3:16   980
And when king David came to *B* 2Sa 16:5   980
and came to a man's house in *B* 2Sa 17:18   980
Gera, a Benjamite, which was of *B* 2Sa 19:16   980
the son of Gera, a Benjamite of *B* 1Kin 2:8   980

BAJITH (ba'-jith) *A temple in Moab.*
He is gone up to *B*, and to Dibon, ... Is 15:2   1006

BAKBAKKAR (bak-bak'-kar) *A Levite who returned from exile.*
And *B*, Heresh, and Galal, and 1Chr 9:15   1230

BAKBUK (bak'-buk) *A family who returned from exile.*
The children of *B*, the children .... Ezr 2:51   1227
The children of *B*, the children .... Neh 7:53   1227

BAKBUKIAH (bak-buk-i'-ah) *A Levite exile who resettled in Jerusalem.*
B the second among his brethren, ... Neh 11:17   1229
Also *B* and Unni, their brethren, ... Neh 12:9   1229
Mattaniah, and *B*, Obadiah, ... Neh 12:25   1229

BAKE
did *b* unleavened bread, and they .... Gen 19:3   644
b that which ye will *b* to day, ... Ex 16:23   644
flour, and *b* twelve cakes thereof .... Lev 24:5   644
ten women shall *b* your bread in .... Lev 26:26   644
did *b* unleavened bread thereof 1Sa 28:24   644
in his sight, and did *b* the cakes 2Sa 13:8   1310
thou shalt *b* it with dung that .... Eze 4:12   5746
where they shall *b* the meat .... Eze 46:20   644

BAKED
they *b* unleavened cakes of the.............. Ex 12:39   644
b it in pans, and made cakes of it .... Num 11:8   1310
and for that which is *b* in the pan 1Chr 23:29   644
also I have *b* bread upon the .... Is 44:19   644

BAKEMEATS
of all manner of *b* for Pharaoh Gen 40:17   3978,4639,644

BAKEN
of a meat offering *b* in the oven .... Lev 2:4   644
be a meat offering *b* in a pan.................. Lev 2:5   644
meat offering *b* in the frying pan........... Lev 2:7   644
It shall not be *b* with leaven.................. Lev 6:17   644
and when it is *b*, thou shalt bring .... Lev 6:21   7246
the *b* pieces of the meat offering............. Lev 6:21   8601
offering that is *b* in the oven .... Lev 7:9   644
they shall be *b* with leaven.................... Lev 23:17   644
there was a cake *b* on the coals............ 1Kin 19:6

BAKER
his *b* had offended their lord the............ Gen 40:1   644
the *b* of the king of Egypt, which............ Gen 40:5   644
When the chief *b* saw that the .... Gen 40:16   644
of the chief *b* among his servants .... Gen 40:20   644
But he hanged the chief *b* .... Gen 40:22   644
house, both me and the chief *b* .... Gen 41:10   644
as an oven heated by the *b* .... Hos 7:4   644
their *b* sleepeth all the night .... Hos 7:6   644

BAKERS
and against the chief of the *b* .... Gen 40:2   644
and to be cooks, and to be *b* 1Sa 8:13   644

BAKERS'
of bread out of the *b* street .... Jer 37:21   644

BAKETH
yea, he kindleth it, and *b* bread .... Is 44:15   644

BALAAM (ba'-la-am) See BALAAM'S. *Son of Beor.*
unto *B* the son of Beor to Pethor............ Num 22:5   1109
and they came unto *B*, and spake .... Num 22:7   1109
the princes of Moab abode with *B*.......... Num 22:8   1109
And God came unto *B*, and said, What . Num 22:9   1109
B said unto God, Balak the son of .... Num 22:10   1109
And God said unto *B*, Thou shalt.......... Num 22:12   1109
B rose up in the morning, and said .... Num 22:13   1109
B refuseth to come with us..................... Num 22:14   1109
And they came to *B*, and said to him .... Num 22:16   1109
B answered and said unto the .... Num 22:18   1109
And God came unto *B* at night .... Num 22:20   1109
B rose up in the morning, and .... Num 22:21   1109
B smote the ass, to turn her into .... Num 22:23   1109
the LORD, she fell down under *B* .... Num 22:27   1109
of the ass, and she said unto *B* .... Num 22:28   1109
B said unto the ass, Because thou .... Num 22:29   1109
And the ass said unto *B*, Am not I .... Num 22:30   1109
the LORD opened the eyes of *B* .... Num 22:31   1109
B said unto the angel of the LORD.......... Num 22:34   1109
the angel of the LORD said unto *B*.......... Num 22:35   1109
So *B* went with the princes of .... Num 22:35   1109
when Balak heard that *B* was come .... Num 22:36   1109
And Balak said unto *B*, Did I not........... Num 22:37   1109
B said unto Balak, Lo, I am come .... Num 22:38   1109
B went with Balak, and they came .... Num 22:39   1109
oxen and sheep, and sent to *B* .... Num 22:40   1109
on the morrow, that Balak took *B* .... Num 22:41   1109
B said unto Balak, Build me here .... Num 23:1   1109
And Balak did as *B* had spoken .... Num 23:2   1109
B offered on every altar a .... Num 23:2   1109
B said unto Balak, Stand by thy .... Num 23:3   1109

And God met *B*	Num 23:4	1109
And Balak said unto *B*, What hast	Num 23:11	1109
And the LORD met *B*, and put a word	Num 22:20	1109
And Balak said unto *B*, Neither	Num 23:25	1109
But *B* answered and said unto Balak	Num 23:26	1109
And Balak said unto *B*, Come, I	Num 23:27	1109
Balak brought *B* unto the top of	Num 23:28	1109
B said unto Balak, Build me here	Num 23:29	1109
And Balak did as *B* had said	Num 23:30	1109
when *B* saw that it pleased the	Num 24:1	1109
B lifted up his eyes, and he saw	Num 24:2	1109
B the son of Beor hath said, and	Num 24:3	1109
anger was kindled against *B*	Num 24:10	1109
and Balak said unto *B*, I called	Num 24:10	1109
B said unto Balak, Spake I not	Num 24:12	1109
B the son of Beor hath said, and	Num 24:15	1109
B rose up, and went and returned to	Num 24:25	1109
B also the son of Beor they slew	Num 31:8	1109
Israel, through the counsel of *B*	Num 31:16	1109
B the son of Beor of Pethor of	Deut 23:4	1109
thy God would not hearken unto *B*	Deut 23:5	1109
B also the son of Beor, the	Josh 13:22	1109
called *B* the son of Beor to curse	Josh 24:9	1109
But I would not hearken unto *B*	Josh 24:10	1109
but hired *B* against them, that he	Neh 13:2	1109
what *B* the son of Beor answered	Mic 6:5	1109
the way of *B* the son of Bosor	2Pet 2:15	*903*
after the error of *B* for reward	Jude 11	*903*
them that hold the doctrine of *B*	Rev 2:14	*903*

BALAAM'S

crushed *B* foot against the wall	Num 22:25	1109
B anger was kindled, and he smote	Num 22:27	1109
And the LORD put a word in *B* mouth	Num 23:5	1109

BALAC (ba'-lak) See BALAK. *Greek form of Balak.*

of Balaam, who taught *B* to cast a	Rev 2:14	*904*

BALADAN (bal'-adan) See BERODACH-BALADAN, MERODACH-BALADAN. *Father of a Babylonian king.*

Berodach-baladan, the son of *B*	2Kin 20:12	1081
Merodach-baladan, the son of *B*	Is 39:1	1081

BALAH (ba'-lah) See BAALAH. *A city in Simeon.*

And Hazar-shual, and *B*, and Azem,	Josh 19:3	1088

BALAK (ba'-lak) See BALAC, BALAK'S. *A king of Moab.*

B the son of Zippor saw all that	Num 22:2	1111
B the son of Zippor was king of	Num 22:4	1111
and spake unto him the words of *B*	Num 22:7	1111
B the son of Zippor, king of Moab	Num 22:10	1111
and said unto the princes of *B*	Num 22:13	1111
Moab rose up, and they went unto *B*	Num 22:14	1111
B sent yet again princes, more,	Num 22:15	1111
Thus saith *B* the son of Zippor,	Num 22:16	1111
and said unto the servants of *B*	Num 22:18	1111
If *B* would give me his house full	Num 22:18	1111
Balaam went with the princes of *B*	Num 22:35	1111
when *B* heard that Balaam was come	Num 22:36	1111
B said unto Balaam, Did I not	Num 22:37	1111
And Balaam said unto *B*, Lo, I am	Num 22:38	1111
And Balaam went with *B*, and they	Num 22:39	1111
B offered oxen and sheep, and sent	Num 22:40	1111
that *B* took Balaam, and brought	Num 22:41	1111
And Balaam said unto *B*, Build me	Num 23:1	1111
B did as Balaam had spoken	Num 23:2	1111
and *B* and Balaam offered on every	Num 23:2	1111
And Balaam said unto *B*, Stand by	Num 23:3	1111
mouth, and said, Return unto *B*	Num 23:5	1111
B the king of Moab hath brought	Num 23:7	1111
B said unto Balaam, What hast	Num 23:11	1111
B said unto him, Come, I pray	Num 23:13	1111
And he said unto *B*, Stand here by	Num 23:15	1111
mouth, and said, Go again unto *B*	Num 23:16	1111
B said unto him, What hath the	Num 23:17	1111
his parable, and said, Rise up, *B*	Num 23:18	1111
B said unto Balaam, Neither curse	Num 23:25	1111
Balaam answered and said unto *B*	Num 23:26	1111
B said unto Balaam, Come, I pray	Num 23:27	1111
B brought Balaam unto the top of	Num 23:28	1111
And Balaam said unto *B*, Build me	Num 23:29	1111
B did as Balaam had said, and	Num 23:30	1111
B said unto Balaam, I called thee	Num 24:10	1111
And Balaam said unto *B*, Spake I	Num 24:12	1111
If *B* would give me his house full	Num 24:13	1111
and *B* also went his way	Num 24:25	1111
Then *B* the son of Zippor, king of	Josh 24:9	1111
better than *B* the son of Zippor	Judg 11:25	1111
remember now what *B* king of Moab	Mic 6:5	1111

BALAK'S (ba'-laks)

B anger was kindled against	Num 24:10	1111

BALANCE

Let me be weighed in an even *b*	Job 31:6	3976
to be laid in the *b*, they are	Ps 62:9	3976
A false *b* is abomination to the	Prov 11:1	3976
A just weight and *b* are the LORD's	Prov 16:11	3976
and a false *b* is not good	Prov 20:23	3976
in scales, and the hills in a *b*	Is 40:12	3976
as the small dust of the *b*	Is 40:15	3976
the bag, and weigh silver in the *b*	Is 46:6	7070

BALANCES

Just *b*, just weights, a just	Lev 19:36	3976
calamity laid in the *b* together	Job 6:2	3976
and weighed him the money in the *b*	Jer 32:10	3976
then take thee *b* to weigh	Eze 5:1	3976
Ye shall have just *b*, and a just	Eze 45:10	3976
Thou art weighed in the *b*	Dan 5:27	3977
the *b* of deceit are in his hand	Hos 12:7	3976
and falsifying the *b* by deceit	Amos 8:5	3976
count them pure with the wicked *b*	Mic 6:11	3976
him had a pair of *b* in his hand	Rev 6:5	

BALANCINGS

thou know the *b* of the clouds	Job 37:16	4657

BALD

the *b* locust after his kind, and	Lev 11:22	5556
is fallen off his head, he is *b*	Lev 13:40	7142
toward his face, he is forehead *b*	Lev 13:41	1371
And if there be in the *b* head	Lev 13:42	7146
or *b* forehead, a white reddish	Lev 13:42	1372
his *b* head, or his *b* forehead	Lev 13:42	1372
b head, or in his *b* forehead	Lev 13:43	1372
said unto him, Go up, thou *b* head	2Kin 2:23	7142
go up, thou *b* head	2Kin 2:23	7142
nor make themselves *b* for them	Jer 16:6	7139
For every head shall be *b*	Jer 48:37	7144
themselves utterly *b* for thee	Eze 27:31	7139
every head was made *b*, and every	Eze 29:18	7139
Make thee *b*, and poll thee for thy	Mic 1:16	7139

BALDNESS

shall not make *b* upon their head	Lev 21:5	7144
nor make any *b* between your eyes	Deut 14:1	7144
and instead of well set hair *b*	Is 3:24	7144
on all their heads shall be *b*	Is 15:2	7144
weeping, and to mourning, and to *b*	Is 22:12	7144
B is come upon Gaza	Jer 47:5	7144
faces, and *b* upon all their heads	Eze 7:18	7144
all loins, and *b* upon every head	Amos 8:10	7144
enlarge thy *b* as the eagle	Mic 1:16	7144

BALL

toss thee like a *b* into a large	Is 22:18	1754

BALM

their camels bearing spicery and *b*	Gen 37:25	6875
the man a present, a little *b*	Gen 43:11	6875
Is there no *b* in Gilead	Jer 8:22	6875
Go up into Gilead, and take *b*	Jer 46:11	6875
take *b* for her pain, if so be she	Jer 51:8	6875
and Pannag, and honey, and oil, and *b*	Eze 27:17	6875

BAMAH (ba'-mah) See BAMOTH. *Places where Israel sacrificed to idols.*

thereof is called *B* unto this day	Eze 20:29	1117

BAMOTH (ba'-moth) See BAMOTH-BAAL. *A city on the Arnon River.*

and from Nahaliel to *B*	Num 21:19	1120
from *B* in the valley, that is in	Num 21:20	1120

BAMOTH-BAAL (ba'-moth-ba'-al) *A Moabite town.*

Dibon, and *B*, and Beth-baal-meon,	Josh 13:17	1120

BAND

with a *b* round about the hole,	Ex 39:23	8193
and there went with him a *b* of men	1Sa 10:26	2428
him, and became captain over a *b*	1Kin 11:24	1416
behold, they spied a *b* of men	2Kin 13:21	1416
and made them captains of the *b*	1Chr 12:18	1416
David against the *b* of the rovers	1Chr 12:21	1416
for the *b* of men that came with	2Chr 22:1	1416
of the king a *b* of soldiers	Ezr 8:22	2428
unicorn with his *b* in the furrow	Job 39:10	5688
the earth, even with a *b* of iron	Dan 4:15	613
the earth, even with a *b* of iron	Dan 4:23	613
unto him the whole *b* of soldiers	Mt 27:27	4686
and they call together the whole *b*	Mk 15:16	4686
then, having received a *b* of men	Jn 18:3	4686
Then the *b* and the captain and	Jn 18:12	4686
of the *b* called the Italian *b*	Acts 10:1	4686
unto the chief captain of the *b*	Acts 21:31	4686
a centurion of Augustus' *b*	Acts 27:1	4686

BANDED
certain of the Jews *b* together .... Acts 23:12   *4160,4963*

BANDS
herds, and the camels, into two *b* .... Gen 32:7   4264
and now I am become two *b* .... Gen 32:10   4264
I have broken the *b* of your yoke .... Lev 26:13   4133
his *b* loosed from off his hands .... Judg 15:14   612
two men that were captains of *b* 2Sa 4:2   1416
So the *b* of Syria came no more 2Kin 6:23   1416
the *b* of the Moabites invaded the 2Kin 13:20   1416
Pharaoh-nechoh put him in *b* at 2Kin 23:33   631
against him *b* of the Chaldees 2Kin 24:2   1416
b of the Syrians, and *b* of the 2Kin 24:2   1416
b of the children of Ammon, and 2Kin 24:2   1416
were *b* of soldiers for war, six 1Chr 7:4   1416
b that were ready armed to the 1Chr 12:23   7218
men, that went out to war by *b* 2Chr 26:11   1416
The Chaldeans made out three *b* .... Job 1:17   7218
Pleiades, or loose the *b* of Orion .... Job 38:31   4189
hath loosed the *b* of the wild ass .... Job 39:5   4147
Let us break their *b* asunder .... Ps 2:3   4147
For there are no *b* in their death .... Ps 73:4   2784
death, and brake their *b* in sunder .... Ps 107:14   4147
The *b* of the wicked have robbed .... Ps 119:61   2256
go they forth all of them by *b* .... Prov 30:27   2683
snares and nets, and her hands as *b* ..... Eccl 7:26   612
lest your *b* be made strong .... Is 28:22   4147
thyself from the *b* of thy neck .... Is 52:2   4147
to loose the *b* of wickedness, to .... Is 58:6   2784
broken thy yoke, and burst thy *b* .... Jer 2:20   4147
they shall put *b* upon thee .... Eze 3:25   5688
behold, I will lay *b* upon thee .... Eze 4:8   5688
him to help him, and all his *b* .... Eze 12:14   102
all his *b* shall fall by the sword .... Eze 17:21   102
I have broken the *b* of their yoke .... Eze 34:27   4133
Gomer, and all his *b* .... Eze 38:6   102
the north quarters, and all his *b* .... Eze 38:6   102
the land, thou, and all thy *b* .... Eze 38:9   102
will rain upon him, and upon his *b* .... Eze 38:22   102
of Israel, thou, and all thy *b* .... Eze 39:4   102
cords of a man, with *b* of love .... Hos 11:4   5688
Beauty, and the other I called *B* .... Zec 11:7   2256
asunder mine other staff, even *B* .... Zec 11:14   2256
and he brake the *b*, and was driven .... Lk 8:29   1199
and every one's *b* were loosed .... Acts 16:26   1199
Jews, he loosed him from his *b* .... Acts 22:30   1199
the sea, and loosed the rudder *b* .... Acts 27:40   2202
b having nourishment ministered, ... Col 2:19   4886

BANI (ba'-ni)
1. A "mighty man" of David.
of Nathan of Zobah, *B* the Gadite, ... 2Sa 23:36   1137
2. A Levite descendant of Merari.
The son of Amzi, the son of *B* 1Chr 6:46   1137
3. A descendant of Pharez.
the son of Imri, the son of *B* 1Chr 9:4   1137
4. A family of exiles.
The children of *B*, six hundred .... Ezr 2:10   1137
And of the sons of *B* .... Ezr 10:29   1137
5. Father whose sons married foreign wives.
Of the sons of *B* .... Ezr 10:34   1137
6. A Jewish descendant of a foreign woman.
And *B*, and Binnui, Shimei, ... Ezr 10:38   1137
7. Father of Rehum.
the Levites, Rehum the son of *B* .... Neh 3:17   1137
Also Jeshua, and *B*, and Sherebiah, ... Neh 8:7   1137
of the Levites, Jeshua, and *B* .... Neh 9:4   1137
Levites, Jeshua, and Kadmiel, *B* .... Neh 9:5   1137
8. A priest who assisted Ezra.
Shebaniah, Bunni, Sherebiah, *B* .... Neh 9:4   1137
Hodijah, *B*, Beninu .... Neh 10:13   1137
9. An Israelite who renewed the covenant under
Nehemiah.
Pahath-moab, Elam, Zatthu, *B* .... Neh 10:14   1137
10. A family of exiles.
Jerusalem was Uzzi the son of *B* .... Neh 11:22   1137

BANISHED
doth not fetch home again his *b* 2Sa 14:13   5080
that his *b* be not expelled from 2Sa 14:14   5080

BANISHMENT
whether it be unto death, or to *b* .... Ezr 7:26   8331
thee false burdens and causes of *b* .... Lam 2:14   4065

BANK
I stood upon the *b* of the river .... Gen 41:17   8193
which is by the *b* of the river .... Deut 4:48   8193
which is upon the *b* of the river .... Josh 12:2   8193
that is upon the *b* of the river .... Josh 13:9   8193
that is on the *b* of the river .... Josh 13:16   8193
they cast up a *b* against the city 2Sa 20:15   5550

back, and stood by the *b* of Jordan 2Kin 2:13   8193
shield, nor cast a *b* against it 2Kin 19:32   5550
shields, nor cast a *b* against it .... Is 37:33   5550
at the *b* of the river were very .... Eze 47:7   8193
by the river upon the *b* thereof .... Eze 47:12   8193
this side of the *b* of the river .... Dan 12:5   8193
that side of the *b* of the river .... Dan 12:5   8193
not thou my money into the *b* .... Lk 19:23   *5132*

BANKS
all his *b* all the time of harvest .... Josh 3:15   1415
place, and flowed over all his *b* .... Josh 4:18   1415
when it had overflown all his *b* 1Chr 12:15   1428
channels, and go over all his *b* .... Is 8:7   1415
man's voice between the *b* of Ulai .... Dan 8:16   1415

BANNER
Thou hast given a *b* to them that .... Ps 60:4   5251
house, and his *b* over me was love .... Song 2:4   1714
Lift ye up a *b* upon the high .... Is 13:2   5251

BANNERS
of our God we will set up our *b* .... Ps 20:5   1713
terrible as an army with *b* .... Song 6:4   1713
and terrible as an army with *b* .... Song 6:10   1713

BANQUET
b that I have prepared for him .... Est 5:4   4960
Haman came to the *b* that Esther .... Est 5:5   4960
said unto Esther at the *b* of wine .... Est 5:6   4960
Haman come to the *b* that I shall .... Est 5:8   4960
the *b* that she had prepared but .... Est 5:12   4960
merrily with the king unto the *b* .... Est 5:14   4960
the *b* that Esther had prepared .... Est 6:14   4960
Haman came to *b* with Esther the .... Est 7:1   8354
the second day at the *b* of wine .... Est 7:2   4960
the king arising from the *b* of .... Est 7:7   4960
into the place of the *b* of wine .... Est 7:8   4960
the companions make a *b* of him .... Job 41:6   3738
his lords, came into the *b* house .... Dan 5:10   4961
the *b* of them that stretched .... Amos 6:7   4797

BANQUETING
He brought me to the *b* house .... Song 2:4   3196

BANQUETINGS
excess of wine, revellings, *b* 1Pet 4:3   4224

BAPTISM
and Sadducees come to his *b* .... Mt 3:7   908
the *b* that I am baptized with .... Mt 20:22   908
be baptized with the *b* that I am .... Mt 20:23   908
The *b* of John, whence was it .... Mt 21:25   908
preach the *b* of repentance for .... Mk 1:4   908
be baptized with the *b* that I am .... Mk 10:38   908
with the *b* that I am baptized .... Mk 10:39   908
The *b* of John, was it from heaven .... Mk 11:30   908
preaching the *b* of repentance for .... Lk 3:3   908
being baptized with the *b* of John .... Lk 7:29   908
But I have a *b* to be baptized .... Lk 12:50   908
The *b* of John, was it from heaven .... Lk 20:4   908
Beginning from the *b* of John .... Acts 1:22   908
after the *b* which John preached .... Acts 10:37   908
preached before his coming the *b* .... Acts 13:24   908
Lord, knowing only the *b* of John .... Acts 18:25   908
And they said, Unto John's *b* .... Acts 19:3   908
baptized with the *b* of repentance .... Acts 19:4   908
buried with him by *b* into death .... Rom 6:4   908
One Lord, one faith, one *b* .... Eph 4:5   908
Buried with him in *b*, wherein .... Col 2:12   908
b doth also now save us (not the 1Pet 3:21   908

BAPTISMS
Of the doctrine of *b*, and of .... Heb 6:2   909

BAPTIST (bap'-tist) See BAPTIST'S. *John, the forerunner*
of Jesus.
In those days came John the *B* .... Mt 3:1   910
risen a greater than John the *B* .... Mt 11:11   910
from the days of John the *B* until .... Mt 11:12   910
his servants, This is John the *B* .... Mt 14:2   910
Some say that thou art John the *B* .... Mt 16:14   910
he spake unto them of John the *B* .... Mt 17:13   910
That John the *B* was risen from .... Mk 6:14   907
she said, The head of John the *B* .... Mk 6:24   910
a charger the head of John the *B* .... Mk 6:25   910
And they answered, John the *B* .... Mk 8:28   910
John *B* hath sent us unto thee, ... Lk 7:20   910
a greater prophet than John the *B* .... Lk 7:28   910
For John the *B* came neither .... Lk 7:33   910
They answering said, John the *B* .... Lk 9:19   910

BAPTIST'S (bap'-tists)
me here John *B* head in a charger .... Mt 14:8   910

B

BAPTIZE

I indeed *b* you with water unto	Mt 3:11	907
he shall *b* you with the Holy	Mt 3:11	907
John did *b* in the wilderness, and	Mk 1:4	907
but he shall *b* you with the Holy	Mk 1:8	907
I indeed *b* you with water	Lk 3:16	907
he shall *b* you with the Holy	Lk 3:16	907
them, saying, I *b* with water	Jn 1:26	907
he that sent me to *b* with water	Jn 1:33	907
For Christ sent me not to *b*	1Cor 1:17	907

BAPTIZED

And were *b* of him in Jordan,	Mt 3:6	907
Jordan unto John, to be *b* of him	Mt 3:13	907
I have need to be *b* of thee	Mt 3:14	907
And Jesus, when he was *b*, went up	Mt 3:16	907
b with the baptism that I am *b*	Mt 20:22	907
b with the baptism that I am *b*	Mt 20:23	907
were all *b* of him in the river of	Mk 1:5	907
I indeed have *b* you with water	Mk 1:8	907
and was *b* of John in Jordan	Mk 1:9	907
b with the baptism that I am *b*	Mk 10:38	907
am *b* withal shall ye be *b*	Mk 10:39	907
believeth and is *b* shall be saved	Mk 16:16	907
that came forth to be *b* of him	Lk 3:7	907
Then came also publicans to be *b*	Lk 3:12	907
Now when all the people were *b*	Lk 3:21	907
to pass, that Jesus also being *b*	Lk 3:21	907
being *b* with the baptism of John	Lk 7:29	907
themselves, being not *b* of him	Lk 7:30	907
But I have a baptism to be *b* with	Lk 12:50	907
there he tarried with them, and *b*	Jn 3:22	907
and they came, and were *b*	Jn 3:23	907
b more disciples than John,	Jn 4:1	907
(Though Jesus himself *b* not	Jn 4:2	907
the place where John at first *b*	Jn 10:40	907
For John truly *b* with water	Acts 1:5	907
but ye shall be *b* with the Holy	Acts 1:5	907
be *b* every one of you in the name	Acts 2:38	907
gladly received his word were *b*	Acts 2:41	907
name of Jesus Christ, they were *b*	Acts 8:12	907
and when he was *b*, he continued	Acts 8:13	907
only they were *b* in the name of	Acts 8:16	907
what doth hinder me to be *b*	Acts 8:36	907
and he *b* him	Acts 8:38	907
forthwith, and arose, and was *b*	Acts 9:18	907
water, that these should not be *b*	Acts 10:47	907
to be *b* in the name of the Lord	Acts 10:48	907
he said, John indeed *b* with water	Acts 11:16	907
but ye shall be *b* with the Holy	Acts 11:16	907
And when she was *b*, and her	Acts 16:15	907
and was *b*, he and all his,	Acts 16:33	907
hearing believed, and were *b*	Acts 18:8	907
them, Unto what then were ye *b*	Acts 19:3	907
John verily *b* with the baptism of	Acts 19:4	907
they were *b* in the name of the	Acts 19:5	907
arise, and be *b*, and wash away thy	Acts 22:16	907
that so many of us as were *b* into	Rom 6:3	907
Christ were *b* into his death	Rom 6:3	907
or were ye *b* in the name of Paul	1Cor 1:13	907
I thank God that I *b* none of you	1Cor 1:14	907
say that I had in mine own name	1Cor 1:15	907
I *b* also the household of	1Cor 1:16	907
I know not whether I *b* any other	1Cor 1:16	907
were all *b* unto Moses in the	1Cor 10:2	907
Spirit are we all *b* into one body	1Cor 12:13	907
they do which are *b* for the dead	1Cor 15:29	907
why are they then *b* for the dead	1Cor 15:29	907
b into Christ have put on Christ	Gal 3:27	907

BAPTIZEST

Why *b* thou then, if thou be not	Jn 1:25	907

BAPTIZETH

is he which *b* with the Holy Ghost	Jn 1:33	907
witness, behold, the same *b*	Jn 3:26	907

BAPTIZING

b them in the name of the Father,	Mt 28:19	907
beyond Jordan, where John was *b*	Jn 1:28	907
therefore am I come to *b* with	Jn 1:31	907
John also was *b* in Aenon near to	Jn 3:23	907

BAR

the middle *b* in the midst of the	Ex 26:28	1280
he made the middle *b* to shoot	Ex 36:33	1280
skins, and shall put it upon a *b*	Num 4:10	4132
skins, and shall put them on a *b*	Num 4:12	4132
posts, and went away with them, *b*	Judg 16:3	1280
them shut the doors, and *b* them	Neh 7:3	270
will break also the *b* of Damascus	Amos 1:5	1280

BARABBAS (ba-rab'-bas) *A criminal released instead of Jesus.*

then a notable prisoner, called *B*	Mt 27:16	912
B, or Jesus which is called	Mt 27:17	912
multitude that they should ask *B*	Mt 27:20	912
They said, *B*	Mt 27:21	912
Then released he *B* unto them	Mt 27:26	912
And there was one named *B*, which	Mk 15:7	912
should rather release *B* unto them	Mk 15:11	912
people, released *B* unto them, and	Mk 15:15	912
this man, and release unto us *B*	Lk 23:18	912
saying, Not this man, but *B*	Jn 18:40	912
Now *B* was a robber	Jn 18:40	912

BARACHEL (bar'-ak-el) *Father of Elihu.*

of Elihu the son of *B* the Buzite	Job 32:2	1292
Elihu the son of *B* the Buzite	Job 32:6	1292

BARACHIAH See BARACHIAS.

BARACHIAS (bar'-ak-i'-as) *Father of Zachariah.*

the blood of Zacharias son of *B*	Mt 23:35	914

BARAK (ba'-rak) *A captain in Deborah's army.*

called *B* the son of Abinoam out	Judg 4:6	1301
B said unto her, If thou wilt go	Judg 4:8	1301
arose, and went with *B* to Kedesh	Judg 4:9	1301
B called Zebulun and Naphtali to	Judg 4:10	1301
they shewed Sisera that *B* the son	Judg 4:12	1301
And Deborah said unto *B*, Up	Judg 4:14	1301
So *B* went down from mount Tabor,	Judg 4:14	1301
the edge of the sword before *B*	Judg 4:15	1301
But *B* pursued after the chariots,	Judg 4:16	1301
as *B* pursued Sisera, Jael came	Judg 4:22	1301
B the son of Abinoam on that day,	Judg 5:1	1301
arise, *B*, and lead thy captivity	Judg 5:12	1301
even Issachar, and also *B*	Judg 5:15	1301
me to tell of Gedeon, and of *B*	Heb 11:32	913

BARAKEL See BARACHEL.

BARBARIAN

be unto him that speaketh a *b*	1Cor 14:11	915
speaketh shall be a *b* unto me	1Cor 14:11	915
nor uncircumcision, *B*, Scythian,	Col 3:11	915

BARBARIANS

when the *b* saw the venomous beast	Acts 28:4	915
both to the Greeks, and to the *B*	Rom 1:14	915

BARBAROUS

the *b* people shewed us no little	Acts 28:2	915

BARBED

thou fill his skin with *b* irons	Job 41:7	7905

BARBER'S

sharp knife, take thee a *b* razor	Eze 5:1	1532

BARE

b Cain, and said, I have gotten a	Gen 4:1	3205
she again *b* his brother Abel	Gen 4:2	3205
and she conceived, and *b* Enoch	Gen 4:17	3205
And Adah *b* Jabal	Gen 4:20	3205
she also *b* Tubal-cain, an	Gen 4:22	3205
she *b* a son, and called his name	Gen 4:25	3205
they *b* children to them, the same	Gen 6:4	3205
b up the ark, and it was lift up	Gen 7:17	5375
Abram's wife *b* him no children	Gen 16:1	3205
And Hagar *b* Abram a son	Gen 16:15	3205
his son's name, which Hagar *b*	Gen 16:15	3205
when Hagar *b* Ishmael to Abram	Gen 16:16	3205
And the firstborn *b* a son, and	Gen 19:37	3205
And the younger, she also *b* a son	Gen 19:38	3205
and they *b* children	Gen 20:17	3205
b Abraham a son in his old age,	Gen 21:2	3205
unto him, whom Sarah *b* to him	Gen 21:3	3205
she *b* also Tebah, and Gaham, and	Gen 22:24	3205
of Milcah, which she *b* unto Nahor	Gen 24:24	3205
Sarah my master's wife *b* a son to	Gen 24:36	3205
son, whom Milcah *b* unto him	Gen 24:47	3205
she *b* him Zimran, and Jokshan, and	Gen 25:2	3205
Sarah's handmaid, *b* unto Abraham	Gen 25:12	3205
years old when she *b* them	Gen 25:26	3205
b a son, and she called his name	Gen 29:32	3205
she conceived again, and *b* a son	Gen 29:33	3205
she conceived again, and *b* a son	Gen 29:34	3205
she conceived again, and *b* a son	Gen 29:35	3205
saw that she *b* Jacob no children	Gen 30:1	3205
conceived, and *b* Jacob a son	Gen 30:5	3205
again, and *b* Jacob a second son	Gen 30:7	3205
Zilpah Leah's maid *b* Jacob a son	Gen 30:10	3205
Leah's maid *b* Jacob a second son	Gen 30:12	3205
and *b* Jacob the fifth son	Gen 30:17	3205
again, and *b* Jacob the sixth son	Gen 30:19	3205
And afterwards she *b* a daughter	Gen 30:21	3205

And she conceived, and *b* a son	Gen 30:23	3205
then all the cattle *b* speckled	Gen 31:8	3205
then *b* all the cattle ringstraked	Gen 31:8	3205
I *b* the loss of it	Gen 31:39	2308
which she *b* unto Jacob, went out	Gen 34:1	3205
And Adah *b* to Esau Eliphaz	Gen 36:4	3205
and Bashemath *b* Reuel	Gen 36:4	3205
And Aholibamah *b* Jeush, and Jaalam,	Gen 36:5	3205
and she *b* to Eliphaz Amalek	Gen 36:12	3205
she *b* to Esau Jeush, and Jaalam,	Gen 36:14	3205
And she conceived, and *b* a son	Gen 38:3	3205
she conceived again, and *b* a son	Gen 38:4	3205
yet again conceived, and *b* a son	Gen 38:5	3205
he was at Chezib, when she *b* him	Gen 38:5	3205
priest of On *b* unto him	Gen 41:50	3205
know that my wife *b* me two sons	Gen 44:27	3205
which she *b* unto Jacob in	Gen 46:15	3205
these she *b* unto Jacob, even	Gen 46:18	3205
priest of On *b* unto him	Gen 46:20	3205
and she *b* these unto Jacob	Gen 46:25	3205
the woman conceived, and *b* a son	Ex 2:2	3205
she *b* him a son, and he called his	Ex 2:22	3205
and she *b* him Aaron and Moses,	Ex 6:20	3205
she *b* him Nadab, and Abihu,	Ex 6:23	3205
and she *b* him Phinehas	Ex 6:25	3205
how I *b* you on eagles' wings, and	Ex 19:4	5375
shall be rent, and his head *b*	Lev 13:45	6544
whether it be *b* within or without	Lev 13:55	7146
they *b* it between two upon a	Num 13:23	5375
whom her mother *b* to Levi in	Num 26:59	3205
she *b* unto Amram Aaron and Moses,	Num 26:59	3205
how that the LORD thy God *b* thee	Deut 1:31	5375
which *b* the ark of the covenant	Deut 31:9	5375
which *b* the ark of the covenant	Deut 31:25	5375
as they that *b* the ark were come	Josh 3:15	5375
the feet of the priests that *b*	Josh 3:15	5375
the priests that *b* the ark of the	Josh 3:17	5375
b the ark of the covenant stood	Josh 4:9	5375
For the priests which *b* the ark	Josh 4:10	5375
when the priests that *b* the ark	Josh 4:18	5375
which *b* the ark of the covenant	Josh 8:33	5375
the people that *b* the present	Judg 3:18	5375
she also *b* him a son, whose name	Judg 8:31	3205
And Gilead's wife *b* him sons	Judg 11:2	3205
and his wife was barren, and *b* not	Judg 13:2	3205
And the woman *b* a son, and called	Judg 13:24	3205
Pharez, whom Tamar *b* unto Judah	Ruth 4:12	3205
her conception, and she *b* a son	Ruth 4:13	3205
had conceived, that she *b* a son	1Sa 1:20	3205
b three sons and two daughters	1Sa 2:21	3205
the young man that *b* his armour	1Sa 14:1	5375
the young man that *b* his armour	1Sa 14:6	5375
the man that *b* the shield went	1Sa 17:41	5375
that when they that *b* the ark of	2Sa 6:13	5375
became his wife, and *b* him a son	2Sa 11:27	3205
that Uriah's wife *b* unto David	2Sa 12:15	3205
she *b* a son, and he called his	2Sa 12:24	3205
ten young men that *b* Joab's	2Sa 18:15	5375
whom she *b* unto Saul, Armoni and	2Sa 21:8	3205
his mother *b* him after Absalom	1Kin 1:6	3205
and ten thousand that *b* burdens	1Kin 5:15	5375
which *b* rule over the people that	1Kin 9:23	7287
train, with camels that *b* spices	1Kin 10:2	5375
Tahpenes him Genubath his son	1Kin 11:20	3205
the LORD, that the guard *b* them	1Kin 14:28	5375
b a son at that season that	2Kin 4:17	3205
and they *b* them before him	2Kin 5:23	5375
she *b* Zimran, and Jokshan, and	1Chr 1:32	3205
his daughter in law *b* him Pharez	1Chr 2:4	3205
And Abigail *b* Amasa	1Chr 2:17	3205
unto him Ephrath, which *b* him Hur	1Chr 2:19	3205
and she *b* him Segub	1Chr 2:21	3205
then Abiah Hezron's wife *b* him	1Chr 2:24	3205
she *b* him Ahban, and Molid	1Chr 2:29	3205
and she *b* him Attai	1Chr 2:35	3205
b Haran, and Moza, and Gazez	1Chr 2:46	3205
concubine, *b* Sheber, and Tirhanah	1Chr 2:48	3205
She *b* also Shaaph the father of	1Chr 2:49	3205
Naarah *b* him Ahuzam, and Hepher,	1Chr 4:6	3205
Because I *b* him with sorrow	1Chr 4:9	3205
she *b* Miriam, and Shammai, and	1Chr 4:17	2029
his wife Jehudijah *b* Jered the	1Chr 4:18	3205
Ashriel, whom she *b*	1Chr 7:14	3205
b Machir the father of Gilead	1Chr 7:14	3205
the wife of Machir *b* a son	1Chr 7:16	3205
And his sister Hammoleketh *b* Ishod	1Chr 7:18	3205
b a son, and he called his name	1Chr 7:23	3205
children of Judah that *b* shield	1Chr 12:24	5375
b the ark of God upon their	1Chr 15:15	5375
God helped the Levites that *b* the	1Chr 15:26	5375
and all the Levites that *b* the ark	1Chr 15:27	5375

that *b* rule over the people	2Chr 8:10	7287
company, and camels that *b* spices	2Chr 9:1	5375
Which *b* him children	2Chr 11:19	3205
which *b* him Abijah, and Attai,	2Chr 11:20	3205
had an army of men that *b* targets	2Chr 14:8	5375
that *b* shields and drew bows, two	2Chr 14:8	5375
the wall, and they that *b* burdens	Neh 4:17	5375
even their servants *b* rule over	Neh 5:15	7980
and bitterness to her that *b* him	Prov 17:25	3205
she that *b* thee shall rejoice	Prov 23:25	3205
the choice one of her that *b* her	Song 6:9	3205
brought thee forth that *b* thee	Song 8:5	3205
and she conceived, and *b* a son	Is 8:3	3205
Elam *b* the quiver with chariots	Is 22:6	5375
strip you, and make you *b*, and gird	Is 32:11	6209
make *b* the leg, uncover the thigh	Is 47:2	2834
father, and unto Sarah that *b* you	Is 51:2	2342
The LORD hath made *b* his holy arm	Is 52:10	2834
he *b* the sin of many, and made	Is 53:12	5375
he *b* them, and carried them all	Is 63:9	5190
discovered, and thy heels made *b*	Jer 13:22	2554
their mothers that *b* them	Jer 16:3	3205
wherein my mother *b* me be blessed	Jer 20:14	3205
out, and thy mother that *b* thee	Jer 22:26	3205
But I have made Esau *b*, I have	Jer 49:10	2834
she that *b* you shall be ashamed	Jer 50:12	3205
I *b* it upon my shoulder in their	Eze 12:7	5375
whereas thou wast naked and *b*	Eze 16:7	6181
youth, when thou wast naked and *b*	Eze 16:22	6181
jewels, and leave thee naked and *b*	Eze 16:39	6181
the sceptres of them that *b* rule	Eze 19:11	4910
and they were mine, and they *b* sons	Eze 23:4	3205
and shall leave thee naked and *b*	Eze 23:29	6181
their sons, whom they *b* unto me	Eze 23:37	3205
which conceived, and *b* him a son	Hos 1:3	3205
conceived again, and *b* a daughter	Hos 1:6	3205
she conceived, and *b* a son	Hos 1:8	3205
he hath made it clean *b*, and cast	Joel 1:7	2834
infirmities, and *b* our sicknesses	Mt 8:17	941
For many *b* false witness against	Mk 14:56	5576
b false witness against him,	Mk 14:57	5576
all *b* him witness, and wondered at	Lk 4:22	3140
they that *b* him stood still	Lk 7:14	941
up, and *b* fruit an hundredfold	Lk 8:8	4160
Blessed is the womb that *b* thee	Lk 11:27	941
barren, and the wombs that never *b*	Lk 23:29	1080
John *b* witness of him, and cried,	Jn 1:15	3140
John *b* record, saying, I saw the	Jn 1:32	3140
b record that this is the Son of	Jn 1:34	3140
And they *b* it	Jn 2:8	5342
he *b* witness unto the truth	Jn 5:33	3140
bag, and *b* what was put therein	Jn 12:6	941
him from the dead, *b* record	Jn 12:17	3140
And he that saw it *b* record	Jn 19:35	3140
b them witness, giving them the	Acts 15:8	3140
but *b* grain, it may chance of	1Cor 15:37	1131
Who his own self *b* our sins in	1Pet 2:24	399
Who *b* record of the word of God,	Rev 1:2	3140
which *b* twelve manner of fruits,	Rev 22:2	4160

BAREFOOT

his head covered, and he went *b*	2Sa 15:30	3182
And he did so, walking naked and *b*	Is 20:2	3182
b three years for a sign and	Is 20:3	3182
young and old, naked and *b*	Is 20:4	3182

BAREST

because thou *b* the ark of the	1Kin 2:26	5375
thou never *b* rule over them	Is 63:19	4910
Jordan, to whom thou *b* witness	Jn 3:26	3140

BARHUMITE (bar'-hu-mite) See BAHARUMITE. *A form of Baharumite.*

the Arbathite, Azmaveth the B	2Sa 23:31	1273

BARIAH (ba-ri'-ah) *Grandson of Shechaniah.*

Hattush, and Igeal, and B, and	1Chr 3:22	1282

BAR-JESUS (bar-je'-sus) See ELYMAS. *Another name of Elymas.*

prophet, a Jew, whose name was B	Acts 13:6	919

BAR-JONA (bar-jo'-nah) See SIMON. *Another name of Simon Peter.*

him, Blessed art thou, Simon B	Mt 16:17	920

BAR-JONAH See BAR-JONA.

BARK

are all dumb dogs, they cannot *b*	Is 56:10	5024

BARKED

my vine waste, and *b* my fig tree	Joel 1:7	7111

BARKOS (bar'-cos) *A family who returned from the exile.*

The children of *B*, the children	Ezr 2:53	1302
The children of *B*, the children	Neh 7:55	1302

BARLEY

And the flax and the *b* was smitten	Ex 9:31	8184
for the *b* was in the ear, and the	Ex 9:31	8184
a homer of *b* seed shall be valued	Lev 27:16	8184
tenth part of an ephah of *b* meal	Num 5:15	8184
A land of wheat, and *b*, and vines,	Deut 8:8	8184
a cake of *b* bread tumbled into	Judg 7:13	8184
in the beginning of *b* harvest	Ruth 1:22	8184
and it was about an ephah of *b*	Ruth 2:17	8184
glean unto the end of *b* harvest	Ruth 2:23	8184
he winnoweth *b* to night in the	Ruth 3:2	8184
it, he measured six measures of *b*	Ruth 3:15	8184
six measures of *b* gave he me	Ruth 3:17	8184
is near mine, and he hath *b* there	2Sa 14:30	8184
earthen vessels, and wheat, and *b*	2Sa 17:28	8184
in the beginning of *b* harvest	2Sa 21:9	8184
B also and straw for the horses and	1Kin 4:28	8184
firstfruits, twenty loaves of *b*	2Kin 4:42	8184
and two measures of *b* for a shekel	2Kin 7:1	8184
and two measures of *b* for a shekel	2Kin 7:16	8184
Two measures of *b* for a shekel	2Kin 7:18	8184
was a parcel of ground full of *b*	1Chr 11:13	8184
and twenty thousand measures of *b*	2Chr 2:10	8184
Now therefore the wheat, and the *b*	2Chr 2:15	8184
of wheat, and ten thousand of *b*	2Chr 27:5	8184
of wheat, and cockle instead of *b*	Job 31:40	8184
wheat and the appointed *b* and the	Is 28:25	8184
in the field, of wheat, and of *b*	Jer 41:8	8184
thou also unto thee wheat, and *b*	Eze 4:9	8184
And thou shalt eat it as *b* cakes	Eze 4:12	8184
among my people for handfuls of *b*	Eze 13:19	8184
part of an ephah of an homer of *b*	Eze 45:13	8184
of *b*, and an half homer of *b*	Hos 3:2	8184
for the wheat and for the *b*	Joel 1:11	8184
here, which hath five *b* loaves	Jn 6:9	2916
fragments of the five *b* loaves	Jn 6:13	2916
three measures of *b* for a penny	Rev 6:6	2915

BARN

thy seed, and gather it into thy *b*	Job 39:12	1637
Is the seed yet in the *b*	Hag 2:19	4035
but gather the wheat into my *b*	Mt 13:30	596
neither have storehouse nor *b*	Lk 12:24	596

BARNABAS (bar'-na-bas) *See* JOSES. *A companion of Paul.*

by the apostles was surnamed *B*	Acts 4:36	921
But *B* took him, and brought him to	Acts 9:27	921
and they sent forth *B*, that he	Acts 11:22	921
Then departed *B* to Tarsus	Acts 11:25	921
to the elders by the hands of *B*	Acts 11:30	921
And *B* and Saul returned from	Acts 12:25	921
as *B*, and Simeon that was called	Acts 13:1	921
Holy Ghost said, Separate me *B*	Acts 13:2	921
who called for *B* and Saul, and	Acts 13:7	921
proselytes followed Paul and *B*	Acts 13:43	921
B waxed bold, and said, It was	Acts 13:46	921
persecution against Paul and *B*	Acts 13:50	921
And they called *B*, Jupiter	Acts 14:12	921
Which when the apostles, *B*	Acts 14:14	921
day he departed with *B* to Derbe	Acts 14:20	921
B had no small dissension and	Acts 15:2	921
they determined that Paul and *B*	Acts 15:2	921
silence, and gave audience to *B*	Acts 15:12	921
company to Antioch with Paul and *B*	Acts 15:22	921
men unto you with our beloved *B*	Acts 15:25	921
B continued in Antioch, teaching	Acts 15:35	921
some days after Paul said unto *B*	Acts 15:36	921
B determined to take with them	Acts 15:37	921
so *B* took Mark, and sailed unto	Acts 15:39	921
Or I only and *B*, have not we power	1Cor 9:6	921
went up again to Jerusalem with *B*	Gal 2:1	921
B the right hands of fellowship	Gal 2:9	921
insomuch that *B* also was carried	Gal 2:13	921
you, and Marcus, sister's son to *B*	Col 4:10	921

BARNFLOOR

out of the *b*, or out of the	2Kin 6:27	1637

BARNS

So shall thy *b* be filled with	Prov 3:10	618
desolate, the *b* are broken down	Joel 1:17	4460
do they reap, nor gather into *b*	Mt 6:26	596
I will pull down my *b*, and build	Lk 12:18	596

BARREL

but an handful of meal in a *b*	1Kin 17:12	3537
The *b* of meal shall not waste,	1Kin 17:14	3537
the *b* of meal wasted not, neither	1Kin 17:16	3537

BARRELS

Fill four *b* with water, and pour	1Kin 18:33	3537

BARREN

But Sarai was *b*	Gen 11:30	6135
for his wife, because she was *b*	Gen 25:21	6135
but Rachel was *b*	Gen 29:31	6135
cast their young, nor be *b*	Ex 23:26	6135
not be male or female *b* among you	Deut 7:14	6135
and his wife was *b*, and bare not	Judg 13:2	6135
unto her, Behold now, thou art *b*	Judg 13:3	6135
so that the *b* hath born seven	1Sa 2:5	6135
water is naught, and the ground *b*	2Kin 2:19	7921
thence any more death or *b* land	2Kin 2:21	7921
entreateth the *b* that beareth not	Job 24:21	6135
and the *b* land his dwellings	Job 39:6	4420
He maketh the *b* woman to keep	Ps 113:9	6135
and the *b* womb	Prov 30:16	6115
twins, and none is *b* among them	Song 4:2	7909
and there is not one *b* among them	Song 6:6	7909
Sing, O *b*, thou that didst not	Is 54:1	6135
and will drive him into a land *b*	Joel 2:20	6723
because that Elisabeth was *b*	Lk 1:7	4722
month with her, who was called *b*	Lk 1:36	4722
they shall say, Blessed are the *b*	Lk 23:29	4722
Rejoice, thou *b* that bearest not	Gal 4:27	4722
you that ye shall neither be *b*	2Pet 1:8	692

BARRENNESS

A fruitful land into *b*, for the	Ps 107:34	4420

BARS

thou shalt make *b* of shittim wood	Ex 26:26	1280
five *b* for the boards of the	Ex 26:27	1280
five *b* for the boards of the side	Ex 26:27	1280
of gold for places for the *b*	Ex 26:29	1280
shalt overlay the *b* with gold	Ex 26:29	1280
his taches, and his boards, his *b*	Ex 35:11	1280
he made *b* of shittim wood	Ex 36:31	1280
five *b* for the boards of the	Ex 36:32	1280
five *b* for the boards of the	Ex 36:32	1280
b, and overlaid the *b* with gold	Ex 36:34	1280
his taches, his boards, his *b*	Ex 39:33	1280
thereof, and put in the *b* thereof	Ex 40:18	1280
the *b* thereof, and the pillars	Num 3:36	1280
the *b* thereof, and the pillars	Num 4:31	1280
with high walls, gates, and *b*	Deut 3:5	1280
into a town that hath gates and *b*	1Sa 23:7	1280
cities with walls and brasen *b*	1Kin 4:13	1280
cities, with walls, gates, and *b*	2Chr 8:5	1280
walls, and towers, gates, and *b*	2Chr 14:7	1280
locks thereof, and the *b* thereof	Neh 3:3	1280
locks thereof, and the *b* thereof	Neh 3:6	1280
the *b* thereof, and a thousand	Neh 3:13	1280
locks thereof, and the *b* thereof	Neh 3:14	1280
the *b* thereof, and the wall of the	Neh 3:15	1280
shall go down to the *b* of the pit	Job 17:16	905
for it my decreed place, and set *b*	Job 38:10	1280
his bones are like *b* of iron	Job 40:18	4800
cut the *b* of iron in sunder	Ps 107:16	1280
strengthened the *b* of thy gates	Ps 147:13	1280
are like the *b* of a castle	Prov 18:19	1280
and cut in sunder the *b* of iron	Is 45:2	1280
which have neither gates nor *b*	Jer 49:31	1280
her *b* are broken	Jer 51:30	1280
he hath destroyed and broken her *b*	Lam 2:9	1280
and having neither *b* nor gates	Eze 38:11	1280
the earth with her *b* was about me	Jonah 2:6	1280
the fire shall devour thy *b*	Nah 3:13	1280

BARSABAS (bar'-sab-as) *See* JOSEPH, JUDAS, JUSTUS.
1. *The successor of Judas as apostle.*

appointed two, Joseph called *B*	Acts 1:23	923

2. *A disciple sent to Antioch with Silas.*

namely, Judas surnamed *B*, and	Acts 15:22	923

BARSABBAS *See* BARSABAS.

BARTHOLOMEW (bar-thol'-o-mew) *See* NATHANAEL.
One of Jesus' twelve disciples.

Philip, and *B*; Thomas, and	Mt 10:3	918
And Andrew, and Philip, and *B*	Mk 3:18	918
James and John, Philip and *B*	Lk 6:14	918
and Andrew, Philip, and Thomas, *B*	Acts 1:13	918

BARTIMAEUS (bar-ti-me'-us) *A blind beggar.*

a great number of people, blind *B*	Mk 10:46	924

BARUCH (ba'-rook)
1. *A son of Zabbai.*

After him *B* the son of Zabbai	Neh 3:20	1263
Daniel, Ginnethon, *B*,	Neh 10:6	1263

2. *A descendant of Perez.*

And Maaseiah the son of *B*, the son	Neh 11:5	1263

3. The scribe of Jeremiah.

purchase unto B the son of Neriah	Jer 32:12	1263
I charged B before them, saying,	Jer 32:13	1263
purchase unto B the son of Neriah	Jer 32:16	1263
called B the son of Neriah	Jer 36:4	1263
B wrote from the mouth of	Jer 36:4	1263
And Jeremiah commanded B, saying,	Jer 36:5	1263
B the son of Neriah did according	Jer 36:8	1263
Then read B in the book the words	Jer 36:10	1263
when B read the book in the ears	Jer 36:13	1263
the son of Cushi, unto B	Jer 36:14	1263
So B the son of Neriah took the	Jer 36:14	1263
So B read it in their ears,	Jer 36:15	1263
both one and other, and said unto B	Jer 36:16	1263
And they asked B, saying, Tell us	Jer 36:17	1263
Then B answered them, He	Jer 36:18	1263
Then said the princes unto B	Jer 36:19	1263
to take B the scribe and Jeremiah	Jer 36:26	1263
the words which B wrote at the	Jer 36:27	1263
roll, and gave it to B the scribe	Jer 36:32	1263
But B the son of Neriah setteth	Jer 43:3	1263
prophet, and B the son of Neriah	Jer 43:6	1263
spake unto B the son of Neriah	Jer 45:1	1263
the God of Israel, unto thee, O B	Jer 45:2	1263

BARZILLAI *(bar-zil'-la-i)*
1. A friend of David.

B the Gileadite of Rogelim,	2Sa 17:27	1271
B the Gileadite came down from	2Sa 19:31	1271
Now B was a very aged man, even	2Sa 19:32	1271
And the king said unto B, Come	2Sa 19:33	1271
B said unto the king, How long	2Sa 19:34	1271
was come over, the king kissed B	2Sa 19:39	1271
unto the sons of B the Gileadite	1Kin 2:7	1271
of Koz, the children of B	Ezr 2:61	1271
the daughters of B the Gileadite	Ezr 2:61	1271
of Koz, the children of B	Neh 7:63	1271
of B the Gileadite to wife	Neh 7:63	1271

2. Husband of Merab.

the son of B the Meholathite	2Sa 21:8	1271

BASE

will be b in mine own sight	2Sa 6:22	8217
cubits was the length of one b	1Kin 7:27	4350
the ledges there was a b above	1Kin 7:29	3653
every b had four brasen wheels,	1Kin 7:30	4350
was round after the work of the b	1Kin 7:31	3653
the wheels were joined to the b	1Kin 7:32	4350
to the four corners of one b	1Kin 7:34	4350
were of the very b itself	1Kin 7:34	4350
in the top of the b was there a	1Kin 7:35	4350
on the top of the b the ledges	1Kin 7:35	4350
of fools, yea, children of b men	Job 30:8	1097,8034
the b against the honourable	Is 3:5	7034
That the kingdom might be b	Eze 17:14	8217
they shall be there a b kingdom	Eze 29:14	8217
and set there upon her own b	Zec 5:11	4369
and b before all the people,	Mal 2:9	8217
b things of the world, and things	1Cor 1:28	36
who in presence am b among you	2Cor 10:1	5011

BASEMATH See BASMATH.

BASER

lewd fellows of the b sort	Acts 17:5	60

BASES

And he made ten b of brass	1Kin 7:27	4350
the work of the b was on this	1Kin 7:28	4350
this manner he made the ten b	1Kin 7:37	4350
every one of the ten b one laver	1Kin 7:38	4350
he put five b on the right side	1Kin 7:39	4350
ten b, and ten lavers on the b	1Kin 7:43	4350
Ahaz cut off the borders of the b	2Kin 16:17	4350
the house of the LORD, and the b	2Kin 25:13	4350
the b which Solomon had made for	2Kin 25:16	4350
b, and lavers made he upon the b	2Chr 4:14	4350
And they set the altar upon his b	Ezr 3:3	4350
the sea, and concerning the b	Jer 27:19	4369
the house of the LORD, and the b	Jer 52:17	4350
bulls that were under the b	Jer 52:20	4350

BASEST

It shall be the b of the kingdoms	Eze 29:15	8217
setteth up over it the b of men	Dan 4:17	8215

BASHAN *(ba'-shan)* See BASHAN-HAVOTH-JAIR. *Kingdom of King Og.*

turned and went up by the way of B	Num 21:33	1316
Og the king of B went out against	Num 21:33	1316
and the kingdom of Og king of B	Num 32:33	1316
in Heshbon, and Og the king of B	Deut 1:4	1316
turned, and went up the way to B	Deut 3:1	1316
Og the king of B came out against	Deut 3:1	1316

our hands Og also, the king of B	Deut 3:3	1316
of Argob, the kingdom of Og in B	Deut 3:4	1316
plain, and all Gilead, and all B	Deut 3:10	1316
cities of the kingdom of Og in B	Deut 3:10	1316
For only Og king of B remained of	Deut 3:11	1316
And the rest of Gilead, and all B	Deut 3:13	1316
the region of Argob, with all B	Deut 3:13	1316
and Golan in B, of the Manassites	Deut 4:43	1316
land, and the land of Og king of B	Deut 4:47	1316
of Heshbon, and Og the king of B	Deut 29:7	1316
lambs, and rams of the breed of B	Deut 32:14	1316
he shall leap from B	Deut 33:22	1316
of Heshbon, and to Og king of B	Josh 9:10	1316
And the coast of Og king of B	Josh 12:4	1316
Hermon, and in Salcah, and in all B	Josh 12:5	1316
Hermon, and all B unto Salcah	Josh 13:11	1316
All the kingdom of Og in B	Josh 13:12	1316
coast was from Mahanaim, all B	Josh 13:30	1316
all the kingdom of Og king of B	Josh 13:30	1316
the towns of Jair, which are in B	Josh 13:30	1316
cities of the kingdom of Og in B	Josh 13:31	1316
war, therefore he had Gilead and B	Josh 17:1	1316
beside the land of Gilead and B	Josh 17:5	1316
Golan in B out of the tribe of	Josh 20:8	1316
the half tribe of Manasseh in B	Josh 21:6	1316
gave Golan in B with her suburbs	Josh 21:27	1316
Moses had given possession in B	Josh 22:7	1316
region of Argob, which is in B	1Kin 4:13	1316
the Amorites, and of Og king of B	1Kin 4:19	1316
the river Arnon, even Gilead and B	2Kin 10:33	1316
in the land of B unto Salchah	1Chr 5:11	1316
next, and Jaanai, and Shaphat in B	1Chr 5:12	1316
And they dwelt in Gilead in B	1Chr 5:16	1316
increased from B unto Baal-hermon	1Chr 5:23	1316
out of the tribe of Manasseh in B	1Chr 6:62	1316
Golan in B with her suburbs, and	1Chr 6:71	1316
and the land of Og king of B	Neh 9:22	1316
strong bulls of B have beset me	Ps 22:12	1316
hill of God is as the hill of B	Ps 68:15	1316
an high hill as the hill of B	Ps 68:15	1316
said, I will bring again from B	Ps 68:22	1316
of the Amorites, and Og king of B	Ps 135:11	1316
And Og the king of B	Ps 136:20	1316
up, and upon all the oaks of B	Is 2:13	1316
and B and Carmel shake off their	Is 33:9	1316
and lift up thy voice in B	Jer 22:20	1316
and he shall feed on Carmel and B	Jer 50:19	1316
Of the oaks of B have they made	Eze 27:6	1316
all of them fatlings of B	Eze 39:18	1316
Hear this word, ye kine of B	Amos 4:1	1316
let them feed in B and Gilead, as	Mic 7:14	1316
B languisheth, and Carmel, and the	Nah 1:4	1316
howl, O ye oaks of B	Zec 11:2	1316

BASHAN-HAVOTH-JAIR *(ba'-shan-ha'-voth-ja'-ur)*
Same as Argob.

them after his own name, B	Deut 3:14	1316,2334

BASHEMATH *(bash'-e-math)* See BASMATH.
1. Daughter of Elon the Hittite.

B the daughter of Elon the	Gen 26:34	1315

2. Daughter of Ishmael.

B Ishmael's daughter, sister of	Gen 36:3	1315
and B bare Reuel	Gen 36:4	1315
the son of B the wife of Esau	Gen 36:10	1315
were the sons of B Esau's wife	Gen 36:13	1315
are the sons of B Esau's wife	Gen 36:17	1315

BASKET

in the uppermost b there was of	Gen 40:17	5536
them out of the b upon my head	Gen 40:17	5536
b, and bring them in the b	Ex 29:3	5536
one wafer out of the b of the	Ex 29:23	5536
and the bread that is in the b	Ex 29:32	5536
rams, and a b of unleavened bread	Lev 8:2	5536
out of the b of unleavened bread,	Lev 8:26	5536
that is in the b of consecrations	Lev 8:31	5536
a b of unleavened bread, cakes of	Num 6:15	5536
with the b of unleavened bread	Num 6:17	5536
one unleavened cake out of the b	Num 6:19	5536
thee, and shalt put it in a b	Deut 26:2	2935
take the b out of thine hand	Deut 26:4	2935
Blessed shall be thy b and thy	Deut 28:5	2935
Cursed shall be thy b and thy	Deut 28:17	2935
the flesh he put in a b, and he	Judg 6:19	5536
One b had very good figs, even	Jer 24:2	1731
the other b had very naughty figs	Jer 24:2	1731
behold a b of summer fruit	Amos 8:1	3619
And I said, A b of summer fruit	Amos 8:2	3619
let him down by the wall in a b	Acts 9:25	4711
through a window in a b was I let	2Cor 11:33	4553

BASKETS

I had three white *b* on my head	Gen 40:16	5536
The three *b* are three days......................	Gen 40:18	5536
persons, and put their heads in *b*...........	2Kin 10:7	1731
as a grapegatherer into the *b*	Jer 6:9	5552
two *b* of figs were set before the	Jer 24:1	1736
that remained twelve *b* full	Mt 14:20	2894
meat that was left seven *b* full	Mt 15:37	4711
and how many *b* ye took up	Mt 16:9	2894
and how many *b* ye took up	Mt 16:10	4711
they took up twelve *b* full of the	Mk 6:43	2894
broken meat that was left seven *b*........	Mk 8:8	4711
how many *b* full of fragments took.......	Mk 8:19	2894
how many *b* full of fragments took.......	Mk 8:20	4711
that remained to them twelve *b*.............	Lk 9:17	2894
and filled twelve *b* with the	Jn 6:13	2894

BASMATH (*bas'-math*) See BASHEMATH. *A daughter of Solomon.*

he also took *B* the daughter of	1Kin 4:15	1315

BASON

it in the blood that is in the *b*	Ex 12:22	5592
with the blood that is in the *b*...............	Ex 12:22	5592
gave gold by weight for every *b*	1Chr 28:17	3713
by weight for every *b* of silver	1Chr 28:17	3713
that he poureth water into a *b*	Jn 13:5	3537

BASONS

half of the blood, and put it in *b*	Ex 24:6	101
ashes, and his shovels, and his *b*	Ex 27:3	4219
pots, and the shovels, and the *b*	Ex 38:3	4219
and the shovels, and the *b*.....................	Num 4:14	4219
Brought beds, and *b*, and earthen	2Sa 17:28	5592
lavers, and the shovels, and the *b*.........	1Kin 7:40	4219
pots, and the shovels, and the *b*	1Kin 7:45	4219
bowls, and the snuffers, and the *b*	1Kin 7:50	4219
LORD bowls of silver, snuffers, *b*	2Kin 12:13	4219
for the golden *b* he gave gold by	1Chr 28:17	3713
And he made an hundred *b* of gold	2Chr 4:8	4219
pots, and the shovels, and the *b*	2Chr 4:11	4219
And the snuffers, and the *b*...................	2Chr 4:22	4219
Thirty *b* of gold, silver *b*	Ezr 1:10	3713
Also twenty *b* of gold, of a	Ezr 8:27	3713
a thousand drams of gold, fifty *b*	Neh 7:70	4219
And the *b*, and the firepans, and the	Jer 52:19	5592

BASTARD

A *b* shall not enter into the	Deut 23:2	4464
a *b* shall dwell in Ashdod, and I	Zec 9:6	4464

BASTARDS

all are partakers, then are ye *b*	Heb 12:8	3541

BAT

kind, and the lapwing, and the *b*	Lev 11:19	5847
kind, and the lapwing, and the *b*	Deut 14:18	5847

BATH

of vineyard shall yield one *b*	Is 5:10	1324
and a just ephah, and a just *b*	Eze 45:10	1324
the *b* shall be of one measure, ...	Eze 45:11	1324
that the *b* may contain the tenth	Eze 45:11	1324
the *b* of oil, ye shall offer the	Eze 45:14	1324
tenth part of a *b* out of the cor	Eze 45:14	1324

BATHE

b himself in water, and be unclean.....	Lev 15:5	7364
b himself in water, and be unclean.........	Lev 15:6	7364
b himself in water, and be unclean.........	Lev 15:7	7364
b himself in water, and be unclean.........	Lev 15:8	7364
b himself in water, and be unclean.........	Lev 15:10	7364
b himself in water, and be unclean.........	Lev 15:11	7364
b his flesh in running water, and	Lev 15:13	7364
they shall both *b* themselves in	Lev 15:18	7364
b himself in water, and be unclean.........	Lev 15:21	7364
b himself in water, and be unclean.........	Lev 15:22	7364
b himself in water, and be unclean.........	Lev 15:27	7364
and *b* his flesh in water, and	Lev 16:26	7364
and *b* his flesh in water, and	Lev 16:28	7364
b himself in water, and be unclean.........	Lev 17:15	7364
he wash them not, nor *b* his flesh...........	Lev 17:16	7364
he shall *b* his flesh in water, and	Num 19:7	7364
b his flesh in water, and shall be	Num 19:8	7364
b himself in water, and shall be	Num 19:19	7364

BATHED

For my sword shall be *b* in heaven	Is 34:5	7301

BATH-RABBIM (*bath-rab'-bim*) *A gate at Heshbon.*

in Heshbon, by the gate of *B*	Song 7:4	1337

BATHS

it contained two thousand *b*...................	1Kin 7:26	1324
one laver contained forty *b*.....................	1Kin 7:38	1324
and twenty thousand *b* of wine	2Chr 2:10	1324

and twenty thousand *b* of oil..................	2Chr 2:10	1324
received and held three thousand *b*	2Chr 4:5	1324
wheat, and to an hundred *b* of wine.......	Ezr 7:22	1325
and to an hundred *b* of oil.......................	Ezr 7:22	1324
cor, which is an homer of ten *b*	Eze 45:14	1324
for ten *b* are an homer...........................	Eze 45:14	1324

BATH-SHEBA (*bath-she'-bah*) See BATH-SHUA. *A wife of David.*

And one said, Is not this *B*	2Sa 11:3	1339
And David comforted *B* his wife	2Sa 12:24	1339
unto *B* the mother of Solomon	1Kin 1:11	1339
B went in unto the king into the	1Kin 1:15	1339
B bowed, and did obeisance unto	1Kin 1:16	1339
David answered and said, Call me *B*......	1Kin 1:28	1339
Then *B* bowed with her face to the	1Kin 1:31	1339
came to *B* the mother of Solomon	1Kin 2:13	1339
And *B* said, Well...................................	1Kin 2:18	1339
B therefore went unto king	1Kin 2:19	1339
him, after he had gone in to *B*	Ps 51:t	1339

BATH-SHUA (*bath'-shu-ah*) See BATH-SHEBA. *A form of Bath-sheba.*

of *B* the daughter of Ammiel	1Chr 3:5	1340

BATS

worship, to the moles and to the *b*	Is 2:20	5847

BATTERED

that were with Joab *b* the wall...............	2Sa 20:15	7843

BATTERING

set *b* rams against it round about..........	Eze 4:2	
to appoint *b* rams against the	Eze 21:22	

BATTLE

they joined *b* with them in the	Gen 14:8	4421
all his people, to the *b* at Edrei...............	Num 21:33	4421
which came from the *b*	Num 31:14	6635,4421
men of war which went to the *b*	Num 31:21	4421
war upon them, who went out to *b*	Num 31:27	6635
men of war which went out to *b*	Num 31:28	6635
for war, before the LORD to *b*	Num 32:27	4421
over Jordan, every man armed to *b*.........	Num 32:29	4421
neither contend with them in *b*	Deut 2:9	4421
it, and contend with him in *b*	Deut 2:24	4421
and all his people, to *b* at Edrei.............	Deut 3:1	4421
out to *b* against thine enemies	Deut 20:1	4421
when ye are come nigh unto the *b*	Deut 20:2	4421
day unto *b* against your enemies	Deut 20:3	4421
his house, lest he die in the *b*.................	Deut 20:5	4421
his house, lest he die in the *b*	Deut 20:6	4421
his house, lest he die in the *b*	Deut 20:7	4421
came out against us unto *b*	Deut 29:7	4421
over before the LORD unto *b*	Josh 4:13	4421
city went out against Israel to *b*	Josh 8:14	4421
all other they took in *b*	Josh 11:19	4421
should come against Israel in *b*	Josh 11:20	4421
intend to go up against them in *b*	Josh 22:33	6635
from *b* before the sun was up	Judg 8:13	4421
to go out to *b* against the	Judg 20:14	4421
to the *b* against the children of.............	Judg 20:18	4421
went out to *b* against Benjamin.............	Judg 20:20	4421
set their *b* again in array in the	Judg 20:22	4421
Shall I go up again to *b* against.............	Judg 20:23	4421
out to *b* against the children of.............	Judg 20:28	4421
of all Israel, and the *b* was sore.............	Judg 20:34	4421
men of Israel retired in the *b*	Judg 20:39	4421
down before us, as in the first *b*	Judg 20:39	4421
but the *b* overtook them	Judg 20:42	4421
out against the Philistines to *b*	1Sa 4:1	4421
and when they joined *b*, Israel was	1Sa 4:2	4421
drew near to *b* against Israel	1Sa 7:10	4421
it came to pass in the day of *b*	1Sa 13:22	4421
themselves, and they came to the *b*	1Sa 14:20	4421
followed hard after them in the *b*	1Sa 14:22	4421
the *b* passed over unto Beth-aven	1Sa 14:23	4421
together their armies to *b*.....................	1Sa 17:1	4421
set the *b* in array against the	1Sa 17:2	4421
come out to set your *b* in array	1Sa 17:8	4421
went and followed Saul to the *b*	1Sa 17:13	4421
the *b* were Eliab the first born	1Sa 17:13	4421
the fight, and shouted for the *b*	1Sa 17:20	4421
had put the *b* in array, army...................	1Sa 17:21	
down that thou mightest see the *b*	1Sa 17:28	4421
for the *b* is the LORD's, and he.................	1Sa 17:47	4421
or he shall descend into *b*	1Sa 26:10	4421
thou shalt go out with me to *b*	1Sa 28:1	4264
let him not go down with us to *b*	1Sa 29:4	4421
lest in the *b* he be an adversary	1Sa 29:4	4421
shall not go up with us to the *b*	1Sa 29:9	4421
part is that goeth down to the *b*	1Sa 30:24	4421
the *b* went sore against Saul, and	1Sa 31:3	4421
the people are fled from the *b*...............	2Sa 1:4	4421

fallen in the midst of the *b*	2Sa 1:25	4421
there was a very sore *b* that day	2Sa 2:17	4421
brother Asahel at Gibeon in the *b*	2Sa 3:30	4421
put the *b* in array at the	2Sa 10:8	4221
of the *b* was against him before	2Sa 10:9	4421
unto the *b* against the Syrians	2Sa 10:13	4421
the time when kings go forth to *b*	2Sa 11:1	
in the forefront of the hottest *b*	2Sa 11:15	4421
make thy *b* more strong against	2Sa 11:25	4421
that thou go to *b* in thine own	2Sa 17:11	7128
the *b* was in the wood of Ephraim	2Sa 18:6	4421
For the *b* was there scattered	2Sa 18:8	4421
steal away when they flee in *b*	2Sa 19:3	4421
we anointed over us, is dead in *b*	2Sa 19:10	4421
shalt go no more out with us to *b*	2Sa 21:17	4421
that there was again a *b* with the	2Sa 21:18	4421
there was again a *b* in Gob with	2Sa 21:19	4421
And there was yet a *b* in Gath	2Sa 21:20	4421
hast girded me with strength to *b*	2Sa 22:40	4421
were there gathered together to *b*	2Sa 23:9	4421
go out to *b* against their enemy	1Kin 8:44	4421
he said, Who shall order the *b*	1Kin 20:14	4421
the seventh day the *b* was joined	1Kin 20:29	4421
went out into the midst of the *b*	1Kin 20:39	7128
go with me to *b* to Ramoth-gilead	1Kin 22:4	4421
I go against Ramoth-gilead to *b*	1Kin 22:6	4421
we go against Ramoth-gilead to *b*	1Kin 22:15	4421
myself, and enter into the *b*	1Kin 22:30	4421
himself, and went into the *b*	1Kin 22:30	4421
And the *b* increased that day	1Kin 22:35	4421
thou go with me against Moab to *b*	2Kin 3:7	4421
that the *b* was too sore for him	2Kin 3:26	4421
for they cried to God in the *b*	1Chr 5:20	4421
fit to go out for war and *b*	1Chr 7:11	4421
to *b* was twenty and six thousand	1Chr 7:40	4421
the *b* went sore against Saul, and	1Chr 10:3	4421
were gathered together to *b*	1Chr 11:13	4421
and men of war fit for the *b*	1Chr 12:8	4421
the Philistines against Saul to *b*	1Chr 12:19	4421
Zebulun, such as went forth to *b*	1Chr 12:33	6635
of Asher, such as went forth to *b*	1Chr 12:36	6635
of instruments of war for the *b*	1Chr 12:37	4421
that then thou shalt go out to *b*	1Chr 14:15	4421
from their cities, and came to *b*	1Chr 19:7	4421
put the *b* in array before the	1Chr 19:9	4421
the *b* was set against him before	1Chr 19:10	4421
before the Syrians unto the *b*	1Chr 19:14	4421
set the *b* in array against them	1Chr 19:17	4421
So when David had put the *b* in	1Chr 19:17	4421
the time that kings go out to *b*	1Chr 20:1	
Abijah set the *b* in array with an	2Chr 13:3	4421
Jeroboam also set the *b* in array	2Chr 13:3	4421
the *b* was before and behind	2Chr 13:14	4421
they set the *b* in array in the	2Chr 14:10	4421
Shall we go to Ramoth-gilead to *b*	2Chr 18:5	4421
shall we go to Ramoth-gilead to *b*	2Chr 18:14	4421
myself, and will go to the *b*	2Chr 18:29	4421
and they went to the *b*	2Chr 18:29	4421
And the *b* increased that day	2Chr 18:34	4421
came against Jehoshaphat to *b*	2Chr 20:1	4421
for the *b* is not yours, but God's	2Chr 20:15	4421
shall not need to fight in this *b*	2Chr 20:17	4421
go, do it, be strong for the *b*	2Chr 25:8	4421
they should not go with him to *b*	2Chr 25:13	4421
him, as a king ready to the *b*	Job 15:24	3593
of trouble, against the day of *b*	Job 38:23	7128
and he smelleth the *b* afar off	Job 39:25	4421
hand upon him, remember the *b*	Job 41:8	4421
me with strength unto the *b*	Ps 18:39	4421
and mighty, the LORD mighty in *b*	Ps 24:8	4421
from the *b* that was against me	Ps 55:18	7128
shield, and the sword, and the *b*	Ps 76:3	4421
bows, turned back in the day of *b*	Ps 78:9	7128
not made him to stand in the *b*	Ps 89:43	4421
covered my head in the day of *b*	Ps 140:7	5402
is prepared against the day of *b*	Prov 21:31	4421
nor the *b* to the strong, neither	Eccl 9:11	4421
For every *b* of the warrior is	Is 9:5	5430
hosts mustereth the host of the *b*	Is 13:4	4421
with the sword, nor dead in *b*	Is 22:2	4421
briers and thorns against me in *b*	Is 27:4	4421
them that turn the *b* to the gate	Is 28:6	4421
his anger, and the strength of *b*	Is 42:25	4421
as the horse rusheth into the *b*	Jer 8:6	4421
men be slain by the sword in *b*	Jer 18:21	4421
and shield, and draw near to *b*	Jer 46:3	4421
against her, and rise up to the *b*	Jer 49:14	4421
A sound of *b* is in the land, and	Jer 50:22	4421
put in array, like a man to the *b*	Jer 50:42	4421
Thou art my *b* ax and weapons of	Jer 51:20	4661
but none goeth to the *b*	Eze 7:14	4421

in the *b* in the day of the LORD	Eze 13:5	4421
neither in anger, nor in *b*	Dan 11:20	4421
stirred up to *b* with a very great	Dan 11:25	4421
by bow, nor by sword, nor by *b*	Hos 1:7	4421
the *b* out of the earth, and will	Hos 2:18	4421
the *b* in Gibeah against the	Hos 10:9	4421
Beth-arbel in the day of *b*	Hos 10:14	4421
as a strong people set in *b* array	Joel 2:5	4421
with shouting in the day of *b*	Amos 1:14	4421
let us rise up against her in *b*	Obad 1	4421
the *b* bow shall be cut off	Zec 9:10	4421
them as his goodly horse in the *b*	Zec 10:3	4421
the nail, out of him the *b* bow	Zec 10:4	4421
the mire of the streets in the *b*	Zec 10:5	4421
nations against Jerusalem to *b*	Zec 14:2	4421
as when he fought in the day of *b*	Zec 14:3	7128
shall prepare himself to the *b*	1Cor 14:8	*4171*
like unto horses prepared unto *b*	Rev 9:7	*4171*
of many horses running to *b*	Rev 9:9	*4171*
to gather them to the *b* of that	Rev 16:14	*4171*
to gather them together to *b*	Rev 20:8	*4171*

BATTLEMENT

thou shalt make a *b* for thy roof	Deut 22:8	4624

BATTLEMENTS

take away her *b*	Jer 5:10	5189

BATTLES

go out before us, and fight our *b*	1Sa 8:20	4421
for me, and fight the LORD's *b*	1Sa 18:17	4421
lord fighteth the *b* of the LORD	1Sa 25:28	4421
Out of the spoils won in *b* did	1Chr 26:27	4421
God to help us, and to fight our *b*	2Chr 32:8	4421
in *b* of shaking will he fight	Is 30:32	4421

BAVAI (*bav'-a-i*) *A descendant of Henadad.*

B the son of Henadad, the ruler	Neh 3:18	942

BAVVAI See BAVAI.

BAY

from the *b* that looketh southward	Josh 15:2	3956
the *b* of the sea at the uttermost	Josh 15:5	3956
b of the salt sea at the south	Josh 18:19	3956
himself like a green *b* tree	Ps 37:35	249
chariot grisled and *b* horses	Zec 6:3	554
the *b* went forth, and sought to go	Zec 6:7	554

BAZLITH (*baz'-lith*) See BAZLUTH. *A family who returned from exile.*

The children of *B*, the children	Neh 7:54	1213

BAZLUTH (*baz'-luth*) See BAZLITH. *A form of Bazlith.*

The children of *B*, the children	Ezr 2:52	1213

BDELLIUM

there is *b* and the onyx stone	Gen 2:12	916
colour thereof as the colour of *b*	Num 11:7	916

BE See APPENDIX.

BEACON

till ye be left as a *b* upon the	Is 30:17	8650

BEALIAH (*be-a-li'-ah*) *A warrior in David's army.*

Eluzai, and Jerimoth, and *B*	1Chr 12:5	1183

BEALOTH (*be'-a-loth*) See ALOTH. *A city in Judah.*

Ziph, and Telem, and *B*,	Josh 15:24	1175

BEAM

went away with the pin of the *b*	Judg 16:14	708
his spear was like a weaver's *b*	1Sa 17:7	4500
whose spear was like a weaver's *b*	2Sa 21:19	4500
the thick *b* were before them	1Kin 7:6	5646
and take thence every man a *b*	2Kin 6:2	6982
But as one was felling a *b*	2Kin 6:5	6982
was a spear like a weaver's *b*	1Chr 11:23	4500
spear staff was like a weaver's *b*	1Chr 20:5	4500
the *b* out of the timber shall	Hab 2:11	3714
but considerest not the *b* that is	Mt 7:3	*1385*
behold, a *b* is in thine own eye	Mt 7:4	*1385*
first cast out the *b* out of thine	Mt 7:5	*1385*
but perceivest not the *b* that is	Lk 6:41	*1385*
the *b* that is in thine own eye	Lk 6:42	*1385*
cast out first the *b* out of thine	Lk 6:42	*1385*

BEAMS

that the *b* should not be fastened	1Kin 6:6	
and covered the house with *b*	1Kin 6:9	1356
hewed stone, and a row of cedar *b*	1Kin 6:36	3773
with cedar *b* upon the pillars	1Kin 7:2	3773
with cedar above upon the *b*	1Kin 7:3	6763
hewed stones, and a row of cedar *b*	1Kin 7:12	3773
He overlaid also the house, the *b*	2Chr 3:7	6982
b for the gates of the palace	Neh 2:8	7136
who also laid the *b* thereof	Neh 3:3	7136
they laid the *b* thereof, and set	Neh 3:6	7136

Who layeth the *b* of his chambers	Ps 104:3	7136
The *b* of our house are cedar, and	Song 1:17	6982

BEANS

and flour, and parched corn, and *b*	2Sa 17:28	6321
unto thee wheat, and barley, and *b*	Eze 4:9	6321

BEAR

is greater than I can *b*	Gen 4:13	5375
the land was not able to *b* them	Gen 13:6	5375
art with child, and shalt *b* a son	Gen 16:11	3205
that is ninety years old, *b*	Gen 17:17	3205
wife shall *b* thee a son indeed	Gen 17:19	3205
which Sarah shall *b* unto thee at	Gen 17:21	3205
Shall I of a surety *b* a child	Gen 18:13	3205
these eight Milcah did *b* to Nahor	Gen 22:23	3205
she shall *b* upon my knees, that I	Gen 30:3	3205
b them because of their cattle	Gen 36:7	5375
then let me *b* the blame for ever	Gen 43:9	2398
then I shall *b* the blame to my	Gen 44:32	2398
and bowed his shoulder to *b*	Gen 49:15	5445
they shall *b* the burden with thee	Ex 18:22	5375
Thou shalt not *b* false witness	Ex 20:16	6030
of the staves to *b* the table	Ex 25:27	5375
two sides of the altar, to *b* it	Ex 27:7	5375
Aaron shall *b* their names before	Ex 28:12	5375
Aaron shall *b* the names of the	Ex 28:29	5375
Aaron shall *b* the judgment of the	Ex 28:30	5375
that Aaron may *b* the iniquity of	Ex 28:38	5375
that they *b* not iniquity, and die	Ex 28:43	5375
for the staves to *b* it withal	Ex 30:4	5375
sides of the ark, to *b* the ark	Ex 37:5	5375
for the staves to *b* the table	Ex 37:14	5375
them with gold, to *b* the table	Ex 37:15	5375
for the staves to *b* it withal	Ex 37:27	5375
of the altar, to *b* it withal	Ex 38:7	5375
it, then he shall *b* his iniquity	Lev 5:1	5375
guilty, and shall *b* his iniquity	Lev 5:17	5375
eateth of it shall *b* his iniquity	Lev 7:18	5375
it you to the iniquity of the	Lev 10:17	5375
But if she *b* a maid child, then	Lev 12:5	3205
the goat shall *b* upon him all	Lev 16:22	5375
then he shall *b* his iniquity	Lev 17:16	5375
eateth it shall *b* his iniquity	Lev 19:8	5375
nor *b* any grudge against the	Lev 19:18	5201
he shall *b* his iniquity	Lev 20:17	5375
they shall *b* their iniquity	Lev 20:19	5375
they shall *b* their sin	Lev 20:20	5375
lest they *b* sin for it, and die	Lev 22:9	5375
Or suffer them to *b* the iniquity	Lev 22:16	5375
curseth his God shall *b* his sin	Lev 24:15	5375
they shall *b* the tabernacle, and	Num 1:50	5375
sons of Kohath shall come to *b* it	Num 4:15	5375
they shall *b* the curtains of the	Num 4:25	5375
this woman shall *b* her iniquity	Num 5:31	5375
should *b* upon their shoulders	Num 7:9	5375
season, that man shall *b* his sin	Num 9:13	5375
I am not able to *b* all this	Num 11:14	5375
they shall *b* the burden of the	Num 11:17	5375
that thou *b* it not thyself alone	Num 11:17	
How long shall I *b* with this evil	Num 14:27	
b your whoredoms, until your	Num 14:33	5375
shall ye *b* your iniquities, even	Num 14:34	5375
b the iniquity of the sanctuary	Num 18:1	5375
thy sons with thee shall *b* the	Num 18:1	5375
the congregation, lest they *b* sin	Num 18:22	5375
they shall *b* their iniquity	Num 18:23	5375
ye shall *b* no sin by reason of it	Num 18:32	5375
then he shall *b* her iniquity	Num 30:15	5375
am not able to *b* you myself alone	Deut 1:9	5375
I myself alone *b* your cumbrance	Deut 1:12	5375
thee, as a man doth *b* his son	Deut 1:31	5375
Neither shalt thou *b* false	Deut 5:20	6030
to *b* the ark of the covenant of	Deut 10:8	5375
her children which she shall *b*	Deut 28:57	3205
that *b* the ark of the covenant	Josh 3:3	5375
that *b* the ark of the LORD	Josh 3:13	5375
that *b* the ark of the testimony	Josh 4:16	5375
seven priests shall *b* before the	Josh 6:4	5375
let seven priests *b* seven	Josh 6:6	5375
thou shalt conceive, and *b* a son	Judg 13:3	3205
thou shalt conceive, and *b* a son	Judg 13:5	3205
thou shalt conceive, and *b* a son	Judg 13:7	3205
to night, and should also *b* sons	Ruth 1:12	3205
and there came a lion, and a *b*	1Sa 17:34	1677
slew both the lion and the *b*	1Sa 17:36	1677
lion, and out of the paw of the *b*	1Sa 17:37	1677
as a *b* robbed of her whelps in	2Sa 17:8	1677
b the king tidings, how that he	2Sa 18:19	1319
Thou shalt not *b* tidings this day	2Sa 18:20	1319
but thou shalt *b* tidings another	2Sa 18:20	1319
this day thou shalt *b* no tidings	2Sa 18:20	1319
it was not my son, which I did *b*	1Kin 3:21	3205
to *b* witness against him, saying,	1Kin 21:10	5749
which thou puttest on me will I *b*	2Kin 18:14	5375
root downward, and *b* fruit upward	2Kin 19:30	6213
men, men able to *b* buckler	1Chr 5:18	5375
and ten thousand men to *b* burdens	2Chr 2:2	5445
should *b* rule in his own house	Est 1:22	8323
I *b* up the pillars of it	Ps 75:3	8505
how I do *b* in my bosom the	Ps 89:50	5375
They shall *b* thee up in their	Ps 91:12	5375
scornest, thou alone shalt *b* it	Prov 9:12	5375
hand of the diligent shall *b* rule	Prov 12:24	4910
Let a *b* robbed of her whelps meet	Prov 17:12	1677
but a wounded spirit who can *b*	Prov 18:14	5375
As a roaring lion, and a ranging *b*	Prov 28:15	1677
and for four which it cannot *b*	Prov 30:21	5375
whereof every one *b* twins	Song 4:2	8382
I am weary to *b* them	Is 1:14	5375
b a son, and shall call his name	Is 7:14	3205
And the cow and the *b* shall feed	Is 11:7	1677
root downward, and *b* fruit upward	Is 37:31	6213
I have made, and I will *b*	Is 46:4	5375
They *b* him upon the shoulder,	Is 46:7	5375
that *b* the vessels of the LORD	Is 52:11	5375
for he shall *b* their iniquities	Is 53:11	5445
O barren, thou that didst not *b*	Is 54:1	5375
the priests *b* rule by their means	Jer 5:31	7287
this is a grief, and I must *b* it	Jer 10:19	5375
b no burden on the sabbath day,	Jer 17:21	5375
not to *b* a burden, even entering	Jer 17:27	5375
to husbands, that they may *b* sons	Jer 29:6	3205
because I did *b* the reproach of	Jer 31:19	5375
that the LORD could no longer *b*	Jer 44:22	5375
was unto me as a *b* lying in wait	Lam 3:10	1677
that he *b* the yoke in his youth	Lam 3:27	5375
it thou shalt *b* their iniquity	Eze 4:4	5375
so shalt thou *b* the iniquity of	Eze 4:5	5375
thou shalt *b* the iniquity of the	Eze 4:6	5375
thou *b* it upon thy shoulders	Eze 12:6	5375
shall *b* upon his shoulder in the	Eze 12:12	5375
they shall *b* the punishment of	Eze 14:10	5375
b thine own shame for thy sins	Eze 16:52	5375
b thy shame, in that thou hast	Eze 16:52	5375
thou mayest *b* thine own shame	Eze 16:54	5375
and that it might *b* fruit	Eze 17:8	5375
b fruit, and be a goodly cedar	Eze 17:23	6213
doth not the son *b* the iniquity	Eze 18:19	5375
The son shall not *b* the iniquity	Eze 18:20	5375
father *b* the iniquity of the son	Eze 18:20	5375
therefore *b* thou also thy	Eze 23:35	5375
ye shall *b* the sins of your idols	Eze 23:49	5375
b their shame with them that go	Eze 32:30	5375
neither *b* the shame of the	Eze 34:29	5375
you, they shall *b* their shame	Eze 36:7	5375
neither shalt thou *b* the reproach	Eze 36:15	5375
they shall even *b* their iniquity	Eze 44:10	5375
they shall *b* their iniquity	Eze 44:12	5375
but they shall *b* their shame	Eze 44:13	5375
that they *b* them not out into the	Eze 46:20	3318
which shall *b* rule over all the	Dan 2:39	7981
beast, a second, like to a *b*	Dan 7:5	1678
dried up, they shall *b* no fruit	Hos 9:16	6213
I will meet them as a *b* that is	Hos 13:8	1677
flee from a lion, and a *b* met him	Amos 5:19	1677
is not able to *b* all his words	Amos 7:10	3557
therefore ye shall *b* the reproach	Mic 6:16	5375
I will *b* the indignation of the	Mic 7:9	5375
all they that *b* silver are cut	Zeph 1:11	5187
If one *b* holy flesh in the skirt	Hag 2:12	5375
me, Whither do these *b* the ephah	Zec 5:10	3212
he shall *b* the glory, and shall	Zec 6:13	5375
whose shoes I am not worthy to *b*	Mt 3:11	941
their hands they shall *b* thee up	Mt 4:6	142
Thou shalt not *b* false witness	Mt 19:18	5576
him they compelled to *b* his cross	Mt 27:32	142
Do not *b* false witness, Defraud	Mk 10:19	5576
and Rufus, to *b* his cross	Mk 15:21	142
wife Elisabeth shall *b* thee a son	Lk 1:13	1080
their hands they shall *b* thee up	Lk 4:11	142
Truly ye *b* witness that ye allow	Lk 11:48	3140
And if it *b* fruit, well	Lk 13:9	4160
And whosoever doth not *b* his cross	Lk 14:27	941
though he *b* long with them	Lk 18:7	3114
Do not *b* false witness, Honour	Lk 18:20	5576
that he might *b* it after Jesus	Lk 23:26	5342
to *b* witness of the Light, that	Jn 1:7	3140
but was sent to *b* witness of that	Jn 1:8	3140
b unto the governor of the feast	Jn 2:8	5342
Ye yourselves *b* me witness	Jn 3:28	3140
If I *b* witness of myself, my	Jn 5:31	3140
b witness of me, that the Father	Jn 5:36	3140

B

Though I *b* record of myself, yet	Jn 8:14	3140
I am one that *b* witness of myself	Jn 8:18	3140
name, they *b* witness of me	Jn 10:25	3140
branch cannot *b* fruit of itself	Jn 15:4	5342
glorified, that ye *b* much fruit	Jn 15:8	5342
And ye also shall *b* witness	Jn 15:27	3140
you, but ye cannot *b* them now	Jn 16:12	941
evil, *b* witness of the evil	Jn 18:23	3140
that I should *b* witness unto the	Jn 18:37	3140
to *b* my name before the Gentiles,	Acts 9:15	941
our fathers nor we were able to *b*	Acts 15:10	941
would that I should *b* with you	Acts 18:14	430
the high priest doth *b* me witness	Acts 22:5	3140
so must thou *b* witness also at	Acts 23:11	3140
could not *b* up into the wind, we	Acts 27:15	503
For I *b* them record that they	Rom 10:2	3140
Thou shalt not *b* false witness	Rom 13:9	5576
to *b* the infirmities of the weak	Rom 15:1	941
hitherto ye were not able to *b* it	1Cor 3:2	
that ye may be able to *b* it	1Cor 10:13	5297
we shall also *b* the image of the	1Cor 15:49	5409
I *b* record, yea, and beyond their	2Cor 3:1	3140
Would to God ye could *b* with me a	2Cor 11:1	430
and indeed *b* with me	2Cor 11:1	430
ye might well *b* with him	2Cor 11:4	430
for I *b* you record, that, if it	Gal 4:15	3140
you shall his judgment,	Gal 5:10	941
B ye one another's burdens, and so	Gal 6:2	941
every man shall *b* his own burden	Gal 6:5	941
for I *b* in my body the marks of	Gal 6:17	941
For I *b* him record, that he hath	Col 4:13	3140
b children, guide the house, give	1Ti 5:14	5041
offered to *b* the sins of many	Heb 9:28	399
my brethren, *b* olive berries	Jas 3:12	4160
b witness, and shew unto you that	1Jn 5:7	3140
are three that *b* record in heaven	1Jn 5:7	3140
are three that *b* witness in earth	1Jn 5:8	3140
yea, and we also *b* record	3Jn 12	
how thou canst not *b* them which	Rev 2:2	941
his feet were as the feet of a *b*	Rev 13:2	715

BEARD

a plague upon the head or the *b*	Lev 13:29	2206
even a leprosy upon the head or *b*	Lev 13:30	2206
his hair off his head and his *b*	Lev 14:9	2206
thou mar the corners of thy *b*	Lev 19:27	2206
shave off the corner of their *b*	Lev 21:5	2206
against me, I caught him by his *b*	1Sa 17:35	2206
his spittle fall down upon his *b*	1Sa 21:13	2206
his feet, nor trimmed his *b*	2Sa 19:24	8222
by the *b* with the right hand to	2Sa 20:9	2206
the hair of my head and of my *b*	Ezr 9:3	2206
upon the *b*, even Aaron's *b*	Ps 133:2	2206
and it shall also consume the *b*	Is 7:20	2206
be baldness, and every *b* cut off	Is 15:2	2206
shall be bald, and every *b* clipped	Jer 48:37	2206
upon thine head and upon thy *b*	Eze 5:1	2206

BEARDS

off the one half of their *b*	2Sa 10:4	2206
at Jericho until your *b* be grown	2Sa 10:5	2206
at Jericho until your *b* be grown	1Chr 19:5	2206
men, having their *b* shaven	Jer 41:5	2206

BEARERS

of them to be *b* of burdens	2Chr 2:18	5449
they were over the *b* of burdens	2Chr 34:13	5449
The strength of the *b* of burdens	Neh 4:10	5449

BEAREST

now, thou art barren, and *b* not	Judg 13:3	3205
that thou *b* unto thy people	Ps 106:4	
him, Thou *b* record of thyself	Jn 8:13	3140
thou *b* not the root, but the root	Rom 11:18	941
Rejoice, thou barren that *b* not	Gal 4:27	5088

BEARETH

whosoever *b* ought of the carcase	Lev 11:25	5375
he that *b* the carcase of them	Lev 11:28	5375
he also that *b* the carcase of it	Lev 11:40	5375
he that *b* any of those things	Lev 15:10	5375
father *b* the sucking child	Num 11:12	5375
b shall succeed in the name of	Deut 25:6	3205
be among you a root that *b* gall	Deut 29:18	6509
that it is not sown, nor *b*	Deut 29:23	6779
taketh them, *b* them on her wings	Deut 32:11	5375
up in me *b* witness to my face	Job 16:8	6030
entreateth the barren that *b* not	Job 24:21	3205
A man that *b* false witness	Prov 25:18	6030
but when the wicked *b* rule	Prov 29:2	4910
whereof every one *b* twins	Song 6:6	8382
spring, for the tree *b* her fruit	Joel 2:22	5375
which also *b* fruit, and bringeth	Mt 13:23	2592

is another that *b* witness of me	Jn 5:32	3140
that sent me *b* witness of me	Jn 8:18	3140
Every branch in me that *b* not	Jn 15:2	5342
and every branch that *b* fruit	Jn 15:2	5342
The Spirit itself *b* witness with	Rom 8:16	4828
for he *b* not the sword in vain	Rom 13:4	5409
B all things, believeth all	1Cor 13:7	4722
But that which *b* thorns and briers	Heb 6:8	1627
it is the Spirit that *b* witness	1Jn 5:6	3140

BEARING

have given you every herb *b* seed	Gen 1:29	2232
LORD hath restrained me from *b*	Gen 16:2	3205
his name Judah; and left *b*	Gen 29:35	3205
When Leah saw that she had left *b*	Gen 30:9	3205
with their camels *b* spicery	Gen 37:25	5375
set forward, *b* the tabernacle	Num 10:17	5375
set forward, *b* the sanctuary	Num 10:21	5375
and the priests the Levites *b* it	Josh 3:3	5375
the priests *b* the ark of the	Josh 3:14	5375
that the seven priests *b* the	Josh 6:8	5375
seven priests *b* seven trumpets of	Josh 6:13	5375
one *b* a shield went before him	1Sa 17:7	5375
b the ark of the covenant of God	2Sa 15:24	5375
b precious seed, shall doubtless	Ps 126:6	5375
you a man *b* a pitcher of water	Mk 14:13	941
meet you, *b* a pitcher of water	Lk 22:10	941
he *b* his cross went forth into a	Jn 19:17	941
their conscience also *b* me witness	Rom 2:15	4828
my conscience also *b* me witness	Rom 9:1	4828
Always *b* about in the body the	2Cor 4:10	4064
God also *b* them witness, both	Heb 2:4	4901
without the camp, *b* his reproach	Heb 13:13	5342

BEARS

forth two she *b* out of the wood	2Kin 2:24	1677
We roar all like *b*, and mourn sore	Is 59:11	1677

BEAST

b of the earth after his kind	Gen 1:24	2416
God made the *b* of the earth after	Gen 1:25	2416
to every *b* of the earth, and to	Gen 1:30	2416
God formed every *b* of the field	Gen 2:19	2416
air, and to every *b* of the field	Gen 2:20	2416
was more subtil than any *b* of the	Gen 3:1	2416
above every *b* of the field	Gen 3:14	2416
both man, and *b*, and the creeping	Gen 6:7	929
Of every clean *b* thou shalt take	Gen 7:2	929
every *b* after his kind, and all	Gen 7:14	2416
of fowl, and of cattle, and of *b*	Gen 7:21	2416
Every *b*, every creeping thing, and	Gen 8:19	2416
and took of every clean *b*, and of	Gen 8:20	929
be upon every *b* of the earth	Gen 9:2	2416
hand of every *b* will I require it	Gen 9:5	2416
of every *b* of the earth with you	Gen 9:10	2416
the ark, to every *b* of the earth	Gen 9:10	2416
every *b* of theirs be ours	Gen 34:23	929
Some evil *b* hath devoured him	Gen 37:20	2416
an evil *b* hath devoured him	Gen 37:33	2416
and it became lice in man, and in *b*	Ex 8:17	929
were lice upon man, and upon *b*	Ex 8:18	929
with blains upon man, and upon *b*	Ex 9:9	929
with blains upon man, and upon *b*	Ex 9:10	929
b which shall be found in the	Ex 9:19	929
of Egypt, upon man, and upon *b*	Ex 9:22	929
was in the field, both man and *b*	Ex 9:25	929
move his tongue, against man or *b*	Ex 11:7	929
the land of Egypt, both man and *b*	Ex 12:12	929
of Israel, both of man and of *b*	Ex 13:2	929
cometh of a *b* which thou hast	Ex 13:12	929
of man, and the firstborn of *b*	Ex 13:15	929
whether it be *b* or man, it shall	Ex 19:13	929
and the dead shall be his	Ex 21:34	
be eaten, and shall put in his *b*	Ex 22:5	1165
or an ox, a sheep, or any *b*	Ex 22:10	929
Whosoever lieth with a *b* shall	Ex 22:19	929
the *b* of the field multiply	Ex 23:29	2416
it be a carcase of an unclean *b*	Lev 5:2	2416
of man, or any unclean *b*, or any	Lev 7:21	929
the fat of the *b* that dieth of	Lev 7:24	5038
whosoever eateth the fat of the *b*	Lev 7:25	929
whether it be of fowl or of *b*	Lev 7:26	929
The carcases of every *b* which	Lev 11:26	929
And if any *b*, of which ye may eat,	Lev 11:39	929
between the *b* that may be eaten	Lev 11:47	2416
the *b* that may not be eaten	Lev 11:47	2416
catcheth any *b* or fowl that may	Lev 17:13	2416
any *b* to defile thyself therewith	Lev 18:23	929
before a *b* to lie down thereto	Lev 18:23	929
And if a man lie with a *b*, he	Lev 20:15	929
and ye shall slay the *b*	Lev 20:15	929
And if a woman approach unto any *b*	Lev 20:16	929

shalt kill the woman, and the *b*	Lev 20:16	929
make your souls abominable by *b*	Lev 20:25	929
he that killeth a *b* shall make it	Lev 24:18	5315,929
shall make it good; *b* for *b*	Lev 24:18	5315
shall make it good; *b* for *b*	Lev 24:18	929
And he that killeth a *b*, he shall	Lev 24:21	929
for the *b* that are in thy land,	Lev 25:7	2416
And if it be a *b*, whereof men	Lev 27:9	929
shall at change a *b* for *b*	Lev 27:10	929
And if it be any unclean *b*	Lev 27:11	929
present the *b* before the priest	Lev 27:11	929
And if it be of an unclean *b*	Lev 27:27	929
that he hath, both of man and *b*	Lev 27:28	929
in Israel, both man and *b*	Num 3:13	929
of Israel are mine, both man and *b*	Num 8:17	929
was taken, both of man and of *b*	Num 31:26	929
of fifty, both of man and of *b*	Num 31:47	929
The likeness of any *b* that is on	Deut 4:17	929
every *b* that parteth the hoof, and	Deut 14:6	929
that lieth with any manner of *b*	Deut 27:21	929
the men of every city, as the *b*	Judg 20:48	929
by a wild *b* that was in Lebanon	2Kin 14:9	2416
by a wild *b* that was in Lebanon	2Chr 25:18	2416
neither was there any *b* with me	Neh 2:12	929
save the *b* that I rode upon	Neh 2:12	929
the *b* that was under me to pass	Neh 2:14	929
or that the wild *b* may break them	Job 39:15	2416
O Lord, thou preservest man and *b*	Ps 36:6	929
For every *b* of the forest is mine	Ps 50:10	2416
I was as a *b* before thee	Ps 73:22	929
the wild *b* of the field doth	Ps 80:13	2123
drink to every *b* of the field	Ps 104:11	2416
of Egypt, both of man and *b*	Ps 135:8	929
He giveth to the *b* his food	Ps 147:9	929
man regardeth the life of his *b*	Prov 12:10	929
man hath no preeminence above a *b*	Eccl 3:19	929
the spirit of the *b* that goeth	Eccl 3:21	929
nor any ravenous *b* shall go up	Is 35:9	2416
The *b* of the field shall honour	Is 43:20	2416
they are a burden to the weary *b*	Is 46:1	
As a *b* goeth down into the valley	Is 63:14	929
this place, upon man, and upon *b*	Jer 7:20	929
of the heavens and the *b* are fled	Jer 9:10	929
of this city, both man and *b*	Jer 21:6	929
the *b* that are upon the ground,	Jer 27:5	929
of man, and with the seed of *b*	Jer 31:27	929
It is desolate without man or *b*	Jer 32:43	929
desolate without man and without *b*	Jer 33:10	929
without inhabitant, and without *b*	Jer 33:10	929
desolate without man and without *b*	Jer 33:12	929
to cease from thence man and *b*	Jer 36:29	929
they shall depart, both man and *b*	Jer 50:3	929
remain in it, neither man nor *b*	Jer 51:62	929
and will cut off man and *b* from it	Eze 14:13	929
that I cut off man and *b* from it	Eze 14:17	929
to cut off from it man and *b*	Eze 14:19	929
and the famine, and the noisome *b*	Eze 14:21	2416
to cut off from it man and *b*	Eze 14:21	929
and will cut off man and *b* from it	Eze 25:13	929
and cut off man and *b* out of thee	Eze 29:8	929
nor foot of *b* shall pass through	Eze 29:11	929
meat to every *b* of the field	Eze 34:8	2416
neither shall the *b* of the land	Eze 34:28	2416
I will multiply upon you man and *b*	Eze 36:11	929
to every *b* of the field, Assemble	Eze 39:17	2416
or torn, whether it be fowl or *b*	Eze 44:31	929
And behold another *b*, a second,	Dan 7:5	2423
the *b* had also four heads	Dan 7:6	2423
visions, and behold a fourth *b*	Dan 7:7	2423
beheld even till the *b* was slain	Dan 7:11	2423
know the truth of the fourth *b*	Dan 7:19	2423
The fourth *b* shall be the fourth	Dan 7:23	2423
the wild *b* shall tear them	Hos 13:8	2416
saying, Let neither man nor *b*	Jonah 3:7	929
b be covered with sackcloth, and	Jonah 3:8	929
bind the chariot to the swift *b*	Mic 1:13	7409
I will consume man and *b*	Zeph 1:3	929
hire for man, nor any hire for *b*	Zec 8:10	929
and wine, and set him on his own *b*	Lk 10:34	2934
the venomous *b* hang on his hand	Acts 28:4	2342
he shook off the *b* into the fire	Acts 28:5	2342
if so much as a *b* touch the	Heb 12:20	2342
the first *b* was like a lion, and	Rev 4:7	2226
the second *b* like a calf	Rev 4:7	2226
the third *b* had a face as a man,	Rev 4:7	2226
the fourth *b* was like a flying	Rev 4:7	2226
seal, I heard the second *b* say	Rev 6:3	2226
seal, I heard the third *b* say	Rev 6:5	2226
the voice of the fourth *b* say	Rev 6:7	2226
the *b* that ascendeth out of the	Rev 11:7	2342
saw a *b* rise up out of the sea,	Rev 13:1	2342

the *b* which I saw was like unto a	Rev 13:2	2342
the world wondered after the *b*	Rev 13:3	2342
which gave power unto the *b*	Rev 13:4	2342
and they worshipped the *b*	Rev 13:4	2342
saying, Who is like unto the *b*	Rev 13:4	2342
I beheld another *b* coming up out	Rev 13:11	2342
power of the first *b* before him	Rev 13:12	2342
therein to worship the first *b*	Rev 13:12	2342
power to do in the sight of the *b*	Rev 13:14	2342
should make an image to the *b*	Rev 13:14	2342
give life unto the image of the *b*	Rev 13:15	2342
image of the *b* should both speak	Rev 13:15	2342
image of the *b* should be killed	Rev 13:15	2342
the mark, or the name of the *b*	Rev 13:17	2342
count the number of the *b*	Rev 13:18	2342
voice, If any man worship the *b*	Rev 14:9	2342
day nor night, who worship the *b*	Rev 14:11	2342
had gotten the victory over the *b*	Rev 15:2	2342
men which had the mark of the *b*	Rev 16:2	2342
his vial upon the seat of the *b*	Rev 16:10	2342
and out of the mouth of the *b*	Rev 16:13	2342
sit upon a scarlet coloured *b*	Rev 17:3	2342
of the *b* that carrieth her, which	Rev 17:7	2342
The *b* that thou sawest was, and is	Rev 17:8	2342
when they behold the *b* that was	Rev 17:8	2342
the *b* that was, and is not, even	Rev 17:11	2342
as kings one hour with the *b*	Rev 17:12	2342
power and strength unto the *b*	Rev 17:13	2342
which thou sawest upon the *b*	Rev 17:16	2342
and give their kingdom unto the *b*	Rev 17:17	2342
And I saw the *b*, and the kings of	Rev 19:19	2342
the *b* was taken, and with him the	Rev 19:20	2342
had received the mark of the *b*	Rev 19:20	2342
and which had not worshipped the *b*	Rev 20:4	2342
of fire and brimstone, where the *b*	Rev 20:10	2342

BEAST'S

let a *b* heart be given unto him	Dan 4:16	2423

BEASTS

of *b* that are not clean by two,	Gen 7:2	929
Of clean *b*, and of *b* that are	Gen 7:8	929
That which was torn of *b* I	Gen 31:39	2966
and his cattle, and all his *b*	Gen 36:6	929
lade your *b*, and go, get you unto	Gen 45:17	1165
and all the firstborn of *b*	Ex 11:5	929
that is torn of *b* in the field	Ex 22:31	2966
what they leave the of the	Ex 23:11	2416
fat of that which is torn with *b*	Lev 7:24	2966
These are the *b* which ye shall	Lev 11:2	2416
all the *b* that are on the earth	Lev 11:2	929
and cheweth the cud, among the *b*	Lev 11:3	929
manner of *b* that go on all four	Lev 11:27	2416
This is the law of the *b*, and of	Lev 11:46	929
or that which was torn with *b*	Lev 17:15	2966
put difference between clean *b*	Lev 20:25	929
of itself, or is torn with *b*	Lev 22:8	2966
I will rid evil *b* out of the land	Lev 26:6	2416
I will also send wild *b* among you	Lev 26:22	2416
Only the firstling of the *b*	Lev 27:26	929
Lord, whether it be of men or *b*	Num 18:15	929
of unclean *b* shalt thou redeem	Num 18:15	929
the congregation and their *b* drink	Num 20:8	1165
drank, and their *b* also	Num 20:11	1165
all the prey, both of men and of *b*	Num 31:11	929
of the flocks, of all manner of *b*	Num 31:30	929
their goods, and for all their *b*	Num 35:3	2416
lest the *b* of the field increase	Deut 7:22	2416
These are the *b* which ye shall	Deut 14:4	929
and cheweth the cud among the *b*	Deut 14:6	929
unto the *b* of the earth, and no	Deut 28:26	929
send the teeth of *b* upon them	Deut 32:24	929
the air, and to the *b* of the field	1Sa 17:44	929
to the wild *b* of the earth	1Sa 17:46	2416
nor the *b* of the field by night	2Sa 21:10	2416
he spake also of *b*, and of fowl,	1Kin 4:33	929
alive, that we lose not all the *b*	1Kin 18:5	929
ye, and your cattle, and your *b*	2Kin 3:17	929
and stalls for all manner of *b*	2Chr 32:28	929
gold, and with goods, and with *b*	Ezr 1:4	929
with gold, with goods, and with *b*	Ezr 1:6	929
be afraid of the *b* of the earth	Job 5:22	2416
the *b* of the field shall be at	Job 5:23	2416
But ask now the *b*, and they shall	Job 12:7	929
Wherefore are we counted as *b*	Job 18:3	929
us more than the *b* of the earth	Job 35:11	929
Then the *b* go into dens, and	Job 37:8	2416
where all the *b* of the field play	Job 40:20	2416
oxen, yea, and the *b* of the field	Ps 8:7	929
he is like the *b* that perish	Ps 49:12	929
not, is like the *b* that perish	Ps 49:20	929
the wild *b* of the field are mine	Ps 50:11	2123

saints unto the *b* of the earth	Ps 79:2	2416
wherein all the *b* of the forest	Ps 104:20	2416
both small and great *b*	Ps 104:25	2416
B, and all cattle	Ps 148:10	2416
She hath killed her *b*	Prov 9:2	2874
A lion which is strongest among *b*	Prov 30:30	929
see that they themselves are *b*	Eccl 3:18	929
the sons of men befalleth *b*	Eccl 3:19	929
of rams, and the fat of fed *b*	Is 1:11	4806
But wild *b* of the desert shall	Is 13:21	6728
the wild *b* of the islands shall	Is 13:22	338
and to the *b* of the earth	Is 18:6	929
all the *b* of the earth shall	Is 18:6	929
The burden of the *b* of the south	Is 30:6	929
The wild *b* of the desert shall	Is 34:14	6728
with the wild *b* of the island	Is 34:14	338
nor the *b* thereof sufficient for	Is 40:16	2416
their idols were upon the *b*	Is 46:1	2416
All ye *b* of the field, come to	Is 56:9	2416
yea, all ye *b* in the forest	Is 56:9	2416
and upon mules, and upon swift *b*	Is 66:20	3753
heaven, and for the *b* of the earth	Jer 7:33	929
the *b* are consumed, and the birds	Jer 12:4	929
assemble all the *b* of the field	Jer 12:9	2416
the *b* of the earth, to devour and	Jer 15:3	929
heaven, and for the *b* of the earth	Jer 16:4	929
heaven, and to the *b* of the earth	Jer 19:7	929
the *b* of the field have I given	Jer 27:6	2416
given him the *b* of the field also	Jer 28:14	2416
heaven, and to the *b* of the earth	Jer 34:20	929
Therefore the wild *b* of the	Jer 50:39	6728
wild *b* of the islands shall dwell	Jer 50:39	338
I send upon you famine and evil *b*	Eze 5:17	2416
creeping things, and abominable *b*	Eze 8:10	929
If I cause noisome *b* to pass	Eze 14:15	2416
may pass through because of the *b*	Eze 14:15	2416
for meat to the *b* of the field	Eze 29:5	2416
b of the field bring forth their	Eze 31:6	2416
all the *b* of the field shall be	Eze 31:13	2416
I will fill the *b* of the whole	Eze 32:4	2416
I will destroy also all the *b*	Eze 32:13	929
nor the hoofs of *b* trouble them	Eze 32:13	929
I give to the *b* to be devoured	Eze 33:27	2416
meat to all the *b* of the field	Eze 34:5	2416
will cause the evil *b* to cease	Eze 34:25	2416
the *b* of the field, and all	Eze 38:20	2416
to the *b* of the field to be	Eze 39:4	2416
the *b* of the field and the fowls	Dan 2:38	2423
the *b* of the field had shadow	Dan 4:12	2423
let the *b* get away from under it,	Dan 4:14	2423
the *b* in the grass of the earth	Dan 4:15	2423
under which the *b* of the field	Dan 4:21	2423
be with the *b* of the field	Dan 4:23	2423
shall be with the *b* of the field	Dan 4:25	2423
shall be with the *b* of the field	Dan 4:32	2423
and his heart was made like the *b*	Dan 5:21	2423
four great *b* came up from the sea	Dan 7:3	2423
all the *b* that were before it	Dan 7:7	2423
As concerning the rest of the *b*	Dan 7:12	2423
These great *b*, which are four,	Dan 7:17	2423
so that no *b* might stand before	Dan 8:4	2416
the *b* of the field shall eat them	Hos 2:12	2416
for them with the *b* of the field	Hos 2:18	2416
with the *b* of the field, and with	Hos 4:3	2416
How do the *b* groan	Joel 1:18	929
The *b* of the field cry also unto	Joel 1:20	929
Be not afraid, ye *b* of the field	Joel 2:22	929
the peace offerings of your fat *b*	Amos 5:22	4806
a lion among the *b* of the forest	Mic 5:8	929
cover thee, and the spoil of *b*	Hab 2:17	929
of her, all the *b* of the nations	Zeph 2:14	2416
a place for *b* to lie down in	Zeph 2:15	2416
of all the *b* that shall be in	Zec 14:15	929
and was with the wild *b*	Mk 1:13	2342
have ye offered to me slain *b*	Acts 7:42	4968
of fourfooted *b* of the earth	Acts 10:12	5074
b of the earth, and wild *b*	Acts 10:12	2342
b of the earth, and wild *b*	Acts 11:6	2342
And provide them, that they may	Acts 23:24	2934
man, and to birds, and fourfooted *b*	Rom 1:23	5074
I have fought with *b* at Ephesus	1Cor 15:32	2341
flesh of men, another flesh of *b*	1Cor 15:39	2934
Cretians are alway liars, evil *b*	Titus 1:12	2342
For the bodies of those *b*	Heb 13:11	2226
For every kind of *b*, and of birds,	Jas 3:7	2342
But these, as natural brute *b*	2Pet 2:12	2226
they know naturally, as brute *b*	Jude 10	2226
were four *b* full of eyes before	Rev 4:6	2226
the four *b* had each of them six	Rev 4:8	2226
And when those *b* give glory,	Rev 4:9	2226
of the throne and of the four *b*	Rev 5:6	2226

he had taken the book, the four *b*	Rev 5:8	2226
round about the throne and the *b*	Rev 5:11	2226
And the four *b* said, Amen	Rev 5:14	2226
thunder, one of the four *b* saying	Rev 6:1	2226
in the midst of the four *b* say	Rev 6:6	2226
death, and with the *b* of the earth	Rev 6:8	2342
and about the elders and the four *b*	Rev 7:11	2226
the throne, and before the four *b*	Rev 14:3	2226
one of the four *b* gave unto the	Rev 15:7	2226
and fine flour, and wheat, and *b*	Rev 18:13	2934
elders and the four *b* fell down and	Rev 19:4	2226

BEAT

thou shalt *b* some of it very	Ex 30:36	7833
they did *b* the gold into thin	Ex 39:3	7554
or *b* it in a mortar, and baked it	Num 11:8	1743
b him above these with many	Deut 25:3	5221
he *b* down the tower of Penuel, and	Judg 8:17	5422
b down the city, and sowed it with	Judg 9:45	5422
b at the door, and spake to the	Judg 19:22	1849
b out that she had gleaned	Ruth 2:17	2251
Then did I *b* them as small as the	2Sa 22:43	7833
they *b* down the cities, and on	2Kin 3:25	2040
Three times did Joash *b* him	2Kin 13:25	5221
of the LORD, did the king *b* down	2Kin 23:12	5422
Then did I *b* them small as the	Ps 18:42	7833
I will *b* down his foes before his	Ps 89:23	3807
Thou shalt *b* him with the rod, and	Prov 23:14	5221
they shall *b* their swords into	Is 2:4	3807
ye that ye *b* my people to pieces	Is 3:15	1792
that the LORD shall *b* off from	Is 27:12	2251
b them small, and shalt make the	Is 41:15	1854
B your plowshares into swords, and	Joel 3:10	3807
the sun *b* upon the head of Jonah,	Jonah 4:8	5221
they shall *b* their swords into	Mic 4:3	3807
thou shalt *b* in pieces many	Mic 4:13	1854
winds blew, and *b* upon that house	Mt 7:25	*4363*
winds blew, and *b* upon that house	Mt 7:27	*4350*
b one, and killed another, and	Mt 21:35	*1194*
the waves *b* into the ship, so	Mk 4:37	*1911*
b him, and sent him away empty	Mk 12:3	*1194*
the stream *b* vehemently upon that	Lk 6:48	*4366*
which the stream did *b* vehemently	Lk 6:49	*4366*
shall begin to *b* the menservants	Lk 12:45	*5180*
but the husbandmen *b* him, and sent	Lk 20:10	*1194*
they *b* him also, and entreated him	Lk 20:11	*1194*
clothes, and commanded to *b* them	Acts 16:22	*4463*
b him before the judgment seat	Acts 18:17	*5180*
b in every synagogue them that	Acts 22:19	*1194*

BEATEN

had set over them, were *b*	Ex 5:14	5221
and, behold, thy servants are *b*	Ex 5:16	5221
of *b* work shalt thou make them,	Ex 25:18	4749
of *b* work shall the candlestick	Ex 25:31	4749
shall be one *b* work of pure gold	Ex 25:36	4749
pure oil olive *b* for the light	Ex 27:20	3795
fourth part of an hin of *b* oil	Ex 29:40	3795
b out of one piece made he them,	Ex 37:7	4749
of *b* work made he the candlestick	Ex 37:17	4749
of it was one *b* work of pure gold	Ex 37:22	4749
even corn *b* out of full ears	Lev 2:14	1643
part of the corn thereof, and	Lev 2:16	1643
full of sweet incense *b* small	Lev 16:12	1851
pure oil olive *b* for the light	Lev 24:2	3795
of the candlestick was of *b* gold	Num 8:4	4749
the flowers thereof, was *b* work	Num 8:4	4749
fourth part of an hin of *b* oil	Num 28:5	3795
the wicked man be worthy to be *b*	Deut 25:2	5221
down, and to be *b* before his face,	Deut 25:2	5221
as if they were *b* before them	Josh 8:15	5060
and Abner was *b*, and the men of	2Sa 2:17	5062
two hundred targets of *b* gold	1Kin 10:16	7820
three hundred shields of *b* gold	1Kin 10:17	7820
thousand measures of *b* wheat	2Chr 2:10	4347
two hundred targets of *b* gold	2Chr 9:15	7820
six hundred shekels of *b* gold	2Chr 9:15	7820
hundred shields made he of *b* gold	2Chr 9:16	7820
had *b* the graven images into	2Chr 34:7	3807
they have *b* me, and I felt it not	Prov 23:35	1986
chalkstones that are *b* in sunder	Is 27:9	5310
fitches are *b* out with a staff	Is 28:27	2251
LORD shall the Assyrian be *b* down	Is 30:31	2865
and their mighty ones are *b* down	Jer 46:5	3807
thereof shall be *b* to pieces	Mic 1:7	3807
in the synagogues ye shall be *b*	Mk 13:9	*1194*
shall be *b* with many stripes	Lk 12:47	*1194*
shall be *b* with few stripes	Lk 12:48	*1194*
b them, they commanded that they	Acts 5:40	*1194*
They have *b* us openly uncondemned	Acts 16:37	*1194*
Thrice was I *b* with rods, once	2Cor 11:25	*4463*

B

BEATEST
When thou *b* thine olive tree,.............. Deut 24:20   2251
for if thou *b* him with the rod,.............. Prov 23:13   5221

BEATETH
I, not as one that *b* the air..................... 1Cor 9:26   *1194*

BEATING
they went on *b* down one another 1Sa 14:16   1986
b some, and killing some .... Mk 12:5   *1194*
the soldiers, they left *b* of Paul .... Acts 21:32   5180

BEAUTIES
in the *b* of holiness from the................... Ps 110:3   1926

BEAUTIFUL
Rachel was *b* and well favoured ..... Gen 29:17   3303,8389
among the captives a *b* woman ...... Deut 21:11   3303,8389
and withal of a *b* countenance.............. 1Sa 16:12   3303
and of a *b* countenance 1Sa 25:3   3303
the woman was very *b* to look upon 2Sa 11:2   2896
and the maid was fair and *b* .... Est 2:7   2896,4758
B for situation, the joy of the .... Ps 48:2   3303
made every thing *b* in his time .... Eccl 3:11   3303
Thou art *b*, O my love, as Tirzah .... Song 6:4   3303
How *b* are thy feet with shoes, O .... Song 7:1   3303
shall the branch of the LORD be *b*.......... Is 4:2   6643
put on thy *b* garments, O .... Is 52:1   8597
How *b* upon the mountains are the .... Is 52:7   4998
our *b* house, where our fathers .... Is 64:11   8597
that was given thee, thy *b* flock .... Jer 13:20   8597
strong staff broken, and the *b* rod .... Jer 48:17   8597
a *b* crown upon thine head .... Eze 16:12   8597
and thou wast exceeding *b*, and thou ... Eze 16:13   3303
b crowns upon their heads .... Eze 23:42   8597
which indeed appear *b* outward .... Mt 23:27   *5611*
of the temple which is called *B* .... Acts 3:2   *5611*
alms at the *B* gate of the temple .... Acts 3:10   *5611*
How *b* are the feet of them that .... Rom 10:15   *5611*

BEAUTIFY
to *b* the house of the LORD which........... Ezr 7:27   6286
he will *b* the meek with salvation .... Ps 149:4   6286
to *b* the place of my sanctuary .... Is 60:13   6286

BEAUTY
thy brother for glory and for *b*.............. Ex 28:2   8597
make for them, for glory and for *b* .... Ex 28:40   8597
The *b* of Israel is slain upon thy 2Sa 1:19   6643
much praised as Absalom for his *b* 2Sa 14:25   3308
the LORD in the *b* of holiness 1Chr 16:29   1927
house with precious stones for *b*........... 2Chr 3:6   8597
should praise the *b* of holiness 2Chr 20:21   1927
the people and the princes her *b* .... Est 1:11   3308
and array thyself with glory and *b* .... Job 40:10   1926
life, to behold the *b* of the LORD .... Ps 27:4   5278
the LORD in the *b* of holiness .... Ps 29:2   1927
thou makest his *b* to consume away ...... Ps 39:11   2530
the king greatly desire thy *b*.................. Ps 45:11   3308
their *b* shall consume in the .... Ps 49:14   6736
Out of Zion, the perfection of *b* .... Ps 50:2   3308
let the *b* of the LORD our God be............ Ps 90:17   5278
and *b* are in his sanctuary .... Ps 96:6   8597
the LORD in the *b* of holiness .... Ps 96:9   1927
not after her *b* in thine heart .... Prov 6:25   3308
the *b* of old men is the grey head .... Prov 20:29   1926
Favour is deceitful, and *b* is vain .... Prov 31:30   3308
and burning instead of *b* .... Is 3:24   3308
the *b* of the Chaldees' excellency .... Is 13:19   8597
whose glorious *b* is a fading.................. Is 28:1   8597
And the glorious *b*, which is on............. Is 28:4   8597
of glory, and for a diadem of *b* .... Is 28:5   8597
eyes shall see the king in his *b* .... Is 33:17   3308
man, according to the *b* of a man .... Is 44:13   8597
there is no *b* that we should .... Is 53:2   4758
to give unto them *b* for ashes .... Is 61:3   6287
of Zion all her *b* is departed................... Lam 1:6   1926
unto the earth the *b* of Israel .... Lam 2:1   8597
that men call The perfection of *b* .... Lam 2:15   3308
As for the *b* of his ornament, he .... Eze 7:20   6643
forth among the heathen for thy *b* .... Eze 16:14   3308
thou didst trust in thine own *b* .... Eze 16:15   3308
hast made thy *b* to be abhorred............ Eze 16:25   3308
thou hast said, I am of perfect *b* .... Eze 27:3   3308
thy builders have perfected thy *b* .... Eze 27:4   3308
they have made thy *b* perfect................ Eze 27:11   3308
against the *b* of thy wisdom .... Eze 28:7   3308
full of wisdom, and perfect in *b* .... Eze 28:12   3308
was lifted up because of thy *b* .... Eze 28:17   3308
of God was like unto him in his *b* .... Eze 31:8   3308
Whom dost thou pass in *b* .... Eze 32:19   5276
his *b* shall be as the olive tree, ... Hos 14:6   1935
goodness, and how great is his *b*........... Zec 9:17   3308

---

the one I called *B*, and the other............ Zec 11:7   5278
And I took my staff, even *B* .... Zec 11:10   5278

BEBAI (beb'-a-i)
   1. Father of returned exiles.
The children of *B*, six hundred .... Ezr 2:11   893
The children of *B*, six hundred .... Neh 7:16   893
   2. Father of returned exiles with Ezra.
And of the sons of *B* .... Ezr 8:11   893
Zechariah the son of *B*, and with........... Ezr 8:11   893
Of the sons also of *B* .... Ezr 10:28   893
   3. One who sealed the covenant.
Bunni, Azgad, *B*, ... Neh 10:15   893

BECAME See APPENDIX.

BECAMEST
and thou, LORD, *b* their God................... 1Chr 17:22   1961
the Lord GOD, and thou *b* mine.............. Eze 16:8   1961

BECAUSE See APPENDIX.

BECHER (be'-ker) See BACHRITES.
   1. A son of Benjamin.
sons of Benjamin were Belah, and *B* ...... Gen 46:21   1071
Bela, and *B*, and Jediael, three 1Chr 7:6   1071
And the sons of *B* 1Chr 7:8   1071
All these are the sons of *B* 1Chr 7:8   1071
   2. A son of Ephraim.
of *B*, the family of the Bachrites .... Num 26:35   1071

BECHERITES See BACHRITES.

BECHORATH (be-ko'-rath) An ancestor of King Saul.
the son of Zeror, the son of *B*................. 1Sa 9:1   1064

BECKONED
for he *b* unto them, and remained .... Lk 1:22   *1269*
they *b* unto their partners, which .... Lk 5:7   *2656*
Simon Peter therefore *b* to him .... Jn 13:24   *3506*
Alexander *b* with the hand, and............. Acts 19:33   *2678*
b with the hand unto the people .... Acts 21:40   *2678*
governor had *b* unto him to speak .... Acts 24:10   *3506*

BECKONING
b unto them with the hand to hold .... Acts 12:17   *2678*
b with his hand said, Men of.................. Acts 13:16   *2678*

BECOME See APPENDIX.

BECOMETH
holiness *b* thine house, O LORD, ... Ps 93:5   4998
He *b* poor that dealeth with a................. Prov 10:4
Excellent speech *b* not a fool .... Prov 17:7   5000
b surety in the presence of his .... Prov 17:18   6148
is born in his kingdom *b* poor................ Eccl 4:14
for thus it *b* us to fulfil all .... Mt 3:15   *4241*
the word, and he *b* unfruitful .... Mt 13:22   *1096*
***b* a tree, so that the birds of.**................ Mt 13:32   *1096*
the word, and it *b* unfruitful............... Mk 4:19   *1096*
***b* greater than all herbs, and.**.............. Mk 4:32   *1096*
as *b* saints, and that ye assist .... Rom 16:2   516
once named among you, as *b* saints....... Eph 5:3   *4241*
be as it *b* the gospel of Christ................ Phil 1:27   516
But (which *b* women professing 1Ti 2:10   516
be in behaviour as *b* holiness................. Titus 2:3   2412

BECORATH See BECHORATH.

BED
himself, and sat upon the *b*................... Gen 48:2   4296
thou wentest up to thy father's *b* .... Gen 49:4   4904
gathered up his feet into the *b* .... Gen 49:33   4296
thy bedchamber, and upon thy *b*............ Ex 8:3   4296
and he die not, but keepeth his *b* .... Ex 21:18   4904
Every *b*, whereon he lieth that .... Lev 15:4   4904
his *b* shall wash his clothes .... Lev 15:5   4904
her *b* shall wash his clothes .... Lev 15:21   4904
And if it be on her *b*, or on any .... Lev 15:23   4904
all the *b* whereon he lieth shall .... Lev 15:24   4904
Every *b* whereon she lieth all the .... Lev 15:26   4904
her as the *b* of her separation .... Lev 15:26   4904
an image, and laid it in the *b*................. 1Sa 19:13   4296
Bring him up to me in the *b* 1Sa 19:15   4296
there was an image in the *b*................... 1Sa 19:16   4296
from the earth, and sat upon the *b* 1Sa 28:23   4296
who lay on a *b* at noon 2Sa 4:5   4904
he lay on his *b* in his bedchamber 2Sa 4:7   4296
in his own house upon his *b* 2Sa 4:11   4904
that David arose from off his *b*............... 2Sa 11:2   4904
b with the servants of his lord 2Sa 11:13   4904
unto him, Lay thee down on thy *b* 2Sa 13:5   4904
the king bowed himself upon the *b* 1Kin 1:47   4904
abode, and laid him upon his own *b* 1Kin 17:19   4296
And he laid him down upon his *b* 1Kin 21:4   4296
that *b* on which thou art gone up 2Kin 1:4   4296
that *b* on which thou art gone up 2Kin 1:6   4296
that *b* on which thou art gone up 2Kin 1:16   4296

and let us set for him there a *b* 2Kin 4:10   4296
laid him on the *b* of the man of............2Kin 4:21   4296
was dead, and laid upon his *b* 2Kin 4:32   4296
as he defiled his father's *b*....................1Chr 5:1   3326
laid him in the *b* which was 2Chr 16:14   4904
the priest, and slew him on his *b* 2Chr 24:25   4296
upon the *b* whereon Esther was............Est 7:8   4296
My *b* shall comfort me, my couch ....Job 7:13   6210
I have made my *b* in the darkness ....Job 17:13   3326
men, in slumberings upon the *b*............Job 33:15   4904
also with pain upon his *b*......................Job 33:19   4904
with your own heart upon your *b* ....Ps 4:4   4904
all the night make I my *b* to swim ....Ps 6:6   4296
He deviseth mischief upon his *b* ....Ps 36:4   4904
him upon the *b* of languishing ....Ps 41:3   6210
make all his *b* in his sickness ....Ps 41:3   4904
When I remember thee upon my *b* ....Ps 63:6   3326
of my house, nor go up into my *b* ...Ps 132:3   6210,3326
if I make my *b* in hell, behold, ...Ps 139:8   3331
I have decked my *b* with coverings ....Prov 7:16   6210
I have perfumed my *b* with myrrh ....Prov 7:17   4904
take away thy *b* from under thee ....Prov 22:27   4904
so doth the slothful upon his *b* ....Prov 26:14   4296
also our *b* is green ....Song 1:16   6210
By night on my *b* I sought him ....Song 3:1   4904
Behold his *b*, which is Solomon's ....Song 3:7   4296
His cheeks are as a *b* of spices..............Song 5:13   6170
For the *b* is shorter than that a..............Is 28:20   4702
high mountain hast thou set thy *b* ......Is 57:7   4904
thou hast enlarged thy *b*, and made ......Is 57:8   4904
thou lovedst their *b* where thou ....Is 57:8   4904
came to her into the *b* of love ....Eze 23:17   4904
And satest upon a stately *b* ....Eze 23:41   4296
They have set her a *b* in the..................Eze 32:25   4904
visions of thy head upon thy *b* ....Dan 2:28   4903
came into thy mind upon thy *b* ....Dan 2:29   4903
afraid, and the thoughts upon my *b* ......Dan 4:5   4903
the visions of mine head in my *b* ....Dan 4:10   4903
the visions of my head upon my *b*..........Dan 4:13   4903
and visions of my head upon his *b* ....Dan 7:1   4903
in Samaria in the corner of a *b* ....Amos 3:12   4296
sick of the palsy, lying on a *b*..................Mt 9:2   2825
the palsy,) Arise, take up thy *b* ....Mt 9:6   2825
they let down the *b* wherein the............Mk 2:4   2895
to say, Arise, and take up thy *b*..............Mk 2:9   2895
thee, Arise, and take up thy *b*................Mk 2:11   2895
he arose, took up the *b*, and went..........Mk 2:12   2895
put under a bushel, or under a *b* ....Mk 4:21   2825
and her daughter laid upon the *b* ....Mk 7:30   2825
men brought in a *b* a man which ....Lk 5:18   2825
a vessel, or putteth it under a *b* ....Lk 8:16   2825
and my children are with me in *b* ....Lk 11:7   2845
there shall be two men in one *b* ....Lk 17:34   2825
unto him, Rise, take up thy *b* ....Jn 5:8   2895
was made whole, and took up his *b* ......Jn 5:9   2895
lawful for thee to carry thy *b* ....Jn 5:10   2895
same said unto me, Take up thy *b* ....Jn 5:11   2895
said unto thee, Take up thy *b*..................Jn 5:12   2895
which had kept his *b* eight years............Acts 9:33   2895
arise, and make thy *b*..............................Acts 9:34   4766
in all, and the *b* undefiled......................Heb 13:4   2845
Behold, I will cast her into a *b* ....Rev 2:22   2825

BEDAD (be'-dad) *Father of Hadad.*
died, and Hadad the son of *B*..................Gen 36:35   911
was dead, Hadad the son of *B* 1Chr 1:46   911

BEDAN (be'-dan)
   1. A judge of Israel.
And the LORD sent Jerubbaal, and *B* 1Sa 12:11   917
   2. A descendant of Manasseh.
And the sons of Ulam; *B*..........................1Chr 7:17   917

BEDCHAMBER
into thine house, and into thy *b* ......Ex 8:3   2315,4904
house, he lay on his bed in his *b*.....2Sa 4:7   2315,4904
words that thou speakest in thy *b* ..2Kin 6:12   2315,4904
in the *b* from Athaliah, so that 2Kin 11:2   2315,4296
and put him and his nurse in a *b* ...2Chr 22:11   2315,4296
and curse not the rich in thy *b* ....Eccl 10:20   2315,4904

BEDEIAH (be-de'-yah) *Married a foreign wife in exile.*
Benaiah, *B*, Chelluh, ...Ezr 10:35   912

BED'S
bowed himself upon the *b* head ....Gen 47:31   4296

BEDS
Brought *b*, and basons, and earthen 2Sa 17:28   4904
the *b* were of gold and silver, ...Est 1:6   4296
let them sing aloud upon their *b*............Ps 149:5   4904
to the *b* of spices, to feed in ....Song 6:2   6170
they shall rest in their *b* ....Is 57:2   4904
when they howled upon their *b*..............Hos 7:14   4904

That lie upon *b* of ivory, and ....Amos 6:4   4296
and work evil upon their *b* ....Mic 2:1   4904
about in *b* those that were sick..............Mk 6:55   2895
the streets, and laid them on *b* ....Acts 5:15   2825

BEDSTEAD
his *b* was a *b* of iron ....Deut 3:11   6210

BEE
for the *b* that is in the land of ....Is 7:18   1682

BEELIADA (be-e-li'-ad-ah) *A son of David.*
And Elishama, and *B*, and Eliphalet 1Chr 14:7   1182

BEELZEBUB (be-el'-ze-bub) See BAAL-ZEBUB. *Chief of evil spirits.*
called the master of the house *B* ....Mt 10:25   954
but by *B* the prince of the devils ....Mt 12:24   954
if I by *B* cast out devils, by ....Mt 12:27   954
from Jerusalem said, He hath *B* ....Mk 3:22   954
through *B* the chief of the devils ....Lk 11:15   954
that I cast out devils through *B* ....Lk 11:18   954
if I by *B* cast out devils, by ....Lk 11:19   954

BEELZEBULL See BEELZEBUB.

BEEN See APPENDIX.

BEER (be'-ur) See BAALITH-BEER, BEER-ELIM, BEER-LAHAI-ROI, BEER-SHEBA.
   1. An Israelite post beyond the Arnon River.
And from thence they went to *B* ....Num 21:16   876
   2. A town in Judah.
ran away, and fled, and went to *B* ....Judg 9:21   876

BEERA (be-e'-rah) *Son of Zophah.*
and Shilshah, and Ithran, and *B* 1Chr 7:37   878

BEERAH (be-e'-rah) *A Reubenite prince.*
B his son, whom Tilgath-pilneser............1Chr 5:6   880

BEER-ELIM (be'-ur-e'-lim) *A well in Moab.*
and the howling thereof unto *B*..............Is 15:8   879

BEERI (be-e'-ri)
   1. Father of Judith.
the daughter of *B* the Hittite ....Gen 26:34   882
   2. Father of Hosea.
came unto Hosea, the son of *B* ....Hos 1:1   882

BEER-LAHAI-ROI (be'-ur-la'-hahe-ro'-e) *A well.*
Wherefore the well was called *B* ....Gen 16:14   883

BEEROTH (be-e'-roth) See BEROTHITE.
   1. An Israelite encampment during the Exodus.
B of the children of Jaakan to ....Deut 10:6   881
   2. A Hivite city in Canaan.
were Gibeon, and Chephirah, and *B*.......Josh 9:17   881
Gibeon, and Ramah, and *B*,....................Josh 18:25   881
(for *B* also was reckoned to 2Sa 4:2   881
of Kirjath-arim, Chephirah, and *B* ....Ezr 2:25   881
Kirjath-jearim, Chephirah, and *B* ....Neh 7:29   881

BEEROTHITE (be-er'-o-thite) See BEEROTHITES, BEROTHITE. *An inhabitant of Beeroth.*
Rechab, the sons of Rimmon a *B* 2Sa 4:2   886
And the sons of Rimmon the *B* 2Sa 4:5   886
brother, the sons of Rimmon the *B* 2Sa 4:9   886
Zelek the Ammonite, Nahari the *B* 2Sa 23:37   886

BEEROTHITES (be-er'-o-thites)
the *B* fled to Gittaim, and were..............2Sa 4:3   886

BEER-SHEBA (be-ur'-she-bah) *A Canaanite city.*
wandered in the wilderness of *B* ....Gen 21:14   884
Wherefore he called that place *B* ....Gen 21:31   884
Thus they made a covenant at *B* ....Gen 21:32   884
And Abraham planted a grove in *B* ....Gen 21:33   884
rose up and went together to *B*................Gen 22:19   884
and Abraham dwelt at *B* ....Gen 22:19   884
And he went up from thence to *B* ....Gen 26:23   884
of the city is *B* unto this day ....Gen 26:33   884
And Jacob went out from *B*, and went....Gen 28:10   884
all that he had, and came to *B*................Gen 46:1   884
And Jacob rose up from *B*........................Gen 46:5   884
And Hazar-shual, and *B*, and ....Josh 15:28   884
they had in their inheritance *B* ....Josh 19:2   884
as one man, from Dan even to *B* ....Judg 20:1   884
even to *B* knew that Samuel was............1Sa 3:20   884
they were judges in *B*..............................1Sa 8:2   884
and over Judah, from Dan even to *B* 2Sa 3:10   884
unto thee, from Dan even to *B* 2Sa 17:11   884
of Israel, from Dan even to *B* 2Sa 24:2   884
to the south of Judah, even to *B* 2Sa 24:7   884
even to *B* seventy thousand men 2Sa 24:15   884
his fig tree, from Dan even to *B*..............1Kin 4:25   884
went for his life, and came to *B* 1Kin 19:3   884
his mother's name was Zibiah of *B*..........2Kin 12:1   884
burned incense, from Geba to *B*..............2Kin 23:8   884

B.

And they dwelt at *B*, and Moladah, ... 1Chr 4:28   884
number Israel from *B* even to Dan 1Chr 21:2   884
people from *B* to mount Ephraim 2Chr 19:4   884
name also was Zibiah of *B* 2Chr 24:1   884
from *B* even to Dan, that they 2Chr 30:5   884
And at Hazar-shual, and at *B* .... Neh 11:27   884
they dwelt from *B* unto the valley .... Neh 11:30   884
into Gilgal, and pass not to *B* .... Amos 5:5   884
and, The manner of *B* liveth .... Amos 8:14   884

BEES
you, and chased you, as *b* do .... Deut 1:44   1682
behold, there was a swarm of *b* .... Judg 14:8   1682
They compassed me about like *b* .... Ps 118:12   1682

BE-ESHTARAH See BEESH-TERAH.

BEESH-TERAH *(be-esh'-te-rah)* See ASHTAROTH. *A Levit-ical city in Manasseh.*
and *B* with her suburbs .... Josh 21:27   1203

BEETLE
the *b* after his kind, and the .... Lev 11:22   2728

BEEVES
a male without blemish, of the *b* .... Lev 22:19   1241
a freewill offering in *b* or sheep .... Lev 22:21   1241
both of the persons, and of the *b* .... Num 31:28   1241
fifty, of the persons, of the *b* .... Num 31:30   1241
threescore and twelve thousand *b* ...... Num 31:33   1241
the *b* were thirty and six thousand ...... Num 31:38   1241
And thirty and six thousand *b* .... Num 31:44   1241

BEFALL
Lest peradventure mischief *b* him ...... Gen 42:4   7122
if mischief *b* him by the way in .... Gen 42:38   7122
also from me, and mischief *b* him .... Gen 44:29   7136
shall *b* you in the last days .... Gen 49:1   7122
evils and troubles shall *b* them .... Deut 31:17   4672
evil will *b* you in the latter .... Deut 31:29   7122
There shall no evil *b* thee .... Ps 91:10   579
b thy people in the latter days .... Dan 10:14   7136
the things that shall *b* me there .... Acts 20:22   4876

BEFALLEN
and such things have *b* me .... Lev 10:19   7122
all the travel that hath *b* us .... Num 20:14   4672
many evils and troubles are *b* them ..... Deut 31:21   4672
us, why then is all this *b* us .... Judg 6:13   4672
he thought, Something hath *b* him 1Sa 20:26   4745
every thing that had *b* him .... Est 6:13   7136
what was *b* to the possessed of .... Mt 8:33   4876

BEFALLETH
b the sons of men *b* beasts .... Eccl 3:19   4745
even one thing *b* them .... Eccl 3:19   4745

BEFELL
and told him all that *b* unto them .... Gen 42:29   7136
told him all things that *b* them .... Josh 2:23   4672
thee than all the evil that *b* 2Sa 19:7   935
that saw it told them how it *b* to .... Mk 5:16   1096
which *b* me by the lying in wait .... Acts 20:19   4819

BEFORE See APPENDIX.

BEFOREHAND See APPENDIX.

BEFORETIME
The Horims also dwelt in Seir *b* .... Deut 2:12   6440
for Hazor *b* was the head of all .... Josh 11:10   6440
unwittingly, and hated him not *b* .... Josh 20:5   8543,8032
(*B* in Israel, when a man went to 1Sa 9:9   6440
a Prophet was called a Seer 1Sa 9:9   6440
when all that knew him *b* saw that 1Sa 10:11   865,832
afflict them any more, as *b* 2Sa 7:10   7223
Israel dwelt in their tents, as *b* 2Kin 13:5   8543,8032
Now I had not been *b* sad in his .... Neh 2:1
and *b*, that we may say, He is .... Is 41:26   6440
which *b* in the same city used .... Acts 8:9   4391

BEG
be continually vagabonds, and *b* .... Ps 109:10   7592
therefore shall he *b* in harvest .... Prov 20:4   7592
to *b* I am ashamed .... Lk 16:3   *1871*

BEGAN See APPENDIX.

BEGAT
and Irad *b* Mehujael .... Gen 4:18   3205
and Mehujael *b* Methusael .... Gen 4:18   3205
and Methusael *b* Lamech .... Gen 4:18   3205
b a son in his own likeness, ... Gen 5:3   3205
and he *b* sons and daughters .... Gen 5:4   3205
hundred and five years, and *b* Enos ..... Gen 5:6   3205
after he *b* Enos eight hundred .... Gen 5:7   3205
years, and *b* sons and daughters .... Gen 5:7   3205
lived ninety years, and *b* Cainan .... Gen 5:9   3205
Enos lived after he *b* Cainan .... Gen 5:10   3205

years, and *b* sons and daughters .... Gen 5:10   3205
seventy years, and *b* Mahalaleel .... Gen 5:12   3205
And Cainan lived after he *b* .... Gen 5:13   3205
years, and *b* sons and daughters .... Gen 5:13   3205
sixty and five years, and *b* Jared .... Gen 5:15   3205
after he *b* Jared eight hundred .... Gen 5:16   3205
years, and *b* sons and daughters .... Gen 5:16   3205
sixty and two years, and he *b* Enoch ..... Gen 5:18   3205
Jared lived after he *b* Enoch .... Gen 5:19   3205
years, and *b* sons and daughters .... Gen 5:19   3205
and five years, and *b* Methuselah .... Gen 5:21   3205
b Methuselah three hundred years .... Gen 5:22   3205
and *b* sons and daughters .... Gen 5:22   3205
and seven years, and *b* Lamech .... Gen 5:25   3205
Methuselah lived after he *b* .... Gen 5:26   3205
two years, and *b* sons and daughters ..... Gen 5:26   3205
eighty and two years, and *b* a son .... Gen 5:28   3205
Lamech lived after he *b* Noah five .... Gen 5:30   3205
years, and *b* sons and daughters .... Gen 5:30   3205
and Noah *b* Shem, Ham, and Japheth ... Gen 5:32   3205
Noah *b* three sons, Shem, Ham, and ... Gen 6:10   3205
And Cush *b* Nimrod .... Gen 10:8   3205
And Mizraim *b* Ludim, and Anamim, ... Gen 10:13   3205
Canaan *b* Sidon his firstborn, and .... Gen 10:15   3205
And Arphaxad *b* Salah .... Gen 10:24   3205
and Salah *b* Eber .... Gen 10:24   3205
Joktan *b* Almodad, and Sheleph, and... Gen 10:26   3205
b Arphaxad two years after the .... Gen 11:10   3205
Shem lived after he *b* Arphaxad .... Gen 11:11   3205
years, and *b* sons and daughters .... Gen 11:11   3205
five and thirty years, and *b* Salah .... Gen 11:12   3205
after he *b* Salah four hundred .... Gen 11:13   3205
years, and *b* sons and daughters .... Gen 11:13   3205
lived thirty years, and *b* Eber .... Gen 11:14   3205
after he *b* Eber four hundred .... Gen 11:15   3205
years, and *b* sons and daughters .... Gen 11:15   3205
four and thirty years, and *b* Peleg .... Gen 11:16   3205
after he *b* Peleg four hundred .... Gen 11:17   3205
years, and *b* sons and daughters .... Gen 11:17   3205
lived thirty years, and *b* Reu .... Gen 11:18   3205
lived after he *b* Reu two hundred .... Gen 11:19   3205
years, and *b* sons and daughters .... Gen 11:19   3205
two and thirty years, and *b* Serug .... Gen 11:20   3205
after he *b* Serug two hundred .... Gen 11:21   3205
years, and *b* sons and daughters .... Gen 11:21   3205
lived thirty years, and *b* Nahor .... Gen 11:22   3205
Serug lived after he *b* Nahor two .... Gen 11:23   3205
years, and *b* sons and daughters .... Gen 11:23   3205
nine and twenty years, and *b* Terah ..... Gen 11:24   3205
lived after he *b* Terah an hundred .... Gen 11:25   3205
years, and *b* sons and daughters .... Gen 11:25   3205
and *b* Abram, Nahor, and Haran .... Gen 11:26   3205
Terah *b* Abram, Nahor, and Haran .... Gen 11:27   3205
and Haran *b* Lot .... Gen 11:27   3205
And Bethuel *b* Rebekah .... Gen 22:23   3205
And Jokshan *b* Sheba, and Dedan .... Gen 25:3   3205
Abraham *b* Isaac .... Gen 25:19   3205
which they *b* in your land .... Lev 25:45   3205
and Machir *b* Gilead .... Num 26:29   3205
And Kohath *b* Amram .... Num 26:58   3205
Of the Rock that *b* thee thou art .... Deut 32:18   3205
and Gilead *b* Jephthah .... Judg 11:1   3205
Pharez *b* Hezron .... Ruth 4:18   3205
And Hezron *b* Ram .... Ruth 4:19   3205
and Ram *b* Amminadab .... Ruth 4:19   3205
And Amminadab *b* Nahshon, and .... Ruth 4:20   3205
Nahshon, and Nahshon *b* Salmon .... Ruth 4:20   3205
Salmon *b* Boaz, and Boaz *b* Obed ...... Ruth 4:21   3205
Obed *b* Jesse .... Ruth 4:22   3205
and Jesse *b* David .... Ruth 4:22   3205
And Cush *b* Nimrod 1Chr 1:10   3205
And Mizraim *b* Ludim, and Anamim, ... 1Chr 1:11   3205
Canaan *b* Zidon his firstborn, and 1Chr 1:13   3205
And Arphaxad *b* Shelah 1Chr 1:18   3205
and Shelah *b* Eber 1Chr 1:18   3205
Joktan *b* Almodad, and Sheleph, and.... 1Chr 1:20   3205
And Abraham *b* Isaac 1Chr 1:34   3205
And Ram *b* Amminadab 1Chr 2:10   3205
and Amminadab *b* Nahshon, prince of .. 1Chr 2:10   3205
And Nahshon *b* Salma 1Chr 2:11   3205
and Salma *b* Boaz 1Chr 2:11   3205
Boaz *b* Obed, and Obed *b* Jesse, ... 1Chr 2:12   3205
Jesse *b* his firstborn Eliab, and 1Chr 2:13   3205
Caleb the son of Hezron *b* 1Chr 2:18   3205
Hur *b* Uri, and Uri *b* Bezaleel 1Chr 2:20   3205
And Segub *b* Jair, who had three and 1Chr 2:22   3205
Attai *b* Nathan 1Chr 2:36   3205
and Nathan *b* Zabad 1Chr 2:36   3205
Zabad *b* Ephlal 1Chr 2:37   3205
Ephlal *b* Obed 1Chr 2:37   3205
And Obed *b* Jehu 1Chr 2:38   3205

and Jehu b Azariah	1Chr 2:38	3205
And Azariah b Helez	1Chr 2:39	3205
and Helez b Eleasah	1Chr 2:39	3205
And Eleasah b Sisamai	1Chr 2:40	3205
and Sisamai b Shallum	1Chr 2:40	3205
Shallum b Jekamiah	1Chr 2:41	3205
and Jekamiah b Elishama	1Chr 2:41	3205
And Shema b Raham, the father of	1Chr 2:44	3205
and Rekem b Shammai	1Chr 2:44	3205
and Haran b Gazez	1Chr 2:46	3205
Reaiah the son of Shobal b Jahath	1Chr 4:2	3205
and Jahath b Ahumai, and Lahad	1Chr 4:2	3205
Coz b Anub, and Zobebah, and the	1Chr 4:8	3205
the brother of Shuah b Mehir	1Chr 4:11	3205
Eshton b Beth-rapha, and Paseah,	1Chr 4:12	3205
And Meonothai b Ophrah	1Chr 4:14	3205
and Seraiah b Joab, the father of	1Chr 4:14	3205
Eleazar b Phinehas	1Chr 6:4	3205
Phinehas b Abishua	1Chr 6:4	3205
And Abishua b Bukki	1Chr 6:5	3205
and Bukki b Uzzi	1Chr 6:5	3205
And Uzzi b Zerahiah	1Chr 6:6	3205
and Zerahiah b Meraioth	1Chr 6:6	3205
Meraioth b Amariah	1Chr 6:7	3205
and Amariah b Ahitub	1Chr 6:7	3205
And Ahitub b Zadok	1Chr 6:8	3205
and Zadok b Ahimaaz	1Chr 6:8	3205
And Ahimaaz b Azariah	1Chr 6:9	3205
and Azariah b Johanan	1Chr 6:9	3205
And Johanan b Azariah, (he it is	1Chr 6:10	3205
And Azariah b Amariah	1Chr 6:11	3205
and Amariah b Ahitub	1Chr 6:11	3205
And Ahitub b Zadok	1Chr 6:12	3205
and Zadok b Shallum	1Chr 6:12	3205
And Shallum b Hilkiah	1Chr 6:13	3205
and Hilkiah b Azariah	1Chr 6:13	3205
And Azariah b Seraiah	1Chr 6:14	3205
and Seraiah b Jehozadak	1Chr 6:14	3205
Heber b Japhlet, and Shomer, and	1Chr 7:32	3205
Now Benjamin b Bela his firstborn	1Chr 8:1	3205
them, and b Uzza, and Ahihud	1Chr 8:7	3205
Shaharaim b children in the	1Chr 8:8	3205
he b of Hodesh his wife, Jobab,	1Chr 8:9	3205
And of Hushim he b Abitub, and	1Chr 8:11	3205
And Mikloth b Shimeah	1Chr 8:32	3205
And Ner b Kish, and Kish b Saul	1Chr 8:33	3205
Saul b Jonathan, and Malchi-shua,	1Chr 8:33	3205
and Merib-baal b Micah	1Chr 8:34	3205
And Ahaz b Jehoadah	1Chr 8:36	3205
and Jehoadah b Alemeth, and	1Chr 8:36	3205
and Zimri b Moza,	1Chr 8:36	3205
And Moza b Binea	1Chr 8:37	3205
And Mikloth b Shimeam	1Chr 9:38	3205
And Ner b Kish	1Chr 9:39	3205
and Kish b Saul	1Chr 9:39	3205
Saul b Jonathan, and Malchi-shua,	1Chr 9:39	3205
and Merib-baal b Micah	1Chr 9:40	3205
And Ahaz b Jarah	1Chr 9:42	3205
Jarah b Alemeth, and Azmaveth, and	1Chr 9:42	3205
and Zimri b Moza	1Chr 9:42	3205
And Moza b Binea	1Chr 9:43	3205
David b more sons and daughters	2Chr 14:3	3205
b twenty and eight sons, and	2Chr 11:21	3205
b twenty and two sons, and sixteen	2Chr 13:21	3205
and he b sons and daughters	2Chr 24:3	3205
Jeshua b Joiakim	Neh 12:10	3205
Joiakim also b Eliashib	Neh 12:10	3205
and Eliashib b Joiada	Neh 12:10	3205
Joiada b Jonathan	Neh 12:11	3205
and Jonathan b Jaddua	Neh 12:11	3205
unto thy father that b thee	Prov 23:22	3205
fathers that b them in this land	Jer 16:3	3205
brought her, and he that b her	Dan 11:6	3205
his mother that b him shall say	Zec 13:3	3205
his mother that b him shall	Zec 13:3	3205
Abraham b Isaac	Mt 1:2	1080
and Isaac b Jacob	Mt 1:2	1080
and Jacob b Judas and his brethren	Mt 1:2	1080
Judas b Phares and Zara of Thamar	Mt 1:3	1080
and Phares b Esrom	Mt 1:3	1080
and Esrom b Aram	Mt 1:3	1080
And Aram b Aminadab	Mt 1:4	1080
and Aminadab b Naasson	Mt 1:4	1080
and Naasson b Salmon	Mt 1:4	1080
And Salmon b Booz of Rachab	Mt 1:5	1080
and Booz b Obed of Ruth	Mt 1:5	1080
and Obed b Jesse	Mt 1:5	1080
And Jesse b David the king	Mt 1:6	1080
David the king b Solomon of her	Mt 1:6	1080
And Solomon b Roboam	Mt 1:7	1080
and Roboam b Abia	Mt 1:7	1080

and Abia b Asa	Mt 1:7	1080
And Asa b Josaphat	Mt 1:8	1080
and Josaphat b Joram	Mt 1:8	1080
and Joram b Ozias	Mt 1:8	1080
And Ozias b Joatham	Mt 1:9	1080
and Joatham b Achaz	Mt 1:9	1080
and Achaz b Ezekias	Mt 1:9	1080
And Ezekias b Manasses	Mt 1:10	1080
and Manasses b Amon	Mt 1:10	1080
and Amon b Josias	Mt 1:10	1080
Josias b Jechonias and his	Mt 1:11	1080
to Babylon, Jechonias b Salathiel	Mt 1:12	1080
and Salathiel b Zorobabel	Mt 1:12	1080
And Zorobabel b Abiud	Mt 1:13	1080
and Abiud b Eliakim	Mt 1:13	1080
and Eliakim b Azor	Mt 1:13	1080
And Azor b Sadoc	Mt 1:14	1080
and Sadoc b Achim	Mt 1:14	1080
and Achim b Eliud	Mt 1:14	1080
And Eliud b Eleazar	Mt 1:15	1080
and Eleazar b Matthan	Mt 1:15	1080
and Matthan b Jacob	Mt 1:15	1080
Jacob b Joseph the husband of	Mt 1:16	1080
and so Abraham b Isaac, and	Acts 7:8	1080
and Isaac b Jacob	Acts 7:8	
Jacob b the twelve patriarchs	Acts 7:8	1080
of Madian, where he b two sons	Acts 7:29	1080
Of his own will b he us with the	Jas 1:18	616
that b loveth him also that is	1Jn 5:1	1080

BEGET

twelve princes shall he b	Gen 17:20	3205
When thou shalt b children	Deut 4:25	3205
Thou shalt b sons and daughters,	Deut 28:41	3205
from thee, which thou shalt b	2Kin 20:18	3205
If a man b an hundred children,	Eccl 6:3	3205
from thee, which thou shall b	Is 39:7	3205
ye wives, and b sons and daughters	Jer 29:6	3205
If he b a son that is a robber, a	Eze 18:10	3205
Now, lo, if he b a son, that	Eze 18:14	3205
which shall b children among you	Eze 47:22	3205

BEGETTEST

issue, which thou b after them	Gen 48:6	3205
unto his father, What b thou	Is 45:10	3205

BEGETTETH

He that b a fool doeth it to his	Prov 17:21	3205
he that b a wise child shall have	Prov 23:24	3205
he b a son, and there is nothing	Eccl 5:14	3205

BEGGAR

lifteth up the b from the	1Sa 2:8	34
was a certain b named Lazarus	Lk 16:20	4434
it came to pass, that the b died	Lk 16:22	4434

BEGGARLY

b elements, whereunto ye desire	Gal 4:9	4434

BEGGED

to Pilate, and b the body of Jesus	Mt 27:58	154
Pilate, and b the body of Jesus	Lk 23:52	154
Is not this he that sat and b	Jn 9:8	4319

BEGGING

forsaken, nor his seed b bread	Ps 37:25	1245
sat by the highway side b	Mk 10:46	4319
blind man sat by the way side b	Lk 18:35	4319

BEGIN See APPENDIX.

BEGINNEST

weeks from such time as thou b to	Deut 16:9	2490

BEGINNING See APPENDIX.

BEGINNINGS

in the b of your months, ye shall	Num 10:10	7218
in the b of your months ye shall	Num 28:11	7218
do better unto you than at your b	Eze 36:11	7221
these are the b of sorrows	Mk 13:8	746

BEGOTTEN

b Seth were eight hundred years	Gen 5:4	3205
b of thy father, she is thy	Lev 18:11	4138
have I b them, that thou	Num 11:12	3205
The children that are b of them	Deut 23:8	3205
and ten sons of his body b	Judg 8:30	3318
or who hath b the drops of dew	Job 38:28	3205
this day have I b thee	Ps 2:7	3205
thine heart, Who hath b me these	Is 49:21	3205
for they have b strange children	Hos 5:7	3205
as of the only b of the Father	Jn 1:14	3439
the only b Son, which is in the	Jn 1:18	3439
that he gave his only b Son	Jn 3:16	3439
the name of the only b Son of God	Jn 3:18	3439
my Son, this day have I b thee	Acts 13:33	1080

I have *b* you through the gospel 1Cor 4:15   *1080*
whom I have *b* in my bonds .... Philem 10   *1080*
my Son, this day have I *b* thee .... Heb 1:5   *1080*
art my Son, to day have I *b* thee .... Heb 5:5   *1080*
offered up his only *b* son .... Heb 11:17   *3439*
to his abundant mercy hath *b* us 1Pet 1:3   *313*
his only *b* Son into the world. 1Jn 4:9   *3439*
loveth him also that is *b* of him 1Jn 5:1   *1080*
but he that is *b* of God keepeth 1Jn 5:18   *1080*
the first *b* of the dead, and the .... Rev 1:5   *4416*

BEGUILE
lest any man should *b* you with .... Col 2:4   *3884*
Let no man *b* you of your reward .... Col 2:18   *2603*

BEGUILED
the woman said, The serpent *b* me .... Gen 3:13   *5377*
wherefore then hast thou *b* me .... Gen 29:25   *7411*
wherewith they have *b* you in the .... Num 25:18   *5230*
saying, Wherefore have ye *b* us .... Josh 9:22   *7411*
as the serpent *b* Eve through his 2Cor 11:3   *1818*

BEGUILING
b unstable souls 2Pet 2:14   *1185*

BEGUN See APPENDIX.

BEHALF
the *b* of the children of Israel .... Ex 27:21   *854*
sent messengers to David on his *b* 2Sa 3:12   *8478*
to shew himself strong in the *b* 2Chr 16:9   *5973*
I have yet to speak on God's *b* .... Job 36:2
own *b* shall cause the reproach .... Dan 11:18
I am glad therefore on your *b* .... Rom 16:19   *1909*
I thank my God always on your *b* 1Cor 1:4   *4012*
may be given by many on our *b* 2Cor 1:11   *5228*
you occasion to glory on our *b* 2Cor 5:12   *5228*
and of our boasting on your *b* 2Cor 8:24   *5228*
you should be in vain in this *b* 2Cor 9:3   *3313*
it is given in the *b* of Christ .... Phil 1:29   *5228*
but let him glorify God on this *b* 1Pet 4:16   *3313*

BEHAVE
should *b* themselves strangely .... Deut 32:27   *5234*
let us *b* ourselves valiantly for 1Chr 19:13   *2388*
I will *b* myself wisely in a .... Ps 101:2   *7919*
the child shall *b* himself proudly .... Is 3:5   *7292*
Doth not *b* itself unseemly, ... 1Cor 13:5   *807*
know how thou oughtest to *b* 1Ti 3:15   *390*

BEHAVED
sent him, and *b* himself wisely 1Sa 18:5   *7919*
David *b* himself wisely in all his 1Sa 18:14   *7919*
saw that he *b* himself very wisely 1Sa 18:15   *7919*
that David *b* himself more wisely 1Sa 18:30   *7919*
I *b* myself as though he had been .... Ps 35:14   *1980*
Surely I have *b* and quieted myself .... Ps 131:2   *7737*
as they have *b* themselves ill in .... Mic 3:4   *7489*
unblameably we *b* ourselves among 1Th 2:10   *1096*
for we *b* not ourselves disorderly 2Th 3:7   *812*

BEHAVETH
he *b* himself uncomely toward his 1Cor 7:36   *807*

BEHAVIOUR
And he changed his *b* before them 1Sa 21:13   *2940*
he changed his *b* before Abimelech .... Ps 34:*t*   *2940*
wife, vigilant, sober, of good *b* 1Ti 3:2   *2887*
that they be in *b* as becometh .... Titus 2:3   *2688*

BEHEADED
heifer that is *b* in the valley .... Deut 21:6   *6202*
b him, and took his head, and 2Sa 4:7   *5493,7218*
he sent, and *b* John in the prison .... Mt 14:10   *607*
he said, It is John, whom I *b* .... Mk 6:16   *607*
he went and *b* him in the prison, ... Mk 6:27   *607*
And Herod said, John have I *b* .... Lk 9:9   *607*
were *b* for the witness of Jesus .... Rev 20:4   *3990*

BEHELD
the Egyptians *b* the woman that .... Gen 12:14   *7200*
b all the plain of Jordan, that .... Gen 13:10   *7200*
all the land of the plain, and *b* .... Gen 19:28   *7200*
Jacob *b* the countenance of Laban, ... Gen 31:2   *7200*
Israel *b* Joseph's sons, and said, ... Gen 48:8   *7200*
when he *b* the serpent of brass, ... Num 21:9   *5027*
He hath not *b* iniquity in Jacob, ... Num 23:21   *5027*
that *b* while Samson made sport............. Judg 16:27   *7200*
David *b* the place where Saul lay, ... 1Sa 26:5   *7200*
as he was destroying, the LORD *b* 1Chr 21:15   *7200*
If I *b* the sun when it shined, or............ Job 31:26   *7200*
I *b* the transgressors, and was .... Ps 119:158   *7200*
I looked on my right hand, and *b* .... Ps 142:4   *7200*
b among the simple ones, I.................... Prov 7:7   *7200*
Then I *b* all the work of God, ... Eccl 8:17   *7200*
For I *b*, and there was no man .... Is 41:28   *7200*

I *b* the earth, and, lo, it was .... Jer 4:23   *7200*
I *b* the mountains, and, lo, they .... Jer 4:24   *7200*
I *b*, and, lo, there was no man, and .... Jer 4:25   *7200*
I *b*, and, lo, the fruitful place............... Jer 4:26   *7200*
Upon this I awaked, and *b* .... Jer 31:26   *7200*
Now as I *b* the living creatures,............. Eze 1:15   *7200*
Then I *b*, and lo a likeness as the .... Eze 8:2   *7200*
And when I *b*, lo, the sinews and .... Eze 37:8   *7200*
I *b* till the wings thereof were .... Dan 7:4   *2370,934*
After this I *b*, and lo another, ... Dan 7:6   *2370,934*
I *b* till the thrones were cast .... Dan 7:9   *2370,934*
I *b* then because of the voice of .... Dan 7:11   *2370,934*
I *b* even till the beast was slain ...... Dan 7:11   *2370,934*
I *b*, and the same horn made war... Dan 7:21   *2370,934*
he *b*, and drove asunder the.................. Hab 3:6   *7200*
But Jesus *b* them, and said unto .... Mt 19:26   *1689*
all the people, when they *b* said .... Mk 9:15   *1492*
b how the people cast money into.......... Mk 12:41   *2334*
of Joses *b* where he was laid .... Mk 15:47   *2334*
I *b* Satan as lightning fall from .... Lk 10:18   *2334*
he *b* the city, and wept over it, ... Lk 19:41   *1492*
he *b* them, and said, What is this .... Lk 20:17   *1689*
But a certain maid *b* him as he .... Lk 22:56   *1492*
b the sepulchre, and how his body .... Lk 23:55   *2300*
he *b* the linen clothes laid by .... Lk 24:12   *991*
we *b* his glory, the glory as of .... Jn 1:14   *2300*
And when Jesus *b* him, he said,............. Jn 1:42   *1689*
spoken these things, while they *b*........... Acts 1:9   *991*
b your devotions, I found an................... Acts 17:23   *333*
And I *b*, and, lo, in the midst of............. Rev 5:6   *1492*
And I *b*, and I heard the voice of .... Rev 5:11   *1492*
And I *b*, and lo a black horse................ Rev 6:5   *1492*
I *b* when he had opened the sixth .... Rev 6:12   *1492*
After this I *b*, and, lo, a great.............. Rev 7:9   *1492*
And I *b*, and heard an angel flying .... Rev 8:13   *1492*
and their enemies *b* them .... Rev 11:12   *2334*
I *b* another beast coming up out .... Rev 13:11   *1492*

BEHEMOTH
Behold now *b*, which I made with........... Job 40:15   *930*

BEHIND See APPENDIX.

BEHOLD
And God said, *B*, I have given you.......... Gen 1:29   *2009*
thing that he had made, and, *b*.............. Gen 1:31   *2009*
And the LORD God said, *B*, the man ...... Gen 3:22   *2005*
B, thou hast driven me out this .... Gen 4:14   *2005*
God looked upon the earth, and, *b*......... Gen 6:12   *2009*
and, *b*, I will destroy them with .... Gen 6:13   *2005*
And, *b*, I, even I, do bring a .... Gen 6:17   *2005*
of the ark, and looked, and, *b* .... Gen 8:13   *2009*
And I, *b*, I establish my covenant.......... Gen 9:9   *2005*
And the LORD said, *B*, the people .... Gen 11:6   *2005*
B now, I know that thou art a .... Gen 12:11   *2009*
now therefore *b* thy wife, take............... Gen 12:19   *2009*
And Abram said, *B*, to me thou hast ...... Gen 15:3   *2005*
And, *b*, the word of the LORD came........ Gen 15:4   *2009*
b a smoking furnace, and a burning...... Gen 15:17   *2009*
B now, the LORD hath restrained .... Gen 16:2   *2009*
But Abram said unto Sarai, *B*................ Gen 16:6   *2009*
of the LORD said unto her, *B*................. Gen 16:11   *2009*
b, it is between Kadesh and Bered .... Gen 16:14   *2009*
As for me, *b*, my covenant is with .... Gen 17:4   *2009*
B, I have blessed him, and will .... Gen 17:20   *2009*
And he said, *B*, in the tent .... Gen 18:9   *2009*
B now, I have taken upon me to............. Gen 18:27   *2009*
B now, I have taken upon me to............. Gen 18:31   *2009*
B now, my lords, turn in, I pray .... Gen 19:2   *2009*
B now, I have two daughters which .... Gen 19:8   *2009*
B now, thy servant hath found .... Gen 19:19   *2009*
B now, this city is near to flee .... Gen 19:20   *2009*
said unto the younger, *B*, I lay .... Gen 19:34   *2005*
dream by night, and said to him, *B* .... Gen 20:3   *2009*
And Abimelech said, *B*, my land is .... Gen 20:15   *2009*
And unto Sarah he said, *B*, I have .... Gen 20:16   *2009*
b, he is to thee a covering of .... Gen 20:16   *2009*
and he said, *B*, here I am....................... Gen 22:1   *2009*
he said, *B* the fire and the wood .... Gen 22:7   *2009*
b behind him a ram caught in a .... Gen 22:13   *2009*
it was told Abraham, saying, *B* .... Gen 22:20   *2009*
B, I stand here by the well of .... Gen 24:13   *2009*
he had done speaking, that, *b*............... Gen 24:15   *2009*
and, *b*, he stood by the camels at .... Gen 24:30   *2009*
B, I stand by the well of water .... Gen 24:43   *2009*
done speaking in mine heart, *b* .... Gen 24:45   *2009*
B, Rebekah is before thee, take............. Gen 24:51   *2009*
lifted up his eyes, and saw, and, *b*........ Gen 24:63   *2009*
to be delivered were fulfilled, *b*............. Gen 25:24   *2009*
And Esau said, *B*, I am at the .... Gen 25:32   *2009*
out at a window, and saw, and, *b*.......... Gen 26:8   *2009*
called Isaac, and said, *B*, of a .... Gen 26:9   *2009*

and he said unto him, *B*, here am I	Gen 27:1	2009
B now, I am old, I know not the	Gen 27:2	2009
unto Jacob her son, saying, *B*	Gen 27:6	2009
said to Rebekah his mother, *B*	Gen 27:11	2005
and, *b*, now he hath taken away my	Gen 27:36	2009
answered and said unto Esau, *B*	Gen 27:37	2005
answered and said unto him, *B*	Gen 27:39	2009
younger son, and said unto him, *B*	Gen 27:42	2009
b a ladder set up on the earth,	Gen 28:12	2009
b the angels of God ascending and	Gen 28:12	2009
And, *b*, the LORD stood above it,	Gen 28:13	2009
And, *b*, I am with thee, and will	Gen 28:15	2009
b a well in the field, and, lo,	Gen 29:2	2009
and, *b*, Rachel his daughter cometh	Gen 29:6	2009
to pass, that in the morning, *b*	Gen 29:25	2009
B my maid Bilhah, go in unto her	Gen 30:3	2009
And Laban said, *B*, I would it	Gen 30:34	2005
the countenance of Laban, and, *b*	Gen 31:2	2009
eyes, and saw in a dream, and, *b*	Gen 31:10	2009
B this heap, and *b* this	Gen 31:51	2009
and, *b*, also he is behind us	Gen 32:18	2009
And say ye moreover, *B*, thy	Gen 32:20	2009
up his eyes, and looked, and, *b*	Gen 33:1	2009
for the land, *b*, it is large	Gen 34:21	2009
For, *b*, we were binding sheaves	Gen 37:7	2009
and, *b*, your sheaves stood round	Gen 37:7	2009
told it his brethren, and said, *B*	Gen 37:9	2009
and, *b*, the sun and the moon and the	Gen 37:9	2009
And a certain man found him, and, *b*	Gen 37:15	2009
And they said one to another, *B*	Gen 37:19	2009
up their eyes and looked, and, *b*	Gen 37:25	2009
and, *b*, Joseph was not in the pit	Gen 37:29	2009
B thy father in law gathered up to	Gen 38:13	2009
b, I sent this kid, and thou hast	Gen 38:23	2009
and also, *b*, she is with child by	Gen 38:24	2009
the time of her travail, that, *b*	Gen 38:27	2009
as he drew back his hand, that, *b*	Gen 38:29	2009
and said unto his master's wife, *B*	Gen 39:8	2005
and looked upon them, and, *b*	Gen 40:6	2009
and said to him, In my dream, *b*	Gen 40:9	2009
I also was in my dream, and, *b*	Gen 40:16	2009
and, *b*, he stood by the river	Gen 41:1	2009
And, *b*, there came up out of the	Gen 41:2	2009
And, *b*, seven other kine came up	Gen 41:3	2009
and, *b*, seven ears of corn came up	Gen 41:5	2009
And, *b*, seven thin ears and blasted	Gen 41:6	2009
And Pharaoh awoke, and, *b*, it was a	Gen 41:7	2009
said unto Joseph, In my dream, *b*	Gen 41:17	2005
And, *b*, there came up out of the	Gen 41:18	2009
And, *b*, seven other kine came up	Gen 41:19	2009
And I saw in my dream, and, *b*	Gen 41:22	2009
And, *b*, seven ears, withered, thin	Gen 41:23	2009
B, there come seven years of	Gen 41:29	2009
And he said, *B*, I have heard that	Gen 42:2	2009
and, *b*, the youngest is this day	Gen 42:13	2009
therefore, *b*, also his blood is	Gen 42:22	2009
for, *b*, it was in his sack's	Gen 42:27	2009
they emptied their sacks, that, *b*	Gen 42:35	2009
that we opened our sacks, and, *b*	Gen 43:21	2009
B, the money, which we found in	Gen 44:8	2005
b, we are my lord's servants,	Gen 44:16	2009
And, *b*, your eyes see, and the eyes	Gen 45:12	2009
and, *b*, they are in the land of	Gen 47:1	2009
Joseph said unto the people, *B*	Gen 47:23	2009
things, that one told Joseph, *B*	Gen 48:1	2009
And one told Jacob, and said, *B*	Gen 48:2	2009
And said unto me, *B*, I will make	Gen 48:4	2005
And Israel said unto Joseph, *B*	Gen 48:21	2009
and they said, *B*, we be thy	Gen 50:18	2009
And he said unto his people, *B*	Ex 1:9	2009
and, *b*, the babe wept	Ex 2:6	2009
he went out the second day, *b*	Ex 2:13	2009
and he looked, and, *b*, the bush	Ex 3:2	2009
Now therefore, *b*, the cry of the	Ex 3:9	2009
And Moses said unto God, *B*	Ex 3:13	2009
And Moses answered and said, But, *b*	Ex 4:1	2005
and when he took it out, *b*	Ex 4:6	2009
it out of his bosom, and, *b*	Ex 4:7	2009
And also, *b*, he cometh forth to	Ex 4:14	2009
if thou refuse to let him go, *b*	Ex 4:23	2009
And Pharaoh said, *B*, the people of	Ex 5:5	2005
and, *b*, thy servants are beaten	Ex 5:16	2009
spake before the LORD, saying, *B*	Ex 6:12	2005
And Moses said before the LORD, *B*	Ex 6:30	2005
and, *b*, hitherto thou wouldest not	Ex 7:16	2009
b, I will smite with the rod that	Ex 7:17	2009
if thou refuse to let them go, *b*	Ex 8:2	2009
thou wilt not let my people go, *b*	Ex 8:21	2005
And Moses said, *B*, I go out from	Ex 8:29	2009
B, the hand of the LORD is upon	Ex 9:3	2009
And Pharaoh sent, and, *b*, there was	Ex 9:7	2009
B, to morrow about this time I	Ex 9:18	2005
refuse to let my people go, *b*	Ex 10:4	2005
lifted up their eyes, and, *b*	Ex 14:10	2009
And I, *b*, I will harden the hearts	Ex 14:17	2005
Then said the LORD unto Moses, *B*	Ex 16:4	2005
toward the wilderness, and, *b*	Ex 16:10	2009
the dew that lay was gone up, *b*	Ex 16:14	2009
B, I will stand before thee there	Ex 17:6	2005
B, I send an Angel before thee,	Ex 23:20	2009
B the blood of the covenant,	Ex 24:8	2009
and, *b*, Aaron and Hur are with you	Ex 24:14	2009
And I, *b*, I have given with him	Ex 31:6	2009
I have seen this people, and, *b*	Ex 32:9	2009
b, mine Angel shall go before	Ex 32:34	2009
And the LORD said, *B*, there is a	Ex 33:21	2009
And he said, *B*, I make a covenant	Ex 34:10	2009
b, I drive out before thee the	Ex 34:11	2005
children of Israel saw Moses, *b*	Ex 34:30	2009
did look upon all the work, and, *b*	Ex 39:43	2009
goat of the sin offering, and, *b*	Lev 10:16	2009
B, the blood of it was not	Lev 10:18	2005
And Aaron said unto Moses, *B*	Lev 10:19	2005
and, *b*, if the plague in his sight	Lev 13:5	2009
and, *b*, if the plague be somewhat	Lev 13:6	2009
And if the priest see that, *b*	Lev 13:8	2009
and, *b*, if the rising be white in	Lev 13:10	2009
and, *b*, if the leprosy have	Lev 13:13	2009
and, *b*, if the plague be turned	Lev 13:17	2009
if, when the priest seeth it, *b*	Lev 13:20	2009
if the priest look on it, and, *b*	Lev 13:21	2009
and, *b*, if the hair in the bright	Lev 13:25	2009
if the priest look on it, and, *b*	Lev 13:26	2009
and, *b*, if it be in sight deeper	Lev 13:30	2009
on the plague of the scall, and, *b*	Lev 13:31	2009
and, *b*, if the scall spread not,	Lev 13:32	2009
and, *b*, if the scall be not spread	Lev 13:34	2009
and, *b*, if the scall be spread in	Lev 13:36	2009
and, *b*, if the bright spots in the	Lev 13:39	2009
and, *b*, if the rising of the sore	Lev 13:43	2009
if the priest shall look, and, *b*	Lev 13:53	2009
and, *b*, if the plague have not	Lev 13:55	2009
And if the priest look, and, *b*	Lev 13:56	2009
and the priest shall look, and, *b*	Lev 14:3	2009
shall look on the plague, and, *b*	Lev 14:37	2009
and, *b*, if the plague be spread in	Lev 14:39	2009
priest shall come and look, and, *b*	Lev 14:44	2009
come in, and look upon it, and, *b*	Lev 14:48	2009
b, we shall not sow, nor gather	Lev 25:20	2005
And I, *b*, I have taken the Levites	Num 3:12	2009
similitude of the LORD shall he *b*	Num 12:8	5027
and, *b*, Miriam became leprous,	Num 12:10	2009
Aaron looked upon Miriam, and, *b*	Num 12:10	2009
and, *b*, the cloud covered it, and	Num 16:42	2009
and, *b*, the plague was begun among	Num 16:47	2009
and, *b*, the rod of Aaron for the	Num 17:8	2009
spake unto Moses, saying, *B*	Num 17:12	2005
And I, *b*, I have taken your	Num 18:6	2009
And the LORD spake unto Aaron, *B*	Num 18:8	2009
And, *b*, I have given the children	Num 18:21	2009
and, *b*, we are in Kadesh, a city	Num 20:16	2009
people, to call him, saying, *B*	Num 22:5	2009
b, they cover the face of the	Num 22:5	2009
B, there is a people come out of	Num 22:11	2009
b, I went out to withstand thee,	Num 22:32	2009
him, and from the hills I *b* him	Num 23:9	7789
thee to curse mine enemies, and, *b*	Num 23:11	2009
And when he came to him, *b*	Num 23:17	2009
B, I have received commandment to	Num 23:20	2009
B, the people shall rise up as a	Num 23:24	2005
thee to curse mine enemies, and, *b*	Num 24:10	2009
And now, *b*, I go unto my people	Num 24:14	2005
I shall *b* him, but not nigh	Num 24:17	7789
And, *b*, one of the children of	Num 25:6	2009
Wherefore say, *B*, I give unto him	Num 25:12	2009
B, these caused the children of	Num 31:16	2005
and the land of Gilead, that, *b*	Num 32:1	2009
And, *b*, ye are risen up in your	Num 32:14	2009
But if ye will not do so, *b*	Num 32:23	2009
B, I have set the land before you	Deut 1:8	7200
God hath multiplied you, and, *b*	Deut 1:10	2009
B, the LORD thy God hath set the	Deut 1:21	7200
b, I have given into thine hand	Deut 2:24	7200
And the LORD said unto me, *B*	Deut 2:31	7200
b, his bedstead was a bedstead of	Deut 3:11	2009
eastward, and *b* it with thine eyes	Deut 3:27	2009
B, I have taught you statutes and	Deut 4:5	7200
And ye said, *B*, the LORD our God	Deut 5:24	2005
I have seen this people, and, *b*	Deut 9:13	2009
And I looked, and, *b*, ye had sinned	Deut 9:16	2009
B, the heaven and the heaven of	Deut 10:14	2005
B, I set before you this day a	Deut 11:26	7200

and, *b*, if it be truth, and the	Deut 13:14	2009
it, and enquired diligently, and, *b*	Deut 17:4	2009
and, *b*, if the witness be a false	Deut 19:18	2009
And now, *b*, I have brought the	Deut 26:10	2009
And the LORD said unto Moses, *B*	Deut 31:14	2005
And the LORD said unto Moses, *B*	Deut 31:16	2009
b, while I am yet alive with you	Deut 31:27	2005
b the land of Canaan, which I	Deut 32:49	7200
the king of Jericho, saying, *B*	Josh 2:2	2009
B, when we come into the land,	Josh 2:18	2009
B, the ark of the covenant of the	Josh 3:11	2009
up his eyes and looked, and, *b*	Josh 5:13	2009
and, *b*, they are hid in the earth	Josh 7:21	2009
and, *b*, it was hid in his tent, and	Josh 7:22	2009
And he commanded them, saying, *B*	Josh 8:4	7200
behind them, they saw, and *b*	Josh 8:20	2009
but now, *b*, it is dry, and it is	Josh 9:12	2009
and, *b*, they be rent	Josh 9:13	2009
And now, *b*, we are in thine hand	Josh 9:25	2005
And now, *b*, the LORD hath kept me	Josh 14:10	2009
children of Israel heard say, *B*	Josh 22:11	2009
B the pattern of the altar of the	Josh 22:28	7200
B, I have divided unto you by lot	Josh 23:4	7200
And, *b*, this day I am going the	Josh 23:14	2009
said unto all the people, *B*	Josh 24:27	2009
b, I have delivered the land into	Judg 1:2	2009
and when they saw that, *b*, the	Judg 3:24	2009
and, *b*, he opened not the doors of	Judg 3:25	2009
and, *b*, their lord was fallen down	Judg 3:25	2009
And, *b*, as Barak pursued Sisera,	Judg 4:22	2009
And when he came into her tent, *b*	Judg 4:22	2009
b, my family is poor in Manasseh,	Judg 6:15	2009
arose early in the morning, *b*	Judg 6:28	2009
B, I will put a fleece of wool in	Judg 6:37	2009
And when Gideon was come, *b*	Judg 7:13	2009
dream unto his fellow, and said, *B*	Judg 7:13	2009
and, *b*, when I come to the outside	Judg 7:17	2009
B Zebah and Zalmunna, with whom ye	Judg 8:15	2009
unto Abimelech privily, saying, *B*	Judg 9:31	2009
and, *b*, they fortify the city	Judg 9:31	2009
and, *b*, when he and the people that	Judg 9:33	2009
the people, he said to Zebul, *B*	Judg 9:36	2009
in the field, and looked, and, *b*	Judg 9:43	2009
to Mizpeh unto his house, and, *b*	Judg 11:34	2009
B now, thou art barren, and	Judg 13:3	2009
But he said unto me, *B*, thou	Judg 13:7	2009
her husband, and said unto him, *B*	Judg 13:10	2009
and, *b*, a young lion roared	Judg 14:5	2009
and, *b*, there was a swarm of bees	Judg 14:8	2009
And he said unto her, *B*, I have	Judg 14:16	2009
And Delilah said unto Samson, *B*	Judg 16:10	2009
spakest of also in mine ears, *b*	Judg 17:2	2009
for we have seen the land, and, *b*	Judg 18:9	2009
b, it is behind Kirjath-jearim	Judg 18:12	2009
damsel's father, said unto him, *B*	Judg 19:9	2009
b, the day groweth to an end,	Judg 19:9	2009
And, *b*, there came an old man from	Judg 19:16	2009
were making their hearts merry, *b*	Judg 19:22	2009
B, here is my daughter a maiden,	Judg 19:24	2009
and, *b*, the woman his concubine	Judg 19:27	2009
B, ye are all children of Israel	Judg 20:7	2009
looked behind them, and, *b*	Judg 20:40	2009
And, *b*, there came none to the	Judg 21:8	2009
the people were numbered, and, *b*	Judg 21:9	2009
Then they said, there is a	Judg 21:19	2009
And see, and, *b*, if the daughters	Judg 21:21	2009
And she said, *B*, thy sister in law	Ruth 1:15	2009
And, *b*, Boaz came from Beth-lehem,	Ruth 2:4	2009
B, he winnoweth barley to night	Ruth 3:2	2009
and, *b*, a woman lay at his feet	Ruth 3:8	2009
and, *b*, the kinsman of whom Boaz	Ruth 4:1	2009
B, the days come, that I will cut	1Sa 2:31	2009
And the LORD said to Samuel, *B*	1Sa 3:11	2009
arose early on the morrow, *b*	1Sa 5:3	2009
early on the morrow morning, *b*	1Sa 5:4	2009
And said unto him, *B*, thou art old	1Sa 8:5	2009
B now, there is in this city a	1Sa 9:6	2009
said Saul to his servant, But, *b*	1Sa 9:7	2009
answered Saul again, and said, *B*	1Sa 9:8	2009
b, he is before you	1Sa 9:12	2009
they were come into the city, *b*	1Sa 9:14	2009
B the man whom I spake to thee of	1Sa 9:17	2009
Samuel said, *B* that which is left	1Sa 9:24	2009
and, *b*, I will come down unto thee	1Sa 10:8	2009
they came thither to the hill, *b*	1Sa 10:10	2009
knew him beforetime saw that, *b*	1Sa 10:11	2009
And the LORD answered, *B*, he hath	1Sa 10:22	2009
And, *b*, Saul came after the herd	1Sa 11:5	2009
And Samuel said unto all Israel, *B*	1Sa 12:1	2009
And now, *b*, the king walketh	1Sa 12:2	2009
and, *b*, my sons are with you	1Sa 12:2	2009

B, here I am	1Sa 12:3	2009
Now therefore *b* the king whom ye	1Sa 12:13	2009
and, *b*, the LORD hath set a king	1Sa 12:13	2009
of offering the burnt offering, *b*	1Sa 13:10	2009
b, I am with thee according to	1Sa 14:7	2005
Then said Jonathan, *B*, we will	1Sa 14:8	2009
and the Philistines said, *B*	1Sa 14:11	2009
and, *b*, the multitude melted away,	1Sa 14:16	2009
And when they had numbered, *b*	1Sa 14:17	2009
and, *b*, every man's sword was	1Sa 14:20	2009
people were come into the wood, *b*	1Sa 14:26	2009
Then they told Saul, saying, *B*	1Sa 14:33	2009
Saul came to Carmel, and, *b*	1Sa 15:12	2009
B, to obey is better than	1Sa 15:22	2009
remaineth yet the youngest, and, *b*	1Sa 16:11	2009
B now, an evil spirit from God	1Sa 16:15	2009
one of the servants, and said, *B*	1Sa 16:18	2009
And as he talked with them, *b*	1Sa 17:23	2009
B my elder daughter Merab, her	1Sa 18:17	2009
with David secretly, and say, *B*	1Sa 18:22	2009
the messengers were come in, *b*	1Sa 19:16	2009
And it was told Saul, saying, *B*	1Sa 19:19	2009
And one said, *B*, they be at Naioth	1Sa 19:22	2009
b, my father will do nothing	1Sa 20:2	2009
And David said unto Jonathan, *B*	1Sa 20:5	2009
any time, or the third day, and, *b*	1Sa 20:12	2009
And, *b*, I will send a lad, saying,	1Sa 20:21	2009
I expressly say unto the lad, *B*	1Sa 20:21	2009
I say thus unto the young man, *B*	1Sa 20:22	2009
which thou and I have spoken of, *b*	1Sa 20:23	2009
slewest in the valley of Elah, *b*	1Sa 21:9	2009
Then they told David, saying, *B*	1Sa 23:1	2009
And David's men said unto him, *B*	1Sa 23:3	2009
that it was told him, saying, *B*	1Sa 24:1	2009
B the day of which the LORD said	1Sa 24:4	2009
which the LORD said unto thee, *B*	1Sa 24:4	2009
thou men's words, saying, *B*	1Sa 24:9	2009
B, this day thine eyes have seen	1Sa 24:10	2009
And now, *b*, I know well that thou	1Sa 24:20	2009
Abigail, Nabal's wife, saying, *B*	1Sa 25:14	2009
b, I come after you	1Sa 25:19	2005
by the covert of the hill, and, *b*	1Sa 25:20	2009
and, *b*, he held a feast in his	1Sa 25:36	2009
her face to the earth, and said, *B*	1Sa 25:41	2009
and, *b*, Saul lay sleeping within	1Sa 26:7	2009
b, I have played the fool, and	1Sa 26:21	2009
and said, *B* the king's spear	1Sa 26:22	2009
And, *b*, as thy life was much set	1Sa 26:24	2009
And his servants said to him, *B*	1Sa 28:7	2009
And the woman said unto him, *B*	1Sa 28:9	2009
troubled, and said unto him, *B*	1Sa 28:21	2009
his men came to the city, and, *b*	1Sa 30:3	2009
when he had brought him down, *b*	1Sa 30:16	2009
B a present for you of the spoil	1Sa 30:26	2009
to pass on the third day, that, *b*	2Sa 1:2	2009
by chance upon mount Gilboa, *b*	2Sa 1:6	2009
b, it is written in the book of	2Sa 1:18	2009
Make thy league with me, and, *b*	2Sa 3:12	2009
And, *b*, the servants of David and	2Sa 3:22	2009
b, Abner came unto thee	2Sa 3:24	2009
B the head of Ish-bosheth the son	2Sa 4:8	2009
When one told me, saying, *B*	2Sa 4:10	2009
unto Hebron, and spake, saying, *B*	2Sa 5:1	2005
And Ziba said unto the king, *B*	2Sa 9:4	2009
And he answered, *B* thy servant	2Sa 9:6	2009
Thus saith the LORD, *B*, I will	2Sa 12:11	2005
for they said, *B*, while the child	2Sa 12:18	2009
and said, *B* now, thy servant hath	2Sa 13:24	2009
up his eyes, and looked, and, *b*	2Sa 13:34	2009
And Jonadab said unto the king, *B*	2Sa 13:35	2009
made an end of speaking, that, *b*	2Sa 13:36	2009
And, *b*, the whole family is risen	2Sa 14:7	2009
B now, I have done this thing	2Sa 14:21	2009
And Absalom answered Joab, *B*	2Sa 14:32	2009
servants said unto the king, *B*	2Sa 15:15	2009
b, here am I, let him do to me as	2Sa 15:26	2005
mount, where he worshipped God, *b*	2Sa 15:32	2009
B, they have there with them	2Sa 15:36	2009
past the top of the hill, *b*	2Sa 16:1	2009
And Ziba said unto the king, *B*	2Sa 16:3	2009
Then said the king to Ziba, *B*	2Sa 16:4	2009
king David came to Bahurim, *b*	2Sa 16:5	2009
and, *b*, thou art taken in thy	2Sa 16:8	2009
and to all his servants, *B*	2Sa 16:11	2009
B, he is hid now in some pit, or	2Sa 17:9	2009
saw it, and told Joab, and said, *B*	2Sa 18:10	2009
unto the man that told him, And, *b*	2Sa 18:11	2009
looked, and *b* a man running alone	2Sa 18:24	2009
B another man running alone	2Sa 18:26	2009
And, *b*, Cushi came	2Sa 18:31	2009
And it was told Joab, *B*, the king	2Sa 19:1	2009

B

unto all the people, saying, B	2Sa 19:8	2009
therefore, b, I am come the first	2Sa 19:20	2009
But b thy servant Chimham	2Sa 19:37	2009
And, b, all the men of Israel came	2Sa 19:41	2009
And the woman said unto Joab, B	2Sa 20:21	2009
b, here be oxen for burnt	2Sa 24:22	7200
B, while thou yet talkest there	1Kin 1:14	2009
And now, B, Adonijah reigneth	1Kin 1:18	2009
saying, B Nathan the prophet	1Kin 1:23	2009
and, b, they eat and drink before	1Kin 1:25	2009
And while he yet spake, b,	1Kin 1:42	2009
And it was told Solomon, saying, B	1Kin 1:51	2009
And, b, thou hast with thee Shimei	1Kin 2:8	2009
and, b, he is by the altar	1Kin 2:29	2009
And they told Shimei, saying, B	1Kin 2:39	2009
B, I have done according to thy	1Kin 3:12	2009
and, b, it was a dream	1Kin 3:15	2009
morning to give my child suck, b	1Kin 3:21	2009
considered it in the morning, b	1Kin 3:21	2009
And, b, I purpose to build an	1Kin 5:5	2005
b, the heaven and heaven of	1Kin 8:27	2009
and, b, the half was not told me	1Kin 10:7	2009
hast thou lacked with me, that, b	1Kin 11:22	2009
the Lord, the God of Israel, B	1Kin 11:31	2005
b thy gods, O Israel, which	1Kin 12:28	2009
And, b, there came a man of God	1Kin 13:1	2009
B, a child shall be born unto the	1Kin 13:2	2009
B, the altar shall be rent, and	1Kin 13:3	2009
And, b, men passed by, and saw the	1Kin 13:25	2009
b, there is Ahijah the prophet,	1Kin 14:2	2009
And the Lord said unto Ahijah, B	1Kin 14:5	2009
Therefore, b, I will bring evil	1Kin 14:10	2005
he warred, and how he reigned, b	1Kin 14:19	2009
b, I have sent unto thee a	1Kin 15:19	2009
B, I will take away the posterity	1Kin 16:3	2005
b, I have commanded a widow woman	1Kin 17:9	2009
came to the gate of the city, b	1Kin 17:10	2009
and, b, I am gathering two sticks,	1Kin 17:12	2005
And as Obadiah was in the way, b	1Kin 18:7	2009
go, tell thy lord, B, Elijah is	1Kin 18:8	2009
thou sayest, Go, tell thy lord, B	1Kin 18:11	2009
thou sayest, Go, tell thy lord, B	1Kin 18:14	2009
the seventh time, that he said, B	1Kin 18:44	2009
and slept under a juniper tree, b	1Kin 19:5	2009
And he looked, and, b, there was a	1Kin 19:6	2009
and, b, the word of the Lord came	1Kin 19:9	2009
And, b, the Lord passed by, and a	1Kin 19:11	2009
And, b, there came a voice unto	1Kin 19:13	2009
And, b, there came a prophet unto	1Kin 20:13	2009
b, I will deliver it into thine	1Kin 20:13	2005
B now, we have heard that the	1Kin 20:31	2009
obeyed the voice of the Lord, b	1Kin 20:36	2009
and, b, a man turned aside, and	1Kin 20:39	2009
b, he is in the vineyard of	1Kin 21:18	2009
B, I will bring evil upon thee,	1Kin 21:21	2005
B now, the words of the prophets	1Kin 22:13	2009
Now therefore, b, the Lord hath	1Kin 22:23	2009
And Micaiah said, B, thou shalt	1Kin 22:25	2009
and, b, he sat on the top of an	2Kin 1:9	2009
B, there came fire down from	2Kin 1:14	2009
still went on, and talked, that, b	2Kin 2:11	2009
B now, there be with thy servants	2Kin 2:16	2009
of the city said unto Elisha, B	2Kin 2:19	2009
offering was offered, that, b	2Kin 3:20	2009
B now, I perceive that this is an	2Kin 4:9	2009
unto him, Say now unto her, B	2Kin 4:13	2009
he said to Gehazi his servant, B	2Kin 4:25	2009
Elisha was come into the house, b	2Kin 4:32	2009
this letter is come unto thee, b	2Kin 5:6	2009
wroth, and went away, and said, B	2Kin 5:11	2009
and he said, B, now I know that	2Kin 5:15	2009
of Elisha the man of God, said, B	2Kin 5:20	2009
My master hath sent me, saying, B	2Kin 5:22	2009
B now, the place where we dwell	2Kin 6:1	2009
And it was told him, saying, B	2Kin 6:13	2009
was risen early, and gone forth, b	2Kin 6:15	2009
and, b, the mountain was full of	2Kin 6:17	2009
and, b, they were in the midst of	2Kin 6:20	2009
and, b, they besieged it, until an	2Kin 6:25	2009
wall, and the people looked, and, b	2Kin 6:30	2009
while he yet talked with them, b	2Kin 6:33	2009
and he said, B, this evil is of	2Kin 6:33	2009
the man of God, and said, B	2Kin 7:2	2009
And he said, B, thou shalt see it	2Kin 7:2	2009
part of the camp of Syria, b	2Kin 7:5	2009
to the camp of the Syrians, and, b	2Kin 7:10	2009
which are left in the city, (b	2Kin 7:13	2009
b, I say, they are even as all	2Kin 7:13	2009
the man of God, and said, Now, b	2Kin 7:19	2009
And he said, B, thou shalt see it	2Kin 7:19	2009
a dead body to life, that, b	2Kin 8:5	2009

And when he came, b, the captains	2Kin 9:5	2009
exceedingly afraid, and said, B	2Kin 10:4	2009
b, I conspired against my master,	2Kin 10:9	2009
And when she looked, b, the king	2Kin 11:14	2009
they were burying a man, that, b	2Kin 13:21	2009
rest of the acts of Zachariah, b	2Kin 15:11	2009
his conspiracy which he made, b	2Kin 15:15	2009
Pekahiah, and all that he did, b	2Kin 15:26	2009
of Pekah, and all that he did, b	2Kin 15:31	2009
hath sent lions among them, and, b	2Kin 17:26	2009
Now, b, thou trustest upon the	2Kin 18:21	2009
B, I will send a blast upon him,	2Kin 19:7	2005
of Tirhakah king of Ethiopia, B	2Kin 19:9	2009
B, thou hast heard what the kings	2Kin 19:11	2009
arose early in the morning, b	2Kin 19:35	2009
b, I will heal thee	2Kin 20:5	2005
B, the days come, that all that	2Kin 20:17	2009
saith the Lord God of Israel, B	2Kin 21:12	2009
Thus saith the Lord, B, I will	2Kin 22:16	2005
B therefore, I will gather thee	2Kin 22:20	2005
and, b, they were written in the	1Chr 9:1	2009
to David unto Hebron, saying, B	1Chr 11:1	2009
B, he was honourable among the	1Chr 11:25	2009
B, a son shall be born to thee,	1Chr 22:9	2009
Now, b, in my trouble I have	1Chr 22:14	2009
And, b, the courses of the priests	1Chr 28:21	2009
David the king, first and last, b	1Chr 29:29	2009
B, I build an house to the name	2Chr 2:4	2009
and, b, my servants shall be with	2Chr 2:8	2009
And, b, I will give to thy	2Chr 2:10	2009
b, heaven and the heaven of	2Chr 6:18	2009
and, b, the one half of the	2Chr 9:6	2009
And, b, God himself is with us for	2Chr 13:12	2009
And when Judah looked back, b	2Chr 13:14	2009
b, I have sent thee silver and	2Chr 16:3	2009
And, b, the acts of Asa, first and	2Chr 16:11	2009
Micaiah spake to him, saying, B	2Chr 18:12	2009
Now therefore, b, the Lord hath	2Chr 18:22	2009
And Micaiah said, B, thou shalt	2Chr 18:24	2009
And, b, Amariah the chief priest	2Chr 19:11	2009
and, b, they be in Hazazon-tamar,	2Chr 20:2	2009
And now, b, the children of Ammon	2Chr 20:10	2009
B, I say, how they reward us, to	2Chr 20:11	2009
b, they come up by the cliff of	2Chr 20:16	2009
looked unto the multitude, and, b	2Chr 20:24	2009
of Jehoshaphat, first and last, b	2Chr 20:34	2009
B, with a great plague will the	2Chr 21:14	2009
And he said unto them, B, the	2Chr 23:3	2009
And she looked, and, b, the king	2Chr 23:13	2009
repairing of the house of God, b	2Chr 24:27	2009
acts of Amaziah, first and last, b	2Chr 25:26	2009
priests, looked upon him, and, b	2Chr 26:20	2009
to Samaria, and said unto them, B	2Chr 28:9	2009
of all his ways, first and last, b	2Chr 28:26	2009
we prepared and sanctified, and, b	2Chr 29:19	2009
of Hezekiah, and his goodness, b	2Chr 32:32	2009
name of the Lord God of Israel, b	2Chr 33:18	2009
b, they are written among the	2Chr 33:19	2009
Thus saith the Lord, B, I will	2Chr 34:24	2005
B, I will gather thee to thy	2Chr 34:28	2005
and, b, they are written in the	2Chr 35:25	2009
And his deeds, first and last, b	2Chr 35:27	2009
and that which was found in him, b	2Chr 36:8	2009
b, we are before thee in our	Ezr 9:15	2005
B, we are servants this day, and	Neh 9:36	2009
thereof and the good thereof, b	Neh 9:36	2009
king's servants said unto him, B	Est 6:5	2009
B also, the gallows fifty cubits	Est 7:9	2009
queen and to Mordecai the Jew, B	Est 8:7	2009
And the Lord said unto Satan, B	Job 1:12	2009
And, b, there came a great wind	Job 1:19	2009
And the Lord said unto Satan, B	Job 2:6	2009
B, thou hast instructed many, and	Job 4:3	2009
B, he put no trust in his	Job 4:18	2005
B, happy is the man whom God	Job 5:17	2009
B, this is the joy of his way, and	Job 8:19	2005
B, God will not cast away a	Job 8:20	2005
B, he taketh away, who can hinder	Job 9:12	2005
B, he breaketh down, and it cannot	Job 12:14	2005
B, he withholdeth the waters, and	Job 12:15	2005
B now, I have ordered my cause	Job 13:18	2009
B, he putteth no trust in his	Job 15:15	2005
Also now, b, my witness is in	Job 16:19	2009
B, I cry out of wrong, but I am	Job 19:7	2005
for myself, and mine eyes shall b	Job 19:27	7200
shall his place any more b him	Job 20:9	7789
B, I know your thoughts, and the	Job 21:27	2005
b the height of the stars, how	Job 22:12	7200
B, I go forward, but he is not	Job 23:8	2005
he doth work, but I cannot b him	Job 23:9	2372
B, as wild asses in the desert,	Job 24:5	2005

B even to the moon, and it shineth	Job 25:5	2005
B, all ye yourselves have seen it	Job 27:12	2005
And unto man he said, *B*, the fear	Job 28:28	2005
b, my desire is, that the	Job 31:35	2005
B, I waited for your words	Job 32:11	2005
Yea, I attended unto you, and, *b*	Job 32:12	2009
B, my belly is as wine which hath	Job 32:19	2005
B, now I have opened my mouth, my	Job 33:2	2009
B, I am according to thy wish in	Job 33:6	2005
B, my terror shall not make thee	Job 33:7	2009
B, he findeth occasions against	Job 33:10	2005
B, in this thou art not just	Job 33:12	2005
his face, who then can *b* him	Job 34:29	2009
b the clouds which are higher	Job 35:5	7789
B, God is mighty, and despiseth	Job 36:5	7789
B, God exalteth by his power	Job 36:22	2005
magnify his work, which men *b*	Job 36:24	7891
man may *b* it afar off	Job 36:25	5027
B, God is great, and we know him	Job 36:26	2005
B, he spreadeth his light upon it	Job 36:30	2005
the prey, and her eyes *b* afar off	Job 39:29	5027
B, I am vile	Job 40:4	2005
b every one that is proud, and	Job 40:11	7200
B now behemoth, which I made with	Job 40:15	2009
B, he drinketh up a river, and	Job 40:23	2005
B, the hope of him is in vain	Job 41:9	2005
B, he travaileth with iniquity,	Ps 7:14	2009
his eyes *b*, his eyelids try, the	Ps 11:4	2372
countenance doth *b* the upright	Ps 11:7	2372
let thine eyes *b* the things that	Ps 17:2	2372
As for me, I will *b* thy face in	Ps 17:15	2372
to *b* the beauty of the LORD, and	Ps 27:4	2372
B, the eye of the LORD is upon	Ps 33:18	2009
the perfect man, and *b* the upright	Ps 37:37	7200
B, thou hast made my days as an	Ps 39:5	2009
b the works of the LORD, what	Ps 46:8	2372
B, I was shapen in iniquity	Ps 51:5	2005
B, thou desirest truth in the	Ps 51:6	2005
B, God is mine helper	Ps 54:4	2009
awake to help me, and *b*	Ps 59:4	7200
B, they belch out with their	Ps 59:7	2009
his eyes *b* the nations	Ps 66:7	6822
B, these are the ungodly, who	Ps 73:12	2009
b, I should offend against the	Ps 73:15	2009
B, he smote the rock, that the	Ps 78:20	2005
look down from heaven, and *b*	Ps 80:14	7200
B, O God our shield, and look upon	Ps 84:9	7200
b Philistia, and Tyre, with	Ps 87:4	2009
Only with thine eyes shalt thou *b*	Ps 91:8	5027
heaven did the LORD *b* the earth	Ps 102:19	5027
Who humbleth himself to *b* the	Ps 113:6	7200
that I may *b* wondrous things out	Ps 119:18	5027
B, I have longed after thy	Ps 119:40	2009
B, he that keepeth Israel shall	Ps 121:4	2009
B, as the eyes of servants look	Ps 123:2	2009
B, that thus shall the man be	Ps 128:4	2009
B, how good and how pleasant it is	Ps 133:1	2009
B, bless ye the LORD, all ye	Ps 134:1	2009
if I make my bed in hell, *b*	Ps 139:8	2009
b, I will pour out my spirit unto	Prov 1:23	2009
And, *b*, there met him a woman with	Prov 7:10	2009
B, the righteous shall be	Prov 11:31	2009
Thine eyes shall *b* strange women	Prov 23:33	7200
If thou sayest, *B*, we knew it not	Prov 24:12	2005
and, *b*, all is vanity and vexation	Eccl 1:14	2009
and, *b*, this also is vanity	Eccl 2:1	2009
and, *b*, all was vanity and vexation	Eccl 2:11	2009
And I turned myself to *b* wisdom	Eccl 2:12	7200
b the tears of such as were	Eccl 4:1	2009
B that which I have seen	Eccl 5:18	2009
B, this have I found, saith the	Eccl 7:27	7200
it is for the eyes to *b* the sun	Eccl 11:7	7200
B, thou art fair, my love	Song 1:15	2009
b, thou art fair	Song 1:15	2009
B, thou art fair, my beloved, yea	Song 1:16	2009
b, he cometh leaping upon the	Song 2:8	2009
b, he standeth behind our wall,	Song 2:9	2009
B his bed, which is Solomon's	Song 3:7	2009
b king Solomon with the crown	Song 3:11	7200
B, thou art fair, my love	Song 4:1	2009
b, thou art fair	Song 4:1	2009
For, *b*, the Lord, the Lord of	Is 3:1	2009
for judgment, but *b* oppression	Is 5:7	2009
for righteousness, but *b* a cry	Is 5:7	2009
and, *b*, they shall come with speed	Is 5:26	2009
b darkness and sorrow, and the	Is 5:30	2009
B, a virgin shall conceive, and	Is 7:14	2009
Now therefore, *b*, the Lord	Is 8:7	2009
B, I and the children whom the	Is 8:18	2009
B trouble and darkness, dimness of	Is 8:22	2009
B, the Lord, the LORD of hosts,	Is 10:33	2009

B, God is my salvation	Is 12:2	2009
B, the day of the LORD cometh,	Is 13:9	2009
B, I will stir up the Medes	Is 13:17	2005
B, Damascus is taken away from	Is 17:1	2009
And *b* at eveningtide trouble	Is 17:14	2009
B, the LORD rideth upon a swift	Is 19:1	2009
isle shall say in that day, *B*	Is 20:6	2009
And, *b*, here cometh a chariot of	Is 21:9	2009
b joy and gladness, slaying oxen	Is 22:13	2009
B, the LORD will carry thee away	Is 22:17	2009
B the land of the Chaldeans	Is 23:13	2005
B, the LORD maketh the earth	Is 24:1	2009
will not *b* the majesty of the	Is 26:10	7200
For, *b*, the LORD cometh out of	Is 26:21	2009
B, the Lord hath a mighty and	Is 28:2	2009
thus saith the Lord GOD, *B*	Is 28:16	2005
an hungry man dreameth, and, *b*	Is 29:8	2009
a thirsty man dreameth, and, *b*	Is 29:8	2009
but he awaketh, and, *b*, he is	Is 29:8	2009
Therefore, *b*, I will proceed to	Is 29:14	2005
B, the name of the LORD cometh	Is 30:27	2009
B, a king shall reign in	Is 32:1	2005
B, their valiant ones shall cry	Is 33:7	2005
they shall *b* the land that is	Is 33:17	7200
b, it shall come down upon Idumea	Is 34:5	2009
b, your God will come with	Is 35:4	2009
B, I will send a blast upon him,	Is 37:7	2005
B, thou hast heard what the kings	Is 37:11	2009
arose early in the morning, *b*	Is 37:36	2009
b, I will add unto thy days	Is 38:5	2005
B, I will bring again the shadow	Is 38:8	2005
I shall *b* man no more with the	Is 38:11	7200
B, for peace I had great	Is 38:17	2009
B, the days come, that all that	Is 39:6	2009
the cities of Judah, *B* your God	Is 40:9	2009
B, the Lord GOD will come with	Is 40:10	2009
b, his reward is with him, and his	Is 40:10	2009
B, the nations are as a drop of a	Is 40:15	2005
b, he taketh up the isles as a	Is 40:15	2005
b who hath created these things,	Is 40:26	7200
B, all they that were incensed	Is 41:11	2005
B, I will make thee a new sharp	Is 41:15	2009
may be dismayed, and *b* it together	Is 41:23	7200
B, ye are of nothing, and your	Is 41:24	2005
shall say to Zion, *B* them	Is 41:27	2009
B, they are all vanity	Is 41:29	2005
B my servant, whom I uphold	Is 42:1	2005
B, the former things are come to	Is 42:9	2009
B, I will do a new thing	Is 43:19	2005
B, all his fellows shall be	Is 44:11	2005
B, they shall be as stubble	Is 47:14	2009
lest thou shouldest say, *B*	Is 48:7	2009
B, I have refined thee, but not	Is 48:10	2009
B, these shall come from far	Is 49:12	2009
B, I have graven thee upon the	Is 49:16	2005
up thine eyes round about, and *b*	Is 49:18	7200
B, I was left alone	Is 49:21	2005
Thus saith the Lord GOD, *B*	Is 49:22	2009
B, for your iniquities have ye	Is 50:1	2005
b, at my rebuke I dry up the sea,	Is 50:2	2005
B, the Lord GOD will help me	Is 50:9	2005
B, all ye that kindle a fire,	Is 50:11	2005
the cause of his people, *B*	Is 51:22	2009
b, it is I	Is 52:6	2009
B, my servant shall deal	Is 52:13	2009
with tempest, and not comforted, *b*	Is 54:11	2009
B, they shall surely gather	Is 54:15	2005
B, I have created the smith that	Is 54:16	2005
B, I have given him for a witness	Is 55:4	2005
B, thou shalt call a nation that	Is 55:5	2005
neither let the eunuch say, *B*	Is 56:3	2005
B, in the day of your fast ye	Is 58:3	2005
B, ye fast for strife and debate,	Is 58:4	2005
B, the LORD's hand is not	Is 59:1	2005
wait for light, but *b* obscurity	Is 59:9	2009
For, *b*, the darkness shall cover	Is 60:2	2009
B, the LORD hath proclaimed unto	Is 62:11	2009
Say ye to the daughter of Zion, *B*	Is 62:11	2009
b, his reward is with him, and his	Is 62:11	2009
b from the habitation of thy	Is 63:15	7200
b, thou art wroth	Is 64:5	2005
b, see, we beseech thee, we are	Is 64:9	2005
B me, *b* me, unto a nation	Is 65:1	2009
b me, unto a nation that was not	Is 65:1	2005
B, it is written before me	Is 65:6	2009
thus saith the Lord GOD, *B*	Is 65:13	2009
b, my servants shall drink, but	Is 65:13	2009
b, my servants shall rejoice, but	Is 65:13	2009
B, my servants shall sing for joy	Is 65:14	2009
For, *b*, I create new heavens and a	Is 65:17	2005
for, *b*, I create Jerusalem a	Is 65:18	2005

For thus saith the LORD, B	Is 66:12	2005
For, b, the LORD will come with	Is 66:15	2009
b, I cannot speak	Jer 1:6	2009
And the LORD said unto me, B	Jer 1:9	2009
For, b, I have made thee this day	Jer 1:18	2009
B, I will plead with thee,	Jer 2:35	2005
B, thou hast spoken and done evil	Jer 3:5	2009
B, we come unto thee	Jer 3:22	2005
B, he shall come up as clouds, and	Jer 4:13	2009
b, publish against Jerusalem,	Jer 4:16	2009
Because ye speak this word, b	Jer 5:14	2005
b, their ear is uncircumcised, and	Jer 6:10	2009
b, the word of the LORD is unto	Jer 6:10	2009
b, I will bring evil upon this	Jer 6:19	2009
Therefore thus saith the LORD, B	Jer 6:21	2005
Thus saith the LORD, B, a people	Jer 6:22	2009
B, ye trust in lying words, that	Jer 7:8	2009
B, even I have seen it, saith the	Jer 7:11	2009
B, mine anger and my fury shall be	Jer 7:20	2009
Therefore, b, the days come,	Jer 7:32	2009
a time of health, and b trouble	Jer 8:15	2009
For, b, I will send serpents,	Jer 8:17	2005
B the voice of the cry of the	Jer 8:19	2009
thus saith the LORD of hosts, B	Jer 9:7	2005
B, I will feed them, even this	Jer 9:15	2005
B, the days come, saith the LORD,	Jer 9:25	2009
For thus saith the LORD, B	Jer 10:18	2005
B, the noise of the bruit is come	Jer 10:22	2009
Therefore thus saith the LORD, B	Jer 11:11	2005
thus saith the LORD of hosts, B	Jer 11:22	2005
B, I will pluck them out of their	Jer 12:14	2005
and, b, the girdle was marred, it	Jer 13:7	2009
unto them, Thus saith the LORD, B	Jer 13:13	2005
b them that come from the north	Jer 13:20	7200
b, the prophets say unto them, Ye	Jer 14:13	2009
then b the slain with the sword	Jer 14:18	2009
then b them that are sick with	Jer 14:18	2009
the time of healing, and b trouble	Jer 14:19	2009
B, I will cause to cease out of	Jer 16:9	2005
for, b, ye walk every one after	Jer 16:12	2009
Therefore, b, the days come,	Jer 16:14	2009
B, I will send for many fishers,	Jer 16:16	2005
Therefore, b, I will this once	Jer 16:21	2005
B, they say unto me, Where is the	Jer 17:15	2009
down to the potter's house, and, b	Jer 18:3	2009
B, as the clay is in the potter's	Jer 18:6	2009
B, I frame evil against you, and	Jer 18:11	2009
B, I will bring evil upon this	Jer 19:3	2005
Therefore, b, the days come,	Jer 19:6	2009
B, I will bring upon this city and	Jer 19:15	2005
For thus saith the LORD, B	Jer 20:4	2005
enemies, and thine eyes shall b it	Jer 20:4	7200
B, I will turn back the weapons	Jer 21:4	2005
B, I set before you the way of	Jer 21:8	2005
B, I am against thee, O	Jer 21:13	2005
b, I will visit upon you the evil	Jer 23:2	2005
B, the days come, saith the LORD,	Jer 23:5	2009
Therefore, b, the days come,	Jer 23:7	2009
B, I will feed them with wormwood	Jer 23:15	2005
B, a whirlwind of the LORD is	Jer 23:19	2009
Therefore, b, I am against thee,	Jer 23:30	2005
B, I am against the prophets,	Jer 23:31	2005
B, I am against them that	Jer 23:32	2005
Therefore, b, I, even I will	Jer 23:39	2005
The LORD shewed me, and, b	Jer 24:1	2009
B, I will send and take all the	Jer 25:9	2005
Thus saith the LORD of hosts, B	Jer 25:32	2009
As for me, b, I am in your hand	Jer 26:14	2005
that prophesy unto you, saying, B	Jer 27:16	2009
B, I will cast them from off the	Jer 28:16	2005
B, I will send upon them the	Jer 29:17	2005
B, I will deliver them into the	Jer 29:21	2009
B, I will punish Shemaiah the	Jer 29:32	2005
neither shall he b the good that	Jer 29:32	7200
B, I will bring again the	Jer 30:18	2005
B, the whirlwind of the LORD	Jer 30:23	2009
B, I will bring them from the	Jer 31:8	2005
B, the days come, saith the LORD,	Jer 31:27	2009
B, the days come, saith the LORD,	Jer 31:31	2009
B, the days come, saith the LORD,	Jer 31:38	2009
and say, Thus saith the LORD, B	Jer 32:3	2005
and his eyes shall b his eyes	Jer 32:4	7200
B, Hanameel the son of Shallum	Jer 32:7	2009
b, thou hast made the heaven and	Jer 32:17	2009
B the mounts, they are come unto	Jer 32:24	2009
and, b, thou seest it	Jer 32:24	2009
B, I am the LORD, the God of all	Jer 32:27	2009
B, I will give this city into the	Jer 32:28	2005
B, I will gather them out of all	Jer 32:37	2005
B, I will bring it health and cure	Jer 33:6	2005
B, the days come, saith the LORD,	Jer 33:14	2009

B, I will give this city into the	Jer 34:2	2005
thine eyes shall b the eyes of	Jer 34:3	7200
b, I proclaim a liberty for you,	Jer 34:17	2005
B, I will command, saith the LORD	Jer 34:22	2005
B, I will bring upon Judah and	Jer 35:17	2005
B, Pharaoh's army, which is come	Jer 37:7	2005
Then Zedekiah the king said, B	Jer 38:5	2009
And, b, all the women that are	Jer 38:22	2009
B, I will bring my words upon	Jer 39:16	2005
And now, b, I loose thee this day	Jer 40:4	2009
b, all the land is before thee	Jer 40:4	7200
As for me, b, I will dwell at	Jer 40:10	2005
of many, as thine eyes do b us	Jer 42:2	7200
b, I will pray unto the LORD your	Jer 42:4	2005
B, I will send and take	Jer 43:10	2005
and, b, this day they are a	Jer 44:2	2009
B, I will set my face against you	Jer 44:11	2005
B, I have sworn by my great name,	Jer 44:26	2005
B, I will watch over them for	Jer 44:27	2005
B, I will give Pharaoh-hophra	Jer 44:30	2005
B, that which I have built will I	Jer 45:4	2009
for, b, I will bring evil upon	Jer 45:5	2005
B, I will punish the multitude of	Jer 46:25	2005
for, b, I will save thee from	Jer 46:27	2005
B, waters rise up out of the	Jer 47:2	2009
Therefore, b, the days come,	Jer 48:12	2009
B, he shall fly as an eagle, and	Jer 48:40	2009
Therefore, b, the days come,	Jer 49:2	2009
B, I will bring a fear upon thee,	Jer 49:5	2005
B, they whose judgment was not to	Jer 49:12	2009
B, he shall come up like a lion	Jer 49:19	2009
B, he shall come up and fly as the	Jer 49:22	2009
B, I will break the bow of Elam,	Jer 49:35	2005
b, the hindermost of the nations	Jer 50:12	2009
B, I will punish the king of	Jer 50:18	2005
B, I am against thee, O thou most	Jer 50:31	2005
B, a people shall come from the	Jer 50:41	2009
B, he shall come up like a lion	Jer 50:44	2009
B, I will raise up against	Jer 51:1	2005
B, I am against thee, O	Jer 51:25	2005
B, I will plead thy cause, and	Jer 51:36	2005
Therefore, b, the days come, that	Jer 51:47	2009
Wherefore, b, the days come,	Jer 51:52	2009
O LORD, b my affliction	Lam 1:9	7200
b, and see if there be any sorrow	Lam 1:12	5027
you, all people, and b my sorrow	Lam 1:18	7200
B, O LORD	Lam 1:20	7200
B, O LORD, and consider to whom	Lam 2:20	7200
LORD look down, and b from heaven	Lam 3:50	7200
B their sitting down, and their	Lam 3:63	5027
consider, and b our reproach	Lam 5:1	7200
And I looked, and, b, a whirlwind	Eze 1:4	2009
b one wheel upon the earth by the	Eze 1:15	2009
And when I looked, b, an hand was	Eze 2:9	2009
B, I have made thy face strong	Eze 3:8	2009
and, b, the glory of the LORD	Eze 3:23	2009
But thou, O son of man, b	Eze 3:25	2009
And, b, I will lay bands upon thee	Eze 4:8	2009
b, my soul hath not been polluted	Eze 4:14	2009
he said unto me, Son of man, b	Eze 4:16	2005
B, I, even I, am against thee, and	Eze 5:8	2005
B, I, even I, will bring a sword	Eze 6:3	2005
An evil, an only evil, b, is come	Eze 7:5	2009
b, it is come	Eze 7:6	2009
B the day, b, it is come	Eze 7:10	2009
And, b, the glory of the God of	Eze 8:4	2009
b northward at the gate of the	Eze 8:5	2009
I looked, b a hole in the wall	Eze 8:7	2009
had digged in the wall, b a door	Eze 8:8	2009
b the wicked abominations that	Eze 8:9	7200
b every form of creeping things,	Eze 8:10	2009
and, b, there sat women weeping	Eze 8:14	2009
court of the LORD's house, and, b	Eze 8:16	2009
And, b, six men came from the way	Eze 9:2	2009
And, b, the man clothed with linen	Eze 9:11	2009
Then I looked, and, b, in the	Eze 10:1	2009
looked, b the four wheels by the	Eze 10:9	2009
b at the door of the gate five and	Eze 11:1	2009
Son of man, b, they of the house	Eze 12:27	2009
and seen lies, therefore, b	Eze 13:8	2005
B, I am against your pillows,	Eze 13:20	2005
Yet, b, therein shall be left a	Eze 14:22	2009
b, they shall come forth unto you	Eze 14:22	2009
B, it is cast into the fire for	Eze 15:4	2009
B, when it was whole, it was meet	Eze 15:5	2009
by thee, and looked upon thee, b	Eze 16:8	2009
B, therefore I have stretched out	Eze 16:27	2009
B, therefore I will gather all	Eze 16:37	2009
b, therefore I also will	Eze 16:43	1887
B, every one that useth proverbs	Eze 16:44	2009
B, this was the iniquity of thy	Eze 16:49	2009

and, *b*, this vine did bend her .... Eze 17:7   2009
Yea, *b*, being planted, shall it .... Eze 17:10   2009
tell them, B, the king of Babylon .... Eze 17:12   2009
B, all souls are mine .... Eze 18:4   2005
B, I will kindle a fire in thee, ... Eze 20:47   2005
B, I am against thee, and will .... Eze 21:3   2005
b, it cometh, and shall be brought .... Eze 21:7   2009
B, the princes of Israel, every .... Eze 22:6   2009
B, therefore I have smitten mine .... Eze 22:13   2009
ye are all become dross, *b* .... Eze 22:19   2005
B, I will raise up thy lovers .... Eze 23:22   2005
B, I will deliver thee into the .... Eze 23:28   2005
Son of man, *b*, I take away from .... Eze 24:16   2005
B, I will profane my sanctuary, ... Eze 24:21   2005
B, therefore I will deliver thee .... Eze 25:4   2005
B, therefore I will stretch out .... Eze 25:7   2005
that Moab and Seir do say, B .... Eze 25:8   2009
Therefore, *b*, I will open the .... Eze 25:9   2005
B, I will stretch out mine hand .... Eze 25:16   2005
B, I am against thee, O Tyrus, and .... Eze 26:3   2005
B, I will bring upon Tyrus .... Eze 26:7   2005
B, thou art wiser than Daniel .... Eze 28:3   2009
B, therefore I will bring .... Eze 28:7   2005
kings, that they may *b* thee .... Eze 28:17   7200
the sight of all them that *b* thee .... Eze 28:18   7200
B, I am against thee, O Zidon .... Eze 28:22   2005
B, I am against thee, Pharaoh .... Eze 29:3   2005
B, I will bring a sword upon thee .... Eze 29:8   2005
B, therefore I am against thee, ... Eze 29:10   2005
B, I will give the land of Egypt .... Eze 29:19   2005
B, I am against Pharaoh king of .... Eze 30:22   2005
B, the Assyrian was a cedar in .... Eze 31:3   2009
B, I am against the shepherds .... Eze 34:10   2005
B, I, even I, will both search my .... Eze 34:11   2005
B, I judge between cattle and .... Eze 34:17   2005
B, I, even I, will judge between .... Eze 34:20   2005
B, O mount Seir, I am against .... Eze 35:3   2005
B, I have spoken in my jealousy .... Eze 36:6   2005
For, *b*, I am for you, and I will .... Eze 36:9   2005
and, *b*, there were very many in .... Eze 37:2   2009
B, I will cause breath to enter .... Eze 37:5   2009
b a shaking, and the bones came .... Eze 37:7   2009
b, they say, Our bones are dried, ... Eze 37:11   2009
B, O my people, I will open your .... Eze 37:12   2009
B, I will take the stick of .... Eze 37:19   2009
B, I will take the children of .... Eze 37:21   2009
B, I am against thee, O Gog, the .... Eze 38:3   2005
B, I am against thee, O Gog, the .... Eze 39:1   2005
B, it is come, and it is done, ... Eze 39:8   2009
And he brought me thither, and, *b* ..... Eze 40:3   2009
b with thine eyes, and hear with .... Eze 40:4   7200
b a wall on the outside of the .... Eze 40:5   2009
b a gate toward the south .... Eze 40:24   2009
And, *b*, the glory of the God of .... Eze 43:2   2009
and, *b*, the glory of the LORD .... Eze 43:5   2009
B, this is the law of the house .... Eze 43:12   2009
and I looked, and, *b*, the glory of .... Eze 44:4   2009
b with thine eyes, and hear with .... Eze 44:5   7200
and, *b*, there was a place on the .... Eze 46:19   2009
and, *b*, in every corner of the .... Eze 46:21   2009
and, *b*, waters issued out from .... Eze 47:1   2009
and, *b*, there ran out waters on .... Eze 47:2   2009
Now when I had returned, *b* .... Eze 47:7   2009
king, sawest, and *b* a great image .... Dan 2:31   431
b a tree in the midst of the .... Dan 4:10   431
of my head upon my bed, and, *b* .... Dan 4:13   431
saw in my vision by night, and, *b* ...... Dan 7:2   2009
b another beast, a second, like .... Dan 7:5   718
b a fourth beast, dreadful and .... Dan 7:7   718
I considered the horns, and, *b* .... Dan 7:8   431
and, *b*, in this horn were eyes .... Dan 7:8   431
I saw in the night visions, and, *b* .... Dan 7:13   718
up mine eyes, and saw, and, *b* .... Dan 8:3   2009
And as I was considering, *b* .... Dan 8:5   2009
sought for the meaning, then, *b* .... Dan 8:15   2009
And he said, B, I will make thee .... Dan 8:19   2005
b our desolations, and the city .... Dan 9:18   7200
b a certain man clothed in linen, ... Dan 10:5   2009
And, *b*, an hand touched me, which ...... Dan 10:10   2009
And, *b*, one like the similitude of .... Dan 10:16   2009
B, there shall stand up yet three .... Dan 11:2   2009
Then I Daniel looked, and, *b* .... Dan 12:5   2009
Therefore, *b*, I will hedge up thy .... Hos 2:6   2005
Therefore, *b*, I will allure her, ... Hos 2:14   2009
answer and say unto his people, B .... Joel 2:19   2005
For, *b*, in those days, and in that .... Joel 3:1   2009
B, I will raise them out of the .... Joel 3:7   2005
B, I am pressed under you, as a .... Amos 2:13   2009
b the great tumults in the midst .... Amos 3:9   7200
For, *b*, the LORD commandeth, and .... Amos 6:11   2009
But, *b*, I will raise up against .... Amos 6:14   2005

and, *b*, he formed grasshoppers in .... Amos 7:1   2009
and, *b*, the Lord GOD called to .... Amos 7:4   2009
and, *b*, the Lord stood upon a wall .... Amos 7:7   2009
Then said the Lord, B, I will set .... Amos 7:8   2005
b a basket of summer fruit .... Amos 8:1   2009
B, the days come, saith the Lord .... Amos 8:11   2009
B, the eyes of the Lord GOD are .... Amos 9:8   2009
B, the days come, saith the LORD, ... Amos 9:13   2009
B, I have made thee small among .... Obad 2   2009
For, *b*, the LORD cometh forth out .... Mic 1:3   2009
B, against this family do I .... Mic 2:3   2005
I shall *b* his righteousness .... Mic 7:9   7200
mine eyes shall *b* her .... Mic 7:10   7200
B upon the mountains the feet of .... Nah 1:15   2209
B, I am against thee, saith the .... Nah 2:13   2205
B, I am against thee, saith the .... Nah 3:5   2205
B, thy people in the midst of .... Nah 3:13   2009
and cause me to *b* grievance .... Hab 1:3   5027
B ye among the heathen, and regard .... Hab 1:5   7200
art of purer eyes than to *b* evil .... Hab 1:13   7200
B, his soul which is lifted up is .... Hab 2:4   2009
B, is it not of the LORD of hosts .... Hab 2:13   2009
B, it is laid over with gold and .... Hab 2:19   2009
B, at that time I will undo all .... Zeph 3:19   2005
b a man riding upon a red horse, ... Zec 1:8   2009
and fro through the earth, and, *b* .... Zec 1:11   2009
eyes, and saw, and *b* four horns .... Zec 1:18   2009
b a man with a measuring line in .... Zec 2:1   2009
And, *b*, the angel that talked with .... Zec 2:3   2009
For, *b*, I will shake mine hand .... Zec 2:9   2005
And unto him he said, B, I have .... Zec 3:4   7200
for, *b*, I will bring forth my .... Zec 3:8   2005
For *b* the stone that I have laid .... Zec 3:9   2009
b, I will engrave the graving .... Zec 3:9   2005
b a candlestick all of gold, with .... Zec 4:2   2005
and looked, and *b* a flying roll .... Zec 5:1   2009
And, *b*, there was lifted up a .... Zec 5:7   2009
I up mine eyes, and looked, and, *b* ..... Zec 5:9   2009
up mine eyes, and looked, and, *b* .... Zec 6:1   2009
me, and spake unto me, saying, B .... Zec 6:8   7200
B the man whose name is The .... Zec 6:12   2009
B, I will save my people from the .... Zec 8:7   2005
B, the Lord will cast her out, and .... Zec 9:4   2009
b, thy King cometh unto thee .... Zec 9:9   2009
B, I will make Jerusalem a cup of .... Zec 12:2   2009
B, the day of the LORD cometh, and ...... Zec 14:1   2009
Ye said also, B, what a weariness .... Mal 1:13   2009
B, I will corrupt your seed, and .... Mal 2:3   2005
B, I will send my messenger, and .... Mal 3:1   2005
b, he shall come, saith the LORD .... Mal 3:1   2009
For, *b*, the day cometh, that .... Mal 4:1   2009
B, I will send you Elijah the .... Mal 4:5   2009
he thought on these things, *b* .... Mt 1:20   2400
B, a virgin shall be with child, ... Mt 1:23   2400
in the days of Herod the king, *b* .... Mt 2:1   2400
And when they were departed, *b* .... Mt 2:13   2400
But when Herod was dead, *b* .... Mt 2:19   2400
Then the devil leaveth him, and, *b* ..... Mt 4:11   2400
B the fowls of the air .... Mt 6:26   *1689*
and, *b*, a beam is in thine own eye ...... Mt 7:4   2400
And, *b*, there came a leper and .... Mt 8:2   2400
And, *b*, there arose a great .... Mt 8:24   2400
And, *b*, they cried out, saying, ... Mt 8:29   2400
and, *b*, the whole herd of swine .... Mt 8:32   2400
And, *b*, the whole city came out to .... Mt 8:34   2400
And, *b*, they brought to him a man ...... Mt 9:2   2400
And, *b*, certain of the scribes .... Mt 9:3   2400
Jesus sat at meat in the house, *b* .... Mt 9:10   2400
spake these things unto them, *b* .... Mt 9:18   2400
And, *b*, a woman, which was .... Mt 9:20   2400
As they went out, *b*, they brought .... Mt 9:32   2400
B, I send you forth as sheep in .... Mt 10:16   2400
b, they that wear soft clothing .... Mt 11:8   2400
is he, of whom it is written, B .... Mt 11:10   2400
say, B a man gluttonous, and a .... Mt 11:19   2400
saw it, they said unto him, B .... Mt 12:2   2400
And, *b*, there was a man which had ..... Mt 12:10   2400
B my servant, whom I have chosen ...... Mt 12:18   2400
and, *b*, a greater than Jonas is .... Mt 12:41   2400
and, *b*, a greater than Solomon is ...... Mt 12:42   2400
he yet talked to the people, *b* .... Mt 12:46   2400
Then one said unto him, B .... Mt 12:47   2400
B my mother and my brethren .... Mt 12:49   2400
unto them in parables, saying, B .... Mt 13:3   2400
And, *b*, a woman of Canaan came out ... Mt 15:22   2400
And, *b*, there appeared unto them .... Mt 17:3   2400
While he yet spake, *b*, a bright .... Mt 17:5   2400
b a voice out of the cloud, which .... Mt 17:5   2400
heaven their angels do always *b* .... Mt 18:10   *991*
And, *b*, one came and said unto him, ... Mt 19:16   2400
Peter and said unto him, B .... Mt 19:27   2400

B, we go up to Jerusalem	Mt 20:18	2400
And, *b*, two blind men sitting by	Mt 20:30	2400
Tell ye the daughter of Sion, *B*	Mt 21:5	2400
Tell them which are bidden, *B*	Mt 22:4	2400
Wherefore, *b*, I send unto you	Mt 23:34	2400
B, your house is left unto you	Mt 23:38	2400
B, I have told you before	Mt 24:25	2400
if they shall say unto you, *B*	Mt 24:26	2400
b, he is in the secret chambers	Mt 24:26	2400
midnight there was a cry made, *B*	Mt 25:6	2400
b, I have gained beside them five	Mt 25:20	2396
b, I have gained two other	Mt 25:22	2396
b, the hour is at hand, and the	Mt 26:45	2400
b, he is at hand that doth betray	Mt 26:46	2400
And, *b*, one of them which were	Mt 26:51	2400
b, now ye have heard his	Mt 26:65	2396
And, *b*, the veil of the temple was	Mt 27:51	2400
And, *b*, there was a great	Mt 28:2	2400
and, *b*, he goeth before you into	Mt 28:7	2400
went to tell his disciples, *b*	Mt 28:9	2400
Now when they were going, *b*	Mt 28:11	2400
it is written in the prophets, *B*	Mk 1:2	2400
And the Pharisees said unto him, *B*	Mk 2:24	2396
him, and they said unto him, *B*	Mk 3:32	2396
B my mother and my brethren	Mk 3:34	2396
B, there went out a sower to sow	Mk 4:3	2400
And, *b*, there cometh one of the	Mk 5:22	2400
Saying, *B*, we go up to Jerusalem	Mk 10:33	2400
saith unto him, Master, *b*	Mk 11:21	2396
b, I have foretold you all things	Mk 13:23	2400
b, the Son of man is betrayed	Mk 14:41	2400
b how many things they witness	Mk 15:4	2396
by, when they heard it said, *B*	Mk 15:35	2400
b the place where they laid him	Mk 16:6	2396
And, *b*, thou shalt be dumb, and not	Lk 1:20	2400
And, *b*, thou shalt conceive in thy	Lk 1:31	2400
And, *b*, thy cousin Elisabeth, she	Lk 1:36	2400
B the handmaid of the Lord	Lk 1:38	2400
for, *b*, from henceforth all	Lk 1:48	2400
for, *b*, I bring you good tidings	Lk 2:10	2400
And, *b*, there was a man in	Lk 2:25	2400
and said unto Mary his mother, *B*	Lk 2:34	2400
b, thy father and I have sought	Lk 2:48	2400
city, *b* a man full of leprosy	Lk 5:12	2400
And, *b*, men brought in a bed a man	Lk 5:18	2400
for, *b*, your reward is great in	Lk 6:23	2400
nigh to the gate of the city, *b*	Lk 7:12	2400
B, they which are gorgeously	Lk 7:25	2400
is he, of whom it is written, *B*	Lk 7:27	2400
ye say, *B* a gluttonous man, and a	Lk 7:34	2400
And, *b*, a woman in the city, which	Lk 7:37	2400
And, *b*, there came a man named	Lk 8:41	2400
And, *b*, there talked with him two	Lk 9:30	2400
And, *b*, a man of the company cried	Lk 9:38	2400
b, I send you forth as lambs	Lk 10:3	2400
B, I give unto you power to tread	Lk 10:19	2400
And, *b*, a certain lawyer stood up,	Lk 10:25	2400
and, *b*, a greater than Solomon is	Lk 11:31	2400
and, *b*, a greater than Jonas is	Lk 11:32	2400
and, *b*, all things are clean unto	Lk 11:41	2400
the dresser of his vineyard, *B*	Lk 13:7	2400
And, *b*, there was a woman which	Lk 13:11	2400
And, *b*, there are last which shall	Lk 13:30	2400
them, Go ye, and tell that fox, *B*	Lk 13:32	2400
B, your house is left unto you	Lk 13:35	2400
And, *b*, there was a certain man	Lk 14:2	2400
all that *b* it begin to mock him,	Lk 14:29	2334
for, *b*, the kingdom of God is	Lk 17:21	2400
the twelve, and said unto them, *B*	Lk 18:31	2400
And, *b*, there was a man named	Lk 19:2	2400
B, Lord, the half of my goods I	Lk 19:8	2400
And another came, saying, Lord, *b*	Lk 19:20	2400
As for these things which ye *b*	Lk 21:6	2334
B the fig tree, and all the trees	Lk 21:29	1492
And he said unto them, *B*, when ye	Lk 22:10	2400
But, *b*, the hand of him that	Lk 22:21	2400
And the Lord said, Simon, Simon, *b*	Lk 22:31	2400
And they said, Lord, *b*, here are	Lk 22:38	2400
b a multitude, and he that was	Lk 22:47	2400
and, *b*, I, having examined him	Lk 23:14	2400
For, *b*, the days are coming, in	Lk 23:29	2400
And, *b*, there was a man named	Lk 23:50	2400
were much perplexed thereabout, *b*	Lk 24:4	2400
And, *b*, two of them that same	Lk 24:13	2400
B my hands and my feet, that it is	Lk 24:39	1492
And, *b*, I send the promise of my	Lk 24:49	2400
B the Lamb of God, which taketh	Jn 1:29	2396
he saith, The Lamb of God	Jn 1:36	2396
B an Israelite indeed, in whom is	Jn 1:47	2396
to whom thou barest witness, *b*	Jn 3:26	2396
b, I say unto you, Lift up your	Jn 4:35	2400
the temple, and said unto him, *B*	Jn 5:14	2396
sent unto him, saying, Lord, *b*	Jn 11:3	2396
said the Jews, *B* how he loved him	Jn 11:36	2396
b, thy King cometh, sitting on an	Jn 12:15	2400
b, the world is gone after him	Jn 12:19	2396
B, the hour cometh, yea, is now	Jn 16:32	2400
that they may *b* my glory, which	Jn 17:24	2334
b, they know what I said	Jn 18:21	2396
again, and saith unto them, *B*	Jn 19:4	2396
Pilate saith unto them, *B* the man	Jn 19:5	2396
saith unto the Jews, *B* your King	Jn 19:14	2396
unto his mother, Woman, *b* thy son	Jn 19:26	2400
he to the disciple, *B* thy mother	Jn 19:27	2400
hither thy finger, and *b* my hands	Jn 20:27	2396
toward heaven as he went up, *b*	Acts 1:10	2400
saying one to another, *B*	Acts 2:7	2400
now, Lord, *b* their threatenings	Acts 4:29	1896
b, the feet of them which have	Acts 5:9	2400
came one and told them, saying, *B*	Acts 5:25	2400
and, *b*, ye have filled Jerusalem	Acts 5:28	2400
and as he drew near to *b* it	Acts 7:31	2657
Moses trembled, and durst not *b*	Acts 7:32	2657
And said, *B*, I see the heavens	Acts 7:56	2400
and, *b*, a man of Ethiopia, an	Acts 8:27	2400
And he said, *B*, I am here, Lord	Acts 9:10	2400
for, *b*, he prayeth	Acts 9:11	2400
which he had seen should mean, *b*	Acts 10:17	2400
the Spirit said unto him, *B*	Acts 10:19	2400
and said, *B*, I am he whom ye seek	Acts 10:21	2400
hour I prayed in my house, and, *b*	Acts 10:30	2400
And, *b*, immediately there were	Acts 11:11	2400
And, *b*, the angel of the Lord came	Acts 12:7	2400
And now, *b*, the hand of the Lord	Acts 13:11	2400
But, *b*, there cometh one after me	Acts 13:25	2400
B, ye despisers, and wonder, and	Acts 13:41	1492
and, *b*, a certain disciple was	Acts 16:1	2400
And now, *b*, I go bound in the	Acts 20:22	2400
And now, *b*, I know that ye all,	Acts 20:25	2400
B, thou art called a Jew, and	Rom 2:17	2396
As it is written, *B*, I lay in	Rom 9:33	2400
B therefore the goodness and	Rom 11:22	1492
B Israel after the flesh	1Cor 10:18	991
B, I shew you a mystery	1Cor 15:51	2400
of Israel could not stedfastly *b*	2Cor 3:7	816
b, all things are become new	2Cor 5:17	2400
b, now is the accepted time	2Cor 6:2	2400
b, now is the day of salvation	2Cor 6:2	2400
as dying, and, *b*, we live	2Cor 6:9	2400
For *b* this selfsame thing, that	2Cor 7:11	2400
B, the third time I am ready to	2Cor 12:14	2400
things which I write unto you, *b*	Gal 1:20	2400
B, I Paul say unto you, that if	Gal 5:2	2396
B I and the children which God	Heb 2:13	2400
fault with them, he saith, *B*	Heb 8:8	2400
B, we put bits in the horses'	Jas 3:3	2400
B also the ships, which though	Jas 3:4	2400
B, how great a matter a little	Jas 3:5	2400
B, the hire of the labourers who	Jas 5:4	2400
B, the husbandman waiteth for the	Jas 5:7	2400
b, the judge standeth before the	Jas 5:9	2400
B, we count them happy which	Jas 5:11	2400
is contained in the scripture, *B*	1Pet 2:6	2400
good works, which they shall *b*	1Pet 2:12	2029
While they *b* your chaste	1Pet 3:2	2029
B, what manner of love the Father	1Jn 3:1	1492
prophesied of these, saying, *B*	Jude 14	2400
B, he cometh with clouds	Rev 1:7	2400
and, *b*, I am alive for evermore,	Rev 1:18	2400
b, the devil shall cast some of	Rev 2:10	2400
B, I will cast her into a bed, and	Rev 2:22	2400
b, I have set before thee an open	Rev 3:8	2400
B, I will make them of the	Rev 3:9	2400
b, I will make them to come and	Rev 3:9	2400
B, I come quickly	Rev 3:11	2400
B, I stand at the door, and knock	Rev 3:20	2400
After this I looked, and, *b*	Rev 4:1	2400
and, *b*, a throne was set in heaven	Rev 4:2	2400
b, the Lion of the tribe of Juda,	Rev 5:5	2400
And I saw, and *b* a white horse	Rev 6:2	2400
And I looked, and *b* a pale horse	Rev 6:8	2400
and, *b*, there come two woes more	Rev 9:12	2400
and, *b*, the third woe cometh	Rev 11:14	2400
b a great red dragon, having	Rev 12:3	2400
b a white cloud, and upon the	Rev 14:14	2400
And after that I looked, and, *b*	Rev 15:5	2400
B, I come as a thief	Rev 16:15	2400
when they *b* the beast that was,	Rev 17:8	991
heaven opened, and *b* a white horse	Rev 19:11	2400
voice out of heaven saying, *B*	Rev 21:3	2400
that sat upon the throne said, *B*	Rev 21:5	2400

B, I come quickly .... Rev 22:7   2400
And, *b*, I come quickly .... Rev 22:12   2400

BEHOLDEST
for thou *b* mischief and spite, to .... Ps 10:14   5027
why *b* thou the mote that is in .... Mt 7:3   991
why *b* thou the mote that is in .... Lk 6:41   991
when thou thyself *b* not the beam .... Lk 6:42   991

BEHOLDETH
he *b* not the way of the vineyards .... Job 24:18   6437
He *b* all high things .... Job 41:34   7200
he *b* all the sons of men .... Ps 33:13   7200
For he *b* himself, and goeth his............... Jas 1:24   2657

BEHOLDING
Turn away mine eyes from *b* vanity....... Ps 119:37   7200
place, *b* the evil and the good............... Prov 15:3   6822
saving the *b* of them with their .... Eccl 5:11   7200
many women were there *b* afar off ...... Mt 27:55   2334
Then Jesus *b* him loved him, and .... Mk 10:21   1689
And the people stood .... Lk 23:35   2334
b the things which were done,................ Lk 23:48   2334
stood afar off, *b* these things .... Lk 23:49   3708
b the man which was healed .... Acts 4:14   991
b the miracles and signs which .... Acts 8:13   2334
who stedfastly *b* him, and .... Acts 14:9   816
earnestly *b* the council, said,................. Acts 23:1   816
with open face *b* as in a glass 2Cor 3:18   2734
b your order, and the stedfastness .... Col 2:5   991
he is like unto a man *b* his .... Jas 1:23   2657

BEHOVED
thus it *b* Christ to suffer, and to .... Lk 24:46   *1163*
Wherefore in all things it *b* him .... Heb 2:17   *3784*

BEING See APPENDIX.

BEKAH
A *b* for every man, that is, half.............. Ex 38:26   1235

BEKERITE See BACHRITES.

BEL *(bel)* See BAAL. *A Babylonian god.*
B boweth down, Nebo stoopeth, ... Is 46:1   1078
B is confounded, Merodach is .... Jer 50:2   1078
And I will punish *B* in Babylon .... Jer 51:44   1078

BELA *(be'-lah)* See BELAH, BELAITES.
   1. Another name for Zoar.
king of Zeboiim, and the king of *B* .... Gen 14:2   1106
the king of *B* (the same is Zoar .... Gen 14:8   1106
   2. An Edomite king.
B the son of Beor reigned in Edom .... Gen 36:32   1106
B died, and Jobab the son of Zerah .... Gen 36:33   1106
B the son of Beor 1Chr 1:43   1106
when *B* was dead, Jobab the son of........ 1Chr 1:44   1106
   3. A son of Benjamin.
of *B*, the family of the Belaites .... Num 26:38   1106
And the sons of *B* were Ard.................... Num 26:40   1106
B, and Becher, and Jediael, three........... 1Chr 7:6   1106
And the sons of *B* 1Chr 7:7   1106
Benjamin begat *B* his firstborn 1Chr 8:1   1106
And the sons of *B* were, Addar, and....... 1Chr 8:3   1106
   4. A son of Azaz the Reubenite.
B the son of Azaz, the son of.................. 1Chr 5:8   1106

BELAH *(be'-lah)* See BELA. *A form of Bela.*
And the sons of Benjamin were *B* .... Gen 46:21   1106

BELAITES *(be'-lah-ites) Descendants of Bela.*
of Bela, the family of the *B* .... Num 26:38   1108

BELCH
they *b* out with their mouth .... Ps 59:7   5042

BELIAL *(be'-le-al) A title for a "worthless person."*
Certain men, the children of *B* .... Deut 13:13   1100
of the city, certain sons of *B* .... Judg 19:22   1100
us the men, the children of *B* .... Judg 20:13   1100
handmaid for a daughter of *B* 1Sa 1:16   1100
the sons of Eli were sons of *B*................. 1Sa 2:12   1100
But the children of *B* said....................... 1Sa 10:27   1100
for he is such a son of *B* 1Sa 25:17   1100
I pray thee, regard this man of *B* 1Sa 25:25   1100
all the wicked men and men of *B* 1Sa 30:22   1100
thou bloody man, and thou man of *B*...... 2Sa 16:7   1100
happened to be there a man of *B* 2Sa 20:1   1100
But the sons of *B* shall be all of 2Sa 23:6   1100
And set two men, sons of *B* 1Kin 21:10   1100
came in two men, children of *B*.............. 1Kin 21:13   1100
the men of *B* witnessed against.............. 1Kin 21:13   1100
him vain men, the children of *B*............. 2Chr 13:7   1100
what concord hath Christ with *B* 2Cor 6:15   955

BELIED
They have *b* the LORD, and said, It .... Jer 5:12   3584

BELIEF
of the Spirit and *b* of the truth............... 2Th 2:13   4102

BELIEVE
But, behold, they will not *b* me .... Ex 4:1   539
That they may *b* that the LORD God....... Ex 4:5   539
to pass, if they will not *b* thee .... Ex 4:8   539
that they will *b* the voice of the .... Ex 4:8   539
if they will not *b* also these two .... Ex 4:9   539
with thee, and *b* thee for ever .... Ex 19:9   539
how long will it be ere they *b* me .... Num 14:11   539
ye did not *b* the LORD your God .... Deut 1:32   539
that did not *b* in the LORD their 2Kin 17:14   539
B in the LORD your God, so shall 2Chr 20:20   539
b his prophets, so shall ye 2Chr 20:20   539
on this manner, neither yet *b* him........... 2Chr 32:15   539
yet would I not *b* that he had .... Job 9:16   539
Wilt thou *b* him, that he will .... Job 39:12   539
When he speaketh fair, *b* him not .... Prov 26:25   539
If ye will not *b*, surely ye shall .... Is 7:9   539
b me, and understand that I am he........ Is 43:10   539
b them not, though they speak .... Jer 12:6   539
in your days, which ye will not *b* .... Hab 1:5   539
B ye that I am able to do this .... Mt 9:28   4100
these little ones which *b* in me .... Mt 18:6   4100
us, Why did ye not then *b* him............... Mt 21:25   4100
afterward, that ye might *b* him .... Mt 21:32   4100
b it not... Mt 24:23   4100
b it not... Mt 24:26   4100
from the cross, and we will *b* him........... Mt 27:42   4100
repent ye, and *b* the gospel .... Mk 1:15   4100,*1722*
synagogue, Be not afraid, only *b*............ Mk 5:36   4100
said unto him, If thou canst *b* .... Mk 9:23   4100
and said with tears, Lord, I *b*................. Mk 9:24   4100
of these little ones that *b* in me .... Mk 9:42   4100
but shall *b* that those things .... Mk 11:23   4100
b that ye receive them, and ye .... Mk 11:24   4100
say, Why then did ye not *b* him .... Mk 11:31   4100
b him not .... Mk 13:21   4100
the cross, that we may see and *b* .... Mk 15:32   4100
signs shall follow them that *b* .... Mk 16:17   4100
their hearts, lest they should *b*............... Lk 8:12   4100
have no root, which for a while *b*........... Lk 8:13   4100
b only, and she shall be made .... Lk 8:50   4100
If I tell you, ye will not *b* .... Lk 22:67   4100
slow of heart to *b* all that the .... Lk 24:25   4100,*1909*
that all men through him might *b* .... Jn 1:7   4100
even to them that *b* on his name .... Jn 1:12   4100
and ye *b* not, how shall ye *b* .... Jn 3:12   4100
b me, the hour cometh, when ye .... Jn 4:21   4100
And said unto the woman, Now we *b* .... Jn 4:42   4100
signs and wonders, ye will not *b* .... Jn 4:48   4100
whom he hath sent, him ye *b* not .... Jn 5:38   4100
How can ye *b*, which receive................. Jn 5:44   4100
But if ye *b* not his writings.................... Jn 5:47   4100
how shall ye *b* my words....................... Jn 5:47   4100
that ye *b* on him whom he hath .... Jn 6:29   4100
then, that we may see, and *b* thee .... Jn 6:30   4100
ye also have seen me, and *b* not .... Jn 6:36   4100
there are some of you that *b* not............. Jn 6:64   4100
And we *b* and are sure that thou art....... Jn 6:69   4100
neither did his brethren *b* in him .... Jn 7:5   4100
which they that *b* on him should .... Jn 7:39   4100
for if ye *b* not that I am he, ye................ Jn 8:24   4100
I tell you the truth, ye *b* me not .... Jn 8:45   4100
say the truth, why do ye not *b* me.......... Jn 8:46   4100
the Jews did not *b* concerning him .... Jn 9:18   4100
Dost thou *b* on the Son of God .... Jn 9:35   4100
he, Lord, that I might *b* on him............... Jn 9:36   4100
And he said, Lord, I *b* .... Jn 9:38   4100
But ye *b* not, because ye are not .... Jn 10:26   4100
the works of my Father, *b* me not .... Jn 10:37   4100
ye *b* not me, *b* the works .... Jn 10:38   4100
that ye may know, and *b*, that the.......... Jn 10:38   4100
not there, to the intent ye may *b* .... Jn 11:15   4100
I *b* that thou art the Christ, the .... Jn 11:27   4100
thee, that, if thou wouldest *b* .... Jn 11:40   4100
that they may *b* that thou hast .... Jn 11:42   4100
thus alone, all men will *b* on him .... Jn 11:48   4100
b in the light, that ye may be .... Jn 12:36   4100
Therefore they could not *b*..................... Jn 12:39   4100
words, and *b* not, I judge him not .... Jn 12:47   4100
to pass, ye may *b* that I am he .... Jn 13:19   4100
ye *b* in God, *b* also in me.................... Jn 14:1   4100
B me that I am in the Father, and .... Jn 14:11   4100
or else *b* me for the very works' .... Jn 14:11   4100
it is come to pass, ye might *b* .... Jn 14:29   4100
Of sin, because they *b* not on me .... Jn 16:9   4100
by this we *b* that thou camest................ Jn 16:30   4100
answered them, Do ye now *b*................. Jn 16:31   4100
shall *b* on me through their word .... Jn 17:20   4100

that the world may *b* that thou .... Jn 17:21   4100
he saith true, that ye might *b* .... Jn 19:35   4100
hand into his side, I will not *b* .... Jn 20:25   4100
that ye might *b* that Jesus is the .... Jn 20:31   4100
I *b* that Jesus Christ is the Son .... Acts 8:37   4100
by him all that *b* are justified .... Acts 13:39   4100
work which ye shall in no wise *b* .... Acts 13:41   4100
hear the word of the gospel, and *b* .... Acts 15:7   4100
But we *b* that through the grace .... Acts 15:11   4100
B on the Lord Jesus Christ, and Acts,16:31   4100
that they should *b* on him which .... Acts 19:4   4100
of Jews there are which *b* .... Acts 21:20   4100
As touching the Gentiles which *b* .... Acts 21:25   4100
for I *b* God, that it shall be .... Acts 27:25   4100
For what if some did not *b* .... Rom 3:3   569
unto all and upon all them that *b* .... Rom 3:22   4100
be the father of all them that *b* .... Rom 4:11   4100
if we *b* on him that raised up .... Rom 4:24   4100
we *b* that we shall also live with .... Rom 6:8   4100
shalt in thine heart that God .... Rom 10:9   4100
how shall they *b* in him of whom .... Rom 10:14   4100
from them that do not *b* in Judaea .... Rom 15:31   544
of preaching to save them that *b* 1Cor 1:21   4100
If any of them that *b* not bid you 1Cor 10:27   571
and I partly *b* it 1Cor 11:18   4100
for a sign, not to them that *b* 1Cor 14:22   4100
but to them that *b* not 1Cor 14:22   571
serveth not for them that *b* 1Cor 14:22   571
but for them which *b* 1Cor 14:22   4100
the minds of them which *b* not 2Cor 4:4   571
we also *b*, and therefore speak 2Cor 4:13   4100
might be given to them that *b* .... Gal 3:22   4100
of his power to us-ward who *b* .... Eph 1:19   4100
of Christ, not only to *b* on him .... Phil 1:29   4100
to all that *b* in Macedonia 1Th 1:7   4100
ourselves among you that *b* 1Th 2:10   4100
worketh also in you that *b* 1Th 2:13   4100
For if we *b* that Jesus died and 1Th 4:14   4100
b (because our testimony among 2Th 1:10   4100
that they should *b* a lie 2Th 2:11   4100
b on him to life everlasting 1Ti 1:16   4100
with thanksgiving of them which *b* 1Ti 4:3   4103
men, specially of those that *b* 1Ti 4:10   4103
If we *b* not, yet he abideth 2Ti 2:13   569
but of them that *b* to the saving .... Heb 10:39   4102
cometh to God must *b* that he is .... Heb 11:6   4100
the devils also *b*, and tremble .... Jas 2:19   4100
Who by him do *b* in God, that 1Pet 1:21   4100
therefore which *b* he is precious 1Pet 2:7   4100
That we should *b* on the name of 1Jn 3:23   4100
b not every spirit, but try the 1Jn 4:1   4100
have I written unto you that *b* on 1Jn 5:13   4100
that ye may *b* on the name of the 1Jn 5:13   4100

BELIEVED

And he *b* in the LORD .... Gen 15:6   539
heart fainted, for he *b* them not .... Gen 45:26   539
And the people *b* .... Ex 4:31   539
b the LORD, and his servant Moses .... Ex 14:31   539
and Aaron, Because ye *b* me not .... Num 20:12   539
ye *b* him not, nor hearkened to .... Deut 9:23   539
And Achish *b* David, saying, He 1Sa 27:12   539
Howbeit I *b* not the words, until 1Kin 10:7   539
Howbeit I *b* not their words, ... 2Chr 9:6   539
I laughed on them, they *b* it not .... Job 29:24   539
unless I had *b* to see the .... Ps 27:13   539
Because they *b* not in God .... Ps 78:22   539
b not for his wondrous works .... Ps 78:32   539
Then *b* they his words .... Ps 106:12   539
land, they *b* not his word .... Ps 106:24   539
I *b*, therefore have I spoken .... Ps 116:10   539
for I have *b* thy commandments .... Ps 119:66   539
Who hath *b* our report .... Is 53:1   539
the son of Ahikam *b* them not .... Jer 40:14   539
would not have *b* that the .... Lam 4:12   539
upon him, because he *b* in his God .... Dan 6:23   540
So the people of Nineveh *b* God .... Jonah 3:5   539
and as thou hast *b*, so be it done .... Mt 8:13   4100
of righteousness, and ye *b* him not .... Mt 21:32   4100
publicans and the harlots *b* him .... Mt 21:32   4100
and had been seen of her, *b* not .... Mk 16:11   569
neither *b* they them .... Mk 16:13   4100
because they *b* not them which had ...... Mk 16:14   4100
which are most surely *b* among us .... Lk 1:1   4135
And blessed is she that *b* .... Lk 1:45   4100
will say, Why then *b* ye him not .... Lk 20:5   4100
as idle tales, and they *b* them not .... Lk 24:11   569
And while they yet *b* not for joy .... Lk 24:41   569
and his disciples *b* on him .... Jn 2:11   4100
they *b* the scripture, and the word .... Jn 2:22   4100
many *b* in his name, when they saw ...... Jn 2:23   4100

because he hath not *b* in the name .... Jn 3:18   4100
b on him for the saying of the .... Jn 4:39   4100
many more *b* because of his own .... Jn 4:41   4100
the man *b* the word that Jesus had .... Jn 4:50   4100
and himself *b*, and his whole house .... Jn 4:53   4100
b Moses, ye would have *b* me .... Jn 5:46   4100
who they were that *b* not, and who .... Jn 6:64   4100
And many of the people *b* on him .... Jn 7:31   4100
or of the Pharisees *b* on him .... Jn 7:48   4100
spake these words, many *b* on him .... Jn 8:30   4100
to those Jews which *b* on him .... Jn 8:31   4100
them, I told you, and ye *b* not .... Jn 10:25   4100
And many *b* on him there .... Jn 10:42   4100
things which Jesus did, and *b* on him .... Jn 11:45   4100
the Jews went away, and *b* on Jesus ...... Jn 12:11   4100
them, yet they *b* not on him .... Jn 12:37   4100
Lord, who hath *b* our report .... Jn 12:38   4100
chief rulers also many *b* on him .... Jn 12:42   4100
have *b* that I came out from God .... Jn 16:27   4100
they have *b* that thou didst send .... Jn 17:8   4100
to the sepulchre, and he saw, and *b* ...... Jn 20:8   4100
thou hast seen me, thou hast *b* .... Jn 20:29   4100
that have not seen, and yet have *b* .... Jn 20:29   4100
all that *b* were together, and had .... Acts 2:44   4100
of them which heard the word *b* .... Acts 4:4   4100
of them that *b* were of one heart .... Acts 4:32   4100
But when they *b* Philip preaching .... Acts 8:12   4100
Then Simon himself *b* also .... Acts 8:13   4100
b not that he was a disciple .... Acts 9:26   4100
and many *b* in the Lord .... Acts 9:42   4100
which *b* were astonished, as many .... Acts 10:45   4103
who *b* on the Lord Jesus Christ .... Acts 11:17   4100
and a great number *b*, and turned .... Acts 11:21   4100
when he saw what was done, *b* .... Acts 13:12   4100
were ordained to eternal life *b* .... Acts 13:48   4100
the Jews and also of the Greeks *b* .... Acts 14:1   4100
them to the Lord, on whom they *b* .... Acts 14:23   4100
the sect of the Pharisees which *b* .... Acts 15:5   4100
woman, which was a Jewess, and *b* .... Acts 16:1   4103
And some of them *b*, and consorted ...... Acts 17:4   3982
But the Jews which *b* not, moved .... Acts 17:5   544
Therefore many of them *b* .... Acts 17:12   4100
certain men clave unto him, and *b* .... Acts 17:34   4100
b on the Lord with all his house .... Acts 18:8   4100
many of the Corinthians hearing *b* .... Acts 18:8   4100
much which had *b* through grace .... Acts 18:27   4100
the Holy Ghost since ye *b* .... Acts 19:2   4100
b not, but spake evil of that way .... Acts 19:9   544
And many that *b* came, and confessed .. Acts 19:18   4100
synagogue them that *b* on thee .... Acts 22:19   4100
the centurion *b* the master .... Acts 27:11   3982
some *b* the things which were .... Acts 28:24   3982
which were spoken, and some *b* not ...... Acts 28:24   544
b God, and it was counted .... Rom 4:3   569,4100
nations,) before him whom he *b* .... Rom 4:17   4100
Who against hope *b* in hope .... Rom 4:18   4100
on him in whom they have not *b* .... Rom 10:14   4100
Lord, who hath *b* our report .... Rom 10:16   4100
ye in times past have not *b* God .... Rom 11:30   544
Even so have these also now not *b* .... Rom 11:31   544
salvation nearer than when we *b* .... Rom 13:11   4100
but ministers by whom ye *b* 1Cor 3:5   4100
you, unless ye *b* in vain 1Cor 15:2   4100
or they, so we preach, and so ye *b* 1Cor 15:11   4100
according as it is written, I *b* 2Cor 4:13   4100
even we have *b* in Jesus Christ, ... Gal 2:16   4100
Even as Abraham *b* God, and it was ...... Gal 3:6   4100
in whom also after that ye *b* .... Eph 1:13   4100
among you was *b*) in that day 2Th 1:10   4100
be damned who *b* not the truth 2Th 2:12   4100
b on in the world, received up 1Ti 3:16   4100
for I know whom I have *b*, and am 2Ti 1:12   4100
that they which have *b* in God .... Titus 3:8   4100
his rest, but to them that *b* not .... Heb 3:18   544
For we which have *b* do enter into .... Heb 4:3   4100
perished not with them that *b* not .... Heb 11:31   544
which saith, Abraham *b* God .... Jas 2:23   4100
b the love that God hath to us 1Jn 4:16   4100
destroyed them that *b* not .... Jude 5   4100

BELIEVERS

b were the more added to the Lord .... Acts 5:14   4100
but be thou an example of the *b* 1Ti 4:12   4103

BELIEVEST

because thou *b* not my words .... Lk 1:20   4100
thee under the fig tree, *b* thou .... Jn 1:50   4100
B thou this .... Jn 11:26   4100
B thou not that I am in the .... Jn 14:10   4100
If thou *b* with all thine heart, ... Acts 8:37   4100
King Agrippa, *b* thou the prophets .... Acts 26:27   4100

B

I know that thou *b*	Acts 26:27	*4100*
Thou *b* that there is one God	Jas 2:19	*4100*

BELIEVETH

He *b* not that he shall return out	Job 15:22	*539*
neither *b* he that it is the sound	Job 39:24	*539*
The simple *b* every word	Prov 14:15	*539*
he that *b* shall not make haste	Is 28:16	*539*
things are possible to him that *b*	Mk 9:23	*4100*
He that *b* and is baptized shall be	Mk 16:16	*4100*
but he that *b* not shall be damned	Mk 16:16	*569*
That whosoever *b* in him should	Jn 3:15	*4100*
that whosoever *b* in him should	Jn 3:16	*4100*
He that *b* on him is not condemned	Jn 3:18	*4100*
but he that *b* not is condemned	Jn 3:18	*4100*
He that *b* on the Son hath	Jn 3:36	*4100*
he that *b* not the Son shall not	Jn 3:36	*544*
b on him that sent me, hath	Jn 5:24	*4100*
he that *b* on me shall never	Jn 6:35	*4100*
b on him, may have everlasting	Jn 6:40	*4100*
He that *b* on me hath everlasting	Jn 6:47	*4100*
He that *b* on me, as the scripture	Jn 7:38	*4100*
he that *b* in me, though he were	Jn 11:25	*4100*
liveth and *b* in me shall never die	Jn 11:26	*4100*
cried and said, He that *b* on me	Jn 12:44	*4100*
b not on me, but on him that sent	Jn 12:44	*4100*
that whosoever *b* on me should not	Jn 12:46	*4100*
I say unto you, He that *b* on me	Jn 14:12	*4100*
b in him shall receive remission	Acts 10:43	*4100*
salvation to every one that *b*	Rom 1:16	*4100*
justifier of him which *b* in Jesus	Rom 3:26	*1537,4102*
but *b* on him that justifieth the	Rom 4:5	*4100*
whosoever *b* on him shall not be	Rom 9:33	*4100*
righteousness to every one that *b*	Rom 10:4	*4100*
heart man to *b* unto righteousness	Rom 10:10	*4100*
Whosoever *b* on him shall not be	Rom 10:11	*4100*
For one *b* that he may eat all	Rom 14:2	*4100*
brother hath a wife that *b* not	1Cor 7:12	*571*
which hath an husband that *b* not	1Cor 7:13	*571*
b all things, hopeth all things	1Cor 13:7	*4100*
and there come in one that *b* not	1Cor 14:24	*571*
hath he that *b* with an infidel	2Cor 6:15	*4103*
man or woman that *b* have widows	1Ti 5:16	*4103*
he that *b* on him shall not be	1Pet 2:6	*4100*
Whosoever *b* that Jesus is the	1Jn 5:1	*4100*
but he that *b* that Jesus is the	1Jn 5:5	*4100*
He that *b* on the Son of God hath	1Jn 5:10	*4100*
he that *b* not God hath made him a	1Jn 5:10	*4100*
because he *b* not the record that	1Jn 5:10	*4100*

BELIEVING

ye shall ask in prayer, *b*	Mt 21:22	*4100*
and be not faithless, but *b*	Jn 20:27	*4103*
that *b* ye might have life through	Jn 20:31	*4100*
b in God with all his house	Acts 16:34	*4100*
b all things which are written in	Acts 24:14	*4100*
you with all joy and peace in *b*	Rom 15:13	*4100*
And they that have *b* masters	1Ti 6:2	*4103*
though now ye see him not, yet *b*	1Pet 1:8	*4100*

BELL

A golden *b* and a pomegranate	Ex 28:34	*6472*
and a pomegranate, a golden *b*	Ex 28:34	*6472*
A *b* and a pomegranate, a *b* and a	Ex 39:26	*6472*

BELLIES

alway liars, evil beasts, slow *b*	Titus 1:12	*1064*

BELLOW

heifer at grass, and *b* as bulls	Jer 50:11	*6670*

BELLOWS

The *b* are burned, the lead is	Jer 6:29	*4647*

BELLS

b of gold between them round	Ex 28:33	*6472*
they made *b* of pure gold	Ex 39:25	*6472*
and put the *b* between the	Ex 39:25	*6472*
there be upon the *b* of the horses	Zec 14:20	*4698*

BELLY

upon thy *b* shalt thou go, and dust	Gen 3:14	*1512*
Whatsoever goeth upon the *b*	Lev 11:42	*1512*
thigh to rot, and thy *b* to swell	Num 5:21	*990*
bowels, to make thy *b* to swell	Num 5:22	*990*
her *b* shall swell, and her thigh	Num 5:27	*990*
and the woman through her *b*	Num 25:8	*6897*
thigh, and thrust it into his *b*	Judg 3:21	*990*
not draw the dagger out of his *b*	Judg 3:22	*990*
over against the *b* which was by	1Kin 7:20	*990*
ghost when I came out of the *b*	Job 3:11	*990*
fill his *b* with the east wind	Job 15:2	*990*
and their *b* prepareth deceit	Job 15:35	*990*
God shall cast them out of his *b*	Job 20:15	*990*
shall not feel quietness in his *b*	Job 20:20	*990*

When he is about to fill his *b*	Job 20:23	990
my *b* is as wine which hath no	Job 32:19	990
force is in the navel of his *b*	Job 40:16	990
whose *b* thou fillest with thy hid	Ps 17:14	990
art my God from my mother's *b*	Ps 22:10	990
with grief, yea, my soul and my *b*	Ps 31:9	990
our *b* cleaveth unto the earth	Ps 44:25	990
but the *b* of the wicked shall	Prov 13:25	990
into the innermost parts of the *b*	Prov 18:8	990
A man's *b* shall be satisfied with	Prov 18:20	990
all the inward parts of the *b*	Prov 20:27	990
stripes the inward parts of the *b*	Prov 20:30	990
into the innermost parts of the *b*	Prov 26:22	990
his *b* is as bright ivory overlaid	Song 5:14	4578
thy *b* is like an heap of wheat	Song 7:2	990
which are borne by me from the *b*	Is 46:3	990
formed thee in the *b* I knew thee	Jer 1:5	990
filled his *b* with my delicates	Jer 51:34	3770
Son of man, cause thy *b* to eat	Eze 3:3	990
and his arms of silver, his *b*	Dan 2:32	4577
Jonah was in the *b* of the fish	Jonah 1:17	4578
LORD his God out of the fish's *b*	Jonah 2:1	4578
out of the *b* of hell cried I, and	Jonah 2:2	990
When I heard, my *b* trembled	Hab 3:16	990
and three nights in the whale's *b*	Mt 12:40	*2836*
in at the mouth goeth into the *b*	Mt 15:17	*2836*
into his heart, but into the *b*	Mk 7:19	*2836*
b with the husks that the swine	Lk 15:16	*2836*
out of his *b* shall flow rivers of	Jn 7:38	*2836*
Jesus Christ, but their own *b*	Rom 16:18	*2836*
Meats for the *b*, and the *b* for	1Cor 6:13	*2836*
destruction, whose God is their *b*	Phil 3:19	*2836*
and it shall make thy *b* bitter	Rev 10:9	*2836*
I had eaten it, my *b* was bitter	Rev 10:10	*2836*

BELONG

Do not interpretations *b* to God	Gen 40:8	
the possession of the land did *b*	Lev 27:24	
and over all things that *b* to it	Num 1:50	
The secret things *b* unto the LORD	Deut 29:29	
which are revealed *b* unto us	Deut 29:29	
shields of the earth *b* unto God	Ps 47:9	
unto GOD the Lord *b* the issues	Ps 68:20	
These things also *b* to the wise	Prov 24:23	
To the Lord our God *b* mercies	Dan 9:9	
my name, because ye *b* to Christ	Mk 9:41	*1510*
the things which *b* unto thy peace	Lk 19:42	
for the things that *b* to the Lord	1Cor 7:32	

BELONGED

on the border of Manasseh *b* to	Josh 17:8	
of the herdmen that *b* to Saul	1Sa 21:7	
the mighty men which *b* to David	1Kin 1:8	
which *b* to the Philistines	1Kin 15:27	
which *b* to the Philistines	1Kin 16:15	
which *b* to Judah, for Israel, are	2Kin 14:28	
All these *b* to the sons of Machir	1Chr 2:23	
which *b* to Judah, to bring up	1Chr 13:6	
the burial which *b* to the kings	2Chr 26:23	
house which *b* to king Ahasuerus	Est 1:9	
with such things as *b* to her	Est 2:9	*4490*
he *b* unto Herod's jurisdiction	Lk 23:7	*1510*

BELONGEST

said unto him, To whom *b* thou	1Sa 30:13	

BELONGETH

This is it that *b* unto the	Num 8:24	
To me *b* vengeance, and recompence	Deut 32:35	
by Gibeah, which *b* to Benjamin	Judg 19:14	
into Gibeah that *b* to Benjamin	Judg 20:4	
which *b* to Judah, and pitched	1Sa 17:1	
upon the coast which *b* to Judah	1Sa 30:14	
which *b* to Zidon, and dwell there	1Kin 17:9	
which *b* to Judah, and left his	1Kin 19:3	
at Beth-shemesh, which *b* to Judah	2Kin 14:11	
at Beth-shemesh, which *b* to Judah	2Chr 25:21	
for this matter *b* unto thee	Ezr 10:4	
Salvation *b* unto the LORD	Ps 3:8	
that power *b* unto God	Ps 62:11	
Also unto thee, O Lord, *b* mercy	Ps 62:12	
O LORD God, to whom vengeance *b*	Ps 94:1	
O God, to whom vengeance *b*	Ps 94:1	
O Lord, righteousness *b* unto thee	Dan 9:7	
to us *b* confusion of face, to our	Dan 9:8	
But strong meat *b* to them that	Heb 5:14	*1510*
hath said, Vengeance *b* unto me	Heb 10:30	

BELONGING

the service of the sanctuary *b*	Num 7:9	
a part of the field *b* unto Boaz	Ruth 2:3	
Philistines *b* to the five lords	1Sa 6:18	

meddleth with strife *b* not to him .... Prov 26:17
b to the city called Bethsaida .... Lk 9:10

BELOVED

If a man have two wives, one *b* .... Deut 21:15	157
born him children, both the *b* .... Deut 21:15	157
he may not make the son of the *b* .... Deut 21:16	157
The *b* of the LORD shall dwell in............ Deut 33:12	3039
who was *b* of his God, and God made ... Neh 13:26	157
That thy *b* may be delivered .... Ps 60:5	3039
That thy *b* may be delivered .... Ps 108:6	3039
for so he giveth his *b* sleep.................... Ps 127:2	3039
only *b* in the sight of my mother .... Prov 4:3	
My *b* is unto me as a cluster of .... Song 1:14	1730
Behold, thou art fair, my *b*.................... Song 1:16	157
so is my *b* among the sons .... Song 2:3	1730
The voice of my *b*................................ Song 2:8	1730
My *b* is like a roe or a young .... Song 2:9	1730
My *b* spake, and said unto me, Rise ..... Song 2:10	1730
My *b* is mine, and I am his .... Song 2:16	1730
the shadows flee away, turn, my *b*........ Song 2:17	1730
Let my *b* come into his garden, and ...... Song 4:16	1730
drink, yea, drink abundantly, O *b*.......... Song 5:1	1730
the voice of my *b* that knocketh .... Song 5:2	1730
My *b* put in his hand by the hole .... Song 5:4	1730
I rose up to open to my *b* .... Song 5:5	1730
I opened to my *b* .... Song 5:6	1730
but my *b* had withdrawn himself,.......... Song 5:6	1730
of Jerusalem, if ye find my *b* .... Song 5:8	1730
thy *b* more than another *b* .... Song 5:9	1730
thy *b* more than another *b* .... Song 5:9	1730
My *b* is white and ruddy, the .... Song 5:10	1730
This is my *b*, and this is my .... Song 5:16	1730
Whither is thy *b* gone, O thou.............. Song 6:1	1730
whither is thy *b* turned aside .... Song 6:1	1730
My *b* is gone down into his garden .... Song 6:2	1730
am my beloved's, and my *b* is mine ...... Song 6:3	1730
mouth like the best wine for my *b*......... Song 7:9	1730
Come, my *b*, let us go forth into .... Song 7:11	1730
I have laid up for thee, O my *b* .... Song 7:13	1730
wilderness, leaning upon her *b*............. Song 8:5	1730
Make haste, my *b*, and be thou like ...... Song 8:14	1730
of my *b* touching his vineyard................ Is 5:1	1730
What hath my *b* to do in mine .... Jer 11:15	3039
I have given the dearly *b* of my .... Jer 12:7	3033
for thou art greatly *b*.......................... Dan 9:23	2530
me, O Daniel, a man greatly *b* .... Dan 10:11	2530
And said, O man greatly *b*, fear .... Dan 10:19	2530
love a woman *b* of her friend, yet.......... Hos 3:1	157
even the *b* fruit of their womb.............. Hos 9:16	4261
heaven, saying, This is my *b* Son .... Mt 3:17	27
my *b*, in whom my soul is well .... Mt 12:18	27
which said, This is my *b* Son .... Mt 17:5	27
heaven, saying, Thou art my *b* Son .... Mk 1:11	27
cloud, saying, This is my *b* Son........... Mk 9:7	27
which said, Thou art my *b* Son............. Lk 3:22	27
cloud, saying, This is my *b* Son............ Lk 9:35	27
I will send my *b* son .... Lk 20:13	27
men unto you with our *b* Barnabas........ Acts 15:25	27
b of God, called to be saints .... Rom 1:7	27
and her *b*, which was not *b* .... Rom 9:25	27
they are *b* for the fathers' sakes .... Rom 11:28	27
Dearly *b*, avenge not yourselves, ... Rom 12:19	27
Greet Amplias my *b* in the Lord............ Rom 16:8	27
helper in Christ, and Stachys my *b* .... Rom 16:9	27
Salute the *b* Persis, which .... Rom 16:12	27
but as my *b* sons I warn you 1Cor 4:14	27
you Timotheus, who is my *b* son........... 1Cor 4:17	27
Wherefore, my dearly *b*, flee from 1Cor 10:14	27
my *b* brethren, be ye stedfast, ... 1Cor 15:58	27
therefore these promises dearly *b* 2Cor 7:1	27
but we do all things, dearly *b* 2Cor 12:19	27
he hath made us accepted in the *b* .... Eph 1:6	25
a *b* brother and faithful minister .... Eph 6:21	27
Wherefore, my *b*, as ye have .... Phil 2:12	27
Therefore, my brethren dearly *b*............ Phil 4:1	27
fast in the Lord, my dearly *b*............... Phil 4:1	27
as the elect of God, holy and *b* .... Col 3:12	25
unto you, who is a *b* brother .... Col 4:7	27
b brother, who is one of you .... Col 4:9	27
the *b* physician, and Demas, greet .... Col 4:14	27
Knowing, brethren *b*, your 1Th 1:4	25
brethren *b* of the Lord, because............ 2Th 2:13	25
because they are faithful and *b* 1Ti 6:2	27
To Timothy, my dearly *b* son 2Ti 1:2	27
unto Philemon our dearly *b*.................. Philem 1	27
And to our *b* Apphia, and Archippus ..... Philem 2	27
but above a servant, a brother *b* .... Philem 16	27
But, *b*, we are persuaded better .... Heb 6:9	27
Do not err, my *b* brethren .... Jas 1:16	27
my *b* brethren, let every man be .... Jas 1:19	27

my *b* brethren, Hath not God .... Jas 2:5	27
Dearly *b*, I beseech you as 1Pet 2:11	27
B, think it not strange............................ 1Pet 4:12	27
excellent glory, This is my *b* Son 2Pet 1:17	27
This second epistle, *b*, I now 2Pet 3:1	27
But, *b*, be not ignorant of this 2Pet 3:8	27
Wherefore, *b*, seeing that ye look 2Pet 3:14	27
even as our *b* brother Paul also............. 2Pet 3:15	27
Ye therefore, *b*, seeing ye know 2Pet 3:17	27
B, now are we the sons of God, and 1Jn 3:2	27
B, if our heart condemn us not, ... 1Jn 3:21	27
B, believe not every spirit, but 1Jn 4:1	27
B, let us love one another 1Jn 4:7	27
B, if God so loved us, we ought............. 1Jn 4:11	27
B, I wish above all things that 3Jn 2	27
B, thou doest faithfully 3Jn 5	27
B, follow not that which is evil 3Jn 11	27
B, when I gave all diligence to .... Jude 3	27
But, *b*, remember ye the words .... Jude 17	27
But ye, *b*, building up yourselves........... Jude 20	27
the saints about, and the *b* city .... Rev 20:9	25

BELOVED'S

I am my *b*, and my beloved is mine .... Song 6:3	1730
I am my *b*, and his desire is................... Song 7:10	1730

BELSHAZZAR *(bel-shaz'-ar) A Babylonian king.*

B the king made a great feast to........... Dan 5:1	1113
B, whiles he tasted the wine,................ Dan 5:2	1113
Then was king *B* greatly troubled,......... Dan 5:9	1113
And thou his son, O *B*, hast not .... Dan 5:22	1113
Then commanded *B*, and they clothed ... Dan 5:29	1113
In that night was *B* the king of.............. Dan 5:30	1113
In the first year of *B* king of .... Dan 7:1	1113
king *B* a vision appeared unto me.......... Dan 8:1	1113

BELTESHAZZAR *(bel-te-shaz'-ar)* See DANIEL. *The Babylonian name given to Daniel.*

he gave unto Daniel the name of *B* .... Dan 1:7	1095
said to Daniel, whose name was *B* .... Dan 2:26	1096
in before me, whose name was *B* .... Dan 4:8	1096
O *B*, master of the magicians, ... Dan 4:9	1096
Now thou, O *B*, declare the .... Dan 4:18	1096
Then Daniel, whose name was *B* .... Dan 4:19	1096
The king spake, and said, *B* .... Dan 4:19	1096
B answered and said, My lord, the .... Dan 4:19	1096
Daniel, whom the king named *B* .... Dan 5:12	1096
Daniel, whose name was called *B* .... Dan 10:1	1095

BEMOAN

or who shall *b* thee .... Jer 15:5	5110
neither go to lament nor *b* them .... Jer 16:5	5110
not for the dead, neither *b* him .... Jer 22:10	5110
All ye that are about him, *b* him .... Jer 48:17	5110
who will *b* her .... Nah 3:7	5110

BEMOANED

and they *b* him, and comforted him .... Job 42:11	5110

BEMOANING

heard Ephraim *b* himself thus .... Jer 31:18	5110

BEN *(ben) A Levite.*

the second degree, Zechariah, *B*............ 1Chr 15:18	1122

BENAIAH *(ben-ay'-ah)*

1. An officer of David.

B the son of Jehoiada was over 2Sa 8:18	1141
B the son of Jehoiada was over 2Sa 20:23	1141
B the son of Jehoiada, the son of 2Sa 23:20	1141
These things did *B* the son of................ 2Sa 23:22	1141
B the son of Jehoiada, and Nathan 1Kin 1:8	1141
But Nathan the prophet, and *B*.............. 1Kin 1:10	1141
B the son of Jehoiada, and thy.............. 1Kin 1:26	1141
prophet, and *B* the son of Jehoiada 1Kin 1:32	1141
B the son of Jehoiada answered 1Kin 1:36	1141
B the son of Jehoiada, and the 1Kin 1:38	1141
B the son of Jehoiada, and the 1Kin 1:44	1141
the hand of *B* the son of Jehoiada 1Kin 2:25	1141
Then Solomon sent *B* the son of 1Kin 2:29	1141
B came to the tabernacle of the............. 1Kin 2:30	1141
B brought the king word again,............. 1Kin 2:30	1141
So *B* the son of Jehoiada went up,......... 1Kin 2:34	1141
the king put *B* the son of 1Kin 2:35	1141
commanded *B* the son of Jehoiada 1Kin 2:46	1141
B the son of Jehoiada was over 1Kin 4:4	1141
B the son of Jehoiada, the son of 1Chr 11:22	1141
These things did *B* the son of 1Chr 11:24	1141
B the son of Jehoiada was over 1Chr 18:17	1141
month was *B* the son of Jehoiada 1Chr 27:5	1141
This is that *B*, who was mighty 1Chr 27:6	1141

2. A "mighty man" of David.

B the Pirathonite, Hiddai of the 2Sa 23:30	1141
of Benjamin, *B* the Pirathonite, ... 1Chr 11:31	1141
month was *B* the Pirathonite 1Chr 27:14	1141

3. A Simeonite family chief.
and Adiel, and Jesimiel, and *B* 1Chr 4:36 1141
4. A priest of David.
and Jehiel, and Unni, Eliab, and *B* 1Chr 15:18 1141
Unni, and Eliab, and Maaseiah, and *B* ..1Chr 15:20 1141
and Amasai, and Zechariah, and *B* 1Chr 15:24 1141
and Mattithiah, and Eliab, and *B* 1Chr 16:5 1141
B also and Jahaziel the priests..............1Chr 16:6 1141
5. Father of Jehoida.
was Jehoiada the son of *B* 1Chr 27:34 1141
6. Grandfather of Jehaziel.
son of Zechariah, the son of *B* 2Chr 20:14 1141
7. A Levite during Hezekiah's reign.
and Ismachiah, and Mahath, and *B* 2Chr 31:13 1141
8. A descendant of Parosh.
and Eleazar, and Malchijah, and *B* ....Ezr 10:25 1141
9. A son of Pahath-moab.
Adna, and Chelal, *B*, Maaseiah, ...Ezr 10:30 1141
10. A son of Bani.
B, Bedeiah, Chelluh,...............................Ezr 10:35 1141
11. A son of Nebo.
Zabad, Zebina, Jadau, and Joel, *B*..........Ezr 10:43 1141
12. Father of Pelatiah.
of Azur, and Pelatiah the son of *B* ....Eze 11:1 1141
that Pelatiah the son of *B* died ....Eze 11:13 1141

BEN-AMMI *(ben-am'-mi) A son of Lot.*
bare a son, and called his name *B* ....Gen 19:38 1151

BENCHES
have made thy *b* of ivory, brought ....Eze 27:6 7175

BEND
For, lo, the wicked *b* their bow ....Ps 11:2 1869
b their bows to shoot their ....Ps 64:3 1869
they *b* their tongues like their.................Jer 9:3 1869
Lydians, that handle and *b* the bow ......Jer 46:9 1869
all ye that *b* the bow, shoot at................Jer 50:14 1869
all ye that *b* the bow, camp ....Jer 50:29 1869
bendeth let the archer *b* his bow ....Jer 51:3 1869
this vine did *b* her roots toward ....Eze 17:7 3719

BEN DEKER See DEKAR.

BENDETH
when he *b* his bow to shoot his..............Ps 58:7 1869
Against him that *b* let the archer ....Jer 51:3 1869

BENDING
thee shall come *b* unto thee ....Is 60:14 7817

BENEATH See APPENDIX.

BENE BARAK See BENE-BERAK.

BENE-BERAK *(be'-ne-be'-rak) A city in Dan.*
And Jehud, and *B*, and Gath-rimmon, ...Josh 19:45 1138

BENEFACTORS
authority upon them are called *b* ....Lk 22:25 2110

BENEFIT
according to the *b* done unto him...........2Chr 32:25 1576
wherewith I said I would *b* them.............Jer 18:10 3190
that ye might have a second *b* 2Cor 1:15 5485
and beloved, partakers of the *b* 1Ti 6:2 2108
that thy *b* should not be as it ....Philem 14 18

BENEFITS
Lord, who daily loadeth us with *b* ....Ps 68:19
my soul, and forget not all his *b* ....Ps 103:2 1576
the LORD for all his *b* toward me............Ps 116:12 8408

BENE JAAKAN See BENE-JAAKAN.

BENE-JAAKAN *(be'-ne-ja'-a-kan) Namesake of several wells.*
from Moseroth, and pitched in *B* ....Num 33:31 1142
And they removed from *B*, and ....Num 33:32 1142

BENEVOLENCE
render unto the wife due *b* 1Cor 7:3 2133

BEN-HADAD *(ben'-ha-dad)*
1. A Syrian king, son of Tabrimon.
and king Asa sent them to *B* 1Kin 15:18 1131
So *B* hearkened unto king Asa, and.......1Kin 15:20 1131
sent to *B* king of Syria, that 2Chr 16:2 1130
B hearkened unto king Asa, and 2Chr 16:4 1130
2. A Syrian king during Ahab's reign.
B the king of Syria gathered all 1Kin 20:1 1131
and said unto him, Thus saith *B* 1Kin 20:2 1131
again, and said, Thus speaketh *B* 1Kin 20:5 1131
he said unto the messengers of *B* 1Kin 20:9 1131
B sent unto him, and said, The 1Kin 20:10 1131
when *B* heard this message, as he 1Kin 20:12
But *B* was drinking himself drunk 1Kin 20:16 1130
B sent out, and they told him, ...1Kin 20:17 1130
B the king of Syria escaped on an 1Kin 20:20 1130

that *B* numbered the Syrians, and 1Kin 20:26 1130
B fled, and came into the city,................1Kin 20:30 1130
and said, Thy servant *B* saith 1Kin 20:32 1130
and they said, Thy brother *B*...................1Kin 20:32 1130
Then *B* came forth to him 1Kin 20:33 1130
B said unto him, The cities, ...1Kin 20:34
that *B* king of Syria gathered all 2Kin 6:24 1130
B the king of Syria was sick 2Kin 8:7 1130
Thy son *B* king of Syria hath sent 2Kin 8:9 1130
3. A Syrian king, son of Hazael.
into the hand of *B* the son of 2Kin 13:3 1130
B his son reigned in his stead................2Kin 13:24 1130
of *B* the son of Hazael the cities 2Kin 13:25 1130
shall devour the palaces of *B* ....Amos 1:4 1130
4. A title for all the Syrian kings.
it shall consume the palaces of *B* ....Jer 49:27 1130

BEN-HAIL *(ben-ha'-il) A prince of Judah.*
he sent to his princes, even to *B* 2Chr 17:7 1134

BEN-HANAN *(ben-ha'-nan) A son of Shimon.*
Shimon were, Amnon, and Rinnah, *B* 1Chr 4:20 1135

BENINU *(ben'-i-nu) A Levite who renewed the covenant.*
Hodijah, Bani, *B* ....Neh 10:13 1148

BENJAMIN *(ben'-ja-min)* See BENJAMIN'S, BENJAMITE.
1. Youngest son of Jacob.
but his father called him *B*......................Gen 35:18 1144
Joseph, and *B* ....Gen 35:24 1144
But *B*, Joseph's brother, Jacob ....Gen 42:4 1144
is not, and ye will take *B* away ....Gen 42:36 1144
away your other brother, and *B* ....Gen 43:14 1144
double money in their hand, and *B* ....Gen 43:15 1144
And when Joseph saw *B* with them ....Gen 43:16 1144
up his eyes, and saw his brother *B* ....Gen 43:29 1144
see, and the eyes of my brother *B* ....Gen 45:12 1144
and *B* wept upon his neck ....Gen 45:14 1144
but to *B* he gave three hundred ....Gen 45:22 1144
Joseph, and *B* ....Gen 46:19 1144
And the sons of *B* were Belah ....Gen 46:21 1144
Issachar, Zebulun, and *B*, ...Ex 1:3 1144
Dan, Joseph, and *B*, Naphtali, Gad,.......1Chr 2:2 1144
The sons of *B* 1Chr 7:6 1144
Now *B* begat Bela his firstborn, ...1Chr 8:1 1144
2. One of the twelve tribes comprising Israel.
B shall ravin as a wolf: ....Gen 49:27 1144
Of *B* ....Num 1:11 1144
Of the children of *B*, by their ....Num 1:36 1144
of them, even of the tribe of *B* ....Num 1:37 1144
Then the tribe of *B* ....Num 2:22 1144
of *B* shall be Abidan the son of ....Num 2:22 1144
prince of the children of *B* ....Num 7:60 1144
B was Abidan the son of Gideoni ....Num 10:24 1144
Of the tribe of *B*, Palti the son ....Num 13:9 1144
The sons of *B* after their ....Num 26:38 1144
sons of *B* after their families ....Num 26:41 1144
Of the tribe of *B*, Elidad the son ....Num 34:21 1144
and Issachar, and Joseph, and *B* ....Deut 27:12 1144
of *B* he said, The beloved of the ....Deut 33:12 1144
of *B* came up according to their ....Josh 18:11 1144
inheritance of the children of *B* ....Josh 18:20 1144
of *B* according to their families...............Josh 18:21 1144
of *B* according to their families...............Josh 18:28 1144
Simeon, and out of the tribe of *B* ....Josh 21:4 1144
And out of the tribe of *B*, Gibeon ....Josh 21:17 1144
the children of *B* did not drive ....Judg 1:21 1144
of *B* in Jerusalem unto this day ....Judg 1:21 1144
after thee, *B*, among thy people ....Judg 5:14 1144
also against Judah, and against *B* ....Judg 10:9 1144
by Gibeah, which belongeth to *B* ....Judg 19:14 1144
(Now the children of *B* heard that ....Judg 20:3 1144
into Gibeah that belongeth to *B* ....Judg 20:4 1144
do, when they come to Gibeah of *B* ....Judg 20:10 1144
men through all the tribe of *B* ....Judg 20:12 1144
But the children of *B* would not ....Judg 20:13 1144
But the children of *B* gathered ....Judg 20:14 1144
the children of *B* were numbered ....Judg 20:15 1144
And the men of Israel, beside *B* ....Judg 20:17 1144
battle against the children of *B* ....Judg 20:18 1144
went out to battle against *B*...................Judg 20:20 1144
the children of *B* came forth out ....Judg 20:21 1144
the children of *B* my brother ....Judg 20:23 1144
the children of *B* the second day............Judg 20:24 1144
B went forth against them out of............Judg 20:25 1144
the children of *B* my brother ....Judg 20:28 1144
children of *B* on the third day ....Judg 20:30 1144
the children of *B* went out ....Judg 20:31 1144
And the children of *B* said.......................Judg 20:32 1144
And the LORD smote *B* before Israel.......Judg 20:35 1144
So the children of *B* saw that ....Judg 20:36 1144
B began to smite and kill of the..............Judg 20:39 1144
again, the men of *B* were amazed ....Judg 20:41 1144

there fell of *B* eighteen thousand ....Judg 20:44 1144
fell that day of *B* were twenty ....Judg 20:46 1144
again upon the children of *B* ....Judg 20:48 1144
give his daughter unto *B* to wife ....Judg 21:1 1144
repented them for *B* their brother ....Judg 21:6 1144
to speak to the children of *B* ....Judg 21:13 1144
B came again at that time ....Judg 21:14 1144
And the people repented them for *B* ......Judg 21:15 1144
the women are destroyed out of *B* ....Judg 21:16 1144
for them that be escaped of *B* ....Judg 21:17 1144
be he that giveth a wife to *B* ....Judg 21:18 1144
they commanded the children of *B* ....Judg 21:20 1144
of Shiloh, and go to the land of *B* ....Judg 21:21 1144
And the children of *B* did so ....Judg 21:23 1144
ran a man of *B* out of the army 1Sa 4:12 1144
Now there was a man of *B*, whose............1Sa 9:1 1144
thee a man out of the land of *B* 1Sa 9:16 1144
the families of the tribe of *B* 1Sa 9:21 1144
in the border of *B* 1Sa 10:2 1144
near, the tribe of *B* was taken 1Sa 10:20 1144
B to come near by their families 1Sa 10:21 1144
were with Jonathan in Gibeah of *B* 1Sa 13:2 1144
up from Gilgal unto Gibeah of *B* 1Sa 13:15 1144
with them, abode in Gibeah of *B* 1Sa 13:16 1144
of Saul in Gibeah of *B* looked 1Sa 14:16 1144
and over Ephraim, and over *B* 2Sa 2:9 1144
went over by number twelve of *B* 2Sa 2:15 1144
the children of *B* gathered 2Sa 2:25 1144
of David had smitten of *B* 2Sa 2:31 1144
Abner also spake in the ears of *B*............2Sa 3:19 1144
good to the whole house of *B* 2Sa 3:19 1144
Beerothite, of the children of *B* 2Sa 4:2 1144
Beeroth also was reckoned to *B* 2Sa 4:2 1144
were a thousand men of *B* with him 2Sa 19:17 1144
they in the country of *B* in Zelah 2Sa 21:14 1144
of Gibeah of the children of *B* 2Sa 23:29 1144
Shimei the son of Elah, in *B* 1Kin 4:18 1144
of Judah, with the tribe of *B* 1Kin 12:21 1144
unto all the house of Judah and *B* 1Kin 12:23 1144
Asa built with them Geba of *B* 1Kin 15:22 1144
And out of the tribe of *B* 1Chr 6:60 1144
of the tribe of the children of *B* 1Chr 6:65 1144
All these are of the sons of *B* 1Chr 8:40 1144
of Judah, and of the children of *B* 1Chr 9:3 1144
And of the sons of *B* 1Chr 9:7 1144
pertained to the children of *B* 1Chr 11:31 1144
bow, even of Saul's brethren of *B* 1Chr 12:2 1144
there came of the children of *B* 1Chr 12:16 1144
And of the children of *B*, the 1Chr 12:29 1144
B counted he not among them 1Chr 21:6 1144
of *B*, Jaasiel the son of Abner 1Chr 27:21 1144
B an hundred and fourscore 2Chr 11:1 1144
and to all Israel in Judah and *B* 2Chr 11:3 1144
in Judah and in *B* fenced cities 2Chr 11:10 1144
having Judah and *B* on his side 2Chr 11:12 1144
all the countries of Judah and *B* 2Chr 11:23 1144
and out of *B*, that bare shields and 2Chr 14:8 1144
ye me, Asa, and all Judah and *B* 2Chr 15:2 1144
out of all the land of Judah and *B* 2Chr 15:8 1144
And he gathered all Judah and *B* 2Chr 15:9 1144
And of *B* 2Chr 17:17 1144
throughout all Judah and *B* 2Chr 25:5 1144
the altars out of all Judah and *B* 2Chr 31:1 1144
of Israel, and of all Judah and *B* 2Chr 34:9 1144
in Jerusalem and *B* to stand to it............2Chr 34:32 1144
of the fathers of Judah and *B* ....Ezr 1:5 1144
B heard that the children of the............Ezr 4:1 1144
B gathered themselves together ....Ezr 10:9 1144
of Judah, and of the children of *B* ....Neh 11:4 1144
And these are the sons of *B* ....Neh 11:7 1144
The children also of *B* from Geba............Neh 11:31 1144
were divisions in Judah, and in *B* ....Neh 11:36 1144
There is little *B* with their ....Ps 68:27 1144
Before Ephraim and *B* and Manasseh .....Ps 80:2 1144
were in Anathoth in the land of *B* ....Jer 1:1 1144
O ye children of *B*, gather ....Jer 6:1 1144
Jerusalem, and from the land of *B*...........Jer 17:26 1144
which is in the country of *B* ....Jer 32:8 1144
take witnesses in the land of *B* ....Jer 32:44 1144
of the south, and in the land of *B* ....Jer 33:13 1144
to go into the land of *B*, to ....Jer 37:12 1144
of Judah and the border of *B* ....Eze 48:22 1144
west side, *B* shall have a portion ....Eze 48:23 1144
And by the border of *B*, from the ....Eze 48:24 1144
one gate of Joseph, one gate of *B*...........Eze 48:32 1144
at Beth-aven, after thee, O *B* ....Hos 5:8 1144
and *B* shall possess Gilead ....Obad 19 1144
of Cis, a man of the tribe of *B* ....Acts 13:21 953
of Abraham, of the tribe of *B* ....Rom 11:1 953
of Israel, of the tribe of *B* ....Phil 3:5 953
Of the tribe of *B* were sealed ....Rev 7:8 953

3. Great-grandson of Benjamin 1.
Jeush, and *B*, and Ehud, and...................1Chr 7:10 1144
4. A descendant of Harim.
B, Malluch, and Shemariah.....................Ezr 10:32 1144
5. A repairer of the Jerusalem wall.
After him repaired *B* and Hashub ....Neh 3:23 1144
6. Purified the Jerusalem wall.
Judah, and *B*, and Shemaiah, and..........Neh 12:34 1144
7. A gate of Jerusalem.
that were in the high gate of *B* ....Jer 20:2 1144
And when he was in the gate of *B* ....Jer 37:13 1144
then sitting in the gate of *B*....................Jer 38:7 1144

BENJAMIN'S (ben'-ja-mins)
1. Refers to Benjamin 1.
but *B* mess was five times so much ....Gen 43:34 1144
and the cup was found in *B* sack............Gen 44:12 1144
he fell upon his brother *B* neck..............Gen 45:14 1144
2. Refers to Benjamin 7.
from *B* gate unto the place of the ....Zec 14:10 1144

BENJAMITE (ben'-ja-mite) See BENJAMITES. *A descendant of Benjamin.*
Ehud the son of Gera, a *B* ....Judg 3:15 1145
Bechorath, the son of Aphiah, a *B* 1Sa 9:1 1145
answered and said, Am not I a *B* 1Sa 9:21 1145
much more now may this *B* do it 2Sa 16:11 1145
And Shimei the son of Gera, a *B* 2Sa 19:16 1145
was Sheba, the son of Bichri, a *B* 2Sa 20:1 1145
a *B* of Bahurim, which cursed me 1Kin 2:8 1145
of Shimei, the son of Kish, a *B* ....Est 2:5 1145
the words of Cush the *B* ....Ps 7:t 1145

BENJAMITES (ben'-ja-mites)
but the men of the place were *B* ....Judg 19:16 1145
of the *B* that day twenty and five...........Judg 20:35 1145
men of Israel gave place to the *B* ....Judg 20:36 1145
the *B* looked behind them, and,..............Judg 20:40 1145
they inclosed the *B* round about ....Judg 20:43 1145
passed through the land of the *B* 1Sa 9:4 1145
stood about him, Hear now, ye *B* 1Sa 22:7 1145
Abiezer the Anetothite, of the *B*.............1Chr 27:12 1145

BENO (be'-no) *A descendant of Merari.*
sons of Jaaziah; *B* 1Chr 24:26 1121
B, and Shoham, and Zaccur, and Ibri.....1Chr 24:27 1121

BEN-ONI (ben-o'-ni) *Rachel's second son.*
died) that she called his name *B* ....Gen 35:18 1126

BENT
he hath *b* his bow, and made it ....Ps 7:12 1869
have *b* their bow, to cast down ....Ps 37:14 1869
are sharp, and all their bows *b*...............Is 5:28 1869
drawn sword, and from the *b* bow ....Is 21:15 1869
He hath *b* his bow like an enemy ....Lam 2:4 1869
He hath *b* his bow, and set me as a........Lam 3:12 1869
my people are *b* to backsliding...............Hos 11:7 8511
When I have *b* Judah for me,...................Zec 9:13 1869

BEN-ZOHETH (ben-zo'-heth) *A descendant of Caleb.*
sons of Ishi were, Zoheth, and *B* 1Chr 4:20 1132

BEON (be'-on) *A place east of the Jordan River.*
and Shebam, and Nebo, and *B* ....Num 32:3 1194

BEOR (be'-or)
1. Father of Bela.
Bela the son of *B* reigned in Edom ....Gen 36:32 1160
Bela the son of *B* 1Chr 1:43 1160
2. Father of Balaam.
Balaam the son of *B* to Pethor ....Num 22:5 1160
Balaam the son of *B* hath said.................Num 24:3 1160
Balaam the son of *B* hath said.................Num 24:15 1160
Balaam the son of *B* they ....Num 31:8 1160
son of *B* of Pethor of Mesopotamia........Deut 23:4 1160
Balaam also the son of *B*, the ....Josh 13:22 1160
Balaam the son of *B* to curse you...........Josh 24:9 1160
what Balaam the son of *B* answered ......Mic 6:5 1160

BERA (be'-rah) *King of Sodom.*
made war with *B* king of Sodom ....Gen 14:2 1298

BERACAH See BERACHAH.

BERACHAH (ber'-a-kah)
1. A Benjamite warrior in David's army.
and *B*, and Jehu the Antothite, ...1Chr 12:3 1294
2. A valley in Judah.
themselves in the valley of *B* 2Chr 20:26 1294
place was called, The valley of *B* 2Chr 20:26 1294

BERACHIAH (ber-a-ki'-ah) See BERECHIAH. *Father of Asaph.*
hand, even Asaph the son of *B*................1Chr 6:39 1296

BERAIAH (ber-a-i'-ah) *A son of Shimhi.*
And Adaiah, and *B*, and Shimrath, the ..1Chr 8:21 1256

BERAKIAH See BERACHIAH.

BEREA (be-re'-a) *A city in Macedonia.*
Paul and Silas by night unto *B* .... Acts 17:10   960
of God was preached of Paul at *B* .... Acts 17:13   960
him into Asia Sopater of *B* .... Acts 20:4   960

BEREAVE
do I labour, and *b* my soul of good .... Eccl 4:8   2637
I will *b* them of children, I will .... Jer 15:7   7921
evil beasts, and they shall *b* thee .... Eze 5:17   7921
no more henceforth *b* them of men .... Eze 36:12   7921
neither *b* thy nations any more, ... Eze 36:14   3782,(7921)
their children, yet will I *b* them .... Hos 9:12   7921

BEREAVED
Me have ye *b* of my children .... Gen 42:36   7921
b of my children, I am *b* .... Gen 43:14   7921
wives be *b* of their children .... Jer 18:21   7909
up men, and hast *b* thy nations .... Eze 36:13   7921
as a bear that is *b* of her whelps .... Hos 13:8   7909

BEREAVETH
abroad the sword *b*, at home there .... Lam 1:20   7921

BERECHIAH (ber-e-ki'-ah) See BERACHIAH.
1. A descendant of King Jehoiakim.
And Hashubah, and Ohel, and *B* 1Chr 3:20   1296
2. Same as Berachiah.
his brethren, Asaph the son of *B* 1Chr 15:17   1296
3. A Levite near Jerusalem.
B the son of Asa, the son of 1Chr 9:16   1296
4. A Levite doorkeeper.
And *B* and Elkanah were doorkeepers .. 1Chr 15:23   1296
5. An Ephraimite.
B the son of Meshillemoth, and 2Chr 28:12   1296
6. Father of Meshullam.
repaired Meshullam the son of *B* .... Neh 3:4   1296
son of *B* over against his chamber .... Neh 3:30   1296
of Meshullam the son of *B* .... Neh 6:18   1296
7. Father of Zechariah.
LORD unto Zechariah, the son of *B* .... Zec 1:1   1296
LORD unto Zechariah, the son of *B* .... Zec 1:7   1296

BERED (be'-red)
1. A place in southern Canaan.
behold, it is between Kadesh and *B* .... Gen 16:14   1260
2. An Ephraimite.
B his son, and Tahath his son, and 1Chr 7:20   1260

BEREKIAH See BERECHIAH.

BERI (be'-ri) See BERITES. *Son of Zophah.*
and Harnepher, and Shual, and *B* 1Chr 7:36   1275

BERIAH (be-ri'-ah) See BERIITES.
1. A son of Asher.
Jimnah, and Ishuah, and Isui, and *B* ..... Gen 46:17   1283
and the sons of *B* .... Gen 46:17   1283
of *B*, the family of the Beriites .... Num 26:44   1283
Of the sons of *B* .... Num 26:45   1283
Imnah, and Isuah, and Ishuai, and *B* 1Chr 7:30   1283
And the sons of *B* 1Chr 7:31   1283
2. A son of Ephraim.
a son, and he called his name *B* 1Chr 7:23   1283
3. A son of Elpaal.
B also, and Shema, who were heads 1Chr 8:13   1283
and Ispah, and Joha, the sons of *B* 1Chr 8:16   1283
4. A Levite.
Jahath, Zina, and Jeush, and *B* 1Chr 23:10   1283
but Jeush and *B* had not many sons 1Chr 23:11   1283

BERIITES (be-ri'-ites) *Descendants of Beriah 1.*
of Beriah, the family of the *B* .... Num 26:44   1284

BERITES (be'-rites) *Descendants of Beri.*
and to Beth-maachah, and all the *B* 2Sa 20:14   1276

BERITH (be'-rith) See BAAL-BERITH. *Idol at Shechem.*
an hold of the house of the god *B* .... Judg 9:46   1286

BERNICE (bur-ni'-see) *Daughter of Herod Agrippa.*
B came unto Caesarea to salute .... Acts 25:13   959
when Agrippa was come, and *B* .... Acts 25:23   959
rose up, and the governor, and *B* .... Acts 26:30   959

BERODACH-BALADAN (ber-o'-dak-bal'-a-dan) See
MERODACH-BALADAN. *A king of Babylon.*
At that time *B*, the son of 2Kin 20:12   1255

BEROEA See BEREA.

BEROTHAH (ber-o'-thah) See BEROTHAI, BEROTHITE. *A city near Hamath.*
Hamath, *B*, Sibraim, which is .... Eze 47:16   1268

BEROTHAI (ber-o'-thahee) See BEROTHAH. *A city of Hadadezer.*
And from Betah, and from *B*, cities 2Sa 8:8   1268

BEROTHITE (be'-ro-thite) See BEEROTHITE. *A native of Beeroth.*
Zelek the Ammonite, Naharai the *B* 1Chr 11:39   1307

BERRIES
two or three *b* in the top of the .... Is 17:6   1620
tree, my brethren, bear olive *b* .... Jas 3:12   1636

BERYL
And the fourth row a *b*, and an onyx ..... Ex 28:20   8658
And the fourth row, a *b*, an onyx, ... Ex 39:13   8658
are as gold rings set with the *b* .... Song 5:14   8658
was like unto the colour of a *b* .... Eze 1:16   8658
was as the colour of a *b* stone .... Eze 10:9   8658
topaz, and the diamond, the *b* .... Eze 28:13   8658
His body also was like the *b* .... Dan 10:6   8658
the eighth, *b* .... Rev 21:20   969

BESAI (be'-sahee) *A family of exiles.*
of Paseah, the children of *B* .... Ezr 2:49   1153
The children of *B*, the children .... Neh 7:52   1153

BESEECH
we *b* thee, three days' journey .... Ex 3:18   4994
I *b* thee, shew me thy glory .... Ex 33:18   4994
I *b* thee, lay not the sin upon us .... Num 12:11   4994
Heal her now, O God, I *b* thee .... Num 12:13   4994
I *b* thee, let the power of my .... Num 14:17   4994
I *b* thee, the iniquity of this .... Num 14:19   4994
I *b* thee, tell thy servant 1Sa 23:11   4994
I *b* thee, and his servants go with 2Sa 13:24   4994
I humbly *b* thee that I may find 2Sa 16:4
I *b* thee, O LORD, take away the 2Sa 24:10   4994
I *b* thee, save thou us out of his 2Kin 19:19   4994
I *b* thee, O LORD, remember now 2Kin 20:3   577
I *b* thee, do away the iniquity of 1Chr 21:8   4994
I *b* thee, thine eyes be open, and 2Chr 6:40   4994
I *b* thee, O LORD God of heaven, ... Neh 1:5   577
I *b* thee, the word that thou .... Neh 1:8   4994
I *b* thee, let now thine ear be .... Neh 1:11   577
I *b* thee, that thou hast made me .... Job 10:9   4994
I *b* thee, and I will speak .... Job 42:4   4994
we *b* thee, O God of hosts .... Ps 80:14   4994
I *b* thee, deliver my soul .... Ps 116:4   577
Save now, I *b* thee, O LORD .... Ps 118:25   577
I *b* thee, send now prosperity .... Ps 118:25   577
I *b* thee, the freewill offerings .... Ps 119:108   4994
I *b* thee, how I have walked .... Is 38:3   577
we *b* thee, we are all thy people .... Is 64:9   4994
We *b* thee, let this man be put to .... Jer 38:4   4994
I *b* thee, the voice of the LORD, ... Jer 38:20   4994
we *b* thee, our supplication be .... Jer 42:2   4994
thy servants, I *b* thee, ten days .... Dan 1:12   4994
I *b* thee, let thine anger and thy .... Dan 9:16   4994
O Lord GOD, forgive, I *b* thee .... Amos 7:2   4994
I, O Lord GOD, cease, I *b* thee .... Amos 7:5   4994
We *b* thee, O LORD, we *b* .... Jonah 1:14   577
I *b* thee, my life from me .... Jonah 4:3   4994
b God that he will be gracious .... Mal 1:9   2470,6440
they *b* him to put his hand upon .... Mk 7:32   3870
I *b* thee, torment me not .... Lk 8:28   1189
I *b* thee, look upon my son .... Lk 9:38   1189
I *b* thee, suffer me to speak unto .... Acts 21:39   1189
wherefore I *b* thee to hear me .... Acts 26:3   1189
I *b* you therefore, brethren, by .... Rom 12:1   3870
Now I *b* you, brethren, for the .... Rom 15:30   3870
Now I *b* you, brethren, mark them .... Rom 16:17   3870
Now I *b* you, brethren, by the 1Cor 1:10   3870
Wherefore I *b* you, be ye 1Cor 4:16   3870
I *b* you, brethren, (ye know the 1Cor 16:15   3870
Wherefore I *b* you that ye would 2Cor 2:8   3870
as though God did *b* you by us 2Cor 5:20   3870
b you also that ye receive not 2Cor 6:1   3870
Now I Paul myself *b* you by the 2Cor 10:1   3870
But I *b* you, that I may not be 2Cor 10:2   1189
Brethren, I *b* you, be as I am .... Gal 4:12   1189
b you that ye walk worthy of the .... Eph 4:1   3870
I *b* Euodias, and *b* Syntyche .... Phil 4:2   3870
b Syntyche, that they be of the .... Phil 4:2   3870
Furthermore then we *b* you 1Th 4:1   2065
but we *b* you, brethren, that ye 1Th 4:10   3870
we *b* you, brethren, to know them 1Th 5:12   2065
Now we *b* you, brethren, by the 2Th 2:1   2065
for love's sake I rather *b* thee .... Philem 9   3870
I *b* thee for my son Onesimus, ... Philem 10   3870
But I *b* you the rather to do this .... Heb 13:19   3870
I *b* you, brethren, suffer the .... Heb 13:22   3870
I *b* you as strangers and pilgrims, ... 1Pet 2:11   3870
And now I *b* thee, lady, not as 2Jn 5   2065

BESEECHING
came unto him a centurion, *b* him,........ Mt 8:5   3870
b him, and kneeling down to him, ... Mk 1:40   3870
b him that he would come and heal .... Lk 7:3   2065

BESET
b the house round about, and beat........ Judg 19:22 5437
b the house round about upon me .... Judg 20:5   5437
bulls of Bashan have *b* me round .... Ps 22:12   3803
Thou hast *b* me behind and before, ... Ps 139:5   6696
own doings have *b* them about .... Hos 7:2   5437
the sin which doth so easily *b* us .... Heb 12:1   2139

BESIDE See APPENDIX.

BESIDES See APPENDIX.

BESIEGE
thee, then thou shalt *b* it .... Deut 20:12 6696
When thou shalt *b* a city a long............ Deut 20:19 6696
he shall *b* thee in all thy gates,.......... Deut 28:52 6887
he shall *b* thee in all thy gates,.......... Deut 28:52 6887
to Keilah, to *b* David and his men 1Sa 23:8   6696
if thine enemy *b* them in the land 1Kin 8:37   6887
city, and his servants did *b* it 2Kin 24:11 6696
if their enemies *b* them in the 2Chr 6:28   6696
b, O Media .... Is 21:2   6696
which *b* you without the walls, and .... Jer 21:4   6696
to the Chaldeans that *b* you................ Jer 21:9   6696

BESIEGED
children of Ammon, and *b* Rabbah........ 2Sa 11:1   6696
b him in Abel of Beth-maachah, and...... 2Sa 20:15   6696
Israel with him, and they *b* Tirzah....... 1Kin 16:17   6696
b Samaria, and warred against it 1Kin 20:1   6696
host, and went up, and *b* Samaria 2Kin 6:24   6696
and, behold, they *b* it, until an 2Kin 6:25   6696
and they *b* Ahaz, but could not........... 2Kin 16:5   6696
to Samaria, and *b* it three years 2Kin 17:5   6696
came up against Samaria, and *b* it....... 2Kin 18:9   6696
up all the rivers of *b* places 2Kin 19:24   4693
Jerusalem, and the city was *b*........ 2Kin 24:10   935,4692
the city was *b* unto the eleventh 2Kin 25:2   935,4692
of Ammon, and came and *b* Rabbah 1Chr 20:1   6696
b it, and built great bulwarks............ Eccl 9:14   5437
garden of cucumbers, as a *b* city.......... Is 1:8   5341
up all the rivers of the *b* places .... Is 37:25   4693
of Babylon's army *b* Jerusalem............ Jer 32:2   6696
when the Chaldeans that *b* .... Jer 37:5   6696
against Jerusalem, and they *b* it .... Jer 39:1   6696
So the city was *b* unto the............. Jer 52:5   935,4692
face against it, and it shall be *b* .... Eze 4:3   4692
is *b* shall die by the famine............... Eze 6:12   5341
Babylon unto Jerusalem, and *b* it .... Dan 1:1   6696

BESODEIAH (bes-o-di'-ah) *A repairer of Jerusalem's walls.*
Paseah, and Meshullam the son of *B* ..... Neh 3:6   1152

BESOM
it with the *b* of destruction .... Is 14:23   4292

BESOR (be'-sor) *A brook in southern Judah.*
with him, and came to the brook *B* 1Sa 30:9   1308
could not go over the brook *B* 1Sa 30:10   1308
made also to abide at the brook *B* 1Sa 30:21   1308

BESOUGHT
anguish of his soul, when he *b* us........... Gen 42:21   2603
Moses the LORD his God, and said ..... Ex 32:11   2470
I *b* the LORD at that time, saying .... Deut 3:23   2603
David therefore *b* God for the 2Sa 12:16   1245
And the man of God *b* the LORD 1Kin 13:6   2470
b him, and said unto him, O man of...... 2Kin 1:13   2603
And Jehoahaz *b* the LORD, and the....... 2Kin 13:4   2603
he *b* the LORD his God, and humbled 2Chr 33:12   2470
we fasted and *b* our God for this .... Ezr 8:23   1245
b him with tears to put away the........... Est 8:3   2603
b the LORD, and the LORD repented .... Jer 26:19   2470
So the devils *b* him, saying, If.............. Mt 8:31   3870
they *b* him that he would depart .... Mt 8:34   3870
b him that they might only touch .... Mt 14:36   3870
b him, saying, Send her away .... Mt 15:23   2065
b him, saying, Have patience with ...... Mt 18:29   3870
he *b* him much that he would not .... Mk 5:10   3870
And all the devils *b* him, saying,......... Mk 5:12   3870
b him greatly, saying, My little .... Mk 5:23   3870
b him that they might touch if it .... Mk 6:56   3870
she *b* him that he would cast .... Mk 7:26   2065
unto him, and *b* him to touch him .... Mk 8:22   3870
and they *b* him for her .... Lk 4:38   2065
b him, saying, Lord, if thou wilt .... Lk 5:12   1189
they *b* him instantly, saying, ... Lk 7:4   3870
they *b* him that he would not .... Lk 8:31   3870
they *b* him that he would suffer .... Lk 8:32   3870

about *b* him to depart from them .... Lk 8:37   2065
b him that he might be with him .... Lk 8:38   1189
b him that he would come into his......... Lk 8:41   3870
I *b* thy disciples to cast him out .... Lk 9:40   1189
a certain Pharisee *b* him to dine .... Lk 11:37   2065
they *b* him that he would tarry .... Jn 4:40   2065
b him that he would come down, and..... Jn 4:47   2065
b Pilate that his legs might .... Jn 19:31   2065
b Pilate that he might take away .... Jn 19:38   2065
the Gentiles *b* that these words .... Acts 13:42   3870
and her household, she *b* us .... Acts 16:15   3870
b them, and brought them out, and .... Acts 16:39   3870
b him not to go up to Jerusalem........... Acts 21:12   3870
him against Paul, and *b* him, ... Acts 25:2   3870
Paul *b* them all to take meat, ... Acts 27:33   3870
this thing I *b* the Lord thrice 2Cor 12:8   3870
As I *b* thee to abide still at................. 1Ti 1:3   3870

BEST
take of the *b* fruits in the land .... Gen 43:11   2173
in the *b* of the land make thy .... Gen 47:6   4315
in the *b* of the land, in the land............ Gen 47:11   4315
of the *b* of his own field .... Ex 22:5   4315
of the *b* of his own vineyard, ... Ex 22:5   4315
All the *b* of the oil .... Num 18:12   2459
all the *b* of the wine, and of the .... Num 18:12   2459
of the LORD, of all the *b* thereof............ Num 18:29   2459
have heaved the *b* thereof from it .... Num 18:30   2459
have heaved from it the *b* of it .... Num 18:32   2459
them marry to whom they think *b* .... Num 36:6   2896
thy gates, where it liketh him *b* .... Deut 23:16   2896
oliveyards, even the *b* of them 1Sa 8:14   2896
the *b* of the sheep, and the 1Sa 9:2   4315
people spared the *b* of the sheep 1Sa 15:15   4315
What seemeth you *b* I will do 2Sa 18:4   3190
and overlaid it with the *b* gold 1Kin 10:18   6338
Look even out the *b* and meetest of........ 2Kin 10:3   2896
her maids unto the *b* place of the .... Est 2:9   2896
verily every man at his *b* state .... Ps 39:5   5324
like the *b* wine for my beloved .... Song 7:9   2896
b of Lebanon, and that drink .... Eze 31:16   2896
The *b* of them is as a brier .... Mic 7:4   2896
servants, Bring forth the *b* robe .... Lk 15:22   4413
But covet earnestly the *b* gifts 1Cor 12:31   2909

BESTEAD
shall pass through it, hardly *b*................ Is 8:21

BESTIR
that then thou shalt *b* thyself................. 2Sa 5:24   2782

BESTOW
that he may *b* upon you a blessing .... Ex 32:29   5414
thou shalt *b* that money for .... Deut 14:26   5414
the LORD did they *b* upon Baalim 2Chr 24:7   6213
thou shalt have occasion to *b*................ Ezr 7:20   5415
b it out of the king's treasure............... Ezr 7:20   5415
have no room where to *b* my fruits ...... Lk 12:17   4863
there will I *b* all my fruits and............ Lk 12:18   4863
upon these we *b* more abundant............ 1Cor 12:23   4060
though I *b* all my goods to feed 1Cor 13:3   5595

BESTOWED
whom he *b* in the cities for 1Kin 10:26   3240
hand, and *b* them in the house 2Kin 5:24   6485
the money to be *b* on workmen 2Kin 12:15   5414
b upon him such royal majesty as.......... 1Chr 29:25   5414
whom he *b* in the chariot cities, ... 2Chr 9:25   3240
to all that the LORD hath *b* on us .... Is 63:7   1580
which he hath *b* on them according .... Is 63:7   1580
reap that whereon ye *b* no labour ...... Jn 4:38   2872
Mary, who *b* much labour on us .... Rom 16:6   2872
his grace which was *b* upon me was 1Cor 15:11   5485
that for the gift *b* upon us by 2Cor 1:11
b on the churches of Macedonia............ 2Cor 8:1   1325
lest I have *b* upon you labour in .... Gal 4:11   2872
of love the Father hath *b* upon us 1Jn 3:1   1325

BETAH (be'-tah) *A city of Hadadezer.*
And from *B*, and from Berothai,............. 2Sa 8:8   984

BETEN (be'-ten) *A city in Asher.*
border was Helkath, and Hali, and *B* ..... Josh 19:25   991

BETHABARA (beth-ab'-ar-ah) See BETHBARAH. *A place east of the Jordan River.*
were done in *B* beyond Jordan .... Jn 1:28   962

BETH ACACIA See BETH-SHITTAH.

BETH-ANATH (beth'-a-nath) *A city in Naphtali.*
Iron, and Migdal-el, Horem, and *B* .... Josh 19:38   1043
nor the inhabitants of *B*...................... Judg 1:33   1043
of *B* became tributaries unto them........ Judg 1:33   1043

BETH-ANOTH *(beth'-a-noth) A city in Judah.*
And Maarath, and *B*, and Eltekon .... Josh 15:59   1042

BETHANY *(beth'-a-ny) A village near Jerusalem.*
and went out of the city into *B* .... Mt 21:17   963
Now when Jesus was in *B*, in the........... Mt 26:6   963
to Jerusalem, unto Bethphage and *B* ..... Mk 11:1   963
went out unto *B* with the twelve .... Mk 11:11   963
when they were come from *B* .... Mk 11:12   963
being in *B* in the house of Simon .... Mk 14:3   963
was come nigh to Bethphage and *B* .... Lk 19:29   963
And he led them out as far as to *B* .... Lk 24:50   963
man was sick, named Lazarus, of *B*....... Jn 11:1   963
Now *B* was nigh unto Jerusalem, ... Jn 11:18   963
before the passover came to *B* .... Jn 12:1   963

BETH APHRAH See APHRAH.

BETH-ARABAH *(beth-ar'-ab-ah) A city of the Arabah.*
and passed along by the north of *B*........ Josh 15:6   1026
In the wilderness, *B*, Middin, and .... Josh 15:61   1026
And *B*, and Zemaraim, and Beth-el, ... Josh 18:22   1026

BETH-ARAM *(beth'-a-ram) A city in Gad.*
And in the valley, *B*, and................... Josh 13:27   1027

BETH-ARBEL *(beth-ar'-bel) A city destroyed by the As-syrians.*
as Shalman spoiled *B* in the day .... Hos 10:14   1009

BETH ASHBEA See ASHBEA.

BETH-AVEN *(beth-a'-ven) A town in Benjamin.*
Jericho to Ai, which is beside *B* .... Josh 7:2   1007
were at the wilderness of *B*................. Josh 18:12   1007
in Michmash, eastward from *B* 1Sa 13:5   1007
and the battle passed over unto *B*.......... 1Sa 14:23   1007
Gilgal, neither go ye up to *B* .... Hos 4:15   1007
cry aloud at *B*, after thee, O................. Hos 5:8   1007
fear because of the calves of *B* .... Hos 10:5   1007

BETH-AZMAVETH *(beth-az'-maveth) See AZMAVETH. A village in Judah.*
The men of *B*, forty and two .... Neh 7:28   1041

BETH-BAAL-MEON *(beth-ba'-al-me'-on) A Moabite town.*
Dibon, and Bamoth-baal, and *B*............. Josh 13:17   1010

BETH-BARAH *(beth-ba'-rah) See BETHABARA. A place in Gad.*
before them the waters unto *B* .... Judg 7:24   1012
and took the waters unto *B* .... Judg 7:24   1012

BETH-BIREI *(beth-bir'-e-i) See BETH-LEBAOTH. A town in Simeon.*
and Hazar-susim, and at *B*, and at........ 1Chr 4:31   1011

BETH BIRI See BETH-BIREI.

BETH-CAR *(beth'-car) A Philistine stronghold in Judah.*
them, until they came under *B* 1Sa 7:11   1033

BETH-DAGON *(beth-da'-gon)*
   1. A town in Judah.
And Gederoth, *B*, and Naamah, and ...... Josh 15:41   1016
   2. A town in Asher.
turneth toward the sunrising to *B* .... Josh 19:27   1016

BETH-DIBLATHAIM *(beth-dib-lath-a'-im) A Moabite town.*
Dibon, and upon Nebo, and upon *B* .... Jer 48:22   1015

BETH-EL
unto a mountain on the east of *B* .... Gen 12:8   1008
having *B* on the west, and Hai on .... Gen 12:8   1008
journeys from the south even to *B* .... Gen 13:3   1008
been at the beginning, between *B* .... Gen 13:3   1008
called the name of that place *B* .... Gen 28:19   1008
I am the God of *B*, where thou .... Gen 31:13   1008
unto Jacob, Arise, go up to *B* .... Gen 35:1   1008
And let us arise, and go up to *B* .... Gen 35:3   1008
in the land of Canaan, that is, *B*........... Gen 35:6   1008
was buried beneath *B* under an oak .... Gen 35:8   1008
place where God spake with him, *B*....... Gen 35:15   1008
And they journeyed from *B* .... Gen 35:16   1008
Beth-aven, on the east side of *B* .... Josh 7:2   1008
lie in ambush, and abode between *B*....... Josh 8:9   1008
them to lie in ambush between *B* .... Josh 8:12   1008
was not a man left in Ai or *B* .... Josh 8:17   1008
the king of Ai, which is beside *B*........... Josh 12:9   1008
the king of *B*, one .... Josh 12:16   1008
from Jericho throughout mount *B* .... Josh 16:1   1008
And goeth out from *B* to Luz .... Josh 16:2   1008
to the side of Luz, which is *B* .... Josh 18:13   1008
Beth-arabah, and Zemaraim, and *B*....... Josh 18:22   1008
they also went up against *B*................. Judg 1:22   1008
house of Joseph sent to descry *B* .... Judg 1:23   1008
Ramah and *B* in mount Ephraim........... Judg 4:5   1008

which is on the north side of *B*.............. Judg 21:19   1008
that goeth up from *B* to Shechem .... Judg 21:19   1008
from year to year in circuit to *B* 1Sa 7:16   1008
three men going up to God to *B* 1Sa 10:3   1008
Saul in Michmash and in mount *B*........ 1Sa 13:2   1008
To them which were in *B*, and to 1Sa 30:27   1008
And he set the one in *B*, and the........... 1Kin 12:29   1008
So did he in *B*, sacrificing unto............. 1Kin 12:32   1008
he placed in *B* the priests of the........... 1Kin 12:32   1008
the altar which he had made in *B* 1Kin 12:33   1008
by the word of the LORD unto *B* 1Kin 13:1   1008
had cried against the altar in *B* 1Kin 13:4   1008
not by the way that he came to *B* 1Kin 13:10   1008
there dwelt an old prophet in *B*............. 1Kin 13:11   1008
man of God had done that day in *B* 1Kin 13:11   1008
the LORD against the altar in *B* 1Kin 13:32   1008
for the LORD hath sent me to *B* 2Kin 2:2   1008
So they went down to *B* 2Kin 2:2   1008
were at *B* came forth to Elisha 2Kin 2:3   1008
And he went up from thence unto *B*....... 2Kin 2:23   1008
the golden calves that were in *B*............ 2Kin 10:29   1008
from Samaria came and dwelt in *B* 2Kin 17:28   1008
carried the ashes of them unto *B* 2Kin 23:4   1008
Moreover the altar that was at *B* 2Kin 23:15   1008
hast done against the altar of *B* 2Kin 23:17   1008
the acts that he had done in *B* 2Kin 23:19   1008
and habitations were, *B* and the 1Chr 7:28   1008
B with the towns thereof, and 2Chr 13:19   1008
The men of *B* and Ai, two hundred........ Ezr 2:28   1008
The men of *B* and Ai, an hundred.......... Neh 7:32   1008
dwelt at Michmash, and Aija, and *B* ..... Neh 11:31   1008
was ashamed of *B* their confidence .... Jer 48:13   1008
So shall *B* do unto you because of......... Hos 10:15   1008
he found him in *B*, and there he .... Hos 12:4   1008
I will also visit the altars of *B* .... Amos 3:14   1008
Come to *B*, and transgress .... Amos 4:4   1008
But seek not *B*, nor enter into .... Amos 5:5   1008
and *B* shall come to nought................. Amos 5:5   1008
there be none to quench it in *B* .... Amos 5:6   1008
Then Amaziah the priest of *B* sent........ Amos 7:10   1008
prophesy not again any more at *B* .... Amos 7:13   1008

BETH-ELITE *(beth'-el-ite) A native of Beth-el.*
days did Hiel the *B* build Jericho 1Kin 16:34   1017

BETH-EMEK *(beth-e'-mek) A town in Asher.*
toward the north side of *B*.................. Josh 19:27   1025

BETHER *(be'-thur) A district in the Jordan valley.*
hart upon the mountains of *B* .... Song 2:17   1336

BETHESDA *(beth-ez'-dah) A pool in Jerusalem.*
is called in the Hebrew tongue *B* .... Jn 5:2   964

BETH-EZEL *(beth-e'-zel) A city in Judah.*
not forth in the mourning of *B* .... Mic 1:11   1018

BETH-GADER *(beth-ga'-der) See GEDER. A descendant of Caleb.*
Hareph the father of *B* 1Chr 2:51   1013

BETH-GAMUL *(beth-ga'-mul) A Moabite town.*
And upon Kiriathaim, and upon *B* .... Jer 48:23   1014

BETH-HACCEREM *(beth-hak'se-rem) A town in Judah.*
of Rechab, the ruler of part of *B* .... Neh 3:14   1021
and set up a sign of fire in *B*................. Jer 6:1   1021

BETH HAKKEREM See BETH-HACCEREM.

BETH-HARAN *(beth-ha'-ran) See ELON-BETH-HARAN. A city in Gad.*
And Beth-nimrah, and *B*, fenced............ Num 32:36   1028

BETH-HOGLA *(beth-hog'-lah) See BETH-HOGLAH. A city in Benjamin.*
And the border went up to *B*................. Josh 15:6   1031

BETH HOGLAH See BETH-HOGLA.

BETH-HOGLAH *(beth-hog'-lah) See BETH-HOGLAH. Same as Beth-hogla.*
along to the side of *B* northward............ Josh 18:19   1031
their families were Jericho, and *B*.......... Josh 18:21   1031

BETH-HORON *(beth-ho'-ron) Two cities in Ephraim, near Benjamin.*
along the way that goeth up to *B* .... Josh 10:10   1032
and went in the going down to *B* .... Josh 10:11   1032
unto the coast of *B* the nether.............. Josh 16:3   1032
Ataroth-addar, unto *B* the upper........... Josh 16:5   1032
on the south side of the nether *B* .... Josh 18:13   1032
that lieth before *B* southward .... Josh 18:14   1032
suburbs, and *B* with her suburbs........... Josh 21:22   1032
company turned the way to *B* 1Sa 13:18   1032
built Gezer, and *B* the nether, ... 1Kin 9:17   1032
suburbs, and *B* with her suburbs, ... 1Chr 6:68   1032

who built B the nether, and the	1Chr 7:24	1032
Also he built B the upper	2Chr 8:5	1032
B the nether, fenced cities, with	2Chr 8:5	1032
Judah, from Samaria even unto B	2Chr 25:13	1032

BETHINK

if they shall b themselves in	1Kin 8:47	7725,413,3820
Yet if they b themselves in the	2Chr 6:37	7725,413,3820

BETH JESHIMOTH See JESIMOTH.

BETH-JESHIMOTH (beth-jesh'-im-oth) See BETH-JESIMOTH. Same as Beth-jesimoth.

sea on the east, the way to B	Josh 12:3	1020
and Ashdoth-pisgah, and B,	Josh 13:20	1020
the glory of the country, B	Eze 25:9	1020

BETH-JESIMOTH (beth-jes'-im-oth) See BETH-JESHIMOTH. A Moabite city.

from B even unto Abel-shittim in	Num 33:49	1020

BETH-LE-APHRAH See APHRAH.

BETH-LEBAOTH (beth-leb'-a-oth) See BETH-BISEI. A town in Simeon.

And B, and Sharuhen	Josh 19:6	1034

BETH-LEHEM (beth'-le-hem) See BETH-LEHEMITE, BETH-LEHEM-JUDAH.

1. A city in Judah.

in the way to Ephrath, which is B	Gen 35:19	1035
the same is B	Gen 48:7	1035
two went until they came to B	Ruth 1:19	1035
to pass, when they were come to B	Ruth 1:19	1035
they came to B in the beginning	Ruth 1:22	1035
And, behold, Boaz came from B	Ruth 2:4	1035
in Ephratah, and be famous in B	Ruth 4:11	1035
the LORD spake, and came to B	1Sa 16:4	1035
to feed his father's sheep at B	1Sa 17:15	1035
that he might run to B his city	1Sa 20:6	1035
asked leave of me to go to B	1Sa 20:28	1035
of his father, which was in B	2Sa 2:32	1035
of the Philistines was then in B	2Sa 23:14	1035
of the water of the well of B	2Sa 23:15	1035
drew water out of the well of B	2Sa 23:16	1035
Elhanan the son of Dodo of B	2Sa 23:24	1035
garrison was then at B	1Chr 11:16	1035
of the water of the well of B	1Chr 11:17	1035
drew water out of the well of B	1Chr 11:18	1035
Elhanan the son of Dodo of B	1Chr 11:26	1035
He built even B, and Etam, and	2Chr 11:6	1035
The children of B, an hundred	Ezr 2:21	1035
The men of B and Netophah, an	Neh 7:26	1035
B Ephratah, though thou be little	Mic 5:2	1035

2. A town in Zebulun.

and Shimron, and Idalah, and B	Josh 19:15	1035

3. A town in Ephraim.

him Ibzan of B judged Israel	Judg 12:8	1035
died Ibzan, and was buried at B	Judg 12:10	1035

4. A descendant of Caleb.

Salma the father of B, Hareph the	1Chr 2:51	1035
B, and the Netophathites, Ataroth,	1Chr 2:54	1035
of Ephratah, the father of B	1Chr 4:4	1035

BETHLEHEM A town in Judea.

of Chimham, which is by B	Jer 41:17	1035
Now when Jesus was born in B of	Mt 2:1	965
said unto him, In B of Judaea	Mt 2:5	965
And thou B, in the land of Juda,	Mt 2:6	965
And he sent them to B, and said, Go	Mt 2:8	965
all the children that were in B	Mt 2:16	965
city of David, which is called B	Lk 2:4	965
Let us now go even unto B	Lk 2:15	965
of David, and out of the town of B	Jn 7:42	965

BETH-LEHEMITE (beth'-le-hem-ite) A native of Beth-lehem.

I will send thee to Jesse the B	1Sa 16:1	1022
I have seen a son of Jesse the B	1Sa 16:18	1022
son of thy servant Jesse the B	1Sa 17:58	1022
the son of Jaare-oregim, a B	2Sa 21:19	1022

BETH-LEHEM-JUDAH (beth'-le-hem-ju'-dah) Same as Beth-lehem 1.

out of B of the family of Judah	Judg 17:7	1035
departed out of the city from B	Judg 17:8	1035
said unto him, I am a Levite of B	Judg 17:9	1035
took to him a concubine out of B	Judg 19:1	1035
him unto her father's house to B	Judg 19:2	1035
We are passing from B toward the	Judg 19:18	1035
and I went to B, but I am now	Judg 19:18	1035
a certain man of B went to	Ruth 1:1	1035
and Chilion, Ephrathites of B	Ruth 1:2	1035
the son of that Ephrathite of B	1Sa 17:12	1035

BETH MAACAH

BETH-MAACAH (beth-ma'-a-kah) See ABEL-BETH-MAACAH. A city in Manasseh.

of Israel unto Abel, and to B	2Sa 20:14	1038
came and besieged him in Abel of B	2Sa 20:15	1038

BETH-MARCABOTH (beth-mar'-cab-oth) A city in Judah.

And Ziklag, and B, and Hazar-susah,	Josh 19:5	1024
And at B, and Hazar-susim, and at	1Chr 4:31	1024

BETH-MEON (beth-me'-on) See BETH-BAAL-MEON. A Moabite city.

and upon Beth-gamul, and upon B	Jer 48:23	1010

BETH-NIMRAH (beth-nim'-rah) See NIMRAH. A city in Gad.

And B, and Beth-haran, fenced	Num 32:36	1039
And in the valley, Beth-aram, and B	Josh 13:27	1039

BETH OPHRAH See APHRAH.

BETH-PALET (beth-pa'-let) See BETH-PELET. A town in Judah.

Hazar-gaddah, and Heshmon, and B	Josh 15:27	1046

BETH-PAZZEZ (beth-paz'-zez) A town in Issachar.

and En-haddah, and B	Josh 19:21	1048

BETH PELET See BETH-PALET.

BETH-PEOR (beth-pe'-or) A Moabite city.

in the valley over against B	Deut 3:29	1047
in the valley over against B	Deut 4:46	1047
the land of Moab, over against B	Deut 34:6	1047
And B, and Ashdoth-pisgah, and	Josh 13:20	1047

BETHPHAGE (beth'-fa-je) A village near Jerusalem.

unto Jerusalem, and were come to B	Mt 21:1	967
came nigh to Jerusalem, unto B	Mk 11:1	967
pass, when he was come nigh to B	Lk 19:29	967

BETH-PHELET (beth'-fe-let) See BETH-PALET. A town in Judah.

at Jeshua, and at Moladah, and at B	Neh 11:26	1046

BETH-RAPHA (beth'-ra-fah) Son of Eshton.

And Eshton begat B, and Paseah, and	1Chr 4:12	1051

BETH-REHOB (beth'-re-hob) A place in northern Canaan.

was in the valley that lieth by B	Judg 18:28	1050
sent and hired the Syrians of B	2Sa 10:6	1050

BETHSAIDA (beth-sa'-dah)

1. A city in Galilee.

woe unto thee, B	Mt 11:21	966
to the other side before unto B	Mk 6:45	966
woe unto thee, B	Lk 10:13	966
Now Philip was of B, the city of	Jn 1:44	966
Philip, which was of B of Galilee	Jn 12:21	966

2. A place east of Lake Gennesareth.

And he cometh to B	Mk 8:22	966
belonging to the city called B	Lk 9:10	966

BETH SHAN See BETH-SHEAN.

BETH-SHAN (beth'-shan) See BETH-SHEAN. A city in Manasseh.

his body to the wall of B	1Sa 31:10	1052
of his sons from the wall of B	1Sa 31:12	1052
stolen them from the street of B	2Sa 21:12	1052

BETH-SHEAN (beth-she'-an) See BETH-SHAN. Same as Beth-shan.

had in Issachar and in Asher B	Josh 17:11	1052
of iron, both they who are of B	Josh 17:16	1052
drive out the inhabitants of B	Judg 1:27	1052
Taanach and Megiddo, and all B	1Kin 4:12	1052
from B to Abel-meholah, even unto	1Kin 4:12	1052
of the children of Manasseh, B	1Chr 7:29	1052

BETH SHEMESH See SHEMESH.

BETH-SHEMESH (beth'-she-mesh) See BETH-SHEMITE.

1. A town in Judah.

the north side, and went down to B	Josh 15:10	1053
suburbs, and B with her suburbs	Josh 21:16	1053
by the way of his own coast to B	1Sa 6:9	1053
the straight way to the way of B	1Sa 6:12	1053
after them unto the border of B	1Sa 6:12	1053
they of B were reaping their	1Sa 6:13	1053
the men of B offered burnt	1Sa 6:15	1053
And he smote the men of B, because	1Sa 6:19	1053
And the men of B said, Who is able	1Sa 6:20	1053
in Makaz, and in Shaalbim, and B	1Kin 4:9	1053
one another in the face at B	2Kin 14:11	1053
Jehoash the son of Ahaziah, at B	2Kin 14:13	1053
suburbs, and B with her suburbs	1Chr 6:59	1053
he and Amaziah king of Judah, at B	2Chr 25:21	1053

Joash, the son of Jehoahaz, at *B* 2Chr 25:23 1053
south of Judah, and had taken *B* 2Chr 28:18 1053
    2. A city in Issachar.
to Tabor, and Shahazimah, and *B* ....Josh 19:22 1053
    3. A city in Naphtali.
Horem, and Beth-anath, and *B* ....Josh 19:38 1053
drive out the inhabitants of *B* ....Judg 1:33 1053
nevertheless the inhabitants of *B* ....Judg 1:33 1053
    4. A temple in Egypt.
shall break also the images of *B* ....Jer 43:13 1053

BETH-SHEMITE (beth'-shem-ite) *An inhabitant of Beth-shemesh.*
into the field of Joshua, a *B* 1Sa 6:14 1030
day in the field of Joshua, the *B* 1Sa 6:18 1030

BETH-SHITTAH (beth-shit'-tah) *A place in the Jordan valley.*
and the host fled to *B* in Zererath ....Judg 7:22 1029

BETH-TAPPUAH (beth-tap'-pu-ah) *A city in Judah.*
And Janum, and *B*, and Aphekah, ...Josh 15:53 1054

BETHUEL (beth-u'-el) See BETHUL.
    1. Son of Nahor.
and Pildash, and Jidlaph, and *B* ....Gen 22:22 1328
And *B* begat Rebekah............Gen 22:23 1328
came out, who was born to *B* ....Gen 24:15 1328
daughter of *B* the son of Milcah............Gen 24:24 1328
And she said, The daughter of *B* ....Gen 24:47 1328
B answered and said, The thing ....Gen 24:50 1328
the daughter of *B* the Syrian of ....Gen 25:20 1328
to the house of *B* thy mother's ....Gen 28:2 1328
son of *B* the Syrian, the brother ....Gen 28:5 1328
    2. A town in Simeon.
And at *B*, and at Hormah, and at 1Chr 4:30 1328

BETHUL (beth'-ul) See BETHUEL. *A city in Simeon.*
And Eltolad, and *B*, and Hormah,............Josh 19:4 1329

BETHZATHA See BETHESDA.

BETHZOR See BETH-ZUR.

BETH-ZUR (beth'-zur)
    1. A town in Judah.
Halhul, *B*, and Gedor,............Josh 15:58 1049
And *B*, and Shoco, and Adullam, ...2Chr 11:7 1049
the ruler of the half part of *B* ....Neh 3:16 1049
    2. A descendant of Caleb.
and Maon was the father of *B* 1Chr 2:45 1049

BETIMES
they rose up *b* in the morning, and ....Gen 26:31 7925
by his messengers, rising up *b* 2Chr 36:15 7925
If thou wouldest seek unto God *b* ....Job 8:5 7836
rising *b* for a prey ....Job 24:5 7836
that loveth him chasteneth him *b* ....Prov 13:24 7836

BETONIM (bet'-o-nim) *A town in Gad.*
Heshbon unto Ramath-mizpeh, and *B* ...Josh 13:26 993

BETRAY
be come to *b* me to mine enemies............1Chr 12:17 7411
shall *b* one another, and shall ....Mt 24:10 3860
he sought opportunity to *b* him ....Mt 26:16 3860
you, that one of you shall *b* me ....Mt 26:21 3860
in the dish, the same shall *b* me ....Mt 26:23 3860
he is at hand that doth *b* me............Mt 26:46 3860
shall *b* the brother to death ....Mk 13:12 3860
chief priests, to *b* him unto them ....Mk 14:10 3860
how he might conveniently *b* him ....Mk 14:11 3860
which eateth with me shall *b* me ....Mk 14:18 3860
how he might *b* him unto them ....Lk 22:4 3860
sought opportunity to *b* him unto ....Lk 22:6 3860
believed not, and who should *b* him ....Jn 6:64 3860
for he it was that should *b* him ....Jn 6:71 3860
Simon's son, which should *b* him ....Jn 12:4 3860
Iscariot, Simon's son, to *b* him ....Jn 13:2 3860
For he knew who should *b* him ....Jn 13:11 3860
you, that one of you shall *b* me ....Jn 13:21 3860

BETRAYED
and Judas Iscariot, who also *b* him........Mt 10:4 3860
shall be *b* into the hands of men ....Mt 17:22 3860
shall be *b* to the chief priests ....Mt 20:18 3860
Son of man is *b* to be crucified............Mt 26:2 3860
man by whom the Son of man is *b* ....Mt 26:24 3860
Then Judas, which *b* him, answered......Mt 26:25 3860
the Son of man is *b* into the............Mt 26:45 3860
Now he that *b* him gave them a ....Mt 26:48 3860
that I have *b* the innocent blood ....Mt 27:4 3860
Judas Iscariot, which also *b* him ....Mk 3:19 3860
man by whom the Son of man is *b* ....Mk 14:21 3860
the Son of man is *b* into the............Mk 14:41 3860
he that *b* him had given them a ....Mk 14:44 3860
ye shall be *b* both by parents, and........Lk 21:16 3860

woe unto that man by whom he is *b* ......Lk 22:22 *3860*
And Judas also, which *b* him ....Jn 18:2 *3860*
And Judas also, which *b* him ....Jn 18:5 *3860*
in which he was *b* took bread 1Cor 11:23 *3860*

BETRAYERS
of whom ye have been now the *b* ......Acts 7:52 *4273*

BETRAYEST
b thou the Son of man with a kiss ....Lk 22:48 *3860*

BETRAYETH
Then Judas, which had *b* him ....Mt 27:3 *3860*
lo, he that *b* me is at hand ....Mk 14:42 *3860*
the hand of him that *b* me is with ....Lk 22:21 *3860*
Lord, which is he that *b* thee ....Jn 21:20 *3860*

BETROTH
Thou shalt *b* a wife, and another ....Deut 28:30 *781*
I will *b* thee unto me for ever ....Hos 2:19 *781*
yea, I will *b* thee unto me in............Hos 2:19 *781*
I will even *b* thee unto me in ....Hos 2:20 *781*

BETROTHED
who hath *b* her to himself, then ....Ex 21:8 *3259*
if he have *b* her unto his son, he ....Ex 21:9 *3259*
a man entice a maid that is not *b* ....Ex 22:16 *781*
b to an husband, and not at all ....Lev 19:20 *2778*
man is there that hath *b* a wife ....Deut 20:7 *781*
is a virgin be *b* unto an husband............Deut 22:23 *781*
man find a *b* damsel in the field ....Deut 22:25 *781*
the *b* damsel cried, and there was............Deut 22:27 *781*
that is a virgin, which is not *b* ....Deut 22:28 *781*

BETTER See APPENDIX.

BETTERED
that she had, and was nothing *b* ....Mk 5:26 *5623*

BETWEEN See APPENDIX.

BETWIXT
be a token of the covenant *b* me ....Gen 17:11 996
what is that *b* me and thee ....Gen 23:15 996
now an oath *b* us, even *b* us............Gen 26:28 996
set three days' journey *b* himself ....Gen 30:36 996
that they may judge *b* us both ....Gen 31:37 996
see, God is witness *b* me and thee ....Gen 31:50 996
pillar, which I have cast *b* me ....Gen 31:51 996
God of their father, judge *b* us ....Gen 31:53 996
before me, and put a space *b* drove ......Gen 32:16 996
Neither is there any daysman *b* us........Job 9:33 996
shine by the cloud that cometh *b* ....Job 36:32 6293
shall lie all night *b* my breasts ....Song 1:13 996
I pray you, *b* me and my vineyard ....Is 5:3 996
by the gate *b* the two walls ....Jer 39:4 996
For I am in a strait *b* two ....Phil 1:23 1537

BEULAH (be-u'-lah) *A name of restored Israel.*
called Hephzi-bah, and thy land *B* ....Is 62:4 1166

BEWAIL
b the burning which the LORD hath ......Lev 10:6 1058
b her father and her mother a full ....Deut 21:13 1058
b my virginity, I and my fellows ....Judg 11:37 1058
Therefore I will *b* with the ....Is 16:9 1058
that I shall *b* many which have 2Cor 12:21 3996
deliciously with her, shall *b* her ....Rev 18:9 2799

BEWAILED
and *b* her virginity upon the ....Judg 11:38 1058
And all wept, and *b* her ....Lk 8:52 2875
people, and of women, which also *b* ......Lk 23:27 2875

BEWAILETH
that *b* herself, that spreadeth ....Jer 4:31 3306

BEWARE
B thou that thou bring not my son ....Gen 24:6 8104
B of him, and obey his voice,............Ex 23:21 8104
Then *b* lest thou forget the LORD, ...Deut 6:12 8104
B that thou forget not the LORD ....Deut 8:11 8104
B that there be not a thought in ....Deut 15:9 8104
Now therefore *b*, I pray thee, and ....Judg 13:4 8104
I said unto the woman let her *b* ....Judg 13:13 8104
B that none touch the young man......2Sa 18:12 8104
B that thou pass not such a place 2Kin 6:9 8104
b lest he take thee away with his ....Job 36:18
a scorner, and the simple will *b* ....Prov 19:25 6191
B lest Hezekiah persuade you,............Is 36:18
B of false prophets, which come ....Mt 7:15 4337
But *b* of men ....Mt 10:17 4337
b of the leaven of the Pharisees ....Mt 16:6 4337
that ye should *b* of the leaven of ....Mt 16:11 4337
them not *b* of the leaven of bread ....Mt 16:12 4337
b of the leaven of the Pharisees, ...Mk 8:15 991
B of the scribes, which love to ....Mk 12:38 991
B ye of the leaven of the ....Lk 12:1 4337

B

Take heed, and *b* of covetousness .... Lk 12:15   *5442*
B of the scribes, which desire to .... Lk 20:46   *4337*
B therefore, lest that come upon .... Acts 13:40   *991*
B of dogs, *b* of evil workers .... Phil 3:2   *991*
b of the concision .... Phil 3:2   *991*
B lest any man spoil you through .... Col 2:8   *991*
b lest ye also, being led away 2Pet 3:17   *5442*

BEWITCHED
b the people of Samaria, giving.............. Acts 8:9   *1839*
time he had *b* them with sorceries .... Acts 8:11   *1839*
foolish Galatians, who hath *b* you.......... Gal 3:1   *940*

BEWRAY
b not him that wandereth...................... Is 16:3   *1540*

BEWRAYETH
of his right hand, which *b* itself .... Prov 27:16   *7121*
he heareth cursing, and *b* it not .... Prov 29:24   *5046*
for thy speech *b* thee .... Mt 26:73   *1212,4160*

BEYOND See APPENDIX.

BEZAI (be'-zahee)
  1. A family of exiles.
The children of *B*, three hundred .... Ezr 2:17   *1209*
The children of *B*, three hundred .... Neh 7:23   *1209*
  2. A family who renewed the covenant.
Hodijah, Hashum, *B*,.......................... Neh 10:18   *1209*

BEZALEEL (be-zal'-e-el)
  1. A craftsman.
called by name *B* the son of Uri .... Ex 31:2   *1212*
called by name *B* the son of Uri .... Ex 35:30   *1212*
Then wrought *B* and Aholiab, and.......... Ex 36:1   *1212*
And Moses called *B* and Aholiab, and ... Ex 36:2   *1212*
B made the ark of shittim wood .... Ex 37:1   *1212*
B the son of Uri, the son of Hur,.......... Ex 38:22   *1212*
And Hur begat Uri, and Uri begat *B*...... 1Chr 2:20   *1212*
that *B* the son of Uri, the son of 2Chr 1:5   *1212*
  2. Married a foreign wife in exile.
Benaiah, Maaseiah, Mattaniah, *B*.......... Ezr 10:30   *1212*

BEZALEL See BEZALEEL.

BEZEK (be'-zek) See ADONI-BEZEK. *A place in the Jordan valley.*
of them in *B* ten thousand men .... Judg 1:4   *966*
And they found Adoni-bezek in *B* .... Judg 1:5   *966*
And when he numbered them in *B* 1Sa 11:8   *966*

BEZER (be'-zer)
  1. A city of refuge.
B in the wilderness, in the plain .... Deut 4:43   *1221*
they assigned *B* in the wilderness .... Josh 20:8   *1221*
B with her suburbs, and Jahazah........ Josh 21:36   *1221*
B in the wilderness with her 1Chr 6:78   *1221*
  2. A son of Liph.
B, and Hod, and Shamma, ... 1Chr 7:37   *1221*

BICHRI (bik'-ri) *Father of Sheba.*
name was Sheba, the son of *B* 2Sa 20:1   *1075*
and followed Sheba the son of *B* 2Sa 20:2   *1075*
son of *B* do us more harm than did........ 2Sa 20:6   *1075*
pursue after Sheba the son of *B* 2Sa 20:7   *1075*
pursued after Sheba the son of *B* 2Sa 20:10   *1075*
pursue after Sheba the son of *B* 2Sa 20:13   *1075*
Sheba the son of *B* by name.................... 2Sa 20:21   *1075*
the head of Sheba the son of *B* 2Sa 20:22   *1075*

BICHRITES See BERITES.

BICRI See BICHRI.

BID
b them that they make them.................... Num 15:38   *559*
until the day I *b* you shout.................... Josh 6:10   *559*
B the servant pass on before us,............ 1Sa 9:27   *559*
ere thou *b* the people return from 2Sa 2:26   *559*
riding for me, except I *b* thee 2Kin 4:24   *559*
if the prophet had *b* thee do some 2Kin 5:13   *1696*
will do all that thou shalt *b* us................ 2Kin 10:5   *1696*
it the preaching that I *b* thee .... Jonah 3:2   *1696*
a sacrifice, he hath *b* his guests .... Zeph 1:7   *6942*
b me come unto thee on the water........ Mt 14:28   *2753*
ye shall find, *b* to the marriage .... Mt 22:9   *2564*
whatsoever they *b* you observe .... Mt 23:3   *2036*
let me first go *b* them farewell .... Lk 9:61   *657*
b her therefore that she help me .... Lk 10:40   *2036*
lest they also *b* thee again.................... Lk 14:12   *479*
that believe not *b* you to a feast 1Cor 10:27   *2564*
house, neither *b* him God speed 2Jn 10   *3004*

BIDDEN
and afterwards they eat that be *b* 1Sa 9:13   *7121*
place among them that were *b* 1Sa 9:22   *7121*
for the LORD hath *b* him 2Sa 16:11   *559*
the angel of the Lord had *b* him .... Mt 1:24   *4367*

them that were *b* to the wedding............ Mt 22:3   *2564*
saying, Tell them which are *b* .... Mt 22:4   *2564*
they which were *b* were not worthy ...... Mt 22:8   *2564*
Pharisee which had *b* him saw it .... Lk 7:39   *2564*
a parable to those which were *b*.............. Lk 14:7   *2564*
When thou art *b* of any man to a .... Lk 14:8   *2564*
man than thou be *b* of him .... Lk 14:8   *2564*
But when thou art *b*, go and sit.............. Lk 14:10   *2564*
time to say to them that were *b* .... Lk 14:17   *2564*
were *b* shall taste of my supper .... Lk 14:24   *2564*

BIDDETH
For he that *b* him God speed is 2Jn 11   *3004*

BIDDING
son in law, and goeth at thy *b*................ 1Sa 22:14   *4928*

BIDKAR (bid'-kar) *A captain of Jehu.*
Then said Jehu to *B* his captain 2Kin 9:25   *920*

BIER
king David himself followed the *b* 2Sa 3:31   *4296*
And he came and touched the *b* .... Lk 7:14   *4673*

BIGTHA (big'-thah) *A servant of Ahasuerus.*
Mehuman, Biztha, Harbona, *B* .... Est 1:10   *903*

BIGTHAN (big'-than) See BIGTHANA. *A conspirator against Ahasuerus.*
two of the king's chamberlains, *B*.......... Est 2:21   *904*

BIGTHANA (big'-than-ah) See BIGTHAN. *Same as Bigthan.*
that Mordecai had told of *B* .... Est 6:2   *904*

BIGVAI (big'-vahee)
  1. A family chief with Zerubbabel.
Mordecai, Bilshan, Mizpar, *B* .... Ezr 2:2   *902*
Mordecai, Bilshan, Mispereth, *B* .... Neh 7:7   *902*
  2. A family of exiles with Zerubbabel.
The children of *B*, two thousand .... Ezr 2:14   *902*
The children of *B*, two thousand .... Neh 7:19   *902*
  3. A family of exiles with Ezra.
Of the sons also of *B*............................ Ezr 8:14   *902*
  4. A family who renewed the covenant.
Adonijah, *B*, Adin,................................ Neh 10:16   *902*

BILDAD (bil'-dad) *A friend of Job.*
B the Shuhite, and Zophar the .... Job 2:11   *1085*
Then answered *B* the Shuhite .... Job 8:1   *1085*
Then answered *B* the Shuhite .... Job 18:1   *1085*
Then answered *B* the Shuhite .... Job 25:1   *1085*
B the Shuhite and Zophar the................ Job 42:9   *1085*

BILEAM (bil'-e-am) See IBLEAM. *A Levitical city in Manasseh.*
B with her suburbs, for the...................... 1Chr 6:70   *1109*

BILGAH (bil'-gah)
  1. A priest during David's time.
The fifteenth to *B*, the sixteenth 1Chr 24:14   *1083*
  2. A priest with Zerubbabel.
Miamin, Maadiah, *B*,.............................. Neh 12:5   *1083*
Of *B*, Shammua.................................... Neh 12:18   *1083*

BILGAI (bil'-gahee) *A priest with Zerubbabel.*
Maaziah, *B*, Shemaiah .... Neh 10:8   *1084*

BILHAH (bil'-hah) See BALAH.
  1. Mother of Dan and Naphtali.
B his handmaid to be her maid.............. Gen 29:29   *1090*
And she said, Behold my maid *B* .... Gen 30:3   *1090*
she gave him *B* her handmaid to .... Gen 30:4   *1090*
B conceived, and bare Jacob a son .... Gen 30:5   *1090*
B Rachel's maid conceived again,............ Gen 30:7   *1090*
lay with *B* his father's concubine .... Gen 35:22   *1090*
And the sons of *B*, Rachel's .... Gen 35:25   *1090*
and the lad was with the sons of *B*........ Gen 37:2   *1090*
These are the sons of *B*, which .... Gen 46:25   *1090*
Jezer, and Shallum, the sons of *B* 1Chr 7:13   *1090*
  2. A town in Simeon.
And at *B*, and at Ezem, and at Tolad, ... 1Chr 4:29   *1090*

BILHAN (bil'-han)
  1. Son of Ezer.
B, and Zaavan, and Akan.................... Gen 36:27   *1092*
B, and Zavan, and Jakan........................ 1Chr 1:42   *1092*
  2. Son of Jediael.
also of Jediael; *B* 1Chr 7:10   *1092*
and the sons of *B*.................................. 1Chr 7:10   *1092*

BILL
him write her a *b* of divorcement .... Deut 24:1   *5612*
write her a *b* of divorcement, and.......... Deut 24:3   *5612*
Where is the *b* of your mother's.............. Is 50:1   *5612*
away, and given her a *b* of divorce .... Jer 3:8   *5612*
to write a *b* of divorcement .... Mk 10:4   *975*
And he said unto him, Take thy *b* .... Lk 16:6   *1121*
And he said unto him, Take thy *b*.......... Lk 16:7   *1121*

BILLOWS

waves and thy *b* are gone over me	Ps 42:7	1530
all thy *b* and thy waves passed	Jonah 2:3	4867

BILSHAN (bil'-shan) *A Jewish prince with Zerubbabel.*

Seraiah, Reelaiah, Mordecai, *B*	Ezr 2:2	1114
Raamiah, Nahamani, Mordecai, *B*	Neh 7:7	1114

BIMHAL (bim'-hal) *A son of Japlet.*

Pasach, and *B*, and Ashvath	1Chr 7:33	1118

BIND

they shall *b* the breastplate by	Ex 28:28	7405
they did *b* the breastplate by his	Ex 39:21	7405
or swear an oath to *b* his soul	Num 30:2	631
b herself by a bond, being in her	Num 30:3	631
thou shalt *b* them for a sign upon	Deut 6:8	7194
b them for a sign upon your hand,	Deut 11:18	7194
b up the money in thine hand, and	Deut 14:25	6887
thou shalt *b* this line of scarlet	Josh 2:18	7194
To *b* Samson are we come up, to do	Judg 15:10	631
him, We are come down to *b* thee	Judg 15:12	631
but we will *b* thee fast, and	Judg 15:13	631
that we may *b* him to afflict him	Judg 16:5	631
If they *b* me with seven green	Judg 16:7	631
If they *b* me fast with new ropes	Judg 16:11	631
and *b* it as a crown to me	Job 31:36	6029
Canst thou *b* the sweet influences	Job 38:31	7194
Canst thou *b* the unicorn with his	Job 39:10	7194
and *b* their faces in secret	Job 40:13	2280
or wilt thou *b* him for thy	Job 41:5	7194
To *b* his princes at his pleasure	Ps 105:22	631
b the sacrifice with cords, even	Ps 118:27	631
To *b* their kings with chains, and	Ps 149:8	631
b them about thy neck	Prov 3:3	7194
B them continually upon thine	Prov 6:21	7194
B them upon thy fingers, write	Prov 7:3	7194
B up the testimony, seal the law	Is 8:16	6887
b them on thee, as a bride doeth	Is 49:18	7194
he hath sent me to *b* up the	Is 61:1	2280
that thou shalt *b* a stone to it	Jer 51:63	7164
shall *b* thee with them, and thou	Eze 3:25	631
number, and *b* them in thy skirts	Eze 5:3	6887
b the tire of thine head upon	Eze 24:17	2280
healed, to put a roller to *b* it	Eze 30:21	2280
will *b* up that which was broken,	Eze 34:16	2280
were in his army to *b* Shadrach	Dan 3:20	3729
hath smitten, and he will *b* us up	Hos 6:1	2280
when they shall *b* themselves in	Hos 10:10	631
b the chariot to the swift beast	Mic 1:13	7573
except he first *b* the strong man	Mt 12:29	1210
***b* them in bundles to burn them**	Mt 13:30	1210
whatsoever thou shalt *b* on earth	Mt 16:19	1210
Whatsoever ye shall *b* on earth	Mt 18:18	1210
***B* him hand and foot, and take him**	Mt 22:13	1210
For they *b* heavy burdens and	Mt 23:4	1195
he will first *b* the strong man	Mk 3:27	1210
and no man could *b* him, no, not	Mk 5:3	1210
to *b* all that call on thy name	Acts 9:14	1210
Gird thyself, and *b* on thy sandals	Acts 12:8	5265
So shall the Jews at Jerusalem *b*	Acts 21:11	1210

BINDETH

For he maketh sore, and *b* up	Job 5:18	2280
He *b* up the waters in his thick	Job 26:8	6887
He *b* the floods from overflowing	Job 28:11	2280
it he about as the collar of my	Job 30:18	247
they cry not when he *b* them	Job 36:13	631
nor he that *b* sheaves his bosom	Ps 129:7	6014
in heart, and *b* up their wounds	Ps 147:3	2280
As he that *b* a stone in a sling,	Prov 26:8	6887
in the day that the Lord *b* up the	Is 30:26	2280

BINDING

we were *b* sheaves in the field,	Gen 37:7	481
B his foal unto the vine, and his	Gen 49:11	681
it shall have a *b* of woven work	Ex 28:32	8193
every *b* oath to afflict the soul,	Num 30:13	632
this way unto the death, *b*	Acts 22:4	1195

BINEA (bin'-e-ah) *A son of Moza.*

And Moza begat *B*	1Chr 8:37	1150
And Moza begat *B*	1Chr 9:43	1150

BINNUI (bin'-nu-ee)
1. *A Levite who returned from exile.*

Jeshua, and Noadiah the son of *B*	Ezr 8:33	1131

2. *A descendant of Pahath-moab.*

Mattaniah, Bezaleel, and *B*	Ezr 10:30	1131

3. *A descendant of Bani.*

And Bani, and *B*, Shimei,	Ezr 10:38	1131

4. *A descendant of Henadad.*

After him repaired *B* the son of	Neh 3:24	1131

B of the sons of Henadad, Kadmiel	Neh 10:9	1131

5. *A family who returned from exile.*

The children of *B*, six hundred	Neh 7:15	1131

6. *A Levite with Zerubbabel.*

Jeshua, *B*, Kadmiel, Sherebiah,	Neh 12:8	1131

BIRD

his kind, every *b* of every sort	Gen 7:14	6833
As for the living *b*, he shall	Lev 14:6	6833
the living *b* in the blood of the	Lev 14:6	6833
of the *b* that was killed over the	Lev 14:6	6833
shall let the living *b* loose into	Lev 14:7	6833
and the scarlet, and the living *b*	Lev 14:51	6833
them in the blood of the slain *b*	Lev 14:51	6833
the house with the blood of the *b*	Lev 14:52	6833
water, and with the living *b*	Lev 14:52	6833
b out of the city into the open	Lev 14:53	6833
thou play with him as with a *b*	Job 41:5	6833
Flee as a *b* to your mountain	Ps 11:1	6833
Our soul is escaped as a *b* out of	Ps 124:7	6833
is spread in the sight of any *b*	Prov 1:17	1167,3671
as a *b* from the hand of the	Prov 6:5	6833
as a *b* hasteth to the snare, and	Prov 7:23	6833
As the *b* by wandering, as the	Prov 26:2	6833
As a *b* that wandereth from her	Prov 27:8	6833
for a *b* of the air shall carry	Eccl 10:20	5775
rise up at the voice of the *b*	Eccl 12:4	6833
as a wandering *b* cast out of the	Is 16:2	5775
a ravenous *b* from the east	Is 46:11	5861
is unto me as a speckled *b*	Jer 12:9	5861
enemies chased me sore, like a *b*	Lam 3:52	6833
glory shall fly away like a *b*	Hos 9:11	5775
shall tremble as a *b* out of Egypt	Hos 11:11	6833
Can a *b* fall in a snare upon the	Amos 3:5	6833
of every unclean and hateful *b*	Rev 18:2	3732

BIRD'S

If a *b* nest chance to be before	Deut 22:6	6833

BIRDS

but the *b* divided he not	Gen 15:10	6833
the *b* did eat them out of the	Gen 40:17	5775
the *b* shall eat thy flesh from	Gen 40:19	5775
is to be cleansed two *b* alive	Lev 14:4	6833
shall command that one of the *b*	Lev 14:5	6833
take to cleanse the house two *b*	Lev 14:49	6833
the *b* in an earthen vessel over	Lev 14:50	6833
Of all clean *b* ye shall eat	Deut 14:11	6833
suffered neither the *b* of the air	2Sa 21:10	5775
Where the *b* make their nests	Ps 104:17	6833
as the *b* that are caught in the	Eccl 9:12	6833
time of the singing of *b* is come	Song 2:12	
As *b* flying, so will the Lord of	Is 31:5	6833
all the *b* of the heavens were	Jer 4:25	5775
As a cage is full of *b*, so are	Jer 5:27	5775
the *b* are consumed, and the	Jer 12:4	5775
the *b* round about are against her	Jer 12:9	5861
unto the ravenous *b* of every sort	Eze 39:4	6833
the *b* of the air have nests	Mt 8:20	4071
so that the *b* of the air come and	Mt 13:32	4071
holes, and *b* of the air have nests	Lk 9:58	4071
like to corruptible man, and to *b*	Rom 1:23	4071
of fishes, and another of *b*	1Cor 15:39	4421
For every kind of beasts, and of *b*	Jas 3:7	4071

BIRDS'

and his nails like *b* claws	Dan 4:33	6853

BIRSHA (bur'-shah) *A king of Gomorrah.*

with *B* king of Gomorrah, Shinab	Gen 14:2	1306

BIRTH

other stone, according to their *b*	Ex 28:10	8435
the children are come to the *b*	2Kin 19:3	4866
hidden untimely *b* I had not been	Job 3:16	5309
like the untimely *b* of a woman	Ps 58:8	5309
that an untimely *b* is better than	Eccl 6:3	5309
of death than the day of one's *b*	Eccl 7:1	3205
the children are come to the *b*	Is 37:3	4866
Shall I bring to the *b*, and not	Is 66:9	7665
Thy *b* and thy nativity is of the	Eze 16:3	4351
fly away like a bird, from the *b*	Hos 9:11	3205
Now the *b* of Jesus Christ was on	Mt 1:18	1083
and many shall rejoice at his *b*	Lk 1:14	1083
a man which was blind from his *b*	Jn 9:1	1079
of whom I travail in *b* again	Gal 4:19	5605
with child cried, travailing in *b*	Rev 12:2	5605

BIRTHDAY

third day, which was Pharaoh's *b*	Gen 40:20	3117,3205
But when Herod's *b* was kept	Mt 14:6	1077
that Herod on his *b* made a supper	Mk 6:21	1077

BIRTHRIGHT
said, Sell me this day thy *b* .... Gen 25:31 — 1062
what profit shall this *b* do to me .... Gen 25:32 — 1062
and he sold his *b* unto Jacob .... Gen 25:33 — 1062
thus Esau despised his *b* .... Gen 25:34 — 1062
he took away my *b* .... Gen 27:36 — 1062
the firstborn according to his *b* .... Gen 43:33 — 1062
his *b* was given unto the sons of .... 1Chr 5:1 — 1062
is not to be reckoned after the *b* .... 1Chr 5:1 — 1062
but the *b* was Joseph's .... 1Chr 5:2 — 1062
for one morsel of meat sold his *b* .... Heb 12:16 — *4415*

BIRZAITH See BIRZAVITH.

BIRZAVITH (bur'-za-vith) *A descendant of Asher.*
Malchiel, who is the father of B .... 1Chr 7:31 — 1269

BISHLAM (bish'-lam) *A commissioner of Artaxerxes.*
in the days of Artaxerxes wrote B .... Ezr 4:7 — 1312

BISHOP
If a man desire the office of a *b* .... 1Ti 3:1 — *1984*
A *b* then must be blameless, the .... 1Ti 3:2 — *1985*
ordained the first *b* of the .... 2Ti *s* — *1985*
For a *b* must be blameless, as the .... Titus 1:7 — *1985*
ordained the first *b* of the .... Titus 1:5 — *1985*
the Shepherd and B of your souls .... 1Pet 2:25 — *1985*

BISHOPRICK
and his *b* let another take .... Acts 1:20 — *1984*

BISHOPS
which are at Philippi, with the *b* .... Phil 1:1 — *1985*

BIT
the people, and they *b* the people .... Num 21:6 — 5391
mouth must be held in with *b* .... Ps 32:9 — 4964
on the wall, and a serpent *b* him .... Amos 5:19 — 5391

BITE
an hedge, a serpent shall *b* him .... Eccl 10:8 — 5391
will *b* without enchantment .... Eccl 10:11 — 5391
be charmed, and they shall *b* you........... Jer 8:17 — 5391
the serpent, and he shall *b* them .... Amos 9:3 — 5391
that *b* with their teeth, and cry,............. Mic 3:5 — 5391
up suddenly that shall *b* thee.................. Hab 2:7 — 5391
But if ye *b* and devour one another .... Gal 5:15 — *1143*

BITETH
that *b* the horse heels, so that .... Gen 49:17 — 5391
At the last it *b* like a serpent .... Prov 23:32 — 5391

BITHIA See BITHIAH.

BITHIAH (bith-i'-ah) *Daughter of Pharaoh.*
these are the sons of B the .... 1Chr 4:18 — 1332

BITHRON (bith'-ron) *A district in Arabah.*
Jordan, and went through all B .... 2Sa 2:29 — 1338

BITHYNIA (bith-in'-e-ah) *A Roman province in Asia*
Minor.
Mysia, they assayed to go into B .... Acts 16:7 — *978*
Galatia, Cappadocia, Asia, and B .... 1Pet 1:1 — *978*

BITS
we put *b* in the horses' mouths, ... Jas 3:3 — *5469*

BITTEN
to pass, that every one that is *b* .... Num 21:8 — 5391
that if a serpent had *b* any man .... Num 21:9 — 5391

BITTER
with a great and exceeding *b* cry .... Gen 27:34 — 4751
their lives *b* with hard bondage .... Ex 1:14 — 4843
with *b* herbs they shall eat it .... Ex 12:8 — 4844
waters of Marah, for they were *b* .... Ex 15:23 — 4751
shall have in his hand the *b* .... Num 5:18 — 4751
be thou free from this *b* water .... Num 5:19 — 4751
blot them out with the *b* water .... Num 5:23 — 4751
b water that causeth the curse .... Num 5:24 — 4751
shall enter into her, and become *b* .... Num 5:24 — 4751
shall enter into her, and become *b* .... Num 5:27 — 4751
with unleavened bread and *b* herbs ...... Num 9:11 — 4844
heat, and with *b* destruction .... Deut 32:24 — 4815
of gall, their clusters are *b* .... Deut 32:32 — 4846
of Israel, that it was very *b* .... 2Kin 14:26 — 4784
and cried with a loud and a *b* cry .... Est 4:1 — 4751
and life unto the *b* in soul .... Job 3:20 — 4751
For thou writest *b* things against .... Job 13:26 — 4846
Even to day is my complaint *b*................. Job 23:2 — 4805
shoot their arrows, even *b* words .... Ps 64:3 — 4751
But her end is *b* as wormwood................. Prov 5:4 — 4751
soul every *b* thing is sweet .... Prov 27:7 — 4751
I find more *b* than death the .... Eccl 7:26 — 4751
b for sweet, and sweet for *b* .... Is 5:20 — 4751
shall be to them that drink it, ... Is 24:9 — 4843
see that it is an evil thing and *b*............. Jer 2:19 — 4751
thy wickedness, because it is *b* .... Jer 4:18 — 4751

an only son, most *b* lamentation .... Jer 6:26 — 8563
Ramah, lamentation, and *b* weeping ...... Jer 31:15 — 8563
bitterness of heart and *b* wailing .... Eze 27:31 — 4751
and the end thereof as a *b* day .... Amos 8:10 — 4751
I raise up the Chaldeans, that *b* .... Hab 1:6 — 4751
wives, and be not *b* against them........... Col 3:19 — *4087*
the same place sweet water and *b* .... Jas 3:11 — *4089*
But if ye have *b* envying and .... Jas 3:14 — *4089*
waters, because they were made *b* .... Rev 8:11 — *4087*
and it shall make thy belly *b* .... Rev 10:9 — *4087*
as I had eaten it, my belly was *b* .... Rev 10:10 — *4087*

BITTERLY
curse ye *b* the inhabitants....................... Judg 5:23 — 779
hath dealt very *b* with me .... Ruth 1:20 — 4843
I will weep *b*, labour not to .... Is 22:4 — 4843
ambassadors of peace shall weep *b* .... Is 33:7 — 4751
against thee, and shall cry *b* .... Eze 27:30 — 4751
provoked him to anger most *b* .... Hos 12:14 — 8563
the mighty man shall cry there *b* .... Zeph 1:14 — 4751
And he went out, and wept *b* .... Mt 26:75 — 4090
And Peter went out, and wept *b* .... Lk 22:62 — 4090

BITTERN
make it a possession for the *b* .... Is 14:23 — 7090
and the *b* shall possess it .... Is 34:11 — 7090
the *b* shall lodge in the upper .... Zeph 2:14 — 7090

BITTERNESS
And she was in *b* of soul, and .... 1Sa 1:10 — 4751
Surely the *b* of death is past .... 1Sa 15:32 — 4751
it will be *b* in the latter end.................... 2Sa 2:26 — 4751
will complain in the *b* of my soul........... Job 7:11 — 4751
my breath, but filleth me with *b* .... Job 9:18 — 4472
I will speak in the *b* of my soul.............. Job 10:1 — 4751
dieth in the *b* of his soul .... Job 21:25 — 4751
The heart knoweth his own *b*.................. Prov 14:10 — 4751
father, and *b* to her that bare him .... Prov 17:25 — 4470
all my years in the *b* of my soul .... Is 38:15 — 4751
Behold, for peace I had great *b* .... Is 38:17 — 4843
are afflicted, and she is in *b*.................... Lam 1:4 — 4843
He hath filled me with *b*, he hath .... Lam 3:15 — 4844
and took me away, and I went in *b* .... Eze 3:14 — 4751
with *b* sigh before their eyes .... Eze 21:6 — 4814
weep for thee with *b* of heart .... Eze 27:31 — 4751
son, and shall be in *b* for him .... Zec 12:10 — 4843
that is in *b* for his firstborn .... Zec 12:10 — 4843
that thou art in the gall of *b* .... Acts 8:23 — 4088
mouth is full of cursing and *b* .... Rom 3:14 — 4088
Let all *b*, and wrath, and anger, and ... Eph 4:31 — 4088
lest any root of *b* springing up .... Heb 12:15 — 4088

BIZIOTHIAH See BIZJOTHJAH.

BIZJOTHJAH (biz-joth'-jah) *A town in Judah.*
Hazar-shual, and Beer-sheba, and B ..... Josh 15:28 — 964

BIZTHA (biz'-thah) *An eunuch of Ahasuerus.*
wine, he commanded Mehuman, B .... Est 1:10 — 968

BLACK
and that there is no *b* hair in it............... Lev 13:31 — 7838
that there is *b* hair grown up .... Lev 13:37 — 7838
that the heaven was *b* with clouds .... 1Kin 18:45 — 6937
of red, and blue, and white, and *b*......... Est 1:6 — 5508
My skin is *b* upon me, and my bones.... Job 30:30 — 7835
in the evening, in the *b* .... Prov 7:9 — 380
I am *b*, but comely, O ye .... Song 1:5 — 7838
Look not upon me, because I am *b* .... Song 1:6 — 7840
locks are bushy, and *b* as a raven .... Song 5:11 — 7838
mourn, and the heavens above be *b*....... Jer 4:28 — 6937
I am *b*.. Jer 8:21 — 6937
they are *b* unto the ground...................... Jer 14:2 — 6937
Our skin was *b* like an oven .... Lam 5:10 — 3648
and in the second chariot *b* horses........ Zec 6:2 — 7838
The *b* horses which are therein go .... Zec 6:6 — 7838
not make one hair white or *b* .... Mt 5:36 — *3189*
And I beheld, and lo a *b* horse .... Rev 6:5 — *3189*
the sun became *b* as sackcloth of .... Rev 6:12 — *3189*

BLACKER
Their visage is *b* than a coal .... Lam 4:8 — 2821

BLACKISH
Which are *b* by reason of the ice,........... Job 6:16 — 6937

BLACKNESS
let the *b* of the day terrify it .... Job 3:5 — 3650
I clothe the heavens with *b* .... Is 50:3 — 6940
all faces shall gather *b* .... Joel 2:6 — 6289
and the faces of them all gather *b* .... Nah 2:10 — 6289
that burned with fire, nor unto *b* .... Heb 12:18 — 1105
the *b* of darkness for ever .... Jude 13 — 2217

BLADE
the haft also went in after the *b* .... Judg 3:22 — 3851
and the fat closed upon the *b* .... Judg 3:22 — 3851

mine arm fall from my shoulder *b* .... Job 31:22	7929
But when the *b* was sprung up, and ..... Mt 13:26	5528
first the *b*, then the ear, after .... Mk 4:28	5528

BLAINS
breaking forth with *b* upon man .... Ex 9:9 — 76
breaking forth with *b* upon man .... Ex 9:10 — 76

BLAME
then let me bear the *b* for ever .... Gen 43:9 — 2398
bear the *b* to my father for ever .... Gen 44:32 — 2398
that no man should *b* us in this .... 2Cor 8:20 — 3469
without *b* before him in love................... Eph 1:4 — 299

BLAMED
thing, that the ministry be not *b* .... 2Cor 6:3 — 3469
the face, because he was to be *b* .... Gal 2:11 — 2607

BLAMELESS
and ye shall be *b*.................................. Gen 44:10 — 5355
We will be *b* of this thine oath .... Josh 2:17 — 5355
Now shall I be more *b* than .... Judg 15:3 — 5352
profane the sabbath, and are *b* .... Mt 12:5 — 338
and ordinances of the Lord *b* .... Lk 1:6 — 273
that ye may be *b* in the day of .... 1Cor 1:8 — 410
That ye may be *b* and harmless, the ..... Phil 2:15 — 273
which is in the law, *b* .... Phil 3:6 — 273
body be preserved *b* unto the .... 1Th 5:23 — 274
A bishop then must be *b*, the .... 1Ti 3:2 — 423
office of a deacon, being found *b* .... 1Ti 3:10 — 410
in charge, that they may be *b* .... 1Ti 5:7 — 423
If any be *b*, the husband of one .... Titus 1:6 — 410
For a bishop must be *b*, as the .... Titus 1:7 — 410
him in peace, without spot, and *b* .... 2Pet 3:14 — 298

BLASPHEME
to the enemies of the LORD to *b* .... 2Sa 12:14 — 5006
him, saying, Thou didst *b* God .... 1Kin 21:10 — 1288
people, saying, Naboth did *b* God .... 1Kin 21:13 — 1288
shall the enemy *b* thy name for .... Ps 74:10 — 5006
wherewith soever they shall *b* .... Mk 3:28 — 987
But he that shall *b* against the .... Mk 3:29 — 987
synagogue, and compelled them to *b*... Acts 26:11 — 987
that they may learn not to *b* .... 1Ti 1:20 — 987
Do not they *b* that worthy name by .... Jas 2:7 — 987
to *b* his name, and his tabernacle, ... Rev 13:6 — 987

BLASPHEMED
son *b* the name of the LORD.................... Lev 24:11 — 5344
of the king of Assyria have *b* me .... 2Kin 19:6 — 1442
Whom hast thou reproached and *b*...... 2Kin 19:22 — 1442
foolish people have *b* thy name .... Ps 74:18 — 5006
of the king of Assyria have *b* me .... Is 37:6 — 1442
Whom hast thou reproached and *b*........ Is 37:23 — 1442
name continually every day is *b* .... Is 52:5 — 5006
mountains, and *b* me upon the hills .... Is 65:7 — 2778
in this your fathers have *b* me .... Eze 20:27 — 1442
they opposed themselves, and *b*............ Acts 18:6 — 987
For the name of God is *b* among .... Rom 2:24 — 987
of God and his doctrine be not *b* .... 1Ti 6:1 — 987
that the word of God be not *b* .... Titus 2:5 — 987
b the name of God, which hath .... Rev 16:9 — 987
b the God of heaven because of............. Rev 16:11 — 987
men *b* God because of the plague .... Rev 16:21 — 987

BLASPHEMER
Who was before a *b*, and a .... 1Ti 1:13 — 989

BLASPHEMERS
nor yet *b* of your goddess .... Acts 19:37 — 987
covetous, boasters, proud, *b* .... 2Ti 3:2 — 989

BLASPHEMEST
and sent into the world, Thou *b* .... Jn 10:36 — 987

BLASPHEMETH
he that *b* the name of the LORD,............. Lev 24:16 — 5344
when he *b* the name of the LORD, ... Lev 24:16 — 5344
of him that reproacheth and *b* .... Ps 44:16 — 1442
within themselves, This man *b* .... Mt 9:3 — 987
but unto him that *b* against the .... Lk 12:10 — 987

BLASPHEMIES
that I have heard all thy *b* which .... Eze 35:12 — 5007
thefts, false witness, *b* .... Mt 15:19 — 988
Why doth this man thus speak *b* .... Mk 2:7 — 988
b wherewith soever they shall .... Mk 3:28 — 988
Who is this which speaketh *b*................. Lk 5:21 — 988
mouth speaking great things and *b* .... Rev 13:5 — 988

BLASPHEMING
by Paul, contradicting and *b* .... Acts 13:45 — 987

BLASPHEMOUS
him speak *b* words against Moses .... Acts 6:11 — 989
b words against this holy place .... Acts 6:13 — 989

BLASPHEMOUSLY
many other things *b* spake they .... Lk 22:65 — 987

BLASPHEMY
of trouble, and of rebuke, and *b* .... 2Kin 19:3 — 5007
of trouble, and of rebuke, and of *b*......... Is 37:3 — 5007
b shall be forgiven unto men................... Mt 12:31 — 988
but the *b* against the Holy Ghost .... Mt 12:31 — 988
clothes, saying, He hath spoken *b* .... Mt 26:65 — 987
behold, now ye have heard his *b*............. Mt 26:65 — 988
lasciviousness, an evil eye, *b* .... Mk 7:22 — 988
Ye have heard the *b* .... Mk 14:64 — 988
stone thee not; but for *b*......................... Jn 10:33 — 988
anger, wrath, malice, *b*, filthy.................. Col 3:8 — 988
I know the *b* of them which say .... Rev 2:9 — 988
and upon his heads the name of *b* .... Rev 13:1 — 988
opened his mouth in *b* against God .... Rev 13:6 — 988
beast, full of names of *b* .... Rev 17:3 — 988

BLAST
with the *b* of thy nostrils the .... Ex 15:8 — 7307
make a long *b* with the ram's horn......... Josh 6:5 —
at the *b* of the breath of his.................... 2Sa 22:16 — 5397
Behold, I will send a *b* upon him .... 2Kin 19:7 — 7307
By the *b* of God they perish, and .... Job 4:9 — 5397
at the *b* of the breath of thy .... Ps 18:15 — 5397
when the *b* of the terrible ones .... Is 25:4 — 7307
Behold, I will send a *b* upon him .... Is 37:7 — 7307

BLASTED
b with the east wind sprung up .... Gen 41:6 — 7710
b with the east wind, sprung up............. Gen 41:23 — 7710
the seven empty ears *b* with the .... Gen 41:27 — 7710
as corn *b* before it be grown up .... 2Kin 19:26 — 7711
as corn *b* before it be grown up .... Is 37:27 — 7709

BLASTING
and with the sword, and with *b* .... Deut 28:22 — 7711
famine, if there be pestilence, *b*............. 1Kin 8:37 — 7711
be pestilence, if there be *b* .... 2Chr 6:28 — 7711
I have smitten you with *b* .... Amos 4:9 — 7711
I smote you with *b* and with mildew ...... Hag 2:17 — 7711

BLASTUS (blas'-tus) A servant of Herod Agrippa I.
him, and, having made *B* the king's .... Acts 12:20 — 986

BLAZE
to *b* abroad the matter, insomuch .... Mk 1:45 — 1310

BLEATING
What meaneth then this *b* of the........... 1Sa 15:14 — 6963

BLEATINGS
to hear the *b* of the flocks .... Judg 5:16 — 8292

BLEMISH
Your lamb shall be without *b* .... Ex 12:5 — 8549
bullock, and two rams without *b* .... Ex 29:1 — 8549
let him offer a male without *b*................. Lev 1:3 — 8549
shall bring it a male without *b* .... Lev 1:10 — 8549
it without *b* before the LORD .... Lev 3:1 — 8549
he shall offer it without *b* .... Lev 3:6 — 8549
without *b* unto the LORD for a sin .... Lev 4:3 — 8549
of the goats, a male without *b* .... Lev 4:23 — 8549
of the goats, a female without *b* .... Lev 4:28 — 8549
shall bring it a female without *b* .... Lev 4:32 — 8549
a ram without *b* out of the flocks .... Lev 5:15 — 8549
a ram without *b* out of the flock .... Lev 5:18 — 8549
a ram without *b* out of the flock, ... Lev 6:6 — 8549
for a burnt offering, without *b* .... Lev 9:2 — 8549
both of the first year, without *b* .... Lev 9:3 — 8549
shall take two he lambs without *b*.......... Lev 14:10 — 8549
lamb of the first year without *b* .... Lev 14:10 — 8549
their generations that hath any *b* .... Lev 21:17 — 3971
man he be that hath a *b*, he shall .... Lev 21:18 — 3971
or that hath a *b* in his eye...................... Lev 21:20 — 8400
No man that hath a *b* of the seed .... Lev 21:21 — 3971
he hath a *b* .... Lev 21:21 — 3971
the altar, because he hath a *b* .... Lev 21:23 — 3971
at your own will a male without *b* .... Lev 22:19 — 8549
But whatsoever hath a *b*, that .... Lev 22:20 — 3971
there shall be no *b* therein...................... Lev 22:21 — 3971
the sheaf an he lamb without *b* of .... Lev 23:12 — 8549
lambs without *b* of the first year .... Lev 23:18 — 8549
a man cause a *b* in his neighbour .... Lev 24:19 — 3971
as he hath caused a *b* in a man .... Lev 24:20 — 3971
without *b* for a burnt offering................. Num 6:14 — 8549
year without *b* for a sin offering .... Num 6:14 — 8549
one ram without *b* for peace .... Num 6:14 — 8549
without spot, wherein is no *b* .... Num 19:2 — 3971
they shall be unto you without *b* .... Num 28:19 — 8549
they shall be unto you without *b*) .... Num 28:31 — 8549
lambs of the first year without *b* .... Num 29:2 — 8549
they shall be unto you without *b* .... Num 29:8 — 8549
they shall be without *b* .... Num 29:13 — 8549

lambs of the first year without *b*	Num 29:20	8549
lambs of the first year without *b*	Num 29:23	8549
lambs of the first year without *b*	Num 29:29	8549
lambs of the first year without *b*	Num 29:32	8549
lambs of the first year without *b*	Num 29:36	8549
And if there be any *b* therein	Deut 15:21	3971
lame, or blind, or have any ill *b*	Deut 15:21	3971
bullock, or sheep, wherein is *b*	Deut 17:1	3971
of his head there was no *b* in him	2Sa 14:25	3971
without *b* for a sin offering	Eze 43:22	8549
offer a young bullock without *b*	Eze 43:23	8549
a ram out of the flock without *b*	Eze 43:23	8549
a ram out of the flock, without *b*	Eze 43:25	8549
take a young bullock without *b*	Eze 45:18	8549
seven rams without *b* daily the	Eze 45:23	8549
day shall be six lambs without *b*	Eze 46:4	8549
b, and a ram without *b*	Eze 46:4	8549
be a young bullock without *b*	Eze 46:6	8549
they shall be without *b*	Eze 46:6	8549
lamb of the first year without *b*	Eze 46:13	8549
Children in whom was no *b*	Dan 1:4	3971
it should be holy and without *b*	Eph 5:27	299
of Christ, as of a lamb without *b*	1Pet 1:19	299

BLEMISHES

is in them, and *b* be in them	Lev 22:25	3971
Spots they are and *b*, sporting	2Pet 2:13	3470

BLESS

a great nation, and I will *b* thee	Gen 12:2	1288
And I will *b* them that *b* thee	Gen 12:3	1288
And I will *b* her, and give thee a	Gen 17:16	1288
yea, I will *b* her, and she shall	Gen 17:16	1288
That in blessing I will *b* thee	Gen 22:17	1288
will be with thee, and will *b* thee	Gen 26:3	1288
I am with thee, and will *b* thee	Gen 26:24	1288
that my soul may *b* thee before I	Gen 27:4	1288
b thee before the LORD before my	Gen 27:7	1288
that he may *b* thee before his	Gen 27:10	1288
venison, that thy soul may *b* me	Gen 27:19	1288
venison, that my soul may *b* thee	Gen 27:25	1288
venison, that thy soul may *b* me	Gen 27:31	1288
B me, even me also, O my father	Gen 27:34	1288
b me, even me also, O my father	Gen 27:38	1288
And God Almighty *b* thee, and make	Gen 28:3	1288
not let thee go, except thou *b* me	Gen 32:26	1288
thee, unto me, and I will *b* them	Gen 48:9	1288
me from all evil, *b* the lads	Gen 48:16	1288
saying, In thee shall Israel *b*	Gen 48:20	1288
who shall *b* thee with blessings	Gen 49:25	1288
and *b* me also	Ex 12:32	1288
come unto thee, and I will *b* thee	Ex 20:24	1288
he shall *b* thy bread, and thy	Ex 23:25	1288
On this wise ye shall *b* the	Num 6:23	1288
The LORD *b* thee, and keep thee	Num 6:24	1288
and I will *b* them	Num 6:27	1288
I have received commandment to *b*	Num 23:20	1288
them at all, nor *b* them at all	Num 23:25	1288
it pleased the LORD to *b* Israel	Num 24:1	1288
b you, as he hath promised you	Deut 1:11	1288
thee, and *b* thee, and multiply thee	Deut 7:13	1288
he will also *b* the fruit of thy	Deut 7:13	1288
then thou shalt *b* the LORD thy	Deut 8:10	1288
to *b* in his name, unto this day	Deut 10:8	1288
that the LORD thy God may *b* thee	Deut 14:29	1288
for the LORD shall greatly *b* thee	Deut 15:4	1288
God shall *b* thee in all thy works	Deut 15:10	1288
the LORD thy God shall *b* thee in	Deut 15:18	1288
b thee in all thine increase	Deut 16:15	1288
to *b* in the name of the LORD	Deut 21:5	1288
that the LORD thy God may *b* thee	Deut 23:20	1288
in his own raiment, and *b* thee	Deut 24:13	1288
that the LORD thy God may *b* thee	Deut 24:19	1288
b thy people Israel, and the land	Deut 26:15	1288
mount Gerizim to *b* the people	Deut 27:12	1288
he shall *b* thee in the land which	Deut 28:8	1288
to *b* all the work of thine hand	Deut 28:12	1288
that he *b* himself in his heart,	Deut 29:19	1288
the LORD thy God shall *b* thee in	Deut 30:16	1288
B, LORD, his substance, and accept	Deut 33:11	1288
that they should *b* the people of	Josh 8:33	1288
B ye the LORD	Judg 5:9	1288
answered him, The LORD *b* thee	Ruth 2:4	1288
because he doth *b* the sacrifice	1Sa 9:13	1288
David returned to *b* his household	2Sa 6:20	1288
to *b* the house of thy servant	2Sa 7:29	1288
to *b* him, because he had fought	2Sa 8:10	1288
that ye may *b* the inheritance of	2Sa 21:3	1288
came to *b* our lord king David	1Kin 1:47	1288
Oh that thou wouldest *b* me indeed	1Chr 4:10	1288
and David returned to *b* his house	1Chr 16:43	1288
to *b* the house of thy servant	1Chr 17:27	1288

to *b* in his name for ever	1Chr 23:13	1288
Now *b* the LORD your God	1Chr 29:20	1288
b the LORD your God for ever and	Neh 9:5	1288
thou, LORD, wilt *b* the righteous	Ps 5:12	1288
I will *b* the LORD, who hath given	Ps 16:7	1288
congregations will I *b* the LORD	Ps 26:12	1288
people, and *b* thine inheritance	Ps 28:9	1288
the LORD will *b* his people with	Ps 29:11	1288
I will *b* the LORD at all times	Ps 34:1	1288
they *b* with their mouth, but they	Ps 62:4	1288
Thus will I *b* thee while I live	Ps 63:4	1288
O *b* our God, ye people, and make	Ps 66:8	1288
God be merciful unto us, and *b* us	Ps 67:1	1288
God, even our own God, shall *b* us	Ps 67:6	1288
God shall *b* us	Ps 67:7	1288
B ye God in the congregations,	Ps 68:26	1288
Sing unto the LORD, *b* his name	Ps 96:2	1288
thankful unto him, and *b* his name	Ps 100:4	1288
B the LORD, O my soul	Ps 103:1	1288
is within me, *b* his holy name	Ps 103:1	
B the LORD, O my soul, and forget	Ps 103:2	1288
B the LORD, ye his angels, that	Ps 103:20	1288
B ye the LORD, all ye his hosts	Ps 103:21	1288
B the LORD, all his works in all	Ps 103:22	1288
b the LORD, O my soul	Ps 103:22	1288
B the LORD, O my soul	Ps 104:1	1288
B thou the LORD, O my soul	Ps 104:35	1288
Let them curse, but *b* thou	Ps 109:28	1288
he will *b* us	Ps 115:12	1288
he will *b* the house of Israel	Ps 115:12	1288
he will *b* the house of Aaron	Ps 115:12	1288
He will *b* them that fear the LORD	Ps 115:13	1288
But we will *b* the LORD from this	Ps 115:18	1288
The LORD shall *b* thee out of Zion	Ps 128:5	1288
we *b* you in the name of the LORD	Ps 129:8	1288
I will abundantly *b* her provision	Ps 132:15	1288
b ye the LORD, all ye servants of	Ps 134:1	1288
in the sanctuary, and *b* the LORD	Ps 134:2	1288
and earth *b* thee out of Zion	Ps 134:3	1288
B the LORD, O house of Israel	Ps 135:19	1288
b the LORD, O house of Aaron	Ps 135:19	1288
B the LORD, O house of Levi	Ps 135:20	1288
ye that fear the LORD, *b* the LORD	Ps 135:20	1288
I will *b* thy name for ever and	Ps 145:1	1288
Every day will I *b* thee	Ps 145:2	1288
and thy saints shall *b* thee	Ps 145:10	1288
let all flesh *b* his holy name for	Ps 145:21	1288
and doth not *b* their mother	Prov 30:11	1288
Whom the LORD of hosts shall *b*	Is 19:25	1288
himself in the earth shall *b*	Is 65:16	1288
nations shall *b* themselves in him	Jer 4:2	1288
The LORD *b* thee, O habitation of	Jer 31:23	1288
from this day will I *b* you	Hag 2:19	1288
b them that curse you, do good to	Mt 5:44	2127
B them that curse you, and pray	Lk 6:28	2127
his Son Jesus, sent him to *b* you	Acts 3:26	2127
B them which persecute you	Rom 12:14	2127
b, and curse not	Rom 12:14	2127
being reviled, we *b*	1Cor 4:12	2127
The cup of blessing which we *b*	1Cor 10:16	2127
when thou shalt *b* with the spirit	1Cor 14:16	2127
Surely blessing I will *b* thee	Heb 6:14	2127
Therewith *b* we God, even the	Jas 3:9	2127

BLESSED

God *b* them, saying, Be fruitful,	Gen 1:22	1288
God *b* them, and God said unto them	Gen 1:28	1288
God *b* the seventh day, and	Gen 2:3	1288
b them, and called their name Adam	Gen 5:2	1288
God *b* Noah and his sons, and said	Gen 9:1	1288
B be the LORD God of Shem	Gen 9:26	1288
all families of the earth be *b*	Gen 12:3	1288
he *b* him, and said	Gen 14:19	1288
B be Abram of the most high God,	Gen 14:19	1288
b be the most high God, which	Gen 14:20	1288
Behold, I have *b* him, and will	Gen 17:20	1288
of the earth shall be *b* in him	Gen 18:18	1288
all the nations of the earth be *b*	Gen 22:18	1288
the LORD had *b* Abraham in all	Gen 24:1	1288
B be the LORD God of my master	Gen 24:27	1288
said, Come in, thou *b* of the LORD	Gen 24:31	1288
the LORD hath *b* my master greatly	Gen 24:35	1288
b the LORD God of my master	Gen 24:48	1288
they *b* Rebekah, and said unto her,	Gen 24:60	1288
Abraham, that God *b* his son Isaac	Gen 25:11	1288
all the nations of the earth be *b*	Gen 26:4	1288
and the LORD *b* him	Gen 26:12	1288
thou art now the *b* of the LORD	Gen 26:29	1288
so he *b* him	Gen 27:23	1288
b him, and said, See, the smell of	Gen 27:27	1288
of a field which the LORD hath *b*	Gen 27:27	1288

B

b be he that blesseth thee	Gen 27:29	1288
before thou camest, and have *b* him	Gen 27:33	1288
yea, and he shall be *b*	Gen 27:33	1288
wherewith his father *b* him	Gen 27:41	1288
b him, and charged him, and said	Gen 28:1	1288
Esau saw that Isaac had *b* Jacob	Gen 28:6	1288
that as he *b* him he gave him a	Gen 28:6	1288
the families of the earth be *b*	Gen 28:14	1288
for the daughters will call me *b*	Gen 30:13	833
the LORD hath *b* me for thy sake	Gen 30:27	1288
the LORD hath *b* thee since my	Gen 30:30	1288
sons and his daughters, and *b* them	Gen 31:55	1288
And he *b* him there	Gen 32:29	1288
came out of Padan-aram, and *b* him	Gen 35:9	1288
that the LORD *b* the Egyptian's	Gen 39:5	1288
and Jacob *b* Pharaoh	Gen 47:7	1288
Jacob *b* Pharaoh, and went out from	Gen 47:10	1288
in the land of Canaan, and *b* me,	Gen 48:3	1288
he *b* Joseph, and said, God, before	Gen 48:15	1288
he *b* them that day, saying, In	Gen 48:20	1288
father spake unto them, and *b* them	Gen 49:28	1288
to his blessing he *b* them	Gen 49:28	1288
B be the LORD, who hath delivered	Ex 18:10	1288
the LORD *b* the sabbath day	Ex 20:11	1288
and Moses *b* them	Ex 39:43	1288
b them, and came down from	Lev 9:22	1288
and came out, and *b* the people	Lev 9:23	1288
that he whom thou blessest is *b*	Num 22:6	1288
for they are *b*	Num 22:12	1288
thou hast *b* them altogether	Num 23:11	1288
and he hath *b*	Num 23:20	1288
B is he that blesseth thee, and	Num 24:9	1288
thou hast altogether *b* them these	Num 24:10	1288
For the LORD thy God hath *b* thee	Deut 2:7	1288
Thou shalt be *b* above all people	Deut 7:14	1288
the LORD thy God hath *b* thee	Deut 12:7	1288
when the LORD thy God hath *b* thee	Deut 14:24	1288
b thee thou shalt give unto him	Deut 15:14	1288
as the LORD thy God hath *b* thee	Deut 16:10	1288
B shalt thou be in the city, and	Deut 28:3	1288
b shalt thou be in the field	Deut 28:3	1288
B shall be the fruit of thy body,	Deut 28:4	1288
B shall be thy basket and thy	Deut 28:5	1288
B shalt thou be when thou comest	Deut 28:6	1288
b shalt thou be when thou goest	Deut 28:6	1288
b the children of Israel before	Deut 33:1	1288
B of the LORD be his land, for	Deut 33:13	1288
B be he that enlargeth Gad	Deut 33:20	1288
Let Asher be *b* with children	Deut 33:24	1288
And Joshua *b* him, and gave unto	Josh 14:13	1288
as the LORD hath *b* me hitherto	Josh 17:14	1288
So Joshua *b* them, and sent them	Josh 22:6	1288
unto their tents, then he *b* them	Josh 22:7	1288
and the children of Israel *b* God	Josh 22:33	1288
therefore he *b* you still	Josh 24:10	1288
B above women shall Jael the wife	Judg 5:24	1288
b shall she be above women in the	Judg 5:24	1288
the child grew, and the LORD *b* him	Judg 13:24	1288
B be thou of the LORD, my son	Judg 17:2	1288
b be he that did take knowledge	Ruth 2:19	1288
B be he of the LORD, who hath not	Ruth 2:20	1288
B be thou of the LORD, my	Ruth 3:10	1288
B be the LORD, which hath not	Ruth 4:14	1288
Eli *b* Elkanah and his wife, and	1Sa 2:20	1288
unto him, *B* be thou of the LORD	1Sa 15:13	1288
And Saul said, *B* be ye of the LORD	1Sa 23:21	1288
B be the LORD God of Israel,	1Sa 25:32	1288
b be thy advice, and *b* be	1Sa 25:33	1288
B be the LORD, that hath pleaded	1Sa 25:39	1288
to David, *B* be thou, my son David	1Sa 26:25	1288
B be ye of the LORD, that ye have	2Sa 2:5	1288
the LORD *b* Obed-edom, and all his	2Sa 6:11	1288
The LORD hath *b* the house of	2Sa 6:12	1288
he *b* the people in the name of	2Sa 6:18	1288
of thy servant be *b* for ever	2Sa 7:29	1288
he would not go, but he *b* him	2Sa 13:25	1288
B be the LORD thy God, which hath	2Sa 18:28	1288
king kissed Barzillai, and *b* him	2Sa 19:39	1288
and *b* be my rock	2Sa 22:47	1288
B be the LORD God of Israel,	1Kin 1:48	1288
And king Solomon shall be *b*	1Kin 2:45	1288
B be the LORD this day, which	1Kin 5:7	1288
b all the congregation of Israel	1Kin 8:14	1288
B be the LORD God of Israel,	1Kin 8:15	1288
b all the congregation of Israel	1Kin 8:55	1288
B be the LORD, that hath given	1Kin 8:56	1288
they *b* the king, and went unto	1Kin 8:66	1288
B be the LORD thy God, which	1Kin 10:9	1288
the LORD *b* the house of Obed-edom	1Chr 13:14	1288
he *b* the people in the name of	1Chr 16:2	1288
B be the LORD God of Israel for	1Chr 16:36	1288
O LORD, and it shall be *b* for ever	1Chr 17:27	1288
for God *b* him	1Chr 26:5	1288
Wherefore David *b* the LORD before	1Chr 29:10	1288
B be thou, LORD God of Israel our	1Chr 29:10	1288
all the congregation *b* the LORD	1Chr 29:20	1288
B be the LORD God of Israel, that	2Chr 2:12	1288
b the whole congregation of	2Chr 6:3	1288
B be the LORD God of Israel, who	2Chr 6:4	1288
B be the LORD thy God, which	2Chr 9:8	1288
for there they *b* the LORD	2Chr 20:26	1288
the Levites arose and *b* the people	2Chr 30:27	1288
they *b* the LORD, and his people	2Chr 31:8	1288
for the LORD hath *b* his people	2Chr 31:10	1288
B be the LORD God of our fathers,	Ezr 7:27	1288
Ezra *b* the LORD, the great God	Neh 8:6	1288
b be thy glorious name, which is	Neh 9:5	1288
the people *b* all the men, that	Neh 11:2	1288
thou hast *b* the work of his hands	Job 1:10	1288
b be the name of the LORD	Job 1:21	1288
the ear heard me, then it *b* me	Job 29:11	833
If his loins have not *b* me	Job 31:20	1288
So the LORD *b* the latter end of	Job 42:12	1288
B is the man that walketh not in	Ps 1:1	835
B are all they that put their	Ps 2:12	835
and *b* be my rock	Ps 18:46	1288
hast made him most *b* for ever	Ps 21:6	1293
B be the LORD, because he hath	Ps 28:6	1288
B be the LORD	Ps 31:21	1288
B is he whose transgression is	Ps 32:1	835
B is the man unto whom the LORD	Ps 32:2	835
B is the nation whose God is the	Ps 33:12	835
b is the man that trusteth in him	Ps 34:8	835
For such as be *b* of him shall	Ps 37:22	1288
and his seed is *b*	Ps 37:26	1293
B is that man that maketh the	Ps 40:4	835
B is he that considereth the poor	Ps 41:1	835
he shall be *b* upon the earth	Ps 41:2	833
B be the LORD God of Israel from	Ps 41:13	1288
God hath *b* thee for ever	Ps 45:2	1288
while he lived he *b* his soul	Ps 49:18	1288
B is the man whom thou choosest,	Ps 65:4	835
B be God, which hath not turned	Ps 66:20	1288
B be the Lord, who daily loadeth	Ps 68:19	1288
B be God	Ps 68:35	1288
and men shall be *b* in him	Ps 72:17	1288
all nations shall call him *b*	Ps 72:17	833
B be the LORD God, the God of	Ps 72:18	1288
b be his glorious name for ever	Ps 72:19	1288
B are they that dwell in thy	Ps 84:4	835
B is the man whose strength is in	Ps 84:5	835
b is the man that trusteth in	Ps 84:12	835
B is the people that know the	Ps 89:15	835
B be the LORD for evermore	Ps 89:52	1288
B is the man whom thou chastenest,	Ps 94:12	835
B are they that keep judgment, and	Ps 106:3	835
B be the LORD God of Israel from	Ps 106:48	1288
B is the man that feareth the	Ps 112:1	835
of the upright shall be *b*	Ps 112:2	1288
B be the name of the LORD from	Ps 113:2	1288
Ye are *b* of the LORD which made	Ps 115:15	1288
B be he that cometh in the name	Ps 118:26	1288
we have *b* you out of the house of	Ps 118:26	1288
B are the undefiled in the way,	Ps 119:1	835
B are they that keep his	Ps 119:2	835
B art thou, O LORD	Ps 119:12	1288
B be the LORD, who hath not given	Ps 124:6	1288
B is every one that feareth the	Ps 128:1	835
man be *b* that feareth the LORD	Ps 128:4	1288
B be the LORD out of Zion, which	Ps 135:21	1288
B be the LORD my strength, which	Ps 144:1	1288
he hath *b* thy children within	Ps 147:13	1288
Let thy fountain be *b*	Prov 5:18	1288
for *b* are they that keep my ways	Prov 8:32	835
B is the man that heareth me,	Prov 8:34	835
The memory of the just is *b*	Prov 10:7	1293
his children are *b* after him	Prov 20:7	835
the end thereof shall not be *b*	Prov 20:21	1288
hath a bountiful eye shall be *b*	Prov 22:9	1288
children arise up, and call her *b*	Prov 31:28	833
B art thou, O land, when thy king	Eccl 10:17	835
The daughters saw her, and *b* her	Song 6:9	833
B be Egypt my people, and Assyria	Is 19:25	1288
b are all they that wait for him	Is 30:18	835
B are ye that sow beside all	Is 32:20	835
alone, and *b* him, and increased him	Is 51:2	1288
B is the man that doeth this, and	Is 56:2	835
the seed which the LORD hath *b*	Is 61:9	1288
are the seed of the *b* of the LORD	Is 65:23	1288
incense, as if he *b* an idol	Is 66:3	1288
B is the man that trusteth in the	Jer 17:7	1288
wherein my mother bare me be *b*	Jer 20:14	1288

B be the glory of the LORD from	Eze 3:12	1288
Then Daniel *b* the God of heaven	Dan 2:19	1289
B be the name of God for ever and	Dan 2:20	1289
B be the God of Shadrach, Meshach	Dan 3:28	1289
I *b* the most High, and I praised	Dan 4:34	1289
B is he that waiteth, and cometh	Dan 12:12	835
that sell them say, *B* be the LORD	Zec 11:5	1288
And all nations shall call you *b*	Mal 3:12	833
B are the poor in spirit	Mt 5:3	3107
B are they that mourn	Mt 5:4	3107
B are the meek	Mt 5:5	3107
B are they which do hunger and	Mt 5:6	3107
B are the merciful	Mt 5:7	3107
B are the pure in heart	Mt 5:8	3107
B are the peacemakers	Mt 5:9	3107
B are they which are persecuted	Mt 5:10	3107
B are ye, when men shall revile	Mt 5:11	3107
b is he, whosoever shall not be	Mt 11:6	3107
But *b* are your eyes, for they see	Mt 13:16	3107
and looking up to heaven, he *b*	Mt 14:19	2127
B art thou, Simon Bar-jona	Mt 16:17	3107
B is he that cometh in the name	Mt 21:9	2127
B is he that cometh in the name	Mt 23:39	2127
B is that servant, whom his lord	Mt 24:46	3107
ye *b* of my Father, inherit the	Mt 25:34	2127
b it, and brake it, and gave it to	Mt 26:26	2127
he looked up to heaven, and *b*	Mk 6:41	2127
and he *b*, and commanded to set them	Mk 8:7	2127
his hands upon them, and *b* them	Mk 10:16	2127
B is he that cometh in the name	Mk 11:9	2127
B be the kingdom of our father	Mk 11:10	2127
did eat, Jesus took bread, and *b*	Mk 14:22	2127
thou the Christ, the Son of the *B*	Mk 14:61	2128
b art thou among women	Lk 1:28	2127
B art thou among women, and	Lk 1:42	2127
b is the fruit of thy womb	Lk 1:42	2127
And *b* is she that believed	Lk 1:45	3107
all generations shall call me *b*	Lk 1:48	3106
B be the Lord God of Israel	Lk 1:68	2128
in his arms, and *b* God, and said,	Lk 2:28	2127
And Simeon *b* them, and said unto	Lk 2:34	2127
disciples, and said, *B* be ye poor	Lk 6:20	3107
B are ye that hunger now	Lk 6:21	3107
B are ye that weep now	Lk 6:21	3107
B are ye, when men shall hate you	Lk 6:22	3107
b is he, whosoever shall not be	Lk 7:23	3107
he *b* them, and brake, and gave to	Lk 9:16	2127
B are the eyes which see the	Lk 10:23	3107
B is the womb that bare thee, and	Lk 11:27	3107
b are they that hear the word of	Lk 11:28	3107
B are those servants, whom the	Lk 12:37	3107
them so, *b* are those servants	Lk 12:38	3107
B is that servant, whom his lord	Lk 12:43	3107
B is he that cometh in the name	Lk 13:35	2127
And thou shalt be *b*	Lk 14:14	3107
B is he that shall eat bread in	Lk 14:15	3107
B be the King that cometh in the	Lk 19:38	2127
B are the barren, and the wombs	Lk 23:29	3107
b it, and brake, and gave to them	Lk 24:30	2127
he lifted up his hands, and *b* them	Lk 24:50	2127
it came to pass, while he *b* them	Lk 24:51	2127
B is the King of Israel that	Jn 12:13	2127
b are they that have not seen, and	Jn 20:29	3107
the kindreds of the earth be *b*	Acts 3:25	1757
It is more *b* to give than to	Acts 20:35	3107
the Creator, who is *b* for ever	Rom 1:25	2128
B are they whose iniquities are	Rom 4:7	3107
B is the man to whom the Lord	Rom 4:8	3107
who is over all, God *b* for ever	Rom 9:5	2128
B be God, even the Father of our	2Cor 1:3	2128
which is *b* for evermore, knoweth	2Cor 11:31	2128
In thee shall all nations be *b*	Gal 3:8	1757
faith are *b* with faithful Abraham	Gal 3:9	2127
B be the God and Father of our	Eph 1:3	2128
who hath *b* us with all spiritual	Eph 1:3	2127
the glorious gospel of the *b* God	1Ti 1:11	3107
times he shall shew, who is the *b*	1Ti 6:15	3107
Looking for that *b* hope, and the	Titus 2:13	3107
slaughter of the kings, and *b* him	Heb 7:1	2127
b him that had the promises	Heb 7:6	2127
the less is *b* of the better	Heb 7:7	2127
By faith Isaac *b* Jacob and Esau	Heb 11:20	2127
b both the sons of Joseph	Heb 11:21	2127
B is the man that endureth	Jas 1:12	3107
this man shall be *b* in his deed	Jas 1:25	3107
B be the God and Father of our	1Pet 1:3	2128
B is he that readeth, and they	Rev 1:3	3107
B are the dead which die in the	Rev 14:13	3107
B is he that watcheth, and keepeth	Rev 16:15	3107
B are they which are called unto	Rev 19:9	3107
B and holy is he that hath part in	Rev 20:6	3107

b is he that keepeth the sayings	Rev 22:7	3107
B are they that do his	Rev 22:14	3107

BLESSEDNESS

also describeth the *b* of the man	Rom 4:6	3108
Cometh this *b* then upon the	Rom 4:9	3108
Where is then the *b* ye spake of	Gal 4:15	3108

BLESSEST

that he whom thou *b* is blessed	Num 22:6	1288
for thou *b*, O LORD, and it shall	1Chr 17:27	1288
thou *b* the springing thereof	Ps 65:10	1288

BLESSETH

and blessed be he that *b* thee	Gen 27:29	1288
Blessed is he that *b* thee	Num 24:9	1288
For the LORD thy God *b* thee	Deut 15:6	1288
b the covetous, whom the LORD	Ps 10:3	1288
He *b* them also, so that they are	Ps 107:38	1288
but he *b* the habitation of the	Prov 3:33	1288
He that *b* his friend with a loud	Prov 27:14	1288
That he who *b* himself in the	Is 65:16	1288

BLESSING

and thou shalt be a *b*	Gen 12:2	1293
That in *b* I will bless thee, and	Gen 22:17	1288
bring a curse upon me, and not a *b*	Gen 27:12	1293
Isaac had made an end of *b* Jacob	Gen 27:30	1293
and hath taken away thy *b*	Gen 27:35	1293
now he hath taken away my *b*	Gen 27:36	1293
Hast thou not reserved a *b* for me	Gen 27:36	1293
his father, Hast thou but one *b*	Gen 27:38	1293
b wherewith his father blessed	Gen 27:41	1293
And give thee the *b* of Abraham	Gen 28:4	1293
my *b* that is brought to thee	Gen 33:11	1293
the *b* of the LORD was upon all	Gen 39:5	1293
to his *b* he blessed them	Gen 49:28	1293
may bestow upon you a *b* this day	Ex 32:29	1293
Then I will command my *b* upon you	Lev 25:21	1293
I set before you this day a *b*	Deut 11:26	1293
A *b*, if ye obey the commandments	Deut 11:27	1293
put the *b* upon mount Gerizim	Deut 11:29	1293
according to the *b* of the LORD	Deut 12:15	1293
according to the *b* of the LORD	Deut 16:17	1293
the curse into a *b* unto thee	Deut 23:5	1293
The LORD shall command the *b* upon	Deut 28:8	1293
things are come upon thee, the *b*	Deut 30:1	1293
set before you life and death, *b*	Deut 30:19	1293
And this is the *b*, wherewith Moses	Deut 33:1	1293
And this is the *b* of Judah	Deut 33:7	
let the *b* come upon the head of	Deut 33:16	
and full with the *b* of the LORD	Deut 33:23	1293
Who answered, Give me a *b*	Josh 15:19	1293
And she said unto him, Give me a *b*	Judg 1:15	1293
now this *b* which thine handmaid	1Sa 25:27	1293
with thy *b* let the house of thy	2Sa 7:29	1293
thee, take a *b* of thy servant	2Kin 5:15	1293
which is exalted above all *b*	Neh 9:5	1293
our God turned the curse into a *b*	Neh 13:2	1293
The *b* of him that was ready to	Job 29:13	1293
thy *b* is upon thy people	Ps 3:8	1293
shall receive the *b* from the LORD	Ps 24:5	1293
as he delighted not in *b*, so let	Ps 109:17	1293
The *b* of the LORD be upon you	Ps 129:8	1293
there the LORD commanded the *b*	Ps 133:3	1293
The *b* of the LORD, it maketh rich	Prov 10:22	1293
By the *b* of the upright the city	Prov 11:11	1293
but *b* shall be upon the head of	Prov 11:26	1293
a good *b* shall come upon them	Prov 24:25	1293
even a *b* in the midst of the land	Is 19:24	1293
my *b* upon thine offspring	Is 44:3	1293
for a *b* is in it	Is 65:8	1293
places round about my hill a *b*	Eze 34:26	1293
there shall be showers of *b*	Eze 34:26	1293
that he may cause the *b* to rest	Eze 44:30	1293
repent, and leave a *b* behind him	Joel 2:14	1293
I save you, and ye shall be a *b*	Zec 8:13	1293
of heaven, and pour you out a *b*	Mal 3:10	1293
in the temple, praising and *b* God	Lk 24:53	2127
of the *b* of the gospel of Christ	Rom 15:29	2129
The cup of *b* which we bless, is	1Cor 10:16	2129
That the *b* of Abraham might come	Gal 3:14	2129
is dressed, receiveth *b* from God	Heb 6:7	2129
Surely *b* I will bless thee, and	Heb 6:14	2129
he would have inherited the *b*	Heb 12:17	2129
of the same mouth proceedeth *b*	Jas 3:10	2129
but contrariwise	1Pet 3:9	2129
that ye should inherit a *b*	1Pet 3:9	2129
and honour, and glory, and *b*	Rev 5:12	2129
are in them, heard I saying, *B*	Rev 5:13	2129
B, and glory, and wisdom, and	Rev 7:12	2129

BLESSINGS

bless thee with *b* of heaven above	Gen 49:25	1293
b of the deep that lieth under,	Gen 49:25	1293
b of the breasts, and of the womb	Gen 49:25	1293
The *b* of thy father have	Gen 49:26	1293
the *b* of my progenitors unto the	Gen 49:26	1293
all these *b* shall come on thee,	Deut 28:2	1293
all the words of the law, the *b*	Josh 8:34	1293
him with the *b* of goodness	Ps 21:3	1293
B are upon the head of the just	Prov 10:6	1293
faithful man shall abound with *b*	Prov 28:20	1293
upon you, and I will curse your *b*	Mal 2:2	1293
b in heavenly places in Christ	Eph 1:3	2129

BLEW

the LORD, and *b* with the trumpets	Josh 6:8	8628
priests that *b* with the trumpets	Josh 6:9	8628
and *b* with the trumpets	Josh 6:13	8628
when the priests *b* with the	Josh 6:16	8628
the priests *b* with the trumpets	Josh 6:20	8628
that he *b* a trumpet in the	Judg 3:27	8628
upon Gideon, and he *b* a trumpet	Judg 6:34	8628
they *b* the trumpets, and brake the	Judg 7:19	8628
three companies *b* the trumpets	Judg 7:20	8628
the three hundred *b* the trumpets	Judg 7:22	8628
Saul *b* the trumpet throughout all	1Sa 13:3	8628
So Joab *b* a trumpet, and all the	2Sa 2:28	8628
Joab *b* the trumpet, and the people	2Sa 18:16	8628
he *b* a trumpet, and said, We have	2Sa 20:1	8628
he *b* a trumpet, and they retired	2Sa 20:22	8628
And they *b* the trumpet	1Kin 1:39	8628
b with trumpets, saying, Jehu is	2Kin 9:13	8628
land rejoiced, and *b* with trumpets	2Kin 11:14	8628
the floods came, and the winds	Mt 7:25	4154
the floods came, and the winds *b*	Mt 7:27	4154
by reason of a great wind that *b*	Jn 6:18	4154
And when the south wind *b* softly	Acts 27:13	5285
and after one day the south wind *b*	Acts 28:13	1920

BLIND

or deaf, or the seeing, or the *b*	Ex 4:11	5787
put a stumblingblock before the *b*	Lev 19:14	5787
a *b* man, or a lame, or he that	Lev 21:18	5787
B, or broken, or maimed, or	Lev 22:22	5788
therein, as if it be lame, or *b*	Deut 15:21	5787
for a gift doth the eyes of the	Deut 16:19	5786
the *b* to wander out of the way	Deut 27:18	5787
as the *b* gropeth in darkness, and	Deut 28:29	5787
bribe to *b* mine eyes therewith	1Sa 12:3	5956
Except thou take away the *b*	2Sa 5:6	5787
Jebusites, and the lame and the *b*	2Sa 5:8	5787
Wherefore they said, The *b*	2Sa 5:8	5787
I was eyes to the *b*, and feet was	Job 29:15	5787
LORD openeth the eyes of the *b*	Ps 146:8	5787
the eyes of the *b* shall see out	Is 29:18	5787
the eyes of the *b* shall be opened	Is 35:5	5787
To open the *b* eyes, to bring out	Is 42:7	5787
I will bring the *b* by a way that	Is 42:16	5787
and look, ye *b*, that ye may see	Is 42:18	5787
Who is *b*, but my servant	Is 42:19	5787
who is *b* as he that is perfect,	Is 42:19	5787
and *b* as the LORD's servant	Is 42:19	5787
Bring forth the *b* people that	Is 43:8	5787
His watchmen are *b*	Is 56:10	5787
We grope for the wall like the *b*	Is 59:10	5787
of the earth, and with them the *b*	Jer 31:8	5787
wandered as *b* men in the streets	Lam 4:14	5787
that they shall walk like *b* men	Zeph 1:17	5787
if ye offer the *b* for sacrifice	Mal 1:8	5787
two *b* men followed him, crying,	Mt 9:27	5185
the house, the *b* men came to him	Mt 9:28	5185
The *b* receive their sight, and the	Mt 11:5	5185
him one possessed with a devil, *b*	Mt 12:22	5185
healed him, insomuch that the *b*	Mt 12:22	5185
they be *b* leaders of the *b*	Mt 15:14	5185
they be *b* leaders of the *b*	Mt 15:14	5185
if the *b* lead the *b*, both	Mt 15:14	5185
And if the *b* lead the *b*	Mt 15:14	5185
with them those that were lame, *b*	Mt 15:30	5185
the lame to walk, and the *b* to see	Mt 15:31	5185
two *b* men sitting by the way side	Mt 20:30	5185
And the *b* and the lame came to him	Mt 21:14	5185
ye *b* guides, which say, Whosoever	Mt 23:16	5185
Ye fools and *b*:	Mt 23:17	5185
Ye fools and *b*:	Mt 23:19	5185
Ye *b* guides, which strain at a	Mt 23:24	5185
Thou *b* Pharisee, cleanse first	Mt 23:26	5185
and they bring a *b* man unto him	Mk 8:22	5185
he took the *b* man by the hand, and	Mk 8:23	5185
b Bartimaeus, the son of Timaeus	Mk 10:46	5185
And they call the *b* man, saying	Mk 10:49	5185
The *b* man said unto him, Lord,	Mk 10:51	5185

and recovering of sight to the *b*	Lk 4:18	5185
them, Can the *b* lead the *b*	Lk 6:39	5185
many that were *b* he gave sight	Lk 7:21	5185
how that the *b* see, the lame walk	Lk 7:22	5185
poor, the maimed, the lame, the *b*	Lk 14:13	5185
the maimed, and the halt, and the *b*	Lk 14:21	5185
a certain *b* man sat by the way	Lk 18:35	5185
multitude of impotent folk, of *b*	Jn 5:3	5185
a man which was *b* from his birth	Jn 9:1	5185
his parents, that he was born *b*	Jn 9:2	5185
eyes of the *b* man with the clay	Jn 9:6	5185
before had seen him that he was *b*	Jn 9:8	5185
him that aforetime was *b*	Jn 9:13	5185
They say unto the *b* man again	Jn 9:17	5185
him, that he had been *b*, and	Jn 9:18	5185
your son, who ye say was born *b*	Jn 9:19	5185
is our son, and that he was born *b*	Jn 9:20	5185
called they the man that was *b*	Jn 9:24	5185
I know, that, whereas I was *b*	Jn 9:25	5185
the eyes of one that was born *b*	Jn 9:32	5185
they which see might be made *b*	Jn 9:39	5185
and said unto him, Are we *b* also	Jn 9:40	5185
said unto them, If ye were *b*	Jn 9:41	5185
a devil open the eyes of the *b*	Jn 10:21	5185
which opened the eyes of the *b*	Jn 11:37	5185
is upon thee, and thou shalt be *b*	Acts 13:11	5185
thou thyself art a guide of the *b*	Rom 2:19	5185
he that lacketh these things is *b*	2Pet 1:9	5185
and miserable, and poor, and *b*	Rev 3:17	5185

BLINDED

He hath *b* their eyes, and hardened	Jn 12:40	5186
obtained it, and the rest were *b*	Rom 11:7	4456
But their minds were *b*	2Cor 3:14	4456
b the minds of them which believe	2Cor 4:4	5186
that darkness hath *b* his eyes	1Jn 2:11	5186

BLINDETH

for the gift *b* the wise, and	Ex 23:8	5786

BLINDFOLDED

And when they had *b* him, they	Lk 22:64	4028

BLINDNESS

at the door of the house with *b*	Gen 19:11	5575
smite thee with madness, and *b*	Deut 28:28	5788
this people, I pray thee, with *b*	2Kin 6:18	5575
he smote them with *b* according to	2Kin 6:18	5575
every horse of the people with *b*	Zec 12:4	5788
that *b* in part is happened to	Rom 11:25	4457
because of the *b* of their heart	Eph 4:18	4457

BLOOD

the voice of thy brother's *b*	Gen 4:10	1818
thy brother's *b* from thy hand	Gen 4:11	1818
thereof, which is the *b* thereof	Gen 9:4	1818
surely your *b* of your lives will	Gen 9:5	1818
Whoso sheddeth man's *b*,	Gen 9:6	1818
by man shall his *b* be shed	Gen 9:6	1818
Reuben said unto them, Shed no *b*	Gen 37:22	1818
our brother, and conceal his *b*	Gen 37:26	1818
and dipped the coat in the *b*	Gen 37:31	1818
behold, also his *b* is required	Gen 42:22	1818
and his clothes in the *b* of grapes	Gen 49:11	1818
shall become *b* upon the dry land	Ex 4:9	1818
and they shall be turned to *b*	Ex 7:17	1818
of water, that they may become *b*	Ex 7:19	1818
that there may be *b* throughout	Ex 7:19	1818
in the river were turned to *b*	Ex 7:20	1818
there was *b* throughout all the	Ex 7:21	1818
And they shall take of the *b*	Ex 12:7	1818
the *b* shall be to you for a token	Ex 12:13	1818
and when I see the *b*, I will pass	Ex 12:13	1818
dip it in the *b* that is in the	Ex 12:22	1818
with the *b* that is in the bason	Ex 12:22	1818
he seeth the *b* upon the lintel	Ex 12:23	1818
there shall no *b* be shed for him	Ex 22:2	1818
there shall be *b* shed for him	Ex 22:3	1818
Thou shalt not offer the *b* of my	Ex 23:18	1818
And Moses took half of the *b*	Ex 24:6	1818
half of the *b* he sprinkled on the	Ex 24:6	1818
And Moses took the *b*, and sprinkled	Ex 24:8	1818
Behold the *b* of the covenant,	Ex 24:8	1818
take of the *b* of the bullock	Ex 29:12	1818
pour all the *b* beside the bottom	Ex 29:12	1818
the ram, and thou shalt take his *b*	Ex 29:16	1818
kill the ram, and take of his *b*	Ex 29:20	1818
sprinkle the *b* upon the altar	Ex 29:20	1818
of the *b* that is upon the altar	Ex 29:21	1818
with the *b* of the sin offering of	Ex 30:10	1818
Thou shalt not offer the *b* of my	Ex 34:25	1818
Aaron's sons, shall bring the *b*	Lev 1:5	1818
sprinkle the *b* round about upon	Lev 1:5	1818

shall sprinkle his *b* round about	Lev 1:11	1818
the *b* thereof shall be wrung out	Lev 1:15	1818
the *b* upon the altar round about	Lev 3:2	1818
b thereof round about upon the	Lev 3:8	1818
of Aaron shall sprinkle the *b*	Lev 3:13	1818
that ye eat neither fat nor *b*	Lev 3:17	1818
shall take of the bullock's *b*	Lev 4:5	1818
shall dip his finger in the *b*	Lev 4:6	1818
sprinkle of the *b* seven times	Lev 4:6	1818
priest shall put some of the *b*	Lev 4:7	1818
shall pour all the *b* of the	Lev 4:7	1818
b to the tabernacle of the	Lev 4:16	1818
dip his finger in some of the *b*	Lev 4:17	1818
he shall put some of the *b* upon	Lev 4:18	1818
shall pour out all the *b* at the	Lev 4:18	1818
b of the sin offering with his	Lev 4:25	1818
shall pour out his *b* at the	Lev 4:25	1818
of the *b* thereof with his finger	Lev 4:30	1818
shall pour out all the *b* thereof	Lev 4:30	1818
b of the sin offering with his	Lev 4:34	1818
shall pour out all the *b* thereof	Lev 4:34	1818
he shall sprinkle of the *b* of the	Lev 5:9	1818
the rest of the *b* shall be wrung	Lev 5:9	1818
of the *b* thereof upon any garment	Lev 6:27	1818
whereof any of the *b* is brought	Lev 6:30	1818
the *b* thereof shall he sprinkle	Lev 7:2	1818
the *b* of the peace offerings	Lev 7:14	1818
ye shall eat no manner of *b*	Lev 7:26	1818
it be that eateth any manner of *b*	Lev 7:27	1818
that offereth the *b* of the peace	Lev 7:33	1818
and Moses took the *b*, and put it	Lev 8:15	1818
poured the *b* at the bottom of the	Lev 8:15	1818
Moses sprinkled the *b* upon the	Lev 8:19	1818
and Moses took of the *b* of it	Lev 8:23	1818
Moses put of the *b* upon the tip	Lev 8:24	1818
Moses sprinkled the *b* upon the	Lev 8:24	1818
of the *b* which was upon the altar	Lev 8:30	1818
of Aaron brought the *b* unto him	Lev 9:9	1818
and he dipped his finger in the *b*	Lev 9:9	1818
poured out the *b* at the bottom of	Lev 9:9	1818
sons presented unto him the *b*	Lev 9:12	1818
sons presented unto him the *b*	Lev 9:18	1818
the *b* of it was not brought in	Lev 10:18	1818
in the *b* of her purifying three	Lev 12:4	1818
she shall continue in the *b* of	Lev 12:5	1818
cleansed from the issue of her *b*	Lev 12:7	1818
the living bird in the *b* of the	Lev 14:6	1818
of the *b* of the trespass offering	Lev 14:14	1818
upon the *b* of the trespass	Lev 14:17	1818
of the *b* of the trespass offering	Lev 14:25	1818
upon the place of the *b* of the	Lev 14:28	1818
dip them in the *b* of the slain	Lev 14:51	1818
the house with the *b* of the bird	Lev 14:52	1818
and her issue in her flesh be *b*	Lev 15:19	1818
b many days out of the time of	Lev 15:25	1818
take of the *b* of the bullock	Lev 16:14	1818
the *b* with his finger seven times	Lev 16:14	1818
bring his *b* within the vail, and	Lev 16:15	1818
do with that *b* as he did with the	Lev 16:15	1818
he did with the *b* of the bullock	Lev 16:15	1818
take of the *b* of the bullock	Lev 16:18	1818
of the *b* of the goat, and put it	Lev 16:18	1818
he shall sprinkle of the *b* upon	Lev 16:19	1818
whose *b* was brought in to make	Lev 16:27	1818
b shall be imputed unto that man	Lev 17:4	1818
he hath shed *b*	Lev 17:4	1818
b upon the altar of the LORD at	Lev 17:6	1818
you, that eateth any manner of *b*	Lev 17:10	1818
against that soul that eateth *b*	Lev 17:10	1818
the life of the flesh is in the *b*	Lev 17:11	1818
for it is the *b* that maketh an	Lev 17:11	1818
No soul of you shall eat *b*	Lev 17:12	1818
that sojourneth among you eat *b*	Lev 17:12	1818
shall even pour out the *b* thereof	Lev 17:13	1818
the *b* of it is for the life	Lev 17:14	1818
Ye shall eat the *b* of no manner	Lev 17:14	1818
of all flesh is the *b* thereof	Lev 17:14	1818
against the *b* of thy neighbour	Lev 19:16	1818
not eat any thing with the *b*	Lev 19:26	1818
his *b* shall be upon him	Lev 20:9	1818
their *b* shall be upon them	Lev 20:11	1818
their *b* shall be upon them	Lev 20:12	1818
their *b* shall be upon them	Lev 20:13	1818
their *b* shall be upon them	Lev 20:16	1818
uncovered the fountain of her *b*	Lev 20:18	1818
their *b* shall be upon them	Lev 20:27	1818
sprinkle their *b* upon the altar	Num 18:17	1818
take of her *b* with his finger	Num 19:4	1818
sprinkle of the *b* directly before	Num 19:4	1818
her skin, and her flesh, and her *b*	Num 19:5	1818
prey, and drink the *b* of the slain	Num 23:24	1818
The revenger of *b* himself shall	Num 35:19	1818
the revenger of *b* shall slay the	Num 35:21	1818
the revenger of *b* according to	Num 35:24	1818
of the hand of the revenger of *b*	Num 35:25	1818
the revenger of *b* find him	Num 35:27	1818
the revenger of *b* kill the slayer	Num 35:27	1818
he shall not be guilty of *b*	Num 35:27	1818
for *b* it defileth the land	Num 35:33	1818
of the *b* that is shed therein	Num 35:33	1818
but by the *b* of him that shed it	Num 35:33	1818
Only ye shall not eat the *b*	Deut 12:16	1818
be sure that thou eat not the *b*	Deut 12:23	1818
for the *b* is the life	Deut 12:23	1818
offerings, the flesh and the *b*	Deut 12:27	1818
the *b* of thy sacrifices shall be	Deut 12:27	1818
thou shalt not eat the *b* thereof	Deut 15:23	1818
in judgment, between *b* and *b*	Deut 17:8	1818
of the *b* pursue the slayer	Deut 19:6	1818
That innocent *b* be not shed in	Deut 19:10	1818
inheritance, and so *b* be upon thee	Deut 19:10	1818
into the hand of the avenger of *b*	Deut 19:12	1818
guilt of innocent *b* from Israel	Deut 19:13	1818
Our hands have not shed this *b*	Deut 21:7	1818
lay not innocent *b* unto thy	Deut 21:8	1818
the *b* shall be forgiven them	Deut 21:8	1818
of innocent *b* from among you	Deut 21:9	1818
thou bring not *b* upon thine house	Deut 22:8	1818
drink the pure *b* of the grape	Deut 32:14	1818
make mine arrows drunk with *b*	Deut 32:42	1818
and that with the *b* of the slain	Deut 32:42	1818
will avenge the *b* of his servants	Deut 32:43	1818
his *b* shall be upon his head, and	Josh 2:19	1818
his *b* shall be on our head, if	Josh 2:19	1818
your refuge from the avenger of *b*	Josh 20:3	1818
the avenger of *b* pursue after him	Josh 20:5	1818
by the hand of the avenger of *b*	Josh 20:9	1818
their *b* be laid upon Abimelech	Judg 9:24	1818
people did eat them with the *b*	1Sa 14:32	1818
LORD, in that they eat with the *b*	1Sa 14:33	1818
the LORD in eating with the *b*	1Sa 14:34	1818
wilt thou sin against innocent *b*	1Sa 19:5	1818
thee from coming to shed *b*	1Sa 25:26	1818
that thou hast shed *b* causeless	1Sa 25:31	1818
me this day from coming to shed *b*	1Sa 25:33	1818
let not my *b* fall to the earth	1Sa 26:20	1818
unto him, Thy *b* be upon thy head	2Sa 1:16	1818
From the *b* of the slain, from the	2Sa 1:22	1818
for the *b* of Asahel his brother	2Sa 3:27	1818
the *b* of Abner the son of Ner	2Sa 3:28	1818
now require his *b* of your hand	2Sa 4:11	1818
of *b* to destroy any more, lest	2Sa 4:11	1818
all the *b* of the house of Saul	2Sa 16:8	1818
Amasa wallowed in *b* in the midst	2Sa 20:12	1818
is not this the *b* of the men that	2Sa 23:17	1818
shed the *b* of war in peace, and	1Kin 2:5	1818
put the *b* of war upon his girdle	1Kin 2:5	1818
thou down to the grave with *b*	1Kin 2:9	1818
mayest take away the innocent *b*	1Kin 2:31	1818
return his *b* upon his own head	1Kin 2:32	1818
Their *b* shall therefore return	1Kin 2:33	1818
thy *b* shall be upon thine own	1Kin 2:37	1818
till the *b* gushed out upon them	1Kin 18:28	1818
b of Naboth shall dogs lick thy	1Kin 21:19	1818
of Naboth shall dogs lick thy *b*	1Kin 21:19	1818
the *b* ran out of the wound into	1Kin 22:35	1818
and the dogs licked up his *b*	1Kin 22:38	1818
on the other side as red as *b*	2Kin 3:22	1818
And they said, This is *b*	2Kin 3:23	1818
that I may avenge the *b* of my	2Kin 9:7	1818
the *b* of all the servants of the	2Kin 9:7	1818
seen yesterday the *b* of Naboth	2Kin 9:26	1818
the *b* of his sons, saith the LORD	2Kin 9:26	1818
some of her *b* was sprinkled on	2Kin 9:33	1818
sprinkled the *b* of his peace	2Kin 16:13	1818
all the *b* of the burnt offering	2Kin 16:15	1818
all the *b* of the sacrifice	2Kin 16:15	1818
shed innocent *b* very much	2Kin 21:16	1818
for the innocent *b* that he shed	2Kin 24:4	1818
filled Jerusalem with innocent *b*	2Kin 24:4	1818
shall I drink the *b* of these men	1Chr 11:19	1818
Thou hast shed *b* abundantly	1Chr 22:8	1818
much *b* upon the earth in my sight	1Chr 22:8	1818
been a man of war, and hast shed *b*	1Chr 28:3	1818
their cities, between *b* and *b*	2Chr 19:10	1818
the *b* of the sons of Jehoiada the	2Chr 24:25	1818
and the priests received the *b*	2Chr 29:22	1818
sprinkled the *b* upon the altar	2Chr 29:22	1818
sprinkled the *b* upon the altar	2Chr 29:22	1818
with their *b* upon the altar	2Chr 29:24	1818
the priests sprinkled the *b*	2Chr 30:16	1818
sprinkled the *b* from their hands	2Chr 35:11	1818

O earth, cover not thou my *b*	Job 16:18	1818
Her young ones also suck up *b*	Job 39:30	1818
When he maketh inquisition for *b*	Ps 9:12	1818
offerings of *b* will I not offer	Ps 16:4	1818
What profit is there in my *b*	Ps 30:9	1818
of bulls, or drink the *b* of goats	Ps 50:13	1818
his feet in the *b* of the wicked	Ps 58:10	1818
dipped in the *b* of thine enemies	Ps 68:23	1818
shall their *b* be in his sight	Ps 72:14	1818
And had turned their rivers into *b*	Ps 78:44	1818
Their *b* have they shed like water	Ps 79:3	1818
b of thy servants which is shed	Ps 79:10	1818
and condemn the innocent *b*	Ps 94:21	1818
He turned their waters into *b*	Ps 105:29	1818
And shed innocent *b*	Ps 106:38	1818
even the *b* of their sons and of	Ps 106:38	1818
and the land was polluted with *b*	Ps 106:38	1818
with us, let us lay wait for *b*	Prov 1:11	1818
to evil, and make haste to shed *b*	Prov 1:16	1818
And they lay wait for their own *b*	Prov 1:18	1818
and hands that shed innocent *b*	Prov 6:17	1818
wicked are to lie in wait for *b*	Prov 12:6	1818
man that doeth violence to the *b*	Prov 28:17	1818
of the nose bringeth forth *b*	Prov 30:33	1818
delight not in the *b* of bullocks	Is 1:11	1818
your hands are full of *b*	Is 1:15	1818
shall have purged the *b* of	Is 4:4	1818
noise, and garments rolled in *b*	Is 9:5	1818
of Dimon shall be full of *b*	Is 15:9	1818
earth also shall disclose her *b*	Is 26:21	1818
his ears from hearing of *b*	Is 33:15	1818
shall be melted with their *b*	Is 34:3	1818
of the LORD is filled with *b*	Is 34:6	1818
fatness, and with the *b* of lambs	Is 34:6	1818
their land shall be soaked with *b*	Is 34:7	1818
shall be drunken with their own *b*	Is 49:26	1818
For your hands are defiled with *b*	Is 59:3	1818
make haste to shed innocent *b*	Is 59:7	1818
their *b* shall be sprinkled upon	Is 63:3	5332
as if he offered swine's *b*	Is 66:3	1818
the *b* of the souls of the poor	Jer 2:34	1818
shed not innocent *b* in this place	Jer 7:6	1818
pour out their *b* by the force of	Jer 18:21	
place with the *b* of innocents	Jer 19:4	1818
shed innocent *b* in this place	Jer 22:3	1818
and for to shed innocent *b*	Jer 22:17	1818
bring innocent *b* upon yourselves	Jer 26:15	1818
and made drunk with their *b*	Jer 46:10	1818
keepeth back his sword from *b*	Jer 48:10	1818
my *b* upon the inhabitants of	Jer 51:35	1818
that have shed the *b* of the just	Lam 4:13	1818
have polluted themselves with *b*	Lam 4:14	1818
but his *b* will I require at thine	Eze 3:18	1818
but his *b* will I require at thine	Eze 3:20	1818
b shall pass through thee	Eze 5:17	1818
great, and the land is full of *b*	Eze 9:9	1818
and pour out my fury upon it in *b*	Eze 14:19	1818
saw thee polluted in thine own *b*	Eze 16:6	1818
unto thee when thou wast in thy *b*	Eze 16:6	1818
unto thee when thou wast in thy *b*	Eze 16:6	1818
washed away thy *b* from thee	Eze 16:9	1818
bare, and wast polluted in thy *b*	Eze 16:22	1818
by the *b* of thy children, which	Eze 16:36	1818
wedlock is shed and *b* are judged	Eze 16:38	1818
and I will give thee *b* in fury	Eze 16:38	1818
that is a robber, a shedder of *b*	Eze 18:10	1818
his *b* shall be upon him	Eze 18:13	1818
mother is like a vine in thy *b*	Eze 19:10	1818
thy *b* shall be in the midst of	Eze 21:32	1818
The city sheddeth *b* in the midst	Eze 22:3	1818
in thy *b* that thou hast shed	Eze 22:4	1818
in thee to their power to shed *b*	Eze 22:6	1818
men that carry tales to shed *b*	Eze 22:9	1818
have they taken gifts to shed *b*	Eze 22:12	1818
at thy *b* which hath been in the	Eze 22:13	1818
ravening the prey, to shed *b*	Eze 22:27	1818
b is in their hands, and with	Eze 23:37	1818
the manner of women that shed *b*	Eze 23:45	1818
and *b* is in their hands	Eze 23:45	1818
For her *b* is in the midst of her	Eze 24:7	1818
I have set her *b* upon the top of	Eze 24:8	1818
pestilence, and *b* into her street	Eze 28:23	1818
I will also water with thy *b* the	Eze 32:6	1818
his *b* shall be upon his own head	Eze 33:4	1818
his *b* shall be upon him	Eze 33:5	1818
but his *b* will I require at the	Eze 33:6	1818
but his *b* will I require at thine	Eze 33:8	1818
Ye eat with the *b*, and lift up	Eze 33:25	1818
eyes toward your idols, and shed *b*	Eze 33:25	1818
hast shed the *b* of the children	Eze 35:5	
b, and *b* shall pursue thee	Eze 35:6	1818
b, even *b* shall pursue thee	Eze 35:6	1818
my fury upon them for the *b* that	Eze 36:18	1818
him with pestilence and with *b*	Eze 38:22	1818
that ye may eat flesh, and drink *b*	Eze 39:17	1818
drink the *b* of the princes of the	Eze 39:18	1818
drink *b* till ye be drunken, of my	Eze 39:19	1818
thereon, and to sprinkle *b* thereon	Eze 43:18	1818
thou shalt take of the *b* thereof	Eze 43:20	1818
offer my bread, the fat and the *b*	Eze 44:7	1818
to offer unto me the fat and the *b*	Eze 44:15	1818
take of the *b* of the sin offering	Eze 45:19	1818
I will avenge the *b* of Jezreel	Hos 1:4	1818
break out, and *b* toucheth *b*	Hos 4:2	1818
iniquity, and is polluted with *b*	Hos 6:8	1818
shall he leave his *b* upon him	Hos 12:14	1818
in the heavens and in the earth, *b*	Joel 2:30	1818
into darkness, and the moon into *b*	Joel 2:31	1818
shed innocent *b* in their land	Joel 3:19	1818
their *b* that I have not cleansed	Joel 3:21	1818
and lay not upon us innocent *b*	Jonah 1:14	1818
They build up Zion with *b*	Mic 3:10	1818
they all lie in wait for *b*	Mic 7:2	1818
because of men's *b*, and for the	Hab 2:8	1818
him that buildeth a town with *b*	Hab 2:12	1818
them afraid, because of men's *b*	Hab 2:17	1818
their *b* shall be poured out as	Zeph 1:17	1818
take away his *b* out of his mouth	Zec 9:7	1818
by the *b* of thy covenant I have	Zec 9:11	1818
with an issue of *b* twelve years	Mt 9:20	131
b hath not revealed it unto thee,	Mt 16:17	129
them in the *b* of the prophets.	Mt 23:30	129
righteous *b* shed upon the earth	Mt 23:35	129
b of righteous Abel unto the *b*	Mt 23:35	129
For this is my *b* of the new	Mt 26:28	129
I have betrayed the innocent *b*	Mt 27:4	129
because it is the price of *b*	Mt 27:6	129
field was called, The field of *b*	Mt 27:8	129
of the *b* of this just person	Mt 27:24	129
His *b* be on us, and on our	Mt 27:25	129
had an issue of *b* twelve years	Mk 5:25	129
fountain of her *b* was dried up	Mk 5:29	129
This is my *b* of the new testament	Mk 14:24	129
having an issue of *b* twelve years	Lk 8:43	129
her issue of *b* stanched	Lk 8:44	129
That the *b* of all the prophets,	Lk 11:50	129
From the *b* of Abel unto the *b*	Lk 11:51	129
whose *b* Pilate had mingled with	Lk 13:1	129
cup is the new testament in my *b*	Lk 22:20	129
of *b* falling down to the ground	Lk 22:44	129
Which were born, not of *b*	Jn 1:13	129
of the Son of man, and drink his *b*	Jn 6:53	129
eateth my flesh, and drinketh my *b*	Jn 6:54	129
indeed, and my *b* is drink indeed	Jn 6:55	129
eateth my flesh, and drinketh my *b*	Jn 6:56	129
and forthwith came there out *b*	Jn 19:34	129
that is to say, The field of *b*	Acts 1:19	129
b, and fire, and vapour of smoke	Acts 2:19	129
into darkness, and the moon into *b*	Acts 2:20	129
to bring this man's *b* upon us	Acts 5:28	129
from things strangled, and from *b*	Acts 15:20	129
meats offered to idols, and from *b*	Acts 15:29	129
hath made of one *b* all nations of	Acts 17:26	129
Your *b* be upon your own heads	Acts 18:6	129
I am pure from the *b* of all men	Acts 20:26	129
he hath purchased with his own *b*	Acts 20:28	129
offered to idols, and from *b*	Acts 21:25	129
when the *b* of thy martyr Stephen	Acts 22:20	129
Their feet are swift to shed *b*	Rom 3:15	129
through faith in his *b*, to	Rom 3:25	129
being now justified by his *b*	Rom 5:9	129
the communion of the *b* of Christ	1Cor 10:16	129
cup is the new testament in my *b*	1Cor 11:25	129
of the body and *b* of the Lord	1Cor 11:27	129
b cannot inherit the kingdom of	1Cor 15:50	129
I conferred not with flesh and *b*	Gal 1:16	129
we have redemption through his *b*	Eph 1:7	129
are made nigh by the *b* of Christ	Eph 2:13	129
we wrestle not against flesh and *b*	Eph 6:12	129
we have redemption through his *b*	Col 1:14	129
peace through the *b* of his cross	Col 1:20	129
are partakers of flesh and *b*	Heb 2:14	129
once every year, not without *b*	Heb 9:7	129
Neither by the *b* of goats	Heb 9:12	129
but by his own *b* he entered in	Heb 9:12	129
For if the *b* of bulls and of goats	Heb 9:13	129
much more shall the *b* of Christ	Heb 9:14	129
testament was dedicated without *b*	Heb 9:18	129
the law, he took the *b* of calves	Heb 9:19	129
This is the *b* of the testament	Heb 9:20	129
with *b* both the tabernacle	Heb 9:21	129
are by the law purged with *b*	Heb 9:22	129

shedding of *b* is no remission.................. Heb 9:22   130
place every year with *b* of others .... Heb 9:25   129
not possible that the *b* of bulls............... Heb 10:4   129
the holiest by the *b* of Jesus .... Heb 10:19   129
counted the *b* of the covenant .... Heb 10:29   129
passover, and the sprinkling of *b* .... Heb 11:28   129
Ye have not yet resisted unto *b*.............. Heb 12:4   129
to the *b* of sprinkling, that .... Heb 12:24   129
whose *b* is brought into the .... Heb 13:11   129
the people with his own *b*....................... Heb 13:12   129
through the *b* of the everlasting .... Heb 13:20   129
of the *b* of Jesus Christ 1Pet 1:2   129
But with the precious *b* of Christ 1Pet 1:19   129
the *b* of Jesus Christ his Son 1Jn 1:7   129
is he that came by water and *b*............... 1Jn 5:6   129
by water only, but by water and *b*.......... 1Jn 5:6   129
spirit, and the water, and the *b* 1Jn 5:8   129
us from our sins in his own *b*.................. Rev 1:5   129
God by thy *b* out of every kindred.......... Rev 5:9   129
avenge our *b* on them that dwell .... Rev 6:10   129
of hair, and the moon became as *b*........ Rev 6:12   129
them white in the *b* of the Lamb............ Rev 7:14   129
hail and fire mingled with *b*................... Rev 8:7   129
third part of the sea became *b* .... Rev 8:8   129
over waters to turn them to *b* .... Rev 11:6   129
overcame him by the *b* of the Lamb ...... Rev 12:11   129
b came out of the winepress, even .... Rev 14:20   129
it became as the *b* of a dead man .... Rev 16:3   129
and they became *b*................................... Rev 16:4   129
they have shed the *b* of saints .... Rev 16:6   129
thou hast given them *b* to drink .... Rev 16:6   129
drunken with the *b* of the saints .... Rev 17:6   129
with the *b* of the martyrs of .... Rev 17:6   129
her was found the *b* of prophets............. Rev 18:24   129
hath avenged the *b* of his .... Rev 19:2   129
with a vesture dipped in *b* .... Rev 19:13   129

BLOODGUILTINESS
Deliver me from *b*, O God, thou.............. Ps 51:14   1818

BLOODTHIRSTY
The *b* hate the upright..................... Prov 29:10   582,1818

BLOODY
Surely a *b* husband art thou to me .... Ex 4:25   1818
A *b* husband thou art, because of........... Ex 4:26   1818
Come out, come out, thou *b* man 2Sa 16:7   1818
because thou art a *b* man 2Sa 16:8   1818
is for Saul, and for his *b* house 2Sa 21:1   1818
the Lord will abhor the *b* .... Ps 5:6   1818
sinners, nor my life with *b* men .... Ps 26:9   1818
b and deceitful men shall not live........... Ps 55:23   1818
iniquity, and save me from *b* men........... Ps 59:2   1818
from me therefore, ye *b* men .... Ps 139:19   1818
for the land is full of *b* crimes .... Eze 7:23   1818
judge, wilt thou judge the *b* city............ Eze 22:2   1818
Woe to the *b* city, to the pot................... Eze 24:6   1818
Woe to the *b* city .... Eze 24:9   1818
Woe to the *b* city .... Nah 3:1   1818
sick of a fever and of a *b* flux................. Acts 28:8   1420

BLOOMED
b blossoms, and yielded almonds .... Num 17:8   6692

BLOSSOM
rod, whom I shall choose, shall *b* .... Num 17:5   6524
their *b* shall go up as dust .... Is 5:24   6525
Israel shall *b* and bud, and fill............... Is 27:6   6692
shall rejoice, and *b* as the rose .... Is 35:1   6524
It shall *b* abundantly, and rejoice .... Is 35:2   6524
Although the fig tree shall not *b* .... Hab 3:17   6524

BLOSSOMED
the rod hath *b*, pride hath budded......... Eze 7:10   6692

BLOSSOMS
it budded, and her *b* shot forth .... Gen 40:10   5322
brought forth buds, and bloomed *b* .... Num 17:8   6731

BLOT
b me, I pray thee, out of thy .... Ex 32:32   4229
him will I *b* out of my book .... Ex 32:33   4229
he shall *b* them out with the .... Num 5:23   4229
b out their name from under .... Deut 9:14   4229
that thou shalt *b* out the......................... Deut 25:19   4229
the Lord shall *b* out his name .... Deut 29:20   4229
b out the name of Israel from 2Kin 14:27   4229
if any *b* hath cleaved to mine .... Job 31:7   3971
mercies *b* out my transgressions .... Ps 51:1   4229
b out all mine iniquities.......................... Ps 51:9   4229
a wicked man getteth himself a *b* .... Prov 9:7   3971
neither *b* out their sin from thy.............. Jer 18:23   4229
I will not *b* out his name out of.............. Rev 3:5   1813

BLOTTED
sin be *b* out from before thee .... Neh 4:5   4229
Let them be *b* out of the book of............ Ps 69:28   4229
following let their name be *b* out .... Ps 109:13   4229
the sin of his mother be *b* out .... Ps 109:14   4229
I have *b* out, as a thick cloud, ... Is 44:22   4229
that your sins may be *b* out .... Acts 3:19   1813

BLOTTETH
I, even I, am he that *b* out thy .... Is 43:25   4229

BLOTTING
B out the handwriting of......................... Col 2:14   1813

BLOW
Thou didst *b* with thy wind, the .... Ex 15:10   5398
And when they shall *b* with them .... Num 10:3   8628
if they *b* but with one trumpet .... Num 10:4   8628
When ye *b* an alarm, then the .... Num 10:5   8628
When ye *b* an alarm the second .... Num 10:6   8628
they shall *b* an alarm for their............... Num 10:6   8628
be gathered together, ye shall *b*............. Num 10:7   8628
shall *b* with the trumpets .... Num 10:8   8628
then ye shall *b* an alarm with the .... Num 10:9   7321
ye shall *b* with the trumpets over .... Num 10:10   8628
and the trumpets to *b* in his hand......... Num 31:6   8643
priests shall *b* with the trumpets........... Josh 6:4   8628
When I *b* with a trumpet, I and all .... Judg 7:18   8628
then ye *b* the trumpets also on .... Judg 7:18   8628
in their right hands to *b* withal.............. Judg 7:20   8628
b ye with the trumpet, and say, ... 1Kin 1:34   8628
did *b* with the trumpets before 1Chr 15:24   2690
consumed by the *b* of thine hand .... Ps 39:10   8409
an east wind to *b* in the heaven............. Ps 78:26   5265
B up the trumpet in the new moon, ... Ps 81:3   8628
he causeth his wind to *b*, and the.......... Ps 147:18   5380
b upon my garden, that the spices .... Song 4:16   6315
and he shall also *b* upon them................ Is 40:24   5398
B ye the trumpet in the land .... Jer 4:5   8628
b the trumpet in Tekoa, and set up .... Jer 6:1   8628
breach, with a very grievous *b*............... Jer 14:17   4347
b the trumpet among the nations, ... Jer 51:27   8628
I will *b* against thee in the fire .... Eze 21:31   6315
to *b* the fire upon it, to melt it .... Eze 22:20   5301
b upon you in the fire of my .... Eze 22:21   5301
he *b* the trumpet, and warn the .... Eze 33:3   8628
b not the trumpet, and the people .... Eze 33:6   8628
B ye the cornet in Gibeah, and the........ Hos 5:8   8628
B ye the trumpet in Zion, and .... Joel 2:1   8628
B the trumpet in Zion, sanctify a .... Joel 2:15   8628
brought it home, I did *b* upon it .... Hag 1:9   5301
the Lord God shall *b* the trumpet.......... Zec 9:14   8628
And when ye see the south wind *b* .... Lk 12:55   *4154*
wind should not *b* on the earth .... Rev 7:1   *4154*

BLOWETH
when he *b* a trumpet, hear ye .... Is 18:3   8628
the spirit of the Lord *b* upon it.............. Is 40:7   5380
that *b* the coals in the fire...................... Is 54:16   5301
The wind *b* where it listeth, and........ Jn 3:8   *4154*

BLOWING
a memorial of *b* of trumpets .... Lev 23:24   8643
it is a day of *b* the trumpets................... Num 29:1   8643
going on, and *b* with the trumpets .... Josh 6:9   8628
going on, and *b* with the trumpets .... Josh 6:13   8628

BLOWN
a fire not *b* shall consume him .... Job 20:26   5301
that the great trumpet shall be *b* .... Is 27:13   8628
They have *b* the trumpet, even to .... Eze 7:14   8628
Shall a trumpet be *b* in the city............. Amos 3:6   8628

BLUE
And *b*, and purple, and scarlet, and ...... Ex 25:4   8504
of fine twined linen, and *b* .... Ex 26:1   8504
of *b* upon the edge of the one .... Ex 26:4   8504
And thou shalt make a vail of *b*............. Ex 26:31   8504
for the door of the tent, of *b* .... Ex 26:36   8504
an hanging of twenty cubits, of *b* .... Ex 27:16   8504
And they shall take gold, and *b* .... Ex 28:5   8504
make the ephod of gold, of *b* .... Ex 28:6   8504
even of gold, of *b*, and purple, and........ Ex 28:8   8504
of gold, of *b*, and of purple, and .... Ex 28:15   8504
of the ephod with a lace of *b*.................. Ex 28:28   8504
the robe of the ephod all of *b* .... Ex 28:31   8504
thou shalt make pomegranates of *b* ...... Ex 28:33   8504
And thou shalt put it on a *b* lace .... Ex 28:37   8504
And *b*, and purple, and scarlet, and ...... Ex 35:6   8504
every man, with whom was found *b* .... Ex 35:23   8504
which they had spun, both of *b* .... Ex 35:25   8504
and of the embroiderer, in *b* .... Ex 35:35   8504
of fine twined linen, and *b* .... Ex 36:8   8504
he made loops of *b* on the edge of .... Ex 36:11   8504

B

And he made a vail of *b*, and purple	Ex 36:35	8504
for the tabernacle door of *b*	Ex 36:37	8504
of the court was needlework, of *b*	Ex 38:18	8504
workman, and an embroiderer in *b*	Ex 38:23	8504
And of the *b*, and purple, and	Ex 39:1	8504
And he made the ephod of gold, *b*	Ex 39:2	8504
into wires, to work it in the *b*	Ex 39:3	8504
of gold, *b*, and purple, and scarlet	Ex 39:5	8504
of gold, *b*, and purple, and scarlet	Ex 39:8	8504
of the ephod with a lace of *b*	Ex 39:21	8504
the ephod of woven work, all of *b*	Ex 39:22	8504
of the robe pomegranates of *b*	Ex 39:24	8504
girdle of fine twined linen, and *b*	Ex 39:29	8504
And they tied unto it a lace of *b*	Ex 39:31	8504
over it a cloth wholly of *b*	Num 4:6	8504
they shall spread a cloth of *b*.................	Num 4:7	8504
And they shall take a cloth of *b*	Num 4:9	8504
they shall spread a cloth of *b*.................	Num 4:11	8504
and put them in a cloth of *b*...................	Num 4:12	8504
of the borders a ribband of *b*	Num 15:38	8504
and in purple, and crimson, and *b*	2Chr 2:7	8504
and in timber, in purple, in *b*.................	2Chr 2:14	8504
And he made the vail of *b*, and	2Chr 3:14	8504
Where were white, green, and *b*	Est 1:6	8504
upon a pavement of red, and *b*	Est 1:6	8504
of the king in royal apparel of *b*	Est 8:15	8504
b and purple is their clothing	Jer 10:9	8504
Which were clothed with *b*	Eze 23:6	8504
b and purple from the isles of	Eze 27:7	8504
in *b* clothes, and broidered work, ...	Eze 27:24	8504

BLUENESS

The *b* of a wound cleanseth away...........	Prov 20:30	2250

BLUNT

If the iron be *b*, and he do not.................	Eccl 10:10	6949

BLUSH

b to lift up my face to thee, my...............	Ezr 9:6	3637
all ashamed, neither could they *b*...........	Jer 6:15	3637
all ashamed, neither could they *b*...........	Jer 8:12	3637

BOANERGES (*bo-an-er'-jees*) *Surname of James and John, the sons of Zebedee.*

and he surnamed them *B*, which is, ...	Mk 3:17	993

BOAR

The *b* out of the wood doth waste...........	Ps 80:13	2386

BOARD

cubits shall be the length of a *b*.............	Ex 26:16	7175
shall be the breadth of one *b*	Ex 26:16	7175
tenons shall there be in one *b*	Ex 26:17	7175
under one *b* for his two tenons	Ex 26:19	7175
another *b* for his two tenons	Ex 26:19	7175
two sockets under one *b*	Ex 26:21	7175
and two sockets under another *b*	Ex 26:21	7175
two sockets under one *b*	Ex 26:25	7175
and two sockets under another *b*	Ex 26:25	7175
The length of a *b* was ten cubits	Ex 36:21	7175
and the breadth of a *b* one cubit	Ex 36:21	7175
One *b* had two tenons, equally	Ex 36:22	7175
under one *b* for his two tenons	Ex 36:24	7175
another *b* for his two tenons	Ex 36:24	7175
two sockets under one *b*	Ex 36:26	7175
and two sockets under another *b*	Ex 36:26	7175
silver, under every *b* two sockets	Ex 36:30	7175

BOARDS

thou shalt make *b* for the	Ex 26:15	7175
for all the *b* of the tabernacle	Ex 26:17	7175
make the *b* for the tabernacle	Ex 26:18	7175
twenty *b* on the south side	Ex 26:18	7175
of silver under the twenty *b*...................	Ex 26:19	7175
side there shall be twenty *b*	Ex 26:20	7175
westward thou shalt make six *b*	Ex 26:22	7175
two *b* shalt thou make for the	Ex 26:23	7175
And they shall be eight *b*, and	Ex 26:25	7175
five for the *b* of the one side of	Ex 26:26	7175
five bars for the *b* of the other	Ex 26:27	7175
five bars for the *b* of the side	Ex 26:27	7175
the *b* shall reach from end to end	Ex 26:28	7175
shalt overlay the *b* with gold	Ex 26:29	7175
Hollow with *b* shalt thou make it	Ex 27:8	3871
covering, his taches, and his *b*...............	Ex 35:11	7175
he made *b* for the tabernacle of	Ex 36:20	7175
for all the *b* of the tabernacle	Ex 36:22	7175
he made *b* for the tabernacle	Ex 36:23	7175
twenty *b* for the south side	Ex 36:23	7175
silver he made under the twenty *b*	Ex 36:24	7175
north corner, he made twenty *b*	Ex 36:25	7175
tabernacle westward he made six *b*........	Ex 36:27	7175
two *b* made he for the corners of	Ex 36:28	7175
And there were eight *b*	Ex 36:30	7175

five for the *b* of the one side of	Ex 36:31	7175
five bars for the *b* of the other	Ex 36:32	7175
five bars for the *b* of the	Ex 36:32	7175
b from the one end to the other	Ex 36:33	7175
And he overlaid the *b* with gold	Ex 36:34	7175
he made the altar hollow with *b*	Ex 38:7	3871
his furniture, his taches, his *b*	Ex 39:33	7175
sockets, and set up the *b* thereof	Ex 40:18	7175
shall be the *b* of the tabernacle	Num 3:36	7175
the *b* of the tabernacle, and the.............	Num 4:31	7175
house with beams and *b* of cedar...........	1Kin 6:9	7713
the house within with *b* of cedar	1Kin 6:15	6763
and the walls with *b* of cedar.................	1Kin 6:16	6763
will inclose her with *b* of cedar	Song 8:9	3871
thy ship *b* of fir trees of Senir	Eze 27:5	3871
And the rest, some on *b*, and some	Acts 27:44	4548

BOAST

b himself as he that putteth it	1Kin 20:11	1984
thine heart lifteth thee up to *b*	2Chr 25:19	3513
soul shall make her *b* in the LORD	Ps 34:2	1984
In God we *b* all the day long, and..........	Ps 44:8	1984
b themselves in the multitude of............	Ps 49:6	1984
workers of iniquity *b* themselves	Ps 94:4	559
that *b* themselves of idols	Ps 97:7	1984
B not thyself of to morrow......................	Prov 27:1	1984
Shall the ax *b* itself against him	Is 10:15	6286
their glory being ye *b* yourselves............	Is 61:6	3235
the law, and makest thy *b* of God	Rom 2:17	2744
Thou that makest thy *b* of the law	Rom 2:23	2744
B not against the branches	Rom 11:18	2620
But if thou *b*, thou bearest not	Rom 11:18	
for which I *b* of you to them of...............	2Cor 9:2	2744
For though I should *b* somewhat............	2Cor 10:8	2744
But we will not *b* of things	2Cor 10:13	2744
not to *b* in another man's line of	2Cor 10:16	2744
that I may *b* myself a little.....................	2Cor 11:16	2744
of works, lest any man should *b*	Eph 2:9	2744

BOASTED

your mouth ye have *b* against me	Eze 35:13	1431
For if I have *b* any thing to him.............	2Cor 7:14	2744

BOASTERS

of God, despiteful, proud, *b*	Rom 1:30	213
of their own selves, covetous, *b*..............	2Ti 3:2	213

BOASTEST

Why *b* thou thyself in mischief, O	Ps 52:1	1984

BOASTETH

For the wicked *b* of his heart's	Ps 10:3	1984
he is gone his way, then he *b*	Prov 20:14	1984
Whoso *b* himself of a false gift	Prov 25:14	1984
little member, and *b* great things...........	Jas 3:5	3166

BOASTING

Theudas, *b* himself to be somebody	Acts 5:36	3004
Where is *b* then..	Rom 3:27	2746
to you in truth, even so our *b*.................	2Cor 7:14	2746
love, and of our *b* on your behalf...........	2Cor 8:24	2746
lest our *b* of you should be in.................	2Cor 9:3	2745
ashamed in this same confident *b*..........	2Cor 9:4	2746
Not *b* of things without our	2Cor 10:15	2744
this *b* in the regions of Achaia	2Cor 11:10	2746
in this confidence of *b*............................	2Cor 11:17	2746

BOASTINGS

But now ye rejoice in your *b*	Jas 4:16	212

BOAT

there went over a ferry *b* to	2Sa 19:18	5679
that there was none other *b* there...........	Jn 6:22	4142
not with his disciples into the *b*	Jn 6:22	4142
we had much work to come by the *b*.......	Acts 27:16	4627
had let down the *b* into the sea	Acts 27:30	4627
cut off the ropes of the *b*	Acts 27:32	4627

BOATS

(Howbeit there came other *b* from	Jn 6:23	4142

BOAZ (*bo'-az*) See BOOZ.

1. Husband of Ruth.

and his name was *B*.................................	Ruth 2:1	1162
of the field belonging unto *B*	Ruth 2:3	1162
B came from Beth-lehem, and said..........	Ruth 2:4	1162
Then said *B* unto his servant that	Ruth 2:5	1162
Then said *B* unto Ruth, Hearest	Ruth 2:8	1162
B answered and said unto her, It	Ruth 2:11	1162
B said unto her, At mealtime come	Ruth 2:14	1162
B commanded his young men, saying	Ruth 2:15	1162
with whom I wrought to day is *B*............	Ruth 2:19	1162
B to glean unto the end of barley	Ruth 2:23	1162
now is not *B* of our kindred, with	Ruth 3:2	1162
when *B* had eaten and drunk, and his ...	Ruth 3:7	1162
Then went *B* up to the gate, and............	Ruth 4:1	1162

kinsman of whom *B* spake came by	Ruth 4:1	1162
Then said *B*, What day thou buyest	Ruth 4:5	1162
Therefore the kinsman said unto *B*	Ruth 4:8	1162
B said unto the elders, and unto	Ruth 4:9	1162
So *B* took Ruth, and she was his	Ruth 4:13	1162
And Salmon begat *B*	Ruth 4:21	1162
and *B* begat Obed	Ruth 4:21	1162
begat Salma, and Salma begat *B*	1Chr 2:11	1162
B begat Obed, and Obed begat Jesse	1Chr 2:12	1162

  2. A pillar in Solomon's Temple.

and called the name thereof *B*	1Kin 7:21	1162
and the name of that on the left *B*	2Chr 3:17	1162

BOCHERU (bok'-er-u) *A relative of Saul.*

whose names are these, Azrikam, *B*	1Chr 8:38	1074
whose names are these, Azrikam, *B*	1Chr 9:44	1074

BOCHIM (bo'-kim) *A place near Gilgal.*

the LORD came up from Gilgal to *B*	Judg 2:1	1066
called the name of that place *B*	Judg 2:5	1066

BODIES

the sight of my lord, but our *b*	Gen 47:18	1472
the *b* of his sons from the wall	1Sa 31:12	1472
the *b* of his sons, and brought	1Chr 10:12	1480
they were dead *b* fallen to the	2Chr 20:24	6297
both riches with the dead *b*	2Chr 20:25	6297
they have dominion over our *b*	Neh 9:37	1472
ashes, your *b* to to *b* of clay	Job 13:12	1354
ashes, your *b* to to *b* of clay	Job 13:12	1472
The dead *b* of thy servants have	Ps 79:2	5038
fill the places with the dead *b*	Ps 110:6	1472
And the whole valley of the dead *b*	Jer 31:40	6297
fill them with the dead *b* of men	Jer 33:5	6297
their dead *b* shall be for meat	Jer 34:20	5038
cast all the dead *b* of the men	Jer 41:9	6297
another, and two covered their *b*	Eze 1:11	1472
covered on that side, their *b*	Eze 1:23	1472
upon whose *b* the fire had no	Dan 3:27	1655
king's word, and yielded their *b*	Dan 3:28	1655
be many dead *b* in every place	Amos 8:3	6297
many of the saints which slept	Mt 27:52	4983
that the *b* should not remain upon	Jn 19:31	4983
their own *b* between themselves	Rom 1:24	4983
b by his Spirit that dwelleth in	Rom 8:11	4983
present your *b* a living sacrifice	Rom 12:1	4983
Know ye not that your *b* are the	1Cor 6:15	4983
There are also celestial *b*	1Cor 15:40	4983
and *b* terrestrial	1Cor 15:40	4983
love their wives as their own *b*	Eph 5:28	4983
our *b* washed with pure water	Heb 10:22	4983
For the *b* of those beasts, whose	Heb 13:11	4983
their dead *b* shall lie in the	Rev 11:8	4430
shall see their dead *b* three days	Rev 11:9	4430
their dead *b* to be put in graves	Rev 11:9	4430

BODILY

in a *b* shape like a dove upon him	Lk 3:22	4984
but his *b* presence is weak, and	2Cor 10:10	4983
all the fulness of the Godhead *b*	Col 2:9	4985
For *b* exercise profiteth little	1Ti 4:8	4984

BODY

as it were the *b* of heaven in his	Ex 24:10	6106
shall he go in to any dead *b*	Lev 21:11	5315
LORD he shall come at no dead *b*	Num 6:6	5315
defiled by the dead *b* of a man	Num 9:6	5315
defiled by the dead *b* of a man	Num 9:7	5315
be unclean by reason of a dead *b*	Num 9:10	5315
He that toucheth the dead *b* of	Num 19:11	5315
dead *b* of any man that is dead	Num 19:13	5315
in the open fields, or a dead *b*	Num 19:16	5315
His *b* shall not remain all night	Deut 21:23	5038
shall be the fruit of thy *b*	Deut 28:4	990
in goods, in the fruit of thy *b*	Deut 28:11	990
shall be the fruit of thy *b*	Deut 28:18	990
eat the fruit of thine own *b*	Deut 28:53	990
thine hand, in the fruit of thy *b*	Deut 30:9	990
and ten sons of his *b* begotten	Judg 8:30	3409
they fastened his *b* to the wall	1Sa 31:10	1472
all night, and took the *b* of Saul	1Sa 31:12	1472
he had restored a dead *b* to life	2Kin 8:5	
men, and took away the *b*	1Chr 10:12	1480
the children's sake of mine own *b*	Job 19:17	990
my skin worms destroy this *b*	Job 19:26	
is drawn, and cometh out of the *b*	Job 20:25	1465
Of the fruit of thy *b* will I set	Ps 132:11	990
thy flesh and thy *b* are consumed,	Prov 5:11	7607
fruitful field, both soul and *b*	Is 10:18	1320
with my dead *b* shall they arise	Is 26:19	5038
hast laid thy *b* as the ground	Is 51:23	1460
cast his dead *b* into the graves	Jer 26:23	5038
his dead *b* shall be cast out in	Jer 36:30	5038

were more ruddy in *b* than rubies	Lam 4:7	6106
And their whole *b*, and their backs,	Eze 10:12	1320
his *b* was wet with the dew of	Dan 4:33	1655
his *b* was wet with the dew of	Dan 5:21	1655
his *b* destroyed, and given to the	Dan 7:11	1655
in my spirit in the midst of my *b*	Dan 7:15	5085
His *b* also was like the beryl, and	Dan 10:6	1472
the fruit of my *b* for the sin of	Mic 6:7	990
by a dead *b* touch any of these	Hag 2:13	5315
not that thy whole *b* should be	Mt 5:29	4983
not that thy whole *b* should be	Mt 5:30	4983
The light of the *b* is the eye	Mt 6:22	4983
thy whole *b* shall be full of	Mt 6:22	4983
thy whole *b* shall be full of	Mt 6:23	4983
nor yet for your *b*, what ye shall	Mt 6:25	4983
than meat, and the *b* than raiment	Mt 6:25	4983
And fear not them which kill the *b*	Mt 10:28	4983
to destroy both soul and *b* in hell	Mt 10:28	4983
disciples came, and took up the *b*	Mt 14:12	4983
hath poured this ointment on my *b*	Mt 26:12	4983
this is my *b*	Mt 26:26	4983
Pilate, and begged the *b* of Jesus	Mt 27:58	4983
commanded the *b* to be delivered	Mt 27:58	4983
And when Joseph had taken the *b*	Mt 27:59	4983
she felt in her *b* that she was	Mk 5:29	4983
to anoint my *b* to the burying	Mk 14:8	4983
this is my *b*	Mk 14:22	4983
cloth cast about his naked *b*	Mk 14:51	4983
Pilate, and craved the *b* of Jesus	Mk 15:43	4983
he gave the *b* to Joseph	Mk 15:45	4983
The light of the *b* is the eye	Lk 11:34	4983
thy whole *b* also is full of light	Lk 11:34	4983
thy *b* also is full of darkness	Lk 11:34	4983
If thy whole *b* therefore be full	Lk 11:36	4983
afraid of them that kill the *b*	Lk 12:4	4983
neither for the *b*, what ye shall	Lk 12:22	4983
the *b* is more than raiment	Lk 12:23	4983
unto them, Wheresoever the *b* is	Lk 17:37	4983
This is my *b* which is given for	Lk 22:19	4983
Pilate, and begged the *b* of Jesus	Lk 23:52	4983
sepulchre, and how his *b* was laid	Lk 23:55	4983
found not the *b* of the Lord Jesus	Lk 24:3	4983
And when they found not his *b*	Lk 24:23	4983
he spake of the temple of his *b*	Jn 2:21	4983
he might take away the *b* of Jesus	Jn 19:38	4983
therefore, and took the *b* of Jesus	Jn 19:38	4983
Then took they the *b* of Jesus	Jn 19:40	4983
where the *b* of Jesus had lain	Jn 20:12	4983
and turning him to the *b* said	Acts 9:40	4983
So that from his *b* were brought	Acts 19:12	5559
considered not his own *b* now dead	Rom 4:19	4983
that the *b* of sin might be	Rom 6:6	4983
therefore reign in your mortal *b*	Rom 6:12	4983
to the law by the *b* of Christ	Rom 7:4	4983
me from the *b* of this death	Rom 7:24	4983
the *b* is dead because of sin	Rom 8:10	4983
do mortify the deeds of the *b*	Rom 8:13	4983
to wit, the redemption of our *b*	Rom 8:23	4983
as we have many members in one *b*	Rom 12:4	4983
are one *b* in Christ, and every one	Rom 12:5	4983
For I verily, as absent in *b*	1Cor 5:3	4983
Now the *b* is not for fornication,	1Cor 6:13	4983
and the Lord for the *b*	1Cor 6:13	4983
is joined to an harlot is one *b*	1Cor 6:16	4983
that a man doeth is without the *b*	1Cor 6:18	4983
sinneth against his own *b*	1Cor 6:18	4983
know ye not that your *b* is the	1Cor 6:19	4983
therefore glorify God in your *b*	1Cor 6:20	4983
wife hath not power of her own *b*	1Cor 7:4	4983
hath not power of his own *b*	1Cor 7:4	4983
that she may be holy both in *b*	1Cor 7:34	4983
But I keep under my *b*, and bring	1Cor 9:27	4983
the communion of the *b* of Christ	1Cor 10:16	4983
many are one bread, and one *b*	1Cor 10:17	4983
this is my *b*, which is broken for	1Cor 11:24	4983
shall be guilty of the *b*	1Cor 11:27	4983
not discerning the Lord's *b*	1Cor 11:29	4983
For as the *b* is one, and hath many	1Cor 12:12	4983
one *b*, being many, are one *b*	1Cor 12:12	4983
are we all baptized into one *b*	1Cor 12:13	4983
For the *b* is not one member, but	1Cor 12:14	4983
not the hand, I am not of the *b*	1Cor 12:15	4983
is it therefore not of the *b*	1Cor 12:15	4983
am not the eye, I am not of the *b*	1Cor 12:16	4983
is it therefore not of the *b*	1Cor 12:16	4983
If the whole *b* were an eye	1Cor 12:17	4983
every one of them in the *b*	1Cor 12:18	4983
all one member, where were the *b*	1Cor 12:19	4983
they many members, yet but one *b*	1Cor 12:20	4983
much more those members of the *b*	1Cor 12:22	4983
And those members of the *b*	1Cor 12:23	4983

God hath tempered the *b* together 1Cor 12:24   4983
should be no schism in the *b* 1Cor 12:25   4983
Now ye are the *b* of Christ 1Cor 12:27   4983
though I give my *b* to be burned 1Cor 13:3   4983
and with what *b* do they come 1Cor 15:35   4983
sowest not that *b* that shall be 1Cor 15:37   4983
But God giveth it a *b* as it hath 1Cor 15:38   4983
him, and to every seed his own *b* 1Cor 15:38   4983
It is sown a natural *b* 1Cor 15:44   4983
it is raised a spiritual *b* 1Cor 15:44   4983
There is a natural *b* 1Cor 15:44   4983
and there is a spiritual *b* 1Cor 15:44   4983
the *b* the dying of the Lord Jesus 2Cor 4:10   4983
might be made manifest in our *b* 2Cor 4:10   4983
whilst we are at home in the *b* 2Cor 5:6   4983
rather to be absent from the *b* 2Cor 5:8   4983
receive the things done in his *b* 2Cor 5:10   4983
years ago, (whether in the *b* 2Cor 12:2   4983
or whether out of the *b*, I cannot 2Cor 12:2   4983
in the *b*, or out of the *b* 2Cor 12:3   4983
for I bear in my *b* the marks of .... Gal 6:17   4983
Which is his *b*, the fulness of .... Eph 1:23   4983
unto God in one *b* by the cross .... Eph 2:16   4983
be fellowheirs, and of the same *b* .... Eph 3:6   4954
There is one *b*, and one Spirit, ... Eph 4:4   4983
the edifying of the *b* of Christ .... Eph 4:12   4983
From whom the whole *b* fitly .... Eph 4:16   4983
maketh increase of the *b* unto the .... Eph 4:16   4983
and he is the saviour of the *b* .... Eph 5:23   4983
For we are members of his *b* .... Eph 5:30   4983
Christ shall be magnified in my *b* .... Phil 1:20   4983
Who shall change our vile *b*, ... Phil 3:21   4983
like unto his glorious *b*, ... Phil 3:21   4983
And he is the head of the *b* .... Col 1:18   4983
In the *b* of his flesh through .... Col 1:22   4983
in putting off the *b* of the sins .... Col 2:11   4983
but the *b* is of Christ .... Col 2:17   4983
from which all the *b* by joints .... Col 2:19   4983
humility, and neglecting of the *b* .... Col 2:23   4983
which also ye are called in one *b* .... Col 3:15   4983
b be preserved blameless unto the 1Th 5:23   4983
but a *b* hast thou prepared me .... Heb 10:5   4983
through the offering of the *b* of .... Heb 10:10   4983
as being yourselves also in the *b* .... Heb 13:3   4983
things which are needful to the *b* .... Jas 2:16   4983
For as the *b* without the spirit .... Jas 2:26   4983
able also to bridle the whole *b* .... Jas 3:2   4983
and we turn about their whole *b* .... Jas 3:3   4983
that it defileth the whole *b* .... Jas 3:6   4983
our sins in his own *b* on the tree 1Pet 2:24   4983
he disputed about the *b* of Moses .... Jude 9   4983

BODY'S
Christ in my flesh for his *b* sake .... Col 1:24   4983

BOHAN (bo'-han) *A namesake of a border stone.*
the stone of *B* the son of Reuben .... Josh 15:6   932
the stone of *B* the son of Reuben .... Josh 18:17   932

BOIL
shall be a *b* breaking forth with .... Ex 9:9   7822
it became a *b* breaking forth with .... Ex 9:10   7822
for the *b* was upon the magicians, ... Ex 9:11   7822
B the flesh at the door of the .... Lev 8:31   1310
even in the skin thereof, was a *b* .... Lev 13:18   7822
in the place of the *b* there be a .... Lev 13:19   7822
of leprosy broken out of the *b* .... Lev 13:20   7822
and spread not, it is a burning *b* .... Lev 13:23   7822
And they took and laid it on the *b* 2Kin 20:7   7822
maketh the deep to *b* like a pot .... Job 41:31   7570
lay it for a plaister upon the *b* .... Is 38:21   7822
the fire causeth the waters to *b* .... Is 64:2   1158
bones under it, and make it *b* well .... Eze 24:5   7570
shall *b* the trespass offering .... Eze 46:20   1310
are the places of them that *b* .... Eze 46:24   1310
b the sacrifice of the people .... Eze 46:24   1310

BOILED
them, and *b* their flesh with the 1Kin 19:21   1310
So we *b* my son, and did eat him 2Kin 6:29   1310
My bowels *b*, and rested not .... Job 30:27   7570

BOILING
it was made with *b* places under .... Eze 46:23   4018

BOILS
before Moses because of the *b* .... Ex 9:11   7822
smote Job with sore *b* from the .... Job 2:7   7822

BOISTEROUS
But when he saw the wind *b* .... Mt 14:30   2478

BOKERU See BOCHERU.

BOKIM See BOCHIM.

BOLD
but the righteous are *b* as a lion .... Prov 28:1   982
Then Paul and Barnabas waxed *b* .... Acts 13:46   3955
But Esaias is very *b*, and saith, I............ Rom 10:20   662
but being absent am *b* toward you 2Cor 10:1   2292
that I may not be *b* when I am 2Cor 10:2   2292
I think to be *b* against some 2Cor 10:2   5111
Howbeit whereinsoever any is *b* 2Cor 11:21   5111
(I speak foolishly,) I am *b* also............... 2Cor 11:21   5111
are much more *b* to speak the word .... Phil 1:14   5111
we were *b* in our God to speak 1Th 2:2   3955
though I might be much *b* in .... Philem 8   3954

BOLDLY
sword, and came upon the city *b* .... Gen 34:25   983
went in *b* unto Pilate, and craved .... Mk 15:43   5111
But, lo, he speaketh *b*, and they .... Jn 7:26   3954
how he had preached *b* at Damascus ...... Acts 9:27   3955
he spake *b* in the name of .... Acts 9:29   3955
abode they speaking *b* in the Lord .... Acts 14:3   3955
began to speak *b* in the synagogue .... Acts 18:26   3955
spake *b* for the space of three .... Acts 19:8   3955
the more *b* unto you in some sort .... Rom 15:15   5112
me, that I may open my mouth *b* .... Eph 6:19   3954
that therein I may speak *b* .... Eph 6:20   3955
Let us therefore come *b* unto the .... Heb 4:16   3954
So that we may *b* say, The Lord is.......... Heb 13:6   2292

BOLDNESS
the *b* of his face shall be........................ Eccl 8:1   5797
Now when they saw the *b* of Peter.......... Acts 4:13   3954
that with all *b* they may speak .... Acts 4:29   3954
they spake the word of God with *b*.......... Acts 4:31   3954
Great is my *b* of speech toward 2Cor 7:4   3954
In whom we have *b* and access with ...... Eph 3:12   3954
be ashamed, but that with all *b*.............. Phil 1:20   3954
great *b* in the faith which is in............... 1Ti 3:13   3954
b to enter into the holiest by .... Heb 10:19   3954
that we may have *b* in the day of........... 1Jn 4:17   3954

BOLLED
was in the ear, and the flax was *b* .... Ex 9:31   1392

BOLSTER
a pillow of goats' hair for his *b* 1Sa 19:13   4763
a pillow of goats' hair for his *b* 1Sa 19:16   4763
stuck in the ground at his *b* 1Sa 26:7   4763
now the spear that is at his *b* 1Sa 26:11   4763
the cruse of water from Saul's *b* 1Sa 26:12   4763
cruse of water that was at his *b* 1Sa 26:16   4763

BOLT
from me, and *b* the door after her 2Sa 13:17   5274

BOLTED
her out, and *b* the door after her 2Sa 13:18   5274

BOND
an oath to bind his soul with a *b* .... Num 30:2   632
the LORD, and bind herself by a *b* .... Num 30:3   632
her *b* wherewith she hath bound .... Num 30:4   632
every *b* wherewith she hath bound .... Num 30:4   632
her soul by a *b* with an oath .... Num 30:10   632
every *b* wherewith she bound her .... Num 30:11   632
or concerning the *b* of her soul .... Num 30:12   632
He looseth the *b* of kings .... Job 12:18   4148
you into the *b* of the covenant .... Eze 20:37   4562
from this *b* on the sabbath day .... Lk 13:16   1199
and in the *b* of iniquity .... Acts 8:23   4886
Gentiles, whether we be *b* or free 1Cor 12:13   1401
there is neither *b* nor free .... Gal 3:28   1401
of the Spirit in the *b* of peace .... Eph 4:3   4886
the Lord, whether he be *b* or free .... Eph 6:8   1401
Barbarian, Scythian, *b* nor free.............. Col 3:11   1401
which is the *b* of perfectness .... Col 3:14   4886
and great, rich and poor, free and *b*....... Rev 13:16   1401
flesh of all men, both free and *b*............ Rev 19:18   1401

BONDAGE
their lives bitter with hard *b* .... Ex 1:14   5656
Israel sighed by reason of the *b* .... Ex 2:23   5656
up unto God by reason of the *b* .... Ex 2:23   5656
whom the Egyptians keep in *b* .... Ex 6:5   5647
and I will rid you out of their *b* .... Ex 6:6   5656
anguish of spirit, and for cruel *b* .... Ex 6:9   5656
from Egypt, out of the house of *b* .... Ex 13:3   5650
from Egypt, from the house of *b* .... Ex 13:14   5650
of Egypt, out of the house of *b* .... Ex 20:2   5650
of Egypt, from the house of *b* .... Deut 5:6   5650
of Egypt, from the house of *b* .... Deut 6:12   5650
of Egypt, from the house of *b* .... Deut 8:14   5650
you out of the house of *b* .... Deut 13:5   5650
of Egypt, from the house of *b* .... Deut 13:10   5650
us, and laid upon us hard *b* .... Deut 26:6   5656
of Egypt, from the house of *b*................. Josh 24:17   5650

you forth out of the house of *b*	Judg 6:8	5650
us a little reviving in our *b*	Ezr 9:8	5659
God hath not forsaken us in our *b*	Ezr 9:9	5659
and, lo, we bring into *b* our sons	Neh 5:5	3533
are brought unto *b* already	Neh 5:5	3533
because the *b* is heavy upon this	Neh 5:18	5656
a captain to return to their *b*	Neh 9:17	5659
from the hard *b* wherein thou wast	Is 14:3	5656
and were never in *b* to any man	Jn 8:33	1398
they should bring them into *b*	Acts 7:6	1402
they shall be in *b* will I judge	Acts 7:7	1398
the spirit of *b* again to fear	Rom 8:15	1397
shall be delivered from the *b* of	Rom 8:21	1397
is not under *b* in such cases	1Cor 7:15	1402
suffer, if a man bring you into *b*	2Cor 11:20	2615
that they might bring us into *b*	Gal 2:4	2615
were in *b* under the elements of	Gal 4:3	1402
ye desire again to be in *b*	Gal 4:9	1398
mount Sinai, which gendereth to *b*	Gal 4:24	1397
is in *b* with her children	Gal 4:25	1398
again with the yoke of *b*	Gal 5:1	1397
all their lifetime subject to *b*	Heb 2:15	1397
of the same is he brought in *b*	2Pet 2:19	1402

BONDMAID

with a woman, that is a *b*	Lev 19:20	8198
had two sons, the one by a *b*	Gal 4:22	3814

BONDMAIDS

Both thy bondmen, and thy *b*	Lev 25:44	519
of them shall ye buy bondmen and *b*	Lev 25:44	519

BONDMAN

instead of the lad a *b* to my lord	Gen 44:33	5650
wast a *b* in the land of Egypt	Deut 15:15	5650
that thou wast a *b* in Egypt	Deut 16:12	5650
that thou wast a *b* in Egypt	Deut 24:18	5650
wast a *b* in the land of Egypt	Deut 24:22	5650
and the mighty men, and every *b*	Rev 6:15	1401

BONDMEN

and fall upon us, and take us for *b*	Gen 43:18	5650
and we also will be my lord's *b*	Gen 44:9	5650
they shall not be sold as *b*	Lev 25:42	5650
Both thy *b*, and thy bondmaids,	Lev 25:44	5650
of them shall ye buy *b* and	Lev 25:44	5650
they shall be your *b* for ever	Lev 25:46	5647
that ye should not be their *b*	Lev 26:13	5650
son, We were Pharaoh's *b* in Egypt	Deut 6:21	5650
you out of the house of *b*	Deut 7:8	5650
be sold unto your enemies for *b*	Deut 28:68	5650
none of you be freed from being *b*	Josh 9:23	5650
of Israel did Solomon make no *b*	1Kin 9:22	5650
take unto him my two sons to be *b*	2Kin 4:1	5650
of Judah and Jerusalem for *b*	2Chr 28:10	5650
For we were *b*	Ezr 9:9	5650
But if we had been sold for *b*	Est 7:4	5650
of Egypt, out of the house of *b*	Jer 34:13	5650

BONDS

or of her *b* wherewith she hath	Num 30:5	632
her *b* wherewith she bound her	Num 30:7	632
all her vows, or all her *b*	Num 30:14	632
thou hast loosed my *b*	Ps 116:16	4147
broken the yoke, and burst the *b*	Jer 5:5	4147
Make thee *b* and yokes, and put them	Jer 27:2	4147
off thy neck, and will burst thy *b*	Jer 30:8	4147
and will burst thy *b* in sunder	Nah 1:13	4147
in every city, saying that *b*	Acts 20:23	1199
charge worthy of death or of *b*	Acts 23:29	1199
a certain man left in *b* by Felix	Acts 25:14	1198
such as I am, except these *b*	Acts 26:29	1199
nothing worthy of death or of *b*	Acts 26:31	1199
For which I am an ambassador in *b*	Eph 6:20	254
inasmuch as both in my *b*, and in	Phil 1:7	1199
So that my *b* in Christ are	Phil 1:13	1199
Lord, waxing confident by my *b*	Phil 1:14	1199
to add affliction to my *b*	Phil 1:16	1199
Christ, for which I am also in *b*	Col 4:3	1210
Remember my *b*	Col 4:18	1199
as an evil doer, even unto *b*	2Ti 2:9	1199
whom I have begotten in my *b*	Philem 10	1199
unto me in the *b* of the gospel	Philem 13	1199
ye had compassion of me in my *b*	Heb 10:34	1199
and scourgings, yea, moreover of *b*	Heb 11:36	1199
Remember them that are in *b*	Heb 13:3	1198

BONDSERVANT

not compel him to serve as a *b*	Lev 25:39	5656,5650

BONDSERVICE

levy a tribute of *b* unto this day	1Kin 9:21	5647

BONDWOMAN

unto Abraham, Cast out this *b*	Gen 21:10	519
for the son of this *b* shall not	Gen 21:10	519
of the lad, and because of thy *b*	Gen 21:12	519
son of the *b* will I make a nation	Gen 21:13	519
But he who was of the *b* was born	Gal 4:23	3814
Cast out the *b* and her son	Gal 4:30	3814
for the son of the *b* shall not be	Gal 4:30	3814
we are not children of the *b*	Gal 4:31	3814

BONDWOMEN

your enemies for bondmen and *b*	Deut 28:68	8198
for bondmen and *b* unto you	2Chr 28:10	8198
we had been sold for bondmen and *b*	Est 7:4	8198

BONE

said, This is now *b* of my bones	Gen 2:23	6106
said to him, Surely thou art my *b*	Gen 29:14	6106
shall ye break a *b* thereof	Ex 12:46	6106
morning, nor break any *b* of it	Num 9:12	6106
or a *b* of a man, or a grave,	Num 19:16	6106
and upon him that touched a *b*	Num 19:18	6106
remember also that I am your *b*	Judg 9:2	6106
saying, Behold, we are thy *b*	2Sa 5:1	6106
ye to Amasa, Art thou not of my *b*	2Sa 19:13	6106
saying, Behold, we are thy *b*	1Chr 11:1	6106
thine hand now, and touch his *b*	Job 2:5	6106
My *b* cleaveth to my skin and to my	Job 19:20	6106
and mine arm be broken from the *b*	Job 31:22	7070
all mine enemies upon the cheek *b*	Ps 3:7	
and a soft tongue breaketh the *b*	Prov 25:15	1634
came together, *b* to his *b*	Eze 37:7	6106
land, when any seeth a man's *b*	Eze 39:15	6106
A *b* of him shall not be broken	Jn 19:36	3747

BONES

said, This is now bone of my *b*	Gen 2:23	6106
ye shall carry up my *b* from hence	Gen 50:25	6106
Moses took the *b* of Joseph with	Ex 13:19	6106
carry up my *b* away hence with you	Ex 13:19	6106
enemies, and shall break their *b*	Num 24:8	6106
the *b* of Joseph, which the	Josh 24:32	6106
divided her, together with her *b*	Judg 19:29	6106
And they took their *b*, and buried	1Sa 31:13	6106
Ye are my brethren, ye are my *b*	2Sa 19:12	6106
David went and took the *b* of Saul	2Sa 21:12	6106
the *b* of Jonathan his son from	2Sa 21:12	6106
up from thence the *b* of Saul	2Sa 21:13	6106
the *b* of Jonathan his son	2Sa 21:13	6106
they gathered the *b* of them that	2Sa 21:13	6106
the *b* of Saul and Jonathan his son	2Sa 21:14	6106
men's *b* shall be burnt upon thee	1Kin 13:2	6106
lay my *b* beside his *b*	1Kin 13:31	6106
down, and touched the *b* of Elisha	2Kin 13:21	6106
their places with the *b* of men	2Kin 23:14	6106
took the *b* out of the sepulchres,	2Kin 23:16	6106
let no man move his *b*	2Kin 23:18	6106
So they let his *b* alone	2Kin 23:18	6106
with the *b* of the prophet that	2Kin 23:18	6106
and burned men's *b* upon them	2Kin 23:20	6106
buried their *b* under the oak in	1Chr 10:12	6106
he burnt the *b* of the priests	2Chr 34:5	6106
which maketh all my *b* to shake	Job 4:14	6106
flesh, and hast fenced me with *b*	Job 10:11	6106
His *b* are full of the sin of his	Job 20:11	6106
his *b* are moistened with marrow	Job 21:24	6106
My *b* are pierced in me in the	Job 30:17	6106
my *b* are burned with heat	Job 30:30	6106
of his *b* with strong pain	Job 33:19	6106
his *b* that were not seen stick	Job 33:21	6106
His *b* are as strong pieces of	Job 40:18	6106
his *b* are like bars of iron	Job 40:18	1634
for my *b* are vexed	Ps 6:2	6106
all my *b* are out of joint	Ps 22:14	6106
I may tell all my *b*	Ps 22:17	6106
iniquity, and my *b* are consumed	Ps 31:10	6106
my *b* waxed old through my roaring	Ps 32:3	6106
He keepeth all his *b*	Ps 34:20	6106
All my *b* shall say, LORD, who is	Ps 35:10	6106
rest in my *b* because of my sin	Ps 38:3	6106
As with a sword in my *b*, mine	Ps 42:10	6106
that the *b* which thou hast broken	Ps 51:8	6106
for God hath scattered the *b* of	Ps 53:5	6106
my *b* are burned as an hearth	Ps 102:3	6106
groaning my *b* cleave to my skin	Ps 102:5	6106
water, and like oil into his *b*	Ps 109:18	6106
Our *b* are scattered at the	Ps 141:7	6106
to thy navel, and marrow to thy *b*	Prov 3:8	6106
ashamed is as rottenness in my *b*	Prov 12:4	6106
but envy the rottenness of the *b*	Prov 14:30	6106
and a good report maketh the *b* fat	Prov 15:30	6106
to the soul, and health to the *b*	Prov 16:24	6106

but a broken spirit drieth the *b*	Prov 17:22	1634
nor how the *b* do grow in the womb	Eccl 11:5	6106
a lion, so will he break all my *b*	Is 38:13	6106
in drought, and make fat thy *b*	Is 58:11	6106
your *b* shall flourish like an	Is 66:14	6106
out the *b* of the kings of Judah	Jer 8:1	6106
the *b* of his princes, and the	Jer 8:1	6106
the *b* of the priests, and the	Jer 8:1	6106
the *b* of the prophets, and the	Jer 8:1	6106
the *b* of the inhabitants of	Jer 8:1	6106
as a burning fire shut up in my *b*	Jer 20:9	6106
all my *b* shake	Jer 23:9	6106
king of Babylon hath broken his *b*	Jer 50:17	6106
above hath he sent fire into my *b*	Lam 1:13	6106
he hath broken my *b*	Lam 3:4	6106
their skin cleaveth to their *b*	Lam 4:8	6106
I will scatter your *b* round about	Eze 6:5	6106
fill it with the choice *b*	Eze 24:4	6106
and burn also the *b* under it	Eze 24:5	6106
them seethe the *b* of it therein	Eze 24:5	6106
it well, and let the *b* be burned	Eze 24:10	6106
iniquities shall be upon their *b*	Eze 32:27	6106
of the valley which was full of *b*	Eze 37:1	6106
me, Son of man, can these *b* live	Eze 37:3	6106
unto me, Prophesy upon these *b*	Eze 37:4	6106
and say unto them, O ye dry *b*	Eze 37:4	6106
saith the Lord GOD unto these *b*	Eze 37:5	6106
the *b* came together, bone to his	Eze 37:7	6106
these *b* are the whole house of	Eze 37:11	6106
Our *b* are dried, and our hope is	Eze 37:11	6106
brake all their *b* in pieces or	Dan 6:24	1635
because he burned the *b* of the	Amos 2:1	6106
bring out the *b* out of the house	Amos 6:10	6106
and their flesh from off their *b*	Mic 3:2	6106
and they break their *b*, and chop	Mic 3:3	6106
rottenness entered into my *b*	Hab 3:16	6106
gnaw not the *b* till the morrow	Zeph 3:3	1633
are within full of dead men's *b*	Mt 23:27	3747
for a spirit hath not flesh and *b*	Lk 24:39	3747
ancle *b* received strength	Acts 3:7	4974
body, of his flesh, and of his *b*	Eph 5:30	3747
gave commandment concerning his *b*	Heb 11:22	3747

BONNETS

b shalt thou make for them, for	Ex 28:40	4021
and his sons, and put the *b* on them	Ex 29:9	4021
goodly *b* of fine linen, and linen	Ex 39:28	4021
with girdles, and put *b* upon them	Lev 8:13	4021
The *b*, and the ornaments of the	Is 3:20	6287
have linen *b* upon their heads	Eze 44:18	6287

BOOK

This is the *b* of the generations	Gen 5:1	5612
Write this for a memorial in a *b*	Ex 17:14	5612
he took the *b* of the covenant, and	Ex 24:7	5612
out of thy *b* which thou hast	Ex 32:32	5612
me, him will I blot out of my *b*	Ex 32:33	5612
shall write these curses in a *b*	Num 5:23	5612
in the *b* of the wars of the LORD	Num 21:14	5612
him a copy of this law in a *b* out	Deut 17:18	5612
law that are written in this *b*	Deut 28:58	5612
not written in the *b* of this law	Deut 28:61	5612
in this *b* shall lie upon him	Deut 29:20	5612
are written in this *b* of the law	Deut 29:21	5612
curses that are written in this *b*	Deut 29:27	5612
are written in the *b* of the law	Deut 30:10	5612
the words of this law in a *b*	Deut 31:24	5612
Take this *b* of the law, and put it	Deut 31:26	5612
This *b* of the law shall not	Josh 1:8	5612
in the *b* of the law of Moses	Josh 8:31	5612
is written in the *b* of the law	Josh 8:34	5612
this written in the *b* of Jasher	Josh 10:13	5612
by cities into seven parts in a *b*	Josh 18:9	5612
in the *b* of the law of Moses	Josh 23:6	5612
words in the *b* of the law of God	Josh 24:26	5612
the kingdom, and wrote it in a *b*	1Sa 10:25	5612
it is written in the *b* of Jasher	2Sa 1:18	5612
in the *b* of the acts of Solomon	1Kin 11:41	5612
they are written in the *b* of the	1Kin 14:19	5612
are they not written in the *b* of	1Kin 14:29	5612
are they not written in the *b* of	1Kin 15:7	5612
are they not written in the *b* of	1Kin 15:23	5612
are they not written in the *b* of	1Kin 15:31	5612
are they not written in the *b* of	1Kin 16:5	5612
are they not written in the *b* of	1Kin 16:14	5612
are they not written in the *b* of	1Kin 16:20	5612
are they not written in the *b* of	1Kin 16:27	5612
are they not written in the *b* of	1Kin 22:39	5612
are they not written in the *b* of	1Kin 22:45	5612
are they not written in the *b* of	2Kin 1:18	5612
are they not written in the *b* of	2Kin 8:23	5612
are they not written in the *b* of	2Kin 10:34	5612
are they not written in the *b* of	2Kin 12:19	5612
are they not written in the *b* of	2Kin 13:8	5612
are they not written in the *b* of	2Kin 13:12	5612
in the *b* of the law of Moses	2Kin 14:6	5612
are they not written in the *b* of	2Kin 14:15	5612
are they not written in the *b* of	2Kin 14:18	5612
are they not written in the *b* of	2Kin 14:28	5612
are they not written in the *b* of	2Kin 15:6	5612
they are written in the *b* of the	2Kin 15:11	5612
they are written in the *b* of the	2Kin 15:15	5612
are they not written in the *b* of	2Kin 15:21	5612
they are written in the *b* of the	2Kin 15:26	5612
they are written in the *b* of the	2Kin 15:31	5612
are they not written in the *b* of	2Kin 15:36	5612
are they not written in the *b* of	2Kin 16:19	5612
are they not written in the *b* of	2Kin 20:20	5612
are they not written in the *b* of	2Kin 21:17	5612
b of the chronicles of the kings	2Kin 21:25	5612
I have found the *b* of the law in	2Kin 22:8	5612
And Hilkiah gave the *b* to Shaphan	2Kin 22:8	5612
the priest hath delivered me a *b*	2Kin 22:10	5612
the words of the *b* of the law	2Kin 22:11	5612
the words of this *b* that is found	2Kin 22:13	5612
unto the words of this *b*, to do	2Kin 22:13	5612
even all the words of the *b* which	2Kin 22:16	5612
b of the covenant which was found	2Kin 23:2	5612
that were written in this *b*	2Kin 23:3	5612
written in the *b* of this covenant	2Kin 23:21	5612
b that Hilkiah the priest found	2Kin 23:24	5612
are they not written in the *b* of	2Kin 23:28	5612
are they not written in the *b* of	2Kin 24:5	5612
in the *b* of the kings of Israel	1Chr 9:1	5612
in the *b* of Samuel the seer	1Chr 29:29	1697
in the *b* of Nathan the prophet,	1Chr 29:29	1697
in the *b* of Gad the seer,	1Chr 29:29	1697
in the *b* of Nathan the prophet	2Chr 9:29	1697
in the *b* of Shemaiah the prophet	2Chr 12:15	1697
in the *b* of the kings of Judah	2Chr 16:11	5612
had the *b* of the law of the LORD	2Chr 17:9	5612
they are written in the *b* of Jehu	2Chr 20:34	1697
in the *b* of the kings of Israel	2Chr 20:34	5612
the story of the *b* of the kings	2Chr 24:27	5612
in the law in the *b* of Moses	2Chr 25:4	5612
in the *b* of the kings of Judah	2Chr 25:26	5612
in the *b* of the kings of Israel	2Chr 27:7	5612
in the *b* of the kings of Judah	2Chr 28:26	5612
in the *b* of the kings of Judah and	2Chr 32:32	5612
in the *b* of the kings of Israel	2Chr 33:18	1697
Hilkiah the priest found a *b* of	2Chr 34:14	5612
I have found the *b* of the law in	2Chr 34:15	5612
delivered the *b* to Shaphan	2Chr 34:15	5612
Shaphan carried the *b* to the king	2Chr 34:16	5612
the priest hath given me a *b*	2Chr 34:18	5612
the words of the *b* that is found	2Chr 34:21	5612
all that is written in this *b*	2Chr 34:21	5612
curses that are written in the *b*	2Chr 34:24	5612
b of the covenant that was found	2Chr 34:30	5612
which are written in this *b*	2Chr 34:31	5612
it is written in the *b* of Moses	2Chr 35:12	5612
in the *b* of the kings of Israel	2Chr 35:27	5612
in the *b* of the kings of Israel	2Chr 36:8	5612
b of the records of thy fathers	Ezr 4:15	5609
thou find in the *b* of the records	Ezr 4:15	5609
it is written in the *b* of Moses	Ezr 6:18	5609
bring the *b* of the law of Moses	Neh 8:1	5612
attentive unto the *b* of the law	Neh 8:3	5612
Ezra opened the *b* in the sight of	Neh 8:5	5612
So being read in the *b* in the law	Neh 8:8	5612
he read in the *b* of the law of	Neh 8:18	5612
read in the *b* of the law of the	Neh 9:3	5612
in the *b* of the chronicles	Neh 12:23	5612
On that day they read in the *b* of	Neh 13:1	5612
it was written in the *b* of the	Est 2:23	5612
he commanded to bring the *b* of	Est 6:1	5612
and it was written in the *b*	Est 9:32	5612
are they not written in the *b* of	Est 10:2	5612
oh that they were printed in a *b*	Job 19:23	5612
mine adversary had written a *b*	Job 31:35	5612
of the *b* it is written of me	Ps 40:7	5612
are they not in thy *b*	Ps 56:8	5612
out of the *b* of the living	Ps 69:28	5612
in thy *b* all my members were	Ps 139:16	5612
the words of a *b* that is sealed	Is 29:11	5612
the *b* is delivered to him that is	Is 29:12	5612
the deaf hear the words of the *b*	Is 29:18	5612
in a table, and note it in a *b*	Is 30:8	5612
Seek ye out of the *b* of the LORD	Is 34:16	5612
all that is written in this *b*	Jer 25:13	5612
I have spoken unto thee in a *b*	Jer 30:2	5612
subscribed the *b* of the purchase	Jer 32:12	5612
Take thee a roll of a *b*, and write	Jer 36:2	5612

unto him, upon a roll of a *b*	Jer 36:4	5612
reading in the *b* the words of the	Jer 36:8	5612
Then read Baruch in the *b*	Jer 36:10	5612
had heard out of the *b* all the	Jer 36:11	5612
when Baruch read the *b* in the	Jer 36:13	5612
and I wrote them with ink in the *b*	Jer 36:18	5612
b which Jehoiakim king of Judah	Jer 36:32	5612
in a *b* at the mouth of Jeremiah	Jer 45:1	5612
So Jeremiah wrote in a *b* all the	Jer 51:60	5612
made an end of reading this *b*	Jer 51:63	5612
and, lo, a roll of a *b* was therein	Eze 2:9	5612
shall be found written in the *b*	Dan 12:1	5612
shut up the words, and seal the *b*	Dan 12:4	5612
The *b* of the vision of Nahum the	Nah 1:1	5612
a *b* of remembrance was written	Mal 3:16	5612
The *b* of the generation of Jesus	Mt 1:1	976
ye not read in the *b* of Moses	Mk 12:26	976
As it is written in the *b* of the	Lk 3:4	976
him the *b* of the prophet Esaias	Lk 4:17	975
And when he had opened the *b*	Lk 4:17	975
And he closed the *b*, and he gave it	Lk 4:20	975
himself saith in the *b* of Psalms	Lk 20:42	976
which are not written in this *b*	Jn 20:30	975
it is written in the *b* of Psalms	Acts 1:20	976
written in the *b* of the prophets	Acts 7:42	976
in the *b* of the law to do them	Gal 3:10	975
whose names are in the *b* of life	Phil 4:3	976
hyssop, and sprinkled both the *b*	Heb 9:19	975
of the *b* it is written of me	Heb 10:7	975
and, What thou seest, write in a *b*	Rev 1:11	975
out his name out of the *b* of life	Rev 3:5	976
on the throne a *b* written within	Rev 5:1	975
Who is worthy to open the *b*	Rev 5:2	975
the earth, was able to open the *b*	Rev 5:3	975
worthy to open and to read the *b*	Rev 5:4	975
hath prevailed to open the *b*	Rev 5:5	975
took the *b* out of the right hand	Rev 5:7	975
And when he had taken the *b*	Rev 5:8	975
Thou art worthy to take the *b*	Rev 5:9	975
had in his hand a little *b* open	Rev 10:2	974
take the little *b* which is open	Rev 10:8	974
unto him, Give me the little *b*	Rev 10:9	974
I took the little *b* out of the	Rev 10:10	974
names are not written in the *b* of	Rev 13:8	976
names were not written in the *b*	Rev 17:8	976
another *b* was opened	Rev 20:12	976
which is the *b* of life	Rev 20:12	976
was not found written in the *b* of	Rev 20:15	976
written in the Lamb's *b* of life	Rev 21:27	975
sayings of the prophecy of this *b*	Rev 22:7	975
which keep the sayings of this *b*	Rev 22:9	975
sayings of the prophecy of this *b*	Rev 22:10	975
words of the prophecy of this *b*	Rev 22:18	975
that are written in this *b*	Rev 22:18	975
words of the *b* of this prophecy	Rev 22:19	976
his part out of the *b* of life	Rev 22:19	976
which are written in this *b*	Rev 22:19	975

BOOKS

of making many *b* there is no end	Eccl 12:12	5612
was set, and the *b* were opened	Dan 7:10	5609
by the number of the years	Dan 9:2	5612
the *b* that should be written	Jn 21:25	975
arts brought their *b* together	Acts 19:19	976
comest, bring with thee, and the *b*	2Ti 4:13	975
and the *b* were opened	Rev 20:12	975
which were written in the *b*	Rev 20:12	975

BOOTH

as a *b* that the keeper maketh	Job 27:18	5521
the city, and there made him a *b*	Jonah 4:5	5521

BOOTHS

house, and made *b* for his cattle	Gen 33:17	5521
Ye shall dwell in *b* seven days	Lev 23:42	5521
Israelites born shall dwell in *b*	Lev 23:42	5521
children of Israel to dwell in *b*	Lev 23:43	5521
of Israel should dwell in *b* in	Neh 8:14	5521
of thick trees, to make *b*	Neh 8:15	5521
them, and made themselves *b*	Neh 8:16	5521
made *b*, and sat under the *b*	Neh 8:17	5521

BOOTIES

and thou shalt be for *b* unto them	Hab 2:7	4933

BOOTY

And the *b*, being the rest of the	Num 31:32	4455
And their camels shall be a *b*	Jer 49:32	957
their goods shall become a *b*	Zeph 1:13	4953

BOOZ (bo'-oz) See BOAZ. *Greek form of Boaz.*

And Salmon begat *B* of Rachab	Mt 1:5	1003
and *B* begat Obed of Ruth	Mt 1:5	1003
of Obed, which was the son of *B*	Lk 3:32	1003

BOR ASHAN See CHOR-ASHAN.

BORDER

the *b* of the Canaanites was from	Gen 10:19	1366
his *b* shall be unto Zidon	Gen 49:13	3411
the mount, or touch the *b* of it	Ex 19:12	7097
thou shalt make unto it a *b* of an	Ex 25:25	4526
to the *b* thereof round about	Ex 25:25	4526
Over against the *b* shall the	Ex 25:27	4526
the breastplate in the *b* thereof	Ex 28:26	8193
Also he made thereunto a *b* of an	Ex 37:12	4526
for the *b* thereof round about	Ex 37:12	4526
Over against the *b* were the rings	Ex 37:14	4526
the breastplate, upon the *b* of it	Ex 39:19	8193
a city in the uttermost of thy *b*	Num 20:16	1366
give Israel passage through his *b*	Num 20:21	1366
for Arnon is the *b* of Moab	Num 21:13	1366
Ar, and lieth upon the *b* of Moab	Num 21:15	1366
Israel to pass through his *b*	Num 21:23	1366
for the *b* of the children of	Num 21:24	1366
Moab, which is in the *b* of Arnon	Num 22:36	1366
in Ije-abarim, in the *b* of Moab	Num 33:44	1366
your south *b* shall be the outmost	Num 34:3	1366
your *b* shall turn from the south	Num 34:4	1366
the *b* shall fetch a compass from	Num 34:5	1366
And as for the western *b*, ye shall	Num 34:6	1366
even have the great sea for a *b*	Num 34:6	1366
this shall be your west *b*	Num 34:6	1366
And this shall be your north *b*	Num 34:7	1366
b unto the entrance of Hamath	Num 34:8	
forth of the *b* shall be to Zedad	Num 34:8	1366
the *b* shall go on to Ziphron, and	Num 34:9	1366
this shall be your north *b*	Num 34:9	1366
east *b* from Hazar-enan to Shepham	Num 34:10	1366
the *b* shall descend, and shall	Num 34:11	1366
the *b* shall go down to Jordan, and	Num 34:12	1366
the *b* of the city of his refuge	Num 35:26	1366
the *b* even unto the river Jabbok,	Deut 3:16	1366
which is the *b* of the children of	Deut 3:16	1366
LORD thy God shall enlarge thy *b*	Deut 12:20	1366
Gilgal, in the east *b* of Jericho	Josh 4:19	7097
which is the *b* of the children of	Josh 12:2	1366
unto the *b* of the Geshurites and	Josh 12:5	1366
the *b* of Sihon king of Heshbon	Josh 12:5	1366
unto the *b* of the children of	Josh 13:10	1366
the *b* of the Geshurites and	Josh 13:11	1366
the *b* of the children of Reuben	Josh 13:23	1366
was Jordan, and the *b* thereof	Josh 13:23	1366
from Mahanaim unto the *b* of Debir	Josh 13:26	1366
king of Heshbon, Jordan and his *b*	Josh 13:27	1366
even to the *b* of Edom the	Josh 15:1	1366
their south *b* was from the shore	Josh 15:2	1366
the east *b* was the salt sea, even	Josh 15:5	1366
their *b* in the north quarter was	Josh 15:5	1366
the *b* went up to Beth-hogla, and	Josh 15:6	1366
the *b* went up to the stone of	Josh 15:6	1366
the *b* went up toward Debir from	Josh 15:7	1366
the *b* passed toward the waters of	Josh 15:7	1366
the *b* went up by the valley of	Josh 15:8	1366
the *b* went up to the top of the	Josh 15:8	1366
the *b* was drawn from the top of	Josh 15:9	1366
the *b* was drawn to Baalah, which	Josh 15:9	1366
the *b* compassed from Baalah	Josh 15:10	1366
the *b* went out unto the side of	Josh 15:11	1366
the *b* was drawn to Shicron, and	Josh 15:11	1366
out of the *b* were at the sea	Josh 15:11	1366
the west *b* was to the great sea,	Josh 15:12	1366
the great sea, and the *b* thereof	Josh 15:47	1366
the *b* of the children of Ephraim	Josh 16:5	1366
even the *b* of their inheritance	Josh 16:5	1366
the *b* went out toward the sea to	Josh 16:6	1366
the *b* went about eastward unto	Josh 16:6	1366
The *b* went out from Tappuah	Josh 16:8	1366
the *b* went along on the right	Josh 17:7	1366
but Tappuah unto the *b* of Manasseh	Josh 17:8	1366
Manasseh's, and the sea is his *b*	Josh 17:10	1366
their *b* on the north side was	Josh 18:12	1366
the *b* went up to the side of	Josh 18:12	1366
the *b* went over from thence	Josh 18:13	1366
the *b* descended to Ataroth-adar,	Josh 18:13	1366
the *b* was drawn thence, and	Josh 18:14	1366
the *b* went out on the west, and	Josh 18:15	1366
the *b* came down to the end of the	Josh 18:16	1366
the *b* passed along to the side of	Josh 18:19	1366
the outgoings of the *b* were at	Josh 18:19	1366
Jordan was the *b* of it on the	Josh 18:20	1379
the *b* of their inheritance was	Josh 19:10	1366
their *b* went up toward the sea,	Josh 19:11	1366
unto the *b* of Chisloth-tabor	Josh 19:12	1366
the *b* compasseth it on the north	Josh 19:14	1366
their *b* was toward Jezreel, and	Josh 19:18	1366

of their *b* were at Jordan	Josh 19:22	1366
their *b* was Helkath, and Hali, and	Josh 19:25	1366
Rakkon, with the *b* before Japho	Josh 19:46	1366
hath made Jordan a *b* between us	Josh 22:25	1366
in the *b* of his inheritance in	Josh 24:30	1366
in the *b* of his inheritance in	Judg 2:9	1366
to the *b* of Abel-meholah, unto	Judg 7:22	8193
but came not within the *b* of Moab	Judg 11:18	1366
for Arnon was the *b* of Moab	Judg 11:18	1366
them unto the *b* of Beth-shemesh	1Sa 6:12	1366
in the *b* of Benjamin at Zelzah	1Sa 10:2	1366
turned to the way of the *b* that	1Sa 13:18	1366
his *b* at the river Euphrates	2Sa 8:3	3027
and unto the *b* of Egypt	1Kin 4:21	1366
and upward, and stood in the *b*	2Kin 3:21	1366
Philistines, and to the *b* of Egypt	2Chr 9:26	1366
them to the *b* of his sanctuary	Ps 78:54	1366
will establish the *b* of the widow	Prov 15:25	1366
a pillar at the *b* thereof to the	Is 19:19	1366
enter into the height of his *b*	Is 37:24	7093
shall come again to their own *b*	Jer 31:17	1366
against her from the utmost *b*	Jer 50:26	7093
will judge you in the *b* of Israel	Eze 11:10	1366
will judge you in the *b* of Israel	Eze 11:11	1366
Syene even unto the *b* of Ethiopia	Eze 29:10	1366
the *b* thereof by the edge thereof	Eze 43:13	1366
the *b* about it shall be half a	Eze 43:17	1366
settle, and upon the *b* round about	Eze 43:20	1366
the west *b* unto the east *b*	Eze 45:7	1366
This shall be the *b*, whereby ye	Eze 47:13	1366
this shall be the *b* of the land	Eze 47:15	1366
is between the *b* of Damascus	Eze 47:16	1366
of Damascus and the *b* of Hamath	Eze 47:16	1366
the *b* from the sea shall be	Eze 47:17	1366
the *b* of Damascus, and the north	Eze 47:17	1366
northward, and the *b* of Hamath	Eze 47:17	1366
from the *b* unto the east sea	Eze 47:18	1366
shall be the great sea from the *b*	Eze 47:20	1366
the *b* of Damascus northward, to	Eze 48:1	1366
And by the *b* of Dan, from the east	Eze 48:2	1366
by the *b* of Asher, from the east	Eze 48:3	1366
by the *b* of Naphtali, from the	Eze 48:4	1366
by the *b* of Manasseh, from the	Eze 48:5	1366
by the *b* of Ephraim, from the	Eze 48:6	1366
by the *b* of Reuben, from the east	Eze 48:7	1366
by the *b* of Judah, from the east	Eze 48:8	1366
most holy by the *b* of the Levites	Eze 48:12	1366
over against the *b* of the priests	Eze 48:13	1366
of the oblation toward the east *b*	Eze 48:21	1366
twenty thousand toward the west *b*	Eze 48:21	1366
prince's, between the *b* of Judah	Eze 48:22	1366
the *b* of Benjamin, shall be for	Eze 48:22	1366
by the *b* of Benjamin, from the	Eze 48:24	1366
by the *b* of Simeon, from the east	Eze 48:25	1366
by the *b* of Issachar, from the	Eze 48:26	1366
by the *b* of Zebulun, from the	Eze 48:27	1366
And by the *b* of Gad, at the south	Eze 48:28	1366
the *b* shall be even from Tamar	Eze 48:28	1366
remove them far from their *b*	Joel 3:6	1366
that they might enlarge their *b*	Amos 1:13	1366
their *b* greater than your *b*	Amos 6:2	1366
have brought the even to the *b*	Obad 7	1366
themselves against their *b*	Zeph 2:8	1366
And Hamath also shall *b* thereby	Zec 9:2	1379
The *b* of wickedness, and, The	Mal 1:4	1366
be magnified from the *b* of Israel	Mal 1:5	1366
it were but the *b* of his garment	Mk 6:56	2899
touched the *b* of his garment	Lk 8:44	2899

BORDERS

were in all the *b* round about	Gen 23:17	1366
to cities from one end of the *b*	Gen 47:21	1366
I will smite all thy *b* with frogs	Ex 8:2	1366
unto the *b* of the land of Canaan	Ex 16:35	7097
before thee, and enlarge thy *b*	Ex 34:24	1366
b of their garments throughout	Num 15:38	3671
fringe of the *b* a ribband of blue	Num 15:38	3671
left, until we have passed thy *b*	Num 20:17	1366
high way, until we be past thy *b*	Num 21:22	1366
the *b* of the city of his refuge	Num 35:27	1366
in the *b* of Dor on the west,	Josh 11:2	5299
all the *b* of the Philistines, and	Josh 13:2	1552
Egypt, even unto the *b* of Ekron	Josh 13:3	1366
Aphek, to the *b* of the Amorites	Josh 13:4	1366
unto the *b* of Archi to Ataroth	Josh 16:2	1366
they came unto the *b* of Jordan	Josh 22:10	1552
in the *b* of Jordan, at the	Josh 22:11	1552
they had *b*, and the *b* were	1Kin 7:28	4526
on the *b* that were between the	1Kin 7:29	4526
of it were gravings with their *b*	1Kin 7:31	4526
under the *b* were four wheels	1Kin 7:32	4526

the *b* thereof were of the same	1Kin 7:35	4526
on the *b* thereof, he graved	1Kin 7:36	4526
Ahaz cut off the *b* of the bases	2Kin 16:17	4526
the *b* thereof, from the tower of	2Kin 18:8	1366
enter into the lodgings of his *b*	2Kin 19:23	7093
suburbs of Sharon, upon their *b*	1Chr 5:16	8444
by the *b* of the children of	1Chr 7:29	3027
hast set all the *b* of the earth	Ps 74:17	1367
He maketh peace in thy *b*, and	Ps 147:14	1366
We will make thee *b* of gold with	Song 1:11	8447
is gone round about the *b* of Moab	Is 15:8	1366
all thy *b* of pleasant stones	Is 54:12	1366
nor destruction within thy *b*	Is 60:18	1366
all thy sins, even in all thy *b*	Jer 15:13	1366
for sin, throughout all thy *b*	Jer 17:3	1366
Thy *b* are in the midst of the	Eze 27:4	1366
in all the *b* thereof round about	Eze 45:1	1366
and when he treadeth within our *b*	Mic 5:6	1366
in the *b* of Zabulon and Nephthalim	Mt 4:13	3725
enlarge the *b* of their garments,	Mt 23:5	2899
arose, and went into the *b* of Tyre	Mk 7:24	3181

BORE

his master shall *b* his ear	Ex 21:6	7527
or *b* his jaw through with a thorn	Job 41:2	5344

BORED

b a hole in the lid of it, and set	2Kin 12:9	5344

BORN

And unto Enoch was *b* Irad	Gen 4:18	3205
to him also there was *b* a son	Gen 4:26	3205
and daughters were *b* unto them	Gen 6:1	3205
them were sons *b* after the flood	Gen 10:1	3205
even to him were children *b*	Gen 10:21	3205
And unto Eber were *b* two sons	Gen 10:25	3205
b in his own house, three hundred	Gen 14:14	3211
one in my house is mine heir	Gen 15:3	1121
he that is *b* in the house, or	Gen 17:12	3211
He that is *b* in thy house, and he	Gen 17:13	3211
Shall a child be *b* unto him that	Gen 17:17	3205
and all that were *b* in his house	Gen 17:23	3211
b in the house, and bought with	Gen 17:27	3211
of his son that was *b* unto him	Gen 21:3	3205
when his son Isaac was *b* unto him	Gen 21:5	3205
for I have *b* him a son in his old	Gen 21:7	3205
which she had *b* unto Abraham	Gen 21:9	3205
she hath also *b* children unto thy	Gen 22:20	3205
who was *b* to Bethuel, son of	Gen 24:15	3205
because I have *b* him three sons	Gen 29:34	3205
me, because I have *b* him six sons	Gen 30:20	3205
to pass, when Rachel had *b* Joseph	Gen 30:25	3205
their children which they have *b*	Gen 31:43	3205
which were *b* to him in Padan-aram	Gen 35:26	3205
which were *b* unto him in the land	Gen 36:5	3205
unto Joseph were *b* two sons	Gen 41:50	3205
the land of Egypt were *b* Manasseh	Gen 46:20	3205
of Rachel, which were *b* to Jacob	Gen 46:22	3205
which were *b* him in Egypt, were	Gen 46:27	3205
which were *b* unto thee in the	Gen 48:5	3205
Every son that is *b* ye shall cast	Ex 1:22	3209
be a stranger, or *b* in the land	Ex 12:19	249
be as one that is *b* in the land	Ex 12:48	249
she have *b* him sons or daughters	Ex 21:4	3205
conceived seed, and *b* a man child	Lev 12:2	3205
that hath a male or a female	Lev 12:7	3205
mother, whether she be *b* at home	Lev 18:9	4138
or *b* abroad, even their nakedness	Lev 18:9	4138
be unto you as one *b* among you	Lev 19:34	249
he that is *b* in his house	Lev 22:11	3211
b shall dwell in booths	Lev 23:42	249
as he that is *b* in the land	Lev 24:16	249
and for him that was *b* in the land	Num 9:14	249
All that are *b* of the country	Num 15:13	249
both for him that is *b* among the	Num 15:29	249
whether he be in the land	Num 15:30	249
And unto Aaron was *b* Nadab	Num 26:60	3205
they have *b* him children, then	Deut 21:15	3205
but all the people that were *b* in	Josh 5:5	3209
as he that was *b* among them	Josh 8:33	249
do unto the child that shall be *b*	Judg 13:8	3205
father, who was *b* unto Israel	Judg 18:29	3205
thee than seven sons, hath *b* him	Ruth 4:15	3205
saying, There is a son *b* to Naomi	Ruth 4:17	3205
so that the barren hath *b* seven	1Sa 2:5	3205
for thou hast *b* a son	1Sa 4:20	3205
the battle were Eliab the first *b*	1Sa 17:13	3205
unto David were sons *b* in Hebron	2Sa 3:2	3205
These were *b* to David in Hebron	2Sa 3:5	3205
yet sons and daughters *b* to David	2Sa 5:13	3205
that were *b* unto him in Jerusalem	2Sa 5:14	3209
the child also that is *b* unto	2Sa 12:14	3209

Absalom there were *b* three sons	2Sa 14:27	3205
he also was *b* to the giant	2Sa 21:20	3205
These four were *b* to the giant in	2Sa 21:22	3205
a child shall be *b* unto the house	1Kin 13:2	3205
And unto Eber were *b* two sons	1Chr 1:19	3205
which three were *b* unto him of	1Chr 2:3	3205
of Hezron, that were *b* unto him	1Chr 2:9	3205
which were *b* unto him in Hebron	1Chr 3:1	3205
These six were *b* unto him in	1Chr 3:4	3205
And these were *b* unto him in	1Chr 3:5	3205
that were *b* in that land slew	1Chr 7:21	3205
These were *b* unto the giant in	1Chr 20:8	3205
Behold, a son shall be *b* to thee	1Chr 22:9	3205
unto Shemaiah his son were sons *b*	1Chr 26:6	3205
wives, and such as are *b* of them	Ezr 10:3	3205
there were *b* unto him seven sons	Job 1:2	3205
the day perish wherein I was *b*	Job 3:3	3205
Yet man is *b* unto trouble, as the	Job 5:7	3205
though man be *b* like a wild ass's	Job 11:12	3205
Man that is *b* of a woman is of	Job 14:1	3205
Art thou the first man that was *b*	Job 15:7	3205
and he which is *b* of a woman	Job 15:14	3205
he be clean that is *b* of a woman	Job 25:4	3205
thou it, because thou wast then *b*	Job 38:21	3205
unto a people that shall be *b*	Ps 22:31	3205
go astray as soon as they be *b*	Ps 58:3	990
the children which should be *b*	Ps 78:6	3205
this man was *b* there	Ps 87:4	3205
This and that man was *b* in her	Ps 87:5	3205
people, that this man was *b* there	Ps 87:6	3205
a brother is *b* for adversity	Prov 17:17	3205
and had servants *b* in my house	Eccl 2:7	1121
A time to be *b*, and a time to die	Eccl 3:2	3205
whereas also he that is *b* in his	Eccl 4:14	3205
For unto us a child is *b*, unto us	Is 9:6	3205
or shall a nation be *b* at once	Is 66:8	3205
that are *b* in this place, and	Jer 16:3	3205
Cursed be the day wherein I was *b*	Jer 20:14	3205
A man child is *b* unto thee	Jer 20:15	3205
country, where ye were not *b*	Jer 22:26	3205
in the day thou wast *b* thy navel	Eze 16:4	3205
in the day that thou wast *b*	Eze 16:5	3205
you as *b* in the country among the	Eze 47:22	249
her as in the day that she was *b*	Hos 2:3	3205
of Mary, of whom was *b* Jesus	Mt 1:16	1080
Now when Jesus was *b* in Bethlehem	Mt 2:1	1080
is he that is *b* King of the Jews	Mt 2:2	5088
of them where Christ should be *b*	Mt 2:4	1080
Among them that are *b* of women	Mt 11:11	1084
which were so *b* from their	Mt 19:12	1080
for that man if he had not been *b*	Mt 26:24	1080
that man if he had never been *b*	Mk 14:21	1080
that holy thing which shall be *b*	Lk 1:35	1080
For unto you is *b* this day in the	Lk 2:11	5088
Among those that are *b* of women	Lk 7:28	1084
Which were *b*, not of blood, nor	Jn 1:13	1080
thee, Except a man be *b* again	Jn 3:3	1080
How can a man be *b* when he is old	Jn 3:4	1080
into his mother's womb, and be *b*	Jn 3:4	1080
thee, Except a man be *b* of water	Jn 3:5	1080
That which is *b* of the flesh is	Jn 3:6	1080
that which is *b* of the Spirit is	Jn 3:6	1080
unto thee, Ye must be *b* again	Jn 3:7	1080
every one that is *b* of the Spirit	Jn 3:8	1080
We be not *b* of fornication	Jn 8:41	1080
his parents, that he was *b* blind	Jn 9:2	1080
your son, who ye say was *b* blind	Jn 9:19	1080
our son, and that he was *b* blind	Jn 9:20	1080
the eyes of one that was *b* blind	Jn 9:32	1080
Thou wast altogether *b* in sins	Jn 9:34	1080
that a man is *b* into the world	Jn 16:21	1080
To this end was I *b*, and for this	Jn 18:37	1080
our own tongue, wherein we were *b*	Acts 2:8	1080
In which time Moses was *b*	Acts 7:20	1080
b in Pontus, lately come from	Acts 18:2	1085
b at Alexandria, an eloquent man,	Acts 18:24	1085
b in Tarsus, a city in Cilicia,	Acts 22:3	1080
And Paul said, But I was free *b*	Acts 22:28	1080
(For the children being not yet *b*	Rom 9:11	1080
as of one *b* out of due time	1Cor 15:8	1626
bondwoman was *b* after the flesh	Gal 4:23	1080
But as then he that was *b* after	Gal 4:29	1080
him that was *b* after the Spirit	Gal 4:29	
By faith Moses, when he was *b*	Heb 11:23	1080
Being *b* again, not of corruptible	1Pet 1:23	313
doeth righteousness is *b* of him	1Jn 2:29	1080
Whosoever is *b* of God doth not	1Jn 3:9	1080
sin, because he is *b* of God	1Jn 3:9	1080
every one that loveth is *b* of God	1Jn 4:7	1080
Jesus is the Christ is *b* of God	1Jn 5:1	1080
For whatsoever is *b* of God	1Jn 5:4	1080
whosoever is *b* of God sinneth not	1Jn 5:18	1080
her child as soon as it was *b*	Rev 12:4	5088

BORNE

that the ark may be *b* with them	Ex 25:14	5375
that the table may be *b* with them	Ex 25:28	5375
stood, and on which it was *b* up	Judg 16:29	5564
I have *b* chastisement, I will not	Job 34:31	5375
then I could have *b* it	Ps 55:12	5375
for thy sake I have *b* reproach	Ps 69:7	5375
which are *b* by me from the belly,	Is 46:3	6006
Surely he hath *b* our griefs	Is 53:4	5375
ye shall be *b* upon her sides, and	Is 66:12	5375
they must needs be *b*, because	Jer 10:5	5375
She that hath *b* seven languisheth	Jer 15:9	3205
that thou hast *b* me a man of	Jer 15:10	3205
because he hath *b* it upon him	Lam 3:28	5190
we have *b* their iniquities	Lam 5:7	5445
whom thou hast *b* unto me	Eze 16:20	3205
Thou hast *b* thy lewdness and thine	Eze 16:58	5375
yet have they *b* their shame with	Eze 32:24	5375
yet have they *b* their shame with	Eze 32:25	5375
because ye have *b* the shame of	Eze 36:6	5375
that they have *b* their shame	Eze 39:26	5375
But ye have *b* the tabernacle of	Amos 5:26	5375
unto us, which have *b* the burden	Mt 20:12	941
heavy burdens and grievous to be *b*	Mt 23:4	1418
of the palsy, which was *b* of four	Mk 2:3	142
men with burdens grievous to be *b*	Lk 11:46	1418
sent me, hath *b* witness of me	Jn 5:37	
Sir, if thou have *b* him hence	Jn 20:15	941
that he was *b* of the soldiers for	Acts 21:35	941
as we have *b* the image of the	1Cor 15:49	5409
Which have *b* witness of thy	3Jn 6	
And hast *b*, and hast patience, and	Rev 2:3	941

BORROW

woman shall *b* of her neighbour	Ex 3:22	7592
let every man *b* of his neighbour,	Ex 11:2	7592
if a man *b* ought of his neighbour	Ex 22:14	7592
nations, but thou shalt not *b*	Deut 15:6	5670
many nations, and thou shalt not *b*	Deut 28:12	3867
b thee vessels abroad of all thy	2Kin 4:3	7592
b not a few	2Kin 4:3	
from him that would *b* of thee	Mt 5:42	1155

BORROWED

they *b* of the Egyptians jewels of	Ex 12:35	7592
for it was *b*	2Kin 6:5	7592
We have *b* money for the king's	Neh 5:4	3867

BORROWER

the *b* is servant to the lender	Prov 22:7	3867
as with the lender, so with the *b*	Is 24:2	3867

BORROWETH

The wicked *b*, and payeth not again	Ps 37:21	3867

BORSHAN See Chor-ashan.

BOSCATH *(bos'-cath)* See Bosketh. *A city in Judah.*

the daughter of Adaiah of B	2Kin 22:1	1218

BOSOM

I have given my maid into thy *b*	Gen 16:5	2436
Put now thine hand into thy *b*	Ex 4:6	2436
And he put his hand into his *b*	Ex 4:6	2436
Put thine hand into thy *b* again	Ex 4:7	2436
he put his hand into his *b* again	Ex 4:7	2436
and plucked it out of his *b*	Ex 4:7	2436
say unto me, Carry them in thy *b*	Num 11:12	2436
daughter, or the wife of thy *b*	Deut 13:6	2436
and toward the wife of his *b*	Deut 28:54	2436
evil toward the husband of her *b*	Deut 28:56	2436
the child, and laid it in her *b*	Ruth 4:16	2436
of his own cup, and lay in his *b*	2Sa 12:3	2436
and thy master's wives into thy *b*	2Sa 12:8	2436
him, and let her lie in thy *b*	1Kin 1:2	2436
slept, and laid it in her *b*	1Kin 3:20	2436
and laid her dead child in my *b*	1Kin 3:20	2436
And he took him out of her *b*	1Kin 17:19	2436
by hiding mine iniquity in my *b*	Job 31:33	2243
prayer returned into mine own *b*	Ps 35:13	2436
pluck it out of thy *b*	Ps 74:11	2436
into their *b* their reproach	Ps 79:12	2436
how I do bear in my *b* the	Ps 89:50	2436
nor he that bindeth sheaves his *b*	Ps 129:7	2683
embrace the *b* of a stranger	Prov 5:20	2436
Can a man take fire in his *b*	Prov 6:27	2436
man taketh a gift out of the *b* to	Prov 17:23	2436
man hideth his hand in his *b*	Prov 19:24	6747
and a reward in the *b* strong wrath	Prov 21:14	2436
slothful hideth his hand in his *b*	Prov 26:15	6747
anger resteth in the *b* of fools	Eccl 7:9	2436
his arm, and carry them in his *b*	Is 40:11	2436

even recompense into their *b*	Is 65:6	2436
their former work into their *b*	Is 65:7	2436
of the fathers into the *b* of	Jer 32:18	2436
poured out into their mothers' *b*	Lam 2:12	2436
from her that lieth in thy *b*	Mic 7:5	2436
over, shall men give into your *b*	Lk 6:38	2859
by the angels into Abraham's *b*	Lk 16:22	2859
afar off, and Lazarus in his *b*	Lk 16:23	2859
which is in the *b* of the Father	Jn 1:18	2859
on Jesus' *b* one of his disciples	Jn 13:23	2859

BOSOR (bo'-sor) Greek form of Besor.

the way of Balaam the son of B	2Pet 2:15	1007

BOSSES

upon the thick *b* of his bucklers	Job 15:26	1354

BOTCH

smite thee with the *b* of Egypt	Deut 28:27	7822
with a sore that cannot be	Deut 28:35	7822

BOTH See APPENDIX.

BOTTLE

a *b* of water, and gave it unto	Gen 21:14	2573
And the water was spent in the *b*	Gen 21:15	2573
went, and filled the *b* with water	Gen 21:19	2573
And she opened a *b* of milk	Judg 4:19	4997
a *b* of wine, and brought him unto	1Sa 1:24	5035
and another carrying a *b* of wine	1Sa 10:3	5035
a *b* of wine, and a kid, and sent	1Sa 16:20	4997
of summer fruits, and a *b* of wine	2Sa 16:1	5035
put thou my tears into thy *b*	Ps 56:8	4997
I am become like a *b* in the smoke	Ps 119:83	4997
Every *b* shall be filled with wine	Jer 13:12	5035
every *b* shall be filled with wine	Jer 13:12	5035
Go and get a potter's earthen *b*	Jer 19:1	1228
Then shalt thou break the *b* in	Jer 19:10	1228
drink, that puttest thy *b* to him	Hab 2:15	2573

BOTTLES

sacks upon their asses, and wine *b*	Josh 9:4	4997
these *b* of wine, which we filled,	Josh 9:13	4997
two *b* of wine, and five sheep	1Sa 25:18	5035
it is ready to burst like new *b*	Job 32:19	178
or who can stay the *b* of heaven	Job 38:37	5035
his vessels, and break their *b*	Jer 48:12	5035
have made him sick with *b* of wine	Hos 7:5	2573
do men put new wine into old *b*	Mt 9:17	779
else the *b* break, and the wine	Mt 9:17	779
wine runneth out, and the *b* perish	Mt 9:17	779
but they put new wine into new *b*	Mt 9:17	779
man putteth new wine into old *b*	Mk 2:22	779
the new wine doth burst the *b*	Mk 2:22	779
spilled, and the *b* will be marred	Mk 2:22	779
new wine must be put into new *b*	Mk 2:22	779
man putteth new wine into old *b*	Lk 5:37	779
the new wine will burst the *b*	Lk 5:37	779
be spilled, and the *b* shall perish	Lk 5:37	779
new wine must be put into new *b*	Lk 5:38	779

BOTTOM

they sank into the *b* as a stone	Ex 15:5	4688
blood beside the *b* of the altar	Ex 29:12	3247
the *b* of the altar of the burnt	Lev 4:7	3247
the *b* of the altar of the burnt	Lev 4:18	3247
b of the altar of burnt offering	Lev 4:25	3247
thereof at the *b* of the altar	Lev 4:30	3247
thereof at the *b* of the altar	Lev 4:34	3247
wrung out at the *b* of the altar	Lev 5:9	3247
the blood at the *b* of the altar	Lev 8:15	3247
the blood at the *b* of the altar	Lev 9:9	3247
it, and covereth the *b* of the sea	Job 36:30	8328
the *b* thereof of gold, the	Song 3:10	7507
even the *b* shall be a cubit, and	Eze 43:13	2436
from the *b* upon the ground even	Eze 43:14	2436
the *b* thereof shall be a cubit	Eze 43:17	3247
they came at the *b* of the den	Dan 6:24	773
from my sight in the *b* of the sea	Amos 9:3	7172
myrtle trees that were in the *b*	Zec 1:8	4699
in twain from the top to the *b*	Mt 27:51	2736
in twain from the top to the *b*	Mk 15:38	2736

BOTTOMLESS

was given the key of the *b* pit	Rev 9:1	12
And he opened the *b* pit	Rev 9:2	12
which is the angel of the *b* pit	Rev 9:11	12
b pit shall make war against them	Rev 11:7	12
and shall ascend out of the *b* pit	Rev 17:8	12
having the key of the *b* pit	Rev 20:1	12
And cast him into the *b* pit	Rev 20:3	12

BOTTOMS

down to the *b* of the mountains	Jonah 2:6	7095

BOUGH

Joseph is a fruitful *b*	Gen 49:22	1121
even a fruitful *b* by a well	Gen 49:22	1121
cut down a *b* from the trees, and	Judg 9:48	7754
likewise cut down every man his *b*	Judg 9:49	7754
shall lop the *b* with terror	Is 10:33	6288
in the top of the uppermost *b*	Is 17:6	534
strong cities be as a forsaken *b*	Is 17:9	2793

BOUGHS

first day the *b* of goodly trees	Lev 23:40	6529
the *b* of thick trees, and willows	Lev 23:40	6057
shalt not go over the *b* again	Deut 24:20	6288
under the thick *b* of a great oak	2Sa 18:9	7730
bring forth *b* like a plant	Job 14:9	7105
the *b* thereof were like the	Ps 80:10	6057
She sent out her *b* unto the sea	Ps 80:11	7105
I will take hold of the *b* thereof	Song 7:8	5577
When the *b* thereof are withered,	Is 27:11	7105
and it shall bring forth *b*	Eze 17:23	6057
and his top was among the thick *b*	Eze 31:3	5688
his *b* were multiplied, and his	Eze 31:5	5634
heaven made their nests in his *b*	Eze 31:6	5589
the fir trees were not like his *b*	Eze 31:8	5589
shot up his top among the thick *b*	Eze 31:10	5688
his *b* are broken by all the	Eze 31:12	6288
up their top among the thick *b*	Eze 31:14	5688
the heaven dwelt in the *b* thereof	Dan 4:12	6056

BOUGHT

or *b* with money of any stranger,	Gen 17:12	4736
he that is *b* with thy money, must	Gen 17:13	4736
all that were *b* with his money,	Gen 17:23	4736
b with money of the stranger,	Gen 17:27	4736
he *b* a parcel of a field, where	Gen 33:19	7069
b him of the hands of the	Gen 39:1	7069
Canaan, for the corn which they *b*	Gen 47:14	7666
Joseph *b* all the land of Egypt	Gen 47:20	7069
the land of the priests *b* he not	Gen 47:22	7069
I have *b* you this day and your	Gen 47:23	7069
which Abraham *b* with the field of	Gen 49:30	7069
which Abraham *b* with the field	Gen 50:13	7069
man's servant that is *b* for money	Ex 12:44	4736
b it until the year of jubile	Lev 25:28	7069
for ever to him that *b* it	Lev 25:30	7069
b him from the year that he was	Lev 25:50	7069
of the money that he was *b* for	Lev 25:51	4736
the LORD a field which he hath *b*	Lev 27:22	4736
return unto him of whom it was *b*	Lev 27:24	7069
he thy father that hath *b* thee	Deut 32:6	7069
a parcel of ground which Jacob *b*	Josh 24:32	7069
that I have *b* all that was	Ruth 4:9	7069
little ewe lamb, which he had *b*	2Sa 12:3	7069
So David *b* the threshingfloor and	2Sa 24:24	7069
he *b* the hill Samaria of Shemer	1Kin 16:24	7069
this wall, neither *b* we any land	Neh 5:16	7069
Thou hast *b* me no sweet cane with	Is 43:24	7069
I *b* the field of Hanameel my	Jer 32:9	7069
And fields shall be *b* in this land	Jer 32:43	7069
So I *b* her to me for fifteen	Hos 3:2	3739
and sold all that he had, and *b* it	Mt 13:46	59
b in the temple, and overthrew the	Mt 21:12	59
b with them the potter's field,	Mt 27:7	59
b in the temple, and overthrew the	Mk 11:15	59
he *b* fine linen, and took him down	Mk 15:46	59
had *b* sweet spices, that they	Mk 16:1	59
I have *b* a piece of ground, and I	Lk 14:18	59
I have *b* five yoke of oxen, and I	Lk 14:19	59
they did eat, they drank, they *b*	Lk 17:28	59
that sold therein, and them that *b*	Lk 19:45	59
in the sepulchre that Abraham *b*	Acts 7:16	5608
For ye are *b* with a price	1Cor 6:20	59
Ye are *b* with a price	1Cor 7:23	59
even denying the Lord that *b* them	2Pet 2:1	59

BOUND

b Isaac his son, and laid him on	Gen 22:9	6123
b upon his hand a scarlet thread,	Gen 38:28	7194
where the king's prisoners were *b*	Gen 39:20	631
the place where Joseph was *b*	Gen 40:3	631
which were *b* in the prison	Gen 40:5	631
be *b* in the house of your prison	Gen 42:19	631
and *b* him before their eyes	Gen 42:24	631
life is *b* up in the lad's life	Gen 44:30	7194
utmost *b* of the everlasting hills	Gen 49:26	8379
their kneadingtroughs being *b* up	Ex 12:34	6887
ephod, and *b* it unto him therewith	Lev 8:7	640
which hath no covering *b* upon it	Num 19:15	6616
wherewith she hath *b* her soul	Num 30:4	631
she hath *b* her soul shall stand	Num 30:4	631
wherewith she hath *b* her soul	Num 30:5	631
lips, wherewith she *b* her soul	Num 30:6	631

she *b* her soul shall stand	Num 30:7	631
lips, wherewith she *b* her soul	Num 30:8	631
wherewith have *b* their souls	Num 30:9	631
or *b* her soul by a bond with an	Num 30:10	631
she *b* her soul shall stand	Num 30:11	631
she *b* the scarlet line in the	Josh 2:21	7194
bottles, old, and rent, and *b* up	Josh 9:4	6887
they *b* him with two new cords, and	Judg 15:13	631
mightest be *b* to afflict thee	Judg 16:6	631
dried, and she *b* him with them	Judg 16:8	631
wherewith thou mightest be *b*	Judg 16:10	631
b him therewith, and said unto him	Judg 16:12	631
me wherewith thou mightest be *b*	Judg 16:13	631
b him with fetters of brass	Judg 16:21	631
the soul of my lord shall be *b* in	1Sa 25:29	6887
Thy hands were not *b*, nor thy	2Sa 3:34	631
b two talents of silver in two	2Kin 5:23	6887
shut him up, and *b* him in prison	2Kin 17:4	631
b him with fetters of brass, and	2Kin 25:7	631
b him with fetters, and carried	2Chr 33:11	631
b him in fetters, to carry him to	2Chr 36:6	631
And if they be *b* in fetters	Job 36:8	631
take it to the *b* thereof, and that	Job 38:20	1366
out those which are *b* with chains	Ps 68:6	615
Thou hast set a *b* that they may	Ps 104:9	1366
being *b* in affliction and iron	Ps 107:10	615
Foolishness is *b* in the heart of	Prov 22:15	7194
who hath *b* the waters in a	Prov 30:4	6887
not been closed, neither *b* up	Is 1:6	2280
they are *b* by the archers	Is 22:3	631
are found in thee are *b* together	Is 22:3	631
of the prison to them that are *b*	Is 61:1	631
the *b* of the sea by a perpetual	Jer 5:22	1366
cause, that thou mayest be *b* up	Jer 30:13	4205
b him with chains, to carry him	Jer 39:7	631
when he had taken him being *b* in	Jer 40:1	631
king of Babylon *b* him in chains	Jer 52:11	631
transgressions is *b* by his hand	Lam 1:14	8244
b with cords, and made of cedar,	Eze 27:24	2280
it shall not be *b* up to be healed	Eze 30:21	2280
neither have ye *b* up that which	Eze 34:4	2280
these men were *b* in their coats	Dan 3:21	3729
fell down *b* into the midst of the	Dan 3:23	3729
Did not we cast three men *b* into	Dan 3:24	3729
The wind hath *b* her up in her	Hos 4:19	6887
were like them that remove the *b*	Hos 5:10	1366
Though I have *b* and strengthened	Hos 7:15	3256
The iniquity of Ephraim is *b* up	Hos 13:12	6887
her great men were *b* in chains	Nah 3:10	7576
b him, and put him in prison for	Mt 14:3	1210
on earth shall be *b* in heaven	Mt 16:19	1210
on earth shall be *b* in heaven	Mt 18:18	1210
And when they had *b* him, they led	Mt 27:2	1210
he had been often *b* with fetters	Mk 5:4	1210
b him in prison for Herodias'	Mk 6:17	1210
b Jesus, and carried him away, and	Mk 15:1	1210
which lay *b* with them that had	Mk 15:7	1210
and he was kept *b* with chains	Lk 8:29	1196
b up his wounds, pouring in oil	Lk 10:34	2611
of Abraham, whom Satan hath *b*	Lk 13:16	1210
b hand and foot with graveclothes	Jn 11:44	1210
his face was *b* about with a	Jn 11:44	4019
of the Jews took Jesus, and him,	Jn 18:12	1210
Now Annas had sent him *b* unto	Jn 18:24	1210
might bring them *b* unto Jerusalem	Acts 9:2	1210
them *b* unto the chief priests	Acts 9:21	1210
two soldiers, *b* with two chains	Acts 12:6	1210
I go *b* in the spirit unto	Acts 20:22	1210
b his own hands and feet, and said,	Acts 21:11	1210
for I am ready not to be *b* only	Acts 21:13	1210
him to be *b* with two chains	Acts 21:33	1210
which were there *b* unto Jerusalem	Acts 22:5	1210
as they *b* him with thongs, Paul	Acts 22:25	4385
a Roman, and because he had *b* him	Acts 22:29	1210
b themselves under a curse,	Acts 23:12	332
We have *b* ourselves under a great	Acts 23:14	332
which have *b* themselves with an	Acts 23:21	332
the Jews a pleasure, left Paul *b*	Acts 24:27	1210
of Israel I am *b* with this chain	Acts 28:20	4029
is *b* by the law to her husband so	Rom 7:2	1210
Art thou *b* unto a wife	1Cor 7:27	1210
The wife is *b* by the law as long	1Cor 7:39	1210
We are *b* to thank God always for	2Th 1:3	3784
But we are *b* to give thanks alway	2Th 2:13	3784
but the word of God is not *b*	2Ti 2:9	1210
that are in bonds, as *b* with them	Heb 13:3	4887
b in the great river Euphrates	Rev 9:14	1210
Satan, and *b* him a thousand years,	Rev 20:2	1210

BOUNDS

thou shalt set *b* unto the people	Ex 19:12	1379
Set *b* about the mount, and	Ex 19:23	1379
I will set thy *b* from the Red sea	Ex 23:31	1366
he set the *b* of the people	Deut 32:8	1367
his *b* that he cannot pass	Job 14:5	2706
hath compassed the waters with *b*	Job 26:10	2706
have removed the *b* of the people	Is 10:13	1367
the *b* of their habitation	Acts 17:26	3734

BOUNTIFUL

He that hath a *b* eye shall be	Prov 22:9	2896
nor the churl said to be *b*	Is 32:5	7771

BOUNTIFULLY

because he hath dealt *b* with me	Ps 13:6	1580
the LORD hath dealt *b* with thee	Ps 116:7	1580
Deal *b* with thy servant, that I	Ps 119:17	1580
for thou shalt deal *b* with me	Ps 142:7	1580
soweth *b* shall reap also *b*	2Cor 9:6	2129

BOUNTIFULNESS

enriched in every thing to all *b*	2Cor 9:11	572

BOUNTY

Solomon gave her of his royal *b*	1Kin 10:13	3027
you, and make up beforehand your *b*	2Cor 9:5	2129
might be ready, as a matter of *b*	2Cor 9:5	2129

BOW See also WORSHIP.

I do set my *b* in the cloud, and it	Gen 9:13	7198
that the *b* shall be seen in the	Gen 9:14	7198
the *b* shall be in the cloud	Gen 9:16	7198
thy weapons, thy quiver and thy *b*	Gen 27:3	7198
thee, and nations *b* down to thee	Gen 27:29	7812
thy mother's sons *b* down to thee	Gen 27:29	7812
thy brethren indeed come to *b*	Gen 37:10	7812
they cried before him, *B* the knee	Gen 41:43	86
with my sword and with my *b*	Gen 48:22	7198
children shall *b* down before thee	Gen 49:8	7812
But his *b* abode in strength, and	Gen 49:24	7198
b down themselves unto me, saying	Ex 11:8	7812
Thou shalt not *b* down thyself to	Ex 20:5	7812
Thou shalt not *b* down to their	Ex 23:24	7812
in your land, to *b* down unto it	Lev 26:1	7812
Thou shalt not *b* down thyself	Deut 5:9	7812
nor *b* yourselves unto them	Josh 23:7	7812
with thy sword, nor with thy *b*	Josh 24:12	7198
them, and to *b* down unto them	Judg 2:19	7812
even to his sword, and to his *b*	1Sa 18:4	7198
of Judah the use of the *b*	2Sa 1:18	7198
the *b* of Jonathan turned not back	2Sa 1:22	7198
so that a *b* of steel is broken by	2Sa 22:35	7198
certain man drew a *b* at a venture	1Kin 22:34	7198
I *b* myself in the house of Rimmon	2Kin 5:18	7812
when I *b* down myself in the house	2Kin 5:18	7812
with thy sword and with thy *b*	2Kin 6:22	7198
Jehu drew a *b* with his full	2Kin 9:24	7198
And Elisha said unto him, Take *b*	2Kin 13:15	7198
And he took unto him *b* and arrows	2Kin 13:15	7198
Israel, Put thine hand upon the *b*	2Kin 13:16	7198
nor *b* yourselves to them, nor	2Kin 17:35	7812
b down thine ear, and hear	2Kin 19:16	5186
and sword, and to shoot with *b*	1Chr 5:18	7198
and shooting arrows out of a *b*	1Chr 12:2	7198
and with him armed men with *b*	2Chr 17:17	7198
certain man drew a *b* at a venture	2Chr 18:33	7198
the *b* of steel shall strike him	Job 20:24	7198
my *b* was renewed in my hand	Job 29:20	7198
let others *b* down upon her	Job 31:10	3766
They *b* themselves, they bring	Job 39:3	3766
he hath bent his *b*, and made it	Ps 7:12	7198
For, lo, the wicked bend their *b*	Ps 11:2	7198
so that a *b* of steel is broken by	Ps 18:34	7198
to the dust shall *b* before him	Ps 22:29	3766
B down thine ear to me	Ps 31:2	5186
the sword, and have bent their *b*	Ps 37:14	7198
For I will not trust in my *b*	Ps 44:6	7198
he breaketh the *b*, and cutteth the	Ps 46:9	7198
bendeth his *b* to shoot his arrows	Ps 58:7	
the wilderness shall *b* before him	Ps 72:9	3766
brake he the arrows of the *b*	Ps 76:3	7198
turned aside like a deceitful *b*	Ps 78:57	7198
B down thine ear, O LORD, hear me	Ps 86:1	5186
O come, let us worship and *b* down	Ps 95:6	3766
B thy heavens, O LORD, and come	Ps 144:5	5186
b thine ear to my understanding	Prov 5:1	5186
The evil *b* before the good	Prov 14:19	7817
B down thine ear, and hear the	Prov 22:17	5186
the strong men shall *b* themselves	Eccl 12:3	5791
Without me they shall *b* down	Is 10:4	3766
drawn sword, and from the bent *b*	Is 21:15	7198
and as driven stubble to his *b*	Is 41:2	7198

B

That unto me every knee shall *b*	Is 45:23	3766
They stoop, they *b* down together	Is 46:2	3766
they shall *b* down to thee with	Is 49:23	7812
B down, that we may go over	Is 51:23	7812
is it to *b* down his head as a	Is 58:5	3721
they that despised thee shall *b*	Is 60:14	7812
ye shall all *b* down to the	Is 65:12	3766
Pul, and Lud, that draw the *b*	Is 66:19	7198
They shall lay hold on *b* and spear	Jer 6:23	7198
tongues like their *b* for lies	Jer 9:3	7198
that handle and bend the *b*	Jer 46:9	7198
I will break the *b* of Elam	Jer 49:35	7198
all ye that bend the *b*, shoot at	Jer 50:14	7198
all ye that bend the *b*, camp	Jer 50:29	7198
They shall hold the *b* and the	Jer 50:42	7198
bendeth let the archer bend his *b*	Jer 51:3	7198
He hath bent his *b* like an enemy	Lam 2:4	7198
He hath bent his *b*, and set me as	Lam 3:12	7198
As the appearance of the *b* that	Eze 1:28	7198
I will smite thy *b* out of thy	Eze 39:3	7198
that I will break the *b* of Israel	Hos 1:5	7198
God, and will not save them by *b*	Hos 1:7	7198
and I will break the *b* and the	Hos 2:18	7198
they are like a deceitful *b*	Hos 7:16	7198
he stand that handleth the *b*	Amos 2:15	7198
b myself before the high God	Mic 6:6	3721
the perpetual hills did *b*	Hab 3:6	7817
Thy *b* was made quite naked,	Hab 3:9	7198
the battle *b* shall be cut off	Zec 9:10	7198
filled the *b* with Ephraim, and	Zec 9:13	7198
the nail, out of him the battle *b*	Zec 10:4	7198
see, and *b* down their back alway	Rom 11:10	4781
Lord, every knee shall *b* to me	Rom 14:11	2578
For this cause I *b* my knees unto	Eph 3:14	2578
name of Jesus every knee should *b*	Phil 2:10	2578
and he that sat on him had a *b*	Rev 6:2	5115

BOWED

b himself toward the ground,	Gen 18:2	7812
he *b* himself with his face toward	Gen 19:1	7812
b himself to the people of the	Gen 23:7	7812
Abraham *b* down himself before the	Gen 23:12	7812
the man *b* down his head, and	Gen 24:26	6915
I *b* down my head, and worshipped	Gen 24:48	6915
b himself to the ground seven	Gen 33:3	7812
children, and they *b* themselves	Gen 33:6	7812
came near, and *b* themselves	Gen 33:7	7812
and Rachel, and they *b* themselves	Gen 33:7	7812
b down themselves before him with	Gen 42:6	7812
b themselves to him to the earth	Gen 43:26	7812
they *b* down their heads, and made	Gen 43:28	6915
Israel *b* himself upon the bed's	Gen 47:31	7812
he *b* himself with his face to the	Gen 48:12	7812
b his shoulder to bear, and became	Gen 49:15	5186
then they *b* their heads and	Ex 4:31	6915
And the people *b* the head and	Ex 12:27	6915
b his head toward the earth, and	Ex 34:8	6915
he *b* down his head, and fell flat	Num 22:31	6915
did eat, and *b* down to their gods	Num 25:2	7812
gods, and *b* yourselves unto them	Josh 23:16	7812
b themselves unto them, and	Judg 2:12	7812
gods, and *b* themselves unto them	Judg 2:17	7812
At her feet he *b*, he fell, he lay	Judg 5:27	3766
at her feet he *b*, he fell	Judg 5:27	3766
where he *b*, there he fell down	Judg 5:27	3766
b down upon their knees to drink	Judg 7:6	3766
he *b* himself with all his might	Judg 16:30	5186
b herself to the ground, and said	Ruth 2:10	7812
she *b* herself and travailed	1Sa 4:19	3766
ground, and *b* himself three times	1Sa 20:41	7812
face to the earth, and *b* himself	1Sa 24:8	7812
face, and *b* herself to the ground,	1Sa 25:23	7812
b herself on her face to the	1Sa 25:41	7812
face to the ground, and *b* himself	1Sa 28:14	7812
he *b* himself, and said, What is	2Sa 9:8	7812
b himself, and thanked the king	2Sa 14:22	7812
b himself on his face to the	2Sa 14:33	7812
Cushi *b* himself unto Joab, and ran	2Sa 18:21	7812
he *b* the heart of all the men of	2Sa 19:14	5186
He *b* the heavens also, and came	2Sa 22:10	5186
b himself before the king on his	2Sa 24:20	7812
And Bath-sheba *b*, and did obeisance	1Kin 1:16	6915
he *b* himself to the king with	1Kin 1:23	7812
Then Bath-sheba *b* with her face	1Kin 1:31	6915
the king *b* himself upon the bed	1Kin 1:47	7812
b himself to king Solomon	1Kin 1:53	7812
b himself unto her, and sat down	1Kin 2:19	7812
knees which have not *b* unto Baal	1Kin 19:18	3766
b themselves to the ground before	2Kin 2:15	7812
b herself to the ground, and took	2Kin 4:37	7812
b himself to David with his face	1Chr 21:21	7812

b down their heads, and worshipped	1Chr 29:20	6915
they *b* themselves with their	2Chr 7:3	3766
Jehoshaphat *b* his head with his	2Chr 20:18	6915
b down himself before them, and	2Chr 25:14	7812
present with him *b* themselves	2Chr 29:29	3766
they *b* their heads and worshipped	2Chr 29:30	6915
they *b* their heads, and worshipped	Neh 8:6	6915
that were in the king's gate, *b*	Est 3:2	3766
But Mordecai *b* not, nor did him	Est 3:2	3766
Haman saw that Mordecai *b* not	Est 3:5	3766
He *b* the heavens also, and came	Ps 18:9	5186
I *b* down heavily, as one that	Ps 35:14	7817
I am *b* down greatly,	Ps 38:6	7817
For our soul is *b* down to the	Ps 44:25	7743
my soul is *b* down	Ps 57:6	3721
up all those that be *b* down	Ps 145:14	3721
LORD raiseth them that are *b* down	Ps 146:8	3721
of men shall be *b* down, and the	Is 2:11	7817
loftiness of man shall be *b* down	Is 2:17	7817
I was *b* down at the hearing of it	Is 21:3	5791
they *b* the knee before him, and	Mt 27:29	1120
was *b* together, and could in no	Lk 13:11	4794
b down their faces to the earth,	Lk 24:5	2827
he *b* his head, and gave up the	Jn 19:30	2827
who have not *b* the knee to the	Rom 11:4	2578

BOWELS

thine own *b* shall be thine heir	Gen 15:4	4578
shall be separated from thy *b*	Gen 25:23	4578
for his *b* did yearn upon his	Gen 43:30	7358
the curse shall go into thy *b*	Num 5:22	4578
which shall proceed out of thy *b*	2Sa 7:12	4578
my son, which came forth of my *b*	2Sa 16:11	4578
shed out his *b* to the ground, and	2Sa 20:10	4578
for her *b* yearned upon her son,	1Kin 3:26	7358
sickness by disease of thy *b*	2Chr 21:15	4578
until thy *b* fall out by reason of	2Chr 21:15	4578
his *b* with an incurable disease	2Chr 21:18	4578
his *b* fell out by reason of his	2Chr 21:19	4578
b slew him there with the sword	2Chr 32:21	4578
Yet his meat in his *b* is turned	Job 20:14	4578
My *b* boiled, and rested not	Job 30:27	4578
it is melted in the midst of my *b*	Ps 22:14	4578
that took me out of my mother's *b*	Ps 71:6	4578
let it come into his *b* like water	Ps 109:18	7130
door, and my *b* were moved for him	Song 5:4	4578
Wherefore my *b* shall sound like	Is 16:11	4578
the offspring of thy *b* like the	Is 48:19	4578
from the *b* of my mother hath he	Is 49:1	4578
strength, the sounding of thy *b*	Is 63:15	4578
My *b*, my *b*	Jer 4:19	4578
therefore my *b* are troubled for	Jer 31:20	4578
my *b* are troubled	Lam 1:20	4578
my *b* are troubled, my liver is	Lam 2:11	4578
fill thy *b* with this roll that I	Eze 3:3	4578
their souls, neither fill their *b*	Eze 7:19	4578
midst, and all his *b* gushed out	Acts 1:18	4698
ye are straitened in your own *b*	2Cor 6:12	4698
you all in the *b* of Jesus Christ	Phil 1:8	4698
of the Spirit, if any *b* and	Phil 2:1	4698
beloved, *b* of mercies, kindness,	Col 3:12	4698
because the *b* of the saints are	Philem 7	4698
receive him, that is, mine own *b*	Philem 12	4698
refresh my *b* in the Lord	Philem 20	4698
shutteth up his *b* of compassion	1Jn 3:17	4698

BOWETH

likewise every one that *b* down	Judg 7:5	3766
And the mean man *b* down, and the	Is 2:9	7817
Bel *b* down, Nebo stoopeth, their	Is 46:1	3766

BOWING

the LORD, *b* himself to the earth	Gen 24:52	
their eyes *b* down to the ground	Ps 17:11	5186
as a *b* wall shall ye be, and as a	Ps 62:3	5186
b their knees worshipped him	Mk 15:19	5087

BOWL

one silver *b* of seventy shekels,	Num 7:13	4219
one silver *b* of seventy shekels,	Num 7:19	4219
one silver *b* of seventy shekels,	Num 7:25	4219
one silver *b* of seventy shekels,	Num 7:31	4219
one silver *b* of seventy shekels,	Num 7:37	4219
a silver *b* of seventy shekels,	Num 7:43	4219
one silver *b* of seventy shekels,	Num 7:49	4219
one silver *b* of seventy shekels,	Num 7:55	4219
one silver *b* of seventy shekels,	Num 7:61	4219
one silver *b* of seventy shekels,	Num 7:67	4219
one silver *b* of seventy shekels,	Num 7:73	4219
one silver *b* of seventy shekels,	Num 7:79	4219
and thirty shekels, each *b* seventy	Num 7:85	4219
of the fleece, a *b* full of water	Judg 6:38	5602
loosed, or the golden *b* be broken	Eccl 12:6	1543

with a *b* upon the top of it, and	Zec 4:2	1543
one upon the right side of the *b*	Zec 4:3	1543

BOWLS

b thereof, to cover withal	Ex 25:29	4518
his shaft, and his branches, his *b*	Ex 25:31	1375
Three *b* made like unto almonds,	Ex 25:33	1375
three *b* made like almonds in the	Ex 25:33	1375
be four *b* made like unto almonds	Ex 25:34	1375
dishes, and his spoons, and his *b*	Ex 37:16	4518
his shaft, and his branch, his *b*	Ex 37:17	1375
Three *b* made after the fashion of	Ex 37:19	1375
three *b* made like almonds in	Ex 37:19	1375
were four *b* made like almonds	Ex 37:20	1375
dishes, and the spoons, and the *b*	Num 4:7	4518
of silver, twelve silver *b*	Num 7:84	4219
the two *b* of the chapiters that	1Kin 7:41	1543
to cover the two *b* of the	1Kin 7:41	1543
to cover the two *b* of the	1Kin 7:42	1543
And the *b*, and the snuffers, and the	1Kin 7:50	5592
the house of the Lord *b* of silver	2Kin 12:13	5592
And the firepans, and the *b*	2Kin 25:15	4219
gold for the fleshhooks, and the *b*	1Chr 28:17	4219
and the snuffers, and the *b*	Jer 52:18	4219
basons, and the firepans, and the *b*	Jer 52:19	4219
That drink wine in *b*, and anoint	Amos 6:6	4219
and they shall be filled like *b*	Zec 9:15	4219
be like the *b* before the altar	Zec 14:20	4219

BOWMEN

the noise of the horsemen and *b*	Jer 4:29	7411,7198

BOWS

The *b* of the mighty men are	1Sa 2:4	7198
They were armed with *b*, and could	1Chr 12:2	7198
that bare shields and drew *b*	2Chr 14:8	7198
and helmets, and habergeons, and *b*	2Chr 26:14	7198
swords, their spears, and their *b*	Neh 4:13	7198
the spears, the shields, and the *b*	Neh 4:16	7198
heart, and their *b* shall be broken	Ps 37:15	7198
bend their *b* to shoot their	Ps 64:3	
being armed, and carrying *b*	Ps 78:9	7198
are sharp, and all their *b* bent	Is 5:28	7198
with *b* shall men come thither	Is 7:24	7198
Their *b* also shall dash the young	Is 13:18	7198
every one of their *b* is broken	Jer 51:56	7198
shields and the bucklers, the *b*	Eze 39:9	7198

BOWSHOT

a good way off, as it were a *b*	Gen 21:16	2909,7198

BOX

take this *b* of oil in thine hand,	2Kin 9:1	6378
Then take the *b* of oil, and pour	2Kin 9:3	6378
the pine, and the *b* tree together	Is 41:19	8391
the *b* together, to beautify the	Is 60:13	8391
b of very precious ointment	Mt 26:7	211
a woman having an alabaster *b* of	Mk 14:3	211
and she brake the *b*, and poured it	Mk 14:3	211
an alabaster *b* of ointment	Lk 7:37	211

BOY

have given a *b* for an harlot, and	Joel 3:3	3206

BOYS

And the *b* grew	Gen 25:27	5288
of the city shall be full of *b*	Zec 8:5	3206

BOZEZ (bo'-zez) *A rock near Michmash.*

and the name of the one was *B*	1Sa 14:4	949

BOZKATH (boz'-kath) *A city in Judah.*

Lachish, and *B*, and Eglon,	Josh 15:39	1218

BOZRAH (boz'-rah)
1. *The capital city of Edom.*

Zerah of *B* reigned in his stead	Gen 36:33	1224
Zerah of *B* reigned in his stead	1Chr 1:44	1224
the Lord hath a sacrifice in *B*	Is 34:6	1224
Edom, with dyed garments from *B*	Is 63:1	1224
that *B* shall become a desolation,	Jer 49:13	1224
eagle, and spread his wings over *B*	Jer 49:22	1224
shall devour the palaces of *B*	Amos 1:12	1224
them together as the sheep of *B*	Mic 2:12	1224

2. *A place in Moab.*

And upon Kerioth, and upon *B*	Jer 48:24	1224

BRACELET

the *b* that was on his arm, and	2Sa 1:10	685

BRACELETS

two *b* for her hands of ten	Gen 24:22	6781
b upon his sister's hands, and	Gen 24:30	6781
her face, and the *b* upon her hands	Gen 24:47	6781
And she said, Thy signet, and thy *b*	Gen 38:18	6616
whose are these, the signet, and *b*	Gen 38:25	6616
willing hearted, and brought *b*	Ex 35:22	2397

of jewels of gold, chains, and *b*	Num 31:50	6781
The chains, and the *b*, and the	Is 3:19	8285
I put *b* upon thy hands, and a	Eze 16:11	6781
which put *b* upon their hands, and	Eze 23:42	6781

BRAKE

b every tree of the field	Ex 9:25	7665
all the people *b* off the golden	Ex 32:3	6561
and *b* them beneath the mount	Ex 32:19	7665
hands, and *b* them before your eyes	Deut 9:17	7665
b the pitchers that were in their	Judg 7:19	5310
b the pitchers, and held the lamps	Judg 7:20	7665
head, and all to *b* his skull	Judg 9:53	7533
he *b* the withs, as a thread of	Judg 16:9	5423
he *b* them from off his arms like	Judg 16:12	5423
side of the gate, and his neck *b*	1Sa 4:18	7665
the three mighty men *b* through	2Sa 23:16	1234
b in pieces the rocks before the	1Kin 19:11	7665
they *b* down the image of Baal, and	2Kin 10:27	5422
b down the house of Baal, and made	2Kin 10:27	5422
the house of Baal, and *b* it down	2Kin 11:18	5422
his images *b* they in pieces	2Kin 11:18	7665
b down the wall of Jerusalem from	2Kin 14:13	6555
b the images, and cut down the	2Kin 18:4	7665
b in pieces the brasen serpent	2Kin 18:4	3807
he *b* down the houses of the	2Kin 23:7	5422
b down the high places of the	2Kin 23:8	5422
b them down from thence, and cast	2Kin 23:12	7323
he *b* in pieces the images, and cut	2Kin 23:14	7665
altar and the high place he *b* down	2Kin 23:15	5422
b down the walls of Jerusalem	2Kin 25:10	5422
the three *b* through the host of	1Chr 11:18	1234
b down the images, and cut down	2Chr 14:3	7665
b into it, and carried away all	2Chr 21:17	1234
b it down, and *b* his altars and	2Chr 23:17	5422
b down the wall of Jerusalem from	2Chr 25:23	6555
b down the wall of Gath, and the	2Chr 26:6	6555
b the images in pieces, and cut	2Chr 31:1	7665
they *b* down the altars of Baalim	2Chr 34:4	5422
he *b* in pieces, and made dust of	2Chr 34:4	7665
b down the wall of Jerusalem, and	2Chr 36:19	5422
I *b* the jaws of the wicked, and	Job 29:17	7665
sea with doors, when it *b* forth	Job 38:8	1518
b up for it my decreed place, and	Job 38:10	7665
There *b* he the arrows of the bow,	Ps 76:3	7665
he *b* the whole staff of bread	Ps 105:16	7665
b the trees of their coasts	Ps 105:33	7665
the plague *b* in upon them	Ps 106:29	6555
death, and *b* their bands in sunder	Ps 107:14	5423
prophet Jeremiah's neck, and *b* it	Jer 28:10	7665
which my covenant they *b*,	Jer 31:32	6565
b down the walls of Jerusalem	Jer 39:8	5422
b down all the walls of Jerusalem	Jer 52:14	5422
of the Lord, the Chaldeans *b*	Jer 52:17	7665
despised, and whose covenant he *b*	Eze 17:16	6565
troubled, and his sleep *b* from him	Dan 2:1	1961
iron and clay, and *b* them to pieces	Dan 2:34	1855
that it *b* in pieces the iron, the	Dan 2:45	1855
b all their bones in pieces or	Dan 6:24	1855
b in pieces, and stamped the	Dan 7:7	1855
b in pieces, and stamped the	Dan 7:19	1855
smote the ram, and *b* his two horns	Dan 8:7	7665
up to heaven, he blessed, and *b*	Mt 14:19	2806
b them, and gave to his disciples,	Mt 15:36	2806
b it, and gave it to the disciples	Mt 26:26	2806
b the loaves, and gave them to his	Mk 6:41	2622
loaves, and gave thanks, and *b*	Mk 8:6	2806
When I *b* the five loaves among	Mk 8:19	2806
she *b* the box, and poured it on	Mk 14:3	4937
b it and gave to them, and said,	Mk 14:22	2806
and their net *b*	Lk 5:6	1284
he *b* the bands, and was driven of	Lk 8:29	1284
to heaven, he blessed them, and *b*	Lk 9:16	2622
b it, and gave unto them, saying,	Lk 22:19	2806
took bread, and blessed it, and *b*	Lk 24:30	2806
b the legs of the first, and of	Jn 19:32	2608
dead already, they *b* not his legs	Jn 19:33	2608
when he had given thanks, he *b* it	1Cor 11:24	2806

BRAKEST

in the first tables, which thou *b*	Ex 34:1	7665
in the first tables which thou *b*	Deut 10:2	7665
thou *b* the heads of the dragons	Ps 74:13	7665
Thou *b* the heads of leviathan in	Ps 74:14	7533
they leaned upon thee, thou *b*	Eze 29:7	7665

BRAMBLE

said all the trees unto the *b*	Judg 9:14	329
the *b* said unto the trees, If in	Judg 9:15	329
not, let fire come out of the *b*	Judg 9:15	329
nor of a *b* bush gather they	Lk 6:44	942

B

BRAMBLES

b in the fortresses thereof	Is 34:13	2336

BRANCH

with a knop and a flower in one *b*	Ex 25:33	7070
made like almonds in the other *b*	Ex 25:33	7070
his shaft, and his *b*, his bowls,	Ex 37:17	7070
the fashion of almonds in one *b*	Ex 37:19	7070
made like almonds in another *b*	Ex 37:19	7070
cut down from thence a *b* with one	Num 13:23	2156
his *b* shooteth forth in his	Job 8:16	3127
that the tender *b* thereof will	Job 14:7	
time, and his *b* shall not be green	Job 15:32	3712
and above shall his *b* be cut off	Job 18:16	7105
the dew lay all night upon my *b*	Job 29:19	7105
the *b* that thou madest strong for	Ps 80:15	1121
righteous shall flourish as a *b*	Prov 11:28	5929
In that day shall the *b* of the	Is 4:2	6780
off from Israel head and tail, *b*	Is 9:14	3712
a *B* shall grow out of his roots	Is 11:1	5342
of thy grave like an abominable *b*	Is 14:19	5342
forsaken bough, and an uppermost *b*	Is 17:9	534
head or tail, *b* or rush, may do	Is 19:15	3712
the *b* of the terrible ones shall	Is 25:5	2158
the *b* of my planting, the work of	Is 60:21	5342
raise unto David a righteous *B*	Jer 23:5	6780
that time, will I cause the *B* of	Jer 33:15	6780
they put the *b* to their nose	Eze 8:17	2156
or than a *b* which is among the	Eze 15:2	2156
took the highest *b* of the high cedar	Eze 17:3	6788
the highest *b* of the high cedar	Eze 17:22	6788
But out of a *b* of her roots shall	Dan 11:7	5342
will bring forth my servant the *B*	Zec 3:8	6780
the man whose name is The *B*	Zec 6:12	6780
leave them neither root nor *b*	Mal 4:1	6057
When his *b* is yet tender, and	Mt 24:32	2798
When her *b* is yet tender, and	Mk 13:28	2798
Every *b* in me that beareth not	Jn 15:2	2814
every *b* that beareth fruit, he	Jn 15:2	
As the *b* cannot bear fruit of	Jn 15:4	2814
in me, he is cast forth as a *b*	Jn 15:6	2814

BRANCHES

And in the vine were three *b*	Gen 40:10	8299
The three *b* are three days	Gen 40:12	8299
whose *b* run over the wall	Gen 49:22	1121
his shaft, and his *b*, his bowls,	Ex 25:31	7070
six *b* shall come out of the sides	Ex 25:32	7070
three *b* of the candlestick out of	Ex 25:32	7070
three *b* of the candlestick out of	Ex 25:32	7070
so in the six *b* that come out of	Ex 25:33	7070
be a knop under two *b* of the same	Ex 25:35	7070
and a knop under two *b* of the same	Ex 25:35	7070
and a knop under two *b* of the same	Ex 25:35	7070
according to the six *b* that	Ex 25:35	7070
their *b* shall be of the same	Ex 25:36	7070
six *b* going out of the sides	Ex 37:18	7070
three *b* of the candlestick out of	Ex 37:18	7070
three *b* of the candlestick out of	Ex 37:18	7070
so throughout the six *b* going out	Ex 37:19	7070
And a knop under two *b* of the same	Ex 37:21	7070
and a knop under two *b* of the same	Ex 37:21	7070
and a knop under two *b* of the same	Ex 37:21	7070
to the six *b* going out of it	Ex 37:21	7070
knops and their *b* were of the same	Ex 37:22	7070
b of palm trees, and the boughs of	Lev 23:40	3709
fetch olive *b*, and pine *b*	Neh 8:15	5929
and myrtle *b*, and palm *b*	Neh 8:15	5929
b of thick trees, to make booths,	Neh 8:15	5929
the flame shall dry up his *b*	Job 15:30	3127
the sea, and her *b* unto the river	Ps 80:11	3127
which sing among the *b*	Ps 104:12	6073
her *b* are stretched out, they are	Is 16:8	7976
in the outmost fruitful *b* thereof	Is 17:6	5585
and take away and cut down the *b*	Is 18:5	5189
down, and consume the *b* thereof	Is 27:10	5585
it, and the *b* of it are broken	Jer 11:16	1808
whose *b* turned toward him, and the	Eze 17:6	1808
became a vine, and brought forth *b*	Eze 17:6	905
and shot forth her *b* toward him	Eze 17:7	1808
that it might bring forth *b*	Eze 17:8	6057
in the shadow of the *b* thereof	Eze 17:23	1808
full of *b* by reason of many	Eze 19:10	6058
was exalted among the thick *b*	Eze 19:11	5688
with the multitude of her *b*	Eze 19:11	1808
is gone out of a rod of her *b*	Eze 19:14	905
a cedar in Lebanon with fair *b*	Eze 31:3	6057
his *b* became long because of the	Eze 31:5	6288
under his *b* did all the beasts of	Eze 31:6	6288
greatness, in the length of his *b*	Eze 31:7	1808
chesnut trees were not like his *b*	Eze 31:8	6288
fair by the multitude of his *b*	Eze 31:9	1808

all the valleys his *b* are fallen	Eze 31:12	1808
of the field shall be upon his *b*	Eze 31:13	6288
ye shall shoot forth your *b*	Eze 36:8	6057
down the tree, and cut off his *b*	Dan 4:14	6056
under it, and the fowls from his *b*	Dan 4:14	6056
upon whose *b* the fowls of the	Dan 4:21	6056
cities, and shall consume his *b*	Hos 11:6	905
His *b* shall spread, and his beauty	Hos 14:6	3127
the *b* thereof are made white	Joel 1:7	8299
them out, and marred their vine *b*	Nah 2:2	2156
What be these two olive *b* which	Zec 4:12	7641
come and lodge in the *b* thereof	Mt 13:32	2798
others cut down *b* from the trees	Mt 21:8	2798
herbs, and shooteth out great *b*	Mk 4:32	2798
others cut down *b* off the trees	Mk 11:8	4746
of the air lodged in the *b* of it	Lk 13:19	2798
Took *b* of palm trees, and went	Jn 12:13	902
I am the vine, ye are the *b*	Jn 15:5	2814
if the root be holy, so are the *b*	Rom 11:16	2798
And if some of the *b* be broken off	Rom 11:17	2798
Boast not against the *b*	Rom 11:18	2798
The *b* were broken off, that I	Rom 11:19	2798
if God spared not the natural *b*	Rom 11:21	2798
these, which be the natural *b*	Rom 11:24	

BRAND

is not this a *b* plucked out of	Zec 3:2	181

BRANDISH

when I shall *b* my sword before	Eze 32:10	5774

BRANDS

And when he had set the *b* on fire	Judg 15:5	3940

BRASEN

four *b* rings in the four corners	Ex 27:4	5178
burnt offering, with his *b* grate	Ex 35:16	5178
he made for the altar a *b* grate	Ex 38:4	5178
twenty, and their *b* sockets twenty	Ex 38:10	5178
the *b* altar, and the *b* grate	Ex 38:30	5178
The *b* altar, and his grate of	Ex 39:39	5178
and if it be sodden in a *b* pot	Lev 6:28	5178
the priest took the *b* censers	Num 16:39	5178
great cities with walls and *b* bars	1Kin 4:13	5178
And every base had four *b* wheels	1Kin 7:30	5178
because the *b* altar that was	1Kin 8:64	5178
made in their stead *b* shields	1Kin 14:27	5178
And he brought also the *b* altar	2Kin 16:14	5178
the *b* altar shall be for me to	2Kin 16:15	5178
off the *b* oxen that were under it	2Kin 16:17	5178
brake in pieces the *b* serpent	2Kin 18:4	5178
the *b* sea that was in the house	2Kin 25:13	5178
wherewith Solomon made the *b* sea	1Chr 18:8	5178
Moreover the *b* altar, that	2Chr 1:5	5178
to the *b* altar before the LORD	2Chr 1:6	5178
For Solomon had made a *b* scaffold	2Chr 6:13	5178
because the *b* altar which Solomon	2Chr 7:7	5178
b walls against the whole land,	Jer 1:18	5178
unto this people a fenced *b* wall	Jer 15:20	5178
the *b* sea that was in the house	Jer 52:17	5178
twelve *b* bulls that were under	Jer 52:20	5178
in, and stood beside the *b* altar	Eze 9:2	5178
and pots, *b* vessels, and of tables	Mk 7:4	5473

BRASS

of every artificer in *b* and iron	Gen 4:22	5178
gold, and silver, and, *b*,	Ex 25:3	5178
thou shalt make fifty taches of *b*	Ex 26:11	5178
cast five sockets of *b* for them	Ex 26:37	5178
and thou shalt overlay it with *b*	Ex 27:2	5178
thereof thou shalt make of *b*	Ex 27:3	5178
for it a grate of network of *b*	Ex 27:4	5178
wood, and overlay them with *b*	Ex 27:6	5178
twenty sockets shall be of *b*	Ex 27:10	5178
and their sockets of *b*	Ex 27:11	5178
of silver, and their sockets of *b*	Ex 27:17	5178
linen, and their sockets of *b*	Ex 27:18	5178
pins of the court, shall be of *b*	Ex 27:19	5178
Thou shalt also make a laver of *b*	Ex 30:18	5178
and his foot also of *b*	Ex 30:18	5178
in gold, and in silver, and in *b*	Ex 31:4	5178
gold, and silver, and, *b*,	Ex 35:5	5178
b brought the LORD's offering	Ex 35:24	5178
in gold, and in silver, and in *b*	Ex 35:32	5178
he made fifty taches of *b* to	Ex 36:18	5178
but their five sockets were of *b*	Ex 36:38	5178
and he overlaid it with *b*	Ex 38:2	5178
the vessels thereof made he of *b*	Ex 38:3	5178
the four ends of the grate of *b*	Ex 38:5	5178
wood, and overlaid them with *b*	Ex 38:6	5178
And he made the laver of *b*	Ex 38:8	5178
and the foot of it of *b*	Ex 38:8	5178
and their sockets of *b* twenty	Ex 38:11	5178

sockets for the pillars were of *b*	Ex 38:17	5178
four, and their sockets of *b* four	Ex 38:19	5178
the court round about, were of *b*	Ex 38:20	5178
the *b* of the offering was seventy	Ex 38:29	5178
brasen altar, and his grate of *b*	Ex 39:39	5178
as iron, and your earth as *b*	Lev 26:19	5154
And Moses made a serpent of *b*	Num 21:9	5178
when he beheld the serpent of *b*	Num 21:9	5178
the gold, and the silver, the *b*	Num 31:22	5178
of whose hills thou mayest dig *b*	Deut 8:9	5178
that is over thy head shall be *b*	Deut 28:23	5178
Thy shoes shall be iron and *b*	Deut 33:25	5178
silver, and gold, and vessels of *b*	Josh 6:19	5178
and the gold, and the vessels of *b*	Josh 6:24	5178
silver, and with gold, and with *b*	Josh 22:8	5178
and bound him with fetters of *b*	Judg 16:21	5178
had an helmet of *b* upon his head	1Sa 17:5	5178
was five thousand shekels of *b*	1Sa 17:5	5178
he had greaves of *b* upon his legs	1Sa 17:6	5178
a target of *b* between his	1Sa 17:6	5178
put an helmet of *b* upon his head	1Sa 17:38	5178
king David took exceeding much *b*	2Sa 8:8	5178
vessels of gold, and vessels of *b*	2Sa 8:10	5178
hundred shekels of *b* in weight	2Sa 21:16	5178
was a man of Tyre, a worker in *b*	1Kin 7:14	5178
and cunning to work all works in *b*	1Kin 7:14	5178
For he cast two pillars of *b*	1Kin 7:15	5178
he made two chapiters of molten *b*	1Kin 7:16	5178
And he made ten bases of *b*	1Kin 7:27	5178
brasen wheels, and plates of *b*	1Kin 7:30	5178
Then made he ten lavers of *b*	1Kin 7:38	5178
of the LORD, were of bright *b*	1Kin 7:45	5178
was the weight of the *b* found out	1Kin 7:47	5178
and bound him with fetters of *b*	2Kin 25:7	5178
the pillars of *b* that were in the	2Kin 25:13	5178
carried the *b* of them to Babylon	2Kin 25:13	5178
all the vessels of *b* wherewith	2Kin 25:14	5178
the *b* of all these vessels was	2Kin 25:16	5178
and the chapiter upon it was *b*	2Kin 25:17	5178
chapiter round about, all of *b*	2Kin 25:17	5178
to sound with cymbals of *b*	1Chr 15:19	5178
brought David very much *b*	1Chr 18:8	5178
the pillars, and the vessels of *b*	1Chr 18:8	5178
of vessels of gold and silver and *b*	1Chr 18:10	5178
b in abundance without weight	1Chr 22:3	5178
and of *b* and iron without weight	1Chr 22:14	5178
Of the gold, the silver, and the *b*	1Chr 22:16	5178
and the *b* for things of *b*	1Chr 29:2	5178
of *b* eighteen thousand talents,	1Chr 29:7	5178
in gold, and in silver, and in *b*	2Chr 2:7	5178
work in gold, and in silver, in *b*	2Chr 2:14	5178
Moreover he made an altar of *b*	2Chr 4:1	5178
overlaid the doors of them with *b*	2Chr 4:9	5178
the house of the LORD of bright *b*	2Chr 4:16	5178
for the weight of the *b* could not	2Chr 4:18	5178
king Rehoboam made shields of *b*	2Chr 12:10	5178
b to mend the house of the LORD	2Chr 24:12	5178
or is my flesh of *b*	Job 6:12	5153
b is molten out of the stone	Job 28:2	5154
bones are as strong pieces of *b*	Job 40:18	5154
as straw, and *b* as rotten wood	Job 41:27	5154
For he hath broken the gates of *b*	Ps 107:16	5154
break in pieces the gates of *b*	Is 45:2	5154
is an iron sinew, and thy brow *b*	Is 48:4	5154
For *b* I will bring gold, and for	Is 60:17	5178
will bring silver, and for wood *b*	Is 60:17	5178
they are *b* and iron	Jer 6:28	5178
Also the pillars of *b* that were in	Jer 52:17	5178
carried all the *b* of them to	Jer 52:17	5178
all the vessels of *b* wherewith	Jer 52:18	5178
the *b* of all these vessels was	Jer 52:20	5178
And a chapiter of *b* was upon it	Jer 52:22	5178
chapiters round about, all of *b*	Jer 52:22	5178
like the colour of burnished *b*	Eze 1:7	5178
all they are *b*, and tin, and iron,	Eze 22:18	5178
As they gather silver, and *b*	Eze 22:20	5178
that the *b* of it may be hot, and	Eze 24:11	5178
vessels of *b* in thy market	Eze 27:13	5178
was like the appearance of *b*	Eze 40:3	5178
his belly and his thighs of *b*	Dan 2:32	5174
was the iron, the clay, the *b*	Dan 2:35	5174
and another third kingdom of *b*	Dan 2:39	5174
brake in pieces the iron, the *b*	Dan 2:45	5174
even with a band of iron and *b*	Dan 4:15	5174
even with a band of iron and *b*	Dan 4:23	5174
gods of gold, and of silver, of *b*	Dan 5:4	5174
the gods of silver, and gold, of *b*	Dan 5:23	5174
were of iron, his nails of *b*	Dan 7:19	5174
feet like in colour to polished *b*	Dan 10:6	5178
iron, and I will make thy hoofs *b*	Mic 4:13	5154
the mountains were mountains of *b*	Zec 6:1	5178

nor silver, nor *b* in your purses,	Mt 10:9	5475
I am become as sounding *b*	1Cor 13:1	5475
And his feet like unto fine *b*	Rev 1:15	5474
fire, and his feet are like fine *b*	Rev 2:18	5474
and idols of gold, and silver, and *b*	Rev 9:20	5470
of most precious wood, and of *b*	Rev 18:12	5475

BRAVERY

the *b* of their tinkling ornaments	Is 3:18	8597

BRAWLER

but patient, not a *b*, not	1Ti 3:3	269

BRAWLERS

speak evil of no man, to be no *b*	Titus 3:2	269

BRAWLING

the housetop, than with a *b* woman	Prov 21:9	4090
the housetop, than with a *b* woman	Prov 25:24	4090

BRAY

Doth the wild ass *b* when he hath	Job 6:5	5101
Though thou shouldest *b* a fool in	Prov 27:22	3806

BRAYED

Among the bushes they *b*	Job 30:7	5101

BREACH

this *b* be upon thee	Gen 38:29	6556
B for *b*, eye for eye, tooth	Lev 24:20	7667
and ye shall know my *b* of promise	Num 14:34	8569
made a *b* in the tribes of Israel	Judg 21:15	6556
before me, as the *b* of waters	2Sa 5:20	6556
the LORD had made a *b* upon Uzzah	2Sa 6:8	6556
wheresoever any *b* shall be found	2Kin 12:5	919
the LORD had made a *b* upon Uzza	1Chr 13:11	6556
the LORD our God made a *b* upon us	1Chr 15:13	6555
that there was no *b* left therein	Neh 6:1	6556
He breaketh me with *b* upon *b*	Job 16:14	6556
chosen stood before him in the *b*	Ps 106:23	6556
therein is a *b* in the spirit	Prov 15:4	7667
let us make a *b* therein for us,	Is 7:6	1234
be to you as a *b* ready to fall	Is 30:13	6556
bindeth up the *b* of his people	Is 30:26	7667
be called, The repairer of the *b*	Is 58:12	6556
people is broken with a great *b*	Jer 14:17	7667
for thy *b* is great like the sea	Lam 2:13	7667
into a city wherein is made a *b*	Eze 26:10	1234

BREACHES

the sea shore, and abode in his *b*	Judg 5:17	4664
repaired the *b* of the city of	1Kin 11:27	6556
them repair the *b* of the house	2Kin 12:5	919
not repaired the *b* of the house	2Kin 12:6	919
repair ye not the *b* of the house	2Kin 12:7	919
deliver it for the *b* of the house	2Kin 12:7	919
to repair the *b* of the house	2Kin 12:8	919
the *b* of the house of the LORD	2Kin 12:12	919
to repair the *b* of the house	2Kin 22:5	919
that the *b* began to be stopped,	Neh 4:7	6555
heal the *b* thereof	Ps 60:2	7667
also the *b* of the city of David	Is 22:9	1233
And ye shall go out at the *b*	Amos 4:3	6556
will smite the great house with *b*	Amos 6:11	7447
fallen, and close up the *b* thereof	Amos 9:11	6556

BREAD

of thy face shalt thou eat *b*	Gen 3:19	3899
king of Salem brought forth *b*	Gen 14:18	3899
And I will fetch a morsel of *b*	Gen 18:5	3899
a feast, and did bake unleavened *b*	Gen 19:3	3899
early in the morning, and took *b*	Gen 21:14	3899
Then Jacob gave Esau *b* and pottage	Gen 25:34	3899
gave the savoury meat and the *b*	Gen 27:17	3899
I go, and will give me *b* to eat.	Gen 28:20	3899
and called his brethren to eat *b*	Gen 31:54	3899
and they did eat *b*, and tarried all	Gen 31:54	3899
And they sat down to eat *b*	Gen 37:25	3899
save the *b* which he did eat	Gen 39:6	3899
all the land of Egypt there was *b*	Gen 41:54	3899
the people cried to Pharaoh for *b*	Gen 41:55	3899
that they should eat *b* there	Gen 43:25	3899
himself, and said, Set on *b*	Gen 43:31	3899
might not eat *b* with the Hebrews	Gen 43:32	3899
she asses laden with corn and *b*	Gen 45:23	3899
his father's household, with *b*	Gen 45:23	3899
there was no *b* in all the land	Gen 47:13	3899
unto Joseph, and said, Give us *b*	Gen 47:15	3899
Joseph gave them in exchange	Gen 47:17	3899
he fed them with *b* for all their	Gen 47:17	3899
buy us and our land for *b*, and we	Gen 47:19	3899
Out of Asher his *b* shall be fat	Gen 49:20	3899
call him, that he may eat *b*	Ex 2:20	3899
roast with fire, and unleavened *b*	Ex 12:8	3899
days shall ye eat unleavened *b*	Ex 12:15	

b from the first day until the .... Ex 12:15
observe the feast of unleavened *b* .... Ex 12:17
even, ye shall eat unleavened *b* .... Ex 12:18
shall ye eat unleavened *b* .... Ex 12:20
shall no leavened *b* be eaten.................. Ex 13:3
days thou shalt eat unleavened *b* .... Ex 13:6
Unleavened *b* shall be eaten seven........ Ex 13:7
no leavened *b* be seen with thee............ Ex 13:7
and when we did eat *b* to the full .... Ex 16:3
I will rain *b* from heaven for you .... Ex 16:4   3899
and in the morning *b* to the full............ Ex 16:8   3899
morning ye shall be filled with *b* .... Ex 16:12   3899
This is the *b* which the Lord hath .... Ex 16:15   3899
day they gathered twice as much *b* .... Ex 16:22   3899
the sixth day the *b* of two days .... Ex 16:29   3899
that they may see the *b* wherewith .... Ex 16:32   3899
to eat *b* with Moses' father in .... Ex 18:12   3899
keep the feast of unleavened *b* .... Ex 23:15
shalt eat unleavened *b* seven days .... Ex 23:15
of my sacrifice with leavened *b* .... Ex 23:18
your God, and he shall bless thy *b* .... Ex 23:25   3899
And unleavened *b*, and cakes .... Ex 29:2   3899
one loaf of *b*, and one cake of oiled .... Ex 29:23   3899
b that is before the Lord .... Ex 29:23
the *b* that is in the basket, by .... Ex 29:32   3899
of the consecrations, or of the *b*............ Ex 29:34   3899
of unleavened *b* shalt thou keep .... Ex 34:18
days thou shalt eat unleavened *b* .... Ex 34:18
he did neither eat *b*, nor drink .... Ex 34:28   3899
he set the *b* in order upon it .... Ex 40:23   3899
with unleavened *b* shall it be .... Lev 6:16
leavened *b* with the sacrifice of .... Lev 7:13   3899
rams, and a basket of unleavened *b* ...... Lev 8:2
out of the basket of unleavened *b*.......... Lev 8:26
cake, and a cake of oiled .... Lev 8:26
there eat it with the *b* that is .... Lev 8:31   3899
of the *b* shall ye burn with fire .... Lev 8:32   3899
the *b* of their God, they do offer .... Lev 21:6   3899
for he offereth the *b* of thy God .... Lev 21:8   3899
to offer the *b* of his God......................... Lev 21:17   3899
nigh to offer the *b* of his God .... Lev 21:21   3899
He shall eat the *b* of his God .... Lev 21:22   3899
hand shall ye offer the *b* of your .... Lev 22:25   3899
of unleavened *b* unto the Lord .... Lev 23:6
days ye must eat unleavened *b*............... Lev 23:6
And ye shall eat neither *b* .... Lev 23:14   3899
ye shall offer with the *b* seven .... Lev 23:18   3899
b of the first fruits for a wave .... Lev 23:20   3899
it may be on the *b* for a memorial .... Lev 24:7   3899
ye shall eat your *b* to the full .... Lev 26:5   3899
I have broken the staff of your *b*........... Lev 26:26   3899
shall bake your *b* in one oven................ Lev 26:26   3899
you your *b* again by weight.................... Lev 26:26   3899
the continual *b* shall be thereon .... Num 4:7   3899
And a basket of unleavened *b* .... Num 6:15
of unleavened *b* anointed with oil.......... Num 6:15
with the basket of unleavened *b* .... Num 6:17
it, and eat it with unleavened *b* .... Num 9:11
for they are *b* for us .... Num 14:9   3899
when ye eat of the *b* of the land .... Num 15:19   3899
for there is no *b*, neither is................... Num 21:5   3899
and our soul loatheth this light *b*.......... Num 21:5   3899
my *b* for my sacrifices made by .... Num 28:2   3899
days shall unleavened *b* be eaten.......... Num 28:17
that man doth not live by *b* only .... Deut 8:3   3899
shalt eat *b* without scarceness.............. Deut 8:9   3899
neither did eat *b* nor drink water.......... Deut 9:9   3899
I did neither eat *b*, nor drink................ Deut 9:18   3899
shalt eat no leavened *b* with it .... Deut 16:3
thou eat unleavened *b* therewith .... Deut 16:3
even the *b* of affliction........................... Deut 16:3   3899
there shall be no leavened *b* seen.......... Deut 16:4
days thou shalt eat unleavened *b* .... Deut 16:8
in the feast of unleavened *b* .... Deut 16:16
Because they met you not with *b*........... Deut 23:4   3899
Ye have not eaten *b*, neither have .... Deut 29:6   3899
all the *b* of their provision was .... Josh 9:5   3899
This our *b* we took hot for our .... Josh 9:12   3899
a cake of barley *b* tumbled into............. Judg 7:13   3899
loaves of *b* unto the people that............ Judg 8:5   3899
we should give *b* unto thine army .... Judg 8:6   3899
that we should give *b* unto thy.............. Judg 8:15   3899
me, I will not eat of thy *b* .... Judg 13:16   3899
thine heart with a morsel of *b* .... Judg 19:5   3899
and there is *b* and wine also for me ...... Judg 19:19   3899
his people in giving them *b*.................... Ruth 1:6   3899
come thou hither, and eat of the *b* .... Ruth 2:14   3899
have hired out themselves for *b* 1Sa 2:5   3899
piece of silver and a morsel of *b* 1Sa 2:36   3899
that I may eat a piece of *b* 1Sa 2:36   3899
for the *b* is spent in our vessels 1Sa 9:7   3899

carrying three loaves of *b* 1Sa 10:3   3899
and give thee two loaves of *b*................. 1Sa 10:4   3899
And Jesse took an ass laden with *b* 1Sa 16:20   3899
me five loaves of *b* in mine hand 1Sa 21:3   3899
is no common *b* under mine hand 1Sa 21:4   3899
but there is hallowed *b* 1Sa 21:4   3899
the *b* is in a manner common, yea,......... 1Sa 21:5
So the priest gave him hallowed *b* 1Sa 21:6
for there was no *b* there but the............ 1Sa 21:6   3899
to put hot *b* in the day when it 1Sa 21:6   3899
in that thou hast given him *b* 1Sa 22:13   3899
Shall I then take my *b*, and my 1Sa 25:11   3899
for he had eaten no *b* all the day 1Sa 28:20   3899
me set a morsel of *b* before thee............ 1Sa 28:22   3899
and did bake unleavened *b* thereof 1Sa 28:24
him to David, and gave him *b*................. 1Sa 30:11   3899
for he had eaten no *b*, nor drunk........... 1Sa 30:12   3899
on the sword, or that lacketh *b* 2Sa 3:29   3899
to me, and more also, if I taste *b*........... 2Sa 3:35   3899
as men, to every one a cake of *b*............ 2Sa 6:19   3899
thou shalt eat *b* at my table 2Sa 9:7   3899
son shall eat *b* alway at my table.......... 2Sa 9:10   3899
neither did he eat *b* with them............... 2Sa 12:17   3899
they set *b* before him, and he did 2Sa 12:20   3899
dead, thou didst rise and eat *b* 2Sa 12:21   3899
upon them two hundred loaves of *b* 2Sa 16:1   3899
and the *b* and summer fruit for the 2Sa 16:2   3899
neither will I eat *b* nor drink................. 1Kin 13:8   3899
of the Lord, saying, Eat no *b* 1Kin 13:9   3899
him, Come home with me, and eat *b* 1Kin 13:15   3899
neither will I eat *b* nor drink................. 1Kin 13:16   3899
Thou shalt eat no *b* nor drink 1Kin 13:17   3899
thine house, that he may eat *b* 1Kin 13:18   3899
did eat *b* in his house, and drank.......... 1Kin 13:19   3899
But camest back, and hast eaten *b* 1Kin 13:22   3899
Lord did say to thee, Eat no *b* 1Kin 13:22   3899
to pass, after he had eaten *b* 1Kin 13:23   3899
And the ravens brought him *b*................ 1Kin 17:6   3899
and flesh in the morning, and *b*............. 1Kin 17:6   3899
a morsel of *b* in thine hand 1Kin 17:11   3899
in a cave, and fed them with *b*............... 1Kin 18:4   3899
in a cave, and fed them with *b*............... 1Kin 18:13   3899
away his face, and would eat no *b* 1Kin 21:4   3899
so sad, that thou eatest no *b* 1Kin 21:5   3899
arise, and eat *b*, and let thine 1Kin 21:7   3899
and feed him with *b* of affliction............ 1Kin 22:27   3899
and she constrained him to eat *b* 2Kin 4:8   3899
by, he turned in thither to eat *b*............ 2Kin 4:8   3899
man of God *b* of the firstfruits 2Kin 4:42   3899
set *b* and water before them, that......... 2Kin 6:22   3899
land of corn and wine, a land of *b*......... 2Kin 18:32   3899
unleavened *b* among their brethren 2Kin 23:9
there was no *b* for the people of............ 2Kin 25:3   3899
he did eat *b* continually before.............. 2Kin 25:29   3899
brought *b* on asses, and on camels, ... 1Chr 12:40   3899
woman, to every one a loaf of *b* 1Chr 16:3   3899
even in the feast of unleavened *b* 2Chr 8:13
and feed him with *b* of affliction............ 2Chr 18:26   3899
unleavened *b* in the second month 2Chr 30:13
kept the feast of unleavened *b* 2Chr 30:21
feast of unleavened *b* seven days 2Chr 35:17
unleavened *b* seven days with joy .... Ezr 6:22
he came thither, he did eat no *b*............ Ezr 10:6   3899
not eaten the *b* of the governor .... Neh 5:14   3899
people, and had taken of them *b* .... Neh 5:15   3899
not I the *b* of the governor.................... Neh 5:18   3899
gavest them *b* from heaven for .... Neh 9:15   3899
not the children of Israel with *b* .... Neh 13:2   3899
He wandereth abroad for *b* .... Job 15:23   3899
hast withholden *b* from the hungry .... Job 22:7   3899
shall not be satisfied with *b* .... Job 27:14   3899
for the earth, out of it cometh *b*............ Job 28:5   3899
So that his life abhorreth *b* .... Job 33:20   3899
did eat *b* with him in his house .... Job 42:11   3899
eat up my people as they eat *b*.............. Ps 14:4   3899
forsaken, nor his seed begging *b* .... Ps 37:25   3899
I trusted, which did eat of my *b*............ Ps 41:9   3899
eat up my people as they eat *b*.............. Ps 53:4   3899
can he give *b* also .... Ps 78:20   3899
feedest them with the *b* of tears .... Ps 80:5   3899
so that I forget to eat my *b* .... Ps 102:4   3899
For I have eaten ashes like *b* .... Ps 102:9   3899
b which strengtheneth man's heart .... Ps 104:15   3899
he brake the whole staff of *b* .... Ps 105:16   3899
them with the *b* of heaven..................... Ps 105:40   3899
let them seek their *b* also out of........... Ps 109:10
up late, to eat the *b* of sorrows .... Ps 127:2   3899
I will satisfy her poor with *b* .... Ps 132:15   3899
For they eat the *b* of wickedness .... Prov 4:17   3899
a man is brought to a piece of *b* .... Prov 6:26   3899
Come, eat of my *b*, and drink of .... Prov 9:5   3899

b eaten in secret is pleasant	Prov 9:17	3899
honoureth himself, and lacketh *b*	Prov 12:9	3899
land shall be satisfied with *b*	Prov 12:11	3899
and thou shalt be satisfied with *b*	Prov 20:13	3899
B of deceit is sweet to a man	Prov 20:17	3899
he giveth of his *b* to the poor	Prov 22:9	3899
Eat thou not the *b* of him that	Prov 23:6	3899
be hungry, give him *b* to eat	Prov 25:21	3899
his land shall have plenty of *b*	Prov 28:19	3899
for for a piece of *b* that man	Prov 28:21	3899
and eateth not the *b* of idleness	Prov 31:27	3899
eat thy *b* with joy, and drink thy	Eccl 9:7	3899
strong, neither yet *b* to the wise	Eccl 9:11	3899
Cast thy *b* upon the waters	Eccl 11:1	3899
and the staff, the whole stay of *b*	Is 3:1	3899
house is neither *b* nor clothing	Is 3:7	3899
saying, We will eat our own *b*	Is 4:1	3899
with their *b* him that fled	Is 21:14	3899
B corn is bruised	Is 28:28	3899
Lord give you the *b* of adversity	Is 30:20	3899
b of the increase of the earth,	Is 30:23	3899
b shall be given him	Is 33:16	3899
land of corn and wine, a land of *b*	Is 36:17	3899
yea, he kindleth it, and baketh *b*	Is 44:15	3899
also I have baked *b* upon the	Is 44:19	3899
pit, nor that his *b* should fail	Is 51:14	3899
money for that which is not *b*	Is 55:2	3899
to the sower, and *b* to the eater	Is 55:10	3899
not to deal thy *b* to the hungry	Is 58:7	3899
eat up thine harvest, and thy *b*	Jer 5:17	3899
of *b* out of the bakers' street	Jer 37:21	3899
until all the *b* in the city were	Jer 37:21	3899
there is no more *b* in the city	Jer 38:9	3899
they did eat *b* together in Mizpah	Jer 41:1	3899
the trumpet, nor have hunger of *b*	Jer 42:14	3899
so that there was no *b* for the	Jer 52:6	3899
he did continually eat *b* before	Jer 52:33	3899
All her people sigh, they seek *b*	Lam 1:11	3899
the young children ask *b*, and no	Lam 4:4	3899
Assyrians, to be satisfied with *b*	Lam 5:6	3899
We gat our *b* with the peril of	Lam 5:9	3899
vessel, and make thee *b* thereof	Eze 4:9	3899
defiled *b* among the Gentiles	Eze 4:13	3899
shalt prepare thy *b* therewith	Eze 4:15	3899
break the staff of *b* in Jerusalem	Eze 4:16	3899
and they shall eat *b* by weight	Eze 4:16	3899
That they may want *b* and water, and	Eze 4:17	3899
and will break your staff of *b*	Eze 5:16	3899
eat thy *b* with quaking, and drink	Eze 12:18	3899
eat their *b* with carefulness	Eze 12:19	3899
of barley and for pieces of *b*	Eze 13:19	3899
break the staff of the *b* thereof	Eze 14:13	3899
sister Sodom, pride, fulness of *b*	Eze 16:49	3899
hath given his *b* to the hungry	Eze 18:7	3899
hath given his *b* to the hungry	Eze 18:16	3899
thy lips, and eat not the *b* of men	Eze 24:17	3899
your lips, nor eat the *b* of men	Eze 24:22	3899
in it to eat *b* before the LORD	Eze 44:3	3899
even my house, when ye offer my *b*	Eze 44:7	3899
unleavened *b* shall be eaten	Eze 45:21	
I ate no pleasant *b*, neither came	Dan 10:3	3899
my lovers, that give me my *b*	Hos 2:5	3899
be unto them as the *b* of mourners	Hos 9:4	3899
for their *b* for their soul shall	Hos 9:4	3899
want of *b* in all your places	Amos 4:6	3899
the land of Judah, and there eat *b*	Amos 7:12	3899
in the land, not a famine of *b*	Amos 8:11	3899
they that eat thy *b* have laid a	Obad 7	3899
and with his skirt do touch *b*	Hag 2:12	3899
offer polluted *b* upon mine altar	Mal 1:7	3899
that these stones be made *b*	Mt 4:3	740
Man shall not live by *b* alone	Mt 4:4	740
Give us this day our daily *b*	Mt 6:11	740
of you, whom if his son ask *b*	Mt 7:9	740
not their hands when they eat *b*	Mt 15:2	740
not meet to take the children's *b*	Mt 15:26	740
have so much *b* in the wilderness	Mt 15:33	740
they had forgotten to take *b*	Mt 16:5	740
It is because we have taken no *b*	Mt 16:7	740
because ye have brought no *b*	Mt 16:8	740
spake it not to you concerning *b*	Mt 16:11	740
not beware of the leaven of *b*	Mt 16:12	740
b the disciples came to Jesus	Mt 26:17	
as they were eating, Jesus took *b*	Mt 26:26	740
they could not so much as eat *b*	Mk 3:20	740
no scrip, no *b*, no money in their	Mk 6:8	740
the villages, and buy themselves *b*	Mk 6:36	740
buy two hundred pennyworth of *b*	Mk 6:37	740
his disciples eat *b* with defiled	Mk 7:2	740
but eat *b* with unwashen hands	Mk 7:5	740
not meet to take the children's *b*	Mk 7:27	740

men with *b* here in the wilderness	Mk 8:4	740
disciples had forgotten to take *b*	Mk 8:14	740
It is because we have no *b*	Mk 8:16	740
reason ye, because ye have no *b*	Mk 8:17	740
the passover, and of unleavened *b*	Mk 14:1	
And the first day of unleavened *b*	Mk 14:12	
And as they did eat, Jesus took *b*	Mk 14:22	740
this stone that it be made *b*	Lk 4:3	740
man shall not live by *b* alone	Lk 4:4	740
eating *b* nor drinking wine	Lk 7:33	740
staves, nor scrip, neither *b*	Lk 9:3	740
Give us day by day our daily *b*	Lk 11:3	740
If a son shall ask *b* of any of	Lk 11:11	740
to eat *b* on the sabbath day	Lk 14:1	740
shall eat *b* in the kingdom of God	Lk 14:15	740
of my father's have *b* enough	Lk 15:17	740
feast of unleavened *b* drew nigh	Lk 22:1	
Then came the day of unleavened *b*	Lk 22:7	
And he took *b*, and gave thanks, and	Lk 22:19	740
sat at meat with them, he took *b*	Lk 24:30	740
known of them in breaking of *b*	Lk 24:35	740
Philip, Whence shall we buy *b*	Jn 6:5	740
Two hundred pennyworth of *b* is	Jn 6:7	740
the place where they did eat *b*	Jn 6:23	740
He gave them *b* from heaven to eat	Jn 6:31	740
gave you not that *b* from heaven	Jn 6:32	740
giveth you the true *b* from heaven	Jn 6:32	740
For the *b* of God is he which	Jn 6:33	740
Lord, evermore give us this *b*	Jn 6:34	740
unto them, I am the *b* of life	Jn 6:35	740
I am the *b* which came down from	Jn 6:41	740
I am that *b* of life	Jn 6:48	740
This is the *b* which cometh down	Jn 6:50	740
I am the living *b* which came down	Jn 6:51	740
if any man eat of this *b*, he	Jn 6:51	740
the *b* that I will give is my	Jn 6:51	740
This is that *b* which came down	Jn 6:58	740
of this *b* shall live for ever	Jn 6:58	740
He that eateth *b* with me hath	Jn 13:18	740
there, and fish laid thereon, and *b*	Jn 21:9	740
Jesus then cometh, and taketh *b*	Jn 21:13	740
fellowship, and in breaking of *b*	Acts 2:42	740
breaking *b* from house to house,	Acts 2:46	740
were the days of unleavened *b*	Acts 12:3	
after the days of unleavened *b*	Acts 20:6	
came together to break *b*, Paul	Acts 20:7	740
come up again, and had broken *b*	Acts 20:11	740
he had thus spoken, he took *b*	Acts 27:35	740
the unleavened *b* of sincerity	1Cor 5:8	
The *b* which we break, is it not	1Cor 10:16	740
For we being many are one *b*	1Cor 10:17	740
are all partakers of that one *b*	1Cor 10:17	740
in which he was betrayed took *b*	1Cor 11:23	740
For as often as ye eat this *b*	1Cor 11:26	740
whosoever shall eat this *b*	1Cor 11:27	740
and so let him eat of that *b*	1Cor 11:28	740
both minister *b* for your food	2Cor 9:10	740
did we eat any man's *b* for nought	2Th 3:8	740
they work, and eat their own *b*	2Th 3:12	740

BREADTH

the *b* of it fifty cubits, and the	Gen 6:15	7341
length of it and in the *b* of it	Gen 13:17	7341
a cubit and a half the *b* thereof	Ex 25:10	7341
a cubit and a half the *b* thereof	Ex 25:17	7341
thereof, and a cubit the *b* thereof	Ex 25:23	7341
a border of an hand *b* round about	Ex 25:25	2948
the *b* of one curtain four cubits	Ex 26:2	7341
the *b* of one curtain four cubits	Ex 26:8	7341
half shall be the *b* of one board	Ex 26:16	7341
for the *b* of the court on the	Ex 27:12	7341
the *b* of the court on the east	Ex 27:13	7341
the *b* fifty every where, and the	Ex 27:18	7341
and a span shall be the *b* thereof	Ex 28:16	7341
thereof, and a cubit the *b* thereof	Ex 30:2	7341
the *b* of one curtain four cubits	Ex 36:9	7341
cubits was the *b* of one curtain	Ex 36:15	7341
the *b* of a board one cubit and a	Ex 36:21	7341
and a cubit and a half the *b* of it	Ex 37:1	7341
one cubit and a half the *b* thereof	Ex 37:6	7341
thereof, and a cubit the *b* thereof	Ex 37:10	7341
a cubit, and the *b* of it a cubit	Ex 37:25	7341
and five cubits the *b* thereof	Ex 38:1	7341
height in the *b* was five cubits	Ex 38:18	7341
thereof, and a span the *b* thereof	Ex 39:9	7341
and four cubits the *b* thereof	Deut 3:11	7341
could sling stones at an hair *b*	Judg 20:16	
the *b* thereof twenty cubits, and	1Kin 6:2	7341
according to the *b* of the house	1Kin 6:3	7341
ten cubits was the *b* thereof	1Kin 6:3	7341
in length, and twenty cubits in *b*	1Kin 6:20	7341

B

the *b* thereof fifty cubits, and	1Kin 7:2	7341
the *b* thereof thirty cubits	1Kin 7:6	7341
And it was an hand *b* thick	1Kin 7:26	2947
and four cubits the *b* thereof	1Kin 7:27	7341
cubits, and the *b* twenty cubits	2Chr 3:3	7341
according to the *b* of the house	2Chr 3:4	7341
according to the *b* of the house	2Chr 3:8	7341
the *b* thereof twenty cubits	2Chr 3:8	7341
and twenty cubits the *b* thereof	2Chr 4:1	7341
the *b* threescore cubits	Ezr 6:3	6613
the *b* of the waters is straitened	Job 37:10	7341
thou perceived the *b* of the earth	Job 38:18	7338
shall fill the *b* of thy land	Is 8:8	7341
long by the cubit and an hand *b*	Eze 40:5	2948
he measured the *b* of the building	Eze 40:5	7341
he measured the *b* of the entry of	Eze 40:11	7341
the *b* was five and twenty cubits,	Eze 40:13	7341
Then he measured the *b* from the	Eze 40:19	7341
length thereof, and the *b* thereof	Eze 40:20	7341
the *b* five and twenty cubits	Eze 40:21	7341
the *b* five and twenty cubits	Eze 40:25	7341
the *b* five and twenty cubits	Eze 40:36	7341
the *b* of the gate was three	Eze 40:48	7341
cubits, and the *b* eleven cubits	Eze 40:49	7341
which was the *b* of the tabernacle	Eze 41:1	7341
the *b* of the door was ten cubits	Eze 41:2	7341
and the *b*, twenty cubits	Eze 41:2	7341
the *b* of the door, seven cubits	Eze 41:3	7341
and the *b*, twenty cubits, before	Eze 41:4	7341
the *b* of every side chamber, four	Eze 41:5	7341
therefore the *b* of the house was	Eze 41:7	7341
the *b* of the place that was left	Eze 41:11	7341
Also the *b* of the face of the	Eze 41:14	7341
door, and the *b* was fifty cubits	Eze 42:2	7341
was a walk of ten cubits *b* inward	Eze 42:4	7341
The cubit is a cubit and an hand *b*	Eze 43:13	2948
the *b* a cubit, and the border	Eze 43:13	7341
be two cubits, and the *b* one cubit	Eze 43:14	7341
four cubits, and the *b* one cubit	Eze 43:14	7341
the *b* shall be ten thousand	Eze 45:1	7341
in length, with five hundred in *b*	Eze 45:2	7341
and the *b* of ten thousand	Eze 45:3	7341
length, and the ten thousand of *b*	Eze 45:5	7341
and twenty thousand reeds in *b*	Eze 48:8	7341
length, and of ten thousand in *b*	Eze 48:9	7341
toward the west ten thousand in *b*	Eze 48:10	7341
toward the east ten thousand in *b*	Eze 48:10	7341
in length, and ten thousand in *b*	Eze 48:13	7341
thousand, and the *b* ten thousand	Eze 48:13	7341
that are left in the *b* over	Eze 48:15	7341
and the *b* thereof six cubits	Dan 3:1	6613
march through the *b* of the land	Hab 1:6	4800
to see what is the *b* thereof	Zec 2:2	7341
and the *b* thereof ten cubits	Zec 5:2	7341
with all saints what is the *b*	Eph 3:18	4114
went up on the *b* of the earth	Rev 20:9	4114
the length is as large as the *b*	Rev 21:16	4114
The length and the *b* and the height	Rev 21:16	4114

BREAK

Lot, and came near to *b* the door	Gen 19:9	7665
that thou shalt *b* his yoke from	Gen 27:40	6561
neither shall ye *b* a bone thereof	Ex 12:46	7665
it, then thou shalt *b* his neck	Ex 13:13	6202
lest they *b* through unto the Lord	Ex 19:21	2040
lest the Lord *b* forth upon them	Ex 19:22	6555
the people *b* through to come up	Ex 19:24	2040
lest he *b* forth upon them	Ex 19:24	6555
If fire *b* out, and catch in thorns	Ex 22:6	3318
quite *b* down their images	Ex 23:24	7665
B off the golden earrings, which	Ex 32:2	6561
hath any gold, let them *b* it off	Ex 32:24	6561
b their images, and cut down their	Ex 34:13	7665
not, then shalt thou *b* his neck	Ex 34:20	6202
and ye shall *b* it	Lev 11:33	7665
if a leprosy *b* out abroad in the	Lev 13:12	6524
b out in the place, after that he	Lev 14:43	6524
he shall *b* down the house, the	Lev 14:45	5422
but that ye *b* my covenant	Lev 26:15	6565
I will *b* the pride of your power	Lev 26:19	7665
to *b* my covenant with them	Lev 26:44	6565
the morning, nor *b* any bone of it	Num 9:12	7665
shall *b* their bones, and pierce	Num 24:8	1633
he shall not *b* his word, he shall	Num 30:2	2490
b down their images, and cut down	Deut 7:5	7665
b their pillars, and burn their	Deut 12:3	7665
b my covenant which I have made	Deut 31:16	6565
and provoke me, and *b* my covenant	Deut 31:20	6565
I will never *b* my covenant with	Judg 2:1	6565
peace, I will *b* down this tower	Judg 8:9	5422
many servants now a days that *b*	1Sa 25:10	6555

they came to Hebron at *b* of day	2Sa 2:32	215
b thy league with Baasha king of	1Kin 15:19	6565
to *b* through even unto the king	2Kin 3:26	1234
did the Chaldees *b* in pieces	2Kin 25:13	7665
b thy league with Baasha king of	2Chr 16:3	6565
Should we again *b* thy	Ezr 9:14	6565
he shall even *b* down their stone	Neh 4:3	6565
Wilt thou *b* a leaf driven to and	Job 13:25	6206
b me in pieces with words	Job 19:2	1792
He shall *b* in pieces mighty men	Job 34:24	7489
or that the wild beast may *b* them	Job 39:15	1758
Let us *b* their bands asunder, and	Ps 2:3	5423
Thou shalt *b* them with a rod of	Ps 2:9	7489
B thou the arm of the wicked and	Ps 10:15	7665
B their teeth, O God, in their	Ps 58:6	2040
b out the great teeth of the	Ps 58:6	5422
shall *b* in pieces the oppressor	Ps 72:4	1792
But now they *b* down the carved	Ps 74:6	1986
If they *b* my statutes, and keep	Ps 89:31	2490
My covenant will I not *b*, nor	Ps 89:34	2490
They *b* in pieces thy people, O	Ps 94:5	1792
oil, which shall not *b* my head	Ps 141:5	5106
a time to *b* down, and a time to	Eccl 3:3	6555
Until the day *b*, and the shadows	Song 2:17	6315
Until the day *b*, and the shadows	Song 4:6	6315
b down the wall thereof, and it	Is 5:5	6555
they *b* forth into singing	Is 14:7	6476
That I will *b* the Assyrian in my	Is 14:25	7665
b the clods of his ground	Is 28:24	7702
nor *b* it with the wheel of his	Is 28:28	2000
he shall *b* it as the breaking of	Is 30:14	7665
the wilderness shall waters *b* out	Is 35:6	1234
so will he *b* all my bones	Is 38:13	7665
A bruised reed shall he not *b*	Is 42:3	7665
b forth into singing, ye	Is 44:23	6476
I will *b* in pieces the gates of	Is 45:2	7665
b forth into singing, O mountains	Is 49:13	6476
B forth into joy, sing together,	Is 52:9	6476
b forth into singing, and cry	Is 54:1	6476
For thou shalt *b* forth on the	Is 54:3	6555
the hills shall *b* forth before	Is 55:12	6476
go free, and that ye *b* every yoke	Is 58:6	5423
thy light *b* forth as the morning	Is 58:8	1234
b forth upon all the inhabitants	Jer 1:14	6605
B up your fallow ground, and sow	Jer 4:3	5214
b not thy covenant with us	Jer 14:21	6565
Shall iron *b* the northern iron and	Jer 15:12	7489
Then shalt thou *b* the bottle in	Jer 19:10	7665
Even so will I *b* this people	Jer 19:11	7665
for I will *b* the yoke of the king	Jer 28:4	7665
Even so will I *b* the yoke of	Jer 28:11	7665
that I will *b* his yoke from off	Jer 30:8	7665
to *b* down, and to throw down, and	Jer 31:28	5422
If ye can *b* my covenant of the	Jer 33:20	6565
He shall *b* also the images of	Jer 43:13	7665
which I have built will I *b* down	Jer 45:4	2040
his vessels, and *b* their bottles	Jer 48:12	5310
I will *b* the bow of Elam, the	Jer 49:35	7665
for with thee will I *b* in pieces	Jer 51:20	5310
with thee will I *b* in pieces the	Jer 51:21	5310
with thee will I *b* in pieces the	Jer 51:21	5310
thee also will I *b* in pieces man	Jer 51:22	5310
with thee will I *b* in pieces old	Jer 51:22	5310
with thee will I *b* in pieces the	Jer 51:22	5310
I will also *b* in pieces with thee	Jer 51:23	5310
with thee will I *b* in pieces the	Jer 51:23	5310
with thee will I *b* in pieces	Jer 51:23	5310
I will *b* the staff of bread in	Eze 4:16	7665
will *b* your staff of bread	Eze 5:16	7665
So will I *b* down the wall that ye	Eze 13:14	2040
will *b* the staff of the bread	Eze 14:13	7665
thee, as women that *b* wedlock	Eze 16:38	5003
shall *b* down thy high places	Eze 16:39	5422
or shall he *b* the covenant, and be	Eze 17:15	6565
thou shalt *b* the sherds thereof,	Eze 23:34	1633
of Tyrus, and *b* down her towers	Eze 26:4	2040
axes he shall *b* down thy towers	Eze 26:9	5422
they shall *b* down thy walls, and	Eze 26:12	2040
of thee by thy hand, thou didst *b*	Eze 29:7	7533
when I shall *b* there the yokes of	Eze 30:18	7665
will *b* his arms, the strong, and	Eze 30:22	7665
but I will *b* Pharaoh's arms, and	Eze 30:24	7665
shall it *b* in pieces and bruise	Dan 2:40	1854
people, but it shall *b* in pieces	Dan 2:44	1854
b off thy sins by righteousness,	Dan 4:27	6562
tread it down, and *b* it in pieces	Dan 7:23	1854
that I will *b* the bow of Israel	Hos 1:5	7665
I will *b* the bow and the sword and	Hos 2:18	7665
committing adultery, they *b* out	Hos 4:2	6555
he shall *b* down their altars, he	Hos 10:2	6202
plow, and Jacob shall *b* his clods	Hos 10:11	7702

b up your fallow ground	Hos 10:12	5214
and they shall not *b* their ranks	Joel 2:7	5670
I will also the bar of Damascus	Amos 1:5	7665
lest he *b* out like fire in the	Amos 5:6	6743
they *b* their bones, and chop them	Mic 3:3	6746
For now will I *b* his yoke from	Nah 1:13	7665
that I might *b* my covenant which	Zec 11:10	6565
that I might *b* the brotherhood	Zec 11:14	6565
Whosoever therefore shall *b* one	Mt 5:19	3089
and where thieves *b* through	Mt 6:19	1358
do not *b* through nor steal	Mt 6:20	1358
else the bottles *b*, and the wine	Mt 9:17	4486
A bruised reed shall he not *b*	Mt 12:20	2608
came together to *b* bread, Paul	Acts 20:7	2806
a long while, even till *b* of day	Acts 20:11	827
ye to weep and to *b* mine heart	Acts 21:13	4919
The bread which we *b*, is it not	1Cor 10:16	2806
b forth and cry, thou that	Gal 4:27	4486

BREAKER

The *b* is come up before them	Mic 2:13	6555
but if thou be a *b* of the law	Rom 2:25	3848

BREAKEST

Thou *b* the ships of Tarshish with	Ps 48:7	7665

BREAKETH

he said, Let me go, for the day *b*	Gen 32:26	5927
For he *b* me with a tempest, and	Job 9:17	7779
he *b* down, and it cannot be built	Job 12:14	2040
He *b* me with breach upon breach	Job 16:14	6555
The flood *b* out from the	Job 28:4	6555
voice of the LORD *b* the cedars	Ps 29:5	7665
the LORD *b* the cedars of Lebanon	Ps 29:5	7665
he *b* the bow, and cutteth the	Ps 46:9	7665
My soul *b* for the longing that it	Ps 119:20	1638
and a soft tongue *b* the bone	Prov 25:15	7665
whoso *b* an hedge, a serpent shall	Eccl 10:8	6555
is crushed *b* out into a viper	Is 59:5	1234
as one *b* a potter's vessel, that	Jer 19:11	7665
hammer that *b* the rock in pieces	Jer 23:29	6327
bread, and no man *b* it unto them	Lam 4:4	6566
forasmuch as iron *b* in pieces	Dan 2:40	1855
and as iron that *b* all these	Dan 2:40	7940

BREAKING

with him until the *b* of the day	Gen 32:24	5927
shall be a boil *b* forth with	Ex 9:9	6524
it became a boil *b* forth with	Ex 9:10	6524
If a thief be found *b* up, and be	Ex 22:2	4290
hand like the *b* forth of waters	1Chr 14:11	6556
upon me as a wide *b* in of waters	Job 30:14	6556
that there be no *b* in, nor going	Ps 144:14	6556
b down the walls, and of crying to	Is 22:5	6979
whose *b* cometh suddenly at an	Is 30:13	7667
he shall break it as the *b* of the	Is 30:14	7667
the oath in *b* the covenant	Eze 16:59	6565
the oath by *b* the covenant	Eze 17:18	6565
of man, with the *b* of thy loins	Eze 21:6	7670
place of the *b* forth of children	Hos 13:13	4866
was known of them in *b* of bread	Lk 24:35	2800
in *b* of bread, and in prayers	Acts 2:42	2800
b bread from house to house, did	Acts 2:46	2806
through *b* the law dishonourest	Rom 2:23	3847

BREAKINGS

by reason of *b* they purify	Job 41:25	7667

BREAST

thou shalt take the *b* of the ram	Ex 29:26	2373
the *b* of the wave offering	Ex 29:27	2373
made by fire, the fat with the *b*	Lev 7:30	2373
that the *b* may be waved for a	Lev 7:30	2373
but the *b* shall be Aaron's and his	Lev 7:31	2373
For the wave *b* and the heave	Lev 7:34	2373
And Moses took the *b*, and waved it	Lev 8:29	2373
And the wave *b* and heave shoulder	Lev 10:14	2373
the wave *b* shall they bring with	Lev 10:15	2373
for the priest, with the wave *b*	Num 6:20	2373
shall be thine, as the wave *b*	Num 18:18	2373
pluck the fatherless from the *b*	Job 24:9	7699
and shalt suck the *b* of kings	Is 60:16	7699
the sea monsters draw out the *b*	Lam 4:3	7699
head was of fine gold, his *b*	Dan 2:32	2306
unto heaven, but smote upon his *b*	Lk 18:13	4738
lying on Jesus' *b* saith unto him	Jn 13:25	4738
also leaned on his *b* at supper	Jn 21:20	4738

BREASTPLATE

be set in the ephod, and in the *b*	Ex 25:7	2833
a *b*, and an ephod, and a robe, and a	Ex 28:4	2833
thou shalt make the *b* of judgment	Ex 28:15	2833
thou shalt make upon the *b* chains	Ex 28:22	2833
make upon the *b* two rings of gold	Ex 28:23	2833

rings on the two ends of the *b*	Ex 28:23	2833
which are on the two ends of the *b*	Ex 28:24	2833
of the *b* in the border thereof	Ex 28:26	2833
they shall bind the *b* by the	Ex 28:28	2833
that the *b* be not loosed from the	Ex 28:28	2833
the *b* of judgment upon his heart	Ex 28:29	2833
put in the *b* of judgment the Urim	Ex 28:30	2833
the ephod, and the ephod, and the *b*	Ex 29:5	2833
set for the ephod, and for the *b*	Ex 35:9	2833
set, for the ephod, and for the *b*	Ex 35:27	2833
he made the *b* of cunning work,	Ex 39:8	2833
they made the *b* double	Ex 39:9	2833
upon the *b* chains at the ends	Ex 39:15	2833
rings in the two ends of the *b*	Ex 39:16	2833
two rings on the ends of the *b*	Ex 39:17	2833
put them on the two ends of the *b*	Ex 39:19	2833
they did bind the *b* by his rings	Ex 39:21	2833
that the might not be loosed	Ex 39:21	2833
And he put the *b* upon him	Lev 8:8	2833
also he put in the *b* the Urim	Lev 8:8	2833
he put on righteousness as a *b*	Is 59:17	8302
having on the *b* of righteousness	Eph 6:14	2382
sober, putting on the *b* of faith	1Th 5:8	2382

BREASTPLATES

And they had *b*	Rev 9:9	2382
as it were *b* of iron	Rev 9:9	2382
having *b* of fire, and of jacinth,	Rev 9:17	2382

BREASTS

lieth under, blessings of the *b*	Gen 49:25	7699
And they put the fat upon the *b*	Lev 9:20	2373
And the *b* and the right shoulder	Lev 9:21	2373
or why the *b* that I should suck	Job 3:12	7699
His *b* are full of milk, and his	Job 21:24	5845
when I was upon my mother's *b*	Ps 22:9	7699
let her *b* satisfy thee at all	Prov 5:19	1717
shall lie all night betwixt my *b*	Song 1:13	7699
Thy two *b* are like two young roes	Song 4:5	7699
Thy two *b* are like two young roes	Song 7:3	7699
thy *b* to clusters of grapes	Song 7:7	7699
now also thy *b* shall be as	Song 7:8	7699
that sucked the *b* of my mother	Song 8:1	7699
a little sister, and she hath no *b*	Song 8:8	7699
I am a wall, and my *b* like towers	Song 8:10	7699
the milk, and drawn from the *b*	Is 28:9	7699
with the *b* of her consolations	Is 66:11	7699
thy *b* are fashioned, and thine	Eze 16:7	7699
there were their *b* pressed	Eze 23:3	7699
bruised the *b* of her virginity	Eze 23:8	1717
thereof, and pluck off thine own *b*	Eze 23:34	7699
her adulteries from between her *b*	Hos 2:2	7699
them a miscarrying womb and dry *b*	Hos 9:14	7699
and those that suck the *b*	Joel 2:16	7699
of doves, tabering upon their *b*	Nah 2:7	3824
which were done, smote their *b*	Lk 23:48	4738
having their *b* girded with golden	Rev 15:6	4738

BREATH

into his nostrils the *b* of life	Gen 2:7	5397
flesh, wherein is the *b* of life	Gen 6:17	7307
flesh, wherein is the *b* of life	Gen 7:15	7307
whose nostrils was the *b* of life	Gen 7:22	5397
blast of the *b* of his nostrils	2Sa 22:16	7307
that there was no *b* left in him	1Kin 17:17	5397
by the *b* of his nostrils are they	Job 4:9	7307
will not suffer me to take my *b*	Job 9:18	7307
thing, and the *b* of all mankind	Job 12:10	7307
by the *b* of his mouth shall he go	Job 15:30	7307
My *b* is corrupt, my days are	Job 17:1	7307
My *b* is strange to my wife,	Job 19:17	7307
All the while my *b* is in me	Job 27:3	5397
the *b* of the Almighty hath given	Job 33:4	5397
unto himself his spirit and his *b*	Job 34:14	5397
By the *b* of God frost is given	Job 37:10	5397
His *b* kindleth coals, and a flame	Job 41:21	5315
blast of the *b* of thy nostrils	Ps 18:15	7307
of them by the *b* of his mouth	Ps 33:6	7307
thou takest away their *b*, they	Ps 104:29	7307
is there any *b* in their mouths	Ps 135:17	7307
His *b* goeth forth, he returneth	Ps 146:4	7307
thing that hath *b* praise the LORD	Ps 150:6	5397
yea, they have all one *b*	Eccl 3:19	7307
whose *b* is in his nostrils	Is 2:22	5397
with the *b* of his lips shall he	Is 11:4	7307
And his *b*, as an overflowing	Is 30:28	7307
the *b* of the LORD, like a stream	Is 30:33	5397
your *b*, as fire, shall devour you	Is 33:11	7307
he that giveth *b* unto the people	Is 42:5	5397
and there is no *b* in them	Jer 10:14	7307
and there is no *b* in them	Jer 51:17	7307
The *b* of our nostrils, the	Lam 4:20	7307

I will cause *b* to enter into you,	Eze 37:5	7307
put *b* in you, and ye shall live	Eze 37:6	7307
but there was no *b* in them	Eze 37:8	7307
Come from the four winds, O *b*	Eze 37:9	7307
the *b* came into them, and they	Eze 37:10	7307
me, neither is there *b* left in me	Dan 5:23	5396
there is no *b* at all in the midst	Dan 10:17	5397
he giveth to all life, and *b*	Hab 2:19	7307
	Acts 17:25	4157

BREATHE

there was not any left to *b*	Josh 11:11	5397
them, neither left they any to *b*	Josh 11:14	5397
me, and such as *b* out cruelty	Ps 27:12	3307
b upon these slain, that they may	Eze 37:9	5301

BREATHED

b into his nostrils the breath of	Gen 2:7	5301
but utterly destroyed all that *b*	Josh 10:40	5397
left not to Jeroboam any that *b*	1Kin 15:29	5397
he *b* on them, and saith unto them,	Jn 20:22	1720

BREATHETH

shalt save alive nothing that *b*	Deut 20:16	5397

BREATHING

hide not thine ear at my *b*	Lam 3:56	7309
yet *b* out threatenings and	Acts 9:1	1709

BRED

morning, and it *b* worms, and stank	Ex 16:20	7311

BREECHES

linen *b* to cover their nakedness	Ex 28:42	4370
linen *b* of fine twined linen,	Ex 39:28	4370
his linen *b* shall he put upon his	Lev 6:10	4370
have the linen *b* upon his flesh	Lev 16:4	4370
have linen *b* upon their loins	Eze 44:18	4370

BREED

that they may *b* abundantly in the	Gen 8:17	8317
lambs, and rams of the *b* of Bashan	Deut 32:14	1121

BREEDING

even the *b* of nettles, and	Zeph 2:9	4476

BRETHREN

father, and told his two *b* without	Gen 9:22	251
servants shall he be unto his *b*	Gen 9:25	251
for we be *b*	Gen 13:8	251
in the presence of all his *b*	Gen 16:12	251
And said, I pray you, *b*, do not so	Gen 19:7	251
me to the house of my master's *b*	Gen 24:27	251
died in the presence of all his *b*	Gen 25:18	251
be lord over thy *b*, and let thy	Gen 27:29	251
all his *b* have I given to him for	Gen 27:37	251
And Jacob said unto them, My *b*	Gen 29:4	251
And he took his *b* with him	Gen 31:23	251
Laban with his *b* pitched in the	Gen 31:25	251
before our *b* discern thou what is	Gen 31:32	251
here before my *b* and thy *b*	Gen 31:37	251
And Jacob said unto his *b*, Gather	Gen 31:46	251
called his *b* to eat bread	Gen 31:54	251
unto her father and unto her *b*	Gen 34:11	251
Jacob, Simeon and Levi, Dinah's *b*	Gen 34:25	251
was feeding the flock with his *b*	Gen 37:2	251
when his *b* saw that their father	Gen 37:4	251
loved him more than all his *b*	Gen 37:4	251
a dream, and he told it his *b*	Gen 37:5	251
his *b* said to him, Shalt thou	Gen 37:8	251
another dream, and told it his *b*	Gen 37:9	251
it to his father, and to his *b*	Gen 37:10	251
thy *b* indeed come to bow down	Gen 37:10	251
And his *b* envied him	Gen 37:11	251
his *b* went to feed their father's	Gen 37:12	251
Do not thy *b* feed the flock in	Gen 37:13	251
see whether it be well with thy *b*	Gen 37:14	251
And he said, I seek my *b*	Gen 37:16	251
And Joseph went after his *b*	Gen 37:17	251
when Joseph was come unto his *b*	Gen 37:23	251
And Judah said unto his *b*, What	Gen 37:26	251
And his *b* were content	Gen 37:27	251
And he returned unto his *b*	Gen 37:30	251
that Judah went down from his *b*	Gen 38:1	251
he die also, as his *b* did	Gen 38:11	251
Joseph's ten *b* went down to buy	Gen 42:3	251
Jacob sent not with his *b*	Gen 42:4	251
and Joseph's *b* came, and bowed down	Gen 42:6	251
And Joseph saw his *b*, and he knew	Gen 42:7	251
And Joseph knew his *b*, but they	Gen 42:8	251
said, Thy servants are twelve *b*	Gen 42:13	251
let one of your *b* be bound in the	Gen 42:19	251
And he said unto his *b*, My money	Gen 42:28	251
We be twelve *b*, sons of our	Gen 42:32	251
leave one of your *b* here with me	Gen 42:33	251

his *b* came to Joseph's house	Gen 44:14	251
and let the lad go up with his *b*	Gen 44:33	251
made himself known unto his *b*	Gen 45:1	251
And Joseph said unto his *b*	Gen 45:3	251
his *b* could not answer him	Gen 45:3	251
And Joseph said unto his *b*	Gen 45:4	251
Moreover he kissed all his *b*	Gen 45:15	251
after that his *b* talked with him	Gen 45:15	251
saying, Joseph's *b* are come	Gen 45:16	251
said unto Joseph, Say unto thy *b*	Gen 45:17	251
So he sent his *b* away, and they	Gen 45:24	251
And Joseph said unto his *b*	Gen 46:31	251
Pharaoh, and say unto him, My *b*	Gen 46:31	251
and said, My father and my *b*	Gen 47:1	251
And he took some of his *b*, even	Gen 47:2	251
And Pharaoh said unto his *b*	Gen 47:3	251
and thy *b* are come unto thee	Gen 47:5	251
make thy father and *b* to dwell	Gen 47:6	251
Joseph placed his father and his *b*	Gen 47:11	251
nourished his father, and his *b*	Gen 47:12	251
of their *b* in their inheritance	Gen 48:6	251
to thee one portion above thy *b*	Gen 48:22	251
Simeon and Levi are *b*	Gen 49:5	251
art he whom thy *b* shall praise	Gen 49:8	251
him that was separate from his *b*	Gen 49:26	251
all the house of Joseph, and his *b*	Gen 50:8	251
returned into Egypt, he, and his *b*	Gen 50:14	251
when Joseph's *b* saw that their	Gen 50:15	251
thee now, the trespass of thy *b*	Gen 50:17	251
his *b* also went and fell down	Gen 50:18	251
And Joseph said unto his *b*	Gen 50:24	251
And Joseph died, and all his *b*	Ex 1:6	251
that he went out unto his *b*	Ex 2:11	251
smiting an Hebrew, one of his *b*	Ex 2:11	251
return unto my *b* which are in	Ex 4:18	251
carry your *b* from before the	Lev 10:4	251
but let your *b*, the whole house	Lev 10:6	251
is the high priest among his *b*	Lev 21:10	251
but over your *b* the children of	Lev 25:46	251
one of his *b* may redeem him	Lev 25:48	251
their *b* in the tabernacle of the	Num 8:26	251
all thy *b* the sons of Levi with	Num 16:10	251
thy *b* also of the tribe of Levi,	Num 18:2	251
I have taken your *b* the Levites	Num 18:6	251
when our *b* died before the LORD	Num 20:3	251
brought unto his *b* a Midianitish	Num 25:6	251
among the *b* of our father	Num 27:4	251
among their father's *b*	Num 27:7	251
give his inheritance unto his *b*	Num 27:9	251
And if he have no *b*, then ye shall	Num 27:10	251
inheritance unto his father's *b*	Num 27:10	251
And if his father have no *b*	Num 27:11	251
of Reuben, Shall your *b* go to war	Num 32:6	251
Hear the causes between your *b*	Deut 1:16	251
our *b* have discouraged our heart,	Deut 1:28	251
of your *b* the children of Esau	Deut 2:4	251
from our *b* the children of Esau	Deut 2:8	251
your *b* the children of Israel	Deut 3:18	251
LORD have given rest unto your *b*	Deut 3:20	251
part nor inheritance with his *b*	Deut 10:9	251
you a poor man of one of thy *b*	Deut 15:7	251
one from among thy *b* shalt thou	Deut 17:15	251
be not lifted up above his *b*	Deut 17:20	251
have no inheritance among their *b*	Deut 18:2	251
as all his *b* the Levites do,	Deut 18:7	251
from the midst of thee, of thy *b*	Deut 18:15	251
up a Prophet from among their *b*	Deut 18:18	251
his *b* of the children of Israel	Deut 24:7	251
and weary, whether he be of thy *b*	Deut 24:14	251
If *b* dwell together, and one of	Deut 25:5	251
neither did he acknowledge his *b*	Deut 33:9	251
him that was separated from his *b*	Deut 33:16	251
let him be acceptable to his *b*	Deut 33:24	251
ye shall pass before your *b* armed	Josh 1:14	251
the LORD have given your *b* rest	Josh 1:15	251
my father, and my mother, and my *b*	Josh 2:13	251
father, and thy mother, and thy *b*	Josh 2:18	251
father, and her mother, and her *b*	Josh 6:23	251
Nevertheless my *b* that went up	Josh 14:8	251
us an inheritance among our *b*	Josh 17:4	251
among the *b* of their father	Josh 17:4	251
Ye have not left your *b* these	Josh 22:3	251
God hath given rest unto your *b*	Josh 22:4	251
b on this side Jordan westward	Josh 22:7	251
spoil of your enemies with your *b*	Josh 22:8	251
And he said, They were my *b*	Judg 8:19	251
to Shechem unto his mother's *b*	Judg 9:1	251
his mother's *b* spake of him in	Judg 9:3	251
slew his *b* the sons of Jerubbaal,	Judg 9:5	251
aided him in the killing of his *b*	Judg 9:24	251
the son of Ebed came with his *b*	Judg 9:26	251

B

Ebed and his *b* be come to Shechem	Judg 9:31	251
and Zebul thrust out Gaal and his *b*	Judg 9:41	251
father, in slaying his seventy *b*	Judg 9:56	251
Then Jephthah fled from his *b*	Judg 11:3	251
among the daughters of thy *b*	Judg 14:3	251
Then his *b* and all the house of	Judg 16:31	251
they came unto their *b* to Zorah	Judg 18:8	251
their *b* said unto them, What say	Judg 18:8	251
of Laish, and said unto their *b*	Judg 18:14	251
and said unto them, Nay, my *b*	Judg 19:23	251
of their *b* the children of Israel	Judg 20:13	251
their *b* come unto us to complain	Judg 21:22	251
be not cut off from among his *b*	Ruth 4:10	251
him in the midst of his *b*	1Sa 16:13	251
Take now for thy *b* an ephah of	1Sa 17:17	251
and run to the camp to thy *b*	1Sa 17:17	251
thousand, and look how thy *b* fare	1Sa 17:18	251
army, and came and saluted his *b*	1Sa 17:22	251
away, I pray thee, and see my *b*	1Sa 20:29	251
and when his *b* and all his father's	1Sa 22:1	251
David, Ye shall not do so, my *b*	1Sa 30:23	251
return from following their *b*	2Sa 2:26	251
of Saul thy father, to his *b*	2Sa 3:8	251
return thou, and take back thy *b*	2Sa 15:20	251
Ye are my *b*, ye are my bones and	2Sa 19:12	251
Why have our *b* the men of Judah	2Sa 19:41	251
called all his *b* the king's sons,	1Kin 1:9	251
your *b* the children of Israel	1Kin 12:24	251
him arise up from among his *b*	2Kin 9:2	251
Jehu met with the *b* of Ahaziah	2Kin 10:13	251
answered, We are the *b* of Ahaziah	2Kin 10:13	251
unleavened bread among their *b*	2Kin 23:9	251
was more honourable than his *b*	1Chr 4:9	251
but his *b* had not many children,	1Chr 4:27	251
For Judah prevailed above his *b*	1Chr 5:2	251
his *b* by their families, when the	1Chr 5:7	251
their *b* of the house of their	1Chr 5:13	251
their *b* the sons of Merari stood	1Chr 6:44	251
Their *b* also the Levites were	1Chr 6:48	251
their *b* among all the families of	1Chr 7:5	251
his *b* came to comfort him	1Chr 7:22	251
dwelt with their *b* in Jerusalem	1Chr 8:32	251
Jeuel, and their *b*, six hundred and	1Chr 9:6	251
And their *b*, according to their	1Chr 9:9	251
And their *b*, heads of the house of	1Chr 9:13	251
and Talmon, and Ahiman, and their *b*	1Chr 9:17	251
the son of Korah, and his *b*	1Chr 9:19	251
And their *b*, which were in their	1Chr 9:25	251
And other of their *b*, of the sons	1Chr 9:32	251
dwelt with their *b* at Jerusalem	1Chr 9:38	251
over against their *b*	1Chr 9:38	251
bow, even of Saul's *b* of Benjamin	1Chr 12:2	251
all their *b* were at their	1Chr 12:32	251
for their *b* had prepared for them	1Chr 12:39	251
abroad unto our *b* every where	1Chr 13:2	251
his *b* an hundred and twenty	1Chr 15:5	251
his *b* two hundred and twenty	1Chr 15:6	251
his *b* an hundred and thirty	1Chr 15:7	251
the chief, and his *b* two hundred	1Chr 15:8	251
the chief, and his *b* fourscore	1Chr 15:9	251
his *b* an hundred and twelve	1Chr 15:10	251
yourselves, both ye and your *b*	1Chr 15:12	251
their *b* to be the singers with	1Chr 15:16	251
and of his *b*, Asaph the son of	1Chr 15:17	251
and of the sons of Merari their *b*	1Chr 15:17	251
with them their *b* of the second	1Chr 15:18	251
into the hand of Asaph and his *b*	1Chr 16:7	251
of the LORD Asaph and his *b*	1Chr 16:37	251
And Obed-edom with their *b*	1Chr 16:38	251
his *b* the priests, before the	1Chr 16:39	251
their *b* the sons of Kish took	1Chr 23:22	251
of the sons of Aaron their *b*	1Chr 23:32	251
their *b* the sons of Aaron in the	1Chr 24:31	251
over against their younger *b*	1Chr 24:31	251
with their *b* that were instructed	1Chr 25:7	251
to Gedaliah, who with his *b*	1Chr 25:9	251
to Zaccur, he, his sons, and his *b*	1Chr 25:10	251
to Izri, he, his sons, and his *b*	1Chr 25:11	251
Nethaniah, he, his sons, and his *b*	1Chr 25:12	251
Bukkiah, he, his sons, and his *b*	1Chr 25:13	251
he, his sons, and his *b*, were	1Chr 25:14	251
Jeshaiah, he, his sons, and his *b*	1Chr 25:15	251
Mattaniah, he, his sons, and his *b*	1Chr 25:16	251
to Shimei, he, his sons, and his *b*	1Chr 25:17	251
Azareel, he, his sons, and his *b*	1Chr 25:18	251
Hashabiah, he, his sons, and his *b*	1Chr 25:19	251
Shubael, he, his sons, and his *b*	1Chr 25:20	251
he, his sons, and his *b*, were	1Chr 25:21	251
Jeremoth, he, his sons, and his *b*	1Chr 25:22	251
Hananiah, he, his sons, and his *b*	1Chr 25:23	251
he, his sons, and his *b*, were	1Chr 25:24	251
to Hanani, he, his sons, and his *b*	1Chr 25:25	251
Mallothi, he, his sons, and his *b*	1Chr 25:26	251
Eliathah, he, his sons, and his *b*	1Chr 25:27	251
to Hothir, he, his sons, and his *b*	1Chr 25:28	251
Giddalti, he, his sons, and his *b*	1Chr 25:29	251
Mahazioth, he, his sons, and his *b*	1Chr 25:30	251
he, his sons, and his *b*, were	1Chr 25:31	251
whose *b* were strong men, Elihu,	1Chr 26:7	251
they and their sons and their *b*	1Chr 26:8	251
And Meshelemiah had sons and *b*	1Chr 26:9	251
sons and *b* of Hosah were thirteen	1Chr 26:11	251
And his *b* by Eliezer	1Chr 26:25	251
his *b* were over all the treasures	1Chr 26:26	251
hand of Shelomith, and of his *b*	1Chr 26:28	251
Hebronites, Hashabiah and his *b*	1Chr 26:30	251
And his *b*, men of valour, were two	1Chr 26:32	251
Elihu, one of the *b* of David	1Chr 27:18	251
his feet, and said, Hear me, my *b*	1Chr 28:2	251
with their sons and their *b*	2Chr 5:12	251
go up, nor fight against your *b*	2Chr 11:4	251
chief, to be ruler among his *b*	2Chr 11:22	251
shall come to you of your *b* that	2Chr 19:10	251
come upon you, and upon your *b*	2Chr 19:10	251
he had *b* the sons of Jehoshaphat,	2Chr 21:2	251
slew all his *b* with the sword, and	2Chr 21:4	251
also hast slain thy *b* of thy	2Chr 21:13	251
and the sons of the *b* of Ahaziah	2Chr 22:8	251
of their *b* two hundred thousand	2Chr 28:8	251
ye have taken captive of your *b*	2Chr 28:11	251
city of palm trees, to their *b*	2Chr 28:15	251
And they gathered their *b*, and	2Chr 29:15	251
wherefore their *b* the Levites did	2Chr 29:34	251
like your fathers, and like your *b*	2Chr 30:7	251
turn again unto the LORD, your *b*	2Chr 30:9	251
to give to their *b* by courses	2Chr 31:15	251
the fathers of your *b* the people	2Chr 35:5	251
yourselves, and prepare your *b*	2Chr 35:6	251
and Shemaiah and Nethaneel, his *b*	2Chr 35:9	251
for their *b* the Levites prepared	2Chr 35:15	251
his *b* the priests, and Zerubbabel	Ezr 3:2	251
the son of Shealtiel, and his *b*	Ezr 3:2	251
remnant of their *b* the priests	Ezr 3:8	251
Jeshua with his sons and his *b*	Ezr 3:9	251
their sons and their *b* the Levites	Ezr 3:9	251
for their *b* the priests, and for	Ezr 6:20	251
seem good to thee, and to thy *b*	Ezr 7:18	252
to his *b* the Nethinims, at the	Ezr 8:17	251
Sherebiah, with his sons and his *b*	Ezr 8:18	251
of the sons of Merari, his *b*	Ezr 8:19	251
and ten of their *b* with them	Ezr 8:24	251
the son of Jozadak, and his *b*	Ezr 10:18	251
That Hanani, one of my *b*, came,	Neh 1:2	251
rose up with his *b* the priests	Neh 3:1	251
After him repaired their *b*	Neh 3:18	251
And he spake before his *b* and the	Neh 4:2	251
and terrible, and fight for your *b*	Neh 4:14	251
So neither I, nor my *b*, nor my	Neh 4:23	251
wives against their *b* the Jews	Neh 5:1	251
flesh is as the flesh of our *b*	Neh 5:5	251
have redeemed our *b* the Jews	Neh 5:8	251
and will ye even sell your *b*	Neh 5:8	251
I likewise, and my *b*, and my	Neh 5:10	251
my *b* have not eaten the bread of	Neh 5:14	251
And their *b*, Shebaniah, Hodijah,	Neh 10:10	251
They clave to their *b*, their	Neh 10:29	251
their *b* that did the work of the	Neh 11:12	251
And his *b*, chief of the fathers,	Neh 11:13	251
And their *b*, mighty men of valour,	Neh 11:14	251
Bakbukiah the second among his *b*	Neh 11:17	251
their *b* that kept the gates, were	Neh 11:19	251
of their *b* in the days of Jeshua	Neh 12:7	251
the thanksgiving, he and his *b*	Neh 12:8	251
Also Bakbukiah and Unni, their *b*	Neh 12:9	251
with their *b* over against them,	Neh 12:24	251
And his *b*, Shemaiah, and Azarael,	Neh 12:36	251
was to distribute unto their *b*	Neh 13:13	251
of the multitude of his *b*	Est 10:3	251
My *b* have dealt deceitfully as a	Job 6:15	251
He hath put my *b* far from me	Job 19:13	251
came there unto him all his *b*	Job 42:11	251
them inheritance among their *b*	Job 42:15	251
I will declare thy name unto my *b*	Ps 22:22	251
I am become a stranger unto my *b*	Ps 69:8	251
For my *b* and companions' sakes, I	Ps 122:8	251
how pleasant it is for *b* to dwell	Ps 133:1	251
and he that soweth discord among *b*	Prov 6:19	251
of the inheritance among the *b*	Prov 17:2	251
All the *b* of the poor do hate him	Prov 19:7	251
Your *b* that hated you, that cast	Is 66:5	251
they shall bring all your *b* for	Is 66:20	251
as I have cast out all your *b*	Jer 7:15	251

For even thy *b*, and the house of	Jer 12:6	251
of your *b* that are not gone forth	Jer 29:16	251
the son of Habaziniah, and his *b*	Jer 35:3	251
and slew them not among their *b*	Jer 41:8	251
his seed is spoiled, and his *b*	Jer 49:10	251
of man, thy *b*, even thy *b*	Eze 11:15	251
Say ye unto your *b*, Ammi	Hos 2:1	251
Though he be fruitful among his *b*	Hos 13:15	251
then the remnant of his *b* shall	Mic 5:3	251
and Jacob begat Judas and his *b*	Mt 1:2	80
Josias begat Jechonias and his *b*	Mt 1:11	80
by the sea of Galilee, saw two *b*	Mt 4:18	80
from thence, he saw other two *b*	Mt 4:21	80
And if ye salute your *b* only	Mt 5:47	80
his *b* stood without, desiring to	Mt 12:46	80
thy *b* stand without, desiring to	Mt 12:47	80
and who are my *b*	Mt 12:48	80
and said, Behold my mother and my *b*	Mt 12:49	80
and his *b*, James, and Joses, and	Mt 13:55	80
that hath forsaken houses, or *b*	Mt 19:29	80
indignation against the two *b*	Mt 20:24	80
Now there were with us seven *b*	Mt 22:25	80
and all ye are *b*	Mt 23:8	80
one of the least of these my *b*	Mt 25:40	80
go tell my *b* that they go into	Mt 28:10	80
There came then his *b* and his	Mk 3:31	80
thy *b* without seek for thee	Mk 3:32	80
saying, Who is my mother, or my *b*	Mk 3:33	80
and said, Behold my mother and my *b*	Mk 3:34	80
no man that hath left house, or *b*	Mk 10:29	80
now in this time, houses, and *b*	Mk 10:30	80
Now there were seven *b*	Mk 12:20	80
came to him his mother and his *b*	Lk 8:19	80
thy *b* stand without, desiring to	Lk 8:20	80
my *b* are these which hear the	Lk 8:21	80
call not thy friends, nor thy *b*	Lk 14:12	80
and wife, and children, and *b*	Lk 14:26	80
For I have five *b*	Lk 16:28	80
hath left house, or parents, or *b*	Lk 18:29	80
There were therefore seven *b*	Lk 20:29	80
be betrayed both by parents, and *b*	Lk 21:16	80
art converted, strengthen thy *b*	Lk 22:32	80
he, and his mother, and his *b*	Jn 2:12	80
His *b* therefore said unto him,	Jn 7:3	80
neither did his *b* believe in him	Jn 7:5	80
But when his *b* were gone up	Jn 7:10	80
but go to my *b*, and say unto them,	Jn 20:17	80
this saying abroad among the *b*	Jn 21:23	80
mother of Jesus, and with his *b*	Acts 1:14	80
Men and *b*, this scripture must	Acts 1:16	80
Men and *b*, let me freely speak	Acts 2:29	80
rest of the apostles, Men and *b*	Acts 2:37	80
And now, *b*, I wot that through	Acts 3:17	80
God raise up unto you of your *b*	Acts 3:22	80
Wherefore, *b*, look ye out among	Acts 6:3	80
And he said, Men, *b*, and fathers,	Acts 7:2	80
Joseph was made known to his *b*	Acts 7:13	80
his *b* the children of Israel	Acts 7:23	80
For he supposed his *b* would have	Acts 7:25	80
one again, saying, Sirs, ye are *b*	Acts 7:26	80
God raise up unto you of your *b*	Acts 7:37	80
Which when the *b* knew, they	Acts 9:30	80
certain *b* from Joppa accompanied	Acts 10:23	80
b that were in Judaea heard that	Acts 11:1	80
these six *b* accompanied me	Acts 11:12	80
unto the *b* which dwelt in Judaea	Acts 11:29	80
things unto James, and to the *b*	Acts 12:17	80
unto them, saying, Ye men and *b*	Acts 13:15	80
Men and *b*, children of the stock	Acts 13:26	80
unto you therefore, men and *b*	Acts 13:38	80
minds evil affected against the *b*	Acts 14:2	80
down from Judaea taught the *b*	Acts 15:1	80
caused great joy unto all the *b*	Acts 15:3	80
up, and said unto them, Men and *b*	Acts 15:7	80
James answered, saying, Men and *b*	Acts 15:13	80
and Silas, chief men among the *b*	Acts 15:22	80
b send greeting unto the *b*	Acts 15:23	80
exhorted the *b* with many words,	Acts 15:32	80
from the *b* unto the apostles	Acts 15:33	80
visit our *b* in every city where	Acts 15:36	80
by the *b* unto the grace of God	Acts 15:40	80
of by the *b* that were at Lystra	Acts 16:2	80
and when they had seen the *b*	Acts 16:40	80
certain *b* unto the rulers of the	Acts 17:6	80
the *b* immediately sent away Paul	Acts 17:10	80
then immediately the *b* sent away	Acts 17:14	80
and then took his leave of the *b*	Acts 18:18	80
the *b* wrote, exhorting the	Acts 18:27	80
And now, *b*, I commend you to God,	Acts 20:32	80
to Ptolemais, and saluted the *b*	Acts 21:7	80
the *b* received us gladly	Acts 21:17	80

Men, *b*, and fathers, hear ye my	Acts 22:1	80
I received letters unto the *b*	Acts 22:5	80
the council, said, Men and *b*	Acts 23:1	80
Then said Paul, I wist not, *b*	Acts 23:5	80
out in the council, Men and *b*	Acts 23:6	80
Where we found *b*, and were desired	Acts 28:14	80
when the *b* heard of us, they came	Acts 28:15	80
he said unto them, Men and *b*	Acts 28:17	80
neither any of the *b* that came	Acts 28:21	80
I would not have you ignorant, *b*	Rom 1:13	80
Know ye not, *b*, (for I speak to	Rom 7:1	80
Wherefore, my *b*, ye also are	Rom 7:4	80
Therefore, *b*, we are debtors, not	Rom 8:12	80
be the firstborn among many *b*	Rom 8:29	80
accursed from Christ for my *b*	Rom 9:3	80
B, my heart's desire and prayer to	Rom 10:1	80
For I would not, *b*, that ye	Rom 11:25	80
I beseech you therefore, *b*	Rom 12:1	80
also am persuaded of you, my *b*	Rom 15:14	80
Nevertheless, *b*, I have written	Rom 15:15	80
Now I beseech you, *b*, for the	Rom 15:30	80
the *b* which are with them	Rom 16:14	80
Now I beseech you, *b*, mark them	Rom 16:17	80
Now I beseech you, *b*, by the name	1Cor 1:10	80
declared unto me of you, my *b*	1Cor 1:11	80
For ye see your calling, *b*	1Cor 1:26	80
And I, *b*, when I came to you, came	1Cor 2:1	80
And I, *b*, could not speak unto you	1Cor 3:1	80
And these things, *b*, I have in a	1Cor 4:6	80
be able to judge between his *b*	1Cor 6:5	80
wrong, and defraud, and that your *b*	1Cor 6:8	80
B, let every man, wherein he is	1Cor 7:24	80
But this I say, *b*, the time is	1Cor 7:29	80
But when ye sin so against the *b*	1Cor 8:12	80
as the *b* of the Lord, and Cephas	1Cor 9:5	80
Moreover, *b*, I would not that ye	1Cor 10:1	80
Now I praise you, *b*, that ye	1Cor 11:2	80
Wherefore, my *b*, when ye come	1Cor 11:33	80
Now concerning spiritual gifts, *b*	1Cor 12:1	80
Now, *b*, if I come unto you	1Cor 14:6	80
B, be not children in	1Cor 14:20	80
How is it then, *b*	1Cor 14:26	80
Wherefore, *b*, covet to prophesy,	1Cor 14:39	80
Moreover, *b*, I declare unto you	1Cor 15:1	80
of above five hundred *b* at once	1Cor 15:6	80
Now this I say, *b*, that flesh and	1Cor 15:50	80
Therefore, my beloved *b*, be ye	1Cor 15:58	80
for I look for him with the *b*	1Cor 16:11	80
him to come unto you with the *b*	1Cor 16:12	80
I beseech you, *b*, (ye know the	1Cor 16:15	80
All the *b* greet you	1Cor 16:20	80
For we would not, *b*, have you	2Cor 1:8	80
Moreover, *b*, we do you to wit of	2Cor 8:1	80
or our *b* be enquired of, they are	2Cor 8:23	80
Yet have I sent the *b*, lest our	2Cor 9:3	80
it necessary to exhort the *b*	2Cor 9:5	80
the *b* which came from Macedonia	2Cor 11:9	80
the sea, in perils among false *b*	2Cor 11:26	5569
Finally, *b*, farewell	2Cor 13:11	80
all the *b* which are with me, unto	Gal 1:2	80
But I certify you, *b*, that the	Gal 1:11	80
of false *b* unawares brought in	Gal 2:4	5569
B, I speak after the manner of	Gal 3:15	80
B, I beseech you, be as I am	Gal 4:12	80
Now we, *b*, as Isaac was, are the	Gal 4:28	80
So then, *b*, we are not children	Gal 4:31	80
And I, *b*, if I yet preach	Gal 5:11	80
For, *b*, ye have been called unto	Gal 5:13	80
B, if a man be overtaken in a	Gal 6:1	80
B, the grace of our Lord Jesus	Gal 6:18	80
Finally, my *b*, be strong in the	Eph 6:10	80
Peace to the *b*, and love with	Eph 6:23	80
I would ye should understand, *b*	Phil 1:12	80
And many of the *b* in the Lord	Phil 1:14	80
Finally, my *b*, rejoice in the	Phil 3:1	80
B, I count not myself to have	Phil 3:13	80
B, be followers together of me,	Phil 3:17	80
my *b* dearly beloved and longed for	Phil 4:1	80
Finally, *b*, whatsoever things are	Phil 4:8	80
The *b* which are with me greet you	Phil 4:21	80
faithful *b* in Christ which are at	Col 1:2	80
Salute the *b* which are in	Col 4:15	80
b beloved, your election of God	1Th 1:4	80
For yourselves, *b*, know our	1Th 2:1	80
For ye remember, *b*, our labour and	1Th 2:9	80
For ye, *b*, became followers of	1Th 2:14	80
But we, *b*, being taken from you	1Th 2:17	80
Therefore, *b*, we were comforted	1Th 3:7	80
then we beseech you, *b*, and exhort	1Th 4:1	80
the *b* which are in all Macedonia	1Th 4:10	80
but we beseech you, *b*, that ye	1Th 4:10	80

not have you to be ignorant, *b*	1Th 4:13	80
of the times and the seasons, *b*	1Th 5:1	80
But ye, *b*, are not in darkness,	1Th 5:4	80
And we beseech you, *b*, to know	1Th 5:12	80
Now we exhort you, *b*, warn them	1Th 5:14	80
B, pray for us	1Th 5:25	80
Greet all the *b* with an holy kiss	1Th 5:26	80
be read unto all the holy *b*	1Th 5:27	80
to thank God always for you, *b*	2Th 1:3	80
Now we beseech you, *b*, by the	2Th 2:1	80
b beloved of the Lord, because	2Th 2:13	80
Therefore, *b*, stand fast, and hold	2Th 2:15	80
Finally, *b*, pray for us, that the	2Th 3:1	80
Now we command you, *b*, in the	2Th 3:6	80
But ye, *b*, be not weary in well	2Th 3:13	80
If thou put the *b* in remembrance	1Ti 4:6	80
and the younger men as *b*	1Ti 5:1	80
despise them, because they are *b*	1Ti 6:2	80
Linus, and Claudia, and all the *b*	2Ti 4:21	80
he is not ashamed to call them *b*	Heb 2:11	80
I will declare thy name unto my *b*	Heb 2:12	80
him to be made like unto his *b*	Heb 2:17	80
Wherefore, holy *b*, partakers of	Heb 3:1	80
Take heed, *b*, lest there be in	Heb 3:12	80
to the law, that is, of their *b*	Heb 7:5	80
Having therefore, *b*, boldness to	Heb 10:19	80
And I beseech you, *b*, suffer the	Heb 13:22	80
My *b*, count it all joy when ye	Jas 1:2	80
Do not err, my beloved *b*	Jas 1:16	80
Wherefore, my beloved *b*, let	Jas 1:19	80
My *b*, have not the faith of our	Jas 2:1	80
Hearken, my beloved *b*, Hath not	Jas 2:5	80
What doth it profit, my *b*	Jas 2:14	80
My *b*, be not many masters,	Jas 3:1	80
My *b*, these things ought not so	Jas 3:10	80
Can the fig tree, my *b*, bear	Jas 3:12	80
Speak not evil one of another, *b*	Jas 4:11	80
Be patient therefore, *b*, unto the	Jas 5:7	80
Grudge not one against another, *b*	Jas 5:9	80
Take, my *b*, the prophets, who	Jas 5:10	80
But above all things, my *b*	Jas 5:12	80
B, if any of you do err from the	Jas 5:19	80
unto unfeigned love of the *b*	1Pet 1:22	5360
one of another, love as *b*	1Pet 3:8	5361
in your *b* that are in the world	1Pet 5:9	81
Wherefore the rather, *b*, give	2Pet 1:10	80
B, I write no new commandment	1Jn 2:7	80
Marvel not, my *b*, if the world	1Jn 3:13	80
unto life, because we love the *b*	1Jn 3:14	80
to lay down our lives for the *b*	1Jn 3:16	80
rejoiced greatly, when the *b* came	3Jn 3	80
whatsoever thou doest to the *b*	3Jn 5	80
doth he himself receive the *b*	3Jn 10	80
fellowservants also and their *b*	Rev 6:11	80
the accuser of our *b* is cast down	Rev 12:10	80
of thy *b* that have the testimony	Rev 19:10	80
of thy *b* the prophets, and of them	Rev 22:9	80

BRETHREN'S

lest his *b* heart faint as well as	Deut 20:8	251

BRIBE

b to blind mine eyes therewith	1Sa 12:3	3724
afflict the just, they take a *b*	Amos 5:12	3724

BRIBERY

consume the tabernacles of *b*	Job 15:34	7810

BRIBES

aside after lucre, and took *b*	1Sa 8:3	7810
and their right hand is full of *b*	Ps 26:10	7810
his hands from holding of *b*	Is 33:15	7810

BRICK

to another, Go to, let us make *b*	Gen 11:3	3835
they had *b* for stone, and slime	Gen 11:3	3843
hard bondage, in morter, and in *b*	Ex 1:14	3843
give the people straw to make *b*	Ex 5:7	3835
task in making *b* both yesterday	Ex 5:14	3835
and they say to us, Make *b*	Ex 5:16	3843
burneth incense upon altars of *b*	Is 65:3	3843

BRICKKILN

and made them pass through the *b*	2Sa 12:31	4404
and hide them in the clay in the *b*	Jer 43:9	4404
the morter, make strong the *b*	Nah 3:14	4404

BRICKS

And the tale of the *b*, which they	Ex 5:8	3843
shall ye deliver the tale of *b*	Ex 5:18	3843
from your *b* of your daily task	Ex 5:19	3843
The *b* are fallen down, but we	Is 9:10	3843

BRIDE

bind them on thee, as a *b* doeth	Is 49:18	3618
as a *b* adorneth herself with her	Is 61:10	3618
bridegroom rejoiceth over the *b*	Is 62:5	3618
her ornaments, or a *b* her attire	Jer 2:32	3618
bridegroom, and the voice of the *b*	Jer 7:34	3618
bridegroom, and the voice of the *b*	Jer 16:9	3618
bridegroom, and the voice of the *b*	Jer 25:10	3618
bridegroom, and the voice of the *b*	Jer 33:11	3618
and the *b* out of her closet	Joel 2:16	3618
He that hath the *b* is the	Jn 3:29	3565
of the *b* shall be heard no more	Rev 18:23	3565
prepared as a *b* adorned for her	Rev 21:2	3565
hither, I will shew thee the *b*	Rev 21:9	3565
And the Spirit and the *b* say	Rev 22:17	3565

BRIDECHAMBER

Can the children of the *b* mourn	Mt 9:15	3567
Can the children of the *b* fast	Mk 2:19	3567
make the children of the *b* fast	Lk 5:34	3567

BRIDEGROOM

Which is as a *b* coming out of his	Ps 19:5	2860
as a *b* decketh himself with	Is 61:10	2860
as the *b* rejoiceth over the bride	Is 62:5	2860
of gladness, the voice of the *b*	Jer 7:34	2860
of gladness, the voice of the *b*	Jer 16:9	2860
of gladness, the voice of the *b*	Jer 25:10	2860
of gladness, the voice of the *b*	Jer 33:11	2860
let the *b* go forth of his chamber	Joel 2:16	2860
as long as the *b* is with them	Mt 9:15	3566
when the *b* shall be taken from	Mt 9:15	3566
and went forth to meet the *b*	Mt 25:1	3566
While the *b* tarried, they all	Mt 25:5	3566
a cry made, Behold, the *b* cometh	Mt 25:6	3566
they went to buy, the *b* came	Mt 25:10	3566
fast, while the *b* is with them	Mk 2:19	3566
long as they have the *b* with them	Mk 2:19	3566
when the *b* shall be taken away	Mk 2:20	3566
fast, while the *b* is with them	Lk 5:34	3566
when the *b* shall be taken away	Lk 5:35	3566
of the feast called the *b*	Jn 2:9	3566
He that hath the bride is the *b*	Jn 3:29	3566
but the friend of the *b*, which	Jn 3:29	3566
and the voice of the *b* and of the	Rev 18:23	3566

BRIDEGROOM'S

greatly because of the *b* voice	Jn 3:29	3566

BRIDLE

my *b* in thy lips, and I will turn	2Kin 19:28	4964
also let loose the *b* before me	Job 30:11	7448
can come to him with his double *b*	Job 41:13	7448
must be held in with bit and *b*	Ps 32:9	7448
I will keep my mouth with a *b*	Ps 39:1	4269
a *b* for the ass, and a rod for the	Prov 26:3	4964
there shall be a *b* in the jaws of	Is 30:28	7448
my *b* in thy lips, and I will turn	Is 37:29	4964
able also to *b* the whole body	Jas 3:2	5469

BRIDLES

winepress, even unto the horse *b*	Rev 14:20	5469

BRIDLETH

b not his tongue, but deceiveth	Jas 1:26	5468

BRIEFLY

it is *b* comprehended in this	Rom 13:9	346
as I suppose, I have written *b*	1Pet 5:12	1223,3641

BRIER

instead of the *b* shall come up	Is 55:13	5636
b unto the house of Israel	Eze 28:24	5544
The best of them is as a *b*	Mic 7:4	2312

BRIERS

of the wilderness and with *b*	Judg 8:7	1303
and thorns of the wilderness and *b*	Judg 8:16	1303
but there shall come up *b*	Is 5:6	8068
it shall even be for *b* and thorns	Is 7:23	8068
all the land shall become *b*	Is 7:24	8068
not come thither the fear of *b*	Is 7:25	8068
it shall devour the *b* and thorns,	Is 9:18	8068
his thorns and his *b* in one day	Is 10:17	8068
who would set the *b* and thorns	Is 27:4	8068
people shall come up thorns and *b*	Is 32:13	8068
afraid of their words, though *b*	Eze 2:6	5621
b is rejected, and is nigh unto	Heb 6:8	5146

BRIGANDINE

that lifteth himself up in his *b*	Jer 51:3	5630

BRIGANDINES

the spears, and put on the *b*	Jer 46:4	5630

B

BRIGHT

or *b* spot, and it be in the skin	Lev 13:2	934
If the *b* spot be white in the	Lev 13:4	934
be a white rising, or a *b* spot	Lev 13:19	934
But if the *b* spot stay in his	Lev 13:23	934
that burneth have a white *b* spot	Lev 13:24	934
if the hair in the *b* spot be	Lev 13:25	934
be no white hair in the *b* spot	Lev 13:26	934
if the *b* spot stay in his place	Lev 13:28	934
b spots, even white *b* spots	Lev 13:38	934
if the *b* spots in the skin of	Lev 13:39	934
and for a scab, and for a *b* spot	Lev 14:56	934
of the LORD, were of *b* brass	1Kin 7:45	4803
the house of the LORD of *b* brass	2Chr 4:16	4838
he scattereth his *b* cloud	Job 37:11	216
now men see not the *b* light which	Job 37:21	925
his belly is as *b* ivory overlaid	Song 5:14	6247
Make *b* the arrows	Jer 51:11	1305
and the fire was *b*, and out of the	Eze 1:13	5051
it is made *b*, it is wrapped up	Eze 21:15	1300
he made his arrows *b*, he	Eze 21:21	7043
b iron, cassia, and calamus, were	Eze 27:19	6219
All the *b* lights of heaven will I	Eze 32:8	3974
lifteth up both the *b* sword	Nah 3:3	3851
so the LORD shall make *b* clouds	Zec 10:1	2385
a *b* cloud overshadowed them	Mt 17:5	5460
as when the *b* shining of a candle	Lk 11:36	*796*
man stood before me in *b* clothing	Acts 10:30	*2986*
the offspring of David, and the *b*	Rev 22:16	*2986*

BRIGHTNESS

Through the *b* before him were	2Sa 22:13	5051
shined, or the moon walking in *b*	Job 31:26	3368
At the *b* that was before him his	Ps 18:12	5051
for *b*, but we walk in darkness	Is 59:9	5054
kings to the *b* of thy rising	Is 60:3	5051
neither for *b* shall the moon give	Is 60:19	5051
thereof go forth as *b*, and the	Is 62:1	5051
a *b* was about it, and out of the	Eze 1:4	5051
of fire, and it had *b* round about	Eze 1:27	5051
appearance of the *b* round about	Eze 1:28	5051
upward, as the appearance of *b*	Eze 8:2	2096
full of the *b* of the LORD's glory	Eze 10:4	5051
and they shall defile thy *b*	Eze 28:7	3314
thy wisdom by reason of thy *b*	Eze 28:17	3314
whose *b* was excellent, stood	Dan 2:31	2122
mine honour and *b* returned unto me	Dan 4:36	2122
shine as the *b* of the firmament	Dan 12:3	2096
even very dark, and no *b* in it	Amos 5:20	5051
And his *b* was as the light	Hab 3:4	5051
above the *b* of the sun, shining	Acts 26:13	*2987*
destroy with the *b* of his coming	2Th 2:8	*2015*
Who being the *b* of his glory	Heb 1:3	*541*

BRIM

were dipped in the *b* of the water	Josh 3:15	7097
from the one *b* to the other	1Kin 7:23	8193
under the *b* of it round about	1Kin 7:24	8193
the *b* thereof was wrought like	1Kin 7:26	8193
was wrought like the *b* of a cup	1Kin 7:26	8193
sea of ten cubits from *b* to *b*	2Chr 4:2	8193
the *b* of it like the work of the	2Chr 4:5	8193
like the work of the *b* of a cup	2Chr 4:5	8193
And they filled them up to the *b*	Jn 2:7	*507*

BRIMSTONE

upon Sodom and upon Gomorrah *b*	Gen 19:24	1614
that the whole land thereof is *b*	Deut 29:23	1614
b shall be scattered upon his	Job 18:15	1614
he shall rain snares, fire and *b*	Ps 11:6	1614
of the LORD, like a stream of *b*	Is 30:33	1614
pitch, and the dust thereof into *b*	Is 34:9	1614
and great hailstones, fire, and *b*	Eze 38:22	1614
b from heaven, and destroyed them	Lk 17:29	*2303*
of fire, and of jacinth, and *b*	Rev 9:17	*2306*
mouths issued fire and smoke and *b*	Rev 9:17	*2303*
and by the smoke, and by the *b*	Rev 9:18	*2303*
b in the presence of the holy	Rev 14:10	*2303*
a lake of fire burning with *b*	Rev 19:20	*2303*
cast into the lake of fire and *b*	Rev 20:10	*2303*
lake which burneth with fire and *b*	Rev 21:8	*2303*

BRING See APPENDIX.

BRINGERS

the *b* up of the children, sent to	2Kin 10:5	539

BRINGEST

a valiant man, and *b* good tidings	1Kin 1:42	1319
b me into judgment with thee	Job 14:3	935
that *b* good tidings, get thee up	Is 40:9	1319
that *b* good tidings, lift up thy	Is 40:9	1319
For thou *b* certain strange things	Acts 17:20	*1533*

BRINGETH See APPENDIX.

BRINGING See APPENDIX.

BRINK

kine upon the *b* of the river	Gen 41:3	8193
it in the flags by the river's *b*	Ex 2:3	8193
by the river's *b* against he come	Ex 7:15	8193
which is by the *b* of the river of	Deut 2:36	8193
to the *b* of the water of Jordan	Josh 3:8	7097
to return to the *b* of the river	Eze 47:6	8193

BROAD

cubits long, and five cubits *b*	Ex 27:1	7341
let them make them *b* plates for a	Num 16:38	7555
they were made *b* plates for a	Num 16:39	7554
chamber was five cubits *b*	1Kin 6:6	7341
and the middle was six cubits *b*	1Kin 6:6	7341
and the third was seven cubits *b*	1Kin 6:6	7341
cubits long, and five cubits *b*	2Chr 6:13	7341
Jerusalem unto the *b* wall	Neh 3:8	7342
the furnaces even unto the *b* wall	Neh 12:38	7342
out of the strait into a *b* place	Job 36:16	7338
thy commandment is exceeding *b*	Ps 119:96	7342
in the *b* ways I will seek him	Song 3:2	7339
be unto us a place of *b* rivers	Is 33:21	7338,3027
seek in the *b* places thereof, if	Jer 5:1	7339
The *b* walls of Babylon shall be	Jer 51:58	7342
of the gate, which was one reed *b*	Eze 40:6	7341
of the gate, which was one reed *b*	Eze 40:6	7341
was one reed long, and one reed *b*	Eze 40:7	7341
long, and five and twenty cubits *b*	Eze 40:29	7341
cubits long, and five cubits *b*	Eze 40:30	7341
long, and five and twenty cubits *b*	Eze 40:33	7341
long, and a cubit and an half *b*	Eze 40:42	7341
And within were hooks, an hand *b*	Eze 40:43	
long, and an hundred cubits *b*	Eze 40:47	7341
six cubits *b* on the one side, and	Eze 41:1	7341
six cubits *b* on the other side,	Eze 41:1	7341
the west was seventy cubits *b*	Eze 41:12	7341
as long as they, and as *b* as they	Eze 42:11	7342
reeds long, and five hundred *b*	Eze 42:20	7341
be twelve cubits long, twelve *b*	Eze 43:16	7341
fourteen *b* in the four squares	Eze 43:17	7341
of the city five thousand *b*	Eze 45:6	7341
of forty cubits long and thirty *b*	Eze 46:22	7341
one against another in the *b* ways	Nah 2:4	7339
b is the way, that leadeth to	Mt 7:13	*2149*
they make *b* their phylacteries,	Mt 23:5	*4115*

BROADER

than the earth, and *b* than the sea	Job 11:9	7342

BROIDED

not with *b* hair, or gold, or	1Ti 2:9	*4117*

BROIDERED

a *b* coat, a mitre, and a girdle	Ex 28:4	8665
I clothed thee also with *b* work	Eze 16:10	7553
of fine linen, and silk, and *b* work	Eze 16:13	7553
And tookest thy *b* garments	Eze 16:18	7553
and put off their *b* garments	Eze 26:16	7553
Fine linen with *b* work from Egypt	Eze 27:7	7553
b work, and fine linen, and coral,	Eze 27:16	7553
b work, and in chests of rich	Eze 27:24	7553

BROILED

they gave him a piece of a *b* fish	Lk 24:42	*3702*

BROKEN

fountains of the great deep *b* up	Gen 7:11	1234
he hath *b* my covenant	Gen 17:14	6565
she said, How hast thou *b* forth	Gen 38:29	6555
wherein it is sodden shall be *b*	Lev 6:28	7665
for pots, they shall be *b* down	Lev 11:35	5422
of leprosy *b* out of the boil	Lev 13:20	6524
it is a leprosy *b* out of the	Lev 13:25	6524
which hath the issue, shall be *b*	Lev 15:12	7665
or scabbed, or hath his stones *b*	Lev 21:20	4790
Blind, or *b*, or maimed, or having	Lev 22:22	7665
is bruised, or crushed, or *b*	Lev 22:24	5423
I have *b* the bands of your yoke	Lev 26:13	7665
when I have *b* the staff of your	Lev 26:26	7665
hath *b* his commandment, that soul	Num 15:31	6565
Then were the horsehoofs *b* by the	Judg 5:22	1986
as a thread of tow is *b* when it	Judg 16:9	5423
The bows of the mighty men are *b*	1Sa 2:4	2844
of the LORD shall be *b* to pieces	1Sa 2:10	2865
The LORD hath *b* forth upon mine	2Sa 5:20	6555
a bow of steel is *b* by mine arms	2Sa 22:35	5181
altar of the LORD that was *b* down	1Kin 18:30	2040
the ships were *b* at Ezion-geber	1Kin 22:48	7665
the house, that it be not *b* down	2Kin 11:6	4535
And the city was *b* up, and all the	2Kin 25:4	1234
God hath *b* in upon mine enemies	1Chr 14:11	6555

the LORD hath *b* thy works	2Chr 20:37	6555
And the ships were *b*, that they	2Chr 20:37	7665
had *b* up the house of God	2Chr 24:7	6555
that they all were *b* in pieces	2Chr 25:12	1234
built up all the wall that was *b*	2Chr 32:5	6555
Hezekiah his father had *b* down	2Chr 33:3	5422
when he had *b* down the altars and	2Chr 34:7	5422
wall of Jerusalem also is *b* down	Neh 1:3	6555
of Jerusalem, which were *b* down	Neh 2:13	6555
teeth of the young lions, are *b*	Job 4:10	5421
my skin is *b*, and become loathsome	Job 7:5	7280
at ease, but he hath *b* me asunder	Job 16:12	6565
are past, my purposes are *b* off	Job 17:11	5423
of the fatherless have been *b*	Job 22:9	1792
wickedness shall be *b* as a tree	Job 24:20	7665
mine arm be *b* from the bone	Job 31:22	7665
and the high arm shall be *b*	Job 38:15	7665
thou hast *b* the teeth of the	Ps 3:7	7665
a bow of steel is *b* by mine arms	Ps 18:34	5181
I am like a *b* vessel	Ps 31:12	6
unto them that are of a *b* heart	Ps 34:18	7665
not one of them is *b*	Ps 34:20	7665
heart, and their bows shall be *b*	Ps 37:15	7665
the arms of the wicked shall be *b*	Ps 37:17	7665
I am feeble and sore *b*	Ps 38:8	1794
Though thou hast sore *b* us in the	Ps 44:19	1794
which thou hast *b* may rejoice	Ps 51:8	1794
sacrifices of God are a *b* spirit	Ps 51:17	7665
a *b* and a contrite heart, O God,	Ps 51:17	7665
he hath *b* his covenant	Ps 55:20	2490
thou hast *b* it	Ps 60:2	6480
Reproach hath *b* my heart	Ps 69:20	7665
hast thou then *b* down her hedges	Ps 80:12	6555
Thou hast *b* Rahab in pieces, as	Ps 89:10	1792
Thou hast *b* down all his hedges	Ps 89:40	6555
For he hath *b* the gates of brass,	Ps 107:16	7665
he might even slay the *b* in heart	Ps 109:16	5218
the snare is *b*, and we are escaped	Ps 124:7	7665
He healeth the *b* in heart	Ps 147:3	7665
his knowledge the depths are *b* up	Prov 3:20	1234
shall he be *b* without remedy	Prov 6:15	7665
of the heart the spirit is *b*	Prov 15:13	5218
but a *b* spirit drieth the bones	Prov 17:22	5218
the stone wall thereof was *b* down	Prov 24:31	2040
time of trouble is like a *b* tooth	Prov 25:19	7465
is like a city that is *b* down	Prov 25:28	6555
a threefold cord is not quickly *b*	Eccl 4:12	5423
loosed, or the golden bowl be *b*	Eccl 12:6	7533
the pitcher be *b* at the fountain	Eccl 12:6	7665
or the wheel *b* at the cistern	Eccl 12:6	7533
the latchet of their shoes be *b*	Is 5:27	5423
and five years shall Ephraim be *b*	Is 7:8	2844
and ye shall be *b* in pieces	Is 8:9	2844
and ye shall be *b* in pieces	Is 8:9	2844
and ye shall be *b* in pieces	Is 8:9	2844
shall stumble, and fall, and be *b*	Is 8:15	7665
For thou hast *b* the yoke of his	Is 9:4	2865
The LORD hath *b* the staff of the	Is 14:5	7665
rod of him that smote thee is *b*	Is 14:29	7665
have *b* down the principal plants	Is 16:8	1986
they shall be *b* in the purposes	Is 19:10	1792
gods he hath *b* unto the ground	Is 21:9	7665
the houses have ye *b* down to	Is 22:10	5422
b the everlasting covenant	Is 24:5	6565
The city of confusion is *b* down	Is 24:10	7665
The earth is utterly *b* down	Is 24:19	7489
are withered, they shall be *b* off	Is 27:11	7665
go, and fall backward, and be *b*	Is 28:13	7665
vessel that is *b* in pieces	Is 30:14	3807
he hath *b* the covenant, he hath	Is 33:8	6565
any of the cords thereof be *b*	Is 33:20	5423
in the staff of this *b* reed	Is 36:6	7533
b cisterns, that can hold no	Jer 2:13	7665
Tahapanes have *b* the crown of thy	Jer 2:16	7462
For of old time I have *b* thy yoke	Jer 2:20	7665
b down at the presence of the	Jer 4:26	5422
these have altogether *b* the yoke	Jer 5:5	7665
is spoiled, and all my cords are *b*	Jer 10:20	5423
the house of Judah have *b* my	Jer 11:10	6565
it, and the branches of it are *b*	Jer 11:16	7489
people is *b* with a great breach	Jer 14:17	7665
this man Coniah a despised *b* idol	Jer 22:28	5310
me is *b* because of the prophets	Jer 23:9	7665
I have *b* the yoke of the king of	Jer 28:2	7665
b the yoke from off the neck of	Jer 28:12	7665
Thou hast *b* the yokes of wood	Jer 28:13	7665
be *b* with David my servant	Jer 33:21	6565
b up from Jerusalem for fear of	Jer 37:11	5927
of the month, the city was *b* up	Jer 39:2	1234
say, How is the strong staff *b*	Jer 48:17	7665
for it is *b* down	Jer 48:20	2865

Moab is cut off, and his arm is *b*	Jer 48:25	7665
for I have *b* Moab like a vessel	Jer 48:38	7665
howl, saying, How is it *b* down	Jer 48:39	2865
Merodach is *b* in pieces	Jer 50:2	2844
her images are *b* in pieces	Jer 50:2	2865
king of Babylon hath *b* his bones	Jer 50:17	6105
whole earth cut in asunder and *b*	Jer 50:23	7665
her bars are *b*	Jer 51:30	7665
every one of their bows is *b*	Jer 51:56	2865
of Babylon shall be utterly *b*	Jer 51:58	6209
Then the city was *b* up, and all	Jer 52:7	1234
he hath destroyed and *b* her bars	Lam 2:9	7665
he hath *b* my bones	Lam 3:4	7665
He hath also *b* my teeth with	Lam 3:16	1638
and your images shall be *b*	Eze 6:4	7665
desolate, and your idols may be *b*	Eze 6:6	7665
because I am *b* with their whorish	Eze 6:9	7665
and my covenant that he hath *b*	Eze 17:19	6331
her strong rods were *b* and	Eze 19:12	6531
she is *b* that was the gates of	Eze 26:2	7665
the east wind hath *b* thee in the	Eze 27:26	7665
be *b* by the seas in the depths of	Eze 27:34	7665
her foundations shall be *b* down	Eze 30:4	2040
I have *b* the arm of Pharaoh king	Eze 30:21	7665
the strong, and that which was *b*	Eze 30:22	7665
his boughs are *b* by all the	Eze 31:12	7665
thou shalt be *b* in the midst of	Eze 32:28	7665
have ye bound up that which was *b*	Eze 34:4	7665
and will bind up that which was *b*	Eze 34:16	7665
when I have *b* the bands of their	Eze 34:27	7665
they have *b* my covenant because	Eze 44:7	6565
b to pieces together, and became	Dan 2:35	1854
be partly strong, and partly *b*	Dan 2:42	8406
was strong, the great horn was *b*	Dan 8:8	7665
Now that being *b*, whereas four	Dan 8:22	7665
but he shall be *b* without hand	Dan 8:25	7665
stand up, his kingdom shall be *b*	Dan 11:4	7665
from before him, and shall be *b*	Dan 11:22	7665
b in judgment, because he	Hos 5:11	7533
of Samaria shall be *b* in pieces	Hos 8:6	7616
desolate, the barns are *b* down	Joel 1:17	2040
so that the ship was like to be *b*	Jonah 1:4	7665
they have *b* up, and have passed	Mic 2:13	6555
And it was *b* in that day	Zec 11:11	6565
one, nor heal that that is *b*	Zec 11:16	7665
they took up of the *b* meat that	Mt 15:37	2801
fall on this stone shall be *b*	Mt 21:44	4917
suffered his house to be *b* up	Mt 24:43	1358
and when they had *b* it up, they	Mk 2:4	1846
him, and the fetters in pieces	Mk 5:4	4937
they took up of the *b* meat that	Mk 8:8	2801
his house to be *b* through	Lk 12:39	1358
fall upon that stone shall be *b*	Lk 20:18	4917
he not only had *b* the sabbath	Jn 5:18	3089
the law of Moses should not be *b*	Jn 7:23	3089
and the scripture cannot be *b*	Jn 10:35	3089
Pilate that their legs might be *b*	Jn 19:31	2608
A bone of him shall not be *b*	Jn 19:36	4937
so many, yet was not the net *b*	Jn 21:11	4977
when the congregation was *b* up	Acts 13:43	3089
had *b* bread, and eaten, and talked	Acts 20:11	2806
and when he had *b* it, he began to	Acts 27:35	2806
but the hinder part was *b* with	Acts 27:41	3089
some on *b* pieces of the ship	Acts 27:44	
if some of the branches be *b* off	Rom 11:17	1575
say then, The branches were *b* off	Rom 11:19	1575
of unbelief they were *b* off	Rom 11:20	1575
is my body, which is *b* for you	1Cor 11:24	2806
hath *b* down the middle wall of	Eph 2:14	3089
potter shall they be *b* to shivers	Rev 2:27	4937

BROKENFOOTED

Or a man that is *b*, or	Lev 21:19	7667,7272

BROKENHANDED

a man that is brokenfooted, or *b*	Lev 21:19	7667,3027

BROKENHEARTED

he hath sent me to bind up the *b*	Is 61:1	7665,3820
he hath sent me to heal the *b*	Lk 4:18	4937,2588

BROOD

doth gather her *b* under her wings	Lk 13:34	3555

BROOK

them, and sent them over the *b*	Gen 32:23	5158
thick trees, and willows of the *b*	Lev 23:40	5158
And they came unto the *b* of Eshcol	Num 13:23	5158
The place was called the *b* Eshcol	Num 13:24	5158
I, and get you over the *b* Zered	Deut 2:13	5158
And we went over the *b* Zered	Deut 2:13	5158
we were come over the *b* Zered	Deut 2:14	5158
cast the dust thereof into the *b*	Deut 9:21	5158

B

five smooth stones out of the *b*	1Sa 17:40	5158
with him, and came to the *b* Besor	1Sa 30:9	5158
could not go over the *b* Besor	1Sa 30:10	5158
made also to abide at the *b* Besor	1Sa 30:21	5158
himself passed over the *b* Kidron	2Sa 15:23	5158
They be gone over the *b* of water	2Sa 17:20	4323
out, and passest over the *b* Kidron	1Kin 2:37	5158
idol, and burnt it by the *b* Kidron	1Kin 15:13	5158
and hide thyself by the *b* Cherith	1Kin 17:3	5158
that thou shalt drink of the *b*	1Kin 17:4	5158
he went and dwelt by the *b* Cherith	1Kin 17:5	5158
and he drank of the *b*	1Kin 17:6	5158
a while, that the *b* dried up	1Kin 17:7	5158
brought them down to the *b* Kishon	1Kin 18:40	5158
Jerusalem, unto the *b* Kidron	2Kin 23:6	5158
and burned it at the *b* Kidron	2Kin 23:6	5158
dust of them into the *b* Kidron	2Kin 23:12	5158
it, and burnt it at the *b* Kidron	2Chr 15:16	5158
find them at the end of the *b*	2Chr 20:16	5158
it out abroad into the *b* Kidron	2Chr 29:16	5158
and cast them into the *b* Kidron	2Chr 30:14	5158
the *b* that ran through the midst	2Chr 32:4	5158
went I up in the night by the *b*	Neh 2:15	5158
have dealt deceitfully as a *b*	Job 6:15	5158
of the *b* compass him about	Job 40:22	5158
as to Jabin, at the *b* of Kison	Ps 83:9	5158
shall drink of the *b* in the way	Ps 110:7	5158
of wisdom as a flowing *b*	Prov 18:4	5158
away to the *b* of the willows	Is 15:7	5158
the fields unto the *b* of Kidron	Jer 31:40	5158
his disciples over the *b* Cedron	Jn 18:1	5493

BROOKS

Red sea, and in the *b* of Arnon,	Num 21:14	5158
at the stream of the *b* that goeth	Num 21:15	5158
a good land, a land of *b* of water	Deut 8:7	5158
Hiddai of the *b* of Gaash	2Sa 23:30	5158
fountains of water, and unto all *b*	1Kin 18:5	5158
Hurai of the *b* of Gaash, Abiel	1Chr 11:32	5158
as the stream of *b* they pass away	Job 6:15	5158
floods, the *b* of honey and butter	Job 20:17	5158
of Ophir as the stones of the *b*	Job 22:24	5158
hart panteth after the water *b*	Ps 42:1	650
the *b* of defence shall be emptied	Is 19:6	2975
the *b*, by the mouth of the	Is 19:7	2975
and every thing sown by the *b*	Is 19:7	2975
angle into the *b* shall lament	Is 19:8	2975

BROTH

basket, and he put the *b* in a pot	Judg 6:19	4839
upon this rock, and pour out the *b*	Judg 6:20	4839
b of abominable things is in	Is 65:4	6564

BROTHER

And she again bare his *b* Abel	Gen 4:2	251
And Cain talked with Abel his *b*	Gen 4:8	251
Cain rose up against Abel his *b*	Gen 4:8	251
unto Cain, Where is Abel thy *b*	Gen 4:9	251
at the hand of every man's *b* will	Gen 9:5	251
the *b* of Japheth the elder, even	Gen 10:21	251
b of Eshcol, and *b* of Aner	Gen 14:13	251
b of Eshcol, and *b* of Aner	Gen 14:13	251
that his *b* was taken captive	Gen 14:14	251
and also brought again his *b* Lot	Gen 14:16	251
even she herself said, He is my *b*	Gen 20:5	251
shall come, say of me, He is my *b*	Gen 20:13	251
I have given thy *b* a thousand	Gen 20:16	251
born children unto thy *b* Nahor	Gen 22:20	251
Huz his firstborn, and Buz his *b*	Gen 22:21	251
did bear to Nahor, Abraham's *b*	Gen 22:23	251
the wife of Nahor, Abraham's *b*	Gen 24:15	251
And Rebekah had a *b*, and his name	Gen 24:29	251
he gave also to her *b* and to her	Gen 24:53	251
And her *b* and her mother said, Let	Gen 24:55	251
And after that came his *b* out	Gen 25:26	251
thy father speak unto Esau thy *b*	Gen 27:6	251
Esau my *b* is a hairy man, and I am	Gen 27:11	251
were hairy, as his *b* Esau's hands	Gen 27:23	251
that Esau his *b* came in from his	Gen 27:30	251
Thy *b* came with subtilty, and hath	Gen 27:35	251
thou live, and shalt serve thy *b*	Gen 27:40	251
then will I slay my *b* Jacob	Gen 27:41	251
thy *b* Esau, as touching thee,	Gen 27:42	251
flee thou to Laban my *b* to Haran	Gen 27:43	251
daughters of Laban thy mother's *b*	Gen 28:2	251
the *b* of Rebekah, Jacob's and	Gen 28:5	251
daughter of Laban his mother's *b*	Gen 29:10	251
the sheep of Laban his mother's *b*	Gen 29:10	251
the flock of Laban his mother's *b*	Gen 29:10	251
Rachel that he was her father's *b*	Gen 29:12	251
unto Jacob, Because thou art my *b*	Gen 29:15	251
Esau his *b* unto the land of Seir	Gen 32:3	251

saying, We came to thy *b* Esau	Gen 32:6	251
pray thee, from the hand of my *b*	Gen 32:11	251
his hand a present for Esau his *b*	Gen 32:13	251
When Esau my *b* meeteth thee	Gen 32:17	251
until he came near to his *b*	Gen 33:3	251
And Esau said, I have enough, my *b*	Gen 33:9	251
from the face of Esau thy *b*	Gen 35:1	251
he fled from the face of his *b*	Gen 35:7	251
from the face of his *b* Jacob	Gen 36:6	251
profit is it if we slay our *b*	Gen 37:26	251
for he is our *b* and our flesh	Gen 37:27	251
her, and raise up seed to thy *b*	Gen 38:8	251
that he should give seed to his *b*	Gen 38:9	251
that, behold, his *b* came out	Gen 38:29	251
And afterward came out his *b*	Gen 38:30	251
But Benjamin, Joseph's *b*, Jacob	Gen 42:4	251
your youngest *b* come hither	Gen 42:15	251
of you, and let him fetch your *b*	Gen 42:16	251
But bring your youngest *b* unto me	Gen 42:20	251
verily guilty concerning our *b*	Gen 42:21	251
And bring your youngest *b* unto me	Gen 42:34	251
so will I deliver you your *b*	Gen 42:34	251
for his *b* is dead, and he is left	Gen 42:38	251
face, except your *b* be with you	Gen 43:3	251
If thou wilt send our *b* with us	Gen 43:4	251
face, except your *b* be with you	Gen 43:5	251
the man whether ye had yet a *b*	Gen 43:6	251
have ye another *b*	Gen 43:7	251
he would say, Bring your *b* down	Gen 43:7	251
Take also your *b*, and arise, go	Gen 43:13	251
he may send away your other *b*	Gen 43:14	251
saw his *b* Benjamin, his mother's	Gen 43:29	251
and said, Is this your younger *b*	Gen 43:29	251
his bowels did yearn upon his *b*	Gen 43:30	251
saying, Have ye a father, or a *b*	Gen 44:19	251
his *b* is dead, and he alone is	Gen 44:20	251
youngest *b* come down with you	Gen 44:23	251
if our youngest *b* be with us	Gen 44:26	251
except our youngest *b* be with us	Gen 44:26	251
And he said, I am Joseph your *b*	Gen 45:4	251
see, and the eyes of my *b* Benjamin	Gen 45:12	251
fell upon his *b* Benjamin's neck	Gen 45:14	251
but truly his younger *b* shall be	Gen 48:19	251
Is not Aaron the Levite thy *b*	Ex 4:14	251
Aaron thy *b* shall be thy prophet	Ex 7:1	251
Aaron thy *b* shall speak unto	Ex 7:2	251
take thou unto thee Aaron thy *b*	Ex 28:1	251
for Aaron thy *b* for glory	Ex 28:2	251
holy garments for Aaron thy *b*	Ex 28:4	251
shalt put them upon Aaron thy *b*	Ex 28:41	251
the camp, and slay every man his *b*	Ex 32:27	251
man upon his son, and upon his *b*	Ex 32:29	251
Moses, Speak unto Aaron thy *b*	Lev 16:2	251
the nakedness of thy father's *b*	Lev 18:14	251
not hate thy *b* in thine heart	Lev 19:17	251
and for his daughter, and for his *b*	Lev 21:2	251
If thy *b* be waxen poor, and hath	Lev 25:25	251
he redeem that which his *b* sold	Lev 25:25	251
if thy *b* be waxen poor, and fallen	Lev 25:35	251
that thy *b* may live with thee	Lev 25:36	251
if thy *b* that dwelleth by thee be	Lev 25:39	251
thy *b* that dwelleth by him wax	Lev 25:47	251
or for his mother, for his *b*	Num 6:7	251
together, thou, and Aaron thy *b*	Num 20:8	251
of Edom, Thus saith thy *b* Israel	Num 20:14	251
as Aaron thy *b* was gathered	Num 27:13	251
our *b* unto his daughters	Num 36:2	251
between every man and his *b*	Deut 1:16	251
If thy *b*, the son of thy mother,	Deut 13:6	251
it of his neighbour, or of his *b*	Deut 15:2	251
thy *b* thine hand shall release	Deut 15:3	251
shut thine hand from thy poor *b*	Deut 15:7	251
eye be evil against thy poor *b*	Deut 15:9	251
open thine hand wide unto thy *b*	Deut 15:11	251
And if thy *b*, an Hebrew man, or an	Deut 15:12	251
over thee, which is not thy *b*	Deut 17:15	251
testified falsely against his *b*	Deut 19:18	251
thought to have done unto his *b*	Deut 19:19	251
case bring them again unto thy *b*	Deut 22:1	251
if thy *b* be not nigh unto thee,	Deut 22:2	251
thee until thy *b* seek after it	Deut 22:2	251
for he is thy *b*	Deut 23:7	251
not lend upon usury to thy *b*	Deut 23:19	251
but unto thy *b* thou shalt not	Deut 23:20	251
thou dost lend thy *b* any thing	Deut 24:10	7453
then thy *b* should seem vile unto	Deut 25:3	251
her husband's *b* shall go in unto	Deut 25:5	2993
duty of an husband's *b* unto her	Deut 25:5	2992
the name of his *b* which is dead	Deut 25:6	251
My husband's *b* refuseth to raise	Deut 25:7	2993
up unto his *b* a name in Israel	Deut 25:7	251

the duty of my husband's *b*	Deut 25:7	2992
eye shall be evil toward his *b*	Deut 28:54	251
as Aaron thy *b* died in mount Hor,	Deut 32:50	251
of Kenaz, the *b* of Caleb, took it	Josh 15:17	251
And Judah said unto Simeon his *b*	Judg 1:3	251
son of Kenaz, Caleb's younger *b*	Judg 1:13	251
And Judah went with Simeon his *b*	Judg 1:17	251
son of Kenaz, Caleb's younger *b*	Judg 3:9	251
for they said, He is our *b*	Judg 9:3	251
of Shechem, because he is your *b*	Judg 9:18	251
for fear of Abimelech his *b*	Judg 9:21	251
be laid upon Abimelech their *b*	Judg 9:24	251
the children of Benjamin my *b*	Judg 20:23	251
the children of Benjamin my *b*	Judg 20:28	251
them for Benjamin their *b*	Judg 21:6	251
land, which was our *b* Elimelech's	Ruth 4:3	251
the son of Ahitub, I-chabod's *b*	1Sa 14:3	251
Eliab his eldest *b* heard when he	1Sa 17:28	251
and my *b*, he hath commanded me to	1Sa 20:29	251
b to Joab, saying, Who will go	1Sa 26:6	251
for thee, my *b* Jonathan	2Sa 1:26	251
I hold up my face to Joab thy *b*	2Sa 2:22	251
up every one from following his *b*	2Sa 2:27	251
for the blood of Asahel his *b*	2Sa 3:27	251
Joab and Abishai his *b* slew Abner	2Sa 3:30	251
because he had slain their *b*	2Sa 3:30	251
Rechab and Baanah his *b* escaped	2Sa 4:6	251
answered Rechab and Baanah his *b*	2Sa 4:9	251
into the hand of Abishai his *b*	2Sa 10:10	251
the son of Shimeah David's *b*	2Sa 13:3	251
love Tamar, my *b* Absalom's sister	2Sa 13:4	251
Go now to thy *b* Amnon's house	2Sa 13:7	251
Tamar went to her *b* Amnon's house	2Sa 13:8	251
into the chamber to Amnon her *b*	2Sa 13:10	251
And she answered him, Nay, my *b*	2Sa 13:12	251
Absalom her *b* said unto her	2Sa 13:20	251
Hath Amnon thy *b* been with thee	2Sa 13:20	251
he is thy *b*	2Sa 13:20	251
desolate in her *b* Absalom's house	2Sa 13:20	251
Absalom spake unto his *b* Amnon	2Sa 13:22	251
let my *b* Amnon go with us	2Sa 13:26	251
the son of Shimeah David's *b*	2Sa 13:32	251
Deliver him that smote his *b*	2Sa 14:7	251
the life of his *b* whom he slew	2Sa 14:7	251
the son of Zeruiah, Joab's *b*	2Sa 18:2	251
Amasa, Art thou in health, my *b*	2Sa 20:9	251
Abishai his *b* pursued after Sheba	2Sa 20:10	251
slew the *b* of Goliath the Gittite	2Sa 21:19	251
Shimeah the *b* of David slew him	2Sa 21:21	251
the *b* of Joab, the son of Zeruiah	2Sa 23:18	251
Asahel the *b* of Joab was one of	2Sa 23:24	251
the mighty men, and Solomon his *b*	1Kin 1:10	251
I fled because of Absalom thy *b*	1Kin 2:7	251
given to Adonijah thy *b* to wife	1Kin 2:21	251
for he is mine elder *b*	1Kin 2:22	251
which thou hast given me, my *b*	1Kin 9:13	251
over him, saying, Alas, my *b*	1Kin 13:30	251
he is my *b*	1Kin 20:32	251
and they said, Thy *b* Ben-hadad	1Kin 20:33	251
his father's *b* king in his stead	2Kin 24:17	251
the sons of Jada the *b* of Shammai	1Chr 2:32	251
of Caleb the *b* of Jerahmeel were	1Chr 2:42	251
Chelub the *b* of Shuah begat Mehir	1Chr 4:11	251
his *b* Asaph, who stood on his	1Chr 6:39	251
and the name of his *b* was Sheresh	1Chr 7:16	251
And the sons of his *b* Helem	1Chr 7:35	251
And the sons of Eshek his *b* were	1Chr 8:39	251
And Abishai the *b* of Joab, he was	1Chr 11:20	251
armies unto Asahel the *b* of Joab	1Chr 11:26	251
Joel the *b* of Nathan, Mibhar the	1Chr 11:38	251
the son of Shimri, and Joha his *b*	1Chr 11:45	251
unto the hand of Abishai his *b*	1Chr 19:11	251
fled before Abishai his *b*	1Chr 19:15	251
the *b* of Goliath the Gittite	1Chr 20:5	251
son of Shimea David's *b* slew him	1Chr 20:7	251
The *b* of Michah was Isshiah	1Chr 24:25	1730
Zetham, and Joel his *b*, which were	1Chr 26:22	251
month was Asahel the *b* of Joab	1Chr 27:7	251
Shimei his *b* was the next	2Chr 31:12	251
hand of Cononiah and Shimei his *b*	2Chr 31:13	251
Eliakim his *b* king over Judah	2Chr 36:4	251
And Necho took Jehoahaz his *b*	2Chr 36:4	251
Zedekiah his *b* king over Judah	2Chr 36:10	251
exact usury, every one of his *b*	Neh 5:7	251
That I gave my *b* Hanani, and	Neh 7:2	251
a pledge from thy *b* for nought	Job 22:6	251
I am a *b* to dragons, and a	Job 30:29	251
though he had been my friend or *b*	Ps 35:14	251
can by any means redeem his *b*	Ps 49:7	251
sittest and speakest against thy *b*	Ps 50:20	251
a *b* is born for adversity	Prov 17:17	251
b to him that is a great waster	Prov 18:9	251
A *b* offended is harder to be won	Prov 18:19	251
that sticketh closer than a *b*	Prov 18:24	251
that is near than a *b* far off	Prov 27:10	251
yea, he hath neither child nor *b*	Eccl 4:8	251
O that thou wert as my *b*, that	Song 8:1	251
his *b* of the house of his father	Is 3:6	251
no man shall spare his *b*	Is 9:19	251
fight every one against his *b*	Is 19:2	251
and every one said to his *b*	Is 41:6	251
and trust ye not in any *b*	Jer 9:4	251
for every *b* will utterly supplant	Jer 9:4	251
lament for him, saying, Ah my *b*	Jer 22:18	251
neighbour, and every one to his *b*	Jer 23:35	251
his neighbour, and every man his *b*	Jer 31:34	251
of them, to wit, of a Jew his *b*	Jer 34:9	251
ye go every man his *b* an Hebrew	Jer 34:14	251
liberty, every one to his *b*	Jer 34:17	251
spoiled his *b* by violence	Eze 18:18	251
to another, every one to his *b*	Eze 33:30	251
sword shall be against his *b*	Eze 38:21	251
for son, or for daughter, for *b*	Eze 44:25	251
He took his *b* by the heel in the	Hos 12:3	251
did pursue his *b* with the sword	Amos 1:11	251
b Jacob shame shall cover thee	Obad 10	251
thy *b* in the day that he became a	Obad 12	251
hunt every man his *b* with a net	Mic 7:2	251
every one by the sword of his *b*	Hag 2:22	251
and compassions every man to his *b*	Zec 7:9	251
evil against his *b* in your heart	Zec 7:10	251
Was not Esau Jacob's *b*	Mal 1:2	251
every man against his *b*, by	Mal 2:10	251
called Peter, and Andrew his *b*	Mt 4:18	80
the son of Zebedee, and John his *b*	Mt 4:21	80
his *b* without a cause shall be in	Mt 5:22	80
and whosoever shall say to his *b*	Mt 5:22	80
thy *b* hath ought against thee	Mt 5:23	80
first be reconciled to thy *b*	Mt 5:24	80
Or how wilt thou say to thy *b*	Mt 7:4	80
is called Peter, and Andrew his *b*	Mt 10:2	80
the son of Zebedee, and John his *b*	Mt 10:2	80
b deliver up the *b* to death	Mt 10:21	80
is in heaven, the same is my *b*	Mt 12:50	80
sake, his *b* Philip's wife	Mt 14:3	80
Peter, James, and John his *b*	Mt 17:1	80
Moreover if thy *b* shall trespass	Mt 18:15	80
hear thee, thou hast gained thy *b*	Mt 18:15	80
how oft shall my *b* sin against me	Mt 18:21	80
every one his *b* their trespasses	Mt 18:35	80
his *b* shall marry his wife	Mt 22:24	80
and raise up seed unto his *b*	Mt 22:24	80
issue, left his wife unto his *b*	Mt 22:25	80
Andrew his *b* casting a net into	Mk 1:16	80
the son of Zebedee, and John his *b*	Mk 1:19	80
Zebedee, and John the *b* of James	Mk 3:17	80
the will of God, the same is my *b*	Mk 3:35	80
and James, and John the *b* of James	Mk 5:37	80
the *b* of James, and Joses, and of	Mk 6:3	80
sake, his *b* Philip's wife	Mk 6:17	80
wrote unto us, If a man's *b* die	Mk 12:19	80
that his *b* should take his wife,	Mk 12:19	80
and raise up seed unto his *b*	Mk 12:19	80
b shall betray the *b* to death	Mk 13:12	80
his *b* Philip tetrarch of Ituraea	Lk 3:1	80
for Herodias his *b* Philip's wife	Lk 3:19	80
named Peter,) and Andrew his *b*	Lk 6:14	80
And Judas the *b* of James, and Judas	Lk 6:16	80
canst thou say to thy *b*, B.	Lk 6:42	80
unto him, Master, speak to my *b*	Lk 12:13	80
he said unto him, Thy *b* is come	Lk 15:27	80
for this thy *b* was dead, and is	Lk 15:32	80
If thy *b* trespass against thee,	Lk 17:3	80
wrote unto us, If any man's *b* die	Lk 20:28	80
that his *b* should take his wife,	Lk 20:28	80
wife, and raise up seed unto his *b*	Lk 20:28	80
him, was Andrew, Simon Peter's *b*	Jn 1:40	80
He first findeth his own *b* Simon	Jn 1:41	80
Andrew, Simon Peter's *b*, saith	Jn 6:8	80
hair, whose *b* Lazarus was sick	Jn 11:2	80
comfort them concerning their *b*	Jn 11:19	80
been here, my *b* had not died	Jn 11:21	80
unto her, Thy *b* shall rise again	Jn 11:23	80
been here, my *b* had not died	Jn 11:32	80
Zelotes, and Judas the *b* of James	Acts 1:13	80
B Saul, the Lord, even Jesus,	Acts 9:17	80
he killed James the *b* of John	Acts 12:2	80
and said unto him, Thou seest, *b*	Acts 21:20	80
B Saul, receive thy sight	Acts 22:13	80
But why dost thou judge thy *b*	Rom 14:10	80
why dost thou set at nought thy *b*	Rom 14:10	80
But if thy *b* be grieved with thy	Rom 14:15	80

any thing whereby thy *b* stumbleth........Rom 14:21   80
city saluteth you, and Quartus a *b*.........Rom 16:23   80
will of God, and Sosthenes our *b*...............1Cor 1:1   80
is called a *b* be a fornicator 1Cor 5:11   80
But *b* goeth to law with *b*,......................1Cor 6:6   80
If any *b* hath a wife that.............................1Cor 7:12   80
A *b* or a sister is not under 1Cor 7:15   80
knowledge shall the weak *b* perish 1Cor 8:11   80
if meat make my *b* to offend 1Cor 8:13   80
lest I make my *b* to offend.......................1Cor 8:13   80
As touching our *b* Apollos 1Cor 16:12   80
the will of God, and Timothy our *b* 2Cor 1:1   80
because I found not Titus my *b* 2Cor 2:13   80
And we have sent with him the *b* 2Cor 8:18   80
And we have sent with them our *b* 2Cor 8:22   80
Titus, and with him I sent a *b* 2Cor 12:18   80
I none, save James the Lord's *b* ....Gal 1:19   80
how I do, Tychicus, a beloved *b* ....Eph 6:21   80
to send to you Epaphroditus, my *b*.........Phil 2:25   80
will of God, and Timothy our *b* ....Col 1:1   80
unto you, who is a beloved *b*....................Col 4:7   80
Onesimus, a faithful and beloved *b* ....Col 4:9   80
And sent Timotheus, our *b*, and.............1Th 3:2   80
defraud his *b* in any matter....................1Th 4:6   80
every *b* that walketh disorderly 2Th 3:6   80
an enemy, but admonish him as a *b* 2Th 3:15   80
of Jesus Christ, and Timothy our *b* ......Philem 1   80
saints are refreshed by thee, *b*,...........Philem 7   80
a *b* beloved, specially to me, but.........Philem 16   80
Yea, *b*, let me have joy of thee............Philem 20   80
his neighbour, and every man his *b* ......Heb 8:11   80
Know ye that our *b* Timothy is set ....Heb 13:23   80
Let the *b* of low degree rejoice ....Jas 1:9   80
If a *b* or sister be naked, and................Jas 2:15   80
He that speaketh evil of his *b* ....Jas 4:11   80
of his *b*, and judgeth his *b* ....Jas 4:11   80
Silvanus, a faithful *b* unto you..............1Pet 5:12   80
even as our beloved *b* Paul also............2Pet 3:15   80
is in the light, and hateth his *b* 1Jn 2:9   80
He that loveth his *b* abideth in 1Jn 2:10   80
that hateth his *b* is in darkness..............1Jn 2:11   80
neither he that loveth not his *b* 1Jn 3:10   80
of that wicked one, and slew his *b*..........1Jn 3:12   80
loveth not his *b* abideth in death 1Jn 3:14   80
hateth his *b* is a murderer.....................1Jn 3:15   80
good, and seeth his *b* have need.............1Jn 3:17   80
say, I love God, and hateth his *b* 1Jn 4:20   80
not his *b* whom he hath seen 1Jn 4:20   80
he who loveth God love his *b* also 1Jn 4:21   80
If any man see his *b* sin a sin..................1Jn 5:16   80
b of James, to them that are ....Jude 1   80
I John, who also am your *b* ....Rev 1:9   80

BROTHERHOOD
I might break the *b* between Judah ....Zec 11:14   264
Love the *b* 1Pet 2:17   *81*

BROTHERLY
and remembered not the *b* covenant......Amos 1:9   251
one to another with *b* love ....Rom 12:10   5360
But as touching *b* love ye need 1Th 4:9   5360
Let *b* love continue ....Heb 13:1   5360
And to godliness *b* kindness 2Pet 1:7   5360
and to *b* kindness charity.........................2Pet 1:7   5360

BROTHER'S
Am I my *b* keeper ....Gen 4:9   251
the voice of thy *b* blood crieth ....Gen 4:10   251
receive thy *b* blood from thy hand ....Gen 4:11   251
And his *b* name was Jubal ....Gen 4:21   251
and his *b* name was Joktan....................Gen 10:25   251
Sarai his wife, and Lot his his son ....Gen 12:5   251
And they took Lot, Abram's *b* son ....Gen 14:12   251
master's *b* daughter unto his son...........Gen 24:48   251
until thy *b* fury turn away ....Gen 27:44   251
Until thy *b* anger turn away from ....Gen 27:45   251
unto Onan, Go in unto thy *b* wife ....Gen 38:8   251
when he went in unto his *b* wife ....Gen 38:9   251
the nakedness of thy *b* wife ....Lev 18:16   251
it is thy *b* nakedness................................Lev 18:16   251
And if a man shall take his *b* wife ....Lev 20:21   251
he hath uncovered his *b* nakedness ....Lev 20:21   251
Thou shalt not see thy *b* ox or ....Deut 22:1   251
and with all lost things of thy *b* ....Deut 22:3   251
Thou shalt not see thy *b* ass or..............Deut 22:4   251
man like not to take his *b* wife ....Deut 25:7   2994
then let his *b* wife go up to the ....Deut 25:7   2994
Then shall his *b* wife come unto ....Deut 25:9   2994
will not build up his *b* house ....Deut 25:9   251
turned about, and is become my *b* 1Kin 1:19   251
and his *b* name was Joktan.....................1Chr 1:19   251
wine in their eldest *b* house ....Job 1:13   251

wine in their eldest *b* house ....Job 1:18   251
neither go into thy *b* house in ....Prov 27:10   251
the mote that is in thy *b* eye ....Mt 7:3   *80*
out the mote out of thy *b* eye ....Mt 7:5   *80*
for thee to have thy *b* wife ....Mk 6:18   *80*
the mote that is in thy *b* eye ....Lk 6:41   *80*
out the mote that is in thy *b* eye...........Lk 6:42   *80*
an occasion to fall in his *b* way ....Rom 14:13   *80*
were evil, and his *b* righteous 1Jn 3:12   *80*

BROTHERS'
unto their father's *b* sons ....Num 36:11   1730

BROUGHT See APPENDIX.

BROUGHTEST See APPENDIX.

BROW
is an iron sinew, and thy *b* brass ....Is 48:4   *4696*
led him unto the *b* of the hill.................Lk 4:29   *3790*

BROWN
all the *b* cattle among the sheep, ...Gen 30:32   2345
b among the sheep, that shall be............Gen 30:33   2345
all the *b* among the sheep, and ....Gen 30:35   2345
all the *b* in the flock of Laban................Gen 30:40   2345

BRUISE
it shall *b* thy head, and thou ....Gen 3:15   7779
head, and thou shalt *b* his heel...............Gen 3:15   7779
nor *b* it with his horsemen ....Is 28:28   1854
Yet it pleased the LORD to *b* him..............Is 53:10   1792
Thy *b* is incurable, and thy wound ....Jer 30:12   7667
shall it break in pieces and *b*..................Dan 2:40   7490
There is no healing of thy *b*......................Nah 3:19   7667
the God of peace shall *b* Satan ....Rom 16:20   *4937*

BRUISED
unto the LORD that which is *b* ....Lev 22:24   4600
upon the staff of this *b* reed...................2Kin 18:21   7533
Bread corn is *b*..Is 28:28   1854
A *b* reed shall he not break, and ....Is 42:3   7533
he was *b* for our iniquities ....Is 53:5   1792
there they *b* the teats of their ....Eze 23:3   6213
they *b* the breasts of her..........................Eze 23:8   6213
A *b* reed shall he not break, and ....Mt 12:20   *4937*
to set at liberty them that are *b* ....Lk 4:18   *2352*

BRUISES
but wounds, and *b*, and putrifying.........Is 1:6   2250

BRUISING
in *b* thy teats by the Egyptians ....Eze 23:21   6213
b him hardly departeth from him ....Lk 9:39   *4937*

BRUIT
the noise of the *b* is come ....Jer 10:22   8052
all that hear the *b* of thee shall ....Nah 3:19   8088

BRUTE
But these, as natural *b* beasts 2Pet 2:12   *249*
as *b* beasts, in those things they ....Jude 10   *249*

BRUTISH
the *b* person perish, and leave ....Ps 49:10   1197
A *b* man knoweth not ....Ps 92:6   1197
Understand, ye *b* among the people ....Ps 94:8   1197
but he that hateth reproof is *b*.............Prov 12:1   1197
Surely I am more *b* than any man ....Prov 30:2   1197
of Pharaoh is become *b* ....Is 19:11   1197
But they are altogether *b* ....Jer 10:8   1197
Every man is *b* in his knowledge...........Jer 10:14   1197
For the pastors are become *b* ....Jer 10:21   1197
Every man is *b* by his knowledge ....Jer 51:17   1197
thee into the hand of *b* men ....Eze 21:31   1197

BUCKET
the nations are as a drop of a *b*..............Is 40:15   1805

BUCKETS
shall pour the water out of his *b* ....Num 24:7   1805

BUCKLER
he is a *b* to all them that trust 2Sa 22:31   4043
valiant men, men able to bear *b* 1Chr 5:18   4043
that could handle shield and *b*................1Chr 12:8   7420
my *b*, and the horn of my salvation ....Ps 18:2   4043
he is a *b* to all those that trust ....Ps 18:30   4043
Take hold of shield and *b*, and ....Ps 35:2   6793
truth shall be thy shield and *b* ....Ps 91:4   5507
he is a *b* to them that walk ....Prov 2:7   4043
Order ye the *b* and shield, and draw ....Jer 46:3   4043
which shall set against thee *b* ....Eze 23:24   6793
lift up the *b* against thee ....Eze 26:8   6793

BUCKLERS
captains of hundreds spears, and *b* 2Chr 23:9   4043
upon the thick bosses of his *b* ....Job 15:26   4043
whereon there hang a thousand *b* ....Song 4:4   4043

B

even a great company with *b*	Eze 38:4	6793
both the shields and the *b*	Eze 39:9	6793

BUD

the scent of water it will *b*	Job 14:9	6524
to cause the *b* of the tender herb	Job 38:27	4161
I make the horn of David to *b*	Ps 132:17	6779
and the pomegranates *b* forth	Song 7:12	5132
when the *b* is perfect, and the	Is 18:5	6525
Israel shall blossom and *b*	Is 27:6	6524
and maketh it bring forth and *b*	Is 55:10	6779
as the earth bringeth forth her *b*	Is 61:11	6779
to multiply as the *b* of the field	Eze 16:7	6779
of the house of Israel to *b* forth	Eze 29:21	6779
the *b* shall yield no meal	Hos 8:7	6779

BUDDED

and it was as though it *b*, and her	Gen 40:10	6524
Aaron for the house of Levi was *b*	Num 17:8	6524
flourished, and the pomegranates *b*	Song 6:11	5132
rod hath blossomed, pride hath *b*	Eze 7:10	6524
had manna, and Aaron's rod that *b*	Heb 9:4	985

BUDS

was budded, and brought forth *b*	Num 17:8	6525

BUFFET

to *b* him, and to say unto him,	Mk 14:65	2852
the messenger of Satan to *b* me	2Cor 12:7	2852

BUFFETED

they spit in his face, and *b* him	Mt 26:67	2852
and thirst, and are naked, and are *b*	1Cor 4:11	2852
when ye be *b* for your faults, ye	1Pet 2:20	2852

BUILD

let us *b* us a city and a tower,	Gen 11:4	1129
and they left off to *b* the city	Gen 11:8	1129
thou shalt not *b* it of hewn stone	Ex 20:25	1129
B me here seven altars, and	Num 23:1	1129
B me here seven altars, and	Num 23:29	1129
We will *b* sheepfolds here for our	Num 32:16	1129
B you cities for your little ones	Num 32:24	1129
thou shalt *b* bulwarks against the	Deut 20:20	1129
will not *b* up thy brother's house	Deut 25:9	1129
there shalt thou *b* an altar unto	Deut 27:5	1129
Thou shalt *b* the altar of the	Deut 27:6	1129
thou shalt *b* an house, and thou	Deut 28:30	1129
us now prepare to *b* us an altar	Josh 22:26	1129
to *b* an altar for burnt offerings	Josh 22:29	1129
b an altar unto the LORD thy God	Judg 6:26	1129
which two did *b* the house of	Ruth 4:11	1129
I will *b* him a sure house	1Sa 2:35	1129
Shalt thou *b* me an house for me	2Sa 7:5	1129
Why ye not me an house of cedar	2Sa 7:7	1129
He shall *b* an house for my name,	2Sa 7:13	1129
saying, I will *b* thee an house	2Sa 7:27	1129
to *b* an altar unto the LORD, that	2Sa 24:21	1129
B thee an house in Jerusalem, and	1Kin 2:36	1129
b an house unto the name of the	1Kin 5:3	1129
I purpose to *b* an house unto the	1Kin 5:5	1129
he shall *b* an house unto my name	1Kin 5:5	1129
timber and stones to *b* the house	1Kin 5:18	1129
that he began to *b* the house of	1Kin 6:1	1129
tribes of Israel to *b* an house	1Kin 8:16	1129
to *b* an house for the name of the	1Kin 8:17	1129
heart to *b* an house unto my name	1Kin 8:18	1129
thou shalt not *b* the house	1Kin 8:19	1129
he shall *b* the house unto my name	1Kin 8:19	1129
for to *b* the house of the LORD,	1Kin 9:15	1129
Solomon desired to *b* in Jerusalem	1Kin 9:19	1129
then did he *b* Millo	1Kin 9:24	1129
Then did Solomon *b* an high place	1Kin 11:7	1129
b thee a sure house, as I built	1Kin 11:38	1129
did Hiel the Beth-elite *b* Jericho	1Kin 16:34	1129
and carpenters, to *b* him an house	1Chr 14:1	1129
Thou shalt not *b* me an house to	1Chr 17:4	1129
the LORD will *b* thee an house	1Chr 17:10	1129
He shall *b* me an house, and I will	1Chr 17:12	1129
that thou wilt *b* him an house	1Chr 17:25	1129
that I may *b* an altar therein	1Chr 21:22	1129
stones to *b* the house of God	1Chr 22:2	1129
charged him to *b* an house for the	1Chr 22:6	1129
it was in my mind to *b* an house	1Chr 22:7	1129
thou shalt not *b* an house unto my	1Chr 22:8	1129
He shall *b* an house for my name	1Chr 22:10	1129
b the house of the LORD thy God,	1Chr 22:11	1129
b ye the sanctuary of the LORD	1Chr 22:19	1129
I had in mine heart to *b* an house	1Chr 28:2	1129
Thou shalt not *b* an house for my	1Chr 28:3	1129
thy son, he shall *b* my house	1Chr 28:6	1129
to *b* an house for the sanctuary	1Chr 28:10	1129
to *b* thee an house for thine holy	1Chr 29:16	1129
to *b* the palace, for the which I	1Chr 29:19	1129

Solomon determined to *b* an house	2Chr 2:1	1129
didst send him cedars to *b* him an	2Chr 2:3	1129
I *b* an house to the name of the	2Chr 2:4	1129
And the house which I *b* is great	2Chr 2:5	1129
But who is able to *b* him an house	2Chr 2:6	1129
that I should *b* him an house	2Chr 2:6	1129
to *b* shall be wonderful great	2Chr 2:9	1129
that might *b* an house for the	2Chr 2:12	1129
Then Solomon began to *b* the house	2Chr 3:1	1129
he began to *b* in the second day	2Chr 3:2	1129
tribes of Israel to *b* an house in	2Chr 6:5	1129
to *b* an house for the name of the	2Chr 6:7	1129
heart to *b* an house for my name	2Chr 6:8	1129
thou shalt not *b* the house	2Chr 6:9	1129
he shall *b* the house for my name	2Chr 6:9	1129
Solomon desired to *b* in Jerusalem	2Chr 8:6	1129
Let us *b* these cities, and make	2Chr 14:7	1129
son of David king of Israel did *b*	2Chr 35:3	1129
he hath charged me to *b* him an	2Chr 36:23	1129
he hath charged me to *b* him an	Ezr 1:2	1129
b the house of the LORD God of	Ezr 1:3	1129
to go up to *b* the house of the	Ezr 1:5	1129
said unto them, Let us *b* with you	Ezr 4:2	1129
us to *b* an house unto our God	Ezr 4:3	1129
b unto the LORD God of Israel	Ezr 4:3	1129
began to *b* the house of God which	Ezr 5:2	1124
commanded you to *b* this house	Ezr 5:3	1124
Who commanded you to *b* this house	Ezr 5:9	1124
b the house that was builded	Ezr 5:11	1129
a decree to *b* this house of God	Ezr 5:13	1124
was made of Cyrus the king to *b*	Ezr 5:17	1124
the elders of the Jews this	Ezr 6:7	1124
sepulchres, that I may *b* it	Neh 2:5	1129
let us *b* up the wall of Jerusalem	Neh 2:17	1129
And they said, Let us rise up and *b*	Neh 2:18	1129
we his servants will arise and *b*	Neh 2:20	1129
gate did the sons of Hassenaah *b*	Neh 3:3	1129
he said, Even that which they *b*	Neh 4:3	1129
we are not able to *b* the wall	Neh 4:10	1129
destroy them, and not *b* them up	Ps 28:5	1129
b thou the walls of Jerusalem	Ps 51:18	1129
will *b* the cities of Judah	Ps 69:35	1129
ever, and *b* up thy throne to all	Ps 89:4	1129
When the LORD shall *b* up Zion	Ps 102:16	1129
Except the LORD *b* the house	Ps 127:1	1129
they labour in vain that *b* it	Ps 127:1	1129
The LORD doth *b* up Jerusalem	Ps 147:2	1129
and afterwards *b* thine house	Prov 24:27	1129
to break down, and a time to *b* up	Eccl 3:3	1129
we will *b* upon her a palace of	Song 8:9	1129
but we will *b* with hewn stones	Is 9:10	1129
he shall *b* my city, and he shall	Is 45:13	1129
thee shall *b* the old waste places	Is 58:12	1129
of strangers shall *b* up thy walls	Is 60:10	1129
they shall *b* the old wastes, they	Is 61:4	1129
And they shall *b* houses, and	Is 65:21	1129
They shall not *b*, and another	Is 65:22	1129
is the house that ye *b* unto me	Is 66:1	1129
destroy, and to throw down, to *b*	Jer 1:10	1129
and concerning a kingdom, to *b*	Jer 18:9	1129
I will *b* me a wide house and large	Jer 22:14	1129
and I will *b* them, and not pull	Jer 24:6	1129
B ye houses, and dwell in them	Jer 29:5	1129
b ye houses, and dwell in them	Jer 29:28	1129
Again I will *b* thee, and thou	Jer 31:4	1129
so will I watch over them, to *b*	Jer 31:28	1129
Israel to return, and will *b* them	Jer 33:7	1129
Neither shall ye *b* house, nor sow	Jer 35:7	1129
Nor to *b* houses for us to dwell	Jer 35:9	1129
in this land, then will I *b* you	Jer 42:10	1129
b a fort against it, and cast a	Eze 4:2	1129
let us *b* houses	Eze 11:3	1129
to cast a mount, and to *b* a fort	Eze 21:22	1129
and shall *b* houses, and plant	Eze 28:26	1129
I the LORD *b* the ruined places	Eze 36:36	1129
to *b* Jerusalem unto the Messiah	Dan 9:25	1129
I will *b* it as in the days of old	Amos 9:11	1129
they shall *b* the waste cities, and	Amos 9:14	1129
They *b* up Zion with blood, and	Mic 3:10	1129
they shall also *b* houses, but not	Zeph 1:13	1129
and bring wood, and *b* the house	Hag 1:8	1129
To *b* it an house in the land of	Zec 5:11	1129
he shall *b* the temple of the LORD	Zec 6:12	1129
Even he shall *b* the temple of the	Zec 6:13	1129
b in the temple of the LORD, and	Zec 6:15	1129
Tyrus did *b* herself a strong hold	Zec 9:3	1129
return and *b* the desolate places	Mal 1:4	1129
the LORD of hosts, They shall *b*	Mal 1:4	1129
upon this rock I will *b* my church	Mt 16:18	3618
because ye *b* the tombs of the	Mt 23:29	3618
of God, and to *b* it in three days	Mt 26:61	3618

within three days I will *b*	Mk 14:58	3618
Woe unto you! for ye *b* the	Lk 11:47	3618
them, and ye *b* their sepulchres	Lk 11:48	3618
pull down my barns, and *b* greater	Lk 12:18	3618
of you, intending to *b* a tower	Lk 14:28	3618
Saying, This man began to *b*	Lk 14:30	3618
what house will ye *b* me	Acts 7:49	3618
will *b* again the tabernacle of	Acts 15:16	456
I will *b* again the ruins thereof,	Acts 15:16	456
grace, which is able to *b* you up	Acts 20:32	2026
lest I should *b* upon another	Rom 15:20	3618
Now if any man *b* upon this	1Cor 3:12	2026
For if I *b* again the things which	Gal 2:18	3618

BUILDED

he *b* a city, and called the name	Gen 4:17	1129
Noah *b* an altar unto the LORD	Gen 8:20	1129
b Nineveh, and the city Rehoboth,	Gen 10:11	1129
which the children of men *b*	Gen 11:5	1129
there *b* he an altar unto the LORD	Gen 12:7	1129
there he *b* an altar unto the LORD	Gen 12:8	1129
he *b* an altar there, and called	Gen 26:25	1129
b an altar under the hill, and	Ex 24:4	1129
unto the cities which they *b*	Num 32:38	1129
in that ye have *b* you an altar	Josh 22:16	1129
less this house that I have *b*	1Kin 8:27	1129
that this house, which I have *b*	1Kin 8:43	1129
thereof, wherewith Baasha had *b*	1Kin 15:22	1129
b for Ashtoreth the abomination	2Kin 23:13	1129
the house that is to be *b* for the	1Chr 22:5	1129
b the altar of the God of Israel,	Ezr 3:2	1129
the children of the captivity *b*	Ezr 4:1	1129
the king, that, if this city be *b*	Ezr 4:13	1124
that, if this city be *b* again	Ezr 4:16	1124
cease, and that this city be not *b*	Ezr 4:21	1124
which is *b* with great stones, and	Ezr 5:8	1124
that was *b* these many years ago	Ezr 5:11	1124
which a great king of Israel *b*	Ezr 5:11	1124
house of God be *b* in his place	Ezr 5:15	1124
at Jerusalem, Let the house be *b*	Ezr 6:3	1124
And the elders of the Jews *b*	Ezr 6:14	1124
And they *b*, and finished it,	Ezr 6:14	1124
priests, and they *b* the sheep gate	Neh 3:1	1129
next unto him *b* the men of	Neh 3:2	1129
next to them *b* Zaccur the son of	Neh 3:2	1129
heard that we *b* the wall, he was	Neh 4:1	1129
They which *b* on the wall, and they	Neh 4:17	1129
sword girded by his side, and so *b*	Neh 4:18	1129
heard that I had *b* the wall	Neh 6:1	1129
therein, and the houses were not *b*	Neh 7:4	1129
for the singers had *b* them	Neh 12:29	1129
away an house which he *b* not	Job 20:19	1129
Jerusalem is *b* as a city that is	Ps 122:3	1129
Wisdom hath *b* her house, she hath	Prov 9:1	1129
Through wisdom is an house *b*	Prov 24:3	1129
I *b* me houses	Eccl 2:4	1129
tower of David *b* for an armoury	Song 4:4	1129
city shall be *b* upon her own heap	Jer 30:18	1129
He hath *b* against me, and	Lam 3:5	1129
and the wastes shall be *b*	Eze 36:10	1129
cities, and the wastes shall be *b*	Eze 36:33	1129
they sold, they planted, they *b*	Lk 17:28	3618
In whom ye also are *b* together	Eph 2:22	4925
inasmuch as he who hath *b* the	Heb 3:3	2680
For every house is *b* by some man	Heb 3:4	2680

BUILDEDST

goodly cities, which thou *b* not	Deut 6:10	1129

BUILDER

which hath foundations, whose *b*	Heb 11:10	5079

BUILDERS

Solomon's *b* and Hiram's *b*	1Kin 5:18	1129
it out to the carpenters and *b*	2Kin 12:11	1129
Unto carpenters, and *b*, and masons,	2Kin 22:6	1129
b gave they it, to buy hewn stone	2Chr 34:11	1129
when the *b* laid the foundation of	Ezr 3:10	1129
thee to anger before the *b*	Neh 4:5	1129
For the *b*, every one had his	Neh 4:18	1129
The stone which the *b* refused is	Ps 118:22	1129
thy *b* have perfected thy beauty	Eze 27:4	1129
The stone which the *b* rejected	Mt 21:42	3618
The stone which the *b* rejected is	Mk 12:10	3618
The stone which the *b* rejected	Lk 20:17	3618
which was set at nought of you *b*	Acts 4:11	3618
the stone which the *b* disallowed	1Pet 2:7	3618

BUILDEST

When thou *b* a new house, then	Deut 22:8	1129
for which cause thou *b* the wall	Neh 6:6	1129
In that thou *b* thine eminent	Eze 16:31	1129

b it in three days, save thyself	Mt 27:40	3618
temple, and *b* it in three days,	Mk 15:29	3618

BUILDETH

riseth up and *b* this city Jericho	Josh 6:26	1129
He *b* his house as a moth, and as a	Job 27:18	1129
Every wise woman *b* her house	Prov 14:1	1129
Woe unto him that *b* his house by	Jer 22:13	1129
forgotten his Maker, and *b* temples	Hos 8:14	1129
It is he that *b* his stories in	Amos 9:6	1129
Woe to him that *b* a town with	Hab 2:12	1129
foundation, and another *b* thereon	1Cor 3:10	2026
man take heed how he *b* thereupon	1Cor 3:10	2026

BUILDING

in *b* you an altar beside the	Josh 22:19	1129
made an end of *b* his own house	1Kin 3:1	1129
And the house, when it was in *b*	1Kin 6:7	1129
in the house, while it was in *b*	1Kin 6:7	1129
this house which thou art in *b*	1Kin 6:12	1129
So was he seven years in *b* it	1Kin 6:38	1129
But Solomon was *b* his own house	1Kin 7:1	1129
the *b* of the house of the LORD	1Kin 9:1	1129
that he left off *b* of Ramah	1Kin 15:21	1129
God, and had made ready for the *b*	1Chr 28:2	1129
for the *b* of the house of God	2Chr 3:3	1129
it, that he left off *b* of Ramah	2Chr 16:5	1129
thereof, wherewith Baasha was *b*	2Chr 16:6	1129
of Judah, and troubled them in *b*	Ezr 4:4	1129
b the rebellious and the bad city,	Ezr 4:12	1124
names of the men that make this *b*	Ezr 5:4	1147
even until now hath it been in *b*	Ezr 5:16	1124
for the *b* of this house of God	Ezr 6:8	1124
much slothfulness the *b* decayeth	Eccl 10:18	4746
b forts, to cut off many persons	Eze 17:17	1129
he measured the breadth of the *b*	Eze 40:5	1146
Now the *b* that was before the	Eze 41:12	1146
the wall of the *b* was five cubits	Eze 41:12	1146
and the separate place, and the *b*	Eze 41:13	1140
he measured the length of the *b*	Eze 41:15	1146
was before the *b* toward the north	Eze 42:1	1146
and than the middlemost of the *b*	Eze 42:5	1146
therefore the *b* was straitened	Eze 42:6	
place, and over against the *b*	Eze 42:10	1146
there was a row of *b* round about	Eze 46:23	
and six years was this temple in *b*	Jn 2:20	3618
God's husbandry, ye are God's *b*	1Cor 3:9	3619
dissolved, we have a *b* of God	2Cor 5:1	3619
In whom all the *b* fitly framed	Eph 2:21	3619
that is to say, not of this *b*	Heb 9:11	2937
b up yourselves on your most holy	Jude 20	2026
the *b* of the wall of it was of	Rev 21:18	1739

BUILDINGS

to shew him the *b* of the temple	Mt 24:1	3619
of stones and what *b* are here	Mk 13:1	3619
him, Seest thou these great *b*	Mk 13:2	3619

BUILT

b there an altar unto the LORD	Gen 13:18	1129
Abraham *b* an altar there, and laid	Gen 22:9	1129
b him an house, and made booths	Gen 33:17	1129
he *b* there an altar, and called	Gen 35:7	1129
they *b* for Pharaoh treasure	Ex 1:11	1129
Moses *b* an altar, and called the	Ex 17:15	1129
saw it, he *b* an altar before it	Ex 32:5	1129
(Now Hebron was *b* seven years	Num 13:22	1129
let the city of Sihon be *b*	Num 21:27	1129
b seven altars, and offered a	Num 23:14	1129
And the children of Gad *b* Dibon	Num 32:34	1129
the children of Reuben *b* Heshbon	Num 32:37	1129
hast *b* goodly houses, and dwelt	Deut 8:12	1129
it shall not be *b* again	Deut 13:16	1129
is there that hath *b* a new house	Deut 20:5	1129
Then Joshua *b* an altar unto the	Josh 8:30	1129
he *b* the city, and dwelt therein	Josh 19:50	1129
b there an altar by Jordan	Josh 22:10	1129
b an altar over against the land	Josh 22:11	1129
That we have *b* us an altar to	Josh 22:23	1129
labour, and cities which ye *b* not	Josh 24:13	1129
b a city, and called the name	Judg 1:26	1129
Then Gideon *b* an altar there unto	Judg 6:24	1129
offered upon the altar that was *b*	Judg 6:28	1129
they *b* a city, and dwelt therein	Judg 18:28	1129
b there an altar, and offered	Judg 21:4	1129
there he *b* an altar unto the LORD	1Sa 7:17	1129
Saul *b* an altar unto the LORD	1Sa 14:35	1129
altar that he *b* unto the LORD	1Sa 14:35	1129
David *b* round about from Millo and	2Sa 5:9	1129
and they *b* David an house	2Sa 5:11	1129
David *b* there an altar unto the	2Sa 24:25	1129
house *b* unto the name of the LORD	1Kin 3:2	1129
which king Solomon *b* for the LORD	1Kin 6:2	1129

house he *b* chambers round about	1Kin 6:5	1129
was *b* of stone made ready before	1Kin 6:7	1129
So he *b* the house, and finished it	1Kin 6:9	1129
then he *b* chambers against all	1Kin 6:10	1129
So Solomon *b* the house, and	1Kin 6:14	1129
he *b* the walls of the house	1Kin 6:15	1129
he *b* twenty cubits on the sides	1Kin 6:16	1129
he even *b* them for it within,	1Kin 6:16	1129
he *b* the inner court with three	1Kin 6:36	1129
He *b* also the house of the forest	1Kin 7:2	1129
I have surely *b* thee an house to	1Kin 8:13	1129
have an house for the name of	1Kin 8:20	1129
house that I have *b* for thy name	1Kin 8:44	1129
house which I have *b* for thy name	1Kin 8:48	1129
this house, which thou hast *b*	1Kin 9:3	1129
when Solomon had *b* the two houses	1Kin 9:10	1129
And Solomon *b* Gezer, and Beth-horon	1Kin 9:17	1129
house which Solomon had *b* for her	1Kin 9:24	1129
altar which he *b* unto the Lord	1Kin 9:25	1129
and the house that he had *b*	1Kin 10:4	1129
Solomon *b* Millo, and repaired the	1Kin 11:27	1129
as I *b* for David, and will give	1Kin 11:38	1129
Then Jeroboam *b* Shechem in mount	1Kin 12:25	1129
went out from thence, and *b* Penuel	1Kin 12:25	1129
For they also *b* them high places,	1Kin 14:23	1129
b Ramah, that he might not suffer	1Kin 15:17	1129
king Asa *b* with them Geba of	1Kin 15:22	1129
he did, and the cities which he *b*	1Kin 15:23	1129
b on the hill, and called the name	1Kin 16:24	1129
the name of the city which he *b*	1Kin 16:24	1129
Baal, which he had *b* in Samaria	1Kin 16:32	1129
with the stones he *b* an altar in	1Kin 18:32	1129
made, and all the cities that he *b*	1Kin 22:39	1129
He *b* Elath, and restored it to	2Kin 14:22	1129
He *b* the higher gate of the house	2Kin 15:35	1129
Urijah the priest *b* an altar	2Kin 16:11	1129
that they had *b* in the house	2Kin 16:18	1129
they *b* them high places in all	2Kin 17:9	1129
For he *b* up again the high places	2Kin 21:3	1129
he *b* altars in the house of the	2Kin 21:4	1129
he *b* altars for all the host of	2Kin 21:5	1129
they *b* forts against it round	2Kin 25:1	1129
that Solomon *b* in Jerusalem	1Chr 6:10	1129
until Solomon had *b* the house of	1Chr 6:32	1129
who *b* Beth-horon the nether, and	1Chr 7:24	1129
and Misham, and Shamed, who *b* Ono	1Chr 8:12	1129
he *b* the city round about, even	1Chr 11:8	1129
Why have ye not *b* me an house of	1Chr 17:6	1129
David *b* there an altar unto the	1Chr 21:26	1129
to be *b* to the name of the Lord	1Chr 22:19	1129
But I have *b* an house of	2Chr 6:2	1129
have *b* the house for the name of	2Chr 6:10	1129
less this house which I have *b*	2Chr 6:18	1129
I have *b* is called by thy name	2Chr 6:33	1129
house which I have *b* for thy name	2Chr 6:34	1129
house which I have *b* for thy name	2Chr 6:38	1129
wherein Solomon had *b* the house	2Chr 8:1	1129
to Solomon, Solomon *b* them	2Chr 8:2	1129
he *b* Tadmor in the wilderness, and	2Chr 8:4	1129
cities, which he *b* in Hamath	2Chr 8:4	1129
Also he *b* Beth-horon the upper,	2Chr 8:5	1129
the house that he had *b* for her	2Chr 8:11	1129
which he had *b* before the porch,	2Chr 8:12	1129
and the house that he had *b*	2Chr 9:3	1129
b cities for defence in Judah	2Chr 11:5	1129
He *b* even Beth-lehem, and Etam, and	2Chr 11:6	1129
he *b* fenced cities in Judah	2Chr 14:6	1129
So they *b* and prospered	2Chr 14:7	1129
b Ramah, to the intent that he	2Chr 16:1	1129
he *b* therewith Geba and Mizpah	2Chr 16:6	1129
he *b* in Judah castles, and cities	2Chr 17:12	1129
have *b* a sanctuary therein	2Chr 20:8	1129
He *b* Eloth, and restored it to	2Chr 26:2	1129
b cities about Ashdod, and among	2Chr 26:6	1129
Moreover Uzziah *b* towers in	2Chr 26:9	1129
Also he *b* towers in the desert,	2Chr 26:10	1129
He *b* the high gate of the house	2Chr 27:3	1129
and on the wall of Ophel he *b* much	2Chr 27:3	1129
Moreover he *b* cities in the	2Chr 27:4	1129
and in the forests *b* castles	2Chr 27:4	1129
b up all the wall that was broken	2Chr 32:5	1129
For he *b* again the high places	2Chr 33:3	1129
Also he *b* altars in the house of	2Chr 33:4	1129
he *b* altars for all the host of	2Chr 33:5	1129
Now after this he *b* a wall	2Chr 33:14	1129
all the altars that he had *b* in	2Chr 33:15	1129
places wherein he *b* high places	2Chr 33:19	1129
they *b* it, and set up the doors	Neh 3:13	1129
he *b* it, and set up the doors	Neh 3:14	1129
he *b* it, and covered it, and set up	Neh 3:15	1129
So *b* we the wall	Neh 4:6	1129

came to pass, when the wall was *b*	Neh 7:1	1129
which *b* desolate places for	Job 3:14	1129
down, and it cannot be *b* again	Job 12:14	1129
the Almighty, thou shalt be *b* up	Job 22:23	1129
he *b* his sanctuary like high	Ps 78:69	1129
Mercy shall be *b* up for ever	Ps 89:2	1129
b great bulwarks against it	Eccl 9:14	1129
b a tower in the midst of it, and	Is 5:2	1129
it shall never be *b*	Is 25:2	1129
cities of Judah, Ye shall be *b*	Is 44:26	1129
to Jerusalem, Thou shalt be *b*	Is 44:28	1129
they have *b* the high places of	Jer 7:31	1129
then shall they be *b* in the midst	Jer 12:16	1129
They have *b* also the high places	Jer 19:5	1129
build thee, and thou shalt be *b*	Jer 31:4	1129
that the city shall be *b* to the	Jer 31:38	1129
that they *b* it even unto this day	Jer 32:31	1129
they *b* the high places of Baal,	Jer 32:35	1129
which I have *b* will I break down	Jer 45:4	1129
b forts against it round about	Jer 52:4	1129
one *b* up a wall, and, lo, others	Eze 13:10	1129
That thou hast also *b* unto thee	Eze 16:24	1129
Thou hast *b* thy high place at	Eze 16:25	1129
thou shalt be *b* no more	Eze 26:14	1129
that I have *b* for the house of	Dan 4:30	1124
the street shall be *b* again	Dan 9:25	1129
ye have *b* houses of hewn stone,	Amos 5:11	1129
day that thy walls are to be *b*	Mic 7:11	1129
that the Lord's house should be *b*	Hag 1:2	1129
my house shall be *b* in it	Zec 1:16	1129
laid, that the temple might be *b*	Zec 8:9	1129
which *b* his house upon a rock	Mt 7:24	3618
which *b* his house upon the sand	Mt 7:26	3618
b a tower, and let it out to	Mt 21:33	3618
b a tower, and let it out to	Mk 12:1	3618
the hill whereon their city was *b*	Lk 4:29	3618
He is like a man which *b* an house	Lk 6:48	3618
b an house upon the earth	Lk 6:49	3618
and he hath *b* us a synagogue	Lk 7:5	3618
But Solomon *b* him an house	Acts 7:47	3618
abide which he hath *b* thereupon	1Cor 3:14	2026
are *b* upon the foundation of the	Eph 2:20	2026
b up in him, and stablished in the	Col 2:7	2026
but he that *b* all things is God	Heb 3:4	2680
are *b* up a spiritual house, an	1Pet 2:5	3618

BUKKI *(buk'-ki)*
  1. A high priest.

And Abishua begat B	1Chr 6:5	1231
and B begat Uzzi	1Chr 6:5	1231
B his son, Uzzi his son, Zerahiah	1Chr 6:51	1231
the son of Uzzi, the son of B	Ezr 7:4	1231

  2. A Danite prince.

of Dan, B the son of Jogli	Num 34:22	1231

BUKKIAH *(buk-ki'-ah) A Levite musician.*

B, Mattaniah, Uzziel, Shebuel, and	1Chr 25:4	1232
The sixth to B, he, his sons, and	1Chr 25:13	1232

BUL *(bul) Eighth month of the Hebrew year.*

the eleventh year, in the month B	1Kin 6:38	945

BULL

Their *b* gendereth, and faileth not	Job 21:10	7794
the streets, as a wild *b* in a net	Is 51:20	8377

BULLOCK

Take one young *b*, and two rams	Ex 29:1	6499
them in the basket, with the *b*	Ex 29:3	6499
thou shalt cause a *b* to be	Ex 29:10	6499
hands upon the head of the *b*	Ex 29:10	6499
shalt kill the *b* before the Lord	Ex 29:11	6499
shalt take of the blood of the *b*	Ex 29:12	6499
But the flesh of the *b*, and his	Ex 29:14	6499
day a *b* for a sin offering for	Ex 29:36	6499
shall kill the *b* before the Lord	Lev 1:5	1121,1241
a young *b* without blemish unto	Lev 4:3	6499
he shall bring the *b* unto the	Lev 4:4	6499
kill the *b* before the Lord	Lev 4:4	6499
b at the bottom of the altar of	Lev 4:7	6499
fat of the *b* for the sin offering	Lev 4:8	6499
the *b* of the sacrifice of peace	Lev 4:10	7794
And the skin of the *b*, and all his	Lev 4:11	6499
Even the whole *b* shall he carry	Lev 4:12	6499
shall offer a young *b* for the sin	Lev 4:14	6499
the head of the *b* before the Lord	Lev 4:15	6499
the *b* shall be killed before the	Lev 4:15	6499
he shall do with the *b* as he did	Lev 4:20	6499
did with the *b* for a sin offering	Lev 4:20	6499
forth the *b* without the camp	Lev 4:21	6499
burn him as he burned the first *b*	Lev 4:21	6499
a *b* for the sin offering, and two	Lev 8:2	6499
he brought the *b* for the sin	Lev 8:14	6499

of the *b* for the sin offering	Lev 8:14	6499
But the *b*, and his hide, his flesh	Lev 8:17	6499
Also a *b* and a ram for peace	Lev 9:4	7794
He slew also the *b* and the ram for	Lev 9:18	7794
And the fat of the *b* and of the ram	Lev 9:19	7794
with a young *b* for a sin offering	Lev 16:3	6499
offer his *b* of the sin offering	Lev 16:6	6499
bring the *b* of the sin offering	Lev 16:11	6499
shall kill the *b* of the sin	Lev 16:11	6499
shall take of the blood of the *b*	Lev 16:14	6499
as he did with the blood of the *b*	Lev 16:15	6499
shall take of the blood of the *b*	Lev 16:18	6499
the *b* for the sin offering, and	Lev 16:27	6499
Either a *b* or a lamb that hath	Lev 22:23	7794
When a *b*, or a sheep, or a goat,	Lev 22:27	7794
of the first year, and one young *b*	Lev 23:18	6499
One young *b*, one ram, one lamb of	Num 7:15	6499
One young *b*, one ram, one lamb of	Num 7:21	6499
One young *b*, one ram, one lamb of	Num 7:27	6499
One young *b*, one ram, one lamb of	Num 7:33	6499
One young *b*, one ram, one lamb of	Num 7:39	6499
One young *b*, one ram, one lamb of	Num 7:45	6499
One young *b*, one ram, one lamb of	Num 7:51	6499
One young *b*, one ram, one lamb of	Num 7:57	6499
One young *b*, one ram, one lamb of	Num 7:63	6499
One young *b*, one ram, one lamb of	Num 7:69	6499
One young *b*, one ram, one lamb of	Num 7:75	6499
One young *b*, one ram, one lamb of	Num 7:81	6499
a young *b* with his meat offering	Num 8:8	6499
another young *b* shalt thou take	Num 8:8	6499
a *b* for a burnt offering, or for	Num 15:8	1121,1241
Then shall he bring with a *b* a	Num 15:9	1121,1241
Thus shall it be done for one *b*	Num 15:11	7794
one young *b* for a burnt offering	Num 15:24	6499
Balaam offered on every altar a *b*	Num 23:2	6499
have offered upon every altar a *b*	Num 23:4	6499
seven altars, and offered a *b*	Num 23:14	6499
Balaam had said, and offered a *b*	Num 23:30	6499
mingled with oil, for one *b*	Num 28:12	6499
be half an hin of wine unto a *b*	Num 28:14	6499
deals shall ye offer for a *b*	Num 28:20	6499
oil, three tenth deals unto one *b*	Num 28:28	6499
one young *b*, one ram, and seven	Num 29:2	6499
oil, three tenth deals for a *b*	Num 29:3	6499
one young *b*, one ram, and seven	Num 29:8	6499
oil, three tenth deals to a *b*	Num 29:9	6499
every *b* of the thirteen bullocks	Num 29:14	6499
one *b*, one ram, seven lambs of	Num 29:36	6499
their drink offerings for the *b*	Num 29:37	6499
work with the firstling of thy *b*	Deut 15:19	7794
unto the Lord thy God any *b*	Deut 17:1	7794
is like the firstling of his *b*	Deut 33:17	7794
him, Take thy father's young *b*	Judg 6:25	6499
even the second *b* of seven years	Judg 6:25	6499
place, and take the second *b*	Judg 6:26	6499
the second *b* was offered upon the	Judg 6:28	6499
And they slew a *b*, and brought the	1Sa 1:25	6499
them choose one *b* for themselves	1Kin 18:23	6499
and I will dress the other *b*	1Kin 18:23	6499
Choose you one *b* for yourselves	1Kin 18:25	6499
they took the *b* which was given	1Kin 18:26	6499
cut the *b* in pieces, and laid him	1Kin 18:33	6499
consecrate himself with a young *b*	2Chr 13:9	6499
I will take no *b* out of thy house	Ps 50:9	6499
than an ox or *b* that hath horns	Ps 69:31	6499
lion shall eat straw like the *b*	Is 65:25	1241
as a *b* unaccustomed to the yoke	Jer 31:18	5695
a young *b* for a sin offering	Eze 43:19	6499
Thou shalt take the *b* also of the	Eze 43:21	6499
as they did cleanse it with the *b*	Eze 43:22	6499
offer a young *b* without blemish	Eze 43:23	6499
they shall also prepare a young *b*	Eze 43:25	6499
take a young *b* without blemish	Eze 45:18	6499
the land a *b* for a sin offering	Eze 45:22	6499
meat offering of an ephah for a *b*	Eze 45:24	6499
be a young *b* without blemish	Eze 46:6	6499
a meat offering, an ephah for a *b*	Eze 46:7	6499
offering shall be an ephah to a *b*	Eze 46:11	6499

BULLOCK'S

lay his hand upon the *b* head	Lev 4:4	6499
shall take of the *b* blood	Lev 4:5	6499
b blood to the tabernacle of the	Lev 4:16	6499

BULLOCKS

the burnt offering were twelve *b*	Num 7:87	6499
offerings were twenty and four *b*	Num 7:88	6499
hands upon the heads of the *b*	Num 8:12	6499
and prepare me here seven *b*	Num 23:29	6499
two young *b*, and one ram, seven	Num 28:11	6499
two young *b*, and one ram, and seven	Num 28:19	6499
two young *b*, one ram, seven lambs	Num 28:27	6499

thirteen young *b*, two rams, and	Num 29:13	6499
every bullock of the thirteen *b*	Num 29:14	6499
day ye shall offer twelve young *b*	Num 29:17	6499
their drink offerings for the *b*	Num 29:18	6499
And on the third day eleven *b*	Num 29:20	6499
their drink offerings for the *b*	Num 29:21	6499
And on the fourth day ten *b*	Num 29:23	6499
their drink offerings for the *b*	Num 29:24	6499
And on the fifth day nine *b*	Num 29:26	6499
their drink offerings for the *b*	Num 29:27	6499
And on the sixth day eight *b*	Num 29:29	6499
their drink offerings for the *b*	Num 29:30	6499
And on the seventh day seven *b*	Num 29:32	6499
their drink offerings for the *b*	Num 29:33	6499
him up with her, with three *b*	1Sa 1:24	6499
Let them therefore give us two *b*	1Kin 18:23	6499
Lord, that they offered seven *b*	1Chr 15:26	6499
after that day, even a thousand *b*	1Chr 29:21	6499
And they brought seven *b*, and seven	2Chr 29:21	6499
So they killed the *b*, and the	2Chr 29:22	1241
brought, was threescore and ten *b*	2Chr 29:32	1241
to the congregation a thousand *b*	2Chr 30:24	6499
to the congregation a thousand *b*	2Chr 30:24	6499
thousand, and three thousand *b*	2Chr 35:7	1241
they have need of, both young *b*	Ezr 6:9	8450
of this house of God an hundred *b*	Ezr 6:17	8450
buy speedily with this money *b*	Ezr 7:17	8450
twelve *b* for all Israel, ninety	Ezr 8:35	6499
take unto you now seven *b*	Job 42:8	6499
they offer *b* upon thine altar	Ps 51:19	6499
I will offer *b* with goats	Ps 66:15	1241
I delight not in the blood of *b*	Is 1:11	6499
them, and the *b* with the bulls	Is 34:7	6499
in the midst of her like fatted *b*	Jer 46:21	5695
Slay all her *b*	Jer 50:27	6499
rams, of lambs, and of goats, of *b*	Eze 39:18	6499
offering to the Lord, seven *b*	Eze 45:23	6499
they sacrifice *b* in Gilgal	Hos 12:11	7794

BULLS

their colts, forty kine, and ten *b*	Gen 32:15	6499
Many *b* have compassed me	Ps 22:12	6499
strong *b* of Bashan have beset me	Ps 22:12	
Will I eat the flesh of *b*	Ps 50:13	47
spearmen, the multitude of the *b*	Ps 68:30	47
them, and the bullocks with the *b*	Is 34:7	47
heifer at grass, and bellow as *b*	Jer 50:11	47
twelve brasen *b* that were under	Jer 52:20	1241
For if the blood of *b* and of goats	Heb 9:13	5022
not possible that the blood of *b*	Heb 10:4	5022

BULRUSH

is it to bow down his head as a *b*	Is 58:5	100

BULRUSHES

him, she took for him an ark of *b*	Ex 2:3	1573
in vessels of *b* upon the waters	Is 18:2	1573

BULWARKS

thou shalt build *b* against the	Deut 20:20	4692
to be on the towers and upon the *b*	2Chr 26:15	6438
Mark ye well her *b*, consider her	Ps 48:13	2430
it, and built great *b* against it	Eccl 9:14	4685
will God appoint for walls and *b*	Is 26:1	2426

BUNAH (boo'-nah) *Son of Jerahmeel.*

were, Ram the firstborn, and B	1Chr 2:25	946

BUNCH

And ye shall take a *b* of hyssop	Ex 12:22	92

BUNCHES

bread, and an hundred *b* of raisins	2Sa 16:1	6778
b of raisins, and wine, and oil, and	1Chr 12:40	6778
treasures upon the *b* of camels	Is 30:6	1707

BUNDLE

every man's *b* of money was in his	Gen 42:35	6872
b of life with the Lord thy God	1Sa 25:29	6872
A *b* of myrrh is my wellbeloved	Song 1:13	6872
Paul had gathered a *b* of sticks	Acts 28:3	4128

BUNDLES

their father saw the *b* of money	Gen 42:35	6872
and bind them in *b* to burn them	Mt 13:30	1197

BUNNI (bun'-ni)
  1. *A Levite with Ezra.*

and Bani, Kadmiel, Shebaniah, B	Neh 9:4	1137

  2. *Father of Hashabiah.*

son of Hashabiah, the son of B	Neh 11:15	1137

  3. *A family who renewed the covenant.*

B, Azgad, Bebai,	Neh 10:15	1137

BURDEN

they shall bear the *b* with thee	Ex 18:22	
hateth thee lying under his *b*	Ex 23:5	4853

These things are the *b* of the	Num 4:15	4853
one to his service and to his *b*	Num 4:19	4853
And this is the charge of their *b*	Num 4:31	4853
of the charge of their *b*	Num 4:32	4853
the service of the *b* in the	Num 4:47	4853
service, and according to his *b*	Num 4:49	4853
that thou layest the *b* of all	Num 11:11	4853
they shall bear the *b* of the	Num 11:17	4853
bear your cumbrance, and your *b*	Deut 1:12	4853
then thou shalt be a *b* unto me	2Sa 15:33	4853
be yet a *b* unto my lord the king	2Sa 19:35	4853
thy servant two mules' *b* of earth	2Kin 5:17	4853
of Damascus, forty camels' *b*	2Kin 8:9	4853
the LORD laid this *b* upon him	2Kin 9:25	4853
it shall not be a *b* upon your	2Chr 35:3	4853
that there should no *b* be brought	Neh 13:19	4853
thee, so that I am a *b* to myself	Job 7:20	4853
as an heavy *b* they are too heavy	Ps 38:4	4853
Cast thy *b* upon the LORD, and he	Ps 55:22	3053
I removed his shoulder from the *b*	Ps 81:6	5449
and the grasshopper shall be a *b*	Eccl 12:5	5445
hast broken the yoke of his *b*	Is 9:4	5448
that his *b* shall be taken away	Is 10:27	5448
The *b* of Babylon, which Isaiah	Is 13:1	4853
his *b* depart from off their	Is 14:25	5448
that king Ahaz died was this *b*	Is 14:28	4853
The *b* of Moab	Is 15:1	4853
The *b* of Damascus	Is 17:1	4853
The *b* of Egypt	Is 19:1	4853
The *b* of the desert of the sea	Is 21:1	4853
The *b* of Dumah	Is 21:11	4853
The *b* upon Arabia	Is 21:13	4853
The *b* of the valley of vision	Is 22:1	4853
the *b* that was upon it shall be	Is 22:25	4853
The *b* of Tyre	Is 23:1	4853
The *b* of the beasts of the south	Is 30:6	4853
anger, and the *b* thereof is heavy	Is 30:27	4858
they are a *b* to the weary beast	Is 46:1	4853
they could not deliver the *b*	Is 46:2	4853
bear no *b* on the sabbath day, nor	Jer 17:21	4853
Neither carry forth a *b* out of	Jer 17:22	4853
to bring in no *b* through the	Jer 17:24	4853
sabbath day, and not to bear a *b*	Jer 17:27	4853
saying, What is the *b* of the LORD	Jer 23:33	4853
shalt then say unto them, What *b*	Jer 23:33	4853
The *b* of the LORD, I will even	Jer 23:34	4853
the *b* of the LORD shall ye	Jer 23:36	4853
every man's word shall be his *b*	Jer 23:36	4853
since ye say, The *b* of the LORD	Jer 23:38	4853
The *b* of the LORD, and I have sent	Jer 23:38	4853
shall not say, The *b* of the LORD	Jer 23:38	4853
This *b* concerneth the prince in	Eze 12:10	4853
for the *b* of the king of princes	Hos 8:10	4853
The *b* of Nineveh	Nah 1:1	4853
The *b* which Habakkuk the prophet	Hab 1:1	4853
whom the reproach of it was a *b*	Zeph 3:18	4864
The *b* of the word of the LORD in	Zec 9:1	4853
The *b* of the word of the LORD for	Zec 12:1	4853
all that *b* themselves with it	Zec 12:3	6006
The *b* of the word of the LORD to	Mal 1:1	4853
my yoke is easy, and my *b* is light	Mt 11:30	*5413*
unto us, which have borne the *b*	Mt 20:12	*922*
to lay upon you no greater *b* than	Acts 15:28	*922*
the ship was to unlade her *b*	Acts 21:3	*1117*
But be it so, I did not *b* you	2Cor 12:16	*2599*
every man shall bear his own *b*	Gal 6:5	*5413*
I will put upon you none other *b*	Rev 2:24	*922*

BURDENED

this tabernacle do groan, being *b*	2Cor 5:4	*916*
that other men be eased, and ye *b*	2Cor 8:13	*2347*

BURDENS

ass couching down between two *b*	Gen 49:14	4942
to afflict them with their *b*	Ex 1:11	5450
brethren, and looked on their *b*	Ex 2:11	5450
get you unto your *b*	Ex 5:4	5450
and ye make them rest from their *b*	Ex 5:5	5450
from under the *b* of the Egyptians	Ex 6:6	5450
from under the *b* of the Egyptians	Ex 6:7	5450
Gershonites, to serve, and for *b*	Num 4:24	4853
the Gershonites, in all their *b*	Num 4:27	4853
unto them in charge all their *b*	Num 4:27	4853
and ten thousand that bare *b*	1Kin 5:15	5449
and ten thousand men to bear *b*	2Chr 2:2	5449
of them to be bearers of *b*	2Chr 2:18	5449
greatness of the *b* laid upon him	2Chr 24:27	4853
they were over the bearers of *b*	2Chr 34:13	5449
of the bearers of *b* is decayed	Neh 4:10	5449
on the wall, and they that bare *b*	Neh 4:17	5447
and figs, and all manner of *b*	Neh 13:15	4853
wickedness, to undo the heavy *b*	Is 58:6	92

but have seen for thee false *b*	Lam 2:14	4864
and ye take from him *b* of wheat	Amos 5:11	4864
For they bind heavy *b* and grievous	Mt 23:4	*5413*
men with *b* grievous to be borne	Lk 11:46	*5413*
the *b* with one of your fingers	Lk 11:46	*5413*
Bear ye one another's *b*, and so	Gal 6:2	*922*

BURDENSOME

a *b* stone for all people	Zec 12:3	4614
kept myself from being *b* unto you	2Cor 11:9	*4*
be that I myself was not *b* to you	2Cor 12:13	*2655*
and I will not be *b* to you	2Cor 12:14	*2655*
when we might have been *b*	1Th 2:6	*1722,922*

BURIAL

the *b* which belonged to the kings	2Chr 26:23	6900
good, and also that he have no *b*	Eccl 6:3	6900
not be joined with them in *b*	Is 14:20	6900
be buried with the *b* of an ass	Jer 22:19	6900
on my body, she did it for my *b*	Mt 26:12	*1779*
men carried Stephen to his *b*	Acts 8:2	

BURIED

thou shalt be *b* in a good old age	Gen 15:15	6912
Abraham *b* Sarah his wife in the	Gen 23:19	6912
Ishmael *b* him in the cave of	Gen 25:9	6912
there was Abraham *b*, and Sarah his	Gen 25:10	6912
she was *b* beneath Beth-el under	Gen 35:8	6912
was *b* in the way to Ephrath	Gen 35:19	6912
and his sons Esau and Jacob *b* him	Gen 35:29	6912
I *b* her there in the way of	Gen 48:7	6912
There they *b* Abraham and Sarah his	Gen 49:31	6912
there they *b* Isaac and Rebekah his	Gen 49:31	6912
and there I *b* Leah	Gen 49:31	6912
b him in the cave of the field of	Gen 50:13	6912
father, after he had *b* his father	Gen 50:14	6912
because there they *b* the people	Num 11:34	6912
Miriam died there, and was *b* there	Num 20:1	6912
For the Egyptians *b* all their	Num 33:4	6912
Aaron died, and there he was *b*	Deut 10:6	6912
he *b* him in a valley in the land	Deut 34:6	6912
they *b* him in the border of his	Josh 24:30	6912
b they in Shechem, in a parcel of	Josh 24:32	6912
they *b* him in a hill that	Josh 24:33	6912
they *b* him in the border of his	Judg 2:9	6912
was *b* in the sepulchre of Joash	Judg 8:32	6912
and died, and was *b* in Shamir	Judg 10:2	6912
And Jair died, and was *b* in Camon	Judg 10:5	6912
was *b* in one of the cities of	Judg 12:7	6912
Ibzan, and was *b* at Beth-lehem	Judg 12:10	6912
was *b* in Aijalon in the country	Judg 12:12	6912
was *b* in Pirathon in the land of	Judg 12:15	6912
b him between Zorah and Eshtaol in	Judg 16:31	6912
will I die, and there will I be *b*	Ruth 1:17	6912
b him in his house at Ramah	1Sa 25:1	6912
b him in Ramah, even in his own	1Sa 28:3	6912
b them under a tree at Jabesh, and	1Sa 31:13	6912
were they that *b* Saul	2Sa 2:4	6912
even unto Saul, and have *b* him	2Sa 2:5	6912
b him in the sepulchre of his	2Sa 2:32	6912
And they *b* Abner in Hebron	2Sa 3:32	6912
b it in the sepulchre of Abner in	2Sa 4:12	6912
was *b* in the sepulchre of his	2Sa 17:23	6912
be *b* by the grave of my father and	2Sa 19:37	
Jonathan his son *b* they in the	2Sa 21:14	6912
was *b* in the city of David	1Kin 2:10	6912
he was *b* in his own house in the	1Kin 2:34	6912
was *b* in the city of David his	1Kin 11:43	6912
came to pass, after he had *b* him	1Kin 13:31	6912
wherein the man of God is *b*	1Kin 13:31	6912
And they *b* him	1Kin 14:18	6912
was *b* with his fathers in the	1Kin 14:31	6912
they *b* him in the city of David	1Kin 15:8	6912
was *b* with his fathers in the	1Kin 15:24	6912
his fathers, and was *b* in Tirzah	1Kin 16:6	6912
his fathers, and was *b* in Samaria	1Kin 16:28	6912
they *b* the king in Samaria	1Kin 22:37	6912
was *b* with his fathers in the	1Kin 22:50	6912
was *b* with his fathers in the	2Kin 8:24	6912
b him in his sepulchre with his	2Kin 9:28	6912
and they *b* him in Samaria	2Kin 10:35	6912
they *b* him with his fathers in	2Kin 12:21	6912
and they *b* him in Samaria	2Kin 13:9	6912
Joash was *b* in Samaria with the	2Kin 13:13	6912
And Elisha died, and they *b* him	2Kin 13:20	6912
was *b* in Samaria with the kings	2Kin 14:16	6912
he was *b* at Jerusalem with his	2Kin 14:20	6912
they *b* him with his fathers in	2Kin 15:7	6912
was *b* with his fathers in the	2Kin 15:38	6912
was *b* with his fathers in the	2Kin 16:20	6912
was *b* in the garden of his own	2Kin 21:18	6912
he was *b* in his sepulchre in the	2Kin 21:26	6912

b him in his own sepulchre	2Kin 23:30	6912
b their bones under the oak in	1Chr 10:12	6912
he was *b* in the city of David his	2Chr 9:31	6912
was *b* in the city of David	2Chr 12:16	6912
they *b* him in the city of David	2Chr 14:1	6912
they *b* him in his own sepulchres,	2Chr 16:14	6912
was *b* with his fathers in the	2Chr 21:1	6912
Howbeit they *b* him in the city of	2Chr 21:20	6912
they had slain him, they *b* him	2Chr 22:9	6912
they *b* him in the city of David	2Chr 24:16	6912
they *b* him in the city of David,	2Chr 24:25	6912
but they *b* him not in the	2Chr 24:25	6912
b him with his fathers in the	2Chr 25:28	6912
they *b* him with his fathers in	2Chr 26:23	6912
they *b* him in the city of David	2Chr 27:9	6912
they *b* him in the city, even in	2Chr 28:27	6912
they *b* him in the chiefest of the	2Chr 32:33	6912
they *b* him in his own house	2Chr 33:20	6912
was *b* in one of the sepulchres of	2Chr 35:24	6912
remain of him shall be *b* in death	Job 27:15	6912
And so I saw the wicked *b*, who had	Eccl 8:10	6912
shall not be gathered, nor be *b*	Jer 8:2	6912
neither shall they be *b*	Jer 16:4	6912
they shall not be *b*, neither	Jer 16:6	6912
shalt die, and shalt be *b* there	Jer 20:6	6912
He shall be *b* with the burial of	Jer 22:19	6912
lamented, neither gathered, nor *b*	Jer 25:33	6912
till the buriers have *b* it in the	Eze 39:15	6912
b it, and went and told Jesus	Mt 14:12	2290
the rich man also died, and was *b*	Lk 16:22	2290
David, that he is both dead and *b*	Acts 2:29	2290
up, and carried him out, and *b* him	Acts 5:6	2290
b thy husband are at the door	Acts 5:9	2290
her forth, *b* her by her husband	Acts 5:10	2290
Therefore we are *b* with him by	Rom 6:4	4916
And that he was *b*, and that he rose	1Cor 15:4	2290
B with him in baptism, wherein	Col 2:12	4916

BURIERS

till the *b* have buried it in the	Eze 39:15	6912

BURN

make brick, and *b* them throughly	Gen 11:3	8313
thine anger *b* against thy servant	Gen 44:18	2734
the morning ye shall *b* with fire	Ex 12:10	8313
to cause the lamp to *b* always	Ex 27:20	5927
them, and *b* them upon the altar	Ex 29:13	6999
shalt thou *b* with fire without	Ex 29:14	8313
thou shalt *b* the whole ram upon	Ex 29:18	6999
b them upon the altar for a burnt	Ex 29:25	6999
then thou shalt *b* the remainder	Ex 29:34	8313
make an altar to *b* incense upon	Ex 30:1	4729
Aaron shall *b* thereon sweet	Ex 30:7	6999
he shall *b* incense upon it,	Ex 30:7	6999
he shall *b* incense upon it, a	Ex 30:8	6999
to *b* offering made by fire unto	Ex 30:20	6999
priest shall *b* all on the altar	Lev 1:9	6999
it all, and *b* it upon the altar	Lev 1:13	6999
his head, and *b* it on the altar	Lev 1:15	6999
the priest shall *b* it upon the	Lev 1:17	6999
the priest shall *b* the memorial	Lev 2:2	6999
shall *b* it upon the altar	Lev 2:9	6999
for ye shall *b* no leaven, nor any	Lev 2:11	6999
the priest shall *b* the memorial	Lev 2:16	6999
Aaron's sons shall *b* it on the	Lev 3:5	6999
the priest shall *b* it upon the	Lev 3:11	6999
the priest shall *b* them upon the	Lev 3:16	6999
the priest shall *b* them upon the	Lev 4:10	6999
b him on the wood with fire	Lev 4:12	8313
from him, and *b* it upon the altar	Lev 4:19	6999
b him as he burned the first	Lev 4:21	8313
he shall *b* all his fat upon the	Lev 4:26	6999
the priest shall *b* it upon the	Lev 4:31	6999
the priest shall *b* them upon the	Lev 4:35	6999
b it on the altar, according to	Lev 6:12	6999
the priest shall *b* wood on it	Lev 6:12	1197
he shall *b* thereon the fat of the	Lev 6:12	6999
shall *b* it upon the altar for a	Lev 6:15	6999
the priest shall *b* them upon the	Lev 7:5	6999
the priest shall *b* the fat upon	Lev 7:31	6999
of the bread shall ye *b* with fire	Lev 8:32	8313
He shall therefore *b* that garment	Lev 13:52	8313
thou shalt *b* it in the fire	Lev 13:55	8313
thou shalt *b* that wherein the	Lev 13:57	8313
shall he *b* upon the altar	Lev 16:25	6999
they shall *b* in the fire their	Lev 16:27	8313
b the fat for a sweet savour unto	Lev 17:6	6999
cause the lamps to *b* continually	Lev 24:2	5927
b it upon the altar, and afterward	Num 5:26	6999
shalt *b* their fat for an offering	Num 18:17	6999
one shall *b* the heifer in his	Num 19:5	8313
blood, with her dung, shall he *b*	Num 19:5	8313

(for the mountain did *b* with fire	Deut 5:23	1197
b their graven images with fire	Deut 7:5	8313
their gods shall ye *b* with fire	Deut 7:25	8313
and *b* their groves with fire	Deut 12:3	8313
shalt *b* with fire the city, and	Deut 13:16	8313
shall *b* unto the lowest hell, and	Deut 32:22	3344
b their chariots with fire	Josh 11:6	8313
that did Joshua *b*	Josh 11:13	8313
of the tower to *b* it with fire	Judg 9:52	8313
we will *b* thine house upon thee	Judg 12:1	8313
us the riddle, lest we *b* thee	Judg 14:15	8313
not fail to *b* the fat presently	1Sa 2:16	6999
to *b* incense, to wear an ephod	1Sa 2:28	6999
stood by the altar to *b* incense	1Kin 13:1	6999
places that *b* incense upon the	1Kin 13:2	6999
Upon the great altar *b* the	2Kin 16:15	6999
of Israel did *b* incense to it	2Kin 18:4	6999
b incense in the high places in	2Kin 23:5	6999
to *b* incense before the LORD, to	1Chr 23:13	6999
to *b* before him sweet incense, and	2Chr 2:4	6999
save only to *b* sacrifice before	2Chr 2:6	6999
that they should *b* after the	2Chr 4:20	1197
they *b* unto the LORD every	2Chr 13:11	6999
lamps thereof, to *b* every evening	2Chr 13:11	1197
to *b* incense upon the altar of	2Chr 26:16	6999
to *b* incense unto the LORD, but	2Chr 26:18	6999
that are consecrated to *b* incense	2Chr 26:18	6999
a censer in his hand to *b* incense	2Chr 26:19	6999
to *b* incense unto other gods	2Chr 28:25	6999
minister unto him, and *b* incense	2Chr 29:11	6999
one altar, and *b* incense upon it	2Chr 32:12	6999
to *b* upon the altar of the LORD	Neh 10:34	1197
shall thy jealousy *b* like fire	Ps 79:5	1197
shall thy wrath *b* like fire	Ps 89:46	1197
and they shall both *b* together	Is 1:31	1197
and it shall *b* and devour his	Is 10:17	1197
them, I would *b* them together	Is 27:4	6702
And Lebanon is not sufficient to *b*	Is 40:16	1197
Then shall it be for a man to *b*	Is 44:15	1197
the fire shall *b* them	Is 47:14	8313
b that none can quench it because	Jer 4:4	1197
b incense unto Baal, and walk	Jer 7:9	6999
and it shall *b*, and shall not be	Jer 7:20	1197
Hinnom, to *b* their sons and their	Jer 7:31	8313
even altars to *b* incense unto	Jer 11:13	6999
anger, which shall *b* upon you	Jer 15:14	3344
anger, which shall *b* for ever	Jer 17:4	3344
to *b* their sons with fire for	Jer 19:5	8313
and he shall *b* it with fire	Jer 21:10	8313
b that none can quench it,	Jer 21:12	1197
b it with the houses, upon whose	Jer 32:29	8313
and he shall *b* it with fire	Jer 34:2	8313
so shall they *b* odours for thee	Jer 34:5	8313
and take it, and *b* it with fire	Jer 34:22	8313
king that he would not *b* the roll	Jer 36:25	8313
and take it, and *b* it with fire	Jer 37:8	8313
tent, and *b* this city with fire	Jer 37:10	8313
they shall *b* it with fire, and	Jer 38:18	8313
and he shall *b* them, and carry them	Jer 43:12	8313
Egyptians shall he *b* with fire	Jer 43:13	8313
in that they went to *b* incense	Jer 44:3	6999
to *b* no incense unto other gods	Jer 44:5	6999
to *b* incense unto the queen of	Jer 44:17	6999
But since we left off to *b*	Jer 44:18	6999
to *b* incense to the queen of	Jer 44:25	6999
Thou shalt *b* with fire a third	Eze 5:2	1197
the fire, and *b* them in the fire	Eze 5:4	8313
they shall *b* thine houses with	Eze 16:41	8313
b up their houses with fire	Eze 23:47	8313
b also the bones under it, and	Eze 24:5	1754
brass of it may be hot, and may *b*	Eze 24:11	2787
b the weapons, both the shields	Eze 39:9	5400
they shall *b* them with fire seven	Eze 39:9	1197
for they shall *b* the weapons with	Eze 39:10	1197
he shall *b* it in the appointed	Eze 43:21	8313
b incense upon the hills, under	Hos 4:13	6999
I will *b* her chariots in the	Nah 2:13	1197
b incense unto their drag	Hab 1:16	6999
cometh, that shall *b* as an oven	Mal 4:1	1197
day that cometh shall *b* them up	Mal 4:1	3857
but he will *b* up the chaff with	Mt 3:12	2618
and bind them in bundles to *b* them	Mt 13:30	2618
his lot was to *b* incense when he	Lk 1:9	2370
but the chaff he will *b* with fire	Lk 3:17	2618
Did not our heart *b* within us	Lk 24:32	2545
it is better to marry than to *b*	1Cor 7:9	4448
who is offended, and I *b* not	2Cor 11:29	4448
eat her flesh, and *b* her with fire	Rev 17:16	2618

B

BURNED

the bush *b* with fire, and the bush	Ex 3:2	1197
burn him as he *b* the first	Lev 4:21	8313
Moses *b* it upon the altar	Lev 8:16	6999
the mountain *b* with fire unto the	Deut 4:11	1197
mount, and the mount *b* with fire	Deut 9:15	1197
b them with fire, after they had	Josh 7:25	8313
Israel *b* none of them, save Hazor	Josh 11:13	8313
smitten Ziklag, and *b* it with fire	1Sa 30:1	8313
and, behold, it was *b* with fire	1Sa 30:3	8313
and we *b* Ziklag with fire	1Sa 30:14	8313
and David and his men *b* them	2Sa 5:21	5375
they shall be utterly *b* with fire	2Sa 23:7	8313
of the house of Baal, and *b* them	2Kin 10:26	8313
b incense still in the high	2Kin 15:35	6999
have *b* incense unto other gods,	2Kin 22:17	6999
he *b* them without Jerusalem in	2Kin 23:4	8313
them also that *b* incense unto	2Kin 23:5	6999
b it at the brook Kidron, and	2Kin 23:6	8313
where the priests had *b* incense	2Kin 23:8	6999
b the chariots of the sun with	2Kin 23:11	8313
b the high place, and stamped it	2Kin 23:15	8313
small to powder, and *b* the grove	2Kin 23:15	8313
b them upon the altar, and	2Kin 23:16	8313
b men's bones upon them, and	2Kin 23:20	8313
and they were *b* with fire	1Chr 14:12	8313
them, and *b* incense unto them	2Chr 25:14	6999
have not *b* incense nor offered	2Chr 29:7	6999
have *b* incense unto other gods,	2Chr 34:25	6999
the gates thereof are *b* with fire	Neh 1:3	3341
the gates thereof are *b* with fire	Neh 2:17	3341
heaps of the rubbish which are *b*	Neh 4:2	8313
very wroth, and his anger *b* in him	Est 1:12	1197
hath *b* up the sheep, and the	Job 1:16	1197
me, and my bones are *b* with heat	Job 30:30	2787
while I was musing the fire *b*	Ps 39:3	1197
they have *b* up all the synagogues	Ps 74:8	8313
It is *b* with fire, it is cut down	Ps 80:16	8313
and my bones are *b* as an hearth	Ps 102:3	2787
the flame *b* up the wicked	Ps 106:18	3857
bosom, and his clothes not be *b*	Prov 6:27	8313
hot coals, and his feet not be *b*	Prov 6:28	3554
your cities are *b* with fire	Is 1:7	8313
inhabitants of the earth are *b*	Is 24:6	2787
up shall they be in the fire	Is 33:12	3341
it *b* him, yet he laid it not to	Is 42:25	1197
the fire, thou shalt not be *b*	Is 43:2	3554
I have *b* part of it in the fire	Is 44:19	8314
praised thee, is *b* up with fire	Is 64:11	8316
which have *b* incense upon the	Is 65:7	6999
have *b* incense unto other gods,	Jer 1:16	6999
his cities are *b* without	Jer 2:15	3341
The bellows are *b*, the lead is	Jer 6:29	2787
because they are *b* up, so that	Jer 9:10	3341
is *b* up like a wilderness, that	Jer 9:12	3341
they have *b* incense to vanity, and	Jer 18:15	6999
have *b* incense in it unto other	Jer 19:4	6999
upon whose roofs they have *b*	Jer 19:13	6999
that the king had *b* the roll	Jer 36:27	8313
the king of Judah hath *b*	Jer 36:28	8313
Thou hast *b* this roll, saying,	Jer 36:29	8313
king of Judah had *b* in the fire	Jer 36:32	8313
city shall not be *b* with fire	Jer 38:17	8313
cause this city to be *b* with fire	Jer 38:23	8313
the Chaldeans the king's house,	Jer 39:8	8313
had *b* incense unto other gods	Jer 44:15	6999
when we *b* incense to the queen of	Jer 44:19	6999
The incense that ye *b* in the	Jer 44:21	6999
Because ye have *b* incense	Jer 44:23	6999
daughters shall be *b* with fire	Jer 49:2	3341
they have *b* her dwellingplaces	Jer 51:30	3341
the reeds they have *b* with fire	Jer 51:32	8313
high gates shall be *b* with fire	Jer 51:58	3341
b the house of the Lord, and the	Jer 52:13	8313
of the great men, *b* he with fire	Jer 52:13	8313
he *b* against Jacob like a flaming	Lam 2:3	1197
of it, and the midst of it is *b*	Eze 15:4	2787
fire hath devoured it, and it is *b*	Eze 15:5	2787
to the north shall be *b* therein	Eze 20:47	6866
it well, and let the bones be *b*	Eze 24:10	2787
wherein she *b* incense to them, and	Hos 2:13	6999
b incense to graven images	Hos 11:2	6999
the flame hath *b* all the trees of	Joel 1:19	3857
because he *b* the bones of the	Amos 2:1	8313
thereof shall be *b* with the fire	Mic 1:7	8313
the earth is *b* at his presence,	Nah 1:5	5375
are gathered and *b* in the fire	Mt 13:40	2618
murderers, and *b* up their city,	Mt 22:7	1714
them into the fire, and they are *b*	Jn 15:6	2545
and *b* them before all men	Acts 19:19	2618
b in their lust one toward	Rom 1:27	1572

If any man's work shall be *b*	1Cor 3:15	2618
and though I give my body to be *b*	1Cor 13:3	2545
whose end is to be *b*	Heb 6:8	2740
that *b* with fire, nor unto	Heb 12:18	2545
for sin, are *b* without the camp	Heb 13:11	2618
that are therein shall be *b* up	2Pet 3:10	2618
as if they *b* in a furnace	Rev 1:15	4448
she shall be utterly *b* with fire	Rev 18:8	2618

BURNETH

the quick flesh that *b* have a	Lev 13:24	4348
he that *b* them shall wash his	Lev 16:28	8313
he that *b* her shall wash his	Num 19:8	8313
he *b* the chariot in the fire	Ps 46:9	8313
As the fire *b* a wood, and as the	Ps 83:14	1197
b up his enemies round about	Ps 97:3	3857
For wickedness *b* as the fire	Is 9:18	1197
He *b* part thereof in the fire	Is 44:16	8313
thereof as a lamp that *b*	Is 62:1	1197
As when the melting fire *b*	Is 64:2	6919
b incense upon altars of brick	Is 65:3	6999
nose, a fire that *b* all the day	Is 65:5	3344
he that *b* incense, as if he	Is 66:3	2142
him that *b* incense to his gods	Jer 48:35	6999
morning it *b* as a flaming fire	Hos 7:6	1197
and behind them a flame *b*	Joel 2:3	3857
take him up, and he that *b* him	Amos 6:10	5635
in the lake which *b* with fire	Rev 21:8	2545

BURNING

a *b* lamp that passed between	Gen 15:17	784
B for *b*, wound for wound,	Ex 21:25	3555
B for *b*, wound for wound,	Ex 21:25	3345
because of the *b* upon the altar	Lev 6:9	4169
of the altar shall be *b* in it	Lev 6:9	3344
upon the altar shall be *b* in it	Lev 6:12	3344
shall ever be *b* upon the altar	Lev 6:13	3344
bewail the *b* which the Lord hath	Lev 10:6	8316
and spread not, it is a *b* boil	Lev 13:23	6867
the skin whereof there is a hot *b*	Lev 13:24	4348
is a leprosy broken out of the *b*	Lev 13:25	4348
it is a rising of the *b*, and the	Lev 13:28	4348
it is an inflammation of the *b*	Lev 13:28	4348
of *b* coals of fire from off the	Lev 16:12	784
the *b* ague, that shall consume	Lev 26:16	6920
take up the censers out of the *b*	Num 16:37	8316
the midst of the *b* of the heifer	Num 19:6	8316
and with an extreme *b*, and with	Deut 28:22	2746
is brimstone, and salt, and *b*	Deut 29:23	8316
hunger, and devoured with *b* heat	Deut 32:24	
they made a very great *b* for him	2Chr 16:14	8316
And his people made no *b* for him	2Chr 21:19	8316
like the *b* of his fathers	2Chr 21:19	8316
Out of his mouth go *b* lamps	Job 41:19	3940
Let *b* coals fall upon them	Ps 140:10	784
in his lips as a *b* fire	Prov 16:27	6867
As coals are to *b* coals, and wood	Prov 26:21	1513
B lips and a wicked heart are like	Prov 26:23	1814
and *b* instead of beauty	Is 3:24	3587
judgment, and by the spirit of *b*	Is 4:4	1197
but this shall be with *b* and fuel	Is 9:5	8316
a *b* like	Is 10:16	3350
the *b* of a fire	Is 10:16	3345
b with his anger, and the burden	Is 30:27	1197
land thereof shall become *b* pitch	Is 34:9	1197
as a *b* fire shut up in my bones	Jer 20:9	1197
a fire on the hearth *b* before him	Jer 36:22	1197
b incense unto other gods in the	Jer 44:8	6999
was like *b* coals of fire, and like	Eze 1:13	1197
the midst of a *b* fiery furnace	Dan 3:6	3345
the midst of a *b* fiery furnace	Dan 3:11	3345
the midst of a *b* fiery furnace	Dan 3:15	3345
us from the *b* fiery furnace	Dan 3:17	3345
them into the *b* fiery furnace	Dan 3:20	3345
the midst of the *b* fiery furnace	Dan 3:21	3345
the midst of the *b* fiery furnace	Dan 3:23	3345
the mouth of the *b* fiery furnace	Dan 3:26	3345
flame, and his wheels as *b* fire	Dan 7:9	1815
and given to the *b* flame	Dan 7:11	3346
a firebrand plucked out of the *b*	Amos 4:11	8316
b coals went forth at his feet	Hab 3:5	7565
be girded about, and your lights *b*	Lk 12:35	2545
He was a *b* and a shining light	Jn 5:35	2545
is no sooner risen with a *b* heat	Jas 1:11	2742
lamps of fire *b* before the throne	Rev 4:5	2545
as it were a great mountain *b*	Rev 8:8	2545
b as it were a lamp, and it fell	Rev 8:10	2545
they shall see the smoke of her *b*	Rev 18:9	4451
when they saw the smoke of her *b*	Rev 18:18	4451
a lake of fire *b* with brimstone	Rev 19:20	2545

B

BURNINGS

people shall be as the *b* of lime	Is 33:12	4955
us shall dwell with everlasting *b*	Is 33:14	4168
with the *b* of thy fathers, the	Jer 34:5	4955

BURNISHED

like the colour of *b* brass	Eze 1:7	7044

BURNT

offered *b* offerings on the altar	Gen 8:20	5930
offer him there for a *b* offering	Gen 22:2	5930
clave the wood for the *b* offering	Gen 22:3	5930
took the wood of the *b* offering	Gen 22:6	5930
is the lamb for a *b* offering	Gen 22:7	5930
himself a lamb for a *b* offering	Gen 22:8	5930
offered him up for a *b* offering	Gen 22:13	5930
Bring her forth, and let her be *b*	Gen 38:24	8313
sight, why the bush is not *b*	Ex 3:3	1197
and *b* offerings, that we may	Ex 10:25	5930
took a *b* offering and sacrifices	Ex 18:12	5930
sacrifice thereon thy *b* offerings	Ex 20:24	5930
Israel, which offered *b* offerings	Ex 24:5	5930
it is a *b* offering unto the LORD	Ex 29:18	5930
upon the altar for a *b* offering	Ex 29:25	5930
b offering throughout your	Ex 29:42	5930
nor *b* sacrifice, nor meat	Ex 30:9	5930
the altar of *b* offering with all	Ex 30:28	5930
the altar of *b* offering with all	Ex 31:9	5930
offered *b* offerings, and brought	Ex 32:6	5930
b it in the fire, and ground it to	Ex 32:20	8313
The altar of *b* offering, with his	Ex 35:16	5930
he made the altar of *b* offering	Ex 38:1	5930
b offering before the door of the	Ex 40:6	5930
the altar of the *b* offering	Ex 40:10	5930
he *b* sweet incense thereon	Ex 40:27	6999
he put the altar of *b* offering by	Ex 40:29	5930
and offered upon it the *b* offering	Ex 40:29	5930
If his offering be a *b* sacrifice	Lev 1:3	5930
upon the head of the *b* offering	Lev 1:4	5930
And he shall flay the *b* offering	Lev 1:6	5930
to be a *b* sacrifice, an offering	Lev 1:9	5930
of the goats, for a *b* sacrifice	Lev 1:10	5930
it is a *b* sacrifice, an offering	Lev 1:13	5930
if the *b* sacrifice for his	Lev 1:14	5930
it is a *b* sacrifice, an offering	Lev 1:17	5930
but they shall not be *b* on the	Lev 2:12	5927
on the altar upon the *b* sacrifice	Lev 3:5	5930
of the altar of the *b* offering	Lev 4:7	5930
upon the altar of the *b* offering	Lev 4:10	5930
are poured out shall he be *b*	Lev 4:12	8313
of the altar of the *b* offering	Lev 4:18	5930
the *b* offering before the LORD	Lev 4:24	5930
horns of the altar of *b* offering	Lev 4:25	5930
bottom of the altar of *b* offering	Lev 4:25	5930
in the place of the *b* offering	Lev 4:29	5930
horns of the altar of *b* offering	Lev 4:30	5930
where they kill the *b* offering	Lev 4:33	5930
horns of the altar of *b* offering	Lev 4:34	5930
and the other for a *b* offering	Lev 5:7	5930
offer the second for a *b* offering	Lev 5:10	5930
This is the law of the *b* offering	Lev 6:9	5930
It is the *b* offering, because of	Lev 6:9	5930
with the *b* offering on the altar	Lev 6:10	5930
lay the *b* offering in order upon	Lev 6:12	6999
it shall be wholly *b*	Lev 6:22	6999
for the priest shall be wholly *b*	Lev 6:23	6999
In the place where the *b* offering	Lev 6:25	5930
it shall be *b* in the fire	Lev 6:30	8313
b offering shall they kill the	Lev 7:2	5930
offereth any man's *b* offering	Lev 7:8	5930
b offering which he hath offered	Lev 7:8	5930
third day shall be *b* with fire	Lev 7:17	8313
it shall be *b* with fire.	Lev 7:19	8313
This is the law of the *b* offering	Lev 7:37	5930
he *b* with fire without the camp	Lev 8:17	8313
the ram for the *b* offering	Lev 8:18	5930
Moses *b* the head, and the pieces,	Lev 8:20	6999
Moses *b* the whole ram upon the	Lev 8:21	6999
it was a *b* sacrifice for a sweet	Lev 8:21	5930
b them on the altar upon the	Lev 8:28	6999
on the altar upon the *b* offering	Lev 8:28	5930
and a ram for a *b* offering	Lev 9:2	5930
without blemish, for a *b* offering	Lev 9:3	5930
thy *b* offering, and make an	Lev 9:7	5930
sin offering, he *b* upon the altar	Lev 9:10	5930
the hide he *b* with fire without	Lev 9:11	8313
And he slew the *b* offering	Lev 9:12	5930
presented the *b* offering unto him	Lev 9:13	5930
and he *b* them upon the altar	Lev 9:13	6999
b them upon	Lev 9:14	6999
upon the *b* offering on	Lev 9:14	5930
And he brought the *b* offering	Lev 9:16	5930

b it upon the altar	Lev 9:17	6999
beside the *b* sacrifice of the	Lev 9:17	5930
he *b* the fat upon the altar	Lev 9:20	6999
and the *b* offering, and peace	Lev 9:22	5930
upon the altar the *b* offering	Lev 9:24	5930
offering, and, behold, it was *b*	Lev 10:16	8313
their *b* offering before the LORD	Lev 10:19	5930
the first year for a *b* offering	Lev 12:6	5930
the one for the *b* offering	Lev 12:8	5930
it shall be *b* in the fire	Lev 13:52	8313
the *b* offering, in the holy place	Lev 14:13	5930
he shall kill the *b* offering	Lev 14:19	5930
priest shall offer the *b* offering	Lev 14:20	5930
and the other a *b* offering	Lev 14:22	5930
and the other for a *b* offering	Lev 14:31	5930
and the other for a *b* offering	Lev 15:15	5930
and the other for a *b* offering	Lev 15:30	5930
and a ram for a *b* offering	Lev 16:3	5930
and one ram for a *b* offering	Lev 16:5	5930
forth, and offer his *b* offering	Lev 16:24	5930
the *b* offering of the people, and	Lev 16:24	5930
that offereth a *b* offering or	Lev 17:8	5930
day, it shall be *b* in the fire	Lev 19:6	8313
they shall be *b* with fire	Lev 20:14	8313
she shall be *b* with fire	Lev 21:9	8313
unto the LORD for a *b* offering	Lev 22:18	5930
for a *b* offering unto the LORD	Lev 22:18	5930
they shall be for a *b* offering	Lev 23:12	5930
a *b* offering, and a meat offering,	Lev 23:18	5930
and the other for a *b* offering	Lev 23:37	5930
without blemish for a *b* offering	Num 6:11	5930
sin offering, and his *b* offering	Num 6:14	5930
the first year, for a *b* offering	Num 6:16	5930
the first year, for a *b* offering	Num 7:15	5930
the first year, for a *b* offering	Num 7:21	5930
the first year, for a *b* offering	Num 7:27	5930
the first year, for a *b* offering	Num 7:33	5930
the first year, for a *b* offering	Num 7:39	5930
the first year, for a *b* offering	Num 7:45	5930
the first year, for a *b* offering	Num 7:51	5930
the first year, for a *b* offering	Num 7:57	5930
the first year, for a *b* offering	Num 7:63	5930
the first year, for a *b* offering	Num 7:69	5930
the first year, for a *b* offering	Num 7:75	5930
the first year, for a *b* offering	Num 7:81	5930
All the oxen for the *b* offering	Num 7:87	5930
and the other for a *b* offering	Num 8:12	5930
trumpets over your *b* offerings	Num 10:10	5930
the fire of the LORD *b* among them	Num 11:1	1197
the fire of the LORD *b* among them	Num 11:3	1197
a *b* offering, or a sacrifice in	Num 15:3	5930
with the *b* offering or sacrifice	Num 15:5	5930
a bullock for a *b* offering	Num 15:8	5930
young bullock for a *b* offering	Num 15:24	5930
they that were *b* had offered	Num 16:39	8313
b heifer of purification for sin	Num 19:17	8316
Balak, Stand by thy *b* offering	Num 23:3	5930
lo, he stood by his *b* sacrifice	Num 23:6	5930
Stand here by thy *b* offering	Num 23:15	5930
he stood by his *b* offering	Num 23:17	5930
day, for a continual *b* offering	Num 28:3	5930
It is a continual *b* offering	Num 28:6	5930
This is the *b* offering of every	Num 28:10	5930
beside the continual *b* offering	Num 28:10	5930
offer a *b* offering unto the LORD	Num 28:11	5930
for a *b* offering of a sweet	Num 28:13	5930
this is the *b* offering of every	Num 28:14	5930
beside the continual *b* offering	Num 28:15	5930
for a *b* offering unto the LORD	Num 28:19	5930
the *b* offering in the morning	Num 28:23	5930
is for a continual *b* offering	Num 28:23	5930
beside the continual *b* offering	Num 28:24	5930
But ye shall offer the *b* offering	Num 28:27	5930
beside the continual *b* offering	Num 28:31	5930
ye shall offer a *b* offering for a	Num 29:2	5930
Beside the *b* offering of the	Num 29:6	5930
offering, and the daily *b* offering	Num 29:6	5930
But ye shall offer a *b* offering	Num 29:8	5930
and the continual *b* offering	Num 29:11	5930
And ye shall offer a *b* offering	Num 29:13	5930
beside the continual *b* offering	Num 29:16	5930
beside the continual *b* offering	Num 29:19	5930
beside the continual *b* offering	Num 29:22	5930
beside the continual *b* offering	Num 29:25	5930
beside the continual *b* offering	Num 29:28	5930
beside the continual *b* offering	Num 29:31	5930
beside the continual *b* offering	Num 29:34	5930
But ye shall offer a *b* offering	Num 29:36	5930
beside the continual *b* offering	Num 29:38	5930
for your *b* offerings, and for your	Num 29:39	5930
they *b* all their cities wherein	Num 31:10	8313
b it with fire, and stamped it, and	Deut 9:21	8313

ye shall bring your *b* offerings	Deut 12:6	5930
your *b* offerings, and your	Deut 12:11	5930
b offerings in every place that	Deut 12:13	5930
thou shalt offer thy *b* offerings	Deut 12:14	5930
thou shalt offer thy *b* offerings	Deut 12:27	5930
have *b* in the fire to their gods	Deut 12:31	8313
thou shalt offer *b* offerings	Deut 27:6	5930
They shall be *b* with hunger	Deut 32:24	4198
whole *b* sacrifice upon thine	Deut 33:10	3632
they *b* the city with fire, and all	Josh 6:24	8313
thing shall be *b* with fire	Josh 7:15	8313
And Joshua *b* Ai, and made it an	Josh 8:28	8313
they offered thereon *b* offerings	Josh 8:31	5930
b their chariots with fire	Josh 11:9	8313
and he *b* Hazor with fire	Josh 11:11	8313
or if to offer thereon *b* offering	Josh 22:23	5930
not for *b* offering, nor for	Josh 22:26	5930
before him with our *b* offerings	Josh 22:27	5930
not for *b* offerings, nor for	Josh 22:28	5930
to build an altar for *b* offerings	Josh 22:29	5930
offer a *b* sacrifice with the wood	Judg 6:26	5930
will offer it up for a *b* offering	Judg 11:31	5930
if thou wilt offer a *b* offering	Judg 13:16	5930
not have received a *b* offering	Judg 13:23	5930
b up both the shocks, and also the	Judg 15:5	1197
b her and her father with fire	Judg 15:6	8313
as flax that was *b* with fire	Judg 15:14	1197
sword, and *b* the city with fire	Judg 18:27	8313
offered *b* offerings and peace	Judg 20:26	5930
offered *b* offerings and peace	Judg 21:4	5930
Also before they *b* the fat	1Sa 2:15	6999
offered the kine a *b* offering	1Sa 6:14	5930
Beth-shemesh offered *b* offerings	1Sa 6:15	5930
offered it for a *b* offering	1Sa 7:9	5930
was offering up the *b* offering	1Sa 7:10	5930
to offer *b* offerings, and to	1Sa 10:8	5930
Bring hither a *b* offering to me	1Sa 13:9	5930
And he offered the *b* offering	1Sa 13:9	5930
an end of offering the *b* offering	1Sa 13:10	5930
and offered a *b* offering	1Sa 13:12	5930
as great delight in *b* offerings	1Sa 15:22	5930
came to Jabesh, and *b* them there	1Sa 31:12	8313
and David offered *b* offerings	2Sa 6:17	5930
an end of offering *b* offerings	2Sa 6:18	5930
here be oxen for *b* sacrifice	2Sa 24:22	5930
neither will I offer *b* offerings	2Sa 24:24	5930
offered *b* offerings and peace	2Sa 24:25	5930
and *b* incense in high places	1Kin 3:3	6999
a thousand *b* offerings did	1Kin 3:4	5930
LORD, and offered up *b* offerings	1Kin 3:15	5930
for there he offered *b* offerings	1Kin 8:64	5930
little to receive the *b* offerings	1Kin 8:64	5930
b it with fire, and slain the	1Kin 9:16	8313
did Solomon offer *b* offerings	1Kin 9:25	5930
he *b* incense upon the altar that	1Kin 9:25	6999
which *b* incense and sacrificed	1Kin 11:8	6999
upon the altar, and *b* incense	1Kin 12:33	6999
men's bones shall be *b* upon thee	1Kin 13:2	8313
idol, and *b* it by the brook Kidron	1Kin 15:13	8313
b the king's house over him with	1Kin 16:18	8313
and pour it on the *b* sacrifice	1Kin 18:33	5930
fell, and consumed the *b* sacrifice	1Kin 18:38	5930
b incense yet in the high places	1Kin 22:43	6999
b up the two captains of the	2Kin 1:14	398
offered him for a *b* offering upon	2Kin 3:27	5930
b offering nor sacrifice unto	2Kin 5:17	5930
b offerings, Jehu appointed	2Kin 10:24	5930
an end of offering the *b* offering	2Kin 10:25	5930
b incense in the high places	2Kin 12:3	6999
b incense on the high places	2Kin 14:4	6999
b incense still on the high	2Kin 15:4	6999
b incense in the high places, and	2Kin 16:4	6999
And he his *b* offering	2Kin 16:13	6999
altar burn the morning *b* offering	2Kin 16:15	5930
and the king's *b* sacrifice	2Kin 16:15	5930
with the *b* offering of all the	2Kin 16:15	5930
all the blood of the *b* offering	2Kin 16:15	5930
there they *b* incense in all the	2Kin 17:11	6999
the Sepharvites *b* their children	2Kin 17:31	8313
he *b* the house of the LORD, and	2Kin 25:9	8313
great man's house *b* he with fire	2Kin 25:9	8313
upon the altar of the *b* offering	1Chr 6:49	5930
and they offered *b* sacrifices	1Chr 16:1	5930
end of offering the *b* offerings	1Chr 16:2	5930
To offer *b* offerings unto the	1Chr 16:40	5930
b offering continually morning	1Chr 16:40	5930
the oxen also for *b* offerings	1Chr 21:23	5930
nor offer *b* offerings without	1Chr 21:24	5930
offered *b* offerings and peace	1Chr 21:26	5930
fire upon the altar of *b* offering	1Chr 21:26	5930
and the altar of the *b* offering	1Chr 21:29	5930

of the *b* offering for Israel	1Chr 22:1	5930
to offer all *b* sacrifices unto	1Chr 23:31	5930
offered *b* offerings unto the LORD	1Chr 29:21	5930
a thousand *b* offerings upon it	2Chr 1:6	5930
for the *b* offerings morning and	2Chr 2:4	5930
b offering they washed in them	2Chr 4:6	5930
and consumed the *b* offering	2Chr 7:1	5930
for there he offered *b* offerings	2Chr 7:7	5930
able to receive the *b* offerings	2Chr 7:7	5930
Then Solomon offered *b* offerings	2Chr 8:12	5930
and every evening *b* sacrifices	2Chr 13:11	5930
it, and *b* it at the brook Kidron	2Chr 15:16	8313
to offer the *b* offerings of the	2Chr 23:18	5930
they offered *b* offerings in the	2Chr 24:14	5930
Moreover he *b* incense in the	2Chr 28:3	6999
b his children in the fire, after	2Chr 28:3	1197
b incense in the high places, and	2Chr 28:4	6999
b offerings in the holy place	2Chr 29:7	5930
LORD, and the altar of *b* offering	2Chr 29:18	5930
commanded that the *b* offering	2Chr 29:24	5930
the *b* offering upon the altar	2Chr 29:27	5930
when the *b* offering began, the	2Chr 29:27	5930
until the *b* offering was finished	2Chr 29:28	5930
were of a free heart *b* offerings	2Chr 29:31	5930
And the number of the *b* offerings	2Chr 29:32	5930
were for a *b* offering to the LORD	2Chr 29:32	5930
not flay all the *b* offerings	2Chr 29:34	5930
also the *b* offerings were in	2Chr 29:35	5930
offerings for every *b* offering	2Chr 29:35	5930
brought in the *b* offerings into	2Chr 30:15	5930
and Levites for *b* offerings	2Chr 31:2	5930
his substance for the *b* offerings	2Chr 31:3	5930
evening *b* offerings, and the *b*	2Chr 31:3	5930
he *b* the bones of the priests	2Chr 34:5	8313
And they removed the *b* offerings	2Chr 35:12	5930
busied in offering of *b* offerings	2Chr 35:14	5930
to offer *b* offerings upon the	2Chr 35:16	5930
they *b* the house of God, and brake	2Chr 36:19	8313
b all the palaces thereof with	2Chr 36:19	8313
to offer *b* offerings thereon, as	Ezr 3:2	5930
they offered *b* offerings thereon	Ezr 3:3	5930
even *b* offerings morning and	Ezr 3:3	5930
offered the daily *b* offerings by	Ezr 3:4	5930
offered the continual *b* offering	Ezr 3:5	5930
offer *b* offerings unto the LORD	Ezr 3:6	5930
for the *b* offerings of the God of	Ezr 6:9	5928
offered *b* offerings unto the God	Ezr 8:35	5930
all this was a *b* offering unto	Ezr 8:35	5930
and for the continual *b* offering	Neh 10:33	5930
offered *b* offerings according to	Job 1:5	5930
up for yourselves a *b* offering	Job 42:8	5930
and accept thy *b* sacrifice	Ps 20:3	5930
b offering and sin offering hast	Ps 40:6	5930
thy sacrifices or thy *b* offerings	Ps 50:8	5930
thou delightest not in *b* offering	Ps 51:16	5930
b offering and whole *b* offering	Ps 51:19	5930
into thy house with *b* offerings	Ps 66:13	5930
thee *b* sacrifices of fatlings	Ps 66:15	5930
I am full of the *b* offerings of	Is 1:11	5930
sufficient for a *b* offering	Is 40:16	5930
small cattle of thy *b* offerings	Is 43:23	5930
their *b* offerings and their	Is 56:7	5930
I hate robbery for *b* offering	Is 61:8	5930
your *b* offerings are not	Jer 6:20	5930
Put your *b* offerings unto your	Jer 7:21	5930
concerning *b* offerings or	Jer 7:22	5930
and when they offer *b* offering	Jer 14:12	5930
south, bringing *b* offerings, and	Jer 17:26	5930
fire for *b* offerings unto Baal	Jer 19:5	5930
before me to offer *b* offerings	Jer 33:18	5930
and will make thee a *b* mountain	Jer 51:25	8316
where they washed the *b* offering	Eze 40:38	5930
to slay thereon the *b* offering	Eze 40:39	5930
of hewn stone for the *b* offering	Eze 40:42	5930
they slew the *b* offering and the	Eze 40:42	5930
to offer *b* offerings thereon, and	Eze 43:18	5930
up for a *b* offering unto the LORD	Eze 43:24	5930
your *b* offerings upon the altar	Eze 43:27	5930
they shall slay the *b* offering	Eze 44:11	5930
for a *b* offering, and for peace	Eze 45:15	5930
prince's part to give *b* offerings	Eze 45:17	5930
the *b* offering, and the peace	Eze 45:17	5930
prepare a *b* offering to the LORD	Eze 45:23	5930
according to the *b* offering	Eze 45:25	5930
shall prepare his *b* offering	Eze 46:2	5930
the *b* offering that the prince	Eze 46:4	5930
shall prepare a voluntary *b*	Eze 46:12	5930
he shall prepare his *b* offering	Eze 46:12	5930
Thou shalt daily prepare a *b*	Eze 46:13	5930
for a continual *b* offering	Eze 46:15	5930
of God more than *b* offerings	Hos 6:6	5930

Though ye offer me *b* offerings	Amos 5:22	5930
come before him with *b* offerings	Mic 6:6	5930
more than all whole *b* offerings	Mk 12:33	3646
In *b* offerings and sacrifices for	Heb 10:6	3646
b offerings and offering for sin	Heb 10:8	3646
the third part of trees was *b* up	Rev 8:7	2618
and all green grass was *b* up	Rev 8:7	2618

BURST

it is ready to *b* like new bottles	Job 32:19	1234
presses shall *b* out with new wine	Prov 3:10	6555
broken thy yoke, and *b* thy bands	Jer 2:20	5423
broken the yoke, and *b* the bonds	Jer 5:5	5423
will *b* thy bonds, and strangers	Jer 30:8	5423
will *b* thy bonds in sunder	Nah 1:13	5423
the new wine doth *b* the bottles	Mk 2:22	4486
the new wine will *b* the bottles	Lk 5:37	4486
he *b* asunder in the midst, and all	Acts 1:18	2997

BURSTING

b of it a sherd to take fire from	Is 30:14	4386

BURY

that I may *b* my dead out of my	Gen 23:4	6912
of our sepulchres *b* thy dead	Gen 23:6	6912
but that thou mayest *b* thy dead	Gen 23:6	6912
should *b* my dead out of my sight	Gen 23:8	6912
b thy dead	Gen 23:11	6912
of me, and I will *b* my dead there	Gen 23:13	6912
b therefore thy dead	Gen 23:15	6912
b me not, I pray thee, in Egypt	Gen 47:29	6912
b me in their buryingplace	Gen 47:30	6912
b me with my fathers in the cave	Gen 49:29	6912
of Canaan, there shalt thou *b* me	Gen 50:5	6912
b my father, and I will come again	Gen 50:5	6912
b thy father, according as he	Gen 50:6	6912
And Joseph went up to *b* his father	Gen 50:7	6912
went up with him to *b* his father	Gen 50:14	6912
shalt in any wise *b* him that day	Deut 21:23	6912
said, and fall upon him, and *b* him	1Kin 2:31	6912
host was gone up to *b* the slain	1Kin 11:15	6912
to the city, to mourn and to *b* him	1Kin 13:29	6912
then *b* me in the sepulchre	1Kin 13:31	6912
shall mourn for him, and *b* him	1Kin 14:13	6912
and there shall be none to *b* her	2Kin 9:10	6912
now this cursed woman, and *b* her	2Kin 9:34	6912
And they went to *b* her	2Kin 9:35	6912
and there was none to *b* them	Ps 79:3	6912
for they shall *b* in Tophet	Jer 7:32	6912
and they shall have none to *b* them	Jer 14:16	6912
they shall *b* them in Tophet	Jer 19:11	6912
till there be no place to *b*	Jer 19:11	6912
and there shall they *b* Gog	Eze 39:11	6912
people of the land shall *b* them	Eze 39:13	6912
passing through the land to *b*	Eze 39:14	6912
them up, Memphis shall *b* them	Hos 9:6	6912
me first to go and *b* my father	Mt 8:21	2290
and let the dead *b* their dead	Mt 8:22	2290
potter's field, to *b* strangers in	Mt 27:7	5027
me first to go and *b* my father	Lk 9:59	2290
him, Let the dead *b* their dead	Lk 9:60	2290
as the manner of the Jews is to *b*	Jn 19:40	1779

BURYING

to pass, as they were *b* a man	2Kin 13:21	6912
the house of Israel be *b* of them	Eze 39:12	6912
to anoint my body to the *b*.	Mk 14:8	1780
day of my *b* hath she kept this	Jn 12:7	1780

BURYINGPLACE

me a possession of a *b* with you	Gen 23:4	6913
a possession of a *b* amongst you	Gen 23:9	6913
of a *b* by the sons of Heth	Gen 23:20	6913
of Egypt, and bury me in their *b*	Gen 47:30	6913
Hittite for a possession of a *b*	Gen 49:30	6913
of a *b* of Ephron the Hittite	Gen 50:13	6913
Eshtaol in the *b* of Manoah his	Judg 16:31	6913

BUSH

of fire out of the midst of a *b*	Ex 3:2	5572
the *b* burned with fire	Ex 3:2	5572
and the *b* was not consumed	Ex 3:2	5572
sight, why the *b* is not burnt	Ex 3:3	5572
him out of the midst of the *b*	Ex 3:4	5572
will of him that dwelt in the *b*	Deut 33:16	5572
how in the *b* God spake unto him,	Mk 12:26	942
nor of a bramble *b* gather they	Lk 6:44	942
even Moses shewed at the *b*	Lk 20:37	942
Lord in a flame of fire in a *b*	Acts 7:30	942
which appeared to him in the *b*.	Acts 7:35	942

BUSHEL

a candle, and put it under a *b*	Mt 5:15	3426
brought to be put under a *b*	Mk 4:21	3426
a secret place, neither under a *b*	Lk 11:33	3426

BUSHES

Who cut up mallows by the *b*	Job 30:4	7880
Among the *b* they brayed	Job 30:7	7880
and upon all thorns, and upon all *b*	Is 7:19	5097

BUSHY

most fine gold, his locks are *b*	Song 5:11	8534

BUSIED

b in offering of burnt offerings	2Chr 35:14	

BUSINESS

went into the house to do his *b*	Gen 39:11	4399
shall he be charged with any *b*	Deut 24:5	1697
yours, if ye utter not this our *b*	Josh 2:14	1697
And if thou utter this our *b*	Josh 2:20	1697
and had no *b* with any man	Judg 18:7	1697
they had no *b* with any man	Judg 18:28	1697
thyself when the *b* was in hand	1Sa 20:19	4639
The king hath commanded me a *b*	1Sa 21:2	1697
of the *b* whereabout I send thee	1Sa 21:2	1697
the king's *b* required haste	1Sa 21:8	1697
for the outward *b* over Israel	1Chr 26:29	4399
westward in all the *b* of the LORD	1Chr 26:30	4399
and the Levites wait upon their *b*	2Chr 13:10	4399
he had much *b* in the cities of	2Chr 17:13	4399
Howbeit in the *b* of the	2Chr 32:31	
the outward *b* of the house of God	Neh 11:16	4399
over the *b* of the house of God	Neh 11:22	4399
the Levites, every one in his *b*	Neh 13:30	4399
that have the charge of the *b*	Est 3:9	4399
that do *b* in great waters	Ps 107:23	4399
thou a man diligent in his *b*	Prov 22:29	4399
cometh through the multitude of *b*	Eccl 5:3	6045
to see the *b* that is done upon	Eccl 8:16	6045
I rose up, and did the king's *b*	Dan 8:27	4399
I must be about my Father's *b*	Lk 2:49	
whom we may appoint over this *b*	Acts 6:3	5532
Not slothful in *b*	Rom 12:11	4710
whatsoever *b* she hath need of you	Rom 16:2	4229
to be quiet, and to do your own *b*	1Th 4:11	2398

BUSY

And as thy servant was *b* here	1Kin 20:40	6213

BUSYBODIES

working not at all, but are *b*	2Th 3:11	4020
only idle, but tattlers also and *b*	1Ti 5:13	4021

BUSYBODY

or as a *b* in other men's matters	1Pet 4:15	244

BUT See APPENDIX.

BUTLER

that the *b* of the king of Egypt	Gen 40:1	4945
of his dream, the *b* and the baker	Gen 40:5	4945
the chief *b* told his dream to	Gen 40:9	4945
manner when thou wast his *b*	Gen 40:13	4945
lifted up the head of the chief *b*	Gen 40:20	4945
he restored the chief *b* unto his	Gen 40:21	4945
not the chief *b* remember Joseph	Gen 40:23	4945
spake the chief *b* unto Pharaoh	Gen 41:9	4945

BUTLERS

against the chief of the *b*.	Gen 40:2	4945

BUTLERSHIP

the chief butler unto his *b* again	Gen 40:21	4945

BUTTER

And he took *b*, and milk, and the	Gen 18:8	2529
B of kine, and milk of sheep, with	Deut 32:14	2529
brought forth *b* in a lordly dish	Judg 5:25	2529
And honey, and *b*, and sheep, and	2Sa 17:29	2529
floods, the brooks of honey and *b*	Job 20:17	2529
When I washed my steps with *b*	Job 29:6	2529
of his mouth were smoother than *b*	Ps 55:21	4260
churning of milk bringeth forth *b*	Prov 30:33	2529
B and honey shall he eat, that he	Is 7:15	2529
they shall give, he shall eat *b*	Is 7:22	2529
for *b* and honey shall every one	Is 7:22	2529

BUTTOCKS

in the middle, even to their *b*	2Sa 10:4	8357
in the midst hard by their *b*	1Chr 19:4	4667
even with their *b* uncovered	Is 20:4	8357

BUY

Egypt to Joseph for to *b* corn	Gen 41:57	7666
thither, and *b* for us from thence	Gen 42:2	7666
went down to *b* corn in Egypt	Gen 42:3	7666
to *b* corn among those that came	Gen 42:5	7666
From the land of Canaan to *b* food	Gen 42:7	7666
but to *b* food are thy servants	Gen 42:10	7666
Go again, *b* us a little food	Gen 43:2	7666
we will go down and *b* thee food	Gen 43:4	7666
down at the first time to *b* food	Gen 43:20	7666

down in our hands to *b* food .... Gen 43:22   7666
Go again, and *b* us a little food .... Gen 44:25   7666
b us and our land for bread, and we ...... Gen 47:19   7069
If thou *b* an Hebrew servant, six............ Ex 21:2   7069
But if the priest *b* any soul with .... Lev 22:11   7069
thou shalt *b* of thy neighbour................. Lev 25:15   7069
of them shall ye *b* bondmen .... Lev 25:44   7069
among you, of them shall ye *b* .... Lev 25:45   7069
Ye shall *b* meat of them for money .... Deut 2:6   7666
ye shall also *b* water of them for .... Deut 2:6   3739
bondwomen, and no man shall *b* you ... Deut 28:68   7069
B it before the inhabitants, and .... Ruth 4:4   7069
thou must *b* it also of Ruth the .... Ruth 4:5   7069
said unto Boaz, *B* it for thee.................... Ruth 4:8   7069
To *b* the threshingfloor of thee,............... 2Sa 24:21   7069
but I will surely *b* it of thee at 2Sa 24:24   7069
to *b* timber and hewed stone to 2Kin 12:12   7069
to *b* timber and hewn stone to 2Kin 22:6   7069
but I will verily *b* it for the 1Chr 21:24   7069
to *b* hewn stone, and timber for 2Chr 34:11   7069
That thou mayest *b* speedily with .... Ezr 7:17   7066
and houses, that we might *b* corn .... Neh 5:3   3947
that we would not *b* it of them on .... Neh 10:31   3947
B the truth, and sell it not .... Prov 23:23   7069
come ye, *b*, and eat .... Is 55:1   7666
b wine and milk without money and ...... Is 55:1   7666
B thee my field that is in .... Jer 32:7   7069
of redemption is thine to *b* it .... Jer 32:7   7069
B my field, I pray thee, that is................. Jer 32:8   7069
b it for thyself .... Jer 32:8   7069
B thee the field for money, and.............. Jer 32:25   7069
Men shall *b* fields for money, and .... Jer 32:44   7069
That we may *b* the poor for silver .... Amos 8:6   7069
and *b* themselves victuals .... Mt 14:15   59
that sell, and *b* for yourselves .... Mt 25:9   59
And while they went to *b*, the............... Mt 25:10   59
villages, and *b* themselves bread .... Mk 6:36   59
b two hundred pennyworth of bread ...... Mk 6:37   59
b meat for all this people........................ Lk 9:13   59
him sell his garment, and *b* one .... Lk 22:36   59
gone away unto the city to *b* meat .... Jn 4:8   59
Philip, Whence shall we *b* bread........... Jn 6:5   59

B those things that we have need............ Jn 13:29   59
and they that *b*, as though they 1Cor 7:30   59
and continue there a year, and *b* .... Jas 4:13   *1710*
I counsel thee to *b* of me gold................ Rev 3:18   59
And that no man might *b* or sell .... Rev 13:17   59

BUYER
naught, it is naught, saith the *b*............. Prov 20:14   7069
as with the *b*, so with the seller .... Is 24:2   7069
let not the *b* rejoice, nor the .... Eze 7:12   7069

BUYEST
or *b* ought of thy neighbour's .... Lev 25:14   7069
What day thou *b* the field of the .... Ruth 4:5   7069

BUYETH
She considereth a field, and *b* it .... Prov 31:16   3947
all that he hath, and *b* that field........... Mt 13:44   *59*
for no man *b* their merchandise .... Rev 18:11   *59*

BUZ *(buz)*
1. Son of Nahor.
B his brother, and Kemuel the .... Gen 22:21   938
2. A Gadite.
the son of Jahdo, the son of *B* 1Chr 5:14   938
3. A tribe in northern Arabia.
Dedan, and Tema, and *B*, and all that ... Jer 25:23   938

BUZI *(boo'-zi)* See BUZITE. *Father of Ezekiel.*
Ezekiel the priest, the son of *B* .... Eze 1:3   941

BUZITE *(boo'-zite)* *A member of Buz 3.*
Elihu the son of Barachel the *B* .... Job 32:2   940
son of Barachel the *B* answered .... Job 32:6   940

BY See APPENDIX.

BYWAYS
the travellers walked through *b* ...... Judg 5:6   734,6128

BYWORD
astonishment, a proverb, and a *b* .... Deut 28:37   8148
a proverb and a *b* among all people....... 1Kin 9:7   8148
proverb and a *b* among all nations 2Chr 7:20   8148
made me also a *b* of the people.............. Job 17:6   4914
I their song, yea, I am their *b* .... Job 30:9   4405
Thou makest us a *b* among the .... Ps 44:14   4912

C

CAB
the fourth part of a *c* of dove's 2Kin 6:25   6894

CABBON *(cab'-bon)* *A town in Judah.*
And *C*, and Lahmam, and Kithlish, ... Josh 15:40   3522

CABINS
into the dungeon, and into the *c* .... Jer 37:16   2588

CABUL *(ca'-bul)* *A town in Asher.*
goeth out to *C* on the left hand, ... Josh 19:27   3521
them the land of *C* unto this day 1Kin 9:13   3521

CAESAR *(se'-zur)* See CAESAR'S. *Title for the Roman Emperor.*
it lawful to give tribute unto *C*................ Mt 22:17   2541
Render therefore unto *C* the .... Mt 22:21   2541
Is it lawful to give tribute to *C*................ Mk 12:14   2541
Render to *C* the things that are .... Mk 12:17   2541
went out a decree from *C* Augustus ...... Lk 2:1   2541
year of the reign of Tiberius *C* .... Lk 3:1   2541
for us to give tribute unto *C*.................... Lk 20:22   2541
Render therefore unto *C* the .... Lk 20:25   2541
forbidding to give tribute to *C*................. Lk 23:2   2541
himself a king speaketh against *C*......... Jn 19:12   2541
answered, We have no king but *C* .... Jn 19:15   2541
to pass in the days of Claudius *C*.......... Acts 11:28   2541
do contrary to the decrees of *C*.............. Acts 17:7   2541
the temple, nor yet against *C*.................. Acts 25:8   2541
I appeal unto *C* .... Acts 25:11   2541
Hast thou appealed unto *C* .... Acts 25:12   2541
unto *C* shalt thou go .... Acts 25:12   2541
kept till I might send him to *C* .... Acts 25:21   2541
if he had not appealed unto *C* .... Acts 26:32   2541
thou must be brought before *C* .... Acts 27:24   2541
was constrained to appeal unto *C* .... Acts 28:19   2541

CAESAREA *(ses-a-re'-ah)*
1. A town north of Galilee.
into the coasts of *C* Philippi .... Mt 16:13   2542
into the towns of *C* Philippi .... Mk 8:27   2542
2. A Judean Mediterranean port.
all the cities, till he came to *C*................ Acts 8:40   2542
knew, they brought him down to *C* .... Acts 9:30   2542
certain man in *C* called Cornelius.......... Acts 10:1   2542
morrow after they entered into *C*............ Acts 10:24   2542

where I was, sent from *C* unto me .... Acts 11:11   2542
And he went down from Judaea to *C* ..... Acts 12:19   2542
And when he had landed at *C* .... Acts 18:22   2542
company departed, and came unto *C*..... Acts 21:8   2542
certain of the disciples of *C*.................... Acts 21:16   2542
two hundred soldiers to go to *C*............. Acts 23:23   2542
Who, when they came to *C*, and............ Acts 23:33   2542
he ascended from *C* to Jerusalem .... Acts 25:1   2542
that Paul should be kept at *C*................. Acts 25:4   2542
ten days, he went down unto *C* .... Acts 25:6   2542
came unto *C* to salute Festus .... Acts 25:13   2542

CAESAR'S *(se'-zurs)*
They say unto him, *C*.............................. Mt 22:21   2541
Caesar the things which are *C*............... Mt 22:21   2541
And they said unto him, *C*...................... Mk 12:16   2541
to Caesar the things that are *C*............. Mk 12:17   2541
They answered and said, *C* .... Lk 20:24   2541
unto Caesar the things which be *C* .... Lk 20:25   2541
man go, thou art not *C* friend .... Jn 19:12   2541
I stand at *C* judgment seat, where......... Acts 25:10   2541
they that are of *C* household .... Phil 4:22   2541

CAGE
As a *c* is full of birds, so are.................. Jer 5:27   3619
a *c* of every unclean and hateful............ Rev 18:2   5438

CAIAPHAS *(cah'-ya-fus)* *A High Priest during Jesus' time.*
the high priest, who was called *C*........... Mt 26:3   2533
led him away to *C* the high priest .... Mt 26:57   2533
C being the high priests, the................... Lk 3:2   2533
And one of them, named *C*, being .... Jn 11:49   2533
for he was father in law to *C*.................. Jn 18:13   2533
Now *C* was he, which gave counsel .... Jn 18:14   2533
him bound unto *C* the high priest .... Jn 18:24   2533
Then led they Jesus from *C* unto .... Jn 18:28   2533
And Annas the high priest, and *C*.......... Acts 4:6   2533

CAIN See TUBAL-CAIN.
1. Eldest son of Adam and Eve.
and she conceived, and bare *C*.............. Gen 4:1   7014
but *C* was a tiller of the ground .... Gen 4:2   7014
that *C* brought of the fruit of.................. Gen 4:3   7014
But unto *C* and to his offering he .... Gen 4:5   7014
And *C* was very wroth, and his............... Gen 4:5   7014

And the LORD said unto *C*, Why art .... Gen 4:6   7014
C talked with Abel his brother.............. Gen 4:8   7014
that *C* rose up against Abel his .... Gen 4:8   7014
And the LORD said unto *C*, Where is ...... Gen 4:9   7014
And *C* said unto the LORD, My .... Gen 4:13   7014
Therefore whosoever slayeth *C* .... Gen 4:15   7014
And the LORD set a mark upon *C* .... Gen 4:15   7014
C went out from the presence of .... Gen 4:16   7014
And *C* knew his wife .... Gen 4:17   7014
If *C* shall be avenged sevenfold,.......... Gen 4:24   7014
seed instead of Abel, whom *C* slew .... Gen 4:25   7014
a more excellent sacrifice than *C* .... Heb 11:4   2535
Not as *C*, who was of that wicked 1Jn 3:12   2535
they have gone in the way of *C* .... Jude 11   2535
   2. *A town in Judah.*
C, Gibeah, and Timnah .... Josh 15:57   7014

CAINAN (ca'-nun) See KENAN. *Son of Enos.*
lived ninety years, and begat *C* .... Gen 5:9   7018
after he begat *C* eight hundred............. Gen 5:10   7018
C lived seventy years, and begat .... Gen 5:12   7018
C lived after he begat Mahalaleel .... Gen 5:13   7018
all the days of *C* were nine .... Gen 5:14   7018
Which was the son of *C*, which was ...... Lk 3:36   2536
Maleleel, which was the son of *C*.......... Lk 3:37   2536

CAKE
one *c* of oiled bread, and one .... Ex 29:23   2471
LORD, he took one unleavened *c* .... Lev 8:26   2471
a *c* of oiled bread, and one wafer, ... Lev 8:26   2471
two tenth deals shall be in one *c* .... Lev 24:5   2471
one unleavened *c* out of the .... Num 6:19   2471
Ye shall offer up a *c* of the .... Num 15:20   2471
a *c* of barley bread tumbled into .... Judg 7:13   6742
gave him a piece of a *c* of figs............. 1Sa 30:12   1690
as men, to every one a *c* of bread 2Sa 6:19   2471
thy God liveth, I have not a *c*............... 1Kin 17:12   4580
make me thereof a little *c* first 1Kin 17:13   5692
there was a *c* baken on the coals,......... 1Kin 19:6   5692
Ephraim is a *c* not turned .... Hos 7:8   5692

CAKES
it, and make *c* upon the hearth............. Gen 18:6   5692
they baked unleavened *c* of the .... Ex 12:39   5692
c unleavened tempered with oil, ... Ex 29:2   2471
it shall be unleavened *c* of fine .... Lev 2:4   2471
unleavened *c* mingled with oil .... Lev 7:12   2471
c mingled with oil, of fine flour .... Lev 7:12   2471
Besides the *c*, he shall offer for .... Lev 7:13   2471
flour, and bake twelve *c* thereof .... Lev 24:5   2471
c of fine flour mingled with oil, ... Num 6:15   2471
baked it in pans, and made *c* of it .... Num 11:8   5692
after the passover, unleavened *c*............ Josh 5:11   4682
unleavened *c* of an ephah of flour .... Judg 6:19   4682
the flesh and the unleavened *c* .... Judg 6:20   4682
the flesh and the unleavened *c* .... Judg 6:21   4682
the flesh and the unleavened *c* .... Judg 6:21   2471
raisins, and two hundred *c* of figs 1Sa 25:18   1690
make me a couple of *c* in my sight 2Sa 13:6   3834
made *c* in his sight, and did bake 2Sa 13:8   3823
in his sight, and did bake the *c* 2Sa 13:8   3834
Tamar took the *c* which she had 2Sa 13:10   3834
c of figs, and bunches of raisins 1Chr 12:40   1690
offering, and for the unleavened *c* 1Chr 23:29   7550
to make a *c* to the queen of heaven,...... Jer 7:18   3561
did we make her *c* to worship her.......... Jer 44:19   3561
And thou shalt eat it as barley *c* .... Eze 4:12   5692

CALAH (ca'-lah) *An Assyrian city.*
and the city Rehoboth, and *C*, ... Gen 10:11   3625
And Resen between Nineveh and *C* .... Gen 10:12   3625

CALAMITIES
refuge, until these *c* be overpast .... Ps 57:1   1942
prayer also shall be in their *c* .... Ps 141:5   7451
he that is glad at *c* shall not be .... Prov 17:5   343

CALAMITY
for the day of their *c* is at hand............. Deut 32:35   343
prevented me in the day of my *c*............. 2Sa 22:19   343
my *c* laid in the balances .... Job 6:2   1942
my path, they set forward my *c* .... Job 30:13   1942
prevented me in the day of my *c* .... Ps 18:18   343
I also will laugh at your *c* .... Prov 1:26   343
shall his *c* come suddenly .... Prov 6:15   343
son is the *c* of his father....................... Prov 19:13   1942
For their *c* shall rise suddenly .... Prov 24:22   343
house in the day of thy *c* .... Prov 27:10   343
the face, in the day of their *c* .... Jer 18:17   343
day of their *c* was come upon them .... Jer 46:21   343
The *c* of Moab is near to come, and .... Jer 48:16   343
will bring the *c* of Esau upon him.......... Jer 49:8   343
I will bring their *c* from all .... Jer 49:32   343
the sword in the time of their *c* .... Eze 35:5   343

my people in the day of their *c* .... Obad 13   343
affliction in the day of their *c* .... Obad 13   343
substance in the day of their *c* .... Obad 13   343

CALAMUS
of sweet *c* two hundred and fifty .... Ex 30:23   7070
c and cinnamon, with all trees of .... Song 4:14   7070
bright iron, cassia, and *c* .... Eze 27:19   7070

CALCOL (cal'-col) See CHALCOL. *A son of Zerah.*
Zimri, and Ethan, and Heman, and *C* 1Chr 2:6   3633

CALDRON
it into the pan, or kettle, or *c* 1Sa 2:14   7037
as out of a seething pot or *c* .... Job 41:20   100
this city is the *c*, and we be the............. Eze 11:3   5518
the flesh, and this city is the *c* .... Eze 11:7   5518
This city shall not be your *c* .... Eze 11:11   5518
the pot, and as flesh within the *c* .... Mic 3:3   7037

CALDRONS
sod they in pots, and in *c* 2Chr 35:13   1731
The *c* also, and the shovels, and .... Jer 52:18   5518
firepans, and the bowls, and the *c* .... Jer 52:19   5518

CALEB (ca'-leb) See CALEB'S, CALEB-EPHRATAH, CHELUBAI.
   1. *A son of Jephunneh.*
of Judah, *C* the son of Jephunneh .... Num 13:6   3612
C stilled the people before Moses .... Num 13:30   3612
C the son of Jephunneh, which .... Num 14:6   3612
But my servant *C*, because he had .... Num 14:24   3612
save *C* the son of Jephunneh, and.......... Num 14:30   3612
C the son of Jephunneh, which .... Num 14:38   3612
save *C* the son of Jephunneh, and.......... Num 26:65   3612
Save *C* the son of Jephunneh the .... Num 32:12   3612
of Judah, *C* the son of Jephunneh .... Num 34:19   3612
Save *C* the son of Jephunneh .... Deut 1:36   3612
C the son of Jephunneh the .... Josh 14:6   3612
gave unto *C* the son of Jephunneh .... Josh 14:13   3612
of *C* the son of Jephunneh the .... Josh 14:14   3612
unto *C* the son of Jephunneh he .... Josh 15:13   3612
C drove thence the three sons of .... Josh 15:14   3612
And *C* said, He that smiteth .... Josh 15:16   3612
son of Kenaz, the brother of *C* .... Josh 15:17   3612
C said unto her, What wouldest .... Josh 15:18   3612
gave they to *C* the son of .... Josh 21:12   3612
And *C* said, He that smiteth .... Judg 1:12   3612
C said unto her, What wilt thou .... Judg 1:14   3612
C gave her the upper springs and .... Judg 1:15   3612
And they gave Hebron unto *C* .... Judg 1:20   3612
and he was of the house of *C* 1Sa 25:3   3612
to Judah, and upon the south of *C*......... 1Sa 30:14   3612
and the daughter of *C* was Achsa 1Chr 2:49   3612
And the sons of *C* the son of 1Chr 4:15   3612
they gave to *C* the son of 1Chr 6:56   3612
   2. *A son of Hezron.*
C the son of Hezron begat.................... 1Chr 2:18   3612
C took unto him Ephrath, which............ 1Chr 2:19   3612
Now the sons of *C* the brother of 1Chr 2:42   3612
   3. *A son of Hur.*
were the sons of *C* the son of Hur.......... 1Chr 2:50   3612

CALEB-EPHRATAH (ca'-leb-ef'-ra-tah) *The place where Hezron died.*
after that Hezron was dead in *C* 1Chr 2:24   3613

CALEB-EPHRATHAH See CALEB-EPHRATAH.

CALEB'S (ca'-lebs) *Refers to Caleb 1.*
C younger brother, took it .... Judg 1:13   3612
son of Kenaz, *C* younger brother .... Judg 3:9   3612
C concubine, bare Haran, and Moza,..... 1Chr 2:46   3612
C concubine, bare Sheber, and 1Chr 2:48   3612

CALF
the herd, and fetch a *c* tender .... Gen 18:7   1121,1241
the *c* which he had dressed, and .... Gen 18:8   1121,1241
after he had made it a molten *c* .... Ex 32:4   5695
they have made them a molten *c* .... Ex 32:8   5695
unto the camp, that he saw the *c*........... Ex 32:19   5695
he took the *c* which they had made .... Ex 32:20   5695
fire, and there came out this *c* .... Ex 32:24   5695
people, because they made the *c* .... Ex 32:35   5695
Take thee a young *c* for a sin .... Lev 9:2   5695
and a *c* and a lamb, both of the .... Lev 9:3   5695
slew the *c* of the sin offering, ... Lev 9:8   5695
God, and had made you a molten *c* .... Deut 9:16   5695
the *c* which ye had made, and burnt ...... Deut 9:21   5695
woman had a fat *c* in the house 1Sa 28:24   5695
they had made them a molten *c* .... Neh 9:18   5695
cow calveth, and casteth not her *c* .... Job 21:10
maketh them also to skip like a *c* .... Ps 29:6   5695
They made a *c* in Horeb, and .... Ps 106:19   5695
and the *c* and the young lion and the .... Is 11:6   5695
there shall the *c* feed, and there .... Is 27:10   5695
me, when they cut the *c* in twain .... Jer 34:18   5695

passed between the parts of the c .... Jer 34:19 | 5695
Thy c, O Samaria, hath cast thee .... Hos 8:5 | 5695
but the c of Samaria shall be .... Hos 8:6 | 5695
And bring hither the fatted c .... Lk 15:23 | 3448
father hath killed the fatted c .... Lk 15:27 | 3448
hast killed for him the fatted c .... Lk 15:30 | 3448
they made a c in those days, and ...... Acts 7:41 | 3447
and the second beast like a c .... Rev 4:7 | 3448

CALF'S

was like the sole of a c foot .... Eze 1:7 | 5695

CALKERS

men thereof were in thee thy c .... Eze 27:9 | 2388,919
mariners, and thy pilots, thy c .... Eze 27:27 | 2388,919

CALL

Adam to see what he would c them .... Gen 2:19 | 7121
then began men to c upon the name .... Gen 4:26 | 7121
son, and shalt c his name Ishmael .... Gen 16:11 | 7121
thou shalt not c her name Sarai .... Gen 17:15 | 7121
thou shalt c his name Isaac .... Gen 17:19 | 7121
We will c the damsel, and enquire .... Gen 24:57 | 7121
the daughters will c me blessed .... Gen 30:13 | 833
to pass, when Pharaoh shall c you .... Gen 46:33 | 7121
c to thee a nurse of the Hebrew .... Ex 2:7 | 7121
c him, that he may eat bread .... Ex 2:20 | 7121
one c thee, and thou eat of his .... Ex 34:15 | 7121
And Moses sent to c Dathan .... Num 16:12 | 7121
to c him, saying, Behold, there .... Num 22:5 | 7121
him, If thee come to c thee .... Num 22:20 | 7121
send unto thee to c thee .... Num 22:37 | 7121
but the Moabites c them Emims .... Deut 2:11 | 7121
the Ammonites c them Zamzummims ... Deut 2:20 | 7121
Hermon the Sidonians c Sirion .... Deut 3:9 | 7121
and the Amorites c it Shenir .... Deut 3:9 | 7121
all things that we c upon him for .... Deut 4:7 | 7121
I c heaven and earth to witness .... Deut 4:26 | 5749
elders of his city shall c him .... Deut 25:8 | 7121
thou shalt c them to mind among .... Deut 30:1 | 7725
I c heaven and earth to record .... Deut 30:19 | 5749
c Joshua, and present yourselves .... Deut 31:14 | 7121
c heaven and earth to record .... Deut 31:28 | 5749
They shall c the people unto the .... Deut 33:19 | 7121
didst not c us to go with thee .... Judg 12:1 | 7121
C for Samson, that he may make us ...... Judg 16:25 | 7121
and to c peaceably unto them .... Judg 21:13 | 7121
C me not Naomi, call me Mara .... Ruth 1:20 | 7121
why then c ye me Naomi, seeing .... Ruth 1:21 | 7121
for thou didst c me .... 1Sa 3:6 | 7121
for thou didst c me .... 1Sa 3:8 | 7121
and it shall be, if he c thee .... 1Sa 3:9 | 7121
I will c unto the LORD, and he .... 1Sa 12:17 | 7121
c Jesse to the sacrifice, and I .... 1Sa 16:3 | 7121
sent to c Ahimelech the priest .... 1Sa 22:11 | 7121
C now Hushai the Archite also, and ...... 2Sa 17:5 | 7121
I will c on the LORD, who is .... 2Sa 22:4 | 7121
answered and said, C me Bath-sheba ...... 1Kin 1:28 | 7121
C me Zadok the priest, and Nathan ...... 1Kin 1:32 | 7121
in all that they c for unto thee .... 1Kin 8:52 | 7121
me to c my sin to remembrance .... 1Kin 17:18 | 2142
c ye on the name of your gods, and .... 1Kin 18:24 | 7121
I will c on the name of the LORD .... 1Kin 18:24 | 7121
c on the name of your gods, but .... 1Kin 18:25 | 7121
gone to c Micaiah spake unto him .... 1Kin 22:13 | 7121
his servant, C this Shunammite .... 2Kin 4:12 | 7121
And he said, C her .... 2Kin 4:15 | 7121
and said, C this Shunammite .... 2Kin 4:36 | 7121
c on the name of the LORD his God ...... 2Kin 5:11 | 7121
Now therefore c unto me all the .... 2Kin 10:19 | 7121
c upon his name, make known his .... 1Chr 16:8 | 7121
went to c Micaiah spake to him .... 2Chr 18:12 | 7121
C now, if there be any that will .... Job 5:1 | 7121
Then c thou, and I will answer .... Job 13:22 | 7121
Thou shalt c, and I will answer .... Job 14:15 | 7121
will he always c upon God .... Job 27:10 | 7121
Hear me when I c, O God of my .... Ps 4:1 | 7121
LORD will hear when I c unto him .... Ps 4:3 | 7121
eat bread, and c not upon the LORD ...... Ps 14:4 | 7121
I will c upon the LORD, who is .... Ps 18:3 | 7121
let the king hear us when we c .... Ps 20:9 | 7121
they c their lands after their .... Ps 49:11 | 7121
He shall c to the heavens from .... Ps 50:4 | 7121
c upon me in the day of trouble .... Ps 50:15 | 7121
As for me, I will c upon God .... Ps 55:16 | 7121
all nations shall c him blessed .... Ps 72:17 | 833
I c to remembrance my song in the ...... Ps 77:6 | 2142
us, and we will c upon thy name .... Ps 80:18 | 7121
unto all them that c upon thee .... Ps 86:5 | 7121
of my trouble I will c upon thee .... Ps 86:7 | 7121
He shall c upon me, and I will .... Ps 91:15 | 7121
among them that c upon his name .... Ps 99:6 | 7121

in the day when I c answer me .... Ps 102:2 | 7121
c upon his name .... Ps 105:1 | 7121
therefore will I c upon him as .... Ps 116:2 | 7121
c upon the name of the LORD .... Ps 116:13 | 7121
will c upon the name of the LORD .... Ps 116:17 | 7121
unto all them that c upon him .... Ps 145:18 | 7121
to all that c upon him in truth .... Ps 145:18 | 7121
Then shall they c upon me .... Prov 1:28 | 7121
c understanding thy kinswoman .... Prov 7:4 | 7121
Unto you, O men, I c .... Prov 8:4 | 7121
To c passengers who go right on .... Prov 9:15 | 7121
arise up, and c her blessed...................... Prov 31:28 | 833
Woe unto them that c evil good.............. Is 5:20 | 559
shall c his name Immanuel.................... Is 7:14 | 7121
C his name Maher-shalal-hash-baz ...... Is 8:3 | 7121
c upon his name, declare his .... Is 12:4 | 7121
Lord GOD of hosts c to weeping .... Is 22:12 | 7121
that I will c my servant Eliakim .... Is 22:20 | 7121
will not c back his words........................ Is 31:2 | 5493
They shall c the nobles thereof .... Is 34:12 | 7121
the sun shall he c upon my name .... Is 41:25 | 7121
another shall c himself by the................ Is 44:5 | 7121
And who, as I, shall c, and shall .... Is 44:7 | 7121
which c thee by thy name, am the........... Is 45:3 | 7121
For they c themselves of the holy .... Is 48:2 | 7121
when I c unto them, they stand up .... Is 48:13 | 7121
thou shalt c a nation that thou .... Is 55:5 | 7121
c ye upon him while he is near .... Is 55:6 | 7121
wilt thou c this a fast, and an .... Is 58:5 | 7121
Then shalt thou c, and the LORD .... Is 58:9 | 7121
c the sabbath a delight, the holy .... Is 58:13 | 7121
and they shall c thee, The city of .... Is 60:14 | 7121
but thou shalt c thy walls .... Is 60:18 | 7121
shall c you the Ministers of our .... Is 61:6 | 7121
And they shall c them, The holy .... Is 62:12 | 7121
c his servants by another name .... Is 65:15 | 7121
come to pass, that before they c .... Is 65:24 | 7121
I will c all the families of the.................. Jer 1:15 | 7121
At that time they shall c.......................... Jer 3:17 | 7121
and I said, Thou shalt c me .... Jer 3:19 | 7121
Reprobate silver shall men c them .... Jer 6:30 | 7121
thou shalt also c unto them................... Jer 7:27 | 7121
c for the mourning women, that .... Jer 9:17 | 7121
families that c not on thy name .... Jer 10:25 | 7121
for I will c for a sword upon all .... Jer 25:29 | 7121
Then shall ye c upon me, and ye .... Jer 29:12 | 7121
C unto me, and I will answer thee, ... Jer 33:3 | 7121
C together the archers against .... Jer 50:29 | 8085
c together against her the .... Jer 51:27 | 8085
men c The perfection of beauty .... Lam 2:15 | 559
but he will c to remembrance the .... Eze 21:23 | 2142
I will c for the corn, and will .... Eze 36:29 | 7121
I will c for a sword against him .... Eze 38:21 | 7121
they shall c it The valley of................... Eze 39:11 | 7121
king commanded to c the magicians ...... Dan 2:2 | 7121
said unto him, C his name Jezreel.......... Hos 1:4 | 7121
unto him, C her name Lo-ruhamah .... Hos 1:6 | 7121
Then said God, C his name Lo-ammi ..... Hos 1:9 | 7121
LORD, that thou shalt c me Ishi .... Hos 2:16 | 7121
and shalt c me no more Baali .... Hos 2:16 | 7121
they c to Egypt, they go to .... Hos 7:11 | 7121
c a solemn assembly, gather the .... Joel 1:14 | 7121
a fast, c a solemn assembly .... Joel 2:15 | 7121
that whosoever shall c on the .... Joel 2:32 | 7121
the remnant whom the LORD shall c .... Joel 2:32 | 7121
they shall c the husbandman to............. Amos 5:16 | 7121
c upon thy God, if so be that God .... Jonah 1:6 | 7121
that they may all c upon the name......... Zeph 3:9 | 7121
hosts, shall ye c every man his .... Zec 3:10 | 7121
they shall c on my name, and I .... Zec 13:9 | 7121
and they shall c them, The border .... Mal 1:4 | 7121
all nations shall c you blessed .... Mal 3:12 | 833
And now we c the proud happy .... Mal 3:15 | 833
thou shalt c his name JESUS .... Mt 1:21 | 2564
they shall c his name Emmanuel,.......... Mt 1:23 | 2564
I am not come to c the righteous .... Mt 9:13 | 2564
they c them of his household .... Mt 10:25 | 2564
C the labourers, and give them .... Mt 20:8 | 2564
sent forth his servants to c them .... Mt 22:3 | 2564
doth David in spirit c him Lord .... Mt 22:43 | 2564
If David then c him Lord .... Mt 22:45 | 2564
c no man your father upon the .... Mt 23:9 | 2564
I came not to c the righteous .... Mk 2:17 | 2564
they c the blind man, saying unto .... Mk 10:49 | 5455
whom ye c the King of the Jews .... Mk 15:12 | 3004
they c together the whole band .... Mk 15:16 | 4779
thou shalt c his name John .... Lk 1:13 | 2564
a son, and shalt c his name JESUS........ Lk 1:31 | 2564
generations shall c me blessed .... Lk 1:48 | 3106
I came not to c the righteous .... Lk 5:32 | 2564
why c ye me, Lord, Lord, and do .... Lk 6:46 | 2564

C

c not thy friends, nor thy	Lk 14:12	5455
c the poor, the maimed, the lame,	Lk 14:13	2564
c thy husband, and come hither	Jn 4:16	5455
Ye c me Master and Lord	Jn 13:13	5455
Henceforth I c you not servants	Jn 15:15	3004
that whosoever shall c on the	Acts 2:21	1941
many as the Lord our God shall c	Acts 2:39	4341
to bind all that c on thy name	Acts 9:14	1941
c for one Simon, whose surname is	Acts 10:5	3343
cleansed, that c not thou common	Acts 10:15	2840
not c any man common or unclean	Acts 10:28	3004
c hither Simon, whose surname is	Acts 10:32	3333
cleansed, that c not thou common	Acts 11:9	2840
c for Simon, whose surname is	Acts 11:13	3343
took upon them to c over them	Acts 19:13	3687
after the way which they c heresy	Acts 24:14	3004
season, I will c for thee	Acts 24:25	3333
I will c them my people, which	Rom 9:25	2564
is rich unto all that c upon him	Rom 10:12	1941
For whosoever shall c upon the	Rom 10:13	1941
How then shall they c on him in	Rom 10:14	1941
with all that in every place c	1Cor 1:2	1941
Moreover I c God for a record	2Cor 1:23	1941
When I c to remembrance the	2Ti 1:5	1941
with them that c on the Lord out	2Ti 2:22	2983
is not ashamed to c them brethren	Heb 2:11	2564
But c to remembrance the former	Heb 10:32	363
let him c for the elders of the	Jas 5:14	4341
if ye c on the Father, who	1Pet 1:17	1941

CALLED

God c the light Day, and the	Gen 1:5	7121
Day, and the darkness he c Night	Gen 1:5	7121
God c the firmament Heaven	Gen 1:8	7121
And God c the dry land Earth	Gen 1:10	7121
together of the waters c he Seas	Gen 1:10	7121
whatsoever Adam c every living	Gen 2:19	7121
she shall be c Woman, because she	Gen 2:23	7121
And the LORD God c unto Adam	Gen 3:9	7121
Adam c his wife's name Eve	Gen 3:20	7121
c the name of the city, after the	Gen 4:17	7121
bare a son, and c his name Seth	Gen 4:25	7121
and he c his name Enos	Gen 4:26	7121
c their name Adam, in the day	Gen 5:2	7121
and c his name Seth	Gen 5:3	7121
he c his name Noah, saying, This	Gen 5:29	7121
is the name of it c Babel	Gen 11:9	7121
c upon the name of the LORD	Gen 12:8	7121
And Pharaoh c Abram, and said	Gen 12:18	7121
there Abram c on the name of the	Gen 13:4	7121
she c the name of the LORD that	Gen 16:13	7121
the well was c Beer-lahai-roi	Gen 16:14	7121
Abram c his son's name, which	Gen 16:15	7121
thy name any more be c Abram	Gen 17:5	7121
they c unto Lot, and said unto him	Gen 19:5	7121
the name of the city was c Zoar	Gen 19:22	7121
bare a son, and c his name Moab	Gen 19:37	7121
a son, and c his name Ben-ammi	Gen 19:38	7121
c all his servants, and told all	Gen 20:8	7121
Then Abimelech c Abraham, and said	Gen 20:9	7121
Abraham c the name of his son	Gen 21:3	7121
for in Isaac shall thy seed be c	Gen 21:12	7121
the angel of God c to Hagar out	Gen 21:17	7121
Wherefore he c that place	Gen 21:31	7121
c there on the name of the LORD,	Gen 21:33	7121
the angel of the LORD c unto him	Gen 22:11	7121
Abraham c the name of that place	Gen 22:14	7121
the angel of the LORD c unto	Gen 22:15	7121
they c Rebekah, and said unto her,	Gen 24:58	7121
and they c his name Esau	Gen 25:25	7121
and his name was c Jacob	Gen 25:26	7121
therefore was his name c Edom	Gen 25:30	7121
And Abimelech c Isaac, and said,	Gen 26:9	7121
he c their names after the names	Gen 26:18	7121
by which his father had c them	Gen 26:18	7121
he c the name of the well Esek	Gen 26:20	7121
he c the name of it Sitnah	Gen 26:21	7121
he c the name of it Rehoboth	Gen 26:22	7121
c upon the name of the LORD, and	Gen 26:25	7121
And he c it Shebah	Gen 26:33	7121
he c Esau his eldest son, and said	Gen 27:1	7121
c Jacob her younger son, and said	Gen 27:42	7121
And Isaac c Jacob, and blessed him,	Gen 28:1	7121
he c the name of that place	Gen 28:19	7121
that city was c Luz at the first	Gen 28:19	7121
a son, and she c his name Reuben	Gen 29:32	7121
and she c his name Simeon	Gen 29:33	7121
therefore was his name c Levi	Gen 29:34	7121
therefore she c his name Judah	Gen 29:35	7121
therefore c she his name Dan	Gen 30:6	7121
and she c his name Naphtali	Gen 30:8	7121

and she c his name Gad	Gen 30:11	7121
and she c his name Asher	Gen 30:13	7121
and she c his name Issachar	Gen 30:18	7121
and she c his name Zebulun	Gen 30:20	7121
a daughter, and c her name Dinah	Gen 30:21	7121
And she c his name Joseph	Gen 30:24	7121
c Rachel and Leah to the field	Gen 31:4	7121
Laban c it Jegar-sahadutha	Gen 31:47	7121
but Jacob c it Galeed	Gen 31:47	7121
was the name of it c Galeed	Gen 31:48	7121
c his brethren to eat bread	Gen 31:54	7121
he c the name of that place	Gen 32:2	7121
Thy name shall be c no more Jacob	Gen 32:28	559
Jacob c the name of the place	Gen 32:30	7121
name of the place is c Succoth	Gen 33:17	7121
an altar, and c it El-elohe-Israel	Gen 33:20	7121
altar, and c the place El-beth-el	Gen 35:7	7121
name of it was c Allon-bachuth	Gen 35:8	7121
shall not be c any more Jacob	Gen 35:10	7121
and he c his name Israel	Gen 35:10	7121
Jacob c the name of the place	Gen 35:15	7121
died) that she c his name Ben-oni	Gen 35:18	7121
but his father c him Benjamin	Gen 35:18	7121
and he c his name Er	Gen 38:3	7121
and she c his name Onan	Gen 38:4	7121
and c his name Shelah	Gen 38:5	7121
therefore his name was c Pharez	Gen 38:29	7121
and his name was c Zarah	Gen 38:30	7121
That she c unto the men of her	Gen 39:14	7121
c for all the magicians of Egypt,	Gen 41:8	7121
c Joseph, and they brought him	Gen 41:14	7121
And Pharaoh c Joseph's name	Gen 41:45	7121
And Joseph c the name of the	Gen 41:51	7121
name of the second c he Ephraim	Gen 41:52	7121
he c his son Joseph, and said unto	Gen 47:29	7121
shall be c after the name of	Gen 48:6	7121
Jacob c unto his sons, and said,	Gen 49:1	7121
the name of it was c Abel-mizraim	Gen 50:11	7121
king of Egypt c for the midwives	Ex 1:18	7121
maid went and c the child's mother	Ex 2:8	7121
And she c his name Moses	Ex 2:10	7121
a son, and he c his name Gershom	Ex 2:22	7121
God c unto him out of the midst	Ex 3:4	7121
Then Pharaoh also c the wise men	Ex 7:11	7121
Then Pharaoh c for Moses and Aaron	Ex 8:8	7121
Pharaoh c for Moses and for Aaron	Ex 8:25	7121
c for Moses and Aaron, and said	Ex 9:27	7121
Then Pharaoh c for Moses and Aaron	Ex 10:16	7121
Pharaoh c unto Moses, and said, Go	Ex 10:24	7121
Then Moses c for all the elders	Ex 12:21	7121
he c for Moses and Aaron by night,	Ex 12:31	7121
the name of it was c Marah	Ex 15:23	7121
the house of Israel c the name	Ex 16:31	7121
he c the name of the place Massah	Ex 17:7	7121
c the name of it Jehovah-nissi	Ex 17:15	7121
the LORD c unto him out of the	Ex 19:3	7121
c for the elders of the people,	Ex 19:7	7121
the LORD c Moses up to the top of	Ex 19:20	7121
the seventh day he c unto Moses	Ex 24:16	7121
I have c by name Bezaleel the son	Ex 31:2	7121
c it the Tabernacle of the	Ex 33:7	7121
And Moses c unto them	Ex 34:31	7121
the LORD hath c by name Bezaleel	Ex 35:30	7121
Moses c Bezaleel and Aholiab, and	Ex 36:2	7121
the LORD c unto Moses, and spake	Lev 1:1	7121
eighth day, that Moses c Aaron	Lev 9:1	7121
Moses c Mishael and Elzaphan, and	Lev 10:4	7121
he c the name of the place	Num 11:3	7121
he c the name of that place	Num 11:34	7121
tabernacle, and c Aaron and Miriam	Num 12:5	7121
Moses c Oshea the son of Nun	Num 13:16	7121
The place was c the brook Eshcol,	Num 13:24	7121
he c the name of the place Hormah	Num 21:3	7121
I c thee to curse mine enemies,	Num 24:10	7121
they c the people unto the	Num 25:2	7121
thereof, and c them Havoth-jair	Num 32:41	7121
c it Nobah, after his own name	Num 32:42	7121
which was c the land of giants	Deut 3:13	7121
c them after his own name,	Deut 3:14	7121
Moses c all Israel, and said unto	Deut 5:1	7121
because it is c the LORD's	Deut 15:2	7121
And his name shall be c in Israel	Deut 25:10	7121
art c by the name of the LORD	Deut 28:10	7121
Moses c unto all Israel, and said	Deut 29:2	7121
Moses c unto Joshua, and said unto	Deut 31:7	7121
Then Joshua c the twelve men,	Josh 4:4	7121
place is c Gilgal unto this day	Josh 5:9	7121
the son of Nun c the priests	Josh 6:6	7121
the name of that place was c	Josh 7:26	7121
c together to pursue after them	Josh 8:16	2199
Joshua c for them, and he spake	Josh 9:22	7121

that Joshua c for all the men of	Josh 10:24	7121
c Leshem, Dan, after the name of	Josh 19:47	7121
Then Joshua c the Reubenites, and	Josh 22:1	7121
children of Gad c the altar Ed	Josh 22:34	7121
Joshua c for all Israel, and for	Josh 23:2	7121
c for the elders of Israel, and	Josh 24:1	7121
c Balaam the son of Beor to curse	Josh 24:9	7121
the name of the city was c Hormah	Judg 1:17	7121
a city, and c the name thereof Luz	Judg 1:26	7121
they c the name of that place	Judg 2:5	7121
c Barak the son of Abinoam out of	Judg 4:6	7121
Barak c Zebulun and Naphtali to	Judg 4:10	2199
the LORD, and c it Jehovah-shalom	Judg 6:24	7121
on that day he c him Jerubbaal	Judg 6:32	7121
a son, whose name he c Abimelech	Judg 8:31	7760
Then he c hastily unto the young	Judg 9:54	7121
which are c Havoth-jair unto this	Judg 10:4	7121
and when I c you, ye delivered me	Judg 12:2	2199
bare a son, and c his name Samson	Judg 13:24	7121
have ye c us to take that we have	Judg 14:15	7121
hand, and c that place Ramath-lehi	Judg 15:17	7121
c on the LORD, and said, Thou hast	Judg 15:18	7121
wherefore he c the name thereof	Judg 15:19	7121
sent and c for the lords of the	Judg 16:18	7121
she c for a man, and she caused	Judg 16:19	7121
they c for Samson out of the	Judg 16:25	7121
Samson c unto the LORD, and said,	Judg 16:28	7121
wherefore they c that place	Judg 18:12	7121
they c the name of the city Dan,	Judg 18:29	7121
and they c his name Obed	Ruth 4:17	7121
c his name Samuel, saying,	1Sa 1:20	7121
That the LORD c Samuel	1Sa 3:4	7121
And he said, I c not	1Sa 3:5	7121
the LORD c yet again, Samuel	1Sa 3:6	7121
And he answered, I c not, my son	1Sa 3:6	7121
the LORD c Samuel again the third	1Sa 3:8	7121
that the LORD had c the child	1Sa 3:8	7121
c as at other times, Samuel,	1Sa 3:10	7121
Then Eli c Samuel, and said,	1Sa 3:16	7121
the Philistines c for the priests	1Sa 6:2	7121
c the name of it Eben-ezer,	1Sa 7:12	7121
for he that is now c a Prophet	1Sa 9:9	
a Prophet was beforetime c a Seer	1Sa 9:9	7121
that Samuel c Saul to the top of	1Sa 9:26	7121
Samuel c the people together unto	1Sa 10:17	6817
So Samuel c unto the LORD	1Sa 12:18	7121
the people were c together after	1Sa 13:4	6817
sons, and c them to the sacrifice	1Sa 16:5	7121
Then Jesse c Abinadab, and made	1Sa 16:8	7121
And Jonathan c David, and Jonathan	1Sa 19:7	7121
Saul c all the people together to	1Sa 23:8	8085
therefore they c that place	1Sa 23:28	7121
therefore I c thee, that	1Sa 28:15	7121
Then Achish c David, and said unto	1Sa 29:6	7121
him, he saw me, and c unto me	2Sa 1:7	7121
David c one of the young men, and	2Sa 1:15	7121
that place was c Helkath-hazzurim	2Sa 2:16	7121
Then Abner c to Joab, and said,	2Sa 2:26	7121
fort, and c it the city of David	2Sa 5:9	7121
Therefore he c the name of that	2Sa 5:20	7121
whose name is c by the name of	2Sa 6:2	7121
he c the name of the place	2Sa 6:8	7121
when they had c him unto David,	2Sa 9:2	7121
Then the king c to Ziba, Saul's	2Sa 9:9	7121
And when David had c him, he did	2Sa 11:13	7121
a son, and he c his name Solomon	2Sa 12:24	7121
he c his name Jedidiah, because	2Sa 12:25	7121
city, and it be c after my name	2Sa 12:28	7121
Then he c his servant that	2Sa 13:17	7121
and when he had c for Absalom	2Sa 14:33	7121
judgment, then Absalom c unto him	2Sa 15:2	7121
men out of Jerusalem, that were c	2Sa 15:11	7121
he c the pillar after his own	2Sa 18:18	7121
it is c unto this day, Absalom's	2Sa 18:18	7121
the watchman c unto the porter,	2Sa 18:26	7121
And Ahimaaz c, and said unto the	2Sa 18:28	7121
the king c the Gibeonites, and	2Sa 21:2	7121
In my distress I c upon the LORD	2Sa 22:7	7121
c all his brethren the king's	1Kin 1:9	7121
and Solomon his brother, he c not	1Kin 1:10	7121
hath c all the sons of the king,	1Kin 1:19	7121
Solomon thy servant hath he not c	1Kin 1:19	7121
hath c all the king's sons, and	1Kin 1:25	7121
servant Solomon, hath he not c	1Kin 1:26	7121
c for Shimei, and said unto him,	1Kin 2:36	7121
c for Shimei, and said unto him,	1Kin 2:42	7121
c the name thereof Jachin	1Kin 7:21	7121
and c the name thereof Boaz	1Kin 7:21	7121
I have builded, is c by thy name	1Kin 8:43	7121
he c them the land of Cabul unto	1Kin 9:13	7121
That they sent and c him	1Kin 12:3	7121

c him unto the congregation, and	1Kin 12:20	7121
c the name of the city which he	1Kin 16:24	7121
he c to her, and said, Fetch me, I	1Kin 17:10	7121
he c to her, and said, Bring me, I	1Kin 17:11	7121
Ahab c Obadiah, which was the	1Kin 18:3	7121
c on the name of Baal from	1Kin 18:26	7121
Then the king of Israel c all the	1Kin 20:7	7121
the king of Israel c an officer	1Kin 22:9	7121
that the LORD hath c these three	2Kin 3:10	7121
for the LORD hath c these three	2Kin 3:13	7121
And when he had c her, she stood	2Kin 4:12	7121
And when he had c her, she stood	2Kin 4:15	7121
she c unto her husband, and said,	2Kin 4:22	7121
he c Gehazi, and said, Call this	2Kin 4:36	7121
So he c her	2Kin 4:36	7121
he c his servants, and said unto	2Kin 6:11	7121
c unto the porter of the city	2Kin 7:10	7121
And he c the porters	2Kin 7:11	7121
for the LORD hath c for a famine	2Kin 8:1	7121
Elisha the prophet c one of the	2Kin 9:1	7121
Then king Jehoash c for Jehoiada	2Kin 12:7	7121
c the name of it Joktheel unto	2Kin 14:7	7121
and he c it Nehushtan	2Kin 18:4	7121
And when they had c to the king	2Kin 18:18	7121
his mother c his name Jabez	1Chr 4:9	7121
Jabez c on the God of Israel,	1Chr 4:10	7121
which are c by their names	1Chr 6:65	7121
a son, and she c his name Peresh	1Chr 7:16	7121
he c his name Beriah, because it	1Chr 7:23	7121
therefore they c it the city of	1Chr 11:7	7121
cherubims, whose name is c on it	1Chr 13:6	7121
place is c Perez-uzza to this day	1Chr 13:11	7121
therefore they c the name of that	1Chr 14:11	7121
David c for Zadok and Abiathar the	1Chr 15:11	7121
offerings, and c upon the LORD	1Chr 21:26	7121
Then c for Solomon his son, and	1Chr 22:6	7121
c the name of that on the right	2Chr 3:17	7121
I have built is c by thy name	2Chr 6:33	7121
which are c by my name, shall	2Chr 7:14	7121
And they sent and c him	2Chr 10:3	7121
the king of Israel c for one of	2Chr 18:8	7121
the name of the same place was c	2Chr 20:26	7121
the king c for Jehoiada the chief	2Chr 24:6	7121
and was c after their name	Ezr 2:61	7121
Then I c the priests, and took an	Neh 5:12	7121
wife, and was c after their name	Neh 7:63	7121
her, and that she were c by name	Est 2:14	7121
c on the thirteenth day of the	Est 3:12	7121
Then c Esther for Hatach, one of	Est 4:5	7121
the inner court, who is not c	Est 4:11	7121
but I have not been c to come in	Est 4:11	7121
c for his friends, and Zeresh his	Est 5:10	935
Then were the king's scribes c at	Est 8:9	7121
Wherefore they c these days Purim	Est 9:26	7121
c for their three sisters to eat	Job 1:4	7121
If I had c, and he had answered me	Job 9:16	7121
I c my servant, and he gave me no	Job 19:16	7121
he c the name of the first,	Job 42:14	7121
I have c upon thee, for thou wilt	Ps 17:6	7121
In my distress I c upon the LORD	Ps 18:6	7121
for I have c upon thee	Ps 31:17	7121
c the earth from the rising of	Ps 50:1	7121
they have not c upon God	Ps 53:4	7121
that have not c upon thy name	Ps 79:6	7121
I have c daily upon thee, I have	Ps 88:9	7121
they c upon the LORD, and he	Ps 99:6	7121
Moreover he c for a famine upon	Ps 105:16	7121
Then c I upon the name of the	Ps 116:4	7121
I c upon the LORD in distress	Ps 118:5	7121
Because I have c, and ye refused	Prov 1:24	7121
wise in heart shall be c prudent	Prov 16:21	7121
shall be c a mischievous person	Prov 24:8	7121
I c him, but he gave me no answer	Song 5:6	7121
afterward thou shalt be c	Is 1:26	7121
only let us be c by thy name	Is 4:1	7121
in Jerusalem, shall be c holy	Is 4:3	559
and his name shall be c Wonderful	Is 9:6	7121
I have also c my mighty ones for	Is 13:3	7121
one shall be c, The city of	Is 19:18	559
shepherds is c forth against him	Is 31:4	7121
person shall be no more c liberal	Is 32:5	7121
it shall be c The way of holiness	Is 35:8	7121
c him to his foot, gave the	Is 41:2	7121
c thee from the chief men thereof	Is 41:9	7121
I the LORD have c thee in	Is 42:6	7121
I have c thee by thy name	Is 43:1	7121
every one that is c by my name	Is 43:7	7121
But thou hast not c upon me	Is 43:22	7121
I have even c thee by thy name	Is 45:4	7121
thou shalt no more be c tender	Is 47:1	7121
for thou shalt no more be c	Is 47:5	7121

which are c by the name of Israel	Is 48:1	7121
wast c a transgressor from the	Is 48:8	7121
unto me, O Jacob and Israel, my c	Is 48:12	7121
yea, I have c him	Is 48:15	7121
The LORD hath c me from the womb	Is 49:1	7121
when I c, was there none to	Is 50:2	7121
for I c him alone, and blessed him	Is 51:2	7121
of the whole earth shall he be c	Is 54:5	7121
For the LORD hath c thee as a	Is 54:6	7121
for mine house shall be c an	Is 56:7	7121
and thou shalt be c, The repairer	Is 58:12	7121
that they might be c trees of	Is 61:3	7121
and thou shalt be c by a new name	Is 62:2	7121
but thou shalt be c Hephzi-bah	Is 62:4	7121
and thou shalt be c, Sought out, A	Is 62:12	7121
they were not c by thy name	Is 63:19	7121
nation that was not c by my name	Is 65:1	7121
because when I c, ye did not	Is 65:12	7121
because when I c, none did answer	Is 66:4	7121
which is c by my name, and say, We	Jer 7:10	7121
which is c by my name, become a	Jer 7:11	7121
I c you, but ye answered not	Jer 7:13	7121
which is c by my name, wherein ye	Jer 7:14	7121
the house which is c by my name	Jer 7:30	7121
that it shall no more be c Tophet	Jer 7:32	559
The LORD c thy name, A green	Jer 11:16	7121
they have c a multitude after	Jer 12:6	7121
of us, and we are c by thy name	Jer 14:9	7121
for I am c by thy name, O LORD	Jer 15:16	7121
place shall no more be c Tophet	Jer 19:6	7121
LORD hath not c thy name Pashur	Jer 20:3	7121
is his name whereby he shall be c	Jer 23:6	7121
on the city which is c by my name	Jer 25:29	7121
because they c thee an Outcast,	Jer 30:17	7121
which is c by my name, to defile	Jer 32:34	7121
the name wherewith she shall be c	Jer 33:16	7121
the house which is c by my name	Jer 34:15	7121
I have c unto them, but they have	Jer 35:17	7121
Then Jeremiah c Baruch the son of	Jer 36:4	7121
Then c he Johanan the son of	Jer 42:8	7121
he hath c an assembly against me	Lam 1:15	7121
I c for my lovers, but they	Lam 1:19	7121
bring the day that thou hast c	Lam 1:21	7121
Thou hast c as in a solemn day my	Lam 2:22	7121
I c upon thy name, O LORD, out of	Lam 3:55	7121
in the day that I c upon thee	Lam 3:57	7121
he c to the man clothed with	Eze 9:3	7121
thereof is c Bamah unto this day	Eze 20:29	7121
now let Daniel be c, and he will	Dan 5:12	7123
the banks of Ulai, which c	Dan 8:16	7121
the city which is c by thy name	Dan 9:18	7121
and thy people are c by thy name	Dan 9:19	7121
whose name was c Belteshazzar	Dan 10:1	7121
him, and c my son out of Egypt	Hos 11:1	7121
As they c them, so they went from	Hos 11:2	7121
though they c them to the most	Hos 11:7	7121
the Lord GOD c to contend by fire	Amos 7:4	7121
which are c by my name, saith the	Amos 9:12	7121
I c for a drought upon the land,	Hag 1:11	7121
shall be c a city of truth	Zec 8:3	7121
two staves; the one I c Beauty	Zec 11:7	7121
Beauty, and the other I c Bands	Zec 11:7	7121
was born Jesus, who is c Christ	Mt 1:16	3004
and he c his name JESUS	Mt 1:25	2564
he had privily c the wise men	Mt 2:7	2564
Out of Egypt have I c my son	Mt 2:15	2564
and dwelt in a city c Nazareth	Mt 2:23	3004
He shall be c a Nazarene	Mt 2:23	2564
saw two brethren, Simon c Peter	Mt 4:18	3004
and he c them	Mt 4:21	2564
for they shall be c the children	Mt 5:9	2564
he shall be c the least in the	Mt 5:19	2564
the same shall be c great in the	Mt 5:19	2564
when he had c unto him his twelve	Mt 10:1	4341
The first, Simon, who is c Peter	Mt 10:2	3004
If they have c the master of the	Mt 10:25	2564
is not his mother c Mary	Mt 13:55	3004
he c the multitude, and said unto	Mt 15:10	4341
Then Jesus c his disciples unto	Mt 15:32	4341
Jesus c a little child unto him,	Mt 18:2	4341
his lord, after that he had c him	Mt 18:32	4341
for many be c, but few chosen	Mt 20:16	2822
But Jesus c them unto him, and	Mt 20:25	4341
c them, and said, What will ye	Mt 20:32	5455
My house shall be c the house of	Mt 21:13	2564
For many are c, but few are	Mt 22:14	2822
to be c of men, Rabbi, Rabbi	Mt 23:7	2564
But be not ye c Rabbi	Mt 23:8	2564
Neither be ye c masters	Mt 23:10	2564
who c his own servants, and	Mt 25:14	2564
high priest, who was c Caiaphas,	Mt 26:3	3004

c Judas Iscariot, went unto the	Mt 26:14	3004
them unto a place c Gethsemane	Mt 26:36	3004
Wherefore that field was c	Mt 27:8	2564
a notable prisoner, c Barabbas	Mt 27:16	3004
or Jesus which is c Christ	Mt 27:17	3004
then with Jesus which is c Christ	Mt 27:22	3004
were come unto a place c Golgotha	Mt 27:33	3004
And straightway he c them	Mk 1:20	2564
he c them unto him, and said unto	Mk 3:23	4341
he c unto him the twelve, and	Mk 6:7	4341
when he had c all the people unto	Mk 7:14	4341
Jesus c his disciples unto him,	Mk 8:1	4341
when he had c the people unto him	Mk 8:34	4341
c the twelve, and saith unto them,	Mk 9:35	5455
But Jesus c them to him, and saith	Mk 10:42	4341
still, and commanded him to be c	Mk 10:49	5455
My house shall be c of all	Mk 11:17	2564
he c unto him his disciples, and	Mk 12:43	4341
Peter c to mind the word that	Mk 14:72	363
away into the hall, c Praetorium	Mk 15:16	3739,2076
shall be c the Son of the Highest	Lk 1:32	
of thee shall be c the Son of God	Lk 1:35	2564
month with her, who was c barren	Lk 1:36	2564
they c him Zacharias, after the	Lk 1:59	2564
but he shall be c John	Lk 1:60	2564
kindred that is c by this name	Lk 1:61	2564
father, how he would have him c	Lk 1:62	2564
shalt be c the prophet of the	Lk 1:76	2564
of David, which is c Bethlehem	Lk 2:4	2564
the child, his name was c JESUS	Lk 2:21	2564
womb shall be c holy to the Lord	Lk 2:23	2564
he c unto him his disciples	Lk 6:13	4377
of Alphaeus, and Simon c Zelotes	Lk 6:15	2564
that he went into a city c Nain	Lk 7:11	2564
Mary c Magdalene, out of whom	Lk 8:2	2564
and took her by the hand, and c	Lk 8:54	5455
Then he c his twelve disciples	Lk 9:1	4779
belonging to the city c Bethsaida	Lk 9:10	2564
And she had a sister c Mary	Lk 10:39	2564
he c her to him, and said unto her	Lk 13:12	4377
am no more worthy to be c thy son	Lk 15:19	2564
am no more worthy to be c thy son	Lk 15:21	2564
he c one of the servants, and	Lk 15:26	4341
he c him, and said unto him, How	Lk 16:2	5455
So he c every one of his lord's	Lk 16:5	4341
But Jesus c them unto him, and	Lk 18:16	4341
he c his ten servants, and	Lk 19:13	2564
these servants to be c unto him	Lk 19:15	5455
at the mount c the mount of	Lk 19:29	2564
that is c the mount of Olives	Lk 21:37	2564
nigh, which is c the Passover	Lk 22:1	3004
upon them are c benefactors	Lk 22:25	2564
multitude, and he that was c Judas	Lk 22:47	3004
when he had c together the chief	Lk 23:13	4779
to the place, which is c Calvary	Lk 23:33	2564
same day to a village c Emmaus	Lk 24:13	3686
thou shalt be c Cephas, which is	Jn 1:42	2564
him, Before that Philip c thee	Jn 1:48	5455
And both Jesus was c, and his	Jn 2:2	2564
of the feast c the bridegroom	Jn 2:9	5455
of Samaria, which is c Sychar	Jn 4:5	3004
Messias cometh, which is c Christ	Jn 4:25	3044
which is c in the Hebrew tongue	Jn 5:2	1951
A man that is c Jesus made clay,	Jn 9:11	3004
until the parents of him	Jn 9:18	5455
Then again c they the man that	Jn 9:24	5455
If he c them gods, unto whom the	Jn 10:35	2036
said Thomas, which is c Didymus	Jn 11:16	3004
c Mary her sister secretly,	Jn 11:28	5455
wilderness, into a city c Ephraim	Jn 11:54	3004
he c Lazarus out of his grave	Jn 12:17	5455
but I have c you friends	Jn 15:15	2046
c Jesus, and said unto him, Art	Jn 18:33	5455
in a place that is c the Pavement	Jn 19:13	3004
a place the place of a skull	Jn 19:17	3004
which is c in the Hebrew Golgotha	Jn 19:17	3004
c Didymus, was not with them when	Jn 20:24	3004
Thomas c Didymus, and Nathanael of	Jn 21:2	3004
Jerusalem from the mount c Olivet	Acts 1:12	2564
field is c in their proper tongue	Acts 1:19	2564
Joseph c Barsabas, who was	Acts 1:23	2564
the temple which is c Beautiful	Acts 3:2	3004
in the porch that is c Solomon's	Acts 3:11	2564
And they c them, and commanded	Acts 4:18	2564
c the council together, and all	Acts 5:21	4779
and when they had c the apostles	Acts 5:40	4341
Then the twelve c the multitude	Acts 6:2	4341
which is c the synagogue of the	Acts 6:9	3004
c his father Jacob to him, and all	Acts 7:14	3333
c Simon, which beforetime in the	Acts 8:9	3686
the street which is c Straight	Acts 9:11	2564

the house of Judas for one c Saul	Acts 9:11	3686
which c on this name in Jerusalem	Acts 9:21	1941
by interpretation is c Dorcas..................	Acts 9:36	3004
up, and when he had c the saints	Acts 9:41	5455
man in Caesarea c Cornelius..................	Acts 10:1	3686
of the band c the Italian band................	Acts 10:1	2564
he c two of his household......................	Acts 10:7	5455
And c, and asked whether Simon, ...	Acts 10:18	5455
Then c he them in, and lodged them	Acts 10:23	1528
had c together his kinsmen and..............	Acts 10:24	4779
the disciples were c Christians	Acts 11:26	5537
and Simeon that was c Niger..................	Acts 13:1	2564
the work whereunto I have c them	Acts 13:2	4341
who c for Barnabas and Saul, and	Acts 13:7	4341
Then Saul, (who also is c Paul...............	Acts 13:9	
And they c Barnabas, Jupiter	Acts 14:12	2564
Gentiles, upon whom my name is c	Acts 15:17	1941
had c us for to preach the gospel	Acts 16:10	4341
Then he c for a light, and sprang...........	Acts 16:29	154
Whom he c together with the..................	Acts 19:25	4867
be c in question for this day's...............	Acts 19:40	1458
Paul c unto him the disciples, and	Acts 20:1	4341
c the elders of the church	Acts 20:17	3333
of the dead I am c in question	Acts 23:6	2919
Then Paul c one of the centurions	Acts 23:17	4341
Paul the prisoner c me unto him	Acts 23:18	4341
he c unto him two centurions, ...	Acts 23:23	4341
And when he was c forth, Tertullus	Acts 24:2	2564
am c in question by you this day	Acts 24:21	2919
place which is c The fair havens...........	Acts 27:8	2564
a tempestuous wind, c Euroclydon	Acts 27:14	2564
certain island which is c Clauda............	Acts 27:16	2564
knew that the island was c Melita	Acts 28:1	2564
that after three days Paul c the	Acts 28:17	4779
cause therefore have I c for you	Acts 28:20	3870
c to be an apostle, separated.................	Rom 1:1	2822
are ye also the c of Jesus Christ	Rom 1:6	2822
beloved of God, c to be saints	Rom 1:7	2822
Behold, thou art c a Jew, and	Rom 2:17	2028
she shall be c an adulteress	Rom 7:3	5537
to them who are the c according	Rom 8:28	2822
did predestinate, them he also c...........	Rom 8:30	2564
and whom he c, them he also..............	Rom 8:30	2564
but, In Isaac shall thy seed be c............	Rom 9:7	2564
Even us, whom he hath c, not of	Rom 9:24	2564
there shall they be c the	Rom 9:26	2564
c to be an apostle of Jesus	1Cor 1:1	2822
c to be saints, with all that in	1Cor 1:2	2822
by whom ye were c unto the	1Cor 1:9	2564
But unto them which are c	1Cor 1:24	2822
mighty, not many noble, are c...............	1Cor 1:26	
if any man that is c a brother be	1Cor 5:11	3687
but God hath c us to peace	1Cor 7:15	2564
man, as the Lord hath c every one	1Cor 7:17	2564
Is any man c being circumcised............	1Cor 7:18	2564
Is any c in uncircumcision	1Cor 7:18	2564
the same calling wherein he was c	1Cor 7:20	2564
Art thou c being a servant	1Cor 7:21	2564
For he that is c in the Lord....................	1Cor 7:22	2564
likewise also he that is c......................	1Cor 7:22	2564
let every man, wherein he is c...............	1Cor 7:24	2564
though there be that are c gods.............	1Cor 8:5	3004
am not meet to be c an apostle	1Cor 15:9	2564
c you into the grace of Christ.................	Gal 1:6	2564
womb, and c me by his grace, ...	Gal 1:15	2564
ye have been c unto liberty	Gal 5:13	2564
who are c Uncircumcision by that	Eph 2:11	3004
c the Circumcision in the flesh	Eph 2:11	3004
the vocation wherewith ye are c	Eph 4:1	2564
even as ye are c in one hope of	Eph 4:4	2564
which also ye are c in one body.............	Col 3:15	2564
And Jesus, which is c Justus.................	Col 4:11	3004
who hath c you unto his kingdom..........	1Th 2:12	2564
For God hath not c us unto	1Th 4:7	2564
himself above all that is c God	2Th 2:4	3004
Whereunto he c you by our gospel, ...	2Th 2:14	2564
life, whereunto thou art also c	1Ti 6:12	2564
of science falsely so c..........................	1Ti 6:20	5581
c us with an holy calling, not	2Ti 1:9	2564
daily, while it is c To day	Heb 3:13	2564
himself, but he that is c of God.............	Heb 5:4	2564
C of God an high priest after the	Heb 5:10	4316
not be c after the order of Aaron	Heb 7:11	3004
which is c the sanctuary.......................	Heb 9:2	3004
which is c the Holiest of all	Heb 9:3	3004
they which are c might receive	Heb 9:15	2564
when he was c to go out into a	Heb 11:8	2564
is not ashamed to be c their God	Heb 11:16	1941
That in Isaac shall thy seed be c...........	Heb 11:18	2564
refused to be c the son of	Heb 11:24	3004
worthy name by the which ye are c.......	Jas 2:7	1941

he was c the Friend of God..................	Jas 2:23	2564
as he which hath c you is holy	1Pet 1:15	2564
the praises of him who hath c you........	1Pet 2:9	2564
For even hereunto were ye c.................	1Pet 2:21	2564
knowing that ye are thereunto c	1Pet 3:9	2564
who hath c us unto his eternal	1Pet 5:10	2564
of him that hath c us to glory	2Pet 1:3	2564
we should be c the sons of God............	1Jn 3:1	2564
preserved in Jesus Christ, and	Jude 1	2822
was in the isle that is c Patmos............	Rev 1:9	2564
name of the star is c Wormwood...........	Rev 8:11	3004
which spiritually is c Sodom	Rev 11:8	2564
c the Devil, and Satan, which	Rev 12:9	2564
them together into a place c in	Rev 16:16	2564
and they that are with him are c	Rev 17:14	2822
Blessed are they which are c unto	Rev 19:9	2564
that sat upon him was c Faithful	Rev 19:11	2564
his name is c The Word of God.............	Rev 19:13	2564

CALLEDST

us thus, that thou c us not....................	Judg 8:1	7121
for thou c me....................................	1Sa 3:5	7121
Thou c in trouble, and I delivered.........	Ps 81:7	7121
Thus thou c to remembrance the	Eze 23:21	6485

CALLEST

said unto him, Why c thou me good	Mt 19:17	3004
said unto him, Why c thou me good	Mk 10:18	3004
said unto him, Why c thou me good	Lk 18:19	3004

CALLETH

that the stranger c to thee for	1Kin 8:43	7121
that the stranger c to thee for	2Chr 6:33	7121
who c upon God, and he answereth	Job 12:4	7121
Deep c unto deep at the noise of..........	Ps 42:7	7121
he c them all by their names................	Ps 147:4	7121
and his mouth c for strokes.................	Prov 18:6	7121
He c to me out of Seir, Watchman, ...	Is 21:11	7121
he c them all by names by the	Is 40:26	7121
None c for justice, nor any	Is 59:4	7121
is none that c upon thy name...............	Is 64:7	7121
is none among them that c unto me	Hos 7:7	7121
that c for the waters of the sea, ...	Amos 5:8	7121
he that c for the waters of the	Amos 9:6	7121
that, said, This man c for Elias.............	Mt 27:47	5455
and c unto him whom he would	Mk 3:13	4341
he c thee...................................	Mk 10:49	5455
therefore himself c him Lord	Mk 12:37	3004
heard it said, Behold, he c Elias...........	Mk 15:35	5455
he c together his friends and	Lk 15:6	4779
it, she c her friends and her................	Lk 15:9	4779
when he c the Lord the God of..............	Lk 20:37	3004
David therefore c him Lord	Lk 20:44	2564
he c his own sheep by name, and	Jn 10:3	2564
The Master is come, and c for thee........	Jn 11:28	5455
c those things which be not as	Rom 4:17	2564
not of works, but of him that c..............	Rom 9:11	2564
Spirit of God c Jesus accursed	1Cor 12:3	3004
cometh not of him that c you	Gal 5:8	2564
Faithful is he that c you......................	1Th 5:24	2564
which c herself a prophetess, to	Rev 2:20	3004

CALLING

them for the c of the assembly	Num 10:2	4744
the c of assemblies, I cannot	Is 1:13	7121
c the generations from the...................	Is 41:4	7121
C a ravenous bird from the east, ...	Is 46:11	7121
in c to remembrance the days of..........	Eze 23:19	2142
markets, and c unto their fellows,........	Mt 11:16	4377
without, sent unto him, c him..............	Mk 3:31	5455
Peter c to remembrance saith unto	Mk 11:21	363
c unto him the centurion, he	Mk 15:44	4341
John c unto him two of his	Lk 7:19	4341
c one to another, and saying, We	Lk 7:32	4377
c upon God, and saying, Lord Jesus	Acts 7:59	1941
c on the name of the Lord....................	Acts 22:16	1941
c of God are without repentance	Rom 11:29	2821
For ye see your c, brethren, how	1Cor 1:26	2821
the same c wherein he was called	1Cor 7:20	2821
know what is the hope of his c.............	Eph 1:18	2821
are called in one hope of your c...........	Eph 4:4	2821
the high c of God in Christ Jesus	Phil 3:14	2821
would count you worthy of this c	2Th 1:11	2821
us, and called us with an holy c	2Ti 1:9	2821
partakers of the heavenly c..................	Heb 3:1	2821
Sarah obeyed Abraham, c him lord	1Pet 3:6	2564
give diligence to make your c	2Pet 1:10	2821

CALM

He maketh the storm a c, so that	Ps 107:29	1827
that the sea may be c unto us..............	Jonah 1:11	8367
so shall the sea be c unto you.............	Jonah 1:12	8367
and there was a great c	Mt 8:26	1055

ceased, and there was a great *c* .... Mk 4:39   *1055*
and they ceased, and there was a *c* .... Lk 8:24   *1055*

CALNEH (cal'-neh) See CALNO, CANNEH. *A center of Babylonian worship.*
Babel, and Erech, and Accad, and *C* .... Gen 10:10   *3641*
Pass ye unto *C*, and see .... Amos 6:2   *3641*

CALNO (cal'-no) See CALNEH. *Same as Calneh.*
Is not *C* as Carchemish .... Is 10:9   *3641*

CALVARY
to the place, which is called *C* .... Lk 23:33   *2898*

CALVE
thou mark when the hinds do *c* .... Job 39:1   *2342*
of the LORD maketh the hinds to *c* .... Ps 29:9   *2342*

CALVED
Yea, the hind also *c* in the field .... Jer 14:5   *3205*

CALVES
bring their *c* home from them 1Sa 6:7   *1121*
cart, and shut up their *c* at home 1Sa 6:10   *1121*
and took sheep, and oxen, and *c* 1Sa 14:32   *1121,1241*
counsel, and made two *c* of gold 1Kin 12:28   *5695*
unto the *c* that he had made 1Kin 12:32   *5695*
the golden *c* that were in Beth-el 2Kin 10:29   *5695*
them molten images, even two *c* 2Kin 17:16   *5695*
for the *c* which he had made 2Chr 11:15   *5695*
and there are with you golden *c* 2Chr 13:8   *5695*
with the *c* of the people, till .... Ps 68:30   *5695*
because of the *c* of Beth-aven .... Hos 10:5   *5697*
the men that sacrifice kiss the *c* .... Hos 13:2   *5695*
will we render the *c* of our lips .... Hos 14:2   *6499*
the *c* out of the midst of the .... Amos 6:4   *5695*
offerings, with *c* of a year old .... Mic 6:6   *5695*
grow up as *c* of the stall .... Mal 4:2   *5695*
by the blood of goats and *c* .... Heb 9:12   *3448*
the law, he took the blood of *c* .... Heb 9:19   *3448*

CALVETH
their cow *c*, and casteth not her .... Job 21:10   *6403*

CAME See APPENDIX.

CAMEL
saw Isaac, she lighted off the *c* .... Gen 24:64   *1581*
as the *c*, because he cheweth the .... Lev 11:4   *1581*
as the *c*, and the hare, and the .... Deut 14:7   *1581*
and suckling, ox and sheep, *c* 1Sa 15:3   *1581*
the horse, of the mule, of the *c* .... Zec 14:15   *1581*
It is easier for a *c* to go .... Mt 19:24   *2574*
strain at a gnat, and swallow a *c* .... Mt 23:24   *2574*
It is easier for a *c* to go .... Mk 10:25   *2574*
For it is easier for a *c* to go .... Lk 18:25   *2574*

CAMEL'S
and put them in the *c* furniture .... Gen 31:34   *1581*
John had his raiment of *c* hair .... Mt 3:4   *2574*
And John was clothed with *c* hair .... Mk 1:6   *2574*

CAMELS
maidservants, and she asses, and *c* .... Gen 12:16   *1581*
ten of the *c* of his master .... Gen 24:10   *1581*
he made his *c* to kneel down .... Gen 24:11   *1581*
and I will give thy *c* drink also .... Gen 24:14   *1581*
I will draw water for thy *c* also .... Gen 24:19   *1581*
draw water, and drew for all his *c* .... Gen 24:20   *1581*
as the *c* had done drinking, that .... Gen 24:22   *1581*
he stood by the *c* at the well .... Gen 24:30   *1581*
the house, and room for the *c* .... Gen 24:31   *1581*
and he ungirded his *c* .... Gen 24:32   *1581*
gave straw and provender for the *c* .... Gen 24:32   *1581*
and maidservants, and *c*, and asses ...... Gen 24:35   *1581*
and I will also draw for thy *c* .... Gen 24:44   *1581*
and I will give thy *c* drink also .... Gen 24:46   *1581*
and she made the *c* drink also .... Gen 24:46   *1581*
damsels, and they rode upon the *c* .... Gen 24:61   *1581*
and, behold, the *c* were coming .... Gen 24:63   *1581*
and menservants, *c*, and asses .... Gen 30:43   *1581*
set his sons and his wives upon *c* .... Gen 31:17   *1581*
and the flocks, and herds, and the *c* ..... Gen 32:7   *1581*
Thirty milch *c* with their colts, ... Gen 32:15   *1581*
with their bearing spicery .... Gen 37:25   *1581*
upon the asses, upon the *c* .... Ex 9:3   *1581*
their *c* were without number .... Judg 6:5   *1581*
their *c* were without number, as .... Judg 7:12   *1581*
the oxen, and the asses, and the *c* 1Sa 27:9   *1581*
young men, which rode upon *c* 1Sa 30:17   *1581*
with *c* that bare spices, and very 1Kin 10:2   *1581*
of their *c* fifty thousand, and of 1Chr 5:21   *1581*
brought bread on asses, and on *c* 1Chr 12:40   *1581*
Over the *c* also was Obil the 1Chr 27:30   *1581*
c that bare spices, and gold in 2Chr 9:1   *1581*
c in abundance, and returned to 2Chr 14:15   *1581*
Their *c*, four hundred thirty and .... Ezr 2:67   *1581*

Their *c*, four hundred thirty and .... Neh 7:69   *1581*
horseback, and riders on mules, *c* .... Est 8:10   *327*
c went out, being hastened and .... Est 8:14   *327*
sheep, and three thousand *c* .... Job 1:3   *1581*
three bands, and fell upon the *c* .... Job 1:17   *1581*
thousand sheep, and six thousand *c* .... Job 42:12   *1581*
of asses, and a chariot of *c* .... Is 21:7   *1581*
treasures upon the bunches of *c* .... Is 30:6   *1581*
multitude of *c* shall cover thee .... Is 60:6   *1581*
and all their vessels, and their *c* .... Jer 49:29   *1581*
their *c* shall be a booty, and the .... Jer 49:32   *1581*
I will make Rabbah a stable for *c* .... Eze 25:5   *1581*

CAMELS'
that were on their *c* necks .... Judg 8:21   *1581*
that were about their *c* necks .... Judg 8:26   *1581*
forty *c* burden, and came and stood 2Kin 8:9   *1581*

CAMEST See APPENDIX.

CAMON (ca'-mon) *A town in Gilead.*
And Jair died, and was buried in *C* .... Judg 10:5   *7056*

CAMP
which went before the *c* of Israel .... Ex 14:19   *4264*
between the *c* of the Egyptians .... Ex 14:20   *4264*
the Egyptians and the *c* of Israel .... Ex 14:20   *4264*
quails came up, and covered the *c* .... Ex 16:13   *4264*
people that was in the *c* trembled .... Ex 19:16   *4264*
out of the *c* to meet with God .... Ex 19:17   *4264*
thou burn with fire without the *c* .... Ex 29:14   *4264*
There is a noise of war in the *c* .... Ex 32:17   *4264*
soon as he came nigh unto the *c* .... Ex 32:19   *4264*
Moses stood in the gate of the *c* .... Ex 32:26   *4264*
gate to gate throughout the *c* .... Ex 32:27   *4264*
the *c*, afar off from the *c* .... Ex 33:7   *4264*
which was without the *c* .... Ex 33:7   *4264*
And he turned again into the *c* .... Ex 33:11   *4264*
to be proclaimed throughout the *c* .... Ex 36:6   *4264*
without the *c* unto a clean place .... Lev 4:12   *4264*
forth the bullock without the *c* .... Lev 4:21   *4264*
without the *c* unto a clean place .... Lev 6:11   *4264*
he burnt with fire without the *c* .... Lev 8:17   *4264*
he burnt with fire without the *c* .... Lev 9:11   *4264*
before the sanctuary out of the *c* .... Lev 10:4   *4264*
them in their coats out of the *c* .... Lev 10:5   *4264*
without the *c* shall his .... Lev 13:46   *4264*
shall go forth out of the *c* .... Lev 14:3   *4264*
that he shall come into the *c* .... Lev 14:8   *4264*
and afterward come into the *c* .... Lev 16:26   *4264*
one carry forth without the *c* .... Lev 16:27   *4264*
he shall come into the *c* .... Lev 16:28   *4264*
an ox, or lamb, or goat, in the *c* .... Lev 17:3   *4264*
or that killeth it out of the *c* .... Lev 17:3   *4264*
Israel strove together in the *c* .... Lev 24:10   *4264*
that hath cursed without the *c* .... Lev 24:14   *4264*
him that had cursed out of the *c* .... Lev 24:23   *4264*
tents, every man by his own *c* .... Num 1:52   *4264*
they of the standard of the *c* .... Num 2:3   *4264*
in the *c* of Judah were an hundred .... Num 2:9   *4264*
c of Reuben according to their .... Num 2:10   *4264*
the *c* of Reuben were an hundred .... Num 2:16   *4264*
shall set forward with the *c* of .... Num 2:17   *4264*
the Levites in the midst of the *c* .... Num 2:17   *4264*
shall be the standard of the *c* of .... Num 2:18   *4264*
the *c* of Ephraim were an hundred .... Num 2:24   *4264*
The standard of the *c* of Dan .... Num 2:25   *4264*
they that were numbered in the *c* .... Num 2:31   *4264*
when the *c* setteth forward, Aaron .... Num 4:5   *4264*
as the *c* is to set forward .... Num 4:15   *4264*
they put out of the *c* every leper .... Num 5:2   *4264*
without the *c* shall ye put them .... Num 5:3   *4264*
so, and put them out without the *c* .... Num 5:4   *4264*
of the *c* of the children of Judah .... Num 10:14   *4264*
the standard of the *c* of Reuben .... Num 10:18   *4264*
the standard of the *c* of the .... Num 10:22   *4264*
the standard of the *c* of the .... Num 10:25   *4264*
day, when they went out of the *c* .... Num 10:34   *4264*
in the uttermost parts of the *c* .... Num 11:1   *4264*
dew fell upon the *c* in the night .... Num 11:9   *4264*
remained two of the men in the *c* .... Num 11:26   *4264*
and they prophesied in the *c* .... Num 11:26   *4264*
and Medad do prophesy in the *c* .... Num 11:27   *4264*
And Moses gat him into the *c* .... Num 11:30   *4264*
sea, and let them fall by the *c* .... Num 11:31   *4264*
the other side, round about the *c* .... Num 11:31   *4264*
for themselves round about the *c* .... Num 11:32   *4264*
be shut out from the *c* seven days .... Num 12:14   *4264*
shut out from the *c* seven days .... Num 12:15   *4264*
Moses, departed not out of the *c* .... Num 14:44   *4264*
him with stones without the *c* .... Num 15:35   *4264*
brought him without the *c* .... Num 15:36   *4264*
may bring her forth without the *c* .... Num 19:3   *4264*

C

he shall come into the *c*, and the	Num 19:7	4264
up without the *c* in a clean place	Num 19:9	4264
unto the *c* at the plains of Moab,	Num 31:12	4264
forth to meet them without the *c*	Num 31:13	4264
ye abide without the *c* seven days	Num 31:19	4264
ye shall come into the *c*	Num 31:24	4264
shall he go abroad out of the *c*	Deut 23:10	4264
he shall not come within the *c*	Deut 23:10	4264
he shall come into the *c* again	Deut 23:11	4264
have a place also without the *c*	Deut 23:12	4264
God walketh in the midst of thy *c*	Deut 23:14	4264
therefore shall thy *c* be holy	Deut 23:14	4264
and thy stranger that is in thy *c*	Deut 29:11	4264
abode in their places in the *c*	Josh 5:8	4264
into the *c*, and lodged in the *c*	Josh 6:11	4264
city once, and returned into the *c*	Josh 6:14	4264
make the *c* of Israel a curse, and	Josh 6:18	4264
left them without the *c* of Israel	Josh 6:23	4264
to Joshua unto the *c* at Gilgal	Josh 9:6	4264
unto Joshua to the *c* to Gilgal	Josh 10:6	4264
with him, unto the *c* to Gilgal	Josh 10:15	4264
c to Joshua at Makkedah in peace	Josh 10:21	4264
with him, unto the *c* to Gilgal	Josh 10:43	4264
I come to the outside of the *c*	Judg 7:17	4264
also on every side of all the *c*	Judg 7:18	4264
came unto the outside of the *c* in	Judg 7:19	4264
in his place round about the *c*	Judg 7:21	4264
in the *c* of Dan between Zorah	Judg 13:25	4264
there came none to the *c* from	Judg 21:8	4264
brought them unto the *c* to Shiloh	Judg 21:12	4264
the people were come into the *c*	1Sa 4:3	4264
of the LORD came into the *c*	1Sa 4:5	4264
shout in the *c* of the Hebrews	1Sa 4:6	4264
of the LORD was come into the *c*	1Sa 4:6	4264
they said, God is come into the *c*	1Sa 4:7	4264
the *c* of the Philistines in three	1Sa 13:17	4264
went up with them into the *c* from	1Sa 14:21	4264
out of the *c* of the Philistines	1Sa 17:4	4264
run to the *c* to thy brethren	1Sa 17:17	4264
go down with me to Saul to the *c*	1Sa 26:6	4264
a man came out of the *c* from Saul	2Sa 1:2	4264
Out of the *c* of Israel am I	2Sa 1:3	4264
over Israel that day in the *c*	1Kin 16:16	4264
when they came to the *c* of Israel	2Kin 3:24	4264
and such a place shall be my *c*	2Kin 6:8	8466
to go unto the *c* of the Syrians	2Kin 7:5	4264
uttermost part of the *c* of Syria	2Kin 7:5	4264
even the *c* as it was, and fled for	2Kin 7:7	4264
to the uttermost part of the *c*	2Kin 7:8	4264
We came to the *c* of the Syrians	2Kin 7:10	4264
are they gone out of the *c* to	2Kin 7:12	4264
smote in the *c* of the Assyrians	2Kin 19:35	4264
to the *c* had slain all the eldest	2Chr 22:1	4264
captains in the *c* of the king of	2Chr 32:21	4264
it fall in the midst of their *c*	Ps 78:28	4264
They envied Moses also in the *c*	Ps 106:16	4264
I will *c* against thee round about	Is 29:3	2583
smote in the *c* of the Assyrians	Is 37:36	4264
the bow, *c* against it round about	Jer 50:29	2583
set the *c* also against it, and set	Eze 4:2	4264
for his *c* is very great	Joel 2:11	4264
which *c* in the hedges in the cold	Nah 3:17	2583
for sin, are burned without the *c*	Heb 13:11	3925
therefore unto him without the *c*	Heb 13:13	3925
compassed the *c* of the saints	Rev 20:9	3925

CAMPED
there Israel *c* before the mount	Ex 19:2	2583

CAMPHIRE
is unto me as a cluster of *c* in	Song 1:14	3724
c, with spikenard,	Song 4:13	3724

CAMPS
c throughout their hosts were six	Num 2:32	4264
that they defile not their *c*	Num 5:3	4264
and for the journeying of the *c*	Num 10:2	4264
then the *c* that lie on the east	Num 10:5	4264
then the *c* that lie on the south	Num 10:6	4264
all the *c* throughout their hosts	Num 10:25	4264
c to come up unto your nostrils	Amos 4:10	4264

CAN See APPENDIX.

CANA (*ca'-nah*) A village in Galilee.
was a marriage in *C* of Galilee	Jn 2:1	2580
did Jesus in *C* of Galilee	Jn 2:11	2580
came again into *C* of Galilee	Jn 4:46	2580
and Nathanael of *C* in Galilee	Jn 21:2	2580

CANAAN (*ca'-na-an*) See CANAANITE.
1. Son of Ham.
and Ham is the father of *C*	Gen 9:18	3667
And Ham, the father of *C*, saw the	Gen 9:22	3667

And he said, Cursed be *C*	Gen 9:25	3667
and *C* shall be his servant	Gen 9:26	3667
and *C* shall be his servant	Gen 9:27	3667
Cush, and Mizraim, and Phut, and *C*	Gen 10:6	3667
C begat Sidon his firstborn, and	Gen 10:15	3667
Cush, and Mizraim, Put, and *C*	1Chr 1:8	3667
C begat Zidon his firstborn, and	1Chr 1:13	3667

2. Place where Canaanites dwell.
to go into the land of *C*	Gen 11:31	3667
forth to go into the land of *C*	Gen 12:5	3667
and into the land of *C* they came	Gen 12:5	3667
Abram dwelled in the land of *C*	Gen 13:12	3667
dwelt ten years in the land of *C*	Gen 16:3	3667
art a stranger, all the land of *C*	Gen 17:8	3667
same is Hebron in the land of *C*	Gen 23:2	3667
same is Hebron in the land of *C*	Gen 23:19	3667
take a wife of the daughters of *C*	Gen 28:1	3667
take a wife of the daughters of *C*	Gen 28:6	3667
of *C* pleased not Isaac his father	Gen 28:8	3667
Isaac his father in the land of *C*	Gen 31:18	3667
which is in the land of *C*	Gen 33:18	3667
to Luz, which is in the land of *C*	Gen 35:6	3667
his wives of the daughters of *C*	Gen 36:2	3667
born unto him in the land of *C*	Gen 36:5	3667
which he had got in the land of *C*	Gen 36:6	3667
was a stranger, in the land of *C*	Gen 37:1	3667
the famine was in the land of *C*	Gen 42:5	3667
From the land of *C* to buy food	Gen 42:7	3667
sons of one man in the land of *C*	Gen 42:13	3667
their father unto the land of *C*	Gen 42:29	3667
with our father in the land of *C*	Gen 42:32	3667
unto thee out of the land of *C*	Gen 44:8	3667
and go, get you unto the land of *C*	Gen 45:17	3667
came into the land of *C* unto	Gen 45:25	3667
they had gotten in the land of *C*	Gen 46:6	3667
Er and Onan died in the land of *C*	Gen 46:12	3667
which were in the land of *C*	Gen 46:31	3667
are come out of the land of *C*	Gen 47:1	3667
famine is sore in the land of *C*	Gen 47:4	3667
all the land of *C* fainted by	Gen 47:13	3667
of Egypt, and in the land of *C*	Gen 47:14	3667
of Egypt, and in the land of *C*	Gen 47:15	3667
unto me at Luz in the land of *C*	Gen 48:3	3667
by me in the land of *C* in the way	Gen 48:7	3667
is before Mamre, in the land of *C*	Gen 49:30	3667
digged for me in the land of *C*	Gen 50:5	3667
carried him into the land of *C*	Gen 50:13	3667
them, to give them the land of *C*	Ex 6:4	3667
inhabitants of *C* shall melt away	Ex 15:15	3667
unto the borders of the land of *C*	Ex 16:35	3667
ye be come into the land of *C*	Lev 14:34	3667
after the doings of the land of *C*	Lev 18:3	3667
Egypt, to give you the land of *C*	Lev 25:38	3667
they may search the land of *C*	Num 13:2	3667
them to spy out the land of *C*	Num 13:17	3667
Er and Onan died in the land of *C*	Num 26:19	3667
among you in the land of *C*	Num 32:30	3667
the LORD into the land of *C*	Num 32:32	3667
in the south in the land of *C*	Num 33:40	3667
over Jordan into the land of *C*	Num 33:51	3667
When ye come into the land of *C*	Num 34:2	3667
even the land of *C* with the	Num 34:2	3667
of Israel in the land of *C*	Num 34:29	3667
over Jordan into the land of *C*	Num 35:10	3667
shall ye give in the land of *C*	Num 35:14	3667
and behold the land of *C*, which I	Deut 32:49	3667
fruit of the land of *C* that year	Josh 5:12	3667
Israel inherited in the land of *C*	Josh 14:1	3667
them at Shiloh in the land of *C*	Josh 21:2	3667
Shiloh, which is in the land of *C*	Josh 22:9	3667
Jordan, that are in the land of *C*	Josh 22:10	3667
altar over against the land of *C*	Josh 22:11	3667
of Gilead, unto the land of *C*	Josh 22:32	3667
him throughout all the land of *C*	Josh 24:3	3667
had not known all the wars of *C*	Judg 3:1	3667
into the hand of Jabin king of *C*	Judg 4:2	3667
C before the children of Israel	Judg 4:23	3667
against Jabin the king of *C*	Judg 4:24	3667
had destroyed Jabin king of *C*	Judg 4:24	3667
then fought the kings of *C* in	Judg 5:19	3667
Shiloh, which is in the land of *C*	Judg 21:12	3667
thee will I give the land of *C*	1Chr 16:18	3667
thee will I give the land of *C*	Ps 105:11	3667
sacrificed unto the idols of *C*	Ps 106:38	3667
Bashan, and all the kingdoms of *C*	Ps 135:11	3667
of Egypt speak the language of *C*	Is 19:18	3667
thy nativity is of the land of *C*	Eze 16:3	3667
in the land of *C* unto Chaldea	Eze 16:29	3667
O *C*, the land of the Philistines,	Zeph 2:5	3667
a woman of *C* came out of the same	Mt 15:22	5478

CANAANITE (*ca'-na-an-ite*) See CANAANITES, CANAAN-ITESS, CANAANITISH, ZELOTES. *Descendants of Canaan.*

the *C* was then in the land	Gen 12:6	3669
and the *C* and the Perizzite dwelled	Gen 13:7	3669
there a daughter of a certain *C*	Gen 38:2	3669
shall drive out the Hivite, the *C*	Ex 23:28	3669
and I will drive out the *C*	Ex 33:2	3669
before the Amorite, and the *C*	Ex 34:11	3669
And when king Arad the *C*, which	Num 21:1	3669
And king Arad the *C*, which dwelt	Num 33:40	3669
Hittite, and the Amorite, the *C*	Josh 9:1	3669
to the *C* on the east and on the	Josh 11:3	3669
which is counted to the *C*	Josh 13:3	3669
the *C* in the house of the LORD of	Zec 14:21	3669
Simon the *C*, and Judas Iscariot,	Mt 10:4	2581
and Thaddaeus, and Simon the *C*	Mk 3:18	2581

CANAANITES (*ca'-na-an-ites*)

families of the *C* spread abroad	Gen 10:18	3669
border of the *C* was from Sidon	Gen 10:19	3669
And the Amorites, and the *C*	Gen 15:21	3669
my son of the daughters of the *C*	Gen 24:3	3669
my son of the daughters of the *C*	Gen 24:37	3669
of the land, among the *C* and the	Gen 34:30	3669
inhabitants of the land, the *C*	Gen 50:11	3669
unto the place of the *C*, and the	Ex 3:8	3669
of Egypt into the land of the *C*	Ex 3:17	3669
bring thee into the land of the *C*	Ex 13:5	3669
bring thee into the land of the *C*	Ex 13:11	3669
and the Perizzites, and the *C*	Ex 23:23	3669
the *C* dwell by the sea, and by the	Num 13:29	3669
the *C* dwelt in the valley	Num 14:25	3669
the *C* are there before you, and ye	Num 14:43	3669
the *C* which dwelt in that hill	Num 14:45	3669
of Israel, and delivered up the *C*	Num 21:3	3669
sea side, to the land of the *C*	Deut 1:7	3669
and the Amorites, and the *C*	Deut 7:1	3669
goeth down, in the land of the *C*	Deut 11:30	3669
Hittites, and the Amorites, the *C*	Deut 20:17	3669
drive out from before you the *C*	Josh 3:10	3669
and all the kings of the *C*	Josh 5:1	3669
For the *C* and all the inhabitants	Josh 7:9	3669
Hittites, the Amorites, and the *C*	Josh 12:8	3669
the south, all the land of the *C*	Josh 13:4	3669
not out the *C* that dwelt in Gezer	Josh 16:10	3669
but the *C* dwell among the	Josh 16:10	3669
but the *C* would dwell in that	Josh 17:12	3669
that they put the *C* to tribute	Josh 17:13	3669
all the *C* that dwelt in the land	Josh 17:16	3669
for thou shalt drive out the *C*	Josh 17:18	3669
and the Perizzites, and the *C*	Josh 24:11	3669
go up for us against the *C* first	Judg 1:1	3669
that we may fight against the *C*	Judg 1:3	3669
and the LORD delivered the *C*	Judg 1:4	3669
against him, and they slew the *C*	Judg 1:5	3669
went down to fight against the *C*	Judg 1:9	3669
the *C* that dwelt in Hebron	Judg 1:10	3669
they slew the *C* that inhabited	Judg 1:17	3669
but the *C* would dwell in that	Judg 1:27	3669
that they put the *C* to tribute	Judg 1:28	3669
out the *C* that dwelt in Gezer	Judg 1:29	3669
but the *C* dwelt in Gezer among	Judg 1:29	3669
but the *C* dwelt among them, and	Judg 1:30	3669
the Asherites dwelt among the *C*	Judg 1:32	3669
but he dwelt among the *C*, the	Judg 1:33	3669
of the Philistines, and all the *C*	Judg 3:3	3669
of Israel dwelt among the *C*	Judg 3:5	3669
of the Hivites, and of the *C*	2Sa 24:7	3669
slain the *C* that dwelt in the	1Kin 9:16	3669
their abominations, even of the *C*	Ezr 9:1	3669
him to give the land of the *C*	Neh 9:8	3669
inhabitants of the land, the *C*	Neh 9:24	3669
shall possess that of the *C*	Obad 20	3669

CANAANITESS (*ca'-na-an-ite-ess*)

him of the daughter of Shua the *C*	1Chr 2:3	3669

CANAANITISH (*ca'-na-an-i-tish*)

and Shaul the son of a *C* woman	Gen 46:10	3669
and Shaul the son of a *C* woman	Ex 6:15	3669

CANDACE (*can'-da-see*) Name for a dynasty of Ethiopian queens.

under *C* queen of the Ethiopians	Acts 8:27	2582

CANDLE

his *c* shall be put out with him	Job 18:6	5216
How oft is the *c* of the wicked	Job 21:17	5216
When his *c* shined upon my head,	Job 29:3	5216
For thou wilt light my *c*	Ps 18:28	5216
of man is the *c* of the LORD	Prov 20:27	5216
the *c* of the wicked shall be put	Prov 24:20	5216

her *c* goeth not out by night	Prov 31:18	5216
millstones, and the light of the *c*	Jer 25:10	5216
Neither do men light a *c*, and put	Mt 5:15	*3088*
Is a *c* brought to be put under a	Mk 4:21	*3088*
No man, when he hath lighted a *c*	Lk 8:16	*3088*
No man, when he hath lighted a *c*	Lk 11:33	*3088*
of a *c* doth give thee light	Lk 11:36	*3088*
one piece, doth not light a *c*	Lk 15:8	*3088*
the light of a *c* shall shine no	Rev 18:23	*3088*
and they need no *c*, neither light	Rev 22:5	*3088*

CANDLES

I will search Jerusalem with *c*	Zeph 1:12	5216

CANDLESTICK

thou shalt make a *c* of pure gold	Ex 25:31	4501
beaten work shall the *c* be made	Ex 25:31	4501
of the *c* out of the one side	Ex 25:32	4501
of the *c* out of the other side	Ex 25:32	4501
branches that come out of the *c*	Ex 25:33	4501
in the *c* shall be four bowls made	Ex 25:34	4501
that proceed out of the *c*	Ex 25:35	4501
the *c* over against the table on	Ex 26:35	4501
and all his vessels, and the *c*	Ex 30:27	4501
the pure *c* with all his furniture	Ex 31:8	4501
The *c* also for the light, and his	Ex 35:14	4501
he made the *c* of pure gold	Ex 37:17	4501
of beaten work made he the *c*	Ex 37:17	4501
three branches of the *c* out of	Ex 37:18	4501
three branches of the *c* out of	Ex 37:18	4501
six branches going out of the *c*	Ex 37:19	4501
in the *c* were four bowls made	Ex 37:20	4501
The pure *c*, with the lamps	Ex 39:37	4501
and thou shalt bring in the *c*	Ex 40:4	4501
he put the *c* in the tent of the	Ex 40:24	4501
c before the LORD continually	Lev 24:4	4501
the ark, and the table, and the *c*	Num 3:31	4501
cover the *c* of the light, and his	Num 4:9	4501
give light over against the *c*	Num 8:2	4501
lamps thereof over against the *c*	Num 8:3	4501
this work of the *c* was of beaten	Num 8:4	4501
shewed Moses, so he made the *c*	Num 8:4	4501
and a table, and a stool, and a *c*	2Kin 4:10	4501
of gold, by weight for every *c*	1Chr 28:15	4501
silver by weight, both for the *c*	1Chr 28:15	4501
according to the use of every *c*	1Chr 28:15	4501
the *c* of gold with the lamps	2Chr 13:11	4501
wrote over against the *c* upon the	Dan 5:5	5043
behold a *c* all of gold, with a	Zec 4:2	4501
upon the right side of the *c*	Zec 4:11	4501
put it under a bushel, but on a *c*	Mt 5:15	*3087*
and not to be set on a *c*	Mk 4:21	*3087*
but setteth it on a *c*, that they	Lk 8:16	*3087*
under a bushel, but on a *c*	Lk 11:33	*3087*
the first, wherein was the *c*	Heb 9:2	*3087*
will remove thy *c* out of his	Rev 2:5	*3087*

CANDLESTICKS

the *c* of pure gold, five on the	1Kin 7:49	4501
Even the weight for the *c* of gold	1Chr 28:15	4501
for the *c* of silver by weight,	1Chr 28:15	4501
he made ten *c* of gold according	2Chr 4:7	4501
Moreover the *c* with their lamps,	2Chr 4:20	4501
bowls, and the caldrons, and the *c*	Jer 52:19	4501
turned, I saw seven golden *c*	Rev 1:12	*3087*
in the midst of the seven *c* one	Rev 1:13	*3087*
right hand, and the seven golden *c*	Rev 1:20	*3087*
the seven *c* which thou sawest are	Rev 1:20	*3087*
the midst of the seven golden *c*	Rev 2:1	*3087*
the two *c* standing before the God	Rev 11:4	*3087*

CANE

bought me no sweet *c* with money	Is 43:24	7070
the sweet *c* from a far country	Jer 6:20	7070

CANKER

their word will eat as doth a *c*	2Ti 2:17	*1044*

CANKERED

Your gold and silver is *c*	Jas 5:3	*2728*

CANKERWORM

locust hath left hath the *c* eaten	Joel 1:4	3218
that which the *c* hath left hath	Joel 1:4	3218
that the locust hath eaten, the *c*	Joel 2:25	3218
it shall eat thee up like the *c*	Nah 3:15	3218
make thyself many as the *c*	Nah 3:15	3218
the *c* spoileth, and fleeth away	Nah 3:16	3218

CANNEH (*can'-neh*) See CALNEH. *A place in southern Arabia.*

Haran, and *C*, and Eden, the	Eze 27:23	3656

CANNOT See APPENDIX.

CANST See APPENDIX.

CAPERNAUM (ca-pur'-na-um) A city in Galilee.

Nazareth, he came and dwelt in *C*	Mt 4:13	2584
And when Jesus was entered into *C*	Mt 8:5	2584
And thou, *C*, which art exalted	Mt 11:23	2584
And when they were come to *C*	Mt 17:24	2584
And they went into *C*	Mk 1:21	2584
he entered into *C* after some days	Mk 2:1	2584
And he came to *C*	Mk 9:33	2584
we have heard done in *C*, do also	Lk 4:23	2584
And came down to *C*, a city of	Lk 4:31	2584
of the people, he entered into *C*	Lk 7:1	2584
And thou, *C*, which art exalted to	Lk 10:15	2584
After this he went down to *C*	Jn 2:12	2584
nobleman, whose son was sick at *C*	Jn 4:46	2584
and went over the sea toward *C*	Jn 6:17	2584
also took shipping, and came to *C*	Jn 6:24	2584
the synagogue, as he taught in *C*	Jn 6:59	2584

CAPHTHORIM (caf-tho-rim) See CAPHTORIM. People of Caphtor.

whom came the Philistines,) and *C*	1Chr 1:12	3732

CAPHTOR (caf-tor) See CAPHTORIM. Original land of the Philistines.

which came forth out of *C*	Deut 2:23	3731
the remnant of the country of *C*	Jer 47:4	3731
and the Philistines from *C*	Amos 9:7	3731

CAPHTORIM (caf-to-rim) See CAPHTHORIM, CAPHTORIMS. Same as Caphtorim.

out of whom came Philistim,) and *C*	Gen 10:14	3732

CAPHTORIMS (caf'-to-rims) See CAPHTORIM.

Hazerim, even unto Azzah, the *C*	Deut 2:23	3732

CAPHTORITES See CAPHTORIMS.

CAPPADOCIA (cap-pa-do'-she-ah) A Roman province in Asia Minor.

Mesopotamia, and in Judaea, and *C*	Acts 2:9	2587
throughout Pontus, Galatia, *C*	1Pet 1:1	2587

CAPTAIN

Phichol the chief *c* of his host	Gen 21:22	8269
Phichol the chief *c* of his host	Gen 21:32	8269
Phichol the chief *c* of his army	Gen 26:26	8269
of Pharaoh's, and *c* of the guard	Gen 37:36	8269
c of the guard, an Egyptian,	Gen 39:1	8269
the house of the *c* of the guard	Gen 40:3	8269
the *c* of the guard charged Joseph	Gen 40:4	8269
in the *c* of the guard's house	Gen 41:10	8269
servant to the *c* of the guard	Gen 41:12	8269
be *c* of the children of Judah	Num 2:3	5387
the son of Zuar shall be *c* of the	Num 2:5	5387
be *c* of the children of Zebulun	Num 2:7	5387
the *c* of the children of Reuben	Num 2:10	5387
the *c* of the children of Simeon	Num 2:12	5387
the *c* of the sons of Gad shall be	Num 2:14	5387
the *c* of the sons of Ephraim	Num 2:18	5387
the *c* of the children of Manasseh	Num 2:20	5387
the *c* of the sons of Benjamin	Num 2:22	5387
the *c* of the children of Dan	Num 2:25	5387
the *c* of the children of Asher	Num 2:27	5387
the *c* of the children of Naphtali	Num 2:29	5387
one to another, Let us make a *c*	Num 14:4	7218
but as *c* of the host of the LORD	Josh 5:14	8269
the *c* of the LORD's host said	Josh 5:15	8269
the *c* of whose host was Sisera	Judg 4:2	8269
the *c* of Jabin's army, with his	Judg 4:7	8269
unto Jephthah, Come, and be our *c*	Judg 11:6	7101
made him head and *c* over them	Judg 11:11	7101
him to be *c* over my people Israel	1Sa 9:16	5057
thee to be *c* over his inheritance	1Sa 10:1	5057
c of the host of Hazor, and into	1Sa 12:9	8269
him to be *c* over his people	1Sa 13:14	5057
the name of the *c* of his host was	1Sa 14:50	8269
unto the *c* of their thousand	1Sa 17:18	8269
the *c* of the host, Abner, whose	1Sa 17:55	8269
made him his *c* over a thousand	1Sa 18:13	8269
and he became a *c* over them	1Sa 22:2	8269
the son of Ner, the *c* of his host	1Sa 26:5	8269
of Ner, *c* of Saul's host, took	2Sa 2:8	8269
and thou shalt be a *c* over Israel	2Sa 5:2	5057
soul, he shall be chief and *c*	2Sa 5:8	
Shobach the *c* of the host of	2Sa 10:16	8269
smote Shobach the *c* of their host	2Sa 10:18	8269
Absalom made Amasa *c* of the host	2Sa 17:25	5921
if thou be not *c* of the host	2Sa 19:13	8269
therefore he was their *c*	2Sa 23:19	8269
said to Joab the *c* of the host	2Sa 24:2	8269
priest, and Joab the *c* of the host	1Kin 1:19	8269
c of the host of Israel, and Amasa	1Kin 2:32	8269
of Jether, *c* of the host of Judah	1Kin 2:32	8269
Joab the *c* of the host was gone	1Kin 11:15	8269

that Joab the *c* of the host was	1Kin 11:21	8269
became *c* over a band, when David	1Kin 11:24	8269
c of half his chariots, conspired	1Kin 16:9	8269
the *c* of the host, king over	1Kin 16:16	8269
him a *c* of fifty with his fifty	2Kin 1:9	8269
and said to the *c* of fifty	2Kin 1:10	8269
another *c* of fifty with his fifty	2Kin 1:11	8269
he sent again a *c* of the third	2Kin 1:13	8269
the third *c* of fifty went up, and	2Kin 1:13	8269
the king, or to the *c* of the host	2Kin 4:13	8269
c of the host of the king of	2Kin 5:1	8269
I have an errand to thee, O *c*	2Kin 9:5	8269
And he said, To thee, O *c*	2Kin 9:5	8269
Then said Jehu to Bidkar his *c*	2Kin 9:25	7991
a *c* of his, conspired against him	2Kin 15:25	7991
one *c* of the least of my master's	2Kin 18:24	6346
tell Hezekiah the *c* of my people	2Kin 20:5	5057
c of the guard, a servant of the	2Kin 25:8	7227
that were with the *c* of the guard	2Kin 25:10	7227
did Nebuzar-adan the *c* of the	2Kin 25:11	7227
But the *c* of the guard left of	2Kin 25:12	7227
the *c* of the guard took away	2Kin 25:15	7227
the *c* of the guard took Seraiah	2Kin 25:18	7227
Nebuzar-adan *c* of the guard took	2Kin 25:20	7227
first shall be chief and *c*	1Chr 11:6	8269
for he was their *c*	1Chr 11:21	8269
a *c* of the Reubenites, and thirty	1Chr 11:42	7218
Shophach the *c* of the host of	1Chr 19:16	8269
killed Shophach the *c* of the host	1Chr 19:18	8269
The third *c* of the host for the	1Chr 27:5	8269
The fourth *c* for the fourth month	1Chr 27:7	
The fifth *c* for the fifth month	1Chr 27:8	8269
The sixth *c* for the sixth month	1Chr 27:9	
The seventh *c* for the seventh	1Chr 27:10	
The eighth *c* for the eighth month	1Chr 27:11	
The ninth *c* for the ninth month	1Chr 27:12	
The tenth *c* for the tenth month	1Chr 27:13	
The eleventh *c* for the eleventh	1Chr 27:14	
The twelfth *c* for the twelfth	1Chr 27:15	
God himself is with us for our *c*	2Chr 13:12	7218
next to him was Jehohanan the *c*	2Chr 17:15	8269
a *c* to return to their bondage	Neh 9:17	7218
The *c* of fifty, and the honourable	Is 3:3	8269
one *c* of the least of my master's	Is 36:9	6346
a *c* of the ward was there, whose	Jer 37:13	1167
Then Nebuzar-adan the *c* of the	Jer 39:9	7227
But Nebuzar-adan the *c* of the	Jer 39:10	
Nebuzar-adan the *c* of the guard	Jer 39:11	7227
the *c* of the guard sent, and	Jer 39:13	7227
the *c* of the guard had let him go	Jer 40:1	7227
the *c* of the guard took Jeremiah,	Jer 40:2	7227
So the *c* of the guard gave him	Jer 40:5	7227
whom Nebuzar-adan the *c* of the	Jer 41:10	7227
the *c* of the guard had left with	Jer 43:6	7227
appoint a *c* against her	Jer 51:27	2951
c of the guard, which served the	Jer 52:12	7227
that were with the *c* of the guard	Jer 52:14	7227
Then Nebuzar-adan the *c* of the	Jer 52:15	7227
But Nebuzar-adan the *c* of the	Jer 52:16	7227
took the *c* of the guard away	Jer 52:19	7227
the *c* of the guard took Seraiah	Jer 52:24	7227
So Nebuzar-adan the *c* of the	Jer 52:26	7227
the *c* of the guard carried away	Jer 52:30	7227
Arioch the *c* of the king's guard	Dan 2:14	7229
and said to Arioch the king's *c*	Dan 2:15	7990
Then the band and the *c* and	Jn 18:12	5506
the *c* of the temple, and the	Acts 4:1	4755
the *c* of the temple and the chief	Acts 5:24	4755
Then went the *c* with the officers	Acts 5:26	4755
came unto the chief *c* of the band	Acts 21:31	5506
and when they saw the chief *c*	Acts 21:32	5506
Then the chief *c* came near	Acts 21:33	5506
castle, he said unto the chief *c*	Acts 21:37	5506
The chief *c* commanded him to be	Acts 22:24	5506
that, he went and told the chief *c*	Acts 22:26	5506
Then the chief *c* came, and said	Acts 22:27	5506
And the chief *c* answered, With a	Acts 22:28	5506
the chief *c* also was afraid,	Acts 22:29	5506
a great dissension, the chief *c*	Acts 23:10	5506
council signify to the chief *c*	Acts 23:15	5506
this young man unto the chief *c*	Acts 23:17	5506
and brought him to the chief *c*	Acts 23:18	5506
Then the chief *c* took him by the	Acts 23:19	5506
So the chief *c* then let the young	Acts 23:22	5506
But the chief *c* Lysias came upon	Acts 24:7	5506
the chief *c* shall come down	Acts 24:22	5506
prisoners to the *c* of the guard	Acts 28:16	4759
to make the *c* of their salvation	Heb 2:10	747

C

CAPTAINS

and *c* over every one of them	Ex 14:7	7991
his chosen *c* also are drowned in	Ex 15:4	7991
with the *c* over thousands, and	Num 31:14	8269
c over hundreds, which came from	Num 31:14	8269
the *c* of thousands, and *c*	Num 31:48	8269
c of hundreds, came near unto	Num 31:48	8269
of the *c* of thousands, and of the	Num 31:52	8269
of the *c* of hundreds, was sixteen	Num 31:52	8269
the gold of the *c* of thousands	Num 31:54	8269
c over thousands, and *c*	Deut 1:15	8269
c over hundreds, and *c* over	Deut 1:15	8269
c over fifties, and *c* over	Deut 1:15	8269
c over tens, and officers among	Deut 1:15	8269
that they shall make *c* of the	Deut 20:9	8269
your *c* of your tribes, your	Deut 29:10	7218
said unto the *c* of the men of war	Josh 10:24	7101
will appoint him *c* over thousands	1Sa 8:12	8269
over thousands, and *c* over fifties	1Sa 8:12	8269
and make you all *c* of thousands	1Sa 22:7	8269
of thousands, and *c* of hundreds	1Sa 22:7	8269
had two men that were *c* of bands	2Sa 4:2	8269
set *c* of thousands and *c* of	2Sa 18:1	8269
and *c* of hundreds over them	2Sa 18:1	8269
the *c* charge concerning Absalom	2Sa 18:5	8269
in the seat, chief among the *c*	2Sa 23:8	7991
and against the *c* of the host	2Sa 24:4	8269
the *c* of the host went out from	2Sa 24:4	8269
the *c* of the host, and Abiathar	1Kin 1:25	8269
the two *c* of the hosts of Israel	1Kin 2:5	8269
and his princes, and his *c*	1Kin 9:22	7991
sent the *c* of the hosts which he	1Kin 15:20	8269
place, and put *c* in their rooms	1Kin 20:24	6346
two *c* that had rule over his	1Kin 22:31	8269
when the *c* of the chariots saw	1Kin 22:32	8269
when the *c* of the chariots	1Kin 22:33	8269
burnt up the two *c* of the former	2Kin 1:14	8269
about, and the *c* of the chariots	2Kin 8:21	8269
the *c* of the host were sitting	2Kin 9:5	8269
said to the guard and to the *c*	2Kin 10:25	7991
the *c* cast them out, and went to	2Kin 10:25	7991
rulers over hundreds, with the *c*	2Kin 11:4	3746
the *c* over the hundreds did	2Kin 11:9	8269
to the *c* over hundreds did the	2Kin 11:10	8269
commanded the *c* of the hundreds	2Kin 11:15	8269
rulers over hundreds, and the *c*	2Kin 11:19	3746
when all the *c* of the armies	2Kin 25:23	8269
the *c* of the armies, arose, and	2Kin 25:26	8269
Seir, having for their *c* Pelatiah	1Chr 4:42	8269
a Hachmonite, the chief of the *c*	1Chr 11:11	7991
Now three of the thirty *c* went	1Chr 11:15	7218
of the sons of Gad, *c* of the host	1Chr 12:14	7218
Amasai, who was chief of the *c*	1Chr 12:18	7991
them, and made them *c* of the band	1Chr 12:18	7218
c of the thousands that were of	1Chr 12:20	7218
of valour, and were *c* in the host	1Chr 12:21	8269
father's house twenty and two *c*	1Chr 12:28	8269
And of Naphtali a thousand *c*	1Chr 12:34	8269
consulted with the *c* of thousands	1Chr 13:1	8269
the *c* over thousands, went to	1Chr 15:25	8269
the *c* of the host separated to	1Chr 25:1	8269
the *c* over thousands and hundreds,	1Chr 26:26	8269
the *c* of the host, had dedicated	1Chr 26:26	8269
c of thousands and hundreds, and	1Chr 27:1	8269
Perez was the chief of all the *c*	1Chr 27:3	8269
the *c* of the companies that	1Chr 28:1	8269
the *c* over the thousands, and	1Chr 28:1	8269
c over the hundreds, and the	1Chr 28:1	8269
the *c* of thousands and of hundreds	1Chr 28:1	8269
to the *c* of thousands and of	2Chr 1:2	8269
men of war, and chief of his *c*	2Chr 8:9	7991
c of his chariots and horsemen	2Chr 8:9	8269
put *c* in them, and store of	2Chr 11:11	5057
sent the *c* of his armies against	2Chr 16:4	8269
Of Judah, the *c* of thousands	2Chr 17:14	8269
c of the chariots that were with	2Chr 18:30	8269
when the *c* of the chariots saw	2Chr 18:31	8269
when the *c* of the chariots	2Chr 18:32	8269
him in, and the *c* of the chariots	2Chr 21:9	8269
took the *c* of hundreds, Azariah	2Chr 23:1	8269
to the *c* of hundreds spears	2Chr 23:9	8269
the priest brought out the *c* of	2Chr 23:14	8269
And he took the *c* of hundreds	2Chr 23:20	8269
made them *c* over thousands, and	2Chr 25:5	8269
c over hundreds, according to the	2Chr 25:5	8269
of Hananiah, one of the king's *c*	2Chr 26:11	8269
he set *c* of war over the people,	2Chr 32:6	8269
c in the camp of the king of	2Chr 32:21	8269
the *c* of the host of the king of	2Chr 33:11	8269
put *c* of war in all the fenced	2Chr 33:14	8269
the king had sent *c* of the army	Neh 2:9	8269

afar off, the thunder of the *c*	Job 39:25	8269
for thou hast taught them to be *c*	Jer 13:21	441
Now when all the *c* of the forces	Jer 40:7	8269
all the *c* of the forces that were	Jer 40:13	8269
all the *c* of the forces that were	Jer 41:11	8269
all the *c* of the forces that were	Jer 41:13	8269
all the *c* of the forces that were	Jer 41:16	8269
Then all the *c* of the forces, and	Jer 42:1	8269
all the *c* of the forces which	Jer 42:8	8269
all the *c* of the forces, and all	Jer 43:4	8269
all the *c* of the forces, took all	Jer 43:5	8269
thee will I break in pieces *c*	Jer 51:23	6346
the *c* thereof, and all the rulers	Jer 51:28	6346
princes, and her wise men, her *c*	Jer 51:57	6346
for Jerusalem, to appoint *c*	Eze 21:22	3733
Which were clothed with blue, *c*	Eze 23:6	6346
the Assyrians her neighbours, *c*	Eze 23:12	6346
of them desirable young men, *c*	Eze 23:23	6346
princes, the governors, and the *c*	Dan 3:2	6347
the princes, the governors, and *c*	Dan 3:3	6347
And the princes, governors, and *c*	Dan 3:27	6347
the counsellors, and the *c*	Dan 6:7	6347
thy *c* as the great grasshoppers,	Nah 3:17	2951
a supper to his lords, high *c*	Mk 6:21	5506
with the chief priests and *c*	Lk 22:4	4755
c of the temple, and the elders,	Lk 22:52	4755
of hearing, with the chief *c*	Acts 25:23	5506
and the rich men, and the chief *c*	Rev 6:15	5506
flesh of kings, and the flesh of *c*	Rev 19:18	5506

CAPTIVE

that his brother was taken *c*	Gen 14:14	7617
ones, and their wives took they *c*	Gen 34:29	7617
of the *c* that was in the dungeon	Ex 12:29	7628
Asshur shall carry thee away *c*	Num 24:22	7617
hands, and thou hast taken them *c*	Deut 21:10	7617
Barak, and lead thy captivity *c*	Judg 5:12	7617
enemies, which led them away *c*	1Kin 8:48	7617
before them who carried them *c*	1Kin 8:50	7617
had brought away *c* out of the	2Kin 5:2	7617
thou hast taken *c* with thy sword	2Kin 6:22	7617
and carried them *c* to Assyria	2Kin 15:29	1540
carried the people of it *c* to Kir	2Kin 16:9	1540
of Babylon brought *c* to Babylon	2Kin 24:16	1473
king of Assyria carried away *c*	1Chr 5:6	1540
land whither they are carried *c*	2Chr 6:37	7617
children of Judah carry away *c*	2Chr 25:12	7617
c of their brethren two hundred	2Chr 28:8	7617
ye have taken *c* of your brethren	2Chr 28:11	7617
before them that lead them *c*	2Chr 30:9	7617
high, thou hast led captivity *c*	Ps 68:18	7617
us away *c* required of us a song	Ps 137:3	7617
my children, and am desolate, a *c*	Is 49:21	1473
mighty, or the lawful *c* delivered	Is 49:24	7628
The *c* exile hasteneth that he may	Is 51:14	6808
of thy neck, O *c* daughter of Zion	Is 52:2	7628
of Jerusalem *c* in the fifth month	Jer 1:3	1540
LORD's flock is carried away *c*	Jer 13:17	7617
shall be carried away *c* all of it	Jer 13:19	1540
it shall be wholly carried away *c*	Jer 13:19	1540
shall carry them *c* into Babylon	Jer 20:4	1540
place whither they have led him *c*	Jer 22:12	1540
of Babylon had carried away *c*	Jer 24:1	1540
that are carried away *c* of Judah	Jer 24:5	1546
when he carried away *c* Jeconiah	Jer 27:20	1540
and all that is carried away *c*	Jer 28:6	1473
away *c* from Jerusalem to Babylon	Jer 29:1	1473
I caused you to be carried away *c*	Jer 29:14	1540
of the guard carried away *c* into	Jer 39:9	1540
were carried away *c* of Jerusalem	Jer 40:1	1546
were carried away *c* unto Babylon	Jer 40:1	1540
not carried away *c* to Babylon	Jer 40:7	1540
Then Ishmael carried away *c* all	Jer 41:10	7617
of Nethaniah carried them away *c*	Jer 41:10	7617
away from Mizpah cast about	Jer 41:14	7617
of the guard carried away *c*	Jer 52:15	1540
away *c* out of his own land	Jer 52:27	1540
Nebuchadrezzar carried away *c*	Jer 52:28	1540
c from Jerusalem eight hundred	Jer 52:29	1540
of the guard carried away *c* of	Jer 52:30	1540
away *c* the whole captivity	Amos 1:6	1540
Therefore now shall they go *c*	Amos 6:7	1540
c with the first that go *c*	Amos 6:7	1540
led away *c* out of their own land	Amos 7:11	1540
carried away *c* his forces	Obad 11	7617
And Huzzab shall be led away *c*	Nah 2:7	1540
be led away *c* into all nations	Lk 21:24	*163*
up on high, he led captivity *c*	Eph 4:8	*162*
who are taken *c* by him at his	2Ti 2:26	*2221*
lead *c* silly women laden with	2Ti 3:6	*162*

CAPTIVES

as *c* taken with the sword	Gen 31:26	7617
took all the women of Midian *c*	Num 31:9	7617
And they brought the, *c*, and the	Num 31:12	7628
your *c* on the third day, and on	Num 31:19	7628
seest among the *c* a beautiful	Deut 21:11	7633
blood of the slain and of the *c*	Deut 32:42	7633
And had taken the women *c*, that	1Sa 30:2	7617
and their daughters, were taken *c*	1Sa 30:3	7617
And David's two wives were taken *c*	1Sa 30:5	7617
away *c* unto the land of the enemy	1Kin 8:46	7617
land whither they were carried *c*	1Kin 8:47	7617
land of them that carried them *c*	1Kin 8:47	7617
of valour, even ten thousand *c*	2Kin 24:14	1540
they carry them away *c* unto a	2Chr 6:36	7617
whither they have carried them *c*	2Chr 6:38	7617
away a great multitude of them *c*	2Chr 28:5	7633
therefore, and deliver the *c* again	2Chr 28:11	7633
shall not bring in the *c* hither	2Chr 28:13	7633
So the armed men left the *c*	2Chr 28:14	7633
by name rose up, and took the *c*	2Chr 28:15	7633
smitten Judah, and carried away *c*	2Chr 28:17	7628
of all those that carried them *c*	Ps 106:46	7617
and they shall take them *c*	Is 14:2	7617
them *c*, whose *c* they were	Is 14:2	7617
prisoners, and the Ethiopians *c*	Is 20:4	1546
my city, and he shall let go my *c*	Is 45:13	1546
Even the *c* of the mighty shall be	Is 49:25	7628
to proclaim liberty to the *c*	Is 61:1	7628
of Judah, with all the *c* of Judah	Jer 28:4	1546
elders which were carried away *c*	Jer 29:1	1473
unto all that are carried away *c*	Jer 29:4	1473
caused you to be carried away *c*	Jer 29:7	1540
and carry us away *c* into Babylon	Jer 43:3	1540
burn then, and carry them away *c*	Jer 43:12	7617
for thy sons are taken *c*, and thy	Jer 48:46	7628
c, and thy daughters *c*	Jer 48:46	7633
that took them *c* held them fast	Jer 50:33	7617
as I was among the *c* by the river	Eze 1:1	1473
whither they shall be carried *c*	Eze 6:9	7617
of thy *c* in the midst of them	Eze 16:53	7628
found a man of the *c* of Judah	Dan 2:25	1123,1547
shall also carry *c* into Egypt	Dan 11:8	7628
to preach deliverance to the *c*	Lk 4:18	*164*

CAPTIVITY

into *c* unto Sihon king of the	Num 21:29	7628
the raiment of her *c* from off her	Deut 21:13	7633
for they shall go into *c*	Deut 28:41	7628
the LORD thy God will turn thy *c*	Deut 30:3	7622
Barak, and lead thy *c* captive	Judg 5:12	7628
the day of the *c* of the land	Judg 18:30	1546
those carried he into *c* from	2Kin 24:15	1540
thirtieth year of the *c* of	2Kin 25:27	1546
dwelt in their steads until the *c*	1Chr 5:22	1473
And Jehozadak went into *c*, when	1Chr 6:15	
unto thee in the land of their *c*	2Chr 6:37	7633
their soul in the land of their *c*	2Chr 6:38	7617
and our wives are in *c* for this	2Chr 29:9	7628
the *c* that were brought up from	Ezr 1:11	1473
that went up out of the *c*	Ezr 2:1	7628
come out of the *c* unto Jerusalem	Ezr 3:8	7628
the *c* builded the temple unto the	Ezr 4:1	1473
the rest of the children of the *c*	Ezr 6:16	1547
the children of the *c* kept the	Ezr 6:19	1473
for all the children of the *c*	Ezr 6:20	1473
which were come again out of *c*	Ezr 6:21	1473
which were come out of the *c*	Ezr 8:35	7628
of the lands, to the sword, to *c*	Ezr 9:7	7628
unto all the children of the *c*	Ezr 10:7	1473
And the children of the *c* did so	Ezr 10:16	1473
escaped, which were left of the *c*	Neh 1:2	7628
c there in the province are in	Neh 1:3	7628
them for a prey in the land of *c*	Neh 4:4	7633
that went up out of the *c*	Neh 7:6	7628
again out of the *c* made booths	Neh 8:17	7628
the *c* which had been carried away	Est 2:6	1473
And the LORD turned the *c* of Job	Job 42:10	7622
bringeth back the *c* of his people	Ps 14:7	7622
bringeth back the *c* of his people	Ps 53:6	7622
on high, thou hast led *c* captive	Ps 68:18	7628
And delivered his strength into *c*	Ps 78:61	7628
hast brought back the *c* of Jacob	Ps 85:1	7622
LORD turned again the *c* of Zion	Ps 126:1	7622
Turn again our *c*, O LORD, as the	Ps 126:4	7622
my people are gone into *c*	Is 5:13	1540
carry thee away with a mighty *c*	Is 22:17	2925
but themselves are gone into *c*	Is 46:2	7628
are for the *c*, to the *c*	Jer 15:2	7628
in thine house shall go into *c*	Jer 20:6	7628
and thy lovers shall go into *c*	Jer 22:22	7628

and I will turn away your *c*	Jer 29:14	7622
not gone forth with you into *c*	Jer 29:16	1473
word of the LORD, all ye of the *c*	Jer 29:20	1473
c of Judah which are in Babylon	Jer 29:22	1546
Babylon, saying, This *c* is long	Jer 29:28	
Send to all them of the *c*	Jer 29:31	1473
again the *c* of my people Israel	Jer 30:3	7622
thy seed from the land of their *c*	Jer 30:10	7628
one of them, shall go into *c*	Jer 30:16	7633
again the *c* of Jacob's tents	Jer 30:18	7622
when I shall bring again their *c*	Jer 31:23	7622
I will cause their *c* to return	Jer 32:44	7622
And I will cause the *c* of Judah	Jer 33:7	7622
the *c* of Israel to return, and	Jer 33:7	7622
cause to return the *c* of the land	Jer 33:11	7622
I will cause their *c* to return	Jer 33:26	7622
and such as are for *c* to *c*	Jer 43:11	7628
and such as are for *c* to *c*	Jer 43:11	7628
furnish thyself to go into *c*	Jer 46:19	1473
thy seed from the land of their *c*	Jer 46:27	7633
go forth into *c* with his priests	Jer 48:7	1473
neither hath he gone into *c*	Jer 48:11	1473
the *c* of Moab in the latter days	Jer 48:47	7622
for their king shall go into *c*	Jer 49:3	1473
I will bring again the *c* of the	Jer 49:6	7622
I will bring again the *c* of Elam	Jer 49:39	7622
thirtieth year of the *c* of	Jer 52:31	1546
Judah is gone into *c* because of	Lam 1:3	1540
are gone into *c* before the enemy	Lam 1:5	7628
and my young men are gone into *c*	Lam 1:18	7628
iniquity, to turn away thy *c*	Lam 2:14	7622
no more carry thee away into *c*	Lam 4:22	1540
fifth year of king Jehoiachin's *c*	Eze 1:2	1546
And go, get thee to them of the *c*	Eze 3:11	1473
came to them of the *c* at Tel-abib	Eze 3:15	1473
into Chaldea, to them of the *c*	Eze 11:24	1473
c all the things that the LORD	Eze 11:25	1473
as they that go forth into *c*	Eze 12:4	1473
my stuff by day, as stuff for *c*	Eze 12:7	1473
they shall remove and go into *c*	Eze 12:11	7628
When I shall bring again their *c*	Eze 16:53	7622
the *c* of Sodom and her daughters,	Eze 16:53	7622
the *c* of Samaria and her daughters	Eze 16:53	7622
then will I bring again the *c* of	Eze 16:53	7622
of Judah, when they went into *c*	Eze 25:3	1473
I will bring again the *c* of Egypt	Eze 29:14	7622
and these cities shall go into *c*	Eze 30:17	7628
and her daughters shall go into *c*	Eze 30:18	7628
pass in the twelfth year of our *c*	Eze 33:21	1546
went into *c* for their iniquity	Eze 39:23	1540
will I bring again the *c* of Jacob	Eze 39:25	7622
be led into *c* among the heathen	Eze 39:28	1473
five and twentieth year of our *c*	Eze 40:1	1546
of the children of the *c* of Judah	Dan 5:13	1547
of the children of the *c* of Judah	Dan 6:13	1547
by the sword, and by flame, by *c*	Dan 11:33	7628
I returned the *c* of my people	Hos 6:11	7622
shall bring again the *c* of Judah	Joel 3:1	7622
of Syria shall go into *c* unto Kir	Amos 1:5	1540
carried away captive the whole *c*	Amos 1:6	1546
delivered up the whole *c* to Edom	Amos 1:9	1546
And their king shall go into *c*	Amos 1:15	1473
for Gilgal shall surely go into *c*	Amos 5:5	1540
you to go into *c* beyond Damascus	Amos 5:27	1540
go into *c* forth of his land	Amos 7:17	1540
though they go into *c* before	Amos 9:4	7628
the *c* of my people of Israel	Amos 9:14	7622
the *c* of this host of the	Obad 20	1546
the *c* of Jerusalem, which is in	Obad 20	1546
they are gone into *c* from thee	Mic 1:16	1540
she carried away, she went into *c*	Nah 3:10	7628
shall gather the *c* as the sand	Hab 1:9	7628
visit them, and turn away their *c*	Zeph 2:7	7622
turn back your *c* before your eyes	Zeph 3:20	7622
Take of them of the *c*, even of	Zec 6:10	1473
of the city shall go forth into *c*	Zec 14:2	1473
bringing me into *c* to the law of	Rom 7:23	*163*
bringing into *c* every thought to	2Cor 10:5	*163*
he led *c* captive, and gave gifts	Eph 4:8	*161*
into *c* shall go into *c*	Rev 13:10	*161*

CARBUNCLE

be a sardius, a topaz, and a *c*	Ex 28:17	1304
was a sardius, a topaz, and a *c*	Ex 39:10	1304
sapphire, the emerald, and the *c*	Eze 28:13	1304

CARBUNCLES

of agates, and thy gates of *c*	Is 54:12	68,688

CARCAS (car'-cas) A servant of King Ahasuerus.

Bigtha, and Abagtha, Zethar, and C	Est 1:10	3752

C

CARCASE

whether it be a *c* of an unclean	Lev 5:2	5038
or a *c* of unclean cattle, or the	Lev 5:2	5038
or the *c* of unclean creeping	Lev 5:2	5038
their *c* shall ye not touch	Lev 11:8	5038
whosoever toucheth the *c* of them	Lev 11:24	5038
c of them shall wash his clothes	Lev 11:25	5038
whoso toucheth their *c* shall be	Lev 11:27	5038
he that beareth the *c* of them	Lev 11:28	5038
their *c* falleth shall be unclean	Lev 11:35	5038
toucheth their *c* shall be unclean	Lev 11:36	5038
if any part of their *c* fall upon	Lev 11:37	5038
any part of their *c* fall thereon	Lev 11:38	5038
he that toucheth the *c* thereof	Lev 11:39	5038
he that eateth of the *c* of it	Lev 11:40	5038
he also that beareth the *c* of it	Lev 11:40	5038
flesh, nor touch their dead *c*	Deut 14:8	5038
thy *c* shall be meat unto all	Deut 28:26	5038
take his *c* down from the tree	Josh 8:29	5038
aside to see the *c* of the lion	Judg 14:8	4658
and honey in the *c* of the lion	Judg 14:8	1472
honey out of the *c* of the lion	Judg 14:9	1472
thy *c* shall not come unto the	1Kin 13:22	5038
his *c* was cast in the way, and the	1Kin 13:24	5038
it, the lion also stood by the *c*	1Kin 13:24	5038
saw the *c* cast in the way	1Kin 13:25	5038
and the lion standing by the *c*	1Kin 13:25	5038
found his *c* cast in the way, and	1Kin 13:28	5038
ass and the lion standing by the *c*	1Kin 13:28	5038
the lion had not eaten the *c*	1Kin 13:28	5038
took up the *c* of the man of God	1Kin 13:29	5038
he laid his *c* in his own grave	1Kin 13:30	5038
the *c* of Jezebel shall be as dung	2Kin 9:37	5038
as a *c* trodden under feet	Is 14:19	6297
For wheresoever the *c* is, there	Mt 24:28	4430

CARCASES

the fowls came down upon the *c*	Gen 15:11	6297
shall have their *c* in abomination	Lev 11:11	5038
The *c* of every beast which	Lev 11:26	6297
cast your *c* upon the *c* of	Lev 26:30	6297
Your *c* shall fall in this	Num 14:29	6297
But as for you, your *c*, they	Num 14:32	6297
until your *c* be wasted in the	Num 14:33	6297
I will give the *c* of the host of	1Sa 17:46	6297
their *c* were torn in the midst of	Is 5:25	5038
shall come up out of their *c*	Is 34:3	6297
look upon the *c* of the men that	Is 66:24	6297
the *c* of this people shall be	Jer 7:33	5038
Even the *c* of men shall fall as	Jer 9:22	5038
their *c* shall be meat for the	Jer 16:4	5038
with the *c* of their detestable	Jer 16:18	5038
their *c* will I give to be meat	Jer 19:7	5038
I will lay the dead *c* of the	Eze 6:5	6297
nor by the *c* of their kings in	Eze 43:7	6297
the *c* of their kings, far from me	Eze 43:9	6297
of slain, and a great number of *c*	Nah 3:3	6297
whose *c* fell in the wilderness	Heb 3:17	2966

CARCHEMISH (car'-ke-mish) See CHARCHEMISH. *A city on the Euphrates River.*

Is not Calno as *C*	Is 10:9	3751
was by the river Euphrates in *C*	Jer 46:2	3751

CARE

hath left the *c* of the asses	1Sa 10:2	1697
flee away, they will not *c* for us	2Sa 18:3	7760,3820
of us die, will they *c* for us	2Sa 18:3	7760,3820
careful for us with all this *c*	2Kin 4:13	2731
nation, that dwelleth without *c*	Jer 49:31	983
eat bread by weight, and with *c*	Eze 4:16	1674
the *c* of this world, and the	Mt 13:22	3308
him to an inn, and took *c* of him	Lk 10:34	1959
and said unto him, Take *c* of him	Lk 10:35	1959
dost thou not *c* that my sister	Lk 10:40	3199
c not for it	1Cor 7:21	3199
Doth God take *c* for oxen	1Cor 9:9	3199
have the same *c* one for another	1Cor 12:25	3309
but that our *c* for you in the	2Cor 7:12	4710
which put the same earnest *c* into	2Cor 8:16	4710
the *c* of all the churches	2Cor 11:28	3308
will naturally *c* for your state	Phil 2:20	3309
that now at the last your *c* of me	Phil 4:10	5426
how shall he take *c* of the church	1Ti 3:5	1959
Casting all your *c* upon him	1Pet 5:7	3308

CAREAH (ca-re'-ah) See KAREAH. *Father of Johanan.*

and Johanan the son of *C*, and	2Kin 25:23	7143

CARED

no man *c* for my soul	Ps 142:4	1875
not that he *c* for the poor	Jn 12:6	3199
Gallio *c* for none of those things	Acts 18:17	3199

CAREFUL

thou hast been *c* for us with all	2Kin 4:13	2729
shall not be *c* in the year of	Jer 17:8	1672
we are not *c* to answer thee in	Dan 3:16	2818
her, Martha, Martha, thou art *c*	Lk 10:41	3309
Be *c* for nothing	Phil 4:6	3309
wherein ye were also *c*, but ye	Phil 4:10	5426
might be *c* to maintain good works	Titus 3:8	5431

CAREFULLY

Only if thou *c* hearken unto the	Deut 15:5	8085
of Maroth waited *c* for good	Mic 1:12	2470
I sent him therefore the more *c*	Phil 2:28	4708
though he sought it *c* with tears	Heb 12:17	1567

CAREFULNESS

water with trembling and with *c*	Eze 12:18	1674
They shall eat their bread with *c*	Eze 12:19	1674
But I would have you without *c*	1Cor 7:32	275
what *c* it wrought in you, yea,	2Cor 7:11	4710

CARELESS

were therein, how they dwelt *c*	Judg 18:7	983
hear my voice, ye *c* daughters	Is 32:9	982
shall ye be troubled, ye *c* women	Is 32:10	982
be troubled, ye *c* ones	Is 32:11	982
to make the *c* Ethiopians afraid	Eze 30:9	983

CARELESSLY

to pleasures, that dwellest *c*	Is 47:8	983
them that dwell *c* in the isles	Eze 39:6	983
the rejoicing city that dwelt *c*	Zeph 2:15	983

CARES

the *c* of this world, and the	Mk 4:19	3303
go forth, and are choked with *c*	Lk 8:14	3303
c of this life, and so that day	Lk 21:34	3303

CAREST

neither *c* thou for any man	Mt 22:16	3199
c thou not that we perish	Mk 4:38	3199
thou art true, and *c* for no man	Mk 12:14	3199

CARETH

land which the LORD thy God *c* for	Deut 11:12	1875
hireling, and *c* not for the sheep	Jn 10:13	3199
He that is unmarried *c* for the	1Cor 7:32	3309
But he that is married *c* for the	1Cor 7:33	3309
The unmarried woman *c* for the	1Cor 7:34	3309
but she that is married *c* for the	1Cor 7:34	3309
for he *c* for you	1Pet 5:7	3199

CARING

my father leave *c* for the asses	1Sa 9:5	

CARKAS See CARCAS.

CARMEL (car'-mel) See CARMELITE.
1. A mountain range in Canaan.

the king of Jokneam of *C*, one	Josh 12:22	3760
and reacheth to *C* westward	Josh 19:26	3760
Samuel, saying, Saul came to *C*	1Sa 15:12	3760
to me all Israel unto mount *C*	1Kin 18:19	3760
prophets together unto mount *C*	1Kin 18:20	3760
And Elijah went up to the top of *C*	1Kin 18:42	3760
And he went from thence to mount *C*	2Kin 2:25	3760
unto the man of God to mount *C*	2Kin 4:25	3760
and into the forest of his *C*	2Kin 19:23	3760
in the mountains, and in *C*	2Chr 26:10	3760
Thine head upon thee is like *C*	Song 7:5	3760
and *C* shake off their fruits	Is 33:9	3760
unto it, the excellency of *C*	Is 35:2	3760
border, and the forest of his *C*	Is 37:24	3760
as *C* by the sea, so shall he come	Jer 46:18	3760
habitation, and he shall feed on *C*	Jer 50:19	3760
the top of *C* shall wither	Amos 1:2	3760
hide themselves in the top of *C*	Amos 9:3	3760
in the wood, in the midst of *C*	Mic 7:14	3760
Bashan languisheth, and *C*, and the	Nah 1:4	3760

2. A town in Judah.

Maon, *C*, and Ziph, and Juttah,	Josh 15:55	3760
Maon, whose possessions were in *C*	1Sa 25:2	3760
and he was shearing his sheep in *C*	1Sa 25:2	3760
the young men, Get you up to *C*	1Sa 25:5	3760
all the while they were in *C*	1Sa 25:7	3760
David were come to Abigail to *C*	1Sa 25:40	3760

CARMELITE (car'-mel-ite) See CARMELITESS. *An inhabitant of Carmel 2.*

Abigail the wife of Nabal the *C*	1Sa 30:5	3761
and Abigail Nabal's wife the *C*	2Sa 2:2	3761
Abigail the wife of Nabal the *C*	2Sa 3:3	3761
Hezrai the *C*, Paarai the Arbite,	2Sa 23:35	3761
Hezro the *C*, Naarai the son of	1Chr 11:37	3761

CARMELITESS (car'-mel-i-tess)

Jezreelitess, and Abigail the C	1Sa 27:3	3762
second Daniel, of Abigail the C	1Chr 3:1	3762

CARMI (car'-mi) See CARMITES.

1. Father of Achan.

for Achan, the son of C, the son	Josh 7:1	3756
and Achan, the son of C, the son	Josh 7:18	3756
And the sons of C	1Chr 2:7	3756
Pharez, Hezron, and C, and Hur, and	1Chr 4:1	3756

2. A son of Reuben.

and Phallu, and Hezron, and C	Gen 46:9	3756
Hanoch, and Pallu, Hezron, and C	Ex 6:14	3756
of C, the family of the Carmites	Num 26:6	3756
Hanoch, and Pallu, Hezron, and C	1Chr 5:3	3756

CARMITES (car'-mites) Descendants of Carmi 2.

of Carmi, the family of the C	Num 26:6	3757

CARNAL

but I am c, sold under sin	Rom 7:14	4559
Because the c mind is enmity	Rom 8:7	4561
to minister unto them in c things	Rom 15:27	4559
as unto spiritual, but as unto c	1Cor 3:1	4559
For ye are yet c	1Cor 3:3	4559
and divisions, are ye not c	1Cor 3:3	4559
are ye not c?	1Cor 3:4	4559
if we shall reap your c things	1Cor 9:11	4559
weapons of our warfare are not c	2Cor 10:4	4559
after the law of a c commandment	Heb 7:16	4559
c ordinances, imposed on them	Heb 9:10	4561

CARNALLY

lie with thy neighbour's wife	Lev 18:20	7903,2233
whosoever lieth c with a woman	Lev 19:20	7902,2233
a man lie with her c, and it be	Num 5:13	7902,2233
For to be c minded is death	Rom 8:6	4561

CARPENTER

So the c encouraged the goldsmith	Is 41:7	2796
The c stretcheth out his rule	Is 44:13	2796,6086
Is not this the c, the son of	Mk 6:3	5045

CARPENTER'S

Is not this the c son	Mt 13:55	5045

CARPENTERS

to David, and cedar trees, and c	2Sa 5:11	2796,6086
and they laid it out to the c	2Kin 12:11	6086
Unto c, and builders, and masons	2Kin 22:6	2796
of cedars, with masons and c	1Chr 14:1	2796,6086
c to repair the house of the LORD	2Chr 24:12	2796
also unto the masons, and to the c	Ezr 3:7	2796
the princes of Judah, with the c	Jer 24:1	2796
of Judah and Jerusalem, and the c	Jer 29:2	2796
And the LORD shewed me four c	Zec 1:20	2796

CARPUS (car'-pus) A friend of Paul.

cloke that I left at Troas with C	2Ti 4:13	2591

CARRIAGE

the cattle and the c before them	Judg 18:21	3520
David left his c in the hand of	1Sa 17:22	3627
the hand of the keeper of the c	1Sa 17:22	3627

CARRIAGES

at Michmash he hath laid up his c	Is 10:28	3627
your c were heavy loaden	Is 46:1	5385
after those days we took up our c	Acts 21:15	643

CARRIED

he c away all his cattle, and all	Gen 31:18	5090
c away my daughters, as captives	Gen 31:26	5090
of Israel to Jacob their father	Gen 46:5	5375
For his sons c him into the land	Gen 50:13	5375
c them in their coats out of the	Lev 10:5	5375
c them over with them unto the	Josh 4:8	5674
c them up to the top of an hill	Judg 16:3	5927
of Israel be c about unto Gath	1Sa 5:8	5437
they c the ark of the God of	1Sa 5:8	5437
that, after they had c it about	1Sa 5:9	5437
but c them away, and went on their	1Sa 30:2	5090
that the Amalekites had c away	1Sa 30:18	3947
but David c it aside into the	2Sa 6:10	5186
Abiathar c the ark of God again	2Sa 15:29	7725
land whither they were c captives	1Kin 8:47	7617
land of them that c them captives	1Kin 8:47	7617
before them who c them captive	1Kin 8:50	7617
c him up into a loft, where he	1Kin 17:19	5927
Then they c him forth out of the	1Kin 21:13	3318
c thence silver, and gold, and	2Kin 7:8	5375
c thence also, and went and hid it	2Kin 7:8	5375
his servants c him in a chariot	2Kin 9:28	7392
c them captive to Assyria	2Kin 15:29	1540
c the people of it captive to Kir	2Kin 16:9	1540
c Israel away into Assyria, and	2Kin 17:6	1540

whom the LORD c away before them	2Kin 17:11	1540
So was Israel c away out of their	2Kin 17:23	1540
they had c away from Samaria came	2Kin 17:28	1540
whom they c away from thence	2Kin 17:33	1540
this day, shall be c into Babylon	2Kin 20:17	5375
c the ashes of them unto Beth-el	2Kin 23:4	5375
his servants c him in a chariot	2Kin 23:30	7392
he c out thence all the treasures	2Kin 24:13	3318
he c away all Jerusalem, and all	2Kin 24:14	1540
he c away Jehoiachin to Babylon	2Kin 24:15	1540
those c he into captivity from	2Kin 24:15	1980
of brass, and c him to Babylon	2Kin 25:7	935
c the brass of them to Babylon	2Kin 25:13	5375
So Judah was c away out of their	2Kin 25:21	1540
king of Assyria c away captive	1Chr 5:6	1540
and he c them away, even the	1Chr 5:26	1540
when the LORD c away Judah	1Chr 6:15	1540
who were c away to Babylon for	1Chr 9:1	1540
they c the ark of God in a new	1Chr 13:7	7392
but c it aside into the house of	1Chr 13:13	5186
land whither they are c captive	2Chr 6:37	7617
whither they have c them captives	2Chr 6:38	7617
he c away also the shields of	2Chr 12:9	3947
they c away very much spoil	2Chr 14:13	5375
c away sheep and camels in	2Chr 14:15	7617
they c away the stones of Ramah	2Chr 16:6	5375
c away all the substance that was	2Chr 21:17	7617
it, and c it to his place again	2Chr 24:11	7725
c away a great multitude of them	2Chr 28:5	7617
the children of Israel c away	2Chr 28:8	7617
c all the feeble of them upon	2Chr 28:15	5095
smitten Judah, and c away captives	2Chr 28:17	7617
with fetters, and c him to Babylon	2Chr 33:11	3212
Shaphan c the book to the king	2Chr 34:16	935
his brother, and c him to Egypt	2Chr 36:4	935
Nebuchadnezzar also c of the	2Chr 36:7	935
the sword c he away to Babylon	2Chr 36:20	1473
of those which had been c away	Ezr 2:1	1540
Babylon had c away unto Babylon	Ezr 2:1	1540
c the people away into Babylon	Ezr 5:12	1541
of those that had been c away	Ezr 8:35	1473
of those that had been c away	Ezr 9:4	1473
of them that had been c away	Ezr 10:6	1473
of those that had been c away	Ezr 10:8	1473
of those that had been c away	Neh 7:6	1473
the king of Babylon had c away	Neh 7:6	1540
Who had been c away from	Est 2:6	1540
been c away with Jeconiah king of	Est 2:6	1540
the king of Babylon had c away	Est 2:6	1540
have c them away, yea, and slain	Job 1:17	3947
of the froward is c headlong	Job 5:13	4116
I should have been c from the	Job 10:19	2986
though the mountains be c into	Ps 46:2	4131
of all those that c them captives	Ps 106:46	7617
For there they that c us away	Ps 137:3	7617
this day, shall be c to Babylon	Is 39:6	5375
which are c from the womb	Is 46:3	5375
shall be c upon their shoulders	Is 49:22	5375
our griefs, and c our sorrows	Is 53:4	5445
c them all the days of old	Is 63:9	5375
LORD's flock is c away captive	Jer 13:17	7617
Judah shall be c away captive all	Jer 13:19	1540
it shall be wholly c away captive	Jer 13:19	1540
king of Babylon had c away	Jer 24:1	1540
that are c away captive of Judah	Jer 24:5	1546
when he c away captive Jeconiah	Jer 27:20	1546
They shall be c to Babylon	Jer 27:22	935
this place, and c them to Babylon	Jer 28:3	935
all that is c away captive, from	Jer 28:6	1473
elders which were c away captives	Jer 29:1	1473
c away captive from Jerusalem to	Jer 29:1	1540
unto all that are c away captives	Jer 29:4	1473
to be c away from Jerusalem unto	Jer 29:4	1540
caused you to be c away captives	Jer 29:7	1540
I caused you to be c away captive	Jer 29:14	1540
the captain of the guard c away	Jer 39:9	1540
were c away captive of Jerusalem	Jer 40:1	1546
which were c away captive unto	Jer 40:1	1540
of them that were not c away	Jer 40:7	1540
Then Ishmael c away captive all	Jer 41:10	7617
of Nethaniah c them away captive	Jer 41:10	7617
c away captive from Mizpah cast	Jer 41:14	7617
c him up unto the king of Babylon	Jer 52:9	5927
c him to Babylon, and put him in	Jer 52:11	935
the captain of the guard c away	Jer 52:15	1540
c all the brass of them to	Jer 52:17	5375
Thus Judah was c away captive out	Jer 52:27	1540
Nebuchadrezzar c away captive	Jer 52:28	1540
year of Nebuchadrezzar he c away	Jer 52:29	
the captain of the guard c away	Jer 52:30	1540
whither they shall be c captives	Eze 6:9	7617

C

c it into a land of traffick......................Eze 17:4 — 935
c me out in the spirit of the ....Eze 37:1 — 3318
which he *c* into the land of ....Dan 1:2 — 935
the wind *c* them away, that no ....Dan 2:35 — 5376
It shall be also *c* unto Assyria ....Hos 10:6 — 2986
Assyrians, and oil is *c* into Egypt ......Hos 12:1 — 2986
have *c* into your temples my ....Joel 3:5 — 935
because they *c* away captive the ....Amos 1:6 — 1540
c away captive his forces......................Obad 11 — 7617
Yet was she *c* away, she went into ....Nah 3:10 — 1473
time they were *c* away to Babylon ....Mt 1:11 — 3350
c him away, and delivered him to ....Mk 15:1 — 667
there was a dead man *c* out ....Lk 7:12 — 1580
died, and was *c* by the angels into......Lk 16:22 — 667
from them, and *c* up into heaven ....Lk 24:51 — 339
lame from his mother's womb was *c*.....Acts 3:2 — 941
up, and *c* him out, and buried him ....Acts 5:6 — 1627
were *c* over into Sychem, and laid ....Acts 7:16 — 3346
devout men *c* Stephen to his..................Acts 8:2 — 4792
him to be *c* into the castle ....Acts 21:34 — 71
c away unto these dumb idols, ...1Cor 12:2 — 520
c away with their dissimulation ....Gal 2:13 — 4879
c about with every wind of ....Eph 4:14 — 4064
Be not *c* about with divers and ....Heb 13:9 — 4064
clouds that are *c* with a tempest ....2Pet 2:17 — 1643
without water, *c* about of winds ....Jude 12 — 4064
her to be *c* away of the flood ....Rev 12:15 — 4216
So he *c* me away in the spirit ....Rev 17:3 — 667
he *c* me away in the spirit to a ....Rev 21:10 — 667

CARRIEST
Thou *c* them away as with a flood ....Ps 90:5 — 2229

CARRIETH
and as chaff that the storm *c* away ....Job 21:18 — 1589
The east wind *c* him away, and he ....Job 27:21 — 5375
woman, and of the beast that *c* her ....Rev 17:7 — 941

CARRY
going to *c* it down to Egypt ....Gen 37:25 — 3381
c corn for the famine of your..................Gen 42:19 — 935
c down the man a present, a....................Gen 43:11 — 3381
sacks, *c* it again in your hand...............Gen 43:12 — 7725
with food, as much as they can *c*...........Gen 44:1 — 5375
which Joseph had sent to *c* him............Gen 45:27 — 5375
which Pharaoh had sent to *c* him ....Gen 46:5 — 5375
thou shalt *c* me out of Egypt, and ....Gen 47:30 — 5375
ye shall *c* up my bones from hence........Gen 50:25 — 5927
thou shalt not *c* forth ought of ....Ex 12:46 — 3318
ye shall *c* up my bones away hence........Ex 13:19 — 5927
to *c* us forth out of Egypt ....Ex 14:11 — 3318
go not with me, *c* us not up hence ....Ex 33:15 — 5927
c forth without the camp unto a ....Lev 4:12 — 3318
he shall *c* forth the bullock....................Lev 4:21 — 3318
c forth the ashes without the..................Lev 6:11 — 3318
c your brethren from before the ....Lev 10:4 — 5375
he shall *c* them forth out of the ....Lev 14:45 — 3318
shall one *c* forth without the ....Lev 16:27 — 3318
C them in thy bosom, as a nursing ....Num 11:12 — 5375
Asshur shall *c* thee away captive ....Num 24:22 — 7617
so that thou art not able to *c* it ....Deut 14:24 — 5375
Thou shalt *c* much seed out into ....Deut 28:38 — 3318
ye shall *c* them over with you, and ....Josh 4:3 — 5674
c these ten cheeses unto the ....1Sa 17:18 — 935
unto him, Go, *c* them to the city ....1Sa 20:40 — 935
C back the ark of God into the ....2Sa 15:25 — 7725
to *c* over the king's household ....2Sa 19:18 — 5674
so that they *c* them away captives ....1Kin 8:46 — 7617
shall *c* thee whither I know not ....1Kin 18:12 — 5375
then *c* him out, and stone him, ...1Kin 21:10 — 3318
c him back unto Amon the governor ......1Kin 22:26 — 7725
hand, and *c* me out of the host ....1Kin 22:34 — 3318
to a lad, *C* him to his mother ....2Kin 4:19 — 5375
c him to an inner chamber ....2Kin 9:2 — 935
C thither one of the priests whom..........2Kin 17:27 — 1980
the king of Assyria did *c* away ....2Kin 18:11 — 1540
the captain of the guard *c* away ....2Kin 25:11 — 1540
to *c* tidings unto their idols, and ....1Chr 10:9 — 1319
None ought to *c* the ark of God ....1Chr 15:2 — 5375
LORD chosen to *c* the ark of God...........1Chr 15:2 — 5375
shall no more *c* the tabernacle..............1Chr 23:26 — 5375
thou shalt *c* it up to Jerusalem ....2Chr 2:16 — 5927
they *c* them away captives unto a ....2Chr 6:36 — 7617
c him back to Amon the governor ....2Chr 18:25 — 7725
that thou mayest *c* me out of the ....2Chr 18:33 — 3318
more than they could *c* away ....2Chr 20:25 — 4853
children of Judah *c* away captive..........2Chr 25:12 — 7617
c forth the filthiness out of the ....2Chr 29:5 — 3318
to *c* it out abroad into the brook ....2Chr 29:16 — 3318
in fetters, to *c* him to Babylon ....2Chr 36:6 — 3212
c them into the temple that is in ....Ezr 5:15 — 5182
to *c* the silver and gold, which...............Ezr 7:15 — 2987

Why doth thine heart *c* thee away ....Job 15:12 — 3947
he dieth he shall *c* nothing away ....Ps 49:17 — 3947
which he may *c* away in his hand...........Eccl 5:15 — 3212
bird of the air shall *c* the voice ....Eccl 10:20 — 3212
shall *c* it away safe, and none ....Is 5:29 — 6403
shall they *c* away to the brook of ....Is 15:7 — 5375
the LORD will *c* thee away with a ....Is 22:17 — 2904
her own feet shall *c* her afar off ....Is 23:7 — 2986
they will *c* their riches upon the ....Is 30:6 — 5375
c them in his bosom, and shall ....Is 40:11 — 5375
and the wind shall *c* them away ....Is 41:16 — 5375
even to hoar hairs will I *c* you ....Is 46:4 — 5445
even I will *c*, and will deliver..................Is 46:4 — 5445
him upon the shoulder, they *c* him ....Is 46:7 — 5445
the wind shall *c* them all away ....Is 57:13 — 5375
Neither *c* forth a burden out of ....Jer 17:22 — 3318
he shall *c* them captive into ....Jer 20:4 — 1540
take them, and *c* them to Babylon ....Jer 20:5 — 935
with chains, to *c* him to Babylon ....Jer 39:7 — 935
that he should *c* him home ....Jer 39:14 — 3318
c us away captives into Babylon ....Jer 43:3 — 1540
them, and *c* them away captives............Jer 43:12 — 7617
he will no more *c* thee away into............Lam 4:22 — 1540
in their sight, and *c* out thereby ....Eze 12:5 — 3318
c it forth in the twilight ....Eze 12:6 — 3318
through the wall to *c* out thereby ....Eze 12:12 — 3318
men that *c* tales to shed blood ....Eze 22:9 — 7400
to *c* away silver and gold, to take...........Eze 38:13 — 5375
shall also *c* captives into Egypt ....Dan 11:8 — 935
began to *c* about in beds those ....Mk 6:55 — 4046
c any vessel through the temple ....Mk 11:16 — 1308
C neither purse, nor scrip, nor ....Lk 10:4 — 941
not lawful for thee to *c* thy bed.............Jn 5:10 — 142
c thee whither thou wouldest not ....Jn 21:18 — 5342
at the door, and shall *c* thee out............Acts 5:9 — 1627
I will *c* you away beyond Babylon ....Acts 7:43 — 3351
is certain we can *c* nothing out ....1Ti 6:7 — 1627

CARRYING
one *c* three kids, and another................1Sa 10:3 — 5375
another *c* three loaves of bread, ...1Sa 10:3 — 5375
another *c* a bottle of wine......................1Sa 10:3 — 5375
c bows, turned back in the day of.........Ps 78:9 — 7411
unto the *c* away of Jerusalem ....Jer 1:3 — 1540
from David until the *c* away into ....Mt 1:17 — 3350
from the *c* away into Babylon unto ....Mt 1:17 — 3350
c her forth, buried her by her ....Acts 5:10 — 1627

CARSHENA (car-she'-nah) A Persian prince.
And the next unto him was *C*..................Est 1:14 — 3771

CART
Now therefore make a new *c* ....1Sa 6:7 — 5699
no yoke, and tie the kine to the *c*...........1Sa 6:7 — 5699
of the LORD, and lay it upon the *c*..........1Sa 6:8 — 5699
milch kine, and tied them to the *c* ....1Sa 6:10 — 5699
the ark of the LORD upon the *c* ....1Sa 6:11 — 5699
the *c* came into the field of ....1Sa 6:14 — 5699
and they clave the wood of the *c* ....1Sa 6:14 — 5699
set the ark of God upon a new *c* ....2Sa 6:3 — 5699
sons of Abinadab, drave the new *c*.........2Sa 6:3 — 5699
c out of the house of Abinadab ....1Chr 13:7 — 5699
and Uzza and Ahio drave the *c* ....1Chr 13:7 — 5699
and sin as it were with a *c* rope.............Is 5:18 — 5699
neither is a *c* wheel turned about ....Is 28:27 — 5699
break it with the wheel of his *c*..............Is 28:28 — 5699
as a *c* is pressed that is full of ....Amos 2:13 — 5699

CARVED
house, and fetched the *c* image..............Judg 18:18 — 6459
the house within was *c* with knops ....1Kin 6:18 — 4734
he *c* all the walls of the house ....1Kin 6:29 — 7049
about with *c* figures of cherubims ....1Kin 6:29 — 6603
he *c* upon them carvings of ....1Kin 6:32 — 7049
he *c* thereon cherubims and palm...........1Kin 6:35 — 7049
with gold fitted upon the *c* work ....1Kin 6:35 — 2707
And he set a *c* image, the idol ....2Chr 33:7 — 6459
the *c* images which Manasseh his..........2Chr 33:22 — 6456
the *c* images, and the molten ....2Chr 34:3 — 6456
the *c* images, and the molten ....2Chr 34:4 — 6456
But now they break down the *c* ....Ps 74:6 — 6603
with *c* works, with fine linen of ....Prov 7:16 — 2405

CARVING
in *c* of timber, to work in all ....Ex 31:5 — 2799
in *c* of wood, to make any manner ....Ex 35:33 — 2799

CARVINGS
carved upon them *c* of cherubims..........1Kin 6:32 — 4734

CASE
did see that they were in evil *c* ....Ex 5:19 —
this is the *c* of the slayer, ...Deut 19:4 — 1697
thou shalt in any *c* bring them...............Deut 22:1 — 7725

In any *c* thou shalt deliver him .... Deut 24:13   7725
that people, that is in such a *c* .... Ps 144:15   3602
ye shall in no *c* enter into the .... Mt 5:20   *3364*
If the *c* of the man be so with .... Mt 19:10   *156*
been now a long time in that *c* .... Jn 5:6

CASEMENT
of my house I looked through my *c* .... Prov 7:6   822

CASES
is not under bondage in such *c* 1Cor 7:15

CASIPHIA *(cas-if'-e-ah) A place in Syria.*
Iddo the chief at the place *C* .... Ezr 8:17   3703
the Nethinims, at the place *C* .... Ezr 8:17   3703

CASLUHIM *(cas'-loo-him) Descendants of Mizraim.*
And Pathrusim, and *C*, (out of whom ...... Gen 10:14   3695
And Pathrusim, and *C*, (of whom came .. 1Chr 1:12   3695

CASLUHITES See CASLUHIM.

CASSIA
of *c* five hundred shekels, after .... Ex 30:24   6916
smell of myrrh, and aloes, and *c* .... Ps 45:8   7102
bright iron, *c*, and calamus, were .... Eze 27:19   6916

CAST See APPENDIX.

CASTAWAY
to others, I myself should be a *c* 1Cor 9:27   *96*

CASTEDST
thou *c* them down into destruction .... Ps 73:18   5307

CASTEST
thou *c* off fear, and restrainest .... Job 15:4   6565
and *c* my words behind thee .... Ps 50:17   7993
LORD, why *c* thou off my soul .... Ps 88:14   2186

CASTETH
cow calveth, and *c* not her calf .... Job 21:10   7921
he *c* the wicked down to the .... Ps 147:6   8213
He *c* forth his ice like morsels .... Ps 147:17   7993
but he *c* away the substance of .... Prov 10:3   1920
Slothfulness *c* into a deep sleep .... Prov 19:15   5307
c down the strength of the .... Prov 21:22   3381
As a mad man who *c* firebrands .... Prov 26:18   3384
with gold, and *c* silver chains .... Is 40:19   6884
As a fountain *c* out her waters, ... Jer 6:7   6979
so she *c* out her wickedness .... Jer 6:7   6979
He *c* out devils through the .... Mt 9:34   1544
of the devils *c* he out devils .... Mk 3:22   1544
He *c* out devils through Beelzebub .... Lk 11:15   1544
but perfect love *c* out fear 1Jn 4:18   906
and *c* them out of the church 3Jn 10   1544
as a fig tree *c* her untimely figs .... Rev 6:13   906

CASTING
c them down to the ground 2Sa 8:2   7901
all of them had one *c*, one 1Kin 7:37   4165
c himself down before the house .... Ezr 10:1   5307
ye see my *c* down, and are afraid .... Job 6:21   2866
they have defiled by *c* down the .... Ps 74:7
his crown by *c* it to the ground .... Ps 89:39
by *c* up mounts, and building forts ..... Eze 17:17   8210
thy *c* down shall be in the midst .... Mic 6:14   3445
his brother, *c* a net into the sea .... Mt 4:18   906
and parted his garments, *c* lots .... Mt 27:35   906
his brother *c* a net into the sea .... Mk 1:16   906
we saw one *c* out devils in thy .... Mk 9:38   1544
c away his garment, rose, and came .. Mk 10:50   577
c lots upon them, what every man .... Mk 15:24   906
we saw one *c* out devils in thy .... Lk 9:49   1544
he was *c* out a devil, and it was .... Lk 11:14   1544
saw the rich men *c* their gifts .... Lk 21:1   906
poor widow *c* in thither two mites .... Lk 21:2   906
For if the *c* away of them be the .... Rom 11:15   580
C down imaginations, and every 2Cor 10:5   2507
C all your care upon him 1Pet 5:7   1977

CASTLE
David took the *c* of Zion, which 1Chr 11:5   4686
And David dwelt in the *c* 1Chr 11:7   4679
are like the bars of a *c* .... Prov 18:19   759
him to be carried into the *c* .... Acts 21:34   3925
as Paul was to be led into the *c* .... Acts 21:37   3925
him to be brought into the *c* .... Acts 22:24   3925
them, and to bring him into the *c* .... Acts 23:10   3925
he went and entered into the *c* .... Acts 23:16   3925
go with him, and returned to the *c* ...... Acts 23:32   3925

CASTLES
by their towns, and by their *c* .... Gen 25:16   2918
they dwelt, and all their goodly *c* .... Num 31:10   2918
their *c* in their coasts, of the 1Chr 6:54   2918
and in the villages, and in the *c* 1Chr 27:25   4026

and he built in Judah *c*, and cities 2Chr 17:12   1003
and in the forests he built *c* 2Chr 27:4   1003

CASTOR *(cas'-tor) Patron god of sailors.*
in the isle, whose sign was *C* .... Acts 28:11   *1359*

CATCH
c in thorns, so that the stacks .... Ex 22:6   4672
c you every man his wife of the .... Judg 21:21   2414
from him, and did hastily *c* it 1Kin 20:33   2480
we shall *c* them alive, and get 2Kin 7:12   8610
he lieth in wait to *c* the poor .... Ps 10:9   2414
he doth *c* the poor, when he .... Ps 10:9   2414
net that he hath hid *c* himself .... Ps 35:8   3920
extortioner *c* all that he hath .... Ps 109:11   5367
they set a trap, they *c* men .... Jer 5:26   3920
lion, and it learned to *c* the prey .... Eze 19:3   2963
lion, and learned to *c* the prey .... Eze 19:6   2963
they *c* them in their net, and .... Hab 1:15   1641
Herodians, to *c* him in his words .... Mk 12:13   64
from henceforth thou shalt *c* men .... Lk 5:10   *2221*
seeking to *c* something out of his .... Lk 11:54   *2340*

CATCHETH
c any beast or fowl that may be .... Lev 17:13   6679
c away that which was sown in his ...... Mt 13:19   *726*
and the wolf *c* them, and scattereth ...... Jn 10:12   *726*

CATERPILLER
mildew, locust, or if there be *c* 1Kin 8:37   2625
also their increase unto the *c* .... Ps 78:46   2625
like the gathering of the *c* .... Is 33:4   2625
hath left hath the *c* eaten .... Joel 1:4   2625
eaten, the cankerworm, and the *c* .... Joel 2:25   2625

CATERPILLERS
or mildew, locusts, or *c* 2Chr 6:28   2625
spake, and the locusts came, and *c* .... Ps 105:34   3218
fill thee with men, as with *c* .... Jer 51:14   3218
horses to come up as the rough *c* .... Jer 51:27   3218

CATTLE
living creature after his kind, *c* .... Gen 1:24   929
c after their kind, and every .... Gen 1:25   929
fowl of the air, and over the *c* .... Gen 1:26   929
And Adam gave names to all *c* .... Gen 2:20   929
this, thou art cursed above all *c* .... Gen 3:14   929
in tents, and of such as have *c* .... Gen 4:20   4735
of *c* after their kind, of every .... Gen 6:20   929
all the *c* after their kind, and .... Gen 7:14   929
the earth, both of fowl, and of *c* .... Gen 7:21   929
of the ground, both man, and *c* .... Gen 7:23   929
all the *c* that was with him in .... Gen 8:1   929
all flesh, both of fowl, and of *c* .... Gen 8:17   929
with you, and the fowl, of the *c* .... Gen 9:10   929
And Abram was very rich in *c* .... Gen 13:2   4735
c and the herdmen of Lot's *c* .... Gen 13:7   4735
the *c* should be gathered together .... Gen 29:7   4735
thee, and how thy *c* was with me .... Gen 30:29   4735
all the speckled and spotted *c* .... Gen 30:32   7716
all the brown *c* among the sheep .... Gen 30:32   7716
and brought forth *c* ringstraked .... Gen 30:39   6629
and put them not unto Laban's *c* .... Gen 30:40   6629
the stronger *c* did conceive .... Gen 30:41   6629
the eyes of the *c* in the gutters .... Gen 30:41   6629
But when the *c* were feeble .... Gen 30:42   6629
exceedingly, and had much *c* .... Gen 30:43   6629
then all the *c* bare speckled .... Gen 31:8   6629
then bare all the *c* ringstraked .... Gen 31:8   6629
taken away the *c* of your father .... Gen 31:9   4735
at the time that the *c* conceived .... Gen 31:10   6629
upon the *c* were ringstraked .... Gen 31:10   6629
leap upon the *c* are ringstraked .... Gen 31:12   6629
And he carried away all his *c* .... Gen 31:18   4735
the *c* of his getting, which he .... Gen 31:18   4735
daughters, and six years for thy *c* .... Gen 31:41   6629
these are my *c*, and all .... Gen 31:43   6629
according as the *c* that goeth .... Gen 33:14   4399
house, and made booths for his *c* .... Gen 33:17   4735
sons were with his *c* in the field .... Gen 34:5   4735
Shall not their *c* and their .... Gen 34:23   4735
persons of his house, and his *c* .... Gen 36:6   4735
not bear them because of their *c* .... Gen 36:7   4735
And they took their *c*, and their .... Gen 46:6   4735
their trade hath been to feed *c* .... Gen 46:32   4735
c from our youth even until now .... Gen 46:34   4735
then make them rulers over my *c* .... Gen 47:6   4735
And Joseph said, Give your *c* .... Gen 47:16   4735
and I will give you for your *c* .... Gen 47:16   4735
they brought their *c* unto Joseph .... Gen 47:17   4735
for the *c* of the herds, and for .... Gen 47:17   4735
for all their *c* for that year .... Gen 47:17   4735
my lord also hath our herds of *c* .... Gen 47:18   929
upon thy *c* which is in the field .... Ex 9:3   4735

sever between the c of Israel	Ex 9:4	4735
of Israel and the c of Egypt	Ex 9:4	4735
and all the c of Egypt died	Ex 9:6	4735
but of the c of the children of	Ex 9:6	4735
of the c of the Israelites dead	Ex 9:7	4735
therefore now, and gather thy c	Ex 9:19	4735
his c flee into the houses	Ex 9:20	4735
servants and his c in the field	Ex 9:21	4735
Our c also shall go with us	Ex 10:26	4735
and all the firstborn of c	Ex 12:29	929
and herds, even very much c	Ex 12:38	4735
our children and our c with thirst	Ex 17:3	4735
nor thy maidservant, nor thy c	Ex 20:10	929
and every firstling among thy c	Ex 34:19	4735
bring your offering of the c	Lev 1:2	929
beast, or a carcase of unclean c	Lev 5:2	929
Thou shalt not let thy c gender	Lev 19:19	929
And for thy c, and for the beast	Lev 25:7	929
your children, and destroy your c	Lev 26:22	929
the c of the Levites instead of	Num 3:41	929
the c of the children of Israel	Num 3:41	929
the c of the Levites instead of	Num 3:45	929
of the Levites instead of their c	Num 3:45	926
that we and our c should die there	Num 20:4	1165
my c drink of thy water, then I	Num 20:19	4735
and took the spoil of all their c	Num 31:9	929
had a very great multitude of c	Num 32:1	4735
the place was a place for c	Num 32:1	4735
c, and thy servants have c	Num 32:4	4735
build sheepfolds here for our c	Num 32:16	4735
wives, our flocks, and all our c	Num 32:26	929
of them shall be for their c	Num 35:3	929
Only the c we took for a prey	Deut 2:35	929
But all the c, and the spoil of	Deut 3:7	929
and your little ones, and your c	Deut 3:19	4735
(for I know that ye have much c	Deut 3:19	4735
nor thine ass, nor any of thy c	Deut 5:14	929
barren among you, or among your c	Deut 7:14	929
grass in thy fields for thy c	Deut 11:15	929
the c thereof, with the edge of	Deut 13:15	929
and the little ones, and the c	Deut 20:14	929
thy ground, and the fruit of thy c	Deut 28:4	929
body, and in the fruit of thy c	Deut 28:11	929
he shall eat the fruit of thy c	Deut 28:51	929
body, and in the fruit of thy c	Deut 30:9	929
your little ones, and your c	Josh 1:14	4735
the c thereof, shall ye take for	Josh 8:2	929
Only the c and the spoil of that	Josh 8:27	929
spoil of these cities, and the c	Josh 11:14	929
with their suburbs for their c	Josh 14:4	4735
the suburbs thereof for our c	Josh 21:2	929
your tents, and with very much c	Josh 22:8	4735
For they came up with their c	Judg 6:5	4735
and put the little ones and the c	Judg 18:21	4735
and brought away their c, and	1Sa 23:5	4735
they drave before those other c	1Sa 30:20	4735
fat c by the stone of Zoheleth,	1Kin 1:9	4806
And he hath slain oxen and fat c	1Kin 1:19	4806
day, and hath slain oxen and fat c	1Kin 1:25	4806
for the c that followed them	2Kin 3:9	929
ye may drink, both ye, and your c	2Kin 3:17	4735
because their c were multiplied	1Chr 5:9	4735
And they took away their c	1Chr 5:21	929
came down to take away their c	1Chr 7:21	929
They smote also the tents of c	2Chr 14:15	929
for he had much c, both in the	2Chr 26:10	929
thousand and six hundred small c	2Chr 35:8	929
offerings five thousand small c	2Chr 35:9	929
over our bodies, and over our c	Neh 9:37	929
of our sons, and of our c, as it	Neh 10:36	929
the c also concerning the vapour	Job 36:33	4735
the c upon a thousand hills	Ps 50:10	929
gave up their c also to the hail	Ps 78:48	1165
the grass to grow for the c	Ps 104:14	929
suffereth not their c to decrease	Ps 107:38	929
Beasts, and all c	Ps 148:10	929
small c above all that were in	Eccl 2:7	4735
and for the treading of lesser c	Is 7:25	7716
in that day shall thy c feed in	Is 30:23	4735
small c of thy burnt offerings	Is 43:23	7716
upon the beasts, and upon the c	Is 46:1	929
can men hear the voice of the c	Jer 9:10	4735
the multitude of their c a spoil	Jer 49:32	4734
I judge between c and c	Eze 34:17	7716
fat c and between the lean c	Eze 34:20	7716
I will judge between c and c	Eze 34:22	7716
the nations, which have gotten c	Eze 38:12	4735
silver and gold, to take away c	Eze 38:13	4735
the herds of c are perplexed	Joel 1:18	1241
and also much c	Jonah 4:11	929
forth, and upon men, and upon c	Hag 1:11	929

the multitude of men and c therein	Zec 2:4	929
taught me to keep c from my youth	Zec 13:5	7069
a servant plowing or feeding c	Lk 17:7	*4165*
and his children, and his c	Jn 4:12	*2353*

CAUDA See CLAUDA.

CAUGHT

behold behind him a ram c in a	Gen 22:13	270
she c him by his garment, saying,	Gen 39:12	8610
c it, and it became a rod in his	Ex 4:4	2388
prey which the men of war had c	Num 31:32	962
c him, and cut off his thumbs and	Judg 1:6	270
c a young man of the men of	Judg 8:14	3920
c three hundred foxes, and took	Judg 15:4	3920
of them that danced, whom they c	Judg 21:23	1497
I c him by his beard, and smote	1Sa 17:35	2388
they c every one his fellow by	2Sa 2:16	2388
his head c hold of the oak, and he	2Sa 18:9	2388
c hold on the horns of the altar	1Kin 1:50	2388
he hath c hold on the horns of	1Kin 1:51	270
c hold on the horns of the altar	1Kin 2:28	2388
Ahijah c the new garment that was	1Kin 11:30	8610
the hill, she c him by the feet	2Kin 4:27	2388
and they c him, (for he was hid in	2Chr 22:9	3920
So she c him, and kissed him, and	Prov 7:13	2388
the birds that are c in the snare	Eccl 9:12	270
thou art found, and also c	Jer 50:24	8610
c him, and said unto him, O thou	Mt 14:31	*1949*
And they c him, and cast him out of	Mt 21:39	*2983*
And they c him, and beat him, and	Mk 12:3	*2983*
For oftentimes it had c him	Lk 8:29	*4884*
and that night they c nothing	Jn 21:3	*4084*
of the fish which ye have now c	Jn 21:10	*4084*
c him, and brought him to the	Acts 6:12	*4884*
Spirit of the Lord c away Philip	Acts 8:39	726
their gains was gone, they c Paul	Acts 16:19	*1949*
and having c Gaius and Aristarchus,	Acts 19:29	*4884*
the Jews c me in the temple	Acts 26:21	*4815*
And when the ship was c, and could	Acts 27:15	*4884*
such an one c up to the third	2Cor 12:2	726
How that he was c up into	2Cor 12:4	726
being crafty, I c you with guile	2Cor 12:16	*2983*
remain shall be c up together	1Th 4:17	726
and her child was c up unto God	Rev 12:5	726

CAUL

the c that is above the liver, and	Ex 29:13	3508
the c above the liver, and the two	Ex 29:22	3508
the c above the liver, with the	Lev 3:4	3508
the c above the liver, with the	Lev 3:10	3508
the c above the liver, with the	Lev 3:15	3508
the c above the liver, with the	Lev 4:9	3508
the c that is above the liver,	Lev 7:4	3508
the c above the liver, and the two	Lev 8:16	3508
the c above the liver, and the two	Lev 8:25	3508
the c above the liver of the sin	Lev 9:10	3508
kidneys, and the c above the liver	Lev 9:19	3508
will rend the c of their heart,	Hos 13:8	5458

CAULS

about their feet, and their c	Is 3:18	7636

CAUSE See APPENDIX.

CAUSED See APPENDIX.

CAUSELESS

that thou hast shed blood c	1Sa 25:31	2600
so the curse c shall not come	Prov 26:2	2600

CAUSES

thou mayest bring the c unto God	Ex 18:19	1697
the hard c they brought unto	Ex 18:26	1697
Hear the c between your brethren,	Deut 1:16	
when for all the c whereby	Jer 3:8	182
false burdens and c of banishment	Lam 2:14	
hast pleaded the c of my soul	Lam 3:58	7379
For these c the Jews caught me in	Acts 26:21	*1752*

CAUSEST

thou c me to ride upon it, and	Job 30:22	
c to approach unto thee, that he	Ps 65:4	

CAUSETH See APPENDIX.

CAUSEWAY

by the c of the going up, ward	1Chr 26:16	4546
At Parbar westward, four at the c	1Chr 26:18	4546

CAUSING

c the lips of those that are	Song 7:9	
jaws of the people, c them to err	Is 30:28	
in c you to return to this place	Jer 29:10	
c their flocks to lie down	Jer 33:12	

CAVE

and he dwelt in a *c*, he and his two	Gen 19:30	4631
he may give me the *c* of Machpelah	Gen 23:9	4631
the *c* that is therein, I give it	Gen 23:11	4631
the *c* which was therein, and all	Gen 23:17	4631
the *c* of the field of Machpelah	Gen 23:19	4631
the *c* that is therein, were made	Gen 23:20	4631
buried him in the *c* of Machpelah	Gen 25:9	4631
c that is in the field of Ephron	Gen 49:29	4631
In the *c* that is in the field of	Gen 49:30	4631
of the *c* that is therein was from	Gen 49:32	4631
buried him in the *c* of the field	Gen 50:13	4631
hid themselves in a *c* at Makkedah	Josh 10:16	4631
are found hid in a *c* at Makkedah	Josh 10:17	4631
stones upon the mouth of the *c*	Josh 10:18	4631
Joshua, Open the mouth of the *c*	Josh 10:22	4631
five kings unto me out of the *c*	Josh 10:22	4631
five kings unto him out of the *c*	Josh 10:23	4631
cast them into the *c* wherein they	Josh 10:27	4631
and escaped to the *c* Adullam	1Sa 22:1	4631
by the way, where was a *c*	1Sa 24:3	4631
remained in the sides of the *c*	1Sa 24:3	4631
But Saul rose up out of the *c*	1Sa 24:7	4631
afterward, and went out of the *c*	1Sa 24:8	4631
to day into mine hand in the *c*	1Sa 24:10	4631
time unto the *c* of Adullam	2Sa 23:13	4631
and hid them by fifty in a *c*	1Kin 18:4	4631
LORD's prophets by fifty in a *c*	1Kin 18:13	4631
And he came thither unto a *c*	1Kin 19:9	4631
stood in the entering in of the *c*	1Kin 19:13	4631
to David, into the *c* of Adullam	1Chr 11:15	4631
when he fled from Saul in the *c*	Ps 57:*t*	4631
A Prayer when he was in the *c*	Ps 142:*t*	4631
It was a *c*, and a stone lay upon	Jn 11:38	4693

CAVE'S

laid great stones in the *c* mouth	Josh 10:27	4631

CAVES

which are in the mountains, and *c*	Judg 6:2	4631
people did hide themselves in *c*	1Sa 13:6	4631
in *c* of the earth, and in the	Job 30:6	2356
into the *c* of the earth, for fear	Is 2:19	4247
in the *c* shall die of the	Eze 33:27	4631
and in dens and *c* of the earth	Heb 11:38	3692

CEASE

and day and night shall not *c*	Gen 8:22	7673
and the thunder shall *c*, neither	Ex 9:29	2308
shall *c* waiting upon the service	Num 8:25	7725
they prophesied, and did not *c*	Num 11:25	3254
I will make to *c* from me the	Num 17:5	7918
shall never *c* out of the land	Deut 15:11	2308
of them to *c* from among men	Deut 32:26	7673
children *c* from fearing the LORD	Josh 22:25	7673
of you, and after that I will *c*	Judg 15:7	2308
Benjamin my brother, or shall I *c*	Judg 20:28	2308
C not to cry unto the LORD our	1Sa 7:8	2790
of Ramah, and let his work *c*	2Chr 16:5	7673
to cause these men to *c*, and that	Ezr 4:21	989
Jews, and made them to *c* by force	Ezr 4:23	989
they could not cause them to *c*	Ezr 5:5	989
slay them, and cause the work to *c*	Neh 4:11	7673
why should the work *c*, whilst I	Neh 6:3	7673
There the wicked *c* from troubling	Job 3:17	2308
c then, and let me alone, that I	Job 10:20	2308
tender branch thereof will not *c*	Job 14:7	2308
C from anger, and forsake wrath	Ps 37:8	7503
He maketh wars to *c* unto the end	Ps 46:9	7673
cause thine anger toward us to *c*	Ps 85:4	6565
Thou hast made his glory to *c*	Ps 89:44	7673
The lot causeth contentions to *c*	Prov 18:18	7673
C, my son, to hear the	Prov 19:27	2308
honour for a man to *c* from strife	Prov 20:3	7647
yea, strife and reproach shall *c*	Prov 22:10	7673
c from thine own wisdom	Prov 23:4	2308
the grinders *c* because they are	Eccl 12:3	988
c to do evil	Is 1:16	2308
C ye from man, whose breath is in	Is 2:22	2308
while, and the indignation shall *c*	Is 10:25	3615
the arrogancy of the proud to *c*	Is 13:11	7673
made their vintage shouting to *c*	Is 16:10	7673
also shall *c* from Ephraim	Is 17:3	7673
sighing thereof have I made to *c*	Is 21:2	7673
One of Israel to *c* from before us	Is 30:11	7673
when thou shalt *c* to spoil	Is 33:1	8552
Then will I cause to *c* from the	Jer 7:34	7673
night and day, and let them not *c*	Jer 14:17	1820
I will cause to *c* out of this	Jer 16:9	7673
neither shall *c* from yielding	Jer 17:8	4185
c from being a nation before me	Jer 31:36	7673
shall cause to *c* from thence man	Jer 36:29	7673

I will cause to *c* in Moab	Jer 48:35	7673
let not the apple of thine eye *c*	Lam 2:18	1826
and your idols may be broken and *c*	Eze 6:6	7673
make the pomp of the strong to *c*	Eze 7:24	7673
I will make this proverb to *c*	Eze 12:23	7673
I will cause thee to *c* from	Eze 16:41	7673
make thy lewdness to *c* from thee	Eze 23:27	7673
lewdness to *c* out of the land	Eze 23:48	7673
cause the noise of thy songs to *c*	Eze 26:13	7673
c by the hand of Nebuchadrezzar	Eze 30:10	7673
their images to *c* out of Noph	Eze 30:13	7673
of her strength shall *c* in her	Eze 30:18	7673
the pomp of her strength shall *c*	Eze 33:28	7673
cause them to *c* from feeding the	Eze 34:10	7673
evil beasts to *c* out of the land	Eze 34:25	7673
sacrifice and the oblation to *c*	Dan 9:27	7673
the reproach offered by him to *c*	Dan 11:18	7673
will cause to *c* the kingdom of	Hos 1:4	7673
also cause all her mirth to *c*	Hos 2:11	7673
Then said I, O Lord GOD, *c*	Amos 7:5	2308
wilt thou not *c* to pervert the	Acts 13:10	3973
there be tongues, they shall *c*	1Cor 13:8	3973
C not to give thanks for you,	Eph 1:16	3973
do not *c* to pray for you, and to	Col 1:9	3973
and that cannot *c* from sin	2Pet 2:14	180

CEASED

it *c* to be with Sarah after the	Gen 18:11	2308
and the thunders and hail *c*	Ex 9:33	2308
the hail and the thunders were *c*	Ex 9:34	2308
the manna *c* on the morrow after	Josh 5:12	7673
they *c* not from their own doings	Judg 2:19	5307
The inhabitants of the villages *c*	Judg 5:7	2308
they *c* in Israel, until that I	Judg 5:7	2308
and they that were hungry *c*	1Sa 2:5	2308
words in the name of David, and *c*	1Sa 25:9	5117
Then *c* the work of the house of	Ezr 4:24	989
So it *c* unto the second year of	Ezr 4:24	1934,989
these three men *c* to answer Job	Job 32:1	7673
they did tear me, and *c* not	Ps 35:15	1826
sore ran in the night, and *c* not	Ps 77:2	6313
and say, How hath the oppressor *c*	Is 14:4	7673
the golden city *c*	Is 14:4	7673
The elders have *c* from the gate	Lam 5:14	7673
The joy of our heart is *c*	Lam 5:15	7673
the sea *c* from her raging	Jonah 1:15	5975
come into the ship, the wind *c*	Mt 14:32	2869
And the wind *c*, and there was a	Mk 4:39	2869
and the wind *c*	Mk 6:51	2869
in hath not *c* to kiss my feet	Lk 7:45	1257
and they *c*, and there was a calm	Lk 8:24	3973
in a certain place, when he *c*	Lk 11:1	3973
they *c* not to teach and preach	Acts 5:42	3973
And after the uproar was *c*	Acts 20:1	3973
I *c* not to warn every one night	Acts 20:31	3973
he would not be persuaded, we *c*	Acts 21:14	2270
is the offence of the cross *c*	Gal 5:11	2673
he also hath *c* from his own works	Heb 4:10	2664
they not have *c* to be offered	Heb 10:2	3973
in the flesh hath *c* from sin	1Pet 4:1	3973

CEASETH

for the godly man *c*	Ps 12:1	1584
is precious, and it *c* for ever	Ps 49:8	2308
is no talebearer, the strife *c*	Prov 26:20	8367
is at an end, the spoiler *c*	Is 16:4	3615
The mirth of tabrets *c*, the noise	Is 24:8	7673
endeth, the joy of the harp *c*	Is 24:8	7673
lie waste, the wayfaring man *c*	Is 33:8	7673
c not, without any intermission	Lam 3:49	1820
who *c* from raising after he hath	Hos 7:4	7673
said, This man *c* not to speak	Acts 6:13	3973

CEASING

the LORD in *c* to pray for you	1Sa 12:23	2308
but prayer was made without *c* of	Acts 12:5	1618
that without *c* I make mention of	Rom 1:9	89
without *c* your work of faith	1Th 1:3	89
cause also thank we God without *c*	1Th 2:13	89
Pray without *c*	1Th 5:17	89
that without *c* I have remembrance	2Ti 1:3	83

CEDAR

c wood, and scarlet, and hyssop	Lev 14:4	730
the *c* wood, and the scarlet, and	Lev 14:6	730
c wood, and scarlet, and hyssop	Lev 14:49	730
And he shall take the *c* wood	Lev 14:51	730
living bird, and with the *c* wood	Lev 14:52	730
And the priest shall take *c* wood	Num 19:6	730
as *c* trees beside the waters	Num 24:6	730
c trees, and carpenters, and masons	2Sa 5:11	730
See now, I dwell in an house of *c*	2Sa 7:2	730
Why build ye not me an house of *c*	2Sa 7:7	730

CEDARS

from the c tree that is in	1Kin 4:33	730
hew me c trees out of Lebanon	1Kin 5:6	730
thy desire concerning timber of c	1Kin 5:8	730
So Hiram gave Solomon c trees	1Kin 5:10	730
house with beams and boards of c	1Kin 6:9	730
on the house with timber of c	1Kin 6:10	730
the house within with boards of c	1Kin 6:15	730
and the walls with boards of c	1Kin 6:16	730
the c of the house within was	1Kin 6:18	730
all was c	1Kin 6:18	730
covered the altar which was of c	1Kin 6:20	730
hewed stone, and a row of c beams	1Kin 6:36	730
upon four rows of c pillars	1Kin 7:2	730
with c beams upon the pillars	1Kin 7:2	730
it was covered with c above upon	1Kin 7:3	730
it was covered with c from one	1Kin 7:7	730
hewed stones, and a row of c beams	1Kin 7:12	730
furnished Solomon with c trees	1Kin 9:11	730
sent to the c that was in Lebanon	2Kin 14:9	730
cut down the tall c trees thereof	2Kin 19:23	730
Also c trees in abundance	1Chr 22:4	730
Tyre brought much c wood to David	1Chr 22:4	730
c trees made he as the sycomore	2Chr 1:15	730
Send me also c trees, fir trees,	2Chr 2:8	730
c trees made he as the sycomore	2Chr 9:27	730
sent to the c that was in Lebanon	2Chr 25:18	730
to bring c trees from Lebanon to	Ezr 3:7	730
He moveth his tail like a c	Job 40:17	730
he shall grow like a c in Lebanon	Ps 92:12	730
The beams of our house are c	Song 1:17	730
will inclose her with boards of c	Song 8:9	730
plant in the wilderness the c	Is 41:19	730
and it is cieled with c, and	Jer 22:14	730
because thou closest thyself in c	Jer 22:15	730
took the highest branch of the c	Eze 17:3	730
the highest branch of the high c	Eze 17:22	730
and bear fruit, and be a goodly c	Eze 17:23	730
bound with cords, and made of c	Eze 27:24	729
the Assyrian was a c in Lebanon	Eze 31:3	730
for he shall uncover the c work	Zeph 2:14	731
for the c is fallen	Zec 11:2	730

CEDARS

and devour the c of Lebanon	Judg 9:15	730
measures of hewed stones, and c	1Kin 7:11	730
c made he to be as the sycomore	1Kin 10:27	730
to David, and timber of c, with	1Chr 14:1	730
Lo, I dwell in an house of c	1Chr 17:1	730
ye not built me an house of c	1Chr 17:6	730
didst send him c to build him an	2Chr 2:3	730
voice of the LORD breaketh the c	Ps 29:5	730
LORD breaketh the c of Lebanon	Ps 29:5	730
thereof were like the goodly c	Ps 80:10	730
the c of Lebanon, which he hath	Ps 104:16	730
fruitful trees, and all c	Ps 148:9	730
is as Lebanon, excellent as the c	Song 5:15	730
And upon all the c of Lebanon	Is 2:13	730
but we will change them into c	Is 9:10	730
the c of Lebanon, saying, Since	Is 14:8	730
will cut down the tall c thereof	Is 37:24	730
He heweth him down c, and taketh	Is 44:14	730
they shall cut down thy choice c	Jer 22:7	730
that makest thy nest in the c	Jer 22:23	730
they have taken c from Lebanon to	Eze 27:5	730
The c in the garden of God could	Eze 31:8	730
was like the height of the c	Amos 2:9	730
that the fire may devour thy c	Zec 11:1	730

CEDRON (se'-drun) See KIDRON. Same as Kidron.

his disciples over the brook C	Jn 18:1	2748

CELEBRATE

even, shall ye c your sabbath	Lev 23:32	7673
ye shall c it in the seventh	Lev 23:41	2278
praise thee, death can not c thee	Is 38:18	1984

CELESTIAL

There are also c bodies, and	1Cor 15:40	2032
but the glory of the c is one	1Cor 15:40	2032

CELLARS

wine c was Zabdi the Shiphmite	1Chr 27:27	214
over the c of oil was Joash	1Chr 27:28	214

CENCHREA (sen'-kre-ah) Harbor city for Corinth.

having shorn his head in C	Acts 18:18	2747
of the church which is at C	Rom 16:1	2747
Phebe servant of the church at C	Rom s	

CENCHREAE See CENCHREA.

CENSER

Aaron, took either of them his c	Lev 10:1	4289
he shall take a c full of burning	Lev 16:12	4289
And take every man his c, and put	Num 16:17	4289

before the LORD every man his c	Num 16:17	4289
also, and Aaron, each of you his c	Num 16:17	4289
And they took every man his c	Num 16:18	4289
Moses said unto Aaron, Take a c	Num 16:46	4289
had a c in his hand to burn	2Chr 26:19	4730
with every man his c in his hand	Eze 8:11	4730
Which had the golden c, and the	Heb 9:4	2369
at the altar, having a golden c	Rev 8:3	3031
And the angel took the c, and	Rev 8:5	3031

CENSERS

minister about it, even the c	Num 4:14	4289
Take you c, Korah, and all his	Num 16:6	4289
censer, two hundred and fifty c	Num 16:17	4289
take up the c out of the burning	Num 16:37	4289
The c of these sinners against	Num 16:38	4289
the priest took the brasen c	Num 16:39	4289
the spoons, and the c of pure gold	1Kin 7:50	4289
basons, and the spoons, and the c	2Chr 4:22	4289

CENTURION

there came unto him a c,	Mt 8:5	1543
The c answered and said, Lord, I	Mt 8:8	1543
And Jesus said unto the c, Go thy	Mt 8:13	1543
Now when the c, and they that were	Mt 27:54	1543
And when the c, which stood over	Mk 15:39	2760
and calling unto him the c	Mk 15:44	2760
And when he knew it of the c	Mk 15:45	2760
the c sent friends to him, saying	Lk 7:6	1543
Now when the c saw what was done,	Lk 23:47	1543
a c of the band called the	Acts 10:1	1543
And they said, Cornelius the c	Acts 10:22	1543
said unto the c that stood by	Acts 22:25	1543
When the c heard that, he went and	Acts 22:26	1543
And he commanded a c to keep Paul	Acts 24:23	1543
Julius, a c of Augustus' band	Acts 27:1	1543
there the c found a ship of	Acts 27:6	1543
Nevertheless the c believed the	Acts 27:11	1543
Paul said to the c and to the	Acts 27:31	1543
But the c, willing to save Paul,	Acts 27:43	1543
the c delivered the prisoners to	Acts 28:16	1543

CENTURION'S

And a certain c servant, who was	Lk 7:2	1543

CENTURIONS

immediately took soldiers and c	Acts 21:32	1543
Paul called one of the c unto him	Acts 23:17	1543
And he called unto him two c	Acts 23:23	1543

CEPHAS (se'-fas) See PETER. Name given to Simon Peter.

thou shalt be called C, which is	Jn 1:42	2786
and I of C	1Cor 1:12	2786
Whether Paul, or Apollos, or C	1Cor 3:22	2786
as the brethren of the Lord, and C	1Cor 9:5	2786
And that he was seen of C, then of	1Cor 15:5	2786
And when James, C, and John, who	Gal 2:9	2786

CEREMONIES

and according to all the c thereof	Num 9:3	4941

CERTAIN

And he lighted upon a c place	Gen 28:11	
a c man found him, and, behold, he	Gen 37:15	
and turned in to a c Adullamite	Gen 38:1	376
there a daughter of a c Canaanite	Gen 38:2	376
gather a c rate every day, that I	Ex 16:4	1697
And there were c men, who were	Num 9:6	
with c of the children of Israel,	Num 16:2	582
C men, the children of Belial,	Deut 13:13	
if it be truth, and the thing c	Deut 13:14	3559
it be true, and the thing c	Deut 17:4	3559
to his fault, by a c number	Deut 25:2	
a c woman cast a piece of a	Judg 9:53	259
there was a c man of Zorah, of	Judg 13:2	259
that there was a c Levite	Judg 19:1	376
c sons of Belial, beset the house	Judg 19:22	582
a c man of Beth-lehem-judah went	Ruth 1:1	
Now there was a c man of	1Sa 1:1	259
Now a c man of the servants of	1Sa 21:7	
a c man saw it, and told Joab, and	2Sa 18:10	259
thou shalt know for c that thou	1Kin 2:37	3045
unto thee, saying, Know for a c	1Kin 2:42	3045
oxen were c additions made of	1Kin 7:29	
c Edomites of his father's	1Kin 11:17	582
a c man of the sons of the	1Kin 20:35	259
a c man drew a bow at a venture,	1Kin 22:34	
Now there cried a c woman of the	2Kin 4:1	259
appointed unto her a c officer	2Kin 8:6	259
c of them had the charge of the	1Chr 9:28	
he appointed c of the Levites to	1Chr 16:4	
Then there went c, and told David	1Chr 19:5	
Even after a c rate every day,	2Chr 8:13	1697

after *c* years he went down to 2Chr 18:2
a *c* man drew a bow at a venture, ... 2Chr 18:33
Then *c* of the heads of the 2Chr 28:12   592
with *c* chief of the fathers, ... Ezr 10:16   592
came, he and *c* men of Judah .... Neh 1:2
down and wept, and mourned *c* days ..... Neh 1:4
at Jerusalem dwelt *c* of the.................... Neh 11:4
that a *c* portion should be for .... Neh 11:23
c of the priests' sons with .... Neh 12:35
after *c* days obtained I leave of .... Neh 13:6
smote *c* of them, and plucked off .... Neh 13:25   582
the palace there was a *c* Jew .... Est 2:5   376
There is a *c* people scattered .... Est 3:8   259
But know ye for *c*, that if ye put .... Jer 26:15   3045
Then rose up *c* of the elders of .... Jer 26:17   582
c men with him into Egypt .... Jer 26:22
That there came *c* from Shechem .... Jer 41:5   582
c of the poor of the people .... Jer 52:15
c of the poor of the land for .... Jer 52:16
Then came *c* of the elders of.................. Eze 14:1   582
that *c* of the elders of Israel .... Eze 20:1   582
that he should bring *c* of the .... Dan 1:3
and the dream is *c*, and the .... Dan 2:45   3330
that time *c* Chaldeans came near .... Dan 3:8   1400
There are *c* Jews whom thou hast .... Dan 3:12   1400
unto that *c* saint which spake .... Dan 8:13   6422
fainted, and was sick *c* days.................. Dan 8:27
behold a *c* man clothed in linen, ... Dan 10:5   259
after *c* years with a great army .... Dan 11:13   6256
a *c* scribe came, and said unto him .... Mt 8:19   1520
c of the scribes said within .... Mt 9:3   5100
behold, there came a *c* ruler .... Mt 9:18
Then *c* of the scribes and of the .... Mt 12:38   5100
there came to him a *c* man .... Mt 17:14
of heaven likened unto a *c* king .... Mt 18:23   444
desiring a *c* thing of him .... Mt 20:20   5100
A *c* man had two sons .... Mt 21:28
There was a *c* householder .... Mt 21:33   444,5100
of heaven is like unto a *c* king .... Mt 22:2   444
But there were *c* of the scribes .... Mk 2:6   5100
a *c* woman, which had an issue of.......... Mk 5:25   5100
synagogue's house *c* which said .... Mk 5:35
c of the scribes, which came from .... Mk 7:1   5100
For a *c* woman, whose young .... Mk 7:25
c of them that stood there said .... Mk 11:5   5100
A *c* man planted a vineyard, and .... Mk 12:1
send unto him *c* of the Pharisees........... Mk 12:13   5100
And there came a *c* poor widow .... Mk 12:42   1520
there followed him a *c* young man .... Mk 14:51   5100
And there arose *c*, and bare false .... Mk 14:57   5100
a *c* priest named Zacharias, of .... Lk 1:5   5100
to pass, when he was in a *c* city .... Lk 5:12   1520
And it came to pass on a *c* day .... Lk 5:17   1520
c of the Pharisees said unto them........... Lk 6:2   5100
a *c* centurion's servant, who was .... Lk 7:2   5100
There was a *c* creditor which had .... Lk 7:41   5100
c women, which had been healed of .... Lk 8:2   5100
it was told him by *c* which said .... Lk 8:20
Now it came to pass on a *c* day .... Lk 8:22   1520
met him out of the city a *c* man.............. Lk 8:27   5100
a *c* man said unto him, Lord, I............... Lk 9:57   5100
a *c* lawyer stood up, and tempted .... Lk 10:25   5100
A *c* man went down from Jerusalem ...... Lk 10:30   5100
came down a *c* priest that way .... Lk 10:31   5100
But a *c* Samaritan, as he .... Lk 10:33   5100
that he entered into a *c* village .... Lk 10:38   5100
a *c* woman named Martha received....... Lk 10:38   5100
as he was praying in a *c* place............... Lk 11:1   5100
a *c* woman of the company lifted .... Lk 11:27   5100
a *c* Pharisee besought him to dine .... Lk 11:37   5100
The ground of a *c* rich man .... Lk 12:16   5100
A *c* man had a fig tree planted in .... Lk 13:6   5100
day there came *c* of the Pharisees .... Lk 13:31   5100
there was a *c* man before him .... Lk 14:2   5100
A *c* man made a great supper, and .... Lk 14:16   5100
And he said, A *c* man had two sons....... Lk 15:11   5100
disciples, There was a *c* rich man .... Lk 16:1   5100
There was a *c* rich man, which was .... Lk 16:19   5100
there was a *c* beggar named .... Lk 16:20   5100
And as he entered into a *c* village .... Lk 17:12   5100
he spake this parable unto *c*.................... Lk 18:9   5100
a *c* ruler asked him, saying, Good.......... Lk 18:18   5100
a *c* blind man sat by the way side .... Lk 18:35   5100
A *c* nobleman went into a far .... Lk 19:12   5100
A *c* man planted a vineyard, and .... Lk 20:9   5100
came to him *c* of the Sadducees .... Lk 20:27   5100
Then *c* of the scribes answering .... Lk 20:39   5100
he saw also a *c* poor widow................... Lk 21:2   5100
But a *c* maid beheld him as he sat .... Lk 22:56   5100
(Who for a *c* sedition made in the .... Lk 23:19   5100
prepared, and *c* others with them .... Lk 24:1

c women also of our company made ...... Lk 24:22   5100
c of them which were with us went......... Lk 24:24   5100
And there was a *c* nobleman................... Jn 4:46   5100
down at a *c* season into the pool .... Jn 5:4
a *c* man was there, which had an .... Jn 5:5   5100
Now a *c* man was sick, named .... Jn 11:1   5100
there were *c* Greeks among them .... Jn 12:20   5100
a *c* man lame from his mother's .... Acts 3:2   5100
But a *c* man named Ananias, with........ Acts 5:1   5100
privy to it, and brought a *c* part............. Acts 5:2   5100
there arose *c* of the synagogue .... Acts 6:9   5100
But there was a *c* man, called................. Acts 8:9   5100
way, they came unto a *c* water .... Acts 8:36   5100
there was a *c* disciple at .... Acts 9:10   5100
Then was Saul *c* days with the .... Acts 9:19   5100
he found a *c* man named Aeneas .... Acts 9:33   5100
Joppa a *c* disciple named Tabitha .... Acts 9:36   5100
There was a *c* man in Caesarea .... Acts 10:1   5100
a *c* vessel descending unto him, ... Acts 10:11   5100
c brethren from Joppa accompanied ...... Acts 10:23   5100
prayed they him to tarry *c* days .... Acts 10:48   5100
A *c* vessel descend, as it had .... Acts 11:5   5100
his hands to vex *c* of the church .... Acts 12:1   5100
that was at Antioch *c* prophets .... Acts 13:1   5100
Paphos, they found a *c* sorcerer .... Acts 13:6   5100
there sat a *c* man at Lystra, ... Acts 14:8   5100
came thither *c* Jews from Antioch .... Acts 14:19
c men which came down from Judaea ...... Acts 15:1   5100
c other of them, should go up to .... Acts 15:2   5100
But there rose up *c* of the sect .... Acts 15:5   5100
that *c* which went out from us .... Acts 15:24   5100
a *c* disciple was there, named .... Acts 16:1   5100
Timotheus, the son of a *c* woman .... Acts 16:1   5100
were in that city abiding *c* days .... Acts 16:12   5100
a *c* woman named Lydia, a seller .... Acts 16:14   5100
a *c* damsel possessed with a .... Acts 16:16   5100
took unto them *c* lewd fellows of .... Acts 17:5   5100
c brethren unto the rulers of the............. Acts 17:6   5100
Then *c* philosophers of the..................... Acts 17:18   5100
For thou bringest *c* strange .... Acts 17:20   5100
as *c* also of your own poets have .... Acts 17:28   5100
Howbeit *c* men clave unto him, and .... Acts 17:34   5100
found a *c* Jew named Aquila, born .... Acts 18:2   5100
and entered into a *c* man's house .... Acts 18:7   5100
a *c* Jew named Apollos, born at .... Acts 18:24   5100
and finding *c* disciples, ... Acts 19:1   5100
Then *c* of the vagabond Jews, ... Acts 19:13   5100
For a *c* man named Demetrius, a .... Acts 19:24   5100
c of the chief of Asia, which .... Acts 19:31   5100
there sat in a window a *c* young .... Acts 20:9   5100
came down from Judaea a *c* prophet ...... Acts 21:10   5100
There went with us also *c* of the .... Acts 21:16   5100
c of the Jews banded together, and......... Acts 23:12   5100
for he hath a *c* thing to tell him .... Acts 23:17   5100
with a *c* orator named Tertullus,............ Acts 24:1   5100
Whereupon *c* Jews from Asia found ...... Acts 24:18   5100
And after *c* days, when Felix came .... Acts 24:24   5100
after *c* days king Agrippa and .... Acts 25:13   5100
There is a *c* man left in bonds by............ Acts 25:14   5100
But had *c* questions against him .... Acts 25:19   5100
Of whom I have no *c* thing to .... Acts 25:26   804
c other prisoners unto one named .... Acts 27:1   5100
running under a *c* island which is .... Acts 27:16   5100
we must be cast upon a *c* island............. Acts 27:26   5100
discovered a *c* creek with a shore .... Acts 27:39   5100
Achaia to make a *c* contribution............ Rom 15:26   5100
have no *c* dwellingplace........................ 1Cor 4:11   790
For before that *c* came from James .... Gal 2:12   5100
it is *c* we can carry nothing out 1Ti 6:7   1212
But one in a *c* place testified,.................. Heb 2:6   4225
For he spake in a *c* place of the .... Heb 4:4   4225
Again, he limiteth a *c* day .... Heb 4:7   5100
But a *c* fearful looking for of .... Heb 10:27   5100
For there are *c* men crept in .... Jude 4   5100

CERTAINLY

I will *c* return unto thee.......................... Gen 18:10
We saw *c* that the LORD was with .... Gen 26:28
could we *c* know that he would say .... Gen 43:7
that such a man as I can *c* divine .... Gen 44:15
will *c* requite us all the evil .... Gen 50:15
And he said, C I will be with thee........... Ex 3:12   3588
If the theft be *c* found in his .... Ex 22:4
he hath *c* trespassed against the .... Lev 5:19
congregation shall *c* stone him .... Lev 24:16
Because it was *c* told you .... Josh 9:24
if ye can *c* declare it me within.............. Judg 14:12
Thy father *c* knoweth that I have 1Sa 20:3
for if I knew *c* that evil were 1Sa 20:9
thy servant hath *c* heard that 1Sa 23:10
for the LORD will *c* make my lord 1Sa 25:28

even so will I *c* do this day 1Kin 1:30
unto him, Thou mayest *c* recover 2Kin 8:10
If thou *c* return in peace, then 2Chr 18:27
for riches *c* make themselves .... Prov 23:5
Lo, *c* in vain made he it .... Jer 8:8   403
Do we *c* not know that every .... Jer 13:12
Ye shall *c* drink .... Jer 25:28
The king of Babylon shall *c* come .... Jer 36:29
Dost thou *c* know that Baalis the .... Jer 40:14
know *c* that I have admonished you .... Jer 42:19
Now therefore know *c* that ye .... Jer 42:22
But we will *c* do whatsoever thing .... Jer 44:17
c this is the day that we looked .... Lam 2:16   389
and one shall *c* come, and overflow, ... Dan 11:10
shall *c* come after certain years .... Dan 11:13
C this was a righteous man .... Lk 23:47   3689

CERTAINTY
Know for a *c* that the LORD your .... Josh 23:13
and come ye again to me with the *c* 1Sa 23:23   3559
know the *c* of the words of truth .... Prov 22:21   7189
I know of *c* that ye would gain .... Dan 2:8   3330
know the *c* of those things .... Lk 1:4   803
not know the *c* for the tumult .... Acts 21:34   804
c wherefore he was accused of the .... Acts 22:30   804

CERTIFIED
have we sent and *c* the king .... Ezr 4:14   3064
Esther *c* the king thereof in .... Est 2:22   559

CERTIFY
there come word from you to *c* me 2Sa 15:28   5046
We *c* the king that, if this city .... Ezr 4:16   3046
to *c* thee, that we might write .... Ezr 5:10   3046
Also we *c* you, that touching any .... Ezr 7:24   3046
But I *c* you, brethren, that the .... Gal 1:11   1107

CHAFED
they be *c* in their minds, as a 2Sa 17:8   4751

CHAFF
as *c* that the storm carrieth away .... Job 21:18   4671
but are like the *c* which the wind .... Ps 1:4   4671
Let them be as *c* before the wind .... Ps 35:5   4671
and the flame consumeth the *c* .... Is 5:24   2842
shall be chased as the *c* of the .... Is 17:13   4671
shall be as *c* that passeth away .... Is 29:5   4671
Ye shall conceive *c*, ye shall .... Is 33:11   2842
and shalt make the hills as *c* .... Is 41:15   4671
What is the *c* to the wheat .... Jer 23:28   8401
became like the *c* of the summer .... Dan 2:35   5784
as the *c* that is driven with the .... Hos 13:3   4671
before the day pass as the *c* .... Zeph 2:2   4671
up the *c* with unquenchable fire .... Mt 3:12   892
but the *c* he will burn with fire .... Lk 3:17   892

CHAIN
put a gold *c* about his neck .... Gen 41:42   7242
work, and wreaths of *c* work 1Kin 7:17   8333
compasseth them about as a *c* .... Ps 73:6   6059
eyes, with one *c* of thy neck .... Song 4:9   6060
he hath made my *c* heavy .... Lam 3:7   5178
Make a *c* .... Eze 7:23   7659
thy hands, and a *c* on thy neck, ... Eze 16:11   7242
have a *c* of gold about his neck, ... Dan 5:7   2002
have a *c* of gold about thy neck, ... Dan 5:16   2002
put a *c* of gold about his neck, ... Dan 5:29   2002
of Israel I am bound with this *c* .... Acts 28:20   254
me, and was not ashamed of my *c* 2Ti 1:16   254
pit and a great *c* in his hand .... Rev 20:1   254

CHAINS
two *c* of pure gold at the ends .... Ex 28:14   8333
the wreathen *c* to the ouches .... Ex 28:14   8333
c at the ends of wreathen work of .... Ex 28:22   8337
c of gold in the two rings which .... Ex 28:24   5688
c thou shalt fasten in the two .... Ex 28:25
the breastplate at the ends .... Ex 39:15   8333
they put the two wreathen *c* of .... Ex 39:17   5688
two ends of the two wreathen *c* .... Ex 39:18   5688
hath gotten, of jewels of gold, *c* .... Num 31:50   685
beside the *c* that were about .... Judg 8:26   6060
the *c* of gold before the oracle 1Kin 6:21   7569
and set thereon palm trees and *c* 2Chr 3:5   8333
And he made *c*, as in the oracle, ... 2Chr 3:16   8333
and put them on the 2Chr 3:16   8333
out those which are bound with *c* .... Ps 68:6   3574
To bind their kings with *c* .... Ps 149:8   2131
thy head, and *c* about thy neck .... Prov 1:9   6060
jewels, thy neck with *c* of gold .... Song 1:10   2737
The *c*, and the bracelets, and the .... Is 3:19   5188
with gold, and casteth silver *c* .... Is 40:19   7569
in *c* they shall come over, and .... Is 45:14   2131
eyes, and bound him with *c* .... Jer 39:7   5178

in *c* among all that were carried .... Jer 40:1   246
the *c* which were upon thine hand .... Jer 40:4   246
king of Babylon bound him in *c* .... Jer 52:11   5178
they brought him with *c* unto the .... Eze 19:4   2397
And they put him in ward in *c* .... Eze 19:9   2397
all her great men were bound in *c* .... Nah 3:10   2131
could bind him, no, not with *c* .... Mk 5:3   254
often bound with fetters and *c* .... Mk 5:4   254
the *c* had been plucked asunder by .... Mk 5:4   254
and he was kept bound with *c* .... Lk 8:29   254
two soldiers, bound with two *c* .... Acts 12:6   254
his *c* fell off from his hands .... Acts 12:7   254
him to be bound with two *c* .... Acts 21:33   254
delivered them into *c* of darkness 2Pet 2:4   4577
c under darkness unto the...................... Jude 6   1199

CHALCEDONY
the third, a *c* .... Rev 21:19   5472

CHALCOL (kal'-kol) See CALCOL. *Son of Mahol.*
the Ezrahite, and Heman, and *C* 1Kin 4:31   3633

CHALDAEANS (kal-de'-uns) See CHALDEANS. *Inhabitants of southern Babylonia.*
came he out of the land of the *C* .... Acts 7:4   5466

CHALDEA (kal-de'-ah) See BABYLON, CHALDEAN. *Southern portion of Babylonia.*
And *C* shall be a spoil .... Jer 50:10   3778
to all the inhabitants of *C* all .... Jer 51:24   3778
blood upon the inhabitants of *C* .... Jer 51:35   3778
by the Spirit of God into *C* .... Eze 11:24   3778
in the land of Canaan unto *C* .... Eze 16:29   3778
manner of the Babylonians of *C* .... Eze 23:15   3778
sent messengers unto them into *C* .... Eze 23:16   3778

CHALDEAN (kal-de'-un) See BABYLONIAN, CHALDEANS, CHALDEANS'.
the king of Babylon, the *C* .... Ezr 5:12   3777
any magician, or astrologer, or *C* .... Dan 2:10   3777

CHALDEANS (kal-de'-uns) See BABYLONIANS, CHALDAEANS, CHALDEANS', CHALDEES. *Same as Chaldaeans.*
The *C* made out three bands, and .... Job 1:17   3778
Behold the land of the *C* .... Is 23:13   3778
down all their nobles, and the *C* .... Is 43:14   3778
is no throne, O daughter of the *C* .... Is 47:1   3778
darkness, O daughter of the *C* .... Is 47:5   3778
and his arm shall be on the *C* .... Is 48:14   3778
of Babylon, flee ye from the *C* .... Is 48:20   3778
king of Babylon, and against the *C* .... Jer 21:4   3778
falleth to the *C* that besiege you .... Jer 21:9   3778
and into the hand of the *C* .... Jer 22:25   3778
the land of the *C* for their good .... Jer 24:5   3778
iniquity, and the land of the *C* .... Jer 25:12   3778
escape out of the hand of the *C* .... Jer 32:4   3778
though ye fight with the *C* .... Jer 32:5   3778
is given into the hand of the *C* .... Jer 32:24   3778
is given into the hand of the *C* .... Jer 32:25   3778
this city into the hand of the *C* .... Jer 32:28   3778
And the *C*, that fight against this .... Jer 32:29   3778
is given into the hand of the *C* .... Jer 32:43   3778
They come to fight with the *C* .... Jer 33:5   3778
for fear of the army of the *C* .... Jer 35:11   3778
and when the *C* that besieged .... Jer 37:5   3778
the *C* shall come again, and fight .... Jer 37:8   3778
The *C* shall surely depart from us .... Jer 37:9   3778
of the *C* that fight against you .... Jer 37:10   3778
that when the army of the *C* was .... Jer 37:11   3778
Thou fallest away to the *C* .... Jer 37:13   3778
I fall not away to the *C* .... Jer 37:14   3778
goeth forth to the *C* shall live .... Jer 38:2   3778
be given into the hand of the *C* .... Jer 38:18   3778
the Jews that are fallen to the *C* .... Jer 38:19   3778
wives and thy children to the *C* .... Jer 38:23   3778
the *C* burned the king's house, and ...... Jer 39:8   3778
saying, Fear not to serve the *C* .... Jer 40:9   3778
dwell at Mizpah to serve the *C* .... Jer 40:10   3778
the *C* that were found there, and .... Jer 41:3   3778
Because of the *C*.................................... Jer 41:18   3778
deliver us into the hand of the *C* .... Jer 43:3   3778
of the *C* by Jeremiah the prophet .... Jer 50:1   3778
go forth out of the land of the *C* .... Jer 50:8   3778
GOD of hosts in the land of the *C* .... Jer 50:25   3778
A sword is upon the *C*, saith the .... Jer 50:35   3778
against the land of the *C* .... Jer 50:45   3778
shall fall in the land of the *C* .... Jer 51:4   3778
from the land of the *C* .... Jer 51:54   3778
(now the *C* were by the city round .... Jer 52:7   3778
But the army of the *C* pursued .... Jer 52:8   3779
And all the army of the *C*, that .... Jer 52:14   3779
the *C* brake, and carried all the............. Jer 52:17   3779
in the land of the *C* by the river .... Eze 1:3   3779

to Babylon to the land of the *C*	Eze 12:13	3779
the images of the *C* portrayed	Eze 23:14	3779
The Babylonians, and all the *C*	Eze 23:23	3779
learning and the tongue of the *C*	Dan 1:4	3779
and the sorcerers, and the *C*	Dan 2:2	3779
Then spake the *C* to the king in	Dan 2:4	3779
king answered and said to the *C*	Dan 2:5	3779
The *C* answered before the king,	Dan 2:10	3779
at that time certain *C* came near	Dan 3:8	3779
magicians, the astrologers, the *C*	Dan 4:7	3779
bring in the astrologers, the *C*	Dan 5:7	3779
of the magicians, astrologers, *C*	Dan 5:11	3779
the king of the *C* slain	Dan 5:30	3779
made king over the realm of the *C*	Dan 9:1	3778
For, lo, I raise up the *C*	Hab 1:6	3778

CHALDEANS' *(kal-de'-uns)*

But the *C* army pursued after them	Jer 39:5	3778

CHALDEES *(kal'-dees)* See CHALDEES'. Same as Chaldeans.

of his nativity, in Ur of the *C*	Gen 11:28	3778
forth with them from Ur of the *C*	Gen 11:31	3778
brought thee out of Ur of the *C*	Gen 15:7	3778
sent against him bands of the *C*	2Kin 24:2	3778
(now the *C* were against the city	2Kin 25:4	3778
the army of the *C* pursued after	2Kin 25:5	3778
And all the army of the *C*, that	2Kin 25:10	3778
did the *C* break in pieces, and	2Kin 25:13	3778
not to be the servants of the *C*	2Kin 25:24	3778
the *C* that were with him at	2Kin 25:25	3778
for they were afraid of the *C*	2Kin 25:26	3778
upon them the king of the *C*	2Chr 36:17	3778
him forth out of Ur of the *C*	Neh 9:7	3778

CHALDEES' *(kal'-dees)* See CHALDEANS.

the beauty of the *C* excellency	Is 13:19	3778

CHALKSTONES

as *c* that are beaten in sunder	Is 27:9	68,1615

CHALLENGETH

thing, which another *c* to be his	Ex 22:9	559

CHAMBER

and he entered into his *c*, and wept	Gen 43:30	2315
covereth his feet in his summer *c*	Judg 3:24	2315
will go in to my wife into the *c*	Judg 15:1	2315
wait, abiding with her in the *c*	Judg 16:9	2315
liers in wait abiding in the *c*	Judg 16:12	2315
Tamar, Bring the meat into the *c*	2Sa 13:10	2315
into the *c* to Amnon her brother	2Sa 13:10	2315
and went up to the *c* over the gate	2Sa 18:33	5944
went in unto the king into the *c*	1Kin 1:15	2315
The nethermost *c* was five cubits	1Kin 6:6	3326
The door for the middle *c* was in	1Kin 6:8	6763
winding stairs into the middle *c*	1Kin 6:8	2315
them back into the guard	1Kin 14:28	8372
down out of the *c* into the house	1Kin 17:23	5944
into the city, into an inner *c*	1Kin 20:30	2315
into an inner *c* to hide thyself	1Kin 22:25	2315
his upper *c* that was in Samaria	2Kin 1:2	5944
Let us make a little *c*, I pray	2Kin 4:10	5944
thither, and he turned into the *c*	2Kin 4:11	5944
and carry him to an inner *c*	2Kin 9:2	2315
by the *c* of Nathan-melech the	2Kin 23:11	3957
on the top of the upper *c* of Ahaz	2Kin 23:12	5944
them again into the guard *c*	2Chr 12:11	8372
into an inner *c* to hide thyself	2Chr 18:24	2315
went into the *c* of Johanan the	Ezr 10:6	3957
of Berechiah over against his *c*	Neh 3:30	5393
of the *c* of the house of our God	Neh 13:4	3957
he had prepared for him a great *c*	Neh 13:5	3957
in preparing him a *c* in the	Neh 13:7	5393
stuff of Tobiah out of the *c*	Neh 13:8	3957
a bridegroom coming out of his *c*	Ps 19:5	2646
into the *c* of her that conceived	Song 3:4	2315
into the *c* of the sons of Hanan	Jer 35:4	3957
which was by the *c* of the princes	Jer 35:4	2315
which was above the *c* of Maaseiah	Jer 35:4	3957
in the *c* of Gemariah the son of	Jer 36:10	3957
king's house, into the scribe's *c*	Jer 36:12	3957
in the *c* of Elishama the scribe	Jer 36:20	3957
it out of Elishama the scribe's *c*	Jer 36:21	3957
every little *c* was one reed long,	Eze 40:7	8372
little *c* to the roof of another	Eze 40:13	8372
And he said unto me, This *c*	Eze 40:45	3957
the *c* whose prospect is toward	Eze 40:46	3957
and the breadth of every side *c*	Eze 41:5	6763
c to the highest by the midst	Eze 41:7	
which was for the side *c* without	Eze 41:9	6763
he brought me into the *c* that was	Eze 42:1	3957
open in his *c* toward Jerusalem	Dan 6:10	5952
the bridegroom go forth of his *c*	Joel 2:16	2315

they laid her in an upper *c*	Acts 9:37	5253
they brought him into the upper *c*	Acts 9:39	5253
were many lights in the upper *c*	Acts 20:8	5253

CHAMBERING

rioting and drunkenness, not in *c*	Rom 13:13	2845

CHAMBERLAIN

chamber of Nathan-melech the *c*	2Kin 23:11	5631
the custody of Hege the king's *c*	Est 2:3	5631
of Shaashgaz, the king's *c*	Est 2:14	5631
but what Hegai the king's *c*	Est 2:15	5631
the king's *c* their friend	Acts 12:20	1909,3588,2846
Erastus the *c* of the city	Rom 16:23	3623

CHAMBERLAINS

the seven *c* that served in the	Est 1:10	5631
the king's commandment by his *c*	Est 1:12	5631
of the king Ahasuerus by the *c*	Est 1:15	5631
king's gate, two of the king's *c*	Est 2:21	5631
her *c* came and told it her	Est 4:4	5631
for Hatach, one of the king's *c*	Est 4:5	5631
and Teresh, two of the king's *c*	Est 6:2	5631
with him, came the king's *c*	Est 6:14	5631
And Harbonah, one of the *c*	Est 7:9	5631

CHAMBERS

the house he built *c* round about	1Kin 6:5	3326
and he made *c* round about	1Kin 6:5	6763
then he built *c* against all the	1Kin 6:10	3326
set office, and were over the *c*	1Chr 9:26	3957
who remaining in the *c* were free	1Chr 9:33	3957
LORD, in the courts, and in the *c*	1Chr 23:28	3957
and of the upper *c* thereof	1Chr 28:11	5944
of all the *c* round about, of the	1Chr 28:12	3957
he overlaid the upper *c* with gold	2Chr 3:9	5944
c in the house of the LORD	2Chr 31:11	3957
in the *c* of the house of the LORD	Ezr 8:29	3957
to the *c* of the house of our God	Neh 10:37	3957
the house of our God, to the *c*	Neh 10:38	3957
new wine, and the oil, unto the *c*	Neh 10:39	3957
over the *c* for the treasures	Neh 12:44	5393
commanded, and they cleansed the *c*	Neh 13:9	3957
Pleiades, and the *c* of the south	Job 9:9	2315
the beams of his *c* in the waters	Ps 104:3	5944
He watereth the hills from his *c*	Ps 104:13	5944
in the *c* of their kings	Ps 105:30	2315
going down to the *c* of death	Prov 7:27	2315
by knowledge shall the *c* be	Prov 24:4	2315
king hath brought me into his *c*	Song 1:4	2315
my people, enter thou into thy *c*	Is 26:20	2315
and his *c* by wrong	Jer 22:13	5944
build me a wide house and large *c*	Jer 22:14	5944
of the LORD, into one of the *c*	Jer 35:2	3957
every man in the *c* of his imagery	Eze 8:12	2315
which entereth into their privy *c*	Eze 21:14	2315
the little *c* were five cubits	Eze 40:7	8372
the little *c* of the gate eastward	Eze 40:10	8372
c was one cubit on this side	Eze 40:12	8372
the little *c* were six cubits on	Eze 40:12	8372
narrow windows to the little *c*	Eze 40:16	8372
court, and, lo, there were *c*	Eze 40:17	3957
thirty *c* were upon the pavement	Eze 40:17	3957
the little *c* thereof were three	Eze 40:21	8372
And the little *c* thereof, and the	Eze 40:29	8372
And the little *c* thereof, and the	Eze 40:33	8372
The little *c* thereof, the posts	Eze 40:36	8372
And the *c* and the entries thereof	Eze 40:38	3957
the *c* of the singers in the inner	Eze 40:44	3957
the side *c* were three, one over	Eze 41:6	6763
house for the side *c* round about	Eze 41:6	6763
about still upward to the side *c*	Eze 41:7	6763
the foundations of the side *c*	Eze 41:8	6763
of the side *c* that were within	Eze 41:9	6763
between the *c* was the wideness of	Eze 41:10	3957
the doors of the side *c* were	Eze 41:11	6763
and upon the side *c* of the house	Eze 41:26	6763
before the *c* was a walk of ten	Eze 42:4	3957
Now the upper *c* were shorter	Eze 42:5	3957
was without over against the *c*	Eze 42:7	3957
court on the forepart of the *c*	Eze 42:7	3957
For the length of the *c* that were	Eze 42:8	3957
from under these *c* was the entry	Eze 42:9	3957
The *c* were in the thickness of	Eze 42:10	3957
the *c* which were toward the north	Eze 42:11	3957
according to the doors of the *c*	Eze 42:12	3957
Then said he unto me, The north *c*	Eze 42:13	3957
The north *c* and the south *c*	Eze 42:13	3957
separate place, they be holy *c*	Eze 42:13	3957
and lay them in the holy *c*	Eze 44:19	3957
for a possession for twenty	Eze 45:5	3957
into the holy *c* of the priests,	Eze 46:19	3957
behold, he is in the secret *c*	Mt 24:26	5009

CHAMELEON
And the ferret, and the *c*, and the .... Lev 11:30   3581

CHAMOIS
pygarg, and the wild ox, and the *c* .... Deut 14:5   2169

CHAMPAIGN
which dwell in the *c* over against .... Deut 11:30   6160

CHAMPION
there went out a *c* out of the 1Sa 17:4   376,1143
them, behold, there came up the *c* .. 1Sa 17:23   376,1143
Philistines saw their *c* was dead 1Sa 17:51   1368

CHANAAN (ka'-na-un) See CANAAN. *Greek form of Canaan.*
over all the land of Egypt and *C* .... Acts 7:11   5477
seven nations in the land of *C* .... Acts 13:19   5477

CHANCE
If a bird's nest *c* to be before .... Deut 22:6   7122
it was a *c* that happened to us 1Sa 6:9   4745
As I happened by *c* upon mount 2Sa 1:6   7122
time and *c* happeneth to them all .... Eccl 9:11   6294
by *c* there came down a certain .... Lk 10:31   4795
it may *c* of wheat, or of some 1Cor 15:37   5177

CHANCELLOR
Rehum the *c* and Shimshai the .... Ezr 4:8   1169,2942
Then wrote Rehum the *c*, and .... Ezr 4:9   1169,2942
an answer unto Rehum the *c* .... Ezr 4:17   1169,2942

CHANCETH
uncleanness that *c* him by night .... Deut 23:10   4745

CHANGE
and be clean, and *c* your garments .... Gen 35:2   2498
He shall not alter it, nor *c* it .... Lev 27:10   4171
he shall at all *c* beast for beast .... Lev 27:10   4171
or bad, neither shall he *c* it .... Lev 27:33   4171
if he *c* it at all, then both it .... Lev 27:33   4171
the *c* thereof shall be holy .... Lev 27:33   8545
sheets and thirty *c* of garments .... Judg 14:12   2487
sheets and thirty *c* of garments .... Judg 14:13   2487
gave *c* of garments unto them .... Judg 14:19   2487
time will I wait, till my *c* come .... Job 14:14   2487
They *c* the night into day .... Job 17:12   7760
as a vesture shalt thou *c* them .... Ps 102:26   2498
not with them that are given to *c* .... Prov 24:21   8138
but we will *c* them into cedars .... Is 9:10   2498
thou about so much to *c* thy way .... Jer 2:36   8138
Can the Ethiopian *c* his skin .... Jer 13:23   2015
most High, and think to *c* times .... Dan 7:25   8133
therefore will I *c* their glory .... Hos 4:7   4171
Then shall his mind *c*, and he .... Hab 1:11   2498
clothe thee with *c* of raiment .... Zec 3:4   4254
For I am the LORD, I *c* not .... Mal 3:6   8138
shall *c* the customs which Moses............ Acts 6:14   236
for even their women did *c* the .... Rom 1:26   3337
with you now, and to *c* my voice .... Gal 4:20   236
Who shall *c* our vile body, that .... Phil 3:21   3345
of necessity a *c* also of the law .... Heb 7:12   3331

CHANGEABLE
The *c* suits of apparel, and the.............. Is 3:22   4254

CHANGED
me, and *c* my wages ten times .... Gen 31:7   2498
thou hast *c* my wages ten times .... Gen 31:41   2498
c his raiment, and came in unto .... Gen 41:14   2498
be *c* unto white, he shall come .... Lev 13:16   2015
the plague have not *c* his colour .... Lev 13:55   2015
Baal-meon, (their names being *c*............ Num 32:38   5437
he *c* his behaviour before them,............ 1Sa 21:13   8138
c his apparel, and came into the.............. 2Sa 12:20   2498
stead, and *c* his name to Zedekiah........ 2Kin 24:17   5437
And *c* his prison garments 2Kin 25:29   8132
of my disease is my garment *c* .... Job 30:18   2664
when he *c* his behaviour before .... Ps 34:t   8138
change them, and they shall be *c* .... Ps 102:26   2498
Thus they *c* their glory into the .... Ps 106:20   4171
boldness of his face shall be *c*.............. Eccl 8:1   8132
c the ordinance, broken the.................... Is 24:5   2498
Hath a nation *c* their gods .... Jer 2:11   4171
but my people have *c* their glory .... Jer 2:11   4171
in him, and his scent is not *c* .... Jer 48:11   4171
And *c* his prison garments .... Jer 52:33   8138
how is the most fine gold *c* .... Lam 4:1   8132
she hath *c* my judgments into .... Eze 5:6   4171
before me, till the time be *c* .... Dan 2:9   8133
his visage was *c* against Shadrach .... Dan 3:19   8133
neither were their coats *c* .... Dan 3:27   8133
have *c* the king's word, and .... Dan 3:28   8133
Let his heart be *c* from man's .... Dan 4:16   8133
Then the king's countenance was *c* ...... Dan 5:6   8133
and his countenance was *c* in him........ Dan 5:9   8133

nor let thy countenance be *c* .... Dan 5:10   8133
the writing, that it be not *c* .... Dan 6:8   8133
the king establisheth may be *c* .... Dan 6:15   8133
might not be *c* concerning Daniel.......... Dan 6:17   8133
me, and my countenance *c* in me .... Dan 7:28   8133
he hath *c* the portion of my .... Mic 2:4   4171
they *c* their minds, and said that .... Acts 28:6   3328
c the glory of the uncorruptible .... Rom 1:23   236
Who *c* the truth of God into a lie .... Rom 1:25   3337
all sleep, but we shall all be *c* 1Cor 15:51   236
incorruptible, and we shall be *c*.............. 1Cor 15:52   236
are *c* into the same image from 2Cor 3:18   3339
fold them up, and they shall be *c* .... Heb 1:12   236
For the priesthood being *c*.................... Heb 7:12   3346

CHANGERS
doves, and the *c* of money sitting .... Jn 2:14   2773

CHANGERS'
and poured out the *c* money .... Jn 2:15   2855

CHANGES
he gave each man *c* of raiment .... Gen 45:22   2487
of silver, and five *c* of raiment .... Gen 45:22   2487
of gold, and ten *c* of raiment.................. 2Kin 5:5   2487
of silver, and two *c* of garments 2Kin 5:22   2487
with two *c* of garments, and laid 2Kin 5:23   2487
c and war are against me .... Job 10:17   2487
Because they have no *c*, therefore.......... Ps 55:19   2487

CHANGEST
thou *c* his countenance, and.................. Job 14:20   8138

CHANGETH
to his own hurt, and *c* not .... Ps 15:4   4171
he *c* the times and the seasons .... Dan 2:21   8133

CHANGING
redeeming and concerning *c* .... Ruth 4:7   8545

CHANNEL
LORD shall beat off from the *c* of .... Is 27:12   7641

CHANNELS
the *c* of the sea appeared, the.............. 2Sa 22:16   650
Then the *c* of waters were seen, ... Ps 18:15   650
he shall come up over all his *c* .... Is 8:7   650

CHANT
That *c* to the sound of the viol,.............. Amos 6:5   6527

CHAPEL
for it is the king's *c*, and it is .... Amos 7:13   4720

CHAPITER
of the one *c* was five cubits...................... 1Kin 7:16   3805
of the other *c* was five cubits.................. 1Kin 7:16   3805
seven for the one *c* 1Kin 7:17   3805
and seven for the other *c* 1Kin 7:17   3805
and so did he for the other *c* 1Kin 7:18   3805
rows round about upon the other *c* 1Kin 7:20   3805
And the mouth of it within the *c* 1Kin 7:31   3805
and the *c* upon it was brass 2Kin 25:17   3805
the height of the *c* three cubits 2Kin 25:17   3805
upon the *c* round about, all of 2Kin 25:17   3805
the *c* that was on the top of each............ 2Chr 3:15   6858
And a *c* of brass was upon it .... Jer 52:22   3805
height of one *c* was five cubits .... Jer 52:22   3805

CHAPITERS
and he overlaid their *c* and their .... Ex 36:38   7218
overlaying of their *c* of silver .... Ex 38:17   7218
and the overlaying of their *c* .... Ex 38:19   7218
the pillars, and overlaid their *c* .... Ex 38:28   7218
he made two *c* of molten brass, to 1Kin 7:16   3805
for the *c* which were upon the top 1Kin 7:17   3805
to cover the *c* that were upon the 1Kin 7:18   3805
the *c* that were upon the top of 1Kin 7:19   3805
the *c* upon the two pillars had 1Kin 7:20   3805
the two bowls of the *c* that were 1Kin 7:41   3805
to cover the two bowls of the *c* 1Kin 7:41   3805
the *c* that were upon the pillars 1Kin 7:42   3805
the *c* which were on the top of 2Chr 4:12   3805
c which were on the top of the 2Chr 4:12   3805
the *c* which were upon the pillars 2Chr 4:13   3805
upon the *c* round about, all of .... Jer 52:22   3805

CHAPMEN
that which *c* and merchants............ 2Chr 9:14   582,8846

CHAPT
Because the ground is *c*, for .... Jer 14:4   2865

CHARASHIM (car'-a-shim) *Place founded by Joab.*
the father of the valley of *C* 1Chr 4:14   2798

CHARCHEMISH (car'-ke-mish) See CARCHEMISH. *Same as Carchemish.*
to fight against *C* by Euphrates.............. 2Chr 35:20   3751

CHARGE

obeyed my voice, and kept my *c*	Gen 26:5	4931
as he blessed him he gave him a *c*	Gen 28:6	6680
gave them a *c* unto the children	Ex 6:13	6680
c the people, lest they break	Ex 19:21	5749
keep the *c* of the LORD, that ye	Lev 8:35	4931
the Levites shall keep the *c* of	Num 1:53	4931
And they shall keep his *c*, and the	Num 3:7	4931
the *c* of the whole congregation	Num 3:7	4931
the *c* of the children of Israel,	Num 3:8	4931
the *c* of the sons of Gershon in	Num 3:25	4931
keeping the *c* of the sanctuary	Num 3:28	4931
their *c* shall be the ark, and the	Num 3:31	4931
that keep the *c* of the sanctuary	Num 3:32	4931
c of the sons of Merari shall be	Num 3:36	4931
keeping the *c* of the sanctuary	Num 3:38	4931
the *c* of the children of Israel	Num 3:38	4931
unto them in *c* all their burdens	Num 4:27	4931
their *c* shall be under the hand	Num 4:28	4931
this is the *c* of their burden,	Num 4:31	4931
of the *c* of their burden	Num 4:32	4931
the priest shall *c* her by an oath	Num 5:19	7650
Then the priest shall *c* the woman	Num 5:21	7650
the congregation, to keep the *c*	Num 8:26	4931
unto the Levites touching their *c*	Num 8:26	4931
of Israel kept the *c* of the LORD	Num 9:19	4931
they kept the *c* of the LORD	Num 9:23	4931
And they shall keep thy *c*, and the	Num 18:3	4931
the *c* of all the tabernacle	Num 18:3	4931
keep the *c* of the tabernacle of	Num 18:4	4931
shall keep the *c* of the sanctuary	Num 18:5	4931
sanctuary, and the *c* of the altar	Num 18:5	4931
I also have given thee the *c* of	Num 18:8	4931
give him a *c* in their sight	Num 27:19	6680
hands upon him, and gave him a *c*	Num 27:23	6680
Levites, which keep the *c* of the	Num 31:30	4931
Levites, which kept the *c* of the	Num 31:47	4931
men of war which are under our *c*	Num 31:49	3027
But *c* Joshua, and encourage him,	Deut 3:28	6680
the LORD thy God, and keep his *c*	Deut 11:1	4931
unto thy people of Israel's *c*	Deut 21:8	7130
that I may give him a *c*	Deut 31:14	6680
he gave Joshua the son of Nun a *c*	Deut 31:23	6680
but have kept the *c* of the	Josh 22:3	4931
I will give *c* concerning thee	2Sa 14:8	6680
the captains *c* concerning Absalom	2Sa 18:5	6680
keep the *c* of the LORD thy God,	1Kin 2:3	4931
every man according to his *c*	1Kin 4:28	4941
all the *c* of the house of Joseph	1Kin 11:28	5447
leaned to have the *c* of the gate	2Kin 7:17	5921
because the *c* was upon them, and	1Chr 9:27	4931
certain of them had the *c* of the	1Chr 9:28	5921
give thee *c* concerning Israel,	1Chr 22:12	6680
the *c* of the tabernacle of the	1Chr 23:32	4931
the *c* of the holy place, and the	1Chr 23:32	4931
the *c* of the sons of Aaron their	1Chr 23:32	4931
for we keep the *c* of the LORD our	2Chr 13:11	4931
therefore the Levites had the *c*	2Chr 30:17	5921
of the palace, *c* over Jerusalem	Neh 7:2	6680
to *c* ourselves yearly with the	Neh 10:32	5414
that have the *c* of the business	Est 3:9	6213
to *c* her that she should go in	Est 4:8	6680
hath given him a *c* over the earth	Job 34:13	6485
they laid to my *c* things that I	Ps 35:11	7592
shall give his angels *c* over thee	Ps 91:11	6680
I *c* you, O ye daughters of	Song 2:7	7650
I *c* you, O ye daughters of	Song 3:5	7650
I *c* you, O daughters of Jerusalem	Song 5:8	7650
beloved, that thou dost so *c* us	Song 5:9	7650
I *c* you, O daughters of Jerusalem	Song 8:4	7650
of my wrath will I give him a *c*	Is 10:6	6680
king of Babylon gave *c* concerning	Jer 39:11	6680
given it a *c* against Ashkelon	Jer 47:7	6680
which had the *c* of the men of war	Jer 52:25	6496
Cause them that have *c* over the	Eze 9:1	6486
the keepers of the *c* of the house	Eze 40:45	4931
the keepers of the *c* of the altar	Eze 40:46	4931
kept the *c* of mine holy things	Eze 44:8	4931
but ye have set keepers of my *c*	Eze 44:8	4931
having *c* at the gates of the	Eze 44:11	6486
keepers of the *c* of the house	Eze 44:14	4931
that kept the *c* of my sanctuary	Eze 44:15	4931
unto me, and they shall keep my *c*	Eze 44:16	4931
which have kept my *c*, which went	Eze 48:11	4931
ways, and if thou wilt keep my *c*	Zec 3:7	4931
give his angels *c* concerning thee	Mt 4:6	1781
I *c* thee, come out of him, and	Mk 9:25	2004
shall give his angels *c* over thee	Lk 4:10	1781
Lord, lay not this sin to their *c*	Acts 7:60	2476
who had the *c* of all her treasure	Acts 8:27	1909
Who, having received such a *c*	Acts 16:24	3852

his *c* worthy of death or of bonds	Acts 23:29	*1462*
any thing to the *c* of God's elect	Rom 8:33	*1458,2596*
the gospel of Christ without *c*	1Cor 9:18	*77*
I *c* you by the Lord that this	1Th 5:27	*3726*
that thou mightest *c* some that	1Ti 1:3	*3853*
This *c* I commit unto thee, son	1Ti 1:18	*3852*
And these things give in *c*	1Ti 5:7	*3853*
I *c* thee before God, and the Lord	1Ti 5:21	*1263*
I give thee *c* in the sight of God	1Ti 6:13	*3853*
C them that are rich in this	1Ti 6:17	*3853*
I *c* thee therefore before God, and	2Ti 4:1	*1263*
it may not be laid to their *c*	2Ti 4:16	*3049*

CHARGEABLE

now go, lest we be *c* unto thee	2Sa 13:25	3513
before me were *c* unto the people	Neh 5:15	3513
you, and wanted, I was *c* to no man	2Cor 11:9	*2655*
we would not be *c* unto any of you	1Th 2:9	*1912*
we might not be *c* to any of you	2Th 3:8	*1912*

CHARGED

Abimelech *c* all his people,	Gen 26:11	6680
c him, and said unto him, Thou	Gen 28:1	6680
of the guard *c* Joseph with them	Gen 40:4	6485
he *c* them, and said unto them, I	Gen 49:29	6680
Pharaoh *c* all his people, saying,	Ex 1:22	6680
I *c* your judges at that time,	Deut 1:16	6680
shall he be *c* with any business	Deut 24:5	5674,5921
Moses *c* the people the same day,	Deut 27:11	6680
Joshua *c* them that went to	Josh 8:8	6680
the servant of the LORD *c* you	Josh 22:5	6680
have I not *c* the young men that	Ruth 2:9	6680
father *c* the people with the oath	1Sa 14:27	7650
Thy father straitly *c* the people	1Sa 14:28	7650
c the messenger, saying, When	2Sa 11:19	6680
in our hearing the king *c* thee	2Sa 18:12	6680
he *c* Solomon his son, saying,	1Kin 2:1	6680
that I have *c* thee with	1Kin 2:43	6680
For so was it *c* me by the word of	1Kin 13:9	6680
whom the LORD had *c* them, that	2Kin 17:15	6680
c them, saying, Ye shall not fear	2Kin 17:35	6680
c him to build an house for the	1Chr 22:6	6680
judgments which the LORD *c* Moses	1Chr 22:13	6680
he *c* them, saying, Thus shall ye	2Chr 19:9	6680
he hath *c* me to build him an	2Chr 36:23	6485
he hath *c* me to build him an	Ezr 1:2	6485
c that they should not be opened	Neh 13:19	559
for Mordecai had *c* her that she	Est 2:10	6680
as Mordecai had *c* her	Est 2:20	6680
sinned not, nor *c* God foolishly	Job 1:22	5414
and his angels *c* with folly	Job 4:18	7760
I *c* Baruch before them, saying,	Jer 32:13	6680
father in all that he hath *c* us	Jer 35:8	6680
and Jesus straitly *c* them, saying,	Mt 9:30	*1690*
c them that they should not make	Mt 12:16	*2008*
Then *c* he his disciples that they	Mt 16:20	*1291*
from the mountain, Jesus *c* them	Mt 17:9	*1781*
And he straitly *c* him, and	Mk 1:43	*1690*
he straitly *c* them that they	Mk 3:12	*2008*
he *c* them straitly that no man	Mk 5:43	*1291*
he *c* them that they should tell	Mk 7:36	*1291*
but the more he *c* them, so much	Mk 7:36	*1291*
he *c* them, saying, Take heed,	Mk 8:15	*1291*
he *c* them that they should tell	Mk 8:30	*2008*
he *c* them that they should tell	Mk 9:9	*1291*
many *c* him that he should hold	Mk 10:48	*2008*
And he *c* him to tell no man	Lk 5:14	*3853*
but he *c* them that they should	Lk 8:56	*3853*
And he straitly *c* them, and	Lk 9:21	*2008*
c him, See thou tell no man that	Acts 23:22	*3853*
c every one of you, as a father	1Th 2:11	*3146*
them, and let not the church be *c*	1Ti 5:16	*916*

CHARGEDST

for thou *c* us, saying, Set bounds	Ex 19:23	5749

CHARGER

And his offering was one silver *c*	Num 7:13	7086
for his offering one silver *c*	Num 7:19	7086
His offering was one silver *c*	Num 7:25	7086
c of the weight of an hundred	Num 7:31	7086
His offering was one silver *c*	Num 7:37	7086
c of the weight of an hundred	Num 7:43	7086
His offering was one silver *c*	Num 7:49	7086
c of the weight of an hundred	Num 7:55	7086
His offering was one silver *c*	Num 7:61	7086
His offering was one silver *c*	Num 7:67	7086
His offering was one silver *c*	Num 7:73	7086
His offering was one silver *c*	Num 7:79	7086
Each *c* of silver weighing an	Num 7:85	7086
here John Baptist's head in a *c*	Mt 14:8	*4094*
And his head was brought in a *c*	Mt 14:11	*4094*

by in a *c* the head of John the .... Mk 6:25   4094
And brought his head in a *c*. .... Mk 6:28   4094

CHARGERS
twelve *c* of silver, twelve silver ...... Num 7:84   7086
thirty *c* of gold, a thousand .... Ezr 1:9   105
of gold, a thousand *c* of silver .... Ezr 1:9   105

CHARGES
and the Levites to their *c*. 2Chr 8:14   4931
c according to their courses 2Chr 31:16   4931
in their *c* by their courses 2Chr 31:17   4931
And he set the priests in their *c*. 2Chr 35:2   4931
be at *c* with them, that they may ....Acts 21:24   1159
a warfare any time at his own *c* 1Cor 9:7   3800

CHARGEST
that thou *c* me to day with a 2Sa 3:8   6485

CHARGING
c the jailer to keep them safely .... Acts 16:23   3853
c them before the Lord that they 2Ti 2:14   1263

CHARIOT
ride in the second *c* which he had .... Gen 41:43   4818
And Joseph made ready his *c* .... Gen 46:29   4818
And he made ready his *c*, and took....... Ex 14:6   7393
And took off their *c* wheels .... Ex 14:25   4818
Sisera lighted down off his *c* .... Judg 4:15   4818
Why is his *c* so long in coming .... Judg 5:28   7393
and David houghed all the *c* horses 2Sa 8:4   7393
was like the work of a *c* wheel 1Kin 7:33   4818
a *c* came up and went out of Egypt 1Kin 10:29   4818
made speed to get him up to his *c* 1Kin 12:18   4818
up, say unto Ahab, Prepare thy *c* 1Kin 18:44   4818
horse for horse, and *c* for *c*. 1Kin 20:25   7393
horse for horse, and *c* for *c*. 1Kin 20:25   7393
caused him to come up into the *c* 1Kin 20:33   4818
he said unto the driver of his *c* 1Kin 22:34   7395
up in his *c* against the Syrians 1Kin 22:35   4818
the wound into the midst of the *c*...........1Kin 22:35   7393
one washed the *c* in the pool of...........1Kin 22:38   7393
there appeared a *c* of fire 2Kin 2:11   7393
the *c* of Israel, and the horsemen 2Kin 2:12   7393
with his horses and with his *c* 2Kin 5:9   7393
down from the *c* to meet him 2Kin 5:21   4818
again from his *c* to meet thee 2Kin 5:26   4818
They took therefore two *c* horses 2Kin 7:14   7393
So Jehu rode in a *c*, and went to...........2Kin 9:16
And his *c* was made ready 2Kin 9:21   7393
of Judah went out, each in his *c*...........2Kin 9:21   7393
heart, and smote him down in his *c*.......2Kin 9:24   7393
and said, Smite him also in the *c*...........2Kin 9:27   4818
carried him in a *c* to Jerusalem 2Kin 9:28
he took him up to him into the *c* 2Kin 10:15   4818
So they made him ride in his *c* 2Kin 10:16   7393
the *c* of Israel, and the horsemen 2Kin 13:14   7393
him in a *c* dead from Megiddo 2Kin 23:30
also houghed all the *c* horses............1Chr 18:4   7393
pattern of the *c* of the cherubims 1Chr 28:18   4818
which he placed in the *c* cities 2Chr 1:14   7393
a *c* for six hundred shekels of 2Chr 1:17   4818
Solomon had, and all the *c* cities 2Chr 8:6   7393
whom he bestowed in the *c* cities 2Chr 9:25   7393
made speed to get him up to his *c* 2Chr 10:18   4818
therefore he said to his *c* man.................2Chr 18:33   7395
c against the Syrians until the 2Chr 18:34   4818
therefore took him out of that *c* 2Chr 35:24   4818
him in the second *c* that he had 2Chr 35:24   7393
he burneth the *c* in the fire.....................Ps 46:9   5699
O God of Jacob, both the *c*. ....Ps 76:6   7393
who maketh the clouds his *c*...................Ps 104:3   7398
a *c* of the wood of Lebanon ....Song 3:9   668
he saw a *c* with a couple of ....Is 21:7   7393
a *c* of asses, and a *c* of..........................Is 21:7   7393
behold, here cometh a *c* of men............Is 21:9   7393
Which bringeth forth the *c*. ....Is 43:17   7393
thee will I break in pieces the *c*..........Jer 51:21   7393
bind the *c* to the swift beast ....Mic 1:13   4818
In the first *c* were red horses ....Zec 6:2   4818
and in the second *c* black horses..........Zec 6:2   4818
And in the third *c* white horses ....Zec 6:3   4818
and in the fourth *c* grisled ....Zec 6:3   4818
I will cut off the *c* from Ephraim ....Zec 9:10   7393
sitting in his *c* read Esaias the ....Acts 8:28   716
near, and join thyself to this *c*. ....Acts 8:29   716
he commanded the *c* to stand still ....Acts 8:38   716

CHARIOTS
And there went up with him both *c*........ Gen 50:9   7393
And he took six hundred chosen *c*.......... Ex 14:7   7393
all the *c* of Egypt, and captains........... Ex 14:7   7393
c of Pharaoh, and his horsemen, and ..... Ex 14:9   7393
and upon all his host, upon his *c* .... Ex 14:17   7393

honour upon Pharaoh, upon his *c* ....Ex 14:18   7393
even all Pharaoh's horses, his *c* ....Ex 14:23   7393
upon the Egyptians, upon their *c* ....Ex 14:26   7393
waters returned, and covered the *c* ....Ex 14:28   7393
Pharaoh's *c* and his host hath he ....Ex 15:4   4818
of Pharaoh went in with his *c* ....Ex 15:19   7393
unto their horses, and to their *c* ....Deut 11:4   7393
enemies, and seest horses, and *c*...........Deut 20:1   7393
with horses and *c* very many ....Josh 11:4   7393
horses, and burn their *c* with fire ....Josh 11:6   4818
and burnt their *c* with fire ....Josh 11:9   4818
land of the valley have *c* of iron ....Josh 17:16   7393
though they have iron *c*, and ....Josh 17:18   7393
pursued after your fathers with *c* ....Josh 24:6   7393
because they had *c* of iron ....Judg 1:19   7393
for he had nine hundred *c* of iron ....Judg 4:3   7393
of Jabin's army, with his *c* ....Judg 4:13   7393
gathered together all his *c* ....Judg 4:13   7393
even nine hundred *c* of iron................Judg 4:13   7393
discomfited Sisera, and all his *c* ....Judg 4:15   7393
But Barak pursued after the *c* ....Judg 4:16   7393
Why tarry the wheels of his *c* ....Judg 5:28   4818
them for himself, for his *c*. 1Sa 8:11   4818
and some shall run before his *c* 1Sa 8:11   4818
of war, and instruments of his *c* 1Sa 8:12   7393
with Israel, thirty thousand *c*.................1Sa 13:5   7393
and, lo, the *c* and horsemen 2Sa 1:6   7393
David took from him a thousand *c*.........2Sa 8:4
reserved of them for an hundred *c* 2Sa 8:4   7393
of seven hundred *c* of the Syrians 2Sa 10:18   7393
this, that Absalom prepared him *c* 2Sa 15:1   4818
and he prepared him *c* and horsemen,...1Kin 1:5   7393
stalls of horses for his *c* 1Kin 4:26   4817
Solomon had, and cities for his *c* 1Kin 9:19   7393
his captains, and rulers of his *c* 1Kin 9:22   7393
And Solomon gathered together *c* 1Kin 10:26   7393
had a thousand and four hundred *c* 1Kin 10:26   7393
he bestowed in the cities for *c*...............1Kin 10:26   7393
Zimri, captain of half his *c*. 1Kin 16:9   7393
kings with him, and horses, and *c* 1Kin 20:1   7393
out, and smote the horses and *c* 1Kin 20:21   7393
captains that had rule over his *c* 1Kin 22:31   7393
captains of the *c* saw Jehoshaphat 1Kin 22:32   7393
when the captains of the *c* 1Kin 22:33   7393
sent he thither horses, and *c* 2Kin 6:14   7393
the city both with horses and *c*...........2Kin 6:15   7393
c of fire round about Elisha 2Kin 6:17   7393
the Syrians to hear a noise of *c* 2Kin 7:6   7393
to Zair, and all the *c* with him 2Kin 8:21   7393
about, and the captains of the *c* 2Kin 8:21   7393
with you, and there are with you *c*...........2Kin 10:2   7393
but fifty horsemen, and ten *c* 2Kin 13:7   7393
and put thy trust on Egypt for *c*............2Kin 18:24   7393
With the multitude of my *c* I am 2Kin 19:23   7393
burned the *c* of the sun with fire 2Kin 23:11   7393
David took from him a thousand *c* 1Chr 18:4   7393
but reserved of them an hundred *c*...........1Chr 18:4   7393
talents of silver to hire them *c* 1Chr 19:6   7393
hired thirty and two thousand *c* 1Chr 19:7   7393
thousand men which fought in *c* 1Chr 19:18   7393
Solomon gathered *c* and horsemen.........2Chr 1:14   7393
had a thousand and four hundred *c* 2Chr 1:14   7393
captains, and captains of his *c* 2Chr 8:9   7393
thousand stalls for horses and *c* 2Chr 9:25   4818
With twelve hundred *c*, and 2Chr 12:3   7393
thousand, and three hundred *c* 2Chr 14:9   4818
a huge host, with very many *c* 2Chr 16:8   7393
of the *c* that were with him 2Chr 18:30   7393
captains of the *c* saw Jehoshaphat 2Chr 18:31   7393
when the captains of the *c* 2Chr 18:32   7393
princes, and all his *c* with him 2Chr 21:9   7393
him in, and the captains of the *c*...........2Chr 21:9   7393
Some trust in *c*, and some in.................Ps 20:7   7393
The *c* of God are twenty thousand,........Ps 68:17   7393
company of horses in Pharaoh's *c* ....Song 1:9   7393
made me like the *c* of Ammi-nadib ....Song 6:12   4818
is there any end of their *c* ....Is 2:7   4818
bare the quiver with *c* of men ....Is 22:6   7393
valleys shall be full of *c* ....Is 22:7   7393
there the *c* of thy glory shall be ....Is 22:18   4818
and stay on horses, and trust in *c* ....Is 31:1   7393
and put thy trust on Egypt for *c*............Is 36:9   7393
By the multitude of my *c* am I ....Is 37:24   7393
with his *c* like a whirlwind, to ....Is 66:15   4818
all nations upon horses, and in *c*...........Is 66:20   7393
his *c* shall be as a whirlwind ....Jer 4:13   4818
the throne of David, riding in *c* ....Jer 17:25   7393
the throne of David, riding in *c* ....Jer 22:4   7393
and rage, ye *c*. ....Jer 46:9   7393
horses, at the rushing of his *c*...............Jer 47:3   7393
their horses, and upon their *c* ....Jer 50:37   7393

shall come against thee with *c*	Eze 23:24	2021
the north, with horses, and with *c*	Eze 26:7	7393
and of the wheels, and of the *c*	Eze 26:10	7393
in precious clothes for *c*	Eze 27:20	7396
at my table with horses and *c*	Eze 39:20	7393
him like a whirlwind, with *c*	Dan 11:40	7393
Like the noise of *c* on the tops	Joel 2:5	4818
of thee, and I will destroy thy *c*	Mic 5:10	4818
the *c* shall be with flaming	Nah 2:3	7393
The *c* shall rage in the streets	Nah 2:4	7393
and I will burn her *c* in the smoke	Nah 2:13	7393
horses, and of the jumping *c*	Nah 3:2	4818
horses and thy *c* of salvation	Hab 3:8	4818
and I will overthrow the *c*	Hag 2:22	4818
there came four *c* out from	Zec 6:1	4818
of *c* of many horses running to	Rev 9:9	716
beasts, and sheep, and horses, and *c*	Rev 18:13	4480

CHARITABLY
thy meat, now walkest thou not *c*	Rom 14:15	2596,26

CHARITY
puffeth up, but *c* edifieth	1Cor 8:1	26
men and of angels, and have not *c*	1Cor 13:1	26
remove mountains, and have not *c*	1Cor 13:2	26
body to be burned, and have not *c*	1Cor 13:3	26
C suffereth long, and is kind	1Cor 13:4	26
c envieth not	1Cor 13:4	26
c vaunteth not itself, is not	1Cor 13:4	26
C never faileth	1Cor 13:8	26
And now abideth faith, hope, *c*	1Cor 13:13	26
but the greatest of these is *c*	1Cor 13:13	26
Follow after *c*, and desire	1Cor 14:1	26
all your things be done with *c*	1Cor 16:14	26
above all these things put on *c*	Col 3:14	26
good tidings of your faith and *c*	1Th 3:6	26
the *c* of every one of you all	2Th 1:3	26
is *c* out of a pure heart, and of a	1Ti 1:5	26
if they continue in faith and *c*	1Ti 2:15	26
in word, in conversation, in *c*	1Ti 4:12	26
follow righteousness, faith, *c*	2Ti 2:22	26
purpose, faith, longsuffering, *c*	2Ti 3:10	26
temperate, sound in faith, in *c*	Titus 2:2	26
have fervent *c* among yourselves	1Pet 4:8	26
for *c* shall cover the multitude	1Pet 4:8	26
ye one another with a kiss of *c*	1Pet 5:14	26
and to brotherly kindness *c*	2Pet 1:7	26
of thy *c* before the church	3Jn 6	26
are spots in your feasts of *c*	Jude 12	26
I know thy works, and *c*, and	Rev 2:19	26

CHARMED
among you, which will not be *c*	Jer 8:17	3908

CHARMER
Or a *c*, or a consulter with	Deut 18:11	2266,2267

CHARMERS
not hearken to the voice of *c*	Ps 58:5	3907
seek to the idols, and to the *c*	Is 19:3	328

CHARMING
of charmers, *c* never so wisely	Ps 58:5	2266,2267

CHARRAN (car'-ran) See HARAN. Greek form of Haran.
Mesopotamia, before he dwelt in *C*	Acts 7:2	5488
of the Chaldaeans, and dwelt in *C*	Acts 7:4	5488

CHASE
ye shall *c* your enemies, and they	Lev 26:7	7291
And five of you shall *c* an hundred	Lev 26:8	7291
of a shaken leaf shall *c* them	Lev 26:36	7291
How should one *c* a thousand	Deut 32:30	7291
One man of you shall *c* a thousand	Josh 23:10	7291
let the angel of the LORD *c* them	Ps 35:5	1760

CHASED
c you, as bees do, and destroyed	Deut 1:44	7291
for they *c* them from before the	Josh 7:5	7291
wilderness wherein they *c* them	Josh 8:24	7291
c them along the way that goeth	Josh 10:10	7291
c them unto great Zidon, and unto	Josh 11:8	7291
And Abimelech *c* him, and he fled	Judg 9:40	7291
c them, and trode them down with	Judg 20:43	7291
therefore I *c* him from me	Neh 13:28	1272
darkness, and *c* out of the world	Job 18:18	5074
he shall be *c* away as a vision of	Job 20:8	5074
And it shall be as the *c* roe	Is 13:14	5080
shall be *c* as the chaff of the	Is 17:13	7291
Mine enemies *c* me sore, like a	Lam 3:52	6679

CHASETH
c away his mother, is a son that	Prov 19:26	1272

CHASING
from *c* after the Philistines	1Sa 17:53	1814

CHASTE
you as a *c* virgin to Christ	2Cor 11:2	53
To be discreet, *c*, keepers at	Titus 2:5	53
While they behold your *c*	1Pet 3:2	53

CHASTEN
I will *c* him with the rod of men,	2Sa 7:14	3198
anger, neither *c* me in thy hot	Ps 6:1	3256
neither *c* me in thy hot	Ps 38:1	3256
C thy son while there is hope, and	Prov 19:18	3256
to *c* thyself before thy God, thy	Dan 10:12	6031
As many as I love, I rebuke and *c*	Rev 3:19	3811

CHASTENED
and that, when they have *c* him	Deut 21:18	3256
He is *c* also with pain upon his	Job 33:19	3198
c my soul with fasting, that was	Ps 69:10	3256
been plagued, and *c* every morning	Ps 73:14	8433
The LORD hath *c* me sore	Ps 118:18	3256
we are *c* of the Lord, that we	1Cor 11:32	3811
as *c*, and not killed	2Cor 6:9	3811
c us after their own pleasure	Heb 12:10	3811

CHASTENEST
Blessed is the man whom thou *c*	Ps 94:12	3256

CHASTENETH
heart, that, as a man *c* his son	Deut 8:5	3256
son, so the LORD thy God *c* thee	Deut 8:5	3256
he that loveth him *c* him betimes	Prov 13:24	4148
For whom the Lord loveth he *c*	Heb 12:6	3811
son is he whom the father *c* not	Heb 12:7	3811

CHASTENING
not thou the *c* of the Almighty	Job 5:17	4148
despise not the *c* of the LORD	Prov 3:11	4148
a prayer when thy *c* was upon them	Is 26:16	4148
not thou the *c* of the Lord	Heb 12:5	3809
If ye endure *c*, God dealeth with	Heb 12:7	3809
Now no *c* for the present seemeth	Heb 12:11	3809

CHASTISE
will *c* you seven times for your	Lev 26:28	3256
city shall take that man and *c* him	Deut 22:18	3256
but I will *c* you with scorpions	1Kin 12:11	3256
but I will *c* you with scorpions	1Kin 12:14	3256
but I will *c* you with scorpions	2Chr 10:11	
but I will *c* you with scorpions	2Chr 10:14	
I will *c* them, as their	Hos 7:12	3256
in my desire that I should *c* them	Hos 10:10	3256
I will therefore *c* him, and	Lk 23:16	3811
I will therefore *c* him, and let	Lk 23:22	3811

CHASTISED
my father hath *c* you with whips	1Kin 12:11	3256
my father also *c* you with whips	1Kin 12:14	3256
my father *c* you with whips, but I	2Chr 10:11	3256
my father *c* you with whips, but I	2Chr 10:14	3256
hast *c* me, and I was *c*	Jer 31:18	3256

CHASTISEMENT
seen the *c* of the LORD your God	Deut 11:2	4148
be said unto God, I have borne *c*	Job 34:31	
the *c* of our peace was upon him	Is 53:5	4148
with the *c* of a cruel one, for	Jer 30:14	4148
But if ye be without *c*, whereof	Heb 12:8	3809

CHASTISETH
He that *c* the heathen, shall not	Ps 94:10	3256

CHATTER
a crane or a swallow, so did I *c*	Is 38:14	6850

CHEBAR (ke'-bar) A river in Mesopotamia.
the captives by the river of *C*	Eze 1:1	3529
of the Chaldeans by the river *C*	Eze 1:3	3529
that dwelt by the river of *C*	Eze 3:15	3529
which I saw by the river of *C*	Eze 3:23	3529
that I saw by the river of *C*	Eze 10:15	3529
God of Israel by the river *C*	Eze 10:20	3529
which I saw by the river of *C*	Eze 10:22	3529
vision that I saw by the river *C*	Eze 43:3	3529

CHECK
I have heard the *c* of my reproach	Job 20:3	4148

CHECKER
And nets of *c* work, and wreaths of	1Kin 7:17	7639

CHEDORLAOMER (ke'-dor-la'-o-mer) An Elamite king.
C king of Elam, and Tidal king of	Gen 14:1	3540
Twelve years they served *C*	Gen 14:4	3540
And in the fourteenth year came *C*	Gen 14:5	3540
With *C* the king of Elam, and with	Gen 14:9	3540
return from the slaughter of *C*	Gen 14:17	3540

CHEEK
near, and smote Micaiah on the *c*	1Kin 22:24	3895
near, and smote Micaiah upon the *c*	2Chr 18:23	3895

me upon the *c* reproachfully	Job 16:10	3895
all mine enemies upon the *c* bone	Ps 3:7	3895
He giveth his *c* to him that	Lam 3:30	3895
he hath the *c* teeth of a great	Joel 1:6	4973
of Israel with a rod upon the *c*	Mic 5:1	3895
shall smite thee on thy right *c*	Mt 5:39	4600
on the one *c* **offer also the other**	Lk 6:29	4600

CHEEKS

priest the shoulder, and the two *c*	Deut 18:3	3895
Thy *c* are comely with rows of	Song 1:10	3895
His *c* are as a bed of spices, as	Song 5:13	3895
my *c* to them that plucked off the	Is 50:6	3895
night, and her tears are on her *c*	Lam 1:2	3895

CHEER

shall *c* up his wife which he hath	Deut 24:5	8055
let thy heart *c* thee in the days	Eccl 11:9	3190
Son, be of good *c*	Mt 9:2	2293
unto them, saying, Be of good *c*	Mt 14:27	2293
and saith unto them, Be of good *c*	Mk 6:50	2293
but be of good *c*	Jn 16:33	2293
by him, and said, Be of good *c*	Acts 23:11	2293
now I exhort you to be of good *c*	Acts 27:22	2114
Wherefore, sirs, be of good *c*	Acts 27:25	2114
Then were they all of good *c*	Acts 27:36	2114

CHEERETH

I leave my wine, which *c* God	Judg 9:13	8055

CHEERFUL

heart maketh a *c* countenance	Prov 15:13	3190
joy and gladness, and *c* feasts	Zec 8:19	2896
corn shall make the young men *c*	Zec 9:17	5107
for God loveth a *c* giver	2Cor 9:7	2431

CHEERFULLY

I do the more *c* answer for myself	Acts 24:10	2115

CHEERFULNESS

he that sheweth mercy, with *c*	Rom 12:8	2432

CHEESE

c of kine, for David, and for the	2Sa 17:29	8194
out as milk, and curdled me like *c*	Job 10:10	1385

CHEESES

carry these ten *c* unto the	1Sa 17:18	2757,2461

CHELAL (ke'-lal) *Married a foreign wife in exile.*

Adna, and *C*, Benaiah, Maaseiah,	Ezr 10:30	3636

CHELLUH (kel'-loo) *Married a foreign wife in exile.*

Benaiah, Bedeiah, *C*,	Ezr 10:35	3622

CHELUB (ke'-lub)
  1. A descendant of Caleb.

C the brother of Shuah begat	1Chr 4:11	3620

  2. Father of Ezri.

the ground was Ezri the son of *C*	1Chr 27:26	3620

CHELUBAI (ke-loo'-ba-hee) *Son of Hezron.*

Jerahmeel, and Ram, and *C*	1Chr 2:9	3621

CHELUH See CHELLUH.

CHELUHI See CHELLUH.

CHEMARIMS (kem'-a-rims) *Idolatrous priests of Judah.*

the name of the *C* with the	Zeph 1:4	3649

CHEMOSH (ke'-mosh) *A Moabite god.*

thou art undone, O people of *C*	Num 21:29	3645
not thou possess that which *C* thy	Judg 11:24	3645
Solomon build an high place for *C*	1Kin 11:7	3645
C the god of the Moabites, and	1Kin 11:33	3645
for *C* the abomination of the	2Kin 23:13	3645
C shall go forth into captivity	Jer 48:7	3645
And Moab shall be ashamed of *C*	Jer 48:13	3645
the people of *C* perisheth	Jer 48:46	3645

CHENAANAH (ke-na'-a-nah)
  1. Father of Zedekiah.

Zedekiah the son of *C* made him	1Kin 22:11	3668
Zedekiah the son of *C* went near	1Kin 22:24	3668
Zedekiah the son of *C* had made	2Chr 18:10	3668
Zedekiah the son of *C* came near	2Chr 18:23	3668

  2. Brother of Ehud.

Jeush, and Benjamin, and Ehud, and *C*	1Chr 7:10	3668

CHENANI (ken'-a-ni) *A Levite helper of Ezra.*

Bunni, Sherebiah, Bani, and *C*	Neh 9:4	3662

CHENANIAH (ken-a-ni'-ah) See CONONIAH.
  1. A chief Levite during David's reign.

And *C*, chief of the Levites, was	1Chr 15:22	3663
C the master of the song with the	1Chr 15:27	3663

  2. An officer in David's army.

Of the Izharites, *C* and his sons	1Chr 26:29	3663

CHEPHAR-AMMONI See CHEPHAR-HAAMMONAI.

CHEPHAR-HAAMMONAI (ke'-far-ha-am'-mo-nahee) *A town in Benjamin.*

And *C*, and Ophni, and Gaba	Josh 18:24	3726

CHEPHIRAH (ke-fi'-rah) *A Hittite village in Benjamin.*

their cities were Gibeon, and *C*	Josh 9:17	3716
And Mizpeh, and *C*, and Mozah,	Josh 18:26	3716
The children of Kirjath-arim, *C*	Ezr 2:25	3716
The men of Kirjath-jearim, *C*	Neh 7:29	3716

CHERAN (ke'-ran) *Son of Dishon.*

and Eshban, and Ithran, and *C*	Gen 36:26	3763
and Eshban, and Ithran, and *C*	1Chr 1:41	3763

CHERETHIMS (ker'-e-thims) See CHERETHITES. *A Philistine tribe.*

and I will cut off the *C*, and	Eze 25:16	3774

CHERETHITES (ker'-e-thites) See CHERETHIMS.
  1. Same as Cherethims.

invasion upon the south of the *C*	1Sa 30:14	3774
sea coast, the nation of the *C*	Zeph 2:5	3774

  2. Executioners and runners in David's army.

of Jehoiada was over both the *C*	2Sa 8:18	3774
and all the *C*, and all the	2Sa 15:18	3774
after him Joab's men, and the *C*	2Sa 20:7	3774
son of Jehoiada was over the *C*	2Sa 20:23	3774
the son of Jehoiada, and the *C*	1Kin 1:38	3746
the son of Jehoiada, and the *C*	1Kin 1:44	3774
son of Jehoiada was over the *C*	1Chr 18:17	3774

CHERISH

before the king, and let her *c* him	1Kin 1:2	5532

CHERISHED

c the king, and ministered to him	1Kin 1:4	5532

CHERISHETH

c it, even as the Lord the church	Eph 5:29	2282
even as a nurse *c* her children	1Th 2:7	2282

CHERITH (ke'-rith) *A brook in Gilead.*

and hide thyself by the brook *C*	1Kin 17:3	3747
he went and dwelt by the brook *C*	1Kin 17:5	3747

CHERUB (ke'-rub)
  1. A winged celestial being.

make one *c* on the one end, and the	Ex 25:19	3742
the other *c* on the other end	Ex 25:19	3742
One *c* on the end on this side, and	Ex 37:8	3742
another *c* on the other end on	Ex 37:8	3742
And he rode upon a *c*, and did fly	2Sa 22:11	3742
cubits was the one wing of the *c*	1Kin 6:24	3742
cubits the other wing of the *c*	1Kin 6:24	3742
the other *c* was ten cubits	1Kin 6:25	3742
of the one *c* was ten cubits	1Kin 6:26	3742
and so was it of the other *c*	1Kin 6:26	3742
the wing of the other *c* touched	1Kin 6:27	3742
wing of the one *c* was five cubits	2Chr 3:11	
to the wing of the other *c*	2Chr 3:11	3742
of the other *c* was five cubits	2Chr 3:12	3742
to the wing of the other *c*	2Chr 3:12	3742
And he rode upon a *c*, and did fly	Ps 18:10	3742
of Israel was gone up from the *c*	Eze 9:3	3742
the wheels, even under the *c*	Eze 10:2	3742
of the LORD went up from the *c*	Eze 10:4	3742
one *c* stretched forth his hand	Eze 10:7	3742
the cherubims, one wheel by one *c*	Eze 10:9	3742
and another wheel by another *c*	Eze 10:9	3742
first face was of a *c*	Eze 10:14	3742
art the anointed *c* that covereth	Eze 28:14	3742
I will destroy thee, O covering *c*	Eze 28:16	3742
tree was between a *c* and a *c*	Eze 41:18	3742
and every *c* had two faces	Eze 41:18	3742

  2. An exile who returned with Zerubbabel.

up from Tel-melah, Tel-harsa, *C*	Ezr 2:59	3743
from Tel-melah, Tel-haresha, *C*	Neh 7:61	3743

CHERUBIMS

the east of the garden of Eden *C*	Gen 3:24	3742
And thou shalt make two *c* of gold	Ex 25:18	3742
the *c* on the two ends thereof	Ex 25:18	3742
the *c* shall stretch forth their	Ex 25:20	3742
seat shall the faces of the *c* be	Ex 25:20	3742
from between the two *c* which are	Ex 25:22	3742
with *c* of cunning work shalt thou	Ex 26:1	3742
with *c* shall it be made	Ex 26:31	3742
with *c* of cunning work made he	Ex 36:8	3742
with *c* made he it of cunning work	Ex 36:35	3742
And he made two *c* of gold, beaten	Ex 37:7	3742
he the *c* on the two ends thereof	Ex 37:8	3742
the *c* spread out their wings on	Ex 37:9	3742
seatward were the faces of the *c*	Ex 37:9	3742
testimony, from between the two *c*	Num 7:89	3742

which dwelleth between the *c* 1Sa 4:4   3742
hosts that dwelleth between the *c* 2Sa 6:2   3742
he made two *c* of olive tree...................... 1Kin 6:23   3742
both the *c* were of one measure and....... 1Kin 6:25   3742
he set the *c* within the inner.................... 1Kin 6:27   3742
forth the wings of the *c*, so that 1Kin 6:27   3742
And he overlaid the *c* with gold 1Kin 6:28   3742
about with carved figures of *c* 1Kin 6:29   3742
he carved upon them carvings of *c* 1Kin 6:32   3742
gold, and spread gold upon the *c* 1Kin 6:32   3742
And he carved thereon *c* and palm 1Kin 6:35   3742
the ledges were lions, oxen, and *c* 1Kin 7:29   3742
the borders thereof, he graved *c* 1Kin 7:36   3742
even under the wings of the *c* 1Kin 8:6   3742
For the *c* spread forth their two 1Kin 8:7   3742
the *c* covered the ark and the 1Kin 8:7   3742
which dwelleth between the *c*................... 2Kin 19:15   3742
Lord, that dwelleth between the *c* 1Chr 13:6   3742
pattern of the chariot of the *c* 1Chr 28:18   3742
and graved *c* on the walls........................ 2Chr 3:7   3742
house he made two *c* of image work 2Chr 3:10   3742
the wings of the *c* were twenty 2Chr 3:11   3742
The wings of these *c* spread.................... 2Chr 3:13   3742
fine linen, and wrought *c* thereon 2Chr 3:14   3742
even under the wings of the *c* 2Chr 5:7   3742
For the *c* spread forth their 2Chr 5:8   3742
the *c* covered the ark and the 2Chr 5:8   3742
thou that dwellest between the *c* .... Ps 80:1   3742
he sitteth between the *c*.......................... Ps 99:1   3742
that dwellest between the *c* .... Is 37:16   3742
c there appeared over them as it .... Eze 10:1   3742
coals of fire from between the *c* .... Eze 10:2   3742
Now the *c* stood on the right side .... Eze 10:3   3742
the wheels, from between the *c*............... Eze 10:6   3742
c unto the fire that was between .... Eze 10:7   3742
the fire that was between the *c*............... Eze 10:7   3742
there appeared in the *c* the form .... Eze 10:8   3742
behold the four wheels by the *c* .... Eze 10:9   3742
And the *c* were lifted up .... Eze 10:15   3742
And when the *c* went, the wheels .... Eze 10:16   3742
when the *c* lifted up their wings .... Eze 10:16   3742
of the house, and stood over the *c* .... Eze 10:18   3742
the *c* lifted up their wings, and .... Eze 10:19   3742
and I knew that they were the *c* .... Eze 10:20   3742
Then did the *c* lift up their .... Eze 11:22   3742
And it was made with *c* and palm .... Eze 41:18   3742
ground unto above the door were *c* .... Eze 41:20   3742
on the doors of the temple, *c* .... Eze 41:25   3742
over it the *c* of glory shadowing .... Heb 9:5   5502

CHERUBIMS'
the sound of the *c* wings was .... Eze 10:5   3742

CHESALON (kes'-a-lon) *A landmark in Judah.*
side of mount Jearim, which is *C* .... Josh 15:10   3693

CHESED (ke'-sed) *A son of Nahor.*
And *C*, and Hazo, and Pildash, and....... Gen 22:22   3777

CHESIL (ke'-sil) *A Canaanite town.*
And Eltolad, and *C*, and Hormah,.......... Josh 15:30   3686

CHESNUT
poplar, and of the hazel and *c* tree .... Gen 30:37   6196
the *c* trees were not like his .... Eze 31:8   6196

CHEST
But Jehoiada the priest took a *c* 2Kin 12:9   727
there was much money in the *c*............... 2Kin 12:10   727
king's commandment they made a *c* 2Chr 24:8   727
and brought in, and cast into the *c* 2Chr 24:10   727
that at what time the *c* was 2Chr 24:11   727
officer came and emptied the *c*............... 2Chr 24:11   727

CHESTS
in *c* of rich apparel, bound with.............. Eze 27:24   1595

CHESULLOTH (ke-sul'-loth) *See CHISLOTH-TABOR. A town in Issachar.*
border was toward Jezreel, and *C* .... Josh 19:18   3694

CHEW
ye not eat of them that *c* the cud .... Lev 11:4   5927
not eat of them that *c* the cud................ Deut 14:7   5927
for they *c* the cud, but divide .... Deut 14:7   5927

CHEWED
between their teeth, ere it was *c* .... Num 11:33   3772

CHEWETH
c the cud, among the beasts, that .... Lev 11:3   5927
the camel, because he *c* the cud .... Lev 11:4   5927
the coney, because he *c* the cud .... Lev 11:5   5927
And the hare, because he *c* the cud....... Lev 11:6   5927
yet he *c* not the cud................................ Lev 11:7   1647
nor *c* the cud, are unclean unto .... Lev 11:26   5927

c the cud among the beasts, that .... Deut 14:6   5927
yet *c* not the cud, it is unclean .... Deut 14:8

CHEZIB (ke'-zib) *See ACHZIB, CHOZEBA. A Canaanite village.*
and he was at *C*, when she bare him ..... Gen 38:5   3580

CHICKENS
gathereth her *c* under her wings .... Mt 23:37   *3556*

CHIDE
the people did *c* with Moses .... Ex 17:2   7378
said unto them, Why *c* ye with me .... Ex 17:2   7378
they did *c* with him sharply................... Judg 8:1   7378
He will not always *c*.............................. Ps 103:9   7378

CHIDING
because of the *c* of the children............. Ex 17:7   7379

CHIDON (ki'-don) *See NACHON. Place where Uzzah died.*
came unto the threshingfloor of *C* 1Chr 13:9   3592

CHIEF
Phichol the *c* captain of his host .... Gen 21:22
Phichol the *c* captain of his host .... Gen 21:32
Phichol the *c* captain of his army .... Gen 26:26
against the *c* of the butlers, and .... Gen 40:2   8269
against the *c* of the bakers..................... Gen 40:2   8269
the *c* butler told his dream to .... Gen 40:9   8269
When the *c* baker saw that the.............. Gen 40:16   8269
up the head of the *c* butler .... Gen 40:20   8269
of the *c* baker among his servants .... Gen 40:20   8269
he restored the *c* butler unto his .... Gen 40:21   8269
But he hanged the *c* baker .... Gen 40:22   8269
Yet did not the *c* butler remember......... Gen 40:23   8269
Then spake the *c* butler unto .... Gen 41:9   8269
house, both me and the *c* baker............. Gen 41:10   8269
being a *c* man among his people, ... Lev 21:4   1167
the *c* of the house of the father .... Num 3:24   5387
the *c* of the house of the father .... Num 3:30   5387
c over the *c* of the Levites .... Num 3:32   5387
the *c* of the house of the father .... Num 3:35   5387
the *c* of the congregation .... Num 4:34   5387
the *c* of Israel numbered, after.............. Num 4:46   5387
a prince of a *c* house among .... Num 25:14   1
people, and of a *c* house in Midian........ Num 25:15   1
the *c* fathers of the congregation .... Num 31:26   7218
the *c* fathers of the tribes of .... Num 32:28   7218
the *c* fathers of the families of .... Num 36:1   7218
the *c* fathers of the children of .... Num 36:1   7218
So I took the *c* of your tribes,................. Deut 1:15   7218
for the *c* things of the ancient .... Deut 33:15   7218
princes, of each *c* house a prince............ Josh 22:14   1
the *c* of all the people, even of .... Judg 20:2   6438
hither, all the *c* of the people 1Sa 14:38   6438
the *c* of the things which should 1Sa 15:21   7225
of David's soul, he shall be *c* 2Sa 5:8
and David's sons were *c* rulers............... 2Sa 8:18   3548
Jairite was a *c* ruler about David 2Sa 20:26   3548
in the seat, *c* among the captains 2Sa 23:8   7218
three of the thirty *c* went down.............. 2Sa 23:13   7218
son of Zeruiah, was *c* among three........ 2Sa 23:18   7218
Beside the *c* of Solomon's....................... 1Kin 5:16   8269
the *c* of the fathers of the 1Kin 8:1   5387
These were the *c* of the officers 1Kin 9:23   8269
the hands of the *c* of the guard.............. 1Kin 14:27   8269
guard took Seraiah the *c* priest 2Kin 25:18   7218
and of him came the *c* ruler 1Chr 5:2   5059
was reckoned, were the *c*, Jeiel, ... 1Chr 5:7   7218
Joel the *c*, and Shapham the next,......... 1Chr 5:12   7218
c of the house of their fathers................ 1Chr 5:15   7218
all of them *c* men.................................. 1Chr 7:3   7218
men of valour, *c* of the princes 1Chr 7:40   7218
by their generations, *c* men 1Chr 8:28   7218
All these men were *c* of the 1Chr 9:9   7218
Shallum was the *c*................................. 1Chr 9:17   7218
these Levites, the four *c* porters 1Chr 9:26   1368
c of the fathers of the Levites................. 1Chr 9:33   7218
These *c* fathers of the Levites................ 1Chr 9:34   7218
fathers of the Levites were *c*.................. 1Chr 9:34   7218
the Jebusites first shall be *c* 1Chr 11:6   7218
Zeruiah went first up, and was *c* 1Chr 11:6   7218
These also are the *c* of the 1Chr 11:10   7218
Hachmonite, the *c* of the captains 1Chr 11:11   7218
of Joab, he was *c* of the three 1Chr 11:20   7218
The *c* was Ahiezer, then Joash,.............. 1Chr 12:3   7218
who was *c* of the captains, and he......... 1Chr 12:18   7218
Uriel the *c*, and his brethren an............ 1Chr 15:5   8269
Asaiah the *c*, and his brethren two 1Chr 15:6   8269
Joel the *c*, and his brethren an 1Chr 15:7   8269
Shemaiah the *c*, and his brethren 1Chr 15:8   8269
Eliel the *c*, and his brethren 1Chr 15:9   8269
Amminadab the *c*, and his brethren 1Chr 15:10   8269

C

Ye are the *c* of the fathers of	1Chr 15:12	7218
David spake to the *c* of the	1Chr 15:16	8269
c of the Levites, was for song	1Chr 15:22	8269
Asaph the *c*, and next to him	1Chr 16:5	7218
of David were *c* about the king	1Chr 18:17	7223
the *c* was Jehiel, and Zetham, and	1Chr 23:8	7218
These were the *c* of the fathers	1Chr 23:9	7218
And Jahath was the *c*, and Zizah the	1Chr 23:11	7218
of Gershom, Shebuel was the *c*	1Chr 23:16	7218
of Eliezer were, Rehabiah the *c*	1Chr 23:17	7218
Shelomith the *c*	1Chr 23:18	7218
even the *c* of the fathers, as	1Chr 23:24	7218
there were more *c* men found of	1Chr 24:4	7218
c men of the house of their	1Chr 24:4	7218
before the *c* of the fathers of	1Chr 24:6	7218
the *c* of the fathers of the	1Chr 24:31	7218
Simri the *c*, (for though he was	1Chr 26:10	7218
yet his father made him the *c*	1Chr 26:10	7218
the porters, even among the *c* men	1Chr 26:12	7218
c fathers, even of Laadan the	1Chr 26:21	7218
the *c* fathers, the captains over	1Chr 26:26	7218
the Hebronites was Jerijah the *c*	1Chr 26:31	7218
and seven hundred *c* fathers	1Chr 26:32	7218
the *c* fathers and captains of	1Chr 27:1	7218
the children of Perez was the *c*	1Chr 27:3	7218
the son of Jehoiada, a *c* priest	1Chr 27:5	7218
Then the *c* of the fathers and	1Chr 29:6	8269
the Lord to be the *c* governor	1Chr 29:22	5057
all Israel, the *c* of the fathers	2Chr 1:2	7218
the *c* of the fathers of the	2Chr 5:2	5387
c of his captains, and captains of	2Chr 8:9	8269
And these were the *c* of king	2Chr 8:10	8269
Abijah the son of Maachah the *c*	2Chr 11:22	7218
the hands of the *c* of the guard	2Chr 12:10	8269
Adnah the *c*, and with him mighty	2Chr 17:14	8269
of the *c* of the fathers of Israel	2Chr 19:8	7218
Amariah the *c* priest is over you	2Chr 19:11	7218
the *c* of the fathers of Israel,	2Chr 23:2	7218
king called for Jehoiada the *c*	2Chr 24:6	7218
The whole number of the *c* of the	2Chr 26:12	7218
And Azariah the *c* priest, and all	2Chr 26:20	7218
Azariah the *c* priest of the house	2Chr 31:10	7218
c of the Levites, gave unto the	2Chr 35:9	8269
Moreover all the *c* of the priests	2Chr 36:14	8269
Then rose up the *c* of the fathers	Ezr 1:5	7218
some of the *c* of the fathers,	Ezr 2:68	7218
c of the fathers, who were	Ezr 3:12	7218
to the *c* of the fathers, and said	Ezr 4:2	7218
the rest of the *c* of the fathers	Ezr 4:3	7218
the men that were the *c* of them	Ezr 5:10	7217
the son of Aaron the *c* priest	Ezr 7:5	7218
of Israel *c* men to go up with me	Ezr 7:28	7218
are now the *c* of their fathers	Ezr 8:1	7218
and for Meshullam, *c* men	Ezr 8:16	7218
Iddo the *c* at the place Casiphia	Ezr 8:17	7218
twelve of the *c* of the priests	Ezr 8:24	8269
them before the *c* of the priests	Ezr 8:29	8269
c of the fathers of Israel, at	Ezr 8:29	8269
hath been *c* in this trespass	Ezr 9:2	7223
arose Ezra, and made the *c* priests	Ezr 10:5	8269
with certain of the *c* of the fathers,	Ezr 10:16	7218
some of the *c* of the fathers gave	Neh 7:70	7218
some of the *c* of the fathers gave	Neh 7:71	7218
the *c* of the fathers of all the	Neh 8:13	7218
The *c* of the people	Neh 10:14	7218
Now these are the *c* of the	Neh 11:3	7218
c of the fathers, two hundred	Neh 11:13	7218
of the *c* of the Levites, had the	Neh 11:14	7218
These were the *c* of the priests	Neh 12:7	7218
priests, the *c* of the fathers	Neh 12:12	7218
were recorded *c* of the fathers	Neh 12:22	7218
the *c* of the fathers, were	Neh 12:23	7218
And the *c* of the Levites	Neh 12:24	7218
old there were *c* of the singers	Neh 12:46	7218
the *c* of the people of the earth	Job 12:24	7218
I chose out their way, and sat *c*	Job 29:25	7218
He is the *c* of the ways of God	Job 40:19	7225
To the *c* Musician upon Neginoth, A	Ps 4:t	5329
To the *c* Musician upon Nehiloth, A	Ps 5:t	5329
To the *c* Musician on Neginoth	Ps 6:t	5329
To the *c* Musician upon Gittith, A	Ps 8:t	
To the *c* Musician upon	Ps 9:t	5329
To the *c* Musician, A Psalm of	Ps 11:t	5329
To the *c* Musician upon Sheminith,	Ps 12:t	5329
To the *c* Musician, A Psalm of	Ps 13:t	5329
To the *c* Musician, A Psalm of	Ps 14:t	5329
To the *c* Musician, A Psalm of	Ps 18:t	5329
To the *c* Musician, A Psalm of	Ps 19:t	5329
To the *c* Musician, A Psalm of	Ps 20:t	5329
To the *c* Musician, A Psalm of	Ps 21:t	5329
To the *c* Musician upon Aijeleth	Ps 22:t	5329
To the *c* Musician, A Psalm of	Ps 31:t	5329
To the *c* Musician, A Psalm of	Ps 36:t	5329
To the *c* Musician, even to	Ps 39:t	5329
To the *c* Musician, A Psalm of	Ps 40:t	5329
To the *c* Musician, A Psalm of	Ps 41:t	5329
To the *c* Musician, Maschil, for	Ps 42:t	5329
To the *c* Musician for the sons of	Ps 44:t	5329
To the *c* Musician upon Shoshannim	Ps 45:t	5329
To the *c* Musician for the sons of	Ps 46:t	5329
To the *c* Musician, A Psalm for	Ps 47:t	5329
To the *c* Musician, A Psalm of	Ps 49:t	5329
To the *c* Musician, A Psalm of	Ps 51:t	5329
To the *c* Musician, Maschil, A	Ps 52:t	5329
To the *c* Musician upon Mahalath,	Ps 53:t	5329
To the *c* Musician on Neginoth,	Ps 54:t	5329
To the *c* Musician on Neginoth,	Ps 55:t	5329
To the *c* Musician upon	Ps 56:t	5329
To the *c* Musician, Altaschith,	Ps 57:t	5329
To the *c* Musician, Altaschith,	Ps 58:t	5329
To the *c* Musician, Altaschith,	Ps 59:t	5329
To the *c* Musician upon	Ps 60:t	5329
To the *c* Musician upon Neginah, A	Ps 61:t	5329
To the *c* Musician, to Jeduthun, A	Ps 62:t	5329
To the *c* Musician, A Psalm of	Ps 64:t	5329
To the *c* Musician, A Psalm and	Ps 65:t	5329
To the *c* Musician, A Song or	Ps 66:t	5329
To the *c* Musician on Neginoth, A	Ps 67:t	5329
To the *c* Musician, A Psalm or	Ps 68:t	5329
To the *c* Musician upon Shoshannim	Ps 69:t	5329
To the *c* Musician, A Psalm of	Ps 70:t	5329
To the *c* Musician, Altaschith, A	Ps 75:t	5329
To the *c* Musician on Neginoth, A	Ps 76:t	5329
To the *c* Musician, to Jeduthun, A	Ps 77:t	5329
the *c* of their strength in the	Ps 78:51	7725
To the *c* Musician upon	Ps 80:t	5329
To the *c* Musician upon Gittith, A	Ps 81:t	5329
To the *c* Musician upon Gittith, A	Ps 84:t	5329
To the *c* Musician, A Psalm for	Ps 85:t	5329
for the sons of Korah to the *c*	Ps 88:t	5329
the *c* of all their strength	Ps 105:36	7725
To the *c* Musician, A Psalm of	Ps 109:t	5329
not Jerusalem above my *c* joy	Ps 137:6	7218
To the *c* Musician, A Psalm of	Ps 139:t	5329
To the *c* Musician, A Psalm of	Ps 140:t	5329
She crieth in the *c* place of	Prov 1:21	7218
a whisperer separateth *c* friends	Prov 16:28	441
and aloes, with all the *c* spices	Song 4:14	7218
even all the *c* ones of the earth	Is 14:9	6260
thee from the *c* men thereof	Is 41:9	678
to be captains, and as *c* over thee	Jer 13:21	7218
who was also *c* governor in the	Jer 20:1	5051
shout among the *c* of the nations	Jer 31:7	7218
bow of Elam, the *c* of their might	Jer 49:35	7225
guard took Seraiah the *c* priest	Jer 52:24	7218
Her adversaries are the *c*	Lam 1:5	7218
in thy fairs with *c* of all spices	Eze 27:22	7218
the *c* prince of Meshech and Tubal,	Eze 38:2	7218
the *c* prince of Meshech and Tubal	Eze 38:3	7218
the *c* prince of Meshech and Tubal	Eze 39:1	7218
c of the governors over all the	Dan 2:48	7229
lo, Michael, one of the *c* princes	Dan 10:13	7223
the *c* of the children of Ammon	Dan 11:41	7225
which are named *c* of the nations	Amos 6:1	7225
themselves with the *c* ointments	Amos 6:6	7225
To the *c* singer on my stringed	Hab 3:19	5329
he had gathered all the *c* priests	Mt 2:4	749
c priests and scribes, and be	Mt 16:21	749
be betrayed unto the *c* priests	Mt 20:18	749
And whosoever will be *c* among you	Mt 20:27	4413
And when the *c* priests and scribes	Mt 21:15	749
the *c* priests and the elders of	Mt 21:23	749
And when the *c* priests and	Mt 21:45	749
the *c* seats in the synagogues,	Mt 23:6	4410
assembled together the *c* priests	Mt 26:3	749
Iscariot, went unto the *c* priests	Mt 26:14	749
and staves, from the *c* priests	Mt 26:47	749
Now the *c* priests, and elders, and	Mt 26:59	749
was come, all the *c* priests	Mt 27:1	749
pieces of silver to the *c* priests	Mt 27:3	749
the *c* priests took the silver	Mt 27:6	749
he was accused of the *c* priests	Mt 27:12	749
But the *c* priests and elders	Mt 27:20	749
Likewise also the *c* priests	Mt 27:41	749
the *c* priests and Pharisees came	Mt 27:62	749
shewed unto the *c* priests all the	Mt 28:11	749
captains, and *c* estates of Galilee	Mk 6:21	4413
of the *c* priests, and scribes, and	Mk 8:31	749
be delivered unto the *c* priests	Mk 10:33	749
c priests heard it, and sought how	Mk 11:18	749
there come to him the *c* priests	Mk 11:27	749
the *c* seats in the synagogues, and	Mk 12:39	4410

the *c* priests and the scribes .... Mk 14:1   749
twelve, went unto the *c* priests .... Mk 14:10   749
and staves, from the *c* priest .... Mk 14:43   749
were assembled all the *c* priests .... Mk 14:53   749
the *c* priests and all the council .... Mk 14:55   749
the *c* priests held a consultation .... Mk 15:1   749
the *c* priests accused him of many .... Mk 15:3   749
For he knew that the *c* priests .... Mk 15:10   749
But the *c* priests moved the .... Mk 15:11   749
Likewise also the *c* priests .... Mk 15:31   749
c priests and scribes, and be slain .... Lk 9:22   749
Beelzebub the *c* of the devils .... Lk 11:15   758
into the house of one of the *c* .... Lk 14:1   758
how they chose out the *c* rooms .... Lk 14:7   4411
which was the *c* among the .... Lk 19:2   754
But the *c* priests and the scribes .... Lk 19:47   749
the *c* of the people sought to .... Lk 19:47   4413
the *c* priests and the scribes came .... Lk 20:1   749
the *c* priests and the scribes the .... Lk 20:19   749
and the c rooms at feasts .... Lk 20:46   4411
the *c* priests and scribes sought .... Lk 22:2   749
and communed with the *c* priests .... Lk 22:4   749
and he that is c, as he that doth .... Lk 22:26   2233
Jesus said unto the *c* priests .... Lk 22:52   749
the *c* priests and the scribes came .... Lk 22:66   749
Then said Pilate to the *c* priests .... Lk 23:4   749
the *c* priests and scribes stood and .... Lk 23:10   749
had called together the *c* priests .... Lk 23:13   749
of the *c* priests prevailed .... Lk 23:23   749
And how the *c* priests and our .... Lk 24:20   749
the *c* priests sent officers to .... Jn 7:32   749
the officers to *c* priests .... Jn 7:45   749
Then gathered the *c* priests .... Jn 11:47   749
Now both the *c* priests and the .... Jn 11:57   749
But the *c* priests consulted that .... Jn 12:10   749
Nevertheless among the *c* rulers .... Jn 12:42   758
and officers from the *c* priests .... Jn 18:3   749
the *c* priests have delivered thee .... Jn 18:35   749
When the *c* priests therefore and .... Jn 19:6   749
The *c* priests answered, We have .... Jn 19:15   749
Then said the *c* priests of the .... Jn 19:21   749
reported all that the *c* priests .... Acts 4:23   749
the *c* priests heard these things, ... Acts 5:24   749
c priests to bind all that call .... Acts 9:14   749
them bound unto the *c* priests .... Acts 9:21   749
the *c* men of the city, and raised .... Acts 13:50   4413
because he was the *c* speaker .... Acts 14:12   2233
Silas, *c* men among the brethren .... Acts 15:22   2233
which is the *c* city of that part .... Acts 16:12   4413
and of the *c* women not a few .... Acts 17:4   4413
the *c* ruler of the synagogue, ... Acts 18:8   752
the *c* ruler of the synagogue, and .... Acts 18:17   752
c of the priests, which did so .... Acts 19:14   749
And certain of the *c* of Asia .... Acts 19:31   775
unto the *c* captain of the band .... Acts 21:31   5506
and when they saw the *c* captain .... Acts 21:32   5506
Then the *c* captain came near, and .... Acts 21:33   5506
he said unto the *c* captain .... Acts 21:37   5506
The *c* captain commanded him to be .... Acts 22:24   5506
he went and told the *c* captain .... Acts 22:26   5506
Then the *c* captain came, and said .... Acts 22:27   5506
the *c* captain answered, With a .... Acts 22:28   5506
the *c* captain also was afraid, ... Acts 22:29   5506
bands, and commanded the *c* priests ..... Acts 22:30   749
the *c* captain, fearing lest Paul .... Acts 23:10   5506
And they came to the *c* priests .... Acts 23:14   749
c captain that he bring him down .... Acts 23:15   5506
this young man unto the *c* captain .... Acts 23:17   5506
and brought him to the *c* captain .... Acts 23:18   5506
Then the *c* captain took him by .... Acts 23:19   5506
So the *c* captain then let the .... Acts 23:22   5506
But the *c* captain Lysias came .... Acts 24:7   5506
When the *c* captain Lysias shall .... Acts 24:22   5506
the *c* of the Jews informed him .... Acts 25:2   4413
the *c* priests and the elders of .... Acts 25:15   749
of hearing, with the *c* captains .... Acts 25:23   5506
authority from the *c* priests .... Acts 26:10   749
and commission from the *c* priests .... Acts 26:12   749
of the *c* man of the island .... Acts 28:7   4413
called the *c* of the Jews together .... Acts 28:17   4413
himself being the *c* corner stone .... Eph 2:20   204
of whom I am *c* 1Ti 1:15   4413
I lay in Sion a *c* corner stone 1Pet 2:6   204
when the *c* Shepherd shall appear, ... 1Pet 5:4   750
the *c* captains, and the mighty men ...... Rev 6:15   5506

CHIEFEST

c of all the offerings of Israel 1Sa 2:29   7225
made them sit in the *c* place 1Sa 9:22   7218
the *c* of the herdmen that 1Sa 21:7   47
they buried him in the *c* of the 2Chr 32:33   4608

ruddy, the *c* among ten thousand .... Song 5:10   1713
And whosoever of you will be the c .... Mk 10:44   *4413*
a whit behind the very *c* apostles ... 2Cor 11:5   5228,3029
am I behind the very *c* apostles 2Cor 12:11   5228,3029
the *c* city of Phrygia Pacatiana .... 1Ti s   3390

CHIEFLY

c, because that unto them were .... Rom 3:2   4412
c they that are of Caesar's .... Phil 4:22   3122
But *c* them that walk after the 2Pet 2:10   3122

CHILD

she had no *c* .... Gen 11:30   2056
unto her, Behold, thou art with *c* .... Gen 16:11   2030
Every man *c* among you shall be .... Gen 17:10
every man *c* in your generations, ... Gen 17:12
the uncircumcised *c* whose .... Gen 17:14
Shall a *c* be born unto him that .... Gen 17:17
Shall I of a surety bear a *c* .... Gen 18:13
of Lot with *c* by their father .... Gen 19:36   2029
the *c* grew, and was weaned .... Gen 21:8   3206
it on her shoulder, and the *c* .... Gen 21:14   3206
she cast the *c* under one of the .... Gen 21:15   3206
Let me not see the death of the *c* .... Gen 21:16   3206
brethren, and said, The *c* is not .... Gen 37:30   3206
behold, she is with *c* by whoredom .... Gen 38:24   2030
man, whose these are, am I with *c* .... Gen 38:25   2030
saying, Do not sin against the *c* .... Gen 42:22   3206
a *c* of his old age, a little one .... Gen 44:20   3206
saw him that he was a goodly *c* .... Ex 2:2
with pitch, and put the *c* therein .... Ex 2:3   3206
she had opened it, she saw the *c* .... Ex 2:6   3206
that she may nurse the *c* for thee .... Ex 2:7   3206
said unto her, Take this *c* away .... Ex 2:9   3206
And the woman took the *c*, and .... Ex 2:9   3206
the *c* grew, and she brought him .... Ex 2:10   3206
strive, and hurt a woman with *c* .... Ex 21:22   2030
any widow, or fatherless *c* .... Ex 22:22
conceived seed, and born a man *c* .... Lev 12:2
But if she bear a maid *c*, then .... Lev 12:5
widow, or divorced, and have no *c* .... Lev 22:13   2233
father beareth the sucking *c* .... Num 11:12
and one of them die, and have no *c* .... Deut 25:5   1121
and she was his only *c* .... Judg 11:34   3173
for the *c* shall be a Nazarite .... Judg 13:5   5288
for the *c* shall be a Nazarite to .... Judg 13:7   5288
do unto the *c* that shall be born .... Judg 13:8   5288
How shall we order the *c*, and how .... Judg 13:12   5288
the *c* grew, and the LORD blessed .... Judg 13:24   5288
And Naomi took the *c*, and laid it .... Ruth 4:16   3206
give unto thine handmaid a man *c* 1Sa 1:11   2233
not go up until the *c* be weaned 1Sa 1:22   5288
and the *c* was young 1Sa 1:24   5288
bullock, and brought the *c* to Eli 1Sa 1:25   5288
For this *c* I prayed 1Sa 1:27   5288
the *c* did minister unto the LORD 1Sa 2:11   5288
before the LORD, being a *c* 1Sa 2:18   5288
the *c* Samuel grew before the LORD 1Sa 2:21   5288
the *c* Samuel grew on, and was in 1Sa 2:26   5288
the *c* Samuel ministered unto the 1Sa 3:1   5288
that the LORD had called the *c* 1Sa 3:8   5288
law, Phinehas' wife, was with *c* 1Sa 4:19   2030
And she named the *c* I-chabod 1Sa 4:21   5288
no *c* unto the day of her death 2Sa 6:23   3206
told David, and said, I am with *c* 2Sa 11:5   2030
the *c* also that is born unto thee 2Sa 12:14   1121
the LORD struck the *c* that 2Sa 12:15   3206
therefore besought God for the *c* 2Sa 12:16   5288
the seventh day, that the *c* died 2Sa 12:18   3206
to tell him that the *c* was dead 2Sa 12:18   3206
while the *c* was yet alive, we 2Sa 12:18   3206
if we tell him that the *c* is dead 2Sa 12:18   3206
perceived that the *c* was dead 2Sa 12:19   3206
unto his servants, Is the *c* dead 2Sa 12:19   3206
thou didst fast and weep for the *c* 2Sa 12:21   3206
but when the *c* was dead, thou 2Sa 12:21   3206
While the *c* was yet alive, I 2Sa 12:22   3206
to me, that the *c* may live 2Sa 12:22   3206
and I am but a little *c* 1Kin 3:7   5288
I was delivered of a *c* with her 1Kin 3:17   3205
this woman's *c* died in the night 1Kin 3:19   1121
and laid her dead *c* in my bosom 1Kin 3:20   1121
in the morning to give my *c* suck 1Kin 3:21   1121
said, Divide the living *c* in two 1Kin 3:25   3206
the living *c* was unto the king 1Kin 3:26   1121
O my lord, give her the living *c* 1Kin 3:26   3205
and said, Give her the living *c* 1Kin 3:27   3205
Hadad being yet a little *c* 1Kin 11:17   5288
a *c* shall be born unto the house 1Kin 13:2   1121
thee what shall become of the *c* 1Kin 14:3   5288
into the city, the *c* shall die 1Kin 14:12   3206
threshold of the door, the *c* died 1Kin 14:17   5288

himself upon the *c* three times 1Kin 17:21   3206
the soul of the *c* came into him 1Kin 17:21   3206
And Elijah took the *c*, and brought 1Kin 17:23   3206
answered, Verily she hath no *c* 2Kin 4:14   1121
when the *c* was grown, it fell on 2Kin 4:18   3206
is it well with the *c* 2Kin 4:26   3206
my staff upon the face of the *c* 2Kin 4:29   5288
And the mother of the *c* said 2Kin 4:30   5288
the staff upon the face of the *c* 2Kin 4:31   5288
him, saying, The *c* is not awaked 2Kin 4:31   5288
the *c* was dead, and laid upon his 2Kin 4:32   5288
And he went up, and lay upon the *c* 2Kin 4:34   3206
he stretched himself upon the *c* 2Kin 4:34
and the flesh of the *c* waxed warm 2Kin 4:34   3206
the *c* sneezed seven times 2Kin 4:35   5288
and the *c* opened his eyes 2Kin 4:35   5288
like unto the flesh of a little *c* 2Kin 5:14   5288
and rip up their women with *c* 2Kin 8:12   2030
that were with *c* he ripped up 2Kin 15:16   2030
said, There is a man *c* conceived .... Job 3:3
as a *c* that is weaned of his .... Ps 131:2
my soul is even as a weaned *c* .... Ps 131:2
Even a *c* is known by his doings, ... Prov 20:11   5288
Train up a *c* in the way he should .... Prov 22:6   5288
is bound in the heart of a *c* .... Prov 22:15   5288
not correction from the *c* .... Prov 23:13   5288
a wise *c* shall have joy of him .... Prov 23:24
but a *c* left to himself bringeth .... Prov 29:15   5288
a *c* shall have him become his son .... Prov 29:21   5290
he hath neither *c* nor brother .... Eccl 4:8   1121
a wise *c* than an old and foolish ......,..... Eccl 4:13   3206
with the second *c* that shall .... Eccl 4:15   3206
O land, when thy king is a *c* .... Eccl 10:16   5288
in the womb of her that is with *c* .... Eccl 11:5   4392
the *c* shall behave himself .... Is 3:5   5288
For before the *c* shall know to .... Is 7:16   5288
For before the *c* shall have .... Is 8:4   5288
For unto us a *c* is born, unto us .... Is 9:6   3206
be few, that a *c* may write them .... Is 10:19   5288
a little *c* shall lead them .... Is 11:6   5288
the sucking *c* shall play on the .... Is 11:8
the weaned *c* shall put his hand .... Is 11:8
Like as a woman with *c*, that .... Is 26:17   2030
We have been with *c*, we have been ...... Is 26:18   2029
Can a woman forget her sucking *c* .... Is 49:15
that didst not travail with *c* .... Is 54:1
for the *c* shall die an hundred .... Is 65:20   5288
she was delivered of a man *c* .... Is 66:7
for I am a *c* .... Jer 1:6   5288
said unto me, Say not, I am a *c* .... Jer 1:7   5288
that bringeth forth her first *c* .... Jer 4:31
A man *c* is born unto thee .... Jer 20:15   1121
whether a man doth travail with *c* .... Jer 30:6   3205
and the lame, the woman with *c* .... Jer 31:8   2030
that travaileth with *c* together .... Jer 31:8   3205
is he a pleasant *c* .... Jer 31:20   3206
cut off from you man and woman, *c* ...... Jer 44:7   5768
The tongue of the sucking *c* .... Lam 4:4
When Israel was a *c*, then I loved .... Hos 11:1   5288
their women with *c* shall be .... Hos 13:16   2030
up the women with *c* of Gilead .... Amos 1:13   2030
found with *c* of the Holy Ghost .... Mt 1:18   1722,1064,2192
a virgin shall be with *c* .... Mt 1:23   1722,1064,2192
search diligently for the young *c* .... Mt 2:8   3813
stood over where the young *c* was .... Mt 2:9   3813
they saw the young *c* with Mary .... Mt 2:11   3813
Arise, and take the young *c* .... Mt 2:13   3813
seek the young *c* to destroy him .... Mt 2:13   3813
he arose, he took the young *c* .... Mt 2:14   3813
Arise, and take the young *c* .... Mt 2:20   3813
And he arose, and took the young *c* ...... Mt 2:21   3813
to death, and the father the *c* .... Mt 10:21   5043
the *c* was cured from that very .... Mt 17:18   3816
Jesus called a little *c* unto him .... Mt 18:2   3813
humble himself as this little *c* .... Mt 18:4   3813
little *c* in my name receiveth me ...... Mt 18:5   3813
the *c* of hell than yourselves .... Mt 23:15   5207
woe unto them that are with *c* Mt 24:19   1722,1064,2192
And he said, Of a *c* .... Mk 9:21   3812
the father of the *c* cried out .... Mk 9:24   3813
And he took a *c*, and set him in the ...... Mk 9:36   3813
the kingdom of God as a little *c* .... Mk 10:15   3813
woe to them that are with *c* ..... Mk 13:17   1722,1064,2192
And they had no *c*, because that .... Lk 1:7   5043
day they came to circumcise the *c* .... Lk 1:59   3813
What manner of *c* shall this be .... Lk 1:66   3813
And thou, *c*, shalt be called the .... Lk 1:76   3813
the *c* grew, and waxed strong in .... Lk 1:80   3813
espoused wife, being great with *c* .... Lk 2:5   1471
was told them concerning this *c* .... Lk 2:17   3813
for the circumcising of the *c* .... Lk 2:21   3813

parents brought in the *c* Jesus .... Lk 2:27   3813
this *c* is set for the fall and .... Lk 2:34
the *c* grew, and waxed strong in .... Lk 2:40   3813
the *c* Jesus tarried behind in .... Lk 2:43   3816
for he is mine only *c* .... Lk 9:38   3439
unclean spirit, and healed the *c* .... Lk 9:42   3816
thought of their heart, took a *c* .... Lk 9:47   3813
this *c* in my name receiveth me .... Lk 9:48   3813
c shall in no wise enter therein .... Lk 18:17   3813
woe unto them that are with *c* Lk 21:23   1722,1064,2192
him, Sir, come down ere my *c* die .... Jn 4:49   3813
soon as she is delivered of the *c* ...... Jn 16:21   3813
a truth against thy holy *c* Jesus .... Acts 4:27   3816
by the name of thy holy *c* Jesus .... Acts 4:30   3816
him, when as yet he had no *c* .... Acts 7:5   5043
thou *c* of the devil, thou enemy .... Acts 13:10   5207
I was a *c*, I spake as a *c* 1Cor 13:11   3516
I understood as a *c* 1Cor 13:11   3516
I thought as a *c* 1Cor 13:11   3516
the heir, as long as he is a *c* .... Gal 4:1   3516
travail upon a woman with *c* ... 1Th 5:3   1722,1064,2192
that from a *c* thou hast known the 2Ti 3:15   1025
was delivered of a *c* when she was .... Heb 11:11   5088
they saw he was a proper *c* .... Heb 11:23   3813
And she being with *c* cried ...... Rev 12:2   1722,1064,2192
for to devour her *c* as soon as it .... Rev 12:4   5043
And she brought forth a man *c* .... Rev 12:5   5207
her *c* was caught up unto God, and .... Rev 12:5   5043
which brought forth the man *c* .... Rev 12:13

CHILDBEARING
she shall be saved in *c*, if they 1Ti 2:15   5042

CHILDHOOD
you from my *c* unto this day 1Sa 12:2   5271
for *c* and youth are vanity .... Eccl 11:10   3208

CHILDISH
became a man, I put away *c* things 1Cor 13:11   3516

CHILDLESS
wilt thou give me, seeing I go *c* .... Gen 15:2   6185
they shall die *c* .... Lev 20:20   6185
they shall be *c* .... Lev 20:21   6185
As thy sword hath made women *c* 1Sa 15:33   7921
shall thy mother be *c* among women 1Sa 15:33   7921
the LORD, Write ye this man *c* .... Jer 22:30   6185
took her to wife, and he died *c* .... Lk 20:30   815

CHILDREN
sorrow thou shalt bring forth *c* .... Gen 3:16   1121
of men, and they bare *c* to them .... Gen 6:4
the father of all the *c* of Eber .... Gen 10:21   1121
elder, even to him were *c* born .... Gen 10:21
The *c* of Shem .... Gen 10:22   1121
And the *c* of Aram .... Gen 10:23   1121
which the *c* of men builded .... Gen 11:5   1121
Sarai Abram's wife bare him no *c* .... Gen 16:1
may be that I may obtain *c* by her .... Gen 16:2   1129
him, that he will command his *c* .... Gen 18:19   1121
of the *c* of Ammon unto this day .... Gen 19:38   1121
and they bare *c* .... Gen 20:17
Sarah should have given *c* suck .... Gen 21:7   1121
she hath also born *c* unto thy .... Gen 22:20   1121
the *c* of Heth answered Abraham, ... Gen 23:5   1121
the land, even to the *c* of Heth .... Gen 23:7   1121
Ephron dwelt among the *c* of Heth .... Gen 23:10   1121
in the audience of the *c* of Heth .... Gen 23:10   1121
in the presence of the *c* of Heth .... Gen 23:18   1121
All these were the *c* of Keturah .... Gen 25:4   1121
the *c* struggled together within .... Gen 25:22   1121
saw that she bare Jacob no *c* .... Gen 30:1
and said unto Jacob, Give me *c* .... Gen 30:1   1121
that I may also have *c* by her .... Gen 30:3   1129
Give me my wives and my *c*, for .... Gen 30:26   3206
and these *c* are my *c* .... Gen 31:43   1121
or unto their *c* which they have .... Gen 31:43   1121
me, and the mother with the *c* .... Gen 32:11   1121
Therefore the *c* of Israel eat not............ Gen 32:32   1121
And he divided the *c* unto Leah .... Gen 33:1   3206
their *c* foremost, and Leah and her .... Gen 33:2   3206
her *c* after, and Rachel and Joseph .... Gen 33:2   3206
eyes, and saw the women and the *c* .... Gen 33:5   3206
The *c* which God hath graciously .... Gen 33:5   3206
came near, they and their *c* .... Gen 33:6   3206
And Leah also with her *c* came near ..... Gen 33:7   3206
knoweth that the *c* are tender .... Gen 33:13   3206
the *c* be able to endure, until I .... Gen 33:14   3206
at the hand of the *c* of Hamor .... Gen 33:19   1121
the *c* of Seir in the land of Edom .... Gen 36:21   1121
the *c* of Lotan were Hori and Hemam .... Gen 36:22   1121
the *c* of Shobal were these...................... Gen 36:23   1121
And these are the *c* of Zibeon .... Gen 36:24   1121

And the c of Anah were these	Gen 36:25	1121
And these are the c of Dishon	Gen 36:26	1121
The c of Ezer are these	Gen 36:27	1121
The c of Dishan are these	Gen 36:28	1121
any king over the c of Israel	Gen 36:31	1121
loved Joseph more than all his c	Gen 37:3	1121
them, Me have ye bereaved of my c	Gen 42:36	
If I be bereaved of my c, I am	Gen 43:14	
thy c, and thy children's c	Gen 45:10	1121
And the c of Israel did so	Gen 45:21	1121
are the names of the c of Israel	Gen 46:8	1121
thy father's c shall bow down	Gen 49:8	1121
is therein was from the c of Heth	Gen 49:32	1121
Joseph saw Ephraim's c of the	Gen 50:23	1121
the c also of Machir the son of	Gen 50:23	1121
took an oath of the c of Israel	Gen 50:25	1121
are the names of the c of Israel	Ex 1:1	1121
the c of Israel be fruitful, and	Ex 1:7	1121
the people of the c of Israel are	Ex 1:9	1121
because of the c of Israel	Ex 1:12	1121
the Egyptians made the c of	Ex 1:13	1121
them, but saved the men c alive	Ex 1:17	3206
and have saved the men c alive	Ex 1:18	3206
This is one of the Hebrews' c	Ex 2:6	3206
the c of Israel sighed by reason	Ex 2:23	1121
God looked upon the c of Israel	Ex 2:25	1121
the cry of the c of Israel is	Ex 3:9	1121
the c of Israel out of Egypt	Ex 3:10	1121
the c of Israel out of Egypt	Ex 3:11	1121
when I come unto the c of Israel	Ex 3:13	1121
thou say unto the c of Israel	Ex 3:14	1121
thou say unto the c of Israel	Ex 3:15	1121
all the elders of the c of Israel	Ex 4:29	1121
Lord had visited the c of Israel	Ex 4:31	1121
the officers of the c of Israel	Ex 5:14	1121
officers of the c of Israel came	Ex 5:15	1121
the officers of the c of Israel	Ex 5:19	1121
the groaning of the c of Israel	Ex 6:5	1121
say unto the c of Israel, I am	Ex 6:6	1121
spake so unto the c of Israel	Ex 6:9	1121
that he let the c of Israel go	Ex 6:11	1121
Behold, the c of Israel have not	Ex 6:12	1121
a charge unto the c of Israel	Ex 6:13	1121
to bring the c of Israel out of	Ex 6:13	1121
Bring out the c of Israel from	Ex 6:26	1121
to bring out the c of Israel from	Ex 6:27	1121
that he send the c of Israel out	Ex 7:2	1121
and my people the c of Israel	Ex 7:4	1121
bring out the c of Israel from	Ex 7:5	1121
of the c of Israel died not one	Ex 9:6	1121
where the c of Israel were, was	Ex 9:26	1121
would he let the c of Israel go	Ex 9:35	1121
would not let the c of Israel go	Ex 10:20	1121
but all the c of Israel had light	Ex 10:23	1121
But against any of the c of	Ex 11:7	1121
c of Israel go out of his land	Ex 11:10	1121
when your c shall say unto you,	Ex 12:26	1121
of the c of Israel in Egypt	Ex 12:27	1121
the c of Israel went away, and did	Ex 12:28	1121
both ye and the c of Israel	Ex 12:31	1121
the c of Israel did according to	Ex 12:35	1121
the c of Israel journeyed from	Ex 12:37	1121
on foot that were men, beside c	Ex 12:37	2945
the sojourning of the c of Israel	Ex 12:40	1121
c of Israel in their generations	Ex 12:42	1121
Thus did all the c of Israel	Ex 12:50	1121
that the Lord did bring the c of	Ex 12:51	1121
the womb among the c of Israel	Ex 13:2	1121
man among thy c shalt thou redeem	Ex 13:13	1121
the firstborn of my c I redeem	Ex 13:15	1121
the c of Israel went up harnessed	Ex 13:18	1121
straitly sworn the c of Israel	Ex 13:19	1121
Speak unto the c of Israel	Ex 14:2	1121
will say of the c of Israel	Ex 14:3	1121
he pursued after the c of Israel	Ex 14:8	1121
the c of Israel went out with an	Ex 14:8	1121
the c of Israel lifted up their	Ex 14:10	1121
the c of Israel cried out unto	Ex 14:10	1121
speak unto the c of Israel	Ex 14:15	1121
the c of Israel shall go on dry	Ex 14:16	1121
the c of Israel went into the	Ex 14:22	1121
But the c of Israel walked upon	Ex 14:29	1121
the c of Israel this song unto	Ex 15:1	1121
but the c of Israel went on dry	Ex 15:19	1121
of the c of Israel came unto the	Ex 16:1	1121
the c of Israel murmured against	Ex 16:2	1121
the c of Israel said unto them,	Ex 16:3	1121
said unto all the c of Israel	Ex 16:6	1121
congregation of the c of Israel	Ex 16:9	1121
congregation of the c of Israel	Ex 16:10	1121
the murmurings of the c of Israel	Ex 16:12	1121

when the c of Israel saw it, they	Ex 16:15	1121
the c of Israel did so, and	Ex 16:17	1121
the c of Israel did eat manna	Ex 16:35	1121
all the congregation of the c of	Ex 17:1	1121
out of Egypt, to kill us and our c	Ex 17:3	1121
of the chiding of the c of Israel	Ex 17:7	1121
when the c of Israel were gone	Ex 19:1	1121
of Jacob, and tell the c of Israel	Ex 19:3	1121
shalt speak unto the c of Israel	Ex 19:6	1121
fathers upon the c unto the third	Ex 20:5	1121
shalt say unto the c of Israel	Ex 20:22	1121
her c shall be her master's, and	Ex 21:4	3206
love my master, my wife, and my c	Ex 21:5	1121
be widows, and your c fatherless	Ex 22:24	1121
sent young men of the c of Israel	Ex 24:5	1121
upon the nobles of the c of	Ex 24:11	1121
in the eyes of the c of Israel	Ex 24:17	1121
Speak unto the c of Israel	Ex 25:2	1121
commandment unto the c of Israel	Ex 25:22	1121
shalt command the c of Israel	Ex 27:20	1121
on the behalf of the c of Israel	Ex 27:21	1121
him, from among the c of Israel	Ex 28:1	1121
them the names of the c of Israel	Ex 28:9	1121
with the names of the c of Israel	Ex 28:11	1121
of memorial unto the c of Israel	Ex 28:12	1121
with the names of the c of Israel	Ex 28:21	1121
shall bear the names of the c of	Ex 28:29	1121
shall bear the judgment of the c	Ex 28:30	1121
which the c of Israel shall	Ex 28:38	1121
for ever from the c of Israel	Ex 29:28	1121
c of Israel of the sacrifice of	Ex 29:28	1121
I will meet with the c of Israel	Ex 29:43	1121
will dwell among the c of Israel	Ex 29:45	1121
c of Israel after their number	Ex 30:12	1121
money of the c of Israel, and	Ex 30:16	1121
the c of Israel before the Lord	Ex 30:16	1121
shalt speak unto the c of Israel	Ex 30:31	1121
thou also unto the c of Israel	Ex 31:13	1121
Wherefore the c of Israel shall	Ex 31:16	1121
me and the c of Israel for ever	Ex 31:17	1121
made the c of Israel drink of it	Ex 32:20	1121
the c of Levi did according to	Ex 32:28	1121
Moses, Say unto the c of Israel	Ex 33:5	1121
And the c of Israel stripped	Ex 33:6	1121
of the fathers upon the c	Ex 34:7	1121
and upon the children's c	Ex 34:7	
men c appear before the Lord God	Ex 34:23	
all the c of Israel saw Moses	Ex 34:30	1121
afterward all the c of Israel	Ex 34:32	1121
spake unto the c of Israel that	Ex 34:34	1121
the c of Israel saw the face of	Ex 34:35	1121
of the c of Israel together	Ex 35:1	1121
congregation of the c of Israel	Ex 35:4	1121
the c of Israel departed from the	Ex 35:20	1121
The c of Israel brought a willing	Ex 35:29	1121
Moses said unto the c of Israel	Ex 35:30	1121
which the c of Israel had brought	Ex 36:3	1121
with the names of the c of Israel	Ex 39:6	1121
for a memorial to the c of Israel	Ex 39:7	1121
to the names of the c of Israel	Ex 39:14	1121
the c of Israel did according to	Ex 39:32	1121
so the c of Israel made all the	Ex 39:42	1121
the c of Israel went onward in	Ex 40:36	1121
Speak unto the c of Israel	Lev 1:2	1121
Speak unto the c of Israel	Lev 4:2	1121
All the males among the c of	Lev 6:18	1121
Speak unto the c of Israel	Lev 7:23	1121
Speak unto the c of Israel	Lev 7:29	1121
of the c of Israel from off the	Lev 7:34	1121
ever from among the c of Israel	Lev 7:34	1121
be given them of the c of Israel	Lev 7:36	1121
the c of Israel to offer their	Lev 7:38	1121
unto the c of Israel thou shalt	Lev 9:3	1121
that ye may teach the c of Israel	Lev 10:11	1121
offerings of the c of Israel	Lev 10:14	1121
Speak unto the c of Israel	Lev 11:2	1121
Speak unto the c of Israel	Lev 12:2	1121
Speak unto the c of Israel	Lev 15:2	1121
the c of Israel from their	Lev 15:31	1121
c of Israel two kids of the goats	Lev 16:5	1121
uncleanness of the c of Israel	Lev 16:16	1121
uncleanness of the c of Israel	Lev 16:19	1121
the iniquities of the c of Israel	Lev 16:21	1121
c of Israel for all their sins	Lev 16:34	1121
sons, and unto all the c of Israel	Lev 17:2	1121
To the end that the c of Israel	Lev 17:5	1121
I said unto the c of Israel	Lev 17:12	1121
man there be of the c of Israel	Lev 17:13	1121
I said unto the c of Israel	Lev 17:14	1121
Speak unto the c of Israel	Lev 18:2	1121
congregation of the c of Israel	Lev 19:2	1121

against the *c* of thy people	Lev 19:18	1121
thou shalt say to the *c* of Israel	Lev 20:2	1121
he be of the *c* of Israel, or of	Lev 20:2	1121
sons, and unto all the *c* of Israel	Lev 21:24	1121
holy things of the *c* of Israel	Lev 22:2	1121
which the *c* of Israel hallow unto	Lev 22:3	1121
holy things of the *c* of Israel	Lev 22:15	1121
sons, and unto all the *c* of Israel	Lev 22:18	1121
be hallowed among the *c* of Israel	Lev 22:32	1121
Speak unto the *c* of Israel	Lev 23:2	1121
Speak unto the *c* of Israel	Lev 23:10	1121
Speak unto the *c* of Israel	Lev 23:24	1121
Speak unto the *c* of Israel	Lev 23:34	1121
may know that I made the *c* of	Lev 23:43	1121
Moses declared unto the *c* of	Lev 23:44	1121
Command the *c* of Israel, that	Lev 24:2	1121
being taken from the *c* of Israel	Lev 24:8	1121
went out among the *c* of Israel	Lev 24:10	1121
shalt speak unto the *c* of Israel	Lev 24:15	1121
And Moses spake to the *c* of Israel	Lev 24:23	1121
the *c* of Israel did as the LORD	Lev 24:23	1121
Speak unto the *c* of Israel	Lev 25:2	1121
possession among the *c* of Israel	Lev 25:33	1121
his *c* with him, and shall return	Lev 25:41	1121
Moreover of the *c* of the	Lev 25:45	1121
inheritance for your *c* after you	Lev 25:46	1121
your brethren the *c* of Israel	Lev 25:46	1121
both he, and his *c* with him	Lev 25:54	1121
For unto me the *c* of Israel are	Lev 25:55	1121
which shall rob you of your *c*	Lev 26:22	
the *c* of Israel in mount Sinai by	Lev 26:46	1121
Speak unto the *c* of Israel	Lev 27:2	1121
the *c* of Israel in mount Sinai	Lev 27:34	1121
congregation of the *c* of Israel	Num 1:2	1121
Of the *c* of Joseph	Num 1:10	1121
the *c* of Reuben, Israel's eldest	Num 1:20	1121
Of the *c* of Simeon, by their	Num 1:22	1121
Of the *c* of Gad, by their	Num 1:24	1121
Of the *c* of Judah, by their	Num 1:26	1121
Of the *c* of Issachar, by their	Num 1:28	1121
Of the *c* of Zebulun, by their	Num 1:30	1121
Of the *c* of Joseph, namely, of	Num 1:32	1121
of the *c* of Ephraim, by their	Num 1:32	1121
Of the *c* of Manasseh, by their	Num 1:34	1121
Of the *c* of Benjamin, by their	Num 1:36	1121
Of the *c* of Dan, by their	Num 1:38	1121
Of the *c* of Asher, by their	Num 1:40	1121
Of the *c* of Naphtali, throughout	Num 1:42	1121
were numbered of the *c* of Israel	Num 1:45	1121
sum of them among the *c* of Israel	Num 1:49	1121
the *c* of Israel shall pitch their	Num 1:52	1121
congregation of the *c* of Israel	Num 1:53	1121
the *c* of Israel did according to	Num 1:54	1121
Every man of the *c* of Israel	Num 2:2	1121
be captain of the *c* of Judah	Num 2:3	1121
be captain of the *c* of Issachar	Num 2:5	1121
be captain of the *c* of Zebulun	Num 2:7	1121
the captain of the *c* of Reuben	Num 2:10	1121
the captain of the *c* of Simeon	Num 2:12	1121
the captain of the *c* of Manasseh	Num 2:20	1121
the captain of the *c* of Dan shall	Num 2:25	1121
the captain of the *c* of Asher	Num 2:27	1121
the captain of the *c* of Naphtali	Num 2:29	1121
which were numbered of the *c* of	Num 2:32	1121
numbered of the *c* of Israel	Num 2:33	1121
the *c* of Israel did according to	Num 2:34	1121
of Sinai, and they had no *c*	Num 3:4	1121
and the charge of the *c* of Israel	Num 3:8	1121
unto him out of the *c* of Israel	Num 3:9	1121
the Levites from among the *c* of	Num 3:12	1121
the matrix among the *c* of Israel	Num 3:12	1121
Number the *c* of Levi after the	Num 3:15	1121
for the charge of the *c* of Israel	Num 3:38	1121
the *c* of Israel from a month old	Num 3:40	1121
firstborn among the *c* of Israel	Num 3:41	1121
the cattle of the *c* of Israel	Num 3:41	1121
firstborn among the *c* of Israel	Num 3:42	1121
firstborn among the *c* of Israel	Num 3:45	1121
the firstborn of the *c* of Israel	Num 3:46	1121
Of the firstborn of the *c* of	Num 3:50	1121
Command the *c* of Israel, that	Num 5:2	1121
the *c* of Israel did so, and put	Num 5:4	1121
Moses, so did the *c* of Israel	Num 5:4	1121
Speak unto the *c* of Israel	Num 5:6	1121
holy things of the *c* of Israel	Num 5:9	1121
Speak unto the *c* of Israel	Num 5:12	1121
Speak unto the *c* of Israel	Num 6:2	1121
ye shall bless the *c* of Israel	Num 6:23	1121
put my name upon the *c* of Israel	Num 6:27	1121
Helon, prince of the *c* of Zebulun	Num 7:24	1121
prince of the *c* of Reuben	Num 7:30	1121
prince of the *c* of Simeon	Num 7:36	1121
of Deuel, prince of the *c* of Gad	Num 7:42	1121
prince of the *c* of Ephraim	Num 7:48	1121
prince of the *c* of Manasseh	Num 7:54	1121
prince of the *c* of Benjamin	Num 7:60	1121
prince of the *c* of Dan, offered	Num 7:66	1121
Ocran, prince of the *c* of Asher	Num 7:72	1121
Enan, prince of the *c* of Naphtali	Num 7:78	1121
from among the *c* of Israel	Num 8:6	1121
of the *c* of Israel together	Num 8:9	1121
the *c* of Israel shall put their	Num 8:10	1121
an offering of the *c* of Israel	Num 8:11	1121
from among the *c* of Israel	Num 8:14	1121
me from among the *c* of Israel	Num 8:16	1121
firstborn of all the *c* of Israel	Num 8:16	1121
of the *c* of Israel are mine	Num 8:17	1121
the firstborn of the *c* of Israel	Num 8:18	1121
sons from among the *c* of Israel	Num 8:19	1121
to do the service of the *c* of	Num 8:19	1121
an atonement for the *c* of Israel	Num 8:19	1121
no plague among the *c* of Israel	Num 8:19	1121
when the *c* of Israel come nigh	Num 8:19	1121
congregation of the *c* of Israel	Num 8:20	1121
so did the *c* of Israel unto them	Num 8:20	1121
Let the *c* of Israel also keep the	Num 9:2	1121
Moses spake unto the *c* of Israel	Num 9:4	1121
Moses, so did the *c* of Israel	Num 9:5	1121
season among the *c* of Israel	Num 9:7	1121
Speak unto the *c* of Israel	Num 9:10	1121
that the *c* of Israel journeyed	Num 9:17	1121
there the *c* of Israel pitched	Num 9:17	1121
LORD the *c* of Israel journeyed	Num 9:18	1121
then the *c* of Israel kept the	Num 9:19	1121
the *c* of Israel abode in their	Num 9:22	1121
the *c* of Israel took their	Num 10:12	1121
the *c* of Judah according to their	Num 10:14	1121
the host of the tribe of the *c* of	Num 10:15	1121
the host of the tribe of the *c* of	Num 10:16	1121
the host of the tribe of the *c* of	Num 10:19	1121
the host of the tribe of the *c* of	Num 10:20	1121
of the *c* of Ephraim set forward	Num 10:22	1121
c of Manasseh was Gamaliel the	Num 10:23	1121
the host of the tribe of the *c* of	Num 10:24	1121
camp of the *c* of Dan set forward	Num 10:25	1121
the host of the tribe of the *c* of	Num 10:26	1121
the host of the tribe of the *c* of	Num 10:27	1121
were the journeyings of the *c* of	Num 10:28	1121
the *c* of Israel also wept again,	Num 11:4	1121
which I give unto the *c* of Israel	Num 13:2	1121
men were heads of the *c* of Israel	Num 13:3	1121
and Talmai, the *c* of Anak, were	Num 13:22	3211
c of Israel cut down from thence	Num 13:24	1121
congregation of the *c* of Israel	Num 13:26	1121
we saw the *c* of Anak there	Num 13:28	3211
had searched unto the *c* of Israel	Num 13:32	1121
all the *c* of Israel murmured	Num 14:2	1121
wives and our *c* should be a prey	Num 14:3	2945
congregation of the *c* of Israel	Num 14:5	1121
the company of the *c* of Israel	Num 14:7	1121
before all the *c* of Israel	Num 14:10	1121
fathers upon the *c* unto the third	Num 14:18	1121
the murmurings of the *c* of Israel	Num 14:27	1121
your *c* shall wander in the	Num 14:33	1121
sayings unto all the *c* of Israel	Num 14:39	1121
Speak unto the *c* of Israel	Num 15:2	1121
Speak unto the *c* of Israel	Num 15:18	1121
congregation of the *c* of Israel	Num 15:25	1121
congregation of the *c* of Israel	Num 15:26	1121
is born among the *c* of Israel	Num 15:29	1121
while the *c* of Israel were in the	Num 15:32	1121
Speak unto the *c* of Israel	Num 15:38	1121
with certain of the *c* of Israel	Num 16:2	1121
and their sons, and their little *c*	Num 16:27	2945
be a sign unto the *c* of Israel	Num 16:38	1121
a memorial unto the *c* of Israel	Num 16:40	1121
the *c* of Israel murmured against	Num 16:41	1121
Speak unto the *c* of Israel	Num 17:2	1121
the murmurings of the *c* of Israel	Num 17:5	1121
Moses spake unto the *c* of Israel	Num 17:6	1121
the LORD unto all the *c* of Israel	Num 17:9	1121
the *c* of Israel spake unto Moses,	Num 17:12	1121
any more upon the *c* of Israel	Num 18:5	1121
from among the *c* of Israel	Num 18:6	1121
things of the *c* of Israel	Num 18:8	1121
wave offerings of the *c* of Israel	Num 18:11	1121
which the *c* of Israel offer unto	Num 18:19	1121
inheritance among the *c* of Israel	Num 18:20	1121
I have given to the *c* of Levi all	Num 18:21	1121
Neither must the *c* of Israel	Num 18:22	1121
that among the *c* of Israel they	Num 18:23	1121
But the tithes of the *c* of Israel	Num 18:24	1121

Among the *c* of Israel they shall	Num 18:24	1121
When ye take of the *c* of Israel	Num 18:26	1121
ye receive of the *c* of Israel	Num 18:28	1121
holy things of the *c* of Israel	Num 18:32	1121
Speak unto the *c* of Israel	Num 19:2	1121
of the *c* of Israel for a water of	Num 19:9	1121
it shall be unto the *c* of Israel	Num 19:10	1121
Then came the *c* of Israel	Num 20:1	1121
me in the eyes of the *c* of Israel	Num 20:12	1121
because the *c* of Israel strove	Num 20:13	1121
the *c* of Israel said unto him, We	Num 20:19	1121
the *c* of Israel, even the whole	Num 20:22	1121
I have given unto the *c* of Israel	Num 20:24	1121
the *c* of Israel set forward, and	Num 21:10	1121
Jabbok, even unto the *c* of Ammon	Num 21:24	1121
of the *c* of Ammon was strong	Num 21:24	1121
the *c* of Israel set forward, and	Num 22:1	1121
because of the *c* of Israel	Num 22:3	1121
the land of the *c* of his people	Num 22:5	1121
and destroy all the *c* of Sheth	Num 24:17	1121
one of the *c* of Israel came and	Num 25:6	1121
congregation of the *c* of Israel	Num 25:6	1121
was stayed from the *c* of Israel	Num 25:8	1121
wrath away from the *c* of Israel	Num 25:11	1121
that I consumed not the *c* of	Num 25:11	1121
an atonement for the *c* of Israel	Num 25:13	1121
congregation of the *c* of Israel	Num 26:2	1121
the *c* of Israel, which went forth	Num 26:4	1121
the *c* of Reuben	Num 26:5	1121
the *c* of Korah died not	Num 26:11	1121
The *c* of Gad after their families	Num 26:15	1121
These are the families of the *c*	Num 26:18	1121
Of the *c* of Asher after their	Num 26:44	1121
the numbered of the *c* of Israel	Num 26:51	1121
numbered among the *c* of Israel	Num 26:62	1121
given them among the *c* of Israel	Num 26:62	1121
who numbered the *c* of Israel in	Num 26:63	1121
when they numbered the *c* of	Num 26:64	1121
shalt speak unto the *c* of Israel	Num 27:8	1121
it shall be unto the *c* of Israel	Num 27:11	1121
I have given unto the *c* of Israel	Num 27:12	1121
the *c* of Israel may be obedient	Num 27:20	1121
all the *c* of Israel with him,	Num 27:21	1121
Command the *c* of Israel, and say	Num 28:2	1121
Moses told the *c* of Israel	Num 29:40	1121
tribes concerning the *c* of Israel	Num 30:1	1121
Avenge the *c* of Israel of the	Num 31:2	1121
the *c* of Israel took all the	Num 31:9	1121
congregation of the *c* of Israel	Num 31:12	1121
these caused the *c* of Israel	Num 31:16	1121
But all the women *c*, that have	Num 31:18	2945
of the *c* of Israel's half, thou	Num 31:30	1121
of the *c* of Israel's half, which	Num 31:42	1121
Even of the *c* of Israel's half,	Num 31:47	1121
for a memorial for the *c* of	Num 31:54	1121
Now the *c* of Reuben and the	Num 32:1	1121
the *c* of Gad had a very great	Num 32:1	1121
The *c* of Gad and the *c* of	Num 32:2	1121
And Moses said unto the *c* of Gad	Num 32:6	1121
to the *c* of Reuben, Shall your	Num 32:6	1121
c of Israel from going over into	Num 32:7	1121
the heart of the *c* of Israel	Num 32:9	1121
armed before the *c* of Israel	Num 32:17	1121
until the *c* of Israel have	Num 32:18	1121
the *c* of Gad and the *c* of	Num 32:25	1121
of the tribes of the *c* of Israel	Num 32:28	1121
said unto them, If the *c* of Gad	Num 32:29	1121
the *c* of Reuben will pass with	Num 32:29	1121
the *c* of Gad and the *c* of	Num 32:31	1121
unto them, even to the *c* of Gad	Num 32:33	1121
to the *c* of Reuben, and unto half	Num 32:33	1121
the *c* of Gad built Dibon, and	Num 32:34	1121
the *c* of Reuben built Heshbon, and	Num 32:37	1121
the *c* of Machir the son of	Num 32:39	1121
the journeys of the *c* of Israel	Num 33:1	1121
morrow after the passover the *c*	Num 33:3	1121
the *c* of Israel removed from	Num 33:5	1121
c of Israel were come out of the	Num 33:38	1121
of the coming of the *c* of Israel	Num 33:40	1121
Speak unto the *c* of Israel	Num 33:51	1121
Command the *c* of Israel, and say	Num 34:2	1121
Moses commanded the *c* of Israel	Num 34:13	1121
For the tribe of the *c* of Reuben	Num 34:14	1121
the tribe of the *c* of Gad	Num 34:14	1121
of the tribe of the *c* of Simeon	Num 34:20	1121
of the tribe of the *c* of Dan	Num 34:22	1121
The prince of the *c* of Joseph	Num 34:23	1121
the tribe of the *c* of Manasseh	Num 34:23	1121
of the tribe of the *c* of Ephraim	Num 34:24	1121
of the tribe of the *c* of Zebulun	Num 34:25	1121
of the tribe of the *c* of Issachar	Num 34:26	1121
of the tribe of the *c* of Asher	Num 34:27	1121
of the tribe of the *c* of Naphtali	Num 34:28	1121
c of Israel in the land of Canaan	Num 34:29	1121
Command the *c* of Israel, that	Num 35:2	1121
the possession of the *c* of Israel	Num 35:8	1121
Speak unto the *c* of Israel	Num 35:10	1121
refuge, both for the *c* of Israel	Num 35:15	1121
LORD dwell among the *c* of Israel	Num 35:34	1121
the families of the *c* of Gilead	Num 36:1	1121
chief fathers of the *c* of Israel	Num 36:1	1121
by lot to the *c* of Israel	Num 36:2	1121
other tribes of the *c* of Israel	Num 36:3	1121
of the *c* of Israel shall be	Num 36:4	1121
Moses commanded the *c* of Israel	Num 36:5	1121
not the inheritance of the *c* of	Num 36:7	1121
for every one of the *c* of Israel	Num 36:7	1121
in any tribe of the *c* of Israel	Num 36:8	1121
that the *c* of Israel may enjoy	Num 36:8	1121
every one of the tribes of the *c*	Num 36:9	1121
by the hand of Moses unto the *c*	Num 36:13	1121
Moses spake unto the *c* of Israel	Deut 1:3	1121
he hath trodden upon, and to his *c*	Deut 1:36	1121
said should be a prey, and your *c*	Deut 1:39	1121
of your brethren the *c* of Esau	Deut 2:4	1121
from our brethren the *c* of Esau	Deut 2:8	1121
the *c* of Lot for a possession	Deut 2:9	1121
but the *c* of Esau succeeded them,	Deut 2:12	1121
nigh over against the *c* of Ammon	Deut 2:19	1121
of the *c* of Ammon any possession	Deut 2:19	1121
the *c* of Lot for a possession	Deut 2:19	1121
As he did to the *c* of Esau	Deut 2:22	1121
(As the *c* of Esau which dwell in	Deut 2:29	1121
of the *c* of Ammon thou camest not	Deut 2:37	1121
destroying the men, women, and *c*	Deut 3:6	2945
not in Rabbah of the *c* of Ammon	Deut 3:11	1121
is the border of the *c* of Ammon	Deut 3:16	1121
your brethren the *c* of Israel	Deut 3:18	1121
and that they may teach their *c*	Deut 4:10	1121
beget *c*, and children's *c*	Deut 4:25	1121
with thy *c* after thee, and that	Deut 4:40	1121
Moses set before the *c* of Israel	Deut 4:44	1121
Moses spake unto the *c* of Israel	Deut 4:45	1121
the *c* of Israel smote, after they	Deut 4:46	1121
fathers upon the *c* unto the third	Deut 5:9	1121
them, and with their *c* for ever	Deut 5:29	1121
teach them diligently unto thy *c*	Deut 6:7	1121
the *c* of the Anakims, whom thou	Deut 9:2	1121
can stand before the *c* of Anak	Deut 9:2	1121
the *c* of Israel took their	Deut 10:6	1121
of the *c* of Jaakan to Mosera	Deut 10:6	1121
with your *c* which have not known	Deut 11:2	1121
And ye shall teach them your *c*	Deut 11:19	1121
multiplied, and the days of your *c*	Deut 11:21	1121
with thy *c* after thee, when thou	Deut 12:25	1121
with thy *c* after thee for ever,	Deut 12:28	1121
the *c* of Belial, are gone out	Deut 13:13	1121
Ye are the *c* of the LORD your God	Deut 14:1	1121
days in his kingdom, he, and his *c*	Deut 17:20	1121
hated, and they have born him *c*	Deut 21:15	1121
The *c* that are begotten of them	Deut 23:8	1121
his brethren the *c* of Israel	Deut 24:7	1121
not be put to death for the *c*	Deut 24:16	1121
neither shall the *c* be put to	Deut 24:16	1121
of his *c* which he shall leave	Deut 28:54	1121
flesh of his *c* whom he shall eat	Deut 28:55	1121
toward her *c* which she shall bear	Deut 28:57	1121
Moses to make with the *c* of	Deut 29:1	1121
c that shall rise up after you	Deut 29:22	1121
to our *c* for ever, that we may do	Deut 29:29	1121
thee this day, thou and thy *c*	Deut 30:2	1121
together, men, and women, and *c*	Deut 31:12	2945
And that their *c*, which have not	Deut 31:13	1121
you, and teach it the *c* of Israel	Deut 31:19	1121
for me against the *c* of Israel	Deut 31:19	1121
day, and taught it the *c* of Israel	Deut 31:22	1121
for thou shalt bring the *c* of	Deut 31:23	1121
spot is not the spot of his *c*	Deut 32:5	1121
to the number of the *c* of Israel	Deut 32:8	1121
generation, *c* in whom is no faith	Deut 32:20	1121
command your *c* to observe to do	Deut 32:46	1121
which I give unto the *c* of Israel	Deut 32:49	1121
the *c* of Israel at the waters of	Deut 32:51	1121
in the midst of the *c* of Israel	Deut 32:51	1121
land which I give the *c* of Israel	Deut 32:52	1121
the *c* of Israel before his death	Deut 33:1	1121
his brethren, nor knew his own *c*	Deut 33:9	1121
said, Let Asher be blessed with *c*	Deut 33:24	1121
the *c* of Israel wept for Moses in	Deut 34:8	1121
the *c* of Israel hearkened unto	Deut 34:9	1121
to them, even to the *c* of Israel	Josh 1:2	1121
the *c* of Israel to search out the	Josh 2:2	1121

all the *c* of Israel, and lodged.................Josh 3:1 1121
Joshua said unto the *c* of Israel ....Josh 3:9 1121
had prepared of the *c* of Israel ....Josh 4:4 1121
of the tribes of the *c* of Israel ....Josh 4:5 1121
that when your *c* ask their ....Josh 4:6 1121
unto the *c* of Israel for ever ....Josh 4:7 1121
the *c* of Israel did so as Joshua ....Josh 4:8 1121
of the tribes of the *c* of Israel ....Josh 4:8 1121
the *c* of Reuben, and the *c* ....Josh 4:12 1121
over armed before the *c* of Israel ....Josh 4:12 1121
And he spake unto the *c* of Israel ....Josh 4:21 1121
When your *c* shall ask their ....Josh 4:21 1121
Then ye shall let your *c* know ....Josh 4:22 1121
from before the *c* of Israel ....Josh 5:1 1121
more, because of the *c* of Israel ....Josh 5:1 1121
circumcise again the *c* of Israel ....Josh 5:2 1121
circumcised the *c* of Israel at ....Josh 5:3 1121
For the *c* of Israel walked forty ....Josh 5:6 1121
And their *c*, whom he raised up in ....Josh 5:7 1121
the *c* of Israel encamped in ....Josh 5:10 1121
neither had the *c* of Israel manna ....Josh 5:12 1121
up because of the *c* of Israel ....Josh 6:1 1121
But the *c* of Israel committed a ....Josh 7:1 1121
kindled against the *c* of Israel ....Josh 7:1 1121
Therefore the *c* of Israel could ....Josh 7:12 1121
and unto all the *c* of Israel ....Josh 7:23 1121
LORD commanded the *c* of Israel ....Josh 8:31 1121
the presence of the *c* of Israel ....Josh 8:32 1121
the *c* of Israel journeyed, and ....Josh 9:17 1121
the *c* of Israel smote them not, ...Josh 9:18 1121
of the hand of the *c* of Israel ....Josh 9:26 1121
Joshua and with the *c* of Israel ....Josh 10:4 1121
c of Israel slew with the sword ....Josh 10:11 1121
Amorites before the *c* of Israel ....Josh 10:12 1121
the *c* of Israel had made an end ....Josh 10:20 1121
against any of the *c* of Israel ....Josh 10:21 1121
the *c* of Israel took for a prey ....Josh 11:14 1121
made peace with the *c* of Israel..............Josh 11:19 1121
in the land of the *c* of Israel ....Josh 11:22 1121
which the *c* of Israel smote, and ....Josh 12:1 1121
is the border of the *c* of Ammon..............Josh 12:2 1121
the LORD and the *c* of Israel smite ....Josh 12:6 1121
the *c* of Israel smote on this ....Josh 12:7 1121
out from before the *c* of Israel................Josh 13:6 1121
unto the border of the *c* of Ammon.........Josh 13:10 1121
Nevertheless the *c* of Israel ....Josh 13:13 1121
gave unto the tribe of the *c* of ....Josh 13:15 1121
did the *c* of Israel slay with the ....Josh 13:22 1121
the border of the *c* of Reuben was ....Josh 13:23 1121
c of Reuben after their families...............Josh 13:23 1121
even unto the *c* of Gad according ....Josh 13:24 1121
half the land of the *c* of Ammon ....Josh 13:25 1121
the *c* of Gad after their families ....Josh 13:28 1121
of the half tribe of the *c* of ....Josh 13:29 1121
were pertaining unto the *c* of ....Josh 13:31 1121
the *c* of Machir by their families..............Josh 13:31 1121
are the countries which the *c* of ....Josh 14:1 1121
of the tribes of the *c* of Israel ....Josh 14:1 1121
For the *c* of Joseph were two ....Josh 14:4 1121
so the *c* of Israel did, and they...............Josh 14:5 1121
Then the *c* of Judah came unto..............Josh 14:6 1121
while the *c* of Israel wandered in ....Josh 14:10 1121
the *c* of Judah by their families...............Josh 15:1 1121
This is the coast of the *c* of ....Josh 15:12 1121
gave a part among the *c* of Judah ....Josh 15:13 1121
Ahiman, and Talmai, the *c* of Anak ....Josh 15:14 3211
the *c* of Judah according to their ....Josh 15:20 1121
cities of the tribe of the *c* of..................Josh 15:21 1121
the *c* of Judah could not drive ....Josh 15:63 1121
the Jebusites dwell with the *c* of ....Josh 15:63 1121
the lot of the *c* of Joseph fell ....Josh 16:1 1121
So the *c* of Joseph, Manasseh and ....Josh 16:4 1121
the border of the *c* of Ephraim ....Josh 16:5 1121
c of Ephraim by their families.................Josh 16:8 1121
the *c* of Ephraim were among the ....Josh 16:9 1121
inheritance of the *c* of Manasseh ....Josh 16:9 1121
c of Manasseh by their families ....Josh 17:2 1121
for the *c* of Abiezer................................Josh 17:2 1121
for the *c* of Helek ....Josh 17:2 1121
for the *c* of Asriel...................................Josh 17:2 1121
for the *c* of Shechem ....Josh 17:2 1121
for the *c* of Hepher ....Josh 17:2 1121
and for the *c* of Shemida ....Josh 17:2 1121
these were the male *c* of Manasseh ....Josh 17:2 1121
belonged to the *c* of Ephraim ....Josh 17:8 1121
Yet the *c* of Manasseh could not ....Josh 17:12 1121
when the *c* of Israel were waxen ....Josh 17:13 1121
the *c* of Joseph spake unto Joshua ....Josh 17:14 1121
the *c* of Joseph said, The hill is ....Josh 17:16 1121
the whole congregation of the *c* ....Josh 18:1 1121
the *c* of Israel seven tribes ....Josh 18:2 1121

Joshua said unto the *c* of Israel ....Josh 18:3 1121
divided the land unto the *c* of ....Josh 18:10 1121
the lot of the tribe of the *c* of.................Josh 18:11 1121
came forth between the *c* of Judah.........Josh 18:11 1121
of Judah and the *c* of Joseph ....Josh 18:11 1121
a city of the *c* of Judah ....Josh 18:14 1121
inheritance of the *c* of Benjamin ....Josh 18:20 1121
c of Benjamin according to their ....Josh 18:21 1121
c of Benjamin according to their ....Josh 18:28 1121
even for the tribe of the *c* of ....Josh 19:1 1121
the inheritance of the *c* of Judah ....Josh 19:1 1121
c of Simeon according to their ....Josh 19:8 1121
Out of the portion of the *c* of.................Josh 19:9 1121
inheritance of the *c* of Simeon.................Josh 19:9 1121
for the part of the *c* of Judah ....Josh 19:9 1121
therefore the *c* of Simeon had ....Josh 19:9 1121
c of Zebulun according to their ....Josh 19:10 1121
c of Zebulun according to their ....Josh 19:16 1121
for the *c* of Issachar according ....Josh 19:17 1121
c of Issachar according to their ....Josh 19:23 1121
the *c* of Asher according to their ....Josh 19:24 1121
the *c* of Asher according to their ....Josh 19:31 1121
lot came out to the *c* of Naphtali ....Josh 19:32 1121
even for the *c* of Naphtali ....Josh 19:32 1121
c of Naphtali according to their ....Josh 19:39 1121
the *c* of Dan according to their ....Josh 19:40 1121
the coast of the *c* of Dan went ....Josh 19:47 1121
therefore the *c* of Dan went up to ....Josh 19:47 1121
the *c* of Dan according to their ....Josh 19:48 1121
coasts, the *c* of Israel gave an ....Josh 19:49 1121
of the tribes of the *c* of Israel ....Josh 19:51 1121
Speak to the *c* of Israel, saying,.............Josh 20:2 1121
appointed for all the *c* of Israel...............Josh 20:9 1121
of the tribes of the *c* of Israel ....Josh 21:1 1121
the *c* of Israel gave unto the...................Josh 21:3 1121
the *c* of Aaron the priest, which ....Josh 21:4 1121
the rest of the *c* of Kohath had ....Josh 21:5 1121
the *c* of Gershon had by lot out ....Josh 21:6 1121
The *c* of Merari by their families ....Josh 21:7 1121
the *c* of Israel gave by lot unto ....Josh 21:8 1121
of the tribe of the *c* of Judah ....Josh 21:9 1121
of the tribe of the *c* of Simeon ....Josh 21:9 1121
Which the *c* of Aaron, being of................Josh 21:10 1121
who were of the *c* of Levi ....Josh 21:10 1121
Thus they gave to the *c* of Aaron ....Josh 21:13 1121
All the cities of the *c* of Aaron ....Josh 21:19 1121
the families of the *c* of Kohath ....Josh 21:20 1121
which remained of the *c* of Kohath ....Josh 21:20 1121
of the *c* of Kohath that remained ....Josh 21:26 1121
unto the *c* of Gershon, of the.................Josh 21:27 1121
the families of the *c* of Merari ....Josh 21:34 1121
So all the cities for the *c* of....................Josh 21:40 1121
of the *c* of Israel were forty ....Josh 21:41 1121
the *c* of Reuben and the *c*....................Josh 22:9 1121
departed from the *c* of Israel out ....Josh 22:9 1121
the *c* of Reuben and the *c* ....Josh 22:10 1121
the *c* of Israel heard say, Behold ....Josh 22:11 1121
the *c* of Reuben and the *c*...................Josh 22:11 1121
at the passage of the *c* of Israel.............Josh 22:11 1121
when the *c* of Israel heard of it, ...Josh 22:12 1121
c of Israel gathered themselves ....Josh 22:12 1121
the *c* of Israel sent unto the ....Josh 22:13 1121
Israel sent unto the *c* of Reuben ....Josh 22:13 1121
and to the *c* of Gad ....Josh 22:13 1121
And they came unto the *c* of Reuben ......Josh 22:15 1121
and to the *c* of Gad ....Josh 22:15 1121
Then the *c* of Reuben and the ....Josh 22:21 1121
the *c* of Gad and the half tribe of ....Josh 22:21 1121
c might speak unto our *c* ....Josh 22:24 1121
ye *c* of Reuben and *c* of Gad................Josh 22:25 1121
so shall your *c* make our *c* ....Josh 22:25 1121
your *c* may not say to our *c*..................Josh 22:27 1121
the words that the *c* of Reuben ....Josh 22:30 1121
the *c* of Gad and the *c* of ....Josh 22:30 1121
c of Reuben, and to the *c* of Gad..........Josh 22:31 1121
to the *c* of Manasseh, This day we ....Josh 22:31 1121
now ye have delivered the *c* of ....Josh 22:31 1121
returned from the *c* of Reuben ....Josh 22:32 1121
and from the *c* of Gad............................Josh 22:32 1121
to the *c* of Israel, and brought ....Josh 22:33 1121
the thing pleased the *c* of Israel ....Josh 22:33 1121
the *c* of Israel blessed God, and ....Josh 22:33 1121
the land wherein the *c* of Reuben ....Josh 22:33 1121
the *c* of Reuben and the *c* of................Josh 22:34 1121
his *c* went down into Egypt ....Josh 24:4 1121
which the *c* of Israel brought up ....Josh 24:32 1121
inheritance of the *c* of Joseph ....Josh 24:32 1121
that the *c* of Israel asked the ....Judg 1:1 1121
Now the *c* of Judah had fought ....Judg 1:8 1121
afterward the *c* of Judah went ....Judg 1:9 1121
the *c* of the Kenite, Moses'......................Judg 1:16 1121

c of Judah into the wilderness of	Judg 1:16	1121
the c of Benjamin did not drive	Judg 1:21	1121
the Jebusites dwell with the c of	Judg 1:21	1121
the Amorites forced the c of Dan	Judg 1:34	1121
words unto all the c of Israel	Judg 2:4	1121
the c of Israel went every man	Judg 2:6	1121
the c of Israel did evil in the	Judg 2:11	1121
of the c of Israel might know	Judg 3:2	1121
the c of Israel dwelt among the	Judg 3:5	1121
the c of Israel did evil in the	Judg 3:7	1121
and the c of Israel served	Judg 3:8	1121
when the c of Israel cried unto	Judg 3:9	1121
up a deliverer to the c of Israel	Judg 3:9	1121
the c of Israel did evil again in	Judg 3:12	1121
gathered unto him the c of Ammon	Judg 3:13	1121
So the c of Israel served Eglon	Judg 3:14	1121
But when the c of Israel cried	Judg 3:15	1121
by him the c of Israel sent a	Judg 3:15	1121
the c of Israel went down with	Judg 3:27	1121
the c of Israel again did evil in	Judg 4:1	1121
the c of Israel cried unto the	Judg 4:3	1121
oppressed the c of Israel	Judg 4:3	1121
the c of Israel came up to her	Judg 4:5	1121
thousand men of the c of Naphtali	Judg 4:6	1121
Naphtali and of the c of Zebulun	Judg 4:6	1121
which was of the c of Hobab the	Judg 4:11	1121
of Canaan before the c of Israel	Judg 4:23	1121
the hand of the c of Israel	Judg 4:24	1121
the c of Israel did evil in the	Judg 6:1	1121
c of Israel made them the dens	Judg 6:2	1121
the c of the east, even they came	Judg 6:3	1121
the c of Israel cried unto the	Judg 6:6	1121
when the c of Israel cried unto	Judg 6:7	1121
a prophet unto the c of Israel	Judg 6:8	1121
the c of the east were gathered	Judg 6:33	1121
all the c of the east lay along	Judg 7:12	1121
the hosts of the c of the east	Judg 8:10	1121
one resembled the c of a king	Judg 8:18	1121
subdued before the c of Israel	Judg 8:28	1121
that the c of Israel turned again	Judg 8:33	1121
the c of Israel remembered not	Judg 8:34	1121
the c of Israel did evil again in	Judg 10:6	1121
and the gods of the c of Ammon	Judg 10:6	1121
into the hands of the c of Ammon	Judg 10:7	1121
and oppressed the c of Israel	Judg 10:8	1121
all the c of Israel that were on	Judg 10:8	1121
Moreover the c of Ammon passed	Judg 10:9	1121
the c of Israel cried unto the	Judg 10:10	1121
Lord said unto the c of Israel	Judg 10:11	1121
the Amorites, from the c of Ammon	Judg 10:11	1121
the c of Israel said unto the	Judg 10:15	1121
Then the c of Ammon were gathered	Judg 10:17	1121
the c of Israel assembled	Judg 10:17	1121
to fight against the c of Ammon	Judg 10:18	1121
that the c of Ammon made war	Judg 11:4	1121
that when the c of Ammon made war	Judg 11:5	1121
we may fight with the c of Ammon	Judg 11:6	1121
and fight against the c of Ammon	Judg 11:8	1121
to fight against the c of Ammon	Judg 11:9	1121
unto the king of the c of Ammon	Judg 11:12	1121
the king of the c of Ammon	Judg 11:13	1121
unto the king of the c of Ammon	Judg 11:14	1121
nor the land of the c of Ammon	Judg 11:15	1121
c of Israel and the c of Ammon	Judg 11:27	1121
Howbeit the king of the c of	Judg 11:28	1121
passed over unto the c of Ammon	Judg 11:29	1121
the c of Ammon into mine hands	Judg 11:30	1121
in peace from the c of Ammon	Judg 11:31	1121
Jephthah passed over unto the c	Judg 11:32	1121
Thus the c of Ammon were subdued	Judg 11:33	1121
subdued before the c of Israel	Judg 11:33	1121
enemies, even of the c of Ammon	Judg 11:36	1121
to fight against the c of Ammon	Judg 12:1	1121
great strife with the c of Ammon	Judg 12:2	1121
over against the c of Ammon	Judg 12:3	1121
the c of Israel did evil again in	Judg 13:1	1121
a riddle unto the c of my people	Judg 14:16	1121
the riddle to the c of her people	Judg 14:17	1121
the c of Dan sent of their family	Judg 18:2	1121
war, which were of the c of Dan	Judg 18:16	1121
and overtook the c of Dan	Judg 18:22	1121
And they cried unto the c of Dan	Judg 18:23	1121
the c of Dan said unto him, Let	Judg 18:25	1121
the c of Dan went their way	Judg 18:26	1121
the c of Dan set up the graven	Judg 18:30	1121
that is not of the c of Israel	Judg 19:12	1121
c of Israel came up out of the	Judg 19:30	1121
Then all the c of Israel went out	Judg 20:1	1121
(Now the c of Benjamin heard that	Judg 20:3	1121
the c of Israel were gone up to	Judg 20:3	1121
Then said the c of Israel	Judg 20:3	1121
Behold, ye are all c of Israel	Judg 20:7	1121
the c of Belial, which are in	Judg 20:13	1121
But the c of Benjamin would not	Judg 20:13	1121
of their brethren the c of Israel	Judg 20:13	1121
But the c of Benjamin gathered	Judg 20:14	1121
to battle against the c of Israel	Judg 20:14	1121
the c of Benjamin were numbered	Judg 20:15	1121
the c of Israel arose, and went up	Judg 20:18	1121
battle against the c of Benjamin	Judg 20:18	1121
the c of Israel rose up in the	Judg 20:19	1121
the c of Benjamin came forth out	Judg 20:21	1121
the c of Israel went up and wept	Judg 20:23	1121
the c of Benjamin my brother	Judg 20:23	1121
the c of Benjamin came near against	Judg 20:24	1121
the c of Benjamin the second day	Judg 20:24	1121
of the c of Israel again eighteen	Judg 20:25	1121
Then all the c of Israel, and all	Judg 20:26	1121
the c of Israel enquired of the	Judg 20:27	1121
the c of Benjamin my brother	Judg 20:28	1121
the c of Israel went up against	Judg 20:30	1121
c of Benjamin on the third day	Judg 20:30	1121
the c of Benjamin went out	Judg 20:31	1121
the c of Benjamin said, They are	Judg 20:32	1121
But the c of Israel said, Let us	Judg 20:32	1121
the c of Israel destroyed of the	Judg 20:35	1121
So the c of Benjamin saw that	Judg 20:36	1121
again upon the c of Benjamin	Judg 20:48	1121
the c of Israel said, Who is	Judg 21:5	1121
the c of Israel repented them for	Judg 21:6	1121
sword, with the women and the c	Judg 21:10	2945
sent some to speak to the c of	Judg 21:13	1121
for the c of Israel have sworn,	Judg 21:18	1121
they commanded the c of Benjamin	Judg 21:20	1121
the c of Benjamin did so, and took	Judg 21:23	1121
the c of Israel departed thence	Judg 21:24	1121
had c, but Hannah had no c	1Sa 1:2	3206
that hath many c is waxed feeble	1Sa 2:5	1121
made by fire of the c of Israel	1Sa 2:28	1121
Then the c of Israel did put away	1Sa 7:4	1121
Samuel judged the c of Israel in	1Sa 7:6	1121
the c of Israel were gathered	1Sa 7:7	1121
when the c of Israel heard it,	1Sa 7:7	1121
the c of Israel said to Samuel,	1Sa 7:8	1121
there was not among the c of	1Sa 9:2	1121
And said unto the c of Israel	1Sa 10:18	1121
But the c of Belial said, How	1Sa 10:27	1121
the c of Israel were three	1Sa 11:8	1121
the c of Ammon came against you	1Sa 12:12	1121
at that time with the c of Israel	1Sa 14:18	1121
Moab, and against the c of Ammon	1Sa 14:47	1121
kindness to all the c of Israel	1Sa 15:6	1121
unto Jesse, Are here all thy c	1Sa 16:11	5288
the c of Israel returned from	1Sa 17:53	1121
the sword, both men and women, c	1Sa 22:19	5768
but if they be the c of men	1Sa 26:19	1121
to every man his wife and his c	1Sa 30:22	1121
the c of Judah the use of the bow	2Sa 1:18	1121
the c of Benjamin gathered	2Sa 2:25	1121
Beerothite, of the c of Benjamin	2Sa 4:2	1121
up the c of Israel out of Egypt	2Sa 7:6	1121
I have walked with all the c of	2Sa 7:7	1121
neither shall the c of wickedness	2Sa 7:10	1121
with the stripes of the c of men	2Sa 7:14	1121
of the c of Ammon, and of the	2Sa 8:12	1121
the king of the c of Ammon died	2Sa 10:1	1121
into the land of the c of Ammon	2Sa 10:2	1121
the princes of the c of Ammon	2Sa 10:3	1121
when the c of Ammon saw that they	2Sa 10:6	1121
the c of Ammon sent and hired the	2Sa 10:6	1121
the c of Ammon came out, and put	2Sa 10:8	1121
in array against the c of Ammon	2Sa 10:10	1121
but if the c of Ammon be too	2Sa 10:11	1121
when the c of Ammon saw that the	2Sa 10:14	1121
Joab returned from the c of Ammon	2Sa 10:14	1121
to help the c of Ammon any more	2Sa 10:19	1121
and they destroyed the c of Ammon	2Sa 11:1	1121
together with him, and with his c	2Sa 12:3	1121
with the sword of the c of Ammon	2Sa 12:9	1121
against Rabbah of the c of Ammon	2Sa 12:26	1121
all the cities of the c of Ammon	2Sa 12:31	1121
of Rabbah of the c of Ammon	2Sa 17:27	1121
were not of the c of Israel	2Sa 21:2	1121
the c of Israel had sworn unto	2Sa 21:2	1121
in his zeal to the c of Israel	2Sa 21:2	1121
of Gibeah of the c of Benjamin	2Sa 23:29	1121
If thy c take heed to their way,	1Kin 2:4	1121
of all the c of the east country	1Kin 4:30	1121
eightieth year after the c of	1Kin 6:1	1121
will dwell among the c of Israel	1Kin 6:13	1121
of the fathers of the c of Israel	1Kin 8:1	1121
a covenant with the c of Israel	1Kin 8:9	1121

C

so that thy *c* take heed to their	1Kin 8:25	1121
the hearts of all the *c* of men	1Kin 8:39	1121
all the *c* of Israel dedicated the	1Kin 8:63	1121
from following me, ye or your *c*	1Kin 9:6	1121
which were not of the *c* of Israel	1Kin 9:20	1121
Their *c* that were left after them	1Kin 9:21	1121
whom the *c* of Israel also were	1Kin 9:21	1121
But of the *c* of Israel did	1Kin 9:22	1121
Lord said unto the *c* of Israel	1Kin 11:2	1121
the abomination of the *c* of Ammon	1Kin 11:7	1121
Milcom the god of the *c* of Ammon	1Kin 11:33	1121
But as for the *c* of Israel which	1Kin 12:17	1121
your brethren the *c* of Israel	1Kin 12:24	1121
a feast unto the *c* of Israel	1Kin 12:33	1121
cast out before the *c* of Israel	1Kin 14:24	1121
sent unto all the *c* of Israel	1Kin 18:20	1121
for the *c* of Israel have forsaken	1Kin 19:10	1121
because the *c* of Israel have	1Kin 19:14	1121
thy wives also and thy *c*, even the	1Kin 20:3	1121
thy gold, and thy wives, and thy *c*	1Kin 20:5	1121
unto me for my wives, and for my *c*	1Kin 20:7	1121
people, even all the *c* of Israel	1Kin 20:15	1121
the *c* of Israel were numbered, and	1Kin 20:27	1121
the *c* of Israel pitched before	1Kin 20:27	1121
the *c* of Israel slew of the	1Kin 20:29	1121
c of Belial, and sat before him	1Kin 21:13	1121
cast out before the *c* of Israel	1Kin 21:26	1121
forth little *c* out of the city	2Kin 2:23	5288
and tare forty and two *c* of them	2Kin 2:24	3206
and live thou and thy *c* of the rest	2Kin 4:7	1121
thou wilt do unto the *c* of Israel	2Kin 8:12	1121
the sword, and wilt dash their *c*	2Kin 8:12	6768
him alway a light, and to his *c*	2Kin 8:19	1121
one of the *c* of the prophets	2Kin 9:1	1121
to them that brought up Ahab's *c*	2Kin 10:1	
also, and the bringers up of the *c*	2Kin 10:5	
down to salute the *c* of the king	2Kin 10:13	1121
of the king and the *c* of the queen	2Kin 10:13	1121
thy *c* of the fourth generation	2Kin 10:30	1121
the *c* of Israel dwelt in their	2Kin 13:5	1121
But the *c* of the murderers he	2Kin 14:6	1121
not be put to death for the *c*	2Kin 14:6	1121
nor the *c* be put to death for the	2Kin 14:6	1121
out from before the *c* of Israel	2Kin 16:3	1121
that the *c* of Israel had sinned	2Kin 17:7	1121
out from before the *c* of Israel	2Kin 17:8	1121
the *c* of Israel did secretly	2Kin 17:9	1121
For the *c* of Israel walked in all	2Kin 17:22	1121
instead of the *c* of Israel	2Kin 17:24	1121
their *c* in fire to Adrammelech	2Kin 17:31	1121
the Lord commanded the *c* of Jacob	2Kin 17:34	1121
c, and their children's *c*	2Kin 17:41	1121
for unto those days the *c* of	2Kin 18:4	1121
for the *c* are come to the birth,	2Kin 19:3	1121
the *c* of Eden which were in	2Kin 19:12	1121
cast out before the *c* of Israel	2Kin 21:2	1121
destroyed before the *c* of Israel	2Kin 21:9	1121
the graves of the *c* of the people	2Kin 23:6	1121
in the valley of the *c* of Hinnom	2Kin 23:10	1121
the abomination of the *c* of Ammon	2Kin 23:13	1121
and bands of the *c* of Ammon	2Kin 24:2	1121
king reigned over the *c* of Israel	1Chr 1:43	1121
Nahshon, prince of the *c* of Judah	1Chr 2:10	1121
Hezron begat *c* of Azubah his wife	1Chr 2:18	1121
but Seled died without *c*	1Chr 2:30	1121
And the *c* of Sheshan	1Chr 2:31	1121
and Jether died without *c*	1Chr 2:32	1121
but his brethren had not many *c*	1Chr 4:27	1121
multiply, like to the *c* of Judah	1Chr 4:27	1121
the *c* of Gad dwelt over against	1Chr 5:11	1121
These are the *c* of Abihail the	1Chr 5:14	1121
the *c* of the half tribe of	1Chr 5:23	1121
And the *c* of Amram	1Chr 6:3	1121
are they that waited with their *c*	1Chr 6:33	1121
the *c* of Israel gave to the	1Chr 6:64	1121
of the tribe of the *c* of Judah	1Chr 6:65	1121
of the tribe of the *c* of Simeon	1Chr 6:65	1121
of the tribe of the *c* of Benjamin	1Chr 6:65	1121
Unto the rest of the *c* of Merari	1Chr 6:77	1121
the *c* of Ir, and Hushim, the sons	1Chr 7:12	1121
the borders of the *c* of Manasseh	1Chr 7:29	1121
In these dwelt the *c* of Joseph	1Chr 7:29	1121
These are the *c* of Japhlet	1Chr 7:33	1121
All these were the *c* of Asher	1Chr 7:40	1121
Shaharaim begat *c* in the country	1Chr 8:8	1121
Jerusalem dwelt of the *c* of Judah	1Chr 9:3	1121
of the *c* of Benjamin	1Chr 9:3	1121
of the *c* of Ephraim, and Manasseh	1Chr 9:3	1121
of the *c* of Pharez the son of	1Chr 9:4	1121
in the companies of the *c* of Levi	1Chr 9:18	1121
their *c* had the oversight of the	1Chr 9:23	1121

pertained to the *c* of Benjamin	1Chr 11:31	1121
there came of the *c* of Benjamin	1Chr 12:16	1121
The *c* of Judah that bare shield	1Chr 12:24	1121
Of the *c* of Simeon, mighty men of	1Chr 12:25	1121
Of the *c* of Levi four thousand and	1Chr 12:26	1121
of the *c* of Benjamin, the kindred	1Chr 12:29	1121
of the *c* of Ephraim twenty	1Chr 12:30	1121
of the *c* of Issachar, which were	1Chr 12:32	1121
his *c* which he had in Jerusalem	1Chr 14:4	3205
And David assembled the *c* of Aaron	1Chr 15:4	1121
the *c* of the Levites bare the ark	1Chr 15:15	1121
ye *c* of Jacob, his chosen ones	1Chr 16:13	1121
neither shall the *c* of wickedness	1Chr 17:9	1121
from Moab, and from the *c* of Ammon	1Chr 18:11	1121
the king of the *c* of Ammon died	1Chr 19:1	1121
land of the *c* of Ammon to Hanun	1Chr 19:2	1121
of the *c* of Ammon said to Hanun	1Chr 19:3	1121
when the *c* of Ammon saw that they	1Chr 19:6	1121
the *c* of Ammon sent a thousand	1Chr 19:6	1121
And the *c* of Ammon gathered	1Chr 19:7	1121
the *c* of Ammon came out, and put	1Chr 19:9	1121
in array against the *c* of Ammon	1Chr 19:11	1121
but if the *c* of Ammon be too	1Chr 19:12	1121
when the *c* of Ammon saw that the	1Chr 19:15	1121
help the *c* of Ammon any more	1Chr 19:19	1121
the country of the *c* of Ammon	1Chr 20:1	1121
all the cities of the *c* of Ammon	1Chr 20:3	1121
that was of the *c* of the giant	1Chr 20:4	3211
before their father, and had no *c*	1Chr 24:2	1121
of the *c* of Merari, had sons	1Chr 26:10	1121
Now the *c* of Israel after their	1Chr 27:1	1121
Of the *c* of Perez was the chief	1Chr 27:3	1121
the Pelonite, of the *c* of Ephraim	1Chr 27:10	1121
Pirathonite, of the *c* of Ephraim	1Chr 27:14	1121
Of the *c* of Ephraim, Hoshea the	1Chr 27:20	1121
for your *c* after you for ever	1Chr 28:8	1121
of the fathers of the *c* of Israel	2Chr 5:2	1121
a covenant with the *c* of Israel	2Chr 5:10	1121
that he made with the *c* of Israel	2Chr 6:11	1121
yet so that thy *c* take heed to	2Chr 6:16	1121
the hearts of the *c* of men	2Chr 6:30	1121
when all the *c* of Israel saw how	2Chr 7:3	1121
caused the *c* of Israel to dwell	2Chr 8:2	1121
But of their *c*, who were left	2Chr 8:8	1121
whom the *c* of Israel consumed not	2Chr 8:8	1121
But of the *c* of Israel did	2Chr 8:9	1121
But as for the *c* of Israel that	2Chr 10:17	1121
the *c* of Israel stoned him with	2Chr 10:18	1121
Which bare him *c*	2Chr 11:19	1121
dispersed of all his *c* throughout	2Chr 11:23	1121
men, the *c* of Belial, and have	2Chr 13:7	1121
O *c* of Israel, fight ye not	2Chr 13:12	1121
the *c* of Israel fled before Judah	2Chr 13:16	1121
Thus the *c* of Israel were brought	2Chr 13:18	1121
the *c* of Judah prevailed, because	2Chr 13:18	1121
this also, that the *c* of Moab	2Chr 20:1	1121
the *c* of Ammon, and with them	2Chr 20:1	1121
the *c* of Ammon and Moab and mount	2Chr 20:10	1121
ones, their wives, and their *c*	2Chr 20:13	1121
of the *c* of the Kohathites, and of	2Chr 20:19	1121
of the *c* of the Korhites, stood	2Chr 20:19	1121
against the *c* of Ammon, Moab, and	2Chr 20:22	1121
For the *c* of Ammon and Moab stood	2Chr 20:23	1121
Lord smite thy people, and thy *c*	2Chr 21:14	1121
But he slew not their *c*, but did	2Chr 25:4	1121
fathers shall not die for the *c*	2Chr 25:4	1121
neither shall the *c* die for the	2Chr 25:4	1121
to wit, with all the *c* of Ephraim	2Chr 25:7	1121
smote the *c* of Seir ten	2Chr 25:11	1121
the *c* of Judah carry away captive	2Chr 25:12	1121
brought the gods of the *c* of Seir	2Chr 25:14	1121
the *c* of Ammon gave him the same	2Chr 27:5	1121
So much did the *c* of Ammon pay	2Chr 27:5	1121
burnt his *c* in the fire, after	2Chr 28:3	1121
cast out before the *c* of Israel	2Chr 28:3	1121
the *c* of Israel carried away	2Chr 28:8	1121
to keep under the *c* of Judah	2Chr 28:10	1121
of the heads of the *c* of Ephraim	2Chr 28:12	1121
Ye *c* of Israel, turn again unto	2Chr 30:6	1121
your *c* shall find compassion	2Chr 30:9	1121
the *c* of Israel that were present	2Chr 30:21	1121
Then all the *c* of Israel returned	2Chr 31:1	1121
the *c* of Israel brought in	2Chr 31:5	1121
And concerning the *c* of Israel	2Chr 31:6	1121
cast out before the *c* of Israel	2Chr 33:2	1121
he caused his *c* to pass through	2Chr 33:6	1121
destroyed before the *c* of Israel	2Chr 33:9	1121
that pertained to the *c* of Israel	2Chr 34:33	1121
the *c* of Israel that were present	2Chr 35:17	1121
Now these are the *c* of the	Ezr 2:1	1121
The *c* of Parosh, two thousand an	Ezr 2:3	1121

The c of Neziah	Neh 7:56	1121
the c of Hatipha	Neh 7:56	1121
The c of Solomon's servants	Neh 7:57	1121
the c of Sotai	Neh 7:57	1121
the c of Sophereth	Neh 7:57	1121
the c of Perida	Neh 7:57	1121
The c of Jaala	Neh 7:58	1121
the c of Darkon	Neh 7:58	1121
the c of Giddel	Neh 7:58	1121
The c of Shephatiah	Neh 7:59	1121
the c of Hattil	Neh 7:59	1121
the c of Pochereth of Zebaim	Neh 7:59	1121
the c of Amon	Neh 7:59	1121
the c of Solomon's servants, were	Neh 7:60	1121
The c of Delaiah	Neh 7:62	1121
the c of Tobiah	Neh 7:62	1121
the c of Nekoda, six hundred	Neh 7:62	1121
the c of Habaiah	Neh 7:63	1121
the c of Koz	Neh 7:63	1121
the c of Barzillai, which took	Neh 7:63	1121
the c of Israel were in their	Neh 7:73	1121
that the c of Israel should dwell	Neh 8:14	1121
had not the c of Israel done so	Neh 8:17	1121
fourth day of this month the c of	Neh 9:1	1121
Their c also multipliedst thou as	Neh 9:23	1121
So the c went in and possessed the	Neh 9:24	1121
For the c of Israel and the	Neh 10:39	1121
the c of Levi shall bring the	Neh 10:39	1121
the c of Solomon's servants	Neh 11:3	1121
dwelt certain of the c of Judah	Neh 11:4	1121
and of the c of Benjamin	Neh 11:4	1121
Of the c of Judah	Neh 11:4	1121
of Mahalaleel, of the c of Perez	Neh 11:4	1121
of the c of Zerah the son of	Neh 11:24	1121
some of the c of Judah dwelt at	Neh 11:25	1121
The c also of Benjamin from Geba	Neh 11:31	1121
the wives also and the c rejoiced	Neh 12:43	3206
them unto the c of Aaron	Neh 12:47	1121
not the c of Israel with bread	Neh 13:2	1121
the sabbath unto the c of Judah	Neh 13:16	1121
their c spake half in the speech	Neh 13:24	1121
Jews, both young and old, little c	Est 3:13	2945
riches, and the multitude of his c	Est 5:11	1121
His c are far from safety, and	Job 5:4	1121
If thy c have sinned against him,	Job 8:4	1121
even the eyes of his c shall fail	Job 17:5	1121
Yea, young c despised me	Job 19:18	
His c shall seek to please the	Job 20:10	1121
like a flock, and their c dance	Job 21:11	3206
layeth up his iniquity for his c	Job 21:19	1121
food for them and for their c	Job 24:5	5288
If his c be multiplied, it is for	Job 27:14	1121
with me, when my c were about me	Job 29:5	5288
They were c of fools	Job 30:8	1121
yea, c of base men	Job 30:8	1121
is a king over all the c of pride	Job 41:34	1121
his eyelids try, the c of men	Ps 11:4	1121
fail from among the c of men	Ps 12:1	1121
from heaven upon the c of men	Ps 14:2	1121
they are full of c, and leave the	Ps 17:14	1121
seed from among the c of men	Ps 21:10	1121
Come, ye c, hearken unto me	Ps 34:11	1121
therefore the c of men put their	Ps 36:7	1121
Thou art fairer than the c of men	Ps 45:2	1121
of thy fathers shall be thy c	Ps 45:16	1121
from heaven upon the c of men	Ps 53:2	1121
in his doing toward the c of men	Ps 66:5	1121
and an alien unto my mother's c	Ps 69:8	1121
he shall save the c of the needy	Ps 72:4	1121
against the generation of thy c	Ps 73:15	1121
will not hide them from their c	Ps 78:4	1121
should make them known to their c	Ps 78:5	1121
even the c which should be born	Ps 78:6	1121
arise and declare them to their c	Ps 78:6	1121
The c of Ephraim, being armed, and	Ps 78:9	1121
all of you are c of the most High	Ps 82:6	1121
they have holpen the c of Lot	Ps 83:8	1121
If his c forsake my law, and walk	Ps 89:30	1121
and sayest, Return, ye c of men	Ps 90:3	1121
and thy glory unto their c	Ps 90:16	1121
The c of thy servants shall	Ps 102:28	1121
his acts unto the c of Israel	Ps 103:7	1121
Like as a father pitieth his c	Ps 103:13	1121
righteousness unto children's c	Ps 103:17	1121
servant, ye c of Jacob his chosen	Ps 105:6	1121
wonderful works to the c of men	Ps 107:8	1121
wonderful works to the c of men	Ps 107:15	1121
wonderful works to the c of men	Ps 107:21	1121
wonderful works to the c of men	Ps 107:31	1121
Let his c be fatherless, and his	Ps 109:9	1121
Let his c be continually	Ps 109:10	1121

be any to favour his fatherless c	Ps 109:12	
and to be a joyful mother of c	Ps 113:9	1121
you more and more, you and your c	Ps 115:14	1121
hath he given to the c of men	Ps 115:16	1121
c are an heritage of the LORD	Ps 127:3	1121
so are c of the youth	Ps 127:4	1121
thy c like olive plants round	Ps 128:3	1121
thou shalt see thy children's c	Ps 128:6	1121
If thy c will keep my covenant and	Ps 132:12	1121
their c shall also sit upon thy	Ps 132:12	1121
the c of Edom in the day of	Ps 137:7	1121
from the hand of strange c	Ps 144:7	1121
me from the hand of strange c	Ps 144:11	1121
he hath blessed thy c within thee	Ps 147:13	1121
old men, and c	Ps 148:12	5288
even of the c of Israel, a people	Ps 148:14	1121
let the c of Zion be joyful in	Ps 149:2	1121
Hear, ye c, the instruction of a	Prov 4:1	1121
Hear me now therefore, O ye c	Prov 5:7	1121
unto me now therefore, O ye c	Prov 7:24	1121
therefore hearken unto me, O ye c	Prov 8:32	1121
inheritance to his children's c	Prov 13:22	1121
his c shall have a place of	Prov 14:26	1121
then the hearts of the c of men	Prov 15:11	1121
Children's c are the crown of old	Prov 17:6	1121
the glory of c are their fathers	Prov 17:6	1121
his c are blessed after him	Prov 20:7	1121
Her c arise up, and call her	Prov 31:28	1121
If a man beget an hundred c	Eccl 6:3	
my mother's c were angry with me	Song 1:6	1121
I have nourished and brought up c	Is 1:2	1121
evildoers, c that are corrupters	Is 1:4	1121
themselves in the c of strangers	Is 2:6	3206
I will give c to be their princes	Is 3:4	5288
c are their oppressors, and women	Is 3:12	5768
the c whom the LORD hath given me	Is 8:18	3206
the c of Ammon shall obey them	Is 11:14	1121
Their c also shall be dashed to	Is 13:16	5768
their eye shall not spare c	Is 13:18	1121
his c for the iniquity of their	Is 14:21	1121
as the glory of the c of Israel	Is 17:3	1121
left because of the c of Israel	Is 17:9	1121
the mighty men of the c of Kedar	Is 21:17	1121
I travail not, nor bring forth c	Is 23:4	
one by one, O ye c of Israel	Is 27:12	1121
But when he seeth his c, the work	Is 29:23	3206
Woe to the rebellious c, saith	Is 30:1	1121
is a rebellious people, lying c	Is 30:9	1121
c that will not hear the law of	Is 30:9	1121
c of Israel have deeply revolted	Is 31:6	1121
for the c are come to the birth,	Is 37:3	1121
the c of Eden which were in	Is 37:12	1121
the father to the c shall make	Is 38:19	1121
shall I know the loss of c	Is 47:8	
moment in one day, the loss of c	Is 47:9	
Thy c shall make haste	Is 49:17	1121
The c which thou hast have,	Is 49:20	1121
me these, seeing I have lost my c	Is 49:21	
with thee, and I will save thy c	Is 49:25	1121
for more are the c of the	Is 54:1	1121
than the c of the married wife	Is 54:1	1121
all thy c shall be taught of the	Is 54:13	1121
great shall be the peace of thy c	Is 54:13	1121
are ye not c of transgression, a	Is 57:4	3206
slaying the c in the valleys	Is 57:5	3206
my people, c that will not lie	Is 63:8	1121
she brought forth her c	Is 66:8	1121
as the c of Israel bring an	Is 66:20	1121
your children's c will I plead	Jer 2:9	1121
Also the c of Noph and Tahapanes	Jer 2:16	1121
In vain have I smitten your c	Jer 2:30	1121
Turn, O backsliding c, saith the	Jer 3:14	1121
How shall I put thee among the c	Jer 3:19	1121
supplications of the c of Israel	Jer 3:21	1121
Return, ye backsliding c, and I	Jer 3:22	1121
they are sottish c, and they have	Jer 4:22	1121
thy c have forsaken me, and sworn	Jer 5:7	1121
O ye c of Benjamin, gather	Jer 6:1	1121
pour it out upon the c abroad	Jer 6:11	5768
The c gather wood, and the fathers	Jer 7:18	1121
For the c of Judah have done evil	Jer 7:30	1121
to cut off the c from without	Jer 9:21	5768
the c of Ammon, and Moab, and all	Jer 9:26	1121
my c are gone forth of me, and	Jer 10:20	1121
I will bereave them of c, I will	Jer 15:7	
that brought up the c of Israel	Jer 16:14	1121
that brought up the c of Israel	Jer 16:15	1121
Whilst their c remember their	Jer 17:2	1121
the gate of the c of the people	Jer 17:19	1121
deliver up their c to the famine	Jer 18:21	1121
wives be bereaved of their c	Jer 18:21	

and they left no *c*, and died	Lk 20:31	5043
The *c* of this world marry, and are	Lk 20:34	5207
and are the *c* of God, being the	Lk 20:36	5207
being the *c* of the resurrection	Lk 20:36	5207
for yourselves, and for your *c*	Lk 23:28	5043
drank thereof himself, and his *c*	Jn 4:12	5207
unto them, If ye were Abraham's *c*	Jn 8:39	5043
the *c* of God that were scattered	Jn 11:52	5043
that ye may be the *c* of light	Jn 12:36	5207
Little *c*, yet a little while I am	Jn 13:33	5040
Then Jesus saith unto them, *C*	Jn 21:5	3813
promise is unto you, and to your *c*	Acts 2:39	5043
Ye are the *c* of the prophets, and	Acts 3:25	5207
all the senate of the *c* of Israel	Acts 5:21	5207
that they cast out their young *c*	Acts 7:19	1025
his brethren the *c* of Israel	Acts 7:23	5207
which said unto the *c* of Israel	Acts 7:37	5207
and kings, and the *c* of Israel	Acts 9:15	5207
God sent unto the *c* of Israel	Acts 10:36	5207
c of the stock of Abraham, and	Acts 13:26	5207
the same unto us their *c*, in that	Acts 13:33	5043
us on our way, with wives and *c*	Acts 21:5	5043
ought not to circumcise their *c*	Acts 21:21	5043
spirit, that we are the *c* of God	Rom 8:16	5043
And if *c*, then heirs	Rom 8:17	5043
glorious liberty of the *c* of God	Rom 8:21	5043
seed of Abraham, are they all *c*	Rom 9:7	5043
They which are the *c* of the flesh	Rom 9:8	5043
these are not the *c* of God	Rom 9:8	5043
but the *c* of the promise are	Rom 9:8	5043
(For the *c* being not yet born,	Rom 9:11	5043
be called the *c* of the living God	Rom 9:26	5207
Though the number of the *c* of	Rom 9:27	5207
else were your *c* unclean	1Cor 7:14	5043
be not *c* in understanding	1Cor 14:20	3813
howbeit in malice be ye *c*	1Cor 14:20	3515
so that the *c* of Israel could not	2Cor 3:7	5207
that the *c* of Israel could not	2Cor 3:13	5207
the same, (I speak as unto my *c*	2Cor 6:13	5043
for the *c* ought not to lay up for	2Cor 12:14	5043
but the parents for the *c*	2Cor 12:14	5043
the same are the *c* of Abraham	Gal 3:7	5207
For ye are all the *c* of God by	Gal 3:26	5207
Even so we, when we were *c*	Gal 4:3	3516
My little *c*, of whom I travail in	Gal 4:19	5040
is, and is in bondage with her *c*	Gal 4:25	5043
than she which hath a husband	Gal 4:27	5043
Isaac was, are the *c* of promise	Gal 4:28	5043
we are not *c* of the bondwoman,	Gal 4:31	5043
us unto the adoption of *c* by	Eph 1:5	5206
worketh in the *c* of disobedience	Eph 2:2	5207
and were by nature the *c* of wrath	Eph 2:3	5043
That we henceforth be no more *c*	Eph 4:14	3516
followers of God, as dear *c*	Eph 5:1	5043
of God upon the *c* of disobedience	Eph 5:6	5207
walk as *c* of light	Eph 5:8	5043
C, obey your parents in the Lord	Eph 6:1	5043
provoke not your *c* to wrath	Eph 6:4	5043
cometh on the *c* of disobedience	Col 3:6	5207
C, obey your parents in all	Col 3:20	5043
provoke not your *c* to anger	Col 3:21	5043
even as a nurse cherisheth her *c*	1Th 2:7	5043
of you, as a father doth his *c*	1Th 2:11	5043
c of light, and the *c* of the day	1Th 5:5	5207
having his *c* in subjection with	1Ti 3:4	5043
of one wife, ruling their *c*	1Ti 3:12	5043
if any widow have *c* or nephews	1Ti 5:4	5043
if she have brought up *c*, if she	1Ti 5:10	5044
the younger women marry, bear *c*	1Ti 5:14	5041
having faithful *c* not accused of	Titus 1:6	5043
their husbands, to love their *c*	Titus 2:4	5388
the *c* which God hath given me	Heb 2:13	3813
Forasmuch then as the *c* are	Heb 2:14	3813
the departing of the *c* of Israel	Heb 11:22	5027
which speaketh unto you as unto *c*	Heb 12:5	5027
As obedient *c*, not fashioning	1Pet 1:14	5043
with covetous practices; cursed *c*	2Pet 2:14	5043
My little *c*, these things write I	1Jn 2:1	5040
I write unto you, little *c*	1Jn 2:12	5040
I write unto you, little *c*	1Jn 2:13	3813
Little *c*, it is the last time	1Jn 2:18	3813
And now, little *c*, abide in him	1Jn 2:28	5040
Little *c*, let no man deceive you	1Jn 3:7	5040
In this the *c* of God are manifest	1Jn 3:10	5043
and the *c* of the devil	1Jn 3:10	5043
My little *c*, let us not love in	1Jn 3:18	5040
Ye are of God, little *c*, and have	1Jn 4:4	5040
we know that we love the *c* of God	1Jn 5:2	5043
Little *c*, keep yourselves from	1Jn 5:21	5040
unto the elect lady and her *c*	2Jn 1	5043
I found of thy *c* walking in truth	2Jn 4	5043

The *c* of thy elect sister greet	2Jn 13	5043
to hear that my *c* walk in truth	3Jn 4	5043
before the *c* of Israel, to eat	Rev 2:14	5207
And I will kill her *c* with death	Rev 2:23	5043
all the tribes of the *c* of Israel	Rev 7:4	5207
twelve tribes of the *c* of Israel	Rev 21:12	5207

CHILDREN'S See APPENDIX.

CHILD'S
maid went and called the *c* mother	Ex 2:8	3206
let this *c* soul come into him	1Kin 17:21	3206
flesh shall be fresher than a *c*	Job 33:25	5290
which sought the young *c* life	Mt 2:20	3813

CHILEAB (kil'-e-ab) See DANIEL. *A son of David.*
And his second, *C*, of Abigail the	2Sa 3:3	3609

CHILION (kil'-e-on) See CHILION'S. *A son of Elimelech.*
name of his two sons Mahlon and *C*	Ruth 1:2	3630
and *C* died also both of them	Ruth 1:5	3630

CHILION'S (kil'-e-ons)
Elimelech's, and all that was *C*	Ruth 4:9	3630

CHILMAD (kil'-mad) *An area between Assyria and Arabia.*
merchants of Sheba, Asshur, and *C*	Eze 27:23	3638

CHIMHAM (kim'-ham) *A servant of David.*
But behold thy servant *C*	2Sa 19:37	3643
C shall go over with me, and I	2Sa 19:38	3643
to Gilgal, and *C* went on with him	2Sa 19:40	3643
and dwelt in the habitation of *C*	Jer 41:17	3643

CHIMNEY
and as the smoke out of the *c*	Hos 13:3	699

CHINNERETH (kin'-ne-reth) See CHINNEROTH, CINNEROTH, GENNESARET. *A district around the Sea of Galilee.*
the side of the sea of *C* eastward	Num 34:11	3672
from *C* even unto the sea of the	Deut 3:17	3672
sea of *C* on the other side Jordan	Josh 13:27	3672
Zer, and Hammath, Rakkath, and *C*	Josh 19:35	3672

CHINNEROTH (kin'-ne-roth) See CHINNERETH. *Same as Chinnereth.*
and of the plains south of *C*	Josh 11:2	3672
plain to the sea of *C* on the east	Josh 12:3	3672

CHIOS (ki'-os) *An island near Greece.*
came the next day over against *C*	Acts 20:15	5508

CHISLEU (kis'-lew) *Ninth month of the Hebrew year.*
And it came to pass in the month *C*	Neh 1:1	3691
day of the ninth month, even in *C*	Zec 7:1	3691

CHISLEV See CHISLEU.

CHISLON (kis'-lon) *Father of Elidad.*
of Benjamin, Elidad the son of *C*	Num 34:21	3692

CHISLOTH-TABOR (kis'-loth-ta'-bor) See CHESULLOTH. *A city in Zebulon.*
sunrising unto the border of *C*	Josh 19:12	3696

CHITTIM (kit'-tim) See KITTIM. *Descendants of Javan.*
come from the coast of *C*	Num 24:24	3794
from the land of *C* it is revealed	Is 23:1	3794
arise, pass over to *C*	Is 23:12	3794
For pass over the isles of *C*	Jer 2:10	3794
brought out of the isles of *C*	Eze 27:6	3794
For the ships of *C* shall come	Dan 11:30	3794

CHIUN (ki'-un) See REMPHAN. *Another name for the god Saturn.*
C your images, the star of your	Amos 5:26	3594

CHLOE (clo'-e) *A Christian acquaintance of Paul.*
them which are of the house of *C*	1Cor 1:11	5514

CHLOE'S See CHLOE.

CHODE
Jacob was wroth, and *c* with Laban	Gen 31:36	7378
And the people *c* with Moses	Num 20:3	7378

CHOICE
in the *c* of our sepulchres bury	Gen 23:6	4005
and his ass's colt unto the *c* vine	Gen 49:11	8321
all your *c* vows which ye vow unto	Deut 12:11	4005
a *c* young man, and a goodly	1Sa 9:2	970
chose of all the *c* men of Israel	2Sa 10:9	977
fenced city, and every *c* city	2Kin 3:19	4005
and the *c* fir trees thereof	2Kin 19:23	4005
heads of their father's house, *c*	1Chr 7:40	1305
chose out of all the *c* of Israel	1Chr 19:10	970
them three hundred thousand *c* men	2Chr 25:5	970
daily was one ox and six *c* sheep	Neh 5:18	1305
and knowledge rather than *c* gold	Prov 8:10	977
and my revenue than *c* silver	Prov 8:19	977

C

tongue of the just is as *c* silver	Prov 10:20	977
she is the *c* one of her that bare	Song 6:9	1249
and the *c* fir trees thereof	Is 37:24	4005
they shall cut down thy *c* cedars	Jer 22:7	4005
fill it with the *c* bones	Eze 24:4	4005
Take the *c* of the flock, and burn	Eze 24:5	4005
and all the trees of Eden, the *c*	Eze 31:16	4005
while ago God made *c* among us	Acts 15:7	1586

CHOICEST

and planted it with the *c* vine	Is 5:2	8321
that thy *c* valleys shall be full	Is 22:7	4055

CHOKE

c the word, and he becometh	Mt 13:22	*4846*
c the word, and it becometh	Mk 4:19	*4846*

CHOKED

the thorns sprung up, and c them	Mt 13:7	*638*
c it, and it yielded no fruit	Mk 4:7	*4846*
and were *c* in the sea	Mk 5:13	4155
thorns sprang up with it, and c it	Lk 8:7	*638*
are c with cares and riches and	Lk 8:14	*4846*
place into the lake, and were *c*	Lk 8:33	*638*

CHOLER

he was moved with *c* against him	Dan 8:7	4843
the south shall be moved with *c*	Dan 11:11	4843

CHOOSE

C us out men, and go out, fight	Ex 17:9	977
that the man whom the LORD doth *c*	Num 16:7	977
the man's rod, whom I shall *c*	Num 17:5	977
set his love upon you, nor *c* you	Deut 7:7	977
c out of all your tribes to put	Deut 12:5	977
c to cause his name to dwell	Deut 12:11	977
LORD shall *c* in one of thy tribes	Deut 12:14	977
which the LORD thy God shall *c*	Deut 12:18	977
the place which the LORD shall *c*	Deut 12:26	977
shall *c* to place his name there	Deut 14:23	977
God shall *c* to set his name there	Deut 14:24	977
which the LORD thy God shall *c*	Deut 14:25	977
the.place which the LORD shall *c*	Deut 15:20	977
shall *c* to place his name there	Deut 16:2	977
God shall *c* to place his name in	Deut 16:6	977
which the LORD thy God shall *c*	Deut 16:7	977
the place which the LORD shall *c*	Deut 16:15	977
God in the place which he shall *c*	Deut 16:16	977
which the LORD shall *c*	Deut 17:8	977
the LORD shall *c* shall shew thee	Deut 17:10	977
whom the LORD thy God shall *c*	Deut 17:15	977
the place which the LORD shall *c*	Deut 18:6	977
he shall *c* in one of thy gates	Deut 23:16	977
shall *c* to place his name there	Deut 26:2	977
therefore *c* life, that both thou	Deut 30:19	977
God in the place which he shall *c*	Deut 31:11	977
in the place which he should *c*	Josh 9:27	977
c you this day whom ye will serve	Josh 24:15	977
did I *c* him out of all the tribes	1Sa 2:28	977
c you a man for you, and let him	1Sa 17:8	1262
and all the men of Israel, *c*	2Sa 16:18	977
Let me now *c* out twelve thousand	2Sa 17:1	977
of Saul, whom the LORD did *c*	2Sa 21:6	972
c thee one of them, that I may do	2Sa 24:12	977
the city which the LORD did *c* out	1Kin 14:21	977
let them *c* one bullock for	1Kin 18:23	977
C you one bullock for yourselves	1Kin 18:25	977
c thee one of them, that I may do	1Chr 21:10	977
him, Thus saith the LORD, *C* thee	1Chr 21:11	6901
LORD the God, who didst *c* Abram	Neh 9:7	977
c out my words to reason with him	Job 9:14	977
Let us *c* to us judgment	Job 34:4	977
thou refuse, or whether thou *c*	Job 34:33	977
teach in the way that he shall *c*	Ps 25:12	977
He shall *c* our inheritance for us	Ps 47:4	977
did not *c* the fear of the LORD	Prov 1:29	977
oppressor, and *c* none of his ways	Prov 3:31	977
to refuse the evil, and *c* the good	Is 7:15	977
c the good, the land that thou	Is 7:16	977
on Jacob, and will yet *c* Israel	Is 14:1	977
One of Israel, and he shall *c* thee	Is 49:7	977
c the things that please me, and	Is 56:4	977
did *c* that wherein I delighted	Is 65:12	977
I also will *c* their delusions, and	Is 66:4	977
c thou a place, *c* it at the	Eze 21:19	1254
c it at the head of the way to	Eze 21:19	1254
Zion, and shall yet *c* Jerusalem	Zec 1:17	977
land, and shall *c* Jerusalem again	Zec 2:12	977
yet what I shall *c* I wot not	Phil 1:22	*138*

CHOOSEST

thou *c* the tongue of the crafty	Job 15:5	977
Blessed is the man whom thou *c*	Ps 65:4	977

CHOOSETH

So that my soul *c* strangling	Job 7:15	977
c a tree that will not rot	Is 40:20	977
an abomination is he that *c* you	Is 41:24	977

CHOOSING

C rather to suffer affliction	Heb 11:25	*138*

CHOP

c them in pieces, as for the pot,	Mic 3:3	6566

CHOR-ASHAN (cor-a'-shan) A town in Judah.

and to them which were in *C*	1Sa 30:30	3565

CHORAZIN (co-ra'-zin) A city near Capernaum.

Woe unto thee, C,	Mt 11:21	5523
Woe unto thee, C,	Lk 10:13	5523

CHOSE

them wives of all which they *c*	Gen 6:2	977
Then Lot *c* him all the plain of	Gen 13:11	977
Moses *c* able men out of all	Ex 18:25	977
therefore he *c* their seed after	Deut 4:37	977
he *c* their seed after them, even	Deut 10:15	977
Joshua *c* out thirty thousand	Josh 8:3	977
They *c* new gods	Judg 5:8	977
Saul *c* him three thousand men of	1Sa 13:2	977
c him five smooth stones out of	1Sa 17:40	977
which *c* me before thy father, and	2Sa 6:21	977
he *c* of all the choice men of	2Sa 10:9	977
I *c* no city out of all the tribes	1Kin 8:16	977
but I *c* David to be over my	1Kin 8:16	977
David my servant's sake, whom I *c*	1Kin 11:34	977
he *c* out of all the choice of	1Chr 19:10	977
c me before all the house of my	1Chr 28:4	977
out of the land of Egypt I *c* no	2Chr 6:5	977
neither *c* I any man to be a ruler	2Chr 6:5	977
I *c* out their way, and sat chief,	Job 29:25	977
c not the tribe of Ephraim	Ps 78:67	977
But *c* the tribe of Judah, the	Ps 78:68	977
He *c* David also his servant, and	Ps 78:70	977
c that in which I delighted not	Is 66:4	977
In the day when I *c* Israel	Eze 20:5	977
and of them he *c* twelve, whom also	Lk 6:13	1586
how they *c* out the chief rooms	Lk 14:7	1586
they *c* Stephen, a man full of	Acts 6:5	1586
people of Israel *c* our fathers	Acts 13:17	1586
Paul *c* Silas, and departed, being	Acts 15:40	1951

CHOSEN

And he took six hundred *c* chariots	Ex 14:7	970
his *c* captains also are drowned	Ex 15:4	4005
even him whom he hath *c* will he	Num 16:5	977
the LORD thy God hath *c* thee to	Deut 7:6	977
which the LORD thy God hath *c* to	Deut 12:21	977
the LORD hath *c* thee to be a	Deut 14:2	977
hath *c* to place his name there	Deut 16:11	977
hath *c* him out of all thy tribes	Deut 18:5	977
God hath *c* to minister unto him	Deut 21:5	977
that ye have *c* you the LORD	Josh 24:22	977
cry unto the gods which ye have *c*	Judg 10:14	977
were numbered seven hundred *c* men	Judg 20:15	970
seven hundred *c* men lefthanded	Judg 20:16	970
thousand *c* men out of all Israel	Judg 20:34	970
king which ye shall have *c* you	1Sa 8:18	977
See ye him whom the LORD hath *c*	1Sa 10:24	977
behold the king whom ye have *c*	1Sa 12:13	977
Neither hath the LORD *c* this	1Sa 16:8	977
Neither hath the LORD *c* this	1Sa 16:9	977
Jesse, the LORD hath not *c* these	1Sa 16:10	977
do not I know that thou hast *c*	1Sa 20:30	977
thousand *c* men out of all Israel	1Sa 24:2	970
having three thousand *c* men of	1Sa 26:2	970
together all the *c* men of Israel	2Sa 6:1	970
of thy people which thou hast *c*	1Kin 3:8	977
toward the city which thou hast *c*	1Kin 8:44	977
the city which thou hast *c*	1Kin 8:48	977
Jerusalem's sake which I have *c*	1Kin 11:13	977
the city which I have *c* out of	1Kin 11:32	977
the city which I have *c* me to put	1Kin 11:36	977
and fourscore thousand *c* men	1Kin 12:21	970
which I have *c* out of all tribes	2Kin 21:7	977
city Jerusalem which I have *c*	2Kin 23:27	977
All these which were *c* to be	1Chr 9:22	1305
for them hath the LORD *c* to carry	1Chr 15:2	977
ye children of Jacob, his *c* ones	1Chr 16:13	972
Jeduthun, and the rest that were *c*	1Chr 16:41	1305
for he hath *c* Judah to be the	1Chr 28:4	977
he hath *c* Solomon my son to sit	1Chr 28:5	977
for I have *c* him to be my son, and	1Chr 28:6	977
for the LORD hath *c* thee to build	1Chr 28:10	977
my son, whom alone God hath *c*	1Chr 29:1	977
But I have *c* Jerusalem, that my	2Chr 6:6	977
have *c* David to be over my people	2Chr 6:6	977

this city which thou hast *c*	2Chr 6:34	977
toward the city which thou hast *c*	2Chr 6:38	977
have *c* this place to myself for	2Chr 7:12	977
For now have I *c* and sanctified	2Chr 7:16	977
and fourscore thousand *c* men	2Chr 11:1	970
the city which the LORD had *c* out	2Chr 12:13	970
even four hundred thousand *c* men	2Chr 13:3	970
with eight hundred thousand *c* men	2Chr 13:3	970
five hundred thousand *c* men	2Chr 13:17	970
for the LORD hath *c* you to stand	2Chr 29:11	970
which I have *c* before all the	2Chr 33:7	970
I have *c* to set my name there	Neh 1:9	970
for this hast thou *c* rather than	Job 36:21	970
he hath *c* for his own inheritance	Ps 33:12	970
and smote down the *c* men of Israel	Ps 78:31	970
I have made a covenant with my *c*	Ps 89:3	972
exalted one *c* out of the people	Ps 89:19	970
ye children of Jacob his *c*	Ps 105:6	972
and Aaron whom he had *c*	Ps 105:26	977
with joy, and his *c* with gladness	Ps 105:43	972
That I may see the good of thy *c*	Ps 106:5	972
had not Moses his *c* stood before	Ps 106:23	972
I have *c* the way of truth	Ps 119:30	977
for I have *c* thy precepts	Ps 119:173	977
For the LORD hath *c* Zion	Ps 132:13	977
For the LORD hath *c* Jacob unto	Ps 135:4	977
rather to be *c* than silver	Prov 16:16	977
rather to be *c* than great riches	Prov 22:1	977
for the gardens that ye have *c*	Is 1:29	977
my servant, Jacob whom I have *c*	Is 41:8	977
I have *c* thee, and not cast thee	Is 41:9	977
LORD, and my servant whom I have *c*	Is 43:10	977
to give drink to my people, my *c*	Is 43:20	972
and Israel, whom I have *c*	Is 44:1	977
and thou, Jesurun, whom I have *c*	Is 44:2	977
I have *c* thee in the furnace of	Is 48:10	977
Is it such a fast that I have *c*	Is 58:5	970
not this the fast that I have *c*	Is 58:6	977
your name for a curse unto my *c*	Is 65:15	972
they have *c* their own ways, and	Is 66:3	977
death shall be *c* rather than life	Jer 8:3	977
families which the LORD hath *c*	Jer 33:24	977
his *c* young men are gone down to	Jer 48:15	4005
and who is a *c* man, that I may	Jer 49:19	970
and who is a *c* man, that I may	Jer 50:44	970
that were the *c* men of Assyria	Eze 23:7	4005
withstand, neither his *c* people	Dan 11:15	4005
for I have *c* thee, saith the LORD	Hag 2:23	977
that hath *c* Jerusalem rebuke thee	Zec 3:2	977
Behold my servant, whom I have *c*	Mt 12:18	140
for many be called, but few *c*	Mt 20:16	1588
many are called, but few are *c*	Mt 22:14	1588
the elect's sake, whom he hath *c*	Mk 13:20	1586
Mary hath *c* that good part, which	Lk 10:42	1586
if he be Christ, the *c* of God	Lk 23:35	1588
them, Have not I *c* you twelve	Jn 6:70	1586
I know whom I have *c*	Jn 13:18	1586
not *c* me, but I have *c* you	Jn 15:16	1586
but I have *c* you out of the world	Jn 15:19	1586
unto the apostles whom he had *c*	Acts 1:2	1586
whether of these two thou hast *c*	Acts 1:24	1586
for he is a *c* vessel unto me, to	Acts 9:15	1589
unto witnesses *c* before of God	Acts 10:41	4401
to send *c* men of their own	Acts 15:22	1586
to send *c* men unto you with our	Acts 15:25	1586
God of our fathers hath *c* thee	Acts 22:14	4400
Salute Rufus *c* in the Lord	Rom 16:13	1588
But God hath *c* the foolish things	1Cor 1:27	1586
God hath *c* the weak things of the	1Cor 1:27	1586
which are despised, hath God *c*	1Cor 1:28	1586
but who was also *c* of the	2Cor 8:19	5500
According as he hath *c* us in him	Eph 1:4	1586
c you to salvation through	2Th 2:13	138
who hath *c* him to be a soldier	2Ti 2:4	4758
Hath not God *c* the poor of this	Jas 2:5	1586
but *c* of God, and precious	1Pet 2:4	1588
But ye are a *c* generation	1Pet 2:9	1588
are with him are called, and *c*	Rev 17:14	1588

CHOZEBA *(ko-ze'-bah)* See CHEZIB. *A city in Judah.*

And Jokim, and the men of *C*	1Chr 4:22	3578

CHRIST *(krist)* See ANTICHRIST, CHRISTIAN, CHRIST'S, CHRISTS, JESUS, MESSIAH. *A title of Jesus of Nazareth; Greek for Messiah.*

book of the generation of Jesus *C*	Mt 1:1	5547
was born Jesus, who is called *C*	Mt 1:16	5547
unto *C* are fourteen generations	Mt 1:17	5547
birth of Jesus *C* was on this wise	Mt 1:18	5547
of them where *C* should be born	Mt 2:4	5547
in the prison the works of *C*	Mt 11:2	5547
answered and said, Thou art the *C*	Mt 16:16	5547

no man that he was Jesus the *C*	Mt 16:20	5547
Saying, What think ye of *C*	Mt 22:42	5547
for one is your Master, even *C*	Mt 23:8	5547
for one is your Master, even *C*	Mt 23:10	5547
come in my name, saying, I am *C*	Mt 24:5	5547
shall say unto you, Lo, here is *C*	Mt 24:23	5547
tell us whether thou be the *C*	Mt 26:63	5547
Saying, Prophesy unto us, thou *C*	Mt 26:68	5547
or Jesus which is called *C*	Mt 27:17	5547
then with Jesus which is called *C*	Mt 27:22	5547
of the gospel of Jesus *C*, the Son	Mk 1:1	5547
and saith unto him, Thou art the *C*	Mk 8:29	5547
my name, because ye belong to *C*	Mk 9:41	5547
that *C* is the son of David	Mk 12:35	5547
come in my name, saying, I am *C*	Mk 13:6	5547
shall say to you, Lo, here is *C*	Mk 13:21	5547
and said unto him, Art thou the *C*	Mk 14:61	5547
Let *C* the King of Israel descend	Mk 15:32	5547
a Saviour, which is *C* the Lord	Lk 2:11	5547
before he had seen the Lord's *C*	Lk 2:26	5547
of John, whether he were the *C*	Lk 3:15	5547
Thou art *C* the Son of God	Lk 4:41	5547
for they knew that he was *C*	Lk 4:41	5547
answering said, The *C* of God	Lk 9:20	5547
say they that *C* is David's son	Lk 20:41	5547
come in my name, saying, I am *C*	Lk 21:8	5547
Art thou the *C*	Lk 22:67	5547
that he himself is *C* a King	Lk 23:2	5547
let him save himself, if he be *C*	Lk 23:35	5547
on him, saying, If thou be *C*	Lk 23:39	5547
Ought not *C* to have suffered	Lk 24:26	5547
and thus it behoved *C* to suffer	Lk 24:46	5547
grace and truth came by Jesus *C*	Jn 1:17	5547
but confessed, I am not the *C*	Jn 1:20	5547
thou then, if thou be not that *C*	Jn 1:25	5547
is, being interpreted, the *C*	Jn 1:41	5547
that I said, I am not the *C*	Jn 3:28	5547
Messias cometh, which is called *C*	Jn 4:25	5547
is not this the *C*	Jn 4:29	5547
and know that this is indeed the *C*	Jn 4:42	5547
and are sure that thou art that *C*	Jn 6:69	5547
indeed that this is the very *C*	Jn 7:26	5547
but when *C* cometh, no man knoweth	Jn 7:27	5547
When *C* cometh, will he do more	Jn 7:31	5547
Others said, This is the *C*	Jn 7:41	5547
Shall *C* come out of Galilee	Jn 7:41	5547
That *C* cometh of the seed of	Jn 7:42	5547
any man did confess that he was *C*	Jn 9:22	5547
If thou be the *C*, tell us plainly	Jn 10:24	5547
I believe that thou art the *C*	Jn 11:27	5547
the law that *C* abideth for ever	Jn 12:34	5547
the only true God, and Jesus *C*	Jn 17:3	5547
might believe that Jesus is the *C*	Jn 20:31	5547
he would raise up *C* to sit on his	Acts 2:30	5547
spake of the resurrection of *C*	Acts 2:31	5547
ye have crucified, both Lord and *C*	Acts 2:36	5547
Jesus *C* for the remission of sins	Acts 2:38	5547
of Jesus *C* of Nazareth rise up	Acts 3:6	5547
that *C* should suffer, he hath so	Acts 3:18	5547
And he shall send Jesus *C*, which	Acts 3:20	5547
the name of Jesus *C* of Nazareth	Acts 4:10	5547
the Lord, and against his *C*	Acts 4:26	5547
not to teach and preach Jesus *C*	Acts 5:42	5547
Samaria, and preached *C* unto them	Acts 8:5	5547
of God, and the name of Jesus *C*	Acts 8:12	5547
that Jesus *C* is the Son of God	Acts 8:37	5547
he preached *C* in the synagogues	Acts 9:20	5547
proving that this is very *C*	Acts 9:22	5547
Jesus *C* maketh thee whole	Acts 9:34	5547
preaching peace by Jesus *C*	Acts 10:36	5547
who believed on the Lord Jesus *C*	Acts 11:17	5547
Lord Jesus *C* we shall be saved	Acts 15:11	5547
for the name of our Lord Jesus *C*	Acts 15:26	5547
of Jesus *C* to come out of her	Acts 16:18	5547
said, Believe on the Lord Jesus *C*	Acts 16:31	5547
that *C* must needs have suffered	Acts 17:3	5547
whom I preach unto you, is *C*	Acts 17:3	5547
to the Jews that Jesus was *C*	Acts 18:5	5547
the scriptures that Jesus was *C*	Acts 18:28	5547
after him, that is, on *C* Jesus	Acts 19:4	5547
and faith toward our Lord Jesus *C*	Acts 20:21	5547
him concerning the faith in *C*	Acts 24:24	5547
That *C* should suffer, and that he	Acts 26:23	5547
which concern the Lord Jesus *C*	Acts 28:31	5547
Paul, a servant of Jesus *C*	Rom 1:1	5547
his Son Jesus *C* our Lord, which	Rom 1:3	5547
are ye also the called of Jesus *C*	Rom 1:6	5547
our Father, and the Lord Jesus *C*	Rom 1:7	5547
God through Jesus *C* for you all	Rom 1:8	5547
am not ashamed of the gospel of *C*	Rom 1:16	5547
by Jesus *C* according to my gospel	Rom 2:16	5547

is by faith of Jesus *C* unto all	Rom 3:22	5547
the redemption that is in *C* Jesus	Rom 3:24	5547
with God through our Lord Jesus *C*	Rom 5:1	5547
in due time *C* died for the	Rom 5:6	5547
were yet sinners, *C* died for us	Rom 5:8	5547
in God through our Lord Jesus *C*	Rom 5:11	5547
which is by one man, Jesus *C*	Rom 5:15	5547
reign in life by one, Jesus *C*	Rom 5:17	5547
eternal life by Jesus *C* our Lord	Rom 5:21	5547
C were baptized into his death	Rom 6:3	5547
that like as *C* was raised up from	Rom 6:4	5547
Now if we be dead with *C*, we	Rom 6:8	5547
Knowing that *C* being raised from	Rom 6:9	5547
unto God through Jesus *C* our Lord	Rom 6:11	5547
life through Jesus *C* our Lord	Rom 6:23	5547
dead to the law by the body of *C*	Rom 7:4	5547
God through Jesus *C* our Lord	Rom 7:25	5547
to them which are in *C* Jesus	Rom 8:1	5547
in *C* Jesus hath made me free from	Rom 8:2	5547
any man have not the Spirit of *C*	Rom 8:9	5547
if *C* be in you, the body is dead	Rom 8:10	5547
he that raised up *C* from the dead	Rom 8:11	5547
of God, and joint-heirs with *C*	Rom 8:17	5477
It is *C* that died, yea rather,	Rom 8:34	5547
separate us from the love of *C*	Rom 8:35	5547
which is in *C* Jesus our Lord	Rom 8:39	5547
I say the truth in *C*, I lie not,	Rom 9:1	5547
accursed from *C* for my brethren	Rom 9:3	5547
as concerning the flesh *C* came	Rom 9:5	5547
For *C* is the end of the law for	Rom 10:4	5547
to bring *C* down from above	Rom 10:6	5547
to bring up *C* again from the dead	Rom 10:7	5547
we, being many, are one body in *C*	Rom 12:5	5547
But put ye on the Lord Jesus *C*	Rom 13:14	5547
For to this end *C* both died	Rom 14:9	5547
before the judgment seat of *C*	Rom 14:10	5547
with thy meat, for whom *C* died	Rom 14:15	5547
serveth *C* is acceptable to God	Rom 14:18	5547
For even *C* pleased not himself	Rom 15:3	5547
another according to *C* Jesus	Rom 15:5	5547
the Father of our Lord Jesus *C*	Rom 15:6	5547
as *C* also received us to the	Rom 15:7	5547
Now I say that Jesus *C* was a	Rom 15:8	5547
of Jesus *C* to the Gentiles	Rom 15:16	5547
I may glory through Jesus *C* in	Rom 15:17	5547
which *C* hath not wrought by me	Rom 15:18	5547
fully preached the gospel of *C*	Rom 15:19	5547
the gospel, not where *C* was named	Rom 15:20	5547
the blessing of the gospel of *C*	Rom 15:29	5547
and Aquila my helpers in *C* Jesus	Rom 16:3	5547
the firstfruits of Achaia unto *C*	Rom 16:5	5547
who also were in *C* before me	Rom 16:7	5547
Salute Urbane, our helper in *C*	Rom 16:9	5547
Salute Apelles approved in *C*	Rom 16:10	5547
The churches of *C* salute you	Rom 16:16	5547
such serve not our Lord Jesus *C*	Rom 16:18	5547
of our Lord Jesus *C* be with you	Rom 16:20	5547
our Lord Jesus *C* be with you all	Rom 16:24	5547
and the preaching of Jesus *C*	Rom 16:25	5547
be glory through Jesus *C* for ever	Rom 16:27	5547
Jesus *C* through the will of God	1Cor 1:1	5547
that are sanctified in *C* Jesus	1Cor 1:2	5547
upon the name of Jesus *C* our Lord	1Cor 1:2	5547
Father, and from the Lord Jesus *C*	1Cor 1:3	5547
God which is given you by Jesus *C*	1Cor 1:4	5547
of *C* was confirmed in you	1Cor 1:6	5547
the coming of our Lord Jesus *C*	1Cor 1:7	5547
in the day of our Lord Jesus *C*	1Cor 1:8	5547
of his Son Jesus *C* our Lord	1Cor 1:9	5547
by the name of our Lord Jesus *C*	1Cor 1:10	5547
and I of *C*	1Cor 1:12	5547
Is *C* divided?	1Cor 1:13	5547
For *C* sent me not to baptize, but	1Cor 1:17	5547
lest the cross of *C* should be	1Cor 1:17	5547
But we preach *C* crucified	1Cor 1:23	5547
C the power of God, and the wisdom	1Cor 1:24	5547
But of him are ye in *C* Jesus	1Cor 1:30	5547
any thing among you, save Jesus *C*	1Cor 2:2	5547
But we have the mind of *C*	1Cor 2:16	5547
carnal, even as unto babes in *C*	1Cor 3:1	5547
that is laid, which is Jesus *C*	1Cor 3:11	5547
and *C* is God's	1Cor 3:23	5547
of us, as of the ministers of *C*	1Cor 4:1	5547
sake, but ye are wise in *C*	1Cor 4:10	5547
ten thousand instructers in *C*	1Cor 4:15	5547
for in *C* Jesus I have begotten	1Cor 4:15	5547
of my ways which be in *C*, as I	1Cor 4:17	5547
In the name of our Lord Jesus *C*	1Cor 5:4	5547
the power of our Lord Jesus *C*	1Cor 5:4	5547
For even *C* our passover is	1Cor 5:7	5547
your bodies are the members of *C*	1Cor 6:15	5547
I then take the members of *C*	1Cor 6:15	5547
and one Lord Jesus *C*, by whom are	1Cor 8:6	5547
brother perish, for whom *C* died	1Cor 8:11	5547
weak conscience, ye sin against *C*	1Cor 8:12	5547
have I not seen Jesus *C* our Lord	1Cor 9:1	5547
we should hinder the gospel of *C*	1Cor 9:12	5547
the gospel of *C* without charge	1Cor 9:18	5547
to God, but under the law to *C*	1Cor 9:21	5547
and that Rock was *C*	1Cor 10:4	5547
Neither let us tempt *C*, as some	1Cor 10:9	5547
the communion of the blood of *C*	1Cor 10:16	5547
the communion of the body of *C*	1Cor 10:16	5547
of me, even as I also am of *C*	1Cor 11:1	5547
that the head of every man is *C*	1Cor 11:3	5547
and the head of *C* is God	1Cor 11:3	5547
so also is *C*	1Cor 12:12	5547
Now ye are the body of *C*, and	1Cor 12:27	5547
how that *C* died for our sins	1Cor 15:3	5547
Now if *C* be preached that he rose	1Cor 15:12	5547
of the dead, then is *C* not risen	1Cor 15:13	5547
if *C* be not risen, then is our	1Cor 15:14	5547
of God that he raised up *C*	1Cor 15:15	5547
rise not, then is not *C* raised	1Cor 15:16	5547
if *C* be not raised, your faith is	1Cor 15:17	5547
fallen asleep in *C* are perished	1Cor 15:18	5547
this life only we have hope in *C*	1Cor 15:19	5547
But now is *C* risen from the dead,	1Cor 15:20	5547
even so in *C* shall all be made	1Cor 15:22	5547
C the firstfruits	1Cor 15:23	5547
which I have in *C* Jesus our Lord	1Cor 15:31	5547
victory through our Lord Jesus *C*	1Cor 15:57	5547
any man love not the Lord Jesus *C*	1Cor 16:22	5547
of our Lord Jesus *C* be with you	1Cor 16:23	5547
love be with you all in *C* Jesus	1Cor 16:24	5547
of Jesus *C* by the will of God	2Cor 1:1	5547
Father, and from the Lord Jesus *C*	2Cor 1:2	5547
the Father of our Lord Jesus *C*	2Cor 1:3	5547
the sufferings of *C* abound in us	2Cor 1:5	5547
consolation also aboundeth by *C*	2Cor 1:5	5547
For the Son of God, Jesus *C*	2Cor 1:19	5547
stablisheth us with you in *C*	2Cor 1:21	5547
forgave I it in the person of *C*	2Cor 2:10	5547
always causeth us to triumph in *C*	2Cor 2:14	5547
are unto God a sweet savour of *C*	2Cor 2:15	5547
in the sight of God speak we in *C*	2Cor 2:17	5547
the epistle of *C* ministered by us	2Cor 3:3	5547
have we through *C* to God-ward	2Cor 3:4	5547
which vail is done away in *C*	2Cor 3:14	5547
light of the glorious gospel of *C*	2Cor 4:4	5547
ourselves, but *C* Jesus the Lord	2Cor 4:5	5547
of God in the face of Jesus *C*	2Cor 4:6	5547
before the judgment seat of *C*	2Cor 5:10	5547
For the love of *C* constraineth us	2Cor 5:14	5547
we have known *C* after the flesh	2Cor 5:16	5547
Therefore if any man be in *C*	2Cor 5:17	5547
us to himself by Jesus *C*, and hath	2Cor 5:18	5547
To wit, that God was in *C*	2Cor 5:19	5547
Now then we are ambassadors for *C*	2Cor 5:20	5547
what concord hath *C* with Belial	2Cor 6:15	5547
the grace of our Lord Jesus *C*	2Cor 8:9	5547
the churches, and the glory of *C*	2Cor 8:23	5547
subjection into the gospel of *C*	2Cor 9:13	5547
the meekness and gentleness of *C*	2Cor 10:1	5547
thought to the obedience of *C*	2Cor 10:5	5547
also in preaching the gospel of *C*	2Cor 10:14	5547
you as a chaste virgin to *C*	2Cor 11:2	5547
from the simplicity that is in *C*	2Cor 11:3	5547
As the truth of *C* is in me	2Cor 11:10	5547
themselves into the apostles of *C*	2Cor 11:13	5547
Are they ministers of *C*	2Cor 11:23	5547
God and Father of our Lord Jesus *C*	2Cor 11:31	5547
I knew a man in *C* above fourteen	2Cor 12:2	5547
the power of *C* may rest upon me	2Cor 12:9	5547
we speak before God in *C*	2Cor 12:19	5547
seek a proof of *C* speaking in me	2Cor 13:3	5547
how that Jesus *C* is in you	2Cor 13:5	5547
The grace of the Lord Jesus *C*	2Cor 13:14	5547
neither by man, but by Jesus *C*	Gal 1:1	5547
Father, and from our Lord Jesus *C*	Gal 1:3	5547
grace of *C* unto another gospel	Gal 1:6	5547
and would pervert the gospel of *C*	Gal 1:7	5547
I should not be the servant of *C*	Gal 1:10	5547
but by the revelation of Jesus *C*	Gal 1:12	5547
of Judaea which were in *C*	Gal 1:22	5547
liberty which we have in *C* Jesus	Gal 2:4	5547
law, but by the faith of Jesus *C*	Gal 2:16	5547
even we have believed in Jesus *C*	Gal 2:16	5547
be justified by the faith of *C*	Gal 2:16	5547
we seek to be justified by *C*	Gal 2:17	5547
is therefore *C* the minister of	Gal 2:17	5547
I am crucified with *C*	Gal 2:20	5547

yet not I, but *C* liveth in me	Gal 2:20	5547
the law, then *C* is dead in vain	Gal 2:21	5547
before whose eyes Jesus *C* hath	Gal 3:1	5547
C hath redeemed us from the curse	Gal 3:13	5547
on the Gentiles through Jesus *C*	Gal 3:14	5547
one, And to thy seed, which is *C*	Gal 3:16	5547
was confirmed before of God in *C*	Gal 3:17	5547
C might be given to them that	Gal 3:22	5547
schoolmaster to bring us unto *C*	Gal 3:24	5547
of God by faith in *C* Jesus	Gal 3:26	5547
baptized into *C* have put on *C*	Gal 3:27	5547
for ye are all one in *C* Jesus	Gal 3:28	5547
then an heir of God through *C*	Gal 4:7	5547
an angel of God, even as *C* Jesus	Gal 4:14	5547
again until *C* be formed in you	Gal 4:19	5547
wherewith *C* hath made us free	Gal 5:1	5547
C shall profit you nothing	Gal 5:2	5547
C is become of no effect unto you	Gal 5:4	5547
For in Jesus *C* neither	Gal 5:6	5547
and so fulfil the law of *C*	Gal 6:2	5547
persecution for the cross of *C*	Gal 6:12	5547
in the cross of our Lord Jesus *C*	Gal 6:14	5547
For in *C* Jesus neither	Gal 6:15	5547
Lord Jesus *C* be with your spirit	Gal 6:18	5547
of Jesus *C* by the will of God	Eph 1:1	5547
and to the faithful in *C* Jesus	Eph 1:1	5547
Father, and from the Lord Jesus *C*	Eph 1:2	5547
God and Father of our Lord Jesus *C*	Eph 1:3	5547
blessings in heavenly places in *C*	Eph 1:3	5547
of children by Jesus *C* to himself	Eph 1:5	5547
together in one all things in *C*	Eph 1:10	5547
his glory, who first trusted in *C*	Eph 1:12	5547
That the God of our Lord Jesus *C*	Eph 1:17	5547
Which he wrought in *C*, when he	Eph 1:20	5547
hath quickened us together with *C*	Eph 2:5	5547
in heavenly places in *C* Jesus	Eph 2:6	5547
toward us through *C* Jesus	Eph 2:7	5547
created in *C* Jesus unto good	Eph 2:10	5547
at that time ye were without *C*	Eph 2:12	5547
But now in *C* Jesus ye who	Eph 2:13	5547
are made nigh by the blood of *C*	Eph 2:13	5547
Jesus *C* himself being the chief	Eph 2:20	5547
of Jesus *C* for you Gentiles	Eph 3:1	5547
my knowledge in the mystery of *C*)	Eph 3:4	5547
of his promise in *C* by the gospel	Eph 3:6	5547
the unsearchable riches of *C*	Eph 3:8	5547
who created all things by Jesus *C*	Eph 3:9	5547
he purposed in *C* Jesus our Lord	Eph 3:11	5547
the Father of our Lord Jesus *C*	Eph 3:14	5547
That *C* may dwell in your hearts	Eph 3:17	5547
And to know the love of *C*, which	Eph 3:19	5547
by *C* Jesus throughout all ages	Eph 3:21	5547
to the measure of the gift of *C*	Eph 4:7	5547
for the edifying of the body of *C*	Eph 4:12	5547
the stature of the fulness of *C*	Eph 4:13	5547
things, which is the head, even *C*	Eph 4:15	5547
But ye have not so learned *C*	Eph 4:20	5547
as *C* also hath loved us, and hath	Eph 5:2	5547
inheritance in the kingdom of *C*	Eph 5:5	5547
dead, and *C* shall give thee light	Eph 5:14	5547
in the name of our Lord Jesus *C*	Eph 5:20	5547
even as *C* is the head of the	Eph 5:23	5547
as the church is subject unto *C*	Eph 5:24	5547
even as *C* also loved the church	Eph 5:25	5547
but I speak concerning *C* and the	Eph 5:32	5547
of your heart, as unto *C*	Eph 6:5	5547
but as the servants of *C*, doing	Eph 6:6	5547
the Father and the Lord Jesus *C*	Eph 6:23	5547
our Lord Jesus *C* in sincerity	Eph 6:24	5547
the servants of Jesus *C*, to all	Phil 1:1	5547
to all the saints in *C* Jesus	Phil 1:1	5547
Father, and from the Lord Jesus *C*	Phil 1:2	5547
it until the day of Jesus *C*	Phil 1:6	5547
you all in the bowels of Jesus *C*	Phil 1:8	5547
without offence till the day of *C*	Phil 1:10	5547
which are by Jesus *C*, unto the	Phil 1:11	5547
So that my bonds in *C* are	Phil 1:13	5547
Some indeed preach *C* even of envy	Phil 1:15	5547
The one preach *C* of contention	Phil 1:16	5547
or in truth, *C* is preached	Phil 1:18	5547
supply of the Spirit of Jesus *C*	Phil 1:19	5547
so now also *C* shall be magnified	Phil 1:20	5547
For to me to live is *C*, and to die	Phil 1:21	5547
desire to depart, and to be with *C*	Phil 1:23	5547
C for me by my coming to you	Phil 1:26	5547
be as it becometh the gospel of *C*	Phil 1:27	5547
it is given in the behalf of *C*	Phil 1:29	5547
be therefore any consolation in *C*	Phil 2:1	5547
in you, which was also in *C* Jesus	Phil 2:5	5547
confess that Jesus *C* is Lord	Phil 2:11	5547
I may rejoice in the day of *C*	Phil 2:16	5547

work of *C* he was nigh unto death	Phil 2:30	5547
the spirit, and rejoice in *C* Jesus	Phil 3:3	5547
to me, those I counted loss for *C*	Phil 3:7	5547
the knowledge of *C* Jesus my Lord	Phil 3:8	5547
them but dung, that I may win *C*	Phil 3:8	5547
which is through the faith of *C*	Phil 3:9	5547
also I am apprehended of *C* Jesus	Phil 3:12	5547
high calling of God in *C* Jesus	Phil 3:14	5547
are the enemies of the cross of *C*	Phil 3:18	5547
for the Saviour, the Lord Jesus *C*	Phil 3:20	5547
hearts and minds through *C* Jesus	Phil 4:7	5547
through *C* which strengtheneth me	Phil 4:13	5547
to his riches in glory by *C* Jesus	Phil 4:19	5547
Salute every saint in *C* Jesus	Phil 4:21	5547
our Lord Jesus *C* be with you all	Phil 4:23	5547
of Jesus *C* by the will of God	Col 1:1	5547
in *C* which are at Colosse	Col 1:2	5547
our Father and the Lord Jesus *C*	Col 1:2	5547
and the Father of our Lord Jesus *C*	Col 1:3	5547
we heard of your faith in *C* Jesus	Col 1:4	5547
for you a faithful minister of *C*	Col 1:7	5547
C in my flesh for his body's sake	Col 1:24	5547
which is *C* in you, the hope of	Col 1:27	5547
every man perfect in *C* Jesus	Col 1:28	5547
of God, and of the Father, and of *C*	Col 2:2	5547
stedfastness of your faith in *C*	Col 2:5	5547
received *C* Jesus the Lord	Col 2:6	5547
of the world, and not after *C*	Col 2:8	5547
flesh by the circumcision of *C*	Col 2:11	5547
but the body is of *C*	Col 2:17	5547
Wherefore if ye be dead with *C*	Col 2:20	5547
If ye then be risen with *C*	Col 3:1	5547
where *C* sitteth on the right hand	Col 3:1	5547
and your life is hid with *C* in God	Col 3:3	5547
When *C*, who is our life, shall	Col 3:4	5547
but *C* is all, and in all	Col 3:11	5547
even as *C* forgave you, so also do	Col 3:13	5547
Let the word of *C* dwell in you	Col 3:16	5547
for ye serve the Lord *C*	Col 3:24	5547
to speak the mystery of *C*	Col 4:3	5547
who is one of you, a servant of *C*	Col 4:12	5547
the Father and in the Lord Jesus *C*	1Th 1:1	5547
our Father, and the Lord Jesus *C*	1Th 1:1	5547
of hope in our Lord Jesus *C*	1Th 1:3	5547
burdensome, as the apostles of *C*	1Th 2:6	5547
which in Judaea are in *C* Jesus	1Th 2:14	5547
of our Lord Jesus *C* at his coming	1Th 2:19	5547
fellowlabourer in the gospel of *C*	1Th 3:2	5547
our Father, and our Lord Jesus *C*	1Th 3:11	5547
Lord Jesus *C* with all his saints	1Th 3:13	5547
the dead in *C* shall rise first	1Th 4:16	5547
salvation by our Lord Jesus *C*	1Th 5:9	5547
of God in *C* Jesus concerning you	1Th 5:18	5547
the coming of our Lord Jesus *C*	1Th 5:23	5547
of our Lord Jesus *C* be with you	1Th 5:28	5547
our Father and the Lord Jesus *C*	2Th 1:1	5547
our Father and the Lord Jesus *C*	2Th 1:2	5547
the gospel of our Lord Jesus *C*	2Th 1:8	5547
Jesus *C* may be glorified in you	2Th 1:12	5547
of our God and the Lord Jesus *C*	2Th 1:12	5547
by the coming of our Lord Jesus *C*	2Th 2:1	5547
as that the day of *C* is at hand	2Th 2:2	5547
of the glory of our Lord Jesus *C*	2Th 2:14	5547
Now our Lord Jesus *C* himself	2Th 2:16	5547
and into the patient waiting for *C*	2Th 3:5	5547
in the name of our Lord Jesus *C*	2Th 3:6	5547
and exhort by our Lord Jesus *C*	2Th 3:12	5547
our Lord Jesus *C* be with you all	2Th 3:18	5547
an apostle of Jesus *C* by the	1Ti 1:1	5547
God our Saviour, and Lord Jesus *C*	1Ti 1:1	5547
our Father and Jesus *C* our Lord	1Ti 1:2	5547
I thank *C* Jesus our Lord, who	1Ti 1:12	5547
faith and love which is in *C* Jesus	1Ti 1:14	5547
that *C* Jesus came into the world	1Ti 1:15	5547
Jesus *C* might shew forth all	1Ti 1:16	5547
God and men, the man *C* Jesus	1Ti 2:5	5547
apostle, (I speak the truth in *C*	1Ti 2:7	5547
in the faith which is in *C* Jesus	1Ti 3:13	5547
be a good minister of Jesus *C*	1Ti 4:6	5547
begun to wax wanton against *C*	1Ti 5:11	5547
before God, and the Lord Jesus *C*	1Ti 5:21	5547
the words of our Lord Jesus *C*	1Ti 6:3	5547
all things, and before *C* Jesus	1Ti 6:13	5547
the appearing of our Lord Jesus *C*	1Ti 6:14	5547
of Jesus *C* by the will of God	2Ti 1:1	5547
of life which is in *C* Jesus	2Ti 1:1	5547
the Father and *C* Jesus our Lord	2Ti 1:2	5547
which was given us in *C* Jesus	2Ti 1:9	5547
appearing of our Saviour Jesus *C*	2Ti 1:10	5547
faith and love which is in *C* Jesus	2Ti 1:13	5547
in the grace that is in *C* Jesus	2Ti 2:1	5547

as a good soldier of Jesus *C*	2Ti 2:3	5547
Remember that Jesus *C* of the seed	2Ti 2:8	5547
is in *C* Jesus with eternal glory	2Ti 2:10	5547
name of *C* depart from iniquity	2Ti 2:19	5547
all that will live godly in *C*	2Ti 3:12	5547
through faith which is in *C* Jesus	2Ti 3:15	5547
before God, and the Lord Jesus *C*	2Ti 4:1	5547
The Lord Jesus *C* be with thy	2Ti 4:22	5547
of God, and an apostle of Jesus *C*	Titus 1:1	5547
and the Lord Jesus *C* our Saviour	Titus 1:4	5547
great God and our Saviour Jesus *C*	Titus 2:13	5547
through Jesus *C* our Saviour	Titus 3:6	5547
Paul, a prisoner of Jesus *C*	Philem 1	5547
our Father and the Lord Jesus *C*	Philem 3	5547
thing which is in you in *C* Jesus	Philem 6	5547
in *C* to enjoin thee that which is	Philem 8	5547
and now also a prisoner of Jesus *C*	Philem 9	5547
my fellowprisoner in *C* Jesus	Philem 23	5547
Lord Jesus *C* be with your spirit	Philem 25	5547
Priest of our profession, *C* Jesus	Heb 3:1	5547
But *C* as a son over his own house	Heb 3:6	5547
For we are made partakers of *C*	Heb 3:14	5547
So also *C* glorified not himself	Heb 5:5	5547
principles of the doctrine of *C*	Heb 6:1	5547
But *C* being come an high priest	Heb 9:11	5547
much more shall the blood of *C*	Heb 9:14	5547
For *C* is not entered into the	Heb 9:24	5547
So *C* was once offered to bear the	Heb 9:28	5547
the body of Jesus *C* once for all	Heb 10:10	5547
of *C* greater riches than the	Heb 11:26	5547
Jesus *C* the same yesterday, and to	Heb 13:8	5547
in his sight, through Jesus *C*	Heb 13:21	5547
of God and of the Lord Jesus *C*	Jas 1:1	5547
not the faith of our Lord Jesus *C*	Jas 2:1	5547
Peter, an apostle of Jesus *C*	1Pet 1:1	5547
of the blood of Jesus *C*	1Pet 1:2	5547
God and Father of our Lord Jesus *C*	1Pet 1:3	5547
of Jesus *C* from the dead,	1Pet 1:3	5547
glory at the appearing of Jesus *C*	1Pet 1:7	5547
manner of time the Spirit of *C*	1Pet 1:11	5547
beforehand the sufferings of *C*	1Pet 1:11	5547
you at the revelation of Jesus *C*	1Pet 1:13	5547
But with the precious blood of *C*	1Pet 1:19	5547
acceptable to God by Jesus *C*	1Pet 2:5	5547
because *C* also suffered for us,	1Pet 2:21	5547
your good conversation in *C*	1Pet 3:16	5547
For *C* also hath once suffered for	1Pet 3:18	5547
by the resurrection of Jesus *C*	1Pet 3:21	5547
Forasmuch then as *C* hath suffered	1Pet 4:1	5547
may be glorified through Jesus *C*	1Pet 4:11	5547
be reproached for the name of *C*	1Pet 4:14	5547
a witness of the sufferings of *C*	1Pet 5:1	5547
unto his eternal glory by *C* Jesus	1Pet 5:10	5547
with you all that are in *C* Jesus	1Pet 5:14	5547
servant and an apostle of Jesus *C*	2Pet 1:1	5547
of God and our Saviour Jesus *C*	2Pet 1:1	5547
the knowledge of our Lord Jesus *C*	2Pet 1:8	5547
of our Lord and Saviour Jesus *C*	2Pet 1:11	5547
our Lord Jesus *C* hath shewed me	2Pet 1:14	5547
and coming of our Lord Jesus *C*	2Pet 1:16	5547
of the Lord and Saviour Jesus *C*	2Pet 2:20	5547
of our Lord and Saviour Jesus *C*	2Pet 3:18	5547
Father, and with his Son Jesus *C*	1Jn 1:3	5547
the blood of Jesus *C* his Son	1Jn 1:7	5547
the Father, Jesus *C* the righteous	1Jn 2:1	5547
that denieth that Jesus is the *C*	1Jn 2:22	5547
on the name of his Son Jesus *C*	1Jn 3:23	5547
that confesseth that Jesus *C* is	1Jn 4:2	5547
C is come in the flesh is not of	1Jn 4:3	5547
Jesus is the *C* is born of God	1Jn 5:1	5547
by water and blood, even Jesus *C*	1Jn 5:6	5547
is true, even in his Son Jesus *C*	1Jn 5:20	5547
Father, and from the Lord Jesus *C*	2Jn 3	5547
that Jesus *C* is come in the flesh	2Jn 7	5547
abideth not in the doctrine of *C*	2Jn 9	5547
that abideth in the doctrine of *C*	2Jn 9	5547
Jude, the servant of Jesus *C*	Jude 1	5547
Father, and preserved in Jesus *C*	Jude 1	5547
Lord God, and our Lord Jesus *C*	Jude 4	5547
the apostles of our Lord Jesus *C*	Jude 17	5547
Lord Jesus *C* unto eternal life	Jude 21	5547
The Revelation of Jesus *C*	Rev 1:1	5547
and of the testimony of Jesus *C*	Rev 1:2	5547
And from Jesus *C*, who is the	Rev 1:5	5547
kingdom and patience of Jesus *C*	Rev 1:9	5547
and for the testimony of Jesus *C*	Rev 1:9	5547
kingdoms of our Lord, and of his *C*	Rev 11:15	5547
of our God, and the power of his *C*	Rev 12:10	5547
and have the testimony of Jesus *C*	Rev 12:17	5547
reigned with *C* a thousand years	Rev 20:4	5547

shall be priests of God and of *C*	Rev 20:6	5547
our Lord Jesus *C* be with you all	Rev 22:21	5547

CHRISTIAN (*kris'-tyan*) See CHRISTIANS. *A follower of Jesus Christ.*

thou persuadest me to be a *C*	Acts 26:28	5546
Yet if any man suffer as a *C*	1Pet 4:16	5546

CHRISTIANS (*kris'-tyans*)

were called *C* first in Antioch	Acts 11:26	5546

CHRIST'S (*krists*)

for the Lord Jesus *C* sake	Rom 15:30	5547
And ye are *C*	1Cor 3:23	5547
We are fools for *C* sake, but ye	1Cor 4:10	5547
called, being free, is *C* servant	1Cor 7:22	5547
they that are *C* at his coming	1Cor 15:23	5547
came to Troas to preach *C* gospel	2Cor 2:12	5547
we pray you in *C* stead, be ye	2Cor 5:20	5547
man trust to himself that he is *C*	2Cor 10:7	5547
he is *C*, even so are we *C*	2Cor 10:7	5547
in distresses for *C* sake	2Cor 12:10	5547
And if ye be *C*, then are ye	Gal 3:29	5547
they that are *C* have crucified	Gal 5:24	5547
even as God for *C* sake hath	Eph 4:32	5547
not the things which are Jesus *C*	Phil 2:21	5547
ye are partakers of *C* sufferings	1Pet 4:13	5547

CHRISTS (*krists*)

For there shall arise false *C*	Mt 24:24	5580
For false *C* and false prophets	Mk 13:22	5580

CHRONICLES

of the *c* of the kings of Israel	1Kin 14:19	1697,3117
of the *c* of the kings of Judah	1Kin 14:29	1697,3117
of the *c* of the kings of Judah	1Kin 15:7	1697,3117
of the *c* of the kings of Judah	1Kin 15:23	1697,3117
of the *c* of the kings of Israel	1Kin 15:31	1697,3117
of the *c* of the kings of Israel	1Kin 16:5	1697,3117
of the *c* of the kings of Israel	1Kin 16:14	1697,3117
of the *c* of the kings of Israel	1Kin 16:20	1697,3117
of the *c* of the kings of Israel	1Kin 16:27	1697,3117
of the *c* of the kings of Israel	1Kin 22:39	1697,3117
of the *c* of the kings of Judah	1Kin 22:45	1697,3117
of the *c* of the kings of Israel	2Kin 1:18	1697,3117
of the *c* of the kings of Judah	2Kin 8:23	1697,3117
of the *c* of the kings of Israel	2Kin 10:34	1697,3117
of the *c* of the kings of Judah	2Kin 12:19	1697,3117
of the *c* of the kings of Israel	2Kin 13:8	1697,3117
of the *c* of the kings of Israel	2Kin 13:12	1697,3117
of the *c* of the kings of Israel	2Kin 14:15	1697,3117
of the *c* of the kings of Judah	2Kin 14:18	1697,3117
of the *c* of the kings of Israel	2Kin 14:28	1697,3117
of the *c* of the kings of Judah	2Kin 15:6	1697,3117
of the *c* of the kings of Israel	2Kin 15:11	1697,3117
of the *c* of the kings of Israel	2Kin 15:15	1697,3117
of the *c* of the kings of Israel	2Kin 15:21	1697,3117
of the *c* of the kings of Israel	2Kin 15:26	1697,3117
of the *c* of the kings of Israel	2Kin 15:31	1697,3117
of the *c* of the kings of Judah	2Kin 15:36	1697,3117
of the *c* of the kings of Judah	2Kin 16:19	1697,3117
of the *c* of the kings of Judah	2Kin 20:20	1697,3117
of the *c* of the kings of Judah	2Kin 21:17	1697,3117
of the *c* of the kings of Judah	2Kin 21:25	1697,3117
of the *c* of the kings of Judah	2Kin 23:28	1697,3117
of the *c* of the kings of Judah	2Kin 24:5	1697,3117
account of the *c* of king David	1Chr 27:24	1697,3117
were written in the book of the *c*	Neh 12:23	1697,3117
the book of the *c* before the king	Est 2:23	1697,3117
the book of records of the *c*	Est 6:1	1697,3117
of the *c* of the kings of Media	Est 10:2	1697,3117

CHRYSOLITE

the seventh, *c*	Rev 21:20	5555

CHRYSOPRASUS

the tenth, a *c*	Rev 21:20	5556

CHUB (*cub*) *Allies of Egypt.*

and all the mingled people, and *C*	Eze 30:5	3552

CHUN (*kun*) *A city in Aran-zobah.*

Likewise from Tibhath, and from *C*	1Chr 18:8	3560

CHURCH

upon this rock I will build my *c*	Mt 16:18	1577
to hear them, tell it unto the *c*	Mt 18:17	1577
but if he neglect to hear the *c*	Mt 18:17	1577
the Lord added to the *c* daily	Acts 2:47	1577
And great fear came upon all the *c*	Acts 5:11	1577
is he, that was in the *c* in the	Acts 7:38	1577
the *c* which was at Jerusalem	Acts 8:1	1577
for Saul, he made havock of the *c*	Acts 8:3	1577
of the *c* which was in Jerusalem	Acts 11:22	1577
assembled themselves with the *c*	Acts 11:26	1577
his hands to vex certain of the *c*	Acts 12:1	1577

ceasing of the *c* unto God for him .... Acts 12:5   *1577*
Now there were in the *c* that was .... Acts 13:1   *1577*
ordained them elders in every *c* .... Acts 14:23   *1577*
and had gathered the *c* together .... Acts 14:27   *1577*
brought on their way by the *c* .... Acts 15:3   *1577*
they were received of the *c* .... Acts 15:4   *1577*
and elders, with the whole *c* .... Acts 15:22   *1577*
and gone up, and saluted the *c* .... Acts 18:22   *1577*
and called the elders of the *c* .... Acts 20:17   *1577*
overseers, to feed the *c* of God .... Acts 20:28   *1577*
of the *c* which is at Cenchrea .... Rom 16:1   *1577*
Likewise greet the *c* that is in .... Rom 16:5   *1577*
mine host, and the whole *c* .... Rom 16:23   *1577*
servant of the *c* at Cenchrea .... Rom *s*   *1577*
Unto the *c* of God which is at 1Cor 1:2   *1577*
as I teach every where in every *c* 1Cor 4:17   *1577*
who are least esteemed in the *c* 1Cor 6:4   *1577*
the Gentiles, nor to the *c* of God 1Cor 10:32   *1577*
when ye come together in the *c* 1Cor 11:18   *1577*
or despise ye the *c* of God 1Cor 11:22   *1577*
And God hath set some in the *c* 1Cor 12:28   *1577*
that prophesieth edifieth the *c* 1Cor 14:4   *1577*
that the *c* may receive edifying 1Cor 14:5   *1577*
excel to the edifying of the *c* 1Cor 14:12   *1577*
Yet in the *c* I had rather speak 1Cor 14:19   *1577*
If therefore the whole *c* be come 1Cor 14:23   *1577*
let him keep silence in the *c* 1Cor 14:28   *1577*
shame for women to speak in the *c* 1Cor 14:35   *1577*
because I persecuted the *c* of God 1Cor 15:9   *1577*
with the *c* that is in their house 1Cor 16:19   *1577*
unto the *c* of God which is at 2Cor 1:1   *1577*
measure I persecuted the *c* of God.... ... Gal 1:13   *1577*
the head over all things to the *c* .... Eph 1:22   *1577*
the *c* the manifold wisdom of God .... Eph 3:10   *1577*
Unto him be glory in the *c* by .... Eph 3:21   *1577*
as Christ is the head of the *c* .... Eph 5:23   *1577*
Therefore as the *c* is subject .... Eph 5:24   *1577*
even as Christ also loved the *c* .... Eph 5:25   *1577*
it to himself a glorious *c* .... Eph 5:27   *1577*
it, even as the Lord the *c* .... Eph 5:29   *1577*
speak concerning Christ and the *c* .... Eph 5:32   *1577*
zeal, persecuting the *c* .... Phil 3:6   *1577*
no *c* communicated with me as .... Phil 4:15   *1577*
he is the head of the body, the *c* .... Col 1:18   *1577*
his body's sake, which is the *c* .... Col 1:24   *1577*
the *c* which is in his house .... Col 4:15   *1577*
also in the *c* of the Laodiceans .... Col 4:16   *1577*
unto the *c* of the Thessalonians 1Th 1:1   *1577*
unto the *c* of the Thessalonians 2Th 1:1   *1577*
he take care of the *c* of God 1Ti 3:5   *1577*
which is the *c* of the living God, ... 1Ti 3:15   *1577*
them, and let not the *c* be charged 1Ti 5:16   *1577*
bishop of the *c* of the Ephesians .... 2Ti *s*   *1577*
bishop of the *c* of the Cretians .... Titus *s*   *1577*
and to the *c* in thy house .... Philem 2   *1577*
in the midst of the *c* will I sing .... Heb 2:12   *1577*
c of the firstborn, which are .... Heb 12:23   *1577*
him call for the elders of the *c* .... Jas 5:14   *1577*
The *c* that is at Babylon, elected 1Pet 5:13   *1577*
of thy charity before the *c* 3Jn 6   *1577*
I wrote unto the *c* 3Jn 9   *1577*
and casteth them out of the *c* 3Jn 10   *1577*
angel of the *c* of Ephesus write .... Rev 2:1   *1577*
angel of the *c* in Smyrna write .... Rev 2:8   *1577*
angel of the *c* in Pergamos write .... Rev 2:12   *1577*
angel of the *c* in Thyatira write .... Rev 2:18   *1577*
angel of the *c* in Sardis write .... Rev 3:1   *1577*
And to the angel of the *c* in .... Rev 3:7   *1577*
unto the angel of the *c* of the .... Rev 3:14   *1577*

CHURCHES

Then had the *c* rest throughout .... Acts 9:31   *1577*
and Cilicia, confirming the *c* .... Acts 15:41   *1577*
so were the *c* established in the .... Acts 16:5   *1577*
which are neither robbers of *c* .... Acts 19:37   *2417*
also all the *c* of the Gentiles .... Rom 16:4   *1577*
The *c* of Christ salute you .... Rom 16:16   *1577*
And so ordain I in all *c* 1Cor 7:17   *1577*
such custom, neither the *c* of God 1Cor 11:16   *1577*
as in all *c* of the saints 1Cor 14:33   *1577*
your women keep silence in the *c* 1Cor 14:34   *1577*
given order to the *c* of Galatia 1Cor 16:1   *1577*
The *c* of Asia salute you 1Cor 16:19   *1577*
bestowed on the *c* of Macedonia 2Cor 8:1   *1577*
the gospel throughout all the *c* 2Cor 8:18   *1577*
the *c* to travel with us with this 2Cor 8:19   *1577*
they are the messengers of the *c* 2Cor 8:23   *1577*
shew ye to them, and before the *c* 2Cor 8:24   *1577*
I robbed other *c*, taking wages of 2Cor 11:8   *1577*
me daily, the care of all the *c* 2Cor 11:28   *1577*
ye were inferior to other *c* 2Cor 12:13   *1577*

with me, unto the *c* of Galatia .... Gal 1:2   *1577*
was unknown by face unto the *c* of ...... Gal 1:22   *1577*
became followers of the *c* of God 1Th 2:14   *1577*
in the *c* of God for your patience 2Th 1:4   *1577*
to the seven *c* which are in Asia .... Rev 1:4   *1577*
the seven *c* which are in Asia .... Rev 1:11   *1577*
are the angels of the seven *c* .... Rev 1:20   *1577*
which thou sawest are the seven *c* .... Rev 1:20   *1577*
what the Spirit saith unto the *c* .... Rev 2:7   *1577*
what the Spirit saith unto the *c* .... Rev 2:11   *1577*
what the Spirit saith unto the *c* .... Rev 2:17   *1577*
all the *c* shall know that I am he .... Rev 2:23   *1577*
what the Spirit saith unto the *c* .... Rev 2:29   *1577*
what the Spirit saith unto the *c* .... Rev 3:6   *1577*
what the Spirit saith unto the *c* .... Rev 3:13   *1577*
what the Spirit saith unto the *c* .... Rev 3:22   *1577*
unto you these things in the *c* .... Rev 22:16   *1577*

CHURL

nor the *c* said to be bountiful .... Is 32:5   *3596*
also of the *c* are evil .... Is 32:7   *3596*

CHURLISH

but the man was *c* and evil in his 1Sa 25:3   *7186*

CHURNING

Surely the *c* of milk bringeth .... Prov 30:33   *4330*

CHUSHAN-RISHATHAIM *(cu'-shan-rish-a-tha'-im) A king of Mesopotamia.*

the hand of C king of Mesopotamia .... Judg 3:8   *3573*
of Israel served C eight years .... Judg 3:8   *3573*
the LORD delivered C king of .... Judg 3:10   *3573*
and his hand prevailed against C............ Judg 3:10   *3573*

CHUZA *(cu'-zah) A steward of Herod Antipas.*

the wife of C Herod's steward .... Lk 8:3   *5529*

CIELED

greater house he *c* with fir tree 2Chr 3:5   *2645*
it is *c* with cedar, and painted .... Jer 22:14   *5603*
c with wood round about, and from .... Eze 41:16   *7824*
O ye, to dwell in your *c* houses .... Hag 1:4   *5603*

CIELING

the house, and the walls of the *c* 1Kin 6:15   *5604*

CILICIA *(sil-ish'-yah) A Roman province in Asia Minor.*

and Alexandrians, and of them of C....... Acts 6:9   *2791*
Gentiles in Antioch and Syria and C...... Acts 15:23   *2791*
And he went through Syria and C .... Acts 15:41   *2791*
am a Jew of Tarsus, a city in C .... Acts 21:39   *2791*
Jew, born in Tarsus, a city in C .... Acts 22:3   *2791*
he understood that he was of C .... Acts 23:34   *2791*
we had sailed over the sea of C .... Acts 27:5   *2791*
into the regions of Syria and C .... Gal 1:21   *2791*

CINNAMON

of sweet *c* half so much, even two .... Ex 30:23   *7076*
my bed with myrrh, aloes, and *c* .... Prov 7:17   *7076*
calamus and *c*, with all trees of .... Song 4:14   *7076*
And *c*, and odours, and ointments, and.. Rev 18:13   *2792*

CINNEROTH *(sin'-ne-roth) See* CHINNEROTH. *Same as Chinneroth.*

and Abel-beth-maachah, and all C 1Kin 15:20   *3672*

CIRCLE

sitteth upon the *c* of the earth .... Is 40:22   *2329*

CIRCUIT

from year to year in *c* to Beth-el 1Sa 7:16   *5437*
and he walketh in the *c* of heaven .... Job 22:14   *2329*
his *c* unto the ends of it .... Ps 19:6   *8622*

CIRCUITS

again according to his *c* .... Eccl 1:6   *5439*

CIRCUMCISE

ye shall *c* the flesh of your .... Gen 17:11   *5243*
C therefore the foreskin of your .... Deut 10:16   *4135*
LORD thy God will *c* thine heart .... Deut 30:6   *4135*
c again the children of Israel .... Josh 5:2   *4135*
is the cause why Joshua did *c* .... Josh 5:4   *4135*
C yourselves to the LORD, and take .... Jer 4:4   *4135*
day they came to *c* the child .... Lk 1:59   *4059*
and ye on the sabbath day *c* a man ..... Jn 7:22   *4059*
That it was needful to *c* them .... Acts 15:5   *4059*
ought not to *c* their children .... Acts 21:21   *4059*

CIRCUMCISED

man child among you shall be *c* .... Gen 17:10   *4135*
days old shall be *c* among you .... Gen 17:12   *4135*
with thy money, must needs be *c* .... Gen 17:13   *4135*
flesh of his foreskin is not *c* .... Gen 17:14   *4135*
c the flesh of their foreskin in .... Gen 17:23   *4135*
when he was *c* in the flesh of his .... Gen 17:24   *4135*
when he was *c* in the flesh of his .... Gen 17:25   *4135*
In the selfsame day was Abraham *c* ...... Gen 17:26   *4135*

C

of the stranger, were *c* with him	Gen 17:27	4135
Abraham *c* his son Isaac being	Gen 21:4	4135
be, that every male of you be *c*	Gen 34:15	4135
will not hearken unto us, to be *c*	Gen 34:17	4135
us be *c*, as they are *c*	Gen 34:22	4135
and every male was *c*, all that	Gen 34:24	4135
for money, when thou hast *c* him	Ex 12:44	4135
the LORD, let all his males be *c*	Ex 12:48	4135
flesh of his foreskin shall be *c*	Lev 12:3	4135
c the children of Israel at the	Josh 5:3	4135
the people that came out were *c*	Josh 5:5	4135
out of Egypt, them they had not *c*	Josh 5:5	4135
up in their stead, them Joshua *c*	Josh 5:7	4135
they had not *c* them by the way	Josh 5:7	4135
are *c* with the uncircumcised	Jer 9:25	4135
Isaac, and *c* him the eighth day	Acts 7:8	4059
Except ye be *c* after the manner	Acts 15:1	4059
your souls, saying, Ye must be *c*	Acts 15:24	4059
c him because of the Jews which	Acts 16:3	4059
believe, though they be not *c*	Rom 4:11	203
Is any man called being *c*	1Cor 7:18	4059
let him not be *c*	1Cor 7:18	4059
a Greek, was compelled to be *c*	Gal 2:3	4059
say unto you, that if ye be *c*	Gal 5:2	4059
again to every man that is *c*	Gal 5:3	4059
flesh, they constrain you to be *c*	Gal 6:12	4059
themselves who are *c* keep the law	Gal 6:13	4059
but desire to have you *c*, that	Gal 6:13	4059
C the eighth day, of the stock of	Phil 3:5	4061
In whom also ye are *c* with the	Col 2:11	4059

CIRCUMCISING

they had done *c* all the people	Josh 5:8	4135
for the *c* of the child, his name	Lk 2:21	4059

CIRCUMCISION

thou art, because of the *c*	Ex 4:26	4139
Moses therefore gave unto you *c*	Jn 7:22	4061
man on the sabbath day receive *c*	Jn 7:23	4061
And he gave him the covenant of *c*	Acts 7:8	4061
they of the *c* which believed were	Acts 10:45	4061
were of the *c* contended with him	Acts 11:2	4061
For *c* verily profiteth, if thou	Rom 2:25	4061
thy *c* is made uncircumcision	Rom 2:25	4061
uncircumcision be counted for *c*	Rom 2:26	4061
c dost transgress the law	Rom 2:27	4061
neither is that *c*, which is	Rom 2:28	4061
c is that of the heart, in the	Rom 2:29	4061
or what profit is there of *c*	Rom 3:1	4061
shall justify the *c* by faith	Rom 3:30	4061
blessedness then upon the *c* only	Rom 4:9	4061
when he was in *c*, or in	Rom 4:10	4061
Not in *c*, but in uncircumcision	Rom 4:10	4061
And he received the sign of *c*	Rom 4:11	4061
the father of *c* to them who are	Rom 4:12	4061
to them who are not of the *c* only	Rom 4:12	4061
of the *c* for the truth of God	Rom 15:8	4061
C is nothing, and uncircumcision	1Cor 7:19	4061
gospel of the *c* was unto Peter	Gal 2:7	4061
Peter to the apostleship of the *c*	Gal 2:8	4061
the heathen, and they unto the *c*	Gal 2:9	4061
fearing them which were of the *c*	Gal 2:12	4061
neither *c* availeth any thing	Gal 5:6	4061
And I, brethren, if I yet preach *c*	Gal 5:11	4061
neither *c* availeth any thing	Gal 6:15	4061
the *C* in the flesh made by hands	Eph 2:11	4061
For we are the *c*, which worship	Phil 3:3	4061
with the *c* made without hands	Col 2:11	4061
of the flesh by the *c* of Christ	Col 2:11	4061
c nor uncircumcision, Barbarian,	Col 3:11	4061
called Justus, who are of the *c*	Col 4:11	4061
specially they of the *c*	Titus 1:10	4061

CIRCUMSPECT

that I have said unto you be *c*	Ex 23:13	8104

CIRCUMSPECTLY

See then that ye walk *c*, not as	Eph 5:15	199

CIS (sis) See KISH. *Father of King Saul.*

gave unto them Saul the son of *C*	Acts 13:21	2797

CISTERN

ye every one the waters of his *c*	2Kin 18:31	953
Drink waters out of thine own *c*	Prov 5:15	953
or the wheel broken at the *c*	Eccl 12:6	953
every one the waters of his own *c*	Is 36:16	953

CISTERNS

hewed them out *c*, broken *c*	Jer 2:13	877

CITIES See APPENDIX.

CITIZEN

himself to a *c* of that country	Lk 15:15	4177
in Cilicia, a *c* of no mean city	Acts 21:39	4177

CITIZENS

But his *c* hated him, and sent a	Lk 19:14	4177

CITY

and he builded a *c*	Gen 4:17	5892
and called the name of the *c*	Gen 4:17	5892
the *c* Rehoboth, and Calah,	Gen 10:11	5892
the same is a great *c*	Gen 10:12	5892
said, Go to, let us build us a *c*	Gen 11:4	5892
the LORD came down to see the *c*	Gen 11:5	5892
and they left off to build the *c*	Gen 11:8	5892
be fifty righteous within the *c*	Gen 18:24	5892
fifty righteous within the *c*	Gen 18:26	5982
all the *c* for lack of five	Gen 18:28	5892
they lay down, the men of the *c*	Gen 19:4	5892
and whatsoever thou hast in the *c*	Gen 19:12	5892
for the LORD will destroy this *c*	Gen 19:14	5892
consumed in the iniquity of the *c*	Gen 19:15	5892
forth, and set him without the *c*	Gen 19:16	5892
this *c* is near to flee unto, and	Gen 19:20	5892
that I will not overthrow this *c*	Gen 19:21	5892
the name of the *c* was called Zoar	Gen 19:22	5892
that went in at the gate of his *c*	Gen 23:10	5892
that went in at the gate of his *c*	Gen 23:18	5892
Mesopotamia, unto the *c* of Nahor	Gen 24:10	5892
to kneel down without the *c* by a	Gen 24:11	5892
of the *c* come out to draw water	Gen 24:13	5892
therefore the name of the *c* is	Gen 26:33	5892
but the name of that *c* was called	Gen 28:19	5892
a *c* of Shechem, which is in the	Gen 33:18	5892
and pitched his tent before the *c*	Gen 33:18	5892
son came unto the gate of their *c*	Gen 34:20	5892
commune with the men of their *c*	Gen 34:20	5892
went out of the gate of his *c*	Gen 34:24	5892
went out of the gate of his *c*	Gen 34:24	5892
sword, and came upon the *c* boldly	Gen 34:25	5892
upon the slain, and spoiled the *c*	Gen 34:27	5892
asses, and that which was in the *c*	Gen 34:28	5892
unto Mamre, unto the *c* of Arbah	Gen 35:27	7151
and the name of his *c* was Dinhabah	Gen 36:32	5892
and the name of his *c* was Avith	Gen 36:35	5892
and the name of his *c* was Pau	Gen 36:39	5892
which was round about every *c*	Gen 41:48	5892
when they were gone out of the *c*	Gen 44:4	5892
man his ass, and returned to the *c*	Gen 44:13	5892
As soon as I am gone out of the *c*	Ex 9:29	5892
went out of the *c* from Pharaoh	Ex 9:33	5892
an unclean place without the *c*	Lev 14:40	5892
the *c* into an unclean place	Lev 14:41	5892
of the *c* into an unclean place	Lev 14:45	5892
out of the *c* into the open fields	Lev 14:53	5892
a dwelling house in a walled *c*	Lev 25:29	5892
c shall be established for ever	Lev 25:30	5892
the *c* of his possession, shall go	Lev 25:33	5892
a *c* in the uttermost of thy	Num 20:16	5892
For Heshbon was the *c* of Sihon	Num 21:26	5892
let the *c* of Sihon be built and	Num 21:27	5892
a flame from the *c* of Sihon	Num 21:28	7151
out to meet him unto a *c* of Moab	Num 22:36	5892
him that remaineth of the *c*	Num 24:19	5892
reach from the wall of the *c*	Num 35:4	5892
c on the east side two thousand	Num 35:5	5892
the *c* shall be in the midst	Num 35:5	5892
him to the *c* of his refuge	Num 35:25	5892
the border of the *c* of his refuge	Num 35:26	5892
borders of the *c* of his refuge	Num 35:27	5892
c of his refuge until the death	Num 35:28	5892
is fled to the *c* of his refuge	Num 35:32	5892
and the little ones, of every *c*	Deut 2:34	5892
from the *c* that is by the river,	Deut 2:36	5892
was not one *c* too strong for us	Deut 2:36	7151
there was not a *c* which we took	Deut 3:4	7151
women, and children, of every *c*	Deut 3:6	5892
the inhabitants of their *c*	Deut 13:13	5892
that *c* with the edge of the sword	Deut 13:15	5892
and shalt burn with fire the *c*	Deut 13:16	5892
the elders of his *c* shall send	Deut 19:12	5892
nigh unto a *c* to fight against it	Deut 20:10	5892
cattle, and all that is in the *c*	Deut 20:14	5892
shalt besiege a *c* a long time	Deut 20:19	5892
the *c* that maketh war with thee	Deut 20:20	5892
that the *c* which is next unto the	Deut 21:3	5892
of that *c* shall take an heifer	Deut 21:3	5892
the elders of that *c* shall bring	Deut 21:4	5892
And all the elders of that *c*	Deut 21:6	5892
him out unto the elders of his *c*	Deut 21:19	5892
say unto the elders of his *c*	Deut 21:20	5892
all the men of his *c* shall stone	Deut 21:21	5892
the elders of the *c* in the gate	Deut 22:15	5892
cloth before the elders of the *c*	Deut 22:17	5892
the elders of that *c* shall take	Deut 22:18	5892

the men of her *c* shall stone her	Deut 22:21	5892
and a man find her in the *c*	Deut 22:23	5892
both out unto the gate of that *c*	Deut 22:24	5892
she cried not, being in the *c*	Deut 22:24	5892
elders of his *c* shall call him	Deut 25:8	5892
Blessed shalt thou be in the *c*	Deut 28:3	5892
Cursed shalt thou be in the *c*	Deut 28:16	5892
the *c* of palm trees, unto Zoar	Deut 34:3	5892
an heap very far from the *c* Adam	Josh 3:16	5892
And ye shall compass the *c*	Josh 6:3	5892
war, and go round about the *c* once	Josh 6:3	5892
shall compass the *c* seven times	Josh 6:4	5892
the wall of the *c* shall fall down	Josh 6:5	5892
people, Pass on, and compass the *c*	Josh 6:7	5892
ark of the LORD compassed the *c*	Josh 6:11	5892
day they compassed the *c* once	Josh 6:14	5892
compassed the *c* after the same	Josh 6:15	5892
they compassed the *c* seven times	Josh 6:15	5892
for the LORD hath given you the *c*	Josh 6:16	5892
the *c* shall be accursed, even it,	Josh 6:17	5892
the people went up into the *c*	Josh 6:20	5892
before him, and they took the *c*	Josh 6:20	5892
destroyed all that was in the *c*	Josh 6:21	5892
And they burnt the *c* with fire	Josh 6:24	5892
up and buildeth this *c* Jericho	Josh 6:26	5892
of Ai, and his people, and his *c*	Josh 8:1	5892
an ambush for the *c* behind it	Josh 8:2	5892
the *c*, even behind the *c*	Josh 8:4	5892
go not very far from the *c*	Josh 8:4	5892
with me, will approach unto the *c*	Josh 8:5	5892
we have drawn them from the *c*	Josh 8:6	5892
the ambush, and seize upon the *c*	Josh 8:7	5892
be, when ye have taken the *c*	Josh 8:8	5892
that ye shall set the *c* on fire	Josh 8:8	5892
drew nigh, and came before the *c*	Josh 8:11	5892
and Ai, on the west side of the *c*	Josh 8:12	5892
that was on the north of the *c*	Josh 8:13	5892
in wait on the west of the *c*	Josh 8:13	5892
the men of the *c* went out against	Josh 8:14	5892
ambush against him behind the *c*	Josh 8:14	5892
and were drawn away from the *c*	Josh 8:16	5892
and they left the *c* open, and	Josh 8:17	5892
he had in his hand toward the *c*	Josh 8:18	5892
and they entered into the *c*	Josh 8:19	5892
and hasted and set the *c* on fire	Josh 8:19	5892
the smoke of the *c* ascended up to	Josh 8:20	5892
that the ambush had taken the *c*	Josh 8:21	5892
that the smoke of the *c* ascended	Josh 8:21	5892
issued out of the *c* against them	Josh 8:22	5892
the spoil of that *c* Israel took	Josh 8:27	5892
the entering of the gate of the *c*	Josh 8:29	5892
because Gibeon was a great *c*	Josh 10:2	5892
There was not a *c* that made peace	Josh 11:19	5892
the *c* that is in the midst of the	Josh 13:9	5892
the *c* that is in the midst of the	Josh 13:16	5892
even the *c* of Arba the father of	Josh 15:13	7151
father of Anak, which *c* is Hebron	Josh 15:13	
the *c* of Salt, and En-gedi	Josh 15:62	5892
a *c* of the children of Judah	Josh 18:14	5892
to Ramah, and to the strong *c* Tyre	Josh 19:29	5892
gave him the *c* which he asked	Josh 19:50	5892
and he built the *c*, and dwelt	Josh 19:50	5892
the entering of the gate of the *c*	Josh 20:4	5892
the ears of the elders of that *c*	Josh 20:4	5892
take him into the *c* unto them	Josh 20:4	5892
And he shall dwell in that *c*	Josh 20:6	5892
return, and come unto his own *c*	Josh 20:6	5892
unto the *c* from whence he fled	Josh 20:6	5892
they gave them the *c* of Arba	Josh 21:11	7151
which *c* is Hebron, in the hill	Josh 21:11	
But the fields of the *c*, and the	Josh 21:12	5892
to be a *c* of refuge for the	Josh 21:13	5892
to be a *c* of refuge for the	Josh 21:21	5892
to be a *c* of refuge for the	Josh 21:27	5892
to be a *c* of refuge for the	Josh 21:32	5892
to be a *c* of refuge for the	Josh 21:38	5892
the sword, and set the *c* on fire	Judg 1:8	5892
went up out of the *c* of palm	Judg 1:16	5892
the name of the *c* was called	Judg 1:17	5892
the name of the *c* before was Luz	Judg 1:23	5892
saw a man come forth out of the *c*	Judg 1:24	5892
thee, the entrance into the *c*	Judg 1:24	5892
them the entrance into the *c*	Judg 1:25	5892
they smote the *c* with the edge of	Judg 1:25	5892
of the Hittites, and built a *c*	Judg 1:26	5892
and possessed the *c* of palm trees	Judg 3:13	5892
household, and the men of the *c*	Judg 6:27	5892
when the men of the *c* arose early	Judg 6:28	5892
the men of the *c* said unto Joash	Judg 6:30	5892
And he took the elders of the *c*	Judg 8:16	5892
Penuel, and slew the men of the *c*	Judg 8:17	5892
ephod thereof, and put it in his *c*	Judg 8:27	5892
when Zebul the ruler of the *c*	Judg 9:30	5892
they fortify the *c* against thee	Judg 9:31	5892
rise early, and set upon the *c*	Judg 9:33	5892
the entering of the gate of the *c*	Judg 9:35	5892
were come forth out of the *c*	Judg 9:43	5892
the entering of the gate of the *c*	Judg 9:44	5892
fought against the *c* all that day	Judg 9:45	5892
and he took the *c*, and slew the	Judg 9:45	5892
was therein, and beat down the *c*	Judg 9:45	5892
was a strong tower within the *c*	Judg 9:51	5892
and women, and all they of the *c*	Judg 9:51	5892
the men of the *c* said unto him on	Judg 14:18	5892
all night in the gate of the *c*	Judg 16:2	5892
the doors of the gate of the *c*	Judg 16:3	5892
of the *c* from Beth-lehem-judah to	Judg 17:8	5892
sword, and burnt the *c* with fire	Judg 18:27	5892
And they built a *c*, and dwelt	Judg 18:28	5892
they called the name of the *c* Dan	Judg 18:29	5892
of the *c* was Laish at the first	Judg 18:29	5892
in into this *c* of the Jebusites	Judg 19:11	5892
hither into the *c* of a stranger	Judg 19:12	5892
sat him down in a street of the *c*	Judg 19:15	5892
man in the street of the *c*	Judg 19:17	5892
merry, behold, the men of the *c*	Judg 19:22	5892
were gathered against the *c*	Judg 20:11	5892
and were drawn away from the *c*	Judg 20:31	5892
them from the *c* unto the highways	Judg 20:32	5892
smote all the *c* with the edge of	Judg 20:37	5892
with smoke rise up out of the *c*	Judg 20:38	5892
of the *c* with a pillar of smoke	Judg 20:40	5892
the flame of the *c* ascended up to	Judg 20:40	5892
sword, as well the men of every *c*	Judg 20:48	5892
that all the *c* was moved about	Ruth 1:19	5892
took it up, and went into the *c*	Ruth 2:18	5892
for all the *c* of my people doth	Ruth 3:11	8179
and she went into the *c*	Ruth 3:15	5892
ten men of the elders of the *c*	Ruth 4:2	5892
up out of his *c* yearly to worship	1Sa 1:3	5892
And when the man came into the *c*	1Sa 4:13	5892
and told it, all the *c* cried out	1Sa 4:13	5892
of the LORD was against the *c*	1Sa 5:9	5892
and he smote the men of the *c*	1Sa 5:9	5892
destruction throughout all the *c*	1Sa 5:11	5892
the cry of the *c* went up to	1Sa 5:12	5892
Go ye every man unto his *c*	1Sa 8:22	5892
there is in this *c* a man of God	1Sa 9:6	5892
So they went unto the *c* where the	1Sa 9:10	5892
as they went up the hill to the *c*	1Sa 9:11	5892
now, for he came to day to the *c*	1Sa 9:12	5892
As soon as ye be come into the *c*	1Sa 9:13	5892
And they went up into the *c*	1Sa 9:14	5892
and when they were come into the *c*	1Sa 9:14	5892
from the high place into the *c*	1Sa 9:25	5892
going down to the end of the *c*	1Sa 9:27	5892
thou art come thither to the *c*	1Sa 10:5	5892
And Saul came to a *c* of Amalek	1Sa 15:5	5892
he might run to Beth-lehem his *c*	1Sa 20:6	5892
family hath a sacrifice in the *c*	1Sa 20:29	5892
unto him, Go, carry them to the *c*	1Sa 20:40	5892
and Jonathan went into the *c*	1Sa 20:42	5892
the *c* of the priests, smote he	1Sa 22:19	5892
to destroy the *c* for my sake	1Sa 23:10	5892
dwell in the royal *c* with thee	1Sa 27:5	5892
him in Ramah, even in his own *c*	1Sa 28:3	5892
So David and his men came to the *c*	1Sa 30:3	5892
the same is the *c* of David	2Sa 5:7	5892
fort, and called it the *c* of David	2Sa 5:9	5892
LORD unto him into the *c* of David	2Sa 6:10	5892
into the *c* of David with gladness	2Sa 6:12	5892
the LORD came into the *c* of David	2Sa 6:16	5892
unto thee, to search the *c*	2Sa 10:3	5892
Abishai, and entered into the *c*	2Sa 10:14	5892
to pass, when Joab observed the *c*	2Sa 11:16	5892
And the men of the *c* went out	2Sa 11:17	5892
nigh unto the *c* when ye did fight	2Sa 11:20	5892
battle more strong against the *c*	2Sa 11:25	5892
him, There were two men in one *c*	2Sa 12:1	5892
of Ammon, and took the royal *c*	2Sa 12:26	5892
and have taken the *c* of waters	2Sa 12:27	5892
together, and encamp against the *c*	2Sa 12:28	5892
lest I take the *c*, and it be	2Sa 12:28	5892
spoil of the *c* in great abundance	2Sa 12:30	5892
him, and said, Of what *c* art thou	2Sa 15:2	5892
David's counsellor, from his *c*	2Sa 15:12	5892
smite the *c* with the edge of the	2Sa 15:14	5892
had done passing out of the *c*	2Sa 15:24	5892
back the ark of God into the *c*	2Sa 15:25	5892
return into the *c* in peace	2Sa 15:27	5892
But if thou return to the *c*	2Sa 15:34	5892
David's friend came into the *c*	2Sa 15:37	5892

if he be gotten into a c	2Sa 17:13	5892
all Israel bring ropes to that c	2Sa 17:13	5892
not be seen to come into the c	2Sa 17:17	5892
him home to his house, to his c	2Sa 17:23	5892
that thou succour us out of the c	2Sa 18:3	5892
by stealth that day into the c	2Sa 19:3	5892
that I may die in mine own c	2Sa 19:37	5892
they cast up a bank against the c	2Sa 20:15	5892
cried a wise woman out of the c	2Sa 20:16	5892
thou seekest to destroy a c	2Sa 20:19	5892
only, and I will depart from the c	2Sa 20:21	5892
and they retired from the c	2Sa 20:22	5892
on the right side of the c that	2Sa 24:5	5892
noise of the c being in an uproar	1Kin 1:41	7151
so that the c rang again	1Kin 1:45	7151
and was buried in the c of David	1Kin 2:10	5892
brought her into the c of David	1Kin 3:1	5892
of the Lord out of the c of David	1Kin 8:1	5892
I chose no c out of all the	1Kin 8:16	5892
the c which thou hast chosen	1Kin 8:44	5892
the c which thou hast chosen, and	1Kin 8:48	5892
Canaanites that dwelt in the c	1Kin 9:16	5892
daughter came up out of the c of	1Kin 9:24	5892
of the c of David his father	1Kin 11:27	5892
the c which I have chosen out of	1Kin 11:32	5892
the c which I have chosen me to	1Kin 11:36	5892
was buried in the c of David his	1Kin 11:43	5892
told it in the c where the old	1Kin 13:25	5892
and the old prophet came to the c	1Kin 13:29	5892
in the c shall the dogs eat	1Kin 14:11	5892
and when thy feet enter into the c	1Kin 14:12	5892
the c which the Lord did choose	1Kin 14:21	5892
his fathers in the c of David	1Kin 14:31	5892
they buried him in the c of David	1Kin 15:8	5892
in the c of David his father	1Kin 15:24	5892
in the c shall the dogs eat	1Kin 16:4	5892
Zimri saw that the c was taken	1Kin 16:18	5892
the name of the c which he built	1Kin 16:24	5892
when he came to the gate of the c	1Kin 17:10	5892
to Ahab king of Israel into the c	1Kin 20:2	5892
themselves in array against the c	1Kin 20:12	5892
the provinces came out of the c	1Kin 20:19	5892
rest fled to Aphek, into the c	1Kin 20:30	5892
fled, and came into the c, into an	1Kin 20:30	5892
to the nobles that were in his c	1Kin 21:8	5892
And the men of his c, even the	1Kin 21:11	5892
who were the inhabitants in his c	1Kin 21:11	5892
carried him forth out of the c	1Kin 21:13	5892
Ahab in the c the dogs shall eat	1Kin 21:24	5892
unto Amon the governor of the c	1Kin 22:26	5892
sun, saying, Every man to his c	1Kin 22:36	5892
in the c of David his father	1Kin 22:50	5892
the men of the c said unto Elisha	2Kin 2:19	5892
situation of this c is pleasant	2Kin 2:19	5892
little children out of the c	2Kin 2:23	5892
And ye shall smite every fenced c	2Kin 3:19	5892
fenced c, and every choice c	2Kin 3:19	5892
night, and compassed the c about	2Kin 6:14	5892
compassed the c both with horses	2Kin 6:15	5892
the way, neither is this the c	2Kin 6:19	5892
we say, We will enter into the c	2Kin 7:4	5892
c, then the famine is in the c	2Kin 7:4	5892
called unto the porter of the c	2Kin 7:10	5892
When they come out of the c	2Kin 7:12	5892
them alive, and get into the c	2Kin 7:12	5892
remain, which are left in the c	2Kin 7:13	
his fathers in the c of David	2Kin 8:24	5892
the c to go to tell it in Jezreel	2Kin 9:15	5892
his fathers in the c of David	2Kin 9:28	5892
and horses, a fenced c also	2Kin 10:2	5892
house, and he that was over the c	2Kin 10:5	5892
were with the great men of the c	2Kin 10:6	5892
went to the c of the house of	2Kin 10:25	5892
rejoiced, and the c was in quiet	2Kin 11:20	5892
his fathers in the c of David	2Kin 12:21	5892
his fathers in the c of David	2Kin 14:20	5892
his fathers in the c of David	2Kin 15:7	5892
in the c of David his father	2Kin 15:38	5892
his fathers in the c of David	2Kin 16:20	5892
of the watchmen to the fenced c	2Kin 17:9	5892
of the watchmen to the fenced c	2Kin 18:8	5892
this c shall not be delivered	2Kin 18:30	5892
the king of the c of Sepharvaim	2Kin 19:13	5892
He shall not come into this c	2Kin 19:32	5892
and shall not come into this c	2Kin 19:33	5892
For I will defend this c, to save	2Kin 19:34	5892
this c out of the hand of the	2Kin 20:6	5892
defend this c for mine own sake	2Kin 20:6	5892
and brought water into the c	2Kin 20:20	5892
of Joshua the governor of the c	2Kin 23:8	5892
left hand at the gate of the c	2Kin 23:8	5892

And the men of the c told him	2Kin 23:17	5892
will cast off this c Jerusalem	2Kin 23:27	5892
Jerusalem, and the c was besieged	2Kin 24:10	5892
of Babylon came against the c	2Kin 24:11	5892
the c was besieged unto the	2Kin 25:2	5892
the famine prevailed in the c	2Kin 25:3	5892
the c was broken up, and all the	2Kin 25:4	5892
were against the c round about	2Kin 25:4	5892
people that were left in the c	2Kin 25:11	5892
out of the c he took an officer	2Kin 25:19	5892
which were found in the c	2Kin 25:19	5892
the land that were found in the c	2Kin 25:19	5892
and the name of his c was Dinhabah	1Chr 1:43	5892
and the name of his c was Avith	1Chr 1:46	5892
and the name of his c was Pai	1Chr 1:50	5892
But the fields of the c, and the	1Chr 6:56	5892
the c of refuge, and Libnah with	1Chr 6:57	5892
of Zion, which is the c of David	1Chr 11:5	5892
they called it the c of David	1Chr 11:7	5892
And he built the c round about	1Chr 11:8	5892
Joab repaired the rest of the c	1Chr 11:8	5892
home to himself to the c of David	1Chr 13:13	5892
made him houses in the c of David	1Chr 15:1	5892
the Lord came to the c of David	1Chr 15:29	5892
in array before the gate of the c	1Chr 19:9	5892
brother, and entered into the c	1Chr 19:15	5892
exceeding much spoil out of the c	1Chr 20:2	5892
of the Lord out of the c of David	2Chr 5:2	5892
c among all the tribes of Israel	2Chr 6:5	5892
this c which thou hast chosen	2Chr 6:34	5892
toward the c which thou hast	2Chr 6:38	5892
daughter of Pharaoh out of the c	2Chr 8:11	5892
in the c of David his father	2Chr 9:31	5892
in every several c he put shields	2Chr 11:12	5892
and Benjamin, unto every fenced c	2Chr 11:23	5892
the c which the Lord had chosen	2Chr 12:13	5892
and was buried in the c of David	2Chr 12:16	5892
they buried him in the c of David	2Chr 14:1	5892
destroyed of nation, and of c	2Chr 15:6	5892
for himself in the c of David	2Chr 16:14	5892
to Amon the governor of the c	2Chr 18:25	5892
fenced cities of Judah, c by c	2Chr 19:5	5892
his fathers in the c of David	2Chr 21:1	5892
they buried him in the c of David	2Chr 21:20	5892
the c was quiet, after that they	2Chr 23:21	5892
they buried him in the c of David	2Chr 24:16	5892
they buried him in the c of David	2Chr 24:25	5892
his fathers in the c of Judah	2Chr 25:28	5892
they buried him in the c of David	2Chr 27:9	5892
the c of palm trees, to their	2Chr 28:15	5892
in every several c of Judah he	2Chr 28:25	5892
and they buried him in the c	2Chr 28:27	5892
and gathered the rulers of the c	2Chr 29:20	5892
the posts passed from c to c	2Chr 30:10	5892
their cities, in every several c	2Chr 31:19	5892
which were without the c	2Chr 32:3	5892
repaired Millo in the c of David	2Chr 32:5	5892
the street of the gate of the c	2Chr 32:6	5892
that they might take the c	2Chr 32:18	5892
the west side of the c of David	2Chr 32:30	5892
a wall without the c of David	2Chr 33:14	5892
and cast them out of the c	2Chr 33:15	5892
and Maaseiah the governor of the c	2Chr 34:8	5892
and Judah, every one unto his c	Ezr 2:1	5892
the rebellious and the bad c	Ezr 4:12	7149
if this c be builded, and the	Ezr 4:13	7149
that this c is a rebellious c	Ezr 4:15	7149
which cause was this c destroyed	Ezr 4:15	7149
if this c be builded again, and	Ezr 4:16	7149
that this c of old time hath made	Ezr 4:19	7149
that this c be not builded, until	Ezr 4:21	7179
with them the elders of every c	Ezr 10:14	5892
my countenance be sad, when the c	Neh 2:3	5892
unto the c of my fathers'	Neh 2:5	5892
house, and for the wall of the c	Neh 2:8	5892
that go down from the c of David	Neh 3:15	5892
Now the c was large and great	Neh 7:4	5892
and to Judah, every one unto his c	Neh 7:6	5892
to dwell in Jerusalem the holy c	Neh 11:1	5892
of Senuah was second over the c	Neh 11:9	5892
holy c were two hundred fourscore	Neh 11:18	5892
by the stairs of the c of David	Neh 12:37	5892
this evil upon us, and upon this c	Neh 13:18	5892
this evil upon us, and upon this c	Est 3:15	5892
but the c Shushan was perplexed	Est 4:1	5892
went out into the midst of the c	Est 4:6	5892
Mordecai unto the street of the c	Est 6:9	5892
through the street of the c	Est 6:11	5892
through the street of the c	Est 8:11	5892
the Jews which were in every c to	Est 8:15	5892
the c of Shushan rejoiced and was	Est 8:17	5892
in every province, and in every c		5892

every province, and every *c*	Est 9:28	5892
Men groan from out of the *c*	Job 24:12	5892
out to the gate through the *c*	Job 29:7	7176
scorneth the multitude of the *c*	Job 39:7	7151
marvellous kindness in a strong *c*	Ps 31:21	5892
shall make glad the *c* of God	Ps 46:4	5892
to be praised in the *c* of our God	Ps 48:1	5892
north, the *c* of the great King	Ps 48:2	7151
in the *c* of the LORD of hosts	Ps 48:8	5892
in the *c* of our God	Ps 48:8	5892
seen violence and strife in the *c*	Ps 55:9	5892
a dog, and go round about the *c*	Ps 59:6	5892
a dog, and go round about the *c*	Ps 59:14	5892
will bring me into the strong *c*	Ps 60:9	5892
they of the *c* shall flourish like	Ps 72:16	5892
are spoken of thee, O *c* of God	Ps 87:3	5892
doers from the *c* of the LORD	Ps 101:8	5892
they found no *c* to dwell in	Ps 107:4	5892
might go to a *c* of habitation	Ps 107:7	5892
may prepare a *c* for habitation	Ps 107:36	5892
will bring me into the strong *c*	Ps 108:10	5892
as a *c* that is compact together	Ps 122:3	5892
except the LORD keep the *c*	Ps 127:1	5892
in the *c* she uttereth her words,	Prov 1:21	5892
the gates, at the entry of the *c*	Prov 8:3	7176
upon the highest places of the *c*	Prov 9:3	7176
seat in the high places of the *c*	Prov 9:14	7176
rich man's wealth is his strong *c*	Prov 10:15	7151
the righteous, the *c* rejoiceth	Prov 11:10	7151
of the upright the *c* is exalted	Prov 11:11	5892
spirit than he that taketh a *c*	Prov 16:32	7176
rich man's wealth is his strong *c*	Prov 18:11	7151
harder to be won than a strong *c*	Prov 18:19	7151
man scaleth the *c* of the mighty	Prov 21:22	5892
is like a *c* that is broken down	Prov 25:28	5892
men bring a *c* into a snare	Prov 29:8	7151
ten mighty men which are in the *c*	Eccl 7:19	5892
in the *c* where they had so done	Eccl 8:10	5892
There was a little *c*, and few men	Eccl 9:14	5892
he by his wisdom delivered the *c*	Eccl 9:15	5892
he knoweth not how to go to the *c*	Eccl 10:15	5892
go about the *c* in the streets, and	Song 3:2	5892
that go about the *c* found me	Song 3:3	5892
that went about the *c* found me	Song 5:7	5892
of cucumbers, as a besieged *c*	Is 1:8	5892
the faithful *c* become an harlot	Is 1:21	7151
The *c* of righteousness, the	Is 1:26	5892
of righteousness, the faithful *c*	Is 1:26	7151
the golden *c* ceased	Is 14:4	4062
cry, O *c*	Is 14:31	5892
is taken away from being a *c*	Is 17:1	5892
c against *c*, and kingdom	Is 19:2	5892
be called, The *c* of destruction	Is 19:18	5892
art full of stirs, a tumultuous *c*	Is 22:2	5892
a joyous *c*: thy slain men	Is 22:2	7151
the breaches of the *c* of David	Is 22:9	5892
Is this your joyous *c*, whose	Is 23:7	5892
against Tyre, the crowning *c*	Is 23:8	5892
against the merchant *c*, to	Is 23:11	
Take an harp, go about the *c*	Is 23:16	5892
The *c* of confusion is broken down	Is 24:10	7151
In the *c* is left desolation, and	Is 24:12	5892
For thou hast made of a *c* an heap	Is 25:2	5892
of a defenced *c* a ruin	Is 25:2	7151
a palace of strangers to be no *c*	Is 25:2	5892
the *c* of the terrible nations	Is 25:3	7151
We have a strong *c*	Is 26:1	5892
the lofty *c*, he layeth it low	Is 26:5	7151
Yet the defenced *c* shall be	Is 27:10	5892
to Ariel, the *c* where David dwelt	Is 29:1	7151
the houses of joy in the joyous *c*	Is 32:13	7151
multitude of the *c* shall be left	Is 32:14	5892
the *c* shall be low in a low place	Is 32:19	5892
Zion, the *c* of our solemnities	Is 33:20	7151
this *c* shall not be delivered	Is 36:15	5892
the king of the *c* of Sepharvaim	Is 37:13	5892
He shall not come into this *c*	Is 37:33	5892
and shall not come into this *c*	Is 37:34	5892
For I will defend this *c* to save	Is 37:35	5892
this *c* out of the hand of the	Is 38:6	5892
and I will defend this *c*	Is 38:6	5892
he shall build my *c*, and he shall	Is 45:13	5892
call themselves of the holy *c*	Is 48:2	5892
garments, O Jerusalem, the holy *c*	Is 52:1	5892
The *c* of the LORD, The Zion of	Is 60:14	5892
Sought out, A *c* not forsaken	Is 62:12	5892
A voice of noise from the *c*	Is 66:6	5892
made thee this day a defenced *c*	Jer 1:18	5892
and I will take you one of a *c*	Jer 3:14	5892
The whole *c* shall flee for the	Jer 4:29	5892
every *c* shall be forsaken, and not	Jer 4:29	5892

this is the *c* to be visited	Jer 6:6	5892
the *c*, and those that dwell	Jer 8:16	5892
and if I enter into the *c*, then	Jer 14:18	5892
suddenly, and terrors upon the *c*	Jer 15:8	5892
of this *c* on the sabbath day	Jer 17:24	5892
into the gates of this *c* kings	Jer 17:25	5892
this *c* shall remain for ever	Jer 17:25	5892
And I will make this *c* desolate	Jer 19:8	5892
I break this people and this *c*	Jer 19:11	5892
and even make this *c* as Tophet	Jer 19:12	5892
Behold, I will bring upon this *c*	Jer 19:15	5892
all the strength of this *c*	Jer 20:5	5892
them into the midst of this *c*	Jer 21:4	5892
smite the inhabitants of this *c*	Jer 21:6	5892
in this *c* from the pestilence	Jer 21:7	5892
in this *c* shall die by the sword	Jer 21:9	5892
my face against this *c* for evil	Jer 21:10	5892
many nations shall pass by this *c*	Jer 22:8	5892
LORD done thus unto this great *c*	Jer 22:8	5892
the *c* that I gave you and your	Jer 23:39	5892
the *c* which is called by my name	Jer 25:29	5892
will make this *c* a curse to all	Jer 26:6	5892
this *c* shall be desolate without	Jer 26:9	5892
he hath prophesied against this *c*	Jer 26:11	5892
against this *c* all the words that	Jer 26:12	5892
upon yourselves, and upon this *c*	Jer 26:15	5892
who prophesied against this *c*	Jer 26:20	5892
should this *c* be laid waste	Jer 27:17	5892
the vessels that remain in this *c*	Jer 27:19	5892
seek the peace of the *c* whither I	Jer 29:7	5892
people that dwelleth in this *c*	Jer 29:16	5892
the *c* shall be builded upon her	Jer 30:18	5892
that the *c* shall be built to the	Jer 31:38	5892
I will give this *c* into the hand	Jer 32:3	5892
are come unto the *c* to take it	Jer 32:24	5892
the *c* is given into the hand of	Jer 32:24	5892
for the *c* is given into the hand	Jer 32:25	5892
I will give this *c* into the hand	Jer 32:28	5892
that fight against this *c*	Jer 32:29	5892
shall come and set fire on this *c*	Jer 32:29	5892
For this *c* hath been to me as a	Jer 32:31	5892
God of Israel, concerning this *c*	Jer 32:36	5892
concerning the houses of this *c*	Jer 33:4	5892
I have hid my face from this *c*	Jer 33:5	5892
I will give this *c* into the hand	Jer 34:2	5892
and cause them to return to this *c*	Jer 34:22	5892
again, and fight against this *c*	Jer 37:8	5892
tent, and burn this *c* with fire	Jer 37:10	5892
all the bread in the *c* were spent	Jer 37:21	5892
in this *c* shall die by the sword	Jer 38:2	5892
This *c* shall surely be given into	Jer 38:3	5892
men of war that remain in this *c*	Jer 38:4	5892
there is no more bread in the *c*	Jer 38:9	5892
this *c* shall not be burned with	Jer 38:17	5892
then shall this *c* be given into	Jer 38:18	5892
thou shalt cause this *c* to be	Jer 38:23	5892
of the month, the *c* was broken up	Jer 39:2	5892
went forth out of the *c* by night	Jer 39:4	5892
the people that remained in the *c*	Jer 39:9	5892
my words upon this *c* for evil	Jer 39:16	5892
they came into the midst of the *c*	Jer 41:7	5892
I will destroy the *c* and the	Jer 46:8	5892
the *c*, and them that dwell therein	Jer 47:2	5892
every *c*, and no *c* shall escape	Jer 48:8	5892
How is the *c* of praise not left,	Jer 49:25	5892
praise not left, the *c* of my joy	Jer 49:25	7151
that his *c* is taken at one end	Jer 51:31	5892
So the *c* was besieged unto the	Jer 52:5	5892
the famine was sore in the *c*	Jer 52:6	5892
Then the *c* was broken up, and all	Jer 52:7	5892
went forth out of the *c* by night	Jer 52:7	5892
were by the *c* round about	Jer 52:7	5892
the people that remained in the *c*	Jer 52:15	5892
took also out of the *c* an eunuch	Jer 52:25	5892
person, which were found in the *c*	Jer 52:25	5892
were found in the midst of the *c*	Jer 52:25	5892
How doth the *c* sit solitary	Lam 1:1	5892
elders gave up the ghost in the *c*	Lam 1:19	5892
swoon in the streets of the *c*	Lam 2:11	7151
wounded in the streets of the *c*	Lam 2:12	5892
Is this the *c* that men call The	Lam 2:15	5892
of all the daughters of my *c*	Lam 3:51	5892
thee, and pourtray upon it the *c*	Eze 4:1	5892
of iron between thee and the *c*	Eze 4:3	5892
third part in the midst of the *c*	Eze 5:2	5892
and he that is in the *c*, famine and	Eze 7:15	5892
the *c* is full of violence	Eze 7:23	5892
charge over the *c* to draw near	Eze 9:1	5892
Go through the midst of the *c*	Eze 9:4	5892
Go ye after him through the *c*	Eze 9:5	5892
they went forth, and slew in the *c*	Eze 9:7	5892

C

the c full of perverseness	Eze 9:9	5892
and scatter them over the c	Eze 10:2	5892
and give wicked counsel in this c	Eze 11:2	5892
this c is the caldron, and we be	Eze 11:3	
multiplied your slain in this c	Eze 11:6	5892
flesh, and this is the caldron	Eze 11:7	
This c shall not be your caldron,	Eze 11:11	
went up from the midst of the c	Eze 11:23	5892
is on the east side of the c	Eze 11:23	5892
he set it in a c of merchants	Eze 17:4	5892
at the head of the way to the c	Eze 21:19	5892
wilt thou judge the bloody c	Eze 22:2	5892
The c sheddeth blood in the midst	Eze 22:3	5892
Woe to the bloody c, to the pot	Eze 24:6	5892
Woe to the bloody c	Eze 24:9	5892
as men enter into a c wherein is	Eze 26:10	5892
of seafaring men, the renowned c	Eze 26:17	5892
I shall make thee a desolate c	Eze 26:19	5892
What c is like Tyrus, like the	Eze 27:32	
unto me, saying, The c is smitten	Eze 33:21	5892
name of the c shall be Hamonah	Eze 39:16	5892
year after that the c was smitten	Eze 40:1	5892
as the frame of a c on the south	Eze 40:2	5892
saw when I came to destroy the c	Eze 43:3	5892
of the c five thousand broad	Eze 45:6	5892
and of the possession of the c	Eze 45:7	5892
and before the possession of the c	Eze 45:7	5892
be a profane place for the c	Eze 48:15	5892
the c shall be in the midst	Eze 48:15	5892
the suburbs of the c shall be	Eze 48:17	5892
food unto them that serve the c	Eze 48:18	5892
they that serve the c shall serve	Eze 48:19	5892
with the possession of the c	Eze 48:20	5892
and of the possession of the c	Eze 48:21	5892
and from the possession of the c	Eze 48:22	5892
out of the c on the north side	Eze 48:30	5892
the gates of the c shall be after	Eze 48:31	5892
the name of the c from that day	Eze 48:35	5892
turned away from thy c Jerusalem	Dan 9:16	5892
the c which is called by thy name	Dan 9:18	5892
for thy c and thy people are	Dan 9:19	5892
thy people and upon thy holy c	Dan 9:24	5892
shall come shall destroy the c	Dan 9:26	5892
Gilead is a c of them that work	Hos 6:8	7151
and I will not enter into the c	Hos 11:9	5892
They shall run to and fro in the c	Joel 2:9	5892
Shall a trumpet be blown in the c	Amos 3:6	5892
shall there be evil in a c	Amos 3:6	5892
and I caused it to rain upon one c	Amos 4:7	5892
it not to rain upon another c	Amos 4:7	5892
three cities wandered unto one c	Amos 4:8	5892
The c that went out by a thousand	Amos 5:3	5892
up the c with all that is therein	Amos 6:8	5892
wife shall be an harlot in the c	Amos 7:17	5892
go to Nineveh, that great c	Jonah 1:2	5892
go unto Nineveh, that great c	Jonah 3:2	5892
great c of three days' journey	Jonah 3:3	5892
enter into the c a day's journey	Jonah 3:4	5892
So Jonah went out of the c	Jonah 4:5	5892
and sat on the east side of the c	Jonah 4:5	5892
see what would become of the c	Jonah 4:5	5892
not I spare Nineveh, that great c	Jonah 4:11	5892
shalt thou go forth out of the c	Mic 4:10	7151
Lord's voice crieth unto the c	Mic 6:9	5892
Woe to the bloody c	Nah 3:1	5892
violence of the land, of the c	Hab 2:8	7151
and stablisheth a c by iniquity	Hab 2:12	7151
violence of the land, of the c	Hab 2:17	7151
rejoicing c that dwelt carelessly	Zeph 2:15	5892
and polluted, to the oppressing c	Zeph 3:1	5892
shall be called a c of truth	Zec 8:3	5892
the streets of the c shall be	Zec 8:5	5892
of one c shall go to another	Zec 8:21	
the c shall be taken, and the	Zec 14:2	5892
half of the c shall go forth into	Zec 14:2	5892
shall not be cut off from the c	Zec 14:2	5892
dwelt in a c called Nazareth	Mt 2:23	4172
taketh him up into the holy c	Mt 4:5	4172
A c that is set on an hill cannot	Mt 5:14	4172
for it is the c of the great King	Mt 5:35	4172
and went their ways into the c	Mt 8:33	4172
the whole c came out to meet	Mt 8:34	4172
over, and came into his own c	Mt 9:1	4172
into any c of the Samaritans	Mt 10:5	4172
into whatsoever c or town ye	Mt 10:11	4172
ye depart out of that house or c	Mt 10:14	4172
day of judgment, than for that c	Mt 10:15	4172
when they persecute you in this c	Mt 10:23	4172
every c or house divided against	Mt 12:25	4172
all the c was moved, saying, Who	Mt 21:10	4172
and went out of the c into Bethany	Mt 21:17	4172

morning as he returned into the c	Mt 21:18	4172
murderers, and burned up their c	Mt 22:7	4172
and persecute them from c to c	Mt 23:34	4172
Go into the c to such a man, and	Mt 26:18	4172
and went into the holy c, and	Mt 27:53	4172
some of the watch came into the c	Mt 28:11	4172
all the c was gathered together	Mk 1:33	4172
no more openly enter into the c	Mk 1:45	4172
swine fled, and told it in the c	Mk 5:14	4172
day of judgment, than for that c	Mk 6:11	4172
was come, he went out of the c	Mk 11:19	4172
saith unto them, Go ye into the c	Mk 14:13	4172
went forth, and came into the c	Mk 14:16	4172
sent from God unto a c of Galilee	Lk 1:26	4172
with haste, into a c of Juda	Lk 1:39	4172
taxed, every one into his own c	Lk 2:3	4172
out of the c of Nazareth	Lk 2:4	4172
into Judaea, unto the c of David	Lk 2:4	4172
day in the c of David a Saviour	Lk 2:11	4172
Galilee, to their own c Nazareth	Lk 2:39	4172
a c of Sidon, unto a woman that	Lk 4:26	
up, and thrust him out of the c	Lk 4:29	4172
hill whereon their c was built	Lk 4:29	4172
a c of Galilee, and taught them on	Lk 4:31	4172
pass, when he was in a certain c	Lk 5:12	4172
that he went into a c called Nain	Lk 7:11	4172
he came nigh to the gate of the c	Lk 7:12	4172
much people of the c was with her	Lk 7:12	4172
And, behold, a woman in the c	Lk 7:37	4172
that he went throughout every c	Lk 8:1	4172
were come to him out of every c	Lk 8:4	4172
him out of the c a certain man	Lk 8:27	4172
fled, and went and told it in the c	Lk 8:34	4172
published throughout the whole c	Lk 8:39	4172
you, when ye go out of that c	Lk 9:5	4172
to the c called Bethsaida	Lk 9:10	4172
two before his face into every c	Lk 10:1	4172
And into whatsoever c ye enter	Lk 10:8	4172
But into whatsoever c ye enter	Lk 10:10	4172
Even the very dust of your c	Lk 10:11	4172
day for Sodom, than for that c	Lk 10:12	4172
the streets and lanes of the c	Lk 14:21	4172
Saying, There was in a c a judge	Lk 18:2	4172
And there was a widow in that c	Lk 18:3	4172
he was come near, he beheld the c	Lk 19:41	4172
when ye are entered into the c	Lk 22:10	4172
a certain sedition made in the c	Lk 23:19	4172
of Arimathaea, a c of the Jews	Lk 23:51	4172
tarry ye in the c of Jerusalem	Lk 24:49	4172
the c of Andrew and Peter	Jn 1:44	4172
Then cometh he to a c of Samaria	Jn 4:5	4172
gone away unto the c to buy meat	Jn 4:8	4172
and went her way into the c	Jn 4:28	4172
Then they went out of the c	Jn 4:30	4172
c believed on him for the saying	Jn 4:39	4172
into a c called Ephraim, and there	Jn 11:54	4172
was crucified was nigh to the c	Jn 19:20	4172
And cast him out of the c, and	Acts 7:58	4172
went down to the c of Samaria	Acts 8:5	4172
And there was great joy in that c	Acts 8:8	4172
in the same c used sorcery	Acts 8:9	4172
unto him, Arise, and go into the c	Acts 9:6	4172
journey, and drew nigh unto the c	Acts 10:9	4172
I was in the c of Joppa praying	Acts 11:5	4172
iron gate that leadeth unto the c	Acts 12:10	4172
day came almost the whole c	Acts 13:44	4172
women, and the chief men of the c	Acts 13:50	4172
multitude of the c was divided	Acts 14:4	4172
Jupiter, which was before their c	Acts 14:13	4172
Paul, drew him out of the c	Acts 14:19	4172
he rose up, and came into the c	Acts 14:20	4172
had preached the gospel to that c	Acts 14:21	4172
in every c them that preach him	Acts 15:21	4172
visit our brethren in every c	Acts 15:36	4172
which is the chief c of that part	Acts 16:12	4172
we were in that c abiding certain	Acts 16:12	4172
went out of the c by a river side	Acts 16:13	4172
of the c of Thyatira, which	Acts 16:14	4172
do exceedingly trouble our c	Acts 16:20	4172
them to depart out of the c	Acts 16:39	4172
set all the c on an uproar, and	Acts 17:5	4172
brethren unto the rulers of the c	Acts 17:6	4173
the people and the rulers of the c	Acts 17:8	4173
when he saw the c wholly given to	Acts 17:16	4172
for I have much people in this c	Acts 18:10	4172
the whole c was filled with	Acts 19:29	4172
that the c of the Ephesians is a	Acts 19:35	4172
Holy Ghost witnesseth in every c	Acts 20:23	4172
till we were out of the c	Acts 21:5	4172
in the c Trophimus an Ephesian	Acts 21:29	4172
all the c was moved, and the	Acts 21:30	4172

a Jew of Tarsus, a *c* in Cilicia	Acts 21:39	
a citizen of no mean *c*	Acts 21:39	4172
born in Tarsus, a *c*	Acts 22:3	
yet brought up in this *c* at the	Acts 22:3	4172
in the synagogues, nor in the *c*	Acts 24:12	4172
and principal men of the *c*	Acts 25:23	4172
we came to Myra, a *c* of Lycia	Acts 27:5	
nigh whereunto was the *c* of Lasea	Acts 27:8	4172
chamberlain of the *c* saluteth you	Rom 16:23	4172
the heathen, in perils in the *c*	2Cor 11:26	4172
the *c* of the Damascenes with a	2Cor 11:32	4172
a *c* of Macedonia, by Titus and	2Cor *s*	
chiefest of Phrygia Pacatiana	1Ti *s*	3390
and ordain elders in every *c*	Titus 1:5	4172
For he looked for a *c* which hath	Heb 11:10	4172
for he hath prepared for them a *c*	Heb 11:16	4172
unto the *c* of the living God, the	Heb 12:22	4172
For here have we no continuing *c*	Heb 13:14	4172
morrow we will go into such a *c*	Jas 4:13	4172
and the name of the *c* of my God	Rev 3:12	4172
the holy *c* shall they tread under	Rev 11:2	4172
lie in the street of the great *c*	Rev 11:8	4172
and the tenth part of the *c* fell	Rev 11:13	4172
fallen, is fallen, that great *c*	Rev 14:8	4172
was trodden without the *c*	Rev 14:20	4172
the great *c* was divided into	Rev 16:19	4172
which thou sawest is that great *c*	Rev 17:18	4172
great *c* Babylon, that mighty *c*	Rev 18:10	4172
saying, Alas, alas that great *c*	Rev 18:16	4172
c is like unto this great *c*	Rev 18:18	4172
saying, Alas, alas that great *c*	Rev 18:19	4172
great *c* Babylon be thrown down	Rev 18:21	4172
saints about, and the beloved *c*	Rev 20:9	4172
And I John saw the holy *c*, new	Rev 21:2	4172
and shewed me that great *c*	Rev 21:10	4172
the wall of the *c* had twelve	Rev 21:14	4172
a golden reed to measure the *c*	Rev 21:15	4172
the *c* lieth foursquare, and the	Rev 21:16	4172
he measured the *c* with the reed	Rev 21:16	4172
the *c* was pure gold, like unto	Rev 21:18	4172
c were garnished with all manner	Rev 21:19	4172
the street of the *c* was pure gold	Rev 21:21	4172
the *c* had no need of the sun,	Rev 21:23	4172
in through the gates into the *c*	Rev 22:14	4172
of life, and out of the holy *c*	Rev 22:19	4172

CLAD

he had *c* himself with a new	1Kin 11:29	3680
was *c* with zeal as a cloke	Is 59:17	5844

CLAMOROUS

A foolish woman is *c*	Prov 9:13	1993

CLAMOUR

and wrath, and anger, and *c*	Eph 4:31	2906

CLAP

Men shall *c* their hands at him,	Job 27:23	5606
O *c* your hands, all ye people	Ps 47:1	8628
Let the floods *c* their hands	Ps 98:8	4222
of the field shall *c* their hands	Is 55:12	4222
All that pass by *c* their hands at	Lam 2:15	5606
thee shall *c* the hands over thee	Nah 3:19	8628

CLAPPED

they *c* their hands, and said, God	2Kin 11:12	5221
Because thou hast *c* thine hands	Eze 25:6	4222

CLAPPETH

he *c* his hands among us, and	Job 34:37	5606

CLAUDA (claw'-dah) *An island near Crete.*

certain island which is called C	Acts 27:16	2802

CLAUDIA (claw'-de-ah) *A Roman Christian.*

thee, and Pudens, and Linus, and C	2Ti 4:21	2803

CLAUDIUS (claw'-de-us)
1. A Roman emperor.

to pass in the days of C Caesar	Acts 11:28	2804
(because that C had commanded all	Acts 18:2	2804

2. A Roman officer in Jerusalem.

C Lysias unto the most excellent	Acts 23:26	2804

CLAVE

c the wood for the burnt offering	Gen 22:3	1234
his soul *c* unto Dinah the	Gen 34:3	1692
that the ground *c* asunder that	Num 16:31	1234
But God *c* an hollow place that	Judg 15:19	1234
but Ruth *c* unto her	Ruth 1:14	1692
they *c* the wood of the cart, and	1Sa 6:14	1234
men of Judah *c* unto their king	2Sa 20:2	1692
his hand *c* unto the sword	2Sa 23:10	1692
Solomon *c* unto these in love	1Kin 11:2	1692
For he *c* to the LORD, and departed	2Kin 18:6	1692
They *c* to their brethren, their	Neh 10:29	2388

He *c* the rocks in the wilderness,	Ps 78:15	1234
he *c* the rock also, and the waters	Is 48:21	1234
Howbeit certain men *c* unto him	Acts 17:34	2853

CLAWS

and cleaveth the cleft into two *c*	Deut 14:6	6541
and his nails like birds' *c*	Dan 4:33	
fat, and tear their *c* in pieces	Zec 11:16	6541

CLAY

in the *c* ground between Succoth	1Kin 7:46	4568
in the *c* ground between Succoth	2Chr 4:17	4568
in them that dwell in houses of *c*	Job 4:19	2563
that thou hast made me as the *c*	Job 10:9	2563
ashes, your bodies to bodies of *c*	Job 13:12	2563
dust, and prepare raiment as the *c*	Job 27:16	2563
I also am formed out of the *c*	Job 33:6	2563
It is turned as *c* to the seal	Job 38:14	2563
horrible pit, out of the miry *c*	Ps 40:2	2916
be esteemed as the potter's *c*	Is 29:16	2563
and as the potter treadeth *c*	Is 41:25	2916
Shall the *c* say to him that	Is 45:9	2563
we are the *c*, and thou our potter	Is 64:8	2563
the vessel that he made of *c* was	Jer 18:4	2563
as the *c* is in the potter's hand,	Jer 18:6	2563
them in the *c* in the brickkiln	Jer 43:9	4423
feet part of iron and part of *c*	Dan 2:33	2635
his feet that were of iron and *c*	Dan 2:34	2635
Then was the iron, the *c*, the	Dan 2:35	2635
feet and toes, part of potters' *c*	Dan 2:41	2635
sawest the iron mixed with miry *c*	Dan 2:41	2635
were part of iron, and part of *c*	Dan 2:42	2635
sawest iron mixed with miry *c*	Dan 2:43	2635
even as iron is not mixed with *c*	Dan 2:43	2635
pieces the iron, the brass, the *c*	Dan 2:45	2635
go into *c*, and tread the morter,	Nah 3:14	2916
that ladeth himself with thick *c*	Hab 2:6	5671
made of the spittle, and he	Jn 9:6	4081
eyes of the blind man with the *c*	Jn 9:6	4081
A man that is called Jesus made *c*	Jn 9:11	4081
sabbath day when Jesus made the *c*	Jn 9:14	4081
He put *c* upon mine eyes, and I	Jn 9:15	4081
not the potter power over the *c*	Rom 9:21	4081

CLEAN

Of every *c* beast thou shalt take	Gen 7:2	2889
of beasts that are not *c* by two	Gen 7:2	2889
Of *c* beasts, and of beasts that	Gen 7:8	2889
and of beasts that are not *c*	Gen 7:8	2889
c beast, and of every *c* fowl	Gen 8:20	2889
gods that are among you, and be *c*	Gen 35:2	2891
without the camp unto a *c* place	Lev 4:12	2889
without the camp unto a *c* place	Lev 6:11	2889
all that be *c* shall eat thereof	Lev 7:19	2889
unholy, and between unclean and *c*	Lev 10:10	2889
shall ye eat in a *c* place	Lev 10:14	2889
is plenty of water, shall be *c*	Lev 11:36	2889
is to be sown, it shall be *c*	Lev 11:37	2889
between the unclean and the *c*	Lev 11:47	2889
for her, and she shall be *c*	Lev 12:8	2891
the priest shall pronounce him *c*	Lev 13:6	2891
shall wash his clothes, and be *c*	Lev 13:6	2891
him *c* that hath the plague	Lev 13:13	2891
he is *c*	Lev 13:13	2889
him *c* that hath the plague	Lev 13:17	2891
he is *c*	Lev 13:17	2889
the priest shall pronounce him *c*	Lev 13:23	2891
the priest shall pronounce him *c*	Lev 13:28	2891
the priest shall pronounce him *c*	Lev 13:34	2891
shall wash his clothes, and be *c*	Lev 13:34	2891
the scall is healed, he is *c*	Lev 13:37	2889
the priest shall pronounce him *c*	Lev 13:37	2891
he is *c*	Lev 13:39	2889
yet is he *c*	Lev 13:40	2889
yet is he *c*	Lev 13:41	2889
the second time, and shall be *c*	Lev 13:58	2891
thing of skins, to pronounce it *c*	Lev 13:59	2891
be cleansed two birds alive and *c*	Lev 14:4	2889
times, and shall pronounce him *c*	Lev 14:7	2891
in water, that he may be *c*	Lev 14:8	2891
flesh in water, and he shall be *c*	Lev 14:9	2891
the priest that maketh him *c*	Lev 14:11	2891
the man that is to be made *c*	Lev 14:11	2891
for him, and he shall be *c*	Lev 14:20	2891
shall pronounce the house *c*	Lev 14:48	2891
and it shall be *c*	Lev 14:53	2891
it is unclean, and when it is *c*	Lev 14:57	2889
the issue spit upon him that is *c*	Lev 15:8	2889
in running water, and shall be *c*	Lev 15:13	2891
and after that shall be *c*	Lev 15:28	2891
that ye may be *c* from all your	Lev 16:30	2891
then shall he be *c*	Lev 17:15	2891

put difference between *c* beasts .... Lev 20:25 2889
and between unclean fowls and *c* .... Lev 20:25 2889
of the holy things, until he be *c* .... Lev 22:4 2891
the sun is down, he shall be *c* .... Lev 22:7 2891
thou shalt not make *c* riddance of .... Lev 23:22
woman be not defiled, but be *c* .... Num 5:28 2889
clothes, and so make themselves *c* .... Num 8:7 2891
But the man that is *c*, and is not .... Num 9:13 2889
every one that is *c* in thy house .... Num 18:11 2889
every one that is *c* in thine .... Num 18:13 2889
a man that is *c* shall gather up .... Num 19:9 2889
up without the camp in a *c* place .... Num 19:9 2889
on the seventh day he shall be *c* .... Num 19:12 2889
the seventh day he shall not be *c* .... Num 19:12 2891
a *c* person shall take hyssop, and .... Num 19:18 2889
the *c* person shall sprinkle upon .... Num 19:19 2889
in water, and shall be *c* at even .... Num 19:19 2891
the fire, and it shall be *c* .... Num 31:23 2891
the seventh day, and ye shall be *c* .... Num 31:24 2891
the *c* may eat thereof, as of the .... Deut 12:15 2889
the *c* shall eat of them alike .... Deut 12:22 2889
Of all *c* birds ye shall eat .... Deut 14:11 2889
But of all *c* fowls ye may eat .... Deut 14:20 2889
the *c* person shall eat it alike, ... Deut 15:22 2889
that is not *c* by reason of .... Deut 23:10 2889
people were passed *c* over Jordan .... Josh 3:17 8552
people were *c* passed over Jordan .... Josh 4:1 8552
all the people were *c* passed over .... Josh 4:11 8552
hath befallen him, he is not *c* 1Sa 20:26 2889
surely he is not *c* 1Sa 20:26 2889
again to thee, and thou shalt be *c* 2Kin 5:10 2891
may I not wash in them, and be *c* 2Kin 5:12 2891
he saith to thee, Wash, and be *c* 2Kin 5:13 2891
of a little child, and he was *c* 2Kin 5:14 2891
for every one that was not *c* 2Chr 30:17 2889
and make my hands never so *c* .... Job 9:30 2141
is pure, and I am *c* in thine eyes .... Job 11:4 1249
Who can bring a *c* thing out of an .... Job 14:4 2889
What is man, that he should be *c* .... Job 15:14 2135
heavens are not *c* in his sight .... Job 15:15 2141
he that hath *c* hands shall be .... Job 17:9 2891
or how can he be *c* that is born .... Job 25:4 2135
I am *c* without transgression, I .... Job 33:9 2134
The fear of the LORD is *c* .... Ps 19:9 2889
He that hath *c* hands, and a pure .... Ps 24:4 5355
me with hyssop, and I shall be *c* .... Ps 51:7 2891
Create in me a *c* heart, O God .... Ps 51:10 2889
even to such as are of a *c* heart .... Ps 73:1 1249
Is his mercy *c* gone for ever .... Ps 77:8 656
Where no oxen are, the crib is *c* .... Prov 14:4 1249
of a man are *c* in his own eyes .... Prov 16:2 2134
can say, I have made my heart *c* .... Prov 20:9 2135
to the good and to the *c*, and to .... Eccl 9:2 2889
Wash you, make you *c* .... Is 1:16 2135
down, the earth is *c* dissolved .... Is 24:19 6565
so that there is no place *c* .... Is 28:8
the ground shall eat *c* provender .... Is 30:24 2548
be ye *c*, that bear the vessels of .... Is 52:11 1305
a *c* vessel into the house of the .... Is 66:20 2889
wilt thou not be made *c* .... Jer 13:27 2891
between the unclean and the *c* .... Eze 22:26 2889
will I sprinkle *c* water upon you .... Eze 36:25 2889
and ye shall be *c* .... Eze 36:25 2891
between the unclean and the *c* .... Eze 44:23 2889
he hath made it *c* bare, and cast .... Joel 1:7
his arm shall be *c* dried up .... Zec 11:17
thou wilt, thou canst make me *c* .... Mt 8:2 2889
be thou *c* .... Mt 8:3 2889
for ye make *c* the outside of the .... Mt 23:25 2889
the outside of them may be *c* also ..... Mt 23:26 2513
he wrapped it in a *c* linen cloth .... Mt 27:59 2513
thou wilt, thou canst make me *c* .... Mk 1:40 2511
be thou *c* .... Mk 1:41 2511
thou wilt, thou canst make me *c* .... Lk 5:12 2511
be thou *c* .... Lk 5:13 2511
make *c* the outside of the cup .... Lk 11:39 2511
behold, all things are *c* unto you ...... Lk 11:41 2513
his feet, but is *c* every whit .... Jn 13:10 2513
and ye are *c*, but not all .... Jn 13:10 2513
said he, Ye are not all *c* .... Jn 13:11 2513
Now ye are *c* through the word .... Jn 15:3 2513
I am *c* .... Acts 18:6 2513
those that were *c* escaped from 2Pet 2:18 3689
be arrayed in fine linen, *c* .... Rev 19:8 2513
clothed in fine linen, white and *c* .... Rev 19:14 2513

CLEANNESS

according to the *c* of my hands 2Sa 22:21 1252
according to my *c* in his eye 2Sa 22:25 1252
according to the *c* of my hands .... Ps 18:20 1252

according to the *c* of my hands in .... Ps 18:24 1252
I also have given you *c* of teeth .... Amos 4:6 5356

CLEANSE

and thou shalt *c* the altar .... Ex 29:36 2398
he shall take to *c* the house two .... Lev 14:49 2398
he shall *c* the house with the .... Lev 14:52 2398
c it, and hallow it from the .... Lev 16:19 2891
to *c* you, that ye may be clean .... Lev 16:30 2891
the children of Israel, and *c* them .... Num 8:6 2891
thou do unto them, to *c* them .... Num 8:7 2891
and thou shalt *c* them, and offer .... Num 8:15 2891
an atonement for them to *c* them .... Num 8:21 2891
to *c* the house of the LORD 2Chr 29:15 2891
of the house of the LORD, to *c* it 2Chr 29:16 2891
that they should *c* themselves .... Neh 13:22 2891
c thou me from secret faults .... Ps 19:12 5352
iniquity, and *c* me from my sin .... Ps 51:2 5352
shall a young man *c* his way .... Ps 119:9 2135
my people, not to fan, nor to *c* .... Jer 4:11 1305
I will *c* them from all their .... Jer 33:8 2891
from all your idols, will I *c* you .... Eze 36:25 2891
they have sinned, and will *c* them .... Eze 37:23 2891
of them, that they may *c* the land .... Eze 39:12 2891
the face of the earth, to *c* it .... Eze 39:14 2891
Thus shall they *c* the land .... Eze 39:16 2891
thus shalt thou *c* and purge it .... Eze 43:20 2398
and they shall *c* the altar .... Eze 43:22 2398
as they did *c* it with the bullock .... Eze 43:22 2398
blemish, and *c* the sanctuary .... Eze 45:18 2398
For I will *c* their blood that I .... Joel 3:21 5352
c the lepers, raise the dead, ... Mt 10:8 2511
c first that which is within the .... Mt 23:26 2511
let us *c* ourselves from all 2Cor 7:1 2511
c it with the washing of water by .... Eph 5:26 2511
C your hands, ye sinners .... Jas 4:8 2511
to *c* us from all unrighteousness 1Jn 1:9 2511

CLEANSED

so it shall be *c* .... Lev 11:32 2891
she shall be *c* from the issue of .... Lev 12:7 2891
that is to be *c* two birds alive .... Lev 14:4 2891
be *c* from the leprosy seven times .... Lev 14:7 2891
he that is to be *c* shall wash his .... Lev 14:8 2891
right ear of him that is to be *c* .... Lev 14:14 2891
right ear of him that is to be *c* .... Lev 14:17 2891
the head of him that is to be *c* .... Lev 14:18 2891
is to be *c* from his uncleanness .... Lev 14:19 2891
right ear of him that is to be *c* .... Lev 14:25 2891
right ear of him that is to be *c* .... Lev 14:28 2891
the head of him that is to be *c* .... Lev 14:29 2891
that is to be *c* before the LORD .... Lev 14:31 2891
hath an issue of *c* of his issue .... Lev 15:13 2891
But if she be *c* of her issue .... Lev 15:28 2891
the land cannot be *c* of the blood .... Num 35:33 3722
which we are not *c* until this day .... Josh 22:17 2891
We have *c* all the house of the 2Chr 29:18 2891
had not *c* themselves, yet did 2Chr 30:18 2891
though he be not *c* according to 2Chr 30:19 2891
altars, and *c* Judah and Jerusalem 2Chr 34:5 2891
commanded, and they *c* the chambers ... Neh 13:9 2891
Thus *c* I them from all strangers, ... Neh 13:30 2891
I have, if I be *c* from my sin .... Job 35:3
Verily I have *c* my heart in vain, ... Ps 73:13 2135
Thou art the land that is not *c* .... Eze 22:24 2891
In the day that I shall have *c* .... Eze 36:33 2891
And after he is *c*, they shall .... Eze 44:26 2893
then shall the sanctuary be *c* .... Dan 8:14 6663
their blood that I have not *c* .... Joel 3:21 5352
And immediately his leprosy was *c* .... Mt 8:3 2511
the lame walk, the lepers are *c* .... Mt 11:5 2511
departed from him, and he was *c* .... Mk 1:42 2511
and none of them was *c*, saving .... Lk 4:27 2511
the lame walk, the lepers are *c* .... Lk 7:22 2511
that, as they went, they were *c* .... Lk 17:14 2511
said, Were there not ten *c* .... Lk 17:17 2511
the second time, What God hath *c* .... Acts 10:15 2511
from heaven, What God hath *c* .... Acts 11:9 2511

CLEANSETH

but the wind passeth, and *c* them .... Job 37:21 2891
blueness of a wound *c* away evil .... Prov 20:30 8562
Christ his Son *c* us from all sin 1Jn 1:7 2511

CLEANSING

been seen of the priest for his *c* .... Lev 13:7 2893
much in the skin after his *c* .... Lev 13:35 2893
of the leper in the day of his *c* .... Lev 14:2 2893
day for his *c* unto the priest .... Lev 14:23 2893
that which pertaineth to his *c* .... Lev 14:32 2893
to himself seven days for his *c* .... Lev 15:13 2893
his head in the day of his *c* .... Num 6:9 2893
thou hast made an end of *c* .... Eze 43:23 2893

C

offer for thy *c* those things .... Mk 1:44   2512
to the priest, and offer for thy *c* .... Lk 5:14   2512

CLEAR

thou shalt be *c* from this my oath .... Gen 24:8   5352
shalt thou be *c* from this my oath .... Gen 24:41   5352
one, thou shalt be *c* from my oath .... Gen 24:41   5355
or how shall we *c* ourselves .... Gen 44:16   6663
will by no means *c* the guilty .... Ex 34:7   5352
the earth by *c* shining after rain 2Sa 23:4
and be *c* when thou judgest .... Ps 51:4   2135
c as the sun, and terrible as an .... Song 6:10   1249
place like a *c* heat upon herbs .... Is 18:4   6703
darken the earth in the *c* day .... Amos 8:9   216
that the light shall not be *c* .... Zec 14:6   3368
yourselves to be *c* in this matter 2Cor 7:11   53
like a jasper stone, *c* as crystal .... Rev 21:11   2929
was pure gold, like unto *c* glass .... Rev 21:18   2513
c as crystal, proceeding out of .... Rev 22:1   2986

CLEARER

age shall be *c* than the noonday .... Job 11:17   6965

CLEARING

and by no means *c* the guilty .... Num 14:18   5352
what *c* of yourselves, yea, what 2Cor 7:11   627

CLEARLY

my lips shall utter knowledge *c* .... Job 33:3   1305
then shalt thou see *c* to cast out .... Mt 7:5   1227
was restored, and saw every man *c* .... Mk 8:25   5081
then shalt thou see *c* to pull out .... Lk 6:42   1227
creation of the world are *c* seen .... Rom 1:20   2529

CLEARNESS

were the body of heaven in his *c* .... Ex 24:10   2892

CLEAVE

mother, and shall *c* unto his wife .... Gen 2:24   1692
he shall *c* it with the wings .... Lev 1:17   8156
But ye that did *c* unto the LORD .... Deut 4:4   1695
serve, and to him shalt thou *c* .... Deut 10:20   1692
in all his ways, and to *c* unto him .... Deut 11:22   1692
ye shall serve him, and *c* unto him .... Deut 13:4   1692
there shall *c* nought of the .... Deut 13:17   1692
make the pestilence *c* unto thee .... Deut 28:21   1692
and they shall *c* unto thee .... Deut 28:60   1692
and that thou mayest *c* unto him .... Deut 30:20   1692
to *c* unto him, and to serve him .... Josh 22:5   1692
But *c* unto the LORD your God, as .... Josh 23:8   1692
c unto the remnant of these .... Josh 23:12   1692
of Naaman shall *c* unto thee 2Kin 5:27   1692
the clods *c* fast together .... Job 38:38   1692
Thou didst *c* the fountain and the .... Ps 74:15   1234
it shall not *c* to me .... Ps 101:3   1692
my groaning my bones *c* to my skin ...... Ps 102:5   1692
let my tongue *c* to the roof of my .... Ps 137:6   1692
they shall *c* to the house of .... Is 14:1   5596
so have I caused to *c* unto me the .... Jer 13:11   1692
I will make thy tongue *c* to the .... Eze 3:26   1692
they shall not *c* one to another .... Dan 2:43   1693
but many shall *c* to them with .... Dan 11:34   3867
Thou didst *c* the earth with .... Hab 3:9   1234
the mount of Olives shall *c* in .... Zec 14:4   1234
and mother, and shall *c* to his wife .... Mt 19:5   4347
and mother, and *c* to his wife .... Mk 10:7   4347
heart they would *c* unto the Lord .... Acts 11:23   4347
c to that which is good .... Rom 12:9   2853

CLEAVED

Nevertheless he *c* unto the sins 2Kin 3:3   1692
their tongue *c* to the roof of .... Job 29:10   1692
if any blot hath *c* to mine hands .... Job 31:7   1692

CLEAVETH

c the cleft into two claws, and .... Deut 14:6   8157
he *c* my reins asunder, and doth .... Job 16:13   6398
My bone *c* to my skin and to my .... Job 19:20   1692
and my tongue *c* to my jaws .... Ps 22:15   1692
say they, *c* fast unto him .... Ps 41:8   3332
our belly *c* unto the earth .... Ps 44:25   1692
My soul *c* unto the dust .... Ps 119:25   1692
cutteth and *c* wood upon the earth .... Ps 141:7   1234
and he that *c* wood shall be .... Eccl 10:9   1234
For as the girdle *c* to the loins .... Jer 13:11   1692
c to the roof of his mouth for .... Lam 4:4   1692
their skin *c* to their bones .... Lam 4:8   6821
dust of your city, which *c* on us .... Lk 10:11   2853

CLEFT

cleaveth the *c* into two claws, and .... Deut 14:6   8156
him, and the valleys shall be *c* .... Mic 1:4   1234

CLEFTS

that art in the *c* of the rock .... Song 2:14   2288
To go into the *c* of the rocks .... Is 2:21   5366

dwellest in the *c* of the rock .... Jer 49:16   2288
and the little house with *c* .... Amos 6:11   1233
dwellest in the *c* of the rock .... Obad 3   2288

CLEMENCY

hear us of thy *c* a few words .... Acts 24:4   1932

CLEMENT (clem'-ent) A companion of Paul.
me in the gospel, with *C* also .... Phil 4:3   2815

CLEOPAS (cle'-o-pas) See ALPHAEUS, CLEOPHAS. A disciple on Emmaus Road.
the one of them, whose name was *C* ...... Lk 24:18   2810

CLEOPHAS (cle'-o-fas) See CLEOPAS. Husband of Mary.
sister, Mary the wife of *C* .... Jn 19:25   2832

CLIFF

they come up by the *c* of Ziz 2Chr 20:16   4608

CLIFFS

To dwell in the *c* of the valleys .... Job 30:6   6178

CLIFT

will put thee in a *c* of the rock .... Ex 33:22   5366

CLIFTS

valleys under the *c* of the rocks .... Is 57:5   5585

CLIMB

thickets, and *c* up upon the rocks .... Jer 4:29   5927
they shall *c* the wall like men of .... Joel 2:7   5927
they shall *c* up upon the houses .... Joel 2:9   5927
though they *c* up to heaven, ... Amos 9:2   5927

CLIMBED

Jonathan *c* up upon his hands and 1Sa 14:13   5927
c up into a sycomore tree to see .... Lk 19:4   305

CLIMBETH

but *c* up some other way, the same .... Jn 10:1   305

CLIPPED

shall be bald, and every beard *c* .... Jer 48:37   1639

CLODS

clothed with worms and *c* of dust .... Job 7:5   1487
The *c* of the valley shall be .... Job 21:33   7263
the *c* cleave fast together .... Job 38:38   7263
break the *c* of his ground .... Is 28:24   7702
plow, and Jacob shall break his *c* .... Hos 10:11   7702
The seed is rotten under their *c* .... Joel 1:17   4053

CLOKE

and was clad with zeal as a *c* .... Is 59:17   4598
thy coat, let him have thy *c* also .... Mt 5:40   2440
him that taketh away thy *c* forbid .... Lk 6:29   2440
now they have no *c* for their sin .... Jn 15:22   4392
ye know, nor a *c* of covetousness 1Th 2:5   4392
The *c* that I left at Troas with 2Ti 4:13   5341
liberty for a *c* of maliciousness 1Pet 2:16   1942

CLOPAS See CLEOPHAS.

CLOSE

eyes of her husband, and be kept *c* .... Num 5:13   5956
be afraid out of their *c* places 2Sa 22:46   4526
while he yet kept himself *c* 1Chr 12:1   6113
kept *c* from the fowls of the air .... Job 28:21   5641
shut up together as with a *c* seal .... Job 41:15   6862
be afraid out of their *c* places .... Ps 18:45   4526
shall follow *c* after you there in .... Jer 42:16   1692
And I saw him come *c* unto the ram ...... Dan 8:7   681
c up the breaches thereof .... Amos 9:11   1443
And they kept it *c*, and told no man ...... Lk 9:36   4601
thence, they sailed *c* by Crete .... Acts 27:13   788

CLOSED

c up the flesh instead thereof .... Gen 2:21   5462
For the LORD had fast *c* up all .... Gen 20:18   6113
the pit, and the earth *c* upon them .... Num 16:33   3680
the fat *c* upon the blade, so that .... Judg 3:22   5462
they have not been *c*, neither .... Is 1:6   2115
deep sleep, and hath *c* your eyes .... Is 29:10   6105
for the words are *c* up and sealed .... Dan 12:9   5640
the depth *c* me round about, the .... Jonah 2:5   5437
and their eyes they have *c* .... Mt 13:15   2576
he *c* the book, and he gave it .... Lk 4:20   4428
and their eyes have they *c* .... Acts 28:27   2576

CLOSER

that sticketh *c* than a brother .... Prov 18:24

CLOSEST

because thou *c* thyself in cedar .... Jer 22:15   8474

CLOSET

and the bride out of her *c* .... Joel 2:16   2646
thou prayest, enter into thy *c* .... Mt 6:6   5009

CLOSETS

in *c* shall be proclaimed upon the .... Lk 12:3   5009

CLOTH

spread over it a *c* wholly of blue ....Num 4:6 899
they shall spread a *c* of blue ....Num 4:7 899
spread upon them a *c* of scarlet ....Num 4:8 899
And they shall take a *c* of blue ....Num 4:9 899
they shall spread a *c* of blue ....Num 4:11 899
and put them in a *c* of blue ....Num 4:12 899
and spread a purple *c* thereon...............Num 4:13 899
they shall spread the *c* before ....Deut 22:17 8071
bolster, and covered it with a *c* 1Sa 19:13 899
wrapped in a *c* behind the ephod 1Sa 21:9 8071
cast a *c* upon him, when he saw 2Sa 20:12 899
morrow, that he took a thick *c* 2Kin 8:15 4346
cast them away as a menstruous *c* ....Is 30:22
of new *c* **unto an old garment** ....Mt 9:16 4470
he wrapped it in a clean linen *c* ....Mt 27:59 4616
piece of new *c* **on an old garment**........Mk 2:21 4470
having a linen *c* cast about his ....Mk 14:51 4616
And he left the linen *c*, and fled ....Mk 14:52 4616

CLOTHE

his sons, and *c* them with coats ....Ex 40:14 3847
and she sent raiment to *c* Mordecai ....Est 4:4 3847
I will also *c* her priests with ....Ps 132:16 3847
His enemies will I *c* with shame ....Ps 132:18 3847
shall *c* a man with rags ....Prov 23:21 3847
I will *c* him with thy robe, and ....Is 22:21 3847
thou shalt surely *c* thee with ....Is 49:18 3847
I *c* the heavens with blackness, ...Is 50:3 3847
they shall *c* themselves with ....Eze 26:16 3847
ye *c* you with the wool, ye kill ....Eze 34:3 3847
ye *c* you, but there is none warm ....Hag 1:6 3847
I will *c* thee with change of ....Zec 3:4 3847
if God so *c* **the grass of the** ....Mt 6:30 294
shall he not much more *c* **you** ....Mt 6:30
If then God so *c* **the grass** ....Lk 12:28 294
how much more will he *c* **you** ....Lk 12:28

CLOTHED

make coats of skins, and *c* them ....Gen 3:21 3847
c him with the robe, and put the ....Lev 8:7 3847
who *c* you in scarlet, with other.............2Sa 1:24 3847
David was *c* with a robe of fine..............1Chr 15:27 3736
who were *c* in sackcloth, fell 1Chr 21:16 3680
be *c* with salvation, and let thy 2Chr 6:41 3847
c in their robes, and they sat in 2Chr 18:9 3847
with the spoil *c* all that were 2Chr 28:15 3847
the king's gate *c* with sackcloth ....Est 4:2 3830
My flesh is *c* with worms and clods ......Job 7:5 3847
hate thee shall be *c* with shame ....Job 8:22 3847
Thou hast *c* me with skin and flesh.........Job 10:11 3847
put on righteousness, and it *c* me ....Job 29:14 3847
hast thou *c* his neck with thunder ....Job 39:19 3847
let them be *c* with shame and ....Ps 35:26 3847
The pastures are *c* with flocks...............Ps 65:13 3847
reigneth, he is *c* with majesty ....Ps 93:1 3847
the LORD is *c* with strength, ...Ps 93:1 3847
thou art *c* with honour and majesty ....Ps 104:1 3847
As he *c* himself with cursing like ....Ps 109:18 3847
mine adversaries be *c* with shame ....Ps 109:29 3847
priests be *c* with righteousness ....Ps 132:9 3847
her household are *c* with scarlet ....Prov 31:21 3847
for he hath *c* me with the ....Is 61:10 3847
prince shall be *c* with desolation ....Eze 7:27 3847
man among them was *c* with linen ....Eze 9:2 3847
he called to the man *c* with linen ....Eze 9:3 3847
the man *c* with linen, which had............Eze 9:11 3847
spake unto the man *c* with linen ....Eze 10:2 3847
commanded the man *c* with linen ....Eze 10:6 3847
of him that was *c* with linen ....Eze 10:7 3847
I *c* thee also with broidered work ....Eze 16:10 3847
Which were *c* with blue, captains..........Eze 23:6 3847
rulers *c* most gorgeously, ...Eze 23:12 3847
all of them *c* with all sorts of ....Eze 38:4 3847
they shall be *c* with linen.....................Eze 44:17 3847
shall be *c* with scarlet, and have ....Dan 5:7 3848
thou shalt be *c* with scarlet ....Dan 5:16 3848
they *c* Daniel with scarlet, and ....Dan 5:29 3848
behold a certain man *c* in linen ....Dan 10:5 3847
And one said to the man *c* in linen ....Dan 12:6 3847
And I heard the man *c* in linen ....Dan 12:7 3847
all such as are *c* with strange...............Zeph 1:8 3847
Now Joshua was *c* with filthy...............Zec 3:3 3847
his head, and *c* him with garments ....Zec 3:5 3847
or, Wherewithal shall we be *c* ....Mt 6:31 4016
A man *c* **in soft raiment** ....Mt 11:8 294
Naked, and ye *c* **me** ....Mt 25:36 4016
or naked, and *c* **thee** ....Mt 25:38 4016
naked, and ye *c* **me not** ....Mt 25:43 4016
John was *c* with camel's hair, and ....Mk 1:6 1746
and had the legion, sitting, and *c* ....Mk 5:15 2439
they *c* him with purple, and ....Mk 15:17 1746

c in a long white garment......................Mk 16:5 4016
A man *c* **in soft raiment** ....Lk 7:25 294
sitting at the feet of Jesus, *c*................Lk 8:35 2439
rich man, which was *c* **in purple** ....Lk 16:19 1737
earnestly desiring to be *c* upon 2Cor 5:2 1902
If so be that being *c* we shall 2Cor 5:3 1746
but *c* upon, that mortality might 2Cor 5:4 1902
to another, and be *c* with humility 1Pet 5:5 1463
c with a garment down to the foot.........Rev 1:13 1746
same shall be *c* in white raiment ....Rev 3:5 4016
raiment, that thou mayest be *c* ....Rev 3:18 4016
sitting, *c* in white raiment.....................Rev 4:4 4016
c with white robes, and palms in ....Rev 7:9 4016
down from heaven, *c* with a cloud ....Rev 10:1 4016
threescore days, *c* in sackcloth ....Rev 11:3 4016
a woman *c* with the sun, and the ....Rev 12:1 4016
c in pure and white linen, and ....Rev 15:6 1746
that was *c* in fine linen, and ....Rev 18:16 4016
he was *c* with a vesture dipped in ....Rev 19:13 4016
c in fine linen, white and clean ....Rev 19:14 1746

CLOTHES

and he rent his *c*...................................Gen 37:29 899
And Jacob rent his *c*, and put ....Gen 37:34 8071
Then they rent their *c*, and laded ....Gen 44:13 8071
his *c* in the blood of grapes ....Gen 49:11 5497
in their *c* upon their shoulders ....Ex 12:34 8071
morrow, and let them wash their *c* ....Ex 19:10 8071
and they washed their *c*........................Ex 19:14 8071
your heads, neither rend your *c* ....Lev 10:6 899
carcase of them shall wash his *c* ....Lev 11:25 899
carcase of them shall wash his *c*...........Lev 11:28 899
carcase of it shall wash his *c* ....Lev 11:40 899
carcase of it shall wash his *c* ....Lev 11:40 899
and he shall wash his *c*, and be ....Lev 13:6 899
and he shall wash his *c*, and be ....Lev 13:34 899
his *c* shall be rent, and his head ....Lev 13:45 899
to be cleansed shall wash his *c* ....Lev 14:8 899
and he shall wash his *c*, also he ....Lev 14:9 899
in the house shall wash his *c* ....Lev 14:47 899
in the house shall wash his *c* ....Lev 14:47 899
toucheth his bed shall wash his *c* ....Lev 15:5 899
hath the issue shall wash his *c* ....Lev 15:6 899
hath the issue shall wash his *c* ....Lev 15:7 899
then he shall wash his *c*, and ....Lev 15:8 899
of those things shall wash his *c* ....Lev 15:10 899
in water, he shall wash his *c*................Lev 15:11 899
for his cleansing, and wash his *c* ....Lev 15:13 899
toucheth her bed shall wash his *c* ....Lev 15:21 899
she sat upon shall wash his *c* ....Lev 15:22 899
be unclean, and shall wash his *c* ....Lev 15:27 899
the scapegoat shall wash his *c* ....Lev 16:26 899
burneth them shall wash his *c*..............Lev 16:28 899
and shall put on the linen *c*.................Lev 16:32 899
he shall both wash his *c* ....Lev 17:15 899
uncover his head, nor rend his *c* ....Lev 21:10 899
flesh, and let them wash their *c* ....Num 8:7 899
purified, and they washed their *c* ....Num 8:21 899
searched the land, rent their *c* ....Num 14:6 899
Then the priest shall wash his *c* ....Num 19:7 899
her shall wash his *c* in water...............Num 19:8 899
of the heifer shall wash his *c*...............Num 19:10 899
purify himself, and wash his *c* ....Num 19:19 899
of separation shall wash his *c* ....Num 19:21 899
wash your *c* on the seventh day ....Num 31:24 899
your *c* are not waxen old upon you.........Deut 29:5 8008
And Joshua rent his *c*, and fell to ....Josh 7:6 8071
he saw her, that he rent his *c* ....Judg 11:35 899
the same day with his *c* rent 1Sa 4:12 4055
And he stript off his *c* also 1Sa 19:24 899
camp from Saul with his *c* rent............2Sa 1:2 899
Then David took hold on his *c*..............2Sa 1:11 899
that were with him, Rend your *c*..........2Sa 3:31 899
stood by with their *c* rent 2Sa 13:31 899
his beard, nor washed his *c* 2Sa 19:24 899
and they covered him with *c* 1Kin 1:1 899
those words, that he rent his *c* 1Kin 21:27 899
and he took hold of his own *c* 2Kin 2:12 899
the letter, that he rent his *c* 2Kin 5:7 899
the king of Israel had rent his *c*..........2Kin 5:8 899
Wherefore hast thou rent thy *c* 2Kin 5:8 899
of the woman, that he rent his *c* 2Kin 6:30 899
and Athaliah rent her *c*, and cried, ...2Kin 11:14 899
to Hezekiah with their *c* rent 2Kin 18:37 899
heard it, that he rent his *c* 2Kin 19:1 899
of the law, that he rent his *c* 2Kin 22:11 899
and a curse, and hast rent thy *c* 2Kin 22:19 899
Then Athaliah rent her *c*, and said 2Chr 23:13 899
of the law, that he rent his *c* 2Chr 34:19 899
before me, and didst rend thy *c*............2Chr 34:27 899
me, none of us put off our *c* ....Neh 4:23 899

their *c* waxed not old, and their	Neh 9:21	8008
was done, Mordecai rent his *c*	Est 4:1	899
mine own *c* shall abhor me	Job 9:31	8008
his bosom, and his *c* not be burned	Prov 6:27	899
to Hezekiah with their *c* rent	Is 36:22	899
heard it, that he rent his *c*	Is 37:1	899
beards shaven, and their *c* rent	Jer 41:5	899
shall strip thee also of thy *c*	Eze 16:39	899
also strip thee out of thy *c*	Eze 23:26	899
in precious *c* for chariots	Eze 27:20	899
in all sorts of things, in blue *c*	Eze 27:24	1545
c laid to pledge by every altar	Amos 2:8	899
the colt, and put on them their *c*	Mt 21:7	2440
field return back to take his *c*	Mt 24:18	2440
Then the high priest rent his *c*	Mt 26:65	2440
said, If I may touch but his *c*	Mk 5:28	2440
press, and said, Who touched my *c*	Mk 5:30	2440
Then the high priest rent his *c*	Mk 14:63	5509
from him, and put his own *c* on him	Mk 15:20	2440
and wrapped him in swaddling *c*	Lk 2:7	4683
the babe wrapped in swaddling *c*	Lk 2:12	4683
devils long time, and ware no *c*	Lk 8:27	2440
they spread their *c* in the way	Lk 19:36	2440
the linen *c* laid by themselves	Lk 24:12	3608
it in linen *c* with the spices	Jn 19:40	3608
looking in, saw the linen *c* lying	Jn 20:5	3608
and seeth the linen *c* lie	Jn 20:6	3608
head, not lying with the linen *c*	Jn 20:7	3608
their *c* at a young man's feet	Acts 7:58	2440
Paul, heard of, they rent their *c*	Acts 14:14	2440
the magistrates rent off their *c*	Acts 16:22	2440
cried out, and cast off their *c*	Acts 22:23	2440

CLOTHEST

Though thou *c* thyself with	Jer 4:30	3847

CLOTHING

and stripped the naked of their *c*	Job 22:6	899
the naked to lodge without *c*	Job 24:7	3830
cause him to go naked without *c*	Job 24:10	3830
seen any perish for want of *c*	Job 31:19	3830
were sick, my *c* was sackcloth	Ps 35:13	3830
her *c* is of wrought gold	Ps 45:13	3830
The lambs are for thy *c*, and the	Prov 27:26	3830
her *c* is silk and purple	Prov 31:22	3830
Strength and honour are her *c*	Prov 31:25	3830
his father, saying, Thou hast *c*	Is 3:6	8071
my house is neither bread nor *c*	Is 3:7	8071
sufficiently, and for durable *c*	Is 23:18	4374
the garments of vengeance for *c*	Is 59:17	8516
blue and purple is their *c*	Jer 10:9	3830
which come to you in sheep's *c*	Mt 7:15	1742
they that wear soft *c* are in	Mt 11:8	
which love to go in long *c*	Mk 12:38	4749
a man stood before me in bright *c*	Acts 10:30	2066
to him that weareth the gay *c*	Jas 2:3	2066

CLOTHS

the *c* of service, and the holy	Ex 31:10	899
The *c* of service, to do service	Ex 35:19	899
they made *c* of service, to do	Ex 39:1	899
The *c* of service to do service in	Ex 39:41	899

CLOUD

I do set my bow in the *c*, and it	Gen 9:13	6051
when I bring a *c* over the earth	Gen 9:14	6051
the bow shall be seen in the *c*	Gen 9:14	6051
And the bow shall be in the *c*	Gen 9:16	6051
them by day in a pillar of a *c*	Ex 13:21	6051
away the pillar of the *c* by day	Ex 13:22	6051
the pillar of the *c* went from	Ex 14:19	6051
and it was a *c* and darkness to them	Ex 14:20	6051
the pillar of fire and of the *c*	Ex 14:24	6051
of the LORD appeared in the *c*	Ex 16:10	6051
Lo, I come unto thee in a thick *c*	Ex 19:9	6051
a thick *c* upon the mount, and the	Ex 19:16	6051
mount, and a *c* covered the mount	Ex 24:15	6051
the *c* covered it six days	Ex 24:16	6051
Moses out of the midst of the *c*	Ex 24:16	6051
went into the midst of the *c*	Ex 24:18	6051
And the LORD descended in the *c*	Ex 34:5	6051
Then a *c* covered the tent of the	Ex 40:34	6051
because the *c* abode thereon, and	Ex 40:35	6051
when the *c* was taken up from over	Ex 40:36	6051
But if the *c* were not taken up,	Ex 40:37	6051
For the *c* of the LORD was upon	Ex 40:38	6051
in the *c* upon the mercy seat	Lev 16:2	6051
that the *c* of the incense may	Lev 16:13	6051
up the *c* covered the tabernacle	Num 9:15	6051
the *c* covered it by day, and the	Num 9:16	6051
when the *c* was taken up from the	Num 9:17	6051
and in the place where the *c* abode	Num 9:17	6051
as long as the *c* abode upon the	Num 9:18	6051

when the *c* tarried long upon the	Num 9:19	6051
when the *c* was a few days upon	Num 9:20	6051
when the *c* abode from even unto	Num 9:21	6051
that the *c* was taken up in the	Num 9:21	6051
by night that the *c* was taken up	Num 9:21	6051
that the *c* tarried upon the	Num 9:22	6051
that the *c* was taken up from off	Num 10:11	6051
the *c* rested in the wilderness of	Num 10:12	6051
the *c* of the LORD was upon them	Num 10:34	6051
And the LORD came down in a *c*	Num 11:25	6051
came down in the pillar of the *c*	Num 12:5	6051
the *c* departed from off the	Num 12:10	6051
that thy *c* standeth over them, and	Num 14:14	6051
by daytime in a pillar of a *c*	Num 14:14	6051
the *c* covered it, and the glory of	Num 16:42	6051
ye should go, and in a *c* by day	Deut 1:33	6051
the midst of the fire, of the *c*	Deut 5:22	6051
the tabernacle in a pillar of a *c*	Deut 31:15	6051
the pillar of the *c* stood over	Deut 31:15	6051
that the *c* filled the house of	1Kin 8:10	6051
to minister because of the *c*	1Kin 8:11	6051
ariseth a little *c* out of the sea	1Kin 18:44	5645
the house was filled with a *c*	2Chr 5:13	6051
to minister by reason of the *c*	2Chr 5:14	6051
the pillar of the *c* departed not	Neh 9:19	6051
let a *c* dwell upon it	Job 3:5	6053
As the *c* is consumed and vanisheth	Job 7:9	6051
can he judge through the dark *c*	Job 22:13	6205
the *c* is not rent under them	Job 26:8	6051
and spreadeth his *c* upon it	Job 26:9	6051
and my welfare passeth away as a *c*	Job 30:15	5645
by the *c* that cometh betwixt	Job 36:32	
watering he wearieth the thick *c*	Job 37:11	5645
he scattereth his bright *c*	Job 37:11	6051
the light of his *c* to shine	Job 37:15	6051
When I made the *c* the garment	Job 38:9	6051
daytime also he led them with a *c*	Ps 78:14	6051
He spread a *c* for a covering	Ps 105:39	6051
is as a *c* of the latter rain	Prov 16:15	5645
Zion, and upon her assemblies, a *c*	Is 4:5	6051
like a *c* of dew in the heat of	Is 18:4	5645
the LORD rideth upon a swift *c*	Is 19:1	5645
the heat with the shadow of a *c*	Is 25:5	5645
I have blotted out, as a thick *c*	Is 44:22	5645
thy transgressions, and, as a *c*	Is 44:22	6051
Who are these that fly as a *c*	Is 60:8	5645
of Zion with a *c* in his anger	Lam 2:1	5743
hast covered thyself with a *c*	Lam 3:44	6051
came out of the north, a great *c*	Eze 1:4	6051
is in the *c* in the day of rain	Eze 1:28	6051
a thick *c* of incense went up	Eze 8:11	6051
the *c* filled the inner court	Eze 10:3	6051
the house was filled with the *c*	Eze 10:4	6051
a *c* shall cover her, and her	Eze 30:18	6051
I will cover the sun with a *c*	Eze 32:7	6051
be like a *c* to cover the land	Eze 38:9	6051
Israel, as a *c* to cover the land	Eze 38:16	6051
your goodness is as a morning *c*	Hos 6:4	6051
they shall be as the morning *c*	Hos 13:3	6051
a bright *c* overshadowed them	Mt 17:5	3507
and behold a voice out of the *c*	Mt 17:5	3507
there was a *c* that overshadowed	Mk 9:7	3507
and a voice came out of the *c*	Mk 9:7	3507
he thus spake, there came a *c*	Lk 9:34	3507
feared as they entered into the *c*	Lk 9:34	3507
there came a voice out of the *c*	Lk 9:35	3507
When ye see a *c* rise out of the	Lk 12:54	3507
of man coming in a *c* with power	Lk 21:27	3507
a *c* received him out of their	Acts 1:9	3507
all our fathers were under the *c*	1Cor 10:1	3507
all baptized unto Moses in the *c*	1Cor 10:2	3507
with so great a *c* of witnesses	Heb 12:1	3509
from heaven, clothed with a *c*	Rev 10:1	3507
they ascended up to heaven in a *c*	Rev 11:12	3507
And I looked, and behold a white *c*	Rev 14:14	3507
upon the *c* one sat like unto the	Rev 14:14	3507
voice to him that sat on the *c*	Rev 14:15	3507
he that sat on the *c* thrust in	Rev 14:16	3507

CLOUDS

midst of heaven, with darkness, *c*	Deut 4:11	6051
dropped, the *c* also dropped water	Judg 5:4	5645
waters, and thick *c* of the skies	2Sa 22:12	5645
riseth, even a morning without *c*	2Sa 23:4	5645
that the heaven was black with *c*	1Kin 18:45	5645
and his head reach unto the *c*	Job 20:6	5645
Thick *c* are a covering to him,	Job 22:14	5645
up the waters in his thick *c*	Job 26:8	5645
behold the *c* which are higher	Job 35:5	7834
Which the *c* do drop and distil	Job 36:28	7834
the spreadings of the *c*, or the	Job 36:29	5645

With *c* he covereth the light	Job 36:32	3709
thou know the balancings of the *c*	Job 37:16	5645
bright light which is in the *c*	Job 37:21	7834
thou lift up thy voice to the *c*	Job 38:34	5645
Who can number the *c* in wisdom	Job 38:37	7834
waters and thick *c* of the skies	Ps 18:11	5645
was before him his thick *c* passed	Ps 18:12	5645
faithfulness reacheth unto the *c*	Ps 36:5	7834
heavens, and thy truth unto the *c*	Ps 57:10	7834
and his strength is in the *c*	Ps 68:34	7834
The *c* poured out water	Ps 77:17	5645
he had commanded the *c* from above	Ps 78:23	7834
C and darkness are round about him	Ps 97:2	6051
who maketh the *c* his chariot	Ps 104:3	5645
and thy truth reacheth unto the *c*	Ps 108:4	7834
Who covereth the heaven with *c*	Ps 147:8	5645
up, and the *c* drop down the dew	Prov 3:20	7834
When he established the *c* above	Prov 8:28	7834
himself of a false gift is like *c*	Prov 25:14	5387
If the *c* be full of rain, they	Eccl 11:3	5645
regardeth the *c* shall not reap	Eccl 11:4	5645
nor the *c* return after the rain	Eccl 12:2	5645
I will also command the *c* that	Is 5:6	5645
ascend above the heights of the *c*	Is 14:14	5645
Behold, he shall come up as *c*	Jer 4:13	6053
of man came with the *c* of heaven	Dan 7:13	6050
and of gloominess, a day of *c*	Joel 2:2	6051
the *c* are the dust of his feet	Nah 1:3	6051
and gloominess, a day of *c*	Zeph 1:15	6051
so the Lord shall make bright *c*	Zec 10:1	2385
in the *c* of heaven with power	Mt 24:30	3507
and coming in the *c* of heaven	Mt 26:64	3507
coming in the *c* with great power	Mk 13:26	3507
and coming in the *c* of heaven	Mk 14:62	3507
up together with them in the *c*	1Th 4:17	3507
c that are carried with a tempest	2Pet 2:17	3507
c they are without water, carried	Jude 12	3507
Behold, he cometh with *c*	Rev 1:7	3507

CLOUDY

the *c* pillar descended, and stood	Ex 33:9	6051
all the people saw the *c* pillar	Ex 33:10	6051
them in the day by a *c* pillar	Neh 9:12	6051
spake unto them in the *c* pillar	Ps 99:7	6051
day of the Lord is near, a *c* day	Eze 30:3	6051
they have been scattered in the *c*	Eze 34:12	6051

CLOUTED

c upon their feet, and old	Josh 9:5	2921

CLOUTS

and took thence old cast *c*	Jer 38:11	5499
Put now these old cast *c*	Jer 38:12	5499

CLOVEN

or of them that divide the *c* hoof	Deut 14:7	8156
them *c* tongues like as of fire	Acts 2:3	1266

CLOVENFOOTED

parteth the hoof, and is *c*	Lev 11:3	8156,8157,6541
he divide the hoof, and be *c*	Lev 11:7	8156,8157,6541
divideth the hoof, and is not *c*	Lev 11:26	8156,8157

CLUSTER

a branch with one *c* of grapes	Num 13:23	811
because of the *c* of grapes which	Num 13:24	811
My beloved is unto me as a *c* of	Song 1:14	811
As the new wine is found in the *c*	Is 65:8	811
there is no *c* to eat	Mic 7:1	811

CLUSTERS

the *c* thereof brought forth ripe	Gen 40:10	811
of gall, their *c* are bitter	Deut 32:32	811
corn, and an hundred *c* of raisins	1Sa 25:18	6778
cake of figs, and two *c* of raisins	1Sa 30:12	6778
and thy breasts to *c* of grapes	Song 7:7	811
breasts shall be as *c* of the vine	Song 7:8	811
gather the *c* of the vine of the	Rev 14:18	1009

CNIDUS (ni'-dus) *A port town in southwestern Asia Minor.*

scarce were come over against *C*	Acts 27:7	2834

COAL

shall quench my *c* which is left	2Sa 14:7	1513
me, having a live *c* in his hand	Is 6:6	7531
there shall not be a *c* to warm at	Is 47:14	1513
Their visage is blacker than a *c*	Lam 4:8	7815

COALS

c of fire from off the altar	Lev 16:12	1513
c were kindled by it	2Sa 22:9	1513
before him were *c* of fire kindled	2Sa 22:13	1513
there was a cake baken on the *c*	1Kin 19:6	7529
His breath kindleth *c*, and a flame	Job 41:21	1513
c were kindled by it	Ps 18:8	1513

passed, hail stones and *c* of fire	Ps 18:12	1513
hail stones and *c* of fire	Ps 18:13	1513
of the mighty, with *c* of juniper	Ps 120:4	1513
Let burning *c* fall upon them	Ps 140:10	1513
Can one go upon hot *c*, and his	Prov 6:28	1513
For thou shalt heap *c* of fire	Prov 25:22	1513
As *c* are to burning *c*, and	Prov 26:21	6352
As *c* are to burning *c*	Prov 26:21	1513
the *c* thereof are *c* of fire	Song 8:6	7565
the tongs both worketh in the *c*	Is 44:12	6352
baked bread upon the *c* thereof	Is 44:19	1513
that bloweth the *c* in the fire	Is 54:16	6352
was like burning *c* of fire	Eze 1:13	1513
fill thine hand with *c* of fire	Eze 10:2	1513
set it empty upon the *c* thereof	Eze 24:11	1513
burning *c* went forth at his feet	Hab 3:5	7565
there, who had made a fire of *c*	Jn 18:18	439
land, they saw a fire of *c* there	Jn 21:9	439
shalt heap *c* of fire on his head	Rom 12:20	440

COAST

I bring the locusts into thy *c*	Ex 10:4	1366
by the sea, and by the *c* of Jordan	Num 13:29	3027
by the *c* of the land of Edom,	Num 20:23	1366
Arnon, which is in the utmost *c*	Num 22:36	1366
come come from the *c* of Chittim	Num 24:24	3027
of Zin along by the *c* of Edom	Num 34:3	3027
c of the salt sea eastward	Num 34:3	7097
the *c* shall go down from Shepham	Num 34:11	1366
Ye are to pass through the *c* of	Deut 2:4	1366
Ar, the *c* of Moab, this day	Deut 2:18	1366
the *c* thereof, from Chinnereth	Deut 3:17	1366
the uttermost sea shall your *c* be	Deut 11:24	1366
with thee in all thy *c* seven days	Deut 16:4	1366
if the Lord thy God enlarge thy *c*	Deut 19:8	1366
down of the sun, shall be your *c*	Josh 1:4	1366
the *c* of Og king of Bashan, which	Josh 12:4	1366
The king of Dor in the *c* of Dor	Josh 12:23	5299
their *c* was from Aroer, that is	Josh 13:16	1366
their *c* was Jazer, and all the	Josh 13:25	1366
their *c* was from Mahanaim, all	Josh 13:30	1366
the uttermost part of the south *c*	Josh 15:1	1366
out of that *c* were at the sea	Josh 15:4	1366
this shall be your south *c*	Josh 15:4	1366
the great sea, and the *c* thereof	Josh 15:12	1366
This is the *c* of the children of	Josh 15:12	1366
children of Judah toward the *c* of	Josh 15:21	1366
westward to the *c* of Japhleti	Josh 16:3	1366
unto the *c* of Beth-horon the	Josh 16:3	1366
the *c* of Manasseh was from Asher	Josh 17:7	1366
the *c* descended unto the river	Josh 17:9	1366
the *c* of Manasseh also was on the	Josh 17:9	1366
abide in their *c* on the south	Josh 18:5	1366
the *c* of their lot came forth	Josh 18:11	1366
this was the south *c*	Josh 18:19	1366
the *c* reacheth to Tabor, and	Josh 19:22	1366
then the *c* turneth to Ramah, and	Josh 19:29	1366
and the *c* turneth to Hosah	Josh 19:29	1366
at the sea from the *c* to Achzib	Josh 19:29	2256
their *c* was from Heleph, from	Josh 19:33	1366
then the *c* turneth westward to	Josh 19:34	1366
the *c* of their inheritance was	Josh 19:41	1366
the *c* of the children of Dan went	Josh 19:47	1366
took Gaza with the *c* thereof	Judg 1:18	1366
and Askelon with the *c* thereof	Judg 1:18	1366
and Ekron with the *c* thereof	Judg 1:18	1366
the *c* of the Amorites was from	Judg 1:36	1366
not Israel to pass through his *c*	Judg 11:20	1366
way of his own *c* to Beth-shemesh	1Sa 6:9	1366
came no more into the *c* of Israel	1Sa 7:13	1366
me any more in any *c* of Israel	1Sa 27:1	1366
upon the *c* which belongeth to	1Sa 30:14	
He restored the *c* of Israel from	2Kin 14:25	1366
bless me indeed, and enlarge my *c*	1Chr 4:10	1366
destroy the remnant of the sea *c*	Eze 25:16	2348
which is by the *c* of Hauran	Eze 47:16	1366
to the *c* of the way of Hethlon	Eze 48:1	3027
northward, to the *c* of Hamath	Eze 48:1	3027
unto the inhabitants of the sea *c*	Zeph 2:5	2256
the sea *c* shall be dwellings and	Zeph 2:6	2256
the *c* shall be for the remnant of	Zeph 2:7	2256
which is upon the sea *c*, in the	Mt 4:13	3864
and from the sea *c* of Tyre	Lk 6:17	3882

COASTS

and rested in all the *c* of Egypt	Ex 10:14	1366
one locust in all the *c* of Egypt	Ex 10:19	1366
out of the *c* of the Amorites	Num 21:13	1366
with the cities thereof in the *c*	Num 32:33	1367
land of Canaan with the *c* thereof	Num 34:2	1367
with the *c* thereof round about	Num 34:12	1367
of Argob unto the *c* of Geshuri	Deut 3:14	1366

divide the *c* of thy land, which	Deut 19:3	1366
olive trees throughout all thy *c*	Deut 28:40	1366
in all the *c* of the great sea	Josh 9:1	2348
abide in their *c* on the north	Josh 18:5	1366
by the *c* thereof round about,	Josh 18:20	1367
land for inheritance by their *c*	Josh 19:49	1367
all the *c* of the Amorites	Judg 11:22	1366
that be along by the *c* of Arnon	Judg 11:26	3027
family five men from their *c*	Judg 18:2	7098
sent her into all the *c* of Israel	Judg 19:29	1366
even Ashdod and the *c* thereof	1Sa 5:6	1366
the *c* thereof did Israel deliver	1Sa 7:14	1366
unto all the *c* of Israel	1Sa 11:3	1366
the *c* of Israel by the hands of	1Sa 11:7	1366
in any of the *c* of Israel	2Sa 21:5	1366
throughout all the *c* of Israel	1Kin 1:3	1366
smote them in all the *c* of Israel	2Kin 10:32	1366
the *c* thereof from Tirzah	2Kin 15:16	1366
their castles in their *c*, of the	1Chr 6:54	1366
c out of the tribe of Ephraim	1Chr 6:66	1366
throughout all the *c* of Israel	1Chr 21:12	1366
to him out of all their *c*	2Chr 11:13	1366
of flies, and lice in all their *c*	Ps 105:31	1366
and brake the trees of their *c*	Ps 105:33	1366
raised up from the *c* of the earth	Jer 25:32	3411
them from the *c* of the earth	Jer 31:8	3411
raised up from the *c* of the earth	Jer 50:41	3411
of the land take a man of their *c*	Eze 33:2	7097
Zidon, and all the *c* of Palestine	Joel 3:4	1552
and in all the *c* thereof, from	Mt 2:16	3725
he would depart out of their *c*	Mt 8:34	3725
and departed into the *c* of Tyre	Mt 15:21	3313
of Canaan came out of the same *c*	Mt 15:22	3725
and came into the *c* of Magdala	Mt 15:39	3725
into the *c* of Caesarea Philippi	Mt 16:13	3313
came into the *c* of Judaea beyond	Mt 19:1	3725
pray him to depart out of their *c*	Mk 5:17	3725
departing from the *c* of Tyre	Mk 7:31	3725
the midst of the *c* of Decapolis	Mk 7:31	3725
cometh into the *c* of Judaea by	Mk 10:1	3725
and expelled them out of their *c*	Acts 13:50	3725
the upper *c* came to Ephesus	Acts 19:1	3313
and throughout all the *c* of Judaea	Acts 26:20	5561
meaning to sail by the *c* of Asia	Acts 27:2	5117

COAT

he made him a *c* of many colours	Gen 37:3	3801
they stript Joseph out of his *c*	Gen 37:23	3801
his *c* of many colours that was on	Gen 37:23	3801
And they took Joseph's *c*, and	Gen 37:31	3801
dipped the *c* in the blood	Gen 37:31	3801
they sent the *c* of many colours,	Gen 37:32	3801
whether it be thy son's *c* or no	Gen 37:32	3801
it, and said, It is my son's *c*	Gen 37:33	3801
and a robe, and a broidered *c*	Ex 28:4	3801
embroider the *c* of fine linen	Ex 28:39	3801
garments, and put upon Aaron the *c*	Ex 29:5	3801
And he put upon him the *c*, and	Lev 8:7	3801
He shall put on the holy linen *c*	Lev 16:4	3801
his mother made him a little *c*	1Sa 2:19	4598
and he was armed with a *c* of mail	1Sa 17:5	8302
the weight of the *c* was five	1Sa 17:5	8302
he armed him with a *c* of mail	1Sa 17:38	8302
came to meet him with his *c* rent	2Sa 15:32	3801
me about as the collar of my *c*	Job 30:18	3801
I have put off my *c*	Song 5:3	3801
at the law, and take away thy *c*	Mt 5:40	5509
forbid not to take thy *c* also	Lk 6:29	5509
and also his *c*	Jn 19:23	5509
now the *c* was without seam, woven	Jn 19:23	5509
he girt his fisher's *c* unto him	Jn 21:7	1903

COATS

did the LORD God make *c* of skins	Gen 3:21	3801
Aaron's sons thou shalt make *c*	Ex 28:40	3801
his sons, and put *c* upon them	Ex 29:8	3801
they made *c* of fine linen of	Ex 39:27	3801
his sons, and clothe them with *c*	Ex 40:14	3801
put *c* upon them, and girded them	Lev 8:13	3801
them in their *c* out of the camp	Lev 10:5	3801
these men were bound in their *c*	Dan 3:21	5622
neither were their *c* changed	Dan 3:27	5622
for your journey, neither two *c*	Mt 10:10	5509
and not put on two *c*	Mk 6:9	5509
unto them, He that hath two *c*	Lk 3:11	5509
neither have two *c* apiece	Lk 9:3	5509
by him weeping, and shewing the *c*	Acts 9:39	5509

COCK

this night, before the *c* crow	Mt 26:34	220
And immediately the *c* crew	Mt 26:74	220
said unto him, Before the *c* crow	Mt 26:75	220

night, before the *c* crow twice	Mk 14:30	220
and the *c* crew	Mk 14:68	220
And the second time the *c* crew	Mk 14:72	220
unto him, Before the *c* crow twice	Mk 14:72	220
the *c* shall not crow this day,	Lk 22:34	220
while he yet spake, the *c* crew	Lk 22:60	220
said unto him, Before the *c* crow	Lk 22:61	220
The *c* shall not crow, till thou	Jn 13:38	220
and immediately the *c* crew	Jn 18:27	220

COCKATRICE

root shall come forth a *c*	Is 14:29	6848

COCKATRICE'

shall put his hand on the *c* den	Is 11:8	6848
They hatch *c* eggs, and weave the	Is 59:5	6848

COCKATRICES

behold, I will send serpents, *c*	Jer 8:17	6848

COCKCROWING

even, or at midnight, or at the *c*	Mk 13:35	219

COCKLE

of wheat, and *c* instead of barley	Job 31:40	890

COFFER

in a *c* by the side thereof	1Sa 6:8	712
the *c* with the mice of gold and	1Sa 6:11	712
the *c* that was with it, wherein	1Sa 6:15	712

COFFIN

and he was put in a *c* in Egypt	Gen 50:26	727

COGITATIONS

my *c* much troubled me, and my	Dan 7:28	7476

COLD

seedtime and harvest, and *c*	Gen 8:22	7120
they have no covering in the *c*	Job 24:7	7135
and *c* out of the north	Job 37:9	7135
who can stand before his *c*	Ps 147:17	7135
will not plow by reason of the *c*	Prov 20:4	2779
As the *c* of snow in the time of	Prov 25:13	6793
away a garment in *c* weather	Prov 25:20	7135
As *c* waters to a thirsty soul, so	Prov 25:25	7119
or shall the *c* flowing waters	Jer 18:14	7119
camp in the hedges in the *c* day	Nah 3:17	7135
of *c* water only in the name of a	Mt 10:42	5593
the love of many shall wax *c*	Mt 24:12	5594
for it was *c*	Jn 18:18	5592
present rain, and because of the *c*	Acts 28:2	5592
thirst, in fastings often, in *c*	2Cor 11:27	5592
that thou art neither *c* nor hot	Rev 3:15	5593
I would thou wert *c* or hot	Rev 3:15	5593
lukewarm, and neither *c* nor hot	Rev 3:16	5593

COLHOZEH (col-ho'-zeh)

repaired Shallun the son of C	Neh 3:15	3626
the son of Baruch, the son of C	Neh 11:5	3626

COLLAR

me about as the *c* of my coat	Job 30:18	6310

COLLARS

beside ornaments, and *c*, and purple	Judg 8:26	5188

COLLECTION

Judah and out of Jerusalem the *c*	2Chr 24:6	4864
to bring in to the LORD the *c*	2Chr 24:9	4864
concerning the *c* for the saints	1Cor 16:1	3048

COLLEGE

she dwelt in Jerusalem in the *c*	2Kin 22:14	4932
she dwelt in Jerusalem in the *c*	2Chr 34:22	4932

COLLOPS

maketh *c* of fat on his flanks	Job 15:27	6371

COLONY

of that part of Macedonia, and a *c*	Acts 16:12	2862

COLORS

I will lay thy stones with fair *c*	Is 54:11	6320

COLOSSE (co-los'-see) See COLOSSIANS. A city in Phrygia.

brethren in Christ which are at C	Col 1:2	2857

COLOSSIANS (co-los'-yans) Residents of Colosse.

from Rome to the C by Tychicus	Col s	2858

COLOUR

the plague have not changed his *c*	Lev 13:55	5869
the *c* thereof as the *c* of	Num 11:7	5869
when it giveth his *c* in the cup	Prov 23:31	5869
midst thereof as the *c* of amber	Eze 1:4	5869
like the *c* of burnished brass	Eze 1:7	5869
was like unto the *c* of a beryl	Eze 1:16	5869
as the *c* of the terrible crystal	Eze 1:22	5869
And I saw as the *c* of amber	Eze 1:27	5869

of brightness, as the *c* of amber	Eze 8:2	5869
was as the *c* of a beryl stone	Eze 10:9	5869
his feet like in *c* to polished	Dan 10:6	5869
under *c* as though they would have	Acts 27:30	4392
arrayed in purple and scarlet *c*	Rev 17:4	

COLOURED
woman sit upon a scarlet *c* beast	Rev 17:3	

COLOURS
and he made him a coat of many *c*	Gen 37:3	6446
coat of many *c* that was on him	Gen 37:23	6446
And they sent the coat of many *c*	Gen 37:32	6446
to Sisera a prey of divers *c*	Judg 5:30	6648
a prey of divers *c* of needlework	Judg 5:30	6648
of divers *c* of needlework on both	Judg 5:30	6648
a garment of divers *c* upon her	2Sa 13:18	6446
of divers *c* that was on her	2Sa 13:19	6446
glistering stones, and of divers *c*	1Chr 29:2	7553
thy high places with divers *c*	Eze 16:16	2921
of feathers, which had divers *c*	Eze 17:3	7553

COLT
his ass's *c* unto the choice vine	Gen 49:11	1121
man be born like a wild ass's *c*	Job 11:12	5895
upon a *c* the foal of an ass	Zec 9:9	5895
find an ass tied, and a *c* with her	Mt 21:2	4454
an ass, and a *c* the foal of an ass	Mt 21:5	4454
And brought the ass, and the *c*	Mt 21:7	4454
into it, ye shall find a *c* tied	Mk 11:2	4454
found the *c* tied by the door	Mk 11:4	4454
them, What do ye, loosing the *c*	Mk 11:5	4454
And they brought the *c* to Jesus	Mk 11:7	4454
entering ye shall find a *c* tied	Lk 19:30	4454
And as they were loosing the *c*	Lk 19:33	4454
unto them, Why loose ye the *c*	Lk 19:33	4454
cast their garments upon the *c*	Lk 19:35	4454
cometh, sitting on an ass's *c*	Jn 12:15	4454

COLTS
Thirty milch camels with their *c*	Gen 32:15	1121
sons rode on thirty ass *c*	Judg 10:4	5895
rode on threescore and ten ass *c*	Judg 12:14	5895

COME See APPENDIX.

COMELINESS
he hath no form nor *c*	Is 53:2	1926
for it was perfect through my *c*	Eze 16:14	1926
they set forth thy *c*	Eze 27:10	1926
for my *c* was turned in me into	Dan 10:8	1935
parts have more abundant *c*	1Cor 12:23	2157

COMELY
a *c* person, and the LORD is with	1Sa 16:18	8389
his power, nor his *c* proportion	Job 41:12	2433
for praise is *c* for the upright	Ps 33:1	5000
and praise is *c*	Ps 147:1	5000
go well, yea, four are *c* in going	Prov 30:29	3190
c for one to eat and to drink, and	Eccl 5:18	3303
I am black, but *c*, O ye daughters	Song 1:5	5000
Thy cheeks are *c* with rows of	Song 1:10	4998
voice, and thy countenance is *c*	Song 2:14	5000
of scarlet, and thy speech is *c*	Song 4:3	5000
c as Jerusalem, terrible as an	Song 6:4	5000
c for them that are escaped of	Is 4:2	8597
the daughter of Zion to a *c*	Jer 6:2	5000
upon you, but for that which is *c*	1Cor 7:35	2158
is it *c* that a woman pray unto	1Cor 11:13	4241
For our *c* parts have no need	1Cor 12:24	2158

COMERS
make the *c* thereunto perfect	Heb 10:1	4334

COMEST See APPENDIX.

COMETH See APPENDIX.

COMFORT
This same shall *c* us concerning	Gen 5:29	5162
of bread, and *c* ye your hearts	Gen 18:5	5582
doth *c* himself, purposing to kill	Gen 27:42	5162
his daughters rose up to *c* him	Gen 37:35	5162
C thine heart with a morsel of	Judg 19:5	5582
C thine heart, I pray thee	Judg 19:8	5582
David sent to *c* him by the hand	2Sa 10:2	5162
and his brethren came to *c* him	1Chr 7:22	5162
David sent messengers to *c* him	1Chr 19:2	5162
of Ammon to Hanun, to *c* him	1Chr 19:2	5162
to mourn with him and to *c* him	Job 2:11	5162
Then should I yet have *c*	Job 6:10	5165
When I say, My bed shall *c* me	Job 7:13	5162
off my heaviness, and *c* myself	Job 9:27	1082
alone, that I may take *c* a little	Job 10:20	1082
How then *c* ye me in vain, seeing	Job 21:34	5162
thy rod and thy staff they *c* me	Ps 23:4	5162

greatness, and *c* me on every side	Ps 71:21	5162
This is my *c* in my affliction	Ps 119:50	5162
thy merciful kindness be for my *c*	Ps 119:76	5162
word, saying, When wilt thou *c* me	Ps 119:82	5162
me with flagons, *c* me with apples	Song 2:5	7502
weep bitterly, labour not to *c* me	Is 22:4	5162
C ye, *c* ye my people, saith	Is 40:1	5162
For the LORD shall *c* Zion	Is 51:3	5162
he will *c* all her waste places	Is 51:3	5162
by whom shall I *c* thee	Is 51:19	5162
Should I receive *c* in these	Is 57:6	5162
to *c* all that mourn	Is 61:2	5162
comforteth, so will I *c* you	Is 66:13	5162
When I would *c* myself against	Jer 8:18	4010
mourning, to *c* them for the dead	Jer 16:7	5162
mourning into joy, and will *c* them	Jer 31:13	5162
her lovers she hath none to *c* her	Lam 1:2	5162
hands, and there is none to *c* her	Lam 1:17	5162
there is none to *c* me	Lam 1:21	5162
equal to thee, that I may *c* thee	Lam 2:13	5162
And they shall *c* you, when ye see	Eze 14:23	5162
in that thou art a *c* unto them	Eze 16:54	5162
and the LORD shall yet *c* Zion	Zec 1:17	5162
they *c* in vain	Zec 10:2	5162
he said, Daughter, be of good *c*	Mt 9:22	2293
saying unto him, Be of good *c*	Mk 10:49	2293
unto her, Daughter, be of good *c*	Lk 8:48	2293
to *c* them concerning their	Jn 11:19	3888
in the *c* of the Holy Ghost, were	Acts 9:31	3874
c of the scriptures might have	Rom 15:4	3874
edification, and exhortation, and *c*	1Cor 14:3	3889
of mercies, and the God of all *c*	2Cor 1:3	3874
that we may be able to *c* them	2Cor 1:4	3870
by the *c* wherewith we ourselves	2Cor 1:4	3874
c him, lest perhaps such a one	2Cor 2:7	3870
I am filled with *c*, I am	2Cor 7:4	3874
we were comforted in your *c*	2Cor 7:13	3874
Be perfect, be of good *c*, be of	2Cor 13:11	3870
and that he might *c* your hearts	Eph 6:22	3870
Christ, if any *c* of love, if any	Phil 2:1	3890
you, that I also may be of good *c*	Phil 2:19	2174
your estate, and *c* your hearts	Col 4:8	3870
God, which have been a *c* unto me	Col 4:11	3931
to *c* you concerning your faith	1Th 3:2	3870
Wherefore *c* one another with	1Th 4:18	3870
Wherefore *c* yourselves together	1Th 5:11	3870
c the feebleminded, support the	1Th 5:14	3888
C your hearts, and stablish you in	2Th 2:17	3870

COMFORTABLE
my lord the king shall now be *c*	2Sa 14:17	4496
me with good words and *c* words	Zec 1:13	5150

COMFORTABLY
speak *c* unto thy servants	2Sa 19:7	5921,3820
Hezekiah spake *c* unto all the	2Chr 30:22	5921,3820
city, and spake *c* to them, saying	2Chr 32:6	5921,3824
Speak ye *c* to Jerusalem, and cry	Is 40:2	5921,3820
wilderness, and speak *c* unto her	Hos 2:14	5921,3820

COMFORTED
Isaac was *c* after his mother's	Gen 24:67	5162
but he refused to be *c*	Gen 37:35	5162
and Judah was *c*, and went up unto	Gen 38:12	5162
he *c* them, and spake kindly unto	Gen 50:21	5162
for that thou hast *c* me, and for	Ruth 2:13	5162
David *c* Bath-sheba his wife, and	2Sa 12:24	5162
for he was *c* concerning Amnon	2Sa 13:39	5162
c him over all the evil that the	Job 42:11	5162
my soul refused to be *c*	Ps 77:2	5162
LORD, hast holpen me, and *c* me	Ps 86:17	5162
and have I myself	Ps 119:52	5162
for the LORD hath *c* his people	Is 49:13	5162
for the LORD hath *c* his people	Is 52:9	5162
tossed with tempest, and not *c*	Is 54:11	5162
ye shall be *c* in Jerusalem	Is 66:13	5162
refused to be *c* for her children	Jer 31:15	5162
to rest upon them, and I will be *c*	Eze 5:13	5162
ye shall be *c* concerning the evil	Eze 14:22	5162
shall be *c* in the nether parts of	Eze 31:16	5162
shall be *c* over all his multitude	Eze 32:31	5162
her children, and would not be *c*	Mt 2:18	3870
for they shall be *c*	Mt 5:4	3870
but now he is *c*, and thou art	Lk 16:25	3870
c her, when they saw Mary, that	Jn 11:31	3888
seen the brethren, they *c* them	Acts 16:40	3870
man alive, and were not a little *c*	Acts 20:12	3870
that I may be *c* together with you	Rom 1:12	4837
all may learn, and all may be *c*	1Cor 14:31	3870
we ourselves are *c* of God	2Cor 1:4	3870
or whether we be *c*, it is for	2Cor 1:6	3870
c us by the coming of Titus	2Cor 7:6	3870

C

wherewith he was *c* in you	2Cor 7:7	3870
we were *c* in your comfort	2Cor 7:13	3870
That their hearts might be *c*	Col 2:2	3870
As ye know how we exhorted and *c*	1Th 2:11	3888
we were *c* over you in all our	1Th 3:7	3870

COMFORTEDST

is turned away, and thou *c* me	Is 12:1	5162

COMFORTER

were oppressed, and they had no *c*	Eccl 4:1	5162
but they had no *c*	Eccl 4:1	
she had no *c*	Lam 1:9	5162
because the *c* that should relieve	Lam 1:16	5162
and he shall give you another *C*	Jn 14:16	3875
But the *C*, which is the Holy	Jn 14:26	3875
But when the *C* is come, whom I	Jn 15:26	3875
the *C* will not come unto you	Jn 16:7	3875

COMFORTERS

that he hath sent *c* unto thee	2Sa 10:3	5162
that he hath sent *c* unto thee	1Chr 19:3	5162
miserable *c* are ye all	Job 16:2	5162
and for *c*, but I found none	Ps 69:20	5162
whence shall I seek *c* for thee	Nah 3:7	5162

COMFORTETH

as one that *c* the mourners	Job 29:25	5162
I, even I, am he that *c* you	Is 51:12	5162
As one whom his mother *c*, so will	Is 66:13	5162
Who *c* us in all our tribulation	2Cor 1:4	3870
that *c* those that are cast down,	2Cor 7:6	3870

COMFORTLESS

I will not leave you *c*	Jn 14:18	3737

COMFORTS

within me thy *c* delight my soul	Ps 94:19	8575
restore *c* unto him and to his	Is 57:18	5150

COMING See APPENDIX.

COMINGS

the *c* in thereof, and all the	Eze 43:11	4126

COMMAND

him, that he will *c* his children	Gen 18:19	6680
according to that which I *c* thee	Gen 27:8	6680
Thy father did *c* before he died	Gen 50:16	6680
shalt speak all that I *c* thee	Ex 7:2	6680
LORD our God, as he shall *c* us	Ex 8:27	559
God *c* thee so, then thou shalt be	Ex 18:23	6680
thou shalt *c* the children of	Ex 27:20	6680
thou that which I *c* thee this day	Ex 34:11	6680
C Aaron and his sons, saying, This	Lev 6:9	6680
Then the priest shall *c* that they	Lev 13:54	6680
Then shall the priest *c* to take	Lev 14:4	6680
the priest shall *c* that one of	Lev 14:5	6680
Then the priest shall *c* that they	Lev 14:36	6680
Then the priest shall *c* that they	Lev 14:40	6680
C the children of Israel, that	Lev 24:2	6680
Then I will *c* my blessing upon	Lev 25:21	6680
C the children of Israel, that	Num 5:2	6680
the LORD will *c* concerning you	Num 9:8	6680
C the children of Israel, and say	Num 28:2	6680
C the children of Israel, and say	Num 34:2	6680
C the children of Israel, that	Num 35:2	6680
c concerning the daughters of	Num 36:6	6680
c thou the people, saying, Ye are	Deut 2:4	6680
add unto the word which I *c* you	Deut 4:2	6680
the LORD your God which I *c* you	Deut 4:2	6680
which I *c* thee this day, that it	Deut 4:40	6680
his commandments, which I *c* thee	Deut 6:2	6680
which I *c* thee this day, shall be	Deut 6:6	6680
which I *c* thee this day, to do	Deut 7:11	6680
All the commandments which I *c*	Deut 8:1	6680
statutes, which I *c* thee this day	Deut 8:11	6680
which I *c* thee this day for thy	Deut 10:13	6680
which I *c* you this day, that ye	Deut 11:8	6680
which I *c* you this day, to love	Deut 11:13	6680
these commandments which I *c* you	Deut 11:22	6680
your God, which I *c* you this day	Deut 11:27	6680
of the way which I *c* you this day	Deut 11:28	6680
shall ye bring all that I *c* you	Deut 12:11	6680
thou shalt do all that I *c* thee	Deut 12:14	6680
all these words which I *c* thee	Deut 12:28	6680
What thing soever I *c* you	Deut 12:32	6680
which I *c* thee this day, to do	Deut 13:18	6680
which I *c* thee this day	Deut 15:5	6680
therefore I *c* thee, saying, Thou	Deut 15:11	6680
therefore I *c* thee this thing to	Deut 15:15	6680
unto them all that I shall *c* him	Deut 18:18	6680
Wherefore I *c* thee, saying, Thou	Deut 19:7	6680
which I *c* thee this day, to love	Deut 19:9	6680
therefore I *c* thee to do this	Deut 24:18	6680

therefore I *c* thee to do this	Deut 24:22	6680
which I *c* you this day	Deut 27:1	6680
which I *c* you this day, in mount	Deut 27:4	6680
statutes, which I *c* thee this day	Deut 27:10	6680
which I *c* thee this day, that the	Deut 28:1	6680
The LORD shall *c* the blessing	Deut 28:8	6680
which I *c* thee this day, to	Deut 28:13	6680
the words which I *c* thee this day	Deut 28:14	6680
statutes which I *c* thee this day	Deut 28:15	6680
to all that I *c* thee this day	Deut 30:2	6680
which I *c* thee this day	Deut 30:8	6680
which I *c* thee this day, it is	Deut 30:11	6680
In that I *c* thee this day to love	Deut 30:16	6680
which ye shall *c* your children to	Deut 32:46	6680
c the people, saying, Prepare you	Josh 1:11	6680
thou shalt *c* the priests that	Josh 3:8	6680
c ye them, saying, Take you hence	Josh 4:3	6680
C the priests that bear the ark	Josh 4:16	6680
servant, so did Moses *c* Joshua	Josh 11:15	6680
Let our lord now *c* thy servants	1Sa 16:16	559
Now therefore *c* thou that they	1Kin 5:6	6680
hearken unto all that I *c* thee	1Kin 11:38	6680
or if I *c* the locusts to devour	2Chr 7:13	6680
Doth the eagle mount up at thy *c*	Job 39:27	6310
Yet the LORD will *c* his	Ps 42:8	6680
c deliverances for Jacob	Ps 44:4	6680
I will also *c* the clouds that	Is 5:6	6680
the work of my hands *c* ye me	Is 45:11	6680
whatsoever I *c* thee thou shalt	Jer 1:7	6680
speak unto them all that I *c* thee	Jer 1:17	6680
according to all which I *c* you	Jer 11:4	6680
all the words that I *c* thee to	Jer 26:2	6680
c them to say unto their masters,	Jer 27:4	6680
Behold, I will *c*, saith the LORD,	Jer 34:22	6680
whom thou didst *c* that they	Lam 1:10	6680
sea, thence will I *c* the serpent	Amos 9:3	6680
thence will I *c* the sword	Amos 9:4	6680
For, lo, I will *c*, and I will sift	Amos 9:9	6680
c that these stones be made bread	Mt 4:3	2036
Why did Moses then *c* to give a	Mt 19:7	1781
C therefore that the sepulchre be	Mt 27:64	2753
unto them, What did Moses *c* you	Mk 10:3	1781
c this stone that it be made	Lk 4:3	2036
c them to go out into the deep	Lk 8:31	2004
wilt thou that we *c* fire to come	Lk 9:54	2036
if ye do whatsoever I *c* you	Jn 15:14	1781
These things I *c* you, that ye	Jn 15:17	1781
Did not we straitly *c* you that ye	Acts 5:28	3853
to *c* them to keep the law of	Acts 15:5	3853
I *c* thee in the name of Jesus	Acts 16:18	3853
And unto the married I *c*, yet not	1Cor 7:10	3853
will do the things which we *c* you	2Th 3:4	3853
Now we *c* you, brethren, in the	2Th 3:6	3853
Now them that are such we *c*	2Th 3:12	3853
These things *c* and teach	1Ti 4:11	3853

COMMANDED

And the LORD God *c* the man	Gen 2:16	6680
whereof I *c* thee that thou	Gen 3:11	6680
of the tree, of which I *c* thee	Gen 3:17	6680
according to all that God *c* him	Gen 6:22	6680
unto all that the LORD *c* him	Gen 7:5	6680
and the female, as God had *c* Noah	Gen 7:9	6680
of all flesh, as God had *c* him	Gen 7:16	6680
Pharaoh *c* his men concerning him	Gen 12:20	6680
eight days old, as God had *c* him	Gen 21:4	6680
he *c* them, saying, Thus shall ye	Gen 32:4	6680
he *c* the foremost, saying, When	Gen 32:17	6680
so *c* he the second, and the third,	Gen 32:19	6680
Then Joseph *c* to fill their sacks	Gen 42:25	6680
he *c* the steward of his house,	Gen 44:1	6680
Now thou art *c*, this do ye	Gen 45:19	6680
land of Rameses, as Pharaoh had *c*	Gen 47:11	6680
Joseph *c* his servants the	Gen 50:2	6680
unto him according as he *c* them	Gen 50:12	6680
not as the king of Egypt *c* them	Ex 1:17	1696
all the signs which he had *c* him	Ex 4:28	6680
Pharaoh *c* the same day the	Ex 5:6	6680
and Aaron did as the LORD *c* them	Ex 7:6	6680
and they did so as the LORD had *c*	Ex 7:10	6680
and Aaron did so, as the LORD *c*	Ex 7:20	6680
and did as the LORD had *c* Moses	Ex 12:28	6680
as the LORD *c* Moses and Aaron, so	Ex 12:50	6680
the thing which the LORD hath *c*	Ex 16:16	6680
As the LORD *c* Moses, so Aaron	Ex 16:34	6680
these words which the LORD *c* him	Ex 19:7	6680
bread seven days, as I *c* thee	Ex 23:15	6680
to all things which I have *c* thee	Ex 29:35	6680
may make all that I have *c* thee	Ex 31:6	6680
that I have *c* thee shall they do	Ex 31:11	6680
out of the way which I *c* them	Ex 32:8	6680

Sinai, as the LORD had c him	Ex 34:4	6680
eat unleavened bread, as I c thee	Ex 34:18	6680
of Israel that which he was c	Ex 34:34	6680
the words which the LORD hath c	Ex 35:1	6680
is the thing which the LORD c	Ex 35:4	6680
and make all that the LORD hath c	Ex 35:10	6680
which the LORD had c to be made	Ex 35:29	6680
to all that the LORD had c	Ex 36:1	6680
work, which the LORD c to make	Ex 36:5	6680
made all that the LORD c Moses	Ex 38:22	6680
as the LORD c Moses	Ex 39:1	6680
as the LORD c Moses	Ex 39:5	6680
as the LORD c Moses	Ex 39:7	6680
as the LORD c Moses	Ex 39:21	6680
as the LORD c Moses	Ex 39:26	6680
as the LORD c Moses	Ex 39:29	6680
as the LORD c Moses	Ex 39:31	6680
to all that the LORD c Moses	Ex 39:32	6680
to all that the LORD c Moses	Ex 39:42	6680
had done it as the LORD had c	Ex 39:43	6680
to all that the LORD c him	Ex 40:16	6680
as the LORD c Moses	Ex 40:19	6680
as the LORD c Moses	Ex 40:21	6680
as the LORD had c Moses	Ex 40:23	6680
as the LORD c Moses	Ex 40:25	6680
as the LORD c Moses	Ex 40:27	6680
as the LORD c Moses	Ex 40:29	6680
as the LORD c Moses	Ex 40:32	6680
Which the LORD c to be given them	Lev 7:36	6680
Which the LORD c Moses in mount	Lev 7:38	6680
in the day that he c the children	Lev 7:38	6680
And Moses did as the LORD c him	Lev 8:4	6680
thing which the LORD c to be done	Lev 8:5	6680
as the LORD c Moses	Lev 8:9	6680
as the LORD c Moses	Lev 8:13	6680
as the LORD c Moses	Lev 8:17	6680
as the LORD c Moses	Lev 8:21	6680
as the LORD c Moses	Lev 8:29	6680
basket of consecrations, as I c	Lev 8:31	6680
day, so the LORD hath c to do	Lev 8:34	6680
for so I am c	Lev 8:35	6680
the LORD c by the hand of Moses	Lev 8:36	6680
c before the tabernacle of the	Lev 9:5	6680
the LORD c that ye should do	Lev 9:6	6680
as the LORD c	Lev 9:7	6680
as the LORD c Moses	Lev 9:10	6680
before the LORD; as Moses c	Lev 9:21	6680
the LORD, which he c them not	Lev 10:1	6680
for so I am c	Lev 10:13	6680
as the LORD hath c	Lev 10:15	6680
it in the holy place, as I c	Lev 10:18	6680
And he did as the LORD c Moses	Lev 16:34	6680
the thing which the LORD hath c	Lev 17:2	6680
of Israel did as the LORD c Moses	Lev 24:23	6680
which the LORD c Moses for the	Lev 27:34	6680
As the LORD c Moses, so he	Num 1:19	6680
to all that the LORD c Moses	Num 1:54	6680
as the LORD c Moses	Num 2:33	6680
to all that the LORD c Moses	Num 2:34	6680
the word of the LORD, as he was c	Num 3:16	6680
Moses numbered, as the LORD c him	Num 3:42	6680
of the LORD, as the LORD c Moses	Num 3:51	6680
of him, as the LORD c Moses	Num 4:49	6680
candlestick, as the LORD c Moses	Num 8:3	6680
unto all that the LORD c Moses	Num 8:20	6680
as the LORD had c Moses	Num 8:22	6680
to all that the LORD c Moses	Num 9:5	6680
hath c you by the hand of Moses	Num 15:23	6680
the day that the LORD c Moses	Num 15:23	6680
as the LORD c Moses	Num 15:36	6680
And Aaron took as Moses c, and ran	Num 16:47	1696
as the LORD c him, so did he	Num 17:11	6680
of the law which the LORD hath c	Num 19:2	6680
from before the LORD, as he c him	Num 20:9	6680
And Moses did as the LORD c	Num 20:27	6680
as the LORD c Moses and the	Num 26:4	6680
of judgment, as the LORD c Moses	Num 27:11	6680
And Moses did as the LORD c him	Num 27:22	6680
as the LORD c by the hand of	Num 27:23	1696
to all that the LORD c Moses	Num 29:40	6680
the thing which the LORD hath c	Num 30:1	6680
statutes, which the LORD c Moses	Num 30:16	6680
Midianites, as the LORD c Moses	Num 31:7	6680
of the law which the LORD c Moses	Num 31:21	6680
priest did as the LORD c Moses	Num 31:31	6680
the priest, as the LORD c Moses	Num 31:41	6680
as the LORD c the priest	Num 31:47	6680
them Moses c Eleazar the priest	Num 32:28	6680
Moses c the children of Israel,	Num 34:13	6680
which the LORD c to give unto the	Num 34:13	6680
These are they whom the LORD c to	Num 34:29	6680
The LORD c my lord to give the	Num 36:2	6680
my lord was c by the LORD to give	Num 36:2	6680
Moses c the children of Israel	Num 36:5	6680
Even as the LORD c Moses, so did	Num 36:10	6680
which the LORD c by the hand of	Num 36:13	6680
I c you at that time all the	Deut 1:18	6680
as the LORD our God c us	Deut 1:19	6680
to all that the LORD our God c us	Deut 1:41	6680
I c you at that time, saying, The	Deut 3:18	6680
I c Joshua at that time, saying,	Deut 3:21	6680
even as the LORD my God c me	Deut 4:5	6680
which he c you to perform, even	Deut 4:13	6680
the LORD c me at that time to	Deut 4:14	6680
as the LORD thy God hath c thee	Deut 5:12	6680
therefore the LORD thy God c thee	Deut 5:15	6680
as the LORD thy God hath c thee	Deut 5:16	6680
as the LORD your God hath c you	Deut 5:32	6680
the LORD your God hath c you	Deut 5:33	6680
the LORD your God c to teach you	Deut 6:1	6680
statutes, which he hath c thee	Deut 6:17	6680
which the LORD our God hath c you	Deut 6:20	6680
the LORD c us to do all these	Deut 6:24	6680
the LORD our God, as he hath c us	Deut 6:25	6680
out of the way which I c them	Deut 9:12	6680
the way which the LORD had c you	Deut 9:16	6680
there they be, as the LORD c me	Deut 10:5	6680
hath given thee, as I have c thee	Deut 12:21	6680
LORD thy God c thee to walk in	Deut 13:5	6680
of heaven, which I have not c	Deut 17:3	6680
which I have not c him to speak	Deut 18:20	6680
as the LORD thy God hath c thee	Deut 20:17	6680
as I c them, so ye shall observe	Deut 24:8	6680
commandments which thou hast c me	Deut 26:13	6680
to all that thou hast c me	Deut 26:14	6680
hath c thee to do these statutes	Deut 26:16	6680
the elders of Israel c the people	Deut 27:1	6680
and his statutes which he c thee	Deut 28:45	6680
which the LORD c Moses to make	Deut 29:1	6680
commandments which I have c you	Deut 31:5	6680
And Moses c them, saying, At the	Deut 31:10	6680
That Moses c the Levites, which	Deut 31:25	6680
from the way which I have c you	Deut 31:29	6680
Moses c us a law, even the	Deut 33:4	6680
him, and did as the LORD c Moses	Deut 34:9	6680
which Moses my servant c thee	Josh 1:7	6680
Have not I c thee	Josh 1:9	6680
Then Joshua c the officers of the	Josh 1:10	6680
the servant of the LORD c you	Josh 1:13	6680
they c the people, saying, When	Josh 3:3	6680
of Israel did so as Joshua c	Josh 4:8	6680
was finished that the LORD c	Josh 4:10	6680
to all that Moses c Joshua	Josh 4:10	6680
Joshua therefore c the priests	Josh 4:17	6680
And Joshua had c the people	Josh 6:10	6680
my covenant which I c them	Josh 7:11	6680
he c them, saying, Behold, ye	Josh 8:4	6680
See, I have c you	Josh 8:8	6680
of the LORD which he c Joshua	Josh 8:27	6680
Joshua c that they should take	Josh 8:29	6680
the LORD c the children of Israel	Josh 8:31	6680
servant of the LORD had c before	Josh 8:33	6680
not a word of all that Moses c	Josh 8:35	6680
how that the LORD thy God c his	Josh 9:24	6680
down of the sun, that Joshua c	Josh 10:27	6680
as the LORD God of Israel c	Josh 10:40	6680
Moses the servant of the LORD c	Josh 11:12	6680
As the LORD c Moses his servant,	Josh 11:15	6680
of all that the LORD c Moses	Josh 11:15	6680
destroy them, as the LORD c Moses	Josh 11:20	6680
an inheritance, as I have c thee	Josh 13:6	6680
as the LORD c by the hand of	Josh 14:2	6680
As the LORD c Moses, so the	Josh 14:5	6680
The LORD c Moses to give us an	Josh 17:4	6680
The LORD c by the hand of Moses	Josh 21:2	6680
as the LORD c by the hand of	Josh 21:8	6680
the servant of the LORD c you	Josh 22:2	6680
my voice in all that I c you	Josh 22:2	6680
the LORD your God, which he c you	Josh 23:16	6680
covenant which I c their fathers	Judg 2:20	6680
which he c their fathers by the	Judg 3:4	6680
Hath not the LORD God of Israel c	Judg 4:6	6680
all that I c her let her observe	Judg 13:14	6680
c them, saying, Go and smite the	Judg 21:10	6680
Therefore they c the children of	Judg 21:20	6680
Boaz c his young men, saying, Let	Ruth 2:15	6680
which I have c in my habitation	1Sa 2:29	6680
the LORD thy God, which he c thee	1Sa 13:13	6680
the LORD hath c him to be captain	1Sa 13:14	6680
kept that which the LORD c thee	1Sa 13:14	6680
took, and went, as Jesse had c him	1Sa 17:20	6680
Saul c his servants, saying,	1Sa 18:22	6680

brother, he hath *c* me to be there	1Sa 20:29	6680
The king hath *c* me a business	1Sa 21:2	6680
send thee, and what I have *c* thee	1Sa 21:2	6680
David *c* his young men, and they	2Sa 4:12	6680
did so, as the LORD *c* him	2Sa 5:25	6680
whom I *c* to feed my people Israel	2Sa 7:7	6680
as since the time that I *c* judges	2Sa 7:11	6680
lord the king hath *c* his servant	2Sa 9:11	6680
Now Absalom had *c* his servants	2Sa 13:28	6680
have not I *c* you	2Sa 13:28	6680
did unto Amnon as Absalom had *c*	2Sa 13:29	6680
And the king *c* Joab and Abishai and	2Sa 18:5	6680
performed all that the king *c*	2Sa 21:14	6680
of Gad, went up as the LORD *c*	2Sa 24:19	6680
So the king *c* Benaiah the son of	1Kin 2:46	6680
And the king *c*, and they brought	1Kin 5:17	6680
judgments, which he *c* our fathers	1Kin 8:58	6680
to all that I have *c* thee	1Kin 9:4	6680
had *c* him concerning this thing,	1Kin 11:10	6680
he kept not that which the LORD *c*	1Kin 11:10	6680
my statutes, which I have *c* thee	1Kin 11:11	6680
which the LORD thy God *c* thee	1Kin 13:21	6680
he *c* him all the days of his life	1Kin 15:5	6680
I have *c* the ravens to feed thee	1Kin 17:4	6680
I have *c* a widow woman there to	1Kin 17:9	6680
the king of Syria *c* his thirty	1Kin 22:31	6680
he *c* them, saying, This is the	2Kin 11:5	6680
things that Jehoiada the priest *c*	2Kin 11:9	6680
But Jehoiada the priest *c* the	2Kin 11:15	6680
law of Moses, wherein the LORD *c*	2Kin 14:6	6680
king Ahaz *c* Urijah the priest,	2Kin 16:15	6680
according to all that king Ahaz *c*	2Kin 16:16	6680
the law which I *c* your fathers	2Kin 17:13	6680
Then the king of Assyria *c*	2Kin 17:27	6680
the LORD *c* the children of Jacob	2Kin 17:34	6680
which the LORD *c* Moses	2Kin 18:6	6680
Moses the servant of the LORD *c*	2Kin 18:12	6680
to all that I have *c* them	2Kin 21:8	6680
law that my servant Moses *c* them	2Kin 21:8	6680
the king *c* Hilkiah the priest, and	2Kin 22:12	6680
the king *c* Hilkiah the high	2Kin 23:4	6680
the king *c* all the people, saying	2Kin 23:21	6680
Moses the servant of God had *c*	1Chr 6:49	6680
David therefore did as God *c* him	1Chr 14:16	6680
as Moses *c* according to the word	1Chr 15:15	6680
the word which he *c* to a thousand	1Chr 16:15	6680
of the LORD, which he *c* Israel	1Chr 16:40	6680
whom I *c* to feed my people,	1Chr 17:6	6680
since the time that I *c* judges to	1Chr 17:10	6680
Is it not I that *c* the people to	1Chr 21:17	559
of the LORD *c* Gad to say to David	1Chr 21:18	559
And the LORD *c* the angel	1Chr 21:27	559
David *c* to gather together the	1Chr 22:2	559
David also *c* all the princes of	1Chr 23:31	
to the order *c* unto them,	1Chr 23:31	
the LORD God of Israel had *c* him	1Chr 24:19	6680
to all that I have *c* thee	2Chr 7:17	6680
for so had David the man of God *c*	2Chr 8:14	4687
c Judah to seek the LORD God of	2Chr 14:4	559
Now the king of Syria had *c* the	2Chr 18:30	6680
that Jehoiada the priest had *c*	2Chr 23:8	6680
book of Moses, where the LORD *c*	2Chr 25:4	6680
he *c* the priests the sons of	2Chr 29:21	559
for the king *c* that the burnt	2Chr 29:24	559
Hezekiah *c* to offer the burnt	2Chr 29:27	559
the princes *c* the Levites to sing	2Chr 29:30	559
Moreover he *c* the people that	2Chr 31:4	559
Then Hezekiah *c* to prepare	2Chr 31:11	559
c Judah and Jerusalem, saying, Ye	2Chr 32:12	559
heed to do all that I have *c* them	2Chr 33:8	6680
c Judah to serve the LORD God of	2Chr 33:16	559
And the king *c* Hilkiah, and Ahikam	2Chr 34:20	6680
for God *c* me to make haste	2Chr 35:21	559
the king of Persia hath *c* us	Ezr 4:3	6680
I *c*, and search hath been made,	Ezr 4:19	7761,2942
Who hath *c* you to build this	Ezr 5:3	7761,2942
c you to build this house, and	Ezr 5:9	7761,2942
Whatsoever is *c* by the God of	Ezr 7:23	4480,2941
Which thou hast *c* by thy servants	Ezr 9:11	6680
which the LORD had *c* to Israel	Neh 8:1	6680
law which the LORD had *c* by Moses	Neh 8:14	6680
which was *c* to be given to the	Neh 13:5	4687
Then I *c*, and they cleansed the	Neh 13:9	559
I *c* that the gates should be shut	Neh 13:19	559
I *c* the Levites that they should	Neh 13:22	559
he *c* Mehuman, Biztha, Harbona,	Est 1:10	559
The king Ahasuerus *c* Vashti the	Est 1:17	559
the king had so *c* concerning him	Est 3:2	6680
had *c* unto the king's lieutenants	Est 3:12	6680
Then Mordecai *c* to answer Esther,	Est 4:13	559
to all that Esther had *c* him	Est 4:17	6680
he *c* to bring the book of records	Est 6:1	559
all that Mordecai *c* unto the Jews	Est 8:9	6680
the king *c* it so to be done	Est 9:14	559
he *c* by letters that his wicked	Est 9:25	559
Hast thou *c* the morning since thy	Job 38:12	6680
did according as the LORD *c* them	Job 42:9	1696
to the judgment that thou hast *c*	Ps 7:6	6680
he *c*, and it stood fast	Ps 33:9	6680
Thy God hath *c* thy strength	Ps 68:28	6680
which he *c* our fathers, that they	Ps 78:5	6680
Though he had *c* the clouds from	Ps 78:23	6680
the word which he *c* to a thousand	Ps 105:8	6680
concerning whom the LORD *c* them	Ps 106:34	559
he hath *c* his covenant for ever	Ps 111:9	6680
Thou hast *c* us to keep thy	Ps 119:4	6680
that thou hast *c* are righteous	Ps 119:138	6680
for there the LORD *c* the blessing	Ps 133:3	6680
for he *c*, and they were created	Ps 148:5	6680
I have *c* my sanctified ones, I	Is 13:3	6680
for my mouth it hath *c*, and his	Is 34:16	6680
and all their host have I *c*	Is 45:12	6680
and my molten image, hath *c* them	Is 48:5	6680
nor *c* them in the day that I	Jer 7:22	6680
But this thing *c* I them, saying,	Jer 7:23	6680
in all the ways that I have *c* you	Jer 7:23	6680
which I *c* them not, neither came	Jer 7:31	6680
Which I *c* your fathers in the day	Jer 11:4	6680
covenant, which I *c* them to do	Jer 11:8	6680
it by Euphrates, as the LORD *c* me	Jer 13:5	6680
which I *c* thee to hide there	Jer 13:6	6680
them not, neither have I *c* them	Jer 14:14	6680
sabbath day, as I *c* your fathers	Jer 17:22	6680
unto Baal, which I *c* not, nor	Jer 19:5	6680
yet I sent them not, nor *c* them	Jer 23:32	6680
had *c* him to speak unto all the	Jer 26:8	6680
my name, which I have not *c* them	Jer 29:23	6680
which I *c* them not, neither came	Jer 32:35	6680
the son of Rechab our father *c* us	Jer 35:6	6680
all that Jonadab our father *c* us	Jer 35:10	6680
that he *c* his sons not to drink	Jer 35:14	6680
of their father, which he *c* them	Jer 35:16	6680
unto all that he hath *c* you	Jer 35:18	6680
And Jeremiah *c* Baruch, saying, I	Jer 36:5	6680
that Jeremiah the prophet *c* him	Jer 36:8	6680
But the king *c* Jerahmeel the son	Jer 36:26	6680
Then Zedekiah the king *c* that	Jer 37:21	6680
Then the king *c* Ebed-melech the	Jer 38:10	6680
these words that the king had *c*	Jer 38:27	6680
to all that I have *c* thee.	Jer 50:21	6680
c Seraiah the son of Neriah	Jer 51:59	6680
the LORD hath *c* concerning Jacob,	Lam 1:17	6680
that he had *c* in the days of old	Lam 2:17	6680
I have done as thou hast *c* me	Eze 9:11	6680
that when he had *c* the man	Eze 10:6	6680
And I did so as I was *c*	Eze 12:7	6680
I did in the morning as I was *c*	Eze 24:18	6680
So I prophesied as I was *c*	Eze 37:7	6680
So I prophesied as he *c* me	Eze 37:10	6680
Then the king *c* to call the	Dan 2:2	559
c to destroy all the wise men of	Dan 2:12	560
c that they should offer an	Dan 2:46	560
cried aloud, To you it is *c*	Dan 3:4	560
fury *c* to bring Shadrach, Meshach	Dan 3:13	560
c that they should heat the	Dan 3:19	560
he *c* the most mighty men that	Dan 3:20	560
whereas they *c* to leave the stump	Dan 4:26	560
c to bring the golden and silver	Dan 5:2	560
Then *c* Belshazzar, and they	Dan 5:29	560
Then the king *c*, and they brought	Dan 6:16	560
c that they should take Daniel up	Dan 6:23	560
And the king *c*, and they brought	Dan 6:24	560
c the prophets, saying, Prophesy	Amos 2:12	6680
which I *c* my servants the	Zec 1:6	6680
which I *c* unto him in Horeb for	Mal 4:4	6680
and offer the gift that Moses *c*	Mt 8:4	4367
c them, saying, Go not into the	Mt 10:5	3853
at meat, he *c* it to be given her	Mt 14:9	2753
he *c* the multitude to sit down on	Mt 14:19	2753
For God *c*, saying, Honour thy	Mt 15:4	1781
he *c* the multitude to sit down on	Mt 15:35	2753
his lord *c* him to be sold, and his	Mt 18:25	2753
went, and did as Jesus *c* them	Mt 21:6	4367
Then Pilate *c* the body to be	Mt 27:58	2753
things whatsoever I have *c* you	Mt 28:20	1781
those things which Moses	Mk 1:44	4367
c that something should be given	Mk 5:43	2036
c them that they should take	Mk 6:8	3853
and *c* his head to be brought	Mk 6:27	2004
he *c* them to make all sit down by	Mk 6:39	2004
he *c* the people to sit down on	Mk 8:6	3853
c to set them also before them	Mk 8:7	2036

still, and c him to be called	Mk 10:49	2036
unto them even as Jesus did c	Mk 11:6	1781
work, and c the porter to watch	Mk 13:34	1781
cleansing, according as Moses c	Lk 5:14	4367
(For he had c the unclean spirit	Lk 8:29	3853
and he c to give her meat	Lk 8:55	1299
c them to tell no man that thing	Lk 9:21	3853
Lord, it is done as thou hast c	Lk 14:22	2004
he did the things that were c him	Lk 17:9	1299
all those things which are c you	Lk 17:10	1299
c him to be brought unto him	Lk 18:40	2750
then he c these servants to be	Lk 19:15	2036
Now Moses in the law c us	Jn 8:5	1781
c them that they should not	Acts 1:4	3853
But when they had c them to go	Acts 4:15	2753
c them not to speak at all nor	Acts 4:18	3853
c to put the apostles forth a	Acts 5:34	2753
they c that they should not speak	Acts 5:40	3853
he c the chariot to stand still	Acts 8:38	2753
all things that are c thee of God	Acts 10:33	4367
he c us to preach unto the people	Acts 10:42	3853
he c them to be baptized in the	Acts 10:48	4367
c that they should be put to	Acts 12:19	2753
For so hath the Lord c us	Acts 13:47	1781
their clothes, and c to beat them	Acts 16:22	2753
(because that Claudius had c all	Acts 18:2	1299
c him to be bound with two chains	Acts 21:33	2753
he c him to be carried into the	Acts 21:34	2753
The chief captain c him to be	Acts 22:24	2753
c the chief priests and all their	Acts 22:30	2753
the high priest Ananias c them	Acts 23:2	2004
c the soldiers to go down, and to	Acts 23:10	2753
the soldiers, as it was c them	Acts 23:31	1299
he c him to be kept in Herod's	Acts 23:35	2753
he c a centurion to keep Paul, and	Acts 24:23	1299
seat c Paul to be brought	Acts 25:6	2753
c the man to be brought forth	Acts 25:17	2753
I c him to be kept till I might	Acts 25:21	2753
c that they which could swim	Acts 27:43	2753
but they are c to be under	1Cor 14:34	
who c the light to shine out of	2Cor 4:6	2036
with your own hands, as we c you	1Th 4:11	3853
we were with you, this we c you	2Th 3:10	3853
could not endure that which was c	Heb 12:20	1291
it was c them that they should	Rev 9:4	4483

COMMANDEDST

which thou c thy servant Moses	Neh 1:7	6680
that thou c thy servant Moses	Neh 1:8	6680
c them precepts, statutes, and	Neh 9:14	6680
of all that thou c them to do	Jer 32:23	6680

COMMANDER

a leader and c to the people	Is 55:4	6680

COMMANDEST

All that thou c us we will do	Josh 1:16	6680
thy words in all that thou c him	Josh 1:18	6680
c me to be smitten contrary to	Acts 23:3	2753

COMMANDETH

is the thing which the Lord c	Ex 16:32	6680
Thy servants will do as my lord c	Num 32:25	6680
Which c the sun, and it riseth not	Job 9:7	559
c that they return from iniquity	Job 36:10	559
c it not to shine by the cloud	Job 36:32	6680
that they may do whatsoever he c	Job 37:12	6680
For he c, and raiseth the stormy	Ps 107:25	559
to pass, when the Lord c it not	Lam 3:37	6680
For, behold, the Lord c, and he	Amos 6:11	6680
for with authority he c even the	Mk 1:27	2004
power he c the unclean spirits,	Lk 4:36	2004
for he c even the winds and water,	Lk 8:25	2004
but now c all men every where to	Acts 17:30	3853

COMMANDING

had made an end of c his sons	Gen 49:33	6680
an end of c his twelve disciples	Mt 11:1	1299
C his accusers to come unto thee	Acts 24:8	2753
c to abstain from meats, which	1Ti 4:3	

COMMANDMENT

according to the c of Pharaoh	Gen 45:21	6310
according to the c of the Lord	Ex 17:1	6310
which I will give thee in c unto	Ex 25:22	6680
he gave them in c all that the	Ex 34:32	6680
And Moses gave c, and they caused	Ex 36:6	6680
according to the c of Moses	Ex 38:21	6310
numbered at the c of the Lord	Num 3:39	6310
the c of the Lord by the hand of	Num 4:37	6310
according to the c of the Lord	Num 4:41	6310
According to the c of the Lord	Num 4:49	6310
At the c of the Lord the children	Num 9:18	6310
at the c of the Lord they pitched	Num 9:18	6310

according to the c of the Lord	Num 9:20	6310
according to the c of the Lord	Num 9:20	6310
At the c of the Lord they rested	Num 9:23	6310
at the c of the Lord they	Num 9:23	6310
at the c of the Lord by the hand	Num 9:23	6310
the c of the Lord by the hand of	Num 10:13	6310
Moses by the c of the Lord sent	Num 13:3	6310
ye transgress the c of the Lord	Num 14:41	6310
of the Lord, and hath broken his c	Num 15:31	4687
I have received c to bless	Num 23:20	
go beyond the c of the Lord	Num 24:13	6310
against my c in the desert of Zin	Num 27:14	6310
journeys by the c of the Lord	Num 33:2	6310
mount Hor at the c of the Lord	Num 33:38	6310
Lord had given him in c unto them	Deut 1:3	6680
the c of the Lord your God	Deut 1:26	6310
against the c of the Lord	Deut 1:43	6310
the c of the Lord your God	Deut 9:23	6310
that he turn not aside from the c	Deut 17:20	4687
For this c which I command thee	Deut 30:11	4687
be that doth rebel against thy c	Josh 1:18	6310
according to the c of the Lord	Josh 8:8	1697
according to the c of the Lord to	Josh 15:13	6310
Therefore according to the c of	Josh 17:4	6310
at the c of the Lord, these	Josh 21:3	6310
of the c of the Lord your God	Josh 22:3	4687
take diligent heed to do the c	Josh 22:5	4687
not rebel against the c of the	1Sa 12:14	6310
rebel against the c of the Lord	1Sa 12:15	6310
kept the c of the Lord thy God	1Sa 13:13	4687
have performed the c of the Lord	1Sa 15:13	1697
transgressed the c of the Lord	1Sa 15:24	6310
thou despised the c of the Lord	2Sa 12:9	1697
the c that I have charged thee	1Kin 2:43	4687
hast not kept the c which the	1Kin 13:21	4687
c which the Lord commanded the	2Kin 17:34	4687
ordinances, and the law, and the c	2Kin 17:37	4687
for the king's c was, saying,	2Kin 18:36	4687
according to the c of Pharaoh	2Kin 23:35	6310
Surely at the c of the Lord came	2Kin 24:3	6310
their brethren were at their c	1Chr 12:32	6310
their gods there, David gave a c	1Chr 14:12	559
people will be wholly at thy c	1Chr 28:21	1697
according to the c of Moses	2Chr 8:13	4687
they departed not from the c of	2Chr 8:15	4687
and to do the law and the c	2Chr 14:4	4687
blood and blood, between law and c	2Chr 19:10	4687
according to the c of Moses the	2Chr 24:6	
at the king's c they made a chest	2Chr 24:8	559
stoned him with stones at the c	2Chr 24:21	4687
according to the c of the king	2Chr 29:15	4687
according to the c of David	2Chr 29:25	4687
for so was the c of the Lord by	2Chr 29:25	4687
and according to the c of the king	2Chr 30:6	4687
one heart to do the c of the king	2Chr 30:12	4687
And as soon as the c came abroad	2Chr 31:5	1697
at the c of Hezekiah the king, and	2Chr 31:13	4662
according to the king's c	2Chr 35:10	4687
according to the c of David	2Chr 35:15	4687
according to the c of king Josiah	2Chr 35:16	4687
Give ye now c to cause these men	Ezr 4:21	2942
until another c shall be given	Ezr 4:21	2941
according to the c of the God of	Ezr 6:14	2941
and according to the c of Cyrus	Ezr 6:14	2942
I sent them with c unto Iddo	Ezr 8:17	3318
that tremble at the c of our God	Ezr 10:3	4687
was the king's c concerning them	Neh 11:23	4687
according to the c of David the	Neh 12:24	4687
according to the c of David	Neh 12:45	4687
the king's c by his chamberlains	Est 1:12	1697
she hath not performed the c of	Est 1:15	3982
let there go a royal c from him	Est 1:19	1697
came to pass, when the king's c	Est 2:8	1697
for Esther did the c of Mordecai	Est 2:20	3982
transgressest thou the king's c	Est 3:3	4687
a c to be given in every province	Est 3:14	1881
being hastened by the king's c	Est 3:15	1697
whithersoever the king's c	Est 4:3	1697
gave him a c to Mordecai, to know	Est 4:5	6680
and gave him c unto Mordecai	Est 4:10	6680
a c to be given in every province	Est 8:13	1881
and pressed on by the king's c	Est 8:14	1697
city, whithersoever the king's c	Est 8:17	1697
of the same, when the king's c	Est 9:1	1697
gone back from the c of his lips	Job 23:12	4687
the c of the Lord is pure,	Ps 19:8	4687
thou hast given c to save me	Ps 71:3	6680
but thy c is exceeding broad	Ps 119:96	4687
He sendeth forth his c upon earth	Ps 147:15	565
My son, keep thy father's c	Prov 6:20	4687
For the c is a lamp	Prov 6:23	4687

the waters should not pass his *c*	Prov 8:29	6310
feareth the *c* shall be rewarded	Prov 13:13	4687
He that keepeth the *c* keepeth his	Prov 19:16	4687
counsel thee to keep the king's *c*	Eccl 8:2	6310
Whoso keepeth the *c* shall feel no	Eccl 8:5	4687
the LORD hath given a *c* against	Is 23:11	6680
for the king's *c* was, saying,	Is 36:21	4687
none, but obey their father's *c*	Jer 35:14	4687
performed the *c* of their father	Jer 35:16	4687
the *c* of Jonadab your father	Jer 35:18	4687
for I have rebelled against his *c*	Lam 1:18	6310
because the king's *c* was urgent	Dan 3:22	4406
supplications the *c* came forth	Dan 9:23	1697
going forth of the *c* to restore	Dan 9:25	1697
he willingly walked after the *c*	Hos 5:11	6673
hath given a *c* concerning thee	Nah 1:14	6680
O ye priests, this *c* is for you	Mal 2:1	4687
that I have sent this *c* unto you	Mal 2:4	4687
he gave *c* to depart unto the	Mt 8:18	2753
the *c* of God by your tradition	Mt 15:3	1785
Thus have ye made the *c* of God of	Mt 15:6	1785
which is the great *c* in the law	Mt 22:36	1785
This is the first and great *c*	Mt 22:38	1785
For laying aside the *c* of God	Mk 7:8	1785
Full well ye reject the *c* of God	Mk 7:9	1785
him, Which is the first *c* of all	Mk 12:28	1785
this is the first *c*	Mk 12:30	1785
none other *c* greater than these	Mk 12:31	1785
transgressed I at any time thy *c*	Lk 15:29	1785
sabbath day according to the *c*	Lk 23:56	1785
This *c* have I received of my	Jn 10:18	1785
and the Pharisees had given a *c*	Jn 11:57	1785
which sent me, he gave me a *c*	Jn 12:49	1785
I know that his *c* is life	Jn 12:50	1785
A new *c* I give unto you, That ye	Jn 13:34	1785
and as the Father gave me *c*	Jn 14:31	1781
This is my *c*, That ye love one	Jn 15:12	1785
to whom we gave no such *c*	Acts 15:24	1291
and receiving a *c* unto Silas	Acts 17:15	1785
gave *c* to his accusers also to	Acts 23:30	3853
at Festus' *c* Paul was brought	Acts 25:23	2753
But sin, taking occasion by the *c*	Rom 7:8	1785
but when the *c* came, sin revived,	Rom 7:9	1785
And the *c*, which was ordained to	Rom 7:10	1785
For sin, taking occasion by the *c*	Rom 7:11	1785
the *c* holy, and just, and good	Rom 7:12	1785
that sin by the *c* might become	Rom 7:13	1785
and if there be any other *c*	Rom 13:9	1785
according to the *c* of the	Rom 16:26	2003
this by permission, and not of *c*	1Cor 7:6	2003
virgins I have no *c* of the Lord	1Cor 7:25	2003
I speak not by *c*, but by occasion	2Cor 8:8	2003
which is the first *c* with promise	Eph 6:2	1785
by the *c* of God our Saviour	1Ti 1:1	2003
Now the end of the *c* is charity	1Ti 1:5	3852
thou keep this *c* without spot	1Ti 6:14	1785
to the *c* of God our Saviour	Titus 1:3	2003
have a *c* to take tithes of the	Heb 7:5	1785
not after the law of a carnal *c*	Heb 7:16	1785
c going before for the weakness	Heb 7:18	1785
gave *c* concerning his bones	Heb 11:22	1781
were not afraid of the king's *c*	Heb 11:23	1297
the holy *c* delivered unto them	2Pet 2:21	1785
of the *c* of us the apostles of	2Pet 3:2	1785
I write not new *c* unto you	1Jn 2:7	1785
but an old *c* which ye had from	1Jn 2:7	1785
The old *c* is the word which ye	1Jn 2:7	1785
a new *c* I write unto you, which	1Jn 2:8	1785
And this is his *c*, That we should	1Jn 3:23	1785
love one another, as he gave us *c*	1Jn 3:23	1785
this *c* have we from him, That he	1Jn 4:21	1785
have received a *c* from the Father	2Jn 4	1785
though I wrote a new *c* unto thee	2Jn 5	1785
This is the *c*, That, as ye have	2Jn 6	1785

COMMANDMENTS

my voice, and kept my charge, my *c*	Gen 26:5	4687
sight, and wilt give ear to his *c*	Ex 15:26	4687
How long refuse ye to keep my *c*	Ex 16:28	4687
them that love me, and keep my *c*	Ex 20:6	4687
a law, and *c* which I have written	Ex 24:12	4687
words of the covenant, the ten *c*	Ex 34:28	1697
ignorance against any of the *c* of	Lev 4:2	4687
somewhat against any of the *c* of	Lev 4:13	4687
ignorance against any of the *c* of	Lev 4:22	4687
somewhat against any of the *c* of	Lev 4:27	4687
to be done by the *c* of the LORD	Lev 5:17	4687
Therefore shall ye keep my *c*	Lev 22:31	4687
walk in my statutes, and keep my *c*	Lev 26:3	4687
me, and will not do all these *c*	Lev 26:14	4687
so that ye will not do all my *c*	Lev 26:15	4687

These are the *c*, which the LORD	Lev 27:34	4687
and not observed all these *c*	Num 15:22	4687
and remember all the *c* of the LORD	Num 15:39	4687
ye may remember, and do all my *c*	Num 15:40	4687
These are the *c* and the judgments,	Num 36:13	4687
that ye may keep the *c* of the	Deut 4:2	4687
you to perform, even ten *c*	Deut 4:13	1697
therefore his statutes, and his *c*	Deut 4:40	4687
of them that love me and keep my *c*	Deut 5:10	4687
fear me, and keep all my *c* always	Deut 5:29	4687
I will speak unto thee all the *c*	Deut 5:31	4687
Now these are the *c*, the statutes	Deut 6:1	4687
to keep all his statutes and his *c*	Deut 6:2	4687
keep the *c* of the LORD your God	Deut 6:17	4687
these *c* before the LORD our God	Deut 6:25	4687
him and keep his *c* to a thousand	Deut 7:9	4687
Thou shalt therefore keep the *c*	Deut 7:11	4687
All the *c* which I command thee	Deut 8:1	4687
whether thou wouldest keep his *c*	Deut 8:2	4687
keep the *c* of the LORD thy God	Deut 8:6	4687
thy God, in not keeping his *c*	Deut 8:11	4687
to the first writing, the ten *c*	Deut 10:4	1697
To keep the *c* of the LORD	Deut 10:13	4687
and his judgments, and his *c*	Deut 11:1	4687
c which I command you this day	Deut 11:8	4687
hearken diligently unto my *c*	Deut 11:13	4687
all these *c* which I command you	Deut 11:22	4687
if ye obey the *c* of the LORD your	Deut 11:27	4687
obey the *c* of the LORD your God	Deut 11:28	4687
God, and fear him, and keep his *c*	Deut 13:4	4687
to keep all his *c* which I command	Deut 13:18	4687
to observe to do all these *c*	Deut 15:5	4687
shalt keep all these *c* to do them	Deut 19:9	4687
according to all thy *c* which thou	Deut 26:13	4687
I have not transgressed thy *c*	Deut 26:13	4687
and to keep his statutes, and his *c*	Deut 26:17	4687
thou shouldest keep all his *c*	Deut 26:18	4687
Keep all the *c* which I command	Deut 27:1	4687
of the LORD thy God, and do his *c*	Deut 27:10	4687
to do all his *c* which I command	Deut 28:1	4687
keep the *c* of the LORD thy God	Deut 28:9	4687
unto the *c* of the LORD thy God	Deut 28:13	4687
God, to observe to do all his *c*	Deut 28:15	4687
the LORD thy God, to keep his *c*	Deut 28:45	4687
do all his *c* which I command thee	Deut 30:8	4687
the LORD thy God, to keep his *c*	Deut 30:10	4687
in his ways, and to keep his *c*	Deut 30:16	4687
the *c* which I have commanded you	Deut 31:5	4687
in all his ways, and to keep his *c*	Josh 22:5	4687
in, obeying the *c* of the LORD	Judg 2:17	4687
hearken unto the *c* of the LORD	Judg 3:4	4687
me, and hath not performed my *c*	1Sa 15:11	1697
to keep his statutes, and his *c*	1Kin 2:3	4687
ways, to keep my statutes and my *c*	1Kin 3:14	4687
keep all my *c* to walk in them	1Kin 6:12	4687
in all his ways, and to keep his *c*	1Kin 8:58	4687
in his statutes, and to keep his *c*	1Kin 8:61	4687
children, and will not keep my *c*	1Kin 9:6	4687
I chose, because he kept my *c*	1Kin 11:34	4687
to keep my statutes and my *c*	1Kin 11:38	4687
my servant David, who kept my *c*	1Kin 14:8	4687
have forsaken the *c* of the LORD	1Kin 18:18	4687
from your evil ways, and keep my *c*	2Kin 17:13	4687
they left all the *c* of the LORD	2Kin 17:16	4687
not the *c* of the LORD their God	2Kin 17:19	4687
following him, but kept his *c*	2Kin 18:6	4687
after the LORD, and to keep his *c*	2Kin 23:3	4687
if he be constant to do my *c*	1Chr 28:7	4687
seek for all the *c* of the LORD	1Chr 28:8	4687
a perfect heart, to keep thy *c*	1Chr 29:19	4687
and forsake my statutes and my *c*	2Chr 7:19	4687
of his father, and walked in his *c*	2Chr 17:4	4687
transgress ye the *c* of the LORD	2Chr 24:20	4687
God, and in the law, and in the *c*	2Chr 31:21	4687
after the LORD, and to keep his *c*	2Chr 34:31	4687
of the words of the *c* of the LORD	Ezr 7:11	4687
for we have forsaken thy *c*	Ezr 9:10	4687
Should we again break thy *c*	Ezr 9:14	4687
that love him and observe his *c*	Neh 1:5	4687
thee, and have not kept the *c*	Neh 1:7	4687
if ye turn unto me, and keep my *c*	Neh 1:9	4687
and true laws, good statutes and *c*	Neh 9:13	4687
necks, and hearkened not to thy *c*	Neh 9:16	4687
and hearkened not unto thy *c*	Neh 9:29	4687
thy law, nor hearkened unto thy *c*	Neh 9:34	4687
do all the *c* of the LORD our Lord	Neh 10:29	4687
the works of God, but keep his *c*	Ps 78:7	4687
my statutes, and keep not my *c*	Ps 89:31	4687
that remember his *c* to do them	Ps 103:18	6490
excel in strength, that do his *c*	Ps 103:20	1697
all his *c* are sure	Ps 111:7	6490

have all they that do his *c*	Ps 111:10	
that delighteth greatly in his *c*	Ps 112:1	4687
I have respect unto all thy *c*	Ps 119:6	4687
O let me not wander from thy *c*	Ps 119:10	4687
hide not thy *c* from me	Ps 119:19	4687
cursed, which do err from thy *c*	Ps 119:21	4687
I will run the way of thy *c*	Ps 119:32	4687
me to go in the path of thy *c*	Ps 119:35	4687
And I will delight myself in thy *c*	Ps 119:47	4687
also will I lift up unto thy *c*	Ps 119:48	4687
and delayed not to keep thy *c*	Ps 119:60	4687
for I have believed thy *c*	Ps 119:66	4687
that I may learn thy *c*	Ps 119:73	4687
All thy *c* are faithful	Ps 119:86	4687
Thou through thy *c* hast made me	Ps 119:98	4687
for I will keep the *c* of my God	Ps 119:115	4687
Therefore I love thy *c* above gold	Ps 119:127	4687
for I longed for thy *c*	Ps 119:131	4687
yet thy *c* are my delights	Ps 119:143	4687
and all thy *c* are truth	Ps 119:151	4687
for thy salvation, and done thy *c*	Ps 119:166	4687
for all thy *c* are righteousness	Ps 119:172	4687
for I do not forget thy *c*	Ps 119:176	4687
my words, and hide my *c* with thee	Prov 2:1	4687
but let thine heart keep my *c*	Prov 3:1	4687
keep my *c*, and live	Prov 4:4	4687
words, and lay up my *c* with thee	Prov 7:1	4687
Keep my *c*, and live	Prov 7:2	4687
The wise in heart will receive *c*	Prov 10:8	4687
Fear God, and keep his *c*	Eccl 12:13	4687
that thou hadst hearkened to my *c*	Is 48:18	4687
him, and to them that keep his *c*	Dan 9:4	4687
the LORD, and have not kept his *c*	Amos 2:4	2706
shall break one of these least *c*	Mt 5:19	1785
for doctrines the *c* of men	Mt 15:9	1778
wilt enter into life, keep the *c*	Mt 19:17	1785
On these two *c* hang all the law	Mt 22:40	1785
for doctrines the *c* of men	Mk 7:7	1778
Thou knowest the *c*, Do not commit	Mk 10:19	1785
him, The first of all the *c* is	Mk 12:29	1785
before God, walking in all the *c*	Lk 1:6	1785
Thou knowest the *c*, Do not commit	Lk 18:20	1785
If ye love me, keep my *c*	Jn 14:15	1785
He that hath my *c*, and keepeth	Jn 14:21	1785
If ye keep my *c*, ye shall abide	Jn 15:10	1785
even as I have kept my Father's *c*	Jn 15:10	1785
the Holy Ghost had given *c* unto	Acts 1:2	1781
but the keeping of the *c* of God	1Cor 7:19	1785
unto you are the *c* of the Lord	1Cor 14:37	1785
even the law of *c* contained in	Eph 2:15	1785
after the *c* and doctrines of men	Col 2:22	1778
(touching whom ye received *c*	Col 4:10	1785
For ye know what *c* we gave you by	1Th 4:2	3852
c of men, that turn from the	Titus 1:14	1785
we know him, if we keep his *c*	1Jn 2:3	1785
I know him, and keepeth not his *c*	1Jn 2:4	1785
of him, because we keep his *c*	1Jn 3:22	1785
keepeth his *c* dwelleth in him	1Jn 3:24	1785
when we love God, and keep his *c*	1Jn 5:2	1785
love of God, that we keep his *c*	1Jn 5:3	1785
and his *c* are not grievous	1Jn 5:3	1785
is love, that we walk after his *c*	2Jn 6	1785
her seed, which keep the *c* of God	Rev 12:17	1785
are they that keep the *c* of God	Rev 14:12	1785
Blessed are they that do his *c*	Rev 22:14	1785

COMMEND

into thy hands I *c* my spirit	Lk 23:46	3908
I *c* you to God, and to the word of	Acts 20:32	3908
c the righteousness of God	Rom 3:5	4921
I *c* unto you Phebe our sister,	Rom 16:1	4921
Do we begin again to *c* ourselves	2Cor 3:1	4921
For we *c* not ourselves again unto	2Cor 5:12	4921
with some that *c* themselves	2Cor 10:12	4921

COMMENDATION

some others, epistles of *c* to you	2Cor 3:1	4956
to you, or letters of *c* from you	2Cor 3:1	4956

COMMENDED

saw her, and *c* her before Pharaoh	Gen 12:15	1984
A man shall be *c* according to his	Prov 12:8	1984
Then I *c* mirth, because a man	Eccl 8:15	7623
the lord *c* the unjust steward,	Lk 16:8	1867
they *c* them to the Lord, on whom	Acts 14:23	3908
for I ought to have been *c* of you	2Cor 12:11	4921

COMMENDETH

But God *c* his love toward us, in	Rom 5:8	4921
But meat *c* us not to God	1Cor 8:8	3936
For not he that *c* himself is	2Cor 10:18	4921
is approved, but whom the Lord *c*	2Cor 10:18	4921

COMMENDING

truth *c* ourselves to every man's	2Cor 4:2	4921

COMMISSION

c from the chief priests,	Acts 26:12	2011

COMMISSIONS

they delivered the king's *c* unto	Ezr 8:36	1881

COMMIT

Thou shalt not *c* adultery	Ex 20:14	5003
If a soul *c* a trespass, and sin	Lev 5:15	4603
c any of these things which are	Lev 5:17	6213
c a trespass against the LORD, and	Lev 6:2	4603
and shall not *c* any of these	Lev 18:26	6213
For whosoever shall *c* any of	Lev 18:29	6213
even the souls that *c* them shall	Lev 18:29	6213
that ye *c* not any one of these	Lev 18:30	6213
to *c* whoredom with Molech, from	Lev 20:5	2181
When a man or woman shall *c*	Num 5:6	6213
any sin that men *c*, to do	Num 5:6	
c a trespass against him,	Num 5:12	4603
the people began to *c* whoredom	Num 25:1	2181
to *c* trespass against the LORD in	Num 31:16	4560
Neither shalt thou *c* adultery	Deut 5:18	5003
shall henceforth *c* no more any	Deut 19:20	6213
c a trespass in the accursed	Josh 22:20	4603
If he *c* iniquity, I will chasten	2Sa 7:14	5753
of Jerusalem to *c* fornication	2Chr 21:11	2181
and unto God would I *c* my cause	Job 5:8	7760
that he should *c* iniquity	Job 34:10	
Into thine hand I *c* my spirit	Ps 31:5	6485
C thy way unto the LORD	Ps 37:5	1556
C thy works unto the LORD, and thy	Prov 16:3	1556
to kings to *c* wickedness	Prov 16:12	6213
I will *c* thy government into his	Is 22:21	5414
shall *c* fornication with all the	Is 23:17	2181
c adultery, and swear falsely, and	Jer 7:9	5003
and weary themselves to *c* iniquity	Jer 9:5	5753
they *c* adultery, and walk in lies	Jer 23:14	5003
c Jeremiah into the court of the	Jer 37:21	6485
Wherefore *c* ye this great evil	Jer 44:7	6213
and *c* iniquity, and I lay a	Eze 3:20	6213
c the abominations which they *c*	Eze 8:17	6213
didst *c* whoredom with them,	Eze 16:17	2181
followeth thee to *c* whoredoms	Eze 16:34	2181
thou shalt not *c* this lewdness	Eze 16:43	6213
c ye whoredom after their	Eze 20:30	2181
the midst of thee they *c* lewdness	Eze 22:9	6213
Will they now *c* whoredoms with	Eze 23:43	2181
and *c* iniquity, all his	Eze 33:13	6213
they shall *c* whoredom, and shall	Hos 4:10	2181
your daughters shall *c* whoredom	Hos 4:13	2181
and your spouses shall *c* adultery	Hos 4:13	5003
daughters when they *c* whoredom	Hos 4:14	2181
your spouses when they *c* adultery	Hos 4:14	5003
for they *c* lewdness	Hos 6:9	6313
for they *c* falsehood	Hos 7:1	6466
time, Thou shalt not *c* adultery	Mt 5:27	3431
causeth her to *c* adultery	Mt 5:32	3429
which is put away doth *c* adultery	Mt 19:9	3429
murder, Thou shalt not *c* adultery	Mt 19:18	3431
Do not *c* adultery, Do not kill,	Mk 10:19	3431
did *c* things worthy of stripes,	Lk 12:48	4160
who will *c* to your trust the true	Lk 16:11	4100
Do not *c* adultery, Do not kill,	Lk 18:20	3431
Jesus did not *c* himself unto them	Jn 2:24	4100
that they which *c* such things are	Rom 1:32	4238
against them which *c* such things	Rom 2:2	4238
a man should not *c* adultery	Rom 2:22	3431
dost thou *c* adultery	Rom 2:22	3431
idols, dost thou *c* sacrilege	Rom 2:22	2416
this, Thou shalt not *c* adultery	Rom 13:9	3431
Neither let us *c* fornication	1Cor 10:8	4203
This charge I *c* unto thee	1Ti 1:18	3908
the same *c* thou to faithful men,	2Ti 2:2	3908
ye *c* sin, and are convinced of the	Jas 2:9	2038
Do not *c* adultery, said also, Do	Jas 2:11	3431
Now if thou *c* no adultery	Jas 2:11	3431
according to the will of God *c*	1Pet 4:19	3908
is born of God doth not *c* sin	1Jn 3:9	4160
unto idols, and to *c* fornication	Rev 2:14	4203
my servants to *c* fornication	Rev 2:20	4203
them that *c* adultery with her	Rev 2:22	3431

COMMITTED

he hath *c* all that he hath to my	Gen 39:8	5414
prison *c* to Joseph's hand all the	Gen 39:22	5414
for his sin that he hath *c*	Lev 4:35	2398
for his trespass, which he hath *c*	Lev 5:7	2398
customs, which were *c* before you	Lev 18:30	6213
of them have *c* an abomination	Lev 20:13	6213
for they *c* all these things, and	Lev 20:23	6213

if ought be c by ignorance	Num 15:24	6213
which have c that wicked thing,	Deut 17:5	6213
if a man have c a sin worthy of	Deut 21:22	1961
c a trespass in the accursed	Josh 7:1	4600
have c against the God of Israel	Josh 22:16	4600
because ye have not c this	Josh 22:31	4600
for they have c lewdness and folly	Judg 20:6	6213
perversely, we have c wickedness	1Kin 8:47	7561
with their sins which they had c	1Kin 14:22	2398
c them unto the hands of the	1Kin 14:27	6485
which he c against the LORD	1Chr 10:13	4600
c them to the hands of the chief	2Chr 12:10	6485
All that was c to thy servants,	2Chr 34:16	5414
we have c iniquity, we have done	Ps 106:6	5753
For my people have c two evils	Jer 2:13	6213
whereby backsliding Israel c	Jer 3:8	5003
c adultery with stones and with	Jer 3:9	5003
to the full, they then c adultery	Jer 5:7	5003
horrible thing is c in the land	Jer 5:30	1961
when they had c abomination	Jer 6:15	6213
when they had c abomination	Jer 8:12	6213
have c against the LORD our God	Jer 16:10	2398
they have c villany in Israel	Jer 29:23	6213
have c adultery with their	Jer 29:23	6213
c him unto Gedaliah the son of	Jer 39:14	5414
had c unto him men, and women, and	Jer 40:7	6485
the captain of the guard had c to	Jer 41:10	6485
have c to provoke me to anger	Jer 44:3	6213
which they have c in the land of	Jer 44:9	6213
the abominations which ye have c	Jer 44:22	6213
have c in all their abominations	Eze 6:9	6213
because they have c a trespass	Eze 15:8	4600
Thou hast also c fornication with	Eze 16:26	2181
and c abomination before me	Eze 16:50	6213
hath Samaria c half of thy sins	Eze 16:51	2398
hast c more abominable than they	Eze 16:52	8581
to the idols, hath c abomination,	Eze 18:12	6213
from all his sins that he hath c	Eze 18:21	6213
his transgressions that he hath c	Eze 18:22	6213
his wickedness that he hath c	Eze 18:27	6213
his transgressions that he hath c	Eze 18:28	6213
in that they have c a trespass	Eze 20:27	4600
for all your evils that ye have c	Eze 20:43	6213
one hath c abomination with his	Eze 22:11	6213
they c whoredoms in Egypt	Eze 23:3	2181
they c whoredoms in their youth	Eze 23:3	2181
Thus she c her whoredoms with	Eze 23:7	5414
That they have c adultery	Eze 23:37	5003
their idols have they c adultery	Eze 23:37	5003
for his iniquity that he hath c	Eze 33:13	6213
c shall be mentioned unto him	Eze 33:16	2398
abominations which they have c	Eze 33:29	6213
abominations that they have c	Eze 43:8	6213
abominations which they have c	Eze 44:13	6213
have c iniquity, and have done	Dan 9:5	5753
the land hath c great whoredom	Hos 1:2	2181
they have c whoredom continually	Hos 4:18	2181
and an abomination is c in Israel	Mal 2:11	6213
c adultery with her already in	Mt 5:28	3431
with him, who had c murder in the	Mk 15:7	4160
and to whom men have c much	Lk 12:48	3908
but hath c all judgment unto the	Jn 5:22	1325
men and women c them to prison	Acts 8:3	3860
or have c any thing worthy of	Acts 25:11	4238
he had c nothing worthy of death	Acts 25:25	4238
they c themselves unto the sea,	Acts 27:40	1439
though I have c nothing against	Acts 28:17	4160
them were c the oracles of God	Rom 3:2	4100
of the gospel is c unto me	1Cor 9:17	4100
fornication, as some of them c	1Cor 10:8	4203
hath c unto us the word of	2Cor 5:19	5087
Have I c an offence in abasing	2Cor 11:7	4160
lasciviousness which they have c	2Cor 12:21	4238
the uncircumcision was c unto me	Gal 2:7	4100
God, which was c to my trust	1Ti 1:11	4100
keep that which is c to thy trust	1Ti 6:20	3872
have c unto him against that day	2Ti 1:12	3866
That good thing which was c unto	2Ti 1:14	3872
which is c unto me according to	Titus 1:3	4100
and if he have c sins, they shall	Jas 5:15	4160
but c himself to him that judgeth	1Pet 2:23	3860
deeds which they have ungodly c	Jude 15	764
of the earth have c fornication	Rev 17:2	4203
earth have c fornication with her	Rev 18:3	4203
who have c fornication and lived	Rev 18:9	4203

COMMITTEST
thou c whoredom, and Israel is	Hos 5:3	2181

COMMITTETH
the man that c adultery with	Lev 20:10	5003
even he that c adultery with his	Lev 20:10	5003

the poor c himself unto thee	Ps 10:14	5800
But whoso c adultery with a woman	Prov 6:32	5003
that the house of Israel c here	Eze 8:6	6213
But as a wife that c adultery	Eze 16:32	5003
c iniquity, and doeth according to	Eze 18:24	6213
c iniquity, and dieth in them	Eze 18:26	6213
c iniquity, he shall even die	Eze 33:18	6213
her that is divorced c adultery	Mt 5:32	3429
shall marry another, c adultery	Mt 19:9	3429
another, c adultery against her	Mk 10:11	3429
to another, she c adultery	Mk 10:12	3429
and marrieth another, c adultery	Lk 16:18	3431
away from her husband c adultery	Lk 16:18	3431
Whosoever c sin is the servant of	Jn 8:34	4160
but he that c fornication sinneth	1Cor 6:18	4203
Whosoever c sin transgresseth	1Jn 3:4	4160
He that c sin is of the devil	1Jn 3:8	4160

COMMITTING
of life, without c iniquity	Eze 33:15	6213
c adultery, they break out, and	Hos 4:2	5003

COMMODIOUS
the haven was not c to winter in	Acts 27:12	428

COMMON
if any one of the c people sin	Lev 4:27	776
men die the c death of all men	Num 16:29	
There is no c bread under mine	1Sa 21:4	2455
and the bread is in a manner c	1Sa 21:5	2455
the sun, and it is c among men	Eccl 6:1	7227
into the graves of the c people	Jer 26:23	1121
and shall eat them as c things	Jer 31:5	2490
with the men of the c sort were	Eze 23:42	7230
took Jesus into the c hall	Mt 27:27	4232
the c people heard him gladly	Mk 12:37	4183
together, and had all things c	Acts 2:44	2839
but they had all things c	Acts 4:32	2839
and put them in the c prison	Acts 5:18	1219
any thing that is c or unclean	Acts 10:14	2839
cleansed, that call not thou c	Acts 10:15	2840
not call any man c or unclean	Acts 10:28	2839
for nothing c or unclean hath at	Acts 11:8	2839
cleansed, that call not thou c	Acts 11:9	2839
taken you but such as is c to man	1Cor 10:13	442
mine own son after the c faith	Titus 1:4	2839
write unto you of the c salvation	Jude 3	2839

COMMONLY
this saying is c reported among	Mt 28:15	1310
It is reported c that there is	1Cor 5:1	3654

COMMONWEALTH
being aliens from the c of Israel	Eph 2:12	4174

COMMOTION
a great c out of the north	Jer 10:22	7494

COMMOTIONS
when ye shall hear of wars and c	Lk 21:9	181

COMMUNE
went out unto Jacob to c with him	Gen 34:6	1696
I will c with thee from above the	Ex 25:22	1696
C with David secretly, and say,	1Sa 18:22	1696
I will c with my father of thee	1Sa 19:3	1696
If we assay to c with thee	Job 4:2	1697
c with your own heart upon your	Ps 4:4	559
they c of laying snares privily	Ps 64:5	5608
I c with mine own heart	Ps 77:6	7878

COMMUNED
he c with them, saying, If it be	Gen 23:8	1696
Hamor c with them, saying, The	Gen 34:8	1696
c with the men of their city,	Gen 34:20	1696
c with them, and took from them	Gen 42:24	1696
they c with him at the door of	Gen 43:19	1696
c with them, and with all the	Judg 9:1	1696
Samuel c with Saul upon the top	1Sa 9:25	1696
c with Abigail, to take her to	1Sa 25:39	1696
she c with him of all that was in	1Kin 10:2	1696
) and they c with her	2Kin 22:14	1696
she c with him of all that was in	2Chr 9:1	1696
I c with mine own heart, saying,	Eccl 1:16	1696
And the king c with them	Dan 1:19	1696
So the angel that c with me said	Zec 1:14	1696
c one with another what they	Lk 6:11	1255
c with the chief priests and	Lk 22:4	4814
pass, that, while they c together	Lk 24:15	3656
him the oftener, and c with him	Acts 24:26	3656

COMMUNICATE
c unto him that teacheth in all	Gal 6:6	2841
that ye did c with my affliction	Phil 4:14	4790
ready to distribute, willing to c	1Ti 6:18	2843
But to do good and to c forget not	Heb 13:16	2842

COMMUNICATED

c unto them that gospel which I	Gal 2:2	394
no church c with me as concerning	Phil 4:15	2841

COMMUNICATION

Abner had c with the elders of	2Sa 3:17	1697
them, Ye know the man, and his c	2Kin 9:11	7879
But let your c be, Yea, yea	Mt 5:37	3056
Let no corrupt c proceed out of	Eph 4:29	3056
filthy c out of your mouth	Col 3:8	148
That the c of thy faith may	Philem 6	2842

COMMUNICATIONS

What manner of c are these that	Lk 24:17	3056
evil c corrupt good manners	1Cor 15:33	3657

COMMUNING

as he had left c with Abraham	Gen 18:33	1696
of c with him upon mount Sinai	Ex 31:18	1696

COMMUNION

is it not the c of the blood of	1Cor 10:16	2842
is it not the c of the body of	1Cor 10:16	2842
what c hath light with darkness	2Cor 6:14	2842
the c of the Holy Ghost, be with	2Cor 13:14	2842

COMPACT

as a city that is c together	Ps 122:3	2266

COMPACTED

c by that which every joint	Eph 4:16	4822

COMPANIED

of these men which have c with us	Acts 1:21	4905

COMPANIES

three hundred men into three c	Judg 7:16	7218
the three c blew the trumpets, and	Judg 7:20	7218
wait against Shechem in four c	Judg 9:34	7218
and divided them into three c	Judg 9:43	7218
the two other c ran upon all the	Judg 9:44	7218
Saul set the people in three c	1Sa 11:11	7218
of the Philistines in three c	1Sa 13:17	7218
And the Syrians had gone out by c	2Kin 5:2	1416
in the c of the children of Levi	1Chr 9:18	4264
the captains of the c that	1Chr 28:1	4256
appointed two great c of them	Neh 12:31	
So stood the two c of them that	Neh 12:40	
the c of Sheba waited for them	Job 6:19	1979
O ye travelling c of Dedanim	Is 21:13	736
criest, let thy c deliver thee	Is 57:13	
chariots, and with horsemen, and c	Eze 26:7	6951
down by c upon the green grass	Mk 6:39	4849

COMPANION

his brother, and every man his c	Ex 32:27	7453
Samson's wife was given to his c	Judg 14:20	4828
therefore I gave her to thy c	Judg 15:2	4828
his wife, and given her to his c	Judg 15:6	4828
the Archite was the king's c	1Chr 27:33	7453
to dragons, and a c to owls	Job 30:29	7453
I am a c of all them that fear	Ps 119:63	2270
but a c of fools shall be	Prov 13:20	7462
but he that is a c of riotous men	Prov 28:7	7462
the same is the c of a destroyer	Prov 28:24	2270
yet is she thy c, and the wife of	Mal 2:14	2278
c in labour, and fellow soldier,	Phil 2:25	4904
c in tribulation, and in the	Rev 1:9	4791

COMPANIONS

and she went with her c, and	Judg 11:38	7464
brought thirty c to be with him	Judg 14:11	4828
Tabeel, and the rest of their c	Ezr 4:7	3675
scribe, and the rest of their c	Ezr 4:9	3675
to the rest of their c that dwelt	Ezr 4:17	3675
Shimshai the scribe, and their c	Ezr 4:23	3675
and Shethar-boznai, and their c	Ezr 5:3	3675
his c the Apharsachites, which	Ezr 5:6	3675
your c the Apharsachites, which	Ezr 6:6	3675
river, Shethar-boznai, and their c	Ezr 6:13	3675
answer thee, and thy c with thee	Job 35:4	7453
Shall the c make a banquet of him	Job 41:6	2271
the virgins her c that follow her	Ps 45:14	7464
aside by the flocks of thy c	Song 1:7	2270
the c hearken to thy voice	Song 8:13	2270
are rebellious, and c of thieves	Is 1:23	2270
for the children of Israel his c	Eze 37:16	2270
for all the house of Israel his c	Eze 37:16	2270
Mishael, and Azariah, his c	Dan 2:17	2269
Paul's c in travel, they rushed	Acts 19:29	4898
whilst ye became c of them that	Heb 10:33	2844

COMPANIONS'

c sakes, I will now say, Peace be	Ps 122:8	7453

COMPANY

said, If Esau come to the one c	Gen 32:8	4264
then the other c which is left	Gen 32:8	4264
lodged that night in the c	Gen 32:21	4264
a c of nations shall be of thee,	Gen 35:11	6951
a c of Ishmeelites came from	Gen 37:25	736
and it was a very great c	Gen 50:9	4264
they spake unto all the c of the	Num 14:7	5712
unto Korah and unto all his c	Num 16:5	5712
you censers, Korah, and all his c	Num 16:6	5712
all thy c are gathered together	Num 16:11	5712
all thy c before the LORD, thou,	Num 16:16	5712
he be not as Korah, and as his c	Num 16:40	5712
Now shall this c lick up all that	Num 22:4	6951
against Aaron in the c of Korah	Num 26:9	
with Korah, when that c died	Num 26:10	5712
he was not in the c of them that	Num 27:3	5712
the LORD in the c of Korah	Num 27:3	5712
another c come along by the plain	Judg 9:37	7218
the c that was with him, rushed	Judg 9:44	7218
that thou comest with such a c	Judg 18:23	2199
that thou shalt meet a c of	1Sa 10:5	2256
behold, a c of prophets met him	1Sa 10:10	2256
one c turned unto the way that	1Sa 13:17	7218
another c turned the way to	1Sa 13:18	7218
another c turned to the way of	1Sa 13:18	7218
when they saw the c of the	1Sa 19:20	3862
thou bring me down to this c	1Sa 30:15	1416
I will bring thee down to this c	1Sa 30:15	1416
delivered the c that came against	1Sa 30:23	1416
the man of God, he and all his c	2Kin 5:15	4264
he spied the c of Jehu as he came	2Kin 9:17	8229
and said, I see a c	2Kin 9:17	8229
at Jerusalem, with a very great c	2Chr 9:1	2428
great c that cometh against us	2Chr 20:12	1995
came with a small c of men	2Chr 24:24	
the other c of them that gave	Neh 12:38	
thou hast made desolate all my c	Job 16:7	5712
Which goeth in c with the workers	Job 34:8	2274
walked unto the house of God in c	Ps 55:14	7285
great was the c of those that	Ps 68:11	6635
Rebuke the c of spearmen, the	Ps 68:30	2416
and covered the c of Abiram	Ps 106:17	5712
And a fire was kindled in their c	Ps 106:18	5712
but he that keepeth c with	Prov 29:3	7462
to a c of horses in Pharaoh's	Song 1:9	
As it were the c of two armies	Song 6:13	4246
a great c shall return thither	Jer 31:8	6951
also bring up a c against thee	Eze 16:40	6951
great c make for him in the war,	Eze 17:17	6951
I will bring up a c upon them	Eze 23:46	6951
the c shall stone them with	Eze 23:47	6951
the c of the Ashurites have made	Eze 27:6	1323
in all thy c which is in the	Eze 27:27	6951
all thy c in the midst of thee	Eze 27:34	6951
over thee with a c of many people	Eze 32:3	6951
Asshur is there and all her c	Eze 32:22	6951
her c is round about her grave	Eze 32:23	6951
even a great c with bucklers and	Eze 38:4	6951
all thy c that are assembled unto	Eze 38:7	6951
gathered thy c to take a prey	Eze 38:13	6951
riding upon horses, a great c	Eze 38:15	6951
so the c of priests murder in the	Hos 6:9	2267
him to have been in the c	Lk 2:44	4923
there was a great c of publicans	Lk 5:29	3793
the c of his disciples, and a	Lk 6:17	3793
shall separate you from their c	Lk 6:22	
them sit down by fifties in a c	Lk 9:14	2828
behold, a man of the c cried out	Lk 9:38	3793
of the c lifted up her voice	Lk 11:27	3793
one of the c said unto him,	Lk 12:13	3793
followed him a great c of people	Lk 23:27	4128
also of our c made us astonished	Lk 24:22	
saw a great c come unto him, he	Jn 6:5	3793
let go, they went to their own c	Acts 4:23	2398
a great c of the priests were	Acts 6:7	3793
for a man that is a Jew to keep c	Acts 10:28	2853
his c loosed from Paphos, they	Acts 13:13	3588,4012
their own c to Antioch with Paul	Acts 15:22	
the baser sort, and gathered a c	Acts 17:5	3792
we that were of Paul's c departed	Acts 21:8	4012
I be somewhat filled with your c	Rom 15:24	
epistle not to c with fornicators	1Cor 5:9	4874
written unto you not to keep c	1Cor 5:11	4874
have no c with him, that he may	2Th 3:14	4874
and to an innumerable c of angels	Heb 12:22	3461
all the c in ships, and sailors,	Rev 18:17	3658

COMPARABLE

c to fine gold, how are they	Lam 4:2	5577

COMPARE

what likeness will ye *c* unto him	Is 40:18	6186
c me, that we may be like	Is 46:5	4911
what comparison shall we *c* it	Mk 4:30	3846
or *c* ourselves with some that	2Cor 10:12	4793

COMPARED

the heaven can be *c* unto the LORD	Ps 89:6	6186
desire are not to be *c* unto her	Prov 3:15	7737
be desired are not to be *c* to it	Prov 8:11	7737
I have *c* thee, O my love, to a	Song 1:9	1819
time are not worthy to be *c* with	Rom 8:18	

COMPARING

c spiritual things with spiritual	1Cor 2:13	4793
c themselves among themselves,	2Cor 10:12	4793

COMPARISON

What have I done now in *c* of you	Judg 8:2	
what was I able to do in *c* of you	Judg 8:3	
your eyes in *c* of it as nothing	Hag 2:3	3644
or with what *c* shall we compare	Mk 4:30	3850

COMPASS

under the *c* of the altar beneath	Ex 27:5	3749
grate of network under the *c*	Ex 38:4	3749
Red sea, to *c* the land of Edom	Num 21:4	5437
the border shall fetch a *c* from	Num 34:5	5437
And ye shall *c* the city, all ye	Josh 6:3	5437
ye shall *c* the city seven times	Josh 6:4	5437
c the city, and let him that is	Josh 6:7	5437
to Adar, and fetched a *c* to Karkaa	Josh 15:3	5437
but fetch a *c* behind them	2Sa 5:23	5437
cubits did *c* either of them about	1Kin 7:15	5437
cubits did *c* it round about	1Kin 7:23	5437
a round *c* of half a cubit high	1Kin 7:35	5439
they fetched a *c* of seven days'	2Kin 3:9	5437
ye shall *c* the king round about,	2Kin 11:8	5362
from brim to brim, round in *c*	2Chr 4:2	5439
cubits did *c* it round about	2Chr 4:2	5437
which did *c* it round about	2Chr 4:3	5437
the Levites shall *c* the king	2Chr 23:7	5362
His archers *c* me round about, he	Job 16:13	5437
willows of the brook *c* him about	Job 40:22	5437
wilt thou *c* him as with a shield	Ps 5:12	5849
of the people *c* thee about	Ps 7:7	5437
my deadly enemies, who *c* me about	Ps 17:9	5362
so will I *c* thine altar, O LORD	Ps 26:6	5437
thou shalt *c* me about with songs	Ps 32:7	5437
the LORD, mercy shall *c* him about	Ps 32:10	5437
of my heels shall *c* me about	Ps 49:5	5437
the head of those that *c* me about	Ps 140:9	4524
the righteous shall *c* me about	Ps 142:7	3803
when he set a *c* upon the face of	Prov 8:27	2329
and he marketh it out with the *c*	Is 44:13	4230
that *c* yourselves about with	Is 50:11	247
the earth, A woman shall *c* a man	Jer 31:22	5437
Gareb, and shall *c* about to Goath	Jer 31:39	5437
fillet of twelve cubits did *c* it	Jer 52:21	5437
wicked doth *c* about the righteous	Hab 1:4	3803
for ye *c* sea and land to make one	Mt 23:15	4013
***c* thee round, and keep thee in on**	Lk 19:43	4033
And from thence we fetched a *c*	Acts 28:13	4022

COMPASSED

c the house round, both old and	Gen 19:4	5437
we *c* mount Seir many days	Deut 2:1	5437
Ye have *c* this mountain long	Deut 2:3	5437
So the ark of the LORD *c* the city	Josh 6:11	5437
second day they *c* the city once	Josh 6:14	5437
c the city after the same manner	Josh 6:15	5437
day they *c* the city seven times	Josh 6:15	5437
the border *c* from Baalah westward	Josh 15:10	5437
c the corner of the sea southward	Josh 18:14	5437
c the land of Edom, and the land	Judg 11:18	5437
they *c* him in, and laid wait for	Judg 16:2	5437
for Saul and his men *c* David	1Sa 23:26	5849
that bare Joab's armour *c* about	2Sa 18:15	5437
When the waves of death *c* me	2Sa 22:5	661
The sorrows of hell *c* me about	2Sa 22:6	5437
by night, and *c* the city about	2Kin 6:14	5362
an host *c* the city both with	2Kin 6:15	5437
the Edomites which *c* him about	2Kin 8:21	5437
Therefore they *c* about him to	2Chr 18:31	5437
smote the Edomites which *c* him in	2Chr 17:5	5437
c about Ophel, and raised it up a	2Chr 33:14	5437
me, and hath *c* me with his net	Job 19:6	5362
He hath *c* the waters with bounds,	Job 26:10	2328
They have now *c* us in our steps	Ps 17:11	5437
The sorrows of death *c* me	Ps 18:4	661
The sorrows of hell *c* me about	Ps 18:5	5437
Many bulls have *c* me	Ps 22:12	5437
For dogs have *c* me	Ps 22:16	5437

innumerable evils have *c* me about	Ps 40:12	661
they *c* me about together	Ps 88:17	5362
They *c* me about also with words	Ps 109:3	5437
The sorrows of death *c* me	Ps 116:3	661
All nations *c* me about	Ps 118:10	5437
They *c* me about	Ps 118:11	5437
yea, they *c* me about	Ps 118:11	5437
They *c* me about like bees	Ps 118:12	5437
me, and *c* me with gall and travail	Lam 3:5	5362
and the floods *c* me about	Jonah 2:3	5437
The waters *c* me about, even to	Jonah 2:5	661
shall see Jerusalem *c* with armies	Lk 21:20	2944
himself also is *c* with infirmity	Heb 5:2	4029
after they were *c* about seven	Heb 11:30	2944
Wherefore seeing we also are *c*	Heb 12:1	4029
c the camp of the saints about,	Rev 20:9	2944

COMPASSEST

Thou *c* my path and my lying down,	Ps 139:3	2219

COMPASSETH

that is it which *c* the whole land	Gen 2:11	5437
the same is it that *c* the whole	Gen 2:13	5437
the border *c* it on the north side	Josh 19:14	5437
Therefore pride *c* them about as a	Ps 73:6	6059
Ephraim *c* me about with lies, and	Hos 11:12	5437

COMPASSING

round about there were knops *c* it	1Kin 7:24	5437
in a cubit, *c* the sea round about	1Kin 7:24	5362
in a cubit, *c* the sea round about	2Chr 4:3	5362

COMPASSION

And she had *c* on him, and said,	Ex 2:6	2550
have *c* upon thee, and multiply	Deut 13:17	7355
have *c* upon thee, and will return	Deut 30:3	7355
for ye have *c* on me	1Sa 23:21	2550
give them *c* before them who	1Kin 8:50	7356
that they may have *c* on them	1Kin 8:50	7355
had *c* on them, and had respect	2Kin 13:23	7355
your children shall find *c* before	2Chr 30:9	7356
because he had *c* on his people	2Chr 36:15	2550
had no *c* upon young man or maiden	2Chr 36:17	2550
But he, being full of *c*, forgave	Ps 78:38	7349
thou, O Lord, art a God full of *c*	Ps 86:15	7349
the LORD is gracious and full of *c*	Ps 111:4	7349
he is gracious, and full of *c*	Ps 112:4	7349
LORD is gracious, and full of *c*	Ps 145:8	7349
not have *c* on the son of her womb	Is 49:15	7355
have *c* on them, and will bring	Jer 12:15	7355
yet will he have *c* according to	Lam 3:32	7355
unto thee, to have *c* upon thee	Eze 16:5	2550
again, he will have *c* upon us	Mic 7:19	7355
he was moved with *c* on them	Mt 9:36	4697
and was moved with *c* toward them	Mt 14:14	4697
I have *c* on the multitude,	Mt 15:32	4697
of that servant was moved with *c*	Mt 18:27	4697
have had *c* on thy fellowservant	Mt 18:33	1653
So Jesus had *c* on them, and	Mt 20:34	4697
And Jesus, moved with *c*, put forth	Mk 1:41	4697
for thee, and hath had *c* on thee	Mk 5:19	1653
and was moved with *c* toward them	Mk 6:34	4697
I have *c* on the multitude,	Mk 8:2	4697
thing, have *c* on us, and help us	Mk 9:22	4697
the Lord saw her, he had *c* on her	Lk 7:13	4697
when he saw him, he had *c* on him	Lk 10:33	4697
off, his father saw him, and had *c*	Lk 15:20	4697
have *c* on whom I will have *c*	Rom 9:15	3627
Who can have *c* on the ignorant,	Heb 5:2	3356
For ye had *c* of me in my bonds,	Heb 10:34	4834
having *c* one of another, love as	1Pet 3:8	4835
up his bowels of *c* from him	1Jn 3:17	
And of some have *c*, making a	Jude 22	1653

COMPASSIONS

consumed, because his *c* fail not	Lam 3:22	7355
c every man to his brother	Zec 7:9	7356

COMPEL

thou shalt not *c* him to serve as	Lev 25:39	5647
none did *c*	Est 1:8	597
whosoever shall *c* thee to go a	Mt 5:41	29
they *c* one Simon a Cyrenian, who	Mk 15:21	29
***c* them to come in, that my house**	Lk 14:23	315

COMPELLED

together with the woman, *c* him	1Sa 28:23	6555
fornication, and *c* Judah thereto	2Chr 21:11	5080
him they *c* to bear his cross	Mt 27:32	29
synagogue, and *c* them to blaspheme	Acts 26:11	315
ye have *c* me	2Cor 12:11	315
a Greek, was *c* to be circumcised	Gal 2:3	315

COMPELLEST

why *c* thou the Gentiles to live	Gal 2:14	315

COMPLAIN

their brethren come unto us to c	Judg 21:22	7378
I will c in the bitterness of my	Job 7:11	7878
the furrows likewise thereof c	Job 31:38	1058
Wherefore doth a living man c	Lam 3:39	596

COMPLAINED

And when the people c, it	Num 11:1	596
I c, and my spirit was overwhelmed	Ps 77:3	7878

COMPLAINERS

These are murmurers, c, walking	Jude 16	3202

COMPLAINING

that there be no c in our streets	Ps 144:14	6682

COMPLAINT

for out of the abundance of my c	1Sa 1:16	7878
me, my couch shall ease my c	Job 7:13	7878
If I say, I will forget my c	Job 9:27	7878
I will leave my c upon myself	Job 10:1	7878
As for me, is my c to man	Job 21:4	7878
Even to day is my c bitter	Job 23:2	7878
I mourn in my c, and make a noise	Ps 55:2	7878
poureth out his c before the Lord	Ps 102:t	7878
I poured out my c before him	Ps 142:2	7878

COMPLAINTS

grievous c against Paul, which	Acts 25:7	157

COMPLETE

seven sabbaths shall be c	Lev 23:15	8549
And ye are c in him, which is the	Col 2:10	4137
and c in all the will of God	Col 4:12	4137

COMPOSITION

other like it, after the c of it	Ex 30:32	4971
according to the c thereof	Ex 30:37	4971

COMPOUND

an ointment c after the art of	Ex 30:25	4842

COMPOUNDETH

Whosoever c any like it, or	Ex 30:33	7543

COMPREHEND

doeth he, which we cannot c	Job 37:5	3045
May be able to c with all saints	Eph 3:18	2638

COMPREHENDED

c the dust of the earth in a	Is 40:12	3557
and the darkness c it not	Jn 1:5	2638
it is briefly c in this saying,	Rom 13:9	346

CONANIAH (co·na·ni'·ah) See CONONIAH. A chief Levite during Josiah's time.

C also, and Shemaiah and Nethaneel,	2Chr 35:9	3562

CONCEAL

slay our brother, and c his blood	Gen 37:26	3680
spare, neither shalt thou c him	Deut 13:8	3680
is with the Almighty will I not c	Job 27:11	3582
I will not c his parts, nor his	Job 41:12	2790
is the glory of God to c a thing	Prov 25:2	5641
publish, and c not	Jer 50:2	3582

CONCEALED

for I have not c the words of the	Job 6:10	3582
I have not c thy lovingkindness	Ps 40:10	3582

CONCEALETH

of a faithful spirit c the matter	Prov 11:13	3680
A prudent man c knowledge	Prov 12:23	3680

CONCEIT

and as an high wall in his own c	Prov 18:11	4906
lest he be wise in his own c	Prov 26:5	5869
thou a man wise in his own c	Prov 26:12	5869
sluggard is wiser in his own c	Prov 26:16	5869
The rich man is wise in his own c	Prov 28:11	5869

CONCEITS

ye should be wise in your own c	Rom 11:25	3844,1438
Be not wise in your own c	Rom 12:16	3844,1438

CONCEIVE

that they should c when they came	Gen 30:38	3179
the stronger cattle did c	Gen 30:41	3179
that they might c among the rods	Gen 30:41	3179
shall be free, and shall c seed	Num 5:28	2232
but thou shalt c, and bear a son	Judg 13:3	2030
For, lo, thou shalt c, and bear a	Judg 13:5	2030
unto him, Behold, thou shalt c	Judg 13:7	2030
They c mischief, and bring forth	Job 15:35	2029
and in sin did my mother c me	Ps 51:5	3179
Behold, a virgin shall c, and bear	Is 7:14	2030
Ye shall c chaff, ye shall bring	Is 33:11	2029
they c mischief, and bring forth	Is 59:4	2029
thou shalt c in thy womb, and	Lk 1:31	4815
received strength to c seed	Heb 11:11	2602

CONCEIVED

and she c, and bare Cain, and said,	Gen 4:1	2030
and she c, and bare Enoch	Gen 4:17	2030
he went in unto Hagar, and she c	Gen 16:4	2030
and when she saw that she had c	Gen 16:4	2030
and when she saw that she had c	Gen 16:5	2030
For Sarah c, and bare Abraham a	Gen 21:2	2030
of him, and Rebekah his wife c	Gen 25:21	2030
And Leah c, and bare a son, and she	Gen 29:32	2030
she c again, and bare a son	Gen 29:33	2030
she c again, and bare a son	Gen 29:34	2030
she c again, and bare a son	Gen 29:35	2030
And Bilhah c, and bare Jacob a son	Gen 30:5	2030
And Bilhah Rachel's maid c again	Gen 30:7	2030
God hearkened unto Leah, and she c	Gen 30:17	2030
Leah c again, and bare Jacob the	Gen 30:19	2030
And she c, and bare a son	Gen 30:23	2030
the flocks c before the rods, and	Gen 30:39	3179
at the time that the cattle c	Gen 31:10	3179
And she c, and bare a son	Gen 38:3	2029
she c again, and bare a son	Gen 38:4	2030
And she yet again c, and bare a son	Gen 38:5	3254
came in unto her, and she c by him	Gen 38:18	2030
And the woman c, and bare a son	Ex 2:2	2030
saying, If a woman have c seed	Lev 12:2	2232
Have I c all this people	Num 11:12	2030
was come about after Hannah had c	1Sa 1:20	2030
visited Hannah, so that she c	1Sa 2:21	2030
And the woman c, and sent and told	2Sa 11:5	2030
And the woman c, and bare a son at	2Kin 4:17	2030
he went in to his wife, she c	1Chr 7:23	2030
was said, There is a man child c	Job 3:3	2030
hath c mischief, and brought forth	Ps 7:14	2030
into the chamber of her that c me	Song 3:4	2030
and she c, and bare a son	Is 8:3	2030
hath c a purpose against you	Jer 49:30	2803
which c, and bare him a son	Hos 1:3	2030
she c again, and bare a daughter	Hos 1:6	2030
she had weaned Lo-ruhamah, she c	Hos 1:8	2030
she that c them hath done	Hos 2:5	2030
for that which is c in her is of	Mt 1:20	1080
those days his wife Elisabeth c	Lk 1:24	4815
she hath also c a son in her old	Lk 1:36	4815
angel before he was c in the womb	Lk 2:21	4815
why hast thou c this thing in	Acts 5:4	5087
when Rebecca also had c by one	Rom 9:10	2845,2192
Then when lust hath c, it	Jas 1:15	4815

CONCEIVING

speaking oppression and revolt, c	Is 59:13	2030

CONCEPTION

multiply thy sorrow and thy c	Gen 3:16	2032
in unto her, the Lord gave her c	Ruth 4:13	2032
and from the womb, and from the c	Hos 9:11	2032

CONCERN

which c the Lord Jesus Christ	Acts 28:31	4012
things which c mine infirmities	2Cor 11:30	4012

CONCERNETH

Lord will perfect that which c me	Ps 138:8	1157
This burden c the prince in	Eze 12:10	

CONCERNING See APPENDIX.

CONCISION

of evil workers, beware of the c	Phil 3:2	2699

CONCLUDE

Therefore we c that a man is	Rom 3:28	3049

CONCLUDED

c that they observe no such thing	Acts 21:25	2919
For God hath c them all in	Rom 11:32	4788
scripture hath c all under sin	Gal 3:22	4788

CONCLUSION

Let us hear the c of the whole	Eccl 12:13	5490

CONCORD

what c hath Christ with Belial	2Cor 6:15	4857

CONCOURSE

crieth in the chief place of c	Prov 1:21	1993
we may give an account of this c	Acts 19:40	4963

CONCUBINE

And his c, whose name was Reumah,	Gen 22:24	6370
and lay with Bilhah his father's c	Gen 35:22	6370
Timna was c to Eliphaz Esau's son	Gen 36:12	6370
his c that was in Shechem, she	Judg 8:31	6370
who took to him a c out of	Judg 19:1	6370
his c played the whore against	Judg 19:2	6370
rose up to depart, he, and his c	Judg 19:9	6370
saddled, his c also was with him	Judg 19:10	6370
is my daughter a maiden, and his c	Judg 19:24	6370

so the man took his *c*, and brought .... Judg 19:25   6370
the woman his *c* was fallen down .... Judg 19:27   6370
a knife, and laid hold on his *c* .... Judg 19:29   6370
belongeth to Benjamin, I and my *c* .... Judg 20:4   6370
my *c* have they forced, that she .... Judg 20:5   6370
And I took my *c*, and cut her in .... Judg 20:6   6370
And Saul had a *c*, whose name was 2Sa 3:7   6370
thou gone in unto my father's *c* 2Sa 3:7   6370
of Aiah, the *c* of Saul, had done 2Sa 21:11   6370
the sons of Keturah, Abraham's *c* 1Chr 1:32   6370
And Ephah, Caleb's *c*, bare Haran, ... 1Chr 2:46   6370
Maachah, Caleb's *c*, bare Sheber, ... 1Chr 2:48   6370
(but his *c* the Aramitess bare 1Chr 7:14   6370

CONCUBINES
But unto the sons of the *c* .... Gen 25:6   6370
And David took him more *c* and wives .. 2Sa 5:13   6370
king left ten women, which were *c* 2Sa 15:16   6370
Go in unto thy father's *c* 2Sa 16:21   6370
went in unto his father's *c* in 2Sa 16:22   6370
thy wives, and the lives of thy *c* 2Sa 19:5   6370
the king took the ten women his *c* 2Sa 20:3   6370
princesses, and three hundred *c* 1Kin 11:3   6370
David, beside the sons of the *c* 1Chr 3:9   6370
above all his wives and his *c* 2Chr 11:21   6370
eighteen wives, and threescore *c* 2Chr 11:21   6370
chamberlain, which kept the *c* .... Est 2:14   6370
threescore queens, and fourscore *c* .... Song 6:8   6370
yea, the queens and the *c*, and they ...... Song 6:9   6370
his princes, his wives, and his *c* .... Dan 5:2   3904
his princes, his wives, and his *c* .... Dan 5:3   3904
and thy lords, thy wives, and thy *c* .... Dan 5:23   3904

CONCUPISCENCE
wrought in me all manner of *c* .... Rom 7:8   1939
inordinate affection, evil *c* .... Col 3:5   1939
Not in the lust of *c*, even as the 1Th 4:5   1939

CONDEMN
and whom the judges shall *c* .... Ex 22:9   7561
the righteous, and *c* the wicked .... Deut 25:1   7561
myself, mine own mouth shall *c* me .... Job 9:20   7561
I will say unto God, Do not *c* me .... Job 10:2   7561
wilt thou *c* him that is most just .... Job 34:17   7561
wilt thou *c* me, that thou mayest .... Job 40:8   7561
nor *c* him when he is judged .... Ps 37:33   7561
and *c* the innocent blood .... Ps 94:21   7561
him from those that *c* his soul .... Ps 109:31   8199
a man of wicked devices will he *c* .... Prov 12:2   7561
who is he that shall *c* me .... Is 50:9   7561
thee in judgment thou shalt *c* .... Is 54:17   7561
this generation, and shall *c* it .... Mt 12:41   2632
this generation, and shall *c* it .... Mt 12:42   2632
they shall *c* him to death, ... Mt 20:18   2632
they shall *c* him to death, and .... Mk 10:33   2632
c not, and ye shall not be .... Lk 6:37   2618
men of this generation, and *c* them .... Lk 11:31   2632
this generation, and shall *c* it .... Lk 11:32   2632
Son into the world to *c* the world .... Jn 3:17   2919
unto her, Neither do I *c* thee .... Jn 8:11   2632
I speak not this to *c* you 2Cor 7:3   2633
For if our heart *c* us, God is 1Jn 3:20   2607
Beloved, if our heart *c* us not 1Jn 3:21   2607

CONDEMNATION
seeing thou art in the same *c* .... Lk 23:40   2917
And this is the *c*, that light is .... Jn 3:19   2920
life, and shall not come into *c* .... Jn 5:24   2920
for the judgment was by one to *c* .... Rom 5:16   2631
judgment came upon all men to *c* .... Rom 5:18   2631
There is therefore now no *c* to .... Rom 8:1   2631
that ye come not together unto *c* 1Cor 11:34   2917
if the ministration of *c* be glory 2Cor 3:9   2633
he fall into the *c* of the devil 1Ti 3:6   2917
we shall receive the greater *c* .... Jas 3:1   2917
lest ye fall into *c* .... Jas 5:12   5272
before of old ordained to this *c* .... Jude 4   2917

CONDEMNED
c the land in an hundred talents 2Chr 36:3   6064
found no answer, and yet had *c* Job .... Job 32:3   7561
he shall be judged, let him be *c* ...... Ps 109:7   3318,7563
the *c* in the house of their god .... Amos 2:8   6064
ye would not have *c* the guiltless .... Mt 12:7   2613
and by thy words thou shalt be *c* .... Mt 12:37   2613
him, when he saw that he was *c* .... Mt 27:3   2632
they all *c* him to be guilty of .... Mk 14:64   2632
condemn not, and ye shall not be *c* .... Lk 6:37   2613
delivered him to be *c* to death .... Lk 24:20   1519,2917
He that believeth on him is not *c* .... Jn 3:18   2919
that believeth not is *c* already .... Jn 3:18   2919
hath no man *c* thee .... Jn 8:10   2632
and for sin, *c* sin in the flesh .... Rom 8:3   2632

we should not be *c* with the world 1Cor 11:32   2632
Sound speech, that cannot be *c* .... Titus 2:8   176
and sinneth, being of himself .... Titus 3:11   843
by the which he *c* the world .... Heb 11:7   2632
Ye have *c* and killed the just .... Jas 5:6   2613
another, brethren, lest ye be *c* .... Jas 5:9   2632
Gomorrah into ashes *c* them with 2Pet 2:6   2632

CONDEMNEST
judgest another, thou *c* thyself .... Rom 2:1   2632

CONDEMNETH
Thine own mouth *c* thee, and not I .... Job 15:6   7561
he that *c* the just, even they .... Prov 17:15   7561
Who is he that *c* .... Rom 8:34   2632
Happy is he that *c* not himself in .... Rom 14:22   4314

CONDEMNING
c the wicked, to bring his way 1Kin 8:32   7561
they have fulfilled them in *c* him .... Acts 13:27   2919

CONDESCEND
but *c* to men of low estate .... Rom 12:16   4879

CONDITION
On this *c* will I make a covenant 1Sa 11:2

CONDITIONS
ambassage, and desireth *c* of peace .... Lk 14:32   4314

CONDUCT
to *c* the king over Jordan 2Sa 19:15   5674
the king, to *c* him over Jordan 2Sa 19:31   7971
but *c* him forth in peace, that he 1Cor 16:11   4311

CONDUCTED
the people of Judah *c* the king 2Sa 19:40   5674
they that *c* Paul brought him unto .... Acts 17:15   2525

CONDUIT
stood by the *c* of the upper pool, ... 2Kin 18:17   8585
and how he made a pool, and a *c* 2Kin 20:20   8585
at the end of the *c* of the upper .... Is 7:3   8585
he stood by the *c* of the upper .... Is 36:2   8585

CONEY
And the *c*, because he cheweth the .... Lev 11:5   8227
the camel, and the hare, and the *c* .... Deut 14:7   8227

CONFECTION
perfume, a *c* after the art of the .... Ex 30:35   7545

CONFECTIONARIES
will take your daughters to be *c* 1Sa 8:13   7543

CONFEDERACY
Say ye not, A *c*, to all them to .... Is 8:12   7195
whom this people shall say, A *c* .... Is 8:12   7195
All the men of thy *c* have brought .... Obad 7   1285

CONFEDERATE
and these were *c* with Abram .... Gen 14:13   1167,1285
they are *c* against thee .... Ps 83:5   1285,3772
saying, Syria is *c* with Ephraim .... Is 7:2   5117

CONFERENCE
somewhat in *c* added nothing to me .... Gal 2:6   4323

CONFERRED
he *c* with Joab the son of Zeruiah... 1Kin 1:7   1961,1697
council, they *c* among themselves, ... Acts 4:15   4820
when he had *c* with the council, ... Acts 25:12   4814
immediately I *c* not with flesh and .... Gal 1:16   4323

CONFESS
that he shall *c* that he hath .... Lev 5:5   3034
c over him all the iniquities of .... Lev 16:21   3034
If they shall *c* their iniquity, ... Lev 26:40   3034
Then they shall *c* their sin which .... Num 5:7   3034
c thy name, and pray, and make 1Kin 8:33   3034
c thy name, and turn from their 1Kin 8:35   3034
c thy name, and pray and make 2Chr 6:24   3034
c thy name, and turn from their 2Chr 6:26   3034
c the sins of the children of .... Neh 1:6   3034
Then will I also *c* unto thee that .... Job 40:14   3034
I will *c* my transgressions unto .... Ps 32:5   3034
therefore shall *c* me before men .... Mt 10:32   3670
him will I *c* also before my .... Mt 10:32   3670
Whosoever shall *c* me before men .... Lk 12:8   3670
also *c* before the angels of God .... Lk 12:8   3670
any man did *c* that he was Christ .... Jn 9:22   3670
the Pharisees they did not *c* him .... Jn 12:42   3670
but the Pharisees *c* both .... Acts 23:8   3670
But this I *c* unto thee, that .... Acts 24:14   3670
That if thou shalt *c* with thy .... Rom 10:9   3670
and every tongue shall *c* to God .... Rom 14:11   1843
For this cause I will *c* to thee .... Rom 15:9   1843
that every tongue should *c* that .... Phil 2:11   1843
C your faults one to another, and .... Jas 5:16   1843
If we *c* our sins, he is faithful 1Jn 1:9   3670

Whosoever shall *c* that Jesus is	1Jn 4:15	3670
who *c* not that Jesus Christ is	2Jn 7	3670
but I will *c* his name before my	Rev 3:5	*1843*

CONFESSED

Ezra had prayed, and when he had *c*	Ezr 10:1	3034
c their sins, and the iniquities	Neh 9:2	3034
and another fourth part they *c*	Neh 9:3	3034
And he *c*, and denied not	Jn 1:20	3670
but *c*, I am not the Christ	Jn 1:20	3670
And many that believed came, and *c*	Acts 19:18	*1843*
c that they were strangers and	Heb 11:13	3670

CONFESSETH

but whoso *c* and forsaketh them	Prov 28:13	3034
Every spirit that *c* that Jesus	1Jn 4:2	3670
every spirit that *c* not that	1Jn 4:3	3670

CONFESSING

c my sin and the sin of my people	Dan 9:20	3034
of him in Jordan, *c* their sins	Mt 3:6	*1843*
the river of Jordan, *c* their sins	Mk 1:5	*1843*

CONFESSION

God of Israel, and make *c* unto him	Josh 7:19	8426
making *c* to the LORD God of their	2Chr 30:22	3034
Now therefore make *c* unto the	Ezr 10:11	8426
the LORD my God, and made my *c*	Dan 9:4	3034
with the mouth *c* is made unto	Rom 10:10	3670
Pontius Pilate witnessed a good *c*	1Ti 6:13	3671

CONFIDENCE

men of Shechem put their *c* in him	Judg 9:26	982
What is *c* this wherein thou	2Kin 18:19	986
Is not this thy fear, thy *c*	Job 4:6	3690
His *c* shall be rooted out of his	Job 18:14	4009
to the fine gold, Thou art my *c*	Job 31:24	4009
who art the *c* of all the ends of	Ps 65:5	4009
in the LORD than to put *c* in man	Ps 118:8	982
the LORD than to put *c* in princes	Ps 118:9	982
For the LORD shall be thy *c*	Prov 3:26	3689
the fear of the LORD is strong *c*	Prov 14:26	4009
the strength of the *c* thereof	Prov 21:22	4009
C in an unfaithful man in time of	Prov 25:19	4009
in *c* shall be your strength	Is 30:15	985
What is *c* this wherein thou	Is 36:4	986
was ashamed of Beth-el their *c*	Jer 48:13	4009
yea, they shall dwell with *c*	Eze 28:26	983
more the *c* of the house of Israel	Eze 29:16	4009
a friend, put ye not *c* in a guide	Mic 7:5	982
the Lord Jesus Christ, with all *c*	Acts 28:31	3954
in this *c* I was minded to come	2Cor 1:15	4006
having *c* in you all, that my joy	2Cor 2:3	3982
I have *c* in you in all things	2Cor 7:16	2292
upon the great *c* which I have in	2Cor 8:22	4006
when I am present with that *c*	2Cor 10:2	4006
foolishly, in this *c* of boasting	2Cor 11:17	5287
I have *c* in you through the Lord,	Gal 5:10	3982
access with *c* by the faith of him	Eph 3:12	4006
And having this *c*, I know that I	Phil 1:25	3982
Jesus, and have no *c* in the flesh	Phil 3:3	3982
I might also have *c* in the flesh	Phil 3:4	4006
we have *c* in the Lord touching	2Th 3:4	3982
Having *c* in thy obedience I wrote	Philem 21	3982
are we, if we hold fast the *c*	Heb 3:6	3954
of our *c* stedfast unto the end	Heb 3:14	5287
Cast not away therefore your *c*	Heb 10:35	3954
he shall appear, we may have *c*	1Jn 2:28	3954
us not, then have we *c* toward God	1Jn 3:21	3954
this is the *c* that we have in him	1Jn 5:14	3954

CONFIDENCES

for the LORD hath rejected thy *c*	Jer 2:37	4009

CONFIDENT

against me, in this will I be *c*	Ps 27:3	982
but the fool rageth, and is *c*	Prov 14:16	982
art *c* that thou thyself art a	Rom 2:19	3982
Therefore we are always *c*	2Cor 5:6	2292
We are *c*, I say, and willing	2Cor 5:8	2292
ashamed in this same *c* boasting	2Cor 9:4	5287
Being *c* of this very thing, that	Phil 1:6	3982
waxing *c* by my bonds, are much	Phil 1:14	3982

CONFIDENTLY

one hour after another *c* affirmed	Lk 22:59	*1340*

CONFIRM

changing, for to *c* all things	Ruth 4:7	6965
in after thee, and *c* thy words	1Kin 1:14	4390
him to *c* the kingdom in his hand	2Kin 15:19	2388
to *c* this second letter of Purim	Est 9:29	6965
To *c* these days of Purim in their	Est 9:31	6965
thou didst *c* thine inheritance	Ps 68:9	3559
weak hands, and *c* the feeble knees	Is 35:3	553

hope that they would *c* the word	Eze 13:6	6965
he shall *c* the covenant with many	Dan 9:27	1396
the Mede, even I, stood to *c*	Dan 11:1	2388
to *c* the promises made unto the	Rom 15:8	950
Who shall also *c* you unto the end	1Cor 1:8	950
ye would *c* your love toward him	2Cor 2:8	2964

CONFIRMATION

c of the gospel, ye all are	Phil 1:7	951
an oath for *c* is to them an end	Heb 6:16	951

CONFIRMED

For thou hast *c* to thyself thy	2Sa 7:24	3559
as the kingdom was *c* in his hand	2Kin 14:5	2388
LORD had *c* him king over Israel	1Chr 14:2	3559
hath *c* the same to Jacob for a	1Chr 16:17	5975
the decree of Esther *c* these	Est 9:32	6965
c the same unto Jacob for a law,	Ps 105:10	5975
he hath *c* his words, which he	Dan 9:12	6965
with many words, and *c* them	Acts 15:32	1991
testimony of Christ was *c* in you	1Cor 1:6	950
a man's covenant, yet if it be *c*	Gal 3:15	2964
that was *c* before of God in	Gal 3:17	4300
was *c* unto us by them that heard	Heb 2:3	950
of his counsel, *c* it by an oath	Heb 6:17	3315

CONFIRMETH

he *c* them, because he held his	Num 30:14	6965
Cursed be he that *c* not all the	Deut 27:26	6965
That *c* the word of his servant,	Is 44:26	6965

CONFIRMING

c the word with signs following	Mk 16:20	950
C the souls of the disciples, and	Acts 14:22	1991
Syria and Cilicia, *c* the churches	Acts 15:41	1991

CONFISCATION

or to *c* of goods, or to	Ezr 7:26	6065

CONFLICT

Having the same *c* which ye saw in	Phil 1:30	73
knew what great *c* I have for you	Col 2:1	73

CONFORMABLE

being made *c* unto his death	Phil 3:10	4832

CONFORMED

to be *c* to the image of his Son	Rom 8:29	4832
And be not *c* to this world	Rom 12:2	4964

CONFOUND

there *c* their language, that they	Gen 11:7	1101
because the LORD did there *c* the	Gen 11:9	1101
lest I *c* thee before them	Jer 1:17	2865
things of the world to *c* the wise	1Cor 1:27	2617
to *c* the things which are mighty	1Cor 1:27	2617

CONFOUNDED

power, they were dismayed and *c*	2Kin 19:26	954
They were *c* because they had	Job 6:20	954
trusted in thee, and were not *c*	Ps 22:5	954
Let them be *c* and put to shame	Ps 35:4	954
c together that seek after my	Ps 40:14	2659
that seek thee be *c* for my sake	Ps 69:6	3637
c that seek after my soul	Ps 70:2	2659
Let them be *c* and consumed that	Ps 71:13	954
for they are *c*, for they are	Ps 71:24	954
Let them be *c* and troubled for	Ps 83:17	954
C be all they that serve graven	Ps 97:7	954
Let them all be *c* and turned back	Ps 129:5	954
ye shall be *c* for the gardens	Is 1:29	2659
that weave networks, shall be *c*	Is 19:9	954
Then the moon shall be *c*, and the	Is 24:23	2659
power, they were dismayed and *c*	Is 37:27	954
thee shall be ashamed and *c*	Is 41:11	3637
They shall be ashamed, and also *c*	Is 45:16	3637
ashamed nor *c* world without end	Is 45:17	3637
therefore shall I not be *c*	Is 50:7	3637
neither be thou *c*	Is 54:4	3637
we are greatly *c*, because we have	Jer 9:19	954
every founder is *c* by the graven	Jer 10:14	3001
they were ashamed and *c*, and	Jer 14:3	3637
she hath been ashamed and *c*	Jer 15:9	2659
Let them be *c* that persecute me,	Jer 17:18	954
but let not me be *c*	Jer 17:18	954
and *c* for all thy wickedness	Jer 22:22	3637
I was ashamed, yea, even *c*	Jer 31:19	3637
The daughter of Egypt shall be *c*	Jer 46:24	3001
Kiriathaim is *c* and taken	Jer 48:1	3001
Misgab is *c* and dismayed	Jer 48:1	3001
Moab is *c*	Jer 48:20	3001
Hamath is *c*, and Arpad	Jer 49:23	954
say, Babylon is taken, Bel is *c*	Jer 50:2	3001
her idols are *c*, her images are	Jer 50:2	3001
Your mother shall be sore *c*	Jer 50:12	954
every founder is *c* by the graven	Jer 51:17	3001

and her whole land shall be *c* .... Jer 51:47 — 954
We are *c*, because we have heard .... Jer 51:51 — 954
yea, be thou *c* also, and bear thy .... Eze 16:52 — 954
mayest be *c* in all that thou hast .... Eze 16:54 — 3637
thou mayest remember, and be *c* .... Eze 16:63 — 954
c for your own ways, O house of .... Eze 36:32 — 3637
be ashamed, and the diviners *c* .... Mic 3:7 — 2659
see and be *c* at all their might .... Mic 7:16 — 954
the riders on horses shall be *c* .... Zec 10:5 — 3001
came together, and were *c*, because ...... Acts 2:6 — 4797
c the Jews which dwelt at .... Acts 9:22 — 4797
believeth on him shall not be *c* .... 1Pet 2:6 — 2617

CONFUSED
of the warrior is with *c* noise .... Is 9:5 — 7494
for the assembly was *c* .... Acts 19:32 — 4797

CONFUSION
it is *c* .... Lev 18:23
they have wrought *c* .... Lev 20:12 — 8397
the son of Jesse to thine own *c* .... 1Sa 20:30 — 8397
unto the *c* of thy mother's .... 1Sa 20:30 — 1322
to *c* of face, as it is this day .... Ezr 9:7 — 1322
I am full of *c* .... Job 10:15 — 1322
brought to *c* that devise my hurt .... Ps 35:4 — 7036
brought to *c* together that .... Ps 35:26 — 2659
My *c* is continually before me, and ...... Ps 44:15 — 2659
be turned backward, and put to *c* .... Ps 70:2 — 3639
let me never be put to *c* .... Ps 71:1 — 3637
cover themselves with their own *c* ..... Ps 109:29 — 954
The city of *c* is broken down .... Is 24:10 — 1322
in the shadow of Egypt your *c* .... Is 30:3 — 8414
stretch out upon it the line of *c* .... Is 34:11 — 3639
their molten images are wind and *c* ..... Is 41:29 — 8414
they shall go to *c* together that .... Is 45:16 — 8414
for *c* they shall rejoice in their .... Is 61:7 — 3639
our shame, and our *c* covereth us .... Jer 3:25 — 3639
to the *c* of their own faces .... Jer 7:19 — 3639
their everlasting *c* shall never .... Jer 20:11 — 1322
unto thee, but unto us *c* of faces .... Dan 9:7 — 3639
O Lord, to us belongeth *c* of face .... Dan 9:8 — 1322
the whole city was filled with *c* .... Acts 19:29 — 1322
For God is not the author of *c* .... 1Cor 14:33 — 4799
envying and strife is, there is *c* .... Jas 3:16 — 181
                                                                                   181

CONGEALED
the depths were *c* in the heart of .... Ex 15:8 — 7087

CONGRATULATE
to *c* him, because he had fought .... 1Chr 18:10 — 1288

CONGREGATION
Speak ye unto all the *c* of Israel .... Ex 12:3 — 5712
the whole assembly of the *c* of .... Ex 12:6 — 5712
be cut off from the *c* of Israel .... Ex 12:19 — 5712
All the *c* of Israel shall keep it .... Ex 12:47 — 5712
all the *c* of the children of .... Ex 16:1 — 5712
the whole *c* of the children of .... Ex 16:2 — 5712
Say unto all the *c* of the .... Ex 16:9 — 5712
whole *c* of the children of Israel .... Ex 16:10 — 5712
and all the rulers of the *c* came .... Ex 16:22 — 5712
all the *c* of the children of .... Ex 17:1 — 5712
of the *c* without the vail .... Ex 27:21 — 4150
in unto the tabernacle of the *c* .... Ex 28:43 — 4150
door of the tabernacle of the *c* .... Ex 29:4 — 4150
before the tabernacle of the *c* .... Ex 29:10 — 4150
door of the tabernacle of the *c* .... Ex 29:11 — 4150
into the tabernacle of the *c* to .... Ex 29:30 — 4150
door of the tabernacle of the *c* .... Ex 29:32 — 4150
of the *c* before the LORD .... Ex 29:42 — 4150
sanctify the tabernacle of the *c* .... Ex 29:44 — 4150
of the tabernacle of the *c* .... Ex 30:16 — 4150
between the tabernacle of the *c* .... Ex 30:18 — 4150
go into the tabernacle of the *c* .... Ex 30:20 — 4150
the tabernacle of the *c* therewith .... Ex 30:26 — 4150
in the tabernacle of the *c* .... Ex 30:36 — 4150
The tabernacle of the *c*, and the .... Ex 31:7 — 4150
called it the Tabernacle of the *c* .... Ex 33:7 — 4150
out unto the tabernacle of the *c* .... Ex 33:7 — 4150
rulers of the *c* returned unto him .... Ex 34:31 — 5712
Moses gathered all the *c* of the .... Ex 35:1 — 5712
Moses spake unto all the *c* of the .... Ex 35:4 — 5712
all the *c* of the children of .... Ex 35:20 — 5712
work of the tabernacle of the *c* .... Ex 35:21 — 4150
door of the tabernacle of the *c* .... Ex 38:8 — 4150
of the *c* was an hundred talents .... Ex 38:25 — 5712
door of the tabernacle of the *c* .... Ex 38:30 — 4150
of the tent of the *c* finished .... Ex 39:32 — 4150
tabernacle, for the tent of the *c* .... Ex 39:40 — 4150
tabernacle of the tent of the *c* .... Ex 40:2 — 4150
tabernacle of the tent of the *c* .... Ex 40:6 — 4150
laver between the tent of the *c* .... Ex 40:7 — 4150
door of the tabernacle of the *c* .... Ex 40:12 — 4150

the table in the tent of the *c* .... Ex 40:22 — 4150
candlestick in the tent of the *c* .... Ex 40:24 — 4150
the tent of the *c* before the vail .... Ex 40:26 — 4150
tabernacle of the tent of the *c* .... Ex 40:29 — 4150
laver between the tent of the *c* .... Ex 40:30 — 4150
they went into the tent of the *c* .... Ex 40:32 — 4150
a cloud covered the tent of the *c* .... Ex 40:34 — 4150
to enter into the tent of the *c* .... Ex 40:35 — 4150
out of the tabernacle of the *c* .... Lev 1:1 — 4150
of the *c* before the LORD .... Lev 1:3 — 4150
door of the tabernacle of the *c* .... Lev 1:5 — 4150
door of the tabernacle of the *c* .... Lev 3:2 — 4150
it before the tabernacle of the *c* .... Lev 3:8 — 4150
it before the tabernacle of the *c* .... Lev 3:13 — 4150
of the *c* before the LORD .... Lev 4:4 — 4150
it to the tabernacle of the *c* .... Lev 4:5 — 4150
is in the tabernacle of the *c* .... Lev 4:7 — 4150
door of the tabernacle of the *c* .... Lev 4:7 — 4150
if the whole *c* of Israel sin .... Lev 4:13 — 5712
then the *c* shall offer a young .... Lev 4:14 — 6951
before the tabernacle of the *c* .... Lev 4:14 — 4150
the elders of the *c* shall lay .... Lev 4:15 — 5712
blood to the tabernacle of the *c* .... Lev 4:16 — 4150
is in the tabernacle of the *c* .... Lev 4:18 — 4150
door of the tabernacle of the *c* .... Lev 4:18 — 4150
it is a sin offering for the *c* .... Lev 4:21 — 6951
of the *c* they shall eat it .... Lev 6:16 — 4150
court of the tabernacle of the *c* .... Lev 6:26 — 4150
into the tabernacle of the *c* to .... Lev 6:30 — 4150
gather thou all the *c* together .... Lev 8:3 — 5712
door of the tabernacle of the *c* .... Lev 8:3 — 4150
door of the tabernacle of the *c* .... Lev 8:4 — 4150
And Moses said unto the *c*, This is ...... Lev 8:5 — 5712
door of the tabernacle of the *c* .... Lev 8:31 — 4150
tabernacle of the *c* in seven days .... Lev 8:33 — 4150
of the tabernacle of the *c* day .... Lev 8:35 — 4150
before the tabernacle of the *c* .... Lev 9:5 — 4150
all the *c* drew near and stood .... Lev 9:5 — 5712
went into the tabernacle of the *c* .... Lev 9:23 — 4150
door of the tabernacle of the *c* .... Lev 10:7 — 4150
go into the tabernacle of the *c* .... Lev 10:9 — 4150
you to bear the iniquity of the *c* .... Lev 10:17 — 5712
door of the tabernacle of the *c* .... Lev 12:6 — 4150
door of the tabernacle of the *c* .... Lev 14:11 — 4150
door of the tabernacle of the *c* .... Lev 14:23 — 4150
door of the tabernacle of the *c* .... Lev 15:14 — 4150
he shall take of the *c* of the .... Lev 15:29 — 4150
door of the tabernacle of the *c* .... Lev 16:5 — 5712
he do for the tabernacle of the *c* .... Lev 16:7 — 4150
the *c* when he goeth in to make an ...... Lev 16:16 — 4150
and for all the *c* of Israel .... Lev 16:17 — 4150
place, and the tabernacle of the *c* .... Lev 16:17 — 6951
come into the tabernacle of the *c* .... Lev 16:20 — 4150
for the tabernacle of the *c* .... Lev 16:23 — 4150
and for all the people of the *c* .... Lev 16:33 — 4150
door of the tabernacle of the *c* .... Lev 16:33 — 6951
door of the tabernacle of the *c* .... Lev 17:4 — 4150
door of the tabernacle of the *c* .... Lev 17:5 — 4150
door of the tabernacle of the *c* .... Lev 17:6 — 4150
door of the tabernacle of the *c* .... Lev 17:9 — 4150
Speak unto all the *c* of the .... Lev 19:2 — 4150
door of the tabernacle of the *c* .... Lev 19:21 — 5712
in the tabernacle of the *c* .... Lev 24:3 — 4150
head, and let all the *c* stone him .... Lev 24:14 — 4150
all the *c* shall certainly stone .... Lev 24:16 — 5712
Sinai, in the tabernacle of the *c* .... Num 1:1 — 5712
the *c* of the children of Israel .... Num 1:2 — 4150
These were the renowned of the *c* .... Num 1:16 — 5712
they assembled all the *c* together .... Num 1:18 — 5712
the *c* of the children of Israel .... Num 1:53 — 5712
of the *c* shall they pitch .... Num 2:2 — 5712
Then the tabernacle of the *c* .... Num 2:17 — 4150
the charge of the whole *c* before .... Num 3:7 — 5712
before the tabernacle of the *c* .... Num 3:7 — 4150
of the tabernacle of the *c* .... Num 3:8 — 4150
of the *c* shall be the tabernacle .... Num 3:25 — 4150
door of the tabernacle of the *c* .... Num 3:25 — 4150
the tabernacle of the *c* eastward .... Num 3:38 — 4150
work in the tabernacle of the *c* .... Num 4:3 — 4150
Kohath in the tabernacle of the *c* .... Num 4:4 — 4150
Kohath in the tabernacle of the *c* .... Num 4:15 — 4150
work in the tabernacle of the *c* .... Num 4:23 — 4150
and the tabernacle of the *c* .... Num 4:25 — 4150
door of the tabernacle of the *c* .... Num 4:25 — 4150
in the tabernacle of the *c* .... Num 4:28 — 4150
work in the tabernacle of the *c* .... Num 4:30 — 4150
in the tabernacle of the *c* .... Num 4:31 — 4150
in the tabernacle of the *c* .... Num 4:33 — 4150
the chief of the *c* numbered the .... Num 4:34 — 5712
work in the tabernacle of the *c* .... Num 4:35 — 4150
in the tabernacle of the *c* .... Num 4:37 — 4150

C

work in the tabernacle of the *c*	Num 4:39	4150
in the tabernacle of the *c*	Num 4:41	4150
work in the tabernacle of the *c*	Num 4:43	4150
burden in the tabernacle of the *c*	Num 4:47	4150
door of the tabernacle of the *c*	Num 6:10	4150
door of the tabernacle of the *c*	Num 6:13	4150
door of the tabernacle of the *c*	Num 6:18	4150
of the tabernacle of the *c*	Num 7:5	4150
of the *c* to speak with him	Num 7:89	4150
before the tabernacle of the *c*	Num 8:9	4150
of the tabernacle of the *c*	Num 8:15	4150
Israel in the tabernacle of the *c*	Num 8:19	4150
all the *c* of the children of	Num 8:20	5712
tabernacle of the *c* before Aaron	Num 8:22	4150
of the tabernacle of the *c*	Num 8:24	4150
in the tabernacle of the *c*	Num 8:26	4150
door of the tabernacle of the *c*	Num 10:3	4150
But when the *c* is to be gathered	Num 10:7	6951
them unto the tabernacle of the *c*	Num 11:16	4150
unto the tabernacle of the *c*	Num 12:4	4150
to all the *c* of the children of	Num 13:26	5712
word unto them, and unto all the *c*	Num 13:26	5712
all the *c* lifted up their voice,	Num 14:1	5712
the whole *c* said unto them, Would	Num 14:2	5712
the *c* of the children of Israel	Num 14:5	5712
But all the *c* bade stone them	Num 14:10	5712
in the tabernacle of the *c* before	Num 14:10	4150
shall I bear with this evil *c*	Num 14:27	5712
surely do it unto all this evil *c*	Num 14:35	5712
made all the *c* to murmur against	Num 14:36	5712
shall be both for you of the *c*	Num 15:15	6951
without the knowledge of the *c*	Num 15:24	5712
that all the *c* shall offer one	Num 15:24	5712
the *c* of the children of Israel	Num 15:25	5712
the *c* of the children of Israel	Num 15:26	5712
Moses and Aaron, and unto all the *c*	Num 15:33	5712
all the *c* shall stone him with	Num 15:35	
all the *c* brought him without the	Num 15:36	5712
of the assembly, famous in the *c*	Num 16:2	4150
you, seeing all the *c* are holy	Num 16:3	5712
above the *c* of the LORD	Num 16:3	6951
you from the *c* of Israel	Num 16:9	5712
to stand before the *c* to minister	Num 16:9	5712
tabernacle of the *c* with Moses	Num 16:18	4150
Korah gathered all the *c* against	Num 16:19	5712
door of the tabernacle of the *c*	Num 16:19	4150
the LORD appeared unto all the *c*	Num 16:19	5712
yourselves from among this *c*	Num 16:21	5712
wilt thou be wroth with all the *c*	Num 16:22	5712
Speak unto the *c*, saying, Get you	Num 16:24	5712
And he spake unto the *c*, saying,	Num 16:26	5712
and they perished from among the *c*	Num 16:33	6951
the *c* of the children of Israel	Num 16:41	5712
when the *c* was gathered against	Num 16:42	5712
toward the tabernacle of the *c*	Num 16:42	4150
before the tabernacle of the *c*	Num 16:43	4150
Get you up from among this *c*	Num 16:45	5712
incense, and go quickly unto the *c*	Num 16:46	5712
and ran into the midst of the *c*	Num 16:47	6951
door of the tabernacle of the *c*	Num 16:50	4150
of the *c* before the testimony	Num 17:4	4150
charge of the tabernacle of the *c*	Num 18:4	4150
of the tabernacle of the *c*	Num 18:6	4150
of the tabernacle of the *c*	Num 18:21	4150
come nigh the tabernacle of the *c*	Num 18:22	4150
of the tabernacle of the *c*	Num 18:23	4150
in the tabernacle of the *c*	Num 18:31	4150
tabernacle of the *c* seven times	Num 19:4	4150
it shall be kept for the *c* of the	Num 19:9	5712
shall be cut off from among the *c*	Num 19:20	6951
of Israel, even the whole *c*	Num 20:1	5712
And there was no water for the *c*	Num 20:2	5712
up the *c* of the LORD into this	Num 20:4	6951
door of the tabernacle of the *c*	Num 20:6	4150
so thou shalt give the *c* and their	Num 20:8	5712
Aaron gathered the *c* together	Num 20:10	6951
the *c* drank, and their beasts also	Num 20:11	5712
ye shall not bring this *c* into	Num 20:12	6951
of Israel, even the whole *c*	Num 20:22	5712
Hor in the sight of all the *c*	Num 20:27	5712
when all the *c* saw that Aaron was	Num 20:29	5712
in the sight of all the *c* of the	Num 25:6	5712
door of the tabernacle of the *c*	Num 25:6	4150
it, he rose up from among the *c*	Num 25:7	5712
Take the sum of all the *c* of the	Num 26:2	5712
which were famous in the *c*	Num 26:9	5712
before the princes and all the *c*	Num 27:2	5712
door of the tabernacle of the *c*	Num 27:2	4150
of Zin, in the strife of the *c*	Num 27:14	5712
all flesh, set a man over the *c*	Num 27:16	5712
that the *c* of the LORD be not as	Num 27:17	5712
the priest, and before all the *c*	Num 27:19	5712
that all the *c* of the children of	Num 27:20	5712
Israel with him, even all the *c*	Num 27:21	5712
the priest, and before all the *c*	Num 27:22	5712
unto the *c* of the children of	Num 31:12	5712
and all the princes of the *c*	Num 31:13	5712
a plague among the *c* of the LORD	Num 31:16	5712
and the chief fathers of the *c*	Num 31:26	5712
to battle, and between all the *c*	Num 31:27	5712
the *c* was three hundred thousand	Num 31:43	5712
it into the tabernacle of the *c*	Num 31:54	4150
and unto the princes of the *c*	Num 32:2	5712
LORD smote before the *c* of Israel	Num 32:4	5712
he stand before the *c* in judgment	Num 35:12	5712
Then the *c* shall judge between	Num 35:24	5712
the *c* shall deliver the slayer	Num 35:25	5712
the *c* shall restore him to the	Num 35:25	5712
not enter into the *c* of the LORD	Deut 23:1	6951
not enter into the *c* of the LORD	Deut 23:2	6951
not enter into the *c* of the LORD	Deut 23:2	6951
not enter into the *c* of the LORD	Deut 23:3	6951
into the *c* of the LORD for ever	Deut 23:3	6951
the *c* of the LORD in their third	Deut 23:8	6951
in the tabernacle of the *c*	Deut 31:14	4150
in the tabernacle of the *c*	Deut 31:14	4150
the *c* of Israel the words of this	Deut 31:30	4150
the inheritance of the *c* of Jacob	Deut 33:4	6952
not before all the *c* of Israel	Josh 8:35	6951
princes of the *c* sware unto them	Josh 9:15	5712
because the princes of the *c* had	Josh 9:18	5712
all the *c* murmured against the	Josh 9:18	5712
the princes said unto all the *c*	Josh 9:19	5712
drawers of water unto all the *c*	Josh 9:21	5712
and drawers of water for the *c*	Josh 9:27	5712
the whole *c* of the children of	Josh 18:1	5712
up the tabernacle of the *c* there	Josh 18:1	4150
door of the tabernacle of the *c*	Josh 19:51	4150
stand before the *c* for judgment	Josh 20:6	5712
until he stood before the *c*	Josh 20:9	5712
the whole *c* of the children of	Josh 22:12	5712
saith the whole *c* of the LORD	Josh 22:16	5712
was a plague in the *c* of the LORD	Josh 22:17	5712
wroth with the whole *c* of Israel	Josh 22:18	5712
wrath fell on all the *c* of Israel	Josh 22:20	5712
priest, and the princes of the *c*	Josh 22:30	5712
the *c* was gathered together as	Judg 20:1	5712
not up with the *c* unto the LORD	Judg 21:5	6951
the *c* sent thither twelve	Judg 21:10	5712
the whole *c* sent some to speak to	Judg 21:13	5712
Then the elders of the *c* said	Judg 21:16	5712
door of the tabernacle of the *c*	1Sa 2:22	4150
LORD, and the tabernacle of the *c*	1Kin 8:4	4150
all the *c* of Israel, that were	1Kin 8:5	5712
and blessed all the *c* of Israel	1Kin 8:14	6951
all the *c* of Israel stood	1Kin 8:14	6951
presence of all the *c* of Israel	1Kin 8:22	6951
blessed all the *c* of Israel with	1Kin 8:55	6951
and all Israel with him, a great *c*	1Kin 8:65	6951
all the *c* of Israel came, and	1Kin 12:3	6951
sent and called him unto the *c*	1Kin 12:20	5712
tabernacle of the *c* with singing	1Chr 6:32	4150
door of the tabernacle of the *c*	1Chr 9:21	4150
said unto all the *c* of Israel	1Chr 13:2	6951
all the *c* said that they would do	1Chr 13:4	6951
charge of the tabernacle of the *c*	1Chr 23:32	4150
of all Israel the *c* of the LORD	1Chr 28:8	6951
the king said unto all the *c*	1Chr 29:1	6951
blessed the LORD before all the *c*	1Chr 29:10	6951
And David said to all the *c*	1Chr 29:20	6951
all the *c* blessed the LORD God of	1Chr 29:20	6951
all the *c* with him, went to the	2Chr 1:3	6951
the tabernacle of the *c* of God	2Chr 1:3	4150
Solomon and the *c* sought unto it	2Chr 1:5	6951
was at the tabernacle of the *c*	2Chr 1:6	4150
before the tabernacle of the *c*	2Chr 1:13	4150
ark, and the tabernacle of the *c*	2Chr 5:5	4150
all the *c* of Israel that were	2Chr 5:6	5712
and blessed the whole *c* of Israel	2Chr 6:3	6951
all the *c* of Israel stood	2Chr 6:3	6951
presence of all the *c* of Israel	2Chr 6:12	6951
knees before all the *c* of Israel	2Chr 6:13	6951
Israel with him, a very great *c*	2Chr 7:8	6951
stood in the *c* of Judah and	2Chr 20:5	6951
of the LORD in the midst of the *c*	2Chr 20:14	6951
all the *c* made a covenant with	2Chr 23:3	6951
of the *c* of Israel, for the	2Chr 24:6	6951
before the princes and all the *c*	2Chr 28:14	6951
offering before the king and the *c*	2Chr 29:23	6951
all the *c* worshipped, and the	2Chr 29:28	6951
the *c* brought in sacrifices and	2Chr 29:31	6951
offerings, which the *c* brought	2Chr 29:32	6951

all the *c* in Jerusalem, to keep 2Chr 30:2   6951
pleased the king and all the *c* 2Chr 30:4   6951
the second month, a very great *c* 2Chr 30:13   6951
in the *c* that were not sanctified 2Chr 30:17   6951
give to the *c* a thousand bullocks 2Chr 30:24   6951
gave to the *c* a thousand bullocks 2Chr 30:24   6951
all the *c* of Judah, with the 2Chr 30:25   6951
all the *c* that came out of Israel............ 2Chr 30:25   6951
daughters, through all the *c* 2Chr 31:18   6951
The whole *c* together was forty and...... Ezr 2:64   6951
of Israel a very great *c* of men .... Ezr 10:1   6951
himself separated from the *c* of .... Ezr 10:8   6951
Then all the *c* answered and said .... Ezr 10:12   6951
now our rulers of all the *c* stand .... Ezr 10:14   6951
And all the *c* said, Amen, and .... Neh 5:13   6951
The whole *c* together was forty and...... Neh 7:66   6951
the law before the *c* both of men.......... Neh 8:2   6951
all the *c* of them that were come .... Neh 8:17   6951
come into the *c* of God for ever .... Neh 13:1   6951
For the *c* of hypocrites shall be .... Job 15:34   5712
I stood up, and I cried in the *c*............. Job 30:28   6951
sinners in the *c* of the righteous............ Ps 1:5   5712
So shall the *c* of the people .... Ps 7:7   5712
midst of the *c* will I praise thee .... Ps 22:22   6951
shall be of thee in the great *c* .... Ps 22:25   6951
I have hated the *c* of evildoers .... Ps 26:5   6951
give thee thanks in the great *c* .... Ps 35:18   6951
righteousness in the great *c* .... Ps 40:9   6951
and thy truth from the great *c* .... Ps 40:10   6951
indeed speak righteousness, O *c* .... Ps 58:1   482
Thy *c* hath dwelt therein .... Ps 68:10   2416
Remember thy *c*, which thou hast .... Ps 74:2   5712
forget not the *c* of thy poor for .... Ps 74:19   2416
the *c* I will judge uprightly .... Ps 75:2   4150
standeth in the *c* of the mighty .... Ps 82:1   5712
also in the *c* of the saints .... Ps 89:5   6951
him also in the *c* of the people .... Ps 107:32   6951
of the upright, and in the *c*................ Ps 111:1   5712
and his praise in the *c* of saints .... Ps 149:1   6951
in all evil in the midst of the *c* .... Prov 5:14   6951
shall remain in the *c* of the dead .... Prov 21:16   6951
be shewed before the whole *c*............ Prov 26:26   6951
sit also upon the mount of the *c*........... Is 14:13   4150
hear, ye nations, and know, O *c* .... Jer 6:18   5712
their *c* shall be established .... Jer 30:20   5712
they should not enter into thy *c* .... Lam 1:10   6951
them, as their *c* hath heard .... Hos 7:12   5712
Gather the people, sanctify the *c* .... Joel 2:16   6951
cord by lot in the *c* of the LORD .... Mic 2:5   6951
Now when the *c* was broken up, ... Acts 13:43   4865

CONGREGATIONS
in the *c* will I bless the LORD .... Ps 26:12   4721
Bless ye God in the *c*, even the .... Ps 68:26   4721
roar in the midst of thy *c*........................ Ps 74:4   4150

CONIAH (*co-ni'-ah*) See JEHOIACHIN. *Another name for Jehoiachin.*
though *C* the son of Jehoiakim .... Jer 22:24   3659
Is this man *C* a despised broken .... Jer 22:28   3659
instead of *C* the son of Jehoiakim .... Jer 37:1   3659

CONIES
and the rocks for the *c*........................... Ps 104:18   8226
The *c* are but a feeble folk, yet............... Prov 30:26   8226

CONONIAH (*co-no-ni'-ah*) See CONANIAH. *A Levite during Hezekiah's time.*
over which *C* the Levite was ruler 2Chr 31:12   3562
overseers under the hand of *C* 2Chr 31:13   3562

CONQUER
he went forth conquering, and to *c* ...... Rev 6:2   3528

CONQUERING
and he went forth *c*, and to conquer ...... Rev 6:2   3528

CONQUERORS
than *c* through him that loved us .... Rom 8:37   5245

CONSCIENCE
being convicted by their own *c* .... Jn 8:9   4893
I have lived in all good *c* before .... Acts 23:1   4893
to have always a *c* void of..................... Acts 24:16   4893
their *c* also bearing witness, and............ Rom 2:15   4893
my *c* also bearing me witness in .... Rom 9:1   4893
for wrath, but also for *c* sake .... Rom 13:5   4893
for some with *c* of the idol unto 1Cor 8:7   4893
their *c* being weak is defiled 1Cor 8:7   4893
shall not the *c* of him which is 1Cor 8:10   4893
brethren, and wound their weak *c*........... 1Cor 8:12   4893
asking no question for *c* sake 1Cor 10:25   4893
asking no question for *c* sake 1Cor 10:27   4893
that shewed it, and for *c* sake 1Cor 10:28   4893
C, I say, not thine own, but of................. 1Cor 10:29   4893

liberty judged of another man's *c* 1Cor 10:29   4893
is this, the testimony of our *c* 2Cor 1:12   4893
every man's *c* in the sight of God 2Cor 4:2   4893
of a pure heart, and of a good *c*............ 1Ti 1:5   4893
Holding faith, and a good *c* 1Ti 1:19   4893
mystery of the faith in a pure *c* 1Ti 3:9   4893
having their *c* seared with a hot 1Ti 4:2   4893
from my forefathers with pure *c* 2Ti 1:3   4893
even their mind and *c* is defiled .... Titus 1:15   4893
perfect, as pertaining to the *c* .... Heb 9:9   4893
purge your *c* from dead works to........... Heb 9:14   4893
should have had no more of *c* of sins ...... Heb 10:2   4893
hearts sprinkled from an evil *c* .... Heb 10:22   4893
for we trust we have a good *c* .... Heb 13:18   4893
if a man for *c* toward God endure 1Pet 2:19   4893
Having a good *c* 1Pet 3:16   4893
the answer of a good *c* toward God 1Pet 3:21   4893

CONSCIENCES
also are made manifest in your *c* 2Cor 5:11   4893

CONSECRATE
make Aaron's garments to *c* him .... Ex 28:3   6942
c them, and sanctify them, that ...... Ex 28:41   4390,3027
shalt *c* Aaron and his sons .... Ex 29:9   4390,3027
the atonement was made, to *c*........ Ex 29:33   4390,3027
seven days shalt thou *c* them .... Ex 29:35   4390,3027
c them, that they may minister .... Ex 30:30   6942
C yourselves to day to the LORD.......... Ex 32:29   4390,3027
for seven days shall he *c* you.......... Lev 8:33   4390,3027
whom he shall *c* to minister in .... Lev 16:32   4390,3027
he shall *c* unto the LORD the days....... Num 6:12   5144
who then is willing to *c* his............. 1Chr 29:5   4390,3027
so that whosoever cometh to *c*....... 2Chr 13:9   4390,3027
and they shall *c* themselves .... Eze 43:26   4390,3027
I will *c* their gain unto the LORD .... Mic 4:13   2763

CONSECRATED
therein, and to be *c* in them .... Ex 29:29   4390,3027
that is *c* to put on the garments,...... Lev 21:10   4390,3027
whom he *c* to minister in the........... Num 3:3   4390,3027
and iron, are *c* unto the LORD........... Josh 6:19   6944
c one of his sons, who became .... Judg 17:5   4390,3027
And Micah *c* the Levite................... Judg 17:12   4390,3027
c him, and he became one of the 1Kin 13:33   4390,3027
that are *c* to burn incense 2Chr 26:18   6942
ye have *c* yourselves unto the 2Chr 29:31   4390,3027
the *c* things were six hundred 2Chr 29:33   6942
were *c* unto the LORD their God 2Chr 31:6   6942
feasts of the LORD that were *c* .... Ezr 3:5   6942
the Son, who is *c* for evermore .... Heb 7:28   5048
way, which he hath *c* for us ...... Heb 10:20   1457

CONSECRATION
for it is a ram of *c*.................................. Ex 29:22   4394
breast of the ram of Aaron's *c*.............. Ex 29:26   4394
is heaved up, of the ram of the *c*......... Ex 29:27   4394
thou shalt take the ram of the *c*........... Ex 29:31   4394
the other ram, the ram of *c* .... Lev 8:22   4394
for of the ram of *c* it was Moses'............ Lev 8:29   4394
the days of your *c* be at an end............. Lev 8:33   4394
because the *c* of his God is upon .... Num 6:7   5145
he hath defiled the head of his *c*............ Num 6:9   5145

CONSECRATIONS
And if ought of the flesh of the *c*....... Ex 29:34   4394
trespass offering, and of the *c*.............. Lev 7:37   4394
they were *c* for a sweet savour .... Lev 8:28   4394
bread that is in the basket of *c*.............. Lev 8:31   4394

CONSENT
But in this will we *c* unto you................. Gen 34:15   225
Only herein will the men *c* unto .... Gen 34:22   225
only let us *c* unto them, and they........... Gen 34:23   225
Thou shalt not *c* unto him .... Deut 13:8   14
but he would not *c*.................................. Judg 11:17   14
and they came out with one *c* 1Sa 11:7   376
him, Hearken not unto him, nor *c*.......... 1Kin 20:8   14
consulted together with one *c* .... Ps 83:5   3820
sinners entice thee, *c* thou not .... Prov 1:10   14
of priests murder in the way by *c*.......... Hos 6:9   7926
the LORD, to serve him with one *c*........... Zeph 3:9   7926
they all with one *c* began to make...... Lk 14:18
I *c* unto the law that it is good .... Rom 7:16   4852
except it be with *c* for a time 1Cor 7:5   4859
c not to wholesome words, even 1Ti 6:3   4334

CONSENTED
the priests *c* to receive no more 2Kin 12:8   225
So he *c* to them in this matter,............... Dan 1:14   8085
The same had not *c* to the counsel .... Lk 23:51   4784
longer with them, he *c* not .... Acts 18:20   1962

CONSENTEDST
a thief, then thou *c* with him .... Ps 50:18   7521

CONSENTING

Saul was c unto his death	Acts 8:1	4909
c unto his death, and kept the	Acts 22:20	4909

CONSIDER

c that this nation is thy people	Ex 33:13	7200
Then the priest shall c	Lev 13:13	7200
c it in thine heart, that the	Deut 4:39	7725
Thou shalt also c in thine heart	Deut 8:5	3045
c the years of many generations	Deut 32:7	995
that they would c their latter	Deut 32:29	995
now therefore c what ye have to	Judg 18:14	3045
c of it, take advice, and speak	Judg 19:30	7760
for c how great things he hath	1Sa 12:24	7200
know and c what thou wilt do	1Sa 25:17	7200
wherefore c, I pray you, and see	2Kin 5:7	3045
will he not then c it	Job 11:11	995
when I c, I am afraid of him	Job 23:15	995
would not c any of his ways	Job 34:27	7919
c the wondrous works of God	Job 37:14	995
c my meditation	Ps 5:1	995
When I c thy heavens, the work of	Ps 8:3	7200
c my trouble which I suffer of	Ps 9:13	7200
C and hear me, O Lord my God	Ps 13:3	5027
C mine enemies	Ps 25:19	7200
thou shalt diligently c his place	Ps 37:10	995
Hearken, O daughter, and c	Ps 45:10	7200
well her bulwarks, c her palaces	Ps 48:13	6448
Now c this, ye that forget God,	Ps 50:22	995
they shall wisely c of his doing	Ps 64:9	7919
but I will c thy testimonies	Ps 119:95	995
C mine affliction, and deliver me	Ps 119:153	7200
C how I love thy precepts	Ps 119:159	7200
c her ways, and be wise	Prov 6:6	7200
c diligently what is before thee	Prov 23:1	995
he that pondereth the heart c it	Prov 24:12	995
for they c not that they do evil	Eccl 5:1	3045
C the work of God	Eccl 7:13	7200
but in the day of adversity c	Eccl 7:14	7200
not know, my people doth not c	Is 1:3	995
neither c the operation of his	Is 5:12	7200
c thee, saying, Is this the man	Is 14:16	995
I will c in my dwelling place	Is 18:4	5027
That they may see, and know, and c	Is 41:20	7760
what they be, that we may c them	Is 41:22	7760,3820
neither c the things of old	Is 43:18	995
they had not heard shall they c	Is 52:15	995
c diligently, and see if there be	Jer 2:10	995
C ye, and call for the mourning	Jer 9:17	995
days ye shall c it perfectly	Jer 23:20	995
in the latter days ye shall c it	Jer 30:24	995
see, O Lord, and c	Lam 1:11	5027
c to whom thou hast done this	Lam 2:20	5027
c, and behold our reproach	Lam 5:1	5027
it may be they will c, though	Eze 12:3	7200
the matter, and c the vision	Dan 9:23	995
they c not in their hearts that I	Hos 7:2	559
C your ways	Hag 1:5	7760,3820,5921
C your ways	Hag 1:7	7760,3820,5921
c from this day and upward, from	Hag 2:15	7760,3820
C now from this day and upward,	Hag 2:18	7760,3820
the Lord's temple was laid, c it	Hag 2:18	7760,3820
C the lilies of the field, how	Mt 6:28	2648
C the ravens	Lk 12:24	2657
C the lilies how they grow	Lk 12:27	2657
Nor c that it is expedient for us	Jn 11:50	1260
together for to c of this matter	Acts 15:6	1492
C what I say	2Ti 2:7	3539
c the Apostle and High Priest of	Heb 3:1	2657
Now c how great this man was,	Heb 7:4	2334
let us c one another to provoke	Heb 10:24	2657
For c him that endured such	Heb 12:3	357

CONSIDERED

but when I had c it in the	1Kin 3:21	995
I have c the things which thou	1Kin 5:8	8085
Hast thou c my servant Job, that	Job 1:8	7760,3820
Hast thou c my servant Job, that	Job 2:3	7760,3820
for thou hast c my trouble	Ps 31:7	7200
I have c the days of old, the	Ps 77:5	2803
Then I saw, and c it well	Prov 24:32	7896,3820
c all the oppressions that are	Eccl 4:1	7200
I c all travail, and every right	Eccl 4:4	7200
I c all the living which walk	Eccl 4:15	7200
For all this I c in my heart even	Eccl 9:1	5414
I c the horns, and, behold, there	Dan 7:8	7920
For they c not the miracle of the	Mk 6:52	4920
I had fastened mine eyes, I c	Acts 11:6	2657
And when he had c the thing	Acts 12:12	4894
he c not his own body now dead,	Rom 4:19	2657

CONSIDEREST

C thou not what this people have	Jer 33:24	7200
but c not the beam that is in	Mt 7:3	2657

CONSIDERETH

he c all their works	Ps 33:15	995
Blessed is he that c the poor	Ps 41:1	7919
wisely c the house of the wicked	Prov 21:12	7919
c not that poverty shall come	Prov 28:22	3045
The righteous c the cause of the	Prov 29:7	3045
She c a field, and buyeth it	Prov 31:16	2161
none c in his heart, neither is	Is 44:19	7725
sins which he hath done, and c	Eze 18:14	7200
Because he c, and turneth away	Eze 18:28	7200

CONSIDERING

none c that the righteous is	Is 57:1	995
And as I was c, behold, an he goat	Dan 8:5	995
c thyself, lest thou also be	Gal 6:1	4648
c the end of their conversation	Heb 13:7	333

CONSIST

things, and by him all things c	Col 1:17	4921

CONSISTETH

for a man's life c not in the	Lk 12:15	2076

CONSOLATION

of c to drink for their father or	Jer 16:7	8575
waiting for the c of Israel	Lk 2:25	3874
for ye have received your c	Lk 6:24	3874
being interpreted, The son of c	Acts 4:36	3874
had read, they rejoiced for the c	Acts 15:31	3874
c grant you to be likeminded one	Rom 15:5	3874
so our c also aboundeth by Christ	2Cor 1:5	3874
we be afflicted, it is for your c	2Cor 1:6	3874
we be comforted, it is for your c	2Cor 1:6	3874
so shall ye be also of the c	2Cor 1:7	3874
but by the c wherewith he was	2Cor 7:7	3874
be therefore any c in Christ	Phil 2:1	3874
and hath given us everlasting c	2Th 2:16	3874
c in thy love, because the bowels	Philem 7	3874
to lie, we might have a strong c	Heb 6:18	3874

CONSOLATIONS

Are the c of God small with thee	Job 15:11	8575
my speech, and let this be your c	Job 21:2	8575
with the breasts of her c	Is 66:11	8575

CONSORTED

believed, and c with Paul and Silas	Acts 17:4	4845

CONSPIRACY

And the c was strong	2Sa 15:12	7195
his servants arose, and made a c	2Kin 12:20	7195
Now they made a c against him in	2Kin 14:19	7195
his c which he made, behold, they	2Kin 15:15	7195
made a c against Pekah the son of	2Kin 15:30	7195
king of Assyria found c in Hoshea	2Kin 17:4	7195
made a c against him in Jerusalem	2Chr 25:27	7195
A c is found among the men of	Jer 11:9	7195
There is a c of her prophets in	Eze 22:25	7195
than forty which had made this c	Acts 23:13	4945

CONSPIRATORS

is among the c with Absalom	2Sa 15:31	7194

CONSPIRED

they c against him to slay him	Gen 37:18	5320
That all of you have c against me	1Sa 22:8	7194
him, Why have ye c against me	1Sa 22:13	7194
house of Issachar, c against him	1Kin 15:27	7194
c against him, as he was in	1Kin 16:9	7194
encamped heard say, Zimri hath c	1Kin 16:16	7194
the son of Nimshi c against Joram	2Kin 9:14	7194
I c against my master, and slew	2Kin 10:9	7194
the son of Jabesh c against him	2Kin 15:10	7194
c against him, and smote him in	2Kin 15:25	7194
servants of Amon c against him	2Kin 21:23	7194
them that had c against king Amon	2Kin 21:24	7194
they c against him, and stoned him	2Chr 24:21	7194
his own servants c against him	2Chr 24:25	7194
these are they that c against him	2Chr 24:26	7194
And his servants c against him	2Chr 33:24	7194
them that had c against king Amon	2Chr 33:25	7194
c all of them together to come and	Neh 4:8	7194
Amos hath c against thee in the	Amos 7:10	7194

CONSTANT

if he be c to do my commandments	1Chr 28:7	2388

CONSTANTLY

the man that heareth speaketh c	Prov 21:28	5331
But she c affirmed that it was	Acts 12:15	1340
things I will that thou affirm c	Titus 3:8	1226

CONSTELLATIONS

the c thereof shall not give	Is 13:10	3685

CONSTRAIN
they c you to be circumcised.................Gal 6:12   315

CONSTRAINED
and she c him to eat bread 2Kin 4:8   2388
straightway Jesus c his disciples ....Mt 14:22   315
straightway he c his disciples to ....Mk 6:45   315
But they c him, saying, Abide ....Lk 24:29   3849
And she c us ....Acts 16:15   3849
I was c to appeal unto Caesar ....Acts 28:19   315

CONSTRAINETH
the spirit within me c me.........................Job 32:18   6693
For the love of Christ c us.......................2Cor 5:14   4912

CONSTRAINT
the oversight thereof, not by c 1Pet 5:2   317

CONSULT
They only c to cast him down from ....Ps 62:4   3289

CONSULTATION
priests held a c with the elders ....Mk 15:1   4824

CONSULTED
king Rehoboam c with the old men, ...1Kin 12:6   3289
c with the young men that were 1Kin 12:8   3289
David c with the captains of 1Chr 13:1   3289
when he had c with the people, he 2Chr 20:21   3289
Then I c with myself, and I.......................Neh 5:7   4427
c against thy hidden ones.........................Ps 83:3   3289
For they have c together with one ....Ps 83:5   3289
he c with images, he looked in ....Eze 21:21   7592
have c together to establish a ....Dan 6:7   3272
now what Balak king of Moab c ....Mic 6:5   3289
Thou hast c shame to thy house by ....Hab 2:10   3289
c that they might take Jesus by ....Mt 26:4   4823
But the chief priests c that they.............Jn 12:10   1011

CONSULTER
or a c with familiar spirits, or ....Deut 18:11   7592

CONSULTETH
c whether he be able with ten ....Lk 14:31   1011

CONSUME
and the famine shall c the land ....Gen 41:30   3615
them, and that I may c them ....Ex 32:10   3615
to c them from the face of the ....Ex 32:12   3615
lest I c thee in the way............................Ex 33:3   3615
of thee in a moment, and c thee.............Ex 33:5   3615
ague, that shall c the eyes.......................Lev 26:16   3615
that I may c them in a moment...............Num 16:21   3615
that I may c them as in a moment...........Num 16:45   3615
for this great fire will c us ....Deut 5:25   398
thou shalt c all the people which ....Deut 7:16   398
thou mayest not c them at once ....Deut 7:22   3615
for the locust shall c it ....Deut 28:38   2628
of thy land shall the locust c ....Deut 28:42   3423
shall c the earth with her ....Deut 32:22   398
c you, after that he hath done ....Josh 24:20   3615
altar, shall be to c thine eyes................1Sa 2:33   3615
heaven, and c thee and thy fifty.............2Kin 1:10   398
heaven, and c thee and thy fifty.............2Kin 1:12   398
thou didst not utterly c them..................Neh 9:31   3615
to c them, and to destroy them...............Est 9:24   2000
fire shall c the tabernacles of................Job 15:34   398
a fire not blown shall c him.....................Job 20:26   398
Drought and heat c the snow waters.....Job 24:19   1497
they shall c...Ps 37:20   3615
into smoke shall they c away...................Ps 37:20   3615
his beauty to c away like a moth ....Ps 39:11   4529
their beauty shall c in the grave ....Ps 49:14   1086
C them in wrath, c them,..........................Ps 59:13   3615
their days did he c in vanity.....................Ps 78:33   3615
and it shall also c the beard....................Is 7:20   5595
shall c the glory of his forest, ...Is 10:18   3615
down, and c the branches thereof ....Is 27:10   3615
I will surely c them, saith the.................Jer 8:13   5486
but I will c them by the sword, ...Jer 14:12   3615
it shall c the palaces of..........................Jer 49:27   398
c away for their iniquity...........................Eze 4:17   4743
hailstones in my fury to c it ....Eze 13:13   3615
them in the wilderness, to c them ....Eze 20:13   3615
to c because of the glittering ....Eze 21:28   398
will c thy filthiness out of thee ....Eze 22:15   8552
c the flesh, and spice it well, and ....Eze 24:10   8552
desolate, they are given us to c............Eze 35:12   402
c all these kingdoms, and it shall ....Dan 2:44   5487
take away his dominion, to c ....Dan 7:26   8046
shall c his branches, and devour ....Hos 11:6   3615
I will utterly c all things from ....Zeph 1:2   5486
I will c man and beast ....Zeph 1:3   5486
I will c the fowls of the heaven, ...Zeph 1:3   5486
shall c it with the timber ....Zec 5:4   3615

Their flesh shall c away while ....Zec 14:12   4743
their eyes shall c away in their ....Zec 14:12   4743
their tongue shall c away in ....Zec 14:12   4743
c them, even as Elias did........................Lk 9:54   355
whom the Lord shall c with the 2Th 2:8   355
that ye may c it upon your lusts ....Jas 4:3   1159

CONSUMED
lest thou be c in the iniquity of..............Gen 19:15   5595
to the mountain, lest thou be c...............Gen 19:17   5595
in the day the drought c me ....Gen 31:40   398
with fire, and the bush was not c...........Ex 3:2   398
wrath, which c them as stubble...............Ex 15:7   398
or the field, be c therewith.....................Ex 22:6   398
the ashes which the fire hath c..............Lev 6:10   398
c upon the altar the burnt ....Lev 9:24   398
c them that were in the uttermost ....Num 11:1   398
half c when he cometh out of his ....Num 12:12   398
this wilderness they shall be c ....Num 14:35   8552
lest ye be c in all their sins ....Num 16:26   5595
c the two hundred and fifty men.............Num 16:35   398
shall we be c with dying ....Num 17:13   8552
it hath c Ar of Moab, and the..................Num 21:28   398
that I c not the children of ....Num 25:11   3615
in the sight of the LORD, was c ....Num 32:13   8552
among the host, until they were c ....Deut 2:15   8552
when all the men of war were c ....Deut 2:16   8552
until he have c thee from off the ....Deut 28:21   3615
which came out of Egypt, were c ....Josh 5:6   8552
of the sword, until they were c ....Josh 8:24   8552
great slaughter, till they were c ....Josh 10:20   8552
c the flesh and the unleavened ....Judg 6:21   398
still do wickedly, ye shall be c 1Sa 12:25   5595
against them until they be c 1Sa 15:18   3615
the king, The man that c us 2Sa 21:5   3615
not again until I had c them 2Sa 22:38   3615
And I have c them, and wounded them ..2Sa 22:39   3615
c the burnt sacrifice, and the 1Kin 18:38   398
Syrians, until thou have c them 1Kin 22:11   3615
heaven, and c him and his fifty 2Kin 1:10   398
heaven, and c him and his fifty 2Kin 1:12   398
of the Israelites that are c.......................2Kin 7:13   8552
in Aphek, till thou have c them 2Kin 13:17   3615
Syria till thou hadst c it..........................2Kin 13:19   3615
c the burnt offering and the....................2Chr 7:1   398
whom the children of Israel c not 2Chr 8:8   3615
shalt push Syria until they be c 2Chr 18:10   3615
with us till thou hadst c us ....Ezr 9:14   3615
the gates thereof are c with fire..............Neh 2:3   398
gates thereof were c with fire ....Neh 2:13   398
sheep, and the servants, and c them ......Job 1:16   398
breath of his nostrils are they c.............Job 4:9   3615
they are c out of their place ....Job 6:17   1846
As the cloud is c and vanisheth ....Job 7:9   3615
though my reins be c within me ....Job 19:27   3615
His flesh is c away, that it.......................Job 33:21   3615
Mine eye is c because of grief ....Ps 6:7   6244
did I turn again till they were c ....Ps 18:37   3615
mine eye is c with grief, yea, my.............Ps 31:9   6244
mine iniquity, and my bones are c ....Ps 31:10   6244
I am c by the blow of thine hand ....Ps 39:10   3615
c that are adversaries to my soul ....Ps 71:13   3615
they are utterly c with terrors.................Ps 73:19   8552
The fire c their young men ....Ps 78:63   398
For we are c by thine anger, and ....Ps 90:7   3615
For my days are c like smoke...................Ps 102:3   3615
the sinners be c out of the earth............Ps 104:35   8552
They had almost c me upon earth...........Ps 119:87   3615
My zeal hath c me, because mine ....Ps 119:139   6789
when thy flesh and thy body are c ....Prov 5:11   3615
that forsake the LORD shall be c ....Is 1:28   3615
oppressors are c out of the land ....Is 16:4   8552
to nought, and the scorner is c...............Is 29:20   3615
thy face from us, and hast c us ....Is 64:7   4127
and the mouse, shall be c together ....Is 66:17   5486
thou hast c them, but they have ....Jer 5:3   3615
burned, the lead is c of the fire ....Jer 6:29   8552
after them, till I have c them..................Jer 9:16   3615
him, and c them, and have made his.......Jer 10:25   3615
the beasts are c, and the birds...............Jer 12:4   5595
famine shall those prophets be c ....Jer 14:15   8552
and they shall be c by the sword ....Jer 16:4   3615
my days should be c with shame ....Jer 20:18   3615
till they be c from off the land ....Jer 24:10   8552
until I have c them by his hand ....Jer 27:8   8552
until all the roll was c in the ....Jer 36:23   8552
there, and they shall all be c ....Jer 44:12   8552
they shall even be c by the sword ....Jer 44:12   8552
have been c by the sword and by ....Jer 44:18   8552
of Egypt shall be c by the sword ....Jer 44:27   8552
after them, till I have c them..................Jer 49:37   3615

and brought up hath mine enemy c .... Lam 2:22 — 3615
LORD's mercies that we are not c .... Lam 3:22 — 8552
they be c in the midst of these .... Eze 5:12 — 3615
ye shall be c in the midst .... Eze 13:14 — 3615
the fire c them .... Eze 19:12 — 398
I have c them with the fire of my .... Eze 22:31 — 3615
it, that the scum of it may be c .... Eze 24:11 — 8552
they shall be no more c with .... Eze 34:29 — 622
wherefore I have c them in mine .... Eze 43:8 — 398
shall the fruit thereof be c .... Eze 47:12 — 8552
which by his hand shall be c .... Dan 11:16 — 3615
ye sons of Jacob are not c .... Mal 3:6 — 3615
that ye be c one of another .... Gal 5:15 — 355

CONSUMETH
And he, as a rotten thing, c .... Job 13:28 — 1086
the remnant of them the fire c .... Job 22:20 — 398
is a fire that c to destruction .... Job 31:12 — 398
stubble, and the flame c the chaff .... Is 5:24 — 7503

CONSUMING
For the LORD thy God is a c fire .... Deut 4:24 — 398
as a c fire he shall destroy them .... Deut 9:3 — 398
For our God is a c fire .... Heb 12:29 — 2654

CONSUMMATION
it desolate, even until the c .... Dan 9:27 — 3617

CONSUMPTION
even appoint over you terror, c .... Lev 26:16 — 7829
LORD shall smite thee with a c .... Deut 28:22 — 7829
the c decreed shall overflow with .... Is 10:22 — 3631
Lord GOD of hosts shall make a c .... Is 10:23 — 3617
from the Lord GOD of hosts a c .... Is 28:22 — 3617

CONTAIN
heaven of heavens cannot c thee .... 1Kin 8:27 — 3557
as great as would c two measures......... 1Kin 18:32 — 1004
and heaven of heavens cannot c him ..... 2Chr 2:6 — 3557
heaven of heavens cannot c thee .... 2Chr 6:18 — 3557
that the bath may c the tenth .... Eze 45:11 — 5375
not c the books that should be .... Jn 21:25 — 5562
But if they cannot c, let them .... 1Cor 7:9 — 1467

CONTAINED
it c two thousand baths .... 1Kin 7:26 — 3557
one laver c forty baths .... 1Kin 7:38 — 3557
by nature the things c in the law .... Rom 2:14
of commandments c in ordinances .... Eph 2:15
also it is c in the scripture .... 1Pet 2:6 — 4023

CONTAINETH
it c much .... Eze 23:32 — 3557

CONTAINING
c two or three firkins apiece .... Jn 2:6 — 5562

CONTEMN
Wherefore doth the wicked c God .... Ps 10:13 — 5006
what if the sword c even the rod............ Eze 21:13 — 3988

CONTEMNED
In whose eyes a vile person is c............. Ps 15:4 — 959
c the counsel of the most High .... Ps 107:11 — 5006
for love, it would utterly be c .... Song 8:7 — 936
and the glory of Moab shall be c .... Is 16:14 — 7034

CONTEMNETH
it c the rod of my son, as every .... Eze 21:10 — 3988

CONTEMPT
Thus shall there arise too much c.......... Est 1:18 — 963
He poureth c upon princes, and............. Job 12:21 — 937
or did the c of families terrify................ Job 31:34 — 937
He poureth c upon princes, and .... Ps 107:40 — 937
Remove from me reproach and c .... Ps 119:22 — 937
we are exceedingly filled with c............. Ps 123:3 — 937
ease, and with the c of the proud .... Ps 123:4 — 937
wicked cometh, then cometh also c .... Prov 18:3 — 937
glory, and to bring into c all the .... Is 23:9 — 7043
and some to shame and everlasting c .... Dan 12:2 — 1860

CONTEMPTIBLE
say, The table of the LORD is c............... Mal 1:7 — 959
thereof, even his meat, is c .... Mal 1:12 — 959
Therefore have I also made you c .... Mal 2:9 — 959
presence is weak, and his speech c .... 2Cor 10:10 — 1848

CONTEMPTUOUSLY
and c against the righteous .... Ps 31:18 — 937

CONTEND
neither c with them in battle .... Deut 2:9 — 1624
it, and c with him in battle .... Deut 2:24 — 1624
If he will c with him, he cannot .... Job 9:3 — 7378
will ye c for God .... Job 13:8 — 7378
such as keep the law c with them .... Prov 28:4 — 1624
neither may he c with him that is .... Eccl 6:10 — 1777
for I will c with him that .... Is 49:25 — 7378

who will c with me .... Is 50:8 — 7378
For I will not c for ever.......................... Is 57:16 — 7378
then how canst thou c with horses .... Jer 12:5 — 8474
the voice of them that c with me .... Jer 18:19 — 3401
the Lord GOD called to c by fire .... Amos 7:4 — 7378
c thou before the mountains, and .... Mic 6:1 — 7378
c for the faith which was once............... Jude 3 — 1864

CONTENDED
Then c I with the rulers, and said.......... Neh 13:11 — 7378
Then I c with the nobles of Judah.......... Neh 13:17 — 7378
I c with them, and cursed them, and...... Neh 13:25 — 7378
maidservant, when they c with me .... Job 31:13 — 7378
them, even them that c with thee .... Is 41:12 — 4695
of the circumcision c with him .... Acts 11:2 — 1252

CONTENDEST
shew me wherefore thou c with me .... Job 10:2 — 7378

CONTENDETH
Shall he that c with the Almighty.......... Job 40:2 — 7378
If a wise man c with a foolish .... Prov 29:9 — 8199
contend with him that c with thee .... Is 49:25 — 3401

CONTENDING
when c with the devil he disputed .... Jude 9 — 1252

CONTENT
And his brethren were c .... Gen 37:27 — 8085
Moses was c to dwell with the man .... Ex 2:21 — 2974
Moses heard that, he was c .... Lev 10:20 — 3190,5869
would to God we had been c .... Josh 7:7 — 2974
the Levite was c to dwell with .... Judg 17:11 — 2974
had said unto the man, Be c .... Judg 19:6 — 2974
And Naaman said, Be c, take two .... 2Kin 5:23 — 2974
And one said, Be c, I pray thee, ... 2Kin 6:3 — 2974
Now therefore be c, look upon me......... Job 6:28 — 2974
neither will he rest c, though .... Prov 6:35 — 14
Pilate, willing to c the people ... Mk 15:15 — 2425,3588,4160
and be c with your wages...................... Lk 3:14 — 714
state I am, therewith to be c .... Phil 4:11 — 842
and raiment let us be therewith c .... 1Ti 6:8 — 714
be c with such things as ye have .... Heb 13:5 — 714
not c therewith, neither doth he .... 3Jn 10 — 714

CONTENTION
Only by pride cometh c......................... Prov 13:10 — 4683
therefore leave off c, before it .... Prov 17:14 — 7379
A fool's lips enter into c .... Prov 18:6 — 7379
the scorner, and c shall go out .... Prov 22:10 — 4066
a man of c to the whole earth .... Jer 15:10 — 4066
are that raise up strife and c .... Hab 1:3 — 4066
the c was so sharp between them, ... Acts 15:39 — 3948
The one preach Christ of c.................... Phil 1:16 — 2052
you the gospel of God with much c .... 1Th 2:2 — 73

CONTENTIONS
The lot causeth c to cease .... Prov 18:18 — 4079
their c are like the bars of a.................. Prov 18:19 — 4079
the c of a wife are a continual............... Prov 19:13 — 4079
who hath c .... Prov 23:29 — 4079
Chloe, that there are c among you .... 1Cor 1:11 — 2054
questions, and genealogies, and c........ Titus 3:9 — 2054

CONTENTIOUS
in the wilderness, than with a c .... Prov 21:19 — 4066
so is a c man to kindle strife .... Prov 26:21 — 4066
rainy day and a c woman are alike .... Prov 27:15 — 4066
But unto them that are c, and do.... Rom 2:8 — 1537,2052
But if any man seem to be c .... 1Cor 11:16 — 5380

CONTENTMENT
godliness with c is great gain .... 1Ti 6:6 — 841

CONTINUAL
This shall be a c burnt offering............. Ex 29:42 — 8548
the c bread shall be thereon.................. Num 4:7 — 8548
by day, for a c burnt offering .... Num 28:3 — 8548
It is a c burnt offering, which .... Num 28:6 — 8548
beside the c burnt offering, and .... Num 28:10 — 8548
beside the c burnt offering, and .... Num 28:15 — 8548
which is for a c burnt offering .... Num 28:23 — 8548
beside the c burnt offering..................... Num 28:24 — 8548
them beside the c burnt offering .... Num 28:31 — 8548
the c burnt offering, and the meat .... Num 29:11 — 8548
beside the c burnt offering, his .... Num 29:16 — 8548
beside the c burnt offering, and .... Num 29:19 — 8548
beside the c burnt offering, and .... Num 29:22 — 8548
beside the c burnt offering, his .... Num 29:25 — 8548
beside the c burnt offering, and .... Num 29:28 — 8548
beside the c burnt offering, his .... Num 29:31 — 8548
beside the c burnt offering, his .... Num 29:34 — 8548
beside the c burnt offering, and .... Num 29:38 — 8548
his allowance was a c allowance .... 2Kin 25:30 — 8548
for the c shewbread, and for the .... 2Chr 2:4 — 8548
offered the c burnt offering................... Ezr 3:5 — 8548

for the c meat offering, and for .... Neh 10:33   8548
for the c burnt offering, of the .... Neh 10:33   8548
of a merry heart hath a c feast .... Prov 15:15   8548
of a wife are a c dropping .... Prov 19:13   2956
A c dropping in a very rainy day .... Prov 27:15   1115,5627
people in wrath with a c stroke .... Is 14:6
of Luhith c weeping shall go up .... Jer 48:5
there was a c diet given him of .... Jer 52:34   8548
sever out men of c employment .... Eze 39:14   8548
morning for a c burnt offering .... Eze 46:15   8548
by her c coming she weary me ..... Lk 18:5   1519,5056
heaviness and c sorrow in my heart....... Rom 9:2   88

CONTINUALLY

of his heart was only evil c .... Gen 6:5   3605,3117
returned from off the earth c .... Gen 8:3   1980,7725
the waters decreased c until the .... Gen 8:5   1980
for a memorial before the LORD c.... Ex 28:29   8548
upon his heart before the LORD c.... Ex 28:30   8548
of the first year day by day c .... Ex 29:38   8548
to cause the lamps to burn c .... Lev 24:2   8548
the morning before the LORD c .... Lev 24:3   8548
candlestick before the LORD c .... Lev 24:4   8548
set it in order before the LORD c .... Lev 24:8   8548
the ark of the LORD went on c .... Josh 6:13   1980
and Saul became David's enemy c . 1Sa 18:29   3605,3117
shalt eat bread at my table c 2Sa 9:7   8548
for he did eat c at the king's 2Sa 9:13   8548
people increased c with Absalom 2Sa 15:12   1980
before me c in the room of Joab.... 2Sa 19:13   3605,3117
which stand c before the 1Kin 10:8   8548
man of God, which passeth by us c....... 2Kin 4:9   8548
he did eat bread c before him all...... 2Kin 25:29   8548
the priests with trumpets c 1Chr 16:6   8548
and his strength, seek his face c 1Chr 16:11   8548
to minister before the ark c 1Chr 16:37   8548
of the burnt offering c morning 1Chr 16:40   8548
unto them, c before the LORD 1Chr 23:31   8548
which stand c before thee 2Chr 9:7   8548
Rehoboam and Jeroboam c 2Chr 12:15   3605,3117
LORD c all the days of Jehoiada 2Chr 24:14   8548
Thus did Job c.. Job 1:5   3605,3117
his praise shall c be in my mouth .... Ps 34:1   8548
yea, let them say c, Let the LORD .... Ps 35:27   8548
halt, and my sorrow is c before me........ Ps 38:17   8548
and thy truth c preserve me .... Ps 40:11   8544
such as love thy salvation say c............ Ps 40:16   8548
while they c say unto me, Where .... Ps 42:3   3605,3117
My confusion is c before me .... Ps 44:15   3605,3117
to have been c before me .... Ps 50:8   8548
the goodness of God endureth c ..... Ps 52:1   3605,3117
melt away as waters which run c........... Ps 58:7
and make their loins c to shake .... Ps 69:23   8548
such as love thy salvation say c .... Ps 70:4   8548
whereunto I may c resort .... Ps 71:3   8548
my praise shall be c of thee .... Ps 71:6   8548
But I will hope c, and will yet .... Ps 71:14   8548
also shall be made for him c .... Ps 72:15   8548
Nevertheless I am c with thee .... Ps 73:23   8548
rise up against thee increaseth c .... Ps 74:23   8548
Let his children be c vagabonds .... Ps 109:10
Let them be before the LORD c .... Ps 109:15   8548
a girdle wherewith he is girded c.......... Ps 109:19   8548
shall I keep thy law c for ever .... Ps 119:44   8548
My soul is c in my hand .... Ps 119:109   8548
have respect unto thy statutes c .... Ps 119:117   8548
c are they gathered together for ..... Ps 140:2   3605,3117
his heart, he deviseth mischief c........... Prov 6:14   6256
Bind them c upon thine heart, and .... Prov 6:21   8548
it whirleth about c, and the wind........... Eccl 1:6
I stand c upon the watchtower in .... Is 21:8
thy walls are c before me .... Is 49:16   8548
hast feared c every day because .... Is 51:13   8548
my name c every day is blasphemed...... Is 52:5   8548
And the LORD shall guide thee c .... Is 58:11   8548
thy gates shall be open c .... Is 60:11   8548
me to anger c to my face .... Is 65:3   8548
before me c is grief and wounds............ Jer 6:7   8548
offerings, and to do sacrifice c .... Jer 33:18   3605,3117
he did c eat bread before him all .... Jer 52:33   8548
a meat offering c by a perpetual........... Eze 46:14   8548
Thy God whom thou servest c .... Dan 6:16   8411
is thy God, whom thou servest c............ Dan 6:20   8411
they have committed whoredom c.......... Hos 4:18
and judgment, and wait on thy God c ... Hos 12:6   8548
so shall all the heathen drink c .... Obad 16   8548
hath not thy wickedness passed c.......... Nah 3:19   8548
not spare c to slay the nations .... Hab 1:17   8548
were c in the temple, praising and.... Lk 24:53   1725
will give ourselves c to prayer.............. Acts 6:4   4342
of them that waited on him c .... Acts 10:7   4342

attending c upon this very thing............ Rom 13:6   4342
abideth a priest c .... Heb 7:3   1519,1336
year c make the comers thereunto.. Heb 10:1   1519,1336
the sacrifice of praise to God c............. Heb 13:15   1275

CONTINUANCE

even great plagues, and of long c .... Deut 28:59   539
and sore sicknesses, and of long c......... Deut 28:59   539
which in c were fashioned, when .... Ps 139:16   3117
in those is c, and we shall be .... Is 64:5   5769
To them who by patient c in well .... Rom 2:7   5281

CONTINUE

if he c a day or two, he shall .... Ex 21:21   5975
she shall then c in the blood of .... Lev 12:4   3427
she shall c in the blood of her .... Lev 12:5   3427
you c following the LORD your God 1Sa 12:14   1961
But now thy kingdom shall not c........... 1Sa 13:14   6965
that it may c for ever before 2Sa 7:29   1961
That the LORD may c his word 1Kin 2:4   6965
neither shall his substance c .... Job 15:29   6965
doth not mine eye c in their .... Job 17:2   3885
O c thy lovingkindness unto them .... Ps 36:10   4900
their houses shall c for ever .... Ps 49:11
children of thy servants shall c .... Ps 102:28   7931
They c this day according to .... Ps 119:91   5975
that c until night, till wine .... Is 5:11   309
vessel, that they may c many days .... Jer 32:14   5975
he shall c more years than the .... Dan 11:8   5975
because they c with me now three ..... Mt 15:32   4357
If ye c in my word, then are ye .... Jn 8:31   3306
c ye in my love .... Jn 15:9   3306
persuaded them to c in the grace.......... Acts 13:43   1961
exhorting them to c in the faith .... Acts 14:22   1696
I c unto this day, witnessing .... Acts 26:22   2476
Shall we c in sin, that grace may .... Rom 6:1   1961
if thou c in his goodness .... Rom 11:22   1961
of the gospel might c with you .... Gal 2:5   1265
abide and c with you all for your .... Phil 1:25   4839
If ye c in the faith grounded and .... Col 1:23   1961
C in prayer, and watch in the same ...... Col 4:2   4342
if they c in faith and charity and 1Ti 2:15   3306
c in them 1Ti 4:16   1961
But c thou in the things which 2Ti 3:14   3306
suffered to c by reason of death .... Heb 7:23   3887
Let brotherly love c .... Heb 13:1   3306
c there a year, and buy and sell, ... Jas 4:13   4160
all things c as they were from 2Pet 3:4   1265
you, ye also shall c in the Son 1Jn 2:24   3306
was given unto him to c forty .... Rev 13:5   4160
cometh, he must c a short space .... Rev 17:10   3306

CONTINUED

and they c a season in ward .... Gen 40:4   1961
Asher c on the sea shore, and .... Judg 5:17   3427
the country of Moab, and c there .... Ruth 1:2   1961
hath c even from the morning................ Ruth 2:7   5975
as she c praying before the LORD,.......... 1Sa 1:12   7235
the ark of the LORD c in the 2Sa 6:11   3427
they c three years without war 1Kin 22:1   3427
all this c until the burnt 2Chr 29:28
also I c in the work of this wall .... Neh 5:16   2388
Moreover Job c his parable .... Job 27:1   3254
Moreover Job c his parable .... Job 29:1   3254
his name shall be c as long as .... Ps 72:17   5125
Daniel c even unto the first year .... Dan 1:21   1961
c all night in prayer to God .... Lk 6:12   1273
Ye are they which have c with me ..... Lk 22:28   1265
they c there not many days .... Jn 2:12   3306
So when they c asking him .... Jn 8:7   1961
there c with his disciples .... Jn 11:54   1304
These all c with one accord in .... Acts 1:14   4342
And they c stedfastly in the .... Acts 2:42   4342
he c with Philip, and wondered.............. Acts 8:13   4342
But Peter c knocking .... Acts 12:16   1961
Barnabas c in Antioch, teaching .... Acts 15:35   1304
he c there a year and six months,.......... Acts 18:11   2523
this c by the space of two years .... Acts 19:10   1096
c his speech until midnight .... Acts 20:7   3905
c fasting, having taken nothing .... Acts 27:33   1300
because they c not in my covenant .... Heb 8:9   1696
would no doubt have c with us 1Jn 2:19   3306

CONTINUETH

fleeth also as a shadow, and c not .... Job 14:2   5975
Cursed is every one that c not in.......... Gal 3:10   1696
c in supplications and prayers 1Ti 5:5   4357
But this man, because he c ever .... Heb 7:24   3306
c therein, he being not a .... Jas 1:25   3887

CONTINUING

forth with fury, a c whirlwind .... Jer 30:23   1641
c daily with one accord in the................ Acts 2:46   4342

c instant in prayer .... Rom 12:12   4342
For here have we no *c* city .... Heb 13:14   3306

CONTRADICTING
which were spoken by Paul, *c* .... Acts 13:45   483

CONTRADICTION
without all *c* the less is blessed .... Heb 7:7   485
such of sinners against himself .... Heb 12:3   485

CONTRARIWISE
So that *c* ye ought rather to 2Cor 2:7   5121
But *c*, when they saw that the .... Gal 2:7   5121
but *c* blessing 1Pet 3:9   5121

CONTRARY
And if ye walk *c* unto me, and will .... Lev 26:21   7147
things, but will walk *c* unto me .... Lev 26:23   7147
Then will I also walk *c* unto you .... Lev 26:24   7147
unto me, but walk *c* unto me .... Lev 26:27   7147
Then I will walk *c* unto you also .... Lev 26:28   7147
also they have walked *c* unto me .... Lev 26:40   7147
I also have walked *c* unto them .... Lev 26:41   7147
(though it was turned to the *c* .... Est 9:1
the *c* is in thee from other women .... Eze 16:34   2016
unto thee, therefore thou art *c* .... Eze 16:34   2016
for the wind was *c* .... Mt 14:24   1727
for the wind was *c* unto them .... Mk 6:48   1727
these all do *c* to the decrees of .... Acts 17:7   561
men to worship God *c* to the law .... Acts 18:13   3844
me to be smitten *c* to the law .... Acts 23:3   3891
things *c* to the name of Jesus of .... Acts 26:9   1727
Cyprus, because the winds were *c* .... Acts 27:4   1727
wert graffed *c* to nature into a .... Rom 11:24   3844
offences *c* to the doctrine which .... Rom 16:17   3844
these are *c* the one to the other .... Gal 5:17   480
was against us, which was *c* to us .... Col 2:14   5227
not God, and are *c* to all men 1Th 2:15   1727
thing that is *c* to sound doctrine 1Ti 1:10   480
is of the *c* part may be ashamed .... Titus 2:8   1727

CONTRIBUTION
Achaia to make a certain *c* for .... Rom 15:26   2842

CONTRITE
saveth such as be of a *c* spirit .... Ps 34:18   1793
a *c* heart, O God, thou wilt not .... Ps 51:17   1794
with him also that is of a *c* .... Is 57:15   1793
to revive the heart of the *c* ones .... Is 57:15   1792
of a *c* spirit, and trembleth at my .... Is 66:2   5223

CONTROVERSIES
judgment of the LORD, and for *c* 2Chr 19:8   7379

CONTROVERSY
matters of *c* within thy gates .... Deut 17:8   7379
the men, between whom the *c* is .... Deut 19:17   7379
and by their word shall every *c* .... Deut 21:5   7379
If there be a *c* between men .... Deut 25:1   7379
that when any man that had a *c* 2Sa 15:2   7379
of recompences for the *c* of Zion .... Is 34:8   7379
LORD hath a *c* with the nations .... Jer 25:31   7379
in *c* they shall stand in judgment .... Eze 44:24   7379
for the LORD hath a *c* with the .... Hos 4:1   7379
The LORD hath also a *c* with Judah .... Hos 12:2   7379
ye, O mountains, the LORD's *c* .... Mic 6:2   7379
the LORD hath a *c* with his people .... Mic 6:2   7379
without *c* great is the mystery of 1Ti 3:16   3672

CONVENIENT
feed me with food *c* for me .... Prov 30:8   2706
c for thee to go, thither go .... Jer 40:4   3477
it seemeth *c* unto thee to go .... Jer 40:5   3477
when a *c* day was come, that Herod ...... Mk 6:21   2121
when I have a *c* season, I will .... Acts 24:25   2540
do those things which are not *c* .... Rom 1:28   2520
come when he shall have *c* time 1Cor 16:12   2119
nor jesting, which are not *c* .... Eph 5:4   433
to enjoin thee that which is *c* .... Philem 8   433

CONVENIENTLY
sought how he might *c* betray him .... Mk 14:11   2122

CONVERSANT
strangers that were *c* among them .... Josh 8:35   1980
as long as we were *c* with them 1Sa 25:15   1980

CONVERSATION
to slay such as be of upright *c* .... Ps 37:14   1870
his *c* aright will I shew the .... Ps 50:23   1870
we have had our *c* in the world 2Cor 1:12   390
For ye have heard of my *c* in time .... Gal 1:13   391
c in times past in the lusts of .... Eph 2:3   390
the former *c* the old man, which .... Eph 4:22   391
Only let your *c* be as it becometh .... Phil 1:27   4176
For our *c* is in heaven .... Phil 3:20   4175
of the believers, in word, in *c* 1Ti 4:12   391

Let your *c* be without .... Heb 13:5   5158
considering the end of their *c* .... Heb 13:7   391
good *c* his works with meekness of .... Jas 3:13   391
so be ye holy in all manner of *c* 1Pet 1:15   391
from your vain *c* received by 1Pet 1:18   391
Having your *c* honest among the 1Pet 2:12   391
word be won by the *c* of the wives 1Pet 3:1   391
your chaste *c* coupled with fear 1Pet 3:2   391
accuse your good *c* in Christ 1Pet 3:16   391
with the filthy *c* of the wicked 2Pet 2:7   391
ought ye to be in all holy *c* 2Pet 3:11   391

CONVERSION
declaring the *c* of the Gentiles .... Acts 15:3   1995

CONVERT
understand with their heart, and *c* .... Is 6:10   7725
err from the truth, and one *c* him .... Jas 5:19   1994

CONVERTED
and sinners shall be *c* unto thee .... Ps 51:13   7725
of the sea shall be *c* unto thee .... Is 60:5   2015
with their heart, and should be *c* .... Mt 13:15   1994
I say unto you, Except ye be *c* .... Mt 18:3   4762
lest at any time they should be *c* .... Mk 4:12   1994
and when thou art *c*, strengthen .... Lk 22:32   1994
with their heart, and be *c* .... Jn 12:40   1994
Repent ye therefore, and be *c* .... Acts 3:19   1994
with their heart, and should be *c* .... Acts 28:27   1994

CONVERTETH
that he which *c* the sinner from .... Jas 5:20   1994

CONVERTING
the LORD is perfect, *c* the soul .... Ps 19:7   7725

CONVERTS
and her *c* with righteousness .... Is 1:27   7725

CONVEY
I will *c* them by sea in floats 1Kin 5:9   7760
that they may *c* me over till I .... Neh 2:7   5674

CONVEYED
for Jesus had *c* himself away .... Jn 5:13   1593

CONVICTED
being *c* by their own conscience, ... Jn 8:9   1651

CONVINCE
to exhort and to *c* the gainsayers .... Titus 1:9   1651
to *c* all that are ungodly among .... Jude 15   1827

CONVINCED
there was none of you that *c* Job .... Job 32:12   3198
For he mightily *c* the Jews .... Acts 18:28   1246
he is *c* of all, he is judged of 1Cor 14:24   1651
are *c* of the law as transgressors .... Jas 2:9   1651

CONVINCETH
Which of you *c* me of sin .... Jn 8:46   1651

CONVOCATION
day there shall be an holy *c* .... Ex 12:16   4744
there shall be an holy *c* to you .... Ex 12:16   4744
is the sabbath of rest, an holy *c* .... Lev 23:3   4744
first day ye shall have an holy *c* .... Lev 23:7   4744
in the seventh day is an holy *c* .... Lev 23:8   4744
that it may be an holy *c* unto you .... Lev 23:21   4744
of blowing of trumpets, an holy *c* .... Lev 23:24   4744
it shall be an holy *c* unto you .... Lev 23:27   4744
the first day shall be an holy *c* .... Lev 23:35   4744
day shall be an holy *c* unto you .... Lev 23:36   4744
the first day shall be an holy *c* .... Num 28:18   4744
day ye shall have an holy *c* .... Num 28:25   4744
be out, ye shall have an holy *c* .... Num 28:26   4744
month, ye shall have an holy *c* .... Num 29:1   4744
of this seventh month an holy *c* .... Num 29:7   4744

CONVOCATIONS
ye shall proclaim to be holy *c* .... Lev 23:2   4744
feasts of the LORD, even holy *c* .... Lev 23:4   4744
ye shall proclaim to be holy *c* .... Lev 23:37   4744

COOK
And Samuel said unto the *c* 1Sa 9:23   2876
the *c* took up the shoulder, and 1Sa 9:24   2876

COOKS
to be confectionaries, and to be *c* 1Sa 8:13   2876

COOL
in the garden in the *c* of the day .... Gen 3:8   7307
finger in water, and *c* my tongue .... Lk 16:24   2711

COOS (co'-os) *An island near Cnidus.*
with a straight course unto *C* .... Acts 21:1   2972

COPIED
of Hezekiah king of Judah *c* out .... Prov 25:1   6275

COPING

from the foundation unto the *c* 1Kin 7:9   2947

COPPER

and two vessels of fine *c*, ...Ezr 8:27   5178

COPPERSMITH

Alexander the *c* did me much evil............2Ti 4:14   *5471*

COPULATION

man's seed of *c* go out from him............Lev 15:16   7902
skin, whereon is the seed of *c* ....Lev 15:17   7902
whom man shall lie with seed of *c* ....Lev 15:18   7902

COPY

that he shall write him a *c* of ....Deut 17:18   4932
stones a *c* of the law of Moses ....Josh 8:32   4932
This is the *c* of the letter that ....Ezr 4:11   6573
Now when the *c* of king ....Ezr 4:23   6573
The *c* of the letter that Tatnai, ...Ezr 5:6   6573
Now this is the *c* of the letter ....Ezr 7:11   6573
The *c* of the writing for a ....Est 3:14   6572
Also he gave him the *c* of the ....Est 4:8   6572
The *c* of the writing for a ....Est 8:13   6572

COR

tenth part of a bath out of the *c*............Eze 45:14   3734

CORAL

No mention shall be made of *c* ....Job 28:18   7215
work, and fine linen, and *c* ....Eze 27:16   7215

CORBAN (cor'-ban) *A sacred gift.*
to his father or mother, It is *C* ....Mk 7:11   *2878*

CORD

down by a *c* through the window ....Josh 2:15   2256
Because he hath loosed my *c*...................Job 30:11   3499
or his tongue with a *c* which thou ....Job 41:1   2256
a threefold *c* is not quickly ....Eccl 4:12   2339
Or ever the silver *c* be loosed...............Eccl 12:6   2256
have none that shall cast a *c* by ....Mic 2:5   2256

CORDS

the pins of the court, and their *c* ....Ex 35:18   4340
hanging for the court gate, his *c* ....Ex 39:40   4340
the *c* of it for all the service...................Num 3:26   4340
and their pins, and their *c* ....Num 3:37   4340
the altar round about, and their *c* ....Num 4:26   4340
and their pins, and their *c* ....Num 4:32   4340
And they bound him with two new *c* ....Judg 15:13   5688
the *c* that were upon his arms ....Judg 15:14   5688
fastened with *c* of fine linen ....Est 1:6   2256
be holden in *c* of affliction ....Job 36:8   2256
and cast away their *c* from us.................Ps 2:3   5688
bind the sacrifice with *c* ....Ps 118:27   5688
cut asunder the *c* of the wicked ....Ps 129:4   5688
have hid a snare for me, and *c*...............Ps 140:5   2256
be holden with the *c* of his sins ....Prov 5:22   2256
draw iniquity with *c* of vanity ....Is 5:18   2256
any of the *c* thereof be broken ....Is 33:20   2256
spare not, lengthen thy *c*...................Is 54:2   4340
spoiled, and all my *c* are broken ....Jer 10:20   4340
and they let down Jeremiah with *c*...........Jer 38:6   2256
let them down by *c* into the ....Jer 38:11   2256
under thine armholes under the *c*...........Jer 38:12   2256
So they drew up Jeremiah with *c* ....Jer 38:13   2256
of rich apparel, bound with *c* ....Eze 27:24   2256
I drew them with *c* of a man ....Hos 11:4   2256
he had made a scourge of small *c* ....Jn 2:15   4979

CORE (co'-ree) See KORAH. *Greek form of Korah.*
perished in the gainsaying of *C* ....Jude 11   *2879*

CORIANDER

and it was like *c* seed, white ....Ex 16:31   1407
And the manna was as *c* seed ....Num 11:7   1407

CORINTH (cor'-inth) See CORINTHIANS, CORINTHUS.
Capital of Achaia.
from Athens, and came to *C* ....Acts 18:1   *2882*
that, while Apollos was at *C* ....Acts 19:1   *2882*
the church of God which is at *C* 1Cor 1:1   *2882*
the church of God which is at *C* 2Cor 1:1   *2882*
you I came not as yet unto *C* 2Cor 1:23   *2882*
Erastus abode at *C*................................2Ti 4:20   *2882*

CORINTHIANS (co-rin'-the-uns) *Residents of Corinth.*
many of the *C* hearing believed, ...Acts 18:8   *2881*
The first epistle to the *C* was ....1Cor *s*   *2881*
O ye *C*, our mouth is open unto 2Cor 6:11   *2881*
the *C* was written from Philippi ....2Cor *s*   *2881*

CORINTHUS (co-rin'-thus) See CORINTH. *Same as Corinth.*
Written to the Romans from *C* ....Rom *s*   *2882*

CORMORANT

And the little owl, and the *c* ....Lev 11:17   7994
and the gier eagle, and the *c*...............Deut 14:17   7994
But the *c* and the bittern shall ....Is 34:11   6893
both the *c* and the bittern shall ....Zeph 2:14   6893

CORN

of the earth, and plenty of *c* ....Gen 27:28   1715
and with *c* and wine have I ....Gen 27:37   1715
seven ears of *c* came up upon one ....Gen 41:5
lay up *c* under the hand of ....Gen 41:35   1250
Joseph gathered *c* as the sand of ....Gen 41:49   1250
into Egypt to Joseph for to buy *c*...........Gen 41:57
saw that there was *c* in Egypt ....Gen 42:1   7668
heard that there is *c* in Egypt ....Gen 42:2   7668
went down to buy *c* in Egypt ....Gen 42:3   1250
to buy *c* among those that came ....Gen 42:5
carry *c* for the famine of your ....Gen 42:19   7668
to fill their sacks with *c* ....Gen 42:25   1250
they laded their asses with the *c* ....Gen 42:26   7668
when they had eaten up the *c* ....Gen 43:2   7668
of the youngest, and his *c* money ....Gen 44:2   7668
and ten she asses laden with *c* ....Gen 45:23   1250
for the *c* which they bought...................Gen 47:14   7668
thorns, so that the stacks of *c*...............Ex 22:6
or the standing *c*, or the field ....Ex 22:6   7054
green ears of *c* dried by the fire ....Lev 2:14
even *c* beaten out of full ears ....Lev 2:14   1643
it, part of the beaten *c* thereof ....Lev 2:16   1643
eat neither bread, nor parched *c* ....Lev 23:14
were the *c* of the threshingfloor ....Num 18:27   1715
and the fruit of thy land, thy *c* ....Deut 7:13   1715
that thou mayest gather in thy *c* ....Deut 11:14   1715
thy gates the tithe of thy *c* ....Deut 12:17   1715
name there, the tithe of thy *c* ....Deut 14:23   1715
to put the sickle to the *c*...................Deut 16:9   7054
that thou hast gathered in thy *c* ....Deut 16:13   1637
The firstfruit also of thy *c*...................Deut 18:4   1715
the standing *c* of thy neighbour ....Deut 23:25   7054
unto thy neighbour's standing *c* ....Deut 23:25   7054
the ox when he treadeth out the *c*...........Deut 25:4
shall not leave thee either *c* ....Deut 28:51   1715
Jacob shall be upon a land of *c* ....Deut 33:28   1715
they did eat of the old *c* of the ....Josh 5:11   5669
parched *c* in the selfsame day ....Josh 5:11
eaten of the old *c* of the land ....Josh 5:12   5669
the standing *c* of the Philistines ....Judg 15:5   7054
shocks, and also the standing *c*...........Judg 15:5   7054
glean ears of *c* after him in ....Ruth 2:2
and he reached her parched *c* ....Ruth 2:14
down at the end of the heap of *c*...........Ruth 3:7   6194
an ephah of this parched *c* 1Sa 17:17
and five measures of parched *c* 1Sa 25:18
mouth, and spread ground *c* thereon 2Sa 17:19   7383
and barley, and flour, and parched *c* 2Sa 17:28
full ears of *c* in the husk 2Kin 4:42   3759
like your own land, a land of *c*...........2Kin 18:32   1715
as *c* blasted before it be grown...............2Kin 19:26
in abundance the firstfruits of *c* 2Chr 31:5   1715
also for the increase of *c* 2Chr 32:28   1715
therefore we take up *c* for them ....Neh 5:2   1715
and houses, that we might buy *c* ....Neh 5:3   1715
might exact of them money and *c* ....Neh 5:10   1715
part of the money, and of the *c*...........Neh 5:11   1715
shall bring the offering of the *c* ....Neh 10:39   1715
vessels, and the tithes of the *c* ....Neh 13:5   1715
all Judah the tithe of the *c*...................Neh 13:12   1715
like as a shock of *c* cometh in in ....Job 5:26
reap every one his *c* in the field ....Job 24:6   1098
off as the tops of the ears of *c* ....Job 24:24
good liking, they grow up with *c* ....Job 39:4   1250
than in the time that their *c* ....Ps 4:7   1715
thou preparest them *c*, when thou ....Ps 65:9   1715
also are covered over with *c* ....Ps 65:13   1250
of *c* in the earth upon the top of ....Ps 72:16   1250
had given them of the *c* of heaven ....Ps 78:24   1715
He that withholdeth *c*, the people ....Prov 11:26   1250
the harvestman gathereth the *c* ....Is 17:5   7054
threshing, and the *c* of my floor ....Is 21:10   1121
Bread *c* is bruised ....Is 28:28
like your own land, a land of *c*...............Is 36:17   1715
as *c* blasted before it be grown ....Is 37:27
c to be meat for thine enemies...............Is 62:8   1715
say to their mothers, Where is *c* ....Lam 2:12
and I will call for the *c*, and will ....Eze 36:29   1715
did not know that I gave her *c* ....Hos 2:8   1715
take away my *c* in the time ....Hos 2:9   1715
And the earth shall hear the *c* ....Hos 2:22   1715
they assemble themselves for *c* ....Hos 7:14   1715
and loveth to tread out the *c*...................Hos 10:11
they shall revive as the *c*...................Hos 14:7   1715

for the *c* is wasted	Joel 1:10	1715
for the *c* is withered	Joel 1:17	1715
people, Behold, I will send you *c*	Joel 2:19	1715
moon be gone, that we may sell *c*	Amos 8:5	7668
like as *c* is sifted in a sieve,	Amos 9:9	
upon the mountains, and upon the *c*	Hag 1:11	1715
c shall make the young men	Zec 9:17	1715
on the sabbath day through the *c*	Mt 12:1	4702
and began to pluck the ears of *c*	Mt 12:1	4719
that he went through the *c* fields	Mk 2:23	4702
they went, to pluck the ears of *c*	Mk 2:23	4719
after that the full *c* in the ear	Mk 4:28	4621
that he went through the *c* fields	Lk 6:1	4702
disciples plucked the ears of *c*	Lk 6:1	4719
Except a *c* of wheat fall into the	Jn 12:24	2848
heard that there was *c* in Egypt	Acts 7:12	4621
of the ox that treadeth out the *c*	1Cor 9:9	
the ox that treadeth out the *c*	1Ti 5:18	

CORNELIUS (*cor-ne′-le-us*) *A Roman centurion converted by Peter.*

certain man in Caesarea called *C*	Acts 10:1	2883
in to him, and saying unto him, *C*	Acts 10:3	2883
which spake unto *C* was departed	Acts 10:7	2883
C had made enquiry for Simon's	Acts 10:17	2883
which were sent unto him from *C*	Acts 10:21	2883
C the centurion, a just man, and	Acts 10:22	2883
C waited for them, and had called	Acts 10:24	2883
C met him, and fell down at his	Acts 10:25	2883
C said, Four days ago I was	Acts 10:30	2883
And said, *C*, thy prayer is heard,	Acts 10:31	2883

CORNER

which is toward the north *c*	Ex 36:25	6285
shave off the *c* of their beard	Lev 21:5	6285
compassed the *c* of the sea	Josh 18:14	6285
from the right *c* of the temple to	2Kin 11:11	3802
to the left *c* of the temple	2Kin 11:11	3802
gate of Ephraim unto the *c* gate	2Kin 14:13	6438
the gate of Ephraim to the *c* gate	2Chr 25:23	6437
towers in Jerusalem at the *c* gate	2Chr 26:9	6438
altars in every *c* of Jerusalem	2Chr 28:24	6438
of the wall, even unto the *c*	Neh 3:24	6438
and to the going up of the *c*	Neh 3:31	6438
between the going up of the *c*	Neh 3:32	6438
or who laid the *c* stone thereof	Job 38:6	6438
is become the head stone of the *c*	Ps 118:22	6438
our daughters may be as *c* stones	Ps 144:12	2106
through the street near her *c*	Prov 7:8	6438
and lieth in wait at every *c*	Prov 7:12	6438
to dwell in a *c* of the housetop	Prov 21:9	6438
to dwell in the *c* of the housetop	Prov 25:24	6438
a tried stone, a precious *c* stone	Is 28:16	6438
be removed into a *c* any more	Is 30:20	3671
Hananeel unto the gate of the *c*	Jer 31:38	6438
unto the *c* of the horse gate	Jer 31:40	6438
and shall devour the *c* of Moab	Jer 48:45	6285
not take of thee a stone for a *c*	Jer 51:26	6438
in every *c* of the court there was	Eze 46:21	4742
in Samaria in the *c* of a bed	Amos 3:12	6285
Out of him came forth the *c*	Zec 10:4	6438
the first gate, unto the *c* gate	Zec 14:10	6434
same is become the head of the *c*	Mt 21:42	1137
is become the head of the *c*	Mk 12:10	1137
same is become the head of the *c*	Lk 20:17	1137
which is become the head of the *c*	Acts 4:11	1137
this thing was not done in a *c*	Acts 26:26	1137
himself being the chief *c* stone	Eph 2:20	204
I lay in Sion a chief *c* stone	1Pet 2:6	204
same is made the head of the *c*	1Pet 2:7	1137

CORNERS

and put them in the four *c* thereof	Ex 25:12	6471
four *c* that are on the four feet	Ex 25:26	6285
c of the tabernacle in the two	Ex 26:23	4742
they shall be for the two *c*	Ex 26:24	4742
of it upon the four *c* thereof	Ex 27:2	6438
rings in the four *c* thereof	Ex 27:4	7098
crown of it, by the two *c* thereof	Ex 30:4	6763
two boards made he for the *c* of	Ex 36:28	4742
did to both of them in both the *c*	Ex 36:29	4742
to be set by the four *c* of it	Ex 37:13	6471
four *c* that were in the four feet	Ex 37:13	6285
crown thereof, by the two *c* of it	Ex 37:27	6763
horns thereof on the four *c* of it	Ex 38:2	7098
wholly reap the *c* of thy field	Lev 19:9	6285
not round the *c* of your heads	Lev 19:27	6285
shalt thou mar the *c* of thy beard	Lev 19:27	6285
c of thy field when thou reapest	Lev 23:22	6285
and shall smite the *c* of Moab	Num 24:17	6285
said, I would scatter them into *c*	Deut 32:26	6284
and the four *c* thereof had	1Kin 7:30	6471

to the four *c* of one base	1Kin 7:34	6438
and didst divide them into *c*	Neh 9:22	6285
and smote the four *c* of the house	Job 1:19	6438
from the four *c* of the earth	Is 11:12	3671
and all that are in the utmost *c*	Jer 9:26	6285
and all that are in the utmost *c*	Jer 25:23	6285
them that are in the utmost *c*	Jer 49:32	6285
come upon the four *c* of the land	Eze 7:2	3671
the *c* thereof, and the length	Eze 41:22	4740
on the four *c* of the settle, and	Eze 43:20	6438
upon the four *c* of the settle of	Eze 45:19	6438
pass by the four *c* of the court	Eze 46:21	4742
In the four *c* of the court there	Eze 46:22	4742
these four *c* were of one measure	Eze 46:22	7106
bowls, and as the *c* of the altar	Zec 9:15	2106
in the *c* of the streets, that	Mt 6:5	1137
a great sheet knit at the four *c*	Acts 10:11	746
let down from heaven by four *c*	Acts 11:5	746
on the four *c* of the earth	Rev 7:1	1137

CORNET

shouting, and with sound of the *c*	1Chr 15:28	7782
sound of *c* make a joyful noise	Ps 98:6	7782
time ye hear the sound of the *c*	Dan 3:5	7162
people heard the sound of the *c*	Dan 3:7	7162
shall hear the sound of the *c*	Dan 3:10	7162
time ye hear the sound of the *c*	Dan 3:15	7162
Blow ye the *c* in Gibeah, and the	Hos 5:8	7782

CORNETS

and on timbrels, and on *c*, and on	2Sa 6:5	4517
and with trumpets, and with *c*	2Chr 15:14	7782

CORNFLOOR

hast loved a reward upon every *c*	Hos 9:1	1637,1715

CORPSE

of it, they came and took up his *c*	Mk 6:29	4430

CORPSES

behold, they were all dead *c*	2Kin 19:35	6297
behold, they were all dead *c*	Is 37:36	6297
and there is none end of their *c*	Nah 3:3	1472
they stumble upon their *c*	Nah 3:3	1472

CORRECT

rebukes dost *c* man for iniquity	Ps 39:11	3256
the heathen, shall not he *c*	Ps 94:10	3198
C thy son, and he shall give thee	Prov 29:17	3256
Thine own wickedness shall *c* thee	Jer 2:19	3256
O LORD, *c* me, but with judgment	Jer 10:24	3256
but I will *c* thee in measure, and	Jer 30:11	3256
of thee, but *c* thee in measure	Jer 46:28	3256

CORRECTED

A servant will not be *c* by words	Prov 29:19	3256
fathers of our flesh which *c* us	Heb 12:9	3810

CORRECTETH

happy is the man whom God *c*	Job 5:17	3198
For whom the LORD loveth he *c*	Prov 3:12	3198

CORRECTION

causeth it to come, whether for *c*	Job 37:13	7626
neither be weary of his *c*	Prov 3:11	8433
as a fool to the *c* of the stocks	Prov 7:22	4148
C is grievous unto him that	Prov 15:10	4148
but the rod of *c* shall drive it	Prov 22:15	4148
Withhold not *c* from the child	Prov 23:13	4148
they received no *c*	Jer 2:30	4148
they have refused to receive *c*	Jer 5:3	4148
LORD their God, nor received *c*	Jer 7:28	4148
thou hast established them for *c*	Hab 1:12	3198
she received not *c*	Zeph 3:2	4148
for doctrine, for reproof, for *c*	2Ti 3:16	1882

CORRUPT

The earth also was *c* before God	Gen 6:11	7843
the earth, and, behold, it was *c*	Gen 6:12	7843
Lest ye *c* yourselves, and make you	Deut 4:16	7843
shall *c* yourselves, and make a	Deut 4:25	7843
ye will utterly *c* yourselves	Deut 31:29	7843
My breath is *c*, my days are	Job 17:1	2254
They are *c*, they have done	Ps 14:1	7843
are *c* because of my foolishness	Ps 38:5	4743
C are they, and have done	Ps 53:1	7843
They are *c*, and speak wickedly	Ps 73:8	4167
troubled fountain, and a *c* spring	Prov 25:26	7843
nor according to your *c* doings	Eze 20:44	7843
she was more *c* in her inordinate	Eze 23:11	7843
c words to speak before me, till	Dan 2:9	7844
covenant shall he *c* by flatteries	Dan 11:32	2610
unto the Lord a *c* thing	Mal 1:14	
I will *c* your seed, and spread	Mal 2:3	1605
earth, where moth and rust doth *c*	Mt 6:19	853
neither moth nor rust doth *c*	Mt 6:20	853

but a *c* tree bringeth forth evil.............. Mt 7:17   4550
neither can a *c* tree bring forth .... Mt 7:18   4550
the tree *c*, and his fruit *c*....................... Mt 12:33   4550
tree bringeth not forth *c* fruit .... Lk 6:43   4550
neither doth a *c* tree bring forth .... Lk 6:43   4550
communications *c* good manners 1Cor 15:33   5351
as many, which *c* the word of God........ 2Cor 2:17   2585
which is *c* according to the .... Eph 4:22   5351
Let no *c* communication proceed........... Eph 4:29   4550
disputings of men of *c* minds 1Ti 6:5   1311
men of *c* minds, reprobate 2Ti 3:8   2704
in those things they *c* themselves.......... Jude 10   5351
which did *c* the earth with her .... Rev 19:2   5351

CORRUPTED

for all flesh had *c* his way upon .... Gen 6:12   7843
the land was *c* by reason of the .... Ex 8:24   7843
land of Egypt, have *c* themselves .... Ex 32:7   7843
out of Egypt have *c* themselves .... Deut 9:12   7843
They have *c* themselves, their .... Deut 32:5   7843
c themselves more than their .... Judg 2:19   7843
thou wast *c* more than they in all .... Eze 16:47   7843
thou hast *c* thy wisdom by reason .... Eze 28:17   7843
They have deeply *c* themselves .... Hos 9:9   7843
rose early, and *c* all their doings........... Zeph 3:7   7843
ye have *c* the covenant of Levi, ... Mal 2:8   7843
wronged no man, we have *c* no man 2Cor 7:2   5351
so your minds should be *c* from 2Cor 11:3   5351
Your riches are *c*, and your .... Jas 5:2   4595

CORRUPTERS

of evildoers, children that are *c*............... Is 1:4   7843
they are all *c*... Jer 6:28   7843

CORRUPTETH

thief approacheth, neither moth *c*.......... Lk 12:33   1311

CORRUPTIBLE

into an image made like to *c* man .... Rom 1:23   5349
they do it to obtain a *c* crown 1Cor 9:25   5349
For this *c* must put on 1Cor 15:53   5349
So when this *c* shall have put on 1Cor 15:54   5349
were not redeemed with *c* things........... 1Pet 1:18   5349
Being born again, not of *c* seed 1Pet 1:23   5349
the heart, in that which is not *c* 1Pet 3:4   862

CORRUPTING

him the daughter of women, *c* her .... Dan 11:17   7843

CORRUPTION

because their *c* is in them .... Lev 22:25   4893
the right hand of the mount of *c* 2Kin 23:13   4889
I have said to *c*, Thou art my .... Job 17:14   7845
suffer thine Holy One to see *c* .... Ps 16:10   7845
still live for ever, and not see *c* .... Ps 49:9   7845
delivered it from the pit of *c* .... Is 38:17   1097
was turned in me into *c*, and I .... Dan 10:8   4889
thou brought up my life from *c* .... Jonah 2:6   7845
suffer thine Holy One to see *c* .... Acts 2:27   1312
hell, neither his flesh did see *c* .... Acts 2:31   1312
dead, now no more to return to *c* .... Acts 13:34   1312
suffer thine Holy One to see *c* .... Acts 13:35   1312
laid unto his fathers, and saw *c* .... Acts 13:36   1312
whom God raised again, saw no *c*........... Acts 13:37   1312
of *c* into the glorious liberty of .... Rom 8:21   5356
It is sown in *c* 1Cor 15:42   5356
neither doth *c* inherit 1Cor 15:50   5356
flesh shall of the flesh reap *c* .... Gal 6:8   5356
having escaped the *c* that is in 2Pet 1:4   5356
utterly perish in their own *c*................... 2Pet 2:12   5356
themselves are the servants of *c*........... 2Pet 2:19   5356

CORRUPTLY

And the people did yet *c* 2Chr 27:2   7843
We have dealt very *c* against thee .... Neh 1:7   2254

COSAM (co'-sam) *Son of Elmodam; ancestor of Jesus*
of Addi, which was the son of *C* .... Lk 3:28   2973

COST

we eaten at all of the king's *c*................. 2Sa 19:42
of that which doth *c* me nothing 2Sa 24:24   2600
offer burnt offerings without *c* 1Chr 21:24   2600
not down first, and counteth the *c* .... Lk 14:28   1160

COSTLINESS

in the sea by reason of her *c* .... Rev 18:19   5094

COSTLY

c stones, and hewed stones, to lay 1Kin 5:17   3368
All these were of *c* stones 1Kin 7:9   3368
And the foundation was of *c* stones 1Kin 7:10   3368
And above were *c* stones, after the 1Kin 7:11   3368
of ointment of spikenard, very *c*............. Jn 12:3   4186
or gold, or pearls, or *c* array 1Ti 2:9   4185

COTES

manner of beasts, and *c* for flocks.......... 2Chr 32:28   220

COTTAGE

Zion is left as a *c* in a vineyard.............. Is 1:8   5521
and shall be removed like a *c* .... Is 24:20   4412

COTTAGES

c for shepherds, and folds for............... Zeph 2:6   3741

COUCH

he went up to my *c*.................................. Gen 49:4   3326
my *c* shall ease my complaint................. Job 7:13   4904
When they *c* in their dens, and............... Job 38:40   7742
I water my *c* with my tears .... Ps 6:6   6210
of a bed, and in Damascus in a *c*............ Amos 3:12   6210
his *c* into the midst before Jesus .... Lk 5:19   2826
thee, Arise, and take up thy *c* .... Lk 5:24   2826

COUCHED

he *c* as a lion, and as an old lion............. Gen 49:9   7257
He *c*, he lay down as a lion, and .... Num 24:9   3766

COUCHES

stretch themselves upon their *c*.............. Amos 6:4   6210
and laid them on beds and *c*................... Acts 5:15   2895

COUCHETH

and for the deep that *c* beneath.............. Deut 33:13   7257

COUCHING

ass *c* down between two burdens .... Gen 49:14   7257

COUCHINGPLACE

and the Ammonites a *c* for flocks .... Eze 25:5   4769

COULD See APPENDIX.

COULDEST

and done evil things as thou *c*................. Jer 3:5   3201
them, and yet *c* not be satisfied .... Eze 16:28
c not thou watch one hour .... Mk 14:37   2480
Thou *c* have no power at all .... Jn 19:11

COULDST

seeing thou *c* reveal this secret .... Dan 2:47   3202

COULTER

every man his share, and his *c* 1Sa 13:20   855

COULTERS

for the mattocks, and for the *c*............... 1Sa 13:21   855

COUNCIL

the princes of Judah and their *c* .... Ps 68:27   7277
Raca, shall be in danger of the *c* .... Mt 5:22   4892
held a *c* against him, how they .... Mt 12:14   4824
priests, and elders, and all the *c* .... Mt 26:59   4892
all the *c* sought for witness .... Mk 14:55   4892
elders and scribes and the whole *c* .... Mk 15:1   4892
together, and led him into their *c*........... Lk 22:66   4892
priests and the Pharisees a *c* .... Jn 11:47   4892
them to go aside out of the *c* .... Acts 4:15   4892
him, and called the *c* together .... Acts 5:21   4892
them, they set them before the *c*............ Acts 5:27   4892
Then stood there up one in the *c* .... Acts 5:34   4892
from the presence of the *c* .... Acts 5:41   4892
him, and brought him to the *c* .... Acts 6:12   4892
And all that sat in the *c*, looking .... Acts 6:15   4892
priests and all their *c* to appear .... Acts 22:30   4892
Paul, earnestly beholding the *c* .... Acts 23:1   4892
Pharisees, he cried out in the *c*.............. Acts 23:6   4892
Now therefore ye with the *c* .... Acts 23:15   4892
down Paul to morrow into the *c* .... Acts 23:20   4892
I brought him forth into their *c* .... Acts 23:28   4892
in me, while I stood before the *c* .... Acts 24:20   4892
when he had conferred with the *c* .... Acts 25:12   4824

COUNCILS

they will deliver you up to the *c*............. Mt 10:17   4891
they shall deliver you up to *c* .... Mk 13:9   4891

COUNSEL

unto my voice, I will give thee *c* .... Ex 18:19   3289
who shall ask *c* for him after the .... Num 27:21
Israel, through the *c* of Balaam .... Num 31:16   1697
For they are a nation void of *c* .... Deut 32:28   6098
asked not *c* at the mouth of the .... Josh 9:14
And they said unto him, Ask *c*............... Judg 18:5
give here your advice and *c* .... Judg 20:7   6098
asked *c* of God, and said, Which of .... Judg 20:18   6098
asked *c* of the LORD, saying, ... Judg 20:23
And Saul asked of God, Shall I 1Sa 14:37
turn the *c* of Ahithophel into 2Sa 15:31   6098
for me defeat the *c* of Ahithophel........... 2Sa 15:34   6098
Give *c* among you what we shall do 2Sa 16:20   6098
the *c* of Ahithophel, which he 2Sa 16:23   6098
so was all the *c* of Ahithophel 2Sa 16:23   6098
The *c* that Ahithophel hath given 2Sa 17:7   6098

Therefore I *c* that all Israel be 2Sa 17:11   3289
The *c* of Hushai the Archite is 2Sa 17:14   6098
better than the *c* of Ahithophel 2Sa 17:14   6098
defeat the good *c* of Ahithophel 2Sa 17:14   6098
and thus did Ahithophel *c* Absalom 2Sa 17:15   3289
saw that his *c* was not followed 2Sa 17:23   6098
They shall surely ask *c* at Abel..............2Sa 20:18
let me, I pray thee, give thee *c* 1Kin 1:12   6098
he forsook the *c* of the old men 1Kin 12:8   6098
What *c* give ye that we may answer 1Kin 12:9   3289
old men's *c* that they gave him 1Kin 12:13   6098
them after the *c* of the young men 1Kin 12:14   6098
Whereupon the king took *c* 1Kin 12:28   3289
took *c* with his servants, saying, ...2Kin 6:8   3289
are but vain words,) I have *c* 2Kin 18:20   6098
also for asking *c* of one that had 1Chr 10:13
king Rehoboam took *c* with the old 2Chr 10:6   3289
What *c* give ye me to return 2Chr 10:6   3289
But he forsook the *c* which the 2Chr 10:8   6098
took *c* with the young men that 2Chr 10:8   3289
forsook the *c* of the old men 2Chr 10:13   6098
He walked also after their *c* 2Chr 22:5   6098
Art thou made of the king's *c*................2Chr 25:16   3289
and hast not hearkened unto my *c*........2Chr 25:16   6098
For the king had taken *c*, and his 2Chr 30:2   3289
the whole assembly took *c* to keep 2Chr 30:23   6098
He took *c* with his princes and his 2Chr 32:3   3289
according to the *c* of my lord ....Ezr 10:3   6098
according to the *c* of the princes ....Ezr 10:8   6098
God had brought their *c* to nought ....Neh 4:15   6098
and let us take *c* together ....Neh 6:7   3289
the *c* of the froward is carried................Job 5:13   6098
and shine upon the *c* of the wicked ....Job 10:3   6098
is wisdom and strength, he hath *c*........Job 12:13   6098
his own *c* shall cast him down ....Job 18:7   6098
the *c* of the wicked is far from ....Job 21:16   6098
but the *c* of the wicked is far ....Job 22:18   6098
waited, and kept silence at my *c*............Job 29:21   6098
c by words without knowledge ....Job 38:2   6098
that hideth *c* without knowledge ....Job 42:3   6098
not in the *c* of the ungodly....................Ps 1:1   6098
and the rulers take *c* together ....Ps 2:2   3245
long shall I take *c* in my soul ....Ps 13:2   6098
Ye have shamed the *c* of the poor ....Ps 14:6   6098
the LORD, who hath given me *c* ....Ps 16:7   3289
own heart, and fulfil all thy *c* ....Ps 20:4   6098
while they took *c* together ....Ps 31:13   3245
The LORD bringeth the *c* of the ....Ps 33:10   6098
The *c* of the LORD standeth for ....Ps 33:11   6098
We took sweet *c* together, and ....Ps 55:14   5475
from the secret *c* of the wicked ....Ps 64:2   5475
wait for my soul take *c* together ....Ps 71:10   3289
Thou shalt guide me with thy *c*..............Ps 73:24   6098
taken crafty *c* against thy people ....Ps 83:3   5475
they waited not for his *c* ....Ps 106:13   6098
they provoked him with their *c* ....Ps 106:43   6098
contemned the *c* of the most High ....Ps 107:11   6098
ye have set at nought all my *c* ....Prov 1:25   6098
They would none of my *c* ....Prov 1:30   6098
C is mine, and sound wisdom................Prov 8:14   6098
Where no *c* is, the people fall ....Prov 11:14   8458
he that hearkeneth unto *c* is wise ....Prov 12:15   6098
Without *c* purposes are ....Prov 15:22   5475
Hear *c*, and receive instruction, ...Prov 19:20   6098
nevertheless the *c* of the LORD ....Prov 19:21   6098
C in the heart of man is like ....Prov 20:5   6098
Every purpose is established by *c*............Prov 20:18   6098
nor *c* against the LORD ....Prov 21:30   6098
For by wise *c* thou shalt make thy ....Prov 24:6   8458
of a man's friend by hearty *c* ....Prov 27:9   6098
I *c* thee to keep the king's................Eccl 8:2
let the of the Holy One of........................Is 5:19   6098
have taken evil *c* against thee ....Is 7:5   3289
Take *c* together, and it shall come..........Is 8:10   6098
and understanding, the spirit of *c* ....Is 11:2   6098
Take *c*, execute judgment ....Is 16:3   6098
and I will destroy the *c* thereof ....Is 19:3   6098
the *c* of the wise counsellors of ....Is 19:11   6098
because of the *c* of the LORD of ....Is 19:17   6098
hath taken this *c* against Tyre ....Is 23:8   3289
of hosts, which is wonderful in *c*............Is 28:29   6098
to hide their *c* from the LORD ....Is 29:15   6098
saith the LORD, that take *c*....................Is 30:1   6098
they are but vain words) I have *c*............Is 36:5   6098
With whom took he *c*, and who ....Is 40:14   3289
and performeth the *c* of his ....Is 44:26   6098
yea, let them take *c* together ....Is 45:21   3289
My *c* shall stand, and I will do................Is 46:10   6098
executeth my *c* from a far country ....Is 46:11   6098
nor *c* from the wise, nor the word ....Jer 18:18   6098
all their *c* against me to slay me ....Jer 18:23   6098

I will make void the *c* of Judah ....Jer 19:7   6098
hath stood in the *c* of the LORD ....Jer 23:18   5475
But if they had stood in my *c*................Jer 23:22   5475
Great in *c*, and mighty in work................Jer 32:19   6098
and if I give thee *c*, wilt thou..................Jer 38:15   3289
is *c* perished from the prudent ....Jer 49:7   6098
Therefore hear the *c* of the LORD ....Jer 49:20   6098
Babylon hath taken *c* against you ....Jer 49:30   6098
hear ye the *c* of the LORD......................Jer 50:45   6098
priest, and *c* from the ancients ....Eze 7:26   6098
give wicked *c* in this city ....Eze 11:2   6098
Then Daniel answered with *c*................Dan 2:14   5843
let my *c* be acceptable unto thee, ...Dan 4:27   4431
My people ask *c* at their stocks, ...Hos 4:12
shall be ashamed of his own *c* ....Hos 10:6   6098
neither understand they his *c*................Mic 4:12   6098
the *c* of peace shall be between ....Zec 6:13   6098
took *c* how they might entangle ....Mt 22:15   4824
elders of the people took *c* ....Mt 27:1   4824
And they took *c*, and bought with ....Mt 27:7   4824
with the elders, and had taken *c*..........Mt 28:12   4824
straightway took *c* with the ....Mk 3:6   4824
lawyers rejected the *c* of God..................Lk 7:30   1012
same had not consented to the *c* ....Lk 23:51   1012
took *c* together for to put him to ....Jn 11:53   4823
which gave *c* to the Jews, that it ....Jn 18:14   4823
delivered by the determinate *c*................Acts 2:23   1012
thy *c* determined before to be ....Acts 4:28   1012
the heart, and took *c* to slay them ....Acts 5:33   1011
for if this *c* or this work be of ....Acts 5:38   1012
the Jews took *c* to kill him ....Acts 9:23   4823
declare unto you all the *c* of God............Acts 20:27   1012
the soldiers' *c* was to kill the ....Acts 27:42   1012
after the *c* of his own will ....Eph 1:11   1012
promise the immutability of his *c* ....Heb 6:17   1012
I *c* thee to buy of me gold tried..............Rev 3:18   4823

COUNSELED
How hast thou *c* him that hath no ....Job 26:3   3289

COUNSELLED
which he *c* in those days, was as 2Sa 16:23   3289
and thus and thus have I *c*....................2Sa 17:15   3289
hath Ahithophel *c* against you 2Sa 17:21   3289

COUNSELLOR
the Gilonite, David's *c*, from his 2Sa 15:12   3289
for Zechariah his son, a wise *c* 1Chr 26:14   3289
Jonathan David's uncle was a *c* 1Chr 27:32   3289
And Ahithophel was the king's *c*..............1Chr 27:33   3289
mother was his *c* to do wickedly 2Chr 22:3   3289
and the honourable man, and the *c*........Is 3:3   3289
name shall be called Wonderful, *C*........Is 9:6   3289
or being his *c* hath taught him ....Is 40:13   6098
among them, and there was no *c* ....Is 41:28   3289
is thy *c* perished? ....Mic 4:9   3289
evil against the LORD, a wicked *c* ....Nah 1:11   3289
of Arimathaea, an honourable *c* ....Mk 15:43   1010
there was a man named Joseph, a *c*.......Lk 23:50   1010
or who hath been his *c* ....Rom 11:34   4825

COUNSELLORS
for they were his *c* after the 2Chr 22:4   3289
And hired *c* against them, to ....Ezr 4:5   3289
of the king, and of his seven *c* ....Ezr 7:14   3272
his *c* have freely offered unto ....Ezr 7:15   3272
unto me before the king, and his *c* ....Ezr 7:28   3289
our God, which the king, and his *c*........Ezr 8:25   3289
c of the earth, which built........................Job 3:14   3289
He leadeth *c* away spoiled, and ....Job 12:17   3289
also are my delight, and my *c*................Ps 119:24   6098
multitude of *c* there is safety ....Prov 11:14   3289
but to the *c* of peace is joy....................Prov 12:20   3289
of *c* they are established........................Prov 15:22   3289
in multitude of *c* there is safety..............Prov 24:6   3289
thy *c* as at the beginning......................Is 1:26   3289
the counsel of the wise *c* of ....Is 19:11   3289
the judges, the treasurers, the *c*............Dan 3:2   1884
the judges, the treasurers, the *c*............Dan 3:3   1884
and spake, and said unto his *c* ....Dan 3:24   1907
and captains, and the king's *c* ....Dan 3:27   1907
and my *c* and my lords sought unto ......Dan 4:36   1907
governors, and the princes, the *c* ....Dan 6:7   1907

COUNSELS
it is turned round about by his *c* ....Job 37:12   8458
let them fall by their own *c* ....Ps 5:10   4156
and they walked in their own *c*..............Ps 81:12   4156
shall attain unto wise *c* ....Prov 1:5   8458
but the *c* of the wicked are....................Prov 12:5   8458
to thee excellent things in *c*..................Prov 22:20   4156
thy *c* of old are faithfulness and ....Is 25:1   6098
wearied in the multitude of thy *c* ....Is 47:13   6098

their ear, but walked in the *c*	Jer 7:24	4156
them, because of their own *c*	Hos 11:6	4156
of Ahab, and ye walk in the heart *c*	Mic 6:16	4156
make manifest the *c* of the hearts	1Cor 4:5	1012

COUNT

shall make your *c* for the lamb	Ex 12:4	
then ye shall *c* the fruit thereof	Lev 19:23	3699
ye shall *c* unto you from the	Lev 23:15	5608
Then let him *c* the years of the	Lev 25:27	2803
jubile, then he shall *c* with him	Lev 25:52	2803
Who can *c* the dust of Jacob, and	Num 23:10	4487
C not thine handmaid for a	1Sa 1:16	5414
and my maids, *c* me for a stranger	Job 19:15	2803
he see my ways, and *c* all my steps	Job 31:4	5608
The LORD shall *c*, when he writeth	Ps 87:6	5608
If I should *c* them, they are more	Ps 139:18	5608
I *c* them mine enemies	Ps 139:22	1961
Shall I *c* them pure with the	Mic 6:11	
neither *c* I my life dear unto	Acts 20:24	2192
I *c* all things but loss for the	Phil 3:8	2233
do *c* them but dung, that I may	Phil 3:8	2233
Brethren, I *c* not myself to have	Phil 3:13	3049
that our God would *c* you worthy	2Th 1:11	515
Yet *c* him not as an enemy, but	2Th 3:15	2233
servants as are under the yoke *c*	1Ti 6:1	2233
If thou *c* me therefore a partner	Philem 17	2192
c it all joy when ye fall into	Jas 1:2	2233
we *c* them happy which endure	Jas 5:11	3106
as they that *c* it pleasure to	2Pet 2:13	2233
promise, as some men *c* slackness	2Pet 3:9	2233
c the number of the beast	Rev 13:18	5585

COUNTED

he *c* it to him for righteousness	Gen 15:6	2803
that shall be *c* stolen with me	Gen 30:33	
Are we not *c* of him strangers	Gen 31:15	2803
of testimony, as it was *c*	Ex 38:21	6485
be *c* as the fields of the country	Lev 25:31	2803
then it shall be *c* unto the	Num 18:30	2803
which is *c* to the Canaanite	Josh 13:3	2803
son Solomon shall be *c* offenders	1Kin 1:21	
be numbered nor *c* for multitude	1Kin 3:8	5608
Benjamin *c* he not among them	1Chr 21:6	6485
as they were *c* by number of names	1Chr 23:24	6485
for they were *c* faithful, and	Neh 13:13	2803
Wherefore are we *c* as beasts	Job 18:3	2803
Darts are *c* as stubble	Job 41:29	2803
we are *c* as sheep for the	Ps 44:22	2803
I am *c* with them that go down	Ps 88:4	2803
And that was *c* unto him for	Ps 106:31	2803
he holdeth his peace, is *c* wise	Prov 17:28	2803
it shall be *c* a curse to him	Prov 27:14	2803
hoofs shall be *c* like flint	Is 5:28	2803
fruitful field be *c* for a forest	Is 32:15	2803
where is he that *c* the towers	Is 33:18	5608
are as the small dust of the	Is 40:15	2803
they are *c* to him less than	Is 40:17	2803
but they were *c* as a strange	Hos 8:12	2803
because they *c* him as a prophet	Mt 14:5	2192
for all men *c* John, that he was a	Mk 11:32	2192
rejoicing that they were *c* worthy	Acts 5:41	2661
they *c* the price of them, and	Acts 19:19	4860
be *c* for circumcision	Rom 2:26	3049
God, and it was *c* unto him for	Rom 4:3	3049
his faith is *c* for righteousness	Rom 4:5	3049
of the promise are *c* for the seed	Rom 9:8	3049
those I *c* loss for Christ	Phil 3:7	2233
that ye may be *c* worthy of the	2Th 1:5	2661
me, for that he *c* me faithful	1Ti 1:12	2233
well be *c* worthy of double honour	1Ti 5:17	515
For this man was *c* worthy of more	Heb 3:3	515
But he whose descent is not *c*	Heb 7:6	1075
hath *c* the blood of the covenant,	Heb 10:29	2233

COUNTENANCE

was very wroth, and his *c* fell	Gen 4:5	6440
and why is thy *c* fallen	Gen 4:6	6440
And Jacob beheld the *c* of Laban	Gen 31:2	6440
unto them, I see your father's *c*	Gen 31:5	6440
Neither shalt thou *c* a poor man	Ex 23:3	1921
The LORD lift up his *c* upon thee	Num 6:26	6440
A nation of fierce *c*, which shall	Deut 28:50	6440
his *c* was like the *c* of	Judg 13:6	4758
did eat, and her *c* was no more sad	1Sa 1:18	6440
unto Samuel, Look not on his *c*	1Sa 16:7	4758
ruddy, and withal of a beautiful *c*	1Sa 16:12	5869
a youth, and ruddy, and of a fair *c*	1Sa 17:42	4758
and of a beautiful *c*	1Sa 25:3	8389
she was a woman of a fair *c*	2Sa 14:27	4758
And he settled his *c* stedfastly	2Kin 8:11	6440
said unto me, Why is thy *c* sad	Neh 2:2	6440

why should not my *c* be sad	Neh 2:3	6440
thou changest his *c*, and sendest	Job 14:20	6440
the light of my *c* they cast not	Job 29:24	6440
up the light of thy *c* upon us	Ps 4:6	6440
through the pride of his *c*	Ps 10:4	639
his *c* doth behold the upright	Ps 11:7	6440
him exceeding glad with thy *c*	Ps 21:6	6440
praise him for the help of his *c*	Ps 42:5	6440
him, who is the health of my *c*	Ps 42:11	6440
him, who is the health of my *c*	Ps 43:5	6440
thine arm, and the light of thy *c*	Ps 44:3	6440
perish at the rebuke of thy *c*	Ps 80:16	6440
O LORD, in the light of thy *c*	Ps 89:15	6440
secret sins in the light of thy *c*	Ps 90:8	6440
A merry heart maketh a cheerful *c*	Prov 15:13	6440
the light of the king's *c* is life	Prov 16:15	6440
so doth an angry *c* a backbiting	Prov 25:23	6440
sharpeneth the *c* of his friend	Prov 27:17	6440
of the *c* the heart is made better	Eccl 7:3	6440
of the stairs, let me see thy *c*	Song 2:14	4758
is thy voice, and thy *c* is comely	Song 2:14	4758
his *c* is as Lebanon, excellent as	Song 5:15	4758
The shew of their *c* doth witness	Is 3:9	6440
they shall be troubled in their *c*	Eze 27:35	6440
the *c* of the children that eat of	Dan 1:13	4758
Then the king's *c* was changed	Dan 5:6	2122
his *c* was changed in him, and his	Dan 5:6	2122
thee, nor let thy *c* be changed	Dan 5:10	2122
me, and my *c* changed in me	Dan 7:28	2122
to the full, a king of fierce *c*	Dan 8:23	6440
as the hypocrites, of a sad *c*	Mt 6:16	4659
His *c* was like lightning, and his	Mt 28:3	2397
the fashion of his *c* was altered	Lk 9:29	4383
make me full of joy with thy *c*	Acts 2:28	4383
of Moses for the glory of his *c*	2Cor 3:7	4383
his *c* was as the sun shineth in	Rev 1:16	3799

COUNTENANCES

Then let our *c* be looked upon	Dan 1:13	4758
ten days their *c* appeared fairer	Dan 1:15	4758

COUNTERVAIL

could not *c* the king's damage	Est 7:4	7737

COUNTETH

he *c* me unto him as one of his	Job 19:11	2803
me, he *c* me for his enemy,	Job 33:10	2803
c the cost, whether he have	Lk 14:28	5585

COUNTING

c one by one, to find out the	Eccl 7:27	

COUNTRIES

after their tongues, in their *c*	Gen 10:20	776
thy seed, I will give all these *c*	Gen 26:3	776
give unto thy seed all these *c*	Gen 26:4	776
all *c* came into Egypt to Joseph	Gen 41:57	776
These are the *c* which Moses did	Josh 13:32	
these are the *c* which the	Josh 14:1	
and her towns, even three *c*	Josh 17:11	5316
they among all the gods of the *c*	2Kin 18:35	776
fame and glory throughout all *c*	1Chr 22:5	776
and over all the kingdoms of the *c*	1Chr 29:30	776
throughout all the *c* of Judah	2Chr 11:23	776
service of the kingdoms of the *c*	2Chr 12:8	776
upon all the inhabitants of the *c*	2Chr 15:5	776
on all the kingdoms of those *c*	2Chr 20:29	776
c that pertained to the children	2Chr 34:33	776
because of the people of those *c*	Ezr 3:3	776
ruled over all *c* beyond the river	Ezr 4:20	
shall wound the heads over many *c*	Ps 110:6	776
and give ear, all ye of far *c*	Is 8:9	776
waste all the nations, and their *c*	Is 37:18	776
all *c* whither I have driven them	Jer 23:3	776
from all *c* whither I had driven	Jer 23:8	776
prophesied both against many *c*	Jer 28:8	776
I will gather them out of all *c*	Jer 32:37	776
Edom, and that were in all the *c*	Jer 40:11	776
c that are round about her	Eze 5:5	776
the *c* that are round about her	Eze 5:6	776
shall be scattered through the *c*	Eze 6:8	776
I have scattered them among the *c*	Eze 11:16	776
in the *c* where they shall come	Eze 11:16	776
assemble you out of the *c* where	Eze 11:17	776
and disperse them in the *c*	Eze 12:15	776
and disperse them through the *c*	Eze 20:23	776
heathen, as the families of the *c*	Eze 20:32	776
of the *c* wherein ye are scattered	Eze 20:34	776
gather you out of the *c* wherein	Eze 20:41	776
heathen, and a mocking to all *c*	Eze 22:4	776
and disperse thee in the *c*	Eze 22:15	776
cause thee to perish out of the *c*	Eze 25:7	776
midst of the *c* that are desolate	Eze 29:12	776

will disperse them through the *c*	Eze 29:12	776
midst of the *c* that are desolate	Eze 30:7	776
will disperse them through the *c*	Eze 30:23	776
and disperse them among the *c*	Eze 30:26	776
into the *c* which thou hast not	Eze 32:9	776
people, and gather them from the *c*	Eze 34:13	776
these two *c* shall be mine, and we	Eze 35:10	776
they were dispersed through the *c*	Eze 36:19	776
and gather you out of all *c*	Eze 36:24	776
through all the *c* whither thou	Dan 9:7	776
and he shall enter into the *c*	Dan 11:40	776
many *c* shall be overthrown	Dan 11:41	
forth his hand also upon the *c*	Dan 11:42	776
they shall remember me in far *c*	Zec 10:9	
that are in the *c* enter thereinto	Lk 21:21	5561

COUNTRY

unto Abram, Get thee out of thy *c*	Gen 12:1	776
smote all the *c* of the Amalekites	Gen 14:7	7704
the smoke of the *c* went up as the	Gen 19:28	776
from thence toward the south *c*	Gen 20:1	776
But thou shalt go unto my *c*	Gen 24:4	776
for he dwelt in the south *c*	Gen 24:62	776
lived, eastward, unto the east *c*	Gen 25:6	776
It must not be so done in our *c*	Gen 29:26	4725
unto mine own place, and to my *c*	Gen 30:25	776
the land of Seir, the *c* of Edom	Gen 32:3	7704
saidst unto me, Return unto thy *c*	Gen 32:9	776
Hamor the Hivite, prince of the *c*	Gen 34:2	776
went into the *c* from the face of	Gen 36:6	776
us, and took us for spies of the *c*	Gen 42:30	776
And the man, the lord of the *c*	Gen 42:33	776
land of Egypt, in the *c* of Goshen	Gen 47:27	776
whether it be one of your own *c*	Lev 16:29	249
whether it be one of your own *c*	Lev 17:15	249
as for one of your own *c*	Lev 24:22	249
be counted as the fields of the *c*	Lev 25:31	776
All that are born of the *c* shall	Num 15:13	249
pass, I pray thee, through thy *c*	Num 20:17	776
valley, that is in the *c* of Moab	Num 21:20	7704
Even the *c* which the LORD smote	Num 32:4	776
the cities of the *c* round about	Num 32:33	776
the *c* of Argob unto the coasts of	Deut 3:14	2256
in the wilderness, in the plain *c*	Deut 4:43	776
that I am come unto the *c* which	Deut 26:3	776
of Israel to search out the *c*	Josh 2:2	776
be come to search out all the *c*	Josh 2:3	776
of the *c* do faint because of us	Josh 2:24	776
two men that had spied out the *c*	Josh 6:22	776
was noised throughout all the *c*	Josh 6:27	776
them, saying, Go up and view the *c*	Josh 7:2	776
Israel, We be come from a far *c*	Josh 9:6	776
From a very far *c* thy servants	Josh 9:9	776
inhabitants of our *c* spake to us	Josh 9:11	776
smote all the *c* of the hills	Josh 10:40	776
all the *c* of Goshen, even unto	Josh 10:41	776
the hills, and all the south *c*	Josh 11:16	
the kings of the *c* which Joshua	Josh 12:7	776
the wilderness, and in the south *c*	Josh 12:8	
of the hill *c* from Lebanon unto	Josh 13:6	
dukes of Sihon, dwelling in the *c*	Josh 13:21	776
then get thee up to the wood *c*	Josh 17:15	
made an end of dividing the *c*	Josh 19:51	776
is Hebron, in the hill *c* of Judah	Josh 21:11	
to go unto the *c* of Gilead	Josh 22:9	776
the *c* was in quietness forty	Judg 8:28	776
the inhabitants of that *c*	Judg 11:21	776
in Aijalon in the *c* of Zebulun	Judg 12:12	776
enemy, and the destroyer of our *c*	Judg 16:24	776
went to spy out the *c* of Laish	Judg 18:14	776
sent her throughout all the *c* of	Judg 20:6	7704
went to sojourn in the *c* of Moab	Ruth 1:1	7704
And they came into the *c* of Moab	Ruth 1:2	7704
might return from the *c* of Moab	Ruth 1:6	7704
for she had heard in the *c* of	Ruth 1:6	7704
returned out of the *c* of Moab	Ruth 1:22	7704
with Naomi out of the *c* of Moab	Ruth 2:6	7704
come again out of the *c* of Moab	Ruth 4:3	7704
the ark of the LORD was in the *c*	1Sa 6:1	7704
of *c* villages, even unto the	1Sa 6:18	6521
the camp from the *c* round about	1Sa 14:21	
me a place in some town in the *c*	1Sa 27:5	7704
time that David dwelt in the *c* of	1Sa 27:7	7704
in the *c* of the Philistines	1Sa 27:11	7704
all the *c* wept with a loud voice,	2Sa 15:23	776
over the face of all the *c*	2Sa 18:8	776
in the *c* of Benjamin in Zelah	2Sa 21:14	776
son of Uri was in the *c* of Gilead	1Kin 4:19	776
in the *c* of Sihon king of the	1Kin 4:19	776
of all the children of the east *c*	1Kin 4:30	
of a far *c* for thy name's sake	1Kin 8:41	776

she turned and went to her own *c*	1Kin 10:13	776
and of the governors of the *c*	1Kin 10:15	776
that I may go to mine own *c*	1Kin 11:21	776
thou seekest to go to thine own *c*	1Kin 11:22	776
but the Syrians filled the *c*	1Kin 20:27	776
city, and every man to his own *c*	1Kin 22:36	776
the *c* was filled with water	2Kin 3:20	776
the Moabites, even in their *c*	2Kin 3:24	
their *c* out of mine hand, that	2Kin 18:35	776
said, They are come from a far *c*	2Kin 20:14	776
begat children in the *c* of Moab	1Chr 8:8	7704
wasted the *c* of the children of	1Chr 20:1	776
but is come from a far *c* for thy	2Chr 6:32	776
governors of the *c* brought gold	2Chr 9:14	776
much cattle, both in the low *c*	2Chr 26:10	
invaded the cities of the low *c*	2Chr 28:18	
to city through the *c* of Ephraim	2Chr 30:10	776
the plain *c* round about Jerusalem	Neh 12:28	
so is good news from a far *c*	Prov 25:25	776
Your *c* is desolate, your cities	Is 1:7	776
They come from a far *c*, from the	Is 13:5	776
thee like a ball into a large *c*	Is 22:18	776
are come from a far *c* unto me	Is 39:3	776
executeth my counsel from a far *c*	Is 46:11	776
I brought you into a plentiful *c*	Jer 2:7	776
that watchers come from a far *c*	Jer 4:16	776
and the sweet cane from a far *c*	Jer 6:20	776
a people cometh from the north *c*	Jer 6:22	776
of them that dwell in a far *c*	Jer 8:19	776
commotion out of the north *c*	Jer 10:22	776
no more, nor see his native *c*	Jer 22:10	776
that bare thee, into another *c*	Jer 22:26	776
of Israel out of the north *c*	Jer 23:8	776
will bring them from the north *c*	Jer 31:8	776
which is in the *c* of Benjamin	Jer 32:8	776
in the *c* of Pathros, saying,	Jer 44:1	776
north *c* by the river Euphrates	Jer 46:10	776
the remnant of the *c* of Caphtor	Jer 47:4	339
judgment is come upon the plain *c*	Jer 48:21	776
of great nations from the north *c*	Jer 50:9	776
us go every one into his own *c*	Jer 51:9	776
out of the *c* where they sojourn	Eze 20:38	776
into the *c* for the which I lifted	Eze 20:42	776
his frontiers, the glory of the *c*	Eze 25:9	776
the *c* shall be destitute of that	Eze 32:15	776
all the inhabited places of the *c*	Eze 34:13	776
issue out toward the east *c*	Eze 47:8	1552
be unto you as born in the *c*	Eze 47:22	249
And Jacob fled into the *c* of Syria	Hos 12:12	7704
what is thy *c*?	Jonah 1:8	776
my saying, when I was yet in my *c*	Jonah 4:2	127
therein go forth into the north *c*	Zec 6:6	776
go forth toward the south *c*	Zec 6:6	776
c have quieted my spirit in the	Zec 6:8	776
quieted my spirit in the north *c*	Zec 6:8	776
east *c*, and from the west *c*	Zec 8:7	776
into their own *c* another way	Mt 2:12	5561
side into the *c* of the Gergesenes	Mt 8:28	5561
abroad his fame in all that *c*	Mt 9:31	1093
when he was come into his own *c*	Mt 13:54	3968
without honour, save in his own *c*	Mt 13:57	3968
out into all that *c* round about	Mt 14:35	4066
husbandmen, and went into a far *c*	Mt 21:33	589
as a man travelling into a far *c*	Mt 25:14	589
into the *c* of the Gadarenes	Mk 5:1	5561
not send them away out of the *c*	Mk 5:10	5561
told in the city, and in the *c*	Mk 5:14	68
thence, and came into his own *c*	Mk 6:1	3968
without honour, but in his own *c*	Mk 6:4	3968
may go into the *c* round about	Mk 6:36	68
into villages, or cities, or *c*	Mk 6:56	68
husbandmen, and went into a far *c*	Mk 12:1	589
passed by, coming out of the *c*	Mk 15:21	68
they walked, and went into the *c*	Mk 16:12	68
went into the hill *c* with haste	Lk 1:39	
all the hill *c* of Judaea	Lk 1:65	
And there were in the same *c*	Lk 2:8	5561
came into all the *c* about Jordan	Lk 3:3	4066
Capernaum, do also here in thy *c*	Lk 4:23	3968
prophet is accepted in his own *c*	Lk 4:24	3968
every place of the *c* round about	Lk 4:37	4066
arrived at the *c* of the Gadarenes	Lk 8:26	5561
told it in the city and in the *c*	Lk 8:34	68
c of the Gadarenes round about	Lk 8:37	4066
c round about, and lodge, and get	Lk 9:12	68
and took his journey into a far *c*	Lk 15:13	5561
himself to a citizen of that *c*	Lk 15:15	5561
a far *c* to receive for himself a	Lk 19:12	5561
went into a far *c* for a long time	Lk 20:9	589
a Cyrenian, coming out of the *c*	Lk 23:26	68
hath no honour in his own *c*	Jn 4:44	3968

unto a *c* near to the wilderness	Jn 11:54	5561
many went out of the *c* up to	Jn 11:55	5561
a Levite, and of the *c* of Cyprus	Acts 4:36	1085
unto him, Get thee out of thy *c*	Acts 7:3	1093
because their *c* was nourished by	Acts 12:20	5561
was nourished by the king's *c*	Acts 12:20	5561
was with the deputy of the *c*	Acts 13:7	
and went over all the *c* of Galatia	Acts 18:23	5561
that they drew near to some *c*	Acts 27:27	5561
of promise, as in a strange *c*	Heb 11:9	
plainly that they seek a *c*	Heb 11:14	3968
that *c* from whence they came out	Heb 11:15	
But now they desire a better *c*	Heb 11:16	

COUNTRYMEN

robbers, in perils by mine own *c*	2Cor 11:26	1085
like things of your own *c*	1Th 2:14	4853

COUPLE

c the curtains together with the	Ex 26:6	2266
thou shalt *c* five curtains by	Ex 26:9	2266
c the tent together, that it may	Ex 26:11	2266
of brass to *c* the tent together	Ex 36:18	2266
for it, to *c* it together	Ex 39:4	2266
servant with him, and a *c* of asses	Judg 19:3	6776
make me a *c* of cakes in my sight,	2Sa 13:6	8147
with a *c* of asses saddled, and	2Sa 16:1	6776
a chariot with a *c* of horsemen	Is 21:7	6776
of men, with a *c* of horsemen	Is 21:9	6776

COUPLED

be *c* together one to another	Ex 26:3	2266
shall be *c* one to another	Ex 26:3	2266
they shall be *c* together beneath,	Ex 26:24	8382
they shall be *c* together above	Ex 26:24	8535
he *c* the five curtains one unto	Ex 36:10	2266
curtains he *c* one unto another	Ex 36:10	2266
c the curtains one unto another	Ex 36:13	2266
he *c* five curtains by themselves,	Ex 36:16	2266
And they were *c* beneath, and	Ex 36:29	8382
c together at the head thereof,	Ex 36:29	8535
the two edges was it *c* together	Ex 39:4	2266
chaste conversation *c* with fear	1Pet 3:2	

COUPLETH

of the curtain which *c* the second	Ex 26:10	2279
of the curtain which *c* the second	Ex 36:17	2279

COUPLING

from the selvedge in the *c*	Ex 26:4	2279
curtain, in the *c* of the second	Ex 26:4	4225
that is in the *c* of the second	Ex 26:5	4225
curtain that is outmost in the *c*	Ex 26:10	2279
over against the other *c* thereof	Ex 28:27	4225
from the selvedge in the *c*	Ex 36:11	4225
curtain, in the *c* of the second	Ex 36:11	4225
which was in the *c* of the second	Ex 36:12	4225
edge of the curtain in the *c*	Ex 36:17	4225
over against the other *c* thereof	Ex 39:20	4225

COUPLINGS

buy hewn stone, and timber for *c*	2Chr 34:11	4226

COURAGE

And be ye of good *c*, and bring of	Num 13:20	2388
Be strong and of a good *c*, fear	Deut 31:6	553
Israel, Be strong and of a good *c*	Deut 31:7	553
and said, Be strong and of a good *c*	Deut 31:23	553
Be strong and of a good *c*	Josh 1:6	553
Be strong and of a good *c*	Josh 1:9	553
only be strong and of a good *c*	Josh 1:18	553
remain any more *c* in any man	Josh 2:11	7307
dismayed, be strong and of good *c*	Josh 10:25	553
Be of good *c*, and let us play the	2Sa 10:12	2388
Be of good *c*, and let us behave	1Chr 19:13	2388
be strong, and of good *c*	1Chr 22:13	553
his son, Be strong and of good *c*	1Chr 28:20	553
of Oded the prophet, he took *c*	2Chr 15:8	2388
be of good *c*, and do it	Ezr 10:4	2388
be of good *c*, and he shall	Ps 27:14	2388
Be of good *c*, and he shall	Ps 31:24	2388
said to his brother, Be of good *c*	Is 41:6	2388
his *c* against the king of the	Dan 11:25	3824
saw, he thanked God, and took *c*	Acts 28:15	2294

COURAGEOUS

Only be thou strong and very *c*	Josh 1:7	553
Be ye therefore very *c* to keep	Josh 23:6	2388
be *c*, and be valiant	2Sa 13:28	2388
Be strong and *c*, be not afraid nor	2Chr 32:7	553
he that is *c* among the mighty	Amos 2:16	533,3820

COURAGEOUSLY

Deal *c*, and the LORD shall be with	2Chr 19:11	2388

COURSE

of every *c* were twenty and four	1Chr 27:1	4256
Over the first *c* for the first	1Chr 27:2	4256
in his *c* were twenty and four	1Chr 27:2	4256
over the *c* of the second month	1Chr 27:4	4256
of his *c* was Mikloth also the	1Chr 27:4	4256
in his *c* likewise were twenty and	1Chr 27:4	4256
in his *c* were twenty and four	1Chr 27:5	4256
in his *c* was Ammizabad his son	1Chr 27:6	4256
in his *c* were twenty and four	1Chr 27:7	4256
in his *c* were twenty and four	1Chr 27:8	4256
in his *c* were twenty and four	1Chr 27:9	4256
in his *c* were twenty and four	1Chr 27:10	4256
in his *c* were twenty and four	1Chr 27:11	4256
in his *c* were twenty and four	1Chr 27:12	4256
in his *c* were twenty and four	1Chr 27:13	4256
in his *c* were twenty and four	1Chr 27:14	4256
in his *c* were twenty and four	1Chr 27:15	4256
that ministered to the king by *c*	1Chr 28:1	4256
and did not then wait by *c*	2Chr 5:11	4256
sang together by *c* in praising	Ezr 3:11	
of the earth are out of *c*	Ps 82:5	4131
every one turned to his *c*	Jer 8:6	4794
their *c* is evil, and their force	Jer 23:10	4794
named Zacharias, of the *c* of Abia	Lk 1:5	2183
before God in the order of his *c*	Lk 1:8	2183
And as John fulfilled his *c*	Acts 13:25	1408
with a straight *c* to Samothracia	Acts 16:11	2113
that I might finish my *c* with joy	Acts 20:24	1408
came with a straight *c* unto Coos	Acts 21:1	4144
we had finished our *c* from Tyre	Acts 21:7	4144
the most by three, and that by *c*	1Cor 14:27	3313
according to the *c* of this world	Eph 2:2	165
word of the Lord may have free *c*	2Th 3:1	5143
good fight, I have finished my *c*	2Ti 4:7	1408
setteth on fire the *c* of nature	Jas 3:6	5164

COURSES

the stars in their *c* fought	Judg 5:20	4546
ten thousand a month by *c*	1Kin 5:14	2487
into *c* among the sons of Levi	1Chr 23:6	4256
the king in any matter of the *c*	1Chr 27:1	4256
Also for the *c* of the priests and	1Chr 28:13	4256
the *c* of the priests and the	1Chr 28:21	4256
the *c* of the priests to their	2Chr 8:14	4256
also by their *c* at every gate	2Chr 8:14	4256
the priest dismissed not the *c*	2Chr 23:8	4256
appointed the *c* of the priests	2Chr 31:2	4256
and the Levites after their *c*	2Chr 31:2	4256
to give to their brethren by *c*	2Chr 31:15	4256
charges according to their *c*	2Chr 31:16	4256
in their charges by their *c*	2Chr 31:17	4256
of your fathers, after your *c*	2Chr 35:4	4256
place, and the Levites in their *c*	2Chr 35:10	4256
and the Levites in their *c*	Ezr 6:18	4255
grass, as willows by the water *c*	Is 44:4	2988

COURT

make the *c* of the tabernacle	Ex 27:9	2691
the *c* of fine twined linen of an	Ex 27:9	2691
for the breadth of the *c* on the	Ex 27:12	2691
the breadth of the *c* on the east	Ex 27:13	2691
for the gate of the *c* shall be an	Ex 27:16	2691
c shall be filleted with silver	Ex 27:17	2691
The length of the *c* shall be an	Ex 27:18	2691
thereof, and all the pins of the *c*	Ex 27:19	2691
The hangings of the *c*, his	Ex 35:17	2691
the hanging for the door of the *c*	Ex 35:17	2691
tabernacle, and the pins of the *c*	Ex 35:18	2691
And he made the *c*	Ex 38:9	2691
the *c* were of fine twined linen	Ex 38:9	2691
for the other side of the *c* gate	Ex 38:15	2691
All the hangings of the *c* round	Ex 38:16	2691
all the pillars of the *c* were	Ex 38:17	2691
the gate of the *c* was needlework	Ex 38:18	2691
to the hangings of the *c*	Ex 38:18	2691
of the *c* round about, were of	Ex 38:20	2691
the sockets of the *c* round about	Ex 38:31	2691
and the sockets of the *c* gate	Ex 38:31	2691
all the pins of the *c* round about	Ex 38:31	2691
The hangings of the *c*, his	Ex 39:40	2691
and the hanging for the *c* gate	Ex 39:40	2691
shalt set up the *c* round about	Ex 40:8	2691
hang up the hanging at the *c* gate	Ex 40:8	2691
he reared up the *c* round about	Ex 40:33	2691
set up the hanging of the *c* gate	Ex 40:33	2691
in the *c* of the tabernacle of the	Lev 6:16	2691
in the *c* of the tabernacle of the	Lev 6:26	2691
And the hangings of the *c*, and the	Num 3:26	2691
the curtain for the door of the *c*	Num 3:26	2691
the pillars of the *c* round about	Num 3:37	2691
And the hangings of the *c*, and the	Num 4:26	2691

for the door of the gate of the *c*	Num 4:26	2691
the pillars of the *c* round about	Num 4:32	2691
which had a well in his *c*	2Sa 17:18	2691
he built the inner *c* with three	1Kin 6:36	2691
had another *c* within the porch	1Kin 7:8	2691
on the outside toward the great *c*	1Kin 7:9	2691
the great *c* round about was with	1Kin 7:12	2691
both for the inner *c* of the house	1Kin 7:12	2691
c that was before the house of	1Kin 8:64	2691
was gone out into the middle *c*	2Kin 20:4	5892
he made the *c* of the priests	2Chr 4:9	2691
great *c*, and doors for the *c*	2Chr 4:9	5835
had set it in the midst of the *c*	2Chr 6:13	5835
hallowed the middle of the *c* that	2Chr 7:7	2691
of the Lord, before the new *c*	2Chr 20:5	2691
in the *c* of the house of the Lord	2Chr 24:21	2691
the *c* of the house of the Lord	2Chr 29:16	2691
that was by the *c* of the prison	Neh 3:25	2691
in the *c* of the garden of the	Est 1:5	2691
before the *c* of the women's house	Est 2:11	2691
unto the king into the inner *c*	Est 4:11	2691
stood in the inner *c* of the	Est 5:1	2691
the queen standing in the *c*	Est 5:2	2691
And the king said, Who is in the *c*	Est 6:4	2691
the outward *c* of the king's house	Est 6:4	2691
Behold, Haman standeth in the *c*	Est 6:5	2691
of dragons, and a *c* for owls	Is 34:13	2681
he stood in the *c* of the Lord's	Jer 19:14	2691
Stand in the *c* of the Lord's	Jer 26:2	2691
shut up in the *c* of the prison	Jer 32:2	2691
uncle's son came to me in the *c*	Jer 32:8	2691
that sat in the *c* of the prison	Jer 32:12	2691
shut up in the *c* of the prison	Jer 33:1	2691
the scribe, in the higher *c*	Jer 36:10	2691
went in to the king into the *c*	Jer 36:20	2691
Jeremiah into the *c* of the prison	Jer 37:21	2691
remained in the *c* of the prison	Jer 37:21	2691
that was in the *c* of the prison	Jer 38:6	2691
remained in the *c* of the prison	Jer 38:13	2691
So Jeremiah abode in the *c* of the	Jer 38:28	2691
out of the *c* of the prison	Jer 39:14	2691
shut up in the *c* of the prison	Jer 39:15	2691
brought me to the door of the *c*	Eze 8:7	2691
the inner *c* of the Lord's house	Eze 8:16	2691
and the cloud filled the inner *c*	Eze 10:3	2691
the *c* was full of the brightness	Eze 10:4	2691
was heard even to the outer *c*	Eze 10:5	2691
of the *c* round about the gate	Eze 40:14	2691
brought he me into the outward *c*	Eze 40:17	2691
made for the *c* round about	Eze 40:17	2691
forefront of the inner *c* without	Eze 40:19	2691
the gate of the outward *c* that	Eze 40:20	2691
the gate of the inner *c* was over	Eze 40:23	2691
in the inner *c* toward the south	Eze 40:27	2691
to the inner *c* by the south gate	Eze 40:28	2691
thereof were toward the utter *c*	Eze 40:31	2691
into the inner *c* toward the east	Eze 40:32	2691
thereof were toward the outward *c*	Eze 40:34	2691
thereof were toward the utter *c*	Eze 40:37	2691
of the singers in the inner *c*	Eze 40:44	2691
So he measured the *c*, an hundred	Eze 40:47	2691
temple, and the porches of the *c*	Eze 41:15	2691
brought me forth into the utter *c*	Eze 42:1	2691
cubits which were for the inner *c*	Eze 42:3	2691
which was for the utter *c*	Eze 42:3	2691
toward the utter *c* on the	Eze 42:7	2691
in the utter *c* was fifty cubits	Eze 42:8	2691
goeth into them from the utter *c*	Eze 42:9	2691
the wall of the *c* toward the east	Eze 42:10	2691
the holy place into the utter *c*	Eze 42:14	2691
and brought me into the inner *c*	Eze 43:5	2691
in at the gates of the inner *c*	Eze 44:17	2691
in the gates of the inner *c*	Eze 44:17	2691
they go forth into the utter *c*	Eze 44:19	2691
into the utter *c* to the people	Eze 44:19	2691
when they enter into the inner *c*	Eze 44:21	2691
the sanctuary, unto the inner *c*	Eze 44:27	2691
posts of the gate of the inner *c*	Eze 45:19	2691
The gate of the inner *c* that	Eze 46:1	2691
them not out into the utter *c*	Eze 46:20	2691
brought me forth into the utter *c*	Eze 46:21	2691
pass by the four corners of the *c*	Eze 46:21	2691
corner of the *c* there was a *c*	Eze 46:21	2691
In the four corners of the *c*	Eze 46:22	2691
chapel, and it is the king's *c*	Amos 7:13	1004
But the *c* which is without the	Rev 11:2	833

COURTEOUS

as brethren, be pitiful, be *c*	1Pet 3:8	5391

COURTEOUSLY

Julius *c* entreated Paul, and gave	Acts 27:3	5364
us, and lodged us three days *c*	Acts 28:7	5390

COURTS

two *c* of the house of the Lord	2Kin 21:5	2691
two *c* of the house of the Lord	2Kin 23:12	2691
the house of the Lord, in the *c*	1Chr 23:28	2691
he shall build my house and my *c*	1Chr 28:6	2691
of the *c* of the house of the Lord	1Chr 28:12	2691
in the *c* of the house of the Lord	2Chr 23:5	2691
two *c* of the house of the Lord	2Chr 33:5	2691
roof of his house, and in their *c*	Neh 8:16	2691
in the *c* of the house of God, and	Neh 8:16	2691
in the *c* of the house of God	Neh 13:7	2691
thee, that he may dwell in thy *c*	Ps 65:4	2691
fainteth for the *c* of the Lord	Ps 84:2	2691
For a day in thy *c* is better than	Ps 84:10	2691
flourish in the *c* of our God	Ps 92:13	2691
an offering, and come into his *c*	Ps 96:8	2691
and into his *c* with praise	Ps 100:4	2691
In the *c* of the Lord's house, in	Ps 116:19	2691
in the *c* of the house of our God,	Ps 135:2	2691
this at your hand, to tread my *c*	Is 1:12	2691
drink it in the *c* of my holiness	Is 62:9	2691
fill the *c* with the slain	Eze 9:7	2691
pillars as the pillars of the *c*	Eze 42:6	2691
c joined of forty cubits long	Eze 46:22	2691
my house, and shalt also keep my *c*	Zec 3:7	2691
live delicately, are in kings' *c*	Lk 7:25	

COUSIN

thy *c* Elisabeth, she hath also	Lk 1:36	4773

COUSINS

her *c* heard how the Lord had	Lk 1:58	4773

COVENANT

with thee will I establish my *c*	Gen 6:18	1285
behold, I establish my *c* with you	Gen 9:9	1285
And I will establish my *c* with you	Gen 9:11	1285
of the *c* which I make between me	Gen 9:12	1285
be for a token of a *c* between me	Gen 9:13	1285
And I will remember my *c*, which is	Gen 9:15	1285
the everlasting *c* between God	Gen 9:16	1285
Noah, This is the sign of the *c*	Gen 9:17	1285
day the Lord made a *c* with Abram	Gen 15:18	1285
And I will make my *c* between me	Gen 17:2	1285
my *c* is with thee, and thou shalt	Gen 17:4	1285
I will establish my *c* between me	Gen 17:7	1285
generations for an everlasting *c*	Gen 17:7	1285
Thou shalt keep my *c* therefore	Gen 17:9	1285
This is my *c*, which ye shall keep	Gen 17:10	1285
be a token of the *c* betwixt me	Gen 17:11	1285
my *c* shall be in your flesh for	Gen 17:13	1285
your flesh for an everlasting *c*	Gen 17:13	1285
he hath broken my *c*	Gen 17:14	1285
I will establish my *c* with him	Gen 17:19	1285
with him for an everlasting *c*	Gen 17:19	1285
But my *c* will I establish with	Gen 17:21	1285
and both of them made a *c*	Gen 21:27	1285
Thus they made a *c* at Beer-sheba	Gen 21:32	1285
and let us make a *c* with thee	Gen 26:28	1285
come thou, let us make a *c*	Gen 31:44	1285
God remembered his *c* with Abraham	Ex 2:24	1285
also established my *c* with them	Ex 6:4	1285
and I have remembered my *c*	Ex 6:5	1285
my voice indeed, and keep my *c*	Ex 19:5	1285
Thou shalt make no *c* with them	Ex 23:32	1285
And he took the book of the *c*	Ex 24:7	1285
said, Behold the blood of the *c*	Ex 24:8	1285
generations, for a perpetual *c*	Ex 31:16	1285
And he said, Behold, I make a *c*	Ex 34:10	1285
lest thou make a *c* with the	Ex 34:12	1285
Lest thou make a *c* with the	Ex 34:15	1285
words I have made a *c* with thee	Ex 34:27	1285
the tables the words of the *c*	Ex 34:28	1285
thou suffer the salt of the *c* of	Lev 2:13	1285
of Israel by an everlasting *c*	Lev 24:8	1285
you, and establish my *c* with you	Lev 26:9	1285
but that ye break my *c*	Lev 26:15	1285
shall avenge the quarrel of my *c*	Lev 26:25	1285
will I remember my *c* with Jacob	Lev 26:42	1285
also my *c* with Isaac	Lev 26:42	1285
also my *c* with Abraham will I	Lev 26:42	1285
and to break my *c* with them	Lev 26:44	1285
remember the *c* of their ancestors	Lev 26:45	1285
the ark of the *c* of the Lord went	Num 10:33	1285
the ark of the *c* of the Lord	Num 14:44	1285
it is a *c* of salt for ever before	Num 18:19	1285
I give unto him my *c* of peace	Num 25:12	1285
even the *c* of an everlasting	Num 25:13	1285
And he declared unto you his *c*	Deut 4:13	1285

unto thee an everlasting c	Eze 16:60	1285
for daughters, but not by thy c	Eze 16:61	1285
I will establish my c with thee	Eze 16:62	1285
made a c with him, and hath taken	Eze 17:13	1285
keeping of his c it might stand	Eze 17:14	1285
or shall he break the c, and be	Eze 17:15	1285
whose c he brake, even with him	Eze 17:16	1285
the oath by breaking the c	Eze 17:18	1285
my c that he hath broken, even it	Eze 17:19	1285
bring you into the bond of the c	Eze 20:37	1285
will make with them a c of peace	Eze 34:25	1285
will make a c of peace with them	Eze 37:26	1285
be an everlasting c with them	Eze 37:26	1285
broken my c because of all your	Eze 44:7	1285
and dreadful God, keeping the c	Dan 9:4	1285
he shall confirm the c with many	Dan 9:27	1285
yea, also the prince of the c	Dan 11:22	1285
heart shall be against the holy c	Dan 11:28	1285
indignation against the holy c	Dan 11:30	1285
with them that forsake the holy c	Dan 11:30	1285
c shall he corrupt by flatteries	Dan 11:32	1285
in that day will I make a c for	Hos 2:18	1285
like men have transgressed the c	Hos 6:7	1285
they have transgressed my c	Hos 8:1	1285
swearing falsely in making a c	Hos 10:4	1285
they do make a c with the	Hos 12:1	1285
and remembered not the brotherly c	Amos 1:9	1285
by the blood of thy c I have sent	Zec 9:11	1285
that I might break my c which I	Zec 11:10	1285
that my c might be with Levi,	Mal 2:4	1285
My c was with him of life and	Mal 2:5	1285
ye have corrupted the c of Levi	Mal 2:8	1285
by profaning the c of our fathers	Mal 2:10	1285
companion, and the wife of thy c	Mal 2:14	1285
even the messenger of the c	Mal 3:1	1285
and to remember his holy c	Lk 1:72	1242
of the c which God made with our	Acts 3:25	1242
he gave him the c of circumcision	Acts 7:8	1242
For this is my c unto them	Rom 11:27	1242
Though it be but a man's c	Gal 3:15	1242
And this I say, that the c	Gal 3:17	1242
he is the mediator of a better c	Heb 8:6	1242
For if that first c had been	Heb 8:7	
when I will make a new c with the	Heb 8:8	1242
Not according to the c that I	Heb 8:9	1242
they continued not in my c	Heb 8:9	1242
For this is the c that I will	Heb 8:10	1242
In that he saith, A new c	Heb 8:13	
Then verily the first c had also	Heb 9:1	
the ark of the c overlaid round	Heb 9:4	1242
budded, and the tables of the c	Heb 9:4	1242
This is the c that I will make	Heb 10:16	1242
hath counted the blood of the c	Heb 10:29	1242
Jesus the mediator of the new c	Heb 12:24	1242
the blood of the everlasting c	Heb 13:20	1242

COVENANTBREAKERS
Without understanding, c, without	Rom 1:31	802

COVENANTED
according as I have c with David	2Chr 7:18	3772
I c with you when ye came out of	Hag 2:5	3772
they c with him for thirty pieces	Mt 26:15	2476
were glad, and c to give him money	Lk 22:5	4934

COVENANTS
adoption, and the glory, and the c	Rom 9:4	1242
for these are the two c	Gal 4:24	1242
strangers from the c of promise	Eph 2:12	1242

COVER
they shall c the face of the	Ex 10:5	3680
man shall dig a pit, and not c it	Ex 21:33	3680
and bowls thereof, to c withal	Ex 25:29	5258
side and on that side, to c it	Ex 26:13	3680
breeches to c their nakedness	Ex 28:42	3680
will c thee with my hand while I	Ex 33:22	5526
bowls, and his covers to c withal	Ex 37:16	5258
and c the ark with the vail	Ex 40:3	5526
the leprosy c all the skin of him	Lev 13:12	3680
the cloud of the incense may c	Lev 16:13	3680
blood thereof, and c it with dust	Lev 17:13	3680
c the ark of testimony with it	Num 4:5	3680
the bowls, and covers to c withal	Num 4:7	5258
c the same with a covering of	Num 4:8	3680
c the candlestick of the light,	Num 4:9	3680
c it with a covering of badgers'	Num 4:11	3680
c them with a covering of	Num 4:12	3680
they c the face of the earth, and	Num 22:5	3680
c that which cometh from thee	Deut 23:13	3680
the Lord shall c him all the day	Deut 33:12	2645
and Saul went in to c his feet	1Sa 24:3	5526
to c the chapiters that were upon	1Kin 7:18	3680

to c the two bowls of the	1Kin 7:41	3680
to c the two bowls of the	1Kin 7:42	3680
the two wreaths to c the two	2Chr 4:12	3680
to c the two pommels of the	2Chr 4:13	3680
c not their iniquity, and let not	Neh 4:5	3680
c not thou my blood, and let my	Job 16:18	3680
dust, and the worms shall c them	Job 21:26	3680
and abundance of waters c thee	Job 22:11	3680
abundance of waters may c thee	Job 38:34	3680
The shady trees c him with their	Job 40:22	3680
He shall c thee with his feathers	Ps 91:4	5526
turn not again to c the earth	Ps 104:9	3680
let them c themselves with their	Ps 109:29	5844
Surely the darkness shall c me	Ps 139:11	7779
mischief of their own lips c them	Ps 140:9	3680
the Lord, as the waters c the sea	Is 11:9	3680
under thee, and the worms c thee	Is 14:11	4374
captivity, and will surely c thee	Is 22:17	5844
and shall no more c her slain	Is 26:21	3680
that c with a covering, but not	Is 30:1	5258
seest the naked, that thou c him	Is 58:7	3680
neither shall they c themselves	Is 59:6	3680
the darkness shall c the earth	Is 60:2	3680
multitude of camels shall c thee	Is 60:6	3680
I will go up, and will c the earth	Jer 46:8	3680
sackcloth, and horror shall c them	Eze 7:18	3680
thou shalt c thy face, that thou	Eze 12:6	3680
he shall c his face, that he see	Eze 12:12	3680
the ground, to c it with dust	Eze 24:7	3680
c not thy lips, and eat not the	Eze 24:17	5844
ye shall not c your lips, nor eat	Eze 24:22	5844
horses their dust shall c thee	Eze 26:10	3680
and great waters shall c them	Eze 26:19	3680
as for her, a cloud shall c her	Eze 30:18	3680
I will c the heaven, and make the	Eze 32:7	3680
I will c the sun with a cloud, and	Eze 32:7	3680
c you with skin, and put breath in	Eze 37:6	7159
be like a cloud to c the land	Eze 38:9	3680
Israel, as a cloud to c the land	Eze 38:16	3680
my flax given to c her nakedness	Hos 2:9	3680
shall say to the mountains, C us	Hos 10:8	3680
brother Jacob shame shall c thee	Obad 10	3680
yea, they shall all c their lips	Mic 3:7	5844
shame shall c her which said unto	Mic 7:10	3680
the Lord, as the waters c the sea	Hab 2:14	3680
violence of Lebanon shall c thee	Hab 2:17	3680
to c his face, and to buffet him,	Mk 14:65	4028
and to the hills, C us	Lk 23:30	2572
indeed ought not to c his head	1Cor 11:7	2619
for charity shall c the multitude	1Pet 4:8	2572

COVERED
under the whole heaven, were c	Gen 7:19	3680
and the mountains were c	Gen 7:20	3680
c the nakedness of their father	Gen 9:23	3680
she took a vail, and c herself	Gen 24:65	3680
c her with a vail, and wrapped	Gen 38:14	3680
because she had c her face	Gen 38:15	3680
came up, and c the land of Egypt	Ex 8:6	3680
For they c the face of the whole	Ex 10:15	3680
c the chariots, and the horsemen,	Ex 14:28	3680
The depths have c them	Ex 15:5	3680
with thy wind, the sea c them	Ex 15:10	3680
the quails came up, and c the camp	Ex 16:13	3680
the mount, and a cloud c the mount	Ex 24:15	3680
Sinai, and the cloud c it six days	Ex 24:16	3680
c with their wings over the mercy	Ex 37:9	5526
c the ark of the testimony	Ex 40:21	5526
Then a cloud c the tent of the	Ex 40:34	3680
the leprosy have c all his flesh	Lev 13:13	3680
to see when the holy things are c	Num 4:20	1104
six c wagons, and twelve oxen	Num 7:3	6632
up the cloud c the tabernacle	Num 9:15	3680
the cloud c it by day, and the	Num 9:16	3680
and, behold, the cloud c it	Num 16:42	3680
thick, thou art c with fatness	Deut 32:15	3780
the sea upon them, and c them	Josh 24:7	3680
the tent, she c him with a mantle	Judg 4:18	3680
milk, and gave him drink, and c him	Judg 4:19	3680
his bolster, and c it with a cloth	1Sa 19:13	3680
and he is c with a mantle	1Sa 28:14	5844
as he went up, and had his head c	2Sa 15:30	2645
was with him c every man his head	2Sa 15:30	2645
But the king c his face, and the	2Sa 19:4	3813
they c him with clothes, but he	1Kin 1:1	3680
c the house with beams and boards	1Kin 6:9	5603
he c them on the inside with wood	1Kin 6:15	6823
c the floor of the house with	1Kin 6:15	6823
so c the altar which was of cedar	1Kin 6:20	6823
c them with gold fitted upon the	1Kin 6:35	6823
it was c with cedar above upon	1Kin 7:3	5603

it was c with cedar from one side	1Kin 7:7	5603
ark, and the cherubims c the ark	1Kin 8:7	5526
c himself with sackcloth, and went	2Kin 19:1	3680
c with sackcloth, to Isaiah the	2Kin 19:2	3680
c the ark of the covenant of the	1Chr 28:18	5526
ark, and the cherubims c the ark	2Chr 5:8	3680
c it, and set up the doors thereof	Neh 3:15	2926
mourning, and having his head c	Est 6:12	2645
king's mouth, they c Haman's face	Est 7:8	2645
neither hath he c the darkness	Job 23:17	3680
If I c my transgressions as Adam	Job 31:33	3680
is forgiven, whose sin is c	Ps 32:1	3680
and the shame of my face hath c me	Ps 44:15	3680
c us with the shadow of death	Ps 44:19	3680
valleys also are c over with corn	Ps 65:13	5848
the wings of a dove c with silver	Ps 68:13	2645
shame hath c my face	Ps 69:7	3680
let them be c with reproach and	Ps 71:13	5844
The hills were c with the shadow	Ps 80:10	3680
thou hast c all their sin	Ps 85:2	3680
thou hast c him with shame	Ps 89:45	5844
the waters c their enemies	Ps 106:11	3680
and c the company of Abiram	Ps 106:17	3680
thou hast c me in my mother's	Ps 139:13	5526
thou hast c my head in the day of	Ps 140:7	5526
nettles had c the face thereof	Prov 24:31	3680
a potsherd c with silver dross	Prov 26:23	6823
Whose hatred is c by deceit	Prov 26:26	3680
his name shall be c with darkness	Eccl 6:4	3680
with twain he c his face	Is 6:2	3680
and with twain he c his feet	Is 6:2	3680
your rulers, the seers hath he c	Is 29:10	3680
c himself with sackcloth, and went	Is 37:1	3680
of the priests c with sackcloth	Is 37:2	3680
I have c thee in the shadow of	Is 51:16	3680
he hath c me with the robe of	Is 61:10	3271
and confounded, and c their heads	Jer 14:3	2645
were ashamed, they c their heads	Jer 14:4	2645
she is c with the multitude of	Jer 51:42	3680
shame hath c our faces	Jer 51:51	3680
How hath the Lord c the daughter	Lam 2:1	5743
stones, he hath c me with ashes	Lam 3:16	3728
Thou hast c with anger, and	Lam 3:43	5526
Thou hast c thyself with a cloud	Lam 3:44	5526
to another, and two c their bodies	Eze 1:11	3680
which c on this side, and every	Eze 1:23	3680
which c on that side, their	Eze 1:23	3680
over thee, and c thy nakedness	Eze 16:8	3680
fine linen, and I c thee with silk	Eze 16:10	3680
hath c the naked with a garment	Eze 18:7	3680
hath c the naked with a garment	Eze 18:16	3680
a rock, that it should not be c	Eze 24:8	3680
of Elishah was that which c thee	Eze 27:7	4374
I c the deep for him, and I	Eze 31:15	3680
them, and the skin c them above	Eze 37:8	7159
windows, and the windows were c	Eze 41:16	3680
c him with sackcloth, and sat in	Jonah 3:6	3680
beast be c with sackcloth, and cry	Jonah 3:8	3680
His glory c the heavens, and the	Hab 3:3	3680
the ship was c with the waves	Mt 8:24	2572
for there is nothing c, that	Mt 10:26	2572
For there is nothing c, that	Lk 12:2	4780
are forgiven, and whose sins are c	Rom 4:7	1943
or prophesying, having her head c	1Cor 11:4	2596
For if the woman be not c	1Cor 11:6	2619
be shorn or shaven, let her be c	1Cor 11:6	2619

COVEREDST

Thou c it with the deep as with a	Ps 104:6	3680
thy broidered garments, and c them	Eze 16:18	

COVEREST

vesture, wherewith thou c thyself	Deut 22:12	3680
Who c thyself with light as with	Ps 104:2	5844

COVERETH

all the fat that c the inwards	Ex 29:13	3680
and the fat that c the inwards	Ex 29:22	3680
the fat that c the inwards	Lev 3:3	3680
and the fat that c the inwards	Lev 3:9	3680
the fat that c the inwards	Lev 3:14	3680
the fat that c the inwards	Lev 4:8	3680
and the fat that c the inwards	Lev 7:3	3680
that which c the inwards, and the	Lev 9:19	4374
which c the face of the earth	Num 22:11	3680
Surely he c his feet in his	Judg 3:24	5526
he c the faces of the judges	Job 9:24	4374
Because he c his face with his	Job 15:27	3680
it, and c the bottom of the sea	Job 36:30	3680
With clouds he c the light	Job 36:32	3680
violence c them as a garment	Ps 73:6	5848
him as the garment which c him	Ps 109:19	5844

Who c the heaven with clouds, who	Ps 147:8	3680
but violence c the mouth of the	Prov 10:6	3680
but violence c the mouth of the	Prov 10:11	3680
but love c all sins	Prov 10:12	3680
but a prudent man c shame	Prov 12:16	3680
He that c a transgression seeketh	Prov 17:9	3680
He that c his sins shall not	Prov 28:13	3680
our shame, and our confusion c us	Jer 3:25	3680
art the anointed cherub that c	Eze 28:14	5526
for one c violence with his	Mal 2:16	3680
c it with a vessel, or putteth it	Lk 8:16	2572

COVERING

and Noah removed the c of the ark	Gen 8:13	4372
he is to thee a c of the eyes	Gen 20:16	3682
For that is his c only, it is his	Ex 22:27	3682
c the mercy seat with their wings	Ex 25:20	5526
to be a c upon the tabernacle	Ex 26:7	168
thou shalt make a c for the tent	Ex 26:14	4372
a c above of badgers' skins	Ex 26:14	4372
tabernacle, his tent, and his c	Ex 35:11	4372
mercy seat, and the vail of the c	Ex 35:12	4539
he made a c for the tent of rams'	Ex 36:19	4372
a c of badgers' skins above that	Ex 36:19	4372
the c of rams' skins dyed red, and	Ex 39:34	4372
the c of badgers' skins	Ex 39:34	4372
and the vail of the c	Ex 39:34	4539
put the c of the tent above upon	Ex 40:19	4372
and set up the vail of the c	Ex 40:21	4539
he shall put a c upon his upper	Lev 13:45	5844
the c thereof, and the hanging for	Num 3:25	4372
they shall take down the c vail	Num 4:5	4539
thereon the c of badgers' skins	Num 4:6	3681
same with a c of badgers' skins	Num 4:8	4372
within a c of badgers' skins	Num 4:10	4372
cover it with a c of badgers'	Num 4:11	4372
them with a c of badgers' skins	Num 4:12	4372
upon it a c of badgers' skins	Num 4:14	3681
made an end of c the sanctuary	Num 4:15	3680
of the congregation, his c	Num 4:25	4372
the c of the badgers' skins that	Num 4:25	4372
broad plates for a c of the altar	Num 16:38	6826
broad plates for a c of the altar	Num 16:39	6826
which hath no c bound upon it	Num 19:15	6781
spread a c over the well's mouth,	2Sa 17:19	4539
Thick clouds are a c to him	Job 22:14	5643
that they have no c in the cold	Job 24:7	3682
him, and destruction hath no c	Job 26:6	3682
clothing, or any poor without c	Job 31:19	3682
He spread a cloud for a c	Ps 105:39	4539
the c of it of purple, the midst	Song 3:10	4817
And he discovered the c of Judah	Is 22:8	4539
of the c cast over all people	Is 25:7	3875
the c narrower than that he can	Is 28:20	4541
and that cover with a c, but not	Is 30:1	4541
Ye shall defile also the c of thy	Is 30:22	6826
and I make sackcloth their c	Is 50:3	3682
every precious stone was thy c	Eze 28:13	4540
O c cherub, from the midst of the	Eze 28:16	5526
c the altar of the LORD with	Mal 2:13	3680
for her hair is given her for a c	1Cor 11:15	4018

COVERINGS

decked my bed with c of tapestry	Prov 7:16	4765
She maketh herself c of tapestry	Prov 31:22	4765

COVERS

c thereof, and bowls thereof, to	Ex 25:29	7184
his c to cover withal, of pure	Ex 37:16	7184
the bowls, and c to cover withal	Num 4:7	7184

COVERT

came down by the c of the hill	1Sa 25:20	5643
the c for the sabbath that they	2Kin 16:18	4329
abide in the c to lie in wait	Job 38:40	5521
in the c of the reed, and fens	Job 40:21	5643
will trust in the c of thy wings	Ps 61:4	5643
for a c from storm and from rain	Is 4:6	4563
be thou a c to them from the face	Is 16:4	5643
the wind, and a c from the tempest	Is 32:2	5643
He hath forsaken his c, as the	Jer 25:38	5520

COVET

Thou shalt not c thy neighbour's	Ex 20:17	2530
thou shalt not c thy neighbour's	Ex 20:17	2530
wife, neither shalt thou c thy	Deut 5:21	183
they c fields, and take them by	Mic 2:2	2530
law had said, Thou shalt not c	Rom 7:7	1937
false witness, Thou shalt not c	Rom 13:9	1937
But c earnestly the best gifts	1Cor 12:31	2206
c to prophesy, and forbid not to	1Cor 14:39	2206

COVETED
shekels weight, then I c them .... Josh 7:21   2530
I have c no man's silver, or gold .... Acts 20:33   1937
which while some c after, they 1Ti 6:10   3713

COVETETH
He c greedily all the day long .... Prov 21:26   183
Woe to him that c an evil .... Hab 2:9   1214

COVETOUS
heart's desire, and blesseth the c .... Ps 10:3   1214
And the Pharisees also, who were c .... Lk 16:14   5366
of this world, or with the c................. 1Cor 5:10   4123
a brother be a fornicator, or c 1Cor 5:11   4123
Nor thieves, nor c, nor drunkards 1Cor 6:10   4123
nor unclean person, nor c man .... Eph 5:5   4123
but patient, not a brawler, not c 1Ti 3:3   866
be lovers of their own selves, c............... 2Ti 3:2   5366
have exercised with c practices 2Pet 2:14   4124

COVETOUSNESS
fear God, men of truth, hating c .... Ex 18:21   1215
unto thy testimonies, and not to c .... Ps 119:36   1215
but he that hateth c shall .... Prov 28:16   1215
the iniquity of his c was I wroth .... Is 57:17   1215
of them every one is given to c .... Jer 6:13   1215
unto the greatest is given to c............... Jer 8:10   1215
thine heart are not but for thy c .... Jer 22:17   1215
is come, and the measure of thy c .... Jer 51:13   1215
their heart goeth after their c .... Eze 33:31   1215
coveteth an evil c to his house .... Hab 2:9   1215
Thefts, c, wickedness, deceit, ... Mk 7:22   4124
them, Take heed, and beware of c .... Lk 12:15   4124
fornication, wickedness, c.................... Rom 1:29   4124
matter of bounty, and not as of c 2Cor 9:5   4124
and all uncleanness, or c .... Eph 5:3   4124
evil concupiscence, and c .... Col 3:5   4124
as ye know, nor a cloke of c................. 1Th 2:5   4124
your conversation be without c .... Heb 13:5   866
through c shall they with feigned 2Pet 2:3   4124

COVOCATION
month ye shall have an holy c .... Num 29:12

COW
And whether it be c or ewe...................... Lev 22:28   7794
But the firstling of a c, or the .... Num 18:17   7794
their c calveth, and casteth not .... Job 21:10   6510
a man shall nourish a young c................ Is 7:21   5697
And the c and the bear shall feed .... Is 11:7   6510
every c at that which is before .... Amos 4:3

COW'S
I have given thee c dung for .... Eze 4:15   1241

COZ (coz) A descendant of Caleb.
C begat Anub, and Zobebah, and the..... 1Chr 4:8   6976

COZBI (coz'-bi) A Midianite woman.
woman that was slain was C .... Num 25:15   3579
of Peor, and in the matter of C .... Num 25:18   3579

COZEBA See CHOZEBA.

CRACKLING
For as the c of thorns under a .... Eccl 7:6   6963

CRACKNELS
take with thee ten loaves, and c............. 1Kin 14:3   5350

CRAFT
cause c to prosper in his hand................ Dan 8:25   4820
how they might take him by c .... Mk 14:1   1388
And because he was of the same c .... Acts 18:3   3673
that by this c we have our wealth .... Acts 19:25   2039
our c is in danger to be set at .... Acts 19:27   3313
craftsman, of whatsoever c he be .... Rev 18:22   5078

CRAFTINESS
He taketh the wise in their own c.......... Job 5:13   6193
But he perceived their c, and said .... Lk 20:23   3834
He taketh the wise in their own c......... 1Cor 3:19   3834
of dishonesty, not walking in c 2Cor 4:2   3834
the sleight of men, and cunning c.......... Eph 4:14   3834

CRAFTSMAN
the work of the hands of the c............... Deut 27:15   2976
and no c, of whatsoever craft he .... Rev 18:22   5079

CRAFTSMEN
thousand captives, and all the c 2Kin 24:14   2796
might, even seven thousand, and c......... 2Kin 24:16   2796
for they were c................................. 1Chr 4:14   2796
Lod, and Ono, the valley of c.................. Neh 11:35   2796
all of it the work of the c...................... Hos 13:2   2796
brought no small gain unto the c .... Acts 19:24   5079
the c which are with him, have a............ Acts 19:38   5079

CRAFTY
the devices of the c, so that .... Job 5:12   6175
thou choosest the tongue of the c .... Job 15:5   6175
They have taken c counsel against .... Ps 83:3   6191
nevertheless, being c, I caught 2Cor 12:16   3835

CRAG
upon the c of the rock, and the .... Job 39:28   8127

CRANE
Like a c or a swallow, so did I .... Is 38:14   5483
and the turtle and the c and the .... Jer 8:7   5483

CRASHING
and a great c from the hills.................... Zeph 1:10   7667

CRAVED
Pilate, and c the body of Jesus............... Mk 15:43   154

CRAVETH
for his mouth c it of him .... Prov 16:26   404

CREATE
C in me a clean heart, O God .... Ps 51:10   1254
the Lord will c upon every .... Is 4:5   1254
I form the light, and c darkness............. Is 45:7   1254
I make peace, and c evil........................ Is 45:7   1254
I c the fruit of the lips .... Is 57:19   1254
I c new heavens and a new earth .... Is 65:17   1254
for ever in that which I c .... Is 65:18   1254
I c Jerusalem a rejoicing, and her.......... Is 65:18   1254

CREATED
In the beginning God c the heaven .... Gen 1:1   1254
God c great whales, and every .... Gen 1:21   1254
So God c man in his own image .... Gen 1:27   1254
in the image of God c he him .... Gen 1:27   1254
male and female c he them .... Gen 1:27   1254
from all his work which God c .... Gen 2:3   1254
and of the earth when they were c .... Gen 2:4   1254
In the day that God c man .... Gen 5:1   1254
Male and female c he them .... Gen 5:2   1254
Adam, in the day when they were c....... Gen 5:2   1254
have c from the face of the earth........... Gen 6:7   1254
day that God c man upon the earth........ Deut 4:32   1254
and the south thou hast c them .... Ps 89:12   1254
shall be c shall praise the Lord............. Ps 102:18   1254
forth thy spirit, they are c .... Ps 104:30   1254
for he commanded, and they were c .... Ps 148:5   1254
and behold who hath c these things ...... Is 40:26   1254
the Holy One of Israel hath c it .... Is 41:20   1254
he that c the heavens, and.................... Is 42:5   1254
thus saith the Lord that c thee.............. Is 43:1   1254
for I have c him for my glory, I .... Is 43:7   1254
I the Lord have c it .... Is 45:8   1254
made the earth, and c man upon it .... Is 45:12   1254
saith the Lord that c the heavens .... Is 45:18   1254
he c it not in vain, he formed it............. Is 45:18   1254
They are c now, and not from the .... Is 48:7   1254
I have c the smith that bloweth .... Is 54:16   1254
I have c the waster to destroy .... Is 54:16   1254
for the Lord hath c a new thing .... Jer 31:22   1254
in the place where thou wast c .... Eze 21:30   1254
thee in the day that thou wast c .... Eze 28:13   1254
from the day that thou wast c .... Eze 28:15   1254
hath not one God c us........................... Mal 2:10   1254
which God c unto this time .... Mk 13:19   2936
was the man c for the woman 1Cor 11:9   2936
c in Christ Jesus unto good works.......... Eph 2:10   2936
who c all things by Jesus Christ .... Eph 3:9   2936
after God is c in righteousness .... Eph 4:24   2936
For by him were all things c................... Col 1:16   2936
all things were c by him, and for .... Col 1:16   2936
after the image of him that c him.......... Col 3:10   2936
which God hath c to be received 1Ti 4:3   2936
for thou hast c all things .... Rev 4:11   2936
thy pleasure they are and were c........... Rev 4:11   2936
who c heaven, and the things that........ Rev 10:6   2936

CREATETH
c the wind, and declareth unto man....... Amos 4:13   1254

CREATION
of the c God made them male .... Mk 10:6   2937
the c which God created unto this .... Mk 13:19   2937
things of him from the c of the............... Rom 1:20   2937
we know that the whole c groaneth .... Rom 8:22   2937
were from the beginning of the c 2Pet 3:4   2937
the beginning of the c of God .... Rev 3:14   2937

CREATOR
Remember now thy C in the days of .... Eccl 12:1   1254
the C of the ends of the earth,................ Is 40:28   1254
the c of Israel, your King....................... Is 43:15   1254
the creature more than the C .... Rom 1:25   2936
well doing, as unto a faithful C 1Pet 4:19   2939

CREATURE

the moving c that hath life	Gen 1:20	8318
and every living c that moveth	Gen 1:21	5315
forth the living c after his kind	Gen 1:24	5315
Adam called every living c	Gen 2:19	5315
every living c that is with you	Gen 9:10	5315
every living c that is with you,	Gen 9:12	5315
and every living c of all flesh	Gen 9:15	5315
every living c of all flesh that	Gen 9:16	5315
of every living c that moveth in	Lev 11:46	5315
of every c that creepeth upon the	Lev 11:46	5315
of the living c was in the wheels	Eze 1:20	2416
of the living c was in the wheels	Eze 1:21	2416
living c was as the colour of the	Eze 1:22	2416
This is the living c that I saw	Eze 10:15	2416
of the living c was in them	Eze 10:17	2416
This is the living c that I saw	Eze 10:20	2416
and preach the gospel to every c	Mk 16:15	2937
served the c more than the	Rom 1:25	2937
c waiteth for the manifestation	Rom 8:19	2937
For the c was made subject to	Rom 8:20	2937
Because the c itself also shall	Rom 8:21	2937
nor depth, nor any other c	Rom 8:39	2937
man be in Christ, he is a new c	2Cor 5:17	2937
nor uncircumcision, but a new c	Gal 6:15	2937
God, the firstborn of every c	Col 1:15	2937
to every c which is under heaven	Col 1:23	2937
For every c of God is good, and	1Ti 4:4	2938
Neither is there any c that is	Heb 4:13	2937
every c which is in heaven, and on	Rev 5:13	2938

CREATURES

houses shall be full of doleful c	Is 13:21	255
the likeness of four living c	Eze 1:5	2416
for the likeness of the living c	Eze 1:13	2416
up and down among the living c	Eze 1:13	2416
And the living c ran and returned	Eze 1:14	2416
Now as I beheld the living c	Eze 1:15	2416
upon the earth by the living c	Eze 1:15	2416
And when the living c went	Eze 1:19	2416
when the living c were lifted up	Eze 1:19	2416
living c that touched one another	Eze 3:13	2416
be a kind of firstfruits of his c	Jas 1:18	2938
of the c which were in the sea	Rev 8:9	2938

CREDITOR

Every c that lendeth ought	Deut 15:2	1167,4874,3027
the c is come to take unto him my	2Kin 4:1	5383
There was a certain c which had	Lk 7:41	1157

CREDITORS

or which of my c is it to whom I	Is 50:1	5383

CREEK

a certain c with a shore, into	Acts 27:39	2859

CREEP

All fowls that c, going upon all	Lev 11:20	8318
things that c upon the earth	Lev 11:29	8317
unclean to you among all that c	Lev 11:31	8318
things that c upon the earth	Lev 11:42	8317
beasts of the forest do c forth	Ps 104:20	7430
things that c upon the earth	Eze 38:20	7430
sort are they which c into houses	2Ti 3:6	1744,1519

CREEPETH

every thing that c upon the earth	Gen 1:25	7431
thing that c upon the earth	Gen 1:26	7430
every thing that c upon the earth	Gen 1:30	7430
every thing that c upon the earth	Gen 7:8	7430
every creeping thing that c upon	Gen 7:14	7430
thing that c upon the earth	Gen 7:21	8317
thing that c upon the earth	Gen 8:17	7430
whatsoever c upon the earth,	Gen 8:19	7430
every creeping thing that c upon	Lev 11:41	8317
with any creeping thing that c	Lev 11:43	8317
thing that c upon the earth	Lev 11:44	7430
creature that c upon the earth	Lev 11:46	8317
living thing that c on the ground	Lev 20:25	7430
of any thing that c on the ground	Deut 4:18	7430

CREEPING

c thing, and beast of the earth	Gen 1:24	7431
over every c thing that creepeth	Gen 1:26	7431
the c thing, and the fowls of the	Gen 6:7	7431
of every c thing of the earth	Gen 6:20	7431
every creeping thing that creepeth upon	Gen 7:14	7431
of every c thing that creepeth	Gen 7:21	8318
the c things, and the fowl of the	Gen 7:23	7431
of every c thing that creepeth	Gen 8:17	7431
Every beast, every c thing	Gen 8:19	7431
the carcase of unclean c things	Lev 5:2	8318
may ye eat of every flying c	Lev 11:21	8318
But all other flying c things	Lev 11:23	8318

the c things that creep upon the	Lev 11:29	8318
every c thing that creepeth upon	Lev 11:41	8318
hath more feet among all c things	Lev 11:42	8318
with any c thing that creepeth	Lev 11:43	8318
of c thing that creepeth upon the	Lev 11:44	8318
Or whosoever toucheth any c thing	Lev 22:5	8318
every c thing that flieth is	Deut 14:19	8318
of c things, and of fishes	1Kin 4:33	7431
wherein are things c innumerable	Ps 104:25	7431
c things, and flying fowl	Ps 148:10	7431
and behold every form of c things	Eze 8:10	7431
all c things that creep upon the	Eze 38:20	7431
with the c things of the ground	Hos 2:18	7431
of the sea, as the c things	Hab 1:14	7431
c things, and fowls of the air	Acts 10:12	2062
c things, and fowls of the air	Acts 11:6	2062
and fourfooted beasts, and c things	Rom 1:23	2062

CREPT

are certain men c in unawares	Jude 4	3921

CRESCENS (cres'-sens) A companion of Paul.

C to Galatia, Titus unto Dalmatia	2Ti 4:10	2913

CRETE (creet) See CRETES. An island south of Greece.

suffering us, we sailed under C	Acts 27:7	2914
which is an haven of C, and lieth	Acts 27:12	2914
thence, they sailed close by C	Acts 27:13	2914
me, and not have loosed from C	Acts 27:21	2914
For this cause left I thee in C	Titus 1:5	2914

CRETES (creets) See CRETIANS. Inhabitants of Crete.

C and Arabians, we do hear them	Acts 2:11	2912

CRETIANS (cre'-shuns) See CRETES. Same as Cretes.

The C are alway liars, evil	Titus 1:12	2912
bishop of the church of the C	Titus s	2912

CREW

And immediately the cock c	Mt 26:74	5455
and the cock c	Mk 14:68	5455
And the second time the cock c	Mk 14:72	5455
while he yet spake, the cock c	Lk 22:60	5455
and immediately the cock c	Jn 18:27	5455

CRIB

to serve thee, or abide by thy c	Job 39:9	18
Where no oxen are, the c is clean	Prov 14:4	18
owner, and the ass his master's c	Is 1:3	18

CRIED

he c with a great and exceeding	Gen 27:34	6817
with me, and I c with a loud voice	Gen 39:14	7121
that I lifted up my voice and c	Gen 39:15	7121
as I lifted up my voice and c	Gen 39:18	7121
they c before him, Bow the knee	Gen 41:43	7121
the people c to Pharaoh for bread	Gen 41:55	6817
and he c, Cause every man to go	Gen 45:1	7121
reason of the bondage, and they c	Ex 2:23	2199
c unto Pharaoh, saying, Wherefore	Ex 5:15	6817
Moses c unto the LORD because of	Ex 8:12	6817
of Israel c out unto the LORD	Ex 14:10	6817
And he c unto the LORD	Ex 15:25	6817
Moses c unto the LORD, saying,	Ex 17:4	6817
And the people c unto Moses	Num 11:2	6817
Moses c unto the LORD, saying,	Num 12:13	6817
lifted up their voice, and c	Num 14:1	5414
when we c unto the LORD, he heard	Num 20:16	6817
the damsel, because she c not	Deut 22:24	6817
field, and the betrothed damsel c	Deut 22:27	6817
when we c unto the LORD God of	Deut 26:7	6817
when they c unto the LORD, he put	Josh 24:7	6817
of Israel c unto the LORD	Judg 3:9	2199
of Israel c unto the LORD	Judg 3:15	2199
of Israel c unto the LORD	Judg 4:3	6817
c through the lattice, Why is his	Judg 5:28	2980
of Israel c unto the LORD	Judg 6:6	2199
when the children of Israel c	Judg 6:7	2199
and they c, The sword of the LORD,	Judg 7:20	7121
and all the host ran, and c	Judg 7:21	7321
and lifted up his voice, and c	Judg 9:7	7121
of Israel c unto the LORD	Judg 10:10	2199
ye c to me, and I delivered you	Judg 10:12	6817
they c unto the children of Dan	Judg 18:23	7121
and told it, all the city c out	1Sa 4:13	2199
Ekron, that the Ekronites c out	1Sa 5:10	2199
Samuel c unto the LORD for Israel	1Sa 7:9	2199
your fathers c unto the LORD,	1Sa 12:8	2199
they c unto the LORD, and said, We	1Sa 12:10	2199
he c unto the LORD all night	1Sa 15:11	2199
c unto the armies of Israel, and	1Sa 17:8	7121
Jonathan c after the lad, and said	1Sa 20:37	7121
Jonathan c after the lad, Make	1Sa 20:38	7121
c after Saul, saying, My lord the	1Sa 24:8	7121
David c to the people, and to	1Sa 26:14	7121

CRIES

Samuel, she *c* with a loud voice .... 1Sa 28:12 — 2199
And the watchman *c*, and told the .... 2Sa 18:25 — 7121
the king *c* with a loud voice, O .... 2Sa 19:4 — 2199
Then *c* a wise woman out of the .... 2Sa 20:16 — 7121
upon the LORD, and *c* to my God .... 2Sa 22:7 — 7121
he *c* against the altar in the .... 1Kin 13:2 — 7121
which had *c* against the altar in .... 1Kin 13:4 — 7121
he *c* unto the man of God that .... 1Kin 13:21 — 7121
For the saying which he *c* by the .... 1Kin 13:32 — 7121
he *c* unto the LORD, and said, O .... 1Kin 17:20 — 7121
c unto the LORD, and said, O LORD .... 1Kin 17:21 — 7121
they *c* aloud, and cut themselves .... 1Kin 18:28 — 7121
passed by, he *c* unto the king .... 1Kin 20:39 — 6817
and Jehoshaphat *c* out .... 1Kin 22:32 — 2199
And Elisha saw it, and he *c* .... 2Kin 2:12 — 6817
Now there *c* a certain woman of .... 2Kin 4:1 — 6817
of the pottage, that they *c* out .... 2Kin 4:40 — 6817
and he *c*, and said, Alas, master .... 2Kin 6:5 — 6817
there *c* a woman unto him, saying, ... 2Kin 6:26 — 6817
c to the king for her house and .... 2Kin 8:5 — 6817
Athaliah rent her clothes, and *c* .... 2Kin 11:14 — 7121
c with a loud voice in the Jews' .... 2Kin 18:28 — 7121
the prophet *c* unto the LORD .... 2Kin 20:11 — 7121
for they *c* to God in the battle, ... 1Chr 5:20 — 2199
they *c* unto the LORD, and the .... 2Chr 13:14 — 6817
Asa *c* unto the LORD his God, and .... 2Chr 14:11 — 7121
but Jehoshaphat *c* out, and the .... 2Chr 18:31 — 2199
Then they *c* with a loud voice in .... 2Chr 32:18 — 7121
of Amoz, prayed and *c* to heaven .... 2Chr 32:20 — 2199
c with a loud voice unto the LORD .... Neh 9:4 — 2199
trouble, when they *c* unto thee .... Neh 9:27 — 6817
c unto thee, thou heardest them .... Neh 9:28 — 2199
c with a loud and a bitter cry .... Est 4:1 — 2199
I delivered the poor that *c* .... Job 29:12 — 7768
(they *c* after them as after a .... Job 30:5 — 7321
up, and I *c* in the congregation .... Job 30:28 — 7768
I *c* unto the LORD with my voice, ... Ps 3:4 — 7121
upon the LORD, and *c* unto my God ...... Ps 18:6 — 7768
They *c*, but there was none to .... Ps 18:41 — 7768
They *c* unto thee, and were .... Ps 22:5 — 2199
but when he *c* unto him, he heard .... Ps 22:24 — 7768
I *c* unto thee, and thou hast .... Ps 30:2 — 7768
I *c* to thee, O LORD .... Ps 30:8 — 7121
supplications when I *c* unto thee .... Ps 31:22 — 7768
This poor man *c*, and the LORD .... Ps 34:6 — 7121
I *c* unto him with my mouth, and he ...... Ps 66:17 — 7121
I *c* unto God with my voice, even .... Ps 77:1 — 6817
God of my salvation, I have *c* day .... Ps 88:1 — 6817
But unto thee have I *c*, O LORD .... Ps 88:13 — 7768
Then they *c* unto the LORD in .... Ps 107:6 — 6817
Then they *c* unto the LORD in .... Ps 107:13 — 2199
I *c* with my whole heart .... Ps 119:145 — 7121
I *c* unto thee .... Ps 119:146 — 7121
the dawning of the morning, and *c* .... Ps 119:147 — 7768
In my distress I *c* unto the LORD .... Ps 120:1 — 7121
of the depths have I *c* unto thee .... Ps 130:1 — 7121
In the day when I *c* thou .... Ps 138:3 — 7121
I *c* unto the LORD with my voice .... Ps 142:1 — 2199
I *c* unto thee, O LORD .... Ps 142:5 — 2199
one *c* unto another, and said, Holy .... Is 6:3 — 7121
moved at the voice of him that *c* .... Is 6:4 — 7121
And he *c*, A lion .... Is 21:8 — 7121
have I *c* concerning this, Their .... Is 30:7 — 7121
c with a loud voice in the Jews' .... Is 36:13 — 7121
Destruction upon destruction is *c* .... Jer 4:20 — 7121
I *c* out, I *c* violence and .... Jer 20:8 — 2199
c out, I *c* violence and spoil .... Jer 20:8 — 2199
Their heart *c* unto the Lord, O .... Lam 2:18 — 6817
They *c* unto them, Depart ye .... Lam 4:15 — 7121
He *c* also in mine ears with a .... Eze 9:1 — 7121
that I fell upon my face, and *c* .... Eze 9:8 — 2199
it was *c* unto them in my hearing, ... Eze 10:13 — 7121
c with a loud voice, and said, Ah .... Eze 11:13 — 2199
Then an herald *c* aloud, To you it .... Dan 3:4 — 7123
He *c* aloud, and said thus, Hew .... Dan 4:14 — 7123
The king *c* aloud to bring in the .... Dan 5:7 — 7123
he *c* with a lamentable voice unto .... Dan 6:20 — 2200
they have not *c* unto me with .... Hos 7:14 — 2199
c every man unto his god, and cast ...... Jonah 1:5 — 2199
Wherefore they *c* unto the LORD .... Jonah 1:14 — 7121
I *c* by reason of mine affliction .... Jonah 2:2 — 7121
out of the belly of hell I *c* .... Jonah 2:2 — 7768
the city a day's journey, and he *c* .... Jonah 3:4 — 7121
whom the former prophets have *c* .... Zec 1:4 — 7121
Then he upon me, and spake unto ...... Zec 6:8 — 2199
hath *c* by the former prophets .... Zec 7:7 — 7121
it is come to pass, that as he *c* .... Zec 7:13 — 7121
so they *c*, and I would not hear, ... Zec 7:13 — 7121
And, behold, they *c* out, saying, ... Mt 8:29 — 2896
and they *c* out for fear .... Mt 14:26 — 2896
and beginning to sink, he *c* .... Mt 14:30 — 2896

c unto him, saying, Have mercy on .... Mt 15:22 — 2905
c out, saying, Have mercy on us, ... Mt 20:30 — 2896
but they *c* the more, saying, Have .... Mt 20:31 — 2896
went before, and that followed, *c* .... Mt 21:9 — 2896
But they *c* out the more, saying, ... Mt 27:23 — 2896
hour Jesus *c* with a loud voice .... Mt 27:46 — 310
when he had *c* again with a loud .... Mt 27:50 — 2896
an unclean spirit; and he *c* out .... Mk 1:23 — 349
c with a loud voice, he came out .... Mk 1:26 — 2896
him, fell down before him, and *c* .... Mk 3:11 — 2896
c with a loud voice, and said, ... Mk 5:7 — 2896
it had been a spirit, and *c* out .... Mk 6:49 — 349
the father of the child *c* out .... Mk 9:24 — 2896
And the spirit *c*, and rent him sore ...... Mk 9:26 — 2896
but he *c* the more a great deal, ... Mk 10:48 — 2896
before, and they that followed, *c* .... Mk 11:9 — 2896
they *c* out again, Crucify him .... Mk 15:13 — 2896
they *c* out the more exceedingly, ... Mk 15:14 — 2896
hour Jesus *c* with a loud voice .... Mk 15:34 — 994
Jesus *c* with a loud voice, and .... Mk 15:37 — 863
against him, saw that he so *c* out .... Mk 15:39 — 2896
and *c* out with a loud voice, ... Lk 4:33 — 349
he had said these things, he *c* .... Lk 8:8 — 5455
he *c* out, and fell down before him ...... Lk 8:28 — 349
a man of the company *c* out .... Lk 9:38 — 310
And he *c* and said, Father Abraham, .. Lk 16:24 — 5455
And he *c*, saying, Jesus, thou son .... Lk 18:38 — 994
but he *c* so much the more, Thou .... Lk 18:39 — 2896
they *c* out all at once, saying, ... Lk 23:18 — 349
But they *c*, saying, Crucify him, ... Lk 23:21 — 2019
when Jesus had *c* with a loud .... Lk 23:46 — 5455
John bare witness of him, and *c* .... Jn 1:15 — 2896
Then *c* Jesus in the temple as he .... Jn 7:28 — 2896
of the feast, Jesus stood and *c* .... Jn 7:37 — 2896
he *c* with a loud voice, Lazarus, ... Jn 11:43 — 2905
and went forth to meet him, and *c* ...... Jn 12:13 — 2896
Jesus *c* and said, He that .... Jn 12:44 — 2896
Then *c* they all again, saying, ... Jn 18:40 — 2905
and officers saw him, they *c* out .... Jn 19:6 — 2905
but the Jews *c* out, saying, If .... Jn 19:12 — 2896
But they *c* out, Away with him, ... Jn 19:15 — 2905
Then they *c* out with a loud voice .... Acts 7:57 — 2896
c with a loud voice, Lord, lay .... Acts 7:60 — 2896
same followed Paul and us, and *c* .... Acts 16:17 — 2896
But Paul *c* with a loud voice, ... Acts 16:28 — 5455
c out, saying, Great is Diana of .... Acts 19:28 — 2896
Some therefore *c* one thing .... Acts 19:32 — 2896
the space of two hours *c* out .... Acts 19:34 — 2896
some *c* one thing, some another, ... Acts 21:34 — 994
And as they *c* out, and cast off .... Acts 22:23 — 2905
wherefore they *c* so against him .... Acts 22:24 — 2019
he *c* out in the council, Men and .... Acts 23:6 — 2896
that I *c* standing among them, ... Acts 24:21 — 2896
they *c* with a loud voice, saying, ... Rev 6:10 — 2896
he *c* with a loud voice to the .... Rev 7:2 — 2896
c with a loud voice, saying, ... Rev 7:10 — 2896
c with a loud voice, as when a .... Rev 10:3 — 2896
and when he had *c*, seven thunders ...... Rev 10:3 — 2896
And she being with child *c* .... Rev 12:2 — 2896
c with a loud cry to him that had .... Rev 14:18 — 5455
he *c* mightily with a strong voice .... Rev 18:2 — 2896
c when they saw the smoke of her .... Rev 18:18 — 2896
cast dust on their heads, and *c* .... Rev 18:19 — 2896
he *c* with a loud voice, saying to .... Rev 19:17 — 2896

CRIES

the *c* of them which have reaped .... Jas 5:4 — 995

CRIEST

Moses, Wherefore *c* thou unto me .... Ex 14:15 — 6817
Who art thou that *c* to the king .... 1Sa 26:14 — 7121
if thou *c* after knowledge, and .... Prov 2:3 — 7121
When thou *c*, let thy companies .... Is 57:13 — 2199
Why *c* thou for thine affliction .... Jer 30:15 — 2199

CRIETH

blood *c* unto me from the ground .... Gen 4:10 — 6817
come to pass, when he *c* unto me .... Ex 22:27 — 6817
and the soul of the wounded *c* out .... Job 24:12 — 7768
shall deliver the needy when he *c*.......... Ps 72:12 — 7768
my flesh *c* out for the living God .... Ps 84:2 — 7442
Wisdom *c* without .... Prov 1:20 — 7442
She *c* in the chief place of .... Prov 1:21 — 7121
She *c* at the gates, at the entry .... Prov 8:3 — 7442
she *c* upon the highest places of .... Prov 9:3 — 7121
is in pain, and *c* out in her pangs .... Is 26:17 — 2199
of him that *c* in the wilderness .... Is 40:3 — 7121
it *c* out against me .... Jer 12:8 — 5414,6963
The LORD's voice *c* unto the city .... Mic 6:9 — 7121
for she *c* after us .... Mt 15:23 — 2896
taketh him, and he suddenly *c* out .... Lk 9:39 — 2896

Esaias also *c* concerning Israel, ...	Rom 9:27	2896
is of you kept back by fraud, *c*	Jas 5:4	2896

CRIME

For this is an heinous *c*	Job 31:11	2154
concerning the *c* laid against him	Acts 25:16	1462

CRIMES

for the land is full of bloody *c*	Eze 7:23	4941
to signify the *c* laid against him	Acts 25:27	156

CRIMSON

and in iron, and in purple, and *c* 2Chr 2:7		3758
blue, and in fine linen, and in *c*..............2Chr 2:14		3758
the vail of blue, and purple, and *c* 2Chr 3:14		3758
though they be red like *c*	Is 1:18	8438
thou clothest thyself with *c*	Jer 4:30	8144

CRIPPLE

being a *c* from his mother's womb, ...	Acts 14:8	5560

CRISPING

and the wimples, and the *c* pins, ...	Is 3:22	2754

CRISPUS (cris'-pus) *A convert of Paul.*

And *C*, the chief ruler of the	Acts 18:8	2921
I baptized none of you, but *C*	1Cor 1:14	2921

CROOKBACKT

Or *c*, or a dwarf, or that hath a	Lev 21:20	1384

CROOKED

are a perverse and *c* generation	Deut 32:5	6618
hand hath formed the *c* serpent...............	Job 26:13	1281
as turn aside unto their *c* ways...............	Ps 125:5	6128
Whose ways are *c*, and they froward	Prov 2:15	6141
That which is *c* cannot be made	Eccl 1:15	5791
straight, which he hath made *c*	Eccl 7:13	5791
even leviathan that *c* serpent	Is 27:1	6129
the *c* shall be made straight, and	Is 40:4	6121
before them, and *c* things straight.........	Is 42:16	4625
make the *c* places straight	Is 45:2	1921
they have made them *c* paths	Is 59:8	6140
stone, he hath made my paths *c*	Lam 3:9	5753
the *c* shall be made straight, and	Lk 3:5	4646
rebuke, in the midst of a *c*	Phil 2:15	4646

CROP

away his *c* with his feathers	Lev 1:16	4760
I will *c* off from the top of his	Eze 17:22	6998

CROPPED

He *c* off the top of his young	Eze 17:4	6998

CROSS

And he that taketh not his *c*	Mt 10:38	4716
deny himself, and take up his *c*	Mt 16:24	4716
him they compelled to bear his *c*...........	Mt 27:32	4716
Son of God, come down from the *c*	Mt 27:40	4716
let him now come down from the *c*	Mt 27:42	4716
deny himself, and take up his *c*	Mk 8:34	4716
and come, take up the *c*, and follow	Mk 10:21	4716
Alexander and Rufus, to bear his *c*	Mk 15:21	4716
thyself, and come down from the *c*	Mk 15:30	4716
of Israel descend now from the *c*	Mk 15:32	4716
himself, and take up his *c* daily.............	Lk 9:23	4716
And whosoever doth not bear his *c*........	Lk 14:27	4716
and on him they laid the *c*......................	Lk 23:26	4716
he bearing his *c* went forth into	Jn 19:17	4716
wrote a title, and put it on the *c*	Jn 19:19	4716
by the *c* of Jesus his mother	Jn 19:25	4716
upon the *c* on the sabbath day	Jn 19:31	4716
lest the *c* of Christ should be..................	1Cor 1:17	4716
of the *c* is to them that perish	1Cor 1:18	4716
is the offence of the *c* ceased	Gal 5:11	4716
persecution for the *c* of Christ	Gal 6:12	4716
save in the *c* of our Lord Jesus..............	Gal 6:14	4716
unto God in one body by the *c*	Eph 2:16	4716
death, even the death of the *c*	Phil 2:8	4716
the enemies of the *c* of Christ	Phil 3:18	4716
peace through the blood of his *c*	Col 1:20	4716
of the way, nailing it to his *c*	Col 2:14	4716
was set before him endured the *c*	Heb 12:2	4716

CROSSWAY

thou have stood in the *c*, to cut..............	Obad 14	6563

CROUCH

c to him for a piece of silver and	1Sa 2:36	7812

CROUCHETH

He *c*, and humbleth himself, that...........	Ps 10:10	1794

CROW

this night, before the cock *c*	Mt 26:34	5455
said unto him, Before the cock *c*	Mt 26:75	5455
night, before the cock *c* twice.................	Mk 14:30	5455
unto him, Before the cock *c* twice	Mk 14:72	5455
the cock shall not *c* this day	Lk 22:34	5455

said unto him, Before the cock *c*	Lk 22:61	5455
unto thee, The cock shall not *c*	Jn 13:38	5455

CROWN

on the *c* of the head of him that..............	Gen 49:26	6936
upon it a *c* of gold round about	Ex 25:11	2213
make thereto a *c* of gold round	Ex 25:24	2213
thou shalt make a golden *c* to the..........	Ex 25:25	2213
put the holy *c* upon the mitre	Ex 29:6	5145
unto it a *c* of gold round about	Ex 30:3	2213
thou make to it under the *c* of it	Ex 30:4	2213
made a *c* of gold to it round	Ex 37:2	2213
made thereunto a *c* of gold round	Ex 37:11	2213
made a *c* of gold for the border	Ex 37:12	2213
unto it a *c* of gold round about...............	Ex 37:26	2213
gold for it under the *c* thereof................	Ex 37:27	2213
plate of the holy *c* of pure gold..............	Ex 39:30	5145
put the golden plate, the holy *c*..............	Lev 8:9	5145
for the *c* of the anointing oil of...............	Lev 21:12	5145
the arm with the *c* of the head...............	Deut 33:20	6936
I took the *c* that was upon his................	2Sa 1:10	5145
their king's *c* from off his head	2Sa 12:30	5850
to the *c* of his head there was no	2Sa 14:25	6936
put the *c* upon him, and gave him	2Kin 11:12	5145
David took the *c* of their king	1Chr 20:2	5850
king's son, and put upon him the *c*........	2Chr 23:11	5145
before the king with the *c* royal	Est 1:11	3804
he set the royal *c* upon her head	Est 2:17	3804
the *c* royal which is set upon his	Est 6:8	3804
white, and with a great *c* of gold	Est 8:15	5850
the sole of his foot unto his *c*	Job 2:7	6936
and taken the *c* from my head	Job 19:9	5850
shoulder, and bind it as a *c* to me	Job 31:36	5850
thou settest a *c* of pure gold on.............	Ps 21:3	5850
thou hast profaned his *c* by....................	Ps 89:39	5145
upon himself shall his *c* flourish............	Ps 132:18	5145
a *c* of glory shall she deliver to	Prov 4:9	5850
woman is a *c* to her husband	Prov 12:4	5850
The *c* of the wise is their riches	Prov 14:24	5850
The hoary head is a *c* of glory...............	Prov 16:31	5850
children are the *c* of old men.................	Prov 17:6	5850
doth *c* endure to every	Prov 27:24	5145
c wherewith his mother crowned	Song 3:11	5850
c of the head of the daughters of	Is 3:17	6936
Woe to the *c* of pride, to the	Is 28:1	5850
The *c* of pride, the drunkards of	Is 28:3	5850
LORD of hosts be for a *c* of glory	Is 28:5	5850
Thou shalt also be a *c* of glory	Is 62:3	5850
have broken the *c* of thy head	Jer 2:16	6936
down, even the *c* of your glory	Jer 13:18	5850
Moab, and the *c* of the head of the	Jer 48:45	6936
The *c* is fallen from our head	Lam 5:16	5850
a beautiful *c* upon thine head	Eze 16:12	5850
the diadem, and take off the *c*	Eze 21:26	5850
shall be as the stones of a *c*	Zec 9:16	5145
they had platted a *c* of thorns................	Mt 27:29	4735
purple, and platted a *c* of thorns	Mk 15:17	4735
soldiers platted a *c* of thorns	Jn 19:2	4735
forth, wearing the *c* of thorns................	Jn 19:5	4735
do it to obtain a corruptible *c*	1Cor 9:25	4735
and longed for, my joy and *c*..................	Phil 4:1	4735
hope, or joy, or *c* of rejoicing	1Th 2:19	4735
up for me a *c* of righteousness	2Ti 4:8	4735
he shall receive the *c* of life	Jas 1:12	4735
ye shall receive a *c* of glory	1Pet 5:4	4735
and I will give thee a *c* of life	Rev 2:10	4735
thou hast, that no man take thy *c*	Rev 3:11	4735
and a *c* was given unto him	Rev 6:2	4735
upon her head a *c* of twelve stars	Rev 12:1	4735
having on his head a golden *c*................	Rev 14:14	4735

CROWNED

hast *c* him with glory and honour...........	Ps 8:5	5849
the prudent are *c* with knowledge	Prov 14:18	3803
the crown wherewith his mother *c*..........	Song 3:11	5849
Thy *c* are as the locusts, and thy...........	Nah 3:17	4502
for masteries, yet is he not *c*	2Ti 2:5	4737
of death, *c* with glory and honour	Heb 2:9	4737

CROWNEDST

thou *c* him with glory and honour, ...	Heb 2:7	4737

CROWNEST

Thou *c* the year with thy goodness.........	Ps 65:11	5849

CROWNETH

who *c* thee with lovingkindness and	Ps 103:4	5849

CROWNING

the *c* city, whose merchants are.............	Is 23:8	5849

CROWNS

beautiful *c* upon their heads	Eze 23:42	5850
take silver and gold, and make *c*	Zec 6:11	5850

the c shall be to Helem, and to	Zec 6:14	5850
they had on their heads c of gold	Rev 4:4	4735
cast their c before the throne,	Rev 4:10	4735
heads were as it were c like gold	Rev 9:7	4735
horns, and seven c upon his heads	Rev 12:3	1238
horns, and upon his horns ten c	Rev 13:1	1238
fire, and on his head were many c	Rev 19:12	1238

CRUCIFIED

Son of man is betrayed to be c	Mt 26:2	4717
all say unto him, Let him be c	Mt 27:22	4717
the more, saying, Let him be c	Mt 27:23	4717
Jesus, he delivered him to be c	Mt 27:26	4717
And they c him, and parted his	Mt 27:35	4717
were there two thieves c with him	Mt 27:38	4717
also, which were c with him	Mt 27:44	4957
that ye seek Jesus, which was c	Mt 28:5	4717
when he had scourged him, to be c	Mk 15:15	4717
And when they had c him, they	Mk 15:24	4717
was the third hour, and they c him	Mk 15:25	4717
they that were c with him reviled	Mk 15:32	4957
Jesus of Nazareth, which was c	Mk 16:6	4717
requiring that he might be c	Lk 23:23	4717
called Calvary, there they c him	Lk 23:33	4717
the hands of sinful men, and be c	Lk 24:7	4717
condemned to death, and have c him	Lk 24:20	4717
him therefore unto them to be c	Jn 19:16	4717
Where they c him, and two others	Jn 19:18	4717
Jesus was c was nigh to the city	Jn 19:20	4717
soldiers, when they had c Jesus	Jn 19:23	4717
of the other which was c with him	Jn 19:32	4957
where he was c there was a garden	Jn 19:41	4717
taken, and by wicked hands have c	Acts 2:23	4362
that same Jesus, whom ye have c	Acts 2:36	4717
Christ of Nazareth, whom ye c	Acts 4:10	4717
that our old man is c with him	Rom 6:6	4957
was Paul c for you?	1Cor 1:13	4717
But we preach Christ c, unto the	1Cor 1:23	4717
you, save Jesus Christ, and him c	1Cor 2:2	4717
not have c the Lord of glory	1Cor 2:8	4717
though he was c through weakness	2Cor 13:4	4717
I am c with Christ	Gal 2:20	4957
evidently set forth, c among you	Gal 3:1	4717
they that are Christ's have the c	Gal 5:24	4717
by whom the world is c unto me	Gal 6:14	4717
Egypt, where also our Lord was c	Rev 11:8	4717

CRUCIFY

mock, and to scourge, and to c him	Mt 20:19	4717
some of them ye shall kill and c	Mt 23:34	4717
on him, and led him away to c him	Mt 27:31	4717
And they cried out again, C him	Mk 15:13	4717
out the more exceedingly, C him	Mk 15:14	4717
on him, and led him out to c him	Mk 15:20	4717
And with him they c two thieves	Mk 15:27	4717
cried, saying, C him, c him	Lk 23:21	4717
out, saying, C him, c him	Jn 19:6	4717
unto them, Take ye him, and c him	Jn 19:6	4717
not that I have power to c thee	Jn 19:10	4717
with him, away with him, c him	Jn 19:15	4717
unto them, Shall I c your King	Jn 19:15	4717
seeing they c to themselves the	Heb 6:6	388

CRUEL

and their wrath, for it was c	Gen 49:7	7185
of spirit, and for c bondage	Ex 6:9	7185
dragons, and the c venom of asps	Deut 32:33	393
Thou art become c to me	Job 30:21	393
and they hate me with c hatred	Ps 25:19	2555
hand of the unrighteous and c man	Ps 71:4	2556
others, and thy years unto the c	Prov 5:9	394
but he that is c troubleth his	Prov 11:17	394
mercies of the wicked are c	Prov 12:10	394
therefore a c messenger shall be	Prov 17:11	394
Wrath is c, and anger is	Prov 27:4	395
jealousy is c as the grave	Song 8:6	
c both with wrath and fierce anger	Is 13:9	394
over into the hand of a c lord	Is 19:4	7186
they are c, and have no mercy	Jer 6:23	394
with the chastisement of a c one	Jer 30:14	394
they are c, and will not shew	Jer 50:42	394
daughter of my people is become c	Lam 4:3	393
And others had trial of c mockings	Heb 11:36	

CRUELLY

father, because he c oppressed	Eze 18:18	6233

CRUELTY

instruments of c are in their	Gen 49:5	2555
That the c done to the threescore	Judg 9:24	2555
me, and such as breathe out c	Ps 27:12	2555
are full of the habitations of c	Ps 74:20	2555
with c have ye ruled them	Eze 34:4	6531

CRUMBS

yet the dogs eat of the c which	Mt 15:27	5589
the table eat of the children's c	Mk 7:28	5589
desiring to be fed with the c	Lk 16:21	5589

CRUSE

the c of water, and let us go	1Sa 26:11	6835
the c of water from Saul's	1Sa 26:12	6835
the c of water that was at his	1Sa 26:16	6835
a c of honey, and go to him	1Kin 14:3	1228
a barrel, and a little oil in a c	1Kin 17:12	6835
neither shall the c of oil fail	1Kin 17:14	6835
neither did the c of oil fail	1Kin 17:16	6835
and a c of water at his head	1Kin 19:6	6835
And he said, Bring me a new c	2Kin 2:20	6746

CRUSH

that the foot may c them, or that	Job 39:15	2115
against me to c my young men	Lam 1:15	7665
To c under his feet all the	Lam 3:34	1792
which c the needy, which say to	Amos 4:1	7533

CRUSHED

Lord that which is bruised, or c	Lev 22:24	3807
c Balaam's foot against the wall	Num 22:25	3905
be only oppressed and c alway	Deut 28:33	7533
which are c before the moth	Job 4:19	1792
they are c in the gate, neither	Job 5:4	1792
that which is c breaketh out into	Is 59:5	2116
hath devoured me, he hath c me	Jer 51:34	2000

CRY

Lord said, Because the c of Sodom	Gen 18:20	2201
according to the c of it, which	Gen 18:21	6818
because the c of them is waxen	Gen 19:13	6818
a great and exceeding bitter c	Gen 27:34	6818
their c came up unto God by	Ex 2:23	7775
have heard their c by reason of	Ex 3:7	6818
the c of the children of Israel	Ex 3:9	6818
therefore they c, saying, Let us	Ex 5:8	6817
And there shall be a great c	Ex 11:6	6818
and there was a great c in Egypt	Ex 12:30	6818
they c at all unto me	Ex 22:23	6817
I will surely hear their c	Ex 22:23	6818
of them that c for being overcome	Ex 32:18	6030
upon his upper lip, and shall c	Lev 13:45	7121
about him that fled at the c of them	Num 16:34	6963
he c unto the Lord against thee,	Deut 15:9	7121
lest he c against thee unto the	Deut 24:15	7121
c unto the gods which ye have	Judg 10:14	2199
the c of the city went up to	1Sa 5:12	7775
Cease not to c unto the Lord our	1Sa 7:8	2199
ye shall c out in that day	1Sa 8:18	2199
because their c is come unto me	1Sa 9:16	6818
I yet to c any more unto the king	2Sa 19:28	2199
my c did enter into his ears	2Sa 22:7	7775
my God, to hearken unto the c	1Kin 8:28	7440
mocked them, and said, C aloud	1Kin 18:27	7121
she went forth to c unto the king	2Kin 8:3	6817
my God, to hearken unto the c	2Chr 6:19	7440
trumpets to c alarm against you	2Chr 13:12	7321
c unto thee in our affliction,	2Chr 20:9	2199
there was a great c of the people	Neh 5:1	6818
very angry when I heard their c	Neh 5:6	2201
heardest their c by the Red sea	Neh 9:9	2201
cried with a loud and a bitter c	Est 4:1	2201
of the fastings and their c	Est 9:31	2201
blood, and let my c have no place	Job 16:18	2201
I c out of wrong, but I am not	Job 19:7	6817
I c aloud, but there is no	Job 19:7	7768
Will God hear his c when trouble	Job 27:9	6818
I c unto thee, and thou dost not	Job 30:20	7768
though they c in his destruction	Job 30:24	7769
If my land c against me, or that	Job 31:38	2199
So that they cause the c of the	Job 34:28	6818
he heareth the c of the afflicted	Job 34:28	6818
they make the oppressed to c	Job 35:9	2199
they c out by reason of the arm	Job 35:9	7768
There they c, but none giveth	Job 35:12	6817
they c not when he bindeth them	Job 36:13	7768
when his young ones c unto God	Job 38:41	7768
Hearken unto the voice of my c	Ps 5:2	7773
not the c of the humble	Ps 9:12	6818
right, O Lord, attend unto my c	Ps 17:1	7440
my c came before him, even into	Ps 18:6	7775
I c in the daytime, but thou	Ps 22:2	7121
O Lord, when I c with my voice	Ps 27:7	7121
Unto thee will I c, O Lord my	Ps 28:1	7121
when I c unto thee, when I lift	Ps 28:2	7768
and his ears are open unto their c	Ps 34:15	7775
The righteous c, and the Lord	Ps 34:17	6817
O Lord, and give ear unto my c	Ps 39:12	7775
inclined unto me, and heard my c	Ps 40:1	7775

at noon, will I pray, and *c* aloud.............. Ps 55:17 | 1993
When I *c* unto thee, then shall................ Ps 56:9 | 7121
I will *c* unto God most high................... Ps 57:2 | 7121
Hear my *c*, O God.............................. Ps 61:1 | 7440
of the earth will I *c* unto thee................ Ps 61:2 | 7121
for I *c* unto thee daily......................... Ps 86:3 | 7121
incline thine ear unto my *c*................... Ps 88:2 | 7440
He shall *c* unto me, Thou art my............ Ps 89:26 | 7121
LORD, and let my *c* come unto thee........ Ps 102:1 | 7775
affliction, when he heard their *c*............. Ps 106:44 | 7440
Then they *c* unto the LORD in............... Ps 107:19 | 2199
Then they *c* unto the LORD in............... Ps 107:28 | 6817
Let my *c* come near before thee, O........ Ps 119:169 | 7440
Lord, I *c* unto thee............................. Ps 141:1 | 7121
unto my voice, when I *c* unto thee......... Ps 141:1 | 7121
Attend unto my *c*.............................. Ps 142:6 | 7440
he also will hear their *c*...................... Ps 145:19 | 7775
and to the young ravens which *c*........... Ps 147:9 | 7121
Doth not wisdom *c*............................ Prov 8:1 | 7121
his ears at the *c* of the poor................ Prov 21:13 | 2201
he also shall *c* himself....................... Prov 21:13 | 7121
heard in quiet more than the *c* of.......... Eccl 9:17 | 2201
for righteousness, but behold a *c*.......... Is 5:7 | 6818
child shall have knowledge to *c*............ Is 8:4 | 7121
C out and shout, thou inhabitant........... Is 12:6 | 6670
shall *c* in their desolate houses............ Is 13:22 | 6030
c, O city.. Is 14:31 | 2199
And Heshbon shall *c*, and Elealeh........ Is 15:4 | 2199
soldiers of Moab shall *c* out................. Is 15:4 | 7321
My heart shall *c* out for Moab.............. Is 15:5 | 2199
shall raise up a *c* of destruction........... Is 15:5 | 2201
For the *c* is gone round about the......... Is 15:8 | 2201
for they shall *c* unto the LORD.............. Is 19:20 | 6817
they shall *c* aloud from the sea............ Is 24:14 | 6670
c ye out, and *c*.............................. Is 29:9 | 8173
unto thee at the voice of thy *c*.............. Is 30:19 | 2201
valiant ones shall *c* without................. Is 33:7 | 6817
the satyr shall *c* to his fellow.............. Is 34:14 | 7121
c unto her, that her warfare is............. Is 40:2 | 7121
The voice said, *C*.............................. Is 40:6 | 7121
And he said, What shall I *c*.................. Is 40:6 | 7121
He shall not *c*, nor lift up, nor............. Is 42:2 | 6817
he shall *c*, yea, roar......................... Is 42:13 | 7321
now will I *c* like a travailing............... Is 42:14 | 6463
whose *c* is in the ships...................... Is 43:14 | 7440
yea, one shall *c* unto him.................... Is 46:7 | 6817
c aloud, thou that didst not................. Is 54:1 | 6670
C aloud, spare not, lift up thy.............. Is 58:1 | 7121
thou shalt *c*, and he shall say,............. Is 58:9 | 7768
but ye shall *c* for sorrow of................. Is 65:14 | 6817
c in the ears of Jerusalem,.................. Jer 2:2 | 7121
thou not from this time *c* unto me......... Jer 3:4 | 7121
c, gather together, and say,................ Jer 4:5 | 7121
neither lift up *c* nor prayer for............. Jer 7:16 | 7440
Behold the voice of the *c* of the........... Jer 8:19 | 7775
and though they shall *c* unto me........... Jer 11:11 | 2199
c unto the gods unto whom they........... Jer 11:12 | 2199
neither lift up a *c* or prayer for............ Jer 11:14 | 7440
they *c* unto me for their trouble............ Jer 11:14 | 7121
the *c* of Jerusalem is gone up.............. Jer 14:2 | 6682
fast, I will not hear their *c*.................. Jer 14:12 | 7440
Let a *c* be heard from their................. Jer 18:22 | 2201
let him hear the *c* in the morning......... Jer 20:16 | 2201
Go up to Lebanon, and *c*.................... Jer 22:20 | 6817
in Bashan, and *c* from the passages...... Jer 22:20 | 6817
Howl, ye shepherds, and *c*.................. Jer 25:34 | 2199
A voice of the *c* of the shepherds......... Jer 25:36 | 6818
upon the mount Ephraim shall *c*........... Jer 31:6 | 7121
thy *c* hath filled the land.................... Jer 46:12 | 6682
They did *c* there, Pharaoh king of......... Jer 46:17 | 7121
then the men shall *c*, and all the.......... Jer 47:2 | 2199
ones have caused a *c* to be heard........ Jer 48:4 | 2201
have heard a *c* of destruction.............. Jer 48:5 | 6818
howl and *c*; tell ye it in Arnon............. Jer 48:20 | 2199
I will *c* out for all Moab..................... Jer 48:31 | 2199
From the *c* of Heshbon even unto.......... Jer 48:34 | 2201
c, ye daughters of Rabbah, gird........... Jer 49:3 | 6817
at the *c* the noise thereof was............. Jer 49:21 | 6818
and they shall *c* unto them................. Jer 49:29 | 7121
the *c* is heard among the nations......... Jer 50:46 | 2201
A sound of a *c* cometh from................ Jer 51:54 | 2201
Arise, *c* out in the night..................... Lam 2:19 | 7442
Also when I *c* and shout, he................ Lam 3:8 | 2199
ear at my breathing, at my *c*............... Lam 3:56 | 7775
though they *c* in mine ears with a........ Eze 8:18 | 7121
that *c* for all the abominations............. Eze 9:4 | 602
C and howl, son of man..................... Eze 21:12 | 2199
Forbear to *c*, make no mourning.......... Eze 24:17 | 602
of thy fall, when the wounded *c*........... Eze 26:15 | 602
the sound of the *c* of thy pilots............ Eze 27:28 | 2201
shall *c* bitterly, and shall cast............. Eze 27:30 | 2199

c aloud at Beth-aven, after thee, ... Hos 5:8 | 7321
Israel shall *c* unto me, My God,............ Hos 8:2 | 2199
your God, and *c* unto the LORD, ... Joel 1:14 | 2199
O LORD, to thee will I *c* .... Joel 1:19 | 7121
of the field *c* also unto thee .... Joel 1:20 | 6165
a young lion *c* out of his den .... Amos 3:4 | 5414,6963
that great city, and *c* against it............ Jonah 1:2 | 7121
sackcloth, and *c* mightily unto God....... Jonah 3:8 | 7121
Then shall they *c* unto the LORD .... Mic 3:4 | 2199
that bite with their teeth, and *c* .... Mic 3:5 | 7121
Now why dost thou *c* out aloud .... Mic 4:9 | 7321
Stand, stand, shall they *c* .... Nah 2:8 |
O LORD, how long shall I *c* .... Hab 1:2 | 7768
even *c* out unto thee of violence,......... Hab 1:2 | 2199
the stone shall *c* out of the wall .... Hab 2:11 | 2199
noise of a *c* from the fish gate............. Zeph 1:10 | 6818
mighty man shall *c* there bitterly .... Zeph 1:14 | 6873
C thou, saying, Thus saith the .... Zec 1:14 | 7121
C yet, saying, Thus saith the .... Zec 1:17 | 7121
He shall not strive, nor *c* .... Mt 12:19 | 2905
And at midnight there was a *c* made.... Mt 25:6 | 2906
of Nazareth, he began to *c* out .... Mk 10:47 | 2896
avenge his own elect, which *c* day...... Lk 18:7 | 994
stones would immediately *c* out......... Lk 19:40 | 2896
And there arose a great *c* .... Acts 23:9 | 2906
Spirit of adoption, whereby we *c* .... Rom 8:15 | 2896
break forth and *c*, thou that................ Gal 4:27 | 994
cried with a loud *c* to him that............. Rev 14:18 | 2906

CRYING

when Eli heard the noise of the *c* .... 1Sa 4:14 | 6818
hand on her head, and went on *c*.......... 2Sa 13:19 | 2201
regardeth he the *c* of the driver .... Job 39:7 | 8663
I am weary of my *c* .... Ps 69:3 | 7121
let not thy soul spare for his *c* .... Prov 19:18 | 4191
horseleach hath two daughters, *c* .... Prov 30:15 |
walls, and of *c* to the mountains .... Is 22:5 | 7771
There is a *c* for wine in the................. Is 24:11 | 6682
heard in her, nor the voice of *c* .... Is 65:19 | 2201
A voice of *c* shall be from .... Jer 48:3 | 6818
thereof with shoutings, *c*.................... Zec 4:7 |
with weeping, and with *c* out .... Mal 2:13 | 603
The voice of one *c* in the .... Mt 3:3 | 994
two blind men followed him, *c*............. Mt 9:27 | 2896
the children *c* in the temple, and .... Mt 21:15 | 2896
The voice of one *c* in the .... Mk 1:3 | 994
the mountains, and in the tombs, *c*....... Mk 5:5 | 2896
the multitude *c* aloud began to .... Mk 15:8 | 310
The voice of one *c* in the .... Lk 3:4 | 994
c out, and saying, Thou art Christ........ Lk 4:41 | 2896
voice of one *c* in the wilderness .... Jn 1:23 | 994
c with loud voice, came out of .... Acts 8:7 | 994
ran in among the people, *c* out,........... Acts 14:14 | 2896
unto the rulers of the city, *c*................ Acts 17:6 | 994
C out, Men of Israel, help .... Acts 21:28 | 2896
of the people followed after, *c* .... Acts 21:36 | 2896
c that he ought not to live any .... Acts 25:24 | 1916
of his Son into your hearts, *c* .... Gal 4:6 | 2896
and supplications with strong *c* .... Heb 5:7 | 2906
c with a loud voice to him that .... Rev 14:15 | 2896
more death, neither sorrow, nor *c* .... Rev 21:4 | 2906

CRYSTAL

The gold and the *c* cannot equal it .... Job 28:17 | 2137
as the colour of the terrible *c* .... Eze 1:22 | 7140
was a sea of glass like unto *c* .... Rev 4:6 | 2930
like a jasper stone, clear as *c* .... Rev 21:11 | 2929
of water of life, clear as *c*.................. Rev 22:1 | 2930

CUBIT

in a *c* shalt thou finish it above .... Gen 6:16 | 520
be the length thereof, and a *c* .... Ex 25:10 | 520
half the breadth thereof, and a *c* .... Ex 25:10 | 520
be the length thereof, and a *c* .... Ex 25:17 | 520
c the breadth thereof, and a *c* .... Ex 25:23 | 520
a *c* on the one side, and a *c* .... Ex 26:13 | 520
be the length of a board, and a *c*......... Ex 26:16 | 520
A *c* shall be the length thereof, ... Ex 30:2 | 520
and a *c* the breadth thereof................ Ex 30:2 | 520
and the breadth of a board one *c* .... Ex 36:21 | 520
half was the length of it, and a *c* .... Ex 37:1 | 520
a half the breadth of it, and a *c* .... Ex 37:1 | 520
was the length thereof, and one *c* .... Ex 37:6 | 520
c the breadth thereof, and a *c* .... Ex 37:10 | 520
a *c*, and the breadth of it a *c* .... Ex 37:25 | 520
of it, after the *c* of a man .... Deut 3:11 | 520
had two edges, of a *c* length............... Judg 3:16 | 1574
knops compassing it, ten in a *c* .... 1Kin 7:24 | 520
the chapiter and above was a *c* .... 1Kin 7:31 | 520
after the work of the base, a *c* .... 1Kin 7:31 | 520
a wheel was a *c* and half a *c* .... 1Kin 7:32 | 520
a round compass of half a *c* high .... 1Kin 7:35 | 520

door were five *c* on the one side .... Eze 41:2   520
and five *c* on the other side .... Eze 41:2   520
the length thereof, forty *c* .... Eze 41:2   520
and the breadth, twenty *c* .... Eze 41:2   520
the post of the door, two *c* .... Eze 41:3   520
and the door, six *c* .... Eze 41:3   520
the breadth of the door, seven *c* .... Eze 41:3   520
the length thereof, twenty *c* .... Eze 41:4   520
and the breadth, twenty *c*, before .... Eze 41:4   520
the wall of the house, six *c* .... Eze 41:5   520
of every side chamber, four *c* .... Eze 41:5   520
were a full reed of six great *c* .... Eze 41:8   520
side chamber without, was five *c* .... Eze 41:9   520
was the wideness of twenty *c* .... Eze 41:10   520
was left was five *c* round about .... Eze 41:11   520
the west was seventy *c* broad .... Eze 41:12   520
was five *c* thick round about .... Eze 41:12   520
and the length thereof ninety *c* .... Eze 41:12   520
the house, an hundred *c* long .... Eze 41:13   520
walls thereof, an hundred *c* long .... Eze 41:13   520
toward the east, an hundred *c* .... Eze 41:14   520
on the other side, an hundred *c* .... Eze 41:15   520
altar of wood was three *c* high .... Eze 41:22   520
and the length thereof two *c* .... Eze 41:22   520
an hundred *c* was the north door .... Eze 42:2   520
and the breadth was fifty *c* .... Eze 42:2   520
Over against the twenty *c* which .... Eze 42:3
a walk of ten *c* breadth inward .... Eze 42:4   520
the length thereof was fifty *c* .... Eze 42:7   520
in the utter court was fifty *c* .... Eze 42:8   520
the temple were an hundred *c* .... Eze 42:8   520
measures of the altar after the *c* .... Eze 43:13   520
the lower settle shall be two *c* .... Eze 43:14   520
greater settle shall be four *c* .... Eze 43:14   520
So the altar shall be four *c* .... Eze 43:15   520
the altar shall be twelve *c* long .... Eze 43:16
settle shall be fourteen *c* long .... Eze 43:17
fifty *c* round about for the .... Eze 45:2   520
courts joined of forty *c* long .... Eze 46:22
he measured a thousand *c* .... Eze 47:3   520
whose height was threescore *c* .... Dan 3:1   521
and the breadth thereof six *c* .... Dan 3:1   521
the length thereof is twenty *c* .... Zec 5:2   520
and the breadth thereof ten *c* .... Zec 5:2   520
but as it were two hundred .... Jn 21:8   4088
an hundred and forty and four *c* .... Rev 21:17   4088

CUCKOW
owl, and the night hawk, and the *c* .... Lev 11:16   7828
owl, and the night hawk, and the *c* .... Deut 14:15   7828

CUCUMBERS
the *c*, and the melons, and the .... Num 11:5   7180
as a lodge in a garden of *c* .... Is 1:8   4750

CUD
is clovenfooted, and cheweth the *c* .... Lev 11:3   1625
not eat of them that chew the *c* .... Lev 11:4   1625
camel, because he cheweth the *c* .... Lev 11:4   1625
coney, because he cheweth the *c* .... Lev 11:5   1625
hare, because he cheweth the *c* .... Lev 11:6   1625
yet he cheweth not the *c* .... Lev 11:7   1625
clovenfooted, nor cheweth the *c* .... Lev 11:26   1625
cheweth the *c* among the beasts, ... Deut 14:6   1625
not eat of them that chew the *c* .... Deut 14:7   1625
for they chew the *c*, but divide .... Deut 14:7   1625
the hoof, yet cheweth not the *c* .... Deut 14:8   1625

CUMBERED
But Martha was *c* about much .... Lk 10:40   4049

CUMBERETH
why *c* it the ground .... Lk 13:7   2673

CUMBRANCE
can I myself alone bear your *c* .... Deut 1:12   2960

CUMI (coo'-mi)
hand, and said unto her, Talitha *c* .... Mk 5:41   2891

CUMMIN
the fitches, and scatter the *c* .... Is 28:25   3646
wheel turned about upon the *c* .... Is 28:27   3646
with a staff, and the *c* with a rod .... Is 28:27   3646
pay tithe of mint and anise and *c* .... Mt 23:23   2951

CUN See CHUN.

CUNNING
and Esau was a *c* hunter, a man of .... Gen 25:27   3045
with cherubims of *c* work shalt .... Ex 26:1   2803
and fine twined linen of *c* work .... Ex 26:31   2803
and fine twined linen, with *c* work .... Ex 28:6   2803
of judgment with *c* work .... Ex 28:15   2803
To devise *c* works, to work in .... Ex 31:4   4284
to make any manner of *c* work .... Ex 35:33   4284

of the *c* workman, and of the .... Ex 35:35   2803
and of those that devise *c* work .... Ex 35:35   4284
cherubims of *c* work made he them .... Ex 36:8   2803
cherubims made he it of *c* work .... Ex 36:35   2803
a *c* workman, and an embroider in .... Ex 38:23   2803
and in the fine linen, with *c* work .... Ex 39:3   2803
he made the breastplate of *c* work .... Ex 39:8   2803
who is a *c* player on an harp 1Sa 16:16   3045
that is *c* in playing, and a mighty 1Sa 16:18   3045
c to work all works in brass 1Kin 7:14   1847
all manner of *c* men for every 1Chr 22:15   2450
of the LORD, even all that were *c* 1Chr 25:7   995
therefore a man *c* to work in gold 2Chr 2:7   2450
can skill to grave with the *c* men 2Chr 2:7   2450
And now I have sent a *c* man 2Chr 2:13   2450
be put to him, with thy *c* men 2Chr 2:14   2450
with the *c* men of my lord David 2Chr 2:14   2450
engines, invented by *c* men 2Chr 26:15   2803
let my right hand forget her *c* .... Ps 137:5
work of the hands of a *c* workman .... Song 7:1   542
the *c* artificer, and the eloquent .... Is 3:3   2450
he seeketh unto him a *c* workman .... Is 40:20   2450
and send for *c* women, that they .... Jer 9:17   2450
they are all the work of *c* men .... Jer 10:9   2450
c in knowledge, and understanding .... Dan 1:4   2450
c craftiness, whereby they lie in .... Eph 4:14   3045

CUNNINGLY
not followed *c* devised fables 2Pet 1:16

CUP
Pharaoh's *c* was in my hand .... Gen 40:11   3563
and pressed them into Pharaoh's *c* .... Gen 40:11   3563
I gave the *c* into Pharaoh's hand .... Gen 40:11   3563
deliver Pharaoh's *c* into his hand .... Gen 40:13   3563
he gave the *c* into Pharaoh's hand .... Gen 40:21   3563
And put my *c*, the silver *c* .... Gen 44:2   1375
the *c* was found in Benjamin's .... Gen 44:12   1375
he also with whom the *c* is found .... Gen 44:16   1375
man in whose hand the *c* is found .... Gen 44:17   1375
own meat, and drank of his own *c* 2Sa 12:3   3563
was wrought like the brim of a *c* 1Kin 7:26   3563
like the work of the brim of a *c* 2Chr 4:5   3563
shall be the portion of their *c* .... Ps 11:6   3563
of mine inheritance and of my *c* .... Ps 16:5   3563
my *c* runneth over .... Ps 23:5   3563
waters of a full *c* are wrung out .... Ps 73:10   3563
the hand of the LORD there is a *c* .... Ps 75:8   3563
I will take the *c* of salvation .... Ps 116:13   3563
it giveth his colour in the *c* .... Prov 23:31   3599
of the LORD the *c* of his fury .... Is 51:17   3563
the dregs of the *c* of trembling .... Is 51:17   3563
of thine hand the *c* of trembling .... Is 51:22   3563
the dregs of the *c* of my fury .... Is 51:22   3563
the *c* of consolation to drink for .... Jer 16:7   3563
Take the wine *c* of this fury at .... Jer 25:15   3563
Then took I the *c* at the LORD's .... Jer 25:17   3563
take the *c* at thine hand to drink .... Jer 25:28   3563
of the *c* have assuredly drunken .... Jer 49:12   3563
a golden *c* in the LORD's hand .... Jer 51:7   3563
the *c* also shall pass through .... Lam 4:21   3563
will I give her *c* into thine hand .... Eze 23:31   3563
drink of thy sister's *c* deep .... Eze 23:32   3563
with the *c* of astonishment and .... Eze 23:33   3563
with the *c* of thy sister Samaria .... Eze 23:33   3563
the *c* of the LORD's right hand .... Hab 2:16   3563
I will make Jerusalem a *c* of .... Zec 12:2   5592
c* of cold water only in the name .... Mt 10:42   4221
of the *c* that I shall drink of .... Mt 20:22   4221
Ye shall drink indeed of my *c* .... Mt 20:23   4221
make clean the outside of the *c* .... Mt 23:25   4221
first that which is within the *c* .... Mt 23:26   4221
And he took the *c*, and gave thanks, ... Mt 26:27   4221
possible, let this *c* pass from me .... Mt 26:39   4221
if this *c* may not pass away from .... Mt 26:42   4221
a *c* of water to drink in my name .... Mk 9:41   4221
ye drink of the *c* that I drink of .... Mk 10:38   4221
drink of the *c* that I drink of .... Mk 10:39   4221
And he took the *c*, and when he had ..... Mk 14:23   4221
take away this *c* from me .... Mk 14:36   4221
make clean the outside of the *c* .... Lk 11:39   4221
And he took the *c*, and gave thanks, ... Lk 22:17   4221
Likewise also the *c* after supper .... Lk 22:20   4221
This *c* is the new testament in my ...... Lk 22:20   4221
be willing, remove this *c* from me .... Lk 22:42   4221
the *c* which my Father hath given .... Jn 18:11   4221
The *c* of blessing which we bless 1Cor 10:16   4221
Ye cannot drink the *c* of the Lord 1Cor 10:21   4221
and the *c* of devils 1Cor 10:21   4221
same manner also he took the *c* 1Cor 11:25   4221
This *c* is the new testament in my 1Cor 11:25   4221
eat this bread, and drink this *c* 1Cor 11:26   4221

drink this *c* of the Lord, ... 1Cor 11:27   4221
of that bread, and drink of that *c* 1Cor 11:28   4221
into the *c* of his indignation..................... Rev 14:10   4221
to give unto her the *c* of the .... Rev 16:19   4221
having a golden *c* in her hand................. Rev 17:4   4221
in the *c* which she hath filled.................. Rev 18:6   4221

CUPBEARER
For I was the king's *c* .... Neh 1:11   4945

CUPBEARERS
and their apparel, and his *c* 1Kin 10:5   4945
his *c* also, and their apparel 2Chr 9:4   4945

CUPS
and the bowls, and the *c*...................... 1Chr 28:17   7184
quantity, from the vessels of *c*............... Is 22:24   101
pots full of wine, and *c*, and I............... Jer 35:5   3563
and the spoons, and the *c*..................... Jer 52:19   4518
to hold, as the washing of *c* .... Mk 7:4   4221
men, as the washing of pots and *c* .... Mk 7:8   *4221*

CURDLED
out as milk, and *c* me like cheese .... Job 10:10   7087

CURE
health and *c*, and I will *c* them............... Jer 33:6   7495
heal you, nor *c* you of your wound .... Hos 5:13   1455
and they could not *c* him .... Mt 17:16   2323
over all devils, and to *c* diseases .... Lk 9:1   2323

CURED
for thou shalt not be *c*........................... Jer 46:11   8585
the child was *c* from that very............... Mt 17:18   2323
in that same hour he *c* many of............... Lk 7:21   2323
said unto him that was *c*, It is................ Jn 5:10   2323

CURES
I do *c* to day and to morrow, and .... Lk 13:32   *2392*

CURIOUS
the *c* girdle of the ephod, which .... Ex 28:8
above the *c* girdle of the ephod .... Ex 28:27
above the *c* girdle of the ephod .... Ex 28:28
gird him with the *c* girdle of the .... Ex 29:5
And to devise *c* works, to work in.......... Ex 35:32   4284
the *c* girdle of his ephod, that............... Ex 39:5
above the *c* girdle of the ephod .... Ex 39:20
above the *c* girdle of the ephod .... Ex 39:21
with the *c* girdle of the ephod .... Lev 8:7
used *c* arts brought their books............. Acts 19:19   *4021*

CURIOUSLY
c wrought in the lowest parts of .... Ps 139:15   7551

CURRENT
c money with the merchant .... Gen 23:16   5674

CURSE
I will not again *c* the ground any .... Gen 8:21   7043
thee, and *c* him that curseth thee.......... Gen 12:3   779
and I shall bring a *c* upon me................ Gen 27:12   7045
said unto him, Upon me be thy *c* .... Gen 27:13   7045
nor *c* the ruler of thy people .... Ex 22:28   779
Thou shalt not *c* the deaf .... Lev 19:14   7043
bitter water that causeth the *c*............... Num 5:18   779
bitter water that causeth the *c*............... Num 5:19   779
the woman, The LORD make thee a *c* ..... Num 5:21   423
the *c* shall go into thy bowels................ Num 5:22   779
bitter water that causeth the *c*............... Num 5:24   779
the *c* shall enter into her....................... Num 5:24   779
the *c* shall enter into her....................... Num 5:27   779
shall be a *c* among her people .... Num 5:27   423
I pray thee, *c* me this people .... Num 22:6   779
come now, *c* me them .... Num 22:11   6895
thou shalt not *c* the people .... Num 22:12   779
I pray thee, *c* me this people .... Num 22:17   6895
c me Jacob, and come, defy Israel .... Num 23:7   779
How shall I *c*, whom God hath not .... Num 23:8   5344
I took thee to *c* mine enemies .... Num 23:11   6895
and *c* me them from thence .... Num 23:13   6895
Neither *c* them at all, nor bless............. Num 23:25   6895
thou mayest *c* me them from thence ...... Num 23:27   6895
I called thee to *c* mine enemies .... Num 24:10   6895
you this day a blessing and a *c*.............. Deut 11:26   7045
And a *c*, if ye will not obey the .... Deut 11:28   7045
Gerizim, and the *c* upon mount Ebal .... Deut 11:29   7045
Pethor of Mesopotamia, to *c* thee .... Deut 23:4   7043
the *c* into a blessing unto thee .... Deut 23:5   7045
shall stand upon mount Ebal to *c*......... Deut 27:13   7045
he heareth the words of this *c*............... Deut 29:19   423
upon thee, the blessing and the *c* .... Deut 30:1   7045
and make the camp of Israel a *c* .... Josh 6:18   2764
Balaam the son of Beor to *c* you .... Josh 24:9   7043
C ye Meroz, said the angel of the .... Judg 5:23   779
c ye bitterly the inhabitants .... Judg 5:23   779

upon them came the *c* of Jotham............ Judg 9:57   7045
this dead dog *c* my lord the king 2Sa 16:9   7043
so let him *c*, because the LORD............... 2Sa 16:10   7043
LORD hath said unto him, C David........... 2Sa 16:10   7043
let him alone, and let him *c*................... 2Sa 16:11   7043
c in the day when I went to 1Kin 2:8   7045
should become a desolation and a *c* 2Kin 22:19   7045
their nobles, and entered into a *c*.......... Neh 10:29   423
them, that he should *c* them .... Neh 13:2   7043
God turned the *c* into a blessing .... Neh 13:2   7045
he will *c* thee to thy face....................... Job 1:11   1288
he will *c* thee to thy face....................... Job 2:5   1288
c God, and die .... Job 2:9   1288
Let them *c* it .... Job 3:8   5344
that *c* the day, who are ready .... Job 3:8   779
to sin by wishing a *c* to his soul............ Job 31:30   423
their mouth, but they *c* inwardly .... Ps 62:4   7043
Let them *c*, but bless thou .... Ps 109:28   7043
The *c* of the LORD is in the house .... Prov 3:33   3994
corn, the people shall *c* him .... Prov 11:26   5344
him shall the people *c*, nations .... Prov 24:24   5344
so the *c* causeless shall not come .... Prov 26:2   7045
it shall be counted a *c* to him .... Prov 27:14   7045
his eyes shall have many a *c*.................. Prov 28:27   3994
unto his master, lest he *c* thee.............. Prov 30:10   7043
lest thou hear thy servant *c* thee .... Eccl 7:21   7043
C not the king, no not in thy .... Eccl 10:20   7043
c not the rich in thy bedchamber........... Eccl 10:20   7043
c their king and their God, and .... Is 8:21   7043
hath the *c* devoured the earth................ Is 24:6   423
and upon the people of my *c* .... Is 34:5   2764
and have given Jacob to the *c* .... Is 43:28   2764
your name for a *c* unto my chosen .... Is 65:15   7621
yet every one of them doth *c* me .... Jer 15:10   7043
and a proverb, a taunt and a *c*.............. Jer 24:9   7045
astonishment, an hissing, and a *c* .... Jer 25:18   7045
will make this city a *c* to all.................. Jer 26:6   7045
kingdoms of the earth, to be a *c* .... Jer 29:18   423
of them shall be taken up a *c* by .... Jer 29:22   7045
off, and that ye might be a *c* .... Jer 42:18   7045
and an astonishment, and a *c* .... Jer 44:8   7045
and an astonishment, and a *c* .... Jer 44:12   7045
and an astonishment, and a *c* .... Jer 44:22   7045
a reproach, a waste, and a *c* .... Jer 49:13   7045
sorrow of heart, thy *c* unto them .... Lam 3:65   8381
therefore the *c* is poured upon us .... Dan 9:11   423
This is the *c* that goeth forth .... Zec 5:3   423
as ye were a *c* among the heathen .... Zec 8:13   7045
I will even send a *c* upon you .... Mal 2:2   3994
and I will *c* your blessings..................... Mal 2:2   779
Ye are cursed with a *c*........................... Mal 3:9   3994
come and smite the earth with a *c* .... Mal 4:6   2764
enemies, bless them that *c* you .... Mt 5:44   *2672*
Then began he to *c* and to swear, ... Mt 26:74   2653
But he began to *c* and to swear,............ Mk 14:71   332
Bless them that *c* you, and pray .... Lk 6:28   *2672*
and bound themselves under a *c* .... Acts 23:12   332
bound ourselves under a great *c* .... Acts 23:14   332
bless, and *c* not .... Rom 12:14   2672
works of the law are under the *c* .... Gal 3:10   2671
redeemed us from the *c* of the law .... Gal 3:13   2671
being made a *c* for us .... Gal 3:13   2671
and therewith *c* we men, which are .... Jas 3:9   2672
And there shall be no more *c* .... Rev 22:3   2652

CURSED
thou art *c* above all cattle, and .... Gen 3:14   779
c is the ground for thy sake.................... Gen 3:17   779
now art thou *c* from the earth,.............. Gen 4:11   779
the ground which the LORD hath *c*......... Gen 5:29   779
And he said, *C* be Canaan .... Gen 9:25   779
c be every one that curseth thee,........... Gen 27:29   779
C be their anger, for it was .... Gen 49:7   779
he hath *c* his father or his .... Lev 20:9   7043
the name of the LORD, and *c*................. Lev 24:11   7043
him that hath *c* without the camp .... Lev 24:14   7043
him that had *c* out of the camp .... Lev 24:23   7043
and he whom thou cursest is *c* .... Num 22:6   779
I curse, whom God hath not *c*................ Num 23:8   6895
c is he that curseth thee .... Num 24:9   779
lest thou be a *c* thing like it................... Deut 7:26   2764
for it is a *c* thing .... Deut 7:26   2764
of the *c* thing to thine hand................... Deut 13:17   2764
C be the man that maketh any................ Deut 27:15   779
C be he that setteth light by his .... Deut 27:16   779
C be he that removeth his .... Deut 27:17   779
C be he that maketh the blind to .... Deut 27:18   779
C be he that perverteth the .... Deut 27:19   779
C be he that lieth with his .... Deut 27:20   779
C be he that lieth with any .... Deut 27:21   779
C be he that lieth with his .... Deut 27:22   779

C be he that lieth with his	Deut 27:23	779
C be he that smiteth his	Deut 27:24	779
C be he that taketh reward to	Deut 27:25	779
C be he that confirmeth not all	Deut 27:26	779
C shalt thou be in the city, and	Deut 28:16	779
c shalt thou be in the field	Deut 28:16	779
C shall be thy basket and thy	Deut 28:17	779
C shall be the fruit of thy body,	Deut 28:18	779
C shalt thou be when thou comest	Deut 28:19	779
c shalt thou be when thou goest	Deut 28:19	779
C be the man before the LORD,	Josh 6:26	779
Now therefore ye are *c*, and there	Josh 9:23	779
did eat and drink, and *c* Abimelech	Judg 9:27	7043
C be he that giveth a wife to	Judg 21:18	779
C be the man that eateth any food	1Sa 14:24	779
C be the man that eateth any food	1Sa 14:28	779
the Philistine *c* David by his	1Sa 17:43	779
c be they before the LORD	1Sa 26:19	7043
came forth, and *c* still as he came	2Sa 16:5	779
And thus said Shimei when he *c*	2Sa 16:7	7043
c as he went, and threw stones at	2Sa 16:13	7043
because he *c* the LORD's anointed	2Sa 19:21	7043
which *c* me with a grievous curse	1Kin 2:8	7043
c them in the name of the LORD	2Kin 2:24	7043
and said, Go, see now this *c* woman	2Kin 9:34	779
c them, and smote certain of them,	Neh 13:25	7043
sinned, and *c* God in their hearts	Job 1:5	1288
Job his mouth, and *c* his day	Job 3:1	7043
but suddenly I *c* his habitation	Job 5:3	5344
their portion is *c* in the earth	Job 24:18	7043
they that be *c* of him shall be	Ps 37:22	7043
hast rebuked the proud that are *c*	Ps 119:21	779
thyself likewise hast *c* others	Eccl 7:22	7043
C be the man that obeyeth not the	Jer 11:3	779
C be the man that trusteth in man	Jer 17:5	779
C be the day wherein I was born	Jer 20:14	779
C be the man who brought tidings	Jer 20:15	779
C be he that doeth the work of	Jer 48:10	779
c be he that keepeth back his	Jer 48:10	779
But *c* be the deceiver, which hath	Mal 1:14	779
I have *c* them already, because ye	Mal 2:2	779
Ye are *c* with a curse	Mal 3:9	779
left hand, Depart from me, ye *c*	Mt 25:41	2672
who knoweth not the law are *c*	Jn 7:49	1944
C is every one that continueth	Gal 3:10	1944
C is every one that hangeth on a	Gal 3:13	1944
with covetous practices; *c* children	2Pet 2:14	2671

CURSEDST

from thee, about which thou *c*	Judg 17:2	422
which thou *c* is withered away	Mk 11:21	2672

CURSES

shall write these *c* in a book	Num 5:23	423
that all these *c* shall come upon	Deut 28:15	7045
Moreover all these *c* shall come	Deut 28:45	7045
all the *c* that are written in	Deut 29:20	423
according to all the *c* of the	Deut 29:21	423
to bring upon it all the *c* that	Deut 29:27	7045
all these *c* upon thine enemies	Deut 30:7	423
even all the *c* that are written	2Chr 34:24	423

CURSEST

and he whom thou *c* is cursed	Num 22:6	779

CURSETH

thee, and curse him that *c* thee	Gen 12:3	7043
cursed be every one that *c* thee	Gen 27:29	779
he that *c* his father, or his	Ex 21:17	7043
For every one that *c* his father	Lev 20:9	7043
Whosoever *c* his God shall bear	Lev 24:15	7043
thee, and cursed is he that *c* thee	Num 24:9	779
Whoso *c* his father or his mother,	Prov 20:20	7043
a generation that *c* their father	Prov 30:11	7043
He that *c* father or mother, let	Mt 15:4	2551
Whoso *c* father or mother, let him	Mk 7:10	2551

CURSING

the woman with an oath of *c*	Num 5:21	423
The LORD shall send upon thee *c*	Deut 28:20	3994
you life and death, blessing and *c*	Deut 30:19	7045
me good for his *c* this day	2Sa 16:12	7045
His mouth is full of *c* and deceit	Ps 10:7	423
and for *c* and lying which they	Ps 59:12	423
As he loved *c*, so let it come	Ps 109:17	7045
with *c* like as with his garment	Ps 109:18	7045
he heareth *c*, and bewrayeth it not	Prov 29:24	423
Whose mouth is full of *c* and	Rom 3:14	685
is rejected, and is nigh unto *c*	Heb 6:8	2671
mouth proceedeth blessing and *c*	Jas 3:10	2671

CURSINGS

of the law, the blessings and *c*	Josh 8:34	7045

CURTAIN

length of one *c* shall be eight	Ex 26:2	3407
the breadth of one *c* four cubits	Ex 26:2	3407
one *c* from the selvedge in the	Ex 26:4	3407
the uttermost edge of another *c*	Ex 26:4	3407
shalt thou make in the one *c*	Ex 26:5	3407
thou make in the edge of the *c*	Ex 26:5	3407
The length of one *c* shall be	Ex 26:8	3407
the breadth of one *c* four cubits	Ex 26:8	3407
shalt double the sixth *c* in the	Ex 26:9	3407
loops on the edge of the one *c*	Ex 26:10	3407
the *c* which coupleth the second	Ex 26:10	3407
the half *c* that remaineth, shall	Ex 26:12	3407
The length of one *c* was twenty	Ex 36:9	3407
the breadth of one *c* four cubits	Ex 36:9	3407
of one *c* from the selvedge in the	Ex 36:11	3407
the uttermost side of another *c*	Ex 36:11	3407
Fifty loops made he in one *c*	Ex 36:12	3407
made he in the edge of the *c*	Ex 36:12	3407
the loops held one *c* to another	Ex 36:12	3407
length of one *c* was thirty cubits	Ex 36:15	3407
cubits was the breadth of one *c*	Ex 36:15	3407
edge of the *c* in the coupling	Ex 36:17	3407
the *c* which coupleth the second	Ex 36:17	3407
the *c* for the door of the court,	Num 3:26	4539
out the heavens like a *c*	Ps 104:2	3407
stretcheth out the heavens as a *c*	Is 40:22	1852

CURTAINS

with ten *c* of fine twined linen	Ex 26:1	3407
every one of the *c* shall have one	Ex 26:2	3407
The five *c* shall be coupled	Ex 26:3	3407
other five *c* shall be coupled one	Ex 26:3	3407
couple the *c* together with the	Ex 26:6	3407
thou shalt make *c* of goats' hair	Ex 26:7	3407
eleven *c* shalt thou make	Ex 26:7	3407
the eleven *c* shall be all of one	Ex 26:8	3407
shalt couple five *c* by themselves	Ex 26:9	3407
six *c* by themselves, and shalt	Ex 26:9	3407
remaineth of the *c* of the tent	Ex 26:12	3407
the length of the *c* of the tent	Ex 26:13	3407
made ten *c* of fine twined linen	Ex 36:8	3407
the *c* were all of one size	Ex 36:9	3407
the five *c* one unto another	Ex 36:10	3407
the other five *c* he coupled one	Ex 36:10	3407
coupled the one unto another	Ex 36:13	3407
he made *c* of goats' hair for the	Ex 36:14	3407
eleven *c* he made them	Ex 36:14	3407
the eleven *c* were of one size	Ex 36:15	3407
he coupled five *c* by themselves	Ex 36:16	3407
and six *c* by themselves	Ex 36:16	3407
bear the *c* of the tabernacle	Num 4:25	3407
the ark of God dwelleth within *c*	2Sa 7:2	3407
of the LORD remaineth under *c*	1Chr 17:1	3407
of Kedar, as the *c* of Solomon	Song 1:5	3407
forth the *c* of thine habitations	Is 54:2	3407
spoiled, and my *c* in a moment	Jer 4:20	3407
tent any more, and to set up my *c*	Jer 10:20	3407
shall take to themselves their *c*	Jer 49:29	3407
the *c* of the land of Midian did	Hab 3:7	3407

CUSH (*cush*) See ETHIOPIA.

1. A son of Ham.

C, and Mizraim, and Phut, and	Gen 10:6	3568
the sons of *C*; Seba, and Havilah	Gen 10:7	3568
And *C* begat Nimrod	Gen 10:8	3568
C, and Mizraim, Put, and Canaan	1Chr 1:8	3568
the sons of *C*; Seba, and Havilah	1Chr 1:9	3568
And *C* begat Nimrod	1Chr 1:10	3568

2. A Benjaminite.

the words of *C* the Benjamite	Ps 7:t	3568

3. Land of descendants of Cush.

Egypt, and from Pathros, and from *C*	Is 11:11	3568

CUSHAN (*cu'-shan*) See CHUSHAN-RISHATHAIM. Same as Chushan-rishathaim.

saw the tents of *C* in affliction	Hab 3:7	3572

CUSHI (*cu'-shi*)

1. Messenger of David.

Then said Joab to *C*, Go tell the	2Sa 18:21	3569
C bowed himself unto Joab, and ran	2Sa 18:21	3569
me, I pray thee, also run after *C*	2Sa 18:22	3569
way of the plain, and overran *C*	2Sa 18:23	3569
And, behold, *C* came	2Sa 18:31	3569
C said, Tidings, my lord the king	2Sa 18:31	3569
And the king said unto *C*, Is the	2Sa 18:32	3569
C answered, The enemies of my	2Sa 18:32	3569

2. Ancestor of Jehudi.

son of Shelemiah, the son of *C*	Jer 36:14	3569

3. Father of Zephaniah.

came unto Zephaniah the son of *C*	Zeph 1:1	3569

CUSTODY

And under the c and charge of the	Num 3:36	6486
unto the c of Hege the king's	Est 2:3	3027
to the c of Hegai, that Esther	Est 2:8	3027
to the c of Hegai, keeper of the	Est 2:8	3027
to the c of Shaashgaz, the king's	Est 2:14	3027

CUSTOM

for the c of women is upon me	Gen 31:35	1870
And it was a c in Israel,	Judg 11:39	2706
the priest's c with the people	1Sa 2:13	4941
by number, according to the c	Ezr 3:4	4941
they not pay toll, tribute, and c	Ezr 4:13	1983
and toll, tribute, and c, was paid	Ezr 4:20	1983
to impose toll, tribute, or c	Ezr 7:24	1983
sealed according to the law and c	Jer 32:11	2706
sitting at the receipt of c	Mt 9:9	5058
of the earth take c or tribute	Mt 17:25	5056
sitting at the receipt of c	Mk 2:14	5058
According to the c of the	Lk 1:9	1485
do for him after the c of the law	Lk 2:27	1480
after the c of the feast	Lk 2:42	1485
and, as his c was, he went into	Lk 4:16	3588,1486
Levi, sitting at the receipt of c	Lk 5:27	5058
But ye have a c, that I should	Jn 18:39	4914
c to whom c; fear to whom fear	Rom 13:7	5056
be contentious, we have no such c	1Cor 11:16	4914

CUSTOMS

not any one of these abominable c	Lev 18:30	2708
For the c of the people are vain	Jer 10:3	2708
shall change the c which Moses	Acts 6:14	1485
And teach c, which are not lawful	Acts 16:21	1485
neither to walk after the c	Acts 21:21	1485
I know thee to be expert in all c	Acts 26:3	1485
or c of our fathers, yet was I	Acts 28:17	1485

CUT

neither shall all flesh be c off	Gen 9:11	3772
that soul shall be c off from his	Gen 17:14	3772
c off the foreskin of her son, and	Ex 4:25	3772
thou shalt be c off from the	Ex 9:15	3582
soul shall be c off from Israel	Ex 12:15	3772
even that soul shall be c off	Ex 12:19	3772
and I will c them off	Ex 23:23	3582
thou shalt c the ram in pieces	Ex 29:17	5408
shall even be c off from his	Ex 30:33	3772
shall even be c off from his	Ex 30:38	3772
that soul shall be c off from	Ex 31:14	3772
images, and c down their groves	Ex 34:13	3772
c it into wires, to work it in	Ex 39:3	7112
offering, and c it into his pieces	Lev 1:6	5408
he shall c it into his pieces,	Lev 1:12	5408
shall be c off from his people	Lev 7:20	3772
shall be c off from his people	Lev 7:21	3772
it shall be c off from his people	Lev 7:25	3772
shall be c off from his people	Lev 7:27	3772
And he c the ram into pieces	Lev 8:20	5408
that man shall be c off from	Lev 17:4	3772
even that man shall be c off from	Lev 17:9	3772
will c him off from among his	Lev 17:10	3772
eateth it shall be c off	Lev 17:14	3772
be c off from among his people	Lev 18:29	3772
that soul shall be c off from	Lev 19:8	3772
will c him off from among his	Lev 20:3	3772
will c him off, and all that go a	Lev 20:5	3772
will c him off from among his	Lev 20:6	3772
they shall be c off in the sight	Lev 20:17	3772
both of them shall be c off from	Lev 20:18	3772
that soul shall be c off from my	Lev 22:3	3772
or crushed, or broken, or c	Lev 22:24	3772
he shall be c off from among his	Lev 23:29	3772
c down your images, and cast your	Lev 26:30	3772
C ye not off the tribe of the	Num 4:18	3772
be c off from among his people	Num 9:13	3772
c down thence a branch with	Num 13:23	3772
of Israel c down from thence	Num 13:24	3772
that soul shall be c off from	Num 15:30	3772
that soul shall utterly be c off	Num 15:31	3772
soul shall be c off from Israel	Num 19:13	3772
that soul shall be c off from	Num 19:20	3772
c down their groves, and burn	Deut 7:5	1438
c off the nations from before	Deut 12:29	3772
ye shall not c yourselves	Deut 14:1	1413
thy God hath c off the nations	Deut 19:1	3772
with the axe to c down the tree	Deut 19:5	3772
thou shalt not c them down (for	Deut 20:19	3772
thou shalt destroy and c them down	Deut 20:20	3772
or hath his privy member c off	Deut 23:1	3772
Then thou shalt c off her hand	Deut 25:12	7112
c off from the waters that come	Josh 3:13	3772
salt sea, failed, and were c off	Josh 3:16	3772

were c off before the ark of the	Josh 4:7	3772
the waters of Jordan were c off	Josh 4:7	3772
c off our name from the earth	Josh 7:9	3772
c off the Anakims from the	Josh 11:21	3772
c down for thyself there in the	Josh 17:15	1254
a wood, and thou shalt c it down	Josh 17:18	1254
all the nations that I have c off	Josh 23:4	3772
c off his thumbs and his great	Judg 1:6	7112
thumbs and their great toes c off	Judg 1:7	7112
c down the grove that is by it	Judg 6:25	3772
the grove which thou shalt c down	Judg 6:26	3772
the grove was c down that was by	Judg 6:28	3772
because he hath c down the grove	Judg 6:30	3772
c down a bough from the trees, and	Judg 9:48	3772
all the people likewise c down	Judg 9:49	3772
c her in pieces, and sent her	Judg 20:6	5408
There is one tribe c off from	Judg 21:6	1438
not c off from among his brethren	Ruth 4:10	3772
that I will c off thine arm, and	1Sa 2:31	1438
whom I shall not c off from mine	1Sa 2:33	3772
were c off upon the threshold	1Sa 5:4	3772
him, and c off his head therewith	1Sa 17:51	3772
But also thou shalt not c off thy	1Sa 20:15	3772
not when the LORD hath c off the	1Sa 20:15	3772
c off the skirt of Saul's robe	1Sa 24:4	3772
because he had c off Saul's skirt	1Sa 24:5	3772
for in that I c off the skirt of	1Sa 24:11	3772
that thou wilt not c off my seed	1Sa 24:21	3772
how he hath c off those that have	1Sa 28:9	3772
they c off his head, and stripped	1Sa 31:9	3772
c off their hands and their feet,	2Sa 4:12	7112
have c off all thine enemies out	2Sa 7:9	3772
c off their garments in the	2Sa 10:4	3772
they c off the head of Sheba the	2Sa 20:22	3772
Then will I c off Israel out of	1Kin 9:7	3772
until he had c off every male in	1Kin 11:16	3772
of Jeroboam, even to c it off	1Kin 13:34	3582
will c off from Jeroboam him that	1Kin 14:10	3772
who shall c off the house of	1Kin 14:14	3772
when Jezebel c off the prophets	1Kin 18:4	3772
c it in pieces, and lay it on wood	1Kin 18:23	5408
c themselves after their manner	1Kin 18:28	1413
c the bullock in pieces, and laid	1Kin 18:33	5408
will c off from Ahab him that	1Kin 21:21	3772
came to Jordan, they c down wood	2Kin 6:4	1504
he c down a stick, and cast it in	2Kin 6:6	7094
I will c off from Ahab him that	2Kin 9:8	3772
the LORD began to c Israel short	2Kin 10:32	7096
king Ahaz c off the borders of	2Kin 16:17	7112
c down the groves, and brake in	2Kin 18:4	3772
At that time did Hezekiah c off	2Kin 18:16	7112
will c down the tall cedar trees	2Kin 19:23	3772
c down the groves, and filled	2Kin 23:14	3772
c in pieces all the vessels of	2Kin 24:13	7112
have c off all thine enemies from	1Chr 17:8	3772
c off their garments in the midst	1Chr 19:4	3772
c them with saws, and with harrows	1Chr 20:3	7787
can skill to c timber in Lebanon	2Chr 2:8	3772
the hewers that c timber	2Chr 2:10	3772
we will c wood out of Lebanon, as	2Chr 2:16	3772
the images, and c down the groves	2Chr 14:3	1438
Asa c down her idol, and stamped	2Chr 15:16	3772
to c off the house of Ahab	2Chr 22:7	3772
for he was c off from the house	2Chr 26:21	1504
c in pieces the vessels of the	2Chr 28:24	7112
c down the groves, and threw down	2Chr 31:1	1438
which c off all the mighty men of	2Chr 32:21	3582
on high above them, he c down	2Chr 34:4	1438
c down all the idols throughout	2Chr 34:7	1438
or where were the righteous c off	Job 4:7	3582
let loose his hand, and c me off	Job 6:9	1214
not c down, it withereth before	Job 8:12	6998
Whose hope shall be c off	Job 8:14	6990
If he c off, and shut up, or	Job 11:10	2498
forth like a flower, and is c down	Job 14:2	5243
hope of a tree, if it be c down	Job 14:7	3772
above shall his branch be c off	Job 18:16	5243
his months is c off in the midst	Job 21:21	2686
Which were c down out of time,	Job 22:16	7059
our substance is not c down	Job 22:20	3582
Because I was not c off before	Job 23:17	6780
c off as the tops of the ears of	Job 24:24	5243
Who c up mallows by the bushes,	Job 30:4	6998
when people are c off in their	Job 36:20	5927
The LORD shall c off all	Ps 12:3	3772
I am c off from before thine eyes	Ps 31:22	1629
to c off the remembrance of them	Ps 34:16	3772
soon be c down like the grass	Ps 37:2	5243
For evildoers shall be c off	Ps 37:9	3772
be cursed of him shall be c off	Ps 37:22	3772
seed of the wicked shall be c off	Ps 37:28	3772

when the wicked are *c* off	Ps 37:34	3772
end of the wicked shall be *c* off	Ps 37:38	3772
c them off in thy right	Ps 54:5	6789
let them be as *c* in pieces	Ps 58:7	4135
of the wicked also will I *c* off	Ps 75:10	1438
He shall *c* off the spirit of	Ps 76:12	1219
is burned with fire, it is *c* down	Ps 80:16	3683
let us *c* them off from being a	Ps 83:4	3582
they are *c* off from thy hand	Ps 88:5	1504
thy terrors have *c* me off	Ps 88:16	6789
in the evening it is *c* down	Ps 90:6	4135
for it is soon *c* off, and we fly	Ps 90:10	1504
shall *c* them off in their own	Ps 94:23	6789
the LORD our God shall *c* them off	Ps 94:23	6789
his neighbour, him will I *c* off	Ps 101:5	6789
that I may *c* off all wicked doers	Ps 101:8	3772
c the bars of iron in sunder	Ps 107:16	1438
Let his posterity be *c* off	Ps 109:13	3772
that he may *c* off the memory of	Ps 109:15	3772
he hath *c* asunder the cords of	Ps 129:4	7112
of thy mercy *c* off mine enemies,	Ps 143:12	6789
shall be *c* off from the earth	Prov 2:22	3772
the froward tongue shall be *c* out	Prov 10:31	3772
expectation shall not be *c* off	Prov 23:18	3772
expectation shall not be *c* off	Prov 24:14	3772
the sycomores are *c* down, but we	Is 9:10	1438
LORD will *c* off from Israel head	Is 9:14	3772
and *c* off nations not a few	Is 10:7	3772
he shall *c* down the thickets of	Is 10:34	5362
of Judah shall be *c* off	Is 11:13	3772
how art thou *c* down to the ground	Is 14:12	1438
c off from Babylon the name, and	Is 14:22	3772
be baldness, and every beard *c* off	Is 15:2	1438
he shall both *c* off the sprigs	Is 18:5	3772
take away and *c* down the branches	Is 18:5	8456
be removed, and be *c* down, and fall	Is 22:25	1438
that was upon it shall be *c* off	Is 22:25	3772
that watch for iniquity are *c* off	Is 29:20	3772
as thorns *c* up shall they be	Is 33:12	3683
I will *c* down the tall cedars	Is 37:24	3772
I have *c* off like a weaver my	Is 38:12	7088
he will *c* me off with pining	Is 38:12	1214
c in sunder the bars of iron	Is 45:2	1438
for thee, that I *c* thee not off	Is 48:9	3772
c off nor destroyed from before	Is 48:19	3772
Art thou not it that hath *c* Rahab	Is 51:9	2672
for he was *c* off out of the land	Is 53:8	1504
sign that shall not be *c* off	Is 55:13	3772
name, that shall not be *c* off	Is 56:5	3772
as if he *c* off a dog's neck	Is 66:3	3772
is *c* off from thy mouth	Jer 7:28	3772
C off thine hair, O Jerusalem, and	Jer 7:29	1494
to *c* off the children from	Jer 9:21	3772
let us *c* him off from the land of	Jer 11:19	3772
nor *c* themselves, nor make	Jer 16:6	1413
they shall *c* down thy choice	Jer 22:7	3772
are *c* down because of the fierce	Jer 25:37	1826
when they *c* the calf in twain, and	Jer 34:18	3772
he *c* it with the penknife, and	Jer 36:23	7167
having *c* themselves, with	Jer 41:5	1413
to *c* off from you man and woman,	Jer 44:7	3772
that ye might *c* yourselves off,	Jer 44:8	3772
for evil, and to *c* off all Judah	Jer 44:11	3772
They shall *c* down her forest,	Jer 46:23	3772
to *c* off from Tyrus and Zidon	Jer 47:4	3772
Ashkelon is *c* off with the	Jer 47:5	1820
how long wilt thou *c* thyself	Jer 47:5	1413
let us *c* it off from being a	Jer 48:2	3772
Also thou shalt be *c* down	Jer 48:2	1826
The horn of Moab is *c* off	Jer 48:25	1438
of war shall be *c* off in that day	Jer 49:26	1826
C off the sower from Babylon, and	Jer 50:16	3772
of the whole earth *c* in asunder	Jer 50:23	1438
of war shall be *c* off in that day	Jer 50:30	1826
be not *c* off in her iniquity	Jer 51:6	1826
to *c* it off, that none shall	Jer 51:62	3772
He hath *c* off in his fierce anger	Lam 2:3	1438
They have *c* off my life in the	Lam 3:53	6789
then I said, I am *c* off	Lam 3:54	1504
and your images may be *c* down	Eze 6:6	1438
I will *c* him off from the midst	Eze 14:8	3772
will *c* off man and beast from it	Eze 14:13	3772
so that I *c* off man and beast from	Eze 14:17	3772
to *c* off from it man and beast	Eze 14:19	3772
to *c* off from it man and beast	Eze 14:21	3772
wast born thy navel was not *c*	Eze 16:4	3772
c off the fruit thereof, that it	Eze 17:9	7082
forts, to *c* off many persons	Eze 17:17	3772
and will *c* off from thee the	Eze 21:3	3772
Seeing then that I will *c* off	Eze 21:4	3772
I will *c* thee off from the people	Eze 25:7	3772

will *c* off man and beast from it	Eze 25:13	3772
I will *c* off the Cherethims, and	Eze 25:16	3772
c off man and beast out of thee	Eze 29:8	3772
I will *c* off the multitude of No	Eze 30:15	3772
have *c* him off, and have left him	Eze 31:12	3772
c off from it him that passeth	Eze 35:7	3772
we are *c* off for our parts	Eze 37:11	1504
neither *c* down any out of the	Eze 39:10	2404
thereof, ye shall be *c* in pieces	Dan 2:5	5648
a stone was *c* out without hands	Dan 2:34	1505
was *c* out of the mountain without	Dan 2:45	1505
shall be *c* in pieces, and their	Dan 3:29	5648
c off his branches, shake off his	Dan 4:14	7113
two weeks shall Messiah be *c* off	Dan 9:26	3772
idols, that they may be *c* off	Hos 8:4	3772
her king is *c* off as the foam	Hos 10:7	1820
king of Israel utterly be *c* off	Hos 10:15	1820
for it is *c* off from your mouth	Joel 1:5	3772
the drink offering is *c* off from	Joel 1:9	3772
Is not the meat *c* off before our	Joel 1:16	3772
c off the inhabitant from the	Amos 1:5	3772
I will *c* off the inhabitant from	Amos 1:8	3772
I will *c* off the judge from the	Amos 2:3	3772
horns of the altar shall be *c* off	Amos 3:14	1438
c them in the head, all of them	Amos 9:1	1214
by night, (how art thou *c* off	Obad 5	1820
of Esau may be *c* off by slaughter	Obad 9	3772
and thou shalt be *c* off for ever	Obad 10	3772
to *c* off those of his that did	Obad 14	3772
all thine enemies shall be *c* off	Mic 5:9	3772
that I will *c* off thy horses out	Mic 5:10	3772
I will *c* off the cities of thy	Mic 5:11	3772
I will *c* off witchcrafts out of	Mic 5:12	3772
graven images also will I *c* off	Mic 5:13	3772
yet thus shall they be *c* down	Nah 1:12	1494
will I *c* off the graven image	Nah 1:14	3772
he is utterly *c* off	Nah 1:15	3772
I will *c* off thy prey from the	Nah 2:13	3772
the sword shall *c* thee off	Nah 3:15	3772
shall be *c* off from the fold	Hab 3:17	1504
I will *c* off man from off the	Zeph 1:3	3772
I will *c* off the remnant of Baal	Zeph 1:4	3772
the merchant people are *c* down	Zeph 1:11	1820
they that bear silver are *c* off	Zeph 1:11	3772
I have *c* off the nations	Zeph 3:6	3772
dwelling should not be *c* off	Zeph 3:7	3772
one that stealeth shall be *c* off	Zec 5:3	5352
one that sweareth shall be *c* off	Zec 5:3	5352
I will *c* off the pride of the	Zec 9:6	3772
I will *c* off the chariot from	Zec 9:10	3772
and the battle bow shall be *c* off	Zec 9:10	3772
also I *c* off in one month	Zec 11:8	3582
is to be *c* off, let it be *c* off	Zec 11:9	3582
c it asunder, that I might break	Zec 11:10	1438
Then I *c* asunder mine other staff	Zec 11:14	1438
not visit those that be *c* off	Zec 11:16	3582
with it shall be *c* in pieces	Zec 12:3	8295
that I will *c* off the names of	Zec 13:2	3772
two parts therein shall be *c* off	Zec 13:8	3772
shall not be *c* off from the city	Zec 14:2	3772
The LORD will *c* off the man that	Mal 2:12	3772
c it off, and cast it from thee	Mt 5:30	1581
c them off, and cast them from	Mt 18:8	1581
others *c* down branches from the	Mt 21:8	2875
shall *c* him asunder, and appoint	Mt 24:51	1371
if thy hand offend thee, *c* it off	Mk 9:43	609
if thy foot offend thee, *c* it off	Mk 9:45	609
others *c* down branches off the	Mk 11:8	2875
the high priest, and *c* off his ear	Mk 14:47	581
will *c* him in sunder, and will	Lk 12:46	1371
c it down	Lk 13:7	1581
after that thou shalt *c* it down	Lk 13:9	1581
priest, and *c* off his right ear	Lk 22:50	851
servant, and *c* off his right ear	Jn 18:10	609
his kinsman whose ear Peter *c* off	Jn 18:26	609
they were *c* to the heart, and took	Acts 5:33	1282
they were *c* to the heart, and they	Acts 7:54	1282
Then the soldiers *c* off the ropes	Acts 27:32	609
c it short in righteousness	Rom 9:28	4932
thou also shalt be *c* off	Rom 11:22	1581
For if thou wert *c* out of the	Rom 11:24	1581
that I may *c* off occasion from	2Cor 11:12	1581
were even *c* off which trouble you	Gal 5:12	609

CUTH (cuth) See CUTHAH. *A Babylonian city.*
the men of C made Nergal, and the 2Kin 17:30   3575

CUTHAH (cu'-thah) See CUTH. *Same as Cuth.*
men from Babylon, and from C 2Kin 17:24   3575

CUTTEST
When thou *c* down thine harvest in .... Deut 24:19   7114

CUTTETH

He *c* out rivers among the rocks	Job 28:10	1234
the bow, and *c* the spear in sunder	Ps 46:9	7112
the grave's mouth, as when one *c*	Ps 141:7	6398
the hand of a fool *c* off the feet	Prov 26:6	7096
for one *c* a tree out of the	Jer 10:3	3772
chambers, and *c* him out windows	Jer 22:14	7167

CUTTING

in *c* of stones, to set them, and	Ex 31:5	2799
in the *c* of stones, to set them,	Ex 35:33	2799
I said in the *c* off of my days, I	Is 38:10	1824
to thy house by *c* off many people	Hab 2:10	7096
crying, and *c* himself with stones	Mk 5:5	2629

CUTTINGS

Ye shall not make any *c* in your	Lev 19:28	8296
nor make any *c* in their flesh	Lev 21:5	8296
upon all the hands shall be *c*	Jer 48:37	1417

CUZA See Chuza.

CYMBAL

sounding brass, or a tinkling *c*	1Cor 13:1	2950

CYMBALS

timbrels, and on cornets, and on *c*	2Sa 6:5	6767
and with timbrels, and with *c*	1Chr 13:8	4700
musick, psalteries and harps and *c*	1Chr 15:16	4700
to sound with *c* of brass	1Chr 15:19	4700
and with trumpets, and with *c*,	1Chr 15:28	4700
but Asaph made a sound with *c*	1Chr 16:5	4700
c for those that should make a	1Chr 16:42	4700
harps, with psalteries, and with *c*	1Chr 25:1	4700
in the house of the Lord, with *c*	1Chr 25:6	4700
arrayed in white linen, having *c*	2Chr 5:12	4700
voice with the trumpets and *c*	2Chr 5:13	4700
in the house of the Lord with *c*	2Chr 29:25	4700
Levites the sons of Asaph with *c*	Ezr 3:10	4700
and with singing, with *c*,	Neh 12:27	4700
Praise him upon the loud *c*	Ps 150:5	6767
him upon the high sounding *c*	Ps 150:5	6767

CYPRESS

him down cedars, and taketh the *c*	Is 44:14	8645

CYPRUS (si'-prus) *An island off the Syrian coast.*

a Levite, and of the country of *C*	Acts 4:36	2954
travelled as far as Phenice, and *C*	Acts 11:19	2954

And some of them were men of *C*	Acts 11:20	2954
and from thence they sailed to *C*	Acts 13:4	2954
took Mark, and sailed unto *C*	Acts 15:39	2954
Now when we had discovered *C*	Acts 21:3	2954
brought with them one Mnason of *C*	Acts 21:16	2954
from thence, we sailed under *C*	Acts 27:4	2954

CYRENE (si-re'-ne) See Cyrenian. *A Libyan city.*

came out, they found a man of *C*	Mt 27:32	2957
and in the parts of Libya about *C*	Acts 2:10	2957
of them were men of Cyprus and *C*	Acts 11:20	2957
was called Niger, and Lucius of *C*	Acts 13:1	2957

CYRENIAN (si-re'-ne-an) See Cyrenians. *A native of Cyrene.*

And they compel one Simon a *C*	Mk 15:21	2956
laid hold upon one Simon, a *C*	Lk 23:26	2956

CYRENIANS (si-re'-ne-ans)

synagogue of the Libertines, and *C*	Acts 6:9	2956

CYRENIUS (si-re'-ne-us) *A Roman governor of Syria.*

made when *C* was governor of Syria	Lk 2:2	2958

CYRUS (si'-rus) *Founder of the Persian Empire.*

first year of *C* king of Persia	2Chr 36:22	3566
up the spirit of *C* king of Persia	2Chr 36:22	3566
Thus saith *C* king of Persia, All	2Chr 36:23	3566
first year of *C* king of Persia	Ezr 1:1	3566
up the spirit of *C* king of Persia	Ezr 1:1	3566
Thus saith *C* king of Persia, The	Ezr 1:2	3566
Also *C* the king brought forth the	Ezr 1:7	3566
Even those did *C* king of Persia	Ezr 1:8	3566
that they had of *C* king of Persia	Ezr 3:7	3566
as king *C* the king of Persia hath	Ezr 4:3	3566
all the days of *C* king of Persia	Ezr 4:5	3566
But in the first year of *C* the	Ezr 5:13	3567
C made a decree to build this	Ezr 5:13	3567
those did *C* the king take out of	Ezr 5:14	3567
that a decree was made of *C* the	Ezr 5:17	3567
In the first year of *C* the king	Ezr 6:3	3567
the same *C* the king made a decree	Ezr 6:3	3567
according to the commandment of *C*	Ezr 6:14	3567
That saith of *C*, He is my	Is 44:28	3566
the Lord to his anointed, to *C*	Is 45:1	3566
unto the first year of king *C*	Dan 1:21	3566
and in the reign of *C* the Persian	Dan 6:28	3567
In the third year of *C* king of	Dan 10:1	3566

D

DABAREH (dab'-a-reh) See Daberath. *A Levitical city in Issachar.*

her suburbs, *D* with her suburbs,	Josh 21:28	1705

DABBASHETH (dab'-ba-sheth) *A border city of Issachar.*

sea, and Maralah, and reached to *D*	Josh 19:11	1708

DABBESHETH See Dabbasheth.

DABERATH (dab'-e-rath) See Dabareh. *Same as Dabareh.*

and then goeth out to *D*, and goeth	Josh 19:12	1705
her suburbs, *D* with her suburbs,	1Chr 6:72	1705

DAGGER

made him a *d* which had two edges	Judg 3:16	2719
took the *d* from his right thigh,	Judg 3:21	2719
not draw the *d* out of his belly	Judg 3:22	2719

DAGON See Beth-dagon, Dagon's. *A Philistine god.*

great sacrifice unto *D* their god	Judg 16:23	1712
house of *D*, and set it by *D*	1Sa 5:2	1712
D was fallen upon his face to the	1Sa 5:3	1712
And they took *D*, and set him in his	1Sa 5:3	1712
D was fallen upon his face to the	1Sa 5:4	1712
and the head of *D* and both the	1Sa 5:4	1712
the stump of *D* was left to him	1Sa 5:4	1712
neither the priests of *D*, nor any	1Sa 5:5	1712
of *D* in Ashdod unto this day	1Sa 5:5	1712
sore upon us, and upon *D* our god	1Sa 5:7	1712
his head in the temple of *D*	1Chr 10:10	1712

DAGON'S

nor any that come into *D* house	1Sa 5:5	1712

DAILY

your *d* tasks, as when there was	Ex 5:13	3117
from your bricks of your *d* task	Ex 5:19	3117
be twice as much as they gather *d*	Ex 16:5	3117
the *d* meat offering, and the	Num 4:16	8548
this manner ye shall offer *d*	Num 28:24	3117
the *d* burnt offering, and his meat	Num 29:6	8548
she pressed him *d* with her words	Judg 16:16	3117

a *d* rate for every day, all the	2Kin 25:30	3117
his *d* portion for their service	2Chr 31:16	3117
offered the *d* burnt offerings by	Ezr 3:4	3117
prepared for me *d* was one ox	Neh 5:18	3117,259
pass, when they spake *d* unto him	Est 3:4	3117
soul, having sorrow in my heart *d*	Ps 13:2	3119
they say *d* unto me, Where	Ps 42:10	3605,3117
he fighting *d* oppresseth me	Ps 56:1	3605,3117
enemies would *d* swallow me up	Ps 56:2	3605,3117
that I may *d* perform my vows	Ps 61:8	3117
who *d* loadeth us with benefits,	Ps 68:19	3117
and *d* shall he be praised	Ps 72:15	3605,3117
foolish man reproacheth thee *d*	Ps 74:22	3605,3117
for I cry unto thee *d*	Ps 86:3	3605,3117
Lord, I have called *d* upon thee.	Ps 88:9	3605,3117
round about me *d* like water	Ps 88:17	3605,3117
I was *d* his delight, rejoicing	Prov 8:30	3117
watching *d* at my gates, waiting	Prov 8:34	3117
Yet they seek me *d*, and delight to	Is 58:2	3117
d rising up early and sending them	Jer 7:25	3117
I am in derision *d*, every one	Jer 20:7	3605,3117
unto me, and a derision, *d*	Jer 20:8	3605,3117
that they should give him *d* a	Jer 37:21	3117
and Noph shall have distresses *d*	Eze 30:16	3119
without blemish *d* the seven days	Eze 45:23	3117
of the goats *d* for a sin offering	Eze 45:23	3117
Thou shalt *d* prepare a burnt	Eze 46:13	3117
the king appointed them a *d*	Dan 1:5	3117
by him the *d* sacrifice was taken	Dan 8:11	8548
the *d* sacrifice by reason of	Dan 8:12	8548
vision concerning the *d* sacrifice	Dan 8:13	8548
shall take away the *d* sacrifice	Dan 11:31	8548
And from the time that the *d*	Dan 12:11	8548
he *d* increaseth lies and	Hos 12:1	3605,3117
Give us this day our *d* bread	Mt 6:11	1967
I sat *d* with you teaching in the	Mt 26:55	2596,2250
I was *d* with you in the temple	Mk 14:49	2596,2250
himself, and take up his cross *d*	Lk 9:23	2596,2250
Give us day by day our *d* bread	Lk 11:3	1967
he taught *d* in the temple	Lk 19:47	2596,2250

When I was _d_ with you in the ....Lk 22:53   2596,2250
continuing _d_ with one accord in .....Acts 2:46   2596,2250
church as such as should be saved..Acts 2:47   2596,2250
whom they laid _d_ at the gate of .....Acts 3:2   2596,2250
_d_ in the temple, and in every..........Acts 5:42   3956,2250
neglected in the _d_ ministration...............Acts 6:1   2522
faith, and increased in number _d_ ....Acts 16:5   2596,2250
and searched the scriptures _d_ ....Acts 17:11   2596,2250
in the market _d_ with them ....Acts 17:17   2596,3956,2250
disputing _d_ in the school of one .....Acts 19:9   2596,2250
in Christ Jesus our Lord, I die _d_ ...1Cor 15:31   2596,2250
that which cometh upon me _d_ 2Cor 11:28   2596,2250
But exhort one another _d_, ...Heb 3:13   2596,1538,2250
Who needeth not _d_, as those high...Heb 7:27   2596,2250
priest standeth _d_ ministering.........Heb 10:11   2596,2250
be naked, and destitute of _d_ food ....Jas 2:15   2184

DAINTIES
be fat, and he shall yield royal _d_ ....Gen 49:20   4574
and let me not eat of their _d_ ....Ps 141:4   4516
Be not desirous of his _d_ ....Prov 23:3   4303

DAINTY
bread, and his soul _d_ meat....................Job 33:20   8378
neither desire thou his _d_ meats ....Prov 23:6   3045
thee, and all things which were _d_..........Rev 18:14   3045

DALAIAH (dal-a-i'-ah) See DELAIAH. _A descendant of Judah._
and Akkub, and Johanan, and _D_ 1Chr 3:24   1806

DALE
of Shaveh, which is the king's _d_..............Gen 14:17   6010
pillar, which is in the king's _d_ 2Sa 18:18   6010

DALMANUTHA (dal-ma-nu'-thah) _A village in Galilee._
and came into the parts of _D_ ....Mk 8:10   1148

DALMATIA (dal-ma'-she-ah) _A Roman province west of Macedonia._
Crescens to Galatia, Titus unto _D_ 2Ti 4:10   1149

DALPHON (dal'-fon) _A son of Haman._
And Parshandatha, and _D_, ...Est 9:7   1813

DAM
seven days it shall be with his _d_...............Ex 22:30   517
shall be seven days under the _d_...........Lev 22:27   517
the _d_ sitting upon the young, or ....Deut 22:6   517
not take the _d_ with the young ....Deut 22:6   517
shalt in any wise let the _d_ go ....Deut 22:7   517

DAMAGE
why should _d_ grow to the hurt of............Ezr 4:22   2257
not countervail the king's _d_.....................Est 7:4   5143
off the feet, and drinketh _d_ ....Prov 26:6   2555
and the king should have no _d_ ....Dan 6:2   5142
will be with hurt and much _d_.................Acts 27:10   2209
might receive _d_ by us in nothing............2Cor 7:9   2210

DAMARIS (dam'-a-ris) _An Athenian convert of Paul._
Areopagite, and a woman named _D_.......Acts 17:34   1152

DAMASCENES (dam-as-senes') _Inhabitants of Damascus._
the city of the _D_ with a garrison.............2Cor 11:32   1159

DAMASCUS (da-mas'-cus) See DAMASCENES, SYRIA-DAMASCUS. _A city in Syria._
which is on the left hand of _D_ ....Gen 14:15   1834
of my house is this Eliezer of _D_ ....Gen 15:2   1834
when the Syrians of _D_ came to...............2Sa 8:5   1834
David put garrisons in Syria of _D_ 2Sa 8:6   1834
and they went to _D_, and dwelt...........1Kin 11:24   1834
and dwelt therein, and reigned in _D_.......1Kin 11:24   1834
king of Syria, that dwelt at _D_...............1Kin 15:18   1834
on thy way to the wilderness of _D_.........1Kin 19:15   1834
shalt make streets for thee in _D_ 1Kin 20:34   1834
not Abana and Pharpar, rivers of _D_ 2Kin 5:12   1834
And Elisha came to _D_...........................2Kin 8:7   1834
even of every good thing of _D_ 2Kin 8:9   1834
he warred, and how he recovered _D_.....2Kin 14:28   1834
king of Assyria went up against _D_.........2Kin 16:9   1834
king Ahaz went to _D_ to meet 2Kin 16:10   1834
and saw an altar that was at _D_.............2Kin 16:10   1834
that king Ahaz had sent from _D_ 2Kin 16:11   1834
it against king Ahaz came from _D_ 2Kin 16:11   1834
And when the king was come from _D_ ..2Kin 16:12   1834
when the Syrians of _D_ came to..........1Chr 18:5   1834
king of Syria, that dwelt at _D_................2Chr 16:2   1834
spoil of them unto the king of _D_ 2Chr 24:23   1834
captives, and brought them to _D_ 2Chr 28:5   1834
he sacrificed unto the gods of _D_..........2Chr 28:23   1834
of Lebanon which looketh toward _D_.......Song 7:4   1834
For the head of Syria is _D_ ....Is 7:8   1834
and the head of _D_ is Rezin.....................Is 7:8   1834
and my mother, the riches of _D_ ....Is 8:4   1834

is not Samaria as _D_.............................Is 10:9   1834
The burden of _D_ ....Is 17:1   1834
_D_ is taken away from being a city ....Is 17:1   1834
Ephraim, and the kingdom from _D_ ....Is 17:3   1834
Concerning _D_. Hamath is confounded ...Jer 49:23   1834
_D_ is waxed feeble, and turneth ....Jer 49:24   1834
kindle a fire in the wall of _D_.................Jer 49:27   1834
_D_ was thy merchant in the ....Eze 27:18   1834
which is between the border of _D_ ....Eze 47:16   1834
be Hazar-enan, the border of _D_ ....Eze 47:17   1834
measure from Hauran, and from _D_ ......Eze 47:18   1834
the border of _D_ northward ....Eze 48:1   1834
For three transgressions of _D_ ....Amos 1:3   1834
I will break also the bar of _D_................Amos 1:5   1834
of a bed, and in _D_ in a couch ....Amos 3:12   1833
you to go into captivity beyond _D_.........Amos 5:27   1834
_D_ shall be the rest thereof....................Zec 9:1   1834
letters to _D_ to the synagogues ....Acts 9:2   1154
as he journeyed, he came near _D_ ....Acts 9:3   1154
the hand, and brought him into _D_ ....Acts 9:8   1154
there was a certain disciple at _D_..........Acts 9:10   1154
the disciples which were at _D_ ....Acts 9:19   1154
the Jews which dwelt at _D_....................Acts 9:22   1154
boldly at _D_ in the name of Jesus..........Acts 9:27   1154
unto the brethren, and went to _D_ ....Acts 22:5   1154
was come nigh unto _D_ about noon ....Acts 22:6   1154
said unto me, Arise, and go into _D_ .....Acts 22:10   1154
that were with me, I came into _D_ ....Acts 22:11   1154
as I went to _D_ with authority ....Acts 26:12   1154
But shewed first unto them of _D_ ....Acts 26:20   1154
In _D_ the governor under Aretas.............2Cor 11:32   1154
Arabia, and returned again unto _D_........Gal 1:17   1154

DAMNABLE
privily shall bring in _d_ heresies 2Pet 2:1   684

DAMNATION
ye shall receive the greater _d_ ....Mt 23:14   2917
how can ye escape the _d_ of hell ....Mt 23:33   2920
but is in danger of eternal _d_.................Mk 3:29   2920
these shall receive greater _d_ ....Mk 12:40   2917
the same shall receive greater _d_ ....Lk 20:47   2917
evil, unto the resurrection of _d_..............Jn 5:29   2920
whose _d_ is just...............................Rom 3:8   2917
shall receive to themselves _d_ ....Rom 13:2   2917
drinketh _d_ to himself, not......................1Cor 11:29   2917
Having _d_, because they have cast 1Ti 5:12   2917
not, and their _d_ slumbereth not 2Pet 2:3   684

DAMNED
he that believeth not shall be _d_ ....Mk 16:16   2632
he that doubteth is _d_ if he eat................Rom 14:23   2632
That they all might be _d_ who................2Th 2:12   2919

DAMSEL
that the _d_ to whom I shall say,.................Gen 24:14   5291
the _d_ was very fair to look upon, ...Gen 24:16   5291
And the _d_ ran, and told them of her ......Gen 24:28   5291
Let the _d_ abide with us a few ....Gen 24:55   5291
And they said, We will call the _d_ ....Gen 24:57   5291
of Jacob, and he loved the _d_..................Gen 34:3   5291
and spake kindly unto the _d_ ....Gen 34:3   5291
saying, Get me this _d_ to wife ....Gen 34:4   5291
but give me the _d_ to wife ....Gen 34:8   3207
Then shall the father of the _d_ ....Deut 22:15   5291
them unto the father of the _d_ ....Deut 22:19   5291
virginity be not found for the _d_.............Deut 22:20   5291
the _d_ to the door of her father's ....Deut 22:21   5291
If a _d_ that is a virgin be ....Deut 22:23   5291
the _d_, because she cried not,.................Deut 22:24   5291
find a betrothed _d_ in the field ....Deut 22:25   5291
But unto the _d_ thou shalt do ....Deut 22:26   5291
there is in the _d_ no sin worthy ....Deut 22:26   5291
field, and the betrothed _d_ cried ....Deut 22:27   5291
If a man find a _d_ that is a ....Deut 22:28   5291
to every man a _d_ or two ....Judg 5:30   7356
when the father of the _d_ saw him ....Judg 19:3   5291
over the reapers, Whose _d_ is this ....Ruth 2:5   5291
It is the Moabitish _d_ that came ....Ruth 2:6   5291
So they sought for a fair _d_ 1Kin 1:3   5291
the _d_ was very fair, and cherished 1Kin 1:4   5291
in a charger, and given to the _d_ ....Mt 14:11   2877
a _d_ came unto him, saying, Thou ....Mt 26:69   3814
the _d_ is not dead, but sleepeth ....Mk 5:39   3813
the father and the mother of the _d_.........Mk 5:40   3813
entereth in where the _d_ was lying ....Mk 5:40   3813
And he took the _d_ by the hand ....Mk 5:41   3813
which is, being interpreted, _D_................Mk 5:41   2877
And straightway the _d_ arose ....Mk 5:42   2877
him, the king said unto the _d_ ....Mk 6:22   2877
in a charger, and gave it to the _d_ ....Mk 6:28   2877
the _d_ gave it to her mother ....Mk 6:28   2877
Then saith the _d_ that kept the ....Jn 18:17   3814

D

a *d* came to hearken, named Rhoda ...... Acts 12:13   3814
a certain *d* possessed with a .... Acts 16:16   3814

DAMSEL'S

d virginity unto the elders of................... Deut 22:15   5291
the *d* father shall say unto the .... Deut 22:16   5291
with her shall give unto the *d* .... Deut 22:29   5291
the *d* father, retained him .... Judg 19:4   5291
the *d* father said unto his son in .... Judg 19:5   5291
for the *d* father had said unto .... Judg 19:6   5291
the *d* father said, Comfort thine............ Judg 19:8   5291
the *d* father, said unto him, ... Judg 19:9   5291

DAMSELS

And Rebekah arose, and her *d* .... Gen 24:61   5291
with five of *d* hers that went 1Sa 25:42   5291
among them were the *d* playing .... Ps 68:25   5959

DAN (dan) See DANITES, DAN-JAAN, LAISH, MAHANEH-
    DAN.
    1. A son of Jacob.
therefore called she his name *D* .... Gen 30:6   1835
D, and Naphtali................................... Gen 35:25   1835
And the sons of *D*.................................. Gen 46:23   1835
D shall judge his people, as one............. Gen 49:16   1835
D shall be a serpent by the way,............. Gen 49:17   1835
D, and Naphtali, Gad, and Asher .... Ex 1:4   1835
therein, and called Leshem, *D* .... Josh 19:47   1835
after the name of *D* their father .... Josh 19:47   1835
after the name of *D* their father .... Judg 18:29   1835
D, Joseph, and Benjamin, Naphtali,....... 1Chr 2:2   1835
D also and Javan going to and fro .... Eze 27:19   1835
    2. A city and tribal territory in northern Canaan.
eighteen, and pursued them unto *D*....... Gen 14:14   1835
all the land of Gilead, unto *D*.................. Deut 34:1   1835
called the name of the city *D*.................. Judg 18:29   1835
from *D* even to Beer-sheba, with .... Judg 20:1   1835
all Israel from *D* even to........................ 1Sa 3:20   1835
from *D* even to Beer-sheba 2Sa 3:10   1835
from *D* even to Beer-sheba, as the 2Sa 17:11   1835
from *D* even to Beer-sheba, and 2Sa 24:2   1835
from *D* even to Beer-sheba seventy......... 2Sa 24:15   1835
from *D* even to Beer-sheba, all 1Kin 4:25   1835
Beth-el, and the other put he in *D* 1Kin 12:29   1835
before the one, even unto *D*.................... 1Kin 12:30   1835
of Israel, and smote Ijon, and *D*............. 1Kin 15:20   1835
in Beth-el, and were in *D* 2Kin 10:29   1835
Israel from Beer-sheba even to *D* 1Chr 21:2   1835
and they smote Ijon, and *D*, and 2Chr 16:4   1835
Israel, from Beer-sheba even to *D*........... 2Chr 30:5   1835
For a voice declareth from *D*.................... Jer 4:15   1835
of his horses was heard from *D* .... Jer 8:16   1835
a portion for *D*...................................... Eze 48:1   1835
And by the border of *D*, from the .... Eze 48:2   1835
gate of Benjamin, one gate of *D*.............. Eze 48:32   1835
of Samaria, and say, Thy god, O *D*.......... Amos 8:14   1835
    3. Tribe descended from Dan 1.
of Ahisamach, of the tribe of *D*............... Ex 31:6   1835
of Ahisamach, of the tribe of *D*............... Ex 35:34   1835
of Ahisamach, of the tribe of *D*............... Ex 38:23   1835
of Dibri, of the tribe of *D* .... Lev 24:11   1835
Of *D*; Ahiezer the son .... Num 1:12   1835
Of the children of *D*, by their .... Num 1:38   1835
of them, even of the tribe of *D* .... Num 1:39   1835
The standard of the camp of *D* .... Num 2:25   1835
of *D* shall be Ahiezer the son of.............. Num 2:25   1835
of *D* were an hundred thousand .... Num 2:31   1835
prince of the children of *D* .... Num 7:66   1835
of the children of *D* set forward .... Num 10:25   1835
Of the tribe of *D*, Ammiel the son .... Num 13:12   1835
sons of *D* after their families .... Num 26:42   1835
of *D* after their families .... Num 26:42   1835
of the tribe of the children of *D*.............. Num 34:22   1835
Gad, and Asher, and Zebulun, *D*............ Deut 27:13   1835
Dan he said, *D* is a lion's whelp .... Deut 33:22   1835
of *D* according to their families .... Josh 19:40   1835
of *D* went out too little for them .... Josh 19:47   1835
therefore the children of *D* went .... Josh 19:47   1835
of *D* according to their families .... Josh 19:48   1835
Ephraim, and out of the tribe of *D* .... Josh 21:5   1835
And out of the tribe of *D*, Eltekeh .... Josh 21:23   1835
children of *D* into the mountain .... Judg 1:34   1835
why did *D* remain in ships .... Judg 5:17   1835
in the camp of *D* between Zorah .... Judg 13:25   1835
the children of *D* sent of their .... Judg 18:2   1835
which were of the children of *D* .... Judg 18:16   1835
and overtook the children of *D*................ Judg 18:22   1835
they cried unto the children of *D* .... Judg 18:23   1835
the children of *D* said unto him .... Judg 18:25   1835
the children of *D* went their way .... Judg 18:26   1835
the children of *D* set up the.................... Judg 18:30   1835
were priests to the tribe of *D* .... Judg 18:30   1835

Of *D*, Azareel the son of Jeroham.......... 1Chr 27:22   1835
of a woman of the daughters of *D*........... 2Chr 2:14   1835

DANCE

of Shiloh come out to *d* in dances........... Judg 21:21   2342
like a flock, and their children *d*............. Job 21:11   7540
Let them praise his name in the *d* .... Ps 149:3   4234
Praise him with the timbrel and *d* .... Ps 150:4   4234
a time to mourn, and a time to *d*............. Eccl 3:4   7540
there, and satyrs shall *d* there .... Is 13:21   7540
shall the virgin rejoice in the *d*............... Jer 31:13   4234
our *d* is turned into mourning................. Lam 5:15   4234

DANCED

to their number, of them that *d* .... Judg 21:23   2342
David *d* before the LORD with all 2Sa 6:14   3769
piped unto you, and ye have not *d*...... Mt 11:17   3738
of Herodias *d* before them .... Mt 14:6   3738
the said Herodias came in, and *d* .... Mk 6:22   3738
piped unto you, and ye have not *d*...... Lk 7:32   3738

DANCES

after her with timbrels and with *d* .... Ex 15:20   4246
meet him with timbrels and with *d* .... Judg 11:34   4246
of Shiloh come out to dance in *d* .... Judg 21:21   4246
sing one to another of him in *d* 1Sa 21:11   4246
they sang one to another in *d* 1Sa 29:5   4246
shalt go forth in the *d* of them .... Jer 31:4   4246

DANCING

that he saw the calf, and the *d* .... Ex 32:19   4246
cities of Israel, singing and *d*................. 1Sa 18:6   4246
earth, eating and drinking, and *d* 1Sa 30:16   2287
leaping and *d* before the LORD................ 2Sa 6:16   3769
out at a window saw king David *d* 1Chr 15:29   7540
turned for me my mourning into *d* .... Ps 30:11   4234
the house, he heard musick and *d*...... Lk 15:25   5525

DANDLED

her sides, and be *d* upon her knees .... Is 66:12   8173

DANGER

shall be in *d* of the judgment .... Mt 5:21   1777
shall be in *d* of the judgment .... Mt 5:22   1777
shall be in *d* of the council................... Mt 5:22   1777
shall be in *d* of hell fire .... Mt 5:22   1777
but is in *d* of eternal damnation .... Mk 3:29   1777
craft is in *d* to be set at nought .... Acts 19:27   2793
For we are in *d* to be called in .... Acts 19:40   2793

DANGEROUS

spent, and when sailing was now *d* .... Acts 27:9   2000

DANIEL See BELTESHAZZAR.
    1. A son of David.
the second *D*, of Abigail the 1Chr 3:1   1840
    2. An Israelite who renewed the covenant.
of the sons of Ithamar; *D*....................... Ezr 8:2   1840
D, Ginnethon, Baruch, ... Neh 10:6   1840
    3. A major prophet.
Though these three men, Noah, *D*.......... Eze 14:14   1840
Though Noah, *D*, and Job, were in.......... Eze 14:20   1840
Behold, thou art wiser than *D* .... Eze 28:3   1840
were of the children of Judah, *D* .... Dan 1:6   1840
for he gave unto *D* the name of .... Dan 1:7   1840
But *D* purposed in his heart that .... Dan 1:8   1840
Now God had brought *D* into favour .... Dan 1:9   1840
prince of the eunuchs said unto *D*.......... Dan 1:10   1840
Then said *D* to Melzar, whom the .... Dan 1:11   1840
of the eunuchs had set over *D*................. Dan 1:11   1840
D had understanding in all .... Dan 1:17   1840
them all was found none like *D*............... Dan 1:19   1840
D continued even unto the first .... Dan 1:21   1840
and they sought *D* and his fellows.......... Dan 2:13   1841
Then *D* answered with counsel and .... Dan 2:14   1841
Arioch made the thing known to *D* .... Dan 2:15   1841
Then *D* went in, and desired of the .... Dan 2:16   1841
Then *D* went to his house, and made ...... Dan 2:17   1841
that *D* and his fellows should not .... Dan 2:18   1841
revealed unto *D* in a night vision .... Dan 2:19   1841
Then *D* blessed the God of heaven .... Dan 2:19   1841
D answered and said, Blessed be .... Dan 2:20   1841
Therefore *D* went in unto Arioch,............ Dan 2:24   1841
Then Arioch brought in *D* before............. Dan 2:25   1841
The king answered and said to *D* .... Dan 2:26   1841
D answered in the presence of the .... Dan 2:27   1841
upon his face, and worshipped *D* .... Dan 2:46   1841
The king answered unto *D*, and said...... Dan 2:47   1841
Then the king made *D* a great man .... Dan 2:48   1841
Then *D* requested of the king, and .... Dan 2:49   1841
but *D* sat in the gate of the king............. Dan 2:49   1841
But at the last *D* came in before............. Dan 4:8   1841
Then *D*, whose name was .... Dan 4:19   1841
doubts, were found in the same *D*.......... Dan 5:12   1841
now let *D* be called, and he will.............. Dan 5:12   1841

Then was *D* brought in before the .... Dan 5:13   1841
said unto Daniel, Art thou that *D* ...... Dan 5:13   1841
Then *D* answered and said before .... Dan 5:17   1841
and they clothed *D* with scarlet .... Dan 5:29   1841
of whom *D* was first .... Dan 6:2   1841
Then this *D* was preferred above .... Dan 6:3   1841
against *D* concerning the kingdom .... Dan 6:4   1841
find any occasion against this *D* .... Dan 6:5   1841
Now when *D* knew that the writing ...... Dan 6:10   1841
found *D* praying and making .... Dan 6:11   1841
and said before the king, That *D* ...... Dan 6:13   1841
set his heart on *D* to deliver him .... Dan 6:14   1841
king commanded, and they brought *D*... Dan 6:16   1841
Now the king spake and said unto *D* .... Dan 6:16   1841
might not be changed concerning *D* ..... Dan 6:17   1841
with a lamentable voice unto *D* .... Dan 6:20   1841
king spake and said to Daniel, O *D* .... Dan 6:20   1841
Then said *D* unto the king, O king .... Dan 6:21   1841
should take *D* up out of the den .... Dan 6:23   1841
So *D* was taken up out of the den, ... Dan 6:23   1841
those men which had accused *D* .... Dan 6:24   1841
and fear before the God of *D* .... Dan 6:26   1841
who hath delivered *D* from the .... Dan 6:27   1841
So this *D* prospered in the reign .... Dan 6:28   1841
king of Babylon *D* had a dream. .... Dan 7:1   1841
D spake and said, I saw in my .... Dan 7:2   1841
I *D* was grieved in my spirit in .... Dan 7:15   1841
As for me *D*, my cogitations much .... Dan 7:28   1841
appeared unto me, even unto me *D* .... Dan 8:1   1840
it came to pass, when I, even I *D* .... Dan 8:15   1840
I *D* fainted, and was sick certain .... Dan 8:27   1840
the first year of his reign I *D* .... Dan 9:2   1840
and talked with me, and said, O *D* .... Dan 9:22   1840
a thing was revealed unto *D* .... Dan 10:1   1840
In those days I *D* was mourning .... Dan 10:2   1840
And I *D* alone saw the vision .... Dan 10:7   1840
And he said unto me, O *D*, a man .... Dan 10:11   1840
Then said he unto me, Fear not, *D*........ Dan 10:12   1840
But thou, O *D*, shut up the words, ... Dan 12:4   1840
Then I *D* looked, and, behold, ... Dan 12:5   1840
And he said, Go thy way, *D* .... Dan 12:9   1840
spoken of by *D* the prophet .... Mt 24:15   *1158*
spoken of by *D* the prophet .... Mk 13:14   *1158*

DANITES (dan'-ites) *Descendants of Dan 1.*
of Zorah, of the family of the *D* .... Judg 13:2   1839
D sought them an inheritance to .... Judg 18:1   1839
thence of the family of the *D* .... Judg 18:1   1839
of the *D* expert in war twenty and 1Chr 12:35   1839

DAN-JAAN (dan-ja'-an) *A place between Gilead and Zidon.*
and they came to *D*, and about to 2Sa 24:6   1842

DANNAH (dan'-nah) *A city in Judah.*
And *D*, and Kirjath-sannah, which is ..... Josh 15:49   1837

DARA (da'-rah) See DARDA. *A son of Zerah.*
Ethan, and Heman, and Calcol, and *D* .. 1Chr 2:6   1873

DARDA (dar'-dah) See DARA. *A wise man.*
and Heman, and Chalcol, and *D* 1Kin 4:31   1862

DARE
is so fierce that *d* stir him up .... Job 41:10
good man some would even *d* to die ...... Rom 5:7   *5111*
For I will not to speak of any .... Rom 15:18   *5111*
D any of you, having a matter 1Cor 6:1   *5111*
For we *d* not make ourselves of 2Cor 10:12   *5111*

DARIUS (da-ri'-us)
   1. Darius Hystaspes, king of Persia.
the reign of *D* king of Persia .... Ezr 4:5   1867
of the reign of *D* king of Persia .... Ezr 4:24   1868
cease, till the matter came to *D* .... Ezr 5:5   1868
the river, sent unto *D* the king .... Ezr 5:6   1868
Unto *D* the king, all peace...................... Ezr 5:7   1868
Then *D* the king made a decree, and ..... Ezr 6:1   1868
I *D* have made a decree........................... Ezr 6:12   1868
to that which *D* the king had sent .... Ezr 6:13   1868
to the commandment of Cyrus, and *D* ... Ezr 6:14   1868
year of the reign of *D* the king............... Ezr 6:15   1868
In the second year of *D* the king .... Hag 1:1   1867
in the second year of *D* the king .... Hag 1:15   1867
month, in the second year of *D* .... Hag 2:10   1867
month, in the second year of *D* .... Zec 1:1   1867
Sebat, in the second year of *D* .... Zec 1:7   1867
pass in the fourth year of king *D*........... Zec 7:1   1867
   2. Darius Nothus, king of Persia.
to the reign of *D* the Persian .... Neh 12:22   1867
   3. Cyaxares, king of Media.
D the Median took the kingdom, ... Dan 5:31   1868
It pleased *D* to set over the .... Dan 6:1   1868
and said thus unto him, King *D* .... Dan 6:6   1868

Wherefore king *D* signed the .... Dan 6:9   1868
Then king *D* wrote unto all people .... Dan 6:25   1868
prospered in the reign of *D* .... Dan 6:28   1868
year of *D* the son of Ahasuerus .... Dan 9:1   1867
I in the first year of *D* the Mede .... Dan 11:1   1867

DARK
the sun went down, and it was *d* .... Gen 15:17   5939
if the plague be somewhat *d* .... Lev 13:6   3544
than the skin, but be somewhat *d* .... Lev 13:21   3544
the other skin, but be somewhat *d* .... Lev 13:26   3544
in the skin, but it be somewhat *d* .... Lev 13:28   3544
the plague be somewhat *d* after .... Lev 13:56   3544
apparently, and not in *d* speeches .... Num 12:8   2420
of the gate, when it was *d* .... Josh 2:5   2822
d waters, and thick clouds of the 2Sa 22:12   2841
began to be *d* before the sabbath .... Neh 13:19   6751
of the twilight thereof be *d* .... Job 3:9   2821
They grope in the *d* without light .... Job 12:25   2822
shall be *d* in his tabernacle .... Job 18:6   2821
can he judge through the *d* cloud .... Job 22:13   6205
In the *d* they dig through houses, ... Job 24:16   2822
round about him were *d* waters .... Ps 18:11   2824
Let their way be *d* and slippery .... Ps 35:6   2822
I will open my *d* saying upon the .... Ps 49:4   2420
for the *d* places of the earth are .... Ps 74:20   4285
I will utter *d* sayings of old .... Ps 78:2   2420
thy wonders be known in the *d* .... Ps 88:12   2822
He sent darkness, and made it *d* .... Ps 105:28   2821
of the wise, and their *d* sayings .... Prov 1:6   2420
evening, in the black and night .... Prov 7:9   653
LORD, and their works are in the *d* .... Is 29:15   4285
in a *d* place of the earth .... Is 45:19   2822
feet stumble upon the *d* mountains .... Jer 13:16   5399
He hath set me in *d* places..................... Lam 3:6   4285
the house of Israel do in the *d* .... Eze 8:12   2822
and make the stars thereof *d* .... Eze 32:7   6937
of heaven will I make *d* over thee .... Eze 32:8   6937
scattered in the cloudy and *d* day .... Eze 34:12   6205
and understanding *d* sentences .... Dan 8:23   2420
the sun and the moon shall be *d* .... Joel 2:10   6937
and maketh the day *d* with night .... Amos 5:8   2821
even very *d*, and no brightness in.......... Amos 5:20   651
and it shall be *d* unto you .... Mic 3:6   2821
and the day shall be *d* over them .... Mic 3:6   6937
light shall not be clear, nor *d* .... Zec 14:6   7087
full of light, having no part *d* .... Lk 11:36   *4652*
And it was now *d*, and Jesus was not ..... Jn 6:17   *4653*
early, when it was yet *d*, unto .... Jn 20:1   *4653*
a light that shineth in a *d* place 2Pet 1:19   *850*

DARKEN
I will *d* the earth in the clear .... Amos 8:9   2821

DARKENED
earth, so that the land was *d* .... Ex 10:15   2821
Let their eyes be *d*, that they .... Ps 69:23   2821
the moon, or the stars, be not *d* .... Eccl 12:2   2821
that look out of the windows be *d* .... Eccl 12:3   2821
the light is *d* in the heavens .... Is 5:30   2821
the LORD of hosts is the land *d* .... Is 9:19   6272
the sun shall be *d* in his going .... Is 13:10   2821
all joy is *d*, the mirth of the .... Is 24:11   6150
also the day shall be *d*, when I .... Eze 30:18   2821
The sun and the moon shall be *d* .... Joel 3:15   6937
his right eye shall be utterly *d* .... Zec 11:17   3543
of those days shall the sun be *d* .... Mt 24:29   *4654*
tribulation, the sun shall be *d* .... Mk 13:24   *4654*
And the sun was *d*, and the veil of .... Lk 23:45   *4654*
and their foolish heart was *d* .... Rom 1:21   *4654*
Let their eyes be *d*, that they .... Rom 11:10   *4654*
Having the understanding *d* .... Eph 4:18   *4654*
as the third part of them was *d* .... Rev 8:12   *4654*
the air were *d* by reason of the .... Rev 9:2   *4654*

DARKENETH
Who is this that *d* counsel by................. Job 38:2   2821

DARKISH
skin of their flesh be *d* white .... Lev 13:39   3544

DARKLY
For now we see through a glass, *d* . 1Cor 13:12   *1722,135*

DARKNESS
d was upon the face of the deep .... Gen 1:2   2822
God divided the light from the *d* .... Gen 1:4   2822
Day, and the *d* he called Night .... Gen 1:5   2822
and to divide the light from the *d* .... Gen 1:18   2822
horror of great *d* fell upon him .... Gen 15:12   2825
that there may be *d* over the land .... Ex 10:21   2822
Egypt, even *d* which may be felt .... Ex 10:21   2822
there was a thick *d* in all the .... Ex 10:22   2822
d to them, but it gave light by .... Ex 14:20   2822

unto the thick *d* where God was	Ex 20:21	6205
with *d*, clouds, and thick *d*	Deut 4:11	6205
of the cloud, and of the thick *d*	Deut 5:22	6205
voice out of the midst of the *d*	Deut 5:23	2822
as the blind gropeth in *d*	Deut 28:29	653
he put *d* between you and the	Josh 24:7	3990
the wicked shall be silent in *d*	1Sa 2:9	2822
and *d* was under his feet	2Sa 22:10	6205
he made *d* pavilions round about	2Sa 22:12	2822
and the LORD will lighten my *d*	2Sa 22:29	2822
he would dwell in the thick *d*	1Kin 8:12	6205
he would dwell in the thick *d*	2Chr 6:1	6205
Let that day be *d*	Job 3:4	2822
Let *d* and the shadow of death	Job 3:5	2822
that night, let *d* seize upon it	Job 3:6	652
They meet with *d* in the daytime	Job 5:14	2822
not return, even to the land of *d*	Job 10:21	2822
A land of *d*, as *d* itself	Job 10:22	5890
order, and where the light is as *d*	Job 10:22	652
discovereth deep things out of *d*	Job 12:22	2822
not that he shall return out of *d*	Job 15:22	2822
the day of *d* is ready at his hand	Job 15:23	2822
He shall not depart out of *d*	Job 15:30	2822
the light is short because of the *d*	Job 17:12	2822
I have made my bed in the *d*	Job 17:13	2822
shall be driven from light into *d*	Job 18:18	2822
and he hath set *d* in my paths	Job 19:8	2822
All *d* shall be hid in his secret	Job 20:26	2822
Or *d*, that thou canst not see	Job 22:11	2822
I was not cut off before the *d*	Job 23:17	2822
he covered the *d* from my face	Job 23:17	652
He setteth an end to *d*, and	Job 28:3	2822
the stones of *d*, and the shadow of	Job 28:3	652
by his light I walked through *d*	Job 29:3	2822
I waited for light, there came *d*	Job 30:26	652
There is no *d*, nor shadow of	Job 34:22	2822
order our speech by reason of *d*	Job 37:19	2822
thick *d* a swaddlingband for it,	Job 38:9	6205
and as for *d*, where is the place	Job 38:19	2822
and *d* was under his feet	Ps 18:9	6205
He made *d* his secret place	Ps 18:11	2822
LORD my God will enlighten my *d*	Ps 18:28	2822
they walk on in *d*	Ps 82:5	2825
laid me in the lowest pit, in *d*	Ps 88:6	4285
me, and mine acquaintance into *d*	Ps 88:18	4285
the pestilence that walketh in *d*	Ps 91:6	652
Clouds and *d* are round about him	Ps 97:2	6205
Thou makest *d*, and it is night	Ps 104:20	2822
He sent *d*, and made it dark	Ps 105:28	2822
Such as sit in *d* and in the shadow	Ps 107:10	2822
He brought them out of *d* and the	Ps 107:14	2822
there ariseth light in the *d*	Ps 112:4	2822
Surely the *d* shall cover me	Ps 139:11	2822
the *d* hideth not from thee	Ps 139:12	2822
the *d* and the light are both alike	Ps 139:12	2825
he hath made me to dwell in *d*	Ps 143:3	4285
to walk in the ways of *d*	Prov 2:13	2822
The way of the wicked is as *d*	Prov 4:19	653
shall be put out in obscure *d*	Prov 20:20	2822
as far as light excelleth *d*	Eccl 2:13	2822
but the fool walketh in *d*	Eccl 2:14	2822
All his days also he eateth in *d*	Eccl 5:17	2822
in with vanity, and departeth in *d*	Eccl 6:4	2822
his name shall be covered with *d*	Eccl 6:4	2822
let him remember the days of *d*	Eccl 11:8	2822
that put *d* for light, and light	Is 5:20	2822
for light, and light for *d*	Is 5:20	2822
one look unto the land, behold *d*	Is 5:30	2822
and behold trouble and *d*, dimness	Is 8:22	2825
and they shall be driven to *d*	Is 8:22	653
in *d* have seen a great light	Is 9:2	2822
see out of obscurity, and out of *d*	Is 29:18	2822
them that sit in *d* out of the	Is 42:7	2822
I will make *d* light before them,	Is 42:16	4285
will give thee the treasures of *d*	Is 45:3	2822
I form the light, and create *d*	Is 45:7	2822
thou silent, and get thee into *d*	Is 47:5	2822
to them that are in *d*, Shew	Is 49:9	2822
of his servant, that walketh in *d*	Is 50:10	2825
and thy *d* be as the noonday	Is 58:10	653
for brightness, but we walk in *d*	Is 59:9	653
the *d* shall cover the earth, and	Is 60:2	2822
the earth, and gross *d* the people	Is 60:2	6205
a land of *d*	Jer 2:31	3991
LORD your God, before he cause *d*	Jer 13:16	2821
of death, and make it gross *d*	Jer 13:16	6205
them as slippery ways in the *d*	Jer 23:12	653
hath led me, and brought me into *d*	Lam 3:2	2822
set *d* upon thy land, saith the	Eze 32:8	2822
he knoweth what is in the *d*	Dan 2:22	2816
A day of *d* and of gloominess, a	Joel 2:2	2822

a day of clouds and of thick *d*	Joel 2:2	6205
The sun shall be turned into *d*	Joel 2:31	2822
that maketh the morning *d*	Amos 4:13	5890
the day of the LORD is *d*, and not	Amos 5:18	2822
not the day of the LORD be *d*	Amos 5:20	2822
when I sit in *d*, the LORD shall	Mic 7:8	2822
d shall pursue his enemies	Nah 1:8	2822
and desolation, a day of *d*	Zeph 1:15	2822
a day of clouds and thick *d*	Zeph 1:15	6205
which sat in *d* saw great light	Mt 4:16	4655
thy whole body shall be full of *d*	Mt 6:23	4652
be *d*, how great is that *d*	Mt 6:23	4655
shall be cast out into outer *d*	Mt 8:12	4655
What I tell you in *d*, that speak	Mt 10:27	4653
away, and cast him into outer *d*	Mt 22:13	4655
unprofitable servant into outer *d*	Mt 25:30	4655
was *d* over all the land unto the	Mt 27:45	4655
there was *d* over the whole land	Mk 15:33	4655
give light to them that sit in *d*	Lk 1:79	4655
evil, thy body also is full of *d*	Lk 11:34	4652
light which is in thee be not *d*	Lk 11:35	4655
in *d* shall be heard in the light	Lk 12:3	4653
is your hour, and the power of *d*	Lk 22:53	4655
there was a *d* over all the earth	Lk 23:44	4655
And the light shineth in *d*	Jn 1:5	4653
the *d* comprehended it not	Jn 1:5	4653
men loved *d* rather than light,	Jn 3:19	4655
followeth me shall not walk in *d*	Jn 8:12	4653
the light, lest *d* come upon you	Jn 12:35	4653
for he that walketh in *d* knoweth	Jn 12:35	4653
on me should not abide in *d*	Jn 12:46	4653
The sun shall be turned into *d*	Acts 2:20	4655
there fell on him a mist and a *d*	Acts 13:11	4655
and to turn them from *d* to light	Acts 26:18	4655
a light of them which are in *d*	Rom 2:19	4655
therefore cast off the works of *d*	Rom 13:12	4655
to light the hidden things of *d*	1Cor 4:5	4655
the light to shine out of *d*	2Cor 4:6	4655
what communion hath light with *d*	2Cor 6:14	4655
For ye were sometimes *d*, but now	Eph 5:8	4655
with the unfruitful works of *d*	Eph 5:11	4655
the rulers of the *d* of this world	Eph 6:12	4655
delivered us from the power of *d*	Col 1:13	4655
But ye, brethren, are not in *d*	1Th 5:4	4655
we are not of the night, nor of *d*	1Th 5:5	4655
fire, nor unto blackness, and *d*	Heb 12:18	4655
of *d* into his marvellous light	1Pet 2:9	4655
delivered them into chains of *d*	2Pet 2:4	2217
to whom the mist of *d* is reserved	2Pet 2:17	4655
light, and in him is no *d* at all	1Jn 1:5	4653
fellowship with him, and walk in *d*	1Jn 1:6	4655
because the *d* is past, and the	1Jn 2:8	4653
brother, is in *d* even until now	1Jn 2:9	4653
is in *d*, and walketh in *d*	1Jn 2:11	4653
because that *d* hath blinded his	1Jn 2:11	4653
in everlasting chains under *d*	Jude 6	2217
the blackness of *d* for ever	Jude 13	4655
and his kingdom was full of *d*	Rev 16:10	4656

DARKON (dar'-kon) *A family of exiles.*

of Jaalah, the children of D	Ezr 2:56	1874
of Jaala, the children of D	Neh 7:58	1874

DARLING

my *d* from the power of the dog	Ps 22:20	3173
destructions, my *d* from the lions	Ps 35:17	3173

DART

the spear, the *d*, nor the	Job 41:26	4551
Till a *d* strike through his liver	Prov 7:23	2671
or thrust through with a *d*	Heb 12:20	1002

DARTS

And he took three *d* in his hand	2Sa 18:14	7626
in the city of David, and made *d*	2Chr 32:5	7973
D are counted as stubble	Job 41:29	8455
all the fiery *d* of the wicked	Eph 6:16	956

DASH

wilt *d* their children, and rip up	2Kin 8:12	7376
thou shalt *d* them in pieces like	Ps 2:9	5310
lest thou *d* thy foot against a	Ps 91:12	5062
Their bows also shall *d* the young	Is 13:18	7376
I will *d* them one against another	Jer 13:14	5310
lest at any time thou *d* thy foot	Mt 4:6	4350
lest at any time thou *d* thy foot	Lk 4:11	4350

DASHED

hath *d* in pieces the enemy	Ex 15:6	7492
be *d* to pieces before their eyes	Is 13:16	7376
the mother was *d* in pieces upon	Hos 10:14	7376
infants shall be *d* in pieces	Hos 13:16	7376
her young children also were *d* in	Nah 3:10	7376

DASHETH

d thy little ones against the	Ps 137:9	5310
He that *d* in pieces is come up	Nah 2:1	6327

DATHAN (da´-than) A conspirator against Moses.

of Kohath, the son of Levi, and *D*	Num 16:1	1885
And Moses sent to call *D* and Abiram	Num 16:12	1885
about the tabernacle of Korah, *D*	Num 16:24	1885
And Moses rose up and went unto *D*	Num 16:25	1885
from the tabernacle of Korah, *D*	Num 16:27	1885
D and Abiram came out, and stood	Num 16:27	1885
Nemuel, and *D*, and Abiram	Num 26:9	1885
This is that *D* and Abiram, which	Num 26:9	1885
And what he did unto *D* and Abiram,	Deut 11:6	1885
earth opened and swallowed up *D*	Ps 106:17	1885

DAUB

Say unto them which *d* it with	Eze 13:11	2902

DAUBED

d it with slime and with pitch, and	Ex 2:3	2560
others *d* it with untempered	Eze 13:10	2902
daubing wherewith ye have *d* it	Eze 13:12	2902
ye have *d* with untempered morter	Eze 13:14	2902
upon them that have *d* it with	Eze 13:15	2902
no more, neither they that *d* it	Eze 13:15	2902
her prophets have *d* them with	Eze 22:28	2902

DAUBING

Where is the *d* wherewith ye have	Eze 13:12	2915

DAUGHTER

the *d* of Haran, the father of	Gen 11:29	1323
son's son, and Sarai his *d* in law	Gen 11:31	3618
she is the *d* of my father, but	Gen 20:12	1323
but not the *d* of my mother	Gen 20:12	1323
And said, Whose *d* art thou	Gen 24:23	1323
I am the *d* of Bethuel the son of	Gen 24:24	1323
her, and said, Whose *d* art thou	Gen 24:47	1323
The *d* of Bethuel, Nahor's son,	Gen 24:47	1323
master's brother's *d* unto his son	Gen 24:48	1323
the *d* of Bethuel the Syrian of	Gen 25:20	1323
Judith the *d* of Beeri the Hittite	Gen 26:34	1323
Bashemath the *d* of Elon the	Gen 26:34	1323
the *d* of Ishmael Abraham's son	Gen 28:9	1323
Rachel his *d* cometh with the	Gen 29:6	1323
when Jacob saw Rachel the *d* of	Gen 29:10	1323
years for Rachel thy younger *d*	Gen 29:18	1323
evening, that he took Leah his *d*	Gen 29:23	1323
Laban gave unto his *d* Leah Zilpah	Gen 29:24	1323
him Rachel his *d* to wife also	Gen 29:28	1323
Laban gave to Rachel his *d* Bilhah	Gen 29:29	1323
And afterwards she bare a *d*	Gen 30:21	1323
And Dinah the *d* of Leah, which she	Gen 34:1	1323
clave unto Dinah the *d* of Jacob	Gen 34:3	1323
that he had defiled Dinah his *d*	Gen 34:5	1323
in Israel in lying with Jacob's *d*	Gen 34:7	1323
my son Shechem longeth for your *d*	Gen 34:8	1323
then will we take our *d*, and we	Gen 34:17	1323
he had delight in Jacob's *d*	Gen 34:19	1323
Adah the *d* of Elon the Hittite,	Gen 36:2	1323
Aholibamah the *d* of Anah the	Gen 36:2	1323
Anah the *d* of Zibeon the Hivite	Gen 36:2	1323
And Bashemath Ishmael's *d*, sister	Gen 36:3	1323
d of Anah the *d* of Zibeon	Gen 36:14	1323
came of Aholibamah the *d* of Anah	Gen 36:18	1323
and Aholibamah the *d* of Anah	Gen 36:25	1323
the *d* of Matred, the *d* of	Gen 36:39	1323
Judah saw there a *d* of a certain	Gen 38:2	1323
said Judah to Tamar his *d* in law	Gen 38:11	3618
in process of time the *d* of Shuah	Gen 38:12	1323
not that she was his *d* in law	Gen 38:16	3618
Tamar thy *d* in law hath played	Gen 38:24	3618
the *d* of Poti-pherah priest of On	Gen 41:45	1323
came, which Asenath the *d* of	Gen 41:50	1323
in Padan-aram, with his *d* Dinah	Gen 46:15	1323
whom Laban gave to Leah his *d*	Gen 46:18	1323
Ephraim, which Asenath the *d* of	Gen 46:20	1323
Laban gave unto Rachel his *d*	Gen 46:25	1323
but if it be a *d*, then she shall	Ex 1:16	1323
every *d* ye shall save alive	Ex 1:22	1323
Levi, and took to wife a *d* of Levi	Ex 2:1	1323
the *d* of Pharaoh came down to	Ex 2:5	1323
said his sister to Pharaoh's *d*	Ex 2:7	1323
Pharaoh's *d* said to her, Go	Ex 2:8	1323
Pharaoh's *d* said unto her, Take	Ex 2:9	1323
she brought him unto Pharaoh's *d*	Ex 2:10	1323
and he gave Moses Zipporah his *d*	Ex 2:21	1323
d of Amminadab, sister of Naashon	Ex 6:23	1323
thou, nor thy son, nor thy *d*	Ex 20:10	1323
if a man sell his *d* to be a	Ex 21:7	1323
gored a son, or have gored a *d*	Ex 21:31	1323
fulfilled, for a son, or for a *d*	Lev 12:6	1323

the *d* of thy father, or *d*	Lev 18:9	1323
d, or of thy daughter's *d*	Lev 18:10	1323
of thy father's wife's *d*	Lev 18:11	1323
the nakedness of thy *d* in law	Lev 18:15	3618
the nakedness of a woman and her *d*	Lev 18:17	1323
son's *d*, or her daughter's *d*	Lev 18:17	1323
Do not prostitute thy *d*, to cause	Lev 19:29	1323
And if a man lie with his *d* in law	Lev 20:12	3618
father's *d*, or his mother's *d*	Lev 20:17	1323
and for his son, and for his *d*	Lev 21:2	1323
the *d* of any priest, if she	Lev 21:9	1323
If the priest's *d* also be married	Lev 22:12	1323
But if the priest's *d* be a widow	Lev 22:13	1323
the *d* of Dibri, of the tribe of	Lev 24:11	1323
was slain was Cozbi, the *d* of Zur	Num 25:15	1323
the *d* of a prince of Midian,	Num 25:18	1323
the name of the *d* of Asher was	Num 26:46	1323
the *d* of Levi, whom her mother	Num 26:59	1323
inheritance to pass unto his *d*	Num 27:8	1323
And if he have no *d*, then ye shall	Num 27:9	1323
wife, between the father and his *d*	Num 30:16	1323
And every *d*, that possesseth an	Num 36:8	1323
thou, nor thy son, nor thy *d*	Deut 5:14	1323
thy *d* thou shalt not give unto	Deut 7:3	1323
nor his *d* shalt thou take unto	Deut 7:3	1323
thou, and thy son, and thy *d*	Deut 12:18	1323
thy mother, or thy son, or thy *d*	Deut 13:6	1323
God, thou, and thy son, and thy *d*	Deut 16:11	1323
feast, thou, and thy son, and thy *d*	Deut 16:14	1323
or his *d* to pass through the fire	Deut 18:10	1323
I gave my *d* unto this man to wife	Deut 22:16	1323
saying, I found not thy *d* a maid	Deut 22:17	1323
the *d* of his father, or the	Deut 27:22	1323
father, or the *d* of his mother	Deut 27:22	1323
toward her son, and toward her *d*	Deut 28:56	1323
will I give Achsah my *d* to wife	Josh 15:16	1323
he gave him Achsah his *d* to wife	Josh 15:17	1323
will I give Achsah my *d* to wife	Judg 1:12	1323
he gave him Achsah his *d* to wife	Judg 1:13	1323
his *d* came out to meet him with	Judg 11:34	1323
her he had neither son nor *d*	Judg 11:34	1323
his clothes, and said, Alas, my *d*	Judg 11:35	1323
went yearly to lament the *d* of	Judg 11:40	1323
Behold, here is my *d* a maiden	Judg 19:24	1323
give his *d* unto Benjamin to wife	Judg 21:1	1323
her *d* in law, with her, which	Ruth 1:22	3618
And she said unto her, Go, my *d*	Ruth 2:2	1323
unto Ruth, Hearest thou not, my *d*	Ruth 2:8	1323
And Naomi said unto her *d* in law	Ruth 2:20	3618
d in law, It is good, my *d*	Ruth 2:22	1323
mother in law said unto her, My *d*	Ruth 3:1	1323
Blessed be thou of the LORD, my *d*	Ruth 3:10	1323
And now, my *d*, fear not	Ruth 3:11	1323
law, she said, Who art thou, my *d*	Ruth 3:16	1323
Then said she, Sit still, my *d*	Ruth 3:18	1323
for thy *d* in law, which loveth	Ruth 4:15	3618
thine handmaid for a *d* of Belial	1Sa 1:16	1323
his *d* in law, Phinehas' wife, was	1Sa 4:19	3618
was Ahinoam, the *d* of Ahimaaz	1Sa 14:50	1323
riches, and will give him his *d*	1Sa 17:25	1323
to David, Behold my elder *d* Merab	1Sa 18:17	1323
at the time when Merab Saul's *d*	1Sa 18:19	1323
And Michal Saul's *d* loved David	1Sa 18:20	1323
gave him Michal his *d* to wife	1Sa 18:27	1323
and that Michal Saul's *d* loved him	1Sa 18:28	1323
But Saul had given Michal his *d*	1Sa 25:44	1323
the *d* of Talmai king of Geshur	2Sa 3:3	1323
name was Rizpah, the *d* of Aiah	2Sa 3:7	1323
thou first bring Michal Saul's *d*	2Sa 3:13	1323
Michal Saul's *d* looked through a	2Sa 6:16	1323
Michal the *d* of Saul came out to	2Sa 6:20	1323
Therefore Michal the *d* of Saul	2Sa 6:23	1323
the *d* of Eliam, the wife of Uriah	2Sa 11:3	1323
his bosom, and was unto him as a *d*	2Sa 12:3	1323
were born three sons, and one *d*	2Sa 14:27	1323
in to Abigail the *d* of Nahash	2Sa 17:25	1323
two sons of Rizpah the *d* of Aiah	2Sa 21:8	1323
five sons of Michal the *d* of Saul	2Sa 21:8	1323
Rizpah the *d* of Aiah took	2Sa 21:10	1323
David what Rizpah the *d* of Aiah	2Sa 21:11	1323
of Egypt, and took Pharaoh's *d*	1Kin 3:1	1323
Taphath the *d* of Solomon to wife	1Kin 4:11	1323
Basmath the *d* of Solomon to wife	1Kin 4:15	1323
also an house for Pharaoh's *d*	1Kin 7:8	1323
given it for a present unto his *d*	1Kin 9:16	1323
But Pharaoh's *d* came up out of	1Kin 9:24	1323
together with the *d* of Pharaoh	1Kin 11:1	1323
was Maachah, the *d* of Abishalom	1Kin 15:2	1323
was Maachah, the *d* of Abishalom	1Kin 15:10	1323
the *d* of Ethbaal king of the	1Kin 16:31	1323
name was Azubah the *d* of Shilhi	1Kin 22:42	1323

for the *d* of Ahab was his wife	2Kin 8:18	1323
the *d* of Omri king of Israel	2Kin 8:26	1323
for she is a king's *d*	2Kin 9:34	1323
the *d* of king Joram, sister of	2Kin 11:2	1323
Give thy *d* to my son to wife	2Kin 14:9	1323
name was Jerusha, the *d* of Zadok	2Kin 15:33	1323
also was Abi, the *d* of Zachariah	2Kin 18:2	1323
The virgin the *d* of Zion hath	2Kin 19:21	1323
the *d* of Jerusalem hath shaken	2Kin 19:21	1323
the *d* of Haruz of Jotbah	2Kin 21:19	1323
the *d* of Adaiah of Boscath	2Kin 22:1	1323
his *d* to pass through the fire to	2Kin 23:10	1323
the *d* of Jeremiah of Libnah	2Kin 23:31	1323
the *d* of Pedaiah of Rumah	2Kin 23:36	1323
the *d* of Elnathan of Jerusalem	2Kin 24:8	1323
the *d* of Jeremiah of Libnah	2Kin 24:18	1323
the *d* of Matred, the *d* of	1Chr 1:50	1323
of the *d* of Shua the Canaanitess	1Chr 2:3	1323
Tamar his *d* in law bare him	1Chr 2:4	3618
d of Machir the father of Gilead	1Chr 2:21	1323
Sheshan gave his *d* to Jarha his	1Chr 2:35	1323
and the *d* of Caleb was Achsa	1Chr 2:49	1323
the *d* of Talmai king of Geshur	1Chr 3:2	1323
of Bath-shua the *d* of Ammiel	1Chr 3:5	1323
sons of Bithiah the *d* of Pharaoh	1Chr 4:18	1323
his *d* was Sherah, who built	1Chr 7:24	1323
that Michal the *d* of Saul looking	1Chr 15:29	1323
Solomon brought up the *d* of	2Chr 8:11	1323
Rehoboam took him Mahalath the *d*	2Chr 11:18	1121
Abihail the *d* of Eliab the son of	2Chr 11:18	1323
he took Maachah the *d* of Absalom	2Chr 11:20	1323
Rehoboam loved Maachah the *d* of	2Chr 11:21	1323
Michaiah the *d* of Uriel of Gibeah	2Chr 13:2	1323
name was Azubah the *d* of Shilhi	2Chr 20:31	1323
for he had the *d* of Ahab to wife	2Chr 21:6	1323
also was Athaliah the *d* of Omri	2Chr 22:2	1323
the *d* of the king, took Joash the	2Chr 22:11	
the *d* of king Jehoram, the wife	2Chr 22:11	1323
Give thy *d* to my son to wife	2Chr 25:18	1323
also was Jerusham, the *d* of Zadok	2Chr 27:1	1323
was Abijah, the *d* of Zechariah	2Chr 29:1	1323
the *d* of Meshullam the son of	Neh 6:18	1323
that is, Esther, his uncle's *d*	Est 2:7	1323
were dead, took for his own *d*	Est 2:7	1323
the *d* of Abihail the uncle of	Est 2:15	1323
who had taken her for his *d*	Est 2:15	1323
the *d* of Abihail, and Mordecai the	Est 9:29	1323
in the gates of the *d* of Zion	Ps 9:14	1323
Hearken, O *d*, and consider, and	Ps 45:10	1323
the *d* of Tyre shall be there with	Ps 45:12	1323
The king's *d* is all glorious	Ps 45:13	1323
O *d* of Babylon, who art to be	Ps 137:8	1323
thy feet with shoes, O prince's *d*	Song 7:1	1323
the *d* of Zion is left as a	Is 1:8	1323
Lift up thy voice, O *d* of Gallim	Is 10:30	1323
the mount of the *d* of Zion	Is 10:32	1004
unto the mount of the *d* of Zion	Is 16:1	1323
spoiling of the *d* of my people	Is 22:4	1323
land as a river, O *d* of Tarshish	Is 23:10	1323
thou oppressed virgin, *d* of Zidon	Is 23:12	1323
the *d* of Zion, hath despised thee	Is 37:22	1323
the *d* of Jerusalem hath shaken	Is 37:22	1323
O virgin *d* of Babylon, sit on the	Is 47:1	1323
no throne, O *d* of the Chaldeans	Is 47:1	1323
darkness, O *d* of the Chaldeans	Is 47:5	1323
of thy neck, O captive *d* of Zion	Is 52:2	1323
world, Say ye to the *d* of Zion	Is 62:11	1323
toward the *d* of my people	Jer 4:11	1323
child, the voice of the *d* of Zion	Jer 4:31	1323
I have likened the *d* of Zion to a	Jer 6:2	1323
of the *d* of my people slightly	Jer 6:14	1323
for war against thee, O *d* of Zion	Jer 6:23	1323
O *d* of my people, gird thee with	Jer 6:26	1323
of the *d* of my people slightly	Jer 8:11	1323
the voice of the cry of the *d* of	Jer 8:19	1323
For the hurt of the *d* of my	Jer 8:21	1323
of the *d* of my people recovered	Jer 8:22	1323
the slain of the *d* of my people	Jer 9:1	1323
shall I do for the *d* of my people	Jer 9:7	1323
for the virgin of my people is	Jer 14:17	1323
go about, O thou backsliding *d*	Jer 31:22	1323
balm, O virgin, the *d* of Egypt	Jer 46:11	1323
O thou *d* dwelling in Egypt	Jer 46:19	1323
The *d* of Egypt shall be	Jer 46:24	1323
Thou *d* that dost inhabit Dibon,	Jer 48:18	1323
flowing valley, O backsliding *d*	Jer 49:4	1323
against thee, O *d* of Babylon	Jer 50:42	1323
The *d* of Babylon is like a	Jer 51:33	1323
the *d* of Jeremiah of Libnah	Jer 52:1	1323
from the *d* of Zion all her beauty	Lam 1:6	1323
the *d* of Judah, as in a winepress	Lam 1:15	1323

the *d* of Zion with a cloud in his	Lam 2:1	1323
strong holds of the *d* of Judah	Lam 2:2	1323
the tabernacle of the *d* of Zion	Lam 2:4	1323
in the *d* of Judah mourning	Lam 2:5	1323
destroy the wall of the *d* of Zion	Lam 2:8	1323
The elders of the *d* of Zion sit	Lam 2:10	1323
destruction of the *d* of my people	Lam 2:11	1323
I liken to thee, O *d* of Jerusalem	Lam 2:13	1323
comfort thee, O virgin *d* of Zion	Lam 2:13	1323
their head at the *d* of Jerusalem	Lam 2:15	1323
the Lord, O wall of the *d* of Zion	Lam 2:18	1323
destruction of the *d* of my people	Lam 3:48	1323
the *d* of my people is become	Lam 4:3	1323
of the iniquity of the *d* of my	Lam 4:6	1323
destruction of the *d* of my people	Lam 4:10	1323
O *d* of Edom, that dwellest in the	Lam 4:21	1323
is accomplished, O *d* of Zion	Lam 4:22	1323
visit thine iniquity, O *d* of Edom	Lam 4:22	1323
shall deliver neither son nor *d*	Eze 14:20	1323
As is the mother, so is her *d*	Eze 16:44	1323
Thou art thy mother's *d*, that	Eze 16:45	1323
hath lewdly defiled his *d* in law	Eze 22:11	3618
his sister, his father's *d*	Eze 22:11	1323
for mother, or for son, or for *d*	Eze 44:25	1323
for the king's *d* of the south	Dan 11:6	1323
he shall give him the *d* of women	Dan 11:17	1323
and took Gomer the *d* of Diblaim	Hos 1:3	1323
she conceived again, and bare a *d*	Hos 1:6	1323
of the sin to the *d* of Zion	Mic 1:13	1323
the strong hold of the *d* of Zion	Mic 4:8	1323
shall come to the *d* of Jerusalem	Mic 4:8	1323
O *d* of Zion, like a woman in	Mic 4:10	1323
Arise and thresh, O *d* of Zion	Mic 4:13	1323
thyself in troops, O *d* of troops	Mic 5:1	1323
the *d* riseth up against her	Mic 7:6	1323
the *d* in law against her mother	Mic 7:6	3618
even the *d* of my dispersed, shall	Zeph 3:10	1323
Sing, O *d* of Zion	Zeph 3:14	1323
all the heart, O *d* of Jerusalem	Zeph 3:14	1323
dwellest with the *d* of Babylon	Zec 2:7	1323
Sing and rejoice, O *d* of Zion	Zec 2:10	1323
Rejoice greatly, O *d* of Zion	Zec 9:9	1323
shout, O *d* of Jerusalem	Zec 9:9	1323
married the *d* of a strange god	Mal 2:11	1323
saying, My *d* is even now dead	Mt 9:18	2364
and when he saw her, he said, *D*	Mt 9:22	2364
the *d* against her mother, and the	Mt 10:35	2364
the *d* in law against her mother	Mt 10:35	3565
he that loveth son or *d* more than	Mt 10:37	2364
the *d* of Herodias danced before	Mt 14:6	2364
my *d* is grievously vexed with a	Mt 15:22	2364
her *d* was made whole from that	Mt 15:28	2364
Tell ye the *d* of Sion, Behold,	Mt 21:5	2364
My little *d* lieth at the point of	Mk 5:23	2365
And he said unto her, *D*, thy faith	Mk 5:34	2364
certain which said, Thy *d* is dead	Mk 5:35	2364
when the *d* of the said Herodias	Mk 6:22	2364
whose young *d* had an unclean	Mk 7:25	2365
cast forth the devil out of her *d*	Mk 7:26	2364
the devil is gone out of thy *d*	Mk 7:29	2364
out, and her *d* laid upon the bed	Mk 7:30	2364
the *d* of Phanuel, of the tribe of	Lk 2:36	2364
For he had one only *d*, about	Lk 8:42	2364
And he said unto her, *D*, be of	Lk 8:48	2364
saying to him, Thy *d* is dead	Lk 8:49	2364
the mother against the *d*	Lk 12:53	2364
and the *d* against the mother	Lk 12:53	2364
in law against her *d* in law	Lk 12:53	3565
the *d* in law against her mother	Lk 12:53	3565
being a *d* of Abraham, whom Satan	Lk 13:16	2364
Fear not, *d* of Sion	Jn 12:15	2364
Pharaoh's *d* took him up, and	Acts 7:21	2364
be called the son of Pharaoh's *d*	Heb 11:24	2364

DAUGHTER'S

daughter, or of thy *d* daughter	Lev 18:10	1323
or her *d* daughter, to uncover her	Lev 18:17	1323
are the tokens of my *d* virginity	Deut 22:17	1323

DAUGHTERS

and he begat sons and *d*	Gen 5:4	1121
seven years, and begat sons and *d*	Gen 5:7	1121
fifteen years, and begat sons and *d*	Gen 5:10	1121
forty years, and begat sons and *d*	Gen 5:13	1121
thirty years, and begat sons and *d*	Gen 5:16	1121
hundred years, and begat sons and *d*	Gen 5:19	1121
hundred years, and begat sons and *d*	Gen 5:22	1121
and two years, and begat sons and *d*	Gen 5:26	1121
and five years, and begat sons and *d*	Gen 5:30	1121
earth, and *d* were born unto them,	Gen 6:1	1121
the *d* of men that they were fair	Gen 6:2	1121
of God came in unto the *d* of men	Gen 6:4	1121

hundred years, and begat sons and *d*	Gen 11:11	1121
three years, and begat sons and *d*	Gen 11:13	1121
three years, and begat sons and *d*	Gen 11:15	1121
thirty years, and begat sons and *d*	Gen 11:17	1121
and nine years, and begat sons and *d*	Gen 11:19	1121
seven years, and begat sons and *d*	Gen 11:21	1121
hundred years, and begat sons and *d*	Gen 11:23	1121
years, and begat sons and *d*	Gen 11:25	1121
I have two *d* which have not known	Gen 19:8	1121
son in law, and thy sons, and thy *d*	Gen 19:12	1121
sons in law, which married his *d*	Gen 19:14	1121
take thy wife, and thy two *d*	Gen 19:15	1121
and upon the hand of his two *d*	Gen 19:16	1121
mountain, and his two *d* with him	Gen 19:30	1121
dwelt in a cave, he and his two *d*	Gen 19:30	1121
Thus were both the *d* of Lot with	Gen 19:36	1121
my son of the *d* of the Canaanites	Gen 24:3	1121
the *d* of the men of the city come	Gen 24:13	1121
my son of the *d* of the Canaanites	Gen 24:37	1121
my life because of the *d* of Heth	Gen 27:46	1121
take a wife of the *d* of Heth	Gen 27:46	1121
which are of the *d* of the land	Gen 27:46	1121
take a wife of the *d* of Canaan	Gen 28:1	1121
d of Laban thy mother's brother	Gen 28:2	1121
take a wife of the *d* of Canaan	Gen 28:6	1121
Esau seeing that the *d* of Canaan	Gen 28:8	1121
And Laban had two *d*	Gen 29:16	1121
for the *d* will call me blessed	Gen 30:13	1121
to me, and carried away my *d*	Gen 31:26	1121
me to kiss my sons and my *d*	Gen 31:28	1121
take by force thy *d* from me	Gen 31:31	1121
thee fourteen years for thy two *d*	Gen 31:41	1121
These *d* are my *d*, and	Gen 31:43	1121
Jacob, These *d* are my *d*	Gen 31:43	1121
can I do this day unto these my *d*	Gen 31:43	1121
If thou shalt afflict my *d*	Gen 31:50	1121
take other wives beside my *d*	Gen 31:50	1121
up, and kissed his sons and his *d*	Gen 31:55	1121
went out to see the *d* of the land	Gen 34:1	1121
with us, and give your *d* unto us	Gen 34:9	1121
unto us, and take our *d* unto you	Gen 34:9	1121
Then will we give our *d* unto you	Gen 34:16	1121
and we will take your *d* to us	Gen 34:16	1121
us take their *d* to us for wives	Gen 34:21	1121
and let us give them our *d*	Gen 34:21	1121
took his wives of the *d* of Canaan	Gen 36:2	1121
his wives, and his sons, and his *d*	Gen 36:6	1121
all his *d* rose up to comfort him	Gen 37:35	1121
his *d*, and his sons' *d*	Gen 46:7	1121
his *d* were thirty and three	Gen 46:15	1121
the priest of Midian had seven *d*	Ex 2:16	1121
And he said unto his *d*, And where	Ex 2:20	1121
upon your sons, and upon your *d*	Ex 3:22	1121
one of the *d* of Putiel to wife	Ex 6:25	1121
old, with our sons and with our *d*	Ex 10:9	1121
and she have born him sons or *d*	Ex 21:4	1121
with her after the manner of *d*	Ex 21:9	1121
wives, of your sons, and of your *d*	Ex 32:2	1121
take of their *d* unto thy sons	Ex 34:16	1121
their *d* go a whoring after their	Ex 34:16	1121
and thy sons, and thy *d* with thee	Lev 10:14	1121
the flesh of your *d* shall ye eat	Lev 26:29	1121
to thy *d* with thee, by a statute	Num 18:11	1121
thy *d* with thee, by a statute for	Num 18:19	1121
his sons that escaped, and his *d*	Num 21:29	1121
whoredom with the *d* of Moab	Num 25:1	1121
son of Hepher had no sons, but *d*	Num 26:33	1121
the names of the *d* of Zelophehad	Num 26:33	1121
Then came the *d* of Zelophehad	Num 27:1	1121
and these are the names of his *d*	Num 27:1	1121
The *d* of Zelophehad speak right	Num 27:7	1121
Zelophehad our brother unto his *d*	Num 36:2	1121
concerning the *d* of Zelophehad	Num 36:6	1121
so did the *d* of Zelophehad	Num 36:10	1121
the *d* of Zelophehad, were married	Num 36:11	1121
God, ye, and your sons, and your *d*	Deut 12:12	1121
their *d* they have burnt in the	Deut 12:31	1121
be no whore of the *d* of Israel	Deut 23:17	1121
thy *d* shall be given unto another	Deut 28:32	1121
Thou shalt beget sons and *d*	Deut 28:41	1121
the flesh of thy sons and of thy *d*	Deut 28:53	1121
of his sons, and of his *d*	Deut 32:19	1121
of gold, and his sons, and his *d*	Josh 7:24	1121
of Manasseh, had no sons, but *d*	Josh 17:3	1121
and these are the names of his *d*	Josh 17:3	1121
Because the *d* of Manasseh had an	Josh 17:6	1121
they took their *d* to be their	Judg 3:6	1121
gave their *d* to their sons, and	Judg 3:6	1121
That the *d* of Israel went yearly	Judg 11:40	1121
he had thirty sons, and thirty *d*	Judg 12:9	1121
took in thirty *d* from abroad for	Judg 12:9	1121
of the *d* of the Philistines	Judg 14:1	1121
of the *d* of the Philistines	Judg 14:2	1121
woman among the *d* of thy brethren	Judg 14:3	1121
not give them of our *d* to wives	Judg 21:7	1121
may not give them wives of our *d*	Judg 21:18	1121
if the *d* of Shiloh come out to	Judg 21:21	1121
man his wife of the *d* of Shiloh	Judg 21:21	1121
Then she arose with her *d* in law	Ruth 1:6	3618
her two *d* in law with her	Ruth 1:7	3618
Naomi said unto her two *d* in law	Ruth 1:8	3618
And Naomi said, Turn again, my *d*	Ruth 1:11	1121
Turn again, my *d*, go your way	Ruth 1:12	1121
nay, my *d*	Ruth 1:13	1121
wife, and to all her sons and her *d*	1Sa 1:4	1121
and bare three sons and two *d*	1Sa 2:21	1121
he will take your *d* to be	1Sa 8:13	1121
the names of his two *d* were these	1Sa 14:49	1121
wives, and their sons, and their *d*	1Sa 30:3	1121
man for his sons and for his *d*	1Sa 30:6	1121
nor great, neither sons nor *d*	1Sa 30:19	1121
lest the *d* of the Philistines	2Sa 1:20	1121
lest the *d* of the uncircumcised	2Sa 1:20	1121
Ye *d* of Israel, weep over Saul,	2Sa 1:24	1121
were yet sons and *d* born to David	2Sa 5:13	1121
d that were virgins apparelled	2Sa 13:18	1121
the lives of thy sons and of thy *d*	2Sa 19:5	1121
their *d* to pass through the fire,	2Kin 17:17	1121
Now Sheshan had no sons, but *d*	1Chr 2:34	1121
Shimei had sixteen sons and six *d*	1Chr 4:27	1121
and Zelophehad had *d*	1Chr 7:15	1121
and David begat more sons and *d*	1Chr 14:3	1121
died, and had no sons, but *d*	1Chr 23:22	1121
to Heman fourteen sons and three *d*	1Chr 25:5	1121
son of a woman of the *d* of Dan	2Chr 2:14	1121
and eight sons, and threescore *d*	2Chr 11:21	1121
twenty and two sons, and sixteen *d*	2Chr 13:21	1121
and he begat sons and *d*	2Chr 24:3	1121
thousand, women, sons, and *d*	2Chr 28:8	1121
the sword, and our sons and our *d*	2Chr 29:9	1121
wives, and their sons, and their *d*	2Chr 31:18	1121
which took a wife of the *d* of	Ezr 2:61	1121
taken of their *d* for themselves	Ezr 9:2	1121
give not your *d* unto their sons	Ezr 9:12	1121
take their *d* unto your sons	Ezr 9:12	1121
part of Jerusalem, he and his *d*	Neh 3:12	1121
brethren, your sons, and your *d*	Neh 4:14	1121
that said, We, our sons, and our *d*	Neh 5:2	1121
our *d* to be servants	Neh 5:5	1121
some of our *d* are brought unto	Neh 5:5	1121
which took one of the *d* of	Neh 7:63	1121
wives, their sons, and their *d*	Neh 10:28	1121
that we would not give our *d* unto	Neh 10:30	1121
nor take their *d* for our sons	Neh 10:30	1121
not give your *d* unto their sons	Neh 13:25	1121
nor take their *d* unto your sons	Neh 13:25	1121
unto him seven sons and three *d*	Job 1:2	1121
his *d* were eating and drinking	Job 1:13	1121
thy *d* were eating and drinking	Job 1:18	1121
He had also seven sons and three *d*	Job 42:13	1121
found so fair as the *d* of Job	Job 42:15	1121
Kings' *d* were among thy	Ps 45:9	1121
let the *d* of Judah be glad,	Ps 48:11	1121
the *d* of Judah rejoiced because	Ps 97:8	1121
sons and their *d* unto devils,	Ps 106:37	1121
blood of their sons and of their *d*	Ps 106:38	1121
that our *d* may be as corner	Ps 144:12	1121
The horseleach hath two *d*	Prov 30:15	1121
Many *d* have done virtuously, but	Prov 31:29	1121
all the *d* of musick shall be	Eccl 12:4	1121
O ye *d* of Jerusalem, as the tents	Song 1:5	1121
thorns, so is my love among the *d*	Song 2:2	1121
O ye *d* of Jerusalem, by the roes,	Song 2:7	1121
O ye *d* of Jerusalem, by the roes,	Song 3:5	1121
with love, for the *d* of Jerusalem	Song 3:10	1121
O ye *d* of Zion, and behold king	Song 3:11	1121
O *d* of Jerusalem, if ye find my	Song 5:8	1121
is my friend, O *d* of Jerusalem	Song 5:16	1121
The *d* saw her, and blessed her	Song 6:9	1121
O *d* of Jerusalem, that ye stir	Song 8:4	1121
Because the *d* of Zion are haughty	Is 3:16	1121
of the head of the *d* of Zion	Is 3:17	1121
away the filth of the *d* of Zion	Is 4:4	1121
so the *d* of Moab shall be at the	Is 16:2	1121
hear my voice, ye careless *d*	Is 32:9	1121
my *d* from the ends of the earth	Is 43:6	1121
thy *d* shall be carried upon their	Is 49:22	1121
name better than of sons and of *d*	Is 56:5	1121
thy *d* shall be nursed at thy side	Is 60:4	1121
herds, their sons and their *d*	Jer 3:24	1121
thy sons and thy *d* should eat	Jer 5:17	1121
their sons and their *d* in the fire	Jer 7:31	1121

mouth, and teach your *d* wailing	Jer 9:20	1121
their *d* shall die by famine	Jer 11:22	1121
nor their sons, nor their *d*	Jer 14:16	1121
thou have sons or *d* in this place	Jer 16:2	1121
concerning the *d* that are born in	Jer 16:3	1121
sons and the flesh of their *d*	Jer 19:9	1121
Take ye wives, and beget sons and *d*	Jer 29:6	1121
give your *d* to husbands	Jer 29:6	1121
that they may bear sons and *d*	Jer 29:6	1121
their *d* to pass through the fire	Jer 32:35	1121
our wives, our sons, nor our *d*	Jer 35:8	1121
were in Mizpah, even the king's *d*	Jer 41:10	1121
and children, and the king's *d*	Jer 43:6	1121
taken captives, and thy *d* captives	Jer 48:46	1121
her *d* shall be burned with fire	Jer 49:2	1121
ye *d* of Rabbah, gird you with	Jer 49:3	1121
because of all the *d* of my city	Lam 3:51	1121
face against the *d* of thy people	Eze 13:17	1121
shall deliver neither sons nor *d*	Eze 14:16	1121
shall deliver neither sons nor *d*	Eze 14:18	1121
be brought forth, both sons and *d*	Eze 14:22	1121
thou hast taken thy sons and thy *d*	Eze 16:20	1121
the *d* of the Philistines, which	Eze 16:27	1121
her *d* that dwell at thy left hand	Eze 16:46	1121
thy right hand, is Sodom and her *d*	Eze 16:46	1121
hath not done, she nor her *d*	Eze 16:48	1121
as thou hast done, thou and thy *d*	Eze 16:48	1121
idleness was in her and in her *d*	Eze 16:49	1121
the captivity of Sodom and her *d*	Eze 16:53	1121
the captivity of Samaria and her *d*	Eze 16:53	1121
When thy sisters, Sodom and her *d*	Eze 16:55	1121
her *d* shall return to their	Eze 16:55	1121
thy *d* shall return to your former	Eze 16:55	1121
of thy reproach of the *d* of Syria	Eze 16:57	1121
the *d* of the Philistines, which	Eze 16:57	1121
I will give them unto thee for *d*	Eze 16:61	1121
two women, the *d* of one mother	Eze 23:2	1121
were mine, and they bare sons and *d*	Eze 23:4	1121
they took her sons and her *d*	Eze 23:10	1121
they shall take thy sons and thy *d*	Eze 23:25	1121
shall slay their sons and their *d*	Eze 23:47	1121
your *d* whom ye have left shall	Eze 24:21	1121
minds, their sons and their *d*	Eze 24:25	1121
her *d* which are in the field	Eze 26:6	1121
with the sword thy *d* in the field	Eze 26:8	1121
her *d* shall go into captivity	Eze 30:18	1121
the *d* of the nations shall lament	Eze 32:16	1121
the *d* of the famous nations, unto	Eze 32:18	1121
therefore your *d* shall commit	Hos 4:13	1121
I will not punish your *d* when	Hos 4:14	1121
your *d* shall prophesy, your old	Joel 2:28	1121
your *d* into the hand of the	Joel 3:8	1121
thy *d* shall fall by the sword, and	Amos 7:17	1121
and his wife was of the *d* of Aaron	Lk 1:5	2364
D of Jerusalem, weep not for me,	Lk 23:28	2364
your *d* shall prophesy, and your	Acts 2:17	2364
And the same man had four *d*	Acts 21:9	2364
you, and ye shall be my sons and *d*	2Cor 6:18	2364
whose *d* ye are, as long as ye do	1Pet 3:6	5043

DAVID See DAVID'S. *Second king of Israel.*

father of Jesse, the father of *D*	Ruth 4:17	1732
begat Jesse, and Jesse begat *D*	Ruth 4:22	1732
came upon *D* from that day forward	1Sa 16:13	1732
Jesse, and said, Send me *D* thy son	1Sa 16:19	1732
sent them by *D* his son unto Saul	1Sa 16:20	1732
D came to Saul, and stood before	1Sa 16:21	1732
Saul sent to Jesse, saying, Let *D*	1Sa 16:22	1732
that *D* took an harp, and played	1Sa 16:23	1732
Now *D* was the son of that	1Sa 17:12	1732
And *D* was the youngest	1Sa 17:14	1732
But *D* went and returned from Saul	1Sa 17:15	1732
And Jesse said unto *D* his son	1Sa 17:17	1732
D rose up early in the morning,	1Sa 17:20	1732
D left his carriage in the hand	1Sa 17:22	1732
and *D* heard them	1Sa 17:23	1732
D spake to the men that stood by	1Sa 17:26	1732
anger was kindled against *D*	1Sa 17:28	1732
D said, What have I now done	1Sa 17:29	1732
words were heard which *D* spake	1Sa 17:31	1732
D said to Saul, Let no man's	1Sa 17:32	1732
And Saul said to *D*, Thou art not	1Sa 17:33	1732
D said unto Saul, Thy servant	1Sa 17:34	1732
D said moreover, The LORD that	1Sa 17:37	1732
And Saul said unto *D*, Go, and the	1Sa 17:37	1732
Saul armed *D* with his armour, and	1Sa 17:38	1732
D girded his sword upon his	1Sa 17:39	1732
D said unto Saul, I cannot go	1Sa 17:39	1732
And *D* put them off him	1Sa 17:39	1732
came on and drew near unto *D*	1Sa 17:41	1732
Philistine looked about, and saw *D*	1Sa 17:42	1732
And the Philistine said unto *D*	1Sa 17:43	1732
Philistine cursed *D* by his gods	1Sa 17:43	1732
And the Philistine said to *D*	1Sa 17:44	1732
Then said *D* to the Philistine,	1Sa 17:45	1732
and came and drew nigh to meet *D*	1Sa 17:48	1732
that *D* hasted, and ran toward the	1Sa 17:48	1732
D put his hand in his bag, and	1Sa 17:49	1732
So *D* prevailed over the	1Sa 17:50	1732
was no sword in the hand of *D*	1Sa 17:50	1732
Therefore *D* ran, and stood upon	1Sa 17:51	1732
D took the head of the Philistine	1Sa 17:54	1732
when Saul saw *D* go forth against	1Sa 17:55	1732
as *D* returned from the slaughter	1Sa 17:57	1732
D answered, I am the son of thy	1Sa 17:58	1732
was knit with the soul of *D*	1Sa 18:1	1732
D made a covenant, because he	1Sa 18:3	1732
was upon him, and gave it to *D*	1Sa 18:4	1732
D went out whithersoever Saul	1Sa 18:5	1732
when *D* was returned from the	1Sa 18:6	1732
thousands, and *D* his ten thousands	1Sa 18:7	1732
ascribed unto *D* ten thousands	1Sa 18:8	1732
Saul eyed *D* from that day and	1Sa 18:9	1732
D played with his hand, as at	1Sa 18:10	1732
I will smite *D* even to the wall	1Sa 18:11	1732
D avoided out of his presence	1Sa 18:11	1732
And Saul was afraid of *D*, because	1Sa 18:12	1732
D behaved himself wisely in all	1Sa 18:14	1732
But all Israel and Judah loved *D*	1Sa 18:16	1732
And Saul said to *D*, Behold my	1Sa 18:17	1732
D said unto Saul, Who am I	1Sa 18:18	1732
should have been given to *D*	1Sa 18:19	1732
And Michal Saul's daughter loved *D*	1Sa 18:20	1732
Wherefore Saul said to *D*, Thou	1Sa 18:21	1732
saying, Commune with *D* secretly	1Sa 18:22	1732
those words in the ears of *D*	1Sa 18:23	1732
D said, Seemeth it to you a light	1Sa 18:23	1732
saying, On this manner spake *D*	1Sa 18:24	1732
Saul said, Thus shall ye say to *D*	1Sa 18:25	1732
to make *D* fall by the hand of the	1Sa 18:25	1732
his servants told *D* these words	1Sa 18:26	1732
it pleased *D* well to be the	1Sa 18:26	1732
Wherefore *D* arose and went, he and	1Sa 18:27	1732
D brought their foreskins, and	1Sa 18:27	1732
and knew that the LORD was with *D*	1Sa 18:28	1732
Saul was yet the more afraid of *D*	1Sa 18:29	1732
that *D* behaved himself more	1Sa 18:30	1732
servants, that they should kill *D*	1Sa 19:1	1732
Saul's son delighted much in *D*	1Sa 19:2	1732
and Jonathan told *D*, saying, Saul	1Sa 19:2	1732
good of *D* unto Saul his father	1Sa 19:4	1732
against his servant, against *D*	1Sa 19:4	1732
to slay *D* without a cause	1Sa 19:5	1732
And Jonathan called *D*	1Sa 19:7	1732
And Jonathan brought *D* to Saul	1Sa 19:7	1732
D went out, and fought with the	1Sa 19:8	1732
and *D* played with his hand	1Sa 19:9	1732
Saul sought to smite *D* even to	1Sa 19:10	1732
D fled, and escaped that night	1Sa 19:10	1732
So Michal let *D* down through a	1Sa 19:12	1732
Saul sent messengers to take *D*	1Sa 19:14	1732
the messengers again to see *D*	1Sa 19:15	1732
So *D* fled, and escaped, and came to	1Sa 19:18	1732
Behold, *D* is at Naioth in Ramah	1Sa 19:19	1732
And Saul sent messengers to take *D*	1Sa 19:20	1732
and said, Where are Samuel and *D*	1Sa 19:22	1732
D fled from Naioth in Ramah, and	1Sa 20:1	1732
D sware moreover, and said, Thy	1Sa 20:3	1732
Then said Jonathan unto *D*	1Sa 20:4	1732
D said unto Jonathan, Behold, to	1Sa 20:5	1732
D earnestly asked leave of me	1Sa 20:6	1732
Then said *D* to Jonathan, Who	1Sa 20:10	1732
And Jonathan said unto *D*, Come, and	1Sa 20:11	1732
And Jonathan said unto *D*, O LORD	1Sa 20:12	1732
behold, if there be good toward *D*	1Sa 20:12	1732
hath cut off the enemies of *D*	1Sa 20:15	1732
a covenant with the house of *D*	1Sa 20:16	1732
Jonathan caused *D* to swear again	1Sa 20:17	1732
Then Jonathan said to *D*, To	1Sa 20:18	1732
So *D* hid himself in the field	1Sa 20:24	1732
D earnestly asked leave of me to	1Sa 20:28	1732
of his father to slay *D*	1Sa 20:33	1732
for he was grieved for *D*, because	1Sa 20:34	1732
at the time appointed with *D*	1Sa 20:35	1732
Jonathan and *D* knew the matter	1Sa 20:39	1732
D arose out of a place toward the	1Sa 20:41	1732
with another, until *D* exceeded	1Sa 20:41	1732
And Jonathan said to *D*, Go in	1Sa 20:42	1732
Then came *D* to Nob to Ahimelech	1Sa 21:1	1732
was afraid at the meeting of *D*	1Sa 21:1	1732
D said unto Ahimelech the priest,	1Sa 21:2	1732
And the priest answered *D*, and said	1Sa 21:4	1732

D answered the priest, and said	1Sa 21:5	1732
D said unto Ahimelech, And is	1Sa 21:8	1732
D said, There is none like that	1Sa 21:9	1732
D arose, and fled that day for	1Sa 21:10	1732
Is not this *D* the king of the	1Sa 21:11	1732
thousands, and *D* his ten thousands	1Sa 21:11	1732
D laid up these words in his	1Sa 21:12	1732
D therefore departed thence, and	1Sa 22:1	1732
D went thence to Mizpeh of Moab	1Sa 22:3	1732
the while that *D* was in the hold	1Sa 22:4	1732
And the prophet Gad said unto *D*	1Sa 22:5	1732
Then *D* departed, and came into the	1Sa 22:5	1732
Saul heard that *D* was discovered	1Sa 22:6	1732
among all thy servants as *D*	1Sa 22:14	1732
because their hand also is with *D*	1Sa 22:17	1732
escaped, and fled after *D*	1Sa 22:20	1732
Abiathar shewed *D* that Saul had	1Sa 22:21	1732
D said unto Abiathar, I knew it	1Sa 22:22	1732
Then they told *D*, saying, Behold,	1Sa 23:1	1732
Therefore *D* enquired of the LORD,	1Sa 23:2	1732
And the LORD said unto *D*, Go, and	1Sa 23:2	1732
Then *D* enquired of the LORD yet	1Sa 23:4	1732
So *D* and his men went to Keilah,	1Sa 23:5	1732
So *D* saved the inhabitants of	1Sa 23:5	1732
of Ahimelech fled to *D* to Keilah	1Sa 23:6	1732
Saul that *D* was come to Keilah	1Sa 23:7	1732
go down to Keilah, to besiege *D*	1Sa 23:8	1732
D knew that Saul secretly	1Sa 23:9	1732
Then said *D*, O LORD God of Israel	1Sa 23:10	1732
Then said *D*, Will the men of	1Sa 23:12	1732
Then *D* and his men, which were	1Sa 23:13	1732
it was told Saul that *D* was	1Sa 23:13	1732
D abode in the wilderness in	1Sa 23:14	1732
D saw that Saul was come out to	1Sa 23:15	1732
D was in the wilderness of Ziph	1Sa 23:15	1732
went to *D* into the wood, and	1Sa 23:16	1732
D abode in the wood, and Jonathan	1Sa 23:18	1732
Doth not *D* hide himself with us	1Sa 23:19	1732
but *D* and his men were in the	1Sa 23:24	1732
And they told *D*	1Sa 23:25	1732
he pursued after *D* in the	1Sa 23:25	1732
this side of the mountain, and *D*	1Sa 23:26	1732
D made haste to get away for fear	1Sa 23:26	1732
for Saul and his men compassed *D*	1Sa 23:26	1732
returned from pursuing after *D*	1Sa 23:28	1732
D went up from thence, and dwelt	1Sa 23:29	1732
D is in the wilderness of En-gedi	1Sa 24:1	1732
of all Israel, and went to seek *D*	1Sa 24:2	1732
and *D* and his men remained in the	1Sa 24:3	1732
the men of *D* said unto him,	1Sa 24:4	1732
Then *D* arose, and cut off the	1Sa 24:4	1732
So *D* stayed his servants with	1Sa 24:7	1732
D also arose afterward, and went	1Sa 24:8	1732
D stooped with his face to the	1Sa 24:8	1732
D said to Saul, Wherefore hearest	1Sa 24:9	1732
Behold, *D* seeketh thy hurt	1Sa 24:9	1732
when *D* had made an end of	1Sa 24:16	1732
said, Is this thy voice, my son *D*	1Sa 24:16	1732
And he said to *D*, Thou art more	1Sa 24:17	1732
And *D* sware unto Saul	1Sa 24:22	1732
but *D* and his men gat them up unto	1Sa 24:22	1732
D arose, and went down to the	1Sa 25:1	1732
D heard in the wilderness that	1Sa 25:4	1732
D sent out ten young men, and	1Sa 25:5	1732
D said unto the young men, Get	1Sa 25:5	1732
thy servants, and to thy son *D*	1Sa 25:8	1732
all those words in the name of *D*	1Sa 25:9	1732
servants, and said, Who is *D*	1Sa 25:10	1732
D said unto his men, Gird ye on	1Sa 25:13	1732
D also girded on his sword	1Sa 25:13	1732
there went up after *D* about four	1Sa 25:13	1732
D sent messengers out of the	1Sa 25:14	1732
covert of the hill, and, behold, *D*	1Sa 25:20	1732
Now *D* had said, Surely in vain	1Sa 25:21	1732
also do God unto the enemies of *D*	1Sa 25:22	1732
And when Abigail saw *D*, she hasted	1Sa 25:23	1732
ass, and fell before *D* on her face	1Sa 25:23	1732
D said to Abigail, Blessed be the	1Sa 25:32	1732
So *D* received of her hand that	1Sa 25:35	1732
when *D* heard that Nabal was dead,	1Sa 25:39	1732
D sent and communed with Abigail,	1Sa 25:39	1732
when the servants of *D* were come	1Sa 25:40	1732
D sent us unto thee, to take thee	1Sa 25:40	1732
went after the messengers of *D*	1Sa 25:42	1732
D also took Ahinoam of Jezreel	1Sa 25:43	1732
Doth not *D* hide himself in the	1Sa 26:1	1732
to seek *D* in the wilderness of	1Sa 26:2	1732
But *D* abode in the wilderness, and	1Sa 26:3	1732
D therefore sent out spies, and	1Sa 26:4	1732
D arose, and came to the place	1Sa 26:5	1732
D beheld the place where Saul lay	1Sa 26:5	1732
Then answered *D* and said to	1Sa 26:6	1732
So *D* and Abishai came to the	1Sa 26:7	1732
Then said Abishai to *D*, God hath	1Sa 26:8	1732
D said to Abishai, Destroy him	1Sa 26:9	1732
D said furthermore, As the LORD	1Sa 26:10	1732
So *D* took the spear and the cruse	1Sa 26:12	1732
Then *D* went over to the other	1Sa 26:13	1732
D cried to the people, and to	1Sa 26:14	1732
D said to Abner, Art not thou a	1Sa 26:15	1732
said, Is this thy voice, my son *D*	1Sa 26:17	1732
D said, It is my voice, my lord,	1Sa 26:17	1732
return, my son *D*	1Sa 26:21	1732
D answered and said, Behold the	1Sa 26:22	1732
D, Blessed be thou, my son *D*	1Sa 26:25	1732
So *D* went on his way, and Saul	1Sa 26:25	1732
D said in his heart, I shall now	1Sa 27:1	1732
D arose, and he passed over with	1Sa 27:2	1732
D dwelt with Achish at Gath, he	1Sa 27:3	1732
even *D* with his two wives,	1Sa 27:3	1732
told Saul that *D* was fled to Gath	1Sa 27:4	1732
D said unto Achish, If I have now	1Sa 27:5	1732
the time that *D* dwelt in the	1Sa 27:7	1732
And *D* and his men went up, and	1Sa 27:8	1732
D smote the land, and left neither	1Sa 27:9	1732
D said, Against the south of	1Sa 27:10	1732
D saved neither man nor woman	1Sa 27:11	1732
tell on us, saying, So did *D*	1Sa 27:11	1732
And Achish believed *D*, saying, He	1Sa 27:12	1732
D said to Achish, Surely thou	1Sa 28:1	1732
And Achish said unto *D*, Know thou	1Sa 28:1	1732
And Achish said to *D*, Therefore	1Sa 28:2	1732
it to thy neighbour, even to *D*	1Sa 28:17	1732
but *D* and his men passed on in the	1Sa 29:2	1732
of the Philistines, Is not this *D*	1Sa 29:3	1732
Is not this *D*, of whom they sang	1Sa 29:5	1732
thousands, and *D* his ten thousands	1Sa 29:5	1732
Then Achish called *D*, and said	1Sa 29:6	1732
D said unto Achish, But what have	1Sa 29:8	1732
And Achish answered and said to *D*	1Sa 29:9	1732
So *D* and his men rose up early to	1Sa 29:11	1732
And it came to pass, when *D*	1Sa 30:1	1732
So *D* and his men came to the city,	1Sa 30:3	1732
Then *D* and the people that were	1Sa 30:4	1732
And *D* was greatly distressed	1Sa 30:6	1732
but *D* encouraged himself in the	1Sa 30:6	1732
D said to Abiathar the priest,	1Sa 30:7	1732
brought thither the ephod to *D*	1Sa 30:7	1732
D enquired at the LORD, saying,	1Sa 30:8	1732
So *D* went, he and the six hundred	1Sa 30:9	1732
But *D* pursued, he and four hundred	1Sa 30:10	1732
in the field, and brought him to *D*	1Sa 30:11	1732
And *D* said unto him, To whom	1Sa 30:13	1732
D said to him, Canst thou bring	1Sa 30:15	1732
D smote them from the twilight	1Sa 30:17	1732
And *D* recovered all that the	1Sa 30:18	1732
and *D* rescued his two wives	1Sa 30:18	1732
D recovered all	1Sa 30:19	1732
D took all the flocks and the	1Sa 30:20	1732
D came to the two hundred men,	1Sa 30:21	1732
that they could not follow *D*	1Sa 30:21	1732
and they went forth to meet *D*	1Sa 30:21	1732
when *D* came near to the people,	1Sa 30:21	1732
Belial, of those that went with *D*	1Sa 30:22	1732
Then said *D*, Ye shall not do so,	1Sa 30:23	1732
when *D* came to Ziklag, he sent of	1Sa 30:26	1732
to all the places where *D* himself	1Sa 30:31	1732
when *D* was returned from the	2Sa 1:1	1732
D had abode two days in Ziklag	2Sa 1:1	1732
and so it was, when he came to *D*	2Sa 1:2	1732
D said unto him, From whence	2Sa 1:3	1732
D said unto him, How went the	2Sa 1:4	1732
D said unto the young man that	2Sa 1:5	1732
Then *D* took hold on his clothes,	2Sa 1:11	1732
D said unto the young man that	2Sa 1:13	1732
D said unto him, How wast thou	2Sa 1:14	1732
D called one of the young men, and	2Sa 1:15	1732
D said unto him, Thy blood be	2Sa 1:16	1732
D lamented with this lamentation	2Sa 1:17	1732
that *D* enquired of the LORD,	2Sa 2:1	1732
D said, Whither shall I go up	2Sa 2:1	1732
So *D* went up thither, and his two	2Sa 2:2	1732
that were with him did *D* bring up	2Sa 2:3	1732
there they anointed *D* king over	2Sa 2:4	1732
And they told *D*, saying, That the	2Sa 2:4	1732
D sent messengers unto the men of	2Sa 2:5	1732
But the house of Judah followed *D*	2Sa 2:10	1732
the time that *D* was king in	2Sa 2:11	1732
of Zeruiah, and the servants of *D*	2Sa 2:13	1732
and twelve of the servants of *D*	2Sa 2:15	1732
Israel, before the servants of *D*	2Sa 2:17	1732
But the servants of *D* had smitten	2Sa 2:31	1732

D

D

D

crying, and saying, Thou son of *D*	Mt 9:27	1138
them, Have ye not read what *D* did	Mt 12:3	1138
and said, Is not this the son of *D*	Mt 12:23	1138
on me, O Lord, thou son of *D*	Mt 15:22	1138
on us, O Lord, thou son of *D*	Mt 20:30	1138
on us, O Lord, thou son of *D*	Mt 20:31	1138
saying, Hosanna to the son of *D*	Mt 21:9	1138
saying, Hosanna to the son of *D*	Mt 21:15	1138
They say unto him, The son of *D*	Mt 22:42	1138
How then doth *D* in spirit call	Mt 22:43	1138
If *D* then call him Lord	Mt 22:45	1138
Have ye never read what *D* did	Mk 2:25	1138
out, and say, Jesus, thou son of *D*	Mk 10:47	1138
more a great deal, Thou son of *D*	Mk 10:48	1138
be the kingdom of our father *D*	Mk 11:10	1138
that Christ is the son of *D*	Mk 12:35	1138
For *D* himself said by the Holy	Mk 12:36	1138
D therefore himself calleth him	Mk 12:37	1138
was Joseph, of the house of *D*	Lk 1:27	1138
him the throne of his father *D*	Lk 1:32	1138
us in the house of his servant *D*	Lk 1:69	1138
into Judaea, unto the city of *D*	Lk 2:4	1138
was of the house and lineage of *D*	Lk 2:4	1138
day in the city of *D* a Saviour	Lk 2:11	1138
of Nathan, which was the son of *D*	Lk 3:31	1138
read so much as this, what *D* did	Lk 6:3	1138
saying, Jesus, thou son of *D*	Lk 18:38	1138
so much the more, Thou son of *D*	Lk 18:39	1138
D himself saith in the book of	Lk 20:42	1138
D therefore calleth him Lord, how	Lk 20:44	1138
Christ cometh of the seed of *D*	Jn 7:42	1138
town of Bethlehem, where *D* was	Jn 7:42	1138
D spake before concerning Judas	Acts 1:16	1138
For *D* speaketh concerning him, I	Acts 2:25	1138
speak unto you of the patriarch *D*	Acts 2:29	1138
For *D* is not ascended into the	Acts 2:34	1138
mouth of thy servant *D* hast said	Acts 4:25	1138
our fathers, unto the days of *D*	Acts 7:45	1138
up unto them *D* to be their king	Acts 13:22	1138
I have found *D* the son of Jesse,	Acts 13:22	1138
give you the sure mercies of *D*	Acts 13:34	1138
For *D*, after he had served his	Acts 13:36	1138
build again the tabernacle of *D*	Acts 15:16	1138
seed of *D* according to the flesh	Rom 1:3	1138
Even as *D* also describeth the	Rom 4:6	1138
D saith, Let their table be made	Rom 11:9	1138
of *D* was raised from the dead	2Ti 2:8	1138
a certain day, saying in *D*	Heb 4:7	1138
of *D* also, and Samuel, and of the	Heb 11:32	1138
true, he that hath the key of *D*	Rev 3:7	1138
the tribe of Juda, the Root of *D*	Rev 5:5	1138
am the root and the offspring of *D*	Rev 22:16	1138

DAVID'S

Saul became *D* enemy continually	1Sa 18:29	1732
also sent messengers unto *D* house	1Sa 19:11	1732
Michal *D* wife told him, saying,	1Sa 19:11	1732
it at the hand of *D* enemies	1Sa 20:16	1732
Saul's side, and *D* place was empty	1Sa 20:25	1732
the month, that *D* place was empty	1Sa 20:27	1732
D men said unto him, Behold, we	1Sa 24:3	1732
that *D* heart smote him, because	1Sa 24:5	1732
when *D* young men came, they spake	1Sa 25:9	1732
And Nabal answered *D* servants	1Sa 25:10	1732
So *D* young men turned their way,	1Sa 25:12	1732
D wife, to Phalti the son of	1Sa 25:44	1732
And Saul knew *D* voice, and said, Is	1Sa 26:17	1732
D two wives were taken captives,	1Sa 30:5	1732
cattle, and said, This is *D* spoil	1Sa 30:20	1732
there lacked of *D* servants	2Sa 2:30	1732
sixth, Ithream, by Eglah *D* wife	2Sa 3:5	1732
blind, that are hated of *D* soul	2Sa 5:8	1732
so the Moabites became *D* servants	2Sa 8:2	1732
they of Edom became *D* servants	2Sa 8:14	1732
and *D* sons were chief rulers	2Sa 8:18	1732
D servants came into the land of	2Sa 10:2	1732
Wherefore Hanun took *D* servants	2Sa 10:4	1732
D anger was greatly kindled	2Sa 12:5	1732
and it was set on *D* head	2Sa 12:30	1732
the son of Shimeah *D* brother	2Sa 13:3	1732
the son of Shimeah *D* brother	2Sa 13:32	1732
D counsellor, from his city, even	2Sa 15:12	1732
So Hushai *D* friend came into the	2Sa 15:37	1732
D friend, was come unto Absalom,	2Sa 16:16	1732
all *D* men with him, over Jordan	2Sa 19:41	1732
D heart smote him after that he	2Sa 24:10	1732
the prophet Gad, *D* seer, saying,	2Sa 24:11	1732
Solomon to ride upon king *D* mule	1Kin 1:38	1732
one tribe for my servant *D* sake	1Kin 11:32	1732
Nevertheless for *D* sake did the	1Kin 15:4	1732
did the priest give king *D* spears	2Kin 11:10	1732

sake, and for my servant *D* sake	2Kin 19:34	1732
sake, and for my servant *D* sake	2Kin 20:6	1732
and the Moabites became *D* servants	1Chr 18:2	1732
and the Syrians became *D* servants	1Chr 18:6	1732
the Edomites became *D* servants	1Chr 18:13	1732
Wherefore Hanun took *D* servants	1Chr 19:4	1732
and it was set upon *D* head	1Chr 20:2	1732
son of Shimea *D* brother slew him	1Chr 20:7	1732
spake unto Gad, *D* seer, saying,	1Chr 21:9	1732
of the substance which was king *D*	1Chr 27:31	1732
Also Jonathan *D* uncle was a	1Chr 27:32	1732
and shields, that had been king *D*	2Chr 23:9	1732
For thy servant *D* sake turn not	Ps 132:10	1732
D Psalm of praise	Ps 145:t	1732
sake, and for my servant *D* sake	Is 37:35	1732
the kings that sit upon *D* throne	Jer 13:13	1732
How say they that Christ is *D* son	Lk 20:41	1138

DAWN

as it began to *d* toward the first	Mt 28:1	2020
in a dark place, until the day *d*	2Pet 1:19	1306

DAWNING

rose early about the *d* of the day	Josh 6:15	5927
the woman in the *d* of the day	Judg 19:26	6437
let it see the *d* of the day	Job 3:9	6079
to and fro unto the *d* of the day	Job 7:4	5399
I prevented the *d* of the morning	Ps 119:147	5399

DAY

And God called the light *D*	Gen 1:5	3117
and the morning were the first *d*	Gen 1:5	3117
and the morning were the second *d*	Gen 1:8	3117
and the morning were the third *d*	Gen 1:13	3117
to divide the *d* from the night	Gen 1:14	3117
the greater light to rule the *d*	Gen 1:16	3117
And to rule over the *d* and over the	Gen 1:18	3117
and the morning were the fourth *d*	Gen 1:19	3117
and the morning were the fifth *d*	Gen 1:23	3117
and the morning were the sixth *d*	Gen 1:31	3117
on the seventh *d* God ended his	Gen 2:2	3117
he rested on the seventh *d* from	Gen 2:2	3117
And God blessed the seventh *d*	Gen 2:3	3117
in the *d* that the LORD God made	Gen 2:4	3117
for in the *d* that thou eatest	Gen 2:17	3117
know in the *d* ye eat thereof	Gen 3:5	3117
the garden in the cool of the *d*	Gen 3:8	3117
this *d* from the face of the earth	Gen 4:14	3117
In the *d* that God created man, in	Gen 5:1	3117
in the *d* when they were created	Gen 5:2	3117
the seventeenth *d* of the month	Gen 7:11	3117
the same *d* were all the fountains	Gen 7:11	3117
In the selfsame *d* entered Noah	Gen 7:13	3117
on the seventeenth *d* of the month	Gen 8:4	3117
on the first *d* of the month	Gen 8:5	3117
the first *d* of the month, the	Gen 8:13	3117
twentieth *d* of the month, was the	Gen 8:14	3117
heat, and summer and winter, and *d*	Gen 8:22	3117
In the same of the LORD made a	Gen 15:18	3117
their foreskin in the selfsame *d*	Gen 17:23	3117
In the selfsame *d* was Abraham	Gen 17:26	3117
tent door in the heat of the *d*	Gen 18:1	3117
of the Moabites unto this *d*	Gen 19:37	3117
the children of Ammon unto this *d*	Gen 19:38	3117
the same *d* that Isaac was weaned	Gen 21:8	3117
yet heard I of it, but to *d*	Gen 21:26	3117
Then on the third *d* Abraham	Gen 22:4	3117
as it is said to this *d*, In the	Gen 22:14	3117
thee, send me good speed this *d*	Gen 24:12	3117
I came this *d* unto the well, and	Gen 24:42	3117
Sell me this *d* thy birthright	Gen 25:31	3117
And Jacob said, Swear to me this *d*	Gen 25:33	3117
And it came to pass the same *d*	Gen 26:32	3117
city is Beer-sheba unto this *d*	Gen 26:33	3117
old, I know not the *d* of my death	Gen 27:2	3117
also of you both in one *d*	Gen 27:45	3117
And he said, Lo, it is yet high *d*	Gen 29:7	3117
pass through all thy flock to *d*	Gen 30:32	3117
he removed that *d* the he goats	Gen 30:35	3117
the third *d* that Jacob was fled	Gen 31:22	3117
require it, whether stolen by *d*	Gen 31:39	3117
in the *d* the drought consumed me,	Gen 31:40	3117
what can I do this *d* unto these	Gen 31:43	3117
witness between me and thee this *d*	Gen 31:48	3117
him until the breaking of the *d*	Gen 32:24	7837
Let me go, for the *d* breaketh	Gen 32:26	7837
hollow of the thigh, unto this *d*	Gen 32:32	3117
men should overdrive them one *d*	Gen 33:13	3117
that *d* on his way unto Seir	Gen 33:16	3117
And it came to pass on the third *d*	Gen 34:25	3117
me in the *d* of my distress	Gen 35:3	3117
of Rachel's grave unto this *d*	Gen 35:20	3117

as she spake to Joseph *d* by *d*	Gen 39:10	3117
Wherefore look ye so sadly to *d*	Gen 40:7	3117
And it came to pass the third *d*	Gen 40:20	3117
I do remember my faults this *d*	Gen 41:9	3117
is this *d* with our father	Gen 42:13	3117
Joseph said unto them the third *d*	Gen 42:18	3117
the youngest is this *d* with our	Gen 42:32	3117
Behold, I have bought you this *d*	Gen 47:23	3117
the land of Egypt unto this *d*	Gen 47:26	3117
me all my life long unto this *d*	Gen 48:15	3117
And he blessed them that *d*	Gen 48:20	3117
to bring to pass, as it is this *d*	Gen 50:20	3117
And when he went out the second *d*	Ex 2:13	3117
it that ye are come so soon to *d*	Ex 2:18	3117
Pharaoh commanded the same *d* the	Ex 5:6	3117
brick both yesterday and to *d*	Ex 5:14	3117
it came to pass on the *d* when the	Ex 6:28	3117
in that *d* the land of Goshen	Ex 8:22	3117
since the *d* that they were upon	Ex 10:6	3117
were upon the earth unto this *d*	Ex 10:6	3117
wind upon the land all that *d*	Ex 10:13	3117
for in that *d* thou seest my face	Ex 10:28	3117
In the tenth *d* of this month they	Ex 12:3	3117
fourteenth *d* of the same month	Ex 12:6	
this *d* shall be unto you for a	Ex 12:14	3117
even the first *d* ye shall put	Ex 12:15	3117
the first *d* until the seventh *d*	Ex 12:15	3117
in the first *d* there shall be an	Ex 12:16	3117
in the seventh *d* there shall be	Ex 12:16	3117
for in this selfsame *d* have I	Ex 12:17	3117
this *d* in your generations by an	Ex 12:17	3117
on the fourteenth *d* of the month	Ex 12:18	3117
twentieth *d* of the month at even	Ex 12:18	3117
the selfsame *d* it came to pass	Ex 12:41	3117
And it came to pass the selfsame *d*	Ex 12:51	3117
unto the people, Remember this *d*	Ex 13:3	3117
This *d* came ye out in the month	Ex 13:4	3117
in the seventh *d* shall be a feast	Ex 13:6	3117
thou shalt shew thy son in that *d*	Ex 13:8	3117
them by *d* in a pillar of a cloud	Ex 13:21	3119
to go by *d* and night	Ex 13:21	3119
away the pillar of the cloud by *d*	Ex 13:22	3119
which he will shew to you to *d*	Ex 14:13	3117
Egyptians whom ye have seen to *d*	Ex 14:13	3117
that *d* out of the hand of the	Ex 14:30	3117
on the fifteenth *d* of the second	Ex 16:1	3117
and gather a certain rate every *d*	Ex 16:4	3117
that on the sixth *d* they shall	Ex 16:5	3117
that on the sixth *d* they gathered	Ex 16:22	3117
bake that which ye will bake to *d*	Ex 16:23	
And Moses said, Eat that to *d*	Ex 16:25	3117
for to *d* is a sabbath unto the	Ex 16:25	3117
to *d* ye shall not find it in the	Ex 16:25	3117
but on the seventh *d*, which is	Ex 16:26	3117
on the seventh *d* for to gather	Ex 16:27	3117
the sixth *d* the bread of two days	Ex 16:29	3117
out of his place on the seventh *d*	Ex 16:29	3117
people rested on the seventh *d*	Ex 16:30	3117
the same *d* came they into the	Ex 19:1	3117
the people, and sanctify them to *d*	Ex 19:10	3117
And be ready against the third *d*	Ex 19:11	3117
for the third *d* the LORD will	Ex 19:11	3117
Be ready against the third *d*	Ex 19:15	3117
on the third *d* in the morning	Ex 19:16	3117
Remember the sabbath *d*, to keep	Ex 20:8	3117
But the seventh *d* is the sabbath	Ex 20:10	3117
them is, and rested the seventh *d*	Ex 20:11	3117
the LORD blessed the sabbath *d*	Ex 20:11	3117
if he continue a *d* or two	Ex 21:21	3117
on the eighth *d* thou shalt give	Ex 22:30	3117
on the seventh *d* thou shalt rest	Ex 23:12	3117
the seventh *d* he called unto	Ex 24:16	3117
thou shalt offer every *d* a	Ex 29:36	3117
first year *d* by *d* continually	Ex 29:38	3117
doeth any work in the sabbath *d*	Ex 31:15	3117
and on the seventh *d* he rested	Ex 31:17	3117
that *d* about three thousand men	Ex 32:28	3117
yourselves to *d* to the LORD	Ex 32:29	
bestow upon you a blessing this *d*	Ex 32:29	3117
nevertheless in the *d* when I	Ex 32:34	3117
that which I command thee this *d*	Ex 34:11	3117
on the seventh *d* thou shalt rest	Ex 34:21	3117
but on the seventh *d* there shall	Ex 35:2	3117
there shall be to you an holy *d*	Ex 35:2	
habitations upon the sabbath *d*	Ex 35:3	3117
On the first *d* of the first month	Ex 40:2	3117
year, on the first *d* of the month	Ex 40:17	
till the *d* that it was taken up	Ex 40:37	3117
LORD was upon the tabernacle by *d*	Ex 40:38	3119
in the *d* of his trespass offering	Lev 6:5	3119
LORD in the *d* when he is anointed	Lev 6:20	3119
the same *d* that it is offered	Lev 7:15	3119
it shall be eaten the same *d* that	Lev 7:16	3119
third *d* shall be burnt with fire	Lev 7:17	3119
be eaten at all on the third *d*	Lev 7:18	3119
in the *d* when he presented them	Lev 7:35	3119
in the *d* that he anointed them,	Lev 7:36	3119
in the *d* that he commanded them	Lev 7:38	3119
As he hath done this *d*, so the	Lev 8:34	3117
tabernacle of the congregation	Lev 8:35	3119
it came to pass on the eighth *d*	Lev 9:1	3117
for to *d* the LORD will appear	Lev 9:4	3117
this *d* have they offered their	Lev 10:19	3117
I had eaten the sin offering to *d*	Lev 10:19	3117
in the eighth *d* the flesh of his	Lev 12:3	3117
shall look on him the seventh *d*	Lev 13:5	3117
look on him again the seventh *d*	Lev 13:6	3117
shall look upon him the seventh *d*	Lev 13:27	3117
in the seventh *d* the priest shall	Lev 13:32	3117
in the seventh *d* the priest shall	Lev 13:34	3117
on the plague on the seventh *d*	Lev 13:51	3117
leper in the *d* of his cleansing	Lev 14:2	3117
But it shall be on the seventh *d*	Lev 14:9	3117
on the eighth *d* he shall take two	Lev 14:10	3117
d for his cleansing unto the	Lev 14:23	3117
shall come again the seventh *d*	Lev 14:39	3117
on the eighth *d* he shall take to	Lev 15:14	3117
on the eighth *d* she shall take	Lev 15:29	3117
on the tenth *d* of the month	Lev 16:29	
For on that *d* shall the priest	Lev 16:30	3117
be eaten the same *d* ye offer it	Lev 19:6	3117
if ought remain until the third *d*	Lev 19:6	3117
it be eaten at all on the third *d*	Lev 19:7	3117
and from the eighth *d* and	Lev 22:27	3117
it and her young both in one *d*	Lev 22:28	3117
On the same *d* it shall be eaten	Lev 22:30	3117
but the seventh *d* is the sabbath	Lev 23:3	3117
In the fourteenth *d* of the first	Lev 23:5	
on the fifteenth *d* of the same	Lev 23:6	3117
In the first *d* ye shall have an	Lev 23:7	3117
in the seventh *d* is an holy	Lev 23:8	3117
ye shall offer that *d* when ye	Lev 23:12	3117
until the selfsame *d* that ye have	Lev 23:14	3117
from the *d* that ye brought the	Lev 23:15	3117
shall proclaim on the selfsame *d*	Lev 23:21	3117
in the first *d* of the month	Lev 23:24	
Also on the tenth *d* of this	Lev 23:27	
there shall be a *d* of atonement	Lev 23:27	3117
shall do no work in that same *d*	Lev 23:28	3117
for it is a *d* of atonement, to	Lev 23:28	3117
not be afflicted in that same *d*	Lev 23:29	3117
doeth any work in that same *d*	Lev 23:30	3117
in the ninth *d* of the month at	Lev 23:32	
The fifteenth *d* of this seventh	Lev 23:34	3117
On the first *d* shall be an holy	Lev 23:35	3117
on the eighth *d* shall be an holy	Lev 23:36	3117
offerings, every thing upon his *d*	Lev 23:37	3117
fifteenth *d* of the seventh month	Lev 23:39	3117
on the first *d* shall be a sabbath	Lev 23:39	3117
on the eighth *d* shall be a	Lev 23:39	3117
d the boughs of goodly trees	Lev 23:40	3117
the tenth *d* of the seventh month	Lev 25:9	
in the *d* of atonement shall ye	Lev 25:9	3117
give thine estimation in that *d*	Lev 27:23	3117
on the first *d* of the second month	Num 1:1	
the first *d* of the second month	Num 1:18	
Moses in the *d* that the LORD	Num 3:1	3117
for on the *d* that I smote all the	Num 3:13	3117
head in the *d* of his cleansing	Num 6:9	3117
on the seventh *d* shall he shave	Num 6:9	3117
on the eighth *d* he shall bring	Num 6:10	3117
shall hallow his head that same *d*	Num 6:11	3117
it came to pass on the *d* that	Num 7:1	3117
in the *d* that it was anointed	Num 7:10	3117
offering, each prince on his *d*	Num 7:11	3117
first *d* was Nahshon the son of	Num 7:12	3117
On the second *d* Nethaneel the son	Num 7:18	3117
On the third *d* Eliab the son of	Num 7:24	3117
On the fourth *d* Elizur the son of	Num 7:30	3117
On the fifth *d* Shelumiel the son	Num 7:36	3117
On the sixth *d* Eliasaph the son	Num 7:42	3117
On the seventh *d* Elishama the son	Num 7:48	3117
On the eighth *d* offered Gamaliel	Num 7:54	3117
On the ninth *d* Abidan the son of	Num 7:60	3117
On the tenth *d* Ahiezer the son of	Num 7:66	3117
On the eleventh *d* Pagiel the son	Num 7:72	3117
On the twelfth *d* Ahira the son of	Num 7:78	3117
in the *d* when it was anointed, by	Num 7:84	3117
on the *d* that I smote every	Num 8:17	3117
In the fourteenth *d* of this month	Num 9:3	3117
d of the first month at even in	Num 9:5	3117
not keep the passover on that *d*	Num 9:6	3117

D

Moses and before Aaron on that *d*	Num 9:6	3117
The fourteenth *d* of the second	Num 9:11	3117
on the *d* that the tabernacle was	Num 9:15	3117
the cloud covered it by *d*	Num 9:16	
whether it was by *d* or by night	Num 9:21	3119
Also in the *d* of your gladness,	Num 10:10	3117
twentieth *d* of the second month	Num 10:11	
of the LORD was upon them by *d*	Num 10:34	3119
Ye shall not eat one *d*, nor two	Num 11:19	3117
And the people stood up all that *d*	Num 11:32	3117
all that night, and all the next *d*	Num 11:32	3117
each *d* for a year, shall ye bear	Num 14:34	3117
Moses, from the *d* that the LORD	Num 15:23	3117
sticks upon the sabbath *d*	Num 15:32	3117
himself with it on the third *d*	Num 19:12	3117
on the seventh *d* he shall be	Num 19:12	3117
he purify not himself the third *d*	Num 19:12	3117
then the seventh *d* he shall not	Num 19:12	3117
third *d*, and on the seventh *d*	Num 19:19	3117
on the seventh *d* he shall purify	Num 19:19	3117
since I was thine unto this *d*	Num 22:30	3117
which was slain in the *d* of the	Num 25:18	3117
first year without spot *d* by *d*	Num 28:3	3117
on the sabbath *d* two lambs of the	Num 28:9	3117
in the fourteenth *d* of the first	Num 28:16	3117
in the fifteenth *d* of this month	Num 28:17	3117
In the first *d* shall be an holy	Num 28:18	3117
on the seventh *d* ye shall have an	Num 28:25	3117
Also in the *d* of the firstfruits,	Num 28:26	3117
on the first *d* of the month	Num 29:1	
it is a *d* of blowing the trumpets	Num 29:1	3117
ye shall have on the tenth *d* of	Num 29:7	
on the fifteenth *d* of the seventh	Num 29:12	3117
on the second *d* ye shall offer	Num 29:17	3117
on the third *d* eleven bullocks	Num 29:20	3117
And on the fourth *d* ten bullocks	Num 29:23	3117
on the fifth *d* nine bullocks, two	Num 29:26	3117
on the sixth *d* eight bullocks,	Num 29:29	3117
on the seventh *d* seven bullocks	Num 29:32	3117
On the eighth *d* ye shall have a	Num 29:35	3117
her in the *d* that he heareth	Num 30:5	3117
at her in the *d* that he heard it	Num 30:7	3117
her on the *d* that he heard it	Num 30:8	3117
them void on the *d* he heard them	Num 30:12	3117
his peace at her from *d* to *d*	Num 30:14	3117
her in the *d* that he heard them	Num 30:14	3117
third *d*, and on the seventh *d*	Num 31:19	3117
your clothes on the seventh *d*	Num 31:24	3117
on the fifteenth *d* of the first	Num 33:3	3117
in the first *d* of the fifth month	Num 33:38	
on the first *d* of the month	Deut 1:3	
ye are this *d* as the stars of	Deut 1:10	3117
ye should go, and in a cloud by *d*	Deut 1:33	3119
which in that *d* had no knowledge	Deut 1:39	3117
Ar, the coast of Moab, this *d*	Deut 2:18	3117
in their stead even unto this *d*	Deut 2:22	3117
This *d* will I begin to put the	Deut 2:25	3117
thy hand, as appeareth this *d*	Deut 2:30	3117
Bashan-havoth-jair, unto this *d*	Deut 3:14	3117
are alive every one of you this *d*	Deut 4:4	3117
which I set before you this *d*	Deut 4:8	3117
Specially the *d* that thou	Deut 4:10	3117
no manner of similitude on the *d*	Deut 4:15	3117
of inheritance, as ye are this *d*	Deut 4:20	3117
to witness against you this *d*	Deut 4:26	3117
since the *d* that God created man	Deut 4:32	3117
an inheritance, as it is this *d*	Deut 4:38	3117
Know therefore this *d*, and	Deut 4:39	3117
which I command thee this *d*	Deut 4:40	3117
which I speak in your ears this *d*	Deut 5:1	3117
are all of us here alive this *d*	Deut 5:3	3117
Keep the sabbath *d* to sanctify it	Deut 5:12	3117
But the seventh *d* is the sabbath	Deut 5:14	3117
thee to keep the sabbath *d*	Deut 5:15	3117
we have seen this *d* that God doth	Deut 5:24	3117
which I command thee this *d*	Deut 6:6	3117
us alive, as it is at this *d*	Deut 6:24	3117
which I command thee this *d*	Deut 7:11	3117
this *d* shall ye observe to do	Deut 8:1	3117
which I command thee this *d*	Deut 8:11	3117
unto thy fathers, as it is this *d*	Deut 8:18	3117
I testify against you this *d*	Deut 8:19	3117
art to pass over Jordan this *d*	Deut 9:1	3117
Understand therefore this *d*	Deut 9:3	3117
from the *d* that thou didst depart	Deut 9:7	3117
the fire in the *d* of the assembly	Deut 9:10	3117
LORD from the *d* that I knew you	Deut 9:24	3117
the fire in the *d* of the assembly	Deut 10:4	3117
to bless in his name, unto this *d*	Deut 10:8	3117
command thee this *d* for thy good	Deut 10:13	3117
above all people, as it is this *d*	Deut 10:15	3117

And know ye this *d*	Deut 11:2	3117
hath destroyed them unto this *d*	Deut 11:4	3117
which I command you this *d*	Deut 11:8	3117
which I command you this *d*	Deut 11:13	3117
set before you this *d* a blessing	Deut 11:26	3117
God, which I command you this *d*	Deut 11:27	3117
way which I command you this *d*	Deut 11:28	3117
which I set before you this *d*	Deut 11:32	3117
the things that we do here this *d*	Deut 12:8	3117
which I command thee this *d*	Deut 13:18	3117
which I command thee this *d*	Deut 15:5	3117
I command thee this thing to *d*	Deut 15:15	3117
d when thou camest forth out of	Deut 16:3	3117
sacrificedst the first *d* at even	Deut 16:4	3117
on the seventh *d* shall be a	Deut 16:8	3117
in Horeb in the *d* of the assembly	Deut 18:16	3117
them, which I command thee this *d*	Deut 19:9	3117
ye approach this *d* unto battle	Deut 20:3	3117
shalt in any wise bury him that *d*	Deut 21:23	3117
At his *d* thou shalt give him his	Deut 24:15	3117
I profess this *d* unto the LORD	Deut 26:3	3117
This *d* the LORD thy God hath	Deut 26:16	3117
the LORD this *d* to be thy God	Deut 26:17	3117
this *d* to be his peculiar people	Deut 26:18	3117
which I command you this *d*	Deut 27:1	3117
it shall be on the *d* when ye	Deut 27:2	3117
which I command you this *d*	Deut 27:4	3117
this *d* thou art become the people	Deut 27:9	3117
which I command thee this *d*	Deut 27:10	3117
charged the people the same *d*	Deut 27:11	3117
which I command thee this *d*	Deut 28:1	3117
God, which I command thee this *d*	Deut 28:13	3117
words which I command thee this *d*	Deut 28:14	3117
which I command thee this *d*	Deut 28:15	3117
longing for them all the *d* long	Deut 28:32	3117
and thou shalt fear *d* and night, and	Deut 28:66	3119
see, and ears to hear, unto this *d*	Deut 29:4	3117
Ye stand this *d* all of you before	Deut 29:10	3117
thy God maketh with thee this *d*	Deut 29:12	3117
to *d* for a people unto himself	Deut 29:13	3117
us this *d* before the LORD our God	Deut 29:15	3117
that is not here with us this *d*	Deut 29:15	3117
away this *d* from the LORD our God	Deut 29:18	3117
another land, as it is this *d*	Deut 29:28	3117
to all that I command thee this *d*	Deut 30:2	3117
which I command thee this *d*	Deut 30:8	3117
which I command thee this *d*	Deut 30:11	3117
have set before thee this *d* life	Deut 30:15	3117
this *d* to love the LORD thy God	Deut 30:16	3117
I denounce unto you this *d*	Deut 30:18	3117
to record this *d* against you	Deut 30:19	3117
and twenty years old this *d*	Deut 31:2	3117
be kindled against them in that *d*	Deut 31:17	3117
so that they will say in that *d*	Deut 31:17	3117
surely hide my face in that *d* for	Deut 31:18	3117
wrote this song that *d*	Deut 31:22	3117
I am yet alive with you this *d*	Deut 31:27	3117
for the *d* of their calamity is at	Deut 32:35	3117
which I testify among you this *d*	Deut 32:46	3117
spake unto Moses that selfsame *d*	Deut 32:48	3117
shall cover him all the *d* long	Deut 33:12	3117
of his sepulchre unto this *d*	Deut 34:6	3117
but thou shalt meditate therein *d*	Josh 1:8	3119
This *d* will I begin to magnify	Josh 3:7	3117
and they are there unto this *d*	Josh 4:9	3117
On that *d* the LORD magnified	Josh 4:14	3117
on the tenth *d* of the first month	Josh 4:19	
This *d* have I rolled away the	Josh 5:9	3117
is called Gilgal unto this *d*	Josh 5:9	3117
d of the month at even in the	Josh 5:10	3117
and parched corn in the selfsame *d*	Josh 5:11	3117
the seventh *d* ye shall compass	Josh 6:4	3117
until the *d* I bid you shout	Josh 6:10	3117
the second *d* they compassed the	Josh 6:14	3117
it came to pass on the seventh *d*	Josh 6:15	3117
early about the dawning of the *d*	Josh 6:15	7837
only on that *d* they compassed the	Josh 6:15	3117
in Israel even unto this *d*	Josh 6:25	3117
LORD shall trouble thee this *d*	Josh 7:25	3117
great heap of stones unto this *d*	Josh 7:26	3117
The valley of Achor, unto this *d*	Josh 7:26	3117
it was, that all that fell that *d*	Josh 8:25	3117
even a desolation unto this *d*	Josh 8:28	3117
that remaineth unto this *d*	Josh 8:29	3117
out of our houses on the *d* we	Josh 9:12	3117
unto their cities on the third *d*	Josh 9:17	3117
made them that *d* hewers of wood	Josh 9:27	3117
of the LORD, even unto this *d*	Josh 9:27	3117
d when the LORD delivered up the	Josh 10:12	3117
not to go down about a whole *d*	Josh 10:13	3117
there was no *d* like that before	Josh 10:14	3117

which remain until this very d	Josh 10:27	3117
that d Joshua took Makkedah, and	Josh 10:28	3117
which took it on the second d	Josh 10:32	3117
And they took it on that d	Josh 10:35	3117
he utterly destroyed that d	Josh 10:35	3117
among the Israelites until this d	Josh 13:13	3117
And Moses sware on that d, saying,	Josh 14:9	3117
and now, lo, I am this d fourscore	Josh 14:10	3117
As yet I am as strong this d as I	Josh 14:11	3117
I was in the d that Moses sent me	Josh 14:11	3117
whereof the LORD spake in that d	Josh 14:12	3117
for thou heardest in that d how	Josh 14:12	3117
the Kenezite unto this d, because	Josh 14:14	3117
of Judah at Jerusalem unto this d	Josh 15:63	3117
among the Ephraimites unto this d	Josh 16:10	3117
these many days unto this d	Josh 22:3	3117
Israel, to turn away this d from	Josh 22:16	3117
rebel this d against the LORD	Josh 22:16	3117
we are not cleansed until this d	Josh 22:17	3117
this d from following the LORD	Josh 22:18	3117
ye rebel to d against the LORD	Josh 22:18	3117
the LORD, (save us not this d	Josh 22:22	3117
turn this d from following the	Josh 22:29	3117
This d we perceive that the LORD	Josh 22:31	3117
God, as ye have done unto this d	Josh 23:8	3117
to stand before you unto this d	Josh 23:9	3117
this d I am going the way of all	Josh 23:14	3117
choose you this d whom ye will	Josh 24:15	3117
a covenant with the people that d	Josh 24:25	3117
Benjamin in Jerusalem unto this d	Judg 1:21	3117
is the name thereof unto this d	Judg 1:26	3117
that d under the hand of Israel	Judg 3:30	3117
for this is the d in which the	Judg 4:14	3117
So God subdued on that d Jabin	Judg 4:23	3117
the son of Abinoam on that d	Judg 5:1	3117
unto this d it is yet in Ophrah	Judg 6:24	3117
that he could not do it by d	Judg 6:27	3119
Therefore on that d he called him	Judg 6:32	3117
against my father's house this d	Judg 9:18	3117
and with his house this d, then	Judg 9:19	3117
against the city all that d	Judg 9:45	3117
called Havoth-jair unto this d	Judg 10:4	3117
us only, we pray thee, this d	Judg 10:15	3117
LORD the Judge be judge this d	Judg 11:27	3117
are ye come up unto me this d	Judg 12:3	3117
the womb to the d of his death	Judg 13:7	3117
me, that came unto me the other d	Judg 13:10	3117
it came to pass on the seventh d	Judg 14:15	3117
it came to pass on the seventh d	Judg 14:17	3117
d before the sun went down	Judg 14:18	3117
which is in Lehi unto this d	Judg 15:19	3117
In the morning, when it is d	Judg 16:2	1242
for unto that d all their	Judg 18:1	3117
place Mahaneh-dan unto this d	Judg 18:12	3117
d of the captivity of the land	Judg 18:30	3117
it came to pass on the fourth d	Judg 19:5	3117
morning on the fifth d to depart	Judg 19:8	3117
now the d draweth toward evening,	Judg 19:9	3117
the d groweth to an end, lodge	Judg 19:9	3117
by Jebus, the d was far spent	Judg 19:11	3117
when the d began to spring, they	Judg 19:25	7837
the woman in the dawning of the d	Judg 19:26	1242
the d that the children of Israel	Judg 19:30	3117
of the land of Egypt unto this d	Judg 19:30	3117
of the Israelites that d twenty	Judg 20:21	3117
themselves in array the first d	Judg 20:22	3117
children of Benjamin the second d	Judg 20:24	3117
them out of Gibeah the second d	Judg 20:25	3117
LORD, and fasted that d until even	Judg 20:26	3117
of Benjamin on the third d	Judg 20:30	3117
of the Benjamites that d twenty	Judg 20:35	3117
that d of Benjamin were twenty	Judg 20:46	3117
that there should be to d one	Judg 21:3	3117
tribe cut off from Israel this d	Judg 21:6	3117
her, Where hast thou gleaned to d	Ruth 2:19	3117
with whom I wrought to d is Boaz	Ruth 2:19	3117
he have finished the thing this d	Ruth 3:18	3117
What d thou buyest the field of	Ruth 4:5	3117
people, Ye are witnesses this d	Ruth 4:9	3117
ye are witnesses this d	Ruth 4:10	3117
thee this d without a kinsman	Ruth 4:14	3117
in one d they shall die both of	1Sa 2:34	3117
In that d I will perform against	1Sa 3:12	3117
us to d before the Philistines	1Sa 4:3	3117
the same d with his clothes rent	1Sa 4:12	3117
I fled to d out of the army	1Sa 4:16	3117
of Dagon in Ashdod unto this d	1Sa 5:5	3117
the same d unto the LORD	1Sa 6:15	3117
they returned to Ekron the same d	1Sa 6:16	3117
this d in the field of Joshua	1Sa 6:18	3117
the LORD, and fasted on that d	1Sa 7:6	3117
on that d upon the Philistines	1Sa 7:10	3117
d that I brought them up out of	1Sa 8:8	3117
up out of Egypt even unto this d	1Sa 8:8	3117
ye shall cry out in that d	1Sa 8:18	3117
LORD will not hear you in that d	1Sa 8:18	3117
now, for he came to d to the city	1Sa 9:12	3117
the people to d in the high place	1Sa 9:12	3117
in his ear a d before Saul came	1Sa 9:15	3117
for ye shall eat with me to d	1Sa 9:19	3117
Saul did eat with Samuel that d	1Sa 9:24	3117
to pass about the spring of the d	1Sa 9:26	7837
thou art departed from me to d	1Sa 10:2	3117
those signs came to pass that d	1Sa 10:9	3117
ye have this d rejected your God,	1Sa 10:19	3117
Ammonites until the heat of the d	1Sa 11:11	3117
not a man be put to death this d	1Sa 11:13	3117
for to d the LORD hath wrought	1Sa 11:13	3117
you from my childhood unto this d	1Sa 12:2	3117
and his anointed is witness this d	1Sa 12:5	3117
Is it not wheat harvest to d	1Sa 12:17	3117
LORD sent thunder and rain that d	1Sa 12:18	3117
came to pass in the d of battle	1Sa 13:22	3117
Now it came to pass upon a d	1Sa 14:1	3117
So the LORD saved Israel that d	1Sa 14:23	3117
of Israel were distressed that d	1Sa 14:24	3117
man that eateth any food this d	1Sa 14:28	3117
d of the spoil of their enemies	1Sa 14:30	3117
that d from Michmash to Aijalon	1Sa 14:31	3117
roll a great stone unto me this d	1Sa 14:33	3117
But he answered him not that d	1Sa 14:37	3117
wherein this sin hath been this d	1Sa 14:38	3117
he hath wrought with God this d	1Sa 14:45	3117
of Israel from thee this d	1Sa 15:28	3117
see Saul until the d of his death	1Sa 15:35	3117
upon David from that d forward	1Sa 16:13	3117
defy the armies of Israel this d	1Sa 17:10	3117
This d will the LORD deliver thee	1Sa 17:46	3117
this d unto the fowls of the air	1Sa 17:46	3117
And Saul took him that d, and would	1Sa 18:2	3117
And Saul eyed David from that d	1Sa 18:9	3117
Thou shalt this d be my son in	1Sa 18:21	3117
and lay down naked all that d	1Sa 19:24	3117
field unto the third d at even	1Sa 20:5	
morrow any time, or the third d	1Sa 20:12	
Saul spake not any thing that d	1Sa 20:26	3117
was the second d of the month	1Sa 20:27	
meat, neither yesterday, nor to d	1Sa 20:27	3117
no meat the second d of the month	1Sa 20:34	3117
sanctified this d in the vessel	1Sa 21:5	3117
in the d when it was taken away	1Sa 21:6	3117
servants of Saul was there that d	1Sa 21:7	3117
fled that d for fear of Saul, and	1Sa 21:10	3117
me, to lie in wait, as at this d	1Sa 22:8	3117
me, to lie in wait, as at this d	1Sa 22:13	3117
and slew on that d fourscore	1Sa 22:18	3117
unto Abiathar, I knew it that d	1Sa 22:22	3117
And Saul sought him every d	1Sa 23:14	3117
Behold the d of which the LORD	1Sa 24:4	3117
this d thine eyes have seen how	1Sa 24:10	3117
to d into mine hand in the cave	1Sa 24:10	3117
thou hast shewed this d how that	1Sa 24:18	3117
thou hast done unto me this d	1Sa 24:19	3117
for we come in a good d	1Sa 25:8	3117
a wall unto us both by night and d	1Sa 25:16	3119
which sent thee this d to meet me	1Sa 25:32	3117
which hast kept me this d from	1Sa 25:33	3117
enemy into thine hand this d	1Sa 26:8	3117
or his d shall come to die	1Sa 26:10	3117
they have driven me out this d	1Sa 26:19	3117
was precious in thine eyes this d	1Sa 26:21	3117
delivered thee into my hand to d	1Sa 26:23	3117
much set by this d in mine eyes	1Sa 26:24	3117
perish one d by the hand of Saul	1Sa 27:1	3117
Achish gave him Ziklag that d	1Sa 27:6	3117
the kings of Judah unto this d	1Sa 27:6	3117
Whither have ye made a road to d	1Sa 27:10	3117
done this thing unto thee this d	1Sa 28:18	3117
he had eaten no bread all the d	1Sa 28:20	3117
since he fell unto me unto this d	1Sa 29:3	3117
found evil in thee since the d of	1Sa 29:6	3117
of thy coming unto me unto this d	1Sa 29:6	3117
I have been with thee unto this d	1Sa 29:8	3117
come to Ziklag on the third d	1Sa 30:1	3117
unto the evening of the next d	1Sa 30:17	4283
And it was so from that d forward	1Sa 30:25	3117
ordinance for Israel unto this d	1Sa 30:25	3117
all his men, that same d together	1Sa 31:6	3117
came even to pass on the third d	2Sa 1:2	3117
was a very sore battle that d	2Sa 2:17	3117
they came to Hebron at break of d	2Sa 2:32	215
this d unto the house of Saul thy	2Sa 3:8	3117

that thou chargest me to *d* with a	2Sa 3:8	3117
to eat meat while it was yet *d*	2Sa 3:35	3117
all Israel understood that *d* that	2Sa 3:37	3117
great man fallen this *d* in Israel	2Sa 3:38	3117
And I am this *d* weak, though	2Sa 3:39	3117
sojourners there until this *d*	2Sa 4:3	3117
came about the heat of the *d* to	2Sa 4:5	3117
my lord the king this *d* of Saul	2Sa 4:8	3117
And David said on that *d*,	2Sa 5:8	3117
the place Perez-uzzah to this *d*	2Sa 6:8	3117
was afraid of the LORD that *d*	2Sa 6:9	3117
to *d* in the eyes of the handmaids	2Sa 6:20	3117
no child unto the *d* of her death	2Sa 6:23	3117
out of Egypt, even to this *d*	2Sa 7:6	3117
to Uriah, Tarry here to *d* also	2Sa 11:12	3117
Uriah abode in Jerusalem that *d*	2Sa 11:12	3117
it came to pass on the seventh *d*	2Sa 12:18	3117
king's son, lean from *d* to *d*	2Sa 13:4	1242
king's son, lean from *d* to *d*	2Sa 13:4	1242
hath been determined from the *d*	2Sa 13:32	3117
David mourned for his son every *d*	2Sa 13:37	3117
should I this *d* make thee go up	2Sa 15:20	3117
me good for his cursing this *d*	2Sa 16:12	3117
that *d* of twenty thousand men	2Sa 18:7	3117
that *d* than the sword devoured	2Sa 18:8	3117
and it is called unto this *d*	2Sa 18:18	3117
shalt not bear tidings this *d*	2Sa 18:20	3117
thou shalt bear tidings another *d*	2Sa 18:20	3117
but this *d* thou shalt bear no	2Sa 18:20	3117
this *d* of all them that rose up	2Sa 18:31	3117
the victory that *d* was turned	2Sa 19:2	3117
d how the king was grieved for	2Sa 19:2	3117
by stealth that *d* into the city	2Sa 19:3	3117
said Thou hast shamed this *d* the	2Sa 19:5	3117
which this *d* have saved thy life,	2Sa 19:5	3117
For thou hast declared this *d*	2Sa 19:6	3117
for this *d* I perceive, that if	2Sa 19:6	3117
lived, and all we had died this *d*	2Sa 19:6	3117
d that my lord the king went out	2Sa 19:19	3117
I am come the first this *d* of all	2Sa 19:20	3117
Zeruiah, that ye should this *d* be	2Sa 19:22	3117
be put to death this *d* in Israel	2Sa 19:22	3117
that I am this *d* king over Israel	2Sa 19:22	3117
from the *d* the king departed	2Sa 19:24	3117
the *d* he came again in peace	2Sa 19:24	3117
I am this *d* fourscore years old	2Sa 19:35	3117
shut up unto the *d* of their death	2Sa 20:3	3117
of the air to rest on them by *d*	2Sa 21:10	3119
in the *d* that the LORD had	2Sa 22:1	3117
me in the *d* of my calamity	2Sa 22:19	3117
wrought a great victory that *d*	2Sa 23:10	3117
And Gad came that *d* to David	2Sa 24:18	3117
For he is gone down this *d*	1Kin 1:25	3117
so will I certainly do this *d*	1Kin 1:30	3117
one to sit on my throne this *d*	1Kin 1:48	3117
me to *d* that he will not slay his	1Kin 1:51	3117
in the *d* when I went to Mahanaim	1Kin 2:8	3117
shall be put to death this *d*	1Kin 2:24	3117
that on the *d* thou goest out, and	1Kin 2:37	3117
on the *d* thou goest out, and	1Kin 2:42	3117
on his throne, as it is this *d*	1Kin 3:6	3117
it came to pass the third *d* after	1Kin 4:22	3117
one *d* was thirty measures of fine	1Kin 4:22	3117
said, Blessed be the LORD this *d*	1Kin 5:7	3117
and there they are unto this *d*	1Kin 8:8	3117
Since the *d* that I brought forth	1Kin 8:16	3117
with thine hand, as it is this *d*	1Kin 8:24	3117
servant prayeth before thee to *d*	1Kin 8:28	3117
open toward this house night and *d*	1Kin 8:29	3117
be nigh unto the LORD our God *d*	1Kin 8:59	3119
his commandments, as at this *d*	1Kin 8:61	3117
The same *d* did the king hallow	1Kin 8:64	3117
On the eighth *d* he sent the	1Kin 8:66	3117
the land of Cabul unto this *d*	1Kin 9:13	3117
of bondservice unto this *d*	1Kin 9:21	3117
trees, nor were seen unto this *d*	1Kin 10:12	3117
a servant unto this people this *d*	1Kin 12:7	3117
came to Rehoboam the third *d*	1Kin 12:12	3117
Come to me again the third *d*	1Kin 12:12	3117
the house of David unto this *d*	1Kin 12:19	3117
on the fifteenth *d* of the month	1Kin 12:32	3117
fifteenth *d* of the eighth month	1Kin 12:33	3117
And he gave a sign the same *d*	1Kin 13:3	3117
of God had done that *d* in Beth-el	1Kin 13:11	3117
off the house of Jeroboam that *d*	1Kin 14:14	3117
over Israel that *d* in the camp	1Kin 16:16	3117
until the *d* that the LORD sendeth	1Kin 17:14	3117
surely shew myself unto him to *d*	1Kin 18:15	3117
let it be known this *d* that thou	1Kin 18:36	3117
deliver it into thine hand this *d*	1Kin 20:13	3117
that in the seventh *d* the battle	1Kin 20:29	3117

hundred thousand footmen in one *d*	1Kin 20:29	3117
at the word of the LORD to *d*	1Kin 22:5	3117
Behold, thou shalt see in that *d*	1Kin 22:25	3117
And the battle increased that *d*	1Kin 22:35	3117
thy master from thy head to *d*	2Kin 2:3	3117
thy master from thy head to *d*	2Kin 2:5	3117
waters were healed unto this *d*	2Kin 2:22	3117
And it fell on a *d*, that Elisha	2Kin 4:8	3117
And it fell on a *d*, that he came	2Kin 4:11	3117
child was grown, it fell on a *d*	2Kin 4:18	3117
wilt thou go to him to *d*	2Kin 4:23	3117
thy son, that we may eat him to *d*	2Kin 6:28	3117
and I said unto her on the next *d*	2Kin 6:29	3117
Shaphat shall stand on him this *d*	2Kin 6:31	3117
this *d* is a *d* of good tidings,	2Kin 7:9	3117
this *d* is a *d* of good tidings,	2Kin 7:9	3117
the *d* that she left the land	2Kin 8:6	3117
the hand of Judah unto this *d*	2Kin 8:22	3117
it a draught house unto this *d*	2Kin 10:27	3117
name of it Joktheel unto this *d*	2Kin 14:7	3117
a leper unto the *d* of his death	2Kin 15:5	3117
Elath, and dwelt there unto this *d*	2Kin 16:6	3117
own land to Assyria unto this *d*	2Kin 17:23	3117
Unto this *d* they do after the	2Kin 17:34	3117
fathers, so do they unto this *d*	2Kin 17:41	3117
This *d* is a *d* of trouble	2Kin 19:3	3117
on the third *d* thou shalt go up	2Kin 20:5	3117
the house of the LORD the third *d*	2Kin 20:8	3117
have laid up in store unto this *d*	2Kin 20:17	3117
since the *d* their fathers came	2Kin 21:15	3117
out of Egypt, even to this *d*	2Kin 21:15	3117
in the tenth *d* of the month	2Kin 25:1	3117
on the ninth *d* of the fourth	2Kin 25:3	
on the seventh *d* of the month	2Kin 25:8	
twentieth *d* of the month, that	2Kin 25:27	
king, a daily rate for every *d*	2Kin 25:30	3117
them utterly unto this *d*, and	1Chr 4:41	3117
and dwelt there unto this *d*	1Chr 4:43	3117
to the river Gozan, unto this *d*	1Chr 5:26	3117
they were employed in that work *d*	1Chr 9:33	3119
slew a lion in a pit in a snowy *d*	1Chr 11:22	3117
For at that time *d* by *d* there	1Chr 12:22	3117
is called Perez-uzza to this *d*	1Chr 13:11	3117
And David was afraid of God that *d*	1Chr 13:12	3117
Then on that *d* David delivered	1Chr 16:7	3117
shew forth from *d* to his	1Chr 16:23	3117
forth from *d* to *d* his salvation	1Chr 16:23	3117
d that I brought up Israel unto	1Chr 17:5	3117
I brought up Israel unto this *d*	1Chr 17:5	3117
four a *d*, southward four a *d*	1Chr 26:17	3117
and my judgments, as at this *d*	1Chr 28:7	3117
his service this *d* unto the LORD	1Chr 29:5	3117
LORD, on the morrow after that *d*	1Chr 29:21	3117
on that *d* with great gladness	1Chr 29:22	3117
the second *d* of the second month	2Chr 3:2	
And there it is unto this *d*	2Chr 5:9	3117
Since the *d* that I brought forth	2Chr 6:5	3117
with thine hand, as it is this *d*	2Chr 6:15	3117
may be open upon this house *d*	2Chr 6:20	3119
in the eighth *d* they made a	2Chr 7:9	3117
twentieth *d* of the seventh month	2Chr 7:10	3117
make to pay tribute until this *d*	2Chr 8:8	3117
Even after a certain rate every *d*	2Chr 8:13	3117
as the duty of every *d* required	2Chr 8:14	3117
Solomon was prepared unto the *d*	2Chr 8:16	3117
came to Rehoboam on the third *d*	2Chr 10:12	3117
Come again to me on the third *d*	2Chr 10:12	3117
the house of David unto this *d*	2Chr 10:19	3117
at the word of the LORD to *d*	2Chr 18:4	3117
thou shalt see on that *d* when	2Chr 18:24	3117
And the battle increased that *d*	2Chr 18:34	3117
on the fourth *d* they assembled	2Chr 20:26	3117
valley of Berachah, unto this *d*	2Chr 20:26	3117
the hand of Judah unto this *d*	2Chr 21:10	3117
reason of the sickness by *d*	2Chr 21:15	3117
Thus they did *d* by *d*, and	2Chr 24:11	3117
a leper unto the *d* of his death	2Chr 26:21	3117
and twenty thousand in one *d*	2Chr 28:6	3117
Now they began on the first *d* of	2Chr 29:17	
on the eighth *d* of the month came	2Chr 29:17	
in the sixteenth *d* of the first	2Chr 29:17	
fourteenth *d* of the second month	2Chr 30:15	
priests praised the LORD *d* by *d*	2Chr 30:21	3117
fourteenth *d* of the first month	2Chr 35:1	
the LORD was prepared the same *d*	2Chr 35:16	
I come not against thee this *d*	2Chr 35:21	
in their lamentations to this *d*	2Chr 35:25	
as the duty of every *d* required	Ezr 3:4	3117
From the first *d* of the seventh	Ezr 3:6	3117
given them *d* by *d* without fail	Ezr 6:9	3118
on the third *d* of the month Adar	Ezr 6:15	3118

fourteenth *d* of the first month	Ezr 6:19	let it see the dawning of the *d*	Job 3:9	7837
For upon the first *d* of the first	Ezr 7:9	and fro unto the dawning of the *d*	Job 7:4	5399
on the first *d* of the fifth month	Ezr 7:9	accomplish, as an hireling, his *d*	Job 14:6	3117
the twelfth *d* of the first month	Ezr 8:31	he knoweth that the *d* of darkness	Job 15:23	3117
on the fourth *d* was the silver	Ezr 8:33	They change the night into *d*	Job 17:12	3117
in a great trespass unto this *d*	Ezr 9:7	him shall be astonied at his *d*	Job 18:20	3117
of face, as it is this *d*	Ezr 9:7	at the latter *d* upon the earth	Job 19:25	
yet escaped, as it is this *d*	Ezr 9:15	flow away in the *d* of his wrath	Job 20:28	3117
on the twentieth *d* of the month	Ezr 10:9	reserved to the *d* of destruction	Job 21:30	3117
is this a work of one *d* or two	Ezr 10:13	brought forth to the *d* of wrath	Job 21:30	3117
sat down in the first *d* of the	Ezr 10:16	Even to *d* is my complaint bitter	Job 23:2	3117
by the first *d* of the first month	Ezr 10:17	waters with bounds, until the *d*	Job 26:10	216
which I pray before thee now, *d*	Neh 1:6	trouble, against the *d* of battle	Job 38:23	3117
I pray thee, thy servant this *d*	Neh 1:11	and in his law doth he meditate *d*	Ps 1:2	3119
will they make an end in a *d*	Neh 4:2	this *d* have I begotten thee	Ps 2:7	3117
and set a watch against them *d*	Neh 4:9	is angry with the wicked every *d*	Ps 7:11	3117
a guard to us, and labour on the *d*	Neh 4:22	the *d* that the LORD delivered him	Ps 18:*t*	3117
I pray you, to them, even this *d*	Neh 5:11	me in the *d* of my calamity	Ps 18:18	3117
fifth *d* of the month Elul, in	Neh 6:15	*D* unto *d* uttereth speech, and	Ps 19:2	3117
upon the first *d* of the seventh	Neh 8:2	*D* unto *d* uttereth speech, and	Ps 19:2	3117
This *d* is holy unto the LORD your	Neh 8:9	hear thee in the *d* of trouble	Ps 20:1	3117
for this *d* is holy unto our Lord	Neh 8:10	on thee do I wait all the *d*	Ps 25:5	3117
your peace, for the *d* is holy	Neh 8:11	through my roaring all the *d* long	Ps 32:3	3117
on the second *d* were gathered	Neh 8:13	For *d* and night thy hand was heavy	Ps 32:4	3119
d had not the children of Israel	Neh 8:17	and of thy praise all the *d* long	Ps 35:28	3117
Also *d* by *d*, from the first *d*	Neh 8:18	for he seeth that his *d* is coming	Ps 37:13	3117
the first *d* unto the last *d*	Neh 8:18	I go mourning all the *d* long	Ps 38:6	3117
on the eighth *d* was a solemn	Neh 8:18	and imagine deceits all the *d* long	Ps 38:12	3117
fourth *d* of this month the	Neh 9:1	My tears have been my meat *d*	Ps 42:3	3119
God one fourth part of the *d*	Neh 9:3	In God we boast all the *d* long	Ps 44:8	3117
get thee a name, as it is this *d*	Neh 9:10	sake are we killed all the *d* long	Ps 44:22	3117
them in the *d* by a cloudy pillar	Neh 9:12	call upon me in the *d* of trouble	Ps 50:15	3117
cloud departed not from them by *d*	Neh 9:19	*D* and night they go about it upon	Ps 55:10	3119
the kings of Assyria unto this *d*	Neh 9:32	Every *d* they wrest my words	Ps 56:5	3117
Behold, we are servants this *d*	Neh 9:36	and refuge in the *d* of my trouble	Ps 59:16	3117
victuals on the sabbath *d* to sell	Neh 10:31	and with thy honour all the *d*	Ps 71:8	3117
on the sabbath, or on the holy *d*	Neh 10:31	and thy salvation all the *d*	Ps 71:15	3117
for the singers, due for every *d*	Neh 11:23	thy righteousness all the *d* long	Ps 71:24	3117
Also that *d* they offered great	Neh 12:43	For all the *d* long have I been	Ps 73:14	3117
the porters, every *d* his portion	Neh 12:47	The *d* is thine, the night also is	Ps 74:16	3117
On that *d* they read in the book	Neh 13:1	In the *d* of my trouble I sought	Ps 77:2	3117
into Jerusalem on the sabbath *d*	Neh 13:15	turned back in the *d* of battle	Ps 78:9	3117
the *d* wherein they sold victuals	Neh 13:15	nor the *d* when he delivered them	Ps 78:42	3117
ye do, and profane the sabbath *d*	Neh 13:17	appointed, on our solemn feast *d*	Ps 81:3	3117
be brought in on the sabbath *d*	Neh 13:19	For a *d* in thy courts is better	Ps 84:10	3117
gates, to sanctify the sabbath *d*	Neh 13:22	In the *d* of my trouble I will	Ps 86:7	3117
On the seventh *d*, when the heart	Est 1:10	of my salvation, I have cried *d*	Ps 88:1	3117
Media say this *d* unto all the	Est 1:18	name shall they rejoice all the *d*	Ps 89:16	3117
Mordecai walked every *d* before	Est 2:11	for the arrow that flieth by *d*	Ps 91:5	3119
lot, before Haman from *d* to *d*	Est 3:7	A Psalm or Song for the sabbath *d*	Ps 92:*t*	3117
lot, before Haman from *d* to *d*	Est 3:7	To *d* if ye will hear his voice,	Ps 95:7	3117
thirteenth *d* of the first month	Est 3:12	as in the *d* of temptation in the	Ps 95:8	3117
children and women, in one *d*	Est 3:13	forth his salvation from *d* to *d*	Ps 96:2	3117
thirteenth *d* of the twelfth month	Est 3:13	me in the *d* when I am in trouble	Ps 102:2	3117
should be ready against that *d*	Est 3:14	in the *d* when I call answer me	Ps 102:2	3117
nor drink three days, night or *d*	Est 4:16	enemies reproach me all the *d*	Ps 102:8	3117
it came to pass on the third *d*	Est 5:1	be willing in the *d* of thy power	Ps 110:3	3117
Haman come this *d* unto the	Est 5:4	kings in the *d* of his wrath	Ps 110:5	3117
went Haman forth that *d* joyful	Est 5:9	This is the *d* which the LORD hath	Ps 118:24	3117
second *d* at the banquet of wine	Est 7:2	They continue this *d* according to	Ps 119:91	3117
On that *d* did the king Ahasuerus	Est 8:1	it is my meditation all the *d*	Ps 119:97	3117
the three and twentieth *d* thereof	Est 8:9	Seven times a *d* do I praise thee	Ps 119:164	3117
Upon one *d* in all the provinces	Est 8:12	The sun shall not smite thee by *d*	Ps 121:6	3119
upon the thirteenth *d* of the	Est 8:12	The sun to rule by *d*	Ps 136:8	3117
should be ready against that *d* to	Est 8:13	of Edom in the *d* of Jerusalem	Ps 137:7	3117
and gladness, a feast and a good *d*	Est 8:17	In the *d* when I cried thou	Ps 138:3	3117
on the thirteenth *d* of the same	Est 9:1	but the night shineth as the *d*	Ps 139:12	3117
in the *d* that the enemies of the	Est 9:1	my head in the *d* of battle	Ps 140:7	3117
On that *d* the number of those	Est 9:11	Every *d* will I bless thee	Ps 145:2	3117
d also of the month Adar, and slew	Est 9:15	in that very *d* his thoughts	Ps 146:4	3117
thirteenth *d* of the month Adar	Est 9:17	more and more unto the perfect *d*	Prov 4:18	3117
on the fourteenth *d* of the same	Est 9:17	not spare in the *d* of vengeance	Prov 6:34	3117
made it a *d* of feasting and	Est 9:17	this *d* have I payed my vows	Prov 7:14	3117
on the thirteenth *d* thereof	Est 9:18	will come home at the *d* appointed	Prov 7:20	3117
on the fifteenth *d* of the same	Est 9:18	profit not in the *d* of wrath	Prov 11:4	3117
made it a *d* of feasting and	Est 9:18	even the wicked for the *d* of evil	Prov 16:4	3117
made the fourteenth *d* of the	Est 9:19	covoteth greedily all the *d* long	Prov 21:26	3117
of the month Adar a *d* of gladness	Est 9:19	prepared against the *d* of battle	Prov 21:31	3117
gladness and feasting, and a good *d*	Est 9:19	I have made known to thee this *d*	Prov 22:19	3117
fourteenth *d* of the month Adar	Est 9:21	fear of the LORD all the *d* long	Prov 23:17	3117
and the fifteenth *d* of the same	Est 9:21	thou faint in the *d* of adversity	Prov 24:10	3117
and from mourning into a good *d*	Est 9:22	not what a *d* may bring forth	Prov 27:1	3117
in their houses, every one his *d*	Job 1:4	house in the *d* of thy calamity	Prov 27:10	3117
Now there was a *d* when the sons	Job 1:6	dropping in a very rainy *d*	Prov 27:15	3117
there was a *d* when his sons and	Job 1:13	the *d* of death than the *d* of	Eccl 7:1	3117
Again there was a *d* when the sons	Job 2:1	death than the *d* of one's birth	Eccl 7:1	3117
Job his mouth, and cursed his *d*	Job 3:1	In the *d* of prosperity be joyful,	Eccl 7:14	3117
Let the *d* perish wherein I was	Job 3:3	but in the *d* of adversity	Eccl 7:14	3117
Let that *d* be darkness	Job 3:4	hath he power in the *d* of death	Eccl 8:8	3117
the blackness of the *d* terrify it	Job 3:5	*d* nor night seeth sleep with his	Eccl 8:16	3117
them curse it that curse the *d*	Job 3:8	In the *d* when the keepers of the	Eccl 12:3	3117

D

Until the *d* break, and the shadows	Song 2:17	3117
him in the *d* of his espousals	Song 3:11	3117
in the *d* of the gladness of his	Song 3:11	3117
Until the *d* break, and the shadows	Song 4:6	3117
we do for our sister in the *d*	Song 8:8	3117
alone shall be exalted in that *d*	Is 2:11	3117
For the *d* of the LORD of hosts	Is 2:12	3117
alone shall be exalted in that *d*	Is 2:17	3117
In that *d* a man shall cast his	Is 2:20	3117
In that *d* shall he swear, saying,	Is 3:7	3117
In that *d* the Lord will take away	Is 3:18	3117
in that *d* seven women shall take	Is 4:1	3117
In that *d* shall the branch of the	Is 4:2	3117
assemblies, a cloud and smoke by *d*	Is 4:5	3119
in that *d* they shall roar against	Is 5:30	3117
from the *d* that Ephraim departed	Is 7:17	3117
it shall come to pass in that *d*	Is 7:18	3117
In the same *d* shall the Lord	Is 7:20	3117
it shall come to pass in that *d*	Is 7:21	3117
it shall come to pass in that *d*	Is 7:23	3117
oppressor, as in the *d* of Midian	Is 9:4	3117
and tail, branch and rush, in one *d*	Is 9:14	3117
will ye do in the *d* of visitation	Is 10:3	3117
his thorns and his briers in one *d*	Is 10:17	3117
it shall come to pass in that *d*	Is 10:20	3117
it shall come to pass in that *d*	Is 10:27	3117
yet shall he remain at Nob that *d*	Is 10:32	3117
in that *d* there shall be a root	Is 11:10	3117
it shall come to pass in that *d*	Is 11:11	3117
d that he came up out of the land	Is 11:16	3117
in that *d* thou shalt say, O LORD,	Is 12:1	3117
in that *d* shall ye say, Praise	Is 12:4	3117
for the *d* of the LORD is at hand	Is 13:6	3117
the *d* of the LORD cometh, cruel	Is 13:9	3117
in the *d* of his fierce anger	Is 13:13	3117
it shall come to pass in the *d*	Is 14:3	3117
in that *d* it shall come to pass,	Is 17:4	3117
At that *d* shall a man look to his	Is 17:7	3117
In that *d* shall his strong cities	Is 17:9	3117
In the *d* shalt thou make thy	Is 17:11	3117
shall be a heap in the *d* of grief	Is 17:11	3117
In that *d* shall Egypt be like	Is 19:16	3117
In that *d* shall five cities in	Is 19:18	3117
In that *d* shall there be an altar	Is 19:19	3117
shall know the LORD in that *d*	Is 19:21	3117
In that *d* shall there be a	Is 19:23	3117
In that *d* shall Israel be the	Is 19:24	3117
of this isle shall say in that *d*	Is 20:6	3117
For it is a *d* of trouble, and of	Is 22:5	3117
thou didst look in that *d* to the	Is 22:8	3117
in that *d* did the Lord GOD of	Is 22:12	3117
it shall come to pass in that *d*	Is 22:20	3117
In that *d*, saith the LORD of	Is 22:25	3117
it shall come to pass in that *d*	Is 23:15	3117
it shall come to pass in that *d*	Is 24:21	3117
And it shall be said in that *d*	Is 25:9	3117
In that *d* shall this song be sung	Is 26:1	3117
In that *d* the LORD with his sore	Is 27:1	3117
In that *d* sing ye unto her, A	Is 27:2	3117
it, I will keep it night and *d*	Is 27:3	3117
wind in the *d* of the east wind	Is 27:8	3117
it shall come to pass in that *d*	Is 27:12	3117
it shall come to pass in that *d*	Is 27:13	3117
In that *d* shall the LORD of hosts	Is 28:5	3117
morning shall it pass over, by *d*	Is 28:19	3117
the plowman plow all *d* to sow	Is 28:24	3117
in that *d* shall the deaf hear the	Is 29:18	3117
in that *d* shall thy cattle feed	Is 30:23	3117
in the *d* of the great slaughter	Is 30:25	3117
in the *d* that the LORD bindeth up	Is 30:26	3117
For in that *d* every man shall	Is 31:7	3117
For it is the *d* of the LORD's	Is 34:8	3117
shall not be quenched night nor *d*	Is 34:10	3119
This *d* is a *d* of trouble, and of	Is 37:3	3117
This *d* is a *d* of trouble	Is 37:3	3117
from *d* even to night wilt thou	Is 38:12	3117
from *d* even to night wilt thou	Is 38:13	3117
shall praise thee, as I do this *d*	Is 38:19	3117
laid up in store until this *d*	Is 39:6	3117
Yea, before the *d* was I am he	Is 43:13	3117
come to thee in a moment in one *d*	Is 47:9	3117
even before the *d* when thou	Is 48:7	3117
in a *d* of salvation have I helped	Is 49:8	3117
d because of the fury of the	Is 51:13	3117
continually every *d* is blasphemed	Is 52:5	3117
they shall know in that *d* that I	Is 52:6	3117
and to morrow shall be as this *d*	Is 56:12	3117
in the *d* of your fast ye find	Is 58:3	3117
ye shall not fast as ye do this *d*	Is 58:4	3117
a *d* for a man to afflict his soul	Is 58:5	3117
and an acceptable *d* to the LORD	Is 58:5	3117
doing thy pleasure on my holy *d*	Is 58:13	3117
shall not be shut *d* nor night	Is 60:11	3119
shall be no more thy light by *d*	Is 60:19	3117
the *d* of vengeance of our God	Is 61:2	3117
hold their peace *d* nor night	Is 62:6	3117
For the *d* of vengeance is in mine	Is 63:4	3117
the *d* unto a rebellious people	Is 65:2	3117
a fire that burneth all the *d*	Is 65:5	3117
be made to bring forth in one *d*	Is 66:8	3117
I have this *d* set thee over the	Jer 1:10	3117
made thee this *d* a defenced city	Jer 1:18	3117
from our youth even unto this *d*	Jer 3:25	3117
it shall come to pass at that *d*	Jer 4:9	3117
for the *d* goeth away, for the	Jer 6:4	3117
nor commanded them in the *d* that	Jer 7:22	3117
Since the *d* that your fathers	Jer 7:25	3117
d I have even sent unto you all	Jer 7:25	3117
of tears, that I might weep *d*	Jer 9:1	3119
d that I brought them forth out	Jer 11:4	3117
milk and honey, as it is this *d*	Jer 11:5	3117
unto your fathers in the *d* that I	Jer 11:7	3117
land of Egypt, even unto this *d*	Jer 11:7	3117
them for the *d* of slaughter	Jer 12:3	3117
run down with tears night and *d*	Jer 14:17	3119
is gone down while it was yet *d*	Jer 15:9	3119
there shall ye serve other gods *d*	Jer 16:13	3119
my refuge in the *d* of affliction	Jer 16:19	3117
have I desired the woeful *d*	Jer 17:16	3117
thou art my hope in the *d* of evil	Jer 17:17	3117
bring upon them the *d* of evil	Jer 17:18	3117
bear no burden on the sabbath *d*	Jer 17:21	3117
of your houses on the sabbath *d*	Jer 17:22	3117
work, but hallow ye the sabbath *d*	Jer 17:22	3117
of this city on the sabbath *d*	Jer 17:24	3117
but hallow the sabbath *d*	Jer 17:24	3117
unto me to hallow the sabbath *d*	Jer 17:27	3117
of Jerusalem on the sabbath *d*	Jer 17:27	3117
in the *d* of their calamity	Jer 18:17	3117
Cursed be the *d* wherein I was	Jer 20:14	3117
let not the *d* wherein my mother	Jer 20:14	3117
king of Judah, even unto this *d*	Jer 25:3	3117
as it is this *d*	Jer 25:18	3117
of the LORD shall be at that *d*	Jer 25:33	3117
be until the *d* that I visit them	Jer 27:22	3117
for that *d* is great, so that none	Jer 30:7	3117
it shall come to pass in that *d*	Jer 30:8	3117
For there shall be a *d*, that the	Jer 31:6	3117
made with their fathers in the *d*	Jer 31:32	3117
giveth the sun for a light by *d*	Jer 31:35	3119
land of Egypt, even unto this *d*	Jer 32:20	3119
made thee a name, as at this *d*	Jer 32:20	3119
of my fury from the *d* that they	Jer 32:31	3119
they built it even unto this *d*	Jer 32:31	3119
ye can break my covenant of the *d*	Jer 33:20	3117
and that there should not be *d*	Jer 33:20	3119
If my covenant be not with *d*	Jer 33:25	3119
with your fathers in the *d* that I	Jer 34:13	3117
for unto this *d* they drink none,	Jer 35:14	3117
from the *d* I spake unto thee,	Jer 36:2	3117
days of Josiah, even into this *d*	Jer 36:2	3117
LORD's house upon the fasting *d*	Jer 36:6	3117
be cast out in the *d* to the heat	Jer 36:30	3117
the *d* that Jerusalem was taken	Jer 38:28	3117
the ninth *d* of the month, the	Jer 39:2	3117
in that *d* before thee	Jer 39:16	3117
But I will deliver thee in that *d*	Jer 39:17	3117
I loose thee this *d* from the	Jer 40:4	3117
it came to pass the second *d*	Jer 41:4	3117
that I have admonished you this *d*	Jer 42:19	3117
now I have this *d* declared it to	Jer 42:21	3117
this *d* they are a desolation, and	Jer 44:2	3117
wasted and desolate, as at this *d*	Jer 44:6	3117
are not humbled even unto this *d*	Jer 44:10	3117
an inhabitant, as at this *d*	Jer 44:22	3117
happened unto you, as at this *d*	Jer 44:23	3117
For this is the *d* of the Lord GOD	Jer 46:10	3117
a *d* of vengeance, that he may	Jer 46:10	3117
because the *d* of their calamity	Jer 46:21	3117
Because of the *d* that cometh to	Jer 47:4	3117
that *d* shall be as the heart of a	Jer 48:41	3117
at that *d* shall the heart of the	Jer 49:22	3117
of war shall be cut off in that *d*	Jer 49:26	3117
for their *d* is come, the time of	Jer 50:27	3117
of war shall be cut off in that *d*	Jer 50:30	3117
for thy *d* is come, the time that	Jer 50:31	3117
for in the *d* of trouble they	Jer 51:2	3117
in the tenth *d* of the month	Jer 52:4	
in the ninth *d* of the month	Jer 52:6	
in prison till the *d* of his death	Jer 52:11	3117
in the tenth *d* of the month	Jer 52:12	
twentieth *d* of the month, that	Jer 52:31	

D

The *d* following Jesus would go..............Jn 1:43
the third *d* there was a marriage ....Jn 2:1   1887
at the passover, in the feast of ....Jn 2:23   2250
on the same *d* was the sabbath ....Jn 5:9   2250
was cured, It is the sabbath *d*..............Jn 5:10
these things on the sabbath *d*..............Jn 5:16
The *d* following, when the people ....Jn 6:22   1887
raise it up again at the last *d*..............Jn 6:39   2250
I will raise him up at the last *d* ....Jn 6:40   2250
I will raise him up at the last *d* ....Jn 6:44   2250
I will raise him up at the last *d* ....Jn 6:54   2250
on the sabbath *d* **circumcise a man**..............Jn 7:22
sabbath *d* **receive circumcision**..............Jn 7:23
every whit whole on the sabbath *d* ....Jn 7:23
In the last *d*, that great of ....Jn 7:37   2250
Abraham rejoiced to see my *d*..............Jn 8:56   2250
him that sent me, while it is *d*..............Jn 9:4   2250
it was the sabbath *d* when Jesus ....Jn 9:14
he keepeth not the sabbath *d* ....Jn 9:16
there not twelve hours in the *d* ....Jn 11:9   2250
If any man walk in the *d***, he**..............Jn 11:9   2250
in the resurrection at the last *d*..............Jn 11:24   2250
Then from that *d* forth they took ....Jn 11:53   2250
against the *d* **of my burying hath**..............Jn 12:7   2250
On the next *d* much people that ....Jn 12:12   1887
shall judge him in the last *d*..............Jn 12:48   2250
At that *d* ye shall know that I am ....Jn 14:20   2250
in that *d* **ye shall ask me nothing**..............Jn 16:23   2250
At that *d* ye shall ask in my name ....Jn 16:26   2250
upon the cross on the sabbath *d* ....Jn 19:31
that sabbath *d* was an high *d*..............Jn 19:31
of the Jews' preparation *d* ....Jn 19:42
The first *d* of the week cometh ....Jn 20:1
Then the same *d* at evening ....Jn 20:19
being the first *d* of the week ....Jn 20:19   2250
Until the *d* in which he was taken ....Acts 1:2   2250
unto that same *d* that he was ....Acts 1:22   2250
when the *d* of Pentecost was fully ....Acts 2:1   2250
it is but the third hour of the *d* ....Acts 2:15   2250
notable *d* of the Lord come ....Acts 2:20   2250
sepulchre is with us unto this *d*..........Acts 2:29   2250
the same *d* there were added unto ....Acts 2:41   2250
put them in hold unto the next *d* ....Acts 4:3   839
If we this *d* be examined of the..........Acts 4:9   4594
and circumcised him the eighth *d*..........Acts 7:8   2250
the next *d* he shewed himself unto ....Acts 7:26   2250
And they watched the gates *d* ....Acts 9:24   2250
about the ninth hour of the *d* an ....Acts 10:3   2250
Him God raised up the third *d* ....Acts 10:40   2250
Now as soon as it was *d*, there ....Acts 12:18   2250
And upon a set *d* Herod, arrayed in ....Acts 12:21   2250
the synagogue on the sabbath *d* ....Acts 13:14   2250
which are read every sabbath *d* ....Acts 13:27
this *d* have I begotten thee ....Acts 13:33   4594
the next sabbath *d* came almost ....Acts 13:44
the next *d* he departed with ....Acts 14:20   1887
in the synagogues every sabbath *d*..........Acts 15:21
and the next *d* to Neapolis ....Acts 16:11
And when it was *d*, the magistrates ....Acts 16:35   2250
Because he hath appointed a *d* ....Acts 17:31   2250
And upon the first *d* of the week ....Acts 20:7
long while, even till break of *d*..........Acts 20:11   827
came the next *d* over against ....Acts 20:15
the next *d* we arrived at Samos, ...Acts 20:15
the next *d* we came to Miletus ....Acts 20:15
at Jerusalem the *d* of Pentecost ....Acts 20:16   2250
from the first *d* that I came into ....Acts 20:18   2250
I take you to record this *d*..........Acts 20:26   4594
every one night and *d* with tears ....Acts 20:31   2250
the *d* following unto Rhodes, and ....Acts 21:1
and abode with them one *d*..........Acts 21:7   2250
the next *d* we that were of Paul's ....Acts 21:8
the *d* following Paul went in with ....Acts 21:18
the next *d* purifying himself with ....Acts 21:26   2250
toward God, as ye all are this *d* ....Acts 22:3   4594
before God until this *d*..........Acts 23:1   2250
And when it was *d*, certain of the ....Acts 23:12   2250
called in question by you this *d*..........Acts 24:21   2250
the next *d* sitting on the ....Acts 25:6   1887
d before these touching all the ....Acts 26:2   4594
tribes, instantly serving God *d* ....Acts 26:7   2250
of God, I continue unto this *d* ....Acts 26:22   2250
but also all that hear me this *d* ....Acts 26:29   4594
the next *d* we touched at Sidon ....Acts 27:3
the next *d* they lightened the ....Acts 27:18
the third *d* we cast out with our ....Acts 27:19
of the stern, and wished for the *d* ....Acts 27:29   2250
while the *d* was coming on, Paul ....Acts 27:33   2250
meat, saying, This *d*..........Acts 27:33   4594
fourteenth *d* that ye have tarried ....Acts 27:33   2250
And when it was *d*, they knew not ....Acts 27:39

after one *d* the south wind blew, ...Acts 28:13   2250
and we came the next *d* to Puteoli ....Acts 28:13   2250
when they had appointed him a *d*..........Acts 28:23   2250
wrath against the *d* of wrath ....Rom 2:5   2250
In the *d* when God shall judge the ....Rom 2:16   2250
sake we are killed all the *d* long ....Rom 8:36   2250
All *d* long I have stretched forth ....Rom 10:21   2250
should not hear;) unto this *d* ....Rom 11:8   4594,2250
is far spent, the *d* is at hand ....Rom 13:12   2250
Let us walk honestly, as in the *d* ....Rom 13:13   2250
man esteemeth one *d* above another ....Rom 14:5   2250
another esteemeth every *d* alike ....Rom 14:5   2250
He that regardeth the *d* ....Rom 14:6   2250
and he that regardeth not the *d* ....Rom 14:6   2250
in the *d* of our Lord Jesus Christ 1Cor 1:8   2250
for the *d* shall declare it, ...1Cor 3:13   2250
of all things unto this *d* 1Cor 4:13   737
saved in the *d* of the Lord Jesus 1Cor 5:5   2250
committed, and fell in one *d* three 1Cor 10:8   2250
d according to the scriptures 1Cor 15:4   2250
Upon the first *d* of the week let 1Cor 16:2
ours in the *d* of the Lord Jesus 2Cor 1:14   2250
for until this *d* remaineth the 2Cor 3:14   4594
But even unto this *d*, when Moses 2Cor 3:15   4594
inward man is renewed *d* by *d*..........2Cor 4:16   2250
in the *d* of salvation have I 2Cor 6:2   2250
now is the *d* of salvation 2Cor 6:2   2250
a *d* I have been in the deep 2Cor 11:25   3574
sealed unto the *d* of redemption ....Eph 4:30   2250
able to withstand in the evil *d* ....Eph 6:13   2250
gospel from the first *d* until now ....Phil 1:5   2250
it until the *d* of Jesus Christ ....Phil 1:6   2250
offence till the *d* of Christ ....Phil 1:10   2250
I may rejoice in the *d* of Christ ....Phil 2:16   2250
Circumcised the eighth *d*, of the ....Phil 3:5   2250
since the *d* ye heard of it, and ....Col 1:6   2250
since the *d* we heard it, do not ....Col 1:9   2250
for labouring night and *d*, because 1Th 2:9   2250
d praying exceedingly that we 1Th 3:10   2250
know perfectly that the *d* of the 1Th 5:2   2250
that that *d* should overtake you 1Th 5:4   2250
light, and the children of the *d* 1Th 5:5   2250
But let us, who are of the *d* 1Th 5:8   2250
among you was believed) in that *d* 2Th 1:10   2250
as that the *d* of Christ is at 2Th 2:2   2250
for that *d* shall not come, except 2Th 2:3
with labour and travail night and *d* 2Th 3:8   2250
and prayers night and *d* 1Ti 5:5   2250
of thee in my prayers night and *d* 2Ti 1:3   2250
committed unto him against that *d* 2Ti 1:12   2250
find mercy of the Lord in that *d*..........2Ti 1:18   2250
judge, shall give me at that *d* 2Ti 4:8   2250
this *d* have I begotten thee ....Heb 1:5   4594
To *d* if ye will hear his voice, ...Heb 3:7   4594
in the *d* of temptation in the ....Heb 3:8   2250
daily, while it is called To *d* ....Heb 3:13   4594
To *d* if ye will hear his voice, ...Heb 3:15   4594
of the seventh *d* on this wise ....Heb 4:4
the seventh *d* from all his works ....Heb 4:4   2250
Again, he limiteth a certain *d* ....Heb 4:7   2250
saying in David, To *d* ....Heb 4:7   4594
To *d* if ye will hear his voice, ...Heb 4:7   4594
have spoken of another *d* ....Heb 4:8   2250
to *d* have I begotten thee ....Heb 5:5   4594
in the *d* when I took them by the ....Heb 8:9   2250
more, as ye see the *d* approaching ....Heb 10:25   2250
the same yesterday, and to *d* ....Heb 13:8   4594
To *d* or to morrow we will go into ....Jas 4:13   4594
hearts, as in a *d* of slaughter ....Jas 5:5   2250
God in the *d* of visitation 1Pet 2:12   2250
in a dark place, until the *d* dawn 2Pet 1:19   2250
the *d* star arise in your hearts 2Pet 1:19   5459
from *d* to *d* with their unlawful 2Pet 2:8   2250
to *d* with their unlawful deeds 2Pet 2:8   2250
the *d* of judgment to be punished 2Pet 2:9   2250
fire against the *d* of judgment 2Pet 3:7   2250
that one *d* is with the Lord as a 2Pet 3:8   2250
and a thousand years as one *d* 2Pet 3:8   2250
But the *d* of the Lord will come 2Pet 3:10   2250
unto the coming of the *d* of God 2Pet 3:12   2250
boldness in the *d* of judgment 1Jn 4:17   2250
unto the judgment of the great *d* ....Jude 6   2250
was in the Spirit on the Lord's *d* ....Rev 1:10   2250
and they rest not *d* and night, ...Rev 4:8   2250
For the great *d* of his wrath is ....Rev 6:17   2250
the throne of God, and serve him *d* ....Rev 7:15   2250
the *d* shone not for a third part ....Rev 8:12   2250
were prepared for an hour, and a *d* ....Rev 9:15   2250
accused them before our God *d* ....Rev 12:10   2250
and they have no rest *d* nor night ....Rev 14:11   2250
of that great *d* of God Almighty ....Rev 16:14   2250

D

shall her plagues come in one *d* .... Rev 18:8   2250
are, and shall be tormented *d* .... Rev 20:10   2250
it shall not be shut at all by *d* .... Rev 21:25   2250

DAY'S See APPENDIX.

DAYS See APPENDIX.

DAYS' See APPENDIX.

DAYSMAN
  Neither is there any *d* betwixt us .... Job 9:33   3198

DAYSPRING
  caused the *d* to know his place .... Job 38:12   7837
  whereby the *d* from on high hath .... Lk 1:78   395

DAYTIME
  by *d* in a pillar of a cloud, and .... Num 14:14   3119
  They meet with darkness in the *d* .... Job 5:14   3119
  marked for themselves in the *d* .... Job 24:16   3119
  O my God, I cry in the *d*, but .... Ps 22:2   3119
  his lovingkindness in the *d* .... Ps 42:8   3119
  In the *d* also he led them with a .... Ps 78:14   3119
  a shadow in the *d* from the heat .... Is 4:6   3119
  upon the watchtower in the *d* .... Is 21:8   3119
  it pleasure to riot in the *d* 2Pet 2:13

DEACON
  let them use the office of a *d* 1Ti 3:10   1247
  a *d* well purchase to themselves a 1Ti 3:13   1247

DEACONS
  Philippi, with the bishops and *d* .... Phil 1:1   1249
  Likewise must the *d* be grave 1Ti 3:8   1249
  Let the *d* be the husbands of one 1Ti 3:12   1249

DEAD
  him, Behold, thou art but a *d* man .... Gen 20:3   4191
  stood up from before his *d* .... Gen 23:3   4191
  I may bury my *d* out of my sight .... Gen 23:4   4191
  of our sepulchres bury thy *d* .... Gen 23:6   4191
  but that thou mayest bury thy *d* .... Gen 23:6   4191
  should bury my *d* out of my sight .... Gen 23:8   4191
  bury thy *d* .... Gen 23:11   4191
  of me, and I will bury my *d* there .... Gen 23:13   4191
  bury therefore thy *d* .... Gen 23:15   4191
  for his brother is *d*, and he is .... Gen 42:38   4191
  and his brother is *d*, and he alone .... Gen 44:20   4191
  saw that their father was *d* .... Gen 50:15   4191
  for all the men are *d* which .... Ex 4:19   4191
  of the cattle of the Israelites *d* .... Ex 9:7   4191
  a house where there was not one *d* ...... Ex 12:30   4191
  for they said, We be all *d* men .... Ex 12:33   4191
  Egyptians *d* upon the sea shore .... Ex 14:30   4191
  and the *d* beast shall be his .... Ex 21:34   4191
  the *d* ox also they shall divide .... Ex 21:35   4191
  and the *d* shall be his own .... Ex 21:36   4191
  doth touch them, when they be *d* .... Lev 11:31   4194
  any of them, when they are *d* .... Lev 11:32   4194
  cuttings in your flesh for the *d* .... Lev 19:28   5315
  for the *d* among his people .... Lev 21:1   5315
  shall he go in to any *d* body .... Lev 21:11   4191
  thing that is unclean by the *d* .... Lev 22:4   5315
  and whosoever is defiled by the *d* .... Num 5:2   5315
  LORD he shall come at no *d* body .... Num 6:6   4191
  him, for that he sinned by the *d* .... Num 6:11   4191
  defiled by the *d* body of a man .... Num 9:6   5315
  defiled by the *d* body of a man .... Num 9:7   5315
  be unclean by reason of a *d* body .... Num 9:10   5315
  Let her not be as one *d*, of whom .... Num 12:12   4191
  And he stood between the *d* .... Num 16:48   4191
  He that toucheth the *d* body of .... Num 19:11   4191
  Whosoever toucheth the *d* body of .... Num 19:13   4191
  d body of any man that is .... Num 19:13   4191
  in the open fields, or a *d* body .... Num 19:16   4191
  a bone, or one slain, or one *d* .... Num 19:18   4191
  congregation saw that Aaron was *d* ...... Num 20:29   1478
  and *d* from among the people, ... Deut 2:16   4191
  between your eyes for the *d* .... Deut 14:1   4191
  flesh, nor touch their *d* carcase .... Deut 14:8   5038
  the wife of the *d* shall not marry .... Deut 25:5   4191
  name of his brother which is *d* .... Deut 25:6   4191
  nor given ought thereof for the *d* .... Deut 26:14   4191
  Moses my servant is *d* .... Josh 1:2   4191
  to pass, when the judge was *d* .... Judg 2:19   4191
  was fallen down *d* on the earth.............. Judg 3:25   4191
  of the LORD, when Ehud was *d* .... Judg 4:1   4191
  her tent, behold, Sisera lay *d* .... Judg 4:22   4191
  he bowed, there he fell down *d* .... Judg 5:27   7703
  to pass, as soon as Gideon was *d* .... Judg 8:33   4191
  Israel saw that Abimelech was *d* .... Judg 9:55   4191
  So the *d* which he slew at his .... Judg 16:30   4191
  have they forced, that she is *d* .... Judg 20:5   4191
  you, as ye have dealt with the *d* .... Ruth 1:8   4191

to the living and to the *d* .... Ruth 2:20   4191
the Moabitess, the wife of the *d* .... Ruth 4:5   4191
of the *d* upon his inheritance .... Ruth 4:5   4191
of the *d* upon his inheritance .... Ruth 4:10   4191
that the name of the *d* be not cut .... Ruth 4:10   4191
also, Hophni and Phinehas, are *d* 1Sa 4:17   4191
in law and her husband were *d* 1Sa 4:19   4191
saw their champion was *d*, they 1Sa 17:51   4191
after a *d* dog, after a flea 1Sa 24:14   4191
when David heard that Nabal was *d* 1Sa 25:39   4191
Now Samuel was *d*, and all Israel 1Sa 28:3   4191
armourbearer saw that Saul was *d* 1Sa 31:5   4191
and that Saul and his sons were *d* 1Sa 31:7   4191
the people also are fallen and *d* 2Sa 1:4   4191
and Jonathan his son are *d* also............ 2Sa 1:4   4191
Saul and Jonathan his son be *d* 2Sa 1:5   4191
for your master Saul is *d* 2Sa 2:7   4191
heard that Abner was *d* in Hebron 2Sa 4:1   4191
me, saying, Behold, Saul is *d* 2Sa 4:10   4191
look upon such a *d* dog as I am 2Sa 9:8   4191
Uriah the Hittite is *d* also 2Sa 11:21   4191
some of the king's servants be *d* 2Sa 11:24   4191
Uriah the Hittite is *d* also 2Sa 11:24   4191
that Uriah her husband was *d* 2Sa 11:26   4191
to tell him that the child was *d* 2Sa 12:18   4191
we tell him that the child is *d* 2Sa 12:18   4191
perceived that the child was *d* 2Sa 12:19   4191
unto his servants, Is the child *d* 2Sa 12:19   4191
And they said, He is *d* 2Sa 12:19   4191
but when the child was *d*, thou 2Sa 12:21   4191
But now he is *d*, wherefore should 2Sa 12:23   4191
for Amnon only is *d* 2Sa 13:32   4191
that all the king's sons are *d* 2Sa 13:33   4191
for Amnon only is *d* 2Sa 13:33   4191
concerning Amnon, seeing he was *d* 2Sa 13:39   4191
had a long time mourned for the *d* 2Sa 14:2   4191
widow woman, and mine husband is *d* .. 2Sa 14:5   4191
Why should this *d* dog curse my 2Sa 16:9   4191
because the king's son is *d* 2Sa 18:20   4191
anointed over us, is *d* in battle 2Sa 19:10   4191
but *d* men before my lord the king 2Sa 19:28   4194
laid her *d* child in my bosom.................. 1Kin 3:20   4191
my child suck, behold, it was *d* 1Kin 3:21   4191
is my son, and the *d* is thy son 1Kin 3:22   4191
but the *d* is thy son, and the 1Kin 3:22   4191
that liveth, and thy son is the *d* 1Kin 3:23   4191
but thy son is *d*, and my son.................. 1Kin 3:23   4191
the captain of the host was *d* 1Kin 11:21   4191
to his sons, saying, When I am *d* 1Kin 13:31   4191
saying, Naboth is stoned, and is *d* 1Kin 21:14   4191
that Naboth was stoned, and was *d* 1Kin 21:15   4191
for Naboth is not alive, but *d* 1Kin 21:15   4191
when Ahab heard that Naboth was *d* 1Kin 21:16   4191
it came to pass, when Ahab was *d* 2Kin 3:5   4194
house, behold, the child was *d* 2Kin 4:1   4191
Thy servant thy husband is *d* 2Kin 4:32   4191
he had restored a *d* body to life............ 2Kin 8:5   4191
of Ahaziah saw that her son was *d* 2Kin 11:1   4191
behold, they were all *d* corpses 2Kin 19:35   4191
him in a chariot *d* from Megiddo 2Kin 23:30   4191
And when Bela was *d*, Jobab the son 1Chr 1:44   4191
And when Jobab was *d*, Husham of 1Chr 1:45   4191
And when Husham was *d*, Hadad the ... 1Chr 1:46   4191
And when Hadad was *d*, Samlah of 1Chr 1:47   4191
And when Samlah was *d*, Shaul of 1Chr 1:48   4191
And when Shaul was *d*, Baal-hanan 1Chr 1:49   4191
And when Baal-hanan was *d*, Hadad...... 1Chr 1:50   4191
And when Azubah was *d*, Caleb took 1Chr 2:19   4191
Hezron was *d* in Caleb-ephratah 1Chr 2:24   4194
armourbearer saw that Saul was *d* 1Chr 10:5   4191
and that Saul and his sons were *d* 1Chr 10:7   4191
they were *d* bodies fallen to the 2Chr 20:24   6297
both riches with the *d* bodies................ 2Chr 20:25   6297
of Ahaziah saw that her son was *d* 2Chr 22:10   4191
when her father and mother were *d* ...... Est 2:7   4194
upon the young men, and they are *d* ...... Job 1:19   4191
D things are formed from under .... Job 26:5   7496
forgotten as a *d* man out of mind .... Ps 31:12   4191
and horse are cast into a *d* sleep............ Ps 76:6
The *d* bodies of thy servants have .... Ps 79:2   5038
Free among the *d*, like the slain .... Ps 88:5   4191
Wilt thou shew wonders to the *d* .... Ps 88:10   4191
shall the *d* arise and praise thee .... Ps 88:10   7496
and ate the sacrifices of the *d*................ Ps 106:28   4191
fill the places with the *d* bodies .... Ps 110:6   1472
The *d* praise not the LORD, ... Ps 115:17   4191
as those that have been long *d* .... Ps 143:3   4191
death, and her paths unto the *d* .... Prov 2:18   7496
knoweth not that the *d* are there .... Prov 9:18   7496
in the congregation of the *d* .... Prov 21:16   7496
Wherefore I praised the *d* which .... Eccl 4:2   4191

the *d* which are already *d* more	Eccl 4:2	4191
and after that they go to the *d*	Eccl 9:3	4191
dog is better than a *d* lion	Eccl 9:4	4191
but the *d* know not any thing,	Eccl 9:5	4191
D flies cause the ointment of the	Eccl 10:1	4194
for the living to the *d*	Is 8:19	4191
it stirreth up the *d* for thee	Is 14:9	7496
with the sword, nor *d* in battle	Is 22:2	4191
They are *d*, they shall not live	Is 26:14	4191
Thy *d* men shall live, together	Is 26:19	4191
together with my *d* body shall	Is 26:19	5038
and the earth shall cast out the *d*	Is 26:19	7496
behold, they were all *d* corpses	Is 37:36	4191
are in desolate places as *d* men	Is 59:10	4191
to comfort them for the *d*	Jer 16:7	4191
Weep ye not for the *d*, neither	Jer 22:10	4191
cast his *d* body into the graves	Jer 26:23	5038
the whole valley of the *d* bodies	Jer 31:40	6297
them with the *d* bodies of men	Jer 33:5	6297
their *d* bodies shall be for meat	Jer 34:20	5038
his *d* body shall be cast out in	Jer 36:30	5038
cast all the *d* bodies of the men	Jer 41:9	6297
places, as they that be *d* of old	Lam 3:6	4191
I will lay the *d* carcases of the	Eze 6:5	
cry, make no mourning for the *d*	Eze 24:17	4191
they shall come at no *d* person to	Eze 44:25	4191
of any thing that is *d* of itself	Eze 44:31	5038
there shall be many *d* bodies in	Amos 8:3	6297
by a *d* body touch any of these	Hag 2:13	
But when Herod was *d*, behold, an	Mt 2:19	5053
for they are *d* which sought the	Mt 2:20	2348
and let the *d* bury their *d*	Mt 8:22	3498
saying, My daughter is even now *d*	Mt 9:18	5053
for the maid is not *d*, but	Mt 9:24	599
cleanse the lepers, raise the *d*	Mt 10:8	3498
the *d* are raised up, and the poor	Mt 11:5	3498
he is risen from the *d*	Mt 14:2	3498
of man be risen again from the *d*	Mt 17:9	3498
the resurrection from the *d*	Mt 22:31	3498
God is not the God of the *d*	Mt 22:32	3498
are within full of *d* men's bones	Mt 23:27	3498
people, He is risen from the *d*	Mt 27:64	3498
did shake, and became as *d* men	Mt 28:4	3498
that he is risen from the *d*	Mt 28:7	3498
which said, Thy daughter is *d*	Mk 5:35	599
the damsel is not *d*, but sleepeth	Mk 5:39	599
the Baptist was risen from the *d*	Mk 6:14	3498
he is risen from the *d*	Mk 6:16	3498
Son of man were risen from the *d*	Mk 9:9	3498
the rising from the *d* should mean	Mk 9:10	3498
and he was as one *d*	Mk 9:26	3498
insomuch that many said, He is *d*	Mk 9:26	599
when they shall rise from the *d*	Mk 12:25	3498
And as touching the *d*, that they	Mk 12:26	3498
He is not the God of the *d*	Mk 12:27	3498
marvelled if he were already *d*	Mk 15:44	2348
whether he had been any while *d*	Mk 15:44	599
there was a *d* man carried out,	Lk 7:12	2348
And he that was *d* sat up, and began	Lk 7:15	3498
the *d* are raised, to the poor	Lk 7:22	3498
saying to him, Thy daughter is *d*	Lk 8:49	2348
she is not *d*, but sleepeth	Lk 8:52	599
to scorn, knowing that she was *d*	Lk 8:53	599
that John was risen from the *d*	Lk 9:7	3498
Let the *d* bury their *d*	Lk 9:60	3498
and departed, leaving him half *d*	Lk 10:30	2258
For this my son was *d*, and is	Lk 15:24	3498
for this thy brother was *d*	Lk 15:32	3498
if one went unto them from the *d*	Lk 16:30	3498
though one rose from the *d*	Lk 16:31	3498
and the resurrection from the *d*	Lk 20:35	3498
Now that the *d* are raised	Lk 20:37	3498
For he is not a God of the *d*	Lk 20:38	3498
seek ye the living among the *d*	Lk 24:5	3498
to rise from the *d* the third day	Lk 24:46	3498
therefore he was risen from the *d*	Jn 2:22	3498
as the Father raiseth up the *d*	Jn 5:21	3498
when the *d* shall hear the voice	Jn 5:25	3498
manna in the wilderness, and are *d*	Jn 6:49	599
fathers did eat manna, and are *d*	Jn 6:58	599
Abraham is *d*, and the prophets	Jn 8:52	599
our father Abraham, which is *d*	Jn 8:53	599
and the prophets are *d*	Jn 8:53	599
unto the people plainly, Lazarus is *d*	Jn 11:14	599
believeth in me, though he were *d*	Jn 11:25	599
the sister of him that was *d*	Jn 11:39	2348
for he hath been *d* four days	Jn 11:39	
the place where the *d* was laid	Jn 11:41	2348
And he that was *d* came forth	Jn 11:44	2348
Lazarus was which had been *d*	Jn 12:1	2348
d, whom he raised from the *d*	Jn 12:1	3498

whom he had raised from the *d*	Jn 12:9	3498
grave, and raised him from the *d*	Jn 12:17	3498
and saw that he was *d* already	Jn 19:33	2348
he must rise again from the *d*	Jn 20:9	3498
that he was risen from the *d*	Jn 21:14	3498
David, that he is both *d* and	Acts 2:29	5053
whom God hath raised from the *d*	Acts 3:15	3498
Jesus the resurrection from the *d*	Acts 4:2	3498
whom God raised from the *d*	Acts 4:10	3498
young men came in, and found her *d*	Acts 5:10	3498
thence, when his father was *d*	Acts 7:4	599
with him after he rose from the *d*	Acts 10:41	3498
God to be the Judge of quick and *d*	Acts 10:42	3498
But God raised him from the *d*	Acts 13:30	3498
that he raised him up from the *d*	Acts 13:34	3498
the city, supposing he had been *d*	Acts 14:19	2348
and risen again from the *d*	Acts 17:3	3498
he hath raised him from the *d*	Acts 17:31	3498
of the resurrection of the *d*	Acts 17:32	3498
the third loft, and was taken up *d*	Acts 20:9	3498
resurrection of the *d* I am called	Acts 23:6	3498
shall be a resurrection of the *d*	Acts 24:15	3498
the resurrection of the *d* I am	Acts 24:21	3498
and of one Jesus, which was *d*	Acts 25:19	2348
you, that God should raise the *d*	Acts 26:8	3498
first that should rise from the *d*	Acts 26:23	3498
or fallen down *d* suddenly	Acts 28:6	3498
by the resurrection from the *d*	Rom 1:4	3498
even God, who quickeneth the *d*	Rom 4:17	3498
considered not his own body now *d*	Rom 4:19	3499
up Jesus our Lord from the *d*	Rom 4:24	3498
the offence of one many be *d*	Rom 5:15	599
How shall we, that are *d* to sin	Rom 6:2	599
the *d* by the glory of the Father	Rom 6:4	3498
For he that is *d* is freed from	Rom 6:7	599
Now if we be *d* with Christ	Rom 6:8	599
raised from the *d* dieth no more	Rom 6:9	3498
to be *d* indeed unto sin, but	Rom 6:11	599
those that are alive from the *d*	Rom 6:13	3498
but if the husband be *d*, she is	Rom 7:2	599
but if her husband be *d*, she is	Rom 7:3	599
ye also are become *d* to the law	Rom 7:4	2289
to him who is raised from the *d*	Rom 7:4	3498
that being *d* wherein we were held	Rom 7:6	599
For without the law sin was *d*	Rom 7:8	3498
the body is *d* because of sin	Rom 8:10	3498
up Jesus from the *d* dwell in you	Rom 8:11	3498
d shall also quicken your mortal	Rom 8:11	3498
bring up Christ again from the *d*	Rom 10:7	3498
God hath raised him from the *d*	Rom 10:9	3498
of them be, but life from the *d*	Rom 11:15	3498
he might be Lord both of the *d*	Rom 14:9	3498
but if her husband be *d*, she is	1Cor 7:39	2837
preached that he rose from the *d*	1Cor 15:12	3498
there is no resurrection of the *d*	1Cor 15:12	3498
there be no resurrection of the *d*	1Cor 15:13	3498
up, if so be that the *d* rise not	1Cor 15:15	3498
For if the *d* rise not, then is	1Cor 15:16	3498
now is Christ risen from the *d*	1Cor 15:20	3498
also the resurrection of the *d*	1Cor 15:21	3498
do which are baptized for the *d*	1Cor 15:29	3498
if the *d* rise not at all	1Cor 15:29	3498
are they then baptized for the *d*	1Cor 15:29	3498
it me, if the *d* rise not	1Cor 15:32	3498
will say, How are the *d* raised up	1Cor 15:35	3498
also is the resurrection of the *d*	1Cor 15:42	3498
sound, and the *d* shall be raised	1Cor 15:52	3498
but in God which raiseth the *d*	2Cor 1:9	3498
one died for all, then were all *d*	2Cor 5:14	599
Father, who raised him from the *d*	Gal 1:1	3498
I through the law am *d* to the law	Gal 2:19	599
the law, then Christ is *d* in vain	Gal 2:21	599
when he raised him from the *d*	Eph 1:20	3498
who were *d* in trespasses and sins	Eph 2:1	3498
Even when we were *d* in sins	Eph 2:5	3498
sleepest, and arise from the *d*	Eph 5:14	3498
unto the resurrection of the *d*	Phil 3:11	3498
the firstborn from the *d*	Col 1:18	3498
who hath raised him from the *d*	Col 2:12	3498
being *d* in your sins and the	Col 2:13	3498
Wherefore if ye be *d* with Christ	Col 2:20	599
For ye are *d*, and your life is hid	Col 3:3	599
heaven, whom he raised from the *d*	1Th 1:10	3498
the *d* in Christ shall rise first	1Th 4:16	3498
in pleasure is *d* while she liveth	1Ti 5:6	2348
from the *d* according to my gospel	2Ti 2:8	3498
For if we be *d* with him, we shall	2Ti 2:11	4880
the *d* at his appearing and his	2Ti 4:1	3498
of repentance from *d* works	Heb 6:1	3498
and of resurrection of the *d*	Heb 6:2	3498
purge your conscience from *d*	Heb 9:14	3498

D

is of force after men are *d*	Heb 9:17	3498
and by it he being *d* yet speaketh	Heb 11:4	599
even of one, and him as good as *d*	Heb 11:12	3498
to raise him up, even from the *d*	Heb 11:19	3498
their *d* raised to life again	Heb 11:35	3498
again from the *d* our Lord Jesus	Heb 13:20	3498
faith, if it hath not works, is *d*	Jas 2:17	3498
that faith without works is *d*	Jas 2:20	3498
the body without the spirit is *d*	Jas 2:26	3498
so faith without works is *d* also	Jas 2:26	3498
of Jesus Christ from the *d*	1Pet 1:3	3498
that raised him up from the *d*	1Pet 1:21	3498
being *d* to sins, should live unto	1Pet 2:24	581
ready to judge the quick and the *d*	1Pet 4:5	3498
preached also to them that are *d*	1Pet 4:6	3498
withereth, without fruit, twice *d*	Jude 12	599
and the first begotten of the *d*	Rev 1:5	3498
saw him, I fell at his feet as *d*	Rev 1:17	3498
I am he that liveth, and was *d*	Rev 1:18	3498
first and the last, which was *d*	Rev 2:8	3498
a name that thou livest, and art *d*	Rev 3:1	3498
their *d* bodies shall lie in the	Rev 11:8	4430
see their *d* bodies three days	Rev 11:9	4430
shall not suffer their *d* bodies	Rev 11:9	4430
is come, and the time of the *d*	Rev 11:18	3498
Blessed are the *d* which die in	Rev 14:13	3498
it became as the blood of a *d* man	Rev 16:3	3498
But the rest of the *d* lived not	Rev 20:5	3498
And I saw the *d*, small and great,	Rev 20:12	3498
the *d* were judged out of those	Rev 20:12	3498
gave up the *d* which were in it	Rev 20:13	3498
up the *d* which were in them	Rev 20:13	3498

DEADLY

for there was a *d* destruction	1Sa 5:11	4194
oppress me, from my *d* enemies	Ps 17:9	5315
the groanings of a *d* wounded man	Eze 30:24	
and if they drink any *d* thing	Mk 16:18	2286
an unruly evil, full of *d* poison	Jas 3:8	2287
and his *d* wound was healed	Rev 13:3	2288
beast, whose *d* wound was healed	Rev 13:12	2288

DEADNESS

neither yet the *d* of Sarah's womb	Rom 4:19	3500

DEAF

or who maketh the dumb, or *d*	Ex 4:11	2795
Thou shalt not curse the *d*	Lev 19:14	2795
But I, as a *d* man, heard not	Ps 38:13	2795
they are like the *d* adder that	Ps 58:4	2795
in that day shall the *d* hear the	Is 29:18	2795
the ears of the *d* shall be	Is 35:5	2795
Hear, ye *d*	Is 42:18	2795
or as my messenger that I sent	Is 42:19	2795
eyes, and the *d* that have ears	Is 43:8	2795
mouth, their ears shall be *d*	Mic 7:16	2790
the *d* hear, the dead are raised	Mt 11:5	2974
bring unto him one that was *d*	Mk 7:32	2974
he maketh both the *d* to hear	Mk 7:37	2974
d spirit, I charge thee, come out	Mk 9:25	2974
the *d* hear, the dead are raised,	Lk 7:22	2974

DEAL

now will we *d* worse with thee,	Gen 19:9	
thou wilt not falsely with me	Gen 21:23	
And now if ye will *d* kindly	Gen 24:49	6213
and I will *d* well with thee	Gen 32:9	
Should he *d* with our sister as	Gen 34:31	6213
d kindly and truly with me	Gen 47:29	6213
let us *d* wisely with them	Ex 1:10	
but let not Pharaoh *d* deceitfully	Ex 8:29	
he shall *d* with her after the	Ex 21:9	6213
thou shalt *d* with thy vineyard	Ex 23:11	6213
tenth *d* of flour mingled with the	Ex 29:40	
one tenth *d* of fine flour mingled	Lev 14:21	
not steal, neither *d* falsely	Lev 19:11	
if thou *d* thus with me, kill me,	Num 11:15	6213
tenth *d* of flour mingled with the	Num 15:4	
a several tenth *d* of flour	Num 28:13	
A several tenth *d* shalt thou	Num 28:21	
A several tenth *d* unto one lamb	Num 28:29	
one tenth *d* for one lamb,	Num 29:4	
A several tenth *d* for one lamb	Num 29:10	
a several tenth *d* to each lamb of	Num 29:15	
But thus shall ye *d* with them	Deut 7:5	6213
the land, that we will *d* kindly	Josh 2:14	6213
the LORD *d* kindly with you, as ye	Ruth 1:8	6213
Therefore thou shalt *d* kindly	1Sa 20:8	6213
D gently for my sake with the	2Sa 18:5	
As thou didst *d* with David my	2Chr 2:3	
dwell therein, even so *d* with me	2Chr 2:3	
D courageously, and the LORD shall	2Chr 19:11	6213
lest I *d* with you after your	Job 42:8	6213

unto the fools, *D* not foolishly	Ps 75:4	
to *d* subtilly with his servants	Ps 105:25	
D bountifully with thy servant,	Ps 119:17	1580
D with thy servant according unto	Ps 119:124	6213
for thou shalt *d* bountifully with	Ps 142:7	1580
but they that *d* truly are his	Prov 12:22	6213
of uprightness he will *d* unjustly	Is 26:10	
make an end to *d* treacherously	Is 33:1	
they shall *d* treacherously with	Is 33:1	
wouldest *d* very treacherously	Is 48:8	
my servant shall *d* prudently	Is 52:13	
Is it not to *d* thy bread to the	Is 58:7	6536
happy that *d* very treacherously	Jer 12:1	
d thus with them in the time of	Jer 18:23	6213
if so be that the LORD will *d*	Jer 21:2	6213
Therefore will I also *d* in fury	Eze 8:18	6213
I will even *d* with thee as thou	Eze 16:59	6213
kept my judgments, to *d* truly	Eze 18:9	6213
the days that I shall *d* with thee	Eze 22:14	6213
they shall *d* furiously with thee	Eze 23:25	6213
they shall *d* with thee hatefully,	Eze 23:29	6213
he shall surely *d* with him	Eze 31:11	6213
thou seest, *d* with thy servants	Dan 1:13	6213
shall *d* against them, and shall	Dan 11:7	6213
upon them that *d* treacherously	Hab 1:13	
why do we *d* treacherously every	Mal 2:10	
let none *d* treacherously against	Mal 2:15	
that ye *d* not treacherously	Mal 2:16	
more a great *d* they published it	Mk 7:36	4054
but he cried the more a great *d*	Mk 10:48	

DEALER

the treacherous *d* dealeth	Is 21:2	

DEALERS

the treacherous *d* have dealt	Is 24:16	
the treacherous *d* have dealt very	Is 24:16	

DEALEST

Wherefore *d* thou thus with thy	Ex 5:15	6213
d treacherously, and they dealt	Is 33:1	

DEALETH

thus with Micah with me, and hath	Judg 18:4	6213
told me that he *d* very subtilly	1Sa 23:22	
poor that *d* with a slack hand	Prov 10:4	6213
prudent man *d* with knowledge	Prov 13:16	6213
He that is soon angry *d* foolishly	Prov 14:17	6213
is his name, who *d* in proud wrath	Prov 21:24	6213
dealer *d* treacherously, and the	Is 21:2	
the priest every one *d* falsely	Jer 6:13	6213
the priest every one *d* falsely	Jer 8:10	6213
God *d* with you as with sons	Heb 12:7	4374

DEALING

his violent *d* shall come down	Ps 7:16	

DEALINGS

of your evil *d* by all this people	1Sa 2:23	1697
have no *d* with the Samaritans	Jn 4:9	4798

DEALS

three tenth *d* of fine flour for a	Lev 14:10	
thereof shall be two tenth *d* of	Lev 23:13	
two wave loaves of two tenth *d*	Lev 23:17	
two tenth *d* shall be in one cake	Lev 24:5	
for a meat offering two tenth *d*	Num 15:6	
d of flour mingled with half an	Num 15:9	
two tenth *d* of flour for a meat	Num 28:9	
three tenth *d* of flour for a meat	Num 28:12	
two tenth *d* of flour for a meat	Num 28:12	
three tenth *d* shall ye offer for	Num 28:20	
bullock, and two tenth *d* for a ram	Num 28:20	
three tenth *d* unto one bullock,	Num 28:28	
two tenth *d* unto one ram,	Num 28:28	
three tenth *d* for a bullock	Num 29:3	
and two tenth *d* for a ram	Num 29:3	
three tenth *d* to a bullock	Num 29:9	
and two tenth *d* to one ram,	Num 29:9	
three tenth *d* unto every bullock	Num 29:14	
two tenth *d* to each ram of the	Num 29:14	

DEALT

when Sarai *d* hardly with her, she	Gen 16:6	
because God hath *d* graciously	Gen 33:11	
Wherefore *d* ye so ill with me, as	Gen 43:6	
Therefore God *d* well with the	Ex 1:20	
hast thou *d* thus with us, to	Ex 14:11	6213
they proudly he was above them	Ex 18:11	
seeing he hath *d* deceitfully with	Ex 21:8	
if ye have *d* well with Jerubbaal	Judg 9:16	6213
If ye then have *d* truly and	Judg 9:19	6213
and the men of Shechem *d*	Judg 9:23	
as ye have *d* with the dead, and	Ruth 1:8	6213
hath *d* very bitterly with me	Ruth 1:20	

how that thou hast *d* well with me .... 1Sa 24:18 | 6213
shall have *d* well with my lord 1Sa 25:31
he *d* among all the people, even .... 2Sa 6:19 | 2505
for they *d* faithfully .... 2Kin 12:15 | 6213
d with familiar spirits and .... 2Kin 21:6 | 6213
hand, because they *d* faithfully............... 2Kin 22:7 | 6213
he *d* to every one of Israel, both .... 1Chr 16:3 | 2505
Even so *d* David with all the.................. 1Chr 20:3 | 6213
done amiss, and have *d* wickedly 2Chr 6:37
he *d* wisely, and dispersed of all 2Chr 11:23
d with a familiar spirit, and with........... 2Chr 33:6 | 6213
We have *d* very corruptly against .... Neh 1:7
that they *d* proudly against them .... Neh 9:10
But they and our fathers *d* proudly .... Neh 9:16
yet they *d* proudly, and hearkened .... Neh 9:29
My brethren have *d* deceitfully as........ Job 6:15
because he hath *d* bountifully................. Ps 13:6 | 1580
neither have we *d* falsely in thy .... Ps 44:17
d unfaithfully like their fathers .... Ps 78:57
He hath not *d* with us after our .... Ps 103:10 | 6213
for the LORD hath *d* bountifully............... Ps 116:7 | 1580
Thou hast *d* well with thy servant .... Ps 119:65 | 6213
for they *d* perversely with me .... Ps 119:78
He hath not *d* so with any nation .... Ps 147:20 | 6213
dealers have *d* treacherously .... Is 24:16
dealers have *d* very treacherously .... Is 24:16
they *d* not treacherously with .... Is 33:1
so have ye *d* treacherously with .... Jer 3:20
the house of Judah have *d* very .... Jer 5:11
even they have *d* treacherously .... Jer 12:6
all her friends have *d* .... Lam 1:2
in the midst of thee have they *d* .... Eze 22:7 | 6213
Because that Edom hath *d* against .... Eze 25:12 | 6213
the Philistines have *d* by revenge .... Eze 25:15 | 6213
They have *d* treacherously against .... Hos 5:7
there have they *d* treacherously............. Hos 6:7
that hath *d* wondrously with you .... Joel 2:26 | 6213
our doings, so hath he *d* with us .... Zec 1:6 | 6213
Judah hath *d* treacherously, and an ...... Mal 2:11
whom thou hast *d* treacherously .... Mal 2:14
Thus hath the Lord *d* with me in .... Lk 1:25 | 4160
Son, why hast thou thus *d* with us .... Lk 2:48 | 4160
The same *d* subtilly with our .... Acts 7:19 | 2686
of the Jews have *d* with me .... Acts 25:24 | 1793
according as God hath *d* to every .... Rom 12:3 | 3307

DEAR

Is Ephraim my *d* son .... Jer 31:20 | 3357
who was *d* unto him, was sick, and .... Lk 7:2 | 1784
count I my life *d* unto myself .... Acts 20:24 | 5093
followers of God, as *d* children .... Eph 5:1 | 27
of Epaphras our *d* fellowservant .... Col 1:7 | 27
us into the kingdom of his *d* Son .... Col 1:13 | 26
souls, because ye were *d* unto us........... 1Th 2:8 | 27

DEARLY

I have given the *d* beloved of my .... Jer 12:7
D beloved, avenge not yourselves, ... Rom 12:19
my *d* beloved, flee from idolatry 1Cor 10:14
these promises *d* beloved, let us 2Cor 7:1
d beloved, for your edifying 2Cor 12:19
Therefore, my brethren *d* beloved .... Phil 4:1
fast in the Lord, my *d* beloved .... Phil 4:1
To Timothy, my *d* beloved son................ 2Ti 1:2
unto Philemon our *d* beloved .... Philem 1
D beloved, I beseech you as 1Pet 2:11

DEARTH

seven years of *d* began to come............. Gen 41:54 | 7458
and the *d* was in all lands .... Gen 41:54 | 7458
and there was a *d* in the land .... 2Kin 4:38 | 7458
If there be *d* in the land.......................... 2Chr 6:28 | 7458
might buy corn, because of the *d* .... Neh 5:3 | 7458
came to Jeremiah concerning the *d* ...... Jer 14:1 | 1226
Now there came a *d* over all the............ Acts 7:11 | 3042
great *d* throughout all the world .... Acts 11:28 | 3042

DEATH

Let me not see the *d* of the child .... Gen 21:16 | 4194
comforted after his mother's *d* .... Gen 24:67
to pass after the *d* of Abraham............... Gen 25:11 | 4194
his wife shall surely be put to *d* .... Gen 26:11 | 4191
them after the *d* of Abraham.................. Gen 26:18 | 4194
old, I know not the day of my *d* .... Gen 27:2 | 4194
thee before the LORD before my *d*.......... Gen 27:7 | 4194
he may bless thee before his *d* .... Gen 27:10 | 4194
may take away from me this *d* only .... Ex 10:17 | 4194
mount shall be surely put to *d*............... Ex 19:12 | 4191
he die, shall be surely put to *d* .... Ex 21:12 | 4191
mother, shall be surely put to *d* .... Ex 21:15 | 4191
hand, he shall surely be put to *d* .... Ex 21:16 | 4191
mother, shall surely be put to *d* .... Ex 21:17 | 4191
his owner also shall be put to *d*............. Ex 21:29 | 4191

a beast shall surely be put to *d* .... Ex 22:19 | 4191
it shall surely be put to *d* .... Ex 31:14 | 4191
day, he shall surely be put to *d*.............. Ex 31:15 | 4191
work therein shall be put to *d* .... Ex 35:2 | 4191
the *d* of the two sons of Aaron .... Lev 16:1 | 4194
they shall not be put to *d* .... Lev 19:20 | 4191
he shall surely be put to *d* .... Lev 20:2 | 4191
mother shall be surely put to *d* .... Lev 20:9 | 4191
shall surely be put to *d*.......................... Lev 20:10 | 4191
of them shall surely be put to *d* .... Lev 20:11 | 4191
of them shall surely be put to *d* .... Lev 20:12 | 4191
they shall surely be put to *d* .... Lev 20:13 | 4191
he shall surely be put to *d* .... Lev 20:15 | 4191
they shall surely be put to *d* .... Lev 20:16 | 4191
wizard, shall surely be put to *d* .... Lev 20:27 | 4191
LORD, he shall surely be put to *d* .... Lev 24:16 | 4191
of the LORD, shall be put to *d* .... Lev 24:16 | 4191
any man shall surely be put to *d*............ Lev 24:17 | 4191
a man, he shall be put to *d* .... Lev 24:21 | 4191
but shall surely be put to *d* .... Lev 27:29 | 4191
cometh nigh shall be put to *d* .... Num 1:51 | 4191
cometh nigh shall be put to *d* .... Num 3:10 | 4191
cometh nigh shall be put to *d* .... Num 3:38 | 4191
The man shall be surely put to *d* .... Num 15:35 | 4191
men die the common *d* of all men.......... Num 16:29 | 4194
cometh nigh shall be put to *d* .... Num 18:7 | 4191
Let me die the *d* of the righteous .... Num 23:10 | 4194
murderer shall surely be put to *d* .... Num 35:16 | 4191
murderer shall surely be put to *d* .... Num 35:17 | 4191
murderer shall surely be put to *d* .... Num 35:18 | 4191
him shall surely be put to *d* .... Num 35:21 | 4191
it unto the *d* of the high priest .... Num 35:25 | 4194
until the *d* of the high priest .... Num 35:28 | 4194
but after the *d* of the high .... Num 35:28 | 4194
to *d* by the mouth of witnesses .... Num 35:30 | 7523
a murderer, which is guilty of *d* .... Num 35:31 | 4191
but he shall be surely put to *d* .... Num 35:31 | 4194
until the *d* of the priest .... Num 35:32 | 4194
of dreams, shall be put to *d* .... Deut 13:5 | 4191
be first upon him to put him to *d* .... Deut 13:9 | 4191
is worthy of *d* be put to *d* .... Deut 17:6 | 4191
witness he shall not be put to *d* .... Deut 17:6 | 4191
be first upon him to put him to *d* .... Deut 17:7 | 4191
whereas he was not worthy of *d* .... Deut 19:6 | 4194
have committed a sin worthy of *d* .... Deut 21:22 | 4194
and he be to be put to *d* .... Deut 21:22 | 4191
in the damsel no sin worthy of *d* .... Deut 22:26 | 4194
not be put to *d* for the children............. Deut 24:16 | 4191
be put to *d* for the fathers .... Deut 24:16 | 4191
shall be put to *d* for his own sin .... Deut 24:16 | 4191
thee this day life and good, and *d* .... Deut 30:15 | 4194
I have set before you life and *d* .... Deut 30:19 | 4194
and how much more after my *d* .... Deut 31:27 | 4194
my *d* ye will utterly corrupt .... Deut 31:29 | 4194
children of Israel before his *d* .... Deut 33:1 | 4194
Now after the *d* of Moses the.................. Josh 1:1 | 4194
him, he shall be put to *d* .... Josh 1:18 | 4191
have, and deliver our lives from *d* .... Josh 2:13 | 4194
until the *d* of the high priest .... Josh 20:6 | 4194
Now after the *d* of Joshua it came.......... Judg 1:1 | 4194
jeoparded their lives unto the *d* .... Judg 5:18 | 4194
let him be put to *d* whilst it is .... Judg 6:31 | 4191
from the womb to the day of his *d* .... Judg 13:7 | 4194
so that his soul was vexed unto *d*........... Judg 16:16 | 4191
d were more than they which he............. Judg 16:30 | 4194
Gibeah, that we may put them to *d* .... Judg 20:13 | 4191
He shall surely be put to *d*..................... Judg 21:5 | 4191
also, if ought but *d* part thee .... Ruth 1:17 | 4194
law since the *d* of thine husband .... Ruth 2:11 | 4194
about the time of her *d* the women .... 1Sa 4:20 | 4191
men, that we may put them to *d* .... 1Sa 11:12 | 4191
not a man be put to *d* this day .... 1Sa 11:13 | 4191
the bitterness of *d* is past .... 1Sa 15:32 | 4194
see Saul until the day of his *d*................ 1Sa 15:35 | 4194
is but a step between me and *d* .... 1Sa 20:3 | 4194
I have occasioned the *d* of all 1Sa 22:22
came to pass after the *d* of Saul .... 2Sa 1:1 | 4194
in their *d* they were not divided .... 2Sa 1:23 | 4194
no child unto the day of her *d* .... 2Sa 6:23 | 4194
two lines measured he to put to *d* .... 2Sa 8:2 | 4191
shall be, whether in *d* or life .... 2Sa 15:21 | 4194
not Shimei be put to *d* for this .... 2Sa 19:21 | 4191
be put to *d* this day in Israel .... 2Sa 19:22 | 4191
shut up unto the day of their *d* .... 2Sa 20:3 | 4191
were put to *d* in the days of................... 2Sa 21:9 | 4194
When the waves of *d* compassed me...... 2Sa 22:5 | 4194
the snares of *d* prevented me .... 2Sa 22:6 | 4194
not put thee to *d* with the sword............ 1Kin 2:8 | 4191
shall be put to *d* this day .... 1Kin 2:24 | 4194
for thou art worthy of *d* .... 1Kin 2:26 | 4194
not at this time put thee to *d* .... 1Kin 2:26 | 4191

D

in Egypt until the *d* of Solomon	1Kin 11:40	4194
Israel after the *d* of Ahab	2Kin 1:1	4194
thence any more *d* or barren land	2Kin 2:21	4194
man of God, there is *d* in the pot	2Kin 4:40	4194
not be put to *d* for the children	2Kin 14:6	4191
be put to *d* for the fathers	2Kin 14:6	4191
shall be put to *d* for his own sin	2Kin 14:6	4191
king of Judah lived after the *d*	2Kin 14:17	4194
was a leper unto the day of his *d*	2Kin 15:5	4194
days was Hezekiah sick unto *d*	2Kin 20:1	4191
prepared abundantly before his *d*	1Chr 22:5	4194
God of Israel should be put to *d*	2Chr 15:13	4191
after the *d* of his father to his	2Chr 22:4	4194
the house, he shall be put to *d*	2Chr 23:7	4191
Now after the *d* of Jehoiada came	2Chr 24:17	4194
d of Joash son of Jehoahaz king	2Chr 25:25	4194
was a leper unto the day of his *d*	2Chr 26:21	4194
days Hezekiah was sick to the *d*	2Chr 32:24	4191
Jerusalem did him honour at his *d*	2Chr 32:33	4194
upon him, whether it be unto *d*	Ezr 7:26	4193
is one law of his to put him to *d*	Est 4:11	4191
and the shadow of *d* stain it	Job 3:5	6757
Which long for *d*, but it cometh	Job 3:21	4194
he shall redeem thee from *d*	Job 5:20	4194
and *d* rather than my life	Job 7:15	4194
of darkness and the shadow of *d*	Job 10:21	6757
and of the shadow of *d*, without	Job 10:22	6757
out to light the shadow of *d*	Job 12:22	6757
on my eyelids is the shadow of *d*	Job 16:16	6757
even the firstborn of *d* shall	Job 18:13	4194
to them even as the shadow of *d*	Job 24:17	6757
in the terrors of the shadow of *d*	Job 24:17	6757
of him shall be buried in *d*	Job 27:15	4194
of darkness, and the shadow of *d*	Job 28:3	6757
d say, We have heard the fame	Job 28:22	4194
know that thou wilt bring me to *d*	Job 30:23	4194
is no darkness, nor shadow of *d*	Job 34:22	6757
Have the gates of *d* been opened	Job 38:17	4194
seen the doors of the shadow of *d*	Job 38:17	6757
For in *d* there is no remembrance	Ps 6:5	4194
for him the instruments of *d*	Ps 7:13	4194
liftest me up from the gates of *d*	Ps 9:13	4194
eyes, lest I sleep the sleep of *d*	Ps 13:3	4194
The sorrows of *d* compassed me	Ps 18:4	4194
the snares of *d* prevented me	Ps 18:5	4194
brought me into the dust of *d*	Ps 22:15	4194
the valley of the shadow of *d*	Ps 23:4	6757
To deliver their soul from *d*	Ps 33:19	4194
covered us with the shadow of *d*	Ps 44:19	6757
he will be our guide even unto *d*	Ps 48:14	4192
d shall feed on them	Ps 49:14	4194
the terrors of *d* are fallen upon	Ps 55:4	4194
Let *d* seize upon them, and let	Ps 55:15	4194
hast delivered my soul from *d*	Ps 56:13	4194
the Lord belong the issues from *d*	Ps 68:20	4194
For there are no bands in their *d*	Ps 73:4	4194
he spared not their soul from *d*	Ps 78:50	4194
that liveth, and shall not see *d*	Ps 89:48	4194
those that are appointed to *d*	Ps 102:20	8546
in darkness and in the shadow of *d*	Ps 107:10	6757
of darkness and the shadow of *d*	Ps 107:14	6757
draw near unto the gates of *d*	Ps 107:18	4194
The sorrows of *d* compassed me	Ps 116:3	4194
hast delivered my soul from *d*	Ps 116:8	4194
the LORD is the *d* of his saints	Ps 116:15	4194
he hath not given me over unto *d*	Ps 118:18	4194
For her house inclineth unto *d*	Prov 2:18	4194
Her feet go down to *d*	Prov 5:5	4194
going down to the chambers of *d*	Prov 7:27	4194
all they that hate me love *d*	Prov 8:36	4194
righteousness delivereth from *d*	Prov 10:2	4194
righteousness delivereth from *d*	Prov 11:4	4194
evil pursueth it to his own *d*	Prov 11:19	4194
the pathway thereof there is no *d*	Prov 12:28	4194
to depart from the snares of *d*	Prov 13:14	4194
the end thereof are the ways of *d*	Prov 14:12	4194
to depart from the snares of *d*	Prov 14:27	4194
the righteous hath hope in his *d*	Prov 14:32	4194
of a king is as messengers of *d*	Prov 16:14	4194
the end thereof are the ways of *d*	Prov 16:25	4194
D and life are in the power of the	Prov 18:21	4194
to and fro of them that seek *d*	Prov 21:6	4194
them that are drawn unto *d*	Prov 24:11	4194
casteth firebrands, arrows, and *d*	Prov 26:18	4194
the day of *d* than the day of	Eccl 7:1	4194
find more bitter than *d* the woman	Eccl 7:26	4194
hath he power in the day of *d*	Eccl 8:8	4194
for love is strong as *d*	Song 8:6	4194
in the land of the shadow of *d*	Is 9:2	6757
He will swallow up *d* in victory	Is 25:8	4194
We have made a covenant with *d*	Is 28:15	4194
your covenant with *d* shall be	Is 28:18	4194
days was Hezekiah sick unto *d*	Is 38:1	4191
thee, *d* can not celebrate thee	Is 38:18	4194
wicked, and with the rich in his *d*	Is 53:9	4194
hath poured out his soul unto *d*	Is 53:12	4194
of drought, and of the shadow of *d*	Jer 2:6	6757
d shall be chosen rather than	Jer 8:3	4194
For *d* is come up into our windows	Jer 9:21	4194
he turn it into the shadow of *d*	Jer 13:16	6757
Such as are for *d*, to *d*	Jer 15:2	4194
Such as are for *d*, to *d*	Jer 15:2	4194
and let their men be put to *d*	Jer 18:21	4194
the way of life, and the way of *d*	Jer 21:8	4194
certain, that if ye put me to *d*	Jer 26:15	4191
and all Judah put him at all to *d*	Jer 26:19	4191
the king sought to put him to *d*	Jer 26:21	4191
of the people to put him to *d*	Jer 26:24	4191
thee, let this man be put to *d*	Jer 38:4	4191
wilt thou not surely put me to *d*	Jer 38:15	4191
soul, I will not put thee to *d*	Jer 38:16	4191
us, and we will not put thee to *d*	Jer 38:25	4191
that they might put us to *d*	Jer 43:3	4191
such as are for *d* to *d*	Jer 43:11	4194
in prison till the day of his *d*	Jer 52:11	4194
put them to *d* in Riblah in the	Jer 52:27	4191
a portion until the day of his *d*	Jer 52:34	4194
bereaveth, at home there is as *d*	Lam 1:20	4194
in the *d* of him that dieth	Eze 18:32	4194
for they are all delivered unto *d*	Eze 31:14	4194
pleasure in the *d* of the wicked	Eze 33:11	4194
I will redeem them from *d*	Hos 13:14	4194
O *d*, I will be thy plagues	Hos 13:14	4194
the shadow of *d* into the morning	Amos 5:8	6757
do well to be angry, even unto *d*	Jonah 4:9	4194
his desire as hell, and is as *d*	Hab 2:5	4194
And was there until the *d* of Herod	Mt 2:15	5054
shadow of *d* light is sprung up	Mt 4:16	2288
shall deliver up the brother to *d*	Mt 10:21	2288
and cause them to be put to *d*	Mt 10:21	2289
when he would have put them to *d*	Mt 14:5	615
or mother, let him die the *d*	Mt 15:4	2288
here, which shall not taste of *d*	Mt 16:28	2288
and they shall condemn him to *d*	Mt 20:18	2288
exceeding sorrowful, even unto *d*	Mt 26:38	2288
against Jesus, to put him to *d*	Mt 26:59	2289
and said, He is guilty of *d*	Mt 26:66	2288
against Jesus to put him to *d*	Mt 27:1	2289
daughter lieth at the point of *d*	Mk 5:23	2079
or mother, let him die the *d*	Mk 7:10	2288
here, which shall not taste of *d*	Mk 9:1	2288
and they shall condemn him to *d*	Mk 10:33	2288
shall betray the brother to *d*	Mk 13:12	2288
shall cause them to be put to *d*	Mk 13:12	2289
him by craft, and put him to *d*	Mk 14:1	615
is exceeding sorrowful unto *d*	Mk 14:34	2288
against Jesus to put him to *d*	Mk 14:55	2289
condemned him to be guilty of *d*	Mk 14:64	2288
in darkness and in the shadow of *d*	Lk 1:79	2288
Ghost, that he should not see *d*	Lk 2:26	2288
here, which shall not taste of *d*	Lk 9:27	2288
scourge him, and put him to *d*	Lk 18:33	615
shall they cause to be put to *d*	Lk 21:16	2289
thee, both into prison, and to *d*	Lk 22:33	2288
worthy of *d* is done unto him	Lk 23:15	2288
I have found no cause of *d* in him	Lk 23:22	2288
led with him to be put to *d*	Lk 23:32	337
him to be condemned to *d*, and have	Lk 24:20	2288
for he was at the point of *d*	Jn 4:47	599
but is passed from *d* unto life	Jn 5:24	2288
my saying, he shall never see *d*	Jn 8:51	2288
saying, he shall never taste of *d*	Jn 8:52	2288
said, This sickness is not unto *d*	Jn 11:4	2288
Howbeit Jesus spake of his *d*	Jn 11:13	2288
together for to put him to *d*	Jn 11:53	615
they might put Lazarus also to *d*	Jn 12:10	615
signifying what *d* he should die	Jn 12:33	2288
lawful for us to put any man to *d*	Jn 18:31	615
signifying what *d* he should die	Jn 18:32	2288
signifying by what *d* he should	Jn 21:19	2288
up, having loosed the pains of *d*	Acts 2:24	2288
And Saul was consenting unto his *d*	Acts 8:1	336
that should be put to *d*	Acts 12:19	520
they found no cause of *d* in him	Acts 13:28	2288
I persecuted this way unto the *d*	Acts 22:4	2288
by, and consenting unto his *d*	Acts 22:20	336
charge worthy of *d* or of bonds	Acts 23:29	336
committed any thing worthy of *d*	Acts 25:11	336
had committed nothing worthy of *d*	Acts 25:25	336
and when they were put to *d*	Acts 26:10	337
nothing worthy of *d* or of bonds	Acts 26:31	2288
there was no cause of *d* in me	Acts 28:18	2288

such things are worthy of *d* .... Rom 1:32 2288
to God by the *d* of his Son.................... Rom 5:10 2288
into the world, and *d* by sin................. Rom 5:12 2288
so *d* passed upon all men, for .... Rom 5:12 2288
Nevertheless *d* reigned from Adam .... Rom 5:14 2288
man's offence *d* reigned by one .... Rom 5:17 2288
That as sin hath reigned unto *d* .... Rom 5:21 2288
Christ were baptized into his *d* .... Rom 6:3 2288
buried with him by baptism into *d* .... Rom 6:4 2288
together in the likeness of his *d* .... Rom 6:5 2288
d hath no more dominion over him .... Rom 6:9 2288
whether of sin unto *d*, or of .... Rom 6:16 2288
for the end of those things is *d* .... Rom 6:21 2288
For the wages of sin is *d* .... Rom 6:23 2288
to bring forth fruit unto *d* .... Rom 7:5 2288
to life, I found to be unto *d* .... Rom 7:10 2288
that which is good made *d* unto me .... Rom 7:13 2288
working *d* in me by that which is .... Rom 7:13 2288
me from the body of this *d* .... Rom 7:24 2288
me free from the law of sin and *d* .... Rom 8:2 2288
For to be carnally minded is *d* .... Rom 8:6 2288
I am persuaded, that neither *d* .... Rom 8:38 2288
or the world, or life, or *d* 1Cor 3:22 2288
last, as it were appointed to *d* 1Cor 4:9 1935
do shew the Lord's *d* till he come 1Cor 11:26 2288
For since by man came *d*, by man......... 1Cor 15:21 2288
that shall be destroyed is *d* 1Cor 15:26 2288
D is swallowed up in victory 1Cor 15:54 2288
O *d*, where is thy sting 1Cor 15:55 2288
The sting of *d* is sin 1Cor 15:56 2288
the sentence of *d* in ourselves 2Cor 1:9 2288
delivered us from so great a *d* 2Cor 1:10 2288
we are the savour of *d* unto *d* 2Cor 2:16 2288
we are the savour of *d* unto *d* 2Cor 2:16 2288
But if the ministration of *d* 2Cor 3:7 2288
delivered unto *d* for Jesus' sake............ 2Cor 4:11 2288
So then *d* worketh in us, but life 2Cor 4:12 2288
the sorrow of the world worketh *d*......... 2Cor 7:10 2288
whether it be by life, or by *d* .... Phil 1:20 2288
and became obedient unto *d* .... Phil 2:8 2288
even the *d* of the cross .... Phil 2:8 2288
indeed he was sick nigh unto *d* .... Phil 2:27 2288
work of Christ he was nigh unto *d* .... Phil 2:30 2288
being made conformable unto his *d*........ Phil 3:10 2288
the body of his flesh through *d* .... Col 1:22 2288
Christ, who hath abolished *d* 2Ti 1:10 2288
the angels for the suffering of *d* .... Heb 2:9 2288
God should taste *d* for every man .... Heb 2:9 2288
that through *d* he might destroy .... Heb 2:14 2288
him that had the power of *d* .... Heb 2:14 2288
them who through fear of *d* were .... Heb 2:15 2288
that was able to save him from *d* .... Heb 5:7 2288
to continue by reason of *d* .... Heb 7:23 2288
new testament, that by means of *d*........ Heb 9:15 2288
be the *d* of the testator .... Heb 9:16 2288
that he should not see *d* .... Heb 11:5 2288
it is finished, bringeth forth *d* .... Jas 1:15 2288
his way shall save a soul from *d* .... Jas 5:20 2288
God, being put to *d* in the flesh 1Pet 3:18 2288
we have passed from *d* unto life 1Jn 3:14 2289
not his brother abideth in *d* 1Jn 3:14 2288
sin a sin which is not unto *d* 1Jn 5:16 2288
life for him that sin not unto *d* 1Jn 5:16 2288
There is a sin unto *d* 1Jn 5:16 2288
and there is a sin not unto *d* 1Jn 5:17 2288
and have the keys of hell and of *d* ...... Rev 1:18 2288
be thou faithful unto *d*, and I .... Rev 2:10 2288
shall not be hurt of the second *d* .... Rev 2:11 2288
I will kill her children with *d* .... Rev 2:23 2288
and his name that sat on him was *D* ..... Rev 6:8 2288
sword, and with hunger, and with *d* ...... Rev 6:8 2288
And in those days shall men seek *d* ...... Rev 9:6 2288
to die, and *d* shall flee from them.......... Rev 9:6 2288
loved not their lives unto the *d* .... Rev 12:11 2288
his heads as it were wounded to *d* .... Rev 13:3 2288
her plagues come in one day, *d*............. Rev 18:8 2288
such the second *d* hath no power .... Rev 20:6 2288
and *d* and hell delivered up the .... Rev 20:13 2288
And *d* and hell were cast into the .... Rev 20:14 2288
This is the second *d* .... Rev 20:14 2288
and there shall be no more *d* .... Rev 21:4 2288
which is the second *d* .... Rev 21:8 2288

DEATHS
They shall die of grievous *d* .... Jer 16:4 4463
thou shalt die the *d* of them that .... Eze 28:8 4463
Thou shalt die the *d* of the .... Eze 28:10 4194
prisons more frequent, in *d* oft 2Cor 11:23 2288

DEBASE
didst *d* thyself even unto hell .... Is 57:9 8213

DEBATE
D thy cause with thy neighbour .... Prov 25:9 7378
forth, thou wilt *d* with it..................... Is 27:8 7378
Behold, ye fast for strife and *d* .... Is 58:4 4683
full of envy, murder, *d*, deceit, ... Rom 1:29 2054

DEBATES
lest there be *d*, envyings, wraths 2Cor 12:20 2054

DEBIR (de'-bur) See Kirjath-sannah, Kirjath-sepher.
  1. An Amorite king.
unto *D* king of Eglon, saying,............... Josh 10:3 1688
  2. A city in Judah.
and all Israel with him, to *D* .... Josh 10:38 1688
done to Hebron, so he did to *D*............. Josh 10:39 1688
mountains, from Hebron, from *D* .... Josh 11:21 1688
The king of *D*, one .... Josh 12:13 1688
toward *D* from the valley of Achor......... Josh 15:7 1688
up thence to the inhabitants of *D* .... Josh 15:15 1688
and the name of *D* before was .... Josh 15:15 1688
and Kirjath-sannah, which is *D* .... Josh 15:49 1688
suburbs, and *D* with her suburbs,.......... Josh 21:15 1688
went against the inhabitants of *D* .... Judg 1:11 1688
and the name of *D* before was .... Judg 1:11 1688
her suburbs, *D* with her suburbs, ... 1Chr 6:58 1688
  3. The boundary of Gad.
Mahanaim unto the border of *D* .... Josh 13:26 1688

DEBORAH (deb'-o-rah)
  1. Rebekah's nurse.
But *D* Rebekah's nurse died, and .... Gen 35:8 1683
  2. A judge of Israel.
And *D*, a prophetess, the wife of............ Judg 4:4 1683
the palm tree of *D* between Ramah .... Judg 4:5 1683
D arose, and went with Barak to .... Judg 4:9 1683
and *D* went up with him .... Judg 4:10 1683
And *D* said unto Barak, Up................... Judg 4:14 1683
Then sang *D* and Barak the son of .... Judg 5:1 1683
in Israel, until that I *D* arose .... Judg 5:7 1683
Awake, awake, *D* .... Judg 5:12 1683
princes of Issachar were with *D* .... Judg 5:15 1683

DEBT
and every one that was in *d* 1Sa 22:2 5378
Go, sell the oil, and pay thy *d* 2Kin 4:7 5386
year, and the exaction of every *d* .... Neh 10:31 3027
loosed him, and forgave him the *d* ...... Mt 18:27 1156
prison, till he should pay the *d* .... Mt 18:27 3784
I forgave thee all that *d* .... Mt 18:32 3782
not reckoned of grace, but of *d* .... Rom 4:4 3783

DEBTOR
hath restored to the *d* his pledge .... Eze 18:7 2326
the gold of the temple, he is a *d* .... Mt 23:16 3784
I am *d* both to the Greeks, and to .... Rom 1:14 3781
that he is a *d* to do the whole.............. Gal 5:3 3781

DEBTORS
us our debts, as we forgive our *d* .... Mt 6:12 3781
certain creditor which had two *d* .... Lk 7:41 5533
one of his lord's *d* unto him .... Lk 16:5 5533
Therefore, brethren, we are *d* .... Rom 8:12 3781
and their *d* they are.......................... Rom 15:27 3781

DEBTS
of them that are sureties for *d* .... Prov 22:26 4859
And forgive us our *d*, as we.............. Mt 6:12 3783

DECAPOLIS (de-cap'-o-lis) A district east of the Jordan
River.
of people from Galilee, and from *D* .... Mt 4:25 1179
began to publish in *D* how great .... Mk 5:20 1179
the midst of the coasts of *D* .... Mk 7:31 1179

DECAY
poor, and fallen in *d* with thee .... Lev 25:35 4131

DECAYED
of the bearers of burdens is *d* .... Neh 4:10 3782
raise up the *d* places thereof................ Is 44:26 2723

DECAYETH
fail from the sea, and the flood *d*........... Job 14:11 2717
much slothfulness the building *d* .... Eccl 10:18 4355
Now that which *d* and waxeth old is ...... Heb 8:13 3822

DECEASE
spake of his *d* which he should .... Lk 9:31 1841
that ye may be able after my *d* to 2Pet 1:15 1841

DECEASED
they are *d*, they shall not rise .... Is 26:14 7496
when he had married a wife, *d*.............. Mt 22:25 5053

DECEIT
and their belly prepareth *d* .... Job 15:35 4820
wickedness, nor my tongue utter *d* .... Job 27:4 7423
or if my foot hath hasted to *d* .... Job 31:5 4820

DECEITFUL

His mouth is full of cursing and *d*	Ps 10:7	4820
of his mouth are iniquity and *d*	Ps 36:3	4820
to evil, and thy tongue frameth *d*	Ps 50:19	4820
d and guile depart not from her	Ps 55:11	8496
He shall redeem their soul from *d*	Ps 72:14	8496
He that worketh *d* shall not dwell	Ps 101:7	7423
for their *d* is falsehood	Ps 119:118	8649
the counsels of the wicked are *d*	Prov 12:5	4820
but a false witness *d*	Prov 12:17	4820
D is in the heart of them that	Prov 12:20	4820
but the folly of fools is *d*	Prov 14:8	4820
Bread of *d* is sweet to a man	Prov 20:17	8267
lips, and layeth up *d* within him	Prov 26:24	4820
Whose hatred is covered by *d*	Prov 26:26	4860
neither was any *d* in his mouth	Is 53:9	4820
so are their houses full of *d*	Jer 5:27	4820
they hold fast *d*, they refuse to	Jer 8:5	8649
habitation is in the midst of *d*	Jer 9:6	4820
through *d* they refuse to know me,	Jer 9:6	4820
it speaketh *d*	Jer 9:8	4820
nought, and the *d* of their heart	Jer 14:14	8649
of the *d* of their own heart	Jer 23:26	8649
and the house of Israel are *d*	Hos 11:12	4820
the balances of *d* are in his hand	Hos 12:7	4820
and falsifying the balances by *d*	Amos 8:5	4820
houses with violence and *d*	Zeph 1:9	4820
covetousness, wickedness, *d*	Mk 7:22	1388
full of envy, murder, debate, *d*	Rom 1:29	1388
their tongues they have used *d*	Rom 3:13	1387
you through philosophy and vain *d*	Col 2:8	539
For our exhortation was not of *d*	1Th 2:3	4106

DECEITFUL

will abhor the bloody and *d* man	Ps 5:6	4820
but they devise *d* matters against	Ps 35:20	4820
O deliver me from the *d* and unjust	Ps 43:1	4820
devouring words, O thou *d* tongue	Ps 52:4	4820
d men shall not live out half	Ps 55:23	4820
were turned aside like a *d* bow	Ps 78:57	7423
the mouth of the *d* are opened	Ps 109:2	4820
lying lips, and from a *d* tongue	Ps 120:2	7423
The wicked worketh a *d* work	Prov 11:18	8267
but a *d* witness speaketh lies	Prov 14:25	4820
for they are *d* meat	Prov 23:3	3577
but the kisses of an enemy are *d*	Prov 27:6	6280
poor and the *d* man meet together	Prov 29:13	8501
Favour is *d*, and beauty is vain	Prov 31:30	8267
The heart is *d* above all things,	Jer 17:9	6121
they are like a *d* bow	Hos 7:16	7423
and with the bag of *d* weights	Mic 6:11	4820
their tongue is *d* in their mouth	Mic 6:12	7423
neither shall a *d* tongue be found	Zeph 3:13	8649
apostles, *d* workers, transforming	2Cor 11:13	1386
corrupt according to the *d* lusts	Eph 4:22	539

DECEITFULLY

Shechem and Hamor his father *d*	Gen 34:13	4820
but let not Pharaoh deal *d* any	Ex 8:29	2048
seeing he hath dealt *d* with her	Ex 21:8	898
the thing which he hath *d* gotten	Lev 6:4	6231
brethren have dealt *d* as a brook	Job 6:15	898
and talk *d* for him	Job 13:7	7423
his soul unto vanity, nor sworn *d*	Ps 24:4	4820
like a sharp razor, working *d*	Ps 52:2	7423
that doeth the work of the LORD *d*	Jer 48:10	7423
made with him he shall work *d*	Dan 11:23	4820
nor handling the word of God *d*	2Cor 4:2	1389

DECEITFULNESS

the *d* of riches, choke the word,	Mt 13:22	539
the *d* of riches, and the lusts of	Mk 4:19	539
be hardened through the *d* of sin	Heb 3:13	539

DECEITS

imagine *d* all the day long	Ps 38:12	4820
unto us smooth things, prophesy *d*	Is 30:10	4123

DECEIVABLENESS

with all *d* of unrighteousness in	2Th 2:10	539

DECEIVE

of Ner, that he came to *d* thee	2Sa 3:25	6601
did I not say, Do not *d* me	2Kin 4:28	7952
the king, Let not Hezekiah *d* you	2Kin 18:29	5377
God in whom thou trustest *d* thee	2Kin 19:10	5377
therefore let not Hezekiah *d* you	2Chr 32:15	5377
and *d* not with thy lips	Prov 24:28	6601
the king, Let not Hezekiah *d* you	Is 36:14	5377
d thee, saying, Jerusalem shall	Is 37:10	5377
they will *d* every one his	Jer 9:5	2048
d you, neither hearken to your	Jer 29:8	5377
D not yourselves, saying, The	Jer 37:9	5377
they wear a rough garment to *d*	Zec 13:4	3884
them, Take heed that no man *d* you	Mt 24:4	4105

and shall *d* many	Mt 24:5	4105
shall rise, and shall *d* many	Mt 24:11	4105
they shall *d* the very elect	Mt 24:24	4105
say, Take heed lest any man *d* you	Mk 13:5	4105
and shall *d* many	Mk 13:6	4105
fair speeches *d* the hearts of the	Rom 16:18	1818
Let no man *d* himself	1Cor 3:18	1818
whereby they lie in wait to *d*	Eph 4:14	4106
Let no man *d* you with vain words	Eph 5:6	538
Let no man *d* you by any means	2Th 2:3	1818
we *d* ourselves, and the truth is	1Jn 1:8	4105
Little children, let no man *d* you	1Jn 3:7	4105
that he should *d* the nations no	Rev 20:3	4105
shall go out to *d* the nations	Rev 20:8	4105

DECEIVED

And your father hath *d* me, and	Gen 31:7	2048
violence, or hath *d* his neighbour	Lev 6:2	6231
that your heart be not *d*	Deut 11:16	6601
Michal, Why hast thou *d* me so	1Sa 19:17	7411
Saul, saying, Why hast thou *d* me	1Sa 28:12	7411
My lord, O king, my servant *d* me	2Sa 19:26	7411
the *d* and the deceiver are his	Job 12:16	7683
not him that is *d* trust in vanity	Job 15:31	8582
mine heart have been *d* by a woman	Job 31:9	6601
whosoever is *d* thereby is not	Prov 20:1	7686
fools, the princes of Noph are *d*	Is 19:13	5377
a *d* heart hath turned him aside,	Is 44:20	2048
thou hast greatly *d* this people	Jer 4:10	5377
O LORD, thou hast *d* me, and I was	Jer 20:7	6601
thou hast *d* me, and I was *d*	Jer 20:7	6601
Thy terribleness hath *d* thee	Jer 49:16	5377
for my lovers, but they *d* me	Lam 1:19	7411
if the prophet be *d* when he hath	Eze 14:9	6601
I the LORD have *d* that prophet	Eze 14:9	6601
pride of thine heart hath *d* thee	Obad 3	5377
at peace with thee have *d* thee	Obad 7	5377
said, Take heed that ye be not *d*	Lk 21:8	4105
them the Pharisees, Are ye also *d*	Jn 7:47	4105
d me, and by it slew me	Rom 7:11	1818
Be not *d*: neither fornicators	1Cor 6:9	4105
Be not *d*: evil communications	1Cor 15:33	4105
Be not *d*; God is not	Gal 6:7	4105
And Adam was not *d*, but the woman	1Ti 2:14	538
but the woman being *d* was in the	1Ti 2:14	538
and worse, deceiving, and being *d*	2Ti 3:13	4105
sometimes foolish, disobedient, *d*	Titus 3:3	4105
thy sorceries were all nations *d*	Rev 18:23	4105
with which he *d* them that had	Rev 19:20	4105
the devil that *d* them was cast	Rev 20:10	4105

DECEIVER

me, and I shall seem to him as a *d*	Gen 27:12	8591
the deceived and the *d* are his	Job 12:16	7686
But cursed be the *d*, which hath	Mal 1:14	5230
Sir, we remember that that *d* said	Mt 27:63	4108
This is a *d* and an antichrist	2Jn 7	4108

DECEIVERS

as *d*, and yet true	2Cor 6:8	4108
many unruly and vain talkers and *d*	Titus 1:10	5423
For many *d* are entered into the	2Jn 7	4108

DECEIVETH

is the man that *d* his neighbour	Prov 26:19	7411
but he *d* the people	Jn 7:12	4105
when he is nothing, he *d* himself	Gal 6:3	5422
but *d* his own heart, this man's	Jas 1:26	538
and Satan, which *d* the whole world	Rev 12:9	4105
d them that dwell on the earth by	Rev 13:14	4105

DECEIVING

shall wax worse and worse, *d*	2Ti 3:13	4105
hearers only, *d* your own selves	Jas 1:22	3884

DECEIVINGS

own *d* while they feast with you	2Pet 2:13	539

DECENTLY

Let all things be done *d* and in	1Cor 14:40	2156

DECIDED

thyself hast *d* it	1Kin 20:40	2782

DECISION

multitudes in the valley of *d*	Joel 3:14	2742
LORD is near in the valley of *d*	Joel 3:14	2742

DECK

D thyself now with majesty and	Job 40:10	5710
They *d* it with silver and with	Jer 10:4	3302

DECKED

I have *d* my bed with coverings of	Prov 7:16	7234
I *d* thee also with ornaments, and	Eze 16:11	5710
Thus wast thou *d* with gold	Eze 16:13	5710

she *d* herself with her earrings .... Hos 2:13   5710
d with gold and precious stones and ...... Rev 17:4   5558
d with gold, and precious stones, ... Rev 18:16   5558

DECKEDST
d thy high places with divers .... Eze 16:16   6213
d thyself with ornaments, ... Eze 23:40   5710

DECKEST
though thou *d* thee with ornaments .... Jer 4:30   5710

DECKETH
as a bridegroom *d* himself with .... Is 61:10   3547

DECLARATION
the *d* of the greatness of .... Est 10:2   6575
my speech, and my *d* with your ears ..... Job 13:17   262
d of those things which are most .... Lk 1:1   *1335*
Lord, and *d* of your ready mind 2Cor 8:19

DECLARE
was none that could *d* it to me .... Gen 41:24   5046
Moab, began Moses to *d* this law .... Deut 1:5   874
shall *d* his cause in the ears of .... Josh 20:4   1696
if ye can certainly *d* it me .... Judg 14:12   5046
But if ye cannot *d* it me, then .... Judg 14:13   5046
that he may *d* unto us the riddle, ... Judg 14:15   5046
the words of the prophets *d* good 1Kin 22:13
D his glory among the heathen 1Chr 16:24   5608
d good to the king with one 2Chr 18:12
to *d* it unto her, and to charge .... Est 4:8   5046
of the sea shall *d* unto thee .... Job 12:8   5608
that which I have seen I will *d* .... Job 15:17   5608
Who shall *d* his way to his face .... Job 21:31   5046
Then did he see it, and *d* it .... Job 28:27   5608
I would *d* unto him the number of .... Job 31:37   5046
d, if thou hast understanding .... Job 38:4   5046
d if thou knowest it all .... Job 38:18   5046
demand of thee, and *d* thou unto me ..... Job 40:7   3045
demand of thee, and *d* thou unto me ...... Job 42:4   3045
I will *d* the decree .... Ps 2:7   5608
d among the people his doings .... Ps 9:11   5046
The heavens *d* the glory of God .... Ps 19:1   5608
I will *d* thy name unto my .... Ps 22:22   5608
shall *d* his righteousness unto a .... Ps 22:31   5046
shall it *d* thy truth. .... Ps 30:9   5046
For I will *d* mine iniquity .... Ps 38:18   5046
if I would *d* and speak of them, ... Ps 40:5   5046
heavens shall *d* his righteousness .... Ps 50:6   5046
hast thou to do to *d* my statutes. .... Ps 50:16   5608
fear, and shall *d* the work of God .... Ps 64:9   5046
I will *d* what he hath done for my .... Ps 66:16   5608
that I may *d* all thy works. .... Ps 73:28   5608
name is near thy wondrous works *d* ...... Ps 75:1   5608
But I will *d* for ever .... Ps 75:9   5046
arise and *d* them to their children .... Ps 78:6   5608
D his glory among the heathen, ... Ps 96:3   5608
The heavens *d* his righteousness, ... Ps 97:6   5046
To *d* the name of the LORD in Zion .... Ps 102:21   5608
d his works with rejoicing .... Ps 107:22   5608
live, and *d* the works of the LORD .... Ps 118:17   5608
and shall *d* thy mighty acts .... Ps 145:4   5046
and I will *d* thy greatness .... Ps 145:6   5608
in my heart even to *d* all this .... Eccl 9:1   952
they *d* their sin as Sodom, they .... Is 3:9   5046
d his doings among the people, ... Is 12:4   3045
watchman, let him *d* what he seeth .... Is 21:6   5046
or *d* us things for to come .... Is 41:22   8085
to pass, and new things do I *d* .... Is 42:9   5046
d his praise in the islands .... Is 42:12   5046
who among them can *d* this .... Is 43:9   5046
d thou, that thou mayest be .... Is 43:26   5608
as I, shall call, and shall *d* it .... Is 44:7   5046
I *d* things that are right .... Is 45:19   5046
and will not ye *d* it .... Is 48:6   5046
with a voice of singing *d* ye .... Is 48:20   5046
who shall *d* his generation .... Is 53:8   7878
I will *d* thy righteousness, and .... Is 57:12   5046
they shall *d* my glory among the .... Is 66:19   5046
D ye in Judah, and publish in .... Jer 4:5   5046
D this in the house of Jacob, and .... Jer 5:20   5046
hath spoken, that he may *d* it .... Jer 9:12   5046
d it in the isles afar off, and .... Jer 31:10   5046
If I *d* it unto thee, wilt thou .... Jer 38:15   5046
D unto us now what thou hast said .... Jer 38:25   5046
answer you, I will *d* it unto you .... Jer 42:4   5046
so *d* unto us, and we will do it .... Jer 42:20   5046
D ye in Egypt, and publish in .... Jer 46:14   5046
D ye among the nations, and .... Jer 50:2   5046
to *d* in Zion the vengeance of the .... Jer 50:28   5046
let us *d* in Zion the work of the .... Jer 51:10   5608
that they may *d* all their .... Eze 12:16   5608
d unto them their abominations .... Eze 23:36   5046

d all that thou seest to the .... Eze 40:4   5046
d the interpretation thereof, ... Dan 4:18   560
D ye it not at Gath, weep ye not .... Mic 1:10   5046
to *d* unto Jacob his transgression .... Mic 3:8   5046
even to day do I *d* that I will .... Zec 9:12   5046
D unto us the parable of the .... Mt 13:36   *5419*
unto him, *D* unto us this parable. .... Mt 15:15   *5419*
unto them thy name, and will *d* it .... Jn 17:26   *1107*
who shall *d* his generation .... Acts 8:33   *1334*
we *d* unto you glad tidings, how .... Acts 13:32   *2097*
though a man *d* it unto you .... Acts 13:41   *1555*
worship, him *d* I unto you .... Acts 17:23   *2605*
For I have not shunned to *d* unto .... Acts 20:27   *312*
to *d* his righteousness for the .... Rom 3:25   *1732*
To *d*, I say, at this time his .... Rom 3:26   *1732*
for the day shall *d* it, because 1Cor 3:13   *1213*
Now in this that I *d* unto you I 1Cor 11:17   *3853*
I *d* unto you the gospel which I 1Cor 15:1   *1107*
state shall Tychicus *d* unto you. .... Col 4:7   *1107*
I will *d* thy name unto my .... Heb 2:12   *518*
things *d* plainly that they seek a .... Heb 11:14   *1718*
heard *d* we unto you, that ye also 1Jn 1:3   *518*
d unto you, that God is light, and 1Jn 1:5   *312*

DECLARED
that my name may be *d* throughout ...... Ex 9:16   5608
Moses *d* unto the children of .... Lev 23:44   1696
they *d* their pedigrees after .... Num 1:18
because it was not *d* what should .... Num 15:34   6567
he *d* unto you his covenant, which .... Deut 4:13   5046
For thou hast *d* this day, that 2Sa 19:6   5046
the words that were *d* unto them .... Neh 8:12   3045
plentifully *d* the thing as it is .... Job 26:3   3045
I have *d* thy faithfulness and thy .... Ps 40:10   559
hitherto have I *d* thy wondrous .... Ps 71:17   5046
thou hast *d* thy strength among .... Ps 77:14   3045
lovingkindness be *d* in the grave .... Ps 88:11   5608
With my lips have I *d* all the .... Ps 119:13   5608
I have *d* my ways, and thou .... Ps 119:26   5608
A grievous vision is *d* unto me .... Is 21:2   5046
God of Israel, have I *d* unto you .... Is 21:10   5046
Who hath *d* from the beginning, ... Is 41:26   5046
I have *d*, and have saved, and I .... Is 43:12   5046
thee from that time, and have *d* it .... Is 44:8   5046
who hath *d* this from ancient time .... Is 45:21   8085
I have *d* the former things from .... Is 48:3   5046
from the beginning *d* it to thee .... Is 48:5   5046
among them hath *d* these things .... Is 48:14   5046
Then Michaiah *d* unto them all the .... Jer 36:13   5046
now I have this day *d* it to you .... Jer 42:21   5046
she *d* unto him before all the .... Lk 8:47   *518*
of the Father, he hath *d* him .... Jn 1:18   *1834*
I have *d* unto them thy name, and .... Jn 17:26   *1107*
d unto them how he had seen the .... Acts 9:27   *1334*
when he had *d* all these things .... Acts 10:8   *1834*
d unto them how the Lord had .... Acts 12:17   *1334*
they *d* all things that God had .... Acts 15:4   *312*
Simeon hath *d* how God at the .... Acts 15:14   *1834*
he *d* particularly what things God .... Acts 21:19   *1834*
Festus *d* Paul's cause unto the .... Acts 25:14   *394*
d to be the Son of God with power .... Rom 1:4   *3724*
thee, and that my name might be *d* .... Rom 9:17   *1229*
For it hath been *d* unto me of you 1Cor 1:11   *1213*
d to be the epistle of Christ 2Cor 3:3   *5319*
Who also *d* unto us your love in .... Col 1:8   *1213*
as he hath *d* to his servants the .... Rev 10:7   *2097*

DECLARETH
yea, there is none that *d* .... Is 41:26   5046
For a voice *d* from Dan, and .... Jer 4:15   5046
and their staff *d* unto them .... Hos 4:12   5046
d unto man what is his thought, ... Amos 4:13   5046

DECLARING
D the end from the beginning, and .... Is 46:10   5046
d the conversion of the Gentiles .... Acts 15:3   *1555*
d what miracles and wonders God .... Acts 15:12   *1834*
d unto you the testimony of God 1Cor 2:1   *2605*

DECLINE
to *d* after many to wrest judgment .... Ex 23:2   5186
thou shalt not *d* from the .... Deut 17:11   5493
yet do I not *d* from thy .... Ps 119:157   5186
neither *d* from the words of my .... Prov 4:5   5186
Let not thine heart *d* to her ways .... Prov 7:25   7847

DECLINED
d neither to the right hand, nor 2Chr 34:2   5493
his way have I kept, and not *d* .... Job 23:11   5186
have our steps *d* from thy way .... Ps 44:18   5186
yet have I not *d* from thy law .... Ps 119:51   5186

D

DECLINETH
My days are like a shadow that *d*	Ps 102:11	5186
am gone like the shadow when it *d*	Ps 109:23	5186

DECREASE
suffereth not their cattle to *d*	Ps 107:38	4591
He must increase, but I must *d*	Jn 3:30	1642

DECREASED
the waters *d* continually until	Gen 8:5	2637

DECREE
So they established a *d* to make	2Chr 30:5	1697
a *d* to build this house of God	Ezr 5:13	2942
that a *d* was made of Cyrus the	Ezr 5:17	2942
Then Darius the king made a *d*	Ezr 6:1	2942
d concerning the house of God at	Ezr 6:3	2942
Moreover I make a *d* what ye shall	Ezr 6:8	2942
Also I have made a *d*, that	Ezr 6:11	2942
I Darius have made a *d*	Ezr 6:12	2942
I make a *d*, that all they of the	Ezr 7:13	2942
do make a *d* to all the treasurers	Ezr 7:21	2942
when the king's *d* which he shall	Est 1:20	6599
his *d* was heard, and when many	Est 2:8	1881
the *d* was given in Shushan the	Est 3:15	1881
his *d* came, there was great	Est 4:3	1881
d that was given at Shushan to	Est 4:8	1881
the *d* was given at Shushan the	Est 8:14	1881
his *d* came, the Jews had joy and	Est 8:17	1881
his *d* drew near to be put in	Est 9:1	1881
also according unto this day's *d*	Est 9:13	1881
the *d* was given at Shushan	Est 9:14	1881
the *d* of Esther confirmed these	Est 9:32	3982
Thou shalt also *d* a thing	Job 22:28	1504
When he made a *d* for the rain	Job 28:26	2706
I will declare the *d*	Ps 2:7	2706
he hath made a *d* which shall not	Ps 148:6	2706
kings reign, and princes *d* justice	Prov 8:15	2710
When he gave to the sea his *d*	Prov 8:29	2706
Woe unto them that *d* unrighteous	Is 10:1	2710
bound of the sea by a perpetual *d*	Jer 5:22	2706
dream, there is but one *d* for you	Dan 2:9	1882
the *d* went forth that the wise	Dan 2:13	1882
Why is the *d* so hasty from the	Dan 2:15	1882
Thou, O king, hast made a *d*	Dan 3:10	2942
Therefore I make a *d*, That every	Dan 3:29	2942
Therefore made I a *d* to bring in	Dan 4:6	2942
is by the *d* of the watchers	Dan 4:17	1510
this is the *d* of the most High	Dan 4:24	1510
statute, and to make a firm *d*	Dan 6:7	633
Now, O king, establish the *d*	Dan 6:8	633
signed the writing and the *d*	Dan 6:9	633
the king concerning the king's *d*	Dan 6:12	633
Hast thou not signed a *d*, that	Dan 6:12	633
nor the *d* that thou hast signed,	Dan 6:13	633
That no *d* nor statute which the	Dan 6:15	633
I make a *d*, That in every	Dan 6:26	2942
Nineveh by the *d* of the king	Jonah 3:7	2940
day shall the *d* be far removed	Mic 7:11	2706
Before the *d* bring forth, before	Zeph 2:2	2706
went out a *d* from Caesar Augustus	Lk 2:1	1378

DECREED
done, and what was *d* against her	Est 2:1	1504
as they had *d* for themselves and	Est 9:31	6965
And brake up for it my *d* place	Job 38:10	2706
the consumption *d* shall overflow	Is 10:22	2782
hath so *d* in his heart that he	1Cor 7:37	2919

DECREES
them that decree unrighteous *d*	Is 10:1	2711
delivered them the *d* for to keep	Acts 16:4	1378
do contrary to the *d* of Caesar	Acts 17:7	1378

DEDAN (de'-dan) See DEDANIM.
1. A grandson of Cush.
sons of Raamah; Sheba, and *D*	Gen 10:7	1719
sons of Raamah; Sheba, and *D*	1Chr 1:9	1719

2. A son of Jokshan.
And Jokshan begat Sheba, and *D*	Gen 25:3	1719
the sons of *D* were Asshurim, and	Gen 25:3	1719
sons of Jokshan; Sheba, and *D*	1Chr 1:32	1719

3. A district between Sela and the Salt Sea.
D, and Tema, and Buz, and all that	Jer 25:23	1719
dwell deep, O inhabitants of *D*	Jer 49:8	1719
they of *D* shall fall by the sword	Eze 25:13	1719
The men of *D* were thy merchants	Eze 27:15	1719
D was thy merchant in precious	Eze 27:20	1719
Sheba, and *D*, and the merchants of	Eze 38:13	1719

DEDANIM (ded'-a-nim) See DODANIM. *Descendants of Raamah.*
O ye travelling companies of *D*	Is 21:13	1720

DEDANITES See DEDANIM.

DEDICATE
the battle, and another man *d* it	Deut 20:5	2596
king David did *d* unto the LORD	2Sa 8:11	6942
d to maintain the house of the	1Chr 26:27	6942
to *d* it to him, and to burn before	2Chr 2:4	6942

DEDICATED
a new house, and hath not *d* it	Deut 20:5	2596
I had wholly *d* the silver unto	Judg 17:3	6942
gold that he had *d* of all nations	2Sa 8:11	6942
which David his father had *d*	1Kin 7:51	6944
of Israel *d* the house of the LORD	1Kin 8:63	2596
the things which his father had *d*	1Kin 15:15	6944
and the things which himself had *d*	1Kin 15:15	6944
All the money of the *d* things	2Kin 12:4	6944
fathers, kings of Judah, had *d*	2Kin 12:18	6942
also king David *d* unto the LORD	1Chr 18:11	6942
the treasures of the *d* things	1Chr 26:20	6944
all the treasures of the *d* things	1Chr 26:26	6944
the captains of the host, had *d*	1Chr 26:26	6942
and Joab the son of Zeruiah, had *d*	1Chr 26:28	6942
and whosoever had *d* any thing	1Chr 26:28	6942
of the treasuries of the *d* things	1Chr 28:12	6944
that David his father had *d*	2Chr 5:1	6944
all the people the house of God	2Chr 7:5	2596
the things that his father had *d*	2Chr 15:18	6944
and that he himself had *d*	2Chr 15:18	6944
also all the *d* things of the	2Chr 24:7	6944
tithes and the *d* things faithfully	2Chr 31:12	6944
every *d* thing in Israel shall be	Eze 44:29	2764
testament was *d* without blood	Heb 9:18	1457

DEDICATING
the princes offered for *d* of the	Num 7:10	2598
his day, for the *d* of the altar	Num 7:11	2598

DEDICATION
This was the *d* of the altar	Num 7:84	2598
This was the *d* of the altar	Num 7:88	2598
for they kept the *d* of the altar	2Chr 7:9	2598
kept the *d* of this house of God	Ezr 6:16	2597
offered at the *d* of this house of	Ezr 6:17	2597
at the *d* of the wall of Jerusalem	Neh 12:27	2598
to keep the *d* with gladness, both	Neh 12:27	2598
Song at the *d* of the house of	Ps 30:t	2598
to come to the *d* of the image	Dan 3:2	2597
unto the *d* of the image that	Dan 3:3	2597
at Jerusalem the feast of the *d*	Jn 10:22	1456

DEED
What *d* is this that ye have done	Gen 44:15	4639
in very *d* for this cause have I	Ex 9:16	199
There was no such *d* done nor seen	Judg 19:30	
For in very *d*, as the LORD God of	1Sa 25:34	199
that Saul was come in very *d*	1Sa 26:4	3559
because by this *d* thou hast given	2Sa 12:14	1697
But will God in very *d* dwell with	2Chr 6:18	
For this *d* of the queen shall	Est 1:17	1697
have heard of the *d* of the queen	Est 1:18	1697
to the counsel and *d* of them	Lk 23:51	4334
which was a prophet mighty in *d*	Lk 24:19	2041
good *d* done to the impotent man	Acts 4:9	2108
Gentiles obedient, by word and *d*	Rom 15:18	2041
that he that hath done this *d*	1Cor 5:2	2041
him that hath so done this *d*	1Cor 5:3	
be also in *d* when we are present	2Cor 10:11	2041
And whatsoever ye do in word or *d*	Col 3:17	2041
man shall be blessed in his *d*	Jas 1:25	4162
but in *d* and in truth	1Jn 3:18	2041

DEEDS
thou hast done *d* unto me that	Gen 20:9	4639
make known his *d* among the people	1Chr 16:8	5949
And his *d*, first and last, behold,	2Chr 35:27	1697
is come upon us for our evil *d*	Ezr 9:13	4639
reported his good *d* before me	Neh 6:19	
wipe not out my good *d* that I	Neh 13:14	
Give them according to their *d*	Ps 28:4	6467
make known his *d* among the people	Ps 105:1	5949
According to their *d*, accordingly	Is 59:18	1578
they overpass the *d* of the wicked	Jer 5:28	1697
them according to their *d*	Jer 25:14	6467
ye allow the *d* of your fathers	Lk 11:48	2041
receive the due reward of our *d*	Lk 23:41	3739,4238
light, because their *d* were evil	Jn 3:19	2041
lest his *d* should be reproved	Jn 3:20	2041
that his *d* may be made manifest,	Jn 3:21	2041
Ye do the *d* of your father	Jn 8:41	2041
and was mighty in words and in *d*	Acts 7:22	2041
and confessed, and shewed their *d*	Acts 19:18	4234
that very worthy *d* are done unto	Acts 24:2	2735
to every man according to his *d*	Rom 2:6	2041
Therefore by the *d* of the law	Rom 3:20	2041

by faith without the *d* of the law .... Rom 3:28   2041
do mortify the *d* of the body.................... Rom 8:13   4234
in signs, and wonders, and mighty *d* 2Cor 12:12   1411
put off the old man with his *d* .... Col 3:9   4234
day to day with their unlawful *d* 2Pet 2:8   2041
speed is partaker of his evil *d* 2Jn 11   2041
remember his *d* which he doeth 3Jn 10   2041
ungodly of all their ungodly *d* ...... Jude 15   2041
hatest the *d* of the Nicolaitanes .... Rev 2:6   2041
except they repent of their *d* .... Rev 2:22   2041
sores, and repented not of their *d*.......... Rev 16:11   2041

DEEMED
about midnight the shipmen *d* that........ Acts 27:27   5282

DEEP
was upon the face of the *d* .... Gen 1:2   8415
the Lord God caused a *d* sleep to .... Gen 2:21   8639
of the great *d* broken up, and the .... Gen 7:11   8415
The fountains also of the *d*.................... Gen 8:2   8415
a *d* sleep fell upon Abram .... Gen 15:12   8639
of the *d* that lieth under .... Gen 49:25   8415
for the *d* that coucheth beneath,............ Deut 33:13   8415
because a *d* sleep from the Lord 1Sa 26:12   8639
when *d* sleep falleth on men,...................... Job 4:13   8639
He discovereth *d* things out of .... Job 12:22   6013
when *d* sleep falleth upon men, in .... Job 33:15   8639
and the face of the *d* is frozen .... Job 38:30   8415
He maketh the *d* to boil like a .... Job 41:31   4688
one would think the *d* to be hoary .... Job 41:32   8415
thy judgments are a great *d*.................. Ps 36:6   8415
D calleth unto *d* at the noise.................. Ps 42:7   8415
D calleth unto *d* at the noise.................. Ps 42:7   8415
one of them, and the heart, is *d* .... Ps 64:6   6013
I sink in *d* mire, where there is .... Ps 69:2   4688
I am come into *d* waters, where .... Ps 69:2   4615
hate me, and out of the *d* waters .... Ps 69:14   4615
neither let the *d* swallow me up .... Ps 69:15   4688
and didst cause it to take *d* root .... Ps 80:9   8328
and thy thoughts are very *d*.................... Ps 92:5   6009
are the *d* places of the earth.................. Ps 95:4   4278
it with the *d* as with a garment .... Ps 104:6   8415
the Lord, and his wonders in the *d* .... Ps 107:24   4688
in the seas, and all *d* places.................. Ps 135:6   8415
into *d* pits, that they rise not.................. Ps 140:10   4113
the fountains of the *d* .... Prov 8:28   8415
of a man's mouth are as *d* waters .... Prov 18:4   6013
casteth into a *d* sleep............................ Prov 19:15   8639
the heart of man is like *d* water............ Prov 20:5   6013
mouth of strange women is a *d* pit .... Prov 22:14   6013
For a whore is a *d* ditch.......................... Prov 23:27   6013
which is far off, and exceeding *d* .... Eccl 7:24   6013
upon you the spirit of *d* sleep .... Is 29:10   8639
Woe unto them that seek *d* to hide .... Is 29:15   6009
he hath made it *d* and large .... Is 30:33   6009
That saith to the *d*, Be dry, and I .... Is 44:27   6683
sea, the waters of the great *d* .... Is 51:10   8415
That led them through the *d* .... Is 63:13   8415
Flee ye, turn back, dwell *d* .... Jer 49:8   6009
Flee, get you far off, dwell *d* .... Jer 49:30   6009
shalt drink of thy sister's cup *d* .... Eze 23:32   6013
I shall bring up the *d* upon thee .... Eze 26:19   8415
the *d* set him up on high with her .... Eze 31:4   8415
I covered the *d* for him, and I .... Eze 31:15   8415
Then will I make their waters *d*............ Eze 32:14   8257
and to have drunk of the *d* waters .... Eze 34:18   4950
He revealeth the *d* and secret .... Dan 2:22   5994
I was in a *d* sleep on my face................ Dan 8:18   7290
then was I in a *d* sleep on my .... Dan 10:9   7290
fire, and it devoured the great *d* .... Amos 7:4   8415
For thou hadst cast me into the *d* .... Jonah 2:3   4688
the *d* uttered his voice, and...................... Hab 3:10   8415
unto Simon, Launch out into the *d*........ Lk 5:4   899
built an house, and digged a .... Lk 6:48   2532,900
command them to go out into the *d* .... Lk 8:31   12
to draw with, and the well is *d*.............. Jn 4:11   901
being fallen into a *d* sleep .... Acts 20:9   901
Or, Who shall descend into the *d* .... Rom 10:7   12
things, yea, the *d* things of God............ 1Cor 2:10   899
their *d* poverty abounded unto the 2Cor 8:2   899
and a day I have been in the *d* 2Cor 11:25   1037

DEEPER
the plague in sight be *d* than the .... Lev 13:3   6013
in sight be not *d* than the skin................ Lev 13:4   6013
and it be in sight *d* than the skin .... Lev 13:25   6013
if it be in sight *d* than the skin .... Lev 13:30   6013
be not in sight *d* than the skin................ Lev 13:31   6013
be not in sight *d* than the skin .... Lev 13:32   6013
nor be in sight *d* than the skin................ Lev 13:34   6013
d than hell; what canst thou know? ...... Job 11:8   6013
a people of a *d* speech than thou .... Is 33:19   6012

DEEPLY
of Israel have *d* revolted .... Is 31:6   6009
They have *d* corrupted themselves,........ Hos 9:9   6009
he sighed *d* in his spirit, and.................. Mk 8:12   389

DEEPNESS
because they had no *d* of earth .... Mt 13:5   899

DEEPS
thou threwest into the *d*, as a .... Neh 9:11   4688
lowest pit, in darkness, in the *d* .... Ps 88:6   4688
the earth, ye dragons, and all *d*.............. Ps 148:7   8415
all the *d* of the river shall dry .... Zec 10:11   4688

DEER
and the roebuck, and the fallow *d* .... Deut 14:5   3180

DEFAMED
Being *d*, we intreat.................................... 1Cor 4:13   987

DEFAMING
For I heard the *d* of many .... Jer 20:10   1681

DEFEAT
then mayest thou for me *d* the 2Sa 15:34   6565
For the Lord had appointed to *d* 2Sa 17:14   6565

DEFENCE
their *d* is departed from them, and .... Num 14:9   6738
and built cities for *d* in Judah 2Chr 11:5   4692
Yea, the Almighty shall be thy *d* .... Job 22:25   1220
My *d* is of God, which saveth the .... Ps 7:10   4043
for an house of *d* to save me .... Ps 31:2   4686
for God is my *d* .... Ps 59:9   4869
for thou hast been my *d* and refuge ...... Ps 59:16   4869
for God is my *d*, and the God of my ...... Ps 59:17   4869
he is my *d* .... Ps 62:2   4869
he is my *d* .... Ps 62:6   4869
For the Lord is our *d* .... Ps 89:18   4043
But the Lord is my *d* .... Ps 94:22   4869
For wisdom is a *d*.................................... Eccl 7:12   6738
and money is a *d* .... Eccl 7:12   6738
upon all the glory shall be a *d*................ Is 4:5   2646
the brooks of *d* shall be emptied .... Is 19:6   4692
his place of *d* shall be the .... Is 33:16   4869
and the *d* shall be prepared.................... Nah 2:5   5526
have made his *d* unto the people .... Acts 19:33   626
hear ye my *d* which I make now .... Acts 22:1   627
as both in my bonds, and in the *d* .... Phil 1:7   627
I am set for the *d* of the gospel.............. Phil 1:17   627

DEFENCED
of a *d* city a ruin .... Is 25:2   1219
Yet the *d* city shall be desolate,............ Is 27:10   1219
against all the *d* cities of Judah .... Is 36:1   1219
waste *d* cities into ruinous heaps .... Is 37:26   1219
have made thee this day a *d* city............ Jer 1:18   4013
and let us go into the *d* cities................ Jer 4:5   4013
and let us enter into the *d* cities .... Jer 8:14   4013
for these *d* cities remained of................ Jer 34:7   4013
and to Judah in Jerusalem the *d* .... Eze 21:20   1219

DEFEND
to *d* Israel Tola the son of Puah............ Judg 10:1   3467
For I will *d* this city, to save 2Kin 19:34   1598
I will *d* this city for mine own 2Kin 20:6   1598
name of the God of Jacob *d* thee .... Ps 20:1   7682
d me from them that rise up .... Ps 59:1   7682
D the poor and fatherless .... Ps 82:3   8199
the Lord of hosts *d* Jerusalem .... Is 31:5   1598
For I will *d* this city to save it .... Is 37:35   1598
and I will *d* this city................................ Is 38:6   1598
The Lord of hosts shall *d* them .... Zec 9:15   1598
In that day shall the Lord *d* the .... Zec 12:8   1598

DEFENDED
d it, and slew the Philistines 2Sa 23:12   5337
he it, him, and avenged him that was .... Acts 7:24   292

DEFENDEST
for joy, because thou *d* them .... Ps 5:11   5526

DEFENDING
d also he will deliver it .... Is 31:5   1598

DEFER
a vow unto God, *d* not to pay it .... Eccl 5:4   309
name's sake will I *d* mine anger .... Is 48:9   748
d not, for thine own sake, O my .... Dan 9:19   309

DEFERRED
the young man *d* not to do the................ Gen 34:19   309
Hope *d* maketh the heart sick, but .... Prov 13:12   4900
he *d* them, and said, When Lysias........ Acts 24:22   306

DEFERRETH
discretion of a man *d* his anger............ Prov 19:11   748

DEFIED

I defy, whom the LORD hath not d	Num 23:8	2194
seeing he hath d the armies of	1Sa 17:36	2778
of Israel, whom thou hast d	1Sa 17:45	2778
And when he d Israel, Jonathan the	2Sa 21:21	2778
when they d the Philistines that	2Sa 23:9	2778
But when he d Israel, Jonathan	1Chr 20:7	2778

DEFILE

neither shall ye d yourselves	Lev 11:44	2930
when they d my tabernacle that is	Lev 15:31	2930
wife, to d thyself with her	Lev 18:20	2930
any beast to d thyself therewith	Lev 18:23	2930
D not ye yourselves in any of	Lev 18:24	2930
not you out also, when ye d it	Lev 18:28	2930
that ye not yourselves therein	Lev 18:30	2930
to d my sanctuary, and to profane	Lev 20:3	2930
But he shall not d himself	Lev 21:4	2930
nor d himself for his father, or	Lev 21:11	2930
not eat to d himself therewith	Lev 22:8	2930
that they d not their camps, in	Num 5:3	2930
D not therefore the land which ye	Num 35:34	2930
children of Ammon, did the king d	2Kin 23:13	2930
how shall I d them?	Song 5:3	2936
Ye shall d also the covering of	Is 30:22	2930
is called by my name, to d it	Jer 32:34	2930
shall enter into it, and d it	Eze 7:22	2490
D the house, and fill the courts	Eze 9:7	2930
d not yourselves with the idols	Eze 20:7	2930
nor d yourselves with their idols	Eze 20:18	2930
against herself to d herself	Eze 22:3	2930
they shall d thy brightness	Eze 28:7	2490
ye d every one his neighbour's	Eze 33:26	2930
Neither shall they d themselves	Eze 37:23	2930
the house of Israel no more d	Eze 43:7	2930
at no dead person to d themselves	Eze 44:25	2930
no husband, they may d themselves	Eze 44:25	2930
in his heart that he would not d	Dan 1:8	1351
that he might not d himself	Dan 1:8	1351
and they d the man	Mt 15:18	*2840*
are the things which d a man	Mt 15:20	*2840*
that entering into him can d him	Mk 7:15	*2840*
those are they that d the man	Mk 7:15	*2840*
into the man, it cannot d him	Mk 7:18	*2840*
come from within, and d the man	Mk 7:23	*2840*
If any man d the temple of God,	1Cor 3:17	*5351*
for them that d themselves with	1Ti 1:10	*733*
these filthy dreamers d the flesh	Jude 8	*3392*

DEFILED

her, and lay with her, and d her	Gen 34:2	6031
that he had d Dinah his daughter	Gen 34:5	2930
because he had d Dinah their	Gen 34:13	2930
because they had d their sister	Gen 34:27	2930
be that a man shall be d withal	Lev 5:3	2930
them, that ye should be d thereby	Lev 11:43	2933
shall be in him he shall be d	Lev 13:46	2930
goeth from him, and is d therewith	Lev 15:32	2930
are d which I cast out before you	Lev 18:24	2930
And the land is d	Lev 18:25	2930
were before you, and the land is d	Lev 18:27	2930
after wizards, to be d by them	Lev 19:31	2930
There shall none be d for the	Lev 21:1	2930
for her may he be d	Lev 21:3	2930
and whosoever is d by the dead	Num 5:2	2931
and be kept close, and she be d	Num 5:13	2930
jealous of his wife, and she be d	Num 5:14	2930
of his wife, and she be not d	Num 5:14	2930
of thy husband, and if thou be d	Num 5:20	2930
come to pass, that, if she be d	Num 5:27	2930
And if the woman be not d, but be	Num 5:28	2930
instead of her husband, and is d	Num 5:29	2930
he hath d the head of his	Num 6:9	2930
because his separation was d	Num 6:12	2930
who were d by the dead body of a	Num 9:6	2931
We are d by the dead body of a	Num 9:7	2931
because he hath d the sanctuary	Num 19:20	2930
that thy land be not d, which	Deut 21:23	2930
the fruit of thy vineyard, be d	Deut 22:9	6942
be his wife, after that she is d	Deut 24:4	2930
d the high places where the	2Kin 23:8	2930
he d Topheth, which is in the	2Kin 23:10	2930
forasmuch as he d his father's	1Chr 5:1	2490
they have d the priesthood	Neh 13:29	1351
my skin, and d my horn in the dust	Job 16:15	5953
they have d by casting down the	Ps 74:7	2490
thy holy temple have they d	Ps 79:1	2930
Thus were they d with their own	Ps 106:39	2930
The earth also is d under the	Is 24:5	2610
For your hands are d with blood	Is 59:3	1351
ye d my land, and made mine	Jer 2:7	2930
her whoredom, that she the land	Jer 3:9	2610

because they have d my land	Jer 16:18	2490
shall be d as the place of Tophet	Jer 19:13	2931
their d bread among the Gentiles	Eze 4:13	2931
because thou hast d my sanctuary	Eze 5:11	2930
and their holy places shall be d	Eze 7:24	2490
neither hath d his neighbour's	Eze 18:6	2930
and d his neighbour's wife,	Eze 18:11	2930
hath not d his neighbour's wife,	Eze 18:15	2930
doings, wherein ye have been d	Eze 20:43	2930
hast d thyself in thine idols	Eze 22:4	2930
hath lewdly d his daughter in law	Eze 22:11	2930
all their idols she d herself	Eze 23:7	2930
Then I saw that she was d	Eze 23:13	2930
they d her with their whoredom,	Eze 23:17	2930
they have d my sanctuary in the	Eze 23:38	2930
Thou hast d thy sanctuaries by	Eze 28:18	2490
they d it by their own way and by	Eze 36:17	2930
they have even d my holy name by	Eze 43:8	2930
whoredom, and Israel is d	Hos 5:3	2930
whoredom of Ephraim, Israel is d	Hos 6:10	2930
thee, that say, Let her be d	Mic 4:11	2610
of his disciples eat bread with d	Mk 7:2	*2839*
hall, lest they should be d	Jn 18:28	*3392*
their conscience being weak is d	1Cor 8:7	*3435*
but unto them that are d and	Titus 1:15	*3392*
their mind and conscience is d	Titus 1:15	*3392*
trouble you, and thereby many be d	Heb 12:15	*3392*
which have not d their garments	Rev 3:4	*3435*
they which were not d with women	Rev 14:4	*3435*

DEFILEDST

then d thou it	Gen 49:4	2490

DEFILETH

every one that d it shall surely	Ex 31:14	2490
d the tabernacle of the LORD	Num 19:13	2930
for blood it d the land	Num 35:33	2610
goeth into the mouth d a man	Mt 15:11	*2840*
out of the mouth, this d a man	Mt 15:11	*2840*
with unwashen hands d not a man	Mt 15:20	*2840*
out of the man, that d the man	Mk 7:20	*2840*
that it d the whole body, and	Jas 3:6	*4695*
enter into it any thing that d	Rev 21:27	*2840*

DEFRAUD

Thou shalt not d thy neighbour	Lev 19:13	6231
D not, Honour thy father and	Mk 10:19	*650*
Nay, ye do wrong, and d, and that	1Cor 6:8	*650*
D ye not one the other, except it	1Cor 7:5	*650*
d his brother in any matter	1Th 4:6	*4122*

DEFRAUDED

or whom have I d?	1Sa 12:3	6231
And they said, Thou hast not d us	1Sa 12:4	6231
rather suffer yourselves to be d	1Cor 6:7	*650*
no man, we have d no man	2Cor 7:2	*4122*

DEFY

curse me Jacob, and come, d Israel	Num 23:7	2194
or how shall I d, whom the LORD	Num 23:8	2194
I d the armies of Israel this day	1Sa 17:10	2778
surely to d Israel is he come up	1Sa 17:25	2778
that he should d the armies of	1Sa 17:26	2778

DEGENERATE

then art thou turned into the d	Jer 2:21	5494

DEGREE

their brethren of the second d	1Chr 15:18	
to the estate of a man of high d	1Chr 17:17	
Surely men of low d are vanity	Ps 62:9	
and men of high d are a lie	Ps 62:9	
seats, and exalted them of low d	Lk 1:52	*5011*
purchase to themselves a good d	1Ti 3:13	*898*
Let the brother of low d rejoice	Jas 1:9	*5011*

DEGREES

shall the shadow go forward d	2Kin 20:9	4609
or go back ten d	2Kin 20:9	4609
for the shadow to go down ten d	2Kin 20:10	4609
the shadow return backward ten d	2Kin 20:10	4609
brought the shadow ten d backward	2Kin 20:11	4609
A Song of d	Ps 120:t	4609
A Song of d	Ps 121:t	4609
A Song of d	Ps 122:t	4609
A Song of d of David	Ps 122:t	4609
A Song of d	Ps 123:t	4609
A Song of d of David	Ps 124:t	4609
A Song of d	Ps 125:t	4609
A Song of d	Ps 126:t	4609
A Song of d for Solomon	Ps 127:t	4609
A Song of d	Ps 128:t	4609
A Song of d	Ps 129:t	4609
A Song of d	Ps 130:t	4609
A Song of d	Ps 131:t	4609
A Song of d of David	Ps 131:t	4609
A Song of d	Ps 132:t	4609

A Song of d of David	Ps 133:t	4609
A Song of d	Ps 134:t	4609
bring again the shadow of the d	Is 38:8	4609
sun dial of Ahaz, ten d backward	Is 38:8	4609
So the sun returned ten d	Is 38:8	4609
by which d it was gone down	Is 38:8	4609

DEHAVITES (de-ha´-vites) *Foreign settlers in Samaria.*
the Susanchites, the D, and the	Ezr 4:9	1723

DEKAR (de´-kar) *Father of an officer of Solomon.*
The son of D, in Makaz, and in	1Kin 4:9	1857

DELAIAH (del-a-i´ah) See DALAIAH.
1. A priest of David.
The three and twentieth to D	1Chr 24:18	1806

2. A family with a lost genealogy.
The children of D, the children	Ezr 2:60	1806
The children of D, the children	Neh 7:62	1806

3. An opponent of Nehemiah.
son of D the son of Mehetabeel	Neh 6:10	1806

4. A prince of Judah.
D the son of Shemaiah, and	Jer 36:12	1806
Nevertheless Elnathan and D	Jer 36:25	1806

DELAY
Thou shalt not d to offer the	Ex 22:29	309
he would not d to come to them	Acts 9:38	3635
without any d on the morrow I sat	Acts 25:17	311

DELAYED
d to come down out of the mount	Ex 32:1	954
d not to keep thy commandments	Ps 119:60	4102

DELAYETH
his heart, My lord d his coming	Mt 24:48	5549
his heart, My lord d his coming	Lk 12:45	5549

DELECTABLE
their d things shall not profit	Is 44:9	2530

DELICACIES
through the abundance of her d	Rev 18:3	4764

DELICATE
is tender among you, and very d	Deut 28:54	6028
d woman among you, which would	Deut 28:56	6028
no more be called tender and d	Is 47:1	6028
of Zion to a comely and d woman	Jer 6:2	6026
and poll thee for thy d children	Mic 1:16	8588

DELICATELY
And Agag came unto him d	1Sa 15:32	4574
He that d bringeth up his servant	Prov 29:21	6445
They that did feed d are desolate	Lam 4:5	4574
gorgeously apparelled, and live d	Lk 7:25	5172

DELICATENESS
of her foot upon the ground for d	Deut 28:56	6026

DELICATES
hath filled his belly with my d	Jer 51:34	5730

DELICIOUSLY
glorified herself, and lived d	Rev 18:7	4763
lived d with her, shall bewail	Rev 18:9	4763

DELIGHT
because he had d in Jacob's	Gen 34:19	2654
If the LORD d in us, then he will	Num 14:8	2654
Only the LORD had a d in thy	Deut 10:15	2836
be, if thou have no d in her	Deut 21:14	2654
as great d in burnt offerings	1Sa 15:22	2656
Behold, the king hath d in thee	1Sa 18:22	2654
he thus say, I have no d in thee	2Sa 15:26	2654
my lord the king d in this thing	2Sa 24:3	2654
To whom would the king d to do	Est 6:6	2654
thou have thy d in the Almighty	Job 22:26	6026
Will he d himself in the Almighty	Job 27:10	6026
that he should d himself with God	Job 34:9	7521
But his d is in the law of the	Ps 1:2	2656
excellent, in whom is all my d	Ps 16:3	2656
D thyself also in the LORD	Ps 37:4	6026
shall d themselves in the	Ps 37:11	6026
I d to do thy will, O my God	Ps 40:8	2654
they d in lies	Ps 62:4	7521
thou the people that d in war	Ps 68:30	2654
within me thy comforts d my soul	Ps 94:19	8173
I will d myself in thy statutes	Ps 119:16	8173
Thy testimonies also are my d	Ps 119:24	8191
for therein do I d	Ps 119:35	2654
And I will d myself in thy	Ps 119:47	8173
but I d in thy law	Ps 119:70	8173
for thy law is my d	Ps 119:77	8173
and thy law is my d	Ps 119:174	8191
the scorners d in their scorning,	Prov 1:22	2531
d in the frowardness of the	Prov 2:14	1523
and I was daily his d, rejoicing	Prov 8:30	8191

but a just weight is his d	Prov 11:1	7522
upright in their way are his d	Prov 11:20	7522
they that deal truly are his d	Prov 12:22	7522
prayer of the upright is his d	Prov 15:8	7522
Righteous lips are the d of kings	Prov 16:13	7522
A fool hath no d in understanding	Prov 18:2	2654
D is not seemly for a fool	Prov 19:10	8588
them that rebuke him shall be d	Prov 24:25	5276
he shall give d unto thy soul	Prov 29:17	4574
under his shadow with great d	Song 2:3	2530
I d not in the blood of bullocks	Is 1:11	2654
for gold, they shall not d in it	Is 13:17	2654
let your soul d itself in fatness	Is 55:2	6026
d to know my ways, as a nation	Is 58:2	2654
they take d in approaching to God	Is 58:2	2654
and call the sabbath a d, the holy	Is 58:13	6027
Then shalt thou d thyself in the	Is 58:14	6026
they have no d in it	Jer 6:10	2654
for in these things I d, saith	Jer 9:24	2654
of the covenant, whom ye d in	Mal 3:1	2655
For I d in the law of God after	Rom 7:22	4913

DELIGHTED
Saul's son d much in David	1Sa 19:2	2654
delivered me, because he d in me	2Sa 22:20	2654
which d in thee, to set thee on	1Kin 10:9	2654
which d in thee, to set thee on	2Chr 9:8	2654
d themselves in thy great	Neh 9:25	5727
no more, except the king d in her	Est 2:14	2654
delivered me, because he d in me	Ps 18:19	2654
deliver him, seeing he d in him	Ps 22:8	2654
as he d not in blessing, so let	Ps 109:17	2654
did choose that wherein I d not	Is 65:12	2654
and chose that in which I d not	Is 66:4	2654
be d with the abundance of her	Is 66:11	6026

DELIGHTEST
thou d not in burnt offering	Ps 51:16	7521

DELIGHTETH
the man whom the king d to honour	Est 6:6	2654
the man whom the king d to honour	Est 6:7	2654
withal whom the king d to honour	Est 6:9	2654
the man whom the king d to honour	Est 6:9	2654
the man whom the king d to honour	Est 6:11	2654
and he d in his way	Ps 37:23	2654
the LORD, that d greatly in his	Ps 112:1	2654
He d not in the strength of the	Ps 147:10	2654
as a father the son in whom he d	Prov 3:12	7521
mine elect, in whom my soul d	Is 42:1	7521
for the LORD d in thee, and thy	Is 62:4	2654
ways, and their soul d in their	Is 66:3	2654
for ever, because he d in mercy	Mic 7:18	2654
of the LORD, and he d in them	Mal 2:17	2654

DELIGHTS
you in scarlet, with other d	2Sa 1:24	5730
Unless thy law had been my d	Ps 119:92	8191
yet thy commandments are my d	Ps 119:143	8191
my d were with the sons of men	Prov 8:31	8191
the d of the sons of men, as	Eccl 2:8	8588
pleasant art thou, O love, for d	Song 7:6	8588

DELIGHTSOME
for ye shall be a d land, saith	Mal 3:12	2656

DELILAH (de-li´-lah) *Woman who betrayed Samson.*
valley of Sorek, whose name was D	Judg 16:4	1807
D said to Samson, Tell me, I pray	Judg 16:6	1807
D said unto Samson, Behold, thou	Judg 16:10	1807
D therefore took new ropes, and	Judg 16:12	1807
D said unto Samson, Hitherto thou	Judg 16:13	1807
when D saw that he had told her	Judg 16:18	1807

DELIVER
D me, I pray thee, from the hand	Gen 32:11	5337
to d him to his father again	Gen 37:22	7725
thou shalt d Pharaoh's cup into	Gen 40:13	5414
so will I d you your brother, and	Gen 42:34	5414
d him into my hand, and I will	Gen 42:37	5414
I am come down to d them out of	Ex 3:8	5337
yet shall ye d the tale of bricks	Ex 5:18	5414
but God d him into his hand	Ex 21:13	579
If a man shall d unto his	Ex 22:7	5414
If a man d unto his neighbour an	Ex 22:10	5414
thou shalt d it unto him by that	Ex 22:26	7725
for I will d the inhabitants of	Ex 23:31	5414
they shall d you your bread again	Lev 26:26	7725
If thou wilt indeed d this people	Num 21:2	5414
the congregation shall the	Num 35:25	5337
to d us into the hand of the	Deut 1:27	5414
that he might d him into thy hand	Deut 2:30	5414
for I will d him, and all his	Deut 3:2	5414
thy God shall d them before thee	Deut 7:2	5414

the LORD thy God shall *d* thee	Deut 7:16	5414
thy God shall *d* them unto thee	Deut 7:23	5414
he shall *d* their kings into thine	Deut 7:24	5414
d him into the hand of the	Deut 19:12	5414
to *d* thee; and to give up thine	Deut 23:14	5337
Thou shalt not *d* unto his master	Deut 23:15	5462
In any case thou shalt *d* him the	Deut 24:13	7725
d her husband out of the hand of	Deut 25:11	5337
any that can *d* out of my hand	Deut 32:39	5337
have, and *d* our lives from death	Josh 2:13	5337
to *d* us into the hand of the	Josh 7:7	5414
your God will *d* it into your hand	Josh 8:7	5414
morrow about this time will I *d*	Josh 11:6	5414
then they shall not *d* the slayer	Josh 20:5	5462
I will *d* him into thine hand	Judg 4:7	5414
d the Midianites into thine hand	Judg 7:7	5414
Israel, Did not I *d* you from the	Judg 10:11	3467
wherefore I will *d* you no more	Judg 10:13	3467
let them *d* you in the time of	Judg 10:14	3467
d us only, we pray thee, this day	Judg 10:15	5337
the LORD *d* them before me, shall	Judg 11:9	5414
If thou shalt without fail *d* the	Judg 11:30	5414
he shall begin to *d* Israel out of	Judg 13:5	3467
that we may *d* thee into the hand	Judg 15:12	5414
fast, and *d* thee into their hand	Judg 15:13	5414
Now therefore *d* us the men	Judg 20:13	5414
I will *d* them into thine hand	Judg 20:28	5414
who shall *d* us out of the hand of	1Sa 4:8	5337
he will *d* you out of the hand of	1Sa 7:3	5337
Israel *d* out of the hands of the	1Sa 7:14	5337
but now *d* us out of the hand of	1Sa 12:10	5337
things, which cannot profit nor *d*	1Sa 12:21	5337
wilt thou *d* them into the hand of	1Sa 14:37	5414
he will *d* me out of the hand of	1Sa 17:37	5337
the LORD *d* thee into mine hand	1Sa 17:46	5462
for I will *d* the Philistines into	1Sa 23:4	5414
of Keilah *d* me up into his hand	1Sa 23:11	5462
Will the men of Keilah *d* me	1Sa 23:12	5462
LORD said, They will *d* thee up	1Sa 23:12	5462
our part shall be to *d* him into	1Sa 23:20	5462
I will *d* thine enemy into thine	1Sa 24:4	5414
cause, and *d* me out of thine hand	1Sa 24:15	8199
LORD, and let him *d* me out of all	1Sa 26:24	5337
Moreover the LORD will also *d*	1Sa 28:19	5414
the LORD also shall the host of	1Sa 28:19	5414
nor *d* me into the hands of my	1Sa 30:15	5462
D me my wife Michal, which I	2Sa 3:14	5414
wilt thou *d* them into mine hand	2Sa 5:19	5414
for I will doubtless *d* the	2Sa 5:19	5414
D him that smote his brother,	2Sa 14:7	5414
to *d* his handmaid out of the hand	2Sa 14:16	5337
d him only, and I will depart from	2Sa 20:21	5414
d them to the enemy, so that they	1Kin 8:46	5414
that thou wouldest *d* thy servant	1Kin 18:9	5414
Thou shalt *d* me thy silver, and	1Kin 20:5	5414
I will *d* it into thine hand this	1Kin 20:13	5414
therefore will I *d* all this great	1Kin 20:28	5414
for the Lord shall *d* it into the	1Kin 22:6	5414
for the LORD shall *d* it into the	1Kin 22:12	5414
for the LORD shall *d* it into the	1Kin 22:15	5414
to *d* them into the hand of Moab	2Kin 3:10	5414
to *d* them into the hand of Moab	2Kin 3:13	5414
he will *d* the Moabites also into	2Kin 3:18	5414
but *d* it for the breaches of the	2Kin 12:7	5414
he shall *d* you out of the hand of	2Kin 17:39	5337
I will *d* thee two thousand horses	2Kin 18:23	5414
be able to *d* you out of his hand	2Kin 18:29	5337
saying, The LORD will surely *d* us	2Kin 18:30	5337
you, saying, The LORD will *d* us	2Kin 18:32	5337
that the LORD should *d* Jerusalem	2Kin 18:35	5337
and I will *d* thee and this city out	2Kin 20:6	5337
d them into the hand of their	2Kin 21:14	5414
let them *d* it into the hand of	2Kin 22:5	5414
wilt thou *d* them into mine hand	1Chr 14:10	5414
for I will *d* them into thine hand	1Chr 14:10	5414
d us from the heathen, that we	1Chr 16:35	5337
d them over before their enemies,	2Chr 6:36	5414
for God will *d* it into the king's	2Chr 18:5	5414
for the LORD shall *d* it into the	2Chr 18:11	5414
which could not *d* their own	2Chr 25:15	5337
that he might *d* them into the	2Chr 25:20	5414
d the captives again, which ye	2Chr 28:11	7725
The LORD our God shall *d* us out	2Chr 32:11	5337
to *d* their lands out of mine hand	2Chr 32:13	5337
that could *d* his people out of	2Chr 32:14	5337
be able to *d* you out of mine hand	2Chr 32:14	5337
to *d* his people out of mine hand	2Chr 32:15	5337
your God *d* you out of mine hand	2Chr 32:17	5337
d his people out of mine hand	Ezr 7:19	8000
those *d* thou before the God of	Neh 9:28	5337
many times didst thou *d* them		5337

neither is there any to *d* them	Job 5:4	5337
He shall *d* thee in six troubles	Job 5:19	5337
D me from the enemy's hand	Job 6:23	4422
none that can *d* out of thine hand	Job 10:7	5337
He shall *d* the island of the	Job 22:30	4422
D him from going down to the pit	Job 33:24	6308
He will *d* his soul from going	Job 33:28	6299
then a great ransom cannot *d* thee	Job 36:18	5186
Return, O LORD, *d* my soul	Ps 6:4	2502
them that persecute me, and *d* me	Ps 7:1	5337
pieces, while there is none to *d*	Ps 7:2	5337
d my soul from the wicked, which	Ps 17:13	6403
trusted, and thou didst *d* them	Ps 22:4	6403
on the LORD that he would *d* him	Ps 22:8	6403
let him *d* him, seeing he	Ps 22:8	5337
D my soul from the sword	Ps 22:20	5337
O keep my soul, and *d* me	Ps 25:20	5337
D me not over unto the will of	Ps 27:12	5414
d me in thy righteousness	Ps 31:1	6403
d me speedily	Ps 31:2	5337
d me from the hand of mine	Ps 31:15	5337
neither shall he *d* any by his	Ps 33:17	4422
To *d* their soul from death, and to	Ps 33:19	5337
LORD shall help them, and *d* them	Ps 37:40	6403
he shall *d* them from the wicked,	Ps 37:40	6403
D me from all my transgressions	Ps 39:8	5337
Be pleased, O LORD, to *d* me	Ps 40:13	5337
the LORD will *d* him in time of	Ps 41:1	4422
thou wilt not *d* him unto the will	Ps 41:2	5414
O *d* me from the deceitful and	Ps 43:1	6403
I will *d* thee, and thou shalt	Ps 50:15	2502
in pieces, and there be none to *d*	Ps 50:22	5337
D me from bloodguiltiness, O God,	Ps 51:14	5337
wilt not thou *d* my feet from	Ps 56:13	5337
D me from mine enemies, O my God	Ps 59:1	5337
D me from the workers of iniquity	Ps 59:2	5337
D me out of the mire, and let me	Ps 69:14	5337
d me because of mine enemies	Ps 69:18	6299
Make haste, O God, to *d* me	Ps 70:1	5337
D me in thy righteousness, and	Ps 71:2	5337
D me, O my God, out of the hand	Ps 71:4	6403
for there is none to *d* him	Ps 71:11	5337
For he shall *d* the needy when he	Ps 72:12	5337
O *d* not the soul of thy	Ps 74:19	5414
d us, and purge away our sins, for	Ps 79:9	5337
D the poor and needy	Ps 82:4	6403
shall he *d* his soul from the hand	Ps 89:48	4422
Surely he shall *d* thee from the	Ps 91:3	5337
upon me, therefore will I *d* him	Ps 91:14	6403
I will *d* him, and honour him	Ps 91:15	2502
Many times did he *d* them	Ps 106:43	5337
thy mercy is good, *d* thou me	Ps 109:21	5337
O LORD, I beseech thee, *d* my soul	Ps 116:4	4422
D me from the oppression of man	Ps 119:134	6299
Consider mine affliction, and *d* me	Ps 119:153	2502
Plead my cause, and *d* me	Ps 119:154	1350
d me according to thy word	Ps 119:170	5337
D my soul, O LORD, from lying	Ps 120:2	5337
D me, O LORD, from the evil man	Ps 140:1	2502
d me from my persecutors	Ps 142:6	5337
D me, O LORD, from mine enemies	Ps 143:9	5337
d me out of great waters, from	Ps 144:7	5337
d me from the hand of strange	Ps 144:11	5337
To *d* thee from the way of the	Prov 2:12	5337
To *d* thee from the strange woman,	Prov 2:16	5337
of glory shall she *d* to thee	Prov 4:9	4042
d thyself, when thou art come	Prov 6:3	5337
D thyself as a roe from the hand	Prov 6:5	5337
of the upright shall *d* them	Prov 11:6	5337
mouth of the upright shall *d* them	Prov 12:6	5337
for if thou *d* him, yet thou must	Prov 19:19	5337
shalt *d* his soul from hell	Prov 23:14	5337
If thou forbear to *d* them that	Prov 24:11	5337
neither shall wickedness *d* those	Eccl 8:8	4422
it away safe, and none shall *d* it	Is 5:29	5337
a great one, and he shall *d* them	Is 19:20	5337
which men *d* to one that is	Is 29:11	5414
defending also he will *d* it	Is 31:5	5337
for he shall not be able to *d* you	Is 36:14	5337
saying, The LORD will surely *d* us	Is 36:15	5337
you, saying, The LORD will *d* us	Is 36:18	5337
that the LORD should *d* Jerusalem	Is 36:20	5337
And I will *d* thee and this city out	Is 38:6	5337
is none that can *d* out of my hand	Is 43:13	5337
prayeth unto it, and saith, *D* me	Is 44:17	5337
aside, that he cannot *d* his soul	Is 44:20	5337
they could not *d* the burden	Is 46:2	4422
even I will carry, and will *d* you	Is 46:4	4422
they shall not *d* themselves from	Is 47:14	5337
or have I no power to *d*	Is 50:2	5337
criest, let thy companies *d* thee	Is 57:13	5337

for I am with thee to d thee	Jer 1:8	5337
thee, saith the LORD, to d thee	Jer 1:19	5337
I d to the sword before their	Jer 15:9	5414
to d thee, saith the LORD	Jer 15:20	5337
I will d thee out of the hand of	Jer 15:21	5337
Therefore d up their children to	Jer 18:21	5414
Moreover I will d all the	Jer 20:5	5414
I will d Zedekiah king of Judah,	Jer 21:7	5414
d him that is spoiled out of the	Jer 21:12	5337
d the spoiled out of the hand of	Jer 22:3	5337
I will d them to be removed into	Jer 24:9	5414
will d them to be removed to all	Jer 29:18	5414
I will d them into the hand of	Jer 29:21	5414
lest they d me into their hand,	Jer 38:19	5414
said, They shall not d thee	Jer 38:20	5414
But I will d thee in that day,	Jer 39:17	5337
For I will surely d thee, and thou	Jer 39:18	4422
you, and to d you from his hand	Jer 42:11	5337
for to d us into the hand of the	Jer 43:3	5414
d such as are for death to death	Jer 43:11	
I will d them into the hand of	Jer 46:26	5414
Babylon, and d every man his soul	Jer 51:6	4422
d ye every man his soul from the	Jer 51:45	4422
that doth d us out of their hand	Lam 5:8	6561
d them in the day of the wrath of	Eze 7:19	5337
d you into the hands of strangers	Eze 11:9	5414
d my people out of your hand, and	Eze 13:21	5337
for I will d my people out of	Eze 13:23	5337
they should d but their own souls	Eze 14:14	5337
they shall d neither sons nor	Eze 14:16	5337
they shall d neither sons nor	Eze 14:18	5337
they shall d neither son nor	Eze 14:20	5337
they shall but d their own souls	Eze 14:20	5337
d thee into the hand of brutish	Eze 21:31	5414
I will d thee into the hand of	Eze 23:28	5414
therefore I will d thee to the	Eze 25:4	5414
will d thee for a spoil to the	Eze 25:7	5414
taketh warning shall d his soul	Eze 33:5	4422
shall not d him in the day of his	Eze 33:12	5337
for I will d my flock from their	Eze 34:10	5337
will d them out of all places	Eze 34:12	5337
that shall d you out of my hands	Dan 3:15	7804
to d us from the burning fiery	Dan 3:17	7804
he will d us out of thine hand, O	Dan 3:17	7804
God that can d after this sort	Dan 3:29	5338
set his heart on Daniel to d him	Dan 6:14	7804
going down of the sun to d him	Dan 6:14	5338
continually, he will d thee	Dan 6:16	7804
able to d thee from the lions	Dan 6:20	7804
any that could d out of his hand	Dan 8:4	5337
could d the ram out of his hand	Dan 8:7	5337
none shall d her out of mine hand	Hos 5:14	5337
how shall I d thee, Israel	Hos 11:8	4042
captivity, to d them up to Edom	Amos 1:6	5462
shall the mighty d himself	Amos 2:14	4422
swift of foot shall not d himself	Amos 2:15	4422
that rideth the horse d himself	Amos 2:15	4422
therefore will I d up the city	Amos 6:8	5462
his head, to d him from his grief	Jonah 4:6	5337
thus shall he d us from the	Mic 5:6	5337
teareth in pieces, and none can d	Mic 5:8	5337
shalt take hold, but shalt not d	Mic 6:14	6403
d them in the day of the LORD's	Zeph 1:18	5337
D thyself, O Zion, that dwellest	Zec 2:7	4422
I will d the men every one into	Zec 11:6	4672
of their hand I will not d them	Zec 11:6	5337
the adversary d thee to the judge	Mt 5:25	*3860*
the judge d thee to the officer,	Mt 5:25	*3860*
temptation, but d us from evil	Mt 6:13	*4506*
for they will d you up to	Mt 10:17	*3860*
But when they d you up, take no	Mt 10:19	*3860*
the brother d up the	Mt 10:21	*3860*
shall d him to the Gentiles to	Mt 20:19	*3860*
Then shall they d you up to be	Mt 24:9	*3860*
give me, and I will d him unto you	Mt 26:15	*3860*
let him d him now, if he will	Mt 27:43	*4506*
shall d him to the Gentiles	Mk 10:33	*3860*
for they shall d you up to.	Mk 13:9	*3860*
d you up, take no thought	Mk 13:11	*3860*
but d us from evil	Lk 11:4	*4506*
the judge d thee to the officer.	Lk 12:58	*3860*
they might d him unto the power	Lk 20:20	*3860*
that God by his hand would d them	Acts 7:25	*1325*
and am come down to d them	Acts 7:34	*1807*
shall d him into the hands of the	Acts 21:11	*3860*
no man may d me unto them	Acts 25:11	*5483*
of the Romans to d any man to die	Acts 25:16	*5483*
who shall d me from the body of	Rom 7:24	*4506*
To d such a one unto Satan for	1Cor 5:5	*3860*
from so great a death, and doth d	2Cor 1:10	*4506*
we trust that he will yet d us	2Cor 1:10	*4506*
that he might d us from this	Gal 1:4	*1807*
the Lord shall d me from every	2Ti 4:18	*4506*
d them who through fear of death	Heb 2:15	*525*
The Lord knoweth how to d the	2Pet 2:9	*4506*

DELIVERANCE

to save your lives by a great d	Gen 45:7	6413
Thou hast given this great d into	Judg 15:18	8668
the LORD had given d unto Syria	2Kin 5:1	8668
said, The arrow of the LORD's d	2Kin 13:17	8668
and the arrow of d from Syria	2Kin 13:17	8668
the LORD saved them by a great d	1Chr 11:14	8668
but I will grant them some d	2Chr 12:7	6413
and hast given us such d as this	Ezr 9:13	6413
d arise to the Jews from another	Est 4:14	2020
Great d giveth he to his king	Ps 18:50	3444
compass me about with songs of d	Ps 32:7	6405
not wrought any d in the earth	Is 26:18	3444
Zion and in Jerusalem shall be d	Joel 2:32	6413
But upon mount Zion shall be d	Obad 17	6413
to preach d to the captives, and	Lk 4:18	*859*
were tortured, not accepting d	Heb 11:35	*629*

DELIVERANCES

command d for Jacob	Ps 44:4	3444

DELIVERED

into your hand are they d	Gen 9:2	5414
which hath d thine enemies into	Gen 14:20	4042
her days to be d were fulfilled	Gen 25:24	3205
he d them into the hand of his	Gen 32:16	5414
he d him out of their hands	Gen 37:21	5337
are d ere the midwives come in	Ex 1:19	3205
An Egyptian d us out of the hand	Ex 2:19	5337
hast thou d thy people at all	Ex 5:23	5337
the Egyptians, and d our houses	Ex 12:27	5337
d me from the sword of Pharaoh	Ex 18:4	5337
the way, and how the LORD d them	Ex 18:8	5337
whom he had d out of the hand of	Ex 18:9	5337
who hath d you out of the hand of	Ex 18:10	5337
who hath d the people from under	Ex 18:10	5337
in that which was d him to keep	Lev 6:2	6487
or that which was d him to keep	Lev 6:4	6487
ye shall be d into the hand of	Lev 26:25	5414
of Israel, and d up the Canaanites	Num 21:3	5414
for I have d him into thy hand,	Num 21:34	5414
So there were d out of the	Num 31:5	4560
the LORD our God d him before us	Deut 2:33	5414
the LORD our God d all unto us	Deut 2:36	5414
So the LORD our God d into our	Deut 3:3	5414
of stone, and d them unto me	Deut 5:22	5414
the LORD d unto me two tables of	Deut 9:10	5414
God hath d it into thine hands	Deut 20:13	5414
God hath d them into thine hands	Deut 21:10	5414
d it unto the priests the sons of	Deut 31:9	5414
Truly the LORD hath d into our	Josh 2:24	5414
d them out of the hand of the	Josh 9:26	5337
for I have d them into thine hand	Josh 10:8	5414
LORD d up the Amorites before the	Josh 10:12	5414
God hath d them into your hand	Josh 10:19	5414
And the LORD d it also, and the	Josh 10:30	5414
the LORD d Lachish into the hand	Josh 10:32	5414
the LORD d them into the hand of	Josh 11:8	5414
the LORD d all their enemies into	Josh 21:44	5414
now ye have d the children of	Josh 22:31	5337
so I d you out of his hand	Josh 24:10	5337
and I d them into your hand	Josh 24:11	5414
I have d the land into his hand	Judg 1:2	5414
the LORD d the Canaanites and the	Judg 1:4	5414
he d them into the hands of	Judg 2:14	5414
which d them out of the hand of	Judg 2:16	3467
d them out of the hand of their	Judg 2:18	3467
neither d he them into the hand	Judg 2:23	5414
who d them, even Othniel the son	Judg 3:9	3467
the LORD d Chushan-rishathaim	Judg 3:10	5414
for the LORD hath d your enemies	Judg 3:28	5414
and he also d Israel	Judg 3:31	3467
hath d Sisera into thine hand	Judg 4:14	5414
They that are d from the noise of	Judg 5:11	
the LORD d them into the hand of	Judg 6:1	5414
I d you out of the hand of the	Judg 6:9	5337
d us into the hands of the	Judg 6:13	5414
for I have d it into thine hand	Judg 7:9	5414
into his hand hath God d Midian	Judg 7:14	5414
for the LORD hath d into your	Judg 7:15	5414
God hath d into your hands the	Judg 8:3	5414
when the LORD hath d Zebah	Judg 8:7	5414
for thou hast d us from the hand	Judg 8:22	3467
who had d them out of the hands	Judg 8:34	5337
d you out of the hand of Midian	Judg 9:17	5337
I d you out of their hand	Judg 10:12	3467
And the LORD God of Israel d Sihon	Judg 11:21	5414

D

the Lord d them into his hands	Judg 11:32	5414
ye d me not out of their hands	Judg 12:2	3467
And when I saw that ye d me not	Judg 12:3	3467
the Lord d them into my hand	Judg 12:3	5414
the Lord d them into the hand of	Judg 13:1	5414
Our god hath d Samson our enemy	Judg 16:23	5414
Our god hath d into our hands our	Judg 16:24	5414
was with child, near to be d	1Sa 4:19	3205
d you out of the hand of the	1Sa 10:18	5337
d you out of the hand of your	1Sa 12:11	5337
for the Lord hath d them into our	1Sa 14:10	5414
for the Lord hath d them into the	1Sa 14:12	5414
d Israel out of the hands of them	1Sa 14:48	5337
him, and d it out of his mouth	1Sa 17:35	5337
The Lord that d me out of the paw	1Sa 17:37	5337
God hath d him into mine hand	1Sa 23:7	5234
but God him not into his hand	1Sa 23:14	5414
d thee to day into mine hand in	1Sa 24:10	5414
the Lord had d me into thine hand	1Sa 24:18	5462
God hath d thine enemy into thine	1Sa 26:8	5462
for the Lord d thee into my hand	1Sa 26:23	5414
d the company that came against	1Sa 30:23	5414
have not d thee into the hand of	2Sa 3:8	4672
the rest of the people he d into	2Sa 10:10	5414
I d thee out of the hand of Saul	2Sa 12:7	5337
the Lord hath d the kingdom into	2Sa 16:8	5414
which hath d up the men that	2Sa 18:28	5462
he d us out of the hand of the	2Sa 19:9	4422
men of his sons be d unto us	2Sa 21:6	5414
he d them into the hands of the	2Sa 21:9	5414
in the day that the Lord had d	2Sa 22:1	5337
He d me from my strong enemy, and	2Sa 22:18	5337
he d me, because he delighted in	2Sa 22:20	2502
Thou also hast d me from the	2Sa 22:44	6403
thou hast d me from the violent	2Sa 22:49	5337
I was d of a child with her in	1Kin 3:17	3205
the third day after that I was d	1Kin 3:18	3205
that this woman was d also	1Kin 3:18	3205
the Lord hath d him unto the lion	1Kin 13:26	5414
d them into the hand of his	1Kin 15:18	5414
house, and d him unto his mother	1Kin 17:23	5414
into whose hand they d the money	2Kin 12:15	5414
he d them into the hand of Hazael	2Kin 13:3	5414
d them into the hand of spoilers,	2Kin 17:20	5414
this city shall not be d into the	2Kin 18:30	5337
any of the gods of the nations d	2Kin 18:33	5337
have they d Samaria out of mine	2Kin 18:34	5337
that have d their country out of	2Kin 18:35	5337
Jerusalem shall not be d into the	2Kin 19:10	5414
and shalt thou be d	2Kin 19:11	5337
d them which my fathers have	2Kin 19:12	5337
money that was d into their hand	2Kin 22:7	5414
have d it into the hand of them	2Kin 22:9	5414
the priest hath d me a book	2Kin 22:10	5414
Hagarites were d into their hand	1Chr 5:20	5414
d it, and slew the Philistines	1Chr 11:14	5337
Then on that day David d first	1Chr 16:7	5414
the rest of the people he d unto	1Chr 19:11	5414
God d them into thine hand	2Chr 13:16	5414
he d them into thine hand	2Chr 16:8	5414
they shall be d into your hand	2Chr 18:14	5414
d to the captains of hundreds	2Chr 23:9	5414
the Lord d a very great host into	2Chr 24:24	5414
Wherefore the Lord his God d him	2Chr 28:5	5414
he was also d into the hand of	2Chr 28:5	5414
he hath d them into your hand, and	2Chr 28:9	5414
he hath d them to trouble, to	2Chr 29:8	5414
d their people out of mine hand	2Chr 32:17	5337
they d the money that was brought	2Chr 34:9	5414
Hilkiah d the book to Shaphan	2Chr 34:15	5414
have d it into the hand of the	2Chr 34:17	5414
Babylon, and they were d unto one	Ezr 5:14	3052
he d us from the hand of the	Ezr 8:31	5337
they d the king's commissions	Ezr 8:36	5414
been d into the hand of the kings	Ezr 9:7	5414
horse be d to the hand of one of	Est 6:9	5414
God hath d me to the ungodly, and	Job 16:11	5462
it is d by the pureness of thine	Job 22:30	4422
so should I be d for ever from my	Job 23:7	6403
Because I d the poor that cried,	Job 29:12	4422
I have d him that without cause	Ps 7:4	2502
d him from the hand of all his	Ps 18:t	5337
He d me from my strong enemy, and	Ps 18:17	5337
he d me, because he delighted in	Ps 18:19	2502
Thou hast d me from the strivings	Ps 18:43	6403
thou hast d me from the violent	Ps 18:48	5337
They cried unto thee, and were d	Ps 22:5	4422
man is not d by much strength	Ps 33:16	5337
me, and d me from all my fears	Ps 34:4	5337
For he hath d me out of all	Ps 54:7	5337
He hath d my soul in peace from	Ps 55:18	6299

For thou hast d my soul from	Ps 56:13	5337
That thy beloved may be d	Ps 60:5	2502
let me be d from them that hate	Ps 69:14	5337
day when he d them from the enemy	Ps 78:42	6299
d his strength into captivity, and	Ps 78:61	5414
his hands were d from the pots	Ps 81:6	5674
calledst in trouble, and I d thee	Ps 81:7	2502
thou hast d my soul from the	Ps 86:13	5337
he d them out of their distresses	Ps 107:6	5337
d them from their destructions	Ps 107:20	4422
That thy beloved may be d	Ps 108:6	2502
For thou hast d my soul from	Ps 116:8	2502
The righteous is d out of trouble	Prov 11:8	2502
knowledge shall the just be d	Prov 11:9	2502
seed of the righteous shall be d	Prov 11:21	4422
walketh wisely, he shall be d	Prov 28:26	4422
and he by his wisdom d the city	Eccl 9:15	4422
to be d to the king of Assyria	Is 20:6	5337
the book is d to him that is not	Is 29:12	5414
he hath d them to the slaughter	Is 34:2	5414
this city shall not be d into the	Is 36:15	5414
any of the gods of the nations d	Is 36:18	5337
have they d Samaria out of my	Is 36:19	5337
that have d their land out of my	Is 36:20	5337
and shalt thou be d	Is 37:11	5337
d them which my fathers have	Is 37:12	5337
thou hast in love to my soul d it	Is 38:17	
mighty, or the lawful captive d	Is 49:24	4422
prey of the terrible shall be d	Is 49:25	4422
came, she was d of a man child	Is 66:7	4422
and say, We are d to do all these	Jer 7:10	5337
for he hath d the soul of the	Jer 20:13	5337
but shall surely be d into the	Jer 32:4	5414
Now when I had d the evidence of	Jer 32:16	5414
It shall be d into the hand of	Jer 32:36	5414
be taken, and d into his hand	Jer 34:3	5414
thou shalt be d into the hand of	Jer 37:17	5414
she shall be d into the hand of	Jer 46:24	5414
the Lord hath d me into their	Lam 1:14	5414
but thou hast d thy soul	Eze 3:19	5337
also thou hast d thy soul	Eze 3:21	5337
they only shall be d, but the	Eze 14:16	5337
they only shall be d themselves	Eze 14:18	5337
d them to cause them to pass	Eze 16:21	5414
d thee unto the will of them that	Eze 16:27	5414
he break the covenant, and be d	Eze 17:15	4422
Wherefore I have d her into the	Eze 23:9	5414
I have therefore d him into the	Eze 31:11	5414
for they are all d unto death	Eze 31:14	5414
she is d to the sword	Eze 32:20	5414
but thou hast d thy soul	Eze 33:9	5337
d them out of the hand of those	Eze 34:27	5337
d his servants that trusted in	Dan 3:28	7804
who hath d Daniel from the power	Dan 6:27	7804
that time thy people shall be d	Dan 12:1	4422
the name of the Lord shall be d	Joel 2:32	4422
because they d up the whole	Amos 1:9	5462
escapeth of them shall not be d	Amos 9:1	4422
neither shouldest thou have d up	Obad 14	5462
there shalt thou be d	Mic 4:10	5337
that he may be d from the power	Hab 2:9	5337
they that tempt God are even d	Mal 3:15	4422
All things are d unto me of my	Mt 11:27	3860
d him to the tormentors, till he	Mt 18:34	3860
and d unto him his goods	Mt 25:14	3860
d him to Pontius Pilate the	Mt 27:2	3860
knew that for envy they had d him	Mt 27:18	3860
Jesus, and d him to be crucified	Mt 27:26	3860
Pilate commanded the body to be d	Mt 27:58	591
your tradition, which ye have d	Mk 7:13	3860
The Son of man is d into the	Mk 9:31	3860
shall be d unto the chief priests	Mk 10:33	3860
him away, and d him to Pilate	Mk 15:1	3860
chief priests had d him for envy	Mk 15:10	3860
d Jesus, when he had scourged him	Mk 15:15	3860
Even as they d them unto us	Lk 1:2	3860
time came that she should be d	Lk 1:57	5088
being d out of the hand of our	Lk 1:74	4506
accomplished that she should be d	Lk 2:6	5088
for that is d unto me	Lk 4:6	3860
there was d unto him the book of	Lk 4:17	1929
And he d him to his mother	Lk 7:15	1325
d him again to his father	Lk 9:42	591
shall be d into the hands of men	Lk 9:44	3860
All things are d to me of my	Lk 10:22	3860
that thou mayest be d from him	Lk 12:58	525
For he shall be d unto the	Lk 18:32	3860
d them ten pounds, and said unto	Lk 19:13	1825
but he d Jesus to their will	Lk 23:25	3860
The Son of man must be d into the	Lk 24:7	3860
our rulers d him to be condemned	Lk 24:20	3860

as soon as she is *d* of the child	Jn 16:21	1080
would not have *d* him up unto thee	Jn 18:30	3860
chief priests have *d* thee unto me	Jn 18:35	3860
I should not be *d* to the Jews	Jn 18:36	3860
therefore he that *d* me unto thee	Jn 19:11	3860
Then *d* he him therefore unto them	Jn 19:16	3860
being *d* by the determinate	Acts 2:23	1560
whom ye *d* up, and denied him in	Acts 3:13	3860
the customs which Moses *d* us	Acts 6:14	3860
d him out of all his afflictions,	Acts 7:10	1807
d him to four quaternions of	Acts 12:4	3860
hath *d* me out of the hand of	Acts 12:11	1807
together, they *d* the epistle	Acts 15:30	1929
they *d* them the decrees for to	Acts 16:4	3860
d the epistle to the governor,	Acts 23:33	325
sail into Italy, they *d* Paul	Acts 27:1	3860
the centurion *d* the prisoners to	Acts 28:16	3860
yet was I *d* prisoner from	Acts 28:17	3860
Who was *d* for our offences, and	Rom 4:25	3860
form of doctrine which was *d* you	Rom 6:17	3860
But now we are *d* from the law	Rom 7:6	2673
creature itself also shall be *d*	Rom 8:21	1659
but *d* him up for us all, how	Rom 8:32	3860
That I may be *d* from them that do	Rom 15:31	4506
ordinances, as I *d* them to you	1Cor 11:2	3860
Lord that which also I *d* unto you	1Cor 11:23	3860
For I *d* unto you first of all	1Cor 15:3	3860
when he shall have *d* up the	1Cor 15:24	3860
Who *d* us from so great a death,	2Cor 1:10	4506
d unto death for Jesus' sake	2Cor 4:11	3860
Who hath *d* us from the power of	Col 1:13	4506
which *d* us from the wrath to come	1Th 1:10	4506
And that we may be *d* from	2Th 3:2	4506
whom I have *d* unto Satan, that	1Ti 1:20	3860
but out of them all the Lord *d* me	2Ti 3:11	4506
I was *d* out of the mouth of the	2Ti 4:17	4506
was *d* of a child when she was	Heb 11:11	5088
d them into chains of darkness,	2Pet 2:4	3860
d just Lot, vexed with the filthy	2Pet 2:7	4506
the holy commandment *d* unto them	2Pet 2:21	3860
which was once *d* unto the saints	Jude 3	3860
in birth, and pained to be *d*	Rev 12:2	5088
the woman which was ready to be *d*	Rev 12:4	5088
hell *d* up the dead which were in	Rev 20:13	1325

DELIVEREDST

Therefore thou *d* them into the	Neh 9:27	5414
thou *d* unto me five talents	Mt 25:20	3860
thou *d* unto me two talents	Mt 25:22	3860

DELIVERER

the Lord raised up a *d* to the	Judg 3:9	3467
Lord, the Lord raised them up a *d*	Judg 3:15	3467
And there was no *d*, because it was	Judg 18:28	5337
my rock, and my fortress, and my *d*	2Sa 22:2	6403
my rock, and my fortress, and my *d*	Ps 18:2	6403
thou art my help and my *d*	Ps 40:17	6403
thou art my help and my *d*	Ps 70:5	6403
my high tower, and my *d*	Ps 144:2	6403
a *d* by the hand of the angel	Acts 7:35	3086
shall come out of Sion the *D*	Rom 11:26	4506

DELIVEREST

which *d* the poor from him that is	Ps 35:10	5337
that which thou *d* will I give up	Mic 6:14	6403

DELIVERETH

He *d* the poor in his affliction,	Job 36:15	2502
He *d* me from mine enemies	Ps 18:48	6403
them that fear him, and *d* them	Ps 34:7	2502
d them out of all their troubles	Ps 34:17	5337
but the Lord *d* him out of them	Ps 34:19	5337
he *d* them out of the hand of the	Ps 97:10	5337
who *d* David his servant from the	Ps 144:10	6475
but righteousness *d* from death	Prov 10:2	5337
but righteousness *d* from death	Prov 11:4	5337
A true witness *d* souls	Prov 14:25	5337
d girdles unto the merchant	Prov 31:24	5414
they are for a prey, and none *d*	Is 42:22	5337
He *d* and rescueth, and he worketh	Dan 6:27	7804

DELIVERING

d you up to the synagogues, and	Lk 21:12	3860
d into prisons both men and women	Acts 22:4	3860
D thee from the people, and from	Acts 26:17	1807

DELIVERY

draweth near the time of her *d*	Is 26:17	3205

DELUSION

God shall send them strong *d*	2Th 2:11	4106

DELUSIONS

I also will choose their *d*	Is 66:4	8586

DEMAND

for I will *d* of thee, and answer	Job 38:3	7592
I will *d* of thee, and declare thou	Job 40:7	7592
I will *d* of thee, and declare thou	Job 42:4	7592
the *d* by the word of the holy	Dan 4:17	7595

DEMANDED

set over them, were beaten, and *d*	Ex 5:14	559
David *d* of him how Joab did, and	2Sa 11:7	7592
king hath *d* cannot the wise men	Dan 2:27	7593
he *d* of them where Christ should	Mt 2:4	4441
And the soldiers likewise *d* of him	Lk 3:14	1905
when he was *d* of the Pharisees,	Lk 17:20	1905
d who he was, and what he had done	Acts 21:33	4441

DEMAS (de'-mas) *A companion of Paul.*

Luke, the beloved physician, and *D*	Col 4:14	1214
For *D* hath forsaken me, having	2Ti 4:10	1214
Marcus, Aristarchus, *D*, Lucas, my	Philem 24	1214

DEMETRIUS (de-me'-tre-us)
   1. *An opponent of Paul.*

For a certain man named *D*	Acts 19:24	1216
Wherefore if *D*, and the craftsmen	Acts 19:38	1216

   2. *Disciple commended by John.*

D hath good report of all men, and	3Jn 12	1216

DEMONSTRATION

but in *d* of the Spirit and of	1Cor 2:4	585

DEN

wait secretly as a lion in his *d*	Ps 10:9	5520
put his hand on the cockatrice' *d*	Is 11:8	3975
become a *d* of robbers in your	Jer 7:11	4631
heaps, and a *d* of dragons	Jer 9:11	4583
Judah desolate, and a *d* of dragons	Jer 10:22	4583
shall be cast into the *d* of lions	Dan 6:7	1358
shall be cast into the *d* of lions	Dan 6:12	1358
and cast him into the *d* of lions	Dan 6:16	1358
and laid upon the mouth of the *d*	Dan 6:17	1358
went in haste unto the *d* of lions	Dan 6:19	1358
And when he came to the *d*, he	Dan 6:20	1358
take Daniel up out of the *d*	Dan 6:23	1358
Daniel was taken up out of the *d*	Dan 6:23	1358
cast them into the *d* of lions	Dan 6:24	1358
they came at the bottom of the *d*	Dan 6:24	1358
a young lion cry out of his *d*	Amos 3:4	4585
ye have made it a *d* of thieves	Mt 21:13	4693
ye have made it a *d* of thieves	Mk 11:17	4693
ye have made it a *d* of thieves	Lk 19:46	4693

DENIED

Then Sarah *d*, saying, I laughed	Gen 18:15	3584
and I *d* him not	1Kin 20:7	4513
for I should have *d* the God that	Job 31:28	3584
But he *d* before them all, saying,	Mt 26:70	720
again he *d* with an oath, I do not	Mt 26:72	720
But he *d*, saying, I know not,	Mk 14:68	720
And he *d* it again	Mk 14:70	720
When all *d*, Peter and they that	Lk 8:45	720
be *d* before the angels of God	Lk 12:9	533
he *d* him, saying, Woman, I know	Lk 22:57	720
And he confessed, and *d* not	Jn 1:20	720
crow, till thou hast *d* me thrice	Jn 13:38	533
He *d* it, and said, I am not	Jn 18:25	720
Peter then *d* again	Jn 18:27	720
d him in the presence of Pilate,	Acts 3:13	720
But ye *d* the Holy One and the Just	Acts 3:14	720
he hath *d* the faith, and is worse	1Ti 5:8	720
my name, and hast not *d* my faith	Rev 2:13	720
my word, and hast not *d* my name	Rev 3:8	720

DENIETH

But he that *d* me before men shall	Lk 12:9	720
that *d* that Jesus is the Christ	1Jn 2:22	720
that *d* the Father and the Son	1Jn 2:22	720
Whosoever *d* the Son, the same	1Jn 2:23	720

DENOUNCE

I *d* unto you this day, that ye	Deut 30:18	5046

DENS

of Israel made them the *d* which	Judg 6:2	4492
Then the beasts go into *d*	Job 37:8	695
When they couch in their *d*	Job 38:40	4585
and lay them down in their *d*	Ps 104:22	4585
and Hermon, from the lions' *d*	Song 4:8	4585
and towers shall be for *d* for ever	Is 32:14	4631
with prey, and his *d* with ravin	Nah 2:12	4585
deserts, and in mountains, and in *d*	Heb 11:38	4693
free man, hid themselves in the *d*	Rev 6:15	4693

DENY

unto you, lest ye *d* your God	Josh 24:27	3584
one petition of thee, *d* me not	1Kin 2:16	7725
his place, then it shall *d* him	Job 8:18	3584

D

d me them not before I die	Prov 30:7	4513
d thee, and say, Who is the LORD	Prov 30:9	3584
whosoever shall *d* me before men	Mt 10:33	720
him will I also *d* before my	Mt 10:33	720
come after me, let him *d* himself	Mt 16:24	533
cock crow, thou shalt *d* me thrice	Mt 26:34	533
with thee, yet will I not *d* thee	Mt 26:35	533
cock crow, thou shalt *d* me thrice	Mt 26:75	533
come after me, let him *d* himself	Mk 8:34	533
twice, thou shalt *d* me thrice	Mk 14:30	533
I will not *d* thee in any wise	Mk 14:31	533
twice, thou shalt *d* me thrice	Mk 14:72	533
come after me, let him *d* himself	Lk 9:23	533
which *d* that there is any	Lk 20:27	483
thrice *d* that thou knowest me	Lk 22:34	533
cock crow, thou shalt *d* me thrice	Lk 22:61	533
and we cannot *d* it	Acts 4:16	720
if we *d* him, he also will *d* us	2Ti 2:12	720
if we *d* him, he also will *d* us	2Ti 2:12	720
he cannot *d* himself	2Ti 2:13	720
but in works they *d* him, being	Titus 1:16	720

DENYING

but *d* the power thereof	2Ti 3:5	720
d ungodly and worldly lusts,	Titus 2:12	720
even the *d* Lord that bought them,	2Pet 2:1	720
d the only Lord God, and our Lord	Jude 4	720

DEPART

or if thou *d* to the right hand,	Gen 13:9	
sceptre shall not *d* from Judah	Gen 49:10	5493
And the frogs shall *d* from thee	Ex 8:11	5493
of flies may *d* from Pharaoh	Ex 8:29	5493
And Moses let his father in law *d*	Ex 18:27	7971
so that her fruit *d* from her	Ex 21:22	3318
And the LORD said unto Moses, *D*	Ex 33:1	3212
And then shall he *d* from thee	Lev 25:41	3318
but I will *d* to mine own land, and	Num 10:30	3212
unto the congregation, saying, *D*	Num 16:26	5493
lest they *d* from thy heart all	Deut 4:9	5493
didst *d* out of the land of Egypt	Deut 9:7	3318
law shall not *d* out of thy mouth	Josh 1:8	4185
So Joshua let the people *d*	Josh 24:28	7971
D not hence, I pray thee, until I	Judg 6:18	4185
d early from mount Gilead	Judg 7:3	6852
the morning, that he rose up to *d*	Judg 19:5	3212
And when the man rose up to *d*	Judg 19:7	3212
the morning on the fifth day to *d*	Judg 19:8	3212
And when the man rose up to *d*	Judg 19:9	3212
Saul said unto the Kenites, Go, *d*	1Sa 15:6	5493
d, and get thee into the land of	1Sa 22:5	3212
in the morning, and have light, *d*	1Sa 29:10	3212
rose up early to *d* in the morning	1Sa 29:11	3212
they may lead them away, and *d*	1Sa 30:22	3212
mercy shall not *d* away from him	2Sa 7:15	5493
and to morrow I will let thee *d*	2Sa 11:12	7971
shall never *d* from thine house	2Sa 12:10	5493
make speed to *d*, lest he overtake	2Sa 15:14	3212
only, and I will *d* from the city	2Sa 20:21	3212
statutes, I did not *d* from them	2Sa 22:23	5493
Hadad said to Pharaoh, Let me *d*	1Kin 11:21	7971
D yet for three days, then come	1Kin 12:5	3212
of the LORD, and returned to *d*	1Kin 12:24	3212
of Israel, that he may *d* from me	1Kin 15:19	5927
of Israel, that he may *d* from him	2Chr 16:3	5927
and God moved them to *d* from him	2Chr 18:31	
they might not *d* from their	2Chr 35:15	5493
How long wilt thou not *d* from me	Job 7:19	8159
He shall not *d* out of darkness	Job 15:30	5493
The increase of his house shall *d*	Job 20:28	1540
they say unto God, *D* from us	Job 21:14	5493
Which said unto God, *D* from us	Job 22:17	5493
to *d* from evil is understanding	Job 28:28	5493
D from me, all ye workers of	Ps 6:8	5493
D from evil, and do good	Ps 34:14	5493
D from evil, and do good	Ps 37:27	5493
guile *d* not from her streets	Ps 55:11	4185
A froward heart shall *d* from me	Ps 101:4	5493
D from me, ye evildoers	Ps 119:115	5493
d from me therefore, ye bloody	Ps 139:19	5493
fear the LORD, and *d* from evil	Prov 3:7	5493
let not them *d* from thine eyes	Prov 3:21	3868
Let them not *d* from thine eyes	Prov 4:21	3868
d not from the words of my mouth	Prov 5:7	5493
to *d* from the snares of death	Prov 13:14	5493
to fools to *d* from evil	Prov 13:19	5493
to *d* from the snares of death	Prov 14:27	5493
that he may *d* from hell beneath	Prov 15:24	5493
fear of the LORD men *d* from evil	Prov 16:6	5493
of the upright is to *d* from evil	Prov 16:17	5493
evil shall not *d* from his house	Prov 17:13	4185
he is old, he will not *d* from it	Prov 22:6	5493

not his foolishness *d* from him	Prov 27:22	5493
The envy also of Ephraim shall *d*	Is 11:13	5493
shall his yoke *d* from off them	Is 14:25	5493
his burden *d* from off their	Is 14:25	5493
D ye, *d* ye, go ye out from	Is 52:11	5493
d ye, go ye out from thence,	Is 52:11	5493
For the mountains shall *d*	Is 54:10	4185
my kindness shall not *d* from thee	Is 54:10	4185
shall not *d* out of thy mouth, nor	Is 59:21	4185
lest my soul *d* from thee	Jer 6:8	3363
they that *d* from me shall be	Jer 17:13	3249
those ordinances *d* from before me	Jer 31:36	4185
that they shall not *d* from me	Jer 32:40	5493
Chaldeans shall surely *d* from us	Jer 37:9	1980
for they shall not *d*	Jer 37:9	1980
they shall remove, they shall *d*	Jer 50:3	1980
They cried unto them, *D* ye	Lam 4:15	5493
d, *d*, touch not	Lam 4:15	5493
d, *d*, touch not	Lam 4:15	5493
and my jealousy shall *d* from thee	Eze 16:42	5493
also to them when I *d* from them	Hos 9:12	5493
Arise ye, and *d*	Mic 2:10	3212
the sceptre of Egypt shall *d* away	Zec 10:11	5493
d from me, ye that work iniquity	Mt 7:23	672
to *d* unto the other side	Mt 8:18	565
he would *d* out of their coasts	Mt 8:34	3327
when ye *d* out of that house or	Mt 10:14	1831
said unto them, They need not *d*	Mt 14:16	565
D from me, ye cursed, into	Mt 25:41	4198
pray him to *d* out of their coasts	Mk 5:17	565
abide till ye *d* from that place	Mk 6:10	1831
nor hear you, when ye *d* thence	Mk 6:11	1607
thou thy servant *d* in peace	Lk 2:29	630
that he should not *d* from them	Lk 4:42	4198
Jesus' knees, saying, *D* from me	Lk 5:8	1831
about besought him to *d* from them	Lk 8:37	565
into, there abide, and thence *d*	Lk 9:4	1831
thee, thou shalt not *d* thence	Lk 12:59	1831
d from me, all ye workers of	Lk 13:27	868
him, Get thee out, and *d* hence	Lk 13:31	4198
are in the midst of it *d* out	Lk 21:21	1633
D hence, and go into Judaea, that	Jn 7:3	3327
D out of this world unto the	Jn 13:1	3327
but if I *d*, I will send him unto	Jn 16:7	4198
they should not *d* from Jerusalem	Acts 1:4	5562
now therefore *d*, and go in peace	Acts 16:36	1831
desired them to *d* out of the city	Acts 16:39	1831
commanded all Jews to *d* from Rome	Acts 18:2	5562
them, ready to *d* on the morrow	Acts 20:7	1826
And he said unto me, *D*	Acts 22:21	4198
captain then let the young man *d*	Acts 23:22	630
himself would *d* shortly thither	Acts 25:4	1607
part advised to *d* thence also	Acts 27:12	321
not the wife *d* from her husband	1Cor 7:10	5562
But and if she *d*, let her remain	1Cor 7:11	5562
But if the unbelieving *d*, let him	1Cor 7:15	5562
the unbelieving *d*, let him *d*	1Cor 7:15	5562
thrice, that it might *d* from me	2Cor 12:8	868
betwixt two, having a desire to *d*	Phil 1:23	360
times some shall *d* from the faith	1Ti 4:1	868
name of Christ *d* from iniquity	2Ti 2:19	868
D in peace, be ye warmed and	Jas 2:16	5217

DEPARTED

So Abram *d*, as the LORD had	Gen 12:4	3212
years old when he *d* out of Haran	Gen 12:4	3318
in Sodom, and his goods, and *d*	Gen 14:12	3212
and she *d*, and wandered in the	Gen 21:14	3212
of the camels of his master, and *d*	Gen 24:10	3212
Isaac *d* thence, and pitched his	Gen 26:17	3212
away, and they *d* from him in peace	Gen 26:31	3212
my sleep *d* from mine eyes	Gen 31:40	5074
and Laban *d*, and returned unto his	Gen 31:55	5265
And the man said, They are *d* hence	Gen 37:17	5265
asses *d* with the corn, and *d* thence	Gen 42:26	3212
sent his brethren away, and they *d*	Gen 45:24	3212
For they were *d* from Rephidim	Ex 19:2	5265
d not out of the tabernacle	Ex 33:11	4185
of the children of Israel *d* from	Ex 35:20	3318
if the plague be *d* from them	Lev 13:58	5493
they *d* from the mount of the LORD	Num 10:33	5265
kindled against them; and he *d*	Num 12:9	3212
And the cloud *d* from off the	Num 12:10	5493
their defence is *d* from them	Num 14:9	5493
and Moses, *d* not out of the camp	Num 14:44	4185
the elders of Midian *d* with the	Num 22:7	3212
they *d* from Rameses in the first	Num 33:3	5265
they *d* from Succoth, and pitched	Num 33:6	5265
they *d* from before Pi-hahiroth,	Num 33:8	5265
they *d* from Dophkah, and encamped	Num 33:13	5265
they *d* from Rephidim, and pitched	Num 33:15	5265

D

they *d* from Kibroth-hattaavah, and	Num 33:17	5265
they *d* from Hazeroth, and pitched	Num 33:18	5265
they *d* from Rithmah, and pitched	Num 33:19	5265
they *d* from Rimmon-parez, and	Num 33:20	5265
they *d* from Tahath, and pitched at	Num 33:27	5265
they *d* from Hashmonah, and	Num 33:30	5265
they *d* from Moseroth, and pitched	Num 33:31	5265
they *d* from Ebronah, and encamped	Num 33:35	5265
they *d* from mount Hor, and pitched	Num 33:41	5265
they *d* from Zalmonah, and pitched	Num 33:42	5265
they *d* from Punon, and pitched in	Num 33:43	5265
they *d* from Oboth, and pitched in	Num 33:44	5265
they *d* from Iim, and pitched in	Num 33:45	5265
they *d* from the mountains of	Num 33:48	5265
when we *d* from Horeb, we went	Deut 1:19	5265
when she is *d* out of his house,	Deut 24:2	3318
And she sent them away, and they *d*	Josh 2:21	3212
d from the children of Israel out	Josh 22:9	3212
of the LORD *d* out of his sight	Judg 6:21	1980
they *d* every man unto his place	Judg 9:55	3212
not that the LORD was *d* from him	Judg 16:20	5493
the man *d* out of the city from	Judg 17:8	3212
Then the five men *d*, and came to	Judg 18:7	3212
So they turned and *d*, and put the	Judg 18:21	3212
that night, but he rose up and *d*	Judg 19:10	3212
of Israel *d* thence at that time	Judg 21:24	1980
The glory is *d* from Israel	1Sa 4:21	1540
said, The glory is *d* from Israel	1Sa 4:22	1540
not let the people go, and they *d*	1Sa 6:6	3212
When thou art *d* from me to day,	1Sa 10:2	3212
So the Kenites *d* from among the	1Sa 15:6	5493
Spirit of the LORD *d* from Saul	1Sa 16:14	5493
and the evil spirit *d* from him	1Sa 16:23	5493
was with him, and was *d* from Saul	1Sa 18:12	5493
And he arose and *d*	1Sa 20:42	3212
David therefore *d* thence, and	1Sa 22:1	3212
Then David *d*, and came into the	1Sa 22:5	3212
arose and *d* out of Keilah, and went	1Sa 23:13	3318
God is *d* from me, and answereth me	1Sa 28:15	5493
seeing the LORD is *d* from thee	1Sa 28:16	5493
So all the people *d* every one to	2Sa 6:19	3212
Uriah *d* out of the king's house,	2Sa 11:8	3318
And Nathan *d* unto his house	2Sa 12:15	3212
came to pass, after they were *d*	2Sa 17:21	3212
from the day the king *d* until the	2Sa 19:24	3212
have not wickedly *d* from my God	2Sa 22:22	
And the people *d*	1Kin 12:5	3212
So Israel *d* unto their tents	1Kin 12:16	3212
And Jeroboam's wife arose, and *d*	1Kin 14:17	3212
So he *d* thence, and found Elisha	1Kin 19:19	3212
And the messengers *d*, and brought	1Kin 20:9	3212
as soon as thou art *d* from me	1Kin 20:36	1980
And as soon as he was *d* from him	1Kin 20:36	3212
So the prophet *d*, and waited for	1Kin 20:38	3212
And Elijah *d*	2Kin 1:4	3212
he *d* not therefrom	2Kin 3:3	5493
they *d* from him, and returned to	2Kin 3:27	5265
And he *d*, and took with him ten	2Kin 5:5	3212
So he *d* from him a little way	2Kin 5:19	3212
and he let the men go, and they *d*	2Kin 5:24	3212
So he *d* from Elisha, and came to	2Kin 8:14	3212
And he arose and *d*, and came to	2Kin 10:12	935
And when he was *d* thence, he	2Kin 10:15	3212
Jehu *d* not from after them, to	2Kin 10:29	5493
for he *d* not from the sins of	2Kin 10:31	5493
he *d* not therefrom	2Kin 13:2	5493
Nevertheless they *d* not from the	2Kin 13:6	5493
he *d* not from all the sins of	2Kin 13:11	5493
he *d* not from all the sins of	2Kin 14:24	5493
he *d* not from the sins of	2Kin 15:9	5493
he *d* not all his days from the	2Kin 15:18	5493
he *d* not from the sins of	2Kin 15:24	5493
he *d* not from the sins of	2Kin 15:28	5493
they *d* not from them	2Kin 17:22	5493
d not from following him, but	2Kin 18:6	5493
heard that he was *d* from Lachish	2Kin 19:8	5265
So Sennacherib king of Assyria *d*	2Kin 19:36	5265
all the people *d* every man to his	1Chr 16:43	3212
Wherefore Joab *d*, and went	1Chr 21:4	3318
they *d* not from the commandment	2Chr 8:15	5493
And the people *d*	2Chr 10:5	3212
d not from it, doing that which	2Chr 20:32	5493
years, and *d* without being desired	2Chr 21:20	3212
And when they were *d* from him,	2Chr 24:25	3212
all his days they *d* not from	2Chr 34:33	5493
Then we *d* from the river of Ahava	Ezr 8:31	5265
the cloud *d* not from them by day	Neh 9:19	5493
have not wickedly *d* from my God	Ps 18:21	
who drove him away, and he *d*	Ps 34:*t*	3212
Egypt was glad when they *d*	Ps 105:38	3318
I have not *d* from thy judgments	Ps 119:102	5493
the day that Ephraim *d* from Judah	Is 7:17	5493
heard that he was *d* from Lachish	Is 37:8	5265
So Sennacherib king of Assyria *d*	Is 37:37	5265
Mine age is *d*, and is removed from	Is 38:12	5265
the smiths, were *d* from Jerusalem	Jer 29:2	3318
of them, they *d* from Jerusalem	Jer 37:5	5927
d to go over to the Ammonites	Jer 41:10	3212
And they *d*, and dwelt in the	Jer 41:17	3212
of Zion all her beauty is *d*	Lam 1:6	3318
heart, which hath *d* from me	Eze 6:9	5493
Then the glory of the LORD *d* from	Eze 10:18	3318
The kingdom is *d* from thee	Dan 4:31	5709
thereof, because it is *d* from it	Hos 10:5	1540
But ye are *d* out of the way	Mal 2:8	5493
they had heard the king, they *d*	Mt 2:9	4198
they *d* into their own country	Mt 2:12	402
And when they were *d*, behold, the	Mt 2:13	402
mother by night, and *d* into Egypt	Mt 2:14	402
into prison, he *d* into Galilee	Mt 4:12	402
And he arose, and *d* to his house	Mt 9:7	565
And when Jesus *d* thence, two blind	Mt 9:27	3855
But they, when they were *d*	Mt 9:31	1831
he *d* thence to teach and to preach	Mt 11:1	3327
And as they *d*, Jesus began to say	Mt 11:7	4198
And when he was *d* thence, he went	Mt 12:9	3327
these parables, he *d* thence	Mt 13:53	3332
he *d* thence by ship into a desert	Mt 14:13	402
d into the coasts of Tyre and	Mt 15:21	402
Jesus *d* from thence, and came nigh	Mt 15:29	3327
And he left them, and *d*	Mt 16:4	565
and he *d* out of him	Mt 17:18	1831
he *d* from Galilee, and came into	Mt 19:1	3332
his hands on them, and *d* thence	Mt 19:15	4198
as they *d* from Jericho, a great	Mt 20:29	1607
went out, and *d* from the temple	Mt 24:1	4198
of silver in the temple, and *d*	Mt 27:5	402
the door of the sepulchre, and *d*	Mt 27:60	565
they *d* quickly from the sepulchre	Mt 28:8	1831
d into a solitary place, and there	Mk 1:35	565
the leprosy *d* from him, and he was	Mk 1:42	565
And he *d*, and began to publish in	Mk 5:20	565
they *d* into a desert place by	Mk 6:32	565
he *d* into a mountain to pray	Mk 6:46	565
ship again *d* to the other side	Mk 8:13	565
they *d* thence, and passed through	Mk 9:30	1831
he *d* to his own house	Lk 1:23	565
And the angel *d* from her	Lk 1:38	565
which *d* not from the temple, but	Lk 2:37	868
he *d* from him for a season	Lk 4:13	868
And when it was day, he *d* and went	Lk 4:42	1831
the leprosy *d* from him	Lk 5:13	565
d to his own house, glorifying	Lk 5:25	565
the messengers of John were *d*	Lk 7:24	565
out of whom the devils were *d*	Lk 8:35	1831
d besought him that he might be	Lk 8:38	1831
And they *d*, and went through the	Lk 9:6	1831
as they *d* from him, Peter said	Lk 9:33	1316
his raiment, and wounded him, and *d*	Lk 10:30	565
And on the morrow when he *d*	Lk 10:35	1831
clothes laid by themselves, and *d*	Lk 24:12	565
Judaea, and *d* again into Galilee	Jn 4:3	565
Now after two days he *d* thence	Jn 4:43	565
The man *d*, and told the Jews that	Jn 5:15	565
he *d* again into a mountain	Jn 6:15	402
These things spake Jesus, and *d*	Jn 12:36	565
they *d* from the presence of the	Acts 5:41	4198
which spake unto Cornelius was *d*	Acts 10:7	565
Then *d* Barnabas to Tarsus, for to	Acts 11:25	1831
and forthwith the angel *d* from him	Acts 12:10	868
And he *d*, and went into another	Acts 12:17	1831
the Holy Ghost, *d* unto Seleucia	Acts 13:4	2718
But when they *d* from Perga	Acts 13:14	1330
the next day he *d* with Barnabas	Acts 14:20	1831
who *d* from them from Pamphylia,	Acts 15:38	868
that they *d* in asunder one from	Acts 15:39	673
And Paul chose Silas, and *d*	Acts 15:40	1831
they comforted them, and *d*	Acts 16:40	1831
to him with all speed, they *d*	Acts 17:15	1826
So Paul *d* from among them	Acts 17:33	1831
these things Paul *d* from Athens	Acts 18:1	5562
he *d* thence, and entered into a	Acts 18:7	1831
had spent some time there, he *d*	Acts 18:23	1831
he *d* from them, and separated the	Acts 19:9	868
and the diseases *d* from them	Acts 19:12	525
d for to go into Macedonia	Acts 20:1	1831
even till break of day, so he *d*	Acts 20:11	1831
had accomplished those days, we *d*	Acts 21:5	1831
we that were of Paul's company *d*	Acts 21:8	1831
Then straightway they *d* from him	Acts 22:29	868
and when we *d*, they laded us with	Acts 28:10	321
after three months we *d* in a ship	Acts 28:11	321

DEPARTETH (continued)

not among themselves, they *d* .... Acts 28:25   630
had said these words, the Jews *d* .... Acts 28:29   565
when I *d* from Macedonia, no .... Phil 4:15   1831
world, and is *d* unto Thessalonica 2Ti 4:10   4198
he therefore *d* for a season .... Philem 15   5563
the heaven *d* as a scroll when it .... Rev 6:14   673
soul lusted after are *d* from thee .... Rev 18:14   565
dainty and goodly are *d* from thee .... Rev 18:14   565

DEPARTETH

wind carrieth him away, and he *d* .... Job 27:21   3212
wise man feareth, and *d* from evil........... Prov 14:16   5493
d in darkness, and his name shall.......... Eccl 6:4   3212
he that *d* from evil maketh.................... Is 59:15   5493
treacherously *d* from her husband .... Jer 3:20
whose heart *d* from the LORD .... Jer 17:5   5493
the prey *d* not .... Nah 3:1   4185
and bruising him hardly *d* from him...... Lk 9:39   672

DEPARTING

to pass, as her soul was in *d* .... Gen 35:18   3318
their *d* out of the land of Egypt .... Ex 16:1   3318
d away from our God, speaking.............. Is 59:13   5253
even by *d* from thy precepts and .... Dan 9:5   5493
transgressed thy law, even by *d* .... Dan 9:11   5493
great whoredom, *d* from the LORD .... Hos 1:2
And the people saw them *d*, and many .. Mk 6:33   5217
d from the coasts of Tyre and .... Mk 7:31   1831
John *d* from them returned to................. Acts 13:13   672
that after my *d* shall grievous............... Acts 20:29   867
in *d* from the living God .... Heb 3:12   868
made mention of the *d* of the .... Heb 11:22   1841

DEPARTURE

sea shall be troubled at thy *d* .... Eze 26:18   3318
and the time of my *d* is at hand............. 2Ti 4:6   359

DEPOSED

he was *d* from his kingly throne, ... Dan 5:20   5182

DEPRIVED

why should I be *d* also of you .... Gen 27:45   7921
Because God hath *d* her of wisdom........ Job 39:17   5382
I am *d* of the residue of my years........... Is 38:10   6485

DEPTH

The *d* saith, It is not in me .... Job 28:14   8415
walked in the search of the *d* .... Job 38:16   8415
he layeth up the *d* in storehouses........... Ps 33:7   8415
a compass upon the face of the *d* .... Prov 8:27   8415
for height, and the earth for *d* .... Prov 25:3   6012
ask it either in the *d*, or in the .... Is 7:11   6009
the *d* closed me round about, the .... Jonah 2:5   8415
were drowned in the *d* of the sea .... Mt 18:6   3989
up, because it had no *d* of earth .... Mk 4:5   899
Nor height, nor *d*, nor any other .... Rom 8:39   899
O the *d* of the riches both of the .... Rom 11:33   899
is the breadth, and length, and *d* .... Eph 3:18   899

DEPTHS

The *d* have covered them .... Ex 15:5   8415
the *d* were congealed in the heart .... Ex 15:8   8415
d that spring out of valleys and.............. Deut 8:7   8415
again from the *d* of the sea .... Ps 68:22   4688
up again from the *d* of the earth .... Ps 71:20   8415
the *d* also were troubled .... Ps 77:16   8415
them drink as out of the great *d* .... Ps 78:15   8415
so he led them through the *d*................. Ps 106:9   8415
they go down again to the *d* .... Ps 107:26   8415
Out of the *d* have I cried unto................ Ps 130:1   4615
his knowledge the *d* are broken up .... Prov 3:20   8415
When there were no *d*, I was .... Prov 8:24   8415
her guests are in the *d* of hell .... Prov 9:18   6010
that hath made the *d* of the sea a .... Is 51:10   4615
be broken by the seas in the *d* of.......... Eze 27:34   4615
their sins into the *d* of the sea .... Mic 7:19   4688
have not known the *d* of Satan.............. Rev 2:24   899

DEPUTED

but there is no man *d* of the king 2Sa 15:3

DEPUTIES

and to the lieutenants, and the *d* .... Est 8:9   6346
and the lieutenants, and the *d* .... Est 9:3   6346
the law is open, and there are *d* .... Acts 19:38   446

DEPUTY

a *d* was king.................................... 1Kin 22:47   5324
was with the *d* of the country .... Acts 13:7   446
to turn away the *d* from the faith .... Acts 13:8   446
Then the *d*, when he saw what was ...... Acts 13:12   446
when Gallio was the *d* of Achaia........... Acts 18:12   446

DERBE (der'-by) A south Galatian town.

of it, and fled unto Lystra and *D*........... Acts 14:6   1191
he departed with Barnabas to *D* .... Acts 14:20   1191

Then came he to *D* and Lystra................ Acts 16:1   1191
and Gaius of *D*, and Timotheus .... Acts 20:4   1191

DERIDE

they shall *d* every strong hold .... Hab 1:10   7832

DERIDED

and they *d* him .... Lk 16:14   1592
the rulers also with them *d* him .... Lk 23:35   1592

DERISION

are younger than I have me in *d* .... Job 30:1   7832
the Lord shall have them in *d* .... Ps 2:4   3932
a *d* to them that are round about........... Ps 44:13   7047
shalt have all the heathen in *d* .... Ps 59:8   3932
d to them that are round about us .... Ps 79:4   7047
proud have had me greatly in *d*.............. Ps 119:51   3887
I am in *d* daily, every one .... Jer 20:7   7814
made a reproach unto me, and a *d* .... Jer 20:8   7047
vomit, and he also shall be in *d*............. Jer 48:26   7814
For was not Israel a *d* unto thee............ Jer 48:27   7814
so shall Moab be a *d* and a.................. Jer 48:39   7814
I was a *d* to all my people .... Lam 3:14   7814
be laughed to scorn and had in *d*........... Eze 23:32   3932
d to the residue of the heathen .... Eze 36:4   3932
this shall be their *d* in the land .... Hos 7:16   3932

DESCEND

and the border shall *d*, and shall.......... Num 34:11   3381
or he shall *d* into battle 1Sa 26:10   3381
his glory shall not *d* after him .... Ps 49:17   3381
that rejoiceth, shall *d* into it .... Is 5:14   3381
with them that *d* into the pit .... Eze 26:20   3381
with them that *d* into the pit .... Eze 31:16   3381
of Israel *d* now from the cross .... Mk 15:32   2597
saw a vision, A certain vessel *d*............. Acts 11:5   2597
Who shall *d* into the deep .... Rom 10:7   2597
shall *d* from heaven with a shout 1Th 4:16   2597

DESCENDED

the LORD *d* upon it in fire .... Ex 19:18   3381
tabernacle, the cloudy pillar *d* .... Ex 33:9   3381
the LORD *d* in the cloud, and stood .... Ex 34:5   3381
the brook that *d* out of the mount .... Deut 9:21   3381
d from the mountain, and passed.......... Josh 2:23   3381
the coast *d* unto the river Kanah,.......... Josh 17:9   3381
the border *d* to Ataroth-adar,................ Josh 18:13   3381
d to the valley of Hinnom, to the .... Josh 18:16   3381
on the south, and *d* to En-rogel,............ Josh 18:16   3381
d to the stone of Bohan the son .... Josh 18:17   3381
as the dew that *d* upon the .... Ps 133:3   3381
ascended up into heaven, or *d* .... Prov 30:4   3381
And the rain *d*, and the floods came ..... Mt 7:25   2597
And the rain *d*, and the floods came ..... Mt 7:27   2597
angel of the Lord *d* from heaven............ Mt 28:2   2597
the Holy Ghost *d* in a bodily .... Lk 3:22   2597
the high priest *d* with the elders............ Acts 24:1   2597
what is it but that he also *d* .... Eph 4:9   2597
He that *d* is the same also that .... Eph 4:10   2597

DESCENDETH

This wisdom *d* not from above, but .... Jas 3:15   2718

DESCENDING

of God ascending and *d* on it .... Gen 28:12   3381
the Spirit of God *d* like a dove .... Mt 3:16   2597
the Spirit like a dove *d* upon him .... Mk 1:10   2597
I saw the Spirit *d* from heaven.............. Jn 1:32   2597
whom thou shalt see the Spirit *d* .... Jn 1:33   2597
and *d* upon the Son of man .... Jn 1:51   2597
and a certain vessel *d* unto him .... Acts 10:11   2597
d out of heaven from God,..................... Rev 21:10   2597

DESCENT

even now at the *d* of the mount of .... Lk 19:37   2600
father, without mother, without *d* .... Heb 7:3   35
But he whose *d* is not counted.............. Heb 7:6   1075

DESCRIBE

d it according to the inheritance .... Josh 18:4   3789
Ye shall therefore *d* the land .... Josh 18:6   3789
them that went to *d* the land.................. Josh 18:8   3789
d it, and come again to me, that I .... Josh 18:8   3789

DESCRIBED

d it by cities into seven parts .... Josh 18:9   3789
he *d* unto him the princes of .... Judg 8:14   3789

DESCRIBETH

Even as David also *d* the....................... Rom 4:6   3004
For Moses *d* the righteousness .... Rom 10:5   1125

DESCRIPTION

bring the *d* hither to me, that I .... Josh 18:6

DESCRY

house of Joseph sent to *d* Beth-el........... Judg 1:23   8446

DESERT

flock to the backside of the *d*	Ex 3:1	4057
three days' journey into the *d*	Ex 5:3	4057
and were come to the *d* of Sinai	Ex 19:2	4057
from the *d* unto the river	Ex 23:31	4057
into the *d* of Zin in the first	Num 20:1	4057
my commandment in the *d* of Zin	Num 27:14	4057
they removed from the *d* of Sinai	Num 33:16	4057
He found him in a *d* land, and in	Deut 32:10	4057
Also he built towers in the *d*	2Chr 26:10	4057
Behold, as wild asses in the *d*	Job 24:5	4057
render to them their *d*	Ps 28:4	1576
and grieve him in the *d*	Ps 78:40	3452
I am like an owl of the *d*	Ps 102:6	2723
and tempted God in the *d*	Ps 106:14	3452
beasts of the *d* shall lie there	Is 13:21	6728
The burden of the *d* of the sea	Is 21:1	4057
so it cometh from the *d*, from a	Is 21:1	4057
The wild beasts of the *d* shall	Is 34:14	6728
the *d* shall rejoice, and blossom	Is 35:1	6160
break out, and streams in the *d*	Is 35:6	6160
make straight in the *d* a highway	Is 40:3	6160
I will set in the *d* the fir tree	Is 41:19	6160
wilderness, and rivers in the *d*	Is 43:19	3452
wilderness, and rivers in the *d*	Is 43:20	3452
her *d* like the garden of the LORD	Is 51:3	6160
shall be like the heath in the *d*	Jer 17:6	6160
people that dwell in the *d*	Jer 25:24	4057
a wilderness, a dry land, and a *d*	Jer 50:12	6160
the wild beasts of the *d* with the	Jer 50:39	6728
country, and go down into the *d*	Eze 47:8	6160
by ship into a *d* place apart	Mt 14:13	2048
to him, saying, This is a *d* place	Mt 14:15	2048
unto you, Behold, he is in the *d*	Mt 24:26	2048
city, but was without in *d* places	Mk 1:45	2048
yourselves apart into a *d* place	Mk 6:31	2048
they departed into a *d* place by	Mk 6:32	2048
him, and said, This is a *d* place	Mk 6:35	2048
departed and went into a *d* place	Lk 4:42	2048
a *d* place belonging to the city	Lk 9:10	2048
for we are here in a *d* place	Lk 9:12	2048
fathers did eat manna in the *d*	Jn 6:31	2048
Jerusalem unto Gaza, which is *d*	Acts 8:26	2048

DESERTS

when he led them through the *d*	Is 48:21	2723
wilderness, through a land of *d*	Jer 2:6	6160
to their *d* will I judge them	Eze 7:27	4941
are like the foxes in the *d*	Eze 13:4	2723
was in the *d* till the day of his	Lk 1:80	2048
they wandered in *d*, and in	Heb 11:38	2047

DESERVE

us less than our iniquities *d*	Ezr 9:13	

DESERVETH

thee less than thine iniquity *d*	Job 11:6	

DESERVING

according to the *d* of his hands	Judg 9:16	1576

DESIRABLE

rulers, all of them *d* young men	Eze 23:6	2531
horses, all of them *d* young men	Eze 23:12	2531
all of them *d* young men, captains	Eze 23:23	2531

DESIRE

thy *d* shall be to thy husband, and	Gen 3:16	8669
And unto thee shall be his *d*	Gen 4:7	8669
for that ye did *d*	Ex 10:11	1245
neither shall any man *d* thy land	Ex 34:24	2530
Neither shalt thou *d* thy	Deut 5:21	2530
thou shalt not *d* the silver or	Deut 7:25	2530
come with all the *d* of his mind	Deut 18:6	183
hast a *d* unto her, that thou	Deut 21:11	2836
I would *d* a request of you, that	Judg 8:24	7592
And on whom is all the *d* of Israel	1Sa 9:20	2532
the *d* of thy soul to come down	1Sa 23:20	183
is all my salvation, and all my *d*	2Sa 23:5	2656
I *d* one small petition of thee	1Kin 2:20	7592
I will do all thy *d* concerning	1Kin 5:8	2656
and thou shalt accomplish my *d*	1Kin 5:9	2656
fir trees according to all his *d*	1Kin 5:10	2656
all Solomon's *d* which he was	1Kin 9:1	2837
with gold, according to all his *d*	1Kin 9:11	2656
unto the queen of Sheba all her *d*	1Kin 10:13	2656
said, Did I a son of my lord	1Kin 4:28	7592
to the queen of Sheba all her *d*	2Chr 9:12	2656
and sought him with their whole *d*	2Chr 15:15	7522
servants, who *d* to fear thy name	Neh 1:11	2655
and I *d* to reason with God	Job 13:3	2654
thou wilt have a *d* to the work of	Job 14:15	3700
for we *d* not the knowledge of thy	Job 21:14	2654
withheld the poor from their *d*	Job 31:16	2656

behold, my *d* is, that the	Job 31:35	8420
speak, for I *d* to justify thee	Job 33:32	2654
My *d* is that Job may be tried	Job 34:36	15
D not the night, when people are	Job 36:20	7602
wicked boasteth of his heart's *d*	Ps 10:3	8378
hast heard the *d* of the humble	Ps 10:17	8378
Thou hast given him his heart's *d*	Ps 21:2	8378
Lord, all my *d* is before thee	Ps 38:9	8378
and offering thou didst not *d*	Ps 40:6	2654
the king greatly thy beauty	Ps 45:11	183
hath seen his *d* upon mine enemies	Ps 54:7	
let me see my *d* upon mine enemies	Ps 59:10	
put to confusion, that *d* my hurt	Ps 70:2	2655
upon earth that I *d* beside thee	Ps 73:25	2654
for he gave them their own *d*	Ps 78:29	8378
shall see my *d* on mine enemies	Ps 92:11	
mine ears shall hear my *d* of the	Ps 92:11	
he see his *d* upon his enemies	Ps 112:8	
the *d* of the wicked shall perish	Ps 112:10	8378
I see my *d* upon them that hate me	Ps 118:7	
satisfiest the *d* of every living	Ps 145:16	7522
He will fulfil the *d* of them that	Ps 145:19	7522
all the things thou canst *d* are	Prov 3:15	2656
but the *d* of the righteous shall	Prov 10:24	8378
The *d* of the righteous is only	Prov 11:23	8378
heart sick, but when the *d* cometh	Prov 13:12	8378
The *d* accomplished is sweet to	Prov 13:19	8378
Through *d* a man, having separated	Prov 18:1	8378
The *d* of a man is his kindness	Prov 19:22	8378
The *d* of the slothful killeth him	Prov 21:25	8378
neither *d* thou his dainty meats	Prov 23:6	183
neither *d* to be with them	Prov 24:1	183
eyes than the wandering of the *d*	Eccl 6:9	5315
be a burden, and *d* shall fail	Eccl 12:5	35
beloved's, and his *d* is toward me	Song 7:10	8669
the *d* of our soul is to thy name,	Is 26:8	8378
is no beauty that we should *d* him	Is 53:2	2530
land whereunto they *d* to return	Jer 22:27	5375,5315
in the place whither ye *d* to go	Jer 42:22	2654
have a *d* to return to dwell there	Jer 44:14	5375,5315
I take away from thee the *d* of	Eze 24:16	4261
the *d* of your eyes, and that which	Eze 24:21	4261
the *d* of their eyes, and that	Eze 24:25	4261
That they would *d* mercies of the	Dan 2:18	1156
nor the *d* of women, nor regard	Dan 11:37	2532
It is in my *d* that I should	Hos 10:10	183
Woe unto you that *d* the day of	Amos 5:18	183
he uttereth his mischievous *d*	Mic 7:3	5315
home, who enlargeth his *d* as hell	Hab 2:5	5315
the *d* of all nations shall come	Hag 2:7	2532
If any man *d* to be first, the	Mk 9:35	2309
do for us whatsoever we shall *d*	Mk 10:35	154
unto you, What things soever ye *d*	Mk 11:24	154
d him to do as he had ever done	Mk 15:8	154
when ye shall *d* to see one of the	Lk 17:22	1937
which *d* to walk in long robes, and	Lk 20:46	2309
With *d* I have desired to eat this	Lk 22:15	1939
The Jews have agreed to *d* thee	Acts 23:20	2065
But we *d* to hear of thee what	Acts 28:22	515
Brethren, my heart's *d* and prayer	Rom 10:1	2107
having a great *d* these many years	Rom 15:23	1974
d spiritual gifts, but rather	1Cor 14:1	2206
when he told us your earnest *d*	2Cor 7:7	1972
what fear, yea, what vehement *d*	2Cor 7:11	1972
from them which *d* occasion	2Cor 11:12	2309
For though I would *d* to glory	2Cor 12:6	2309
whereunto ye *d* again to be in	Gal 4:9	2309
I *d* to be present with you now,	Gal 4:20	2309
ye that *d* to be under the law, do	Gal 4:21	2309
As many as *d* to make a fair shew	Gal 6:12	2309
but *d* to have you circumcised,	Gal 6:13	2309
Wherefore I *d* that ye faint not	Eph 3:13	154
having a *d* to depart, and to be	Phil 1:23	1939
Not because I *d* a gift	Phil 4:17	1934
but I *d* fruit that may abound to	Phil 4:17	1934
to *d* that ye might be filled with	Col 1:9	154
to see your face with great *d*	1Th 2:17	1939
If a man *d* the office of a bishop	1Ti 3:1	3713
we *d* that every one of you do	Heb 6:11	1937
But now they *d* a better country,	Heb 11:16	3713
d to have, and cannot obtain	Jas 4:2	2206
things the angels *d* to look into	1Pet 1:12	1937
d the sincere milk of the word,	1Pet 2:2	1971
shall *d* to die, and death shall	Rev 9:6	1937

DESIRED

a tree to be *d* to make one wise,	Gen 3:6	2530
ye have chosen, and whom ye have *d*	1Sa 12:13	7592
that which Solomon *d* to build in	1Kin 9:19	2836
all that Solomon *d* to build in	2Chr 8:6	2836
And he *d* many wives	2Chr 11:23	7592

D

and departed without being *d*	2Chr 21:20	2532
whatsoever she *d* was given her to	Est 2:13	559
shall not save of that which he *d*	Job 20:20	2530
More to be *d* are they than gold,	Ps 19:10	2530
One thing have I *d* of the LORD	Ps 27:4	7592
bringeth them unto their *d* haven	Ps 107:30	2656
he hath *d* it for his habitation	Ps 132:13	183
for I have *d* it	Ps 132:14	183
all the things that may be *d* are	Prov 8:11	2656
There is treasure to be *d*	Prov 21:20	2530
mine eyes *d* I kept not from them	Eccl 2:10	7592
of the oaks which ye have *d*	Is 1:29	2530
soul have I *d* thee in the night	Is 26:9	183
neither have I *d* the woeful day	Jer 17:16	183
d of the king that he would give	Dan 2:16	1156
unto me now what we *d* of thee	Dan 2:23	1156
For I *d* mercy, and not sacrifice	Hos 6:6	2654
my soul the firstripe fruit	Mic 7:1	183
gather together, O nation not *d*	Zeph 2:1	3700
righteous men have *d* to see those	Mt 13:17	*1939*
tempting *d* him that he would shew	Mt 16:1	*1905*
one prisoner, whomsoever they *d*	Mk 15:6	*154*
one of the Pharisees *d* him that	Lk 7:36	*2065*
And he *d* to see him	Lk 9:9	*2212*
kings have *d* to see those things	Lk 10:24	*2309*
With desire I have *d* to eat this	Lk 22:15	*1937*
Satan hath *d* to have you, that he	Lk 22:31	*1809*
cast into prison, whom they had *d*	Lk 23:25	*154*
d him, saying, Sir, we would see	Jn 12:21	*2065*
d a murderer to be granted unto	Acts 3:14	*154*
d to find a tabernacle for the	Acts 7:46	*154*
he *d* Philip that he would come up	Acts 8:31	*3870*
d of him letters to Damascus to	Acts 9:2	*154*
chamberlain their friend, *d* peace	Acts 12:20	*154*
d to hear the word of God	Acts 13:7	*1934*
And afterward they *d* a king	Acts 13:21	*154*
yet *d* they Pilate that he should	Acts 13:28	*154*
d them to depart out of the city	Acts 16:39	*2065*
When they *d* him to tarry longer	Acts 18:20	*2065*
d favour against him, that he	Acts 25:3	*154*
were *d* to tarry with them seven	Acts 28:14	*3870*
I greatly *d* him to come unto you	1Cor 16:12	*3870*
Insomuch that we *d* Titus, that as	2Cor 8:6	*3870*
I *d* Titus, and with him I sent a	2Cor 12:18	*3870*
the petitions that we *d* of him	1Jn 5:15	*154*

DESIREDST

According to all that thou *d* of	Deut 18:16	7592
all that debt, because thou *d* me	Mt 18:32	*3870*

DESIRES

give thee the *d* of thine heart	Ps 37:4	4862
not, O LORD, the *d* of the wicked	Ps 140:8	3970
fulfilling the *d* of the flesh	Eph 2:3	2307

DESIREST

thou *d* truth in the inward parts	Ps 51:6	2654
For thou *d* not sacrifice	Ps 51:16	2654

DESIRETH

or for whatsoever thy soul *d*	Deut 14:26	7592
then take as much as thy soul *d*	1Sa 2:16	8378
The king *d* not any dowry, but an	1Sa 18:25	2656
unto David, Whatsoever thy soul *d*	1Sa 20:4	559
reign over all that thine heart *d*	2Sa 3:21	8378
according to all that thy soul *d*	1Kin 11:37	8378
a servant earnestly *d* the shadow	Job 7:2	7602
And what his soul *d*, even that he	Job 23:13	183
What man is he that *d* life	Ps 34:12	2655
the hill which God *d* to dwell in	Ps 68:16	2530
The wicked *d* the net of evil men	Prov 12:12	2530
The soul of the sluggard *d*	Prov 13:4	183
The soul of the wicked *d* evil	Prov 21:10	183
for his soul of all that he *d*	Eccl 6:2	183
drunk old wine straightway *d* new	Lk 5:39	*2309*
and *d* conditions of peace	Lk 14:32	*2065*
of a bishop, he *d* a good work	1Ti 3:1	*1937*

DESIRING

without, *d* to speak with him	Mt 12:46	*2212*
without, *d* to speak with thee	Mt 12:47	*2212*
him, and *d* a certain thing of him	Mt 20:20	*154*
stand without, *d* to see thee	Lk 8:20	*2309*
d* to be fed with the crumbs which	Lk 16:21	*1937*
d him that he would not delay to	Acts 9:38	*3870*
d him that he would not adventure	Acts 19:31	*3870*
d to have judgment against him	Acts 25:15	*154*
earnestly *d* to be clothed upon	2Cor 5:2	*1971*
d greatly to see us, as we also	1Th 3:6	*1971*
D to be teachers of the law	1Ti 1:7	*2309*
Greatly *d* to see thee, being	2Ti 1:4	*1971*

DESIROUS

Be not *d* of his dainties	Prov 23:3	183
for he was *d* to see him of a long	Lk 23:8	*2309*
knew that they were *d* to ask him	Jn 16:19	*2309*
a garrison, *d* to apprehend me	2Cor 11:32	*2309*
Let us not be *d* of vain glory	Gal 5:26	*2755*
So being affectionately *d* of you	1Th 2:8	*2442*

DESOLATE

not die, that the land be not *d*	Gen 47:19	3456
lest the land become *d*, and the	Ex 23:29	8077
and your high ways shall be *d*	Lev 26:22	8074
and your land shall be *d*, and your	Lev 26:33	8077
sabbaths, as long as it lieth *d*	Lev 26:34	8074
long as it lieth *d* it shall rest	Lev 26:35	8074
while she lieth *d* without them	Lev 26:43	8074
So Tamar remained *d* in her	2Sa 13:20	8076
as she lay *d* she kept sabbath	2Chr 36:21	8074
earth, which built *d* places for	Job 3:14	2723
And he dwelleth in *d* cities	Job 15:28	3582
of hypocrites shall be *d*, and fire	Job 15:34	1565
thou hast made *d* all my company	Job 16:7	8074
the wilderness in former time *d*	Job 30:3	7722
To satisfy the *d* and waste ground	Job 38:27	7722
for I am *d* and afflicted	Ps 25:16	3173
hate the righteous shall be *d*	Ps 34:21	816
them that trust in him shall be *d*	Ps 34:22	816
Let them be *d* for a reward of	Ps 40:15	8074
Let their habitation be *d*	Ps 69:25	8074
bread also out of their *d* places	Ps 109:10	2723
my heart within me is *d*	Ps 143:4	8074
Your country is *d*, your cities	Is 1:7	8077
it in your presence, and it is *d*	Is 1:7	8077
she being *d* shall sit upon the	Is 3:26	5352
Of a truth many houses shall be *d*	Is 5:9	8047
man, and the land be utterly *d*	Is 6:11	8077
rest all of them in the *d* valleys	Is 7:19	1327
fierce anger, to lay the land *d*	Is 13:9	8047
shall cry in their *d* houses	Is 13:22	490
the waters of Nimrim shall be *d*	Is 15:6	4923
and they that dwell therein are *d*	Is 24:6	816
Yet the defenced city shall be *d*	Is 27:10	910
cause to inherit the *d* heritages	Is 49:8	8076
thy *d* places, and the land of thy	Is 49:19	8074
I have lost my children, and am *d*	Is 49:21	1565
of the *d* than the children of the	Is 54:1	8074
make the *d* cities to be inhabited	Is 54:3	8077
we are in *d* places as dead men	Is 59:10	820
thy land any more be termed *D*	Is 62:4	8077
be horribly afraid, be ye very *d*	Jer 2:12	2717
from his place to make thy land *d*	Jer 4:7	8047
said, The whole land shall be *d*	Jer 4:27	8077
lest I make thee *d*, a land not	Jer 6:8	8077
for the land shall be *d*	Jer 7:34	2723
I will make the cities of Judah *d*	Jer 9:11	8077
to make the cities of Judah *d*	Jer 10:22	8077
and have made his habitation *d*	Jer 10:25	8074
pleasant portion a *d* wilderness	Jer 12:10	8077
They have made it *d*	Jer 12:11	8074
being *d* it mourneth unto me	Jer 12:11	8077
the whole land is made *d*, because	Jer 12:11	8074
To make their land *d*, and a	Jer 18:16	8047
And I will make this city *d*	Jer 19:8	8047
for their land is *d* because of	Jer 25:38	8047
this city shall be *d* without an	Jer 26:9	2717
It is *d* without man or beast	Jer 32:43	8077
ye say shall be *d* without man	Jer 33:10	2717
streets of Jerusalem, that are *d*	Jer 33:10	8074
which is *d* without man and without	Jer 33:12	2717
and they are wasted and *d*, as at	Jer 44:6	8077
waste and *d* without an inhabitant	Jer 46:19	3341
for the cities thereof shall be *d*	Jer 48:9	8047
waters also of Nimrim shall be *d*	Jer 48:34	4923
and it shall be a *d* heap, and her	Jer 49:2	8077
their habitations *d* with them	Jer 49:20	8074
her, which shall make her land *d*	Jer 50:3	8047
but it shall be wholly *d*	Jer 50:13	8077
make their habitation *d* with them	Jer 50:45	8074
but thou shalt be *d* for ever	Jer 51:26	8077
but that it shall be *d* for ever	Jer 51:62	8077
all her gates are *d*	Lam 1:4	8076
he hath made me *d* and faint all	Lam 1:13	8076
my children are *d*, because the	Lam 1:16	8076
he hath made me *d*	Lam 3:11	8074
delicately are *d* in the streets	Lam 4:5	8074
the mountain of Zion, which is *d*	Lam 5:18	8074
And your altars shall be *d*	Eze 6:4	8074
and the high places shall be *d*	Eze 6:6	3456
may be laid waste and made *d*	Eze 6:6	816
upon them, and make the land *d*	Eze 6:14	8077
more *d* than the wilderness toward	Eze 6:14	8047

that her land may be *d* from all	Eze 12:19	3456
waste, and the land shall be *d*	Eze 12:20	8077
and they spoil it, so that it be *d*	Eze 14:15	8077
but the land shall be *d*	Eze 14:16	8077
And I will make the land *d*	Eze 15:8	8077
And he knew their *d* palaces	Eze 19:7	490
and the land was *d*, and the fulness	Eze 19:7	3456
womb, that I might make them *d*	Eze 20:26	8074
the land of Israel, when it was *d*	Eze 25:3	8074
And I will make it *d* from Teman	Eze 25:13	2723
When I shall make thee a *d* city	Eze 26:19	2717
of the earth, in places *d* of old	Eze 26:20	2723
And the land of Egypt shall be *d*	Eze 29:9	8077
land of Egypt utterly waste and *d*	Eze 29:10	8077
d in the midst of the countries	Eze 29:12	8077
midst of the countries that are *d*	Eze 29:12	8074
laid waste shall be *d* forty years	Eze 29:12	8077
they shall be *d* in the midst of	Eze 30:7	8074
midst of the countries that are *d*	Eze 30:7	8074
And I will make Pathros *d*, and will	Eze 30:14	8074
I shall make the land of Egypt *d*	Eze 32:15	8077
For I will lay the land most *d*	Eze 33:28	8077
mountains of Israel shall be *d*	Eze 33:28	8074
land most *d* because of all their	Eze 33:29	8077
thee, and I will make thee most *d*	Eze 35:3	8077
cities waste, and thou shalt be *d*	Eze 35:4	8077
will I make mount Seir most *d*	Eze 35:7	8077
Israel, saying, They are laid *d*	Eze 35:12	8074
rejoiceth, I will make thee *d*	Eze 35:14	8077
house of Israel, because it was *d*	Eze 35:15	8074
thou shalt be *d*, O mount Seir, and	Eze 35:15	8077
Because they have made you *d*	Eze 36:3	8074
to the valleys, to the *d* wastes	Eze 36:4	8076
the *d* land shall be tilled	Eze 36:34	8074
whereas it lay *d* in the sight of	Eze 36:34	8077
This land that was *d* is become	Eze 36:35	8074
and the waste and *d* and ruined	Eze 36:35	8074
places, and plant that that was *d*	Eze 36:36	8074
to turn thine hand upon the *d*	Eze 38:12	2723
upon thy sanctuary that is *d*	Dan 9:17	8074
abominations he shall make it *d*	Dan 9:27	8074
shall be poured upon the *d*	Dan 9:27	8076
the abomination that maketh *d*	Dan 11:31	8074
abomination that maketh *d* set up	Dan 12:11	8074
Ephraim shall be *d* in the day of	Hos 5:9	8047
Samaria shall become *d*	Hos 13:16	816
clods, the garners are laid *d*	Joel 1:17	8074
the flocks of sheep are made *d*	Joel 1:18	816
and behind them a *d* wilderness	Joel 2:3	8077
drive him into a land barren and *d*	Joel 2:20	8077
and Edom shall be a *d* wilderness	Joel 3:19	8077
high places of Isaac shall be *d*	Amos 7:9	8074
the idols thereof will I lay *d*	Mic 1:7	8077
in making thee *d* because of thy	Mic 6:13	8074
the land shall be *d* because of	Mic 7:13	8077
their towers are *d*	Zeph 3:6	8074
Thus the land was *d* after them	Zec 7:14	8074
for they laid the pleasant land *d*	Zec 7:14	8047
will return and build the *d* places	Mal 1:4	2723
your house is left unto you *d*	Mt 23:38	2048
your house is left unto you *d*	Lk 13:35	2048
Psalms, Let his habitation be *d*	Acts 1:20	2048
for the *d* hath many more children	Gal 4:27	2048
she that is a widow indeed, and *d*	1Ti 5:5	3443
the whore, and shall make her *d*	Rev 17:16	2049
for in one hour is she made *d*	Rev 18:19	2049

DESOLATION

and bring your sanctuaries unto *d*	Lev 26:31	8074
And I will bring the land into *d*	Lev 26:32	8074
for ever, even a *d* unto this day	Josh 8:28	8077
that they should become a *d*	2Kin 22:19	8047
who therefore gave them up to *d*	2Chr 30:7	8047
in the *d* which they rolled themselves	Job 30:14	7722
How are they brought into *d*	Ps 73:19	8047
When your fear cometh as a *d*	Prov 1:27	7584
neither of the *d* of the wicked	Prov 3:25	7722
in the *d* which shall come from	Is 10:3	7722
and there shall be *d*	Is 17:9	8077
In the city is left *d*, and the	Is 24:12	8047
d shall come upon thee suddenly,	Is 47:11	7722
d, and destruction, and the famine,	Is 51:19	7701
is a wilderness, Jerusalem a *d*	Is 64:10	8077
that this house shall become a *d*	Jer 22:5	2723
And this whole land shall be a *d*	Jer 25:11	2723
princes thereof, to make them a *d*	Jer 25:18	2723
Judah a *d* without an inhabitant	Jer 34:22	8077
and, behold, this day they are a *d*	Jer 44:2	2723
therefore is your land a *d*	Jer 44:22	2723
that Bozrah shall become a *d*	Jer 49:13	8047
Also Edom shall be a *d*	Jer 49:17	8047

for dragons, and a *d* for ever	Jer 49:33	8077
become a *d* among the nations	Jer 50:23	8047
Babylon a *d* without an inhabitant	Jer 51:29	8047
Her cities are a *d*, a dry land,	Jer 51:43	8047
and a snare is come upon us, *d*	Lam 3:47	7612
prince shall be clothed with *d*	Eze 7:27	8077
with the cup of astonishment and *d*	Eze 23:33	8077
and the transgression of *d*	Dan 8:13	8074
he daily increaseth lies and *d*	Hos 12:1	7701
Egypt shall be a *d*, and Edom shall	Joel 3:19	8077
that I should make thee a *d*	Mic 6:16	8047
a booty, and their houses a *d*	Zeph 1:13	8074
distress, a day of wasteness and *d*	Zeph 1:15	4875
be forsaken, and Ashkelon a *d*	Zeph 2:4	8077
and saltpits, and a perpetual *d*	Zeph 2:9	8077
and will make Nineveh a *d*, and dry	Zeph 2:13	8077
d shall be in the thresholds	Zeph 2:14	2721
how is she become a *d*, a place	Zeph 2:15	8047
against itself is brought to *d*	Mt 12:25	2049
shall see the abomination of *d*	Mt 24:15	2050
ye shall see the abomination of *d*	Mk 13:14	2050
against itself is brought to *d*	Lk 11:17	2049
know that the *d* thereof is nigh	Lk 21:20	2050

DESOLATIONS

God, and to repair the *d* thereof	Ezr 9:9	2723
what *d* he hath made in the earth	Ps 46:8	8047
up thy feet unto the perpetual *d*	Ps 74:3	4876
they shall raise up the former *d*	Is 61:4	8074
the *d* of many generations	Is 61:4	8074
and an hissing, and perpetual *d*	Jer 25:9	2723
and will make it perpetual *d*	Jer 25:12	8077
I will make thee perpetual *d*	Eze 35:9	8077
years in the *d* of Jerusalem	Dan 9:2	2723
open thine eyes, and behold our *d*	Dan 9:18	8074
end of the war *d* are determined	Dan 9:26	8074

DESPAIR

and Saul shall *d* of me, to seek me	1Sa 27:1	2976
d of all the labour which I took	Eccl 2:20	2976
we are perplexed, but not in *d*	2Cor 4:8	1820

DESPAIRED

insomuch that we *d* even of life	2Cor 1:8	1820

DESPERATE

and the speeches of one that is *d*	Job 6:26	2976
the day of grief and of *d* sorrow	Is 17:11	605

DESPERATELY

above all things, and *d* wicked	Jer 17:9	605

DESPISE

And if ye shall *d* my statutes	Lev 26:15	3988
they that *d* me shall be lightly	1Sa 2:30	959
why then did ye *d* us, that our	2Sa 19:43	7043
so that they shall *d* their	Est 1:17	959
therefore *d* not thou the	Job 5:17	3988
I would *d* my life	Job 9:21	3988
that thou shouldest *d* the work of	Job 10:3	3988
If I did *d* the cause of my	Job 31:13	3988
heart, O God, thou wilt not *d*	Ps 51:17	959
awakest, thou shalt *d* their image	Ps 73:20	959
destitute, and not *d* their prayer	Ps 102:17	959
but fools *d* wisdom and instruction	Prov 1:7	936
d not the chastening of the LORD	Prov 3:11	3988
Men do not *d* a thief, if he steal	Prov 6:30	936
for he will *d* the wisdom of thy	Prov 23:9	936
d not thy mother when she is old	Prov 23:22	936
of Israel, Because ye *d* this word	Is 30:12	3988
thy lovers will *d* thee, they will	Jer 4:30	3988
say still unto them that *d* me	Jer 23:17	5006
all that honoured her *d* her	Lam 1:8	2107
which *d* thee round about	Eze 16:57	7590
that *d* them round about them	Eze 28:26	7590
I *d* your feast days, and I will	Amos 5:21	3988
you, O priests, that *d* my name	Mal 1:6	959
hold to the one, and *d* the other	Mt 6:24	2706
Take heed that ye *d* not one of	Mt 18:10	2706
hold to the one, and *d* the other	Lk 16:13	2706
that eateth *d* him that eateth not	Rom 14:3	1848
or *d* ye the church of God, and	1Cor 11:22	2706
Let no man therefore *d* him	1Cor 16:11	1848
D not prophesyings	1Th 5:20	1848
Let no man *d* thy youth	1Ti 4:12	2706
masters, let them not *d* them	1Ti 6:2	2706
Let no man *d* thee	Titus 2:15	4065
d not thou the chastening of the	Heb 12:5	3643
of uncleanness, and *d* government	2Pet 2:10	2706
d dominion, and speak evil of	Jude 8	114

DESPISED

her mistress was *d* in her eyes	Gen 16:4	7043
conceived, I was *d* in her eyes	Gen 16:5	7043

D

thus Esau *d* his birthright	Gen 25:34	959
even because they *d* my judgments	Lev 26:43	3988
because that ye have *d* the LORD	Num 11:20	3988
know the land which ye have *d*	Num 14:31	3988
Because he hath *d* the word of the	Num 15:31	959
this the people that thou hast *d*	Judg 9:38	3988
And they *d* him, and brought him no	1Sa 10:27	959
and she *d* him in her heart	2Sa 6:16	959
Wherefore hast thou *d* the	2Sa 12:9	959
because thou hast *d* me, and hast	2Sa 12:10	959
the daughter of Zion hath *d* thee	2Kin 19:21	959
and she *d* him in her heart	1Chr 15:29	959
d his words, and misused his	2Chr 36:16	959
d us, and said, What is this thing	Neh 2:19	959
for we are *d*	Neh 4:4	939
d in the thought of him that is	Job 12:5	937
Yea, young children *d* me	Job 19:18	3988
of men, and *d* of the people	Ps 22:6	959
For he hath not *d* nor abhorred	Ps 22:24	959
to shame, because God hath *d* them	Ps 53:5	3988
they *d* the pleasant land, they	Ps 106:24	3988
I am small and *d*	Ps 119:141	959
they *d* all my reproof	Prov 1:30	5006
and my heart *d* reproof	Prov 5:12	5006
is of a perverse heart shall be *d*	Prov 12:8	937
He that is *d*, and hath a servant,	Prov 12:9	7034
the poor man's wisdom is *d*	Eccl 9:16	959
yea, I should not be *d*	Song 8:1	937
d the word of the Holy One of	Is 5:24	5006
he hath *d* the cities, he	Is 33:8	3988
the daughter of Zion, hath *d* thee	Is 37:22	959
He is *d* and rejected of men	Is 53:3	959
he was *d*, and we esteemed him not	Is 53:3	959
all they that *d* thee shall bow	Is 60:14	5006
this man Coniah a *d* broken idol	Jer 22:28	959
thus they have *d* my people	Jer 33:24	5006
among the heathen, and *d* among men	Jer 49:15	959
hath *d* in the indignation of his	Lam 2:6	5006
which hast *d* the oath in breaking	Eze 16:59	959
made him king, whose oath he *d*	Eze 17:16	959
Seeing he *d* the oath by breaking	Eze 17:18	959
surely mine oath that he hath *d*	Eze 17:19	959
they *d* my judgments, which if a	Eze 20:13	3988
Because they *d* my judgments	Eze 20:16	3988
but had *d* my statutes, and had	Eze 20:24	3988
Thou hast *d* mine holy things, and	Eze 22:8	959
are round about them, that *d* them	Eze 28:24	7590
because they have *d* the law of	Amos 2:6	3988
thou art greatly *d*	Obad 2	959
For who hath *d* the day of small	Zec 4:10	937
say, Wherein have we *d* thy name	Mal 1:6	959
they were righteous, and *d* others	Lk 18:9	1848
goddess Diana should be *d*	Acts 19:27	1519,3762,3049
the world, and things which are *d*	1Cor 1:28	1848
ye are honourable, but we are *d*	1Cor 4:10	820
which was in my flesh ye *d* not	Gal 4:14	1848
He that *d* Moses' law died without	Heb 10:28	114
But ye have *d* the poor	Jas 2:6	818

DESPISERS

Behold, ye *d*, and wonder, and	Acts 13:41	2707
d of those that are good,	2Ti 3:3	865

DESPISEST

Or *d* thou the riches of his	Rom 2:4	2706

DESPISETH

God is mighty, and *d* not any	Job 36:5	3988
the poor, and *d* not his prisoners	Ps 69:33	959
is void of wisdom *d* his neighbour	Prov 11:12	936
Whoso *d* the word shall be	Prov 13:13	936
is perverse in his ways *d* him	Prov 14:2	959
He that *d* his neighbour sinneth	Prov 14:21	936
A fool *d* his father's instruction	Prov 15:5	5006
but a foolish man *d* his mother	Prov 15:20	959
instruction *d* his own soul	Prov 15:32	3988
but he that *d* his ways shall die	Prov 19:16	959
d to obey his mother, the ravens	Prov 30:17	959
he that *d* the gain of oppressions	Is 33:15	3988
his Holy One, to him whom man *d*	Is 49:7	960
he that *d* you *d* me	Lk 10:16	114
***d* me *d* him that sent me**	Lk 10:16	114
He therefore that *d*, *d* not man	1Th 4:8	114

DESPISING

d the shame, and is set down at	Heb 12:2	2706

DESPITE

thy *d* against the land of Israel	Eze 25:6	7589
hath done *d* unto the Spirit of	Heb 10:29	1796

DESPITEFUL

taken vengeance with a *d* heart	Eze 25:15	7589
with *d* minds, to cast it out for	Eze 36:5	7589
Backbiters, haters of God,	Rom 1:30	5197

DESPITEFULLY

and pray for them which *d* use you	Mt 5:44	1908
and pray for them which *d* use you	Lk 6:28	1908
with their rulers, to use them *d*	Acts 14:5	5195

DESTITUTE

who hath not left *d* my master of	Gen 24:27	5800
will regard the prayer of the *d*	Ps 102:17	6199
leave not my soul *d*	Ps 141:8	6168
is joy to him that is *d* of wisdom	Prov 15:21	2638
the country shall be *d* of that	Eze 32:15	8047
d of the truth, supposing that	1Ti 6:5	650
being *d*, afflicted, tormented	Heb 11:37	5302
be naked, and *d* of daily food,	Jas 2:15	3007

DESTROY

I will *d* man whom I have created	Gen 6:7	4229
I will *d* them with the earth	Gen 6:13	7843
to *d* all flesh, wherein is the	Gen 6:17	7843
that I have made will I *d* from	Gen 7:4	4229
more be a flood to *d* the earth	Gen 9:11	7843
become a flood to *d* all flesh	Gen 9:15	7843
Wilt thou also *d* the righteous	Gen 18:23	5595
wilt thou also *d* and not spare the	Gen 18:24	5595
wilt thou *d* all the city for lack	Gen 18:28	7843
forty and five, I will not *d* it	Gen 18:28	7843
I will not *d* it for twenty's sake	Gen 18:31	7843
I will not *d* it for ten's sake	Gen 18:32	7843
For we will *d* this place, because	Gen 19:13	7843
and the LORD hath sent us to *d* it	Gen 19:13	7843
for the LORD will *d* this city	Gen 19:14	7843
to *d* the frogs from thee and thy	Ex 8:9	3772
shall not be upon you to *d* you	Ex 12:13	4889
my sword, my hand shall *d* them	Ex 15:9	3423
will *d* all the people to whom	Ex 23:27	2000
But ye shall *d* their altars	Ex 34:13	5422
the same soul will I *d* from among	Lev 23:30	6
d your cattle, and make you few in	Lev 26:22	3772
I will *d* your high places, and cut	Lev 26:30	8045
to *d* them utterly, and to break my	Lev 26:44	3615
I will utterly *d* their cities	Num 21:2	2763
d all the children of Sheth	Num 24:17	6979
shall *d* him that remaineth of the	Num 24:19	6
ye shall *d* all this people	Num 32:15	7843
d all their pictures, and *d*	Num 33:52	6
the hand of the Amorites, to *d* us	Deut 1:27	8045
to *d* them from among the host,	Deut 2:15	2000
not forsake thee, neither *d* thee	Deut 4:31	7843
d thee from off the face of the	Deut 6:15	8045
smite them, and utterly *d* them	Deut 7:2	2763
against you, and *d* thee suddenly	Deut 7:4	8045
ye shall *d* their altars, and break	Deut 7:5	5422
hate him to their face, to *d* them	Deut 7:10	6
shall *d* them with a mighty	Deut 7:23	2000
thou shalt *d* their name from	Deut 7:24	6
a consuming fire he shall *d* them	Deut 9:3	8045
d them quickly, as the LORD hath	Deut 9:3	6
Let me alone, that I may *d* them	Deut 9:14	8045
was wroth against you to *d* you	Deut 9:19	8045
the LORD had said he would *d* you	Deut 9:25	8045
d not thy people and thine	Deut 9:26	7843
and the LORD would not *d* thee	Deut 10:10	7843
Ye shall utterly *d* all the places	Deut 12:2	6
d the names of them out of that	Deut 12:3	6
But thou shalt utterly *d* them	Deut 20:17	2763
thou shalt not *d* the trees	Deut 20:19	7843
not trees for meat, thou shalt *d*	Deut 20:20	7843
will rejoice over you to *d* you	Deut 28:63	6
he will *d* these nations from	Deut 31:3	8045
shall *d* both the young man and the	Deut 32:25	7921
and shall say, *D* them	Deut 33:27	8045
the hand of the Amorites, to *d* us	Josh 7:7	6
except ye *d* the accursed from	Josh 7:12	8045
to *d* all the inhabitants of the	Josh 9:24	8045
that he might *d* them utterly	Josh 11:20	2763
favour, but that he might *d* them	Josh 11:20	8045
to *d* the land wherein the	Josh 22:33	7843
entered into the land to *d* it	Judg 6:5	7843
do, Ye shall utterly *d* every male	Judg 21:11	2763
utterly *d* all that they have, and	1Sa 15:3	2763
lest I *d* you with them	1Sa 15:6	622
good, and would not utterly *d* them	1Sa 15:9	2763
utterly *d* the sinners the	1Sa 15:18	2763
to *d* the city for my sake	1Sa 23:10	7843
that thou wilt not *d* my name out	1Sa 24:21	8045
David said to Abishai, *D* him not	1Sa 26:9	7843
people in to *d* the king thy lord	1Sa 26:15	7843

hand to *d* the Lord's anointed	2Sa 1:14	7843
and we will *d* the heir also	2Sa 14:7	8045
revengers of blood to *d* any more	2Sa 14:11	7843
lest they *d* my son	2Sa 14:11	8045
hand of the man that would *d* me	2Sa 14:16	8045
thou seekest to *d* a city and a	2Sa 20:19	4191
me, that I should swallow up or *d*	2Sa 20:20	7843
that I might *d* them that hate me	2Sa 22:41	6789
his hand upon Jerusalem to *d* it	2Sa 24:16	7843
also were not able utterly to *d*	1Kin 9:21	2763
to *d* it from off the face of the	1Kin 13:34	8045
Thus did Zimri *d* all the house of	1Kin 16:12	8045
Yet the Lord would not *d* Judah	2Kin 8:19	7843
might *d* the worshippers of Baal	2Kin 10:19	6
and Jacob, and would not *d* them	2Kin 13:23	7843
Lord against this place to *d* it	2Kin 18:25	7843
Go up against this land, and *d* it	2Kin 18:25	7843
sent them against Judah to *d* it	2Kin 24:2	6
an angel unto Jerusalem to *d* it	1Chr 21:15	7843
therefore I will not *d* them	2Chr 12:7	7843
he would not *d* him altogether	2Chr 12:12	7843
Seir, utterly to slay and *d* them	2Chr 20:23	8045
every one helped to *d* another	2Chr 20:23	4889
would not *d* the house of David	2Chr 21:7	7843
God hath determined to *d* thee	2Chr 25:16	7843
is with me, that he *d* thee not	2Chr 35:21	7843
name to dwell there *d* all kings	Ezr 6:12	4049
to *d* this house of God which is	Ezr 6:12	2255
to *d* all the Jews that were	Est 3:6	8045
all the king's provinces, to *d*	Est 3:13	8045
for the Jews, to *d* them	Est 4:7	6
was given at Shushan to *d* them	Est 4:8	8045
which he wrote to *d* the Jews	Est 8:5	
and to stand for their life, to *d*	Est 8:11	8045
against the Jews to *d* them	Est 9:24	6
to consume them, and to *d* them	Est 9:24	6
him, to *d* him without cause	Job 2:3	1104
that it would please God to *d* me	Job 6:9	1792
If he *d* him from his place, then	Job 8:18	1104
yet thou dost *d* me	Job 10:8	1104
after my skin worms *d* this body	Job 19:26	5362
Thou shalt *d* them that speak	Ps 5:6	6
D thou them, O God	Ps 5:10	816
that I might *d* them that hate me	Ps 18:40	6789
fruit shalt thou *d* from the earth	Ps 21:10	6
of his hands, he shall *d* them	Ps 28:5	2040
that seek after my soul to *d* it	Ps 40:14	5595
shall likewise *d* thee for ever	Ps 52:5	5422
D, O Lord, and divide their	Ps 55:9	1104
those that seek my soul, to *d* it	Ps 63:9	7722
they that would *d* me, being mine	Ps 69:4	6789
hearts, Let us *d* them together	Ps 74:8	3238
I will early *d* all the wicked of	Ps 101:8	6789
he said that he would *d* them	Ps 106:23	8045
his wrath, lest he should *d* them	Ps 106:23	7843
They did not *d* the nations	Ps 106:34	8045
name of the Lord will I *d* them	Ps 118:10	4135
name of the Lord I will *d* them	Ps 118:11	4135
name of the Lord I will *d* them	Ps 118:12	4135
wicked have waited for me to *d* me	Ps 119:95	6
d all them that afflict my soul	Ps 143:12	6
shoot out thine arrows, and *d* them	Ps 144:6	1949
but all the wicked will he *d*	Ps 145:20	8045
prosperity of fools shall *d* them	Prov 1:32	6
of transgressors shall *d* them	Prov 11:3	7703
The Lord will *d* the house of the	Prov 15:25	5255
of the wicked shall *d* them	Prov 21:7	1641
d the work of thine hands	Eccl 5:6	2254
why shouldest thou *d* thyself	Eccl 7:16	8074
to err, and *d* the way of thy paths	Is 3:12	1104
but it is in his heart to *d*	Is 10:7	8045
nor *d* in all my holy mountain	Is 11:9	7843
the Lord shall utterly *d* the	Is 11:15	2763
indignation, to *d* the whole land	Is 13:5	2254
he shall *d* the sinners thereof	Is 13:9	8045
I will *d* the counsel thereof	Is 19:3	1104
to *d* the strong holds thereof	Is 23:11	8045
he will *d* in this mountain the	Is 25:7	1104
to *d* the poor with lying words	Is 32:7	2254
Lord against this land to *d* it	Is 36:10	7843
Go up against this land, and *d* it	Is 36:10	7843
I will *d* and devour at once	Is 42:14	5395
as if he were ready to *d*	Is 51:13	7843
and I have created the waster to *d*	Is 54:16	2254
cluster, and one saith, *D* it not	Is 65:8	7843
sakes, that I may not *d* them all	Is 65:8	7843
nor *d* in all my holy mountain	Is 65:25	7843
out, and to pull down, and to *d*	Jer 1:10	6
Go ye up upon her walls, and *d*	Jer 5:10	7843
by night, and let us *d* her palaces	Jer 6:5	7843
Let us *d* the tree with the fruit	Jer 11:19	7843

d that nation, saith the Lord	Jer 12:17	6
spare, nor have mercy, but *d* them	Jer 13:14	7843
of the earth, to devour and *d*	Jer 15:3	7843
my hand against thee, and *d* thee	Jer 15:6	7843
I will *d* my people, since they	Jer 15:7	6
d them with double destruction	Jer 17:18	7665
up, and to pull down, and to *d* it	Jer 18:7	6
Woe be unto the pastors that *d*	Jer 23:1	6
about, and will utterly *d* them	Jer 25:9	2763
down, and to throw down, and to *d*	Jer 31:28	6
d this land, and shall cause to	Jer 36:29	7843
I will *d* the city and the	Jer 46:8	6
he shall *d* thy strong holds	Jer 48:18	7843
they will *d* till they have enough	Jer 49:9	7843
will *d* from thence the king and	Jer 49:38	6
utterly *d* after them, saith the	Jer 50:21	7843
her up as heaps, and *d* her utterly	Jer 50:26	2763
d ye utterly all her host	Jer 51:3	2763
is against Babylon, to *d* it	Jer 51:11	7843
and with thee will I *d* kingdoms	Jer 51:20	7843
The Lord hath purposed to *d* the	Lam 2:8	7843
d them in anger from under the	Lam 3:66	8045
and which I will send to *d* you	Eze 5:16	7843
I will *d* your high places	Eze 6:3	6
wilt thou *d* all the residue of	Eze 9:8	7843
will *d* him from the midst of my	Eze 14:9	8045
of brutish men, and skilful to *d*	Eze 21:31	4889
to *d* souls, to get dishonest gain	Eze 22:27	6
the land, that I should not *d* it	Eze 22:30	7843
I will *d* thee	Eze 25:7	8045
to *d* it for the old hatred	Eze 25:15	4889
d the remnant of the sea coast	Eze 25:16	9
they shall *d* the walls of Tyrus	Eze 26:4	7843
walls, and *d* thy pleasant houses	Eze 26:12	5422
and I will *d* thee, O covering	Eze 28:16	6
shall be brought to *d* the land	Eze 30:11	7843
I will also *d* the idols, and I	Eze 30:13	6
I will also *d* all the beasts	Eze 32:13	6
but I will *d* the fat and the	Eze 34:16	8045
I saw when I came to *d* the city	Eze 43:3	7843
commanded to *d* all the wise men	Dan 2:12	7
to *d* the wise men of Babylon	Dan 2:24	7
D not the wise men of Babylon	Dan 2:24	7
Hew the tree down, and *d* it	Dan 4:23	2255
consume and to *d* it unto the end	Dan 7:26	7
he shall *d* wonderfully, and shall	Dan 8:24	7843
shall *d* the mighty and the holy	Dan 8:24	7843
heart, and by peace shall *d* many	Dan 8:25	7843
that shall come shall *d* the city	Dan 9:26	7843
portion of his meat shall *d* him	Dan 11:26	7665
go forth with great fury to *d*	Dan 11:44	8045
I will *d* her vines and her fig	Hos 2:12	8074
the night, and I will *d* thy mother	Hos 4:5	1820
I will not return to *d* Ephraim	Hos 11:9	7843
I will *d* it from off the face of	Amos 9:8	8045
not utterly *d* the house of Jacob	Amos 9:8	8045
even the wise men out of Edom,	Obad 8	6
it is polluted, it shall *d* you	Mic 2:10	2254
of thee, and I will *d* thy chariots	Mic 5:10	6
so will I *d* thy cities	Mic 5:14	8045
Philistines, I will even *d* thee	Zeph 2:5	6
against the north, and *d* Assyria	Zeph 2:13	6
I will *d* the strength of the	Hag 2:22	8045
that I will seek to *d* all the	Zec 12:9	8045
he shall not *d* the fruits of your	Mal 3:11	7843
seek the young child to *d* him	Mt 2:13	622
not that I am come to *d* the law	Mt 5:17	2647
I am not come to *d*, but to fulfil	Mt 5:17	2647
him which is able to *d* both soul	Mt 10:28	622
against him, how they might *d* him	Mt 12:14	622
will miserably *d* those wicked men	Mt 21:41	622
I am able to *d* the temple of God,	Mt 26:61	2647
should ask Barabbas, and *d* Jesus	Mt 27:20	622
art thou come to *d* us	Mk 1:24	622
against him, how they might *d* him	Mk 3:6	622
and into the waters, to *d* him	Mk 9:22	622
and sought how they might *d* him	Mk 11:18	622
d* the husbandmen, and will give	Mk 12:9	622
I will *d* this temple that is made	Mk 14:58	2647
art thou come to *d* us	Lk 4:34	622
to save life, or to *d* it	Lk 6:9	622
man is not come to *d* men's lives	Lk 9:56	622
of the people sought to *d* him	Lk 19:47	622
d* these husbandmen, and shall give	Lk 20:16	622
D this temple, and in three days I	Jn 2:19	3089
for to steal, and to kill, and to *d*	Jn 10:10	622
of Nazareth shall *d* this place	Acts 6:14	2647
D not him with thy meat, for whom	Rom 14:15	622
For meat *d* not the work of God	Rom 14:20	2647
I will *d* the wisdom of the wise,	1Cor 1:19	622
temple of God, him shall God *d*	1Cor 3:17	5351

D

but God shall *d* both it and them	1Cor 6:13	2673
shall *d* with the brightness of	2Th 2:8	2673
that through death he might *d* him	Heb 2:14	2673
who is able to save and to *d*	Jas 4:12	622
that he might *d* the works of the	1Jn 3:8	3089
d them which *d* the earth	Rev 11:18	1311

DESTROYED

every living substance was *d*	Gen 7:23	4229
they were *d* from the earth	Gen 7:23	4229
where, before the LORD *d* Sodom	Gen 13:10	7843
when God *d* the cities of the	Gen 19:29	7843
and I shall be *d*, I and my house	Gen 34:30	8045
thou not yet that Egypt is *d*	Ex 10:7	6
LORD only, he shall be utterly *d*	Ex 22:20	2763
and they utterly *d* them and their	Num 21:3	2763
d you in Seir, even unto Hormah	Deut 1:44	3807
when they had *d* them from before	Deut 2:12	8045
but the LORD *d* them before them	Deut 2:21	8045
when he *d* the Horims from before	Deut 2:22	8045
d them, and dwelt in their stead	Deut 2:23	8045
that time, and utterly *d* the men	Deut 2:34	2763
And we utterly *d* them, as we did	Deut 3:6	2763
God hath *d* them from among you	Deut 4:3	8045
upon it, but shall utterly be *d*	Deut 4:26	8045
hide themselves from thee, be *d*	Deut 7:20	6
destruction, until they be *d*	Deut 7:23	8045
thee, until thou have *d* them	Deut 7:24	8045
was angry with you to have *d* you	Deut 9:8	8045
angry with Aaron to have *d* him	Deut 9:20	8045
how the LORD hath *d* them unto	Deut 11:4	6
that they be *d* from before thee	Deut 12:30	8045
unto for to do, until thou be *d*	Deut 28:20	8045
down upon thee, until thou be *d*	Deut 28:24	8045
and overtake thee, till thou be *d*	Deut 28:45	8045
thy neck, until he have *d* thee	Deut 28:48	8045
of thy land, until thou be *d*	Deut 28:51	8045
thy sheep, until he have *d* thee	Deut 28:51	6
bring upon thee, until thou be *d*	Deut 28:61	8045
unto the land of them, whom he *d*	Deut 31:4	8045
Sihon and Og, whom ye utterly *d*	Josh 2:10	2763
they utterly *d* all that was in	Josh 6:21	2763
until he had utterly *d* all the	Josh 8:26	2763
had taken Ai, and had utterly *d* it	Josh 10:1	2763
and the king thereof he utterly *d*	Josh 10:28	2763
therein he utterly *d* that day	Josh 10:35	2763
but *d* it utterly, and all the	Josh 10:37	2763
utterly *d* all the souls that were	Josh 10:39	2763
but utterly *d* all that breathed,	Josh 10:40	2763
the sword, and he utterly *d* them	Josh 11:12	2763
the sword, until they had *d* them	Josh 11:14	8045
Joshua *d* them utterly with their	Josh 11:21	2763
until he have *d* you from off this	Josh 23:15	8045
and I *d* them from before you	Josh 24:8	8045
Zephath, and utterly *d* it	Judg 1:17	2763
until they had *d* Jabin king of	Judg 4:24	3772
d the increase of the earth, till	Judg 6:4	7843
d down to the ground of the	Judg 20:21	7843
d down to the ground of the	Judg 20:25	7843
the children of Israel *d* of the	Judg 20:35	7843
they *d* in the midst of them	Judg 20:42	7843
the women are *d* out of Benjamin	Judg 21:16	8045
a tribe be not *d* out of Israel	Judg 21:17	4229
he *d* them, and smote them with	1Sa 5:6	8074
utterly *d* all the people with the	1Sa 15:8	2763
and refuse, that they *d* utterly	1Sa 15:9	2763
and the rest we have utterly *d*	1Sa 15:15	2763
have utterly *d* the Amalekites	1Sa 15:18	2763
which should have been utterly *d*	1Sa 15:21	2764
they *d* the children of Ammon, and	2Sa 11:1	7843
be *d* from remaining in any of the	2Sa 21:5	8045
pursued mine enemies, and *d* them	2Sa 22:38	8045
to the angel that *d* the people	2Sa 24:16	7843
Asa *d* her idol, and burnt it by	1Kin 15:13	3772
that breathed, until he had *d* him	1Kin 15:29	8045
in Samaria, till he had *d* him	2Kin 10:17	8045
Thus Jehu *d* Baal out of Israel	2Kin 10:28	8045
she arose and *d* all the seed royal	2Kin 11:1	6
for the king of Syria had *d* them	2Kin 13:7	6
them which my fathers have *d*	2Kin 19:12	843
of Assyria have *d* the nations	2Kin 19:17	2717
therefore they have *d* them	2Kin 19:18	6
which Hezekiah his father had *d*	2Kin 21:3	6
d before the children of Israel	2Kin 21:9	8045
d them utterly unto this day, and	1Chr 4:41	2763
the land, whom God *d* before them	1Chr 5:25	8045
And Joab smote Rabbah, and *d* it	1Chr 20:1	2040
months to be *d* before thy foes	1Chr 21:12	5595
evil, and said to the angel that *d*	1Chr 21:15	7843
for they were *d* before the LORD,	2Chr 14:13	7665
And nation was *d* of nation	2Chr 15:6	3807

turned from them, and *d* them not	2Chr 20:10	8045
d all the seed royal of the house	2Chr 22:10	1696
d all the princes of the people	2Chr 24:23	7843
until they had utterly *d* them all	2Chr 31:1	3615
nations that my fathers utterly *d*	2Chr 32:14	2763
whom the LORD had *d* before the	2Chr 33:9	8045
which the kings of Judah had *d*	2Chr 34:11	7843
d all the goodly vessels thereof	2Chr 36:19	7843
for which cause was this city *d*	Ezr 4:15	2718
who *d* this house, and carried the	Ezr 5:12	5642
it be written that they may be *d*	Est 3:9	6
and thy father's house shall be *d*	Est 4:14	6
are sold, I and my people, to be *d*	Est 7:4	8045
Jews slew and *d* five hundred men	Est 9:6	6
d five hundred men in Shushan the	Est 9:12	6
They are *d* from morning to	Job 4:20	3807
He hath *d* me on every side, and I	Job 19:10	5422
in the night, so that they are *d*	Job 34:25	1792
thou hast *d* the wicked, thou hast	Ps 9:5	6
and thou hast *d* cities	Ps 9:6	5428
If the foundations be *d*, what can	Ps 11:3	2040
transgressors shall be *d* together	Ps 37:38	8045
thou hast *d* all them that go a	Ps 73:27	6789
their iniquity, and *d* them not	Ps 78:38	7843
and frogs, which *d* them	Ps 78:45	7843
He *d* their vines with hail, and	Ps 78:47	2026
is that they shall be *d* for ever	Ps 92:7	8045
of Babylon, who art to be *d*	Ps 137:8	7703
despiseth the word shall be *d*	Prov 13:13	2254
a companion of fools shall be *d*	Prov 13:20	7321
is that is *d* for want of judgment	Prov 13:23	5595
his neck, shall suddenly be *d*	Prov 29:1	7665
they that are led of them are *d*	Is 9:16	1104
the yoke shall be *d* because of	Is 10:27	2254
and *d* the cities thereof	Is 14:17	2040
because thou hast *d* thy land	Is 14:20	7843
d them, and made all their memory	Is 26:14	8045
he hath utterly *d* them, he hath	Is 34:2	2763
them which my fathers have *d*	Is 37:12	7843
therefore they have *d* them	Is 37:19	6
been cut off nor *d* from before me	Is 48:19	8045
Many pastors have *d* my vineyard	Jer 12:10	7843
for all thy lovers are *d*	Jer 22:20	7665
Moab is *d*	Jer 48:4	7665
perish, and the plain shall be *d*	Jer 48:8	8045
Moab shall be *d* from being a	Jer 48:42	8045
Babylon is suddenly fallen and *d*	Jer 51:8	7665
d out of her the great voice	Jer 51:55	6
he hath *d* his strong holds, and	Lam 2:5	7843
he hath *d* his places of the	Lam 2:6	7843
he hath *d* and broken her bars	Lam 2:9	6
and say to thee, How art thou *d*	Eze 26:17	6
like the *d* in the midst of the	Eze 27:32	1822
when all her helpers shall be *d*	Eze 30:8	7665
the multitude thereof shall be *d*	Eze 32:12	8045
a kingdom, which shall never be *d*	Dan 2:44	2255
kingdom that which shall not be *d*	Dan 6:26	2255
beast was slain, and his body *d*	Dan 7:11	7
kingdom that which shall not be *d*	Dan 7:14	2255
but within few days he shall be *d*	Dan 11:20	7665
My people are *d* for lack of	Hos 4:6	1820
the sin of Israel, shall be *d*	Hos 10:8	8045
O Israel, thou hast *d* thyself	Hos 13:9	7843
Yet *d* I the Amorite before them,	Amos 2:9	8045
yet I *d* his fruit from above, and	Amos 2:9	8045
their cities are *d*, so that there	Zeph 3:6	6658
d those murderers, and burned up	Mt 22:7	622
and the flood came, and *d* them all	Lk 17:27	622
from heaven, and *d* them all	Lk 17:29	622
shall be *d* from among the people	Acts 3:23	1842
Is not this he that *d* them which	Acts 9:21	4199
when he had *d* seven nations in	Acts 13:19	2507
and her magnificence should be *d*	Acts 19:27	2507
that the body of sin might be *d*	Rom 6:6	2673
tempted, and were *d* of serpents	1Cor 10:9	622
and were *d* of the destroyer	1Cor 10:10	622
enemy that shall be *d* is death	1Cor 15:26	2673
cast down, but not *d*	2Cor 4:9	622
the faith which once he *d*	Gal 1:23	4199
build again the things which I *d*	Gal 2:18	2647
lest he that *d* the firstborn	Heb 11:28	3645
beasts, made to be taken and *d*	2Pet 2:12	5356
afterward *d* them that believed	Jude 5	622
third part of the ships were *d*	Rev 8:9	1311

DESTROYER

will not suffer the *d* to come in	Ex 12:23	7843
the *d* of our country, which slew	Judg 16:24	2717
in prosperity the *d* shall come	Job 15:21	7703
kept me from the paths of the *d*	Ps 17:4	6530
the same is the companion of a *d*	Prov 28:24	7843

the *d* of the Gentiles is on his .... Jer 4:7   7843
and were destroyed of the *d* 1Cor 10:10   *3644*

DESTROYERS
the grave, and his life to the *d* .... Job 33:22   4191
thy *d* and they that made thee .... Is 49:17   2040
And I will prepare *d* against thee .... Jer 22:7   7843
O ye *d* of mine heritage, because .... Jer 50:11   8154

DESTROYEST
and thou *d* the hope of man .... Job 14:19   6
the LORD, which *d* all the earth .... Jer 51:25   7843
Thou that *d* the temple, and.................. Mt 27:40   *2647*
thou that *d* the temple, and.................. Mk 15:29   *2647*

DESTROYETH
which the LORD *d* before your face .... Deut 8:20   6
He *d* the perfect and the wicked............ Job 9:22   3615
increaseth the nations, and *d* them....... Job 12:23   6
he that doeth it *d* his own soul .... Prov 6:32   7843
with his mouth *d* his neighbour.............. Prov 11:9   7843
thy ways to that which *d* kings .... Prov 31:3   4229
and a gift of the heart .... Eccl 7:7   6
but one sinner *d* much good.................. Eccl 9:18   6

DESTROYING
of Heshbon, utterly *d* the men .... Deut 3:6   2763
d it utterly, and all that is.................... Deut 13:15   2763
edge of the sword, utterly *d* them .... Josh 11:11   2763
to all lands, by *d* them utterly............... 2Kin 19:11   2763
land, and the angel of the LORD *d*.......... 1Chr 21:12   7843
and as he was *d*, the LORD beheld, ... 1Chr 21:15   7843
a *d* storm, as a flood of mighty.............. Is 28:2   6986
to all lands by *d* them utterly .... Is 37:11   2763
your prophets, like a *d* lion.................... Jer 2:30   7843
that rise up against me, a *d* wind .... Jer 51:1   7843
O *d* mountain, saith the LORD,............... Jer 51:25   4889
not withdrawn his hand from *d* .... Lam 2:8   1104
man with his *d* weapon in his hand ...... Eze 9:1   4892
mine eye spared them from *d* them .... Eze 20:17   7843

DESTRUCTION
destroy them with a mighty *d*................ Deut 7:23   4103
burning heat, and with bitter *d*............. Deut 32:24   6986
the city with a very great *d*.................... 1Sa 5:9   4103
for there was a deadly *d* 1Sa 5:11   4103
a man whom I appointed to utter *d* 1Kin 20:42   2764
the death of his father to his *d*.............. 2Chr 22:4   4889
the *d* of Ahaziah was of God by 2Chr 22:7   8395
his heart was lifted up to his *d*.............. 2Chr 26:16   7843
endure to see the *d* of my kindred......... Est 8:6   13
of the sword, and slaughter, and *d*........ Est 9:5   12
be afraid of *d* when it cometh .... Job 5:21   7701
At *d* and famine thou shalt laugh.......... Job 5:22   7701
d shall be ready at his side.................... Job 18:12   343
how oft cometh their *d* upon them......... Job 21:17   343
His eyes shall see his *d*, and he .... Job 21:20   3589
is reserved to the day of *d*.................... Job 21:30   343
before him, and *d* hath no covering....... Job 26:6   11
D and death say, We have heard the...... Job 28:22   11
up against me the ways of their *d*.......... Job 30:12   343
grave, though they cry in his *d*.............. Job 30:24   6365
Is not *d* to the wicked .... Job 31:3   343
it is a fire that consumeth to *d*.............. Job 31:12   11
For *d* from God was a terror to me......... Job 31:23   343
at the *d* of him that hated me .... Job 31:29   6365
Let *d* come upon him at unawares .... Ps 35:8   7722
into that very *d* let him fall .... Ps 35:8   7722
bring them down into the pit of *d*.......... Ps 55:23   7845
thou castedst them down into *d* .... Ps 73:18   4876
or thy faithfulness in *d*.......................... Ps 88:11   11
Thou turnest man to *d*........................... Ps 90:3   1793
nor for the *d* that wasteth at................. Ps 91:6   6986
Who redeemeth thy life from *d*............... Ps 103:4   7845
your *d* cometh as a whirlwind .... Prov 1:27   343
mouth of the foolish is near *d* .... Prov 10:14   4288
the *d* of the poor is their....................... Prov 10:15   4288
but *d* shall be to the workers of *d*........ Prov 10:29   4288
wide his lips shall have *d* .... Prov 13:3   4288
of people is the *d* of the prince............. Prov 14:28   4288
Hell and *d* are before the LORD.............. Prov 15:11   11
Pride goeth before *d*, and an................. Prov 16:18   7667
that exalteth his gate seeketh *d* .... Prov 17:19   7667
A fool's mouth is his *d*, and his .... Prov 18:7   4288
Before *d* the heart of man is .... Prov 18:12   7667
but *d* shall be to the workers of *d*........ Prov 21:15   4288
For their heart studieth *d* .... Prov 24:2   7701
Hell and *d* are never full........................ Prov 27:20   10
of all such as are appointed to *d* .... Prov 31:8   2475
the *d* of the transgressors and of.......... Is 1:28   7667
cease, and mine anger in their *d* .... Is 10:25   8399
come as a *d* from the Almighty .... Is 13:6   7701
will sweep it with the besom of *d*.......... Is 14:23   8045

they shall raise up a cry of *d* .... Is 15:5   7667
shall be called, The city of *d* .... Is 19:18   2041
and the gate is smitten with *d* .... Is 24:12   7591
places, and the land of thy *d*................. Is 49:19   2035
desolation, and *d*, and the famine,........ Is 51:19   7667
wasting and *d* are in their paths .... Is 59:7   7667
wasting nor *d* within thy borders .... Is 60:18   7667
evil from the north, and a great *d*.......... Jer 4:6   7667
D upon *d* is cried................................. Jer 4:20   7667
out of the north, and great *d* .... Jer 6:1   7667
and destroy them with double *d* .... Jer 17:18   7670
a very fair heifer, but *d* cometh............. Jer 46:20   7171
Horonaim, spoiling and great *d*............. Jer 48:3   7667
the enemies have heard a cry of *d* .... Jer 48:5   7667
is in the land, and of great *d*................. Jer 50:22   7667
great *d* from the land of the .... Jer 51:54   7667
for the *d* of the daughter of my .... Lam 2:11   7667
is come upon us, desolation and *d*......... Lam 3:47   7667
d of the daughter of my people............. Lam 3:48   7667
they were their meat in the *d* of............ Lam 4:10   7667
which shall be for their *d* .... Eze 5:16   4889
D cometh; and they shall seek .... Eze 7:25   7089
bring thy *d* among the nations .... Eze 32:9   7667
fled from me: *d* unto them..................... Hos 7:13   7701
lo, they are gone because of *d*............... Hos 9:6   7701
O grave, I will be thy *d*.......................... Hos 13:14   6987
as a *d* from the Almighty shall it........... Joel 1:15   7701
of Judah in the day of their *d* .... Obad 12   6
destroy you, even with a sore *d* .... Mic 2:10   2256
and there shall be no more utter *d* .... Zec 14:11   2764
is the way, that leadeth to *d*............. Mt 7:13   684
D and misery are in their ways .... Rom 3:16   *4938*
the vessels of wrath fitted to *d*............. Rom 9:22   *684*
unto Satan for the *d* of the flesh 1Cor 5:5   *3639*
edification, and not for your *d* 2Cor 10:8   *2506*
me to edification, and not to *d* 2Cor 13:10   *2506*
Whose end is *d*, whose God is............... Phil 3:19   *684*
then sudden *d* cometh upon them, ... 1Th 5:3   *3639*
be punished with everlasting *d*............. 2Th 1:9   *3639*
lusts, which drown men in *d* 1Ti 6:9   *3639*
and bring upon themselves swift *d* 2Pet 2:1   *684*
scriptures, unto their own *d*.................. 2Pet 3:16   *684*

DESTRUCTIONS
d are come to a perpetual end............... Ps 9:6   2723
rescue my soul from their *d*................... Ps 35:17   7722
and delivered them from their *d* .... Ps 107:20   7825

DETAIN
LORD, I pray thee, let us *d* thee.............. Judg 13:15   6113
unto Manoah, Though thou *d* me .... Judg 13:16   6113

DETAINED
there that day, *d* before the LORD........... 1Sa 21:7   6113

DETERMINATE
being delivered by the *d* counsel .... Acts 2:23   *3724*

DETERMINATION
for my *d* is to gather the nations .... Zeph 3:8   4941

DETERMINE
and he shall pay as the judges *d* .... Ex 21:22

DETERMINED
be sure that evil is *d* by him 1Sa 20:7   3615
d by my father to come upon thee 1Sa 20:9   3615
Jonathan knew that it was *d* of............. 1Sa 20:33   3615
for evil is *d* against our master, ... 1Sa 25:17   3615
of Absalom this hath been *d* from 2Sa 13:32   7760
Solomon to build an house for 2Chr 2:1   559
that God hath *d* to destroy thee 2Chr 25:16   3289
evil *d* against him by the king .... Est 7:7   3615
Seeing his days are *d*, the number .... Job 14:5   2782
shall make a consumption, even *d* .... Is 10:23   2782
hosts, which he hath *d* against it .... Is 19:17   3289
even *d* upon the whole earth .... Is 28:22   2782
weeks are *d* upon thy people .... Dan 9:24   2852
end of the war desolations are *d*........... Dan 9:26   2782
that *d* shall be poured upon the .... Dan 9:27   2782
for that that is *d* shall be done.............. Dan 11:36   2782
the Son of man goeth, as it was *d*...... Lk 22:22   *3724*
when he was *d* to let him go .... Acts 3:13   *2919*
thy counsel *d* before to be done .... Acts 4:28   *4309*
d to send relief unto the........................ Acts 11:29   *3724*
they *d* that Paul and Barnabas, and ..... Acts 15:2   *5021*
Barnabas *d* to take with them John ...... Acts 15:37   *1011*
hath *d* the times before appointed......... Acts 17:26   *3724*
it shall be *d* in a lawful......................... Acts 19:39   *1956*
For Paul had *d* to sail by Ephesus .... Acts 20:16   *2919*
to Augustus, I have *d* to send him......... Acts 25:25   *2919*
when it was *d* that we should sail.......... Acts 27:1   *2919*
For I *d* not to know any thing 1Cor 2:2   *2919*

But I *d* this with myself, that I .... 2Cor 2:1 — 2919
for I have *d* there to winter .... Titus 3:12 — 2919

DETEST
but thou shalt utterly *d* it .... Deut 7:26 — 8262

DETESTABLE
with the carcases of their *d* .... Jer 16:18 — 8251
sanctuary with all thy *d* things .... Eze 5:11 — 8251
of their *d* things therein........................... Eze 7:20 — 8251
away all the *d* things thereof................... Eze 11:18 — 8251
after the heart of their *d* things .... Eze 11:21 — 8251
idols, nor with their *d* things .... Eze 37:23 — 8251

DEUEL *(de-oo'-el)* See REUEL. *Father of Eliasaph.*
Eliasaph the son of *D*.................... Num 1:14 — 1845
sixth day Eliasaph the son of .... Num 7:42 — 1845
offering of Eliasaph the son of *D* .... Num 7:47 — 1845
of Gad was Eliasaph the son of *D* .... Num 10:20 — 1845

DEVICE
to find out every *d* which shall................ 2Chr 2:14 — 4284
his *d* that he had devised against .... Est 8:3 — 4284
by letters that his wicked *d* .... Est 9:25 — 4284
they imagined a mischievous *d* .... Ps 21:11 — 4284
further not his wicked *d* .... Ps 140:8 — 4284
for there is no work, nor *d* .... Eccl 9:10 — 2808
you, and devise a *d* against you .... Jer 18:11 — 4284
for his *d* is against Babylon, to .... Jer 51:11 — 4284
their *d* against me all the day............... Lam 3:62 — 1902
stone, graven by art and man's *d* .... Acts 17:29 — 1761

DEVICES
disappointeth the *d* of the crafty .... Job 5:12 — 4284
the *d* which ye wrongfully imagine .... Job 21:27 — 4209
in the *d* that they have imagined............ Ps 10:2 — 4209
he maketh the *d* of the people of .... Ps 33:10 — 4284
man who bringeth wicked *d* to pass ...... Ps 37:7 — 4209
and be filled with their own *d* .... Prov 1:31 — 4156
a man of wicked *d* will he condemn .... Prov 12:2 — 4209
and a man of wicked *d* is hated .... Prov 14:17 — 4209
There are many *d* in a man's heart........ Prov 19:21 — 4284
he deviseth wicked *d* to destroy .... Is 32:7 — 2154
they had devised *d* against me .... Jer 11:19 — 4284
but we will walk after our own *d* .... Jer 18:12 — 4284
let us devise *d* against Jeremiah .... Jer 18:18 — 4284
he shall forecast his *d* against................ Dan 11:24 — 4284
they shall forecast *d* against him .... Dan 11:25 — 4284
for we are not ignorant of his *d* .... 2Cor 2:11 — 3540

DEVIL
wilderness to be tempted of the *d*........... Mt 4:1 — 1228
Then the *d* taketh him up into the.......... Mt 4:5 — 1228
the *d* taketh him up into an .... Mt 4:8 — 1228
Then the *d* leaveth him, and, ... Mt 4:11 — 1228
him a dumb man possessed with a *d* ..... Mt 9:32 — 1139
when the *d* was cast out, the dumb .... Mt 9:33 — 1140
and they say, He hath a *d* .... Mt 11:18 — 1140
unto him one possessed with a *d* .... Mt 12:22 — 1139
enemy that sowed them is the *d* .... Mt 13:39 — 1228
is grievously vexed with a *d* .... Mt 15:22 — 1139
And Jesus rebuked the *d* .... Mt 17:18 — 1140
fire, prepared for the *d* and his............... Mt 25:41 — 1228
him that was possessed with the *d* .... Mk 5:15 — 1139
him that was possessed with the *d* .... Mk 5:16 — 1139
the *d* prayed him that he might be......... Mk 5:18 — 1139
forth the *d* out of her daughter .... Mk 7:26 — 1140
the *d* is gone out of thy daughter .... Mk 7:29 — 1140
house, she found the *d* gone out .... Mk 7:30 — 1140
Being forty days tempted of the *d* .... Lk 4:2 — 1228
the *d* said unto him, If thou be .... Lk 4:3 — 1228
And the *d*, taking him up into an .... Lk 4:5 — 1228
the *d* said unto him, All this................... Lk 4:6 — 1228
when the *d* had ended all the................. Lk 4:13 — 1228
had a spirit of an unclean *d* .... Lk 4:33 — 1140
when the *d* had thrown him in the .... Lk 4:35 — 1140
and ye say, He hath a *d* .... Lk 7:33 — 1140
then cometh the *d*, and taketh away ...... Lk 8:12 — 1228
was driven of the *d* into the .... Lk 8:29 — 1142
the *d* threw him down, and tare him ...... Lk 9:42 — 1140
And he was casting out a *d* .... Lk 11:14 — 1140
when the *d* was gone out, the dumb ...... Lk 11:14 — 1140
you twelve, and one of you is a *d* .... Jn 6:70 — 1228
answered and said, Thou hast a *d*.......... Jn 7:20 — 1140
Ye are of your father the *d* .... Jn 8:44 — 1228
thou art a Samaritan, and hast a *d* ...... Jn 8:48 — 1140
Jesus answered, I have not a *d* .... Jn 8:49 — 1140
Now we know that thou hast a *d* .... Jn 8:52 — 1140
And many of them said, He hath a *d* ..... Jn 10:20 — 1140
the words of him that hath a *d* .... Jn 10:21 — 1139
Can a *d* open the eyes of the................. Jn 10:21 — 1140
the *d* having now put into the .... Jn 13:2 — 1228
all that were oppressed of the *d* .... Acts 10:38 — 1228
all mischief, thou child of the *d* .... Acts 13:10 — 1228

Neither give place to the *d*..................... Eph 4:27 — 1228
stand against the wiles of the *d* .... Eph 6:11 — 1228
into the condemnation of the *d* .... 1Ti 3:6 — 1228
reproach and the snare of the *d* .... 1Ti 3:7 — 1228
out of the snare of the *d* .... 2Ti 2:26 — 1228
power of death, that is, the *d* .... Heb 2:14 — 1228
Resist the *d*, and he will flee .... Jas 4:7 — 1228
because your adversary the *d* .... 1Pet 5:8 — 1228
that committeth sin is of the *d*................ 1Jn 3:8 — 1228
for the *d* sinneth from the .... 1Jn 3:8 — 1228
might destroy the works of the *d* .... 1Jn 3:8 — 1228
and the children of the *d* .... 1Jn 3:10 — 1228
when contending with the *d* he .... Jude 9 — 1228
the *d* shall cast some of you into .... Rev 2:10 — 1228
that old serpent, called the *D* .... Rev 12:9 — 1228
for the *d* is come down unto you, ... Rev 12:12 — 1228
that old serpent, which is the *D* .... Rev 20:2 — 1228
the *d* that deceived them was cast .... Rev 20:10 — 1228

DEVILISH
above, but is earthly, sensual, *d* .... Jas 3:15 — 1141

DEVILS
offer their sacrifices unto *d* .... Lev 17:7 — 8163
They sacrificed unto *d*, not to .... Deut 32:17 — 7700
for the high places, and for the *d* .... 2Chr 11:15 — 8163
sons and their daughters unto *d* .... Ps 106:37 — 7700
those which were possessed with *d*....... Mt 4:24 — 1139
and in thy name have cast out *d* .... Mt 7:22 — 1140
many that were possessed with *d* .... Mt 8:16 — 1139
met him two possessed with *d* .... Mt 8:28 — 1139
So the *d* besought him, saying, If .... Mt 8:31 — 1142
to the possessed of the *d* .... Mt 8:33 — 1139
He casteth out *d* through the .... Mt 9:34 — 1140
through the prince of the *d* .... Mt 9:34 — 1140
raise the dead, cast out *d*.................... Mt 10:8 — 1140
This fellow doth not cast out *d* .... Mt 12:24 — 1140
by Beelzebub the prince of the *d* .... Mt 12:24 — 1140
And if I by Beelzebub cast out *d* .... Mt 12:27 — 1140
But if I cast out *d* by the Spirit............ Mt 12:28 — 1140
them that were possessed with *d* .... Mk 1:32 — 1140
diseases, and cast out many *d* .... Mk 1:34 — 1140
and suffered not the *d* to speak............. Mk 1:34 — 1140
all Galilee, and cast out *d* .... Mk 1:39 — 1140
heal sicknesses, and to cast out *d* .... Mk 3:15 — 1140
of the *d* casteth he out *d* .... Mk 3:22 — 1140
all the *d* besought him, saying, ... Mk 5:12 — 1142
And they cast out many *d*, and.............. Mk 6:13 — 1140
saw one casting out *d* in thy name .... Mk 9:38 — 1140
out of whom he had cast seven *d* .... Mk 16:9 — 1140
In my name shall they cast out *d* .... Mk 16:17 — 1140
d also came out of many, crying............ Lk 4:41 — 1140
out of whom went seven *d* .... Lk 8:2 — 1140
man, which had *d* long time................... Lk 8:27 — 1140
because many *d* were entered into .... Lk 8:30 — 1140
Then went the *d* out of the man, ... Lk 8:33 — 1140
out of whom the *d* were departed .... Lk 8:35 — 1140
was possessed of the *d* was healed .... Lk 8:36 — 1139
Now the man out of whom the *d* .... Lk 8:38 — 1140
power and authority over all *d* .... Lk 9:1 — 1140
saw one casting out *d* in thy name .... Lk 9:49 — 1140
even the *d* are subject unto us............... Lk 10:17 — 1140
said, He casteth out *d* through .... Lk 11:15 — 1140
Beelzebub the chief of the *d* .... Lk 11:15 — 1140
I cast out *d* through Beelzebub .... Lk 11:18 — 1140
And if I by Beelzebub cast out *d* .... Lk 11:19 — 1140
with the finger of God cast out *d* .... Lk 11:20 — 1140
that fox, Behold, I cast out *d* .... Lk 13:32 — 1140
sacrifice, they sacrifice to *d* .... 1Cor 10:20 — 1140
ye should have fellowship with *d* .... 1Cor 10:20 — 1140
cup of the Lord, and the cup of *d* .... 1Cor 10:21 — 1140
table, and of the table of *d* .... 1Cor 10:21 — 1140
spirits, and doctrines of *d*....................... 1Ti 4:1 — 1140
the *d* also believe, and tremble .... Jas 2:19 — 1140
that they should not worship *d* .... Rev 9:20 — 1140
For they are the spirits of *d*.................... Rev 16:14 — 1140
and is become the habitation of *d* .... Rev 18:2 — 1142

DEVISE
To *d* cunning works, to work in .... Ex 31:4 — 2803
to *d* curious works, to work in .... Ex 35:32 — 2803
and of those that *d* cunning work .... Ex 35:35 — 2803
yet doth he *d* means, that his .... 2Sa 14:14 — 2803
to confusion that *d* my hurt .... Ps 35:4 — 2803
but they *d* deceitful matters................... Ps 35:20 — 2803
against me do they *d* my hurt .... Ps 41:7 — 2803
D not evil against thy neighbour, ... Prov 3:29 — 2790
Do they not err that *d* evil..................... Prov 14:22 — 2790
shall be to them that *d* good.................. Prov 14:22 — 2790
his eyes to *d* froward things .... Prov 16:30 — 2803
you, and a device against you .... Jer 18:11 — 2803
let us devise *d* devices against Jeremiah .... Jer 18:18 — 2803

these are the men that *d* mischief .... Eze 11:2   2803
Woe to them that *d* iniquity .... Mic 2:1   2803
this family do I *d* an evil .... Mic 2:3   2803

DEVISED

that *d* against us that we should 2Sa 21:5   1819
which he had *d* of his own heart 1Kin 12:33   908
that he had *d* against the Jews............. Est 8:3   2803
d by Haman the son of Hammedatha.... Est 8:5   4284
had *d* against the Jews to destroy .... Est 9:24   2803
which he *d* against the Jews, ... Est 9:25   2803
they *d* to take away my life .... Ps 31:13   2161
they had *d* devices against me .... Jer 11:19   2803
they have *d* evil against it .... Jer 48:2   2803
for the Lord hath both *d* and done........ Jer 51:12   2161
hath done that which he had *d* .... Lam 2:17   2161
not followed cunningly *d* fables 2Pet 1:16   4679

DEVISETH

He *d* mischief upon his bed................... Ps 36:4   2803
Thy tongue *d* mischiefs......................... Ps 52:2   2803
he *d* mischief continually...................... Prov 6:14   2790
An heart that *d* wicked .... Prov 6:18   2790
A man's heart *d* his way....................... Prov 16:9   2803
He that *d* to do evil shall be .... Prov 24:8   2803
he *d* wicked devices to destroy .... Is 32:7   3289
But the liberal *d* liberal things.............. Is 32:8   3289

DEVOTE

that a man shall *d* unto the Lord .... Lev 27:28   2763

DEVOTED

holy unto the Lord, as a field *d* .... Lev 27:21   2764
Notwithstanding no *d* thing .... Lev 27:28   2764
every *d* thing is most holy unto............. Lev 27:28   2764
None *d*, which shall be .... Lev 27:29   2764
which shall be of men............................. Lev 27:29   2763
Every thing *d* in Israel shall be .... Num 18:14   2764
thy servant, who is *d* to thy fear .... Ps 119:38

DEVOTIONS

as I passed by, and beheld your *d* .... Acts 17:23   4574

DEVOUR

the morning he shall *d* the prey............ Gen 49:27   398
blood, and my sword shall *d* flesh .... Deut 32:42   398
and *d* the cedars of Lebanon .... Judg 9:15   398
d the men of Shechem, and the .... Judg 9:20   398
house of Millo, and *d* Abimelech .... Judg 9:20   398
said, Shall the sword *d* for ever 2Sa 2:26   398
command the locusts to *d* the land 2Chr 7:13   398
It shall *d* the strength of his.................. Job 18:13   398
of death shall *d* his strength................. Job 18:13   398
wrath, and the fire shall *d* them .... Ps 21:9   398
a fire shall *d* before him .... Ps 50:3   398
wild beast of the field doth *d* it .... Ps 80:13   7462
to *d* the poor from off the earth, ... Prov 30:14   398
strangers *d* it in your presence, ... Is 1:7   398
they shall *d* Israel with open .... Is 9:12   398
it shall *d* the briers and thorns, ... Is 9:18   398
d his thorns and his briers in one .... Is 10:17   398
of thine enemies shall *d* them .... Is 26:11   398
not of a mean man, shall *d* him .... Is 31:8   398
your breath, as fire, shall *d* you............ Is 33:11   398
I will destroy and *d* at once................... Is 42:14   7602
ye beasts of the field, come to *d*........... Is 56:9   398
all that *d* him shall offend .... Jer 2:3   398
people wood, and it shall *d* them .... Jer 5:14   398
beasts of the field, come to *d* .... Jer 12:9   402
d from the one end of the land .... Jer 12:12   398
and the beasts of the earth, to *d* .... Jer 15:3   398
it shall *d* the palaces of .... Jer 17:27   398
it shall *d* all things round about .... Jer 21:14   398
that *d* thee shall be devoured .... Jer 30:16   398
and the sword shall *d*, and it shall .... Jer 46:10   398
sword shall *d* round about thee .... Jer 46:14   398
shall *d* the corner of Moab, and............ Jer 48:45   398
it shall *d* all round about him .... Jer 50:32   398
famine and pestilence shall *d* him .... Eze 7:15   398
and another fire shall *d* them .... Eze 15:7   398
it shall *d* every green tree in .... Eze 20:47   398
them through the fire, to *d* them .... Eze 23:37   402
midst of thee, it shall *d* thee................. Eze 28:18   398
the beast of the land *d* them .... Eze 34:28   398
thou shalt *d* men no more, neither .... Eze 36:14   398
thus unto it, Arise, *d* much flesh........... Dan 7:5   399
shall *d* the whole earth, and shall .... Dan 7:23   399
now shall a month *d* them with .... Hos 5:7   398
it shall *d* the palaces thereof................. Hos 8:14   398
d them, because of their own .... Hos 11:6   398
there will I *d* them like a lion .... Hos 13:8   398
which shall *d* the palaces of.................. Amos 1:4   398
which shall *d* the palaces thereof.......... Amos 1:7   398
which shall *d* the palaces thereof.......... Amos 1:10   398

which shall *d* the palaces of.................. Amos 1:12   398
it shall *d* the palaces thereof, ... Amos 1:14   398
it shall *d* the palaces of Kirioth .... Amos 2:2   398
it shall *d* the palaces of .... Amos 2:5   398
d it, and there be none to quench .... Amos 5:6   398
shall kindle in them, and *d* them .... Obad 18   398
the sword shall *d* thy young lions .... Nah 2:13   398
the fire shall *d* thy bars........................ Nah 3:13   398
There shall the fire *d* thee .... Nah 3:15   398
was as to *d* the poor secretly .... Hab 3:14   398
and they shall *d*, and subdue with........ Zec 9:15   398
that the fire may *d* thy cedars .... Zec 11:1   398
they shall *d* all the people round .... Zec 12:6   398
for ye *d* widows' houses, and for a ...... Mt 23:14   2719
Which *d* widows' houses, and for a ...... Mk 12:40   2719
Which *d* widows' houses, and for a ...... Lk 20:47   2719
you into bondage, if a man *d* you........... 2Cor 11:20   2719
d one another, take heed that ye............ Gal 5:15   2719
which shall *d* the adversaries .... Heb 10:27   2068
about, seeking whom he may *d* 1Pet 5:8   2666
for to *d* her child as soon as it .... Rev 12:4   2719

DEVOURED

hath quite *d* also our money .... Gen 31:15   398
say, Some evil beast hath *d* him............ Gen 37:20   398
an evil beast hath *d* him .... Gen 37:33   398
seven thin ears *d* the seven rank.......... Gen 41:7   1104
the thin ears *d* the seven good.............. Gen 41:24   1104
d them, and they died before the .... Lev 10:2   398
what time the fire *d* two hundred .... Num 26:10   398
from them, and they shall be *d* .... Deut 31:17   398
d with burning heat, and with .... Deut 32:24   3898
the wood *d* more people that day 2Sa 18:8   398
people that day than the sword *d* 2Sa 18:8   398
and fire out of his mouth *d*................... 2Sa 22:9   398
and fire out of his mouth *d*................... Ps 18:8   398
of flies among them, which *d* them .... Ps 78:45   398
For they have *d* Jacob, and laid .... Ps 79:7   398
d the fruit of their ground .... Ps 105:35   398
ye shall be *d* with the sword .... Is 1:20   398
hath the curse *d* the earth .... Is 24:6   398
own sword hath *d* your prophets........... Jer 2:30   398
For shame hath *d* the labour of .... Jer 3:24   398
have *d* the land, and all that is .... Jer 8:16   398
d him, and consumed him, and have .... Jer 10:25   398
they that devour thee shall be *d* .... Jer 30:16   398
All that found them have *d* them .... Jer 50:7   398
the king of Assyria hath *d* him .... Jer 50:17   398
the king of Babylon hath *d* me.............. Jer 51:34   398
it hath *d* the foundations thereof .... Lam 4:11   398
any work, when the fire hath *d* it .... Eze 15:5   398
thou sacrificed unto them to be *d* .... Eze 16:20   398
to catch the prey; it *d* men .... Eze 19:3   398
to catch the prey, and *d* men .... Eze 19:6   398
branches, which hath *d* her fruit .... Eze 19:14   398
they have *d* souls................................. Eze 22:25   398
residue shall be *d* by the fire................. Eze 23:25   398
will I give to the beasts to be *d* .... Eze 33:27   398
the beasts of the field to be *d*............... Eze 39:4   402
it *d* and brake in pieces, and................ Dan 7:7   399
which *d*, brake in pieces, and .... Dan 7:19   399
an oven, and have *d* their judges .... Hos 7:7   398
Strangers have *d* his strength............... Hos 7:9   398
for the fire hath *d* the pastures............. Joel 1:19   398
the fire hath *d* the pastures of.............. Joel 1:20   398
increased, the palmerworm *d* them .... Amos 4:9   398
it *d* the great deep, and did eat............. Amos 7:4   398
they shall be *d* as stubble fully .... Nah 1:10   398
be *d* by the fire of his jealousy .... Zeph 1:18   398
for all the earth shall be *d* with .... Zeph 3:8   398
and she shall be *d* with fire................... Zec 9:4   398
and the fowls came and *d* them up...... Mt 13:4   2719
fowls of the air came and *d* it up .... Mk 4:4   2719
and the fowls of the air *d* it .... Lk 8:5   2719
which hath *d* thy living with .... Lk 15:30   2719
from God out of heaven, and *d* them ...... Rev 20:9   2719

DEVOURER

will rebuke the *d* for your sakes .... Mal 3:11   398

DEVOUREST

say unto you, Thou land *d* up men .... Eze 36:13   398

DEVOURETH

for the sword *d* one as well as................ 2Sa 11:25   398
mouth of the wicked *d* iniquity .... Prov 19:28   1104
the man who *d* that which is holy .... Prov 20:25   3216
as the fire *d* the stubble....................... Is 5:24   398
flaming fire, which *d* round about.......... Lam 2:3   398
the fire *d* both the ends of it, ... Eze 15:4   398
A fire *d* before them.............................. Joel 2:3   398
flame of fire that *d* the stubble .... Joel 2:5   398

D

thy tongue when the wicked *d* the	Hab 1:13	1104
their mouth, and *d* their enemies	Rev 11:5	2719

DEVOURING

the glory of the LORD was like *d*	Ex 24:17	398
Thou lovest all *d* words, O thou	Ps 52:4	1105
tempest, and the flame of *d* fire	Is 29:6	398
and his tongue as a *d* fire	Is 30:27	398
and with the flame of a *d* fire	Is 30:30	398
us shall dwell with the *d* fire	Is 33:14	398

DEVOUT

and the same man was just and *d*	Lk 2:25	2126
d men, out of every nation under	Acts 2:5	2126
d men carried Stephen to his	Acts 8:2	2126
A *d* man, and one that feared God	Acts 10:2	2152
a *d* soldier of them that waited	Acts 10:7	2152
But the Jews stirred up the *d*	Acts 13:50	4576
of the *d* Greeks a great multitude	Acts 17:4	4576
the Jews, and with the *d* persons	Acts 17:17	4576
a *d* man according to the law,	Acts 22:12	2152

DEW

God give thee of the *d* of heaven	Gen 27:28	2919
of the *d* of heaven from above	Gen 27:39	2919
in the morning the *d* lay round	Ex 16:13	2919
when the *d* that lay was gone up,	Ex 16:14	2919
when the *d* fell upon the camp in	Num 11:9	2919
my speech shall distil as the *d*	Deut 32:2	2919
things of heaven, for the *d*	Deut 33:13	2919
his heavens shall drop down *d*	Deut 33:28	2919
if the *d* be on the fleece only,	Judg 6:37	2919
wringed the *d* out of the fleece,	Judg 6:38	2919
all the ground let there be *d*	Judg 6:39	2919
there was *d* on all the ground	Judg 6:40	2919
of Gilboa, let there be no *d*	2Sa 1:21	2919
as the *d* falleth on the ground	2Sa 17:12	2919
there shall not be *d* nor rain	1Kin 17:1	2919
the *d* lay all night upon my	Job 29:19	2919
who hath begotten the drops of *d*	Job 38:28	2919
thou hast the *d* of thy youth	Ps 110:3	2919
As the *d* of Hermon, and as the *d*	Ps 133:3	2919
up, and the clouds drop down the *d*	Prov 3:20	2919
his favour is as *d* upon the grass	Prov 19:12	2919
for my head is filled with *d*	Song 5:2	2919
like a cloud of *d* in the heat of	Is 18:4	2919
for thy *d* is as the *d* of herbs,	Is 26:19	2919
it be wet with the *d* of heaven	Dan 4:15	2920
it be wet with the *d* of heaven	Dan 4:23	2920
wet thee with the *d* of heaven	Dan 4:25	2920
body was wet with the *d* of heaven	Dan 4:33	2920
body was wet with the *d* of heaven	Dan 5:21	2920
as the early *d* it goeth away	Hos 6:4	2919
as the early *d* that passeth away,	Hos 13:3	2919
I will be as the *d* unto Israel	Hos 14:5	2919
many people as a *d* from the LORD,	Mic 5:7	2919
heaven over you is stayed from *d*	Hag 1:10	2919
and the heavens shall give their *d*	Zec 8:12	2919

DIADEM

my judgment was as a robe and a *d*	Job 29:14	6797
for a *d* of beauty, unto the	Is 28:5	6843
a royal *d* in the hand of thy God	Is 62:3	6797
Remove the *d*, and take off the	Eze 21:26	4701

DIAL

it had gone down in the *d* of Ahaz	2Kin 20:11	4609
is gone down in the sun *d* of Ahaz	Is 38:8	4609

DIAMOND

be an emerald, a sapphire, and a *d*	Ex 28:18	3095
an emerald, a sapphire, and a *d*	Ex 39:11	3095
of iron, and with the point of a *d*	Jer 17:1	8068
the sardius, topaz, and the *d*	Eze 28:13	3095

DIANA *(di-an'-ah) A Greek goddess.*

which made silver shrines for *D*	Acts 19:24	735
goddess *D* should be despised	Acts 19:27	735
Great is *D* of the Ephesians	Acts 19:28	735
Great is *D* of the Ephesians	Acts 19:34	735
worshipper of the great goddess *D*	Acts 19:35	735

DIBLAH See DIBLATH.

DIBLAIM *(dib'-la-im) Father of Gomer.*

and took Gomer the daughter of *D*	Hos 1:3	1691

DIBLATH *(dib'-lath) A place in northern Canaan.*

than the wilderness toward *D*	Eze 6:14	1689

DIBON *(di'-bon)* See DIBON-GAD, DIMON.
 1. A Moabite city.

Heshbon is perished even unto *D*	Num 21:30	1769
Ataroth, and *D*, and Jazer, and	Num 32:3	1769
And the children of Gad built *D*	Num 32:34	1769
and all the plain of Medeba unto *D*	Josh 13:9	1769

D, and Bamoth-baal, and	Josh 13:17	1769
Thou daughter that dost inhabit *D*	Jer 48:18	1769
upon *D*, and upon Nebo, and upon	Jer 48:22	1769
He is gone up to Bajith, and to *D*	Is 15:2	1769

 2. A town in Judah.

in the villages thereof, and at *D*	Neh 11:25	1769

DIBON-GAD *(di'-bon-gad') An encampment during the Exodus.*

from Iim, and pitched in *D*	Num 33:45	1769
And they removed from *D*, and	Num 33:46	1769

DIBRI *(dib'-ri) Father of Shelomith.*

was Shelomith, the daughter of *D*	Lev 24:11	1704

DID See APPENDIX.

DIDDEST

as thou *d* the Egyptian yesterday	Acts 7:28	387

DIDST See APPENDIX.

DIDYMUS *(did'-i-mus)* See THOMAS. *Another name for Thomas the apostle.*

said Thomas, which is called *D*	Jn 11:16	1324
one of the twelve, called *D*	Jn 20:24	1324
Simon Peter, and Thomas called *D*	Jn 21:2	1324

DIE

thereof thou shalt surely *d*	Gen 2:17	4191
shall ye touch it, lest ye *d*	Gen 3:3	4191
the woman, Ye shall not surely *d*	Gen 3:4	4191
that is in the earth shall *d*	Gen 6:17	1478
lest some evil take me, and I *d*	Gen 19:19	4191
thou that thou shalt surely *d*	Gen 20:7	4191
Behold, I am at the point to *d*	Gen 25:32	4191
Because I said, Lest I *d* for her	Gen 26:9	4191
my soul may bless thee before I *d*	Gen 27:4	4191
Give me children, or else I *d*	Gen 30:1	4191
one day, all the flock will *d*	Gen 33:13	4191
said, Lest peradventure he *d* also	Gen 38:11	4191
that we may live, and not *d*	Gen 42:2	4191
be verified, and ye shall not *d*	Gen 42:20	4191
that we may live, and not *d*	Gen 43:8	4191
it be found, both let him *d*	Gen 44:9	4191
his father, his father would *d*	Gen 44:22	4191
is not with us, that he will *d*	Gen 44:31	4191
I will go and see him before I *d*	Gen 45:28	4191
said unto Joseph, Now let me *d*	Gen 46:30	4191
why should we *d* in thy presence	Gen 47:15	4191
shall we *d* before thine eyes	Gen 47:19	4191
seed, that we may live, and not *d*	Gen 47:19	4191
time drew nigh that Israel must *d*	Gen 47:29	4191
said unto Joseph, Behold, I *d*	Gen 48:21	4191
made me swear, saying, Lo, I *d*	Gen 50:5	4191
said unto his brethren, I *d*	Gen 50:24	4191
fish that is in the river shall *d*	Ex 7:18	4191
there shall nothing *d* of all that	Ex 9:4	4191
down upon them, and they shall *d*	Ex 9:19	4191
thou seest my face thou shalt *d*	Ex 10:28	4191
in the land of Egypt shall *d*	Ex 11:5	4191
us away to *d* in the wilderness	Ex 14:11	4191
we should *d* in the wilderness	Ex 14:12	4191
not God speak with us, lest we *d*	Ex 20:19	4191
that smiteth a man, so that he *d*	Ex 21:12	4191
from mine altar, that he may *d*	Ex 21:14	4191
he *d* not, but keepeth his bed	Ex 21:18	4191
a rod, and he *d* under his hand	Ex 21:20	4191
a man or a woman, that they *d*	Ex 21:28	4191
ox hurt another's, that he *d*	Ex 21:35	4191
up, and be smitten that he *d*	Ex 22:2	4191
and it *d*, or be hurt, or driven	Ex 22:10	4191
neighbour, and it be hurt, or *d*	Ex 22:14	4191
when he cometh out, that he *d* not	Ex 28:35	4191
that they bear not iniquity, and *d*	Ex 28:43	4191
wash with water, that they *d* not	Ex 30:20	4191
and their feet, that they *d* not	Ex 30:21	4191
charge of the LORD, that ye *d* not	Lev 8:35	4191
lest ye *d*, and lest wrath come	Lev 10:6	4191
of the congregation, lest ye *d*	Lev 10:7	4191
of the congregation, lest ye *d*	Lev 10:9	4191
any beast, of which ye may eat, *d*	Lev 11:39	4191
that they *d* not in their	Lev 15:31	4191
that he *d* not	Lev 16:2	4191
upon the testimony, that he *d* not	Lev 16:13	4191
they shall *d* childless	Lev 20:20	4191
d therefore, if they profane it	Lev 21:9	4191
touch any holy thing, lest they *d*	Num 4:15	4191
that they may live, and not *d*	Num 4:19	4191
things are covered, lest they *d*	Num 4:20	4191
or for his sister, when they *d*	Num 6:7	4194
if any man *d* very suddenly by him	Num 6:9	4191
consumed, and there they shall *d*	Num 14:35	4191
If these men *d* the common death	Num 16:29	4191

from me, that they *d* not	Num 17:10	4191
unto Moses, saying, Behold, we *d*	Num 17:12	1478
tabernacle of the LORD shall *d*	Num 17:13	4191
that neither they, nor ye also, *d*	Num 18:3	4191
lest they bear sin, and *d*	Num 18:22	4191
the children of Israel, lest ye *d*	Num 18:32	4191
we and our cattle should *d* there	Num 20:4	4191
unto his people, and shall *d* there	Num 20:26	4191
of Egypt to *d* in the wilderness	Num 21:5	4191
Let me *d* the death of the	Num 23:10	4191
shall surely *d* in the wilderness	Num 26:65	4191
of Israel, saying, If a man *d*	Num 27:8	4191
that the manslayer *d* not, until	Num 35:12	4191
instrument of iron, so that he *d*	Num 35:16	4191
wherewith he may *d*, and he *d*	Num 35:17	4191
wherewith he may *d*, and he *d*	Num 35:18	4191
him by laying of wait, that he *d*	Num 35:20	4191
him with his hand, that he *d*	Num 35:21	4191
any stone, wherewith a man may *d*	Num 35:23	4191
and cast it upon him, that he *d*	Num 35:23	4191
any person to cause him to *d*	Num 35:30	4191
But I must *d* in this land, I must	Deut 4:22	4191
Now therefore why should we *d*	Deut 5:25	4191
our God any more, then we shall *d*	Deut 5:25	4191
stone him with stones, that he *d*	Deut 13:10	4191
them with stones, till they *d*	Deut 17:5	4191
the judge, even that man shall *d*	Deut 17:12	4191
great fire any more, that I *d* not	Deut 18:16	4191
gods, even that prophet shall *d*	Deut 18:20	4191
upon his neighbour, that he *d*	Deut 19:5	4191
and smite him mortally that he *d*	Deut 19:11	4191
avenger of blood, that he may *d*	Deut 19:12	4191
lest he *d* in the battle, and	Deut 20:5	4191
lest he *d* in the battle, and	Deut 20:6	4191
lest he *d* in the battle, and	Deut 20:7	4191
stone him with stones, that he *d*	Deut 21:21	4191
stone her with stones that she *d*	Deut 22:21	4191
then they shall both of them *d*	Deut 22:22	4191
them with stones that they *d*	Deut 22:24	4191
only that lay with her shall *d*	Deut 22:25	4191
or if the latter husband *d*	Deut 24:3	4191
then that thief shall *d*	Deut 24:7	4191
dwell together, and one of them *d*	Deut 25:5	4191
days approach that thou must *d*	Deut 31:14	4191
d in the mount whither thou goest	Deut 32:50	4191
Let Reuben live, and not *d*	Deut 33:6	4191
not *d* by the hand of the avenger	Josh 20:9	4191
thou shalt not *d*	Judg 6:23	4191
Bring out thy son, that he may *d*	Judg 6:30	4191
unto his wife, We shall surely *d*	Judg 13:22	4191
and now shall I *d* for thirst	Judg 15:18	4191
Let me *d* with the Philistines	Judg 16:30	4191
Where thou diest, will I *d*	Ruth 1:17	4191
d in the flower of their age	1Sa 2:33	4191
one day they shall *d* both of them	1Sa 2:34	4191
the LORD thy God, that we *d* not	1Sa 12:19	4191
my son, he shall surely *d*	1Sa 14:39	4191
in mine hand, and, lo, I must *d*	1Sa 14:43	4191
for thou shalt surely *d*, Jonathan	1Sa 14:44	4191
said unto Saul, Shall Jonathan *d*	1Sa 14:45	4191
thou shalt not *d*	1Sa 20:2	4191
of the LORD, that I *d* not	1Sa 20:14	4191
unto me, for he shall surely *d*	1Sa 20:31	4191
king, Thou shalt surely *d*	1Sa 22:16	4191
or his day shall come to *d*	1Sa 26:10	4191
LORD liveth, ye are worthy to *d*	1Sa 26:16	4194
for my life, to cause me to *d*	1Sa 28:9	4191
him, that he may be smitten, and *d*	2Sa 11:15	4191
done this thing shall surely *d*	2Sa 12:5	4194
thou shalt not *d*	2Sa 12:13	4191
is born unto thee shall surely *d*	2Sa 12:14	4191
For we must needs *d*, and are as	2Sa 14:14	4191
neither if half of us *d*, will	2Sa 18:3	4191
unto Shimei, Thou shalt not *d*	2Sa 19:23	4191
that I may *d* in mine own city, and	2Sa 19:37	4191
shall be found in him, he shall *d*	1Kin 1:52	4191
David drew nigh that he should *d*	1Kin 2:1	4191
but I will *d* here	1Kin 2:30	4191
certain that thou shalt surely *d*	1Kin 2:37	4191
whither, that thou shalt surely *d*	1Kin 2:42	4191
into the city, the child shall *d*	1Kin 14:12	4191
my son, that we may eat it, and *d*	1Kin 17:12	4191
for himself that he might *d*	1Kin 19:4	4191
out, and stone him, that he may *d*	1Kin 21:10	4191
art gone up, but shalt surely *d*	2Kin 1:4	4191
art gone up, but shalt surely *d*	2Kin 1:6	4191
art gone up, but shalt surely *d*	2Kin 1:16	4191
Why sit we here until we *d*	2Kin 7:3	4191
in the city, and we shall *d* there	2Kin 7:4	4191
if we sit still here, we *d* also	2Kin 7:4	4191
if they kill us, we shall but *d*	2Kin 7:4	4191
shewed me that he shall surely *d*	2Kin 8:10	4191
honey, that ye may live, and not *d*	2Kin 18:32	4191
for thou shalt *d*, and not live	2Kin 20:1	4191
shall not *d* for the children	2Chr 25:4	4191
the children *d* for the fathers	2Chr 25:4	4191
every man shall *d* for his own sin	2Chr 25:4	4191
over yourselves to *d* by famine	2Chr 32:11	4191
curse God, and *d*	Job 2:9	4191
they *d*, even without wisdom	Job 4:21	4191
and wisdom shall *d* with you	Job 12:2	4191
the stock thereof *d* in the ground	Job 14:8	4191
If a man *d*, shall he live again	Job 14:14	4191
till I *d* I will not remove mine	Job 27:5	1478
I shall *d* in my nest, and I shall	Job 29:18	1478
In a moment shall they *d*, and the	Job 34:20	4191
they shall *d* without knowledge	Job 36:12	1478
They *d* in youth, and their life is	Job 36:14	4191
speak evil of me, When shall he *d*	Ps 41:5	4191
For he seeth that wise men *d*	Ps 49:10	4191
those that are appointed to *d*	Ps 79:11	8546
But ye shall *d* like men, and fall	Ps 82:7	4191
ready to *d* from my youth up	Ps 88:15	1478
takest away their breath, they *d*	Ps 104:29	1478
I shall not *d*, but live, and	Ps 118:17	4191
He shall *d* without instruction	Prov 5:23	4191
but fools *d* for want of wisdom	Prov 10:21	4191
and he that hateth reproof shall *d*	Prov 15:10	4191
that despiseth his ways shall *d*	Prov 19:16	4191
him with the rod, he shall not *d*	Prov 23:13	4191
deny me them not before I *d*	Prov 30:7	4191
A time to be born, and a time to *d*	Eccl 3:2	4191
shouldest thou *d* before thy time	Eccl 7:17	4191
the living know that they shall *d*	Eccl 9:5	4191
for to morrow we shall *d*	Is 22:13	4191
not be purged from you till ye *d*	Is 22:14	4191
there shalt thou *d*, and there the	Is 22:18	4191
for thou shalt *d*, and not live	Is 38:1	4191
therein shall *d* in like manner	Is 51:6	4191
be afraid of a man that shall *d*	Is 51:12	4191
that he should not *d* in the pit	Is 51:14	4191
for the child shall *d* an hundred	Is 65:20	4191
for their worm shall not *d*	Is 66:24	4191
that thou *d* not by our hand	Jer 11:21	4191
young men shall *d* by the sword	Jer 11:22	4191
their daughters shall *d* by famine	Jer 11:22	4191
They shall *d* of grievous deaths	Jer 16:4	4191
and the small shall *d* in this land	Jer 16:6	4191
to Babylon, and there thou shalt *d*	Jer 20:6	4191
they shall *d* of a great	Jer 21:6	4191
in this city shall *d* by the sword	Jer 21:9	4191
But he shall *d* in the place	Jer 22:12	4191
and there shall ye *d*	Jer 22:26	4191
him, saying, Thou shalt surely *d*	Jer 26:8	4191
saying, This man is worthy to *d*	Jer 26:11	4194
This man is not worthy to *d*	Jer 26:16	4194
Why will ye *d*, thou and thy people	Jer 27:13	4191
this year thou shalt *d*, because	Jer 28:16	4191
But every one shall *d* for his own	Jer 31:30	4191
Thou shalt not *d* by the sword	Jer 34:4	4191
But thou shalt *d* in peace	Jer 34:5	4191
the scribe, lest I *d* there	Jer 37:20	4191
in this city shall *d* by the sword	Jer 38:2	4191
he is like to *d* for hunger in the	Jer 38:9	4191
out of the dungeon, before he *d*	Jer 38:10	4191
these words, and thou shalt not *d*	Jer 38:24	4191
to Jonathan's house, to *d* there	Jer 38:26	4191
and there ye shall *d*	Jer 42:16	4191
they shall *d* by the sword, by the	Jer 42:17	4191
that ye shall *d* by the sword	Jer 42:22	4191
they shall *d*, from the least even	Jer 44:12	4191
the wicked, Thou shalt surely *d*	Eze 3:18	4191
man shall *d* in his iniquity	Eze 3:18	4191
he shall *d* in his iniquity	Eze 3:19	4191
before him, he shall *d*	Eze 3:20	4191
he shall *d* in his sin, and his	Eze 3:20	4191
thee shall *d* with the pestilence	Eze 5:12	4191
far off shall *d* of the pestilence	Eze 6:12	4191
is besieged shall *d* by the famine	Eze 6:12	4191
the field shall *d* with the sword	Eze 7:15	4191
see it, though he shall *d* there	Eze 12:13	4191
slay the souls that should not *d*	Eze 13:19	4191
the midst of Babylon he shall *d*	Eze 17:16	4191
the soul that sinneth, it shall *d*	Eze 18:4	4191
he shall surely *d*	Eze 18:13	4191
he shall not *d* for the iniquity	Eze 18:17	4191
even he shall *d* in his iniquity	Eze 18:18	4191
The soul that sinneth, it shall *d*	Eze 18:20	4191
shall surely live, he shall not *d*	Eze 18:21	4191
at all that the wicked should *d*	Eze 18:23	4194
hath sinned, in them shall he *d*	Eze 18:24	4191
that he hath done shall he *d*	Eze 18:26	4191

D

shall surely live, he shall not d	Eze 18:28	4191
for why will ye d, O house of	Eze 18:31	4191
thou shalt d the deaths of them	Eze 28:8	4191
Thou shalt d the deaths of the	Eze 28:10	4191
O wicked man, thou shalt surely d	Eze 33:8	4191
man shall d in his iniquity	Eze 33:8	4191
he shall d in his iniquity	Eze 33:9	4191
for why will ye d, O house of	Eze 33:11	4191
hath committed, he shall d for it	Eze 33:13	4191
the wicked, Thou shalt surely d	Eze 33:14	4191
shall surely live, he shall not d	Eze 33:15	4191
iniquity, he shall even d thereby	Eze 33:18	4191
caves shall d of the pestilence	Eze 33:27	4191
Moab shall d with tumult, with	Amos 2:2	4191
in one house, that they shall d	Amos 6:9	4191
Jeroboam shall d by the sword	Amos 7:11	4191
thou shalt d in a polluted land	Amos 7:17	4191
of my people shall d by the sword	Amos 9:10	4191
better for me to d than to live	Jonah 4:3	4194
and wished in himself to d	Jonah 4:8	4191
better for me to d than to live	Jonah 4:8	4191
we shall not d	Hab 1:12	4191
that that dieth, let it d	Zec 11:9	4191
therein shall be cut off and d	Zec 13:8	1478
or mother, let him d the death	Mt 15:4	5053
Master, Moses said, If a man d	Mt 22:24	599
him, Though I should d with thee	Mt 26:35	599
or mother, let him d the death	Mk 7:10	5053
unto us, If a man's brother d	Mk 12:19	599
If I should d with thee, I will	Mk 14:31	4880
unto him, was sick, and ready to d	Lk 7:2	5053
unto us, If any man's brother d	Lk 20:28	599
he d without children, that his	Lk 20:28	599
Neither can they d any more	Lk 20:36	599
Sir, come down ere my child d	Jn 4:49	599
a man may eat thereof, and not d	Jn 6:50	599
seek me, and shall d in your sins	Jn 8:21	599
you, that ye shall d in your sins	Jn 8:24	599
I am he, ye shall d in your sins	Jn 8:24	599
also go, that we may d with him	Jn 11:16	599
and believeth in me shall never d	Jn 11:26	599
one man should d for the people	Jn 11:50	599
Jesus should d for that nation	Jn 11:51	599
wheat fall into the ground and d	Jn 12:24	599
but if it d, it bringeth forth	Jn 12:24	599
signifying what death he should d	Jn 12:33	599
one man should d for the people	Jn 18:14	622
signifying what death he should d	Jn 18:32	599
law, and by our law he ought to d	Jn 19:7	599
that that disciple should not d	Jn 21:23	599
said not unto him, He shall not d	Jn 21:23	599
but also to d at Jerusalem for	Acts 21:13	599
of death, I refuse not to d	Acts 25:11	599
Romans to deliver any man to d	Acts 25:16	684
for a righteous man will one d	Rom 5:7	599
man some would even dare to d	Rom 5:7	599
live after the flesh, ye shall d	Rom 8:13	599
we d, we d unto the Lord	Rom 14:8	599
whether we live therefore, or d	Rom 14:8	599
for it were better for me to d	1Cor 9:15	599
For as in Adam all d, even so in	1Cor 15:22	599
Christ Jesus our Lord, I d daily	1Cor 15:31	599
for to morrow we d	1Cor 15:32	599
is not quickened, except it d	1Cor 15:36	599
that ye are in our hearts to d	2Cor 7:3	4880
live is Christ, and to d is gain	Phil 1:21	599
here men that d receive tithes	Heb 7:8	599
is appointed unto men once to d	Heb 9:27	599
which remain, that are ready to d	Rev 3:2	599
and shall desire to d, and death	Rev 9:6	599
Blessed are the dead which d in	Rev 14:13	599

DIED

and thirty years: and he d	Gen 5:5	4191
and twelve years: and he d	Gen 5:8	4191
and five years: and he d	Gen 5:11	4191
and ten years: and he d	Gen 5:14	4191
and five years: and he d	Gen 5:17	4191
and two years: and he d	Gen 5:20	4191
and nine years: and he d	Gen 5:27	4191
and seven years: and he d	Gen 5:31	4191
all flesh d that moved upon the	Gen 7:21	1478
all that was in the dry land, d	Gen 7:22	4191
and fifty years: and he d	Gen 9:29	4191
Haran d before his father Terah	Gen 11:28	4191
and Terah d in Haran	Gen 11:32	4191
And Sarah d in Kirjath-arba	Gen 23:2	4191
d in a good old age, an old man,	Gen 25:8	4191
and he gave up the ghost and d	Gen 25:17	4191
he d in the presence of all his	Gen 25:18	5307
But Deborah Rebekah's nurse d	Gen 35:8	4191

(for she d) that she called his	Gen 35:18	4191
And Rachel d, and was buried in the	Gen 35:19	4191
And Isaac gave up the ghost, and d	Gen 35:29	4191
And Bela d, and Jobab the son of	Gen 36:33	4191
And Jobab d, and Husham of the land	Gen 36:34	4191
And Husham d, and Hadad the son of	Gen 36:35	4191
Hadad d, and Samlah of Masrekah	Gen 36:36	4191
And Samlah d, and Saul of Rehoboth	Gen 36:37	4191
And Saul d, and Baal-hanan the son	Gen 36:38	4191
And Baal-hanan the son of Achbor d	Gen 36:39	4191
daughter of Shuah Judah's wife d	Gen 38:12	4191
Onan d in the land of Canaan	Gen 46:12	4191
Rachel d by me in the land of	Gen 48:7	4194
father did command before he d	Gen 50:16	4191
So Joseph d, being an hundred and	Gen 50:26	4191
And Joseph d, and all his brethren,	Ex 1:6	4191
of time, that the king of Egypt d	Ex 2:23	4191
the fish that was in the river d	Ex 7:21	4191
the frogs d out of the houses,	Ex 8:13	4191
and all the cattle of Egypt d	Ex 9:6	4191
the children of Israel d not one	Ex 9:6	4191
Would to God we had d by the hand	Ex 16:3	4191
them, and they d before the LORD	Lev 10:2	4191
offered before the LORD, and d	Lev 16:1	4191
eateth that which d of itself	Lev 17:15	5038
Abihu d before the LORD, when	Num 3:4	4191
we had d in the land of Egypt	Num 14:2	4191
God we had d in this wilderness	Num 14:2	4191
d by the plague before the LORD	Num 14:37	4191
stoned him with stones, and he d	Num 15:36	4191
Now they that d in the plague	Num 16:49	4191
beside them that d about the	Num 16:49	4191
and Miriam d there, and was buried	Num 20:1	4191
Would God that we had d when our	Num 20:3	1478
our brethren d before the LORD	Num 20:3	1478
Aaron d there in the top of the	Num 20:28	4191
and much people of Israel d	Num 21:6	4191
those that d in the plague were	Num 25:9	4191
with Korah, when that company d	Num 26:10	4194
the children of Korah d not	Num 26:11	4191
Onan d in the land of Canaan	Num 26:19	4191
And Nadab and Abihu d, when they	Num 26:61	4191
Our father d in the wilderness	Num 27:3	4191
but d in his own sin, and had no	Num 27:3	4191
d there, in the fortieth year	Num 33:38	4191
years old when he d in mount Hor	Num 33:39	4194
there Aaron d, and there he was	Deut 10:6	4191
Aaron thy brother d in mount Hor	Deut 32:50	4191
LORD d there in the land of Moab	Deut 34:5	4191
and twenty years old when he d	Deut 34:7	4194
d in the wilderness by the way,	Josh 5:4	4191
upon them unto Azekah, and they d	Josh 10:11	4191
they were more which d with	Josh 10:11	4191
Nun, the servant of the LORD, d	Josh 24:29	4191
And Eleazar the son of Aaron d	Josh 24:33	4191
him to Jerusalem, and there he d	Judg 1:7	4191
Nun, the servant of the LORD, d	Judg 2:8	4191
which Joshua left when he d	Judg 2:21	4191
And Othniel the son of Kenaz d	Judg 3:11	4191
asleep and weary. So he d	Judg 4:21	4191
son of Joash in a good old age	Judg 8:32	4191
of the tower of Shechem d also	Judg 9:49	4191
man thrust him through, and he d	Judg 9:54	4191
twenty and three years, and d	Judg 10:2	4191
And Jair d, and was buried in Camon	Judg 10:5	4191
Then d Jephthah the Gileadite, and	Judg 12:7	4191
Then d Ibzan, and was buried at	Judg 12:10	4191
And Elon the Zebulonite d, and was	Judg 12:12	4191
son of Hillel the Pirathonite d	Judg 12:15	4191
And Elimelech Naomi's husband d	Ruth 1:3	4191
Chilion d also both of them	Ruth 1:5	4191
gate, and his neck brake, and he d	1Sa 4:18	4191
the men that d not were smitten	1Sa 5:12	4191
rescued Jonathan, that he d not	1Sa 14:45	4191
And Samuel d; and all the Israelites	1Sa 25:1	4191
that his heart d within him	1Sa 25:37	4191
the LORD smote Nabal, that he d	1Sa 25:38	4191
upon his sword, and d with him	1Sa 31:5	4191
So Saul d, and his three sons, and	1Sa 31:6	4191
And he smote him that he d	2Sa 1:15	4191
there, and d in the same place	2Sa 2:23	4191
Asahel fell down and d stood still	2Sa 2:23	4191
three hundred and threescore men d	2Sa 2:31	4191
under the fifth rib, that he d	2Sa 3:27	4191
and said, D Abner as a fool dieth	2Sa 3:33	4191
there he d by the ark of God	2Sa 6:7	4191
king of the children of Ammon d	2Sa 10:1	4191
of their host, who d there	2Sa 10:18	4191
and Uriah the Hittite d also	2Sa 11:17	4191
the wall, that he d in Thebez	2Sa 11:21	4191
the seventh day, that the child d	2Sa 12:18	4191

D

in order, and hanged himself, and *d*	2Sa 17:23	4191
would God I had *d* for thee	2Sa 18:33	4191
lived, and all we had *d* this day	2Sa 19:6	4191
him not again; and he *d*	2Sa 20:10	4191
there *d* of the people from Dan	2Sa 24:15	4191
and he fell upon him that he *d*	1Kin 2:25	4191
out, and fell upon him, that he *d*	1Kin 2:46	4191
this woman's child *d* in the night	1Kin 3:19	4191
stoned him with stones, that he *d*	1Kin 12:18	4191
of the door, the child *d*	1Kin 14:17	4191
house over him with fire, and *d*	1Kin 16:18	4191
so Tibni *d*, and Omri reigned	1Kin 16:22	4191
stoned him with stones, that he *d*	1Kin 21:13	4191
against the Syrians, and *d* at even	1Kin 22:35	4191
So the king *d*, and was brought to	1Kin 22:37	4191
So he *d* according to the word of	2Kin 4:14	4191
on her knees till noon, and then *d*	2Kin 4:20	4191
upon him in the gate, and he *d*	2Kin 7:17	4191
upon him in the gate, and he *d*	2Kin 7:20	4191
it on his face, so that he *d*	2Kin 8:15	4191
And he fled to Megiddo, and *d* there	2Kin 9:27	4191
his servants, smote him, and he *d*	2Kin 12:21	4191
sick of his sickness whereof he *d*	2Kin 13:14	4191
And Elisha *d*, and they buried him	2Kin 13:20	4191
So Hazael king of Syria *d*	2Kin 13:24	4191
and he came to Egypt, and *d* there	2Kin 23:34	4191
him, and smote Gedaliah, that he *d*	2Kin 25:25	4191
Hadad *d* also. And the dukes	1Chr 1:51	4191
but Seled *d* without children	1Chr 2:30	4191
Jether *d* without children	1Chr 2:32	4191
fell likewise on the sword, and *d*	1Chr 10:5	4191
So Saul *d*, and his three sons	1Chr 10:6	4191
and all his house *d* together	1Chr 10:6	4191
So Saul *d* for his transgression	1Chr 10:13	4191
and there he *d* before God	1Chr 13:10	4191
king of the children of Ammon *d*	1Chr 19:1	4191
And Eleazar *d*, and had no sons, but	1Chr 23:22	4191
Abihu *d* before their father, and	1Chr 24:2	4191
he *d* in a good old age, full of	1Chr 29:28	4191
stoned him with stones, that he *d*	2Chr 10:18	4191
and the LORD struck him, and he *d*	2Chr 13:20	4191
d in the one and fortieth year of	2Chr 16:13	4191
time of the sun going down he *d*	2Chr 18:34	4191
so he *d* of sore diseases	2Chr 21:19	4191
and was full of days when he *d*	2Chr 24:15	4191
thirty years old was he when he *d*	2Chr 24:15	4194
And when he *d*, he said, The LORD	2Chr 24:22	4191
and slew him on his bed, and he *d*	2Chr 24:25	4191
brought him to Jerusalem, and he *d*	2Chr 35:24	4191
Why *d* I not from the womb	Job 3:11	4191
So Job *d*, being old and full of	Job 42:17	4191
d I saw also the Lord sitting	Is 6:1	4194
that king Ahaz *d* was this burden	Is 14:28	4194
So Hananiah the prophet *d* the	Jer 28:17	4191
Pelatiah the son of Benaiah *d*	Eze 11:13	4191
and at even my wife *d*	Eze 24:18	4191
when he offended in Baal, he *d*	Hos 13:1	4191
And last of all the woman *d* also	Mt 22:27	599
And the second took her, and *d*	Mk 12:21	599
last of all the woman *d* also	Mk 12:22	599
came to pass, that the beggar *d*	Lk 16:22	599
the rich man also *d*, and was	Lk 16:22	599
a wife, and *d* without children	Lk 20:29	599
her to wife, and he *d* childless	Lk 20:30	599
and they left no children, and *d*	Lk 20:31	599
Last of all the woman *d* also	Lk 20:32	599
been here, my brother had not *d*	Jn 11:21	599
been here, my brother had not *d*	Jn 11:32	599
even this man should not have *d*	Jn 11:37	599
Jacob went down into Egypt, and *d*	Acts 7:15	5053
days, that she was sick, and *d*	Acts 9:37	599
due time Christ *d* for the ungodly	Rom 5:6	599
were yet sinners, Christ *d* for us	Rom 5:8	599
that he *d*, he *d* unto sin once	Rom 6:10	599
came, sin revived, and I *d*	Rom 7:9	599
It is Christ that *d*, yea rather,	Rom 8:34	599
For to this end Christ both *d*	Rom 14:9	599
with thy meat, for whom Christ *d*	Rom 14:15	599
brother perish, for whom Christ *d*	1Cor 8:11	599
how that Christ *d* for our sins	1Cor 15:3	599
thus judge, that if one *d* for all	2Cor 5:14	599
And that he *d* for all, that they	2Cor 5:15	599
but unto him which *d* for them	2Cor 5:15	599
For if we believe that Jesus *d*	1Th 4:14	599
Who *d* for us, that, whether we	1Th 5:10	599
law without mercy under two or	Heb 10:28	599
These all *d* in faith, not having	Heb 11:13	599
By faith Joseph, when he *d*	Heb 11:22	5053
were in the sea, and had life, *d*	Rev 8:9	599
many men *d* of the waters, because	Rev 8:11	599
and every living soul *d* in the sea	Rev 16:3	599

DIEST
Where thou *d*, will I die, and	Ruth 1:17	4191

DIET
And for his *d*, there was a	Jer 52:34	737
there was a continual *d* given him	Jer 52:34	737

DIETH
fat of the beast that *d* of itself	Lev 7:24	5038
That which *d* of itself, or is	Lev 22:8	5038
the law, when a man *d* in a tent	Num 19:14	4191
eat of any thing that *d* of itself	Deut 14:21	5038
and said, Died Abner as a fool *d*	2Sa 3:33	4194
Him that of Jeroboam in the	1Kin 14:11	4191
him that *d* in the field shall the	1Kin 14:11	4191
Him that *d* of Baasha in the city	1Kin 16:4	4191
him that *d* of his in the fields	1Kin 16:4	4191
Him that *d* of Ahab in the city	1Kin 21:24	4191
him that *d* in the field shall the	1Kin 21:24	4191
But man *d*, and wasteth away	Job 14:10	4191
One *d* in his full strength, being	Job 21:23	4191
another *d* in the bitterness of	Job 21:25	4191
For when he *d* he shall carry	Ps 49:17	4194
When a wicked man *d*, his	Prov 11:7	4194
And how *d* the wise man	Eccl 2:16	4191
as the one *d*, so the other	Eccl 3:19	4194
is no water, and *d* for thirst	Is 50:2	4191
he that eateth of their eggs *d*	Is 59:5	4191
eaten of that which *d* of itself	Eze 4:14	5038
committeth iniquity, and *d* in them	Eze 18:26	4191
in the death of him that *d*	Eze 18:32	4191
that that *d*, let it die	Zec 11:9	4191
Where their worm *d* not, and the	Mk 9:44	5053
Where their worm *d* not, and the	Mk 9:46	5053
Where their worm *d* not, and the	Mk 9:48	5053
raised from the dead *d* no more	Rom 6:9	599
himself, and no man *d* to himself	Rom 14:7	599

DIFFER
who maketh thee to *d* from another	1Cor 4:7	1252

DIFFERENCE
put a *d* between the Egyptians	Ex 11:7	6395
And that ye may put *d* between holy	Lev 10:10	914
To make a *d* between the unclean	Lev 11:47	914
put *d* between clean beasts	Lev 20:25	914
have put no *d* between the holy	Eze 22:26	
they shewed *d* between the unclean	Eze 22:26	
my people the *d* between the holy	Eze 44:23	
put no *d* between us and them,	Acts 15:9	1252
for there is no *d*	Rom 3:22	1293
For there is no *d* between the Jew	Rom 10:12	1293
There is also between a wife and	1Cor 7:34	3307
some have compassion, making a *d*	Jude 22	1252

DIFFERENCES
there are *d* of administrations,	1Cor 12:5	1243

DIFFERETH
for one star *d* from another star	1Cor 15:41	1308
d nothing from a servant, though	Gal 4:1	1308

DIFFERING
Having then gifts *d* according to	Rom 12:6	1313

DIG
a pit, or if a man shall *d* a pit	Ex 21:33	3738
whose hills thou mayest *d* brass	Deut 8:9	2672
abroad, thou shalt *d* therewith	Deut 23:13	2658
d for it more than for hid	Job 3:21	2658
ye *d* a pit for your friend	Job 6:27	3738
yea, thou shalt *d* about thee	Job 11:18	2658
In the dark they *d* through houses	Job 24:16	2864
me, Son of man, *d* now in the wall	Eze 8:8	2864
D thou through the wall in their	Eze 12:5	2864
they shall *d* through the wall to	Eze 12:12	2864
Though they *d* into hell, thence	Amos 9:2	2864
also, till I shall *d* about it	Lk 13:8	4626
I cannot *d*	Lk 16:3	4626

DIGGED
unto me, that I have *d* this well	Gen 21:30	2658
had *d* in the days of Abraham his	Gen 26:15	2658
Isaac *d* again the wells of water,	Gen 26:18	2658
which they had *d* in the days of	Gen 26:18	2658
Isaac's servants *d* in the valley	Gen 26:19	2658
they *d* another well, and strove	Gen 26:21	2658
from thence, and *d* another well	Gen 26:22	2658
there Isaac's servants *d* a well	Gen 26:25	3738
the well which they had *d*	Gen 26:32	2658
their selfwill they *d* down a wall	Gen 49:6	6131
in my grave which I have *d* for me	Gen 50:5	3738
all the Egyptians *d* round about	Ex 7:24	2658
The princes *d* the well	Num 21:18	2658
the nobles of the people *d* it	Num 21:18	3738

thou filledst not, and wells *d*	Deut 6:11	2672
I have *d* and drunk strange waters,	2Kin 19:24	5365
in the desert, and *d* many wells	2Chr 26:10	2672
houses full of all goods, wells *d*	Neh 9:25	2672
d it, and is fallen into the ditch	Ps 7:15	2658
cause they have *d* for my soul	Ps 35:7	2658
they have *d* a pit before me, into	Ps 57:6	3738
until the pit be *d* for the wicked	Ps 94:13	3738
The proud have *d* pits for me	Ps 119:85	3738
it shall not be pruned, nor *d*	Is 5:6	5737
that shall be *d* with the mattock	Is 7:25	5737
I have *d*, and drunk water	Is 37:25	5365
hole of the pit whence ye are *d*	Is 51:1	5365
Then I went to Euphrates, and *d*	Jer 13:7	2658
for they have *d* a pit for my soul	Jer 18:20	3738
for they have *d* a pit to take me,	Jer 18:22	3738
when I had *d* in the wall, behold	Eze 8:8	2864
in the even I *d* through the wall	Eze 12:7	2864
d a winepress in it, and built a	Mt 21:33	3736
d in the earth, and hid his lord's	Mt 25:18	3736
d a place for the winefat, and	Mk 12:1	3736
d deep, and laid the foundation on	Lk 6:48	4626
prophets, and *d* down thine altars	Rom 11:3	2679

DIGGEDST
and wells digged, which thou *d* not	Deut 6:11	2672

DIGGETH
An ungodly man *d* up evil	Prov 16:27	3738
Whoso *d* a pit shall fall therein	Prov 26:27	3738
He that *d* a pit shall fall into	Eccl 10:8	2658

DIGNITIES
are not afraid to speak evil of *d*	2Pet 2:10	1891
dominion, and speak evil of *d*	Jude 8	1891

DIGNITY
my strength, the excellency of *d*	Gen 49:3	7613
d hath been done to Mordecai for	Est 6:3	1420
Folly is set in great *d*, and the	Eccl 10:6	4791
and their *d* shall proceed of	Hab 1:7	7613

DIKLAH (dik'-lah) A son of Joktan.
And Hadoram, and Uzal, and *D*	Gen 10:27	1853
Hadoram also, and Uzal, and *D*	1Chr 1:21	1853

DILEAN (dil'-e-an) A city in Judah.
And *D*, and Mizpeh, and Joktheel,	Josh 15:38	1810

DILIGENCE
Keep thy heart with all *d*	Prov 4:23	4929
give d that thou mayest be	Lk 12:58	2039
he that ruleth, with *d*	Rom 12:8	4710
and knowledge, and in all *d*	2Cor 8:7	4710
Do thy *d* to come shortly unto me	2Ti 4:9	4704
Do thy *d* to come before winter	2Ti 4:21	4704
one of you do shew the same *d* to	Heb 6:11	4710
And beside this, giving all *d*	2Pet 1:5	4710
give *d* to make your calling and	2Pet 1:10	4710
when I gave all *d* to write unto	Jude 3	4710

DILIGENT
judges shall make *d* inquisition	Deut 19:18	3190
But take *d* heed to do the	Josh 22:5	3966
they accomplish a *d* search	Ps 64:6	
and my spirit made *d* search	Ps 77:6	
but the hand of the *d* maketh rich	Prov 10:4	2742
The hand of the *d* shall bear rule	Prov 12:24	2742
substance of a *d* man is precious	Prov 12:27	2742
soul of the *d* shall be made fat	Prov 13:4	2742
The thoughts of the *d* tend only	Prov 21:5	2742
thou a man *d* in his business	Prov 22:29	4106
Be thou *d* to know the state of	Prov 27:23	
proved *d* in many things	2Cor 8:22	4705
but now much more *d*	2Cor 8:22	4707
be *d* to come unto me to Nicopolis	Titus 3:12	4704
be *d* that ye may be found of him	2Pet 3:14	4704

DILIGENTLY
If thou wilt *d* hearken to the	Ex 15:26	
Moses *d* sought the goat of the	Lev 10:16	
to thyself, and keep thy soul *d*	Deut 4:9	3966
teach them *d* unto thy children	Deut 6:7	8150
Ye shall *d* keep the commandments	Deut 6:17	
if ye shall hearken *d* unto my	Deut 11:13	
For if ye shall *d* keep all these	Deut 11:22	
enquire, and make search, and ask *d*	Deut 13:14	3190
hast heard of it, and enquired *d*	Deut 17:4	3190
of leprosy, that thou observe *d*	Deut 24:8	3966
if thou shalt hearken *d* unto the	Deut 28:1	
Now the men did *d* observe whether	1Kin 20:33	5172
let it be *d* done for the house of	Ezr 7:23	149
Hear *d* my speech, and my	Job 13:17	
Hear *d* my speech, and let this be	Job 21:2	
thou shalt *d* consider his place,	Ps 37:10	995

us to keep thy precepts *d*	Ps 119:4	3966
d to seek thy face, and I have	Prov 7:15	7836
He that *d* seeketh good procureth	Prov 11:27	7836
consider *d* what is before thee	Prov 23:1	
he hearkened *d* with much heed	Is 21:7	7182
hearken *d* unto me, and eat ye that	Is 55:2	
and send unto Kedar, and consider *d*	Jer 2:10	3966
if they will *d* learn the ways of	Jer 12:16	
if ye *d* hearken unto me, saith	Jer 17:24	
if ye will *d* obey the voice of	Zec 6:15	
enquired of them *d* what time the	Mt 2:7	
search *d* for the young child	Mt 2:8	199
he had *d* enquired of the wise men	Mt 2:16	
house, and seek d till she find it	Lk 15:8	1960
taught *d* the things of the Lord,	Acts 18:25	199
if she have *d* followed every good	1Ti 5:10	
in Rome, he sought me out very *d*	2Ti 1:17	4706
and Apollos on their journey *d*	Titus 3:13	4709
rewarder of them that *d* seek him	Heb 11:6	1567
Looking *d* lest any man fail of	Heb 12:15	
have enquired and searched *d*	1Pet 1:10	

DIM
Isaac was old, and his eyes were *d*	Gen 27:1	3543
the eyes of Israel were *d* for age	Gen 48:10	3513
his eye was not *d*, nor his	Deut 34:7	3543
place, and his eyes began to wax *d*	1Sa 3:2	3544
and his eyes were *d*, that he could	1Sa 4:15	6965
Mine eye also is *d* by reason of	Job 17:7	3543
of them that see shall not be *d*	Is 32:3	8159
How is the gold become *d*	Lam 4:1	6004
for these things our eyes are *d*	Lam 5:17	2821

DIMINISH
ye shall not *d* ought thereof	Ex 5:8	1639
duty of marriage, shall he not *d*	Ex 21:10	1639
thou shalt *d* the price of it	Lev 25:16	4591
neither shall ye *d* ought from it	Deut 4:2	1639
not add thereto, nor *d* from it	Deut 12:32	1639
d not a word	Jer 26:2	1639
therefore will I also *d* thee	Eze 5:11	1639
for I will *d* them, that they	Eze 29:15	4591

DIMINISHED
not ought of your work shall be *d*	Ex 5:11	1639
gotten by vanity shall be *d*	Prov 13:11	4591
the children of Kedar, shall be *d*	Is 21:17	4591
may be increased there, and not *d*	Jer 29:6	4591
have *d* thine ordinary food, and	Eze 16:27	1639

DIMINISHING
the *d* of them the riches of the	Rom 11:12	2275

DIMNAH (dim'-nah) A Levitical city in Zebulun.
D with her suburbs, Nahalal with	Josh 21:35	1829

DIMNESS
trouble and darkness, *d* of anguish	Is 8:22	4588
Nevertheless the *d* shall not be	Is 9:1	4155

DIMON (di'-mon) See DIBON, DIMONAH. A Moabite city.
For the waters of *D* shall be full	Is 15:9	1775
for I will bring more upon *D*	Is 15:9	1775

DIMONAH (di-mo'-nah) See DIMON. A city in Judah.
And Kinah, and *D*, and Adadah,	Josh 15:22	1776

DINAH See DINAH'S. A daughter of Jacob.
a daughter, and called her name *D*	Gen 30:21	1783
D the daughter of Leah, which she	Gen 34:1	1783
his soul clave unto *D* the	Gen 34:3	1783
he had defiled *D* his daughter	Gen 34:5	1783
he had defiled *D* their sister	Gen 34:13	1783
took *D* out of Shechem's house, and	Gen 34:26	1783
Padan-aram, with his daughter *D*	Gen 46:15	1783

DINAH'S
D brethren, took each man his	Gen 34:25	1783

DINAITES (di'-na-ites) Foreign settlers in Samaria.
the *D*, the Apharsathchites, the	Ezr 4:9	1784

DINE
these men shall *d* with me at noon	Gen 43:16	398
besought him to *d* with him	Lk 11:37	709
Jesus saith unto them, Come and d	Jn 21:12	709

DINED
So when they had *d*, Jesus saith	Jn 21:15	709

DINHABAH (din'-ha-bah) Capital of Edom.
and the name of his city was *D*	Gen 36:32	1838
and the name of his city was *D*	1Chr 1:43	1838

DINNER
Better is a *d* of herbs where love	Prov 15:17	737
Behold, I have prepared my d	Mt 22:4	712
he had not first washed before *d*	Lk 11:38	712
When thou makest a d or a supper	Lk 14:12	712

DIONYSIUS (di-on-ish'-yus) *An Athenian convert of Paul.*
the which was *D* the Areopagite............ Acts 17:34   *1354*

DIOTREPHES (di-ot'-re-feez) *A believer condemned by John.*
but *D*, who loveth to have the 3Jn 9   *1361*

DIP
d it in the blood that is in the .... Ex 12:22   2881
the priest shall *d* his finger in................ Lev 4:6   2881
the priest shall *d* his finger in............... Lev 4:17   2881
and the hyssop, and shall *d* them ...... Lev 14:6   2881
the priest shall *d* his right .... Lev 14:16   2881
d them in the blood of the slain ...... Lev 14:51   2881
d it in the water, and sprinkle it............ Num 19:18   2881
let him *d* his foot in oil .... Deut 33:24   2881
d thy morsel in the vinegar .... Ruth 2:14   2881
that he may *d* the tip of his .... Lk 16:24   *911*

DIPPED
goats, and *d* the coat in the blood .... Gen 37:31   2881
he *d* his finger in the blood, and .... Lev 9:9   2881
were *d* in the brim of the water............ Josh 3:15   2881
d it in an honeycomb, and put his 1Sa 14:27   2881
d himself seven times in Jordan, ... 2Kin 5:14   2881
d it in water, and spread it on 2Kin 8:15   2881
That thy foot may be *d* in the .... Ps 68:23   4272
give a sop, when I have *d* it .... Jn 13:26   *911*
And when he had *d* the sop, he gave...... Jn 13:26   *1686*
clothed with a vesture *d* in blood .... Rev 19:13   *911*

DIPPETH
He that *d* his hand with me in the........ Mt 26:23   *1686*
that *d* with me in the dish .... Mk 14:20   *1686*

DIRECT
to *d* his face unto Goshen .... Gen 46:28   3384
will I *d* my prayer unto thee................ Ps 5:3   6186
him, and he shall *d* thy paths .... Prov 3:6   3474
of the perfect shall *d* his way .... Prov 11:5   3474
but wisdom is profitable to *d* .... Eccl 10:10   3787
and I will *d* all his ways........................... Is 45:13   3474
I will *d* their work in truth, and........ Is 61:8   5414
man that walketh to *d* his steps .... Jer 10:23   3559
Jesus Christ, *d* our way unto you 1Th 3:11   2720
the Lord *d* your hearts into the.............. 2Th 3:5   2720

DIRECTED
Now he hath not *d* his words .... Job 32:14   6186
O that my ways were *d* to keep thy........ Ps 119:5   3559
Who hath *d* the Spirit of the LORD........ Is 40:13   8505

DIRECTETH
He *d* it under the whole heaven, ... Job 37:3   3474
but the LORD *d* his steps .... Prov 16:9   3559
as for the upright, he *d* his way .... Prov 21:29   3559

DIRECTION
by the *d* of the lawgiver, with .... Num 21:18

DIRECTLY
sprinkle of her blood *d* before .... Num 19:4   *413,5227*
even the way *d* before the wall.............. Eze 42:12   *1903*

DIRT
and the *d* came out .... Judg 3:22   6574
them out as the *d* in the streets............ Ps 18:42   2916
whose waters cast up mire and *d*.......... Is 57:20   2916

DISALLOW
But if her father *d* her in the .... Num 30:5   5106

DISALLOWED
her, because her father *d* her .... Num 30:5   5106
But if her husband *d* her on the .... Num 30:8   5106
his peace at her, and *d* her not .... Num 30:11   5106
d indeed of men, but chosen of 1Pet 2:4   *593*
the stone which the builders *d* 1Pet 2:7   *593*

DISANNUL
Wilt thou also *d* my judgment .... Job 40:8   6565
hath purposed, and who shall *d* it.......... Is 14:27   6565
and thirty years after, cannot *d* .... Gal 3:17   *208*

DISANNULLED
covenant with death shall be *d*.............. Is 28:18   3722

DISANNULLETH
yet if it be confirmed, no man *d* .... Gal 3:15   *114*

DISANNULLING
For there is verily a *d* of the .... Heb 7:18   *115*

DISAPPOINT
O LORD, *d* him, cast him down............... Ps 17:13   6923

DISAPPOINTED
Without counsel purposes are *d* .... Prov 15:22   6565

DISAPPOINTETH
He *d* the devices of the crafty,................. Job 5:12   6565

DISCERN
before our brethren *d* thou what .... Gen 31:32   5234
and she said, *D*, I pray thee,................... Gen 38:25   5234
so is my lord the king to *d* good 2Sa 14:17   8085
can I *d* between good and evil 2Sa 19:35   3045
that I may *d* between good and bad 1Kin 3:9   995
understanding to *d* judgment................. 1Kin 3:11   8085
So that the people could not *d* .... Ezr 3:13   5234
but I could not *d* the form .... Job 4:16   5234
cannot my taste *d* perverse things .... Job 6:30   995
cause them to *d* between the .... Eze 44:23   3045
cannot *d* between their right hand .... Jonah 4:11   3045
d between the righteous and the .... Mal 3:18   7200
ye can *d* the face of the sky .... Mt 16:3   *1252*
but can ye not *d* the signs of the........... Mt 16:3
ye can *d* the face of the sky and .... Lk 12:56   *1381*
is it that ye do not *d* this time .... Lk 12:56
senses exercised to *d* both good .... Heb 5:14   *1253*

DISCERNED
he *d* him not, because his hands .... Gen 27:23   5234
the king of Israel *d* him that he............ 1Kin 20:41   5234
I *d* among the youths, a young man...... Prov 7:7   995
because they are spiritually *d*.............. 1Cor 2:14   *350*

DISCERNER
is a *d* of the thoughts and intents .... Heb 4:12   *2924*

DISCERNETH
and a wise man's heart *d* both time .... Eccl 8:5   3045

DISCERNING
to himself, not *d* the Lord's body 1Cor 11:29   *1252*
to another *d* of spirits 1Cor 12:10   *1253*

DISCHARGE
and there is no *d* in that war .... Eccl 8:8   4917

DISCHARGED
and will cause them to be *d* there 1Kin 5:9   5310

DISCIPLE
The *d* is not above his master, ... Mt 10:24   *3101*
It is enough for the *d* that he be........... Mt 10:25   *3101*
water only in the name of a *d* .... Mt 10:42   *3101*
who also himself was Jesus' *d* .... Mt 27:57   *3100*
The *d* is not above his master .... Lk 6:40   *3101*
own life also, he cannot be my *d* .... Lk 14:26   *3101*
and come after me, cannot be my *d* ...... Lk 14:27   *3101*
that he hath, he cannot be my *d* .... Lk 14:33   *3101*
him, and said, Thou art his *d* .... Jn 9:28   *3101*
Jesus, and so did another *d*................... Jn 18:15   *3101*
that *d* was known unto the high .... Jn 18:15   *3101*
Then went out that other *d* .... Jn 18:16   *3101*
the *d* standing by, whom he loved, ... Jn 19:26   *3101*
Then saith he to the *d*, Behold .... Jn 19:27   *3101*
from that hour that *d* took her .... Jn 19:27   *3101*
being a *d* of Jesus, but secretly.............. Jn 19:38   *3101*
to Simon Peter, and to the other *d* .... Jn 20:2   *3101*
went forth, and that other *d* .... Jn 20:3   *3101*
the other *d* did outrun Peter, and............ Jn 20:4   *3101*
Then went in also that other *d* .... Jn 20:8   *3101*
Therefore that *d* whom Jesus loved .... Jn 21:7   *3101*
seeth the *d* whom Jesus loved............... Jn 21:20   *3101*
that that *d* should not die .... Jn 21:23   *3101*
This is the *d* which testifieth of .... Jn 21:24   *3101*
there was a certain *d* at Damascus .... Acts 9:10   *3101*
and believed not that he was a *d*............ Acts 9:26   *3101*
Joppa a certain *d* named Tabitha.......... Acts 9:36   *3102*
and, behold, a certain *d* was there .... Acts 16:1   *3101*
one Mnason of Cyprus, an old *d*............ Acts 21:16   *3101*

DISCIPLES
seal the law among my *d* .... Is 8:16   3928
he was set, his *d* came unto him .... Mt 5:1   *3101*
And another of his *d* said unto him .... Mt 8:21   *3101*
into a ship, his *d* followed him .... Mt 8:23   *3101*
his *d* came to him, and awoke him, ... Mt 8:25   *3101*
and sat down with him and his *d* .... Mt 9:10   *3101*
saw it, they said unto his *d* .... Mt 9:11   *3101*
Then came to him the *d* of John .... Mt 9:14   *3101*
fast oft, but thy *d* fast not..................... Mt 9:14   *3101*
and followed him, and so did his *d* .... Mt 9:19   *3101*
Then saith he unto his *d*, The .... Mt 9:37   *3101*
had called unto him his twelve *d*............ Mt 10:1   *3101*
an end of commanding his twelve *d* ...... Mt 11:1   *3101*
of Christ, he sent two of his *d* .... Mt 11:2   *3101*
his *d* were an hungred, and began .... Mt 12:1   *3101*
thy *d* do that which is not lawful .... Mt 12:2   *3101*
forth his hand toward his *d*................... Mt 12:49   *3101*
the *d* came, and said unto him, Why ..... Mt 13:10   *3101*
his *d* came unto him, saying, ... Mt 13:36   *3101*

D

his *d* came, and took up the body,	Mt 14:12	*3101*
his *d* came to him, saying, This	Mt 14:15	*3101*
and gave the loaves to his *d*	Mt 14:19	*3101*
and the *d* to the multitude	Mt 14:19	*3101*
his *d* to get into a ship, and to	Mt 14:22	*3101*
when the *d* saw him walking on the	Mt 14:26	*3101*
Why do thy *d* transgress the	Mt 15:2	*3101*
Then came his *d*, and said unto him	Mt 15:12	*3101*
his *d* came and besought him,	Mt 15:23	*3101*
Then Jesus called his *d* unto him	Mt 15:32	*3101*
his *d* say unto him, Whence should	Mt 15:33	*3101*
and brake them, and gave to his *d*	Mt 15:36	*3101*
and the *d* to the multitude	Mt 15:36	*3101*
when his *d* were come to the other	Mt 16:5	*3101*
Caesarea Philippi, he asked his *d*	Mt 16:13	*3101*
Then charged he his *d* that they	Mt 16:20	*3101*
began Jesus to shew unto his *d*	Mt 16:21	*3101*
Then said Jesus unto his *d*	Mt 16:24	*3101*
And when the *d* heard it, they fell	Mt 17:6	*3101*
his *d* asked him, saying, Why then	Mt 17:10	*3101*
Then the *d* understood that he	Mt 17:13	*3101*
And I brought him to thy *d*	Mt 17:16	*3101*
Then came the *d* to Jesus apart,	Mt 17:19	*3101*
same time came the *d* unto Jesus	Mt 18:1	*3101*
His *d* say unto him, If the case	Mt 19:10	*3101*
and the *d* rebuked them	Mt 19:13	*3101*
Then said Jesus unto his *d*	Mt 19:23	*3101*
When his *d* heard it, they were	Mt 19:25	*3101*
the twelve *d* apart in the way	Mt 20:17	*3101*
of Olives, then sent Jesus two *d*	Mt 21:1	*3101*
the *d* went, and did as Jesus	Mt 21:6	*3101*
And when the *d* saw it, they	Mt 21:20	*3101*
him their *d* with the Herodians	Mt 22:16	*3101*
to the multitude, and to his *d*	Mt 23:1	*3101*
his *d* came to him for to shew him	Mt 24:1	*3101*
the *d* came unto him privately,	Mt 24:3	*3101*
these sayings, he said unto his *d*	Mt 26:1	*3101*
But when his *d* saw it, they had	Mt 26:8	*3101*
bread the *d* came to Jesus	Mt 26:17	*3101*
passover at thy house with my *d*	Mt 26:18	*3101*
the *d* did as Jesus had appointed	Mt 26:19	*3101*
and brake it, and gave it to the *d*	Mt 26:26	*3101*
Likewise also said all the *d*	Mt 26:35	*3101*
Gethsemane, and saith unto the *d*	Mt 26:36	*3101*
And he cometh unto the *d*, and	Mt 26:40	*3101*
Then cometh he to his *d*, and saith	Mt 26:45	*3101*
Then all the *d* forsook him	Mt 26:56	*3101*
lest his *d* come by night, and	Mt 27:64	*3101*
tell his *d* that he is risen from	Mt 28:7	*3101*
and did run to bring his *d* word	Mt 28:8	*3101*
And as they went to tell his *d*	Mt 28:9	*3101*
His *d* came by night, and stole him	Mt 28:13	*3101*
Then the eleven *d* went away into	Mt 28:16	*3101*
also together with Jesus and his *d*	Mk 2:15	*3101*
and sinners, they said unto his *d*	Mk 2:16	*3101*
the *d* of John and of the Pharisees	Mk 2:18	*3101*
unto him, Why do the *d* of John	Mk 2:18	*3101*
fast, but thy *d* fast not	Mk 2:18	*3101*
his *d* began, as they went, to	Mk 2:23	*3101*
himself with his *d* to the sea	Mk 3:7	*3101*
And he spake to his *d*, that a	Mk 3:9	*3101*
he expounded all things to his *d*	Mk 4:34	*3101*
his *d* said unto him, Thou seest	Mk 5:31	*3101*
and his *d* follow him	Mk 6:1	*3101*
when his *d* heard of it, they came	Mk 6:29	*3101*
his *d* came unto him, and said,	Mk 6:35	*3101*
gave them to his *d* to set before	Mk 6:41	*3101*
his *d* to get into the ship	Mk 6:45	*3101*
of his *d* eat bread with defiled	Mk 7:2	*3101*
Why walk not thy *d* according to	Mk 7:5	*3101*
his *d* asked him concerning the	Mk 7:17	*3101*
eat, Jesus called his *d* unto him	Mk 8:1	*3101*
his *d* answered him, From whence	Mk 8:4	*3101*
gave to his *d* to set before them	Mk 8:6	*3101*
he entered into a ship with his *d*	Mk 8:10	*3101*
Now the *d* had forgotten to take	Mk 8:14	
And Jesus went out, and his *d*	Mk 8:27	*3101*
and by the way he asked his *d*	Mk 8:27	*3101*
turned about and looked on his *d*	Mk 8:33	*3101*
people unto him with his *d* also	Mk 8:34	*3101*
And when he came to his *d*, he saw	Mk 9:14	*3101*
I spake to thy *d* that they should	Mk 9:18	*3101*
his *d* asked him privately, Why	Mk 9:28	*3101*
For he taught his *d*, and said unto	Mk 9:31	*3101*
in the house his *d* asked him	Mk 10:10	*3101*
his *d* rebuked those that brought	Mk 10:13	*3101*
round about, and saith unto his *d*	Mk 10:23	*3101*
the *d* were astonished at his	Mk 10:24	*3101*
he went out of Jericho with his *d*	Mk 10:46	*3101*
he sendeth forth two of his *d*	Mk 11:1	*3101*
And his *d* heard it	Mk 11:14	*3101*
And he called unto him his *d*	Mk 12:43	*3101*
one of his *d* saith unto him,	Mk 13:1	*3101*
his *d* said unto him, Where wilt	Mk 14:12	*3101*
And he sendeth forth two of his *d*	Mk 14:13	*3101*
shall eat the passover with my *d*	Mk 14:14	*3101*
his *d* went forth, and came into	Mk 14:16	*3101*
and he saith to his *d*, Sit ye here	Mk 14:32	*3101*
But go your way, tell his *d*	Mk 16:7	*3101*
Pharisees murmured against his *d*	Lk 5:30	*3101*
Why do the *d* of John fast often,	Lk 5:33	*3101*
likewise the *d* of the Pharisees	Lk 5:33	
his *d* plucked the ears of corn,	Lk 6:1	*3101*
was day, he called unto him his *d*	Lk 6:13	*3101*
plain, and the company of his *d*	Lk 6:17	*3101*
And he lifted up his eyes on his *d*	Lk 6:20	*3101*
many of his *d* went with him, and	Lk 7:11	*3101*
the *d* of John shewed him of all	Lk 7:18	*3101*
two of his *d* sent them to Jesus	Lk 7:19	*3101*
his *d* asked him, saying, What	Lk 8:9	*3101*
he went into a ship with his *d*	Lk 8:22	*3101*
he called his twelve *d* together	Lk 9:1	*3101*
And he said to his *d*, Make them	Lk 9:14	*3101*
gave to the *d* to set before the	Lk 9:16	*3101*
praying, his *d* were with him	Lk 9:18	*3101*
I besought thy *d* to cast him out	Lk 9:40	*3101*
Jesus did, he said unto his *d*	Lk 9:43	*3101*
And when his *d* James and John saw	Lk 9:54	*3101*
And he turned him unto his *d*	Lk 10:23	*3101*
one of his *d* said unto him, Lord,	Lk 11:1	*3101*
pray, as John also taught his *d*	Lk 11:1	*3101*
to say unto his *d* first of all	Lk 12:1	*3101*
And he said unto his *d*, Therefore	Lk 12:22	*3101*
And he said also unto his *d*	Lk 16:1	*3101*
Then said he unto the *d*, It is	Lk 17:1	*3101*
And he said unto the *d*, The days	Lk 17:22	*3101*
but when his *d* saw it, they	Lk 18:15	*3101*
of Olives, he sent two of his *d*	Lk 19:29	*3101*
of the *d* began to rejoice	Lk 19:37	*3101*
unto him, Master, rebuke thy *d*	Lk 19:39	*3101*
all the people he said unto his *d*	Lk 20:45	*3101*
shall eat the passover with my *d*	Lk 22:11	*3101*
and his *d* also followed him	Lk 22:39	*3101*
from prayer, and was come to his *d*	Lk 22:45	*3101*
after John stood, and two of his *d*	Jn 1:35	*3101*
the two *d* heard him speak, and	Jn 1:37	*3101*
both Jesus was called, and his *d*	Jn 2:2	*3101*
and his *d* believed on him	Jn 2:11	*3101*
mother, and his brethren, and his *d*	Jn 2:12	*3101*
his *d* remembered that it was	Jn 2:17	*3101*
his *d* remembered that he had said	Jn 2:22	*3101*
his *d* into the land of Judaea	Jn 3:22	*3101*
question between some of John's *d*	Jn 3:25	*3101*
made and baptized more *d* than John	Jn 4:1	*3101*
himself baptized not, but his *d*	Jn 4:2	*3101*
(For his *d* were gone away unto	Jn 4:8	*3101*
And upon this came his *d*, and	Jn 4:27	*3101*
the mean while his *d* prayed him	Jn 4:31	*3101*
said the *d* one to another	Jn 4:33	*3101*
and there he sat with his *d*	Jn 6:3	*3101*
One of his *d*, Andrew, Simon	Jn 6:8	*3101*
thanks, he distributed to the *d*	Jn 6:11	*3101*
the *d* to them that were set down	Jn 6:11	*3101*
were filled, he said unto his *d*	Jn 6:12	*3101*
his *d* went down unto the sea,	Jn 6:16	*3101*
one whereinto his *d* were entered	Jn 6:22	*3101*
went not with his *d* into the boat	Jn 6:22	*3101*
but that his *d* were gone away	Jn 6:22	*3101*
was not there, neither his *d*	Jn 6:24	*3101*
Many therefore of his *d*, when	Jn 6:60	*3101*
himself that his *d* murmured at it	Jn 6:61	*3101*
that time many of his *d* went back	Jn 6:66	*3101*
that thy *d* also may see the works	Jn 7:3	*3101*
my word, then are ye my *d* indeed	Jn 8:31	*3101*
his *d* asked him, saying, Master,	Jn 9:2	*3101*
will ye also be his *d*	Jn 9:27	*3101*
but we are Moses' *d*	Jn 9:28	*3101*
Then after that saith he to his *d*	Jn 11:7	*3101*
His *d* say unto him, Master, the	Jn 11:8	*3101*
Then said his *d*, Lord, if he	Jn 11:12	*3101*
and there continued with his *d*	Jn 11:54	*3101*
Then saith one of his *d*, Judas	Jn 12:4	*3101*
understood not his *d* at the first	Jn 12:16	*3101*
Then the *d* looked one on another,	Jn 13:22	*3101*
on Jesus' bosom one of his *d*	Jn 13:23	*3101*
all men know that ye are my *d*	Jn 13:35	*3101*
so shall ye be my *d*	Jn 15:8	*3101*
some of his *d* among themselves	Jn 16:17	*3101*
His *d* said unto him, Lo, now	Jn 16:29	*3101*
with his *d* over the brook Cedron	Jn 18:1	*3101*
the which he entered, and his *d*	Jn 18:1	*3101*
resorted thither with his *d*	Jn 18:2	*3101*

not thou also one of this man's *d* .... Jn 18:17 — 3101
priest then asked Jesus of his *d* .... Jn 18:19 — 3101
Art not thou also one of his *d* .... Jn 18:25 — 3101
Then the *d* went away again unto .... Jn 20:10 — 3101
told the *d* that she had seen the .... Jn 20:18 — 3101
the doors were shut where the *d* .... Jn 20:19 — 3101
Then were the *d* glad, when they .... Jn 20:20 — 3101
The other *d* therefore said unto .... Jn 20:25 — 3101
days again his *d* were within .... Jn 20:26 — 3101
Jesus in the presence of his *d* .... Jn 20:30 — 3101
to the *d* at the sea of Tiberias .... Jn 21:1 — 3101
of Zebedee, and two other of his *d* .... Jn 21:2 — 3101
but the *d* knew not that it was .... Jn 21:4 — 3101
the other *d* came in a little ship............ Jn 21:8 — 3101
none of the *d* durst ask him, Who .... Jn 21:12 — 3101
Jesus shewed himself to his *d* .... Jn 21:14 — 3101
stood up in the midst of the *d* .... Acts 1:15 — 3101
number of the *d* was multiplied .... Acts 6:1 — 3101
the multitude of the *d* unto them .... Acts 6:2 — 3101
the number of the *d* multiplied in .... Acts 6:7 — 3101
against the *d* of the Lord .... Acts 9:1 — 3101
with the *d* which were at Damascus ...... Acts 9:19 — 3101
Then the *d* took him by night, and .... Acts 9:25 — 3101
assayed to join himself to the *d* .... Acts 9:26 — 3101
the *d* had heard that Peter was .... Acts 9:38 — 3101
the *d* were called Christians .... Acts 11:26 — 3101
Then the *d*, every man according .... Acts 11:29 — 3101
the *d* were filled with joy, and .... Acts 13:52 — 3101
as the *d* stood round about him,........... Acts 14:20 — 3101
Confirming the souls of the *d*............... Acts 14:22 — 3101
they abode long time with the *d* .... Acts 14:28 — 3101
put a yoke upon the neck of the *d* .... Acts 15:10 — 3101
in order, strengthening all the *d* .... Acts 18:23 — 3101
exhorting the *d* to receive him .... Acts 18:27 — 3101
and finding certain *d*, ... Acts 19:1 — 3101
from them, and separated the *d* .... Acts 19:9 — 3101
people, the *d* suffered him not .... Acts 19:30 — 3101
Paul called unto him the *d* .... Acts 20:1 — 3101
when the *d* came together to break .... Acts 20:7 — 3101
things, to draw away *d* after them .... Acts 20:30 — 3101
And finding *d*, we tarried there............. Acts 21:4 — 3101
also certain of the *d* of Caesarea .... Acts 21:16 — 3101

DISCIPLES'
and began to wash the *d* feet .... Jn 13:5 — 3101

DISCIPLINE
He openeth also their ear to *d* .... Job 36:10 — 4148

DISCLOSE
the earth also shall *d* her blood............. Is 26:21 — 1540

DISCOMFITED
And Joshua *d* Amalek and his people.... Ex 17:13 — 2522
them, and *d* them, even unto Hormah ... Num 14:45 — 3807
the Lord *d* them before Israel, and .... Josh 10:10 — 1949
And the Lord *d* Sisera, and all his .... Judg 4:15 — 2000
and Zalmunna, and *d* all the host .... Judg 8:12 — 2729
upon the Philistines, and *d* them .... 1Sa 7:10 — 1949
lightning, and *d* them .... 2Sa 22:15 — 2000
he shot out lightnings, and *d* them .... Ps 18:14 — 1949
and his young men shall be *d* .... Is 31:8 — 4522

DISCOMFITURE
and there was a very great *d* .... 1Sa 14:20 — 4103

DISCONTENTED
in debt, and every one that was *d*... 1Sa 22:2 — 4751,5315

DISCONTINUE
shalt *d* from thine heritage that............. Jer 17:4 — 8058

DISCORD
he soweth *d*.. Prov 6:14 — 4066
he that soweth *d* among brethren .... Prov 6:19 — 4090

DISCOURAGE
wherefore *d* ye the heart of the .... Num 32:7 — 5106

DISCOURAGED
was much *d* because of the way............. Num 21:4 — 7114
they *d* the heart of the children .... Num 32:9 — 5106
fear not, neither be *d* .... Deut 1:21 — 2865
our brethren have *d* our heart .... Deut 1:28 — 4549
He shall not fail nor be *d* .... Is 42:4 — 7533
children to anger, lest they be *d*............ Col 3:21 — 120

DISCOVER
wife, nor *d* his father's skirt .... Deut 22:30 — 1540
we will *d* ourselves unto them .... 1Sa 14:8 — 1540
Who can *d* the face of his garment .... Job 41:13 — 1540
but that his heart may *d* itself .... Prov 18:2 — 1540
d not a secret to another....................... Prov 25:9 — 1540
the Lord will *d* their secret .... Is 3:17 — 6168
Therefore will I *d* thy skirts .... Jer 13:26 — 2834
he will *d* thy sins .... Lam 4:22 — 1540

will *d* thy nakedness unto them,.......... Eze 16:37 — 1540
now will I *d* her lewdness in the .... Hos 2:10 — 1540
I will *d* the foundations thereof............ Mic 1:6 — 1540
I will *d* thy skirts upon thy face............ Nah 3:5 — 1540

DISCOVERED
thy nakedness be not *d* thereon .... Ex 20:26 — 1540
he hath *d* her fountain, and she .... Lev 20:18 — 6168
both of them *d* themselves unto .... 1Sa 14:11 — 1540
When Saul heard that David was *d* ...... 1Sa 22:6 — 3045
foundations of the world were *d* .... 2Sa 22:16 — 1540
of the world were *d* at thy rebuke .... Ps 18:15 — 1540
he *d* the covering of Judah, and............ Is 22:8 — 1540
for thou hast *d* thyself to .... Is 57:8 — 1540
thine iniquity are thy skirts *d* .... Jer 13:22 — 1540
they have not *d* thine iniquity, ... Lam 2:14 — 1540
the foundation thereof shall be *d* .... Eze 13:14 — 1540
thy nakedness *d* through thy .... Eze 16:36 — 1540
Before thy wickedness was *d* .... Eze 16:57 — 1540
in that your transgressions are *d* .... Eze 21:24 — 1540
In thee have they *d* their .... Eze 22:10 — 1540
These *d* her nakedness .... Eze 23:10 — 1540
So she *d* her whoredoms, and .... Eze 23:18 — 1540
her whoredoms, and *d* her nakedness .... Eze 23:18 — 1540
of thy whoredoms shall be *d* .... Eze 23:29 — 1540
the iniquity of Ephraim was *d*............... Hos 7:1 — 1540
Now when we had *d* Cyprus, we left ...... Acts 21:3 — 398
but they *d* a certain creek with a .... Acts 27:39 — 2657

DISCOVERETH
He *d* deep things out of darkness, ... Job 12:22 — 1540
hinds to calve, and *d* the forests .... Ps 29:9 — 2834

DISCOVERING
by *d* the foundation unto the neck .... Hab 3:13 — 6168

DISCREET
let Pharaoh look out a man *d* .... Gen 41:33 — 995
thee all this, there is none so *d* .... Gen 41:39 — 995
To be *d*, chaste, keepers at home, ... Titus 2:5 — 4998

DISCREETLY
when Jesus saw that he answered *d* ...... Mk 12:34 — 3562

DISCRETION
he will guide his affairs with *d* .... Ps 112:5 — 4941
to the young man knowledge and *d* .... Prov 1:4 — 4209
D shall preserve thee,............................. Prov 2:11 — 4209
keep sound wisdom and *d* .... Prov 3:21 — 4209
That thou mayest regard *d* .... Prov 5:2 — 4209
a fair woman which is without *d* .... Prov 11:22 — 2940
The *d* of a man deferreth his................... Prov 19:11 — 7922
his God doth instruct him to *d* .... Is 28:26 — 4941
out the heavens by his *d*........................ Jer 10:12 — 8394

DISDAINED
about, and saw David, he *d* him .... 1Sa 17:42 — 959
whose fathers I would have *d* to .... Job 30:1 — 3988

DISEASE
whether I shall recover of this *d* .... 2Kin 1:2 — 2483
saying, Shall I recover of this *d* .... 2Kin 8:8 — 2483
saying, Shall I recover of this *d* .... 2Kin 8:9 — 2483
until his *d* was exceeding great .... 2Chr 16:12 — 2483
yet in his *d* he sought not to the .... 2Chr 16:12 — 2483
great sickness by *d* of thy bowels .... 2Chr 21:15 — 4245
in his bowels with an incurable *d*........... 2Chr 21:18 — 2483
of my *d* is my garment changed .... Job 30:18
are filled with a loathsome *d* .... Ps 38:7
An evil *d*, say they, cleaveth.................. Ps 41:8 — 1697
is vanity, and it is an evil *d* .... Eccl 6:2 — 2483
all manner of *d* among the people .... Mt 4:23 — 3119
and every *d* among the people .... Mt 9:35 — 3119
of sickness and all manner of *d* .... Mt 10:1 — 3119
made whole of whatsoever *d* he had ...... Jn 5:4 — 3553

DISEASED
his old age he was *d* in his feet............. 1Kin 15:23 — 2470
of his reign was *d* in his feet .... 2Chr 16:12 — 2470
The *d* have ye not strengthened,............ Eze 34:4 — 2456
pushed all the *d* with your horns,........... Eze 34:21 — 2456
which was *d* with an issue of................ Mt 9:20
brought unto him all that were *d*.... Mt 14:35 — 2560,2192
brought unto him all that were *d*.... Mk 1:32 — 2560,2192
which he did on them that were *d* .... Jn 6:2 — 770

DISEASES
put none of these *d* upon thee .... Ex 15:26 — 4245
put none of the evil *d* of Egypt.............. Deut 7:15 — 4064
upon thee all the *d* of Egypt .... Deut 28:60 — 4064
so he died of sore *d*............................... 2Chr 21:19 — 8463
(for they left him in great *d*................... 2Chr 24:25 — 4251
who healeth all thy *d* .... Ps 103:3 — 8463
that were taken with divers *d* .... Mt 4:24 — 3554
many that were sick of divers *d* .... Mk 1:34 — 3554
divers *d* brought them unto him .... Lk 4:40 — 3554

that thou *d* not the lords of the	1Sa 29:7	6213,7451,5869
Joab, Let not this thing *d* thee	2Sa 11:25	7489,5869
it *d* him, and he turn away his	Prov 24:18	7489,5869

DISPLEASED

thing which he did *d* the LORD	Gen 38:10	7489,5869
the head of Ephraim, it *d* him	Gen 48:17	7489,5869
people complained, it *d* the LORD	Num 11:1	7451,241
Moses also was *d*	Num 11:10	
the thing *d* Samuel, when they	1Sa 8:6	7489,5869
very wroth, and the saying *d* him	1Sa 18:8	7489,5869
And David was *d*, because the LORD	2Sa 6:8	2734
that David had done *d* the LORD	2Sa 11:27	7489,5869
his father had not *d* him at any	1Kin 1:6	6087
went to his house heavy and *d*	1Kin 20:43	2198
d because of the word which	1Kin 21:4	2198
And David was *d*, because the LORD	1Chr 13:11	2734
God was *d* with this thing	1Chr 21:7	3415,5869
scattered us, thou hast been *d*	Ps 60:1	599
it *d* him that there was no	Is 59:15	7489,5869
was sore *d* with himself, and set	Dan 6:14	888
it *d* Jonah exceedingly, and he	Jonah 4:1	7489,5869
Was the LORD *d* against the rivers	Hab 3:8	2734
been sore *d* with your fathers	Zec 1:2	7107
I am very sore *d* with the heathen	Zec 1:15	7107
for I was but a little *d*, and they	Zec 1:15	7107
they were sore *d*,	Mt 21:15	23
when Jesus saw it, he was much *d*	Mk 10:14	23
began to be much *d* with James	Mk 10:41	23
Herod was highly *d* with them of	Acts 12:20	2371

DISPLEASURE

was afraid of the anger and hot *d*	Deut 9:19	2534
Philistines, though I do them a *d*	Judg 15:3	7451
wrath, and vex them in his sore *d*	Ps 2:5	2740
neither chasten me in thy hot *d*	Ps 6:1	2534
neither chasten me in thy hot *d*	Ps 38:1	2534

DISPOSED

Or who hath *d* the whole world	Job 34:13	7760
Dost thou know when God *d* them	Job 37:15	7760
when he was *d* to pass into Achaia	Acts 18:27	1014
you to a feast, and ye be *d* to go	1Cor 10:27	2309

DISPOSING

but the whole *d* thereof is of the	Prov 16:33	4941

DISPOSITION

the law by the *d* of angels	Acts 7:53	1296

DISPOSSESS

ye shall *d* the inhabitants of the	Num 33:53	3423
how can I *d* them	Deut 7:17	3423

DISPOSSESSED

d the Amorite which was in it	Num 32:39	3423
d the Amorites from before his	Judg 11:23	3423

DISPUTATION

d with them, they determined that	Acts 15:2	4803

DISPUTATIONS

receive ye, but not to doubtful *d*	Rom 14:1	1253

DISPUTE

the righteous might *d* with him	Job 23:7	3198

DISPUTED

What was it that ye *d* among	Mk 9:33	1260
way they had *d* among themselves	Mk 9:34	1256
Jesus, and *d* against the Grecians	Acts 9:29	4802
Therefore *d* he in the synagogue	Acts 17:17	1256
he *d* about the body of Moses	Jude 9	1256

DISPUTER

where is the *d* of this world	1Cor 1:20	4804

DISPUTING

and of Asia, *d* with Stephen	Acts 6:9	4802
And when there had been much *d*	Acts 15:7	4803
for the space of three months, *d*	Acts 19:8	1256
d daily in the school of one	Acts 19:9	1256
me in the temple *d* with any man	Acts 24:12	1256

DISPUTINGS

things without murmurings and *d*	Phil 2:14	1261
Perverse *d* of men of corrupt	1Ti 6:5	3859

DISQUIET

d the inhabitants of Babylon	Jer 50:34	7264

DISQUIETED

said to Saul, Why hast thou *d* me	1Sa 28:15	7264
surely they are *d* in vain	Ps 39:6	1993
and why art thou *d* in me	Ps 42:5	1993
and why art thou *d* within me	Ps 42:11	1993
and why art thou *d* within me	Ps 43:5	1993
For three things the earth is *d*	Prov 30:21	7264

DISQUIETNESS

by reason of the *d* of my heart	Ps 38:8	5100

DISSEMBLED

d also, and they have put it even	Josh 7:11	3584
For ye *d* in your hearts, when ye	Jer 42:20	8582
the other Jews *d* likewise with	Gal 2:13	4942

DISSEMBLERS

neither will I go in with *d*	Ps 26:4	5956

DISSEMBLETH

He that hateth *d* with his lips	Prov 26:24	5234

DISSENSION

Paul and Barnabas had no small *d*	Acts 15:2	4714
there arose a *d* between the	Acts 23:7	4714
And when there arose a great *d*	Acts 23:10	4714

DISSIMULATION

Let love be without *d*	Rom 12:9	505
was carried away with their *d*	Gal 2:13	5272

DISSOLVE

make interpretations, and *d* doubts	Dan 5:16	8271

DISSOLVED

all the inhabitants thereof are *d*	Ps 75:3	4127
thou, whole Palestina, art *d*	Is 14:31	4127
broken down, the earth is clean *d*	Is 24:19	6565
all the host of heaven shall be *d*	Is 34:4	4743
opened, and the palace shall be *d*	Nah 2:6	4127
house of this tabernacle were *d*	2Cor 5:1	2647
that all these things shall be *d*	2Pet 3:11	3089
heavens being on fire shall be *d*	2Pet 3:12	3089

DISSOLVEST

ride upon it, and *d* my substance	Job 30:22	4127

DISSOLVING

d of doubts, were found in the	Dan 5:12	8271

DISTAFF

spindle, and her hands hold the *d*	Prov 31:19	6418

DISTANT

equally *d* one from another	Ex 36:22	7947

DISTIL

my speech shall *d* as the dew	Deut 32:2	5140
do drop and *d* upon man abundantly	Job 36:28	7491

DISTINCTION

they give a *d* in the sounds	1Cor 14:7	1293

DISTINCTLY

in the book in the law of God *d*	Neh 8:8	6567

DISTRACTED

while I suffer thy terrors I am *d*	Ps 88:15	6323

DISTRACTION

attend upon the Lord without *d*	1Cor 7:35	563

DISTRESS

answered me in the day of my *d*	Gen 35:3	6869
therefore is this *d* come upon us	Gen 42:21	6869
D not the Moabites, neither	Deut 2:9	6696
d them not, nor meddle with them	Deut 2:19	6696
thine enemies shall *d* thee	Deut 28:53	6693
shall *d* thee in all thy gates	Deut 28:55	6693
enemy shall *d* thee in thy gates	Deut 28:57	6693
come unto me now when ye are in *d*	Judg 11:7	6887
And every one that was in *d*	1Sa 22:2	4689
In my *d* I called upon the LORD	2Sa 22:7	6862
redeemed my soul out of all *d*	1Kin 1:29	6869
in the time of his *d* did he	2Chr 28:22	6693
Ye see the *d* that we are in, how	Neh 2:17	7451
pleasure, and we are in great *d*	Neh 9:37	6869
hast enlarged me when I was in *d*	Ps 4:1	6862
In my *d* I called upon the LORD,	Ps 18:6	6862
I called upon the LORD in *d*	Ps 118:5	4712
In my *d* I cried unto the LORD, and	Ps 120:1	6869
when *d* and anguish cometh upon you	Prov 1:27	6869
a strength to the needy in his *d*	Is 25:4	6862
Yet I will *d* Ariel, and there	Is 29:2	6693
and her munition, and that her *d*	Is 29:7	6693
land at this once, and will *d* them	Jer 10:18	6887
for I am in *d*	Lam 1:20	6887
spoken proudly in the day of *d*	Obad 12	6869
that did remain in the day of *d*	Obad 14	6869
of wrath, a day of trouble and *d*	Zeph 1:15	4691
And I will bring *d* upon men	Zeph 1:17	6887
shall be great *d* in the land	Lk 21:23	318
and upon the earth *d* of nations	Lk 21:25	4928
shall tribulation, or *d*, or	Rom 8:35	4730
this is good for the present *d*	1Cor 7:26	318
our affliction and *d* by your faith	1Th 3:7	318

D

DISTRESSED

Jacob was greatly afraid and d .... Gen 32:7 — 3334
Moab was d because of the .... Num 22:3 — 6973
and they were greatly d .... Judg 2:15 — 3334
so that Israel was sore d .... Judg 10:9 — 3334
a strait, (for the people were d .... 1Sa 13:6 — 5065
the men of Israel were d that day .... 1Sa 14:24 — 5065
And Saul answered, I am sore d .... 1Sa 28:15 — 6887
And David was greatly d .... 1Sa 30:6 — 3334
I am d for thee, my brother .... 2Sa 1:26 — 6887
d him, but strengthened him not .... 2Chr 28:20 — 6696
troubled on every side, yet not d .... 2Cor 4:8 — 4729

DISTRESSES

O bring thou me out of my d .... Ps 25:17 — 4691
he delivered them out of their d .... Ps 107:6 — 4691
and he saved them out of their d .... Ps 107:13 — 4691
and he saveth them out of their d .... Ps 107:19 — 4691
he bringeth them out of their d .... Ps 107:28 — 4691
and Noph shall have d daily .... Eze 30:16 — 6862
afflictions, in necessities, in d .... 2Cor 6:4 — 4730
in d for Christ's sake .... 2Cor 12:10 — 4730

DISTRIBUTE

d for inheritance in the plains .... Josh 13:32 — 5157
to d the oblations of the LORD, ... 2Chr 31:14 — 5414
was to d unto their brethren .... Neh 13:13 — 2505
d unto the poor, and thou shalt .... Lk 18:22 — 1239
be rich in good works, ready to d .... 1Ti 6:18 — 2130

DISTRIBUTED

d for inheritance to them .... Josh 14:1 — 5157
And David d them, both Zadok of .... 1Chr 24:3 — 2505
whom David had d in the house of .... 2Chr 23:18 — 2505
he d to the disciples, and the .... Jn 6:11 — 1239
But as God hath d to every man .... 1Cor 7:17 — 3307
the rule which God hath d to us .... 2Cor 10:13 — 3307

DISTRIBUTETH

God d sorrows in his anger .... Job 21:17 — 2505

DISTRIBUTING

D to the necessity of saints .... Rom 12:13 — 2841

DISTRIBUTION

d was made unto every man .... Acts 4:35 — 1239
and for your liberal d unto them .... 2Cor 9:13 — 2842

DITCH

Yet shalt thou plunge me in the d .... Job 9:31 — 7845
fallen into the d which he made .... Ps 7:15 — 7845
For a whore is a deep d .... Prov 23:27 — 7745
Ye made also a d between the two .... Is 22:11 — 4724
blind, both shall fall into the d .... Mt 15:14 — 999
they not both fall into the d .... Lk 6:39 — 999

DITCHES

LORD, Make this valley full of d .... 2Kin 3:16 — 1356

DIVERS

not sow thy vineyard with d seeds .... Deut 22:9 — 3610
not wear a garment of d sorts .... Deut 22:11 — 8162
not have in thy bag d weights .... Deut 25:13
have in thine house d measures .... Deut 25:14
to Sisera a prey of d colours .... Judg 5:30 — 6648
a prey of d colours of needlework .... Judg 5:30 — 6648
of d colours of needlework on .... Judg 5:30 — 6648
a garment of d colours upon her .... 2Sa 13:18 — 6446
rent her garment of d colours .... 2Sa 13:19 — 6446
of d colours, and all manner of .... 1Chr 29:2 — 7553
d kinds of spices prepared by the 2Chr 16:14
d also of the princes of Israel 2Chr 21:4
Nevertheless d of Asher and .... 2Chr 30:11 — 582
He sent d sorts of flies among .... Ps 78:45
there came d sorts of flies, and .... Ps 105:31
D weights, and d measures, ... Prov 20:10
D weights are an abomination unto .... Prov 20:23
words there are also d vanities .... Eccl 5:7
thy high places with d colours .... Eze 16:16 — 2921
of feathers, which had d colours .... Eze 17:3 — 7553
that were taken with d diseases .... Mt 4:24 — 4164
and earthquakes, in d places .... Mt 24:7
many that were sick of d diseases .... Mk 1:34 — 4164
for d of them came from far .... Mk 8:3 — 5100
shall be earthquakes in d places ...... Mk 13:8
d diseases brought them unto him .... Lk 4:40 — 4164
earthquakes shall be in d places ...... Lk 21:11
But when d were hardened, and .... Acts 19:9 — 5100
to another d kinds of tongues 1Cor 12:10
with sins, led away with d lusts .... 2Ti 3:6 — 4164
deceived, serving d lusts .... Titus 3:3 — 4164
in d manners spake in time past .... Heb 1:1 — 4187
with d miracles, and gifts of the .... Heb 2:4 — 4164
d washings, and carnal ordinances, ... Heb 9:10 — 1313

Be not carried about with d .... Heb 13:9 — 4164
when ye fall into d temptations .... Jas 1:2 — 4164

DIVERSE

thy cattle gender with a d kind .... Lev 19:19 — 3610
vessels being d one from another .... Est 1:7 — 8138
their laws are d from all people .... Est 3:8 — 8138
from the sea, d one from another .... Dan 7:3 — 8133
it was d from all the beasts that .... Dan 7:7 — 8133
which was d from all the others, ... Dan 7:19 — 8133
which shall be d from all, ... Dan 7:23 — 8133
he shall be d from the first, and .... Dan 7:24 — 8133

DIVERSITIES

Now there are d of gifts, but the .... 1Cor 12:4 — 1243
there are d of operations, but it .... 1Cor 12:6 — 1243
helps, governments, d of tongues .... 1Cor 12:28 — 1085

DIVIDE

let it d the waters from the .... Gen 1:6 — 914
to d the day from the night .... Gen 1:14 — 914
to d the light from the darkness .... Gen 1:18 — 914
I will d them in Jacob, and .... Gen 49:7 — 2505
and at night he shall d the spoil .... Gen 49:27 — 2505
thine hand over the sea, and d it .... Ex 14:16 — 1234
will overtake, I will d the spoil .... Ex 15:9 — 2505
the live ox, and the money of it .... Ex 21:35 — 2673
and the dead ox also they shall d .... Ex 21:35 — 2673
the vail shall d unto you between .... Ex 26:33 — 914
but shall not d it asunder .... Lev 1:17 — 914
neck, but shall not d it asunder .... Lev 5:8 — 914
cud, or of them that d the hoof .... Lev 11:4 — 6536
the swine, though he d the hoof .... Lev 11:7 — 6536
d the prey into two parts .... Num 31:27 — 2673
ye shall d the land by lot for an .... Num 33:54 — 5157
which shall d the land unto you .... Num 34:17 — 5157
to d the land by inheritance .... Num 34:18 — 5157
to d the inheritance unto the .... Num 34:29
or of them that d the cloven hoof .... Deut 14:7 — 6536
chew the cud, but d not the hoof .... Deut 14:7 — 6536
d the coasts of thy land, which .... Deut 19:3
d for an inheritance the land .... Josh 1:6
only d thou it by lot unto the .... Josh 13:6 — 5307
Now therefore d this land for an .... Josh 13:7 — 2505
they shall d it into seven parts .... Josh 18:5 — 2505
d the spoil of your enemies with .... Josh 22:8 — 2505
said, Thou and Ziba d the land .... 2Sa 19:29 — 2505
D the living child in two, and .... 1Kin 3:25 — 1504
neither mine nor thine, but d it .... 1Kin 3:26 — 1504
thou didst d the sea before them, ... Neh 9:11 — 1234
didst d them into corners .... Neh 9:22 — 2505
the innocent shall d the silver .... Job 27:17 — 2505
O Lord, and d their tongues .... Ps 55:9 — 6385
I will d Shechem, and mete out the ...... Ps 60:6 — 2505
Thou didst d the sea by thy .... Ps 74:13 — 6565
I will d Shechem, and mete out the ...... Ps 108:7 — 2505
than to d the spoil with the .... Prov 16:19 — 2505
men rejoice when they d the spoil .... Is 9:3 — 2505
Therefore will I d him a portion .... Is 53:12 — 5312
he shall d the spoil with the .... Is 53:12 — 5312
balances to weigh, and d the hair .... Eze 5:1 — 2505
when ye shall d by lot the land .... Eze 45:1 — 5307
So shall ye d this land unto you .... Eze 47:21 — 2505
that ye shall d it by lot for an .... Eze 47:22 — 5307
shall d by lot unto the tribes of .... Eze 48:29 — 5307
shall d the land for gain .... Dan 11:39 — 2505
that he d the inheritance with me .... Lk 12:13 — 3307
this, and d it among yourselves .... Lk 22:17 — 1266

DIVIDED

God d the light from the darkness .... Gen 1:4 — 914
d the waters which were under the .... Gen 1:7 — 914
of the Gentiles d in their lands .... Gen 10:5 — 6504
for in his days was the earth d .... Gen 10:25 — 6385
by these were the nations d in .... Gen 10:32 — 5504
he d himself against them, he and .... Gen 14:15 — 2505
d them in the midst, and laid each .... Gen 15:10 — 1334
but the birds he d not .... Gen 15:10 — 1334
he d the people that was with him .... Gen 32:7 — 2673
he d the children unto Leah, and .... Gen 33:1 — 2673
dry land, and the waters were d .... Ex 14:21 — 1234
Unto these the land shall be d .... Num 26:53 — 2505
the land shall be d by lot .... Num 26:55 — 2505
thereof be d between many .... Num 26:56 — 2505
which Moses d from the men that .... Num 31:42 — 2673
hath d unto all nations under the .... Deut 4:19 — 2505
When the Most High d to the .... Deut 32:8
of Israel did, and they d the land .... Josh 14:5 — 2505
there Joshua d the land unto the .... Josh 18:10 — 2505
d for an inheritance by lot in .... Josh 19:51
I have d unto you by lot these .... Josh 23:4 — 5307
have they not d the prey .... Judg 5:30 — 2505
he d the three hundred men into .... Judg 7:16 — 2673

_d_ them into three companies, and	Judg 9:43	2673
_d_ her, together with her bones,	Judg 19:29	5408
and in their death they were not _d_	2Sa 1:23	6504
people of Israel _d_ into two parts	1Kin 16:21	2505
So they _d_ the land between them	1Kin 18:6	2505
the waters, and they were _d_ hither	2Kin 2:8	2673
in his days the earth was _d_	1Chr 1:19	6385
David _d_ them into courses among	1Chr 23:6	2505
and thus were they _d_	1Chr 24:4	2505
Thus were they _d_ by lot, one sort	1Chr 24:5	2505
_d_ them speedily among all the	2Chr 35:13	7323
Who hath _d_ a watercourse for the	Job 38:25	6385
that tarried at home _d_ the spoil	Ps 68:12	2505
He _d_ the sea, and caused them to	Ps 78:13	1234
_d_ them an inheritance by line, and	Ps 78:55	5307
To him which _d_ the Red sea into	Ps 136:13	1504
is the prey of a great spoil _d_	Is 33:23	2505
his hand hath _d_ it unto them by	Is 34:17	2505
that _d_ the sea, whose waves	Is 51:15	7280
The anger of the LORD hath _d_ them	Lam 4:16	2505
neither shall they be _d_ into two	Eze 37:22	2673
of iron, the kingdom shall be _d_	Dan 2:41	6386
Thy kingdom is _d_, and given to the	Dan 5:28	6537
shall be _d_ toward the four winds	Dan 11:4	2673
Their heart is _d_	Hos 10:2	2505
and thy land shall be _d_ by line	Amos 7:17	2505
turning away he hath _d_ our fields	Mic 2:4	2505
thy spoil shall be _d_ in the midst	Zec 14:1	2505
Every kingdom _d_ against itself is	Mt 12:25	_3307_
every city or house _d_ against	Mt 12:25	_3307_
Satan, he is _d_ against himself	Mt 12:26	_3307_
if a kingdom be _d_ against itself	Mk 3:24	_3307_
if a house be _d_ against itself,	Mk 3:25	_3307_
rise up against himself, and be _d_	Mk 3:26	_3307_
the two fishes _d_ he among them	Mk 6:41	_3307_
Every kingdom _d_ against itself is	Lk 11:17	_1266_
a house _d_ against a house falleth	Lk 11:17	_1266_
Satan also be _d_ against himself	Lk 11:18	_1266_
shall be five in one house _d_	Lk 12:52	_1266_
father shall be _d_ against the son	Lk 12:53	_1266_
he _d_ unto them his living	Lk 15:12	_1244_
he _d_ their land to them by lot	Acts 13:19	2624
the multitude of the city was _d_	Acts 14:4	_4977_
and the multitude was _d_	Acts 23:7	_4977_
Is Christ _d_?	1Cor 1:13	_3307_
great city was _d_ into three parts	Rev 16:19	_1096_

DIVIDER

made me a judge or a _d_ over you	Lk 12:14	_3312_

DIVIDETH

the cud, but _d_ not the hoof	Lev 11:4	6536
the cud, but _d_ not the hoof	Lev 11:5	6536
the cud, but _d_ not the hoof	Lev 11:6	6536
of every beast which _d_ the hoof	Lev 11:26	6536
the swine, because it _d_ the hoof	Deut 14:8	6536
He _d_ the sea with his power, and	Job 26:12	7280
of the LORD _d_ the flames of fire	Ps 29:7	2672
which _d_ the sea when the waves	Jer 31:35	7280
as a shepherd _d_ his sheep from	Mt 25:32	_873_
he trusted, and _d_ his spoils	Lk 11:22	_1239_

DIVIDING

of _d_ the land for inheritance by	Josh 19:49	
they made an end of _d_ the country	Josh 19:51	2505
_d_ the water before them, to make	Is 63:12	1234
a time and times and the _d_ of time	Dan 7:25	6387
_d_ to every man severally as he	1Cor 12:11	_1244_
rightly _d_ the word of truth	2Ti 2:15	_3718_
even to the _d_ asunder of soul	Heb 4:12	_3311_

DIVINATION

the rewards of _d_ in their hand	Num 22:7	7081
is there any _d_ against Israel	Num 23:23	7081
through the fire, or that useth _d_	Deut 18:10	7081
pass through the fire, and used _d_	2Kin 17:17	7081
unto you a false vision and _d_	Jer 14:14	7081
_d_ within the house of Israel	Eze 12:24	4738
They have seen vanity and lying _d_	Eze 13:6	7081
and have ye not spoken a lying _d_	Eze 13:7	4738
head of the two ways, to use _d_	Eze 21:21	7081
hand was the _d_ for Jerusalem	Eze 21:22	7081
them as a false _d_ in their sight	Eze 21:23	7080
with a spirit of _d_ met us	Acts 16:16	4436

DIVINATIONS

see no more vanity, nor divine _d_	Eze 13:23	7081

DIVINE

such a man as I can certainly _d_	Gen 44:15	5172
_d_ unto me by the familiar spirit,	1Sa 28:8	7080
A _d_ sentence is in the lips of	Prov 16:10	7081
that see vanity, and that _d_ lies	Eze 13:9	7080
no more vanity, nor _d_ divinations	Eze 13:23	7181

whiles they _d_ a lie unto thee, to	Eze 21:29	7080
unto you, that ye shall not _d_	Mic 3:6	7080
the prophets thereof _d_ for money	Mic 3:11	7080
had also ordinances of _d_ service	Heb 9:1	2999
According as his _d_ power hath	2Pet 1:3	2304
be partakers of the _d_ nature	2Pet 1:4	2304

DIVINERS

observers of times, and unto _d_	Deut 18:14	7080
called for the priests and the _d_	1Sa 6:2	7080
of the liars, and maketh _d_ mad	Is 44:25	7080
to your prophets, nor to your _d_	Jer 27:9	7080
Let not your prophets and your _d_	Jer 29:8	7080
be ashamed, and the _d_ confounded	Mic 3:7	7080
the _d_ have seen a lie, and have	Zec 10:2	7080

DIVINETH

drinketh, and whereby indeed he _d_	Gen 44:5	5172

DIVINING

_d_ lies unto them, saying, Thus	Eze 22:28	7080

DIVISION

I will put a _d_ between my people	Ex 8:23	6304
after the _d_ of the families of	2Chr 35:5	2515
you, Nay; but rather _d_	Lk 12:51	_1267_
So there was a _d_ among the people	Jn 7:43	_4978_
And there was a _d_ among them	Jn 9:16	_4978_
There was a _d_ therefore again	Jn 10:19	_4978_

DIVISIONS

to their _d_ by their tribes	Josh 11:23	4256
a possession according to their _d_	Josh 12:7	4256
of Israel according to their _d_	Josh 18:10	4256
For the _d_ of Reuben there were	Judg 5:15	6391
For the _d_ of Reuben there were	Judg 5:16	6391
Now these are the _d_ of the sons	1Chr 24:1	4256
Concerning the _d_ of the porters	1Chr 26:1	4256
these were the _d_ of the porters	1Chr 26:12	4256
These are the _d_ of the porters	1Chr 26:19	4256
_d_ of the families of the fathers	2Chr 35:5	6391
might give according to the _d_ of	2Chr 35:12	4653
they set the priests in their _d_	Ezr 6:18	6392
And of the Levites were _d_ in Judah	Neh 11:36	4256
brethren, mark them which cause _d_	Rom 16:17	1370
and that there be no _d_ among you	1Cor 1:10	_4978_
you envying, and strife, and _d_	1Cor 3:3	1370
I hear that there be _d_ among you	1Cor 11:18	_4978_

DIVORCE

away, and given her a bill of _d_	Jer 3:8	3748

DIVORCED

or a _d_ woman, or profane, or an	Lev 21:14	1644
daughter be a widow, or _d_	Lev 22:13	1644
of a widow, and of her that is _d_	Num 30:9	1644
her that is _d_ committeth adultery	Mt 5:32	_630_

DIVORCEMENT

let him write her a bill of _d_	Deut 24:1	3748
her, and write her a bill of _d_	Deut 24:3	3748
is the bill of your mother's _d_	Is 50:1	3748
let him give her a writing of _d_	Mt 5:31	_647_
command to give a writing of _d_	Mt 19:7	_647_
suffered to write a bill of _d_	Mk 10:4	_647_

DIZAHAB (diz'-a-hab) _A place in the Sinai wilderness._

and Laban, and Hazeroth, and _D_	Deut 1:1	1774

DO See APPENDIX.

DOCTOR

a _d_ of the law, had in reputation	Acts 5:34	_3547_

DOCTORS

sitting in the midst of the _d_	Lk 2:46	_1320_
_d_ of the law sitting by, which	Lk 5:17	_3547_

DOCTRINE

My _d_ shall drop as the rain, my	Deut 32:2	3948
My _d_ is pure, and I am clean in	Job 11:4	3948
For I give you good _d_, forsake ye	Prov 4:2	3948
shall he make to understand _d_	Is 28:9	8052
they that murmured shall learn _d_	Is 29:24	3948
the stock is a _d_ of vanities	Jer 10:8	4148
people were astonished at his _d_	Mt 7:28	_1322_
but of the _d_ of the Pharisees and	Mt 16:12	_1322_
they were astonished at his _d_	Mt 22:33	_1322_
And they were astonished at his _d_	Mk 1:22	_1322_
what new _d_ is this	Mk 1:27	_1322_
and said unto them in his _d_	Mk 4:2	_1322_
people was astonished at his _d_	Mk 11:18	_1322_
And he said unto them in his _d_	Mk 12:38	_1322_
And they were astonished at his _d_	Lk 4:32	_1322_
My _d_ is not mine, but his that	Jn 7:16	_1322_
his will, he shall know of the _d_	Jn 7:17	_1322_
of his disciples, and of his _d_	Jn 18:19	_1322_
stedfastly in the apostles' _d_	Acts 2:42	_1322_

have filled Jerusalem with your *d*	Acts 5:28	1322
astonished at the *d* of the Lord	Acts 13:12	1322
May we know what this new *d*	Acts 17:19	1322
form of *d* which was delivered you	Rom 6:17	1322
to the *d* which ye have learned	Rom 16:17	1322
or by prophesying, or by *d*	1Cor 14:6	1322
one of you hath a psalm, hath a *d*	1Cor 14:26	1322
about with every wind of *d*	Eph 4:14	1319
some that they teach no other *d*	1Ti 1:3	
thing that is contrary to sound *d*	1Ti 1:10	1319
the words of faith and of good *d*	1Ti 4:6	1319
to reading, to exhortation, to *d*	1Ti 4:13	1319
heed unto thyself, and unto the *d*	1Ti 4:16	1319
they who labour in the word and *d*	1Ti 5:17	1319
of God and his *d* be not blasphemed	1Ti 6:1	1319
to the *d* which is according to	1Ti 6:3	1319
But thou hast fully known my *d*	2Ti 3:10	1319
of God, and is profitable for *d*	2Ti 3:16	1319
with all longsuffering and *d*	2Ti 4:2	1322
when they will not endure sound *d*	2Ti 4:3	1319
be able by sound *d* both to exhort	Titus 1:9	1319
the things which become sound *d*	Titus 2:1	1319
in *d* shewing uncorruptness	Titus 2:7	1319
that they may adorn the *d* of God	Titus 2:10	1319
the principles of the *d* of Christ	Heb 6:1	3056
Of the *d* of baptisms, and of	Heb 6:2	1322
and abideth not in the *d* of Christ	2Jn 9	1322
that abideth in the *d* of Christ	2Jn 9	1322
any unto you, and bring not this *d*	2Jn 10	1322
them that hold the *d* of Balaam	Rev 2:14	1322
hold the *d* of the Nicolaitanes	Rev 2:15	1322
as many as have not this *d*	Rev 2:24	1322

DOCTRINES
teaching for *d* the commandments	Mt 15:9	1319
teaching for *d* the commandments	Mk 7:7	1319
the commandments and of men	Col 2:22	1319
seducing spirits, and of *d* of devils	1Ti 4:1	1319
about with divers and strange *d*	Heb 13:9	1322

DODAI (*do'-dahee*) See DODO. *A captain in David's army.*
the second month was *D* an Ahohite	1Chr 27:4	1739

DODANIM (*do'-da-nim*) See RODANIM. *Descendants of Javan.*
and Tarshish, Kittim, and *D*	Gen 10:4	1721
and Tarshish, Kittim, and *D*	1Chr 1:7	1721

DODAVAH (*do'-da-vah*) *Father of Eliezer.*
Then Eliezer the son of *D* of	2Chr 20:37	1735

DODAVAHU See DODAVAH.

DODO (*do'-do*) See DODAI.
1. Grandfather of Tola.
the son of Puah, the son of *D*	Judg 10:1	1734

2. Father of Eleazar.
Eleazar the son of *D* the Ahohite	2Sa 23:9	1734
him was Eleazar the son of *D*	1Chr 11:12	1734

3. Father of Elhanan.
the son of *D* of Beth-lehem	2Sa 23:24	1734
the son of *D* of Beth-lehem	1Chr 11:26	1734

DOEG (*do'-eg*) *Chief herdsman of King Saul.*
and his name was *D*, an Edomite,	1Sa 21:7	1673
Then answered *D* the Edomite	1Sa 22:9	1673
And the king said to *D*, Turn thou,	1Sa 22:18	1673
D the Edomite turned, and he fell	1Sa 22:18	1673
when *D* the Edomite was there,	1Sa 22:22	1673
when *D* the Edomite came and told	Ps 52:t	1673

DOER
did there, he was the *d* of it	Gen 39:22	6218
the *d* of evil according to his	2Sa 3:39	6218
plentifully rewardeth the proud *d*	Ps 31:23	6218
A wicked *d* giveth heed to false	Prov 17:4	
I suffer trouble, as an evil *d*	2Ti 2:9	2557
a hearer of the word, and not a *d*	Jas 1:23	4163
but a *d* of the work, this man	Jas 1:25	4163
law, thou art not a *d* of the law	Jas 4:11	4163

DOERS
the hand of the *d* of the work	2Kin 22:5	6213
let them give it to the *d* of the	2Kin 22:5	6213
neither will he help the evil *d*	Job 8:20	
d from the city of the LORD	Ps 101:8	6466
but the *d* of the law shall be	Rom 2:13	4163
But be ye *d* of the word, and not	Jas 1:22	4163

DOEST See APPENDIX.

DOETH See APPENDIX.

DOG
shall not a *d* move his tongue	Ex 11:7	3611
of a whore, or the price of a *d*	Deut 23:18	3611

as a *d* lappeth, him shalt thou	Judg 7:5	3611
said unto David, Am I a *d*	1Sa 17:43	3611
after a dead *d*, after a flea	1Sa 24:14	3611
look upon such a dead *d* as I am	2Sa 9:8	3611
Why should this dead *d* curse my	2Sa 16:9	3611
But what, is thy servant a *d*	2Kin 8:13	3611
darling from the power of the *d*	Ps 22:20	3611
they make a noise like a *d*	Ps 59:6	3611
and let them make a noise like a *d*	Ps 59:14	3611
As a *d* returneth to his vomit, so	Prov 26:11	3611
one that taketh a *d* by the ears	Prov 26:17	3611
for a living *d* is better than a	Eccl 9:4	3611
The *d* is turned to his own vomit	2Pet 2:22	2965

DOG'S
and said, Am I a *d* head, which	2Sa 3:8	3611
a lamb, as if he cut off a *d* neck	Is 66:3	3611

DOGS
ye shall cast it to the *d*	Ex 22:31	3611
in the city shall the *d* eat	1Kin 14:11	3611
in the city shall the *d* eat	1Kin 16:4	3611
In the place where *d* licked the	1Kin 21:19	3611
of Naboth shall *d* lick thy blood	1Kin 21:19	3611
The *d* shall eat Jezebel by the	1Kin 21:23	3611
Ahab in the city the *d* shall eat	1Kin 21:24	3611
the *d* licked up his blood	1Kin 22:38	3611
the *d* shall eat Jezebel in the	2Kin 9:10	3611
shall *d* eat the flesh of Jezebel	2Kin 9:36	3611
have set with the *d* of my flock	Job 30:1	3611
For *d* have compassed me	Ps 22:16	3611
the tongue of thy *d* in the same	Ps 68:23	3611
all ignorant, they are all dumb *d*	Is 56:10	3611
they are greedy *d* which can never	Is 56:11	3611
the *d* to tear, and the fowls of	Jer 15:3	3611
not that which is holy unto the *d*	Mt 7:6	2965
bread, and to cast it to *d*	Mt 15:26	2952
yet the *d* eat of the crumbs which	Mt 15:27	2952
bread, and to cast it unto the *d*	Mk 7:27	2952
yet the *d* under the table eat of	Mk 7:28	2952
moreover the *d* came and licked his	Lk 16:21	2965
Beware of *d*, beware of evil	Phil 3:2	2965
For without are *d*, and sorcerers,	Rev 22:15	2965

DOING See APPENDIX.

DOINGS See APPENDIX.

DOLEFUL
shall be full of *d* creatures	Is 13:21	255
and lament with a *d* lamentation	Mic 2:4	5093

DOMINION
let them have *d* over the fish of	Gen 1:26	7287
have *d* over the fish of the sea,	Gen 1:28	7287
pass when thou shalt have the *d*	Gen 27:40	7300
shalt thou indeed have *d* over us	Gen 37:8	4910
shall come he that shall have *d*	Num 24:19	7287
have *d* over the nobles among the	Judg 5:13	7287
made me have *d* over the mighty	Judg 5:13	7287
the Philistines had *d* over Israel	Judg 14:4	4910
For he had *d* over all the region	1Kin 4:24	7287
and in all the land of his *d*	1Kin 9:19	4475
in his house, nor in all his *d*	1Chr 4:22	1166
and Saraph, who had the *d* in Moab	1Chr 4:22	1166
his *d* by the river Euphrates	1Chr 18:3	3027
throughout all the land of his *d*	2Chr 8:6	4475
from under the *d* of Judah	2Chr 21:8	3027
so that they had the *d* over them	Neh 9:28	7287
also they have *d* over our bodies,	Neh 9:37	4910
D and fear are with him	Job 25:2	4910
canst thou set the *d* thereof in	Job 38:33	4896
Thou madest him to have *d* over	Ps 8:6	4910
let them not have *d* over me	Ps 19:13	4910
the upright shall have *d* over	Ps 49:14	7287
He shall have *d* also from sea to	Ps 72:8	7287
his works in all places of his *d*	Ps 103:22	4475
his sanctuary, and Israel his *d*	Ps 114:2	4475
not any iniquity have *d* over me	Ps 119:133	7980
thy *d* endureth throughout all	Ps 145:13	4475
besides thee have had *d* over us	Is 26:13	1196
in his house, nor in all his *d*	Is 39:2	4475
kingdoms of the earth of his *d*	Jer 34:1	4475
thereof, and all the land of his *d*	Jer 51:28	4475
his *d* is from generation to	Dan 4:3	7985
thy *d* to the end of the earth	Dan 4:22	7985
whose *d* is an everlasting *d*	Dan 4:34	7985
That in every *d* of my kingdom men	Dan 6:26	7985
his *d* shall be even unto the end	Dan 6:26	7985
and *d* was given to it	Dan 7:6	7985
they had their *d* taken away	Dan 7:12	7985
And there was given him *d*, and	Dan 7:14	7985
his *d* is an everlasting *d*,	Dan 7:14	7985
and they shall take away his *d*	Dan 7:26	7985

And the kingdom and *d*, and the	Dan 7:27	7985
up, that shall rule with great *d*	Dan 11:3	4474
according to his *d* which he ruled	Dan 11:4	4915
be strong above him, and have *d*	Dan 11:5	4910
his *d* shall be a great *d*	Dan 11:5	4474
shall it come, even the first *d*	Mic 4:8	4475
his *d* shall be from sea even to	Zec 9:10	4915
the Gentiles exercise *d* over them	Mt 20:25	2634
death hath no more *d* over him	Rom 6:9	2961
For sin shall not have *d* over you	Rom 6:14	2961
how that the law hath *d* over a	Rom 7:1	2961
that we have *d* over your faith	2Cor 1:24	2961
and power, and might, and *d*	Eph 1:21	2963
be praise and *d* for ever and ever	1Pet 4:11	2904
be glory and *d* for ever and ever	1Pet 5:11	2904
defile the flesh, despise *d*	Jude 8	2963
Saviour, be glory and majesty, *d*	Jude 25	2904
be glory and *d* for ever and ever	Rev 1:6	2904

DOMINIONS

all *d* shall serve and obey him	Dan 7:27	7985
whether they be thrones, or *d*	Col 1:16	2963

DONE See APPENDIX.

DOOR

not well, sin lieth at the *d*	Gen 4:7	6607
the *d* of the ark shalt thou set	Gen 6:16	6607
he sat in the tent *d* in the heat	Gen 18:1	6607
ran to meet them from the tent *d*	Gen 18:2	6607
And Sarah heard it in the tent *d*	Gen 18:10	6607
Lot went out at the *d* unto them	Gen 19:6	6607
and shut the *d* after him	Gen 19:6	1817
Lot, and came near to break the *d*	Gen 19:9	1817
house to them, and shut to the *d*	Gen 19:10	1817
the *d* of the house with blindness	Gen 19:11	6607
wearied themselves to find the *d*	Gen 19:11	6607
with him at the *d* of the house	Gen 43:19	1817
on the upper *d* post of the houses	Ex 12:7	4947
d of his house until the morning	Ex 12:22	6607
the LORD will pass over the *d*	Ex 12:23	6607
he shall also bring him to the *d*	Ex 21:6	1817
or unto the *d* post	Ex 21:6	4201
an hanging for the *d* of the tent	Ex 26:36	6607
the *d* of the tabernacle of the	Ex 29:4	6607
by the *d* of the tabernacle of the	Ex 29:11	6607
by the *d* of the tabernacle of the	Ex 29:32	6607
your generations at the *d* of the	Ex 29:42	6607
and stood every man at his tent *d*	Ex 33:8	6607
stood at the *d* of the tabernacle,	Ex 33:9	6607
pillar stand at the tabernacle *d*	Ex 33:10	6607
every man in his tent *d*	Ex 33:10	6607
the hanging for the *d* at the	Ex 35:15	6607
hanging for the *d* of the court	Ex 35:17	8179
for the tabernacle *d* of blue	Ex 36:37	6607
which assembled at the *d* of the	Ex 38:8	6607
to the *d* of the tabernacle of the	Ex 38:30	6607
the hanging for the tabernacle *d*	Ex 39:38	6607
of the *d* to the tabernacle	Ex 40:5	6607
d of the tabernacle of the tent	Ex 40:6	6607
his sons unto the *d* of the	Ex 40:12	6607
at the *d* of the tabernacle	Ex 40:28	6607
d of the tabernacle of the tent	Ex 40:29	6607
at the *d* of the tabernacle of the	Lev 1:3	6607
by the *d* of the tabernacle of the	Lev 1:5	6607
and kill it at the *d* of the	Lev 3:2	6607
the *d* of the tabernacle of the	Lev 4:4	6607
which is at the *d* of the	Lev 4:7	6607
which is at the *d* of the	Lev 4:18	6607
the *d* of the tabernacle of the	Lev 8:3	6607
the *d* of the tabernacle of the	Lev 8:4	6607
Boil the flesh at the *d* of the	Lev 8:31	6607
of the *d* of the tabernacle of the	Lev 8:33	6607
at the *d* of the tabernacle of the	Lev 8:35	6607
the *d* of the tabernacle of the	Lev 10:7	6607
unto the *d* of the tabernacle of	Lev 12:6	6607
at the *d* of the tabernacle of the	Lev 14:11	6607
unto the *d* of the tabernacle of	Lev 14:23	6607
the house to the *d* of the house	Lev 14:38	6607
the *d* of the tabernacle of the	Lev 15:14	6607
to the *d* of the tabernacle of the	Lev 15:29	6607
at the *d* of the tabernacle of the	Lev 16:7	6607
the *d* of the tabernacle of the	Lev 17:4	6607
unto the *d* of the tabernacle of	Lev 17:5	6607
at the *d* of the tabernacle of the	Lev 17:6	6607
the *d* of the tabernacle of the	Lev 17:9	6607
unto the *d* of the tabernacle of	Lev 19:21	6607
the hanging for the *d* of the	Num 3:25	6607
curtain for the *d* of the court	Num 3:26	6607
the hanging for the *d* of the	Num 4:25	6607
the hanging for the *d* of the gate	Num 4:26	6607
to the *d* of the tabernacle of the	Num 6:10	6607

the *d* of the tabernacle of the	Num 6:13	6607
at the *d* of the tabernacle of the	Num 6:18	6607
at the *d* of the tabernacle of the	Num 10:3	6607
every man in the *d* of his tent	Num 11:10	6607
stood in the *d* of the tabernacle,	Num 12:5	6607
stood in the *d* of the tabernacle	Num 16:18	6607
against them unto the *d* of the	Num 16:19	6607
stood in the *d* of their tents, and	Num 16:27	6607
the *d* of the tabernacle of the	Num 16:50	6607
the *d* of the tabernacle of the	Num 20:6	6607
the *d* of the tabernacle of the	Num 25:6	6607
by the *d* of the tabernacle of the	Num 27:2	6607
upon the *d* posts of thine house	Deut 11:20	4201
it through his ear unto the *d*	Deut 15:17	1817
to the *d* of her father's house	Deut 22:21	6607
over the *d* of the tabernacle	Deut 31:15	6607
at the *d* of the tabernacle of the	Josh 19:51	6607
her, Stand in the *d* of the tent	Judg 4:20	6607
went hard unto the *d* of the tower	Judg 9:52	6607
round about, and beat at the *d*	Judg 19:22	1817
fell down at the *d* of the man's	Judg 19:26	6607
fallen down at the *d* of the house	Judg 19:27	6607
at the *d* of the tabernacle of the	1Sa 2:22	6607
But Uriah slept at the *d* of the	2Sa 11:9	6607
from me, and bolt the *d* after her	2Sa 13:17	1817
out, and bolted the *d* after her	2Sa 13:18	1817
The *d* for the middle chamber was	1Kin 6:8	6907
So also made he for the *d* of the	1Kin 6:31	6907
leaves of the one *d* were folding	1Kin 6:34	1817
of the other *d* were folding	1Kin 6:34	1817
her feet, as she came in at the *d*	1Kin 14:6	6607
came to the threshold of the *d*	1Kin 14:17	1004
which kept the *d* of the king's	1Kin 14:27	6607
thou shalt shut the *d* upon thee	2Kin 4:4	1817
from him, and shut the *d* upon her	2Kin 4:5	1817
called her, she stood in the *d*	2Kin 4:15	6607
of God, and shut the *d* upon him	2Kin 4:21	
shut the *d* upon them twain, and	2Kin 4:33	1817
stood at the *d* of the house of	2Kin 5:9	6607
d, and hold him fast at the *d*	2Kin 6:32	1817
Then open the *d*, and flee, and	2Kin 9:3	1817
And he opened the *d*, and fled	2Kin 9:10	1817
the priests that kept the *d* put	2Kin 12:9	5592
which the keepers of the *d* have	2Kin 22:4	5592
order, and the keepers of the *d*	2Kin 23:4	5592
and the three keepers of the *d*	2Kin 25:18	5592
of the *d* of the tabernacle of the	1Chr 9:21	6607
d of the house of Eliashib the	Neh 3:20	6607
from the *d* of the house of	Neh 3:21	6607
Teresh, of those which kept the *d*	Est 2:21	5592
the keepers of the *d*, who sought	Est 6:2	5592
laid wait at my neighbour's *d*	Job 31:9	6607
silence, and went not out of the *d*	Job 31:34	6607
Keep the *d* of my lips	Ps 141:3	1817
come not nigh the *d* of her house	Prov 5:8	6607
she sitteth at the *d* of her house	Prov 9:14	6607
As the *d* turneth upon his hinges,	Prov 26:14	1817
in his hand by the hole of the *d*	Song 5:4	6607
and if she be a *d*, we will inclose	Song 8:9	1817
the posts of the *d* moved at the	Is 6:4	5592
of Shallum, the keeper of the *d*	Jer 35:4	5592
and the three keepers of the *d*	Jer 52:24	5592
to the *d* of the inner gate, that	Eze 8:3	6607
brought me to the *d* of the court	Eze 8:7	6607
digged in the wall, behold a *d*	Eze 8:8	6607
Then he brought me to the *d* of	Eze 8:14	6607
at the *d* of the temple of the	Eze 8:16	6607
every one stood at the *d* of the	Eze 10:19	6607
behold at the *d* of the gate five	Eze 11:1	6607
and twenty cubits, *d* against *d*	Eze 40:13	6607
breadth of the *d* was ten cubits	Eze 41:2	6607
the sides of the *d* were five	Eze 41:2	6607
and measured the post of the *d*	Eze 41:3	6607
and the *d*, six cubits	Eze 41:3	6607
and the breadth of the *d*, seven	Eze 41:3	6607
one *d* toward the north, and	Eze 41:11	6607
another *d* toward the south	Eze 41:11	6607
The *d* posts, and the narrow	Eze 41:16	5592
three stories, over against the *d*	Eze 41:16	5592
To that above the *d*, even unto	Eze 41:17	6607
unto above the *d* were cherubims	Eze 41:20	6607
two leaves for the one *d*	Eze 41:24	1817
and two leaves for the other *d*	Eze 41:24	1817
an hundred cubits was the north *d*	Eze 42:2	6607
was a *d* in the head of the way	Eze 42:12	6607
the land shall worship at the *d*	Eze 46:3	6607
me again unto the *d* of the house	Eze 47:1	6607
valley of Achor for a *d* of hope	Hos 2:15	6607
said, Smite the lintel of the *d*	Amos 9:1	
and when thou hast shut thy *d*	Mt 6:6	2374
and the *d* was shut	Mt 25:10	2374

D

DOORKEEPER (continued)

stone to the *d* of the sepulchre	Mt 27:60	2374
rolled back the stone from the *d*	Mt 28:2	2374
was gathered together at the *d*	Mk 1:33	2374
no, not so much as about the *d*	Mk 2:2	2374
found the colt tied by the *d*	Mk 11:4	2374
stone unto the *d* of the sepulchre	Mk 15:46	2374
stone from the *d* of the sepulchre	Mk 16:3	2374
the *d* is now shut, and my children	Lk 11:7	2374
risen up, and hath shut to the *d*	Lk 13:25	2374
without, and to knock at the *d*	Lk 13:25	2374
not by the *d* into the sheepfold	Jn 10:1	2374
***d* is the shepherd of the sheep**	Jn 10:2	2374
unto you, I am the *d* of the sheep	Jn 10:7	2374
I am the *d*	Jn 10:9	2374
But Peter stood at the *d* without	Jn 18:16	2374
and spake unto her that kept the *d*	Jn 18:16	2377
damsel that kept the *d* unto Peter	Jn 18:17	2377
buried thy husband are at the *d*	Acts 5:9	2374
before the *d* kept the prison	Acts 12:6	2374
knocked at the *d* of the gate	Acts 12:13	
and when they had opened the *d*	Acts 12:16	
how he had opened the *d* of faith	Acts 14:27	2374
For a great *d* and effectual is	1Cor 16:9	2374
a *d* was opened unto me of the	2Cor 2:12	2374
open unto us a *d* of utterance	Col 4:3	2374
the judge standeth before the *d*	Jas 5:9	2374
I have set before thee an open *d*	Rev 3:8	2374
Behold, I stand at the *d*, and	Rev 3:20	2374
man hear my voice, and open the *d*	Rev 3:20	2374
behold, a *d* was opened in heaven	Rev 4:1	2374

DOORKEEPER

I had rather be a *d* in the house	Ps 84:10	5605

DOORKEEPERS

and Elkanah were *d* for the ark	1Chr 15:23	7778
and Jehiah were *d* for the ark	1Chr 15:24	7778

DOORS

d of thy house into the street	Josh 2:19	1817
shut the *d* of the parlour upon	Judg 3:23	1817
the *d* of the parlour were locked,	Judg 3:24	1817
opened not the *d* of the parlour	Judg 3:25	1817
of the *d* of my house to meet me	Judg 11:31	1817
took the *d* of the gate of the	Judg 16:3	1817
opened the *d* of the house, and	Judg 19:27	1817
opened the *d* of the house of the	1Sa 3:15	1817
and scrabbled on the *d* of the gate	1Sa 21:13	1817
oracle he made *d* of olive tree	1Kin 6:31	1817
The two *d* also were of olive tree	1Kin 6:32	1817
the two *d* were of fir tree	1Kin 6:34	1817
And all the *d* and posts were square	1Kin 7:5	6607
both for the *d* of the inner house	1Kin 7:50	1817
for the *d* of the house, to wit,	1Kin 7:50	1817
the *d* of the temple of the LORD	2Kin 18:16	1817
the nails for the *d* of the gates	1Chr 22:3	1817
and the *d* thereof, with gold	2Chr 3:7	1817
great court, and *d* for the court	2Chr 4:9	1817
overlaid *d* of them with brass	2Chr 4:9	1817
the inner *d* thereof for the most	2Chr 4:22	1817
the *d* of the house of the temple,	2Chr 4:22	1817
shall be porters of the *d*	2Chr 23:4	5592
shut up the *d* of the house of the	2Chr 28:24	1817
opened the *d* of the house of the	2Chr 29:3	1817
have shut up the *d* of the porch	2Chr 29:7	1817
the *d* had gathered of the hand of	2Chr 34:9	5592
it, and set up the *d* of it	Neh 3:1	1817
thereof, and set up the *d* thereof	Neh 3:3	1817
thereof, and set up the *d* thereof	Neh 3:6	1817
built it, and set up the *d* thereof	Neh 3:13	1817
build it, and set up the *d* thereof	Neh 3:14	1817
it, and set up the *d* thereof	Neh 3:15	1817
not set up the *d* upon the gates	Neh 6:1	1817
let us shut the *d* of the temple	Neh 6:10	1817
was built, and I had set up the *d*	Neh 7:1	1817
stand by, let them shut the *d*	Neh 7:3	1817
not up the *d* of my mother's womb	Job 3:10	1817
but I opened my *d* to the	Job 31:32	1817
Or who shut up the sea with *d*	Job 38:8	1817
decreed place, and set bars and *d*	Job 38:10	1817
or hast thou seen the *d* of the	Job 38:17	8179
Who can open the *d* of his face	Job 41:14	1817
be ye lifted up, ye everlasting *d*	Ps 24:7	6607
lift them up, ye everlasting *d*	Ps 24:9	6607
above, and opened the *d* of heaven	Ps 78:23	1817
city, at the coming in at the *d*	Prov 8:3	6607
waiting at the posts of my *d*	Prov 8:34	6607
the *d* shall be shut in the	Eccl 12:4	1817
and shut thy *d* about thee	Is 26:20	1817
Behind the *d* also and the posts	Is 57:8	1817
in the *d* of the houses, and speak	Eze 33:30	6607
the *d* of the side chambers were	Eze 41:11	6607
temple and the sanctuary had two *d*	Eze 41:23	1817
the *d* had two leaves apiece, two	Eze 41:24	1817
on the *d* of the temple, cherubims	Eze 41:25	1817
and their *d* toward the north	Eze 42:4	6607
fashions, and according to their *d*	Eze 42:11	6607
according to the *d* of the	Eze 42:12	6607
keep the *d* of thy mouth from her	Mic 7:5	6607
Open thy *d*, O Lebanon, that the	Zec 11:1	1817
that would shut the *d* for nought	Mal 1:10	1817
that it is near, even at the *d*	Mt 24:33	2374
that it is nigh, even at the *d*	Mk 13:29	2374
when the *d* were shut where the	Jn 20:19	2374
the *d* being shut, and stood in the	Jn 20:26	2374
Lord by night opened the prison *d*	Acts 5:19	2374
standing without before the *d*	Acts 5:23	2374
immediately all the *d* were opened	Acts 16:26	2374
and seeing the prison *d* open	Acts 16:27	2374
and forthwith the *d* were shut	Acts 21:30	2374

DOPHKAH *(dof-kah) An encampment during the Exodus.*

of Sin, and encamped in *D*	Num 33:12	1850
And they departed from *D*, and	Num 33:13	1850

DOR *(dor)* See EN-DOR. *A Canaanite city.*

in the borders of *D* on the west	Josh 11:2	1756
The king of *D* in the coast of	Josh 12:23	1756
towns, and the inhabitants of *D*	Josh 17:11	1756
towns, nor the inhabitants of *D*	Judg 1:27	1756
Abinadab, in all the region of *D*	1Kin 4:11	1756
towns, Megiddo and her towns, *D*	1Chr 7:29	1756

DORCAS *(dor-cas)* See TABITHA. *Disciple raised from the dead by Peter.*

by interpretation is called *D*	Acts 9:36	1393
coats and garments which *D* made	Acts 9:39	1393

DOST

it that thou *d* ask after my name	Gen 32:29	
when thou *d* overtake them, say	Gen 44:4	
d thou go to possess their land	Deut 9:5	
When thou *d* lend thy brother any	Deut 24:10	
the man to whom thou *d* lend shall	Deut 24:11	
Thou *d* but hate me, and lovest me	Judg 14:16	
after whom *d* thou pursue	1Sa 24:14	
Wherefore then *d* thou ask of me	1Sa 28:16	
why *d* thou ask Abishag the	1Kin 2:22	
D thou now govern the kingdom of	1Kin 21:7	
Now on whom *d* thou trust, that	2Kin 18:20	
sin, when thou *d* afflict them	2Chr 6:26	
For what *d* thou make request	Neh 2:4	
D thou still retain thine	Job 2:9	
And why *d* not pardon my	Job 7:21	
yet thou *d* destroy me	Job 10:8	
d thou open thine eyes upon such	Job 14:3	
d thou not watch over my sin	Job 14:16	
d thou restrain wisdom to thyself	Job 15:8	
unto thee, and thou *d* not hear me	Job 30:20	
Why *d* thou strive against him	Job 33:13	
D thou know when God disposed	Job 37:15	
D thou know the balancings of the	Job 37:16	
When thou with rebukes *d* correct	Ps 39:11	
why *d* thou cast me off	Ps 43:2	
d not increase thy wealth by	Ps 44:12	
thou *d* establish equity, thou	Ps 99:4	
honour, when thou *d* embrace her	Prov 4:8	
for thou *d* not enquire wisely	Eccl 7:10	
beloved, that thou *d* so charge us	Song 5:9	
d weigh the path of the just	Is 26:7	
now on whom *d* thou trust, that	Is 36:5	
Wherefore *d* thou prophesy, and say	Jer 32:3	
D thou certainly know that Baalis	Jer 40:14	
daughter that *d* inhabit Dibon	Jer 48:18	
Wherefore *d* thou forget us for	Lam 5:20	
thou *d* dwell among scorpions	Eze 2:6	
Whom *d* thou pass in beauty	Eze 32:19	
if thou *d* not speak to warn the	Eze 33:8	
Now why *d* thou cry out aloud	Mic 4:9	
Why *d* thou shew me iniquity, and	Hab 1:3	
d thou not care that my sister	Lk 10:40	
D not thou fear God, seeing thou	Lk 23:40	
what *d* thou work?	Jn 6:30	
born in sins, and *d* thou teach us	Jn 9:34	
D thou believe on the Son of God	Jn 9:35	
How long *d* thou make us to doubt	Jn 10:24	
him, Lord, *d* thou wash my feet	Jn 13:6	
should not steal, *d* thou steal	Rom 2:21	
adultery, *d* thou commit adultery	Rom 2:22	
idols, *d* thou commit sacrilege	Rom 2:22	
circumcision *d* transgress the law	Rom 2:27	
But why *d* thou judge thy brother	Rom 14:10	
or why *d* thou set at nought thy	Rom 14:10	

why *d* thou glory, as if thou.....................1Cor 4:7
d thou not judge and avenge our ....Rev 6:10

DOTE
and they shall *d*: a sword is.....................Jer 50:36   2973

DOTED
she *d* on her lovers, on the......................Eze 23:5   5689
and with all on whom she *d* ....Eze 23:7   5689
of the Assyrians, upon whom she *d* ....Eze 23:9   5689
She *d* upon the Assyrians her..................Eze 23:12   5689
eyes, she *d* upon them, and sent.............Eze 23:16   5689
For she *d* upon their paramours, ...Eze 23:20   5689

DOTH
For God *d* know that in the day ye........Gen 3:5
d comfort himself, purposing to..............Gen 27:42
d my father yet live ....Gen 45:3
d put a difference between the ....Ex 11:7
I am the Lord that *d* sanctify you ....Ex 31:13
why *d* thy wrath wax hot against...........Ex 32:11
whosoever *d* touch them, when they ......Lev 11:31
d fall, it shall be unclean ....Lev 11:32
of the fruits *d* he sell unto thee ....Lev 25:16
when the Lord *d* make thy thigh to ....Num 5:21
the man whom the Lord *d* choose...........Num 16:7
the Lord *d* command concerning the .....Num 36:6
the Lord our God *d* give unto us............Deut 1:20
which the Lord our God *d* give us ....Deut 1:25
as a man *d* bear his son, in all ....Deut 1:31
this day that God *d* talk with man........Deut 5:24
that man *d* not live by bread only ....Deut 8:3
the mouth of the Lord *d* man live ....Deut 8:3
of these nations the Lord *d* drive ....Deut 9:4
these nations the Lord thy God *d* ....Deut 9:5
what *d* the Lord thy God require ....Deut 10:12
He *d* execute the judgment of the ....Deut 10:18
for a gift *d* blind the eyes of ....Deut 16:19
abominations the Lord thy God *d*...........Deut 18:12
which the Lord thy God *d* give............Deut 20:16
God, he it is that *d* go with thee ....Deut 31:6
he it is that *d* go before thee ....Deut 31:8
Whosoever he be that *d* rebel ....Josh 1:18
when he that *d* flee unto one of ....Josh 20:4
it shall be, when any man *d* come ....Judg 4:20
d know that thou art a virtuous ....Ruth 3:11
because he *d* bless the sacrifice 1Sa 9:13
D not David hide himself with us 1Sa 23:19
D not David hide himself in the.............1Sa 26:1
Wherefore *d* my lord thus pursue 1Sa 26:18
as when one *d* hunt a partridge in 1Sa 26:20
that David *d* honour thy father 2Sa 10:3
for the king *d* speak this thing 2Sa 14:13
in that the king *d* not fetch home 2Sa 14:13
neither *d* God respect any person 2Sa 14:14
yet *d* he devise means, that his 2Sa 14:14
the king *d* sit in the gate 2Sa 19:8
For thy servant *d* know that I 2Sa 19:20
but why *d* my lord the king 2Sa 24:3
of that which *d* cost me nothing 2Sa 24:24
the son of Haggith *d* reign 1Kin 1:11
why then *d* Adonijah reign 1Kin 1:13
for he *d* not prophesy good 1Kin 22:8
spirit of Elijah *d* rest on Elisha 2Kin 2:15
that this man *d* send unto me to 2Kin 5:7
that David *d* honour thy father 1Chr 19:3
why then *d* my lord require this 1Chr 21:3
as *d* thy people Israel, and may............2Chr 6:33
D not Hezekiah persuade you to 2Chr 32:11
D Job fear God for nought ....Job 1:9
D not their excellency which is ....Job 4:21
neither *d* trouble spring out of ....Job 5:6
D the wild ass bray when he hath ....Job 6:5
but what *d* your arguing reprove ....Job 6:25
D God pervert judgment ....Job 8:3
or *d* the Almighty pervert justice ....Job 8:3
D not the ear try words ....Job 12:11
Why *d* thine heart carry thee away ....Job 15:12
my reins asunder, and *d* not spare ....Job 16:13
d not mine eye continue in their ....Job 17:2
And thou sayest, How *d* God know ....Job 22:13
On the left hand, where he *d* work ....Job 23:9
so *d* the grave those which have.............Job 24:19
upon whom *d* not his light arise ....Job 25:3
D not he see my ways, and count ....Job 31:4
Therefore *d* Job open his mouth in ....Job 35:16
he *d* establish them for ever, and............Job 36:7
D the hawk fly by thy wisdom, and ....Job 39:26
D the eagle mount up at thy ....Job 39:27
By his neesings a light *d* shine ....Job 41:18
in his law *d* he meditate day and............Ps 1:2
in his pride *d* persecute the poor............Ps 10:2

in the secret places *d* he murder ....Ps 10:8
he *d* catch the poor, when he ....Ps 10:9
Wherefore *d* the wicked contemn ....Ps 10:13
his countenance *d* behold the ....Ps 11:7
in his temple *d* every one speak ....Ps 29:9
because mine enemy *d* not triumph ......Ps 41:11
D not David hide himself with us ....Ps 54:t
for who, say they, *d* hear ....Ps 59:7
he *d* send out his voice, and that...........Ps 68:33
And they say, How *d* God know ....Ps 73:11
why *d* thine anger smoke against ....Ps 74:1
d his promise fail for evermore ....Ps 77:8
boar out of the wood *d* waste it ....Ps 80:13
beast of the field *d* devour it ....Ps 80:13
neither *d* a fool understand this ....Ps 92:6
therefore *d* my soul keep them ....Ps 119:129
wait for the Lord, my soul *d* wait ....Ps 130:5
The Lord *d* build up Jerusalem ....Ps 147:2
These six things *d* the Lord hate ....Prov 6:16
D not wisdom cry? ....Prov 8:1
a stranger *d* not intermeddle with ....Prov 14:10
he that *d* keep his soul shall be ....Prov 22:5
d not he that pondereth the heart ....Prov 24:12
thy soul, *d* not he know it ....Prov 24:12
so *d* an angry countenance a..................Prov 25:23
so *d* the slothful upon his bed ....Prov 26:14
so *d* the sweetness of a man's ....Prov 27:9
d the crown endure to every ....Prov 27:24
but the righteous *d* sing and ....Prov 29:6
and *d* not bless their mother ....Prov 30:11
her husband *d* safely trust in her ....Prov 31:11
so *d* a little folly him that is ....Eccl 10:1
and his right hand *d* embrace me ....Song 2:6
but Israel *d* not know ....Is 1:3
my people *d* not consider ....Is 1:3
neither *d* the cause of the widow ....Is 1:23
d take away from Jerusalem and............Is 3:1
d witness against them ....Is 3:9
neither *d* his heart think so.....................Is 10:7
D the plowman plow all day to sow ......Is 28:24
d he open and break the clods of ....Is 28:24
d he not cast abroad the fitches, ...Is 28:25
For his God *d* instruct him to ....Is 28:26
him to discretion, and *d* teach him ....Is 28:26
stream of brimstone, *d* kindle it.............Is 30:33
the villages that Kedar *d* inhabit ....Is 42:11
an ash, and the rain *d* nourish it ....Is 44:14
day that I am he that *d* speak ....Is 52:6
neither *d* justice overtake us ....Is 59:9
glory for that which *d* not profit ....Jer 2:11
for to thee *d* it appertain ....Jer 10:7
Wherefore *d* the way of the wicked ....Jer 12:1
the Lord *d* not accept them ....Jer 14:10
yet every one of them *d* curse me ....Jer 15:10
that none *d* return from his.....................Jer 23:14
see whether a man *d* travail with ....Jer 30:6
him, as a shepherd *d* his flock ....Jer 31:10
why then *d* their king inherit Gad ....Jer 49:1
neither *d* any son of man pass................Jer 51:43
How *d* the city sit solitary, that..............Lam 1:1
For he *d* not afflict willingly ....Lam 3:33
Wherefore *d* a living man complain ....Lam 3:39
there is none that *d* deliver us ....Lam 5:8
When a righteous man *d* turn from ......Eze 3:20
he *d* not sin, he shall surely ....Eze 3:21
d not the son bear the iniquity ....Eze 18:19
of me, *D* he not speak parables ....Eze 20:49
that *d* not understand shall fall ....Hos 4:14
of Israel *d* testify to his face ....Hos 5:5
what *d* the Lord require of thee, ...Mic 6:8
judgment *d* never go forth ....Hab 1:4
for the wicked *d* compass about ....Hab 1:4
every morning *d* he bring his.................Zeph 3:5
rust *d* corrupt, and where thieves........Mt 6:19
neither moth nor rust *d* corrupt...........Mt 6:20
This fellow *d* not cast out devils ....Mt 12:24
D not your master pay tribute ....Mt 17:24
d he not leave the ninety and nine ....Mt 18:12
is put away *d* commit adultery ....Mt 19:9
How then *d* David in spirit call..............Mt 22:43
not what hour your Lord *d* come ....Mt 24:42
he is at hand that *d* betray me ....Mt 26:46
Why *d* this man thus speak....................Mk 2:7
the new wine *d* burst the bottles...........Mk 2:22
Why *d* this generation seek after...........Mk 8:12
My soul *d* magnify the Lord,...................Lk 1:46
neither *d* a corrupt tree bring ....Lk 6:43
of a candle *d* give thee light..................Lk 11:36
d not each one of you on the ....Lk 13:15
as a hen *d* gather her brood under ....Lk 13:34
whosoever *d* not bear his cross, ...Lk 14:27

d not leave the ninety and nine in	Lk 15:4	
d not light a candle, and sweep	Lk 15:8	
D he thank that servant because	Lk 17:9	
that is chief, as he that *d* serve	Lk 22:26	
beginning *d* set forth good wine	Jn 2:10	
said unto them, D this offend you	Jn 6:61	
D our law judge any man, before	Jn 7:51	
how then *d* he now see	Jn 9:19	
Therefore *d* my Father love me,	Jn 10:17	
even by him *d* this man stand here	Acts 4:10	
what *d* hinder me to be baptized	Acts 8:36	
the high priest *d* bear me witness	Acts 22:5	
much learning *d* make thee mad	Acts 26:24	
man seeth, why *d* he yet hope for	Rom 8:24	
unto me, Why *d* he yet find fault	Rom 9:19	
to the Lord he *d* not regard it	Rom 14:6	
D God take care for oxen	1Cor 9:9	
D not even nature itself teach	1Cor 11:14	
D not behave itself unseemly,	1Cor 13:5	
neither *d* corruption inherit	1Cor 15:50	
so great a death, and *d* deliver	2Cor 1:10	
much more *d* the ministration of	2Cor 3:9	
for whatsoever *d* make manifest is	Eph 5:13	
as it *d* also in you, since the	Col 1:6	
as a father *d* his children,	1Th 2:11	
of iniquity *d* already work	2Th 2:7	
their word will eat as *d* a canker	2Ti 2:17	
all shall wax old as *d* a garment	Heb 1:11	
the sin which *d* so easily beset	Heb 12:1	
What *d* it profit, my brethren,	Jas 2:14	
to the body; what *d* it profit?	Jas 2:16	
D a fountain send forth at the	Jas 3:11	
and he *d* not resist you	Jas 5:6	
d also now save us (not the	1Pet 3:21	
and so *d* Marcus my son	1Pet 5:13	
it *d* not yet appear what we shall	1Jn 3:2	
is born of God *d* not commit sin	1Jn 3:9	
neither *d* he himself receive the	3Jn 10	
and in righteousness he *d* judge	Rev 19:11	

DOTHAN (do'-than) *A city in Manasseh.*

I heard them say, Let us go to D	Gen 37:17	1886
his brethren, and found them in D	Gen 37:17	1886
him, saying, Behold, he is in D	2Kin 6:13	1886

DOTING

but *d* about questions and strifes	1Ti 6:4	3552

DOUBLE

take *d* money in your hand	Gen 43:12	4932
they took *d* money in their hand,	Gen 43:15	4932
he shall restore *d*	Ex 22:4	8147
the thief be found, let him pay *d*	Ex 22:7	8147
he shall pay *d* unto his neighbour	Ex 22:9	8147
shalt *d* the sixth curtain in the	Ex 26:9	3717
they made the breastplate *d*	Ex 39:9	3717
worth a *d* hired servant to thee	Deut 15:18	4932
by giving him a *d* portion of	Deut 21:17	8147
let a *d* portion of thy spirit be	2Kin 2:9	8147
they were not of *d* heart	1Chr 12:33	
that they are *d* to that which is	Job 11:6	3718
can come to him with his *d* bridle	Job 41:13	3718
with a *d* heart do they speak	Ps 12:2	
LORD's hand *d* for all her sins	Is 40:2	3718
For your shame ye shall have *d*	Is 61:7	4932
land they shall possess the *d*	Is 61:7	4932
their iniquity and their sin *d*	Jer 16:18	4932
destroy them with *d* destruction	Jer 17:18	4932
that I will render *d* unto thee	Zec 9:12	4932
be counted worthy of *d* honour	1Ti 5:17	1362
A *d* minded man is unstable in all	Jas 1:8	1374
purify your hearts, ye *d* minded	Jas 4:8	1374
d unto her *d* according to	Rev 18:6	3588,1362
she hath filled fill to her *d*	Rev 18:6	1362

DOUBLED

dream was *d* unto Pharaoh twice	Gen 41:32	8138
Foursquare it shall be being *d*	Ex 28:16	3717
span the breadth thereof, being *d*	Ex 39:9	3717
let the sword be *d* the third time	Eze 21:14	3717

DOUBLETONGUED

must the deacons be grave, not *d*	1Ti 3:8	1351

DOUBT

is without *d* rent in pieces	Gen 37:33	
life shall hang in *d* before thee	Deut 28:66	
No *d* but ye are the people, and	Job 12:2	551
faith, wherefore didst thou *d*	Mt 14:31	1365
d not, ye shall not only do this	Mt 21:21	1252
shall not *d* in his heart, but	Mk 11:23	1252
no *d* the kingdom of God is come	Lk 11:20	686
How long dost thou make us to *d*	Jn 10:24	142,5590
were all amazed, and were in *d*	Acts 2:12	1280

No *d* this man is a murderer, whom	Acts 28:4	3843
For our sakes, no *d*, this is	1Cor 9:10	1063
for I stand in *d* of you	Gal 4:20	639
they would no *d* have continued	1Jn 2:19	

DOUBTED

but some *d*	Mt 28:17	1365
they *d* of them whereunto this	Acts 5:24	1280
Now while Peter *d* in himself what	Acts 10:17	1280
because I *d* of such manner of	Acts 25:20	639

DOUBTETH

he that *d* is damned if he eat	Rom 14:23	1252

DOUBTFUL

drink, neither be ye of *d* mind	Lk 12:29	3349
but not to *d* disputations	Rom 14:1	1261

DOUBTING

on another, *d* of whom he spake	Jn 13:22	639
down, and go with them, *d* nothing	Acts 10:20	1252
bade me go with them, nothing *d*	Acts 11:12	1252
up holy hands, without wrath and *d*	1Ti 2:8	1261

DOUBTLESS

D ye shall not come into the land	Num 14:30	518
for I will *d* deliver the	2Sa 5:19	
shall *d* come again with rejoicing	Ps 126:6	
D thou art our father, though	Is 63:16	3588
unto others, yet *d* I am to you	1Cor 9:2	1065
not expedient for me *d* to glory	2Cor 12:1	1211
Yea *d*, and I count all things but	Phil 3:8	3304

DOUBTS

sentences, and dissolving of *d*	Dan 5:12	7001
interpretations, and dissolve *d*	Dan 5:16	7001

DOUGH

the people took their *d* before it	Ex 12:34	1217
baked unleavened cakes of the *d*	Ex 12:39	1217
of your *d* for an heave offering	Num 15:20	6182
Of the first of your *d* ye shall	Num 15:21	6182
bring the firstfruits of our *d*	Neh 10:37	6182
fire, and the women knead their *d*	Jer 7:18	1217
the priest the first of your *d*	Eze 44:30	6182
after he hath kneaded the *d*	Hos 7:4	1217

DOVE

Also he sent forth a *d* from him	Gen 8:8	3123
But the *d* found no rest for the	Gen 8:9	3123
sent forth the *d* out of the ark	Gen 8:10	3123
the *d* came in to him in the	Gen 8:11	3123
and sent forth the *d*	Gen 8:12	3123
Oh that I had wings like a *d*	Ps 55:6	3123
wings of a *d* covered with silver	Ps 68:13	3123
O my *d*, that art in the clefts of	Song 2:14	3123
to me, my sister, my love, my *d*	Song 5:2	3123
My *d*, my undefiled is but one	Song 6:9	3123
I did mourn as a *d*	Is 38:14	3123
be like the *d* that maketh her	Jer 48:28	3123
is like a silly *d* without heart	Hos 7:11	3123
as a *d* out of the land of Assyria	Hos 11:11	3123
Spirit of God descending like a *d*	Mt 3:16	4058
the Spirit like a *d* descending	Mk 1:10	4058
a bodily shape like a *d* upon him	Lk 3:22	4058
descending from heaven like a *d*	Jn 1:32	4058

DOVE'S

the fourth part of a cab of *d*	2Kin 6:25	1686

DOVES

eyes of *d* by the rivers of waters	Song 5:12	3123
like bears, and mourn sore like *d*	Is 59:11	3123
as the *d* to their windows	Is 60:8	3123
mountains like *d* of the valleys	Eze 7:16	3123
lead her as with the voice of *d*	Nah 2:7	3123
as serpents, and harmless as *d*	Mt 10:16	4058
and the seats of them that sold *d*	Mt 21:12	4058
and the seats of them that sold *d*	Mk 11:15	4058
that sold oxen and sheep and *d*	Jn 2:14	4058
And said unto them that sold *d*	Jn 2:16	4058

DOVES'

thou art fair; thou hast *d* eyes	Song 1:15	3123
thou hast *d* eyes within thy locks	Song 4:1	3123

DOWN See APPENDIX.

DOWNSITTING

Thou knowest my *d* and mine	Ps 139:2	3427

DOWNWARD

Judah shall yet again take root *d*	2Kin 19:30	4295
beast that goeth *d* to the earth	Eccl 3:21	4295
of Judah shall again take root *d*	Is 37:31	4295
appearance of his loins even *d*	Eze 1:27	4295
appearance of his loins even *d*	Eze 8:2	4295

<table>
<tr><td colspan="3">

DOWRY
God hath endued me with a good *d*	Gen 30:20	2065
Ask me never so much *d* and gift,	Gen 34:12	4119
according to the *d* of virgins	Ex 22:17	4119
The king desireth not any *d*	1Sa 18:25	4119

DRAG
net, and gather them in their *d*	Hab 1:15	4365
net, and burn incense unto their *d*	Hab 1:16	4365

DRAGGING
cubits,) *d* the net with fishes	Jn 21:8	4951

DRAGON
valley, even before the *d* well	Neh 2:13	8577
the *d* shalt thou trample under	Ps 91:13	8577
he shall slay the *d* that is in	Is 27:1	8577
hath cut Rahab, and wounded the *d*	Is 51:9	8577
he hath swallowed me up like a *d*	Jer 51:34	8577
the great *d* that lieth in the	Eze 29:3	8577
and behold a great red *d*, having	Rev 12:3	1404
the *d* stood before the woman	Rev 12:4	1404
his angels fought against the *d*	Rev 12:7	1404
the *d* fought and his angels,	Rev 12:7	1404
the great *d* was cast out, that	Rev 12:9	1404
when the *d* saw that he was cast	Rev 12:13	1404
which the *d* cast out of his mouth	Rev 12:16	1404
the *d* was wroth with the woman,	Rev 12:17	1404
the *d* gave him his power, and his	Rev 13:2	1404
they worshipped the *d* which gave	Rev 13:4	1404
like a lamb, and he spake as a *d*	Rev 13:11	1404
come out of the mouth of the *d*	Rev 16:13	1404
And he laid hold on the *d*, that	Rev 20:2	1404

DRAGONS
Their wine is the poison of *d*	Deut 32:33	8577
I am a brother to *d*, and a	Job 30:29	8577
sore broken us in the place of *d*	Ps 44:19	8577
the heads of the *d* in the waters	Ps 74:13	8577
the LORD from the earth, ye *d*	Ps 148:7	8577
d in their pleasant palaces	Is 13:22	8577
and it shall be an habitation of *d*	Is 34:13	8577
in the habitation of *d*, where	Is 35:7	8577
the field shall honour me, the *d*	Is 43:20	8577
Jerusalem heaps, and a den of *d*	Jer 9:11	8577
of Judah desolate, and a den of *d*	Jer 10:22	8577
they snuffed up the wind like *d*	Jer 14:6	8577
Hazor shall be a dwelling for *d*	Jer 49:33	8577
heaps, a dwelling place for *d*	Jer 51:37	8577
I will make a wailing like the *d*	Mic 1:8	8577
waste for the *d* of the wilderness	Mal 1:3	8568

DRAMS
talents and ten thousand *d*	1Chr 29:7	150
and one thousand *d* of gold	Ezr 2:69	1871
basons of gold, of a thousand *d*	Ezr 8:27	150
the treasure a thousand *d* of gold	Neh 7:70	1871
work twenty thousand *d* of gold	Neh 7:71	1871
was twenty thousand *d* of gold	Neh 7:72	1871

DRANK
he *d* of the wine, and was drunken	Gen 9:21	8354
so I *d*, and she made the camels	Gen 24:46	8354
and he brought him wine, and he *d*	Gen 27:25	8354
And they *d*, and were merry with him	Gen 43:34	8354
abundantly, and the congregation *d*	Num 20:11	8354
d the wine of their drink	Deut 32:38	8354
d of his own cup, and lay in his	2Sa 12:3	8354
bread in his house, and *d* water	1Kin 13:19	8354
and he *d* of the brook	1Kin 17:6	
meat, and of the wine which he *d*	Dan 1:5	4960
nor with the wine which he *d*	Dan 1:8	4960
d wine before the thousand	Dan 5:1	8355
and his concubines, in them *d*	Dan 5:3	8355
They *d* wine, and praised the gods	Dan 5:4	8355
and they all *d* of it	Mk 14:23	4095
They did eat, they *d*, they,	Lk 17:27	4095
they did eat, they *d*, they bought	Lk 17:28	4095
d thereof himself, and his	Jn 4:12	4095
for they *d* of that spiritual Rock	1Cor 10:4	4095

DRAUGHT
made it a *d* house unto this day	2Kin 10:27	4280
belly, and is cast out into the *d*	Mt 15:17	856
belly, and goeth out into the *d*	Mk 7:19	856
and let down your nets for a *d*	Lk 5:4	61
at the *d* of the fishes which they	Lk 5:9	61

DRAVE
wheels, that they *d* them heavily	Ex 14:25	5090
they *d* not out the Canaanites	Josh 16:10	3423
which *d* out from before you,	Josh 24:12	1644
the LORD *d* out from before us all	Josh 24:18	1644
he *d* out the inhabitants of the	Judg 1:19	3423
d them out from before you, and	Judg 6:9	1644

</td><td colspan="3">

which they *d* before those other	1Sa 30:20	5090
sons of Abinadab, *d* the new cart	2Sa 6:3	5090
Syria, and *d* the Jews from Elath	2Kin 16:6	5394
Jeroboam *d* Israel from following	2Kin 17:21	5071
and Uzza and Ahio *d* the cart	1Chr 13:7	5090
whom God *d* out before the face of	Acts 7:45	1856
he *d* them from the judgment seat	Acts 18:16	556

DRAW
time that women go out to *d* water	Gen 24:11	7579
of the city come out to *d* water	Gen 24:13	7579
I will *d* water for thy camels	Gen 24:19	7579
again unto the well to *d* water	Gen 24:20	7579
virgin cometh forth to *d* water	Gen 24:43	7579
I will also *d* for thy camels	Gen 24:44	7579
And he said, *D* not nigh hither	Ex 3:5	
them, *D* out and take you a lamb	Ex 12:21	4900
I will *d* my sword, my hand shall	Ex 15:9	7324
will *d* out a sword after you	Lev 26:33	7324
so that he could not *d* the dagger	Judg 3:22	8025
d toward mount Tabor, and take	Judg 4:6	4900
I will *d* unto thee to the river	Judg 4:7	4900
D thy sword, and slay me, that men	Judg 9:54	8025
let us *d* near to one of these	Judg 19:13	
d them from the city unto the	Judg 20:32	5423
maidens going out to *d* water	1Sa 9:11	7579
Let us *d* near hither unto God	1Sa 14:36	7579
D ye near hither, all the chief	1Sa 14:38	
D thy sword, and thrust me through	1Sa 31:4	8025
we will *d* it into the river,	2Sa 17:13	5498
D thy sword, and thrust me through	1Chr 10:4	8025
and every man shall *d* after him	Job 21:33	4900
he trusteth that he can *d* up	Job 40:23	1518
Canst thou *d* out leviathan with	Job 41:1	4900
D me not away with the wicked, and	Ps 28:3	4900
D out also the spear, and stop the	Ps 35:3	7324
D nigh unto my soul, and redeem it	Ps 69:18	
is good for me to *d* near to God	Ps 73:28	
wilt thou *d* out thine anger to	Ps 85:5	4900
they *d* near unto the gates of	Ps 107:18	
They *d* nigh that follow after	Ps 119:150	
of understanding will *d* it out	Prov 20:5	1802
come not, nor the years *d* nigh	Eccl 12:1	
D me, we will run after thee	Song 1:4	4900
Woe unto them that *d* iniquity	Is 5:18	4900
of the Holy One of Israel *d* nigh	Is 5:19	
ye *d* water out of the wells of	Is 12:3	7579
people *d* near me with their mouth	Is 29:13	
d near together, ye that are	Is 45:20	
But *d* near hither, ye sons of the	Is 57:3	
a wide mouth, and *d* out the tongue	Is 57:4	748
if thou *d* out thy soul to the	Is 58:10	6329
that *d* the bow, to Tubal, and	Is 66:19	4900
and I will cause him to *d* near	Jer 30:21	
and shield, and *d* near to battle	Jer 46:3	
of the flock shall *d* them out	Jer 49:20	5498
of the flock shall *d* them out	Jer 50:45	5498
the sea monsters *d* out the breast	Lam 4:3	2502
I will *d* out a sword after them	Eze 5:2	7324
I will *d* out a sword after them	Eze 5:12	7324
charge over the city to *d* near	Eze 9:1	
I will *d* out the sword after them	Eze 12:14	7324
will *d* forth my sword out of his	Eze 21:3	3318
hast caused thy days to *d* near	Eze 22:4	
they shall *d* their swords against	Eze 28:7	7324
they shall *d* their swords against	Eze 30:11	7324
d her and all her multitudes	Eze 32:20	4900
let all the men of war *d* near	Joel 3:9	
D thee waters for the siege,	Nah 3:14	7579
to *d* out fifty vessels out of the	Hag 2:16	2834
D out now, and bear unto the	Jn 2:8	501
a woman of Samaria to *d* water	Jn 4:7	501
Sir, thou hast nothing to *d* with	Jn 4:11	502
not, neither come hither to *d*	Jn 4:15	501
Father which hath sent me *d* him	Jn 6:44	1670
the earth, will *d* all men unto me	Jn 12:32	1670
now they were not able to *d* it	Jn 21:6	1670
to *d* away disciples after them	Acts 20:30	645
by the which we *d* nigh unto God	Heb 7:19	
Let us *d* near with a true heart	Heb 10:22	4334
but if any man *d* back, my soul	Heb 10:38	5288
of them who *d* back unto perdition	Heb 10:39	5289
d you before the judgment seats	Jas 2:6	1670
D nigh to God, and he will *d*	Jas 4:8	

DRAWER
thy wood unto the *d* of thy water	Deut 29:11	7579

DRAWERS
wood and *d* of water unto all the	Josh 9:21	7579
d of water for the house of my	Josh 9:23	7579
d of water for the congregation,	Josh 9:27	7579

</td></tr>
</table>

D

DRAWETH

the wife of the one *d* near for to.............Deut 25:11
now the day *d* toward evening, I.............Judg 19:9   7503
He *d* also the mighty with his.................Job 24:22   4900
his soul *d* near unto the grave, ...Job 33:22
when he *d* him into his net.....................Ps 10:9   4900
my life *d* nigh unto the grave..................Ps 88:3
that *d* near the time of her ....Is 26:17
The time is come, the day *d* near ....Eze 7:12
This people *d* nigh unto me with ....Mt 15:8
and the time *d* near ....Lk 21:8
for your redemption *d* nigh ....Lk 21:28
for the coming of the Lord *d* nigh ....Jas 5:8

DRAWING

archers in the places of *d* water ....Judg 5:11   4857
the sea, and *d* nigh unto the ship ....Jn 6:19   *1096*

DRAWN

way, and his sword *d* in his hand...........Num 22:23   8025
way, and his sword *d* in his hand...........Num 22:31   8025
and which hath not *d* in the yoke ....Deut 21:3   4900
not hear, but shalt be *d* away ....Deut 30:17   5080
him with his sword *d* in his hand ....Josh 5:13   8025
till we have *d* them from the city ....Josh 8:6   5423
were *d* away from the city ....Josh 8:16   5423
the border was *d* from the top of ....Josh 15:9   8388
and the border was *d* to Baalah ....Josh 15:9   8388
and the border was *d* to Shicron ....Josh 15:11   8388
And the border was *d* thence ....Josh 18:14   8388
was *d* from the north, and went.............Josh 18:17   8388
were *d* away from the city ....Judg 20:31   5423
that which the young men have *d* ....Ruth 2:9   7579
having a *d* sword in his hand 1Chr 21:16   8025
It is *d*, and cometh out of the ....Job 20:25   8025
The wicked *d* out the sword ....Ps 37:14   6605
than oil, yet were they *d* swords ....Ps 55:21   6609
them that are *d* unto death.....................Prov 24:11   3947
from the swords, from the *d* sword ....Is 21:15   5203
the milk, and *d* from the breasts ....Is 28:9   6267
with the burial of an ass, *d* ....Jer 22:19   5498
with lovingkindness have I *d* thee ....Jer 31:3   4900
he hath *d* back his right hand ....Lam 2:3   7725
have *d* forth my sword out of his ....Eze 21:5   3318
thou, The sword, the sword is *d* ....Eze 21:28   6605
all were *d* up again into heaven ....Acts 11:10   *385*
when he is *d* away of his own lust ....Jas 1:14   *1828*

DREAD

the *d* of you shall be upon every ....Gen 9:2   2844
Fear and *d* shall fall upon them............Ex 15:16   6343
D not, neither be afraid of them............Deut 1:29   6206
will I begin to put the *d* of thee ....Deut 2:25   6343
the *d* of you upon all the land ....Deut 11:25   4172
d not, nor be dismayed 1Chr 22:13   3372
and his *d* fall upon you ....Job 13:11   6343
let not thy *d* make me afraid ....Job 13:21   367
your fear, and let him be your *d* ....Is 8:13   6206

DREADFUL

and said, How *d* is this place ....Gen 28:17   3372
A *d* sound is in his ears..........................Job 15:21   6343
were so high that they were *d*................Eze 1:18   3374
and behold a fourth beast, *d* ....Dan 7:7   1763
from all the others, exceeding *d* ....Dan 7:19   1763
d God, keeping the covenant and ....Dan 9:4   3372
They are terrible and *d*..........................Hab 1:7   3372
my name is *d* among the heathen ....Mal 1:14   3372
of the great and *d* day of the LORD ....Mal 4:5   3372

DREAM

came to Abimelech in a *d* by night........Gen 20:3   2472
And God said unto him in a *d* ....Gen 20:6   2472
up mine eyes, and saw in a *d* ....Gen 31:10   2472
angel of God spake unto me in a *d* ....Gen 31:11   2472
Laban the Syrian in a *d* by night ....Gen 31:24   2472
And Joseph dreamed a *d*, and he told ....Gen 37:5   2472
this *d* which I have dreamed ....Gen 37:6   2472
And he dreamed yet another *d* ....Gen 37:9   2472
Behold, I have dreamed a *d* more..........Gen 37:9   2472
What is this *d* that thou hast.................Gen 37:10   2472
And they dreamed a *d* both of them ......Gen 40:5   2472
each man his *d* in one night ....Gen 40:5   2472
to the interpretation of his *d* ....Gen 40:5   2472
unto him, We have dreamed a *d* ....Gen 40:8   2472
chief butler told his *d* to Joseph ....Gen 40:9   2472
and said to him, In my *d* ....Gen 40:9   2472
unto Joseph, I also was in my *d*............Gen 40:16   2472
awoke, and, behold, it was a *d* ....Gen 41:7   2472
and Pharaoh told them his *d*..................Gen 41:8   2472
And we dreamed a *d* in one night ....Gen 41:11   2472
to the interpretation of his *d* ....Gen 41:11   2472
to his *d* he did interpret ....Gen 41:12   2472

unto Joseph, I have dreamed a *d*............Gen 41:15   2472
understand a *d* to interpret it ....Gen 41:15   2472
Pharaoh said unto Joseph, In my *d*........Gen 41:17   2472
And I saw in my *d*, and, behold, ...Gen 41:22   2472
Pharaoh, The *d* of Pharaoh is one ....Gen 41:26   2472
are seven years: the *d* is one ....Gen 41:26   2472
for that the *d* was doubled unto ....Gen 41:32   2472
and will speak unto him in a *d* ....Num 12:6   2472
man that told a *d* unto his fellow ....Judg 7:13   2472
and said, Behold, I dreamed a *d* ....Judg 7:13   2472
Gideon heard the telling of the *d* ....Judg 7:15   2472
to Solomon in a *d* by night 1Kin 3:5   2472
and, behold, it was a *d* 1Kin 3:15   2472
He shall fly away as a *d*, and ....Job 20:8   2472
In a *d*, in a vision of the night,...............Job 33:15   2472
As a *d* when one awaketh ....Ps 73:20   2472
of Zion, we were like them that *d* ....Ps 126:1   2472
For a *d* cometh through the ....Eccl 5:3   2472
shall be as a *d* of a night vision.............Is 29:7   2472
hath a *d*, let him tell a *d* ....Jer 23:28   2472
unto them, I have dreamed a *d* ....Dan 2:3   2472
spirit was troubled to know the *d* ....Dan 2:3   2472
tell thy servants the *d*, and we ....Dan 2:4   2493
will not make known unto me the *d* ......Dan 2:5   2493
But if ye shew the *d*, and the ....Dan 2:6   2493
therefore shew me the *d*, and the ....Dan 2:6   2493
the king tell his servants the *d* ....Dan 2:7   2493
will not make known unto me the *d* ......Dan 2:9   2493
therefore tell me the *d*, and I ....Dan 2:9   2493
unto me the *d* which I have seen ....Dan 2:26   2493
Thy *d*, and the visions of thy head ....Dan 2:28   2493
This is the *d*; and we will.......................Dan 2:36   2493
and the *d* is certain, and the ....Dan 2:45   2493
I saw a *d* which made me afraid, ...Dan 4:5   2493
me the interpretation of the *d* ....Dan 4:6   2493
and I told the *d* before them ....Dan 4:7   2493
and before him I told the *d* ....Dan 4:8   2493
visions of my *d* that I have seen ....Dan 4:9   2493
This *d* I king Nebuchadnezzar have.......Dan 4:18   2493
said, Belteshazzar, let not the *d*............Dan 4:19   2493
the *d* be to them that hate thee, ...Dan 4:19   2493
king of Babylon Daniel had a *d* ....Dan 7:1   2493
then he wrote the *d*, and told the...........Dan 7:1   2493
your old men shall *d* dreams..................Joel 2:28   2492
the Lord appeared unto him in a *d* ....Mt 1:20   3677
being warned of God in a *d* that ....Mt 2:12   3677
Lord appeareth to Joseph in a *d*............Mt 2:13   3677
in a *d* to Joseph in Egypt ....Mt 2:19   3677
being warned of God in a *d* ....Mt 2:22   3677
this day in a *d* because of him................Mt 27:19   3677
and your old men shall *d* dreams ....Acts 2:17   *1798*

DREAMED

And he *d*, and behold a ladder set........Gen 28:12   2492
Joseph *d* a dream, and he told it............Gen 37:5   2492
you, this dream which I have *d* ....Gen 37:6   2492
he *d* yet another dream, and told ....Gen 37:9   2492
Behold, I have *d* a dream more..............Gen 37:9   2492
is this dream that thou hast *d* ....Gen 37:10   2492
they *d* a dream both of them, each ....Gen 40:5   2492
said unto him, We have *d* a dream ....Gen 40:8   2492
of two full years, that Pharaoh *d* ....Gen 41:1   2492
And he slept and *d* the second time ......Gen 41:5   2492
we *d* a dream in one night, I and............Gen 41:11   2492
we *d* each man according to the ....Gen 41:11   2492
I have *d* a dream, and there is ....Gen 41:15   2492
the dreams which he *d* of them ....Gen 42:9   2492
I *d* a dream, and, lo, a cake of ....Judg 7:13   2492
saying, I have *d*, I have *d* ....Jer 23:25   2492
dreams which ye cause to be *d* ....Jer 29:8   2492
Nebuchadnezzar *d* dreams, ...Dan 2:1   2492
I have a dream, and my spirit ....Dan 2:3   2492

DREAMER

to another, Behold, this *d* cometh ...Gen 37:19   1167,2472
or a *d* of dreams, and giveth thee ....Deut 13:1   2492
that prophet, or that *d* of dreams ....Deut 13:3   2492
or that *d* of dreams, shall be put ....Deut 13:5   2492

DREAMERS

to your diviners, nor to your *d* ....Jer 27:9   2492
these filthy *d* defile the flesh ....Jude 8   *1797*

DREAMETH

even be as when an hungry man *d* ....Is 29:8   2492
or as when a thirsty man *d*.....................Is 29:8   2492

DREAMS

hated him yet the more for his *d* ....Gen 37:8   2472
see what will become of his *d* ....Gen 37:20   2472
and he interpreted to us our *d* ....Gen 41:12   2472
Joseph remembered the *d* which he ......Gen 42:9   2472
you a prophet, or a dreamer of *d*............Deut 13:1   2472

prophet, or that dreamer of *d*	Deut 13:3	2472
prophet, or that dreamer of *d*	Deut 13:5	2472
answered him not, neither by *d*	1Sa 28:6	2472
neither by prophets, nor by *d*	1Sa 28:15	2472
Then thou scarest me with *d*	Job 7:14	2472
For in the multitude of *d*	Eccl 5:7	2472
to forget my name by their *d*	Jer 23:27	2472
them that prophesy false *d*	Jer 23:32	2472
neither hearken to your *d* which	Jer 29:8	2472
understanding in all visions and *d*	Dan 1:17	2472
Nebuchadnezzar dreamed *d*	Dan 2:1	2472
for to shew the king his *d*	Dan 2:2	2472
understanding, interpreting of *d*	Dan 5:12	2493
your old men shall dream *d*	Joel 2:28	2472
seen a lie, and have told false *d*	Zec 10:2	2472
and your old men shall dream *d*	Acts 2:17	1797

DREGS

but the *d* thereof, all the wicked	Ps 75:8	8105
thou hast drunken the *d* of the	Is 51:17	6907
even the *d* of the cup of my fury	Is 51:22	6907

DRESS

into the garden of Eden to *d* it	Gen 2:15	5647
and he hasted to *d* it	Gen 18:7	6213
d them, but shalt neither drink	Deut 28:39	5647
to *d* for the wayfaring man that	2Sa 12:4	6213
d the meat in my sight, that I	2Sa 13:5	6213
Amnon's house, and *d* him meat	2Sa 13:7	6213
d it for me and my son, that we	1Kin 17:12	6213
I will *d* the other bullock, and	1Kin 18:23	6213
for yourselves, and *d* it first	1Kin 18:25	6213

DRESSED

milk, and the calf which he had *d*	Gen 18:8	6213
all that is *d* in the fryingpan,	Lev 7:9	6213
of wine, and five sheep ready *d*	1Sa 25:18	6213
d it for the man that was come to	2Sa 12:4	6213
king, and had neither *d* his feet	2Sa 19:24	6213
was given them, and they *d* it	1Kin 18:26	6213
meet for them by whom it is *d*	Heb 6:7	1090

DRESSER

he unto the *d* of his vineyard	Lk 13:7	289

DRESSERS

vine in the mountains, and in	2Chr 26:10	3755

DRESSETH

when he *d* the lamps, he shall	Ex 30:7	3190

DREW

And Abraham *d* near, and said, Wilt	Gen 18:23	
water, and *d* for all his camels	Gen 24:20	8025
down unto the well, and *d* water	Gen 24:45	7579
and they *d* and lifted up Joseph out	Gen 37:28	4900
as he *d* back his hand, that,	Gen 38:29	7725
the time *d* nigh that Israel must	Gen 47:29	
Because I *d* him out of the water,	Ex 2:10	4871
d water, and filled the troughs to	Ex 2:16	1802
also *d* water enough for us, and	Ex 2:19	1802
And when Pharaoh *d* nigh, the	Ex 14:10	
Moses *d* near unto the thick	Ex 20:21	
and all the congregation *d* near	Lev 9:5	
d nigh, and came before the city,	Josh 8:11	
For Joshua *d* not his hand back,	Josh 8:26	7725
twenty thousand men that *d* sword	Judg 8:10	8025
But the youth *d* not his sword	Judg 8:20	8025
thousand footmen that *d* sword	Judg 20:2	8025
and six thousand men that *d* sword	Judg 20:15	8025
hundred thousand men that *d* sword	Judg 20:17	8025
all these *d* the sword	Judg 20:25	8025
all these *d* the sword	Judg 20:35	8025
liers in wait *d* themselves along	Judg 20:37	4900
thousand men that *d* the sword	Judg 20:46	8025
So he *d* off his shoe	Ruth 4:8	8025
d water, and poured it out before	1Sa 7:6	7579
the Philistines *d* near to battle	1Sa 7:10	
Then Saul *d* near to Samuel in the	1Sa 9:18	
And the Philistine *d* near morning	1Sa 17:16	
he *d* near to the Philistine	1Sa 17:40	
came on and *d* near unto David	1Sa 17:41	
d nigh to meet David, that David	1Sa 17:48	
d it out of the sheath thereof,	1Sa 17:51	8025
And Joab *d* nigh, and the people	2Sa 10:13	
And he came apace, and *d* near	2Sa 18:25	
he *d* me out of many waters	2Sa 22:17	4871
d water out of the well of	2Sa 23:16	7579
valiant men that *d* the sword	2Sa 24:9	8025
Now the days of David *d* nigh that	1Kin 2:1	
they *d* out the staves, that the	1Kin 8:8	748
a certain man *d* a bow at a	1Kin 22:34	4900
seven hundred men that *d* swords	2Kin 3:26	8025
Jehu *d* a bow with his full	2Kin 9:24	

d water out of the well of	1Chr 11:18	7579
d nigh before the Syrians unto	1Chr 19:14	
d forth the Syrians that were	1Chr 19:16	3318
hundred thousand men that *d* sword	1Chr 21:5	8025
and ten thousand men that *d* sword	1Chr 21:5	8025
they *d* out the staves of the ark,	2Chr 5:9	748
d bows, two hundred and fourscore	2Chr 14:8	1869
a certain man *d* a bow at a	2Chr 18:33	4900
So Esther *d* near, and touched the	Est 5:2	
his decree *d* near to be put in	Est 9:1	
he *d* me out of many waters	Ps 18:16	4871
were afraid, *d* near, and came	Is 41:5	
So they *d* up Jeremiah with cords,	Jer 38:13	4900
I *d* them with cords of a man,	Hos 11:4	4900
she *d* not near to her God	Zeph 3:2	
they *d* to shore, and sat down, and	Mt 13:48	307
when they *d* nigh unto Jerusalem,	Mt 21:1	
when the time of the fruit *d* near	Mt 21:34	
d his sword, and struck a servant	Mt 26:51	645
of Gennesaret, and *d* to the shore	Mk 6:53	4358
of them that stood by *d* a sword	Mk 14:47	4685
Then *d* near unto him all the	Lk 15:1	
d nigh to the house, he heard	Lk 15:25	
feast of unleavened bread *d* nigh	Lk 22:1	
d near unto Jesus to kiss him	Lk 22:47	
preparation, and the sabbath *d* on	Lk 23:54	2020
and reasoned, Jesus himself *d* near	Lk 24:15	
they *d* nigh unto the village,	Lk 24:28	
servants which *d* the water knew	Jn 2:9	501
Simon Peter having a sword *d* it	Jn 18:10	1670
d the net to land full of great	Jn 21:11	1670
d away much people after him	Acts 5:37	868
the time of the promise *d* nigh	Acts 7:17	
as he *d* near to behold it, the	Acts 7:31	4334
d nigh unto the city, Peter went	Acts 10:9	
d him out of the city, supposing	Acts 14:19	4951
d them into the marketplace unto	Acts 16:19	1670
he *d* out his sword, and would have	Acts 16:27	4685
they *d* Jason and certain brethren	Acts 17:6	4951
they *d* Alexander out of the	Acts 19:33	4264
Paul, and *d* him out of the temple	Acts 21:30	1670
that they *d* near to some country	Acts 27:27	4317
his tail *d* the third part of the	Rev 12:4	4951

DREWEST

Thou *d* near in the day that I	Lam 3:57	

DRIED

were *d* up from off the earth	Gen 8:7	3001
the waters were *d* up from off the	Gen 8:13	2717
day of the month, was the earth *d*	Gen 8:14	3001
green ears of corn *d* by the fire	Lev 2:14	7033
nor eat moist grapes, or *d*	Num 6:3	3002
But now our soul is *d* away	Num 11:6	3001
For we have heard how the LORD *d*	Josh 2:10	3001
For the LORD your God *d* up the	Josh 4:23	3001
which he *d* up from before us,	Josh 4:23	3001
heard that the LORD had *d* up the	Josh 5:1	3001
green withs that were never *d*	Judg 16:7	2717
green withs which had not been *d*	Judg 16:8	2717
d up, so that he could not pull	1Kin 13:4	3001
a while, that the brook *d* up	1Kin 17:7	3001
I *d* up all the rivers of besieged	2Kin 19:24	2717
His roots shall be *d* up beneath	Job 18:16	3001
they are *d* up, they are gone away	Job 28:4	1809
My strength is *d* up like a	Ps 22:15	3001
my throat is *d*	Ps 69:3	2787
the Red sea also, and it was *d* up	Ps 106:9	2717
their multitude *d* up with thirst	Is 5:13	6704
the river shall be wasted and *d* up	Is 19:5	3001
defence shall be emptied and *d* up	Is 19:6	2717
have I *d* up all the rivers of the	Is 37:25	2717
thou not it which hath *d* the sea	Is 51:10	2717
places of the wilderness are *d* up	Jer 23:10	3001
and they shall be *d* up	Jer 50:38	3001
have *d* up the green tree, and have	Eze 17:24	3001
and the east wind *d* up her fruit	Eze 19:12	3001
behold, they say, Our bones are *d*	Eze 37:11	3001
is smitten, their root is *d* up	Hos 9:16	3001
and his fountain shall be *d* up	Hos 13:15	2717
the new wine is *d* up, the oil	Joel 1:10	3001
The vine is *d* up, and the fig tree	Joel 1:12	3001
for the rivers of waters are *d* up	Joel 1:20	3001
his arm shall be clean *d* up	Zec 11:17	3001
fountain of her blood was *d* up	Mk 5:29	3583
the fig tree *d* up from the roots	Mk 11:20	3583
and the water thereof was *d* up	Rev 16:12	3583

DRIEDST

thou *d* up mighty rivers	Ps 74:15	3001

DRIETH

and the flood decayeth and *d* up	Job 14:11	3001
but a broken spirit *d* the bones	Prov 17:22	3001
it dry, and *d* up all the rivers	Nah 1:4	3001

DRINK

let us make our father *d* wine	Gen 19:32	8248
their father *d* wine that night	Gen 19:33	8248
let us make him *d* wine this night	Gen 19:34	8248
father *d* wine that night also	Gen 19:35	8248
with water, and gave the lad *d*	Gen 21:19	8248
I pray thee, that I may *d*	Gen 24:14	8354
and she shall say, D	Gen 24:14	8354
and I will give thy camels *d* also	Gen 24:14	8248
d a little water of thy pitcher	Gen 24:17	1572
And she said, D, my lord	Gen 24:18	8354
upon her hand, and gave him *d*	Gen 24:18	8248
And when she had done giving him *d*	Gen 24:19	8248
little water of thy pitcher to *d*	Gen 24:43	8248
And she say to me, Both *d* thou	Gen 24:44	8354
and I said unto her, Let me *d*	Gen 24:45	8248
from her shoulder, and said, D	Gen 24:46	8354
and I will give thy camels *d* also	Gen 24:46	8248
and she made the camels *d* also	Gen 24:46	8354
And they did eat and *d*, he and the	Gen 24:54	8354
and he did eat and *d*, and rose up,	Gen 25:34	8354
a feast, and they did eat and *d*	Gen 26:30	8354
troughs when the flocks came to *d*	Gen 30:38	8354
conceive when they came to *d*	Gen 30:38	8354
he poured a *d* offering thereon,	Gen 35:14	5262
to *d* of the water of the river	Ex 7:18	8354
the Egyptians could not *d* of the	Ex 7:21	8354
about the river for water to *d*	Ex 7:24	8354
for they could not *d* of the water	Ex 7:24	8354
they could not *d* of the waters of	Ex 15:23	8354
Moses, saying, What shall we *d*	Ex 15:24	8354
was no water for the people to *d*	Ex 17:1	8354
said, Give us water that we may *d*	Ex 17:2	8354
out of it, that the people may *d*	Ex 17:6	8354
they saw God, and did eat and *d*	Ex 24:11	8354
an hin of wine for a *d* offering	Ex 29:40	5262
to the *d* offering thereof	Ex 29:41	5262
shall ye pour *d* offering thereon	Ex 30:9	5262
people sat down to eat and to *d*	Ex 32:6	8354
the children of Israel *d* of it	Ex 32:20	8248
neither eat bread, nor *d* water	Ex 34:28	8354
Do not *d* wine nor strong *d*,	Lev 10:9	8354
Do not *d* wine nor strong *d*	Lev 10:9	7941
all *d* that may be drunk in every	Lev 11:34	4945
the *d* offering thereof shall be	Lev 23:13	5262
their *d* offerings, even an	Lev 23:18	5262
d offerings, every thing upon his	Lev 23:37	5262
he shall cause the woman to *d* the	Num 5:24	8248
cause the woman to *d* the water	Num 5:26	8248
he hath made her to *d* the water	Num 5:27	8248
himself from wine and strong *d*	Num 6:3	7941
shall *d* no vinegar of wine, or	Num 6:3	8354
of wine, or vinegar of strong *d*	Num 6:3	7941
neither shall he *d* any liquor of	Num 6:3	8354
offering, and their *d* offerings	Num 6:15	5262
meat offering, and his *d* offering	Num 6:17	5262
that the Nazarite may *d* wine	Num 6:20	8354
a *d* offering shalt thou prepare	Num 15:5	5262
for a *d* offering thou shalt offer	Num 15:7	5262
thou shalt bring for a *d* offering	Num 15:10	5262
his *d* offering, according to the	Num 15:24	5262
neither is there any water to *d*	Num 20:5	8354
congregation and their beasts *d*	Num 20:8	8248
neither will we *d* of the water of	Num 20:17	8354
my cattle *d* of thy water, then I	Num 20:19	8354
we will not *d* of the waters of	Num 21:22	8354
prey, and *d* the blood of the slain	Num 23:24	8354
the *d* offering thereof shall be	Num 28:7	5262
unto the LORD for a *d* offering	Num 28:7	5262
as the *d* offering thereof, thou	Num 28:8	5262
oil, and the *d* offering thereof	Num 28:9	5262
burnt offering, and his *d* offering	Num 28:10	5262
their *d* offerings shall be half	Num 28:14	5262
burnt offering, and his *d* offering	Num 28:15	5262
burnt offering, and his *d* offering	Num 28:24	5262
blemish) and their *d* offerings	Num 28:31	5262
their *d* offerings, according unto	Num 29:6	5262
of it, and their *d* offerings	Num 29:11	5262
meat offering, and his *d* offering	Num 29:16	5262
their *d* offerings for the	Num 29:18	5262
thereof, and their *d* offerings	Num 29:19	5262
their *d* offerings for the	Num 29:21	5262
meat offering, and his *d* offering	Num 29:22	5262
their *d* offerings for the	Num 29:24	5262
meat offering, and his *d* offering	Num 29:25	5262
their *d* offerings for the	Num 29:27	5262

meat offering, and his *d* offering	Num 29:28	5262
their *d* offerings for the	Num 29:30	5262
meat offering, and his *d* offering	Num 29:31	5262
their *d* offerings for the	Num 29:33	5262
meat offering, and his *d* offering	Num 29:34	5262
their *d* offerings for the	Num 29:37	5262
meat offering, and his *d* offering	Num 29:38	5262
for your *d* offerings, and for your	Num 29:39	5262
was no water for the people to *d*	Num 33:14	8354
of them for money, that ye may *d*	Deut 2:6	8354
me water for money, that I may *d*	Deut 2:28	8354
neither did eat bread nor *d* water	Deut 9:9	8354
nor *d* water, because of all your	Deut 9:18	8354
or for wine, or for strong *d*	Deut 14:26	7941
but shalt neither *d* of the wine	Deut 28:39	8354
have ye drunk wine or strong *d*	Deut 29:6	7941
thou didst *d* the pure blood of	Deut 32:14	8354
the wine of their *d* offerings	Deut 32:38	5257
I pray thee, a little water to *d*	Judg 4:19	8248
a bottle of milk, and gave him *d*	Judg 4:19	8248
boweth down upon his knees to *d*	Judg 7:5	8354
down upon their knees to *d* water	Judg 7:6	8354
of their god, and did eat and *d*	Judg 9:27	8354
d not wine nor strong *d*	Judg 13:4	8354
and *d* not wine nor strong *d*	Judg 13:4	7941
now *d* no wine nor strong	Judg 13:7	7941
no wine nor strong *d*	Judg 13:7	8354
neither let her *d* wine or strong	Judg 13:14	8354
let her *d* wine or strong *d*	Judg 13:14	7941
so they did eat and *d*, and lodged	Judg 19:4	8354
eat and *d* both of them together	Judg 19:6	8354
their feet, and did eat and *d*	Judg 19:21	8354
d of that which the young men	Ruth 2:9	8354
drunken neither wine nor strong *d*	1Sa 1:15	7941
and they made him *d* water	1Sa 30:11	8248
into mine house, to eat and to *d*	2Sa 11:11	8354
him, he did eat and *d* before him	2Sa 11:13	8354
be faint in the wilderness may *d*	2Sa 16:2	8354
taste what I eat or what I *d*	2Sa 19:35	8354
Oh that one would give me *d* of	2Sa 23:15	8248
he would not *d* thereof, but	2Sa 23:16	8354
therefore he would not *d* it	2Sa 23:17	8354
d before him, and say, God save	1Kin 1:25	8354
bread nor *d* water in this place	1Kin 13:8	8354
nor *d* water, nor turn again by	1Kin 13:9	8354
neither will I eat bread nor *d*	1Kin 13:16	8354
eat no bread nor *d* water there	1Kin 13:17	8354
that he may eat bread and *d* water	1Kin 13:18	8354
thee, Eat no bread, and *d* no water	1Kin 13:22	8354
that thou shalt *d* of the brook	1Kin 17:4	8354
water in a vessel, that I may *d*	1Kin 17:10	8354
unto Ahab, Get thee up, eat and *d*	1Kin 18:41	8354
So Ahab went up to eat and to *d*	1Kin 18:42	8354
And he did eat and *d*, and laid him	1Kin 19:6	8354
And he arose, and did eat and *d*	1Kin 19:8	8354
filled with water, that ye may *d*	2Kin 3:17	8354
them, that they may eat and *d*	2Kin 6:22	8354
into one tent, and did eat and *d*	2Kin 7:8	8354
he was come in, he did eat and *d*	2Kin 9:34	8354
and poured his *d* offering	2Kin 16:13	5262
offering, and their *d* offerings	2Kin 16:15	5262
d their own piss with you	2Kin 18:27	8354
d ye every one the waters of his	2Kin 18:31	8354
Oh that one would give me *d* of	1Chr 11:17	8248
but David would not *d* of it	1Chr 11:18	8354
shall I *d* the blood of these men	1Chr 11:19	8354
Therefore he would not *d* it	1Chr 11:19	8354
lambs, with their *d* offerings	1Chr 29:21	5262
d before the LORD on that day	1Chr 29:22	8353
them, and gave them to eat and to *d*	2Chr 28:15	8248
the *d* offerings for every burnt	2Chr 29:35	5262
and meat, and, and *d*, and oil, unto them	Ezr 3:7	4960
their *d* offerings, and offer them	Ezr 7:17	5261
he did eat no bread, nor *d* water	Ezr 10:6	8354
d the sweet, and send portions	Neh 8:10	8354
went their way to eat, and to *d*	Neh 8:12	8354
they gave them *d* in vessels of	Est 1:7	8248
the king and Haman sat down to *d*	Est 3:15	8354
and neither eat nor *d* three days	Est 4:16	8354
sisters to eat and to *d* with them	Job 1:4	8354
he shall *d* of the wrath of the	Job 21:20	8354
not given water to the weary to *d*	Job 22:7	8248
their *d* offerings of blood will I	Ps 16:4	5262
thou shalt make them *d* of the	Ps 36:8	8248
of bulls, or *d* the blood of goats	Ps 50:13	8354
thou hast made us to *d* the wine	Ps 60:3	8248
thirst they gave me vinegar to *d*	Ps 69:21	8248
shall wring them out, and *d* them	Ps 75:8	8354
gave them *d* as out of the great	Ps 78:15	8248
floods, that they could not *d*	Ps 78:44	8354
them tears to *d* in great measure	Ps 80:5	8248

mingled my *d* with weeping,	Ps 102:9	8249
They give *d* to every beast of the	Ps 104:11	8248
He shall *d* of the brook in the	Ps 110:7	8354
and *d* the wine of violence	Prov 4:17	8354
D waters out of thine own cistern	Prov 5:15	8354
d of the wine which I have	Prov 9:5	8354
is a mocker, strong *d* is raging	Prov 20:1	7941
Eat and *d*, saith he to thee	Prov 23:7	8354
be thirsty, give him water to *d*	Prov 25:21	8248
it is not for kings to *d* wine	Prov 31:4	8354
nor for princes strong *d*	Prov 31:4	7941
Lest they *d*, and forget the law,	Prov 31:5	8354
Give strong *d* unto him that is	Prov 31:6	7941
Let him *d*, and forget his poverty,	Prov 31:7	8354
man, than that he should eat and *d*	Eccl 2:24	8354
that every man should eat and *d*	Eccl 3:13	8354
and comely for one to eat and to *d*	Eccl 5:18	8354
the sun, than to eat, and to *d*	Eccl 8:15	8354
d thy wine with a merry heart	Eccl 9:7	8354
d, yea, *d* abundantly, O	Song 5:1	8354
yea, *d* abundantly, O beloved	Song 5:1	7937
I would cause thee to *d* of spiced	Song 8:2	8248
that they may follow strong *d*	Is 5:11	7941
them that are mighty to *d* wine	Is 5:22	8354
of strength to mingle strong *d*	Is 5:22	7941
watch in the watchtower, eat, *d*	Is 21:5	8354
let us eat and *d*	Is 22:13	8354
They shall not *d* wine with a song	Is 24:9	8354
strong *d* shall be bitter to them	Is 24:9	7941
shall be bitter to them that *d* it	Is 24:9	8354
through strong *d* are out of the	Is 28:7	7941
have erred through strong *d*	Is 28:7	7941
out of the way through strong *d*	Is 28:7	7941
stagger, but not with strong *d*	Is 29:9	7941
he will cause the *d* of the	Is 32:6	4945
d their own piss with you	Is 36:12	8354
d ye every one the waters of his	Is 36:16	8354
to give *d* to my people, my chosen	Is 43:20	8248
thou shalt no more *d* it again	Is 51:22	8354
will fill ourselves with strong *d*	Is 56:12	7941
hast thou poured a *d* offering	Is 57:6	5262
the stranger shall not *d* thy wine	Is 62:8	8354
have brought it together shall *d*	Is 62:9	8354
that furnish *d* offering unto	Is 65:11	4469
behold, my servants shall *d*	Is 65:13	8354
Egypt, to *d* the waters of Sihor	Jer 2:18	8354
to *d* the waters of the river	Jer 2:18	8354
to pour out *d* offerings unto	Jer 7:18	5262
and given us water of gall to *d*	Jer 8:14	8248
and give them water of gall to *d*	Jer 9:15	8248
d for their father or for their	Jer 16:7	8248
to sit with them to eat and to *d*	Jer 16:8	8354
have poured out *d* offerings unto	Jer 19:13	5262
did not thy father eat and *d*	Jer 22:15	8354
make them *d* the water of gall	Jer 23:15	8354
to whom I send thee, to *d* it	Jer 25:15	8248
And they shall *d*, and be moved, and	Jer 25:16	8354
and made all the nations to *d*	Jer 25:17	8248
of Sheshach shall *d* after them	Jer 25:26	8354
take the cup at thine hand to *d*	Jer 25:28	8354
Ye shall certainly *d*	Jer 25:28	8354
poured out *d* offerings unto other	Jer 32:29	5262
chambers, and give them wine to *d*	Jer 35:2	8248
and I said unto them, D ye wine	Jer 35:5	8354
But they said, We will *d* no wine	Jer 35:6	8354
us, saying, Ye shall *d* no wine	Jer 35:6	8354
to *d* no wine all our days, we,	Jer 35:8	8354
commanded his sons not to *d* wine	Jer 35:14	8354
for unto this day they *d* none	Jer 35:14	8354
to pour out *d* offerings unto her,	Jer 44:17	5262
to pour out *d* offerings unto her,	Jer 44:18	5262
poured out *d* offerings unto her,	Jer 44:19	5262
pour out *d* offerings unto her,	Jer 44:19	5262
to pour out *d* offerings unto her	Jer 44:25	5262
to *d* of the cup have assuredly	Jer 49:12	8354
but thou shalt surely *d* of it	Jer 49:12	8354
Thou shalt *d* also water by	Eze 4:11	8354
from time to time shalt thou *d*	Eze 4:11	8354
they shall *d* water by measure, and	Eze 4:16	8354
d thy water with trembling and	Eze 12:18	8354
d their water with astonishment,	Eze 12:19	8354
out there their *d* offerings	Eze 20:28	5262
Thou shalt *d* of thy sister's cup	Eze 23:32	8354
Thou shalt even *d* it and suck it	Eze 23:34	8354
fruit, and they shall *d* thy milk	Eze 25:4	8354
in their height, all that *d* water	Eze 31:14	8354
best of Lebanon, all that *d* water	Eze 31:16	8354
they *d* that which ye have fouled	Eze 34:19	8354
that ye may eat flesh, and *d* blood	Eze 39:17	8354
d the blood of the princes of the	Eze 39:18	8354

d blood till ye be drunken, of my	Eze 39:19	8354
Neither shall any priest *d* wine	Eze 44:21	8354
d offerings, in the feasts, and in	Eze 45:17	5262
appointed your meat and your *d*	Dan 1:10	4960
us pulse to eat, and water to *d*	Dan 1:12	8354
and the wine that they should *d*	Dan 1:16	4960
his concubines, might *d* therein	Dan 5:2	8355
wool and my flax, mine oil and my *d*	Hos 2:5	8250
Their *d* is sour	Hos 4:18	5435
the *d* offering is cut off from	Joel 1:9	5262
the *d* offering is withholden from	Joel 1:13	5262
a *d* offering unto the LORD your	Joel 2:14	5262
girl for wine, that they might *d*	Joel 3:3	8354
they *d* the wine of the condemned	Amos 2:8	8354
ye gave the Nazarites wine to *d*	Amos 2:12	8248
their masters, Bring, and let us *d*	Amos 4:1	8354
unto one city, to *d* water	Amos 4:8	8354
but ye shall not *d* wine of them	Amos 5:11	8354
That *d* wine in bowls, and anoint	Amos 6:6	8354
vineyards, and *d* the wine thereof	Amos 9:14	8354
d continually, yea, they shall *d*	Obad 16	8354
let them not feed, nor *d* water	Jonah 3:7	8354
unto thee of wine and of strong *d*	Mic 2:11	7941
sweet wine, but shalt not *d* wine	Mic 6:15	8354
him that giveth his neighbour *d*	Hab 2:15	8248
d thou also, and let thy foreskin	Hab 2:16	8354
but not *d* the wine thereof	Zeph 1:13	8354
ye *d*, but ye are not filled with	Hag 1:6	8354
but ye are not filled with *d*	Hag 1:6	7937
when ye did eat, and when ye did *d*	Zec 7:6	8354
yourselves, and *d* for yourselves	Zec 7:6	8354
and they shall *d*, and make a noise	Zec 9:15	8354
ye shall eat, or what ye shall *d*	Mt 6:25	4095
or, What shall we *d*	Mt 6:31	4095
whosoever shall give to *d* unto	Mt 10:42	4222
of the cup that I shall *d*	Mt 20:22	4095
Ye shall *d* indeed of my cup, and	Mt 20:23	4095
and to eat and *d* with the drunken	Mt 24:49	4095
I was thirsty, and ye gave me *d*	Mt 25:35	4222
or thirsty, and gave thee *d*	Mt 25:37	4222
I was thirsty, and ye gave me no *d*	Mt 25:42	4222
to them, saying, D ye all of it	Mt 26:27	4095
I will not *d* henceforth of this	Mt 26:29	4095
until that day when I *d* it new	Mt 26:29	4095
pass away from me, except I *d* it	Mt 26:42	4095
vinegar to *d* mingled with gall	Mt 27:34	4095
tasted thereof, he would not *d*	Mt 27:34	4095
it on a reed, and gave him to *d*	Mt 27:48	4095
a cup of water to *d* in my name	Mk 9:41	4222
can ye *d* of the cup that I *d*	Mk 10:38	4095
d of the cup that I *d* of	Mk 10:39	4095
I will *d* no more of the fruit of	Mk 14:25	4095
until that day that I *d* it new in	Mk 14:25	4095
they gave him to *d* wine mingled	Mk 15:23	4095
it on a reed, and gave him to *d*	Mk 15:36	4222
if they *d* any deadly thing, it	Mk 16:18	4095
shall *d* neither wine nor strong	Lk 1:15	4095
neither wine nor strong *d*	Lk 1:15	4608
d with publicans and sinners	Lk 5:30	4095
but thine eat and *d*	Lk 5:33	4095
take thine ease, eat, *d*, and be	Lk 12:19	4095
ye shall eat, or what ye shall *d*	Lk 12:29	4095
and maidens, and to eat and *d*	Lk 12:45	4095
and afterward thou shalt eat and *d*	Lk 17:8	4095
I will not *d* of the fruit of the	Lk 22:18	4095
d at my table in my kingdom, and	Lk 22:30	4095
saith unto her, Give me to *d*	Jn 4:7	4095
thou, being a Jew, askest *d* of me	Jn 4:9	4095
that saith to thee, Give me to *d*	Jn 4:10	4095
d his blood, ye have no life in	Jn 6:53	4095
indeed, and my blood is *d* indeed	Jn 6:55	4213
let him come unto me, and *d*	Jn 7:37	4095
hath given me, shall I not *d* it	Jn 18:11	4095
sight, and neither did eat nor *d*	Acts 9:9	4095
d with him after he rose from the	Acts 10:41	4844
nor *d* till they had killed Paul	Acts 23:12	4095
nor *d* till they have killed him	Acts 23:21	4095
if he thirst, give him *d*	Rom 12:20	4222
kingdom of God is not meat and *d*	Rom 14:17	4213
to eat flesh, nor to *d* wine	Rom 14:21	4095
Have we not power to eat and to *d*	1Cor 9:4	4095
all *d* the same spiritual *d*	1Cor 10:4	4095
all *d* the same spiritual *d*	1Cor 10:4	4188
The people sat down to eat and *d*	1Cor 10:7	4095
Ye cannot *d* the cup of the Lord,	1Cor 10:21	4095
Whether therefore ye eat, or *d*	1Cor 10:31	4095
ye not houses to eat and to *d* in	1Cor 11:22	4095
this do ye, as oft as ye *d* it	1Cor 11:25	4095
d this cup, ye do shew the Lord's	1Cor 11:26	4095
bread, and *d* this cup of the Lord,	1Cor 11:27	4095
of that bread, and *d* of that cup.	1Cor 11:28	4095

D

all made to *d* into one Spirit	1Cor 12:13	4222
let us eat and *d*	1Cor 15:32	4095
judge you in meat, or in *d*	Col 2:16	4213
D no longer water, but use a	1Ti 5:23	5202
because she made all nations *d* of	Rev 14:8	4222
The same shall *d* of the wine of	Rev 14:10	4095
thou hast given them blood to *d*	Rev 16:6	4095

DRINKERS
all ye *d* of wine, because of the	Joel 1:5	8354

DRINKETH
Is not this it in which my lord *d*	Gen 44:5	8354
d water of the rain of heaven	Deut 11:11	8354
the poison whereof *d* up my spirit	Job 6:4	8354
which *d* iniquity like water	Job 15:16	8354
who *d* up scorning like water	Job 34:7	8354
he *d* up a river, and hasteth not	Job 40:23	6231
cutteth off the feet, and *d* damage	Prov 26:6	8354
man dreameth, and, behold, he *d*	Is 29:8	8354
he *d* no water, and is faint	Is 44:12	8354
d with publicans and sinners	Mk 2:16	4095
Whosoever *d* of this water shall	Jn 4:13	4095
But whosoever *d* of the water that	Jn 4:14	4095
d my blood, hath eternal life	Jn 6:54	4095
d my blood, dwelleth in me, and I	Jn 6:56	4095
d unworthily, eateth and	1Cor 11:29	4095
For the earth which *d* in the rain	Heb 6:7	4095

DRINKING
also, until they have done *d*	Gen 24:19	8354
to pass, as the camels had done *d*	Gen 24:22	8354
he shall have done eating and *d*	Ruth 3:3	8354
upon all the earth, eating and *d*	1Sa 30:16	8354
the sea in multitude, eating and *d*	1Kin 4:20	8354
all king Solomon's *d* vessels were	1Kin 10:21	4945
d himself drunk in the house of	1Kin 16:9	8354
heard this message, as he was *d*	1Kin 20:12	8354
But Ben-hadad was *d* himself drunk	1Kin 20:16	8354
David three days, eating and *d*	1Chr 12:39	8354
all the *d* vessels of king Solomon	2Chr 9:20	4945
the *d* was according to the law	Est 1:8	8360
d wine in their eldest brother's	Job 1:13	8354
d wine in their eldest brother's	Job 1:18	8354
sheep, eating flesh, and *d*	Is 22:13	8354
John came neither eating nor *d*	Mt 11:18	4095
The Son of man came eating and *d*	Mt 11:19	4095
the flood they were eating and *d*	Mt 24:38	4095
neither eating bread nor *d* wine	Lk 7:33	4095
Son of man is come eating and *d*	Lk 7:34	4095
d such things as they give	Lk 10:7	4095

DRINKS
Which stood only in meats and *d*	Heb 9:10	4188

DRIVE
shall he *d* them out of his land	Ex 6:1	1644
which shall *d* out the Hivite, the	Ex 23:28	1644
I will not *d* out from before thee	Ex 23:29	1644
little I will *d* them out from	Ex 23:30	1644
thou shalt *d* them out before thee	Ex 23:31	1644
I will *d* out the Canaanite, the	Ex 33:2	1644
I *d* out before thee the Amorite,	Ex 34:11	1644
that I may *d* them out of the land	Num 22:6	1644
to overcome them, and *d* them out	Num 22:11	1644
Then ye shall *d* out all the	Num 33:52	3423
But if ye will not *d* out the	Num 33:55	3423
To *d* out nations from before thee	Deut 4:38	3423
so shalt thou *d* them out, and	Deut 9:3	3423
doth *d* them out from before thee	Deut 9:4	3423
doth *d* them out from before thee	Deut 9:5	3423
Then will the LORD *d* out all	Deut 11:23	3423
the LORD thy God doth *d* them out	Deut 18:12	3423
fail *d* out from before you the	Josh 3:10	3423
them will I *d* out from before the	Josh 13:6	3423
I shall be able to *d* them out	Josh 14:12	3423
of Judah could not *d* them out	Josh 15:63	3423
d out the inhabitants of those	Josh 17:12	3423
but did not utterly *d* them out	Josh 17:13	3423
for thou shalt *d* out the	Josh 17:18	3423
d them from out of your sight	Josh 23:5	3423
d out any of these nations from	Josh 23:13	3423
but could not *d* out the	Judg 1:19	3423
did not *d* out the Jebusites that	Judg 1:21	3423
Neither did Manasseh *d* out the	Judg 1:27	3423
and did not utterly *d* them out	Judg 1:28	3423
Neither did Ephraim *d* out the	Judg 1:29	3423
Neither did Zebulun *d* out the	Judg 1:30	3423
Neither did Asher *d* out the	Judg 1:31	3423
for they did not *d* them out	Judg 1:32	3423
Neither did Naphtali *d* out the	Judg 1:33	3423
I will not *d* them out from before	Judg 2:3	1644
I also will not henceforth *d* out	Judg 2:21	3423

God shall *d* out from before us	Judg 11:24	3423
an ass, and said to her servant, *D*	2Kin 4:24	5090
who didst *d* out the inhabitants	2Chr 20:7	3423
side, and shall *d* him to his feet	Job 18:11	6327
They *d* away the ass of the	Job 24:3	5090
How thou didst *d* out the heathen	Ps 44:2	3423
is driven away, so *d* them away	Ps 68:2	5086
shall *d* it far from him	Prov 22:15	
I will *d* thee from thy station,	Is 22:19	1920
all places whither I shall *d* them	Jer 24:9	5080
and that I should *d* you out	Jer 27:10	5080
that I might *d* you out, and that	Jer 27:15	5080
not, because the LORD did *d* them	Jer 46:15	1920
Gentiles, whither I will *d* them	Eze 4:13	5080
That they shall *d* thee from men	Dan 4:25	2957
they shall *d* thee from men, and	Dan 4:32	2957
I will *d* them out of mine house	Hos 9:15	1644
will *d* him into a land barren and	Joel 2:20	5080
they shall *d* out Ashdod at the	Zeph 2:4	1644
up into the wind, we let her *d*	Acts 27:15	*1929*

DRIVEN
thou hast *d* me out this day from	Gen 4:14	1644
they were *d* out from Pharaoh's	Ex 10:11	1644
or *d* away, no man seeing it	Ex 22:10	7617
until he hath *d* out his enemies	Num 32:21	3423
shouldest be *d* to worship them,	Deut 4:19	5080
the LORD thy God hath *d* thee	Deut 30:1	5080
If any of thine be *d* out unto the	Deut 30:4	5080
For the LORD hath *d* out from	Josh 23:9	3423
for they have *d* me out this day	1Sa 26:19	1644
is wisdom *d* quite from me	Job 6:13	5080
Wilt thou break a leaf *d* to	Job 13:25	5086
He shall be *d* from light into	Job 18:18	1920
They were *d* forth from among men,	Job 30:5	1644
let them be *d* backward and put to	Ps 40:14	5472
As smoke is *d* away, so drive them	Ps 68:2	5086
Jordan was *d* back	Ps 114:3	5437
Jordan, that thou wast *d* back	Ps 114:5	5437
The wicked is *d* away in his	Prov 14:32	1760
and they shall be *d* to darkness	Is 8:22	5080
wither, be *d* away, and be no more	Is 19:7	5086
sword, and as *d* stubble to his bow	Is 41:2	5086
the places whither I have *d* them	Jer 8:3	5080
the lands whither he had *d* them	Jer 16:15	5080
d them away, and have not visited	Jer 23:2	5080
countries whither I have *d* them	Jer 23:3	5080
countries whither I had *d* them	Jer 23:8	5080
they shall be *d* on, and fall	Jer 23:12	1760
the places whither I have *d* you	Jer 29:14	5080
the nations whither I have *d* them	Jer 29:18	5080
whither I have *d* them in mine	Jer 32:37	5080
of all places whither they were *d*	Jer 40:12	5080
nations, whither they had been *d*	Jer 43:5	5080
the nations whither I have *d* thee	Jer 46:28	5080
ye shall be *d* out every man right	Jer 49:5	5080
the lions have *d* him away	Jer 50:17	5080
I have *d* him out for his	Eze 31:11	1644
again that which was *d* away	Eze 34:4	5080
bring again that which was *d* away	Eze 34:16	5080
he was *d* from men, and did eat	Dan 4:33	2957
he was *d* from the sons of men	Dan 5:21	2957
whither thou hast *d* them, because	Dan 9:7	5080
as the chaff that is *d* with the	Hos 13:3	5590
I will gather her that is *d* out	Mic 4:6	5080
and gather her that was *d* out	Zeph 3:19	5080
was *d* of the devil into the	Lk 8:29	*1643*
strake sail, and so were *d*	Acts 27:17	5342
night was come, as we were *d* up	Acts 27:27	*1308*
a wave of the sea *d* with the wind	Jas 1:6	*416*
are *d* of fierce winds, yet are	Jas 3:4	*1643*

DRIVER
he said unto the *d* of his chariot	1Kin 22:34	7395
regardeth he the crying of the *d*	Job 39:7	5065

DRIVETH
for he *d* furiously	2Kin 9:20	5090
the chaff which the wind *d* away	Ps 1:4	5086
The north wind *d* away rain	Prov 25:23	2342
immediately the spirit *d* him into	Mk 1:12	*1544*

DRIVING
without *d* them out hastily	Judg 2:23	3423
the *d* is like the *d* of Jehu	2Kin 9:20	4491
the *d* is like the *d* of Jehu	2Kin 9:20	4491
by *d* out nations from before thy	1Chr 17:21	1644

DROMEDARIES
d brought they unto the place	1Kin 4:28	7409
on mules, camels, and young *d*	Est 8:10	7424
thee, the *d* of Midian and Ephah	Is 60:6	1070

DROMEDARY
thou art a swift *d* traversing her ....Jer 2:23   1072

DROP
My doctrine shall *d* as the rain ....Deut 32:2   6201
also his heavens shall *d* down dew ....Deut 33:28   6201
Which the clouds do *d* and distil ....Job 36:28   5140
and thy paths of fatness........................Ps 65:11   7491
They *d* upon the pastures of the ....Ps 65:12   7491
the clouds *d* down the dew ....Prov 3:20   7491
a strange woman *d* as an honeycomb ....Prov 5:3   5197
O my spouse, *d* as the honeycomb ....Song 4:11   5197
nations are as a *d* of a bucket ....Is 40:15   4752
D down, ye heavens, from above,...........Is 45:8   7491
d thy word toward the south, and..........Eze 20:46   5197
d thy word toward the holy places.........Eze 21:2   5197
mountains shall *d* down new wine ....Joel 3:18   5197
d not thy word against the house ....Amos 7:16   5197
the mountains shall *d* sweet wine ....Amos 9:13   5197

DROPPED
earth trembled, and the heavens *d*........Judg 5:4   5197
the clouds also *d* water ....Judg 5:4   5197
the wood, behold, the honey *d*..............1Sa 14:26   1982
of harvest until water *d* upon................2Sa 21:10   5413
and my speech *d* upon them..................Job 29:22   5197
the heavens also *d* at the ....Ps 68:8   5197
my hands *d* with myrrh, and my ....Song 5:5   5197

DROPPETH
of the hands the house *d* through ....Eccl 10:18   1811

DROPPING
of a wife are a continual *d* ....Prov 19:13   1812
A continual *d* in a very rainy day ....Prov 27:15   1812
lilies, *d* sweet smelling myrrh ....Song 5:13   5197

DROPS
he maketh small the *d* of water ....Job 36:27   5197
or who hath begotten the *d* of dew ....Job 38:28   96
my locks with the *d* of the night ....Song 5:2   7447
d of blood falling down to the ....Lk 22:44   *2361*

DROPSY
man before him which had the *d* ....Lk 14:2   *5203*

DROSS
the wicked of the earth like *d* ....Ps 119:119   5509
Take away the *d* from the silver, ...Prov 25:4   5509
a potsherd covered with silver *d*............Prov 26:23   5509
Thy silver is become *d*, thy wine ....Is 1:22   5509
thee, and purely purge away thy *d* ....Is 1:25   5509
house of Israel is to me become *d* ....Eze 22:18   5509
they are even the *d* of silver ....Eze 22:18   5509
Because ye are all become *d*.................Eze 22:19   5509

DROUGHT
in the day the *d* consumed me ....Gen 31:40   2721
serpents, and scorpions, and *d* ....Deut 8:15   6774
D and heat consume the snow waters ....Job 24:19   6723
is turned into the *d* of summer ....Ps 32:4   2725
and satisfy thy soul in *d* ....Is 58:11   6710
and of pits, through a land of *d* ....Jer 2:6   6723
not be careful in the year of *d* ....Jer 17:8   1226
A *d* is upon her waters.........................Jer 50:38   2721
in the land of great *d* ....Hos 13:5   8514
And I called for a *d* upon the land ....Hag 1:11   2721

DROVE
So he *d* out the man ....Gen 3:24   1644
the carcases, Abram *d* them away ....Gen 15:11   5380
servants, every *d* by themselves ....Gen 32:16   5739
me, and put a space betwixt *d* ....Gen 32:16   5739
and put a space betwixt *d* and *d* ....Gen 32:16   5739
thou by all this *d* which I met...............Gen 33:8   4264
the shepherds came and *d* them away ...Ex 2:17   1644
d out the Amorites that were ....Num 21:32   3423
Caleb *d* thence the three sons of ....Josh 15:14   3423
who *d* away the inhabitants of...............1Chr 8:13   1272
who *d* him away, and he departed ....Ps 34:*t*   1644
beheld, and *d* asunder the nations ....Hab 3:6   5425
he *d* them all out of the temple, ...Jn 2:15   *1544*

DROVES
third, and all that followed the *d* ....Gen 32:19   5739

DROWN
love, neither can the floods *d* it............Song 8:7   7857
which *d* men in destruction and 1Ti 6:9   *1036*

DROWNED
also are *d* in the Red sea ....Ex 15:4   2823
and it shall be cast out and *d* ....Amos 8:8   8248
and shall be *d*, as by the flood of..........Amos 9:5   8248
that he were *d* in the depth of ....Mt 18:6   *2670*
Egyptians assaying to do were *d* ....Heb 11:29   *2666*

DROWSINESS
d shall clothe a man with rags ....Prov 23:21   5124

DRUNK
all drink that may be *d* in every ....Lev 11:34   8354
neither have ye *d* wine or strong ....Deut 29:6   8354
make mine arrows *d* with blood ....Deut 32:42   7937
and when he had *d*, his spirit came ....Judg 15:19   8354
And when Boaz had eaten and *d* ....Ruth 3:7   8354
in Shiloh, and after they had *d* 1Sa 1:9   8354
nor *d* any water, three days and 1Sa 30:12   8354
and he made him *d*.............................2Sa 11:13   7937
d water in the place, of the...................1Kin 13:22   8354
eaten bread, and after he had *d* 1Kin 13:23   8354
drinking himself *d* in the house 1Kin 16:9   7910
himself *d* in the pavilions 1Kin 20:16   7910
and when they had eaten and *d* 2Kin 6:23   8354
d strange waters, and with the 2Kin 19:24   8354
I have *d* my wine with my milk ....Song 5:1   8354
I have digged, and *d* water...................Is 37:25   8354
which hast *d* at the hand of the ....Is 51:17   8354
make them *d* in my fury, and I will ....Is 63:6   7937
and made *d* with their blood..................Jer 46:10   7301
And I will make *d* her princes ....Jer 51:57   7937
to have *d* of the deep waters, but ....Eze 34:18   8354
concubines, have *d* wine in them ....Dan 5:23   8355
For as ye have *d* upon my holy ....Obad 16   8354
No man also having *d* old wine...........Lk 5:39   *4095*
***d* in thy presence, and thou hast**........Lk 13:26   *4095*
and when men have well *d*, then ....Jn 2:10   *3184*
be not *d* with wine, wherein is ....Eph 5:18   *3182*
been made *d* with the wine of her ....Rev 17:2   *3182*
For all nations have *d* of the.................Rev 18:3   *3182*

DRUNKARD
he is a glutton, and a *d*........................Deut 21:20   5435
For the *d* and the glutton shall ....Prov 23:21   5435
goeth up into the hand of a *d* ....Prov 26:9   7910
shall reel to and fro like a *d*.................Is 24:20   7910
an idolater, or a railer, or a *d*...............1Cor 5:11   *3183*

DRUNKARDS
and I was the song of the *d* ....Ps 69:12   8354,7941
to the *d* of Ephraim, whose ....Is 28:1   7910
the *d* of Ephraim, shall be ....Is 28:3   7910
Awake, ye *d*, and weep.........................Joel 1:5   7910
and while they are drunken as *d* ....Nah 1:10   7910
Nor thieves, nor covetous, nor *d* 1Cor 6:10   *3183*

DRUNKEN
And he drank of the wine, and was *d* ....Gen 9:21   7943
Eli thought she had been *d* 1Sa 1:13   7910
unto her, How long wilt thou be *d* 1Sa 1:14   7937
I have *d* neither wine nor strong............1Sa 1:15   7937
within him for he was very *d*.................1Sa 25:36   7910
them to stagger like a *d* man................Job 12:25   7910
and fro, and stagger like a *d* man ....Ps 107:27   7910
as a *d* man staggereth in his ....Is 19:14   7910
they are *d*, but not with wine ....Is 29:9   7937
they shall be *d* with their own ....Is 49:26   7937
thou hast *d* the dregs of the cup...........Is 51:17   8354
now this, thou afflicted, and *d* ....Is 51:21   7937
I am like a *d* man, and like a man ....Jer 23:9   7910
Drink ye, and be *d*, and spue, and ....Jer 25:27   7937
Make ye him *d*: for he magnified ....Jer 48:26   7937
drink of the cup have assuredly *d*..........Jer 49:12   7937
hand, that made all the earth *d*.............Jer 51:7   7937
the nations have *d* of her wine ....Jer 51:7   8354
feasts, and I will make them *d* ....Jer 51:39   7937
he hath made me *d* with wormwood ......Lam 3:15   7301
thou shalt be *d*, and shalt make ....Lam 4:21   7937
We have *d* our water for money ....Lam 5:4   8354
full, and drink blood till ye be *d* ....Eze 39:19   7943
and while they are *d* as drunkards ....Nah 1:10   5435
Thou also shalt be *d* ....Nah 3:11   7937
to him, and makest him *d* also ....Hab 2:15   7937
and to eat and drink with the *d* ....Mt 24:49   *3184*
and to eat and drink, and to be *d* ....Lk 12:45   *3182*
serve me, till I have eaten and *d*..........Lk 17:8   *4095*
For these are not *d*, as ye ....Acts 2:15   *3184*
and one is hungry, and another is *d* 1Cor 11:21   *3184*
be *d* are *d* in the night........................1Th 5:7   *3184*
I saw the woman *d* with the blood ....Rev 17:6   *3184*

DRUNKENNESS
of mine heart, to add *d* to thirst ....Deut 29:19   7302
for strength, and not for *d* ....Eccl 10:17   8358
inhabitants of Jerusalem, with *d* ....Jer 13:13   7943
Thou shalt be filled with *d*....................Eze 23:33   7943
overcharged with surfeiting, and *d* ....Lk 21:34   *3178*
not in rioting and *d*, not in ....Rom 13:13   *3178*
Envyings, murders, *d*, revellings, ...Gal 5:21   *3178*

DRUSILLA (dru-sil'-lah) Wife of Felix.
when Felix came with his wife D .... Acts 24:24   *1409*

DRY
place, and let the *d* land appear .... Gen 1:9   3004
And God called the *d* land Earth .... Gen 1:10   3004
of all that was in the *d* land .... Gen 7:22   2724
the face of the ground was *d* .... Gen 8:13   2720
river, and pour it upon the *d* land .... Ex 4:9   3004
become blood upon the *d* land .... Ex 4:9   3006
children of Israel shall go on *d* .... Ex 14:16   3004
night, and made the sea *d* land .... Ex 14:21   2724
of the sea upon the *d* ground .... Ex 14:22   3004
d land in the midst of the sea .... Ex 14:29   3004
on *d* land in the midst of the sea .... Ex 15:19   3004
offering, mingled with oil, and *d* .... Lev 7:10   2720
it is a scall, even a leprosy .... Lev 13:30   5424
of the Lord stood firm on *d* .... Josh 3:17   2724
passed over on *d* ground, until .... Josh 3:17   2724
were lifted up unto the *d* land .... Josh 4:18   2724
came over this Jordan on *d* land .... Josh 4:22   3004
bread of their provision was *d* .... Josh 9:5   3004
but now, behold, it is *d*, and it .... Josh 9:12   3001
it be *d* upon all the earth beside .... Judg 6:37   2721
let it now be *d* only upon the .... Judg 6:39   2721
for it was *d* upon the fleece only .... Judg 6:40   2721
they two went over on *d* ground 2Kin 2:8   2724
midst of the sea on the *d* land .... Neh 9:11   3004
the waters, and they *d* up .... Job 12:15   3001
and wilt thou pursue the *d* stubble .... Job 13:25   3002
the flame shall *d* up his branches .... Job 15:30   3001
my flesh longeth for thee in a *d* .... Ps 63:1   6723
He turned the sea into *d* land .... Ps 66:6   3004
the rebellious dwell in a *d* land .... Ps 68:6   6707
and his hands formed the *d* land .... Ps 95:5   3006
they ran in the *d* places like a .... Ps 105:41   6723
and the watersprings into *d* ground .... Ps 107:33   6774
d ground into watersprings .... Ps 107:35   6723
Better is a *d* morsel, and .... Prov 17:1   2720
as the heat in a *d* place .... Is 25:5   6724
as rivers of water in a *d* place .... Is 32:2   6724
the *d* land springs of water .... Is 41:18   6723
and hills, and *d* up all their herbs .... Is 42:15   3001
islands, and I will *d* up the pools .... Is 42:15   3001
and floods upon the *d* ground .... Is 44:3   3004
That saith to the deep, Be *d* .... Is 44:27   2717
and I will *d* up thy rivers .... Is 44:27   3001
at my rebuke I *d* up the sea .... Is 50:2   2717
and as a root out of a *d* ground .... Is 53:2   6723
eunuch say, Behold, I am a *d* tree .... Is 56:3   3002
A *d* wind of the high places in .... Jer 4:11   6703
wilderness, a *d* land, and a desert .... Jer 50:12   6723
I will *d* up her sea .... Jer 51:36   2717
and make her springs *d* .... Jer 51:36   3001
a *d* land, and a wilderness, a land .... Jer 51:43   6723
have made the *d* tree to flourish .... Eze 17:24   3002
planted in the wilderness, in a *d* .... Eze 19:13   6723
tree in thee, and every *d* tree .... Eze 20:47   3002
And I will make the rivers *d* .... Eze 30:12   2724
and, lo, they were very *d* .... Eze 37:2   3002
O ye *d* bones, hear the word of .... Eze 37:4   3002
and set her like a *d* land .... Hos 2:3   6723
a miscarrying womb and *d* breasts .... Hos 9:14   6784
and his spring shall become *d* .... Hos 13:15   954
hath made the sea and the *d* land .... Jonah 1:9   3004
vomited out Jonah upon the *d* land ...... Jonah 2:10   3004
rebuketh the sea, and maketh it *d* .... Nah 1:4   3001
be devoured as stubble fully *d* .... Nah 1:10   3002
and *d* like a wilderness .... Zeph 2:13   6723
earth, and the sea, and the *d* land .... Hag 2:6   2724
the deeps of the river shall *d* up .... Zec 10:11   3001
man, he walketh through *d* places .... Mt 12:43   *504*
man, he walketh through *d* places .... Lk 11:24   *504*
tree, what shall be done in the *d* .... Lk 23:31   *3584*
through the Red sea as by *d* land .... Heb 11:29   *3584*

DRYSHOD
streams, and make men go over *d* .... Is 11:15   5275

DUE
it is thy *d*, and thy sons' *d* .... Lev 10:13   2706
they be thy *d*, and thy sons' *d* .... Lev 10:14   2706
I will give you rain in *d* season .... Lev 26:4
offer unto me in their *d* season .... Num 28:2
rain of your land in his *d* season .... Deut 11:14
be the priest's *d* from the people .... Deut 18:3   4941
their foot shall slide in *d* time .... Deut 32:35
sought him not after the *d* order 1Chr 15:13
Lord the glory *d* unto his name.............. 1Chr 16:29
for the singers, *d* for every day .... Neh 11:23   *1697*
Lord the glory *d* unto his name.............. Ps 29:2
Lord the glory *d* unto his name.............. Ps 96:8

give them their meat in *d* season .... Ps 104:27
them their meat in *d* season .... Ps 145:15
good from them to whom it is *d* .... Prov 3:27   1167
and a word spoken in *d* season .... Prov 15:23
and thy princes eat in *d* season.............. Eccl 10:17
pay all that was *d* unto him .... Mt 18:34   *3784*
to give them meat in *d* season .... Mt 24:45
their portion of meat in *d* season .... Lk 12:42
for we receive the *d* reward of .... Lk 23:41   *514*
in *d* time Christ died for the .... Rom 5:6
tribute to whom tribute is *d* .... Rom 13:7
unto the wife *d* benevolence 1Cor 7:3   *3784*
as of one born out of *d* time 1Cor 15:8
for in *d* season we shall reap, if .... Gal 6:9   *2398*
all, to be testified in *d* time 1Ti 2:6   *2398*
But hath in *d* times manifested .... Titus 1:3   *2398*
that he may exalt you in *d* time 1Pet 5:6

DUES
Render therefore to all their *d* .... Rom 13:7   *3782*

DUKE
firstborn son of Esau; *d* Teman.............. Gen 36:15   441
d Omar, *d* Zepho, *d* Kenaz,.............. Gen 36:15   441
D Korah, *d* Gatam, and *d* .... Gen 36:16   441
D Korah, *d* Gatam, and *d* Amalek........ Gen 36:16   441
d Nahath, *d* Zerah .... Gen 36:17   441
d Shammah, ... Gen 36:17   441
d Jeush, *d* Jaalam, *d* Korah .... Gen 36:18   441
came of the Horites; *d* Lotan.................. Gen 36:29   441
d Shobal, *d* Zibeon, *d* Anah, ... Gen 36:29   441
D Dishon, *d* Ezer, *d* Dishan .... Gen 36:30   441
by their names; *d* Timnah .... Gen 36:40   441
d Alvah, *d* Jetheth .... Gen 36:40   441
D Aholibamah, *d* Elah, *d* Pinon .... Gen 36:41   441
D Kenaz, *d* Teman, *d* Mibzar, ... Gen 36:42   441
D Magdiel, *d* Iram.............................. Gen 36:43   441
of Edom were; *d* Timnah 1Chr 1:51   441
d Aliah, *d* Jetheth 1Chr 1:51   441
D Aholibamah, *d* Elah, *d* Pinon 1Chr 1:52   441
D Kenaz, *d* Teman, *d* Mibzar, ... 1Chr 1:53   441
D Magdiel, *d* Iram.............................. 1Chr 1:54   441

DUKES
These were *d* of the sons of Esau .... Gen 36:15   441
these are the *d* that came of .... Gen 36:16   441
these are the *d* that came of .... Gen 36:17   441
these were the *d* that came of .... Gen 36:18   441
who is Edom, and these are their *d* .... Gen 36:19   441
these are the *d* of the Horites, ... Gen 36:21   441
These are the *d* that came of the .... Gen 36:29   441
these are the *d* that came of Hori .... Gen 36:30   441
among their *d* in the land of Seir .... Gen 36:30   441
names of the *d* that came of Esau .... Gen 36:40   441
these be the *d* of Edom, according .... Gen 36:43   441
Then the *d* of Edom shall be .... Ex 15:15   441
and Reba, which were *d* of Sihon .... Josh 13:21   5257
And the *d* of Edom were 1Chr 1:51   441
These are the *d* of Edom 1Chr 1:54

DULCIMER
flute, harp, sackbut, psaltery, *d* .... Dan 3:5   5481
harp, sackbut, psaltery, and *d* .... Dan 3:10   5481
harp, sackbut, psaltery, and *d* .... Dan 3:15   5481

DULL
and their ears are *d* of hearing.............. Mt 13:15   *917*
and their ears are *d* of hearing .... Acts 28:27   *917*
seeing ye are *d* of hearing...................... Heb 5:11   *3576*

DUMAH (doo'-mah)
   1. Son of Ishmael.
And Mishma, and *D*, and Massa, ... Gen 25:14   1746
Mishma, and *D*, Massa, Hadad, and 1Chr 1:30   1746
   2. A city in Judah.
Arab, and *D*, and Eshean, ... Josh 15:52   1746
   3. An undetermined city.
The burden of *D*. He calleth to................ Is 21:11   1746

DUMB
or who maketh the *d*, or deaf, or .... Ex 4:11   483
I was as a *d* man that openeth not .... Ps 38:13   483
I was *d* with silence, I held my................ Ps 39:2   481
I was *d*, I opened not my mouth .... Ps 39:9   481
Open thy mouth for the *d* in the .... Prov 31:8   483
hart, and the tongue of the *d* sing .... Is 35:6   483
a sheep before her shearers is *d* .... Is 53:7   481
all ignorant, they are all *d* dogs.............. Is 56:10   483
thy mouth, that thou shalt be *d* .... Eze 3:26   481
thou shalt speak, and be no more *d* ...... Eze 24:27   481
was opened, and I was no more *d* .... Eze 33:22   481
toward the ground, and I became *d* .... Dan 10:15   481
trusteth therein, to make *d* idols .... Hab 2:18   483
to the *d* stone, Arise, it shall .... Hab 2:19   1748

they brought to him a *d* man .... Mt 9:32   2974
devil was cast out, the *d* spake .... Mt 9:33   2974
with a devil, blind, and *d* .... Mt 12:22   2974
the blind and *d* both spake and saw ..... Mt 12:22   2974
those that were lame, blind, *d* .... Mt 15:30   2974
when they saw the *d* to speak .... Mt 15:31   2974
deaf to hear, and the *d* to speak .... Mk 7:37   216
my son, which hath a *d* spirit .... Mk 9:17   216
spirit, saying unto him, Thou *d* .... Mk 9:25   216
And, behold, thou shalt be *d* .... Lk 1:20   4623
casting out a devil, and it was *d* .... Lk 11:14   2974
devil was gone out, the *d* spake .... Lk 11:14   2974
like a lamb *d* before his shearer, ... Acts 8:32   880
carried away unto these *d* idols 1Cor 12:2   880
the *d* ass speaking with man's 2Pet 2:16   880

DUNG

bullock, and his skin, and his *d* .... Ex 29:14   6569
legs, and his inwards, and his *d* .... Lev 4:11   6569
and his hide, his flesh, and his *d* .... Lev 8:17   6569
skins, and their flesh, and their *d* .... Lev 16:27   6569
flesh, and her blood, with her *d* .... Num 19:5   6569
Jeroboam, as a man taketh away *d* 1Kin 14:10   1557
d for five pieces of silver 2Kin 6:25   2755
d upon the face of the field in 2Kin 9:37   1828
that they may eat their own *d* .... 2Kin 18:27   2716,(6675)
the dragon well, and to the *d* port .... Neh 2:13   830
on the wall unto the *d* gate .... Neh 3:13   830
But the *d* gate repaired Malchiah .... Neh 3:14   830
upon the wall toward the *d* gate .... Neh 12:31   830
perish for ever like his own *d* .... Job 20:7   1561
they became as *d* for the earth .... Ps 83:10   1828
that they may eat their own *d* .... Is 36:12   2716,(6675)
they shall be for *d* upon the face .... Jer 8:2   1828
fall as *d* upon the open field .... Jer 9:22   1828
but they shall be as *d* upon the .... Jer 16:4   1828
they shall be *d* upon the ground .... Jer 25:33   1828
it with *d* that cometh out of man .... Eze 4:12   1561
given thee cow's *d* for man's *d* .... Eze 4:15   6832
given thee cow's *d* for man's *d* .... Eze 4:15   1561
as dust, and their flesh as the *d* .... Zeph 1:17   1561
spread *d* upon your faces .... Mal 2:3   6569
even the *d* of your solemn feasts .... Mal 2:3   6569
I shall dig about it, and *d* it .... Lk 13:8   906,2874
things, and do count them but *d* .... Phil 3:8   4657

DUNGEON

they should put me into the *d* .... Gen 40:15   953
brought him hastily out of the *d* .... Gen 41:14   953
of the captive that was in the *d* .... Ex 12:29   953
Jeremiah was entered into the *d* .... Jer 37:16   953
cast him into the *d* of Malchiah .... Jer 38:6   953
in the *d* there was no water, but .... Jer 38:6   953
they had put Jeremiah in the *d* .... Jer 38:7   953
whom they have cast into the *d* .... Jer 38:9   953
Jeremiah the prophet out of the *d* .... Jer 38:10   953
by cords into the *d* to Jeremiah .... Jer 38:11   953
and took him up out of the *d* .... Jer 38:13   953
have cut off my life in the *d* .... Lam 3:53   953
name, O Lord, out of the low *d* .... Lam 3:55   953

DUNGHILL

lifteth up the beggar from the *d* 1Sa 2:8   830
his house be made a *d* for this .... Ezr 6:11   5122
and lifteth the needy out of the *d* .... Ps 113:7   830
straw is trodden down for the *d* .... Is 25:10   4087
and your houses shall be made a *d* .... Dan 2:5   5122
and their houses shall be made a *d* .... Dan 3:29   5122
for the land, nor yet for the *d* .... Lk 14:35   2874

DUNGHILLS

brought up in scarlet embrace *d* .... Lam 4:5   830

DURA *(doo'-rah) A plain in Babylonia.*
he set it up in the plain of *D* .... Dan 3:1   1757

DURABLE

d riches and righteousness .... Prov 8:18   6276
sufficiently, and for *d* clothing .... Is 23:18   6266

DURETH

in himself, but *d* for a while .... Mt 13:21   2076

DURST

that *d* presume in his heart to do .... Est 7:5
d not shew you mine opinion .... Job 32:6   3372
neither *d* any man from that day .... Mt 22:46   5111
no man after that *d* ask him any .... Mk 12:34   5111
after that they *d* not ask him any .... Lk 20:40   5111
none of the disciples *d* ask him .... Jn 21:12   5111
of the rest *d* no man join himself .... Acts 5:13   5111
Moses trembled, and *d* not behold .... Acts 7:32   5111
d not bring against him a railing .... Jude 9   5111

DUST

formed man of the *d* of the ground .... Gen 2:7   6083
d shalt thou eat all the days of .... Gen 3:14   6083
for *d* thou art, and unto *d* .... Gen 3:19   6083
thy seed as the *d* of the earth .... Gen 13:16   6083
man can number the *d* of the earth .... Gen 13:16   6083
unto the Lord, which am but *d* .... Gen 18:27   6083
shall be as the *d* of the earth .... Gen 28:14   6083
smite the *d* of the land, that it .... Ex 8:16   6083
smote the *d* of the earth, and it .... Ex 8:17   6083
all the *d* of the land became lice .... Ex 8:17   6083
it shall become small *d* in all .... Ex 9:9   80
they shall pour out the *d* that .... Lev 14:41   6083
blood thereof, and cover it with *d* .... Lev 17:13   6083
of the *d* that is in the floor of .... Num 5:17   6083
Who can count the *d* of Jacob .... Num 23:10   6083
even until it was as small as *d* .... Deut 9:21   6083
I cast the *d* thereof into the .... Deut 9:21   6083
the rain of thy land powder and *d* .... Deut 28:24   6083
the poison of serpents of the *d* .... Deut 32:24   6083
Israel, and put *d* upon their heads .... Josh 7:6   6083
raiseth up the poor out of the *d* 1Sa 2:8   6083
and threw stones at him, and cast *d* 2Sa 16:13   6083
as small as the *d* of the earth 2Sa 22:43   6083
as I exalted thee out of the *d* 1Kin 16:2   6083
the wood, and the stones, and the *d* 1Kin 18:38   6083
if the *d* of Samaria shall suffice 1Kin 20:10   6083
made them like the *d* by threshing 2Kin 13:7   6083
cast the *d* of them into the brook 2Kin 23:12   6083
the *d* of the earth in multitude 2Chr 1:9   6083
made *d* of them, and strowed it 2Chr 34:4   1854
sprinkled *d* upon their heads .... Job 2:12   6083
whose foundation is in the *d* .... Job 4:19   6083
cometh not forth of the *d* .... Job 5:6   6083
clothed with worms and clods of *d* .... Job 7:5   6083
for now shall I sleep in the *d* .... Job 7:21   6083
wilt thou bring me into *d* again .... Job 10:9   6083
grow out of the *d* of the earth .... Job 14:19   6083
skin, and defiled my horn in the *d* .... Job 16:15   6083
our rest together is in the *d* .... Job 17:16   6083
shall lie down with him in the *d* .... Job 20:11   6083
shall lie down alike in the *d* .... Job 21:26   6083
Then shalt thou lay up gold as *d* .... Job 22:24   6083
Though he heap up silver as the *d* .... Job 27:16   6083
and it hath *d* of gold .... Job 28:6   6083
the mire, and I am become like *d* .... Job 30:19   6083
and man shall turn again unto *d* .... Job 34:15   6083
When the *d* groweth into hardness, ... Job 38:38   6083
earth, and warmeth them in the *d* .... Job 39:14   6083
Hide them in the *d* together .... Job 40:13   6083
I abhor myself, and repent in *d* .... Job 42:6   6083
and lay mine honour in the *d* .... Ps 7:5   6083
small as the *d* before the wind .... Ps 18:42   6083
brought me into the *d* of death .... Ps 22:15   6083
to the *d* shall bow before him .... Ps 22:29   6083
shall the *d* praise thee .... Ps 30:9   6083
our soul is bowed down to the *d* .... Ps 44:25   6083
and his enemies shall lick the *d* .... Ps 72:9   6083
rained flesh also upon them as *d* .... Ps 78:27   6083
stones, and favour the *d* thereof .... Ps 102:14   6083
he remembereth that we are *d* .... Ps 103:14   6083
they die, and return to their *d* .... Ps 104:29   6083
raiseth up the poor out of the *d* .... Ps 113:7   6083
My soul cleaveth unto the *d* .... Ps 119:25   6083
part of the *d* of the world .... Prov 8:26   6083
the *d*, and all turn to *d* again .... Eccl 3:20   6083
Then shall the *d* return to the .... Eccl 12:7   6083
the rock, and hide thee in the *d* .... Is 2:10   6083
and their blossom shall go up as *d* .... Is 5:24   80
to the ground, even to the *d* .... Is 25:12   6083
he bringeth it even to the *d* .... Is 26:5   6083
Awake and sing, ye that dwell in *d* .... Is 26:19   6083
speech shall be low out of the *d* .... Is 29:4   6083
speech shall whisper out of the *d* .... Is 29:4   6083
strangers shall be like small *d* .... Is 29:5   80
their *d* made fat with fatness .... Is 34:7   6083
the *d* thereof into brimstone, and .... Is 34:9   6083
comprehended the *d* of the earth .... Is 40:12   6083
as the small *d* of the balance .... Is 40:15   7834
gave them as the *d* to his sword .... Is 41:2   6083
Come down, and sit in the *d* .... Is 47:1   6083
and lick up the *d* of thy feet .... Is 49:23   6083
Shake thyself from the *d* .... Is 52:2   6083
d shall be the serpent's meat .... Is 65:25   6083
have cast up *d* upon their heads .... Lam 2:10   6083
He putteth his mouth in the *d* .... Lam 3:29   6083
the ground, to cover it with *d* .... Eze 24:7   6083
I will also scrape her *d* from her .... Eze 26:4   6083
horses their *d* shall cover thee .... Eze 26:10   80
thy *d* in the midst of the water .... Eze 26:12   6083
shall cast up *d* upon their heads, ... Eze 27:30   6083

in the *d* of the earth shall awake	Dan 12:2	6083
That pant after the *d* of the	Amos 2:7	6083
of Aphrah roll thyself in the *d*	Mic 1:10	6083
shall lick the *d* like a serpent	Mic 7:17	6083
the clouds are the *d* of his feet	Nah 1:3	80
thy nobles shall dwell in the *d*	Nah 3:18	
for they shall heap, and take it	Hab 1:10	6083
blood be poured out as *d*	Zeph 1:17	6083
and heaped up silver as the *d*	Zec 9:3	6083
shake off the *d* of your feet	Mt 10:14	*2868*
shake off the *d* under your feet	Mk 6:11	*5522*
shake off the very *d* from your	Lk 9:5	*2868*
Even the very *d* of your city	Lk 10:11	*2868*
But they shook off the *d* of their	Acts 13:51	*2868*
clothes, and threw *d* into the air,	Acts 22:23	*2868*
they cast *d* on their heads, and	Rev 18:19	*5522*

DUTIES

And that doeth not any of those *d*	Eze 18:11	

DUTY

her *d* of marriage, shall he not	Ex 21:10	
perform the *d* of an husband's	Deut 25:5	
the *d* of my husband's brother	Deut 25:7	
as the *d* of every day required	2Chr 8:14	1697
as the *d* of every day required	Ezr 3:4	1697
for this is the whole *d* of man	Eccl 12:13	
done that which was our *d* to do	Lk 17:10	*3784*
their *d* is also to minister unto	Rom 15:27	*3784*

DWARF

Or crookbackt, or a *d*, or that	Lev 21:20	1851

DWELL

the father of such as *d* in tents	Gen 4:20	3427
he shall *d* in the tents of Shem	Gen 9:27	7931
them, that they might *d* together	Gen 13:6	3427
so that they could not *d* together	Gen 13:6	3427
he shall *d* in the presence of all	Gen 16:12	7931
for he feared to *d* in Zoar	Gen 19:30	3427
d where it pleaseth thee	Gen 20:15	3427
of the Canaanites, among whom I *d*	Gen 24:3	3427
the Canaanites, in whose land I *d*	Gen 24:37	3427
d in the land which I shall tell	Gen 26:2	7931
now will my husband *d* with me	Gen 30:20	2082
And ye shall *d* with us	Gen 34:10	3427
d and trade ye therein, and get you	Gen 34:10	3427
we will *d* with you, and we will	Gen 34:16	3427
therefore let them *d* in the land	Gen 34:21	3427
consent unto us for to *d* with us	Gen 34:22	3427
unto them, and they will *d* with us	Gen 34:23	3427
go up to Beth-el, and *d* there	Gen 35:1	3427
than that they might *d* together	Gen 36:7	3427
thou shalt *d* in the land of	Gen 45:10	3427
that ye may *d* in the land of	Gen 46:34	3427
let thy servants *d* in the land of	Gen 47:4	3427
make thy father and brethren to *d*	Gen 47:6	3427
in the land of Goshen let them *d*	Gen 47:6	3427
Zebulun shall *d* at the haven of	Gen 49:13	7931
was content to *d* with the man	Ex 2:21	3427
of Goshen, in which my people *d*	Ex 8:22	5975
thou hast made for thee to *d* in	Ex 15:17	3427
They shall not *d* in thy land	Ex 23:33	3427
that I may *d* among them	Ex 25:8	7931
I will *d* among the children of	Ex 29:45	7931
of Egypt, that I may *d* among them	Ex 29:46	7931
he shall *d* alone	Lev 13:46	3427
whither I bring you to *d* therein	Lev 20:22	3427
Ye shall *d* in booths seven days	Lev 23:42	3427
Israelites born shall *d* in booths	Lev 23:42	3427
children of Israel to *d* in booths	Lev 23:43	3427
ye shall *d* in the land in safety	Lev 25:18	3427
your fill, and *d* therein in safety	Lev 25:19	3427
full, and in your land safely	Lev 26:5	3427
your enemies which *d* therein	Lev 26:32	3427
camps, in the midst whereof I *d*	Num 5:3	7931
what the land is that they *d* in	Num 13:19	3427
cities they be that they *d* in	Num 13:19	3427
be strong that *d* in the land	Num 13:28	3427
The Amalekites *d* in the land of	Num 13:29	3427
the Amorites, *d* in the mountains	Num 13:29	3427
and the Canaanites *d* by the sea	Num 13:29	3427
I sware to make you *d* therein	Num 14:30	7931
lo, the people shall *d* alone	Num 23:9	7931
our little ones shall *d* in the	Num 32:17	3427
of the land, and *d* therein	Num 33:53	3427
vex you in the land wherein ye *d*	Num 33:55	3427
their possession cities to *d* in	Num 35:2	3427
cities shall they have to *d* in	Num 35:3	3427
come again to *d* in the land	Num 35:32	3427
ye shall inhabit, wherein I *d*	Num 35:34	7931
for I the LORD *d* among the	Num 35:34	7931
children of Esau, which *d* in Seir	Deut 2:4	3427

children of Esau which *d* in Seir	Deut 2:29	3427
and the Moabites which *d* in Ar	Deut 2:29	3427
which *d* in the champaign over	Deut 11:30	3427
ye shall possess it, and *d* therein	Deut 11:31	3427
d in the land which the LORD your	Deut 12:10	3427
about, so that ye *d* in safety	Deut 12:10	3427
to cause his name to *d* there	Deut 12:11	7931
God hath given thee to *d* there	Deut 13:12	3427
shalt *d* therein, and shalt say, I	Deut 17:14	3427
He shall *d* with thee, even among	Deut 23:16	3427
If brethren *d* together, and one of	Deut 25:5	3427
and thou shalt not *d* therein	Deut 28:30	3427
that thou mayest *d* in the land	Deut 30:20	3427
the LORD shall *d* in safety by him	Deut 33:12	7931
he shall *d* between his shoulders	Deut 33:12	7931
then shall *d* in safety alone	Deut 33:28	7931
Peradventure ye *d* among us	Josh 9:7	3427
when ye *d* among us	Josh 9:22	3427
d in the mountains are gathered	Josh 10:6	3427
the Maachathites *d* among the	Josh 13:13	3427
in the land, save cities to *d* in	Josh 14:4	3427
but the Jebusites *d* with the	Josh 15:63	3427
but the Canaanites *d* among the	Josh 16:10	3427
Canaanites would *d* in that land	Josh 17:12	3427
all the Canaanites that *d* in the	Josh 17:16	3427
a place, that he may *d* among them	Josh 20:4	3427
he shall *d* in that city, until he	Josh 20:6	3427
Moses to give us cities to *d* in	Josh 21:2	3427
ye built not, and ye *d* in them	Josh 24:13	3427
the Amorites, in whose land ye *d*	Josh 24:15	3427
but the Jebusites *d* with the	Judg 1:21	3427
Canaanites would *d* in that land	Judg 1:27	3427
But the Amorites would *d* in mount	Judg 1:35	3427
the Amorites, in whose land ye *d*	Judg 6:10	3427
that they should not *d* in Shechem	Judg 9:41	3427
D with me, and be unto me a father	Judg 17:10	3427
was content to *d* with the man	Judg 17:11	3427
them an inheritance to *d* in	Judg 18:1	3427
made them *d* in this place	1Sa 12:8	3427
the country, that I may *d* there	1Sa 27:5	3427
for why should thy servant *d* in	1Sa 27:5	3427
I *d* in an house of cedar, but the	2Sa 7:2	3427
build me an house for me to *d* in	2Sa 7:5	3427
that they may *d* in a place of	2Sa 7:10	7931
d there, and go not forth thence	1Kin 2:36	3427
this woman *d* in one house	1Kin 3:17	3427
I will *d* among the children of	1Kin 6:13	7931
he would *d* in the thick darkness	1Kin 8:12	7931
built thee an house to *d* in	1Kin 8:13	2073
will God indeed *d* on the earth	1Kin 8:27	3427
belongeth to Zidon, and *d* there	1Kin 17:9	3427
I *d* among mine own people	2Kin 4:13	3427
the place where we *d* with thee is	2Kin 6:1	3427
us a place there, where we may *d*	2Kin 6:2	3427
d there, and let him teach them	2Kin 17:27	3427
d in the land, and serve the king	2Kin 25:24	3427
I *d* in an house of cedars, but	1Chr 17:1	3427
not build me an house to *d* in	1Chr 17:4	3427
they shall *d* in their place, and	1Chr 17:9	7931
that they may *d* in Jerusalem for	1Chr 23:25	7931
build him an house to *d* therein	2Chr 2:3	3427
he would *d* in the thick darkness	2Chr 6:1	7931
very deed *d* with men on the earth	2Chr 6:18	3427
the children of Israel to *d* there	2Chr 8:2	3427
My wife shall not *d* in the house	2Chr 8:11	3427
brethren that *d* in their cities	2Chr 19:10	3427
companions that *d* in Samaria	Ezr 4:17	3488
name to *d* there destroy all kings	Ezr 6:12	7932
d in booths in the feast of the	Neh 8:14	3427
to bring one of ten to *d* in	Neh 11:1	3427
nine parts to *d* in other cities	Neh 11:1	3427
themselves to *d* at Jerusalem	Neh 11:2	3427
let a cloud *d* upon it	Job 3:5	7931
in them that *d* in houses of clay	Job 4:19	7931
wickedness *d* in thy tabernacles	Job 11:14	7931
It shall *d* in his tabernacle,	Job 18:15	7931
They that *d* in mine house, and my	Job 19:15	1481
To *d* in the cliffs of the valleys	Job 30:6	7931
LORD, only makest me *d* in safety	Ps 4:8	3427
neither shall evil *d* with thee	Ps 5:4	1481
who shall *d* in thy holy hill	Ps 15:1	7931
I will *d* in the house of the LORD	Ps 23:6	3427
the world, and they that *d* therein	Ps 24:1	3427
His soul shall *d* at ease	Ps 25:13	3885
that I may *d* in the house of the	Ps 27:4	3427
so shalt thou *d* in the land	Ps 37:3	7931
and *d* for evermore	Ps 37:27	7931
the land, and *d* therein for ever	Ps 37:29	7931
that he may *d* in thy courts	Ps 65:4	7931
They also that *d* in the uttermost	Ps 65:8	3427
the rebellious *d* in a dry land	Ps 68:6	7931

hill which God desireth to *d* in	Ps 68:16	3427
the LORD will *d* in it for ever	Ps 68:16	7931
the LORD God might *d* among them	Ps 68:18	7931
let none *d* in their tents	Ps 69:25	3427
that they may *d* there, and have it	Ps 69:35	3427
love his name shall *d* therein	Ps 69:36	7931
They that *d* in the wilderness	Ps 72:9	
of Israel to *d* in their tents	Ps 78:55	7931
are they that *d* in thy house	Ps 84:4	3427
than to *d* in the tents of	Ps 84:10	1752
that glory may *d* in our land	Ps 85:9	7931
the world, and they that *d* therein	Ps 98:7	3427
the land, that they may *d* with me	Ps 101:6	3427
shall not *d* within my house	Ps 101:7	3427
they found no city to *d* in	Ps 107:4	4186
wickedness of them that *d* therein	Ps 107:34	3427
there he maketh the hungry to *d*	Ps 107:36	3427
that I *d* in the tents of Kedar	Ps 120:5	7931
here will I *d*; for I have	Ps 132:14	3427
brethren to *d* together in unity	Ps 133:1	3427
d in the uttermost parts of the	Ps 139:9	7931
upright shall *d* in thy presence	Ps 140:13	3427
he hath made me to *d* in darkness	Ps 143:3	3427
hearkeneth unto me shall *d* safely	Prov 1:33	7931
the upright shall *d* in the land	Prov 2:21	7931
I wisdom *d* with prudence, and find	Prov 8:12	7931
It is better to *d* in a corner of	Prov 21:9	3427
It is better to *d* in the	Prov 21:19	3427
It is better to *d* in the corner	Prov 25:24	3427
I *d* in the midst of a people of	Is 6:5	3427
they that *d* in the land of the	Is 9:2	3427
wolf also shall *d* with the lamb	Is 11:6	1481
and owls shall *d* there, and satyrs	Is 13:21	7931
Let mine outcasts *d* with thee	Is 16:4	1481
for them that *d* in the wilderness	Is 23:13	
for them that *d* before the LORD	Is 23:18	3427
they that *d* therein are desolate	Is 24:6	3427
bringeth down them that *d* on high	Is 26:5	3427
Awake and sing, ye that *d* in dust	Is 26:19	7931
shall *d* in Zion at Jerusalem	Is 30:19	3427
shall *d* in the wilderness	Is 32:16	7931
my people shall *d* in a peaceable	Is 32:18	3427
Who among us shall *d* with the	Is 33:14	1481
who among us shall *d* with	Is 33:14	1481
He shall *d* on high	Is 33:16	7931
the people that *d* therein shall	Is 33:24	3427
also and the raven shall *d* in it	Is 34:11	7931
generation shall they *d* therein	Is 34:17	7931
them out as a tent to *d* in	Is 40:22	3427
give place to me that I may *d*	Is 49:20	3427
they that *d* therein shall die in	Is 51:6	3427
I *d* in the high and holy place,	Is 57:15	7931
The restorer of paths to *d* in	Is 58:12	3427
it, and my servants shall *d* there	Is 65:9	7931
forsaken, and not a man *d* therein	Jer 4:29	3427
will cause you to *d* in this place	Jer 7:3	7931
I cause you to *d* in this place	Jer 7:7	7931
the city, and those that *d* therein	Jer 8:16	3427
of them that *d* in a far country	Jer 8:19	
corners, that *d* in the wilderness	Jer 9:26	3427
wickedness of them that *d* therein	Jer 12:4	3427
all that *d* in thine house shall	Jer 20:6	3427
saved, and Israel shall *d* safely	Jer 23:6	7931
they shall *d* in their own land	Jer 23:8	3427
them that *d* in the land of Egypt	Jer 24:8	3427
d in the land that the LORD hath	Jer 25:5	3427
people that *d* in the desert	Jer 25:24	7931
they shall till it, and *d* therein	Jer 27:11	3427
Build ye houses, and *d* in them	Jer 29:5	3427
build ye houses, and *d* in them	Jer 29:28	3427
have a man to *d* among this people	Jer 29:32	3427
there shall in Judah itself, and	Jer 31:24	3427
and I will cause them to *d* safely	Jer 32:37	3427
and Jerusalem shall *d* safely	Jer 33:16	7931
all your days ye shall *d* in tents	Jer 35:7	3427
to build houses for us to *d* in	Jer 35:9	3427
so we *d* at Jerusalem	Jer 35:11	3427
ye shall *d* in the land which I	Jer 35:15	3427
d with him among the people	Jer 40:5	3427
d in the land, and serve the king	Jer 40:9	3427
I will *d* at Mizpah to serve the	Jer 40:10	3427
d in your cities that ye have	Jer 40:10	3427
We will not *d* in this land,	Jer 42:13	3427
and there will we *d*	Jer 42:14	3427
to *d* in the land of Judah	Jer 43:4	3427
to *d* in the land of Judah	Jer 43:5	1481
Jews which *d* in the land of Egypt	Jer 44:1	3427
which *d* at Migdol, and at	Jer 44:1	3427
of Egypt, whither ye be gone to *d*	Jer 44:8	1481
them that *d* in the land of Egypt	Jer 44:13	3427
a desire to return to *d* there	Jer 44:14	3427
all Judah that *d* in the land of	Jer 44:26	3427
the city, and them that *d* therein	Jer 47:2	3427
without any to *d* therein	Jer 48:9	3427
O ye that *d* in Moab, leave the	Jer 48:28	3427
d in the rock, and be like the	Jer 48:28	7931
his people in his cities	Jer 49:1	3427
d deep, O inhabitants of Dedan	Jer 49:8	3427
shall a son of man *d* in it	Jer 49:18	1481
d deep, O ye inhabitants of Hazor	Jer 49:30	3427
gates nor bars, which *d* alone	Jer 49:31	7931
there, nor any son of man *d* in it	Jer 49:33	1481
desolate, and none shall *d* therein	Jer 50:3	3427
of the islands shall *d* there	Jer 50:39	3427
and the owls shall *d* therein	Jer 50:39	3427
shall any son of man *d* therein	Jer 50:40	1481
against them that *d* in the midst	Jer 51:1	3427
thou dost *d* among scorpions	Eze 2:6	3427
of all them that *d* therein	Eze 12:19	3427
daughters that *d* at thy left hand	Eze 16:46	3427
under it shall *d* all fowl of	Eze 17:23	7931
the branches thereof shall they *d*	Eze 17:23	7931
then shall they *d* in their land	Eze 28:25	3427
they shall *d* safely therein, and	Eze 28:26	3427
they shall *d* with confidence,	Eze 28:26	3427
smite all them that *d* therein	Eze 32:15	3427
they shall *d* safely in the	Eze 34:25	3427
but they shall *d* safely, and none	Eze 34:28	3427
ye shall *d* in the land that I	Eze 36:28	3427
also cause you to *d* in the cities	Eze 36:33	3427
they shall *d* in the land that I	Eze 37:25	3427
and they shall *d* therein, even	Eze 37:25	3427
they shall *d* safely all of them	Eze 38:8	3427
that *d* safely, all of them	Eze 38:11	3427
that *d* in the midst of the land	Eze 38:12	3427
among them that *d* carelessly in	Eze 39:6	3427
they that *d* in the cities of	Eze 39:9	3427
where I will *d* in the midst of	Eze 43:7	7931
I will *d* in the midst of them for	Eze 43:9	7931
wheresoever the children of men *d*	Dan 2:38	1753
that *d* in all the earth	Dan 4:1	1753
that *d* in all the earth	Dan 6:25	1753
They shall not *d* in the LORD's	Hos 9:3	3427
yet make thee to *d* in tabernacles	Hos 12:9	3427
They that *d* under his shadow	Hos 14:7	3427
But Judah shall *d* for ever	Joel 3:20	3427
of Israel be taken out that *d* in	Amos 3:12	3427
stone, but ye shall not *d* in them	Amos 5:11	3427
all that *d* therein shall mourn	Amos 9:5	
thou shalt *d* in the field, and	Mic 4:10	7931
because of them that *d* therein	Mic 7:13	3427
which *d* solitarily in the wood,	Mic 7:14	7931
the world, and all that *d* therein	Nah 1:5	3427
thy nobles shall *d* in the dust	Nah 3:18	7931
city, and of all that *d* therein	Hab 2:8	3427
city, and of all that *d* therein	Hab 2:17	3427
of all them that *d* in the land	Zeph 1:18	3427
to *d* in your cieled houses, and	Hag 1:4	3427
I will *d* in the midst of thee,	Zec 2:10	7931
I will *d* in the midst of thee, and	Zec 2:11	7931
will *d* in the midst of Jerusalem	Zec 8:3	7931
old women *d* in the streets of	Zec 8:4	3427
they shall *d* in the midst of	Zec 8:8	7931
And a bastard shall *d* in Ashdod	Zec 9:6	3427
And men shall *d* in it, and there	Zec 14:11	3427
and they enter in and *d* there	Mt 12:45	*2730*
and they enter in, and *d* there	Lk 11:26	*2730*
***d* on the face of the whole earth**	Lk 21:35	*2521*
desolate, and let no man *d* therein	Acts 1:20	*2730*
all ye that *d* at Jerusalem, be	Acts 2:14	*2730*
to all them that *d* in Jerusalem	Acts 4:16	*2730*
into this land, wherein ye now *d*	Acts 7:4	*2730*
For they that *d* at Jerusalem	Acts 13:27	*2730*
to *d* on all the face of the earth	Acts 17:26	*2730*
but Paul was suffered to *d* by	Acts 28:16	*3306*
that the Spirit of God *d* in you	Rom 8:9	*3611*
up Jesus from the dead *d* in you	Rom 8:11	*3611*
and she be pleased to *d* with him	1Cor 7:12	*3611*
and if he be pleased to *d* with her	1Cor 7:13	*3611*
I will *d* in them, and walk in them	2Cor 6:16	*1774*
That Christ may *d* in your hearts	Eph 3:17	*2730*
that in him should all fulness *d*	Col 1:19	*2730*
Let the word of Christ *d* in you	Col 3:16	*1774*
d with them according to	1Pet 3:7	*4924*
Hereby know we that we *d* in him	1Jn 4:13	*3306*
to try them that *d* upon the earth	Rev 3:10	*2730*
blood on them that *d* on the earth	Rev 6:10	*2730*
on the throne shall *d* among them	Rev 7:15	*4637*
they that *d* upon the earth shall	Rev 11:10	*2730*
ye heavens, and ye that *d* in them	Rev 12:12	*4637*
and them that *d* in heaven	Rev 13:6	*4637*
all that *d* upon the earth shall	Rev 13:8	*2730*

D

them which *d* therein to worship	Rev 13:12	*2730*
deceiveth them that *d* on the	Rev 13:14	*2730*
to them that *d* on the earth	Rev 13:14	*2730*
unto them that *d* on the earth	Rev 14:6	*2730*
they that *d* on the earth shall	Rev 17:8	*2730*
he will *d* with them, and they	Rev 21:3	*4637*

DWELLED

the Perizzite *d* then in the land	Gen 13:7	*3427*
Abram *d* in the land of Canaan, and	Gen 13:12	*3427*
Lot *d* in the cities of the plain,	Gen 13:12	*3427*
d between Kadesh and Shur, and	Gen 20:1	*3427*
they *d* there about ten years	Ruth 1:4	*3427*
on every side, and ye *d* safe	1Sa 12:11	*3427*

DWELLERS

d on the earth, see ye, when he	Is 18:3	*7931*
known unto all the *d* at Jerusalem	Acts 1:19	*2730*
the *d* in Mesopotamia, and in	Acts 2:9	*2730*

DWELLEST

them, and *d* in their land	Deut 12:29	*3427*
d in their cities, and in their	Deut 19:1	*3427*
and possessest it, and *d* therein	Deut 26:1	*3427*
which *d* between the cherubims,	2Kin 19:15	*3427*
thou that *d* between the cherubims	Ps 80:1	*3427*
O thou that *d* in the heavens	Ps 123:1	*3427*
Thou that *d* in the gardens, the	Song 8:13	*3427*
hosts, O my people that *d* in Zion	Is 10:24	*3427*
that *d* between the cherubims,	Is 37:16	*3427*
that *d* carelessly, that sayest in	Is 47:8	*3427*
O thou that *d* in the clefts of	Jer 49:16	*7931*
O thou that *d* upon many waters,	Jer 51:13	*7931*
of Edom, that *d* in the land of Uz	Lam 4:21	*3427*
thee, O thou that *d* in the land	Eze 7:7	*3427*
of man, thou *d* in the midst of a	Eze 12:2	*3427*
thou that *d* in the clefts of the	Obad 3	*7931*
that *d* with the daughter of	Zec 2:7	*3427*
Master,) where *d* thou	Jn 1:38	*3306*
I know thy works, and where thou *d*	Rev 2:13	*2730*

DWELLETH

But the stranger that *d* with you	Lev 19:34	*1481*
if thy brother that *d* by thee be	Lev 25:39	*3427*
brother that *d* by him wax poor	Lev 25:47	*3427*
and the people that *d* therein	Num 13:18	*3427*
he *d* as a lion, and teareth the	Deut 33:20	*7931*
she *d* in Israel even unto this	Josh 6:25	*3427*
wherein the LORD's tabernacle *d*	Josh 22:19	*7931*
which *d* between the cherubims	1Sa 4:4	*3427*
while he *d* in the country of the	1Sa 27:11	*3427*
that *d* between the cherubims,	2Sa 6:2	*3427*
the ark of God *d* within curtains	2Sa 7:2	*3427*
that *d* between the cherubims,	1Chr 13:6	*3427*
he *d* in desolate cities, and in	Job 15:28	*7931*
Where is the way where light *d*	Job 38:19	*7931*
She *d* and abideth on the rock,	Job 39:28	*7931*
to the LORD, which *d* in Zion	Ps 9:11	*3427*
and the place where thine honour *d*	Ps 26:8	*4908*
He that *d* in the secret place of	Ps 91:1	*3427*
the LORD our God, who *d* on high,	Ps 113:5	*3427*
out of Zion, which *d* at Jerusalem	Ps 135:21	*7931*
seeing he *d* securely by thee	Prov 3:29	*3427*
of hosts, which *d* in mount Zion	Is 8:18	*7931*
for he *d* on high	Is 33:5	*7931*
the people that *d* in this city	Jer 29:16	*3427*
desolation, and no man *d* therein,	Jer 44:2	*3427*
that *d* without care, saith the	Jer 49:31	*3427*
a land wherein no man *d*, neither	Jer 51:43	*3427*
she *d* among the heathen, she	Lam 1:3	*3427*
that *d* at thy right hand, is	Eze 16:46	*3427*
the king *d* that made him king	Eze 17:16	
when my people of Israel *d* safely	Eze 38:14	*3427*
darkness, and the light *d* with him	Dan 2:22	*8271*
every one that *d* therein shall	Hos 4:3	*3427*
for the LORD *d* in Zion	Joel 3:21	*7931*
and every one mourn that *d* therein	Amos 8:8	*3427*
by it, and by him that *d* therein	Mt 23:21	*2730*
my blood, *d* in me, and I in him	Jn 6:56	*3306*
but the Father that *d* in me	Jn 14:10	*3306*
for he *d* with you, and shall be in	Jn 14:17	*3306*
Howbeit the most High *d* not in	Acts 7:48	*2730*
d not in temples made with hands	Acts 17:24	*2730*
that do it, but sin that *d* in me	Rom 7:17	*3611*
is, in my flesh,) *d* no good thing	Rom 7:18	*3611*
that do it, but sin that *d* in me	Rom 7:20	*3611*
by his Spirit that *d* in you	Rom 8:11	*1774*
that the Spirit of God *d* in you	1Cor 3:16	*3611*
For in him *d* all the fulness of	Col 2:9	*2730*
by the Holy Ghost which *d* in us	2Ti 1:14	*1774*
The spirit that *d* in us lusteth	Jas 4:5	*2730*
earth, wherein *d* righteousness	2Pet 3:13	*2730*
how *d* the love of God in him	1Jn 3:17	*3306*

keepeth his commandments *d* in him	1Jn 3:24	*3306*
God *d* in us, and his love is	1Jn 4:12	*3306*
God *d* in him, and he in God	1Jn 4:15	*3306*
he that *d* in love is in God	1Jn 4:16	*3306*
the truth's sake, which *d* in us	2Jn 2	*3306*
slain among you, where Satan *d*	Rev 2:13	*2730*

DWELLING

their *d* was from Mesha, as thou	Gen 10:30	*4186*
Jacob was a plain man, *d* in tents	Gen 25:27	*3427*
thy *d* shall be the fatness of the	Gen 27:39	*4186*
if a man sell a *d* house in a	Lev 25:29	*4186*
that goeth down to the *d* of Ar	Num 21:15	*3427*
dukes of Sihon, *d* in the country	Josh 13:21	*3427*
hear thou in heaven thy *d* place	1Kin 8:30	*3427*
hear thou in heaven thy *d* place	1Kin 8:39	*3427*
Hear thou in heaven thy *d* place	1Kin 8:43	*3427*
in heaven thy *d* place, and	1Kin 8:49	*3427*
were in his city, *d* with Naboth	1Kin 21:8	*3427*
at the beginning of their *d* there	2Kin 17:25	*4186*
they ministered before the *d*	1Chr 6:32	*4908*
Now these are their *d* places	1Chr 6:54	*4186*
and a place for thy *d* for ever	2Chr 6:2	*3427*
hear thou from thy *d* place	2Chr 6:21	*3427*
hear thou from heaven thy *d* place	2Chr 6:30	*3427*
heavens, even from thy *d* place	2Chr 6:33	*3427*
heavens, even from thy *d* place	2Chr 6:39	*3427*
came up to his holy *d* place	2Chr 30:27	*4583*
on his people, and on his *d* place	2Chr 36:15	*4583*
the *d* place of the wicked shall	Job 8:22	*168*
where are the *d* places of the	Job 21:28	*4908*
their *d* places to all generations	Ps 49:11	*4908*
consume in the grave from their *d*	Ps 49:14	*2073*
and pluck thee out of thy *d* place	Ps 52:5	*168*
defiled by casting down the *d*	Ps 74:7	*4908*
and his *d* place in Zion	Ps 76:2	*4585*
Jacob, and laid waste his *d* place	Ps 79:7	*5116*
thou hast been our *d* place in all	Ps 90:1	*4583*
shall any plague come nigh thy *d*	Ps 91:10	*168*
and oil in the *d* of the wise	Prov 21:20	*5116*
against the *d* of the righteous	Prov 24:15	*5116*
upon every *d* place of mount Zion	Is 4:5	*4349*
I will consider in my *d* place	Is 18:4	*4349*
O thou daughter *d* in Egypt	Jer 46:19	*3427*
And Hazor shall be a *d* for dragons	Jer 49:33	*4583*
a *d* place for dragons, an	Jer 51:37	*3427*
all of them *d* without walls, and	Eze 38:11	*3427*
profane place for the city, for *d*	Eze 48:15	*4186*
whose *d* is not with flesh	Dan 2:11	*4070*
thy *d* shall be with the beasts of	Dan 4:25	*4070*
thy *d* shall be with the beasts of	Dan 4:32	*4070*
his *d* was with the wild asses	Dan 5:21	*4070*
I am the LORD your God *d* in Zion	Joel 3:17	*7931*
Where is the *d* of the lions	Nah 2:11	*4583*
so their *d* should not be cut off,	Zeph 3:7	*4583*
Who had his *d* among the tombs	Mk 5:3	*2731*
there were at Jerusalem Jews	Acts 2:5	*2730*
Jews and Greeks also *d* at Ephesus	Acts 19:17	*2730*
d in the light which no man can	1Ti 6:16	*3611*
d in tabernacles with Isaac and	Heb 11:9	*2730*
that righteous man *d* among them	2Pet 2:8	*1460*

DWELLINGPLACE

parable, and said, Strong is thy *d*	Num 24:21	*4186*
and have no certain *d* place	1Cor 4:11	*790*

DWELLINGPLACES

tents, and have mercy on his *d*	Jer 30:18	*4908*
they have burned her *d*	Jer 51:30	*4908*
In all your *d* the cities shall be	Eze 6:6	*4186*
will save them out of all their *d*	Eze 37:23	*4186*
to possess the *d* that are not	Hab 1:6	*4908*

DWELLINGS

of Israel had light in their *d*	Ex 10:23	*4186*
generations throughout all your *d*	Lev 3:17	*4186*
or of beast, in any of your *d*	Lev 7:26	*4186*
sabbath of the LORD in all your *d*	Lev 23:3	*4186*
your generations in all your *d*	Lev 23:14	*4186*
d throughout your generations	Lev 23:21	*4186*
your generations in all your *d*	Lev 23:31	*4186*
your generations in all your *d*	Num 35:29	*4186*
nor any remaining in his *d*	Job 18:19	*4033*
such are the *d* of the wicked	Job 18:21	*4908*
and the barren land his *d*	Job 39:6	*4908*
for wickedness is in their *d*	Ps 55:15	*4033*
Zion more than all the *d* of Jacob	Ps 87:2	*4908*
habitation, and in sure *d*, and in	Is 32:18	*4908*
because our *d* have cast us out	Jer 9:19	*4908*
in thee, and make their *d* in thee	Eze 25:4	*4908*
And the sea coast shall be *d*	Zeph 2:6	*5116*

DWELT

d in the land of Nod, on the east	Gen 4:16	3427
and they d there	Gen 11:2	3427
they came unto Haran, and d there	Gen 11:31	3427
d in the plain of Mamre, which is	Gen 13:18	3427
Amorites, that d in Hazezon-tamar	Gen 14:7	3427
who d in Sodom, and his goods, and	Gen 14:12	3427
for he d in the plain of Mamre	Gen 14:13	7931
after Abram had d ten years in	Gen 16:3	3427
the cities in the which Lot d	Gen 19:29	3427
d in the mountain, and his two	Gen 19:30	3427
he d in a cave, he and his two	Gen 19:30	3427
d in the wilderness, and became an	Gen 21:20	3427
he d in the wilderness of Paran	Gen 21:21	3427
and Abraham d at Beer-sheba	Gen 22:19	3427
Ephron d among the children of	Gen 23:10	3427
for he d in the south country	Gen 24:62	3427
Isaac d by the well Lahai-roi	Gen 25:11	3427
they d from Havilah unto Shur,	Gen 25:18	7931
And Isaac d in Gerar	Gen 26:6	3427
the valley of Gerar, and d there	Gen 26:17	3427
when Israel d in that land, that	Gen 35:22	7931
Thus d Esau in mount Seir	Gen 36:8	3427
Jacob d in the land wherein his	Gen 37:1	3427
went and d in her father's house	Gen 38:11	3427
Israel d in the land of Egypt, in	Gen 47:27	3427
Joseph d in Egypt, he, and his	Gen 50:22	3427
and d in the land of Midian	Ex 2:15	3427
who d in Egypt, was four hundred	Ex 12:40	3427
the land of Egypt, where ye d	Lev 18:3	3427
your sabbaths, when ye d upon it	Lev 26:35	3427
and the Canaanites d in the valley	Num 14:25	3427
Canaanites which d in their hill	Num 14:45	3427
we have d in Egypt a long time	Num 20:15	3427
which d in the south, heard tell	Num 21:1	3427
Israel d in all the cities of the	Num 21:25	3427
Thus Israel d in the land of the	Num 21:31	3427
the Amorites, which d at Heshbon	Num 21:34	3427
all their cities wherein they d	Num 31:10	4186
and he d therein	Num 32:40	3427
which d in the south in the land	Num 33:40	3427
which d in Heshbon, and Og the	Deut 1:4	3427
which d at Astaroth in Edrei	Deut 1:4	3427
Ye have d long enough in this	Deut 1:6	3427
which d in that mountain, came	Deut 1:44	3427
which d in Seir, through the way	Deut 2:8	3427
The Emims d therein in times past	Deut 2:10	3427
The Horims also d in Seir	Deut 2:12	3427
before them, and d in their stead	Deut 2:12	3427
giants d therein in old time	Deut 2:20	3427
them, and d in their stead	Deut 2:21	3427
of Esau, which d in Seir, when he	Deut 2:22	3427
d in their stead even unto this	Deut 2:22	3427
And the Avims which d in Hazerim	Deut 2:23	3427
them, and d in their stead	Deut 2:23	3427
the Amorites, which d at Heshbon	Deut 3:2	3427
who d at Heshbon, whom Moses and	Deut 4:46	3427
built goodly houses, and d therein	Deut 8:12	3427
we have d in the land of Egypt	Deut 29:16	3427
will of him that d in the bush	Deut 33:16	7931
town wall, and she d upon the wall	Josh 2:15	3427
d on the other side Jordan	Josh 7:7	3427
and that they d among them	Josh 9:16	3427
who d in Heshbon, and ruled from	Josh 12:2	3427
that d at Ashtaroth and at Edrei,	Josh 12:4	3427
the Canaanites that d in Gezer	Josh 16:10	3427
d therein, and called Leshem, Dan,	Josh 19:47	3427
he built the city, and d therein	Josh 19:50	3427
they possessed it, and d therein	Josh 21:43	3427
the children of Reuben and Gad d	Josh 22:33	3427
Your fathers d on the other side	Josh 24:2	3427
ye d in the wilderness a long	Josh 24:7	3427
which d on the other side Jordan	Josh 24:8	3427
the Amorites which d in the land	Josh 24:18	3427
that d in the mountain, and in the	Judg 1:9	3427
the Canaanites that d in Hebron	Judg 1:10	3427
they went and d among the people	Judg 1:16	3427
the Canaanites that d in Gezer	Judg 1:29	3427
but the Canaanites d in Gezer	Judg 1:29	3427
but the Canaanites d among them	Judg 1:30	3427
But the Asherites d among the	Judg 1:32	3427
but he d among the Canaanites,	Judg 1:33	3427
Hivites that d in mount Lebanon	Judg 3:3	3427
of Israel d among the Canaanites	Judg 3:5	3427
which d in Harosheth of the	Judg 4:2	3427
she d under the palm tree of	Judg 4:5	3427
d in tents on the east of Nobah	Judg 8:11	7931
Joash went and d in his own house	Judg 8:29	3427
d there, for fear of Abimelech	Judg 9:21	3427
And Abimelech d at Arumah	Judg 9:41	3427
he d in Shamir in mount Ephraim	Judg 10:1	3427
brethren, and d in the land of Tob	Judg 11:3	3427
While Israel d in Heshbon	Judg 11:26	3427
d in the top of the rock Etam	Judg 15:8	3427
were therein, how they d careless	Judg 18:7	3427
they built a city, and d therein	Judg 18:28	3427
repaired the cities, and d in them	Judg 21:23	3427
and d with her mother in law	Ruth 2:23	3427
he and Samuel went and d in Naioth	1Sa 19:18	3427
they d with him all the while	1Sa 22:4	3427
d in strong holds at En-gedi	1Sa 23:29	3427
David d with Achish at Gath, he	1Sa 27:3	3427
the time that David d in the	1Sa 27:7	3427
the Philistines came and d in them	1Sa 31:7	3427
they d in the cities of Hebron	2Sa 2:3	3427
So David d in the fort, and called	2Sa 5:9	3427
Whereas I have not d in any house	2Sa 7:6	3427
all that d in the house of Ziba	2Sa 9:12	4186
So Mephibosheth d in Jerusalem	2Sa 9:13	3427
So Absalom d two full years in	2Sa 14:28	3427
Shimei d in Jerusalem many days	1Kin 2:38	3427
And Judah and Israel d safely	1Kin 4:25	3427
his house where he d had another	1Kin 7:8	3427
the Canaanites that d in the city,	1Kin 9:16	3427
d therein, and reigned in Damascus	1Kin 11:24	3427
Solomon, and Jeroboam d in Egypt	1Kin 12:2	3427
which d in the cities of Judah	1Kin 12:17	3427
in mount Ephraim, and d therein	1Kin 12:25	3427
Now there d an old prophet in	1Kin 13:11	3427
the city where the old prophet d	1Kin 13:25	3427
that d at Damascus, saying,	1Kin 15:18	3427
building of Ramah, and d in Tirzah	1Kin 15:21	3427
d by the brook Cherith, that is	1Kin 17:5	3427
of Israel d in their tents	2Kin 13:5	3427
death, and d in a several house	2Kin 15:5	3427
Elath, and d there unto this day	2Kin 16:6	3427
and d in the cities thereof	2Kin 17:24	3427
d in Beth-el, and taught them how	2Kin 17:28	3427
in their cities wherein they d	2Kin 17:29	3427
went and returned, and d at Nineveh	2Kin 19:36	3427
(now she d in Jerusalem in the	2Kin 22:14	3427
of the scribes which d at Jabez	1Chr 2:55	3427
those that d among plants and	1Chr 4:23	3427
there they d with the king for	1Chr 4:23	3427
they d at Beer-sheba, and Moladah,	1Chr 4:28	3427
they of Ham had d there of old	1Chr 4:40	3427
this day, and d in their rooms	1Chr 4:41	3427
escaped, and d there unto this day	1Chr 4:43	3427
who d in Aroer, even unto Nebo and	1Chr 5:8	3427
they d in their tents throughout	1Chr 5:10	3427
of Gad d over against them	1Chr 5:11	3427
they d in Gilead in Bashan, and in	1Chr 5:16	3427
they d in their steads until the	1Chr 5:22	3427
tribe of Manasseh d in the land	1Chr 5:23	3427
In these d the children of Joseph	1Chr 7:29	3427
These d in Jerusalem	1Chr 8:28	3427
at Gibeon d the father of Gibeon	1Chr 8:29	3427
these also d with their brethren	1Chr 8:32	3427
d in their possessions in their	1Chr 9:2	3427
in Jerusalem d of the children of	1Chr 9:3	3427
that d in the villages of the	1Chr 9:16	3427
these d at Jerusalem	1Chr 9:34	3427
in Gibeon d the father of Gibeon,	1Chr 9:35	3427
they also d with their brethren	1Chr 9:38	3427
the Philistines came and d in them	1Chr 10:7	3427
And David d in the castle	1Chr 11:7	3427
For I have not d in an house	1Chr 17:5	3427
that d in the cities of Judah	2Chr 10:17	3427
Rehoboam in Jerusalem, and built	2Chr 11:5	3427
that d at Damascus, saying,	2Chr 16:2	3427
Jehoshaphat d at Jerusalem	2Chr 19:4	3427
they d therein, and have built	2Chr 20:8	3427
the Arabians that d in Gur-baal	2Chr 26:7	3427
d in a several house, being a	2Chr 26:21	3427
and they d there	2Chr 28:18	3427
that d in Judah, rejoiced	2Chr 30:25	3427
that d in Jerusalem to give the	2Chr 31:4	3427
that d in the cities of Judah,	2Chr 31:6	3427
(now she d in Jerusalem in the	2Chr 34:22	3427
d in their cities, and all Israel	Ezr 2:70	3427
Moreover the Nethinims d in Ophel	Neh 3:26	3427
the Jews which d by them came	Neh 4:12	3427
and all Israel, d in their cities	Neh 7:73	3427
of the people d at Jerusalem	Neh 11:1	3427
the province that d in Jerusalem	Neh 11:3	3427
but in the cities of Judah d	Neh 11:3	3427
at Jerusalem d certain of the	Neh 11:4	3427
All the sons of Perez that d at	Neh 11:6	3427
But the Nethinims d in Ophel	Neh 11:21	3427
of Judah d at Kirjath-arba	Neh 11:25	3427
they d from Beer-sheba unto the	Neh 11:30	2583
Benjamin from Geba d at Michmash	Neh 11:31	

There *d* men of Tyre also therein,	Neh 13:16	3427
that *d* in the unwalled towns,	Est 9:19	3427
and the honourable man *d* in it	Job 22:8	3427
d as a king in the army, as one	Job 29:25	7931
Thy congregation hath *d* therein	Ps 68:10	3427
mount Zion, wherein thou hast *d*	Ps 74:2	7931
my soul had almost *d* in silence	Ps 94:17	7931
My soul hath long *d* with him that	Ps 120:6	7931
neither shall it be *d* in from	Is 13:20	7931
to Ariel, the city where David *d*	Is 29:1	2583
went and returned, and *d* at Nineveh	Is 37:37	3427
passed through, and where no man *d*	Jer 2:6	3427
But we have *d* in tents, and have	Jer 35:10	3427
so he *d* among the people	Jer 39:14	3427
d with him among the people that	Jer 40:6	3427
d in the habitation of Chimham,	Jer 41:17	3427
that *d* in the land of Egypt	Jer 44:15	3427
neither shall it be *d* in from	Jer 50:39	7931
that *d* by the river of Chebar, and	Eze 3:15	3427
under his shadow *d* all great	Eze 31:6	3427
that *d* under his shadow in the	Eze 31:17	3427
of Israel *d* in their own land	Eze 36:17	3427
wherein your fathers have *d*	Eze 37:25	3427
when they *d* safely in their land,	Eze 39:26	3427
heaven *d* in the boughs thereof,	Dan 4:12	1753
which the beasts of the field *d*	Dan 4:21	1753
rejoicing city that *d* carelessly	Zeph 2:15	3427
d in a city called Nazareth	Mt 2:23	2730
d in Capernaum, which is upon the	Mt 4:13	2730
on all that *d* round about them	Lk 1:65	4039

above all men that *d* in Jerusalem	Lk 13:4	2730
d among us, (and we beheld his	Jn 1:14	4637
They came and saw where he *d*	Jn 1:39	3306
before he *d* in Charran,	Acts 7:2	2730
the Chaldaeans, and *d* in Charran	Acts 7:4	2730
the Jews which *d* at Damascus	Acts 9:22	2730
to the saints which *d* at Lydda	Acts 9:32	2730
And all that *d* at Lydda and Saron.	Acts 9:35	2730
the brethren which *d* in Judaea	Acts 11:29	2730
d as strangers in the land of	Acts 13:17	3940
so that all they which *d* in Asia	Acts 19:10	2730
of all the Jews which *d* there	Acts 22:12	2730
Paul two whole years in his own	Acts 28:30	3306
which *d* first in thy grandmother	2Ti 1:5	1774
them that *d* on the earth	Rev 11:10	2730

DYED

And rams' skins *d* red, and badgers'	Ex 25:5	
for the tent of rams' skins *d* red	Ex 26:14	
And rams' skins *d* red, and badgers'	Ex 35:7	
for the tent of rams' skins *d* red	Ex 36:19	
the covering of rams' skins *d* red	Ex 39:34	
with *d* garments from Bozrah	Is 63:1	2556
exceeding in *d* attire upon their	Eze 23:15	2871

DYING

shall we be consumed with *d*	Num 17:13	1478
took a wife, and *d* left no seed	Mk 12:20	599
years of age, and she lay a *d*	Lk 8:42	599
the body the *d* of the Lord Jesus	2Cor 4:10	3500
as *d*, and, behold, we live	2Cor 6:9	599
By faith Jacob, when he was a *d*	Heb 11:21	599

E

EACH See APPENDIX.

EAGLE

the *e*, and the ossifrage, and the	Lev 11:13	5404
and the pelican, and the gier *e*	Lev 11:18	7360
the *e*, and the ossifrage, and the	Deut 14:12	5404
And the pelican, and the gier *e*	Deut 14:17	7360
earth, as swift as the *e* flieth	Deut 28:49	5404
As an *e* stirreth up her nest,	Deut 32:11	5404
as the *e* that hasteth to the prey	Job 9:26	5404
Doth the *e* mount up at thy	Job 39:27	5404
fly away as an *e* toward heaven	Prov 23:5	5404
The way of an *e* in the air	Prov 30:19	5404
Behold, he shall fly as an *e*	Jer 48:40	5404
make thy nest as high as the *e*	Jer 49:16	5404
he shall come up and fly as the *e*	Jer 49:22	5404
four also had the face of an *e*	Eze 1:10	5404
and the fourth the face of an *e*	Eze 10:14	5404
A great *e* with great wings,	Eze 17:3	5404
another great *e* with great wings	Eze 17:7	5404
He shall come as an *e* against the	Hos 8:1	5404
thou exalt thyself as the *e*	Obad 4	5404
enlarge thy baldness as the *e*	Mic 1:16	5404
fly as the *e* that hasteth to eat	Hab 1:8	5404
fourth beast was like a flying *e*	Rev 4:7	105
were given two wings of a great *e*	Rev 12:14	105

EAGLE'S

thy youth is renewed like the *e*	Ps 103:5	5404
was like a lion, and had *e* wings	Dan 7:4	5403

EAGLES

they were swifter than *e*, they	2Sa 1:23	5404
out, and the young *e* shall eat it	Prov 30:17	5404
shall mount up with wings as *e*	Is 40:31	5404
his horses are swifter than *e*	Jer 4:13	5404
swifter than the *e* of the heaven	Lam 4:19	5404
there will the *e* be gathered	Mt 24:28	105
thither will the *e* be gathered	Lk 17:37	105

EAGLES'

and how I bare you on *e* wings	Ex 19:4	5404
hairs were grown like *e* feathers	Dan 4:33	5403

EAR

for the barley was in the *e*	Ex 9:31	24
wilt give *e* to his commandments,	Ex 15:26	238
bore his *e* through with an aul	Ex 21:6	241
the tip of the right *e* of Aaron	Ex 29:20	241
tip of the right *e* of his sons	Ex 29:20	241
upon the tip of Aaron's right *e*	Lev 8:23	241
upon the tip of their right *e*	Lev 8:24	241
it upon the tip of the right *e* of	Lev 14:14	241
e of him that is to be cleansed	Lev 14:17	241
it upon the tip of the right *e* of	Lev 14:25	241
e of him that is to be cleansed	Lev 14:28	241
your voice, nor give *e* unto you	Deut 1:45	238

it through his *e* unto the door	Deut 15:17	241
Give *e*, O ye heavens, and I will	Deut 32:1	238
give *e*, O ye princes,	Judg 5:3	238
and will set them to *e* his ground	1Sa 8:12	2790
in his *e* a day before Saul came	1Sa 9:15	241
LORD, bow down thine *e*, and hear	2Kin 19:16	241
but they would not give *e*	2Chr 24:19	238
Let thine *e* now be attentive, and	Neh 1:6	241
let now thine *e* be attentive to	Neh 1:11	241
yet would they not give *e*	Neh 9:30	238
mine *e* received a little thereof	Job 4:12	241
Doth not the *e* try words	Job 12:11	241
mine *e* hath heard and understood	Job 13:1	241
When the *e* heard me, then it	Job 29:11	241
Unto me men gave *e*, and waited, and	Job 29:21	8085
I gave *e* to your reasons, whilst	Job 32:11	238
give *e* unto me, ye that have	Job 34:2	238
For the *e* trieth words, as the	Job 34:3	241
also their *e* to discipline	Job 36:10	241
of thee by the hearing of the *e*	Job 42:5	241
Give *e* to my words, O LORD	Ps 5:1	238
thou wilt cause thine *e* to hear	Ps 10:17	241
give *e* unto my prayer, that goeth	Ps 17:1	238
incline thine *e* unto me, and hear	Ps 17:6	241
Bow down thine *e* to me	Ps 31:2	241
O LORD, and give *e* unto my cry	Ps 39:12	238
and consider, and incline thine *e*	Ps 45:10	241
give *e*, all ye inhabitants of the	Ps 49:1	238
will incline mine *e* to a parable	Ps 49:4	241
give *e* to the words of my mouth	Ps 54:2	238
Give *e* to my prayer, O God	Ps 55:1	238
deaf adder that stoppeth her *e*	Ps 58:4	241
incline thine *e* unto me, and save	Ps 71:2	241
and he gave *e* unto me	Ps 77:1	238
Give *e*, O my people, to my law	Ps 78:1	238
Give *e*, O Shepherd of Israel,	Ps 80:1	238
give *e*, O God of Jacob	Ps 84:8	238
Bow down thine *e*, O LORD, hear me	Ps 86:1	241
Give *e*, O LORD, unto my prayer	Ps 86:6	238
incline thine *e* unto my cry	Ps 88:2	241
He that planted the *e*, shall he	Ps 94:9	241
incline thine *e* unto me	Ps 102:2	241
he hath inclined his *e* unto me	Ps 116:2	241
give *e* unto my voice, when I cry	Ps 141:1	238
give *e* to my supplications	Ps 143:1	238
thou incline thine *e* unto wisdom	Prov 2:2	241
incline thine *e* unto my sayings	Prov 4:20	241
bow thine *e* to my understanding	Prov 5:1	241
nor inclined mine *e* to them that	Prov 5:13	241
The *e* that heareth the reproof of	Prov 15:31	241
a liar giveth *e* to a naughty	Prov 17:4	238
the *e* of the wise seeketh	Prov 18:15	241
The hearing *e*, and the seeing eye,	Prov 20:12	241
Bow down thine *e*, and hear the	Prov 22:17	241

wise reprover upon an obedient *e*	Prov 25:12	241
away his *e* from hearing the law	Prov 28:9	241
nor the *e* filled with hearing	Eccl 1:8	241
Hear, O heavens, and give *e*	Is 1:2	238
give *e* unto the law of our God,	Is 1:10	238
and give *e*, all ye of far	Is 8:9	238
Give ye *e*, and hear my voice	Is 28:23	238
the young asses that *e* the ground	Is 30:24	5647
give *e* unto my speech	Is 32:9	238
Incline thine *e*, O LORD, and hear	Is 37:17	241
Who among you will give *e* to this	Is 42:23	238
time that thine *e* was not opened	Is 48:8	241
he wakeneth mine *e* to hear as the	Is 50:4	241
The Lord GOD hath opened mine *e*	Is 50:5	241
give *e* unto me, O my nation	Is 51:4	238
Incline your *e*, and come unto me	Is 55:3	241
neither his *e* heavy, that it	Is 59:1	241
not heard, nor perceived by the *e*	Is 64:4	238
their *e* is uncircumcised, and they	Jer 6:10	241
not unto me, nor inclined their *e*	Jer 7:24	241
not unto me, nor inclined their *e*	Jer 7:26	241
let your *e* receive the word of	Jer 9:20	241
obeyed not, nor inclined their *e*	Jer 11:8	241
Hear ye, and give *e*	Jer 13:15	238
not, neither inclined their *e*	Jer 17:23	241
nor inclined your *e* to hear	Jer 25:4	241
unto me, neither inclined their *e*	Jer 34:14	241
but ye have not inclined your *e*	Jer 35:15	241
nor inclined their *e* to turn from	Jer 44:5	241
hide not thine *e* at my breathing,	Lam 3:56	241
O my God, incline thine *e*	Dan 9:18	241
and give ye *e*, O house of the king	Hos 5:1	238
Hear this, ye old men, and give *e*	Joel 1:2	238
lion two legs, or a piece of an *e*	Amos 3:12	241
and what ye hear in the *e*, that	Mt 10:27	3775
high priest's, and smote off his *e*	Mt 26:51	5621
first the blade, then the *e*	Mk 4:28	4719
after that the full corn in the *e*	Mk 4:28	4719
the high priest, and cut off his *e*	Mk 14:47	5621
which ye have spoken in the *e* in	Lk 12:3	3775
priest, and cut off his right *e*	Lk 22:50	3775
And he touched his *e*, and healed	Lk 22:51	5621
servant, and cut off his right *e*	Jn 18:10	5621
his kinsman whose *e* Peter cut off	Jn 18:26	5621
nor *e* heard, neither have entered	1Cor 2:9	3775
if the *e* shall say, Because I am	1Cor 12:16	3775
He that hath an *e*, let him hear	Rev 2:7	3775
He that hath an *e*, let him hear	Rev 2:11	3775
He that hath an *e*, let him hear	Rev 2:17	3775
He that hath an *e*, let him hear	Rev 2:29	3775
He that hath an *e*, let him hear	Rev 3:6	3775
He that hath an *e*, let him hear	Rev 3:13	3775
He that hath an *e*, let him hear	Rev 3:22	3775
If any man have an *e*, let him	Rev 13:9	3775

EARED

which is neither *e* nor sown	Deut 21:4	5647

EARING

shall neither be *e* nor harvest	Gen 45:6	2758
in *e* time and in harvest thou	Ex 34:21	2758

EARLY

your feet, and ye shall rise up *e*	Gen 19:2	7925
Abraham gat up *e* in the morning	Gen 19:27	7925
Abimelech rose *e* in the morning	Gen 20:8	7925
Abraham rose up *e* in the morning	Gen 21:14	7925
Abraham rose up *e* in the morning	Gen 22:3	7925
Jacob rose up *e* in the morning,	Gen 28:18	7925
e in the morning Laban rose up,	Gen 31:55	7925
Rise up *e* in the morning, and	Ex 8:20	7925
Rise up *e* in the morning, and	Ex 9:13	7925
rose up *e* in the morning, and	Ex 24:4	7925
they rose up *e* on the morrow, and	Ex 32:6	7925
Moses rose up *e* in the morning,	Ex 34:4	7925
they rose up *e* in the morning, and	Num 14:40	7925
Joshua rose *e* in the morning	Josh 3:1	7925
Joshua rose *e* in the morning, and	Josh 6:12	7925
that they rose *e* about the	Josh 6:15	7925
Joshua rose up *e* in the morning	Josh 7:16	7925
Joshua rose up *e* in the morning	Josh 8:10	7925
it, that they hasted and rose up *e*	Josh 8:14	7925
the city arose *e* in the morning	Judg 6:28	7925
for he rose up *e* on the morrow	Judg 6:38	7925
that were with him, rose up *e*	Judg 7:1	7925
depart *e* from mount Gilead	Judg 7:3	6852
the sun is up, thou shalt rise *e*	Judg 9:33	7925
when they arose *e* in the morning	Judg 19:5	7925
he arose *e* in the morning on the	Judg 19:8	7925
to morrow get you *e* on your way	Judg 19:9	7925
morrow, that the people rose *e*	Judg 21:4	7925
And they rose up in the morning *e*	1Sa 1:19	7925

of Ashdod arose *e* on the morrow	1Sa 5:3	7925
when they arose *e* on the morrow	1Sa 5:4	7925
And they arose *e*	1Sa 9:26	7925
when Samuel rose *e* to meet Saul	1Sa 15:12	7925
David rose up *e* in the morning,	1Sa 17:20	7925
Wherefore now rise up *e* in the	1Sa 29:10	7925
soon as ye be up *e* in the morning,	1Sa 29:10	7925
his men rose up *e* to depart in	1Sa 29:11	7925
And Absalom rose up *e*, and stood	2Sa 15:2	7925
they rose up *e* in the morning, and	2Kin 3:22	7925
of the man of God was risen *e*	2Kin 6:15	7925
when they arose *e* in the morning	2Kin 19:35	7925
they rose *e* in the morning, and	2Chr 20:20	7925
Then Hezekiah the king rose *e*	2Chr 29:20	7925
rose up *e* in the morning, and	Job 1:5	7925
shall help her, and that right *e*	Ps 46:5	1242
I myself will awake *e*	Ps 57:8	7837
e will I seek thee	Ps 63:1	7836
returned and enquired *e* after God	Ps 78:34	7836
O satisfy us *e* with thy mercy	Ps 90:14	1242
I will *e* destroy all the wicked	Ps 101:8	1242
I myself will awake *e*	Ps 108:2	7837
It is vain for you to rise up *e*	Ps 127:2	7925
they shall seek me *e*, but they	Prov 1:28	7836
that seek me *e* shall find me	Prov 8:17	7836
rising *e* in the morning, it shall	Prov 27:14	7925
Let us get up *e* to the vineyards	Song 7:12	7925
that rise up *e* in the morning	Is 5:11	7925
within me will I seek thee *e*	Is 26:9	7836
when they arose *e* in the morning	Is 37:36	7925
and I spake unto you, rising up *e*	Jer 7:13	7925
the prophets, daily rising up *e*	Jer 7:25	7925
even unto this day, rising up *e*	Jer 11:7	7925
I have spoken unto you, rising *e*	Jer 25:3	7925
servants the prophets, rising *e*	Jer 25:4	7925
I sent unto you, both rising up *e*	Jer 26:5	7925
the prophets, rising up *e*	Jer 29:19	7925
though I taught them, rising up *e*	Jer 32:33	7925
I have spoken unto you, rising *e*	Jer 35:14	7925
the prophets, rising up *e*	Jer 35:15	7925
servants the prophets, rising *e*	Jer 44:4	7925
king arose very *e* in the morning	Dan 6:19	8238
affliction they will seek me *e*	Hos 5:15	7836
as the *e* dew it goeth away	Hos 6:4	7925
as the *e* dew that passeth away,	Hos 13:3	7925
but they rose *e*, and corrupted all	Zeph 3:7	7925
which went out *e* in the morning	Mt 20:1	260,4404
very *e* in the morning the first	Mk 16:2	4404
Now when Jesus was risen *e* the	Mk 16:9	4404
all the people came *e* in the	Lk 21:38	3719
very *e* in the morning, they came	Lk 24:1	3722
which were *e* at the sepulchre	Lk 24:22	3721
e in the morning he came again	Jn 8:2	3722
of judgment: and it was *e*	Jn 18:28	4405
the week cometh Mary Magdalene *e*	Jn 20:1	4404
into the temple *e* in the morning	Acts 5:21	3722
for it, until he receive the *e*	Jas 5:7	4406

EARNEST

For the *e* expectation of the	Rom 8:19	603
given the *e* of the Spirit in our	2Cor 1:22	728
given unto us the *e* of the Spirit	2Cor 5:5	728
when he told us your *e* desire	2Cor 7:7	1972
which put the same *e* care into	2Cor 8:16	4710
Which is the *e* of our inheritance	Eph 1:14	728
According to my *e* expectation,	Phil 1:20	603
we ought to give the more *e* heed	Heb 2:1	4056

EARNESTLY

Did I not *e* send unto thee to	Num 22:37	
David *e* asked leave of me that he	1Sa 20:6	
David *e* asked leave of me to go	1Sa 20:28	
Zabbai *e* repaired the other piece	Neh 3:20	2734
As a servant *e* desireth the	Job 7:2	
For I *e* protested unto your	Jer 11:7	
I do *e* remember him still	Jer 31:20	
may do evil with both hands *e*	Mic 7:3	3190
in an agony he prayed more *e*	Lk 22:44	1617
e looked upon him, and said, This	Lk 22:56	816
or why look ye so *e* on us	Acts 3:12	816
e beholding the council, said,	Acts 23:1	816
But covet *e* the best gifts	1Cor 12:31	2206
e desiring to be clothed upon	2Cor 5:2	1971
he prayed *e* that it might not	Jas 5:17	4335
exhort you that ye should *e*	Jude 3	1864

EARNETH

he that *e* wages *e* wages to	Hag 1:6	7936

EARRING

golden *e* of half a shekel weight	Gen 24:22	5141
came to pass, when he saw the *e*	Gen 24:30	5141
I put the *e* upon her face, and the	Gen 24:47	5141

E

EARRINGS

money, and every one an *e* of gold	Job 42:11	5141
As an *e* of gold, and an ornament	Prov 25:12	5141

EARRINGS

all their *e* which were in their	Gen 35:4	5141
unto them, Break off the golden *e*	Ex 32:2	5141
golden *e* which were in their ears	Ex 32:3	5141
and brought bracelets, and *e*	Ex 35:22	5141
chains, and bracelets, rings, *e*	Num 31:50	5694
me every man the *e* of his prey	Judg 8:24	5141
(For they had golden *e*, because	Judg 8:24	5141
every man the *e* of his prey	Judg 8:25	5141
golden *e* that he requested was a	Judg 8:26	5141
and the tablets, and the *e*	Is 3:20	3908
e in thine ears, and a beautiful	Eze 16:12	5694
and she decked herself with her *e*	Hos 2:13	5141

EARS

told all these things in their *e*	Gen 20:8	241
earrings which were in their *e*	Gen 35:4	241
seven *e* of corn came up upon one	Gen 41:5	7641
And, behold, seven thin *e* and	Gen 41:6	7641
the seven thin *e* devoured the	Gen 41:7	7641
devoured the seven rank and full *e*	Gen 41:7	7641
seven *e* came up in one stalk	Gen 41:22	7641
And, behold, seven *e*, withered,	Gen 41:23	7641
e devoured the seven good *e*	Gen 41:24	7641
the seven good *e* are seven years	Gen 41:26	7641
the seven empty *e* blasted with	Gen 41:27	7641
thee, speak a word in my lord's *e*	Gen 44:18	241
in the *e* of Pharaoh, saying,	Gen 50:4	241
mayest tell in the *e* of thy son	Ex 10:2	241
Speak now in the *e* of the people	Ex 11:2	241
and rehearse it in the *e* of Joshua	Ex 17:14	241
which are in the *e* of your wives	Ex 32:2	241
earrings which were in their *e*	Ex 32:3	241
of thy firstfruits green *e* of	Lev 2:14	24
even beaten out of full *e*	Lev 2:14	3759
nor parched corn, nor green *e*	Lev 23:14	3759
ye have wept in the *e* of the LORD	Num 11:18	241
LORD, as ye have spoken in mine *e*	Num 14:28	241
which I speak in your *e* this day	Deut 5:1	241
pluck the *e* with thine hand	Deut 23:25	4425
see, and *e* to hear, unto this day	Deut 29:4	241
may speak these words in their *e*	Deut 31:28	241
Moses spake in the *e* of all the	Deut 31:30	241
this song in the *e* of the people	Deut 32:44	241
the *e* of the elders of that city	Josh 20:4	241
proclaim in the *e* of the people	Judg 7:3	241
in the *e* of all the men of	Judg 9:2	241
brethren spake of him in the *e* of	Judg 9:3	241
and spakest of also in mine *e*	Judg 17:2	241
glean of corn after him in	Ruth 2:2	7641
at which both the *e* of every one	1Sa 3:11	241
them in the *e* of the LORD	1Sa 8:21	241
tidings in the *e* of the people	1Sa 11:4	241
bleating of the sheep in mine *e*	1Sa 15:14	241
those words in the *e* of David	1Sa 18:23	241
also spake in the *e* of Benjamin	2Sa 3:19	241
the *e* of David in Hebron all that	2Sa 3:19	241
all that we have heard with our *e*	2Sa 7:22	241
and my cry did enter into his *e*	2Sa 22:7	241
full of corn in the husk	2Kin 4:42	3759
e of the people that are on the	2Kin 18:26	241
thy tumult is come up into mine *e*	2Kin 19:28	241
of it, both his *e* shall tingle	2Kin 21:12	241
he read in their *e* all the words	2Kin 23:2	241
all that we have heard with our *e*	1Chr 17:20	241
let thine *e* be attent unto the	2Chr 6:40	241
mine *e* attent unto the prayer	2Chr 7:15	241
he read in their *e* all the words	2Chr 34:30	241
the *e* of all the people were	Neh 8:3	241
and my declaration with your *e*	Job 13:17	241
A dreadful sound is in his *e*	Job 15:21	241
off as the tops of the *e* of corn	Job 24:24	7641
heard the fame thereof with our *e*	Job 28:22	241
Then he openeth the *e* of men	Job 33:16	241
and openeth their *e* in oppression	Job 36:15	241
came before him, even into his *e*	Ps 18:6	241
his *e* are open unto their cry	Ps 34:15	241
mine *e* hast thou opened	Ps 40:6	241
We have heard with our *e*, O God	Ps 44:1	241
incline thine *e* to the words of my	Ps 78:1	241
mine *e* shall hear my desire of	Ps 92:11	241
They have *e*, but they hear not	Ps 115:6	241
let thine *e* be attentive to the	Ps 130:2	241
They have *e*, but they hear not	Ps 135:17	241
Whoso stoppeth his *e* at the cry	Prov 21:13	241
Speak not in the *e* of a fool	Prov 23:9	241
thine *e* to the words of knowledge	Prov 23:12	241
one that taketh a dog by the *e*	Prov 26:17	241
In mine *e* said the LORD of hosts,	Is 5:9	241

people fat, and make their *e* heavy	Is 6:10	241
their eyes, and hear with their *e*	Is 6:10	241
after the hearing of his *e*	Is 11:3	241
reapeth the *e* with his arm	Is 17:5	7641
e in the valley of Rephaim	Is 17:5	7641
in mine *e* by the LORD of hosts	Is 22:14	241
thine *e* shall hear a word behind	Is 30:21	241
the *e* of them that hear shall	Is 32:3	241
that stoppeth his *e* from hearing	Is 33:15	241
the *e* of the deaf shall be	Is 35:5	241
in the *e* of the people that are	Is 36:11	241
tumult, is come up into mine *e*	Is 37:29	241
opening the *e*, but he heareth not	Is 42:20	241
eyes, and the deaf that have *e*	Is 43:8	241
other, shall say again in thine *e*	Is 49:20	241
cry in the *e* of Jerusalem, saying	Jer 2:2	241
which have *e*, and hear not	Jer 5:21	241
heareth, his *e* shall tingle	Jer 19:3	241
as ye have heard with your *e*	Jer 26:11	241
speak all these words in your *e*	Jer 26:15	241
this word that I speak in thine *e*	Jer 28:7	241
in the *e* of all the people	Jer 28:7	241
in the *e* of Jeremiah the prophet	Jer 29:29	241
the *e* of the people in the LORD's	Jer 36:6	241
thou shalt read them in the *e* of	Jer 36:6	241
in the *e* of all the people	Jer 36:10	241
the book in the *e* of the people	Jer 36:13	241
hast read in the *e* of the people	Jer 36:14	241
Sit down now, and read it in our *e*	Jer 36:15	241
So Baruch read it in their *e*	Jer 36:15	241
the words in the *e* of the king	Jer 36:20	241
read it in the *e* of the king	Jer 36:21	241
in the *e* of all the princes which	Jer 36:21	241
thine heart, and hear with thine *e*	Eze 3:10	241
cry in mine *e* with a loud voice	Eze 8:18	241
also in mine *e* with a loud voice	Eze 9:1	241
they have *e* to hear, and hear not	Eze 12:2	241
forehead, and earrings in thine *e*	Eze 16:12	241
take away thy nose and thine *e*	Eze 23:25	241
thee to hear it with thine *e*	Eze 24:26	241
thine eyes, and hear with thine *e*	Eze 40:4	241
hear with thine *e* all that I say	Eze 44:5	241
mouth, their *e* shall be deaf	Mic 7:16	241
the shoulder, and stopped their *e*	Zec 7:11	241
He that hath *e* to hear, let him	Mt 11:15	3775
and began to pluck the *e* of corn	Mt 12:1	4719
Who hath *e* to hear, let him hear	Mt 13:9	3775
their *e* are dull of hearing, and	Mt 13:15	3775
their eyes, and hear with their *e*	Mt 13:15	3775
and your *e*, for they hear	Mt 13:16	3775
Who hath *e* to hear, let him hear	Mt 13:43	3775
if this come to the governor's *e*	Mt 28:14	191
they went, to pluck the *e* of corn	Mk 2:23	4719
unto them, He that hath *e* to hear	Mk 4:9	3775
If any man have *e* to hear	Mk 4:23	3775
If any man have *e* to hear	Mk 7:16	3775
and put his fingers into his *e*	Mk 7:33	3775
And straightway his *e* were opened	Mk 7:35	189
and having *e*, hear ye not	Mk 8:18	3775
thy salutation sounded in mine *e*	Lk 1:44	3775
scripture fulfilled in your *e*	Lk 4:21	3775
disciples plucked the *e* of corn	Lk 6:1	4719
he cried, He that hath *e* to hear	Lk 8:8	3775
sayings sink down into your *e*	Lk 9:44	3775
He that hath *e* to hear, let him	Lk 14:35	3775
and uncircumcised in heart and *e*	Acts 7:51	3775
a loud voice, and stopped their *e*	Acts 7:57	3775
the *e* of the church which was in	Acts 11:22	3775
certain strange things to our *e*	Acts 17:20	189
their *e* are dull of hearing, and	Acts 28:27	3775
their eyes, and hear with their *e*	Acts 28:27	3775
e that they should not hear	Rom 11:8	3775
teachers, having itching *e*	2Ti 4:3	189
turn away their *e* from the truth	2Ti 4:4	189
into the *e* of the Lord of Sabaoth	Jas 5:4	3775
his *e* are open unto their prayers	1Pet 3:12	3775

EARTH

God created the heaven and the *e*	Gen 1:1	776
the *e* was without form, and void	Gen 1:2	776
And God called the dry land *E*	Gen 1:10	776
Let the *e* bring forth grass, the	Gen 1:11	776
seed is in itself, upon the *e*	Gen 1:11	776
the *e* brought forth grass, and	Gen 1:12	776
heaven to give light upon the *e*	Gen 1:15	776
heaven to give light upon the *e*	Gen 1:17	776
fowl that may fly above the *e* in	Gen 1:20	776
and let fowl multiply in the *e*	Gen 1:22	776
Let the *e* bring forth the living	Gen 1:24	776
beast of the *e* after his kind	Gen 1:24	776
the beast of the *e* after his kind	Gen 1:25	776

upon the *e* after his kind	Gen 1:25	127
the cattle, and over all the *e*	Gen 1:26	776
thing that creepeth upon the *e*	Gen 1:26	776
and multiply, and replenish the *e*	Gen 1:28	776
thing that moveth upon the *e*	Gen 1:28	776
is upon the face of all the *e*	Gen 1:29	776
And to every beast of the *e*	Gen 1:30	776
thing that creepeth upon the *e*	Gen 1:30	776
the *e* were finished, and all the	Gen 2:1	776
of the *e* when they were created,	Gen 2:4	776
day that the LORD God made the *e*	Gen 2:4	776
the field before it was in the *e*	Gen 2:5	776
not caused it to rain upon the *e*	Gen 2:5	776
there went up a mist from the *e*	Gen 2:6	776
And now art thou cursed from the *e*	Gen 4:11	127
a vagabond shalt thou be in the *e*	Gen 4:12	776
this day from the face of the *e*	Gen 4:14	127
a fugitive and a vagabond in the *e*	Gen 4:14	776
to multiply on the face of the *e*	Gen 6:1	127
giants in the *e* in those days	Gen 6:4	776
of man was great in the *e*	Gen 6:5	776
that he had made man on the *e*	Gen 6:6	776
created from the face of the *e*	Gen 6:7	127
The *e* also was corrupt before God	Gen 6:11	776
the *e* was filled with violence	Gen 6:11	776
And God looked upon the *e*, and,	Gen 6:12	776
had corrupted his way upon the *e*	Gen 6:12	776
for the *e* is filled with violence	Gen 6:13	776
I will destroy them with the *e*	Gen 6:13	776
a flood of waters upon the *e*	Gen 6:17	776
thing that is in the *e* shall die	Gen 6:17	776
thing of the *e* after his kind	Gen 6:20	127
alive upon the face of all the *e*	Gen 7:3	776
it to rain upon the *e* forty days	Gen 7:4	776
from off the face of the *e*	Gen 7:4	127
flood of waters was upon the *e*	Gen 7:6	776
thing that creepeth upon the *e*	Gen 7:8	127
of the flood were upon the *e*	Gen 7:10	776
rain was upon the *e* forty days	Gen 7:12	776
upon the *e* after his kind	Gen 7:14	776
flood was forty days upon the *e*	Gen 7:17	776
and it was lift up above the *e*	Gen 7:17	776
were increased greatly upon the *e*	Gen 7:18	776
prevailed exceedingly upon the *e*	Gen 7:19	776
flesh died that moved upon the *e*	Gen 7:21	776
thing that creepeth upon the *e*	Gen 7:21	776
and they were destroyed from the *e*	Gen 7:23	776
prevailed upon the *e* an hundred	Gen 7:24	776
made a wind to pass over the *e*	Gen 8:1	776
from off the *e* continually	Gen 8:3	776
were dried up from off the *e*	Gen 8:7	776
were on the face of the whole *e*	Gen 8:9	776
waters were abated from off the *e*	Gen 8:11	776
were dried up from off the *e*	Gen 8:13	776
day of the month, was the *e* dried	Gen 8:14	776
thing that creepeth upon the *e*	Gen 8:17	776
may breed abundantly in the *e*	Gen 8:17	776
fruitful, and multiply upon the *e*	Gen 8:17	776
and whatsoever creepeth upon the *e*	Gen 8:19	776
While the *e* remaineth, seedtime	Gen 8:22	776
and multiply, and replenish the *e*	Gen 9:1	776
be upon every beast of the *e*	Gen 9:2	776
upon all that moveth upon the *e*	Gen 9:2	127
bring forth abundantly in the *e*	Gen 9:7	776
of every beast of the *e* with you	Gen 9:10	776
the ark, to every beast of the *e*	Gen 9:10	776
more be a flood to destroy the *e*	Gen 9:11	776
of a covenant between me and the *e*	Gen 9:13	776
when I bring a cloud over the *e*	Gen 9:14	776
of all flesh that is upon the *e*	Gen 9:16	776
and all flesh that is upon the *e*	Gen 9:17	776
them was the whole *e* overspread	Gen 9:19	776
began to be a mighty one in the *e*	Gen 10:8	776
for in his days was the *e* divided	Gen 10:25	776
divided in the *e* after the flood	Gen 10:32	776
the whole *e* was of one language,	Gen 11:1	776
upon the face of the whole *e*	Gen 11:4	776
thence upon the face of all the *e*	Gen 11:8	776
the language of all the *e*	Gen 11:9	776
abroad upon the face of all the *e*	Gen 11:9	776
all families of the *e* be blessed	Gen 12:3	127
thy seed as the dust of the *e*	Gen 13:16	776
man can number the dust of the *e*	Gen 13:16	776
God, possessor of heaven and *e*	Gen 14:19	776
God, the possessor of heaven and *e*	Gen 14:22	776
all the nations of the *e* shall be	Gen 18:18	776
the Judge of all the *e* do right	Gen 18:25	776
the *e* when Lot entered into Zoar	Gen 19:23	776
there is not a man in the *e* to	Gen 19:31	776
us after the manner of all the *e*	Gen 19:31	776
the nations of the *e* be blessed	Gen 22:18	776
of heaven, and the God of the *e*	Gen 24:3	776
the LORD, bowing himself to the *e*	Gen 24:52	776
the nations of the *e* be blessed	Gen 26:4	776
them, and filled them with *e*	Gen 26:15	6083
heaven, and the fatness of the *e*	Gen 27:28	776
shall be the fatness of the *e*	Gen 27:39	776
behold a ladder set up on the *e*	Gen 28:12	776
shall be as the dust of the *e*	Gen 28:14	776
the families of the *e* be blessed	Gen 28:14	127
down ourselves to thee to the *e*	Gen 37:10	776
the *e* brought forth by handfuls	Gen 41:47	776
was over all the face of the *e*	Gen 41:56	776
him with their faces to the *e*	Gen 42:6	776
bowed themselves to him to the *e*	Gen 43:26	776
preserve you a posterity in the *e*	Gen 45:7	776
himself with his face to the *e*	Gen 48:12	776
a multitude in the midst of the *e*	Gen 48:16	776
rod, and smote the dust of the *e*	Ex 8:17	776
am the LORD in the midst of the *e*	Ex 8:22	776
is none like me in all the *e*	Ex 9:14	776
thou shalt be cut off from the *e*	Ex 9:15	776
be declared throughout all the *e*	Ex 9:16	776
know how that the *e* is the LORD's	Ex 9:29	776
rain was not poured upon the *e*	Ex 9:33	776
shall cover the face of the *e*	Ex 10:5	776
one cannot be able to see the *e*	Ex 10:5	776
were upon the *e* unto this day	Ex 10:6	127
covered the face of the whole *e*	Ex 10:15	776
right hand, the *e* swallowed them	Ex 15:12	776
for all the *e* is mine	Ex 19:5	776
or that is in the *e* beneath	Ex 20:4	776
that is in the water under the *e*	Ex 20:4	776
days the LORD made heaven and *e*	Ex 20:11	776
An altar of *e* thou shalt make	Ex 20:24	127
days the LORD made heaven and *e*	Ex 31:17	776
them from the face of the *e*	Ex 32:12	127
that are upon the face of the *e*	Ex 33:16	127
and bowed his head toward the *e*	Ex 34:8	776
have not been done in all the *e*	Ex 34:10	776
all the beasts that are on the *e*	Lev 11:2	776
feet, to leap withal upon the *e*	Lev 11:21	776
things that creep upon the *e*	Lev 11:29	776
the *e* shall be an abomination	Lev 11:41	776
things that creep upon the *e*	Lev 11:42	776
thing that creepeth upon the *e*	Lev 11:44	776
creature that creepeth upon the *e*	Lev 11:46	776
And the vessel of *e*, that he	Lev 15:12	2789
as iron, and your *e* as brass	Lev 26:19	776
high upon the face of the *e*	Num 11:31	776
which were upon the face of the *e*	Num 12:3	127
all the *e* shall be filled with	Num 14:21	776
the *e* open her mouth, and swallow	Num 16:30	127
the *e* opened her mouth, and	Num 16:32	776
pit, and the *e* closed upon them	Num 16:33	776
Lest the *e* swallow us up also	Num 16:34	776
they cover the face of the *e*	Num 22:5	776
which covereth the face of the *e*	Num 22:11	776
the *e* opened her mouth, and	Num 26:10	776
God is there in heaven or in *e*	Deut 3:24	776
that they shall live upon the *e*	Deut 4:10	127
of any beast that is on the *e*	Deut 4:17	776
is in the waters beneath the *e*	Deut 4:18	776
e to witness against you this day	Deut 4:26	776
that God created man upon the *e*	Deut 4:32	776
upon *e* he shewed thee his great	Deut 4:36	776
above, and upon the *e* beneath	Deut 4:39	776
prolong thy days upon the *e*	Deut 4:40	127
or that is in the *e* beneath	Deut 5:8	776
is in the waters beneath the *e*	Deut 5:8	776
thee from off the face of the *e*	Deut 6:15	127
that are upon the face of the *e*	Deut 7:6	127
the *e* also, with all that therein	Deut 10:14	776
how the *e* opened her mouth, and	Deut 11:6	776
as the days of heaven upon the *e*	Deut 11:21	776
the days that ye live upon the *e*	Deut 12:1	127
shall pour it upon the *e* as water	Deut 12:16	776
as long as thou livest upon the *e*	Deut 12:19	127
shalt pour it upon the *e* as water	Deut 12:24	776
from the one end of the *e* even	Deut 13:7	776
even unto the other end of the *e*	Deut 13:7	776
the nations that are upon the *e*	Deut 14:2	127
first of all the fruit of the *e*	Deut 26:2	127
high above all nations of the *e*	Deut 28:1	776
all people of the *e* shall see	Deut 28:10	776
the *e* that is under thee shall be	Deut 28:23	776
into all the kingdoms of the *e*	Deut 28:25	776
air, and unto the beasts of the *e*	Deut 28:26	776
from far, from the end of the *e*	Deut 28:49	776
end of the *e* even unto the other	Deut 28:64	776
e to record this day against you,	Deut 30:19	776
and *e* to record against them	Deut 31:28	776

and hear, O *e*, the words of my	Deut 32:1	776
ride on the high places of the *e*	Deut 32:13	776
consume the *e* with her increase	Deut 32:22	776
for the precious things of the *e*	Deut 33:16	776
together to the ends of the *e*	Deut 33:17	776
in heaven above, and in *e* beneath	Josh 2:11	776
e passeth over before you into	Josh 3:11	776
the LORD, the Lord of all the *e*	Josh 3:13	776
That all the people of the *e*	Josh 4:24	776
Joshua fell on his face to the *e*	Josh 5:14	776
fell to the *e* upon his face	Josh 7:6	776
and cut off our name from the *e*	Josh 7:9	776
they are hid in the *e* in the	Josh 7:21	776
I am going the way of all the *e*	Josh 23:14	776
was fallen down dead on the *e*	Judg 3:25	776
the *e* trembled, and the heavens	Judg 5:4	776
destroyed the increase of the *e*	Judg 6:4	776
it be dry upon all the *e* beside	Judg 6:37	776
of any thing that is in the *e*	Judg 18:10	776
pillars of the *e* are the LORD's	1Sa 2:8	776
shall judge the ends of the *e*	1Sa 2:10	776
shout, so that the *e* rang again	1Sa 4:5	776
rent, and with *e* upon his head	1Sa 4:12	127
the *e* before the ark of the LORD	1Sa 5:3	776
also trembled, and the *e* quaked	1Sa 14:15	776
and to the wild beasts of the *e*	1Sa 17:46	776
that all the *e* may know that	1Sa 17:46	776
and he fell upon his face to the *e*	1Sa 17:49	776
every one from the face of the *e*	1Sa 20:15	127
stooped with his face to the *e*	1Sa 24:8	776
herself on her face to the *e*	1Sa 25:41	776
the spear even to the *e* at once	1Sa 26:8	776
the *e* before the face of the LORD	1Sa 26:20	776
I saw gods ascending out of the *e*	1Sa 28:13	776
straightway all along on the *e*	1Sa 28:20	776
So he arose from the *e*, and sat	1Sa 28:23	776
were spread abroad upon all the *e*	1Sa 30:16	776
clothes rent, and *e* upon his head	2Sa 1:2	127
to David, that he fell to the *e*	2Sa 1:2	776
hand, and take you away from the *e*	2Sa 4:11	776
the great men that are in the *e*	2Sa 7:9	776
in the *e* is like thy people	2Sa 7:23	776
in, and lay all night upon the *e*	2Sa 12:16	776
him, to raise him up from the *e*	2Sa 12:17	776
Then David arose from the *e*	2Sa 12:20	776
his garments, and lay on the *e*	2Sa 13:31	776
name nor remainder upon the *e*	2Sa 14:7	127
one hair of thy son fall to the *e*	2Sa 14:11	776
know all things that are in the *e*	2Sa 14:20	776
his coat rent, and *e* upon his head	2Sa 15:32	127
up between the heaven and the *e*	2Sa 18:9	776
he fell down to the *e* upon his	2Sa 18:28	776
Then the *e* shook and trembled	2Sa 22:8	776
as small as the dust of the *e*	2Sa 22:43	776
grass springing out of the *e* by	2Sa 23:4	776
bowed with her face to the *e*	1Kin 1:31	776
so that the *e* rent with the sound	1Kin 1:40	776
not an hair of him fall to the *e*	1Kin 1:52	776
I go the way of all the *e*	1Kin 2:2	776
Solomon, from kings of the *e*	1Kin 4:34	776
or on *e* beneath, who keepest	1Kin 8:23	776
will God indeed dwell on the *e*	1Kin 8:27	776
people of the *e* may know thy name	1Kin 8:43	776
among all the people of the *e*	1Kin 8:53	776
That all the people of the *e* may	1Kin 8:60	776
all the kings of the *e* for riches	1Kin 10:23	776
all the *e* sought to Solomon, to	1Kin 10:24	776
it from off the face of the *e*	1Kin 13:34	127
the LORD sendeth rain upon the *e*	1Kin 17:14	127
and I will send rain upon the *e*	1Kin 18:1	127
he cast himself down upon the *e*	1Kin 18:42	776
that there is no God in all the *e*	2Kin 5:15	776
servant two mules' burden of *e*	2Kin 5:17	127
that there shall fall unto the *e*	2Kin 10:10	776
of all the kingdoms of the *e*	2Kin 19:15	776
thou hast made heaven and *e*	2Kin 19:15	776
that all the kingdoms of the *e*	2Kin 19:19	776
he began to be mighty upon the *e*	1Chr 1:10	776
in his days the *e* was divided	1Chr 1:19	776
his judgments are in all the *e*	1Chr 16:14	776
Sing unto the LORD, all the *e*	1Chr 16:23	776
Fear before him, all the *e*	1Chr 16:30	776
be glad, and let the *e* rejoice	1Chr 16:31	776
because he cometh to judge the *e*	1Chr 16:33	776
the great men that are in the *e*	1Chr 17:8	776
what one nation in the *e* is like	1Chr 17:21	776
of the LORD stand between the *e*	1Chr 21:16	776
much blood upon the *e* in my sight	1Chr 22:8	776
the heaven and in the *e* is thine	1Chr 29:11	776
our days on the *e* are as a shadow	1Chr 29:15	776
the dust of the *e* in multitude	2Chr 1:9	776
of Israel, that made heaven and *e*	2Chr 2:12	776
thee in the heaven, nor in the *e*	2Chr 6:14	776
very deed dwell with men on the *e*	2Chr 6:18	776
people of the *e* may know thy name	2Chr 6:33	776
all the kings of the *e* in riches	2Chr 9:22	776
all the kings of the *e* sought the	2Chr 9:23	776
to and fro throughout the whole *e*	2Chr 16:9	776
were dead bodies fallen to the *e*	2Chr 20:24	776
the gods of the people of the *e*	2Chr 32:19	776
All the kingdoms of the *e* hath	2Chr 36:23	776
me all the kingdoms of the *e*	Ezr 1:2	776
of the God of heaven and *e*	Ezr 5:11	772
with sackclothes, and *e* upon them	Neh 9:1	127
with all their host, the *e*	Neh 9:6	776
From going to and fro in the *e*	Job 1:7	776
there is none like him in the *e*	Job 1:8	776
From going to and fro in the *e*	Job 2:2	776
there is none like him in the *e*	Job 2:3	776
kings and counsellors of the *e*	Job 3:14	776
Who giveth rain upon the *e*	Job 5:10	776
be afraid of the beasts of the *e*	Job 5:22	776
offspring as the grass of the *e*	Job 5:25	776
an appointed time to man upon *e*	Job 7:1	776
our days upon *e* are a shadow	Job 8:9	776
out of the *e* shall others grow	Job 8:19	6083
shaketh the *e* out of her place	Job 9:6	776
The *e* is given into the hand of	Job 9:24	776
thereof is longer than the *e*	Job 11:9	776
Or speak to the *e*, and it shall	Job 12:8	776
them out, and they overturn the *e*	Job 12:15	776
the chief of the people of the *e*	Job 12:24	776
the root thereof wax old in the *e*	Job 14:8	776
grow out of the dust of the *e*	Job 14:19	776
Unto whom alone the *e* was given	Job 15:19	776
the perfection thereof upon the *e*	Job 15:29	776
O *e*, cover not thou my blood, and	Job 16:18	776
shall the *e* be forsaken for thee	Job 18:4	776
shall perish from the *e*, and he	Job 18:17	776
at the latter day upon the *e*	Job 19:25	6083
old, since man was placed upon *e*	Job 20:4	776
the *e* shall rise up against him	Job 20:27	776
for the mighty man, he had the *e*	Job 22:8	776
the poor of the *e* hide themselves	Job 24:4	776
their portion is cursed in the *e*	Job 24:18	776
hangeth the *e* upon nothing	Job 26:7	776
Iron is taken out of the *e*	Job 28:2	6083
As for the *e*, out of it cometh	Job 28:5	776
he looketh to the ends of the *e*	Job 28:24	776
of the valleys, in caves of the *e*	Job 30:6	6083
they were viler than the *e*	Job 30:8	776
given him a charge over the *e*	Job 34:13	776
us more than the beasts of the *e*	Job 35:11	776
lightning unto the ends of the *e*	Job 37:3	776
to the snow, Be thou on the *e*	Job 37:6	776
the face of the world in the *e*	Job 37:12	776
quieteth the *e* by the south wind	Job 37:17	776
I laid the foundations of the *e*	Job 38:4	776
take hold of the ends of the *e*	Job 38:13	776
perceived the breadth of the *e*	Job 38:18	776
the east wind upon the *e*	Job 38:24	776
To cause it to rain on the *e*	Job 38:26	776
set the dominion thereof in the *e*	Job 38:33	776
Which leaveth her eggs in the *e*	Job 39:14	776
Upon *e* there is not his like, who	Job 41:33	6083
The kings of the *e* set themselves	Ps 2:2	776
parts of the *e* for thy possession	Ps 2:8	776
be instructed, ye judges of the *e*	Ps 2:10	776
him tread down my life upon the *e*	Ps 7:5	127
is thy name in all the *e*	Ps 8:1	776
is thy name in all the *e*	Ps 8:9	776
man of the *e* may no more oppress	Ps 10:18	776
as silver tried in a furnace of *e*	Ps 12:6	776
to the saints that are in the *e*	Ps 16:3	776
their eyes bowing down to the *e*	Ps 17:11	776
Then the *e* shook and trembled	Ps 18:7	776
is gone out through all the *e*	Ps 19:4	776
shalt thou destroy from the *e*	Ps 21:10	776
they that be fat upon *e* shall eat	Ps 22:29	776
The *e* is the LORD's, and the	Ps 24:1	776
and his seed shall inherit the *e*	Ps 25:13	776
the *e* is full of the goodness of	Ps 33:5	776
Let all the *e* fear the LORD	Ps 33:8	776
upon all the inhabitants of the *e*	Ps 33:14	776
remembrance of them from the *e*	Ps 34:16	776
LORD, they shall inherit the *e*	Ps 37:9	776
But the meek shall inherit the *e*	Ps 37:11	776
of him shall inherit the *e*	Ps 37:22	776
and he shall be blessed upon the *e*	Ps 41:2	776
our belly cleaveth unto the *e*	Ps 44:25	776
mayest make princes in all the *e*	Ps 45:16	776
we fear, though the *e* be removed	Ps 46:2	776

uttered his voice, the *e* melted	Ps 46:6	776
desolations he hath made in the *e*	Ps 46:8	776
to cease unto the end of the *e*	Ps 46:9	776
I will be exalted in the *e*	Ps 46:10	776
he is a great King over all the *e*	Ps 47:2	776
For God is the King of all the *e*	Ps 47:7	776
shields of the *e* belong unto God	Ps 47:9	776
situation, the joy of the whole *e*	Ps 48:2	776
thy praise unto the ends of the *e*	Ps 48:10	776
called the *e* from the rising of	Ps 50:1	776
heavens from above, and to the *e*	Ps 50:4	776
let thy glory be above all the *e*	Ps 57:5	776
let thy glory be above all the *e*	Ps 57:11	776
violence of your hands in the *e*	Ps 58:2	776
he is a God that judgeth in the *e*	Ps 58:11	776
in Jacob unto the ends of the *e*	Ps 59:13	776
Thou hast made the *e* to tremble	Ps 60:2	776
From the end of the *e* will I cry	Ps 61:2	776
go into the lower parts of the *e*	Ps 63:9	776
of all the ends of the *e*, and of	Ps 65:5	776
Thou visitest the *e*, and waterest	Ps 65:9	776
All the *e* shall worship thee, and	Ps 66:4	776
That thy way may be known upon *e*	Ps 67:2	776
and govern the nations upon *e*	Ps 67:4	776
Then shall the *e* yield her	Ps 67:6	776
the ends of the *e* shall fear him	Ps 67:7	776
The *e* shook, the heavens also	Ps 68:8	776
unto God, ye kingdoms of the *e*	Ps 68:32	776
e praise him, the seas, and every	Ps 69:34	776
up again from the depths of the *e*	Ps 71:20	776
as showers that water the *e*	Ps 72:6	776
the river unto the ends of the *e*	Ps 72:8	776
be an handful of corn in the *e*	Ps 72:16	776
flourish like grass of the *e*	Ps 72:16	776
let the whole *e* be filled with	Ps 72:19	776
tongue walketh through the *e*	Ps 73:9	776
there is none upon *e* that I	Ps 73:25	776
salvation in the midst of the *e*	Ps 74:12	776
hast set all the borders of the *e*	Ps 74:17	776
for the dark places of the *e* are	Ps 74:20	776
The *e* and all the inhabitants	Ps 75:3	776
of the *e* shall wring them out	Ps 75:8	776
the *e* feared, and was still,	Ps 76:8	776
to save all the meek of the *e*	Ps 76:9	776
is terrible to the kings of the *e*	Ps 76:12	776
the *e* trembled and shook	Ps 77:18	776
palaces, like the *e* which he hath	Ps 78:69	776
saints unto the beasts of the *e*	Ps 79:2	776
of the *e* are out of course	Ps 82:5	776
Arise, O God, judge the *e*	Ps 82:8	776
they became as dung for the *e*	Ps 83:10	127
art the most high over all the *e*	Ps 83:18	776
Truth shall spring out of the *e*	Ps 85:11	776
are thine, the *e* also is thine	Ps 89:11	776
higher than the kings of the *e*	Ps 89:27	776
or ever thou hadst formed the *e*	Ps 90:2	776
up thyself, thou judge of the *e*	Ps 94:2	776
hand are the deep places of the *e*	Ps 95:4	776
sing unto the LORD, all the *e*	Ps 96:1	776
fear before him, all the *e*	Ps 96:9	776
rejoice, and let the *e* be glad	Ps 96:11	776
for he cometh to judge the *e*	Ps 96:13	776
let the *e* rejoice	Ps 97:1	776
the *e* saw, and trembled	Ps 97:4	776
of the LORD of the whole *e*	Ps 97:5	776
LORD, art high above all the *e*	Ps 97:9	776
all the ends of the *e* have seen	Ps 98:3	776
noise unto the LORD, all the *e*	Ps 98:4	776
for he cometh to judge the *e*	Ps 98:9	776
let the *e* be moved	Ps 99:1	776
all the kings of the *e* thy glory	Ps 102:15	776
heaven did the LORD behold the *e*	Ps 102:19	776
thou laid the foundation of the *e*	Ps 102:25	776
as the heaven is high above the *e*	Ps 103:11	776
Who laid the foundations of the *e*	Ps 104:5	776
turn not again to cover the *e*	Ps 104:9	776
the *e* is satisfied with the fruit	Ps 104:13	776
may bring forth food out of the *e*	Ps 104:14	776
the *e* is full of thy riches	Ps 104:24	776
thou renewest the face of the *e*	Ps 104:30	127
He looketh on the *e*, and it	Ps 104:32	776
sinners be consumed out of the *e*	Ps 104:35	776
his judgments are in all the *e*	Ps 105:7	776
The *e* opened and swallowed up	Ps 106:17	776
and thy glory above all the *e*	Ps 108:5	776
off the memory of them from the *e*	Ps 109:15	776
His seed shall be mighty upon *e*	Ps 112:2	776
that are in heaven, and in the *e*	Ps 113:6	776
Tremble, thou *e*, at the presence	Ps 114:7	776
the LORD which made heaven and *e*	Ps 115:15	776
but the *e* hath he given to the	Ps 115:16	776
I am a stranger in the *e*	Ps 119:19	776
The *e*, O LORD, is full of thy	Ps 119:64	776
had almost consumed me upon *e*	Ps 119:87	776
thou hast established the *e*	Ps 119:90	776
the wicked of the *e* like dross	Ps 119:119	776
the LORD, which made heaven and *e*	Ps 121:2	776
of the LORD, who made heaven and *e*	Ps 124:8	776
and *e* bless thee out of Zion	Ps 134:3	776
that did he in heaven, and in *e*	Ps 135:6	776
to ascend from the ends of the *e*	Ps 135:7	776
out the *e* above the waters	Ps 136:6	776
kings of the *e* shall praise thee	Ps 138:4	776
in the lowest parts of the *e*	Ps 139:15	776
speaker be established in the *e*	Ps 140:11	776
and cleaveth wood upon the *e*	Ps 141:7	776
forth, he returneth to his *e*	Ps 146:4	127
Which made heaven, and *e*, the sea,	Ps 146:6	776
who prepareth rain for the *e*	Ps 147:8	776
forth his commandment upon *e*	Ps 147:15	776
Praise the LORD from the *e*	Ps 148:7	776
Kings of the *e*, and all people	Ps 148:11	776
princes, and all judges of the *e*	Ps 148:11	776
his glory is above the *e* and	Ps 148:13	776
shall be cut off from the *e*	Prov 2:22	776
LORD by wisdom hath founded the *e*	Prov 3:19	776
even all the judges of the *e*	Prov 8:16	776
the beginning, or ever the *e* was	Prov 8:23	776
as yet he had not made the *e*	Prov 8:26	776
the foundations of the *e*	Prov 8:29	776
in the habitable part of his *e*	Prov 8:31	776
wicked shall not inhabit the *e*	Prov 10:30	776
shall be recompensed in the *e*	Prov 11:31	776
a fool are in the ends of the *e*	Prov 17:24	776
the *e* for depth, and the heart of	Prov 25:3	776
established all the ends of the *e*	Prov 30:4	776
to devour the poor from off the *e*	Prov 30:14	776
the *e* that is not filled with	Prov 30:16	776
three things the *e* is disquieted	Prov 30:21	776
which are little upon the *e*	Prov 30:24	776
but the *e* abideth for ever	Eccl 1:4	776
that goeth downward to the *e*	Eccl 3:21	776
God is in heaven, and thou upon *e*	Eccl 5:2	776
the profit of the *e* is for all	Eccl 5:9	776
there is not a just man upon *e*	Eccl 7:20	776
a vanity which is done upon the *e*	Eccl 8:14	776
business that is done upon the *e*	Eccl 8:16	776
walking as servants upon the *e*	Eccl 10:7	776
not what evil shall be upon the *e*	Eccl 11:2	776
they empty themselves upon the *e*	Eccl 11:3	776
dust return to the *e* as it was	Eccl 12:7	776
The flowers appear on the *e*	Song 2:12	776
Hear, O heavens, and give ear, O *e*	Is 1:2	776
rocks, and into the caves of the *e*	Is 2:19	6083
ariseth to shake terribly the *e*	Is 2:19	776
ariseth to shake terribly the *e*	Is 2:21	776
the fruit of the *e* shall be	Is 4:2	776
alone in the midst of the *e*	Is 5:8	776
unto them from the end of the *e*	Is 5:26	776
the whole *e* is full of his glory	Is 6:3	776
And they shall look unto the *e*	Is 8:22	776
left, have I gathered all the *e*	Is 10:14	776
with equity for the meek of the *e*	Is 11:4	776
he shall smite the *e* with the rod	Is 11:4	776
for the *e* shall be full of the	Is 11:9	776
from the four corners of the *e*	Is 11:12	776
this is known in all the *e*	Is 12:5	776
the *e* shall remove out of her	Is 13:13	776
The whole *e* is at rest, and is	Is 14:7	776
even all the chief ones of the *e*	Is 14:9	776
man that made the *e* to tremble	Is 14:16	776
that is purposed upon the whole *e*	Is 14:26	776
the world, and dwellers on the *e*	Is 18:3	776
and to the beasts of the *e*	Is 18:6	776
all the beasts of the *e* shall	Is 18:6	776
are the honourable of the *e*	Is 23:8	776
all the honourable of the *e*	Is 23:9	776
the world upon the face of the *e*	Is 23:17	127
the LORD maketh the *e* empty	Is 24:1	776
The *e* mourneth and fadeth away,	Is 24:4	776
people of the *e* do languish	Is 24:4	776
The *e* also is defiled under the	Is 24:5	776
hath the curse devoured the *e*	Is 24:6	776
inhabitants of the *e* are burned	Is 24:6	776
part of the *e* have we heard songs	Is 24:16	776
upon thee, O inhabitant of the *e*	Is 24:17	776
the foundations of the *e* do shake	Is 24:18	776
The *e* is utterly broken down	Is 24:19	776
the *e* is clean dissolved, the	Is 24:19	776
the *e* is moved exceedingly	Is 24:19	776
The *e* shall reel to and fro like a	Is 24:20	776
the kings of the *e* upon the *e*	Is 24:21	127

of all the families of the e .... Amos 3:2 127
a bird fall in a snare upon the e .... Amos 3:5 776
one take up a snare from the e .... Amos 3:5 127
upon the high places of the e .... Amos 4:13 776
leave off righteousness in the e .... Amos 5:7 776
them out upon the face of the e .... Amos 5:8 776
darken the e in the clear day .... Amos 8:9 776
hath founded his troop in the e .... Amos 9:6 776
them out upon the face of the e .... Amos 9:6 776
it from off the face of the e .... Amos 9:8 127
the least grain fall upon the e .... Amos 9:9 776
the e with her bars was about me .... Jonah 2:6 776
hearken, O e, and all that therein .... Mic 1:2 776
upon the high places of the e .... Mic 1:3 776
unto the Lord of the whole e .... Mic 4:13 776
be great unto the ends of the e .... Mic 5:4 776
and ye strong foundations of the e .... Mic 6:2 776
good man is perished out of the e .... Mic 7:2 776
their holes like worms of the e .... Mic 7:17 776
the e is burned at his presence, ... Nah 1:5 776
will cut off thy prey from the e .... Nah 2:13 776
For the e shall be filled with .... Hab 2:14 776
let all the e keep silence before .... Hab 2:20 776
the e was full of his praise .... Hab 3:3 776
He stood, and measured the e .... Hab 3:6 776
didst cleave the e with rivers .... Hab 3:9 776
ye the LORD, all ye meek of the e .... Zeph 2:3 776
will famish all the gods of the e .... Zeph 2:11 776
for all the e shall be devoured .... Zeph 3:8 776
praise among all people of the e .... Zeph 3:20 776
the e is stayed from her fruit .... Hag 1:10 776
will shake the heavens, and the e .... Hag 2:6 776
I will shake the heavens and the e .... Hag 2:21 776
to walk to and fro through the e .... Zec 1:10 776
walked to and fro through the e .... Zec 1:11 776
all the e sitteth still, and is at .... Zec 1:11 776
run to and fro through the whole e .... Zec 4:10 776
stand by the Lord of the whole e .... Zec 4:14 776
over the face of the whole e .... Zec 5:3 776
resemblance through all the e .... Zec 5:6 776
lifted up the ephah between the e .... Zec 5:9 776
before the Lord of all the e .... Zec 6:5 776
walk to and fro through the e .... Zec 6:7 776
walk to and fro through the e .... Zec 6:7 776
walked to and fro through the e .... Zec 6:7 776
river even to the ends of the e .... Zec 9:10 776
and layeth the foundation of the e .... Zec 12:1 776
though all the people of the e be .... Zec 12:3 776
LORD shall be king over all the e .... Zec 14:9 776
e unto Jerusalem to worship the .... Zec 14:17 776
come and smite the e with a curse .... Mal 4:6 776
for they shall inherit the e .... Mt 5:5 1093
Ye are the salt of the e .... Mt 5:13 1093
e pass, one jot or one tittle .... Mt 5:18 1093
Nor by the e; for it is .... Mt 5:35 1093
Thy will be done in e, as it is .... Mt 6:10 1093
for yourselves treasures upon e .... Mt 6:19 1093
hath power on e to forgive sins .... Mt 9:6 1093
that I am come to send peace on e .... Mt 10:34 1093
O Father, Lord of heaven and e .... Mt 11:25 1093
nights in the heart of the e .... Mt 12:40 1093
e to hear the wisdom of Solomon .... Mt 12:42 1093
places, where they had not much e .... Mt 13:5 1093
because they had no deepness of e .... Mt 13:5 1093
on e shall be bound in heaven .... Mt 16:19 1093
on e shall be loosed in heaven .... Mt 16:19 1093
of the e take custom or tribute .... Mt 17:25 1093
on e shall be bound in heaven .... Mt 18:18 1093
on e shall be loosed in heaven .... Mt 18:18 1093
if two of you shall agree on e as .... Mt 18:19 1093
no man your father upon the e .... Mt 23:9 1093
righteous blood shed upon the e .... Mt 23:35 1093
all the tribes of the e mourn .... Mt 24:30 1093
e shall pass away, but my words .... Mt 24:35 1093
one went and digged in the e .... Mt 25:18 1093
went and hid thy talent in the e .... Mt 25:25 1093
the e did quake, and the rocks .... Mt 27:51 1093
given unto me in heaven and in e .... Mt 28:18 1093
hath power on e to forgive sins .... Mk 2:10 1093
ground, where it had not much e .... Mk 4:5 1093
up, because it had no depth of e .... Mk 4:5 1093
For the e bringeth forth fruit of .... Mk 4:28 1093
which, when it is sown in the e .... Mk 4:31 1093
all the seeds that be in the e .... Mk 4:31 1093
as no fuller on e can white them .... Mk 9:3 1093
from the uttermost part of the e .... Mk 13:27 1093
Heaven and e shall pass away .... Mk 13:31 1093
on e peace, good will toward men .... Lk 2:14 1093
hath power upon e to forgive sins .... Lk 5:24 1093
built an house upon the e .... Lk 6:49 1093
O Father, Lord of heaven and e .... Lk 10:21 1093
be done, as in heaven, so in e .... Lk 11:2 1093
from the utmost parts of the e to .... Lk 11:31 1093
I am come to send fire on the e .... Lk 12:49 1093
that I am come to give peace on e .... Lk 12:51 1093
the face of the sky and of the e .... Lk 12:56 1093
e to pass, than one tittle of the .... Lk 16:17 1093
shall he find faith on the e .... Lk 18:8 1093
upon the e distress of nations, ... Lk 21:25 1093
things which are coming on the e .... Lk 21:26 3625
Heaven and e shall pass away .... Lk 21:33 1093
dwell on the face of the whole e .... Lk 21:35 1093
all the e until the ninth hour .... Lk 23:44 1093
bowed down their faces to the e .... Lk 24:5 1093
he that is of the e is earthly .... Jn 3:31 1093
is earthly, and speaketh of the e .... Jn 3:31 1093
I, if I be lifted up from the e .... Jn 12:32 1093
I have glorified thee on the e .... Jn 17:4 1093
unto the uttermost part of the e .... Acts 1:8 1093
above, and signs in the e beneath .... Acts 2:19 1093
the kindreds of the e be blessed .... Acts 3:25 1093
God, which hast made heaven, and e .... Acts 4:24 1093
The kings of the e stood up .... Acts 4:26 1093
my throne, and e is my footstool .... Acts 7:49 1093
for his life is taken from the e .... Acts 8:33 1093
And he fell to the e, and heard a .... Acts 9:4 1093
And Saul arose from the e .... Acts 9:8 1093
corners, and let down to the e .... Acts 10:11 1093
of fourfooted beasts of the e .... Acts 10:12 1093
and saw fourfooted beasts of the e .... Acts 11:6 1093
salvation unto the ends of the e .... Acts 13:47 1093
God, which made heaven, and e .... Acts 14:15 1093
that he is Lord of heaven and e .... Acts 17:24 1093
to dwell on all the face of the e .... Acts 17:26 1093
with such a fellow from the e .... Acts 22:22 1093
when we were all fallen to the e .... Acts 26:14 1093
be declared throughout all the e .... Rom 9:17 1093
will the Lord make upon the e .... Rom 9:28 1093
their sound went into all the e .... Rom 10:18 1093
gods, whether in heaven or in e 1Cor 8:5 1093
For the e is the Lord's, and the 1Cor 10:26 1093
for the e is the Lord's, and the 1Cor 10:28 1093
The first man is of the e 1Cor 15:47 1093
are in heaven, and which are on e .... Eph 1:10 1093
family in heaven and e is named, ... Eph 3:15 1093
into the lower parts of the e .... Eph 4:9 1093
and thou mayest live long on the e .... Eph 6:3 1093
things in heaven, and things in e .... Phil 2:10 1919
and things under the e .... Phil 2:10 2709
are in heaven, and that are in e .... Col 1:16 1093
say, whether they be things in e .... Col 1:20 1093
above, not on things on the e .... Col 3:2 1093
your members which are upon the e .... Col 3:5 1093
silver, but also of wood and of e 2Ti 2:20 3749
hast laid the foundation of the e .... Heb 1:10 1093
For the e which drinketh in the .... Heb 6:7 1093
For if he were on e, he should .... Heb 8:4 1093
strangers and pilgrims on the e .... Heb 11:13 1093
and in dens and caves of the e .... Heb 11:38 1093
who refused him that spake on e .... Heb 12:25 1093
Whose voice then shook the e .... Heb 12:26 1093
once more I shake not the e only .... Heb 12:26 1093
have lived in pleasure on the e .... Jas 5:5 1093
for the precious fruit of the e .... Jas 5:7 1093
by heaven, neither by the e .... Jas 5:12 1093
it rained not on the e by the .... Jas 5:17 1093
the e brought forth her fruit .... Jas 5:18 1093
the e standing out of the water 2Pet 3:5 1093
But the heavens and the e, which 2Pet 3:7 1093
the e also and the works that are 2Pet 3:10 1093
look for new heavens and a new e 2Pet 3:13 1093
are three that bear witness in e 1Jn 5:8 1093
the prince of the kings of the e .... Rev 1:5 1093
all kindreds of the e shall wail .... Rev 1:7 1093
to try them that dwell upon the e .... Rev 3:10 1093
nor in e, neither under the e .... Rev 5:3 1093
of God sent forth into all the e .... Rev 5:6 1093
and we shall reign on the e .... Rev 5:10 1093
and on the e, and under the e .... Rev 5:13 1093
thereon to take peace from the e .... Rev 6:4 1093
over the fourth part of the e .... Rev 6:8 1093
and with the beasts of the e .... Rev 6:8 1093
blood on them that dwell on the e .... Rev 6:10 1093
stars of heaven fell unto the e .... Rev 6:13 1093
And the kings of the e, and the .... Rev 6:15 1093
on the four corners of the e .... Rev 7:1 1093
holding the four winds of the e .... Rev 7:1 1093
the wind should not blow on the e .... Rev 7:1 1093
whom it was given to hurt the e .... Rev 7:2 1093
Saying, Hurt not the e, neither .... Rev 7:3 1093
the altar, and cast it into the e .... Rev 8:5 1093
and they were cast upon the e .... Rev 8:7 1093

to the inhabiters of the *e* by	Rev 8:13	1093
star fall from heaven unto the *e*	Rev 9:1	1093
of the smoke locusts upon the *e*	Rev 9:3	1093
the scorpions of the *e* have power	Rev 9:3	1093
not hurt the grass of the *e*	Rev 9:4	1093
sea, and his left foot on the *e*	Rev 10:2	1093
upon the *e* lifted up his hand to	Rev 10:5	1093
things that therein are, and the *e*	Rev 10:6	1093
upon the sea and upon the *e*	Rev 10:8	1093
standing before the God of the *e*	Rev 11:4	1093
to smite the *e* with all plagues,	Rev 11:6	1093
the *e* shall rejoice over them	Rev 11:10	1093
them that dwelt on the *e*	Rev 11:10	1093
destroy them which destroy the *e*	Rev 11:18	1093
heaven, and did cast them to the *e*	Rev 12:4	1093
he was cast out into the *e*	Rev 12:9	1093
Woe to the inhabiters of the *e*	Rev 12:12	1093
saw that he was cast unto the *e*	Rev 12:13	1093
the *e* helped the woman	Rev 12:16	1093
the *e* opened her mouth, and	Rev 12:16	1093
upon the *e* shall worship him	Rev 13:8	1093
beast coming up out of the *e*	Rev 13:11	1093
before him, and causeth the *e*	Rev 13:12	1093
on the *e* in the sight of men	Rev 13:13	1093
them that dwell on the *e* by the	Rev 13:14	1093
to them that dwell on the *e*	Rev 13:14	1093
which were redeemed from the *e*	Rev 14:3	1093
unto them that dwell on the *e*	Rev 14:6	1093
him that made heaven, and *e*	Rev 14:7	1093
for the harvest of the *e* is ripe	Rev 14:15	1093
thrust in his sickle on the *e*	Rev 14:16	1093
and the *e* was reaped	Rev 14:16	1093
the clusters of the vine of the *e*	Rev 14:18	1093
thrust in his sickle into the *e*	Rev 14:19	1093
and gathered the vine of the *e*	Rev 14:19	1093
of the wrath of God upon the *e*	Rev 16:1	1093
and poured out his vial upon the *e*	Rev 16:2	1093
go forth unto the kings of the *e*	Rev 16:14	1093
was not since men were upon the *e*	Rev 16:18	1093
the *e* have committed fornication	Rev 17:2	1093
the inhabitants of the *e* have	Rev 17:2	1093
AND ABOMINATIONS OF THE *E*	Rev 17:5	1093
that dwell on the *e* shall wonder	Rev 17:8	1093
reigneth over the kings of the *e*	Rev 17:18	1093
the *e* was lightened with his	Rev 18:1	1093
the kings of the *e* have committed	Rev 18:3	1093
the merchants of the *e* are waxed	Rev 18:3	1093
And the kings of the *e*, who have	Rev 18:9	1093
the merchants of the *e* shall weep	Rev 18:11	1093
were the great men of the *e*	Rev 18:23	1093
of all that were slain upon the *e*	Rev 18:24	1093
the *e* with her fornication	Rev 19:2	1093
the beast, and the kings of the *e*	Rev 19:19	1093
are in the four quarters of the *e*	Rev 20:8	1093
went up on the breadth of the *e*	Rev 20:9	1093
sat on it, from whose face the *e*	Rev 20:11	1093
And I saw a new heaven and a new *e*	Rev 21:1	1093
the first *e* were passed away	Rev 21:1	1093
the kings of the *e* do bring their	Rev 21:24	1093

EARTHEN

But the *e* vessel wherein it is	Lev 6:28	2789
every *e* vessel, whereinto any of	Lev 11:33	2789
in an *e* vessel over running water	Lev 14:5	2789
in an *e* vessel over running water	Lev 14:50	2789
take holy water in an *e* vessel	Num 5:17	2789
e vessels, and wheat, and barley,	2Sa 17:28	3335
Go and get a potter's *e* bottle	Jer 19:1	2789
and put them in an *e* vessel	Jer 32:14	2789
are they esteemed as *e* pitchers	Lam 4:2	2789
have this treasure in *e* vessels	2Cor 4:7	3749

EARTHLY

If I have told you *e* things	Jn 3:12	1919
he that is of the earth is *e*	Jn 3:31	1537,3588,1093
For we know that if our *e* house	2Cor 5:1	1919
in their shame, who mind *e* things	Phil 3:19	1919
not from above, but is *e*, sensual	Jas 3:15	1919

EARTHQUAKE

and after the wind an *e*	1Kin 19:11	7494
but the LORD was not in the *e*	1Kin 19:11	7494
And after the *e* a fire	1Kin 19:12	7494
of hosts with thunder, and with *e*	Is 29:6	7494
of Israel, two years before the *e*	Amos 1:1	7494
e in the days of Uzziah king of	Zec 14:5	7494
him, watching Jesus, saw the *e*	Mt 27:54	4578
And, behold, there was a great *e*	Mt 28:2	4578
And suddenly there was a great *e*	Acts 16:26	4578
seal, and, lo, there was a great *e*	Rev 6:12	4578
and lightnings, and an *e*	Rev 8:5	4578
the same hour was there a great *e*	Rev 11:13	4578

in the *e* were slain of men seven	Rev 11:13	4578
voices, and thunderings, and an *e*	Rev 11:19	4578
and there was a great *e*, such as	Rev 16:18	4578
upon the earth, so mighty an *e*	Rev 16:18	4578

EARTHQUAKES

be famines, and pestilences, and *e*	Mt 24:7	4578
there shall be *e* in divers places	Mk 13:8	4578
great *e* shall be in divers places	Lk 21:11	4578

EARTHY

The first man is of the earth, *e*	1Cor 15:47	5517
As is the *e*, such are they also	1Cor 15:48	5517
such are they also that are *e*	1Cor 15:48	5517
we have borne the image of the *e*	1Cor 15:49	5517

EASE

when thou wilt *e* thyself abroad	Deut 23:13	3427
nations shalt thou find no *e*	Deut 28:65	7280
trode them down with *e* over	Judg 20:43	4496
now therefore *e* thou somewhat the	2Chr 10:4	7043
E somewhat the yoke that thy	2Chr 10:9	7043
me, my couch shall *e* my complaint	Job 7:13	5375
the thought of him that is at *e*	Job 12:5	7600
I was at *e*, but he hath broken me	Job 16:12	7961
full strength, being wholly at *e*	Job 21:23	7946
His soul shall dwell at *e*	Ps 25:13	2896
scorning of those that are at *e*	Ps 123:4	7600
I will *e* me of mine adversaries,	Is 1:24	5162
Rise up, ye women that are at *e*	Is 32:9	7600
Tremble, ye women that are at *e*	Is 32:11	7600
return, and be in rest and at *e*	Jer 46:27	7599
hath been at *e* from his youth	Jer 48:11	7599
multitude being at *e* was with her	Eze 23:42	7961
Woe to them that are at *e* in Zion	Amos 6:1	7600
with the heathen that are at *e*	Zec 1:15	7600
take thine *e*, eat, drink, and be	Lk 12:19	373

EASED

and though I forbear, what am I *e*	Job 16:6	1980
I mean not that other men be *e*	2Cor 8:13	425

EASIER

so shall it be *e* for thyself	Ex 18:22	7043
For whether is *e*, to say, Thy	Mt 9:5	2123
It is *e* for a camel to go through	Mt 19:24	2123
Whether is it *e* to say to the	Mk 2:9	2123
It is *e* for a camel to go through	Mk 10:25	2123
Whether is *e*, to say, Thy sins be	Lk 5:23	2123
it is *e* for heaven and earth to	Lk 16:17	2123
For it is *e* for a camel to go	Lk 18:25	2123

EASILY

is not *e* provoked, thinketh no	1Cor 13:5	
the sin which doth so *e* beset us	Heb 12:1	

EAST

goeth toward the *e* of Assyria	Gen 2:14	6926
he placed at the *e* of the garden	Gen 3:24	6924
the land of Nod, on the *e* of Eden	Gen 4:16	6926
unto Sephar a mount of the *e*	Gen 10:30	6924
as they journeyed from the *e*	Gen 11:2	6924
a mountain on the *e* of Beth-el	Gen 12:8	6924
on the west, and Hai on the *e*	Gen 12:8	6924
and Lot journeyed *e*	Gen 13:11	6924
eastward, unto the *e* country	Gen 25:6	6924
abroad to the west, and to the *e*	Gen 28:14	6924
the land of the people of the *e*	Gen 29:1	6924
blasted with the *e* wind sprung up	Gen 41:6	6921
thin, and blasted with the *e* wind	Gen 41:23	6921
empty ears blasted with the *e*	Gen 41:27	6921
the LORD brought an *e* wind upon	Ex 10:13	6921
the *e* wind brought the locusts	Ex 10:13	6921
by a strong *e* wind all that night	Ex 14:21	6921
e side eastward shall be fifty	Ex 27:13	6924
for the *e* side eastward fifty	Ex 38:13	6924
it beside the altar on the *e* part	Lev 1:16	6924
on the *e* side on the rising	Num 2:3	6924
the tabernacle toward the *e*	Num 3:38	6924
on the *e* parts shall go forward	Num 10:5	6924
out of the mountains of the *e*	Num 23:7	6924
ye shall point out your *e* border	Num 34:10	6924
to Riblah, on the *e* side of Ain	Num 34:11	6924
on the *e* side two thousand cubits	Num 35:5	6924
in the *e* border of Jericho	Josh 4:19	4217
on the *e* side of Beth-el, and	Josh 7:2	6924
And to the Canaanite on the *e*	Josh 11:3	4217
Hermon, and all the plain on the *e*	Josh 12:1	4217
to the sea of Chinneroth on the *e*	Josh 12:3	4217
plain, even the salt sea on the *e*	Josh 12:3	4217
the *e* border was the salt sea	Josh 15:5	6924
the water of Jericho on the *e*	Josh 16:1	4217
on the *e* side was Ataroth-addar	Josh 16:5	4217
passed by it on the *e* to Janohah	Josh 16:6	4217

north, and in Issachar on the *e*	Josh 17:10	4217
beyond Jordan on the *e*, which	Josh 18:7	4217
the border of it on the *e* side	Josh 18:20	6924
along on the *e* to Gittah-hepher	Josh 19:13	6924
and the children of the *e*	Judg 6:3	6924
the children of the *e* were	Judg 6:33	6924
all the children of the *e* lay	Judg 7:12	6924
hosts of the children of the *e*	Judg 8:10	6924
dwelt in tents on the *e* of Nobah	Judg 8:11	6924
came by the *e* side of the land of	Judg 11:18	4217,8121
on the *e* side of the highway that	Judg 21:19	4217,8121
all the children of the *e* country	1Kin 4:30	6924
and three looking toward the *e*	1Kin 7:25	4217
even unto the *e* side of the	1Chr 4:39	4217
all the *e* land of Gilead	1Chr 5:10	4217
on the *e* side of Jordan, were	1Chr 6:78	4217
were the porters, toward the *e*	1Chr 9:24	4217
of the valleys, both toward the *e*	1Chr 12:15	4217
and three looking toward the *e*	2Chr 4:4	4217
on the right side of the *e* end	2Chr 4:10	6924
stood at the *e* end of the altar,	2Chr 5:12	4217
them together into the *e* street	2Chr 29:4	4217
Levite, the porter toward the *e*	2Chr 31:14	4217
the water gate toward the *e*	Neh 3:26	4217
the keeper of the *e* gate	Neh 3:29	4217
greatest of all the men of the *e*	Job 1:3	6924
and fill his belly with the *e* wind	Job 15:2	6921
The *e* wind carrieth him away, and	Job 27:21	6921
the *e* wind upon the earth	Job 38:24	6921
ships of Tarshish with an *e* wind	Ps 48:7	6921
cometh neither from the *e*	Ps 75:6	4161
He caused an *e* wind to blow in	Ps 78:26	6921
As far as the *e* is from the west,	Ps 103:12	4217
them out of the lands, from the *e*	Ps 107:3	4217
they be replenished from the *e*	Is 2:6	6924
spoil them of the *e* together	Is 11:14	6924
wind in the day of the *e* wind	Is 27:8	6921
up the righteous man from the *e*	Is 41:2	4217
I will bring my seed from the *e*	Is 43:5	4217
a ravenous bird from the *e*	Is 46:11	4217
with an *e* wind before the enemy	Jer 18:17	6921
is by the entry of the *e* gate	Jer 19:2	2777
of the horse gate toward the *e*	Jer 31:40	4217
Kedar, and spoil the men of the *e*	Jer 49:28	6924
LORD, and their faces toward the *e*	Eze 8:16	6924
worshipped the sun toward the *e*	Eze 8:16	6924
of the *e* gate of the LORD's house	Eze 10:19	6931
brought me unto the *e* gate of the	Eze 11:1	6931
is on the *e* side of the city	Eze 11:23	6924
when the *e* wind toucheth it	Eze 17:10	6921
the *e* wind dried up her fruit	Eze 19:12	6921
the men of the *e* for a possession	Eze 25:4	6924
men of the *e* with the Ammonites	Eze 25:10	6924
the *e* wind hath broken thee in	Eze 27:26	6921
passengers on the *e* of the sea	Eze 39:11	6926
gate which looketh toward the *e*	Eze 40:6	6921
gate that looketh toward the *e*	Eze 40:22	6921
toward the north, and toward the *e*	Eze 40:23	6921
into the inner court toward the *e*	Eze 40:32	6921
one at the side of the *e* gate	Eze 40:44	6921
the separate place toward the *e*	Eze 41:14	6921
was the entry on the *e* side	Eze 42:9	6921
wall of the court toward the *e*	Eze 42:10	6921
before the wall toward the *e*	Eze 42:12	6921
whose prospect is toward the *e*	Eze 42:15	6921
He measured the *e* side with the	Eze 42:16	6921
gate that looketh toward the *e*	Eze 43:1	6921
Israel came from the way of the *e*	Eze 43:2	6921
whose prospect is toward the *e*	Eze 43:4	6921
stairs shall look toward the *e*	Eze 43:17	6921
which looketh toward the *e*	Eze 44:1	6921
and from the *e* side eastward	Eze 45:7	6924
the west border unto the *e* border	Eze 45:7	6921
e shall be shut the six working	Eze 46:1	6921
gate that looketh toward the *e*	Eze 46:12	6921
of the house stood toward the *e*	Eze 47:1	6921
issue out toward the *e* country	Eze 47:8	6930
the *e* side ye shall measure from	Eze 47:18	6921
from the border unto the *e* sea	Eze 47:18	6931
And this is the *e* side	Eze 47:18	6921
for these are his sides *e*	Eze 48:1	6921
from the *e* side unto the west	Eze 48:2	6921
from the *e* side even unto the	Eze 48:3	6921
from the *e* side unto the west	Eze 48:4	6921
from the *e* side unto the west	Eze 48:5	6921
from the *e* side even unto the	Eze 48:6	6921
from the *e* side unto the west	Eze 48:7	6921
from the *e* side unto the west	Eze 48:8	6921
from the *e* side unto the west	Eze 48:8	6921
toward the *e* ten thousand in	Eze 48:10	6921
on the *e* side four thousand and	Eze 48:16	6921

toward the *e* two hundred and fifty	Eze 48:17	6921
the oblation toward the *e* border	Eze 48:21	6921
from the *e* side unto the west	Eze 48:23	6921
from the *e* side unto the west	Eze 48:24	6921
from the *e* side unto the west	Eze 48:25	6921
from the *e* side unto the west	Eze 48:26	6921
from the *e* side unto the west	Eze 48:27	6921
at the *e* side four thousand and	Eze 48:32	6921
toward the south, and toward the *e*	Dan 8:9	4217
But tidings out of the *e* and out	Dan 11:44	4217
and followeth after the *e* wind	Hos 12:1	6921
an *e* wind shall come, the wind of	Hos 13:15	6921
with his face toward the *e* sea	Joel 2:20	6931
and from the north even to the *e*	Amos 8:12	4217
sat on the *e* side of the city, and	Jonah 4:5	6924
God prepared a vehement *e* wind	Jonah 4:8	6921
faces shall sup up as the *e* wind	Hab 1:9	6921
save my people from the *e* country	Zec 8:7	4217
is before Jerusalem on the *e*	Zec 14:4	6924
in the midst thereof toward the *e*	Zec 14:4	4217
wise men from the *e* to Jerusalem	Mt 2:1	395
we have seen his star in the *e*	Mt 2:2	395
the star, which they saw in the *e*	Mt 2:9	395
That many shall come from the *e*	Mt 8:11	395
the lightning cometh out of the *e*	Mt 24:27	395
And they shall come from the *e*	Lk 13:29	395
angel ascending from the *e*	Rev 7:2	395
kings of the *e* might be prepared	Rev 16:12	395
On the *e* three gates	Rev 21:13	395

EASTER *Passover.*

intending after *E* to bring him	Acts 12:4	3957

EASTWARD

God planted a garden *e* in Eden	Gen 2:8	6924
art northward, and southward, and *e*	Gen 13:14	6924
his son, while he yet lived, *e*	Gen 25:6	6924
east side *e* shall be fifty cubits	Ex 27:13	4217
for the east side *e* fifty cubits	Ex 38:13	4217
his finger upon the mercy seat *e*	Lev 16:14	6924
tabernacle of the congregation *e*	Num 3:38	4217
to us on this side Jordan *e*	Num 32:19	4217
outmost coast of the salt sea *e*	Num 34:3	6924
side of the sea of Chinnereth *e*	Num 34:11	6924
this side Jordan near Jericho *e*	Num 34:15	6924
salt sea, under Ashdoth-pisgah *e*	Deut 3:17	4217
and northward, and southward, and *e*	Deut 3:27	4217
the plain on this side Jordan *e*	Deut 4:49	4217
and unto the valley of Mizpeh *e*	Josh 11:8	4217
Moses gave them, beyond Jordan *e*	Josh 13:8	4217
on the other side Jordan *e*	Josh 13:27	4217
other side Jordan, by Jericho, *e*	Josh 13:32	4217
went about *e* unto Taanath-shiloh	Josh 16:6	4217
turned from Sarid *e* toward the	Josh 19:12	6924
other side Jordan by Jericho *e*	Josh 20:8	4217
in Michmash, *e* from Beth-aven	1Sa 13:5	6926
house *e* over against the south	1Kin 7:39	6924
Get thee hence, and turn thee *e*	1Kin 17:3	6924
From Jordan *e*, all the land of	2Kin 10:33	4217,8121
And he said, Open the window *e*	2Kin 13:17	6924
e he inhabited unto the entering	1Chr 5:9	4217
e Naaran, and westward Gezer, with	1Chr 7:28	4217
waited in the king's gate *e*	1Chr 9:18	4217
the lot *e* fell to Shelemiah	1Chr 26:14	4217
E were six Levites, northward	1Chr 26:17	4217
David, even unto the water gate *e*	Neh 12:37	4217
the LORD's house, which looketh *e*	Eze 11:1	6921
gate *e* were three on this side	Eze 40:10	1870,6921
without, an hundred cubits *e*	Eze 40:19	6921
westward, and from the east side *e*	Eze 45:7	6921
the threshold of the house *e*	Eze 47:1	6921
gate by the way that looketh *e*	Eze 47:2	6921
the line in his hand went forth *e*	Eze 47:3	6921
portion shall be ten thousand *e*	Eze 48:18	6921

EASY

but knowledge is *e* unto him that	Prov 14:6	7043
For my yoke is *e*, and my burden is	Mt 11:30	5543
tongue words *e* to be understood	1Cor 14:9	2154
e to be intreated, full of mercy	Jas 3:17	2138

EAT

the garden thou mayest freely *e*	Gen 2:16	398
and evil, thou shalt not *e* of it	Gen 2:17	398
Ye shall not *e* of every tree of	Gen 3:1	398
We may *e* of the fruit of the	Gen 3:2	398
hath said, Ye shall not *e* of it	Gen 3:3	398
know that in the day ye *e* thereof	Gen 3:5	398
of the fruit thereof, and did *e*	Gen 3:6	398
and he did *e*	Gen 3:6	398
thee that thou shouldest not *e*	Gen 3:11	398
gave me of the tree, and I did *e*	Gen 3:12	398
serpent beguiled me, and I did *e*	Gen 3:13	398

E

dust shalt thou *e* all the days of	Gen 3:14	398
saying, Thou shalt not *e* of it	Gen 3:17	398
in sorrow shalt thou *e* of it all	Gen 3:17	398
thou shalt *e* the herb of the	Gen 3:18	398
of thy face shalt thou *e* bread	Gen 3:19	398
also of the tree of life, and *e*	Gen 3:22	398
the blood thereof, shall ye not *e*	Gen 9:4	398
under the tree, and they did *e*	Gen 18:8	398
unleavened bread, and they did *e*	Gen 19:3	398
was set meat before him to *e*	Gen 24:33	398
but he said, I will not *e*	Gen 24:33	398
And they did *e* and drink, he and the	Gen 24:54	398
because he did *e* of his venison	Gen 25:28	6310
and he did *e* and drink, and rose up,	Gen 25:34	398
made them a feast, and they did *e*	Gen 26:30	398
and bring it to me, that I may *e*	Gen 27:4	398
me savoury meat, that I may *e*	Gen 27:7	398
it to thy father, that he may *e*	Gen 27:10	398
e of my venison, that thy soul	Gen 27:19	398
I will *e* of my son's venison,	Gen 27:25	398
it near to him, and he did *e*	Gen 27:25	398
e of his son's venison, that thy	Gen 27:31	398
I go, and will give me bread to *e*	Gen 28:20	398
they did *e* there upon the heap	Gen 31:46	398
and called his brethren to *e* bread	Gen 31:54	398
and they did *e* bread, and tarried	Gen 31:54	398
the children of Israel *e* not of	Gen 32:32	398
And they sat down to *e* bread	Gen 37:25	398
save the bread which he did *e*	Gen 39:6	398
the birds did *e* them out of the	Gen 40:17	398
the birds shall *e* thy flesh from	Gen 40:19	398
leanfleshed kine did *e* up the	Gen 41:4	398
the ill favoured kine did *e* up	Gen 41:20	398
that they should *e* bread there	Gen 43:25	398
Egyptians, which did *e* with him	Gen 43:32	398
not *e* bread with the Hebrews	Gen 43:32	398
ye shall *e* the fat of the land	Gen 45:18	398
did *e* their portion which Pharaoh	Gen 47:22	398
call him, that he may *e* bread	Ex 2:20	398
they shall *e* the residue of that	Ex 10:5	398
shall *e* every tree which groweth	Ex 10:5	398
e every herb of the land, even	Ex 10:12	398
they did *e* every herb of the land	Ex 10:15	398
houses, wherein they shall *e* it	Ex 12:7	398
they shall *e* the flesh in that	Ex 12:8	398
with bitter herbs they shall *e* it	Ex 12:8	398
E not of it raw, nor sodden at	Ex 12:9	398
And thus shall ye *e*	Ex 12:11	398
and ye shall *e* it in haste	Ex 12:11	398
days shall ye *e* unleavened bread	Ex 12:15	398
save that which every man must *e*	Ex 12:16	398
ye shall *e* unleavened bread,	Ex 12:18	398
Ye shall *e* nothing leavened	Ex 12:20	398
shall ye *e* unleavened bread	Ex 12:20	398
There shall no stranger *e* thereof	Ex 12:43	398
him, then shall he *e* thereof	Ex 12:44	398
hired servant shall not *e* thereof	Ex 12:45	398
person shall *e* thereof	Ex 12:48	398
thou shalt *e* unleavened bread	Ex 13:6	398
when we did *e* bread to the full	Ex 16:3	398
you in the evening flesh to *e*	Ex 16:8	398
saying, At even ye shall *e* flesh	Ex 16:12	398
the LORD hath given you to *e*	Ex 16:15	402
And Moses said, *E* that to day	Ex 16:25	398
of Israel did *e* manna forty years	Ex 16:35	398
they did *e* manna, until they came	Ex 16:35	398
to *e* bread with Moses' father in	Ex 18:12	398
neither shall ye *e* any flesh that	Ex 22:31	398
that the poor of thy people may *e*	Ex 23:11	398
the beasts of the field shall *e*	Ex 23:11	398
(thou shalt *e* unleavened bread	Ex 23:15	398
also they saw God, and did *e*	Ex 24:11	398
his sons shall *e* the flesh of the	Ex 29:32	398
they shall *e* those things	Ex 29:33	398
a stranger shall not *e* thereof	Ex 29:33	398
and the people sat down to *e*	Ex 32:6	398
thee, and thou *e* of his sacrifice	Ex 34:15	398
thou shalt *e* unleavened bread	Ex 34:18	398
he did neither *e* bread, nor drink	Ex 34:28	398
that ye *e* neither fat nor blood	Lev 3:17	398
thereof shall Aaron and his sons *e*	Lev 6:16	398
the congregation they shall *e* it	Lev 6:16	398
children of Aaron shall *e* of it	Lev 6:18	398
offereth it for sin shall *e* it	Lev 6:26	398
among the priests shall *e* thereof	Lev 6:29	398
among the priests shall *e* thereof	Lev 7:6	398
all that be clean shall *e* thereof	Lev 7:19	398
e of the flesh of the sacrifice	Lev 7:21	398
Ye shall *e* no manner of fat, of	Lev 7:23	398
but ye shall in no wise *e* of it	Lev 7:24	398
Moreover ye shall *e* no manner of	Lev 7:26	398

there *e* it with the bread that is	Lev 8:31	398
Aaron and his sons shall *e* it	Lev 8:31	398
e it without leaven beside the	Lev 10:12	398
ye shall *e* it in the holy place,	Lev 10:13	398
shall ye *e* in a clean place	Lev 10:14	398
e among all the beasts that are	Lev 11:2	398
among the beasts, that shall ye *e*	Lev 11:3	398
not *e* of them that chew the cud	Lev 11:4	398
Of their flesh shall ye not *e*	Lev 11:8	398
These shall ye *e* of all that are	Lev 11:9	398
and in the rivers, them shall ye *e*	Lev 11:9	398
ye shall not *e* of their flesh,	Lev 11:11	398
Yet these may ye *e* of every	Lev 11:21	398
Even these of them ye may *e*	Lev 11:22	398
if any beast, of which ye may *e*.	Lev 11:39	402
the earth, them ye shall not *e*	Lev 11:42	398
No soul of you shall *e* blood	Lev 17:12	398
that sojourneth among you *e* blood	Lev 17:12	398
Ye shall *e* the blood of no manner	Lev 17:14	398
shall ye *e* of the fruit thereof	Lev 19:25	398
Ye shall not *e* any thing with the	Lev 19:26	398
He shall *e* the bread of his God,	Lev 21:22	398
he shall not *e* of the holy things	Lev 22:4	398
shall not *e* of the holy things,	Lev 22:6	398
shall afterward *e* of the holy	Lev 22:7	398
he shall not *e* to defile himself	Lev 22:8	398
no stranger *e* of the holy thing	Lev 22:10	398
shall not *e* of the holy thing	Lev 22:10	398
with his money, he shall *e* of it	Lev 22:11	398
they shall *e* of his meat	Lev 22:11	398
she may not *e* of an offering of	Lev 22:12	398
she shall *e* of her father's meat	Lev 22:13	398
there shall no stranger *e* thereof	Lev 22:13	398
if a man *e* of the holy thing	Lev 22:14	398
when they *e* their holy things	Lev 22:16	398
days ye must *e* unleavened bread	Lev 23:6	398
ye shall *e* neither bread, nor	Lev 23:14	398
they shall *e* it in the holy place	Lev 24:9	398
ye shall *e* the increase thereof	Lev 25:12	398
ye shall *e* your fill, and dwell	Lev 25:19	398
What shall we *e* the seventh year	Lev 25:20	398
e yet of old fruit until the	Lev 25:22	398
in ye shall *e* of the old store	Lev 25:22	398
ye shall *e* your bread to the full	Lev 26:5	398
ye shall *e* old store, and bring	Lev 26:10	398
vain, for your enemies shall *e* it	Lev 26:16	398
and ye shall *e*, and not be	Lev 26:26	398
ye shall *e* the flesh of your sons	Lev 26:29	398
of your daughters shall ye *e*	Lev 26:29	398
of your enemies shall *e* you up	Lev 26:38	398
nor *e* moist grapes, or dried	Num 6:3	398
he *e* nothing that is made of the	Num 6:4	398
e it with unleavened bread and	Num 9:11	398
Who shall give us flesh to *e*	Num 11:4	398
which we did *e* in Egypt freely	Num 11:5	398
Give us flesh, that we may *e*	Num 11:13	398
to morrow, and ye shall *e* flesh	Num 11:18	398
Who shall give us flesh to *e*	Num 11:18	398
give you flesh, and ye shall *e*	Num 11:18	398
Ye shall not *e* one day, nor two	Num 11:19	398
that they may *e* a whole month	Num 11:21	398
when ye *e* of the bread of the	Num 15:19	398
most holy place shalt thou *e* it	Num 18:10	398
every male shall *e* it	Num 18:10	398
clean in thy house shall *e* of it	Num 18:11	398
in thine house shall *e* of it	Num 18:13	398
ye shall *e* it in every place, ye	Num 18:31	398
lie down until he *e* of the prey	Num 23:24	398
he shall *e* up the nations his	Num 24:8	398
and the people did *e*, and bowed	Num 25:2	398
of them for money, that ye may *e*	Deut 2:6	398
me meat for money, that I may *e*	Deut 2:28	398
neither see, nor hear, nor *e*	Deut 4:28	398
shalt *e* bread without scarceness	Deut 8:9	398
I neither did *e* bread nor drink	Deut 9:9	398
I did neither *e* bread, nor drink	Deut 9:18	398
thy cattle, that thou mayest *e*	Deut 11:15	398
there ye shall *e* before the LORD	Deut 12:7	398
e flesh in all thy gates,	Deut 12:15	398
and the clean may *e* thereof	Deut 12:15	398
Only ye shall not *e* the blood	Deut 12:16	398
Thou mayest not *e* within thy	Deut 12:17	398
But thou must *e* them before the	Deut 12:18	398
and thou shalt say, I will *e* flesh	Deut 12:20	398
thy soul longeth to *e* flesh	Deut 12:20	398
thou mayest *e* flesh, whatsoever	Deut 12:20	398
thou shalt *e* in thy gates	Deut 12:21	398
is eaten, so thou shalt *e* them	Deut 12:22	398
the clean shall *e* of them alike	Deut 12:22	398
be sure that thou *e* not the blood	Deut 12:23	398
thou mayest not *e* the life with	Deut 12:23	398

Thou shalt not *e* it	Deut 12:24	398
Thou shalt not *e* it	Deut 12:25	398
God, and thou shalt *e* the flesh	Deut 12:27	398
Thou shalt not *e* any abominable	Deut 14:3	398
are the beasts which ye shall *e*	Deut 14:4	398
among the beasts, that ye shall *e*	Deut 14:6	398
not *e* of them that chew the cud	Deut 14:7	398
ye shall not *e* of their flesh	Deut 14:8	398
These ye shall *e* of all that are	Deut 14:9	398
have fins and scales shall ye *e*	Deut 14:9	398
not fins and scales ye may not *e*	Deut 14:10	398
Of all clean birds ye shall *e*	Deut 14:11	398
are they of which ye shall not *e*	Deut 14:12	398
But of all clean fowls ye may *e*	Deut 14:20	398
Ye shall not *e* of any thing that	Deut 14:21	398
is in thy gates, that he may *e* it	Deut 14:21	398
thou shalt *e* before the Lord thy	Deut 14:23	398
thou shalt *e* there before the	Deut 14:26	398
thy gates, shall come, and shall *e*	Deut 14:29	398
Thou shalt *e* it before the Lord	Deut 15:20	398
Thou shalt *e* it within thy gates	Deut 15:22	398
the clean person shall *e* it alike	Deut 15:22	398
shalt not *e* the blood thereof	Deut 15:23	398
Thou shalt *e* no leavened bread	Deut 16:3	398
seven days shalt thou *e*	Deut 16:3	398
e it in the place which the Lord	Deut 16:7	398
thou shalt *e* unleavened bread	Deut 16:8	398
they shall *e* the offerings of the	Deut 18:1	398
shall have like portions to *e*	Deut 18:8	398
battle, and another man *e* of it	Deut 20:6	2490
thou shalt *e* the spoil of thine	Deut 20:14	398
for thou mayest *e* of them	Deut 20:19	398
then thou mayest *e* grapes thy	Deut 23:24	398
that they may *e* within thy gates	Deut 26:12	398
peace offerings, and shalt *e* there	Deut 27:7	398
eyes, and thou shalt not *e* thereof	Deut 28:31	398
which thou knowest not *e* up	Deut 28:33	398
for the worms shall *e* them	Deut 28:39	398
he shall *e* the fruit of thy	Deut 28:51	398
thou shalt *e* the fruit of thine	Deut 28:53	398
of his children whom he shall *e*	Deut 28:55	398
for she shall *e* them for want of	Deut 28:57	398
that he might *e* the increase of	Deut 32:13	398
Which did *e* the fat of their	Deut 32:38	398
they did *e* of the old corn of the	Josh 5:11	398
but they did *e* of the fruit of	Josh 5:12	398
which ye planted not do ye *e*	Josh 24:13	398
the house of their god, and did *e*	Judg 9:27	398
drink, and *e* not any unclean thing	Judg 13:4	398
neither *e* any unclean thing	Judg 13:7	398
She may not *e* of any thing that	Judg 13:14	398
drink, nor *e* any unclean thing	Judg 13:14	398
I will not *e* of thy bread	Judg 13:16	398
and gave them, and they did *e*	Judg 14:9	398
so they did *e* and drink, and lodged	Judg 19:4	398
And they sat down, and did *e*	Judg 19:6	398
and they did *e* both of them	Judg 19:8	398
they washed their feet, and did *e*	Judg 19:21	398
e of the bread, and dip thy morsel	Ruth 2:14	398
her parched corn, and she did *e*	Ruth 2:14	398
therefore she wept, and did not *e*	1Sa 1:7	398
the woman went her way, and did *e*	1Sa 1:18	398
that I may *e* a piece of bread	1Sa 2:36	398
he go up to the high place to *e*	1Sa 9:13	398
people will not *e* until he come	1Sa 9:13	398
afterwards they *e* that be bidden	1Sa 9:13	398
for ye shall *e* with me to day, and	1Sa 9:19	398
set it before thee, and *e*	1Sa 9:24	398
So Saul did *e* with Samuel that	1Sa 9:24	398
the people did *e* them with the	1Sa 14:32	398
in that they *e* with the blood	1Sa 14:33	398
sheep, and slay them here, and *e*	1Sa 14:34	398
the king sat him down to *e* meat	1Sa 20:24	398
did *e* no meat the second day of	1Sa 20:34	398
and *e*, that thou mayest have	1Sa 28:22	398
he refused, and said, I will not *e*	1Sa 28:23	398
and they did *e*	1Sa 28:25	398
and gave him bread, and he did *e*	1Sa 30:11	398
to *e* meat while it was yet day	2Sa 3:35	1262
thou shalt *e* bread at my table	2Sa 9:7	398
master's son may have food to *e*	2Sa 9:10	398
thy master's son shall *e* bread	2Sa 9:10	398
he shall *e* at my table, as one of	2Sa 9:11	398
for he did *e* continually at the	2Sa 9:13	398
I then go into mine house, to *e*	2Sa 11:11	398
David had called him, he did *e*	2Sa 11:13	398
it did *e* of his own meat, and	2Sa 12:3	398
neither did he *e* bread with them	2Sa 12:17	1262
set bread before him, and he did *e*	2Sa 12:20	398
dead, thou didst rise and *e* bread	2Sa 12:21	398
I may see it, and *e* it at her hand	2Sa 13:5	398

sight, that I may *e* at her hand	2Sa 13:6	1262
but he refused to *e*	2Sa 13:9	398
that I may *e* of thine hand	2Sa 13:10	1262
had brought them unto him to *e*	2Sa 13:11	398
fruit for the young men to *e*	2Sa 16:2	398
people that were with him, to *e*	2Sa 17:29	398
that did *e* at thine own table	2Sa 19:28	398
taste what I *e* or what I drink	2Sa 19:35	398
and, behold, they *e* and drink	1Kin 1:25	398
be of those that *e* at thy table	1Kin 2:7	398
E no bread, nor drink water, nor	1Kin 13:8	398
Come home with me, and *e* bread	1Kin 13:9	398
neither will I *e* bread nor drink	1Kin 13:15	398
Thou shalt *e* no bread nor drink	1Kin 13:16	398
thine house, that he may *e* bread	1Kin 13:17	398
did *e* bread in his house, and	1Kin 13:18	398
E no bread, and drink no water	1Kin 13:19	398
in the city shall the dogs *e*	1Kin 13:22	398
shall the fowls of the air *e*	1Kin 14:11	398
in the city shall the dogs *e*	1Kin 14:11	398
shall the fowls of the air *e*	1Kin 16:4	398
me and my son, that we may *e* it	1Kin 16:4	398
he, and her house, did *e* many days	1Kin 17:12	398
which *e* at Jezebel's table	1Kin 17:15	398
said unto Ahab, Get thee up, *e*	1Kin 18:19	398
So Ahab went up to *e* and to drink	1Kin 18:41	398
him, and said unto him, Arise and *e*	1Kin 18:42	398
And he did *e* and drink, and laid him	1Kin 19:5	398
touched him, and said, Arise and *e*	1Kin 19:6	398
And he arose, and did *e* and drink	1Kin 19:7	398
unto the people, and they did *e*	1Kin 19:8	398
his face, and would *e* no bread	1Kin 19:21	398
e bread, and let thine heart be	1Kin 21:4	398
The dogs shall *e* Jezebel by the	1Kin 21:7	398
Ahab in the city the dogs shall *e*	1Kin 21:23	398
shall the fowls of the air *e*	1Kin 21:24	398
and she constrained him to *e* bread	1Kin 21:24	398
he turned in thither to *e* bread	2Kin 4:8	398
they poured out for the men to *e*	2Kin 4:8	398
And they could not *e* thereof	2Kin 4:40	398
for the people, that they may *e*	2Kin 4:40	398
unto the people, that they may *e*	2Kin 4:41	398
Give the people, that they may *e*	2Kin 4:42	398
thus saith the Lord, They shall *e*	2Kin 4:43	398
set it before them, and they did *e*	2Kin 4:43	398
before them, that they may *e*	2Kin 4:44	398
thy son, that we may *e* him to day	2Kin 6:22	398
we will *e* my son to morrow	2Kin 6:28	398
So we boiled my son, and did *e* him	2Kin 6:28	398
Give thy son, that we may *e* him	2Kin 6:29	398
eyes, but shalt not *e* thereof	2Kin 6:29	398
they went into one tent, and did *e*	2Kin 7:2	398
eyes, but shalt not *e* thereof	2Kin 7:8	398
the dogs shall *e* Jezebel in the	2Kin 7:19	398
And when he was come in, he did *e*	2Kin 9:10	398
shall dogs *e* the flesh of Jezebel	2Kin 9:34	398
that they may *e* their own dung,	2Kin 9:36	398
then *e* ye every man of his own	2Kin 18:27	398
Ye shall *e* this year such things	2Kin 18:31	398
and *e* the fruits thereof	2Kin 19:29	398
but they did *e* of the unleavened	2Kin 19:29	398
he did *e* bread continually before	2Kin 23:9	398
And did *e* and drink before the Lord	2Kin 25:29	398
and shod them, and gave them to *e*	1Chr 29:22	398
yet did they *e* the passover	2Chr 28:15	398
they did *e* throughout the feast	2Chr 30:18	398
the Lord, we have had enough to *e*	2Chr 30:22	398
that they should not *e* of the	2Chr 31:10	398
the Lord God of Israel, did *e*	Ezr 2:63	398
e the good of the land, and leave	Ezr 6:21	398
he did *e* no bread, nor drink	Ezr 9:12	398
up corn for them, that we may *e*	Ezr 10:6	398
that they should not *e* of the	Neh 5:2	398
e the fat, and drink the sweet, and	Neh 7:65	398
the people went their way to *e*	Neh 8:10	398
so they did *e*, and were filled, and	Neh 8:12	398
fathers to *e* the fruit thereof	Neh 9:25	398
neither *e* nor drink three days,	Neh 9:36	398
for their three sisters to *e*	Est 4:16	398
For my sighing cometh before I *e*	Job 1:4	398
Then let me sow, and let another *e*	Job 3:24	3899
did *e* bread with him in his house	Job 31:8	398
e up my people as they *e* bread	Job 42:11	398
The meek shall *e* and be satisfied	Ps 14:4	398
that be fat upon earth shall *e*	Ps 22:26	398
came upon me to *e* up my flesh	Ps 22:29	398
which did *e* of my bread, hath	Ps 27:2	398
Will I *e* the flesh of bulls, or	Ps 41:9	398
e up my people as they *e* bread	Ps 50:13	398
rained down manna upon them to *e*	Ps 53:4	398
	Ps 78:24	398

E

Man did *e* angels' food	Ps 78:25	398
So they did *e*, and were well	Ps 78:29	398
so that I forget to *e* my bread	Ps 102:4	398
did *e* up all the herbs in their	Ps 105:35	398
to *e* the bread of sorrows	Ps 127:2	398
For thou shalt *e* the labour of	Ps 128:2	398
let me not *e* of their dainties	Ps 141:4	3898
Therefore shall they *e* of the	Prov 1:31	398
For they *e* the bread of	Prov 4:17	3898
e of my bread, and drink of the	Prov 9:5	3898
A man shall *e* good by the fruit	Prov 13:2	398
transgressors shall *e* violence	Prov 13:2	398
love it shall *e* the fruit thereof	Prov 18:21	398
thou sittest to *e* with a ruler	Prov 23:1	3898
E thou not the bread of him that	Prov 23:6	3898
E and drink, saith he to thee	Prov 23:7	398
e thou honey, because it is good	Prov 24:13	398
e so much as is sufficient for	Prov 25:16	398
be hungry, give him bread to *e*	Prov 25:21	398
It is not good to *e* much honey	Prov 25:27	398
tree shall *e* the fruit thereof	Prov 27:18	398
and the young eagles shall *e* it	Prov 30:17	398
for a man, than that he should *e*	Eccl 2:24	398
For who can *e*, or who else can	Eccl 2:25	398
And also that every man should *e*	Eccl 3:13	398
they are increased that *e* them	Eccl 5:11	398
whether he *e* little or much	Eccl 5:12	398
it is good and comely for one to *e*	Eccl 5:18	398
hath given him power to *e* thereof	Eccl 5:19	398
giveth him not power to *e* thereof	Eccl 6:2	398
thing under the sun, than to *e*	Eccl 8:15	398
e thy bread with joy, and drink	Eccl 9:7	398
thy princes *e* in the morning	Eccl 10:16	398
thy princes *e* in due season, for	Eccl 10:17	398
garden, and *e* his pleasant fruits	Song 4:16	398
e, O friends	Song 5:1	398
ye shall *e* the good of the land	Is 1:19	398
for they shall *e* the fruit of	Is 3:10	398
We will *e* our own bread, and wear	Is 4:1	398
of the fat ones shall strangers *e*	Is 5:17	398
Butter and honey shall he *e*	Is 7:15	398
shall give, he shall *e* butter	Is 7:22	398
honey shall every one *e* that is	Is 7:22	398
he shall *e* on the left hand, and	Is 9:20	398
they shall *e* every man the flesh	Is 9:20	398
the lion shall *e* straw like the	Is 11:7	398
table, watch in the watchtower, *e*	Is 21:5	398
let us *e* and drink	Is 22:13	398
to *e* sufficiently, and for durable	Is 23:18	398
ground shall *e* clean provender	Is 30:24	398
that they may *e* their own dung,	Is 36:12	398
e ye every one of his vine, and	Is 36:16	398
Ye shall *e* this year such as	Is 37:30	398
vineyards, and *e* the fruit thereof	Is 37:30	398
the moth shall *e* them up	Is 50:9	398
For the moth shall *e* them up like	Is 51:8	398
the worm shall *e* them like wool	Is 51:8	398
come ye, buy, and *e*	Is 55:1	398
e ye that which is good, and let	Is 55:2	398
ye shall *e* the riches of the	Is 61:6	398
that have gathered it shall *e* it	Is 62:9	398
which *e* swine's flesh, and broth	Is 65:4	398
God, Behold, my servants shall *e*	Is 65:13	398
vineyards, and *e* the fruit of them	Is 65:21	398
shall not plant, and another *e*	Is 65:22	398
the lion shall *e* straw like the	Is 65:25	398
to *e* the fruit thereof and the	Jer 2:7	398
they shall *e* up thine harvest, and	Jer 5:17	398
sons and thy daughters should *e*	Jer 5:17	398
they shall *e* up thy flocks and	Jer 5:17	398
they shall *e* up thy vines and thy	Jer 5:17	398
unto your sacrifices, and *e* flesh	Jer 7:21	398
words were found, and I did *e* them	Jer 15:16	398
feasting, to sit with them to *e*	Jer 16:8	398
I will cause them to *e* the flesh	Jer 19:9	398
they shall *e* every one the flesh	Jer 19:9	398
did not thy father *e* and drink, and	Jer 22:15	398
The wind shall *e* up all thy	Jer 22:22	7462
gardens, and *e* the fruit of them	Jer 29:5	398
gardens, and *e* the fruit of them	Jer 29:28	398
shall *e* them as common things	Jer 31:5	
there they did *e* bread together	Jer 41:1	398
he did continually *e* bread before	Jer 52:33	398
Shall the women *e* their fruit	Lam 2:20	398
thy mouth, and *e* that I give thee	Eze 2:8	398
Son of man, *e* that thou findest	Eze 3:1	398
e this roll, and go speak unto the	Eze 3:1	398
and he caused me to *e* that roll	Eze 3:2	398
Son of man, cause thy belly to *e*	Eze 3:3	398
Then did I *e* it	Eze 3:3	398
ninety days shalt thou *e* thereof	Eze 4:9	398
thou shalt *e* shall be by weight	Eze 4:10	398
from time to time shalt thou *e* it	Eze 4:10	398
thou shalt *e* it as barley cakes,	Eze 4:12	398
shall the children of Israel *e*	Eze 4:13	398
they shall *e* bread by weight, and	Eze 4:16	398
Therefore the fathers shall *e* the	Eze 5:10	398
and the sons shall *e* their fathers	Eze 5:10	398
e thy bread with quaking, and	Eze 12:18	398
They shall *e* their bread with	Eze 12:19	398
thou didst *e* fine flour, and honey	Eze 16:13	398
in thee they *e* upon the mountains	Eze 22:9	398
lips, and *e* not the bread of men	Eze 24:17	398
your lips, nor *e* the bread of men	Eze 24:22	398
they shall *e* thy fruit, and they	Eze 25:4	398
Ye *e* with the blood, and lift up	Eze 33:25	398
Ye *e* the fat, and ye clothe you	Eze 34:3	398
they *e* that which ye have trodden	Eze 34:19	7462
of Israel, that ye may *e* flesh	Eze 39:17	398
Ye shall *e* the flesh of the	Eze 39:18	398
ye shall *e* fat till ye be full,	Eze 39:19	398
Lord shall *e* the most holy things	Eze 42:13	398
in it to *e* bread before the Lord	Eze 44:3	398
They shall *e* the meat offering,	Eze 44:29	398
The priests shall not *e* of any	Eze 44:31	398
and let them give us pulse to *e*	Dan 1:12	398
of the children that *e* of the	Dan 1:13	398
e the portion of the king's meat	Dan 1:15	398
make thee to *e* grass as oxen	Dan 4:25	2939
make thee to *e* grass as oxen	Dan 4:32	2939
did *e* grass as oxen, and his body	Dan 4:33	399
beasts of the field shall *e* them	Hos 2:12	398
They *e* up the sin of my people,	Hos 4:8	398
For they shall *e*, and not have	Hos 4:10	398
of mine offerings, and *e* it	Hos 8:13	398
they shall *e* unclean things in	Hos 9:3	398
all that *e* thereof shall be	Hos 9:4	398
ye shall *e* in plenty, and be	Joel 2:26	398
e the lambs out of the flock, and	Amos 6:4	398
great deep, and did *e* up a part	Amos 7:4	398
land of Judah, and there *e* bread	Amos 7:12	398
gardens, and *e* the fruit of them	Amos 9:14	398
they that *e* thy bread have laid a	Obad 7	
Who also *e* the flesh of my people	Mic 3:3	398
Thou shalt *e*, but not be	Mic 6:14	398
there is no cluster to *e*	Mic 7:1	398
it shall *e* thee up like the	Nah 3:15	398
as the eagle that hasteth to *e*	Hab 1:8	398
ye *e*, but ye have not enough	Hag 1:6	398
And when ye did *e*, and when ye did	Zec 7:6	398
did not ye *e* for yourselves, and	Zec 7:6	398
let the rest *e* every one the	Zec 11:9	398
but he shall *e* the flesh of the	Zec 11:16	398
for your life, what ye shall *e*	Mt 6:25	*5315*
thought, saying, What shall we *e*	Mt 6:31	*5315*
pluck the ears of corn, and to *e*	Mt 12:1	*2068*
did *e* the shewbread, which was	Mt 12:4	*5315*
which was not lawful for him to *e*	Mt 12:4	*5315*
give ye them to *e*	Mt 14:16	*5315*
And they did all *e*, and were filled	Mt 14:20	*5315*
not their hands when they *e* bread	Mt 15:2	*2068*
but to *e* with unwashen hands	Mt 15:20	*5315*
yet the dogs *e* of the crumbs	Mt 15:27	*2068*
three days, and have nothing to *e*	Mt 15:32	*5315*
And they did all *e*, and were filled	Mt 15:37	*5315*
they that did *e* were four	Mt 15:38	*2068*
smite his fellowservants, and to *e*	Mt 24:49	*2068*
for thee to *e* the passover	Mt 26:17	*5315*
And as they did *e*, he said, Verily	Mt 26:21	*2068*
the disciples, and said, Take, *e*	Mt 26:26	*5315*
he did *e* locusts and wild honey	Mk 1:6	*2068*
saw him *e* with publicans and	Mk 2:16	*2068*
did *e* the shewbread, which is not	Mk 2:26	*5315*
lawful to *e* but for the priests	Mk 2:26	*5315*
they could not so much as *e* bread	Mk 3:20	*5315*
should be given her to *e*	Mk 5:43	*5315*
had no leisure so much as to *e*	Mk 6:31	*5315*
for they have nothing to *e*	Mk 6:36	*5315*
said unto them, Give ye them to *e*	Mk 6:37	*5315*
of bread, and give them to *e*	Mk 6:37	*5315*
And they did all *e*, and were filled	Mk 6:42	*5315*
they that did *e* of the loaves	Mk 6:44	*5315*
disciples *e* bread with defiled	Mk 7:2	*2068*
e not, holding the tradition of	Mk 7:3	*2068*
except they wash, they *e* not	Mk 7:4	*2068*
but *e* bread with unwashen hands	Mk 7:5	*2068*
table *e* of the children's crumbs	Mk 7:28	*2068*
great, and having nothing to *e*	Mk 8:1	*5315*
three days, and have nothing to *e*	Mk 8:2	*5315*
So they did *e*, and were filled	Mk 8:8	*5315*
No man *e* fruit of thee hereafter	Mk 11:14	*5315*
that thou mayest *e* the passover	Mk 14:12	*5315*

where I shall *e* the passover with	Mk 14:14	5315
And as they sat and did *e*, Jesus	Mk 14:18	2068
And as they did *e*, Jesus took	Mk 14:22	2068
and gave to them, and said, Take, e...	Mk 14:22	5315
And in those days he did *e* nothing	Lk 4:2	5315
disciples, saying, Why do ye *e*	Lk 5:30	2068
but thine *e* and drink	Lk 5:33	2068
the ears of corn, and did *e*	Lk 6:1	2068
e the shewbread, and gave also to	Lk 6:4	5315
to *e* but for the priests alone	Lk 6:4	5315
him that he would *e* with him	Lk 7:36	2068
said unto them, Give ye them to	Lk 9:13	5315
And they did *e*, and were all filled	Lk 9:17	5315
e such things as are set before	Lk 10:8	2068
take thine ease, e, drink, and be	Lk 12:19	5315
for your life, what ye shall *e*	Lk 12:22	5315
And seek not ye what ye shall *e*	Lk 12:29	5315
menservants and maidens, and to *e*	Lk 12:45	2068
to *e* bread on the sabbath day	Lk 14:1	5315
Blessed is he that shall *e* bread	Lk 14:15	5315
the husks that the swine did *e*	Lk 15:16	5315
and let us *e*, and be merry	Lk 15:23	5315
and afterward thou shalt *e*	Lk 17:8	5315
They did *e*, they drank, they	Lk 17:27	2068
they did *e*, they drank, they	Lk 17:28	2068
us the passover, that we may *e*	Lk 22:8	5315
where I shall *e* the passover with	Lk 22:11	5315
With desire I have desired to *e*	Lk 22:15	5315
I will not any more *e* thereof	Lk 22:16	5315
That ye may *e* and drink at my	Lk 22:30	2068
he took it, and did *e* before them	Lk 24:43	5315
prayed him, saying, Master, *e*	Jn 4:31	5315
I have meat to *e* that ye know not	Jn 4:32	5315
any man brought him ought to *e*	Jn 4:33	5315
we buy bread, that these may *e*	Jn 6:5	5315
the place where they did *e* bread	Jn 6:23	5315
because ye did *e* of the loaves	Jn 6:26	5315
Our fathers did *e* manna in the	Jn 6:31	5315
gave them bread from heaven to *e*	Jn 6:31	5315
Your fathers did *e* manna in the	Jn 6:49	5315
heaven, that a man may *e* thereof	Jn 6:50	5315
if any man *e* of this bread, he	Jn 6:51	5315
this man give us his flesh to *e*	Jn 6:52	5315
Except ye *e* the flesh of the Son	Jn 6:53	5315
not as your fathers did *e* manna	Jn 6:58	5315
that they might *e* the passover	Jn 18:28	5315
did *e* their meat with gladness and	Acts 2:46	3335
sight, and neither did *e* nor drink	Acts 9:9	5315
Rise, Peter; kill, and *e*	Acts 10:13	5315
of God, even to us, who did *e*	Acts 10:41	4906
and didst *e* with them	Acts 11:3	4906
Arise, Peter; slay and *e*	Acts 11:7	5315
e nor drink till they had killed	Acts 23:12	5315
that we will *e* nothing until we	Acts 23:14	1089
that they will neither *e* nor	Acts 23:21	5315
he had broken it, he began to *e*	Acts 27:35	2068
that he may *e* all things	Rom 14:2	5315
It is good neither to *e* flesh	Rom 14:21	5315
that doubteth is damned if he *e*	Rom 14:23	5315
with such an one, no not to *e*	1Cor 5:11	4906
of the idol unto this hour *e* it	1Cor 8:7	2068
for neither, if we *e*, are we the	1Cor 8:8	5315
neither, if we *e* not, are we the	1Cor 8:8	5315
e those things which are offered	1Cor 8:10	2068
I will *e* no flesh while the world	1Cor 8:13	5315
Have we not power to *e* and to	1Cor 9:4	5315
did all *e* the same spiritual meat	1Cor 10:3	5315
written, The people sat down to *e*	1Cor 10:7	5315
are not they which *e* of the	1Cor 10:18	2068
is sold in the shambles, that *e*	1Cor 10:25	2068
whatsoever is set before you, *e*	1Cor 10:27	2068
e not for his sake that shewed it	1Cor 10:28	2068
Whether therefore ye *e*, or drink,	1Cor 10:31	2068
this is not to *e* the Lord's	1Cor 11:20	2068
have ye not houses to *e* and to	1Cor 11:22	2068
he brake it, and said, Take, e.	1Cor 11:24	5315
For as often as ye *e* this bread	1Cor 11:26	2068
whosoever shall *e* this bread	1Cor 11:27	2068
so let him *e* of that bread, and	1Cor 11:28	2068
when ye come together to *e*	1Cor 11:33	5315
any man hunger, let him *e* at home	1Cor 11:34	2068
let us *e* and drink	1Cor 15:32	5315
he did *e* with the Gentiles	Gal 2:12	4906
Neither did we *e* any man's bread	2Th 3:8	5315
not work, neither should he *e*	2Th 3:10	2068
they work, and *e* their own bread	2Th 3:12	2068
their word will *e* as doth a	2Ti 2:17	3542,2192
to *e* which serve the tabernacle	Heb 13:10	5315
shall *e* your flesh as it were	Jas 5:3	5315
I give to *e* of the tree of life	Rev 2:7	5315
to *e* **things sacrificed unto idols**	Rev 2:14	5315

I give to *e* of the hidden manna	Rev 2:17	5315
to *e* things sacrificed unto idols	Rev 2:20	5315
said unto me, Take it, and *e* it up	Rev 10:9	2719
shall *e* her flesh, and burn her	Rev 17:16	5315
That ye may *e* the flesh of kings,	Rev 19:18	5315

EATEN

Hast thou *e* of the tree, whereof	Gen 3:11	398
hast *e* of the tree, of which I.	Gen 3:17	398
unto thee of all food that is *e*	Gen 6:21	398
that which the young men have *e*	Gen 14:24	398
I have *e* of all before thou	Gen 27:33	398
rams of thy flock have I not *e*	Gen 31:38	398
And when they had *e* them up.	Gen 41:21	935,413,7130
known that they had *e* them,	Gen 41:21	935,413,7130
when they had *e* up the corn which	Gen 43:2	398
In one house shall it be *e*	Ex 12:46	398
shall no leavened bread be *e*	Ex 13:3	398
bread shall be *e* seven days	Ex 13:7	398
and his flesh shall not be *e*	Ex 21:28	398
cause a field or vineyard to be *e*	Ex 22:5	1197
it shall not be *e*, because it is	Ex 29:34	398
shall it be *e* in the holy place	Lev 6:16	398
it shall not be *e*	Lev 6:23	398
in the holy place shall it be *e*	Lev 6:26	398
in the holy place, shall be *e*	Lev 6:30	398
it shall be *e* in the holy place	Lev 7:6	398
for thanksgiving shall be the *e*	Lev 7:15	398
it shall be *e* the same day that	Lev 7:16	398
the remainder of it shall be *e*	Lev 7:16	398
be *e* at all on the third day	Lev 7:18	398
any unclean thing shall not be *e*	Lev 7:19	398
Wherefore have ye not *e* the sin	Lev 10:17	398
have *e* it in the holy place	Lev 10:18	398
if I had *e* the sin offering to	Lev 10:19	398
they shall not be *e*, they are an	Lev 11:13	398
Of all meat which may be *e*	Lev 11:34	398
it shall not be *e*	Lev 11:41	398
between the beast that may be *e*	Lev 11:47	398
and the beast that may not be *e*	Lev 11:47	398
any beast or fowl that may be *e*	Lev 17:13	398
It shall be *e* the same day ye	Lev 19:6	398
if it be *e* at all on the third	Lev 19:7	398
it shall not be *e* of.	Lev 19:23	398
On the same day it shall be *e* up	Lev 22:30	398
days until unleavened bread be *e*	Num 28:17	398
when thou shalt have *e* and be full	Deut 6:11	398
When thou hast *e* and art full,	Deut 8:10	398
Lest when thou hast *e* and art full	Deut 8:12	398
as the roebuck and the hart is *e*	Deut 12:22	398
they shall not be *e*	Deut 14:19	398
vineyard, and hath not yet *e* of it	Deut 20:6	2490
I have not *e* thereof in my	Deut 26:14	398
Ye have not *e* bread, neither have	Deut 29:6	398
and they shall have *e* and filled	Deut 31:20	398
had *e* of the old corn of the land	Josh 5:12	398
And when Boaz had *e* and drunk, and	Ruth 3:7	398
up after they had *e* in Shiloh	1Sa 1:9	398
if haply the people had *e* freely	1Sa 14:30	398
for he had *e* no bread all the day	1Sa 28:20	398
and when he had *e*, his spirit came	1Sa 30:12	398
for he had *e* no bread, nor drunk	1Sa 30:12	398
have we *e* at all of the king's	2Sa 19:42	398
hast *e* bread and drunk water in	1Kin 13:22	398
to pass, after he had *e* bread	1Kin 13:23	398
the lion had not *e* the carcase	1Kin 13:28	398
and when they had *e* and drunk, he	2Kin 6:23	398
my brethren have not *e* the bread	Neh 5:14	398
is unsavoury is *e* without salt	Job 6:6	398
as a garment that is moth *e*	Job 13:28	398
Or have *e* my morsel myself alone,	Job 31:17	398
the fatherless hath not *e* thereof	Job 31:17	398
If I have *e* the fruits thereof	Job 31:39	398
zeal of thine house hath *e* me up	Ps 69:9	398
For I have *e* ashes like bread, and	Ps 102:9	398
bread *e* in secret is pleasant	Prov 9:17	398
thou hast *e* shalt thou vomit up	Prov 23:8	398
I have *e* my honeycomb with my	Song 5:1	398
for ye have *e* up the vineyard	Is 3:14	398
thereof, and it shall be *e* up	Is 5:5	398
and it shall return, and shall be *e*	Is 6:13	1197
I have roasted flesh, and *e* it	Is 44:19	398
for they have *e* up Jacob, and	Jer 10:25	398
figs, which could not be *e*	Jer 24:2	398
evil, very evil, that cannot be *e*	Jer 24:3	398
the evil figs, which cannot be *e*	Jer 24:8	398
like vile figs, that cannot be *e*	Jer 29:17	398
The fathers have *e* a sour grape	Jer 31:29	398
up even till now have I not *e* of	Eze 4:14	398
The fathers have *e* sour grapes	Eze 18:2	398
hath not *e* upon the mountains,	Eze 18:6	398

duties, but even hath *e* upon the .... Eze 18:11   398
That hath not *e* upon the........................ Eze 18:15   398
you to have *e* up the good pasture .... Eze 34:18   7462
unleavened bread shall be *e* .... Eze 45:21   398
ye have *e* the fruit of lies .... Hos 10:13   398
hath left hath the locust *e* .... Joel 1:4   398
hath left hath the cankerworm *e* .... Joel 1:4   398
hath left hath the caterpiller *e* .... Joel 1:4   398
the years that the locust hath *e* .... Joel 2:25   398
they that had *e* were about five .... Mt 14:21   2068
they that had *e* were about four............. Mk 8:9   5315
shall ye begin to say, We have *e* .... Lk 13:26   5315
and serve me, till I have *e* .... Lk 17:8   5315
zeal of thine house hath *e* me up.......... Jn 2:17   2719
and above unto them that had *e*............. Jn 6:13   977
very hungry, and would have *e*................ Acts 10:10   1089
for I have never *e* any thing that .... Acts 10:14   5315
he was *e* of worms, and gave up the ...... Acts 12:23   4662
again, and had broken bread, and *e* ...... Acts 20:11   1089
And when they had *e* enough................. Acts 27:38   2880
and as soon as I had *e* it, my .... Rev 10:10   5315

EATER
Out of the *e* came forth meat, and.......... Judg 14:14   398
to the sower, and bread to the *e* .... Is 55:10   398
even fall into the mouth of the *e* .... Nah 3:12   398

EATERS
among riotous *e* of flesh .... Prov 23:20   2151

EATEST
for in the day that thou *e*...................... Gen 2:17   398
and why *e* thou not 1Sa 1:8   398
so sad, that thou *e* no bread 1Kin 21:5   398

EATETH
for whosoever *e* leavened bread.............. Ex 12:15   398
for whosoever *e* that which is.................. Ex 12:19   398
the soul that *e* of it shall bear .... Lev 7:18   398
But the soul that *e* of the flesh .... Lev 7:20   398
For whosoever *e* the fat of the .... Lev 7:25   398
even the soul that *e* it shall be .... Lev 7:25   398
it be that *e* any manner of blood .... Lev 7:27   398
he that *e* of the carcase of it .... Lev 11:40   398
he that *e* in the house shall wash .... Lev 14:47   398
that *e* any manner of blood .... Lev 17:10   398
against that soul that *e* blood .... Lev 17:10   398
whosoever *e* it shall be cut off.............. Lev 17:14   398
every soul that *e* that which died .... Lev 17:15   398
Therefore every one that *e* it .... Lev 19:8   398
it, is a land that *e* up the .... Num 13:32   398
man that *e* any food until evening........ 1Sa 14:24   398
the man that *e* any food this day 1Sa 14:28   398
Whose harvest the hungry *e* up .... Job 5:5   398
soul, and never *e* with pleasure .... Job 21:25   398
he *e* grass as an ox .... Job 40:15   398
similitude of an ox that *e* grass .... Ps 106:20   398
The righteous *e* to the satisfying .... Prov 13:25   398
she *e*, and wipeth her mouth, and.......... Prov 30:20   398
e not the bread of idleness .... Prov 31:27   398
together, and *e* his own flesh.................. Eccl 4:5   398
his days also he *e* in darkness .... Eccl 5:17   398
eat thereof, but a stranger *e* it .... Eccl 6:2   398
it is yet in his hand he *e* it up .... Is 28:4   1104
man dreameth, and, behold, he *e*.......... Is 29:8   398
with part thereof he *e* flesh .... Is 44:16   398
he that *e* of their eggs dieth, and .... Is 59:5   398
every man that *e* the sour grape .... Jer 31:30   398
Why *e* your Master with publicans .... Mt 9:11   2068
disciples, How is it that he *e* .... Mk 2:16   2068
One of you which *e* with me shall........ Mk 14:18   2068
receiveth sinners, and *e* with them........ Lk 15:2   4906
Whoso *e* my flesh, and drinketh my .... Jn 6:54   5176
He that *e* my flesh, and drinketh .... Jn 6:56   5176
so he that *e* me, even he shall .... Jn 6:57   5176
he that *e* of this bread shall .... Jn 6:58   5176
He that *e* bread with me hath .... Jn 13:18   5176
another, who is weak, *e* herbs .... Rom 14:2   2068
e despise him that *e* not...................... Rom 14:3   2068
which *e* not judge him that *e* .... Rom 14:3   2068
He that *e*, *e* to the Lord...................... Rom 14:6   2068
e not, to the Lord he *e* not.................. Rom 14:6   2068
for that man who *e* with offence .... Rom 14:20   2068
because he *e* not of faith...................... Rom 14:23   2068
e not of the fruit thereof...................... 1Cor 9:7   2068
e not of the milk of the flock 1Cor 9:7   2068
e and drinketh unworthily, *e*.............. 1Cor 11:29   2068

EATING
every man according to his *e*.................. Ex 12:4   400
it every man according to his *e*.............. Ex 16:16   400
every man according to his *e*.................. Ex 16:18   400
every man according to his *e* .... Ex 16:21   400

in his hands, and went on *e*.................... Judg 14:9   398
man, until he shall have done *e* .... Ruth 3:3   398
the LORD in *e* with the blood 1Sa 14:34   398
abroad upon all the earth, *e*.................. 1Sa 30:16   398
it as they had made an end of *e*............ 1Kin 1:41   398
is by the sea in multitude, *e* 1Kin 4:20   398
as they were *e* of the pottage, ... 2Kin 4:40   398
were with David three days, *e* 1Chr 12:39   398
his sons and his daughters were *e* .... Job 1:13   398
Thy sons and thy daughters were *e* ...... Job 1:18   398
rain it upon him while he is *e* .... Job 20:23   3894
e flesh, and drinking wine .... Is 22:13   398
midst, *e* swine's flesh, and the.............. Is 66:17   398
an end of *e* the grass of the land .... Amos 7:2   398
John came neither *e* nor drinking ...... Mt 11:18   2068
The Son of man came *e* and drinking .. Mt 11:19   2068
were before the flood they were *e* ...... Mt 24:38   5176
And as they were *e*, Jesus took .... Mt 26:26   2068
neither *e* bread nor drinking wine .... Lk 7:33   2068
The Son of man is come *e* and .... Lk 7:34   2068
And in the same house remain, *e* .... Lk 10:7   2068
the *e* of those things that are 1Cor 8:4   1035
For in *e* every one taketh before............ 1Cor 11:21   5315

EBAL (e'-bal) *Son of Shobal.*
Alvan, and Manahath, and *E*, Shepho, ... Gen 36:23   5858
and the curse upon mount *E* .... Deut 11:29   5858
command you this day, in mount *E* .... Deut 27:4   5858
shall stand upon mount *E* to curse........ Deut 27:13   5858
the LORD God of Israel in mount *E* .... Josh 8:30   5858
half of them over against mount *E* .... Josh 8:33   5858
And *E*, and Abimael, and Sheba, ... 1Chr 1:22   5858
Alian, and Manahath, and *E*, Shephi, ... 1Chr 1:40   5858

EBED (e'-bed) See EBED-MELECH.
   1. Father of Gaal.
Gaal the son of *E* came with his............ Judg 9:26   5651
And Gaal the son of *E* said .... Judg 9:28   5651
the words of Gaal the son of *E* .... Judg 9:30   5651
saying, Behold, Gaal the son of *E* .... Judg 9:31   5651
And Gaal the son of *E* went out .... Judg 9:35   5651
   2. A family of exiles.
E the son of Jonathan, and with .... Ezr 8:6   5651

EBED-MELECH (e'-bed-me'-lek) *An Ethiopian eunuch.*
Now when *E* the Ethiopian, one of.......... Jer 38:7   5663
E went forth out of the king's .... Jer 38:8   5663
king commanded *E* the Ethiopian .... Jer 38:10   5663
So *E* took the men with him, and .... Jer 38:11   5663
E the Ethiopian said unto...................... Jer 38:12   5663
speak to *E* the Ethiopian, saying,.......... Jer 39:16   5663

EBEN-EZER *A Philistine city.*
to battle, and pitched beside *E* 1Sa 4:1   72
and brought it from *E* unto Ashdod........ 1Sa 5:1   72
Shen, and called the name of it *E*.......... 1Sa 7:12   72

EBER (e'-bur) See HEBER.
   1. A great-grandson of Shem.
father of all the children of *E* .... Gen 10:21   5677
and Salah begat *E* .... Gen 10:24   5677
unto *E* were born two sons .... Gen 10:25   5677
lived thirty years, and begat *E* .... Gen 11:14   5677
after he begat *E* four hundred .... Gen 11:15   5677
E lived four and thirty years, and .... Gen 11:16   5677
E lived after he begat Peleg four .... Gen 11:17   5677
begat Shelah, and Shelah begat *E*........ 1Chr 1:18   5677
unto *E* were born two sons 1Chr 1:19   5677
E, Peleg, Reu, ... 1Chr 1:25   5677
   2. Descendants of Eber 1.
Asshur, and shall afflict *E* .... Num 24:24   5677
   3. Son of Elpaal.
E, and Misham, and Shamed, who.......... 1Chr 8:12   5677
   4. A priest of the Amok family.
Kallai; of Amok, *E* .... Neh 12:20   5677

EBEZ See ABEZ.

EBIASAPH (e-bi'-a-saf) See ABIASAPH. *A great-grandson of Korah.*
E his son, and Assir his son, ... 1Chr 6:23   43
the son of Assir, the son of *E* 1Chr 6:37   43
the son of Kore, the son of *E* 1Chr 9:19   43

EBONY
for a present horns of ivory and *e*.......... Eze 27:15   1894

EBRONAH (eb-ro'-nah) *An encampment during the Exodus.*
from Jotbathah, and encamped at *E* ...... Num 33:34   5684
And they departed from *E*, and .... Num 33:35   5684

ECBATANA See ACHMETHA.

ED (ed) *Name of an altar.*
of Gad called the altar *E* .... Josh 22:34

EDAR (e'-dar) See EDER. *A name of a watchtower.*

his tent beyond the tower of *E*	Gen 35:21	5740

EDEN (e'-dun)

1. *Original land of Adam and Eve.*

planted a garden eastward in *E*	Gen 2:8	5731
went out of *E* to water the garden	Gen 2:10	5731
into the garden of *E* to dress it	Gen 2:15	5731
him forth from the garden of *E*	Gen 3:23	5731
east of the garden of *E* Cherubim	Gen 3:24	5731
the land of Nod, on the east of *E*	Gen 4:16	5731
will make her wilderness like *E*	Is 51:3	5731
hast been in *E* the garden of God	Eze 28:13	5731
so that all the trees of *E*	Eze 31:9	5731
and all the trees of *E*, the choice	Eze 31:16	5731
in greatness among the trees of *E*	Eze 31:18	5731
of *E* unto the nether parts of the	Eze 31:18	5731
is become like the garden of *E*	Eze 36:35	5731
is as the garden of *E* before them	Joel 2:3	5731

2. *An undetermined place.*

the children of *E* which were in	2Kin 19:12	5731
the children of *E* which were in	Is 37:12	5731
Haran, and Canneh, and *E*, the	Eze 27:23	5731
the sceptre from the house of *E*	Amos 1:5	5731

3. *Son of Joah.*

of Zimmah, and *E* the son of Joah	2Chr 29:12	5731

4. *A Levite during Hezekiah's time.*

And next him were *E*, and Miniamin,	2Chr 31:15	5731

EDER (e'-dur) See EDAR. *A city in southern Judah.*

Edom southward were Kabzeel, and *E*	Josh 15:21	5740

2. *A grandson of Merari.*

Mahli, and *E*, and Jeremoth, three	1Chr 23:23	5740
Mahli, and *E*, and Jerimoth	1Chr 24:30	5740

EDGE

his son with the *e* of the sword	Gen 34:26	6310
in the *e* of the wilderness	Ex 13:20	7097
people with the *e* of the sword	Ex 17:13	5310
the *e* of the one curtain from the	Ex 26:4	8193
uttermost *e* of another curtain	Ex 26:4	8193
loops shalt thou make in the *e* of	Ex 26:5	7097
the *e* of the one curtain that is	Ex 26:10	8193
the *e* of the curtain which is in the	Ex 26:10	8193
fifty loops on the *e* of the	Ex 26:10	8193
on the *e* of one curtain from the	Ex 36:11	8193
fifty loops made he in the *e* of	Ex 36:12	7097
e of the curtain in the coupling	Ex 36:17	7097
fifty loops made he upon the *e* of	Ex 36:17	7097
smote him with the *e* of the sword	Num 21:24	6310
Etham, which is in the *e* of the	Num 33:6	7097
in the *e* of the land of Edom	Num 33:37	7097
that city with the *e* of the sword	Deut 13:15	6310
thereof, with the *e* of the sword	Deut 13:15	6310
thereof with the *e* of the sword	Deut 20:13	6310
and ass, with the *e* of the sword	Josh 6:21	6310
all fallen on the *e* of the sword	Josh 8:24	6310
smote it with the *e* of the sword	Josh 8:24	6310
smote it with the *e* of the sword	Josh 10:28	6310
smote it with the *e* of the sword	Josh 10:30	6310
smote it with the *e* of the sword	Josh 10:32	6310
smote it with the *e* of the sword	Josh 10:35	6310
smote it with the *e* of the sword	Josh 10:37	6310
them with the *e* of the sword	Josh 10:39	6310
therein with the *e* of the sword	Josh 11:11	6310
them with the *e* of the sword	Josh 11:12	6310
smote with the *e* of the sword	Josh 11:14	6310
even unto the *e* of the sea of	Josh 13:27	7097
smote it with the *e* of the sword	Josh 19:47	6310
it with the *e* of the sword	Judg 1:8	6310
the city with the *e* of the sword	Judg 1:25	6310
with the *e* of the sword before	Judg 4:15	6310
fell upon the *e* of the sword	Judg 4:16	6310
them with the *e* of the sword	Judg 18:27	6310
the city with the *e* of the sword	Judg 20:37	6310
them with the *e* of the sword	Judg 20:48	6310
with the *e* of the sword, with the	Judg 21:10	6310
people with the *e* of the sword	1Sa 15:8	6310
smote he with the *e* of the sword	1Sa 22:19	6310
and sheep, with the *e* of the sword	1Sa 22:19	6310
the city with the *e* of the sword	2Sa 15:14	6310
them with the *e* of the sword	2Kin 10:25	6310
servants with the *e* of the sword	Job 1:15	6310
servants with the *e* of the sword	Job 1:17	6310
also turned the *e* of his sword	Ps 89:43	6697
be blunt, and he do not whet the *e*	Eccl 10:10	6440
them with the *e* of the sword	Jer 21:7	6310
the children's teeth are set on *e*	Jer 31:29	6949
his teeth shall be set on *e*	Jer 31:30	6949
the children's teeth are set on *e*	Eze 18:2	6949
the border thereof by the *e*	Eze 43:13	

shall fall by the *e* of the sword	Lk 21:24	4750
escaped the *e* of the sword, out	Heb 11:34	4750

E

EDGES

joined at the two *e* thereof	Ex 28:7	7098
by the two *e* was it coupled	Ex 39:4	7099
made him a dagger which had two *e*	Judg 3:16	6366
hath the sharp sword with two *e*	Rev 2:12	*1366*

EDIFICATION

his neighbour for his good to *e*	Rom 15:2	*3619*
speaketh unto men to *e*, and	1Cor 14:3	*3619*
the Lord hath given us for *e*	2Cor 10:8	*3619*
which the Lord hath given me to *e*	2Cor 13:10	*3619*

EDIFIED

and Galilee and Samaria, and were *e*	Acts 9:31	*3618*
well, but the other is not *e*	1Cor 14:17	*3618*

EDIFIETH

puffeth up, but charity *e*	1Cor 8:1	*3618*
in an unknown tongue *e* himself	1Cor 14:4	*3618*
he that prophesieth *e* the church	1Cor 14:4	*3618*

EDIFY

wherewith one may *e* another	Rom 14:19	*3619*
for me, but all things *e* not	1Cor 10:23	*3618*
e one another, even as also ye do	1Th 5:11	*3618*

EDIFYING

that the church may receive *e*	1Cor 14:5	*3619*
may excel to the *e* of the church	1Cor 14:12	*3619*
Let all things be done unto *e*	1Cor 14:26	*3619*
dearly beloved, for your *e*	2Cor 12:19	*3619*
for the *e* of the body of Christ	Eph 4:12	*3619*
body unto the *e* of itself in love	Eph 4:16	*3619*
which is good to the use of *e*	Eph 4:29	*3619*
than godly *e* which is in faith	1Ti 1:4	*3618*

EDOM (e'-dum) See EDOMITES, ESAU, IDUMEA, OBED-EDOM.

1. *Another name for Esau.*

children of Seir in the land of *E*	Gen 36:21	123
that reigned in the land of *E*	Gen 36:31	123
Bela the son of Beor reigned in *E*	Gen 36:32	123
these be the dukes of *E*,	Gen 36:43	123
the dukes of *E* shall be amazed	Ex 15:15	123
from Kadesh unto the king of *E*	Num 20:14	123
E said unto him, Thou shalt not	Num 20:18	123
E came out against him with much	Num 20:20	123
Thus *E* refused to give Israel	Num 20:21	123
by the coast of the land of *E*	Num 20:23	123
Red sea, to compass the land of *E*	Num 21:4	123
E shall be a possession, Seir	Num 24:18	123
Hor, in the edge of the land of *E*	Num 33:37	123
of Zin along by the coast of *E*	Num 34:3	123
even to the border of *E* the	Josh 15:1	123
coast of *E* southward were Kabzeel	Josh 15:21	123
marchedst out of the field of *E*	Judg 5:4	123
messengers unto the king of *E*	Judg 11:17	123
but the king of *E* would not	Judg 11:17	123
and compassed the land of *E*	Judg 11:18	123
children of Ammon, and against *E*	1Sa 14:47	123
And he put garrisons in *E*	2Sa 8:14	123
throughout all *E* put he garrisons	2Sa 8:14	123
all they of *E* became David's	2Sa 8:14	123
of the Red sea, in the land of *E*	1Kin 9:26	123
he was of the king's seed in *E*	1Kin 11:14	123
came to pass, when David was in *E*	1Kin 11:15	123
he had smitten every male in *E*	1Kin 11:15	123
he had cut off every male in *E*	1Kin 11:16	123
There was then no king in *E*	1Kin 22:47	123
way through the wilderness of *E*	2Kin 3:8	123
king of Judah, and the king of *E*	2Kin 3:9	123
the king of *E* went down to him	2Kin 3:12	123
there came water by the way of *E*	2Kin 3:20	123
through even unto the king of *E*	2Kin 3:26	123
In his days *E* revolted from under	2Kin 8:20	123
Yet *E* revolted from under the	2Kin 8:22	123
He slew of *E* in the valley of	2Kin 14:7	123
Thou hast indeed smitten *E*	2Kin 14:10	123
that reigned in the land of *E*	1Chr 1:43	123
And the dukes of *E* were	1Chr 1:51	123
These are the dukes of *E*	1Chr 1:54	123
from *E*, and from Moab, and from the	1Chr 18:11	123
And he put garrisons in *E*	1Chr 18:13	123
at the sea side in the land of *E*	2Chr 8:17	123
they sought after the gods of *E*	2Chr 25:20	123
smote of *E* in the valley of salt	Ps 60:t	123
over *E* will I cast out my shoe	Ps 60:8	123
who will lead me into *E*	Ps 60:9	123
The tabernacles of *E*, and the	Ps 83:6	123
over *E* will I cast out my shoe	Ps 108:9	123
who will lead me into *E*	Ps 108:10	123

the children of *E* in the day of	Ps 137:7	123
they shall lay their hand upon *E*	Is 11:14	123
Who is this that cometh from *E*	Is 63:1	123
Egypt, and Judah, and *E*, and the	Jer 9:26	123
E, and Moab, and the children of	Jer 25:21	123
And send them to the king of *E*	Jer 27:3	123
and among the Ammonites, and in *E*	Jer 40:11	123
Concerning *E*, thus saith the LORD	Jer 49:7	123
Also *E* shall be a desolation	Jer 49:17	123
that he hath taken against *E*	Jer 49:20	123
E be as the heart of a woman in	Jer 49:22	123
and be glad, O daughter of *E*	Lam 4:21	123
thine iniquity, O daughter of *E*	Lam 4:22	123
Because that *E* hath dealt against	Eze 25:12	123
also stretch out mine hand upon *E*	Eze 25:13	123
I will lay my vengeance upon *E* by	Eze 25:14	123
they shall do in *E* according to	Eze 25:14	123
There is *E*, her kings, and all her	Eze 32:29	123
escape out of his hand, even *E*	Dan 11:41	123
E shall be a desolate wilderness,	Joel 3:19	123
to deliver them up to *E*	Amos 1:6	123
up the whole captivity to *E*	Amos 1:9	123
For three transgressions of *E*	Amos 1:11	123
bones of the king of *E* into lime	Amos 2:1	123
they may possess the remnant of *E*	Amos 9:12	123
saith the Lord GOD concerning *E*	Obad 1	123
destroy the wise men out of *E*	Obad 8	123
Whereas *E* saith, We are	Mal 1:4	123

2. *Descendants of Esau.*

therefore was his name called *E*	Gen 25:30	123
land of Seir, the country of *E*	Gen 32:3	123
the generations of Esau, who is *E*	Gen 36:1	123
Esau is *E*	Gen 36:8	123
came of Eliphaz in the land of *E*	Gen 36:16	123
came of Reuel in the land of *E*	Gen 36:17	123
are the sons of Esau, who is *E*	Gen 36:19	123

EDOMITE (e'-dum-ite) See EDOMITES. *A descendant of Esau.*

Thou shalt not abhor an *E*	Deut 23:7	130
and his name was Doeg, an *E*	1Sa 21:7	130
Then answered Doeg the *E*, which	1Sa 22:9	130
And Doeg the *E* turned, and he fell	1Sa 22:18	130
day, when Doeg the *E* was there	1Sa 22:22	130
unto Solomon, Hadad the *E*	1Kin 11:14	130
of David, when Doeg the *E* came	Ps 52:t	130

EDOMITES (e'-dum-ites)

the father of the *E* in mount Seir	Gen 36:9	130
he is Esau the father of the *E*	Gen 36:43	130
of the Moabites, Ammonites, *E*	1Kin 11:1	130
certain *E* of his father's	1Kin 11:17	
smote the *E* which compassed him	2Kin 8:21	130
the son Zeruiah slew of the *E* in	1Chr 18:12	130
all the *E* became David's servants	1Chr 18:13	130
In his days the *E* revolted from	2Chr 21:8	130
smote the *E* which compassed him	2Chr 21:9	130
So the *E* revolted from under the	2Chr 21:10	130
come from the slaughter of the *E*	2Chr 25:14	130
Lo, thou hast smitten the *E*	2Chr 25:19	130
For again the *E* had come and	2Chr 28:17	130

EDREI (ed'-re-i)

1. *A city in Bashan.*

his people, to the battle at *E*	Num 21:33	154
which dwelt at Astaroth at *E*	Deut 1:4	154
and all his people, to battle at *E*	Deut 3:1	154
and all Bashan, unto Salchah and *E*	Deut 3:10	154
that dwelt at Ashtaroth and at *E*	Josh 12:4	154
reigned in Ashtaroth and in *E*	Josh 13:12	154
half Gilead, and Ashtaroth, and *E*	Josh 13:31	154

2. *A city in Naphtali.*

And Kedesh, and *E*, and En-hazor,	Josh 19:37	154

EFFECT

she bound her soul, of none *e*	Num 30:8	6565
and they spake to her to that *e*	2Chr 34:22	
devices of the people of none *e*	Ps 33:10	5106
the *e* of righteousness quietness	Is 32:17	5656
his lies shall not so *e* it	Jer 48:30	6213
at hand, and the *e* of every vision	Eze 12:23	1697
God of none *e* by your tradition	Mt 15:6	208
of none *e* through your tradition	Mk 7:13	208
make the faith of God without *e*	Rom 3:3	2673
and the promise made of none *e*	Rom 4:14	2673
the word of God hath taken none *e*	Rom 9:6	1601
Christ should be made of none *e*	1Cor 1:17	2758
should make the promise of none *e*	Gal 3:17	2673
Christ is become of no *e* unto you	Gal 5:4	2673

EFFECTED

his own house, he prosperously *e*	2Chr 7:11	6743

EFFECTUAL

e is opened unto me, and there are	1Cor 16:9	1756
which is *e* in the enduring of the	2Cor 1:6	1754
me by the *e* working of his power	Eph 3:7	1753
according to the *e* working in the	Eph 4:16	1753
of thy faith may become *e* by the	Philem 6	1756
The *e* fervent prayer of a	Jas 5:16	1754

EFFECTUALLY

(For he that wrought *e* in Peter	Gal 2:8	1754
which *e* worketh also in you that	1Th 2:13	1754

EFFEMINATE

idolaters, nor adulterers, nor *e*	1Cor 6:9	3120

EGG

any taste in the white of an *e*	Job 6:6	2495
Or if he shall ask an *e*, will he	Lk 11:12	5609

EGGS

whether they be young ones, or *e*	Deut 22:6	1000
upon the young, or upon the *e*	Deut 22:6	1000
Which leaveth her *e* in the earth	Job 39:14	1000
as one gathereth *e* that are left	Is 10:14	1000
They hatch cockatrice' *e*, and	Is 59:5	1000
he that eateth of their *e* dieth	Is 59:5	1000
As the partridge sitteth on *e*	Jer 17:11	

EGLAH (eg'-lah) See MICHAL. *A wife of David.*

sixth, Ithream, by *E* David's wife	2Sa 3:5	5698
the sixth, Ithream by *E* his wife	1Chr 3:3	5698

EGLAIM (eg'-la-im) See EN-EGLAIM. *A Moabite city.*

the howling thereof unto *E*	Is 15:8	97

EGLON (eg'-lon)

1. *An Amorite city.*

Lachish, and unto Debir king of *E*	Josh 10:3	5700
king of Lachish, the king of *E*	Josh 10:5	5700
king of Lachish, and the king of *E*	Josh 10:23	5700
from Lachish Joshua passed unto *E*	Josh 10:34	5700
And Joshua went up from *E*, and all	Josh 10:36	5700
to all that he had done to *E*	Josh 10:37	5700
The king of *E*, one	Josh 12:12	5700
Lachish, and Bozkath, and *E*	Josh 15:39	5700

2. *A Moabite king.*

the LORD strengthened *E* the king	Judg 3:12	5700
the children of Israel served *E*	Judg 3:14	5700
a present unto *E* the king of Moab	Judg 3:15	5700
the present unto *E* king of Moab	Judg 3:17	5700
and *E* was a very fat man	Judg 3:17	5700

EGYPT (e'-jipt) See EGYPTIAN, MIZRAIM. *Kingdom in northeast Africa.*

went down into *E* to sojourn there	Gen 12:10	4714
he was come near to enter into *E*	Gen 12:11	4714
that, when Abram was come into *E*	Gen 12:14	4714
And Abram went up out of *E*	Gen 13:1	4714
of the LORD, like the land of *E*	Gen 13:10	4714
from the river of *E* unto the	Gen 15:18	4714
him a wife out of the land of *E*	Gen 21:21	4714
unto Shur, that is before *E*	Gen 25:18	4714
him, and said, Go not down into *E*	Gen 26:2	4714
going to carry it down to *E*	Gen 37:25	4714
and they brought Joseph into *E*	Gen 37:28	4714
sold him into *E* unto Potiphar	Gen 37:36	4714
And Joseph was brought down to *E*	Gen 39:1	4714
that the butler of the king of *E*	Gen 40:1	4714
offended their lord the king of *E*	Gen 40:1	4714
and the baker of the king of *E*	Gen 40:5	4714
called for all the magicians of *E*	Gen 41:8	4714
in all the land of *E* for badness	Gen 41:19	4714
throughout all the land of *E*	Gen 41:29	4714
be forgotten in the land of *E*	Gen 41:30	4714
and set him over the land of *E*	Gen 41:33	4714
of *E* in the seven plenteous years	Gen 41:34	4714
which shall be in the land of *E*	Gen 41:36	4714
set thee over all the land of *E*	Gen 41:41	4714
him ruler over all the land of *E*	Gen 41:43	4714
hand or foot in all the land of *E*	Gen 41:44	4714
went out over all the land of *E*	Gen 41:45	4714
he stood before Pharaoh king of *E*	Gen 41:46	4714
went throughout all the land of *E*	Gen 41:46	4714
which were in the land of *E*	Gen 41:48	4714
that was in the land of *E*	Gen 41:53	4714
all the land of *E* there was bread	Gen 41:54	4714
all the land of *E* was famished	Gen 41:55	4714
waxed sore in the land of *E*	Gen 41:56	4714
all countries came into *E* to	Gen 41:57	4714
saw that there was corn in *E*	Gen 42:1	4714
heard that there is corn in *E*	Gen 42:2	4714
went down to buy corn in *E*	Gen 42:3	4714
which they had brought out of *E*	Gen 43:2	4714
and rose up, and went down to *E*	Gen 43:15	4714
your brother, whom ye sold into *E*	Gen 45:4	4714

throughout all the land of E	Gen 45:8	4714
God hath made me lord of all E	Gen 45:9	4714
my father of all my glory in E	Gen 45:13	4714
you the good of the land of E	Gen 45:18	4714
land of E for your little ones	Gen 45:19	4714
of all the land of E is yours	Gen 45:20	4714
laden with the good things of E	Gen 45:23	4714
And they went up out of E, and came	Gen 45:25	4714
governor over all the land of E	Gen 45:26	4714
fear not to go down into E	Gen 46:3	4714
I will go down with thee into E	Gen 46:4	4714
land of Canaan, and came into E	Gen 46:6	4714
seed brought he with him into E	Gen 46:7	4714
of Israel, which came into E	Gen 46:8	4714
the land of E were born Manasseh	Gen 46:20	4714
souls that came with Jacob into E	Gen 46:26	4714
Joseph, which were born him in E	Gen 46:27	4714
house of Jacob, which came into E	Gen 46:27	4714
The land of E is before thee	Gen 47:6	4714
a possession in the land of E	Gen 47:11	4714
very sore, so that the land of E	Gen 47:13	4714
that was found in the land of E	Gen 47:14	4714
money failed in the land of E	Gen 47:15	4714
all the land of E for Pharaoh	Gen 47:20	4714
E even to the other end thereof	Gen 47:21	4714
over the land of E unto this day	Gen 47:26	4714
And Israel dwelt in the land of E	Gen 47:27	4714
in the land of E seventeen years	Gen 47:28	4714
bury me not, I pray thee, in E	Gen 47:29	4714
and thou shalt carry me out of E	Gen 47:30	4714
of E before I came unto thee into	Gen 48:5	4714
before I came unto thee into E	Gen 48:5	4714
all the elders of the land of E	Gen 50:7	4714
And Joseph returned into E	Gen 50:14	4714
And Joseph dwelt in E, he, and his	Gen 50:22	4714
and he was put in a coffin in E	Gen 50:26	4714
of Israel, which came into E	Ex 1:1	4714
for Joseph was in E already	Ex 1:5	4714
there arose up a new king over E	Ex 1:8	4714
the king of E spake to the Hebrew	Ex 1:15	4714
as the king of E commanded them	Ex 1:17	4714
the king of E called for the	Ex 1:18	4714
of time, that the king of E died	Ex 2:23	4714
of my people which are in E	Ex 3:7	4714
the children of Israel out of E	Ex 3:10	4714
the children of Israel out of E	Ex 3:11	4714
brought forth the people out of E	Ex 3:12	4714
that which is done to you in E	Ex 3:16	4714
E unto the land of the Canaanites	Ex 3:17	4714
of Israel, unto the king of E	Ex 3:18	4714
the king of E will not let you go	Ex 3:19	4714
smite E with all my wonders which	Ex 3:20	4714
unto my brethren which are in E	Ex 4:18	4714
in Midian, Go, return into E	Ex 4:19	4714
and he returned to the land of E	Ex 4:20	4714
When thou goest to return into E	Ex 4:21	4714
the king of E said unto them,	Ex 5:4	4714
throughout all the land of E to	Ex 5:12	4714
in, speak unto Pharaoh king of E	Ex 6:11	4714
Israel, and unto Pharaoh king of E	Ex 6:13	4714
of Israel out of the land of E	Ex 6:13	4714
of E according to their armies	Ex 6:26	4714
which spake to Pharaoh king of E	Ex 6:27	4714
out the children of Israel from E	Ex 6:27	4714
spake unto Moses in the land of E	Ex 6:28	4714
of E all that I say unto thee	Ex 6:29	4714
and my wonders in the land of E	Ex 7:3	4714
that I may lay my hand upon E	Ex 7:4	4714
the land of E by great judgments	Ex 7:4	4714
I stretch forth mine hand upon E	Ex 7:5	4714
now the magicians of E, they also	Ex 7:11	4714
thine hand upon the waters of E	Ex 7:19	4714
throughout all the land of E	Ex 7:19	4714
throughout all the land of E	Ex 7:21	4714
the magicians of E did so with	Ex 7:22	4714
to come up upon the land of E	Ex 8:5	4714
out his hand over the waters of E	Ex 8:6	4714
came up, and covered the land of E	Ex 8:6	4714
up frogs upon the land of E	Ex 8:7	4714
lice throughout all the land of E	Ex 8:16	4714
lice throughout all the land of E	Ex 8:17	4714
houses, and into all the land of E	Ex 8:24	4714
of Israel and the cattle of E	Ex 9:4	4714
and all the cattle of E died	Ex 9:6	4714
small dust in all the land of E	Ex 9:9	4714
throughout all the land of E	Ex 9:9	4714
such as hath not been in E since	Ex 9:18	4714
may be hail in all the land of E	Ex 9:22	4714
field, throughout the land of E	Ex 9:22	4714
rained hail upon the land of E	Ex 9:23	4714
of E since it became a nation	Ex 9:24	4714
of E all that was in the field	Ex 9:25	4714
what things I have wrought in E	Ex 10:2	4714
thou not yet that E is destroyed	Ex 10:7	4714
the land of E for the locusts	Ex 10:12	4714
may come up upon the land of E	Ex 10:12	4714
forth his rod over the land of E	Ex 10:13	4714
went up over all the land of E	Ex 10:14	4714
and rested in all the coasts of E	Ex 10:14	4714
field, through all the land of E	Ex 10:15	4714
one locust in all the coasts of E	Ex 10:19	4714
be darkness over the land of E	Ex 10:21	4714
in all the land of E three days	Ex 10:22	4714
more upon Pharaoh, and upon E	Ex 11:1	4714
was very great in the land of E	Ex 11:3	4714
will I go out into the midst of E	Ex 11:4	4714
in the land of E shall die	Ex 11:5	4714
cry throughout all the land of E	Ex 11:6	4714
be multiplied in the land of E	Ex 11:9	4714
Moses and Aaron in the land of E	Ex 12:1	4714
through the land of E this night	Ex 12:12	4714
the firstborn in the land of E	Ex 12:12	4714
gods of E I will execute judgment	Ex 12:12	4714
you, when I smite the land of E	Ex 12:13	4714
your armies out of the land of E	Ex 12:17	4714
of the children of Israel in E	Ex 12:27	4714
the firstborn in the land of E	Ex 12:29	4714
and there was a great cry in E	Ex 12:30	4714
which they brought forth out of E	Ex 12:39	4714
because they were thrust out of E	Ex 12:39	4714
of Israel, who dwelt in E	Ex 12:40	4714
LORD went out from the land of E	Ex 12:41	4714
them out from the land of E	Ex 12:42	4714
of the land of E by their armies	Ex 12:51	4714
day, in which ye came out from E	Ex 13:3	4714
me when I came forth out of E	Ex 13:8	4714
the LORD brought thee out of E	Ex 13:9	4714
the LORD brought us out from E	Ex 13:14	4714
the firstborn in the land of E	Ex 13:15	4714
LORD brought us forth out of E	Ex 13:16	4714
they see war, and they return to E	Ex 13:17	4714
up harnessed out of the land of E	Ex 13:18	4714
king of E that the people fled	Ex 14:5	4714
and all the chariots of E	Ex 14:7	4714
the heart of Pharaoh king of E	Ex 14:8	4714
Because there were no graves in E	Ex 14:11	4714
us, to carry us forth out of E	Ex 14:11	4714
word that we did tell thee in E	Ex 14:12	4714
departing out of the land of E	Ex 16:1	4714
hand of the LORD in the land of E	Ex 16:3	4714
you out from the land of E	Ex 16:6	4714
you forth from the land of E	Ex 16:32	4714
thou hast brought us up out of E	Ex 17:3	4714
LORD had brought Israel out of E	Ex 18:1	4714
gone forth out of the land of E	Ex 19:1	4714
brought thee out of the land of E	Ex 20:2	4714
were strangers in the land of E	Ex 22:21	4714
were strangers in the land of E	Ex 23:9	4714
for in it thou camest out from E	Ex 23:15	4714
them forth out of the land of E	Ex 29:46	4714
us up out of the land of E	Ex 32:1	4714
thee up out of the land of E	Ex 32:4	4714
broughtest out of the land of E	Ex 32:7	4714
thee up out of the land of E	Ex 32:8	4714
of the land of E with great power	Ex 32:11	4714
us up out of the land of E	Ex 32:23	4714
brought up out of the land of E	Ex 33:1	4714
month Abib thou camest out from E	Ex 34:18	4714
you up out of the land of E	Lev 11:45	4714
After the doings of the land of E	Lev 18:3	4714
were strangers in the land of E	Lev 19:34	4714
brought you out of the land of E	Lev 19:36	4714
brought you out of the land of E	Lev 22:33	4714
brought them out of the land of E	Lev 23:43	4714
you forth out of the land of E	Lev 25:38	4714
forth out of the land of E	Lev 25:42	4714
forth out of the land of E	Lev 25:55	4714
you forth out of the land of E	Lev 26:13	4714
forth out of the land of E in the	Lev 26:45	4714
were come out of the land of E	Num 1:1	4714
of E I hallowed unto me all the	Num 3:13	4714
of E I sanctified them for myself	Num 8:17	4714
were come out of the land of E	Num 9:1	4714
which we did eat in E freely	Num 11:5	4714
for it was well with us in E	Num 11:18	4714
Why came we forth out of E	Num 11:20	4714
seven years before Zoan in E	Num 13:22	4714
that we had died in the land of E	Num 14:2	4714
better for us to return into E	Num 14:3	4714
captain, and let us return into E	Num 14:4	4714
people, from E even until now	Num 14:19	4714
and my miracles, which I did in E	Num 14:22	4714

brought you out of the land of *E*	Num 15:41	4714
ye made us to come up out of *E*	Num 20:5	4714
How our fathers went down into *E*	Num 20:15	4714
and we have dwelt in *E* a long time	Num 20:15	4714
and hath brought us forth out of *E*	Num 20:16	4714
out of *E* to die in the wilderness	Num 21:5	4714
there is a people come out from *E*	Num 22:5	4714
there is a people come out of *E*	Num 22:11	4714
God brought them out of *E*	Num 23:22	4714
God brought him forth out of *E*	Num 24:8	4714
went forth out of the land of *E*	Num 26:4	4714
whom her mother bare to Levi in *E*	Num 26:59	4714
of the men that came up out of *E*	Num 32:11	4714
of *E* with their armies under the	Num 33:1	4714
were come out of the land of *E*	Num 33:38	4714
from Azmon unto the river of *E*	Num 34:5	4714
us forth out of the land of *E*	Deut 1:27	4714
did for you in *E* before your eyes	Deut 1:30	4714
the iron furnace, even out of *E*	Deut 4:20	4714
did for you in *E* before your eyes	Deut 4:34	4714
with his mighty power out of *E*	Deut 4:37	4714
after they came forth out of *E*	Deut 4:45	4714
they were come forth out of *E*	Deut 4:46	4714
brought thee out of the land of *E*	Deut 5:6	4714
wast a servant in the land of *E*	Deut 5:15	4714
thee forth out of the land of *E*	Deut 6:12	4714
We were Pharaoh's bondmen in *E*	Deut 6:21	4714
us out of *E* with a mighty hand	Deut 6:21	4714
and wonders, great and sore, upon *E*	Deut 6:22	4714
the hand of Pharaoh king of *E*	Deut 7:8	4714
none of the evil diseases of *E*	Deut 7:15	4714
did unto Pharaoh, and unto all *E*	Deut 7:18	4714
thee forth out of the land of *E*	Deut 8:14	4714
didst depart out of the land of *E*	Deut 9:7	4714
of *E* have corrupted themselves	Deut 9:12	4714
forth out of *E* with a mighty hand	Deut 9:26	4714
were strangers in the land of *E*	Deut 10:19	4714
went down into *E* with threescore	Deut 10:22	4714
which he did in the midst of *E*	Deut 11:3	4714
unto Pharaoh the king of *E*	Deut 11:3	4714
And what he did unto the army of *E*	Deut 11:4	4714
it, is not as the land of *E*	Deut 11:10	4714
brought you out of the land of *E*	Deut 13:5	4714
brought thee out of the land of *E*	Deut 13:10	4714
wast a bondman in the land of *E*	Deut 15:15	4714
thee forth out of *E* by night	Deut 16:1	4714
out of the land of *E* in haste	Deut 16:3	4714
of *E* all the days of thy life	Deut 16:3	4714
that thou camest forth out of *E*	Deut 16:6	4714
that thou wast a bondman in *E*	Deut 16:12	4714
cause the people to return to *E*	Deut 17:16	4714
thee up out of the land of *E*	Deut 20:1	4714
way, when ye came forth out of *E*	Deut 23:4	4714
that ye were come forth out of *E*	Deut 24:9	4714
that thou wast a bondman in *E*	Deut 24:18	4714
wast a bondman in the land of *E*	Deut 24:22	4714
when ye were come forth out of *E*	Deut 25:17	4714
my father, and he went down into *E*	Deut 26:5	4714
forth out of *E* with a mighty hand	Deut 26:8	4714
smite thee with the botch of *E*	Deut 28:27	4714
upon thee all the diseases of *E*	Deut 28:60	4714
thee into *E* again with ships	Deut 28:68	4714
in the land of *E* unto Pharaoh	Deut 29:2	4714
we have dwelt in the land of *E*	Deut 29:16	4714
them forth out of the land of *E*	Deut 29:25	4714
to do in the land of *E* to Pharaoh	Deut 34:11	4714
for you, when ye came out of *E*	Josh 2:10	4714
All the people that came out of *E*	Josh 5:4	4714
the way, after they came out of *E*	Josh 5:4	4714
way as they came forth out of *E*	Josh 5:5	4714
men of war, which came out of *E*	Josh 5:6	4714
the reproach of *E* from off you	Josh 5:9	4714
of him, and all that he did in *E*	Josh 9:9	4714
From Sihor, which is before *E*	Josh 13:3	4714
and went out unto the river of *E*	Josh 15:4	4714
her villages, unto the river of *E*	Josh 15:47	4714
and his children went down into *E*	Josh 24:4	4714
also and Aaron, and I plagued *E*	Josh 24:5	4714
I brought your fathers out of *E*	Josh 24:6	4714
have seen what I have done in *E*	Josh 24:7	4714
other side of the flood, and in *E*	Josh 24:14	4714
our fathers out of the land of *E*	Josh 24:17	4714
of Israel brought up out of *E*	Josh 24:32	4714
I made you to go up out of *E*	Judg 2:1	4714
brought them out of the land of *E*	Judg 2:12	4714
Israel, I brought you up from *E*	Judg 6:8	4714
not the Lord bring us up from *E*	Judg 6:13	4714
land, when they came up out of *E*	Judg 11:13	4714
But when Israel came up from *E*	Judg 11:16	4714
of the land of *E* unto this day	Judg 19:30	4714
when they were in *E* in Pharaoh's	1Sa 2:27	4714
up out of *E* even unto this day	1Sa 8:8	4714
I brought up Israel out of *E*	1Sa 10:18	4714
fathers up out of the land of *E*	1Sa 12:6	4714
When Jacob was come into *E*	1Sa 12:8	4714
forth your fathers out of *E*	1Sa 12:8	4714
the way, when he came up from *E*	1Sa 15:2	4714
when they came up out of *E*	1Sa 15:6	4714
to Shur, that is over against *E*	1Sa 15:7	4714
to Shur, even unto the land of *E*	1Sa 27:8	4714
And he said, I am a young man of *E*	1Sa 30:13	4713
the children of Israel out of *E*	2Sa 7:6	4714
thou redeemedst to thee from *E*	2Sa 7:23	4714
affinity with Pharaoh king of *E*	1Kin 3:1	4714
and unto the border of *E*	1Kin 4:21	4714
country, and all the wisdom of *E*	1Kin 4:30	4714
were come out of the land of *E*	1Kin 6:1	4714
they came out of the land of *E*	1Kin 8:9	4714
forth my people Israel out of *E*	1Kin 8:16	4714
brought them out of the land of *E*	1Kin 8:21	4714
thou broughtest forth out of *E*	1Kin 8:51	4714
broughtest our fathers out of *E*	1Kin 8:53	4714
in of Hamath unto the river of *E*	1Kin 8:65	4714
fathers out of the land of *E*	1Kin 9:9	4714
For Pharaoh king of *E* had gone up	1Kin 9:16	4714
had horses brought out of *E*	1Kin 10:28	4714
went out of *E* for six hundred	1Kin 10:29	4714
servants with him, to go into *E*	1Kin 11:17	4714
to *E*, unto Pharaoh king of *E*	1Kin 11:18	4714
when Hadad heard in *E* that David	1Kin 11:21	4714
And Jeroboam arose, and fled into *E*	1Kin 11:40	4714
unto Shishak king of *E*	1Kin 11:40	4714
was in *E* until the death of	1Kin 11:40	4714
son of Nebat, who was yet in *E*	1Kin 12:2	4714
Solomon, and Jeroboam dwelt in *E*	1Kin 12:2	4714
thee up out of the land of *E*	1Kin 12:28	4714
that Shishak king of *E* came up	1Kin 14:25	4714
sent messengers to So king of *E*	2Kin 17:4	4714
them up out of the land of *E*	2Kin 17:7	4714
the hand of Pharaoh king of *E*	2Kin 17:7	4714
of the land of *E* with great power	2Kin 17:36	4714
of this bruised reed, even upon *E*	2Kin 18:21	4714
so is Pharaoh king of *E* unto all	2Kin 18:21	4714
put thy trust on *E* for chariots	2Kin 18:24	4714
their fathers came forth out of *E*	2Kin 21:15	4714
of *E* went up against the king of	2Kin 23:29	4714
and he came to *E*, and died there	2Kin 23:34	4714
the king of *E* came not again any	2Kin 24:7	4714
had taken from the river of *E*	2Kin 24:7	4714
that pertained to the king of *E*	2Kin 24:7	4714
the armies, arose, and came to *E*	2Kin 25:26	4714
from Shihor of *E* even unto the	1Chr 13:5	4714
whom thou hast redeemed out of *E*	1Chr 17:21	4714
had horses brought out of *E*	2Chr 1:16	4714
brought forth out of *E* a chariot	2Chr 1:17	4714
Israel, when they came out of *E*	2Chr 5:10	4714
my people out of the land of *E* I	2Chr 6:5	4714
in of Hamath unto the river of *E*	2Chr 7:8	4714
them forth out of the land of *E*	2Chr 7:22	4714
and to the border of *E*	2Chr 9:26	4714
unto Solomon horses out of *E*	2Chr 9:28	4714
the son of Nebat, who was in *E*	2Chr 10:2	4714
that Jeroboam returned out of *E*	2Chr 10:2	4714
of *E* came up against Jerusalem	2Chr 12:2	4714
that came with him out of *E*	2Chr 12:3	4714
So Shishak king of *E* came up	2Chr 12:9	4714
they came out of the land of *E*	2Chr 20:10	4714
even to the entering in of *E*	2Chr 26:8	4714
Necho king of *E* came up to fight	2Chr 35:20	4714
the king of *E* put him down at	2Chr 36:3	4714
the king of *E* made Eliakim his	2Chr 36:4	4714
his brother, and carried him to *E*	2Chr 36:4	4714
affliction of our fathers in *E*	Neh 9:9	4714
God that brought thee up out of *E*	Neh 9:18	4714
Princes shall come out of *E*	Ps 68:31	4714
their fathers, in the land of *E*	Ps 78:12	4714
How he had wrought his signs in *E*	Ps 78:43	4714
And smote all the firstborn in *E*	Ps 78:51	4714
Thou hast brought a vine out of *E*	Ps 80:8	4714
he went out through the land of *E*	Ps 81:5	4714
brought thee out of the land of *E*	Ps 81:10	4714
Israel also came into *E*	Ps 105:23	4714
E was glad when they departed	Ps 105:38	4714
understood not thy wonders in *E*	Ps 106:7	4714
which had done great things in *E*	Ps 106:21	4714
When Israel went out of *E*	Ps 114:1	4714
Who smote the firstborn of *E*	Ps 135:8	4714
into the midst of thee, O *E*	Ps 135:9	4714
To him that smote *E* in their	Ps 136:10	4714
works, with fine linen of *E*	Prov 7:16	4714
uttermost part of the rivers of *E*	Is 7:18	4714
thee, after the manner of *E*	Is 10:24	4714

lift it up after the manner of *E*	Is 10:26	4714
be left, from Assyria, and from *E*	Is 11:11	4714
he came up out of the land of *E*	Is 11:16	4714
The burden of *E*	Is 19:1	4714
swift cloud, and shall come into *E*	Is 19:1	4714
the idols of *E* shall be moved at	Is 19:1	4714
the heart of *E* shall melt in the	Is 19:1	4714
the spirit of *E* shall fail in the	Is 19:3	4714
of hosts hath purposed upon *E*	Is 19:12	4714
they have also seduced *E*, even	Is 19:13	4714
they have caused *E* to err in	Is 19:14	4714
shall there be any work for *E*	Is 19:15	4714
In that day shall *E* be like unto	Is 19:16	4714
of Judah shall be a terror unto *E*	Is 19:17	4714
five cities in the land of *E*	Is 19:18	4714
in the midst of the land of *E*	Is 19:19	4714
LORD of hosts in the land of *E*	Is 19:20	4714
And the LORD shall be known to *E*	Is 19:21	4714
And the LORD shall smite *E*	Is 19:22	4714
be a highway out of *E* to Assyria	Is 19:23	4714
and the Assyrian shall come into *E*	Is 19:23	4714
shall Israel be the third with *E*	Is 19:24	4714
saying, Blessed be *E* my people	Is 19:25	4714
years for a sign and wonder upon *E*	Is 20:3	4714
uncovered, to the shame of *E*	Is 20:4	4714
expectation, and of *E* their glory	Is 20:5	4714
As at the report concerning *E*	Is 23:5	4714
of the river unto the stream of *E*	Is 27:12	4714
and the outcasts in the land of *E*	Is 27:13	4714
That walk to go down into *E*	Is 30:2	4714
and to trust in the shadow of *E*	Is 30:2	4714
in the shadow of *E* your confusion	Is 30:3	4714
them that go down to *E* for help	Is 31:1	4714
staff of this broken reed, on *E*	Is 36:6	4714
so is Pharaoh king of *E* to all	Is 36:6	4714
put thy trust on *E* for chariots	Is 36:9	4714
I gave *E* for thy ransom, Ethiopia	Is 43:3	4714
saith the LORD, The labour of *E*	Is 45:14	4714
aforetime into *E* to sojourn there	Is 52:4	4714
us up out of the land of *E*	Jer 2:6	4714
hast thou to do in the way of *E*	Jer 2:18	4714
thou also shalt be ashamed of *E*	Jer 2:36	4714
brought them out of the land of *E*	Jer 7:22	4714
came forth out of the land of *E*	Jer 7:25	4714
E, and Judah, and Edom, and the	Jer 9:26	4714
them forth out of the land of *E*	Jer 11:4	4714
them up out of the land of *E*	Jer 11:7	4714
of Israel out of the land of *E*	Jer 16:14	4714
of Israel out of the land of *E*	Jer 23:7	4714
them that dwell in the land of *E*	Jer 24:8	4714
Pharaoh king of *E*, and his	Jer 25:19	4714
afraid, and fled, and went into *E*	Jer 26:21	4714
the king sent men into *E*, namely,	Jer 26:22	4714
and certain men with him into *E*	Jer 26:22	4714
fetched forth Urijah out of *E*	Jer 26:23	4714
bring them out of the land of *E*	Jer 31:32	4714
signs and wonders in the land of *E*	Jer 32:20	4714
out of the land of *E* with signs	Jer 32:21	4714
them forth out of the land of *E*	Jer 34:13	4714
army was come forth out of *E*	Jer 37:5	4714
shall return to *E* into their own	Jer 37:7	4714
Bethlehem, to go to enter into *E*	Jer 41:17	4714
but we will go into the land of *E*	Jer 42:14	4714
set your faces to enter into *E*	Jer 42:15	4714
you there in *E* shall follow	Jer 42:16	4714
follow close after you there in *E*	Jer 42:16	4714
to go into *E* to sojourn there	Jer 42:17	4714
you, when ye shall enter into *E*	Jer 42:18	4714
Go ye not into *E*	Jer 42:19	4714
Go not into *E* to sojourn there	Jer 43:2	4714
So they came into the land of *E*	Jer 43:7	4714
he shall smite the land of *E*	Jer 43:11	4714
in the houses of the gods of *E*	Jer 43:12	4714
array himself with the land of *E*	Jer 43:12	4714
that is in the land of *E*	Jer 43:13	4714
Jews which dwell in the land of *E*	Jer 44:1	4714
unto other gods in the land of *E*	Jer 44:8	4714
the land of *E* to sojourn there	Jer 44:12	4714
and fall in the land of *E*	Jer 44:12	4714
them that dwell in the land of *E*	Jer 44:13	4714
the land of *E* to sojourn there	Jer 44:14	4714
that dwelt in the land of *E*	Jer 44:15	4714
Judah that are in the land of *E*	Jer 44:24	4714
Judah that dwell in the land of *E*	Jer 44:26	4714
man of Judah in all the land of *E*	Jer 44:26	4714
Judah that are in the land of *E*	Jer 44:27	4714
land of *E* into the land of Judah	Jer 44:28	4714
the land of *E* to sojourn there	Jer 44:28	4714
give Pharaoh-hophra king of *E*	Jer 44:30	4714
Against *E*, against the army of	Jer 46:2	4714
army of Pharaoh-necho king of *E*	Jer 46:2	4714

E riseth up like a flood, and his	Jer 46:8	4714
balm, O virgin, the daughter of *E*	Jer 46:11	4714
come and smite the land of *E*	Jer 46:13	4714
Declare ye in *E*, and publish in	Jer 46:14	4714
Pharaoh king of *E* is but a noise	Jer 46:17	4714
O thou daughter dwelling in *E*	Jer 46:19	4714
E is like a very fair heifer, but	Jer 46:20	4714
The daughter of *E* shall be	Jer 46:24	4714
multitude of No, and Pharaoh, and *E*	Jer 46:25	4714
in sending his ambassadors into *E*	Eze 17:15	4714
with chains unto the land of *E*	Eze 19:4	4714
known unto them in the land of *E*	Eze 20:5	4714
E into a land that I had espied	Eze 20:6	4714
yourselves with the idols of *E*	Eze 20:7	4714
did they forsake the idols of *E*	Eze 20:8	4714
in the midst of the land of *E*	Eze 20:8	4714
them forth out of the land of *E*	Eze 20:9	4714
to go forth out of the land of *E*	Eze 20:10	4714
the wilderness of the land of *E*	Eze 20:36	4714
And they committed whoredoms in *E*	Eze 23:3	4714
she her whoredoms brought from *E*	Eze 23:8	4714
the harlot in the land of *E*	Eze 23:19	4714
brought from the land of *E*	Eze 23:27	4714
them, nor remember *E* any more	Eze 23:27	4714
E was that which thou spreadest	Eze 27:7	4714
face against Pharaoh king of *E*	Eze 29:2	4714
against him, and against all *E*	Eze 29:2	4714
against thee, Pharaoh king of *E*	Eze 29:3	4714
all the inhabitants of *E* shall	Eze 29:6	4714
the land of *E* shall be desolate	Eze 29:9	4714
make the land of *E* utterly waste	Eze 29:10	4714
I will make the land of *E*	Eze 29:12	4714
bring again the captivity of *E*	Eze 29:14	4714
I will give the land of *E* unto	Eze 29:19	4714
of *E* for his labour wherewith he	Eze 29:20	4714
And the sword shall come upon *E*	Eze 30:4	4714
when the slain shall fall in *E*	Eze 30:4	4714
also that uphold *E* shall fall	Eze 30:6	4714
LORD, when I have set a fire in *E*	Eze 30:8	4714
upon them, as in the day of *E*	Eze 30:9	4714
of *E* to cease by the hand of	Eze 30:10	4714
shall draw their swords against *E*	Eze 30:11	4714
no more a prince of the land of *E*	Eze 30:13	4714
will put a fear in the land of *E*	Eze 30:13	4714
fury upon Sin, the strength of *E*	Eze 30:15	4714
And I will set fire in *E*	Eze 30:16	4714
shall break there the yokes of *E*	Eze 30:18	4714
will I execute judgments in *E*	Eze 30:19	4714
the arm of Pharaoh king of *E*	Eze 30:21	4714
I am against Pharaoh king of *E*	Eze 30:22	4714
stretch it out upon the land of *E*	Eze 30:25	4714
man, speak unto Pharaoh king of *E*	Eze 31:2	4714
lamentation for Pharaoh king of *E*	Eze 32:2	4714
and they shall spoil the pomp of *E*	Eze 32:12	4714
shall make the land of *E* desolate	Eze 32:15	4714
shall lament for her, even for *E*	Eze 32:16	4714
man, wail for the multitude of *E*	Eze 32:18	4714
the land of *E* with a mighty hand	Dan 9:15	4714
carry captives into *E* their gods	Dan 11:8	4714
the land of *E* shall not escape	Dan 11:42	4714
over all the precious things of *E*	Dan 11:43	4714
she came up out of the land of *E*	Hos 2:15	4714
they call to *E*, they go to	Hos 7:11	4714
their derision in the land of *E*	Hos 7:16	4714
they shall return to *E*	Hos 8:13	4714
but Ephraim shall return to *E*	Hos 9:3	4714
E shall gather them up, Memphis	Hos 9:6	4714
him, and called my son out of *E*	Hos 11:1	4714
not return into the land of *E*	Hos 11:5	4714
shall tremble as a bird out of *E*	Hos 11:11	4714
and oil is carried into *E*	Hos 12:1	4714
LORD thy God from the land of *E*	Hos 12:9	4714
the LORD brought Israel out of *E*	Hos 12:13	4714
LORD thy God from the land of *E*	Hos 13:4	4714
E shall be a desolation, and Edom	Joel 3:19	4714
brought you up from the land of *E*	Amos 2:10	4714
I brought up from the land of *E*	Amos 3:1	4714
in the palaces in the land of *E*	Amos 3:9	4714
pestilence after the manner of *E*	Amos 4:10	4714
and drowned, as by the flood of *E*	Amos 8:8	4714
be drowned, as by the flood of *E*	Amos 9:5	4714
up Israel out of the land of *E*	Amos 9:7	4714
thee up out of the land of *E*	Mic 6:4	4714
thy coming out of the land of *E*	Mic 7:15	4714
E were her strength, and it was	Nah 3:9	4714
with you when ye came out of *E*	Hag 2:5	4714
again also out of the land of *E*	Zec 10:10	4714
the sceptre of *E* shall depart	Zec 10:11	4714
And if the family of *E* go not up	Zec 14:18	4714
This shall be the punishment of *E*	Zec 14:19	4714
and his mother, and flee into *E*	Mt 2:13	125

by night, and departed into *E*	Mt 2:14	125
Out of *E* have I called my son	Mt 2:15	125
in a dream to Joseph in *E*	Mt 2:19	125
Phrygia, and Pamphylia, in *E*	Acts 2:10	125
with envy, sold Joseph into *E*	Acts 7:9	125
in the sight of Pharaoh king of *E*	Acts 7:10	125
and he made him governor over *E*	Acts 7:10	125
a dearth over all the land of *E*	Acts 7:11	125
heard that there was corn in *E*	Acts 7:12	125
So Jacob went down into *E*	Acts 7:15	125
people grew and multiplied in *E*	Acts 7:17	125
of my people which is in *E*	Acts 7:34	125
now come, I will send thee into *E*	Acts 7:34	125
wonders and signs in the land of *E*	Acts 7:36	125
hearts turned back again into *E*	Acts 7:39	125
brought us out of the land of *E*	Acts 7:40	125
as strangers in the land of *E*	Acts 13:17	125
all that came out of *E* by Moses	Heb 3:16	125
to lead them out of the land of *E*	Heb 8:9	125
riches that the treasures in *E*	Heb 11:26	125
By faith he forsook *E*, not	Heb 11:27	125
the people out of the land of *E*	Jude 5	125
spiritually is called Sodom and *E*	Rev 11:8	125

EGYPTIAN *(e-jip'-shun)* See EGYPTIAN'S, EGYPTIANS.
   1. An inhabitant of Egypt.

and she had an handmaid, an *E*	Gen 16:1	4713
wife took Hagar her maid the *E*	Gen 16:3	4713
Sarah saw the son of Hagar the *E*	Gen 21:9	4713
Abraham's son, whom Hagar the *E*	Gen 25:12	4713
captain of the guard, an *E*	Gen 39:1	4713
in the house of his master the *E*	Gen 39:2	4713
women are not as the *E* women	Ex 1:19	4713
he smiting an *E* smiting an Hebrew,	Ex 2:11	4713
there was no man, he slew the *E*	Ex 2:12	4713
kill me, as thou killedst the *E*	Ex 2:14	4713
An *E* delivered us out of the hand	Ex 2:19	4713
woman, whose father was an *E*	Lev 24:10	4713
thou shalt not abhor an *E*	Deut 23:7	4713
And they found an *E* in the field	1Sa 30:11	4713
And he slew an *E*, a goodly man	2Sa 23:21	4713
the *E* had a spear in his hand	2Sa 23:21	4713
And Sheshan had a servant, an *E*	1Chr 2:34	4713
And he slew an *E*, a man of great	1Chr 11:23	4713
the *E* into Assyria, and the	Is 19:23	4714
was oppressed, and smote the *E*	Acts 7:24	124
as thou diddest the *E* yesterday	Acts 7:28	124
Art not thou that *E*, which before	Acts 21:38	124

   2. The Red Sea.

destroy the tongue of the *E* sea	Is 11:15	4714

EGYPTIAN'S *(e-jip'-shuns)*

the *E* house for Joseph's sake	Gen 39:5	4713
the spear out of the *E* hand	2Sa 23:21	4713
in the *E* hand was a spear like a	1Chr 11:23	4713
the spear out of the *E* hand	1Chr 11:23	4713

EGYPTIANS *(e-jip'-shuns)*

when the *E* shall see thee, that	Gen 12:12	4713
the *E* beheld the woman that she	Gen 12:14	4713
and Pharaoh said unto all the *E*	Gen 41:55	4714
storehouses, and sold unto the *E*	Gen 41:56	4714
them by themselves, and for the *E*	Gen 43:32	4713
because the *E* might not eat bread	Gen 43:32	4713
that is an abomination unto the *E*	Gen 43:32	4714
and the *E* and the house of Pharaoh	Gen 45:2	4714
is an abomination unto the *E*	Gen 46:34	4714
all the *E* came unto Joseph, and	Gen 47:15	4714
for the *E* sold every man his	Gen 47:20	4714
the *E* mourned for him threescore	Gen 50:3	4714
is a grievous mourning to the *E*	Gen 50:11	4714
the *E* made the children of Israel	Ex 1:13	4714
them out of the hand of the *E*	Ex 3:8	4714
wherewith the *E* oppress them	Ex 3:9	4714
favour in the sight of the *E*	Ex 3:21	4714
and ye shall spoil the *E*	Ex 3:22	4714
whom the *E* keep in bondage	Ex 6:5	4714
from under the burdens of the *E*	Ex 6:6	4714
from under the burdens of the *E*	Ex 6:7	4714
the *E* shall know that I am the	Ex 7:5	4714
the *E* shall lothe to drink of the	Ex 7:18	4714
the *E* could not drink of the	Ex 7:21	4714
all the *E* digged round about the	Ex 7:24	4714
the houses of the *E* shall be full	Ex 8:21	4714
of the *E* to the LORD our God	Ex 8:26	4714
of the *E* before their eyes	Ex 8:26	4714
the magicians, and upon all the *E*	Ex 9:11	4714
and the houses of all the *E*	Ex 10:6	4714
favour in the sight of the *E*	Ex 11:3	4714
put a difference between the *E*	Ex 11:7	4714
will pass through to smite the *E*	Ex 12:23	4714
in Egypt, when he smote the *E*	Ex 12:27	4714

and all his servants, and all the *E*	Ex 12:30	4714
the *E* were urgent upon the people	Ex 12:33	4714
of the *E* jewels of silver	Ex 12:35	4714
favour in the sight of the *E*	Ex 12:36	4714
And they spoiled the *E*	Ex 12:36	4714
that the *E* may know that I am the	Ex 14:4	4714
But the *E* pursued after them, all	Ex 14:9	4714
behold, the *E* marched after them	Ex 14:10	4714
us alone, that we may serve the *E*	Ex 14:12	4714
been better for us to serve the *E*	Ex 14:12	4714
for the *E* whom ye have seen to	Ex 14:13	4714
I will harden the hearts of the *E*	Ex 14:17	4714
the *E* shall know that I am the	Ex 14:18	4714
it came between the camp of the *E*	Ex 14:20	4714
the *E* pursued, and went in after	Ex 14:23	4714
the *E* through the pillar of fire	Ex 14:24	4714
and troubled the host of the *E*	Ex 14:24	4714
so that the *E* said, Let us flee	Ex 14:25	4714
fighteth for them against the *E*	Ex 14:25	4714
waters may come again upon the *E*	Ex 14:26	4714
and the *E* fled against it	Ex 14:27	4714
the LORD overthrew the *E* in the	Ex 14:27	4714
that day out of the hand of the *E*	Ex 14:30	4714
Israel saw the *E* dead upon the	Ex 14:30	4714
which the LORD did upon the *E*	Ex 14:31	4714
which I have brought upon the *E*	Ex 15:26	4714
to the *E* for Israel's sake, and	Ex 18:8	4714
out of the hand of the *E*	Ex 18:9	4714
you out of the hand of the *E*	Ex 18:10	4714
from under the hand of the *E*	Ex 18:10	4714
have seen what I did unto the *E*	Ex 19:4	4714
Wherefore should the *E* speak	Ex 32:12	4714
Then the *E* shall hear it, (for	Num 14:13	4714
the *E* vexed us, and our fathers	Num 20:15	4714
hand in the sight of all the *E*	Num 33:3	4714
For the *E* buried all their	Num 33:4	4714
the *E* evil entreated us, and	Deut 26:6	4713
the *E* pursued after your fathers	Josh 24:6	4714
put darkness between you and the *E*	Josh 24:7	4713
you out of the hand of the *E*	Judg 6:9	4714
Did not I deliver you from the *E*	Judg 10:11	4714
the *E* with all the plagues in the	1Sa 4:8	4714
ye harden your hearts, as the *E*	1Sa 6:6	4714
you out of the hand of the *E*	1Sa 10:18	4714
Hittites, and the kings of the *E*	2Kin 7:6	4714
Ammonites, the Moabites, the *E*	Ezr 9:1	4713
set the *E* against the *E*	Is 19:2	4714
the *E* will I give over into the	Is 19:4	4714
the *E* shall know the LORD in that	Is 19:21	4714
the *E* shall serve with the	Is 19:23	4714
Assyria lead away the *E* prisoners	Is 20:4	4714
For the *E* shall help in vain, and	Is 30:7	4714
Now the *E* are men, and not God	Is 31:3	4714
of the *E* he burn with fire	Jer 43:13	4714
We have given the hand to the *E*	Lam 5:6	4714
with the *E* thy neighbours	Eze 16:26	4714
the *E* for the paps of thy youth	Eze 23:21	4714
scatter the *E* among the nations	Eze 29:12	4714
E from the people whither they	Eze 29:13	4714
scatter the *E* among the nations	Eze 30:23	4714
scatter the *E* among the nations	Eze 30:26	4714
in all the wisdom of the *E*	Acts 7:22	124
which the *E* assaying to do were	Heb 11:29	124

EHI *(e'-hi)* See AHARAH. *A son of Benjamin.*

and Ashbel, Gera, and Naaman, *E*	Gen 46:21	278

EHUD *(e'-hud)*
   1. A son of Gera.

E the son of Gera, a Benjamite, a	Judg 3:15	261
But *E* made him a dagger which had	Judg 3:16	261
And *E* came unto him	Judg 3:20	261
E said, I have a message from God	Judg 3:20	261
E put forth his left hand, and	Judg 3:21	261
Then *E* went forth through the	Judg 3:23	261
E escaped while they tarried, and	Judg 3:26	261
of the LORD, when *E* was dead	Judg 4:1	261

   2. A great-grandson of Benjamin.

Jeush, and Benjamin, and *E*, and	1Chr 7:10	261
And these are the sons of *E*	1Chr 8:6	261

EIGHT

Seth were *e* hundred years	Gen 5:4	8083
after he begat Enos *e* hundred	Gen 5:7	8083
after he begat Cainan *e* hundred	Gen 5:10	8083
he begat Mahalaleel *e* hundred	Gen 5:13	8083
after he begat Jared *e* hundred	Gen 5:16	8083
Mahalaleel were *e* hundred ninety	Gen 5:17	8083
he begat Enoch *e* hundred years	Gen 5:19	8083
he that is *e* days old shall be	Gen 17:12	8083
his son Isaac being *e* days old	Gen 21:4	8083
these *e* Milcah did bear to Nahor,	Gen 22:23	8083

length of one curtain shall be *e* .... Ex 26:2   8083
And they shall be *e* boards................. Ex 26:25   8083
e cubits, and the breadth of one............. Ex 36:9   8083
And there were *e* boards......................... Ex 36:30   8083
e thousand and an hundred, ... Num 2:24   8083
were *e* thousand and six hundred, ... Num 3:28   8083
were *e* thousand and five hundred, ... Num 4:48   8083
e oxen he gave unto the sons of .... Num 7:8   8083
And on the sixth day *e* bullocks........... Num 29:29   8083
shall be forty and *e* cities .... Num 35:7   8083
Zered, was thirty and *e* years .... Deut 2:14   8083
e cities with their suburbs .... Josh 21:41   8083
served Chushan-rishathaim *e* years ...... Judg 3:8   8083
and he judged Israel *e* years .... Judg 12:14   8083
Now Eli was ninety and *e* years old 1Sa 4:15   8083
and he had *e* sons 1Sa 17:12   8083
up his spear against *e* hundred 2Sa 23:8   8083
there were in Israel *e* hundred 2Sa 24:9   8083
ten cubits, and stones of *e* cubits 1Kin 7:10   8083
he reigned *e* years in Jerusalem 2Kin 8:17   8083
in Samaria was twenty and *e* years ... 2Kin 10:36   8083
Josiah was *e* years old when he 2Kin 22:1   8083
e hundred, ready armed to the war....... 1Chr 12:24   8083
e hundred, mighty men of valour, ... 1Chr 12:30   8083
e thousand and six hundred 1Chr 12:35   8083
their brethren, threescore and *e* 1Chr 16:38   8083
by man, was thirty and *e* thousand 1Chr 23:3   8083
e among the sons of Ithamar 1Chr 24:4   8083
was two hundred fourscore and *e* 1Chr 25:7   8083
e sons, and threescore daughters 2Chr 11:21   8083
in array against him with *e* 2Chr 13:3   8083
he reigned *e* years in Jerusalem 2Chr 21:5   8083
he reigned in Jerusalem *e* years 2Chr 21:20   8083
the house of the Lord in *e* days 2Chr 29:17   8083
Josiah was *e* years old when he 2Chr 34:1   8083
Jehoiachin was *e* years old when........ 2Chr 36:9   8083
and Joab, two thousand *e* hundred .... Ezr 2:6   8083
of Ater of Hezekiah, ninety and *e* .... Ezr 2:16   8083
Anathoth, an hundred twenty and *e* ...... Ezr 2:23   8083
of Asaph, an hundred twenty and *e*....... Ezr 2:41   8083
and with him twenty and *e* males .... Ezr 8:11   8083
thousand and *e* hundred and eighteen ... Neh 7:11   8083
of Zattu, *e* hundred forty and five .... Neh 7:13   8083
of Binnui, six hundred forty and *e* .... Neh 7:15   8083
of Bebai, six hundred twenty and *e* .... Neh 7:16   8083
of Ater of Hezekiah, ninety and *e* .... Neh 7:21   8083
Hashum, three hundred twenty and *e*..... Neh 7:22   8083
an hundred fourscore and *e* .... Neh 7:26   8083
Anathoth, an hundred twenty and *e* ...... Neh 7:27   8083
of Asaph, an hundred forty and *e* .... Neh 7:44   8083
of Shobai, an hundred thirty and *e* .... Neh 7:45   8083
threescore and *e* valiant men.................. Neh 11:6   8083
Sallai, nine hundred twenty and *e* .... Neh 11:8   8083
the house were *e* hundred twenty .... Neh 11:12   8083
of valour, an hundred twenty and *e* .... Neh 11:14   8083
a portion to seven, and also to *e* .... Eccl 11:2   8083
escaped from Johanan with *e* men........ Jer 41:15   8083
from Jerusalem *e* hundred thirty .... Jer 52:29   8083
the porch of the gate, *e* cubits .... Eze 40:9   8083
and the going up to it had *e* steps .... Eze 40:31   8083
and the going up to it had *e* steps .... Eze 40:34   8083
and the going up to it had *e* steps .... Eze 40:37   8083
e tables, whereupon they slew............... Eze 40:41   8083
shepherds, and *e* principal men.............. Mic 5:5   8083
when *e* days were accomplished for .... Lk 2:21   *3638*
an *e* days after these sayings.................. Lk 9:28   *3638*
an infirmity thirty and *e* years .... Jn 5:5   *3638*
after *e* days again his disciples............. Jn 20:26   *3638*
which had kept his bed *e* years .... Acts 9:33   *3638*
e souls were saved by water 1Pet 3:20   *3638*

EIGHTEEN
house, three hundred and *e*............. Gen 14:14   8083,6240
Eglon the king of Moab *e* years ...... Judg 3:14   8083,6240
e years, all the children of ....Judg 10:8   8083,6240
of Israel again *e* thousand men ..... Judg 20:25   8083,6240
fell of Benjamin *e* thousand men ..... Judg 20:44   8083,6240
of salt, being *e* thousand men 2Sa 8:13   8083,6240
of brass, of *e* cubits high apiece....... 1Kin 7:15   8083,6240
Jehoiachin was *e* years old when 2Kin 24:8   8083,6240
of the one pillar was *e* cubits............ 2Kin 25:17   8083,6240
tribe of Manasseh *e* thousand........ 1Chr 12:31   8083,6240
in the valley of salt *e* thousand 1Chr 18:12   8083,6240
sons and brethren, strong men, *e* .. 1Chr 26:9   8083,6240
of brass *e* thousand talents, and 1Chr 29:7   7239,8083
(for he took *e* wives, and 2Chr 11:21   8083,6240
with him two hundred and *e* males Ezr 8:9   8083,6240
with his sons and his brethren, *e* ...... Ezr 8:18   8083,6240
thousand and eight hundred and *e*. Neh 7:11   8083,6240
height of one pillar was *e* cubits ..... Jer 52:21   8083,6240
round about *e* thousand measures . Eze 48:35   8083,6240

those *e*, upon whom the tower . Lk 13:4   *1176,2532,3638*
a spirit of infirmity *e* years ...... Lk 13:11   *1176,2532,3638*
hath bound, lo, these *e* years... Lk 13:16   *1176,2532,3638*

EIGHTEENTH
Now in the *e* year of king 1Kin 15:1   8083,6240
over Israel in Samaria the *e* year ... 2Kin 3:1   8083,6240
pass in the *e* year of king Josiah 2Kin 22:3   8083,6240
But in the *e* year of king Josiah, ... 2Kin 23:23   8083,6240
to Hezir, the *e* to Aphses, ... 1Chr 24:15   8083,6240
The *e* to Hanani, he, his sons 1Chr 25:25   8083,6240
Now in the *e* year of king 2Chr 13:1   8083,6240
Now in the *e* year of his reign, ... 2Chr 34:8   8083,6240
In the *e* year of the reign of 2Chr 35:19   8083,6240
of Judah, which was the *e* year of... Jer 32:1   8083,6240
In the *e* year of Nebuchadrezzar .... Jer 52:29   8083,6240

EIGHTH
on the *e* day thou shalt give it .... Ex 22:30   8066
And it came to pass on the *e* day........... Lev 9:1   8066
in the *e* day the flesh of his .... Lev 12:3   8066
on the *e* day he shall take two he .... Lev 14:10   8066
he shall bring them on the *e* day .... Lev 14:23   8066
on the *e* day he shall take to him .... Lev 15:14   8066
on the *e* day she shall take unto .... Lev 15:29   8066
and from the *e* day and thenceforth ...... Lev 22:27   8066
on the *e* day shall be an holy .... Lev 23:36   8066
on the *e* day shall be a sabbath .... Lev 23:39   8066
And ye shall sow the *e* year .... Lev 25:22   8066
on the *e* day he shall bring two .... Num 6:10   8066
On the *e* day offered Gamaliel the........ Num 7:54   8066
On the *e* day ye shall have a .... Num 29:35   8066
month Bul, which is the *e* month 1Kin 6:38   8066
On the *e* day he sent the people............. 1Kin 8:66   8066
ordained a feast in the *e* month 1Kin 12:32   8066
the fifteenth day of the *e* month 1Kin 12:33   8066
e year of Asa king of Judah began ... 1Kin 16:29   8083
e year of Azariah king of Judah 2Kin 15:8   8083
him in the *e* year of his reign 2Kin 24:12   8083
Johanan the *e*, Elzabad the ninth, ... 1Chr 12:12   8066
to Hakkoz, the *e* to Abijah,.................... 1Chr 24:10   8066
The *e* to Jeshaiah, he, his sons, ... 1Chr 25:15   8066
the seventh, Peulthai the *e* 1Chr 26:5   8066
e captain for the *e* month 1Chr 27:11   8066
in the *e* day they made a solemn 2Chr 7:9   8066
on the *e* day of the month came 2Chr 29:17   8066
For in the *e* year of his reign, ... 2Chr 34:3   8083
on the *e* day was a solemn .... Neh 8:18   8066
it shall be, that upon the *e* day .... Eze 43:27   8066
In the *e* month, in the second .... Zec 1:1   8066
that on the *e* day they came to............... Lk 1:59   *3590*
and circumcised him the *e* day .... Acts 7:8   *3590*
Circumcised the *e* day, of the .... Phil 3:5   *3637*
but saved Noah the *e* person 2Pet 2:5   *3590*
was, and is not, even he is the *e*............. Rev 17:11   *3590*
the *e*, beryl .... Rev 21:20   *3590*

EIGHTIETH
e year after the children of 1Kin 6:1   8084

EIGHTY
And Methuselah lived an hundred *e* ...... Gen 5:25   8084
he begat Lamech seven hundred *e* .... Gen 5:26   8084
And Lamech lived an hundred *e* .... Gen 5:28   8084

EITHER See APPENDIX.

EKER (e'-ker) *Descendant of Judah.*
were, Maaz, and Jamin, and 1Chr 2:27   6134

EKRON (ec'-ron) See EKRONITES. *A Philistine city.*
unto the borders of E northward .... Josh 13:3   6138
out unto the side of E northward .... Josh 15:11   6138
E, with her towns and her villages .... Josh 15:45   6138
From E even unto the sea, all .... Josh 15:46   6138
And Elon, and Thimnathah, and E .... Josh 19:43   6138
and E with the coast thereof.................... Judg 1:18   6138
they sent the ark of God to E 1Sa 5:10   6138
pass, as the ark of God came to E 1Sa 5:10   6138
they returned to E the same day 1Sa 6:16   6138
one, for Gath one, for E one..................... 1Sa 6:17   6138
to Israel, from E even unto Gath 1Sa 7:14   6138
the valley, and to the gates of E 1Sa 17:52   6138
even unto Gath, and unto E 1Sa 17:52   6138
of Baal-zebub the god of E...................... 2Kin 1:2   6138
of Baal-zebub the god of E...................... 2Kin 1:3   6138
of Baal-zebub the god of E...................... 2Kin 1:6   6138
of Baal-zebub the god of E...................... 2Kin 1:16   6138
and Ashkelon, and Azzah, and E........... Jer 25:20   6138
I will turn mine hand against E............... Amos 1:8   6138
noonday, and E shall be rooted up .... Zeph 2:4   6138
it, and be very sorrowful, and E............... Zec 9:5   6138
in Judah, and E as a Jebusite .... Zec 9:7   6138

E

EKRONITES *(ek'-ron-ites) Inhabitants of Ekron.*
the Gittites, and the *E* .... Josh 13:3   6139
that the *E* cried out, saying, ... 1Sa 5:10   6139

ELADAH *(el'-a-dah) A descendant of Ephraim.*
E his son, and Tahath his son, ... 1Chr 7:20   497

ELAH *(e'-lah)*
   1. An Edomite prince.
Duke Aholibamah, duke *E*, duke .... Gen 36:41   425
Duke Aholibamah, duke *E*, duke 1Chr 1:52   425
   2. A valley in Judah.
and pitched by the valley of *E* 1Sa 17:2   425
Israel, were in the valley of *E* 1Sa 17:19   425
thou slewest in the valley of *E* 1Sa 21:9   425
   3. Father of Shimei.
Shimei the son of *E*, in Benjamin 1Kin 4:18   425
   4. Son of King Baasha of Israel.
E his son reigned in his stead 1Kin 16:6   425
E the son of Baasha to reign over 1Kin 16:8   425
Baasha, and the sins of *E* his son 1Kin 16:13   425
Now the rest of the acts of *E* 1Kin 16:14   425
   5. Father of King Hoshea of Israel.
Hoshea the son of *E* made a 2Kin 15:30   425
Judah began Hoshea the son of *E* 2Kin 17:1   425
of Hoshea son of *E* king of Israel 2Kin 18:1   425
of Hoshea son of *E* king of Israel 2Kin 18:9   425
   6. A son of Caleb.
of Jephunneh; Iru, *E* 1Chr 4:15   425
and the sons of *E*, even Kenaz 1Chr 4:15   425
   7. A Benjamite.
E the son of Uzzi, the son of 1Chr 9:8   425

ELAM *(e'-lam) See* ELAMITES, PERSIA.
   1. A son of Shem.
E, and Asshur, and Arphaxad, and Lud . Gen 10:22   5867
E, and Asshur, and Arphaxad, and Lud . 1Chr 1:17   5867
   2. Land of the Elamites.
Ellasar, Chedorlaomer king of *E* .... Gen 14:1   5867
With Chedorlaomer the king of *E* .... Gen 14:9   5867
Pathros, and from Cush, and from *E* ...... Is 11:11   5867
Go up, O *E*: .... Is 21:2   5867
E bare the quiver with chariots .... Is 22:6   5867
of Zimri, and all the kings of *E* .... Jer 25:25   5867
E in the beginning of the reign .... Jer 49:34   5867
Behold, I will break the bow of *E* .... Jer 49:35   5867
upon *E* will I bring the four .... Jer 49:36   5867
the outcasts of *E* shall not come .... Jer 49:36   5867
For I will cause *E* to be dismayed .... Jer 49:37   5867
And I will set my throne in *E* .... Jer 49:38   5867
bring again the captivity of *E* .... Jer 49:39   5867
There is *E* and all her multitude .... Eze 32:24   5867
which is in the province of *E* .... Dan 8:2   5867
   3. Son of Shashak.
And Hananiah, and *E*, and Antothijah,... 1Chr 8:24   5867
   4. A son of Meshelemiah.
E the fifth, Jehohanan the sixth,............ 1Chr 26:3   5867
   5. A family of exiles with Zerubbabel.
The children of *E*, a thousand two .... Ezr 2:7   5867
The children of *E*, a thousand two .... Neh 7:12   5867
   6. A family of exiles with Zerubbabel.
The children of the other *E*.................... Ezr 2:31   5867
The children of the other *E* .... Neh 7:34   5867
   7. A family of exiles with Ezra.
And of the sons of *E* .... Ezr 8:7   5867
   8. An ancestor of Shechaniah.
of Jehiel, one of the sons of *E* .... Ezr 10:2   5867
And of the sons of *E* .... Ezr 10:26   5867
   9. A chief who renewed the covenant.
Parosh, Pahath-moab, *E*, Zatthu, ... Neh 10:14   5867
   10. A priest who purified the wall.
and Jehohanan, and Malchijah, and *E*...Neh 12:42   5867

ELAMITES *(e'-lam-ites) See* PERSIANS. *Foreign settlers in Samaria.*
the Dehavites, and the *E*, ... Ezr 4:9   5962
Parthians, and Medes, and *E* .... Acts 2:9   1639

ELASAH *(el'-a-sah) See* ELEASAH.
   1. Married a foreign wife.
Ishmael, Nethaneel, Jozabad, and *E*...... Ezr 10:22   501
   2. An ambassador of Hezekiah.
By the hand of *E* the son of .... Jer 29:3   501

ELATH *(e'-lath) See* ELOTH. *An Elamite port.*
the way of the plain from *E* .... Deut 2:8   359
He built *E*, and restored it to................... 2Kin 14:22   359
of Syria recovered *E* to Syria................. 2Kin 16:6   359
and drave the Jews from *E* 2Kin 16:6   359
and the Syrians came to *E*, and 2Kin 16:6   359

EL-BERITH See BERITH.

EL-BETH-EL *Another name for Bethel.*
an altar, and called the place *E* .... Gen 35:7   416

ELDAAH *(el'-da-ah) A son of Midian.*
Epher, and Hanoch, and Abidah, and *E*.. Gen 25:4   420
Epher, and Henoch, and Abida, and *E* 1Chr 1:33   420

ELDAD *(el'-dad) An elder and prophet with Moses.*
camp, the name of the one was *E* .... Num 11:26   419
man, and told Moses, and said, *E* .... Num 11:27   419

ELDER
the brother of Japheth the *e* .... Gen 10:21   1419
the *e* shall serve the younger .... Gen 25:23   7227
these words of Esau her *e* son .... Gen 27:42   1419
the name of the *e* was Leah .... Gen 29:16   1419
Behold my *e* daughter Merab, her 1Sa 18:17   1419
for he is mine *e* brother 1Kin 2:22   1419
aged men, much *e* than thy father .... Job 15:10
because they were *e* than he .... Job 32:4   2205,3117
thine *e* sister is Samaria, she and .... Eze 16:46   1419
receive thy sisters, thine *e* .... Eze 16:61   1419
names of them were Aholah the *e* .... Eze 23:4   1419
Now his *e* son was in the field .... Lk 15:25   4245
The *e* shall serve the younger .... Rom 9:12   3187
Rebuke not an *e*, but intreat him 1Ti 5:1   4245
The *e* women as mothers 1Ti 5:2   4245
Against an *e* receive not an 1Ti 5:19   4245
you I exhort, who am also an *e*.............. 1Pet 5:5   4850
submit yourselves unto the *e*................. 1Pet 5:5   4245
The *e* unto the elect lady and her 2Jn 1   4245
The *e* unto the wellbeloved Gaius, ... 3Jn 1   4245

ELDERS
of Pharaoh, the *e* of his house .... Gen 50:7   2205
all the *e* of the land of Egypt, ... Gen 50:7   2205
gather the *e* of Israel together, ... Ex 3:16   2205
the *e* of Israel, unto the king of .... Ex 3:18   2205
the *e* of the children of Israel .... Ex 4:29   2205
called for all the *e* of Israel .... Ex 12:21   2205
take with thee of the *e* of Israel .... Ex 17:5   2205
in the sight of the *e* of Israel .... Ex 17:6   2205
all the *e* of Israel, to eat bread............. Ex 18:12   2205
and called for the *e* of the people.......... Ex 19:7   2205
and seventy of the *e* of Israel .... Ex 24:1   2205
and seventy of the *e* of Israel .... Ex 24:9   2205
And he said unto the *e*, Tarry ye .... Ex 24:14   2205
the *e* of the congregation shall .... Lev 4:15   2205
and his sons, and the *e* of Israel .... Lev 9:1   2205
me seventy men of the *e* of Israel .... Num 11:16   2205
knowest to be the *e* of the people.......... Num 11:16   2205
men of the *e* of the people.................... Num 11:24   2205
and gave it unto the seventy *e* .... Num 11:25   2205
the camp, he and the *e* of Israel .... Num 11:30   2205
the *e* of Israel followed him .... Num 16:25   2205
And Moab said unto the *e* of Midian ...... Num 22:4   2205
e of Moab and the *e* of Midian .... Num 22:7   2205
heads of your tribes, and your *e* .... Deut 5:23   2205
Then the *e* of his city shall send .... Deut 19:12   2205
Then thy *e* and thy judges shall .... Deut 21:2   2205
even the *e* of that city shall .... Deut 21:3   2205
the *e* of that city shall bring.................. Deut 21:4   2205
all the *e* of that city, that are................. Deut 21:6   2205
him out unto the *e* of his city .... Deut 21:19   2205
shall say unto the *e* of his city .... Deut 21:20   2205
the *e* of the city in the gate.................... Deut 22:15   2205
father shall say unto the *e* .... Deut 22:16   2205
cloth before the *e* of the city .... Deut 22:17   2205
the *e* of that city shall take.................... Deut 22:18   2205
wife go up to the gate unto the *e* .... Deut 25:7   2205
Then the *e* of his city shall call .... Deut 25:8   2205
unto him in the presence of the *e* .... Deut 25:9   2205
Moses with the *e* of Israel .... Deut 27:1   2205
captains of your tribes, your *e* .... Deut 29:10   2205
LORD, and unto all the *e* of Israel........... Deut 31:9   2205
unto me all the *e* of your tribes .... Deut 31:28   2205
thy *e*, and they will tell thee .... Deut 32:7   2205
the *e* of Israel, and put dust upon .... Josh 7:6   2205
the *e* of Israel, before the .... Josh 8:10   2205
And all Israel, and their *e* .... Josh 8:33   2205
Wherefore our *e* and all the .... Josh 9:11   2205
in the ears of the *e* of that city .... Josh 20:4   2205
for all Israel, and for their *e* .... Josh 23:2   2205
and called for the *e* of Israel .... Josh 24:1   2205
all the days of the *e* that....................... Josh 24:31   2205
all the days of the *e* that .... Judg 2:7   2205
the *e* thereof, even threescore and .... Judg 8:14   2205
And he took the *e* of the city .... Judg 8:16   2205
the *e* of Gilead went to fetch .... Judg 11:5   2205
said unto the *e* of Gilead .... Judg 11:7   2205
the *e* of Gilead said unto .... Judg 11:8   2205
said unto the *e* of Gilead .... Judg 11:9   2205
the *e* of Gilead said unto .... Judg 11:10   2205
went with the *e* of Gilead...................... Judg 11:11   2205
Then the *e* of the congregation .... Judg 21:16   2205

took ten men of the *e* of the city	Ruth 4:2	2205
before the *e* of my people	Ruth 4:4	2205
And Boaz said unto the *e*, and unto	Ruth 4:9	2205
that were in the gate, and the *e*	Ruth 4:11	2205
the *e* of Israel said, Wherefore	1Sa 4:3	2205
Then all the *e* of Israel gathered	1Sa 8:4	2205
the *e* of Jabesh said unto him,	1Sa 11:3	2205
before the *e* of my people, and	1Sa 15:30	2205
the *e* of the town trembled at his	1Sa 16:4	2205
of the spoil unto the *e* of Judah	1Sa 30:26	2205
with the *e* of Israel, saying, Ye	2Sa 3:17	2205
So all the *e* of Israel came to	2Sa 5:3	2205
the *e* of his house arose, and went	2Sa 12:17	2205
well, and all the *e* of Israel	2Sa 17:4	2205
Absalom and the *e* of Israel	2Sa 17:15	2205
saying, Speak unto the *e* of Judah	2Sa 19:11	2205
Solomon assembled the *e* of Israel	1Kin 8:1	2205
all the *e* of Israel came, and the	1Kin 8:3	2205
called all the *e* of the land	1Kin 20:7	2205
And all the *e* and all the people	1Kin 20:8	2205
and sent the letters unto the *e*	1Kin 21:8	2205
the men of his city, even the *e*	1Kin 21:11	2205
his house, and the *e* sat with him	2Kin 6:32	2205
came to him, he said to the *e*	2Kin 6:32	2205
the rulers of Jezreel, to the *e*	2Kin 10:1	2205
the *e* also, and the bringers up of	2Kin 10:5	2205
the *e* of the priests, covered	2Kin 19:2	2205
unto him all the *e* of Judah	2Kin 23:1	2205
Therefore came all the *e* of	1Chr 11:3	2205
the *e* of Israel, and the captains	1Chr 15:25	2205
the *e* of Israel, who were clothed	1Chr 21:16	2205
Solomon assembled the *e* of Israel	2Chr 5:2	2205
And all the *e* of Israel came	2Chr 5:4	2205
together all the *e* of Judah	2Chr 34:29	2205
God was upon the *e* of the Jews	Ezr 5:5	7868
Then asked we those *e*, and said	Ezr 5:9	7868
the *e* of the Jews build this	Ezr 6:7	7868
e of these Jews for the building	Ezr 6:8	7868
the *e* of the Jews builded, and	Ezr 6:14	7868
counsel of the princes and the *e*	Ezr 10:8	2205
and with them the *e* of every city	Ezr 10:14	2205
him in the assembly of the *e*	Ps 107:32	2205
sitteth among the *e* of the land	Prov 31:23	2205
the *e* of the priests covered with	Is 37:2	2205
up certain of the *e* of the land	Jer 26:17	2205
of the *e* which were carried away	Jer 29:1	2205
mine *e* gave up the ghost in the	Lam 1:19	2205
The *e* of the daughter of Zion sit	Lam 2:10	2205
priests, they favoured not the *e*	Lam 4:16	2205
the faces of *e* were not honoured	Lam 5:12	2205
The *e* have ceased from the gate,	Lam 5:14	2205
the *e* of Judah sat before me,	Eze 8:1	2205
of the *e* of Israel unto me	Eze 14:1	2205
that certain of the *e* of Israel	Eze 20:1	2205
man, speak unto the *e* of Israel	Eze 20:3	2205
a solemn assembly, gather the *e*	Joel 1:14	2205
the congregation, assemble the *e*	Joel 2:16	2205
transgress the tradition of the *e*	Mt 15:2	4245
and suffer many things of the *e*	Mt 16:21	4245
the *e* of the people came unto him	Mt 21:23	4245
the *e* of the people, unto the	Mt 26:3	4245
chief priests and *e* of the people	Mt 26:47	4245
scribes and the *e* were assembled	Mt 26:57	4245
Now the chief priests, and *e*	Mt 26:59	4245
e of the people took counsel	Mt 27:1	4245
silver to the chief priests and *e*	Mt 27:3	4245
accused of the chief priests and *e*	Mt 27:12	4245
e persuaded the multitude that	Mt 27:20	4245
him, with the scribes and *e*	Mt 27:41	4245
they were assembled with the *e*	Mt 28:12	4245
holding the tradition of the *e*	Mk 7:3	4245
to the tradition of the *e*	Mk 7:5	4245
things, and be rejected of the *e*	Mk 8:31	4245
priests, and the scribes, and the *e*	Mk 11:27	4245
priest and the scribes and the *e*	Mk 14:43	4245
all the chief priests and the *e*	Mk 14:53	4245
held a consultation with the *e*	Mk 15:1	4245
sent unto him the *e* of the Jews	Lk 7:3	4245
things, and be rejected of the *e*	Lk 9:22	4245
scribes came upon him with the *e*	Lk 20:1	4245
captains of the temple, and the *e*	Lk 22:52	4245
the *e* of the people and the chief	Lk 22:66	4244
morrow, that their rulers, and *e*	Acts 4:5	4245
of the people, and *e* of Israel,	Acts 4:8	4245
priests and *e* had said unto them	Acts 4:23	4245
stirred up the people, and the *e*	Acts 6:12	4245
sent it to the *e* by the hands of	Acts 11:30	4245
ordained them in every church	Acts 14:23	4245
apostles and *e* about this question	Acts 15:2	4245
church, and of the apostles and *e*	Acts 15:4	4245
e came together for to consider	Acts 15:6	4245

Then pleased it the apostles and *e*	Acts 15:22	4245
The apostles and *e* and brethren	Acts 15:23	4245
e which were at Jerusalem	Acts 16:4	4245
called the *e* of the church	Acts 20:17	4245
and all the *e* were present	Acts 21:18	4245
and all the estate of the *e*	Acts 22:5	4244
came to the chief priests and *e*	Acts 23:14	4245
high priest descended with the *e*	Acts 24:1	4245
the *e* of the Jews informed me,	Acts 25:15	4245
Let the *e* that rule well be	1Ti 5:17	4245
ordain *e* in every city, as I had	Titus 1:5	4245
For by it the *e* obtained a good	Heb 11:2	4245
him call for the *e* of the church	Jas 5:14	4245
The *e* which are among you I	1Pet 5:1	4245
twenty *e* sitting, clothed in	Rev 4:4	4245
twenty *e* fall down before him	Rev 4:10	4245
one of the *e* saith unto me, Weep	Rev 5:5	4245
beasts, and in the midst of the *e*	Rev 5:6	4245
twenty *e* fell down before the	Rev 5:8	4245
the throne and the beasts and the *e*	Rev 5:11	4245
twenty *e* fell down and worshipped	Rev 5:14	4245
about the throne, and about the *e*	Rev 7:11	4245
And one of the *e* answered, saying	Rev 7:13	4245
And the four and twenty *e*, which	Rev 11:16	4245
before the four beasts, and the *e*	Rev 14:3	4245
And the four and twenty *e* and the	Rev 19:4	4245

ELDEST

unto his *e* servant of his house	Gen 24:2	2205
not see, he called Esau his *e* son	Gen 27:1	1419
goodly raiment of her *e* son Esau	Gen 27:15	1419
And he searched, and began at the *e*	Gen 44:12	1419
of Reuben, Israel's *e* son	Num 1:20	1060
Reuben, the *e* son of Israel	Num 26:5	1060
the three sons of Jesse went and	1Sa 17:13	1419
the three *e* followed Saul	1Sa 17:14	1419
Eliab his *e* brother heard when he	1Sa 17:28	1419
Then he took his *e* son that	2Kin 3:27	1060
to the camp had slain all the *e*	2Chr 22:1	7223
wine in their *e* brother's house	Job 1:13	1060
wine in their *e* brother's house	Job 1:18	1060
one by one, beginning at the *e*	Jn 8:9	4245

ELEAD (*e'le-ad*) *A descendant of Ephraim.*

Shuthelah his son, and Ezer, and *E*	1Chr 7:21	496

ELEADAH See ELADAH.

ELEALEH (*el-e-a'-leh*) *An Amorite village.*

and Nimrah, and Heshbon, and *E*	Num 32:3	500
of Reuben built Heshbon, and *E*	Num 32:37	500
And Heshbon shall cry, and *E*	Is 15:4	500
with my tears, O Heshbon, and *E*	Is 16:9	500
the cry of Heshbon even unto *E*	Jer 48:34	500

ELEASAH (*el-e'-a-sah*) See ELASAH.
    1. A son of Helez.

begat Helez, and Helez begat *E*	1Chr 2:39	501
E begat Sisamai, and Sisamai begat	1Chr 2:40	501

    2. A descendant of King Saul.

his son, *E* his son, Azel his son	1Chr 8:37	501
his son, *E* his son, Azel his son	1Chr 9:43	501

ELEAZAR (*el-e-a'-zar*)
    1. A son of Aaron.

she bare him Nadab, and Abihu, *E*	Ex 6:23	499
E Aaron's son took him one of the	Ex 6:25	499
even Aaron, Nadab and Abihu, *E*	Ex 28:1	499
Moses said unto Aaron, and unto *E*	Lev 10:6	499
Moses spake unto Aaron, and unto *E*	Lev 10:12	499
and he was angry with *E* and Ithamar	Lev 10:16	499
Nadab the firstborn, and Abihu, *E*	Num 3:2	499
and *E* and Ithamar ministered in the	Num 3:4	499
E the son of Aaron the priest	Num 3:32	499
to the office of *E* the son of	Num 4:16	499
Speak unto *E* the son of Aaron the	Num 16:37	499
E the priest took the brasen	Num 16:39	499
shall give her unto *E* the priest	Num 19:3	499
E the priest shall take of her	Num 19:4	499
E his son, and bring them up unto	Num 20:25	499
and put them upon *E* his son	Num 20:26	499
and put them upon *E* his son	Num 20:28	499
E came down from the mount	Num 20:28	499
And when Phinehas, the son of *E*	Num 25:7	499
Phinehas, the son of *E*, the son	Num 25:11	499
unto *E* the son of Aaron the	Num 26:1	499
E the priest spake with them in	Num 26:3	499
Aaron was born Nadab, and Abihu, *E*	Num 26:60	499
E the priest, who numbered the	Num 26:63	499
before *E* the priest, and before	Num 27:2	499
And set him before *E* the priest	Num 27:19	499
shall stand before *E* the priest	Num 27:21	499
and set him before *E* the priest	Num 27:22	499
Phinehas the son of *E* the priest	Num 31:6	499

E

E the priest, and unto the	Num 31:12	499
E the priest, and all the princes	Num 31:13	499
E the priest said unto the men of	Num 31:21	499
E the priest, and the chief	Num 31:26	499
and give it unto *E* the priest	Num 31:29	499
E the priest did as the LORD	Num 31:31	499
unto *E* the priest, as the LORD	Num 31:41	499
E the priest took the gold of	Num 31:51	499
E the priest took the gold of the	Num 31:54	499
to *E* the priest, and unto the	Num 32:2	499
them Moses commanded *E* the priest	Num 32:28	499
E the priest, and Joshua the son	Num 34:17	499
E his son ministered in the	Deut 10:6	499
which *E* the priest, and Joshua the	Josh 14:1	499
came near before *E* the priest	Josh 17:4	499
which *E* the priest, and Joshua the	Josh 19:51	499
of the Levites unto *E* the priest	Josh 21:1	499
Phinehas the son of *E* the priest	Josh 22:13	499
Phinehas the son of *E* the priest	Josh 22:31	499
Phinehas the son of *E* the priest	Josh 22:32	499
And *E* the son of Aaron died	Josh 24:33	499
And Phinehas, the son of *E*	Judg 20:28	499
Nadab, and Abihu, *E*, and Ithamar	1Chr 6:3	499
E begat Phinehas, Phinehas begat	1Chr 6:4	499
E his son, Phinehas his son,	1Chr 6:50	499
Phinehas the son of *E* was the	1Chr 9:20	499
Nadab, and Abihu, *E*, and Ithamar	1Chr 24:1	499
therefore *E* and Ithamar executed	1Chr 24:2	499
them, both Zadok of the sons of *E*	1Chr 24:3	499
of *E* than of the sons of Ithamar	1Chr 24:4	499
Among the sons of *E* there were	1Chr 24:4	499
of God, were of the sons of *E*	1Chr 24:5	499
household being taken for *E*	1Chr 24:6	499
the son of Phinehas, the son of *E*	Ezr 7:5	499

2. Son of Abinadab.

sanctified *E* his son to keep the	1Sa 7:1	499

3. A son of Dodo.

after him was *E* the son of Dodo	2Sa 23:9	499
after him was *E* the son of Dodo,	1Chr 11:12	499

4. Son of Mahli.

The sons of Mahli; *E*, and Kish	1Chr 23:21	499
E died, and had no sons, but	1Chr 23:22	499
Of Mahli came *E*, who had no sons	1Chr 24:28	499

5. Son of Phinehas.

with him was *E* the son of	Ezr 8:33	499

6. Married a foreign wife.

and Malchiah, and Miamin, and *E*	Ezr 10:25	

7. A priest in Nehemiah's time.

And Maaseiah, and Shemaiah, and *E*	Neh 12:42	499

8. Son of Eliud; ancestor of Jesus.

And Eliud begat *E*	Mt 1:15	1648
and *E* begat Matthan	Mt 1:15	1648

ELECT

mine *e*, in whom my soul	Is 42:1	972
servant's sake, and Israel mine *e*	Is 45:4	972
mine *e* shall inherit it, and my	Is 65:9	972
mine *e* shall long enjoy the work	Is 65:22	972
they shall deceive the very *e*	Mt 24:24	1588
his *e* from the four winds	Mt 24:31	1588
if it were possible, even the *e*	Mk 13:22	1588
his *e* from the four winds	Mk 13:27	1588
And shall not God avenge his own *e*	Lk 18:7	1588
thing to the charge of God's *e*	Rom 8:33	1588
Put on therefore, as the *e* of God	Col 3:12	1588
the *e* angels, that thou observe	1Ti 5:21	1588
according to the faith of God's *e*	Titus 1:1	1588
E according to the foreknowledge	1Pet 1:2	1588
in Sion a chief corner stone, *e*	1Pet 2:6	1588
The elder unto the *e* lady	2Jn 1	1588
of thy *e* sister greet thee	2Jn 13	1588

ELECTED

e together with you, saluteth you	1Pet 5:13	4899

ELECTION

of God according to *e* might stand	Rom 9:11	1589
according to the *e* of grace	Rom 11:5	1589
but the *e* hath obtained it, and	Rom 11:7	1589
but as touching the *e*, they are	Rom 11:28	1589
brethren beloved, your *e* of God	1Th 1:4	1589
to make your calling and *e* sure	2Pet 1:10	1589

ELECT'S

but for the *e* sake those days	Mt 24:22	1588
but for the *e* sake, whom he hath	Mk 13:20	1588
endure all things, for the *e* sakes	2Ti 2:10	1588

EL-ELOHE-ISRAEL (*el-el-o'-he-iz'-rah-el*) *An altar of Ja-cob near Shechem.*

there an altar, and called it *E*	Gen 33:20	415

ELEMENTS

bondage under the *e* of the world	Gal 4:3	4747
again to the weak and beggarly *e*	Gal 4:9	4747
the *e* shall melt with fervent	2Pet 3:10	4747
the *e* shall melt with fervent	2Pet 3:12	4747

ELEPH (*e'-lef*) *A town in Benjamin.*

And Zelah, *E*, and Jebusi, which is	Josh 18:28	507

ELEVEN

his *e* sons, and passed over the	Gen 32:22	259,6240
the *e* stars made obeisance to me	Gen 37:9	259,6240
e curtains shalt thou make	Ex 26:7	6249,6240
the *e* curtains shall be all of	Ex 26:8	6249,6240
e curtains he made them	Ex 36:14	6249,6240
the *e* curtains were of one size	Ex 36:15	6249,6240
And on the third day *e* bullocks	Num 29:20	6249,6240
(There are *e* days' journey from	Deut 1:2	259,6240
e cities with their villages	Josh 15:51	259,6240
of us *e* hundred pieces of silver	Judg 16:5	505,3967
The *e* hundred shekels of silver	Judg 17:2	505,3967
when he had restored the *e*	Judg 17:3	505,3967
he reigned *e* years in Jerusalem	2Kin 23:36	259,6240
he reigned *e* years in Jerusalem	2Kin 24:18	259,6240
he reigned *e* years in Jerusalem	2Chr 36:5	259,6240
reigned *e* years in Jerusalem	2Chr 36:11	259,6240
he reigned *e* years in Jerusalem	Jer 52:1	259,6240
cubits, and the breadth *e* cubits	Eze 40:49	6249,6240
Then the *e* disciples went away	Mt 28:16	1733
unto the *e* as they sat at meat	Mk 16:14	1733
told all these things unto the *e*	Lk 24:9	1733
found the *e* gathered together, and	Lk 24:33	1733
was numbered with the *e* apostles	Acts 1:26	1733
But Peter, standing up with the *e*	Acts 2:14	1733

ELEVENTH

On the *e* day Pagiel the son of	Num 7:72	6249,6240
the fortieth year, in the *e* month	Deut 1:3	6249,6240
And in the *e* year, in the month	1Kin 6:38	259,6240
in the *e* year of Joram the son of	2Kin 9:29	259,6240
unto the *e* year of king Zedekiah	2Kin 25:2	6249,6240
the tenth, Machbanai the *e*	1Chr 12:13	6249,6240
The *e* to Eliashib, the twelfth to	1Chr 24:12	6249,6240
The *e* to Azareel, he, his sons,	1Chr 25:18	6249,6240
The *e* captain for the *e*	1Chr 27:14	6249,6240
unto the end of the *e* year of	Jer 1:3	6249,6240
in the *e* year of Zedekiah, in the	Jer 39:2	6249,6240
unto the *e* year of king Zedekiah	Jer 52:5	6249,6240
And it came to pass in the *e* year	Eze 26:1	6249,6240
And it came to pass in the *e* year	Eze 30:20	259,6240
And it came to pass in the *e* year	Eze 31:1	259,6240
and twentieth day of the *e* month	Zec 1:7	6249,6240
about the *e* hour he went out, and	Mt 20:6	1734
that were hired about the *e* hour	Mt 20:9	1734
the *e*, a jacinth	Rev 21:20	1734

ELHANAN (*el-ha'-nan*)
   1. Son of Jair.

where *E* the son of Jaare-oregim,	2Sa 21:19	445
E the son of Jair slew Lahmi the	1Chr 20:5	445

2. Son of Dodo.

E the son of Dodo of Beth-lehem,	2Sa 23:24	445
E the son of Dodo of Beth-lehem,	1Chr 11:26	445

ELI (*e'-li*) See ELI's, ELOI.
   1. A High Priest of Israel.

And the two sons of *E*, Hophni and	1Sa 1:3	5941
Now *E* the priest sat upon a seat	1Sa 1:9	5941
the LORD, that *E* marked her mouth	1Sa 1:12	5941
therefore *E* thought she had been	1Sa 1:13	5941
E said unto her, How long wilt	1Sa 1:14	5941
Then *E* answered and said, Go in	1Sa 1:17	5941
and brought the child to *E*	1Sa 1:25	5941
unto the LORD before *E* the priest	1Sa 2:11	5941
Now the sons of *E* were sons of	1Sa 2:12	5941
E blessed Elkanah and his wife, and	1Sa 2:20	5941
Now *E* was very old, and heard all	1Sa 2:22	5941
And there came a man of God unto *E*	1Sa 2:27	5941
ministered unto the LORD before *E*	1Sa 3:1	5941
when *E* was laid down in his place	1Sa 3:2	5941
And he ran unto *E*, and said, Here	1Sa 3:5	5941
And Samuel arose and went to *E*	1Sa 3:6	5941
And he arose and went to *E*, and said	1Sa 3:8	5941
E perceived that the LORD had	1Sa 3:8	5941
Therefore *E* said unto Samuel, Go,	1Sa 3:9	5941
E all things which I have spoken	1Sa 3:12	5941
I have sworn unto the house of *E*	1Sa 3:14	5941
feared to shew *E* the vision	1Sa 3:15	5941
Then *E* called Samuel, and said,	1Sa 3:16	5941
and the two sons of *E*, Hophni and	1Sa 4:4	5941
and the two sons of *E*, Hophni and	1Sa 4:11	5941
E sat upon a seat by the wayside	1Sa 4:13	5941
when *E* heard the noise of the	1Sa 4:14	5941

man came in hastily, and told *E* 1Sa 4:14   5941
Now *E* was ninety and eight years 1Sa 4:15   5941
And the man said unto *E*, I am he........1Sa 4:16   5941
the son of Phinehas, the son of *E*..........1Sa 14:3   5941
the house of *E* in Shiloh..........................1Kin 2:27   5941
   2. An Aramaic term for God.
with a loud voice, saying, Eli, *E*............Mt 27:46   2241

ELIAB (e'-le-ab) See ELIAB'S, ELIEL.
   1. Son of Helon.
E the son of Helon ....Num 1:9   446
E the son of Helon shall be......................Num 2:7   446
the third day *E* the son of Helon ....Num 7:24   446
offering of *E* the son of Helon..................Num 7:29   446
of Zebulun was *E* the son of Helon ....Num 10:16   446
   2. Father of Dathan.
Dathan and Abiram, the sons of *E*............Num 16:1   446
Dathan and Abiram, the sons of *E* ....Num 16:12   446
the sons of Pallu; *E*..................................Num 26:8   446
And the sons of *E*.....................................Num 26:9   446
Dathan and Abiram, the sons of *E* ....Deut 11:6   446
   3. A son of Jesse.
were come, that he looked on *E* 1Sa 16:6   446
the battle were *E* the first born...............1Sa 17:13   446
E his eldest brother heard when 1Sa 17:28   446
And Jesse begat his firstborn *E*................1Chr 2:13   446
daughter of *E* the son of Jesse.................2Chr 11:18   446
   4. A Levite ancestor of Samuel.
E his son, Jeroham his son, ...1Chr 6:27   446
   5. A leader in David's army.
Obadiah the second, *E* the third,..............1Chr 12:9   446
   6. A Levite in David's time.
and Jehiel, and Unni, *E*, and 1Chr 15:18   446
and Jehiel, and Unni, and *E* 1Chr 15:20   446
and Jehiel, and Mattithiah, and *E* 1Chr 16:5   446

ELIAB'S (e'-le-abs)
E anger was kindled against David........1Sa 17:28   446

ELIADA (e'-li-a-dah) See ELIADAH.
   1. A son of David.
And Elishama, and *E*, and Eliphalet 2Sa 5:16   450
And Elishama, and *E*, and Eliphelet,......1Chr 3:8   450
E a mighty man of valour, and with 2Chr 17:17   450

ELIADAH (e'-li-a-dah) See ELIADA. *An opponent of King Saul.*
adversary, Rezon the son of *E*..................1Kin 11:23   450

ELIAH (e'-li-ah) See ELIJAH. *A son of Jeroham.*
And Jaresiah, and *E*, and Zichri, the......1Chr 8:27   452
and Abdi, and Jeremoth, and *E*................Ezr 10:26   452

ELIAHBA (e'-li-ah-bah) *A "mighty man" of David.*
E the Shaalbonite, of the sons of 2Sa 23:32   455
Baharumite, *E* the Shaalbonite,..............1Chr 11:33   455

ELIAKIM (e'-li-a-kim) See JEHOIAKIM.
   1. A son of Hilkiah.
out to them *E* the son of Hilkiah.............2Kin 18:18   471
Then said *E* the son of Hilkiah................2Kin 18:26   471
Then came *E* the son of Hilkiah,.............2Kin 18:37   471
And he sent *E*, which was over the 2Kin 19:2   471
my servant *E* the son of Hilkiah ....Is 22:20   471
Then came forth unto him *E* ....Is 36:3   471
Then said *E* and Shebna and Joah ....Is 36:11   471
Then came *E*, the son of Hilkiah,............Is 36:22   471
And he sent *E*, who was over the ....Is 37:2   471
   2. Original name of Jehoiakim.
Pharaoh-nechoh made *E* the son of 2Kin 23:34   471
the king of Egypt made *E* his 2Chr 36:4   471
   3. A priest who dedicated the wall.
E, Maaseiah, Miniamin, Michaiah, ...Neh 12:41   471
   4. Son of Abiud; ancestor of Jesus.
and Abiud begat *E* ....Mt 1:13   *1662*
and *E* begat Azor ....Mt 1:13   *1662*
of Jonan, which was the son of *E* ....Lk 3:30   *1662*

ELIAM (e'-le-am)
   1. Father of Bathsheba.
Bath-sheba, the daughter of *E*.................2Sa 11:3   463
   2. A "mighty man" of David.
E the son of Ahithophel the 2Sa 23:34   463

ELIAS (e-li'-as) See ELIJAH. *Greek form of Elijah.*
if ye will receive it, this is *E*...................Mt 11:14   *2243*
some, *E*; and others, Jeremias ....Mt 16:14   *2243*
them Moses and *E* talking with him ......Mt 17:3   *2243*
and one for Moses, and one for *E* ....Mt 17:4   *2243*
scribes that *E* must first come ....Mt 17:10   *2243*
***E* truly shall first come, and** ....Mt 17:11   *2243*
That *E* is come already, and they ....Mt 17:12   *2243*
said, This man calleth for *E* ....Mt 27:47   *2243*
let us see whether *E* will come to ....Mt 27:49   *2243*
Others said, That it is *E*...........................Mk 6:15   *2243*

but some say, *E*...Mk 8:28   *2243*
appeared unto them *E* with Moses..........Mk 9:4   *2243*
and one for Moses, and one for *E* ....Mk 9:5   *2243*
scribes that *E* must first come ....Mk 9:11   *2243*
***E* verily cometh first, and** ....Mk 9:12   *2243*
That *E* is indeed come, and they...........Mk 9:13   *2243*
it said, Behold, he calleth *E* ....Mk 15:35   *2243*
let us see whether *E* will come to ....Mk 15:36   *2243*
him in the spirit and power of *E* ....Lk 1:17   *2243*
were in Israel in the days of *E*..............Lk 4:25   *2243*
But unto none of them was *E* sent ....Lk 4:26   *2243*
And of some, that *E* had appeared...........Lk 9:8   *2243*
but some say *E* ....Lk 9:19   *2243*
two men, which were Moses and *E* ....Lk 9:30   *2243*
and one for Moses, and one for *E* ....Lk 9:33   *2243*
and consume them, even as *E* did ....Lk 9:54   *2243*
Art thou *E*? ....Jn 1:21   *2243*
if thou be not that Christ, nor *E* ....Jn 1:25   *2243*
not what the scripture saith of *E* ....Rom 11:2   *2243*
E was a man subject to like ....Jas 5:17   *2243*

ELIASAPH (e-li'-a-saf)
   1. A chief of Gad.
E the son of Deuel ....Num 1:14   460
Gad shall be *E* the son of Reuel..............Num 2:14   460
the sixth day *E* the son of Deuel ....Num 7:42   460
offering of *E* the son of Deuel ....Num 7:47   460
of Gad was *E* the son of Deuel ....Num 10:20   460
   2. A Gershonite leader.
shall be *E* the son of Lael ....Num 3:24   460

ELIASHIB (e-li'-a-shib)
   1. A descendant of Judah.
of Elioenai were, Hodaiah, and *E*............1Chr 3:24   475
   2. A priest in David's time.
The eleventh to *E*, the twelfth to 1Chr 24:12   475
   3. Son of Joiakim.
chamber of Johanan the son of *E* ....Ezr 10:6   475
Joiakim, Joiakim also begat *E* ....Neh 12:10   475
and *E* begat Joiada ....Neh 12:10   475
The Levites in the days of *E* ....Neh 12:22   475
the days of Johanan the son of *E* ....Neh 12:23   475
   4. Married a foreign wife.
Of the singers also; *E*...............................Ezr 10:24   475
   5. Son of Zotta.
Elioenai, *E*, Mattaniah, and ....Ezr 10:27   475
   6. Son of Bani.
Vaniah, Meremoth, *E*, ...Ezr 10:36   475
   7. High Priest during Nehemiah's time.
Then *E* the high priest rose up ....Neh 3:1   475
of the house of *E* the high priest ....Neh 3:20   475
from the door of the house of *E*...............Neh 3:21   475
even to the end of the house of *E* ....Neh 3:21   475
this, *E* the priest, having the ....Neh 13:4   475
of the evil that *E* did for Tobiah ....Neh 13:7   475
the son of *E* the high priest, was ....Neh 13:28   475

ELIATHAH (e-li'-a-thah) *A son of Heman.*
and Jerimoth, Hananiah, Hanani, *E*........1Chr 25:4   448
The twentieth to *E*, he, his sons, ...1Chr 25:27   448

ELIDAD (e-li'-dad) *Son of Chislon.*
of Benjamin, *E* the son of Chislon...........Num 34:21   449

ELIEHOENAI See ELIHOENAI.

ELIEL (e'-le-el) See ELIAH.
   1. Head of the house of Manasseh.
even Epher, and Ishi, and *E* 1Chr 5:24   447
   2. Son of Jeroham.
the son of Jeroham, the son of *E* 1Chr 6:34   447
   3. A son of Shimhi.
And Elienai, and Zilthai, and *E*...............1Chr 8:20   447
   4. A son of Shashak.
And Ishpan, and Heber, and *E* 1Chr 8:22   447
   5. A captain in David's army.
E the Mahavite, and Jeribai, and 1Chr 11:46   447
   6. A "mighty man" of David.
E, and Obed, and Jasiel the 1Chr 11:47   447
   7. A Gadite ally of David.
Attai the sixth, *E* the seventh, ...1Chr 12:11   447
   8. A chief of Judah.
E the chief, and his brethren...................1Chr 15:9   447
   9. A chief Levite.
Asaiah, and Joel, Shemaiah, and *E* 1Chr 15:11   447
   10. A Levite in Hezekiah's time.
and Jerimoth, and Jozabad, and *E* 2Chr 31:13   447

ELIENAI (e-li-e'-nahee) *A son of Shimhi.*
And *E*, and Zilthai, and Eliel, ...1Chr 8:20   462

ELIEZER
of my house is this *E* of Damascus ....Gen 15:2   461
And the name of the other was *E* ....Ex 18:4   461
Zemira, and Joash, and *E*, and 1Chr 7:8   461

E

and Zechariah, and Benaiah, and *E* 1Chr 15:24   461
sons of Moses were, Gershom, and *E* 1Chr 23:15   461
And the sons of *E* were, Rehabiah 1Chr 23:17   461
And *E* had none other sons 1Chr 23:17   461
And his brethren by *E* 1Chr 26:25   461
was *E* the son of Zichri 1Chr 27:16   461
Then *E* the son of Dodavah of................ 2Chr 20:37   461
Then sent I for *E*, for Ariel, for .... Ezr 8:16   461
Maaseiah, and *E*, and Jarib, and.......... Ezr 10:18   461
Kelita,) Pethahiah, Judah, and *E*.......... Ezr 10:23   461
E, Ishijah, Malchiah, Shemaiah,.......... Ezr 10:31   461
of Jose, which was the son of *E*............. Lk 3:29   *1663*

ELIHOENAI (e-li-ho-e'-nahee) See ELIOENAI. *A family of exiles.*
E the son of Zerahiah, and with .... Ezr 8:4   454

ELIHOREPH (e-li-ho'-ref) *A scribe of Solomon.*
E and Ahiah, the sons of Shisha, ... 1Kin 4:3   456

ELIHU (e-li'-hew)
1. Great-grandfather of Samuel.
the son of Jeroham, the son of *E* 1Sa 1:1   453
2. A soldier of David.
and Michael, and Jozabad, and *E* 1Chr 12:20   453
3. A Tabernacle servant.
whose brethren were strong men, *E* 1Chr 26:7   453
4. Brother of David.
Of Judah, *E*, one of the brethren............. 1Chr 27:18   453
5. A friend of Job.
Then was kindled the wrath of *E*............ Job 32:2   453
Now *E* had waited till Job had .... Job 32:4   453
When *E* saw that there was no .... Job 32:5   453
E the son of Barachel the Buzite .... Job 32:6   453
Furthermore *E* answered and said, ... Job 34:1   453
E spake moreover, and said,.................... Job 35:1   453
E also proceeded, and said,.................... Job 36:1   453

ELIJAH (e-li'-jah) See ELIAH, ELIAS.
1. The prophet.
E the Tishbite, who was of the 1Kin 17:1   452
E said unto her, Fear not........................ 1Kin 17:13   452
did according to the saying of *E* 1Kin 17:15   452
of the LORD, which he spake by *E* 1Kin 17:16   452
And she said unto *E*, What have I 1Kin 17:18   452
And the LORD heard the voice of *E* 1Kin 17:22   452
E took the child, and brought him 1Kin 17:23   452
E said, See, thy son liveth 1Kin 17:23   452
And the woman said to *E*, Now by 1Kin 17:24   452
LORD came to *E* in the third year 1Kin 18:1   452
E went to shew himself unto Ahab 1Kin 18:2   452
was in the way, behold, *E* met him......... 1Kin 18:7   452
and said, Art thou that my lord *E*......... 1Kin 18:7   452
tell thy lord, Behold, *E* is here 1Kin 18:8   452
tell thy lord, Behold, *E* is here 1Kin 18:11   452
tell thy lord, Behold, *E* is here 1Kin 18:14   452
E said, As the LORD of hosts 1Kin 18:15   452
and Ahab went to meet *E*........................ 1Kin 18:16   452
it came to pass, when Ahab saw *E*......... 1Kin 18:17   452
E came unto all the people, and 1Kin 18:21   452
Then said *E* unto the people, I, ... 1Kin 18:22   452
E said unto the prophets of Baal, ... 1Kin 18:25   452
that *E* mocked them, and said, Cry 1Kin 18:27   452
E said unto all the people, Come 1Kin 18:30   452
E took twelve stones, according............. 1Kin 18:31   452
that *E* the prophet came near, and 1Kin 18:36   452
E said unto them, Take the.................... 1Kin 18:40   452
E brought them down to the brook........ 1Kin 18:40   452
E said unto Ahab, Get thee up,............. 1Kin 18:41   452
E went up to the top of Carmel 1Kin 18:42   452
And the hand of the LORD was on *E* 1Kin 18:46   452
told Jezebel all that *E* had done............ 1Kin 19:1   452
Jezebel sent a messenger unto *E*........... 1Kin 19:2   452
unto him, What doest thou here, *E*........ 1Kin 19:9   452
when *E* heard it, that he wrapped......... 1Kin 19:13   452
and said, What doest thou here, *E* 1Kin 19:13   452
E passed by him, and cast his 1Kin 19:19   452
he left the oxen, and ran after *E* 1Kin 19:20   452
Then he arose, and went after *E*............ 1Kin 19:21   452
the LORD came to *E* the Tishbite 1Kin 21:17   452
And Ahab said to *E*, Hast thou 1Kin 21:20   452
the LORD came to *E* the Tishbite 1Kin 21:28   452
the LORD said to *E* the Tishbite 2Kin 1:3   452
And *E* departed................................... 2Kin 1:4   452
And he said, It is *E* the Tishbite............. 2Kin 1:8   452
E answered and said to the captain 2Kin 1:10   452
E answered and said unto them, If........ 2Kin 1:12   452
and fell on his knees before *E* 2Kin 1:13   452
the angel of the LORD said unto *E*......... 2Kin 1:15   452
of the LORD which *E* had spoken............ 2Kin 1:17   452
up *E* into heaven by a whirlwind 2Kin 2:1   452
that *E* went with Elisha from 2Kin 2:1   452
E said unto Elisha, Tarry here, I 2Kin 2:2   452

E said unto him, Elisha, tarry 2Kin 2:4   452
E said unto him, Tarry, I pray 2Kin 2:6   452
E took his mantle, and wrapped it 2Kin 2:8   452
that *E* said unto Elisha, Ask what 2Kin 2:9   452
E went up by a whirlwind into 2Kin 2:11   452
mantle of *E* that fell from him................ 2Kin 2:13   452
mantle of *E* that fell from him................ 2Kin 2:14   452
said, Where is the LORD God of *E* 2Kin 2:14   452
The spirit of *E* doth rest on 2Kin 2:15   452
poured water on the hands of *E* 2Kin 3:11   452
by his servant *E* the Tishbite 2Kin 9:36   452
which he spake by his servant *E* 2Kin 10:10   452
of the LORD, which he spake to *E*........... 2Kin 10:17   452
writing to him from *E* the prophet 2Chr 21:12   452
I will send you *E* the prophet .... Mal 4:5   452
2. Married a foreign wife.
Maaseiah, and *E*, and Shemaiah, and ... Ezr 10:21   452

ELIKA (e-li'-kah) *A guard of David.*
the Harodite, *E* the Harodite,................. 2Sa 23:25   470

ELIM (e'-lim) See BEER-ELIM. *An encampment during the Exodus.*
And they came to *E*, where were .... Ex 15:27   362
And they took their journey from *E* .... Ex 16:1   362
of Sin, which is between *E* .... Ex 16:1   362
from Marah, and came unto *E*................ Num 33:9   362
in *E* were twelve fountains of .... Num 33:9   362
And they removed from *E*, and .... Num 33:10   362

ELIMELECH (e-lim'-e-lek) See ELIMELECH'S. *Husband of Naomi.*
And the name of the man was *E* .... Ruth 1:2   458
And *E* Naomi's husband died .... Ruth 1:3   458
man of wealth, of the family of *E* .... Ruth 2:1   458
Boaz, who was of the kindred of *E* .... Ruth 2:3   458

ELIMELECH'S
of land, which was our brother *E*............ Ruth 4:3   458
that I have bought all that was *E* .... Ruth 4:9   458

ELIOENAI (e-li-o-e'-nahee) See ELIHOENAI.
1. A son of Neariah.
E, and Hezekiah, and Azrikam, three ... 1Chr 3:23   454
And the sons of *E* were, Hodaiah, ... 1Chr 3:24   454
2. A Simeonite prince.
And *E*, and Jaakobah, and 1Chr 4:36   454
3. A son of Becher.
and Joash, and Eliezer, and *E* 1Chr 7:8   454
4. A Temple servant.
the sixth, *E* the seventh 1Chr 26:3   454
5. Married a foreign wife.
E, Maaseiah, Ishmael, Nethaneel,.......... Ezr 10:22   454
6. A son of Zattu.
E, Eliashib, Mattaniah, and .... Ezr 10:27   454
7. A priest during Nehemiah's time.
Maaseiah, Miniamin, Michaiah, *E* .... Neh 12:41   454

ELIPHAL (el'-i-fal) *A captain in David's army.*
the Hararite, *E* the son of Ur, ... 1Chr 11:35   465

ELIPHALET (e-lif-a-let) See ELIPHELET, ELPALET. *A son of David.*
And Elishama, and Eliada, and *E* 2Sa 5:16   467
And Elishama, and Beeliada, and *E*....... 1Chr 14:7   467

ELIPHAZ (el'-if-az)
1. A son of Esau.
And Adah bare to Esau *E*........................ Gen 36:4   464
E the son of Adah the wife of .... Gen 36:10   464
And the sons of *E* were Teman................ Gen 36:11   464
was concubine to *E* Esau's son............... Gen 36:12   464
and she bare to *E* Amalek...................... Gen 36:12   464
the sons of *E* the firstborn son .... Gen 36:15   464
came of *E* in the land of Edom............... Gen 36:16   464
E, Reuel, and Jeush, and Jaalam, and ... 1Chr 1:35   464
The sons of *E*; Teman, and 1Chr 1:36   464
2. A friend of Job.
E the Temanite, and Bildad the .... Job 2:11   464
Then *E* the Temanite answered and .... Job 4:1   464
Then answered *E* the Temanite............... Job 15:1   464
Then *E* the Temanite answered and .... Job 22:1   464
the LORD said to *E* the Temanite............ Job 42:7   464
So *E* the Temanite and Bildad the .... Job 42:9   464

ELIPHELEH (e-lif-e-leh) *A Levite singer.*
and Maaseiah, and Mattithiah, and *E* ... 1Chr 15:18   466
And Mattithiah, and *E*, and Mikneiah, .. 1Chr 15:21   466

ELIPHELEHU See ELIPHELEH.

ELIPHELET (e-lif-e-let) See ELIPHALET.
1. A "mighty man" of David.
E the son of Ahasbai, the son of 2Sa 23:34   467
2. A son of David.
Ibhar also, and Elishama, and *E* 1Chr 3:6   467

3. Same as Eliphat.
And Elishama, and Eliada, and E 1Chr 3:8 467
   4. A descendant of King Saul.
Jehush the second, and E the third 1Chr 8:39 467
   5. A family of exiles.
whose names are these, E ....Ezr 8:13 467
   6. A son of Hashum.
Mattenai, Mattathah, Zabad, E ....Ezr 10:33 467

ELI'S *(e'-lize) Refers to Eli 1.*
that the iniquity of E house 1Sa 3:14 5941

ELISABETH *(e-liz'-a-beth) See* ELISABETH'S. *Mother of John the Baptist.*
of Aaron, and her name was E ....Lk 1:5 1665
child, because that E was barren ....Lk 1:7 1665
thy wife E shall bear thee a son, ...Lk 1:13 1665
those days his wife E conceived............Lk 1:24 1665
And, behold, thy cousin E, she ....Lk 1:36 1665
house of Zacharias, and saluted E ....Lk 1:40 1665
when E heard the salutation of ....Lk 1:41 1665
E was filled with the Holy Ghost ....Lk 1:41 1665

ELISABETH'S *(e-liz'-a-beths)*
Now E full time came that she..............Lk 1:57 1665

ELISEUS *(el-i-se'-us) See* ELISHA. *Greek form of Elisha.*
in the time of E the prophet ....Lk 4:27 1666

ELISHA *(e-li'-shah) See* ELISEUS. *A prophet.*
and E the son of Shaphat of...................1Kin 19:16 477
the sword of Jehu shall E slay 1Kin 19:17 477
found E the son of Shaphat, who 1Kin 19:19 477
Elijah went with E from Gilgal 2Kin 2:1 477
And Elijah said unto E, Tarry here 2Kin 2:2 477
E said unto him, As the LORD..............2Kin 2:2 477
were at Beth-el came forth to E 2Kin 2:3 477
And Elijah said unto him, E 2Kin 2:4 477
that were at Jericho came to E 2Kin 2:5 477
over, that Elijah said unto E 2Kin 2:9 477
E said, I pray thee, let a double 2Kin 2:9 477
E saw it, and he cried, My father, ...2Kin 2:12 477
and thither: and E went over. 2Kin 2:14 477
spirit of Elijah doth rest on E 2Kin 2:15 477
the men of the city said unto 2Kin 2:19 477
to the saying of E which he spake 2Kin 2:22 477
Here is E the son of Shaphat,.............2Kin 3:11 477
E said unto the king of Israel,..............2Kin 3:13 477
E said, As the LORD of hosts 2Kin 3:14 477
the sons of the prophets unto E 2Kin 4:1 477
E said unto her, What shall I do 2Kin 4:2 477
that E passed to Shunem, where...........2Kin 4:8 477
season that E had said unto her 2Kin 4:17 477
when E was come into the house, ...2Kin 4:32 477
And E came again to Gilgal.................2Kin 4:38 477
when E the man of God had heard 2Kin 5:8 477
at the door of the house of E 2Kin 5:9 477
E sent a messenger unto him, ...2Kin 5:10 477
the servant of E the man of God............2Kin 5:20 477
E said unto him, Whence comest 2Kin 5:25 477
sons of the prophets said unto E 2Kin 6:1 477
but E, the prophet that is in 2Kin 6:12 477
E prayed, and said, LORD, I pray 2Kin 6:17 477
and chariots of fire round about E 2Kin 6:17 477
E prayed unto the LORD, and said,........2Kin 6:18 477
according to the word of E....................2Kin 6:18 477
E said unto them, This is not the 2Kin 6:19 477
come into Samaria, that E said 2Kin 6:20 477
And the king of Israel said unto E.........2Kin 6:21 477
if the head of E the son of 2Kin 6:31 477
But E sat in his house, and the 2Kin 6:32 477
Then E said, Hear ye the word of 2Kin 7:1 477
Then spake E unto the woman, ...2Kin 8:1 477
the great things that E hath done 2Kin 8:4 477
her son, whom E restored to life 2Kin 8:5 477
And E came to Damascus 2Kin 8:7 477
E said unto him, Go, say unto him 2Kin 8:10 477
E answered, The LORD hath shewed 2Kin 8:13 477
So he departed from E, and came to......2Kin 8:14 477
said to him, What said E to thee 2Kin 8:14 477
E the prophet called one of the 2Kin 9:1 477
Now E was fallen sick of his...................2Kin 13:14 477
E said unto him, Take bow and 2Kin 13:15 477
E put his hands upon the king's 2Kin 13:16 477
Then E said, Shoot 2Kin 13:17 477
E died, and they buried him 2Kin 13:20 477
the man into the sepulchre of E.............2Kin 13:21 477
down, and touched the bones of E 2Kin 13:21 477

ELISHAH *(e-li'-shah) A son of Javan.*
E, and Tarshish, Kittim, and ....Gen 10:4 473
E, and Tarshish, Kittim, and 1Chr 1:7 473
purple from the isles of E was...............Eze 27:7 473

ELISHAMA *(e-lish'-a-mah) See* ELISHUA.
   1. Grandfather of Joshua.
E the son of Ammihud ....Num 1:10 476
shall be E the son of Ammihud..............Num 2:18 476
seventh day E the son of Ammihud ....Num 7:48 476
offering of E the son of Ammihud ....Num 7:53 476
over his host was E the son of................Num 10:22 476
son, Ammihud his son, E his son,..........1Chr 7:26 476
   2. A son of David.
And E, and Eliada, and Eliphalet 2Sa 5:16 476
Ibhar also, and E, and Eliphelet, ...1Chr 3:6 476
And E, and Eliada, and Eliphelet, ...1Chr 3:8 476
And E, and Beeliada, and Eliphalet........1Chr 14:7 476
   3. A descendant of Judah.
the son of Nethaniah the son of E ....Jer 41:1 476
   4. Son of Jekamiah.
Jekamiah, and Jekamiah begat E 1Chr 2:41 476
   5. Same as Elishua.
son of Nethaniah, the son of E 2Kin 25:25 476
   6. A priest who taught the law.
and with them E and Jehoram,..............2Chr 17:8 476
   7. A scribe of Jehoiakim.
even E the scribe, and Delaiah the........Jer 36:12 476
in the chamber of E the scribe ....Jer 36:20 476
he took it out of E the scribe's...............Jer 36:21 476

ELISHAPHAT *(e-lish'-a-fat) Assisted in making Joash king.*
E the son of Zichri, into 2Chr 23:1 478

ELISHEBA *(e-lish'-e-bah) Daughter of Amminadab.*
And Aaron took him E, daughter of ....Ex 6:23 472

ELISHUA *(e-lish'-oo-ah) See* ELISHAMA. *A son of David.*
Ibhar also, and E, and Nepheg, and 2Sa 5:15 474
And Ibhar, and E, and Elpalet,..............1Chr 14:5 474

ELIUD *(e-li'-ud) Son of Achim; ancestor of Jesus.*
and Achim begat E ....Mt 1:14 1664
And E begat Eleazar ....Mt 1:15 1664

ELIZABETH *See* ELISABETH.

ELIZAPHAN *(e-liz'-a-fan) See* ELZAPHAN.
   1. Son of Uzziel.
shall be E the son of Uzziel ....Num 3:30 469
Of the sons of E....................................1Chr 15:8 469
   2. Son of Parnach.
of Zebulun, E the son of Parnach...........Num 34:25 469
   3. A family of Levites.
And of the sons of E..............................2Chr 29:13 469

ELIZUR *(e-li'-zur) Son of Shedeur.*
E the son of Shedeur ....Num 1:5 468
shall be E the son of Shedeur ....Num 2:10 468
On the fourth day E the son of...............Num 7:30 468
offering of E the son of Shedeur.............Num 7:35 468
over his host was E the son of................Num 10:18 468

ELKANAH *(el-ka'-nah)*
   1. A grandson of Korah.
Assir, and E, and Abiasaph ....Ex 6:24 511
E his son, and Ebiasaph his son, ...1Chr 6:23 511
   2. Father of Samuel.
mount Ephraim, and his name was E 1Sa 1:1 511
when the time was that E offered 1Sa 1:4 511
Then said E her husband to her, ...1Sa 1:8 511
and E knew Hannah his wife 1Sa 1:19 511
And the man E, and all his house,..........1Sa 1:21 511
E her husband said unto her, Do............1Sa 1:23 511
E went to Ramah to his house 1Sa 2:11 511
And Eli blessed E and his wife, and 1Sa 2:20 511
son, Jeroham his son, E his son 1Chr 6:27 511
The son of E, the son of Jeroham, ...1Chr 6:34 511
   3. A Levite.
the sons of E; Amasai, and....................1Chr 6:25 511
The son of E, the son of Joel, ...1Chr 6:36 511
   4. A descendant of Kohath.
the sons of E 1Chr 6:26 511
The son of Zuph, the son of E................1Chr 6:35 511
   5. Father of Asa.
the son of Asa, the son of E...................1Chr 9:16 511
   6. A soldier in David's army.
E, and Jesiah, and Azareel, and 1Chr 12:6 511
   7. A Levite doorkeeper.
E were doorkeepers for the ark..............1Chr 15:23 511
   8. An officer of King Ahaz.
E that was next to the king 2Chr 28:7 511

ELKOSH *See* ELKOSHITE.

ELKOSHITE
book of the vision of Nahum the E ....Nah 1:1 512

ELLASAR *(el'-la-sar) A Babylonian city.*
king of Shinar, Arioch king of E ....Gen 14:1 495
of Shinar, and Arioch king of E.............Gen 14:9 495

ELMODAM (el-mo'-dam) Son of Er.
of Cosam, which was the son of E .... Lk 3:28   1678

ELMS
hills, under oaks and poplars and e .... Hos 4:13   424

ELNAAM (el-na'-am) Father of two of David's "mighty men."
and Joshaviah, the sons of E 1Chr 11:46   493

ELNATHAN (el-na'-than)
   1. Father of Nehushta.
the daughter of E of Jerusalem 2Kin 24:8   494
E the son of Achbor, and certain............. Jer 26:22   494
E the son of Achbor, and Gemariah .... Jer 36:12   494
Nevertheless E and Delaiah and .... Jer 36:25   494
   2. Name of three Levites during Ezra's time.
for Ariel, for Shemaiah, and for E .... Ezr 8:16   494
and for Jarib, and for E .... Ezr 8:16   494
also for Joiarib, and for E..................... Ezr 8:16   494

ELOI (e-lo'-ee) See ELI. Same as Eli 2.
a loud voice, saying, E, E .... Mk 15:34   1682

ELON (e'-lon) See ELONITES.
   1. Esau's father-in-law.
the daughter of E the Hittite .... Gen 26:34   356
the daughter of E the Hittite .... Gen 36:2   356
   2. A son of Zebulun.
Sered, and E, and Jahleel...................... Gen 46:14   356
of E, the family of the Elonites .... Num 26:26   356
   3. A Danite town.
And E, and Thimnathah, and Ekron, ... Josh 19:43   356
   4. A judge of Israel.
And after him E, a Zebulonite, ... Judg 12:11   356
E the Zebulonite died, and was .... Judg 12:12   356

ELON-BETH-HANAN (e'-lon-beth-ha'-nan) A Danite town.
Shaalbim, and Beth-shemesh, and E 1Kin 4:9   358

ELONITES (e'-lon-ites) Descendants of Elon 2.
of Elon, the family of the E .... Num 26:26   440

ELOQUENT
the LORD, O my Lord, I am not e .... Ex 4:10   376,1697
artificer, and the e orator........................ Is 3:3   995
an e man, and mighty in the .... Acts 18:24   3052

ELOTH (e'-loth) See ELATH. Same as Elath.
in Ezion-geber, which is beside E 1Kin 9:26   359
Solomon to Ezion-geber, and to E............ 2Chr 8:17   359
He built E, and restored it to.................. 2Chr 26:2   359

ELPAAL (el-pa'-al) A son of Shaharaim.
of Hushim he begat Abitub, and E 1Chr 8:11   508
The sons of E; Eber, and Misham 1Chr 8:12   508
Jezliah, and Jobab, the sons of E 1Chr 8:18   508

ELPALET (el-pa'-let) See ELIPHALET. A son of David.
And Ibhar, and Elishua, and E 1Chr 14:5   467

EL-PARAN (el-pa'-ran) A place in southern Canaan.
in their mount Seir, unto E .... Gen 14:6   364

ELPELET See ELPALET.

ELSE See APPENDIX.

ELTEKE See ELTEKEH.

ELTEKEH (el'-te-keh) A Danite city.
And E, and Gibbethon, and Baalath,...... Josh 19:44   514
E with her suburbs, Gibbethon .... Josh 21:23   514

ELTEKON (el'-te-kon) A city in Judah.
And Maarath, and Beth-anoth, and E .... Josh 15:59   515

ELTOLAD (el-to'-lad) A city in Judah.
And E, and Chesil, and Hormah, ... Josh 15:30   513
And E, and Bethul, and Hormah,........... Josh 19:4   513

ELUL (e'-lul) Sixth month of the Hebrew year.
and fifth day of the month E .... Neh 6:15   435

ELUZAI (e-loo'-zahee) A soldier in David's army.
E, and Jerimoth, and Bealiah, and 1Chr 12:5   498

ELYMAS (el'-i-mas) See BAR-JESUS. A sorcerer.
But E the sorcerer (for so is his).............. Acts 13:8   1681

ELZABAD (el'-za-bad)
   1. A soldier in David's army.
Johanan the eighth, E the ninth, ... 1Chr 12:12   443
   2. Son of Shemaiah.
Othni, and Rephael, and Obed, E 1Chr 26:7   443

ELZAPHAN (el'-za-fan) See ELIZAPHAN. A son of Uzziel.
Mishael, and E, and Zithri .... Ex 6:22   469
And Moses called Mishael and E .... Lev 10:4   469

EMBALM
the physicians to e his father .... Gen 50:2   2590

EMBALMED
and the physicians e Israel .... Gen 50:2   2590
the days of those which are e................... Gen 50:3   2590
and they e him, and he was put in a ...... Gen 50:26   2590

EMBOLDENED
of him which is weak be e to eat 1Cor 8:10   3618

EMBOLDENETH
or what e thee that thou .... Job 16:3   4834

EMBRACE
time of life, thou shalt e a son 2Kin 4:16   2263
e the rock for want of a shelter .... Job 24:8   2263
to honour, when thou dost e her .... Prov 4:8   2263
e the bosom of a stranger .... Prov 5:20   2263
a time to e, and a time to refrain............ Eccl 3:5   2263
head, and his right hand doth e me........ Song 2:6   2263
and his right hand should e me............... Song 8:3   2263
brought up in scarlet e dunghills............ Lam 4:5   2263

EMBRACED
e him, and kissed him, and brought .... Gen 29:13   2263
e him, and fell on his neck, and .... Gen 33:4   2263
and he kissed them, and e them .... Gen 48:10   2263
e them, and departed for to go............... Acts 20:1   782
e them, and confessed that they .... Heb 11:13   782

EMBRACING
and a time to refrain from e .... Eccl 3:5   2263
him, and e him said, Trouble not .... Acts 20:10   4843

EMBROIDER
thou shalt e the coat of fine .... Ex 28:39   7660

EMBROIDERER
the cunning workman, and of the e .... Ex 35:35   7551
an e in blue, and in purple, and in.......... Ex 38:23   7551

EMEK KEZIZ See KEZIZ.

EMERALD
And the second row shall be an e .... Ex 28:18   5306
And the second row, an e, a .... Ex 39:11   5306
the jasper, the sapphire, the e .... Eze 28:13   5306
throne, in sight like unto an e .... Rev 4:3   4664
a chalcedony; the fourth, an e .... Rev 21:19   4665

EMERALDS
they occupied in thy fairs with e .... Eze 27:16   5306

EMERODS
the botch of Egypt, and with the e.......... Deut 28:27   6076
them, and smote them with e 1Sa 5:6   6076
they had e in their secret parts 1Sa 5:9   6076
died not were smitten with the e............. 1Sa 5:12   6076
They answered, Five golden e 1Sa 6:4   6076
ye shall make images of your e 1Sa 6:5   6076
of gold and the images of their e 1Sa 6:11   2914
these are the golden e which the 1Sa 6:17   2914

EMIM See EMIMS.

EMIMS (e'-mims) A race of giants.
the E in Shaveh Kiriathaim,................... Gen 14:5   368
The E dwelt therein in times past .... Deut 2:10   368
but the Moabites call them E .... Deut 2:11   368

EMINENT
also built unto thee an e place .... Eze 16:24   1354
In that thou buildest thine e................... Eze 16:31   1354
shall throw down thine e place .... Eze 16:39   1354
it upon an high mountain and e .... Eze 17:22   8524

EMITES See EMIMS.

EMMANUEL (em-man'-uel) See IMMANUEL. A Messianic name.
and they shall call his name E............... Mt 1:23   1694

EMMAUS (em'-ma-us) A village near Jerusalem.
same day to a village called E .... Lk 24:13   1695

EMMOR (em'-mor) See HAMOR. Father of Sychem.
sons of E the father of Sychem .... Acts 7:16   1697

EMPIRE
be published throughout all his e .... Est 1:20   4438

EMPLOY
life) to e them in the siege................ Deut 20:19   935,6440

EMPLOYED
for they were e in that work day 1Chr 9:33   5921
Tikvah were e about this matter............ Ezr 10:15   5975

EMPLOYMENT
sever out men of continual e................... Eze 39:14

EMPTIED

e her pitcher into the trough, and .... Gen 24:20   6168
to pass as they *e* their sacks .... Gen 42:35   7324
e the chest, and took it, and 2Chr 24:11   6168
even thus be he shaken out, and *e*..... Neh 5:13   7386
the brooks of defence shall be *e* .... Is 19:6   1809
The land shall be utterly *e*...................... Is 24:3   1238
hath not been *e* from vessel to .... Jer 48:11   7324
for the emptiers have *e* them out .... Nah 2:2   1238

EMPTIERS

for the *e* have emptied them out, ... Nah 2:2   1238

EMPTINESS

of confusion, and the stones of *e* .... Is 34:11   922

EMPTY

thou hadst sent me away now *e* .... Gen 31:42   7387
and the pit was *e*, there was no .... Gen 37:24   7386
the seven *e* ears blasted with the .... Gen 41:27   7386
when ye go, ye shall not go *e* .... Ex 3:21   7387
and none shall appear before me *e*....... Ex 23:15   7387
And none shall appear before me *e* .... Ex 34:20   7387
command that they *e* the house .... Lev 14:36   6437
thou shalt not let him go away *e* .... Deut 15:13   7387
not appear before the Lord *e* .... Deut 16:16   7387
with *e* pitchers, and lamps within .... Judg 7:16   7385
Lord hath brought me home again *e* ...... Ruth 1:21   7387
Go not *e* unto thy mother in law .... Ruth 3:17   7387
the God of Israel, send it not *e* 1Sa 6:3   7387
because thy seat will be *e* 1Sa 20:18   6485
side, and David's place was *e* 1Sa 20:25   6485
month, that David's place was *e* 1Sa 20:27   6485
the sword of Saul returned not *e* 2Sa 1:22   7387
thy neighbours, even *e* vessels 2Kin 4:3   7385
Thou hast sent widows away *e* .... Job 22:9   7387
out the north over the *e* place .... Job 26:7   8414
they *e* themselves upon the earth .... Eccl 11:3   7324
the Lord maketh the earth *e* .... Is 24:1   1238
but he awaked, and his soul is *e* .... Is 29:8   7385
to make *e* the soul of the hungry, ... Is 32:6   7324
returned with their vessels *e* .... Jer 14:3   7387
shall *e* his vessels, and break .... Jer 48:12   7324
fan her, and shall *e* her land .... Jer 51:2   1238
me, he hath made me an *e* vessel .... Jer 51:34   7385
Then set it *e* upon the coals .... Eze 24:11   7385
Israel is an *e* vine, he bringeth .... Hos 10:1   1238
She is *e*, and void, and waste .... Nah 2:10   950
Shall they therefore *e* their net .... Hab 1:17   7324
pipes *e* the golden oil out of .... Zec 4:12   7324
when he is come, he findeth it *e* .... Mt 12:44   4980
and beat him, and sent him away *e* ..... Mk 12:3   2756
and the rich he hath sent *e* away .... Lk 1:53   2756
beat him, and sent him away *e* .... Lk 20:10   2756
shamefully, and sent him away *e* .... Lk 20:11   2756

EMULATION

to *e* them which are my flesh.................. Rom 11:14   3863

EMULATIONS

witchcraft, hatred, variance, *e* .... Gal 5:20   2205

ENABLED

Jesus our Lord, who hath *e* me 1Ti 1:12   1743

ENAM (e'-nam) A city in Judah.

and En-gannim, Tappuah, and *E* .... Josh 15:34   5879

ENAN (e'-nan) See HAZAR-ENAN. Father of Ahira.

Ahira the son of *E*................................... Num 1:15   5881
shall be Ahira the son of *E*...................... Num 2:29   5881
twelfth day Ahira the son of *E* .... Num 7:78   5881
offering of Ahira the son of *E* .... Num 7:83   5881
Naphtali was Ahira the son of *E* .... Num 10:27   5881

ENCAMP

e before Pi-hahiroth, between .... Ex 14:2   2583
before it shall ye *e* by the sea................ Ex 14:2   2583
it, and shall *e* round about the .... Num 1:50   2583
as they *e*, so shall they set .... Num 2:17   2583
those that *e* by him shall be the .... Num 2:27   2583
But those that *e* before the .... Num 3:38   2583
how we are to *e* in the wilderness.......... Num 10:31   2583
e against the city, and take it................ 2Sa 12:28   2583
e round about my tabernacle.................. Job 19:12   2583
an host should *e* against me .... Ps 27:3   2583
I will *e* about mine house because .... Zec 9:8   2583

ENCAMPED

e in Etham, in the edge of the................ Ex 13:20   2583
they *e* there by the waters .... Ex 15:27   2583
where he *e* at the mount of God .... Ex 18:5   2583
from Elim, and *e* by the Red sea............ Num 33:10   2583
e in the wilderness of Sin .... Num 33:11   2583
of Sin, and *e* in Dophkah .... Num 33:12   2583
from Dophkah, and *e* in Alush .... Num 33:13   2583

e at Rephidim, where was no water .... Num 33:14   2583
and *e* at Hazeroth. .... Num 33:17   2583
mount Shapher, and *e* in Haradah......... Num 33:24   2583
from Makheloth, and *e* at Tahath .... Num 33:26   2583
from Hashmonah, and *e* at Moseroth...... Num 33:30   2583
Bene-jaakan, and *e* at Hor-hagidgad ..... Num 33:32   2583
from Jotbathah, and *e* at Ebronah .... Num 33:34   2583
from Ebronah, and *e* at Ezion-gaber ..... Num 33:35   2583
and *e* in Almon-diblathaim.................... Num 33:46   2583
e in Gilgal, in the east border .... Josh 4:19   2583
children of Israel *e* in Gilgal .... Josh 5:10   2583
e before Gibeon, and made war .... Josh 10:5   2583
e against it, and fought against .... Josh 10:31   2583
they *e* against it, and fought .... Josh 10:34   2583
they *e* against them, and destroyed ...... Judg 6:4   2583
e against Thebez, and took it................ Judg 9:50   2583
gathered together, and *e* in Gilead .... Judg 10:17   2583
together, and *e* in Mizpeh..................... Judg 10:17   2583
the morning, and *e* against Gibeah........ Judg 20:19   2583
up, and *e* against Jabesh-gilead 1Sa 11:1   2583
but the Philistines *e* in Michmash 1Sa 13:16   2583
my lord, are *e* in the open fields............ 2Sa 11:11   2583
the people were *e* against...................... 1Kin 16:15   2583
the people that were *e* heard say 1Kin 16:16   2583
e in the valley of Rephaim..................... 1Chr 11:15   2583
e against the fenced cities, and............. 2Chr 32:1   2583

ENCAMPETH

The angel of the Lord *e* round .... Ps 34:7   2583
bones of him that *e* against thee .... Ps 53:5   2583

ENCAMPING

and overtook them *e* by the sea............ Ex 14:9   2583

ENCHANTER

or an observer of times, or an *e* .... Deut 18:10   5172

ENCHANTERS

to your dreamers, nor to your *e* .... Jer 27:9   6049

ENCHANTMENT

neither shall ye use *e*, nor..................... Lev 19:26   5172
there is no *e* against Jacob.................... Num 23:23   5172
the serpent will bite without *e* .... Eccl 10:11   3908

ENCHANTMENTS

did in like manner with their *e* .... Ex 7:11   3858
of Egypt did so with their *e* .... Ex 7:22   3909
the magicians did so with their *e* .... Ex 8:7   3909
with their *e* to bring forth lice............... Ex 8:18   3909
as at other times, to seek for *e*............. Num 24:1   5172
the fire, and used divination and *e*........ 2Kin 17:17   5172
and observed times, and used *e* 2Kin 21:6   5172
also he observed times, and used *e* 2Chr 33:6   5172
the great abundance of thine *e* .... Is 47:9   2267
Stand now with thine *e*, and with .... Is 47:12   2267

ENCOUNTERED

and of the Stoicks, *e* him .... Acts 17:18   4820

ENCOURAGE

e him: for he shall cause....................... Deut 1:38   2388
and *e* him, and strengthen him.............. Deut 3:28   2388
overthrow it: and *e* thou him 2Sa 11:25   2388
They *e* themselves in an evil.................. Ps 64:5   2388

ENCOURAGED

the men of Israel *e* themselves .... Judg 20:22   2388
but David *e* himself in the Lord............. 1Sa 30:6   2388
that they might be *e* in the law 2Chr 31:4   2388
e them to the service of the 2Chr 35:2   2388
So the carpenter *e* the goldsmith .... Is 41:7   2388

END

The *e* of all flesh is come before............ Gen 6:13   7093
after the *e* of the hundred and .... Gen 8:3   7097
to pass at the *e* of forty days .... Gen 8:6   7093
which is in the *e* of his field .... Gen 23:9   7097
had made an *e* of blessing Jacob........... Gen 27:30   3615
pass at the *e* of two full years .... Gen 41:1   7093
e of the borders of Egypt even to .... Gen 47:21   7097
Egypt even to the other *e* thereof.......... Gen 47:21   7097
made an *e* of commanding his sons .... Gen 49:33   3615
to the *e* thou mayest know that I .... Ex 8:22   4616
pass at the *e* of the four hundred .... Ex 12:41   7093
which is in the *e* of the year .... Ex 23:16   3318
And make one cherub on the one *e*........ Ex 25:19   7098
the other cherub on the other *e* .... Ex 25:19   7098
boards shall reach from *e* to *e* .... Ex 26:28   7097
Moses, when he had made an *e* of......... Ex 31:18   3615
of ingathering at the year's *e* .... Ex 34:22   8622
from the one *e* to the other .... Ex 36:33   7097
One cherub on the *e* on this side .... Ex 37:8   7098
on the other *e* on that side .... Ex 37:8   7098
of your consecration be at an *e*............. Lev 8:33   4390
when he hath made an *e* of.................... Lev 16:20   3615

To the *e* that the children of	Lev 17:5	4616
his sons have made an *e* of	Num 4:15	3615
as he had made an *e* of speaking	Num 16:31	3615
and let my last *e* be like his	Num 23:10	
but his latter *e* shall be that he	Num 24:20	
to do thee good at thy latter *e*	Deut 8:16	
to pass at the *e* of forty days	Deut 9:11	7093
year even unto the *e* of the year	Deut 11:12	319
from the one *e* of the earth even	Deut 13:7	7097
unto the other *e* of the earth	Deut 13:7	7097
At the *e* of three years thou	Deut 14:28	7097
At the *e* of every seven years	Deut 15:1	7093
to the *e* that he should multiply	Deut 17:16	4616
to the *e* that he may prolong his	Deut 17:20	4616
an *e* of speaking unto the people	Deut 20:9	3615
When thou hast made an *e* of	Deut 26:12	3615
from the *e* of the earth, as swift	Deut 28:49	7097
from the one *e* of the earth even	Deut 28:64	7097
At the *e* of every seven years, in	Deut 31:10	7093
when Moses had made an *e* of	Deut 31:24	3615
I will see what their *e* shall be	Deut 32:20	319
would consider their latter *e*	Deut 32:29	
Moses made an *e* of speaking all	Deut 32:45	3615
when Israel had made an *e* of	Josh 8:24	3615
it came to pass at the *e* of three	Josh 9:16	7097
an *e* of slaying them with a very	Josh 10:20	3615
sea, even unto the *e* of Jordan	Josh 15:5	7097
which is at the *e* of the valley	Josh 15:8	7097
was from the *e* of Kirjath-jearim	Josh 18:15	7097
the *e* of the mountain that lieth	Josh 18:16	7097
salt sea at the south *e* of Jordan	Josh 18:19	7097
When they had made an *e* of	Josh 19:49	3615
So they made an *e* of dividing the	Josh 19:51	3615
when he had made an *e* to offer	Judg 3:18	3615
e of the staff that was in his	Judg 6:21	7097
to pass at the *e* of two months	Judg 11:39	7093
when he had made an *e* of speaking	Judg 15:17	3615
behold, the day groweth to an *e*	Judg 19:9	2583
unto the *e* of barley harvest	Ruth 2:23	3615
down at the *e* of the heap of corn	Ruth 3:7	7097
latter *e* than at the beginning	Ruth 3:10	
I begin, I will also make an *e*	1Sa 3:12	3615
going down to the *e* of the city	1Sa 9:27	7097
he had made an *e* of prophesying	1Sa 10:13	3615
e of offering the burnt offering	1Sa 13:10	3615
wherefore he put forth the *e* of	1Sa 14:27	7097
the *e* of the rod that was in mine	1Sa 14:43	7097
when he had made an *e* of speaking	1Sa 18:1	3615
when David had made an *e* of	1Sa 24:16	3615
e of the spear smote him under	2Sa 2:23	
be bitterness in the latter *e*	2Sa 2:26	
an *e* of offering burnt offerings	2Sa 6:18	3615
When thou hast made an *e* of	2Sa 11:19	3615
as he had made an *e* of speaking	2Sa 13:36	3615
every year's *e* that he polled it	2Sa 14:26	7093
Jerusalem at the *e* of nine months	2Sa 24:8	7097
as they had made an *e* of eating	1Kin 1:41	3615
to pass at the *e* of three years	1Kin 2:39	7093
until he had made an *e* of	1Kin 3:1	3615
So Hiram made an *e* of doing all	1Kin 7:40	3615
an *e* of praying all this prayer	1Kin 8:54	3615
to pass at the *e* of twenty years	1Kin 9:10	7097
to pass at the seven years' *e*	2Kin 8:3	7097
was full from the one *e* to another	2Kin 10:21	6310
as soon as he had made an *e* of	2Kin 10:25	3615
at the *e* of three years they took	2Kin 18:10	7097
Jerusalem from one *e* to another	2Kin 21:16	6310
when David had made an *e* of	1Chr 16:2	3615
on the right side of the east *e*	2Chr 4:10	
stood at the east *e* of the altar	2Chr 5:12	
Solomon had made an *e* of praying	2Chr 7:1	3615
to pass at the *e* of twenty years	2Chr 8:1	7093
find them at the *e* of the brook	2Chr 20:16	5490
when they had made an *e* of the	2Chr 20:23	3615
after the *e* of two years, his	2Chr 21:19	7093
chest, until they had made an *e*	2Chr 24:10	3615
came to pass at the *e* of the year	2Chr 24:23	8622
of the first month they made an *e*	2Chr 29:17	3615
they had made an *e* of offering	2Chr 29:29	3615
from one *e* to another with their	Ezr 9:11	6310
they made an *e* with all the men	Ezr 10:17	3615
to the *e* of the house of Eliashib	Neh 3:21	8503
will they make an *e* in a day	Neh 4:2	3615
and what is mine *e*, that I should	Job 6:11	7093
yet thy latter *e* should greatly	Job 8:7	
Shall vain words have an *e*	Job 16:3	7093
it be ye made an *e* of words	Job 18:2	7078
the day and night come to an *e*	Job 26:10	8503
He setteth an *e* to darkness	Job 28:3	7093
that Job may be tried unto the *e*	Job 34:36	5331
e of Job more than his beginning	Job 42:12	

of the wicked come to an *e*	Ps 7:9	1584
are come to a perpetual *e*	Ps 9:6	8552
their words to the *e* of the world	Ps 19:4	7097
forth is from the *e* of the heaven	Ps 19:6	7097
To the *e* that my glory may sing	Ps 30:12	4616
for the *e* of that man is peace	Ps 37:37	319
the *e* of the wicked shall be cut	Ps 37:38	319
LORD, make me to know mine *e*	Ps 39:4	7093
to cease unto the *e* of the earth	Ps 46:9	7097
From the *e* of the earth will I	Ps 61:2	7097
then understood I their *e*	Ps 73:17	319
and thy years shall have no *e*	Ps 102:27	8552
man, and are at their wit's *e*	Ps 107:27	1104
and I shall keep it unto the *e*	Ps 119:33	6118
I have seen an *e* of all	Ps 119:96	8503
statutes alway, even unto the *e*	Ps 119:112	6118
But her *e* is bitter as wormwood,	Prov 5:4	319
but the *e* thereof are the ways of	Prov 14:12	319
the *e* of that mirth is heaviness	Prov 14:13	319
but the *e* thereof are the ways of	Prov 16:25	319
mayest be wise in thy latter *e*	Prov 19:20	
but the *e* thereof shall not be	Prov 20:21	319
For surely there is an *e*	Prov 23:18	319
not what to do in the *e* thereof	Prov 25:8	319
from the beginning to the *e*	Eccl 3:11	5490
yet is there no *e* of all his	Eccl 4:8	7093
There is no *e* of all the people,	Eccl 4:16	7093
for that is the *e* of all men	Eccl 7:2	5490
Better is the *e* of a thing than	Eccl 7:8	319
to the *e* that man should find	Eccl 7:14	1700
the *e* of his talk is mischievous	Eccl 10:13	319
making many books there is no *e*	Eccl 12:12	7093
is there any *e* of their treasures	Is 2:7	7097
is there any *e* of their chariots	Is 2:7	7097
unto them from the *e* of the earth	Is 5:26	7097
at the *e* of the conduit of the	Is 7:3	7097
and peace there shall be no *e*	Is 9:7	7093
from the *e* of heaven, even the	Is 13:5	7093
for the extortioner is at an *e*	Is 16:4	657
after the *e* of seventy years	Is 23:15	7093
pass after the *e* of seventy years	Is 23:17	7093
make an *e* to deal treacherously	Is 33:1	5239
night wilt thou make an *e* of me	Is 38:12	7999
night wilt thou make an *e* of me	Is 38:13	7999
and know the latter *e* of them	Is 41:22	
praise from the *e* of the earth	Is 42:10	7097
confounded world without *e*	Is 45:17	5704,5769,5703
Declaring the *e* from the	Is 46:10	319
didst remember the latter *e* of it	Is 47:7	
it even to the *e* of the earth	Is 48:20	7097
salvation unto the *e* of the earth	Is 49:6	7097
unto the *e* of the world, Say ye	Is 62:11	7097
unto the *e* of the eleventh year	Jer 1:3	8537
will he keep it to the *e*	Jer 3:5	5331
yet will I not make a full *e*	Jer 4:27	3615
but make not a full *e*	Jer 5:10	3615
I will not make a full *e* with you	Jer 5:18	3615
will ye do in the *e* thereof	Jer 5:31	319
said, He shall not see our last *e*	Jer 12:4	
e of the land even to the other	Jer 12:12	7097
even to the other *e* of the land	Jer 12:12	7097
days, and at his *e* shall be a fool	Jer 17:11	319
one *e* of the earth even unto the	Jer 25:33	7097
unto the other *e* of the earth	Jer 25:33	7097
when Jeremiah had made an *e* of	Jer 26:8	3615
evil, to give you an expected *e*	Jer 29:11	319
though I make a full *e* of all	Jer 30:11	3615
will I not make a full *e* of thee	Jer 30:11	3615
And there is hope in thine *e*	Jer 31:17	319
At the *e* of seven years let ye go	Jer 34:14	7093
that when Jeremiah had made an *e*	Jer 43:1	3615
until there be an *e* of them	Jer 44:27	3615
for I will make a full *e* of all	Jer 46:28	3615
I will not make a full *e* of thee	Jer 46:28	3615
thine *e* is come, and the measure	Jer 51:13	7093
that his city is taken at one *e*	Jer 51:31	7097
made an *e* of reading this book	Jer 51:63	3615
she remembereth not her last *e*	Lam 1:9	
our *e* is near, our days are	Lam 4:18	7093
for our *e* is come	Lam 4:18	7093
to pass at the *e* of seven days	Eze 3:16	7097
An *e*, the *e* is come upon thee	Eze 7:2	7093
Now is the *e* come upon thee, and I	Eze 7:3	7093
An *e* is come, the *e* is come	Eze 7:6	7093
wilt thou make a full *e* of the	Eze 11:13	3615
neither did I make an *e* of them	Eze 20:17	3615
to the *e* that they might know	Eze 20:26	4616
when iniquity shall have an *e*	Eze 21:25	7093
their iniquity shall have an *e*	Eze 21:29	7093
At the *e* of forty years will I	Eze 29:13	7093
To the *e* that none of all the	Eze 31:14	4616

time that their iniquity had an *e*	Eze 35:5	7093
after the *e* of seven months shall	Eze 39:14	7097
the separate place at the *e*	Eze 41:12	6285
Now when he had made an *e* of	Eze 42:15	3615
hast made an *e* of cleansing it	Eze 43:23	3615
From the north *e* to the coast of	Eze 48:1	7097
that at the *e* thereof they might	Dan 1:5	7117
at the *e* of ten days their	Dan 1:15	7117
Now at the *e* of the days that the	Dan 1:18	7117
thereof to the *e* of all the earth	Dan 4:11	5491
dominion to the *e* of the earth	Dan 4:22	5491
At the *e* of twelve months he	Dan 4:29	7118
And at the *e* of the days I	Dan 4:34	7118
dominion shall be even unto the *e*	Dan 6:26	5491
and to destroy it unto the *e*	Dan 7:26	5491
Hitherto is the *e* of the matter	Dan 7:28	5491
time of the *e* shall be the vision	Dan 8:17	7093
in the last of the indignation	Dan 8:19	
the time appointed the *e* shall be	Dan 8:19	7093
and to make an *e* of sins, and to	Dan 9:24	2856
the *e* thereof shall be with a	Dan 9:26	7093
unto the *e* of the war desolations	Dan 9:26	7093
in the *e* of years they shall join	Dan 11:6	7093
for yet the *e* shall be at the	Dan 11:27	7093
white, even to the time of the *e*	Dan 11:35	7093
at the time of the *e* shall the	Dan 11:40	7093
yet he shall come to his *e*	Dan 11:45	7093
book, even to the time of the *e*	Dan 12:4	7093
it be to the *e* of these wonders	Dan 12:6	7093
shall be the *e* of these things	Dan 12:8	319
and sealed till the time of the *e*	Dan 12:9	7093
But go thou thy way till the *e* be	Dan 12:13	7093
in thy lot at the *e* of the days	Dan 12:13	7093
the great houses shall have an *e*	Amos 3:15	5486
to what is it for you	Amos 5:18	
that when they had made an *e* of	Amos 7:2	3615
The *e* is come upon my people of	Amos 8:2	7093
the *e* thereof as a bitter day	Amos 8:10	319
to the *e* that every one of the	Obad 9	4616
an utter *e* of the place thereof	Nah 1:8	3615
he will make an utter *e*	Nah 1:9	3615
for there is none *e* of the store	Nah 2:9	7097
there is none *e* of their corpses	Nah 3:3	7097
but at the *e* it shall speak, and	Hab 2:3	7093
endureth to the *e* shall be saved	Mt 10:22	5056
when Jesus had made an *e* of	Mt 11:1	5055
the harvest is the *e* of the world	Mt 13:39	4930
it be in the *e* of this world	Mt 13:40	4930
shall it be at the *e* of the world	Mt 13:49	4930
coming, and of the *e* of the world	Mt 24:3	4930
to pass, but the *e* is not yet	Mt 24:6	5056
he that shall endure unto the *e*	Mt 24:13	5056
and then shall the *e* come	Mt 24:14	5056
from one *e* of heaven to the other	Mt 24:31	206
with the servants, to see the *e*	Mt 26:58	5056
In the *e* of the sabbath, as it	Mt 28:1	3796
even unto the *e* of the world	Mt 28:20	4930
he cannot stand, but hath an *e*	Mk 3:26	5056
but the *e* shall not be yet	Mk 13:7	5056
he that shall endure unto the *e*	Mk 13:13	5056
his kingdom there shall be no *e*	Lk 1:33	5056
a parable unto them to this *e*	Lk 18:1	
but the *e* is not by and by	Lk 21:9	5056
things concerning me have an *e*	Lk 22:37	5056
world, he loved them unto the *e*	Jn 13:1	5056
To this *e* was I born, and for this	Jn 18:37	
to the *e* they might not live	Acts 7:19	1519
to the *e* ye may be established	Rom 1:11	1519
to the *e* the promise might be	Rom 4:16	1519
for the *e* of those things is	Rom 6:21	5056
and the *e* everlasting life	Rom 6:22	5056
For Christ is the *e* of the law	Rom 10:4	5056
For to this *e* Christ both died,	Rom 14:9	
shall also confirm you unto the *e*	1Cor 1:8	5056
Then cometh the *e*, when he shall	1Cor 15:24	5056
shall acknowledge even to the *e*	2Cor 1:13	5056
For to this *e* also did I write,	2Cor 2:9	
the *e* of that which is abolished	2Cor 3:13	5056
whose *e* shall be according to	2Cor 11:15	5056
all ages, world without *e*	Eph 3:21	165,3588,165
Whose *e* is destruction, whose God	Phil 3:19	5056
To the *e* he may stablish your	1Th 3:13	1519
Now the *e* of the commandment is	1Ti 1:5	5056
of the hope firm unto the *e*	Heb 3:6	5056
confidence stedfast unto the *e*	Heb 3:14	5056
whose *e* is to be burned	Heb 6:8	5056
full assurance of hope unto the *e*	Heb 6:11	5056
is to them an *e* of all strife	Heb 6:16	4009
beginning of days, nor *e* of life	Heb 7:3	5056
but now once in the *e* of the	Heb 9:26	4930
considering the *e* of their	Heb 13:7	1545

and have seen the *e* of the Lord	Jas 5:11	5056
Receiving the *e* of your faith	1Pet 1:9	5056
hope to the *e* for the grace that	1Pet 1:13	5049
But the *e* of all things is at	1Pet 4:7	5056
what shall the *e* be of them that	1Pet 4:17	5056
the latter *e* is worse with them	2Pet 2:20	2078
and keepeth my works unto the *e*	Rev 2:26	5056
and Omega, the beginning and the *e*	Rev 21:6	5056
and Omega, the beginning and the *e*	Rev 22:13	5056

ENDAMAGE

so thou shalt *e* the revenue of	Ezr 4:13	5142

ENDANGER

ye make me *e* my head to the king	Dan 1:10	2325

ENDANGERED

cleaveth wood shall be *e* thereby	Eccl 10:9	5533

ENDEAVOUR

Moreover I will *e* that ye may be	2Pet 1:15	4704

ENDEAVOURED

immediately we *e* to go into	Acts 16:10	2212
e the more abundantly to see your	1Th 2:17	4704

ENDEAVOURING

E to keep the unity of the Spirit	Eph 4:3	4704

ENDEAVOURS

to the wickedness of their *e*	Ps 28:4	4611

ENDED

on the seventh day God *e* his work	Gen 2:2	3615
was in the land of Egypt, were *e*	Gen 41:53	3615
When that year was *e*, they came	Gen 47:18	8552
of this song, until they were *e*	Deut 31:30	8552
and mourning for Moses were *e*	Deut 34:8	8552
until they have *e* all my harvest	Ruth 2:21	8552
and so they *e* the matter	2Sa 20:18	8552
So was *e* all the work that king	1Kin 7:51	7999
help them, till the work was *e*	2Chr 29:34	3615
The words of Job are *e*	Job 31:40	8552
of David the son of Jesse are *e*	Ps 72:20	3615
days of thy mourning shall be *e*	Is 60:20	7999
harvest is past, the summer is *e*	Jer 8:20	3615
till thou hast *e* the days of thy	Eze 4:8	3615
when Jesus had *e* these sayings	Mt 7:28	4931
and when they were *e*, he afterward	Lk 4:2	4931
devil had *e* all the temptation	Lk 4:13	4931
Now when he had *e* all his sayings	Lk 7:1	4137
And supper being *e*, the devil	Jn 13:2	1096
After these things were *e*	Acts 19:21	4137
when the seven days were almost *e*	Acts 21:27	4931

ENDETH

the noise of them that rejoice *e*	Is 24:8	2308

ENDING

and Omega, the beginning and the *e*	Rev 1:8	5056

ENDLESS

e genealogies, which minister	1Ti 1:4	562
but after the power of an *e* life	Heb 7:16	179

EN-DOR (en'-dor) *A village near Mt. Tabor.*

towns, and the inhabitants of *E*	Josh 17:11	5874
that hath a familiar spirit at *E*	1Sa 28:7	5874
Which perished at *E*: they became	Ps 83:10	5874

ENDOW

he shall surely *e* her to be his	Ex 22:16	4117

ENDS

in the two *e* of the mercy seat	Ex 25:18	7098
cherubims on the two *e* thereof	Ex 25:19	7098
two chains of pure gold at the *e*	Ex 28:14	4020
e of wreathen work of pure gold	Ex 28:22	1383
on the two *e* of the breastplate	Ex 28:23	7098
are on the *e* of the breastplate	Ex 28:24	7098
the other two *e* of the two	Ex 28:25	7098
two *e* of the breastplate in the	Ex 28:26	7098
on the two *e* of the mercy seat	Ex 37:7	7098
cherubims on the two *e* thereof	Ex 37:8	7099
the four *e* of the grate of brass	Ex 38:5	7099
the breastplate chains at the *e*	Ex 39:15	1383
in the two *e* of the breastplate	Ex 39:16	7098
rings on the *e* of the breastplate	Ex 39:17	7098
the two *e* of the two wreathen	Ex 39:18	7098
on the two *e* of the breastplate	Ex 39:19	7098
together to the *e* of the earth	Deut 33:17	657
shall judge the *e* of the earth	1Sa 2:10	657
that the *e* of the staves were	1Kin 8:8	7218
that the *e* of the staves were	2Chr 5:9	7218
he looketh to the *e* of the earth	Job 28:24	7098
lightning unto the *e* of the earth	Job 37:3	3671
take hold of the *e* of the earth	Job 38:13	3671
and his circuit unto the *e* of it	Ps 19:6	7098

All the *e* of the world shall	Ps 22:27	657
praise unto the *e* of the earth	Ps 48:10	7099
in Jacob unto the *e* of the earth	Ps 59:13	657
of all the *e* of the earth	Ps 65:5	7099
all the *e* of the earth shall fear	Ps 67:7	657
the river unto the *e* of the earth	Ps 72:8	657
all the *e* of the earth have seen	Ps 98:3	657
to ascend from the *e* of the earth	Ps 135:7	7097
a fool are in the *e* of the earth	Prov 17:24	7097
all the *e* of the earth	Prov 30:4	657
far unto all the *e* of the earth	Is 26:15	7097
the Creator of the *e* of the earth	Is 40:28	7098
the *e* of the earth were afraid,	Is 41:5	7098
taken from the *e* of the earth	Is 41:9	7098
daughters from the *e* of the earth	Is 43:6	7097
ye saved, all the *e* of the earth	Is 45:22	657
all the *e* of the earth shall see	Is 52:10	657
to ascend from the *e* of the earth	Jer 10:13	7097
unto thee from the *e* of the earth	Jer 16:19	657
come even to the *e* of the earth	Jer 25:31	7097
to ascend from the *e* of the earth	Jer 51:16	7097
fire devoureth both the *e* of it	Eze 15:4	7098
be great unto the *e* of the earth	Mic 5:4	657
river even to the *e* of the earth	Zec 9:10	657
salvation unto the *e* of the earth	Acts 13:47	2078
words unto the *e* of the world	Rom 10:18	4009
upon whom the *e* of the world are	1Cor 10:11	5056

ENDUED

God hath *e* me with a good dowry	Gen 30:20	2064
e with prudence and understanding,	2Chr 2:12	3045
e with understanding, of Huram my	2Chr 2:13	3045
until ye be *e* with power from on	Lk 24:49	*1746*
e with knowledge among you	Jas 3:13	*1990*

ENDURE

me and the children be able to *e*	Gen 33:14	7272
so, then thou shalt be able to *e*	Ex 18:23	5975
For how can I *e* to see the evil	Est 8:6	3201
or how can I *e* to see the	Est 8:6	3201
hold it fast, but it shall not *e*	Job 8:15	6965
of his highness I could not *e*	Job 31:23	
But the Lᴏʀᴅ shall *e* for ever	Ps 9:7	3427
weeping may *e* for a night	Ps 30:5	3885
thee as long as the sun and moon *e*	Ps 72:5	6440
His name shall *e* for ever	Ps 72:17	1961
also will I make to *e* for ever	Ps 89:29	
His seed shall *e* for ever	Ps 89:36	1961
thou, O Lᴏʀᴅ, shalt *e* for ever	Ps 102:12	3427
shall perish, but thou shalt *e*	Ps 102:26	5975
of the Lᴏʀᴅ shall *e* for ever	Ps 104:31	1961
doth the crown *e* to every	Prov 27:24	
Can thine heart *e*, or can thine	Eze 22:14	5975
But he that shall *e* unto the end	Mt 24:13	5278
and so *e* but for a time	Mk 4:17	2076
but he that shall *e* unto the end	Mk 13:13	5278
and tribulations that ye *e*	2Th 1:4	430
Thou therefore *e* hardness	2Ti 2:3	2553
Therefore I *e* all things for the	2Ti 2:10	5278
they will not *e* sound doctrine	2Ti 4:3	430
e afflictions, do the work of an	2Ti 4:5	2553
If ye *e* chastening, God dealeth	Heb 12:7	5278
(For they could not *e* that which	Heb 12:20	5342
we count them happy which *e*	Jas 5:11	5278
for conscience toward God *e* grief	1Pet 2:19	5297

ENDURED

their time should have *e* for ever	Ps 81:15	1961
e with much longsuffering the	Rom 9:22	5342
what persecutions I *e*	2Ti 3:11	5297
And so, after he had patiently *e*	Heb 6:15	3114
ye *e* a great fight of afflictions	Heb 10:32	5278
for he *e*, as seeing him who is	Heb 11:27	2594
was set before him *e* the cross	Heb 12:2	5278
For consider him that *e* such	Heb 12:3	5278

ENDURETH

for his mercy *e* for ever	1Chr 16:34	
because his mercy *e* for ever	1Chr 16:41	
for his mercy *e* for ever	2Chr 5:13	
for his mercy *e* for ever	2Chr 7:3	
because his mercy *e* for ever	2Chr 7:6	
for his mercy *e* for ever	2Chr 20:21	
for his mercy *e* for ever toward	Ezr 3:11	
For his anger *e* but a moment	Ps 30:5	
the goodness of God *e* continually	Ps 52:1	
of peace so long as the moon *e*	Ps 72:7	1097
his truth *e* to all generations	Ps 100:5	
for his mercy *e* for ever	Ps 106:1	
for his mercy *e* for ever	Ps 107:1	
and his righteousness *e* for ever	Ps 111:3	5975
his praise *e* for ever	Ps 111:10	5975
and his righteousness *e* for ever	Ps 112:3	5975

his righteousness *e* for ever	Ps 112:9	5975
the truth of the Lᴏʀᴅ *e* for ever	Ps 117:2	
because his mercy *e* for ever	Ps 118:1	
say, that his mercy *e* for ever	Ps 118:2	
say, that his mercy *e* for ever	Ps 118:3	
say, that his mercy *e* for ever	Ps 118:4	
for his mercy *e* for ever	Ps 118:29	
righteous judgments *e* for ever	Ps 119:160	
Thy name, O Lᴏʀᴅ, *e* for ever	Ps 135:13	
for his mercy *e* for ever	Ps 136:1	
for his mercy *e* for ever	Ps 136:2	
for his mercy *e* for ever	Ps 136:3	
for his mercy *e* for ever	Ps 136:4	
for his mercy *e* for ever	Ps 136:5	
for his mercy *e* for ever	Ps 136:6	
for his mercy *e* for ever	Ps 136:7	
for his mercy *e* for ever	Ps 136:8	
for his mercy *e* for ever	Ps 136:9	
for his mercy *e* for ever	Ps 136:10	
for his mercy *e* for ever	Ps 136:11	
for his mercy *e* for ever	Ps 136:12	
for his mercy *e* for ever	Ps 136:13	
for his mercy *e* for ever	Ps 136:14	
for his mercy *e* for ever	Ps 136:15	
for his mercy *e* for ever	Ps 136:16	
for his mercy *e* for ever	Ps 136:17	
for his mercy *e* for ever	Ps 136:18	
for his mercy *e* for ever	Ps 136:19	
for his mercy *e* for ever	Ps 136:20	
for his mercy *e* for ever	Ps 136:21	
for his mercy *e* for ever	Ps 136:22	
for his mercy *e* for ever	Ps 136:23	
for his mercy *e* for ever	Ps 136:24	
for his mercy *e* for ever	Ps 136:25	
for his mercy *e* for ever	Ps 136:26	
thy mercy, O Lᴏʀᴅ, *e* for ever	Ps 138:8	
thy dominion *e* throughout all	Ps 145:13	
for his mercy *e* for ever	Jer 33:11	
but he that *e* to the end shall be	Mt 10:22	5278
which *e* unto everlasting life	Jn 6:27	3306
hopeth all things, *e* all things	1Cor 13:7	5278
is the man that *e* temptation	Jas 1:12	5278
the word of the Lord *e* for ever	1Pet 1:25	3306

ENDURING

of the Lᴏʀᴅ is clean, *e* for ever	Ps 19:9	5975
which is effectual in the *e* of	2Cor 1:6	5281
heaven a better and an *e* substance	Heb 10:34	3306

EN-EGLAIM (en-eg'-la-im) A place near the Salt Sea.

upon it from En-gedi even unto *E*	Eze 47:10	5882

ENEMIES

delivered thine *e* into thy hand	Gen 14:20	6862
shall possess the gate of his *e*	Gen 22:17	341
shall be in the neck of thine *e*	Gen 49:8	341
war, they join also unto our *e*	Ex 1:10	8130
I will be an enemy unto thine *e*	Ex 23:22	341
I will make all thine *e* turn	Ex 23:27	341
unto their shame among their *e*	Ex 32:25	6965
And ye shall chase your *e*, and they	Lev 26:7	341
your *e* shall fall before you by	Lev 26:8	341
in vain, for your *e* shall eat it	Lev 26:16	341
ye shall be slain before your *e*	Lev 26:17	341
your *e* which dwell therein shall	Lev 26:32	341
hearts in the lands of their *e*	Lev 26:36	341
no power to stand before your *e*	Lev 26:37	341
land of your *e* shall eat you up	Lev 26:38	341
them into the land of their *e*	Lev 26:41	341
they be in the land of their *e*	Lev 26:44	341
and ye shall be saved from your *e*	Num 10:9	341
Lᴏʀᴅ, and let thine *e* be scattered	Num 10:35	341
ye be not smitten before your *e*	Num 14:42	341
I took thee to curse mine *e*	Num 23:11	341
he shall eat up the nations his *e*	Num 24:8	6862
I called them to curse mine *e*	Num 24:10	341
shall be a possession for his *e*	Num 24:18	341
driven out his *e* from before him	Num 32:21	341
lest ye be smitten before your *e*	Deut 1:42	341
out all thine *e* from before thee	Deut 6:19	341
rest from all your *e* round about	Deut 12:10	341
out to battle against thine *e*	Deut 20:1	341
day unto battle against your *e*	Deut 20:3	341
to fight for you against your *e*	Deut 20:4	341
shalt eat the spoil of thine *e*	Deut 20:14	341
forth to war against thine *e*	Deut 21:10	341
host goeth forth against thine *e*	Deut 23:9	341
and to give up thine *e* before thee	Deut 23:14	341
rest from all thine *e* round about	Deut 25:19	341
The Lᴏʀᴅ shall cause thine *e* that	Deut 28:7	341
thee to be smitten before thine *e*	Deut 28:25	341
sheep shall be given unto thine *e*	Deut 28:31	341

E

e in the land which thou knowest .... Jer 17:4 — 341
fall by the sword before their *e*.................. Jer 19:7 — 341
and straitness, wherewith their *e* .... Jer 19:9 — 341
fall by the sword of their *e*...................... Jer 20:4 — 341
I give into the hand of their *e*................. Jer 20:5 — 341
and into the hand of their *e* .... Jer 21:7 — 341
them into the hand of their *e*.................. Jer 34:20 — 341
I give into the hand of their *e* .... Jer 34:21 — 341
of Egypt into the hand of his *e*............... Jer 44:30 — 341
the going down of Horonaim the *e*........ Jer 48:5 — 6862
to be dismayed before their *e* .... Jer 49:37 — 341
with her, they are become her *e* .... Lam 1:2 — 341
are the chief, her *e* prosper................... Lam 1:5 — 341
all mine *e* have heard of my .... Lam 1:21 — 341
All thine *e* have opened their .... Lam 2:16 — 341
All our *e* have opened their .... Lam 3:46 — 341
Mine *e* chased me sore, like a.............. Lam 3:52 — 341
them into the hand of their *e*................. Eze 39:23 — 6862
interpretation thereof to thine *e*........... Dan 4:19 — 6146
go into captivity before their *e*.............. Amos 9:4 — 341
thee from the hand of thine *e* .... Mic 4:10 — 341
all thine *e* shall be cut off..................... Mic 5:9 — 341
a man's *e* are the men of his own .... Mic 7:6 — 341
and he reserveth wrath for his *e*........... Nah 1:2 — 341
and darkness shall pursue his *e* .... Nah 1:8 — 341
be set wide open unto thine *e* .... Nah 3:13 — 341
which tread down their *e* in the............. Zec 10:5 — 341
But I say unto you, Love your *e* .... Mt 5:44 — 2190
till I make thine *e* thy footstool......... Mt 22:44 — 2190
till I make thine *e* thy footstool.......... Mk 12:36 — 2190
we should be saved from our *e*.............. Lk 1:71 — 2190
out of the hand of our *e* might .... Lk 1:74 — 2190
unto you which hear, Love your *e* ...... Lk 6:27 — 2190
But love ye your *e*, and do good, ... Lk 6:35 — 2190
But those mine *e*, which would not ...... Lk 19:27 — 2190
that thine *e* shall cast a trench .... Lk 19:43 — 2190
Till I make thine *e* thy footstool .... Lk 20:43 — 2190
For if, when we were *e*, we were .... Rom 5:10 — 2190
they are *e* for your sakes....................... Rom 11:28 — 2190
he hath put all *e* under his feet............. 1Cor 15:25 — 2190
that they are the *e* of the cross .... Phil 3:18 — 2190
e in your mind by wicked works, ... Col 1:21 — 2190
I make thine *e* thy footstool.................. Heb 1:13 — 2190
till his *e* be made his footstool .... Heb 10:13 — 2190
their mouth, and devoureth their *e*....... Rev 11:5 — 2190
and their *e* beheld them........................... Rev 11:12 — 2190

ENEMIES'

desolate, and ye be in your *e* land .... Lev 26:34 — 341
in their iniquity in your *e* lands .... Lev 26:39 — 341
them out of their *e* lands .... Eze 39:27 — 341

ENEMY

LORD, hath dashed in pieces the *e* .... Ex 15:6 — 341
The *e* said, I will pursue, I will............... Ex 15:9 — 341
then I will be an *e* unto thine .... Ex 23:22 — 340
delivered into the hand of the *e* .... Lev 26:25 — 341
against the *e* that oppresseth you .... Num 10:9 — 341
that he die, and was not his *e* .... Num 35:23 — 341
wherewith thine *e* shall distress .... Deut 28:57 — 341
that I feared the wrath of the *e* .... Deut 32:27 — 341
beginning of revenges upon the *e* .... Deut 32:42 — 341
thrust out the *e* from before thee.......... Deut 33:27 — 341
Samson our *e* into our hand.................... Judg 16:23 — 341
delivered into our hand our *e*................ Judg 16:24 — 341
shalt see an *e* in my habitation............. 1Sa 2:32 — 6862
Saul became David's *e* continually .... 1Sa 18:29 — 341
me so, and sent away mine *e*................... 1Sa 19:17 — 341
deliver thine *e* into thine hand .... 1Sa 24:4 — 341
For if a man find his *e*, will he............... 1Sa 24:19 — 341
thine *e* into thine hand this day .... 1Sa 26:8 — 341
from thee, and is become thine *e* .... 1Sa 28:16 — 6145
the son of Saul thine *e*, which .... 2Sa 4:8 — 341
He delivered me from my strong *e*........ 2Sa 22:18 — 341
be smitten down before the *e* .... 1Kin 8:33 — 341
if their *e* besiege them in the .... 1Kin 8:37 — 341
go out to battle against their *e* .... 1Kin 8:44 — 341
them, and deliver them to the *e* .... 1Kin 8:46 — 341
captives unto the land of the *e*.............. 1Kin 8:46 — 341
Hast thou found me, O mine *e* .... 1Kin 21:20 — 341
be put to the worse before the *e*............ 2Chr 6:24 — 341
shall make thee fall before the *e*........... 2Chr 25:8 — 341
to help the king against the *e* .... 2Chr 26:13 — 341
help us against the *e* in the way .... Ezr 8:22 — 341
us from the hand of the *e* .... Ezr 8:31 — 341
the Agagite, the Jews' *e*......................... Est 3:10 — 6887
tongue, although the *e* could not........... Est 7:4 — 6862
and *e* is this wicked Haman.................... Est 7:6 — 341
the Jews' *e* unto Esther the queen .... Est 8:1 — 6887
the *e* of the Jews, slew they .... Est 9:10 — 6887
the *e* of all the Jews, had .... Est 9:24 — 6887
face, and holdest me for thine *e* .... Job 13:24 — 341

mine *e* sharpeneth his eyes upon .... Job 16:9 — 6862
Let mine *e* be as the wicked, and .... Job 27:7 — 341
me, he counteth me for his *e* .... Job 33:10 — 341
him that without cause is mine *e*........... Ps 7:4 — 6887
Let the *e* persecute my soul, and .... Ps 7:5 — 341
that thou mightest still the *e*................. Ps 8:2 — 341
O thou *e*, destructions are come .... Ps 9:6 — 341
shall mine *e* be exalted over me .... Ps 13:2 — 341
Lest mine *e* say, I have prevailed........... Ps 13:4 — 341
He delivered me from my strong *e*......... Ps 18:17 — 341
shut me up into the hand of the *e* .... Ps 31:8 — 341
because mine *e* doth not triumph .... Ps 41:11 — 341
of the oppression of the *e*...................... Ps 42:9 — 341
of the oppression of the *e*...................... Ps 43:2 — 341
makest us to turn back from the *e* .... Ps 44:10 — 6862
by reason of the *e* and avenger............. Ps 44:16 — 341
Because of the voice of the *e* .... Ps 55:3 — 341
For it was not an *e* that.......................... Ps 55:12 — 341
me, and a strong tower from the *e* .... Ps 61:3 — 341
my life from fear of the *e* .... Ps 64:1 — 341
even all that the *e* hath done................. Ps 74:3 — 341
shall the *e* blaspheme thy name .... Ps 74:10 — 341
that the *e* hath reproached, O............... Ps 74:18 — 341
when he delivered them from the *e* .... Ps 78:42 — 6862
The *e* shall not exact upon him............... Ps 89:22 — 341
them from the hand of the *e*.................. Ps 106:10 — 341
redeemed from the hand of the *e* .... Ps 107:2 — 6862
For the *e* hath persecuted my soul .... Ps 143:3 — 341
Rejoice not when thine *e* falleth............ Prov 24:17 — 341
If thine *e* be hungry, give him .... Prov 25:21 — 8130
the kisses of an *e* are deceitful .... Prov 27:6 — 8130
When the *e* shall come in like a............. Is 59:19 — 6862
he was turned to be their *e* .... Is 63:10 — 341
for the sword of the *e* and fear is .... Jer 6:25 — 341
verily I will cause the *e* to...................... Jer 15:11 — 341
as with an east wind before the *e*.......... Jer 18:17 — 341
thee with the wound of an *e* .... Jer 30:14 — 341
come again from the land of the *e* .... Jer 31:16 — 341
king of Babylon, his *e*, and that .... Jer 44:30 — 341
gone into captivity before the *e*............. Lam 1:5 — 6862
fell into the hand of the *e*...................... Lam 1:7 — 6862
for the *e* hath magnified himself .... Lam 1:9 — 341
desolate, because the *e* prevailed .... Lam 1:16 — 341
his right hand from before the *e* .... Lam 2:3 — 341
He hath bent his bow like an *e* .... Lam 2:4 — 341
The Lord was as an *e*............................. Lam 2:5 — 341
of the *e* the walls of her palaces............ Lam 2:7 — 341
thine *e* to rejoice over thee .... Lam 2:17 — 341
brought up hath mine *e* consumed......... Lam 2:22 — 341
the *e* should have entered into .... Lam 4:12 — 341
Because the *e* hath said against .... Eze 36:2 — 341
the *e* shall pursue him .... Hos 8:3 — 341
my people is risen up as an *e* .... Mic 2:8 — 341
Rejoice not against me, O mine *e* .... Mic 7:8 — 341
she that is mine *e* shall see it .... Mic 7:10 — 341
seek strength because of the *e*............... Nah 3:11 — 341
he hath cast out thine *e* .... Zeph 3:15 — 341
thy neighbour, and hate thine *e* .... Mt 5:43 — 2190
his *e* came and sowed tares among.... Mt 13:25 — 2190
unto them, An *e* hath done this .... Mt 13:28 — 2190
The *e* that sowed them is the .... Mt 13:39 — 2190
and over all the power of the *e* .... Lk 10:19 — 2190
thou *e* of all righteousness, wilt .... Acts 13:10 — 2190
Therefore if thine *e* hunger .... Rom 12:20 — 2190
The last *e* that shall be .... 1Cor 15:26 — 2190
Am I therefore become your *e*............... Gal 4:16 — 2190
Yet count him not as an *e*...................... 2Th 3:15 — 2190
of the world is the *e* of God .... Jas 4:4 — 2190

ENEMY'S

If thou meet thine *e* ox or his .... Ex 23:4 — 341
Or, Deliver me from the *e* hand .... Job 6:23 — 6862
and his glory into the *e* hand .... Ps 78:61 — 6862

ENFLAMING

E yourselves with idols under .... Is 57:5 — 2552

ENGAGED

for who is this that *e* his heart................ Jer 30:21 — 6148

EN-GANNIM (en-gan'-nim)
1. A city in Judah.
and *E*, Tappuah, and Enam..................... Josh 15:34 — 5873
2. A city in Issachar.
And Remeth, and *E*, and En-haddah, ... Josh 19:21 — 5873
her suburbs, *E* with her suburbs .... Josh 21:29 — 5873

EN-GEDI (en-ghe'-di) See HAZAZON-TAMAR. *A town on the Salt Sea.*
and the city of Salt, and *E*...................... Josh 15:62 — 5872
and dwelt in strong holds at *E* .... 1Sa 23:29 — 5872
David is in the wilderness of *E*............... 1Sa 24:1 — 5872
be in Hazazon-tamar, which is *E* .... 2Chr 20:2 — 5872

of camphire in the vineyards of *E* .... Song 1:14   5872
it from *E* even unto En-eglaim .... Eze 47:10   5872

ENGINES
And he made in Jerusalem *e* 2Chr 26:15   2810
he shall set *e* of war against thy .... Eze 26:9   4239

ENGRAFTED
receive with meekness the *e* word .... Jas 1:21   *1721*

ENGRAVE
shalt thou *e* the two stones with .... Ex 28:11   6605
I will *e* the graving thereof, ... Zec 3:9   6605

ENGRAVEN
e in stones, was glorious, so 2Cor 3:7   *1795*

ENGRAVER
With the work of an *e* in stone .... Ex 28:11   2796
work all manner of work, of the *e* .... Ex 35:35   2796
of the tribe of Dan, an *e* .... Ex 38:23   2796

ENGRAVINGS
like the *e* of a signet, shalt .... Ex 28:11   6603
names, like the *e* of a signet .... Ex 28:21   6603
like the *e* of a signet, HOLINESS .... Ex 28:36   6603
like the *e* of a signet, every one .... Ex 39:14   6603
like to the *e* of a signet .... Ex 39:30   6603

EN-HADDAH (en-had'-dah) *A city in Issachar.*
And Remeth, and En-gannim, and *E* .... Josh 19:21   5876

EN-HAKKORE (en-hak'-ko-re) *A spring.*
he called the name thereof *E* .... Judg 15:19   5875

EN-HAZOR (en-ha'-zor) *A city in Naphtali.*
And Kedesh, and Edrei, and *E* .... Josh 19:37   5877

ENJOIN
e thee that which is convenient .... Philem 8   *2004*

ENJOINED
and Esther the queen had *e* them .... Est 9:31   6965
Who hath *e* him his way .... Job 36:23   6485
which God hath *e* unto you .... Heb 9:20   *1781*

ENJOY
shall the land *e* her sabbaths .... Lev 26:34   7521
the land rest, and *e* her sabbaths .... Lev 26:34   7521
shall *e* her sabbaths, while she .... Lev 26:43   7521
e every man the inheritance of .... Num 36:8   3423
but thou shalt not *e* them .... Deut 28:41   1961
e it, which Moses the LORD's .... Josh 1:15   3423
with mirth, therefore *e* pleasure .... Eccl 2:1   7200
his soul *e* good in his labour .... Eccl 2:24   7200
e the good of all his labour, it .... Eccl 3:13   7200
to *e* the good of all his labour .... Eccl 5:18   7200
mine elect shall long *e* the work .... Is 65:22   1086
that by thee we *e* great quietness .... Acts 24:2   5177
giveth us richly all things to *e* 1Ti 6:17   619
than to *e* the pleasures of sin .... Heb 11:25   *2192,619*

ENJOYED
until the land had *e* her sabbaths 2Chr 36:21   7521

ENLARGE
God shall *e* Japheth, and he shall .... Gen 9:27   6601
before thee, and *e* thy borders .... Ex 34:24   7337
LORD thy God shall *e* thy border .... Deut 12:20   7337
if the LORD thy God *e* thy coast .... Deut 12:20   7337
e my coast, and that thine hand 1Chr 4:10   7235
when thou shalt *e* my heart .... Ps 119:32   7337
E the place of thy tent, and let .... Is 54:2   7337
that they might *e* their border .... Amos 1:13   7337
e thy baldness as the eagle .... Mic 1:16   7337
e the borders of their garments, ... Mt 23:5   *3170*

ENLARGED
my mouth is *e* over mine enemies 1Sa 2:1   7337
Thou hast *e* my steps under me 2Sa 22:37   7337
thou hast *e* me when I was in .... Ps 4:1   7337
Thou hast *e* my steps under me, ... Ps 18:36   7337
The troubles of my heart are *e* .... Ps 25:17   7337
Therefore hell hath *e* herself .... Is 5:14   7337
thou hast *e* thy bed, and made thee ...... Is 57:8   7337
thine heart shall fear, and be *e* .... Is 60:5   7337
is open unto you, our heart is *e* 2Cor 6:11   4115
unto my children,) be ye also *e* 2Cor 6:13   4115
that we shall be *e* by you 2Cor 10:15   *3170*

ENLARGEMENT
at this time, then shall there *e* .... Est 4:14   7305

ENLARGETH
he said, Blessed be he that *e* Gad .... Deut 33:20   7337
he *e* the nations, and straiteneth .... Job 12:23   7849
who *e* his desire as hell, and is .... Hab 2:5   7337

ENLARGING
And there was an *e*, and a winding .... Eze 41:7   7337

ENLIGHTEN
LORD my God will *e* my darkness .... Ps 18:28   5050

ENLIGHTENED
and his eyes were *e* 1Sa 14:27   215
you, how mine eyes have been *e* 1Sa 14:29   215
to be *e* with the light of the .... Job 33:30   215
His lightnings *e* the world .... Ps 97:4   215
of your understanding being *e* .... Eph 1:18   *5461*
for those who were once *e* .... Heb 6:4   *5461*

ENLIGHTENING
of the LORD is pure, *e* the eyes .... Ps 19:8   215

EN-MISHPAT *Another name for Kadesh.*
And they returned, and came to *E* .... Gen 14:7   5880

ENMITY
I will put *e* between thee and the .... Gen 3:15   342
Or in *e* smite him with his hand, ... Num 35:21   342
he thrust him suddenly without *e* .... Num 35:22   342
they were at *e* between themselves .... Lk 23:12   *2189*
the carnal mind is *e* against God .... Rom 8:7   *2189*
abolished in his flesh the *e* .... Eph 2:15   *2189*
cross, having slain the *e* thereby .... Eph 2:16   *2189*
of the world is *e* with God .... Jas 4:4   *2189*

ENOCH (e'-nok) *See* HENOCH.
   1. A son of Cain.
and she conceived, and bare *E* .... Gen 4:17   2585
And unto *E* was born Irad .... Gen 4:18   2585
   2. A city built by Cain.
after the name of his son, *E* .... Gen 4:17   2585
   3. A son of Jared.
sixty and two years, and he begat *E* ...... Gen 5:18   2585
he begat *E* eight hundred years .... Gen 5:19   2585
E lived sixty and five years, and .... Gen 5:21   2585
E walked with God after he begat .... Gen 5:22   2585
all the days of *E* were three .... Gen 5:23   2585
And *E* walked with God .... Gen 5:24   2585
Mathusala, which was the son of *E* .... Lk 3:37   *1802*
By faith *E* was translated that he .... Heb 11:5   *1802*
E also, the seventh from Adam, ... Jude 14   *1802*

ENOS (e'-nos) *See* ENOSH. *Son of Seth.*
and he called his name *E* .... Gen 4:26   583
hundred and five years, and begat *E* ..... Gen 5:6   583
after he begat *E* eight hundred .... Gen 5:7   583
E lived ninety years, and begat .... Gen 5:9   583
E lived after he begat Cainan .... Gen 5:10   583
all the days of *E* were nine .... Gen 5:11   583
Which was the son of *E*, which was .... Lk 3:38   *1800*

ENOSH (e'-nosh) *See* ENOS. *Same as Enos.*
Adam, Sheth, *E*, ... 1Chr 1:1   583

ENOUGH *See* APPENDIX.

ENQUIRE
the damsel, and *e* at her mouth .... Gen 24:57   7592
And she went to *e* of the LORD .... Gen 25:22   1875
people come unto me to *e* of God .... Ex 18:15   1875
that thou *e* not after their gods, ... Deut 12:30   1875
Then shalt thou *e*, and make search ..... Deut 13:14   1875
that shall be in those days, and *e* .... Deut 17:9   1875
e of thee, and say, Is there any .... Judg 4:20   7592
when a man went to *e* of God 1Sa 9:9   1875
E thou whose son the stripling is 1Sa 17:56   7592
I then begin to *e* of God for him 1Sa 22:15   7592
that I may go to her, and *e* of her 1Sa 28:7   1875
said unto the king of Israel, *E* 1Kin 22:5   1875
besides, that we might *e* of him 1Kin 22:7   1875
by whom we may *e* of the LORD 1Kin 22:8   1875
e of Baal-zebub the god of Ekron 2Kin 1:2   1875
that ye go to *e* of Baal-zebub the 2Kin 1:3   1875
that thou sendest to *e* of 2Kin 1:6   1875
e of Baal-zebub the god of Ekron 2Kin 1:16   1875
no God in Israel to *e* of his word 2Kin 1:16   1875
that we may *e* of the LORD by him 2Kin 3:11   1875
e of the LORD by him, saying, ... 2Kin 8:8   1875
altar shall be for me to *e* by 2Kin 16:15   1239
e of the LORD for me, and for the 2Kin 22:13   1875
which sent you to *e* of the LORD 2Kin 22:18   1875
had a familiar spirit, to *e* of it 1Chr 10:13   1875
to *e* of his welfare, and to 1Chr 18:10   7592
not go before it to *e* of God 1Chr 21:30   1875
said unto the king of Israel, *E* 2Chr 18:4   1875
besides, that we might *e* of him 2Chr 18:6   1875
man, by whom we may *e* of the LORD 2Chr 18:7   1875
who sent unto him to *e* of the 2Chr 32:31   1875
e of the LORD for me, and for them 2Chr 34:21   1875
who sent you to *e* of the LORD 2Chr 34:26   1875
to *e* concerning Judah and .... Ezr 7:14   1240
For *e*, I pray thee, of the former .... Job 8:8   7592
the LORD, and to *e* in his temple .... Ps 27:4   1239

for thou dost not *e* wisely	Eccl 7:10	7592
also the night: if ye will *e*	Is 21:12	1158
e ye: return, come	Is 21:12	1158
E, I pray thee, of the LORD for	Jer 21:2	1875
that sent you unto me to *e* of me	Jer 37:7	1875
prophet to *e* of him concerning me	Eze 14:7	1875
of Israel came to *e* of the LORD	Eze 20:1	1875
Are ye come to *e* of me	Eze 20:3	1875
enter, *e* who in it is worthy	Mt 10:11	1833
they began to *e* among themselves,	Lk 22:23	4802
Do ye *e* among yourselves of that	Jn 16:19	2212
e in the house of Judas for one	Acts 9:11	2212
But if ye *e* any thing concerning	Acts 19:39	1934
as though ye would *e* something	Acts 23:15	1231
as though they would *e* somewhat	Acts 23:20	4441
Whether any do *e* of Titus	2Cor 8:23	

ENQUIRED

e diligently, and, behold, it be	Deut 17:4	1875
And when they *e* and asked, they	Judg 6:29	1875
the men of Succoth, and *e* of him	Judg 8:14	7592
children of Israel *e* of the LORD	Judg 20:27	7592
Therefore they *e* of the LORD	1Sa 10:22	7592
he *e* of the LORD for him, and gave	1Sa 22:10	7592
hast *e* of God for him, that he	1Sa 22:13	7592
Therefore David *e* of the LORD	1Sa 23:2	7592
Then David *e* of the LORD yet	1Sa 23:4	7592
when Saul *e* of the LORD, the LORD	1Sa 28:6	7592
David *e* at the LORD, saying,	1Sa 30:8	7592
that David *e* of the LORD, saying,	2Sa 2:1	7592
David *e* of the LORD, saying,	2Sa 5:19	7592
when David *e* of the LORD, he said	2Sa 5:23	7592
David sent and *e* after the woman	2Sa 11:3	1875
was as if a man had *e* at the	2Sa 16:23	7592
and David *e* of the LORD	2Sa 21:1	1245
And *e* not of it	1Chr 10:14	1875
for we *e* not at it in the days of	1Chr 13:3	1875
David *e* of God, saying, Shall I	1Chr 14:10	7592
Therefore David *e* again of God	1Chr 14:14	7592
returned and *e* early after God	Ps 78:34	7836
should I be *e* of at all by them	Eze 14:3	1875
GOD, I will not be *e* of by you	Eze 20:3	1875
and shall I be *e* of by you	Eze 20:31	1875
GOD, I will not be *e* of by you	Eze 20:31	
I will yet for this be *e* of by	Eze 36:37	1875
that the king *e* of him, he	Dan 1:20	1245
sought the LORD, nor *e* for him	Zeph 1:6	1875
e of them diligently what time	Mt 2:7	198
had enquired of the wise men	Mt 2:16	198
Then *e* he of them the hour when	Jn 4:52	4441
or our brethren be *e* of, they are	2Cor 8:23	
salvation the prophets have *e*	1Pet 1:10	1567

ENQUIREST

That thou *e* after mine iniquity,	Job 10:6	1245

ENQUIRY

is holy, and after vows to make *e*	Prov 20:25	1239
had made *e* for Simon's house	Acts 10:17	1331

ENRICH

the king will *e* him with great	1Sa 17:25	6238
thou didst *e* the kings of the	Eze 27:33	6238

ENRICHED

in every thing ye are *e* by him	1Cor 1:5	4148
Being *e* in every thing to all	2Cor 9:11	4148

ENRICHEST

thou greatly *e* it with the river	Ps 65:9	6238

EN-RIMMON (en-rim'-mon) See AIN, RIMMON. *A city in Judah.*

And at *E*, and at Zareah, and at	Neh 11:29	5884

EN-ROGEL (en-ro'-ghel) *A fountain near Jerusalem.*

the goings out thereof were at *E*	Josh 15:7	5883
on the south, and descended to *E*	Josh 18:16	5883
Jonathan and Ahimaaz stayed by *E*	2Sa 17:17	5883
stone of Zoheleth, which is by *E*	1Kin 1:9	5883

ENSAMPLE

walk so as ye have us for an *e*	Phil 3:17	5179
an *e* unto you to follow us	2Th 3:9	
making them an *e* unto those that	2Pet 2:6	5262

ENSAMPLES

things happened unto them for *e*	1Cor 10:11	5179
So that we were *e* to all that	1Th 1:7	5179
but being *e* to the flock	1Pet 5:3	5179

EN-SHEMESH (en-she'-mesh) *A spring.*

passed toward the waters of *E*	Josh 15:7	5885
the north, and went forth to *E*	Josh 18:17	5885

ENSIGN

with the *e* of their father's	Num 2:2	226
he will lift up an *e* to the	Is 5:26	5251
stand for an *e* of the people	Is 11:10	5251
shall set up an *e* for the nations	Is 11:12	5251
lifteth up an *e* on the mountains	Is 18:3	5251
a mountain, and as an *e* on an hill	Is 30:17	5251
princes shall be afraid of the *e*	Is 31:9	5251
lifted up as an *e* upon his land	Zec 9:16	5264

ENSIGNS

they set up their *e* for signs	Ps 74:4	226

ENSNARED

reign not, lest the people be *e*	Job 34:30	4170

ENSUE

let him seek peace, and *e* it	1Pet 3:11	1377

ENTANGLE

how they might *e* him in his talk	Mt 22:15	3802

ENTANGLED

They are *e* in the land, the	Ex 14:3	943
be not *e* again with the yoke of	Gal 5:1	1758
Christ, they are again *e* therein	2Pet 2:20	1707

ENTANGLETH

No man that warreth *e* himself	2Ti 2:4	1707

EN-TAPPUAH (en-tap'-poo-ah) *A town in Manasseh.*

hand unto the inhabitants of *E*	Josh 17:7	5887

ENTER

he was come near to *e* into Egypt	Gen 12:11	935
able to *e* into the tent of the	Ex 40:35	935
all that *e* into the host, to do	Num 4:3	935
all that *e* in to perform the	Num 4:23	935
the curse shall *e* into her	Num 5:24	935
the curse shall *e* into her	Num 5:27	935
for he shall not *e* into the land	Num 20:24	935
shall not *e* into the congregation	Deut 23:1	935
A bastard shall not *e* into the	Deut 23:2	935
e into the congregation of the	Deut 23:2	935
e into the congregation of the	Deut 23:3	935
e into the congregation of the	Deut 23:3	935
e into the congregation of the	Deut 23:8	935
That thou shouldest *e* into	Deut 29:12	5674
them not to *e* into their cities	Josh 10:19	935
go, and to *e* to possess the land	Judg 18:9	935
my cry did *e* into his ears	2Sa 22:7	935
and when thy feet *e* into the city	1Kin 14:12	935
myself, and *e* into the battle	1Kin 22:30	935
We will *e* into the city, then the	2Kin 7:4	935
A third part of you that *e* in on	2Kin 11:5	935
I will *e* into the lodgings of his	2Kin 19:23	935
the priests could not *e* into the	2Chr 7:2	935
unclean in any thing should *e* in	2Chr 23:19	935
e into his sanctuary, which he	2Chr 30:8	935
for the house that I shall *e* into	Neh 2:8	935
for none might *e* into the king's	Est 4:2	935
will he *e* with thee into judgment	Job 22:4	935
that he should *e* into judgment	Job 34:23	1980
Their sword shall *e* into their	Ps 37:15	935
they shall *e* into the king's	Ps 45:15	935
they should not *e* into my rest	Ps 95:11	935
E into his gates with	Ps 100:4	935
into which the righteous shall *e*	Ps 118:20	935
e not into judgment with thy	Ps 143:2	935
E not into the path of the wicked	Prov 4:14	935
A fool's lips *e* into contention,	Prov 18:6	935
e not into the fields of the	Prov 23:10	935
E into the rock, and hide thee in	Is 2:10	935
The LORD will *e* into judgment	Is 3:14	935
which keepeth the truth may *e* in	Is 26:2	935
e thou into thy chambers, and shut	Is 26:20	935
I will *e* into the height of his	Is 37:24	935
He shall *e* into peace	Is 57:2	935
in the street, and equity cannot *e*	Is 59:14	935
that *e* in at these gates to	Jer 7:2	935
let us *e* into the defenced cities	Jer 8:14	935
if I *e* into the city, then behold	Jer 14:18	935
E not into the house of mourning,	Jer 16:5	935
that *e* in by these gates	Jer 17:20	935
Then shall there *e* into the gates	Jer 17:25	935
or who shall *e* into our	Jer 21:13	935
thy people that *e* in by these	Jer 22:2	935
then shall there *e* in by the	Jer 22:4	935
Bethlehem, to go to *e* into Egypt,	Jer 41:17	935
set your faces to *e* into Egypt	Jer 42:15	935
you, when ye shall *e* into Egypt	Jer 42:18	935
not *e* into thy congregation	Lam 1:10	935
of his quiver to *e* into my reins	Lam 3:13	935
for the robbers shall *e* into it	Eze 7:22	935
neither shall they *e* into the	Eze 13:9	935

E

they shall not *e* into the land of	Eze 20:38	935
when he shall *e* into thy gates,	Eze 26:10	935
as men *e* into a city wherein is	Eze 26:10	935
I will cause breath to *e* into you	Eze 37:5	935
When the priests *e* therein	Eze 42:14	935
and no man shall *e* in by it	Eze 44:2	935
he shall *e* by the way of the	Eze 44:3	935
shall *e* into my sanctuary, of any	Eze 44:9	935
They shall *e* into thine house	Eze 44:16	935
that when they *e* in at the gates	Eze 44:17	935
when they *e* into the inner court	Eze 44:21	935
the prince shall *e* by the way of	Eze 46:2	935
And when the prince shall *e*	Eze 46:8	935
shall *e* into the fortress of the	Dan 11:7	935
He shall also set his face to *e*	Dan 11:17	935
He shall *e* peaceably even upon	Dan 11:24	935
he shall *e* into the countries, and	Dan 11:40	935
He shall *e* also into the glorious	Dan 11:41	935
I will not *e* into the city	Hos 11:9	935
they shall *e* in at the windows	Joel 2:9	935
nor *e* into Gilgal, and pass not to	Amos 5:5	935
Jonah began to *e* into the city a	Jonah 3:4	935
it shall *e* into the house of the	Zec 5:4	935
ye shall in no case *e* into the	Mt 5:20	*1525*
***e* into thy closet, and when thou**	Mt 6:6	*1525*
***E* ye in at the strait gate**	Mt 7:13	*1525*
shall *e* into the kingdom of	Mt 7:21	*1525*
city of the Samaritans *e* ye not	Mt 10:5	*1525*
city or town ye shall *e*, enquire	Mt 10:11	*1525*
Or else how can one *e* into a	Mt 12:29	*1525*
wicked than himself, and they *e* in	Mt 12:45	*1525*
ye shall not *e* into the kingdom	Mt 18:3	*1525*
to *e* into life halt or maimed	Mt 18:8	*1525*
thee to *e* into life with one eye	Mt 18:9	*1525*
but if thou wilt *e* into life	Mt 19:17	*1525*
***e* into the kingdom of heaven**	Mt 19:23	*1525*
than for a rich man to *e* into the	Mt 19:24	*1525*
***e* thou into the joy of thy lord**	Mt 25:21	*1525*
***e* thou into the joy of thy lord**	Mt 25:23	*1525*
that ye *e* not into temptation	Mt 26:41	*1525*
no more openly *e* into the city	Mk 1:45	*1525*
No man can *e* into a strong man's	Mk 3:27	*1525*
swine, that we may *e* into them	Mk 5:12	*1525*
place soever ye *e* into a house	Mk 6:10	*1525*
out of him, and *e* no more into him	Mk 9:25	*1525*
for thee to *e* into life maimed	Mk 9:43	*1525*
for thee to *e* halt into life	Mk 9:45	*1525*
it is better for thee to *e* into	Mk 9:47	*1525*
child, he shall not *e* therein	Mk 10:15	*1525*
riches *e* into the kingdom of God	Mk 10:23	*1525*
to *e* into the kingdom of God	Mk 10:24	*1525*
than for a rich man to *e* into the	Mk 10:25	*1525*
into the house, neither *e* therein	Mk 13:15	*1525*
lest ye *e* into temptation	Mk 14:38	*1525*
thou shouldest *e* under my roof	Lk 7:6	*1525*
that they which *e* in may see the	Lk 8:16	*1531*
would suffer them to *e* into them	Lk 8:32	*1525*
And whatsoever house ye *e* into	Lk 9:4	*1525*
And into whatsoever house ye *e*	Lk 10:5	*1525*
And into whatsoever city ye *e*	Lk 10:8	*1525*
But into whatsoever city ye *e*	Lk 10:10	*1525*
and they *e* in, and dwell there	Lk 11:26	*1525*
Strive to *e* in at the strait gate	Lk 13:24	*1525*
I say unto you, will seek to *e* in	Lk 13:24	*1525*
child shall in no wise *e* therein	Lk 18:17	*1525*
riches *e* into the kingdom of God	Lk 18:24	*1525*
than for a rich man to *e* into the	Lk 18:25	*1525*
are in the countries *e* thereinto	Lk 21:21	*1525*
them, Pray that ye *e* not into	Lk 22:40	*1525*
lest ye *e* into temptation	Lk 22:46	*1525*
things, and to *e* into his glory	Lk 24:26	*1525*
can he *e* the second time into his	Jn 3:4	*1525*
he cannot *e* into the kingdom of	Jn 3:5	*1525*
by me if any man *e* in, he shall	Jn 10:9	*1525*
e into the kingdom of God	Acts 14:22	*1525*
grievous wolves *e* in among you	Acts 20:29	*1525*
They shall not *e* into my rest	Heb 3:11	*1525*
they should not *e* into his rest	Heb 3:18	*1525*
not *e* in because of unbelief	Heb 3:19	*1525*
have believed do *e* into rest	Heb 4:3	*1525*
if they shall *e* into my rest	Heb 4:3	*1525*
If they shall *e* into my rest	Heb 4:5	*1525*
that some must *e* therein, and they	Heb 4:6	*1525*
therefore to *e* into that rest	Heb 4:11	*1525*
boldness to *e* into the holiest by	Heb 10:19	*1529*
man was able to *e* into the temple	Rev 15:8	*1525*
there shall in no wise *e* into it	Rev 21:27	*1525*
may *e* in through the gates into	Rev 22:14	*1525*

ENTERED

In the selfsame day *e* Noah	Gen 7:13	935
in unto him, and *e* into his house	Gen 19:3	935
the earth when Lot *e* into Zoar	Gen 19:23	935
tent, and *e* into Rachel's tent	Gen 31:33	935
he *e* into his chamber, and wept	Gen 43:30	935
as Moses *e* into the tabernacle,	Ex 33:9	935
which are *e* into thine house	Josh 2:3	935
they *e* into the city, and took it,	Josh 8:19	935
of them *e* into fenced cities	Josh 10:20	935
they *e* into the land to destroy	Judg 6:5	935
they *e* into an hold of the house	Judg 9:46	935
Abishai, *e* into the city	2Sa 10:14	935
e into another tent, and carried	2Kin 7:8	935
as Jehu *e* in at the gate, she	2Kin 9:31	935
his brother, and *e* into the city	1Chr 19:15	935
when the king *e* into the house of	2Chr 12:11	935
they *e* into a covenant to seek	2Chr 15:12	935
howbeit he *e* not into the temple	2Chr 27:2	935
e into Judah, and encamped against	2Chr 32:1	935
e by the gate of the valley, and	Neh 2:15	935
e into a curse, and into an oath,	Neh 10:29	935
Hast thou *e* into the springs of	Job 38:16	935
Hast thou *e* into the treasures of	Job 38:22	935
but when ye, defiled my land	Jer 2:7	935
is *e* into our palaces, to cut off	Jer 9:21	935
which had *e* into the covenant,	Jer 34:10	935
Jeremiah was *e* into the dungeon	Jer 37:16	935
the heathen was *e* into her sanctuary	Lam 1:10	935
the enemy should have *e* into the	Lam 4:12	935
the spirit *e* into me when he	Eze 2:2	935
Then the spirit *e* into me	Eze 3:24	935
e into a covenant with thee,	Eze 16:8	935
when they *e* unto the heathen,	Eze 36:20	935
they *e* into the wall which was of	Eze 41:6	935
hath *e* in by it, therefore it	Eze 44:2	935
foreigners *e* into his gates, and	Obad 11	935
Thou shouldest not have *e* into	Obad 13	935
rottenness *e* into my bones, and I	Hab 3:16	935
when Jesus was *e* into Capernaum	Mt 8:5	*1525*
And when he was *e* into a ship	Mt 8:23	*1684*
he *e* into a ship, and passed over,	Mt 9:1	*1684*
How he *e* into the house of God,	Mt 12:4	*1525*
the day that Noe *e* into the ark	Mt 24:38	*1525*
day he *e* into the synagogue	Mk 1:21	*1525*
they *e* into the house of Simon and	Mk 1:29	*2064*
again he *e* into Capernaum after	Mk 2:1	*1525*
he *e* again into the synagogue	Mk 3:1	*1525*
so that he *e* into a ship, and sat	Mk 4:1	*1684*
went out, and *e* into the swine	Mk 5:13	*1525*
And whithersoever he *e*, into	Mk 6:56	*1531*
when he was *e* into the house from	Mk 7:17	*1525*
e into an house, and would have no	Mk 7:24	*1525*
straightway he *e* into a ship with	Mk 8:10	*1684*
and as soon as ye *e* into it	Mk 11:2	*1531*
Jesus *e* into Jerusalem, and into	Mk 11:11	*1525*
e into the house of Zacharias, and	Lk 1:40	*1525*
and *e* into Simon's house	Lk 4:38	*1525*
he *e* into one of the ships, which	Lk 5:3	*1684*
that he *e* into the synagogue and	Lk 6:6	*1525*
the people, he *e* into Capernaum	Lk 7:1	*1525*
I *e* into thine house, thou gavest	Lk 7:44	*1525*
many devils were *e* into him	Lk 8:30	*1525*
of the man, and *e* into the swine	Lk 8:33	*1525*
feared as they *e* into the cloud	Lk 9:34	*1525*
went, and *e* into a village of the	Lk 9:52	*1525*
that he *e* into a certain village	Lk 10:38	*1525*
ye *e* not in yourselves, and them	Lk 11:52	*1525*
as he *e* into a certain village,	Lk 17:12	*1525*
the day that Noe *e* into the ark	Lk 17:27	*1525*
And Jesus *e* and passed through	Lk 19:1	*1525*
Then *e* Satan into Judas surnamed	Lk 22:3	*1525*
when ye are *e* into the city,	Lk 22:10	*1525*
And they *e* in, and found not the	Lk 24:3	*1525*
ye are *e* into their labours	Jn 4:38	*1525*
e into a ship, and went over the	Jn 6:17	*1684*
whereinto his disciples were *e*	Jn 6:22	*1684*
And after the sop Satan *e* into him	Jn 13:27	*1525*
was a garden, into the which he *e*	Jn 18:1	*1525*
Then Pilate *e* into the judgment	Jn 18:33	*1525*
e into a ship immediately	Jn 21:3	*305*
of them that *e* into the temple	Acts 3:2	*1531*
e with them into the temple,	Acts 3:8	*1525*
they *e* into the temple early in	Acts 5:21	*1525*
went his way, and *e* into the house	Acts 9:17	*1525*
morrow after they *e* into Caesarea	Acts 10:24	*1525*
hath at any time *e* into my mouth	Acts 11:8	*1525*
we *e* into the man's house	Acts 11:12	*1525*
e into the house of Lydia	Acts 16:40	*1525*
e into a certain man's house,	Acts 18:7	*2064*
but he himself *e* into the	Acts 18:19	*1525*

would have *e* in unto the people............Acts 19:30   1525
we *e* into the house of Philip the ....Acts 21:8   1525
with them *e* into the temple....................Acts 21:26   1524
e into the castle, and told Paul ....Acts 23:16   1525
was *e* into the place of hearing, ...Acts 25:23   1525
to whom Paul *e* in, and prayed, and ......Acts 28:8   1525
by one man sin *e* into the world ....Rom 5:12   1525
Moreover the law *e*, that the ....Rom 5:20   3922
neither have *e* into the heart of 1Cor 2:9   305
e not in because of unbelief....................Heb 4:6   1525
For he that is *e* into his rest ....Heb 4:10   1525
the forerunner is for us *e* ....Heb 6:20   1525
but by his own blood he *e* in once ....Heb 9:12   1525
For Christ is not *e* into the holy.............Heb 9:24   1525
e into the ears of the Lord of ....Jas 5:4   1525
deceivers are *e* into the world 2Jn 7   1525
of life from God *e* into them ....Rev 11:11   1525

ENTERETH
every one that *e* into the service ....Num 4:30   935
every one that *e* into the service ....Num 4:35   935
every one that *e* into the service ....Num 4:39   935
every one that *e* into the service ....Num 4:43   935
even unto every one that *e* into 2Chr 31:16   935
When wisdom *e* into thine heart, ...Prov 2:10   935
A reproof *e* more into a wise man ....Prov 17:10   5181
which *e* into their privy chambers ....Eze 21:14
the east, as one *e* into them ....Eze 42:12   935
he that *e* in by the way of the................Eze 46:9   935
he that *e* by the way of the south..........Eze 46:9   935
that whatsoever *e* in at the mouth.........Mt 15:17   1531
e in where the damsel was lying ....Mk 5:40   1531
thing from without *e* into the man.........Mk 7:18   1531
Because it *e* not into his heart, ...Mk 7:19   1531
him into the house where he *e* in ....Lk 22:10   1531
He that *e* not by the door into ....Jn 10:1   1535
But he that *e* in by the door is ....Jn 10:2   1535
which *e* into that within the veil ....Heb 6:19   1535
as the high priest *e* into the ....Heb 9:25   1535

ENTERING
at the *e* in of the tabernacle ....Ex 35:15   6607
cast it at the *e* of the gate of ....Josh 8:29   6607
Hermon unto the *e* into Hamath ....Josh 13:5   935
at the *e* of the gate of the city ....Josh 20:4   6607
unto there is *e* in of Hamath ....Judg 3:3   935
stood in the *e* of the gate of the ....Judg 9:35   6607
even unto the *e* of the gate ....Judg 9:40   6607
stood in the *e* of the gate of the ....Judg 9:44   6607
Dan, stood by the *e* of the gate ....Judg 18:16   6607
the priest stood in the *e* of the ....Judg 18:17   6607
by *e* into a town that hath gates 1Sa 23:7   935
in array at the *e* in of the gate 2Sa 10:8   6607
them even unto the *e* of the gate 2Sa 11:23   6607
for the *e* of the oracle he made 1Kin 6:31   6607
from the *e* in of Hamath unto the 1Kin 8:65   935
stood in the *e* in of the cave 1Kin 19:13   6607
men at the *e* in of the gate 2Kin 7:3   6607
at the *e* in of the gate until the 2Kin 10:8   6607
the coast of Israel from the *e* of 2Kin 14:25   935
e in of the gate of Joshua the 2Kin 23:8   6607
at the *e* in of the house of the 2Kin 23:11   935
e in of the wilderness from the 1Chr 5:9   935
Egypt even unto the *e* of Hemath 1Chr 13:5   935
from the *e* in of Hamath unto the 2Chr 7:8   935
the *e* in of the gate of Samaria 2Chr 18:9   6607
part of you *e* on the sabbath 2Chr 23:4   935
stood at his pillar at the *e* in 2Chr 23:13   3996
when she was come to the *e* of the 2Chr 23:15   3996
abroad even to the *e* in of Egypt 2Chr 26:8   935
even to the *e* in at the fish gate 2Chr 33:14   935
that there is no house, no *e* in ....Is 23:1   935
the *e* of the gates of Jerusalem ....Jer 1:15   6607
even *e* in at the gates of........................Jer 17:27   935
mark well the *e* in of the house, ...Eze 44:5   3996
e in of Hemath unto the river of............Amos 6:14   935
ye them that are *e* to go in....................Mt 23:13   1525
and the lusts of other things *e* in ....Mk 4:19   1531
that *e* into him can defile him ....Mk 7:15   1531
e into the ship again departed to...........Mk 8:13   1684
e into the sepulchre, they saw a ....Mk 16:5   1525
them that were *e* in ye hindered.............Lk 11:52   1525
in the which at your *e* ye shall...............Lk 19:30   1531
e into every house, and haling men ......Acts 8:3   1531
e into a ship of Adramyttium, we..........Acts 27:2   1910
manner of *e* in we had unto you 1Th 1:9   1529
being left us of *e* into his rest..............Heb 4:1   1525

ENTERPRISE
hands cannot perform their *e*.................Job 5:12   8454

ENTERTAIN
Be not forgetful to *e* strangers ....Heb 13:2   5381

ENTERTAINED
some have *e* angels unawares.................Heb 13:2   3579

ENTICE
if a man *e* a maid that is not..................Ex 22:16   6601
e thee secretly, saying, Let us ....Deut 13:6   5496
E thy husband, that he may ....Judg 14:15   6601
E him, and see wherein his great ....Judg 16:5   6601
Who shall *e* Ahab king of Israel, ...2Chr 18:19   6601
the LORD, and said, I will *e* him,...........2Chr 18:20   6601
the LORD said, Thou shalt *e* him...........2Chr 18:21   6601
My son, if sinners *e* thee.......................Prov 1:10   6601

ENTICED
And my heart hath been secretly *e* ....Job 31:27   6601
saying, Peradventure he will be *e* ....Jer 20:10   6601
drawn away of his own lust, and *e*.........Jas 1:14   1185

ENTICETH
A violent man *e* his neighbour ....Prov 16:29   6601

ENTICING
not with *e* words of man's wisdom 1Cor 2:4   3981
should beguile you with *e* words ....Col 2:4   4086

ENTIRE
work, that ye may be perfect and *e* ....Jas 1:4   3648

ENTRANCE
your border unto the *e* of Hamath ....Num 34:8   935
the *e* into the city, and we will...............Judg 1:24   3996
shewed them the *e* into the city ....Judg 1:25   3996
before Ahab to the *e* of Jezreel 1Kin 18:46   935
in the *e* of the gate of Samaria 1Kin 22:10   6607
And they went to the *e* of Gedor 1Chr 4:39   3996
that kept the *e* of the king's.................2Chr 12:10   6607
The *e* of thy words giveth light ....Ps 119:130   6608
the face of the gate of the *e* ....Eze 40:15   2978
know our *e* in unto you, that it..............1Th 2:1   1529
For so an *e* shall be ministered 2Pet 1:11   1529

ENTRANCES
land of Nimrod in the *e* thereof..............Mic 5:6   6607

ENTREAT
I will cause the enemy to *e* thee ....Jer 15:11   6293
e them evil four hundred years ....Acts 7:6   2559

ENTREATED
he *e* Abram well for her sake ....Gen 12:16
hast thou so evil *e* this people...............Ex 5:22
And the Egyptians evil *e* us ....Deut 26:6
e them spitefully, and slew them ....Mt 22:6   5195
shall be mocked, and spitefully *e*..........Lk 18:32   5195
e him shamefully, and sent him ....Lk 20:11   818
evil *e* our fathers, so that they...............Acts 7:19   2559
And Julius courteously *e* Paul ....Acts 27:3   5530
before, and were shamefully *e* 1Th 2:2   5195

ENTREATETH
He evil *e* the barren that beareth ....Job 24:21

ENTRIES
the *e* thereof were by the posts ....Eze 40:38   6607

ENTRY
house, and the king's *e* without..............2Kin 16:18   3996
the LORD, were keepers of the *e*.............1Chr 9:19   3996
the *e* of the house, the inner 2Chr 4:22   6607
at the *e* of the city, at the ....Prov 8:3   6607
which is by the *e* of the east...................Jer 19:2   6607
sat down in the *e* of the new gate ....Jer 26:10   6607
at the *e* of the new gate of the ....Jer 36:10   6607
e that is in the house of the ....Jer 38:14   3996
which is at the *e* of Pharaoh's ....Jer 43:9   6607
this image of jealousy in the *e* ....Eze 8:5   872
art situate at the *e* of the sea ....Eze 27:3   3996
the breadth of the *e* of the gate ....Eze 40:11   6607
up to the *e* of the north gate ....Eze 40:40   6607
was the *e* on the east side ....Eze 42:9   3996
After he brought me through the *e*.........Eze 46:19   3996

ENVIED
and the Philistines *e* him ....Gen 26:14   7065
no children, Rachel *e* her sister ....Gen 30:1   7065
And his brethren *e* him...........................Gen 37:11   7065
They *e* Moses also in the camp, and ......Ps 106:16   7065
this a man is *e* of his neighbour ....Eccl 4:4   7068
were in the garden of God, *e* him ....Eze 31:9   7065

ENVIES
all guile, and hypocrisies, and *e* 1Pet 2:1   5355

ENVIEST
said unto him, *E* thou for my sake..........Num 11:29   7065

ENVIETH
charity *e* not 1Cor 13:4   2206

ENVIOUS

neither be thou *e* against the .... Ps 37:1   7065
For I was *e* at the foolish, when .... Ps 73:3   7065
Be not thou *e* against evil men, ... Prov 24:1   7065
neither be thou *e* at the wicked........... Prov 24:19   7065

ENVIRON

shall *e* us round, and cut off our .... Josh 7:9   5437

ENVY

man, and *e* slayeth the silly one............ Job 5:2   7068
E thou not the oppressor, and .... Prov 3:31   7065
but *e* the rottenness of the bones .... Prov 14:30   7068
Let not thine heart *e* sinners .... Prov 23:17   7065
but who is able to stand before *e* .... Prov 27:4   7068
love, and their hatred, and their *e* .... Eccl 9:6   7068
The *e* also of Ephraim shall .... Is 11:13   7068
Ephraim shall not *e* Judah .... Is 11:13   7065
ashamed for their *e* at the people .... Is 26:11   7068
according to thine *e* which thou .... Eze 35:11   7068
For he knew that for *e* they had .... Mt 27:18   5355
priests had delivered him for *e* .... Mk 15:10   5355
And the patriarchs, moved with *e* .... Acts 7:9   2206
they were filled with *e*, and .... Acts 13:45   2205
which believed not, moved with *e* .... Acts 17:5   2206
full of *e*, murder, debate, deceit .... Rom 1:29   5355
indeed preach Christ even of *e* .... Phil 1:15   5355
of words, whereof cometh *e* 1Ti 6:4   5355
pleasures, living in malice and *e* .... Titus 3:3   5355
that dwelleth in us lusteth to *e* .... Jas 4:5   5355

ENVYING

and wantonness, not in strife and *e* .... Rom 13:13   2205
for whereas there is among you *e* 1Cor 3:3   2205
one another, *e* one another .... Gal 5:26   5354
But if ye have bitter *e* and strife .... Jas 3:14   2205
For where *e* and strife is, there............... Jas 3:16   2205

ENVYINGS

lest there be debates, *e*, wraths,............. 2Cor 12:20   2205
E, murders, drunkenness,........................ Gal 5:21   5355

EPAENETUS (ep-en'-e-tus) *A Christian acquaintance of Paul.*

Salute my wellbeloved *E*, who is .... Rom 16:5   1866

EPAPHRAS (ep'-a-fras) *A Christian acquaintance of Paul.*

As ye also learned of *E* our dear .... Col 1:7   1889
E, who is one of you, a servant................ Col 4:12   1889
There salute thee *E*, my .... Philem 23   1889

EPAPHRODITUS (e-paf-ro-di'-tus) *A fellow-worker with Paul.*

it necessary to send to you *E* .... Phil 2:25   1891
having received of *E* the things .... Phil 4:18   1891
to the Philippians from Rome by *E* .... Phil s   1891

EPENETUS See Epaenetus.

EPHAH (e'-fah)
    1. A son of Midian; grandson of Abraham.
E, and Epher, and Hanoch, and Abidah... Gen 25:4   5891
E, and Epher, and Henoch, and Abida, ... 1Chr 1:33   5891
the dromedaries of Midian and *E* .... Is 60:6   5891
    2. A concubine of Caleb.
And *E*, Caleb's concubine, bare............... 1Chr 2:46   5891
    3. A son of Jahdai.
Jotham, and Gesham, and Pelet, and *E* . 1Chr 2:47   5891
    4. A grain measure.
an omer is the tenth part of an *e* .... Ex 16:36   374
of an *e* of fine flour for a sin .... Lev 5:11   374
the tenth part of an *e* of fine .... Lev 6:20   374
balances, just weights, a just *e* .... Lev 19:36   374
tenth part of an *e* of barley meal .... Num 5:15   374
a tenth part of an *e* of flour for .... Num 28:5   374
unleavened cakes of an *e* of flour .... Judg 6:19   374
and it was about an *e* of barley .... Ruth 2:17   374
one *e* of flour, and a bottle of.................. 1Sa 1:24   374
an *e* of this parched corn 1Sa 17:17   374
seed of an homer shall yield an *e* .... Is 5:10   374
have just balances, and a just *e*.............. Eze 45:10   374
The *e* and the bath shall be of one .... Eze 45:11   374
the *e* the tenth part of an homer .... Eze 45:11   374
part of an *e* of an homer of wheat .... Eze 45:13   374
of an *e* of an homer of barley .... Eze 45:13   374
offering of an *e* for a bullock .... Eze 45:24   374
an *e* for a ram, and an hin of oil .... Eze 45:24   374
a ram, and an hin of oil for an *e* .... Eze 45:24   374
offering shall be an *e* for a ram .... Eze 46:5   374
to give, and an hin of oil to an *e* .... Eze 46:5   374
an *e* for a bullock, and .... Eze 46:7   374
an *e* for a ram, and for the lambs .... Eze 46:7   374
unto, and an hin of oil to an *e* .... Eze 46:7   374
shall be an *e* to a bullock .... Eze 46:11   374

an *e* to a ram, and to the lambs as........ Eze 46:11   374
to give, and an hin of oil to an *e* .... Eze 46:11   374
morning, the sixth part of an *e* .... Eze 46:14   374
forth wheat, making the *e* small............ Amos 8:5   374
This is an *e* that goeth forth .... Zec 5:6   374
sitteth in the midst of the *e* .... Zec 5:7   374
cast it into the midst of the *e*................. Zec 5:8   374
lifted up the *e* between the earth........... Zec 5:9   374
me, Whither do these bear the *e*........... Zec 5:10   374

EPHAI (e'-fahee) *Family who remained in Jerusalem during captivity.*

the sons of *E* the Netophathite, ... Jer 40:8   5778

EPHER (e'-fur)
    1. A son of Midian; grandson of Abraham.
and *E*, and Hanoch, and Abidah .... Gen 25:4   6081
Ephah, and *E*, and Henoch, and Abida,.. 1Chr 1:33   6081
    2. A descendant of Judah.
Ezra were, Jether, and Mered, and *E* 1Chr 4:17   6081
    3. A chief of Manasseh.
house of their fathers, even *E*................. 1Chr 5:24   6081

EPHES-DAMMIM *A city in Judah.*

between Shochoh and Azekah, in *E* 1Sa 17:1   658

EPHESIAN (e-fe'-zheun) See Ephesians. *A resident of Ephesus.*

him in the city Trophimus an *E* .... Acts 21:29   2180

EPHESIANS (e-fe'-zheuns)

saying, Great is Diana of the *E*.............. Acts 19:28   2180
out, Great is Diana of the *E* .... Acts 19:34   2180
E is a worshipper of the great................ Acts 19:35   2180
from Rome unto the *E* by Tychicus .... Eph s   2180
bishop of the church of the *E* .... 2Ti s   2180

EPHESUS (ef-e-sus) See Ephesian. *Capital of Roman province of Asia.*

And he came to *E*, and left them .... Acts 18:19   2181
And he sailed from *E* .... Acts 18:21   2181
in the scriptures, came to *E* .... Acts 18:24   2181
the upper coasts came to *E* .... Acts 19:1   2181
Jews and Greeks also dwelling at *E* .... Acts 19:17   2181
see and hear, that not alone at *E* .... Acts 19:26   2181
the people, he said, Ye men of *E*............ Acts 19:35   2181
Paul had determined to sail by *E* .... Acts 20:16   2181
And from Miletus he sent to *E* .... Acts 20:17   2181
I have fought with beasts at *E* 1Cor 15:32   2181
I will tarry at *E* until Pentecost 1Cor 16:8   2181
God, to the saints which are at *E* .... Eph 1:1   2181
besought thee to abide still at *E* 1Ti 1:3   2181
things he ministered unto me at *E* 2Ti 1:18   2181
And Tychicus have I sent to *E*................ 2Ti 4:12   2181
unto *E*, and unto Smyrna, and unto....... Rev 1:11   2181
angel of the church of *E* write .... Rev 2:1   2181

EPHLAL (ef-lal) *A descendant of Pharez.*

And Zabad begat *E*, and *E* begat 1Chr 2:37   654
begat *E*, and *E* begat Obed,................... 1Chr 2:37   654

EPHOD (e'-fod)
    1. Father of Hanniel.
of Manasseh, Hanniel the son of *E*......... Num 34:23   641
    2. A priestly garment.
and stones to be set in the *e*.................. Ex 25:7   646
a breastplate, and an *e*, and a robe........ Ex 28:4   646
And they shall make the *e* of gold .... Ex 28:6   646
And the curious girdle of the *e*.............. Ex 28:8   642
upon the shoulders of the *e* for .... Ex 28:12   646
work of the *e* thou shalt make it .... Ex 28:15   646
shoulderpieces of the *e* before it .... Ex 28:25   646
is in the side of the *e* inward .... Ex 28:26   646
the two sides of the *e* underneath .... Ex 28:27   646
above the curious girdle of the *e*........... Ex 28:27   646
of the *e* with a lace of blue .... Ex 28:28   646
above the curious girdle of the *e* .... Ex 28:28   646
be not loosed from the *e* .... Ex 28:28   646
the robe of the *e* all of blue................... Ex 28:31   646
the coat, and the robe of the *e* .... Ex 29:5   646
and the *e*, and the breastplate .... Ex 29:5   646
with the curious girdle of the *e* .... Ex 29:5   646
and stones to be set for the *e* .... Ex 35:9   646
and stones to be set, for the *e* .... Ex 35:27   646
And he made the *e* of gold, blue,........... Ex 39:2   646
And the curious girdle of his *e* .... Ex 39:5   642
them on the shoulders of the *e* .... Ex 39:7   646
work, like the work of the *e* .... Ex 39:8   646
on the shoulderpieces of the *e* .... Ex 39:18   646
was on the side of the *e* inward............. Ex 39:19   646
the two sides of the *e* underneath .... Ex 39:20   646
above the curious girdle of the *e* .... Ex 39:20   646
of the *e* with a lace of blue .... Ex 39:21   646
above the curious girdle of the *e*........... Ex 39:21   646
might not be loosed from the *e* .... Ex 39:21   646

the robe of the *e* of woven work	Ex 39:22	646
put the *e* upon him, and he girded	Lev 8:7	646
with the curious girdle of the *e*	Lev 8:7	646
And Gideon made an *e* thereof	Judg 8:27	646
an house of gods, and made an *e*	Judg 17:5	646
there is in these houses an *e*	Judg 18:14	646
took the graven image, and the *e*	Judg 18:17	646
fetched the carved image, the *e*	Judg 18:18	646
heart was glad, and he took the *e*	Judg 18:20	646
a child, girded with a linen *e*	1Sa 2:18	646
incense, to wear an *e* before me	1Sa 2:28	646
priest in Shiloh, wearing an *e*	1Sa 14:3	646
wrapped in a cloth behind the *e*	1Sa 21:9	646
persons that did wear a linen *e*	1Sa 22:18	646
came down with an *e* in his hand	1Sa 23:6	646
the priest, Bring hither the *e*	1Sa 23:9	646
pray thee, bring me hither the *e*	1Sa 30:7	646
brought thither the *e* to David	1Sa 30:7	646
David was girded with a linen *e*	2Sa 6:14	646
also had upon him an *e* of linen	1Chr 15:27	646
without an image, and without an *e*	Hos 3:4	646

EPHPHATHA

he sighed, and saith unto him, *E*	Mk 7:34	2188

EPHRAIM (*e'-fra-im*) See EPHRAIMITE, EPHRAIM'S,
EPHRAIN.

1. A son of Joseph.

name of the second called he *E*	Gen 41:52	669
of Egypt were born Manasseh and *E*	Gen 46:20	669
him his two sons, Manasseh and *E*	Gen 48:1	669
And now thy two sons, *E* and	Gen 48:5	669
E in his right hand toward	Gen 48:13	669
his right hand upon the head of *E*	Gen 48:17	669
bless, saying, God make thee as *E*	Gen 48:20	669
and he set *E* before Manasseh	Gen 48:20	669
their families were Manasseh and *E*	Num 26:28	669
And the sons of *E*	1Chr 7:20	669
E their father mourned many days, ...	1Chr 7:22	669

2. One of the twelve tribes comprising Israel.

children of Joseph: of *E*	Num 1:10	669
namely, of the children of *E*	Num 1:32	669
of them, even of the tribe of *E*	Num 1:33	669
of *E* according to their armies	Num 2:18	669
the captain of the sons of *E*	Num 2:18	669
of *E* were an hundred thousand	Num 2:24	669
prince of the children of *E*	Num 7:48	669
E set forward according to their	Num 10:22	669
Of the tribe of *E*, Oshea the son	Num 13:8	669
sons of *E* after their families	Num 26:35	669
of *E* according to those that were	Num 26:37	669
of the tribe of the children of *E*	Num 34:24	669
they are the ten thousands of *E*	Deut 33:17	669
And all Naphtali, and the land of *E*	Deut 34:2	669
were two tribes, Manasseh and *E*	Josh 14:4	669
children of Joseph, Manasseh and *E*	Josh 16:4	669
the border of the children of *E*	Josh 16:5	669
children of *E* by their families	Josh 16:8	669
cities for the children of *E* were	Josh 16:9	669
belonged to the children of *E*	Josh 17:8	669
these cities of *E* are among the	Josh 17:9	669
the house of Joseph, even to *E*	Josh 17:17	669
of the families of the tribe of *E*	Josh 21:5	669
their lot out of the tribe of *E*	Josh 21:20	669
Neither did *E* drive out the	Judg 1:29	669
Out of *E* was there a root of them	Judg 5:14	669
Then all the men of *E* gathered	Judg 7:24	669
the men of *E* said unto him, Why	Judg 8:1	669
of *E* better than the vintage of	Judg 8:2	669
and against the house of *E*	Judg 10:9	669
the men of *E* gathered themselves..........	Judg 12:1	669
men of Gilead, and fought with *E*	Judg 12:4	669
and the men of Gilead smote *E*	Judg 12:4	669
of *E* among the Ephraimites	Judg 12:4	669
in Pirathon in the land of *E*	Judg 12:15	669
and over Jezreel, and over *E*	2Sa 2:9	669
coasts out of the tribe of *E*	1Chr 6:66	669
Benjamin, and of the children of *E*	1Chr 9:3	669
the children of *E* twenty thousand	1Chr 12:30	669
Pelonite, of the children of *E*	1Chr 27:10	669
Pirathonite, of the children of *E*	1Chr 27:14	669
Of the children of *E*, Hoshea the	1Chr 27:20	669
the strangers with them out of *E*	2Chr 15:9	669
of Judah, and in the cities of *E*	2Chr 17:2	669
wit, with all the children of *E*	2Chr 25:7	669
that was come to him out of *E*	2Chr 25:10	669
And Zichri, a mighty man of *E*	2Chr 28:7	669
of the heads of the children of *E*	2Chr 28:12	669
Judah, and wrote letters also to *E*	2Chr 30:1	669
to city through the country of *E*	2Chr 30:10	669
of the people, even many of *E*	2Chr 30:18	669
in *E* also and Manasseh, until they	2Chr 31:1	669

in the cities of Manasseh, and *E*..............	2Chr 34:6	669
of the hand of Manasseh and *E*	2Chr 34:9	669
E also is the strength of mine	Ps 60:7	669
The children of *E*, being armed,..............	Ps 78:9	669
and chose not the tribe of *E*	Ps 78:67	669
Before *E* and Benjamin and Manasseh..	Ps 80:2	669
E also is the strength of mine	Ps 108:8	669
Syria is confederate with *E*	Is 7:2	669
Because Syria, *E*, and the son of	Is 7:5	669
and five years shall *E* be broken	Is 7:8	669
And the head of *E* is Samaria	Is 7:9	669
from the day that *E* departed from..........	Is 7:17	669
all the people shall know, even *E*	Is 9:9	669
Manasseh, *E*	Is 9:21	669
and *E*, Manasseh	Is 9:21	669
The envy also of *E* shall depart	Is 11:13	669
E shall not envy Judah	Is 11:13	669
and Judah shall not vex *E*	Is 11:13	669
fortress also shall cease from *E*	Is 17:3	669
of pride, to the drunkards of *E*	Is 28:1	669
of pride, the drunkards of *E*	Is 28:3	669
even the whole seed of *E*	Jer 7:15	669
to Israel, and *E* is my firstborn..............	Jer 31:9	669
I have surely heard *E* bemoaning..........	Jer 31:18	669
Is *E* my dear son	Jer 31:20	669
it, For Joseph, the stick of *E*	Eze 37:16	669
Joseph, which is in the hand of *E*..........	Eze 37:19	669
the west side, a portion for *E*	Eze 48:5	669
And by the border of *E*, from the	Eze 48:6	669
E is joined to idols	Hos 4:17	669
I know *E*, and Israel is not hid	Hos 5:3	669
for now, O *E*, thou committest	Hos 5:3	669
and *E* fall in their iniquity	Hos 5:5	669
E shall be desolate in the day of	Hos 5:9	669
E is oppressed and broken in..................	Hos 5:11	669
will I be unto *E* as a moth	Hos 5:12	669
When *E* saw his sickness, and Judah....	Hos 5:13	669
then went *E* to the Assyrian, and	Hos 5:13	669
For I will be unto *E* as a lion	Hos 5:14	669
O *E*, what shall I do unto thee	Hos 6:4	669
there is the whoredom of *E*....................	Hos 6:10	669
the iniquity of *E* was discovered	Hos 7:1	669
E, he hath mixed himself among	Hos 7:8	669
E is a cake not turned	Hos 7:8	669
E also is like a silly dove	Hos 7:11	669
E hath hired lovers..............................	Hos 8:9	669
Because *E* hath made many altars	Hos 8:11	669
but *E* shall return to Egypt, and............	Hos 9:3	669
The watchman of *E* was with my God ...	Hos 9:8	669
As for *E*, their glory shall fly	Hos 9:11	669
E, as I saw Tyrus, is planted in	Hos 9:13	669
but *E* shall bring forth his	Hos 9:13	669
E is smitten, their root is dried	Hos 9:16	669
E shall receive shame, and Israel..........	Hos 10:6	669
E is as an heifer that is taught, ...	Hos 10:11	669
I will make *E* to ride	Hos 10:11	669
I taught *E* also to go, taking	Hos 11:3	669
How shall I give thee up, *E*	Hos 11:8	669
I will not return to destroy *E*	Hos 11:9	669
E compasseth me about with lies, ...	Hos 11:12	669
E feedeth on wind, and followeth	Hos 12:1	669
E said, Yet I am become rich, I	Hos 12:8	669
E provoked him to anger most	Hos 12:14	669
When *E* spake trembling, he..................	Hos 13:1	669
The iniquity of *E* is bound up	Hos 13:12	669
E shall say, What have I to do	Hos 14:8	669
shall possess the fields of *E*	Obad 19	669
I will cut off the chariot from *E*	Zec 9:10	669
for me, filled the bow with *E*	Zec 9:13	669
they of *E* shall be like a mighty	Zec 10:7	669

3. Mountains in Samaria.

if mount *E* be too narrow for thee	Josh 17:15	669
even Timnath-serah in mount *E*..............	Josh 19:50	669
Naphtali, and Shechem in mount *E*	Josh 20:7	669
with her suburbs in mount *E*	Josh 21:21	669
which is in mount *E*, on the	Josh 24:30	669
which was given him in mount *E*	Josh 24:33	669
Timnath-heres, in the mount of *E*	Judg 2:9	669
a trumpet in the mountain of *E*	Judg 3:27	669
Ramah and Beth-el in mount *E*	Judg 4:5	669
messengers throughout all mount *E*	Judg 7:24	669
and he dwelt in Shamir in mount *E*	Judg 10:1	669
And there was a man of mount *E*	Judg 17:1	669
he came to mount *E* to the house	Judg 17:8	669
who when they came to mount *E*	Judg 18:2	669
they passed thence unto mount *E*	Judg 18:13	669
sojourning on the side of mount *E*	Judg 19:1	669
even, which was also of mount *E*	Judg 19:16	669
toward the side of mount *E*	Judg 19:18	669
of Ramathaim-zophim, of mount *E*	1Sa 1:1	669
And he passed through mount *E*	1Sa 9:4	669

had hid themselves in mount *E*	1Sa 14:22	669
but a man of mount *E*, Sheba the	2Sa 20:21	669
The son of Hur, in mount *E*	1Kin 4:8	669
Jeroboam built Shechem in mount *E*	1Kin 12:25	669
E two young men of the sons of	2Kin 5:22	669
in mount *E* with her suburbs	1Chr 6:67	669
Zemaraim, which is in mount *E*	2Chr 13:4	669
which he had taken from mount *E*	2Chr 15:8	669
people from Beer-sheba to mount *E*	2Chr 19:4	669
affliction from mount *E*	Jer 4:15	669
upon the mount *E* shall cry	Jer 31:6	669
shall be satisfied upon mount *E*	Jer 50:19	669

4. A town near Absalom's farm.

in Baal-hazor, which is beside *E*	2Sa 13:23	669

5. Battle site between David's and Absalom's armies.

the battle was in the wood of *E*	2Sa 18:6	669

6. A northern gate at Jerusalem.

gate of *E* unto the corner gate	2Kin 14:13	669
the gate of *E* to the corner gate	2Chr 25:23	669
and in the street of the gate of *E*	Neh 8:16	669
And from above the gate of *E*	Neh 12:39	669

7. A city near Jerusalem.

wilderness, into a city called *E*	Jn 11:54	2187

EPHRAIMITE *(e'-fra-im-ite)* See EPHRAIMITES. *A descendant of Ephraim.*

said unto him, Art thou an *E*	Judg 12:5	673

EPHRAIMITES *(e'-fra-im-ites)*

dwell among the *E* unto this day	Josh 16:10	669
fugitives of Ephraim among the *E*	Judg 12:4	669
passages of Jordan before the *E*	Judg 12:5	669
that when those *E* which were	Judg 12:5	669
fell at that time of the *E* forty	Judg 12:6	669

EPHRAIM'S *(e'-fra-ims)*
1. Refers to Ephraim 1.

hand, and laid it upon *E* head	Gen 48:14	669
to remove it from *E* head unto	Gen 48:17	669
Joseph saw *E* children of the	Gen 50:23	669

2. Refers to Ephraim 2.

Southward it was *E*, and northward	Josh 17:10	669

EPHRAIN *(e'-fra-in)* See EPHRAIM, EPHRON. *A city in Benjamin.*

and *E* with the towns thereof	2Chr 13:19	6085

EPHRATAH *(ef-rat-ah)* See BETHLEHEM, CALEBEPHRATAH, EPHRATH, EPHRATHITE.
1. Another name for Bethlehem-judah.

and do thou worthily in *E*, and be	Ruth 4:11	672
Lo, we heard of it at *E*	Ps 132:6	672
But thou, Beth-lehem *E*, though	Mic 5:2	672

2. A wife of Caleb.

son of Hur, the firstborn of *E*	1Chr 2:50	672
sons of Hur, the firstborn of *E*	1Chr 4:4	672

EPHRATH *(e'-frath)* See EPHRATAH.
1. A city in Judah.

was but a little way to come to *E*	Gen 35:16	672
and was buried in the way to *E*	Gen 35:19	672
but a little way to come unto *E*	Gen 48:7	672
buried her there in the way of *E*	Gen 48:7	672

2. Same as Ephratah 2.

was dead, Caleb took unto him *E*	1Chr 2:19	672

EPHRATHAH See EPHRATAH.

EPHRATHITE *(ef-rath-ite)* See EPHRATHITES. *An inhabitant of Bethlehem-judah.*

of Tohu, the son of Zuph, an *E*	1Sa 1:1	673
son of that *E* of Beth-lehem-judah	1Sa 17:12	673
an *E* of Zereda, Solomon's servant	1Kin 11:26	673

EPHRATHITES *(ef-rath-ites)*

and Chilion, *E* of Beth-lehem-judah	Ruth 1:2	673

EPHRON *(e'-fron)* See EPHRAIM, EPHRAIN.
1. Son of Zohar.

for me to *E* the son of Zohar	Gen 23:8	6085
E dwelt among the children of	Gen 23:10	6085
E the Hittite answered Abraham in	Gen 23:10	6085
he spake unto *E* in the audience	Gen 23:13	6085
E answered Abraham, saying unto	Gen 23:14	6085
And Abraham hearkened unto *E*	Gen 23:16	6085
Abraham weighed to *E* the silver	Gen 23:16	6085
And the field of *E*, which was in	Gen 23:17	6085
in the field of *E* the son of	Gen 25:9	6085
is in the field of *E* the Hittite	Gen 49:29	6085
bought with the field of *E* the	Gen 49:30	6085
a buryingplace of *E* the Hittite	Gen 50:13	6085

2. A mountain between Judah and Benjamin.

went out to the cities of mount *E*	Josh 15:9	6085

EPICUREANS *(ep-i-cu-re'-ans)* *Followers of the philosopher Epicurus.*

certain philosophers of the *E*	Acts 17:18	1946

EPISTLE

together, they delivered the *e*	Acts 15:30	1992
delivered the *e* to the governor,	Acts 23:33	1992
I Tertius, who wrote this *e*	Rom 16:22	1992
I wrote unto you in an *e* not to	1Cor 5:9	1992
The first *e* to the Corinthians	1Cor *s*	
Ye are our *e* written in our	2Cor 3:2	1992
the *e* of Christ ministered by us	2Cor 3:3	1992
the same *e* hath made you sorry	2Cor 7:8	1992
The second *e* to the Corinthians	2Cor *s*	
when this *e* is read among you,	Col 4:16	1992
likewise read the *e* from Laodicea	Col 4:16	
this *e* be read unto all the holy	1Th 5:27	1992
The first *e* unto the	1Th *s*	
taught, whether by word, or our *e*	2Th 2:15	1992
man obey not our word by this *e*	2Th 3:14	1992
which is the token in every *e*	2Th 3:17	1992
The second *e* to the Thessalonians	2Th *s*	
The second *e* unto Timotheus,	2Ti *s*	
This second *e*, beloved, I now	2Pet 3:1	1992

EPISTLES

e of commendation to you, or	2Cor 3:1	1992
As also in all his *e*, speaking in	2Pet 3:16	1992

EQUAL

gold and the crystal cannot *e* it	Job 28:17	6186
topaz of Ethiopia shall not *e* it	Job 28:19	6186
eyes behold the things that are *e*	Ps 17:2	4339
But it was thou, a man mine *e*	Ps 55:13	6187
The legs of the lame are not *e*	Prov 26:7	1809
will ye liken me, or shall I be *e*	Is 40:25	7737
will ye liken me, and make me *e*	Is 46:5	7737
what shall I *e* to thee, that I	Lam 2:13	7737
say, The way of the Lord is not *e*	Eze 18:25	8505
Is not my way *e*	Eze 18:25	8505
The way of the Lord is not *e*	Eze 18:29	8505
of Israel, are not my ways *e*	Eze 18:29	8505
say, The way of the Lord is not *e*	Eze 33:17	8505
as for them, their way is not *e*	Eze 33:17	8505
say, The way of the Lord is not *e*	Eze 33:20	8505
and thou hast made them *e* unto us	Mt 20:12	2470
for they are *e* unto the angels	Lk 20:36	2465
Father, making himself *e* with God	Jn 5:18	2470
it not robbery to be *e* with God	Phil 2:6	2470
servants that which is just and *e*	Col 4:1	2471
breadth and the height of it are *e*	Rev 21:16	2470

EQUALITY

But by an *e*, that now at this	2Cor 8:14	2471
that there may be *e*	2Cor 8:14	2471

EQUALLY

e distant one from another	Ex 36:22	7947

EQUALS

many my *e* in mine own nation	Gal 1:14	4915

EQUITY

the world, and the people with *e*	Ps 98:9	4339
thou dost establish *e*, thou	Ps 99:4	4339
justice, and judgment, and *e*	Prov 1:3	4339
righteousness, and judgment, and *e*	Prov 2:9	4339
good, nor to strike princes for *e*	Prov 17:26	3476
wisdom, and in knowledge, and in *e*	Eccl 2:21	3788
reprove with *e* for the meek of	Is 11:4	4334
in the street, and *e* cannot enter	Is 59:14	5229
abhor judgment, and pervert all *e*	Mic 3:9	3477
he walked with me in peace and *e*	Mal 2:6	4334

ER *(ur)*
1. A son of Judah.

and he called his name *E*	Gen 38:3	6147
took a wife for *E* his firstborn	Gen 38:6	6147
And *E*, Judah's firstborn, was	Gen 38:7	6147
E, and Onan, and Shelah, and Pharez,	Gen 46:12	6147
but *E* and Onan died in the land of	Gen 46:12	6147
The sons of Judah were *E* and Onan	Num 26:19	6147
and *E* and Onan died in the land of	Num 26:19	6147
E, and Onan, and Shelah	1Chr 2:3	6147
And *E*, the firstborn of Judah, was	1Chr 2:3	6147

2. A son of Shelah.

E the father of Lecah, and Laadah	1Chr 4:21	6147

3. Father of Elmodan; ancestor of Jesus.

Elmodam, which was the son of *E*	Lk 3:28	2262

ERAN *(e'-ran)* See ERANITES. *A son of Shath-elah.*

of *E*, the family of the Eranites	Num 26:36	6197

ERANITES *(e'-ran-ites)* *Descendants of Eran.*

of Eran, the family of the *E*	Num 26:36	6198

ERASTUS *(e-ras'-tus)*
1. A fellow-worker with Paul.

unto him, Timotheus and *E*	Acts 19:22	2037
E abode at Corinth	2Ti 4:20	2037

2. *A Corinthian city official.*
E the chamberlain of the city .... Rom 16:23   2037

ERE
are delivered *e* the midwives come .... Ex 1:19   2962
e it was chewed, the wrath of the .... Num 11:33   2962
long will it be *e* they believe me .... Num 14:11   3808
e the lamp of God went out in me 1Sa 3:3   2962
e thou bid the people return from 2Sa 2:26   3808
but *e* the messenger came to him, ... 2Kin 6:32   2962
How long will it be *e* ye make an .... Job 18:2
long will it be *e* thou be quiet .... Jer 47:6   3808
how long will it be *e* they attain .... Hos 8:5   3808
Sir, come down *e* my child die .... Jn 4:49   4250

ERECH (*e'-rek*) See ARCHEVITES. *A city in Shinar.*
of his kingdom was Babel, and *E* .... Gen 10:10   751

ERECTED
he *e* there an altar, and called it .... Gen 33:20   5324

ERI (*e'-ri*) See ERITES. *A son of Gad.*
and Haggi, Shuni, and Ezbon, *E* .... Gen 46:16   6179
of *E*, the family of the Erites .... Num 26:16   6179

ERITES (*e'-rites*) *Descendants of Eri.*
of Eri, the family of the *E* .... Num 26:16   6180

ERR
the inhabitants of Jerusalem to *e* 2Chr 33:9   8582
a people that do *e* in their heart .... Ps 95:10   8582
which do *e* from thy commandments...... Ps 119:21   7686
all them that *e* from thy statutes .... Ps 119:118   7686
Do they not *e* that devise evil.................. Prov 14:22   8582
to *e* from the words of knowledge .... Prov 19:27   7686
which lead thee cause thee to *e* .... Is 3:12   8582
of this people cause them to *e*................. Is 9:16   8582
Egypt to *e* in every work thereof............. Is 19:14   8582
they *e* in vision, they stumble in .... Is 28:7   7686
of the people, causing them to *e* .... Is 30:28   8582
though fools, shall not *e* therein.............. Is 35:8   8582
thou made us to *e* from thy ways............. Is 63:17   8582
and caused my people Israel to *e* .... Jer 23:13   8582
my people to *e* by their lies .... Jer 23:32   8582
whoredoms hath caused them to *e*........ Hos 4:12   8582
and their lies caused them to *e*............... Amos 2:4   8582
prophets that make my people *e* .... Mic 3:5   8582
and said unto them, Ye do *e*................ Mt 22:29   *4105*
unto them, Do ye not therefore *e* .... Mk 12:24   *4105*
ye therefore do greatly *e*.................... Mk 12:27   *4105*
They do alway *e* in their heart .... Heb 3:10   *4105*
Do not *e*, my beloved brethren .... Jas 1:16   *4105*
if any of you do *e* from the truth .... Jas 5:19   *4105*

ERRAND
not eat, until I have told mine *e* .... Gen 24:33   1697
said, I have a secret *e* unto thee .... Judg 3:19   1697
and he said, I have an *e* to thee.............. 2Kin 9:5   1697

ERRED
his ignorance wherein he *e*...................... Lev 5:18   7683
And if ye have *e*, and not observed......... Num 15:22   7683
the fool, and have *e* exceedingly 1Sa 26:21   7683
me to understand wherein I have *e* .... Job 6:24   7683
And be it indeed that I have *e*................. Job 19:4   7683
yet I *e* not from thy precepts .... Ps 119:110   8582
But they also have *e* through wine .... Is 28:7   7686
the prophet have *e* through strong .... Is 28:7   7686
They also that *e* in spirit shall .... Is 29:24   8582
they have *e* from the faith, and 1Ti 6:10   635
have *e* concerning the faith 1Ti 6:21   795
Who concerning the truth have *e* 2Ti 2:18   795

ERRETH
but he that refuseth reproof *e* .... Prov 10:17   8582
of the month for every one that *e* .... Eze 45:20   7686

ERROR
and God smote him there for his *e* 2Sa 6:7   7944
mine *e* remaineth with myself .... Job 19:4   4879
the angel, that it was an *e* .... Eccl 5:6   7684
as an *e* which proceedeth from the .... Eccl 10:5   7684
to utter *e* against the LORD, to .... Is 32:6   8432
there any *e* or fault found in him .... Dan 6:4   7960
so the last *e* shall be worse than .... Mt 27:64   *4106*
of their *e* which was meet...................... Rom 1:27   *4106*
e of his way shall save a soul .... Jas 5:20   *4106*
escaped from them who live in *e* 2Pet 2:18   *4106*
led away with the *e* of the wicked.......... 2Pet 3:17   *4106*
of truth, and the spirit of *e* 1Jn 4:6   *4106*
after the *e* of Balaam for reward .... Jude 11   *4106*

ERRORS
Who can understand his *e* .... Ps 19:12   7691
They are vanity, and the work of *e* .... Jer 10:15   8595

They are vanity, the work of *e* .... Jer 51:18   8595
and for the *e* of the people .... Heb 9:7   *51*

ESAIAS (*e-sah'-yas*) See ISAIAH. *Greek form of Isaiah.*
was spoken of by the prophet *E* .... Mt 3:3   2268
which was spoken by *E* the prophet .... Mt 4:14   2268
which was spoken by *E* the prophet .... Mt 8:17   2268
which was spoken by *E* the prophet .... Mt 12:17   2268
is fulfilled the prophecy of *E* .... Mt 13:14   2268
well did *E* prophesy of you, ... Mt 15:7   2268
Well hath *E* prophesied of you.............. Mk 7:6   2268
of the words of *E* the prophet .... Lk 3:4   2268
him the book of the prophet *E* .... Lk 4:17   2268
the Lord, as said the prophet *E*............... Jn 1:23   2268
That the saying of *E* the prophet .... Jn 12:38   2268
because that *E* said again....................... Jn 12:39   2268
These things said *E*, when he saw .... Jn 12:41   2268
in his chariot read *E* the prophet............ Acts 8:28   2268
and heard him read the prophet *E* .... Acts 8:30   2268
by *E* the prophet unto our fathers........... Acts 28:25   2268
E also crieth concerning Israel, ... Rom 9:27   2268
as *E* said before, Except the Lord .... Rom 9:29   2268
For *E* saith, Lord, who hath .... Rom 10:16   2268
But *E* is very bold, and saith, I .... Rom 10:20   2268
E saith, There shall be a root of .... Rom 15:12   2268

ESAR-HADDON (*e'-zar-had'-dun*) *An Assyrian king.*
E his son reigned in his stead................ 2Kin 19:37   634
since the days of *E* king of Assur .... Ezr 4:2   634
E his son reigned in his stead................ Is 37:38   634

ESAU (*e'-saw*)
1. *A son of Isaac.*
and they called his name *E*..................... Gen 25:25   6215
E was a cunning hunter, a man of .... Gen 25:27   6215
And Isaac loved *E*, because he did .... Gen 25:28   6215
E came from the field, and he was......... Gen 25:29   6215
E said to Jacob, Feed me, I pray .... Gen 25:30   6215
E said, Behold, I am at the point .... Gen 25:32   6215
Then Jacob gave *E* bread and................ Gen 25:34   6215
thus *E* despised his birthright .... Gen 25:34   6215
E was forty years old when he .... Gen 26:34   6215
he called *E* his eldest son, and.............. Gen 27:1   6215
when Isaac spake to *E* his son............... Gen 27:5   6215
E went to the field to hunt for .... Gen 27:5   6215
father speak unto *E* thy brother .... Gen 27:6   6215
E my brother is a hairy man, and I........ Gen 27:11   6215
raiment of her eldest son *E*.................... Gen 27:15   6215
his father, I am *E* thy firstborn .... Gen 27:19   6215
thou be my very son *E* or not.................. Gen 27:21   6215
but the hands are the hands of *E* .... Gen 27:22   6215
he said, Art thou my very son *E* .... Gen 27:24   6215
that *E* his brother came in from .... Gen 27:30   6215
I am thy son, thy firstborn *E*................... Gen 27:32   6215
when *E* heard the words of his............... Gen 27:34   6215
And Isaac answered and said unto *E*..... Gen 27:37   6215
E said unto his father, Hast thou .... Gen 27:38   6215
E lifted up his voice, and wept .... Gen 27:38   6215
E hated Jacob because of the .... Gen 27:41   6215
E said in his heart, The days of .... Gen 27:41   6215
these words of *E* her elder son .... Gen 27:42   6215
unto him, Behold, thy brother *E*.............. Gen 27:42   6215
When *E* saw that Isaac had blessed ...... Gen 28:6   6215
E seeing that the daughters of .... Gen 28:8   6215
Then went *E* unto Ishmael, and took..... Gen 28:9   6215
to *E* his brother unto the land of............. Gen 32:3   6215
shall ye speak unto my lord *E* .... Gen 32:4   6215
saying, We came to thy brother *E* .... Gen 32:6   6215
If *E* come to the one company, and........ Gen 32:8   6215
of my brother, from the hand of *E*........... Gen 32:11   6215
hand a present for *E* his brother............. Gen 32:13   6215
When *E* my brother meeteth thee, ... Gen 32:17   6215
is a present sent unto my lord *E* .... Gen 32:18   6215
this manner shall ye speak unto *E*......... Gen 32:19   6215
E came, and with him four hundred....... Gen 33:1   6215
E ran to meet him, and embraced.......... Gen 33:4   6215
E said, I have enough, my brother.......... Gen 33:9   6215
E said, Let me now leave with............... Gen 33:15   6215
So *E* returned that day on his way .... Gen 33:16   6215
from the face of *E* thy brother................ Gen 35:1   6215
and his sons *E* and Jacob buried him ... Gen 35:29   6215
these are the generations of *E* .... Gen 36:1   6215
E took his wives of the daughters .... Gen 36:2   6215
And Adah bare to *E* Eliphaz .... Gen 36:4   6215
these are the sons of *E*, which .... Gen 36:5   6215
E took his wives, and his sons, and .... Gen 36:6   6215
E in mount Seir: *E* is Edom.................. Gen 36:8   6215
these are the generations of *E* .... Gen 36:9   6215
the son of Adah the wife of *E* .... Gen 36:10   6215
son of Bashemath the wife of *E* .... Gen 36:10   6215
and she bare to *E* Jeush, and Jaalam ... Gen 36:14   6215
These were dukes of the sons of *E* .... Gen 36:15   6215

of Eliphaz the firstborn son of *E* .... Gen 36:15   6215
These are the sons of *E*, who is .... Gen 36:19   6215
names of the dukes that came of *E* .... Gen 36:40   6215
he is *E* the father of the .... Gen 36:43   6215
And I gave unto Isaac Jacob and *E* .... Josh 24:4   6215
and I gave unto *E* mount Seir .... Josh 24:4   6215
sons of Isaac; *E* and Israel 1Chr 1:34   6215
Was not *E* Jacob's brother .... Mal 1:2   6215
And I hated *E*, and laid his .... Mal 1:3   6215
or profane person, as *E*, who for .... Heb 12:16   2269
   2. *Descendants of Esau.*
your brethren the children of *E* .... Deut 2:4   6215
Seir unto *E* for a possession .... Deut 2:5   6215
our brethren the children of *E* .... Deut 2:8   6215
the children of *E* succeeded them .... Deut 2:12   6215
As he did to the children of *E* .... Deut 2:22   6215
children of *E* which dwell in Seir .... Deut 2:29   6215
The sons of *E* 1Chr 1:35   6215
bring the calamity of *E* upon him .... Jer 49:8   6215
But I have made *E* bare, I have .... Jer 49:10   6215
are the things of *E* searched out .... Obad 6   6215
and the house of *E* for stubble .... Obad 18   6215
any remaining of the house of *E* .... Obad 18   6215
have I loved, but *E* have I hated .... Rom 9:13   2269
E concerning things to come .... Heb 11:20   2269
   3. *A mountain.*
out of the mount of *E* .... Obad 8   6215
of *E* may be cut off by slaughter .... Obad 9   6215
shall possess the mount of *E* .... Obad 19   6215
Zion to judge the mount of *E* .... Obad 21   6215

ESAU'S (*e'-saws*) *Refers to Esau 1.*
and his hand took hold on *E* heel .... Gen 25:26   6215
hairy, his brother *E* hands .... Gen 27:23   6215
of Rebekah, Jacob's and *E* mother .... Gen 28:5   6215
These are the names of *E* sons .... Gen 36:10   6215
was concubine to Eliphaz *E* son .... Gen 36:12   6215
were the sons of Adah *E* wife .... Gen 36:12   6215
were the sons of Bashemath *E* wife .... Gen 36:13   6215
the daughter of Zibeon, *E* wife .... Gen 36:14   6215
these are the sons of Reuel *E* son .... Gen 36:17   6215
are the sons of Bashemath *E* wife .... Gen 36:17   6215
are the sons of Aholibamah *E* wife .... Gen 36:18   6215
the daughter of Anah, *E* wife .... Gen 36:18   6215

ESCAPE
that he said, *E* for thy life .... Gen 19:17   4422
e to the mountain, lest thou be .... Gen 19:17   4422
I cannot *e* to the mountain, lest .... Gen 19:19   4422
let me *e* thither, (is it not a .... Gen 19:20   4422
Haste thee, *e* thither .... Gen 19:22   4422
company which is left shall *e* .... Gen 32:8   6413
they let none of them remain or *e* .... Josh 8:22   6412
speedily *e* into the land of the 1Sa 27:1   4422
so shall I *e* out of his hand 1Sa 27:1   4422
we shall not *e* from Absalom 2Sa 15:14   6413
he get him fenced cities, and *e* us 2Sa 20:6   5337
let not one of them *e* 1Kin 18:40   4422
then let none go forth nor *e* out 2Kin 9:15   6412
I have brought into your hands *e* 2Kin 10:24   4422
they that *e* out of mount Zion 2Kin 19:31   6413
God, to leave us a remnant to *e* .... Ezr 9:8   6413
thou shalt *e* in the king's house .... Est 4:13   4422
shall fail, and they shall not *e* .... Job 11:20   4498,6
I would hasten my *e* from the .... Ps 55:8   4655
Shall they *e* by iniquity .... Ps 56:7   6405
righteousness, and cause me to *e* .... Ps 71:2   6403
own nets, whilst that I withal *e* .... Ps 141:10   5674
he that speaketh lies shall not *e* .... Prov 19:5   4422
pleaseth God shall *e* from her .... Eccl 7:26   4422
and how shall we *e* .... Is 20:6   4422
they that *e* out of mount Zion .... Is 37:32   6413
I will send those that *e* of them .... Is 66:19   6412
which they shall not be able to *e* .... Jer 11:11   3318
the principal of the flock to *e* .... Jer 25:35   6413
not *e* out of the hand of the .... Jer 32:4   4422
thou shalt not *e* out of his hand, ... Jer 34:3   4422
thou shalt not *e* out of their .... Jer 38:18   4422
thou shalt not *e* out of their .... Jer 38:23   4422
none of them shall remain or *e* .... Jer 42:17   6412
shall *e* or remain, that they .... Jer 44:14   6412
shall return but such as shall *e* .... Jer 44:14   6412
Yet a small number that *e* the .... Jer 44:28   6412
flee away, nor the mighty man *e* .... Jer 46:6   4422
every city, and no city shall *e* .... Jer 48:8   4422
e out of the land of Babylon, to .... Jer 50:28   6412
let none thereof *e* .... Jer 50:29   6413
e the sword among the nations .... Eze 6:8   6412
they that *e* of you shall remember .... Eze 6:9   6412
But they that *e* of them shall .... Eze 7:16   6403
shall *e*, and shall be on the .... Eze 7:16   6412
shall he that doeth such things .... Eze 17:15   4422

all these things, he shall not *e* .... Eze 17:18   4422
but these shall *e* out of his hand .... Dan 11:41   4422
and the land of Egypt shall not *e* .... Dan 11:42   6413
yea, and nothing shall *e* them .... Joel 2:3   6413
cut off those of his that did *e* .... Obad 14   6412
how can ye *e* the damnation of ...... Mt 23:33   5343,575
to *e* all these things that shall .... Lk 21:36   1628
any of them should swim out, and *e* ...... Acts 27:42   1309
that thou shalt *e* the judgment of .... Rom 2:3   1628
temptation also make a way to *e* 1Cor 10:13   1545
and they shall not *e* 1Th 5:3   1628
How shall we *e*, if we neglect so .... Heb 2:3   1628
earth, much more shall not we *e* .... Heb 12:25   5343

ESCAPED
And there came one that had *e* .... Gen 14:13   6412
the residue of that which is *e* .... Ex 10:5   6413
he hath given his sons that *e* .... Num 21:29   6412
is *e* from his master unto thee .... Deut 23:15   5337
Ehud *e* while they tarried, and.............. Judg 3:26   4422
the quarries, and *e* unto Seirath............ Judg 3:26   4422
and there *e* not a man .... Judg 3:29   4422
Ephraimites which were *e* said .... Judg 12:5   6412
for them that be *e* of Benjamin .... Judg 21:17   6413
but the people *e* 1Sa 14:41   3318
and David fled, and *e* that night 1Sa 19:10   4422
and he went, and fled, and *e* 1Sa 19:12   4422
away mine enemy, that he is *e* 1Sa 19:17   4422
So David fled, and *e*, and came to 1Sa 19:18   4422
thence, and *e* to the cave Adullam 1Sa 22:1   4422
son of Ahitub, named Abiathar, *e* 1Sa 22:20   4422
Saul that David was *e* from Keilah 1Sa 23:13   4422
there *e* not a man of them, save 1Sa 30:17   4422
Out of the camp of Israel am I *e* 2Sa 1:3   4422
and Rechab and Baanah his brother *e* .. 2Sa 4:6   4422
Ben-hadad the king of Syria *e* on 1Kin 20:20   4422
the remnant that is *e* of the 2Kin 19:30   6413
they *e* into the land of Armenia 2Kin 19:37   4422
of the Amalekites that were *e* 1Chr 4:43   6413
king of Syria *e* out of thine hand 2Chr 16:7   4422
fallen to the earth, and none *e* 2Chr 20:24   4422
that are *e* out of the hand of the 2Chr 30:6   6413
them that had *e* from the sword 2Chr 36:20   7611
for we remain yet *e*, as it is .... Ezr 9:15   6413
concerning the Jews that had *e* .... Neh 1:2   6413
I only am *e* alone to tell thee .... Job 1:15   4422
I only am *e* alone to tell thee .... Job 1:16   4422
I only am *e* alone to tell thee .... Job 1:17   4422
I only am *e* alone to tell thee .... Job 1:19   4422
I am *e* with the skin of my teeth .... Job 19:20   4422
Our soul is *e* as a bird out of................ Ps 124:7   4422
the snare is broken, and we are *e* .... Ps 124:7   4422
for them that are *e* of Israel .... Is 4:2   6413
such as are *e* of the house of .... Is 10:20   6413
the remnant that is *e* of the .... Is 37:31   6413
they *e* into the land of Armenia .... Is 37:38   4422
ye that are *e* of the nations .... Is 45:20   6412
e from Johanan with eight men .... Jer 41:15   4422
Ye that have *e* the sword, go away .... Jer 51:50   6412
LORD'S anger none *e* nor remained .... Lam 2:22
mouth be opened to him which is *e* ...... Eze 24:27   6412
that one that had *e* out of .... Eze 33:21   6412
evening, afore he that was *e* came.......... Eze 33:22   6412
but he *e* out of their hand, ... Jn 10:39   1831
that they *e* all safe to land.................... Acts 27:44   1295
And when they were *e*, then they .... Acts 28:1   1295
whom, though he hath *e* the sea............ Acts 28:4   1295
down by the wall, and *e* his hands 2Cor 11:33   1628
e the edge of the sword, out of .... Heb 11:34   5343
For if they *e* not who refused him .... Heb 12:25   5343
having *e* the corruption that is 2Pet 1:4   668
those that were clean *e* from them 2Pet 2:18   668
For if after they have *e* the 2Pet 2:20   668

ESCAPETH
that him that *e* the sword of 1Kin 19:17   4422
him that *e* from the sword of Jehu 1Kin 19:17   4422
lions upon him that *e* of Moab .... Is 15:9   6413
him that fleeth, and her that *e* .... Jer 48:19   4422
That he that *e* in that day shall .... Eze 24:26   6412
he that *e* of them shall not be .... Amos 9:1   6412

ESCAPING
there should be no remnant nor *e* .... Ezr 9:14   6413

ESCHEW
Let him *e* evil, and do good 1Pet 3:11   1578

ESCHEWED
and one that feared God, and *e* evil ...... Job 1:1   5493

ESCHEWETH
one that feareth God, and *e* evil .... Job 1:8   5493
one that feareth God, and *e* evil .... Job 2:3   5493

E

ESEK (e'-sek) A well in the valley of Geran.
he called the name of the well E ....Gen 26:20   6320

ESHAN See ESHEAN.

ESH-BAAL (esh'-ba-al) See ISH-BOSHETH. A son of King
Saul.
Malchi-shua, and Abinadab, and E 1Chr 8:33   792
Malchi-shua, and Abinadab, and E 1Chr 9:39   792

ESHBAN A son of Dishon.
Hemdan, and E, and Ithran, and ....Gen 36:26   790
and E, and Ithran, and Cheran.............1Chr 1:41   790

ESHCOL (esh'-col)
    1. Brother of Mamre and Aner.
Mamre the Amorite, brother, of E ....Gen 14:13   812
men which went with me, Aner, of E ....Gen 14:24   812
    2. A valley or brook in Hebron.
And they came unto the brook of E ....Num 13:23   812
The place was called the brook E ....Num 13:24   812
they went up unto the valley of E ....Num 32:9   812
and came unto the valley of E ....Deut 1:24   812

ESHEAN (esh'-e-an) A city in Judea.
Arab, and Dumah, and E, ...Josh 15:52   824

ESHEK (e'-shek) A descendant of King Saul.
the sons of E his brother were,...........1Chr 8:39   6232

ESHKALONITES (esh'-ka-lon-ites) Inhabitants of Ashkelon.
and the Ashdothites, the E ....Josh 13:3   832

ESHTAOL (esh'-ta-ol) See ESHTAULITES. A town in
Judah.
And in the valley, E, and Zoreah, ...Josh 15:33   847
their inheritance was Zorah, and E ....Josh 19:41   847
camp of Dan between Zorah and E.......Judg 13:25   847
E in the buryingplace of Manoah ....Judg 16:31   847
of valour, from Zorah, and from E ....Judg 18:2   847
unto their brethren to Zorah and E ....Judg 18:8   847
Danites, out of Zorah and out of E ....Judg 18:11   847

ESHTAOLITES See ESHTAULITES.

ESHTAULITES (esh'-ta-u-lites) Inhabitants of Eshtaol.
came the Zareathites, and the E 1Chr 2:53   848

ESHTEMOA (es-te-mo'-ah) See ESHTEMOH.
    1. A Levitical town in Judah.
suburbs, and E with her suburbs, ...Josh 21:14   851
and to them which were in E 1Sa 30:28   851
with her suburbs, and Jattir, and E 1Chr 6:57   851
    2. A descendant of Ezra.
and Ishbah the father of E 1Chr 4:17   851
the Garmite, and E the Maachathite.....1Chr 4:19   851

ESHTEMOH (esh'-te-moh) See ESHTEMOA. Same as Eshtemoa 1.
And Anab, and E, and Anim, ...Josh 15:50   851

ESHTON (esh'-ton) Grandson of Chelub.
Mehir, which was the father of E 1Chr 4:11   850
E begat Beth-rapha, and Paseah, and....1Chr 4:12   850

ESLI (es'-li) Father of Naum; ancestor of Jesus.
of Naum, which was the son of E ....Lk 3:25   2069

ESPECIALLY
but e among my neighbours, and a ....Ps 31:11   3966
E because I know thee to be ....Acts 26:3   3122
e unto them who are of the ....Gal 6:10   3122
e they who labour in the word and 1Ti 5:17   3122
the books, but e the parchments,..........2Ti 4:13   3122

ESPIED
in the inn, he e his money.................Gen 42:27   7200
into a land that I had e for them ....Eze 20:6   8446

ESPOUSALS
crowned him in the day of his e ....Song 3:11   2861
of thy youth, the love of thine e ....Jer 2:2   3623

ESPOUSED
which I e to me for an hundred.............2Sa 3:14   781
his mother Mary was e to Joseph ....Mt 1:18   3423
To a virgin e to a man whose name ....Lk 1:27   3423
To be taxed with Mary his e wife ....Lk 2:5   3423
for I have e you to one husband, ...2Cor 11:2   718

ESPY
Kadesh-barnea to e out the land............Josh 14:7   7270
of Aroer, stand by the way, and e ....Jer 48:19   6822

ESROM (es'-rom) See HEZRON. Son of Phares; ancestor
of Jesus.
and Phares begat E ....Mt 1:3   2074
and E begat Aram ....Mt 1:3   2074
of Aram, which was the son of E ....Lk 3:33   2074

ESTABLISH
with thee will I e my covenant ....Gen 6:18   6965
I e my covenant with you, and with ......Gen 9:9   6965
I will e my covenant with you ....Gen 9:11   6965
I will e my covenant between me...........Gen 17:7   6965
I will e my covenant with him for ....Gen 17:19   6965
my covenant will I e with Isaac...........Gen 17:21   6965
you, and e my covenant with you ....Lev 26:9   6965
the soul, her husband may e it ....Num 30:13   6965
that he may e his covenant which ....Deut 8:18   6965
The LORD shall e thee an holy ....Deut 28:9   6965
That he may e thee to day for a ....Deut 29:13   6965
only the LORD e his word 1Sa 1:23   6965
bowels, and I will e his kingdom 2Sa 7:12   3559
e it for ever, and do as thou hast.........2Sa 7:25   6965
Then I will e the throne of thy............1Kin 9:5   6965
son after him, and to e Jerusalem 1Kin 15:4   5975
and I will e his kingdom 1Chr 17:11   3559
I will e the throne of his.................1Chr 22:10   3559
Moreover I will e his kingdom for 1Chr 28:7   3559
to e them for ever, therefore 2Chr 9:8   5975
he doth e them for ever, and they ....Job 36:7   3427
but e the just: for the righteous ....Ps 7:9   3559
God will e it for ever ....Ps 48:8   3559
the highest himself shall e her ....Ps 87:5   3559
shalt thou e in the very heavens ....Ps 89:2   3559
Thy seed will I e for ever ....Ps 89:4   3559
e thou the work of our hands upon ....Ps 90:17   3559
the work of our hands e thou it ....Ps 90:17   3559
thou dost e equity, thou..................Ps 99:4   3559
but he will e the border of the ....Prov 15:25   5324
to e it with judgment and with ....Is 9:7   5582
to e the earth, to cause to...............Is 49:8   6965
And give him no rest, till he e ....Is 62:7   3559
the LORD that formed it, to e it ....Jer 33:2   3559
I will e unto thee an everlasting ....Eze 16:60   6965
I will e my covenant with thee ....Eze 16:62   6965
together to e a royal statute ....Dan 6:7   6966
e the decree, and sign the writing ....Dan 6:8   6966
exalt themselves to e the vision ....Dan 11:14   5975
good, and e judgment in the gate ....Amos 5:15   3322
yea, we e the law ....Rom 3:31   2476
going about to e their own ....Rom 10:3   2476
to e you, and to comfort you...............1Th 3:2   4741
first, that he may e the second ....Heb 10:9   2476

ESTABLISHED
which I have e between me ....Gen 9:17   6965
is because the thing is e by God ....Gen 41:32   3559
I have also e my covenant with ....Ex 6:4   6965
O Lord, which thy hands have e ....Ex 15:17   3559
e for ever to him that bought it ....Lev 25:30   6965
witnesses, shall the matter be e ....Deut 19:15   6965
Hath he not thee, and e thee ....Deut 32:6   3559
was e to be a prophet of the LORD 1Sa 3:20   539
e thy kingdom upon Israel for..............1Sa 13:13   3559
the ground, thou shalt not be e 1Sa 20:31   3559
Israel shall be e in thine hand 1Sa 24:20   6965
LORD had e him king over Israel...........2Sa 5:12   3559
shall be e for ever before thee 2Sa 7:16   539
thy throne shall be e for ever 2Sa 7:16   3559
servant David be e before thee 2Sa 7:26   3559
and his kingdom was e greatly 1Kin 2:12   3559
the LORD liveth, which hath e me 1Kin 2:24   3559
be e before the LORD for ever..............1Kin 2:45   3559
the kingdom was e in the hand of 1Kin 2:46   3559
throne shall be e for evermore 1Chr 17:14   3559
his house be e for ever, and do as 1Chr 17:23   539
Let it even be e, that thy name 1Chr 17:24   539
thy servant be e before thee 1Chr 17:24   3559
promise unto David my father be e 2Chr 1:9   539
when Rehoboam had e the kingdom 2Chr 12:1   3559
LORD your God, so shall ye be e............2Chr 20:20   539
when the kingdom was e to him 2Chr 25:3   2388
So they e a decree to make 2Chr 30:5   5975
Their seed is e in their sight ....Job 21:8   3559
thing, and it shall be e unto thee ....Job 22:28   6965
the seas, and e it upon the floods ....Ps 24:2   3559
feet upon a rock, and e my goings ....Ps 40:2   3559
For he e a testimony in Jacob, and ....Ps 78:5   6965
earth which he hath e for ever ....Ps 78:69   3245
With whom my hand shall be e ....Ps 89:21   3559
It shall be e for ever as the ....Ps 89:37   3559
Thy throne is e of old ....Ps 93:2   3559
the world also shall be e that it ....Ps 96:10   3559
their seed shall be e before thee ....Ps 102:28   3559
His heart is e, he shall not be ....Ps 112:8   5564
thou hast e the earth, and it..............Ps 119:90   3559
an evil speaker be e in the earth ....Ps 140:11   3559
hath e the heavens ....Prov 3:19   3559
feet, and let all thy ways be e.............Prov 4:26   3559

When he *e* the clouds above .... Prov 8:28   553
man shall not be *e* by wickedness .... Prov 12:3   3559
lip of truth shall be *e* for ever .... Prov 12:19   3559
of counsellors they are *e* .... Prov 15:22   6965
Lord, and thy thoughts shall be *e* .... Prov 16:3   3559
the throne is *e* by righteousness .... Prov 16:12   3559
Every purpose is *e* by counsel .... Prov 20:18   3559
and by understanding it is *e* .... Prov 24:3   3559
shall be *e* in righteousness .... Prov 25:5   3559
his throne shall be *e* for ever .... Prov 29:14   3559
who hath *e* all the ends of the .... Prov 30:4   6965
be *e* in the top of the mountains .... Is 2:2   3559
believe, surely ye shall not be *e* .... Is 7:9   539
And in mercy shall the throne be *e* .... Is 16:5   3559
he hath it, he created it not .... Is 45:18   3559
In righteousness shalt thou be *e* .... Is 54:14   3559
he hath *e* the world by his wisdom .... Jer 10:12   3559
congregation shall be *e* before me .... Jer 30:20   3559
he hath *e* the world by his wisdom .... Jer 51:15   3559
I was *e* in my kingdom, and .... Dan 4:36   8627
be *e* in the top of the mountains .... Mic 4:1   3559
thou hast *e* them for correction .... Hab 1:12   3245
and it shall be *e*, and set there .... Zec 5:11   3559
witnesses every word may be *e* .... Mt 18:16   2476
were the churches *e* in the faith .... Acts 16:5   4732
gift, to the end ye may be *e* .... Rom 1:11   4741
witnesses shall every word be *e* 2Cor 13:1   2476
which was *e* upon better promises .... Heb 8:6   3549
that the heart be *e* with grace .... Heb 13:9   950
be *e* in the present truth 2Pet 1:12   4741

ESTABLISHETH
then he *e* all her vows, or all .... Num 30:14   6965
The king by judgment *e* the land .... Prov 29:4   5975
which the king *e* may be changed .... Dan 6:15   6966

ESTABLISHMENT
the *e* thereof, Sennacherib king 2Chr 32:1   571

ESTATE
to the *e* of a man of high degree 1Chr 17:17   8448
e unto another that is better .... Est 1:19
Who remembered us in our low *e* .... Ps 136:23
saying, Lo, I am come to great *e* .... Eccl 1:16
the *e* of the sons of men, that .... Eccl 3:18   1700
shall return to their former *e* .... Eze 16:55
shall return to their former *e* .... Eze 16:55   3653
shall return to your former *e* .... Eze 16:55
roots shall one stand up in his *e* .... Dan 11:7   3653
Then shall stand up in his *e* a .... Dan 11:20   3653
in his *e* shall stand up a vile .... Dan 11:21   3653
But in his *e* shall he honour the .... Dan 11:38   3653
the low *e* of his handmaiden .... Lk 1:48
and all the *e* of the elders .... Acts 22:5
but condescend to men of low *e* .... Rom 12:16
that he might know your *e* .... Col 4:8   3588,4012
which kept not their first *e* .... Jude 6

ESTATES
will settle you after your old *e* .... Eze 36:11
captains, and chief *e* of Galilee .... Mk 6:21

ESTEEM
Will he *e* thy riches .... Job 36:19   6186
Therefore I *e* all thy precepts .... Ps 119:128
yet we did *e* him stricken, ... Is 53:4   2803
e other better than themselves .... Phil 2:3   2233
to *e* them very highly in love for 1Th 5:13   2233

ESTEEMED
lightly *e* the Rock of his .... Deut 32:15   5034
despise me shall be lightly *e* 1Sa 2:30   7043
I am a poor man, and lightly *e* 1Sa 18:23   7043
I have *e* the words of his mouth .... Job 23:12   6845
lips is *e* a man of understanding .... Prov 17:28
shall be *e* as the potter's clay .... Is 29:16   2803
field shall be *e* as a forest .... Is 29:17   2803
he was despised, and we *e* him not .... Is 53:3   2803
how are they *e* as earthen .... Lam 4:2   2803
for that which is highly *e* among .... Lk 16:15
who are least *e* in the church 1Cor 6:4   1848

ESTEEMETH
He *e* iron as straw, and brass as .... Job 41:27   2803
One man *e* one day above another .... Rom 14:5   2919
another *e* every day alike .... Rom 14:5   2919
but to him that *e* any thing to be .... Rom 14:14   3049

ESTEEMING
E the reproach of Christ greater .... Heb 11:26   2233

ESTHER (*est'-thur*) See ESTHER'S, HADASSAH. *A Jewish queen.*
brought up Hadassah, that is, *E* .... Est 2:7   635
that *E* was brought also unto the .... Est 2:8   635

E had not shewed her people nor .... Est 2:10   635
women's house, to know how *E* did .... Est 2:11   635
Now when the turn of *E*, the .... Est 2:15   635
E obtained favour in the sight of .... Est 2:15   635
So *E* was taken unto king .... Est 2:16   635
the king loved *E* above all the .... Est 2:17   635
E had not yet shewed her kindred .... Est 2:20   635
for *E* did the commandment of .... Est 2:20   635
who told it unto *E* the queen .... Est 2:22   635
E certified the king thereof in .... Est 2:22   635
Then called *E* for Hatach, one of .... Est 4:5   635
destroy them, to shew it unto *E* .... Est 4:8   635
told *E* the words of Mordecai .... Est 4:9   635
Again *E* spake unto Hatach, and .... Est 4:10   635
Mordecai commanded to answer *E* .... Est 4:13   635
Then *E* bade them return Mordecai .... Est 4:15   635
to all that *E* had commanded him .... Est 4:17   635
that *E* put on her royal apparel, ... Est 5:1   635
when the king saw *E* the queen .... Est 5:2   635
the king held out to *E* the golden .... Est 5:2   635
So *E* drew near, and touched the .... Est 5:2   635
unto her, What wilt thou, queen *E* .... Est 5:3   635
E answered, If it seem good unto .... Est 5:4   635
that he may do as *E* hath said .... Est 5:5   635
the banquet that *E* had prepared .... Est 5:5   635
the king said unto *E* at the .... Est 5:6   635
Then answered *E*, and said, My .... Est 5:7   635
E the queen did let no man come .... Est 5:12   635
the banquet that *E* had prepared .... Est 6:14   635
came to banquet with *E* the queen .... Est 7:1   635
unto *E* on the second day at the .... Est 7:2   635
What is thy petition, queen *E* .... Est 7:2   635
Then *E* the queen answered and said .... Est 7:3   635
answered and said unto *E* the queen .... Est 7:5   635
E said, The adversary and enemy is ..... Est 7:6   635
for his life to *E* the queen .... Est 7:7   635
fallen upon the bed whereon *E* was ...... Est 7:8   635
the Jews' enemy unto *E* the queen .... Est 8:1   635
for *E* had told what he was unto .... Est 8:1   635
E set Mordecai over the house of .... Est 8:2   635
E spake yet again before the king .... Est 8:3   635
out the golden sceptre toward *E* .... Est 8:4   635
So *E* arose, and stood before the .... Est 8:4   635
Ahasuerus said unto *E* the queen .... Est 8:7   635
I have given *E* the house of Haman ...... Est 8:7   635
And the king said unto *E* the queen ..... Est 9:12   635
Then said *E*, If it please the .... Est 9:13   635
But when *E* came before the king, ... Est 9:25   635
Then *E* the queen, the daughter of .... Est 9:29   635
E the queen had enjoined them, and ..... Est 9:31   635
the decree of *E* confirmed these .... Est 9:32   635

ESTHER'S (*es'-thurs*)
and his servants, even *E* feast .... Est 2:18   635
So *E* maids and her chamberlains .... Est 4:4   635
And they told to Mordecai *E* words .... Est 4:12   635

ESTIMATE
Lord, then the priest shall *e* it .... Lev 27:14   6186
as the priest shall *e* it, so .... Lev 27:14   6186

ESTIMATION
with thy *e* by shekels of silver, ... Lev 5:15   6187
out of the flock, with thy *e* .... Lev 5:18   6187
out of the flock, with thy *e* .... Lev 6:6   6187
shall be for the Lord by thy *e* .... Lev 27:2   6187
thy *e* shall be of the male from .... Lev 27:3   6187
even thy *e* shall be fifty shekels .... Lev 27:3   6187
then thy *e* shall be thirty .... Lev 27:4   6187
then thy *e* shall be of the male .... Lev 27:5   6187
then thy *e* shall be of the male .... Lev 27:6   6187
for the female thy *e* shall be .... Lev 27:6   6187
then thy *e* shall be fifteen .... Lev 27:7   6187
But if he be poorer than thy *e* .... Lev 27:8   6187
a fifth part thereof unto thy *e* .... Lev 27:13   6187
of the money of thy *e* unto it .... Lev 27:15   6187
then thy *e* shall be according to .... Lev 27:16   6187
according to the *e* it shall stand .... Lev 27:17   6187
and it shall be abated from thy *e* .... Lev 27:18   6187
of the money of thy *e* unto it .... Lev 27:19   6187
unto him the worth of thy *e* .... Lev 27:23   6187
he shall give thine *e* in that day .... Lev 27:23   6187
redeem it according to thine *e* .... Lev 27:27   6187
shall be sold according to thy *e* .... Lev 27:27   6187
thou redeem, according to thine *e* .... Num 18:16   6187

ESTIMATIONS
all thy *e* shall be according to .... Lev 27:25   6187

ESTRANGED
acquaintance are verily *e* from me .... Job 19:13   2114
The wicked are *e* from the womb .... Ps 58:3   2114
They were not *e* from their lust .... Ps 78:30   2114

E

have *e* this place, and have burned	Jer 19:4	5234
because they are all *e* from me	Eze 14:5	2114

ETAM (*e'-tam*)
1. An area in western Judah.

and dwelt in the top of the rock *E*	Judg 15:8	5862
went to the top of the rock *E*	Judg 15:11	5862

2. A descendant of Judah.

And these were of the father of *E*	1Chr 4:3	5862

3. A village in Simeon.

And their villages were, *E*	1Chr 4:32	5862

4. A town in Judah.

He built even Beth-lehem, and *E*	2Chr 11:6	5862

ETERNAL

The *e* God is thy refuge, and	Deut 33:27	6924
I will make thee an *e* excellency	Is 60:15	5769
I do, that I may have *e* life	Mt 19:16	166
but the righteous into life *e*	Mt 25:46	166
I do that I may inherit *e* life	Mk 10:17	166
but is in danger of *e* **damnation**	Mk 3:29	166
and in the world to come *e* **life**	Mk 10:30	166
what shall I do to inherit *e* life	Lk 10:25	166
what shall I do to inherit *e* life	Lk 18:18	166
not perish, but have *e* **life**	Jn 3:15	166
and gathereth fruit unto life *e*	Jn 4:36	166
in them ye think ye have *e* **life**	Jn 5:39	166
and drinketh my blood, hath *e* **life**	Jn 6:54	166
thou hast the words of *e* life	Jn 6:68	166
And I give unto them *e* life	Jn 10:28	166
world shall keep it unto life *e*	Jn 12:25	166
that he should give *e* **life to as**	Jn 17:2	166
And this is life *e*, **that they**	Jn 17:3	166
were ordained to *e* life believed	Acts 13:48	166
that are made, even his *e* power	Rom 1:20	126
and honour and immortality, *e* life	Rom 2:7	166
through righteousness unto *e* life	Rom 5:21	166
but the gift of God is *e* life	Rom 6:23	166
exceeding and *e* weight of glory	2Cor 4:17	166
things which are not seen are *e*	2Cor 4:18	166
made with hands, *e* in the heavens	2Cor 5:1	166
According to the *e* purpose which	Eph 3:11	165
Now unto the King *e*, immortal,	1Ti 1:17	165
of faith, lay hold on *e* life	1Ti 6:12	166
that they may lay hold on *e* life	1Ti 6:19	166
is in Christ Jesus with *e* glory	2Ti 2:10	166
In hope of *e* life, which God,	Titus 1:2	166
according to the hope of *e* life	Titus 3:7	166
he became the author of *e*	Heb 5:9	166
of the dead, and of *e* judgment	Heb 6:2	166
having obtained *e* redemption for	Heb 9:12	166
who through the *e* Spirit offered	Heb 9:14	166
the promise of *e* inheritance	Heb 9:15	166
unto his *e* glory by Christ Jesus	1Pet 5:10	166
and shew unto you that *e* life	1Jn 1:2	166
he hath promised us, even *e* life	1Jn 2:25	166
hath *e* life abiding in him	1Jn 3:15	166
that God hath given to us *e* life	1Jn 5:11	166
ye may know that ye have *e* life	1Jn 5:13	166
This is the true God, and *e* life	1Jn 5:20	166
suffering the vengeance of *e* fire	Jude 7	166
our Lord Jesus Christ unto *e* life	Jude 21	166

ETERNITY

and lofty One that inhabiteth *e*	Is 57:15	5703

ETHAM (*e'-tham*) *An encampment during the Exodus.*

from Succoth, and encamped in *E*	Ex 13:20	864
from Succoth, and pitched in *E*	Num 33:6	864
And they removed from *E*, and turned	Num 33:7	864
journey in the wilderness of *E*	Num 33:8	864

ETHAN (*e'-than*)
1. A wise man in Solomon's time.

than *E* the Ezrahite, and Heman, and	1Kin 4:31	387
Maschil of *E* the Ezrahite	Ps 89:t	387

2. A son of Zerah.

Zimri, and *E*, and Heman, and Calcol,	1Chr 2:6	387
And the sons of *E*	1Chr 2:8	387

3. A descendant of Gershon.

The son of *E*, the son of Zimmah,	1Chr 6:42	387

4. A descendant of Merari.

E the son of Kishi, the son of	1Chr 6:44	387
brethren, *E* the son of Kushaiah	1Chr 15:17	387
the singers, Heman, Asaph, and *E*	1Chr 15:19	387

ETHANIM (*eth'-a-nim*) *Seventh month of the Hebrew year.*

at the feast in the month *E*	1Kin 8:2	388

ETHBAAL (*eth'-ba-al*) *Father of Jezebel.*

of *E* king of the Zidonians	1Kin 16:31	856

ETHER (*e'-ther*) *A city in Judah.*

Libnah, and *E*, and Ashan,	Josh 15:42	6281
Ain, Remmon, and *E*, and Ashan	Josh 19:7	6281

ETHIOPIA (*e-the-o'-pe-ah*) See CUSH, ETHIOPIAN.
1. The land south of Egypt.

compasseth the whole land of *E*	Gen 2:13	3568
reigned from India even unto *E*	Est 1:1	3568
which are from India unto *E*	Est 8:9	3568
The topaz of *E* shall not equal it	Job 28:19	3568
behold Philistia, and Tyre, with *E*	Ps 87:4	3568
which is beyond the rivers of *E*	Is 18:1	3568
Syene even unto the border of *E*	Eze 29:10	3568
the rivers of *E* my suppliants	Zeph 3:10	3568
and, behold, a man of *E*, an eunuch	Acts 8:27	128

2. Inhabitants of Ethiopia.

heard say of Tirhakah king of *E*	2Kin 19:9	3568
E shall soon stretch out her	Ps 68:31	3568
and wonder upon Egypt and upon *E*	Is 20:3	3568
ashamed of *E* their expectation,	Is 20:5	3568
say concerning Tirhakah king of *E*	Is 37:9	3568
I gave Egypt for thy ransom, *E*	Is 43:3	3568
of Egypt, and merchandise of *E*	Is 45:14	3568
and great pain shall be in *E*	Eze 30:4	3568
E, and Libya, and Lydia, and all the	Eze 30:5	3568
Persia, *E*, and Libya with them	Eze 38:5	3568
E and Egypt were her strength, and	Nah 3:9	3568

ETHIOPIAN

the *E* woman whom he had married	Num 12:1	3569
for he had married an *E* woman	Num 12:1	3569
the *E* with an host of a thousand	2Chr 14:9	3569
Can the *E* change his skin, or the	Jer 13:23	3569
Now when Ebed-melech the *E*	Jer 38:7	3569
king commanded Ebed-melech the *E*	Jer 38:10	3569
Ebed-melech the *E* said unto	Jer 38:12	3569
Go and speak to Ebed-melech the *E*	Jer 39:16	3569

ETHIOPIANS *Inhabitants of Ethiopia.*

the Lubim, the Sukkiims, and the *E*	2Chr 12:3	3569
the LORD smote the *E* before Asa	2Chr 14:12	3569
before Judah; and the *E* fled	2Chr 14:12	3569
the *E* were overthrown, that they	2Chr 14:13	3569
Were not the *E* and the Lubims a	2Chr 16:8	3569
Arabians, that were near the *E*	2Chr 21:16	3569
the *E* captives, young and old,	Is 20:4	3569
the *E* and the Libyans, that handle	Jer 46:9	3569
to make the careless *E* afraid	Eze 30:9	3569
the *E* shall be at his steps	Dan 11:43	3569
not as children of the *E* unto me	Amos 9:7	3569
Ye *E* also, ye shall be slain by	Zeph 2:12	3569
under Candace queen of the *E*	Acts 8:27	128

ETH KAZIN See ITTAH-KAZIN.

ETHNAN (*eth'-nan*) *Grandson of Ashur.*

were, Zereth, and Jezoar, and *E*	1Chr 4:7	869

ETHNI (*eth'-ni*) See JEATERAI. *Ancestor of Asaph.*

The son of *E*, the son of Zerah,	1Chr 6:41	867

EUBULUS (*yu-bu'-lus*) *A Christian acquaintance of Paul.*

E greeteth thee, and Pudens, and	2Ti 4:21	2103

EUNICE (*yu-ni'-see*) *Mother of Timothy.*

grandmother Lois, and thy mother *E*	2Ti 1:5	2131

EUNUCH

neither let the *e* say, Behold, I	Is 56:3	5631
He took also out of the city an *e*	Jer 52:25	5631
an *e* of great authority under	Acts 8:27	2135
the *e* answered Philip, and said, I	Acts 8:34	2135
the *e* said, See, here is water	Acts 8:36	2135
the water, both Philip and the *e*	Acts 8:38	2135
that the *e* saw him no more	Acts 8:39	2135

EUNUCHS

looked out to him two or three *e*	2Kin 9:32	5631
they shall be *e* in the palace of	2Kin 20:18	5631
they shalt be *e* in the palace of	Is 39:7	5631
unto the *e* that keep my sabbaths	Is 56:4	5631
the king, and the queen, and the *e*	Jer 29:2	5631
the princes of Jerusalem, the *e*	Jer 34:19	5631
one of the *e* which was in the	Jer 38:7	5631
women, and the children, and the *e*	Jer 41:16	5631
unto Ashpenaz the master of his *e*	Dan 1:3	5631
the prince of the *e* gave names	Dan 1:7	5631
of the *e* that he might not defile	Dan 1:8	5631
love with the prince of the *e*	Dan 1:9	5631
prince of the *e* said unto Daniel	Dan 1:10	5631
of the *e* had set over Daniel	Dan 1:11	5631
of the *e* brought them in after	Dan 1:18	5631
For there are some *e*, **which were**	Mt 19:12	2135
and there are some *e*, **which were**	Mt 19:12	2134
e, **which were made** *e* **of men**	Mt 19:12	2134

and there be *e*, which have made .... Mt 19:12   2135
which have made themselves *e* for .... Mt 19:12   2134

EUODIAS (*yu-o'·de-as*) *A Christian at Philippi.*
I beseech *E*, and beseech Syntyche,...... Phil 4:2   2136

EUPHRATES (*yu-fra'·teze*) *A river in Mesopotamia.*
And the fourth river is *E*......................... Gen 2:14   6578
unto the great river, the river *E* .... Gen 15:18   6578
unto the great river, the river *E* .... Deut 1:7   6578
from the river, the river *E* .... Deut 11:24   6578
unto the great river, the river *E* .... Josh 1:4   6578
recover his border at the river *E*............ 2Sa 8:3   6578
king of Assyria to the river *E*................. 2Kin 23:29   6578
river of Egypt unto the river *E* 2Kin 24:7   6578
the wilderness from the river *E* 1Chr 5:9   6578
his dominion by the river *E* 1Chr 18:3   6578
to fight against Charchemish by *E*......... 2Chr 35:20   6578
upon thy loins, and arise, go to *E* .... Jer 13:4   6578
So I went, and hid it by *E* .... Jer 13:5   6578
LORD said unto me, Arise, go to *E* .... Jer 13:6   6578
Then I went to *E*, and digged, and....... Jer 13:7   6578
was by the river *E* in Carchemish .... Jer 46:2   6578
toward the north by the river *E* .... Jer 46:6   6578
the north country by the river *E* .... Jer 46:10   6578
and cast it into the midst of *E*................ Jer 51:63   6578
are bound in the great river *E* .... Rev 9:14   2166
his vial upon the great river *E* .... Rev 16:12   2166

EURAQUILO See EUROCLYDON.

EUROCLYDON (*yu-roc'·lid-on*) *A Mediterranean wind.*
it a tempestuous wind, called *E*............. Acts 27:14   2148

EUTYCHUS (*yu'-tik-us*) *Youth restored to life.*
a certain young man named *E* .... Acts 20:9   2161

EVANGELIST
into the house of Philip the *e*................. Acts 21:8   2099
afflictions, do the work of an *e*.............. 2Ti 4:5   2099

EVANGELISTS
and some, *e*; and some, pastors .... Eph 4:11   2099

EVE (*eev*) *Wife of Adam.*
And Adam called his wife's name *E* .... Gen 3:20   2332
And Adam knew *E* his wife .... Gen 4:1   2332
beguiled *E* through his subtilty 2Cor 11:3   2096
For Adam was first formed, then *E*........ 1Ti 2:13   2096

EVEN See APPENDIX.

EVENING
And the *e* and the morning were the ...... Gen 1:5   6153
And the *e* and the morning were the ...... Gen 1:8   6153
And the *e* and the morning were the ...... Gen 1:13   6153
And the *e* and the morning were the ...... Gen 1:19   6153
And the *e* and the morning were the ...... Gen 1:23   6153
And the *e* and the morning were the ...... Gen 1:31   6153
the dove came in to him in the *e*............ Gen 8:11   6153
of water at the time of the *e* .... Gen 24:11   6153
And it came to pass in the *e*................... Gen 29:23   6153
came out of the field in the *e* .... Gen 30:16   6153
of Israel shall kill it in the *e* .... Ex 12:6   6153
give you in the *e* flesh to eat .... Ex 16:8   6153
Moses from the morning unto the *e*....... Ex 18:13   6153
from *e* to morning before the LORD .... Ex 27:21   6153
the *e* unto the morning before the .... Lev 24:3   6153
when *e* cometh on, he shall wash .... Deut 23:11   6153
upon the trees until the *e* .... Josh 10:26   6153
now the day draweth toward *e* .... Judg 19:9   6150
man that eateth any food until *e* 1Sa 14:24   6153
Philistine drew near morning and *e* 1Sa 17:16   6150
even unto the *e* of the next day 1Sa 30:17   6153
and bread and flesh in the *e* 1Kin 17:6   6153
the offering of the *e* sacrifice 1Kin 18:29
the offering of the *e* sacrifice 1Kin 18:36
the *e* meat offering, and the 2Kin 16:15   6153
offering continually morning and *e*....... 1Chr 16:40   6153
the burnt offerings morning and *e* 2Chr 2:4   6153
every *e* burnt sacrifices and sweet......... 2Chr 13:11   6153
lamps thereof, to burn every *e* 2Chr 13:11   6153
e burnt offerings, and the burnt 2Chr 31:3   6153
even burnt offerings morning and *e*...... Ezr 3:3   6153
astonied until the *e* sacrifice .... Ezr 9:4   6153
at the *e* sacrifice I arose up .... Ezr 9:5   6153
In the *e* she went, and on the .... Est 2:14   6153
are destroyed from morning to *e* .... Job 4:20   6153
E, and morning, and at noon, will I .... Ps 55:17   6153
They return at *e*: they make a................ Ps 59:6   6153
And at *e* let them return .... Ps 59:14   6153
of the morning and *e* to rejoice .... Ps 65:8   6153
in the *e* it is cut down, and .... Ps 90:6   6153
work and to his labour until the *e* .... Ps 104:23   6153
up of my hands as the *e* sacrifice .... Ps 141:2   6153
In the twilight, in the *e* .... Prov 7:9   6153

in the *e* withhold not thine hand .... Eccl 11:6   6153
of the *e* are stretched out .... Jer 6:4   6153
of the LORD was upon me in the *e* .... Eze 33:22   6153
shall not be shut until the *e* .... Eze 46:2   6153
And the vision of the *e* and the .... Dan 8:26   6153
about the time of the *e* oblation .... Dan 9:21   6153
are more fierce than the *e* wolves.......... Hab 1:8   6153
shall they lie down in the *e*................... Zeph 2:7   6153
her judges are *e* wolves......................... Zeph 3:3   6153
that at *e* time it shall be light............... Zec 14:7   6153
And when it was *e*, his disciples .... Mt 14:15   3798
and when the *e* was come, he was .... Mt 14:23   3798
and said unto them, When it is *e*........... Mt 16:2   3798
in the *e* he cometh with the .... Mk 14:17   3798
for it is toward *e*, and the day is........... Lk 24:29   2073
Then the same day at *e*, being the......... Jn 20:19   3798
the prophets, from morning till *e* .... Acts 28:23   2073

EVENINGS
a wolf of the *e* shall spoil them, ... Jer 5:6   6160

EVENINGTIDE
And it came to pass in an *e*.................... 2Sa 11:2   6256,6153
And behold at *e* trouble .... Is 17:14   6256,6153

EVENT
that one *e* happeneth to them all........... Eccl 2:14   4745
there is one *e* to the righteous, ... Eccl 9:2   4745
sun, that there is one *e* unto all .... Eccl 9:3   4745

EVENTIDE
to meditate in the field at the *e* .... Gen 24:63   6256,6153
the ark of the LORD until the *e* .... Josh 7:6   6153
of Ai he hanged on a tree until *e* .... Josh 8:29   6256,6153
now the *e* was come, he went out .... Mk 11:11
for it was now *e* .... Acts 4:3   2073

EVER
of life, and eat, and live for *e*................ Gen 3:22   5769
I give it, and to thy seed for *e* .... Gen 13:15   5769
then let me bear the blame for *e*...... Gen 43:9   3605,3117
bear the blame to my father for *e*.... Gen 44:32   3605,3117
this is my name for *e*, and this............. Ex 3:15   5769
it a feast by an ordinance for *e*............. Ex 12:14   5769
generations by an ordinance for *e*......... Ex 12:17   5769
to thee and to thy sons for *e*................. Ex 12:24   5769
see them again no more for *e* .... Ex 14:13   5769
The LORD shall reign for *e* .... Ex 15:18   5769
LORD shall reign for *e* and *e* .... Ex 15:18   5703
with thee, and believe thee for *e* .... Ex 19:9   5769
and he shall serve him for *e* .... Ex 21:6   5769
it shall be a statute for *e* unto .... Ex 27:21   5769
shall be a statute for *e* unto him.......... Ex 28:43   5769
his sons' by a statute for *e* from .... Ex 29:28   5769
shall be a statute for *e* to them............. Ex 30:21   5769
and the children of Israel for *e* .... Ex 31:17   5769
and they shall inherit it for *e* .... Ex 32:13   5769
The fire shall *e* be burning upon........... Lev 6:13   8548
It shall be a statute for *e* in .... Lev 6:18   5769
is a statute for *e* unto the LORD.............. Lev 6:22   5769
for *e* from among the children of........... Lev 7:34   5769
by a statute for *e* throughout .... Lev 7:36   5769
it shall be a statute for *e* .... Lev 10:9   5769
with thee, by a statute for *e*.................. Lev 10:15   5769
shall be a statute for *e* unto you .... Lev 16:29   5769
your souls, by a statute for *e* .... Lev 16:31   5769
for *e* unto them throughout their .... Lev 17:7   5769
it shall be a statute for *e* .... Lev 23:14   5769
for *e* in all your dwellings .... Lev 23:21   5769
it shall be a statute for *e* .... Lev 23:31   5769
statute for *e* in your generations .... Lev 23:41   5769
statute for *e* in your generations.......... Lev 24:3   5769
The land shall not be sold for *e* .... Lev 25:23   6783
for *e* to him that bought it .... Lev 25:30   6783
they shall be your bondmen for *e*.......... Lev 25:46   5769
for *e* throughout your generations .... Num 10:8   5769
an ordinance for *e* in your .... Num 15:15   5769
thy sons, by an ordinance for *e*............. Num 18:8   5769
with thee, by a statute for *e* .... Num 18:11   5769
with thee, by a statute for *e* .... Num 18:19   5769
for *e* before the LORD unto thee .... Num 18:19   5769
it shall be a statute for *e* .... Num 18:23   5769
among them, for a statute for *e*............. Num 19:10   5769
upon which thou hast ridden *e* .... Num 22:30   5750
was I *e* wont to do so unto thee............ Num 22:30
end shall be that he perish for *e*........... Num 24:20   5703
and he also shall perish for *e* .... Num 24:24   5703
Did *e* people hear the voice of .... Deut 4:33
LORD thy God giveth thee, for *e* .... Deut 4:40   3605,3117
and with their children for *e*................. Deut 5:29   5769
thy children after thee for *e*.................. Deut 12:28   5769
and it shall be an heap for *e* .... Deut 13:16   5769
and he shall be thy servant for *e* .... Deut 15:17   5769

E

the LORD, him and his sons for *e*	Deut 18:5	3605,3117
thy God, and to walk in his ways.	Deut 19:9	3605,3117
congregation of the LORD for *e*	Deut 23:3	5769
prosperity all thy days for *e*	Deut 23:6	5769
a wonder, and upon thy seed for *e*	Deut 28:46	5769
unto us and to our children for *e*	Deut 29:29	5769
to heaven, and say, I live for *e*	Deut 32:40	5769
unto the children of Israel for *e*	Josh 4:7	5769
fear the LORD your God for *e*	Josh 4:24	3605,3117
Ai, and made it an heap for *e*	Josh 8:28	5769
and thy children's for *e*, because	Josh 14:9	5769
did he *e* strive against Israel,	Judg 11:25	
or did he *e* fight against them,	Judg 11:25	
the LORD, and there abide for *e*	1Sa 1:22	5769
should walk before me for *e*	1Sa 2:30	5769
an old man in thine house for *e*	1Sa 2:32	3605,3117
walk before mine anointed for *e*	1Sa 2:35	3605,3117
for *e* for the iniquity which he	1Sa 3:13	5769
with sacrifice nor offering for *e*	1Sa 3:14	5769
thy kingdom upon Israel for *e*	1Sa 13:13	5769
thy kindness from my house for *e*	1Sa 20:15	5769
LORD be between thee and me for *e*	1Sa 20:23	5769
between my seed and thy seed for *e*	1Sa 20:42	5769
he shall be my servant for *e*	1Sa 27:12	5769
thee keeper of mine head for *e*	1Sa 28:2	3605,3117
Shall the sword devour for *e*	2Sa 2:26	5331
guiltless before the LORD for *e*	2Sa 3:28	5769
the throne of his kingdom for *e*	2Sa 7:13	5769
be established for *e* before thee	2Sa 7:16	5769
throne shall be established for *e*	2Sa 7:16	5769
to be a people unto thee for *e*	2Sa 7:24	5769
his house, establish it for *e*	2Sa 7:25	5769
let thy name be magnified for *e*	2Sa 7:26	5769
it may continue for *e* before thee	2Sa 7:29	5769
of thy servant be blessed for *e*	2Sa 7:29	5769
Let my lord king David live for *e*	1Kin 1:31	5769
upon the head of his seed for *e*	1Kin 2:33	5769
be peace for *e* from the LORD	1Kin 2:33	5769
established before the LORD for *e*	1Kin 2:45	
for Hiram was *e* a lover of David	1Kin 5:1	3605,3117
place for thee to abide in for *e*	1Kin 8:13	5769
built, to put my name there for *e*	1Kin 9:3	5769
of thy kingdom upon Israel for *e*	1Kin 9:5	5769
the LORD loved Israel for *e*	1Kin 10:9	5769
the seed of David, but not for *e*	1Kin 11:39	3605,3117
they will be thy servants for *e*	1Kin 12:7	3605,3117
unto thee, and unto thy seed for *e*	2Kin 5:27	5769
Israel, will I put my name for *e*	2Kin 21:7	5769
and to minister unto him for *e*	1Chr 15:2	5769
for his mercy endureth for *e*	1Chr 16:34	5769
be the LORD God of Israel for *e*	1Chr 16:36	5769
LORD God of Israel for *e* and *e*	1Chr 16:36	5769
because his mercy endureth for *e*	1Chr 16:41	5769
I will stablish his throne for *e*	1Chr 17:12	5769
mine house and in my kingdom for *e*	1Chr 17:14	5769
thou make thine own people for *e*	1Chr 17:22	5769
his house be established for *e*	1Chr 17:23	5769
thy name may be magnified for *e*	1Chr 17:24	5769
that it may be before thee for *e*	1Chr 17:27	5769
and it shall be blessed for *e*	1Chr 17:27	5769
of his kingdom over Israel for *e*	1Chr 22:10	5769
holy things, he and his sons for *e*	1Chr 23:13	5769
and to bless in his name for *e*	1Chr 23:13	5769
they may dwell in Jerusalem for *e*	1Chr 23:25	5769
to be king over Israel for *e*	1Chr 28:4	5769
will establish his kingdom for *e*	1Chr 28:7	5769
for your children after you for *e*	1Chr 28:8	5769
him, he will cast thee off for *e*	1Chr 28:9	5703
Israel our father, for *e* and	1Chr 29:10	5704,5769
fathers, keep this for *e* in the	1Chr 29:18	5769
is an ordinance for *e* to Israel	2Chr 2:4	5769
for his mercy endureth for *e*	2Chr 5:13	5769
and a place for thy dwelling for *e*	2Chr 6:2	5769
for his mercy endureth for *e*	2Chr 7:3	5769
because his mercy endureth for *e*	2Chr 7:6	5769
that my name may be there for *e*	2Chr 7:16	5769
Israel, to establish them for *e*	2Chr 9:8	5769
they will be thy servants for *e*	2Chr 10:7	3605,3117
over Israel to David for *e*	2Chr 13:5	5769
seed of Abraham thy friend for *e*	2Chr 20:7	5769
for his mercy endureth for *e*	2Chr 20:21	5769
light to him and to his sons for *e*	2Chr 21:7	3605,3117
which he hath sanctified for *e*	2Chr 30:8	5769
Jerusalem shall my name be for *e*	2Chr 33:4	5769
Israel, will I put my name for *e*	2Chr 33:7	5865
endureth for *e* toward Israel	Ezr 3:11	5769
their peace or their wealth for *e*	Ezr 9:12	5769
to your children for *e*	Ezr 9:12	5769
the king, Let him live for *e*	Neh 2:3	5769
the LORD your God for *e* and *e*	Neh 9:5	5769
the congregation of God for *e*	Neh 13:1	5769

who *e* perished, being innocent	Job 4:7	
they perish for *e* without any	Job 4:20	5331
Thou prevailest for *e* against him	Job 14:20	5331
pen and lead in the rock for *e*	Job 19:24	5703
perish for *e* like his own dung	Job 20:7	5331
be delivered for *e* from my judge	Job 23:7	5331
yea, he doth establish them for *e*	Job 36:7	5331
thou take him for a servant for *e*	Job 41:4	5769
let them *e* shout for joy, because	Ps 5:11	5769
hast put out their name for *e*	Ps 9:5	5769
put out their name for *e* and *e*	Ps 9:5	5703
But the LORD shall endure for *e*	Ps 9:7	5769
the poor shall not perish for *e*	Ps 9:18	5703
The LORD is King for *e* and *e*	Ps 10:16	5769
The LORD is King for *e* and *e*	Ps 10:16	5703
them from this generation for *e*	Ps 12:7	5769
forget me, O LORD? for *e*?	Ps 13:1	5331
the LORD is clean, enduring for *e*	Ps 19:9	5703
it him, even length of days for *e*	Ps 21:4	5769
even length of days for *e* and *e*	Ps 21:4	5703
hast made him most blessed for *e*	Ps 21:6	5703
your heart shall live for *e*	Ps 22:26	5703
in the house of the LORD for *e*	Ps 23:6	753,3117
for they have been *e* of old	Ps 25:6	
Mine eyes are *e* toward the LORD	Ps 25:15	8548
them also, and lift them up for *e*	Ps 28:9	5769
yea, the LORD sitteth King for *e*	Ps 29:10	5769
will give thanks unto thee for *e*	Ps 30:12	5769
of the LORD standeth for *e*	Ps 33:11	5769
their inheritance shall be for *e*	Ps 37:18	5769
He is *e* merciful, and lendeth	Ps 37:26	3605,3117
they are preserved for *e*	Ps 37:28	5769
the land, and dwell therein for *e*	Ps 37:29	5703
settest me before thy face for *e*	Ps 41:12	5769
long, and praise thy name for *e*	Ps 44:8	5769
arise, cast us not off for *e*	Ps 44:23	5331
God hath blessed thee for *e*	Ps 45:2	5769
Thy throne, O God, is for *e*	Ps 45:6	5769
throne, O God, is for *e* and *e*	Ps 45:6	5703
the people praise thee for *e*	Ps 45:17	5769
people praise thee for *e* and *e*	Ps 45:17	5703
God will establish it for *e*	Ps 48:8	5769
For this God is our God for *e*	Ps 48:14	5769
this God is our God for *e* and *e*	Ps 48:14	5703
is precious, and it ceaseth for *e*	Ps 49:8	5769
That he should still live for *e*	Ps 49:9	5331
their houses shall continue for *e*	Ps 49:11	5769
and my sin is *e* before me	Ps 51:3	8548
shall likewise destroy thee for *e*	Ps 52:5	5331
I trust in the mercy of God for *e*	Ps 52:8	5769
in the mercy of God for *e* and *e*	Ps 52:8	5703
I will praise thee for *e*, because	Ps 52:9	5769
abide in thy tabernacle for *e*	Ps 61:4	5769
He shall abide before God for *e*	Ps 61:7	5769
I sing praise unto thy name for *e*	Ps 61:8	5703
He ruleth by his power for *e*	Ps 66:7	5769
the LORD will dwell in it for *e*	Ps 68:16	5331
His name shall endure for *e*	Ps 72:17	5769
be his glorious name for *e*	Ps 72:19	5769
of my heart, and my portion for *e*	Ps 73:26	5769
why hast thou cast us off for *e*	Ps 74:1	5331
enemy blaspheme thy name for *e*	Ps 74:10	5331
congregation of thy poor for *e*	Ps 74:19	5331
But I will declare for *e*	Ps 75:9	5769
Will the Lord cast off for *e*	Ps 77:7	5769
Is his mercy clean gone for *e*	Ps 77:8	5331
which he hath established for *e*	Ps 78:69	5769
wilt thou be angry for *e*	Ps 79:5	5331
will give thee thanks for *e*	Ps 79:13	5769
time should have endured for *e*	Ps 81:15	5769
be confounded and troubled for *e*	Ps 83:17	5703
Wilt thou be angry with us for *e*	Ps 85:5	5769
of the mercies of the LORD for *e*	Ps 89:1	5769
Mercy shall be built up for *e*	Ps 89:2	5769
Thy seed will I establish for *e*	Ps 89:4	5769
also will I make to endure for *e*	Ps 89:29	5703
His seed shall endure for *e*	Ps 89:36	5769
be established for *e* as the moon	Ps 89:37	5769
wilt thou hide thyself for *e*	Ps 89:46	5331
or *e* thou hadst formed the earth	Ps 90:2	
they shall be destroyed for *e*	Ps 92:7	5703
thine house, O LORD, for *e*	Ps 93:5	753,3117
thou, O LORD, shalt endure for *e*	Ps 102:12	5769
will he keep his anger for *e*	Ps 103:9	5769
it should not be removed for *e*	Ps 104:5	5769,5703
of the LORD shall endure for *e*	Ps 104:31	5769
remembered his covenant for *e*	Ps 105:8	5769
for his mercy endureth for *e*	Ps 106:1	5769
for his mercy endureth for *e*	Ps 107:1	5769
Thou art a priest for *e* after the	Ps 110:4	5769
his righteousness endureth for *e*	Ps 111:3	5703

he will *e* be mindful of his	Ps 111:5	5769
They stand fast for *e* and *e*, and	Ps 111:8	5703
They stand fast for *e* and *e*	Ps 111:8	5769
hath commanded his covenant for *e*	Ps 111:9	5769
his praise endureth for *e*	Ps 111:10	5769
his righteousness endureth for *e*	Ps 112:3	5703
he shall not be moved for *e*	Ps 112:6	5769
his righteousness endureth for *e*	Ps 112:9	5703
truth of the LORD endureth for *e*	Ps 117:2	5769
because his mercy endureth for *e*	Ps 118:1	5769
that his mercy endureth for *e*	Ps 118:2	5769
that his mercy endureth for *e*	Ps 118:3	5769
that his mercy endureth for *e*	Ps 118:4	5769
for his mercy endureth for *e*	Ps 118:29	5769
I keep thy law continually for *e*	Ps 119:44	5769
thy law continually for *e* and *e*	Ps 119:44	5703
For *e*, O LORD, thy word is	Ps 119:89	5769
for they are of with me	Ps 119:98	5769
have I taken as an heritage for *e*	Ps 119:111	5769
that thou hast founded them for *e*	Ps 119:152	5769
judgments endureth for *e*	Ps 119:160	5769
be removed, but abideth for *e*	Ps 125:1	5769
people from henceforth even for *e*	Ps 125:2	5769
the LORD from henceforth and for *e*	Ps 131:3	5769
This is my rest for *e*	Ps 132:14	5769
Thy name, O LORD, endureth for *e*	Ps 135:13	5703
for his mercy endureth for *e*	Ps 136:1	5769
for his mercy endureth for *e*	Ps 136:2	5769
for his mercy endureth for *e*	Ps 136:3	5769
for his mercy endureth for *e*	Ps 136:4	5769
for his mercy endureth for *e*	Ps 136:5	5769
for his mercy endureth for *e*	Ps 136:6	5769
for his mercy endureth for *e*	Ps 136:7	5769
for his mercy endureth for *e*	Ps 136:8	5769
for his mercy endureth for *e*	Ps 136:9	5769
for his mercy endureth for *e*	Ps 136:10	5769
for his mercy endureth for *e*	Ps 136:11	5769
for his mercy endureth for *e*	Ps 136:12	5769
for his mercy endureth for *e*	Ps 136:13	5769
for his mercy endureth for *e*	Ps 136:14	5769
for his mercy endureth for *e*	Ps 136:15	5769
for his mercy endureth for *e*	Ps 136:16	5769
for his mercy endureth for *e*	Ps 136:17	5769
for his mercy endureth for *e*	Ps 136:18	5769
for his mercy endureth for *e*	Ps 136:19	5769
for his mercy endureth for *e*	Ps 136:20	5769
for his mercy endureth for *e*	Ps 136:21	5769
for his mercy endureth for *e*	Ps 136:22	5769
for his mercy endureth for *e*	Ps 136:23	5769
for his mercy endureth for *e*	Ps 136:24	5769
for his mercy endureth for *e*	Ps 136:25	5769
for his mercy endureth for *e*	Ps 136:26	5769
thy mercy, O LORD, endureth for *e*	Ps 138:8	5769
and I will bless thy name for *e*	Ps 145:1	5769
will bless thy name for *e* and *e*	Ps 145:1	5703
and I will praise thy name for *e*	Ps 145:2	5769
praise thy name for *e* and *e*	Ps 145:2	5703
flesh bless his holy name for *e*	Ps 145:21	5769
bless his holy name for *e* and *e*	Ps 145:21	5703
which keepeth truth for *e*	Ps 146:6	5769
The LORD shall reign for *e*	Ps 146:10	5769
hath also stablished them for *e*	Ps 148:6	5703
stablished them for *e* and *e*	Ps 148:6	5769
the beginning, or *e* the earth was	Prov 8:23	6924
truth shall be established for *e*	Prov 12:19	5703
For riches are not for *e*	Prov 27:24	5769
throne shall be established for *e*	Prov 29:14	5703
but the earth abideth for *e*	Eccl 1:4	5769
wise more than of the fool for *e*	Eccl 2:16	5769
God doeth, it shall be for *e*	Eccl 3:14	5769
they any more a portion for *e* in	Eccl 9:6	5769
Or *e* the silver cord be loosed,	Eccl 12:6	
Or I was aware, my soul made me	Song 6:12	3808
from henceforth even for *e*	Is 9:7	
Trust ye in the LORD for *e*	Is 26:4	5703
he will not *e* be threshing it	Is 28:28	5331
may be for the time to come for *e*	Is 30:8	5703
the time to come for *e* and *e*	Is 30:8	5769
and towers shall be for dens for *e*	Is 32:14	5769
quietness and assurance for *e*	Is 32:17	5769
stakes thereof shall *e* be removed	Is 33:20	5331
smoke thereof shall go up for *e*	Is 34:10	5769
none shall pass through it for *e*	Is 34:10	5769
pass through it for *e* and *e*	Is 34:10	5331
they shall possess it for *e*	Is 34:17	5769
word of our God shall stand for *e*	Is 40:8	5769
saidst, I shall be a lady for *e*	Is 47:7	5769
but my salvation shall be for *e*	Is 51:6	5769
my righteousness shall be for *e*	Is 51:8	5769
For I will not contend for *e*	Is 57:16	5769
LORD, from henceforth and for *e*	Is 59:21	5769

they shall inherit the land for *e*	Is 60:21	5769
neither remember iniquity for *e*	Is 64:9	5703
rejoice for *e* in that which I	Is 65:18	5703
Will he reserve his anger for *e*	Jer 3:5	
and I will not keep anger for *e*	Jer 3:12	5769
to your fathers, for *e* and *e*	Jer 7:7	5769
anger, which shall burn for *e*	Jer 17:4	5769
and this city shall remain for *e*	Jer 17:25	5769
and to your fathers for *e* and *e*	Jer 25:5	5769
being a nation before me for *e*	Jer 31:36	3605,3117
nor thrown down any more for *e*	Jer 31:40	5769
way, that they may fear me for *e*	Jer 32:39	3605,3117
for his mercy endureth for *e*	Jer 33:11	5769
neither ye, nor your sons for *e*	Jer 35:6	5769
a man to stand before me for *e*	Jer 35:19	3605,3117
dragons, and a desolation for *e*	Jer 49:33	5769
shall be no more inhabited for *e*	Jer 50:39	5331
but thou shalt be desolate for *e*	Jer 51:26	5769
that it shall be desolate for *e*	Jer 51:62	5769
the Lord will not cast off for *e*	Lam 3:31	5769
Thou, O LORD, remainest for *e*	Lam 5:19	5769
dost thou forget us for *e*	Lam 5:20	5331
their children's children for *e*	Eze 37:25	5769
David shall be their prince for *e*	Eze 37:25	5769
of the children of Israel for *e*	Eze 43:7	5769
dwell in the midst of them for *e*	Eze 43:9	5769
in Syriack, O king, live for *e*	Dan 2:4	5957
Blessed be the name of God for *e*	Dan 2:20	5957
be the name of God for *e* and *e*	Dan 2:20	5957
kingdoms, and it shall stand for *e*	Dan 2:44	5957
O king, live for *e*	Dan 3:9	5957
and honoured him that liveth for *e*	Dan 4:34	5957
spake and said, O king, live for *e*	Dan 5:10	5957
unto him, King Darius, live for *e*	Dan 6:6	5757
unto the king, O king, live for *e*	Dan 6:21	5957
all their bones in pieces or *e*	Dan 6:24	3809
the living God, and stedfast for *e*	Dan 6:26	5957
the kingdom for *e*, even for *e*	Dan 7:18	5957
for *e*, even for *e* and *e*	Dan 7:18	5957
righteousness as the stars for *e*	Dan 12:3	5769
as the stars for *e* and *e*	Dan 12:3	5703
for *e* that it shall be for a time	Dan 12:7	5769
I will betroth thee unto me for *e*	Hos 2:19	5769
there hath not been *e* the like	Joel 2:2	5769
But Judah shall dwell for *e*	Joel 3:20	5769
and he kept his wrath for *e*	Amos 1:11	5331
and thou shalt be cut off for *e*	Obad 10	5769
with her bars was about me for *e*	Jonah 2:6	5769
have ye taken away my glory for *e*	Mic 2:9	5769
name of the LORD our God for *e*	Mic 4:5	5769
of the LORD our God for *e* and *e*	Mic 4:5	5703
Zion from henceforth, even for *e*	Mic 4:7	5769
he retaineth not his anger for *e*	Mic 7:18	5703
the prophets, do they live for *e*	Zec 1:5	5769
the LORD hath indignation for *e*	Mal 1:4	5769
and the power, and the glory, for *e*	Mt 6:13	165
grow on thee henceforward for *e*	Mt 21:19	165
to this time, no, nor *e* shall be	Mt 24:21	3364
eat fruit of thee hereafter for *e*	Mk 11:14	165
to do as he had *e* done unto them	Mk 15:8	104
over the house of Jacob for *e*	Lk 1:33	165
to Abraham, and to his seed for *e*	Lk 1:55	165
unto him, Son, thou art *e* with me	Lk 15:31	3842
told me all things that I did	Jn 4:29	3745
He told me all that *e* I did	Jn 4:39	3745
this bread, he shall live for *e*	Jn 6:51	165
of this bread shall live for *e*	Jn 6:58	165
abideth not in the house for *e*	Jn 8:35	165
but the Son abideth *e*	Jn 8:35	165
All that *e* came before me are	Jn 10:8	3745
the law that Christ abideth for *e*	Jn 12:34	165
that he may abide with you for *e*	Jn 14:16	165
I *e* taught in the synagogue, and	Jn 18:20	3842
or *e* he come near, are ready to	Acts 23:15	4253
the Creator, who is blessed for *e*	Rom 1:25	165
is over all, God blessed for *e*	Rom 9:5	165
to whom be glory for *e*	Rom 11:36	165
glory through Jesus Christ for *e*	Rom 16:27	165
his righteousness remaineth for *e*	2Cor 9:9	165
To whom be glory for *e* and *e*	Gal 1:5	165
For no man *e* yet hated his own	Eph 5:29	4218
our Father be glory for *e* and *e*	Phil 4:20	165
so shall we *e* be with the Lord	1Th 4:17	3842
but *e* follow that which is good,	1Th 5:15	3842
be honour and glory for *e* and *e*	1Ti 1:17	165
E learning, and never able to come	2Ti 3:7	3842
to whom be glory for *e* and *e*	2Ti 4:18	165
thou shouldest receive him for *e*	Philem 15	166
throne, O God, is for *e* and *e*	Heb 1:8	165
Thou art a priest for *e* after the	Heb 5:6	165
made an high priest for *e* after	Heb 6:20	165

E

Thou art a priest for *e* after the .... Heb 7:17 — 165
Thou art a priest for *e* after the .... Heb 7:21 — 165
this man, because he continueth *e* .... Heb 7:24 — 165
seeing he *e* liveth to make .... Heb 7:25 — 3842
one sacrifice for sins for *e* .... Heb 10:12 — 1336
for *e* them that are sanctified .... Heb 10:14 — 1336
yesterday, and to day, and for *e* .... Heb 13:8 — 165
to whom be glory for *e* and *e* .... Heb 13:21 — 165
which liveth and abideth for *e* .... 1Pet 1:23 — 165
word of the Lord endureth for *e* .... 1Pet 1:25 — 165
praise and dominion for *e* and *e* .... 1Pet 4:11 — 165
glory and dominion for *e* and *e* .... 1Pet 5:11 — 165
of darkness is reserved for *e* .... 2Pet 2:17 — 165
him be glory both now and for *e* .... 2Pet 3:18 — 2250,165
the will of God abideth for *e* .... 1Jn 2:17 — 165
in us, and shall be with us for *e* .... 2Jn 2 — 165
the blackness of darkness for *e* .... Jude 13 — 165
and power, both now and *e* .... Jude 25 — 3956,165
glory and dominion for *e* and *e* .... Rev 1:6 — 165
throne, who liveth for *e* and *e* .... Rev 4:9 — 165
him that liveth for *e* and *e* .... Rev 4:10 — 165
and unto the Lamb for *e* and *e* .... Rev 5:13 — 165
him that liveth for *e* and *e* .... Rev 5:14 — 165
be unto our God for *e* and *e* .... Rev 7:12 — 165
by him that liveth for *e* and *e* .... Rev 10:6 — 165
and he shall reign for *e* and *e* .... Rev 11:15 — 165
ascendeth up for *e* and *e* .... Rev 14:11 — 165
of God, who liveth for *e* and *e* .... Rev 15:7 — 165
her smoke rose up for *e* and *e* .... Rev 19:3 — 165
day and night for *e* and *e* .... Rev 20:10 — 165
and they shall reign for *e* and *e* .... Rev 22:5 — 165

EVERLASTING

the *e* covenant between God .... Gen 9:16 — 5769
generations for an *e* covenant .... Gen 17:7 — 5769
of Canaan, for an *e* possession .... Gen 17:8 — 5769
in your flesh for an *e* covenant .... Gen 17:13 — 5769
with him for an *e* covenant .... Gen 17:19 — 5769
the name of the LORD, the *e* God .... Gen 21:33 — 5769
after thee for an *e* possession .... Gen 48:4 — 5769
the utmost bound of the *e* hills .... Gen 49:26 — 5769
an *e* priesthood throughout their .... Ex 40:15 — 5769
shall be an *e* statute unto you .... Lev 16:34 — 5769
of Israel by an *e* covenant .... Lev 24:8 — 5769
the covenant of an *e* priesthood .... Num 25:13 — 5769
and underneath are the *e* arms .... Deut 33:27 — 5769
hath made with me an *e* covenant .... 2Sa 23:5 — 5769
and to Israel for an *e* covenant .... 1Chr 16:17 — 5769
and be ye lifted up, ye *e* doors .... Ps 24:7 — 5769
even lift them up, ye *e* doors .... Ps 24:9 — 5769
Israel from *e*, and to *e* .... Ps 41:13 — 5769
world, even from *e* to *e* .... Ps 90:2 — 5769
thou art from *e* .... Ps 93:2 — 5769
his mercy is *e* .... Ps 100:5 — 5769
e to *e* upon them that .... Ps 103:17 — 5769
and to Israel for an *e* covenant .... Ps 105:10 — 5769
of Israel from *e* to *e* .... Ps 106:48 — 5769
shall be in *e* remembrance .... Ps 112:6 — 5769
is an *e* righteousness, and thy law .... Ps 119:142 — 5769
of thy testimonies is *e* .... Ps 119:144 — 5769
in me, and lead me in the way *e* .... Ps 139:24 — 5769
Thy kingdom is an *e* kingdom .... Ps 145:13 — 5769
I was set up from *e*, from the .... Prov 8:23 — 5769
the righteous is an *e* foundation .... Prov 10:25 — 5769
The *e* Father, The Prince of Peace .... Is 9:6 — 5703
ordinance, broken the *e* covenant .... Is 24:5 — 5769
in the LORD JEHOVAH is *e* strength ..... Is 26:4 — 5769
us shall dwell with *e* burnings .... Is 33:14 — 5769
songs and *e* joy upon their heads .... Is 35:10 — 5769
thou not heard, that the *e* God .... Is 40:28 — 5769
in the LORD with an *e* salvation .... Is 45:17 — 5769
e joy shall be upon their head .... Is 51:11 — 5769
but with *e* kindness will I have .... Is 54:8 — 5769
I will make an *e* covenant with .... Is 55:3 — 5769
for an *e* sign that shall not be .... Is 55:13 — 5769
I will give them an *e* name .... Is 56:5 — 5769
shall be unto thee an *e* light .... Is 60:19 — 5769
the LORD shall be thine *e* light .... Is 60:20 — 5769
e joy shall be unto them .... Is 61:7 — 5769
I will make an *e* covenant with .... Is 61:8 — 5769
them, to make himself an *e* name .... Is 63:12 — 5769
thy name is from *e* .... Is 63:16 — 5769
is the living God, and an *e* king .... Jer 10:10 — 5769
their *e* confusion shall never be .... Jer 20:11 — 5769
I will bring an *e* reproach upon .... Jer 23:40 — 5769
I have loved thee with an *e* love .... Jer 31:3 — 5769
I will make an *e* covenant with .... Jer 32:40 — 5769
establish unto them an *e* covenant .... Eze 16:60 — 5769
it shall be an *e* covenant with .... Eze 37:26 — 5769
his kingdom is an *e* kingdom .... Dan 4:3 — 5957
whose dominion is an *e* dominion .... Dan 4:34 — 5957

his dominion is an *e* dominion .... Dan 7:14 — 5957
whose kingdom is an *e* kingdom .... Dan 7:27 — 5957
to bring in *e* righteousness, and .... Dan 9:24 — 5769
earth shall awake, some to *e* life .... Dan 12:2 — 5769
and some to shame and *e* contempt ...... Dan 12:2 — 5769
have been from of old, from *e* .... Mic 5:2 — 5769
Art thou not from *e*, O LORD my .... Hab 1:12 — 6924
the *e* mountains were scattered, ... Hab 3:6 — 5703
his ways are *e* .... Hab 3:6 — 5769
two feet to be cast into *e* fire .... Mt 18:8 — 166
and shall inherit *e* life .... Mt 19:29 — 166
from me, ye cursed, into *e* fire .... Mt 25:41 — 166
shall go away into *e* punishment .... Mt 25:46 — 166
receive you into *e* habitations .... Lk 16:9 — 166
and in the world to come life *e* .... Lk 18:30 — 166
not perish, but have *e* life .... Jn 3:16 — 166
believeth on the Son hath *e* life .... Jn 3:36 — 166
of water springing up into *e* life .... Jn 4:14 — 166
on him that sent me, hath *e* life .... Jn 5:24 — 166
meat which endureth unto *e* life .... Jn 6:27 — 166
believeth on him, may have *e* life .... Jn 6:40 — 166
that believeth on me hath *e* life .... Jn 6:47 — 166
that his commandment is life *e* .... Jn 12:50 — 166
yourselves unworthy of *e* life .... Acts 13:46 — 166
unto holiness, and the end *e* life .... Rom 6:22 — 166
to the commandment of the *e* God .... Rom 16:26 — 166
shall of the Spirit reap life *e* .... Gal 6:8 — 166
Who shall be punished with *e* .... 2Th 1:9 — 166
and hath given us *e* consolation .... 2Th 2:16 — 166
believe on him to life *e* .... 1Ti 1:16 — 166
to whom be honour and power *e* .... 1Ti 6:16 — 166
the blood of the *e* covenant .... Heb 13:20 — 166
into the *e* kingdom of our Lord .... 2Pet 1:11 — 166
he hath reserved in *e* chains .... Jude 6 — 126
having the *e* gospel to preach .... Rev 14:6 — 166

EVERMORE

be only oppressed and spoiled *e* ..... Deut 28:29 — 3605,3117
unto David, and to his seed for *e* .... 2Sa 22:51 — 5769
you, ye shall observe to do for *e* ..... 2Kin 17:37 — 3605,3117
throne shall be established for *e* .... 1Chr 17:14 — 5769
hand there are pleasures for *e* .... Ps 16:11 — 5331
to David, and to his seed for *e* .... Ps 18:50 — 5769
and dwell for *e* .... Ps 37:27 — 5769
doth his promise fail for *e* .... Ps 77:8 — 1755
and I will glorify thy name for *e* .... Ps 86:12 — 5769
mercy will I keep for him for *e* .... Ps 89:28 — 5769
Blessed be the LORD for *e* .... Ps 89:52 — 5769
thou, LORD, art most high for *e* .... Ps 92:8 — 5769
seek his face *e* .... Ps 105:4 — 8548
unto all generations for *e* .... Ps 106:31 — 5769
from this time forth and for *e* .... Ps 113:2 — 5769
from this time forth and for *e* .... Ps 115:18 — 5769
this time forth, and even for *e* .... Ps 121:8 — 5769
also sit upon thy throne for *e* .... Ps 132:12 — 5703
the blessing, even life for *e* .... Ps 133:3 — 5769
in the midst of them for *e* .... Eze 37:26 — 5769
be in the midst of them for *e* .... Eze 37:28 — 5769
him, Lord, *e* give us this bread .... Jn 6:34 — 3842
Christ, which is blessed for *e* .... 2Cor 11:31 — 3588,165
Rejoice *e* .... 1Th 5:16 — 3842
the Son, who is consecrated for *e* ... Heb 7:28 — 3588,165
and, behold, I am alive for *e* .... Rev 1:18 — 3588,165

EVERY See APPENDIX.

EVI (*e'-vi*) *A Midian prince.*

namely, *E*, and Rekem, and Zur, and ...... Num 31:8 — 189
with the princes of Midian, *E* .... Josh 13:21 — 189

EVIDENCE

And I subscribed the *e*, and sealed .... Jer 32:10 — 5612
So I took the *e* of the purchase, ... Jer 32:11 — 5612
I gave the *e* of the purchase unto .... Jer 32:12 — 5612
this *e* of the purchase, both .... Jer 32:14 — 5612
sealed, and this *e* which is open .... Jer 32:14 — 5612
Now when I had delivered the *e* of .... Jer 32:16 — 5612
for, the *e* of things not seen .... Heb 11:1 — 1650

EVIDENCES

Take these *e*, this evidence of .... Jer 32:14 — 5612
fields for money, and subscribe *e* .... Jer 32:44 — 5612

EVIDENT

for it is *e* unto you if I lie .... Job 6:28 — 5921,6440
law in the sight of God, it is *e* .... Gal 3:11 — 1212
to them an *e* token of perdition .... Phil 1:28 — 1732
For it is *e* that our Lord sprang .... Heb 7:14 — 4271
And it is yet far more *e* .... Heb 7:15 — 2612

EVIDENTLY

He saw in a vision *e* about the .... Acts 10:3 — 5320
Christ hath been *e* set forth .... Gal 3:1 — 4270

EVIL

tree of knowledge of good and *e*	Gen 2:9	7451
of the knowledge of good and *e*	Gen 2:17	7451
be as gods, knowing good and *e*	Gen 3:5	7451
as one of us, to know good and *e*	Gen 3:22	7451
his heart was only *e* continually	Gen 6:5	7451
man's heart is *e* from his youth	Gen 8:21	7451
the mountain, lest some *e* take me	Gen 19:19	7451
unto his father their *e* report	Gen 37:2	7451
Some *e* beast hath devoured him	Gen 37:20	7451
an *e* beast hath devoured him	Gen 37:33	7451
have ye rewarded *e* for good	Gen 44:4	7451
ye have done *e* in so doing	Gen 44:5	7489
lest peradventure I see the *e*	Gen 44:34	7451
e have the days of the years of	Gen 47:9	7451
which redeemed me from all *e*	Gen 48:16	7451
all the *e* which we did unto him	Gen 50:15	7451
for they did unto thee *e*	Gen 50:17	7451
for you, ye thought *e* against me	Gen 50:20	7451
did see that they were in *e* case	Ex 5:19	7451
thou so *e* entreated this people	Ex 5:22	7489
he hath done *e* to this people	Ex 5:23	7489
for *e* is before you	Ex 10:10	7451
not follow a multitude to do *e*	Ex 23:2	7451
repent of this *e* against thy	Ex 32:12	7451
the LORD repented of the *e* which	Ex 32:14	7451
the people heard these *e* tidings	Ex 33:4	7451
pronouncing with his lips to do *e*	Lev 5:4	7489
I will rid *e* beasts out of the	Lev 26:6	7451
they brought up an *e* report of	Num 13:32	1681
I bear with this *e* congregation	Num 14:27	7451
it unto all this *e* congregation	Num 14:35	7451
up the *e* report upon the land	Num 14:37	7451
to bring us in unto this *e* place	Num 20:5	7451
that had done *e* in the sight of	Num 32:13	7451
not one of these men of this *e*	Deut 1:35	7451
no knowledge between good and *e*	Deut 1:39	7451
shall do *e* in the sight of the	Deut 4:25	7451
none of the *e* diseases of Egypt	Deut 7:15	7451
So shalt thou put the *e* away from	Deut 13:5	7451
thine eye be *e* against thy poor	Deut 15:9	7451
put the *e* away from among you	Deut 17:7	7489
shalt put away the *e* from Israel	Deut 17:12	7451
put the *e* away from among you	Deut 19:19	7451
no more any such *e* among you	Deut 19:20	7451
so shalt thou put *e* away from	Deut 21:21	7451
bring up an *e* name upon her, and	Deut 22:14	7451
an *e* name upon a virgin of Israel	Deut 22:19	7451
so shalt thou put *e* away from	Deut 22:21	7451
shalt thou put away *e* from Israel	Deut 22:22	7451
shalt put away *e* from among you	Deut 22:24	7451
thou shalt put *e* away from among	Deut 24:7	7451
And the Egyptians *e* entreated us	Deut 26:6	7451
his eye shall be *e* toward his	Deut 28:54	7489
her eye shall be *e* toward the	Deut 28:56	7489
LORD shall separate him unto *e*	Deut 29:21	7451
day life and good, and death and *e*	Deut 30:15	7451
e will befall you in the latter	Deut 31:29	7451
because ye will do *e* in the sight	Deut 31:29	7451
LORD bring upon you all *e* things	Josh 23:15	7451
if it seem *e* unto you to serve	Josh 24:15	7489
did *e* in the sight of the LORD	Judg 2:11	7451
the LORD was against them for *e*	Judg 2:15	7451
did *e* in the sight of the LORD	Judg 3:7	7451
the children of Israel did *e*	Judg 3:12	7451
because they had done *e* in the	Judg 3:12	7451
did *e* in the sight of the LORD	Judg 4:1	7451
did *e* in the sight of the LORD	Judg 6:1	7451
Then God sent an *e* spirit between	Judg 9:23	7451
all the *e* of the men of Shechem	Judg 9:57	7451
the children of Israel did *e*	Judg 10:6	7451
the children of Israel did *e*	Judg 13:1	7451
death, and put away *e* from Israel	Judg 20:13	7451
knew not that *e* was near them	Judg 20:34	7451
for they saw that *e* was come upon	Judg 20:41	7451
for I hear of your *e* dealings by	1Sa 2:23	7451
then he hath done us this great *e*	1Sa 6:9	7451
added unto all our sins this *e*	1Sa 12:19	7451
didst *e* in the sight of the LORD	1Sa 15:19	7451
an *e* spirit from the LORD	1Sa 16:14	7451
an *e* spirit from God troubleth	1Sa 16:15	7451
when the *e* spirit from God is	1Sa 16:16	7451
when the *e* spirit from God was	1Sa 16:23	7451
the *e* spirit departed from him	1Sa 16:23	7451
that the *e* spirit from God came	1Sa 18:10	7451
the *e* spirit from the LORD was	1Sa 19:9	7451
then be sure that *e* is determined	1Sa 20:7	7451
for if I knew certainly that *e*	1Sa 20:9	7451
it please my father to do thee *e*	1Sa 20:13	7451
see that there is neither *e* nor	1Sa 24:11	7451
whereas I have rewarded thee *e*	1Sa 24:17	7451
was churlish and *e* in his doings	1Sa 25:3	7451
for *e* is determined against our	1Sa 25:17	7451
and he hath requited me *e* for good	1Sa 25:21	7451
and they that seek *e* to my lord	1Sa 25:26	7451
e hath not been found in thee all	1Sa 25:28	7451
and hath kept his servant from *e*	1Sa 25:39	7451
or what *e* is in mine hand	1Sa 26:18	7451
for I have not found *e* in thee	1Sa 29:6	7451
of *e* according to his wickedness	2Sa 3:39	7451
of the LORD, to do *e* in his sight	2Sa 12:9	7451
I will raise up *e* against thee	2Sa 12:11	7451
this *e* in sending me away is	2Sa 13:16	7451
bring *e* upon us, and smite the	2Sa 15:14	7451
LORD might bring *e* upon Absalom	2Sa 17:14	7451
e that befell thee from thy youth	2Sa 19:7	7451
can I discern between good and *e*	2Sa 19:35	7451
the LORD repented him of the *e*	2Sa 24:16	7451
neither adversary nor *e* occurrent	1Kin 5:4	7451
LORD brought upon them all this *e*	1Kin 9:9	7451
Solomon did *e* in the sight of the	1Kin 11:6	7451
returned not from his *e* way	1Kin 13:33	7451
But hast done *e* above all that	1Kin 14:9	7489
I will bring *e* upon the house of	1Kin 14:10	7451
Judah did *e* in the sight of the	1Kin 14:22	7451
he did *e* in the sight of the LORD	1Kin 15:26	7451
he did *e* in the sight of the LORD	1Kin 15:34	7451
even for all the *e* that he did in	1Kin 16:7	7451
doing *e* in the sight of the LORD	1Kin 16:19	7451
But Omri wrought *e* in the eyes of	1Kin 16:25	7451
Ahab the son of Omri did *e* in the	1Kin 16:30	7451
hast thou also brought *e* upon the	1Kin 17:20	7489
work *e* in the sight of the LORD	1Kin 21:20	7451
Behold, I will bring *e* upon thee	1Kin 21:21	7451
will not bring the *e* in his days	1Kin 21:29	7451
will I bring the *e* upon his house	1Kin 21:29	7451
good concerning me, but *e*	1Kin 22:8	7451
no good concerning me, but *e*	1Kin 22:18	7451
hath spoken *e* concerning thee	1Kin 22:23	7451
he did *e* in the sight of the LORD	1Kin 22:52	7451
Behold, this *e* is of the LORD	2Kin 3:2	7451
Because I know the *e* that thou	2Kin 6:33	7451
he did *e* in the sight of the LORD	2Kin 8:12	7451
did *e* in the sight of the LORD,	2Kin 8:18	7451
he did that which was *e* in the	2Kin 8:27	7451
he did that which was *e* in the	2Kin 13:2	7451
he did that which was *e* in the	2Kin 13:11	7451
he did that which was *e* in the	2Kin 14:24	7451
he did that which was *e* in the	2Kin 15:9	7451
he did that which was *e* in the	2Kin 15:18	7451
he did that which was *e* in the	2Kin 15:24	7451
he did that which was *e* in the	2Kin 15:28	7451
he did that which was *e* in the	2Kin 17:2	7451
saying, Turn ye from your *e* ways	2Kin 17:13	7451
sold themselves to do *e* in the	2Kin 17:17	7451
he did that which was *e* in the	2Kin 21:2	7451
seduced them to do more *e* than	2Kin 21:9	7451
am bringing such *e* upon Jerusalem	2Kin 21:12	7451
done that which was *e* in my sight	2Kin 21:15	7451
in doing that which was *e* in the	2Kin 21:16	7451
he did that which was *e* in the	2Kin 21:20	7451
I will bring *e* upon this place,	2Kin 22:16	7451
eyes shall not see all the *e*	2Kin 22:20	7451
he did that which was *e* in the	2Kin 23:32	7451
he did that which was *e* in the	2Kin 23:37	7451
he did that which was *e* in the	2Kin 24:9	7451
he did that which was *e* in the	2Kin 24:19	7451
was *e* in the sight of the LORD	1Chr 2:3	7451
that thou wouldest keep me from *e*	1Chr 4:10	7451
because it went *e* with his house	1Chr 7:23	7451
and he repented him of the *e*	1Chr 21:15	7451
that have sinned and done *e* indeed	1Chr 21:17	7489
he brought all this *e* upon them	2Chr 7:22	7451
And he did *e*, because he prepared	2Chr 12:14	7451
good unto me, but always *e*	2Chr 18:7	7451
not prophesy good unto me, but *e*	2Chr 18:17	7451
LORD hath spoken *e* against thee	2Chr 18:22	7451
when *e* cometh upon us, as the	2Chr 20:9	7451
was *e* in the eyes of the LORD	2Chr 21:6	7451
Wherefore he did *e* in the sight	2Chr 22:4	7451
done that which was *e* in the eyes	2Chr 29:6	7451
But did that which was *e* in the	2Chr 33:2	7451
he wrought much *e* in the sight of	2Chr 33:6	7451
was *e* in the sight of the LORD	2Chr 33:22	7451
I will bring *e* upon this place,	2Chr 34:24	7451
the *e* that I will bring upon this	2Chr 34:28	7451
he did that which was *e* in the	2Chr 36:5	7451
he did that which was *e* in the	2Chr 36:9	7451
he did that which was *e* in the	2Chr 36:12	7451
is come upon us for our *e* deeds	Ezr 9:13	7451
might have matter for an *e* report	Neh 6:13	7451
they did *e* again before thee	Neh 9:28	7451

understood of the *e* that Eliashib	Neh 13:7	7451
What *e* thing is this that ye do,	Neh 13:17	7451
our God bring all this *e* upon us	Neh 13:18	7451
unto you to do all this great *e*	Neh 13:27	7451
for he saw that there was *e*	Est 7:7	7451
e that shall come unto my people	Est 8:6	7451
that feared God, and eschewed *e*	Job 1:1	7451
that feareth God, and escheweth *e*	Job 1:8	7451
that feareth God, and escheweth *e*	Job 2:3	7451
of God, and shall we not receive *e*	Job 2:10	7451
all this *e* that was come upon him	Job 2:11	7451
seven there shall no *e* touch thee	Job 5:19	7451
neither will he help the *e* doers	Job 8:20	7489
He *e* entreateth the barren that	Job 24:21	7462
to depart from *e* is understanding	Job 28:28	7451
for good, then *e* came unto me	Job 30:26	7451
lifted up myself when *e* found him	Job 31:29	7451
because of the pride of *e* men	Job 35:12	7451
comforted him over all the *e* that	Job 42:11	7451
neither shall *e* dwell with thee	Ps 5:4	7451
If I have rewarded *e* unto him	Ps 7:4	7451
arm of the wicked and the *e* man	Ps 10:15	7451
nor doeth *e* to his neighbour, nor	Ps 15:3	7451
For they intended *e* against thee	Ps 21:11	7451
shadow of death, I will fear no *e*	Ps 23:4	7451
Keep thy tongue from *e*, and thy	Ps 34:13	7451
Depart from *e*, and do good	Ps 34:14	7451
LORD is against them that do *e*	Ps 34:16	7451
E shall slay the wicked	Ps 34:21	7451
They rewarded me *e* for good to	Ps 35:12	7451
he abhorreth not *e*	Ps 36:4	7451
not thyself in any wise to do *e*	Ps 37:8	7489
not be ashamed in the *e* time	Ps 37:19	7451
Depart from *e*, and do good	Ps 37:27	7451
They also that render *e* for good	Ps 38:20	7451
and put to shame that wish me *e*	Ps 40:14	7451
Mine enemies speak *e* of me	Ps 41:5	7451
An *e* disease, say they, cleaveth	Ps 41:8	1100
should I fear in the days of *e*	Ps 49:5	7451
Thou givest thy mouth to *e*	Ps 50:19	7451
and done this *e* in thy sight	Ps 51:4	7451
Thou lovest *e* more than good	Ps 52:3	7451
He shall reward *e* unto mine	Ps 54:5	7451
thoughts are against me for *e*	Ps 56:5	7451
themselves in an *e* matter	Ps 64:5	7451
by sending *e* angels among them	Ps 78:49	7451
the years wherein we have seen *e*	Ps 90:15	7451
There shall no *e* befall thee	Ps 91:10	7451
Ye that love the LORD, hate *e*	Ps 97:10	7451
they have rewarded me *e* for good	Ps 109:5	7451
them that speak *e* against my soul	Ps 109:20	7451
shall not be afraid of *e* tidings	Ps 112:7	7451
my feet from every *e* way, that I	Ps 119:101	7451
shall preserve thee from all *e*	Ps 121:7	7451
me, O LORD, from the *e* man	Ps 140:1	7451
Let not an *e* speaker be	Ps 140:11	
e shall hunt the violent man to	Ps 140:11	7451
not my heart to any *e* thing	Ps 141:4	7451
For their feet run to *e*, and make	Prov 1:16	7451
and shall be quiet from fear of *e*	Prov 1:33	7451
thee from the way of the *e* man	Prov 2:12	7451
Who rejoice to do *e*, and delight	Prov 2:14	7451
fear the LORD, and depart from *e*	Prov 3:7	7451
Devise not *e* against thy	Prov 3:29	7451
and go not in the way of *e* men	Prov 4:14	7451
remove thy foot from *e*	Prov 4:27	7451
in all *e* in the midst of the	Prov 5:14	7451
To keep thee from the *e* woman	Prov 6:24	7451
The fear of the LORD is to hate *e*	Prov 8:13	7451
pride, and arrogancy, and the *e* way	Prov 8:13	7451
so he that pursueth *e* pursueth it	Prov 11:19	7451
wicked desireth the net of *e* men	Prov 12:12	7451
the heart of them that imagine *e*	Prov 12:20	7451
There shall no *e* happen to the	Prov 12:21	205
to fools to depart from *e*	Prov 13:19	7451
E pursueth sinners	Prov 13:21	7451
man feareth, and departeth from *e*	Prov 14:16	7451
The *e* bow before the good	Prov 14:19	7451
Do they not err that devise *e*	Prov 14:22	7451
in every place, beholding the *e*	Prov 15:3	7451
the days of the afflicted are *e*	Prov 15:15	7451
the wicked poureth out *e* things	Prov 15:28	7451
even the wicked for the day of *e*	Prov 16:4	7451
of the LORD men depart from *e*	Prov 16:6	7451
the upright is to depart from *e*	Prov 16:17	7451
An ungodly man diggeth up *e*	Prov 16:27	7451
his lips he bringeth *e* to pass	Prov 16:30	7451
An *e* man seeketh only rebellion	Prov 17:11	7451
Whoso rewardeth *e* for good	Prov 17:13	7451
e shall not depart from his house	Prov 17:13	7451
he shall not be visited with *e*	Prov 19:23	7451

away all *e* with his eyes	Prov 20:8	7451
Say not thou, I will recompense *e*	Prov 20:22	7451
of a wound cleanseth away *e*	Prov 20:30	7451
The soul of the wicked desireth *e*	Prov 21:10	7451
A prudent man foreseeth the *e*	Prov 22:3	7451
bread of him that hath an *e* eye	Prov 23:6	7451
Be not thou envious against *e* men	Prov 24:1	7451
He that deviseth to do *e* shall be	Prov 24:8	7489
Fret not thyself because of *e* men	Prov 24:19	7489
shall be no reward to the *e* man	Prov 24:20	7451
A prudent man foreseeth the *e*	Prov 27:12	7451
E men understand not judgment	Prov 28:5	7451
to go astray in an *e* way, he	Prov 28:10	7451
hasteth to be rich hath an *e* eye	Prov 28:22	7451
of an *e* man there is a snare	Prov 29:6	7451
or if thou hast thought *e*	Prov 30:32	
not *e* all the days of her life	Prov 31:12	7451
This also is vanity and a great *e*	Eccl 2:21	7451
who hath not seen the *e* work that	Eccl 4:3	7451
they consider not that they do *e*	Eccl 5:1	7451
There is a sore *e* which I have	Eccl 5:13	7451
those riches perish by *e* travail	Eccl 5:14	7451
And this also is a sore *e*, that in	Eccl 5:16	7451
There is an *e* which I have seen	Eccl 6:1	7451
is vanity, and it is an *e* disease	Eccl 6:2	7451
stand not in an *e* thing	Eccl 8:3	7451
commandment shall feel no *e* thing	Eccl 8:5	7451
Because sentence against an *e*	Eccl 8:11	7451
men is fully set in them to do *e*	Eccl 8:11	7451
a sinner do *e* an hundred times	Eccl 8:12	7451
This is an *e* among all things	Eccl 9:3	7451
of the sons of men is full of *e*	Eccl 9:3	7451
fishes that are taken in an *e* net	Eccl 9:12	7451
sons of men snared in an *e* time	Eccl 9:12	7451
There is an *e* which I have seen	Eccl 10:5	7451
what *e* shall be upon the earth	Eccl 11:2	7451
put away *e* from thy flesh	Eccl 11:10	7451
while the *e* days come not, nor	Eccl 12:1	7451
it be good, or whether it be *e*	Eccl 12:14	7451
put away the *e* of your doings	Is 1:16	7455
cease to do *e*	Is 1:16	7489
have rewarded *e* unto themselves	Is 3:9	7451
that call *e* good, and good *e*	Is 5:20	7451
have taken *e* counsel against thee	Is 7:5	7451
that he may know to refuse the *e*	Is 7:15	7451
child shall know to refuse the *e*	Is 7:16	7451
will punish the world for their *e*	Is 13:11	7451
he also is wise, and will bring *e*	Is 31:2	7451
also of the churl are *e*	Is 32:7	7451
shutteth his eyes from seeing *e*	Is 33:15	7451
yea, do good, or do *e*, that we	Is 41:23	7489
I make peace, and create *e*	Is 45:7	7451
Therefore shall *e* come upon thee	Is 47:11	7451
keepeth his hand from doing any *e*	Is 56:2	7451
is taken away from the *e* to come	Is 57:1	7451
Their feet run to *e*, and they make	Is 59:7	7451
from *e* maketh himself a prey	Is 59:15	7451
but did *e* before mine eyes, and	Is 65:12	7451
but they did *e* before mine eyes,	Is 66:4	7451
Out of the north an *e* shall break	Jer 1:14	7451
e shall come upon them, saith	Jer 2:3	7451
and see that it is an *e* thing	Jer 2:19	7451
done *e* things as thou couldest	Jer 3:5	7451
the imagination of their *e* heart	Jer 3:17	7451
because of the *e* of your doings	Jer 4:4	7455
for I will bring *e* from the north	Jer 4:6	7451
they are wise to do *e*, but to do	Jer 4:22	7489
neither shall *e* come upon us	Jer 5:12	7451
for *e* appeareth out of the north,	Jer 6:1	7451
I will bring *e* upon this people,	Jer 6:19	7451
the imagination of their *e* heart	Jer 7:24	7451
of Judah have done *e* in my sight	Jer 7:30	7451
them that remain of this *e* family	Jer 8:3	7451
for they proceed from *e* to *e*	Jer 9:3	7451
for they cannot do *e*, neither	Jer 10:5	7489
the imagination of their *e* heart	Jer 11:8	7451
Behold, I will bring *e* upon them	Jer 11:11	7451
when thou doest *e*, then thou	Jer 11:15	7451
hath pronounced *e* against thee	Jer 11:17	7451
for the *e* of the house of Israel	Jer 11:17	7451
for I will bring *e* upon the men	Jer 11:23	7451
against all mine *e* neighbours	Jer 12:14	7451
This *e* people, which refuse to	Jer 13:10	7451
good, that are accustomed to do *e*	Jer 13:23	7489
thee well in the time of *e*	Jer 15:11	7451
all this great *e* against us	Jer 16:10	7451
the imagination of his *e* heart	Jer 16:12	7451
thou art my hope in the day of *e*	Jer 17:17	7451
bring upon them the day of *e*	Jer 17:18	7451
pronounced, turn from their *e*	Jer 18:8	7451
I will repent of the *e* that I	Jer 18:8	7451

If it do *e* in my sight, that it	Jer 18:10	7451
I frame *e* against you, and devise	Jer 18:11	7451
ye now every one from his *e* way	Jer 18:11	7451
do the imagination of his *e* heart	Jer 18:12	7451
Shall *e* be recompensed for good	Jer 18:20	7451
I will bring *e* upon this place,	Jer 19:3	7451
upon all her towns all the *e* that	Jer 19:15	7451
my face against this city for *e*	Jer 21:10	7451
because of the *e* of your doings	Jer 21:12	7455
upon you the *e* of your doings	Jer 23:2	7455
dried up, and their course is *e*	Jer 23:10	7451
for I will bring *e* upon them	Jer 23:12	7451
heart, No *e* shall come upon you	Jer 23:17	7451
have turned them from their *e* way	Jer 23:22	7451
from the *e* of their doings	Jer 23:22	7455
and the *e*, very *e*	Jer 24:3	7451
cannot be eaten, they are so *e*	Jer 24:3	7455
And as the *e* figs, which cannot be	Jer 24:8	7451
cannot be eaten, they are so *e*	Jer 24:8	7455
now every one from his *e* way	Jer 25:5	7451
from the *e* of your doings, and	Jer 25:5	7455
I begin to bring *e* on the city	Jer 25:29	7489
e shall go forth from nation to	Jer 25:32	7451
and turn every man from his *e* way	Jer 26:3	7451
that I may repent me of the *e*	Jer 26:3	7451
because of the *e* of their doings	Jer 26:3	7455
e that he hath pronounced against	Jer 26:13	7451
the LORD repented him of the *e*	Jer 26:19	7451
procure great *e* against our souls	Jer 26:19	7451
great kingdoms, of war, and of *e*	Jer 28:8	7451
thoughts of peace, and not of *e*	Jer 29:11	7451
cannot be eaten, they are so *e*	Jer 29:17	7455
all this *e* to come upon them	Jer 32:23	7451
of Judah have only done *e* before	Jer 32:30	7451
Because of all the *e* of the	Jer 32:32	7451
all this great *e* upon this people	Jer 32:42	7451
ye now every man from his *e* way	Jer 35:15	7451
of Jerusalem all the *e* that I	Jer 35:17	7451
of Judah will hear all the *e*	Jer 36:3	7451
return every man from his *e* way	Jer 36:3	7451
return every one from his *e* way	Jer 36:7	7451
all the *e* that I have pronounced	Jer 36:31	7451
these men have done *e* in all that	Jer 38:9	7489
my words upon this city for *e*	Jer 39:16	7451
pronounced this *e* upon this place	Jer 40:2	7451
heard of all the *e* that Ishmael	Jer 41:11	7451
it be good, or whether it be *e*	Jer 42:6	7451
for I repent me of the *e* that I	Jer 42:10	7451
the *e* that I will bring upon them	Jer 42:17	7451
Ye have seen all the *e* that I	Jer 44:2	7451
this great *e* against your souls	Jer 44:7	7451
set my face against you for *e*	Jer 44:11	7451
and were well, and saw no *e*	Jer 44:17	7451
because of the *e* of your doings	Jer 44:22	7455
therefore this *e* is happened unto	Jer 44:23	7451
I will watch over them for *e*	Jer 44:27	7451
surely stand against you for *e*	Jer 44:29	7451
I will bring *e* upon all flesh,	Jer 45:5	7451
they have devised *e* against it	Jer 48:2	7451
for they have heard *e* tidings	Jer 49:23	7451
and I will bring *e* upon them	Jer 49:37	7451
of Chaldea all their *e* that they	Jer 51:24	7451
wrote in a book all the *e* that	Jer 51:60	7451
shall not rise from the *e* that I	Jer 51:64	7451
he did that which was *e* in the	Jer 52:2	7451
of the most High proceedeth not *e*	Lam 3:38	7451
upon them the *e* arrows of famine	Eze 5:16	7451
e beasts, and they shall bereave	Eze 5:17	7451
that I would do this *e* unto them	Eze 6:10	7451
Alas for all the *e* abominations	Eze 6:11	7451
An *e*, an only *e*, behold, is	Eze 7:5	7451
the *e* that I have brought upon	Eze 14:22	7451
turn ye, turn ye from your *e* ways	Eze 33:11	7451
will cause the *e* beasts to cease	Eze 34:25	7451
shall ye remember your own *e* ways	Eze 36:31	7451
and thou shalt think an *e* thought	Eze 38:10	7451
us, by bringing upon us a great *e*	Dan 9:12	7451
all this *e* is come upon us	Dan 9:13	7451
hath the LORD watched upon the *e*	Dan 9:14	7451
and repenteth him of the *e*	Joel 2:13	7451
shall there be *e* in a city	Amos 3:6	7451
for it is an *e* time	Amos 5:13	7451
Seek good, and not *e*, that ye may	Amos 5:14	7451
Hate the *e*, and love the good, and	Amos 5:15	7451
Ye that put far away the *e* day	Amos 6:3	7451
set mine eyes upon them for *e*	Amos 9:4	7451
The *e* shall not overtake nor	Amos 9:10	7451
for whose cause this *e* is upon us	Jonah 1:7	7451
for whose cause this *e* is upon us	Jonah 1:8	7451
turn every one from his *e* way	Jonah 3:8	7451
that they turned from their *e* way	Jonah 3:10	7451
and God repented of the *e*, that he	Jonah 3:10	7451
and repentest thee of the *e*	Jonah 4:2	7451
but *e* came down from the LORD	Mic 1:12	7451
and work *e* upon their beds	Mic 2:1	7451
this family do I devise an *e*	Mic 2:3	7451
for this time is *e*	Mic 2:3	7451
Who hate the good, and love the *e*	Mic 3:2	7451
none *e* can come upon us	Mic 3:11	7451
That they may do *e* with both	Mic 7:3	7451
that imagineth *e* against the LORD	Nah 1:11	7451
of purer eyes than to behold *e*	Hab 1:13	7451
an *e* covetousness to his house	Hab 2:9	7451
be delivered from the power of *e*	Hab 2:9	7451
not do good, neither will he do *e*	Zeph 1:12	7489
thou shalt not see *e* any more	Zeph 3:15	7451
e ways, and from your *e* doings	Zec 1:4	7451
let none of you imagine *e* against	Zec 7:10	7451
let none of you imagine *e* in your	Zec 8:17	7451
blind for sacrifice, is it not *e*	Mal 1:8	7451
the lame and sick, is it not *e*	Mal 1:8	7451
Every one that doeth *e* is good in	Mal 2:17	7451
manner of *e* against you falsely	Mt 5:11	*4190,4487*
is more than these cometh of *e*	Mt 5:37	*4190*
unto you, That ye resist not *e*	Mt 5:39	*4190*
maketh his sun to rise on the *e*	Mt 5:45	*4190*
temptation, but deliver us from *e*	Mt 6:13	*4190*
But if thine eye be *e*, thy whole	Mt 6:23	*4190*
unto the day is the *e* thereof	Mt 6:34	*2549*
If ye then, being *e*, know how to	Mt 7:11	*4190*
tree bringeth forth *e* fruit	Mt 7:17	*4190*
tree cannot bring forth *e* fruit	Mt 7:18	*4190*
think ye *e* in your hearts	Mt 9:4	*4190*
of vipers, how can ye, being *e*	Mt 12:34	*4190*
an *e* man out of the *e* treasure	Mt 12:35	*4190*
bringeth forth *e* things	Mt 12:35	*4190*
answered and said unto them, An *e*	Mt 12:39	*4190*
of the heart proceed *e* thoughts	Mt 15:19	*4190*
Is thine eye *e*, because I am good	Mt 20:15	*4190*
if that *e* servant shall say in	Mt 24:48	*2556*
said, Why, what *e* hath he done	Mt 27:23	*2556*
on the sabbath days, or to do *e*	Mk 3:4	*2554*
proceed *e* thoughts, adulteries,	Mk 7:21	*2556*
an *e* eye, blasphemy, pride,	Mk 7:22	*4190*
All these *e* things come from	Mk 7:23	*4190*
that can lightly speak *e* of me	Mk 9:39	*2551*
them, Why, what *e* hath he done	Mk 15:14	*2556*
days to do good, or to do *e*	Lk 6:9	*2554*
you, and cast out your name as *e*	Lk 6:22	*4190*
unto the unthankful and to the *e*	Lk 6:35	*4190.*
an *e* man out of the *e* treasure	Lk 6:45	*4190*
bringeth forth that which is *e*	Lk 6:45	*4190*
and plagues, and of *e* spirits	Lk 7:21	*4190*
had been healed of *e* spirits	Lk 8:2	*4190*
but deliver us from *e*	Lk 11:4	*4190*
If ye then, being *e*, know how to	Lk 11:13	*4190*
to say, This is an *e* generation	Lk 11:29	*4190*
but when thine eye is *e*, thy body	Lk 11:34	*4190*
and likewise Lazarus *e* things	Lk 16:25	*2556*
time, Why, what *e* hath he done	Lk 23:22	*2556*
light, because their deeds were *e*	Jn 3:19	*4190*
one that doeth *e* hateth the light	Jn 3:20	*5337*
and they that have done *e*, unto	Jn 5:29	*5337*
it, that the works thereof are *e*	Jn 7:7	*4190*
shouldest keep them from the *e*	Jn 17:15	*4190*
answered him, If I have spoken *e*	Jn 18:23	*2560*
bear witness of the *e*	Jn 18:23	*2556*
entreat them *e* four hundred years	Acts 7:6	*2559*
e entreated our fathers, so that	Acts 7:19	*2559*
how much *e* he hath done to thy	Acts 9:13	*2556*
made their minds *e* affected	Acts 14:2	*2559*
but spake *e* of that way before	Acts 19:9	
the *e* spirits went out of them	Acts 19:12	*4190*
to call over them which had *e*	Acts 19:13	*4190*
the *e* spirit answered and said,	Acts 19:15	*4190*
the man in whom the *e* spirit was	Acts 19:16	*4190*
Thou shalt not speak *e* of the	Acts 23:5	*2560*
saying, We find no *e* in this man	Acts 23:9	*2556*
they have found any *e* doing in me	Acts 24:20	*92*
boasters, inventors of *e* things	Rom 1:30	*2556*
every soul of man that doeth *e*	Rom 2:9	*2556*
affirm that we say,) Let us do *e*	Rom 3:8	*2556*
but the *e* which I would not, that	Rom 7:19	*2556*
do good, *e* is present with me	Rom 7:21	*2556*
neither having done any good or *e*	Rom 9:11	*2556*
Abhor that which is *e*	Rom 12:9	*4190*
Recompense to no man *e* for *e*	Rom 12:17	*2556*
Recompense to no man *e* for *e*	Rom 12:17	*2556*
Be not overcome of *e*	Rom 12:21	*2556*
but overcome *e* with good	Rom 12:21	*2556*
to good works, but to the *e*	Rom 13:3	*2556*
But if thou do that which is *e*	Rom 13:4	*2556*

wrath upor. him that doeth *e* .... Rom 13:4   2556
not then your good be *e* spoken of.......... Rom 14:16
but it is *e* for that man who...................... Rom 14:20   2556
is good, and simple concerning *e* .... Rom 16:19   2556
we should not lust after *e* things 1Cor 10:6   2556
why am I *e* spoken of for that for............ 1Cor 10:30   987
easily provoked, thinketh no *e* 1Cor 13:5   2556
e communications corrupt good 1Cor 15:33   2556
by *e* report and good report 2Cor 6:8   1426
Now I pray to God that ye do no *e* 2Cor 13:7   2556
us from this present *e* world.................... Gal 1:4   4190
e speaking, be put away from you, ... Eph 4:31   988
the time, because the days are *e*.............. Eph 5:16   4190
be able to withstand in the *e* day .... Eph 6:13   4190
of dogs, beware of *e* workers .... Phil 3:2   2556
e concupiscence, and covetousness, ... Col 3:5   2556
See that none render *e* for *e* 1Th 5:15   2556
Abstain from all appearance of *e* 1Th 5:22   4190
stablish you, and keep you from *e* 2Th 3:3   4190
strife, railings, *e* surmisings.................... 1Ti 6:4   4190
of money is the root of all *e* 1Ti 6:10   2556
I suffer trouble, as an *e* doer 2Ti 2:9   2557
But *e* men and seducers shall wax 2Ti 3:13   4190
the coppersmith did me much *e* 2Ti 4:14   2556
deliver me from every *e* work.................... 2Ti 4:18   4190
liars, *e* beasts, slow bellies .... Titus 1:12   2556
having no *e* thing to say of you .... Titus 2:8   5337
To speak *e* of no man, to be no .... Titus 3:2   987
any of you an *e* heart of unbelief............ Heb 3:12   4190
to discern both good and *e*...................... Heb 5:14   2556
sprinkled from an *e* conscience .... Heb 10:22   4190
for God cannot be tempted with *e*.......... Jas 1:13   2556
are become judges of *e* thoughts .... Jas 2:4   4190
it is an unruly *e*, full of deadly .... Jas 3:8   2556
is confusion and every *e* work.................. Jas 3:16   5337
Speak not *e* one of another, ... Jas 4:11   2635
He that speaketh *e* of his brother............ Jas 4:11   2635
speaketh *e* of the law, and judgeth .... Jas 4:11   2635
all such rejoicing is *e*................................ Jas 4:16   4190
and envies, and all *e* speakings.............. 1Pet 2:1   2636
Not rendering *e* for *e*, or 1Pet 3:9   2556
Not rendering *e* for *e*, or 1Pet 3:9   2556
let him refrain his tongue from *e*............ 1Pet 3:10   2556
Let him eschew *e*, and do good 1Pet 3:11   2556
Lord is against them that do *e* 1Pet 3:12   2556
that, whereas they speak *e* of you 1Pet 3:16   2635
for well doing, than for *e* doing 1Pet 3:17   2554
excess of riot, speaking *e* of you 1Pet 4:4   987
on their part he is *e* spoken of 1Pet 4:14   987
way of truth shall be *e* spoken of............ 2Pet 2:2   987
afraid to speak *e* of dignities.................... 2Pet 2:10   987
speak *e* of the things that they 2Pet 2:12   987
Because his own works were *e*................ 1Jn 3:12   4190
speed is partaker of his *e* deeds 2Jn 11   4190
follow not that which is *e*........................ 3Jn 11   2556
he that doeth *e* hath not seen God 3Jn 11   2554
dominion, and speak *e* of dignities .... Jude 8   987
But these speak *e* of those things .... Jude 10   987
canst not bear them which are *e* .... Rev 2:2   2556

EVILDOER
every one is an hypocrite and an *e*........ Is 9:17   7489
or as a thief, or as an *e*............................ 1Pet 4:15   2555

EVILDOERS
have hated the congregation of *e*............ Ps 26:5
Fret not thyself because of *e* .... Ps 37:1   7489
For *e* shall be cut off .... Ps 37:9   7489
will rise up for me against the *e* .... Ps 94:16   7489
Depart from me, ye *e* .... Ps 119:115   7489
laden with iniquity, a seed of *e* .... Is 1:4   7489
the seed of *e* shall never be .... Is 14:20   7489
arise against the house of the *e* .... Is 31:2   7489
of the poor from the hand of *e* .... Jer 20:13   7489
strengthen also the hands of *e* .... Jer 23:14   7489
they speak against you as *e*.................... 1Pet 2:12   2555
by him for the punishment of *e* 1Pet 2:14   2555
they speak evil of you, as of *e* 1Pet 3:16   2555

EVILFAVOUREDNESS
wherein is blemish, or any *e* .... Deut 17:1

EVIL-MERODACH (e'-vil-mer'-o-dak) Son of Nebuchadnezzar
that *E* king of Babylon in the.................... 2Kin 25:27   192
that *E* king of Babylon in the .... Jer 52:31   192

EVILS
they shall be devoured, and many *e*........ Deut 31:17   7451
day, Are not these *e* come upon us .... Deut 31:17   7451
e which they shall have wrought .... Deut 31:18   7451
shall come to pass, when many *e* .... Deut 31:21   7451
For innumerable *e* have compassed........ Ps 40:12   7451

my people have committed two *e*............ Jer 2:13   7451
e which they have committed in .... Eze 6:9   7451
all your *e* that ye have committed .... Eze 20:43   7451
for all the *e* which Herod had.................. Lk 3:19   4190

EWE
Abraham set seven *e* lambs of the.......... Gen 21:28   3535
What mean these seven *e* lambs .... Gen 21:29   3535
For these seven *e* lambs shalt .... Gen 21:30   3535
one *e* lamb of the first year .... Lev 14:10   3535
And whether it be cow or *e* .... Lev 22:28   7716
one *e* lamb of the first year .... Num 6:14   3535
nothing, save one little *e* lamb 2Sa 12:3   3535

EWES
thy *e* and thy she goats have not .... Gen 31:38   7353
and twenty he goats, two hundred *e*...... Gen 32:14   7353
From following the *e* great with .... Ps 78:71   5763

EXACT
he shall not *e* it of his.............................. Deut 15:2   5065
foreigner thou mayest *e* it again............ Deut 15:3   5065
Ye *e* usury, every one of his .... Neh 5:7   5378
might *e* of them money and corn .... Neh 5:10   5383
and the oil, that ye *e* of them .... Neh 5:11   5383
The enemy shall not *e* upon him............ Ps 89:22   5378
pleasure, and *e* all your labours .... Is 58:3   5065
E no more than that which is.................. Lk 3:13   4238

EXACTED
Menahem *e* the money of Israel,............ 2Kin 15:20   3318
he *e* the silver and the gold of 2Kin 23:35   5065

EXACTETH
God *e* of thee less than thine .... Job 11:6   5382

EXACTION
year, and the *e* of every debt .... Neh 10:31   4855

EXACTIONS
take away your *e* from my people .... Eze 45:9   1646

EXACTORS
peace, and thine *e* righteousness............ Is 60:17   5065

EXALT
my father's God, and I will *e* him............ Ex 15:2   7311
e the horn of his anointed........................ 1Sa 2:10   7311
therefore shalt thou not *e* them .... Job 17:4   7311
let us *e* his name together .... Ps 34:3   7311
he shall *e* thee to inherit the.................... Ps 37:34   7311
not the rebellious *e* themselves.............. Ps 66:7   7311
But my horn shalt thou *e* like the .... Ps 92:10   7311
E ye the LORD our God, and worship...... Ps 99:5   7311
E the LORD our God, and worship at ...... Ps 99:9   7311
Let them *e* him also in the .... Ps 107:32   7311
thou art my God, I will *e* thee .... Ps 118:28   7311
lest they *e* themselves .... Ps 140:8   7311
E her, and she shall promote thee.......... Prov 4:8   5549
e the voice unto them, shake the .... Is 13:2   7311
I will *e* my throne above the.................... Is 14:13   7311
I will *e* thee, I will praise thy.................. Is 25:1   7311
e him that is low, and abase him .... Eze 21:26   1361
neither shall it *e* itself any .... Eze 29:15   5375
e themselves for their height .... Eze 31:14   1361
e themselves to establish the .... Dan 11:14   5375
and he shall *e* himself, and magnify ...... Dan 11:36   7311
High, none at all would *e* him .... Hos 11:7   7311
Though thou *e* thyself as the .... Obad 4   1361
whosoever shall *e* himself shall .... Mt 23:12   5312
take of you, if a man *e* himself.............. 2Cor 11:20   1869
that he may *e* you in due time 1Pet 5:6   5312

EXALTED
Agag, and his kingdom shall be *e* .... Num 24:7   5375
LORD, mine horn is *e* in the LORD 1Sa 2:1   7311
that he had *e* his kingdom for his.......... 2Sa 5:12   5375
e be the God of the rock of my................ 2Sa 22:47   7311
the son of Haggith *e* himself 1Kin 1:5   5375
Forasmuch as I *e* thee from among 1Kin 14:7   7311
Forasmuch as I *e* thee out of the............ 1Kin 16:2   7311
whom hast thou *e* thy voice.................... 2Kin 19:22   7311
thou art *e* as head above all.................... 1Chr 29:11   5375
which is *e* above all blessing and .... Neh 9:5   7311
which mourn may be *e* to safety.............. Job 5:11   7682
They are *e* for a little while, ... Job 24:24   7426
them for ever, and they are *e* .... Job 36:7   1361
side, when the vilest men are *e* .... Ps 12:8   7311
shall mine enemy be *e* over me.............. Ps 13:2   7311
let the God of my salvation be *e* .... Ps 18:46   7311
Be thou *e*, LORD, in thine own .... Ps 21:13   7311
I will be *e* among the heathen................ Ps 46:10   7311
I will be *e* in the earth .... Ps 46:10   7311
he is greatly *e*.. Ps 47:9   5927
Be thou *e*, O God, above the .... Ps 57:5   7311
Be thou *e*, O God, above the .... Ps 57:11   7311

horns of the righteous shall be *e*	Ps 75:10	7311
thy righteousness shall they be *e*	Ps 89:16	7311
in thy favour our horn shall be *e*	Ps 89:17	7311
I have *e* one chosen out of the	Ps 89:19	7311
and in my name shall his horn be *e*	Ps 89:24	7311
thou art *e* far above all gods	Ps 97:9	5927
Be thou *e*, O God, above the	Ps 108:5	7311
his horn shall be *e* with honour	Ps 112:9	7311
The right hand of the Lord is *e*	Ps 118:16	7426
of the upright the city is *e*	Prov 11:11	7311
shall be *e* above the hills	Is 2:2	5375
Lord alone shall be *e* in that day	Is 2:11	7682
Lord alone shall be *e* in that day	Is 2:17	7682
of hosts shall be *e* in judgment	Is 5:16	1361
make mention that his name is *e*	Is 12:4	7682
you, and therefore will he be *e*	Is 30:18	7311
The Lord is *e*	Is 33:5	7682
now will I be *e*	Is 33:10	7311
whom hast thou *e* thy voice	Is 37:23	7311
Every valley shall be *e*, and every	Is 40:4	5375
a way, and my highways shall be *e*	Is 49:11	7311
deal prudently, he shall be *e*	Is 52:13	7311
have *e* the low tree, have dried	Eze 17:24	1361
her stature was *e* among the thick	Eze 19:11	1361
Therefore his height was *e* above	Eze 31:5	1361
trembling, he *e* himself in Israel	Hos 13:1	5375
were filled, and their heart was *e*	Hos 13:6	7311
it shall be *e* above the hills	Mic 4:1	5375
which art *e* unto heaven, shalt be	Mt 11:23	5312
shall humble himself shall be *e*	Mt 23:12	5312
seats, and *e* them of low degree	Lk 1:52	5312
Capernaum, which art *e* to heaven	Lk 10:15	5312
that humbleth himself shall be *e*	Lk 14:11	5312
that humbleth himself shall be *e*	Lk 18:14	5312
being by the right hand of God *e*	Acts 2:33	5312
Him hath God *e* with his right	Acts 5:31	5312
e the people when they dwelt as	Acts 13:17	5312
abasing myself that ye might be *e*	2Cor 11:7	5312
lest I should be *e* above measure	2Cor 12:7	5229
lest I should be *e* above measure	2Cor 12:7	5229
God also hath highly *e* him	Phil 2:9	5251
degree rejoice in that he is *e*	Jas 1:9	5311

EXALTEST

As yet *e* thou thyself against my	Ex 9:17	5549

EXALTETH

Behold, God *e* by his power	Job 36:22	7682
He also *e* the horn of his people,	Ps 148:14	7311
that is hasty of spirit *e* folly	Prov 14:29	7311
Righteousness *e* a nation	Prov 14:34	7311
he that *e* his gate seeketh	Prov 17:19	1361
For whosoever *e* himself shall be	Lk 14:11	5312
for every one that *e* himself	Lk 18:14	5312
every high thing that *e* itself	2Cor 10:5	1869
e himself above all that is	2Th 2:4	5229

EXAMINATION

O king Agrippa, that, after *e* had	Acts 25:26	351

EXAMINE

the tenth month to *e* the matter	Ezr 10:16	1875
E me, O Lord, and prove me	Ps 26:2	974
to them that do *e* me is this	1Cor 9:3	350
But let a man *e* himself, and so	1Cor 11:28	1381
E yourselves, whether ye be in	2Cor 13:5	3985

EXAMINED

having *e* him before you, have	Lk 23:14	350
If we this day be *e* of the good	Acts 4:9	350
he *e* the keepers, and commanded	Acts 12:19	350
that he should be *e* by scourging	Acts 22:24	426
from him which should have *e* him	Acts 22:29	426
Who, when they had *e* me, would	Acts 28:18	350

EXAMINING

by *e* of whom thyself mayest take	Acts 24:8	350

EXAMPLE

willing to make her a publick *e*	Mt 1:19	3856
For I have given you an *e*	Jn 13:15	5262
but be thou an *e* of the believers	1Ti 4:12	5179
fall after the same *e* of unbelief	Heb 4:11	5262
Who serve unto the *e* and shadow of	Heb 8:5	5262
for an *e* of suffering affliction,	Jas 5:10	5262
suffered for us, leaving us an *e*	1Pet 2:21	5261
flesh, are set forth for an *e*	Jude 7	1164

EXAMPLES

Now these things were our *e*	1Cor 10:6	5179

EXCEED

stripes he may give him, and not *e*	Deut 25:3	3254
lest, if he should *e*, and beat him	Deut 25:3	3254

shall *e* the righteousness of the	Mt 5:20	4052
of righteousness *e* in glory	2Cor 3:9	4052

EXCEEDED

one with another, until David *e*	1Sa 20:41	1431
So king Solomon *e* all the kings	1Kin 10:23	1431
transgressions that they have *e*	Job 36:9	1396

EXCEEDEST

for thou *e* the fame that I heard	2Chr 9:6	3254

EXCEEDETH

prosperity *e* the fame which I	1Kin 10:7	3254

EXCEEDING

thy shield, and thy *e* great reward	Gen 15:1	3966
And I will make thee *e* fruitful	Gen 17:6	3966
e bitter cry, and said unto his	Gen 27:34	3966
and multiplied, and waxed *e* mighty	Ex 1:7	3966
the voice of the trumpet *e* loud	Ex 19:16	3966
to search it, is an *e* good land	Num 14:7	3966
Talk no more so *e* proudly	1Sa 2:3	
king David took *e* much brass	2Sa 8:8	3966
The rich man had *e* many flocks	2Sa 12:2	3966
wisdom and understanding *e* much	1Kin 4:29	3966
because they were *e* many	1Kin 7:47	3966
he brought also *e* much spoil out	1Chr 20:2	3966
for the Lord must be *e* magnifical	1Chr 22:5	4605
spears, and made them *e* strong	2Chr 11:12	7235,3966
for there was *e* much spoil in	2Chr 14:14	7235
until his disease was *e* great	2Chr 16:12	4605
And Hezekiah had *e* much riches	2Chr 32:27	3966
thou hast made him *e* glad with	Ps 21:6	2302
altar of God, unto God my *e* joy	Ps 43:4	8057
but thy commandment is *e* broad	Ps 119:96	
the earth, but they are *e* wise	Prov 30:24	
e deep, who can find it out	Eccl 7:24	
(he is *e* proud) his loftiness, and	Jer 48:29	3966
of Israel and Judah is *e* great	Eze 9:9	3966
and thou wast *e* beautiful, and thou	Eze 16:13	3966
e in dyed attire upon their heads	Eze 23:15	5628
upon their feet, an *e* great army	Eze 37:10	3966
the fish of the great sea, *e* many	Eze 47:10	3966
was urgent, and the furnace *e* hot	Dan 3:22	2493
Then was the king *e* glad for him	Dan 6:23	7689
e dreadful, whose teeth were of	Dan 7:19	3493
little horn, which waxed *e* great	Dan 8:9	3499
Now Nineveh was an *e* great city	Jonah 3:3	430
So Jonah was *e* glad of the gourd	Jonah 4:6	1419
they rejoiced with *e* great joy	Mt 2:10	4970
was *e* wroth, and sent forth, and	Mt 2:16	3029
him up into an *e* high mountain	Mt 4:8	3029
Rejoice, and be *e* glad	Mt 5:12	
e fierce, so that no man might	Mt 8:28	3029
And they were *e* sorry	Mt 17:23	4970
And they were *e* sorrowful, and	Mt 26:22	4970
unto them, My soul is *e* sorrowful	Mt 26:38	4036
And the king was *e* sorry	Mk 6:26	4036
became shining, *e* white as snow	Mk 9:3	3029
My soul is *e* sorrowful unto death	Mk 14:34	4036
Herod saw Jesus, he was *e* glad	Lk 23:8	3029
was *e* fair, and nourished up in	Acts 7:20	3588,2316
commandment might become *e*	Rom 7:13	2596,5236
worketh for us a far more *e*	2Cor 4:17	1519,5236
comfort, I am *e* joyful in all our	2Cor 7:4	5248
you for the grace of God in you	2Cor 9:14	5235
what is the *e* greatness of his	Eph 1:19	5235
the *e* riches of his grace in his	Eph 2:7	5235
do *e* abundantly above all that we	Eph 3:20	5228
Lord was *e* abundant with faith	1Ti 1:14	5250
ye may be glad also with *e* joy	1Pet 4:13	
Whereby are given unto us *e* great	2Pet 1:4	
presence of his glory with *e* joy	Jude 24	
the plague thereof was *e* great	Rev 16:21	4970

EXCEEDINGLY

waters prevailed *e* upon the earth	Gen 7:19	3966
and sinners before the Lord *e*	Gen 13:13	3966
her, I will multiply thy seed *e*	Gen 16:10	7235
and thee, and will multiply thee *e*	Gen 17:2	3966
fruitful, and will multiply him *e*	Gen 17:20	3966
And Isaac trembled very *e*, and said	Gen 27:33	1419
And the man increased *e*, and had	Gen 30:43	3966
therein, and grew, and multiplied *e*	Gen 47:27	3966
played the fool, and have erred *e*	1Sa 26:21	7235,3966
Then Amnon hated her *e*	2Sa 13:15	1419,3966
But they were *e* afraid, and said,	2Kin 10:4	3966
e in the sight of all Israel	1Chr 29:25	4605
was with him, and magnified him *e*	2Chr 1:1	4605
And Jehoshaphat waxed great *e*	2Chr 17:12	4605
for he strengthened himself *e*	2Chr 26:8	4605
it grieved them *e* that there was	Neh 2:10	1419
Then was the queen *e* grieved	Est 4:4	3966

Which rejoice *e*, and are glad, ...Job 3:22 413,1524
yea, let them *e* rejoice ....Ps 68:3 8057
But lusted *e* in the wilderness, ...Ps 106:14
and I love them *e*.................................Ps 119:167 3966
for we are *e* filled with contempt ....Ps 123:3 7227
Our soul is *e* filled with the ....Ps 123:4 7227
dissolved, the earth is moved *e* ....Is 24:19
dreadful and terrible, and strong *e*........Dan 7:7 3493
Then were the men *e* afraid...............Jonah 1:10 1419
Then the men feared the LORD *e* ......Jonah 1:16 1419
But it displeased Jonah *e* ....Jonah 4:1 1419
heard it, they were *e* amazed ....Mt 19:25 4970
And they feared *e*, and said one to . Mk 4:41 5401,3173
And they cried out the more *e*................Mk 15:14 4056
Jews, do *e* trouble our city, ...Acts 16:20 1613
being *e* mad against them, I ....Acts 26:11 4057
we being *e* tossed with a tempest,.........Acts 27:18 4971
e the more joyed we for the joy 2Cor 7:13 4056
being more *e* zealous of the.....................Gal 1:14 4056
praying *e* that we might see 1Th 3:10 5228,1537,4053
because that your faith groweth *e* 2Th 1:3
Moses said, I *e* fear and quake ....Heb 12:21 1630

EXCEL
as water, thou shalt not *e*.......................Gen 49:4 3498
with harps on the Sheminith to *e* 1Chr 15:21 5329
that *e* in strength, that do his ....Ps 103:20 1368
images did *e* them of Jerusalem ....Is 10:10
seek that ye may *e* to the 1Cor 14:12 4052

EXCELLED
Solomon's wisdom *e* the wisdom of 1Kin 4:30 7227

EXCELLENCY
e of dignity, and the *e* of power ....Gen 49:3 3499
in the greatness of thine *e* thou ....Ex 15:7 1347
thy help, and in his *e* on the sky ....Deut 33:26 1346
and who is the sword of thy *e*.................Deut 33:29 1346
Doth not their *e* which is in them ....Job 4:21 3499
Shall not his *e* make you afraid..............Job 13:11 7613
Though his *e* mount up to the ....Job 20:6 7863
with the voice of his *e* ....Job 37:4 1347
thyself now with majesty and *e* ....Job 40:10 1363
the *e* of Jacob whom he loved ....Ps 47:4 1347
to cast him down from his *e*....................Ps 62:4 7613
his *e* is over Israel, and his.....................Ps 68:34 1346
but the *e* of knowledge is, that ....Eccl 7:12 3504
the beauty of the Chaldees' *e* ....Is 13:19 1347
the *e* of Carmel and Sharon, they ....Is 35:2 1926
of the LORD, and the *e* of our God ....Is 35:2 1926
I will make thee an eternal *e* ....Is 60:15 1347
the *e* of your strength, the ....Eze 24:21 1347
of hosts, I abhor the *e* of Jacob ....Amos 6:8 1347
LORD hath sworn by the *e* of Jacob ....Amos 8:7 1347
hath turned away the *e* of Jacob ....Nah 2:2 1347
of Jacob, as the *e* of Israel ....Nah 2:2 1347
came not with *e* of speech or of 1Cor 2:1 5247
that the *e* of the power may be of 2Cor 4:7 5236
the *e* of the knowledge of Christ ....Phil 3:8 5242

EXCELLENT
honour of his *e* majesty many days ....Est 1:4 1420
he is *e* in power, and in judgment,.........Job 37:23 7689
how *e* is thy name in all the ....Ps 8:1 117
how *e* is thy name in all the ....Ps 8:9 117
are in the earth, and to the ....Ps 16:3 117
How *e* is thy lovingkindness, O ....Ps 36:7 3368
e than the mountains of prey ....Ps 76:4 117
it shall be an *e* oil, which shall ....Ps 141:5 7218
for his name alone is *e*............................Ps 148:13 7682
him according to his *e* greatness...........Ps 150:2 7230
for I will speak of *e* things......................Prov 8:6 5057
is more *e* than his neighbour ....Prov 12:26 8446
E speech becometh not a fool ....Prov 17:7 3499
understanding is of an *e* spirit ....Prov 17:27 7119
to thee *e* things in counsels...................Prov 22:20 7991
is as Lebanon, *e* as the cedars ....Song 5:15 977
the fruit of the earth shall be *e* ....Is 4:2 1347
for he hath done *e* things ....Is 12:5 1348
in counsel, and *e* in working ....Is 28:29 1431
and thou art come to *e* ornaments.........Eze 16:7 5716
image, whose brightness was *e*.............Dan 2:31 3493
e majesty was added unto me..............Dan 4:36 3493
Forasmuch as an *e* spirit, and ....Dan 5:12 3493
e wisdom is found in thee ....Dan 5:14 3493
because an *e* spirit was in him ....Dan 6:3 3493
thee in order, most *e* Theophilus, ...Lk 1:3 2903
Claudius Lysias unto the most *e* ....Acts 23:26 2903
the things that are more *e* ....Rom 2:18 1308
yet shew I unto you a more *e* way...1Cor 12:31 2596,5236
ye may approve things that are *e* ....Phil 1:10 1308
obtained a more *e* name than they ....Heb 1:4 1313
he obtained a more *e* ministry ....Heb 8:6 1313

God a more *e* sacrifice than Cain...........Heb 11:4 4119
a voice to him from the *e* glory 2Pet 1:17 3169

EXCELLEST
virtuously, but thou *e* them all ....Prov 31:29 5927

EXCELLETH
Then I saw that wisdom *e* folly ....Eccl 2:13 3504
as far as light *e* darkness ....Eccl 2:13 3504
by reason of the glory that *e* 2Cor 3:10 5235

EXCEPT See APPENDIX.

EXCEPTED See APPENDIX.

EXCESS
they are full of extortion and *e*...............Mt 23:25 192
not drunk with wine, wherein is *e* ....Eph 5:18 810
lusts, *e* of wine, revellings,.....................1Pet 4:3 3632
with them to the same *e* of riot 1Pet 4:4 401

EXCHANGE
gave them bread in *e* for horses ....Gen 47:17
the *e* thereof shall be holy ....Lev 27:10 8545
the *e* of it shall not be for ....Job 28:17 8545
shall not sell of it, neither *e* ....Eze 48:14 4171
a man give in *e* for his soul ....Mt 16:26 465
a man give in *e* for his soul ....Mk 8:37 465

EXCHANGERS
to have put my money to the *e*...............Mt 25:27 5133

EXCLUDE
yea, they would *e* you, that ye ....Gal 4:17 1576

EXCLUDED
is boasting then? It is *e*..........................Rom 3:27 1576

EXCUSE
with one consent began to make *e* ....Lk 14:18 3868
so that they are without *e* ....Rom 1:20 379
think ye that we *e* ourselves unto 2Cor 12:19 626

EXCUSED
I pray thee have me *e*.............................Lk 14:18 3868
I pray thee have me *e*.............................Lk 14:19 3868

EXCUSING
accusing or else *e* one another..............Rom 2:15 626

EXECRATION
and ye shall be an *e*, and an ....Jer 42:18 423
and they shall be an *e*, and an ....Jer 44:12 423

EXECUTE
gods of Egypt I will *e* judgment ....Ex 12:12 6213
the priest shall *e* upon her all ....Num 5:30 6213
that they may *e* the service of ....Num 8:11 5647
He doth the judgment of the ....Deut 10:18 6213
e my judgments, and keep all my 1Kin 6:12 6213
when wilt thou *e* judgment on them ....Ps 119:84 6213
To *e* vengeance upon the heathen,..........Ps 149:7 6213
To *e* upon them the judgment ....Ps 149:9 6213
Take counsel, *e* judgment ....Is 16:3 6213
if ye throughly *e* judgment ....Jer 7:5 6213
E judgment in the morning, and ....Jer 21:12 1777
E ye judgment and righteousness, ...Jer 22:3 6213
shall *e* judgment and justice in ....Jer 23:5 6213
and he shall *e* judgment and...................Jer 33:15 6213
will *e* judgments in the midst of ....Eze 5:8 6213
I will *e* judgments in thee, and ....Eze 5:10 6213
when I shall *e* judgments in thee ....Eze 5:15 6213
will *e* judgments among you ....Eze 11:9 6213
e judgments upon thee in the ....Eze 16:41 6213
I will *e* judgments upon Moab ....Eze 25:11 6213
I will *e* great vengeance upon ....Eze 25:17 6213
Zoan, and will *e* judgments in No ....Eze 30:14 6213
Thus will I *e* judgments in Egypt ....Eze 30:19 6213
e judgment and justice, take away ....Eze 45:9 6213
I will not *e* the fierceness of ....Hos 11:9 6213
I will *e* vengeance in anger and ....Mic 5:15 6213
my cause, and *e* judgment for me ....Mic 7:9 6213
E true judgment, and shew mercy and ...Zec 7:9 8199
e the judgment of truth and peace ....Zec 8:16 8199
him authority to *e* judgment also ....Jn 5:27 4160
a revenger to *e* wrath upon him.............Rom 13:4
To *e* judgment upon all, and to...............Jude 15 4160

EXECUTED
gods also the LORD *e* judgments ....Num 33:4 6213
he *e* the justice of the LORD, and ....Deut 33:21 6213
David *e* judgment and justice unto 2Sa 8:15 6213
(he it is that *e* the priest's......................1Chr 6:10
e judgment and justice among all 1Chr 18:14 6213
Ithamar *e* the priest's office 1Chr 24:2
So they *e* judgment against Joash 2Chr 24:24 6213
let judgment be *e* speedily upon ....Ezr 7:26 5648
stood up Phinehas, and *e* judgment........Ps 106:30 6213
an evil work is not *e* speedily ....Eccl 8:11 6213

shall not return, until he have *e*.............Jer 23:20   6213
neither *e* my judgments, but have..........Eze 11:12   6213
hath *e* true judgment between man ....Eze 18:8   6213
hath *e* my judgments, hath walked ....Eze 18:17   6213
they had not *e* my judgments................Eze 20:24   6213
for they had *e* judgment upon her..........Eze 23:10   6213
I shall have *e* judgments in her ....Eze 28:22   6213
when I have *e* judgments upon all ....Eze 28:26   6213
see my judgment that I have *e*.............Eze 39:21   6213
that while he *e* the priest's ....Lk 1:8   2407

EXECUTEDST
nor *e* his fierce wrath upon 1Sa 28:18   6213

EXECUTEST
thou *e* judgment and righteousness ....Ps 99:4   6213

EXECUTETH
known by the judgment which he *e* ....Ps 9:16   6213
The LORD *e* righteousness and ....Ps 103:6   6213
Which *e* judgment for the.......................Ps 146:7   6213
the man that *e* my counsel from a ....Is 46:11
if there be any that *e* judgment.............Jer 5:1   6213
for he is strong that *e* his word ....Joel 2:11   6213

EXECUTING
in *e* that which is right in mine 2Kin 10:30   6213
e the priest's office unto the 2Chr 11:14
when Jehu was *e* judgment upon the......2Chr 22:8

EXECUTION
decree drew near to be put in *e*............Est 9:1   6213

EXECUTIONER
And immediately the king sent an *e*.......Mk 6:27   4688

EXEMPTED
throughout all Judah; none was *e* 1Kin 15:22   5355

EXERCISE
neither do I *e* myself in great.................Ps 131:1   1980
the LORD which *e* lovingkindness ....Jer 9:24   6213
the Gentiles *e* dominion over them ....Mt 20:25   2634
are great *e* authority upon them ....Mt 20:25   2715
the Gentiles *e* lordship over them ....Mk 10:42   2634
their great ones *e* authority upon ....Mk 10:42   2715
the Gentiles *e* lordship over them ....Lk 22:25   2961
they that *e* authority upon them............Lk 22:25   1850
And herein do I *e* myself, to have ....Acts 24:16   778
e thyself rather unto godliness...............1Ti 4:7   1128
For bodily *e* profiteth little......................1Ti 4:8   1129

EXERCISED
the sons of man to be *e* therewith.........Eccl 1:13   6031
to the sons of men to be *e* in it...............Eccl 3:10   6031
e robbery, and have vexed the poor ......Eze 22:29
senses *e* to discern both good................Heb 5:14   1128
unto them which are *e* thereby ....Heb 12:11   1128
an heart they have *e* with......................2Pet 2:14   1128

EXERCISETH
he *e* all the power of the first ....Rev 13:12   4160

EXHORT
other words did he testify and *e*.............Acts 2:40   3870
now I *e* you to be of good cheer ....Acts 27:22   3867
it necessary to *e* the brethren................2Cor 9:5   3870
e you by the Lord Jesus, that as 1Th 4:1   3870
Now we *e* you, brethren, warn them.......1Th 5:14   3870
e by our Lord Jesus Christ, that 2Th 3:12   3870
I *e* therefore, that, first of all 1Ti 2:1   3870
These things teach and *e*........................1Ti 6:2   3870
e with all longsuffering and....................2Ti 4:2   3870
able by sound doctrine both to *e* ....Titus 1:9   3870
men likewise *e* to be sober minded.........Titus 2:6   3870
E servants to be obedient unto ....Titus 2:9
These things speak, and *e*, and..............Titus 2:15   3870
But *e* one another daily, while it ....Heb 3:13   3870
elders which are among you I *e* 1Pet 5:1   3870
e you that ye should earnestly ....Jude 3   3870

EXHORTATION
many other things in his *e* ....Lk 3:18   3870
have any word of *e* for the people ....Acts 13:15   3874
parts, and had given them much *e* ....Acts 20:2   3870
Or he that exhorteth, on *e* ....Rom 12:8   3874
unto men to edification, and *e*................1Cor 14:3   3874
For indeed he accepted the *e*..................2Cor 8:17   3874
For our *e* was not of deceit, nor..............1Th 2:3   3874
give attendance to reading, to *e* 1Ti 4:13   3874
ye have forgotten the *e* which ....Heb 12:5   3874
brethren, suffer the word of *e*.................Heb 13:22   3874

EXHORTED
e them all, that with purpose of............Acts 11:23   3870
e the brethren with many words,...........Acts 15:32   3870
As ye know how we *e* and comforted 1Th 2:11   3870

EXHORTETH
Or he that *e*, on exhortation ....Rom 12:8   3870

EXHORTING
e them to continue in the faith, ...Acts 14:22   3870
e the disciples to receive him ....Acts 18:27   4389
but *e* one another ....Heb 10:25   3870
I have written briefly, *e* 1Pet 5:12   3870

EXILE
thou art a stranger, and also an *e* 2Sa 15:19   1540
The captive *e* hasteneth that he ....Is 51:14   6808

EXORCISTS
certain of the vagabond Jews, *e* ....Acts 19:13   1845

EXPECTATION
the *e* of the poor shall not ....Ps 9:18   8615
for my *e* is from him..............................Ps 62:5   8615
but the *e* of the wicked shall ....Prov 10:28   8615
man dieth, his *e* shall perish ....Prov 11:7   8615
but the *e* of the wicked is wrath............Prov 11:23   8615
thine *e* shall not be cut off.....................Prov 23:18   8615
thy *e* shall not be cut off........................Prov 24:14   8615
and ashamed of Ethiopia their *e*............Is 20:5   4007
that day, Behold, such is our *e* ....Is 20:6   4007
for her *e* shall be ashamed.....................Zec 9:5   4007
And as the people were in *e* ....Lk 3:15   4328
from all the *e* of the people of................Acts 12:11   4329
For the earnest *e* of the creature ....Rom 8:19   603
According to my earnest *e* ....Phil 1:20   603

EXPECTED
not of evil, to give you an *e* end ....Jer 29:11   8615

EXPECTING
e to receive something of them ....Acts 3:5   4328
From henceforth *e* till his........................Heb 10:13   1551

EXPEDIENT
Nor consider that it is *e* for us ....Jn 11:50   4851
It is *e* for you that I go away ....Jn 16:7   4851
that it was *e* that one man should ....Jn 18:14   4851
unto me, but all things are not *e*............1Cor 6:12   4851
for me, but all things are not *e* 1Cor 10:23   4851
for this is *e* for you, who have 2Cor 8:10   4851
It is not *e* for me doubtless to 2Cor 12:1   4851

EXPEL
he shall *e* them from before you,............Josh 23:5   1920
e me out of my father's house................Judg 11:7   1644

EXPELLED
of Israel *e* not the Geshurites.................Josh 13:13   3423
he *e* thence the three sons of.................Judg 1:20   3423
his banished be not *e* from him 2Sa 14:14   5080
e them out of their coasts......................Acts 13:50   1544

EXPENCES
let the *e* be given out of the...................Ezr 6:4   5313
forthwith *e* be given unto these ....Ezr 6:8   5313

EXPERIENCE
for I have learned by *e* that the ....Gen 30:27   5172
my heart had great *e* of wisdom............Eccl 1:16   7200
And patience, *e*......................................Rom 5:4   1382
and *e*, hope..Rom 5:4   1382

EXPERIMENT
Whiles by the *e* of this............................2Cor 9:13   1382

EXPERT
e in war, with all instruments of 1Chr 12:33   6186
And of the Danites *e* in war twenty 1Chr 12:35   6186
battle, *e* in war, forty thousand 1Chr 12:36   6186
all hold swords, being *e* in war...............Song 3:8   3925
shall be as of a mighty man.....................Jer 50:9   7919
know thee to be *e* in all customs ....Acts 26:3   1109

EXPIRED
and the days were not *e*.........................1Sa 18:26   4390
to pass, after the year was *e* 2Sa 11:1   8666
when thy days be *e* that thou must 1Chr 17:11   4390
pass, that after the year was *e* 1Chr 20:1   8666
And when the year was *e*, king...............2Chr 36:10   8666
And when these days were *e* ....Est 1:5   4390
And when these days are *e*, it ....Eze 43:27   3615
And when forty years were *e*..................Acts 7:30   4137
And when the thousand years are *e* ....Rev 20:7   5055

EXPLOITS
and he shall do *e*, and return to.............Dan 11:28
God shall be strong, and do *e* ....Dan 11:32

EXPOUND
not in three days *e* the riddle ....Judg 14:14   5046

EXPOUNDED
unto them which *e* the riddle ....Judg 14:19   5046
he *e* all things to his disciples ....Mk 4:34   1956

E

he *e* unto them in all the	Lk 24:27	1329
e it by order unto them, saying,	Acts 11:4	1620
e unto him the way of God more	Acts 18:26	1620
to whom he *e* and testified the	Acts 28:23	1620

EXPRESS

the *e* image of his person, and	Heb 1:3	5481

EXPRESSED

men which are *e* by their names	Num 1:17	5344
thousand, which were *e* by name	1Chr 12:31	5344
were chosen, who were *e* by name	1Chr 16:41	5344
men which were *e* by name rose up	2Chr 28:15	5344
city, the men that were *e* by name	2Chr 31:19	5344
all of them were *e* by name	Ezr 8:20	5344

EXPRESSLY

If I *e* say unto the lad, Behold,	1Sa 20:21	559
came *e* unto Ezekiel the priest	Eze 1:3	
Now the Spirit speaketh *e*	1Ti 4:1	4490

EXTEND

there be none to *e* mercy unto him	Ps 109:12	4900
I will *e* peace to her like a	Is 66:12	5186

EXTENDED

hath *e* mercy unto me before the	Ezr 7:28	5186
but hath *e* mercy unto us in the	Ezr 9:9	5186

EXTENDETH

my goodness *e* not to thee	Ps 16:2	

EXTINCT

breath is corrupt, my days are *e*	Job 17:1	2193
they are *e*, they are quenched as	Is 43:17	1846

EXTOL

I will *e* thee, O Lord	Ps 30:1	7311
e him that rideth upon the	Ps 68:4	5549
I will *e* thee, my God, O king	Ps 145:1	7311
Now I Nebuchadnezzar praise and *e*	Dan 4:37	7313

EXTOLLED

mouth, and he was *e* with my tongue	Ps 66:17	7318
he shall be exalted and *e*	Is 52:13	5375

EXTORTION

gained of thy neighbours by *e*	Eze 22:12	6233
but within they are full of *e*	Mt 23:25	724

EXTORTIONER

Let the *e* catch all that he hath	Ps 109:11	5383
for the *e* is at an end, the	Is 16:4	4160
a railer, or a drunkard, or an *e*	1Cor 5:11	727

EXTORTIONERS

that I am not as other men are, *e*	Lk 18:11	727
world, or with the covetous, or *e*	1Cor 5:10	727
drunkards, nor revilers, nor *e*	1Cor 6:10	727

EXTREME

and with an *e* burning, and with	Deut 28:22	2746

EXTREMITY

yet he knoweth it not in great *e*	Job 35:15	6580

EYE

E for *e*, tooth for tooth, hand	Ex 21:24	5869
a man smite the *e* of his servant	Ex 21:26	5869
or the *e* of his maid, that it	Ex 21:26	5869
or that hath a blemish in his *e*	Lev 21:20	5869
e for *e*, tooth for tooth	Lev 24:20	5869
thine *e* shall have no pity upon	Deut 7:16	5869
neither shall thine *e* pity him	Deut 13:8	5869
thine *e* be evil against thy poor	Deut 15:9	5869
Thine *e* shall not pity him, but	Deut 19:13	5869
And thine *e* shall not pity	Deut 19:21	5869
e for *e*, tooth for tooth, hand	Deut 19:21	5869
thine *e* shall not pity her	Deut 25:12	5869
his *e* shall be evil toward his	Deut 28:54	5869
her *e* shall be evil toward the	Deut 28:56	5869
he kept him as the apple of his *e*	Deut 32:10	5869
his *e* was not dim, nor his	Deut 34:7	5869
but mine *e* spared thee	1Sa 24:10	
to my cleanness in his *e* sight	2Sa 22:25	5869
But the *e* of their God was upon	Ezr 5:5	5870
mine *e* shall no more see good	Job 7:7	5869
The *e* of him that hath seen me	Job 7:8	5869
up the ghost, and no *e* had seen me	Job 10:18	5869
mine *e* hath seen all this, mine	Job 13:1	5869
but mine *e* poureth out tears unto	Job 16:20	5869
doth not mine *e* continue in their	Job 17:2	5869
Mine *e* also is dim by reason of	Job 17:7	5869
The *e* also which saw him shall	Job 20:9	5869
The *e* also of the adulterer	Job 24:15	5869
saying, No *e* shall see me	Job 24:15	5869
the vulture's *e* hath not seen	Job 28:7	5869
his *e* seeth every precious thing	Job 28:10	5869
and when the *e* saw me, it gave	Job 29:11	5869

but now mine *e* seeth thee	Job 42:5	5869
Mine *e* is consumed because of	Ps 6:7	5869
Keep me as the apple of the *e*	Ps 17:8	5869
mine *e* is consumed with grief,	Ps 31:9	5869
I will guide thee with mine *e*	Ps 32:8	5869
the *e* of the Lord is upon them	Ps 33:18	5869
e that hate me without a cause	Ps 35:19	5869
Aha, aha, our *e* hath seen it	Ps 35:21	5869
mine *e* hath seen his desire upon	Ps 54:7	5869
Mine *e* mourneth by reason of	Ps 88:9	5869
Mine *e* also shall see my desire	Ps 92:11	5869
he that formed the *e*, shall he	Ps 94:9	5869
and my law as the apple of thine *e*	Prov 7:2	5869
winketh with the *e* causeth sorrow	Prov 10:10	5869
The hearing ear, and the seeing *e*	Prov 20:12	5869
a bountiful *e* shall be blessed	Prov 22:9	5869
bread of him that hath an evil *e*	Prov 23:6	5869
hasteth to be rich hath an evil *e*	Prov 28:22	5869
The *e* that mocketh at his father,	Prov 30:17	5869
the *e* is not satisfied with	Eccl 1:8	5869
neither is his *e* satisfied with	Eccl 4:8	5869
their *e* shall not spare children	Is 13:18	5869
for they shall see *e* to *e*	Is 52:8	5869
the ear, neither hath the *e* seen	Is 64:4	5869
mine *e* shall weep sore, and run	Jer 13:17	5869
mine *e*, mine *e* runneth down	Lam 1:16	5869
to the *e* in the tabernacle of the	Lam 2:4	5869
not the apple of thine *e* cease	Lam 2:18	5869
Mine *e* runneth down with rivers	Lam 3:48	5869
Mine *e* trickleth down, and ceaseth	Lam 3:49	5869
Mine *e* affecteth mine heart	Lam 3:51	5869
neither shall mine *e* spare	Eze 5:11	5869
mine *e* shall not spare thee,	Eze 7:4	5869
mine *e* shall not spare, neither	Eze 7:9	5869
mine *e* shall not spare, neither	Eze 8:18	5869
let not your *e* spare, neither	Eze 9:5	5869
mine *e* shall not spare, neither	Eze 9:10	5869
None *e* pitied thee, to do any of	Eze 16:5	5869
Nevertheless mine *e* spared them	Eze 20:17	5869
and let our *e* look upon Zion	Mic 4:11	5869
you toucheth the apple of his *e*	Zec 2:8	5869
upon his arm, and upon his right *e*	Zec 11:17	5869
his right *e* shall be utterly	Zec 11:17	5869
And if thy right *e* offend thee	Mt 5:29	3788
hath been said, An *e* for an *e*	Mt 5:38	3788
The light of the body is the *e*	Mt 6:22	3788
if therefore thine *e* be single	Mt 6:22	3788
But if thine *e* be evil, thy whole	Mt 6:23	3788
mote that is in thy brother's *e*	Mt 7:3	3788
the beam that is in thine own *e*	Mt 7:3	3788
pull out the mote out of thine *e*	Mt 7:4	3788
behold, a beam is in thine own *e*	Mt 7:4	3788
out the beam out of thine own *e*	Mt 7:5	3788
the mote out of thy brother's *e*	Mt 7:5	3788
if thine *e* offend thee, pluck it	Mt 18:9	3788
to enter into life with one *e*	Mt 18:9	3442
to go through the *e* of a needle	Mt 19:24	5169
Is thine *e* evil, because I am	Mt 20:15	3788
deceit, lasciviousness, an evil *e*	Mk 7:22	3788
if thine *e* offend thee, pluck it	Mk 9:47	3788
the kingdom of God with one *e*	Mk 9:47	3442
to go through the *e* of a needle	Mk 10:25	5168
mote that is in thy brother's *e*	Lk 6:41	3788
the beam that is in thine own *e*	Lk 6:41	3788
out the mote that is in thine *e*	Lk 6:42	3788
the beam that is in thine own *e*	Lk 6:42	3788
first the beam out of thine own *e*	Lk 6:42	3788
mote that is in thy brother's *e*	Lk 6:42	3788
The light of the body is the *e*	Lk 11:34	3788
therefore when thine *e* is single	Lk 11:34	3788
but when thine *e* is evil, thy	Lk 11:34	3788
camel to go through a needle's *e*	Lk 18:25	5168
E hath not seen, nor ear heard,	1Cor 2:9	3788
shall say, Because I am not the *e*	1Cor 12:16	3788
If the whole body were an *e*	1Cor 12:17	3788
the *e* cannot say unto the hand, I	1Cor 12:21	3788
moment, in the twinkling of an *e*	1Cor 15:52	3788
every *e* shall see him, and they	Rev 1:7	3788

EYEBROWS

his head and his beard and his *e*	Lev 14:9	1354,5869

EYED

Leah was tender *e*	Gen 29:17	5869
Saul *e* David from that day and	1Sa 18:9	5770

EYELIDS

on my *e* is the shadow of death	Job 16:16	6079
are like the *e* of the morning	Job 41:18	6079
his eyes behold, his *e* try	Ps 11:4	6079
mine eyes, or slumber to mine *e*	Ps 132:4	6079
let thine *e* look straight before	Prov 4:25	6079

eyes, nor slumber to thine *e*	Prov 6:4	6079
let her take thee with her *e*	Prov 6:25	6079
and their *e* are lifted up	Prov 30:13	6079
our *e* gush out with waters	Jer 9:18	6079

EYE'S

let him go free for his *e* sake	Ex 21:26	5869

EYES

then your *e* shall be opened, and	Gen 3:5	5869
and that it was pleasant to the *e*	Gen 3:6	5869
the *e* of them both were opened,	Gen 3:7	5869
found grace in the *e* of the LORD	Gen 6:8	5869
And Lot lifted up his *e*, and beheld	Gen 13:10	5869
from him, Lift up now thine *e*	Gen 13:14	5869
mistress was despised in her *e*	Gen 16:4	5869
I was despised in her *e*	Gen 16:5	5869
And he lift up his *e* and looked, and	Gen 18:2	5869
ye to them as is good in your *e*	Gen 19:8	5869
he is to thee a covering of the *e*	Gen 20:16	5869
And God opened her *e*, and she saw a	Gen 21:19	5869
third day Abraham lifted up his *e*	Gen 22:4	5869
And Abraham lifted up his *e*	Gen 22:13	5869
and he lifted up his *e*, and saw, and	Gen 24:63	5869
And Rebekah lifted up her *e*	Gen 24:64	5869
his *e* were dim, so that he could	Gen 27:1	5869
if I have found favour in thine *e*	Gen 30:27	5869
e of the cattle in the gutters	Gen 30:41	5869
that I lifted up mine *e*, and saw	Gen 31:10	5869
And he said, Lift up now thine *e*	Gen 31:12	5869
and my sleep departed from mine *e*	Gen 31:40	5869
And Jacob lifted up his *e*, and	Gen 33:1	5869
And he lifted up his *e*, and saw the	Gen 33:5	5869
Let me find grace in your *e*	Gen 34:11	5869
and they lifted up their *e*	Gen 37:25	5869
wife cast her *e* upon Joseph	Gen 39:7	5869
was good in the *e* of Pharaoh	Gen 41:37	5869
in the *e* of all his servants	Gen 41:37	5869
and bound him before their *e*	Gen 42:24	5869
And he lifted up his *e*, and saw his	Gen 43:29	5869
that I, may set mine *e* upon him	Gen 44:21	5869
And, behold, your *e* see, and the	Gen 45:12	5869
the *e* of my brother Benjamin	Gen 45:12	5869
shall put his hand upon thine *e*	Gen 46:4	5869
shall we die before thine *e*	Gen 47:19	5869
Now the *e* of Israel were dim for	Gen 48:10	5869
His *e* shall be red with wine, and	Gen 49:12	5869
now I have found grace in your *e*	Gen 50:4	5869
be abhorred in the *e* of Pharaoh	Ex 5:21	5869
in the *e* of his servants, to put	Ex 5:21	5869
of the Egyptians before their *e*	Ex 8:26	5869
and for a memorial between thine *e*	Ex 13:9	5869
and for frontlets between thine *e*	Ex 13:16	5869
of Israel lifted up their *e*	Ex 14:10	5869
the *e* of the children of Israel	Ex 24:17	5869
be hid from the *e* of the assembly	Lev 4:13	5869
ways hide their *e* from the man	Lev 20:4	5869
ague, that shall consume the *e*	Lev 26:16	5869
be hid from the *e* of her husband	Num 5:13	5869
thou mayest be to us instead of *e*	Num 10:31	5869
beside this manna, before our *e*	Num 11:6	5869
your own heart and your own *e*	Num 15:39	5869
thou put out the *e* of these men	Num 16:14	5869
ye unto the rock before their *e*	Num 20:8	5869
to sanctify me in the *e* of the	Num 20:12	5869
the LORD opened the *e* of Balaam	Num 22:31	5869
And Balaam lifted up his *e*	Num 24:2	5869
the man whose *e* are open hath	Num 24:3	5869
a trance, but having his *e* open	Num 24:4	5869
the man whose *e* are open hath	Num 24:15	5869
a trance, but having his *e* open	Num 24:16	5869
me at the water before their *e*	Num 27:14	5869
of them shall be pricks in your *e*	Num 33:55	5869
for you in Egypt before your *e*	Deut 1:30	5869
Thine *e* have seen all that the	Deut 3:21	5869
and lift up thine *e* westward	Deut 3:27	5869
and behold it with thine *e*	Deut 3:27	5869
Your *e* have seen what the LORD	Deut 4:3	5869
things which thine *e* have seen	Deut 4:9	5869
thou lift up thine *e* unto heaven	Deut 4:19	5869
for you in Egypt before your *e*	Deut 4:34	5869
be as frontlets between thine *e*	Deut 6:8	5869
all his household, before our *e*	Deut 6:22	5869
temptations which thine *e* saw	Deut 7:19	5869
and brake them before your *e*	Deut 9:17	5869
things, which thine *e* have seen	Deut 10:21	5869
But your *e* have seen all the	Deut 11:7	5869
the *e* of the LORD thy God are	Deut 11:12	5869
be as frontlets between your *e*	Deut 11:18	5869
whatsoever is right in his own *e*	Deut 12:8	5869
in the *e* of the LORD thy God	Deut 13:18	5869
between your *e* for the dead	Deut 14:1	5869
gift doth blind the *e* of the wise	Deut 16:19	5869
blood, neither have our *e* seen it	Deut 21:7	5869
that she find no favour in his *e*	Deut 24:1	5869
ox shall be slain before thine *e*	Deut 28:31	5869
thine *e* shall look, and fail with	Deut 28:32	5869
of thine *e* which thou shalt see	Deut 28:34	5869
trembling heart, and failing of *e*	Deut 28:65	5869
of thine *e* which thou shalt see	Deut 28:67	5869
your *e* in the land of Egypt unto	Deut 29:2	5869
which thine *e* have seen, the	Deut 29:3	5869
e to see, and ears to hear, unto	Deut 29:4	5869
thee to see it with thine *e*	Deut 34:4	5869
Jericho, that he lifted up his *e*	Josh 5:13	5869
your sides, and thorns in your *e*	Josh 23:13	5869
your *e* have seen what I have done	Josh 24:7	5869
took him, and put out his *e*	Judg 16:21	5869
of the Philistines for my two *e*	Judg 16:28	5869
that which was right in his own *e*	Judg 17:6	5869
And when he had lifted up his *e*	Judg 19:17	5869
that which was right in his own *e*	Judg 21:25	5869
Let thine *e* be on the field that	Ruth 2:9	5869
Why have I found grace in thine *e*	Ruth 2:10	5869
shall be to consume thine *e*	1Sa 2:33	5869
his *e* began to wax dim, that he	1Sa 3:2	5869
his *e* were dim, that he could not	1Sa 4:15	5869
and they lifted up their *e*	1Sa 6:13	5869
I may thrust out all your right *e*	1Sa 11:2	5869
bribe to blind mine *e* therewith	1Sa 12:3	5869
the LORD will do before your *e*	1Sa 12:16	5869
and his *e* were enlightened	1Sa 14:27	5869
how mine *e* have been enlightened,	1Sa 14:29	5869
I have found grace in thine *e*	1Sa 20:3	5869
if I have found favour in thine *e*	1Sa 20:29	5869
this day thine *e* have seen how	1Sa 24:10	5869
young men find favour in thine *e*	1Sa 25:8	5869
was precious in thine *e* this day	1Sa 26:21	5869
much set by this day in mine *e*	1Sa 26:24	5869
much set by in the *e* of the LORD	1Sa 26:24	5869
I have now found grace in thine *e*	1Sa 27:5	5869
to day in the *e* of the handmaids	2Sa 6:20	5869
take thy wives before thine *e*	2Sa 12:11	5869
kept the watch lifted up his *e*	2Sa 13:34	5869
find favour in the *e* of the LORD	2Sa 15:25	5869
unto the wall, and lifted up his *e*	2Sa 18:24	5869
therefore what is good in thine *e*	2Sa 19:27	5869
but thine *e* are upon the haughty,	2Sa 22:28	5869
that the *e* of my lord the king	2Sa 24:3	5869
the *e* of all Israel are upon thee	1Kin 1:20	5869
this day, mine *e* even seeing it	1Kin 1:48	5869
That thine *e* may be open toward	1Kin 8:29	5869
That thine *e* may be open unto the	1Kin 8:52	5869
and mine *e* and mine heart shall be	1Kin 9:3	5869
I came, and mine *e* had seen it	1Kin 10:7	5869
do that which is right in mine *e*	1Kin 11:33	5869
for his *e* were set by reason of	1Kin 14:4	5869
only which was right in mine *e*	1Kin 14:8	5869
was right in the *e* of the LORD	1Kin 15:5	5869
was right in the *e* of the LORD	1Kin 15:11	5869
wrought evil in the *e* of the LORD	1Kin 16:25	5869
whatsoever is pleasant in thine *e*	1Kin 20:6	5869
was right in the *e* of the LORD	1Kin 22:43	5869
his *e* upon his *e*, and his hands	2Kin 4:34	5869
times, and the child opened his *e*	2Kin 4:35	5869
LORD, I pray thee, open his *e*	2Kin 6:17	5869
opened the *e* of the young man	2Kin 6:17	5869
open the *e* of these men, that	2Kin 6:20	5869
And the LORD opened their *e*	2Kin 6:20	5869
thou shalt see it with thine *e*	2Kin 7:2	5869
thou shalt see it with thine *e*	2Kin 7:19	5869
that which is good in thine *e*	2Kin 10:5	5869
that which is right in mine *e*	2Kin 10:30	5869
open, LORD, thine *e*, and see	2Kin 19:16	5869
and lifted up thine *e* on high	2Kin 19:22	5869
thine *e* shall not see all the	2Kin 22:20	5869
the sons of Zedekiah before his *e*	2Kin 25:7	5869
and put out the *e* of Zedekiah	2Kin 25:7	5869
right in the *e* of all the people	1Chr 13:4	5869
this was a small thing in thine *e*	1Chr 17:17	5869
And David lifted up his *e*, and saw	1Chr 21:16	5869
do that which is good in his *e*	1Chr 21:23	5869
That thine *e* may be open upon	2Chr 6:20	5869
thine *e* be open, and let thine	2Chr 6:40	5869
Now mine *e* shall be open, and mine	2Chr 7:15	5869
and mine *e* and mine heart shall be	2Chr 7:16	5869
I came, and mine *e* had seen it	2Chr 9:6	5869
right in the *e* of the LORD	2Chr 14:2	5869
For the *e* of the LORD run to and	2Chr 16:9	5869
but our *e* are upon thee	2Chr 20:12	5869
was evil in the *e* of the LORD	2Chr 21:6	5869
evil in the *e* of the LORD our God	2Chr 29:6	5869
to hissing, as ye see with your *e*	2Chr 29:8	5869

neither shall thine *e* see all the .... 2Chr 34:28 | 5869
house was laid before their *e*. .... Ezr 3:12 | 5870
that our God may lighten our *e* .... Ezr 9:8 | 5869
now be attentive, and thine *e* open .... Neh 1:6 | 5869
much cast down in their own *e* .... Neh 6:16 | 5869
despise their husbands in their *e* .... Est 1:17 | 5869
king, and I be pleasing in his *e*. .... Est 8:5 | 5869
they lifted up their *e* afar off .... Job 2:12 | 5869
womb, nor hid sorrow from mine *e* .... Job 3:10 | 5869
an image was before mine *e*. .... Job 4:16 | 5869
thine *e* are upon me, and I am not .... Job 7:8 | 5869
Hast thou *e* of flesh .... Job 10:4 | 5869
is pure, and I am clean in thine *e* .... Job 11:4 | 5869
But the *e* of the wicked shall .... Job 11:20 | 5869
open thine *e* upon such an one .... Job 14:3 | 5869
and what do thy *e* wink at, ... Job 15:12 | 5869
enemy sharpeneth his *e* upon me .... Job 16:9 | 5869
even the *e* of his children shall .... Job 17:5 | 5869
mine *e* shall behold, and not .... Job 19:27 | 5869
and their offspring before their *e* .... Job 21:8 | 5869
His *e* shall see his destruction, ... Job 21:20 | 5869
yet his *e* are upon their ways .... Job 24:23 | 5869
he openeth his *e*, and he is not .... Job 27:19 | 5869
is hid from the *e* of all living .... Job 28:21 | 5869
I was *e* to the blind, and feet was .... Job 29:15 | 5869
I made a covenant with mine *e* .... Job 31:1 | 5869
and mine heart walked after mine *e*. ...... Job 31:7 | 5869
or have caused the *e* of the widow .... Job 31:16 | 5869
he was righteous in his own *e* .... Job 32:1 | 5869
For his *e* are upon the ways of .... Job 34:21 | 5869
not his *e* from the righteous .... Job 36:7 | 5869
prey, and her *e* behold afar off .... Job 39:29 | 5869
He taketh it with his *e* .... Job 40:24 | 5869
his *e* are like the eyelids of the .... Job 41:18 | 5869
his *e* are privily set against the .... Ps 10:8 | 5869
his *e* behold, his eyelids try, ... Ps 11:4 | 5869
lighten mine *e*, lest I sleep the .... Ps 13:3 | 5869
In whose *e* a vile person is .... Ps 15:4 | 5869
let thine *e* behold the things .... Ps 17:2 | 5869
they have set their *e* bowing down .... Ps 17:11 | 5869
LORD is pure, enlightening the *e* .... Ps 19:8 | 5869
Mine *e* are ever toward the LORD............ Ps 25:15 | 5869
lovingkindness is before mine *e* .... Ps 26:3 | 5869
I am cut off from before thine *e* .... Ps 31:22 | 5869
The *e* of the LORD are upon the .... Ps 34:15 | 5869
is no fear of God before his *e* .... Ps 36:1 | 5869
flattereth himself in his own *e* .... Ps 36:2 | 5869
as for the light of mine *e*........................ Ps 38:10 | 5869
set them in order before thine *e* .... Ps 50:21 | 5869
his *e* behold the nations .... Ps 66:7 | 5869
mine *e* fail while I wait for my .... Ps 69:3 | 5869
Let their *e* be darkened, that .... Ps 69:23 | 5869
Their *e* stand out with fatness .... Ps 73:7 | 5869
Thou holdest mine *e* waking.................... Ps 77:4 | 5869
Only with thine *e* shalt thou.................. Ps 91:8 | 5869
set no wicked thing before mine *e* .... Ps 101:3 | 5869
Mine *e* shall be upon the faithful........... Ps 101:6 | 5869
e have they, but they see not .... Ps 115:5 | 5869
mine *e* from tears, and my feet .... Ps 116:8 | 5869
it is marvellous in our *e* .... Ps 118:23 | 5869
Open thou mine *e*, that I may .... Ps 119:18 | 5869
Turn away mine *e* from beholding........... Ps 119:37 | 5869
Mine *e* fail for thy word, saying, ... Ps 119:82 | 5869
Mine *e* fail for thy salvation, and .... Ps 119:123 | 5869
Rivers of waters run down mine *e* .... Ps 119:136 | 5869
Mine *e* prevent the night watches, ... Ps 119:148 | 5869
lift up mine *e* unto the hills .... Ps 121:1 | 5869
Unto thee lift I up mine *e*....................... Ps 123:1 | 5869
as the *e* of servants look unto .... Ps 123:2 | 5869
as the *e* of a maiden unto the.................. Ps 123:2 | 5869
so our *e* wait upon the LORD our .... Ps 123:2 | 5869
is not haughty, nor mine *e* lofty............. Ps 131:1 | 5869
I will not give sleep to mine *e* .... Ps 132:4 | 5869
e have they, but they see not .... Ps 135:16 | 5869
Thine *e* did see my substance, yet .... Ps 139:16 | 5869
But mine *e* are unto thee, O GOD .... Ps 141:8 | 5869
The *e* of all wait upon thee .... Ps 145:15 | 5869
LORD openeth the *e* of the blind .... Ps 146:8 |
Be not wise in thine own *e* .... Prov 3:7 | 5869
let not them depart from thine *e*............ Prov 3:21 | 5869
Let them not depart from thine *e*........... Prov 4:21 | 5869
Let thine *e* look right on, and let............ Prov 4:25 | 5869
man are before the *e* of the LORD........... Prov 5:21 | 5869
Give not sleep to mine *e* .... Prov 6:4 | 5869
He winketh with his *e*, he .... Prov 6:13 | 5869
the teeth, and as smoke to the *e* .... Prov 10:26 | 5869
of a fool is right in his own *e*................. Prov 12:15 | 5869
The *e* of the LORD are in every .... Prov 15:3 | 5869
The light of the *e* rejoiceth the .... Prov 15:30 | 5869
of a man are clean in his own *e*.............. Prov 16:2 | 5869
He shutteth his *e* to devise .... Prov 16:30 | 5869

in the *e* of him that hath it .... Prov 17:8 | 5869
but the *e* of a fool are in the .... Prov 17:24 | 5869
away all evil with his *e* .... Prov 20:8 | 5869
open thine *e*, and thou shalt be............... Prov 20:13 | 5869
of a man is right in his own *e* .... Prov 21:2 | 5869
findeth no favour in his *e* .... Prov 21:10 | 5869
The *e* of the LORD preserve .... Prov 22:12 | 5869
Wilt thou set thine *e* upon that .... Prov 23:5 | 5869
let thine *e* observe my ways .... Prov 23:26 | 5869
who hath redness of *e* .... Prov 23:29 | 5869
Thine *e* shall behold strange .... Prov 23:33 | 5869
the prince whom thine *e* have seen .... Prov 25:7 | 5869
so the *e* of man are never .... Prov 27:20 | 5869
but he that hideth his *e* shall .... Prov 28:27 | 5869
the LORD lighteneth both their *e* .... Prov 29:13 | 5869
that are pure in their own *e* .... Prov 30:12 | 5869
O how lofty are their *e*............................ Prov 30:13 | 5869
whatsoever mine *e* desired I kept .... Eccl 2:10 | 5869
The wise man's *e* are in his head............ Eccl 2:14 | 5869
beholding of them with their *e* .... Eccl 5:11 | 5869
the *e* than the wandering of the .... Eccl 6:9 | 5869
nor night seeth sleep with his *e* .... Eccl 8:16 | 5869
it is for the *e* to behold the sun .... Eccl 11:7 | 5869
heart, and in the sight of thine *e*............. Eccl 11:9 | 5869
thou hast doves' *e* .... Song 1:15 | 5869
hast doves' *e* within thy locks .... Song 4:1 | 5869
my heart with one of thine *e* .... Song 4:9 | 5869
His *e* are as the *e* of doves by................ Song 5:12 | 5869
Turn away thine *e* from me .... Song 6:5 | 5869
thine *e* like the fishpools in .... Song 7:4 | 5869
then was I in his *e* as one that .... Song 8:10 | 5869
I will hide mine *e* from you .... Is 1:15 | 5869
of your doings from before mine *e* .... Is 1:16 | 5869
to provoke the *e* of his glory .... Is 3:8 | 5869
stretched forth necks and wanton *e* .... Is 3:16 | 5869
the *e* of the lofty shall be .... Is 5:15 | 5869
them that are wise in their own *e* .... Is 5:21 | 5869
for mine *e* have seen the King, ... Is 6:5 | 5869
their ears heavy, and shut their *e* .... Is 6:10 | 5869
lest they see with their *e* .... Is 6:10 | 5869
judge after the sight of his *e* .... Is 11:3 | 5869
dashed to pieces before their *e* .... Is 13:16 | 5869
his *e* shall have respect to the................ Is 17:7 | 5869
deep sleep, and hath closed your *e* .... Is 29:10 | 5869
the *e* of the blind shall see out .... Is 29:18 | 5869
but thine *e* shall see thy .... Is 30:20 | 5869
the *e* of them that see shall not .... Is 32:3 | 5869
shutteth his *e* from seeing evil .... Is 33:15 | 5869
Thine *e* shall see the king in his .... Is 33:17 | 5869
thine *e* shall see Jerusalem a .... Is 33:20 | 5869
Then the *e* of the blind shall be.............. Is 35:5 | 5869
open thine *e*, O LORD, and see................. Is 37:17 | 5869
and lifted up thine *e* on high .... Is 37:23 | 5869
mine *e* fail with looking upward .... Is 38:14 | 5869
Lift up your *e* on high, and behold.......... Is 40:26 | 5869
To open the blind *e*, to bring out .... Is 42:7 | 5869
the blind people that have *e* .... Is 43:8 | 5869
for he hath shut their *e*, that .... Is 44:18 | 5869
be glorious in the *e* of the LORD .... Is 49:5 | 5869
Lift up thine *e* round about .... Is 49:18 | 5869
Lift up your *e* to the heavens, and .... Is 51:6 | 5869
arm in the *e* of all the nations .... Is 52:10 | 5869
and we grope as if we had no *e*,.............. Is 59:10 | 5869
Lift up thine *e* round about .... Is 60:4 | 5869
but did evil before mine *e* .... Is 65:12 | 5869
because they are hid from mine *e*............ Is 65:16 | 5869
but they did evil before mine *e* .... Is 66:4 | 5869
Lift up thine *e* unto the high .... Jer 3:2 | 5869
are not thine *e* upon the truth .... Jer 5:3 | 5869
which have *e*, and see not .... Jer 5:21 | 5869
become a den of robbers in your *e* .... Jer 7:11 | 5869
mine *e* a fountain of tears, that .... Jer 9:1 | 5869
that our *e* may run down with .... Jer 9:18 | 5869
Lift up your *e*, and behold them .... Jer 13:20 | 5869
their *e* did fail, because there .... Jer 14:6 | 5869
Let mine *e* run down with tears .... Jer 14:17 | 5869
cease out of this place in your *e* .... Jer 16:9 | 5869
For mine *e* are upon all their.................. Jer 16:17 | 5869
is their iniquity hid from mine *e* .... Jer 16:17 | 5869
and thine *e* shall behold it .... Jer 20:4 | 5869
But thine *e* and thine heart are .... Jer 22:17 | 5869
set mine *e* upon them for good .... Jer 24:6 | 5869
he shall slay them before your *e* .... Jer 29:21 | 5869
weeping, and thine *e* from tears .... Jer 31:16 | 5869
his *e* shall behold his *e* .... Jer 32:4 | 5869
for thine *e* are open upon all the............ Jer 32:19 | 5869
thine *e* shall behold the *e* of.................. Jer 34:3 | 5869
the *e* of the king of Babylon................... Jer 34:3 | 5869
Zedekiah in Riblah before his *e*............... Jer 39:6 | 5869
Moreover he put out Zedekiah's *e* .... Jer 39:7 | 5869
of many, as thine *e* do behold us .... Jer 42:2 | 5869

was evil in the *e* of the LORD	Jer 52:2	5869
the sons of Zedekiah before his *e*	Jer 52:10	5869
Then he put out the *e* of Zedekiah	Jer 52:11	5869
Mine *e* do fail with tears, my	Lam 2:11	5869
our *e* as yet failed for our vain	Lam 4:17	5869
for these things our *e* are dim	Lam 5:17	5869
full of *e* round about them four	Eze 1:18	5869
departed from me, and with their *e*	Eze 6:9	5869
lift up thine *e* now the way	Eze 8:5	5869
So I lifted up mine *e* the way	Eze 8:5	5869
were full of *e* round about	Eze 10:12	5869
house, which have *e* to see	Eze 12:2	5869
he see not the ground with his *e*	Eze 12:12	5869
neither hath lifted up his *e* to	Eze 18:6	5869
hath lifted up his *e* to the idols	Eze 18:12	5869
neither hath lifted up his *e* to	Eze 18:15	5869
man the abominations of his *e*	Eze 20:7	5869
away the abominations of their *e*	Eze 20:8	5869
their *e* were after their fathers'	Eze 20:24	5869
bitterness sigh before their *e*	Eze 21:6	5869
have hid their *e* from my sabbaths	Eze 22:26	5869
soon as she saw them with her *e*	Eze 23:16	5869
not lift up thine *e* unto them	Eze 23:27	5869
wash thyself, paintedst thy *e*	Eze 23:40	5869
desire of thine *e* with a stroke	Eze 24:16	5869
strength, the desire of your *e*	Eze 24:21	5869
glory, the desire of their *e*	Eze 24:25	5869
lift up your *e* toward your idols,	Eze 33:25	5869
sanctified in you before their *e*	Eze 36:23	5869
be in thine hand before their *e*	Eze 37:20	5869
in thee, O Gog, before their *e*	Eze 38:16	5869
be known in the *e* of many nations	Eze 38:23	5869
Son of man, behold with thine *e*	Eze 40:4	5869
mark well, and behold with thine *e*	Eze 44:5	5869
lifted up mine *e* unto heaven	Dan 4:34	5870
in this horn were *e* like the *e*	Dan 7:8	5870
horn were *e* like the *e* of man	Dan 7:8	5870
even of that horn that had *e*	Dan 7:20	5870
Then I lifted up mine *e*, and saw,	Dan 8:3	5869
had a notable horn between his *e*	Dan 8:5	5869
between his *e* is the first king	Dan 8:21	5869
open thine *e*, and behold our	Dan 9:18	5869
Then I lifted up mine *e*, and	Dan 10:5	5869
his *e* as lamps of fire, and his	Dan 10:6	5869
shall be hid from mine *e*	Hos 13:14	5869
not the meat cut off before our *e*	Joel 1:16	5869
I will set mine *e* upon them for	Amos 9:4	5869
the *e* of the Lord GOD are upon	Amos 9:8	5869
mine *e* shall behold her	Mic 7:10	5869
Thou art of purer *e* than to	Hab 1:13	5869
back your captivity before your *e*	Zeph 3:20	5869
is it not in your *e* in comparison	Hag 2:3	5869
Then lifted I up mine *e*, and saw,	Zec 1:18	5869
I lifted up mine *e* again, and	Zec 2:1	5869
upon one stone shall be seven *e*	Zec 3:9	5869
they are the *e* of the LORD	Zec 4:10	5869
I turned, and lifted up mine *e*	Zec 5:1	5869
said unto me, Lift up now thine *e*	Zec 5:5	5869
Then lifted I up mine *e*, and	Zec 5:9	5869
And I turned, and lifted up mine *e*	Zec 6:1	5869
If it be marvellous in the *e* of	Zec 8:6	5869
it also be marvellous in mine *e*	Zec 8:6	5869
when the *e* of man, as of all the	Zec 9:1	5869
for now have I seen with mine *e*	Zec 9:8	5869
I will open mine *e* upon the house	Zec 12:4	5869
their *e* shall consume away in	Zec 14:12	5869
your *e* shall see, and ye shall say	Mal 1:5	5869
Then touched he their *e*, saying,	Mt 9:29	3788
And their *e* were opened	Mt 9:30	3788
and their *e* they have closed	Mt 13:15	3788
time they should see with their *e*	Mt 13:15	3788
But blessed are your *e*, for they	Mt 13:16	3788
when they had lifted up their *e*	Mt 17:8	3788
rather than having two *e* to be	Mt 18:9	3788
Lord, that our *e* may be opened	Mt 20:33	
on them, and touched their *e*	Mt 20:34	
their *e* received sight, and they	Mt 20:34	3788
and it is marvellous in our *e*	Mt 21:42	3788
for their *e* were heavy	Mt 26:43	3788
Having *e*, see ye not	Mk 8:18	3788
and when he had spit on his *e*	Mk 8:23	3659
he put his hands again upon his *e*	Mk 8:25	3788
than having two *e* to be cast into	Mk 9:47	3788
and it is marvellous in our *e*	Mk 12:11	3788
again, (for their *e* were heavy	Mk 14:40	3788
For mine *e* have seen thy	Lk 2:30	3788
the *e* of all them that were in	Lk 4:20	3788
lifted up his *e* on his disciples	Lk 6:20	3788
Blessed are the *e* which see the	Lk 10:23	3788
And in hell he lift up his *e*	Lk 16:23	3788
up so much as his *e* unto heaven	Lk 18:13	3788

but now they are hid from thine *e*	Lk 19:42	3788
But their *e* were holden that they	Lk 24:16	3788
their *e* were opened, and they knew	Lk 24:31	3788
I say unto you, Lift up your *e*	Jn 4:35	3788
When Jesus then lifted up his *e*	Jn 6:5	3788
he anointed the *e* of the blind	Jn 9:6	3788
unto him, How were thine *e* opened	Jn 9:10	3788
made clay, and anointed mine *e*	Jn 9:11	3788
made the clay, and opened his *e*	Jn 9:14	3788
them, He put clay upon mine *e*	Jn 9:15	3788
him, that he hath opened thine *e*	Jn 9:17	3788
or who hath opened his *e*, we know	Jn 9:21	3788
how opened he thine *e*	Jn 9:26	3788
is, and yet he hath opened mine *e*	Jn 9:30	3788
the *e* of one that was born blind	Jn 9:32	3788
a devil open the *e* of the blind	Jn 10:21	3788
which opened the *e* of the blind	Jn 11:37	3788
And Jesus lifted up his *e*, and said	Jn 11:41	3788
He hath blinded their *e*, and	Jn 12:40	3788
they should not see with their *e*	Jn 12:40	3788
and lifted up his *e* to heaven	Jn 17:1	3788
fastening his *e* upon him with	Acts 3:4	
when his *e* were opened, he saw no	Acts 9:8	3788
from his *e* as it had been scales	Acts 9:18	3788
And she opened her *e*	Acts 9:40	3788
which when I had fastened mine *e*	Acts 11:6	
the Holy Ghost, set his *e* on him	Acts 13:9	
To open their *e*, and to turn them	Acts 26:18	3788
and their *e* have they closed	Acts 28:27	3788
lest they should see with their *e*	Acts 28:27	3788
is no fear of God before their *e*	Rom 3:18	3788
e that they should not see, and	Rom 11:8	3788
Let their *e* be darkened, that	Rom 11:10	3788
before whose *e* Jesus Christ hath	Gal 3:1	3788
would have plucked out your own *e*	Gal 4:15	3788
The *e* of your understanding being	Eph 1:18	3788
opened unto the *e* of him with	Heb 4:13	3788
For the *e* of the Lord are over	1Pet 3:12	3788
Having *e* full of adultery, and	2Pet 2:14	3788
which we have seen with our *e*	1Jn 1:1	3788
that darkness hath blinded his *e*	1Jn 2:11	3788
the flesh, and the lust of the *e*	1Jn 2:16	3788
his *e* were as a flame of fire	Rev 1:14	3788
who hath his *e* like unto a flame	Rev 2:18	3788
anoint thine *e* with eyesalve,	Rev 3:18	3788
were four beasts full of *e* before	Rev 4:6	3788
and they were full of *e* within	Rev 4:8	3788
having seven horns and seven *e*	Rev 5:6	3788
wipe away all tears from their *e*	Rev 7:17	3788
His *e* were as a flame of fire, and	Rev 19:12	3788
wipe away all tears from their *e*	Rev 21:4	3788

EYESALVE

and anoint thine eyes with *e*	Rev 3:18	2854

EYESERVICE

Not with *e*, as menpleasers	Eph 6:6	3787
not with *e*, as menpleasers	Col 3:22	3787

EYESIGHT

cleanness of my hands in his *e*	Ps 18:24	5869

EYEWITNESSES

which from the beginning were *e*	Lk 1:2	845
but were of his majesty	2Pet 1:16	2030

EZAR (*e'-zar*) See EZER. *A son of Seir.*

Zibeon, and Anah, and Dishon, and *E*	1Chr 1:38	687

EZBAI (*ez'-bahee*) *Father of Naarai.*

Carmelite, Naarai the son of *E*	1Chr 11:37	229

EZBON (*ez'-bon*)
    1. *Son of Gad.*

Ziphion, and Haggi, Shuni, and *E*	Gen 46:16	675

    2. *Son of Bela.*

E, and Uzzi, and Uzziel, and	1Chr 7:7	675

EZEKIAS (*ez-e-ki'-as*) See HEZEKIAH. *Greek form of Hezekiah.*

and Achaz begat *E*	Mt 1:9	1478
And *E* begat Manasses	Mt 1:10	1478

EZEKIEL *A priest and prophet.*

came expressly unto *E* the priest	Eze 1:3	3168
Thus *E* is unto you a sign	Eze 24:24	3168

EZEL *A boundary stone.*

and shalt remain by the stone *E*	1Sa 20:19	237

EZEM *A city in Judah.*

And at Bilhah, and at *E*, and at	1Chr 4:29	6107

EZER
    1. *Son of Seir the Horite.*

And Dishon, and *E*, and Dishan	Gen 36:21	687
The children of *E* are these	Gen 36:27	687

Duke Dishon, duke E, duke Dishan	Gen 36:30	687
The sons of E; Bilhan	1Chr 1:42	687
2. A descendant of Judah.		
Gedor, and E the father of Hushah	1Chr 4:4	5829
3. A son of Ephraim.		
son, and Shuthelah his son, and E	1Chr 7:21	5827
4. A Gadite who fought for David.		
E the first, Obadiah the second,	1Chr 12:9	5829
5. A Levite who repaired the Jerusalem wall.		
him repaired E the son of Jeshua	Neh 3:19	5829
6. A priest in the time of Nehemiah.		
and Malchijah, and Elam, and E	Neh 12:42	5829

EZION-GABER *Same as Ezion-geber.*
from Ebronah, and encamped at E	Num 33:35	6100
And they removed from E, and	Num 33:36	6100
the plain from Elath, and from E	Deut 2:8	6100
and they made the ships in E	2Chr 20:36	6100

EZION-GEBER *(e'-ze-on-ghe'-bur)* See EZION-GABER. *An Israelite seaport.*
Solomon made a navy of ships in E	1Kin 9:26	6100
for the ships were broken at E	1Kin 22:48	6100
Then went Solomon to E, and to	2Chr 8:17	6100

EZNITE *(ez'-nite) Descendant of Adino.*
the same was Adino the E	2Sa 23:8	6112

EZRA *(ez'-rah)* See AZARIAH, EZRAHITE.
1. A descendant of Judah.
And the sons of E were, Jether, and	1Chr 4:17	5830

2. Priest who led exiles back to Jerusalem.
E the son of Seraiah, the son of	Ezr 7:1	5830
This E went up from Babylon	Ezr 7:6	5830

For E had prepared his heart to	Ezr 7:10	5830
Artaxerxes gave unto E the priest	Ezr 7:11	5830
unto E the priest, a scribe of	Ezr 7:12	5830
that whatsoever E the priest	Ezr 7:21	5830
And thou, E, after the wisdom of	Ezr 7:25	5830
Now when E had prayed, and when he	Ezr 10:1	5830
of Elam, answered and said unto E	Ezr 10:2	5830
Then arose E, and made the chief	Ezr 10:5	5830
Then E rose up from before the	Ezr 10:6	5830
E the priest stood up, and said	Ezr 10:10	5830
E the priest, with certain chief	Ezr 10:16	5830
they spake unto E the scribe to	Neh 8:1	5830
E the priest brought the law	Neh 8:2	5830
E the scribe stood upon a pulpit	Neh 8:4	5830
E opened the book in the sight of	Neh 8:5	5830
E blessed the LORD, the great God	Neh 8:6	5830
E the priest the scribe, and the	Neh 8:9	5830
unto E the scribe, even to	Neh 8:13	5830
Of E, Meshullam	Neh 12:13	5830
of E the priest, the scribe	Neh 12:26	5830
And Azariah, E, and Meshullam,	Neh 12:33	5830
God, and E the scribe before them	Neh 12:36	5830
3. A priest who returned from exile.		
Seraiah, Jeremiah, E,	Neh 12:1	5830

EZRAH See EZRA.

EZRAHITE *(ez'-rah-hite)*
than Ethan the E, and Heman, and	1Kin 4:31	250
Leannoth, Maschil of Heman the E	Ps 88:*t*	250
Maschil of Ethan the E	Ps 89:*t*	250

EZRI *(ez'-ri) A superintendent of David.*
ground was E the son of Chelub	1Chr 27:26	5836

F

FABLES
Neither give heed to *f* and endless	1Ti 1:4	3454
refuse profane and old wives' *f*	1Ti 4:7	3454
truth, and shall be turned unto *f*	2Ti 4:4	3454
Not giving heed to Jewish *f*	Titus 1:14	3454
not followed cunningly devised *f*	2Pet 1:16	3454

FACE
was upon the *f* of the deep	Gen 1:2	6440
moved upon the *f* of the waters	Gen 1:2	6440
is upon the *f* of all the earth	Gen 1:29	6440
watered the whole *f* of the ground	Gen 2:6	6440
In the sweat of thy *f* shalt thou	Gen 3:19	639
this day from the *f* of the earth	Gen 4:14	6440
from thy *f* shall I be hid	Gen 4:14	6440
to multiply on the *f* of the earth	Gen 6:1	6440
created from the *f* of the earth	Gen 6:7	6440
alive upon the *f* of all the earth	Gen 7:3	6440
from off the *f* of the earth	Gen 7:4	6440
ark went upon the *f* of the waters	Gen 7:18	6440
was upon the *f* of the ground	Gen 7:23	6440
from off the *f* of the ground	Gen 8:8	6440
were on the *f* of the whole earth	Gen 8:9	6440
the *f* of the ground was dry	Gen 8:13	6440
upon the *f* of the whole earth	Gen 11:4	6440
upon the *f* of all the earth	Gen 11:8	6440
upon the *f* of all the earth	Gen 11:9	6440
with her, she fled from her *f*	Gen 16:6	6440
I flee from the *f* of my mistress	Gen 16:8	6440
And Abram fell on his *f*	Gen 17:3	6440
Then Abraham fell upon his *f*	Gen 17:17	6440
with his *f* toward the ground	Gen 19:1	639
great before the *f* of the LORD	Gen 19:13	6440
and I put the earring upon her *f*	Gen 24:47	639
come for my hire before thy *f*	Gen 30:33	6440
set his *f* toward the mount Gilead	Gen 31:21	6440
me, and afterward I will see his *f*	Gen 32:20	6440
for I have seen God *f* to *f*	Gen 32:30	6440
for therefore I have seen thy *f*	Gen 33:10	6440
as though I had seen the *f* of God	Gen 33:10	6440
from the *f* of Esau thy brother	Gen 35:1	6440
he fled from the *f* of his brother	Gen 35:7	6440
from the *f* of his brother Jacob	Gen 36:6	6440
because she had covered her *f*	Gen 38:15	6440
was over all the *f* of the earth	Gen 41:56	6440
us, saying, Ye shall not see my *f*	Gen 43:3	6440
unto us, Ye shall not see my *f*	Gen 43:5	6440
And he washed his *f*, and went out,	Gen 43:31	6440
you, ye shall see my *f* no more	Gen 44:23	6440
for we may not see the man's *f*	Gen 44:26	6440
to direct his *f* unto Goshen	Gen 46:28	6440
me die, since I have seen thy *f*	Gen 46:30	6440
I had not thought to see thy *f*	Gen 48:11	6440

himself with his *f* to the earth	Gen 48:12	639
Joseph fell upon his father's *f*	Gen 50:1	6440
went and fell down before his *f*	Gen 50:18	6440
Moses fled from the *f* of Pharaoh	Ex 2:15	6440
And Moses hid his *f*	Ex 3:6	6440
shall cover the *f* of the earth	Ex 10:5	5869
covered the *f* of the whole earth	Ex 10:15	5869
heed to thyself, see my *f* no more	Ex 10:28	6440
thou seest my *f* thou shalt die	Ex 10:28	6440
I will see thy *f* again no more	Ex 10:29	6440
cloud went from before their *f*	Ex 14:19	6440
Let us flee from the *f* of Israel	Ex 14:25	6440
upon the *f* of the wilderness	Ex 16:14	6440
them from the *f* of the earth	Ex 32:12	6440
LORD spake unto Moses *f* to *f*	Ex 33:11	6440
that are upon the *f* of the earth	Ex 33:16	6440
he said, Thou canst not see my *f*	Ex 33:20	6440
but my *f* shall not be seen	Ex 33:23	6440
wist not that the skin of his *f*	Ex 34:29	6440
behold, the skin of his *f* shone	Ex 34:30	6440
with them, he put a vail on his *f*	Ex 34:33	6440
of Israel saw the *f* of Moses	Ex 34:35	6440
that the skin of Moses' *f* shone	Ex 34:35	6440
put the vail upon his *f* again	Ex 34:35	6440
the part of his head toward his *f*	Lev 13:41	6440
I will even set my *f* against that	Lev 17:10	6440
honour the *f* of the old man, and	Lev 19:32	6440
I will set my *f* against that man,	Lev 20:3	6440
I will set my *f* against that man	Lev 20:5	6440
even set my *f* against that soul	Lev 20:6	6440
And I will set my *f* against you	Lev 26:17	6440
LORD make his *f* shine upon thee	Num 6:25	6440
high upon the *f* of the earth	Num 11:31	6440
were upon the *f* of the earth	Num 12:3	6440
her father had but spit in her *f*	Num 12:14	6440
that thou LORD art seen *f* to *f*	Num 14:14	5869
heard it, he fell upon his *f*	Num 16:4	6440
one shall slay her before his *f*	Num 19:3	
they shall cover the *f* of the earth	Num 22:5	5869
which covereth the *f* of the earth	Num 22:11	5869
his head, and fell flat on his *f*	Num 22:31	639
but he set his *f* toward the	Num 24:1	6440
not be afraid of the *f* of man	Deut 1:17	6440
LORD talked with you *f* to *f* in	Deut 5:4	6440
thee from off the *f* of the earth	Deut 6:15	6440
that are upon the *f* of the earth	Deut 7:6	6440
them that hate him to their *f*	Deut 7:10	6440
him, he will repay him to his *f*	Deut 7:10	6440
the LORD destroyeth before your *f*	Deut 8:20	6440
bring them down before thy *f*	Deut 9:3	6440
and to be beaten before his *f*	Deut 25:2	
off his foot, and spit in his *f*	Deut 25:9	6440
thee to be smitten before thy *f*	Deut 28:7	

taken away from before thy *f*	Deut 28:31	
shall give them up before your *f*	Deut 31:5	
and I will hide my *f* from them	Deut 31:17	6440
I will surely hide my *f* in that	Deut 31:18	6440
said, I will hide my *f* from them	Deut 32:20	6440
whom the Lord knew *f* to *f*	Deut 34:10	6440
Joshua fell on his *f* to the earth	Josh 5:14	6440
his *f* before the ark of the Lord	Josh 7:6	6440
liest thou thus upon thy *f*	Josh 7:10	6440
an angel of the Lord *f* to *f*	Judg 6:22	6440
Then she fell on her *f*, and bowed	Ruth 2:10	6440
Dagon was fallen upon his *f* to	1Sa 5:3	6440
Dagon was fallen upon his *f* to	1Sa 5:4	6440
he fell upon his *f* to the earth	1Sa 17:49	6440
every one from the *f* of the earth	1Sa 20:15	6440
fell on his *f* to the ground, and	1Sa 20:41	639
stooped with his *f* to the earth	1Sa 24:8	639
and fell before David on her *f*	1Sa 25:23	6440
herself on her *f* to the earth	1Sa 25:41	639
earth before the *f* of the Lord	1Sa 26:20	6440
stooped with his *f* to the ground	1Sa 28:14	639
hold up my *f* to Joab thy brother	2Sa 2:22	6440
that is, Thou shalt not see my *f*	2Sa 3:13	6440
when thou comest to see my *f*	2Sa 3:13	6440
come unto David, he fell on his *f*	2Sa 9:6	6440
she fell on her *f* to the ground	2Sa 14:4	639
Joab fell to the ground on his *f*	2Sa 14:22	6440
house, and let him not see my *f*	2Sa 14:24	6440
house, and saw not the king's *f*	2Sa 14:24	6440
and saw not the king's *f*	2Sa 14:28	6440
therefore let me see the king's *f*	2Sa 14:32	6440
bowed himself on his *f* to the	2Sa 14:33	639
over the *f* of all the country	2Sa 18:8	6440
earth upon his *f* before the king	2Sa 18:28	639
But the king covered his *f*	2Sa 19:4	6440
the king on his *f* upon the ground	2Sa 24:20	639
the king with his *f* to the ground	1Kin 1:23	639
bowed with her *f* to the earth	1Kin 1:31	639
And the king turned his *f* about	1Kin 8:14	6440
Intreat now the *f* of the Lord thy	1Kin 13:6	6440
it from off the *f* of the earth	1Kin 13:34	6440
and he knew him, and fell on his *f*	1Kin 18:7	6440
put his *f* between his knees	1Kin 18:42	6440
he wrapped his *f* in his mantle	1Kin 19:13	6440
himself with ashes upon his *f*	1Kin 20:38	5869
and took the ashes away from his *f*	1Kin 20:41	5869
his bed, and turned away his *f*	1Kin 21:4	6440
my staff upon the *f* of the child	2Kin 4:29	6440
the staff upon the *f* of the child	2Kin 4:31	6440
in water, and spread it on his *f*	2Kin 8:15	6440
and she painted her *f*, and tired	2Kin 9:30	5869
he lifted up his *f* to the window	2Kin 9:32	6440
shall be as dung upon the *f* of	2Kin 9:37	6440
Hazael set his *f* to go up to	2Kin 12:17	6440
down unto him, and wept over his *f*	2Kin 13:14	6440
let us look one another in the *f*	2Kin 14:8	6440
another in the *f* at Beth-shemesh	2Kin 14:11	6440
then wilt thou turn away the *f* of	2Kin 18:24	6440
Then he turned his *f* to the wall	2Kin 20:2	6440
strength, seek his *f* continually	1Chr 16:11	6440
to David with his *f* to the ground	1Chr 21:21	639
And the king turned his *f*, and	2Chr 6:3	6440
not away the *f* of thine anointed	2Chr 6:42	6440
themselves, and pray, and seek my *f*	2Chr 7:14	6440
his head with his *f* to the ground	2Chr 20:18	639
let us see one another in the *f*	2Chr 25:17	6440
and they saw one another in the *f*	2Chr 25:21	6440
will not turn away his *f* from you	2Chr 30:9	6440
with shame of *f* to his own land	2Chr 32:21	6440
would not turn his *f* from him	2Chr 35:22	6440
and blush to lift up my *f* to thee	Ezr 9:6	6440
to a spoil, and to confusion of *f*	Ezr 9:7	6440
and Media, which saw the king's *f*	Est 1:14	6440
mouth, they covered Haman's *f*	Est 7:8	6440
and he will curse thee to thy *f*	Job 1:11	6440
and he will curse thee to thy *f*	Job 2:5	6440
Then a spirit passed before my *f*	Job 4:15	6440
thou lift up thy *f* without spot	Job 11:15	6440
Wherefore hidest thou thy *f*	Job 13:24	6440
covereth his *f* with his fatness	Job 15:27	6440
up in me beareth witness to my *f*	Job 16:8	6440
My *f* is foul with weeping, and on	Job 16:16	6440
shall declare his way to his *f*	Job 21:31	6440
and shalt lift up thy *f* unto God	Job 22:26	6440
he covered the darkness from my *f*	Job 23:17	6440
and disguiseth his *f*	Job 24:15	6440
holdeth back the *f* of his throne	Job 26:9	6440
me, and spare not to spit in my *f*	Job 30:10	6440
and he shall see his *f* with joy	Job 33:26	6440
and when he hideth his *f*, who then	Job 34:29	6440
the *f* of the world in the earth	Job 37:12	6440

the *f* of the deep is frozen	Job 38:30	6440
can discover the *f* of his garment	Job 41:13	6440
Who can open the doors of his *f*	Job 41:14	6440
make thy way straight before my *f*	Ps 5:8	6440
he hideth his *f*	Ps 10:11	6440
long wilt thou hide thy *f* from me	Ps 13:1	6440
behold thy *f* in righteousness	Ps 17:15	6440
thy strings against the *f* of them	Ps 21:12	6440
hath he hid his *f* from him	Ps 22:24	6440
that seek him, that seek thy *f*	Ps 24:6	6440
When thou saidst, Seek ye my *f*	Ps 27:8	6440
my heart said unto thee, Thy *f*	Ps 27:8	6440
Hide not thy *f* far from me	Ps 27:9	6440
thou didst hide thy *f*, and I was	Ps 30:7	6440
Make thy *f* to shine upon thy	Ps 31:16	6440
The *f* of the Lord is against them	Ps 34:16	6440
settest me before thy *f* for ever	Ps 41:12	6440
the shame of my *f* hath covered me	Ps 44:15	6440
Wherefore hidest thou thy *f*	Ps 44:24	6440
Hide thy *f* from my sins, and blot	Ps 51:9	6440
cause his *f* to shine upon us	Ps 67:1	6440
shame hath covered my *f*	Ps 69:7	6440
hide not thy *f* from thy servant	Ps 69:17	6440
O God, and cause thy *f* to shine	Ps 80:3	6440
of hosts, and cause thy *f* to shine	Ps 80:7	6440
of hosts, cause thy *f* to shine	Ps 80:19	6440
look upon the *f* of thine anointed	Ps 84:9	6440
why hidest thou thy *f* from me	Ps 88:14	6440
and truth shall go before thy *f*	Ps 89:14	6440
beat down his foes before his *f*	Ps 89:23	6440
Hide not thy *f* from me in the day	Ps 102:2	6440
and oil to make his *f* to shine	Ps 104:15	6440
Thou hidest thy *f*, they are	Ps 104:29	6440
thou renewest the *f* of the earth	Ps 104:30	6440
seek his *f* evermore	Ps 105:4	6440
Make thy *f* to shine upon thy	Ps 119:135	6440
not away the *f* of thine anointed	Ps 132:10	6440
hide not thy *f* from me, lest I be	Ps 143:7	6440
with an impudent *f* said unto him	Prov 7:13	6440
thee, diligently to seek thy *f*	Prov 7:15	6440
a compass upon the *f* of the depth	Prov 8:27	6440
A wicked man hardeneth his *f*	Prov 21:29	6440
nettles had covered the *f* thereof	Prov 24:31	6440
As in water *f* answereth to *f*,	Prov 27:19	6440
wisdom maketh his *f* to shine	Eccl 8:1	6440
of his *f* shall be changed	Eccl 8:1	6440
with twain he covered his *f*	Is 6:2	6440
that hideth his *f* from the house	Is 8:17	6440
nor fill the *f* of the world with	Is 14:21	6440
to them from the *f* of the spoiler	Is 16:4	6440
the world upon the *f* of the earth	Is 23:17	6440
destroy in this mountain the *f* of	Is 25:7	6440
fill the *f* of the world with	Is 27:6	6440
he hath made plain the *f* thereof	Is 28:25	6440
neither shall his *f* now wax pale	Is 29:22	6440
then wilt thou turn away the *f* of	Is 36:9	6440
turned his *f* toward the wall	Is 38:2	6440
with their *f* toward the earth	Is 49:23	639
I hid not my *f* from shame	Is 50:6	6440
have I set my *f* like a flint	Is 50:7	6440
I hid my *f* from thee for a moment	Is 54:8	6440
your sins have hid his *f* from you	Is 59:2	6440
for thou hast hid thy *f* from us	Is 64:7	6440
me to anger continually to my *f*	Is 65:3	6440
the *f* thereof is toward the north	Jer 1:13	6440
back unto me, and not their *f*	Jer 2:27	6440
thou rentest thy *f* with painting	Jer 4:30	5869
for dung upon the *f* of the earth	Jer 8:2	6440
I discover thy skirts upon thy *f*	Jer 13:26	6440
as dung upon the *f* of the earth	Jer 16:4	6440
they are not hid from my *f*	Jer 16:17	6440
shew them the back, and not the *f*	Jer 18:17	6440
For I have set my *f* against this	Jer 21:10	6440
hand of them whose *f* thou fearest	Jer 22:25	6440
which are upon the *f* of the earth	Jer 25:26	6440
thee from off the *f* of the earth	Jer 28:16	6440
should remove it from before my *f*	Jer 32:31	6440
unto me the back, and not the *f*	Jer 32:33	6440
I have hid my *f* from this city	Jer 33:5	6440
I will set my *f* against you for	Jer 44:11	6440
water before the *f* of the Lord	Lam 2:19	6440
man before the *f* of the most High	Lam 3:35	6440
they four had the *f* of a man	Eze 1:10	6440
the *f* of a lion, on the right	Eze 1:10	6440
they four had the *f* of an ox on	Eze 1:10	6440
four also had the *f* of an eagle	Eze 1:10	6440
when I saw it, I fell upon my *f*	Eze 1:28	6440
I have made thy *f* strong against	Eze 3:8	6440
and I fell on my *f*	Eze 3:23	6440
set thy *f* against it, and it shall	Eze 4:3	6440
Therefore thou shalt set thy *f*	Eze 4:7	6440

F

set thy *f* toward the mountains of	Eze 6:2	6440
My *f* will I turn also from them,	Eze 7:22	6440
I was left, that I fell upon my *f*	Eze 9:8	6440
first *f* was the *f* of a cherub	Eze 10:14	6440
second *f* was the *f* of a man	Eze 10:14	6440
and the third the *f* of a lion	Eze 10:14	6440
and the fourth the *f* of an eagle	Eze 10:14	6440
Then fell I down upon my *f*	Eze 11:13	6440
thou shalt cover thy *f*, that thou	Eze 12:6	6440
he shall cover his *f*, that he see	Eze 12:12	6440
set thy *f* against the daughters	Eze 13:17	6440
of their iniquity before their *f*	Eze 14:3	6440
of his iniquity before his *f*	Eze 14:4	6440
of his iniquity before his *f*	Eze 14:7	6440
I will set my *f* against that man,	Eze 14:8	6440
And I will set my *f* against them	Eze 15:7	6440
when I set my *f* against them	Eze 15:7	6440
will I plead with you *f* to *f*	Eze 20:35	6440
will I plead with you *f* to *f*	Eze 20:35	6440
set thy *f* toward the south, and	Eze 20:46	6440
set thy *f* toward Jerusalem, and	Eze 21:2	6440
left, whithersoever thy *f* is set	Eze 21:16	6440
set thy *f* against the Ammonites,	Eze 25:2	6440
set thy *f* against Zidon, and	Eze 28:21	6440
set thy *f* against Pharaoh king of	Eze 29:2	6440
upon all the *f* of the earth	Eze 34:6	6440
set thy *f* against mount Seir, and	Eze 35:2	6440
set thy *f* against Gog, the land	Eze 38:2	6440
my fury shall come up in my *f*	Eze 38:18	639
that are upon the *f* of the earth	Eze 38:20	6440
remain upon the *f* of the earth	Eze 39:14	6440
therefore hid I my *f* from them	Eze 39:23	6440
unto them, and hid my *f* from them	Eze 39:24	6440
I hide my *f* any more from them	Eze 39:29	6440
from the *f* of the gate of the	Eze 40:15	6440
gate of the entrance unto the *f*	Eze 40:15	6440
the breadth of the *f* of the house	Eze 41:14	6440
So that the *f* of a man was toward	Eze 41:19	6440
the *f* of a young lion toward the	Eze 41:19	6440
and the *f* of the sanctuary	Eze 41:21	6440
upon the *f* of the porch without	Eze 41:25	6440
and I fell upon my *f*	Eze 43:3	6440
and I fell upon my *f*	Eze 44:4	6440
Nebuchadnezzar fell upon his *f*	Dan 2:46	600
west on the *f* of the whole earth	Dan 8:5	6440
I was afraid, and fell upon my *f*	Dan 8:17	6440
sleep on my *f* toward the ground	Dan 8:18	6440
I set my *f* unto the Lord God, to	Dan 9:3	6440
to us belongeth confusion of *f*	Dan 9:8	6440
cause thy *f* to shine upon thy	Dan 9:17	6440
his *f* as the appearance of	Dan 10:6	6440
was I in a deep sleep on my *f*	Dan 10:9	6440
and my *f* toward the ground	Dan 10:9	6440
I set my *f* toward the ground, and	Dan 10:15	6440
He shall also set his *f* to enter	Dan 11:17	6440
he turn his *f* unto the isles	Dan 11:18	6440
Then he shall turn his *f* toward	Dan 11:19	6440
of Israel doth testify to his *f*	Hos 5:5	6440
their offence, and seek my *f*	Hos 5:15	6440
they are before my *f*	Hos 7:2	6440
of Israel testifieth to his *f*	Hos 7:10	6440
Before their *f* the people shall	Joel 2:6	6440
with his *f* toward the east sea,	Joel 2:20	6440
them out upon the *f* of the earth	Amos 5:8	6440
them out upon the *f* of the earth	Amos 9:6	6440
it from off the *f* of the earth	Amos 9:8	6440
he will even hide his *f* from them	Mic 3:4	6440
in pieces is come up before thy *f*	Nah 2:1	6440
discover thy skirts upon thy *f*	Nah 3:5	6440
over the *f* of the whole earth	Zec 5:3	6440
anoint thine head, and wash thy *f*	Mt 6:17	4383
I send my messenger before thee *f*	Mt 11:10	4383
ye can discern the *f* of the sky	Mt 16:3	4383
his *f* did shine as the sun, and	Mt 17:2	4383
heard it, they fell on their *f*	Mt 17:6	4383
angels do always behold the *f* of	Mt 18:10	4383
little farther, and fell on his *f*	Mt 26:39	4383
Then did they spit in his *f*	Mt 26:67	4383
I send my messenger before thy *f*	Mk 1:2	4383
to spit on him, and to cover his *f*	Mk 14:65	4383
for thou shalt go before the *f* of	Lk 1:76	4383
before the *f* of all people	Lk 2:31	4383
who seeing Jesus fell on his *f*	Lk 5:12	4383
I send my messenger before thy *f*	Lk 7:27	4383
set his *f* to go to Jerusalem	Lk 9:51	4383
And sent messengers before his *f*	Lk 9:52	4383
because his *f* was as though he	Lk 9:53	4383
two before his *f* into every city	Lk 10:1	4383
ye can discern the *f* of the sky	Lk 12:56	4383
And fell down on his *f* at his feet	Lk 17:16	4383
dwell on the *f* of the whole earth	Lk 21:35	4383

him, they struck him on the *f*	Lk 22:64	4383
his *f* was bound about with a	Jn 11:44	3799
the Lord always before my *f*	Acts 2:25	1799
saw his *f* as it had been the *f*	Acts 6:15	4383
out before the *f* of our fathers	Acts 7:45	4383
dwell on all the *f* of the earth	Acts 17:26	4383
of God, shall see my *f* no more	Acts 20:25	4383
they should see his *f* no more	Acts 20:38	4383
have the accusers *f* to *f*	Acts 25:16	4383
but then *f* to *f*	1Cor 13:12	4383
down on his *f* he will worship God	1Cor 14:25	4383
f of Moses for the glory of his	2Cor 3:7	4383
which put a vail over his *f*	2Cor 3:13	4383
with open *f* beholding as in a	2Cor 3:18	4383
of God in the *f* of Jesus Christ	2Cor 4:6	4383
if a man smite you on the *f*	2Cor 11:20	4383
was unknown by *f* unto the	Gal 1:22	4383
Antioch, I withstood him to the *f*	Gal 2:11	4383
have not seen my *f* in the flesh	Col 2:1	4383
to see your *f* with great desire	1Th 2:17	4383
that we might see your *f*, and	1Th 3:10	4383
his natural *f* in a glass	Jas 1:23	4383
but the *f* of the Lord is against	1Pet 3:12	4383
speak *f* to *f*, that our joy may	2Jn 12	4750
come unto you, and speak *f* to *f*	2Jn 12	4750
thee, and we shall speak *f* to *f*	3Jn 14	4750
thee, and we shall speak *f* to *f*	3Jn 14	4750
the third beast had a *f* as a man	Rev 4:7	4383
hide us from the *f* of him that	Rev 6:16	4383
his *f* was as it were the sun, and	Rev 10:1	4383
from the *f* of the serpent	Rev 12:14	4383
sat on it, from whose *f* the earth	Rev 20:11	4383
And they shall see his *f*	Rev 22:4	4383

FACES

their *f* were backward, and they	Gen 9:23	6440
men turned their *f* from thence	Gen 18:22	
set the *f* of the flocks toward	Gen 30:40	6440
him with their *f* to the earth	Gen 42:6	639
laid before their *f* all these	Ex 19:7	6440
his fear may be before your *f*	Ex 20:20	6440
their *f* shall look one to another	Ex 25:20	6440
shall the *f* of the cherubims be	Ex 25:20	6440
with their *f* one to another	Ex 37:9	6440
were the *f* of the cherubims	Ex 37:9	6440
they shouted, and fell on their *f*	Lev 9:24	6440
Aaron fell on their *f* before all	Num 14:5	6440
And they fell upon their *f*	Num 16:22	6440
And they fell upon their *f*	Num 16:45	6440
and they fell upon their *f*	Num 20:6	6440
and fell on their *f* to the ground	Judg 13:20	6440
And they turned their *f*, and said	Judg 18:23	6440
day the *f* of all thy servants	2Sa 19:5	6440
that all Israel set their *f* on me	1Kin 2:15	6440
saw it, they fell on their *f*	1Kin 18:39	6440
f were like the *f* of lions	1Chr 12:8	6440
in sackcloth, fell upon their *f*	1Chr 21:16	6440
feet, and their *f* were inward	2Chr 3:13	6440
bowed themselves with their *f* to	2Chr 7:3	639
have turned away their *f* from the	2Chr 29:6	6440
LORD with their *f* to the ground	Neh 8:6	639
he covereth the *f* of the judges	Job 9:24	6440
and bind their *f* in secret	Job 40:13	6440
and their *f* were not ashamed	Ps 34:5	6440
Fill their *f* with shame	Ps 83:16	6440
and grind the *f* of the poor	Is 3:15	6440
their *f* shall be as flames	Is 13:8	6440
wipe away tears from off all *f*	Is 25:8	6440
we hid as it were our *f* from him	Is 53:3	6440
Be not afraid of their *f*	Jer 1:8	6440
be not dismayed at their *f*	Jer 1:17	6440
made their *f* harder than a rock	Jer 5:3	6440
to the confusion of their own *f*	Jer 7:19	6440
all *f* are turned into paleness	Jer 30:6	6440
set your *f* to enter into Egypt	Jer 42:15	6440
f to go into Egypt to sojourn	Jer 42:17	6440
that have set their *f* to go into	Jer 44:12	6440
to Zion with their *f* thitherward	Jer 50:5	6440
shame hath covered our *f*	Jer 51:51	6440
the *f* of elders were not honoured	Lam 5:12	6440
And every one had four *f*, and every	Eze 1:6	6440
and they four had their *f* and their	Eze 1:8	6440
As for the likeness of their *f*	Eze 1:10	6440
Thus were their *f*	Eze 1:11	6440
living creatures, with his four *f*	Eze 1:15	6440
thy face strong against their *f*	Eze 3:8	6440
and shame shall be upon all *f*	Eze 7:18	6440
LORD, and their *f* toward the east	Eze 8:16	6440
And every one had four *f*	Eze 10:14	6440
Every one had four *f* apiece	Eze 10:21	6440
the likeness of their *f* was the	Eze 10:22	6440

f which I saw by the river of .... Eze 10:22   6440
turn away your *f* from all your .... Eze 14:6   6440
all *f* from the south to the north .... Eze 20:47   6440
and every cherub had two *f* .... Eze 41:18   6440
for why should he see your *f* .... Dan 1:10   6440
thee, but unto us confusion of *f* .... Dan 9:7   6440
all *f* shall gather blackness .... Joel 2:6   6440
and the *f* of them all gather .... Nah 2:10   6440
their *f* shall sup up as the east .... Hab 1:9   6440
seed, and spread dung upon your *f* .... Mal 2:3   6440
for they disfigure their *f* .... Mt 6:16   *4383*
bowed down their *f* to the earth .... Lk 24:5   *4383*
fell before the throne on their *f* .... Rev 7:11   *4383*
their *f* were as the *f* of men .... Rev 9:7   *4383*
on their seats, fell upon their *f* .... Rev 11:16   *4383*

FADE

Strangers shall *f* away, and they 2Sa 22:46   5034
The strangers shall *f* away .... Ps 18:45   5034
and we all do *f* as a leaf .... Is 64:6   5034
the fig tree, and the leaf shall *f* .... Jer 8:13   5034
for meat, whose leaf shall not *f* .... Eze 47:12   5034
the rich man *f* away in his ways .... Jas 1:11   *3133*

FADETH

shall be as an oak whose leaf *f* .... Is 1:30   5034
f away, the world languisheth and .... Is 24:4   5034
f away, the haughty people of the .... Is 24:4   5034
The grass withereth, the flower *f* .... Is 40:7   5034
The grass withereth, the flower *f* .... Is 40:8   5034
that *f* not away, reserved in 1Pet 1:4   *263*
a crown of glory that *f* not away 1Pet 5:4   *262*

FADING

glorious beauty is a *f* flower .... Is 28:1   5034
fat valley, shall be a *f* flower .... Is 28:4   5034

FAIL

you for your cattle, if money *f* .... Gen 47:16   656
f with longing for them all the .... Deut 28:32   3615
he will not *f* thee, nor forsake .... Deut 31:6   7503
be with thee, he will not *f* thee .... Deut 31:8   7503
I will not *f* thee, nor forsake .... Josh 1:5   7503
that he will without *f* drive out .... Josh 3:10
If thou shalt without *f* deliver .... Judg 11:30
Let them not *f* to burn the fat 1Sa 2:16
no man's heart *f* because of him 1Sa 17:32   5307
I should not *f* to sit with the 1Sa 20:5
them, and without *f* recover all 1Sa 30:8
let there not *f* from the house of 2Sa 3:29   3772
there shall not *f* thee (said he) 1Kin 2:4   3772
There shall not *f* thee a man in 1Kin 8:25   3772
There shall not *f* thee a man upon 1Kin 9:5   3772
neither shall the cruse of oil *f* 1Kin 17:14   2637
neither did the cruse of oil *f* 1Kin 17:16   2638
he will not *f* thee, nor forsake 1Chr 28:20   7503
There shall not *f* thee a man in 2Chr 6:16   3772
There shall not *f* thee a man to 2Chr 7:18   3772
heed now that ye *f* not to do this .... Ezr 4:22   7960
given them day by day without *f* .... Ezr 6:9   7960
let nothing *f* of all that thou .... Est 6:10   5307
unto them, so as it should not *f* .... Est 9:27   5674
should not *f* from among the Jews .... Est 9:28   5674
the eyes of the wicked shall *f* .... Job 11:20   3615
As the waters *f* from the sea .... Job 14:11   235
the eyes of his children shall *f* .... Job 17:5   3615
caused the eyes of the widow to *f* .... Job 31:16   3615
for the faithful *f* from among the .... Ps 12:1   6461
mine eyes *f* while I wait for my .... Ps 69:3   3615
doth his promise *f* for evermore .... Ps 77:8   1584
nor suffer my faithfulness to *f* .... Ps 89:33   8266
Mine eyes *f* for thy word, saying .... Ps 119:82   3615
Mine eyes *f* for thy salvation, and .... Ps 119:123   3615
and the rod of his anger shall *f* .... Prov 22:8   3615
be a burden, and desire shall *f* .... Eccl 12:5   6565
shall *f* in the midst thereof .... Is 19:3   1238
the waters shall *f* from the sea .... Is 19:5   5405
and all the glory of Kedar shall *f* .... Is 21:16   3615
and they all shall *f* together .... Is 31:3   3615
the drink of the thirsty to *f* .... Is 32:6   2637
for the vintage shall *f*, the .... Is 32:10   3615
no one of these shall *f*, none .... Is 34:16   5737
mine eyes *f* with looking upward .... Is 38:14   1809
He shall not *f* nor be discouraged .... Is 42:4   3543
pit, nor that his bread should *f* .... Is 51:14   2637
for the spirit should *f* before me .... Is 57:16   5848
of water, whose waters *f* not .... Is 58:11   3576
their eyes did *f*, because there .... Jer 14:6   3615
me as a liar, and as waters that *f* ...... Jer 15:18   3808,539
wine to *f* from the winepresses .... Jer 48:33   7673
Mine eyes do *f* with tears .... Lam 2:11   3615
because his compassions *f* not .... Lam 3:22   3584
and the new wine shall *f* in her .... Hos 9:2   3584

to make the poor of the land to *f* .... Amos 8:4   7673
the labour of the olive shall *f* .... Hab 3:17   3584
that, when ye *f*, they may receive .... Lk 16:9   *1587*
than one tittle of the law to *f* .... Lk 16:17   *4098*
for thee, that thy faith *f* not .... Lk 22:32   *1587*
there be prophecies, they shall *f* 1Cor 13:8   *2673*
same, and thy years shall not *f* .... Heb 1:12   *1587*
for the time would *f* me to tell .... Heb 11:32   *1952*
any man *f* of the grace of God .... Heb 12:15   *5302*

FAILED

and their heart *f* them, and they .... Gen 42:28   3318
when money *f* in the land of Egypt .... Gen 47:15   8552
the plain, even the salt sea, *f* .... Josh 3:16   8552
There *f* not ought of any good .... Josh 21:45   5307
that not one thing hath *f* of all .... Josh 23:14   5307
and not one thing hath *f* thereof .... Josh 23:14   5307
there hath not *f* one word of all 1Kin 8:56   5307
My kinsfolk have *f*, and my .... Job 19:14   2308
refuge *f* me; no man cared .... Ps 142:4   6
my soul *f* when he spake .... Song 5:6   3318
their might hath *f* .... Jer 51:30   5405
our eyes as yet *f* for our vain .... Lam 4:17   3615

FAILETH

for the money *f* .... Gen 47:15   656
Their bull gendereth, and *f* not .... Job 21:10   1602
my strength *f* because of mine .... Ps 31:10   3782
heart panteth, my strength *f* me .... Ps 38:10   5800
therefore my heart *f* me .... Ps 40:12   5800
forsake me not when my strength *f* .... Ps 71:9   3615
My flesh and my heart *f* .... Ps 73:26   3615
and my flesh *f* of fatness .... Ps 109:24   3584
my spirit *f* .... Ps 143:7   3615
by the way, his wisdom *f* him .... Eccl 10:3   2638
hay is withered away, the grass *f* .... Is 15:6   3615
strong in power; not one *f* .... Is 40:26   5737
and their tongue *f* for thirst .... Is 41:17   5405
he is hungry, and his strength *f* .... Is 44:12   369
Yea, truth *f* .... Is 59:15   5737
are prolonged, and every vision *f* .... Eze 12:22   6
his judgment to light, he *f* not .... Zeph 3:5   5737
in the heavens that *f* not .... Lk 12:33   *413*
Charity never *f* 1Cor 13:8   *1601*

FAILING

f of eyes, and sorrow of mind .... Deut 28:65   3631
Men's hearts *f* them for fear, and ...... Lk 21:26   *674*

FAIN

he would *f* flee out of his hand .... Job 27:22   1272
he would *f* have filled his belly .... Lk 15:16   *1937*

FAINT

came from the field, and he was *f* .... Gen 25:29   5889
red pottage; for I am *f* .... Gen 25:30   5889
let not your hearts *f*, fear not, ... Deut 20:3   7401
heart *f* as well as his heart .... Deut 20:8   4549
behind thee, when thou wast *f* .... Deut 25:18   5889
of the land *f* because of you .... Josh 2:9   4127
of the country do *f* because of us .... Josh 2:24   4127
hundred men that were with him, *f* ...... Judg 8:4   5889
for they be *f*, and I am pursuing .... Judg 8:5   5889
And the people were *f* 1Sa 14:28   5774
and the people were very *f* 1Sa 14:31   5774
which were so *f* that they could 1Sa 30:10   6296
which were so *f* that they could 1Sa 30:21   6296
wine, that such as be *f* in the 2Sa 16:2   3287
and David waxed *f* 2Sa 21:15   5774
If thou *f* in the day of adversity .... Prov 24:10   7503
is sick, and the whole heart *f* .... Is 1:5   1742
Therefore shall all hands be *f* .... Is 13:7   7503
he awaketh, and, behold, he is *f* .... Is 29:8   5889
He giveth power to the *f* .... Is 40:29   3287
Even the youths shall *f* and be .... Is 40:30   3286
and they shall walk, and not *f* .... Is 40:31   3286
he drinketh no water, and is *f* .... Is 44:12   3286
sorrow, my heart is *f* in me .... Jer 8:18   1742
And lest your heart *f*, and ye fear .... Jer 51:46   7401
made me desolate and *f* all the day ...... Lam 1:13   1738
sighs are many, and my heart is *f* .... Lam 1:22   1742
that *f* for hunger in the top of .... Lam 2:19   5848
For this our heart is *f* .... Lam 5:17   1739
feeble, and every spirit shall *f* .... Eze 21:7   3543
gates, that their heart may *f* .... Eze 21:15   4127
virgins and young men *f* for thirst .... Amos 8:13   5968
fasting, lest they *f* in the way .... Mt 15:32   *1590*
houses, they will *f* by the way .... Mk 8:3   *1590*
ought always to pray, and not to *f* .... Lk 18:1   *1573*
we have received mercy, we *f* not 2Cor 4:1   *1573*
For which cause we *f* not 2Cor 4:16   *1573*
season we shall reap, if we *f* not .... Gal 6:9   *1590*
Wherefore I desire that ye *f* not .... Eph 3:13   *1573*

F

ye be wearied and *f* in your minds .... Heb 12:3   *1590*
nor *f* when thou art rebuked of .... Heb 12:5   *1590*

FAINTED
And Jacob's heart *f*, for he...................... Gen 45:26   6313
all the land of Canaan *f* by .... Gen 47:13   3856
I had *f*, unless I had believed to............ Ps 27:13
and thirsty, their soul *f* in them .... Ps 107:5   5848
Thy sons have *f*, they lie at the .... Is 51:20   5968
I *f* in my sighing, and I find no .... Jer 45:3   3021
the trees of the field *f* for him .... Eze 31:15   5969
And I Daniel *f*, and was sick .... Dan 8:27   1961
When my soul *f* within me I................... Jonah 2:7   5848
upon the head of Jonah, that he *f* .... Jonah 4:8   5968
on them, because they *f*, and were......... Mt 9:36   *1590*
sake hast laboured, and hast not *f* .... Rev 2:3   2577

FAINTEST
it is come upon thee, and thou *f*............ Job 4:5   3811

FAINTETH
even *f* for the courts of the LORD............ Ps 84:2   3615
My soul *f* for thy salvation .... Ps 119:81   3615
be as when a standard-bearer *f*.............. Is 10:18   4549
earth, *f* not, neither is weary .... Is 40:28   3286

FAINTHEARTED
man is there that is fearful and *f*.... Deut 20:8   7390,3824
neither be *f* for the two tails of........ Is 7:4   3824,7401
they are *f*..................................... Jer 49:23   4127

FAINTNESS
f into their hearts in the lands .... Lev 26:36   4816

FAIR
daughters of men that they were *f*.......... Gen 6:2   2896
thou art a *f* woman to look upon .... Gen 12:11   3303
the woman that she was very *f* .... Gen 12:14   3303
damsel was very *f* to look upon .... Gen 24:16   2896
because she was *f* to look upon .... Gen 26:7   2896
and ruddy, and of a *f* countenance 1Sa 17:42   3303
the son of David had a *f* sister 2Sa 13:1   3303
was a woman of a *f* countenance 2Sa 14:27   3303
So they sought for a *f* damsel 1Kin 1:3   3303
And the damsel was very *f*, and............. 1Kin 1:4   3303
for she was *f* to look on........................... Est 1:11   2896
Let there be *f* young virgins .... Est 2:2   2896,4758
may gather together all the *f* .... Est 2:3   2897,4758
nor mother, and the maid was *f* ...... Est 2:7   3303,8389
F weather cometh out of the north .... Job 37:22   2091
so *f* as the daughters of Job.................... Job 42:15   3303
With her much *f* speech she caused....... Prov 7:21   3948
so is a *f* woman which is without............ Prov 11:22   3303
When he speaketh *f*, believe him........... Prov 26:25   2603
Behold, thou art *f*, my love .... Song 1:15   3302
behold, thou art *f*.................................... Song 1:15   3302
Behold, thou art *f*, my beloved, ... Song 1:16   3302
my love, my *f* one, and come away .... Song 2:10   3302
my love, my *f* one, and come away .... Song 2:13   3302
Behold, thou art *f*, my love .... Song 4:1   3302
behold, thou art *f*.................................... Song 4:1   3302
Thou art all *f*, my love............................. Song 4:7   3302
How *f* is thy love, my sister, my .... Song 4:10   3302
f as the moon, clear as the sun, ... Song 6:10   3303
How *f* and how pleasant art thou, O ...... Song 7:6   3302
be desolate, even great and *f* .... Is 5:9   2896
will lay thy stones with *f* colors .... Is 54:11   6320
in vain shalt thou make thyself *f*............ Jer 4:30   3302
thy name, A green olive tree, *f*................ Jer 11:16   3303
they speak *f* words unto thee .... Jer 12:6   2896
Egypt is like a very *f* heifer .... Jer 46:20   3304
taken thy *f* jewels of my gold.................. Eze 16:17   8597
and shall take thy *f* jewels...................... Eze 16:39   8597
and take away thy *f* jewels .... Eze 23:26   8597
cedar in Lebanon with *f* branches .... Eze 31:3   3303
Thus was he *f* in his greatness,.............. Eze 31:7   3302
I have made him *f* by the .... Eze 31:9   3303
The leaves thereof were *f*........................ Dan 4:12   8209
Whose leaves were *f*, and the fruit .... Dan 4:21   8209
but I passed over upon her *f* neck .... Hos 10:11   2898
In that day shall the *f* virgins .... Amos 8:13   3303
Let them set a *f* mitre upon his .... Zec 3:5   2889
So they set a *f* mitre upon his................. Zec 3:5   2889
ye say, It will be *f* **weather** .... Mt 16:2   2105
was born, and was exceeding *f* .... Acts 7:20   *791*
which is called The *f* havens .... Acts 27:8   *2568*
f speeches deceive the hearts of .... Rom 16:18   *2129*
to make a *f* shew in the flesh .... Gal 6:12   *2146*

FAIRER
not her younger sister *f* than she .... Judg 15:2   2896
Thou art *f* than the children of .... Ps 45:2   3302
their countenances appeared *f*................ Dan 1:15   2896

FAIREST
O thou *f* among women, go thy way .... Song 1:8   3303
beloved, O thou *f* among women............. Song 5:9   3303
gone, O thou *f* among women.................. Song 6:1   3303

FAIRS
and lead, they traded in thy *f* .... Eze 27:12   5801
traded in thy *f* with horses .... Eze 27:14   5801
occupied in thy *f* with emeralds.............. Eze 27:16   5801
going to and fro occupied in thy *f* .... Eze 27:19   5801
they occupied in thy *f* with chief............. Eze 27:22   5801
Thy riches, and thy *f*, thy........................ Eze 27:27   5801

FAITH
children in whom is no *f* .... Deut 32:20   529
but the just shall live by his *f*................. Hab 2:4   530
more clothe you, O ye of little *f* .... Mt 6:30   *3640*
you, I have not found so great *f*............ Mt 8:10   *4102*
are ye fearful, O ye of little *f* .... Mt 8:26   *3640*
Jesus seeing their *f* **said unto**.............. Mt 9:2   *4102*
thy *f* **hath made thee whole** .... Mt 9:22   *4102*
to your *f* **be it unto you** .... Mt 9:29   *4102*
said unto him, O thou of little *f* .... Mt 14:31   *3640*
unto her, O woman, great is thy *f*......... Mt 15:28   *4102*
said unto them, O ye of little *f* .... Mt 16:8   *3640*
If ye have *f* **as a grain of** .... Mt 17:20   *4102*
I say unto you, If ye have *f* .... Mt 21:21   *4102*
of the law, judgment, mercy, and *f* ...... Mt 23:23   *4102*
When Jesus saw their *f*, **he said** .... Mk 2:5   *4102*
how is it that ye have no *f* .... Mk 4:40   *4102*
thy *f* **hath made thee whole** .... Mk 5:34   *4102*
thy *f* **hath made thee whole** .... Mk 10:52   *4102*
saith unto them, Have *f* **in God** .... Mk 11:22   *4102*
And when he saw their *f*, **he said**............ Lk 5:20   *4102*
you, I have not found so great *f*............ Lk 7:9   *4102*
the woman, Thy *f* **hath saved thee** .... Lk 7:50   *4102*
said unto them, Where is your *f* .... Lk 8:25   *4102*
thy *f* **hath made thee whole** .... Lk 8:48   *4102*
he clothe you, O ye of little *f* .... Lk 12:28   *3640*
unto the Lord, Increase our *f* .... Lk 17:5   *4102*
If ye had *f* **as a grain of mustard** .... Lk 17:6   *4102*
thy *f* **hath made thee whole** .... Lk 17:19   *4102*
shall he find *f* **on the earth** .... Lk 18:8   *4102*
thy *f* **hath saved thee** .... Lk 18:42   *4102*
for thee, that thy *f* **fail not** .... Lk 22:32   *4102*
his name through *f* **in his name** .... Acts 3:16   *4102*
the *f* **which is by him hath given** .... Acts 3:16   *4102*
chose Stephen, a man full of *f* .... Acts 6:5   *4102*
priests were obedient to the *f*................ Acts 6:7   *4102*
And Stephen, full of *f* **and power,** .... Acts 6:8   *4102*
and full of the Holy Ghost and of *f* .... Acts 11:24   *4102*
turn away the deputy from the *f*............ Acts 13:8   *4102*
that he had *f* **to be healed** .... Acts 14:9   *4102*
them to continue in the *f* .... Acts 14:22   *4102*
the door of *f* **unto the Gentiles** .... Acts 14:27   *4102*
them, purifying their hearts by *f* .... Acts 15:9   *4102*
the churches established in the *f*............ Acts 16:5   *4102*
f **toward our Lord Jesus Christ** .... Acts 20:21   *4102*
him concerning the *f* **in Christ** .... Acts 24:24   *4102*
are sanctified by *f* **that is in me** .... Acts 26:18   *4102*
to the *f* **among all nations** .... Rom 1:5   *4102*
you all, that your *f* **is spoken of**............ Rom 1:8   *4102*
you by the mutual *f* **both of you** .... Rom 1:12   *4102*
of God revealed from *f* **to** *f* .... Rom 1:17   *4102*
written, The just shall live by *f* .... Rom 1:17   *4102*
make the *f* **of God without effect** .... Rom 3:3   *4102*
of God which is by *f* **of Jesus**................... Rom 3:22   *4102*
through *f* **in his blood, to** .... Rom 3:25   *4102*
but by the law of *f* .... Rom 3:27   *4102*
that a man is justified by *f* .... Rom 3:28   *4102*
justify the circumcision by *f* .... Rom 3:30   *4102*
and uncircumcision through *f* .... Rom 3:30   *4102*
then make void the law through *f* .... Rom 3:31   *4102*
the ungodly, his *f* **is counted for** .... Rom 4:5   *4102*
for we say that *f* **was reckoned to** .... Rom 4:9   *4102*
of the *f* **which he had yet being** .... Rom 4:11   *4102*
of that *f* **of our father Abraham** .... Rom 4:12   *4102*
through the righteousness of *f* .... Rom 4:13   *4102*
f **is made void, and the promise** .... Rom 4:14   *4102*
Therefore it is of *f*, **that it** .... Rom 4:16   *4102*
also which is of the *f* **of Abraham** .... Rom 4:16   *4102*
And being not weak in *f*, **he** .... Rom 4:19   *4102*
but was strong in *f*, **giving glory** .... Rom 4:20   *4102*
Therefore being justified by *f* .... Rom 5:1   *4102*
by *f* **into this grace wherein we** .... Rom 5:2   *4102*
the righteousness which is of *f*................ Rom 9:30   *4102*
Because they sought it not by *f* .... Rom 9:32   *4102*
is of *f* **speaketh on this wise** .... Rom 10:6   *4102*
that is, the word of *f*, **which we** .... Rom 10:8   *4102*
So then *f* **cometh by hearing, and**........... Rom 10:17   *4102*
broken off, and thou standest by *f* .... Rom 11:20   *4102*
to every man the measure of *f* .... Rom 12:3   *4102*

according to the proportion of *f* .... Rom 12:6   4102
that is weak in the *f* receive ye .... Rom 14:1   4102
Hast thou *f*? .... Rom 14:22   4102
eat, because he eateth not of *f* .... Rom 14:23   4102
for whatsoever is not of *f* is sin .... Rom 14:23   4102
nations for the obedience of *f* .... Rom 16:26   4102
That your *f* should not stand in 1Cor 2:5   4102
To another *f* by the same Spirit. 1Cor 12:9   4102
and though I have all *f*, so that I 1Cor 13:2   4102
And now abideth *f*, hope, charity, ... 1Cor 13:13   4102
vain, and your *f* is also vain 1Cor 15:14   4102
be not raised, your *f* is vain 1Cor 15:17   4102
Watch ye, stand fast in the *f* 1Cor 16:13   4102
that we have dominion over your *f* 2Cor 1:24   4102
for by *f* ye stand 2Cor 1:24   4102
We having the same spirit of *f* 2Cor 4:13   4102
(For we walk by *f*, not by sight 2Cor 5:7   4102
as ye abound in every thing, in *f* 2Cor 8:7   4102
when your *f* is increased, that we 2Cor 10:15   4102
whether ye be in the *f* 2Cor 13:5   4102
the *f* which once he destroyed .... Gal 1:23   4102
but by the *f* of Jesus Christ, ... Gal 2:16   4102
be justified by the *f* of Christ .... Gal 2:16   4102
I live by the *f* of the Son of God .... Gal 2:20   4102
the law, or by the hearing of *f* .... Gal 3:2   4102
the law, or by the hearing of *f* .... Gal 3:5   4102
that they which are of *f*, the .... Gal 3:7   4102
justify the heathen through *f* .... Gal 3:8   4102
So then they which be of *f* are .... Gal 3:9   4102
for, The just shall live by *f* .... Gal 3:11   4102
And the law is not of *f* .... Gal 3:12   4102
promise of the Spirit through *f* .... Gal 3:14   4102
that the promise by *f* of Jesus .... Gal 3:22   4102
But before *f* came, we were kept .... Gal 3:23   4102
shut up unto the *f* which should .... Gal 3:23   4102
that we might be justified by *f* .... Gal 3:24   4102
But after that *f* is come, we are .... Gal 3:25   4102
of God by *f* in Christ Jesus .... Gal 3:26   4102
the hope of righteousness by *f* .... Gal 5:5   4102
but *f* which worketh by love .... Gal 5:6   4102
gentleness, goodness, *f*, ... Gal 5:22   4102
who are of the household of *f* .... Gal 6:10   4102
heard of your *f* in the Lord Jesus .... Eph 1:15   4102
by grace are ye saved through *f* .... Eph 2:8   4102
with confidence by the *f* of him .... Eph 3:12   4102
may dwell in your hearts by *f* .... Eph 3:17   4102
One Lord, one *f*, one baptism, ... Eph 4:5   4102
we all come in the unity of the *f* .... Eph 4:13   4102
Above all, taking the shield of *f* .... Eph 6:16   4102
to the brethren, and love with *f* .... Eph 6:23   4102
for your furtherance and joy of *f* .... Phil 1:25   4102
together for the *f* of the gospel .... Phil 1:27   4102
sacrifice and service of your *f* .... Phil 2:17   4102
which is through the *f* of Christ .... Phil 3:9   4102
which is of God by *f* .... Phil 3:9   4102
heard of your *f* in Christ Jesus .... Col 1:4   4102
If ye continue in the *f* grounded .... Col 1:23   4102
stedfastness of your *f* in Christ .... Col 2:5   4102
up in him, and stablished in the *f*. .... Col 2:7   4102
the *f* of the operation of God .... Col 2:12   4102
without ceasing your work of *f* 1Th 1:3   4102
f to God-ward is spread abroad 1Th 1:8   4102
to comfort you concerning your *f* 1Th 3:2   4102
forbear, I sent to know your *f* 1Th 3:5   4102
brought us good tidings of your *f* 1Th 3:6   4102
affliction and distress by your *f* 1Th 3:7   4102
that which is lacking in your *f* 1Th 3:10   4102
putting on the breastplate of *f* 1Th 5:8   4102
because that your *f* groweth 2Th 1:3   4102
f in all your persecutions and 2Th 1:4   4102
and the work of *f* with power 2Th 1:11   4102
for all men have not *f* 2Th 3:2   4102
Unto Timothy, my own son in the *f*. 1Ti 1:2   4102
than godly edifying which is in *f* 1Ti 1:4   4102
conscience, and of *f* unfeigned 1Ti 1:5   4102
was exceeding abundant with *f* 1Ti 1:14   4102
Holding *f*, and a good conscience 1Ti 1:19   4102
concerning *f* have made shipwreck 1Ti 1:19   4102
a teacher of the Gentiles in *f* 1Ti 2:7   4102
if they continue in *f* and charity 1Ti 2:15   4102
of the *f* in a pure conscience 1Ti 3:9   4102
great boldness in the *f* which is 1Ti 3:13   4102
some shall depart from the *f* 1Ti 4:1   4102
nourished up in the words of *f* 1Ti 4:6   4102
in charity, in spirit, in *f* 1Ti 4:12   4102
own house, he hath denied the *f* 1Ti 5:8   4102
they have cast off their first *f* 1Ti 5:12   4102
after, they have erred from the *f* 1Ti 6:10   4102
after righteousness, godliness, *f*. 1Ti 6:11   4102
Fight the good fight of *f* 1Ti 6:12   4102
have erred concerning the *f* 1Ti 6:21   4102

the unfeigned *f* that is in thee 2Ti 1:5   4102
which thou hast heard of me, in *f* 2Ti 1:13   4102
and overthrow the *f* of some 2Ti 2:18   4102
but follow righteousness, *f* 2Ti 2:22   4102
minds, reprobate concerning the *f* 2Ti 3:8   4102
manner of life, purpose, *f* 2Ti 3:10   4102
f which is in Christ Jesus 2Ti 3:15   4102
my course, I have kept the *f* 2Ti 4:7   4102
according to the *f* of God's elect .... Titus 1:1   4102
mine own son after the common *f* .... Titus 1:4   4102
that they may be sound in the *f* .... Titus 1:13   4102
grave, temperate, sound in *f* .... Titus 2:2   4102
Greet them that love us in the *f* .... Titus 3:15   4102
Hearing of thy love and *f*, which. .... Philem 5   4102
thy *f* may become effectual by the .... Philem 6   4102
not being mixed with *f* in them. .... Heb 4:2   4102
dead works, and of *f* toward God, ... Heb 6:1   4102
followers of them who through *f* .... Heb 6:12   4102
true heart in full assurance of *f* .... Heb 10:22   4102
of our *f* without wavering .... Heb 10:23   1680
Now the just shall live by *f* .... Heb 10:38   4102
Now *f* is the substance of things .... Heb 11:1   4102
Through *f* we understand that the .... Heb 11:3   4102
By *f* Abel offered unto God a more .... Heb 11:4   4102
By *f* Enoch was translated that he .... Heb 11:5   4102
But without *f* it is impossible to .... Heb 11:6   4102
By *f* Noah, being warned of God of .... Heb 11:7   4102
the righteousness which is by *f* .... Heb 11:7   4102
By *f* Abraham, when he was called .... Heb 11:8   4102
By *f* he sojourned in the land of. .... Heb 11:9   4102
Through *f* also Sara herself .... Heb 11:11   4102
These all died in *f*, not having .... Heb 11:13   4102
By *f* Abraham, when he was tried, ... Heb 11:17   4102
By *f* Isaac blessed Jacob and Esau ...... Heb 11:20   4102
By *f* Jacob, when he was a dying, ... Heb 11:21   4102
By *f* Joseph, when he died, made .... Heb 11:22   4102
By *f* Moses, when he was born, was ...... Heb 11:23   4102
By *f* Moses, when he was come to .... Heb 11:24   4102
By *f* he forsook Egypt, not .... Heb 11:27   4102
Through *f* he kept the passover, ... Heb 11:28   4102
By *f* they passed through the Red .... Heb 11:29   4102
By *f* the walls of Jericho fell .... Heb 11:30   4102
By *f* the harlot Rahab perished .... Heb 11:31   4102
Who through *f* subdued kingdoms, ... Heb 11:33   4102
obtained a good report through *f* .... Heb 11:39   4102
the author and finisher of our *f* .... Heb 12:2   4102
whose *f* follow, considering the .... Heb 13:7   4102
trying of your *f* worketh patience .... Jas 1:3   4102
But let him ask in *f*, nothing .... Jas 1:6   4102
have not the *f* of our Lord Jesus .... Jas 2:1   4102
the poor of this world rich in *f* .... Jas 2:5   4102
though a man say he hath *f* .... Jas 2:14   4102
can *f* save him? .... Jas 2:14   4102
Even so *f*, if it hath not works, ... Jas 2:17   4102
Yea, a man may say, Thou hast *f* .... Jas 2:18   4102
shew me thy *f* without thy works, ... Jas 2:18   4102
I will shew thee my *f* by my works .... Jas 2:18   4102
that *f* without works is dead .... Jas 2:20   4102
Seest thou how *f* wrought with his .... Jas 2:22   4102
and by works was *f* made perfect .... Jas 2:22   4102
is justified, and not by *f* only .... Jas 2:24   4102
so *f* without works is dead also .... Jas 2:26   4102
the prayer of *f* shall save the .... Jas 5:15   4102
f unto salvation ready to be 1Pet 1:5   4102
That the trial of your *f*, being 1Pet 1:7   4102
Receiving the end of your *f* 1Pet 1:9   4102
that your *f* and hope might be in 1Pet 1:21   4102
Whom resist stedfast in the *f* 1Pet 5:9   4102
precious *f* with us through the 2Pet 1:1   4102
diligence, add to your *f* virtue 2Pet 1:5   4102
overcometh the world, even our *f* 1Jn 5:4   4102
earnestly contend for the *f* which .... Jude 3   4102
up yourselves on your most holy *f* .... Jude 20   4102
my name, and hast not denied my *f* .... Rev 2:13   4102
and charity, and service, and *f* .... Rev 2:19   4102
patience and the *f* of the saints .... Rev 13:10   4102
of God, and the *f* of Jesus .... Rev 14:12   4102

FAITHFUL
who is *f* in all mine house .... Num 12:7   539
thy God, he is God, the *f* God .... Deut 7:9   539
And I will raise me up a *f* priest 1Sa 2:35   539
who is so *f* among all thy 1Sa 22:14   539
that are peaceable and *f* in Israel 2Sa 20:19   539
for he was a *f* man, and feared God ...... Neh 7:2   571
foundest his heart *f* before thee .... Neh 9:8   539
for they were counted *f*, and their .... Neh 13:13   539
for the *f* fail from among the .... Ps 12:1   539
for the Lord preserveth the *f* .... Ps 31:23   539
moon, and as a *f* witness in heaven ...... Ps 89:37   539
shall be upon the *f* of the land .... Ps 101:6   539

F

All thy commandments are *f*	Ps 119:86	530
commanded are righteous and very *f*	Ps 119:138	530
but he that is of a *f* spirit	Prov 11:13	539
but a *f* ambassador is health	Prov 13:17	529
A *f* witness will not lie	Prov 14:5	529
but a *f* man who can find	Prov 20:6	529
so is a *f* messenger to them that	Prov 25:13	539
F are the wounds of a friend	Prov 27:6	539
A *f* man shall abound with	Prov 28:20	539
How is the *f* city become an	Is 1:21	539
city of righteousness, the *f* city	Is 1:26	539
I took unto me *f* witnesses to	Is 8:2	539
because of the LORD that is *f*	Is 49:7	539
f witness between us, if we do	Jer 42:5	539
forasmuch as he was *f*, neither	Dan 6:4	540
with God, and is *f* with the saints	Hos 11:12	539
Who then is a *f* and wise servant	Mt 24:45	4103
Well done, thou good and *f* servant	Mt 25:21	4103
thou hast been *f* over a few	Mt 25:21	4103
him, Well done, good and *f* servant	Mt 25:23	4103
thou hast been *f* over a few	Mt 25:23	4103
the Lord said, Who then is that *f*	Lk 12:42	4103
He that is *f* in that which is	Lk 16:10	4103
which is least is *f* also in much	Lk 16:10	4103
been *f* in the unrighteous mammon	Lk 16:11	4103
if ye have not been *f* in that	Lk 16:12	4103
thou hast been *f* in a very little	Lk 19:17	4103
judged me to be *f* to the Lord	Acts 16:15	4103
God is *f*, by whom ye were called	1Cor 1:9	4103
stewards, that a man be found *f*	1Cor 4:2	4103
f in the Lord, who shall bring	1Cor 4:17	4103
mercy of the Lord to be *f*	1Cor 7:25	4103
but God is *f*, who will not suffer	1Cor 10:13	4103
faith are blessed with *f* Abraham	Gal 3:9	4103
and to the *f* in Christ Jesus	Eph 1:1	4103
f minister in the Lord, shall	Eph 6:21	4103
f brethren in Christ which are at	Col 1:2	4103
who is for you a *f* minister of	Col 1:7	4103
a *f* minister and fellowservant in	Col 4:7	4103
With Onesimus, a *f* and beloved	Col 4:9	4103
F is he that calleth you, who	1Th 5:24	4103
But the Lord is *f*, who shall	2Th 3:3	4103
me, for that he counted me *f*	1Ti 1:12	4103
This is a *f* saying, and worthy of	1Ti 1:15	4103
sober, *f* in all things	1Ti 3:11	4103
This is a *f* saying and worthy of	1Ti 4:9	4103
them service, because they are *f*	1Ti 6:2	4103
the same commit thou to *f* men	2Ti 2:2	4103
It is a *f* saying	2Ti 2:11	4103
we believe not, yet he abideth *f*	2Ti 2:13	4103
having *f* children not accused of	Titus 1:6	4103
Holding fast the *f* word as he	Titus 1:9	4103
This is a *f* saying, and these	Titus 3:8	4103
and *f* high priest in things	Heb 2:17	4103
Who was *f* to him that appointed	Heb 3:2	4103
also Moses was *f* in all his house	Heb 3:2	
verily was *f* in all his house	Heb 3:5	4103
(for he is *f* that promised	Heb 10:23	4103
she judged him *f* who had promised	Heb 11:11	4103
well doing, as unto a *f* Creator	1Pet 4:19	4103
a *f* brother unto you, as I	1Pet 5:12	4103
If we confess our sins, he is *f*	1Jn 1:9	4103
Christ, who is the *f* witness	Rev 1:5	4103
be thou *f* unto death, and I will	Rev 2:10	4103
wherein Antipas was my *f* martyr	Rev 2:13	4103
things saith the Amen, the *f*	Rev 3:14	4103
him are called, and chosen, and *f*	Rev 17:14	4103
he that sat upon him was called F	Rev 19:11	4103
for these words are true and *f*	Rev 21:5	4103
said unto me, These sayings are *f*	Rev 22:6	4103

FAITHFULLY

for they dealt *f*	2Kin 12:15	530
their hand, because they dealt *f*	2Kin 22:7	530
ye do in the fear of the LORD, *f*	2Chr 19:9	530
tithes and the dedicated things *f*	2Chr 31:12	530
And the men did the work *f*	2Chr 34:12	530
The king that *f* judgeth the poor, *f*	Prov 29:14	571
my word, let him speak my word *f*	Jer 23:28	571
thou doest *f* whatsoever thou	3Jn 5	4103

FAITHFULNESS

man his righteousness and his *f*	1Sa 26:23	530
For there is no *f* in their mouth	Ps 5:9	3559
thy *f* reacheth unto the clouds	Ps 36:5	530
I have declared thy *f* and thy	Ps 40:10	530
or thy *f* in destruction	Ps 88:11	530
known thy *f* to all generations	Ps 89:1	530
thy *f* shalt thou establish in the	Ps 89:2	530
thy *f* also in the congregation of	Ps 89:5	530
or to thy *f* round about thee	Ps 89:8	530
But my *f* and my mercy shall be	Ps 89:24	530

from him, nor suffer my *f* to fail	Ps 89:33	530
morning, and thy *f* every night,	Ps 92:2	530
that thou in *f* hast afflicted me	Ps 119:75	530
Thy *f* is unto all generations	Ps 119:90	530
in thy *f* answer me, and in thy	Ps 143:1	530
f the girdle of his reins	Is 11:5	530
thy counsels of old are *f*	Is 25:1	530
great is thy *f*	Lam 3:23	530
even betroth thee unto me in *f*	Hos 2:20	530

FAITHLESS

Then Jesus answered and said, O *f*	Mt 17:17	571
O *f* generation, how long shall I	Mk 9:19	571
And Jesus answering said, O *f*	Lk 9:41	571
and be not *f*, but believing	Jn 20:27	571

FALL

a deep sleep to *f* upon Adam	Gen 2:21	5307
f upon us, and take us for bondmen	Gen 43:18	5307
See that ye *f* not out by the way	Gen 45:24	7264
that his rider shall *f* backward	Gen 49:17	5307
lest he *f* upon us with pestilence	Ex 5:3	6293
Fear and dread shall *f* upon them	Ex 15:16	5307
it, and an ox or an ass *f* therein	Ex 21:33	5307
them, when they are dead, doth *f*	Lev 11:32	5307
if any part of their carcase *f*	Lev 11:37	5307
part of their carcase *f* thereon	Lev 11:38	5307
lest the land *f* to whoredom	Lev 19:29	
they shall *f* before you by the	Lev 26:7	5307
your enemies shall *f* before you	Lev 26:8	5307
they shall *f* when none pursueth	Lev 26:36	5307
they shall *f* one upon another, as	Lev 26:37	3782
let them *f* by the camp, as it	Num 11:31	5203
to *f* by the sword, that our wives	Num 14:3	5307
shall *f* in this wilderness	Num 14:29	5307
they shall *f* in this wilderness	Num 14:32	5307
you, and ye shall *f* by the sword	Num 14:43	5307
f unto you for an inheritance	Num 34:2	5307
ass or his ox *f* down by the way	Deut 22:4	5307
house, if any man *f* from thence	Deut 22:8	5307
of the city shall *f* down flat	Josh 6:5	5307
said, Rise thou, and *f* upon us	Judg 8:21	6293
that ye will not *f* upon me	Judg 15:12	6293
thirst, and *f* into the hand of the	Judg 15:18	5307
let *f* also some of the handfuls	Ruth 2:16	7997
thou know how the matter will *f*	Ruth 3:18	5307
none of his words *f* to the ground	1Sa 3:19	5307
hair of his head *f* to the ground	1Sa 14:45	5307
f by the hand of the Philistines	1Sa 18:25	5307
let his spittle *f* down upon his	1Sa 21:13	3381
not put forth their hand to *f*	1Sa 22:17	6293
Turn thou, and *f* upon the priests	1Sa 22:18	6293
let not my blood *f* to the earth	1Sa 26:20	5307
and said, Go near, and *f* upon him	2Sa 1:15	6293
hair of thy son *f* to the earth	2Sa 14:11	5307
let us *f* now into the hand of the	2Sa 24:14	5307
let me not *f* into the hand of man	2Sa 24:14	5307
not an hair of him *f* to the earth	1Kin 1:52	5307
Jehoiada, saying, Go, *f* upon him	1Kin 2:29	6293
said, and *f* upon him, and bury him	1Kin 2:31	6293
may go up and *f* at Ramoth-gilead	1Kin 22:20	5307
let us *f* unto the host of the	2Kin 7:4	5307
Know now that there shall *f* unto	2Kin 10:10	5307
thy hurt, that thou shouldest *f*	2Kin 14:10	5307
I will cause him to *f* by the	2Kin 19:7	5307
He will *f* to his master Saul to	1Chr 12:19	5307
let me *f* now into the hand of the	1Chr 21:13	5307
but let me not *f* into the hand of	1Chr 21:13	5307
may go up and *f* at Ramoth-gilead	2Chr 18:19	5307
until thy bowels *f* out by reason	2Chr 21:15	3318
make thee *f* before the enemy	2Chr 25:8	3782
thine hurt, that thou shouldest *f*	2Chr 25:19	5307
before whom thou hast begun to *f*	Est 6:13	5307
but shalt surely *f* before him	Est 6:13	5307
and his dread *f* upon you	Job 13:11	5307
Then let mine arm *f* from my	Job 31:22	5307
let them *f* by their own counsels	Ps 5:10	5307
are turned back, they shall *f*	Ps 9:3	3782
that the poor may *f* by his strong	Ps 10:10	5307
that very destruction let him *f*	Ps 35:8	5307
Though he *f*, he shall not be	Ps 37:24	5307
whereby the people *f* under thee	Ps 45:5	5307
They shall *f* by the sword	Ps 63:10	5064
own tongue to *f* upon themselves	Ps 64:8	3782
all kings shall *f* down before him	Ps 72:11	7812
he let it *f* in the midst of their	Ps 78:28	5307
f like one of the princes	Ps 82:7	5307
A thousand shall *f* at thy side	Ps 91:7	5307
thrust sore at me that I might *f*	Ps 118:13	5307
Let burning coals *f* upon them	Ps 140:10	4131
Let the wicked *f* into their own	Ps 141:10	5307
The LORD upholdeth all that *f*	Ps 145:14	5307

away, unless they cause some to *f*	Prov 4:16	3782
but a prating fool shall *f*	Prov 10:8	3832
but a prating fool shall *f*	Prov 10:10	3832
but the wicked shall *f* by his own	Prov 11:5	5307
Where no counsel is, the people *f*	Prov 11:14	5307
trusteth in his riches shall *f*	Prov 11:28	5307
and an haughty spirit before a *f*	Prov 16:18	3783
of the LORD shall *f* therein	Prov 22:14	5307
the wicked shall *f* into mischief	Prov 24:16	3782
diggeth a pit shall *f* therein	Prov 26:27	5307
he shall *f* himself into his own	Prov 28:10	5307
his heart shall *f* into mischief	Prov 28:14	5307
in his ways shall *f* at once	Prov 28:18	5307
the righteous shall see their *f*	Prov 29:16	4658
For if they *f*, the one will lift	Eccl 4:10	5307
diggeth a pit shall *f* into it	Eccl 10:8	5307
if the tree *f* toward the south,	Eccl 11:3	5307
Thy men shall *f* by the sword	Is 3:25	5307
among them shall stumble, and *f*	Is 8:15	5307
they shall *f* under the slain	Is 10:4	5307
Lebanon shall *f* by a mighty one	Is 10:34	5307
unto them shall *f* by the sword	Is 13:15	5307
be removed, and be cut down, and *f*	Is 22:25	5307
of the fear shall *f* into the pit	Is 24:18	5307
and it shall *f*, and not rise again	Is 24:20	5307
f backward, and be broken, and	Is 28:13	3782
be to you as a breach ready to *f*	Is 30:13	5307
slaughter, when the towers *f*	Is 30:25	5307
both he that helpeth shall *f*	Is 31:3	3782
and he that is holpen shall *f* down	Is 31:3	5307
the Assyrian *f* with the sword	Is 31:8	5307
and all their host shall *f* down	Is 34:4	5034
I will cause him to *f* by the	Is 37:7	5307
and the young men shall utterly *f*	Is 40:30	3782
shall I *f* down to the stock of a	Is 44:19	5456
they shall *f* down unto thee, they	Is 45:14	7812
they *f* down, yea, they worship	Is 46:6	5456
and mischief shall *f* upon thee	Is 47:11	5307
against thee shall *f* for thy sake	Is 54:15	5307
cause mine anger to *f* upon you	Jer 3:12	5307
they shall *f* among them that	Jer 6:15	5307
sons together shall *f* upon them	Jer 6:21	3782
Shall they *f*, and not arise	Jer 8:4	5307
shall they *f* among them that *f*	Jer 8:12	5307
f as dung upon the open field	Jer 9:22	5307
caused him to *f* upon it suddenly	Jer 15:8	5307
I will cause them to *f* by the	Jer 19:7	5307
they shall *f* by the sword of	Jer 20:4	5307
shall be driven on, and *f* therein	Jer 23:12	5307
it shall *f* grievously upon the	Jer 23:19	2342
ye, and be drunken, and spue, and *f*	Jer 25:27	5307
ye shall *f* like a pleasant vessel	Jer 25:34	5307
it shall *f* with pain upon the	Jer 30:23	2342
I *f* not away to the Chaldeans	Jer 37:14	5307
and thou shalt not *f* by the sword	Jer 39:18	5307
and *f* in the land of Egypt	Jer 44:12	5307
f toward the north by the river	Jer 46:6	5307
He made many to *f*, yea, one fell	Jer 46:16	3782
the fear shall *f* into the pit	Jer 48:44	5307
is moved at the noise of their *f*	Jer 49:21	5307
young men shall *f* in her streets	Jer 49:26	5307
her young men *f* in the streets	Jer 50:30	5307
the most proud shall stumble and *f*	Jer 50:32	5307
Thus the slain shall *f* in the	Jer 51:4	5307
yea, the wall of Babylon shall *f*	Jer 51:44	5307
slain shall *f* in the midst of her	Jer 51:47	5307
caused the slain of Israel to *f*	Jer 51:49	5307
so at Babylon shall *f* the slain	Jer 51:49	5307
he hath made my strength to *f*	Lam 1:14	3782
a third part shall *f* by the sword	Eze 5:12	5307
the slain shall *f* in the midst of	Eze 6:7	5307
for they shall *f* by the sword	Eze 6:11	5307
that is near shall *f* by the sword	Eze 6:12	5307
Ye shall *f* by the sword	Eze 11:10	5307
morter, that it shall *f*	Eze 13:11	5307
ye, O great hailstones, shall *f*	Eze 13:11	5307
be discovered, and it shall *f*	Eze 13:14	5307
his bands shall *f* by the sword	Eze 17:21	5307
thy remnant shall *f* by the sword	Eze 23:25	5307
let no lot *f* upon it	Eze 24:6	5307
ye have left shall *f* by the sword	Eze 24:21	5307
of Dedan shall *f* by the sword	Eze 25:13	5307
isles shake at the sound of thy *f*	Eze 26:15	4658
isles tremble in the day of thy *f*	Eze 26:18	4658
shall *f* into the midst of the	Eze 27:27	5307
in the midst of thee shall *f*	Eze 27:34	5307
thou shalt *f* upon the open fields	Eze 29:5	5307
when the slain shall *f* in Egypt	Eze 30:4	5307
shall *f* with them by the sword	Eze 30:5	5307
also that uphold Egypt shall *f*	Eze 30:6	5307
shall they *f* in it by the sword	Eze 30:6	5307

of Pi-beseth shall *f* by the sword	Eze 30:17	5307
the sword to *f* out of his hand	Eze 30:22	5307
the arms of Pharaoh shall *f* down	Eze 30:25	5307
to shake at the sound of his *f*	Eze 31:16	4658
his own life, in the day of thy *f*	Eze 32:10	4658
will I cause thy multitude to *f*	Eze 32:12	4658
They shall *f* in the midst of them	Eze 32:12	4658
he shall not *f* thereby in the day	Eze 33:12	3782
the wastes shall *f* by the sword	Eze 33:27	5307
shall they *f* that are slain with	Eze 35:8	5307
cause thy nations to *f* any more	Eze 36:15	3782
down, and the steep places shall *f*	Eze 38:20	5307
every wall shall *f* to the ground	Eze 38:20	5307
arrows to *f* out of thy right hand	Eze 39:3	5307
Thou shalt *f* upon the mountains	Eze 39:4	5307
Thou shalt *f* upon the open field	Eze 39:5	5307
of Israel to *f* into iniquity	Eze 44:12	4383
this land shall *f* unto you for	Eze 47:14	5307
ye *f* down and worship the golden	Dan 3:5	5308
all kinds of musick, shall *f* down	Dan 3:10	5308
ye *f* down and worship the image	Dan 3:15	5308
but they shall *f*	Dan 11:14	3782
but he shall stumble and *f*	Dan 11:19	5307
and many shall *f* down slain	Dan 11:26	5307
yet many shall *f* by the sword	Dan 11:33	3782
Now when they shall *f*, they shall	Dan 11:34	3782
of them of understanding shall *f*	Dan 11:35	3782
Therefore shalt thou *f* in the day	Hos 4:5	3782
shall *f* with thee in the night	Hos 4:5	3782
that doth not understand shall *f*	Hos 4:14	3832
Ephraim *f* in their iniquity	Hos 5:5	3782
Judah also shall *f* with them	Hos 5:5	3782
their princes shall *f* by the	Hos 7:16	5307
and to the hills, F on us	Hos 10:8	5307
they shall *f* by the sword	Hos 13:16	5307
the transgressors shall *f* therein	Hos 14:9	3872
when they *f* upon the sword, they	Joel 2:8	5307
Can a bird *f* in a snare upon the	Amos 3:5	5307
be cut off, and *f* to the ground	Amos 3:14	5307
daughters shall *f* by the sword	Amos 7:17	5307
even they shall *f*, and never rise	Amos 8:14	5307
the least grain *f* upon the earth	Amos 9:9	5307
when I *f*, I shall arise	Mic 7:8	5307
they shall even *f* into the mouth	Nah 3:12	5307
I give thee, if thou wilt *f* down	Mt 4:9	4098
and great was the *f* of it	Mt 7:27	4431
one of them shall not *f* on the	Mt 10:29	4098
if it *f* into a pit on the sabbath	Mt 12:11	1706
both shall *f* into the ditch	Mt 15:14	4098
which *f* from their masters' table	Mt 15:27	4098
whosoever shall *f* on this stone	Mt 21:44	4098
but on whomsoever it shall *f*	Mt 21:44	4098
and the stars shall *f* from heaven	Mt 24:29	4098
And the stars of heaven shall *f*	Mk 13:25	1601
this child is set for the *f*	Lk 2:34	4431
they not both *f* into the ditch	Lk 6:39	4098
and in time of temptation *f* away	Lk 8:13	868
Satan as lightning *f* from heaven	Lk 10:18	4098
Whosoever shall *f* upon that stone	Lk 20:18	4098
but on whomsoever it shall *f*	Lk 20:18	4098
they shall *f* by the edge of the	Lk 21:24	4098
to say to the mountains, F on us	Lk 23:30	4098
a corn of wheat *f* into the ground	Jn 12:24	4098
they should *f* into the quicksands	Acts 27:17	1601
of the boat, and let her *f* off	Acts 27:32	1601
f from the head of any of you	Acts 27:34	4098
they stumbled that they should *f*	Rom 11:11	4098
but rather through their *f*	Rom 11:11	3900
Now if the *f* of them be the	Rom 11:12	3900
or an occasion to *f* in his	Rom 14:13	4625
he standeth take heed lest he *f*	1Cor 10:12	4098
he *f* into the condemnation of the	1Ti 3:6	1706
lest he *f* into reproach and the	1Ti 3:7	
will be rich *f* into temptation	1Ti 6:9	
lest any man *f* after the same	Heb 4:11	4098
If they shall *f* away, to renew	Heb 6:6	3895
It is a fearful thing to *f* into	Heb 10:31	1706
when ye *f* into divers temptations	Jas 1:2	4045
lest ye *f* into condemnation	Jas 5:12	
do these things, ye shall never *f*	2Pet 1:10	4417
f from your own stedfastness	2Pet 3:17	1601
twenty elders *f* down before him	Rev 4:10	4098
F on us, and hide us from the face	Rev 6:16	4098
I saw a star *f* from heaven unto	Rev 9:1	4098

FALLEN

and why is thy countenance *f*	Gen 4:6	5307
man whose hair is *f* off his head	Lev 13:40	4803
he that hath his hair *f* off from	Lev 13:41	4803
poor, and *f* in decay with thee	Lev 25:35	4131,3027
is *f* to us on this side Jordan	Num 32:19	935

F

and that your terror is *f* upon us	Josh 2:9	5307
when they were all *f* on the edge	Josh 8:24	5307
their lord was *f* down dead on the	Judg 3:25	5307
f unto them among the tribes of	Judg 18:1	5307
the woman his concubine was *f*	Judg 19:27	5307
Dagon was *f* upon his face to the	1Sa 5:3	5307
Dagon was *f* upon his face to the	1Sa 5:4	5307
from the LORD was *f* upon them	1Sa 26:12	5307
his three sons *f* in mount Gilboa	1Sa 31:8	5307
and many of the people also are *f*	2Sa 1:4	5307
not live after that he was *f*	2Sa 1:10	5307
because they were *f* by the sword	2Sa 1:12	5307
how are the mighty *f*	2Sa 1:19	5307
How are the mighty *f* in the midst	2Sa 1:25	5307
How are the mighty *f*, and the	2Sa 1:27	5307
a great man *f* this day in Israel	2Sa 3:38	5307
yea, they are *f* under my feet	2Sa 22:39	5307
Now Elisha was *f* sick of his	2Kin 13:14	
his sons *f* in mount Gilboa	1Chr 10:8	5307
were dead bodies *f* to the earth	2Chr 20:24	5307
our fathers have *f* by the sword	2Chr 29:9	5307
Haman was *f* upon the bed whereon	Est 7:8	5307
The fire of God is *f* from heaven	Job 1:16	5307
is *f* into the ditch which he made	Ps 7:15	5307
The lines are *f* unto me in	Ps 16:6	5307
they are *f* under my feet	Ps 18:38	5307
They are brought down and *f*	Ps 20:8	5307
are the workers of iniquity *f*	Ps 36:12	5307
terrors of death are *f* upon me	Ps 55:4	5307
whereof they are *f* themselves	Ps 57:6	5307
reproached thee are *f* upon me	Ps 69:9	5307
is ruined, and Judah is *f*	Is 3:8	5307
The bricks are *f* down, but we	Is 9:10	5307
How art thou *f* from heaven	Is 14:12	5307
fruits and for thy harvest is *f*	Is 16:9	5307
he answered and said, Babylon is *f*	Is 21:9	5307
and said, Babylon is, is *f*	Is 21:9	5307
the inhabitants of the world *f*	Is 26:18	5307
for truth is *f* in the street, and	Is 59:14	3782
Jews that are *f* to the Chaldeans	Jer 38:19	5307
and they are *f* both together	Jer 46:12	5307
the spoiler is *f* upon thy summer	Jer 48:32	5307
her foundations are *f*, her walls	Jer 50:15	5307
Babylon is suddenly *f* and	Jer 51:8	5307
my young men are *f* by the sword	Lam 2:21	5307
The crown is *f* from our head	Lam 5:16	5307
Lo, when the wall is *f*, shall it	Eze 13:12	5307
the valleys his branches are *f*	Eze 31:12	5307
all of them slain, *f* by the sword	Eze 32:22	5307
f by the sword, which caused	Eze 32:23	5307
f by the sword, which are gone	Eze 32:24	5307
that are *f* of the uncircumcised	Eze 32:27	5307
all their kings are *f*	Hos 7:7	5307
for thou hast *f* by thine iniquity	Hos 14:1	3782
The virgin of Israel is *f*	Amos 5:2	5307
the tabernacle of David that is *f*	Amos 9:11	5307
for the cedar is *f*	Zec 11:2	5307
have an ass or an ox *f* into a pit	Lk 14:5	1706
as yet he was *f* upon none of them	Acts 8:16	1968
of David, which is *f* down	Acts 15:16	4098
being *f* into a deep sleep	Acts 20:9	2702
when we were all *f* to the earth	Acts 26:14	2667
lest we should have *f* upon rocks	Acts 27:29	1601
swollen, or *f* down suddenly	Acts 28:6	2667
present, but some are *f* asleep	1Cor 15:6	2837
Then they also which are *f* asleep	1Cor 15:18	2837
ye are *f* from grace	Gal 5:4	1601
which happened unto me have *f* out	Phil 1:12	2064
therefore from whence thou art *f*	Rev 2:5	1601
saying, Babylon is, is *f*	Rev 14:8	4098
five are *f*, and one is, and the	Rev 17:10	4098
Babylon the great is *f*, is *f*	Rev 18:2	4098

FALLEST

Thou *f* away to the Chaldeans	Jer 37:13	5307

FALLETH

when there *f* out any war, they	Ex 1:10	7122
vessel, whereinto any of them *f*	Lev 11:33	5307
their carcase *f* shall be unclean	Lev 11:35	5307
be in the place where his lot *f*	Num 33:54	3918
or that *f* on the sword, or that	2Sa 3:29	5307
as a man *f* before wicked men, so	2Sa 3:34	5307
him as the dew *f* on the ground	2Sa 17:12	5307
night, when deep sleep *f* on men	Job 4:13	5307
night, when deep sleep *f* upon men	Job 33:15	5307
wicked messenger *f* into mischief	Prov 13:17	5307
a perverse tongue *f* into mischief	Prov 17:20	5307
For a just man *f* seven times	Prov 24:16	5307
Rejoice not when thine enemy *f*	Prov 24:17	5307
to him that is alone when he *f*	Eccl 4:10	5307
when it *f* suddenly upon them	Eccl 9:12	5307

in the place where the tree *f*	Eccl 11:3	5307
as the leaf *f* off from the vine,	Is 34:4	5034
a graven image, and *f* down thereto	Is 44:15	5456
he *f* down unto it, and worshippeth	Is 44:17	5456
f to the Chaldeans that besiege	Jer 21:9	5307
whoso *f* not down and worshippeth	Dan 3:6	5308
whoso *f* not down and worshippeth,	Dan 3:11	5308
for ofttimes he *f* into the fire	Mt 17:15	4098
a house divided against a house *f*	Lk 11:17	4098
the portion of goods that *f* to me	Lk 15:12	1911
his own master he standeth or *f*	Rom 14:4	4098
grass, and the flower thereof *f*	Jas 1:11	1601
and the flower thereof *f* away	1Pet 1:24	1601

FALLING

f into a trance, but having his	Num 24:4	5307
f into a trance, but having his	Num 24:16	5307
have upholden him that was *f*	Job 4:4	3782
the mountain *f* cometh to nought	Job 14:18	5307
not thou deliver my feet from *f*	Ps 56:13	1762
from tears, and my feet from *f*	Ps 116:8	1762
A righteous man *f* down before the	Prov 25:26	4131
as a *f* fig from the fig tree	Is 34:4	5034
f down before him, she declared	Lk 8:47	4363
f down to the ground	Lk 22:44	2597
of blood *f* down to the ground	Lk 22:44	2597
f headlong, he burst asunder in	Acts 1:18	4248,1096
f into a place where two seas met	Acts 27:41	4045
so *f* down on his face he will	1Cor 14:25	4098
except there come a *f* away first	2Th 2:3	646
that is able to keep you from *f*	Jude 24	679

FALLOW

the *f* deer, and the wild goat, and	Deut 14:5	3180
Jerusalem, Break up your *f* ground	Jer 4:3	5215
break up your *f* ground	Hos 10:12	5215

FALLOWDEER

beside harts, and roebucks, and *f*	1Kin 4:23	3180

FALSE

Thou shalt not bear *f* witness	Ex 20:16	8267
Thou shalt not raise a *f* report	Ex 23:1	7723
Keep thee far from a *f* matter	Ex 23:7	8267
Neither shalt thou bear *f* witness	Deut 5:20	7723
If a *f* witness rise up against	Deut 19:16	2555
if the witness be a *f* witness	Deut 19:18	8267
And they said, It is *f*	2Kin 9:12	8267
For truly my words shall not be *f*	Job 36:4	8267
for *f* witnesses are risen up	Ps 27:12	8267
f witnesses did rise up	Ps 35:11	2555
therefore I hate every *f* way	Ps 119:104	8267
and I hate every *f* way	Ps 119:128	8267
be done unto thee, thou *f* tongue	Ps 120:3	7423
A *f* witness that speaketh lies	Prov 6:19	8267
A *f* balance is abomination to the	Prov 11:1	4820
but a *f* witness deceit	Prov 12:17	8267
but a *f* witness will utter lies	Prov 14:5	8267
wicked doer giveth heed to *f* lips	Prov 17:4	205
A *f* witness shall not be	Prov 19:5	8267
A *f* witness shall not be	Prov 19:9	8267
and a *f* balance is not good	Prov 20:23	4820
A *f* witness shall perish	Prov 21:28	3577
of a *f* gift is like clouds	Prov 25:14	8267
A man that beareth *f* witness	Prov 25:18	8267
they prophesy unto you a *f* vision	Jer 14:14	8267
them that prophesy *f* dreams	Jer 23:32	8267
Then said Jeremiah, It is *f*	Jer 37:14	8267
but have seen for thee *f* burdens	Lam 2:14	7723
as a *f* divination in their sight	Eze 21:23	7723
and love no *f* oath	Zec 8:17	8267
seen a lie, and have told *f* dreams	Zec 10:2	7723
against *f* swearers, and against	Mal 3:5	8267
Beware of *f* prophets, which come	Mt 7:15	5578
thefts, *f* witness, blasphemies	Mt 15:19	5577
Thou shalt not bear *f* witness	Mt 19:18	5576
many *f* prophets shall rise, and	Mt 24:11	5578
For there shall arise *f* Christs	Mt 24:24	
f prophets, and shall shew great	Mt 24:24	5578
sought *f* witness against Jesus,	Mt 26:59	5580
though many *f* witnesses came, yet	Mt 26:60	5575
At the last came two *f* witnesses	Mt 26:60	5575
not steal, Do not bear *f* witness	Mk 10:19	5576
For *f* Christs and *f* prophets	Mk 13:22	5580
For many bare *f* witness against	Mk 14:56	5576
bare *f* witness against him,	Mk 14:57	5576
their fathers to the *f* prophets	Lk 6:26	5578
not steal, Do not bear *f* witness	Lk 18:20	5576
from any man by *f* accusation	Lk 19:8	4811
set up *f* witnesses, which said,	Acts 6:13	5571
a *f* prophet, a Jew, whose name	Acts 13:6	5578
Thou shalt not bear *f* witness	Rom 13:9	5576
we are found *f* witnesses of God	1Cor 15:15	5575
For such are *f* apostles,	2Cor 11:13	5570

sea, in perils among *f* brethren	2Cor 11:26	5569
that because of *f* brethren	Gal 2:4	5569
f accusers, incontinent, fierce,	2Ti 3:3	1228
not *f* accusers, not given to much	Titus 2:3	1228
But there were *f* prophets also	2Pet 2:1	5578
shall be *f* teachers among you	2Pet 2:1	5572
because many *f* prophets are gone	1Jn 4:1	5578
out of the mouth of the *f* prophet	Rev 16:13	5578
with him the *f* prophet that	Rev 19:20	5578
the *f* prophet are, and shall be	Rev 20:10	5578

FALSEHOOD

wrought *f* against mine own life	2Sa 18:13	8267
in your answers there remaineth *f*	Job 21:34	4604
mischief, and brought forth *f*	Ps 7:14	8267
for their deceit is *f*	Ps 119:118	8267
right hand is a right hand of *f*	Ps 144:8	8267
right hand is a right hand of *f*	Ps 144:11	8267
under *f* have we hid ourselves	Is 28:15	8267
of transgression, a seed of *f*	Is 57:4	8267
from the heart words of *f*	Is 59:13	8267
for his molten image is *f*	Jer 10:14	8267
forgotten me, and trusted in *f*	Jer 13:25	8267
for his molten image is *f*	Jer 51:17	8267
for they commit *f*; and the thief	Hos 7:1	8267
f do lie, saying, I will prophesy	Mic 2:11	8267

FALSELY

that thou wilt not deal *f* with me	Gen 21:23	8266
concerning it, and sweareth *f*	Lev 6:3	5921,8267
that about which he hath sworn *f*	Lev 6:5	8267
shall not steal, neither deal *f*	Lev 19:11	3584
ye shall not swear by my name *f*	Lev 19:12	8267
hath testified *f* against his	Deut 19:18	8267
have we dealt *f* in thy covenant	Ps 44:17	8266
surely they swear *f*	Jer 5:2	8267
The prophets prophesy *f*, and the	Jer 5:31	8267
the priest every one dealeth *f*	Jer 6:13	8267
and commit adultery, and swear *f*	Jer 7:9	8267
the priest every one dealeth *f*	Jer 8:10	8267
For they prophesy *f* unto you in	Jer 29:9	8267
for thou speakest *f* of Ishmael	Jer 40:16	8267
unto Jeremiah, Thou speakest *f*	Jer 43:2	8267
swearing *f* in making a covenant	Hos 10:4	7723
of him that sweareth *f* by my name	Zec 5:4	8267
all manner of evil against you *f*	Mt 5:11	5574
to no man, neither accuse any *f*	Lk 3:14	
of science *f* so called	1Ti 6:20	5581
they may be ashamed that *f* accuse	1Pet 3:16	

FALSIFYING

and *f* the balances by deceit	Amos 8:5	5791

FAME

the *f* thereof was heard in	Gen 45:16	6963
heard the *f* of thee will speak	Num 14:15	8088
his *f* was noised throughout all	Josh 6:27	8089
for we have heard the *f* of him	Josh 9:9	8089
his *f* was in all nations round	1Kin 4:31	8034
f of Solomon concerning the name	1Kin 10:1	8088
exceedeth the *f* which I heard	1Kin 10:7	8052
the *f* of David went out into all	1Chr 14:17	8034
be exceeding magnifical, of *f*	1Chr 22:5	8034
Sheba heard of the *f* of Solomon	2Chr 9:1	8088
thou exceedest the *f* that I heard	2Chr 9:6	8052
his *f* went out throughout all the	Est 9:4	8089
We have heard the *f* therewith	Job 28:22	8088
off, that have not heard my *f*	Is 66:19	8088
We have heard the *f* thereof	Jer 6:24	8089
f in every land where they have	Zeph 3:19	8034
his *f* went throughout all Syria	Mt 4:24	189
the *f* hereof went abroad into all	Mt 9:26	5345
spread abroad his *f* in all that	Mt 9:31	1310
tetrarch heard of the *f* of Jesus	Mt 14:1	189
immediately his *f* spread abroad	Mk 1:28	189
there went out a *f* of him through	Lk 4:14	5345
the *f* of him went out into every	Lk 4:37	2279
more went there a *f* abroad of him	Lk 5:15	3056

FAMILIAR

not them that have *f* spirits	Lev 19:31	
after such as have *f* spirits	Lev 20:6	
or woman that hath a *f* spirit	Lev 20:27	
or a consulter with *f* spirits	Deut 18:11	
put away those that had *f* spirits	1Sa 28:3	
me a woman that hath a *f* spirit	1Sa 28:7	
that hath a *f* spirit at En-dor	1Sa 28:7	
divine unto me by the *f* spirit	1Sa 28:8	
cut off those that have *f* spirits	1Sa 28:9	
and dealt with *f* spirits and	2Kin 21:6	
the workers with *f* spirits	2Kin 23:24	
of one that had a *f* spirit	1Chr 10:13	
and dealt with a *f* spirit	2Chr 33:6	

my *f* friends have forgotten me	Job 19:14	3045
Yea, mine own *f* friend, in whom I	Ps 41:9	7965
unto them that have *f* spirits	Is 8:19	
and to them that have *f* spirits	Is 19:3	
as of one that hath a *f* spirit	Is 29:4	

FAMILIARS

All my *f* watched for my halting,	Jer 20:10	7965

FAMILIES

after his tongue, after their *f*	Gen 10:5	4940
afterward were the *f* of the	Gen 10:18	4940
the sons of Ham, after their *f*	Gen 10:20	4940
the sons of Shem, after their *f*	Gen 10:31	4940
These are the *f* of the sons of	Gen 10:32	4940
in thee shall all *f* of the earth	Gen 12:3	4940
all the *f* of the earth be blessed	Gen 28:14	4940
of Esau, according to their *f*	Gen 36:40	4940
with bread, according to their *f*	Gen 47:12	2945
these be the *f* of Reuben	Ex 6:14	4940
these are the *f* of Simeon	Ex 6:15	4940
and Shimi, according to their *f*	Ex 6:17	4940
these are the *f* of Levi according	Ex 6:19	4940
these are the *f* of the Korhites	Ex 6:24	4940
the Levites according to their *f*	Ex 6:25	4940
you a lamb according to your *f*	Ex 12:21	4940
of their *f* that are with you,	Lev 25:45	4940
children of Israel, after their *f*	Num 1:2	4940
their pedigrees after their *f*	Num 1:18	4940
their generations, after their *f*	Num 1:20	4940
their generations, after their *f*	Num 1:22	4940
their generations, after their *f*	Num 1:24	4940
their generations, after their *f*	Num 1:26	4940
their generations, after their *f*	Num 1:28	4940
their generations, after their *f*	Num 1:30	4940
their generations, after their *f*	Num 1:32	4940
their generations, after their *f*	Num 1:34	4940
their generations, after their *f*	Num 1:36	4940
their generations, after their *f*	Num 1:38	4940
their generations, after their *f*	Num 1:40	4940
their generations, after their *f*	Num 1:42	4940
forward, every one after their *f*	Num 2:34	4940
of their fathers, by their *f*	Num 3:15	4940
of the sons of Gershon by their *f*	Num 3:18	4940
And the sons of Kohath by their *f*	Num 3:19	4940
And the sons of Merari by their *f*	Num 3:20	4940
These are the *f* of the Levites	Num 3:20	4940
these are the *f* of the	Num 3:21	4940
The *f* of the Gershonites shall	Num 3:23	4940
these are the *f* of the Kohathites	Num 3:27	4940
The *f* of the sons of Kohath shall	Num 3:29	4940
the *f* of the Kohathites shall be	Num 3:30	4940
these are the *f* of Merari	Num 3:33	4940
the house of the father of the *f*	Num 3:35	4940
of the LORD, throughout their *f*	Num 3:39	4940
the sons of Levi, after their *f*	Num 4:2	4940
f of the Kohathites from among	Num 4:18	4940
of their fathers, by their *f*	Num 4:22	4940
of the *f* of the Gershonites	Num 4:24	4940
This is the service of the *f* of	Num 4:28	4940
shalt number them after their *f*	Num 4:29	4940
of the *f* of the sons of Merari	Num 4:33	4940
of the Kohathites after their *f*	Num 4:34	4940
were numbered of them by their *f*	Num 4:36	4940
of the *f* of the Kohathites	Num 4:37	4940
of Gershon, throughout their *f*	Num 4:38	4940
of them, throughout their *f*	Num 4:40	4940
of the *f* of the sons of Gershon	Num 4:41	4940
of the *f* of the sons of Merari	Num 4:42	4940
throughout their *f*, by the house	Num 4:42	4940
numbered of them after their *f*	Num 4:44	4940
of the *f* of the sons of Merari	Num 4:45	4940
of Israel numbered, after their *f*	Num 4:46	4940
people weep throughout their *f*	Num 11:10	4940
These are the *f* of the Reubenites	Num 26:7	4940
The sons of Simeon after their *f*	Num 26:12	4940
These are the *f* of the Simeonites	Num 26:14	4940
The children of Gad after their *f*	Num 26:15	4940
These are the *f* of the children	Num 26:18	4940
sons of Judah after their *f* were	Num 26:20	4940
These are the *f* of Judah	Num 26:22	4940
sons of Issachar after their *f*	Num 26:23	4940
These are the *f* of Issachar	Num 26:25	4940
the sons of Zebulun after their *f*	Num 26:26	4940
These are the *f* of the	Num 26:27	4940
after their *f* were Manasseh	Num 26:28	4940
These are the *f* of Manasseh	Num 26:34	4940
the sons of Ephraim after their *f*	Num 26:35	4940
These are the *f* of the sons of	Num 26:37	4940
the sons of Joseph after their *f*	Num 26:37	4940
sons of Benjamin after their *f*	Num 26:38	4940
sons of Benjamin after their *f*	Num 26:41	4940

F

are the sons of Dan after their *f* .... Num 26:42 4940
These are the sons of Dan after .... Num 26:42 4940
the *f* of Dan after their *f* .... Num 26:42 4940
All the *f* of the Shuhamites, ... Num 26:43 4940
children of Asher after their *f* .... Num 26:44 4940
These are the *f* of the sons of .... Num 26:47 4940
sons of Naphtali after their *f* .... Num 26:48 4940
These are the *f* of Naphtali .... Num 26:50 4940
of Naphtali according to their *f* .... Num 26:50 4940
of the Levites after their *f* .... Num 26:57 4940
These are the *f* of the Levites .... Num 26:58 4940
of the *f* of Manasseh the son of .... Num 27:1 4940
for an inheritance among your *f* .... Num 33:54 4940
the chief fathers of the *f* of the .... Num 36:1 4940
of the *f* of the sons of Joseph, ... Num 36:1 4940
they were married into the the *f* of .... Num 36:12 4940
come according to the *f* thereof .... Josh 7:14 4940
inheritance according to their *f* .... Josh 13:15 4940
children of Reuben after their *f*. .... Josh 13:23 4940
children of Gad according to their *f* ..... Josh 13:24 4940
the children of Gad after their *f* .... Josh 13:28 4940
children of Manasseh by their *f* .... Josh 13:29 4940
the children of Machir by their *f* .... Josh 13:31 4940
the children of Judah by their *f*. .... Josh 15:1 4940
round about according to their *f*. .... Josh 15:12 4940
of Judah according to their *f*. .... Josh 15:20 4940
according to their *f* was thus .... Josh 16:5 4940
children of Ephraim by their *f*. .... Josh 16:8 4940
children of Manasseh by their *f* .... Josh 17:2 4940
the son of Joseph by their *f*. .... Josh 17:2 4940
came up according to their *f*. .... Josh 18:11 4940
round about, according to their *f*. .... Josh 18:20 4940
according to their *f* were Jericho .... Josh 18:21 4940
of Benjamin according to their *f*. .... Josh 18:28 4940
of Simeon according to their *f* .... Josh 19:1 4940
of Simeon according to their *f*. .... Josh 19:8 4940
of Zebulun according to their *f* .... Josh 19:10 4940
of Zebulun according to their *f*. .... Josh 19:16 4940
of Issachar according to their *f*. .... Josh 19:17 4940
of Issachar according to their *f*. .... Josh 19:23 4940
of Asher according to their *f*. .... Josh 19:24 4940
of Asher according to their *f*. .... Josh 19:31 4940
of Naphtali according to their *f*. .... Josh 19:32 4940
of Naphtali according to their *f*. .... Josh 19:39 4940
of Dan according to their *f*. .... Josh 19:40 4940
of Dan according to their *f*. .... Josh 19:48 4940
out for the *f* of the Kohathites .... Josh 21:4 4940
of the *f* of the tribe of Ephraim .... Josh 21:5 4940
of the *f* of the tribe of Issachar .... Josh 21:6 4940
f had out of the tribe of Reuben .... Josh 21:7 4940
being of the *f* of the Kohathites, ... Josh 21:10 4940
the *f* of the children of Kohath, ... Josh 21:20 4940
f of the children of Kohath that .... Josh 21:26 4940
of the *f* of the Levites, out of .... Josh 21:27 4940
Gershonites according to their *f* .... Josh 21:33 4940
unto the *f* of the children of .... Josh 21:34 4940
the children of Merari by their *f* .... Josh 21:40 4940
remaining of the *f* of the Levites .... Josh 21:40 4940
the *f* of the tribe of Benjamin 1Sa 9:21 4940
Benjamin to come near by their *f*. 1Sa 10:21 4940
And the *f* of of Kirjath-jearim 1Chr 2:53 4940
the *f* of the scribes which dwelt 1Chr 2:55 4940
These are the *f* of the Zorathites 1Chr 4:2 4940
the *f* of Aharhel the son of Harum 1Chr 4:8 4940
the *f* of the house of them that 1Chr 4:21 4940
names were princes in their *f* 1Chr 4:38 4940
And his brethren by their *f* 1Chr 5:7 4940
these are the *f* of the Levites 1Chr 6:19 4940
of the *f* of the Kohathites 1Chr 6:54 4940
their *f* were thirteen cities 1Chr 6:60 4940
of Gershom throughout their *f* out 1Chr 6:62 4940
given by lot, throughout their *f*. 1Chr 6:63 4940
the residue of the *f* of the sons 1Chr 6:66 4940
their brethren among all the *f* of 1Chr 7:5 4940
to the divisions of the *f* of the 2Chr 35:5 1004,1
division of the *f* of the Levites 2Chr 35:5 1004,1
divisions of the *f* of the people 2Chr 35:12 1004
after their *f* with their swords .... Neh 4:13 4940
did the contempt of *f* terrify me .... Job 31:34 4940
God setteth the solitary in *f* .... Ps 68:6 1004
maketh him *f* like a flock .... Ps 107:41 4940
I will call all the *f* of the .... Jer 1:15 4940
all the *f* of the house of Israel .... Jer 2:4 4940
upon the *f* that call not on thy .... Jer 10:25 4940
and take all the *f* of the north .... Jer 25:9 4940
be the God of all the *f* of Israel .... Jer 31:1 4940
The two *f* which the LORD hath .... Jer 33:24 4940
as the *f* of the countries, to .... Eze 20:32 4940
I known of all the *f* of the earth .... Amos 3:2 4940
f through her witchcrafts .... Nah 3:4 4940

All the *f* that remain, every .... Zec 12:14 4940
will not come up of all the *f* of .... Zec 14:17 4940

FAMILY
that man, and against his *f* .... Lev 20:5 4940
shall return every man unto his *f* .... Lev 25:10 4940
and shall return unto his own *f* .... Lev 25:41 4940
to the stock of the stranger's *f* .... Lev 25:47 4940
unto him of his *f* may redeem him .... Lev 25:49 4940
Gershon was the *f* of the Libnites .... Num 3:21 4940
and the *f* of the Shimites .... Num 3:21 4940
Kohath was the *f* of the Amramites .... Num 3:27 4940
the *f* of the Izeharites, and the .... Num 3:27 4940
the *f* of the Hebronites, and the .... Num 3:27 4940
and the *f* of the Uzzielites .... Num 3:27 4940
Merari was the *f* of the Mahlites .... Num 3:33 4940
and the *f* of the Mushites. .... Num 3:33 4940
cometh the *f* of the Hanochites .... Num 26:5 4940
of Pallu, the *f* of the Palluites .... Num 26:5 4940
Hezron, the *f* of the Hezronites .... Num 26:6 4940
of Carmi, the *f* of the Carmites .... Num 26:6 4940
Nemuel, the *f* of the Nemuelites .... Num 26:12 4940
of Jamin, the *f* of the Jaminites .... Num 26:12 4940
Jachin, the *f* of the Jachinites .... Num 26:12 4940
Of Zerah, the *f* of the Zarhites .... Num 26:13 4940
of Shaul, the *f* of the Shaulites .... Num 26:13 4940
Zephon, the *f* of the Zephonites .... Num 26:15 4940
of Haggi, the *f* of the Haggites .... Num 26:15 4940
of Shuni, the *f* of the Shunites .... Num 26:15 4940
Of Ozni, the *f* of the Oznites .... Num 26:16 4940
of Eri, the *f* of the Erites .... Num 26:16 4940
Of Arod, the *f* of the Arodites .... Num 26:17 4940
of Areli, the *f* of the Arelites .... Num 26:17 4940
Shelah, the *f* of the Shelanites .... Num 26:20 4940
of Pharez, the *f* of the Pharzites .... Num 26:20 4940
of Zerah, the *f* of the Zarhites .... Num 26:20 4940
Hezron, the *f* of the Hezronites .... Num 26:21 4940
of Hamul, the *f* of the Hamulites .... Num 26:21 4940
of Tola, the *f* of the Tolaites .... Num 26:23 4940
of Pua, the *f* of the Punites .... Num 26:23 4940
Jashub, the *f* of the Jashubites .... Num 26:24 4940
Shimron, the *f* of the Shimronites .... Num 26:24 4940
of Sered, the *f* of the Sardites .... Num 26:26 4940
of Elon, the *f* of the Elonites .... Num 26:26 4940
Jahleel, the *f* of the Jahleelites .... Num 26:26 4940
Machir, the *f* of the Machirites .... Num 26:29 4940
come the *f* of the Gileadites .... Num 26:29 4940
Jeezer, the *f* of the Jeezerites .... Num 26:30 4940
of Helek, the *f* of the Helekites .... Num 26:30 4940
Asriel, the *f* of the Asrielites .... Num 26:31 4940
Shechem, the *f* of the Shechemites .... Num 26:31 4940
Shemida, the *f* of the Shemidaites .... Num 26:32 4940
Hepher, the *f* of the Hepherites .... Num 26:32 4940
the *f* of the Shuthalhites .... Num 26:35 4940
of Becher, the *f* of the Bachrites .... Num 26:35 4940
of Tahan, the *f* of the Tahanites .... Num 26:35 4940
of Eran, the *f* of the Eranites .... Num 26:36 4940
of Bela, the *f* of the Belaites .... Num 26:38 4940
Ashbel, the *f* of the Ashbelites .... Num 26:38 4940
Ahiram, the *f* of the Ahiramites .... Num 26:38 4940
Shupham, the *f* of the Shuphamites .... Num 26:39 4940
Hupham, the *f* of the Huphamites .... Num 26:39 4940
of Ard, the *f* of the Ardites .... Num 26:40 4940
of Naaman, the *f* of the Naamites .... Num 26:40 4940
Shuham, the *f* of the Shuhamites .... Num 26:42 4940
of Jimna, the *f* of the Jimnites .... Num 26:44 4940
of Jesui, the *f* of the Jesuites .... Num 26:44 4940
of Beriah, the *f* of the Beriites .... Num 26:44 4940
of Heber, the *f* of the Heberites .... Num 26:45 4940
the *f* of the Malchielites .... Num 26:45 4940
Jahzeel, the *f* of the Jahzeelites .... Num 26:48 4940
of Guni, the *f* of the Gunites .... Num 26:48 4940
Of Jezer, the *f* of the Jezerites .... Num 26:49 4940
Shillem, the *f* of the Shillemites .... Num 26:49 4940
Gershon, the *f* of the Gershonites .... Num 26:57 4940
Kohath, the *f* of the Kohathites .... Num 26:57 4940
of Merari, the *f* of the Merarites. .... Num 26:57 4940
the *f* of the Libnites .... Num 26:58 4940
the *f* of the Hebronites .... Num 26:58 4940
the *f* of the Mahlites .... Num 26:58 4940
the *f* of the Mushites .... Num 26:58 4940
Mushites, the *f* of the Korathites .... Num 26:58 4940
be done away from among his *f* .... Num 27:4 4940
that is next to him of his *f* .... Num 27:11 4940
only to the *f* of the tribe of .... Num 36:6 4940
the *f* of the tribe of her father .... Num 36:8 4940
tribe of the *f* of their father .... Num 36:12 4940
be among you man, or woman, or *f* .... Deut 29:18 4940
the *f* which the LORD shall take .... Josh 7:14 4940
And he brought the *f* of Judah .... Josh 7:17 4940
he took the *f* of the Zarhites .... Josh 7:17 4940

he brought the *f* of the Zarhites	Josh 7:17	4940
they let go the man and all his *f*	Judg 1:25	4940
my *f* is poor in Manasseh, and I am	Judg 6:15	504
with all the *f* of the house of	Judg 9:1	4940
of the *f* of the Danites, whose	Judg 13:2	4940
of the *f* of Judah, who was a	Judg 17:7	4940
f five men from their coasts	Judg 18:2	4940
thence of the *f* of the Danites	Judg 18:11	4940
unto a tribe and a *f* in Israel	Judg 18:19	4940
man to his tribe and to his *f*	Judg 21:24	4940
of wealth, of the *f* of Elimelech	Ruth 2:1	4940
my *f* the least of all the	1Sa 9:21	4940
the *f* of Matri was taken, and Saul	1Sa 10:21	4940
life, or my father's *f* in Israel	1Sa 18:18	4940
sacrifice there for all the *f*	1Sa 20:6	4940
for our *f* hath a sacrifice in the	1Sa 20:29	4940
the whole *f* is risen against	2Sa 14:7	4940
man of the *f* of the house of Saul	2Sa 16:5	4940
neither did all their *f* multiply	1Chr 4:27	4940
were left of the *f* of that tribe	1Chr 6:61	4940
for the *f* of the remnant of the	1Chr 6:70	4940
f of the half tribe of Manasseh	1Chr 6:71	4940
ark of God remained with the *f* of	1Chr 13:14	1004
every generation, every *f*	Est 9:28	4940
you one of a city, and two of a *f*	Jer 3:14	4940
them that remain of this evil *f*	Jer 8:3	4940
against the whole *f* which I	Amos 3:1	4940
against this *f* do I devise an	Mic 2:3	4940
land shall mourn, every *f* apart	Zec 12:12	4940
the *f* of the house of David apart	Zec 12:12	4940
the *f* of the house of Nathan	Zec 12:12	4940
The *f* of the house of Levi apart,	Zec 12:13	4940
the *f* of Shimei apart, and their	Zec 12:13	4940
that remain, every *f* apart	Zec 12:14	4940
if the *f* of Egypt go not up, and	Zec 14:18	4940
Of whom the whole *f* in heaven	Eph 3:15	3965

FAMINE

And there was a *f* in the land	Gen 12:10	7458
for the *f* was grievous in the	Gen 12:10	7458
And there was a *f* in the land	Gen 26:1	7458
beside the first *f* that was in	Gen 26:1	7458
wind shall be seven years of *f*	Gen 41:27	7458
arise after them seven years of *f*	Gen 41:30	7458
the *f* shall consume the land	Gen 41:30	7458
by reason of that *f* following	Gen 41:31	7458
land against the seven years of *f*	Gen 41:36	7458
the land perish not through the *f*	Gen 41:36	7458
sons before the years of *f* came	Gen 41:50	7458
the *f* was over all the face of	Gen 41:56	7458
the *f* waxed sore in the land of	Gen 41:56	7458
because that the *f* was so sore in	Gen 41:57	7458
for the *f* was in the land of	Gen 42:5	7458
corn for the *f* of your houses	Gen 42:19	7459
take food for the *f* of your	Gen 42:33	7459
the *f* was sore in the land	Gen 43:1	7458
years hath the *f* been in the land	Gen 45:6	7458
for yet there are five years of *f*	Gen 45:11	7458
for the *f* is sore in the land of	Gen 47:4	7458
for the *f* was very sore, so that	Gen 47:13	7458
Canaan fainted by reason of the *f*	Gen 47:13	7458
because the *f* prevailed over them	Gen 47:20	7458
that there was a *f* in the land	Ruth 1:1	7458
Then there was a *f* in the days of	2Sa 21:1	7458
Shall seven years of *f* come unto	2Sa 24:13	7458
If there be in the land	1Kin 8:37	7458
And there was a sore *f* in Samaria	1Kin 18:2	7458
And there was a great *f* in Samaria	2Kin 6:25	7458
then the *f* is in the city, and we	2Kin 7:4	7458
for the LORD hath called for a *f*	2Kin 8:1	7458
month the *f* prevailed in the city	2Kin 25:3	7458
Either three years' *f*	1Chr 21:12	7458
judgment, or pestilence, or *f*	2Chr 20:9	7458
give over yourselves to die by *f*	2Chr 32:11	7458
In *f* he shall redeem thee from	Job 5:20	7458
destruction and *f* thou shalt laugh	Job 5:22	3720
For want and *f* they were solitary	Job 30:3	3720
death, and to keep them alive in *f*	Ps 33:19	7458
in the days of *f* they shall be	Ps 37:19	7459
he called for a *f* upon the land	Ps 105:16	7458
and I will kill thy root with *f*	Is 14:30	7458
and destruction, and the *f*	Is 51:19	7458
neither shall we see sword nor *f*	Jer 5:12	7458
and their daughters shall die by *f*	Jer 11:22	7458
them by the sword, and by the *f*	Jer 14:12	7458
sword, neither shall ye have *f*	Jer 14:13	7458
f shall not be in this land	Jer 14:15	7458
f shall those prophets be	Jer 14:15	7458
of Jerusalem because of the *f*	Jer 14:16	7458
behold them that are sick with *f*	Jer 14:18	7458
as are for the *f*, to the *f*	Jer 15:2	7458

be consumed by the sword, and by *f*	Jer 16:4	7458
up their children to the *f*	Jer 18:21	7458
from the sword, and from the *f*	Jer 21:7	7458
die by the sword, and by the *f*	Jer 21:9	7458
And I will send the sword, the *f*	Jer 24:10	7458
with the sword, and with the *f*	Jer 27:8	7458
people, by the sword, by the *f*	Jer 27:13	7458
send upon them the sword, the *f*	Jer 29:17	7458
them with the sword, with the *f*	Jer 29:18	7458
because of the sword, and of the *f*	Jer 32:24	7458
Babylon by the sword, and by the *f*	Jer 32:36	7458
to the pestilence, and by the *f*	Jer 34:17	7458
shall die by the sword, by the *f*	Jer 38:2	7458
in the land of Egypt, and the *f*	Jer 42:16	7458
shall die by the sword, by the *f*	Jer 42:17	7458
shall die by the sword, by the *f*	Jer 42:22	7458
consumed by the sword and by the *f*	Jer 44:12	7458
by the sword and by the *f*	Jer 44:12	7458
Jerusalem, by the sword, by the *f*	Jer 44:13	7458
consumed by the sword and by the *f*	Jer 44:18	7458
consumed by the sword and by the *f*	Jer 44:27	7458
the *f* was sore in the city, so	Jer 52:6	7458
an oven because of the terrible *f*	Lam 5:10	7458
with *f* shall they be consumed in	Eze 5:12	7458
upon them the evil arrows of *f*	Eze 5:16	7458
and I will increase the *f* upon you	Eze 5:16	7458
So will I send upon you *f*	Eze 5:17	7458
shall fall by the sword, by the *f*	Eze 6:11	7458
and is besieged shall die by the *f*	Eze 6:12	7458
and the pestilence and the *f* within	Eze 7:15	7458
and he that is in the city, *f*	Eze 7:15	7458
them from the sword, from the *f*	Eze 12:16	7458
thereof, and will send *f* upon it	Eze 14:13	7458
Jerusalem, the sword, and the *f*	Eze 14:21	7458
increase it, and lay no *f* upon you	Eze 36:29	7458
reproach of *f* among the heathen	Eze 36:30	7458
that I will send a *f* in the land	Amos 8:11	7458
not a *f* of bread, nor a thirst	Amos 8:11	7458
when great *f* was throughout all	Lk 4:25	3042
arose a mighty *f* in that land	Lk 15:14	3042
or distress, or persecution, or *f*	Rom 8:35	3042
one day, death, and mourning, and *f*	Rev 18:8	3042

FAMINES

and there shall be *f*, and	Mt 24:7	3042
places, and there shall be *f*	Mk 13:8	3042
shall be in divers places, and *f*	Lk 21:11	3042

FAMISH

the soul of the righteous to *f*	Prov 10:3	7456
for he will *f* all the gods of the	Zeph 2:11	7329

FAMISHED

when all the land of Egypt was *f*	Gen 41:55	7456
and their honourable men are *f*	Is 5:13	7458

FAMOUS

f in the congregation, men of	Num 16:2	7148
which were *f* in the congregation,	Num 26:9	7121
Ephratah, and be *f* in Beth-lehem	Ruth 4:11	8034
that his name may be *f* in Israel	Ruth 4:14	7121
f men, and heads of the house of	1Chr 5:24	8034
f throughout the house of their	1Chr 12:30	8034
A man was *f* according as he had	Ps 74:5	3045
And slew *f* kings	Ps 136:18	117
and she became *f* among women	Eze 23:10	8034
and the daughters of the *f* nations	Eze 32:18	117

FAN

with the shovel and with the *f*	Is 30:24	4214
Thou shalt *f* them, and the wind	Is 41:16	2219
daughter of my people, not to *f*	Jer 4:11	2219
I will *f* them with a *f* in the	Jer 15:7	2219
Babylon fanners, that shall *f* her	Jer 51:2	2219
Whose *f* is in his hand, and he	Mt 3:12	4425
Whose *f* is in his hand, and he	Lk 3:17	4425

FANNERS

And will send unto Babylon *f*	Jer 51:2	2114

FAR See APPENDIX.

FARE

and look how thy brethren *f*	1Sa 17:18	7965
so he paid the *f* thereof, and went	Jonah 1:3	7939
shall do well. *F* ye well	Acts 15:29	4517

FARED

linen, and *f* sumptuously every day	Lk 16:19	2165

FAREWELL

but let me first go bid them *f*	Lk 9:61	657
But bade them *f*, saying, I must	Acts 18:21	657
what they had against him. *F*	Acts 23:30	4517
Finally, brethren, *f*	2Cor 13:11	5463

F

FARM
and went their ways, one to his *f* .... Mt 22:5   68

FARTHER See APPENDIX.

FARTHING
thou hast paid the uttermost *f* .... Mt 5:26   2835
Are not two sparrows sold for a *f* .... Mt 10:29   787
in two mites, which make a *f* .... Mk 12:42   2835

FARTHINGS
not five sparrows sold for two *f* .... Lk 12:6   787

FASHION
this is the *f* which thou shalt .... Gen 6:15
f thereof which was shewed thee .... Ex 26:30   4941
the *f* of almonds in one branch .... Ex 37:19
and according to all the *f* of it 1Kin 6:38   4941
the priest the *f* of the altar 2Kin 16:10   1823
did not one *f* us in the womb .... Job 31:15   3559
the *f* thereof, and the goings out .... Eze 43:11   8498
saying, We never saw it on this *f* .... Mk 2:12   3778
the *f* of his countenance was .... Lk 9:29   1491
to the *f* that he had seen .... Acts 7:44   5179
for the *f* of this world passeth 1Cor 7:31   4976
And being found in *f* as a man .... Phil 2:8   4976
grace of the *f* of it perisheth .... Jas 1:11   4383

FASHIONED
f it with a graving tool, after .... Ex 32:4   3335
f me together round about .... Job 10:8   6213
Thy hands have made me and *f* me .... Ps 119:73   3559
which in continuance were *f* .... Ps 139:16   3335
unto him that *f* it long ago .... Is 22:11   3335
thy breasts are *f*, and thine hair .... Eze 16:7   3559
that it may be *f* like unto his .... Phil 3:21   4832

FASHIONETH
He *f* their hearts alike .... Ps 33:15   3335
f it with hammers, and worketh it .... Is 44:12   3335
the clay say to him that *f* it .... Is 45:9   3335

FASHIONING
not *f* yourselves according to the 1Pet 1:14   4964

FASHIONS
were both according to their *f* .... Eze 42:11   4941

FAST
For the LORD had *f* closed up all .... Gen 20:18
for he was *f* asleep and weary .... Judg 4:21
but we will bind thee *f*, and .... Judg 15:13
If they bind me *f* with new ropes .... Judg 16:11
but abide here *f* by my maidens .... Ruth 2:8
Thou shalt keep *f* by my young men ...... Ruth 2:21
So she kept *f* by the maidens of .... Ruth 2:23
thou didst *f* and weep for the 2Sa 12:21   6684
he is dead, wherefore should I *f* 2Sa 12:23   6684
the letters, saying, Proclaim a *f* 1Kin 21:9   6685
They proclaimed a *f*, and set 1Kin 21:12   6685
door, and hold him *f* at the door 2Kin 6:32
proclaimed a *f* throughout all 2Chr 20:3   6685
walls, and this work goeth *f* on .... Ezr 5:8   629
Then I proclaimed a *f* there .... Ezr 8:21   6685
f ye for me, and neither eat nor .... Est 4:16   6684
and my maidens will I *f* likewise .... Est 4:16   6684
still he holdeth *f* his integrity .... Job 2:3
he shall hold it *f*, but it shall .... Job 8:15
My righteousness I hold *f* .... Job 27:6
and the clods cleave *f* together .... Job 38:38
he commanded, and it stood *f* .... Ps 33:9
For thine arrows stick *f* in me .... Ps 38:2
say they, cleaveth *f* unto him .... Ps 41:8
strength setteth *f* the mountains .... Ps 65:6
covenant shall stand *f* with him .... Ps 89:28
They stand *f* for ever and ever, and ...... Ps 111:8
Take *f* hold of instruction .... Prov 4:13
day of your *f* ye find pleasure .... Is 58:3   6685
ye *f* for strife and debate, and to .... Is 58:4   6684
ye shall not *f* as ye do this day, ... Is 58:4   6684
Is it such a *f* that I have chosen .... Is 58:5   6685
wilt thou call this a *f*, and an .... Is 58:5   6685
Is not this the *f* that I have .... Is 58:6   6685
they hold *f* deceit, they refuse .... Jer 8:5
When they *f*, I will not hear .... Jer 14:12   6684
that they proclaimed a *f* before .... Jer 36:9   6685
say ye, Stand *f*, and prepare thee .... Jer 46:14
come, and his affliction hasteth *f* .... Jer 48:16   3966
took them captives held them *f* .... Jer 50:33
Sanctify ye a *f*, call a solemn .... Joel 1:14   6685
the trumpet in Zion, sanctify a *f* .... Joel 2:15   6685
and he lay, and was *f* asleep .... Jonah 1:5
believed God, and proclaimed a *f* .... Jonah 3:5   6685
years, did ye at all *f* unto me .... Zec 7:5   6684
The *f* of the fourth month, and the .... Zec 8:19   6685

the *f* of the fifth .... Zec 8:19   6685
the *f* of the seventh .... Zec 8:19   6685
and the *f* of .... Zec 8:19   6685
Moreover when ye *f*, be not, as ...... Mt 6:16   3522
they may appear unto men to *f* .... Mt 6:16   3522
thou appear not unto men to *f* .... Mt 6:18   3522
Why do we and the Pharisees *f* oft .... Mt 9:14   3522
f oft, but thy disciples *f* not .... Mt 9:14   3522
from them, and then shall they *f* .... Mt 9:15   3522
hold him *f* .... Mt 26:48
and of the Pharisees used to *f* .... Mk 2:18   3522
of John and of the Pharisees *f* .... Mk 2:18   3522
but thy disciples *f* not .... Mk 2:18   3522
children of the bridechamber *f* .... Mk 2:19   3522
with them, they cannot *f* .... Mk 2:19   3522
then shall they *f* in those days .... Mk 2:20   3522
do the disciples of John *f* often .... Lk 5:33   3522
children of the bridechamber *f* .... Lk 5:34   3522
then shall they *f* in those days .... Lk 5:35   3522
I *f* twice in the week, I give .... Lk 18:12   3522
made their feet *f* in the stocks .... Acts 16:24   805
because the *f* was now already .... Acts 27:9   3521
and the forepart stuck *f*, and .... Acts 27:41
stand *f* in the faith, quit you 1Cor 16:13
Stand *f* therefore in the liberty .... Gal 5:1
that ye stand *f* in one spirit .... Phil 1:27
so stand *f* in the Lord, my dearly .... Phil 4:1
live, if ye stand *f* in the Lord 1Th 3:8
hold *f* that which is good 1Th 5:21   2722
Therefore, brethren, stand *f* 2Th 2:15
Hold *f* the form of sound words, ... 2Ti 1:13
Holding *f* the faithful word as he .... Titus 1:9   472
if we hold *f* the confidence and .... Heb 3:6   2722
let us hold *f* our profession .... Heb 4:14
Let us hold *f* the profession of .... Heb 10:23   2722
and thou holdest *f* my name .... Rev 2:13
have already hold *f* till I come .... Rev 2:25
hast received and heard, and hold *f* ... Rev 3:3
hold that *f* which thou hast, that .... Rev 3:11

FASTED
f that day until even, and offered .... Judg 20:26   6684
f on that day, and said there, We 1Sa 7:6   6684
a tree at Jabesh, and *f* seven days 1Sa 31:13   6684
f until even, for Saul, and for 2Sa 1:12   6684
and David *f*, and went in, and lay 2Sa 12:16   6684
the child was yet alive, I *f* 2Sa 12:22   6684
sackcloth upon his flesh, and *f* 1Kin 21:27   6684
oak in Jabesh, and *f* seven days 1Chr 10:12   6684
So we *f* and besought our God for .... Ezr 8:23   6684
and mourned certain days, and *f* .... Neh 1:4   6684
Wherefore have we *f*, say they, and ..... Is 58:3   6684
to the priests, saying, When ye *f* .... Zec 7:5   6684
And when he had *f* forty days .... Mt 4:2   3522
they ministered to the Lord, and *f* .... Acts 13:2   3522
And when they had *f* and prayed, and ... Acts 13:3   3522

FASTEN
f the wreathen chains to the .... Ex 28:14   5414
thou shalt *f* in the two ouches .... Ex 28:25   5414
to *f* it on high upon the mitre .... Ex 39:31   5414
I will *f* him as a nail in a sure .... Is 22:23   8628
they *f* it with nails and with .... Jer 10:4   2388

FASTENED
chains they *f* in the two ouches .... Ex 39:18   5414
f his sockets, and set up the .... Ex 40:18   5414
temples, and *f* it into the ground .... Judg 4:21   6795
she *f* it with the pin, and said .... Judg 16:14   8628
they *f* his body to the wall of 1Sa 31:10   8628
f upon his loins in the sheath 2Sa 20:8   6775
be *f* in the walls of the house 1Kin 6:6   270
f his head in the temple of Dagon 1Chr 10:10   8628
which were *f* to the throne, and 2Chr 9:18   270
f with cords of fine linen and .... Est 1:6   270
are the foundations thereof *f* .... Job 38:6   2883
as nails *f* by the masters of .... Eccl 12:11   5193
shall the nail that is *f* in the .... Is 22:25   8628
he *f* it with nails, that it .... Is 41:7   2388
an hand broad, *f* round about .... Eze 40:43   3559
in the synagogue were *f* on him .... Lk 4:20   816
the which when I had *f* mine eyes .... Acts 11:6   816
out of the heat, and *f* on his hand ...... Acts 28:3   2510

FASTENING
f his eyes upon him with John, ... Acts 3:4   816

FASTEST
But thou, when thou *f*, anoint .... Mt 6:17   2522

FASTING
of Israel were assembled with *f* .... Neh 9:1   6685
mourning among the Jews, and *f* .... Est 4:3   6685
I humbled my soul with *f* .... Ps 35:13   6685

wept, and chastened my soul with *f*	Ps 69:10	6685
My knees are weak through *f*	Ps 109:24	6685
the LORD's house upon the *f* day	Jer 36:6	6685
his palace, and passed the night *f*	Dan 6:18	2908
prayer and supplications, with *f*	Dan 9:3	6685
me with all your heart, and with *f*	Joel 2:12	6685
and I will not send them away *f*	Mt 15:32	3523
goeth not out but by prayer and *f*	Mt 17:21	3521
them away *f* to their own houses	Mk 8:3	3523
by nothing, but by prayer and *f*	Mk 9:29	3521
days ago I was *f* until this hour	Acts 10:30	3522
church, and had prayed with *f*	Acts 14:23	3521
ye have tarried and continued *f*	Acts 27:33	777
that ye may give yourselves to *f*	1Cor 7:5	3521

FASTINGS

their seed, the matters of the *f*	Est 9:31	6685
the temple, but served God with *f*	Lk 2:37	3521
in labours, in watchings, in *f*	2Cor 6:5	3521
in *f* often, in cold and nakedness	2Cor 11:27	3521

FAT

of his flock and of the *f* thereof	Gen 4:4	2459
the seven well favoured and *f* kine	Gen 41:4	1277
did eat up the first seven *f* kine	Gen 41:20	1277
and ye shall eat the *f* of the land	Gen 45:18	2459
Out of Asher his bread shall be *f*	Gen 49:20	8082
neither shall the *f* of my	Ex 23:18	2459
thou shalt take all the *f* that	Ex 29:13	2459
the *f* that is upon them, and burn	Ex 29:13	2459
thou shalt take of the ram the *f*	Ex 29:22	2459
the *f* that covereth the inwards,	Ex 29:22	2459
the *f* that is upon them, and the	Ex 29:22	2459
lay the parts, the head, and the *f*	Lev 1:8	6309
pieces, with his head and his *f*	Lev 1:12	6309
the *f* that covereth the inwards,	Lev 3:3	2459
all the *f* that is upon the	Lev 3:3	2459
the *f* that is on them, which is	Lev 3:4	2459
the *f* thereof, and the whole rump,	Lev 3:9	2459
the *f* that covereth the inwards,	Lev 3:9	2459
all the *f* that is upon the	Lev 3:9	2459
the *f* that is upon them, which is	Lev 3:10	2459
the *f* that covereth the inwards,	Lev 3:14	2459
all the *f* that is upon the	Lev 3:14	2459
the *f* that is upon them, which is	Lev 3:15	2459
all the *f* is the LORD's	Lev 3:16	2459
that ye eat neither *f* nor blood	Lev 3:17	2459
the *f* of the bullock for the sin	Lev 4:8	2459
the *f* that covereth the inwards,	Lev 4:8	2459
all the *f* that is upon the	Lev 4:8	2459
the *f* that is upon them, which is	Lev 4:9	2459
he shall take all his *f* from him	Lev 4:19	2459
burn all his *f* upon the altar	Lev 4:26	2459
as the *f* of the sacrifice of	Lev 4:26	2459
shall take away all the *f* thereof	Lev 4:31	2459
as the *f* is taken away from off	Lev 4:31	2459
shall take away all the *f* thereof	Lev 4:35	2459
as the *f* of the lamb is taken	Lev 4:35	2459
the *f* of the peace offerings	Lev 6:12	2459
offer of it all the *f* thereof	Lev 7:3	2459
the *f* that covereth the inwards,	Lev 7:3	2459
the *f* that is on them, which is	Lev 7:4	2459
Ye shall eat no manner of *f*	Lev 7:23	2459
the *f* of the beast that dieth of	Lev 7:24	2459
the *f* of that which is torn with	Lev 7:24	2459
eateth the *f* of the beast	Lev 7:25	2459
the *f* with the breast, it shall	Lev 7:30	2459
shall burn the *f* upon the altar	Lev 7:31	2459
of the peace offerings, and the *f*	Lev 7:33	2459
he took all the *f* that was upon	Lev 8:16	2459
and the two kidneys, and their *f*	Lev 8:16	2459
the head, and the pieces, and the *f*	Lev 8:20	6309
And he took the *f*, and the rump, and	Lev 8:25	2459
all the *f* that was upon the	Lev 8:25	2459
and the two kidneys, and their *f*	Lev 8:25	2459
one wafer, and put them on the *f*	Lev 8:26	2459
But the *f*, and the kidneys, and the	Lev 9:10	2459
the *f* of the bullock and of the	Lev 9:19	2459
they put the *f* upon the breasts,	Lev 9:20	2459
he burnt the *f* upon the altar	Lev 9:20	2459
altar the burnt offering and the *f*	Lev 9:24	2459
offerings made by fire of the *f*	Lev 10:15	2459
the *f* of the sin offering shall	Lev 16:25	2459
burn the *f* for a sweet savour	Lev 17:6	2459
land is, whether it be *f* or lean	Num 13:20	8082
shalt burn their *f* for an	Num 18:17	2459
and filled themselves, and waxen *f*	Deut 31:20	1878
with *f* of lambs, and rams of the	Deut 32:14	2459
with the *f* of kidneys of wheat	Deut 32:14	2459
But Jeshurun waxed *f*, and kicked	Deut 32:15	8080
thou art waxen *f*, thou art grown	Deut 32:15	8080
Which did eat the *f* of their	Deut 32:38	2459

and Eglon was a very *f* man	Judg 3:17	1277
the *f* closed upon the blade, so	Judg 3:22	2459
Also before they burnt the *f*	1Sa 2:15	2459
not fail to burn the *f* presently	1Sa 2:16	2459
to make yourselves *f* with the	1Sa 2:29	1254
and to hearken than the *f* of rams	1Sa 15:22	2459
the woman had a *f* calf in the	1Sa 28:24	4770
from the *f* of the mighty, the bow	2Sa 1:22	2459
f cattle by the stone of Zoheleth	1Kin 1:9	4806
f cattle and sheep in abundance,	1Kin 1:19	4806
f cattle and sheep in abundance,	1Kin 1:25	4806
Ten *f* oxen, and twenty oxen out of	1Kin 4:23	1277
the *f* of the peace offerings	1Kin 8:64	2459
the *f* of the peace offerings	1Kin 8:64	2459
And they found *f* pasture and good,	1Chr 4:40	8082
the *f* of the peace offerings,	2Chr 7:7	2459
and the meat offerings, and the *f*	2Chr 7:7	2459
with the *f* of the peace offerings	2Chr 29:35	2459
offerings and the *f* until night	2Chr 35:14	2459
unto them, Go your way, eat the *f*	Neh 8:10	4924
a *f* land, and possessed houses	Neh 9:25	8082
eat, and were filled, and became *f*	Neh 9:25	8082
f land which thou gavest before	Neh 9:35	8082
maketh collops of *f* on his flanks	Job 15:27	6371
They are inclosed in their own *f*	Ps 17:10	2459
All they that be *f* upon earth	Ps 22:29	1879
LORD shall be as the *f* of lambs	Ps 37:20	3368
they shall be *f* and flourishing	Ps 92:14	1879
Their heart is as *f* as grease	Ps 119:70	2954
The liberal soul shall be made *f*	Prov 11:25	1878
of the diligent shall be made *f*	Prov 13:4	1878
a good report maketh the bones *f*	Prov 15:30	1878
trust in the LORD shall be made *f*	Prov 28:25	1878
of rams, and the *f* of fed beasts	Is 1:11	2459
the waste places of the *f* ones	Is 5:17	4220
Make the heart of this people *f*	Is 6:10	8082
send among his *f* ones leanness	Is 10:16	4924
all people a feast of *f* things	Is 25:6	8081
of *f* things full of marrow, of	Is 25:6	8081
of the *f* valleys of them that are	Is 28:1	8081
is on the head of the *f* valley	Is 28:4	8081
of the earth, and it shall be *f*	Is 30:23	1879
it is made *f* with fatness, and	Is 34:6	1878
with the *f* of the kidneys of rams	Is 34:6	2459
and their dust made *f* with fatness	Is 34:7	1878
me with the *f* of thy sacrifices	Is 43:24	2459
in drought, and make *f* thy bones	Is 58:11	2502
They are waxen *f*, they shine	Jer 5:28	8080
because ye are grown *f* as the	Jer 50:11	6335
Ye eat the *f*, and ye clothe you	Eze 34:3	2459
in a *f* pasture shall they feed	Eze 34:14	8082
but I will destroy the *f* and the	Eze 34:16	8082
will judge between the *f* cattle	Eze 34:20	1277
ye shall eat *f* till ye be full,	Eze 39:19	2459
when ye offer my bread, the *f*	Eze 44:7	2459
before me to offer unto me the *f*	Eze 44:15	2459
out of the *f* pastures of Israel	Eze 45:15	4945
peace offerings of your *f* beasts	Amos 5:22	4806
by them their portion is *f*	Hab 1:16	8082
he shall eat the flesh of the *f*	Zec 11:16	1277

FATFLESHED

seven well favoured kine and *f*	Gen 41:2	1277
up out of the river seven kine, *f*	Gen 41:18	1277

FATHER

Therefore shall a man leave his *f*	Gen 2:24	1
he was the *f* of such as dwell in	Gen 4:20	1
he was the *f* of all such as	Gen 4:21	1
and Ham is the *f* of Canaan	Gen 9:18	1
And Ham, the *f* of Canaan	Gen 9:22	1
saw the nakedness of his *f*	Gen 9:22	1
covered the nakedness of their *f*	Gen 9:23	1
the *f* of all the children of Eber	Gen 10:21	1
Haran died before his *f* Terah in	Gen 11:28	1
the *f* of Milcah, and the *f*	Gen 11:29	1
thou shalt be a *f* of many nations	Gen 17:4	1
for a *f* of many nations have I	Gen 17:5	1
Our *f* is old, and there is not a	Gen 19:31	1
let us make our *f* drink wine	Gen 19:32	1
we may preserve seed of our *f*	Gen 19:32	1
they made their *f* drink wine that	Gen 19:33	1
went in, and lay with her *f*	Gen 19:33	1
I lay yesternight with my *f*	Gen 19:34	1
we may preserve seed of our *f*	Gen 19:34	1
they made their *f* drink wine that	Gen 19:35	1
of Lot with child by their *f*	Gen 19:36	1
the same is the *f* of the Moabites	Gen 19:37	1
the same is the *f* of the children	Gen 19:38	1
she is the daughter of my *f*	Gen 20:12	1
Abraham his *f*, and said, My *f*	Gen 22:7	1
brother, and Kemuel the *f* of Aram	Gen 22:21	1

which I sware unto Abraham thy *f*	Gen 26:3	1
in the days of Abraham his *f*	Gen 26:15	1
in the days of Abraham his *f*	Gen 26:18	1
by which his *f* had called them	Gen 26:18	1
I am the God of Abraham thy *f*	Gen 26:24	1
I heard thy *f* speak unto Esau thy	Gen 27:6	1
make them savoury meat for thy *f*	Gen 27:9	1
And thou shalt bring it to thy *f*	Gen 27:10	1
My *f* peradventure will feel me	Gen 27:12	1
savoury meat, such as his *f* loved	Gen 27:14	1
unto his *f*, and said, My *f*	Gen 27:18	1
And Jacob said unto his *f*, I am	Gen 27:19	1
Jacob went near unto Isaac his *f*	Gen 27:22	1
his *f* Isaac said unto him, Come	Gen 27:26	1
from the presence of Isaac his *f*	Gen 27:30	1
his *f*, and said unto his *f*	Gen 27:31	1
unto his *f*, Let my *f* arise	Gen 27:31	1
Isaac his *f* said unto him, Who	Gen 27:32	1
Esau heard the words of his *f*	Gen 27:34	1
bitter cry, and said unto his *f*	Gen 27:34	1
Bless me, even me also, O my *f*	Gen 27:34	1
And Esau said unto his *f*	Gen 27:38	1
Hast thou but one blessing, my *f*	Gen 27:38	1
bless me, even me also, O my *f*	Gen 27:38	1
And Isaac his *f* answered and said	Gen 27:39	1
wherewith his *f* blessed him	Gen 27:41	1
of mourning for my *f* are at hand	Gen 27:41	1
house of Bethuel thy mother's *f*	Gen 28:2	1
And that Jacob obeyed his *f*	Gen 28:7	1
of Canaan pleased not Isaac his *f*	Gen 28:8	1
am the LORD God of Abraham thy *f*	Gen 28:13	1
and she ran and told her *f*	Gen 29:12	1
the God of my *f* hath been with me	Gen 31:5	1
all my power I have served your *f*	Gen 31:6	1
your *f* hath deceived me, and	Gen 31:7	1
taken away the cattle of your *f*	Gen 31:9	1
which God hath taken from our *f*	Gen 31:16	1
Isaac his *f* in the land of Canaan	Gen 31:18	1
but the God of your *f* spake unto	Gen 31:29	1
And she said to her *f*, Let it not	Gen 31:35	1
Except the God of my *f*, the God	Gen 31:42	1
God of Nahor, the God of their *f*	Gen 31:53	1
sware by the fear of his *f* Isaac	Gen 31:53	1
Jacob said, O God of my *f* Abraham	Gen 32:9	1
and God of my *f* Isaac	Gen 32:9	1
children of Hamor, Shechem's *f*	Gen 33:19	1
And Shechem spake unto his *f* Hamor	Gen 34:4	1
Hamor the *f* of Shechem went out	Gen 34:6	1
And Shechem said unto her *f*	Gen 34:11	1
Hamor his *f* deceitfully, and said,	Gen 34:13	1
than all the house of his *f*	Gen 34:19	1
but his *f* called him Benjamin	Gen 35:18	1
came unto Isaac his *f* unto Mamre	Gen 35:27	1
f of the Edomites in mount Seir	Gen 36:9	1
he fed the asses of Zibeon his *f*	Gen 36:24	1
he is Esau the *f* of the Edomites	Gen 36:43	1
land wherein his *f* was a stranger	Gen 37:1	1
unto his *f* their evil report	Gen 37:2	1
f loved him more than all his	Gen 37:4	1
And he told it to his *f*, and to his	Gen 37:10	1
his *f* rebuked him, and said unto	Gen 37:10	1
but his *f* observed the saying	Gen 37:11	1
to deliver him to his *f* again	Gen 37:22	1
and they brought it to their *f*	Gen 37:32	1
Thus his *f* wept for him	Gen 37:35	1
Behold thy *f* in law goeth up to	Gen 38:13	2524
forth, she sent to her *f* in law	Gen 38:25	2524
youngest is this day with our *f*	Gen 42:13	1
their *f* unto the land of Canaan	Gen 42:29	1
be twelve brethren, sons of our *f*	Gen 42:32	1
with our *f* in the land of Canaan	Gen 42:32	1
their *f* saw the bundles of money,	Gen 42:35	1
Jacob their *f* said unto them, Me	Gen 42:36	1
And Reuben spake unto his *f*	Gen 42:37	1
their *f* said unto them, Go again,	Gen 43:2	1
saying, Is your *f* yet alive	Gen 43:7	1
And Judah said unto Israel his *f*	Gen 43:8	1
their *f* Israel said unto them, If	Gen 43:11	1
your God, and the God of your *f*	Gen 43:23	1
welfare, and said, Is your *f* well	Gen 43:27	1
Thy servant our *f* is in good	Gen 43:28	1
get you up in peace unto your *f*	Gen 44:17	1
his servants, saying, Have ye a *f*	Gen 44:19	1
we said unto my lord, We have a *f*	Gen 44:20	1
his mother, and his *f* loveth him	Gen 44:20	1
lord, The lad cannot leave his *f*	Gen 44:22	1
leave his *f*, his *f* would die	Gen 44:22	1
we came up unto thy servant my *f*	Gen 44:24	1
our *f* said, Go again, and buy us a	Gen 44:25	1
And thy servant my *f* said unto us	Gen 44:27	1
when I come to thy servant my *f*	Gen 44:30	1

our *f* with sorrow to the grave	Gen 44:31	1
surety for the lad unto my *f*	Gen 44:32	1
bear the blame to my *f* for ever	Gen 44:32	1
For how shall I go up to my *f*	Gen 44:34	1
the evil that shall come on my *f*	Gen 44:34	1
doth my *f* yet live	Gen 45:3	1
and he hath made me a *f* to Pharaoh	Gen 45:8	1
Haste ye, and go up to my *f*	Gen 45:9	1
ye shall tell my *f* of all my	Gen 45:13	1
haste and bring down my *f* hither	Gen 45:13	1
And take your *f* and your households	Gen 45:18	1
for your wives, and bring your *f*	Gen 45:19	1
to his *f* he sent after this	Gen 45:23	1
and meat for his *f* by the way	Gen 45:23	1
land of Canaan unto Jacob their *f*	Gen 45:25	1
spirit of Jacob their *f* revived	Gen 45:27	1
unto the God of his *f* Isaac	Gen 46:1	1
said, I am God, the God of thy *f*	Gen 46:3	1
of Israel carried Jacob their *f*	Gen 46:5	1
and went up to meet Israel his *f*	Gen 46:29	1
and told Pharaoh, and said, My *f*	Gen 47:1	1
spake unto Joseph, saying, Thy *f*	Gen 47:5	1
the best of the land make thy *f*	Gen 47:6	1
And Joseph brought in Jacob his *f*	Gen 47:7	1
And Joseph placed his *f* and his	Gen 47:11	1
And Joseph nourished his *f*	Gen 47:12	1
Joseph, Behold, thy *f* is sick	Gen 48:1	1
And Joseph said unto his *f*	Gen 48:9	1
when Joseph saw that his *f* laid	Gen 48:17	1
unto his *f*, Not so, my *f*	Gen 48:18	1
his *f* refused, and said, I know it	Gen 48:19	1
and hearken unto Israel your *f*	Gen 49:2	1
Even by the God of thy *f*, who	Gen 49:25	1
The blessings of thy *f* have	Gen 49:26	1
it that their *f* spake unto them	Gen 49:28	1
the physicians to embalm his *f*	Gen 50:2	1
My *f* made me swear, saying, Lo, I	Gen 50:5	1
go up, I pray thee, and bury my *f*	Gen 50:5	1
said, Go up, and bury thy *f*	Gen 50:6	1
And Joseph went up to bury his *f*	Gen 50:7	1
a mourning for his *f* seven days	Gen 50:10	1
went up with him to bury his *f*	Gen 50:14	1
after he had buried his *f*	Gen 50:14	1
saw that their *f* was dead	Gen 50:15	1
Thy *f* did command before he died,	Gen 50:16	1
the servants of the God of thy *f*	Gen 50:17	1
when they came to Reuel their *f*	Ex 2:18	1
the flock of Jethro his *f* in law	Ex 3:1	2859
he said, I am the God of thy *f*	Ex 3:6	1
returned to Jethro his *f* in law	Ex 4:18	2859
priest of Midian, Moses' *f* in law	Ex 18:1	2859
Then Jethro, Moses' *f* in law	Ex 18:2	2859
for the God of my *f*, said he, was	Ex 18:4	1
And Jethro, Moses' *f* in law	Ex 18:5	2859
I thy *f* in law Jethro am come	Ex 18:6	2859
went out to meet his *f* in law	Ex 18:7	2859
Moses told his *f* in law all that	Ex 18:8	2859
And Jethro, Moses' *f* in law	Ex 18:12	2859
with Moses' *f* in law before God	Ex 18:12	2859
when Moses' *f* in law saw all that	Ex 18:14	2859
And Moses said unto his *f* in law	Ex 18:15	2859
Moses' *f* in law said unto him,	Ex 18:17	2589
to the voice of his *f* in law	Ex 18:24	2859
And Moses let his *f* in law depart	Ex 18:27	2859
Honour thy *f* and thy mother	Ex 20:12	1
And he that smiteth his *f*, or his	Ex 21:15	1
And he that curseth his *f*, or his	Ex 21:17	1
If her *f* utterly refuse to give	Ex 22:17	1
as thou didst anoint their *f*	Ex 40:15	1
The nakedness of thy *f*, or the	Lev 18:7	1
thy sister, the daughter of thy *f*	Lev 18:9	1
daughter, begotten of thy *f*	Lev 18:11	1
every man his mother, and his *f*	Lev 19:3	1
f or his mother shall be surely	Lev 20:9	1
hath cursed his *f* or his mother	Lev 20:9	1
is, for his mother, and for his *f*	Lev 21:2	1
the whore, she profaneth her *f*	Lev 21:9	1
nor defile himself for his *f*	Lev 21:11	1
whose *f* was an Egyptian, went out	Lev 24:10	1121
in the sight of Aaron their *f*	Num 3:4	1
the *f* of the Gershonites shall be	Num 3:24	1
of the *f* of the families of the	Num 3:30	1
f of the families of Merari shall	Num 3:35	1
make himself unclean for his *f*	Num 6:7	1
the Midianite, Moses' *f* in law	Num 10:29	2859
as a nursing *f* beareth the	Num 11:12	1
If her *f* had but spit in her face	Num 12:14	1
tribe of Levi, the tribe of thy *f*	Num 18:2	1
Our *f* died in the wilderness, and	Num 27:3	1
Why should the name of our *f* be	Num 27:4	1
among the brethren of our *f*	Num 27:4	1

of their *f* to pass unto them	Num 27:7	1
if his *f* have no brethren, then	Num 27:11	1
her *f* hear her vow, and her bond	Num 30:4	1
her *f* shall hold his peace at her	Num 30:4	1
But if her *f* disallow her in the	Num 30:5	1
because her *f* disallowed her	Num 30:5	1
a man and his wife, between the *f*.	Num 30:16	1
tribe of their *f* shall they marry	Num 36:6	1
the family of the tribe of her *f*	Num 36:8	1
tribe of the family of their *f*	Num 36:12	1
Honour thy *f* and thy mother, as	Deut 5:16	1
in thine house, and bewail her *f*	Deut 21:13	1
will not obey the voice of his *f*	Deut 21:18	1
Then shall his *f* and his mother	Deut 21:19	1
Then shall the *f* of the damsel	Deut 22:15	1
the damsel's *f* shall say unto the	Deut 22:16	1
them unto the *f* of the damsel	Deut 22:19	1
f fifty shekels of silver	Deut 22:29	1
A Syrian ready to perish was my *f*	Deut 26:5	1
light by his *f* or his mother	Deut 27:16	1
his sister, the daughter of his *f*	Deut 27:22	1
is not he thy *f* that hath bought	Deut 32:6	1
ask thy *f*, and he will shew thee	Deut 32:7	1
Who said unto his *f* and to his	Deut 33:9	1
And that ye will save alive my *f*	Josh 2:13	1
and thou shalt bring thy *f*	Josh 2:18	1
and brought out Rahab, and her *f*	Josh 6:23	1
the city of Arba the *f* of Anak	Josh 15:13	1
moved him to ask of her *f* a field	Josh 15:18	1
of Manasseh, the *f* of Gilead	Josh 17:1	1
among the brethren of their *f*	Josh 17:4	1
after the name of Dan their *f*	Josh 19:47	1
the city of Arba the *f* of Anak	Josh 21:11	1
the *f* of Abraham, and the *f*	Josh 24:2	1
I took your *f* Abraham from the	Josh 24:3	1
the *f* of Shechem for an hundred	Josh 24:32	1
moved him to ask of her *f* a field	Judg 1:14	1
of the Kenite, Moses' *f* in law	Judg 1:16	2859
of Hobab the *f* in law of Moses	Judg 4:11	2859
the altar of Baal that thy *f* hath	Judg 6:25	1
in the sepulchre of Joash his *f*	Judg 8:32	1
of the house of his mother's *f*	Judg 9:1	1
(For my *f* fought for you, and	Judg 9:17	1
the men of Hamor the *f* of Shechem	Judg 9:28	1
which he did unto his *f*, in	Judg 9:56	1
And she said unto him, My *f*	Judg 11:36	1
And she said unto her *f*, Let this	Judg 11:37	1
that she returned unto her *f*	Judg 11:39	1
And he came up, and told his *f*	Judg 14:2	1
Then his *f* and his mother said	Judg 14:3	1
And Samson said unto his *f*	Judg 14:3	1
But his *f* and his mother knew not	Judg 14:4	1
Then went Samson down, and his *f*	Judg 14:5	1
but he told not his *f* or his	Judg 14:6	1
went on eating, and came to his *f*	Judg 14:9	1
So his *f* went down unto the woman	Judg 14:10	1
not told it my *f* nor my mother	Judg 14:16	1
But her *f* would not suffer him to	Judg 15:1	1
her *f* said, I verily thought that	Judg 15:2	1
and burnt her and her *f* with fire	Judg 15:6	1
all the house of his *f* came down	Judg 16:31	1
the buryingplace of Manoah his *f*	Judg 16:31	1
Dwell with me, and be unto me a *f*	Judg 17:10	1
and go with us, and be to us a *f*	Judg 18:19	1
after the name of Dan their *f*	Judg 18:29	1
when the *f* of the damsel saw him,	Judg 19:3	1
his *f* in law, the damsel's *f*	Judg 19:4	2859
his *f* in law, the damsel's *f*	Judg 19:4	1
the damsel's *f* said unto his son	Judg 19:5	1
for the damsel's *f* had said unto	Judg 19:6	1
to depart, his *f* in law urged him	Judg 19:7	2859
and the damsel's *f* said, Comfort	Judg 19:8	1
his *f* in law, the damsel's *f*	Judg 19:9	2859
his *f* in law, the damsel's *f*	Judg 19:9	1
and how thou hast left thy *f*	Ruth 2:11	1
f of Jesse, the *f* of David	Ruth 4:17	1
not unto the voice of their *f*	1Sa 2:25	1
appear unto the house of thy *f*	1Sa 2:27	1
I give unto the house of thy *f*	1Sa 2:28	1
thy house, and the house of thy *f*	1Sa 2:30	1
was taken, and that her *f* in law	1Sa 4:19	2524
taken, and because of her *f* in law	1Sa 4:21	2524
asses of Kish Saul's *f* were lost	1Sa 9:3	1
lest my *f* leave caring for the	1Sa 9:5	1
thy *f* hath left the care of the	1Sa 10:2	1
and said, But who is their *f*	1Sa 10:12	1
But he told not his *f*	1Sa 14:1	1
his *f* charged the people with the	1Sa 14:27	1
Thy *f* straitly charged the people	1Sa 14:28	1
My *f* hath troubled the land	1Sa 14:29	1
And Kish was the *f* of Saul	1Sa 14:51	1

Ner the *f* of Abner was the son of	1Sa 14:51	1
Saul my *f* seeketh to kill thee	1Sa 19:2	1
stand beside my *f* in the field	1Sa 19:3	1
I will commune with my *f* of thee	1Sa 19:3	1
good of David unto Saul his *f*.	1Sa 19:4	1
and what is my sin before thy *f*	1Sa 20:1	1
my *f* will do nothing either great	1Sa 20:2	1
why should my *f* hide this thing	1Sa 20:2	1
Thy *f* certainly knoweth that I	1Sa 20:3	1
If thy *f* at all miss me, then say	1Sa 20:6	1
shouldest thou bring me to thy *f*	1Sa 20:8	1
by my *f* to come upon thee	1Sa 20:9	1
or what if thy *f* answer thee	1Sa 20:10	1
when I have sounded my *f* about to	1Sa 20:12	1
if it please my *f* to do thee evil	1Sa 20:13	1
thee, as he hath been with my *f*	1Sa 20:13	1
And Jonathan answered Saul his *f*	1Sa 20:32	1
determined of his *f* to slay David	1Sa 20:33	1
because his *f* had done him shame	1Sa 20:34	1
unto the king of Moab, Let my *f*	1Sa 22:3	1
nor to all the house of my *f*	1Sa 22:15	1
of Saul my *f* shall not find thee	1Sa 23:17	1
and that also Saul my *f* knoweth	1Sa 23:17	1
Moreover, my *f*, see, yea, see the	1Sa 24:11	1
him in the sepulchre of his *f*	2Sa 2:32	1
day unto the house of Saul thy *f*	2Sa 3:8	1
LORD, which chose me before thy *f*	2Sa 6:21	1
I will be his *f*, and he shall be	2Sa 7:14	1
thee all the land of Saul thy *f*	2Sa 9:7	1
as his *f* shewed kindness unto me	2Sa 10:2	1
hand of his servants for his *f*	2Sa 10:2	1
thou that David doth honour thy *f*	2Sa 10:3	1
when thy *f* cometh to see thee,	2Sa 13:5	1
restore me the kingdom of my *f*	2Sa 16:3	1
that thou art abhorred of thy *f*	2Sa 16:21	1
said Hushai, thou knowest thy *f*	2Sa 17:8	1
thy *f* is a man of war, and will	2Sa 17:8	1
that thy *f* is a mighty man	2Sa 17:10	1
buried in the sepulchre of his *f*	2Sa 17:23	1
and be buried by the grave of my *f*	2Sa 19:37	1
in the sepulchre of Kish his *f*	2Sa 21:14	1
his *f* had not displeased him at	1Kin 1:6	1
upon the throne of David his *f*	1Kin 2:12	1
me on the throne of David my *f*	1Kin 2:24	1
of the Lord GOD before David my *f*	1Kin 2:26	1
in all wherein my *f* was afflicted	1Kin 2:26	1
me, and from the house of my *f*	1Kin 2:31	1
my *f* David not knowing thereof,	1Kin 2:32	1
to, that thou didst to David my *f*	1Kin 2:44	1
in the statutes of David my *f*	1Kin 3:3	1
servant David my *f* great mercy	1Kin 3:6	1
king instead of David my *f*	1Kin 3:7	1
as thy *f* David did walk, then I	1Kin 3:14	1
him king in the room of his *f*	1Kin 5:1	1
f could not build an house unto	1Kin 5:3	1
as the LORD spake unto David my *f*	1Kin 5:5	1
which I spake unto David thy *f*	1Kin 6:12	1
his *f* was a man of Tyre, a worker	1Kin 7:14	1
which David his *f* had dedicated	1Kin 7:51	1
with his mouth unto David my *f*	1Kin 8:15	1
f to build an house for the name	1Kin 8:17	1
And the LORD said unto David my *f*	1Kin 8:18	1
up in the room of David my *f*	1Kin 8:20	1
my *f* that thou promisedst him	1Kin 8:24	1
my *f* that thou promisedst him	1Kin 8:25	1
unto thy servant David my *f*	1Kin 8:26	1
before me, as David thy *f* walked	1Kin 9:4	1
as I promised to David thy *f*	1Kin 9:5	1
as was the heart of David his *f*	1Kin 11:4	1
the LORD, as did David his *f*	1Kin 11:6	1
of the city of David his *f*	1Kin 11:27	1
my judgments, as did David his *f*	1Kin 11:33	1
buried in the city of David his *f*	1Kin 11:43	1
Thy *f* made our yoke grievous	1Kin 12:4	1
the grievous service of thy *f*	1Kin 12:4	1
Solomon his *f* while he yet lived	1Kin 12:6	1
thy *f* did put upon us lighter	1Kin 12:9	1
Thy *f* made our yoke heavy, but	1Kin 12:10	1
now whereas my *f* did lade you	1Kin 12:11	1
my *f* hath chastised you with	1Kin 12:11	1
My *f* made your yoke heavy, and I	1Kin 12:14	1
my *f* also chastised you with	1Kin 12:14	1
them they told also to their *f*	1Kin 13:11	1
their *f* said unto them, What way	1Kin 13:12	1
walked in all the sins of his *f*	1Kin 15:3	1
God, as the heart of David his *f*	1Kin 15:3	1
of the LORD, as did David his *f*	1Kin 15:11	1
things which his *f* had dedicated	1Kin 15:15	1
and between my *f* and thy *f*	1Kin 15:19	1
in the city of David his *f*	1Kin 15:24	1
and walked in the way of his *f*	1Kin 15:26	1

F

Let me, I pray thee, kiss my *f* 1Kin 19:20   1
which my *f* took from thy *f*...................1Kin 20:34   1
Damascus, as my *f* made in Samaria....1Kin 20:34   1
in all the ways of Asa his *f*...................1Kin 22:43   1
remained in the days of his *f* Asa...........1Kin 22:46   1
in the city of David his *f*.......................1Kin 22:50   1
and walked in the way of his *f*...............1Kin 22:52   1
to all that his *f* had done......................1Kin 22:53   1
it, and he cried, My *f*, my *f*..................2Kin 2:12   1
but not like his *f*..................................2Kin 3:2   1
image of Baal that his *f* had made........2Kin 3:2   1
get thee to the prophets of thy *f*...........2Kin 3:13   1
went out to his *f* to the reapers...........2Kin 4:18   1
And he said unto his *f*, My head,.........2Kin 4:19   1
and spake unto him, and said, My *f*......2Kin 5:13   1
Elisha, when he saw them, My *f*............2Kin 6:21   1
rode together after Ahab his *f*...............2Kin 9:25   1
face, and said, O my *f*, my *f*.............2Kin 13:14   1
the hand of Jehoahaz his *f* by war.......2Kin 13:25   1
LORD, yet not like David his *f*.............2Kin 14:3   1
to all things as Joash his *f* did...........2Kin 14:3   1
which had slain the king his *f*..............2Kin 14:5   1
him king instead of his *f* Amaziah........2Kin 14:21   1
all that his *f* Amaziah had done...........2Kin 15:3   1
to all that his *f* Uzziah had done.........2Kin 15:34   1
in the city of David his *f*......................2Kin 15:38   1
LORD his God, like David his *f*.............2Kin 16:2   1
to all that David his *f* did....................2Kin 18:3   1
the LORD, the God of David thy *f*.........2Kin 20:5   1
Hezekiah his *f* had destroyed...............2Kin 21:3   1
the LORD, as his *f* Manasseh did..........2Kin 21:20   1
all the way that his *f* walked in...........2Kin 21:21   1
the idols that his *f* served...................2Kin 21:21   1
in all the way of David his *f*................2Kin 22:2   1
king in the room of Josiah his *f*............2Kin 23:34   1
to all that his *f* had done.....................2Kin 24:9   1
the *f* of Amasa was Jether the 1Chr 2:17   1
of Machir the *f* of Gilead....................1Chr 2:21   1
sons of Machir the *f* of Gilead.............1Chr 2:23   1
bare him Ashur the *f* of Tekoa.............1Chr 2:24   1
which was the *f* of Ziph.......................1Chr 2:42   1
sons of Mareshah the *f* of Hebron.........1Chr 2:42   1
begat Raham, the *f* of Jorkoam............1Chr 2:44   1
and Maon was the *f* of Beth-zur...........1Chr 2:45   1
also Shaaph the *f* of Madmannah..........1Chr 2:49   1
Sheva the *f* of Machbenah, and the......1Chr 2:49   1
of Machbenah, and the *f* of Gibea........1Chr 2:49   1
Shobal the *f* of Kirjath-jearim.............1Chr 2:50   1
Salma the *f* of Beth-lehem...................1Chr 2:51   1
Hareph the *f* of Beth-gader..................1Chr 2:51   1
Shobal the *f* of Kirjath-jearim.............1Chr 2:52   1
the *f* of the house of Rechab................1Chr 2:55   1
And these were the *f* of Etam 1Chr 4:3   1
And Penuel the *f* of Gedor, and Ezer 1Chr 4:4   1
of Gedor, and Ezer the *f* of Hushah.......1Chr 4:4   1
of Ephratah, the *f* of Beth-lehem..........1Chr 4:4   1
Ashur the *f* of Tekoa had two..............1Chr 4:5   1
Mehir, which was the *f* of Eshton..........1Chr 4:11   1
and Tehinnah the *f* of Ir-nahash...........1Chr 4:12   1
the *f* of the valley of Charashim...........1Chr 4:14   1
and Ishbah the *f* of Eshtemoa..............1Chr 4:17   1
bare Jered the *f* of Gedor 1Chr 4:18   1
and Heber the *f* of Socho.....................1Chr 4:18   1
and Jekuthiel the *f* of Zanoah..............1Chr 4:18   1
the *f* of Keilah the Garmite, and..........1Chr 4:19   1
Er the *f* of Lecah...............................1Chr 4:21   1
Laadah the *f* of Mareshah, and the 1Chr 4:21   1
bare Machir the *f* of Gilead..................1Chr 7:14   1
Ephraim their *f* mourned many days 1Chr 7:22   1
who is the *f* of Birzavith.....................1Chr 7:31   1
at Gibeon dwelt the *f* of Gibeon 1Chr 8:29   25
brethren, of the house of his *f*.............1Chr 9:19   1
in Gibeon dwelt the *f* of Gibeon 1Chr 9:35   25
I will be his *f*, and he shall be 1Chr 17:13   25
because his *f* shewed kindness to.........1Chr 19:2   25
to comfort him concerning his *f*...........1Chr 19:2   25
thou that David doth honour thy *f*........1Chr 19:3   25
be my son, and I will be his *f*.............1Chr 22:10   25
and Abihu died before their *f*...............1Chr 24:2   25
their manner, under Aaron their *f*.........1Chr 24:19   25
the hands of their *f* Jeduthun..............1Chr 25:3   25
f for song in the house of the..............1Chr 25:6   25
throughout the house of their *f*............1Chr 26:6   25
yet his *f* made him the chief................1Chr 26:10   25
me before all the house of my *f*............1Chr 28:4   25
house of Judah, the house of my *f*........1Chr 28:4   25
among the sons of my *f* he liked..........1Chr 28:4   25
to be my son, and I will be his *f*.........1Chr 28:6   25
son, know thou the God of thy *f*...........1Chr 28:9   25
be thou, LORD God of Israel our *f*.........1Chr 29:10   25
as king instead of David his *f*..............1Chr 29:23   25

great mercy unto David my *f*.................2Chr 1:8   25
unto David my *f* be established.............2Chr 1:9   25
thou didst deal with David my *f*............2Chr 2:3   25
whom David my *f* did provide................2Chr 2:7   25
his *f* was a man of Tyre, skilful.............2Chr 2:14   25
men of my lord David thy *f*...................2Chr 2:14   25
David his *f* had numbered them.............2Chr 2:17   25
LORD appeared unto David his *f*..............2Chr 3:1   25
did Huram his *f* make to king...............2Chr 4:16   25
that David his *f* had dedicated.............2Chr 5:1   25
with his mouth to my *f* David...............2Chr 6:4   25
f to build an house for the name...........2Chr 6:7   25
But the LORD said to David my *f*...........2Chr 6:8   25
up in the room of David my *f*...............2Chr 6:10   25
f that which thou hast promised............2Chr 6:15   25
f that which thou hast promised............2Chr 6:16   25
before me, as David thy *f* walked 2Chr 7:17   25
have covenanted with David thy *f*..........2Chr 7:18   25
to the order of David his *f*...................2Chr 8:14   25
buried in the city of David his *f*............2Chr 9:31   25
Thy *f* made our yoke grievous...............2Chr 10:4   25
the grievous servitude of thy *f*.............2Chr 10:4   25
Solomon his *f* while he yet lived 2Chr 10:6   25
yoke that thy *f* did put upon us............2Chr 10:9   25
Thy *f* made our yoke heavy, but............2Chr 10:10   25
For whereas my *f* put a heavy yoke........2Chr 10:11   25
my *f* chastised you with whips,.............2Chr 10:11   25
My *f* made your yoke heavy, but I..........2Chr 10:14   25
my *f* chastised you with whips,.............2Chr 10:14   25
things that his *f* had dedicated..............2Chr 15:18   25
was between my *f* and thy *f*...............2Chr 16:3   25
which Asa his *f* had taken....................2Chr 17:2   25
in the first ways of his *f* David.............2Chr 17:3   25
sought to the LORD God of his *f*............2Chr 17:4   25
he walked in the way of Asa his *f*.........2Chr 20:32   25
their *f* gave them great gifts of............2Chr 21:3   25
risen up to the kingdom of his *f*...........2Chr 21:4   25
saith the LORD God of David thy *f*.........2Chr 21:12   25
in the ways of Jehoshaphat thy *f*..........2Chr 21:12   25
death of his *f* to his destruction 2Chr 22:4   25
Jehoiada his *f* had done to him.............2Chr 24:22   25
that had killed the king his *f*................2Chr 25:3   25
king in the room of his *f* Amaziah.........2Chr 26:1   25
to all that his *f* Amaziah did................2Chr 26:4   25
to all that his *f* Uzziah did..................2Chr 27:2   25
of the LORD, like David his *f*................2Chr 28:1   25
to all that David his *f* had done............2Chr 29:2   25
Hezekiah his *f* had broken down............2Chr 33:3
the LORD, as did Manasseh his *f*...........2Chr 33:22   1
which Manasseh his *f* had made...........2Chr 33:22   1
as Manasseh his *f* had humbled............2Chr 33:23   1
walked in the ways of David his *f*..........2Chr 34:2   1
seek after the God of David his *f*...........2Chr 34:3   1
for she had neither *f* nor mother...........Est 2:7   1
whom Mordecai, when her *f*..................Est 2:7   1
aged men, much elder than thy *f*...........Job 15:10   1
said to corruption, Thou art my *f*...........Job 17:14   1
I was a *f* to the poor...........................Job 29:16   1
brought up with me, as with a *f*............Job 31:18   1
Hath the rain a *f*...............................Job 38:28   1
their *f* gave them inheritance...............Job 42:15   1
When my *f* and my mother forsake me ...Ps 27:10   1
A *f* of the fatherless, and a judge ....Ps 68:5   1
shall cry unto me, Thou art my *f*..........Ps 89:26   1
Like as a *f* pitieth his children, ...Ps 103:13   1
hear the instruction of thy *f*................Prov 1:8   1
even as a *f* the son in whom he............Prov 3:12   1
children, the instruction of a *f*..............Prov 4:1   1
A wise son maketh a glad *f*..................Prov 10:1   1
A wise son maketh a glad *f*..................Prov 15:20   1
the *f* of a fool hath no joy....................Prov 17:21   1
A foolish son is a grief to his *f*.............Prov 17:25   1
son is the calamity of his *f*..................Prov 19:13   1
He that wasteth his *f*, and chaseth........Prov 19:26   1
Whoso curseth his *f* or his mother........Prov 20:20   1
unto thy *f* that begat thee...................Prov 23:22   1
The *f* of the righteous shall.................Prov 23:24   1
Thy *f* and thy mother shall be glad........Prov 23:25   1
of riotous men shameth his *f*...............Prov 28:7   1
Whoso robbeth his *f* or his mother........Prov 28:24   1
loveth wisdom rejoiceth his *f*...............Prov 29:3   1
a generation that curseth their *f*...........Prov 30:11   1
The eye that mocketh at his *f*..............Prov 30:17   1
his brother of the house of his *f*...........Is 3:6   1
shall have knowledge to cry, My *f*.........Is 8:4   1
The mighty God, The everlasting *F*.........Is 9:6   1
and he shall be a *f* to the....................Is 22:21   1
the LORD, the God of David thy *f*...........Is 38:5   1
the *f* to the children shall make............Is 38:19   1
Thy first *f* hath sinned, and thy ....Is 43:27   1
unto him that saith unto his *f*..............Is 45:10   1

Look unto Abraham your *f*, and unto	Is 51:2	
with the heritage of Jacob thy *f*	Is 58:14	1
Doubtless thou art our *f*, though	Is 63:16	1
thou, O LORD, art our *f*, our	Is 63:16	1
But now, O LORD, thou art our *f*	Is 64:8	1
Saying to a stock, Thou art my *f*	Jer 2:27	1
from this time cry unto me, My *f*	Jer 3:4	1
I said, Thou shalt call me, My *f*	Jer 3:19	1
brethren, and the house of thy *f*	Jer 12:6	1
for their *f* or for their mother	Jer 16:7	1
man who brought tidings to my *f*	Jer 20:15	1
reigned instead of Josiah his *f*	Jer 22:11	1
did not thy *f* eat and drink, and do	Jer 22:15	1
for I am a *f* to Israel, and	Jer 31:9	1
son of Rechab our *f* commanded us	Jer 35:6	1
Jonadab the son of Rechab our *f*	Jer 35:8	1
that Jonadab our *f* commanded us	Jer 35:10	1
the commandment of their *f*	Jer 35:16	1
the commandment of Jonadab your *f*	Jer 35:18	1
thy *f* was an Amorite, and thy	Eze 16:3	1
an Hittite, and your *f* an Amorite	Eze 16:45	1
as the soul of the *f*, so also the	Eze 18:4	1
not die for the iniquity of his *f*	Eze 18:17	1
As for his *f*, because he cruelly	Eze 18:18	1
son bear the iniquity of the *f*	Eze 18:19	1
not bear the iniquity of the *f*	Eze 18:20	1
neither shall the *f* bear the	Eze 18:20	1
In thee have they set light by *f*	Eze 22:7	1
but for *f*, or for mother, or for	Eze 44:25	1
silver vessels which his *f*	Dan 5:2	2
and in the days of thy *f* light	Dan 5:11	2
the king Nebuchadnezzar thy *f*	Dan 5:11	2
the king, I say, thy *f*	Dan 5:11	2
whom the king my *f* brought out of	Dan 5:13	2
Nebuchadnezzar thy *f* a kingdom	Dan 5:18	2
his *f* will go in unto the same	Amos 2:7	2
For the son dishonoureth the *f*	Mic 7:6	2
shall yet prophesy, then his *f*	Zec 13:3	2
and his *f* and his mother that begat	Zec 13:3	2
A son honoureth his *f*, and a	Mal 1:6	2
if then I be a *f*, where is mine	Mal 1:6	2
Have we not all one *f*	Mal 2:10	2
Judaea in the room of his *f* Herod	Mt 2:22	3962
We have Abraham to our *f*	Mt 3:9	3962
in a ship with Zebedee their *f*	Mt 4:21	3962
left the ship and their *f*, and	Mt 4:22	3962
glorify your *F* which is in heaven	Mt 5:16	3962
of your *F* which is in heaven	Mt 5:45	3962
even as your *F* which is in heaven	Mt 5:48	3962
of your *F* which is in heaven	Mt 6:1	3962
thy *F* which seeth in secret	Mt 6:4	3962
pray to thy *F* which is in secret	Mt 6:6	3962
thy *F* which seeth in secret shall	Mt 6:6	3962
for your *F* knoweth what things ye	Mt 6:8	3962
Our *F* which art in heaven,	Mt 6:9	3962
your heavenly *F* will also forgive	Mt 6:14	3962
neither will your *F* forgive your	Mt 6:15	3962
but unto thy *F* which is in secret	Mt 6:18	3962
and thy *F*, which seeth in secret,	Mt 6:18	3962
yet your heavenly *F* feedeth them	Mt 6:26	3962
for your heavenly *F* knoweth that	Mt 6:32	3962
how much more shall your *F* which	Mt 7:11	3962
will of my *F* which is in heaven	Mt 7:21	3962
me first to go and bury my *f*	Mt 8:21	3962
of your *F* which speaketh in you	Mt 10:20	3962
to death, and the *f* the child	Mt 10:21	3962
fall on the ground without your *F*	Mt 10:29	3962
before my *F* which is in heaven	Mt 10:32	3962
before my *F* which is in heaven	Mt 10:33	3962
a man at variance against his *f*	Mt 10:35	3962
He that loveth *f* or mother more	Mt 10:37	3962
and said, I thank thee, O *F*	Mt 11:25	3962
Even so, *F*; for so it seemed	Mt 11:26	3962
are delivered unto me of my *F*	Mt 11:27	3962
no man knoweth the Son, but the *F*	Mt 11:27	3962
neither knoweth any man the *F*	Mt 11:27	3962
will of my *F* which is in heaven	Mt 12:50	3962
the sun in the kingdom of their *F*	Mt 13:43	3962
commanded, saying, Honour thy *f*	Mt 15:4	3962
and, He that curseth *f* or mother	Mt 15:4	3962
shall say to his *f* or his mother	Mt 15:5	3962
And honour not his *f* or his mother	Mt 15:6	3962
my heavenly *F* hath not planted	Mt 15:13	3962
but my *F* which is in heaven	Mt 16:17	3962
glory of his *F* with his angels	Mt 16:27	3962
face of my *F* which is in heaven	Mt 18:10	3962
will of your *F* which is in heaven	Mt 18:14	3962
them of my *F* which is in heaven	Mt 18:19	3962
my heavenly *F* do also unto you	Mt 18:35	3962
this cause shall a man leave *f*	Mt 19:5	3962
Honour thy *f* and thy mother	Mt 19:19	3962

or brethren, or sisters, or *f*	Mt 19:29	3962
for whom it is prepared of my *F*	Mt 20:23	3962
them twain did the will of his *f*	Mt 21:31	3962
call no man your *f* upon the earth	Mt 23:9	3962
for one is your *F*, which is in	Mt 23:9	3962
angels of heaven, but my *F* only	Mt 24:36	3962
hand, Come, ye blessed of my *F*	Mt 25:34	3962
face, and prayed, saying, O my *F*	Mt 26:39	3962
time, and prayed, saying, O my *F*	Mt 26:42	3962
that I cannot now pray to my *F*	Mt 26:53	3962
them in the name of the *F*.	Mt 28:19	3962
they left their *f* Zebedee in the	Mk 1:20	3962
put them all out, he taketh the *f*	Mk 5:40	3962
For Moses said, Honour thy *f*	Mk 7:10	3962
and, Whoso curseth *f* or mother	Mk 7:10	3962
man shall say to his *f* or mother	Mk 7:11	3962
do ought for his *f* or his mother	Mk 7:12	3962
of his *F* with the holy angels	Mk 8:38	3962
And he asked his *f*, How long is it	Mk 9:21	3962
straightway the *f* of the child	Mk 9:24	3962
cause shall a man leave his *f*	Mk 10:7	3962
Defraud not, Honour thy *f*	Mk 10:19	3962
or brethren, or sisters, or *f*	Mk 10:29	3962
be the kingdom of our *f* David	Mk 11:10	3962
that your *F* also which is in	Mk 11:25	3962
neither will your *F* which is in	Mk 11:26	3962
to death, and the *f* the son	Mk 13:12	3962
neither the Son, but the *F*	Mk 13:32	3962
And he said, Abba, *F*, all things	Mk 14:36	3962
the *f* of Alexander and Rufus, to	Mk 15:21	3962
him the throne of his *f* David	Lk 1:32	3962
after the name of his *f*	Lk 1:59	3962
And they made signs to his *f*	Lk 1:62	3962
his *f* Zacharias was filled with	Lk 1:67	3962
which he sware to our *f* Abraham	Lk 1:73	3962
behold, thy *f* and I have sought	Lk 2:48	3962
We have Abraham to our *f*	Lk 3:8	3962
as your *F* also is merciful	Lk 6:36	3962
and James, and John, and the *f*	Lk 8:51	3962
and delivered him again to his *f*	Lk 9:42	3962
me first to go and bury my *f*	Lk 9:59	3962
and said, I thank thee, O *F*	Lk 10:21	3962
even so, *F*; for so it seemed	Lk 10:21	3962
are delivered to me of my *F*	Lk 10:22	3962
knoweth who the Son is, but the *F*	Lk 10:22	3962
and who the *F* is, but the Son, and	Lk 10:22	3962
Our *F* which art in heaven,	Lk 11:2	3962
bread of any of you that is a *f*	Lk 11:11	3962
F give the Holy Spirit to them	Lk 11:13	3962
your *F* knoweth that ye have need	Lk 12:30	3962
The *f* shall be divided against	Lk 12:53	3962
the son, and the son against the *f*	Lk 12:53	3962
man come to me, and hate not his *f*	Lk 14:26	3962
the younger of them said to his *f*	Lk 15:12	3962
of them said to his *f*, *F*	Lk 15:12	3962
I will arise and go to my *f*	Lk 15:18	3962
and will say unto him, *F*	Lk 15:18	3962
And he arose, and came to his *f*	Lk 15:20	3962
his *f* saw him, and had compassion,	Lk 15:20	3962
And the son said unto him,	Lk 15:21	3962
But the *f* said to his servants,	Lk 15:22	3962
thy *f* hath killed the fatted calf	Lk 15:27	3962
therefore came his *f* out, and	Lk 15:28	3962
And he answering said to his *f*	Lk 15:29	3962
F Abraham, have mercy on me, and	Lk 16:24	3962
he said, I pray thee therefore, *f*	Lk 16:27	3962
And he said, Nay, *f* Abraham	Lk 16:30	3962
bear false witness, Honour thy *f*	Lk 18:20	3962
as my *F* hath appointed unto me	Lk 22:29	3962
Saying, *F*, if thou be willing,	Lk 22:42	3962
Then said Jesus, *F*, forgive them	Lk 23:34	3962
with a loud voice, he said, *F*	Lk 23:46	3962
send the promise of my *F* upon you	Lk 24:49	3962
as of the only begotten of the *F*	Jn 1:14	3962
which is in the bosom of the *F*	Jn 1:18	3962
The *F* loveth the Son, and hath	Jn 3:35	3962
Art thou greater than our *f* Jacob	Jn 4:12	3962
yet at Jerusalem, worship the *F*	Jn 4:21	3962
shall worship the *F* in spirit.	Jn 4:23	3962
for the *F* seeketh such to worship	Jn 4:23	3962
So the *f* knew that it was at the	Jn 4:53	3962
My *F* worketh hitherto, and I work	Jn 5:17	3962
but said also that God was his *F*	Jn 5:18	3962
but what he seeth the *F* do	Jn 5:19	3962
For the *F* loveth the Son, and	Jn 5:20	3962
For as the *F* raiseth up the dead,	Jn 5:21	3962
For the *F* judgeth no man, but	Jn 5:22	3962
Son, even as they honour the *F*	Jn 5:23	3962
not the *F* which hath sent him	Jn 5:23	3962
For as the *F* hath life in himself	Jn 5:26	3962
will of the *F* which hath sent me	Jn 5:30	3962

F

the *F* hath given me to finish	Jn 5:36	3962
of me, that the *F* hath sent me	Jn 5:36	3962
the *F* himself, which hath sent me	Jn 5:37	3962
that I will accuse you to the *F*	Jn 5:45	3962
for him hath God the *F* sealed	Jn 6:27	3962
but my *F* giveth you the true	Jn 6:32	3962
All that the *F* giveth me shall	Jn 6:37	3962
Jesus, the son of Joseph, whose *f*	Jn 6:42	3962
except the *F* which hath sent me	Jn 6:44	3962
heard, and hath learned of the *F*	Jn 6:45	3962
Not that any man hath seen the *F*	Jn 6:46	3962
is of God, he hath seen the *F*	Jn 6:46	3962
As the living *F* hath sent me	Jn 6:57	3962
hath sent me, and I live by the *F*	Jn 6:57	3962
it were given unto him of my *F*	Jn 6:65	3962
but I and the *F* that sent me	Jn 8:16	3962
the *F* that sent me beareth	Jn 8:18	3962
they unto him, Where is thy *F*	Jn 8:19	3962
Ye neither know me, nor my *F*	Jn 8:19	3962
ye should have known my *F* also	Jn 8:19	3962
that he spake to them of the *F*	Jn 8:27	3962
but as my *F* hath taught me, I	Jn 8:28	3962
the *F* hath not left me alone	Jn 8:29	3962
that which I have seen with my *F*	Jn 8:38	3962
which ye have seen with your *F*	Jn 8:38	3962
said unto him, Abraham is our *f*	Jn 8:39	3962
Ye do the deeds of your *f*	Jn 8:41	3962
we have one *F*, even God	Jn 8:41	3962
unto them, If God were your *F*	Jn 8:42	3962
Ye are of your *f* the devil	Jn 8:44	3962
and the lusts of your *f* ye will do	Jn 8:44	3962
for he is a liar, and the *f* of it	Jn 8:44	3962
but I honour my *F*, and ye do	Jn 8:49	3962
thou greater than our *f* Abraham	Jn 8:53	3962
it is my *F* that honoureth me	Jn 8:54	3962
Your *f* Abraham rejoiced to see my	Jn 8:56	3962
As the *F* knoweth me, even so know	Jn 10:15	3962
knoweth me, even so know I the *F*	Jn 10:15	3962
Therefore doth my *F* love me	Jn 10:17	3962
have I received of my *F*	Jn 10:18	3962
My *F*, which gave them me, is	Jn 10:29	3962
I and my *F* are one	Jn 10:30	3962
works have I shewed you from my *F*	Jn 10:32	3962
whom the *F* hath sanctified, and	Jn 10:36	3962
If I do not the works of my *F*	Jn 10:37	3962
and believe, that the *F* is in me	Jn 10:38	3962
lifted up his eyes, and said, *F*	Jn 11:41	3962
serve me, him will my *F* honour	Jn 12:26	3962
F, save me from this hour	Jn 12:27	3962
F, glorify thy name	Jn 12:28	3962
but the *F* which sent me, he gave	Jn 12:49	3962
even as the *F* said unto me, so I	Jn 12:50	3962
out of this world unto the *F*	Jn 13:1	3962
Jesus knowing that the *F* had	Jn 13:3	3962
no man cometh unto the *F*, but by	Jn 14:6	3962
ye should have known my *F* also	Jn 14:7	3962
unto him, Lord, shew us the *F*	Jn 14:8	3962
that hath seen me hath seen the *F*	Jn 14:9	3962
sayest thou then, Shew us the *F*	Jn 14:9	3962
am in the *F*, and the *F* in me	Jn 14:10	3962
but the *F* that dwelleth in me, he	Jn 14:10	3962
am in the *F*, and the *F* in me	Jn 14:11	3962
because I go unto my *F*	Jn 14:12	3962
that the *F* may be glorified in	Jn 14:13	3962
And I will pray the *F*, and he shall	Jn 14:16	3962
ye shall know that I am in my *F*	Jn 14:20	3962
loveth me shall be loved of my *F*	Jn 14:21	3962
my *F* will love him, and we will	Jn 14:23	3962
whom the *F* will send in my name,	Jn 14:26	3962
because I said, I go unto the *F*	Jn 14:28	3962
for my *F* is greater than I	Jn 14:28	3962
world may know that I love the *F*	Jn 14:31	3962
as the *F* gave me commandment,	Jn 14:31	3962
vine, and my *F* is the husbandman	Jn 15:1	3962
Herein is my *F* glorified, that ye	Jn 15:8	3962
As the *F* hath loved me, so have I	Jn 15:9	3962
my *F* I have made known unto you	Jn 15:15	3962
ye shall ask of the *F* in my name	Jn 15:16	3962
that hateth me hateth my *F* also	Jn 15:23	3962
seen and hated both me and my *F*	Jn 15:24	3962
I will send unto you from the *F*	Jn 15:26	3962
which proceedeth from the *F*	Jn 15:26	3962
because they have not known the *F*	Jn 16:3	3962
because I go to my *F*, and ye see	Jn 16:10	3962
things that the *F* hath are mine	Jn 16:15	3962
see me, because I go to the *F*	Jn 16:16	3962
and, Because I go to the *F*	Jn 16:17	3962
ye shall ask the *F* in my name	Jn 16:23	3962
I shall shew you plainly of the *F*	Jn 16:25	3962
that I will pray the *F* for you	Jn 16:26	3962
For the *F* himself loveth you,	Jn 16:27	3962
I came forth from the *F*, and am	Jn 16:28	3962
I leave the world, and go to the *F*	Jn 16:28	3962
alone, because the *F* is with me	Jn 16:32	3962
up his eyes to heaven, and said, *F*	Jn 17:1	3962
And now, O *F*, glorify thou me with	Jn 17:5	3962
Holy *F*, keep through thine own	Jn 17:11	3962
as thou, *F*, art in me, and I in	Jn 17:21	3962
F, I will that they also, whom	Jn 17:24	3962
O righteous *F*, the world hath not	Jn 17:25	3962
the cup which my *F* hath given me	Jn 18:11	3962
for he was *f* in law to Caiaphas	Jn 18:13	3995
for I am not yet ascended to my *F*	Jn 20:17	3962
ascend unto my *F*, and your *F*	Jn 20:17	3962
as my *F* hath sent me, even so	Jn 20:21	3962
but wait for the promise of the *F*	Acts 1:4	3962
which the *F* hath put in his own	Acts 1:7	3962
having received of the *F* the	Acts 2:33	3962
glory appeared unto our *f* Abraham	Acts 7:2	3962
from thence, when his *f* was dead	Acts 7:4	3962
called his *f* Jacob to him, and all	Acts 7:14	3962
the sons of Emmor the *f* of Sychem	Acts 7:16	3962
but his *f* was a Greek	Acts 16:1	3962
knew all that his *f* was a Greek	Acts 16:3	3962
that the *f* of Publius lay sick of	Acts 28:8	3962
to you and peace from God our *F*	Rom 1:7	3962
we say then that Abraham our *f*	Rom 4:1	3962
that he might be the *f* of all	Rom 4:11	3962
the *f* of circumcision to them who	Rom 4:12	3962
of that faith of our *f* Abraham	Rom 4:12	3962
who is the *f* of us all,	Rom 4:16	3962
made thee a *f* of many nations	Rom 4:17	3962
become the *f* of many nations	Rom 4:18	3962
the dead by the glory of the *F*	Rom 6:4	3962
adoption, whereby we cry, Abba, *F*	Rom 8:15	3962
by one, even by our *f* Isaac	Rom 9:10	3962
even the *F* of our Lord Jesus	Rom 15:6	3962
you, and peace, from God our *F*	1Cor 1:3	3962
to us there is but one God, the *F*	1Cor 8:6	3962
up the kingdom to God, even the *F*	1Cor 15:24	3962
be to you and peace from God our *F*	2Cor 1:2	3962
even the *F* of our Lord Jesus	2Cor 1:3	3962
the *F* of mercies, and the God of	2Cor 1:3	3962
And will be a *F* unto you, and ye	2Cor 6:18	3962
F of our Lord Jesus Christ, which	2Cor 11:31	3962
but by Jesus Christ, and God the *F*	Gal 1:1	3962
be to you and peace from God the *F*	Gal 1:3	3962
to the will of God and our *F*	Gal 1:4	3962
until the time appointed of the *F*	Gal 4:2	3962
into your hearts, crying, Abba, *F*	Gal 4:6	3962
to you, and peace, from God our *F*	Eph 1:2	3962
F of our Lord Jesus Christ, who	Eph 1:3	3962
the *F* of glory, may give unto you	Eph 1:17	3962
access by one Spirit unto the *F*	Eph 2:18	3962
the *F* of our Lord Jesus Christ	Eph 3:14	3962
F of all, who is above all, and	Eph 4:6	3962
the *F* in the name of our Lord	Eph 5:20	3962
cause shall a man leave his *f*	Eph 5:31	3962
Honour thy *f* and mother	Eph 6:2	3962
love with faith, from God the *F*	Eph 6:23	3962
you, and peace, from God our *F*	Phil 1:2	3962
Lord, to the glory of God the *F*	Phil 2:11	3962
of him, that, as a son with the *f*	Phil 2:22	3962
our *F* be glory for ever and ever	Phil 4:20	3962
you, and peace, from God our *F*	Col 1:2	3962
the *F* of our Lord Jesus Christ,	Col 1:3	3962
Giving thanks unto the *F*, which	Col 1:12	3962
For it pleased the *F* that in him	Col 1:19	
the mystery of God, and of the *F*	Col 2:2	3962
thanks to God and the *F* by him	Col 3:17	3962
which is in God the *F* and in the	1Th 1:1	3962
you, and peace, from God our *F*	1Th 1:1	3962
in the sight of God and our *F*	1Th 1:3	3962
as a *f* doth his children,	1Th 2:11	3962
Now God himself and our *F*, and our	1Th 3:11	3962
holiness before God, even our *F*	1Th 3:13	3962
of the Thessalonians in God our *F*	2Th 1:1	3962
you, and peace, from God our *F*	2Th 1:2	3962
himself, and God, even our *F*	2Th 2:16	3962
mercy, and peace, from God our *F*,	1Ti 1:2	3962
an elder, but intreat him as a *f*	1Ti 5:1	3962
mercy, and peace, from God the *F*	2Ti 1:2	3962
mercy, and peace, from God our *F*	Titus 1:4	3962
to you, and peace, from God our *F*	Philem 3	3962
And again, I will be to him a *F*	Heb 1:5	3962
Without *f*, without mother,	Heb 7:3	540
he was yet in the loins of his *f*	Heb 7:10	3962
is he whom the *f* chasteneth not	Heb 12:7	3962
subjection unto the *F* of spirits	Heb 12:9	3962
cometh down from the *F* of lights	Jas 1:17	3962

the *F* is this, To visit the .... Jas 1:27 — 3962
Abraham our *f* justified by works .... Jas 2:21 — 3962
bless we God, even the *F* .... Jas 3:9 — 3962
to the foreknowledge of God the *F* .... 1Pet 1:2 — 3962
F of our Lord Jesus Christ, which .... 1Pet 1:3 — 3962
And if ye call on the *F*, who .... 1Pet 1:17 — 3962
he received from God the *F* honour .... 2Pet 1:17 — 3962
life, which was with the *F* .... 1Jn 1:2 — 3962
our fellowship is with the *F* .... 1Jn 1:3 — 3962
we have an advocate with the *F* .... 1Jn 2:1 — 3962
because ye have known the *F* .... 1Jn 2:13 — 3962
the love of the *F* is not in him .... 1Jn 2:15 — 3962
pride of life, is not of the *F* .... 1Jn 2:16 — 3962
is antichrist, that denieth the *F* .... 1Jn 2:22 — 3962
the Son, the same hath not the *F* .... 1Jn 2:23 — 3962
the Son hath the *F* also .... 1Jn 2:23 — 3962
continue in the Son, and in the *F* .... 1Jn 2:24 — 3962
love the *F* hath bestowed upon us .... 1Jn 3:1 — 3962
do testify that the *F* sent the .... 1Jn 4:14 — 3962
that bear record in heaven, the *F* .... 1Jn 5:7 — 3962
mercy, and peace, from God the *F* .... 2Jn 3 — 3962
Jesus Christ, the Son of the *F* .... 2Jn 3 — 3962
received a commandment from the *F* ..... 2Jn 4 — 3962
of Christ, he hath both the *F* .... 2Jn 9 — 3962
that are sanctified by God the *F* .... Jude 1 — 3962
and priests unto God and his *F* .... Rev 1:6 — 3962
even as I received of my *F* .... Rev 2:27 — 3962
will confess his name before my *F* ..... Rev 3:5 — 3962
set down with my *F* in his throne .... Rev 3:21 — 3962

FATHERLESS
not afflict any widow, or *f* child .... Ex 22:22 — 3490
be widows, and your children *f* .... Ex 22:24 — 3490
execute the judgment of the *f* .... Deut 10:18 — 3490
thee,) and the stranger, and the *f* .... Deut 14:29 — 3490
gates, and the stranger, and the *f* .... Deut 16:11 — 3490
Levite, the stranger, and the *f* .... Deut 16:14 — 3490
of the stranger, nor of the *f* .... Deut 24:17 — 3490
be for the stranger, for the *f* .... Deut 24:19 — 3490
be for the stranger, for the *f* .... Deut 24:20 — 3490
be for the stranger, for the *f* .... Deut 24:21 — 3490
the Levite, the stranger, the *f* .... Deut 26:12 — 3490
and unto the stranger, to the *f* .... Deut 26:13 — 3490
the judgment of the stranger, *f* .... Deut 27:19 — 3490
Yea, ye overwhelm the *f*, and ye .... Job 6:27 — 3490
the arms of the *f* have been .... Job 22:9 — 3490
They drive away the ass of the *f* .... Job 24:3 — 3490
They pluck the *f* from the breast, ... Job 24:9 — 3490
the poor that cried, and the *f* .... Job 29:12 — 3490
the *f* hath not eaten thereof .... Job 31:17 — 3490
lifted up my hand against the *f* .... Job 31:21 — 3490
thou art the helper of the *f* .... Ps 10:14 — 3490
To judge the *f* and the oppressed, ... Ps 10:18 — 3490
A father of the *f*, and a judge of .... Ps 68:5 — 3490
Defend the poor and *f* .... Ps 82:3 — 3490
and the stranger, and murder the *f* ..... Ps 94:6 — 3490
Let his children be *f*, and his .... Ps 109:9 — 3490
be any to favour his *f* children .... Ps 109:12 — 3490
he relieveth the *f* and widow .... Ps 146:9 — 3490
not into the fields of the *f* .... Prov 23:10 — 3490
the oppressed, judge the *f* .... Is 1:17 — 3490
they judge not the *f*, neither .... Is 1:23 — 3490
shall have mercy on their *f* .... Is 9:17 — 3490
prey, and that they may rob the *f* .... Is 10:2 — 3490
not the cause, the cause of the *f* .... Jer 5:28 — 3490
oppress not the stranger, the *f* .... Jer 7:6 — 3490
violence to the stranger, the *f* .... Jer 22:3 — 3490
Leave thy *f* children, I will .... Jer 49:11 — 3490
We are orphans and *f*, ... Lam 5:3 — 369,1
in thee have they vexed the *f* .... Eze 22:7 — 3490
for in thee the *f* findeth mercy .... Hos 14:3 — 3490
oppress not the widow, nor the *f* .... Zec 7:10 — 3490
in his wages, the widow, and the *f* ..... Mal 3:5 — 3490
Father is this, To visit the .... Jas 1:27 — 3737

FATHER'S See APPENDIX.

FATHERS See APPENDIX.

FATHERS' See APPENDIX.

FATHOMS
And sounded, and found it twenty .... Acts 27:28 — 3712
again, and found it fifteen *f* .... Acts 27:28 — 3712

FATLING
the young lion and the *f* together .... Is 11:6 — 4806

FATLINGS
and of the oxen, and of the *f* .... 1Sa 15:9 — 4932
paces, he sacrificed oxen and *f* .... 2Sa 6:13 — 4806
unto thee burnt sacrifices of *f* .... Ps 66:15 — 4220
bullocks, all of them *f* of Bashan .... Eze 39:18 — 4806
my *f* are killed, and all things .... Mt 22:4 — 4619

FATNESS
the *f* of the earth, and plenty of .... Gen 27:28 — 4924
shall be the *f* of the earth .... Gen 27:39 — 4924
thick, thou art covered with *f* .... Deut 32:15 —
unto them, Should I leave my *f* .... Judg 9:9 — 1880
he covereth his face with his *f* .... Job 15:27 — 2459
on thy table should be full of *f* .... Job 36:16 — 1880
satisfied with the *f* of thy house .... Ps 36:8 — 1880
be satisfied with marrow and *f* .... Ps 63:5 — 1880
and thy paths drop *f* .... Ps 65:11 — 1880
Their eyes stand out with *f* .... Ps 73:7 — 2459
and my flesh faileth of *f* .... Ps 109:24 — 8081
the *f* of his flesh shall wax lean .... Is 17:4 — 4924
with blood, it is made fat with *f* .... Is 34:6 — 2459
and their dust made fat with *f* .... Is 34:7 — 2459
let your soul delight itself in *f* .... Is 55:2 — 1880
the soul of the priests with *f* .... Jer 31:14 — 1880
the root and *f* of the olive tree .... Rom 11:17 — 4096

FATS
the *f* shall overflow with wine and .... Joel 2:24 — 3342
the press is full, the *f* overflow .... Joel 3:13 — 3342

FATTED
and fallowdeer, and *f* fowl .... 1Kin 4:23 — 75
the midst of her like *f* bullocks .... Jer 46:21 — 4770
And bring hither the *f* calf .... Lk 15:23 — 4618
thy father hath killed the *f* calf ..... Lk 15:27 — 4618
hast killed for him the *f* calf .... Lk 15:30 — 4618

FATTER
f in flesh than all the children .... Dan 1:15 — 1277

FATTEST
upon them, and slew the *f* of them .... Ps 78:31 — 4924
upon the *f* places of the province .... Dan 11:24 — 4924

FAULT
but the *f* is in thine own people .... Ex 5:16 — 2398
his face, according to his *f* .... Deut 25:2 — 7564
I have found no *f* in him since he .... 1Sa 29:3 — 3972
with a *f* concerning this woman .... 2Sa 3:8 — 5771
prepare themselves without my *f* .... Ps 59:4 — 5771
could find none occasion nor *f* .... Dan 6:4 — 7844
there any error or *f* found in him .... Dan 6:4 — 7844
go and tell him his *f* between thee. ... Mt 18:15 — 1651
unwashen, hands, they found *f* .... Mk 7:2 — 3201
people, I find no *f* in this man .... Lk 23:4 — 158
them, I find in him no *f* at all .... Lk 23:14 — 158
them, I find in him no *f* at all .... Jn 18:38 — 156
may know that I find no *f* in him .... Jn 19:4 — 156
for I find no *f* in him .... Jn 19:6 — 156
unto me, Why doth he yet find *f* .... Rom 9:19 — 3201
there is utterly a *f* among you .... 1Cor 6:7 — 2275
if a man be overtaken in a *f* .... Gal 6:1 — 3900
For finding *f* with them, he saith .... Heb 8:8 — 3201
for they are without *f* before the .... Rev 14:5 — 299

FAULTLESS
if that first covenant had been *f* .... Heb 8:7 — 278
to present you *f* before the .... Jude 24 — 299

FAULTS
I do remember my *f* this day .... Gen 41:9 — 2399
cleanse thou me from secret *f* .... Ps 19:12 —
Confess your *f* one to another, and ..... Jas 5:16 — 3900
when ye be buffeted for your *f* .... 1Pet 2:20 — 264

FAULTY
this thing as one which is *f* .... 2Sa 14:13 — 818
now shall they be found *f* .... Hos 10:2 — 816

FAVOUR
now I have found *f* in thy sight .... Gen 18:3 — 2580
if I have found *f* in thine eyes .... Gen 30:27 — 2580
gave him *f* in the sight of the .... Gen 39:21 — 2580
I will give this people *f* in the .... Ex 3:21 — 2580
the LORD gave the people *f* in the ..... Ex 11:3 — 2580
the LORD gave the people *f* in the ..... Ex 12:36 — 2580
have I not found *f* in thy sight .... Num 11:11 — 2580
if I have found *f* in thy sight .... Num 11:15 — 2580
that she find no *f* in his eyes .... Deut 24:1 — 2580
the old, nor shew *f* to the young ..... Deut 28:50 — 2603
O Naphtali, satisfied with *f* .... Deut 33:23 — 7522
and that they might have no *f* .... Josh 11:20 — 8467
Let me find *f* in thy sight, my .... Ruth 2:13 — 2580
was in *f* both with the LORD, and ..... 1Sa 2:26 — 2896
for he hath found *f* in my sight .... 1Sa 16:22 — 2580
if I have found *f* in thine eyes .... 1Sa 20:29 — 2580
young men find *f* in thine eyes .... 1Sa 25:8 — 2580
nevertheless the lords *f* thee not ..... 1Sa 29:6 — 2896
if I shall find *f* in the eyes of .... 2Sa 15:25 — 2580
Hadad found great *f* in the sight ..... 1Kin 11:19 — 2580
servant have found *f* in thy sight ..... Neh 2:5 — 3190
Esther obtained *f* in the sight of ..... Est 2:15 — 2580

f in his sight more than all the	Est 2:17	2617
that she obtained *f* in his sight	Est 5:2	2580
If I have found *f* in the sight of	Est 5:8	2580
If I have found *f* in thy sight	Est 7:3	2580
and if I have found *f* in his sight	Est 8:5	2580
Thou hast granted me life and *f*	Job 10:12	2617
with *f* wilt thou compass him as	Ps 5:12	7522
in his *f* is life	Ps 30:5	7522
by thy *f* thou hast made my	Ps 30:7	7522
that *f* my righteous cause	Ps 35:27	2655
because thou hadst a *f* unto them	Ps 44:3	7520
the people shall intreat thy *f*	Ps 45:12	6440
in thy *f* our horn shall be	Ps 89:17	7522
for the time to *f* her, yea, the	Ps 102:13	2603
her stones, and *f* the dust thereof	Ps 102:14	2603
with the *f* that thou bearest unto	Ps 106:4	7522
any to *f* his fatherless children	Ps 109:12	2603
A good man sheweth *f*, and lendeth	Ps 112:5	2603
I intreated thy *f* with my whole	Ps 119:58	6440
So shalt thou find *f* and good	Prov 3:4	2580
and shall obtain *f* of the LORD	Prov 8:35	7522
seeketh good procureth *f*	Prov 11:27	7522
good man obtaineth *f* of the LORD	Prov 12:2	7522
Good understanding giveth *f*	Prov 13:15	2580
among the righteous there is *f*	Prov 14:9	7522
The king's *f* is toward a wise	Prov 14:35	7522
his *f* is as a cloud of the latter	Prov 16:15	7522
thing, and obtaineth *f* of the LORD	Prov 18:22	7522
will intreat the *f* of the prince	Prov 19:6	6440
but his *f* is as dew upon the	Prov 19:12	7522
findeth no *f* in his eyes	Prov 21:10	2603
loving *f* rather than silver and	Prov 22:1	2580
f than he that flattereth with	Prov 28:23	2580
Many seek the ruler's *f*	Prov 29:26	6440
F is deceitful, and beauty is vain	Prov 31:30	2580
nor yet *f* to men of skill	Eccl 9:11	2580
I in his eyes as one that found *f*	Song 8:10	7965
Let *f* be shewed to the wicked,	Is 26:10	2603
formed them will shew them no *f*	Is 27:11	2603
but in my *f* have I had mercy on	Is 60:10	7522
where I will not shew you *f*	Jer 16:13	2594
Now God had brought Daniel into *f*	Dan 1:9	2617
for thou hast found *f* with God	Lk 1:30	5485
stature, and in *f* with God and man	Lk 2:52	5485
having *f* with all the people	Acts 2:47	5485
his afflictions, and gave him *f*	Acts 7:10	5485
Who found *f* before God, and	Acts 7:46	5485
desired *f* against him, that he	Acts 25:3	5485

FAVOURABLE

Be *f* unto them for our sakes	Judg 21:22	2603
God, and he will be *f* unto him	Job 33:26	7520
and will he be *f* no more	Ps 77:7	7520
thou hast been *f* unto thy land	Ps 85:1	7520

FAVOURED

Rachel was beautiful and well *f*	Gen 29:17	4758
was a goodly person, and well *f*	Gen 39:6	4758
of the river seven well *f* kine	Gen 41:2	4758
them out of the river, ill *f*	Gen 41:3	4758
And the ill *f* and leanfleshed kine	Gen 41:4	4758
kine did eat up the seven well *f*	Gen 41:4	4758
seven kine, fatfleshed and well *f*	Gen 41:18	8389
up after them, poor and very ill *f*	Gen 41:19	8389
the ill *f* kine did eat up the	Gen 41:20	
but they were still ill *f*	Gen 41:21	
ill *f* kine that came up after	Gen 41:27	
priests, they *f* not the elders	Lam 4:16	2603
whom was no blemish, but well *f*	Dan 1:4	4758
Hail, thou that art highly *f*	Lk 1:28	5487

FAVOUREST

By this I know that thou *f* me	Ps 41:11	2654

FAVOURETH

by him, and said, He that *f* Joab	2Sa 20:11	2654

FEAR

the *f* of you and the dread of you	Gen 9:2	4172
in a vision, saying, *F* not, Abram	Gen 15:1	3372
Surely the *f* of God is not in	Gen 20:11	3374
f not; for God hath heard	Gen 21:17	3372
f not, for I am with thee, and	Gen 26:24	3372
the *f* of Isaac, had been with me,	Gen 31:42	6343
Jacob sware by the *f* of his	Gen 31:53	6343
for I *f* him, lest he will come and	Gen 32:11	3373
the midwife said unto her, *F* not	Gen 35:17	3372
for I *f* God	Gen 42:18	3373
he said, Peace be to you, *f* not	Gen 43:23	3372
f not to go down into Egypt	Gen 46:3	3372
And Joseph said unto them, *F* not	Gen 50:19	3372
Now therefore *f* ye not	Gen 50:21	3372
ye will not yet *f* the LORD God	Ex 9:30	3372

F ye not, stand still, and see the	Ex 14:13	3372
F and dread shall fall upon them	Ex 15:16	367
people able men, such as *f* God	Ex 18:21	3373
Moses said unto the people, *F* not	Ex 20:20	3372
that his *f* may be before your	Ex 20:20	3374
I will send my *f* before thee	Ex 23:27	367
Ye shall *f* every man his mother,	Lev 19:3	3372
the blind, but shalt *f* thy God	Lev 19:14	3372
face of the old man, and *f* thy God	Lev 19:32	3372
but thou shalt *f* thy God	Lev 25:17	3372
but *f* thy God	Lev 25:36	3372
but shalt *f* thy God	Lev 25:43	3372
neither *f* ye the people of the	Num 14:9	3372
LORD is with us: *f* them not	Num 14:9	3372
LORD said unto Moses, *F* him not	Num 21:34	3372
f not, neither be discouraged	Deut 1:21	3372
the *f* of thee upon the nations	Deut 2:25	3374
the LORD said unto me, *F* him not	Deut 3:2	3372
Ye shall not *f* them	Deut 3:22	3372
that they may learn to *f* me all	Deut 4:10	3372
in them, that they would *f* me	Deut 5:29	3372
thou mightest *f* the LORD thy God	Deut 6:2	3372
Thou shalt *f* the LORD thy God, and	Deut 6:13	3372
to *f* the LORD our God, for our	Deut 6:24	3372
to walk in his ways, and to *f* him	Deut 8:6	3372
but to *f* the LORD thy God, to	Deut 10:12	3372
Thou shalt *f* the LORD thy God	Deut 10:20	3372
your God shall lay the *f* of you	Deut 11:25	6343
f him, and keep his commandments,	Deut 13:4	3372
And all Israel shall hear, and *f*	Deut 13:11	3372
to *f* the LORD thy God always	Deut 14:23	3372
all the people shall hear, and *f*	Deut 17:13	3372
may learn to *f* the LORD his God	Deut 17:19	3372
which remain thou mayest, and *f*	Deut 19:20	3372
f not, and do not tremble, neither	Deut 20:3	3372
and all Israel shall hear, and *f*	Deut 21:21	3372
that thou mayest *f* this glorious	Deut 28:58	3372
and thou shalt *f* day and night, and	Deut 28:66	6342
for the *f* of thine heart	Deut 28:67	6343
heart wherewith thou shalt *f*	Deut 28:67	6342
f not, nor be afraid of them	Deut 31:6	3372
f not, neither be dismayed	Deut 31:8	3372
f the LORD your God, and observe	Deut 31:12	3372
learn to *f* the LORD your God, as	Deut 31:13	3372
that ye might *f* the LORD your God	Josh 4:24	3372
F not, neither be thou dismayed	Josh 8:1	3372
LORD said unto Joshua, *F* them not	Josh 10:8	3372
F not, nor be dismayed, be strong	Josh 10:25	3372
done it for *f* of this thing	Josh 22:24	1674
Now therefore *f* the LORD, and	Josh 24:14	3372
turn in to me; *f* not	Judg 4:18	3372
f not the gods of the Amorites,	Judg 6:10	3372
f not: thou shalt not die	Judg 6:23	3372
But if thou *f* to go down, go thou	Judg 7:10	3373
for *f* of Abimelech his brother	Judg 9:21	6440
And now, my daughter, *f* not	Ruth 3:11	3372
stood by her said unto her, *F* not	1Sa 4:20	3372
the *f* of the LORD fell on the	1Sa 11:7	6343
If ye will *f* the LORD, and serve	1Sa 12:14	3372
said unto the people, *F* not	1Sa 12:20	3372
Only *f* the LORD, and serve him in	1Sa 12:24	3372
and fled that day for *f* of Saul	1Sa 21:10	6440
Abide thou with me, *f* not	1Sa 22:23	3372
And he said unto him, *F* not	1Sa 23:17	3372
haste to get away for *f* of Saul	1Sa 23:26	6440
And David said unto him, *F* not	2Sa 9:7	3372
then kill him, *f* not	2Sa 13:28	3372
be just, ruling in the *f* of God	2Sa 23:3	3374
That they may *f* thee all the days	1Kin 8:40	3372
to *f* thee, as do thy people	1Kin 8:43	3372
And Elijah said unto her, *F* not	1Kin 17:13	3372
but I thy servant *f* the LORD from	1Kin 18:12	3372
that thy servant did *f* the LORD	2Kin 4:1	3373
And he answered, *F* not	2Kin 6:16	3372
them how they should *f* the LORD	2Kin 17:28	3372
they *f* not the LORD, neither do	2Kin 17:34	3373
saying, Ye shall not *f* other gods	2Kin 17:35	3372
stretched out arm, him shall ye *f*	2Kin 17:36	3372
and ye shall not *f* other gods	2Kin 17:37	3372
neither shall ye *f* other gods	2Kin 17:38	3372
But the LORD your God ye shall *f*	2Kin 17:39	3372
F not to be the servants of the	2Kin 25:24	3372
the LORD brought the *f* of him	1Chr 14:17	6343
F before him, all the earth	1Chr 16:30	2342
f not, nor be dismayed	1Chr 28:20	3372
That they may *f* thee, to walk in	2Chr 6:31	3372
f thee, as doth thy people Israel	2Chr 6:33	3372
for the *f* of the LORD came upon	2Chr 14:14	6343
the *f* of the LORD fell upon all	2Chr 17:10	6343
Wherefore now let the *f* of the	2Chr 19:7	6343
shall ye do in the *f* of the LORD	2Chr 19:9	3374

f not, nor be dismayed	2Chr 20:17	3372
the f of God was on all the	2Chr 20:29	6343
for f was upon them because of	Ezr 3:3	367
who desire to f thy name	Neh 1:11	3372
the f of our God because of the	Neh 5:9	3374
not I, because of the f of God	Neh 5:15	3374
that would have put me in f	Neh 6:14	3372
sent letters to put me in f	Neh 6:19	3372
for the f of the Jews fell upon	Est 8:17	6343
for the f of them fell upon all	Est 9:2	6343
because the f of Mordecai fell	Est 9:3	6343
Doth Job f God for nought	Job 1:9	3372
Is not this thy f, thy confidence	Job 4:6	3374
F came upon me, and trembling,	Job 4:14	6343
forsaketh the f of the Almighty	Job 6:14	3374
me, and let not his f terrify me	Job 9:34	367
Then would I speak, and not f him	Job 9:35	3372
shalt be stedfast, and shalt not f	Job 11:15	3372
Yea, thou castest off f, and	Job 15:4	3374
Their houses are safe from f	Job 21:9	6343
he reprove thee for f of thee	Job 22:4	3374
thee, and sudden f troubleth thee	Job 22:10	6343
Dominion and f are with him	Job 25:2	6343
the f of the Lord, that is wisdom	Job 28:28	3374
Did I f a great multitude, or did	Job 31:34	6206
Men do therefore f him	Job 37:24	3372
her labour is in vain without f	Job 39:16	6343
He mocketh at f, and is not	Job 39:22	6343
his like, who is made without f	Job 41:33	2844
Serve the Lord with f, and rejoice	Ps 2:11	3374
in thy f will I worship toward	Ps 5:7	3374
Put them in f, O Lord	Ps 9:20	4172
There were they in great f	Ps 14:5	6342
he honoureth them that f the Lord	Ps 15:4	3373
The f of the Lord is clean,	Ps 19:9	3374
Ye that f the Lord, praise him	Ps 22:23	3373
f him, all ye the seed of Israel	Ps 22:23	1481
my vows before them that f him	Ps 22:25	3373
shadow of death, I will f no evil	Ps 23:4	3372
the Lord is with them that f him	Ps 25:14	3373
whom shall I f?	Ps 27:1	3372
against me, my heart shall not f	Ps 27:3	3372
and a f to mine acquaintance	Ps 31:11	6343
f was on every side	Ps 31:13	4032
hast laid up for them that f thee	Ps 31:19	3373
Let all the earth f the Lord	Ps 33:8	3372
the Lord is upon them that f him	Ps 33:18	3373
round about them that f him	Ps 34:7	3373
O f the Lord, ye his saints	Ps 34:9	3372
is no want to them that f him	Ps 34:9	3373
will teach you the f of the Lord	Ps 34:11	3374
that there is no f of God before	Ps 36:1	6343
many shall see it, and f, and shall	Ps 40:3	3372
Therefore will not we f, though	Ps 46:2	3372
F took hold upon them there, and	Ps 48:6	7461
Wherefore should I f in the days	Ps 49:5	3372
righteous also shall see, and f	Ps 52:6	3372
There were they in great f	Ps 53:5	6343
in great f, where no f was	Ps 53:5	6343
changes, therefore they f not God	Ps 55:19	3372
I will not f what flesh can do	Ps 56:4	3372
a banner to them that f thee	Ps 60:4	3373
heritage of those that f thy name	Ps 61:5	3373
my life from f of the enemy	Ps 64:1	6343
do they shoot at him, and f not	Ps 64:4	3372
And all men shall f, and shall	Ps 64:9	3372
Come and hear, all ye that f God	Ps 66:16	3373
the ends of the earth shall f him	Ps 67:7	3372
They shall f thee as long as the	Ps 72:5	3372
salvation is nigh them that f him	Ps 85:9	3373
unite my heart to f thy name	Ps 86:11	3372
even according to thy f, so is	Ps 90:11	3374
f before him, all the earth	Ps 96:9	2342
shall f the name of the Lord	Ps 102:15	3372
his mercy toward them that f him	Ps 103:11	3373
the Lord pitieth them that f him	Ps 103:13	3373
everlasting upon them that f him	Ps 103:17	3373
for the f of them fell upon them	Ps 105:38	6343
given meat unto them that f him	Ps 111:5	3373
The f of the Lord is the	Ps 111:10	3374
Ye that f the Lord, trust in the	Ps 115:11	3373
will bless them that f the Lord	Ps 115:13	3373
Let them now that f the Lord say	Ps 118:4	3373
I will not f	Ps 118:6	3372
servant, who is devoted to thy f	Ps 119:38	3374
Turn away my reproach which I f	Ps 119:39	3025
companion of all them that f thee	Ps 119:63	3372
They that f thee will be glad	Ps 119:74	3373
Let those that f thee turn unto	Ps 119:79	3373
My flesh trembleth for f of thee	Ps 119:120	6343
ye that f the Lord, bless the	Ps 135:20	3373

the desire of them that f him	Ps 145:19	3373
pleasure in them that f him	Ps 147:11	3373
The f of the Lord is the	Prov 1:7	3374
I will mock when your f cometh	Prov 1:26	6343
When your f cometh as desolation,	Prov 1:27	6343
did not choose the f of the Lord	Prov 1:29	3374
and shall be quiet from f of evil	Prov 1:33	6343
thou understand the f of the Lord	Prov 2:5	3374
f the Lord, and depart from evil	Prov 3:7	3372
Be not afraid of sudden f	Prov 3:25	6343
The f of the Lord is to hate evil	Prov 8:13	3374
The f of the Lord is the	Prov 9:10	3374
The f of the wicked, it shall	Prov 10:24	4034
The f of the Lord prolongeth days	Prov 10:27	3374
In the f of the Lord is strong	Prov 14:26	3374
The f of the Lord is a fountain	Prov 14:27	3374
Better is little with the f of	Prov 15:16	3374
The f of the Lord is the	Prov 15:33	3374
by the f of the Lord men depart	Prov 16:6	3374
The f of the Lord tendeth to life	Prov 19:23	3374
The f of a king is as the roaring	Prov 20:2	367
the f of the Lord are riches, and	Prov 22:4	3374
but be thou in the f of the Lord	Prov 23:17	3374
f thou the Lord and the king	Prov 24:21	3372
The f of man bringeth a snare	Prov 29:25	2731
it, that men should f before him	Eccl 3:14	3372
but f thou God	Eccl 5:7	3372
be well with them that f God	Eccl 8:12	3373
that f God, which f before him	Eccl 8:12	3372
F God, and keep his commandments	Eccl 12:13	3372
thigh because of f in the night	Song 3:8	6343
for f of the Lord, and for the	Is 2:10	6343
for f of the Lord, and for the	Is 2:19	6343
for f of the Lord, and for the	Is 2:21	6343
f not, neither be fainthearted	Is 7:4	3372
not come thither the f of briers	Is 7:25	3374
neither f ye their f, nor be	Is 8:12	3372
neither f ye their f, nor be	Is 8:12	4172
and let him be your f, and let him	Is 8:13	4172
knowledge and of the f of the Lord	Is 11:2	3374
in the f of the Lord	Is 11:3	3374
from thy sorrow, and from thy f	Is 14:3	7267
f because of the shaking of the	Is 19:16	6342
hath he turned into f unto me	Is 21:4	2731
F, and the pit, and the snare, are	Is 24:17	6343
of the f shall fall into the pit	Is 24:18	6343
the terrible nations shall f thee	Is 25:3	3372
their f toward me is taught by	Is 29:13	3374
shall f the God of Israel	Is 29:23	6206
over to his strong hold for f	Is 31:9	4032
the f of the Lord is his treasure	Is 33:6	3374
a fearful heart, Be strong, f not	Is 35:4	3372
F thou not; for I am	Is 41:10	3372
hand, saying unto thee, F not	Is 41:13	3372
F not, thou worm Jacob, and ye men	Is 41:14	3372
that formed thee, O Israel, F not	Is 43:1	3372
F not: for I am with thee	Is 43:5	3372
F not, O Jacob, my servant	Is 44:2	3372
F ye not, neither be afraid	Is 44:8	6342
yet they shall f, and they shall	Is 44:11	6342
f ye not the reproach of men,	Is 51:7	3372
F not; for thou shalt not be ashamed	Is 54:4	3372
for thou shalt not f	Is 54:14	3372
So shall they f the name of the	Is 59:19	3372
together, and thine heart shall f	Is 60:5	6342
and hardened our heart from thy f	Is 63:17	3374
that my f is not in thee, saith	Jer 2:19	6345
F ye not me? saith the Lord	Jer 5:22	3372
Let us now f the Lord our God,	Jer 5:24	3372
the enemy and f is on every side	Jer 6:25	4032
Who would not f thee, O King of	Jer 10:7	3372
defaming of many, f on every side	Jer 20:10	4032
and they shall f no more, nor be	Jer 23:4	3372
did he not f the Lord, and	Jer 26:19	3373
heard a voice of trembling, of f	Jer 30:5	6343
Therefore f thou not, O my	Jer 30:10	3372
way, that they may f me for ever	Jer 32:39	3372
I will put my f in their hearts	Jer 32:40	3374
and they shall f and tremble for	Jer 33:9	6342
let us go to Jerusalem for f of	Jer 35:11	6440
for f of the army of the Syrians	Jer 35:11	6440
Jerusalem for f of Pharaoh's army	Jer 37:11	6440
F not to serve the Chaldeans	Jer 40:9	3372
for f of Baasha king of Israel	Jer 41:9	6440
for f was round about, saith the	Jer 46:5	4032
But f not thou, O my servant	Jer 46:27	3372
F thou not, O Jacob my servant,	Jer 46:28	3372
F, and the pit, and the snare,	Jer 48:43	6343
the f shall fall into the pit	Jer 48:44	6343
I will bring a f upon thee	Jer 49:5	6343
to flee, and f hath seized on her	Jer 49:24	7374

F

cry unto them, *F* is on every side	Jer 49:29	4032
for *f* of the oppressing sword	Jer 50:16	6440
ye *f* the rumour that shall be	Jer 51:46	3372
F and a snare is come upon us,	Lam 3:47	6343
thou saidst, *F* not	Lam 3:57	3372
f them not, neither be dismayed	Eze 3:9	3372
I will put a *f* in the land of	Eze 30:13	3374
I *f* my lord the king, who hath	Dan 1:10	3373
f before the God of Daniel	Dan 6:26	1763
said he unto me, *F* not, Daniel	Dan 10:12	3372
O man greatly beloved, *f* not	Dan 10:19	3372
shall *f* the LORD and his goodness	Hos 3:5	6342
shall *f* because of the calves of	Hos 10:5	1481
F not, O land	Joel 2:21	3372
lion hath roared, who will not *f*	Amos 3:8	3372
I *f* the LORD, the God of heaven,	Jonah 1:9	3373
God, and shall *f* because of thee	Mic 7:17	3372
I said, Surely thou wilt *f* me	Zeph 3:7	3372
be said to Jerusalem, *F* thou not	Zeph 3:16	3372
the people did *f* before the LORD	Hag 1:12	3372
remaineth among you: *f* ye not	Hag 2:5	3372
f not, but let your hands be	Zec 8:13	3372
to the house of Judah: *f* ye not	Zec 8:15	3372
Ashkelon shall see it, and *f*	Zec 9:5	3372
if I be a master, where is my *f*	Mal 1:6	4172
for the *f* wherewith he feared me	Mal 2:5	4172
f not me, saith the LORD of hosts	Mal 3:5	3372
But unto you that *f* my name shall	Mal 4:2	3373
f not to take unto thee Mary thy	Mt 1:20	5399
F them not therefore	Mt 10:26	5399
f not them which kill the body,	Mt 10:28	5399
but rather f him which is able to	Mt 10:28	5399
F ye not therefore, ye are of	Mt 10:31	5399
and they cried out for *f*	Mt 14:26	5401
we *f* the people	Mt 21:26	5399
for *f* of him the keepers did	Mt 28:4	5401
and said unto the women, *F* not ye	Mt 28:5	5399
quickly from the sepulchre with *f*	Mt 28:8	5401
was troubled, and *f* fell upon him	Lk 1:12	5401
said unto him, *F* not, Zacharias	Lk 1:13	5399
angel said unto her, *F* not, Mary	Lk 1:30	5399
that *f* him from generation to	Lk 1:50	5399
f came on all that dwelt round	Lk 1:65	5401
enemies might serve him without *f*	Lk 1:74	870
the angel said unto them, *F* not	Lk 2:10	5399
And Jesus said unto Simon, *F* not	Lk 5:10	5399
God, and were filled with *f*	Lk 5:26	5401
And there came a *f* on all	Lk 7:16	5401
for they were taken with great *f*	Lk 8:37	5401
he answered him, saying, F not	Lk 8:50	5399
will forewarn you whom ye shall f	Lk 12:5	5399
F him, which after he hath killed	Lk 12:5	5399
yea, I say unto you, F him	Lk 12:5	5399
F not therefore	Lk 12:7	5399
F not, little flock	Lk 12:32	5399
himself, Though I f not God	Lk 18:4	5399
Men's hearts failing them for f	Lk 21:26	5401
him, saying, Dost not thou *f* God	Lk 23:40	5399
openly of him for *f* of the Jews	Jn 7:13	5401
F not, daughter of Sion	Jn 12:15	5399
but secretly for *f* of the Jews	Jn 19:38	5401
were assembled for *f* of the Jews	Jn 20:19	5401
And *f* came upon every soul	Acts 2:43	5401
great *f* came on all them that	Acts 5:5	5401
great *f* came upon all the church,	Acts 5:11	5401
and walking in the *f* of the Lord	Acts 9:31	5401
Men of Israel, and ye that *f* God	Acts 13:16	5399
f fell on them all, and the name	Acts 19:17	5401
Saying, *F* not, Paul	Acts 27:24	5399
There is no *f* of God before their	Rom 3:18	5401
the spirit of bondage again to *f*	Rom 8:15	5401
Be not highminded, but *f*	Rom 11:20	5399
to whom custom; *f* to whom	Rom 13:7	5401
to whom *f*; honour to whom	Rom 13:7	5401
was with you in weakness, and in *f*	1Cor 2:3	5401
that he may be with you without *f*	1Cor 16:10	820
holiness in the *f* of God	2Cor 7:1	5401
what indignation, yea, what *f*	2Cor 7:11	5401
obedience of you all, how with *f*	2Cor 7:15	5401
But I *f*, lest by any means, as	2Cor 11:3	5399
For I *f*, lest, when I come, I	2Cor 12:20	5399
one to another in the *f* of God	Eph 5:21	5401
according to the flesh, with *f*	Eph 6:5	5401
bold to speak the word without *f*	Phil 1:14	870
out your own salvation with *f*	Phil 2:12	5401,2192
all, that others also may *f*	1Ti 5:20	5401
hath not given us the spirit of *f*	2Ti 1:7	1167
through *f* of death were all their	Heb 2:15	5401
Let us therefore *f*, lest, a	Heb 4:1	5399
not seen as yet, moved with *f*	Heb 11:7	2125
that Moses said, I exceedingly *f*	Heb 12:21	1630,1510
with reverence and godly *f*	Heb 12:28	2124
I will not *f* what man shall do	Heb 13:6	5399
time of your sojourning here in *f*	1Pet 1:17	5401
F God. Honour the king	1Pet 2:17	5399
to your masters with all *f*	1Pet 2:18	5401
conversation coupled with *f*	1Pet 3:2	5401
that is in you with meekness and *f*	1Pet 3:15	5401
There is no *f* in love	1Jn 4:18	5401
but perfect love casteth out *f*	1Jn 4:18	5401
because *f* hath torment	1Jn 4:18	5401
you, feeding themselves without *f*	Jude 12	870
And others save with *f*, pulling	Jude 23	5401
upon me, saying unto me, F not	Rev 1:17	5399
F none of those things which thou	Rev 2:10	5399
great *f* fell upon them which saw	Rev 11:11	5401
saints, and them that *f* thy name	Rev 11:18	5399
F God, and give glory to him	Rev 14:7	5399
Who shall not *f* thee, O Lord, and	Rev 15:4	5399
afar off for the *f* of her torment	Rev 18:10	5401
afar off for the *f* of her torment	Rev 18:15	5401
ye his servants, and ye that *f* him	Rev 19:5	5399

FEARED

for he *f* to dwell in Zoar	Gen 19:30	3372
for he *f* to say, She is my wife	Gen 26:7	3372
But the midwives *f* God, and did	Ex 1:17	3372
pass, because the midwives *f* God	Ex 1:21	3372
And Moses *f*, and said, Surely this	Ex 2:14	3372
He that *f* the word of the LORD	Ex 9:20	3373
and the people *f* the LORD, and	Ex 14:31	3372
and he *f* not God	Deut 25:18	3373
newly up, whom your fathers *f* not	Deut 32:17	8175
Were it not that I *f* the wrath of	Deut 32:27	1481
and they *f* him, as they *f*	Josh 4:14	3372
That they *f* greatly, because	Josh 10:2	3372
because he *f* his father's	Judg 6:27	3372
for he *f*, because he was yet a	Judg 8:20	3372
Samuel *f* to shew Eli the vision	1Sa 3:15	3372
all the people greatly *f* the LORD	1Sa 12:18	3372
for the people *f* the oath	1Sa 14:26	3372
because I *f* the people, and obeyed	1Sa 15:24	3372
a word again, because he *f* him	2Sa 3:11	3372
So the Syrians *f* to help the	2Sa 10:19	3372
the servants of David *f* to tell	2Sa 12:18	3372
Adonijah *f* because of Solomon, and	1Kin 1:50	3372
and they *f* the king	1Kin 3:28	3372
(Now Obadiah *f* the LORD greatly	1Kin 18:3	3373
of Egypt, and had *f* other gods,	2Kin 17:7	3372
there, that they *f* not the LORD	2Kin 17:25	3372
So they *f* the LORD, and made unto	2Kin 17:32	3373
They *f* the LORD, and served their	2Kin 17:33	3373
So these nations *f* the LORD	2Kin 17:41	3373
he also is to be *f* above all gods	1Chr 16:25	3372
And Jehoshaphat *f*, and set himself	2Chr 20:3	3372
faithful man, and *f* God above many	Neh 7:2	3372
and upright, and one that *f* God	Job 1:1	3372
which I greatly *f* is come upon me	Job 3:25	6342
Thou, even thou, art to be *f*	Ps 76:7	3372
the earth *f*, and was still,	Ps 76:8	3372
unto him that ought to be *f*	Ps 76:11	4172
on Zion, so that they *f* not	Ps 78:53	6342
God is greatly to be *f* in the	Ps 89:7	6206
he is to be *f* above all gods	Ps 96:4	3372
with thee, that thou mayest be *f*	Ps 130:4	3372
The isles saw it, and *f*	Is 41:5	3372
hast *f* continually every day	Is 51:13	6342
whom hast thou been afraid or *f*	Is 57:11	3372
treacherous sister Judah *f* not	Jer 3:8	3372
pass, that the sword, which ye *f*	Jer 42:16	3373
this day, neither have they *f*	Jer 44:10	3372
Ye have *f* the sword	Eze 11:8	3372
trembled *f* before him	Dan 11:1	1763
because we *f* not the LORD	Hos 10:3	3372
Then the men *f* the LORD	Jonah 1:16	3372
for the fear wherewith he *f* me	Mal 2:5	3372
Then they that *f* the LORD spake	Mal 3:16	3372
him for them that *f* the LORD,	Mal 3:16	3372
he *f* the multitude, because they	Mt 14:5	5399
they *f* the multitude, because	Mt 21:46	5399
they *f* greatly, saying, Truly	Mt 27:54	5399
they *f* exceedingly, and said one	Mk 4:41	5399,5401
For Herod *f* John, knowing that he	Mk 6:20	5399
for they *f* him, because all the	Mk 11:18	5399
they *f* the people	Mk 11:32	5399
lay hold on him, but *f* the people	Mk 12:12	5399
they *f* as they entered into the	Lk 9:34	5399
they *f* to ask him of that saying	Lk 9:45	5399
which f not God, neither regarded	Lk 18:2	5399
For I f thee, because thou art an	Lk 19:21	5399
and they *f* the people	Lk 20:19	5399
for they *f* the people	Lk 22:2	5399

parents, because they *f* the Jews	Jn 9:22	*5399*
for they *f* the people, lest they	Acts 5:26	*5399*
one that *f* God with all his house	Acts 10:2	*5399*
and they *f*, when they heard that	Acts 16:38	*5399*
death, and was heard in that he *f*	Heb 5:7	*2124*

FEAREST

for now I know that thou *f* God	Gen 22:12	3373
even of old, and thou *f* me not	Is 57:11	3372
hand of them whose face thou *f*	Jer 22:25	1481

FEARETH

Behold, Adonijah *f* king Solomon	1Kin 1:51	3372
and an upright man, one that *f* God	Job 1:8	3373
and an upright man, one that *f* God	Job 2:3	3373
What man is he that *f* the LORD	Ps 25:12	3373
is the man that *f* the LORD	Ps 112:1	3372
is every one that *f* the Lord	Ps 128:1	3373
man be blessed that *f* the LORD	Ps 128:4	3373
but he that *f* the commandment	Prov 13:13	3373
in his uprightness *f* the LORD	Prov 14:2	3373
A wise man *f*, and departeth from	Prov 14:16	3373
Happy is the man that *f* alway	Prov 28:14	6342
but a woman that *f* the LORD	Prov 31:30	3373
for he that *f* God shall come	Eccl 7:18	3373
because he *f* not before God	Eccl 8:13	3373
sweareth, as he that *f* an oath	Eccl 9:2	3373
Who is among you that *f* the LORD	Is 50:10	3373
a just man, and one that *f* God	Acts 10:22	*5399*
But in every nation he that *f* him	Acts 10:35	*5399*
and whosoever among you *f* God	Acts 13:26	*5399*
He that *f* is not made perfect in	1Jn 4:18	*5399*

FEARFUL

f in praises, doing wonders	Ex 15:11	3372
say, What man is there that is *f*	Deut 20:8	3373
and *f* name, THE LORD THY GOD	Deut 28:58	3372
people, saying, Whosoever is *f*	Judg 7:3	3373
Say to them that are of a *f* heart	Is 35:4	4116
he saith unto them, Why are ye *f*	Mt 8:26	*1169*
said unto them, Why are ye so *f*	Mk 4:40	*1169*
***f* sights and great signs shall**	Lk 21:11	*5400*
But a certain *f* looking for of	Heb 10:27	*5398*
It is a *f* thing to fall into the	Heb 10:31	*5398*
But the *f*, and unbelieving, and the	Rev 21:8	*1169*

FEARFULLY

for I am *f* and wonderfully made	Ps 139:14	3372

FEARFULNESS

F and trembling are come upon me,	Ps 55:5	3374
My heart panted, *f* affrighted me	Is 21:4	6427
f hath surprised the hypocrites	Is 33:14	7461

FEARING

children cease from *f* the LORD	Josh 22:25	3372
But the woman *f* and trembling,	Mk 5:33	*5399*
f lest Paul should have been	Acts 23:10	*2125*
f lest they should fall into the	Acts 27:17	*5399*
Then *f* lest we should have fallen	Acts 27:29	*5399*
himself, *f* them which were of the	Gal 2:12	*5399*
but in singleness of heart, *f* God	Col 3:22	*5399*
not *f* the wrath of the king	Heb 11:27	*5399*

FEARS

me, and delivered me from all my *f*	Ps 34:4	4035
f shall be in the way, and the	Eccl 12:5	2849
and will bring their *f* upon them	Is 66:4	4035
were fightings, within were *f*	2Cor 7:5	*5401*

FEAST

and he made them a *f*, and did bake	Gen 19:3	4960
Abraham made a great *f* the same	Gen 21:8	4960
And he made them a *f*, and they did	Gen 26:30	4960
the men of the place, and made a *f*	Gen 29:22	4960
that he made a *f* unto all his	Gen 40:20	4960
that they may hold a *f* unto me in	Ex 5:1	2287
we must hold a *f* unto the LORD	Ex 10:9	2282
ye shall keep it a *f* to the LORD	Ex 12:14	2282
ye shall keep it a *f* by an	Ex 12:14	2287
observe the *f* of unleavened bread	Ex 12:17	
day shall be a *f* to the LORD	Ex 13:6	2282
keep a *f* unto me in the year	Ex 23:14	2287
keep the *f* of unleavened bread	Ex 23:15	2282
the *f* of harvest, the firstfruits	Ex 23:16	2282
the *f* of ingathering, which is in	Ex 23:16	2282
To morrow is a *f* to the LORD	Ex 32:5	2282
The *f* of unleavened bread shalt	Ex 34:18	2282
thou shalt observe the *f* of weeks	Ex 34:22	2282
the *f* of ingathering at the	Ex 34:22	2282
shall the sacrifice of the *f* of	Ex 34:25	2282
f of unleavened bread unto the	Lev 23:6	2282
f of tabernacles for seven days	Lev 23:34	2282
ye shall keep a *f* unto the LORD	Lev 23:39	2282
ye shall keep it a *f* unto the	Lev 23:41	2282
day of this month is the *f*	Num 28:17	2282
ye shall keep a *f* unto the LORD	Num 29:12	2282
thou shalt keep the *f* of weeks	Deut 16:10	2282
Thou shalt observe the *f* of	Deut 16:13	2282
And thou shalt rejoice in thy *f*	Deut 16:14	2282
f unto the LORD thy God in the	Deut 16:15	2287
in the *f* of unleavened bread, and	Deut 16:16	2282
bread, and in the *f* of weeks	Deut 16:16	2282
and in the *f* of tabernacles	Deut 16:16	2282
release, in the *f* of tabernacles,	Deut 31:10	2282
and Samson made there a *f*	Judg 14:10	4960
me within the seven days of the *f*	Judg 14:12	4960
seven days, while their *f* lasted	Judg 14:17	4960
there is a *f* of the LORD in	Judg 21:19	2282
he held a *f* in his house, like	1Sa 25:36	4960
his house, like the *f* of a king	1Sa 25:36	4960
and the men that were with him a *f*	2Sa 3:20	4960
made a *f* to all his servants	1Kin 3:15	4960
at the *f* in the month Ethanim	1Kin 8:2	2282
And at that time Solomon held a *f*	1Kin 8:65	2282
ordained a *f* in the eighth month	1Kin 12:32	2282
like unto the *f* that is in Judah,	1Kin 12:32	2282
ordained a *f* unto the children of	1Kin 12:33	2282
f which was in the seventh month	2Chr 5:3	2282
Solomon kept the *f* seven days	2Chr 7:8	2282
seven days, and the *f* seven days	2Chr 7:9	2282
even in the *f* of unleavened bread	2Chr 8:13	2282
bread, and in the *f* of weeks	2Chr 8:13	2282
and in the *f* of tabernacles	2Chr 8:13	2282
much people to keep the *f* of	2Chr 30:13	2282
present at Jerusalem kept the *f*	2Chr 30:21	2282
eat throughout the *f* seven days	2Chr 30:22	4150
the *f* of unleavened bread seven	2Chr 35:17	2282
kept also the *f* of tabernacles	Ezr 3:4	2282
kept the *f* of unleavened bread	Ezr 6:22	2282
in the *f* of the seventh month	Neh 8:14	2282
And they kept the *f* seven days	Neh 8:18	2282
he made a *f* unto all his princes	Est 1:3	4960
the king made a *f* unto all the	Est 1:5	4960
a *f* for the women in the royal	Est 1:9	4960
a great *f* unto all his princes	Est 2:18	4960
and his servants, even Esther's *f*	Est 2:18	4960
the Jews had joy and gladness, a *f*	Est 8:17	4960
appointed, on our solemn *f* day	Ps 81:3	2282
a merry heart hath a continual *f*	Prov 15:15	4960
A *f* is made for laughter, and wine	Eccl 10:19	3899
unto all people a *f* of fat things	Is 25:6	4960
a *f* of wines on the lees, of fat	Is 25:6	4960
LORD, as in the day of a solemn *f*	Lam 2:7	4150
the passover, a *f* of seven days	Eze 45:21	2282
seven days of the *f* he shall	Eze 45:23	2282
like in the *f* of the seven days	Eze 45:25	2282
the king made a great *f* to a	Dan 5:1	3900
her *f* days, her new moons, and her	Hos 2:11	2282
in the day of the *f* of the LORD	Hos 9:5	2282
as in the days of the solemn *f*	Hos 12:9	4150
I hate, I despise your *f* days	Amos 5:21	2282
to keep the *f* of tabernacles	Zec 14:16	2282
up to keep the *f* of tabernacles	Zec 14:18	2282
up to keep the *f* of tabernacles	Zec 14:19	2282
two days is the *f* of the passover	Mt 26:2	
But they said, Not on the *f* day	Mt 26:5	*1859*
of the *f* of unleavened bread the	Mt 26:17	
Now at that *f* the governor was	Mt 27:15	*1859*
days was the *f* of the passover	Mk 14:1	
But they said, Not on the *f* day	Mk 14:2	*1859*
Now at that *f* he released unto	Mk 15:6	*1859*
year at the *f* of the passover	Lk 2:41	*1859*
after the custom of the *f*	Lk 2:42	*1859*
him a great *f* in his own house	Lk 5:29	*1408*
But when thou makest a *f*, call	Lk 14:13	*1408*
Now the *f* of unleavened bread	Lk 22:1	*1859*
release one unto them at the *f*	Lk 23:17	*1859*
bear unto the governor of the *f*	Jn 2:8	*755*
When the ruler of the *f* had	Jn 2:9	*755*
the governor of the *f* called the	Jn 2:9	*755*
at the passover, in the *f* day	Jn 2:23	*1859*
that he did at Jerusalem at the *f*	Jn 4:45	*1859*
for they also went unto the *f*	Jn 4:45	*1859*
this there was a *f* of the Jews	Jn 5:1	*1859*
a *f* of the Jews, was nigh	Jn 6:4	*1859*
Now the Jews' *f* of tabernacles	Jn 7:2	*1859*
Go ye up unto this *f*	Jn 7:8	*1859*
I go not up yet unto this *f*	Jn 7:8	*1859*
then went he also up unto the *f*	Jn 7:10	*1859*
Then the Jews sought him at the *f*	Jn 7:11	*1859*
Now about the midst of the *f*	Jn 7:14	*1859*
last day, that great day of the *f*	Jn 7:37	*1859*
Jerusalem the *f* of the dedication	Jn 10:22	*1456*
that he will not come to the *f*	Jn 11:56	*1859*
people that were come to the *f*	Jn 12:12	*1859*

F

that came up to worship at the *f* ....Jn 12:20　1859
Now before the *f* of the passover, ...Jn 13:1　1859
we have need of against the *f* ....Jn 13:29　1859
this *f* that cometh in Jerusalem ....Acts 18:21　1859
Therefore let us keep the *f*.....................1Cor 5:8　1858
that believe not bid you to a *f* 1Cor 10:27
deceivings while they *f* with you............2Pet 2:13　4910
of charity, when they *f* with you............Jude 12　4910

FEASTED
f in their houses, every one his........Job 1:4　6213,4960

FEASTING
they, and made it a day of *f*.................Est 9:17　4960
rested, and made it a day of *f*.................Est 9:18　4960
month Adar a day of gladness and *f* ......Est 9:19　4960
they should make them days of *f*.............Est 9:22　4960
days of their *f* were gone about...............Job 1:5　4960
than to go to the house of *f*...................Eccl 7:2　4960
not also go into the house of *f*.................Jer 16:8　4960

FEASTS
Concerning the *f* of the LORD ....Lev 23:2　4150
convocations, even these are my *f*.........Lev 23:2　4150
These are the *f* of the LORD ....Lev 23:4　4150
These are the *f* of the LORD ....Lev 23:37　4150
of Israel the *f* of the LORD ....Lev 23:44　4150
offering, or in your solemn *f*...................Num 15:3　4150
do unto the LORD in your set *f*.............Num 29:39　4150
in the new moons, on the set *f* ....1Chr 23:31　4150
on the solemn *f* of the LORD our ....2Chr 2:4　4150
the new moons, and on the solemn *f* ......2Chr 8:13　4150
the new moons, and for the set *f*...........2Chr 31:3　4150
of all the set *f* of the LORD that ....Ezr 3:5　4150
of the new moons, for the set *f* ....Neh 10:33　4150
With hypocritical mockers in *f*.................Ps 35:16　4580
your appointed *f* my soul hateth ....Is 1:14
and pipe, and wine, are in their *f* ....Is 5:12　4960
In their heat I will make their *f*...........Jer 51:39　4960
because none come to the solemn *f*......Lam 1:4　4150
the LORD hath caused the solemn *f*......Lam 2:6　4150
of Jerusalem in her solemn *f*..................Eze 36:38　4150
and drink offerings, in the *f*.....................Eze 45:17　2282
before the LORD in the solemn *f*.............Eze 46:9　4150
And in the *f* and in the solemnities........Eze 46:11　2282
her sabbaths, and all her solemn *f* ......Hos 2:11　4150
I will turn your *f* into mourning ....Amos 8:10　2282
O Judah, keep thy solemn *f*...................Nah 1:15　2282
joy and gladness, and cheerful *f*...........Zec 8:19　4150
even the dung of your solemn *f*..............Mal 2:3　2282
And love the uppermost rooms at *f*......Mt 23:6　1173
and the uppermost rooms at *f*............Mk 12:39　1173
and the chief rooms at *f* ....Lk 20:46　1173
are spots in your *f* of charity..................Jude 12

FEATHERED
f fowls like as the sand of the ....Ps 78:27　3671
Speak unto every *f* fowl, and to ....Eze 39:17　3671

FEATHERS
pluck away his crop with his *f*.................Lev 1:16　5133
or wings and *f* unto the ostrich...............Job 39:13　2624
silver, and her *f* with yellow gold ....Ps 68:13　84
He shall cover thee with his *f*.................Ps 91:4　84
wings, longwinged, full of *f*.....................Eze 17:3　5133
eagle with great wings and many *f*.......Eze 17:7　5133
hairs were grown like eagles' *f* ....Dan 4:33

FED
Jacob *f* the rest of Laban's......................Gen 30:36　7462
as he *f* the asses of Zibeon his ....Gen 36:24　7462
and they *f* in a meadow ....Gen 41:2　7462
and they *f* in a meadow ....Gen 41:18　7462
he *f* them with bread for all ....Gen 47:17　5095
the God which *f* me all my life ....Gen 48:15　7462
I have *f* you in the wilderness ....Ex 16:32　398
f thee with manna, which thou ....Deut 8:3　398
Who *f* thee in the wilderness with ....Deut 8:16　398
f them, but went not in unto them ....2Sa 20:3　3557
f them with bread and water.................1Kin 18:4　3557
f them with bread and water.................1Kin 18:13　3557
over the herds that *f* in Sharon...............1Chr 27:29　7462
land, and verily thou shalt be *f*...............Ps 37:3　7462
So he *f* them according to the.................Ps 78:72　7462
He should have *f* them also with ....Ps 81:16　398
of rams, and the fat of *f* beasts ....Is 1:11　4806
when I had *f* them to the full,.................Jer 5:7
They were as *f* horses in the ....Jer 5:8　2109
oil, and honey, wherewith I *f* thee ....Eze 16:19　398
the wool, ye kill them that are *f*...............Eze 34:3　1277
f themselves, and *f* not my flock ....Eze 34:8　7462
thereof, and all flesh was *f* of it...............Dan 4:12　2110
they *f* him with grass like oxen, ...Dan 5:21　2939
and I *f* the flock ....Zec 11:7　7462

saw we thee an hungred, and *f* thee......Mt 25:37　5142
they that *f* the swine fled, and ....Mk 5:14　1006
When they that *f* them saw what ....Lk 8:34　1006
desiring to be *f* with the crumbs ....Lk 16:21　5526
I have *f* you with milk, and not ....1Cor 3:2　4222

FEEBLE
But when the cattle were *f* ....Gen 30:42　5848
even all that were *f* behind thee ....Deut 25:18　2826
hath many children is waxed *f*.................1Sa 2:5　535
dead in Hebron, his hands were *f*............2Sa 4:1　7503
carried all the *f* of them upon ....2Chr 28:15　3782
and said, What do these *f* Jews ....Neh 4:2　537
hast strengthened the *f* knees................Job 4:4　3766
I am *f* and sore broken ....Ps 38:8　6313
there was not one *f* person among ....Ps 105:37　3782
The conies are but a *f* folk....................Prov 30:26　3808,6099
remnant shall be very small and *f*..........Is 16:14　3808,3524
hands, and confirm the *f* knees..............Is 35:3　3782
our hands wax *f*....................................Jer 6:24　7503
Damascus is waxed *f*, and turneth ....Jer 49:24　7503
of them, and his hands waxed *f*...............Jer 50:43　7503
All hands shall be *f*, and all ....Eze 7:17　7503
melt, and all hands shall be *f*.................Eze 21:7　7503
he that is *f* among them at that ....Zec 12:8　3782
the body, which seem to be more *f*.........1Cor 12:22　772
which hang down, and the *f* knees ....Heb 12:12　3886

FEEBLEMINDED
that are unruly, comfort the *f*.................1Th 5:14　3642

FEEBLENESS
to their children for *f* of hands ....Jer 47:3　7510

FEEBLER
so the *f* were Laban's, and the................Gen 30:42　5848

FEED
F me, I pray thee, with that same ....Gen 25:30　3938
ye the sheep, and go and *f* them ....Gen 29:7　7462
this thing for me, I will again *f* ....Gen 30:31　7462
his brethren went to *f* their ....Gen 37:12　7462
Do not thy brethren *f* the flock ....Gen 37:13　7462
where they *f* their flocks ....Gen 37:16　7462
their trade hath been to *f* cattle ....Gen 46:32　7462
shall *f* in another man's field...................Ex 22:5　1197
nor herds *f* before that mount ....Ex 34:3　7462
Saul to *f* his father's sheep at ....1Sa 17:15　7462
Thou shalt *f* my people Israel, and........2Sa 5:2　7462
I commanded to *f* my people Israel........2Sa 7:7　7462
me, and I will *f* thee with me in ....2Sa 19:33　3557
the ravens to *f* thee there ....1Kin 17:4　3557
f him with bread of affliction and ....1Kin 22:27　398
Thou shalt *f* my people Israel, and ....1Chr 11:2　7462
whom I commanded to *f* my people ....1Chr 17:6　7462
f him with bread of affliction and...........2Chr 18:26　398
take away flocks, and *f* thereof ....Job 24:2　7462
the worm shall *f* sweetly on him ....Job 24:20　7462
f them also, and lift them up for ....Ps 28:9　7462
death shall *f* on them ....Ps 49:14　7462
brought him to *f* Jacob his people ....Ps 78:71　7462
The lips of the righteous *f* many ....Prov 10:21　7462
f me with food convenient for me...........Prov 30:8　2963
f thy kids beside the shepherds' ....Song 1:8　7462
twins, which *f* among the lilies ....Song 4:5　7462
to *f* in the gardens, and to gather ....Song 6:2　7462
the lambs *f* after their manner................Is 5:17　7462
And the cow and the bear shall *f* ....Is 11:7　7462
the firstborn of the poor shall *f*...............Is 14:30　7462
there shall the calf *f*, and there ....Is 27:10　7462
thy cattle *f* in large pastures ....Is 30:23　7462
He shall *f* his flock like a ....Is 40:11　7462
They shall *f* in the ways, and ....Is 49:9　7462
I will *f* them that oppress thee ....Is 49:26　398
f thee with the heritage of Jacob ....Is 58:14　398
f your flocks, and the sons of the ....Is 61:5　7462
wolf and the lamb shall *f* together ....Is 65:25　7462
which shall *f* you with knowledge............Jer 3:15　7462
they shall *f* every one in his ....Jer 6:3　7462
Behold, I will *f* them, even this ....Jer 9:15　398
the pastors that *f* my people ....Jer 23:2　7462
over them which shall *f* them ....Jer 23:4　7462
I will *f* them with wormwood, and ....Jer 23:15　398
he shall *f* on Carmel and Bashan, ...Jer 50:19　7462
They that did *f* delicately are ....Lam 4:5　398
of Israel that do *f* themselves ....Eze 34:2　7462
not the shepherds *f* the flocks ....Eze 34:2　7462
but ye *f* not the flock ....Eze 34:3　7462
shepherds *f* themselves any more ....Eze 34:10　7462
f them upon the mountains of ....Eze 34:13　7462
I will *f* them in a good pasture, ...Eze 34:14　7462
in a fat pasture shall they *f*....................Eze 34:14　7462
I will *f* my flock, and I will ....Eze 34:15　7462

I will *f* them with judgment .... Eze 34:16   7462
over them, and he shall *f* them .... Eze 34:23   7462
he shall *f* them, and he shall be .... Eze 34:23   7462
they that *f* of the portion of his .... Dan 11:26   398
now the LORD will *f* them as a.................. Hos 4:16   7462
and the winepress shall not *f* them .... Hos 9:2   7462
let them not *f*, nor drink water.................... Jonah 3:7   7462
f in the strength of the LORD, in .... Mic 5:4   7462
F thy people with thy rod, the .... Mic 7:14   7462
let them *f* in Bashan and Gilead,........... Mic 7:14   7462
they shall *f* thereupon .... Zeph 2:7   7462
for they shall *f* and lie down, and .... Zeph 3:13   7462
F the flock of the slaughter .... Zec 11:7   7462
I will *f* the flock of slaughter, ... Zec 11:7   7462
Then said I, I will not *f* you .... Zec 11:9   7462
nor *f* that that standeth still .... Zec 11:16   3557
him into his fields to *f* swine .... Lk 15:15   *1006*
He saith unto him, *F* my lambs .... Jn 21:15   *1006*
He saith unto him, *F* my sheep .... Jn 21:16   *4165*
Jesus saith unto him, *F* my sheep .... Jn 21:17   *1006*
to *f* the church of God, which he............ Acts 20:28   *4165*
if thine enemy hunger, *f* him .... Rom 12:20   *5595*
bestow all my goods to *f* the poor 1Cor 13:3   *5595*
F the flock of God which is among 1Pet 5:2   *4165*
midst of the throne shall *f* them............. Rev 7:17   *4165*
that they should *f* her there a .... Rev 12:6   *5142*

FEEDEST

Thou *f* them with the bread of .... Ps 80:5   398
whom my soul loveth, where thou *f* .... Song 1:7   7462

FEEDETH

mouth of fools *f* on foolishness .... Prov 15:14   7462
he *f* among the lilies .... Song 2:16   7462
he *f* among the lilies .... Song 6:3   7462
He *f* on ashes .... Is 44:20   7462
Ephraim *f* on wind, and followeth .... Hos 12:1   7462
yet your heavenly Father *f* them .... Mt 6:26   *5142*
and God *f* them .... Lk 12:24   *5142*
or who *f* a flock, and eateth not.............. 1Cor 9:7   *4165*

FEEDING

was *f* the flock with his brethren .... Gen 37:2   7462
and the asses *f* beside them .... Job 1:14   7462
them to cease from *f* the flock .... Eze 34:10   7462
the *f* place of the young lions, ... Nah 2:11   7462
from them an herd of many swine *f*....... Mt 8:30   *1006*
mountains a great herd of swine *f* .... Mk 5:11   *1006*
of many swine *f* on the mountain........... Lk 8:32   *1006*
a servant plowing or *f* cattle .... Lk 17:7   *4165*
f themselves without fear .... Jude 12   *4165*

FEEL

My father peradventure will *f* me .... Gen 27:12   4959
I pray thee, that I may *f* thee .... Gen 27:21   4184
Suffer me that I may *f* the .... Judg 16:26   4184
Surely he shall not *f* quietness............... Job 20:20   3045
Before your pots can *f* the thorns .... Ps 58:9   995
commandment shall *f* no evil thing .... Eccl 8:5   3045
if haply they might *f* after him .... Acts 17:27   5584

FEELING

Who being past *f* have given .... Eph 4:19   *524*
with the *f* of our infirmities .... Heb 4:15   *4834*

FEET

you, be fetched, and wash your *f* .... Gen 18:4   7272
tarry all night, and wash your *f* .... Gen 19:2   7272
camels, and water to wash his *f*............. Gen 24:32   7272
the men's *f* that were with him............... Gen 24:32   7272
water, and they washed their *f* .... Gen 43:24   7272
nor a lawgiver from between his *f*.......... Gen 49:10   7272
he gathered up his *f* into the bed........... Gen 49:33   7272
put off thy shoes from off thy *f* .... Ex 3:5   7272
of her son, and cast it at his *f* .... Ex 4:25   7272
girded, your shoes on your *f* .... Ex 12:11   7272
there was under his *f* as it were .... Ex 24:10   7272
that are on the four *f* thereof.................. Ex 25:26   7272
their hands and their *f* thereat............... Ex 30:19   7272
shall wash their hands and their *f* .... Ex 30:21   7272
that were in the four *f* thereof .... Ex 37:13   7272
their hands and their *f* thereat............... Ex 40:31   7272
the great toes of their right *f*.................. Lev 8:24   7272
which have legs above their *f* .... Lev 11:21   7272
things, which have four *f*........................ Lev 11:23   7272
or whatsoever hath more *f* among .... Lev 11:42   7272
thing else, go through on my *f* .... Num 20:19   7272
only I will pass through on my *f*............. Deut 2:28   7272
your *f* shall tread shall be yours............ Deut 11:24   7272
cometh out from between her *f* .... Deut 28:57   7272
and they sat down at thy *f* .... Deut 33:3   7272
as soon as the soles of the *f* of .... Josh 3:13   7272
the *f* of the priests that bare .... Josh 3:15   7272
where the priests' *f* stood firm .... Josh 4:3   7272

in the place where the *f* of the .... Josh 4:9   7272
the soles of the priests' *f* were .... Josh 4:18   7272
old shoes and clouted upon their *f*........ Josh 9:5   7272
put your *f* upon the necks of .... Josh 10:24   7272
put their *f* upon the necks of .... Josh 10:24   7272
thy *f* have trodden shall be thine........... Josh 14:9   7272
his *f* in his summer chamber.................. Judg 3:24   7272
up with ten thousand men at his *f* .... Judg 4:10   7272
chariot, and fled away on his *f* .... Judg 4:15   7272
f to the tent of Jael the wife of .... Judg 4:17   7272
At her *f* he bowed, he fell, he .... Judg 5:27   7272
at her *f* he bowed, he fell .... Judg 5:27   7272
and they washed their *f*, and did .... Judg 19:21   7272
shalt go in, and uncover his *f* .... Ruth 3:4   4772
came softly, and uncovered his *f* .... Ruth 3:7   4772
and, behold, a woman lay at his *f* .... Ruth 3:8   4772
she lay at his *f* until the .... Ruth 3:14   4772
He will keep the *f* of his saints 1Sa 2:9   7272
up upon his hands and upon his *f*......... 1Sa 14:13   7272
and Saul went in to cover his *f* 1Sa 24:3   7272
And fell at his *f*, and said, Upon 1Sa 25:24   7272
be a servant to wash the *f* of the 1Sa 25:41   7272
nor thy *f* put into fetters 2Sa 3:34   7272
had a son that was lame of his *f*............ 2Sa 4:4   7272
and cut off their hands and their *f* 2Sa 4:12   7272
yet a son, which is lame on his *f* 2Sa 9:3   7272
and was lame on both his *f*.................... 2Sa 9:13   7272
down to thy house, and wash thy *f* 2Sa 11:8   7272
and had neither dressed his *f* 2Sa 19:24   7272
and darkness was under his *f* 2Sa 22:10   7272
He maketh my *f* like hinds' *f* 2Sa 22:34   7272
so that my *f* did not slip 2Sa 22:37   7166
yea, they are fallen under my *f* 2Sa 22:39   7272
in his shoes that were on his *f* 1Kin 2:5   7272
put them under the soles of his *f* 1Kin 5:3   7272
Ahijah heard the sound of her *f* 1Kin 14:6   7272
when thy *f* enter into the city, ... 1Kin 14:12   7272
old age he was diseased in his *f* 1Kin 15:23   7272
the hill, she caught him by the *f* 2Kin 4:27   7272
she went in, and fell at his *f* 2Kin 4:37   7272
of his master's *f* behind him 2Kin 6:32   7272
of her than the skull, and the *f* 2Kin 9:35   7272
he revived, and stood up on his *f* 2Kin 13:21   7272
with the sole of my *f* have I 2Kin 19:24   6471
Neither will I make the *f* of 2Kin 21:8   7272
the king stood up upon his *f* 1Chr 28:2   7272
and they stood on their *f*, and 2Chr 3:13   7272
his reign was diseased in his *f* 2Chr 16:12   7272
not old, and their *f* swelled not.............. Neh 9:21   7272
the king, and fell down at his *f* .... Est 8:3   7272
f is as a lamp despised in the .... Job 12:5   7272
Thou puttest my *f* also in the .... Job 13:27   7272
a print upon the heels of my *f* .... Job 13:27   7272
is cast into a net by his own *f* .... Job 18:8   7272
side, and shall drive him to his *f* .... Job 18:11   7272
the blind, and *f* was I to the lame .... Job 29:15   7272
they push away my *f*, and they .... Job 30:12   7272
He putteth my *f* in the stocks .... Job 33:11   7272
hast put all things under his *f* .... Ps 8:6   7272
and darkness was under his *f* .... Ps 18:9   7272
He maketh my *f* like hinds' *f*, ... Ps 18:33   7272
under me, that my *f* did not slip .... Ps 18:36   7166
they are fallen under my *f* .... Ps 18:38   7272
they pierced my hands and my *f* .... Ps 22:16   7272
shall pluck my *f* out of the net .... Ps 25:15   7272
hast set my *f* in a large room .... Ps 31:8   7272
clay, and set my *f* upon a rock, and ...... Ps 40:2   7272
us, and the nations under our *f* .... Ps 47:3   7272
thou deliver my *f* from falling .... Ps 56:13   7272
he shall wash his *f* in the blood .... Ps 58:10   6471
suffereth not our *f* to be moved............. Ps 66:9   7272
as for me, my *f* were almost gone .... Ps 73:2   7272
Lift up thy *f* unto the perpetual .... Ps 74:3   6471
dragon shalt thou trample under *f*......... Ps 91:13   7272
Whose *f* they hurt with fetters .... Ps 105:18   7272
f have they, but they walk not .... Ps 115:7   7272
from tears, and my *f* from falling .... Ps 116:8   7272
turned my *f* unto thy testimonies .... Ps 119:59   7272
my *f* from every evil way, that I .... Ps 119:101   7272
Thy word is a lamp unto my *f* .... Ps 119:105   7272
Our *f* shall stand within thy .... Ps 122:2   7272
For their *f* run to evil, and make........... Prov 1:16   7272
Ponder the path of thy *f*, and let .... Prov 4:26   7272
Her *f* go down to death .... Prov 5:5   7272
his eyes, he speaketh with his *f* .... Prov 6:13   7272
f that be swift in running to................... Prov 6:18   7272
hot coals, and his *f* not be burned .... Prov 6:28   7272
her *f* abide not in her house .... Prov 7:11   7272
that hasteth with his *f* sinneth............... Prov 19:2   7272
hand of a fool cutteth off the *f* .... Prov 26:6   7272
spreadeth a net for his *f* .... Prov 29:5   6471

I have washed my *f*	Song 5:3	7272
beautiful are thy *f* with shoes	Song 7:1	6471
and making a tinkling with their *f*	Is 3:16	7272
tinkling ornaments about their *f*	Is 3:18	
and with twain he covered his *f*	Is 6:2	7272
the head, and the hair of the *f*	Is 7:20	7272
as a carcase trodden under *f*	Is 14:19	
her own *f* shall carry her afar	Is 23:7	7272
even the *f* of the poor, and the	Is 26:6	7272
Ephraim, shall be trodden under *f*	Is 28:3	7272
forth thither the *f* of the ox	Is 32:20	7272
with the sole of my *f* have I	Is 37:25	6471
that he had not gone with his *f*	Is 41:3	7272
and lick up the dust of thy *f*	Is 49:23	7272
the *f* of him that bringeth good	Is 52:7	7272
Their *f* run to evil, and they make	Is 59:7	7272
make the place of my *f* glorious	Is 60:13	7272
down at the soles of thy *f*	Is 60:14	7272
before your *f* stumble upon the	Jer 13:16	7272
they have not refrained their *f*	Jer 14:10	7272
take me, and hid snares for my *f*	Jer 18:22	7272
thy *f* are sunk in the mire, and	Jer 38:22	7272
he hath spread a net for my *f*	Lam 1:13	7272
To crush under his *f* all the	Lam 3:34	7272
And their *f* were straight *f*	Eze 1:7	7272
the sole of their *f* was like the	Eze 1:7	7272
me, Son of man, stand upon thy *f*	Eze 2:1	7272
unto me, and set me upon my *f*	Eze 2:2	7272
into me, and set me upon my *f*	Eze 3:24	7272
hast opened thy *f* to every one	Eze 16:25	7272
and put on thy shoes upon thy *f*	Eze 24:17	7272
heads, and your shoes upon your *f*	Eze 24:23	7272
hands, and stamped with the *f*	Eze 25:6	7272
troubledst the waters with thy *f*	Eze 32:2	7272
f the residue of your pastures	Eze 34:18	7272
must foul the residue with your *f*	Eze 34:18	7272
which ye have trodden with your *f*	Eze 34:19	7272
which ye have fouled with your *f*	Eze 34:19	7272
lived, and stood up upon their *f*	Eze 37:10	7272
and the place of the soles of my *f*	Eze 43:7	7272
his *f* part of iron and part of	Dan 2:33	7271
upon his *f* that were of iron	Dan 2:34	7271
And whereas thou sawest the *f*	Dan 2:41	7271
toes of the *f* were part of iron	Dan 2:42	7271
and made stand upon the *f* as a man	Dan 7:4	7271
the residue with the *f* of it	Dan 7:7	7271
and stamped the residue with his *f*	Dan 7:19	7271
his *f* like in colour to polished	Dan 10:6	4772
the clouds are the dust of his *f*	Nah 1:3	7272
the *f* of him that bringeth good	Nah 1:15	7272
burning coals went forth at his *f*	Hab 3:5	7272
will make my *f* like hinds' *f*	Hab 3:19	7272
his *f* shall stand in that day	Zec 14:4	7272
while they stand upon their *f*	Zec 14:12	7272
ashes under the soles of your *f*	Mal 4:3	7272
they trample them under their *f*	Mt 7:6	4228
shake off the dust of your *f*	Mt 10:14	4228
and cast them down at Jesus' *f*	Mt 15:30	4228
two *f* to be cast into everlasting	Mt 18:8	4228
fellowservant fell down at his *f*	Mt 18:29	4228
And they came and held him by the *f*	Mt 28:9	4228
when he saw him, he fell at his *f*	Mk 5:22	4228
***f* for a testimony against them**	Mk 6:11	4228
of him, and came and fell at his *f*	Mk 7:25	4228
than having two *f* to be cast into	Mk 9:45	4228
to guide our *f* into the way of	Lk 1:79	4228
stood at his *f* behind him weeping	Lk 7:38	4228
and began to wash his *f* with tears	Lk 7:38	4228
of her head, and kissed his *f*	Lk 7:38	4228
thou gavest me no water for my *f*	Lk 7:44	4228
she hath washed my *f* with tears	Lk 7:44	4228
in hath not ceased to kiss my *f*	Lk 7:45	4228
hath anointed my *f* with ointment	Lk 7:46	4228
sitting at the *f* of Jesus	Lk 8:35	4228
and he fell down at Jesus' *f*	Lk 8:41	4228
off the very dust from your *f* for	Lk 9:5	4228
Mary, which also sat at Jesus' *f*	Lk 10:39	4228
on his hand, and shoes on his *f*	Lk 15:22	4228
And fell down on his face at his *f*	Lk 17:16	4228
Behold my hands and my *f*, that it	Lk 24:39	4228
he shewed them his hands and his *f*	Lk 24:40	4228
wiped his *f* with her hair, whose	Jn 11:2	4228
saw him, she fell down at his *f*	Jn 11:32	4228
and anointed the *f* of Jesus	Jn 12:3	4228
wiped his *f* with her hair	Jn 12:3	4228
and began to wash the disciples' *f*	Jn 13:5	4228
him, Lord, dost thou wash my *f*	Jn 13:6	4228
him, Thou shalt never wash my *f*	Jn 13:8	4228
unto him, Lord, not my *f* only	Jn 13:9	4228
needeth not save to wash his *f*	Jn 13:10	4228
So after he had washed their *f*	Jn 13:12	4228

and Master, have washed your *f*	Jn 13:14	4228
ought to wash one another's *f*	Jn 13:14	4228
the head, and the other at the *f*	Jn 20:12	4228
and immediately his *f* and ancle	Acts 3:7	939
laid them down at the apostles' *f*	Acts 4:35	4228
and laid it at the apostles' *f*	Acts 4:37	4228
and laid it at the apostles' *f*	Acts 5:2	4228
the *f* of them which have buried	Acts 5:9	4228
she down straightway at his *f*	Acts 5:10	4228
him, Put off thy shoes from thy *f*	Acts 7:33	4228
their clothes at a young man's *f*	Acts 7:58	4228
met him, and fell down at his *f*	Acts 10:25	4228
whose shoes of his *f* I am not	Acts 13:25	4228
the dust of their *f* against them	Acts 13:51	4228
man at Lystra, impotent in his *f*	Acts 14:8	4228
voice, Stand upright on thy *f*	Acts 14:10	4228
made their *f* fast in the stocks	Acts 16:24	4228
and bound his own hands and *f*	Acts 21:11	4228
in this city at the *f* of Gamaliel	Acts 22:3	4228
But rise, and stand upon thy *f*	Acts 26:16	4228
Their *f* are swift to shed blood	Rom 3:15	4228
How beautiful are the *f* of them	Rom 10:15	4228
bruise Satan under your *f* shortly	Rom 16:20	4228
nor again the head to the *f*	1Cor 12:21	4228
hath put all enemies under his *f*	1Cor 15:25	4228
hath put all things under his *f*	1Cor 15:27	4228
hath put all things under his *f*	Eph 1:22	4228
your *f* shod with the preparation	Eph 6:15	4228
if she have washed the saints' *f*	1Ti 5:10	4228
things in subjection under his *f*	Heb 2:8	4228
And make straight paths for your *f*	Heb 12:13	4228
his *f* like unto fine brass, as if	Rev 1:15	4228
saw him, I fell at his *f* as dead	Rev 1:17	4228
his *f* are like fine brass	Rev 2:18	4228
to come and worship before thy *f*	Rev 3:9	4228
sun, and his *f* as pillars of fire	Rev 10:1	4228
them, and they stood upon their *f*	Rev 11:11	4228
the sun, and the moon under her *f*	Rev 12:1	4228
his *f* were as the *f* of a bear	Rev 13:2	4228
I fell at his *f* to worship him	Rev 19:10	4228
f of the angel which shewed me	Rev 22:8	4228

FEIGN

f thyself to be a mourner, and put	2Sa 14:2	
that she shall *f* herself to be	1Kin 14:5	5234
which should *f* themselves just	Lk 20:20	5271

FEIGNED

f himself mad in their hands, and	1Sa 21:13	
that goeth not out of *f* lips	Ps 17:1	4820
covetousness shall they with *f*	2Pet 2:3	4112

FEIGNEDLY

me with her whole heart, but *f*	Jer 3:10	8267

FEIGNEST

why *f* thou thyself to be another	1Kin 14:6	5234
but thou *f* them out of thine own	Neh 6:8	908

FELIX *(fe'-lix)* See FELIX'. *A Roman procurator of Judea.*

him safe unto *F* the governor	Acts 23:24	5344
governor *F* sendeth greeting	Acts 23:26	5344
and in all places, most noble *F*	Acts 24:3	5344
when *F* heard these things, having	Acts 24:22	5344
when *F* came with his wife	Acts 24:24	5344
F trembled, and answered, Go thy	Acts 24:25	5344
and *F*, willing to shew the Jews a	Acts 24:27	5344
a certain man left in bonds by *F*	Acts 25:14	5344

FELIX' *(fe'-lix)*

Porcius Festus came into *F* room	Acts 24:27	5344

FELL

very wroth, and his countenance *f*	Gen 4:5	5307
and Gomorrah fled, and *f* there	Gen 14:10	5307
down, a deep sleep *f* upon Abram	Gen 15:12	5307
of great darkness *f* upon him	Gen 15:12	5307
And Abram *f* on his face	Gen 17:3	5307
Then Abraham *f* upon his face, and	Gen 17:17	5307
f on his neck, and kissed him	Gen 33:4	5307
they *f* before him on the ground	Gen 44:14	5307
he *f* upon his brother Benjamin's	Gen 45:14	5307
he *f* on his neck, and wept on his	Gen 46:29	5307
Joseph *f* upon his father's face	Gen 50:1	5307
went and *f* down before his face	Gen 50:18	5307
there *f* of the people that day	Ex 32:28	5307
they shouted, and *f* on their faces	Lev 9:24	5307
goat upon which the LORD's lot *f*	Lev 16:9	5927
on which the lot *f* to be the	Lev 16:10	5927
that was among them *f* a lusting	Num 11:4	
when the dew *f* upon the camp in	Num 11:9	3381
in the night, the manna *f* upon it	Num 11:9	3381
Aaron *f* on their faces before all	Num 14:5	5307

heard it, he *f* upon his face	Num 16:4	5307
they *f* upon their faces, and said,	Num 16:22	5307
And they *f* upon their faces	Num 16:45	5307
and they *f* upon their faces	Num 20:6	5307
the LORD, she *f* down under Balaam	Num 22:27	7257
his head, and *f* flat on his face	Num 22:31	7812
I *f* down before the LORD, as at	Deut 9:18	5307
Thus I *f* down before the LORD	Deut 9:25	5307
nights, as I *f* down at the first	Deut 9:25	5307
Joshua on his face to the earth	Josh 5:14	5307
shout, that the wall *f* down flat	Josh 6:20	5307
f to the earth upon his face	Josh 7:6	5307
it was, that all that *f* that day	Josh 8:25	5307
and they *f* upon them	Josh 11:7	5307
Joseph *f* from Jordan by Jericho	Josh 16:1	5307
there *f* ten portions to Manasseh	Josh 17:5	3318
wrath *f* on all the congregation	Josh 22:20	5307
all the host of Sisera *f* upon the	Judg 4:16	5307
At her feet he bowed, he *f*,	Judg 5:27	5307
at her feet he bowed, he *f*,	Judg 5:27	5307
he bowed, there he *f* down dead,	Judg 5:27	5307
a tent, and smote it that it *f*	Judg 7:13	5307
for there *f* an hundred and twenty	Judg 8:10	5307
there *f* at that time of the	Judg 12:6	5307
f on their faces to the ground	Judg 13:20	5307
the house *f* upon the lords, and	Judg 16:30	5307
f down at the door of the man's	Judg 19:26	5307
there *f* of Benjamin eighteen	Judg 20:44	5307
So that all which *f* that day of	Judg 20:46	5307
Then she *f* on her face, and bowed	Ruth 2:10	5307
for there *f* of Israel thirty	1Sa 4:10	5307
that he *f* from off the seat	1Sa 4:18	5307
fear of the LORD *f* on the people	1Sa 11:7	5307
and they *f* before Jonathan	1Sa 14:13	5307
he *f* upon his face to the earth	1Sa 17:49	5307
f down by the way to Shaaraim	1Sa 17:52	5307
f on his face to the ground, and	1Sa 20:41	5307
he *f* upon the priests, and slew him	1Sa 22:18	6298
f before David on her face, and	1Sa 25:23	5307
f at his feet, and said, Upon me,	1Sa 25:24	5307
Then Saul *f* straightway all along	1Sa 28:20	5307
since he *f* unto me unto this day	1Sa 29:3	5307
because three days agone I *f* sick	1Sa 30:13	5307
f down slain in mount Gilboa	1Sa 31:1	5307
Saul took a sword, and *f* upon it	1Sa 31:4	5307
he *f* likewise upon his sword, and	1Sa 31:5	5307
that he *f* to the earth, and did	2Sa 1:2	5307
so they *f* down together	2Sa 2:16	5307
he *f* down there, and died in the	2Sa 2:23	5307
to the place where Asahel *f* down	2Sa 2:23	5307
she made haste to flee, that he *f*	2Sa 4:4	5307
David, he *f* on his face, and did	2Sa 9:6	5307
there *f* some of the people of the	2Sa 11:17	5307
that he *f* sick for his sister	2Sa 13:2	
she *f* on her face to the ground,	2Sa 14:4	5307
Joab *f* to the ground on his face,	2Sa 14:22	5307
he *f* down to the earth upon his	2Sa 18:28	7812
of Gera *f* down before the king	2Sa 19:18	5307
and as he went forth it *f* out	2Sa 20:8	5307
they *f* all seven together, and	2Sa 21:9	5307
f by the hand of David, and by the	2Sa 21:22	5307
he *f* upon him that he died	1Kin 2:25	6293
who *f* upon two men more righteous	1Kin 2:32	6293
up, and *f* upon him, and slew him	1Kin 2:34	6293
out, and *f* upon him, that he died	1Kin 2:46	6293
Abijah the son of Jeroboam *f* sick	1Kin 14:1	
the mistress of the house, *f* sick	1Kin 17:17	
f on his face, and said, Art thou	1Kin 18:7	5307
Then the fire of the LORD *f*	1Kin 18:38	5307
saw it, they *f* on their faces	1Kin 18:39	5307
and there a wall *f* upon twenty	1Kin 20:30	5307
Ahaziah *f* down through a lattice	2Kin 1:2	5307
f on his knees before Elijah, and	2Kin 1:13	3766
mantle of Elijah that *f* from him	2Kin 2:13	5307
mantle of Elijah that *f* from him	2Kin 2:14	5307
shall *f* every good tree, and stop	2Kin 3:19	5307
it *f* on a day, that Elisha passed	2Kin 4:8	1961
it *f* on a day, that he came	2Kin 4:11	1961
it *f* on a day, that he went out	2Kin 4:18	1961
f at his feet, and bowed herself	2Kin 4:37	5307
the ax head *f* into the water	2Kin 6:5	5307
the man of God said, Where *f* it	2Kin 6:6	5307
And so it *f* out unto him	2Kin 7:20	1961
the fugitives that *f* away to the	2Kin 25:11	5307
Hagarites, who *f* by their hand	1Chr 5:10	5307
For there *f* down many slain,	1Chr 5:22	5307
f down slain in mount Gilboa	1Chr 10:1	5307
Saul took a sword, and *f* upon it	1Chr 10:4	5307
he *f* likewise on the sword, and	1Chr 10:5	5307
there *f* some of Manasseh to David	1Chr 12:19	5307
there *f* to him of Manasseh, Adnah	1Chr 12:20	5307

they *f* by the hand of David, and	1Chr 20:8	5307
there *f* of Israel seventy	1Chr 21:14	5307
in sackcloth, *f* upon their faces	1Chr 21:16	5307
the lot eastward *f* to Shelemiah	1Chr 26:14	5307
because there *f* wrath for it	1Chr 27:24	1961
so there *f* down slain of Israel	2Chr 13:17	5307
for they *f* to him out of Israel	2Chr 15:9	5307
the fear of the LORD *f* upon all	2Chr 17:10	1961
of Jerusalem *f* before the LORD	2Chr 20:18	5307
his bowels *f* out by reason of his	2Chr 21:19	3318
f upon the cities of Judah, from	2Chr 25:13	6584
I *f* upon my knees, and spread out	Ezr 9:5	3766
f down at his feet, and besought	Est 8:3	5307
the fear of the Jews *f* upon them	Est 8:17	5307
fear of them *f* upon all people	Est 9:2	5307
the fear of Mordecai *f* upon them	Est 9:3	5307
And the Sabeans *f* upon them	Job 1:15	5307
f upon the camels, and have	Job 1:17	6584
it *f* upon the young men, and they	Job 1:19	5307
f down upon the ground, and	Job 1:20	5307
up my flesh, they stumbled and *f*	Ps 27:2	5307
Their priests *f* by the sword	Ps 78:64	5307
for the fear of them *f* upon them	Ps 105:38	5307
they *f* down, and there was none to	Ps 107:12	3782
in the city, and those that *f* away	Jer 39:9	5307
that *f* to him, with the rest of	Jer 39:9	5307
to fall, yea, one *f* upon another	Jer 46:16	5307
in the city, and those that *f* away	Jer 52:15	5307
that *f* to the king of Babylon, and	Jer 52:15	5307
when her people *f* into the hand	Lam 1:7	5307
the children *f* under the wood	Lam 5:13	3782
I *f* upon my face, and I heard a	Eze 1:28	5307
and I *f* on my face	Eze 3:23	5307
of the Lord GOD *f* there upon me	Eze 8:1	5307
that I *f* upon my face, and cried,	Eze 9:8	5307
the Spirit of the LORD *f* upon me	Eze 11:5	5307
Then *f* I down upon my face, and	Eze 11:13	5307
so *f* they all by the sword	Eze 39:23	5307
and I *f* upon my face	Eze 43:3	5307
and I *f* upon my face	Eze 44:4	5307
Nebuchadnezzar *f* upon his face	Dan 2:46	5308
f down and worshipped the golden	Dan 3:7	5308
f down bound into the midst of	Dan 3:23	5308
there *f* a voice from heaven,	Dan 4:31	5308
came up, and before whom three *f*	Dan 7:20	5308
I was afraid, and *f* upon my face	Dan 8:17	5307
but a great quaking *f* upon them	Dan 10:7	5307
lots, and the lot *f* upon Jonah	Jonah 1:7	5307
f down, and worshipped him	Mt 2:11	4098
and it *f* not: for it was founded	Mt 7:25	4098
and it *f*: and great was the fall	Mt 7:27	4098
some seeds *f* by the way side, and	Mt 13:4	4098
Some *f* upon stony places, where	Mt 13:5	4098
And some *f* among thorns	Mt 13:7	4098
But other *f* into good ground, and	Mt 13:8	4098
they *f* on their face, and were	Mt 17:6	4098
The servant therefore *f* down	Mt 18:26	4098
fellowservant *f* down at his feet	Mt 18:29	4098
f on his face, and prayed, saying,	Mt 26:39	4098
f down before him, and cried,	Mk 3:11	4363
some *f* by the way side, and the	Mk 4:4	4098
some *f* on stony ground, where it	Mk 4:5	4098
some *f* among thorns, and the	Mk 4:7	4098
other *f* on good ground, and did	Mk 4:8	4098
he saw him, he *f* at his feet,	Mk 5:22	4098
f down before him, and told him	Mk 5:33	4363
of him, and came and *f* at his feet	Mk 7:25	4363
he *f* on the ground, and wallowed	Mk 9:20	4098
f on the ground, and prayed that,	Mk 14:35	4098
was troubled, and fear *f* upon him	Lk 1:12	1968
he *f* down at Jesus' knees, saying	Lk 5:8	4363
who seeing Jesus *f* on his face	Lk 5:12	4098
vehemently, and immediately it *f*	Lk 6:49	4098
he sowed, some *f* by the way side	Lk 8:5	4098
And some *f* upon a rock	Lk 8:6	4098
And some *f* among thorns	Lk 8:7	4098
other *f* on good ground, and sprang	Lk 8:8	4098
that which *f* among thorns are	Lk 8:14	4098
But as they sailed he *f* asleep	Lk 8:23	
f down before him, and with a loud	Lk 8:28	4363
he *f* down at Jesus' feet, and	Lk 8:41	4098
f among thieves, which stripped	Lk 10:30	4045
unto him that *f* among the thieves	Lk 10:36	1706
upon whom the tower in Siloam *f*	Lk 13:4	4098
f on his neck, and kissed him	Lk 15:20	1968
which *f* from the rich man's table	Lk 16:21	4098
f down on his face at his feet,	Lk 17:16	4098
she *f* down at his feet, saying	Jn 11:32	4098
went backward, and *f* to the ground	Jn 18:6	4098
which Judas by transgression *f*	Acts 1:25	
and the lot *f* upon Matthias	Acts 1:26	4098

F

hearing these words *f* down .... Acts 5:5	4098
Then *f* she down straightway at.............. Acts 5:10	4098
he had said this, he *f* asleep .... Acts 7:60	
he *f* to the earth, and heard a .... Acts 9:4	4098
immediately there *f* from his eyes .... Acts 9:18	634
made ready, he *f* into a trance, ... Acts 10:10	1968
f down at his feet, and worshipped......... Acts 10:25	4098
the Holy Ghost *f* on all them .... Acts 10:44	1968
speak, the Holy Ghost *f* on them .... Acts 11:15	1968
his chains *f* off from his hands................ Acts 12:7	1601
immediately there *f* on him a mist .... Acts 13:11	1968
f on sleep, and was laid unto his............ Acts 13:36	
f down before Paul and Silas,.................. Acts 16:29	4363
fear *f* on them all, and the name .... Acts 19:17	1968
image which *f* down from Jupiter .... Acts 19:35	1356
f down from the third loft, and .... Acts 20:9	4098
f on him, and embracing him said,......... Acts 20:10	1968
f on Paul's neck, and kissed him,.......... Acts 20:37	1968
I *f* unto the ground, and heard a............. Acts 22:7	4098
on them which *f*, severity .... Rom 11:22	4098
them that reproached thee *f* on me .... Rom 15:3	1968
f in one day three and twenty 1Cor 10:8	4098
sinned, whose carcases *f* in the .... Heb 3:17	4098
faith the walls of Jericho *f* down .... Heb 11:30	4098
for since the fathers *f* asleep 2Pet 3:4	
saw him, I *f* at his feet as dead.............. Rev 1:17	4098
twenty elders *f* down before the .... Rev 5:8	4098
the four and twenty elders *f* down .... Rev 5:14	4098
stars of heaven *f* unto the earth .... Rev 6:13	4098
f before the throne on their .... Rev 7:11	4098
there *f* a great star from heaven,........... Rev 8:10	4098
it *f* upon the third part of the .... Rev 8:10	4098
great fear *f* upon them which saw.......... Rev 11:11	4098
and the tenth part of the city *f*.............. Rev 11:13	4098
f upon their faces, and worshipped .... Rev 11:16	4098
there *f* a noisome and grievous .... Rev 16:2	1096
and the cities of the nations *f*................ Rev 16:19	4098
there *f* upon men a great hail out........... Rev 16:21	2597
elders and the four beasts *f* down.......... Rev 19:4	4098
I *f* at his feet to worship him................... Rev 19:10	4098
I *f* down to worship before the .... Rev 22:8	4098

FELLED

of water, and *f* all the good trees 2Kin 3:25	5307

FELLER

no *f* is come up against us .... Is 14:8	3772

FELLEST

before wicked men, so *f* thou.................. 2Sa 3:34	5307

FELLING

But as one was *f* a beam, the ax 2Kin 6:5	5307

FELLOES

and their naves, and their *f*..................... 1Kin 7:33	2839

FELLOW

This one *f* came in to sojourn, and .... Gen 19:9	7453
Wherefore smitest thou thy *f* .... Ex 2:13	7453
man that told a dream unto his *f*........... Judg 7:13	7453
his *f* answered and said, This is............. Judg 7:14	7453
every man's sword against his *f*............. Judg 7:22	7453
man's sword was against his *f* 1Sa 14:20	7453
this *f* to play the mad man in my 1Sa 21:15	
shall this *f* come into my house 1Sa 21:15	
this *f* hath in the wilderness................... 1Sa 25:21	
said unto him, Make this *f* return........... 1Sa 29:4	376
every one his *f* by the head 2Sa 2:16	7453
Put this *f* in the prison, and feed 1Kin 22:27	
wherefore came this mad *f* to thee 2Kin 9:11	
Put this *f* in the prison, and feed 2Chr 18:26	
fall, the one will lift up his *f* .... Eccl 4:10	2270
and the satyr shall cry to his *f* .... Is 34:14	7453
And they said every one to his *f*............ Jonah 1:7	7453
and against the man that is my *f*........... Zec 13:7	5997
This *f* doth not cast out devils,.............. Mt 12:24	
And said, This *f* said, I am able .... Mt 26:61	
This *f* was also with Jesus of .... Mt 26:71	
Of a truth this *f* also was with .... Lk 22:59	
We found this *f* perverting the .... Lk 23:2	
as for this *f*, we know not from .... Jn 9:29	
This *f* persuadeth men to worship.......... Acts 18:13	
Away with such a *f* from the earth .... Acts 22:22	
have found this man a pestilent *f*.......... Acts 24:5	
f soldier, but your messenger, and .... Phil 2:25	
These only are my *f* workers unto .... Col 4:11	

FELLOWCITIZENS

but *f* with the saints, and of the .... Eph 2:19	4847

FELLOWDISCIPLES

is called Didymus, unto his *f*.................. Jn 11:16	4827

FELLOWHEIRS

That the Gentiles should be *f* .... Eph 3:6	4789

FELLOWHELPER

is my partner and *f* concerning you 2Cor 8:23	4904

FELLOWHELPERS

that we might be *f* to the truth............... 3Jn 8	4904

FELLOWLABOURER

our *f* in the gospel of Christ, to 1Th 3:2	4904
Philemon our dearly beloved, and *f*........ Philem 1	4904

FELLOWLABOURERS

Clement also, and with other my *f* .... Phil 4:3	4904
Aristarchus, Demas, Lucas, my *f*........... Philem 24	4904

FELLOWPRISONER

Aristarchus my *f* saluteth you .... Col 4:10	4869
Epaphras, my *f* in Christ Jesus............... Philem 23	4869

FELLOWPRISONERS

and Junia, my kinsmen, and my *f* .... Rom 16:7	4869

FELLOW'S

and thrust his sword in his *f* side 2Sa 2:16	7453

FELLOWS

and bewail my virginity, I and my *f* .... Judg 11:37	7464
lest angry *f* run upon thee, and .... Judg 18:25	582
as one of the vain *f* shamelessly 2Sa 6:20	
the oil of gladness above thy *f*............... Ps 45:7	2270
all his *f* shall be ashamed .... Is 44:11	2270
and the tribes of Israel his *f*.................. Eze 37:19	2270
Daniel and his *f* to be slain.................... Dan 2:13	2269
his *f* should not perish with the .... Dan 2:18	2269
look was more stout than his *f*............... Dan 7:20	2273
thy *f* that sit before thee .... Zec 3:8	7453
markets, and calling unto their *f*........... Mt 11:16	2083
certain lewd *f* of the baser sort .... Acts 17:5	435
the oil of gladness above thy *f*............... Heb 1:9	3353

FELLOWSERVANT

his *f* fell down at his feet, and .... Mt 18:29	4889
also have had compassion on thy *f*........ Mt 18:33	4889
learned of Epaphras our dear *f*............... Col 1:7	4889
minister and *f* in the Lord .... Col 4:7	4889
I am thy *f*, and of thy brethren .... Rev 19:10	4889
for I am thy *f*, and of thy .... Rev 22:9	4889

FELLOWSERVANTS

went out, and found one of his *f* .... Mt 18:28	4889
So when his *f* saw what was done,......... Mt 18:31	4889
And shall begin to smite his *f* .... Mt 24:49	4889
little season, until their *f* also .... Rev 6:11	4889

FELLOWSHIP

delivered him to keep, or in *f*................... Lev 6:2	8667,3027
of iniquity have *f* with thee..................... Ps 94:20	2266
in the apostles' doctrine and *f*................ Acts 2:42	2842
the *f* of his Son Jesus Christ our............. 1Cor 1:9	2842
that ye should have *f* with devils 1Cor 10:20	2844
for what *f* hath righteousness................. 2Cor 6:14	3352
take upon us the *f* of the 2Cor 8:4	2842
and Barnabas the right hands of *f*......... Gal 2:9	2842
see what is the *f* of the mystery...,......... Eph 3:9	2842
have no *f* with the unfruitful .... Eph 5:11	4790
For your *f* in the gospel from the .... Phil 1:5	2842
if any *f* of the Spirit, if any .... Phil 2:1	2842
the *f* of his sufferings, being .... Phil 3:10	2842
that ye also may have *f* with us.............. 1Jn 1:3	2842
truly our *f* is with the Father,................. 1Jn 1:3	2842
If we say that we have *f* with him 1Jn 1:6	2842
we have *f* one with another, and ...,......... 1Jn 1:7	2842

FELLOWSOLDIER

Apphia, and Archippus our *f*.................... Philem 2	4961

FELT

he *f* him, and said, The voice is.............. Gen 27:22	4959
even darkness which may be *f*................. Ex 10:21	4959
have beaten me, and I *f* it not................. Prov 23:35	3045
she *f* in her body that she was .... Mk 5:29	1097
beast into the fire, and *f* no harm........... Acts 28:5	3958

FEMALE

male and *f* created he them .... Gen 1:27	5347
Male and *f* created he them .... Gen 5:2	5347
they shall be male and *f*.......................... Gen 6:19	5347
thee by sevens, the male and his *f*......... Gen 7:2	802
clean by two, the male and his *f*............ Gen 7:2	802
air by sevens, the male and the *f*........... Gen 7:3	5347
into the ark, the male and the *f*............. Gen 7:9	5347
f of all flesh, as God had .... Gen 7:16	5347
whether it be a male or *f*......................... Lev 3:1	5347
male or *f*, he shall offer it .... Lev 3:6	5347
a *f* without blemish, for his sin .... Lev 4:28	5347
bring it a *f* without blemish.................... Lev 4:32	5347

FENCE (continued)

a *f* from the flock, a lamb or a	Lev 5:6	5347
her that hath born a male or a *f*	Lev 12:7	5347
And if it be a *f*, then thy	Lev 27:4	5347
shekels, and for the *f* ten shekels	Lev 27:5	5347
for the *f* thy estimation shall be	Lev 27:6	5347
shekels, and for the *f* ten shekels	Lev 27:7	5347
f shall ye put out, without the	Num 5:3	5347
figure, the likeness of male or *f*	Deut 4:16	5347
not be male or *f* barren among you	Deut 7:14	5347
the beginning made them male and *f*	Mt 19:4	2338
creation God made them male and *f*	Mk 10:6	2338
free, there is neither male nor *f*	Gal 3:28	2338

FENCE

shall ye be, and as a tottering *f*	Ps 62:3	1447

FENCED

in the *f* cities because of the	Num 32:17	4013
and Beth-haran, *f* cities	Num 32:36	4013
cities were *f* with high walls	Deut 3:5	1219
cities great and *f* up to heaven,	Deut 9:1	1219
f walls come down, wherein thou	Deut 28:52	1219
of them entered into *f* cities	Josh 10:20	4013
that the cities were great and *f*	Josh 14:12	1219
the *f* cities are Ziddim, Zer, and	Josh 19:35	4013
the five lords, both of *f* cities	1Sa 6:18	4013
him, lest he get him *f* cities	2Sa 20:6	1211
touch them must be *f* with iron	2Sa 23:7	4390
And ye shall smite every *f* city	2Kin 3:19	4013
horses, a *f* city also, and armour	2Kin 10:2	4013
of the watchmen to the *f* city	2Kin 17:9	4013
of the watchmen to the *f* city	2Kin 18:8	4013
against all the *f* cities of Judah	2Kin 18:13	1219
waste *f* cities into ruinous heaps	2Kin 19:25	1219
f cities, with walls, gates, and	2Chr 8:5	4692
in Judah and Benjamin *f* cities	2Chr 11:10	4694
and Benjamin, unto every *f* city	2Chr 11:23	4694
he took the *f* cities which	2Chr 12:4	4694
he built *f* cities in Judah	2Chr 14:6	4694
in all the *f* cities of Judah	2Chr 17:2	1219
the *f* cities throughout all Judah	2Chr 17:19	4013
all the *f* cities of Judah	2Chr 19:5	1219
things, with *f* cities in Judah	2Chr 21:3	4694
and encamped against the *f* cities	2Chr 32:1	1219
war in all the *f* cities of Judah	2Chr 33:14	1219
hast *f* me with bones and sinews	Job 10:11	7753
He hath *f* up my way that I cannot	Job 19:8	1443
high tower, and upon every *f* wall	Is 2:15	1219
And he *f* it, and gathered out the	Is 5:2	5823
shall impoverish thy *f* cities	Jer 5:17	4013
unto this people a *f* brasen wall	Jer 15:20	1219
and ruined cities are become *f*	Eze 36:35	1219
mount, and take the most *f* cities	Dan 11:15	4013
and Judah hath multiplied *f* cities	Hos 8:14	1219
and alarm against the *f* cities	Zeph 1:16	1219

FENS

in the covert of the reed, and *f*	Job 40:21	1207

FERRET

And the *f*, and the chameleon, and	Lev 11:30	604

FERRY

there went over a *f* boat to carry	2Sa 19:18	5679

FERVENT

being *f* in the spirit, he spake	Acts 18:25	2204
f in spirit; serving the Lord	Rom 12:11	2204
mourning, your *f* mind toward me	2Cor 7:7	2205
The effectual *f* prayer of a	Jas 5:16	
above all things have *f* charity	1Pet 4:8	1618
elements shall melt with *f* heat	2Pet 3:10	
elements shall melt with *f* heat	2Pet 3:12	

FERVENTLY

always labouring *f* for you in	Col 4:12	
one another with a pure heart *f*	1Pet 1:22	1619

FESTUS (*fes'-tus*) See FESTUS'. *A Roman procurator of Judea.*

Porcius *F* came into Felix' room	Acts 24:27	5347
Now when *F* was come into the	Acts 25:1	5347
But *F* answered, that Paul should	Acts 25:4	5347
But *F*, willing to do the Jews a	Acts 25:9	5347
Then *F*, when he had conferred	Acts 25:12	5347
came unto Caesarea to salute *F*	Acts 25:13	5347
F declared Paul's cause unto the	Acts 25:14	5347
Then Agrippa said unto *F*, I would	Acts 25:22	5347
F said, King Agrippa, and all men	Acts 25:24	5347
F said with a loud voice, Paul	Acts 26:24	5347
said, I am not mad, most noble *F*	Acts 26:25	5347
Then said Agrippa unto *F*, This	Acts 26:32	5347

FESTUS' (*fes'-tus*)

at *F* commandment Paul was brought	Acts 25:23	5347

FETCH

I will *f* a morsel of bread, and	Gen 18:5	3947
f me from thence two good kids of	Gen 27:9	3947
obey my voice, and go *f* me them	Gen 27:13	3947
will send, and *f* thee from thence	Gen 27:45	3947
let him *f* your brother, and ye	Gen 42:16	3947
flags, she sent her maid to *f* it	Ex 2:5	3947
must we *f* you water out of this	Num 20:10	3318
the border shall *f* a compass from	Num 34:5	
f him thence, and deliver him into	Deut 19:12	3947
go into his house to *f* his pledge	Deut 24:10	5670
thou shalt not go again to *f* it	Deut 24:19	3947
and from thence will he *f* thee	Deut 30:4	3947
the elders of Gilead went to *f*	Judg 11:5	3947
to *f* victual for the people, that	Judg 20:10	3947
Let us *f* the ark of the covenant	1Sa 4:3	3947
come ye down, and *f* it up to you	1Sa 6:21	5927
said unto Jesse, Send and *f* him	1Sa 16:11	3947
f him unto me, for he shall	1Sa 20:31	3947
the young men come over and *f* it	1Sa 26:22	3947
but *f* a compass behind them, and	2Sa 5:23	
not *f* home again his banished	2Sa 14:13	7725
To *f* about this form of speech	2Sa 14:20	5437
F me, I pray thee, a little water	1Kin 17:10	3947
he is, that I may send and *f* him	1Kin 17:11	3947
F quickly Micaiah the son of Imla	2Chr 18:8	
f olive branches, and pine	Neh 8:15	935
I will *f* my knowledge from afar,	Job 36:3	5375
Come ye, say they, I will *f* wine	Is 56:12	3947
king sent Jehudi to *f* the roll	Jer 36:21	3947
them come themselves and *f* us out	Acts 16:37	1806

FETCHED

a little water, I pray you, be *f*	Gen 18:4	3947
And he went, and *f*, and brought them	Gen 27:14	3947
to Adar, and *f* a compass to Karkaa	Josh 15:3	
f the carved image, the ephod, and	Judg 18:18	3947
And they ran and *f* him thence	1Sa 10:23	3947
as though they would have *f* wheat	2Sa 4:6	3947
f him out of the house of Machir,	2Sa 9:5	3947
f her to his house, and she became	2Sa 11:27	622
f thence a wise woman, and said	2Sa 14:2	3947
sent and *f* Hiram out of Tyre	1Kin 7:13	3947
f from thence gold, four hundred	1Kin 9:28	3947
they *f* a compass of seven days'	2Kin 3:9	
f the rulers over hundreds, with	2Kin 11:4	3947
And they *f* up, and brought forth	2Chr 1:17	5927
f them, and brought them again	2Chr 12:11	5375
they *f* forth Urijah out of Egypt	Jer 26:23	3318
And from thence we *f* a compass	Acts 28:13	

FETCHETH

his hand *f* a stroke with the axe	Deut 19:5	5080

FETCHT

f a calf tender and good, and gave	Gen 18:7	3947

FETTERS

and bound him with *f* of brass	Judg 16:21	5178
bound, nor thy feet put into *f*	2Sa 3:34	5178
and bound him with *f* of brass	2Kin 25:7	5178
the thorns, and bound him with *f*	2Chr 33:11	5178
of Babylon, and bound him in *f*	2Chr 36:6	5178
And if they be bound in *f*, and be	Job 36:8	2131
Whose feet they hurt with *f*	Ps 105:18	3525
and their nobles with *f* of iron	Ps 149:8	3525
he had been often bound with *f*	Mk 5:4	3976
by him, and the *f* broken in pieces	Mk 5:4	3976
kept bound with chains and in *f*	Lk 8:29	3976

FEVER

with a consumption, and with a *f*	Deut 28:22	6920
mother laid, and sick of a *f*	Mt 8:14	4445
her hand, and the *f* left her	Mt 8:15	4446
wife's mother lay sick of a *f*	Mk 1:30	4445
and immediately the *f* left her	Mk 1:31	4446
mother was taken with a great *f*	Lk 4:38	4446
stood over her, and rebuked the *f*	Lk 4:39	4446
the seventh hour the *f* left him	Jn 4:52	4446
father of Publius lay sick of a *f*	Acts 28:8	4446

FEW See APPENDIX.

FEWER See APPENDIX.

FEWEST

for ye were the *f* of all people	Deut 7:7	4592

FEWNESS

according to the *f* of years thou	Lev 25:16	4591

FIDELITY

but shewing all good *f*	Titus 2:10	4102

FIELD

every plant of the *f* before it	Gen 2:5	7704
herb of the *f* before it grew	Gen 2:5	7704
God formed every beast of the *f*	Gen 2:19	7704
air, and to every beast of the *f*	Gen 2:20	7704
the *f* which the LORD God had made	Gen 3:1	7704
and above every beast of the *f*	Gen 3:14	7704
thou shalt eat the herb of the *f*	Gen 3:18	7704
to pass, when they were in the *f*	Gen 4:8	7704
which is in the end of his *f*	Gen 23:9	7704
the *f* give I thee, and the cave	Gen 23:11	7704
I will give thee money for the *f*	Gen 23:13	7704
the *f* of Ephron, which was in	Gen 23:17	7704
which was before Mamre, the *f*	Gen 23:17	7704
all the trees that were in the *f*	Gen 23:17	7704
the *f* of Machpelah before Mamre	Gen 23:19	7704
And the *f*, and the cave that is	Gen 23:20	7704
meditate in the *f* at the eventide	Gen 24:63	7704
that walketh in the *f* to meet us	Gen 24:65	7704
in the *f* of Ephron the son of	Gen 25:9	7704
The *f* which Abraham purchased of	Gen 25:10	7704
a cunning hunter, a man of the *f*	Gen 25:27	7704
and Esau came from the *f*, and he	Gen 25:29	7704
and thy bow, and go out to the *f*	Gen 27:3	7704
Esau went to the *f* to hunt for	Gen 27:5	7704
a *f* which the LORD hath blessed	Gen 27:27	7704
looked, and behold a well in the *f*	Gen 29:2	7704
and found mandrakes in the *f*	Gen 30:14	7704
came out of the *f* in the evening	Gen 30:16	7704
Leah to the *f* unto his flock,	Gen 31:4	7704
And he bought a parcel of a *f*	Gen 33:19	7704
were with his cattle in the *f*	Gen 34:5	7704
out of the *f* when they heard it	Gen 34:7	7704
city, and that which was in the *f*	Gen 34:28	7704
who smote Midian in the *f* of Moab	Gen 36:35	7704
we were binding sheaves in the *f*	Gen 37:7	7704
behold, he was wandering in the *f*	Gen 37:15	7704
he had in the house, and in the *f*	Gen 39:5	7704
the food of the *f*, which was	Gen 41:48	7704
Egyptians sold every man his *f*	Gen 47:20	7704
be your own, for seed of the *f*	Gen 47:24	7704
is in the *f* of Ephron the Hittite	Gen 49:29	7704
that is in the *f* of Machpelah	Gen 49:30	7704
the *f* of Ephron the Hittite for a	Gen 49:30	7704
The purchase of the *f* and of the	Gen 49:32	7704
in the cave of the *f* of Machpelah	Gen 50:13	7704
with the *f* for a possession of a	Gen 50:13	7704
in all manner of service in the *f*	Ex 1:14	7704
upon thy cattle which is in the *f*	Ex 9:3	7704
and all that thou hast in the *f*	Ex 9:19	7704
which shall be found in the *f*	Ex 9:19	7704
servants and his cattle in the *f*	Ex 9:21	7704
and upon every herb of the *f*	Ex 9:22	7704
of Egypt all that was in the *f*	Ex 9:25	7704
hail smote every herb of the *f*	Ex 9:25	7704
and brake every tree of the *f*	Ex 9:25	7704
groweth for you out of the *f*	Ex 10:5	7704
trees, or in the herbs of the *f*	Ex 10:15	7704
day ye shall not find it in the *f*	Ex 16:25	7704
If a man shall cause a *f* or	Ex 22:5	7704
and shall feed in another man's *f*	Ex 22:5	7704
of the best of his own *f*, and of	Ex 22:5	7704
or the standing corn, or the *f*	Ex 22:6	7704
that is torn of beasts in the *f*	Ex 22:31	7704
the beasts of the *f* shall eat	Ex 23:11	7704
which thou hast sown in the *f*	Ex 23:16	7704
in thy labours out of the *f*	Ex 23:16	7704
the beast of the *f* multiply	Ex 23:29	7704
living bird loose into the open *f*	Lev 14:7	7704
which they offer in the open *f*	Lev 17:5	7704
wholly reap the corners of thy *f*	Lev 19:9	7704
not sow thy *f* with mingled seed	Lev 19:19	7704
of thy *f* when thou reapest	Lev 23:22	7704
Six years thou shalt sow thy *f*	Lev 25:3	7704
thou shalt neither sow thy *f*	Lev 25:4	7704
the increase thereof out of the *f*	Lev 25:12	7704
But the *f* of the suburbs of their	Lev 25:34	7704
the trees of the *f* shall yield	Lev 26:4	7704
part of a *f* of his possession	Lev 27:16	7704
If he sanctify his *f* from the	Lev 27:17	7704
sanctify his *f* after the jubile	Lev 27:18	7704
if he that sanctified the *f* will	Lev 27:19	7704
And if he will not redeem the *f*	Lev 27:20	7704
he have sold the *f* to another man	Lev 27:20	7704
But the *f*, when it goeth out in	Lev 27:21	7704
unto the LORD, as a *f* devoted	Lev 27:21	7704
the LORD a *f* which he hath bought	Lev 27:22	7704
f shall return unto him of whom	Lev 27:24	7704
of the *f* of his possession, shall	Lev 27:28	7704
ox licketh up the grass of the *f*	Num 22:4	7704
of the way, and went into the *f*	Num 22:23	7704

brought him into the *f* of Zophim	Num 23:14	7704
thy neighbour's house, his *f*	Deut 5:21	7704
of the *f* increase upon thee	Deut 7:22	7704
that the *f* bringeth forth year by	Deut 14:22	7704
f is man's life) to employ them	Deut 20:19	7704
to possess it, lying in the *f*	Deut 21:1	7704
find a betrothed damsel in the *f*	Deut 22:25	7704
For he found her in the *f*	Deut 22:27	7704
down thine harvest in thy *f*	Deut 24:19	7704
and hast forgot a sheaf in the *f*	Deut 24:19	7704
and blessed shalt thou be in the *f*	Deut 28:3	7704
and cursed shalt thou be in the *f*	Deut 28:16	7704
carry much seed out into the *f*	Deut 28:38	7704
the inhabitants of Ai in the *f*	Josh 8:24	7704
him to ask of her father a *f*	Josh 15:18	7704
him to ask of her father a *f*	Judg 1:14	7704
marchedst out of the *f* of Edom	Judg 5:4	7704
death in the high places of the *f*	Judg 5:18	7704
thee, and lie in wait in the *f*	Judg 9:32	7704
the people went out into the *f*	Judg 9:42	7704
companies, and laid wait in the *f*	Judg 9:43	7704
the woman as she sat in the *f*	Judg 13:9	7704
his work out of the *f* at even	Judg 19:16	7704
and the other to Gibeah in the *f*	Judg 20:31	7704
Naomi, Let me now go to the *f*	Ruth 2:2	7704
gleaned in the *f* after the	Ruth 2:3	7704
part of the *f* belonging unto Boaz	Ruth 2:3	7704
Go not to glean in another *f*	Ruth 2:8	7704
be on the *f* that they do reap	Ruth 2:9	7704
she gleaned in the *f* until even	Ruth 2:17	7704
they meet thee not in any other *f*	Ruth 2:22	7704
buyest the *f* of the hand of Naomi	Ruth 4:5	7704
in the *f* about four thousand men	1Sa 4:2	7704
cart came into the *f* of Joshua	1Sa 6:14	7704
unto this day in the *f* of Joshua	1Sa 6:18	7704
came after the herd out of the *f*	1Sa 11:5	7704
trembling in the host, in the *f*	1Sa 14:15	7704
air, and to the beasts of the *f*	1Sa 17:44	7704
my father in the *f* where thou art	1Sa 19:3	7704
the *f* unto the third day at even	1Sa 20:5	7704
Come, and let us go out into the *f*	1Sa 20:11	7704
went out both of them into the *f*	1Sa 20:11	7704
So David hid himself in the *f*	1Sa 20:24	7704
the *f* at the time appointed with	1Sa 20:35	7704
they found an Egyptian in the *f*	1Sa 30:11	7704
were by themselves in the *f*	2Sa 10:8	7704
and came out unto us into the *f*	2Sa 11:23	7704
they two strove together in the *f*	2Sa 14:6	7704
Joab's *f* is near mine, and he hath	2Sa 14:30	2513
servants set the *f* on fire	2Sa 14:30	2513
thy servants set my *f* on fire	2Sa 14:31	2513
robbed of her whelps in the *f*	2Sa 17:8	7704
out into the *f* against Israel	2Sa 18:6	7704
out of the highway into the *f*	2Sa 20:12	7704
nor the beasts of the *f* by night	2Sa 21:10	7704
and they two were alone in the *f*	1Kin 11:29	7704
him that dieth in the *f* shall the	1Kin 14:11	7704
him that dieth in the *f* shall the	1Kin 21:24	7704
out into the *f* to gather herbs	2Kin 4:39	7704
camp to hide themselves in the *f*	2Kin 7:12	7704
all the fruits of the *f* since the	2Kin 8:6	7704
of the *f* of Naboth the Jezreelite	2Kin 9:25	7704
the *f* in the portion of Jezreel	2Kin 9:37	7704
in the highway of the fuller's *f*	2Kin 18:17	7704
they were as the grass of the *f*	2Kin 19:26	7704
smote Midian in the *f* of Moab	1Chr 1:46	7704
come were by themselves in the *f*	1Chr 19:9	7704
f for tillage of the ground was	1Chr 27:26	7704
him with his fathers in the *f* of	2Chr 26:23	7704
and of all the increase of the *f*	2Chr 31:5	7704
were fled every one to his *f*	Neh 13:10	7704
league with the stones of the *f*	Job 5:23	7704
the beasts of the *f* shall be at	Job 5:23	7704
reap every one his corn in the *f*	Job 24:6	7704
all the beasts of the *f* play	Job 40:20	7704
oxen, yea, and the beasts of the *f*	Ps 8:7	7704
the wild beasts of the *f* are mine	Ps 50:11	7704
land of Egypt, in the *f* of Zoan	Ps 78:12	7704
and his wonders in the *f* of Zoan	Ps 78:43	7704
beast of the *f* doth devour it	Ps 80:13	7704
Let the *f* be joyful, and all that	Ps 96:12	7704
as a flower of the *f*, so he	Ps 103:15	7704
drink to every beast of the *f*	Ps 104:11	7704
make it fit for thyself in the *f*	Prov 24:27	7704
I went to the *f* of the slothful,	Prov 24:30	7704
the goats are the price of the *f*	Prov 27:26	7704
She considereth a *f*, and buyeth it	Prov 31:16	7704
king himself is served by the *f*	Eccl 5:9	7704
roes, and by the hinds of the *f*	Song 2:7	7704
roes, and by the hinds of the *f*	Song 3:5	7704
let us go forth into the *f*	Song 7:11	7704

to house, that lay f to f .... Is 5:8   7704
to house, that lay f to f .... Is 5:8   7704
in the highway of the fuller's f .... Is 7:3   7704
his forest, and of his fruitful f .... Is 10:18
and joy out of the plentiful f .... Is 16:10
shall be turned into a fruitful f .... Is 29:17
the fruitful f shall be esteemed .... Is 29:17
and the wilderness be a fruitful f .... Is 32:15
the fruitful f be counted for a .... Is 32:15
remain in the fruitful f .... Is 32:16
in the highway of the fuller's f .... Is 36:2
they were as the grass of the f .... Is 37:27   7704
thereof is as the flower of the f .... Is 40:6   7704
beast of the f shall honour me .... Is 43:20   7704
all the trees of the f shall clap .... Is 55:12   7704
All ye beasts of the f, come to .... Is 56:9   7704
As keepers of a f, are they .... Jer 4:17   7704
Go not forth into the f, nor walk .... Jer 6:25   7704
beast, and upon the trees of the f .... Jer 7:20   7704
fall as dung upon the open f .... Jer 9:22   7704
and the herbs of every f wither .... Jer 12:4   7704
assemble all the beasts of the f .... Jer 12:9   7704
the hind also calved in the f .... Jer 14:5   7704
If I go forth into the f, then .... Jer 14:18   7704
O my mountain in the f, I will .... Jer 17:3   7704
cometh from the rock of the f .... Jer 18:14   7704
Zion shall be plowed like a f .... Jer 26:18   7704
the beasts of the f have I given .... Jer 27:6   7704
him the beasts of the f also .... Jer 28:14   7704
Buy thee my f that is in Anathoth .... Jer 32:7   7704
LORD, and said unto me, Buy my f .... Jer 32:8   7704
I bought the f of Hanameel my .... Jer 32:9   7704
GOD, Buy thee the f for money .... Jer 32:25   7704
neither have we vineyard, nor f .... Jer 35:9   7704
for we have treasures in the f .... Jer 41:8   7704
is taken from the plentiful f .... Jer 48:33
for want of the fruits of the f .... Lam 4:9   7704
he that is in the f shall die .... Eze 7:15   7704
thou wast cast out in the open f .... Eze 16:5   7704
to multiply as the bud of the f .... Eze 16:7   7704
and planted it in a fruitful f .... Eze 17:5   7704
all the trees of the f shall know .... Eze 17:24   7704
against the forest of the south f .... Eze 20:46   7704
the f shall be slain by the sword .... Eze 26:6   7704
the sword thy daughters in the f .... Eze 26:8   7704
for meat to the beasts of the f .... Eze 29:5   776
unto all the trees of the f .... Eze 31:4   7704
above all the trees of the f .... Eze 31:5   7704
of the f bring forth their young .... Eze 31:6   7704
all the beasts of the f shall be .... Eze 31:13   7704
trees of the f fainted for him .... Eze 31:15   7704
cast them forth upon the open f .... Eze 32:4   7704
him that is in the open f will I .... Eze 33:27   7704
meat to all the beasts of the f .... Eze 34:5   7704
meat to every beast of the f .... Eze 34:8   7704
the tree of the f shall yield her .... Eze 34:27   7704
tree, and the increase of the f .... Eze 36:30   7704
heaven, and the beasts of the f .... Eze 38:20   7704
beasts of the f to be devoured .... Eze 39:4   7704
Thou shalt fall upon the open f .... Eze 39:5   7704
shall take no wood out of the f .... Eze 39:10   7704
fowl, and to every beast of the f .... Eze 39:17   7704
of men dwell, the beasts of the f .... Dan 2:38   1251
the beasts of the f had shadow .... Dan 4:12   1251
in the tender grass of the f .... Dan 4:15   1251
which the beasts of the f dwelt .... Dan 4:21   1251
in the tender grass of the f .... Dan 4:23   1251
be with the beasts of the f .... Dan 4:23   1251
shall be with the beasts of the f .... Dan 4:25   1251
shall be with the beasts of the f .... Dan 4:32   1251
beasts of the f shall eat them .... Hos 2:12   7704
for them with the beasts of the f .... Hos 2:18   7704
with the beasts of the f .... Hos 4:3   7704
hemlock in the furrows of the f .... Hos 10:4   7704
The f is wasted, the land .... Joel 1:10   7704
the harvest of the f is perished .... Joel 1:11   7704
tree, even all the trees of the f .... Joel 1:12   7704
burned all the trees of the f .... Joel 1:19   7704
The beasts of the f cry also unto .... Joel 1:20   7704
Be not afraid, ye beasts of the f .... Joel 2:22   7704
make Samaria as an heap of the f .... Mic 1:6   7704
for your sake be plowed as a f .... Mic 3:12   7704
and thou shalt dwell in the f .... Mic 4:10   7704
rain, to every one grass in the f .... Zec 10:1   7704
fruit before the time in the f .... Mal 3:11   7704
Consider the lilies of the f .... Mt 6:28   68
God so clothe the grass of the f .... Mt 6:30   68
which sowed good seed in his f .... Mt 13:24   68
not thou sow good seed in thy f .... Mt 13:27   68
a man took, and sowed in his f .... Mt 13:31   68
the parable of the tares of the f .... Mt 13:36   68

The f **is the world** .... Mt 13:38   68
is like unto treasure hid in a f .... Mt 13:44   68
that he hath, and buyeth that f .... Mt 13:44   68
f **return back to take his clothes** .... Mt 24:18   68
Then shall two be in the f .... Mt 24:40   68
bought with them the potter's f .... Mt 27:7   68
Wherefore that f was called .... Mt 27:8   68
The f of blood, unto this day .... Mt 27:8   68
And gave them for the potter's f .... Mt 27:10   68
let him that is in the f **not turn** .... Mk 13:16   68
shepherds abiding in the f .... Lk 2:8   68
grass, which is to day in the f .... Lk 12:28   68
Now his elder son was in the f .... Lk 15:25   68
and by, when he is come from the f .. Lk 17:7   68
and he that is in the f**, let him** .... Lk 17:31   68
Two men shall be in the f .... Lk 17:36   68
Now this man purchased a f with .... Acts 1:18   5564
insomuch as that f is called in .... Acts 1:19   5564
that is to say, The f of blood .... Acts 1:19   5564

FIELDS

of the villages, and out of the f .... Ex 8:13   7704
out of the city into the open f .... Lev 14:53   7704
counted as the f of the country .... Lev 25:31   7704
is not of the f of his possession .... Lev 27:22   7704
or given us inheritance of f .... Num 16:14   7704
slain with a sword in the open f .... Num 19:16   7704
we will not pass through the f .... Num 20:17   7704
we will not turn into the f .... Num 21:22   7704
grass in thy f for thy cattle .... Deut 11:15   7704
might eat the increase of the f .... Deut 32:13   7704
of Sodom, and of the f of Gomorrah .. Deut 32:32   7709
But the f of the city, and the .... Josh 21:12   7704
And they went out into the f .... Judg 9:27   7704
all the people that were in the f .... Judg 9:44   7704
And he will take your f, and your 1Sa 8:14   7704
of Jesse give every one of you f 1Sa 22:7   7704
with them, when we were in the f 1Sa 25:15   7704
upon you, nor f of offerings 2Sa 1:21   7704
lord, are encamped in the open f 2Sa 11:11   7704
to Anathoth, unto thine own f 1Kin 2:26   7704
him that dieth of his in the f 1Kin 16:4   7704
Jerusalem in the f of Kidron 2Kin 23:4   7709
But the f of the city, and the 1Chr 6:56   7704
let the f rejoice, and all that is 1Chr 16:32   7704
and over the storehouses in the f 1Chr 27:25   7704
which were in the f of the 2Chr 31:19   7704
And for the villages, with their f .... Neh 11:25   7704
the f thereof, at Azekah, and in .... Neh 11:30   7704
Gilgal, and out of the f of Geba .... Neh 12:29   7704
f of the cities the portions of .... Neh 12:44   7704
and sendeth waters upon the f .... Job 5:10   2351
And sow the f, and plant vineyards, ... Ps 107:37   7704
we found it in the f of the wood .... Ps 132:6   7704
had not made the earth, nor the f .... Prov 8:26   2351
not into the f of the fatherless .... Prov 23:10   7704
For the f of Heshbon languish, and ..... Is 16:8   7709
for the teats, for the pleasant f .... Is 32:12   7704
turned unto others, with their f .... Jer 6:12   7704
their f to them that shall .... Jer 8:10   7704
on the hills in the f .... Jer 13:27   7704
all the f unto the brook of .... Jer 31:40   8309
Houses and f and vineyards shall be ... Jer 32:15   7704
f shall be bought in this land, ... Jer 32:43   7704
Men shall buy f for money .... Jer 32:44   7704
vineyards and f at the same time .... Jer 39:10   3010
of the forces which were in the f .... Jer 40:7   7704
of the forces that were in the f .... Jer 40:13   7704
thou shalt fall upon the open f .... Eze 29:5   7704
as heaps in the furrows of the f .... Hos 12:11   7704
shall possess the f of Ephraim .... Obad 19   7704
of Ephraim, and the f of Samaria .... Obad 19   7704
And they covet f, and take them by .... Mic 2:2   7704
away he hath divided our f .... Mic 2:4   7704
the f shall yield no meat .... Hab 3:17   7709
the corn f on the sabbath day .... Mk 2:23
that he went through the corn f .... Lk 6:1
sent him into his f **to feed swine** .... Lk 15:15   68
up your eyes, and look on the f .... Jn 4:35   5561
who have reaped down your f .... Jas 5:4   5561

FIERCE

be their anger, for it was f .... Gen 49:7   5794
Turn from thy f wrath, and repent ...... Ex 32:12   2740
that the f anger of the LORD may .... Num 25:4   2740
to augment yet the f anger of the .... Num 32:14   2740
A nation of f countenance .... Deut 28:50   5794
arose from the table in f anger 1Sa 20:34   2750
his f wrath upon Amalek 1Sa 28:18   2740
for the f wrath of the LORD is 2Chr 28:11   2740
there is f wrath against Israel 2Chr 28:13   2740
that his f wrath may turn away 2Chr 29:10   2740

F

until the *f* wrath of our God for ....Ezr 10:14   2740
lion, and the voice of the *f* lion.............Job 4:10   7826
Thou huntest me as a *f* lion.....................Job 10:16   7826
nor the *f* lion passed by it.......................Job 28:8   7826
None is so *f* that dare stir him.................Job 41:10   393
Thy *f* wrath goeth over me ....Ps 88:16
for the *f* anger of Rezin with ....Is 7:4   2750
f anger, to lay the land desolate...............Is 13:9   2740
and in the day of his *f* anger ....Is 13:13   2740
a *f* king shall rule over them, ...Is 19:4   5794
Thou shalt not see a *f* people ....Is 33:19   3267
for the *f* anger of the LORD is................Jer 4:8   2740
of the LORD, and by his *f* anger ....Jer 4:26   2740
of the *f* anger of the LORD ....Jer 12:13   2740
of the *f* anger of the LORD ....Jer 25:37   2740
and because of his *f* anger ....Jer 25:38   2740
The *f* anger of the LORD shall not ....Jer 30:24   2740
evil upon them, even my *f* anger ....Jer 49:37   2740
soul from the *f* anger of the LORD ....Jer 51:45   2740
me in the day of his *f* anger ....Lam 1:12   2740
He hath cut off in his *f* anger ....Lam 2:3   2750
he hath poured out his *f* anger ....Lam 4:11   2740
a king of *f* countenance, and................Dan 8:23   5794
and turn away from his *f* anger ....Jonah 3:9   2740
are more *f* than the evening ....Hab 1:8   2300
before the *f* anger of the LORD................Zeph 2:2   2740
indignation, even all my *f* anger ....Zeph 3:8   2740
out of the tombs, exceeding *f* ....Mt 8:28   5467
And they were the more *f*, saying, ...Lk 23:5   2001
false accusers, incontinent, *f*, ...2Ti 3:3   434
great, and are driven of *f* winds.............Jas 3:4   4642

FIERCENESS

may turn from the *f* of his anger ....Deut 13:17   2740
turned from the *f* of his anger..................Josh 7:26   2740
not from the *f* of his great wrath 2Kin 23:26   2740
that the *f* of his wrath may turn 2Chr 30:8   2740
He swalloweth the ground with *f* ....Job 39:24   7494
cast upon them the *f* of his anger............Ps 78:49   2740
thyself from the *f* of thine anger ....Ps 85:3   2740
because of the *f* of the oppressor ....Jer 25:38   2740
not execute the *f* of mine anger ....Hos 11:9   2740
can abide in the *f* of his anger ....Nah 1:6   2740
of the wine of the *f* of his wrath ....Rev 16:19   2372
treadeth the winepress of the *f*................Rev 19:15   2372

FIERCER

f than the words of the men of 2Sa 19:43   7185

FIERY

the LORD sent *f* serpents among.............Num 21:6   8314
unto Moses, Make thee a *f* serpent ......Num 21:8   8314
wherein were *f* serpents, and ....Deut 8:15   8314
right hand went a *f* law for them ....Deut 33:2   799
Thou shalt make them as a *f* oven ....Ps 21:9   784
fruit shall be a *f* flying serpent ....Is 14:29   8314
f flying serpent, they will carry...............Is 30:6   8314
the midst of a burning *f* furnace............Dan 3:6   5135
the midst of a burning *f* furnace............Dan 3:11   5135
the midst of a burning *f* furnace............Dan 3:15   5135
us from the burning *f* furnace................Dan 3:17   5135
them into the burning *f* furnace ....Dan 3:20   5135
midst of the burning *f* furnace ....Dan 3:21   5135
midst of the burning *f* furnace ....Dan 3:23   5135
mouth of the burning *f* furnace ....Dan 3:26   5135
his throne was like the *f* flame................Dan 7:9   5135
A *f* stream issued and came forth ....Dan 7:10   5135
all the *f* darts of the wicked ....Eph 6:16   4448
f indignation, which shall devour...........Heb 10:27   4442
the *f* trial which is to try you 1Pet 4:12   4451

FIFTEEN

f years, and begat sons and ....Gen 5:10   2568,6240
F cubits upward did the waters.........Gen 7:20   2568,6240
an hundred threescore and *f* years Gen 25:7   7657,2568
of the gate shall be *f* cubits ....Ex 27:14   2568,6240
side shall be hangings *f* cubits ....Ex 27:15   2568,6240
side of the gate were *f* cubits ....Ex 38:14   2568,6240
hand, were hangings *f* cubits ......Ex 38:15   2568,6240
f shekels, after the shekel of ....Ex 38:25   7657,2568
thy estimation shall be *f* shekels ....Lev 27:7   2568,6240
six hundred and threescore and *f*.. Num 31:37   7657,2568
about *f* thousand men, all that........Judg 8:10   2568,6240
Now Ziba had *f* sons and twenty 2Sa 9:10   2568,6240
his *f* sons and his twenty servants..2Sa 19:17   2568,6240
on forty five pillars, *f* in a row 1Kin 7:3   2568,6240
Jehoahaz king of Israel *f* years......2Kin 14:17   2568,6240
I will add unto thy days *f* years 2Kin 20:6   2568,6240
Jehoahaz king of Israel *f* years 2Chr 25:25   2568,6240
I will add unto thy days *f* years ......Is 38:5   2568,6240
f shekels, shall be your maneh........Eze 45:12   6235,2568
her to me for *f* pieces of silver ....Hos 3:2   2568,6240
Jerusalem, about *f* furlongs off ....Jn 11:18   1178

kindred, threescore and *f* souls.......Acts 7:14   1440,4002
again, and found it *f* fathoms ....Acts 27:28   1178
Peter, and abode with him *f* days...........Gal 1:18   1178

FIFTEENTH

on the *f* day of the second month .... Ex 16:1   2568,6240
on the *f* day of the same month is ... Lev 23:6   2568,6240
The *f* day of this seventh month ......Lev 23:34   2568,6240
Also in the *f* day of the seventh......Lev 23:39   2568,6240
in the *f* day of this month is the ......Num 28:17   2568,6240
on the *f* day of the seventh month...Num 29:12   2568,6240
on the *f* day of the first month......Num 33:3   2568,6240
on the *f* day of the month, like.........1Kin 12:32   2568,6240
the *f* day of the eighth month 1Kin 12:33   2568,6240
In the *f* year of Amaziah the son 2Kin 14:23   2568,6240
The *f* to Bilgah, the sixteenth to 1Chr 24:14   2568,6240
The *f* to Jeremoth, he, his sons,......1Chr 25:22   2568,6240
in the *f* year of the reign of Asa 2Chr 15:10   2568,6240
on the *f* day of the same they ....Est 9:18   2568,6240
the *f* day of the same, yearly, ...Est 9:21   2568,6240
in the *f* day of the month, that.........Eze 32:17   2568,6240
in the *f* day of the month, shall ....Eze 45:25   2568,6240
Now in the *f* year of the reign of.............Lk 3:1   4003

FIFTH

and the morning were the *f* day ....Gen 1:23   2549
and bare Jacob the *f* son ....Gen 30:17   2549
take up the *f* part of the land of..........Gen 41:34   2567
give the *f* part unto Pharaoh ....Gen 47:24   2549
Pharaoh should have the *f* part ....Gen 47:26   2569
and shall add the *f* part thereto............Lev 5:16   2549
shall add the *f* part more thereto ....Lev 6:5   2549
in the *f* year shall ye eat of the ....Lev 19:25   2549
put the *f* part thereof unto it ....Lev 22:14   2549
then he shall add a *f* part......................Lev 27:13   2549
then he shall add the *f* part of ....Lev 27:15   2549
then he shall add the *f* part of ....Lev 27:19   2549
shall add a *f* part of it thereto..............Lev 27:27   2549
add thereto the *f* part thereof ....Lev 27:31   2549
and add unto it the *f* part thereof ....Num 5:7   2549
On the *f* day Shelumiel the son of ....Num 7:36   2549
on the *f* day nine bullocks, two ....Num 29:26   2549
in the first day of the *f* month ....Num 33:38   2549
the *f* lot came out for the tribe ....Josh 19:24   2549
morning on the *f* day to depart ....Judg 19:8   2549
spear smote him under the *f* rib 2Sa 2:23   2549
and the *f*, Shephatiah the son of 2Sa 3:4   2549
smote him there under the *f* rib............2Sa 3:27   2570
and they smote him under the *f* rib 2Sa 4:6   2570
smote him therewith in the *f* rib 2Sa 20:10   2570
posts were a *f* part of the wall 1Kin 6:31   2549
in the *f* year of king Rehoboam 1Kin 14:25   2549
in the *f* year of Joram the son of............2Kin 8:16   2568
And in the *f* month, on the seventh 2Kin 25:8   2549
the fourth, Raddai the *f*,......................1Chr 2:14   2549
The *f*, Shephatiah of Abital..................1Chr 3:3   2549
Nohah the fourth, and Rapha the *f*.........1Chr 8:2   2549
the fourth, Jeremiah the *f*...................1Chr 12:10   2549
The *f* to Malchijah, the sixth.............1Chr 24:9   2549
The *f* to Nethaniah, he, his sons,..........1Chr 25:12   2549
Elam the *f*, Jehohanan the sixth,..........1Chr 26:3   2549
the fourth, and Nethaneel the *f*............1Chr 26:4   2549
The *f* captain for the *f* month 1Chr 27:8   2549
that in the *f* year of king 2Chr 12:2   2549
came to Jerusalem in the *f* month ....Ezr 7:8   2549
on the first day of the *f* month ....Ezr 7:9   2549
unto me in like manner the *f* time ....Neh 6:5   2549
f day of the month Elul, in fifty ....Neh 6:15   2568
Jerusalem captive in the *f* month ....Jer 1:3   2549
fourth year, and in the *f* month ....Jer 28:1   2549
it came to pass in the *f* year of ....Jer 36:9   2549
Now in the *f* month, in the tenth ....Jer 52:12   2549
in the *f* day of the month, as I ....Eze 1:1   2568
In the *f* day of the month ....Eze 1:2   2568
which was the *f* year of king ....Eze 1:2   2549
in the *f* day of the month, as I ....Eze 8:1   2568
the seventh year, in the *f* month............Eze 20:1   2549
in the *f* day of the month, that ....Eze 33:21   2568
Should I weep in the *f* month ....Zec 7:3   2549
ye fasted and mourned in the *f*.............Zec 7:5   2549
month, and the fast of the *f*..................Zec 8:19   2549
And when he had opened the *f* seal ......Rev 6:9   3991
the *f* angel sounded, and I saw a ....Rev 9:1   3991
the *f* angel poured out his vial...............Rev 16:10   3991
The *f*, sardonyx; the sixth ....Rev 21:20   3991

FIFTIES

rulers of hundreds, rulers of *f* ....Ex 18:21   2572
rulers of hundreds, rulers of *f* ....Ex 18:25   2572
over hundreds, and captains over *f*.......Deut 1:15   2572
thousands, and captains over *f*.............1Sa 8:12   2572
the former *f* with their *f*......................2Kin 1:14   2572

FIFTIETH

in ranks, by hundreds, and by *f*	Mk 6:40	4004
them sit down by *f* in a company	Lk 9:14	4004

FIFTIETH

And ye shall hallow the *f* year	Lev 25:10	2572
shall that *f* year be unto you	Lev 25:11	2572
In the *f* year of Azariah king of	2Kin 15:23	2572
f year of Azariah king of Judah	2Kin 15:27	2572

FIFTY

the breadth of it *f* cubits	Gen 6:15	2572
the earth an hundred and *f* days	Gen 7:24	2572
f days the waters were abated	Gen 8:3	2572
flood three hundred and *f* years	Gen 9:28	2572
Noah were nine hundred and *f* years	Gen 9:29	2572
Peradventure there be *f* righteous	Gen 18:24	2572
the *f* righteous that are therein	Gen 18:24	2572
If I find in Sodom *f* righteous	Gen 18:26	2572
lack five of the *f* righteous	Gen 18:28	2572
F loops shalt thou make in the	Ex 26:5	2572
f loops shalt thou make in the	Ex 26:5	2572
thou shalt make *f* taches of gold	Ex 26:6	2572
thou shalt make *f* loops on the	Ex 26:10	2572
f loops in the edge of the	Ex 26:10	2572
thou shalt make *f* taches of brass	Ex 26:11	2572
shall be hangings of *f* cubits	Ex 27:12	2572
side eastward shall be *f* cubits	Ex 27:13	2572
and the breadth *f* every where	Ex 27:18	2572
f shekels, and of sweet calamus	Ex 30:23	2572
calamus two hundred and *f* shekels,	Ex 30:23	2572
F loops made he in one curtain,	Ex 36:12	2572
f loops made he in the edge of	Ex 36:12	2572
he made *f* taches of gold, and	Ex 36:13	2572
And he made *f* loops upon the	Ex 36:17	2572
f loops made he upon the edge of	Ex 36:17	2572
he made *f* taches of brass to	Ex 36:18	2572
side were hangings of *f* cubits	Ex 38:12	2572
the east side eastward *f* cubits	Ex 38:13	2572
thousand and five hundred and *f* men	Ex 38:26	2572
sabbath shall ye number *f* days	Lev 23:16	2572
shall be *f* shekels of silver	Lev 27:3	2572
be valued at *f* shekels of silver	Lev 27:16	2572
of the tribe of Simeon, were *f*	Num 1:23	2572
and five thousand six hundred and *f*	Num 1:25	2572
of the tribe of Issachar, were *f*	Num 1:29	2572
of the tribe of Zebulun, were *f*	Num 1:31	2572
of the tribe of Naphtali, were *f*	Num 1:43	2572
thousand and five hundred and *f*	Num 1:46	2572
were numbered thereof, were *f*	Num 2:6	2572
were numbered thereof, were *f*	Num 2:8	2572
were numbered of them, were *f*	Num 2:13	2572
five thousand and six hundred and *f*	Num 2:15	2572
were an hundred thousand and *f*	Num 2:16	2572
one thousand and four hundred and *f*	Num 2:16	2572
were numbered of them, were *f*	Num 2:30	2572
Dan were an hundred thousand and *f*	Num 2:31	2572
thousand and five hundred and *f*	Num 2:32	2572
and upward even until *f* years old	Num 4:3	2572
upward until *f* years old shalt	Num 4:23	2572
upward even unto *f* years old	Num 4:30	2572
and upward even unto *f* years old	Num 4:35	2572
two thousand seven hundred and *f*	Num 4:36	2572
and upward unto *f* years old	Num 4:39	2572
and upward even unto *f* years old	Num 4:43	2572
and upward even unto *f* years old	Num 4:47	2572
from the age of *f* years they	Num 8:25	2572
f princes of the assembly, famous	Num 16:2	2572
censer, two hundred and *f* censers	Num 16:17	2572
f men that offered incense	Num 16:35	2572
devoured two hundred and *f* men	Num 26:10	2572
that were numbered of them, *f*	Num 26:34	2572
who were *f* and three thousand and	Num 26:47	2572
thou shalt take one portion of *f*	Num 31:30	2572
half, Moses took one portion of *f*	Num 31:47	2572
seven hundred and *f* shekels	Num 31:52	2572
father *f* shekels of silver	Deut 22:29	2572
wedge of gold of *f* shekels weight	Josh 7:21	2572
he smote of the people *f* thousand	1Sa 6:19	2572
and *f* men to run before him	2Sa 15:1	2572
the oxen for *f* shekels of silver	2Sa 24:24	2572
and *f* men to run before him	1Kin 1:5	2572
and the breadth thereof *f* cubits	1Kin 7:2	2572
the length thereof was *f* cubits	1Kin 7:6	2572
Solomon's work, five hundred and *f*	1Kin 9:23	2572
and an horse for an hundred and *f*	1Kin 10:29	2572
and hid them by *f* in a cave	1Kin 18:4	2572
LORD's prophets by *f* in a cave	1Kin 18:13	2572
of Baal four hundred and *f*	1Kin 18:19	2572
are four hundred and *f* men	1Kin 18:22	2572
him a captain of *f* with his *f*	2Kin 1:9	2572
and said to the captain of *f*	2Kin 1:10	2572
heaven, and consume thee and thy *f*	2Kin 1:10	2572

heaven, and consumed him and his *f*	2Kin 1:10	2572
captain of *f* with his *f*	2Kin 1:11	2572
heaven, and consume thee and thy *f*	2Kin 1:12	2572
heaven, and consumed him and his *f*	2Kin 1:12	2572
of the third *f* with his *f*	2Kin 1:13	2572
And the third captain of *f* went up	2Kin 1:13	2572
the life of these *f* thy servants	2Kin 1:13	2572
f men of the sons of the prophets	2Kin 2:7	2572
be with thy servants *f* strong men	2Kin 2:16	2572
They sent therefore *f* men	2Kin 2:17	2572
people to Jehoahaz but *f* horsemen	2Kin 13:7	2572
two and *f* years in Jerusalem	2Kin 15:2	2572
of each man *f* shekels of silver,	2Kin 15:20	2572
with him *f* men of the Gileadites	2Kin 15:25	2572
he began to reign, and reigned *f*	2Kin 21:1	2572
of their camels *f* thousand	1Chr 5:21	2572
f thousand, and of asses two	1Chr 5:21	2572
and sons' sons, an hundred and *f*	1Chr 8:40	2572
generations, nine hundred and *f*	1Chr 9:9	2572
f thousand, which could keep rank	1Chr 12:33	2572
and an horse for an hundred and *f*	2Chr 1:17	2572
f thousand and three thousand and	2Chr 2:17	2572
the nails was *f* shekels of gold	2Chr 3:9	2572
officers, even two hundred and *f*	2Chr 8:10	2572
f talents of gold, and brought	2Chr 8:18	2572
began to reign, and he reigned *f*	2Chr 26:3	2572
began to reign, and he reigned *f*	2Chr 33:1	2572
of Elam, a thousand two hundred *f*	Ezr 2:7	2572
of Bigvai, two thousand *f*	Ezr 2:14	2572
children of Adin, four hundred *f*	Ezr 2:15	2572
The men of Netophah, *f* and six	Ezr 2:22	2572
The children of Nebo, *f* and two	Ezr 2:29	2572
children of Magbish, an hundred *f*	Ezr 2:30	2572
Elam, a thousand two hundred *f*	Ezr 2:31	2572
children of Immer, a thousand *f*	Ezr 2:37	2572
children of Nekoda, six hundred *f*	Ezr 2:60	2572
of the males an hundred and *f*	Ezr 8:3	2572
of Jonathan, and with him *f* males	Ezr 8:6	2572
f talents of silver, and silver	Ezr 8:26	2572
f of the Jews and rulers, beside	Neh 5:17	2572
fifth day of the month Elul, in *f*	Neh 6:15	2572
children of Arah, six hundred *f*	Neh 7:10	2572
of Elam, a thousand two hundred *f*	Neh 7:12	2572
children of Adin, six hundred *f*	Neh 7:20	2572
The men of the other Nebo, *f*	Neh 7:33	2572
Elam, a thousand two hundred *f*	Neh 7:34	2572
children of Immer, a thousand *f*	Neh 7:40	2572
f basons, five hundred and thirty	Neh 7:70	2572
gallows be made of *f* cubits high	Est 5:14	2572
also, the gallows *f* cubits high	Est 7:9	2572
The captain of *f*, and the	Is 3:3	2572
of the inner gate were *f* cubits	Eze 40:15	2572
the length thereof was *f* cubits	Eze 40:21	2572
the length was *f* cubits, and the	Eze 40:25	2572
it was *f* cubits long, and five and	Eze 40:29	2572
it was *f* cubits long, and five and	Eze 40:33	2572
the length was *f* cubits, and the	Eze 40:36	2572
door, and the breadth was *f* cubits	Eze 42:2	2572
the length thereof was *f* cubits	Eze 42:7	2572
in the utter court was *f* cubits	Eze 42:8	2572
f cubits round about for the	Eze 45:2	2572
toward the north two hundred and *f*	Eze 48:17	2572
toward the south two hundred and *f*	Eze 48:17	2572
toward the east two hundred and *f*	Eze 48:17	2572
toward the west two hundred and *f*	Eze 48:17	2572
out *f* vessels out of the press	Hag 2:16	2572
hundred pence, and the other *f*	Lk 7:41	4004
and sit down quickly, and write *f*	Lk 16:6	4004
him, Thou art not yet *f* years old	Jn 8:57	4004
of great fishes, an hundred and *f*	Jn 21:11	4004
f years, until Samuel the prophet	Acts 13:20	4004
found it *f* thousand pieces of	Acts 19:19	4002,3461

FIG

they sewed *f* leaves together, and	Gen 3:7	8384
and *f* trees, and pomegranates	Deut 8:8	8384
And the trees said to the *f* tree	Judg 9:10	8384
But the *f* tree said unto them,	Judg 9:11	8384
his vine and under his *f* tree	1Kin 4:25	8384
vine, and every one of his *f* tree	2Kin 18:31	8384
their vines also and their *f* trees	Ps 105:33	8384
Whoso keepeth the *f* tree shall	Prov 27:18	8384
The *f* tree putteth forth her	Song 2:13	8384
as a falling *f* from the *f* tree	Is 34:4	8384
vine, and every one of his *f* tree	Is 36:16	8384
eat up thy vines and thy *f* trees	Jer 5:17	8384
the vine, nor figs on the *f* tree	Jer 8:13	8384
her *f* trees, whereof she hath	Hos 2:12	8384
in the *f* tree at her first time	Hos 9:10	8384
vine waste, and barked my *f* tree	Joel 1:7	8384
up, and the *f* tree languisheth	Joel 1:12	8384

the *f* tree and the vine do yield .... Joel 2:22 ... 8384
your *f* trees and your olive trees .... Amos 4:9 ... 8384
his vine and under his *f* tree .... Mic 4:4 ... 8384
f trees with the firstripe figs .... Nah 3:12 ... 8384
Although the *f* tree shall not .... Hab 3:17 ... 8384
the *f* tree, and the pomegranate, ... Hag 2:19 ... 8384
the vine and under the *f* tree.................. Zec 3:10 ... 8384
when he saw the *f* tree in the way,........... Mt 21:19 ... *4808*
presently the *f* tree withered .... Mt 21:19 ... *4808*
How soon is the *f* tree withered .... Mt 21:20 ... *4808*
this which is done to the *f* tree .... Mt 21:21 ... *4808*
Now learn a parable of the *f* tree.......... Mt 24:32 ... *4808*
seeing a *f* tree afar off having................. Mk 11:13 ... *4808*
they saw the *f* tree dried up from .... Mk 11:20 ... *4808*
the *f* tree which thou cursedst is .... Mk 11:21 ... *4808*
Now learn a parable of the *f* tree .... Mk 13:28 ... *4808*
A certain man had a *f* tree .... Lk 13:6 ... *4808*
come seeking fruit on this *f* tree .... Lk 13:7 ... *4808*
Behold the *f* tree, and all the .... Lk 21:29 ... *4808*
when thou wast under the *f* tree .... Jn 1:48 ... *4808*
thee, I saw thee under the *f* tree .... Jn 1:50 ... *4808*
Can the *f* tree, my brethren, bear .... Jas 3:12 ... *4808*
even as a *f* tree casteth her................... Rev 6:13 ... *4808*

FIGHT
f against us, and so get them up .... Ex 1:10 ... 3898
The Lord shall *f* for you, and ye .... Ex 14:14 ... 3898
out men, and go out, to *f* with Amalek ...... Ex 17:9 ... 3898
before you, he shall *f* for you .... Deut 1:30 ... 3898
the Lord, we will go up and *f*................... Deut 1:41 ... 3898
unto them, Go not up, neither *f*............... Deut 1:42 ... 3898
and all his people, to *f* at Jahaz .... Deut 2:32 ... 4421
Lord your God he shall *f* for you .... Deut 3:22 ... 3898
to *f* for you against your enemies .... Deut 20:4 ... 3898
nigh unto a city to *f* against it .... Deut 20:10 ... 3898
to *f* with Joshua and with Israel, ... Josh 9:2 ... 3898
your enemies against whom ye *f* .... Josh 10:25 ... 3898
of Merom, to *f* against Israel.................. Josh 11:5 ... 3898
Dan went up to *f* against Leshem .... Josh 19:47 ... 3898
first, to *f* against them .... Judg 1:1 ... 3898
that we may *f* against the .... Judg 1:3 ... 3898
down to *f* against the Canaanites .... Judg 1:9 ... 3898
wentest to *f* with the Midianites .... Judg 8:1 ... 3898
out, I pray now, and *f* with them .... Judg 9:38 ... 3898
Jordan to *f* also against Judah .... Judg 10:9 ... 3898
man is he that will begin to *f*................. Judg 10:18 ... 3898
that we may *f* with the children .... Judg 11:6 ... 3898
f against the children of Ammon, ... Judg 11:8 ... 3898
If ye bring me home again to *f*............... Judg 11:9 ... 3898
come against me to *f* in my land .... Judg 11:12 ... 3898
or did he ever *f* against them .... Judg 11:25 ... 3898
of Ammon to *f* against them .... Judg 11:32 ... 3898
f against the children of Ammon .... Judg 12:1 ... 3898
unto me this day, to *f* against me .... Judg 12:3 ... 3898
array to *f* against them at Gibeah .... Judg 20:20 ... 4421
quit yourselves like men, and *f*.............. 1Sa 4:9 ... 3898
out before us, and *f* our battles............. 1Sa 8:20 ... 3898
together to *f* with Israel........................ 1Sa 13:5 ... 3898
f against them until they be .... 1Sa 15:18 ... 3898
If he be able to *f* with me .... 1Sa 17:9 ... 3898
me a man, that we may *f* together.......... 1Sa 17:10 ... 3898
the host was going forth to the *f*........... 1Sa 17:20 ... 4634
will go and *f* with this Philistine .... 1Sa 17:32 ... 3898
this Philistine to *f* with him .... 1Sa 17:33 ... 3898
for me, and *f* the Lord's battles............. 1Sa 18:17 ... 3898
the Philistines *f* against Keilah .... 1Sa 23:1 ... 3898
for warfare, to *f* with Israel .... 1Sa 28:1 ... 3898
that I may not go *f* against the .... 1Sa 29:8 ... 3898
nigh unto the city when ye did *f* .... 2Sa 11:20 ... 3898
to *f* against the house of Israel, ... 1Kin 12:21 ... 3898
nor *f* against your brethren the .... 1Kin 12:24 ... 3898
but let us *f* against them in the .... 1Kin 20:23 ... 3898
we will *f* against them in the.................. 1Kin 20:25 ... 3898
up to Aphek, to *f* against Israel............. 1Kin 20:26 ... 4421
F neither with small nor great, ... 1Kin 22:31 ... 3898
F'ye not with small or great, ... 1Kin 22:32 ... 3898
turned aside to *f* against him .... 1Kin 22:32 ... 3898
were come up to *f* against them .... 2Kin 3:21 ... 3898
f for your master's house .... 2Kin 10:3 ... 3898
he is come out to *f* against thee .... 2Kin 19:9 ... 3898
to *f* against Israel, that he...................... 2Chr 11:1 ... 3898
nor *f* against your brethren.................... 2Chr 11:4 ... 3898
f ye not against the Lord God of .... 2Chr 13:12 ... 3898
F ye not with small or great, ... 2Chr 18:30 ... 3898
they compassed about him to *f*............. 2Chr 18:31 ... 3898
not need to *f* in this battle .... 2Chr 20:17 ... 3898
purposed to *f* against Jerusalem .... 2Chr 32:2 ... 4421
to help us, and to *f* our battles .... 2Chr 32:8 ... 3898
up to *f* against Charchemish by .... 2Chr 35:20 ... 3898
himself, that he might *f* with him .... 2Chr 35:22 ... 3898
came to *f* in the valley of .... 2Chr 35:22 ... 3898
to *f* against Jerusalem, and to .... Neh 4:8 ... 3898

f for your brethren, your sons, ... Neh 4:14 ... 3898
our God shall *f* for us............................. Neh 4:20 ... 3898
f against them that *f* against .... Ps 35:1 ... 3898
they be many that *f* against me .... Ps 56:2 ... 3898
hands to war, and my fingers to *f*.......... Ps 144:1 ... 4421
they shall *f* every one against .... Is 19:2 ... 3898
the nations that *f* against Ariel .... Is 29:7 ... 6633
even all that *f* against her .... Is 29:7 ... 6633
that *f* against mount Zion .... Is 29:8 ... 6633
of shaking will he *f* with it .... Is 30:32 ... 3898
come down to *f* for mount Zion .... Is 31:4 ... 6633
they shall *f* against thee .... Jer 1:19 ... 3898
they shall *f* against thee, but .... Jer 15:20 ... 3898
wherewith ye *f* against the king .... Jer 21:4 ... 3898
I myself will *f* against you with .... Jer 21:5 ... 3898
though ye *f* with the Chaldeans, ... Jer 32:5 ... 3898
that *f* against it, because of the .... Jer 32:24 ... 3898
that *f* against this city, shall .... Jer 32:29 ... 3898
They come to *f* with the Chaldeans .... Jer 33:5 ... 3898
and they shall *f* against it .... Jer 34:22 ... 3898
f against this city, and take it, ... Jer 37:8 ... 3898
the Chaldeans that *f* against you .... Jer 37:10 ... 3898
went to *f* with Ishmael the son of .... Jer 41:12 ... 3898
men of Babylon have forborn to *f*.......... Jer 51:30 ... 3898
now will I return to *f* with the .... Dan 10:20 ... 3898
f with him, even with the king of .... Dan 11:11 ... 3898
and they shall *f*, because the Lord .... Zec 10:5 ... 3898
f against those nations, as when .... Zec 14:3 ... 3898
Judah also shall *f* at Jerusalem .... Zec 14:14 ... 3898
world, then would my servants *f* .... Jn 18:36 ... 75
ye be found even to *f* against God .... Acts 5:39 ... 2314
to him, let us not *f* against God............. Acts 23:9 ... 2313
so *f* I, not as one that beateth .... 1Cor 9:26 ... 4438
F the good *f* of faith............................. 1Ti 6:12 ... 73
I have fought a good *f*, I have .... 2Ti 4:7 ... 75
endured a great *f* of afflictions .... Heb 10:32 ... 119
made strong, waxed valiant in *f* .... Heb 11:34 ... 4171
ye *f* and war, yet ye have not, ... Jas 4:2 ... 3164
will *f* against them with the .... Rev 2:16 ... 4170

FIGHTETH
for the Lord *f* for them against.............. Ex 14:25 ... 3898
your God, he it is that *f* for you.............. Josh 23:10 ... 3898
because my lord *f* the battles of............. 1Sa 25:28 ... 3898

FIGHTING
of Elah, *f* with the Philistines .... 1Sa 17:19 ... 3898
Uzziah had an host of *f* men.......... 2Chr 26:11 ... 6213,4421
he *f* daily oppresseth me .... Ps 56:1 ... 3898

FIGHTINGS
without were *f*, within were fears............ 2Cor 7:5 ... *3163*
whence come wars and *f* among you ...... Jas 4:1 ... *3163*

FIGS
of the pomegranates, and of the *f*.......... Num 13:23 ... 8384
it is no place of seed, or of *f* .... Num 20:5 ... 8384
and two hundred cakes of *f*.................... 1Sa 25:18 ...
gave him a piece of a cake of *f* .... 1Sa 30:12 ...
And Isaiah said, Take a lump of *f*........... 2Kin 20:7 ... 8384
oxen, and meat, meal, cakes of *f*............ 1Chr 12:40 ...
as also wine, grapes, and *f* .... Neh 13:15 ... 8384
tree putteth forth her green *f*................. Song 2:13 ... 6291
said, Let them take a lump of *f* .... Is 38:21 ... 8384
nor *f* on the fig tree, and the .... Jer 8:13 ... 8384
two baskets of *f* were set before............ Jer 24:1 ... 8384
One basket had very good *f* .... Jer 24:2 ... 8384
even like the *f* that are first................... Jer 24:2 ... 8384
other basket had very naughty *f* .... Jer 24:2 ... 8384
And I said, *F* .... Jer 24:3 ... 8384
the good *f*, very good .... Jer 24:3 ... 8384
Like these good *f*, so will I..................... Jer 24:5 ... 8384
And as the evil *f*, which cannot be .... Jer 24:8 ... 8384
and will make them like vile *f*................ Jer 29:17 ... 8384
fig trees with the firstripe *f* .... Nah 3:12 ...
of thorns, or *f* of thistles .... Mt 7:16 ... *4810*
for the time of *f* was not yet .... Mk 11:13 ... *4810*
For of thorns men do not gather *f* .... Lk 6:44 ... *4810*
either a vine, *f*? .... Jas 3:12 ... *4810*
a fig tree casteth her untimely *f* .... Rev 6:13 ... *3653*

FIGURE
image, the similitude of any *f*................. Deut 4:16 ... 5566
and maketh it after the *f* of a man .... Is 44:13 ... 8403
who is the *f* of him that was to .... Rom 5:14 ... 5179
I have in a *f* transferred to .... 1Cor 4:6 ... 3345
Which was a *f* for the time then .... Heb 9:9 ... 3850
also he received him in a *f*..................... Heb 11:19 ... 3850
The like *f* whereunto even baptism......... 1Pet 3:21 ... *499*

FIGURES
about with carved *f* of cherubims .... 1Kin 6:29 ... 4734
f which ye made to worship them........... Acts 7:43 ... 5179
which are the *f* of the true..................... Heb 9:24 ... *499*

FILE

Yet they had a *f* for the mattocks ... 1Sa 13:21   6477,6310

FILL

f the waters in the seas, and let	Gen 1:22	4390
to *f* their sacks with corn	Gen 42:25	4390
F the men's sacks with food, as	Gen 44:1	4390
And they shall *f* thy houses	Ex 10:6	4390
F an omer of it to be kept for	Ex 16:32	4393
her fruit, and ye shall eat your *f*	Lev 25:19	7648
thy *f* at thine own pleasure	Deut 23:24	7648
f thine horn with oil, and go, I	1Sa 16:1	4390
F four barrels with water, and	1Kin 18:33	4390
Till he *f* thy mouth with laughing	Job 8:21	4390
f his belly with the east wind	Job 15:2	4390
When he is about to *f* his belly	Job 20:23	4390
f my mouth with arguments	Job 23:4	4390
or *f* the appetite of the young	Job 38:39	4390
Canst thou *f* his skin with barbed	Job 41:7	4390
thy mouth wide, and I will *f* it	Ps 81:10	4390
F their faces with shame	Ps 83:16	4390
he shall *f* the places with the	Ps 110:6	4390
we shall *f* our houses with spoil	Prov 1:13	4390
let us take our *f* of love until	Prov 7:18	7301
and I will *f* their treasures	Prov 8:21	4390
out of his wings shall the *f* the	Is 8:8	4393
nor *f* the face of the world with	Is 14:21	4390
f the face of the world with	Is 27:6	4390
we will *f* ourselves with strong	Is 56:12	4390
I will *f* all the inhabitants of	Jer 13:13	5433
Do not I *f* heaven and earth	Jer 23:24	4390
but it is to *f* them with the dead	Jer 33:5	4390
Surely I will *f* thee with men	Jer 51:14	4390
f thy bowels with this roll that	Eze 3:3	4390
souls, neither *f* their bowels	Eze 7:19	4390
f the courts with the slain	Eze 9:7	4390
f thine hand with coals of fire	Eze 10:2	4390
f it with the choice bones	Eze 24:4	4390
f the land with the slain	Eze 30:11	4390
I will *f* the beasts of the whole	Eze 32:4	7646
f the valleys with thy height	Eze 32:5	4390
I will *f* his mountains with his	Eze 35:8	4390
which *f* their masters' houses	Zeph 1:9	4390
I will *f* this house with glory,	Hag 2:7	4390
for that which is put in to *f* it	Mt 9:16	4138
as to *f* so great a multitude	Mt 15:33	5526
F ye up then the measure of your	Mt 23:32	4137
F the waterpots with water	Jn 2:7	1072
God of hope *f* you with all joy	Rom 15:13	4137
that he might *f* all things	Eph 4:10	4137
f up that which is behind of the	Col 1:24	466
saved, to *f* up their sins alway	1Th 2:16	878
she hath filled *f* to her double	Rev 18:6	2767

FILLED

and the earth was *f* with violence	Gen 6:11	4390
for the earth be *f* with violence	Gen 6:13	4390
f the bottle with water, and gave	Gen 21:19	4390
f her pitcher, and came up	Gen 24:16	4390
them, and *f* them with earth	Gen 26:15	4390
and the land was *f* with them	Ex 1:7	4390
f the troughs to water their	Ex 2:16	4390
morning ye shall be *f* with bread	Ex 16:12	7646
whom I have *f* with the spirit of	Ex 28:3	4390
I have *f* him with the spirit of	Ex 31:3	4390
he hath *f* him with the spirit of	Ex 35:31	4390
Them hath he *f* with wisdom of	Ex 35:35	4390
of the LORD *f* the tabernacle	Ex 40:34	4390
of the LORD *f* the tabernacle	Ex 40:35	4390
all the earth shall be *f* with the	Num 14:21	4390
may eat within thy gates, and be *f*	Deut 26:12	7646
f themselves, and waxen fat	Deut 31:20	7646
these bottles of wine, which we *f*	Josh 9:13	4390
and he was *f* with wisdom, and	1Kin 7:14	4390
that the cloud *f* the house of the	1Kin 8:10	4390
LORD had *f* the house of the LORD	1Kin 8:11	4390
he *f* the trench also with water	1Kin 18:35	4390
but the Syrians *f* the country	1Kin 20:27	4390
that valley shall be *f* with water	2Kin 3:17	4390
and the country was *f* with water	2Kin 3:20	4390
cast every man his stone, and *f* it	2Kin 3:25	4390
till he had *f* Jerusalem from one	2Kin 21:16	4390
f their places with the bones of	2Kin 23:14	4390
for he *f* Jerusalem with innocent	2Kin 24:4	4390
then the house was *f* with a cloud	2Chr 5:13	4390
the LORD had *f* the house of God	2Chr 5:14	4390
the glory of the LORD *f* the house	2Chr 7:1	4390
the LORD had *f* the LORD's house	2Chr 7:2	4390
bed which was *f* with sweet odours	2Chr 16:14	4390
which have *f* it from one end to	Ezr 9:11	4390
so they did eat, and were *f*	Neh 9:25	7646

who *f* their houses with silver	Job 3:15	4390
thou hast *f* me with wrinkles,	Job 16:8	7059
Yet he *f* their houses with good	Job 22:18	4390
For my loins are *f* with a	Ps 38:7	4390
Let my mouth be *f* with thy praise	Ps 71:8	4390
whole earth be *f* with his glory	Ps 72:19	4390
So they did eat, and were well *f*	Ps 78:29	7646
take deep root, and it *f* the land	Ps 80:9	4390
thine hand, they are *f* with good	Ps 104:28	7646
are exceedingly *f* with contempt	Ps 123:3	7646
Our soul is exceedingly *f* with	Ps 123:4	7646
was our mouth *f* with laughter	Ps 126:2	4390
be *f* with their own devices	Prov 1:31	7646
shall thy barns be *f* with plenty	Prov 3:10	4390
strangers be *f* with thy wealth	Prov 5:10	7646
wicked shall be *f* with mischief	Prov 12:21	4390
shall be *f* with his own ways	Prov 14:14	7646
of his lips shall he be *f*	Prov 18:20	7646
his mouth shall be *f* with gravel	Prov 20:17	4390
chambers be *f* with all precious	Prov 24:4	4390
thee, lest thou be *f* therewith	Prov 25:16	7646
earth that is not *f* with water	Prov 30:16	7646
and a fool when he is *f* with meat	Prov 30:22	7646
nor the ear *f* with hearing	Eccl 1:8	4390
and his soul be not *f* with good	Eccl 6:3	7646
and yet the appetite is not *f*	Eccl 6:7	4390
for my head is *f* with dew	Song 5:2	4390
up, and his train *f* the temple	Is 6:1	4390
and the house was *f* with smoke	Is 6:4	4390
are my loins *f* with pain	Is 21:3	4390
he hath *f* Zion with judgment and	Is 33:5	4390
sword of the LORD is *f* with blood	Is 34:6	4390
neither hast thou *f* me with the	Is 43:24	7301
old man that hath not *f* his days	Is 65:20	4390
Every bottle shall be *f* with wine	Jer 13:12	4390
every bottle shall be *f* with wine	Jer 13:12	4390
for thou hast *f* me with	Jer 15:17	4390
they have *f* mine inheritance with	Jer 16:18	4390
have *f* this place with the blood	Jer 19:4	4390
f it with them that were slain	Jer 41:9	4390
shame, and thy cry hath *f* the land	Jer 46:12	4390
though their land was *f* with sin	Jer 51:5	4390
he hath *f* his belly with my	Jer 51:34	4390
He hath *f* me with bitterness, he	Lam 3:15	7646
he is *f* full with reproach	Lam 3:30	7646
for they have *f* the land with	Eze 8:17	4390
the cloud *f* the inner court	Eze 10:3	4390
the house was *f* with the cloud,	Eze 10:4	4390
ye have *f* the streets thereof	Eze 11:6	4390
Thou shalt be *f* with drunkenness	Eze 23:33	4390
of thy merchandise they have *f*	Eze 28:16	4390
cities be *f* with flocks of men	Eze 36:38	4390
Thus ye shall be *f* at my table	Eze 39:20	7646
the glory of the LORD *f* the house	Eze 43:5	4390
the LORD *f* the house of the LORD	Eze 44:4	4390
mountain, and *f* the whole earth	Dan 2:35	4391
to their pasture, so were they *f*	Hos 13:6	7646
they were *f*, and their heart was	Hos 13:6	7646
f his holes with prey, and his	Nah 2:12	4390
For the earth shall be *f* with the	Hab 2:14	4390
Thou art *f* with shame for glory	Hab 2:16	7646
but ye are not *f* with drink	Hag 1:6	
f the bow with Ephraim, and raised	Zec 9:13	4390
and they shall be *f* like bowls	Zec 9:15	4390
for they shall be *f*	Mt 5:6	5526
And they did all eat, and were *f*	Mt 14:20	5526
And they did all eat, and were *f*.	Mt 15:37	5526
f it with vinegar, and put it on a	Mt 27:48	4130
else the new piece that *f* it up	Mk 2:21	4138
And they did all eat, and were *f*.	Mk 6:42	5526
her, Let the children first be *f*	Mk 7:27	5526
So they did eat, and were *f*	Mk 8:8	5526
f a spunge full of vinegar, and	Mk 15:36	1072
he shall be *f* with the Holy Ghost	Lk 1:15	4130
Elisabeth was *f* with the Holy	Lk 1:41	4130
He hath *f* the hungry with good	Lk 1:53	1705
was *f* with the Holy Ghost	Lk 1:67	4130
strong in spirit, and *f* with wisdom	Lk 2:40	4137
Every valley shall be *f*, and every	Lk 3:5	4137
these things, were *f* with wrath,	Lk 4:28	4130
f both the ships, so that they	Lk 5:7	4130
were *f* with fear, saying, We have	Lk 5:26	4130
And they were *f* with madness	Lk 6:11	4130
for ye shall be *f*	Lk 6:21	5526
they were *f* with water, and were	Lk 8:23	4845
And they did eat, and were all *f*	Lk 9:17	5526
come in, that my house may be *f*	Lk 14:23	1072
he would fain have *f* his belly	Lk 15:16	1072
they *f* them up to the brim	Jn 2:7	1072
When they were *f*, he said unto	Jn 6:12	1705

f twelve baskets with the	Jn 6:13	1072
did eat of the loaves, and were *f*	Jn 6:26	5526
the house was *f* with the odour of	Jn 12:3	4137
you, sorrow hath *f* your heart	Jn 16:6	4137
they *f* a spunge with vinegar, and	Jn 19:29	4130
it *f* all the house where they	Acts 2:2	4137
they were all *f* with the Holy	Acts 2:4	4130
they were *f* with wonder and	Acts 3:10	4130
f with the Holy Ghost, said unto	Acts 4:8	4130
they were all *f* with the Holy	Acts 4:31	4130
why hath Satan *f* thine heart to	Acts 5:3	4137
and were *f* with indignation,	Acts 5:17	4137
ye have *f* Jerusalem with your	Acts 5:28	4137
and be *f* with the Holy Ghost	Acts 9:17	4130
f with the Holy Ghost, set his	Acts 13:9	4130
multitudes, they were *f* with envy	Acts 13:45	4130
And the disciples were *f* with joy	Acts 13:52	4137
whole city was *f* with confusion	Acts 19:29	4130
Being *f* with all unrighteousness,	Rom 1:29	4137
f with all knowledge, able also	Rom 15:14	4137
I be somewhat *f* with your company	Rom 15:24	1705
I am *f* with comfort, I am	2Cor 7:4	4137
that ye might be *f* with all the	Eph 3:19	4137
but be *f* with the Spirit	Eph 5:18	4137
Being *f* with the fruits of	Phil 1:11	4137
to desire that ye might be *f* with	Col 1:9	4137
tears, that I may be *f* with joy	2Ti 1:4	4137
in peace, be ye warmed and *f*	Jas 2:16	5526
f it with fire of the altar, and	Rev 8:5	1072
for in them is *f* up the wrath of	Rev 15:1	5055
the temple was *f* with smoke from	Rev 15:8	1072
she hath *f* fill to her double	Rev 18:6	2767
the fowls were *f* with their flesh	Rev 19:21	5526

FILLEDST

all good things, which thou *f* not	Deut 6:11	4390
of the seas, thou *f* many people	Eze 27:33	7646

FILLEST

whose belly thou *f* with thy hid	Ps 17:14	4390

FILLET

a *f* of twelve cubits did compass	Jer 52:21	2339

FILLETED

the court shall be *f* with silver	Ex 27:17	2836
of the court were *f* with silver	Ex 38:17	2836
their chapiters, and *f* them	Ex 38:28	2836

FILLETH

breath, but *f* me with bitterness	Job 9:18	7646
the rain also *f* the pools	Ps 84:6	5844
f the hungry soul with goodness	Ps 107:9	4390
the mower *f* not his hand	Ps 129:7	4390
f thee with the finest of the	Ps 147:14	7646
fulness of him that *f* all in all	Eph 1:23	4131

FILLETS

their *f* shall be of silver	Ex 27:10	2838
the pillars and their *f* of silver	Ex 27:11	2838
chapiters and their *f* with gold	Ex 36:38	2838
pillars and their *f* were of silver	Ex 38:10	2838
the pillars and their *f* of silver	Ex 38:11	2838
the pillars and their *f* of silver	Ex 38:12	2838
the pillars and their *f* of silver	Ex 38:17	2838
chapiters and their *f* of silver	Ex 38:19	2838

FILLING

f our hearts with food and	Acts 14:17	1705

FILTH

the *f* of the daughters of Zion	Is 4:4	6675
will cast abominable *f* upon thee	Nah 3:6	
we are made as the *f* of the world	1Cor 4:13	4027
away of the *f* of the flesh	1Pet 3:21	4509

FILTHINESS

carry forth the *f* out of the holy	2Chr 29:5	5079
the *f* of the heathen of the land	Ezr 6:21	2932
the *f* of the people of the lands	Ezr 9:11	5079
and yet is not washed from their *f*	Prov 30:12	6675
all tables are full of vomit and *f*	Is 28:8	6675
Her *f* is in her skirts	Lam 1:9	2932
Because thy *f* was poured out, and	Eze 16:36	5178
and will consume thy *f* out of thee	Eze 22:15	2932
that the *f* of it may be molten in	Eze 24:11	2932
In thy *f* is lewdness	Eze 24:13	2932
not be purged from thy *f* any more	Eze 24:13	2932
from all your *f*, and from all your	Eze 36:25	2932
ourselves from all *f* of the flesh	2Cor 7:1	3436
Neither *f*, nor foolish talking,	Eph 5:4	151
Wherefore lay apart all *f*	Jas 1:21	4507
and *f* of her fornication	Rev 17:4	168

FILTHY

f is man, which drinketh iniquity	Job 15:16	444
they are all together become *f*	Ps 14:3	444
they are altogether become *f*	Ps 53:3	444
our righteousnesses are as *f* rags	Is 64:6	5708
Woe to her that is *f* and polluted,	Zeph 3:1	4754
was clothed with *f* garments	Zec 3:3	6674
Take away the *f* garments from him	Zec 3:4	6674
f communication out of your mouth	Col 3:8	148
no striker, not greedy of *f* lucre	1Ti 3:3	
much wine, not greedy of *f* lucre	1Ti 3:8	
no striker, not given to *f* lucre	Titus 1:7	150
ought not, for *f* lucre's sake	Titus 1:11	150
not for *f* lucre, but of a ready	1Pet 5:2	147
vexed with the *f* conversation of	2Pet 2:7	766
Likewise also these *f* dreamers	Jude 8	
and he which is *f*, let him be	Rev 22:11	4510
let him be *f* still	Rev 22:11	4510

FINALLY

F, brethren, farewell	2Cor 13:11	3063
F, my brethren, be strong in the	Eph 6:10	3063
F, my brethren, rejoice in the	Phil 3:1	3063
F, brethren, whatsoever things	Phil 4:8	3063
F, brethren, pray for us, that	2Th 3:1	3063
F, be ye all of one mind, having	1Pet 3:8	5056

FIND

If I *f* in Sodom fifty righteous	Gen 18:26	4672
If I *f* there forty and five, I	Gen 18:28	4672
not do it, if I *f* thirty there	Gen 18:30	4672
wearied themselves to *f* the door	Gen 19:11	4672
that I may *f* grace in thy sight	Gen 32:5	4672
ye speak unto Esau, when ye *f* him	Gen 32:19	4672
These are to *f* grace in the sight	Gen 33:8	4672
let me *f* grace in the sight of my	Gen 33:15	4672
Let me *f* grace in your eyes, and	Gen 34:11	4672
to Judah, and said, I cannot *f* her	Gen 38:22	4672
Can we *f* such a one as this is, a	Gen 41:38	4672
let us *f* grace in the sight of my	Gen 47:25	4672
get you straw where ye can *f* it	Ex 5:11	4672
ye shall not *f* it in the field	Ex 16:25	4672
that I may *f* grace in thy sight	Ex 33:13	4672
be sure your sin will *f* you out	Num 32:23	4672
the revenger of blood *f* him	Num 35:27	4672
LORD thy God, thou shalt *f* him	Deut 4:29	4672
a man *f* her in the city, and lie	Deut 22:23	4672
But if a man *f* a betrothed damsel	Deut 22:25	4672
If a man *f* a damsel that is a	Deut 22:28	4672
that she *f* no favour in his eyes	Deut 24:1	4672
nations shalt thou *f* no ease	Deut 28:65	4672
to them as thou shalt *f* occasion	Judg 9:33	4672
f it out, then I will give you	Judg 14:12	4672
sojourn where he could *f* a place	Judg 17:8	4672
to sojourn where I may *f* a place	Judg 17:9	4672
LORD grant you that ye may *f* rest	Ruth 1:9	4672
in whose sight I shall *f* grace	Ruth 2:2	4672
Let me *f* favour in thy sight, my	Ruth 2:13	4672
handmaid *f* grace in thy sight	1Sa 1:18	4672
city, ye shall straightway *f* him	1Sa 9:13	4672
about this time ye shall *f* him	1Sa 9:13	4672
then thou shalt *f* two men by	1Sa 10:2	4672
lad, saying, Go, *f* out the arrows	1Sa 20:21	4672
f out now the arrows which I	1Sa 20:36	4672
Saul my father shall not *f* thee	1Sa 23:17	4672
For if a man *f* his enemy, will he	1Sa 24:19	4672
young men *f* favour in thine eyes	1Sa 25:8	4672
if I shall *f* favour in the eyes	2Sa 15:25	4672
that I may *f* grace in thy sight	2Sa 16:4	4672
had sought and could not *f* them	2Sa 17:20	4672
peradventure we may *f* grass to	1Kin 18:5	4672
and tell Ahab, and he cannot *f* thee	1Kin 18:12	4672
to *f* out every device which shall	2Chr 2:14	2803
ye shall *f* them at the end of the	2Chr 20:16	4672
your children shall *f* compassion	2Chr 30:9	
of Assyria come, and *f* much water	2Chr 32:4	4672
so shalt thou *f* in the book of	Ezr 4:15	7912
gold that thou canst *f* in all the	Ezr 7:16	7912
glad, when they can *f* the grave	Job 3:22	4672
Canst thou by searching *f* out God	Job 11:7	4672
canst thou *f* out the Almighty	Job 11:7	4672
for I cannot *f* one wise man among	Job 17:10	4672
that I knew where I might *f* him	Job 23:3	4672
cause every man to *f* according to	Job 34:11	4672
the Almighty, we cannot *f* him out	Job 37:23	4672
his wickedness till thou *f* none	Ps 10:15	4672
hast tried me, and shalt *f* nothing	Ps 17:3	4672
Thine hand shall *f* out all thine	Ps 21:8	4672
thy right hand shall *f* out those	Ps 21:8	4672
Until I *f* out a place for the	Ps 132:5	4672
We shall *f* all precious substance	Prov 1:13	4672

me early, but they shall not *f* me	Prov 1:28	4672
LORD, and *f* the knowledge of God	Prov 2:5	4672
So shalt thou *f* favour and good	Prov 3:4	4672
are life unto those that *f* them	Prov 4:22	4672
and right to them that *f* knowledge	Prov 8:9	4672
and *f* out knowledge of witty	Prov 8:12	4672
that seek me early shall *f* me	Prov 8:17	4672
a matter wisely shall *f* good	Prov 16:20	4672
understanding shall *f* good	Prov 19:8	4672
but a faithful man who can *f*	Prov 20:6	4672
shall *f* more favour than he that	Prov 28:23	4672
Who can *f* a virtuous woman	Prov 31:10	4672
so that no man can *f* out the work	Eccl 3:11	4672
man should *f* nothing after him	Eccl 7:14	4672
exceeding deep, who can *f* it out	Eccl 7:24	4672
I *f* more bitter than death the	Eccl 7:26	4672
one by one, to *f* out the account	Eccl 7:27	4672
yet my soul seeketh, but I *f* not	Eccl 7:28	4672
that a man cannot *f* out the work	Eccl 8:17	4672
it out, yet he shall not *f* it	Eccl 8:17	4672
yet shall he not be able to *f* it	Eccl 8:17	4672
for thou shalt *f* it after many	Eccl 11:1	4672
sought to *f* out acceptable words	Eccl 12:10	4672
sought him, but I could not *f* him	Song 5:6	4672
if ye *f* my beloved, that ye tell	Song 5:8	4672
when I should *f* thee without	Song 8:1	4672
f for herself a place of rest	Is 34:14	4672
seek them, and shalt not *f* them	Is 41:12	4672
day of your fast ye *f* pleasure	Is 58:3	4672
in her month they shall *f* her	Jer 2:24	4672
places thereof, if ye can *f* a man	Jer 5:1	4672
ye shall *f* rest for your souls	Jer 6:16	4672
them, that they may *f* it so	Jer 10:18	4672
f me, when ye shall search for me	Jer 29:13	4672
in my sighing, and I *f* no rest	Jer 45:3	4672
like harts that *f* no pasture	Lam 1:6	4672
her prophets also *f* no vision	Lam 2:9	4672
princes sought to *f* occasion	Dan 6:4	7912
but they could *f* none occasion	Dan 6:4	7912
We shall not *f* any occasion	Dan 6:5	7912
except we *f* it against him	Dan 6:5	7912
that she shall not *f* her paths	Hos 2:6	4672
seek them, but shall not *f* them	Hos 2:7	4672
but they shall not *f* him	Hos 5:6	4672
in all my labours they shall *f*	Hos 12:8	4672
of the LORD, and shall not *f* it	Amos 8:12	4672
seek, and ye shall *f*	Mt 7:7	2147
life, and few there be that *f* it	Mt 7:14	2147
his life for my sake shall *f* it	Mt 10:39	2147
ye shall *f* rest unto your souls	Mt 11:29	2147
his life for my sake shall *f* it	Mt 16:25	2147
thou shalt *f* a piece of money	Mt 17:27	2147
And if so be that he *f* it, verily	Mt 18:13	2147
ye shall *f* an ass tied, and a colt	Mt 21:2	2147
and as many as ye shall *f*	Mt 22:9	2147
when he cometh shall *f* so doing	Mt 24:46	2147
ye shall *f* a colt tied, whereon	Mk 11:2	2147
he might *f* any thing thereon	Mk 11:13	2147
coming suddenly he *f* you sleeping	Mk 13:36	2147
Ye shall *f* the babe wrapped in	Lk 2:12	2147
when they could not *f* by what way	Lk 5:19	2147
that they might *f* an accusation	Lk 6:7	2147
seek, and ye shall *f*	Lk 11:9	2147
when he cometh shall *f* watching	Lk 12:37	2147
f them so, blessed are those	Lk 12:38	2147
when he cometh shall *f* so doing	Lk 12:43	2147
fruit on this fig tree, and *f* none	Lk 13:7	2147
that which is lost, until he *f* it	Lk 15:4	2147
and seek diligently till she *f* it	Lk 15:8	2147
shall he *f* faith on the earth	Lk 18:8	2147
entering ye shall *f* a colt tied	Lk 19:30	2147
could not *f* what they might do	Lk 19:48	2147
people, I *f* no fault in this man	Lk 23:4	2147
shall seek me, and shall not *f* me	Jn 7:34	2147
he go, that we shall not *f* him	Jn 7:35	2147
shall seek me, and shall not *f* me	Jn 7:36	2147
shall go in and out, and *f* pasture	Jn 10:9	2147
I *f* in him no fault at all	Jn 18:38	2147
may know that I *f* no fault in him	Jn 19:4	2147
for I *f* no fault in him	Jn 19:6	2147
side of the ship, and ye shall *f*	Jn 21:6	2147
desired to *f* a tabernacle for the	Acts 7:46	2147
f him, though he be not far from	Acts 17:27	2147
saying, We *f* no evil in this man	Acts 23:9	2147
that which is good I *f* not	Rom 7:18	2147
I *f* then a law, that, when I	Rom 7:21	2147
unto me, Why doth he yet *f* fault	Rom 9:19	
f you unprepared, we (that we say	2Cor 9:4	2147
I shall not *f* you such as I would	2Cor 12:20	2147
f mercy of the Lord in that day	2Ti 1:18	2147
f grace to help in time of need	Heb 4:16	2147

men seek death, and shall not *f* it	Rev 9:6	2147
thou shalt *f* them no more at all	Rev 18:14	2147

FINDEST

With whomsoever thou *f* thy gods	Gen 31:32	4672
me, Son of man, eat that thou *f*	Eze 3:1	4672

FINDETH

every one that *f* me shall slay me	Gen 4:14	4672
he *f* occasions against me, he	Job 33:10	4672
word, as one that *f* great spoil	Ps 119:162	4672
Happy is the man that *f* wisdom	Prov 3:13	4672
For whoso *f* me *f* life	Prov 8:35	4672
seeketh wisdom, and *f* it not	Prov 14:6	4672
hath a froward heart *f* no good	Prov 17:20	4672
Whoso *f* a wife *f* a good	Prov 18:22	4672
his neighbour *f* no favour in his	Prov 21:10	4672
righteousness and mercy *f* life	Prov 21:21	4672
Whatsoever thy hand *f* to do	Eccl 9:10	4672
among the heathen, she *f* no rest	Lam 1:3	4672
in thee the fatherless *f* mercy	Hos 14:3	
and he that seeketh *f*	Mt 7:8	2147
He that *f* his life shall lose it	Mt 10:39	2147
places, seeking rest, and *f* none	Mt 12:43	2147
is come, he *f* it empty, swept, and	Mt 12:44	2147
f them asleep, and saith unto	Mt 26:40	2147
f them sleeping, and saith unto	Mk 14:37	2147
and he that seeketh *f*	Lk 11:10	2147
he *f* it swept and garnished	Lk 11:25	2147
He first *f* his own brother Simon,	Jn 1:41	2147
f Philip, and saith unto him,	Jn 1:43	2147
Philip *f* Nathanael, and saith unto	Jn 1:45	2147
Afterward Jesus *f* him in the	Jn 5:14	2147

FINDING

lest any *f* him should kill him	Gen 4:15	4672
doeth great things past *f* out	Job 9:10	2714
nor *f* thine own pleasure, nor	Is 58:13	4672
f none, he saith, I will return	Lk 11:24	2147
f nothing how they might punish	Acts 4:21	2147
and *f* certain disciples,	Acts 19:1	2147
f a ship sailing over unto	Acts 21:2	2147
f disciples, we tarried there	Acts 21:4	429
judgments, and his ways past *f* out	Rom 11:33	421
For *f* fault with them, he saith,	Heb 8:8	

FINE

quickly three measures of *f* meal	Gen 18:6	
him in vestures of *f* linen	Gen 41:42	
and *f* linen, and goats' hair,	Ex 25:4	
ten curtains of *f* twined linen	Ex 26:1	
f twined linen of cunning work	Ex 26:31	
f twined linen, wrought with	Ex 26:36	
of *f* twined linen of an hundred	Ex 27:9	
f twined linen, wrought with	Ex 27:16	
five cubits of *f* twined linen	Ex 27:18	
and purple, and scarlet, and *f* linen	Ex 28:5	
f twined linen, with cunning work	Ex 28:6	
and scarlet, and *f* twined linen	Ex 28:8	
of *f* twined linen, shalt thou	Ex 28:15	
embroider the coat of *f* linen	Ex 28:39	
shalt make the mitre of *f* linen	Ex 28:39	
and *f* linen, and goats' hair,	Ex 35:6	
f linen, and goats' hair, and red	Ex 35:23	
and of scarlet, and of *f* linen	Ex 35:25	
in *f* linen, and of the weaver,	Ex 35:35	
ten curtains of *f* twined linen	Ex 36:8	
and scarlet, and *f* twined linen	Ex 36:35	
f twined linen, of needlework	Ex 36:37	
the court were of *f* twined linen	Ex 38:9	
about were of *f* twined linen	Ex 38:16	
and scarlet, and *f* twined linen	Ex 38:18	
purple, and in scarlet, and *f* linen	Ex 38:23	
and scarlet, and *f* twined linen	Ex 39:2	
in the scarlet, and in the *f* linen	Ex 39:3	
and scarlet, and *f* twined linen	Ex 39:5	
and scarlet, and *f* twined linen	Ex 39:8	
they made coats of *f* linen of	Ex 39:27	
And a mitre of *f* linen	Ex 39:28	
and goodly bonnets of *f* linen	Ex 39:28	
linen breeches of *f* twined linen	Ex 39:28	
a girdle of *f* twined linen, and	Ex 39:29	
his offering shall be of *f* flour	Lev 2:1	
cakes of *f* flour mingled with oil	Lev 2:4	
it shall be of *f* flour unleavened	Lev 2:5	
shall be made of *f* flour with oil	Lev 2:7	
of *f* flour for a sin offering	Lev 5:11	
of *f* flour for a meat offering	Lev 6:20	
with oil, of *f* flour, fried	Lev 7:12	
three tenth deals of *f* flour for	Lev 14:10	
one tenth deal of *f* flour mingled	Lev 14:21	
deals of *f* flour mingled with oil	Lev 23:13	
they shall be of *f* flour	Lev 23:17	

And thou shalt take *f* flour .... Lev 24:5
cakes of *f* flour mingled with oil .... Num 6:15
both of them were full of *f* flour .... Num 7:13
both of them full of *f* flour .... Num 7:19
both of them full of *f* flour .... Num 7:25
both of them full of *f* flour .... Num 7:31
both of them full of *f* flour .... Num 7:37
both of them full of *f* flour .... Num 7:43
both of them full of *f* flour .... Num 7:49
both of them full of *f* flour .... Num 7:55
both of them full of *f* flour .... Num 7:61
both of them full of *f* flour .... Num 7:67
both of them full of *f* flour .... Num 7:73
both of them full of *f* flour .... Num 7:79
even *f* flour mingled with oil, and .... Num 8:8
was thirty measures of *f* flour 1Kin 4:22
of *f* flour be sold for a shekel 2Kin 7:1
So a measure of *f* flour was sold 2Kin 7:16
a measure of *f* flour for a shekel 2Kin 7:18
of them that wrought *f* linen 1Chr 4:21
the *f* flour, and the wine, and the 1Chr 9:29
clothed with a robe of *f* linen 1Chr 15:27
for the *f* flour for meat offering 1Chr 23:29
in *f* linen, and in crimson 2Chr 2:14
which he overlaid with *f* gold .... 2Chr 3:5 | 2896
and he overlaid it with *f* gold .... 2Chr 3:8 | 2896
f linen, and wrought cherubims 2Chr 3:14
and two vessels of *f* copper .... Ezr 8:27 | 6668
fastened with cords of *f* linen .... Est 1:6
and with a garment of *f* linen .... Est 8:15
a place for gold where they *f* it .... Job 28:1 | 2212
shall not be for jewels of *f* gold .... Job 28:17
hope, or have said to the *f* gold .... Job 31:24
than gold, yea, than much *f* gold .... Ps 19:10
yea, above *f* gold .... Ps 119:127
and the gain thereof than *f* gold .... Prov 3:14
works, with *f* linen of Egypt .... Prov 7:16
than gold, yea, than *f* gold .... Prov 8:19
of gold, and an ornament of *f* gold .... Prov 25:12
She maketh *f* linen, and selleth it .... Prov 31:24
His head is as the most *f* gold .... Song 5:11
set upon sockets of *f* gold .... Song 5:15
the *f* linen, and the hoods, and the .... Is 3:23
a man more precious than *f* gold .... Is 13:12
Moreover they that work in *f* flax .... Is 19:9 | 8305
how is the most *f* gold changed .... Lam 4:1
of Zion, comparable to *f* gold .... Lam 4:2
I girded thee about with *f* linen .... Eze 16:10
and thy raiment was of *f* linen .... Eze 16:13
thou didst eat *f* flour, and honey, ... Eze 16:13
f flour, and oil, and honey, ... Eze 16:19
F linen with broidered work from .... Eze 27:7
f linen, and coral, and agate .... Eze 27:16
oil, to temper with the *f* flour .... Eze 46:14
This image's head was of *f* gold .... Dan 2:32 | 2869
were girded with *f* gold of Uphaz .... Dan 10:5
f gold as the mire of the streets .... Zec 9:3
And he bought *f* linen, and took him ...... Mk 15:46
f linen, and fared sumptuously .... Lk 16:19
And his feet like unto *f* brass .... Rev 1:15
and his feet are like *f* brass .... Rev 2:18
f linen, and purple, and silk, and .... Rev 18:12
f flour, and wheat, and beasts, and........ Rev 18:13 | 4585
city, that was clothed in *f* linen .... Rev 18:16
she should be arrayed in *f* linen............ Rev 19:8
for the *f* linen is the............................... Rev 19:8
white horses, clothed in *f* linen .... Rev 19:14

FINER
come forth a vessel for the *f* .... Prov 25:4 | 6884

FINEST
them also with the *f* of the wheat .... Ps 81:16 | 2459
thee with the *f* of the wheat .... Ps 147:14 | 2459

FINGER
Pharaoh, This is the *f* of God .... Ex 8:19 | 676
the horns of the altar with thy *f*............. Ex 29:12 | 676
stone, written with the *f* of God .... Ex 31:18 | 676
shall dip his *f* in the blood...................... Lev 4:6 | 676
dip his *f* in some of the blood .... Lev 4:17 | 676
of the sin offering with his *f* .... Lev 4:25 | 676
of the blood thereof with his *f* .... Lev 4:30 | 676
of the sin offering with his *f* .... Lev 4:34 | 676
the altar round about with his *f*.............. Lev 8:15 | 676
and he dipped his *f* in the blood .... Lev 9:9 | 676
f in the oil that is in his left .... Lev 14:16 | 676
his *f* seven times before the LORD .... Lev 14:16 | 676
shall sprinkle with his right *f* .... Lev 14:27 | 676
sprinkle it with his *f* upon the................ Lev 16:14 | 676
the blood with his *f* seven times .... Lev 16:14 | 676
upon it with his *f* seven times .... Lev 16:19 | 676

take of her blood with his *f* .... Num 19:4 | 676
stone written with the *f* of God .... Deut 9:10 | 676
My little *f* shall be thicker than 1Kin 12:10
My little *f* shall be thicker than 2Chr 10:10
yoke, the putting forth of the *f* .... Is 58:9 | 676
But if I with the *f* of God cast .... Lk 11:20 | 1147
may dip the tip of his *f* in water .... Lk 16:24 | 1147
with his *f* wrote on the ground,.............. Jn 8:6 | 1147
put my *f* into the print of the.................. Jn 20:25 | 1147
he to Thomas, Reach hither thy *f* .... Jn 20:27 | 1147

FINGERS
that had on every hand six *f* .... 2Sa 21:20 | 676
a man of great stature, whose *f*............. 1Chr 20:6 | 676
thy heavens, the work of thy *f* .... Ps 8:3 | 676
my hands to war, and my *f* to fight......... Ps 144:1 | 676
his feet, he teacheth with his *f*............... Prov 6:13 | 676
Bind them upon thy *f*, write them .... Prov 7:3 | 676
my *f* with sweet smelling myrrh, ... Song 5:5 | 676
that which their own *f* have made .... Is 2:8 | 676
that which his *f* have made .... Is 17:8 | 676
blood, and your *f* with iniquity............... Is 59:3 | 676
the thickness thereof was four *f* .... Jer 52:21 | 676
hour came forth *f* of a man's hand .... Dan 5:5 | 677
not move them with one of their *f* .... Mt 23:4 | 1147
put his *f* into his ears, and he .... Mk 7:33 | 1147
the burdens with one of your *f* .... Lk 11:46 | 1147

FINING
The *f* pot is for silver, and the .... Prov 17:3 | 4715
As the *f* pot for silver, and the .... Prov 27:21 | 4715

FINISH
in a cubit shalt thou *f* it above .... Gen 6:16 | 3615
to *f* the transgression, and to .... Dan 9:24 | 3607
his hands shall also *f* it .... Zec 4:9 | 1214
he have sufficient to *f* it .... Lk 14:28 | 535
and is not able to *f* it, all that .... Lk 14:29 | 1615
to build, and was not able to *f* .... Lk 14:30 | 1615
that sent me, and to *f* his work .... Jn 4:34 | 5048
the Father hath given me to *f* .... Jn 5:36 | 5048
so that I might *f* my course with .... Acts 20:24 | 5048
For he will *f* the work, and cut it .... Rom 9:28 | 4931
so he would also *f* in you the .... 2Cor 8:6 | 2005

FINISHED
the heavens and the earth were *f* .... Gen 2:1 | 3615
of the tent of the congregation *f*............. Ex 39:32 | 3615
So Moses *f* the work .... Ex 40:33 | 3615
law in a book, until they were *f*.............. Deut 31:24 | 8552
until every thing was *f* that the .... Josh 4:10 | 8552
until he have *f* the thing this .... Ruth 3:18 | 3615
So he built the house, and *f* it .... 1Kin 6:9 | 3615
Solomon built the house, and *f* it .... 1Kin 6:14 | 3615
until he had *f* all the house .... 1Kin 6:22 | 8552
was the house *f* throughout all .... 1Kin 6:38 | 3615
years, and he *f* all his house .... 1Kin 7:1 | 3615
so was the work of the pillars *f*.............. 1Kin 7:22 | 8552
when Solomon had *f* the building .... 1Kin 9:1 | 3615
So he *f* the house................................... 1Kin 9:25 | 7999
began to number, but he *f* not .... 1Chr 27:24 | 3615
until thou hast *f* all the work .... 1Chr 28:20 | 3615
Huram *f* the work that he was to .... 2Chr 4:11 | 3615
for the house of the LORD was *f* .... 2Chr 5:1 | 7999
Thus Solomon *f* the house of the .... 2Chr 7:11 | 3615
of the LORD, and until it was *f* .... 2Chr 8:16 | 3615
And when they had *f* it, they .... 2Chr 24:14 | 3615
until the burnt offering was *f* .... 2Chr 29:28 | 3615
Now when all this was *f*, all .... 2Chr 31:1 | 3615
f them in the seventh month .... 2Chr 31:7 | 3615
in building, and yet it is not *f* .... Ezr 5:16 | 8000
and *f* it, according to the .... Ezr 6:14 | 3635
this house was *f* on the third day .... Ezr 6:15 | 3319
So the wall was *f* in the twenty .... Neh 6:15 | 7999
numbered thy kingdom, and *f* it............. Dan 5:26 | 8000
all these things shall be *f* .... Dan 12:7 | 3615
when Jesus had *f* these parables .... Mt 13:53 | 5055
when Jesus had *f* these sayings .... Mt 19:1 | 5055
when Jesus had *f* all these .... Mt 26:1 | 5055
I have *f* the work which thou .... Jn 17:4 | 5048
the vinegar, he said, It is *f* .... Jn 19:30 | 5055
when we had *f* our course from .... Acts 21:7 | 1274
I have *f* my course, I have kept.............. 2Ti 4:7 | 5055
although the works were *f* from .... Heb 4:3 | 1096
and sin, when it is *f*, bringeth .... Jas 1:15 | 658
the mystery of God should be *f*............... Rev 10:7 | 5055
they shall have *f* their testimony .... Rev 11:7 | 5055
until the thousand years were *f* .... Rev 20:5 | 5055

FINISHER
the author and *f* of our faith................... Heb 12:2 | 5047

FINS

whatsoever hath *f* and scales in	Lev 11:9	5579
And all that have not *f* and scales	Lev 11:10	5579
Whatsoever hath no *f* nor scales	Lev 11:12	5579
all that have *f* and scales shall	Deut 14:9	5579
And whatsoever hath not *f* and	Deut 14:10	5579

FIR

of instruments made of *f* wood	2Sa 6:5	1265
cedar, and concerning timber of *f*	1Kin 5:8	1265
f trees according to all his	1Kin 5:10	1265
of the house with planks of *f*	1Kin 6:15	1265
And the two doors were of *f* tree	1Kin 6:34	1265
f trees, and with gold, according	1Kin 9:11	1265
the choice *f* trees thereof	2Kin 19:23	1265
f trees, and algum trees, out of	2Chr 2:8	1265
house he cieled with *f* tree	2Chr 3:5	1265
the *f* trees are her house	Ps 104:17	1265
are cedar, and our rafters of *f*	Song 1:17	1266
the *f* trees rejoice at thee, and	Is 14:8	1265
the choice *f* trees thereof	Is 37:24	1265
will set in the desert the *f* tree	Is 41:19	1265
thorn shall come up the *f* tree	Is 55:13	1265
the *f* tree, the pine tree, and the	Is 60:13	1265
ship boards of *f* trees of Senir	Eze 27:5	1265
the *f* trees were not like his	Eze 31:8	1265
I am like a green *f* tree	Hos 14:8	1265
the *f* trees shall be terribly	Nah 2:3	1265
Howl, *f* tree	Zec 11:2	1265

FIRE

f from the LORD out of heaven	Gen 19:24	784
and he took the *f* in his hand	Gen 22:6	784
And he said, Behold the *f* and the	Gen 22:7	784
of *f* out of the midst of a bush	Ex 3:2	784
behold, the bush burned with *f*	Ex 3:2	784
the *f* ran along upon the ground	Ex 9:23	784
f mingled with the hail, very	Ex 9:24	784
flesh in that night, roast with *f*	Ex 12:8	784
all with water, but roast with *f*	Ex 12:9	784
the morning ye shall burn with *f*	Ex 12:10	784
and by night in a pillar of *f*	Ex 13:21	784
day, nor the pillar of *f* by night	Ex 13:22	784
Egyptians through the pillar of *f*	Ex 14:24	784
the LORD descended upon it in *f*	Ex 19:18	784
If *f* break out, and catch in	Ex 22:6	784
he that kindled the *f* shall	Ex 22:6	1200
f on the top of the mount in the	Ex 24:17	784
thou burn with *f* without the camp	Ex 29:14	784
offering made by *f* unto the LORD	Ex 29:18	
offering made by *f* unto the LORD	Ex 29:25	
shalt burn the remainder with *f*	Ex 29:34	784
offering made by *f* unto the LORD	Ex 29:41	
offering made by *f* unto the LORD	Ex 30:20	
had made, and burnt it in the *f*	Ex 32:20	784
then I cast it into the *f*	Ex 32:24	784
Ye shall kindle no *f* throughout	Ex 35:3	784
f was on it by night, in the	Ex 40:38	784
priest shall put *f* upon the altar	Lev 1:7	784
lay the wood in order upon the *f*	Lev 1:7	784
on the *f* which is upon the altar	Lev 1:8	784
sacrifice, an offering made by *f*	Lev 1:9	784
on the *f* which is upon the altar	Lev 1:12	784
sacrifice, an offering made by *f*	Lev 1:13	784
upon the wood that is upon the *f*	Lev 1:17	784
sacrifice, an offering made by *f*	Lev 1:17	
to be an offering made by *f*	Lev 2:2	
offerings of the LORD made by *f*	Lev 2:3	
it is an offering made by *f*	Lev 2:9	
offerings of the LORD made by *f*	Lev 2:10	
offering of the LORD made by *f*	Lev 2:11	
green ears of corn dried by the *f*	Lev 2:14	784
offering made by *f* unto the LORD	Lev 2:16	
offering made by *f* unto the LORD	Lev 3:3	
is upon the wood that is on the *f*	Lev 3:5	784
it is an offering made by *f*	Lev 3:5	
offering made by *f* unto the LORD	Lev 3:9	
offering made by *f* unto the LORD	Lev 3:11	
offering made by *f* unto the LORD	Lev 3:14	
made by *f* for a sweet savour	Lev 3:16	
and burn him on the wood with *f*	Lev 4:12	784
offerings made by *f* unto the LORD	Lev 4:35	
offerings made by *f* unto the LORD	Lev 5:12	
the *f* of the altar shall be	Lev 6:9	784
take up the ashes which the *f*	Lev 6:10	784
the *f* upon the altar shall be	Lev 6:12	784
The *f* shall ever be burning upon	Lev 6:13	784
portion of my offerings made by *f*	Lev 6:17	
offerings of the LORD made by *f*	Lev 6:18	
it shall be burnt in the *f*	Lev 6:30	784
offering made by *f* unto the LORD	Lev 7:5	
third day shall be burnt with *f*	Lev 7:17	784

it shall be burnt with *f*	Lev 7:19	784
offering made by *f* unto the LORD	Lev 7:25	
offerings of the LORD made by *f*	Lev 7:30	
offerings of the LORD made by *f*	Lev 7:35	
he burnt with *f* without the camp	Lev 8:17	784
offering made by *f* unto the LORD	Lev 8:21	
offering made by *f* unto the LORD	Lev 8:28	
of the bread shall ye burn with *f*	Lev 8:32	784
he burnt with *f* without the camp	Lev 9:11	784
there came a *f* out from before	Lev 9:24	784
put *f* therein, and put incense	Lev 10:1	784
offered strange *f* before the LORD	Lev 10:1	784
And there went out *f* from the LORD	Lev 10:2	784
offerings of the LORD made by *f*	Lev 10:13	
sacrifices of the LORD made by *f*	Lev 10:13	
offerings made by *f* of the fat	Lev 10:15	
it shall be burnt in the *f*	Lev 13:52	784
thou shalt burn it in the *f*	Lev 13:55	784
that wherein the plague is with *f*	Lev 13:57	784
f from off the altar before the	Lev 16:12	784
upon the *f* before the LORD	Lev 16:13	784
shall burn in the *f* their skins	Lev 16:27	784
seed pass through the *f* to Molech	Lev 18:21	
day, it shall be burnt in the *f*	Lev 19:6	784
they shall be burnt with *f*	Lev 20:14	784
offerings of the LORD made by *f*	Lev 21:6	
she shall be burnt with *f*	Lev 21:9	784
offerings of the LORD made by *f*	Lev 21:21	
nor make an offering by *f* of them	Lev 22:22	
offering made by *f* unto the LORD	Lev 22:27	
by *f* unto the LORD seven days	Lev 23:8	784
an offering made by *f* unto the	Lev 23:13	
even an offering made by *f*	Lev 23:18	
offering made by *f* unto the LORD	Lev 23:25	
offering made by *f* unto the LORD	Lev 23:27	784
offering made by *f* unto the LORD	Lev 23:36	
offering made by *f* unto the LORD	Lev 23:36	
offering made by *f* unto the LORD	Lev 23:37	
offering made by *f* unto the LORD	Lev 24:7	
made by *f* by a perpetual statute	Lev 24:9	
offered strange *f* before the LORD	Num 3:4	784
put it in the *f* which is under	Num 6:18	784
as it were the appearance of *f*	Num 9:15	784
and the appearance of *f* by night	Num 9:16	784
the *f* of the LORD burnt among	Num 11:1	784
unto the LORD, the *f* was quenched	Num 11:2	784
because the *f* of the LORD burnt	Num 11:3	784
and in a pillar of *f* by night	Num 14:14	784
an offering by *f* unto the LORD	Num 15:3	
wine, for an offering made by *f*	Num 15:10	
in offering an offering made by *f*	Num 15:13	
will offer an offering made by *f*	Num 15:14	
sacrifice made by *f* unto the LORD	Num 15:25	
put *f* therein, and put incense in	Num 16:7	784
put *f* in them, and laid incense	Num 16:18	784
there came out a *f* from the LORD	Num 16:35	784
and scatter thou the *f* yonder	Num 16:37	784
put *f* therein from off the altar	Num 16:46	784
holy things, reserved from the *f*	Num 18:9	784
fat for an offering made by *f*	Num 18:17	
For there is a *f* gone out of	Num 21:28	784
what time the *f* devoured two	Num 26:10	784
offered strange *f* before the LORD	Num 26:61	784
bread for my sacrifices made by *f*	Num 28:2	
This is the offering made by *f*	Num 28:3	
sacrifice made by *f* unto the LORD	Num 28:6	
offer it, a sacrifice made by *f*	Num 28:8	
sacrifice made by *f* unto the LORD	Num 28:13	
f for a burnt offering unto the	Num 28:19	
meat of the sacrifice made by *f*	Num 28:24	
sacrifice made by *f* unto the LORD	Num 29:6	
offering, a sacrifice made by *f*	Num 29:13	
offering, a sacrifice made by *f*	Num 29:36	
all their goodly castles, with *f*	Num 31:10	784
Every thing that may abide the *f*	Num 31:23	784
ye shall make it go through the *f*	Num 31:23	784
all that abideth not the *f* ye	Num 31:23	784
in *f* by night, to shew you by	Deut 1:33	784
with *f* unto the midst of heaven	Deut 4:11	784
you out of the midst of the *f*	Deut 4:12	784
Horeb out of the midst of the *f*	Deut 4:15	784
the LORD thy God is a consuming *f*	Deut 4:24	784
out of the midst of the *f*	Deut 4:33	784
earth he shewed thee his great *f*	Deut 4:36	784
words out of the midst of the *f*	Deut 4:36	784
mount out of the midst of the *f*	Deut 5:4	784
ye were afraid by reason of the *f*	Deut 5:5	784
mount out of the midst of the *f*	Deut 5:22	784
(for the mountain did burn with *f*	Deut 5:23	784
voice out of the midst of the *f*	Deut 5:24	784
for this great *f* will consume us	Deut 5:25	784

out of the midst of the *f* .... Deut 5:26   784
burn their graven images with *f* .... Deut 7:5   784
their gods shall ye burn with *f* .... Deut 7:25   784
as a consuming *f* he shall destroy .... Deut 9:3   784
the *f* in the day of the assembly .... Deut 9:10   784
mount, and the mount burned with *f* ...... Deut 9:15   784
ye had made, and burnt it with *f* .... Deut 9:21   784
the *f* in the day of the assembly .... Deut 10:4   784
and burn their groves with *f* .... Deut 12:3   784
have burnt in the *f* to their gods .... Deut 12:31   784
and shalt burn with *f* the city .... Deut 13:16   784
offerings of the Lord made by *f* .... Deut 18:1
daughter to pass through the *f* .... Deut 18:10   784
let me see this great *f* any more .... Deut 18:16   784
For a *f* is kindled in mine anger, ... Deut 32:22   784
set on *f* the foundations of the .... Deut 32:22   3857
And they burnt the city with *f* .... Josh 6:24   784
thing shall be burnt with *f* .... Josh 7:15   784
stones, and burned them with *f* .... Josh 7:25   784
that ye shall set the city on *f* .... Josh 8:8   784
and hasted and set the city on *f* .... Josh 8:19   784
and burn their chariots with *f* .... Josh 11:6   784
and burnt their chariots with *f* .... Josh 11:9   784
and he burnt Hazor with *f* .... Josh 11:11   784
made by *f* are their inheritance .... Josh 13:14
the sword, and set the city on *f* .... Judg 1:8   784
there rose up *f* out of the rock, ... Judg 6:21   784
let *f* come out of the bramble, and .... Judg 9:15   784
let *f* come out from Abimelech, and .... Judg 9:20   784
let *f* come out from the men of .... Judg 9:20   784
and set the hold on *f* upon them .... Judg 9:49   784
of the tower to burn it with *f* .... Judg 9:52   784
burn thine house upon thee with *f* .... Judg 12:1   784
thee and thy father's house with *f* .... Judg 14:15   784
when he had set the brands on *f* .... Judg 15:5   784
and burnt her and her father with *f* .... Judg 15:6   784
as flax that was burnt with *f* .... Judg 15:14   784
is broken when it toucheth the *f* .... Judg 16:9   784
sword, and burnt the city with *f* .... Judg 18:27   784
also they set on *f* all the cities .... Judg 20:48   784
by *f* of the children of Israel 1Sa 2:28
Ziklag, and burned it with *f* 1Sa 30:1   784
and, behold, it was burned with *f* 1Sa 30:3   784
and we burned Ziklag with *f* 1Sa 30:14   784
go and set it on *f* 2Sa 14:30
servants set the field on *f* 2Sa 14:30   784
thy servants set my field on *f* 2Sa 14:31   784
f out of his mouth devoured 2Sa 22:9   784
him were coals of *f* kindled 2Sa 22:13   784
burned with *f* in the same place 2Sa 23:7   784
taken Gezer, and burnt it with *f* 1Kin 9:16   784
the king's house over him with *f* 1Kin 16:18   784
lay it on wood, and put no *f* under 1Kin 18:23   784
lay it on wood, and put no *f* under 1Kin 18:23   784
and the God that answereth by *f* 1Kin 18:24   784
of your gods, but put no *f* under 1Kin 18:25   784
Then the *f* of the Lord fell, and 1Kin 18:38   784
And after the earthquake a *f* 1Kin 19:12   784
but the Lord was not in the *f* 1Kin 19:12   784
after the *f* a still small voice 1Kin 19:12   784
then let *f* come down from heaven, ... 2Kin 1:10   784
And there came down *f* from heaven 2Kin 1:10   784
let *f* come down from heaven, and 2Kin 1:12   784
the *f* of God came down from 2Kin 1:12   784
there came down *f* from heaven, and 2Kin 1:14   784
a chariot of *f*, and horses of *f* 2Kin 2:11   784
chariots of *f* round about Elisha 2Kin 6:17   784
strong holds wilt thou set on *f* 2Kin 8:12   784
his son to pass through the *f* 2Kin 16:3   784
daughters to pass through the *f* 2Kin 17:17   784
children in *f* to Adrammelech 2Kin 17:31   784
have cast their gods into the *f* 2Kin 19:18   784
made his son pass through the *f* 2Kin 21:6   784
to pass through the *f* to Molech 2Kin 23:10   784
the chariots of the sun with *f* 2Kin 23:11   784
great man's house burnt he with *f* 2Kin 25:9   784
and they were burned with *f* 1Chr 14:12   784
by *f* upon the altar of burnt 1Chr 21:26   784
the *f* came down from heaven, and 2Chr 7:1   784
of Israel saw how the *f* came down 2Chr 7:3   784
and burnt his children in the *f* 2Chr 28:3   784
the *f* in the valley of the son of 2Chr 33:6   784
with *f* according to the ordinance 2Chr 35:13   784
all the palaces thereof with *f* 2Chr 36:19   784
gates thereof are burned with *f* .... Neh 1:3   784
gates thereof are consumed with *f* .... Neh 2:3   784
thereof were consumed with *f* .... Neh 2:13   784
gates thereof are burned with *f* .... Neh 2:17   784
and in the night by a pillar of *f* .... Neh 9:12   784
neither the pillar of *f* by night .... Neh 9:19   784
The *f* of God is fallen from .... Job 1:16   784

f shall consume the tabernacles .... Job 15:34   784
spark of his *f* shall not shine .... Job 18:5   784
a *f* not blown shall consume him .... Job 20:26   784
remnant of them the *f* consumeth .... Job 22:20   784
it is turned up as it were *f* .... Job 28:5   784
For it is a *f* that consumeth to .... Job 31:12   784
lamps, and sparks of *f* leap out .... Job 41:19   784
wicked he shall rain snares, *f* .... Ps 11:6   784
f out of his mouth devoured .... Ps 18:8   784
passed, hail stones and coals of *f* .... Ps 18:12   784
hail stones and coals of *f* .... Ps 18:13   784
wrath, and the *f* shall devour them .... Ps 21:9   784
the Lord divideth the flames of *f* .... Ps 29:7   784
while I was musing the *f* burned .... Ps 39:3   784
he burneth the chariot in the *f* .... Ps 46:9   784
a *f* shall devour before him, and .... Ps 50:3   784
even among them that are set on *f* .... Ps 57:4   3857
we went through *f* and through .... Ps 66:12   784
as wax melteth before the *f* .... Ps 68:2   784
They have cast *f* into thy .... Ps 74:7   784
all the night with a light of *f* .... Ps 78:14   784
so a *f* was kindled against Jacob, ... Ps 78:21   784
The *f* consumed their young men .... Ps 78:63   784
shall thy jealousy burn like *f* .... Ps 79:5   784
It is burned with *f*, it is cut .... Ps 80:16   784
As the *f* burneth a wood, and as .... Ps 83:14   784
flame setteth the mountains on *f* .... Ps 83:14   3857
shall thy wrath burn like *f* .... Ps 89:46   784
A *f* goeth before him, and burneth .... Ps 97:3   784
his ministers a flaming *f* .... Ps 104:4   784
rain, and flaming *f* in their land .... Ps 105:32   784
f to give light in the night .... Ps 105:39   784
a *f* was kindled in their company .... Ps 106:18   784
are quenched as the *f* of thorns .... Ps 118:12   784
let them be cast into the *f* .... Ps 140:10   784
F, and hail; snow, and .... Ps 148:8   784
Can a man take *f* in his bosom .... Prov 6:27   784
his lips there is as a burning *f* .... Prov 16:27   784
heap coals of *f* upon his head .... Prov 25:22
no wood is, there the *f* goeth out .... Prov 26:20   784
to burning coals, and wood to *f* .... Prov 26:21   784
the *f* that saith not, It is .... Prov 30:16   784
the coals thereof are coals of *f* .... Song 8:6   784
your cities are burned with *f* .... Is 1:7   784
shining of a flaming *f* by night .... Is 4:5   784
Therefore as the *f* devoureth the .... Is 5:24   784
be with burning and fuel of *f* .... Is 9:5   784
For wickedness burneth as the *f* .... Is 9:18   784
shall be as the fuel of the *f* .... Is 9:19   784
a burning like the burning of a *f* .... Is 10:16   784
light of Israel shall be for a *f* .... Is 10:17   784
the *f* of thine enemies shall .... Is 26:11   784
the women come, and set them on *f* ...... Is 27:11   215
and the flame of devouring *f* .... Is 29:6   784
a sherd to take *f* from the hearth .... Is 30:14   784
and his tongue as a devouring *f* .... Is 30:27   784
with the flame of a devouring *f* .... Is 30:30   784
the pile thereof is *f* and much .... Is 30:33   784
whose *f* is in Zion, and his .... Is 31:9   217
your breath, as *f*, shall devour .... Is 33:11   784
up shall they be burned in the *f* .... Is 33:12   784
shall dwell with the devouring *f* .... Is 33:14   784
have cast their gods into the *f* .... Is 37:19   784
it hath set him on *f* round about .... Is 42:25   3857
when thou walkest through the *f* .... Is 43:2   784
He burneth part thereof in the *f* .... Is 44:16   784
Aha, I am warm, I have seen the *f* .... Is 44:16   217
I have burned part of it in the *f* .... Is 44:19   784
the *f* shall burn them .... Is 47:14   784
warm at, nor *f* to sit before it .... Is 47:14   217
Behold, all ye that kindle a *f* .... Is 50:11   784
walk in the light of your *f* .... Is 50:11   784
that bloweth the coals in the *f* .... Is 54:16   784
As when the melting *f* burneth .... Is 64:2   784
the *f* causeth the waters to boil, ... Is 64:2   784
praised thee, is burned up with *f* .... Is 64:11   784
a *f* that burneth all the day .... Is 65:5   784
behold, the Lord will come with *f* .... Is 66:15   784
and his rebuke with flames of *f* .... Is 66:15   784
For by *f* and by his sword will the .... Is 66:16   784
neither shall their *f* be quenched .... Is 66:24   784
lest my fury come forth like *f* .... Jer 4:4   784
will make my words in thy mouth *f* .... Jer 5:14   784
up a sign of *f* in Beth-haccerem .... Jer 6:1   784
the lead is consumed of the *f* .... Jer 6:29   784
wood, and the fathers kindle the *f* .... Jer 7:18   784
sons and their daughters in the *f* .... Jer 7:31   784
tumult he hath kindled *f* upon it .... Jer 11:16   784
for a *f* is kindled in mine anger, ... Jer 15:14   784
ye have kindled a *f* in mine anger .... Jer 17:4   784
I kindle a *f* in the gates thereof .... Jer 17:27   784

to burn their sons with f for	Jer 19:5	784
a burning f shut up in my bones	Jer 20:9	784
and he shall burn it with f	Jer 21:10	784
lest my fury go out like f	Jer 21:12	784
I will kindle a f in the forest	Jer 21:14	784
cedars, and cast them into the f	Jer 22:7	784
Is not my word like as a f	Jer 23:29	784
king of Babylon roasted in the f	Jer 29:22	784
set f on this city, and burn it	Jer 32:29	784
to pass through the f unto Molech	Jer 32:35	784
and he shall burn it with f	Jer 34:2	784
and take it, and burn it with f	Jer 34:22	784
there was a f on the hearth	Jer 36:22	784
cast it into the f that was on	Jer 36:23	784
in the f that was on the hearth	Jer 36:23	784
king of Judah had burned in the f	Jer 36:32	784
and take it, and burn it with f	Jer 37:8	784
tent, and burn this city with f	Jer 37:10	784
city shall not be burned with f	Jer 38:17	784
and they shall burn it with f	Jer 38:18	784
this city to be burned with f	Jer 38:23	784
the houses of the people, with f	Jer 39:8	784
I will kindle a f in the houses	Jer 43:12	784
Egyptians shall he burn with f	Jer 43:13	784
but a f shall come forth out of	Jer 48:45	784
daughters shall be burned with f	Jer 49:2	784
I will kindle a f in the wall of	Jer 49:27	784
I will kindle a f in his cities	Jer 50:32	784
the reeds they have burned with f	Jer 51:32	784
high gates shall be burned with f	Jer 51:58	784
in vain, and the folk in the f	Jer 51:58	784
the great men, burned he with f	Jer 52:13	784
hath he sent f into my bones	Lam 1:13	784
against Jacob like a flaming f	Lam 2:3	784
he poured out his fury like f	Lam 2:4	784
and hath kindled a f in Zion	Lam 4:11	784
a f infolding itself, and a	Eze 1:4	784
amber, out of the midst of the f	Eze 1:4	784
was like burning coals of f	Eze 1:13	784
living creatures; and the f was bright	Eze 1:13	784
out of the f went forth lightning	Eze 1:13	784
as the appearance of f round	Eze 1:27	784
as it were the appearance of f	Eze 1:27	784
Thou shalt burn with f a third	Eze 5:2	217
cast them into the midst of the f	Eze 5:4	784
and burn them in the f	Eze 5:4	784
for thereof shall a f come forth	Eze 5:4	784
a likeness as the appearance of f	Eze 8:2	784
of his loins even downward, f	Eze 8:2	784
of f from between the cherubims	Eze 10:2	784
Take f from between the wheels,	Eze 10:6	784
f that was between the cherubims	Eze 10:7	784
it is cast into the f for fuel	Eze 15:4	784
the f devoureth both the ends of	Eze 15:4	784
when the f hath devoured it, and	Eze 15:5	784
I have given to the f for fuel	Eze 15:6	784
they shall go out from one f	Eze 15:7	784
another f shall devour them	Eze 15:7	784
to pass through the f for them	Eze 16:21	784
shall burn thine houses with f	Eze 16:41	784
the f consumed them	Eze 19:12	784
f is gone out of a rod of her	Eze 19:14	784
the f all that openeth the womb	Eze 20:26	784
your sons to pass through the f	Eze 20:31	784
Behold, I will kindle a f in thee	Eze 20:47	784
against thee in the f of my wrath	Eze 21:31	784
Thou shalt be fuel for the f	Eze 21:32	784
furnace, to blow the f upon it	Eze 22:20	784
upon you in the f of my wrath	Eze 22:21	784
them with the f of my wrath	Eze 22:31	784
shall be devoured by the f	Eze 23:25	784
to pass for them through the f	Eze 23:37	784
and burn up their houses with f	Eze 23:47	784
even make the pile for f great	Eze 24:9	784
Heap on wood, kindle the f	Eze 24:10	784
her scum shall be in the f	Eze 24:12	784
in the midst of the stones of f	Eze 28:14	784
from the midst of the stones of f	Eze 28:16	784
forth a f from the midst of thee	Eze 28:18	784
when I have set a f in Egypt	Eze 30:8	784
desolate, and will set f in Zoan	Eze 30:14	784
And I will set f in Egypt	Eze 30:16	784
Surely in the f of my jealousy	Eze 36:5	784
in the f of my wrath have I	Eze 38:19	784
rain, and great hailstones,	Eze 38:22	784
And I will send a f on Magog	Eze 39:6	784
shall go forth, and shall set on f	Eze 39:9	784
burn them with f seven years	Eze 39:9	784
shall burn the weapons with f	Eze 39:10	5135
the flame of the f slew those men	Dan 3:22	5135
men bound into the midst of the f	Dan 3:24	5135

walking in the midst of the f	Dan 3:25	5135
came forth of the midst of the f	Dan 3:26	5135
whose bodies the f had no power	Dan 3:27	5135
nor the smell of f had passed on	Dan 3:27	5135
flame, and his wheels as burning f	Dan 7:9	5135
and his eyes as lamps of f	Dan 10:6	784
morning it burneth as a flaming f	Hos 7:6	784
I will send a f upon his cities	Hos 8:14	784
for the f hath devoured the	Joel 1:19	784
the f hath devoured the pastures	Joel 1:20	784
A f devoureth before them	Joel 2:3	784
of f that devoureth the stubble	Joel 2:5	784
and in the earth, blood, and f	Joel 2:30	784
But I will send a f into the	Amos 1:4	784
But I will send a f on the wall	Amos 1:7	784
But I will send a f on the wall	Amos 1:10	784
But I will send a f upon Teman	Amos 1:12	784
But I will kindle a f in the wall	Amos 1:14	784
But I will send a f upon Moab	Amos 2:2	784
But I will send a f upon Judah	Amos 2:5	784
out like f in the house of Joseph	Amos 5:6	784
Lord GOD called to contend by f	Amos 7:4	784
the house of Jacob shall be a f	Obad 18	784
be cleft, as wax before the f	Mic 1:4	784
shall be burned with the f	Mic 1:7	784
his fury is poured out like f	Nah 1:6	784
the f shall devour thy bars	Nah 3:13	784
There shall the f devour thee	Nah 3:15	784
people shall labour in the very f	Hab 2:13	784
devoured by the f of his jealousy	Zeph 1:18	784
with the f of my jealousy	Zeph 3:8	784
unto her a wall of f round about	Zec 2:5	784
this a brand plucked out of the f	Zec 3:2	784
and she shall be devoured with f	Zec 9:4	784
that the f may devour thy cedars	Zec 11:1	784
an hearth of f among the wood	Zec 12:6	784
and like a torch of f in a sheaf	Zec 12:6	784
the third part through the f	Zec 13:9	784
neither do ye kindle f on mine	Mal 1:10	
for he is like a refiner's f	Mal 3:2	784
is hewn down, and cast into the f	Mt 3:10	4442
with the Holy Ghost, and with f	Mt 3:11	4442
up the chaff with unquenchable f	Mt 3:12	4442
shall be in danger of hell f	Mt 5:22	4442
is hewn down, and cast into the f	Mt 7:19	4442
are gathered and burned in the f	Mt 13:40	4442
cast them into a furnace of f	Mt 13:42	4442
cast them into the furnace of f	Mt 13:50	4442
ofttimes he falleth into the f	Mt 17:15	4442
to be cast into everlasting f	Mt 18:8	4442
two eyes to be cast into hell f	Mt 18:9	4442
me, ye cursed, into everlasting f	Mt 25:41	4442
it hath cast him into the f	Mk 9:22	4442
into the f that never shall be	Mk 9:43	4442
not, and the f is not quenched	Mk 9:44	4442
into the f that never shall be	Mk 9:45	4442
not, and the f is not quenched	Mk 9:46	4442
two eyes to be cast into hell f	Mk 9:47	4442
not, and the f is not quenched	Mk 9:48	4442
every one shall be salted with f	Mk 9:49	4442
and warmed himself at the f	Mk 14:54	5457
is hewn down, and cast into the f	Lk 3:9	4442
you with the Holy Ghost and with f	Lk 3:16	4442
he will burn with f unquenchable	Lk 3:17	4442
f to come down from heaven	Lk 9:54	4442
I am come to send f on the earth	Lk 12:49	4442
Lot went out of Sodom it rained f	Lk 17:29	4442
when they had kindled a f in the	Lk 22:55	4442
beheld him as he sat by the f	Lk 22:56	5457
them, and cast them into the f	Jn 15:6	4442
there, who had made a f of coals	Jn 18:18	
they saw a f of coals there, and	Jn 21:9	
them cloven tongues like as of f	Acts 2:3	4442
blood, and f, and vapour of smoke	Acts 2:19	4442
Lord in a flame of f in a bush	Acts 7:30	4442
for they kindled a f, and received	Acts 28:2	4443
of sticks, and laid them on the f	Acts 28:3	4443
he shook off the beast into the f	Acts 28:5	4442
shalt heap coals of f on his head	Rom 12:20	4442
because it shall be revealed by f	1Cor 3:13	4442
the f shall try every man's work	1Cor 3:13	4442
yet so as by f	1Cor 3:15	4442
In flaming f taking vengeance on	2Th 1:8	4442
and his ministers a flame of f	Heb 1:7	4442
Quenched the violence of f	Heb 11:34	4442
be touched, and that burned with f	Heb 12:18	4442
For our God is a consuming f	Heb 12:29	4442
a matter a little f kindleth	Jas 3:5	4442
And the tongue is a f, a world of	Jas 3:6	4442
setteth on f the course of nature	Jas 3:6	5394
and it is set on f of hell	Jas 3:6	5394

F

shall eat your flesh as it were *f* .... Jas 5:3 — 4442
though it be tried with *f* .... 1Pet 1:7 — 4442
reserved unto *f* against the day .... 2Pet 3:7 — 4442
being on *f* shall be dissolved .... 2Pet 3:12 — 4448
the vengeance of eternal *f* .... Jude 7 — 4442
fear, pulling them out of the *f* .... Jude 23 — 4442
and his eyes were as a flame of *f* .... Rev 1:14 — 4442
his eyes like unto a flame of *f* .... Rev 2:18 — 4442
to buy of me gold tried in the *f* .... Rev 3:18 — 4442
of *f* burning before the throne .... Rev 4:5 — 4442
and filled it with *f* of the altar .... Rev 8:5 — 4442
f mingled with blood, and they .... Rev 8:7 — 4442
with *f* was cast into the sea .... Rev 8:8 — 4442
on them, having breastplates of *f* .... Rev 9:17 — 4447
and out of their mouths issued *f* .... Rev 9:17 — 4442
part of men killed, by the *f* .... Rev 9:18 — 4442
sun, and his feet as pillars of *f* .... Rev 10:1 — 4442
f proceedeth out of their mouth, ... Rev 11:5 — 4442
so that he maketh *f* come down .... Rev 13:13 — 4442
and he shall be tormented with *f* .... Rev 14:10 — 4442
the altar, which had power over *f* .... Rev 14:18 — 4442
a sea of glass mingled with *f* .... Rev 15:2 — 4442
unto him to scorch men with *f* .... Rev 16:8 — 4442
eat her flesh, and burn her with *f* .... Rev 17:16 — 4442
shall be utterly burned with *f* .... Rev 18:8 — 4442
His eyes were as a flame of *f* .... Rev 19:12 — 4442
lake of *f* burning with brimstone .... Rev 19:20 — 4442
f came down from God out of .... Rev 20:9 — 4442
them was cast into the lake of *f* .... Rev 20:10 — 4442
hell were cast into the lake of *f* .... Rev 20:14 — 4442
life was cast into the lake of *f* .... Rev 20:15 — 4442
in the lake which burneth with *f* .... Rev 21:8 — 4442

FIREBRAND
put a *f* in the midst between two .... Judg 15:4 — 3940
ye were as a *f* plucked out of the .... Amos 4:11 — 181

FIREBRANDS
three hundred foxes, and took *f* .... Judg 15:4 — 3940
As a mad man who casteth *f* .... Prov 26:18 — 2131
the two tails of these smoking *f* .... Is 7:4 — 181

FIREPANS
and his fleshhooks, and his *f* .... Ex 27:3 — 4289
and the fleshhooks, and the *f* .... Ex 38:3 — 4289
And the *f*, and the bowls, and such ...... 2Kin 25:15 — 4289
And the basons, and the *f*, and the ...... Jer 52:19 — 4289

FIRES
glorify ye the LORD in the *f* .... Is 24:15 — 217

FIRKINS
containing two or three *f* apiece .... Jn 2:6 — 3355

FIRM
f on dry ground in the midst of .... Josh 3:17 — 3559
where the priests' feet stood *f* .... Josh 4:3 — 3559
they are *f* in themselves .... Job 41:23 — 3332
His heart is as *f* as a stone .... Job 41:24 — 3332
but their strength is *f* .... Ps 73:4 — 1277
statute, and to make a *f* decree .... Dan 6:7 — 8631
of the hope *f* unto the end .... Heb 3:6 — 949

FIRMAMENT
Let there be a *f* in the midst of .... Gen 1:6 — 7549
And God made the *f*, and divided the .... Gen 1:7 — 7549
the *f* from the waters which were .... Gen 1:7 — 7549
the waters which were above the *f* .... Gen 1:7 — 7549
And God called the *f* Heaven .... Gen 1:8 — 7549
Let there be lights in the *f* of .... Gen 1:14 — 7549
the *f* of the heaven to give light .... Gen 1:15 — 7549
God set them in the *f* of the .... Gen 1:17 — 7549
the earth in the open *f* of heaven .... Gen 1:20 — 7549
the *f* sheweth his handywork .... Ps 19:1 — 7549
praise him in the *f* of his power .... Ps 150:1 — 7549
the likeness of the *f* upon the .... Eze 1:22 — 7549
under the *f* were their wings .... Eze 1:23 — 7549
the *f* that was over their heads .... Eze 1:25 — 7549
above the *f* that was over their .... Eze 1:26 — 7549
in the *f* that was above the head .... Eze 10:1 — 7549
shine as the brightness of the *f* .... Dan 12:3 — 7549

FIRST
and the morning were the *f* day .... Gen 1:5 — 259
The name of the *f* is Pison .... Gen 2:11 — 259
on the *f* day of the month, were .... Gen 8:5 — 259
and *f* year, in the *f* month .... Gen 8:13 — 7223
the *f* day of the month, the .... Gen 8:13 — 259
which he had made there at the *f* .... Gen 13:4 — 7223
the *f* came out red, all over like .... Gen 25:25 — 7223
beside the *f* famine that was in .... Gen 26:1 — 7223
that city was called Luz at the *f* .... Gen 28:19 — 7223
thread, saying, This came out *f* .... Gen 38:28 — 7223
did eat up the *f* seven fat kine .... Gen 41:20 — 7223
at the *f* time are we brought in .... Gen 43:18 — 8462

down at the *f* time to buy food .... Gen 43:20 — 8462
to the voice of the *f* sign .... Ex 4:8 — 7223
it shall be the *f* month of the .... Ex 12:2 — 7223
blemish, a male of the *f* year .... Ex 12:5 — 1121
even the *f* day ye shall put away .... Ex 12:15 — 7223
the *f* day until the seventh day .... Ex 12:15 — 7223
in the *f* day there shall be an .... Ex 12:16 — 7223
In the *f* month, on the fourteenth .... Ex 12:18 — 7223
to offer the *f* of thy ripe fruits .... Ex 22:29 — 4395
The *f* of the firstfruits of thy .... Ex 23:19 — 7225
the *f* row shall be a sardius, a .... Ex 28:17 — ...
this shall be the *f* row .... Ex 28:17 — 259
two lambs of the *f* year day by .... Ex 29:38 — 1121
tables of stone like unto the *f* .... Ex 34:1 — 7223
words that were in the *f* tables .... Ex 34:1 — 7223
tables of stone like unto the *f* .... Ex 34:4 — 7223
The *f* of the firstfruits of thy .... Ex 34:26 — 7225
the *f* row was a sardius, a topaz, ... Ex 39:10 — ...
this was the *f* row .... Ex 39:10 — 259
On the *f* day of the *f* month .... Ex 40:2 — 7223
On the *f* day of the month .... Ex 40:2 — 259
it came to pass in the *f* month in .... Ex 40:17 — 7223
on the *f* day of the month, that .... Ex 40:17 — 259
him as he burned the *f* bullock .... Lev 4:21 — 7223
which is for the sin offering *f* .... Lev 5:8 — 7223
and a lamb, both of the *f* year .... Lev 9:3 — 1121
and offered it for sin, as the *f* .... Lev 9:15 — 7223
the *f* year for a burnt offering .... Lev 12:6 — 1121
one ewe lamb of the *f* year .... Lev 14:10 — 1323
the *f* month at even is the LORD's .... Lev 23:5 — 7223
In the *f* day ye shall have an .... Lev 23:7 — 7223
f year for a burnt offering unto .... Lev 23:12 — 1121
without blemish of the *f* year .... Lev 23:18 — 1121
two lambs of the *f* year for a .... Lev 23:19 — 1121
the *f* fruits for a wave offering, ... Lev 23:20 — ...
in the *f* day of the month, shall .... Lev 23:24 — 259
On the *f* day shall be an holy .... Lev 23:35 — 7223
on the *f* day shall be a sabbath, ... Lev 23:39 — 7223
ye shall take you on the *f* day .... Lev 23:40 — 7223
on the *f* day of the second month, ... Num 1:1 — 259
on the *f* day of the second month .... Num 1:18 — 259
These shall *f* set forth .... Num 2:9 — 7223
shall bring a lamb of the *f* year .... Num 6:12 — 1121
one he lamb of the *f* year without .... Num 6:14 — 1121
one ewe lamb of the *f* of .... Num 6:14 — 1323
the *f* day was Nahshon the son of .... Num 7:12 — 7223
one ram, one lamb of the *f* year .... Num 7:15 — 1121
goats, five lambs of the *f* year .... Num 7:17 — 1121
one ram, one lamb of the *f* year .... Num 7:21 — 1121
goats, five lambs of the *f* year .... Num 7:23 — 1121
one ram, one lamb of the *f* year .... Num 7:27 — 1121
goats, five lambs of the *f* year .... Num 7:29 — 1121
one ram, one lamb of the *f* year .... Num 7:33 — 1121
goats, five lambs of the *f* year .... Num 7:35 — 1121
one ram, one lamb of the *f* year .... Num 7:39 — 1121
goats, five lambs of the *f* year .... Num 7:41 — 1121
one ram, one lamb of the *f* year .... Num 7:45 — 1121
goats, five lambs of the *f* year .... Num 7:47 — 1121
one ram, one lamb of the *f* year .... Num 7:51 — 1121
goats, five lambs of the *f* year .... Num 7:53 — 1121
one ram, one lamb of the *f* year .... Num 7:57 — 1121
goats, five lambs of the *f* year .... Num 7:59 — 1121
one ram, one lamb of the *f* year .... Num 7:63 — 1121
goats, five lambs of the *f* year .... Num 7:65 — 1121
one ram, one lamb of the *f* year .... Num 7:69 — 1121
goats, five lambs of the *f* year .... Num 7:71 — 1121
one ram, one lamb of the *f* year .... Num 7:75 — 1121
goats, five lambs of the *f* year .... Num 7:77 — 1121
one ram, one lamb of the *f* year .... Num 7:81 — 1121
goats, five lambs of the *f* year .... Num 7:83 — 1121
the lambs of the *f* year twelve .... Num 7:87 — 1121
the lambs of the *f* year sixty .... Num 7:88 — 1121
in the *f* month of the second year .... Num 9:1 — 7223
on the fourteenth day of the *f* .... Num 9:5 — 7223
they *f* took their journey .... Num 10:13 — 7223
In the *f* place went the standard .... Num 10:14 — 7223
the *f* of your dough for an heave .... Num 15:20 — 7225
Of the *f* of your dough ye shall .... Num 15:21 — 7225
of the *f* year for a sin offering .... Num 15:27 — 1323
whatsoever is *f* ripe in the land, ... Num 18:13 — 1061
the desert of Zin in the *f* month .... Num 20:1 — 7223
Amalek was the *f* of the nations .... Num 24:20 — 7225
two lambs of the *f* year without .... Num 28:3 — 1121
lambs of the *f* year without spot .... Num 28:9 — 1121
lambs of the *f* year without spot .... Num 28:11 — 1121
f month is the passover of the .... Num 28:16 — 7223
In the *f* day shall be an holy .... Num 28:18 — 7223
ram, and seven lambs of the *f* year ...... Num 28:19 — 1121
ram, seven lambs of the *f* year .... Num 28:27 — 1121
on the *f* day of the month, ye .... Num 29:1 — 259
seven lambs of the *f* year without .... Num 29:2 — 1121

ram, and seven lambs of the *f* year	Num 29:8	1121
and fourteen lambs of the *f* year	Num 29:13	1121
lambs of the *f* year without spot	Num 29:17	1121
of the *f* year without blemish	Num 29:20	1121
of the *f* year without blemish	Num 29:23	1121
lambs of the *f* year without spot	Num 29:26	1121
of the *f* year without blemish	Num 29:29	1121
of the *f* year without blemish	Num 29:32	1121
seven lambs of the *f* year without	Num 29:36	1121
from Rameses in the *f* month	Num 33:3	7223
the fifteenth day of the *f* month	Num 33:3	7223
in the *f* day of the fifth month	Num 33:38	259
on the *f* day of the month, that	Deut 1:3	259
down before the LORD, as at the *f*	Deut 9:18	7223
nights, as I fell down at the *f*	Deut 9:25	
tables of stone like unto the *f*	Deut 10:1	
the *f* tables which thou brakest	Deut 10:2	7223
tables of stone like unto the *f*	Deut 10:3	7223
according to the *f* writing	Deut 10:4	7223
mount, according to the *f* time	Deut 10:10	7223
the *f* rain and the latter rain,	Deut 11:14	3138
thine hand shall be *f* upon him to	Deut 13:9	7223
sacrificedst the *f* day at even	Deut 16:4	7223
be *f* upon him to put him to death	Deut 17:7	7223
the *f* of the fleece of thy sheep,	Deut 18:4	7225
That thou shalt take of the *f* of	Deut 26:2	7225
he provided the *f* part for	Deut 33:21	7225
on the tenth day of the *f* month	Josh 4:19	7223
come up against us, as at the *f*	Josh 8:5	7223
They flee before us, as at the *f*	Josh 8:6	7223
for theirs was the *f* lot	Josh 21:10	7223
for us against the Canaanites *f*	Judg 1:1	8462
of the city was Laish in the *f*	Judg 18:29	7223
Which of us shall go up *f* to the	Judg 20:18	8462
LORD said, Judah shall go up *f*	Judg 20:18	8462
put themselves in array the *f* day	Judg 20:22	7223
down before us, as at the *f*	Judg 20:32	7223
before us, as in the *f* battle	Judg 20:39	7223
that *f* slaughter, which Jonathan	1Sa 14:14	7223
the same was the *f* altar that he	1Sa 14:35	2490
the battle were Eliab the *f* born	1Sa 17:13	
except thou *f* bring Michal Saul's	2Sa 3:13	6440
of them be overthrown at the *f*	2Sa 17:9	8462
I am come the *f* this day of all	2Sa 19:20	7223
f had in bringing back our king	2Sa 19:43	7223
days of harvest, in the *f* days	2Sa 21:9	7223
he attained not unto the *f* three	2Sa 23:19	
he attained not to the *f* three	2Sa 23:23	
f year of Asa king of Judah began	1Kin 16:23	259
make me thereof a little cake *f*	1Kin 17:13	7223
for yourselves, and dress it *f*	1Kin 18:25	7223
to thy servant at the *f* I will do	1Kin 20:9	7223
of the provinces went out *f*	1Kin 20:17	7223
Now the *f* inhabitants that dwelt	1Chr 9:2	7223
the Jebusites *f* shall be chief	1Chr 11:6	7223
Joab the son of Zeruiah went *f* up	1Chr 11:6	7223
he attained not to the *f* three	1Chr 11:21	
but attained not to the *f* three	1Chr 11:25	
Ezer the *f*, Obadiah the second,	1Chr 12:9	7218
went over Jordan in the *f* month	1Chr 12:15	7223
because ye did it not at the *f*	1Chr 15:13	7223
on that day David delivered *f*	1Chr 16:7	7218
Jeriah the *f*, Amariah the second,	1Chr 23:19	7218
Micah the *f*, and Jesiah the second	1Chr 23:20	7218
Now the *f* lot came forth to	1Chr 24:7	7223
of Rehabiah, the *f* was Isshiah	1Chr 24:21	7218
Jeriah the *f*, Amariah the second,	1Chr 24:23	
Now the *f* lot came forth for	1Chr 25:9	7223
Over the *f* course for the	1Chr 27:2	7223
of the host for the *f* month	1Chr 27:3	7223
Now the acts of David the king, *f*	1Chr 29:29	7223
f measure was threescore cubits	2Chr 3:3	7223
rest of the acts of Solomon, *f*	2Chr 9:29	7223
Now the acts of Rehoboam, *f*	2Chr 12:15	7223
And, behold, the acts of Asa, *f*	2Chr 16:11	7223
in the *f* ways of his father David	2Chr 17:3	7223
of the acts of Jehoshaphat, *f*	2Chr 20:34	7223
rest of the acts of Amaziah, *f*	2Chr 25:26	7223
the rest of the acts of Uzziah, *f*	2Chr 26:22	7223
of his acts and of all his ways, *f*	2Chr 26:28	7223
He in the *f* year of his reign, in	2Chr 29:3	7223
year of his reign, in the *f* month	2Chr 29:3	7223
Now they began on the *f* day of	2Chr 29:17	7223
day of the *f* month to sanctify	2Chr 29:17	7223
of the *f* month they made an end	2Chr 29:17	7223
the fourteenth day of the *f* month	2Chr 35:1	7223
And his deeds, *f* and last, behold,	2Chr 35:27	7223
Now in the *f* year of Cyrus king	2Chr 36:22	259
Now in the *f* year of Cyrus king	Ezr 1:1	259
From the *f* day of the seventh	Ezr 3:6	259
men, that had seen the *f* house	Ezr 3:12	7223

But in the *f* year of Cyrus the	Ezr 5:13	2298
In the *f* year of Cyrus the king	Ezr 6:3	2298
the fourteenth day of the *f* month	Ezr 6:19	7223
For upon the *f* day of the	Ezr 7:9	259
f month began he to go up from	Ezr 7:9	7223
on the *f* day of the fifth month	Ezr 7:9	259
on the twelfth day of the *f* month	Ezr 8:31	7223
sat down in the *f* day of the	Ezr 10:16	259
by the *f* day of the month	Ezr 10:17	259
by the *f* day of the month	Ezr 10:17	7223
of them which came up at the *f*	Neh 7:5	7223
upon the *f* day of the seventh	Neh 8:2	259
from the *f* day unto the last day,	Neh 8:18	7223
which sat the *f* in the kingdom	Est 1:14	7223
In the *f* month, that is, the	Est 3:7	7223
the thirteenth day of the *f* month	Est 3:12	7223
Art thou the *f* man that was born	Job 15:7	7223
And he called the name of the *f*	Job 42:14	7223
He that is *f* in his own cause	Prov 18:17	7223
restore thy judges as at the *f*	Is 1:26	7223
when at the *f* he lightly	Is 9:1	7223
I the LORD, the *f*, and with the	Is 41:4	7223
The *f* shall say to Zion, Behold,	Is 41:27	7223
Thy *f* father hath sinned, and thy	Is 43:27	7223
I am the *f*, and I am the last	Is 44:6	7223
I am the *f*, I also am the last	Is 48:12	7223
me, and the ships of Tarshish *f*	Is 60:9	7223
that bringeth forth her *f* child	Jer 4:31	1069
where I set my name at the *f*	Jer 7:12	7223
f I will recompense their	Jer 16:18	7223
like the figs that are *f* ripe	Jer 24:2	1073
of Judah, that was the *f* year of	Jer 25:1	7224
and will build them, as at the *f*	Jer 33:7	7223
of the land, as at the *f*, saith	Jer 33:11	7223
words that were in the *f* roll	Jer 36:28	7223
f the king of Assyria hath	Jer 50:17	7223
king of Babylon in the *f* year of	Jer 52:31	
the *f* face was the face of a	Eze 10:14	259
in the *f* day of the month, that	Eze 26:1	259
and twentieth year, in the *f* month	Eze 29:17	7223
in the *f* day of the month, the	Eze 29:17	259
the eleventh year, in the *f* month	Eze 30:20	7223
in the *f* day of the month, that	Eze 31:1	259
in the *f* day of the month, that	Eze 32:1	259
after the measure of the *f* gate	Eze 40:21	7223
the *f* of all the firstfruits of	Eze 44:30	7223
the priest the *f* of your dough	Eze 44:30	7225
In the *f* month, in the	Eze 45:18	7223
in the *f* day of the month, thou	Eze 45:18	259
In the *f* month, in the fourteenth	Eze 45:21	7223
of the *f* year without blemish	Eze 46:13	1121
unto the *f* year of king Cyrus	Dan 1:21	259
of whom Daniel was *f*	Dan 6:2	2298
In the *f* year of Belshazzar king	Dan 7:1	2298
The *f* was like a lion, and had	Dan 7:4	6933
whom there were three of the *f*	Dan 7:8	6933
and he shall be diverse from the *f*	Dan 7:24	6933
which appeared unto me at the *f*	Dan 8:1	8462
is between his eyes is the *f* king	Dan 8:21	7223
In the *f* year of Darius the son	Dan 9:1	259
In the *f* year of his reign I	Dan 9:2	259
and twentieth day of the *f* month	Dan 10:4	7223
for from the *f* day that thou	Dan 10:12	7223
Also I in the *f* year of Darius	Dan 11:1	259
will go and return to my *f* husband	Hos 2:7	7223
in the fig tree at her *f* time	Hos 9:10	7225
and the latter rain in the *f* month	Joel 2:23	7223
with the *f* that go captive	Amos 6:7	7218
it come, even the *f* dominion	Mic 4:8	7223
in the *f* day of the month, came	Hag 1:1	259
saw this house in her *f* glory	Hag 2:3	7223
In the *f* chariot were red horses	Zec 6:2	7223
shall save the tents of Judah *f*	Zec 12:7	7223
gate unto the place of the *f* gate	Zec 14:10	7223
f be reconciled to thy brother,	Mt 5:24	*4412*
But seek ye *f* the kingdom of God,	Mt 6:33	*4412*
f cast out the beam out of thine	Mt 7:5	*4412*
unto him, Lord, suffer me *f* to go	Mt 8:21	*4412*
The *f*, Simon, who is called Peter	Mt 10:2	*4412*
except he *f* bind the strong man	Mt 12:29	*4412*
of that man is worse than the *f*	Mt 12:45	*4413*
Gather ye together *f* the tares	Mt 13:30	*4412*
scribes that Elias must *f* come	Mt 17:10	*4412*
them, Elias truly shall *f* come	Mt 17:11	*4412*
take up the fish that *f* cometh up	Mt 17:27	*4413*
But many that are *f* shall be last	Mt 19:30	*4412*
and the last shall be *f*	Mt 19:30	*4413*
from the last unto the *f*	Mt 20:8	*4413*
But when the *f* came, they	Mt 20:10	*4413*
shall be *f*, and the *f* last	Mt 20:16	*4413*
and he came to the *f*, and said, Son	Mt 21:28	*4413*

They say unto him, The *f*	Mt 21:31	4413
other servants more than the *f*	Mt 21:36	4413
and the *f*, when he had married a	Mt 22:25	4413
This is the *f* and great	Mt 22:38	4413
cleanse *f* that which is within	Mt 23:26	4412
Now the *f* day of the feast of	Mt 26:17	4413
error shall be worse than the *f*	Mt 27:64	4413
dawn toward the *f* day of the week	Mt 28:1	3391
except he will *f* bind the strong	Mk 3:27	4412
f the blade, then the ear, after	Mk 4:28	4412
her, Let the children *f* be filled	Mk 7:27	4412
scribes that Elias must *f* come	Mk 9:11	4412
told them, Elias verily cometh *f*	Mk 9:12	4412
them, If any man desire to be *f*	Mk 9:35	4413
But many that are *f* shall be last	Mk 10:31	4413
and the last *f*	Mk 10:31	4413
the *f* took a wife, and dying left	Mk 12:20	4413
Which is the *f* commandment of all	Mk 12:28	4413
The *f* of all the commandments is,	Mk 12:29	4413
this is the *f* commandment	Mk 12:30	4413
the gospel must *f* be published	Mk 13:10	4412
the *f* day of unleavened bread,	Mk 14:12	4413
the morning the *f* day of the week	Mk 16:2	3391
risen early the *f* day of the week	Mk 16:9	4413
he appeared *f* to Mary Magdalene,	Mk 16:9	4412
of all things from the very *f*	Lk 1:3	509
this taxing was *f* made when	Lk 2:2	4413
on the second sabbath after the *f*	Lk 6:1	1207
cast out *f* the beam out of thine	Lk 6:42	4412
he said, Lord, suffer me *f* to go	Lk 9:59	4412
but let me *f* go bid them farewell	Lk 9:61	4412
f say, Peace be to this house	Lk 10:5	4412
of that man is worse than the *f*	Lk 11:26	4413
he had not *f* washed before dinner	Lk 11:38	4412
say unto his disciples *f* of all	Lk 12:1	4412
there are last which shall be *f*	Lk 13:30	4413
there are *f* which shall be last	Lk 13:30	4413
The *f* said unto him, I have	Lk 14:18	4413
build a tower, sitteth not down *f*	Lk 14:28	4412
another king, sitteth not down *f*	Lk 14:31	4412
unto him, and said unto the *f*	Lk 16:5	4413
But *f* must he suffer many things,	Lk 17:25	4412
Then came the *f*, saying, Lord,	Lk 19:16	4413
the *f* took a wife, and died	Lk 20:29	4413
these things must *f* come to pass	Lk 21:9	4412
Now upon the *f* day of the week,	Lk 24:1	3891
He *f* findeth his own brother	Jn 1:41	4413
whosoever then *f* after the	Jn 5:4	4413
let him *f* cast a stone at her	Jn 8:7	4413
place where John at *f* baptized	Jn 10:40	4412
not his disciples at the *f*	Jn 12:16	4412
And led him away to Annas *f*	Jn 18:13	4412
and brake the legs of the *f*	Jn 19:32	4413
which at the *f* came to Jesus by	Jn 19:39	4413
The *f* day of the week cometh Mary	Jn 20:1	3391
Peter, and came *f* to the sepulchre	Jn 20:4	4413
which came *f* to the sepulchre, and	Jn 20:8	4413
being the *f* day of the week, when	Jn 20:19	3391
Unto you *f* God, having raised up	Acts 3:26	4412
Egypt, he sent out our fathers *f*	Acts 7:12	4412
called Christians *f* in Antioch	Acts 11:26	4412
When they were past the *f*	Acts 12:10	4413
When John had *f* preached before	Acts 13:24	
should *f* have been spoken to you	Acts 13:46	4412
at the *f* did visit the Gentiles	Acts 15:14	4412
upon the *f* day of the week, when	Acts 20:7	3391
from the *f* day that I came into	Acts 20:18	4413
which was at the *f* among mine own	Acts 26:4	746
But shewed *f* unto them of	Acts 26:20	4412
that he should be the *f* that	Acts 26:23	4413
cast themselves *f* into the sea	Acts 27:43	4413
F, I thank my God through Jesus	Rom 1:8	4412
to the Jew *f*, and also to the	Rom 1:16	4412
man that doeth evil, of the Jew *f*	Rom 2:9	4412
that worketh good, to the Jew *f*	Rom 2:10	4412
F Moses saith, I will provoke you	Rom 10:19	4413
Or who hath *f* given to him, and it	Rom 11:35	4272
if *f* I be somewhat filled with	Rom 15:24	4412
For *f* of all, when ye come	1Cor 11:18	4412
f apostles, secondarily prophets,	1Cor 12:28	4412
by, let the *f* hold his peace	1Cor 14:30	4413
you *f* of all that which I also	1Cor 15:3	1722,4413
The *f* man Adam was made a living	1Cor 15:45	4413
that was not *f* which is spiritual	1Cor 15:46	4412
The *f* man is of the earth, earthy	1Cor 15:47	4413
Upon the *f* day of the week let	1Cor 16:2	3391
The *f* epistle to the Corinthians	1Cor s	4413
but *f* gave their own selves to	2Cor 8:5	4412
For if there be *f* a willing mind,	2Cor 8:12	4295
the gospel unto you at the *f*	Gal 4:13	4386
glory, who *f* trusted in Christ	Eph 1:12	4276

f into the lower parts of the	Eph 4:9	4412
which is the *f* commandment with	Eph 6:2	4413
gospel from the *f* day until now	Phil 1:5	4413
the dead in Christ shall rise *f*	1Th 4:16	4412
The *f* epistle unto the	1Th s	4413
there come a falling away *f*	2Th 2:3	4412
that in me *f* Jesus Christ might	1Ti 1:16	4413
f of all, supplications, prayers,	1Ti 2:1	4412
For Adam was *f* formed, then Eve	1Ti 2:13	4413
And let these also *f* be proved	1Ti 3:10	4412
let them learn *f* to shew piety at	1Ti 5:4	4412
they have cast off their *f* faith	1Ti 5:12	4413
The *f* to Timothy was written from	1Ti s	4413
which dwelt *f* in thy grandmother	2Ti 1:5	4412
must be *f* partaker of the fruits	2Ti 2:6	4413
At my *f* answer no man stood with	2Ti 4:16	4413
ordained the *f* bishop of the	2Ti s	4413
that is an heretick after the *f*	Titus 3:10	3391
ordained the *f* bishop of the	Titus s	4413
which at the *f* began to be spoken	Heb 2:3	746
they to whom it was *f* preached	Heb 4:6	4386
f principles of the oracles of	Heb 5:12	746
f being by interpretation King of	Heb 7:2	4412
f for his own sins, and then for	Heb 7:27	4386
For if that *f* covenant had been	Heb 8:7	4413
covenant, he hath made the *f* old	Heb 8:13	4413
Then verily the *f* covenant had	Heb 9:1	4413
the *f*, wherein was the	Heb 9:2	4413
went always into the *f* tabernacle	Heb 9:6	4413
while as the *f* tabernacle was yet	Heb 9:8	4413
that were under the *f* testament	Heb 9:15	4413
Whereupon neither the *f* testament	Heb 9:18	4413
He taketh away the *f*, that he may	Heb 10:9	4412
that is from above is *f* pure	Jas 3:17	4412
if it *f* begin at us, what shall	1Pet 4:17	4412
Knowing this *f*, that no prophecy	2Pet 1:20	4412
Knowing this *f*, that there shall	2Pet 3:3	4412
love him, because he *f* loved us	1Jn 4:19	4413
which kept not their *f* estate	Jude 6	746
the *f* begotten of the dead, and	Rev 1:5	4416
I am Alpha and Omega, the *f*	Rev 1:11	4413
I am the *f* and the last	Rev 1:17	4413
because thou hast left thy *f* love	Rev 2:4	4413
and repent, and do the *f* works	Rev 2:5	4413
These things saith the *f* and the	Rev 2:8	4413
and the last to be more than the *f*	Rev 2:19	4413
the *f* voice which I heard was as	Rev 4:1	4413
the *f* beast was like a lion, and	Rev 4:7	4413
The *f* angel sounded, and there	Rev 8:7	4413
power of the *f* beast before him	Rev 13:12	4413
therein to worship the *f* beast	Rev 13:12	4413
the *f* went, and poured out his	Rev 16:2	4413
This is the *f* resurrection	Rev 20:5	4413
hath part in the *f* resurrection	Rev 20:6	4413
f heaven and the *f* earth	Rev 21:1	4413
The *f* foundation was jasper	Rev 21:19	4413
the beginning and the end, the *f*	Rev 22:13	4413

FIRSTBEGOTTEN

bringeth in the *f* into the world	Heb 1:6	4416

FIRSTBORN

And Canaan begat Sidon his *f*	Gen 10:15	1060
the *f* said unto the younger, Our	Gen 19:31	1067
the *f* went in, and lay with her	Gen 19:33	1067
that the *f* said unto the younger,	Gen 19:34	1067
the *f* bare a son, and called his	Gen 19:37	1067
Huz his *f*, and Buz his brother, and	Gen 22:21	1060
the *f* of Ishmael, Nebajoth	Gen 25:13	1060
unto his father, I am Esau thy *f*	Gen 27:19	1060
he said, I am thy son, thy *f* Esau	Gen 27:32	1060
to give the younger before the *f*	Gen 29:26	1067
Reuben, Jacob's *f*, and Simeon, and	Gen 35:23	1060
sons of Eliphaz the *f* son of Esau	Gen 36:15	1060
And Judah took a wife for Er his *f*	Gen 38:6	1060
And Er, Judah's *f*, was wicked in	Gen 38:7	1060
called the name of the *f* Manasseh	Gen 41:51	1060
the *f* according to his birthright	Gen 43:33	1060
Reuben, Jacob's *f*	Gen 46:8	1060
for Manasseh was the *f*	Gen 48:14	1060
for this is the *f*	Gen 48:18	1060
Reuben, thou art my *f*, my might,	Gen 49:3	1060
LORD, Israel is my son, even my *f*	Ex 4:22	1060
I will slay thy son, even thy *f*	Ex 4:23	1060
sons of Reuben the *f* of Israel	Ex 6:14	1060
all the *f* in the land of Egypt	Ex 11:5	1060
from the *f* of Pharaoh that	Ex 11:5	1060
throne, even unto the *f* of the	Ex 11:5	1060
and all the *f* of beasts	Ex 11:5	1060
will smite all the *f* in the land	Ex 12:12	1060
all the *f* in the land of Egypt	Ex 12:29	1060
from the *f* of Pharaoh that sat on	Ex 12:29	1060

f of the captive that was in the	Ex 12:29	1060
and all the *f* of cattle	Ex 12:29	1060
Sanctify unto me all the *f*	Ex 13:2	1060
all the *f* of man among thy	Ex 13:13	1060
all the *f* in the land of Egypt	Ex 13:15	1060
land of Egypt, both the *f* of man	Ex 13:15	1060
of man, and the *f* of beast	Ex 13:15	1060
but all the *f* of my children I	Ex 13:15	1060
the *f* of thy sons shalt thou give	Ex 22:29	1060
All the *f* of thy sons thou shalt	Ex 34:20	1060
Nadab the *f*, and Abihu, Eleazar,	Num 3:2	1060
of Israel instead of all the *f*	Num 3:12	1060
Because all the *f* are mine	Num 3:13	1060
f in the land of Egypt I hallowed	Num 3:13	1060
unto me all the *f* in Israel	Num 3:13	1060
Number all the *f* of the males of	Num 3:40	1060
f among the children of Israel	Num 3:41	1060
all the *f* among the children of	Num 3:42	1060
all the *f* males by the number of	Num 3:43	1060
f among the children of Israel	Num 3:45	1060
thirteen of the *f* of the children	Num 3:46	1060
Of the *f* of the children of	Num 3:50	1060
even instead of all the *f* of all the	Num 8:16	1060
For all the *f* of the children of	Num 8:17	1060
every *f* in the land of Egypt I	Num 8:17	1060
the *f* of the children of Israel	Num 8:18	1060
nevertheless the *f* of man shalt	Num 18:15	1060
the Egyptians buried all their *f*	Num 33:4	1060
if the *f* son be hers that was	Deut 21:15	1060
f before the son of the hated	Deut 21:16	1069
which is indeed the *f*	Deut 21:16	1060
the son of the hated for the *f*	Deut 21:17	1060
the right of the *f* is his	Deut 21:17	1062
that the *f* which she beareth	Deut 25:6	1060
the foundation thereof in his *f*	Josh 6:26	1060
for he was the *f* of Joseph	Josh 17:1	1060
wit, for Machir the *f* of Manasseh	Josh 17:1	1060
And he said unto Jether his *f*	Judg 8:20	1060
Now the name of his *f* was Joel	1Sa 8:2	1060
the name of the *f* Merab, and the	1Sa 14:49	1067
his *f* was Amnon, of Ahinoam the	2Sa 3:2	1060
thereof in Abiram his *f*, and set	1Kin 16:34	1060
And Canaan begat Zidon his *f*	1Chr 1:13	1060
The *f* of Ishmael, Nebaioth	1Chr 1:29	1060
the *f* of Judah, was evil in the	1Chr 2:3	1060
And Jesse begat his *f* Eliab	1Chr 2:13	1060
of Jerahmeel the *f* of Hezron were	1Chr 2:25	1060
Ram the *f*, and Bunah	1Chr 2:25	1060
of Ram the *f* of Jerahmeel were	1Chr 2:27	1060
of Jerahmeel were, Mesha his *f*	1Chr 2:42	1060
the son of Hur, the *f* of Ephratah	1Chr 2:50	1060
the *f* Amnon, of Ahinoam the	1Chr 3:1	1060
the *f* Johanan, the second	1Chr 3:15	1060
the *f* of Ephratah, the father of	1Chr 4:4	1060
sons of Reuben the *f* of Israel	1Chr 5:1	1060
(for he was the *f*;	1Chr 5:1	1060
of Reuben the *f* of Israel were,	1Chr 5:3	1060
the *f* Vashni, and Abiah	1Chr 6:28	1060
Now Benjamin begat Bela his *f*	1Chr 8:1	1060
his *f* son Abdon, and Zur, and Kish,	1Chr 8:30	1060
his brother were, Ulam his *f*	1Chr 8:39	1060
Asaiah the *f*, and his sons	1Chr 9:5	1060
who was the *f* of Shallum the	1Chr 9:31	1060
his *f* son Abdon, then Zur, and	1Chr 9:36	1060
Meshelemiah were, Zechariah the *f*	1Chr 26:2	1060
of Obed-edom were, Shemaiah the *f*	1Chr 26:4	1060
(for though he was not the *f*	1Chr 26:10	1060
because he was the *f*	2Chr 21:3	1060
Also the *f* of our sons, and of our	Neh 10:36	1060
even the *f* of death shall devour	Job 18:13	1060
And smote all the *f* in Egypt	Ps 78:51	1060
Also I will make him my *f*	Ps 89:27	1060
also all the *f* in their land	Ps 105:36	1060
Who smote the *f* of Egypt, both of	Ps 135:8	1060
him that smote Egypt in their *f*	Ps 136:10	1060
the *f* of the poor shall feed, and	Is 14:30	1060
to Israel, and Ephraim is my *f*	Jer 31:9	1060
shall I give my *f* for my	Mic 6:7	1060
that is in bitterness for his *f*	Zec 12:10	1060
she had brought forth her *f* son	Mt 1:25	4416
And she brought forth her *f* son	Lk 2:7	4416
be the *f* among many brethren	Rom 8:29	4416
God, the *f* of every creature	Col 1:15	4416
beginning, the *f* from the dead	Col 1:18	4416
destroyed the *f* should touch them	Heb 11:28	4416
assembly and church of the *f*	Heb 12:23	4416

FIRSTFRUIT

The *f* also of thy corn, of thy	Deut 18:4	7225
For if the *f* be holy, the lump is	Rom 11:16	536

FIRSTFRUITS

the *f* of thy labours, which thou	Ex 23:16	1061
The first of the *f* of thy land	Ex 23:19	1061
of the *f* of wheat harvest, and the	Ex 34:22	1061
The first of the *f* of thy land	Ex 34:26	1061
As for the oblation of the *f*	Lev 2:12	7225
offering of thy *f* unto the LORD	Lev 2:14	1061
for the meat offering of thy *f*	Lev 2:14	1061
ye shall bring a sheaf of the *f*	Lev 23:10	7225
they are the *f* unto the LORD	Lev 23:17	1061
the *f* of them which they shall	Num 18:12	7225
Also in the day of the *f*, when ye	Num 28:26	1061
I have brought the *f* of the land	Deut 26:10	7225
the man of God bread of the *f*	2Kin 4:42	1061
in abundance the *f* of corn	2Chr 31:5	7225
to bring the *f* of our ground, and	Neh 10:35	1061
the *f* of all fruit of all trees,	Neh 10:35	1061
should bring the *f* of our dough	Neh 10:37	7225
for the offerings, for the *f*	Neh 12:44	7225
at times appointed, and for the *f*	Neh 13:31	1061
with the *f* of all thine increase	Prov 3:9	7225
LORD, and the *f* of his increase	Jer 2:3	7225
the *f* of your oblations, with all	Eze 20:40	7225
first of all the *f* of all things	Eze 44:30	1061
nor alienate the *f* of the land	Eze 48:14	7225
which have the *f* of the Spirit	Rom 8:23	536
who is the *f* of Achaia unto	Rom 16:5	536
become the *f* of them that slept	1Cor 15:20	536
Christ the *f*	1Cor 15:23	536
that it is the *f* of Achaia	1Cor 16:15	536
be a kind of *f* of his creatures	Jas 1:18	536
among men, being the *f* unto God	Rev 14:4	536

FIRSTLING

every *f* that cometh of a beast	Ex 13:12	6363
every *f* of an ass thou shalt	Ex 13:13	6363
every *f* among thy cattle, whether	Ex 34:19	6363
But the *f* of an ass thou shalt	Ex 34:20	6363
Only the *f* of the beasts, which	Lev 27:26	1060
which should be the LORD's *f*	Lev 27:26	1069
the *f* of unclean beasts shalt	Num 18:15	1060
of a cow, or the *f*	Num 18:17	1060
or the *f* of a goat, thou shalt	Num 18:17	1060
All the *f* males that come of thy	Deut 15:19	1060
no work with the *f* of thy bullock	Deut 15:19	1060
nor shear the *f* of thy sheep	Deut 15:19	1060
is like the *f* of his bullock	Deut 33:17	1060

FIRSTLINGS

brought of the *f* of his flock	Gen 4:4	1062
all the *f* among the cattle of the	Num 3:41	1060
the *f* of your herds and of your	Deut 12:6	1062
or the *f* of thy herds or of thy	Deut 12:17	1062
the *f* of thy herds and of thy	Deut 14:23	1062
the *f* of our herds and of our	Neh 10:36	1062

FIRSTRIPE

time was the time of the *f* grapes	Num 13:20	1061
I saw your fathers as the *f* in	Hos 9:10	1063
my soul desired the *f* fruit	Mic 7:1	1063
be like fig trees with the *f* figs	Nah 3:12	1063

FISH

dominion over the *f* of the sea	Gen 1:26	1710
dominion over the *f* of the sea	Gen 1:28	1710
the *f* that is in the river shall	Ex 7:18	1710
the *f* that was in the river died	Ex 7:21	1710
We remember the *f*, which we did	Num 11:5	1710
or shall all the *f* of the sea be	Num 11:22	1709
the likeness of any *f* that is in	Deut 4:18	1710
to the entering in at the *f* gate	2Chr 33:14	1709
But the *f* gate did the sons of	Neh 3:3	1709
the old gate, and above the *f* gate	Neh 12:39	1709
also therein, which brought *f*	Neh 13:16	1709
or his head with *f* spears	Job 41:7	1709
the *f* of the sea, and whatsoever	Ps 8:8	1709
into blood, and slew their *f*	Ps 105:29	1710
that make sluices and ponds for *f*	Is 19:10	5315
their *f* stinketh, because there	Is 50:2	1710
the LORD, and they shall *f* them	Jer 16:16	1770
I will cause the *f* of thy rivers	Eze 29:4	1710
all the *f* of thy rivers shall	Eze 29:4	1710
thee and all the *f* of thy rivers	Eze 29:5	1710
be a very great multitude of *f*	Eze 47:9	1710
their *f* shall be according to	Eze 47:10	1710
as the *f* of the great sea,	Eze 47:10	1710
a great *f* to swallow up Jonah	Jonah 1:17	1709
in the belly of the *f* three days	Jonah 1:17	1709
And the LORD spake unto the *f*	Jonah 2:10	1709
noise of a cry from the *f* gate	Zeph 1:10	1709
Or if he ask a *f*, will he give	Mt 7:10	2486
take up the *f* that first cometh	Mt 17:27	2486
or if he ask a *f*.	Lk 11:11	2486

F

will he for a *f* give him a	Lk 11:11	2486
gave him a piece of a broiled *f*	Lk 24:42	2486
and *f* laid thereon, and bread	Jn 21:9	3795
Bring of the *f* which ye have now	Jn 21:10	3795
and giveth them, and *f* likewise	Jn 21:13	3795

FISHERMEN

but the *f* were gone out of them,	Lk 5:2	231

FISHER'S

he girt his *f* coat unto him, (for	Jn 21:7	1903

FISHERS

The *f* also shall mourn, and all	Is 19:8	1771
Behold, I will send for many *f*	Jer 16:16	1728
that the *f* shall stand upon it	Eze 47:10	1728
for they were *f*	Mt 4:18	231
me, and I will make you *f* of men	Mt 4:19	231
for they were *f*	Mk 1:16	231
will make you to become *f* of men	Mk 1:17	231

FISHES

and upon all the *f* of the sea	Gen 9:2	1709
and of creeping things, and of *f*	1Kin 4:33	1709
the *f* of the sea shall declare	Job 12:8	1709
as the *f* that are taken in an	Eccl 9:12	1709
So that the *f* of the sea, and the	Eze 38:20	1709
the *f* of the sea also shall be	Hos 4:3	1709
And makest men as the *f* of the sea	Hab 1:14	1709
and the *f* of the sea, and the	Zeph 1:3	1709
here but five loaves, and two *f*	Mt 14:17	2486
the five loaves, and the two *f*	Mt 14:19	2486
said, Seven, and a few little *f*	Mt 15:34	2485
he took the seven loaves and the *f*	Mt 15:36	2486
knew, they say, Five, and two *f*	Mk 6:38	2486
the five loaves and the two *f*	Mk 6:41	2486
the two *f* divided he among them	Mk 6:41	2486
of the fragments, and of the *f*	Mk 6:43	2486
And they had a few small *f*	Mk 8:7	2485
inclosed a great multitude of *f*	Lk 5:6	2486
of the *f* which they had taken	Lk 5:9	2486
no more but five loaves and two *f*	Lk 9:13	2486
took the five loaves and the two *f*	Lk 9:16	2486
barley loaves, and two small *f*	Jn 6:9	3795
likewise of the *f* as much as they	Jn 6:11	3795
to draw it for the multitude of *f*	Jn 21:6	2486
cubits,) dragging the net with *f*	Jn 21:8	2486
the net to land full of great *f*	Jn 21:11	2486
flesh of beasts, another of *f*	1Cor 15:39	2486

FISHHOOKS

hooks, and your posterity with *f*	Amos 4:2	5518,1729

FISHING

Peter saith unto them, I go a *f*	Jn 21:3	232

FISHPOOLS

thine eyes like the *f* in Heshbon	Song 7:4	1295

FISH'S

LORD his God out of the *f* belly	Jonah 2:1	1710

FIST

with a stone, or with his *f*	Ex 21:18	106
to smite with the *f* of wickedness	Is 58:4	106

FISTS

hath gathered the wind in his *f*	Prov 30:4	2651

FIT

of a *f* man into the wilderness	Lev 16:21	6261
f to go out for war and battle	1Chr 7:11	
men of war *f* for the battle, that	1Chr 12:8	
Is it *f* to say to a king, Thou	Job 34:18	
make it *f* for thyself in the	Prov 24:27	6257
is *f* for the kingdom of God	Lk 9:62	2111
It is neither *f* for the land	Lk 14:35	2111
for it is not *f* that he should	Acts 22:22	2520
husbands, as it is *f* in the Lord	Col 3:18	433

FITCHES

doth he not cast abroad the *f*	Is 28:25	7100
For the *f* are not threshed with a	Is 28:27	7100
but the *f* are beaten out with a	Is 28:27	7100
and lentiles, and millet, and *f*	Eze 4:9	3698

FITLY

A word *f* spoken is like apples of	Prov 25:11	5921,655
washed with milk, and *f* set	Song 5:12	5921,4402
In whom all the building *f* framed	Eph 2:21	4883
the whole body *f* joined together	Eph 4:16	4883

FITTED

with gold *f* upon the carved work	1Kin 6:35	3474
shall withal be *f* in thy lips	Prov 22:18	3559
vessels of wrath *f* to destruction	Rom 9:22	2675

FITTETH

he *f* it with planes, and he	Is 44:13	6213

FIVE

hundred and *f* years, and begat Enos	Gen 5:6	2568
Enos lived nine hundred and *f* years	Gen 5:11	2568
sixty and *f* years, and begat Jared	Gen 5:15	2568
eight hundred ninety and *f* years	Gen 5:17	2568
f years, and begat Methuselah	Gen 5:21	2568
three hundred sixty and *f* years	Gen 5:23	2568
he begat Noah *f* hundred ninety	Gen 5:30	2568
f years, and begat sons and	Gen 5:30	2568
Noah was *f* hundred years old	Gen 5:32	2568
he begat Arphaxad *f* hundred years	Gen 11:11	2568
And Arphaxad lived *f* and thirty	Gen 11:12	2568
Terah were two hundred and *f* years	Gen 11:32	2568
f years old when he departed out	Gen 12:4	2568
Ellasar; four kings with *f*	Gen 14:9	2568
lack *f* of the fifty righteous	Gen 18:28	2568
all the city for lack of *f*	Gen 18:28	2568
said, If I find there forty and *f*	Gen 18:28	2568
but Benjamin's mess was *f* times	Gen 43:34	2568
and yet there are *f* years, in the	Gen 45:6	2568
yet there are *f* years of famine	Gen 45:11	2568
silver, and *f* changes of raiment	Gen 45:22	2568
some of his brethren, even *f* men	Gen 47:2	2568
he shall restore *f* oxen for an ox	Ex 22:1	2568
The *f* curtains shall be coupled	Ex 26:3	2568
other *f* curtains shall be coupled	Ex 26:3	2568
thou shalt couple *f* curtains by	Ex 26:9	2568
f for the boards of the one side	Ex 26:26	2568
f bars for the boards of the	Ex 26:27	2568
f bars for the boards of the side	Ex 26:27	2568
hanging *f* pillars of shittim wood	Ex 26:37	2568
thou shalt cast *f* sockets of	Ex 26:37	2568
f cubits long, and *f* cubits	Ex 27:1	2568
the height *f* cubits of fine	Ex 27:18	2568
of pure myrrh *f* hundred shekels	Ex 30:23	2568
of cassia *f* hundred shekels,	Ex 30:24	2568
he coupled the *f* curtains one	Ex 36:10	2568
the other *f* curtains he coupled	Ex 36:10	2568
And he coupled *f* curtains by	Ex 36:16	2568
f for the boards of the one side	Ex 36:31	2568
f bars for the boards of the	Ex 36:32	2568
f bars for the boards of the	Ex 36:32	2568
the *f* pillars of it with their	Ex 36:38	2568
but their *f* sockets were of brass	Ex 36:38	2568
f cubits was the length thereof,	Ex 38:1	2568
f cubits the breadth thereof	Ex 38:1	2568
in the breadth was *f* cubits	Ex 38:18	2568
and *f* hundred and fifty men	Ex 38:26	2568
f shekels he made hooks for the	Ex 38:28	2568
of you shall chase an hundred,	Lev 26:8	2568
if it be from *f* years old even	Lev 27:5	2568
a month old even unto *f* years old	Lev 27:6	2568
of the male *f* shekels of silver	Lev 27:6	2568
and six thousand and *f* hundred	Num 1:21	2568
f thousand six hundred and fifty	Num 1:25	2568
were forty thousand and *f* hundred	Num 1:33	2568
f thousand and four hundred	Num 1:37	2568
and one thousand and *f* hundred	Num 1:41	2568
thousand and *f* hundred and fifty	Num 1:46	2568
and six thousand and *f* hundred	Num 2:11	2568
f thousand and six hundred and	Num 2:15	2568
were forty thousand and *f* hundred	Num 2:19	2568
f thousand and four hundred	Num 2:23	2568
and one thousand and *f* hundred	Num 2:28	2568
thousand and *f* hundred and fifty	Num 2:32	2568
were seven thousand and *f* hundred	Num 3:22	2568
Thou shalt even take *f* shekels	Num 3:47	2568
f shekels, after the shekel of	Num 3:50	2568
and *f* hundred and fourscore	Num 4:48	2568
f rams, *f* he goats, *f* lambs	Num 7:17	2568
f rams, *f* he goats, *f* lambs	Num 7:23	2568
f rams, *f* he goats, *f* lambs	Num 7:29	2568
f rams, *f* he goats, *f* lambs	Num 7:35	2568
f rams, *f* he goats, *f* lambs	Num 7:41	2568
f rams, *f* he goats, *f* lambs	Num 7:47	2568
f rams, *f* he goats, *f* lambs	Num 7:53	2568
f rams, *f* he goats, *f* lambs	Num 7:59	2568
f rams, *f* he goats, *f* lambs	Num 7:65	2568
f rams, *f* he goats, *f* lambs	Num 7:71	2568
f he goats, *f* lambs of the	Num 7:71	2568
f rams, *f* he goats, *f* lambs	Num 7:77	2568
f rams, *f* he goats, *f* lambs	Num 7:83	2568
f years old and upward they shall	Num 8:24	2568
nor *f* days, neither ten days, nor	Num 11:19	2568
for the money of *f* shekels	Num 18:16	2568
them, forty thousand and *f* hundred	Num 26:18	2568
and sixteen thousand and *f* hundred	Num 26:22	2568
threescore thousand and *f* hundred	Num 26:27	2568
and two thousand and *f* hundred	Num 26:37	2568
f thousand and six hundred	Num 26:41	2568
f thousand and four hundred	Num 26:50	2568

Hur, and Reba, *f* kings of Midian	Num 31:8	2568
one soul of *f* hundred, both of	Num 31:28	2568
thousand and *f* thousand sheep,	Num 31:32	2568
thousand and *f* hundred sheep	Num 31:36	2568
were thirty thousand and *f* hundred	Num 31:39	2568
thousand and *f* hundred sheep,	Num 31:43	2568
thousand asses and *f* hundred,	Num 31:45	2568
And he took about *f* thousand men	Josh 8:12	2568
Therefore the *f* kings of the	Josh 10:5	2568
But these *f* kings fled, and hid	Josh 10:16	2568
The *f* kings are found hid in a	Josh 10:17	2568
bring out those *f* kings unto me	Josh 10:22	2568
brought forth those *f* kings unto	Josh 10:23	2568
them, and hanged them on *f* trees	Josh 10:26	2568
f lords of the Philistines	Josh 13:3	2568
f years, even since the LORD	Josh 14:10	2568
this day fourscore and *f* years old	Josh 14:10	2568
f lords of the Philistines, and	Judg 3:3	2568
family *f* men from their coasts	Judg 18:2	2568
Then the *f* men departed, and came	Judg 18:7	2568
Then answered the *f* men that went	Judg 18:14	2568
the *f* men that went to spy out	Judg 18:17	2568
f thousand and an hundred men	Judg 20:35	2568
in the highways *f* thousand men	Judg 20:45	2568
f thousand men that drew the	Judg 20:46	2568
F golden emerods, and *f* golden	1Sa 6:4	2568
f golden mice, according to the	1Sa 6:4	2568
And when the *f* lords of the	1Sa 6:16	2568
belonging to the *f* lords, both of	1Sa 6:18	2568
was *f* thousand shekels of brass	1Sa 17:5	2568
chose him *f* smooth stones out of	1Sa 17:40	2568
give me *f* loaves of bread in mine	1Sa 21:3	2568
f persons that did wear a linen	1Sa 22:18	2568
f sheep ready dressed, and	1Sa 25:18	2568
f measures of parched corn, and an	1Sa 25:18	2568
with *f* damsels of hers that went	1Sa 25:42	2568
He was *f* years old when the	2Sa 4:4	2568
the *f* sons of Michal the daughter	2Sa 21:8	2568
Judah were *f* hundred thousand men	2Sa 24:9	2568
and his songs were a thousand and *f*	1Kin 4:32	2568
chamber was *f* cubits broad	1Kin 6:6	2568
all the house, *f* cubits high	1Kin 6:10	2568
f cubits was the one wing of the	1Kin 6:24	2568
f cubits the other wing of the	1Kin 6:24	2568
that lay on forty *f* pillars	1Kin 7:3	2568
of the one chapiter was *f* cubits	1Kin 7:16	2568
the other chapiter was *f* cubits	1Kin 7:16	2568
about, and his height was *f* cubits	1Kin 7:23	2568
he put *f* bases on the right side	1Kin 7:39	2568
f on the left side of the house	1Kin 7:39	2568
f on the right side, and *f* on	1Kin 7:49	2568
f on the left, before the oracle,	1Kin 7:49	2568
f hundred and fifty, which bare	1Kin 9:23	2568
f years old when he began to	1Kin 22:42	2568
twenty and *f* years in Jerusalem	1Kin 22:42	2568
dung for *f* pieces of silver	2Kin 6:25	2568
f of the horses that remain,	2Kin 7:13	2568
have smitten *f* or six times	2Kin 13:19	2568
f years old when he began to	2Kin 14:2	2568
F and twenty years old was he when	2Kin 15:33	2568
f years old was he when he began	2Kin 18:2	2568
hundred fourscore and *f* thousand	2Kin 19:35	2568
fifty and *f* years in Jerusalem	2Kin 21:1	2568
f years old when he began to	2Kin 23:36	2568
f men of them that were in the	2Kin 25:19	2568
All the sons of Judah were *f*	1Chr 2:4	2568
f of them in all	1Chr 2:6	2568
and Hasadiah, Jushab-hesed, *f*,	1Chr 3:20	2568
and Tochen, and Ashan, *f* cities	1Chr 4:32	2568
f hundred men, went to mount Seir	1Chr 4:42	2568
and Obadiah, and Joel, Ishiah, *f*,	1Chr 7:3	2568
and Uzziel, and Jerimoth, and Iri, *f*,	1Chr 7:7	2568
of great stature, *f* cubits high	1Chr 11:23	2568
of God of gold *f* thousand talents	1Chr 29:7	2568
of the one cherub was *f* cubits	2Chr 3:11	2568
other wing was likewise *f* cubits	2Chr 3:11	2568
of the other cherub was *f* cubits	2Chr 3:12	2568
the other wing was *f* cubits also	2Chr 3:12	2568
f cubits high, and the chapiter	2Chr 3:15	2568
top of each of them was *f* cubits	2Chr 3:15	2568
f cubits the height thereof	2Chr 4:2	2568
put *f* on the right hand, and	2Chr 4:6	2568
f on the left, to wash in them	2Chr 4:6	2568
f on the right hand, and *f* on	2Chr 4:7	2568
f on the right side, and *f* on	2Chr 4:8	2568
of *f* cubits long, and *f* cubits	2Chr 6:13	2568
f hundred thousand chosen men	2Chr 13:17	2568
there was no more war unto the *f*	2Chr 15:19	2568
f years old when he began to	2Chr 20:31	2568
twenty and *f* years in Jerusalem	2Chr 20:31	2568
f years old when he began to	2Chr 25:1	2568
f hundred, that made war with	2Chr 26:13	2568
f years old when he began to	2Chr 27:1	2568
He was *f* and twenty years old when	2Chr 27:8	2568
began to reign when he was *f*	2Chr 29:1	2568
fifty and *f* years in Jerusalem	2Chr 33:1	2568
offerings *f* thousand small cattle	2Chr 35:9	2568
small cattle, and *f* hundred oxen	2Chr 35:9	2568
f years old when he began to	2Chr 36:5	2568
gold and of silver were *f* thousand	Ezr 1:11	2568
Arah, seven hundred seventy and *f*	Ezr 2:5	2568
of Zattu, nine hundred forty and *f*	Ezr 2:8	2568
children of Gibbar, ninety and *f*	Ezr 2:20	2568
and Ono, seven hundred twenty and *f*	Ezr 2:33	2568
Jericho, three hundred forty and *f*	Ezr 2:34	2568
mules, two hundred forty and *f*	Ezr 2:66	2568
camels, four hundred thirty and *f*	Ezr 2:67	2568
f thousand pound of silver, and	Ezr 2:69	2568
Zattu, eight hundred forty and *f*	Neh 7:13	2568
of Adin, six hundred fifty and *f*	Neh 7:20	2568
children of Gibeon, ninety and *f*	Neh 7:25	2568
Jericho, three hundred forty and *f*	Neh 7:36	2568
f singing men and singing women	Neh 7:67	2568
mules, two hundred forty and *f*	Neh 7:68	2568
camels, four hundred thirty and *f*	Neh 7:69	2568
f hundred and thirty priests'	Neh 7:70	2568
slew and destroyed *f* hundred men	Est 9:6	2568
destroyed *f* hundred men in	Est 9:12	2568
f thousand, but they laid not	Est 9:16	2568
f hundred yoke of oxen, and *f*	Job 1:3	2568
f hundred she asses, and a very	Job 1:3	2568
f years shall Ephraim be broken,	Is 7:8	2568
four or *f* in the outmost fruitful	Is 17:6	2568
In that day shall *f* cities in the	Is 19:18	2568
at the rebuke of *f* shall ye flee	Is 30:17	2568
and fourscore and *f* thousand	Is 37:36	2568
of one chapiter was *f* cubits	Jer 52:22	2568
seven hundred forty and *f* persons	Jer 52:30	2568
in the twelfth month, in the *f*	Jer 52:31	2568
porch and the altar, were about *f*	Eze 8:16	2568
behold at the door of the gate *f*	Eze 11:1	2568
In the *f* and twentieth year of our	Eze 40:1	2568
the little chambers were *f* cubits	Eze 40:7	2568
the breadth was *f* and twenty	Eze 40:13	2568
fifty cubits, and the breadth *f*	Eze 40:21	2568
fifty cubits, and the breadth *f*	Eze 40:25	2568
it was fifty cubits long, and *f*	Eze 40:29	2568
And the arches round about were *f*	Eze 40:30	2568
cubits long, and *f* cubits broad	Eze 40:30	2568
it was fifty cubits long, and *f*	Eze 40:33	2568
fifty cubits, and the breadth *f*	Eze 40:36	2568
f cubits on this side	Eze 40:48	2568
and *f* cubits on that side	Eze 40:48	2568
were *f* cubits on the one side	Eze 41:2	2568
f cubits on the other side	Eze 41:2	2568
chamber without, was *f* cubits	Eze 41:9	2568
was left was *f* cubits round about	Eze 41:11	2568
was *f* cubits thick round about	Eze 41:12	2568
f hundred reeds, with the	Eze 42:16	2568
f hundred reeds, with the	Eze 42:17	2568
f hundred reeds, with the	Eze 42:18	2568
measured *f* hundred reeds with the	Eze 42:19	2568
f hundred reeds long, and	Eze 42:20	2568
f hundred broad, to make a	Eze 42:20	2568
length shall be the length of *f*	Eze 45:1	2568
the sanctuary *f* hundred in length	Eze 45:2	2568
with *f* hundred in breadth, square	Eze 45:2	2568
thou measure the length of *f*	Eze 45:3	2568
And the *f* and twenty thousand of	Eze 45:5	2568
city *f* thousand broad, and *f*	Eze 45:6	2568
twenty shekels, *f* and twenty	Eze 45:12	2568
which ye shall offer of *f*	Eze 48:8	2568
offer unto the LORD shall be of *f*	Eze 48:9	2568
toward the north *f* and twenty	Eze 48:10	2568
in breadth, and toward the south *f*	Eze 48:10	2568
priests the Levites shall have *f*	Eze 48:13	2568
all the length shall be *f*	Eze 48:13	2568
the *f* thousand, that are left in	Eze 48:15	2568
in the breadth over against the *f*	Eze 48:15	2568
f hundred, and the south side four	Eze 48:16	2568
f hundred, and on the east side	Eze 48:16	2568
f hundred, and the west side four	Eze 48:16	2568
side four thousand and *f* hundred	Eze 48:16	2568
be *f* and twenty thousand by *f*	Eze 48:20	2568
of the city, over against the *f*	Eze 48:21	2568
and westward over against the *f*	Eze 48:21	2568
thousand and *f* hundred measures	Eze 48:30	2568
side four thousand and *f* hundred	Eze 48:32	2568
thousand and *f* hundred measures	Eze 48:33	2568
f hundred, with their three gates	Eze 48:34	2568
the thousand three hundred and *f*	Dan 12:12	2568
him, We have here but *f* loaves	Mt 14:17	4002

F

the grass, and took the *f* loaves	Mt 14:19	4002
eaten were about *f* thousand men	Mt 14:21	4000
neither remember the *f* loaves of	Mt 16:9	4002
the *f* thousand, and how many baskets	Mt 16:9	4000
f of them were wise, and *f* were	Mt 25:2	4000
And unto one he gave *f* talents	Mt 25:15	4000
had received the *f* talents went	Mt 25:16	4000
and made them other *f* talents	Mt 25:16	4000
that had received *f* talents came	Mt 25:20	4000
came and brought other *f* talents	Mt 25:20	4000
deliveredst unto me *f* talents	Mt 25:20	4000
gained beside them *f* talents more	Mt 25:20	4000
And when they knew, they say, *f*	Mk 6:38	4000
And when he had taken the *f* loaves	Mk 6:41	4000
loaves were about *f* thousand men	Mk 6:44	4000
When I brake the *f* loaves among	Mk 8:19	4002
f thousand, how many baskets	Mk 8:19	4000
and hid herself *f* months, saying,	Lk 1:24	4002
the one owed *f* hundred pence, and	Lk 7:41	4001
We have no more but *f* loaves	Lk 9:13	4002
they were about *f* thousand men	Lk 9:14	4000
Then he took the *f* loaves	Lk 9:16	4002
Are not *f* sparrows sold for two	Lk 12:6	4002
shall be *f* in one house divided	Lk 12:52	4002
I have bought *f* yoke of oxen	Lk 14:19	4002
For I have *f* brethren	Lk 16:28	4002
thy pound hath gained *f* pounds	Lk 19:18	4002
him, Be thou also over *f* cities	Lk 19:19	4002
For thou hast had *f* husbands	Jn 4:18	4002
tongue Bethesda, having *f* porches	Jn 5:2	4002
which hath *f* barley loaves, and	Jn 6:9	4002
down, in number about *f* thousand	Jn 6:10	4000
fragments of the *f* barley loaves	Jn 6:13	4002
So when they had rowed about *f*	Jn 6:19	4002
of the men was about *f* thousand	Acts 4:4	4002
came unto them to Troas in *f* days	Acts 20:6	4002
after *f* days Ananias the high	Acts 24:1	4002
f words with my understanding	1Cor 14:19	4002
he was seen of above *f* hundred	1Cor 15:6	4001
Of the Jews *f* times received I	2Cor 11:24	3999
they should be tormented *f* months	Rev 9:5	4002
power was to hurt men *f* months	Rev 9:10	4002
f are fallen, and one is, and the	Rev 17:10	4002

FIXED

My heart is *f*, O God, my heart is	Ps 57:7	3559
is *f*, O God, my heart is *f*	Ps 57:7	3559
O God, my heart is *f*	Ps 108:1	3559
his heart is *f*, trusting in the	Ps 112:7	3559
us and you there is a great gulf *f*	Lk 16:26	4741

FLAG

can the *f* grow without water	Job 8:11	260

FLAGON

piece of flesh, and a *f* of wine	2Sa 6:19	809
piece of flesh, and a *f* of wine	1Chr 16:3	809

FLAGONS

Stay me with *f*, comfort me with	Song 2:5	809
even to all the vessels of *f*	Is 22:24	5035
to other gods, and love *f* of wine	Hos 3:1	809

FLAGS

she laid it in the *f* by the	Ex 2:3	5488
when she saw the ark among the *f*	Ex 2:5	5488
the reeds and *f* shall wither	Is 19:6	5488

FLAKES

The *f* of his flesh are joined	Job 41:23	4651

FLAME

a *f* of fire out of the midst of a	Ex 3:2	3827
a *f* from the city of Sihon	Num 21:28	3852
when the *f* went up toward heaven	Judg 13:20	3851
ascended in the *f* of the altar	Judg 13:20	3851
f with smoke rise up out of the	Judg 20:38	4864
But when the *f* began to arise up	Judg 20:40	4864
the *f* of the city ascended up to	Judg 20:40	3632
the *f* shall dry up his branches,	Job 15:30	7957
a *f* goeth out of his mouth	Job 41:21	3851
as the *f* setteth the mountains on	Ps 83:14	3852
the *f* burned up the wicked	Ps 106:18	3852
which hath a most vehement *f*	Song 8:6	7957
the *f* consumeth the chaff, so	Is 5:24	3852
a fire, and his Holy One for a *f*	Is 10:17	3852
and the *f* of devouring fire	Is 29:6	3851
with the *f* of a devouring fire,	Is 30:30	3851
shall the *f* kindle upon thee	Is 43:2	3852
from the power of the *f*	Is 47:14	3852
a *f* from the midst of Sihon, and	Jer 48:45	3852
the flaming *f* shall not be	Eze 20:47	7957
the *f* of the fire slew those men	Dan 3:22	7631
his throne was like the fiery *f*	Dan 7:9	7631

and given to the burning *f*	Dan 7:11	785
shall fall by the sword, and by *f*	Dan 11:33	3852
the *f* hath burned all the trees	Joel 1:19	3852
and behind them a *f* burneth	Joel 2:3	3852
like the noise of a *f* of fire	Joel 2:5	3851
fire, and the house of Joseph a *f*	Obad 18	3852
for I am tormented in this *f*	Lk 16:24	5395
the Lord in a *f* of fire in a bush	Acts 7:30	5395
and his ministers a *f* of fire	Heb 1:7	5395
and his eyes were as a *f* of fire	Rev 1:14	5395
his eyes like unto a *f* of fire	Rev 2:18	5395
His eyes were as a *f* of fire	Rev 19:12	5395

FLAMES

the LORD divideth the *f* of fire	Ps 29:7	3852
their faces shall be as *f*	Is 13:8	3851
and his rebuke with *f* of fire	Is 66:15	3851

FLAMING

a *f* sword which turned every way,	Gen 3:24	3858
his ministers a *f* fire	Ps 104:4	3857
for rain, and *f* fire in their land	Ps 105:32	3852
the shining of a *f* fire by night	Is 4:5	3852
against Jacob like a *f* fire	Lam 2:3	3852
the *f* flame shall not be quenched	Eze 20:47	3852
morning it burneth as a *f* fire	Hos 7:6	3852
with *f* torches in the day of his	Nah 2:3	784
In *f* fire taking vengeance on	2Th 1:8	5395

FLANKS

is on them, which is by the *f*	Lev 3:4	3689
is upon them, which is by the *f*	Lev 3:10	3689
is upon them, which is by the *f*	Lev 3:15	3689
is upon them, which is by the *f*	Lev 4:9	3689
is on them, which is by the *f*	Lev 7:4	3689
and maketh collops of fat on his *f*	Job 15:27	3689

FLASH

appearance of a *f* of lightning	Eze 1:14	965

FLAT

a lame, or he that hath a *f* nose	Lev 21:18	2763
his head, and fell *f* on his face	Num 22:31	
of the city shall fall down *f*	Josh 6:5	8478
shout, that the wall fell down *f*	Josh 6:20	8478

FLATTER

they *f* with their tongue	Ps 5:9	2505
they did *f* him with their mouth	Ps 78:36	6601

FLATTERETH

For he *f* himself in his own eyes,	Ps 36:2	2505
stranger which *f* with her words	Prov 2:16	2505
stranger which *f* with her words	Prov 7:5	2505
not with him that *f* with his lips	Prov 20:19	6601
than he that *f* with the tongue	Prov 28:23	2505
A man that *f* his neighbour	Prov 29:5	2505

FLATTERIES

and obtain the kingdom by *f*	Dan 11:21	2519
covenant shall he corrupt by *f*	Dan 11:32	2514
many shall cleave to them with *f*	Dan 11:34	2519

FLATTERING

let me give *f* titles unto man	Job 32:21	3665
For I know not to give *f* titles	Job 32:22	3665
with *f* lips and with a double	Ps 12:2	2513
The LORD shall cut off all *f* lips	Ps 12:3	2513
with the *f* of her lips she forced	Prov 7:21	2505
and a *f* mouth worketh ruin	Prov 26:28	2509
f divination within the house of	Eze 12:24	2509
at any time used we *f* words	1Th 2:5	2850

FLATTERY

He that speaketh *f* to his friends	Job 17:5	2506
from the *f* of the tongue of a	Prov 6:24	2513

FLAX

And the *f* and the barley was	Ex 9:31	6594
in the ear, and the *f* was bolled	Ex 9:31	6594
and hid them with the stalks of *f*	Josh 2:6	6593
as *f* that was burnt with fire	Judg 15:14	6593
She seeketh wool, and *f*, and	Prov 31:13	6593
Moreover they that work in fine *f*	Is 19:9	6593
the smoking *f* shall he not quench	Is 42:3	6594
with a line of *f* in his hand	Eze 40:3	6593
and my water, my wool and my *f*	Hos 2:5	6593
my *f* given to cover her nakedness	Hos 2:9	6593
smoking *f* shall he not quench,	Mt 12:20	3043

FLAY

he shall *f* the burnt offering, and	Lev 1:6	6584
so that they could not *f* all the	2Chr 29:34	6584
f their skin from off them	Mic 3:3	6584

FLAYED

hands, and the Levites *f* them	2Chr 35:11	6584

FLEA

after a dead dog, after a _f_	1Sa 24:14	6550
of Israel is come out to seek a _f_	1Sa 26:20	6550

FLED

the kings of Sodom and Gomorrah _f_	Gen 14:10	5127
that remained _f_ to the mountain	Gen 14:10	5127
with her, she _f_ from her face	Gen 16:6	1272
in that he told him not that he _f_	Gen 31:20	1272
So he _f_ with all that he had	Gen 31:21	1272
on the third day that Jacob was _f_	Gen 31:22	1272
when he _f_ from the face of his	Gen 35:7	1272
his garment in her hand, and _f_	Gen 39:12	5127
in her hand, and was _f_ forth,	Gen 39:13	5127
he left his garment with me, and _f_	Gen 39:15	5127
his garment with me, and _f_ out	Gen 39:18	5127
But Moses _f_ from the face of	Ex 2:15	1272
and Moses _f_ from before it	Ex 4:3	5127
king of Egypt that the people _f_	Ex 14:5	1272
and the Egyptians _f_ against it	Ex 14:27	5127
about them _f_ at the cry of them	Num 16:34	5127
of his refuge, whither he was _f_	Num 35:25	5127
of his refuge, whither he was _f_	Num 35:26	5127
is _f_ to the city of his refuge	Num 35:32	5127
they _f_ before the men of Ai	Josh 7:4	5127
_f_ by the way of the wilderness	Josh 8:15	5127
and the people that _f_ to the	Josh 8:20	5127
as they _f_ from before Israel, and	Josh 10:11	5127
But these five kings _f_, and hid	Josh 10:16	5127
unto the city from whence he _f_	Josh 20:6	5127
But Adoni-bezek _f_	Judg 1:6	5127
chariot, and _f_ away on his feet	Judg 4:15	5127
Howbeit Sisera _f_ away on his feet	Judg 4:17	5127
all the host ran, and cried, and _f_	Judg 7:21	5127
the host _f_ to Beth-shittah in	Judg 7:22	5127
And when Zebah and Zalmunna _f_	Judg 8:12	5127
And Jotham ran away, and _f_, and went	Judg 9:21	1272
he _f_ before him, and many were	Judg 9:40	5127
thither _f_ all the men and women,	Judg 9:51	5127
Then Jephthah _f_ from his brethren	Judg 11:3	1272
_f_ toward the wilderness unto the	Judg 20:45	5127
_f_ to the wilderness unto the rock	Judg 20:47	5127
they _f_ every man into his tent	1Sa 4:10	5127
I _f_ to day out of the army	1Sa 4:16	5127
and said, Israel is _f_ before the	1Sa 4:17	5127
they heard that the Philistines _f_	1Sa 14:22	5127
_f_ from him, and were sore afraid	1Sa 17:24	5127
their champion was dead, they _f_	1Sa 17:51	5127
and they _f_ from him	1Sa 19:8	5127
and David _f_, and escaped that night	1Sa 19:10	5127
and he went, and _f_, and escaped	1Sa 19:12	1272
So David _f_, and escaped, and came	1Sa 19:18	1272
David _f_ from Naioth in Ramah, and	1Sa 20:1	1272
_f_ that day for fear of Saul, and	1Sa 21:10	1272
and because they knew when he _f_	1Sa 22:17	1272
escaped, and _f_ after David	1Sa 22:20	1272
of Ahimelech _f_ to David to Keilah	1Sa 23:6	1272
Saul that David was _f_ to Gath	1Sa 27:4	1272
men, which rode upon camels, and _f_	1Sa 30:17	5127
the men of Israel _f_ from before	1Sa 31:1	5127
saw that the men of Israel _f_	1Sa 31:7	5127
they forsook the cities, and _f_	1Sa 31:7	5127
the people are _f_ from the battle	2Sa 1:4	5127
And the Beerothites _f_ to Gittaim	2Sa 4:3	1272
and his nurse took him up, and _f_	2Sa 4:4	5127
and they _f_ before him	2Sa 10:13	5127
Ammon saw that the Syrians were _f_	2Sa 10:14	5127
then _f_ they also before Abishai	2Sa 10:14	5127
the Syrians _f_ before Israel	2Sa 10:18	5127
gat him up upon his mule, and _f_	2Sa 13:29	5127
But Absalom _f_. And the young man	2Sa 13:34	1272
But Absalom _f_, and went to Talmai,	2Sa 13:37	1272
So Absalom _f_, and went to Geshur,	2Sa 13:38	1272
all Israel _f_ every one to his	2Sa 18:17	5127
for Israel had _f_ every man to his	2Sa 19:8	5127
now he is _f_ out of the land for	2Sa 19:9	1272
the people _f_ from the Philistines	2Sa 23:11	5127
for so they came to me when I _f_	1Kin 2:7	1272
Joab _f_ unto the tabernacle of the	1Kin 2:28	5127
_f_ unto the tabernacle of the LORD	1Kin 2:29	5127
That Hadad _f_, he and certain	1Kin 11:17	1272
which _f_ from his lord Hadadezer	1Kin 11:23	1272
_f_ into Egypt, unto Shishak king	1Kin 11:40	5127
(for he was _f_ from the presence	1Kin 12:2	1272
and the Syrians _f_	1Kin 20:20	5127
But the rest _f_ to Aphek, into the	1Kin 20:30	5127
And Ben-hadad _f_, and came into the	1Kin 20:30	5127
so that they _f_ before them	2Kin 3:24	5127
_f_ in the twilight, and left their	2Kin 7:7	5127
as it was, and _f_ for their life	2Kin 7:7	5127
the people _f_ into their tents	2Kin 8:21	5127

And he opened the door, and _f_	2Kin 9:10	5127
And Joram turned his hands, and _f_	2Kin 9:23	5127
he _f_ by the way of the garden	2Kin 9:27	5127
he _f_ to Megiddo, and died there	2Kin 9:27	5127
they _f_ every man to their tents	2Kin 14:12	5127
and he _f_ to Lachish	2Kin 14:19	5127
all the men of war _f_ by night by	2Kin 25:4	
the men of Israel _f_ from before	1Chr 10:1	5127
in the valley saw that they _f_	1Chr 10:7	5127
they forsook their cities, and _f_	1Chr 10:7	5127
the people _f_ from before the	1Chr 11:13	5127
and they _f_ before him	1Chr 19:14	5127
Ammon saw that the Syrians were _f_	1Chr 19:15	5127
they likewise _f_ before Abishai	1Chr 19:15	5127
But the Syrians _f_ before Israel	1Chr 19:18	5127
whither he had _f_ from the	2Chr 10:2	1272
children of Israel _f_ before Judah	2Chr 13:16	5127
and the Ethiopians _f_	2Chr 14:12	5127
they _f_ every man to his tent	2Chr 25:22	5127
and he _f_ to Lachish	2Chr 25:27	1272
were _f_ every one to his field	Neh 13:10	1272
when he _f_ from Absalom his son	Ps 3:_t_	1272
that did see me without _f_ from me	Ps 31:11	5074
when he _f_ from Saul in the cave	Ps 57:_t_	1272
At thy rebuke they _f_	Ps 104:7	5127
The sea saw it, and _f_	Ps 114:3	5127
Gibeah of Saul is _f_	Is 10:29	5127
with their bread him that _f_	Is 21:14	5074
For they _f_ from the swords, from	Is 21:15	5074
All thy rulers are _f_ together	Is 22:3	5074
together, which have _f_ from far	Is 22:3	1272
noise of the tumult the people _f_	Is 33:3	5074
the birds of the heavens were _f_	Jer 4:25	5074
of the heavens and the beast are _f_	Jer 9:10	5074
heard it, he was afraid, and _f_	Jer 26:21	1272
all the men of war, then they _f_	Jer 39:4	1272
are _f_ apace, and look not back	Jer 46:5	5127
back, and are _f_ away together	Jer 46:21	5127
They that _f_ stood under the	Jer 48:45	5127
up, and all the men of war _f_	Jer 52:7	1272
when they _f_ away and wandered	Lam 4:15	5132
so that they _f_ to hide themselves	Dan 10:7	1272
for they have _f_ from me	Hos 7:13	5074
Jacob _f_ into the country of Syria	Hos 12:12	1272
For the men knew that he _f_ from	Jonah 1:10	1272
Therefore I _f_ before unto	Jonah 4:2	1272
like as ye _f_ from before the	Zec 14:5	5127
And they that kept them _f_, and went	Mt 8:33	5343
the disciples forsook him, and _f_	Mt 26:56	5343
And they that fed the swine _f_	Mk 5:14	5343
And they all forsook him, and _f_	Mk 14:50	5343
linen cloth, and _f_ from them naked	Mk 14:52	5343
quickly, and _f_ from the sepulchre	Mk 16:8	5343
them saw what was done, they _f_	Lk 8:34	5343
Then Moses at this saying, and	Acts 7:29	5343
_f_ unto Lystra and Derbe, cities of	Acts 14:6	2703
that the prisoners had been _f_	Acts 16:27	1628
so that they _f_ out of that house	Acts 19:16	1628
who have _f_ for refuge to lay hold	Heb 6:18	2703
the woman _f_ into the wilderness,	Rev 12:6	5343
And every island _f_ away, and the	Rev 16:20	5343
the earth and the heaven _f_ away	Rev 20:11	5343

FLEDDEST

thou _f_ from the face of Esau thy	Gen 35:1	1272
thee, O thou sea, that thou _f_	Ps 114:5	5127

FLEE

I _f_ from the face of my mistress	Gen 16:8	1272
now, this city is near to _f_ unto	Gen 19:20	5127
_f_ thou to Laban my brother to	Gen 27:43	1272
didst thou _f_ away secretly	Gen 31:27	1272
his cattle _f_ into the houses	Ex 9:20	5127
Let us _f_ from the face of Israel	Ex 14:25	5127
thee a place whither he shall _f_	Ex 21:13	5127
ye shall _f_ when none pursueth you	Lev 26:17	5127
and they shall _f_, as fleeing from	Lev 26:36	5127
them that hate thee _f_ before thee	Num 10:35	5127
Therefore now _f_ thou to thy place	Num 24:11	1272
manslayer, that he may _f_ thither	Num 35:6	5127
that the slayer may _f_ thither	Num 35:11	5127
any person unawares may _f_ thither	Num 35:15	5127
That the slayer might _f_ thither	Deut 4:42	5127
that every slayer may _f_ thither	Deut 19:3	5127
the slayer, which shall _f_ thither	Deut 19:4	5127
he shall _f_ unto one of those	Deut 19:5	5127
way, and _f_ before these seven ways	Deut 28:7	5127
them, and _f_ seven ways before them	Deut 28:25	5127
first, that we will _f_ before them	Josh 8:5	5127
They _f_ before us, as at the first	Josh 8:6	5127
therefore we will _f_ before them	Josh 8:6	5127
power to _f_ this way or that way	Josh 8:20	5127

and unwittingly may *f* thither	Josh 20:3	5127
when he that doth *f* unto one of	Josh 20:4	5127
at unawares might *f* thither	Josh 20:9	5127
children of Israel said, Let us *f*	Judg 20:32	5127
to pass, as she made haste to *f*	2Sa 4:4	5127
at Jerusalem, Arise, and let us *f*	2Sa 15:14	1227
people that are with him shall *f*	2Sa 17:2	5127
for if we *f* away, they will not	2Sa 18:3	5127
steal away when they *f* in battle	2Sa 19:3	5127
or wilt thou *f* three months	2Sa 24:13	5127
to his chariot, to *f* to Jerusalem	1Kin 12:18	5127
Then open the door, and, *f*, and	2Kin 9:3	5127
to his chariot, to *f* to Jerusalem	2Chr 10:18	5127
I said, Should such a man as I *f*	Neh 6:11	1272
they *f* away, they see no good	Job 9:25	1272
He shall *f* from the iron weapon,	Job 20:24	1272
he would fain *f* out of his hand	Job 27:22	1272
they *f* far from me, and spare not	Job 30:10	7368
The arrow cannot make him *f*	Job 41:28	1272
F as a bird to your mountain	Ps 11:1	5110
all that see them shall *f* away	Ps 64:8	5074
also that hate him *f* before him	Ps 68:1	5127
Kings of armies did *f* apace	Ps 68:12	5074
shall I *f* from thy presence	Ps 139:7	1272
I *f* unto thee to hide me	Ps 143:9	3680
The wicked *f* when no man pursueth	Prov 28:1	5127
of any person shall *f* to the pit	Prov 28:17	5127
day break, and the shadows *f* away	Song 2:17	5127
day break, and the shadows *f* away	Song 4:6	5127
to whom will ye *f* for help	Is 10:3	5127
of Gebim gather themselves to *f*	Is 10:31	
f every one into his own land	Is 13:14	5127
his fugitives shall *f* unto Zoar	Is 15:5	
them, and they shall *f* far off	Is 17:13	5127
whither we *f* for help to be	Is 20:6	5127
for we will *f* upon horses	Is 30:16	5127
therefore shall ye *f*	Is 30:16	5127
One thousand shall *f* at the	Is 30:17	
at the rebuke of five shall ye *f*	Is 30:17	5127
but he shall *f* from the sword, and	Is 31:8	5127
and sorrow and sighing shall *f* away	Is 35:10	5127
f ye from the Chaldeans, with a	Is 48:20	1272
sorrow and mourning shall *f* away	Is 51:11	5127
The whole city shall *f* for the	Jer 4:29	1272
gather yourselves to *f* out of the	Jer 6:1	5756
shepherds shall have no way to *f*	Jer 25:35	4498
Let not the swift *f* away, nor the	Jer 46:6	5127
F, save your lives, and be like	Jer 48:6	5127
wings upon Moab, that it may *f*	Jer 48:9	5323
F ye, turn back, dwell deep, O	Jer 49:8	5127
feeble, and turneth herself to *f*	Jer 49:24	5127
F, get you far off, dwell deep, O	Jer 49:30	5127
they shall *f* every one to his own	Jer 50:16	5127
The voice of them that *f* and	Jer 50:28	5127
F out of the midst of Babylon, and	Jer 51:6	5127
shall *f* away naked in that day	Amos 2:16	5127
As if a man did *f* from a lion	Amos 5:19	5127
f thee away into the land of	Amos 7:12	1272
fleeth of them shall not *f* away	Amos 9:1	5127
But Jonah rose up to *f* unto	Jonah 1:3	1272
yet they shall *f* away	Nah 2:8	5127
look upon them shall *f* from thee	Nah 3:7	5074
when the sun ariseth they *f* away	Nah 3:17	5074
f from the land of the north	Zec 2:6	5127
ye shall *f* to the valley of the	Zec 14:5	5127
yea, ye shall *f*, like as ye fled	Zec 14:5	5127
f into Egypt, and be thou there	Mt 2:13	5343
you to *f* from the wrath to come	Mt 3:7	5343
in this city, *f* ye into another	Mt 10:23	5343
be in Judaea *f* into the mountains	Mt 24:16	5343
be in Judaea *f* to the mountains	Mk 13:14	5343
you to *f* from the wrath to come	Lk 3:7	5343
are in Judaea *f* to the mountains	Lk 21:21	5343
not follow, but will *f* from him	Jn 10:5	5343
were about to *f* out of the ship	Acts 27:30	5343
F fornication	1Cor 6:18	5343
dearly beloved, *f* from idolatry	1Cor 10:14	5343
O man of God, *f* these things	1Ti 6:11	5343
F also youthful lusts	2Ti 2:22	5343
the devil, and he will *f* from you	Jas 4:7	5343
die, and death shall *f* from them	Rev 9:6	5343

FLEECE

the first of the *f* of thy sheep	Deut 18:4	1488
I will put a *f* of wool in the	Judg 6:37	1492
and if the dew be on the *f* only	Judg 6:37	1492
morrow, and thrust the *f* together	Judg 6:38	1492
and wringed the dew out of the *f*	Judg 6:38	1492
thee, but this once with the *f*	Judg 6:39	1492
let it now be dry only upon the *f*	Judg 6:39	1492

for it was dry upon the *f* only	Judg 6:40	1492
not warmed with the *f* of my sheep	Job 31:20	1488

FLEEING

shall flee, as *f* from a sword	Lev 26:36	4499
that *f* unto one of these cities	Deut 4:42	5127
f into the wilderness in former	Job 30:3	6207

FLEETH

f into one of these cities	Deut 19:11	5127
he *f* also as a shadow, and	Job 14:2	1272
that he who *f* from the noise of	Is 24:18	5127
ask him that *f*, and her that	Jer 48:19	5127
He that *f* from the fear shall	Jer 48:44	5211
he that *f* of them shall not flee	Amos 9:1	5127
cankerworm spoileth, and *f* away	Nah 3:16	5775
and leaveth the sheep, and *f*	Jn 10:12	5343
The hireling *f*, because he is an	Jn 10:13	5343

FLESH

closed up the *f* instead thereof	Gen 2:21	1320
of my bones, and *f* of my *f*	Gen 2:23	1320
and they shall be one *f*	Gen 2:24	1320
with man, for that he also is *f*	Gen 6:3	1320
for all *f* had corrupted his way	Gen 6:12	1320
The end of all *f* is come before	Gen 6:13	1320
upon the earth, to destroy all *f*	Gen 6:17	1320
And of every living thing of all *f*	Gen 6:19	1320
into the ark, two and two of all *f*	Gen 7:15	1320
went in male and female of all *f*	Gen 7:16	1320
all *f* died that moved upon the	Gen 7:21	1320
thing that is with thee, of all *f*	Gen 8:17	1320
But *f* with the life thereof,	Gen 9:4	1320
neither shall all *f* be cut off	Gen 9:11	1320
and every living creature of all *f*	Gen 9:15	1320
become a flood to destroy all *f*	Gen 9:15	1320
of all *f* that is upon the earth	Gen 9:16	1320
all *f* that is upon the earth	Gen 9:17	1320
circumcise the *f* of your foreskin	Gen 17:11	1320
f for an everlasting covenant	Gen 17:13	1320
whose *f* of his foreskin is not	Gen 17:14	1320
circumcised the *f* of their	Gen 17:23	1320
in the *f* of his foreskin	Gen 17:24	1320
in the *f* of his foreskin	Gen 17:25	1320
Surely thou art my bone and my *f*	Gen 29:14	1320
for he is our brother and our *f*	Gen 37:27	1320
shall eat thy *f* from off thee	Gen 40:19	1320
was turned again as his other *f*	Ex 4:7	1320
shall eat the *f* in that night	Ex 12:8	1320
of the *f* abroad out of the house	Ex 12:46	1320
Egypt, when we sat by the *f* pots	Ex 16:3	1320
give you in the evening *f* to eat	Ex 16:8	1320
saying, At even ye shall eat *f*	Ex 16:12	1320
and his *f* shall not be eaten	Ex 21:28	1320
neither shall ye eat any *f* that	Ex 22:31	1320
But the *f* of the bullock, and his	Ex 29:14	1320
seethe his *f* in the holy place	Ex 29:31	1320
sons shall eat the *f* of the ram	Ex 29:32	1320
And if ought of the *f* of the	Ex 29:34	1320
Upon man's *f* shall it not be	Ex 30:32	1320
skin of the bullock, and all his *f*	Lev 4:11	1320
breeches shall he put upon his *f*	Lev 6:10	1320
touch the *f* thereof shall be holy	Lev 6:27	1320
the *f* of the sacrifice of his	Lev 7:15	1320
But the remainder of the *f* of the	Lev 7:17	1320
if any of the *f* of the sacrifice	Lev 7:18	1320
the *f* that toucheth any unclean	Lev 7:19	1320
and as for the *f*, all that be	Lev 7:19	1320
the *f* of the sacrifice of peace	Lev 7:20	1320
eat of the *f* of the sacrifice of	Lev 7:21	1320
the bullock, and his hide, his *f*	Lev 8:17	1320
Boil the *f* at the door of the	Lev 8:31	1320
And that which remaineth of the *f*	Lev 8:32	1320
And the *f* and the hide he burnt	Lev 9:11	1320
Of their *f* shall ye not eat, and	Lev 11:8	1320
ye shall not eat of their *f*	Lev 11:11	1320
in the eighth day the *f* of his	Lev 12:3	1320
in the skin of his *f* a rising	Lev 13:2	1320
it be in the skin of his *f* like	Lev 13:2	1320
the plague in the skin of the *f*	Lev 13:3	1320
be deeper than the skin of his *f*	Lev 13:3	1320
be white in the skin of his *f*	Lev 13:4	1320
be quick raw *f* in the rising	Lev 13:10	1320
old leprosy in the skin of his *f*	Lev 13:11	1320
leprosy have covered all his *f*	Lev 13:13	1320
But when raw *f* appeareth in him,	Lev 13:14	1320
And the priest shall see the raw *f*	Lev 13:15	1320
for the raw *f* is unclean	Lev 13:15	1320
Or if the raw *f* turn again	Lev 13:16	1320
The *f* also, in which, even in the	Lev 13:18	1320
Or if there be any *f*, in the skin	Lev 13:24	1320
the quick *f* that burneth have a	Lev 13:24	1320

the skin of their *f* bright spots	Lev 13:38	1320
skin of their *f* be darkish white	Lev 13:39	1320
appeareth in the skin of the *f*	Lev 13:43	1320
also he shall wash his *f* in water	Lev 14:9	1320
hath a running issue out of his *f*	Lev 15:2	1320
whether his *f* run with his issue,	Lev 15:3	1320
or his *f* be stopped from his	Lev 15:3	1320
he that toucheth the *f* of him	Lev 15:7	1320
bathe his *f* in running water, and	Lev 15:13	1320
he shall wash all his *f* in water	Lev 15:16	1320
and her issue in her *f* be blood	Lev 15:19	1320
the linen breeches upon his *f*	Lev 16:4	1320
shall he wash his *f* in water	Lev 16:4	1320
he shall wash his *f* with water in	Lev 16:24	1320
clothes, and bathe his *f* in water	Lev 16:26	1320
the fire their skins, and their *f*	Lev 16:27	1320
clothes, and bathe his *f* in water	Lev 16:28	1320
the life of the *f* is in the blood	Lev 17:11	1320
For it is the life of all *f*	Lev 17:14	1320
eat the blood of no manner of *f*	Lev 17:14	1320
for the life of all *f* is the	Lev 17:14	1320
he wash them not, nor bathe his *f*	Lev 17:16	1320
cuttings in your *f* for the dead	Lev 19:28	1320
nor make any cuttings in their *f*	Lev 21:5	1320
unless he wash his *f* with water	Lev 22:6	1320
ye shall eat the *f* of your sons	Lev 26:29	1320
the *f* of your daughters shall ye	Lev 26:29	1320
and let them shave all their *f*	Num 8:7	1320
said, Who shall give us *f* to eat	Num 11:4	1320
Whence should I have *f* to give	Num 11:13	1320
weep unto me, saying, Give us *f*	Num 11:13	1320
to morrow, and ye shall eat *f*	Num 11:18	1320
Who shall give us *f* to eat	Num 11:18	1320
the LORD will give you *f*, and ye	Num 11:18	1320
hast said, I will give them *f*	Num 11:21	1320
while the *f* was yet between their	Num 11:33	1320
of whom the *f* is half consumed	Num 12:12	1320
the God of the spirits of all *f*	Num 16:22	1320
that openeth the matrix in all *f*	Num 18:15	1320
the *f* of them shall be thine, as	Num 18:18	1320
her skin, and her *f*, and her blood,	Num 19:5	1320
and he shall bathe his *f* in water	Num 19:7	1320
in water, and bathe his *f* in water	Num 19:8	1320
the God of the spirits of all *f*	Num 27:16	1320
For who is there of all *f*	Deut 5:26	1320
kill and eat *f* in all thy gates,	Deut 12:15	1320
and thou shalt say, I will eat *f*	Deut 12:20	1320
because thy soul longeth to eat *f*	Deut 12:20	1320
thou mayest eat *f*, whatsoever thy	Deut 12:20	1320
not eat the life with the *f*	Deut 12:23	1320
offer thy burnt offerings, the *f*	Deut 12:27	1320
thy God, and thou shalt eat the *f*	Deut 12:27	1320
ye shall not eat of their *f*	Deut 14:8	1320
shall there any thing of the *f*	Deut 16:4	1320
the *f* of thy sons and of thy	Deut 28:53	1320
f of his children whom he shall	Deut 28:55	1320
blood, and my sword shall devour *f*	Deut 32:42	1320
the *f* he put in a basket, and he	Judg 6:19	1320
of God said unto him, Take the *f*	Judg 6:20	1320
was in his hand, and touched the *f*	Judg 6:21	1320
of the rock, and consumed the *f*	Judg 6:21	1320
then I will tear your *f* with the	Judg 8:7	1320
that I am your bone and your *f*	Judg 9:2	1320
while the *f* was in seething, with	1Sa 2:13	1320
Give *f* to roast for the priest	1Sa 2:15	1320
he will not have sodden *f* of thee	1Sa 2:15	1320
I will give thy *f* unto the fowls	1Sa 17:44	1320
my *f* that I have killed for my	1Sa 25:11	2878
Behold, we are thy bone and thy *f*	2Sa 5:1	1320
of bread, and a good piece of *f*	2Sa 6:19	829
brethren, ye are my bones and my *f*	2Sa 19:12	1320
thou not of my bone, and of my *f*	2Sa 19:13	1320
f in the morning, and bread and	1Kin 17:6	1320
and bread and *f* in the evening	1Kin 17:6	1320
them, and boiled their *f* with the	1Kin 19:21	1320
and put sackcloth upon his *f*	1Kin 21:27	1320
the *f* of the child waxed warm	2Kin 4:34	1320
thy *f* shall come again to thee,	2Kin 5:10	1320
his *f* came again like unto the	2Kin 5:14	1320
like unto the *f* of a little child	2Kin 5:14	1320
had sackcloth within upon his *f*	2Kin 6:30	1320
shall dogs eat the *f* of Jezebel	2Kin 9:36	1320
Behold, we are thy bone and thy *f*	1Chr 11:1	1320
of bread, and a good piece of *f*	1Chr 16:3	829
With his is an arm of *f*	2Chr 32:8	1320
f is as the *f* of our brethren	Neh 5:5	1320
now, and touch his bone and his *f*	Job 2:5	1320
the hair of my *f* stood up	Job 4:15	1320
or is my *f* of brass	Job 6:12	1320
My *f* is clothed with worms and	Job 7:5	1320
Hast thou eyes of *f*	Job 10:4	1320
hast clothed me with skin and *f*	Job 10:11	1320
do I take my *f* in my teeth	Job 13:14	1320
But his *f* upon him shall have	Job 14:22	1320
cleaveth to my skin and to my *f*	Job 19:20	1320
and are not satisfied with my *f*	Job 19:22	1320
yet in my *f* shall I see God	Job 19:26	1320
and trembling taketh hold on my *f*	Job 21:6	1320
said not, Oh that we had of his *f*	Job 31:31	1320
His *f* is consumed away, that it	Job 33:21	1320
His *f* shall be fresher than a	Job 33:25	1320
All *f* shall perish together, and	Job 34:15	1320
The flakes of his *f* are joined	Job 41:23	1320
my *f* also shall rest in hope	Ps 16:9	1320
foes, came upon me to eat up my *f*	Ps 27:2	1320
in my *f* because of thine anger	Ps 38:3	1320
and there is no soundness in my *f*	Ps 38:7	1320
Will I eat the *f* of bulls	Ps 50:13	1320
not fear what *f* can do unto me	Ps 56:4	1320
my *f* longeth for thee in a dry and	Ps 63:1	1320
unto thee shall all *f* come	Ps 65:2	1320
My *f* and my heart faileth	Ps 73:26	7607
can he provide *f* for his people	Ps 78:20	7607
He rained *f* also upon them as	Ps 78:27	7607
remembered that they were but *f*	Ps 78:39	1320
the *f* of thy saints unto the	Ps 79:2	1320
my *f* crieth out for the living	Ps 84:2	1320
and my *f* faileth of fatness	Ps 109:24	1320
My *f* trembleth for fear of thee	Ps 119:120	1320
Who giveth food to all *f*	Ps 136:25	1320
let all *f* bless his holy name for	Ps 145:21	1320
them, and health to all their *f*	Prov 4:22	1320
mourn at the last, when thy *f*	Prov 5:11	1320
that is cruel troubleth his own *f*	Prov 11:17	7607
sound heart is the life of the *f*	Prov 14:30	1320
among riotous eaters of *f*	Prov 23:20	1320
together, and eateth his own *f*	Eccl 4:5	1320
thy mouth to cause thy *f* to sin	Eccl 5:6	1320
and put away evil from thy *f*	Eccl 11:10	1320
study is a weariness of the *f*	Eccl 12:12	1320
every man the *f* of his own arm	Is 9:20	1320
fatness of his *f* shall wax lean	Is 17:4	1320
oxen, and killing sheep, eating *f*	Is 22:13	1320
and their horses *f*, and not spirit	Is 31:3	1320
all *f* shall see it together	Is 40:5	1320
All *f* is grass, and all the	Is 40:6	1320
with part thereof he eateth *f*	Is 44:16	1320
I have roasted *f*, and eaten it	Is 44:19	1320
oppress thee with their own *f*	Is 49:26	1320
all *f* shall know that I the LORD	Is 49:26	1320
hide not thyself from thine own *f*	Is 58:7	1320
monuments, which eat swine's *f*	Is 65:4	1320
will the LORD plead with all *f*	Is 66:16	1320
in the midst, eating swine's *f*	Is 66:17	1320
shall all *f* come to worship	Is 66:23	1320
shall be an abhorring unto all *f*	Is 66:24	1320
unto your sacrifices, and eat *f*	Jer 7:21	1320
the holy *f* is passed from thee	Jer 11:15	1320
no *f* shall have peace	Jer 12:12	1320
maketh *f* his arm, and whose heart	Jer 17:5	1320
them to eat the *f* of their sons	Jer 19:9	1320
the *f* of their daughters, and they	Jer 19:9	1320
the *f* of his friend in the siege	Jer 19:9	1320
nations, he will plead with all *f*	Jer 25:31	1320
I am the LORD, the God of all *f*	Jer 32:27	1320
I will bring evil upon all *f*	Jer 45:5	1320
to my *f* be upon Babylon, shall	Jer 51:35	7607
My *f* and my skin hath he made old	Lam 3:4	1320
there abominable *f* into my mouth	Eze 4:14	1320
is the caldron, and we be the *f*	Eze 11:3	1320
the midst of it, they are the *f*	Eze 11:7	1320
ye be the *f* in the midst thereof	Eze 11:11	1320
the stony heart out of their *f*	Eze 11:19	1320
and will give them an heart of *f*	Eze 11:19	1320
thy neighbours, great of *f*	Eze 16:26	1320
all *f* shall see that I the LORD	Eze 20:48	1320
all *f* from the south to the north	Eze 21:4	1320
That all *f* may know that I the	Eze 21:5	1320
whose *f* is as the *f* of asses,	Eze 23:20	1320
kindle the fire, consume the *f*	Eze 24:10	1320
I will lay thy *f* upon the	Eze 32:5	1320
the stony heart out of your *f*	Eze 36:26	1320
and I will give you an heart of *f*	Eze 36:26	1320
you, and will bring up *f* upon you	Eze 37:6	1320
the *f* came up upon them, and the	Eze 37:8	1320
of Israel, that ye may eat *f*	Eze 39:17	1320
Ye shall eat the *f* of the mighty	Eze 39:18	1320
tables was the *f* of the offering	Eze 40:43	1320
in heart, and uncircumcised in *f*	Eze 44:7	1320
in heart, nor uncircumcised in *f*	Eze 44:9	1320
fatter in *f* than all the children	Dan 1:15	1320
whose dwelling is not with *f*	Dan 2:11	1321

thereof, and all *f* was fed of it	Dan 4:12	1321
unto it, Arise, devour much *f*	Dan 7:5	1321
neither came *f* nor wine in my	Dan 10:3	1320
They sacrifice *f* for the	Hos 8:13	1320
pour out my spirit upon all *f*	Joel 2:28	1320
their *f* from off their bones	Mic 3:2	7607
Who also eat the *f* of my people	Mic 3:3	7607
pot, and as *f* within the caldron	Mic 3:3	1320
as dust, and their *f* as the dung	Zeph 1:17	3894
If one bear holy *f* in the skirt	Hag 2:12	1320
Be silent, O all *f*, before the	Zec 2:13	1320
eat every one the *f* of another	Zec 11:9	1320
but he shall eat the *f* of the fat	Zec 11:16	1320
Their *f* shall consume away while	Zec 14:12	1320
for *f* and blood hath not revealed	Mt 16:17	4561
and they twain shall be one *f*	Mt 19:5	4561
they are no more twain, but one *f*	Mt 19:6	4561
there should no *f* be saved	Mt 24:22	4561
is willing, but the *f* is weak	Mt 26:41	4561
And they twain shall be one *f*	Mk 10:8	4561
they are no more twain, but one *f*	Mk 10:8	4561
those days, no *f* should be saved	Mk 13:20	4561
truly is ready, but the *f* is weak	Mk 14:38	4561
all *f* shall see the salvation of	Lk 3:6	4561
for a spirit hath not *f* and bones,	Lk 24:39	4561
blood, nor of the will of the *f*	Jn 1:13	4561
And the Word was made *f*, and dwelt	Jn 1:14	4561
which is born of the *f* is	Jn 3:6	4561
which is born of the *f* is *f*	Jn 3:6	4561
bread that I will give is my *f*	Jn 6:51	4561
can this man give us his *f* to eat	Jn 6:52	4561
ye eat the *f* of the Son of man	Jn 6:53	4561
Whoso eateth my *f*, and drinketh my	Jn 6:54	4561
For my *f* is meat indeed, and my	Jn 6:55	4561
He that eateth my *f*, and drinketh	Jn 6:56	4561
the *f* profiteth nothing	Jn 6:63	4561
Ye judge after the *f*	Jn 8:15	4561
hast given him power over all *f*	Jn 17:2	4561
pour out of my Spirit upon all *f*	Acts 2:17	4561
moreover also my *f* shall rest in	Acts 2:26	4561
of his loins, according to the *f*	Acts 2:30	4561
neither his *f* did see corruption	Acts 2:31	4561
seed of David according to the *f*	Rom 1:3	4561
which is outward in the *f*	Rom 2:28	4561
no *f* be justified in his sight	Rom 3:20	4561
father, as pertaining to the *f*	Rom 4:1	4561
of the infirmity of your *f*	Rom 6:19	4561
For when we were in the *f*	Rom 7:5	4561
know that in me (that is, in my *f*	Rom 7:18	4561
but with the *f* the law of sin	Rom 7:25	4561
Jesus, who walk not after the *f*	Rom 8:1	4561
in that it was weak through the *f*	Rom 8:3	4561
Son in the likeness of sinful *f*	Rom 8:3	4561
for sin, condemned sin in the *f*	Rom 8:3	4561
in us, who walk not after the *f*	Rom 8:4	4561
f do mind the things of the *f*	Rom 8:5	4561
are in the *f* cannot please God	Rom 8:8	4561
But ye are not in the *f*, but in	Rom 8:9	4561
to the *f*, to live after the *f*	Rom 8:12	4561
For if ye live after the *f*	Rom 8:13	4561
my kinsmen according to the *f*	Rom 9:3	4561
as concerning the *f* Christ came	Rom 9:5	4561
which are the children of the *f*	Rom 9:8	4561
to emulation them which are my *f*	Rom 11:14	4561
and make not provision for the *f*	Rom 13:14	4561
It is good neither to eat *f*	Rom 14:21	2907
not many wise men after the *f*	1Cor 1:26	4561
That no *f* should glory in his	1Cor 1:29	4561
for the destruction of the *f*	1Cor 5:5	4561
for two, saith he, shall be one *f*	1Cor 6:16	4561
such shall have trouble in the *f*	1Cor 7:28	4561
I will eat no *f* while the world	1Cor 8:13	2907
Behold Israel after the *f*	1Cor 10:18	4561
All *f* is not the same *f*	1Cor 15:39	4561
but there is one kind of *f* of men	1Cor 15:39	4561
another *f* of beasts, another of	1Cor 15:39	4561
Now this I say, brethren, that *f*	1Cor 15:50	4561
do I purpose according to the *f*	2Cor 1:17	4561
be made manifest in our mortal *f*	2Cor 4:11	4561
know we no man after the *f*	2Cor 5:16	4561
we have known Christ after the *f*	2Cor 5:16	4561
from all filthiness of the *f*	2Cor 7:1	4561
our *f* had no rest, but we were	2Cor 7:5	4561
if we walked according to the *f*	2Cor 10:2	4561
For though we walk in the *f*	2Cor 10:3	4561
we do not war after the *f*	2Cor 10:3	4561
that many glory after the *f*	2Cor 11:18	4561
was given to me a thorn in the *f*	2Cor 12:7	4561
I conferred not with *f* and blood	Gal 1:16	4561
the law shall no *f* be justified	Gal 2:16	4561
life which I now live in the *f* I	Gal 2:20	4561

are ye now made perfect by the *f*	Gal 3:3	4561
how through infirmity of the *f* I	Gal 4:13	4561
which in my *f* ye despised not	Gal 4:14	4561
bondwoman was born after the *f*	Gal 4:23	4561
f persecuted him that was born	Gal 4:29	4561
liberty for an occasion to the *f*	Gal 5:13	4561
not fulfil the lust of the *f*	Gal 5:16	4561
For the *f* lusteth against the	Gal 5:17	4561
and the Spirit against the *f*	Gal 5:17	4561
the works of the *f* are manifest	Gal 5:19	4561
the *f* with the affections	Gal 5:24	4561
to his *f* shall of the *f* reap	Gal 6:8	4561
to make a fair shew in the *f*	Gal 6:12	4561
that they may glory in your *f*	Gal 6:13	4561
times past in the lusts of our *f*	Eph 2:3	4561
fulfilling the desires of the *f*	Eph 2:3	4561
in time past Gentiles in the *f*	Eph 2:11	4561
in the *f* made by hands	Eph 2:11	4561
abolished in his *f* the enmity	Eph 2:15	4561
no man ever yet hated his own *f*	Eph 5:29	4561
are members of his body, of his *f*	Eph 5:30	4561
wife, and they two shall be one *f*	Eph 5:31	4561
your masters according to the *f*	Eph 6:5	4561
For we wrestle not against *f*	Eph 6:12	4561
But if I live in the *f*, this is	Phil 1:22	4561
in the *f* is more needful for you	Phil 1:24	4561
and have no confidence in the *f*	Phil 3:3	4561
also have confidence in the *f*	Phil 3:4	4561
whereof he might trust in the *f*	Phil 3:4	4561
the body of his *f* through death	Col 1:22	4561
in my *f* for his body's sake	Col 1:24	4561
as have not seen my face in the *f*	Col 2:1	4561
For though I be absent in the *f*	Col 2:5	4561
f by the circumcision of Christ	Col 2:11	4561
and the uncircumcision of your *f*	Col 2:13	4561
honour to the satisfying of the *f*	Col 2:23	4561
your masters according to the *f*	Col 3:22	4561
God was manifest in the *f*	1Ti 3:16	4561
more unto thee, both in the *f*	Philem 16	4561
the children are partakers of *f*	Heb 2:14	4561
Who in the days of his *f*, when he	Heb 5:7	4561
to the purifying of the *f*	Heb 9:13	4561
the veil, that is to say, his *f*	Heb 10:20	4561
of our *f* which corrected us	Heb 12:9	4561
shall eat your *f* as it were fire	Jas 5:3	4561
For all *f* is as grass, and all the	1Pet 1:24	4561
God, being put to death in the *f*	1Pet 3:18	4561
away of the filth of the *f*	1Pet 3:21	4561
hath suffered for us in the *f*	1Pet 4:1	4561
in the *f* hath ceased from sin	1Pet 4:1	4561
time in the *f* to the lusts of men	1Pet 4:2	4561
judged according to men in the *f*	1Pet 4:6	4561
them that walk after the *f* in the	2Pet 2:10	4561
allure through the lusts of the *f*	2Pet 2:18	4561
in the world, the lust of the *f*	1Jn 2:16	4561
Christ is come in the *f* is of God	1Jn 4:2	4561
is come in the *f* is not of God	1Jn 4:3	4561
Jesus Christ is come in the *f*	2Jn 7	4561
and going after strange *f*	Jude 7	4561
filthy dreamers defile the *f*	Jude 8	4561
even the garment spotted by the *f*	Jude 23	4561
and naked, and shall eat her *f*	Rev 17:16	4561
That ye may eat the *f* of kings	Rev 19:18	4561
the *f* of captains, and the *f*	Rev 19:18	4561
the *f* of mighty men	Rev 19:18	4561
the *f* of horses, and of them that	Rev 19:18	4561
the *f* of all men, both free and	Rev 19:18	4561
fowls were filled with their *f*	Rev 19:21	4561

FLESHHOOK

with a *f* of three teeth in his	1Sa 2:13	4207
all that the *f* brought up the	1Sa 2:14	4207

FLESHHOOKS

shovels, and his basons, and his *f*	Ex 27:3	4207
shovels, and the basons, and the *f*	Ex 38:3	4207
about it, even the censers, the *f*	Num 4:14	4207
Also pure gold for the *f*, and the	1Chr 28:17	4207
also, and the shovels, and the *f*	2Chr 4:16	4207

FLESHLY

sincerity, not with *f* wisdom	2Cor 1:12	4559
vainly puffed up by his *f* mind	Col 2:18	4559
and pilgrims, abstain from *f* lusts	1Pet 2:11	4559

FLESHY

but in *f* tables of the heart	2Cor 3:3	4560

FLEW

the people *f* upon the spoil, and	1Sa 14:32	6213
Then *f* one of the seraphims unto	Is 6:6	5774

FLIES

I will send swarms of *f* upon thee	Ex 8:21	
shall be full of swarms of *f*	Ex 8:21	
no swarms of *f* shall be there	Ex 8:22	
of *f* into the house of Pharaoh	Ex 8:24	
by reason of the swarm of *f*	Ex 8:24	
of *f* may depart from Pharaoh	Ex 8:29	
the swarms of *f* from Pharaoh	Ex 8:31	
sent divers sorts of *f* among them	Ps 78:45	6157
and there came divers sorts of *f*	Ps 105:31	6157
Dead *f* cause the ointment of the	Eccl 10:1	2070

FLIETH

any winged fowl that *f* in the air	Deut 4:17	5774
thing that *f* is unclean unto you	Deut 14:19	5775
earth, as swift as the eagle *f*	Deut 28:49	1675
nor for the arrow that *f* by day	Ps 91:5	5774

FLIGHT

you shall put ten thousand to *f*	Lev 26:8	7291
and two put ten thousand to *f*	Deut 32:30	5127
they put to *f* all them of the	1Chr 12:15	1272
go out with haste, nor go by *f*	Is 52:12	4499
Therefore the *f* shall perish from	Amos 2:14	4498
that your *f* be not in the winter	Mt 24:20	5437
pray ye that your *f* be not in the	Mk 13:18	5437
turned to *f* the armies of the	Heb 11:34	

FLINT

forth water out of the rock of *f*	Deut 8:15	2496
the *f* into a fountain of waters	Ps 114:8	2496
hoofs shall be counted like *f*	Is 5:28	6864
have I set my face like a *f*	Is 50:7	2496
than *f* have I made thy forehead	Eze 3:9	6864

FLINTY

rock, and oil out of the *f* rock	Deut 32:13	2496

FLOATS

I will convey them by sea in *f*	1Kin 5:9	1702

FLOCK

of the firstlings of his *f*	Gen 4:4	6629
ewe lambs of the *f* by themselves	Gen 21:28	6629
Go now to the *f*, and fetch me from	Gen 27:9	6629
watered the *f* of Laban his	Gen 29:10	6629
I will again feed and keep thy *f*	Gen 30:31	6629
pass through all thy *f* to day	Gen 30:32	6629
all the brown in the *f* of Laban	Gen 30:40	6629
and Leah to the field unto his *f*	Gen 31:4	6629
the rams of thy *f* have I not	Gen 31:38	6629
them one day, all the *f* will die	Gen 33:13	6629
was feeding the *f* with his	Gen 37:2	6629
feed their father's *f* in Shechem	Gen 37:12	6629
brethren feed the *f* in Shechem	Gen 37:13	
I will send thee a kid from the *f*	Gen 38:17	6629
troughs to water their father's *f*	Ex 2:16	6629
helped them, and watered their *f*	Ex 2:17	6629
enough for us, and watered the *f*	Ex 2:19	6629
Now Moses kept the *f* of Jethro	Ex 3:1	6629
he led the *f* to the backside of	Ex 3:1	6629
even of the herd, and of the *f*	Lev 1:2	6629
unto the LORD be of the *f*	Lev 3:6	6629
hath sinned, a female from the *f*	Lev 5:6	6629
ram without blemish out of the *f*	Lev 5:18	6629
ram without blemish out of the *f*	Lev 6:6	6629
tithe of the herd, or of the *f*	Lev 27:32	6629
LORD, of the herd, or of the *f*	Num 15:3	6629
of thy herds or thy *f*, nor any	Deut 12:17	6629
kill of thy herd and of thy *f*	Deut 12:21	6629
him liberally out of thy *f*	Deut 15:14	6629
of thy *f* thou shalt sanctify unto	Deut 15:19	6629
unto the LORD thy God, of the *f*	Deut 16:2	6629
bear, and took a lamb out of the *f*	1Sa 17:34	5739
and he spared to take of his own *f*	2Sa 12:4	6629
gave to the people, of the *f*	2Chr 35:7	6629
a ram of the *f* for their trespass	Ezr 10:19	6629
forth their little ones like a *f*	Job 21:11	6629
to have set with the dogs of my *f*	Job 30:1	6629
like a *f* by the hand of Moses	Ps 77:20	6629
them in the wilderness like a *f*	Ps 78:52	5739
thou that leadest Joseph like a *f*	Ps 80:1	6629
and maketh him families like a *f*	Ps 107:41	6629
thou makest thy *f* to rest at noon	Song 1:7	
forth by the footsteps of the *f*	Song 1:8	6629
thy hair is as a *f* of goats	Song 4:1	5739
Thy teeth are like a *f* of sheep	Song 4:2	5739
thy hair is as a *f* of goats that	Song 6:5	5739
Thy teeth are as a *f* of sheep	Song 6:6	5739
shall feed his *f* like a shepherd	Is 40:11	5739
sea with the shepherd of his *f*	Is 63:11	5739
because the LORD's *f* is carried	Jer 13:17	5739
where is the *f* that was given	Jer 13:20	5739
was given thee, thy beautiful *f*	Jer 13:20	6629

Ye have scattered my *f*, and driven	Jer 23:2	6629
f out of all countries whither I	Jer 23:3	6629
the ashes, ye principal of the *f*	Jer 25:34	6629
the principal of the *f* to escape	Jer 25:35	6629
howling of the principal of the *f*	Jer 25:36	6629
him, as a shepherd doth his *f*	Jer 31:10	5739
oil, and for the young of the *f*	Jer 31:12	6629
of the *f* shall draw them out	Jer 49:20	6629
of the *f* shall draw them out	Jer 50:45	6629
with thee the shepherd and his *f*	Jer 51:23	5739
Take the choice of the *f*, and burn	Eze 24:5	6629
but ye feed not the *f*	Eze 34:3	6629
my *f* was scattered upon all the	Eze 34:6	6629
surely because my *f* became a prey	Eze 34:8	6629
my *f* became meat to every beast	Eze 34:8	6629
did my shepherds search for my *f*	Eze 34:8	6629
fed themselves, and fed not my *f*	Eze 34:8	6629
I will require my *f* at their hand	Eze 34:10	6629
them to cease from feeding the *f*	Eze 34:10	6629
deliver my *f* from their mouth	Eze 34:10	6629
As a shepherd seeketh out his *f*	Eze 34:12	5739
I will feed my *f*, and I will cause	Eze 34:15	6629
And as for you, O my *f*, thus saith	Eze 34:17	6629
And as for my *f*, they eat that	Eze 34:19	6629
Therefore will I save my *f*	Eze 34:22	6629
And ye my *f*, the *f* of my	Eze 34:31	6629
the *f* of my pasture, are men, and	Eze 34:31	6629
increase them with men like a *f*	Eze 36:37	6629
As the holy *f*, as the *f* of	Eze 36:38	6629
ram out of the *f* without blemish	Eze 43:23	6629
bullock, and a ram out of the *f*	Eze 43:25	6629
And one lamb out of the *f*, out of	Eze 45:15	6629
and eat the lambs out of the *f*	Amos 6:4	6629
LORD took me as I followed the *f*	Amos 7:15	6629
neither man nor beast, herd nor *f*	Jonah 3:7	6629
as the *f* in the midst of their	Mic 2:12	5739
And thou, O tower of the *f*	Mic 4:8	5739
the *f* of thine heritage, which	Mic 7:14	6629
the *f* shall be cut off from the	Hab 3:17	6629
that day as the *f* of his people	Zec 9:16	6629
they went their way as a *f*	Zec 10:2	6629
visited his *f* the house of Judah	Zec 10:3	5739
Feed the *f* of the slaughter	Zec 11:4	6629
And I will feed the *f* of slaughter	Zec 11:7	6629
even you, O poor of the *f*	Zec 11:7	6629
and I fed the *f*	Zec 11:7	6629
so the poor of the *f* that waited	Zec 11:11	6629
idol shepherd that leaveth the *f*	Zec 11:17	6629
which hath in his *f* a male	Mal 1:14	5739
the sheep of the *f* shall be	Mt 26:31	4167
watch over their *f* by night	Lk 2:8	4167
Fear not, little *f*	Lk 12:32	4168
unto yourselves, and to all the *f*	Acts 20:28	4168
in among you, not sparing the *f*	Acts 20:29	4168
or who feedeth a *f*, and eateth not	1Cor 9:7	4167
eateth not of the milk of the *f*	1Cor 9:7	4167
Feed the *f* of God which is among	1Pet 5:2	4168
but being ensamples to the *f*	1Pet 5:3	4168

FLOCKS

which went with Abram, had *f*	Gen 13:5	6629
and he hath given him *f*, and herds,	Gen 24:35	6629
For he had possession of *f*	Gen 26:14	6629
there were three *f* of sheep lying	Gen 29:2	5739
of that well they watered the *f*	Gen 29:2	5739
thither were all the *f* gathered	Gen 29:3	5739
until all the *f* be gathered	Gen 29:8	5739
Jacob fed the rest of Laban's *f*	Gen 30:36	6629
f in the gutters in the watering	Gen 30:38	6629
troughs when the *f* came to drink	Gen 30:38	6629
the *f* conceived before the rods,	Gen 30:39	6629
set the faces of the *f* toward the	Gen 30:40	6629
and he put his own *f* by themselves	Gen 30:40	5739
And I have oxen, and asses, *f*	Gen 32:5	6629
that was with him, and the *f*	Gen 32:7	6629
the children are tender, and the *f*	Gen 33:13	6629
thy brethren, and well with the *f*	Gen 37:14	6629
thee, where they feed their *f*	Gen 37:16	
thy children's children, and thy *f*	Gen 45:10	6629
and they have brought their *f*	Gen 46:32	6629
father and my brethren, and their *f*	Gen 47:1	6629
have no pasture for their *f*	Gen 47:4	6629
exchange for horses, and for the *f*	Gen 47:17	6629
their little ones, and their *f*	Gen 50:8	6629
and with our daughters, with our *f*	Ex 10:9	6629
only let your *f* and your herds be	Ex 10:24	6629
Also take your *f* and your herds,	Ex 12:32	6629
and *f*, and herds, even very much	Ex 12:38	6629
neither let the *f* nor herds feed	Ex 34:3	6629
And if his offering be of the *f*	Lev 1:10	6629
ram without blemish out of the *f*	Lev 5:15	6629

Shall the *f* and the herds be slain	Num 11:22	6629
all their cattle, and all their *f*	Num 31:9	4735
beeves, of the asses, and of the *f*	Num 31:30	6629
Our little ones, our wives, our *f*	Num 32:26	4735
the *f* of thy sheep, in the land	Deut 7:13	6251
thy *f* multiply, and thy silver and	Deut 8:13	6629
of your herds and of your *f*	Deut 12:6	6629
of thy herds and of thy *f*	Deut 14:23	6629
thy kine, and the *f* of thy sheep	Deut 28:4	6251
thy kine, and the *f* of thy sheep	Deut 28:18	6251
or *f* of thy sheep, until he have	Deut 28:51	6251
to hear the bleatings of the *f*	Judg 5:16	5739
And David took all the *f* and the	1Sa 30:20	6629
The rich man had exceeding many *f*	2Sa 12:2	6629
them like two little *f* of kids	1Kin 20:27	2835
to seek pasture for their *f*	1Chr 4:39	6629
was pasture there for their *f*	1Chr 4:41	6629
over the *f* was Jaziz the Hagerite	1Chr 27:31	6629
and the Arabians brought him *f*	2Chr 17:11	6629
manner of beasts, and cotes for *f*	2Chr 32:28	5739
him cities, and possessions of *f*	2Chr 32:29	6629
of our herds and of our *f*, to	Neh 10:36	6629
they violently take away *f*	Job 24:2	5739
The pastures are clothed with *f*	Ps 65:13	6629
their *f* to hot thunderbolts	Ps 78:48	4735
to know the state of thy *f*	Prov 27:23	6629
aside by the *f* of thy companions	Song 1:7	5739
they shall be for *f*, which shall	Is 17:2	5739
joy of wild asses, a pasture of *f*	Is 32:14	5739
All the *f* of Kedar shall be	Is 60:7	6629
shall stand and feed your *f*	Is 61:5	6629
And Sharon shall be a fold of *f*	Is 65:10	6629
their *f* and their herds, their	Jer 3:24	6629
they shall eat up thy *f* and thine	Jer 5:17	6629
with their *f* shall come unto her	Jer 6:3	5739
all their *f* shall be scattered	Jer 10:21	4830
and they that go forth with *f*	Jer 31:24	5739
causing their *f* to lie down	Jer 33:12	6629
shall the *f* pass again under the	Jer 33:13	6629
their *f* shall they take away	Jer 49:29	6629
be as the he goats before the *f*	Jer 50:8	6629
Ammonites a couchingplace for *f*	Eze 25:5	6629
not the shepherds feed the *f*	Eze 34:2	6629
cities with *f* of men	Eze 36:38	6629
They shall go with their *f*	Hos 5:6	6629
the *f* of sheep are made desolate	Joel 1:18	5739
a young lion among the *f* of sheep	Mic 5:8	5739
for shepherds, and folds for *f*	Zeph 2:6	6629
f shall lie down in the midst of	Zeph 2:14	5739

FLOOD

do bring a *f* of waters upon the	Gen 6:17	3999
f of waters was upon the earth	Gen 7:6	3999
because of the waters of the *f*	Gen 7:7	3999
of the *f* were upon the earth	Gen 7:10	3999
the *f* was forty days upon the	Gen 7:17	3999
off any more by the waters of a *f*	Gen 9:11	3999
more be a *f* to destroy the earth	Gen 9:11	3999
become a *f* to destroy all flesh	Gen 9:15	3999
lived after the *f* three hundred	Gen 9:28	3999
them were sons born after the *f*	Gen 10:1	3999
divided in the earth after the *f*	Gen 10:32	3999
Arphaxad two years after the *f*	Gen 11:10	3999
other side of the *f* in old time	Josh 24:2	5104
from the other side of the *f*	Josh 24:3	5104
served on the other side of the *f*	Josh 24:14	5104
were on the other side of the *f*	Josh 24:15	5104
the *f* decayeth and drieth up	Job 14:11	5104
foundation was overflown with a *f*	Job 22:16	5104
The *f* breaketh out from the	Job 28:4	5158
The LORD sitteth upon the *f*	Ps 29:10	3999
they went through the *f* on foot	Ps 66:6	5104
cleave the fountain and the *f*	Ps 74:15	5158
carriest them away as with a *f*	Ps 90:5	2229
storm, as a *f* of mighty waters	Is 28:2	2230
the enemy shall come in like a *f*	Is 59:19	5104
Who is this that cometh up as a *f*	Jer 46:7	2975
Egypt riseth up like a *f*, and his	Jer 46:8	2975
and shall be an overflowing *f*	Jer 47:2	5158
the end thereof shall be with a *f*	Dan 9:26	7858
with the arms of a *f* shall they	Dan 11:22	7858
and it shall rise up wholly as a *f*	Amos 8:8	2975
and drowned, as by the *f* of Egypt	Amos 8:8	2975
it shall rise up wholly as a *f*	Amos 9:5	2975
be drowned, as by the *f* of Egypt	Amos 9:5	2975
But with an overrunning *f* he will	Nah 1:8	7858
before the *f* they were eating	Mt 24:38	2627
And knew not until the *f* came	Mt 24:39	2627
and when they arose, the stream	Lk 6:48	4182
the *f* came, and destroyed them all	Lk 17:27	2627
bringing in the *f* upon the world	2Pet 2:5	2627

water as a *f* after the woman	Rev 12:15	4215
her to be carried away of the *f*	Rev 12:15	4216
swallowed up the *f* which the	Rev 12:16	4215

FLOODS

the *f* stood upright as an heap,	Ex 15:8	5140
the *f* of ungodly men made me	2Sa 22:5	5158
shall not see the rivers, the *f*	Job 20:17	5104
He bindeth the *f* from overflowing	Job 28:11	5104
the *f* of ungodly men made me	Ps 18:4	5158
and established it upon the *f*	Ps 24:2	5104
surely in the *f* of great waters	Ps 32:6	7858
waters, where the *f* overflow me	Ps 69:2	7641
and their *f*, that they could not	Ps 78:44	5140
The *f* have lifted up, O LORD, the	Ps 93:3	5104
The *f* have lifted up their voice	Ps 93:3	5104
the *f* lift up their waves	Ps 93:3	5104
Let the *f* clap their hands	Ps 98:8	5104
love, neither can the *f* drown it	Song 8:7	5104
thirsty, and *f* upon the dry ground	Is 44:3	5104
and I restrained the *f* thereof	Eze 31:15	5104
and the *f* compassed me about	Jonah 2:3	5104
the *f* came, and the winds blew, and	Mt 7:25	4215
the *f* came, and the winds blew, and	Mt 7:27	4215

FLOOR

saw the mourning in the *f* of Atad	Gen 50:11	1637
of the dust that is in the *f* of	Num 5:17	7172
out of thy flock, and out of thy *f*	Deut 15:14	1637
put a fleece of wool in the *f*	Judg 6:37	1637
thee, and get thee down to the *f*	Ruth 3:3	1637
And she went down unto the *f*	Ruth 3:6	1637
that a woman came into the *f*	Ruth 3:14	1637
both the *f* of the house, and the	1Kin 6:15	7172
covered the *f* of the house with	1Kin 6:15	7172
sides of the house, both the *f*	1Kin 6:16	7172
the *f* of the house he overlaid	1Kin 6:30	7172
one side of the *f* to the other	1Kin 7:7	7172
to *f* the houses which the kings	2Chr 34:11	7136
my threshing, and the corn of my *f*	Is 21:10	1637
The *f* and the winepress shall not	Hos 9:2	1637
with the whirlwind out of the *f*	Hos 13:3	1637
them as the sheaves into the *f*	Mic 4:12	1637
and he will throughly purge his *f*	Mt 3:12	257
and he will throughly purge his *f*	Lk 3:17	257

FLOORS

the *f* shall be full of wheat, and	Joel 2:24	1637

FLOTES

it to thee in *f* by sea to Joppa	2Chr 2:16	7513

FLOUR

of wheaten *f* shalt thou make them	Ex 29:2	5560
the one lamb a tenth deal of *f*	Ex 29:40	5560
his offering shall be of fine *f*	Lev 2:1	5560
his handful of fine *f* thereof	Lev 2:2	5560
cakes of fine *f* mingled with oil	Lev 2:4	5560
it shall be of fine *f* unleavened	Lev 2:5	5560
shall be made of fine *f* with oil	Lev 2:7	5560
of fine *f* for a sin offering	Lev 5:11	5560
of the *f* of the meat offering, and	Lev 6:15	5560
f for a meat offering perpetual	Lev 6:20	5560
cakes mingled with oil, of fine *f*	Lev 7:12	5560
of fine *f* for a meat offering	Lev 14:10	5560
one tenth deal of fine *f* mingled	Lev 14:21	5560
deals of fine *f* mingled with oil	Lev 23:13	5560
they shall be of fine *f*	Lev 23:17	5560
And thou shalt take fine *f*	Lev 24:5	5560
cakes of fine *f* mingled with oil,	Num 6:15	5560
f mingled with oil for a meat	Num 7:13	5560
both of them full of fine *f*	Num 7:19	5560
both of them full of fine *f*	Num 7:25	5560
both of them full of fine *f*	Num 7:31	5560
both of them full of fine *f*	Num 7:37	5560
both of them full of fine *f*	Num 7:43	5560
both of them full of fine *f*	Num 7:49	5560
both of them full of fine *f*	Num 7:55	5560
both of them full of fine *f*	Num 7:61	5560
both of them full of fine *f*	Num 7:67	5560
both of them full of fine *f*	Num 7:73	5560
both of them full of fine *f*	Num 7:79	5560
even fine *f* mingled with oil, and	Num 8:8	5560
offering of a tenth deal of *f*	Num 15:4	5560
offering two tenth deals of *f*	Num 15:6	5560
of three tenth deals of *f* mingled	Num 15:9	5560
an ephah of *f* for a meat offering	Num 28:5	5560
two tenth deals of *f* for a meat	Num 28:9	5560
deals of *f* for a meat offering	Num 28:12	5560
two tenth deals of *f* for a meat	Num 28:12	5560
a several tenth deal of *f* mingled	Num 28:13	5560
shall be of *f* mingled with oil	Num 28:20	5560
offering of *f* mingled with oil	Num 28:28	5560

shall be of *f* mingled with oil	Num 29:3	5560
shall be of *f* mingled with oil	Num 29:9	5560
shall be of *f* mingled with oil	Num 29:14	5560
unleavened cakes of an ephah of *f*	Judg 6:19	7058
three bullocks, and one ephah of *f*.	1Sa 1:24	7058
hasted, and killed it, and took *f*	1Sa 28:24	7058
And she took *f*, and kneaded it, and	2Sa 13:8	1217
and wheat, and barley, and *f*	2Sa 17:28	7058
day was thirty measures of fine *f*	1Kin 4:22	5560
of fine *f* be sold for a shekel	2Kin 7:1	5560
So a measure of fine *f* was sold	2Kin 7:16	5560
a measure of fine *f* for a shekel	2Kin 7:18	5560
of the sanctuary, and the fine *f*	1Chr 9:29	5560
for the fine *f* for meat offering,	1Chr 23:29	5560
thou didst eat fine *f*, and honey,	Eze 16:13	5560
also which I gave thee, fine *f*	Eze 16:19	5560
of oil, to temper with the fine *f*	Eze 46:14	5560
and wine, and oil, and fine *f*	Rev 18:13	4585

FLOURISH

In his days shall the righteous *f*	Ps 72:7	6524
they of the city shall *f* like	Ps 72:16	6692
all the workers of iniquity do *f*	Ps 92:7	6692
shall *f* like the palm tree	Ps 92:12	6524
shall *f* in the courts of our God	Ps 92:13	6524
upon himself shall his crown *f*	Ps 132:18	6692
the righteous shall *f* as a branch	Prov 11:28	6524
tabernacle of the upright shall *f*	Prov 14:11	6524
way, and the almond tree shall *f*	Eccl 12:5	5006
let us see if the vine *f*, whether	Song 7:12	6524
shalt thou make thy seed to *f*	Is 17:11	6524
your bones shall *f* like an herb	Is 66:14	6524
and have made the dry tree to *f*	Eze 17:24	6524

FLOURISHED

and to see whether the vine *f*	Song 6:11	6524
last your care of me hath *f* again	Phil 4:10	330

FLOURISHETH

In the morning it *f*, and groweth	Ps 90:6	6692
as a flower of the field, so he *f*	Ps 103:15	6692

FLOURISHING

they shall be fat and *f*	Ps 92:14	7488
in mine house, and *f* in my palace	Dan 4:4	7487

FLOW

his goods shall *f* away in the day	Job 20:28	5064
his wind to blow, and the waters *f*	Ps 147:18	5140
that the spices thereof may *f* out	Song 4:16	5140
and all nations shall *f* unto it	Is 2:2	5102
he caused the waters to *f* out of	Is 48:21	5140
f together, and thine heart shall	Is 60:5	5102
might *f* down at thy presence	Is 64:1	2151
shall *f* together to the goodness	Jer 31:12	5102
the nations shall not *f* together	Jer 51:44	5102
and the hills shall *f* with milk	Joel 3:18	3212
of Judah shall *f* with waters	Joel 3:18	3212
and people shall *f* unto it	Mic 4:1	5102
shall *f* rivers of living water	Jn 7:38	4482

FLOWED

f over all his banks, as they did	Josh 4:18	3212
the mountains *f* down at thy	Is 64:3	2151
Waters *f* over mine head	Lam 3:54	6687

FLOWER

with a knop and a *f* in one branch	Ex 25:33	6525
other branch, with a knop and a *f*	Ex 25:33	6525
in one branch, a knop and a *f*	Ex 37:19	6525
in another branch, a knop and a *f*	Ex 37:19	6525
shall die in the *f* of their age	1Sa 2:33	582
He cometh forth like a *f*, and is	Job 14:2	6731
shall cast off his *f* as the olive	Job 15:33	5328
as a *f* of the field, so he	Ps 103:15	6731
sour grape is ripening in the *f*	Is 18:5	5328
glorious beauty is a fading *f*	Is 28:1	6731
fat valley, shall be a fading *f*	Is 28:4	6733
thereof is as the *f* of the field	Is 40:6	6731
The grass withereth, the *f* fadeth	Is 40:7	6731
The grass withereth, the *f* fadeth	Is 40:8	6731
the *f* of Lebanon languisheth	Nah 1:4	6525
if she pass the *f* of her age	1Cor 7:36	5230
because as the *f* of the grass he	Jas 1:10	438
the *f* thereof falleth, and the	Jas 1:11	438
glory of man as the *f* of grass	1Pet 1:24	438
the *f* thereof falleth away	1Pet 1:24	438

FLOWERS

his bowls, his knops, and his *f*	Ex 25:31	6525
with their knops and their *f*	Ex 25:34	6525
his bowls, his knops, and his *f*	Ex 37:17	6525
like almonds, his knops, and his *f*	Ex 37:20	6525
her *f* be upon him, he shall be	Lev 15:24	5079
And of her that is sick of her *f*	Lev 15:33	5079

shaft thereof, unto the *f* thereof	Num 8:4	6525
was carved with knops and open *f*	1Kin 6:18	6731
cherubims and palm trees and open *f*	1Kin 6:29	6731
cherubims and palm trees and open *f*	1Kin 6:32	6731
cherubims and palm trees and open *f*	1Kin 6:35	6731
brim of a cup, with *f* of lilies	1Kin 7:26	6525
before the oracle, with the *f*	1Kin 7:49	6525
brim of a cup, with *f* of lilies	2Chr 4:5	6525
And the *f*, and the lamps, and the	2Chr 4:21	6525
The *f* appear on the earth	Song 2:12	5339
as a bed of spices, as sweet *f*	Song 5:13	4026

FLOWETH

it, a land that *f* with milk	Lev 20:24	2100
us, and surely it *f* with milk	Num 13:27	2100
a land which *f* with milk and honey	Num 14:8	2100
up out of a land that *f* with milk	Num 16:13	2100
us into a land that *f* with milk	Num 16:14	2100
in the land that *f* with milk	Deut 6:3	2100
seed, a land that *f* with milk	Deut 11:9	2100
even a land that *f* with milk	Deut 26:9	2100
fathers, a land that *f* with milk	Deut 26:15	2100
thee, a land that *f* with milk	Deut 27:3	2100
that *f* with milk and honey	Deut 31:20	2100
give us, a land that *f* with milk	Josh 5:6	2100

FLOWING

a large, unto a land *f* with milk	Ex 3:8	2100
unto a land *f* with milk and honey	Ex 3:17	2100
a land *f* with milk and honey, that	Ex 13:5	2100
Unto a land *f* with milk and honey	Ex 33:3	2100
wellspring of wisdom as a *f* brook	Prov 18:4	5042
of the Gentiles like a *f* stream	Is 66:12	7857
to give them a land *f* with milk	Jer 11:5	2100
or shall the cold *f* waters that	Jer 18:14	5140
a land *f* with milk and honey	Jer 32:22	2100
thy *f* valley, O backsliding	Jer 49:4	2100
f with milk and honey, which is	Eze 20:6	2100
f with milk and honey, which is	Eze 20:15	2100

FLUTE

hear the sound of the cornet, *f*	Dan 3:5	4953
heard the sound of the cornet, *f*	Dan 3:7	4953
hear the sound of the cornet, *f*	Dan 3:10	4953
hear the sound of the cornet, *f*	Dan 3:15	4953

FLUTTERETH

f over her young, spreadeth	Deut 32:11	7363

FLUX

sick of a fever and of a bloody *f*	Acts 28:8	1420

FLY

fowl that may *f* above the earth	Gen 1:20	5774
but didst *f* upon the spoil, and	1Sa 15:19	5860
he rode upon a cherub, and did *f*	2Sa 22:11	5774
trouble, as the sparks *f* upward	Job 5:7	5774
He shall *f* away as a dream, and	Job 20:8	5774
Doth the hawk *f* by thy wisdom	Job 39:26	82
he rode upon a cherub, and did *f*	Ps 18:10	5774
he did *f* upon the wings of the	Ps 18:10	1675
for then would I *f* away, and be at	Ps 55:6	5774
it is soon cut off, and we *f* away	Ps 90:10	5774
they *f* away as an eagle toward	Prov 23:5	5774
his feet, and with twain he did *f*	Is 6:2	5774
the LORD shall hiss for the *f*	Is 7:18	2070
But they shall *f* upon the	Is 11:14	5774
Who are these that *f* as a cloud	Is 60:8	5774
he shall *f* as an eagle, and shall	Jer 48:40	1675
f as the eagle, and spread his	Jer 49:22	1675
hunt the souls to make them *f*	Eze 13:20	6524
souls that ye hunt to make them *f*	Eze 13:20	6524
being caused to *f* swiftly	Dan 9:21	3286
glory shall *f* away like a bird	Hos 9:11	5774
they shall *f* as the eagle that	Hab 1:8	5774
that she might *f* into the	Rev 12:14	4072
I saw another angel *f* in the	Rev 14:6	4072
that *f* in the midst of heaven	Rev 19:17	4072

FLYING

Yet these may ye eat of every *f*	Lev 11:21	5775
But all other *f* creeping things,	Lev 11:23	5775
creeping things, and *f* fowl	Ps 148:10	3671
by wandering, as the swallow by *f*	Prov 26:2	5774
fruit shall be a fiery *f* serpent	Is 14:29	5774
fiery *f* serpent, they will carry	Is 30:6	5774
As birds *f*, so will the LORD	Is 31:5	5774
and looked, and behold a *f* roll	Zec 5:1	5774
And I answered, I see a *f* roll	Zec 5:2	5774
fourth beast was like a *f* eagle	Rev 4:7	4072
heard an angel *f* through the	Rev 8:13	4072

FOAL

Binding his *f* unto the vine, and	Gen 49:11	5895
and upon a colt the *f* of an ass	Zec 9:9	1121
an ass, and a colt the *f* of an ass	Mt 21:5	5207

FOALS

bulls, twenty she asses, and ten *f*	Gen 32:15	5895

FOAM

cut off as the *f* upon the water	Hos 10:7	7110

FOAMETH

and he *f*, and gnasheth with his	Mk 9:18	875
and it teareth him that he *f* again	Lk 9:39	876

FOAMING

fell on the ground, and wallowed *f*	Mk 9:20	875
of the sea, *f* out their own shame	Jude 13	1890

FODDER

or loweth the ox over his *f*	Job 6:5	1098

FOES

to be destroyed before thy *f*	1Chr 21:12	6862
and slew of their *f* seventy	Est 9:16	8130
wicked, even mine enemies and my *f*	Ps 27:2	341
hast not made my *f* to rejoice	Ps 30:1	341
beat down his *f* before his face	Ps 89:23	6862
a man's *f* shall be they of his	Mt 10:36	2190
Until I make thy *f* thy footstool	Acts 2:35	2190

FOLD

the shepherds make their *f* there	Is 13:20	7257
And Sharon shall be a *f* of flocks	Is 65:10	5116
of Israel shall their *f* be	Eze 34:14	5116
there shall they lie in a good *f*	Eze 34:14	5116
the flock in the midst of their *f*	Mic 2:12	1699
flock shall be cut off from the *f*	Hab 3:17	4356
I have, which are not of this *f*	Jn 10:16	833
and there shall be one *f*, and one	Jn 10:16	4167
as a vesture shalt thou *f* them up	Heb 1:12	1667

FOLDEN

For while they be *f* together as	Nah 1:10	5440

FOLDETH

The fool *f* his hands together, and	Eccl 4:5	2263

FOLDING

two leaves of the one door were *f*	1Kin 6:34	1550
leaves of the other door were *f*	1Kin 6:34	1550
a little *f* of the hands to sleep	Prov 6:10	2264
a little *f* of the hands to sleep	Prov 24:33	2264

FOLDS

little ones, and *f* for your sheep	Num 32:24	1448
and *f* of sheep	Num 32:36	1448
house, nor he goats out of thy *f*	Ps 50:9	4356
will bring them again to their *f*	Jer 23:3	5116
for shepherds, and *f* for flocks	Zeph 2:6	1448

FOLK

some of the *f* that are with me	Gen 33:15	5971
The conies are but a feeble *f*	Prov 30:26	5971
the *f* in the fire, and they shall	Jer 51:58	3816
laid his hands upon a few sick *f*	Mk 6:5	
a great multitude of impotent *f*	Jn 5:3	

FOLKS

unto Jerusalem, bringing sick *f*	Acts 5:16	

FOLLOW

be willing to *f* me unto this land	Gen 24:5	3212,310
will not be willing to *f* thee	Gen 24:8	3212,310
the woman will not *f* me	Gen 24:39	3212,310
his steward, Up, *f* after the men	Gen 44:4	7291
and all the people that *f* thee	Ex 11:8	7272
heart, that he shall *f* after them	Ex 14:4	7291
Egyptians, and they shall *f* them	Ex 14:17	310
from her, and yet no mischief *f*	Ex 21:22	1961
And if any mischief *f*, then thou	Ex 21:23	1961
Thou shalt not *f* a multitude to	Ex 23:2	1961,310
is altogether just shalt thou *f*	Deut 16:20	7291
of the Lord, if the thing *f* not	Deut 18:22	1961
And he said unto them, *F* after me	Judg 3:28	7291
bread unto the people that *f* me	Judg 8:5	7272
hearts inclined to *f* Abimelech	Judg 9:3	935,310
unto the young men that *f* my lord	1Sa 25:27	1980,7272
faint that they could not *f* David	1Sa 30:21	3212,310
among the people that *f* Absalom	2Sa 17:9	310
if the Lord be God, *f* him	1Kin 18:21	3212,310
but if Baal, then *f* him	1Kin 18:21	3212,310
my mother, and then I will *f* thee	1Kin 19:20	3212,310
for all the people that *f* me	1Kin 20:10	7272
f me, and I will bring you to the	2Kin 6:19	3212,310
mercy shall *f* me all the days of	Ps 23:6	7291
because I *f* the thing that good	Ps 38:20	7291
f her shall be brought unto thee	Ps 45:14	310

the upright in heart shall *f* it	Ps 94:15	310
draw nigh that *f* after mischief	Ps 119:150	7291
that they may *f* strong drink	Is 5:11	7291
ye that *f* after righteousness, ye	Is 51:1	7291
from being a pastor to *f* thee	Jer 17:16	310
shall *f* close after you there in	Jer 42:16	1692
that *f* their own spirit, and have	Eze 13:3	1980,310
she shall *f* after her lovers, but	Hos 2:7	7291
if we *f* on to know the Lord	Hos 6:3	7291
***F* me, and I will make you fishers**	Mt 4:19	1205,3694
I will *f* thee whithersoever thou	Mt 8:19	190
But Jesus said unto him, *F* me	Mt 8:22	190
and he saith unto him, *F* me	Mt 9:9	190
and take up his cross, and *f* me	Mt 16:24	190
and come and *f* me	Mt 19:21	190
of custom, and said unto him, *F* me	Mk 2:14	190
And he suffered no man to *f* him	Mk 5:37	4870
and his disciples *f* him	Mk 6:1	190
and take up his cross, and *f* me	Mk 8:34	190
come, take up the cross, and *f* me	Mk 10:21	190
bearing a pitcher of water: *f* him	Mk 14:13	190
signs shall *f* them that believe	Mk 16:17	3877
and he said unto him, *F* me	Lk 5:27	190
take up his cross daily, and *f* me	Lk 9:23	190
I will *f* thee whithersoever thou	Lk 9:57	190
And he said unto another, *F* me	Lk 9:59	190
also said, Lord, I will *f* thee	Lk 9:61	190
go not after them, nor *f* them	Lk 17:23	1377
in heaven: and come, *f* me	Lk 18:22	190
f him into the house where he	Lk 22:10	190
were about him saw what would *f*	Lk 22:49	2071
Philip, and saith unto him, *F* me	Jn 1:43	190
before them, and the sheep *f* him	Jn 10:4	190
And a stranger will they not *f*	Jn 10:5	190
and I know them, and they *f* me	Jn 10:27	190
If any man serve me, let him *f* me	Jn 12:26	190
I go, thou canst not *f* me now	Jn 13:36	190
but thou shalt *f* me afterwards	Jn 13:36	190
Lord, why cannot I *f* thee now	Jn 13:37	190
this, he saith unto him, *F* me	Jn 21:19	190
is that to thee? *f* thou me	Jn 21:22	190
from Samuel and those that *f* after	Acts 3:24	2517
thy garment about thee, and *f* me	Acts 12:8	190
Let us therefore *f* after the	Rom 14:19	1377
F after charity, and desire	1Cor 14:1	1377
but I *f* after, if that I may	Phil 3:12	1377
but ever *f* that which is good,	1Th 5:15	1377
know how ye ought to *f* us	2Th 3:7	3401
an ensample unto you to *f* us	2Th 3:9	3401
and some men they *f* after	1Ti 5:24	1872
f after righteousness, godliness,	1Ti 6:11	1377
but *f* righteousness, faith,	2Ti 2:22	1377
F peace with all men, and holiness	Heb 12:14	1377
whose faith *f*, considering the	Heb 13:7	3401
and the glory that should *f*	1Pet 1:11	3326,5023
that ye should *f* his steps	1Pet 2:21	1872
many shall *f* their pernicious	2Pet 2:2	1811
f not that which is evil, but	3Jn 11	3401
These are they which *f* the Lamb	Rev 14:4	190
and their works do *f* them	Rev 14:13	190

FOLLOWED

upon the camels, and *f* the man	Gen 24:61	3212,310
all that *f* the droves, saying, On	Gen 32:19	1980,310
hath *f* me fully, will I bring	Num 14:24	310
and the elders of Israel *f* him	Num 16:25	3212,310
because they have not wholly *f* me	Num 32:11	310
for they have wholly *f* the Lord	Num 32:12	310
because he hath wholly *f* the Lord	Deut 1:36	310
for all the men that *f* Baal-peor	Deut 4:3	1980,310
the covenant of the Lord *f* them	Josh 6:8	1980,310
but I wholly *f* the Lord my God	Josh 14:8	310
hast wholly *f* the Lord my God	Josh 14:9	310
wholly *f* the Lord God of Israel	Josh 14:14	310
f other gods, of the gods of the	Judg 2:12	3212,310
and light persons, which *f* him	Judg 9:4	3212,310
f Abimelech, and put them to the	Judg 9:49	3212,310
and all the people *f* him trembling	1Sa 13:7	310
even they also *f* hard after them	1Sa 14:22	1692
went and *f* Saul to the battle	1Sa 17:13	1980,310
and the three eldest *f* Saul	1Sa 17:14	1980,310
the Philistines *f* hard upon Saul	1Sa 31:2	1692
horsemen *f* hard after him	2Sa 1:6	1692
But the house of Judah *f* David	2Sa 2:10	1961,310
And king David himself *f* the bier	2Sa 3:31	1980,310
there *f* him a mess of meat from	2Sa 11:8	3318,310
saw that his counsel was not *f*	2Sa 17:23	6213
f Sheba the son of Bichri	2Sa 20:2	310
none that *f* the house of David	1Kin 12:20	310
who *f* me with all his heart, to	1Kin 14:8	1980,310
half of the people *f* Tibni the	1Kin 16:21	1961,310

and half *f* Omri	1Kin 16:21	310
But the people that *f* Omri	1Kin 16:22	310
that *f* Tibni the son of Ginath	1Kin 16:22	310
the LORD, and thou hast *f* Baalim	1Kin 18:18	3212,310
city, and the army which *f* them	1Kin 20:19	310
and for the cattle that *f* them	2Kin 3:9	7272
And he arose, and *f* her	2Kin 4:30	3112,310
So Gehazi *f* after Naaman	2Kin 5:21	7291
Jehu *f* after him, and said, Smite	2Kin 9:27	7291
f the sins of Jeroboam the son of	2Kin 13:2	3212,310
they *f* vanity, and became vain	2Kin 17:15	3212,310
the Philistines *f* hard after Saul	1Chr 10:2	1692
the men of the guard which *f* me	Neh 4:23	310
players on instruments *f* after	Ps 68:25	
whither the head looked they *f* it	Eze 10:11	3212,310
the LORD took me as I *f* the flock	Amos 7:15	310
left their nets, and *f* him	Mt 4:20	190
ship and their father, and *f* him	Mt 4:22	190
there *f* him great multitudes of	Mt 4:25	190
mountain, great multitudes *f* him	Mt 8:1	190
marvelled, and said to them that *f*	Mt 8:10	190
into a ship, his disciples *f* him	Mt 8:23	190
And he arose, and *f* him	Mt 9:9	190
f him, and so did his disciples	Mt 9:19	190
thence, two blind men *f* him	Mt 9:27	190
and great multitudes *f* him	Mt 12:15	190
they *f* him on foot out of the	Mt 14:13	190
And great multitudes *f* him	Mt 19:2	190
we have forsaken all, and *f* thee	Mt 19:27	190
unto you, That ye which have *f* me	Mt 19:28	190
Jericho, a great multitude *f* him	Mt 20:29	190
received sight, and they *f* him	Mt 20:34	190
that went before, and that *f*	Mt 21:9	190
But Peter *f* him afar off unto the	Mt 26:58	190
which *f* Jesus from Galilee,	Mt 27:55	190
that *f* the day of the preparation	Mt 27:62	2076,3326
they forsook their nets, and *f* him	Mk 1:18	190
that were with him *f* after him	Mk 1:36	2614
And he arose and *f* him	Mk 2:14	190
there were many, and they *f* him	Mk 2:15	190
multitude from Galilee *f* him	Mk 3:7	190
and much people *f* him, and thronged	Mk 5:24	190
we have left all, and have *f* thee	Mk 10:28	190
and as they *f*, they were afraid	Mk 10:32	190
his sight, and *f* Jesus in the way	Mk 10:52	190
that went before, and they that *f*	Mk 11:9	190
there *f* him a certain young man	Mk 14:51	190
Peter *f* him afar off, even into	Mk 14:54	190
f him, and ministered unto him	Mk 15:41	190
land, they forsook all, and *f* him	Lk 5:11	190
And he left all, rose up, and *f* him	Lk 5:28	190
said unto the people that *f* him	Lk 7:9	190
people, when they knew it, *f* him	Lk 9:11	190
Lo, we have left all, and *f* thee	Lk 18:28	190
sight, and *f* him, glorifying God	Lk 18:43	190
and his disciples also *f* him	Lk 22:39	190
And Peter *f* afar off	Lk 22:54	190
there *f* him a great company of	Lk 23:27	190
the women that *f* him from Galilee	Lk 23:49	4870
f after, and beheld the sepulchre,	Lk 23:55	2628
heard him speak, and they *f* Jesus	Jn 1:37	190
f him, was Andrew, Simon Peter's	Jn 1:40	190
And a great multitude *f* him	Jn 6:2	190
f her, saying, She goeth unto the	Jn 11:31	190
And Simon Peter *f* Jesus, and so did	Jn 18:15	190
And he went out, and *f* him	Acts 12:9	190
and religious proselytes *f* Paul	Acts 13:43	190
The same *f* Paul and us, and cried,	Acts 16:17	2628
multitude of the people *f* after	Acts 21:36	190
which *f* not after righteousness	Rom 9:30	1377
Israel, which *f* after the law of	Rom 9:31	1377
that spiritual Rock that *f* them	1Cor 10:4	190
have diligently *f* every good work	1Ti 5:10	1872
For we have not *f* cunningly	2Pet 1:16	1811
him was Death, and Hell *f* with him	Rev 6:8	190
angel sounded, and there *f* hail	Rev 8:7	1096
there *f* another angel, saying,	Rev 14:8	190
And the third angel *f* them	Rev 14:9	190
in heaven *f* him upon white horses	Rev 19:14	190

FOLLOWEDST

inasmuch as thou *f* not young men	Ruth 3:10	3212,310

FOLLOWERS

I beseech you, be ye *f* of me	1Cor 4:16	3402
Be ye *f* of me, even as I also am	1Cor 11:1	3402
Be ye therefore *f* of God, as dear	Eph 5:1	3402
be *f* together of me, and mark them	Phil 3:17	4831
And ye became *f* of us, and of the	1Th 1:6	3402
became *f* of the churches of God	1Th 2:14	3402
but *f* of them who through faith	Heb 6:12	3402
if ye be *f* of that which is good	1Pet 3:13	3402

FOLLOWETH

him that *f* her kill with the	2Kin 11:15	935,310
and whoso *f* her, let him be slain	2Chr 23:14	935,310
My soul *f* hard after thee	Ps 63:8	1692
but he that *f* vain persons is	Prov 12:11	7291
him that *f* after righteousness	Prov 15:9	7291
He that *f* after righteousness and	Prov 21:21	7291
but he that *f* after vain persons	Prov 28:19	7291
loveth gifts, and *f* after rewards	Is 1:23	7291
whereas none *f* thee to commit	Eze 16:34	310
on wind, and *f* after the east wind	Hos 12:1	7291
f after me, is not worthy of me	Mt 10:38	190
in thy name, and he *f* not us	Mk 9:38	190
forbad him, because he *f* not us	Mk 9:38	190
him, because he *f* not with us	Lk 9:49	190
he that *f* me shall not walk in	Jn 8:12	190

FOLLOWING

land by reason of that famine *f*	Gen 41:31	310,3651
will turn away thy son from *f* me	Deut 7:4	310
that thou be not snared by *f* them	Deut 12:30	310
away this day from *f* the LORD	Josh 22:16	310
away this day from *f* the LORD	Josh 22:18	310
an altar to turn from *f* the LORD	Josh 22:23	310
and turn this day from *f* the LORD	Josh 22:29	310
in *f* other gods to serve them, and	Judg 2:19	3212,310
or to return from *f* after thee	Ruth 1:16	
you continue *f* the LORD your God	1Sa 12:14	310
turn not aside from *f* the LORD	1Sa 12:20	310
went up from *f* the Philistines	1Sa 14:46	310
for he is turned back from *f* me	1Sa 15:11	310
returned from *f* the Philistines	1Sa 24:1	310
hand nor to the left from *f* Abner	2Sa 2:19	310
not turn aside from *f* of him	2Sa 2:21	310
Asahel, Turn thee aside from *f* me	2Sa 2:22	310
return from *f* their brethren	2Sa 2:26	310
up every one from *f* his brother	2Sa 2:27	310
And Joab returned from *f* Abner	2Sa 2:30	310
from *f* the sheep, to be ruler	2Sa 7:8	310
they *f* Adonijah helped him	1Kin 1:7	310
if ye shall at all turn from *f* me	1Kin 9:6	310
he did very abominably in *f* idols	1Kin 21:26	3212,310
drave Israel from *f* the LORD	2Kin 17:21	310
LORD, and departed not from *f* him	2Kin 18:6	310
sheepcote, even from *f* the sheep	1Chr 17:7	310
f the LORD they made a conspiracy	2Chr 25:27	310
they departed not from *f* the LORD	2Chr 34:33	310
may tell it to the generation *f*	Ps 48:13	314
From *f* the ewes great with young	Ps 78:71	310
in the generation *f* let them	Ps 109:13	312
confirming the word with signs *f*	Mk 16:20	1872
day, and to morrow, and the day *f*	Lk 13:33	2192
Then Jesus turned, and saw them *f*	Jn 1:38	190
The day *f* Jesus would go forth	Jn 1:43	1887
The day *f*, when the people which	Jn 6:22	1887
Then cometh Simon Peter *f* him	Jn 20:6	190
the disciple whom Jesus loved *f*	Jn 21:20	190
the day *f* unto Rhodes, and from	Acts 21:1	1836
the day *f* Paul went in with us	Acts 21:18	1966
the night *f* the Lord stood by him	Acts 23:11	
f the way of Balaam the son of	2Pet 2:15	1811

FOLLY

because he had wrought *f* in	Gen 34:7	5039
she hath wrought *f* in Israel	Deut 22:21	5039
he hath wrought *f* in Israel	Josh 7:15	5039
into mine house, do not this *f*	Judg 19:23	5039
committed lewdness and *f* in Israel	Judg 20:6	5039
according to all the *f* that they	Judg 20:10	5039
is his name, and *f* is with him	1Sa 25:25	5039
do not thou this *f*	2Sa 13:12	5039
and his angels he charged with *f*	Job 4:18	8417
yet God layeth not *f* to them	Job 24:12	8604
lest I deal with you after your *f*	Job 42:8	5039
This their way is their *f*	Ps 49:13	3689
but let them not turn again to *f*	Ps 85:8	3690
of his *f* he shall go astray	Prov 5:23	200
but a fool layeth open his *f*	Prov 13:16	200
but the *f* of fools is deceit	Prov 14:8	200
The simple inherit *f*	Prov 14:18	200
but the foolishness of fools is *f*	Prov 14:24	200
is hasty of spirit exalteth *f*	Prov 14:29	200
F is joy to him that is destitute	Prov 15:21	200
but the instruction of fools is *f*	Prov 16:22	200
man, rather than a fool in his *f*	Prov 17:12	200
before he heareth it, it is *f*	Prov 18:13	200
not a fool according to his *f*	Prov 26:4	200
Answer a fool according to his *f*	Prov 26:5	200
so a fool returneth to his *f*	Prov 26:11	200
wisdom, and to know madness and *f*	Eccl 1:17	5531
and to lay hold on *f*, till I might	Eccl 2:3	5531
behold wisdom, and madness, and *f*	Eccl 2:12	5531

F

I saw that wisdom excelleth _f_	Eccl 2:13	5531
and to know the wickedness of _f_	Eccl 7:25	3689
so doth a little _f_ him that is in	Eccl 10:1	5531
_F_ is set in great dignity, and the	Eccl 10:6	5529
and every mouth speaketh _f_	Is 9:17	5039
I have seen _f_ in the prophets of	Jer 23:13	8604
bear with me a little in my _f_	2Cor 11:1	877
for their _f_ shall be manifest	2Ti 3:9	454

FOOD

to the sight, and good for _f_	Gen 2:9	3978
saw that the tree was good for _f_	Gen 3:6	3978
unto thee of all _f_ that is eaten	Gen 6:21	3978
and it shall be for _f_ for thee	Gen 6:21	402
let them gather all the _f_ of	Gen 41:35	400
and let them keep _f_ in the cities	Gen 41:35	400
that _f_ shall be for store to the	Gen 41:36	400
up all the _f_ of the seven years	Gen 41:48	400
laid up the _f_ in the cities	Gen 41:48	400
the _f_ of the field, which was	Gen 41:48	400
From the land of Canaan to buy _f_	Gen 42:7	400
but to buy _f_ are thy servants	Gen 42:10	400
take _f_ for the famine of your	Gen 42:33	
them, Go again, buy us a little _f_	Gen 43:2	400
us, we will go down and buy thee _f_	Gen 43:4	400
down at the first time to buy _f_	Gen 43:20	400
down in our hands to buy _f_	Gen 43:22	400
Fill the men's sacks with _f_	Gen 44:1	400
Go again, and buy us a little _f_	Gen 44:25	400
seed of the field, and for your _f_	Gen 47:24	400
for _f_ for your little ones	Gen 47:24	398
her _f_, her raiment, and her duty	Ex 21:10	7607
it is the _f_ of the offering made	Lev 3:11	3899
it is the _f_ of the offering made	Lev 3:16	3899
planted all manner of trees for _f_	Lev 19:23	3978
because it is his _f_	Lev 22:7	
the stranger, in giving him _f_	Deut 10:18	3899
that eateth any _f_ until evening	1Sa 14:24	3899
none of the people tasted any _f_	1Sa 14:24	3899
man that eateth any _f_ this day	1Sa 14:28	3899
master's son may have _f_ to eat	2Sa 9:10	3899
in giving _f_ for my household	1Kin 5:9	3899
of wheat for _f_ to his household	1Kin 5:11	4361
mouth more than my necessary _f_	Job 23:12	
wilderness yieldeth _f_ for them	Job 24:5	
Who provideth for the raven his _f_	Job 38:41	6718
the mountains bring him forth _f_	Job 40:20	944
Man did eat angels' _f_	Ps 78:25	3899
bring forth _f_ out of the earth	Ps 104:14	3899
Who giveth _f_ to all flesh	Ps 136:25	3899
which giveth _f_ to the hungry	Ps 146:7	3899
He giveth to the beast his _f_	Ps 147:9	3899
gathereth her _f_ in the harvest	Prov 6:8	3978
Much _f_ is in the tillage of the	Prov 13:23	400
have goats' milk enough for thy _f_	Prov 27:27	3899
for thy _f_ of thy household, and	Prov 27:27	3899
sweeping rain which leaveth no _f_	Prov 28:3	3899
feed me with _f_ convenient for me	Prov 30:8	3899
she bringeth her _f_ from afar	Prov 31:14	3899
have diminished thine ordinary _f_	Eze 16:27	
_f_ unto them that serve the city	Eze 48:18	3899
filling our hearts with _f_	Acts 14:17	5160
both minister bread for your _f_	2Cor 9:10	1035
And having _f_ and raiment let us be	1Ti 6:8	1304
be naked, and destitute of daily _f_	Jas 2:15	5160

FOOL

behold, I have played the _f_	1Sa 26:21	5528
and said, Died Abner as a _f_ dieth	2Sa 3:33	5036
The _f_ hath said in his heart	Ps 14:1	5036
that wise men die, likewise the _f_	Ps 49:10	3684
The _f_ hath said in his heart	Ps 53:1	5036
neither doth a _f_ understand this	Ps 92:6	3684
or as a _f_ to the correction of	Prov 7:22	191
but a prating _f_ shall fall	Prov 10:8	191
but a prating _f_ shall fall	Prov 10:10	191
that uttereth a slander, is a _f_	Prov 10:18	3684
is as sport to a _f_ to do mischief	Prov 10:23	3684
the _f_ shall be servant to the	Prov 11:29	191
The way of a _f_ is right in his	Prov 12:15	191
but a _f_ layeth open his folly	Prov 13:16	3684
but the _f_ rageth, and is confident	Prov 14:16	3684
A _f_ despiseth his father's	Prov 15:5	191
Excellent speech becometh not a _f_	Prov 17:7	5036
than an hundred stripes into a _f_	Prov 17:10	3684
man, rather than a _f_ in his folly	Prov 17:12	3684
in the hand of a _f_ to get wisdom	Prov 17:16	3684
He that begetteth a _f_ doeth it to	Prov 17:21	3684
and the father of a _f_ hath no joy	Prov 17:21	5036
but the eyes of a _f_ are in the	Prov 17:24	3684
Even a _f_, when he holdeth his	Prov 17:28	191
A _f_ hath no delight in	Prov 18:2	3684

perverse in his lips, and is a _f_	Prov 19:1	3684
Delight is not seemly for a _f_	Prov 19:10	3684
but every _f_ will be meddling	Prov 20:3	191
Speak not in the ears of a _f_	Prov 23:9	3684
Wisdom is too high for a _f_	Prov 24:7	191
so honour is not seemly for a _f_	Prov 26:1	3684
Answer not a _f_ according to his	Prov 26:4	3684
Answer a _f_ according to his folly	Prov 26:5	3684
hand of a _f_ cutteth off the feet	Prov 26:6	3684
is he that giveth honour to a _f_	Prov 26:8	3684
all things both rewardeth the _f_	Prov 26:10	3684
so a _f_ returneth to his folly	Prov 26:11	3684
is more hope of a _f_ than of him	Prov 26:12	3684
Though thou shouldest bray a _f_ in	Prov 27:22	191
trusteth in his own heart is a _f_	Prov 28:26	3684
A _f_ uttereth all his mind	Prov 29:11	3684
is more hope of a _f_ than of him	Prov 29:20	3684
a _f_ when he is filled with meat	Prov 30:22	5030
but the _f_ walketh in darkness	Eccl 2:14	3684
heart, As it happeneth to the _f_	Eccl 2:15	3684
wise more than of the _f_ for ever	Eccl 2:16	3684
the wise man? as the _f_	Eccl 2:16	3684
he shall be a wise man or a _f_	Eccl 2:19	5530
The _f_ foldeth his hands together,	Eccl 4:5	3684
hath the wise more than the _f_	Eccl 6:8	3684
pot, so is the laughter of the _f_	Eccl 7:6	3684
when he that is a _f_ walketh by	Eccl 10:3	5530
saith to every one that he is a _f_	Eccl 10:3	5530
but the lips of a _f_ will swallow	Eccl 10:12	3684
A _f_ also is full of words	Eccl 10:14	5536
days, and at his end shall be a _f_	Jer 17:11	5036
the prophet is a _f_, the spiritual	Hos 9:7	191
but whosoever shall say, Thou _f_	Mt 5:22	_3474_
But God said unto him, Thou _f_	Lk 12:20	876
in this world, let him become a _f_	1Cor 3:18	_3474_
Thou _f_, that which thou sowest is	1Cor 15:36	876
again, Let no man think me a _f_	2Cor 11:16	876
yet as a _f_ receive me, that I may	2Cor 11:16	876
(I speak as a _f_) I am more	2Cor 11:23	_3912_
to glory, I shall not be a _f_	2Cor 12:6	876
I am become a _f_ in glorying	2Cor 12:11	876

FOOLISH

the Lord, O _f_ people and unwise	Deut 32:6	5036
them to anger with a _f_ nation	Deut 32:21	5036
as one of the _f_ women speaketh	Job 2:10	5039
For wrath killeth the _f_ man	Job 5:2	191
I have seen the _f_ taking root	Job 5:3	191
The _f_ shall not stand in thy	Ps 5:5	1984
make me not the reproach of the _f_	Ps 39:8	5036
For I was envious at the _f_	Ps 73:3	1984
So _f_ was I, and ignorant	Ps 73:22	1198
that the _f_ people have blasphemed	Ps 74:18	5036
remember how the _f_ man	Ps 74:22	5036
Forsake the _f_, and live	Prov 9:6	6612
A _f_ woman is clamorous	Prov 9:13	3687
but a _f_ son is the heaviness of	Prov 10:1	3684
of the _f_ is near destruction	Prov 10:14	191
but the _f_ plucketh it down with	Prov 14:1	200
mouth of the _f_ is a rod of pride	Prov 14:3	191
Go from the presence of a _f_ man	Prov 14:7	3684
the heart of the _f_ doeth not so	Prov 15:7	3684
but a _f_ man despiseth his mother	Prov 15:20	3684
A _f_ son is a grief to his father	Prov 17:25	3684
A _f_ son is the calamity of his	Prov 19:13	3684
but a _f_ man spendeth it up	Prov 21:20	3684
wise man contendeth with a _f_ man	Prov 29:9	191
_f_ king, who will no more be	Eccl 4:13	3684
much wicked, neither be thou _f_	Eccl 7:17	5530
The labour of the _f_ wearieth	Eccl 10:15	3684
and maketh their knowledge _f_	Is 44:25	5528
For my people is _f_, they have not	Jer 4:22	191
these are poor; they are _f_	Jer 5:4	2973
now this, O _f_ people, and without	Jer 5:21	5530
they are altogether brutish and _f_	Jer 10:8	3688
seen vain and _f_ things for thee	Lam 2:14	8602
Woe unto the _f_ prophets, that	Eze 13:3	5036
the instruments of a _f_ shepherd	Zec 11:15	196
shall be likened unto a _f_ man	Mt 7:26	_3474_
of them were wise, and five were _f_	Mt 25:2	_3474_
They that were _f_ took their lamps	Mt 25:3	_3474_
the _f_ said unto the wise, Give us	Mt 25:8	_3474_
their _f_ heart was darkened	Rom 1:21	801
An instructor of the _f_, a teacher	Rom 2:20	878
by a _f_ nation I will anger you	Rom 10:19	801
hath not God made _f_ the wisdom of	1Cor 1:20	_3471_
But God hath chosen the _f_ things	1Cor 1:27	_3474_
O _f_ Galatians, who hath bewitched	Gal 3:1	453
Are ye so _f_?	Gal 3:3	453
nor _f_ talking, nor jesting, which	Eph 5:4	_3473_
and a snare, and into many _f_	1Ti 6:9	453

But *f* and unlearned questions .... 2Ti 2:23 — 3474
ourselves also were sometimes *f* .... Titus 3:3 — 453
But avoid *f* questions, and .... Titus 3:9 — 3474
to silence the ignorance of *f* men .... 1Pet 2:15 — 878

FOOLISHLY

thou hast now done *f* in so doing .... Gen 31:28 — 5528
upon us, wherein we have done *f* .... Num 12:11 — 2973
said to Saul, Thou hast done *f* .... 1Sa 13:13 — 5528
for I have done very *f* .... 2Sa 24:10 — 5528
for I have done very *f* .... 1Chr 21:8 — 5528
Herein thou hast done *f* .... 2Chr 16:9 — 5528
Job sinned not, nor charged God *f* .... Job 1:22 — 8604
I said unto the fools, Deal not *f* .... Ps 75:4 — 1984
He that is soon angry dealeth *f* .... Prov 14:17 — 200
If thou hast done *f* in lifting up .... Prov 30:32 — 5034
after the Lord, but as it were *f* .... 2Cor 11:17 — 1722,877
any is bold, (I speak *f*,) I am .... 2Cor 11:21 — 1722,877

FOOLISHNESS

the counsel of Ahithophel into *f* .... 2Sa 15:31 — 5528
and are corrupt because of my *f* .... Ps 38:5 — 200
O God, thou knowest my *f* .... Ps 69:5 — 200
the heart of fools proclaimeth *f* .... Prov 12:23 — 200
but the *f* of fools is folly .... Prov 14:24 — 200
the mouth of fools poureth out *f* .... Prov 15:2 — 200
the mouth of fools feedeth on *f* .... Prov 15:14 — 200
The *f* of man perverteth his way .... Prov 19:3 — 200
F is bound in the heart of a .... Prov 22:15 — 200
The thought of *f* is sin .... Prov 24:9 — 200
will not his *f* depart from him .... Prov 27:22 — 200
wickedness of folly, even of *f* .... Eccl 7:25 — 5531
of the words of his mouth is *f* .... Eccl 10:13 — 5531
an evil eye, blasphemy, pride, *f* ...... Mk 7:22 — 877
cross is to them that perish *f* .... 1Cor 1:18 — 3472
it pleased God by the *f* of .... 1Cor 1:21 — 3472
and unto the Greeks *f* .... 1Cor 1:23 — 3472
Because the *f* of God is wiser .... 1Cor 1:25 — 3474
for they are *f* unto him .... 1Cor 2:14 — 3472
of this world is *f* with God .... 1Cor 3:19 — 3472

FOOL'S

A *f* wrath is presently known .... Prov 12:16 — 191
A *f* lips enter into contention, ... Prov 18:6 — 3684
A *f* mouth is his destruction, and .... Prov 18:7 — 3684
the ass, and a rod for the *f* back .... Prov 26:3 — 3684
but a *f* wrath is heavier than .... Prov 27:3 — 191
a *f* voice is known by multitude .... Eccl 5:3 — 3684
but a *f* heart at his left .... Eccl 10:2 — 3684

FOOLS

be as one of the *f* in Israel .... 2Sa 13:13 — 5036
spoiled, and maketh the judges *f* .... Job 12:17 — 1984
They were children of *f*, yea, ... Job 30:8 — 5036
I said unto the *f*, Deal not .... Ps 75:4 — 1984
and ye *f*, when will ye be wise .... Ps 94:8 — 3684
F, because of their transgression .... Ps 107:17 — 191
but *f* despise wisdom and .... Prov 1:7 — 191
scorning, and *f* hate knowledge .... Prov 1:22 — 3684
the prosperity of *f* shall destroy .... Prov 1:32 — 3684
shame shall be the promotion of *f* .... Prov 3:35 — 3684
and, ye *f*, be ye of an .... Prov 8:5 — 3684
but *f* die for want of wisdom .... Prov 10:21 — 191
but the heart of *f* proclaimeth .... Prov 12:23 — 3684
to *f* to depart from evil .... Prov 13:19 — 3684
companion of *f* shall be destroyed .... Prov 13:20 — 3684
but the folly of *f* is deceit .... Prov 14:8 — 3684
F make a mock at sin .... Prov 14:9 — 191
but the foolishness of *f* is folly .... Prov 14:24 — 3684
in the midst of *f* is made known .... Prov 14:33 — 3684
but the mouth of *f* poureth out .... Prov 15:2 — 3684
but the mouth of *f* feedeth on .... Prov 15:14 — 3684
but the instruction of *f* is folly .... Prov 16:22 — 191
and stripes for the back of *f* .... Prov 19:29 — 3684
so is a parable in the mouth of *f* .... Prov 26:7 — 3684
so is a parable in the mouth of *f* .... Prov 26:9 — 3684
than to give the sacrifice of *f* .... Eccl 5:1 — 3684
for he hath no pleasure in *f* .... Eccl 5:4 — 3684
but the heart of *f* is in the .... Eccl 7:4 — 3684
for a man to hear the song of *f* .... Eccl 7:5 — 3684
anger resteth in the bosom of *f* .... Eccl 7:9 — 3684
cry of him that ruleth among *f* .... Eccl 9:17 — 3684
Surely the princes of Zoan are *f* .... Is 19:11 — 191
The princes of Zoan are become *f* .... Is 19:13 — 2973
the wayfaring men, though *f* .... Is 35:8 — 191
Ye *f* and blind .... Mt 23:17 — 3474
Ye *f* and blind .... Mt 23:19 — 3474
Ye *f*, did not he that made that .... Lk 11:40 — 878
Then he said unto them, O *f* .... Lk 24:25 — 453
to be wise, they became *f* .... Rom 1:22 — 3471
We are *f* for Christ's sake, but .... 1Cor 4:10 — 3474
For ye suffer *f* gladly, seeing ye .... 2Cor 11:19 — 878
ye walk circumspectly, not as *f* .... Eph 5:15 — 781

FOOT

no rest for the sole of her *f* .... Gen 8:9 — 7272
or *f* in all the land of Egypt .... Gen 41:44 — 7272
thousand on *f* that were men .... Ex 12:37 — 7273
tooth, hand for hand, *f* for *f*, ... Ex 21:24 — 7272
the great toe of their right *f* .... Ex 29:20 — 7272
his *f* also of brass, to wash .... Ex 30:18 — 3653
vessels, and the laver and his *f* .... Ex 30:28 — 3653
furniture, and the laver and his *f* .... Ex 31:9 — 3653
his vessels, the laver and his *f* .... Ex 35:16 — 3653
the *f* of it of brass, of the .... Ex 38:8 — 3653
his vessels, the laver and his *f* .... Ex 39:39 — 3653
shalt anoint the laver and his *f* .... Ex 40:11 — 3653
vessels, both the laver and his *f* .... Lev 8:11 — 3653
upon the great toe of his right *f* .... Lev 8:23 — 7272
from his head even to his *f* .... Lev 13:12 — 7272
upon the great toe of his right *f* .... Lev 14:14 — 7272
upon the great toe of his right *f* .... Lev 14:17 — 7272
upon the great toe of his right *f* .... Lev 14:25 — 7272
upon the great toe of his right *f* .... Lev 14:28 — 7272
Balaam's *f* against the wall .... Num 22:25 — 7272
thee, neither did thy *f* swell .... Deut 8:4 — 7272
seed, and wateredst it with thy *f* .... Deut 11:10 — 7272
tooth, hand for hand, *f* for *f* .... Deut 19:21 — 7272
and loose his shoe from off his *f* .... Deut 25:9 — 7272
from the sole of thy *f* unto the .... Deut 28:35 — 7272
sole of her *f* upon the ground for .... Deut 28:56 — 7272
shall the sole of thy *f* have rest .... Deut 28:65 — 7272
shoe is not waxen old upon thy *f* .... Deut 29:5 — 7272
their *f* shall slide in due time .... Deut 32:35 — 7272
and let him dip his *f* in oil .... Deut 33:24 — 7272
sole of your *f* shall tread upon .... Josh 1:3 — 7272
Loose thy shoe from off thy *f* .... Josh 5:15 — 7272
he was sent on *f* into the valley .... Judg 5:15 — 7272
was as light of *f* as a wild roe .... 2Sa 2:18 — 7272
from the sole of his *f* even to .... 2Sa 14:25 — 7272
fingers, and on every *f* six toes .... 2Sa 21:20 — 7272
and he trode her under *f* .... 2Kin 9:33 —
on each hand, and six on each *f* .... 1Chr 20:6 —
will I any more remove the *f* of .... 2Chr 33:8 — 7272
the sole of his *f* unto his crown .... Job 2:7 — 7272
My *f* hath held his steps, his way .... Job 23:11 — 7272
the waters forgotten of the *f* .... Job 28:4 — 7272
or if my *f* hath hasted to deceit .... Job 31:5 — 7272
that the *f* may crush them .... Job 39:15 — 7272
they hid is their own *f* taken .... Ps 9:15 — 7272
My *f* standeth in an even place .... Ps 26:12 — 7272
Let not the *f* of pride come .... Ps 36:11 — 7272
when my *f* slippeth, they magnify .... Ps 38:16 — 7272
they went through the flood on *f* .... Ps 66:6 — 7272
That thy *f* may be dipped in the .... Ps 68:23 — 7272
thou dash thy *f* against a stone .... Ps 91:12 — 7272
When I said, My *f* slippeth .... Ps 94:18 — 7272
will not suffer thy *f* to be moved .... Ps 121:3 — 7272
refrain thy *f* from their path .... Prov 1:15 — 7272
and thy *f* shall not stumble .... Prov 3:23 — 7272
shall keep thy *f* from being taken .... Prov 3:26 — 7272
remove thy *f* from evil .... Prov 4:27 — 7272
Withdraw thy *f* from thy .... Prov 25:17 — 7272
broken tooth, and a *f* out of joint .... Prov 25:19 — 7272
Keep thy *f* when thou goest to the .... Eccl 5:1 — 7272
From the sole of the *f* even unto .... Is 1:6 — 7272
my mountains tread him under *f* .... Is 14:25 — 947
meted out and trodden under *f* .... Is 18:7 — 4001
and put off thy shoe from thy *f* .... Is 20:2 — 7272
The *f* shall tread it down, even .... Is 26:6 — 7272
the east, called him to his *f* .... Is 41:2 — 7272
turn away thy *f* from the sabbath .... Is 58:13 — 7272
Withhold thy *f* from being unshod, ... Jer 2:25 — 7272
have trodden my portion under *f* .... Jer 12:10 — 947
The Lord hath trodden under *f* all .... Lam 1:15 — 5541
was like the sole of a calf's *f* .... Eze 1:7 — 7272
thine hand, and stamp with thy *f* .... Eze 6:11 — 7272
No *f* of man shall pass through it .... Eze 29:11 — 7272
nor *f* of beast shall pass through .... Eze 29:11 — 7272
neither shall the *f* of man .... Eze 32:13 — 7272
and the host to be trodden under *f* .... Dan 8:13 — 4823
he that is swift of *f* shall not .... Amos 2:15 — 7272
thou dash thy *f* against a stone .... Mt 4:6 — 4228
and to be trodden under *f* of men .... Mt 5:13 — 2662
him on *f* out of the cities .... Mt 14:13 — 3979
if thy hand or thy *f* offend thee .... Mt 18:8 — 4228
the servants, Bind him hand and *f* ...... Mt 22:13 — 4228
if thy *f* offend thee, cut it off .... Mk 9:45 — 4228
thou dash thy *f* against a stone .... Lk 4:11 — 4228
bound hand and *f* with graveclothes .... Jn 11:44 — 4228
not so much as to set his *f* on .... Acts 7:5 — 4228
If the *f* shall say, Because I am .... 1Cor 12:15 — 4228
trodden under *f* the Son of God .... Heb 10:29 — 2662
with a garment down to the *f* .... Rev 1:13 — 4158
he set his right *f* upon the sea .... Rev 10:2 — 4228

and his left *f* on the earth........................Rev 10:2
shall they tread under *f* forty ....Rev 11:2

FOOTBREADTH
land, no, not so much as a *f*..................Deut 2:5

FOOTMEN
I am, are six hundred thousand *f*...........Num 11:21   7273
thousand *f* that drew sword.............Judg 20:2   376,7273
fell of Israel thirty thousand *f*.................1Sa 4:10   7273
in Telaim, two hundred thousand *f*.........1Sa 15:4   7273
unto the *f* that stood about him..............1Sa 22:17   7328
horsemen, and twenty thousand *f*...2Sa 8:4   376,7273
of Zoba, twenty thousand *f*....................2Sa 10:6   7273
an hundred thousand *f* in one day..........1Kin 20:29   7273
ten chariots, and ten thousand *f*...........2Kin 13:7   7273
horsemen, and twenty thousand *f*...1Chr 18:4   376,7273
in chariots, and forty thousand *f* 1Chr 19:18   376,7273
If thou hast run with the *f*........................Jer 12:5   7273

FOOTSTEPS
in thy paths, that my *f* slip not ....Ps 17:5   6471
waters, and thy *f* are not known ....Ps 77:19   6119
the *f* of thine anointed ....Ps 89:51   6119
way forth by the *f* of the flock ....Song 1:8   6119

FOOTSTOOL
for the *f* of our God, and had made 1Chr 28:2   1916,7272
with a *f* of gold, which were.....................2Chr 9:18   3534
our God, and worship at his *f* ....Ps 99:5   1916,7272
until I make thine enemies thy *f*.....Ps 110:1   1916,7272
we will worship at his *f*....................Ps 132:7   1916,7272
my throne, and the earth is my *f*......Is 66:1   1916,7272
remembered not his *f* in the day .....Lam 2:1   1916,7272
for it is his *f*....................................Mt 5:35   5286,3588,4228
till I make thine enemies thy Mt 22:44   5286,3588,4228
till I make thine enemies thy *f* Mk 12:36   5286,3588,4228
Till I make thine enemies thy
***f*..**Lk 20:43   5286,3588,4228
Until I make thy foes thy *f*.........Acts 2:35   5286,3588,4228
my throne, and earth is my *f*.....Acts 7:49   5286,3588,4228
I make thine enemies thy *f* ......Heb 1:13   5286,3588,4228
till his enemies be made his *f*..Heb 10:13   5286,3588,4228
there, or sit here under my *f*......................Jas 2:3   5286

FOR See APPENDIX.

FORASMUCH
F as God hath shewed thee all ....Gen 41:39   310
f as thou knowest how we are.. Num 10:31   3588,5921,3651
f as he hath no part nor ....Deut 12:12   3588
f as the Lord hath said unto you, ...Deut 17:16
f as the Lord hath blessed me ....Josh 17:14   5704
f as the Lord hath taken ....Judg 11:36   310,834
f as we have sworn both of us in 1Sa 20:42
f as when the Lord had delivered... 1Sa 24:18   854,834
f as my lord the king is come 2Sa 19:30   310,834
F as this is done of thee, and.................1Kin 11:11   3282,834
F as thou hast disobeyed the 1Kin 13:21   3282,834
F as I exalted thee from among 1Kin 14:7   3282,834
F as I exalted thee out of the...........1Kin 16:2   3282,834
F as thou hast sent messengers to..2Kin 1:16   3282,834
f as he defiled his father's bed, ...1Chr 5:1
F as it was in thine heart to 2Chr 6:8
F as thou art sent of the king, . Ezr 7:14   3606,6903,1768
F as this people refuseth the ....Is 8:6   3282,365
F as this people draw near me........Is 29:13   3282,365
F as there is none like unto thee ....Jer 10:6
f as among all the wise men of ....Jer 10:7
f as iron breaketh in pieces ..... Dan 2:40   3606,6903,1768
f as thou sawest the iron .... Dan 2:41   3606,6903,1768
F as thou sawest that the .... Dan 2:45   3606,6903,1768
f as all the wise men of my ..... Dan 4:18   3606,6903,1768
F as an excellent spirit, and... Dan 5:12   3606,6903,1768
f as he was faithful, neither...... Dan 6:4   3606,6903,1768
f as before him innocency was Dan 6:22   3606,6903,1768
F therefore as your treading is............... Amos 5:11   3282
But *f* as he had not to pay, his ...Mt 18:25
F as many have taken in hand to .... Lk 1:1   1895
f as Lydda was nigh to Joppa, and .... Acts 9:38   5607
F then as God gave them the like .... Acts 11:17   1487
F as we have heard, that certain .... Acts 15:24   1894
F then as we are the offspring of .... Acts 17:29
F as I know that thou hast been .... Acts 24:10
f as he is the image and glory of 1Cor 11:7
f as ye are zealous of spiritual................ 1Cor 14:12   1893
f as ye know that your labour is 1Cor 15:58
F as ye are manifestly declared.............. 2Cor 3:3
F then as the children are ....Heb 2:14   1893
F as ye know that ye were not 1Pet 1:18
F then as Christ hath suffered 1Pet 4:1

FORBAD
whatsoever the Lord our God *f* us .... Deut 2:37   6680
But John *f* him, saying, I have .... Mt 3:14   1254
we *f* him, because he followeth.............. Mk 9:38   2967
we *f* him, because he followeth.............. Lk 9:49   2967
f the madness of the prophet 2Pet 2:16   2967

FORBARE
and he *f* to go forth 1Sa 23:13   2308
Then the prophet *f*, and said, I 2Chr 25:16   2308
So he *f*, and slew them not among......... Jer 41:8   2308

FORBEAR
wouldest *f* to help him, thou .... Ex 23:5   2308
But if thou shalt *f* to vow .... Deut 23:22   2308
to battle, or shall I *f* 1Kin 22:6   2308
to battle, or shall we *f*............................. 1Kin 22:15   2308
to battle, or shall I *f*................................ 2Chr 18:5   2308
to battle, or shall I *f*................................ 2Chr 18:14   2308
f; why shouldest thou be smitten 2Chr 25:16   2308
f thee from meddling with God, ... 2Chr 35:21   2308
Yet many years didst thou *f* them.......... Neh 9:30   4900
and though I *f*, what am I eased .... Job 16:6   2308
If thou *f* to deliver them that .... Prov 24:11   2820
to come with me into Babylon, *f*............. Jer 40:4   2308
will hear, or whether they will *f* .... Eze 2:5   2308
will hear, or whether they will *f* .... Eze 2:7   2308
will hear, or whether they will *f* .... Eze 3:11   2308
and he that forbeareth, let him *f* .... Eze 3:27   2308
F to cry, make no mourning for .... Eze 24:17   1826
my price; and if not, *f*.............................. Zec 11:12   2308
have not we power to *f* working 1Cor 9:6   3361
but now I *f*, lest any man should............ 2Cor 12:6   5339
when we could no longer *f* 1Th 3:1   4722
cause, when I could no longer *f*............. 1Th 3:5   4722

FORBEARANCE
the riches of his goodness and *f*............. Rom 2:4   463
are past, through the *f* of God .... Rom 3:25   463

FORBEARETH
f to keep the passover, even the .... Num 9:13   2308
and he that *f*, let him forbear................. Eze 3:27   2310

FORBEARING
By long *f* is a prince persuaded, ... Prov 25:15   639
my bones, and I was weary with *f*.......... Jer 20:9   3557
f one another in love .... Eph 4:2   430
things unto them, *f* threatening .... Eph 6:9   447
F one another, and forgiving one .... Col 3:13   430

FORBID
God *f* that thy servants should do .... Gen 44:7   2486
God *f* that I should do so .... Gen 44:17   2486
and said, My lord Moses, *f* them .... Num 11:28   3607
God *f* that we should rebel...................... Josh 22:29   2486
God *f* that we should forsake the .... Josh 24:16   2486
God *f* that I should sin against 1Sa 12:23   2486
God *f*: as the Lord liveth 1Sa 14:45   2486
And he said unto him, God *f* 1Sa 20:2   2486
The Lord *f* that I should do this 1Sa 24:6   2486
The Lord *f* that I should stretch 1Sa 26:11   2486
said to Ahab, The Lord *f* it me 1Kin 21:3   2486
And said, My God *f* it me, that I 1Chr 11:19   2486
God *f* that I should justify you .... Job 27:5   2486
f them not, to come unto me .... Mt 19:14   2967
But Jesus said, *F* him not .... Mk 9:39   2967
to come unto me, and *f* them not ...... Mk 10:14   2967
cloke *f* not to take thy coat also.......... Lk 6:29   2967
And Jesus said unto him, *F* him not ..... Lk 9:50   2967
to come unto me, and *f* them not .... Lk 18:16   2967
they heard it, they said, God *f*........... Lk 20:16   3361,1096
Can any man *f* water, that these............. Acts 10:47   2967
that he should *f* none of his .... Acts 24:23   2967
God *f*: yea, let God be true...................... Rom 3:4   3361,1096
God *f*: for then how shall God .... Rom 3:6   3361,1096
God *f*: yea, we establish the law .... Rom 3:31   3361,1096
God *f*. How shall we .... Rom 6:2   3361,1096
but under grace? God *f*........................... Rom 6:15   3361,1096
Is the law sin? God *f*............................... Rom 7:7   3361,1096
good made death unto me? God *f*.. Rom 7:13   3361,1096
unrighteousness with God? God *f*.. Rom 9:14   3361,1096
God cast away his people? God *f*.... Rom 11:1   3361,1096
that they should fall? God *f*.............. Rom 11:11   3361,1096
members of an harlot? God *f* 1Cor 6:15
f not to speak with tongues 1Cor 14:39   2967
the minister of sin? God *f*................. Gal 2:17   3361,1096
the promises of God? God *f*.............. Gal 3:21   3361,1096
But God *f* that I should glory,............ Gal 6:14   3361,1096

FORBIDDEN
any of these things which are *f*............... Lev 5:17   3808
the Lord thy God hath *f* thee................... Deut 4:23   6680
were *f* of the Holy Ghost to..................... Acts 16:6   2967

FORBIDDETH
f them that would, and casteth .... 3Jn 10 — 2967

FORBIDDING
f to give tribute to Caesar,........................ Lk 23:2 — 2967
with all confidence, no man *f* him .... Acts 28:31 — 209
F us to speak to the Gentiles .... 1Th 2:16 — 2967
F to marry, and commanding to .... 1Ti 4:3 — 2967

FORBORN
men of Babylon have *f* to fight .... Jer 51:30 — 2308

FORCE
take by *f* thy daughters from me............. Gen 31:31 — 1497
in the field, and the man *f* her............... Deut 22:25 — 2388
not dim, nor his natural *f* abated .... Deut 34:7 — 3893
and if not, I will take it by *f*................. 1Sa 2:16 — 2394
him, Nay, my brother, do not *f* me .... 2Sa 13:12 — 6031
Jews, and made them to cease by *f*....... Ezr 4:23 — 153
Will he *f* the queen also before .... Est 7:8 — 3533
By the great *f* of my disease is .... Job 30:18 — 3581
his *f* is in the navel of his .... Job 40:16 — 202
their blood by the *f* of the sword .... Jer 18:21 — 3027
is evil, and their *f* is not right................ Jer 23:10 — 1369
of Heshbon because of the *f*................... Jer 48:45 — 3581
but with *f* and with cruelty have............ Eze 34:4 — 2394
the *f* of the sword in the time of .... Eze 35:5 — 3027
strong shall not strengthen his *f*............ Amos 2:14 — 3581
and the violent take it by *f*...................... Mt 11:12 — 726
they would come and take him by *f*........ Jn 6:15 — 726
to take him by *f* from among them, ... Acts 23:10 — 726
is of *f* after men are dead .... Heb 9:17 — 949

FORCED
the Amorites *f* the children of .... Judg 1:34 — 3905
and my concubine have they *f*................ Judg 20:5 — 6031
I *f* myself therefore, and offered............. 1Sa 13:12 — 662
than she, *f* her, and lay with her .... 2Sa 13:14 — 6031
because he had *f* his sister Tamar .... 2Sa 13:22 — 6031
day that he *f* his sister Tamar .... 2Sa 13:32 — 6031
flattering of her lips she *f* him .... Prov 7:21 — 5080

FORCES
he placed *f* in all the fenced .... 2Chr 17:2 — 2428
gold, nor all the *f* of strength................. Job 36:19 — 3981
the *f* of the Gentiles shall come.............. Is 60:5 — 2428
unto thee the *f* of the Gentiles................ Is 60:11 — 2428
of the *f* which were in the fields .... Jer 40:7 — 2428
of the *f* that were in the fields .... Jer 40:13 — 2428
of the *f* that were with him .... Jer 41:11 — 2428
of the *f* that were with him .... Jer 41:13 — 2428
of the *f* that were with him .... Jer 41:16 — 2428
Then all the captains of the *f*................... Jer 42:1 — 2428
of the *f* which were with him .... Jer 42:8 — 2428
and all the captains of the *f* .... Jer 43:4 — 2428
and all the captains of the *f* .... Jer 43:5 — 2428
assemble a multitude of great *f* .... Dan 11:10 — 2428
shall he honour the God of *f*................... Dan 11:38 — 4581
carried away captive his *f*....................... Obad 11 — 2428

FORCIBLE
How *f* are right words .... Job 6:25 — 4834

FORCING
thereof by *f* an ax against them .... Deut 20:19 — 5080
so the *f* of wrath bringeth forth .... Prov 30:33 — 4330

FORD
sons, and passed over the *f* Jabbok .... Gen 32:22 — 4569

FORDS
them the way to Jordan unto the *f*.......... Josh 2:7 — 4569
took the *f* of Jordan toward Moab, ... Judg 3:28 — 4569
Moab shall be at the *f* of Arnon............. Is 16:2 — 4569

FORECAST
he shall *f* his devices against .... Dan 11:24 — 2803
for they shall *f* devices against .... Dan 11:25 — 2803

FOREFATHERS
back to the iniquities of their *f*............... Jer 11:10
from my *f* with pure conscience............. 2Ti 1:3 — 4269

FOREFRONT
in the *f* of the tabernacle .... Ex 26:9 — 4136,6640
upon the *f* of the mitre it shall .... Ex 28:37 — 4136,6640
upon the mitre, even upon his *f* ...... Lev 8:9 — 4136,6640
The *f* of the one was situate .... 1Sa 14:5 — 8127
Set ye Uriah in the *f* of the............. 2Sa 11:15 — 4136,6440
from the *f* of the house, from .... 2Kin 16:14 — 6440
and Jehoshaphat in the *f* of them .... 2Chr 20:27 — 7218
the *f* of the lower gate unto the .... Eze 40:19 — 6440
the *f* of the inner court without .... Eze 40:19 — 6440
for the *f* of the house stood..................... Eze 47:1 — 6440

FOREHEAD
And it shall be upon Aaron's *f*............... Ex 28:38 — 4696
and it shall be always upon his *f*........... Ex 28:38 — 4696

toward his face, he is *f* bald .... Lev 13:41 — 1371
be in the bald head, or bald *f*................. Lev 13:42 — 1372
in his bald head, or his bald *f*................ Lev 13:42 — 1372
his bald head, or in his bald *f* .... Lev 13:43 — 1372
and smote the Philistine in his *f*............ 1Sa 17:49 — 4696
that the stone sunk into his *f* .... 1Sa 17:49 — 4696
f before the priests in the house .... 2Chr 26:19 — 4696
behold, he was leprous in his *f* .... 2Chr 26:20 — 4696
and thou hadst a whore's *f*..................... Jer 3:3 — 4696
thy *f* strong against their .... Eze 3:8 — 4696
than flint have I made thy *f* .... Eze 3:9 — 4696
And I put a jewel on thy *f*....................... Eze 16:12 — 639
and receive his mark in his *f*.................. Rev 14:9 — 3359
upon her *f* was a name written, ... Rev 17:5 — 3359

FOREHEADS
forehead strong against their *f*............... Eze 3:8 — 4696
set a mark upon the *f* of the men .... Eze 9:4 — 4696
servants of our God in their *f*................. Rev 7:3 — 3359
not the seal of God in their *f* .... Rev 9:4 — 3359
their right hand, or in their *f*................. Rev 13:16 — 3359
Father's name written in their *f* .... Rev 14:1 — 3359
received his mark upon their *f* .... Rev 20:4 — 3359
and his name shall be in their *f* .... Rev 22:4 — 3359

FOREIGNER
A *f* and an hired servant shall not .... Ex 12:45 — 8453
Of a *f* thou mayest exact it again .... Deut 15:3 — 5237

FOREIGNERS
f entered into his gates, and cast............ Obad 11 — 5237
ye are no more strangers and *f*............... Eph 2:19 — 3941

FOREKNEW
cast away his people which he *f* .... Rom 11:2 — 4267

FOREKNOW
For whom he did *f*, he also did .... Rom 8:29 — 4267

FOREKNOWLEDGE
f of God, ye have taken, and by .... Acts 2:23 — 4268
to the *f* of God the Father .... 1Pet 1:2 — 4268

FOREMOST See APPENDIX.

FOREORDAINED
Who verily was *f* before the .... 1Pet 1:20 — 4267

FOREPART
underneath, toward the *f* thereof .... Ex 28:27 — 6440
underneath, toward the *f* of it .... Ex 39:20 — 6440
the oracle on the *f* was twenty .... 1Kin 6:20 — 6440
court on the *f* of the chambers .... Eze 42:7 — 6440
the *f* stuck fast, and remained .... Acts 27:41 — 4408

FORERUNNER
Whither the *f* is for us entered, ... Heb 6:20 — 4274

FORESAW
I *f* the Lord always before my .... Acts 2:25 — 4308

FORESEEING
f that God would justify the .... Gal 3:8 — 4375

FORESEETH
A prudent man *f* the evil, and .... Prov 22:3 — 7200
A prudent man *f* the evil, and .... Prov 27:12 — 7200

FORESHIP
have cast anchors out of the *f* .... Acts 27:30 — 4408

FORESKIN
circumcise the flesh of your *f*................. Gen 17:11 — 6190
flesh of his *f* is not circumcised .... Gen 17:14 — 6190
of their *f* in the selfsame day .... Gen 17:23 — 6190
circumcised in the flesh of his *f*............. Gen 17:24 — 6190
circumcised in the flesh of his *f*............. Gen 17:25 — 6190
and cut off the *f* of her son .... Ex 4:25 — 6190
of his *f* shall be circumcised .... Lev 12:3 — 6190
therefore the *f* of your heart .... Deut 10:16 — 6190
also, and let thy *f* be uncovered............. Hab 2:16 — 6188

FORESKINS
of Israel at the hill of the *f*.................... Josh 5:3 — 6190
dowry, but an hundred *f* of the.............. 1Sa 18:25 — 6190
and David brought their *f*, and they .... 1Sa 18:27 — 6190
an hundred *f* of the Philistines............... 2Sa 3:14 — 6190
and take away the *f* of your heart........... Jer 4:4 — 6190

FOREST
and came into the *f* of Hareth .... 1Sa 22:5 — 3293
the house of the *f* of Lebanon .... 1Kin 7:2 — 3293
in the house of the *f* of Lebanon .... 1Kin 10:17 — 3293
f of Lebanon were of pure gold............... 1Kin 10:21 — 3293
and into the *f* of his Carmel .... 2Kin 19:23 — 3293
in the house of the *f* of Lebanon .... 2Chr 9:16 — 3293
f of Lebanon were of pure gold............... 2Chr 9:20 — 3293
Asaph the keeper of the king's *f*............. Neh 2:8 — 6508
For every beast of the *f* is mine .... Ps 50:10 — 3293
beasts of the *f* do creep forth .... Ps 104:20 — 3293

F

kindle in the thickets of the f	Is 9:18	3293
shall consume the glory of his f	Is 10:18	3293
the trees of his f shall be few	Is 10:19	3293
the thickets of the f with iron	Is 10:34	3293
In the f in Arabia shall ye lodge	Is 21:13	3293
the armour of the house of the f	Is 22:8	3293
field shall be esteemed as a f	Is 29:17	3293
fruitful field be counted for a f	Is 32:15	3293
shall hail, coming down on the f	Is 32:19	3293
border, and the f of his Carmel	Is 37:24	3293
himself among the trees of the f	Is 44:14	3293
into singing, ye mountains, O f	Is 44:23	3293
yea, all ye beasts in the f	Is 56:9	3293
lion out of the f shall slay them	Jer 5:6	3293
one cutteth a tree out of the f	Jer 10:3	3293
is unto me as a lion in the f	Jer 12:8	3293
kindle a fire in the f thereof	Jer 21:14	3293
house as the high places of a f	Jer 26:18	3293
They shall cut down her f	Jer 46:23	3293
which is among the trees of the f	Eze 15:2	3293
tree among the trees of the f	Eze 15:6	3293
against the f of the south field	Eze 20:46	3293
say to the f of the south, Hear	Eze 20:47	3293
and I will make them a f, and the	Hos 2:12	3293
Will a lion roar in the f	Amos 3:4	3293
house as the high places of the f	Mic 3:12	3293
a lion among the beasts of the f	Mic 5:8	3293
for the f of the vintage is come	Zec 11:2	3293

FORESTS

in the f he built castles and	2Chr 27:4	2793
to calve, and discovereth the f	Ps 29:9	3295
neither cut down any out of the f	Eze 39:10	3293

FORETELL

f you, as if I were present, the	2Cor 13:2	4302

FORETOLD

behold, I have f you all things	Mk 13:23	4280
have likewise f of these days	Acts 3:24	4293

FOREWARN

But I will f you whom ye shall	Lk 12:5	5263

FOREWARNED

all such, as we also have f you	1Th 4:6	4277

FORFEITED

all his substance should be f	Ezr 10:8	2763

FORGAT

butler remember Joseph, but f him	Gen 40:23	7911
f the LORD their God, and served	Judg 3:7	7911
when they f the LORD their God	1Sa 12:9	7911
f his works, and his wonders that	Ps 78:11	7911
They soon f his works	Ps 106:13	7911
They f God their saviour, which	Ps 106:21	7911
I f prosperity	Lam 3:17	5382
lovers, and f me, saith the LORD	Hos 2:13	7911

FORGAVE

f their iniquity, and destroyed	Ps 78:38	3722
and loosed him, and f him the debt	Mt 18:27	863
I f thee all that debt, because	Mt 18:32	863
to pay, he frankly f them both	Lk 7:42	5483
that he, to whom he f most	Lk 7:43	5483
f any thing, to whom I f it	2Cor 2:10	5483
for your sakes f I it in the	2Cor 2:10	
even as Christ f you, so also do	Col 3:13	5483

FORGAVEST

thou f the iniquity of my sin	Ps 32:5	5375
thou wast a God that f them	Ps 99:8	5375

FORGED

The proud have f a lie against me	Ps 119:69	2950

FORGERS

But ye are f of lies, ye are all	Job 13:4	2950

FORGET

he f that which thou hast done to	Gen 27:45	7911
he, hath made me f all my toil	Gen 41:51	5382
lest thou f the things which	Deut 4:9	7911
lest ye f the covenant of the	Deut 4:23	7911
nor f the covenant of thy fathers	Deut 4:31	7911
Then beware lest thou f the LORD	Deut 6:12	7911
Beware that thou f not the LORD	Deut 8:11	7911
thou f the LORD thy God, which	Deut 8:14	7911
thou do at all f the LORD thy God	Deut 8:19	7911
f not, how thou provokedst the	Deut 9:7	7911
thou shalt not f it	Deut 25:19	7911
not f thine handmaid, but wilt	1Sa 1:11	7911
have made with you ye shall not f	2Kin 17:38	7911
are the paths of all that f God	Job 8:13	7911
I will f my complaint, I will	Job 9:27	7911
Because thou shalt f thy misery	Job 11:16	7911

The womb shall f him	Job 24:20	7911
and all the nations that f God	Ps 9:17	7913
f not the humble	Ps 10:12	7911
How long wilt thou f me, O LORD	Ps 13:1	7911
f also thine own people, and thy	Ps 45:10	7911
Now consider this, ye that f God	Ps 50:22	7911
Slay them not, lest my people f	Ps 59:11	7911
f not the congregation of thy	Ps 74:19	7911
F not the voice of thine enemies	Ps 74:23	7911
not f the works of God, but keep	Ps 78:7	7911
so that I f to eat my bread	Ps 102:4	7911
soul, and f not all his benefits	Ps 103:2	7911
I will not f thy word	Ps 119:16	7911
yet do I not f thy statutes	Ps 119:83	7911
I will never f thy precepts	Ps 119:93	7911
yet do I not f thy law	Ps 119:109	7911
yet do not I f thy precepts	Ps 119:141	7911
for I do not f thy law	Ps 119:153	7911
for I do not f thy commandments	Ps 119:176	7911
If I f thee, O Jerusalem	Ps 137:5	7911
let my right hand f her cunning	Ps 137:5	7911
My son, f not my law	Prov 3:1	7911
get understanding: f it not	Prov 4:5	7911
f the law, and pervert the	Prov 31:5	7911
f his poverty, and remember his	Prov 31:7	7911
Can a woman f her sucking child,	Is 49:15	7911
yea, they may f, yet will I not	Is 49:15	7911
may f, yet will I not f thee	Is 49:15	7911
for thou shalt f the shame of thy	Is 54:4	7911
that f my holy mountain, that	Is 65:11	7913
Can a maid f her ornaments, or a	Jer 2:32	7911
think to cause my people to f my	Jer 23:27	7911
I, even I, will utterly f you	Jer 23:39	5382
Wherefore dost thou f us for ever	Lam 5:20	7911
I will also f thy children	Hos 4:6	7911
I will never f any of their works	Amos 8:7	7911
is not unrighteous to f your work	Heb 6:10	1950
do good and to communicate f not	Heb 13:16	1950

FORGETFUL

Be not f to entertain strangers	Heb 13:2	1950
therein, he being not a f hearer	Jas 1:25	1953

FORGETFULNESS

righteousness in the land of f	Ps 88:12	5388

FORGETTEST

face, and f our affliction and our	Ps 44:24	7911
f the LORD thy maker, that hath	Is 51:13	7911

FORGETTETH

f that the foot may crush them,	Job 39:15	7911
he f not the cry of the humble	Ps 9:12	7911
f the covenant of her God	Prov 2:17	7913
straightway f what manner of man	Jas 1:24	1950

FORGETTING

f those things which are behind,	Phil 3:13	1950

FORGIVE

So shall ye say unto Joseph, F	Gen 50:17	5375
f the trespass of the servants of	Gen 50:17	5375
Now therefore f, I pray thee, my	Ex 10:17	5375
Yet now, if thou wilt f their sin	Ex 32:32	5375
and the LORD shall f her, because	Num 30:5	5545
and the LORD shall f her	Num 30:8	5545
and the LORD shall f her	Num 30:12	5545
he will not f your transgressions	Josh 24:19	5375
f the trespass of thine handmaid	1Sa 25:28	5375
and when thou hearest, f	1Kin 8:30	5545
f the sin of thy people Israel,	1Kin 8:34	5545
f the sin of thy servants, and of	1Kin 8:36	5545
heaven thy dwelling place, and f	1Kin 8:39	5545
f thy people that have sinned	1Kin 8:50	5545
and when thou hearest, f	2Chr 6:21	5545
f the sin of thy people Israel,	2Chr 6:25	5545
f the sin of thy servants, and of	2Chr 6:27	5545
heaven thy dwelling place, and f	2Chr 6:30	5545
f thy people which have sinned	2Chr 6:39	5545
will f their sin, and will heal	2Chr 7:14	5545
and f all my sins	Ps 25:18	5375
Lord, art good, and ready to f	Ps 86:5	5546
therefore f them not	Is 2:9	5375
f not their iniquity, neither	Jer 18:23	3722
for I will f their iniquity, and I	Jer 31:34	5545
that I may f their iniquity and	Jer 36:3	5545
O Lord, hear; O Lord, f	Dan 9:19	5545
land, then I said, O Lord GOD, f	Amos 7:2	5545
f us our debts, as we f our	Mt 6:12	863
For if ye f men their trespasses,	Mt 6:14	863
heavenly Father will also f you	Mt 6:14	863
But if ye f not men their	Mt 6:15	863
your Father f your trespasses	Mt 6:15	863
man hath power on earth to f sins	Mt 9:6	863

sin against me, and I *f* him	Mt 18:21	863
if ye from your hearts *f* not	Mt 18:35	863
who can *f* sins but God only	Mk 2:7	863
man hath power on earth to *f* sins	Mk 2:10	863
And when ye stand praying, *f*	Mk 11:25	863
heaven may *f* you your trespasses	Mk 11:25	863
But if ye do not *f*, neither will	Mk 11:26	863
is in heaven *f* your trespasses	Mk 11:26	863
Who can *f* sins, but God alone	Lk 5:21	863
hath power upon earth to *f* sins	Lk 5:24	863
f, and ye shall be forgiven	Lk 6:37	630
And *f* us our sins	Lk 11:4	863
for we also *f* every one that is	Lk 11:4	863
and if he repent, *f* him	Lk 17:3	863
thou shalt *f* him	Lk 17:4	863
Then said Jesus, Father, *f* them	Lk 23:34	863
ye ought rather to *f* him, and	2Cor 2:7	5483
ye *f* any thing, I *f* also	2Cor 2:10	5483
f me this wrong	2Cor 12:13	5483
just to *f* us our sins, and to	1Jn 1:9	863

FORGIVEN

for them, and it shall be *f* them	Lev 4:20	5545
his sin, and it shall be *f* him	Lev 4:26	5545
for him, and it shall be *f* him	Lev 4:31	5545
committed, and it shall be *f* him	Lev 4:35	5545
hath sinned, and it shall be *f* him	Lev 5:10	5545
of these, and it shall be *f* him	Lev 5:13	5545
offering, and it shall be *f* him	Lev 5:16	5545
wist it not, and it shall be *f* him	Lev 5:18	5545
it shall be *f* him for any thing	Lev 6:7	5545
which he hath done shall be *f* him	Lev 19:22	5545
and as thou hast *f* this people	Num 14:19	5375
of Israel, and it shall be *f* them	Num 15:25	5545
And it shall be *f* all the	Num 15:26	5545
and it shall be *f* him	Num 15:28	5545
And the blood shall be *f* them	Deut 21:8	3722
is he whose transgression is *f*	Ps 32:1	5375
Thou hast the iniquity of thy	Ps 85:2	5375
therein shall be *f* their iniquity	Is 33:24	5375
thy sins be *f* thee	Mt 9:2	863
to say, Thy sins be *f* thee	Mt 9:5	863
and blasphemy shall be *f* unto men	Mt 12:31	863
Ghost shall not be *f* unto men	Mt 12:31	863
the Son of man, it shall be *f* him	Mt 12:32	863
Holy Ghost, it shall not be *f* him	Mt 12:32	863
palsy, Son, thy sins be *f* thee	Mk 2:5	863
of the palsy, Thy sins be *f* thee	Mk 2:9	863
All sins shall be *f* unto the sons	Mk 3:28	863
and their sins should be *f* them	Mk 4:12	863
him, Man, thy sins are *f* thee	Lk 5:20	863
to say, Thy sins be *f* thee	Lk 5:23	863
forgive, and ye shall be *f*	Lk 6:37	630
Her sins, which are many, are *f*	Lk 7:47	863
but to whom little is *f*, the same	Lk 7:47	863
he said unto her, Thy sins are *f*	Lk 7:48	863
the Son of man, it shall be *f* him	Lk 12:10	863
the Holy Ghost it shall not be *f*	Lk 12:10	863
of thine heart may be *f* thee	Acts 8:22	863
are they whose iniquities are *f*	Rom 4:7	863
God for Christ's sake hath *f* you	Eph 4:32	5483
having *f* you all trespasses	Col 2:13	5483
sins, they shall be *f* him	Jas 5:15	863
because your sins are *f* you for	1Jn 2:12	863

FORGIVENESS

But there is *f* with thee, that	Ps 130:4	5547
the Holy Ghost hath never *f*	Mk 3:29	859
to Israel, and *f* of sins	Acts 5:31	859
preached unto you the *f* of sins	Acts 13:38	859
that they may receive *f* of sins	Acts 26:18	859
the *f* of sins, according to the	Eph 1:7	859
his blood, even the *f* of sins	Col 1:14	859

FORGIVENESSES

Lord our God belong mercies and *f*	Dan 9:9	5547

FORGIVETH

Who *f* all thine iniquities	Ps 103:3	5545
Who is this that *f* sins also	Lk 7:49	863

FORGIVING

f iniquity and transgression and	Ex 34:7	5375
f iniquity and transgression, and	Num 14:18	5375
f one another, even as God for	Eph 4:32	5483
f one another, if any man have a	Col 3:13	5483

FORGOT

hast *f* a sheaf in the field, thou	Deut 24:19	7911

FORGOTTEN

shall be *f* in the land of Egypt	Gen 41:30	7911
neither have I *f* them	Deut 26:13	7911
for it shall not be *f* out of the	Deut 31:21	7911

hast *f* God that formed thee	Deut 32:18	7911
and my familiar friends have *f* me	Job 19:14	7911
even the waters *f* of the foot	Job 28:4	7911
the needy shall not alway be *f*	Ps 9:18	7911
said in his heart, God hath *f*	Ps 10:11	7911
I am *f* as a dead man out of mind	Ps 31:12	7911
God my rock, Why hast thou *f* me	Ps 42:9	7911
yet have we not *f* thee, neither	Ps 44:17	7911
If we have *f* the name of our God,	Ps 44:20	7911
Hath God *f* to be gracious	Ps 77:9	7911
but I have not *f* thy law	Ps 119:61	7911
mine enemies have *f* thy words	Ps 119:139	7911
the days to come shall all be *f*	Eccl 2:16	7911
they were in the city where	Eccl 8:10	7911
for the memory of them is *f*	Eccl 9:5	7911
Because thou hast *f* the God of	Is 17:10	7911
Tyre shall be *f* seventy years	Is 23:15	7911
thou harlot that hast been *f*	Is 23:16	7911
Israel, thou shalt not be *f* of me	Is 44:21	5382
forsaken me, and my Lord hath *f* me	Is 49:14	7913
because the former troubles are *f*	Is 65:16	7911
yet my people have *f* me days	Jer 2:32	7911
they have *f* the LORD their God	Jer 3:21	7911
because thou hast *f* me, and	Jer 13:25	7911
Because my people hath *f* me	Jer 18:15	7911
confusion shall never be *f*	Jer 20:11	7911
fathers have *f* my name for Baal	Jer 23:27	7911
shame, which shall not be *f*	Jer 23:40	7911
All thy lovers have *f* thee	Jer 30:14	7911
Have ye *f* the wickedness of your	Jer 44:9	7911
covenant that shall not be *f*	Jer 50:5	7911
they have *f* their restingplace	Jer 50:6	7911
and sabbaths to be *f* in Zion	Lam 2:6	7911
by extortion, and hast *f* me	Eze 22:12	7911
Because thou hast *f* me, and cast	Eze 23:35	7911
seeing thou hast *f* the law of thy	Hos 4:6	7911
For Israel hath *f* his Maker	Hos 8:14	7911
therefore have *f* me	Hos 13:6	7911
side, they had *f* to take bread	Mt 16:5	1950
the disciples had *f* to take bread	Mk 8:14	1950
not one of them is *f* before God	Lk 12:6	1950
ye have *f* the exhortation which	Heb 12:5	1585
hath *f* that he was purged from	2Pet 1:9	3024,2983

FORKS

and for the coulters, and for the *f*	1Sa 13:21	7969,7053

FORM

And the earth was without *f*	Gen 1:2	8414
he said unto her, What *f* is he of	1Sa 28:14	8389
To fetch about this *f* of speech	2Sa 14:20	6440
of gold according to their *f*	2Chr 4:7	4941
I could not discern the *f* thereof	Job 4:16	4758
I *f* the light, and create darkness	Is 45:7	3335
his *f* more than the sons of men	Is 52:14	8389
he hath no *f* nor comeliness	Is 53:2	8389
earth, and, lo, it was without *f*	Jer 4:23	8414
And he put forth the *f* of an hand	Eze 8:3	8403
behold every *f* of creeping things	Eze 8:10	8403
the *f* of a man's hand under their	Eze 10:8	8403
shew them the *f* of the house	Eze 43:11	6699
they may keep the whole *f* thereof	Eze 43:11	6699
the *f* thereof was terrible	Dan 2:31	6755
the *f* of his visage was changed	Dan 3:19	6755
the *f* of the fourth is like the	Dan 3:25	7299
in another *f* unto two of them	Mk 16:12	3444
which hast the *f* of knowledge	Rom 2:20	3446
f of doctrine which was delivered	Rom 6:17	5179
Who, being in the *f* of God	Phil 2:6	3444
took upon him the *f* of a servant	Phil 2:7	3444
Hold fast the *f* of sound words,	2Ti 1:13	5296
Having a *f* of godliness, but	2Ti 3:5	3446

FORMED

the LORD God *f* man of the dust of	Gen 2:7	3335
he put the man whom he had *f*	Gen 2:8	3335
God *f* every beast of the field	Gen 2:19	3335
and hast forgotten God that *f* thee	Deut 32:18	2342
of ancient times that I have *f* it	2Kin 19:25	3335
Dead things are *f* from under the	Job 26:5	2342
his hand hath *f* the crooked	Job 26:13	2342
I also am *f* out of the clay	Job 33:6	7169
or ever thou hadst *f* the earth	Ps 90:2	2342
he that *f* the eye, shall he not	Ps 94:9	3335
and his hands *f* the dry land	Ps 95:5	3335
The great God that *f* all things	Prov 26:10	2342
he that *f* them will shew them no	Is 27:11	3335
ancient times, that I have *f* it	Is 37:26	3335
thee, O Jacob, and he that *f* thee	Is 43:1	3335
him for my glory, I have *f* him	Is 43:7	3335
before me there was no God *f*	Is 43:10	3335
This people have I *f* for myself	Is 43:21	3335

F

f thee from the womb, which will	Is 44:2	3335
Who hath f a god, or molten a	Is 44:10	3335
I have f thee	Is 44:21	3335
he that f thee from the womb, I	Is 44:24	3335
God himself that f the earth	Is 45:18	3335
in vain, he f it to be inhabited	Is 45:18	3335
saith the LORD that f me from the	Is 49:5	3335
No weapon that is f against thee	Is 54:17	3335
Before I f thee in the belly I	Jer 1:5	3335
maker thereof, the LORD that f it	Jer 33:2	3335
behold, he f grasshoppers in the	Amos 7:1	3335
Shall the thing f say to him that	Rom 9:20	4110
thing f say to him that f it	Rom 9:20	4110
again until Christ be f in you	Gal 4:19	3445
For Adam was first f, then Eve	1Ti 2:13	4111

FORMER

after the f manner when thou wast	Gen 40:13	7223
fought against the f king of Moab	Num 21:26	7223
Her f husband, which sent her	Deut 24:4	7223
in f time in Israel concerning	Ruth 4:7	6440
him again after the f manner	1Sa 17:30	7223
the f fifties with their fifties	2Kin 1:14	7223
day they do after the f manners	2Kin 17:34	7223
but they did after their f manner	2Kin 17:40	7223
But the f governors that had been	Neh 5:15	7223
I pray thee, of the f age	Job 8:8	7223
the wilderness in f time desolate	Job 30:3	570
not against us f iniquities	Ps 79:8	7223
where are thy f lovingkindnesses,	Ps 89:49	7223
is no remembrance of f things	Eccl 1:11	7223
What is the cause that the f days	Eccl 7:10	7223
let them shew the f things	Is 41:22	7223
the f things are come to pass, and	Is 42:9	7223
declare this, and shew us f things	Is 43:9	7223
Remember ye not the f things	Is 43:18	7223
Remember the f things of old	Is 46:9	7223
I have declared the f things from	Is 48:3	7223
shall raise up the f desolations	Is 61:4	7223
their f work into their bosom	Is 65:7	7223
because the f troubles are	Is 65:16	7223
the f shall not be remembered,	Is 65:17	7223
God, that giveth rain, both the f	Jer 5:24	3138
for he is the f of all things	Jer 10:16	3335
the f kings which were before	Jer 34:5	7223
write in it all the f words that	Jer 36:28	7223
for he is the f of all things	Jer 51:19	3335
shall return to their f estate	Eze 16:55	6927
shall return to their f estate	Eze 16:55	6927
shall return to your f estate	Eze 16:55	6927
a multitude greater than the f	Dan 11:13	7223
but it shall not be as the f	Dan 11:29	7223
latter and f rain unto the earth	Hos 6:3	3138
given you the f rain moderately	Joel 2:23	4175
the f rain, and the latter rain in	Joel 2:23	4175
shall be greater than of the f	Hag 2:9	7223
unto whom the f prophets have	Zec 1:4	7223
LORD hath cried by the f prophets	Zec 7:7	7223
in his spirit by the f prophets	Zec 7:12	7223
of this people as in the f days	Zec 8:11	7223
half of them toward the f sea	Zec 14:8	6931
the days of old, and as in f years	Mal 3:4	6931
The f treatise have I made, O	Acts 1:1	4413
the f conversation the old man	Eph 4:22	4387
call to remembrance the f days	Heb 10:32	4386
to the f lusts in your ignorance	1Pet 1:14	4386
for the f things are passed away	Rev 21:4	4413

FORMETH

he that f the mountains, and	Amos 4:13	3335
f the spirit of man within him	Zec 12:1	3335

FORMS

in thereof, and all the f thereof	Eze 43:11	6699
thereof, and all the f thereof	Eze 43:11	6699

FORNICATION

of Jerusalem to commit f, and	2Chr 21:11	2181
shall commit f with all the	Is 23:17	2181
f with the Egyptians thy	Eze 16:26	2181
thy f in the land of Canaan unto	Eze 16:29	8457
wife, saving for the cause of f	Mt 5:32	4202
away his wife, except it be for f	Mt 19:9	4202
they to him, We be not born of f	Jn 8:41	4202
pollutions of idols, and from f	Acts 15:20	4202
from things strangled, and from f	Acts 15:29	4202
and from strangled, and from f	Acts 21:25	4202
with all unrighteousness, f	Rom 1:29	4202
that there is f among you	1Cor 5:1	4202
such f as is not so much as named	1Cor 5:1	4202
Now the body is not for f	1Cor 6:13	4202
Flee f. Every sin that	1Cor 6:18	4202
but he that committeth f sinneth	1Cor 6:18	4203

Nevertheless, to avoid f, let	1Cor 7:2	4202
Neither let us commit f, as some	1Cor 10:8	4203
repented of the uncleanness and f	2Cor 12:21	4202
Adultery, f, uncleanness,	Gal 5:19	4202
But f, and all uncleanness, or	Eph 5:3	4202
f, uncleanness, inordinate	Col 3:5	4202
that ye should abstain from f	1Th 4:3	4202
giving themselves over to f	Jude 7	1608
unto idols, and to commit f	Rev 2:14	4203
to seduce my servants to commit f	Rev 2:20	4203
gave her space to repent of her f	Rev 2:21	4202
their sorceries, nor of their f	Rev 9:21	4202
of the wine of the wrath of her f	Rev 14:8	4202
of the earth have committed f	Rev 17:2	4203
made drunk with the wine of her f	Rev 17:2	4202
and filthiness of her f	Rev 17:4	4202
of the wine of the wrath of her f	Rev 18:3	4202
earth have committed f with her	Rev 18:3	4203
the earth, who have committed f	Rev 18:9	4203
did corrupt the earth with her f	Rev 19:2	4202

FORNICATIONS

pouredst out thy f on every one	Eze 16:15	8457
thoughts, murders, adulteries, f	Mt 15:19	4202
evil thoughts, adulteries, f	Mk 7:21	4202

FORNICATOR

that is called a brother be a f	1Cor 5:11	4205
Lest there be any f, or profane	Heb 12:16	4205

FORNICATORS

an epistle not to company with f	1Cor 5:9	4205
with the f of this world, or with	1Cor 5:10	4205
neither f, nor idolaters, nor	1Cor 6:9	4205

FORSAKE

he will not f thee, neither	Deut 4:31	7503
f not the Levite as long as thou	Deut 12:19	5800
thou shalt not f him	Deut 14:27	5800
he will not fail thee, nor f thee	Deut 31:6	5800
not fail thee, neither f thee	Deut 31:8	5800
go to be among them, and will f me	Deut 31:16	5800
in that day, and I will f them	Deut 31:17	5800
I will not fail thee, nor f thee	Josh 1:5	5800
forbid that we should f the LORD	Josh 24:16	5800
If ye f the LORD, and serve	Josh 24:20	5800
Should I f my sweetness, and my	Judg 9:11	2308
For the LORD will not f his	1Sa 12:22	5203
will not f my people Israel	1Kin 6:13	5800
let him not leave us, nor f us	1Kin 8:57	5203
I will f the remnant of mine	2Kin 21:14	5203
but if thou f him, he will cast	1Chr 28:9	5800
nor f thee, until thou hast	1Chr 28:20	5800
f my statutes and my commandments,	2Chr 7:19	5800
if ye f him, he will f you	2Chr 15:2	5800
is against all them that f him	Ezr 8:22	5800
utterly consume them, nor f them	Neh 9:31	5203
we will not f the house of our	Neh 10:39	5800
f it not, but keep it still	Job 20:13	5800
leave me not, neither f me	Ps 27:9	5800
When my father and my mother f me	Ps 27:10	5800
Cease from anger, and f wrath	Ps 37:8	5800
F me not, O LORD	Ps 38:21	5800
f me not when my strength faileth	Ps 71:9	5800
and greyheaded, O God, f me not	Ps 71:18	5800
If his children f my law, and walk	Ps 89:30	5800
neither will he f his inheritance	Ps 94:14	5800
O f me not utterly	Ps 119:8	5800
of the wicked that f thy law	Ps 119:53	5800
f not the works of thine own	Ps 138:8	7503
f not the law of thy mother	Prov 1:8	5203
Let not mercy and truth f thee	Prov 3:3	5800
good doctrine, f ye not my law	Prov 4:2	5800
F her not, and she shall preserve	Prov 4:6	5800
f not the law of thy mother	Prov 6:20	5203
F the foolish, and live	Prov 9:6	5800
and thy father's friend, f not	Prov 27:10	5800
They that f the law praise the	Prov 28:4	5800
they that f the LORD shall be	Is 1:28	5800
the God of Israel will not f them	Is 41:17	5800
I do unto them, and not f them	Is 42:16	5800
Let the wicked f his way, and the	Is 55:7	5800
But ye are they that f the LORD	Is 65:11	5800
all that f thee shall be ashamed,	Jer 17:13	5800
I will even f you, saith the LORD	Jer 23:33	5203
forget you, and I will f you	Jer 23:39	5203
f her, and let us go every one	Jer 51:9	5800
us for ever, and f us so long time	Lam 5:20	5800
neither did they f the idols of	Eze 20:8	5800
them that f the holy covenant	Dan 11:30	5800
lying vanities f their own mercy	Jonah 2:8	5800
are among the Gentiles to f Moses	Acts 21:21	646,575
will never leave thee, nor f thee	Heb 13:5	1459

FORSAKEN		
doings, whereby thou hast _f_ me	Deut 28:20	5800
Because they have _f_ the covenant	Deut 29:25	5800
but now the LORD hath _f_ us	Judg 6:13	5203
both because we have _f_ our God	Judg 10:10	5800
Yet ye have _f_ me, and served other	Judg 10:13	5800
day, wherewith they have _f_ me	1Sa 8:8	5800
because we have _f_ the LORD	1Sa 12:10	5800
Because that they have _f_ me	1Kin 11:33	5800
house, in that ye have _f_ the	1Kin 18:18	5800
of Israel have _f_ thy covenant	1Kin 19:10	5800
of Israel have _f_ thy covenant	1Kin 19:14	5800
Because they have _f_ me, and have	2Kin 22:17	5800
Thus saith the LORD, Ye have _f_ me	2Chr 12:5	5800
is our God, and we have not _f_ him	2Chr 13:10	5800
but ye have _f_ him	2Chr 13:11	5800
because he had _f_ the LORD God of	2Chr 21:10	5800
because ye have _f_ the LORD	2Chr 24:20	5800
he hath also _f_ you	2Chr 24:20	5800
because they had _f_ the LORD God	2Chr 24:24	5800
because they had _f_ the LORD God	2Chr 28:6	5800
the LORD our God, and have _f_ him	2Chr 29:6	5800
Because they have _f_ me, and have	2Chr 34:25	5800
God hath not _f_ us in our bondage	Ezr 9:9	5800
for we have _f_ thy commandments,	Ezr 9:10	5800
said, Why is the house of God _f_	Neh 13:11	5800
shall the earth be _f_ for thee	Job 18:4	5800
hath oppressed and hath _f_ the poor	Job 20:19	5800
hast not _f_ them that seek thee	Ps 9:10	5800
God, my God, why hast thou _f_ me	Ps 22:1	5800
have I not seen the righteous _f_	Ps 37:25	5800
Saying, God hath _f_ him	Ps 71:11	5800
they have _f_ the LORD, have	Is 1:4	5800
Therefore thou hast _f_ thy people	Is 2:6	5203
shall be _f_ of both her kings	Is 7:16	5800
The cities of Aroer are _f_	Is 17:2	5800
his strong cities be as a _f_ bough	Is 17:9	5800
be desolate, and the habitation _f_	Is 27:10	7971
Because the palaces shall be _f_	Is 32:14	5203
But Zion said, The LORD hath _f_ me	Is 49:14	5800
hath called thee as a woman _f_	Is 54:6	5800
For a small moment have I _f_ thee	Is 54:7	5800
Whereas thou hast been _f_ and hated	Is 60:15	5800
Thou shalt no more be termed _F_	Is 62:4	5800
called, Sought out, A city not _f_	Is 62:12	5800
their wickedness, who have _f_ me	Jer 1:16	5800
they have _f_ me the fountain of	Jer 2:13	5800
that thou hast _f_ the LORD thy God	Jer 2:17	5800
that thou hast _f_ the LORD thy God	Jer 2:19	5800
every city shall be _f_, and not a	Jer 4:29	5800
thy children have _f_ me, and sworn	Jer 5:7	5800
answer them, Like as ye have _f_ me	Jer 5:19	5800
_f_ the generation of his wrath	Jer 7:29	5203
Because they have _f_ my law which	Jer 9:13	5800
because we have _f_ the land	Jer 9:19	5800
I have _f_ mine house, I have left	Jer 12:7	5800
Thou hast _f_ me, saith the LORD,	Jer 15:6	5203
Because your fathers have _f_ me	Jer 16:11	5800
worshipped them, and have _f_ me	Jer 16:11	5800
because they have _f_ the LORD	Jer 17:13	5800
that come from another place be _f_	Jer 18:14	5428
Because they have _f_ me, and have	Jer 19:4	5800
Because they have _f_ the covenant	Jer 22:9	5800
He hath _f_ his covert, as the lion	Jer 25:38	5800
For Israel hath not been _f_	Jer 51:5	488
the LORD hath _f_ the earth	Eze 8:12	5800
say, The LORD hath _f_ the earth	Eze 9:9	5800
and to the cities that are _f_	Eze 36:4	5800
she is _f_ upon her land	Amos 5:2	5203
For Gaza shall be _f_, and Ashkelon	Zeph 2:4	5800
unto him, Behold, we have _f_ all	Mt 19:27	863
And every one that hath _f_ houses	Mt 19:29	863
God, my God, why hast thou _f_ me	Mt 27:46	1459
God, my God, why hast thou _f_ me	Mk 15:34	1459
Persecuted, but not _f_	2Cor 4:9	1459
For Demas hath _f_ me, having loved	2Ti 4:10	1459
Which have _f_ the right way, and	2Pet 2:15	2641

FORSAKETH		
but he _f_ the fear of the Almighty	Job 6:14	5800
judgment, and _f_ not his saints	Ps 37:28	5800
Which _f_ the guide of her youth,	Prov 2:17	5800
grievous unto him that _f_ the way	Prov 15:10	5800
and _f_ them shall have mercy	Prov 28:13	5800
you that _f_ not all that he hath	Lk 14:33	657

FORSAKING		
there be a great _f_ in the midst	Is 6:12	5805
Not _f_ the assembling of ourselves	Heb 10:25	1459

FORSOMUCH		
_f_ as he also is a son of Abraham	Lk 19:9	2530

FORSOOK		
then he _f_ God which made him, and	Deut 32:15	5203
they _f_ the LORD God of their	Judg 2:12	5800
they _f_ the LORD, and served Baal	Judg 2:13	5800
_f_ the LORD, and served not him	Judg 10:6	5800
they _f_ the cities, and fled	1Sa 31:7	5800
Because they _f_ the LORD their God	1Kin 9:9	5800
But he _f_ the counsel of the old	1Kin 12:8	5800
_f_ the old men's counsel that they	1Kin 12:13	5800
he _f_ the LORD God of his fathers,	2Kin 21:22	5800
then they _f_ their cities, and fled	1Chr 10:7	5800
Because they _f_ the LORD God of	2Chr 7:22	5800
But he _f_ the counsel which the	2Chr 10:8	5800
king Rehoboam _f_ the counsel of	2Chr 10:13	5800
he _f_ the law of the LORD, and all	2Chr 12:1	5800
So that he _f_ the tabernacle of	Ps 78:60	5203
but I _f_ not thy precepts	Ps 119:87	5800
_f_ not the ordinance of their God	Is 58:2	5800
_f_ it, because there was no grass	Jer 14:5	5800
Then all the disciples _f_ him	Mt 26:56	863
And straightway they _f_ their nets	Mk 1:18	863
And they all _f_ him, and fled	Mk 14:50	863
their ships to land, they _f_ all	Lk 5:11	863
stood with me, but all men _f_ me	2Ti 4:16	1459
By faith he _f_ Egypt, not fearing	Heb 11:27	2641

FORSOOKEST		
of great kindness, and _f_ them not	Neh 9:17	5800
_f_ them not in the wilderness	Neh 9:19	5800

FORSWEAR		
time, Thou shalt not _f_ thyself	Mt 5:33	1964

FORT		
So David dwelt in the _f_, and	2Sa 5:9	4686
the fortress of the high _f_ of thy	Is 25:12	4869
build a _f_ against it, and cast a	Eze 4:2	1785
to cast a mount, and to build a _f_	Eze 21:22	1785
and he shall make a _f_ against thee	Eze 26:8	1785
face toward the _f_ of his own land	Dan 11:19	4581

FORTH See APPENDIX.

FORTHWITH		
_f_ expences be given unto these	Ezr 6:8	629
_f_ they sprung up, because they	Mt 13:5	2112
_f_ he came to Jesus, and said, Hail	Mt 26:49	2112
_f_, when they were come out of the	Mk 1:29	2112
charged him, and _f_ sent him away	Mk 1:43	2112
And _f_ Jesus gave them leave	Mk 5:13	2112
_f_ came there out blood and water	Jn 19:34	2117
and he received sight _f_, and arose,	Acts 9:18	3916
_f_ the angel departed from him	Acts 12:10	2112
and _f_ the doors were shut	Acts 21:30	2112

FORTIETH		
in the _f_ year after the children	Num 33:38	705
And it came to pass in the _f_ year	Deut 1:3	705
In the _f_ year of the reign of	1Chr 26:31	705
in the one and _f_ year of his reign	2Chr 16:13	705

FORTIFIED		
he _f_ the strong holds, and put	2Chr 11:11	2388
turning of the wall, and _f_ them	2Chr 26:9	2388
they _f_ Jerusalem unto the broad	Neh 3:8	5800
Assyria, and from the _f_ cities	Mic 7:12	4692

FORTIFY		
they _f_ the city against thee	Judg 9:31	6696
will they _f_ themselves	Neh 4:2	5800
have ye broken down to _f_ the wall	Is 22:10	1219
though she should _f_ the height of	Jer 51:53	1219
strong, _f_ thy power mightily	Nah 2:1	553
for the siege, _f_ thy strong holds	Nah 3:14	2388

FORTRESS		
The LORD is my rock, and my _f_	2Sa 22:2	4686
The LORD is my rock, and my _f_	Ps 18:2	4686
For thou art my rock and my _f_	Ps 31:3	4686
me, for thou art my rock and my _f_	Ps 71:3	4686
the LORD, He is my refuge and my _f_	Ps 91:2	4686
My goodness, and my _f_	Ps 144:2	4686
The _f_ also shall cease from	Is 17:3	4013
the _f_ of the high fort of thy	Is 25:12	4013
a _f_ among my people, that thou	Jer 6:27	4013
the land, O inhabitant of the _f_	Jer 10:17	4693
O LORD, my strength, and my _f_	Jer 16:19	4581
shall enter into the _f_ of the	Dan 11:7	4581
and be stirred up, even to his _f_	Dan 11:10	4581
spoiled shall come against the _f_	Amos 5:9	4013
from the _f_ even to the river, and	Mic 7:12	4693

FORTRESSES		
and brambles in the _f_ thereof	Is 34:13	4013
all thy _f_ shall be spoiled, as	Hos 10:14	4013

F

FORTS
they built *f* against it round 2Kin 25:1   1785
and I will raise *f* against thee.................Is 29:3   4694
the *f* and towers shall be for dens...........Is 32:14   6076
built *f* against it round about ....Jer 52:4   1785
casting up mounts, and building *f* ....Eze 17:17   1785
and they that be in the *f*........................Eze 33:27   4679

FORTUNATUS (for-chu-na'-tus) A Christian acquaintance of Paul.
of the coming of Stephanas and F 1Cor 16:17   5415
from Philippi by Stephanus, and F ....1Cor s   5415

FORTY
f years, and begat sons and ....Gen 5:13   705
it to rain upon the earth *f* days..............Gen 7:4   705
the earth *f* days and *f* nights.................Gen 7:4   705
the earth *f* days and *f* nights.................Gen 7:12   705
the flood was *f* days upon the ....Gen 7:17   705
came to pass at the end of *f* days ....Gen 8:6   705
And he said, If I find there *f*.................Gen 18:28   705
there shall be *f* found there ....Gen 18:29   705
Isaac was *f* years old when he ....Gen 25:20   705
Esau was *f* years old when he took ....Gen 26:34   705
f kine, and ten bulls, twenty she ....Gen 32:15   705
age of Jacob was an hundred an ....Gen 47:28   705
f days were fulfilled for him ....Gen 50:3   705
of Israel did eat manna *f* years..............Ex 16:35   705
the mount *f* days and *f* nights...............Ex 24:18   705
thou shalt make *f* sockets of ....Ex 26:19   705
their *f* sockets of silver ....Ex 26:21   705
the LORD *f* days and *f* nights ....Ex 34:28   705
f sockets of silver he made under ....Ex 36:24   705
their *f* sockets of silver ....Ex 36:26   705
of years shall be unto thee *f*.................Lev 25:8   705
of the tribe of Reuben, were *f*...............Num 1:21   705
even of the tribe of Gad, were *f*............Num 1:25   705
were *f* thousand and five hundred ....Num 1:33   705
of the tribe of Asher, were *f* ....Num 1:41   705
were numbered thereof, were *f* ....Num 2:11   705
were numbered of them, were *f* ....Num 2:15   705
were *f* thousand and five hundred ....Num 2:19   705
were numbered of them, were *f* ....Num 2:28   705
of the land after *f* days ....Num 13:25   705
wander in the wilderness *f* years ....Num 14:33   705
ye searched the land, even *f* days..........Num 14:34   705
even *f* years, and ye shall know my.......Num 14:34   705
that were numbered of them were *f*......Num 26:7   705
f thousand and five hundred ....Num 26:18   705
that were numbered of them were *f*......Num 26:41   705
that were numbered of them were *f*......Num 26:50   705
wander in the wilderness *f* years ....Num 32:13   705
and to them ye shall add *f* ....Num 35:6   705
give to the Levites shall be *f* ....Num 35:7   705
these *f* years the LORD thy God ....Deut 2:7   705
these *f* years in the wilderness..............Deut 8:2   705
did thy foot swell, these *f* years...........Deut 8:4   705
then I abode in the mount *f* days ....Deut 9:9   705
f nights, I neither did eat bread ....Deut 9:9   705
came to pass at the end of *f* days ....Deut 9:11   705
f nights, that the LORD gave me ....Deut 9:11   705
the first, *f* days and *f* nights ....Deut 9:18   705
fell down before the LORD *f* days ....Deut 9:25   705
f nights, as I fell down at the ....Deut 9:25   705
time, *f* days and *f* nights ....Deut 10:10   705
F stripes he may give him, and not ....Deut 25:3   705
I have led you *f* years in the ....Deut 29:5   705
About *f* thousand prepared for war ....Josh 4:13   705
walked *f* years in the wilderness...........Josh 5:6   705
F years old was I when Moses the ....Josh 14:7   705
me alive, as he said, these *f* ....Josh 14:10   705
of the children of Israel were *f*............Josh 21:41   705
And the land had rest *f* years ....Judg 3:11   705
seen among *f* thousand in Israel ....Judg 5:8   705
And the land had rest *f* years ....Judg 5:31   705
f years in the days of Gideon ....Judg 8:28   705
at that time of the Ephraimites *f*.........Judg 12:6   705
And he had *f* sons and thirty ....Judg 12:14   705
hand of the Philistines *f* years ....Judg 13:1   705
And he had judged Israel *f* years 1Sa 4:18   705
and presented himself *f* days 1Sa 17:16   705
was *f* years old when he began to 2Sa 2:10   705
to reign, and he reigned *f* years............2Sa 5:4   705
f thousand horsemen, and smote 2Sa 10:18   705
And it came to pass after *f* years 2Sa 15:7   705
reigned over Israel were *f* years 1Kin 2:11   705
Solomon had *f* thousand stalls of 1Kin 4:26   705
before it, was *f* cubits long 1Kin 6:17   705
that lay on *f* five pillars, ...1Kin 7:3   705
one laver contained *f* baths 1Kin 7:38   705
over all Israel was *f* years 1Kin 11:42   705
Rehoboam was *f* and one years old 1Kin 14:21   705

And *f* and one years reigned he in 1Kin 15:10   705
the strength of that meat *f* days 1Kin 19:8   705
f nights unto Horeb the mount of 1Kin 19:8   705
bears out of the wood, and tare *f*..........2Kin 2:24   705
f camels' burden, and came and 2Kin 8:9   705
shearing house, even two and *f* men 2Kin 10:14   705
f years reigned he in Jerusalem............2Kin 12:1   705
to reign in Samaria, and reigned *f*........2Kin 14:23   705
f thousand seven hundred and..............1Chr 5:18   705
battle, expert in war, *f* thousand 1Chr 12:36   705
f thousand footmen, and killed 1Chr 19:18   705
reigned over Israel was *f* years 1Chr 29:27   705
Jerusalem over all Israel *f* years 2Chr 9:30   705
f years old when he began to 2Chr 12:13   705
F and two years old was Ahaziah...........2Chr 22:2   705
he reigned *f* years in Jerusalem 2Chr 24:1   705
children of Zattu, nine hundred *f*..........Ezr 2:8   705
children of Bani, six hundred *f*.............Ezr 2:10   705
The children of Azmaveth, *f*................Ezr 2:24   705
and Beeroth, seven hundred and *f* ....Ezr 2:25   705
of Jericho, three hundred *f* ....Ezr 2:34   705
Pashur, a thousand two hundred *f* ....Ezr 2:38   705
whole congregation together was *f*. Ezr 2:64   702,7239
their mules, two hundred *f*..................Ezr 2:66   705
beside *f* shekels of silver ....Neh 5:15   705
of Zattu, eight hundred *f*...................Neh 7:13   705
children of Binnui, six hundred *f* ....Neh 7:15   705
The men of Beth-azmaveth, *f*..............Neh 7:28   705
and Beeroth, seven hundred *f* ....Neh 7:29   705
of Jericho, three hundred *f* ....Neh 7:36   705
Pashur, a thousand two hundred *f* ....Neh 7:41   705
children of Asaph, an hundred *f*...........Neh 7:44   705
children of Nekoda, six hundred *f* ....Neh 7:62   705
whole congregation together was *f*. Neh 7:66   702,7239
and they had two hundred *f*................Neh 7:67   705
their mules, two hundred *f*..................Neh 7:68   705
f years didst thou sustain them ....Neh 9:21   705
f years didst thou sustain them ....Neh 11:13   705
of the fathers, two hundred *f*...............Neh 11:13   705
f years, and saw his sons, and his ....Job 42:16   705
F years long was I grieved with ....Ps 95:10   705
of the Jews seven hundred *f*................Jer 52:30   705
of the house of Judah *f* days ....Eze 4:6   705
shall it be inhabited *f* years ....Eze 29:11   705
waste shall be desolate *f* years ....Eze 29:12   705
At the end of *f* years will I ....Eze 29:13   705
the length thereof, *f* cubits ....Eze 41:2   705
courts joined of *f* cubits long ....Eze 46:22   705
led you *f* years through the ....Amos 2:10   705
in the wilderness *f* years ....Amos 5:25   705
Yet *f* days, and Nineveh shall be...........Jonah 3:4   705
And when he had fasted *f* days ....Mt 4:2   5062
f nights, he was afterward an ....Mt 4:2   5062
there in the wilderness *f* days ....Mk 1:13   5062
Being *f* days tempted of the devil ....Lk 4:2   5062
Then said the Jews, F and six ....Jn 2:20   5062
proofs, being seen of them *f* days ....Acts 1:3   5062
For the man was above *f* years old ....Acts 4:22   5062
And when he was full *f* years old ....Acts 7:23   5063
when *f* years were expired, there ....Acts 7:30   5062
sea, and in the wilderness *f* years ....Acts 7:36   5062
of *f* years in the wilderness ....Acts 7:42   5062
about the time of *f* years ....Acts 13:18   5063
Benjamin, by the space of *f* years.........Acts 13:21   5062
they were more than *f* which had ....Acts 23:13   5062
for him of them more than *f* men ....Acts 23:21   5062
received I *f* stripes save one.................2Cor 11:24   5062
me, and saw my works *f* years............Heb 3:9   5062
with whom was he grieved *f* years ....Heb 3:17   5062
there were sealed an hundred and *f*......Rev 7:4   5062
shall they tread under foot *f*................Rev 11:2   5062
was given unto him to continue *f*.........Rev 13:5   5062
Sion, and with him an hundred *f*..........Rev 14:1   5062
that song but the hundred and *f*...........Rev 14:3   5062
the wall thereof, an hundred and *f* ......Rev 21:17   5062

FORTY'S
said, I will not do it for *f* sake ....Gen 18:29   705

FORUM
came to meet us as far as Appii *f*..........Acts 28:15   675

FORWARD
And the man waxed great, and went *f* ...Gen 26:13   1980
of Israel, that they go *f* ....Ex 14:15   5265
And when the tabernacle setteth *f* ....Num 1:51   5265
of the congregation shall set *f*..............Num 2:17   5265
they encamp, so shall they set *f*............Num 2:17   5265
they shall go *f* in the third rank ....Num 2:24   5265
their standards, and so they set *f*..........Num 2:34   5265
And when the camp setteth *f* ....Num 4:5   5265
as the camp is to set *f*......................Num 4:15   5265
lie on the east parts shall go *f* ....Num 10:5   5265

and the sons of Merari set *f* .... Num 10:17 5265
set *f* according to their armies .... Num 10:18 5265
And the Kohathites set *f*, bearing .... Num 10:21 5265
set *f* according to their armies .... Num 10:22 5265
camp of the children of Dan set *f* .... Num 10:25 5265
to their armies, when they set *f* .... Num 10:28 5265
came to pass, when the ark set *f* .... Num 10:35 5265
And the children of Israel set *f* .... Num 21:10 5265
And the children of Israel set *f* .... Num 22:1 5265
them on yonder side Jordan, or *f* .... Num 32:19 1973
that was with him, rushed *f* .... Judg 9:44 6584
shalt thou go on *f* from thence 1Sa 10:3 1973
came upon David from that day *f* 1Sa 16:13 4605
eyed David from that day and *f* 1Sa 18:9 1973
And it was so from that day *f*. 1Sa 30:25 4605
but they went *f* smiting the 2Kin 3:24
to her servant, Drive, and go *f* 2Kin 4:24
shall the shadow go *f* ten degrees 2Kin 20:9
four thousand were to set *f* the 1Chr 23:4 5921
of the Kohathites, to set it *f* 2Chr 34:12 5921
to set the work of the house of .... Ezr 3:8 5921
to set *f* the workmen in the house .... Ezr 3:9 5921
Behold, I go *f*, but he is not .... Job 23:8 6924
they set *f* my calamity, they have .... Job 30:13 3276
heart, and went backward, and not *f* ..... Jer 7:24 6440
they went every one straight *f* .... Eze 1:9 6440
And they went every one straight *f* .... Eze 1:12 6440
they went every one straight *f* .... Eze 10:22 6440
LORD their God from that day and *f* .... Eze 39:22 1973
that upon the eighth day, and so *f* .... Eze 43:27 1973
they helped *f* the affliction .... Zec 1:15
he went *f* a little, and fell on .... Mk 14:35 4281
multitude, the Jews running him *f* .... Acts 19:33 4261
do, but also to be *f* a year ago 2Cor 8:10 2309
but being more *f*, of his own 2Cor 8:17 4707
the same which I also was *f* to do .... Gal 2:10 4704
whom if thou bring *f* on their 3Jn 6 4311

FORWARDNESS

by occasion of the *f* of others 2Cor 8:8 4710
For I know the *f* of your mind 2Cor 9:2 4288

FOUGHT

f with Israel in Rephidim .... Ex 17:8 3898
had said to him, and *f* with Amalek .... Ex 17:10 3898
then he *f* against Israel, and took .... Num 21:1 3898
to Jahaz, and *f* against Israel .... Num 21:23 3898
who had *f* against the former king .... Num 21:26 3898
for the LORD *f* for Israel .... Josh 10:14 3898
unto Libnah, and *f* against Libnah .... Josh 10:29 3898
against it, and *f* against it .... Josh 10:31 3898
against it, and *f* against it .... Josh 10:34 3898
and they *f* against it .... Josh 10:36 3898
to Debir, and *f* against it .... Josh 10:38 3898
LORD God of Israel *f* for Israel .... Josh 10:42 3898
God is he that hath *f* for you .... Josh 23:3 3898
and they *f* with you .... Josh 24:8 3898
the men of Jericho *f* against you .... Josh 24:11 3898
they *f* against him, and they slew .... Judg 1:5 3898
of Judah had *f* against Jerusalem .... Judg 1:8 3898
The kings came and *f* .... Judg 5:19 3898
then *f* the kings of Canaan in .... Judg 5:19 3898
They *f* from heaven .... Judg 5:20 3898
in their courses *f* against Sisera .... Judg 5:20 3898
(For my father *f* for you, and .... Judg 9:17 3898
of Shechem, and *f* with Abimelech .... Judg 9:39 3898
Abimelech *f* against the city all .... Judg 9:45 3898
f against it, and went hard unto .... Judg 9:52 3898
in Jahaz, and *f* against Israel .... Judg 11:20 3898
men of Gilead, and *f* with Ephraim .... Judg 12:4 3898
And the Philistines *f*, and Israel 1Sa 4:10 3898
of Moab, and they *f* against them 1Sa 12:9 3898
f against all his enemies on 1Sa 14:47 3898
f with the Philistines, and slew 1Sa 19:8 3898
f with the Philistines, and 1Sa 23:5 3898
the Philistines *f* against Israel 1Sa 31:1 3898
no more, neither *f* they any more 2Sa 2:28 3898
him, because he had *f* against 2Sa 8:10 3898
against David, and *f* with him 2Sa 10:17 3898
the city went out, and *f* with Joab 2Sa 11:17 3898
Joab *f* against Rabbah of the 2Sa 12:26 3898
I have *f* against Rabbah, and have 2Sa 12:27 3898
and *f* against it, and took it 2Sa 12:29 3898
f against the Philistines 2Sa 21:15 3898
when he *f* against Hazael king of 2Kin 8:29 3898
when he *f* with Hazael king of 2Kin 9:15 3898
f against Gath, and took it 2Kin 12:17 3898
his might wherewith he *f* against 2Kin 13:12 3898
how he *f* with Amaziah king of 2Kin 14:28 3898
the Philistines *f* against Israel 1Chr 10:1 3898
him, because he had *f* against 1Chr 18:10 3898
the Syrians, they *f* with him 1Chr 19:17 3898

thousand men which *f* in chariots 1Chr 19:18
they had heard that the LORD *f* 2Chr 18:31 3898
when he *f* with Hazael king of 2Chr 22:6 3898
He *f* also with the king of the 2Chr 27:5 3898
f against me without a cause .... Ps 109:3 3898
f against Ashdod, and took it .... Is 20:1 3898
their enemy, and he *f* against them ...... Is 63:10 3898
f against Jerusalem, and against .... Jer 34:1 3898
army *f* against Jerusalem, and .... Jer 34:7 3898
as when he *f* in the day of battle .... Zec 14:3 3898
that have *f* against Jerusalem .... Zec 14:12 6633
I have *f* with beasts at Ephesus 1Cor 15:32 2341
I have *f* a good fight, I have 2Ti 4:7 75
his angels *f* against the dragon .... Rev 12:7 4170
and the dragon *f* and his angels, ... Rev 12:7 4170

FOUL

My face is *f* with weeping, and on .... Job 16:16 2560
but ye must *f* the residue with .... Eze 34:18 7515
It will be *f* weather to day .... Mt 16:3 5494
together, he rebuked the *f* spirit .... Mk 9:25 169
and the hold of every *f* spirit .... Rev 18:2 169

FOULED

which ye have *f* with your feet .... Eze 34:19 4833

FOULEDST

with thy feet, and *f* their rivers .... Eze 32:2 7515

FOUND

was not *f* an help meet for him .... Gen 2:20 4672
But Noah *f* grace in the eyes of .... Gen 6:8 4672
But the dove *f* no rest for the .... Gen 8:9 4672
that they *f* a plain in the land .... Gen 11:2 4672
the angel of the LORD *f* her by a .... Gen 16:7 4672
if now I have *f* favour in thy .... Gen 18:3 4672
there shall be forty *f* there .... Gen 18:29 4672
there shall thirty be *f* there .... Gen 18:30 4672
there shall be twenty *f* there .... Gen 18:31 4672
Peradventure ten shall be *f* there .... Gen 18:32 4672
thy servant hath *f* grace in thy .... Gen 19:19 4672
f there a well of springing water .... Gen 26:19 4672
and said unto him, We have *f* water ...... Gen 26:32 4672
it that thou hast *f* it so quickly .... Gen 27:20 4672
f mandrakes in the field, and .... Gen 30:14 4672
if I have *f* favour in thine eyes, ... Gen 30:27 4672
but he *f* them not .... Gen 31:33 4672
all the tent, but *f* them not .... Gen 31:34 4672
he searched, but *f* not the images .... Gen 31:35 4672
what hast thou *f* of all thy .... Gen 31:37 4672
if now I have *f* grace in thy .... Gen 33:10 4672
this was that Anah that *f* the .... Gen 36:24 4672
And a certain man *f* him, and, ... Gen 37:15 4672
his brethren, and *f* them in Dothan ...... Gen 37:17 4672
and said, This have we *f* .... Gen 37:32 4672
but he *f* her not .... Gen 38:20 4672
this kid, and thou hast not *f* her .... Gen 38:23 4672
Joseph *f* grace in his sight, and .... Gen 39:4 4672
which we *f* in our sacks' mouths, ... Gen 44:8 4672
of thy servants it be *f*, both let .... Gen 44:9 4672
he with whom it is *f* shall be my .... Gen 44:10 4672
the cup was *f* in Benjamin's sack .... Gen 44:12 4672
God hath *f* out the iniquity of .... Gen 44:16 4672
and he also with whom the cup is *f* ...... Gen 44:16 4672
man in whose hand the cup is *f* .... Gen 44:17 4672
that was in the land of Egypt .... Gen 47:14 4672
If now I have *f* grace in thy .... Gen 47:29 4672
If now I have *f* grace in your .... Gen 50:4 4672
which shall be *f* in the field .... Ex 9:19 4672
be no leaven *f* in your houses .... Ex 12:19 4672
in the wilderness, and *f* no water .... Ex 15:22 4672
day for to gather, and they *f* none .... Ex 16:27 4672
him, or if he be *f* in his hand .... Ex 21:16 4672
If a thief be *f* breaking up .... Ex 22:2 4672
be certainly *f* in his hand alive .... Ex 22:4 4672
if the thief be *f*, let him pay .... Ex 22:7 4672
If the thief be not *f*, then the .... Ex 22:8 4672
thou hast *f* grace in my .... Ex 33:12 4672
if I have *f* grace in thy sight, ... Ex 33:13 4672
thy people have *f* grace in thy .... Ex 33:16 4672
for thou hast *f* grace in my sight .... Ex 33:17 4672
If now I have *f* grace in thy .... Ex 34:9 4672
every man, with whom was *f* blue .... Ex 35:23 4672
with whom was *f* shittim wood for .... Ex 35:24 4672
Or have *f* that which was lost, and ...... Lev 6:3 4672
or the lost thing which he *f* .... Lev 6:4 4672
have I not *f* favour in thy sight .... Num 11:11 4672
if I have *f* favour in thy sight .... Num 11:15 4672
they *f* a man that gathered sticks .... Num 15:32 4672
they that *f* him gathering sticks .... Num 15:33 4672
if we have *f* grace in thy sight, ... Num 32:5 4672
If there be *f* among you, within .... Deut 17:2 4672
There shall not be *f* among you .... Deut 18:10 4672

that all the people that is *f*	Deut 20:11	4672
If one be *f* slain in the land	Deut 21:1	4672
he hath lost, and thou hast *f*	Deut 22:3	4672
I came to her, I *f* her not a maid	Deut 22:14	4672
I *f* not thy daughter a maid	Deut 22:17	4672
virginity be not *f* for the damsel	Deut 22:20	4672
If a man be *f* lying with a woman	Deut 22:22	4672
For he *f* her in the field, and the	Deut 22:27	4672
and lie with her, and they be *f*	Deut 22:28	4672
his eyes, because he hath *f* some	Deut 24:1	4672
If a man be *f* stealing any of his	Deut 24:7	4672
He *f* him in a desert land, and in	Deut 32:10	4672
shall be *f* liars unto thee	Deut 33:29	4672
all the way, but *f* them not	Josh 2:22	4672
The five kings are *f* hid in a	Josh 10:17	4672
they *f* Adoni-bezek in Bezek	Judg 1:5	4672
If now I have *f* grace in thy	Judg 6:17	4672
ye had not *f* out my riddle	Judg 14:18	4672
he *f* a new jawbone of an ass, and	Judg 15:15	4672
they *f* among the inhabitants of	Judg 21:12	4672
Why have I *f* grace in thine eyes,	Ruth 2:10	4672
of Shalisha, but they *f* them not	1Sa 9:4	4672
Benjamites, but they *f* them not	1Sa 9:4	4672
they *f* young maidens going out to	1Sa 9:11	4672
for they are *f*	1Sa 9:20	4672
which thou wentest to seek are *f*	1Sa 10:2	4672
us plainly that the asses were *f*	1Sa 10:16	4672
sought him, he could not be *f*	1Sa 10:21	4672
ye have not *f* ought in my hand	1Sa 12:5	4672
Now there was no smith *f*	1Sa 13:19	4672
spear *f* in the hand of any of the	1Sa 13:22	4672
with Jonathan his son was there *f*	1Sa 13:22	4672
of their enemies which they *f*	1Sa 14:30	4672
for he hath *f* favour in my sight	1Sa 16:22	4672
that I have *f* grace in thine eyes	1Sa 20:3	4672
if I have *f* favour in thine eyes,	1Sa 20:29	4672
evil hath not been *f* in thee all	1Sa 25:28	4672
If I have now *f* grace in thine	1Sa 27:5	4672
I have *f* no fault in him since he	1Sa 29:3	4672
for I have not *f* evil in thee	1Sa 29:6	4672
what hast thou *f* in thy servant	1Sa 29:8	4672
they *f* an Egyptian in the field,	1Sa 30:11	4672
strip the slain, that they *f* Saul	1Sa 31:8	4672
f in his heart to pray this	2Sa 7:27	4672
that I have *f* grace in thy sight	2Sa 14:22	4672
in some place where he shall be *f*	2Sa 17:12	4672
be not one small stone *f* there	2Sa 17:13	
f Abishag a Shunammite, and	1Kin 1:3	4672
if wickedness shall be *f* in him	1Kin 1:52	4672
was the weight of the brass *f* out	1Kin 7:47	2713
Hadad *f* great favour in the sight	1Kin 11:19	4672
the Shilonite *f* him in the way	1Kin 11:29	4672
f him sitting under an oak	1Kin 13:14	4672
f his carcase cast in the way, and	1Kin 13:28	4672
because in him there is *f* some	1Kin 14:13	4672
and nation, that they *f* thee not	1Kin 18:10	4672
f Elisha the son of Shaphat, who	1Kin 19:19	4672
departed from him, a lion *f* him	1Kin 20:36	4672
Then he *f* another man, and said,	1Kin 20:37	4672
said to Elijah, Hast thou *f* me	1Kin 21:20	4672
And he answered, I have *f* thee	1Kin 21:20	4672
sought three days, but *f* him not	2Kin 2:17	4672
f a wild vine, and gathered	2Kin 4:39	4672
but they *f* no more of her than	2Kin 9:35	4672
wheresoever any breach shall be *f*	2Kin 12:5	4672
told the money that was *f* in the	2Kin 12:10	4672
all the gold that was *f* in the	2Kin 12:18	4672
were *f* in the house of the LORD	2Kin 14:14	4672
gold that was *f* in the house of	2Kin 16:8	4672
the king of Assyria *f* conspiracy	2Kin 17:4	4672
was *f* in the house of the LORD	2Kin 18:15	4672
f the king of Assyria warring	2Kin 19:8	4672
all that was *f* in his treasures	2Kin 20:13	4672
I have *f* the book of the law in	2Kin 22:8	4672
the money that was *f* in the house	2Kin 22:9	4672
the words of this book that is *f*	2Kin 22:13	4672
was *f* in the house of the LORD	2Kin 23:2	4672
priest *f* in the house of the LORD	2Kin 23:24	4672
which were *f* in the city, and the	2Kin 25:19	4672
the land that were *f* in the city	2Kin 25:19	4672
they *f* fat pasture and good, and	1Chr 4:40	4672
the habitations that were *f* there	1Chr 4:41	4672
strip the slain, that they *f* Saul	1Chr 10:8	4672
therefore thy servant hath *f* in	1Chr 17:25	4672
f it to weigh a talent of gold,	1Chr 20:2	4672
there were more chief men *f* of	1Chr 24:4	4672
there were *f* among them mighty	1Chr 26:31	4672
seek him, he will be *f* of thee	1Chr 28:9	4672
f gave them to the treasure of	1Chr 29:8	4672
they were *f* an hundred and fifty	2Chr 2:17	4672
of the brass could not be *f* out	2Chr 4:18	2713
ye seek him, he will be *f* of you	2Chr 15:2	4672
and sought him, he was *f* of them	2Chr 15:4	4672
and he was *f* of them	2Chr 15:15	4672
there are good things *f* in thee	2Chr 19:3	4672
they *f* among them in abundance	2Chr 20:25	4672
that was *f* in the king's house	2Chr 21:17	4672
f the princes of Judah, and the	2Chr 22:8	4672
f them three hundred thousand	2Chr 25:5	4672
were *f* in the house of God with	2Chr 25:24	4672
all the uncleanness that they *f*	2Chr 29:16	4672
Hilkiah the priest *f* a book of	2Chr 34:14	4672
I have *f* the book of the law in	2Chr 34:15	4672
was *f* in the house of the LORD	2Chr 34:17	4672
the words of the book that is *f*	2Chr 34:21	4672
was *f* in the house of the LORD	2Chr 34:30	4672
did, and that which was *f* in him	2Chr 36:8	4672
by genealogy, but they were not *f*	Ezr 2:62	4672
it is *f* that this city of old	Ezr 4:19	7912
there was *f* at Achmetha, in	Ezr 6:2	7912
f there none of the sons of Levi	Ezr 8:15	4672
f that had taken strange wives	Ezr 10:18	4672
have *f* favour in thy sight	Neh 2:5	
peace, and *f* nothing to answer	Neh 5:8	
I *f* a register of the genealogy	Neh 7:5	4672
the first, and *f* written therein,	Neh 7:5	4672
by genealogy, but it was not *f*	Neh 7:64	4672
they *f* written in the law which	Neh 8:14	4672
and therein was *f* written, that	Neh 13:1	4672
made of the matter, it was *f* out	Est 2:23	4672
If I have *f* favour in the sight	Est 5:8	4672
it was *f* written, that Mordecai	Est 6:2	4672
If I have *f* favour in thy sight,	Est 7:3	4672
if I have *f* favour in his sight,	Est 8:5	4672
the root of the matter is *f* in me	Job 19:28	4672
as a dream, and shall not be *f*	Job 20:8	4672
But where shall wisdom be *f*	Job 28:12	4672
neither is it *f* in the land of	Job 28:13	4672
lifted up myself when evil *f* him	Job 31:29	4672
because they had *f* no answer	Job 32:3	4672
should say, We have *f* out wisdom	Job 32:13	4672
I have *f* a ransom	Job 33:24	4672
in all the land were no women *f*	Job 42:15	4672
in a time when thou mayest be *f*	Ps 32:6	4672
his iniquity be *f* to be hateful	Ps 36:2	4672
sought him, but he could not be *f*	Ps 37:36	4672
and for comforters, but I *f* none	Ps 69:20	4672
men of might have *f* their hands	Ps 76:5	4672
Yea, the sparrow hath *f* an house	Ps 84:3	4672
I have *f* David my servant	Ps 89:20	4672
they *f* no city to dwell in	Ps 107:4	4672
I *f* trouble and sorrow	Ps 116:3	4672
we *f* it in the fields of the wood	Ps 132:6	4672
But if he be *f*, he shall restore	Prov 6:31	4672
seek thy face, and I have *f* thee	Prov 7:15	4672
hath understanding wisdom is *f*	Prov 10:13	4672
glory, if it be *f* in the way of	Prov 16:31	4672
when thou hast *f* it, then there	Prov 24:14	4672
Hast thou *f* honey	Prov 25:16	4672
reprove thee, and thou be *f* a liar	Prov 30:6	
curse thee, and thou be *f* guilty	Prov 30:10	
Behold, this have I *f*, saith the	Eccl 7:27	4672
one man among a thousand have I *f*	Eccl 7:28	4672
among all those have I not *f*	Eccl 7:28	4672
Lo, this only have I *f*, that God	Eccl 7:29	4672
Now there was *f* in it a poor wise	Eccl 9:15	4672
I sought him, but I *f* him not ,	Song 3:1	4672
I sought him, but I *f* him not	Song 3:2	4672
that go about the city *f* me	Song 3:3	4672
but I *f* him whom my soul loveth	Song 3:4	4672
that went about the city *f* me	Song 5:7	4672
in his eyes as one that *f* favour	Song 8:10	4672
As my hand hath *f* the kingdoms of	Is 10:10	4672
my hand hath *f* as a nest the	Is 10:14	4672
Every one that is *f* shall be	Is 13:15	4672
all that are *f* in thee are bound	Is 22:3	4672
so that there shall not be *f* in	Is 30:14	4672
thereon, it shall not be *f* there	Is 35:9	4672
f the king of Assyria warring	Is 37:8	4672
all that was *f* in his treasures	Is 39:2	4672
and gladness shall be *f* therein	Is 51:3	4672
ye the LORD while he may be *f*	Is 55:6	4672
thou hast *f* the life of thine	Is 57:10	4672
I am *f* of them that sought me not	Is 65:1	4672
the new wine is *f* in the cluster	Is 65:8	4672
have your fathers *f* in me	Jer 2:5	4672
the thief is ashamed when he is *f*	Jer 2:26	4672
Also in thy skirts is *f* the blood	Jer 2:34	4672
I have not *f* it by secret search,	Jer 2:34	4672
among my people are *f* wicked men	Jer 5:26	4672
A conspiracy is *f* among the men	Jer 11:9	4672
came to the pits, and *f* no water	Jer 14:3	4672

Thy words were *f*, and I did eat	Jer 15:16	4672
house have I *f* their wickedness	Jer 23:11	4672
And I will be *f* of you, saith the	Jer 29:14	4672
sword *f* grace in the wilderness	Jer 31:2	4672
the Chaldeans that were *f* there	Jer 41:3	4672
But ten men were *f* among them	Jer 41:8	4672
f him by the great waters that	Jer 41:12	4672
was he *f* among thieves	Jer 48:27	4672
All that *f* them have devoured	Jer 50:7	4672
of Judah, and they shall not be *f*	Jer 50:20	4672
thou art *f*, and also caught,	Jer 50:24	4672
person, which were *f* in the city	Jer 52:25	4672
that were *f* in the midst of the	Jer 52:25	4672
we have *f*, we have seen it	Lam 2:16	4672
not destroy it: but I *f* none	Eze 22:30	4672
yet shalt thou never be *f* again	Eze 26:21	4672
till iniquity was *f* in thee	Eze 28:15	4672
them all was *f* none like Daniel	Dan 1:19	4672
he *f* them ten times better than	Dan 1:20	4672
I have *f* a man of the captives of	Dan 2:25	4672
that no place was *f* for them	Dan 2:35	7912
wisdom of the gods, was *f* in him	Dan 5:11	7912
were *f* in the same Daniel, whom	Dan 5:12	7912
and excellent wisdom is *f* in thee	Dan 5:14	7912
in the balances, and art *f* wanting	Dan 5:27	7912
there any error or fault *f* in him	Dan 6:4	7912
f Daniel praying and making	Dan 6:11	7912
before him innocency was *f* in me	Dan 6:22	7912
no manner of hurt was *f* upon him	Dan 6:23	7912
stumble and fall, and not be *f*	Dan 11:19	4672
shall be *f* written in the book	Dan 12:1	4672
I *f* Israel like grapes in the	Hos 9:10	4672
now shall they be *f* faulty	Hos 10:2	
he *f* him in Beth-el, and there he	Hos 12:4	
I have *f* me out substance	Hos 12:8	4672
From me is thy fruit *f*.	Hos 14:8	4672
he *f* a ship going to Tarshish	Jonah 1:3	4672
of Israel were *f* in thee	Mic 1:13	4672
tongue be *f* in their mouth	Zeph 3:13	4672
and place shall not be *f* for them	Zec 10:10	4672
and iniquity was not *f* in his lips	Mal 2:6	4672
she was *f* with child of the Holy	Mt 1:18	2147
and when ye have *f* him, bring me	Mt 2:8	2147
I have not *f* so great faith, no,	Mt 8:10	2147
the which when a man hath *f*	Mt 13:44	2147
when he had *f* one pearl of great	Mt 13:46	2147
f one of his fellowservants,	Mt 18:28	2147
f others standing idle, and saith	Mt 20:6	2147
f nothing thereon, but leaves	Mt 21:19	2147
together all as many as they *f*	Mt 22:10	2147
And he came and *f* them asleep again	Mt 26:43	2147
But *f* none: yea, though	Mt 26:60	2147
witnesses came, yet *f* they none	Mt 26:60	2147
they *f* a man of Cyrene, Simon by	Mt 27:32	2147
And when they had *f* him, they said	Mk 1:37	2147
unwashen, hands, they *f* fault	Mk 7:2	
she *f* the devil gone out, and her	Mk 7:30	2147
f the colt tied by the door	Mk 11:4	2147
to it, he *f* nothing but leaves	Mk 11:13	2147
f as he had said unto them	Mk 14:16	2147
he *f* them asleep again, (for	Mk 14:40	2147
and *f* none.	Mk 14:55	2147
for thou hast *f* favour with God	Lk 1:30	2147
f Mary, and Joseph, and the babe	Lk 2:16	429
And when they *f* him not, they	Lk 2:45	2147
days they *f* him in the temple	Lk 2:46	2147
he *f* the place where it was	Lk 4:17	2147
I have not *f* so great faith, no,	Lk 7:9	2147
f the servant whole that had been	Lk 7:10	2147
f the man, out of whom the devils	Lk 8:35	2147
voice was past, Jesus was *f* alone	Lk 9:36	2147
sought fruit thereon, and *f* none	Lk 13:6	2147
And when he hath *f* it, he layeth	Lk 15:5	2147
for I have *f* my sheep which was	Lk 15:6	2147
And when she hath *f* it, she	Lk 15:9	2147
for I have *f* the piece which I	Lk 15:9	2147
he was lost, and is *f*.	Lk 15:24	2147
and was lost, and is *f*.	Lk 15:32	2147
There are not *f* that returned to	Lk 17:18	2147
f even as he had said unto them	Lk 19:32	2147
f as he had said unto them	Lk 22:13	2147
he *f* them sleeping for sorrow,	Lk 22:45	2147
We *f* this fellow perverting the	Lk 23:2	2147
have *f* no fault in this man	Lk 23:14	2147
I have *f* no cause of death in him	Lk 23:22	2147
they *f* the stone rolled away from	Lk 24:2	2147
f not the body of the Lord Jesus	Lk 24:3	2147
when they *f* not his body, they	Lk 24:23	2147
f it even so as the women had	Lk 24:24	2147
f the eleven gathered together,	Lk 24:33	2147
We have *f* the Messias, which is,	Jn 1:41	2147

and saith unto him, We have *f* him	Jn 1:45	2147
f in the temple those that sold	Jn 2:14	2147
when they had *f* him on the other	Jn 6:25	2147
and when he had *f* him, he said	Jn 9:35	2147
he *f* that he had lain in the	Jn 11:17	2147
Jesus, when he had *f* a young ass	Jn 12:14	2147
f her dead, and, carrying her	Acts 5:10	2147
f them not in the prison, they	Acts 5:23	2147
The prison truly *f* we shut with	Acts 5:23	2147
we had opened, we *f* no man within	Acts 5:23	2147
lest haply ye be *f* even to fight	Acts 5:39	2147
our fathers *f* no sustenance	Acts 7:11	2147
Who *f* favour before God, and	Acts 7:46	2147
But Philip was *f* at Azotus	Acts 8:40	2147
that if he *f* any of this way,	Acts 9:2	2147
there he *f* a certain man named	Acts 9:33	2147
f many that were come together	Acts 10:27	2147
And when he had *f* him, he brought	Acts 11:26	2147
f him not, he examined the	Acts 12:19	2147
they *f* a certain sorcerer,	Acts 13:6	2147
I have *f* David the son of Jesse,	Acts 13:22	2147
though they *f* no cause of death	Acts 13:28	2147
And when they *f* them not, they	Acts 17:6	2147
devotions, I *f* an altar with this	Acts 17:23	2147
f a certain Jew named Aquila,	Acts 18:2	2147
f it fifty thousand pieces of	Acts 19:19	2147
For we have *f* this man a	Acts 24:5	2147
they neither *f* me in the temple	Acts 24:12	2147
certain Jews from Asia *f* me	Acts 24:18	2147
if they have *f* any evil doing in	Acts 24:20	2147
But when I *f* that he had	Acts 25:25	2638
there the centurion *f* a ship of	Acts 27:6	2147
sounded, and *f* it twenty fathoms	Acts 27:28	2147
again, and *f* it fifteen fathoms	Acts 27:28	2147
Where we *f* brethren, and were	Acts 28:14	2147
pertaining to the flesh, hath *f*	Rom 4:1	2147
to life, I *f* to be unto death	Rom 7:10	2147
I was *f* of them that sought me	Rom 10:20	2147
that a man be *f* faithful	1Cor 4:2	2147
we are *f* false witnesses of God.	1Cor 15:15	2147
because I *f* not Titus my brother	2Cor 2:13	2147
clothed we shall not be *f* naked	2Cor 5:3	2147
I made before Titus, is *f* a truth.	2Cor 7:14	1096
glory, they may be *f* even as we	2Cor 11:12	2147
that I shall be *f* unto you such	2Cor 12:20	2147
we ourselves also are *f* sinners	Gal 2:17	2147
being *f* in fashion as a man, he	Phil 2:8	2147
be *f* in him, not having mine own	Phil 3:9	2147
of a deacon, being *f* blameless	1Ti 3:10	
me out very diligently, and *f* me	2Ti 1:17	2147
and was not *f*, because God had	Heb 11:5	2147
for he *f* no place of repentance,	Heb 12:17	2147
might be *f* unto praise and honour	1Pet 1:7	2147
neither was guile *f* in his mouth	1Pet 2:22	2147
that ye may be *f* of him in peace	2Pet 3:14	2147
I rejoiced greatly that I *f* of	2Jn 4	2147
and are not, and hast *f* them liars	Rev 2:2	2147
for I have not *f* thy works	Rev 3:2	2147
no man was *f* worthy to open	Rev 5:4	2147
their place *f* any more in heaven	Rev 12:8	2147
And in their mouth was *f* no guile	Rev 14:5	2147
away, and the mountains were not *f*.	Rev 16:20	2147
shall be *f* no more at all.	Rev 18:21	2147
shall be *f* any more in thee.	Rev 18:22	2147
in her was *f* the blood of	Rev 18:24	2147
there was *f* no place for them.	Rev 20:11	2147
whosoever was not *f* written in	Rev 20:15	2147

FOUNDATION

the *f* thereof even until now	Ex 9:18	3245
he shall lay the *f* thereof in his	Josh 6:26	3245
to lay the *f* of the house	1Kin 5:17	3245
In the fourth year was the *f* of	1Kin 6:37	3245
even from the *f* unto the coping,	1Kin 7:9	4527
the *f* was of costly stones, even	1Kin 7:10	3245
he laid the *f* thereof in Abiram	1Kin 16:34	3245
of the *f* of the house of the LORD	2Chr 8:16	4143
a third part at the gate of the *f*	2Chr 23:5	3247
began to lay the *f* of the heaps	2Chr 31:7	3245
But the *f* of the temple of the	Ezr 3:6	3245
the *f* of the temple of the LORD	Ezr 3:10	3245
because the *f* of the house of the	Ezr 3:11	3245
when the *f* of this house was laid	Ezr 3:12	3245
laid the *f* of the house of God	Ezr 5:16	787
whose *f* is in the dust, which are	Job 4:19	3247
whose *f* was overflown with a	Job 22:16	3247
His *f* is in the holy mountains	Ps 87:1	3248
hast thou laid the *f* of the earth	Ps 102:25	3245
rase it, even to the *f* thereof	Ps 137:7	3247
the righteous is an everlasting *f*	Prov 10:25	3247
I lay in Zion for a *f* a stone	Is 28:16	3248

a precious corner stone, a sure f	Is 28:16	4143
the temple, Thy f shall be laid	Is 44:28	3245
also hath laid the f of the earth	Is 48:13	3245
so that the f thereof shall be	Eze 13:14	3247
discovering the f unto the neck	Hab 3:13	3247
even from the day that the f of	Hag 2:18	3245
have laid the f of this house	Zec 4:9	3248
the f of the house of the LORD of	Zec 8:9	3248
layeth the f of the earth, and	Zec 12:1	3248
secret from the f of the world	Mt 13:35	2602
for you from the f of the world	Mt 25:34	2602
deep, and laid the f on a rock	Lk 6:48	2310
is like a man that without a f	Lk 6:49	2310
was shed from the f of the world	Lk 11:50	2602
haply, after he hath laid the f	Lk 14:29	2310
me before the f of the world	Jn 17:24	2602
should build upon another man's f	Rom 15:20	2310
masterbuilder, I have laid the f	1Cor 3:10	2310
For other f can no man lay than	1Cor 3:11	2310
if any man build upon this f gold	1Cor 3:12	2310
in him before the f of the world	Eph 1:4	2602
built upon the f of the apostles	Eph 2:20	2310
a good f against the time to come	1Ti 6:19	2310
Nevertheless the f of God	2Ti 2:19	2310
hast laid the f of the earth	Heb 1:10	2311
finished from the f of the world	Heb 4:3	2602
not laying again the f of	Heb 6:1	2310
suffered since the f of the world	Heb 9:26	2602
before the f of the world	1Pet 1:20	2602
slain from the f of the world	Rev 13:8	2602
of life from the f of the world	Rev 17:8	2602
The first f was jasper	Rev 21:19	2310

FOUNDATIONS

and set on fire the f of the	Deut 32:22	4146
the f of heaven moved and shook,	2Sa 22:8	4146
appeared, the f of the world were	2Sa 22:16	4146
walls thereof, and joined the f	Ezr 4:12	787
let the f thereof be strongly	Ezr 5:8	787
when I laid the f of the earth	Job 38:4	3245
are the f thereof fastened	Job 38:6	134
If the f be destroyed, what can	Ps 11:3	8356
the f also of the hills moved and	Ps 18:7	4146
seen, and the f of the world were	Ps 18:15	4146
all the f of the earth are out of	Ps 82:5	4146
Who laid the f of the earth	Ps 104:5	4349
he appointed the f of the earth	Prov 8:29	4146
for the f of Kir-haresheth shall	Is 16:7	808
the f of the earth do shake	Is 24:18	4146
from the f of the earth	Is 40:21	4146
and laid the f of the earth	Is 51:13	3245
lay the f of the earth, and say	Is 51:16	3245
and lay thy f with sapphires	Is 54:11	3245
up the f of many generations	Is 58:12	4146
the f of the earth searched out	Jer 31:37	4146
her f are fallen, her walls are	Jer 50:15	803
for a corner, nor a stone for f	Jer 51:26	4146
and it hath devoured the f thereof	Lam 4:11	3247
her f shall be broken down	Eze 30:4	3247
the f of the side chambers were a	Eze 41:8	4328
and I will discover the f thereof	Mic 1:6	3247
and ye strong f of the earth	Mic 6:2	4146
so that the f of the prison were	Acts 16:26	2310
he looked for a city which hath f	Heb 11:10	2310
the wall of the city had twelve f	Rev 21:14	2310
the f of the wall of the city	Rev 21:19	2310

FOUNDED

For he hath f it upon the seas,	Ps 24:2	3245
fulness thereof, thou hast f them	Ps 89:11	3245
place which thou hast f for them	Ps 104:8	3245
that thou hast f them for ever	Ps 119:152	3245
LORD by wisdom hath f the earth	Prov 3:19	3245
That the LORD hath f Zion	Is 14:32	3245
til the Assyrian f it for them	Is 23:13	3245
hath f his troop in the earth.	Amos 9:6	3245
for it was f upon a rock	Mt 7:25	2311
for it was f upon a rock	Lk 6:48	2311

FOUNDER

of silver, and gave them to the f	Judg 17:4	6884
the f melteth in vain	Jer 6:29	6884
workman, and of the hands of the f	Jer 10:9	6884
every f is confounded by the	Jer 10:14	6884
every f is confounded by the	Jer 51:17	6884

FOUNDEST

f his heart faithful before thee,	Neh 9:8	4672

FOUNTAIN

by a f of water in the wilderness	Gen 16:7	5869
by the f in the way to Shur	Gen 16:7	5869
Nevertheless a f or pit, wherein	Lev 11:36	4599

he hath discovered her f, and she	Lev 20:18	4726
hath uncovered the f of her blood	Lev 20:18	4726
the f of Jacob shall be upon a	Deut 33:28	5869
the f of the water of Nephtoah	Josh 15:9	4599
by a f which is in Jezreel	1Sa 29:1	5869
I went on to the gate of the f	Neh 2:14	5869
But the gate of the f repaired	Neh 3:15	5869
And at the f gate, which was over	Neh 12:37	5869
For with thee is the f of life	Ps 36:9	4726
the Lord, from the f of Israel	Ps 68:26	4726
Thou didst cleave the f and the	Ps 74:15	4599
the flint into a f of waters	Ps 114:8	4599
Let thy f be blessed	Prov 5:18	4726
law of the wise is a f of life	Prov 13:14	4726
fear of the LORD is a f of life	Prov 14:27	4726
the wicked is as a troubled f	Prov 25:26	4599
or the pitcher be broken at the f	Eccl 12:6	4002
a spring shut up, a f sealed	Song 4:12	4599
A f of gardens, a well of living	Song 4:15	4599
me the f of living waters	Jer 2:13	4726
As a f casteth out her waters, so	Jer 6:7	953
waters, and mine eyes a f of tears	Jer 9:1	4726
the LORD, the f of living waters	Jer 17:13	4726
dry, and his f shall be dried up	Hos 13:15	4599
a f shall come forth of the house	Joel 3:18	4599
a f opened to the house of David	Zec 13:1	4726
straightway the f of her blood	Mk 5:29	4077
Doth a f send forth at the same	Jas 3:11	4077
so can no f both yield salt water	Jas 3:12	4077
the f of the water of life freely	Rev 21:6	4077

FOUNTAINS

the same day were all the f of	Gen 7:11	4599
The f also of the deep and the	Gen 8:2	4599
and in Elim were twelve f of water	Num 33:9	5869
a land of brooks of water, of f	Deut 8:7	5869
the land, unto all f of water	1Kin 18:5	4599
the f which were without the city	2Chr 32:3	5869
together, who stopped all the f	2Chr 32:4	4599
Let thy f be dispersed abroad, and	Prov 5:16	4599
when there were no f abounding	Prov 8:24	4599
he strengthened the f of the deep	Prov 8:28	5869
f in the midst of the valleys	Is 41:18	4599
lead them unto living f of waters	Rev 7:17	4077
rivers, and upon the f of waters	Rev 8:10	4077
and the sea, and the f of waters	Rev 14:7	4077
upon the rivers and f of waters	Rev 16:4	4077

FOUR

parted, and became into f heads	Gen 2:10	702
after he begat Salah f hundred	Gen 11:13	702
after he begat Eber f hundred	Gen 11:15	702
And Eber lived f and thirty years,	Gen 11:16	702
after he begat Peleg f hundred	Gen 11:17	702
f kings with five	Gen 14:9	702
afflict them f hundred years	Gen 15:13	702
the land is worth f hundred	Gen 23:15	702
f hundred shekels of silver,	Gen 23:16	702
thee, and f hundred men with him	Gen 32:6	702
came, and with him f hundred men	Gen 33:1	702
f parts shall be your own, for	Gen 47:24	702
was f hundred and thirty years	Ex 12:40	702
pass at the end of the f hundred	Ex 12:41	702
for an ox, and f sheep for a sheep	Ex 22:1	702
thou shalt cast f rings of gold	Ex 25:12	702
put them in the f corners thereof	Ex 25:12	702
shalt make for it f rings of gold	Ex 25:26	702
put the rings in the f corners	Ex 25:26	702
that are on the f feet thereof	Ex 25:26	702
in the candlestick shall be f	Ex 25:34	702
breadth of one curtain f cubits	Ex 26:2	702
breadth of one curtain f cubits	Ex 26:8	702
it upon f pillars of shittim wood	Ex 26:32	702
upon the f sockets of silver	Ex 26:32	702
of it upon the f corners thereof	Ex 27:2	702
make f brasen rings for it	Ex 27:4	702
shall be f, and their sockets f	Ex 27:16	702
of stones, even f rows of stones	Ex 28:17	702
breadth of one curtain f cubits	Ex 36:9	702
f cubits was the breadth of one	Ex 36:15	702
he made thereunto f pillars of	Ex 36:36	702
he cast for them f sockets of	Ex 36:36	702
And he cast for it f rings of gold	Ex 37:3	702
to be set by the f corners of it	Ex 37:3	702
And he cast for it f rings of gold	Ex 37:13	702
put the rings upon the f corners	Ex 37:13	702
that were in the f feet thereof	Ex 37:13	702
were f bowls made like almonds	Ex 37:20	702
thereof on the f corners of it	Ex 38:2	702
he cast f rings for the f ends	Ex 38:5	702
And their pillars were f,	Ex 38:19	702
and their sockets of brass f	Ex 38:19	702

F

about in them, round about them *f*	Eze 46:23	702
the north side *f* thousand	Eze 48:16	702
and the south side *f* thousand	Eze 48:16	702
and on the east side *f* thousand	Eze 48:16	702
and the west side *f* thousand	Eze 48:16	702
f thousand and five hundred	Eze 48:30	702
And at the east side *f* thousand	Eze 48:32	702
And at the south side *f* thousand	Eze 48:33	702
At the west side *f* thousand	Eze 48:34	702
As for these *f* children, God gave	Dan 1:17	702
I see *f* men loose, walking in the	Dan 3:25	703
the *f* winds of the heaven strove	Dan 7:2	703
f great beasts came up from the	Dan 7:3	703
the back of it *f* wings of a fowl	Dan 7:6	703
the beast had also *f* heads	Dan 7:6	703
These great beasts, which are *f*	Dan 7:17	703
are *f* kings, which shall arise	Dan 7:17	703
for it came up *f* notable ones	Dan 8:8	702
ones toward the *f* winds of heaven	Dan 8:8	702
whereas *f* stood up for it	Dan 8:22	702
f kingdoms shall stand up out of	Dan 8:22	702
And in the *f* and twentieth day of	Dan 10:4	702
toward the *f* winds of heaven	Dan 11:4	702
of Damascus, and for *f*, I will not	Amos 1:3	702
transgressions of Gaza, and for *f*	Amos 1:6	702
transgressions of Tyrus, and for *f*	Amos 1:9	702
transgressions of Edom, and for *f*	Amos 1:11	702
the children of Ammon, and for *f*	Amos 1:13	702
transgressions of Moab, and for *f*	Amos 2:1	702
transgressions of Judah, and for *f*	Amos 2:4	702
of Israel, and for *f*, I will not	Amos 2:6	702
In the *f* and twentieth day of the	Hag 1:15	702
In the *f* and twentieth day of the	Hag 2:10	702
this day and upward, from the *f*	Hag 2:18	702
LORD came unto Haggai in the *f*	Hag 2:20	702
Upon the *f* and twentieth day of	Zec 1:7	702
eyes, and saw, and behold *f* horns	Zec 1:18	702
the LORD shewed me *f* carpenters	Zec 1:20	702
as the *f* winds of the heaven	Zec 2:6	702
there came *f* chariots out from	Zec 6:1	702
These are the *f* spirits of the	Zec 6:5	702
that did eat were *f* thousand men	Mt 15:38	5070
seven loaves of the *f* thousand	Mt 16:10	5070
his elect from the *f* winds	Mt 24:31	5064
the palsy, which was borne of *f*	Mk 2:3	5064
had eaten were about *f* thousand	Mk 8:9	5070
when the seven among *f* thousand	Mk 8:20	5070
his elect from the *f* winds	Mk 13:27	5064
f years, which departed not from	Lk 2:37	5064
not ye, There are yet *f* months	Jn 4:35	5072
lain in the grave *f* days already	Jn 11:17	5064
for he hath been dead *f* days	Jn 11:39	5066
made *f* parts, to every soldier a	Jn 19:23	5064
of men, about *f* hundred, joined	Acts 5:36	5064
entreat them evil *f* hundred years	Acts 7:6	5064
great sheet knit at the *f* corners	Acts 10:11	5064
F days ago I was fasting until	Acts 10:30	5067
let down from heaven by *f* corners	Acts 11:5	5064
delivered him to *f* quaternions of	Acts 12:4	5064
about the space of *f* hundred	Acts 13:20	5071
And the same man had *f* daughters	Acts 21:9	5064
We have *f* men which have a vow on	Acts 21:23	5064
f thousand men that were	Acts 21:38	5070
they cast *f* anchors out of the	Acts 27:29	5064
the law, which was *f* hundred	Gal 3:17	5071
And round about the throne were *f*	Rev 4:4	5064
and upon the seats I saw *f*	Rev 4:4	5064
were *f* beasts full of eyes before	Rev 4:6	5064
the *f* beasts had each of them six	Rev 4:8	5064
The *f* and twenty elders fall down	Rev 4:10	5064
of the throne and of the *f* beasts	Rev 5:6	5064
the *f* beasts and *f* and twenty	Rev 5:8	5064
And the *f* beasts said, Amen	Rev 5:14	5064
And the *f* and twenty elders fell	Rev 5:14	5064
one of the *f* beasts saying, Come	Rev 6:1	5064
in the midst of the *f* beasts say	Rev 6:6	5064
after these things I saw *f* angels	Rev 7:1	5064
on the *f* corners of the earth	Rev 7:1	5064
holding the *f* winds of the earth,	Rev 7:1	5064
with a loud voice to the *f* angels	Rev 7:2	5064
f thousand of all the tribes of	Rev 7:4	5064
the *f* beasts, and fell before the	Rev 7:11	5064
I heard a voice from the *f* horns	Rev 9:13	5064
Loose the *f* angels which are	Rev 9:14	5064
the *f* angels were loosed, which	Rev 9:15	5064
And the *f* and twenty elders, which	Rev 11:16	5064
f thousand, having his Father's	Rev 14:1	5064
throne, and before the *f* beasts	Rev 14:3	5064
f thousand, which were redeemed	Rev 14:3	5064
one of the *f* beasts gave unto the	Rev 15:7	5064
And the *f* and twenty elders and the	Rev 19:4	5064
the *f* beasts fell down and	Rev 19:4	5064
in the *f* quarters of the earth	Rev 20:8	5064
f cubits, according to the	Rev 21:17	5064

FOURFOLD

And he shall restore the lamb *f*	2Sa 12:6	706
false accusation, I restore him *f*	Lk 19:8	5073

FOURFOOTED

manner of *f* beasts of the earth	Acts 10:12	5074
saw *f* beasts of the earth, and	Acts 11:6	5074
f beasts, and creeping things	Rom 1:23	5074

FOURSCORE

And Abram was *f* and six years old,	Gen 16:16	8084
Isaac were an hundred and *f* years	Gen 35:28	8084
And Moses was *f* years old, and	Ex 7:7	8084
f years old, and Aaron *f*	Ex 7:7	8084
f thousand and six hundred and	Num 2:9	8084
thousand and five hundred and *f*	Num 4:48	8084
and now, lo, I am this day *f*	Josh 14:10	8084
And the land had rest *f* years	Judg 3:30	8084
priests, and slew on that day *f*	1Sa 22:18	8084
a very aged man, even *f* years old	2Sa 19:32	8084
I am this day *f* years old	2Sa 19:35	8084
and *f* thousand hewers in the	1Kin 5:15	8084
f thousand chosen men, which were	1Kin 12:21	8084
was sold for *f* pieces of silver	2Kin 6:25	8084
Jehu appointed *f* men without	2Kin 10:24	8084
of the Assyrians an hundred *f*	2Kin 19:35	8084
in all by their genealogies *f*	1Chr 7:5	8084
the chief, and his brethren *f*	1Chr 15:9	8084
were cunning, was two hundred *f*	1Chr 25:7	8084
f thousand to hew in the mountain	2Chr 2:2	8084
f thousand to be hewers in the	2Chr 2:18	8084
f thousand chosen men, which were	2Chr 11:1	8084
bows, two hundred and *f* thousand	2Chr 14:8	8084
him two hundred and *f* thousand	2Chr 17:15	8084
f thousand ready prepared for the	2Chr 17:18	8084
with him *f* priests of the LORD,	2Chr 26:17	8084
of Michael, and with him *f* males	Ezr 8:8	8084
and Netophah, an hundred *f*	Neh 7:26	8084
the holy city were two hundred *f*	Neh 11:18	8084
days, even an hundred and *f* days	Est 1:4	8084
of strength they be *f* years	Ps 90:10	8084
f concubines, and virgins without	Song 6:8	8084
of the Assyrians an hundred and *f*	Is 37:36	8084
and from Samaria, even *f* men	Jer 41:5	8084
And she was a widow of about *f*	Lk 2:37	3589
him, Take thy bill, and write *f*	Lk 16:7	3589

FOURSQUARE

the altar shall be *f*	Ex 27:1	7251
F it shall be being doubled	Ex 28:16	7251
breadth thereof; *f* shall it be	Ex 30:2	7251
of it a cubit; it was *f*	Ex 37:25	7251
the breadth thereof; it was *f*	Ex 38:1	7251
It was *f*; they made the	Ex 39:9	7251
gravings with their borders, *f*	1Kin 7:31	7251
and an hundred cubits broad, *f*	Eze 40:47	7251
shall offer the holy oblation *f*	Eze 48:20	7243
And the city lieth *f*, and the	Rev 21:16	5068

FOURTEEN

I served thee *f* years for thy two	Gen 31:41	702,6240
all the souls were *f*	Gen 46:22	702,6240
f thousand and six hundred	Num 1:27	702,7657
f thousand and six hundred	Num 2:4	702,7657
in the plague were *f* thousand	Num 16:49	702,7657
f lambs of the first year	Num 29:13	702,6246
deal to each lamb of the *f* lambs	Num 29:15	702,6246
f lambs of the first year without	Num 29:17	702,6246
f lambs of the first year without	Num 29:20	702,6246
f lambs of the first year without	Num 29:23	
f lambs of the first year without	Num 29:26	
f lambs of the first year without	Num 29:29	
f lambs of the first year without	Num 29:32	
f cities with their villages	Josh 15:36	
f cities with their villages	Josh 18:28	
days and seven days, even *f* days	1Kin 8:65	
And God gave to Heman *f* sons	1Chr 25:5	
waxed mighty, and married *f* wives	2Chr 13:21	
for he had *f* thousand sheep, and	Job 42:12	
the settle shall be *f* cubits long	Eze 43:17	
f broad in the four squares	Eze 43:17	
to David are *f* generations	Mt 1:17	1180
into Babylon are *f* generations	Mt 1:17	1180
unto Christ are *f* generations	Mt 1:17	1180
a man in Christ above *f* years ago	2Cor 12:2	1180
Then *f* years after I went up	Gal 2:1	1180

FOURTEENTH

in the *f* year came Chedorlaomer,	Gen 14:5	702,6240
until the *f* day of the same month	Ex 12:6	702,6240

on the *f* day of the month at even	Ex 12:18	702,6240
In the *f* day of the first month	Lev 23:5	702,6240
In the *f* day of this month, at	Num 9:3	702,6240
they kept the passover on the *f*	Num 9:5	702,6240
The *f* day of the second month at	Num 9:11	702,6240
in the *f* day of the first month	Num 28:16	702,6240
kept the passover on the *f* day of	Josh 5:10	702,6240
Now in the *f* year of king	2Kin 18:13	702,6240
to Huppah, the *f* to Jeshebeab,	1Chr 24:13	702,6240
The *f* to Mattithiah, he, his sons	1Chr 25:21	702,6240
on the *f* day of the second month	2Chr 30:15	702,6240
on the *f* day of the first month	2Chr 35:1	702,6240
upon the *f* day of the first month	Ezr 6:19	702,6240
the *f* day also of the month Adar	Est 9:15	702,6240
on the *f* day of the same rested	Est 9:17	702,6240
day thereof, and on the *f* thereof	Est 9:18	702,6240
made the *f* day of the month Adar	Est 9:19	702,6240
keep the *f* day of the month Adar	Est 9:21	702,6240
in the *f* year of king Hezekiah	Is 36:1	702,6240
in the *f* year after that the city	Eze 40:1	702,6240
in the *f* day of the month, ye	Eze 45:21	702,6240
But when the *f* night was come, as	Acts 27:27	*5065*
This day is the *f* day that ye	Acts 27:33	*5065*

FOURTH

and the morning were the *f* day	Gen 1:19	7243
And the *f* river is Euphrates	Gen 2:14	7243
But in the *f* generation they	Gen 15:16	7243
f generation of them that hate me	Ex 20:5	7256
the *f* row a beryl, and an onyx, and	Ex 28:20	7243
f part of an hin of beaten oil	Ex 29:40	7253
the *f* part of an hin of wine for	Ex 29:40	7243
the third and to the *f* generation	Ex 34:7	7256
And the *f* row, a beryl, an onyx,	Ex 39:13	7243
But in the *f* year all the fruit	Lev 19:24	7243
be of wine, the *f* part of a hin	Lev 23:13	7243
On the *f* day Elizur the son of	Num 7:30	7243
unto the third and *f* generation	Num 14:18	7256
with the *f* part of an hin of oil	Num 15:4	7243
the *f* part of an hin of wine for	Num 15:5	7243
number of the *f* part of Israel	Num 23:10	7255
mingled with the *f* part of an hin	Num 28:5	7243
offering thereof shall be the *f*	Num 28:7	7243
a *f* part of an hin unto a lamb	Num 28:14	7243
on the *f* day ten bullocks, two	Num 29:23	7243
f generation of them that hate me	Deut 5:9	7256
the *f* lot came out to Issachar,	Josh 19:17	7243
And it came to pass on the *f* day	Judg 19:5	7243
I have here at hand the *f* part of	1Sa 9:8	7253
And the *f*, Adonijah the son of	2Sa 3:4	7243
in the *f* year of Solomon's reign	1Kin 6:1	7243
olive tree, a *f* part of the wall	1Kin 6:33	7243
In the *f* year was the foundation	1Kin 6:37	7243
to reign over Judah in the *f* year	1Kin 22:41	702
the *f* part of a cab of dove's	2Kin 6:25	7255
thy children of the *f* generation	2Kin 10:30	7243
of Israel unto the *f* generation	2Kin 15:12	7243
in the *f* year of king Hezekiah	2Kin 18:9	7243
on the ninth day of the *f* month	2Kin 25:3	
Nethaneel the *f*, Raddai the fifth	1Chr 2:14	7243
the *f*, Adonijah the son of	1Chr 3:2	7243
the third Zedekiah, the *f* Shallum	1Chr 3:15	7243
Nohah the *f*, and Rapha the fifth	1Chr 8:2	7243
Mishmannah the *f*, Jeremiah the	1Chr 12:10	7243
the third, and Jekameam the *f*	1Chr 23:19	7243
third to Harim, the *f* to Seorim,	1Chr 24:8	7243
the third, Jekameam the *f*	1Chr 24:23	7243
The *f* to Izri, he, his sons, and	1Chr 25:11	7243
the third, Jathniel the *f*	1Chr 26:2	7243
Joah the third, and Sacar the *f*	1Chr 26:4	7243
the third, Zechariah the *f*	1Chr 26:11	7243
The *f* captain for the *f*	1Chr 27:7	7243
The *f* captain for the *f*	1Chr 27:7	7243
in the *f* year of his reign	2Chr 3:2	702
on the *f* day they assembled	2Chr 20:26	7243
Now on the *f* day was the silver	Ezr 8:33	7243
f day of this month the children	Neh 9:1	702
their God one *f* part of the day	Neh 9:3	7243
another *f* part they confessed, and	Neh 9:3	7243
f year of Jehoiakim the son of	Jer 25:1	7243
king of Judah, in the *f* year	Jer 28:1	7243
it came to pass in the *f* year of	Jer 36:1	7243
year of Zedekiah, in the *f* month	Jer 39:2	7243
in the *f* year of Jehoiakim the	Jer 45:1	7243
f year of Jehoiakim the son of	Jer 46:2	7243
in the *f* year of his reign	Jer 51:59	7243
And in the *f* month, in the ninth	Jer 52:6	7243
thirtieth year, in the *f* month	Eze 1:1	7243
the *f* the face of an eagle	Eze 10:14	7243
the *f* kingdom shall be strong as	Dan 2:40	7244
the form of the *f* is like the Son	Dan 3:25	7244
visions, and behold a *f* beast	Dan 7:7	7244
know the truth of the *f* beast	Dan 7:19	7244
The *f* beast shall be the *f*	Dan 7:23	7244
the *f* shall be far richer than	Dan 11:2	7243
in the *f* chariot grisled and bay	Zec 6:3	7243
pass in the *f* year of king Darius	Zec 7:1	702
in the *f* day of the ninth month	Zec 7:1	702
The fast of the *f* month, and the	Zec 8:19	7243
in the *f* watch of the night Jesus	Mt 14:25	*5067*
about the *f* watch of the night he	Mk 6:48	*5067*
the *f* beast was like a flying	Rev 4:7	*5067*
And when he had opened the *f* seal	Rev 6:7	*5067*
the voice of the *f* beast say	Rev 6:7	*5067*
them over the *f* part of the earth	Rev 6:8	*5067*
the *f* angel sounded, and the third	Rev 8:12	*5067*
the *f* angel poured out his vial	Rev 16:8	*5067*
the *f*, an emerald	Rev 21:19	*5067*

FOWL

f that may fly above the earth in	Gen 1:20	5775
every winged *f* after his kind	Gen 1:21	5775
let *f* multiply in the earth	Gen 1:22	5775
over the *f* of the air, and over	Gen 1:26	5775
over the *f* of the air, and over	Gen 1:28	5775
to every *f* of the air, and to	Gen 1:30	5775
the field, and every *f* of the air	Gen 2:19	5775
to the *f* of the air, and to every	Gen 2:20	5775
every *f* after his kind, every	Gen 7:14	5775
moved upon the earth, both of *f*	Gen 7:21	5775
things, and the *f* of the heaven	Gen 7:23	5775
thee, of all flesh, both of *f*	Gen 8:17	5775
every creeping thing, and every *f*	Gen 8:19	5775
clean beast, and of every clean *f*	Gen 8:20	5775
earth, and upon every *f* of the air	Gen 9:2	5775
that is with you, of the *f*	Gen 9:10	5775
whether it be of *f* or of beast	Lev 7:26	5775
law of the beasts, and of the *f*	Lev 11:46	5775
any beast or *f* that may be eaten	Lev 17:13	5775
abominable by beast, or by *f*	Lev 20:25	5775
winged *f* that flieth in the air	Deut 4:17	6833
and fallowdeer, and fatted *f*	1Kin 4:23	1257
he spake also of beasts, and of *f*	1Kin 4:33	5775
is a path which no *f* knoweth	Job 28:7	5861
The *f* of the air, and the fish of	Ps 8:8	6833
creeping things, and flying *f*	Ps 148:10	6833
both the *f* of the heavens and the	Jer 9:10	5775
shall dwell all *f* of every wing	Eze 17:23	6833
Speak unto every feathered *f*	Eze 39:17	6833
or torn, whether it be *f* or beast	Eze 44:31	5775
the back of it four wings of a *f*	Dan 7:6	5776

FOWLER

thee from the snare of the *f*	Ps 91:3	3353
as a bird from the hand of the *f*	Prov 6:5	3353
is a snare of a *f* in all his ways	Hos 9:8	3353

FOWLERS

a bird out of the snare of the *f*	Ps 124:7	3369

FOWLS

thing, and the *f* of the air	Gen 6:7	5775
Of *f* after their kind, and of	Gen 6:20	5775
Of *f* also of the air by sevens,	Gen 7:3	5775
that are not clean, and of *f*	Gen 7:8	5775
when the *f* came down upon the	Gen 15:11	5861
his offering to the LORD be of *f*	Lev 1:14	5775
have in abomination among the *f*	Lev 11:13	5775
All *f* that creep, going upon all	Lev 11:20	5775
and unclean, and between unclean *f*	Lev 20:25	5775
But of all clean *f* ye may eat	Deut 14:20	5775
be meat unto all *f* of the air	Deut 28:26	5775
thy flesh unto the *f* of the air	1Sa 17:44	5775
this day unto the *f* of the air	1Sa 17:46	5775
field shall the *f* of the air eat	1Kin 14:11	5775
fields shall the *f* of the air eat	1Kin 16:4	5775
field shall the *f* of the air eat	1Kin 21:24	5775
also *f* were prepared for me, and	Neh 5:18	6833
the *f* of the air, and they shall	Job 12:7	5775
kept close from the *f* of the air	Job 28:21	5775
us wiser than the *f* of heaven	Job 35:11	5775
I know all the *f* of the mountains	Ps 50:11	5775
feathered *f* like as the sand of	Ps 78:27	5775
be meat unto the *f* of the heaven	Ps 79:2	5775
By them shall the *f* of the heaven	Ps 104:12	5775
unto the *f* of the mountains	Is 18:6	5861
the *f* shall summer upon them, and	Is 18:6	5861
be meat for the *f* of the heaven	Jer 7:33	5775
the *f* of the heaven, and the	Jer 15:3	5775
shall be meat for the *f* of heaven	Jer 16:4	5775
be meat for the *f* of the heaven	Jer 19:7	5775
for meat unto the *f* of the heaven	Jer 34:20	5775
field and to the *f* of the heaven	Eze 29:5	5775
All the *f* of heaven made their	Eze 31:6	5775

all the _f_ of the heaven remain .... Eze 31:13   5775
will cause all the _f_ of the .... Eze 32:4   5775
the _f_ of the heaven, and the .... Eze 38:20   5775
the _f_ of the heaven hath he given .... Dan 2:38   5776
the _f_ of the heaven dwelt in the .... Dan 4:12   6853
it, and the _f_ from his branches .... Dan 4:14   6853
the _f_ of the heaven had their .... Dan 4:21   6853
with the _f_ of heaven, and with the .... Hos 2:18   5775
field, and with the _f_ of heaven .... Hos 4:3   5775
them down as the _f_ of the heaven .... Hos 7:12   5775
will consume all the _f_ of the heaven ...... Zeph 1:3   5775
Behold the _f_ of the air .... Mt 6:26   4071
the _f_ came and devoured them up ...... Mt 13:4   4071
the _f_ of the air came and devoured ...... Mk 4:4   4071
so that the _f_ of the air may .... Mk 4:32   4071
the _f_ of the air devoured it .... Lk 8:5   4071
more are ye better than the _f_ .... Lk 12:24   4071
the _f_ of the air lodged in the .... Lk 13:19   4071
creeping things, and _f_ of the air .... Acts 10:12   4071
creeping things, and _f_ of the air .... Acts 11:6   4071
saying to the _f_ that fly in .... Rev 19:17   3732
all the _f_ were filled with their .... Rev 19:21   3732

FOX

if a _f_ go up, he shall even break .... Neh 4:3   7776
unto them, Go ye, and tell that _f_ .... Lk 13:32   258

FOXES

went and caught three hundred _f_ .... Judg 15:4   7776
they shall be a portion for _f_ .... Ps 63:10   7776
Take us the _f_, the little _f_, ... Song 2:15   7776
Take us the _f_, the little _f_ .... Song 2:15   7776
is desolate, the _f_ walk upon it .... Lam 5:18   7776
are like the _f_ in the deserts .... Eze 13:4   7776
The _f_ have holes, and the birds of ...... Mt 8:20   258
_F_ have holes, and birds of the air .... Lk 9:58   258

FRAGMENTS

they took up of the _f_ that .... Mt 14:20   2801
up twelve baskets full of the _f_ .... Mk 6:43   2801
many baskets full of _f_ took ye up .... Mk 8:19   2801
many baskets full of _f_ took ye up .... Mk 8:20   2801
there was taken up of _f_ that .... Lk 9:17   2801
Gather up the _f_ that remain .... Jn 6:12   2801
the _f_ of the five barley loaves .... Jn 6:13   2801

FRAIL

that I may know how _f_ I am .... Ps 39:4   2310

FRAME

for he could not _f_ to pronounce .... Judg 12:6   3559
For he knoweth our _f_ .... Ps 103:14   3336
I _f_ evil against you, and devise a .... Jer 18:11   3335
by which was as the _f_ of a city .... Eze 40:2   4011
They will not _f_ their doings to .... Hos 5:4   5414

FRAMED

or shall the thing _f_ say of him .... Is 29:16   3336
thing _f_ say of him that _f_ it .... Is 29:16   3335
_f_ together groweth unto an holy .... Eph 2:21   4883
worlds were _f_ by the word of God .... Heb 11:3   2675

FRAMETH

to evil, and thy tongue _f_ deceit .... Ps 50:19   6775
which _f_ mischief by a law .... Ps 94:20   3335

FRANKINCENSE

these sweet spices with pure _f_ .... Ex 30:34   3828
oil upon it, and put _f_ thereon .... Lev 2:1   3828
thereof, with all the _f_ thereof .... Lev 2:2   3828
put oil upon it, and lay _f_ thereon .... Lev 2:15   3828
thereof, with all the _f_ thereof .... Lev 2:16   3828
shall he put any _f_ thereon .... Lev 5:11   3828
all the _f_ which is upon the meat .... Lev 6:15   3828
shalt put pure _f_ upon each row .... Lev 24:7   3828
no oil upon it, nor put _f_ thereon .... Num 5:15   3828
and the wine, and the oil, and the _f_ 1Chr 9:29   3828
laid the meat offerings, the _f_ .... Neh 13:5   3828
with the meat offering and the _f_ .... Neh 13:9   3828
smoke, perfumed with myrrh and _f_ ...... Song 3:6   3828
of myrrh, and to the hill of _f_ .... Song 4:6   3828
and cinnamon, with all trees of _f_ .... Song 4:14   3828
gold, and _f_, and myrrh .... Mt 2:11   3030
and odours, and ointments, and _f_ .... Rev 18:13   3030

FRANKLY

to pay, he _f_ forgave them both .... Lk 7:42   5435

FRAUD

is full of cursing and deceit and _f_ .... Ps 10:7   8496
which is of you kept back by _f_ .... Jas 5:4   650

FRAY

and no man shall _f_ them away .... Deut 28:26   2729
and none shall _f_ them away .... Jer 7:33   2729
but these are come to _f_ them .... Zec 1:21   2729

FRECKLED

it is a _f_ spot that groweth in .... Lev 13:39   933

FREE

he shall go out _f_ for nothing .... Ex 21:2   2670
I will not go out _f_ .... Ex 21:5   2670
shall she go out _f_ without money .... Ex 21:11   2600
let him go _f_ for his eye's sake .... Ex 21:26   2670
he shall let him go _f_ for his .... Ex 21:27   2670
him _f_ offerings every morning .... Ex 36:3   5071
to death, because she was not _f_ .... Lev 19:20   2666
be thou _f_ from this bitter water .... Num 5:19   5352
then she shall be _f_, and shall .... Num 5:28   5352
thou shalt let him go _f_ from thee .... Deut 15:12   2670
thou sendest him out _f_ from thee .... Deut 15:13   2670
thou sendest him away _f_ from thee .... Deut 15:18   2670
but he shall be _f_ at home one .... Deut 24:5   5355
his father's house _f_ in Israel 1Sa 17:25   2670
remaining in the chambers were _f_ 1Chr 9:33   6362
as many as were of a _f_ heart 2Chr 29:31   5081
the servant is _f_ from his master .... Job 3:19   2670
Who hath sent out the wild ass _f_ .... Job 39:5   2670
and uphold me with thy _f_ spirit .... Ps 51:12   5082
_F_ among the dead, like the slain .... Ps 88:5   2670
of the people, and let him go _f_ .... Ps 105:20   6605
and to let the oppressed go _f_ .... Is 58:6   2670
an Hebrew or an Hebrewess, go _f_ .... Jer 34:9   2670
every one his maidservant, go _f_ .... Jer 34:10   2670
handmaids, whom they had let go _f_ ...... Jer 34:11   2670
thou shalt let him go _f_ from thee .... Jer 34:14   2670
and publish the _f_ offerings .... Amos 4:5   5071
or his mother, he shall be _f_ .... Mt 15:6
unto him, Then are the children _f_ .... Mt 17:26   _1658_
he shall be _f_ .... Mk 7:11
and the truth shall make you _f_ .... Jn 8:32   _1659_
sayest thou, Ye shall be made _f_ .... Jn 8:33   _1658_
Son therefore shall make you _f_ .... Jn 8:36   _1659_
ye shall be _f_ indeed .... Jn 8:36   _1658_
And Paul said, But I was _f_ born .... Acts 22:28
offence, so also is the _f_ gift .... Rom 5:15   _5486_
but the _f_ gift is of many .... Rom 5:16   _5486_
the _f_ gift came upon all men unto .... Rom 5:18   _1659_
Being then made _f_ from sin .... Rom 6:18   _1659_
ye were _f_ from righteousness .... Rom 6:20   _1658_
But now being made _f_ from sin .... Rom 6:22   _1659_
be dead, she is _f_ from that law .... Rom 7:3   _1658_
made me _f_ from the law of sin .... Rom 8:2   _1659_
but if thou mayest be made _f_ .... 1Cor 7:21   _1658_
also he that is called, being _f_ .... 1Cor 7:22   _1658_
am I not _f_? .... 1Cor 9:1   _1658_
For though I be _f_ from all men .... 1Cor 9:19   _1658_
Gentiles, whether we be bond or _f_ .... 1Cor 12:13   _1658_
there is neither bond nor _f_ .... Gal 3:28   _1658_
But Jerusalem which is above is _f_ .... Gal 4:26   _1658_
heir with the son of the _f_ woman .... Gal 4:30   _1658_
of the bondwoman, but of the _f_ .... Gal 4:31   _1658_
wherewith Christ hath made us _f_ .... Gal 5:1   _1659_
the Lord, whether he be bond or _f_ .... Eph 6:8   _1658_
Barbarian, Scythian, bond nor _f_ .... Col 3:11   _1658_
of the Lord may have _f_ course 2Th 3:1
As _f_, and not using your liberty .... 1Pet 2:16   _1658_
and every bondman, and every _f_ man ...... Rev 6:15   _1658_
small and great, rich and poor, _f_ .... Rev 13:16   _1658_
and the flesh of all men, both _f_ .... Rev 19:18   _1658_

FREED

of you be _f_ from being bondmen .... Josh 9:23   3772
For he that is dead is _f_ from sin .... Rom 6:7   _1344_

FREEDMEN See LIBERTINES.

FREEDOM

at all redeemed, nor _f_ given her .... Lev 19:20   2668
a great sum obtained I this _f_ .... Acts 22:28   4174

FREELY

of the garden thou mayest _f_ eat .... Gen 2:16
fish, which we did eat in Egypt _f_ .... Num 11:5   2600
_f_ to day of the spoil of their 1Sa 14:30
offered _f_ for the house of God to .... Ezr 2:68
his counsellors have _f_ offered .... Ezr 7:15
I will _f_ sacrifice unto thee .... Ps 54:6   5071
backsliding, I will love them _f_ .... Hos 14:4   5071
_f_ ye have received, _f_ give .... Mt 10:8   _1432_
_f_ ye have received, _f_ give .... Mt 10:8   _1432_
let me _f_ speak unto you of the .... Acts 2:29   3326,3954
before whom also I speak _f_ .... Acts 26:26   3955
Being justified _f_ by his grace .... Rom 3:24   _1432_
him also _f_ give us all things .... Rom 8:32
that are _f_ given to us of God 1Cor 2:12
to you the gospel of God _f_ .... 2Cor 11:7   _1432_
fountain of the water of life _f_ .... Rev 21:6   _1432_
let him take the water of life _f_ .... Rev 22:17   _1432_

FREEMAN
being a servant, is the Lord's *f*.............1Cor 7:22   558

FREEWILL
vows, and for all his *f* offerings ....Lev 22:18   5071
or a *f* offering in beeves or ....Lev 22:21   5071
thou offer for a *f* offering ....Lev 22:23   5071
and beside all your *f* offerings................Lev 23:38   5071
or in a *f* offering, or in your ....Num 15:3   5071
your *f* offerings, for your burnt...............Num 29:39   5071
vows, and your *f* offerings, and the........Deut 12:6   5071
nor thy *f* offerings, or heave ....Deut 12:17   5071
of a *f* offering of thine hand...................Deut 16:10   5071
even a *f* offering, according as ....Deut 23:23   5071
was over the *f* offerings of God, ...2Chr 31:14   5071
beside the *f* offering for the ....Ezr 1:4   5071
a *f* offering unto the Lord.......................Ezr 3:5   5071
their own *f* to go up to Jerusalem ....Ezr 7:13   5069
with the *f* offering of the people ....Ezr 7:16   5069
the gold are a *f* offering unto.................Ezr 8:28   5071
the *f* offering of my mouth, O ....Ps 119:108   5071

FREEWOMAN
by a bondmaid, the other by a *f*.............Gal 4:22   1658
but he of the *f* was by promise ....Gal 4:23   1658

FREQUENT
above measure, in prisons more *f*..........2Cor 11:23   4056

FRESH
of it was as the taste of *f* oil ....Num 11:8   3955
My glory was *f* in me, and my bow ....Job 29:20   2319
I shall be anointed with *f* oil ....Ps 92:10   7488
both yield salt water and *f*....................Jas 3:12   1099

FRESHER
flesh shall be *f* than a child's ....Job 33:25   7375

FRET
it is *f* inward, whether it be ....Lev 13:55   6356
her sore, for to make her *f*.....................1Sa 1:6   7481
F not thyself because of..........................Ps 37:1   2734
f not thyself because of him who ....Ps 37:7   2734
f not thyself in any wise to do...............Ps 37:8   2734
F not thyself because of evil men ....Prov 24:19   2734
hungry, they shall *f* themselves ....Is 8:21   7107

FRETTED
but hast *f* me in all these things ....Eze 16:43   7264

FRETTETH
his heart *f* against the Lord ....Prov 19:3   2196

FRETTING
the plague is a *f* leprosy ....Lev 13:51   3992
for it is a *f* leprosy ....Lev 13:52   3992
it is a *f* leprosy in the house ....Lev 14:44   3992

FRIED
with oil, of fine flour, *f*.............................Lev 7:12   7246
the pan, and for that which is *f*..............1Chr 23:29   7246

FRIEND
his *f* Hirah the Adullamite.......................Gen 38:12   7453
the hand of his *f* the Adullamite ....Gen 38:20   7453
as a man speaketh unto his *f*...................Ex 33:11   7453
the wife of thy bosom, or thy *f*................Deut 13:6   7453
whom he had used as his *f*.....................Judg 14:20   7462
But Amnon had a *f*, whose name was 2Sa 13:3   7453
So Hushai David's *f* came into the 2Sa 15:37   7463
Hushai the Archite, David's *f*..................2Sa 16:16   7463
Is this thy kindness to thy *f*.....................2Sa 16:17   7453
why wentest thou not with thy *f* 2Sa 16:17   7453
officer, and the king's *f*............................1Kin 4:5   7463
seed of Abraham thy *f* for ever 2Chr 20:7   157
pity should be shewed from his *f*............Job 6:14   7453
and ye dig a pit for your *f*......................Job 6:27   7451
he had been my *f* or brother ....Ps 35:14   7453
Yea, mine own familiar *f*, in whom ....Ps 41:9   7453
f hast thou put far from me, and ....Ps 88:18   7453
son, if thou be surety for thy *f*...............Prov 6:1   7453
art come into the hand of thy *f*.............Prov 6:3   7453
thyself, and make sure thy *f* ....Prov 6:3   7453
A *f* loveth at all times, and a ....Prov 17:17   7453
surety in the presence of his *f*................Prov 17:18   7453
there is a *f* that sticketh closer ....Prov 18:24   157
every man is a *f* to him that ....Prov 19:6   7453
his lips the king shall be his *f*.................Prov 22:11   7453
Faithful are the wounds of a *f*................Prov 27:6   157
of a man's *f* by hearty counsel ....Prov 27:9   7453
Thine own *f*, and thy father's..................Prov 27:10   7453
own *f*, and thy father's...........................Prov 27:10   7453
blesseth his *f* with a loud voice.............Prov 27:14   7453
the countenance of his *f*..........................Prov 27:17   7453
is my beloved, and this is my *f*..............Song 5:16   7453
chosen, the seed of Abraham my *f*.........Is 41:8   157

neighbour and his *f* shall perish ....Jer 6:21   7453
the flesh of his *f* in the siege ....Jer 19:9   7453
love a woman beloved of her *f* ....Hos 3:1   7453
Trust ye not in a *f*, put ye not................Mic 7:5   7453
a *f* of publicans and sinners ....Mt 11:19   5384
answered one of them, and said, F........Mt 20:13   2083
And he saith unto him, F, how..............Mt 22:12   2083
And Jesus said unto him, F....................Mt 26:50   2083
a *f* of publicans and sinners ....Lk 7:34   5384
them, Which of you shall have a ....Lk 11:5   5384
at midnight, and say unto him, F..........Lk 11:5   5384
For a *f* of mine in his journey is ....Lk 11:6   5384
and give him, because he is his *f*..........Lk 11:8   5384
cometh, he may say unto thee, F...........Lk 14:10   5384
but the *f* of the bridegroom, ...Jn 3:29   5384
unto them, Our *f* Lazarus sleepeth......Jn 11:11   5384
man go, thou art not Caesar's *f*.............Jn 19:12   5384
the king's chamberlain their *f*................Acts 12:20   3982
and he was called the *F* of God ....Jas 2:23   5384
a *f* of the world is the enemy of..............Jas 4:4   5384

FRIENDLY
after her, to speak *f* unto her ....Judg 19:3   3820
hast spoken *f* unto thine handmaid ....Ruth 2:13   3820
hath friends must shew himself *f*...........Prov 18:24   7489

FRIENDS
Gerar, and Ahuzzath one of his *f*...........Gen 26:26   4828
elders of Judah, even to his *f*.................1Sa 30:26   7453
to his brethren, and to his *f*...................2Sa 3:8   4828
thine enemies, and hatest thy *f* 2Sa 19:6   157
of his kinsfolks, nor of his *f*...................1Kin 16:11   7453
home, he sent and called for his *f*..........Est 5:10   157
all his *f* unto him, Let a gallows ....Est 5:14   157
all his *f* every thing that had.................Est 6:13   157
Now when Job's three *f* heard of............Job 2:11   7453
My *f* scorn me ....Job 16:20   7453
that speaketh flattery to his *f*...............Job 17:5   7453
my familiar *f* have forgotten me ....Job 19:14   7453
All my inward *f* abhorred me ....Job 19:19   4962
me, have pity upon me, O ye my *f* ....Job 19:21   7453
his three *f* was his wrath kindled ....Job 32:3   7453
thee, and against thy two *f* ....Job 42:7   7453
of Job, when he prayed for his *f* ....Job 42:10   7453
my *f* stand aloof from my sore ....Ps 38:11   7453
but the rich hath many *f* ....Prov 14:20   157
and a whisperer separateth chief *f*.........Prov 16:28   441
a matter separateth very *f* ....Prov 17:9   441
A man that hath *f* must shew ....Prov 18:24   7453
Wealth maketh many *f*...........................Prov 19:4   7453
more do his *f* go far from him ....Prov 19:7   4828
eat, O *f*; drink, yea ....Song 5:1   7453
to thyself, and to all thy *f* ....Jer 20:4   157
buried there, thou, and all thy *f*............Jer 20:6   157
Thy *f* have set thee on, and have ....Jer 38:22   605,7965
all her *f* have dealt ....Lam 1:2   7453
was wounded in the house of my *f*........Zec 13:6   157
when his *f* heard of it, they went ....Mk 3:21   3588,3844
saith unto him, Go home to thy *f*.........Mk 5:19   4674
the centurion sent *f* to him ....Lk 7:6   5384
And I say unto you my *f*, Be not..........Lk 12:4   5384
or a supper, call not thy *f* ....Lk 14:12   5384
home, he calleth together his *f* ....Lk 15:6   5384
hath found it, she calleth her *f*.............Lk 15:9   5384
that I might make merry with my *f*......Lk 15:29   5384
to yourselves of the mammon of ....Lk 16:9   5384
and brethren, and kinsfolks, and *f*.......Lk 21:16   5384
and Herod were made *f* together ....Lk 23:12   5384
a man lay down his life for his *f*..........Jn 15:13   5384
Ye are my *f*, if ye do whatsoever ....Jn 15:14   5384
but I have called you *f*.........................Jn 15:15   5384
together his kinsmen and near *f*............Acts 10:24   5384
chief of Asia, which were his *f*...............Acts 19:31   5384
go unto his *f* to refresh himself.............Acts 27:3   5384
Our *f* salute thee 3Jn 14   5384
Greet the *f* by name...............................3Jn 14   5384

FRIENDSHIP
Make no *f* with an angry man ....Prov 22:24   7462
know ye not that the *f* of the ....Jas 4:4   5373

FRINGE
that they put upon the *f* of the ....Num 15:38   6734
And it shall be unto you for a *f*.............Num 15:39   6734

FRINGES
them *f* in the borders of their ....Num 15:38   6734
Thou shalt make thee *f* upon the ....Deut 22:12   1434

FRO SEE APPENDIX.

FROGS
will smite all thy borders with *f*.............Ex 8:2   6854
shall bring forth *f* abundantly.................Ex 8:3   6854

the *f* shall come up both on thee, ... Ex 8:4   6854
cause *f* to come up upon the land .... Ex 8:5   6854
the *f* came up, and covered the .... Ex 8:6   6854
brought up *f* upon the land of .... Ex 8:7   6854
he may take away the *f* from me .... Ex 8:8   6854
to destroy the *f* from thee .... Ex 8:9   6854
the *f* shall depart from thee, and .... Ex 8:11   6854
f which he had brought against.............. Ex 8:12   6854
the *f* died out of the houses, out........... Ex 8:13   6854
and *f*, which destroyed them .... Ps 78:45   6854
land brought forth *f* in abundance .... Ps 105:30   6854
f come out of the mouth of the .... Rev 16:13   *944*

FROM See APPENDIX.

FRONT See APPENDIX.

FRONTIERS
his cities which are on his *f*.............. Eze 25:9   7097

FRONTLETS
hand, and for *f* between thine eyes........ Ex 13:16   2903
they shall be as *f* between thine .... Deut 6:8   2903
may be as *f* between your eyes .... Deut 11:18   2903

FROST
consumed me, and the *f* by night........... Gen 31:40   7140
small as the hoar *f* on the ground .... Ex 16:14   3713
By the breath of God *f* is given.............. Job 37:10   7140
and the hoary *f* of heaven, who........... Job 38:29   3713
and their sycomore trees with *f*.............. Ps 78:47   2602
scattereth the hoar *f* like ashes .... Ps 147:16   3713
heat, and in the night to the *f* .... Jer 36:30   7140

FROWARD
for they are a very *f* generation .... Deut 32:20   8419
with the *f* thou wilt shew thyself 2Sa 22:27   6141
the counsel of the *f* is carried .... Job 5:13   6617
thyself pure; and with the *f*..................... Ps 18:26   6141
thou wilt shew thyself *f*........................... Ps 18:26   6617
A *f* heart shall depart from me .... Ps 101:4   6141
the man that speaketh *f* things .... Prov 2:12   8419
crooked, and they *f* in their paths .... Prov 2:15   3868
For the *f* is abomination to the............... Prov 3:32   3868
Put away from thee a *f* mouth................. Prov 4:24   6143
man, walketh with a *f* mouth .... Prov 6:12   6143
there is nothing *f* or perverse in .... Prov 8:8   6617
way, and the *f* mouth, do I hate............. Prov 8:13   8419
but the *f* tongue shall be cut out............ Prov 10:31   8419
They that are of a *f* heart are .... Prov 11:20   6141
A *f* man soweth strife .... Prov 16:28   8419
his eyes to devise *f* things .... Prov 16:30   8419
He that hath a *f* heart findeth no .... Prov 17:20   6141
The way of man is *f* and strange .... Prov 21:8   2019
and snares are in the way of the *f*......... Prov 22:5   6141
good and gentle, but also to the *f*........... 1Pet 2:18   *4646*

FROWARDLY
he went on *f* in the way of his .... Is 57:17   7726

FROWARDNESS
and delight in the *f* of the wicked .... Prov 2:14   8419
F is in his heart, he deviseth .... Prov 6:14   8419
mouth of the wicked speaketh *f*.............. Prov 10:32   8419

FROZEN
and the face of the deep is *f*................... Job 38:30   3920

FRUIT
the *f* tree yielding *f* after................... Gen 1:11   6529
his kind, and the tree yielding *f*........... Gen 1:12   6529
in the which is the *f* of a tree .... Gen 1:29   6529
We may eat of the *f* of the trees............. Gen 3:2   6529
But of the *f* of the tree which is .... Gen 3:3   6529
wise, she took of the *f* thereof .... Gen 3:6   6529
that Cain brought of the *f* of the .... Gen 4:3   6529
from thee the *f* of the womb .... Gen 30:2   6529
all the *f* of the trees which the .... Ex 10:15   6529
so that her *f* depart from her, and........... Ex 21:22   3206
then ye shall count the *f* thereof .... Lev 19:23   6529
But in the fourth year all the *f*............... Lev 19:24   6529
shall ye eat of the *f* thereof.................... Lev 19:25   6529
gathered in the *f* of the land................... Lev 23:39   8393
and gather in the *f* thereof .... Lev 25:3   8393
And the land yield her *f*........................ Lev 25:19   6529
bring forth *f* for three years .... Lev 25:21   8393
eat yet of old *f* until the ninth .... Lev 25:22   8393
of the field shall yield their *f* .... Lev 26:4   6529
or of the *f* of the tree, is the................... Lev 27:30   6529
and bring of the *f* of the land .... Num 13:20   6529
and shewed them the *f* of the land .... Num 13:26   6529
and this is the *f* of it.............................. Num 13:27   6529
they took of the *f* of the land in.............. Deut 1:25   6529
will also bless the *f* of thy womb .... Deut 7:13   6529
the *f* of thy land, thy corn, and .... Deut 7:13   6529
and that the land yield not her *f*............. Deut 11:17   2981

lest the *f* of thy seed which thou .... Deut 22:9   4395
the *f* of thy vineyard, be defiled .... Deut 22:9   8393
first of all the *f* of the earth.................... Deut 26:2   6529
shall be the *f* of thy body........................ Deut 28:4   6529
the *f* of thy ground, and the *f*............... Deut 28:4   6529
the *f* of thy cattle, the increase .... Deut 28:4   6529
in the *f* of thy body, and in the .... Deut 28:11   6529
in the *f* of thy cattle, and in the .... Deut 28:11   6529
in the *f* of thy ground, in the .... Deut 28:11   6529
Cursed shall be the *f* of thy body .... Deut 28:18   6529
the *f* of thy land, the increase .... Deut 28:18   6529
The *f* of thy land, and all thy .... Deut 28:33   6529
for thine olive shall cast his *f*................ Deut 28:40
f of thy land shall the locust .... Deut 28:42   6529
he shall eat the *f* of thy cattle .... Deut 28:51   6529
the *f* of thy land, until thou be .... Deut 28:51   6529
shalt eat the *f* of thine own body .... Deut 28:53   6529
in the *f* of thy body................................ Deut 30:9   6529
in the *f* of thy cattle .... Deut 30:9   6529
in the *f* of thy land, for good.................. Deut 30:9   6529
but they did eat of the *f* of the .... Josh 5:12   8393
my sweetness, and my good *f* .... Judg 9:11   8270
summer *f* for the young men to eat 2Sa 16:2
root downward, and bear *f* upward 2Kin 19:30   6529
and *f* trees in abundance....................... Neh 9:25   3978
our fathers to eat the *f* thereof .... Neh 9:36   6529
firstfruits of all *f* of all trees .... Neh 10:35   6529
the *f* of all manner of trees, of .... Neh 10:37   6529
forth his *f* in his season .... Ps 1:3   6529
Their *f* shalt thou destroy from .... Ps 21:10   6529
the *f* thereof shall shake like .... Ps 72:16   6529
still bring forth *f* in old age .... Ps 92:14   5107
satisfied with the *f* of thy works .... Ps 104:13   6529
devoured the *f* of their ground .... Ps 105:35   6529
the *f* of the womb is his reward............. Ps 127:3   6529
Of the *f* of thy body will I set .... Ps 132:11   6529
eat of the *f* of their own way .... Prov 1:31   6529
My *f* is better than gold, yea, ... Prov 8:19   6529
the *f* of the wicked to sin....................... Prov 10:16   8393
The *f* of the righteous is a tree.............. Prov 11:30   6529
root of the righteous yieldeth *f*............... Prov 12:12   6529
with good by the *f* of his mouth .... Prov 12:14   6529
eat good by the *f* of his mouth .... Prov 13:2   6529
satisfied with the *f* of his mouth .... Prov 18:20   6529
love it shall eat the *f* thereof.................. Prov 18:21   6529
fig tree shall eat the *f* thereof .... Prov 27:18   6529
with the *f* of her hands she .... Prov 31:16   6529
Give her of the *f* of her hands............... Prov 31:31   6529
his *f* was sweet to my taste .... Song 2:3   6529
every one for the *f* thereof was .... Song 8:11   6529
keep the *f* thereof two hundred .... Song 8:12   6529
shall eat the *f* of their doings .... Is 3:10   6529
the *f* of the earth shall be .... Is 4:2   6529
I will punish the *f* of the stout .... Is 10:12   6529
have no pity on the *f* of the womb.......... Is 13:18   6529
his *f* shall be a fiery flying..................... Is 14:29   6529
fill the face of the world with *f*............... Is 27:6   8570
this is all the *f* to take away .... Is 27:9   6529
as the hasty *f* before the summer .... Is 28:4   1061
vineyards, and eat the *f* thereof .... Is 37:30   6529
root downward, and bear *f* upward .... Is 37:31   6529
I create the *f* of the lips .... Is 57:19   5108
vineyards, and eat the *f* of them .... Is 65:21   6529
country, to eat the *f* thereof .... Jer 2:7   6529
even the *f* of their thoughts, ... Jer 6:19   6529
and upon the *f* of the ground .... Jer 7:20   6529
olive tree, fair, and of goodly *f*.............. Jer 11:16   6529
the tree with the *f* thereof...................... Jer 11:19   3899
grow, yea, they bring forth *f*.................. Jer 12:2   6529
shall cease from yielding *f*..................... Jer 17:8   6529
according to the *f* of his doings .... Jer 17:10   6529
according to the *f* of your doings .... Jer 21:14   6529
gardens, and eat the *f* of them .... Jer 29:5   6529
gardens, and eat the *f* of them .... Jer 29:28   6529
according to the *f* of his doings .... Jer 32:19   6529
Shall the women eat their *f*.................... Lam 2:20   6529
branches, and that it might bear *f*......... Eze 17:8   6529
thereof, and cut off the *f* thereof .... Eze 17:9   6529
bring forth boughs, and bear *f*.............. Eze 17:23   6529
and the east wind dried up her *f* .... Eze 19:12   6529
which hath devoured her *f*..................... Eze 19:14   6529
they shall eat thy *f*, and they................. Eze 25:4   6529
of the field shall yield her *f*................... Eze 34:27   6529
yield your *f* to my people of.................... Eze 36:8   6529
and they shall increase and bring *f*....... Eze 36:11   6509
I will multiply the *f* of the tree .... Eze 36:30   6529
neither shall the *f* thereof be .... Eze 47:12   6529
new *f* according to his months .... Eze 47:12   1061
the *f* thereof shall be for meat,.............. Eze 47:12   6529
the *f* thereof much, and in it was .... Dan 4:12   4
off his leaves, and scatter his *f*.............. Dan 4:14   4

the f thereof much, and in it was	Dan 4:21	4
is dried up, they shall bear no f	Hos 9:16	6529
even the beloved f of their womb	Hos 9:16	
he bringeth forth f unto himself	Hos 10:1	6529
to the multitude of his f he hath	Hos 10:1	6529
ye have eaten the f of lies	Hos 10:13	6529
From me is thy f found	Hos 14:8	6529
for the tree beareth her f	Joel 2:22	6529
yet I destroyed his f from above	Amos 2:9	6529
the f of righteousness into	Amos 6:12	6529
and a gatherer of sycomore f	Amos 7:14	
and behold a basket of summer f	Amos 8:1	
And I said, A basket of summer f	Amos 8:2	
gardens, and eat the f of them	Amos 9:14	6529
the f of my body for the sin of	Mic 6:7	6529
my soul desired the firstripe f	Mic 7:1	
for the f of their doings	Mic 7:13	6529
neither shall f be in the vines	Hab 3:17	2981
and the earth is stayed from her f	Hag 1:10	2981
the vine shall give her f	Zec 8:12	6529
the f thereof, even his meat, is	Mal 1:12	5108
shall your vine cast her f before	Mal 3:11	7920
not forth good f is hewn down	Mt 3:10	2590
good tree bringeth forth good f	Mt 7:17	2590
tree bringeth forth evil f	Mt 7:17	2590
tree cannot bring forth evil f	Mt 7:18	2590
a corrupt tree bring forth good f	Mt 7:18	2590
not forth good f is hewn down	Mt 7:19	2590
make the tree good, and his f good	Mt 12:33	2590
tree corrupt, and his f corrupt	Mt 12:33	2590
for the tree is known by his f	Mt 12:33	2590
good ground, and brought forth f	Mt 13:8	2590
which also beareth f, and bringeth	Mt 13:23	2592
was sprung up, and brought forth f	Mt 13:26	2590
unto it, Let no f grow on thee	Mt 21:19	2590
when the time of the f drew near	Mt 21:34	2590
henceforth of this f of the vine	Mt 26:29	1081
and choked it, and it yielded no f	Mk 4:7	2590
did yield f that sprang up and	Mk 4:8	2590
and receive it, and bring forth f	Mk 4:20	2592
earth bringeth forth f of herself	Mk 4:28	2592
But when the f is brought forth,	Mk 4:29	2590
No man eat f of thee hereafter	Mk 11:14	2590
of the f of the vineyard	Mk 12:2	2590
no more of the f of the vine	Mk 14:25	1081
and blessed is the f of thy womb	Lk 1:42	2590
not forth good f is hewn down	Lk 3:9	2590
tree bringeth not forth corrupt f	Lk 6:43	2590
a corrupt tree bring forth good f	Lk 6:43	2590
every tree is known by his own f	Lk 6:44	2590
up, and bare f an hundredfold	Lk 8:8	2590
life, and bring no f to perfection	Lk 8:14	5052
bring forth f with patience	Lk 8:15	2592
sought f thereon, and found none	Lk 13:6	2590
I come seeking f on this fig tree	Lk 13:7	2590
And if it bear f, well	Lk 13:9	2590
give him of the f of the vineyard	Lk 20:10	2590
not drink of the f of the vine	Lk 22:18	1081
gathereth f unto life eternal	Jn 4:36	2590
it die, it bringeth forth much f	Jn 12:24	2590
that beareth not f he taketh away	Jn 15:2	2590
and every branch that beareth f	Jn 15:2	2590
that it may bring forth more f	Jn 15:2	2590
branch cannot bear f of itself	Jn 15:4	2590
the same bringeth forth much f	Jn 15:5	2590
glorified, that ye bear much f	Jn 15:8	2590
ye should go and bring forth f	Jn 15:16	2590
that your f should remain	Jn 15:16	2590
that of the f of his loins,	Acts 2:30	2590
might have some f among you also	Rom 1:13	2590
What f had ye then in those	Rom 6:21	2590
ye have your f unto holiness, and	Rom 6:22	2590
we should bring forth f unto God	Rom 7:4	2592
to bring forth f unto death	Rom 7:5	2592
and have sealed to them this f	Rom 15:28	2590
and eateth not of the f thereof	1Cor 9:7	2590
But the f of the Spirit is love,	Gal 5:22	2590
(For the f of the Spirit is in	Eph 5:9	2590
this is the f of my labour	Phil 1:22	2590
but I desire f that may abound to	Phil 4:17	2590
and bringeth forth f, as it doth	Col 1:6	2592
it yieldeth the peaceable f of	Heb 12:11	2590
the f of our lips giving thanks	Heb 13:15	2590
the f of righteousness is sown in	Jas 3:18	2590
for the precious f of the earth	Jas 5:7	2590
and the earth brought forth her f	Jas 5:18	2590
trees whose f withereth, without	Jude 12	5352
whose f withereth, without f	Jude 12	175
and yielded her f every month	Rev 22:2	2590

FRUITFUL

And God blessed them, saying, Be f	Gen 1:22	6509
them, and God said unto them, Be f	Gen 1:28	6509
abundantly in the earth, and be f	Gen 8:17	6509
his sons, and said unto them, Be f	Gen 9:1	6509
And you, be ye f, and multiply	Gen 9:7	6509
And I will make thee exceeding f	Gen 17:6	6509
blessed him, and will make him f	Gen 17:20	6509
us, and we shall be f in the land	Gen 26:22	6509
bless thee, and make thee f	Gen 28:3	6509
be f and multiply	Gen 35:11	6509
be f in the land of my affliction	Gen 41:52	6509
me, Behold, I will make thee f	Gen 48:4	6509
Joseph is a f bough	Gen 49:22	6509
even a f bough by a well	Gen 49:22	6509
And the children of Israel were f	Ex 1:7	6509
respect unto you, and make you f	Lev 26:9	6509
A f land into barrenness, for the	Ps 107:34	6529
Thy wife shall be as a f vine by	Ps 128:3	6509
f trees, and all cedars	Ps 148:9	6529
hath a vineyard in a very f hill	Is 5:1	1121,8081
of his forest, and of his f field	Is 10:18	3759
in the outmost f branches thereof	Is 17:6	6509
shall be turned into a f field	Is 29:17	3759
the f field shall be esteemed as	Is 29:17	3759
pleasant fields, for the f vine	Is 32:12	6509
and the wilderness be a f field	Is 32:15	3759
remain in the f field	Is 32:15	3759
the f field shall be counted for a	Is 32:16	3759
the f place was a wilderness, and	Jer 4:26	3759
and they shall be f and increase	Jer 23:3	6509
land, and planted it in a f field	Eze 17:5	2233
she was f and full of branches by	Eze 19:10	6509
Though he be f among his brethren	Hos 13:15	6500
f seasons, filling our hearts	Acts 14:17	2593
being f in every good work, and	Col 1:10	2592

FRUITS

take of the best f in the land in	Gen 43:11	2173
to offer the first of thy ripe f	Ex 22:29	4395
and shalt gather in the f thereof	Ex 23:10	8393
with the bread of the first f for	Lev 23:20	1061
of the f he shall sell unto thee	Lev 25:15	8393
of the f doth he sell unto thee	Lev 25:16	8393
until her f come in ye shall eat	Lev 25:22	8393
trees of the land yield their f	Lev 26:20	6529
for the precious f brought forth	Deut 33:14	8393
him, and thou shalt bring in the f	2Sa 9:10	
and an hundred of summer f	2Sa 16:1	
all the f of the field since the	2Kin 8:6	8393
vineyards, and eat the f thereof	2Kin 19:29	6529
If I have eaten the f thereof	Job 31:39	3581
which may yield f of increase	Ps 107:37	6529
trees in them of all kind of f	Eccl 2:5	6529
of pomegranates, with pleasant f	Song 4:13	6529
his garden, and eat his pleasant f	Song 4:16	6529
nuts to see the f of the valley	Song 6:11	
are all manner of pleasant f	Song 7:13	3
for the shouting for thy summer f	Is 16:9	
and Carmel shake off their f	Is 33:9	
ye, gather ye wine, and summer f	Jer 40:10	
wine and summer f very much	Jer 40:12	
is fallen upon thy summer f	Jer 48:32	
for want of the f of the field	Lam 4:9	8570
they have gathered the summer f	Mic 7:1	
not destroy the f of your ground	Mal 3:11	6529
therefore f meet for repentance	Mt 3:8	2590
Ye shall know them by their f	Mt 7:16	2590
by their f ye shall know them	Mt 7:20	2590
they might receive the f of it	Mt 21:34	2590
render him the f in their seasons	Mt 21:41	2590
bringing forth the f thereof	Mt 21:43	2590
therefore f worthy of repentance	Lk 3:8	2590
have no room where to bestow my f	Lk 12:17	2590
and there will I bestow all my f	Lk 12:18	1081
sown, and increase the f of your	2Cor 9:10	1081
with the f of righteousness	Phil 1:11	2590
must be first partaker of the f	2Ti 2:6	2590
full of mercy and good f, without	Jas 3:17	2590
the f that thy soul lusted after	Rev 18:14	3703
which bare twelve manner of f	Rev 22:2	2590

FRUSTRATE

to f their purpose, all the days	Ezr 4:5	656
I do not f the grace of God	Gal 2:21	114

FRUSTRATETH

That f the tokens of the liars,	Is 44:25	6565

FRYING

meat offering baken in the f pan	Lev 2:7	4802

F

FRYINGPAN
and all that is dressed in the *f* .... Lev 7:9   4802

FUEL
be with burning and *f* of fire .... Is 9:5   3980
shall be as the *f* of the fire .... Is 9:19   3980
it is cast into the fire for *f* .... Eze 15:4   402
I have given to the fire for *f* .... Eze 15:6   402
Thou shalt be for *f* to the fire .... Eze 21:32   402

FUGITIVE
a *f* and a vagabond shalt thou be .... Gen 4:12   5128
and I shall be a *f* and a vagabond .... Gen 4:14   5128

FUGITIVES
Ye Gileadites are *f* of Ephraim .... Judg 12:4   6412
the *f* that fell away to the king 2Kin 25:11   5307
his *f* shall flee unto Zoar, an .... Is 15:5   1280
all his *f* with all his bands .... Eze 17:21   4015

FULFIL
F her week, and we will give thee .... Gen 29:27   4390
F your works, your daily tasks, ... Ex 5:13   3615
the number of thy days I will *f* .... Ex 23:26   4390
that he might *f* the word of the 1Kin 2:27   4390
takest heed to *f* the statutes 1Chr 22:13   6213
To *f* the word of the LORD by the 2Chr 36:21   4390
to *f* threescore and ten years 2Chr 36:21   4390
number the months that they *f* .... Job 39:2
own heart, and *f* all thy counsel .... Ps 20:4   4390
the LORD *f* all thy petitions .... Ps 20:5   4390
He will *f* the desire of them that .... Ps 145:19   6213
us to *f* all righteousness .... Mt 3:15   *4137*
am not come to destroy, but to *f*. .... Mt 5:17   *4137*
heart, which shall *f* all my will .... Acts 13:22   4160
if it *f* the law, judge thee, who .... Rom 2:27   5055
the flesh, to *f* the lusts thereof .... Rom 13:14
ye shall not *f* the lust of the .... Gal 5:16   *5055*
and so *f* the law of Christ .... Gal 6:2   378
F ye my joy, that ye be .... Phil 2:2   *4137*
me for you, to *f* the word of God .... Col 1:25   *4137*
in the Lord, that thou *f* it .... Col 4:17   *4137*
f all the good pleasure of his 2Th 1:11   *4137*
If ye *f* the royal law according .... Jas 2:8   *5055*
put in their hearts to *f* his will .... Rev 17:17   4160

FULFILLED
her days to be delivered were *f* .... Gen 25:24   4390
me my wife, for my days are *f* .... Gen 29:21   4390
And Jacob did so, and *f* her week .... Gen 29:28   4390
And forty days were *f* for him .... Gen 50:3   4390
for so are *f* the days of those .... Gen 50:3   4390
Wherefore have ye not *f* your task .... Ex 5:14   3615
And seven days were *f*, after that .... Ex 7:25   4390
the days of her purifying be *f* .... Lev 12:4   4390
the days of her purifying are *f* .... Lev 12:6   4390
until the days be *f*, in the which .... Num 6:5   4390
the days of his separation be *f* .... Num 6:13   4390
And when thy days be *f*, and thou 2Sa 7:12   4390
in that the king hath *f* the 2Sa 14:22   6213
and hath with his hand *f* it 1Kin 8:15   4390
hast *f* it with thine hand, as it 1Kin 8:24   4390
who hath with his hands *f* that 2Chr 6:4   4390
hast *f* it with thine hand, as it 2Chr 6:15   4390
the mouth of Jeremiah might be *f* .... Ezr 1:1   3615
But thou hast *f* the judgment of .... Job 36:17   4390
f with your hand, saying, We will .... Jer 44:25   4390
he hath *f* his word that he had .... Lam 2:17   1214
our end is near, our days are *f* .... Lam 4:18   4390
when the days of the siege are *f* .... Eze 5:2   4390
the thing *f* upon Nebuchadnezzar .... Dan 4:33   5487
till three whole weeks were *f* .... Dan 10:3   4390
that it might be *f* which was .... Mt 1:22   *4137*
that it might be *f* which was .... Mt 2:15   *4137*
Then was *f* that which was spoken .... Mt 2:17   *4137*
that it might be *f* which was .... Mt 2:23   *4137*
That it might be *f* which was .... Mt 4:14   *4137*
pass from the law, till all be *f*. .... Mt 5:18   *1096*
That it might be *f* which was .... Mt 8:17   *4137*
That it might be *f* which was .... Mt 12:17   *4137*
in them is *f* the prophecy of .... Mt 13:14   378
That it might be *f* which was .... Mt 13:35   *4137*
that it might be *f* which was .... Mt 21:4   *4137*
pass, till all these things be *f*. .... Mt 24:34   *1096*
then shall the scriptures be *f* .... Mt 26:54   *4137*
of the prophets might be *f* .... Mt 26:56   *4137*
Then was *f* that which was spoken .... Mt 27:9   *4137*
that it might be *f* which was .... Mt 27:35   *4137*
And saying, The time is *f*, and the .... Mk 1:15   *4137*
when all these things shall be *f* .... Mk 13:4   4931
but the scriptures must be *f* .... Mk 14:49   *4137*
And the scripture was *f*, which .... Mk 15:28   *4137*
which shall be *f* in their season .... Lk 1:20   *4137*

And when they had *f* the days .... Lk 2:43   5048
is this scripture *f* in your ears .... Lk 4:21   *4137*
things which are written may be *f*. ...... Lk 21:22   *4137*
the times of the Gentiles be *f* .... Lk 21:24   *4137*
not pass away, till all be *f* .... Lk 21:32   *1096*
until it be *f* in the kingdom of .... Lk 22:16   *4137*
you, that all things must be *f* .... Lk 24:44   *4137*
this my joy therefore is *f* .... Jn 3:29   *4137*
of Esaias the prophet might be *f* .... Jn 12:38   *4137*
but that the scripture may be *f* .... Jn 13:18   *4137*
that the word might be *f* that is .... Jn 15:25   *4137*
that the scripture might be *f* .... Jn 17:12   *4137*
might have my joy *f* in themselves .... Jn 17:13   *4137*
That the saying might be *f* .... Jn 18:9   *4137*
the saying of Jesus might be *f* .... Jn 18:32   *4137*
that the scripture might be *f* .... Jn 19:24   *4137*
that the scripture might be *f* .... Jn 19:28   5048
that the scripture should be *f* .... Jn 19:36   *4137*
scripture must needs have been *f* .... Acts 1:16   *4137*
should suffer, he hath so *f* .... Acts 3:18   *4137*
And after that many days were *f* .... Acts 9:23   *4137*
when they had *f* their ministry, ... Acts 12:25   *4137*
as John *f* his course, he said, ... Acts 13:25   *4137*
they have *f* them in condemning .... Acts 13:27   *4137*
when they had *f* all that was .... Acts 13:29   5055
God hath *f* the same unto us their .... Acts 13:33   1603
of God for the work which they *f* .... Acts 14:26   *4137*
of the law might be *f* in us .... Rom 8:4   *4137*
loveth another hath *f* the law .... Rom 13:8   *4137*
when your obedience is *f* 2Cor 10:6   *4137*
For all the law is *f* in one word .... Gal 5:14   *4137*
the scripture was *f* which saith .... Jas 2:23   *4137*
killed as they were, should be *f* .... Rev 6:11   *4137*
of the seven angels were *f* .... Rev 15:8   5055
until the words of God shall be *f* .... Rev 17:17   5055
the thousand years should be *f* .... Rev 20:3   5055

FULFILLING
stormy wind *f* his word .... Ps 148:8   6213
love is the *f* of the law .... Rom 13:10   *4138*
f the desires of the flesh and of .... Eph 2:3   *4160*

FULL
vale of Siddim was *f* of slimepits .... Gen 14:10
of the Amorites is not yet *f* .... Gen 15:16   8003
age, an old man, and *f* of years .... Gen 25:8   7649
people, being old and *f* of days .... Gen 35:29   7649
to pass at the end of two *f* years .... Gen 41:1   3117
devoured the seven rank and *f* ears .... Gen 41:7   4392
ears came up in one stalk, *f* .... Gen 41:22   4392
his sack, our money in *f* weight .... Gen 43:21
shall be *f* of swarms of flies .... Ex 8:21   4390
and when we did eat bread to the *f* .... Ex 16:3   7648
and in the morning bread to the *f* .... Ex 16:8   7646
put an omer *f* of manna therein, ... Ex 16:33   4393
for he should make *f* restitution .... Ex 22:3   7999
even corn beaten out of *f* ears .... Lev 2:14   3759
he shall take a censer *f* of .... Lev 16:12   4393
his hands *f* of sweet incense .... Lev 16:12   4393
the land become *f* of wickedness .... Lev 19:29   4390
within a *f* year may he redeem it .... Lev 25:29   3117
within the space of a *f* year .... Lev 25:30   8549
ye shall eat your bread to the *f* .... Lev 26:5   7648
both of them *f* of fine flour .... Num 7:13   4392
ten shekels of gold, *f* of incense .... Num 7:14   4392
both of them *f* of fine flour .... Num 7:19   4392
gold of ten shekels, *f* of incense .... Num 7:20   4392
both of them *f* of fine flour .... Num 7:25   4392
of ten shekels, *f* of incense .... Num 7:26   4392
both of them *f* of fine flour .... Num 7:31   4392
of ten shekels, *f* of incense .... Num 7:32   4392
both of them *f* of fine flour .... Num 7:37   4392
of ten shekels, *f* of incense .... Num 7:38   4392
both of them *f* of fine flour .... Num 7:43   4392
of ten shekels, *f* of incense .... Num 7:44   4392
both of them *f* of fine flour .... Num 7:49   4392
of ten shekels, *f* of incense .... Num 7:50   4392
both of them *f* of fine flour .... Num 7:55   4392
of ten shekels, *f* of incense .... Num 7:56   4392
both of them *f* of fine flour .... Num 7:61   4392
of ten shekels, *f* of incense .... Num 7:62   4392
both of them *f* of fine flour .... Num 7:67   4392
of ten shekels, *f* of incense .... Num 7:68   4392
both of them *f* of fine flour .... Num 7:73   4392
of ten shekels, *f* of incense .... Num 7:74   4392
both of them *f* of fine flour .... Num 7:79   4392
of ten shekels, *f* of incense .... Num 7:80   4392
f of incense, weighing ten .... Num 7:86   4392
give me his house *f* of silver .... Num 22:18   4393
give me his house *f* of silver .... Num 24:13   4393
houses *f* of all good things, ... Deut 6:11   4392
thou shalt have eaten and be *f* .... Deut 6:11   7646

When thou hast eaten and art f .... Deut 8:10 — 7646
when thou hast eaten and art f .... Deut 8:12 — 7646
that thou mayest eat and be f .... Deut 11:15 — 7646
father and her mother a f month .... Deut 21:13
f with the blessing of the Lord, ... Deut 33:23 — 4392
Nun was f of the spirit of wisdom .... Deut 34:9 — 4392
of the fleece, a bowl f of water .... Judg 6:38 — 4392
Now the house was f of men .... Judg 16:27 — 4390
I went out f, and the Lord hath .... Ruth 1:21 — 4392
a f reward be given thee of the .... Ruth 2:12 — 8003
They that were f have hired out .... 1Sa 2:5 — 7646
gave them in f tale to the king .... 1Sa 18:27 — 4390
of the Philistines was a f year .... 1Sa 27:7 — 3117
with one f line to keep alive .... 2Sa 8:2 — 4393
it came to pass after two f years .... 2Sa 13:23 — 3117
dwelt two f years in Jerusalem .... 2Sa 14:28 — 3117
a piece of ground f of lentiles .... 2Sa 23:11 — 4392
Make this valley f of ditches 2Kin 3:16
shalt set aside that which is f .... 2Kin 4:4 — 4392
to pass, when the vessels were f .... 2Kin 4:6 — 4390
thereof wild gourds his lap f .... 2Kin 4:39 — 4393
f ears of corn in the husk 2Kin 4:42
the mountain was f of horses .... 2Kin 6:17 — 4390
lo, all the way was f of garments .... 2Kin 7:15 — 4392
drew a bow with his f strength .... 2Kin 9:24 — 4390
the house of Baal was f from one .... 2Kin 10:21 — 4390
he reigned a f month in Samaria .... 2Kin 15:13 — 3117
a parcel of ground f of barley .... 1Chr 11:13 — 4392
shalt grant it me for the f price .... 1Chr 21:22 — 4392
verily buy it for the f price .... 1Chr 21:24 — 4392
f of days, he made Solomon his .... 1Chr 23:1 — 7646
f of days, riches, and honour .... 1Chr 29:28 — 7646
was f of days when he died .... 2Chr 24:15 — 7646
possessed houses f of all goods .... Neh 9:25 — 4392
then was Haman f of wrath .... Est 3:5 — 4390
he was f of indignation against .... Est 5:9 — 4390
come to thy grave in a f age .... Job 5:26 — 3624
I am f of tossings to and fro unto .... Job 7:4 — 7646
I am f of confusion .... Job 10:15 — 7646
should a man f of talk be .... Job 11:2
is of few days, and f of trouble .... Job 14:1 — 7646
His bones are f of the sin of his .... Job 20:11 — 4390
One dieth in his f strength .... Job 21:23 — 8537
His breasts are f of milk .... Job 21:24 — 4390
For I am f of matter .... Job 32:18 — 4390
thy table should be f of fatness .... Job 36:16 — 4390
Job died, being old and f of days .... Job 42:17 — 7646
His mouth is f of cursing .... Ps 10:7 — 4390
they are f of children, and leave .... Ps 17:14 — 7646
their right hand is f of bribes .... Ps 26:10 — 4390
voice of the Lord is f of majesty .... Ps 29:4
the earth is f of the goodness of .... Ps 33:5 — 4390
right hand is f of righteousness .... Ps 48:10 — 4390
river of God, which is f of water .... Ps 65:9 — 4390
and I am f of heaviness .... Ps 69:20
waters of a f cup are wrung out .... Ps 73:10 — 4392
dark places of the earth are f of .... Ps 74:20 — 4390
it is f of mixture .... Ps 75:8 — 4392
he sent them meat to the f .... Ps 78:25 — 7648
being of compassion, forgave .... Ps 78:38
art a God f of compassion, and .... Ps 86:15
For my soul is f of troubles .... Ps 88:3 — 7654
trees of the Lord are f of sap .... Ps 104:16 — 7654
the earth is f of thy riches .... Ps 104:24 — 4390
is gracious and f of compassion .... Ps 111:4
f of compassion, and righteous .... Ps 112:4
earth, O Lord, is f of thy mercy .... Ps 119:64 — 4390
that hath his quiver f of them .... Ps 127:5 — 4390
That our garners may be f .... Ps 144:13 — 4392
is gracious, and f of compassion .... Ps 145:8
than an house f of sacrifices .... Prov 17:1 — 4392
The f soul loatheth an honeycomb .... Prov 27:7 — 7646
Hell and destruction are never f .... Prov 27:20 — 7646
Lest I be f, and deny thee, and say .... Prov 30:9 — 7646
yet the sea is not f .... Eccl 1:7 — 4392
All things are f of labour .... Eccl 1:8
both the hands f with travail .... Eccl 4:6 — 4393
of the sons of men is f of evil .... Eccl 9:3 — 4390
A fool also is f of words .... Eccl 10:14 — 7235
If the clouds be f of rain .... Eccl 11:3 — 4390
I am f of the burnt offerings of .... Is 1:11 — 7646
your hands are f of blood .... Is 1:15 — 4390
it was f of judgment .... Is 1:21 — 4392
Their land also is f of silver .... Is 2:7 — 4390
their land is also f of horses .... Is 2:7 — 4390
Their land also is f of idols .... Is 2:8 — 4390
the whole earth is f of his glory .... Is 6:3 — 4393
for the earth shall be f of the .... Is 11:9 — 4390
shall be f of doleful creatures .... Is 13:21 — 4390
of Dimon shall be f of blood .... Is 15:9 — 4390
Thou that art f of stirs, a .... Is 22:2 — 4392

valleys shall be f of chariots .... Is 22:7 — 4390
lees, of fat things f of marrow .... Is 25:6
For all tables are f of vomit .... Is 28:8 — 4390
his lips are f of indignation, and .... Is 30:27 — 4390
they are f of the fury of the .... Is 51:20 — 4392
Even a f wind from those places .... Jer 4:12 — 4392
yet will I not make a f end .... Jer 4:27
when I had fed them to the f .... Jer 5:7 — 7646
but make not a f end .... Jer 5:10
I will not make a f end with you .... Jer 5:18
As a cage is f of birds, so are .... Jer 5:27 — 4392
so are their houses f of deceit .... Jer 5:27 — 4392
Therefore I am f of the fury of .... Jer 6:11 — 4392
aged with him that is f of days .... Jer 6:11 — 4390
For the land is f of adulterers .... Jer 23:10 — 4390
Within two f years will I bring .... Jer 28:3 — 3117
within the space of two f years .... Jer 28:11 — 3117
though I make a f end of all .... Jer 30:11
will I not make a f end of thee .... Jer 30:11
of the Rechabites pots f of wine .... Jer 35:5 — 4392
for I will make a f end of all .... Jer 46:28
I will not make a f end of thee .... Jer 46:28
solitary, that was f of people .... Lam 1:1 — 7227
he is filled f with reproach .... Lam 3:30 — 7646
their rings were f of eyes round .... Eze 1:18 — 4392
for the land is f of bloody .... Eze 7:23 — 4390
and the city is f of violence .... Eze 7:23 — 4390
great, and the land is f of blood .... Eze 9:9 — 4390
the city f of perverseness .... Eze 9:9 — 4390
the court was f of the brightness .... Eze 10:4 — 4390
were f of eyes round about, even .... Eze 10:12 — 4392
wilt thou make a f end of the .... Eze 11:13
f of feathers, which had divers .... Eze 17:3 — 4392
f of branches by reason of many .... Eze 19:10
f of wisdom, and perfect in beauty .... Eze 28:12 — 4392
and the rivers shall be f of thee .... Eze 32:6 — 4390
of that whereof it was f, when I .... Eze 32:15 — 4393
the valley which was f of bones .... Eze 37:1 — 4392
And ye shall eat fat till ye be f .... Eze 39:19 — 7654
were a f reed of six great cubits .... Eze 41:8 — 4393
Then was Nebuchadnezzar f of fury .... Dan 3:19 — 4391
transgressors are come to the f .... Dan 8:23 — 8552
Daniel was mourning three f weeks .... Dan 10:2 — 3117
And the floors shall be f of wheat .... Joel 2:24 — 4390
for the press is f, the fats .... Joel 3:13 — 4390
is pressed that is f of sheaves .... Amos 2:13 — 4392
But truly I am f of power by the .... Mic 3:8 — 4390
men thereof are f of violence .... Mic 6:12 — 4390
it is all f of lies and robbery .... Nah 3:1 — 4392
and the earth was f of his praise .... Hab 3:3 — 4390
of the city shall be f of boys .... Zec 8:5 — 4390
whole body shall be f of light .... Mt 6:22 — *5460*
whole body shall be f of darkness .... Mt 6:23 — *5460*
Which, when it was f, they drew .... Mt 13:48 — *4137*
that remained twelve baskets f .... Mt 14:20 — *4134*
that was left seven baskets f .... Mt 15:37 — *4134*
within they are f of extortion .... Mt 23:25 — *1073*
but are within f of dead men's .... Mt 23:27 — *1073*
but within ye are f of hypocrisy .... Mt 23:28 — *3324*
after that the f corn in the ear .... Mk 4:28 — *4134*
the ship, so that it was now f .... Mk 4:37 — *1072*
twelve baskets f of the fragments .... Mk 6:43 — *4134*
F well ye reject the commandment .... Mk 7:9
how many baskets f of fragments .... Mk 8:19 — *4134*
how many baskets f of fragments .... Mk 8:20 — *4138*
and filled a spunge f of vinegar .... Mk 15:36
Now Elisabeth's f time came that .... Lk 1:57 — *4130*
Jesus being f of the Holy Ghost .... Lk 4:1 — *4134*
city, behold a man f of leprosy .... Lk 5:12 — *4134*
Woe unto you that are f .... Lk 6:25 — *1705*
thy whole body also is f of light .... Lk 11:34 — *5460*
thy body also is f of darkness .... Lk 11:34
body therefore be f of light .... Lk 11:36 — *5460*
the whole shall be f of light .... Lk 11:36 — *5460*
your inward part is f of ravening .... Lk 11:39 — *1073*
was laid at his gate, f of sores, ... Lk 16:20
the Father,) f of grace and truth .... Jn 1:14 — *4134*
for my time is not yet f come .... Jn 7:8 — *4137*
you, and that your joy might be f .... Jn 15:11 — *4137*
receive, that your joy may be f .... Jn 16:24 — *4137*
was set a vessel f of vinegar .... Jn 19:29 — *3324*
the net to land f of great fishes .... Jn 21:11 — *3324*
said, These men are f of new wine .... Acts 2:13 — *3325*
thou shalt make me f of joy with .... Acts 2:28 — *4137*
f of the Holy Ghost and wisdom, ... Acts 6:3 — *4134*
a man f of faith and of the Holy .... Acts 6:5 — *4134*
f of faith and power, did great .... Acts 6:8 — *4134*
when he was f forty years old, it .... Acts 7:23 — *4137*
being of the Holy Ghost, looked .... Acts 7:55 — *4134*
this woman was f of good works .... Acts 9:36 — *4134*
f of the Holy Ghost and of faith .... Acts 11:24 — *4134*

F

O *f* of all subtilty and all	Acts 13:10	4134
sayings, they were *f* of wrath	Acts 19:28	4134
f of envy, murder, debate, deceit	Rom 1:29	3324
Whose mouth is *f* of cursing	Rom 3:14	1073
that ye also are *f* of goodness	Rom 15:14	3324
Now ye are *f*, now ye are rich, ye	1Cor 4:8	2880
was *f* of heaviness, because that	Phil 2:26	
I am instructed both to be *f*	Phil 4:12	5526
I am *f*, having received of	Phil 4:18	4137
love, and unto all riches of the *f*	Col 2:2	4136
make *f* proof of thy ministry	2Ti 4:5	4135
to them that are of *f* age	Heb 5:14	5046
f assurance of hope unto the end	Heb 6:11	4136
heart in *f* assurance of faith	Heb 10:22	4136
unruly evil, *f* of deadly poison	Jas 3:8	3324
f of mercy and good fruits	Jas 3:17	3324
joy unspeakable and *f* of glory	1Pet 1:8	
Having eyes *f* of adultery	2Pet 2:14	3324
unto you, that your joy may be *f*	1Jn 1:4	4137
but that we receive a *f* reward	2Jn 8	4134
to face, that our joy may be *f*	2Jn 12	4137
were four beasts *f* of eyes before	Rev 4:6	1073
they were *f* of eyes within	Rev 4:8	1073
and golden vials *f* of odours	Rev 5:8	1073
vials *f* of the wrath of God	Rev 15:7	1073
and his kingdom was *f* of darkness	Rev 16:10	
f of names of blasphemy, having	Rev 17:3	1073
cup in her hand *f* of abominations	Rev 17:4	1073
vials *f* of the seven last plagues	Rev 21:9	1073

FULLER
so as no *f* on earth can white	Mk 9:3	1102

FULLER'S
is in the highway of the *f* field	2Kin 18:17	3526
in the highway of the *f* field	Is 7:3	3526
in the highway of the *f* field	Is 36:2	3526

FULLERS'
a refiner's fire, and like *f* sope	Mal 3:2	3526

FULLY
Moses had *f* set up the tabernacle	Num 7:1	3615
with him, and hath followed me *f*	Num 14:24	4392
It hath *f* been shewed me, all	Ruth 2:11	5046
went not *f* after the LORD, as did	1Kin 11:6	4390
men is *f* set in them to do evil	Eccl 8:11	4390
be devoured as stubble *f* dry	Nah 1:10	4390
the day of Pentecost was *f* come	Acts 2:1	4845
being *f* persuaded that, what he	Rom 4:21	4135
Let every man be *f* persuaded in	Rom 14:5	4135
I have *f* preached the gospel of	Rom 15:19	4137
But thou hast *f* known my doctrine	2Ti 3:10	3877
me the preaching might be *f* known	2Ti 4:17	4135
for her grapes are *f* ripe	Rev 14:18	

FULNESS
as the *f* of the winepress	Num 18:27	4395
f thereof, and for the good will	Deut 33:16	4393
the sea roar, and the *f* thereof	1Chr 16:32	4393
In the *f* of his sufficiency he	Job 20:22	4390
in thy presence is *f* of joy	Ps 16:11	7648
is the LORD's, and the *f* thereof	Ps 24:1	4393
world is mine, and the *f* thereof	Ps 50:12	4393
the *f* thereof, thou hast founded	Ps 89:11	4393
the sea roar, and the *f* thereof	Ps 96:11	4393
the sea roar, and the *f* thereof	Ps 98:7	4393
f of bread, and abundance of	Eze 16:49	7653
the *f* thereof, by the noise of	Eze 19:7	4393
of his *f* have all we received, and	Jn 1:16	4138
how much more then *f* of	Rom 11:12	4138
until the *f* of the Gentiles be	Rom 11:25	4138
I shall come in the *f* of the	Rom 15:29	4138
is the Lord's, and the *f* thereof	1Cor 10:26	4138
is the Lord's, and the *f* thereof	1Cor 10:28	4138
But when the *f* of the time was	Gal 4:4	4138
of the *f* of times he might gather	Eph 1:10	4138
the *f* of him that filleth all in	Eph 1:23	4138
be filled with all the *f* of God	Eph 3:19	4138
of the stature of the *f* of Christ	Eph 4:13	4138
that in him should all *f* dwell	Col 1:19	4138
all the *f* of the Godhead bodily	Col 2:9	4138

FURBISH
f the spears, and put on the	Jer 46:4	4838

FURBISHED
a sword is sharpened, and also *f*	Eze 21:9	4803
it is *f* that it may glitter	Eze 21:10	4803
And he hath given it to be *f*	Eze 21:11	4803
sword is sharpened, and it is *f*	Eze 21:11	4803
for the slaughter it is *f*	Eze 21:28	4803

FURIOUS
with a *f* man thou shalt not go	Prov 22:24	2534
strife, and a *f* man aboundeth in	Prov 29:22	2534
anger and in fury and in *f* rebukes	Eze 5:15	2534
upon them the *f* rebukes	Eze 25:17	2534
the king was angry and very *f*	Dan 2:12	7108
the LORD revengeth, and is *f*	Nah 1:2	1167,2534

FURIOUSLY
for he driveth *f*	2Kin 9:20	7697
and they shall deal *f* with thee	Eze 23:25	2534

FURLONGS
from Jerusalem about threescore *f*	Lk 24:13	4712
about five and twenty or thirty *f*	Jn 6:19	4712
Jerusalem, about fifteen *f* off	Jn 11:18	4712
of a thousand and six hundred *f*	Rev 14:20	4712
with the reed, twelve thousand *f*	Rev 21:16	4712

FURNACE
it was dark, behold a smoking *f*	Gen 15:17	8574
went up as the smoke of a *f*	Gen 19:28	3536
to you handfuls of ashes of the *f*	Ex 9:8	3536
And they took ashes of the *f*	Ex 9:10	3536
ascended as the smoke of a *f*	Ex 19:18	3536
you forth out of the iron *f*	Deut 4:20	3564
from the midst of the *f* of iron	1Kin 8:51	3564
as silver tried in a *f* of earth	Ps 12:6	5948
is for silver, and the *f* for gold	Prov 17:3	3564
pot for silver, and the *f* for gold	Prov 27:21	3564
is in Zion, and his *f* in Jerusalem	Is 31:9	8574
thee in the *f* of affliction	Is 48:10	3564
land of Egypt, from the iron *f*	Jer 11:4	3564
and lead, in the midst of the *f*	Eze 22:18	3564
and tin, into the midst of the *f*	Eze 22:20	3564
is melted in the midst of the *f*	Eze 22:22	3564
the midst of a burning fiery *f*	Dan 3:6	861
the midst of a burning fiery *f*	Dan 3:11	861
the midst of a burning fiery *f*	Dan 3:15	861
us from the burning fiery *f*	Dan 3:17	861
that they should heat the *f* one	Dan 3:19	861
them into the burning fiery *f*	Dan 3:20	861
the midst of the burning fiery *f*	Dan 3:21	861
the *f* exceeding hot, the flame of	Dan 3:22	861
the midst of a burning fiery *f*	Dan 3:23	861
the mouth of the burning fiery *f*	Dan 3:26	861
shall cast them into a *f* of fire	Mt 13:42	2575
cast them into the *f* of fire	Mt 13:50	2575
brass, as if they burned in a *f*	Rev 1:15	2575
pit, as the smoke of a great *f*	Rev 9:2	2575

FURNACES
piece, and the tower of the *f*	Neh 3:11	8574
of the *f* even unto the broad wall	Neh 12:38	8574

FURNISH
Thou shalt *f* him liberally out of	Deut 15:14	6059
said, Can God *f* a table in the	Ps 78:19	6186
that *f* the drink offering unto	Is 65:11	4390
f thyself to go into captivity	Jer 46:19	6213,3627

FURNISHED
had *f* Solomon with cedar trees	1Kin 9:11	5375
she hath also *f* her table	Prov 9:2	6186
and the wedding was *f* with guests	Mt 22:10	4130
shew you a large upper room *f*	Mk 14:15	4766
shew you a large upper room *f*	Lk 22:12	4766
throughly *f* unto all good works	2Ti 3:17	1822

FURNITURE
and put them in the camel's *f*	Gen 31:34	3733
all the *f* of the tabernacle,	Ex 31:7	3627
And the table and his *f*, and the	Ex 31:8	3627
pure candlestick with all his *f*	Ex 31:8	3627
of burnt offering with all his *f*	Ex 31:9	3627
also for the light, and his *f*	Ex 35:14	3627
Moses, the tent, and all his *f*	Ex 39:33	3627
glory out of all the pleasant *f*	Nah 2:9	3627

FURROW
unicorn with his band in the *f*	Job 39:10	8525

FURROWS
or that the *f* likewise thereof	Job 31:38	8525
thou settlest the *f* thereof	Ps 65:10	1417
they made long their *f*	Ps 129:3	4618
it by the *f* of her plantation	Eze 17:7	6170
wither in the *f* where it grew	Eze 17:10	6170
as hemlock in the *f* of the field	Hos 10:4	8525
bind themselves in their two *f*	Hos 10:10	5869
as heaps in the *f* of the fields	Hos 12:11	8525

FURTHER See APPENDIX.

FURTHERANCE
rather unto the *f* of the gospel	Phil 1:12	4297
continue with you all for your *f*	Phil 1:25	4297

FURTHERED

they *f* the people, and the house .... Ezr 8:36 — 5375

FURTHERMORE See APPENDIX.

FURY

until thy brother's *f* turn away .... Gen 27:44 — 2534
walk contrary unto you also in *f* .... Lev 26:28 — 2534
God shall cast the *f* of his wrath .... Job 20:23 — 2740
F is not in me .... Is 27:4 — 2534
his *f* upon all their armies .... Is 34:2 — 2534
upon him the *f* of his anger .... Is 42:25 — 2534
because of the *f* of the oppressor .... Is 51:13 — 2534
where is the *f* of the oppressor .... Is 51:13 — 2534
hand of the LORD the cup of his *f* .... Is 51:17 — 2534
are full of the *f* of the LORD .... Is 51:20 — 2534
even the dregs of the cup of my *f* .... Is 51:22 — 2534
f to his adversaries, recompence .... Is 59:18 — 2534
anger, and trample them in my *f* .... Is 63:3 — 2534
and my *f*, it upheld me .... Is 63:5 — 2534
anger, and make them drunk in my *f* ..... Is 63:6 — 2534
to render his anger with *f* .... Is 66:15 — 2534
lest my *f* come forth like fire, ... Jer 4:4 — 2534
I am full of the *f* of the LORD .... Jer 6:11 — 2534
my *f* shall be poured out upon .... Jer 7:20 — 2534
Pour out thy *f* upon the heathen .... Jer 10:25 — 2534
arm, even in anger, and in *f* .... Jer 21:5 — 2534
lest my *f* go out like fire, and .... Jer 21:12 — 2534
of the LORD is gone forth in *f* .... Jer 23:19 — 2534
the wine cup of this *f* at my hand .... Jer 25:15 — 2534
of the LORD goeth forth with *f* .... Jer 30:23 — 2534
of my *f* from the day that they .... Jer 32:31 — 2534
them in mine anger, and in my *f* .... Jer 32:37 — 2534
slain in mine anger and in my *f* .... Jer 33:5 — 2534
anger and the *f* that the LORD hath .... Jer 36:7 — 2534
my *f* hath been poured forth upon .... Jer 42:18 — 2534
so shall my *f* be poured forth .... Jer 42:18 — 2534
Wherefore my *f* and mine anger was ..... Jer 44:6 — 2534

he poured out his *f* like fire .... Lam 2:4 — 2534
The LORD hath accomplished his *f* .... Lam 4:11 — 2534
I will cause my *f* to rest upon .... Eze 5:13 — 2534
I have accomplished my *f* in them .... Eze 5:13 — 2534
in thee in anger and in *f* and in .... Eze 5:15 — 2534
will I accomplish my *f* upon them .... Eze 6:12 — 2534
I shortly pour out my *f* upon thee .... Eze 7:8 — 2534
Therefore will I also deal in *f* .... Eze 8:18 — 2534
out of thy *f* upon Jerusalem .... Eze 9:8 — 2534
it with a stormy wind in my *f* .... Eze 13:13 — 2534
hailstones in my *f* to consume it .... Eze 13:13 — 2534
pour out my *f* upon it in blood, ... Eze 14:19 — 2534
and I will give thee blood in *f* .... Eze 16:38 — 2534
So will I make my *f* toward thee .... Eze 16:42 — 2534
But she was plucked up in *f* .... Eze 19:12 — 2534
I will pour out my *f* upon them .... Eze 20:8 — 2534
I would pour out my *f* upon them .... Eze 20:13 — 2534
I would pour out my *f* upon them .... Eze 20:21 — 2534
with *f* poured out, will I rule .... Eze 20:33 — 2534
out arm, and with *f* poured out .... Eze 20:34 — 2534
and I will cause my *f* to rest .... Eze 21:17 — 2534
you in mine anger and in my *f* .... Eze 22:20 — 2534
have poured out my *f* upon you .... Eze 22:22 — 2534
That it might cause *f* to come up .... Eze 24:8 — 2534
caused my *f* to rest upon thee .... Eze 24:13 — 2534
mine anger and according to my *f* .... Eze 25:14 — 2534
And I will pour my *f* upon Sin .... Eze 30:15 — 2534
spoken in my jealousy and in my *f* .... Eze 36:6 — 2534
Wherefore I poured my *f* upon them ...... Eze 36:18 — 2534
that my *f* shall come up in my .... Eze 38:18 — 2534
f commanded to bring Shadrach, ... Dan 3:13 — 2528
Then was Nebuchadnezzar full of *f* .... Dan 3:19 — 2528
unto him in the *f* of his power .... Dan 8:6 — 2534
thy *f* be turned away from thy .... Dan 9:16 — 2534
go forth with great *f* to destroy .... Dan 11:44 — 2534
f upon the heathen, such as they .... Mic 5:15 — 2534
his *f* is poured out like fire, and .... Nah 1:6 — 2534
was jealous for her with great *f* .... Zec 8:2 — 2534

G

GAAL (ga'-al) A son of Ebed.

G the son of Ebed came with his .... Judg 9:26 — 1603
G the son of Ebed said, Who is .... Judg 9:28 — 1603
the words of *G* the son of Ebed .... Judg 9:30 — 1603
G the son of Ebed and his brethren .... Judg 9:31 — 1603
G the son of Ebed went out, and .... Judg 9:35 — 1603
when *G* saw the people, he said to .... Judg 9:36 — 1603
G spake again and said, See there .... Judg 9:37 — 1603
G went out before the men of .... Judg 9:39 — 1603
and Zebul thrust out *G* and his .... Judg 9:41 — 1603

GAASH (ga'-ash) A mountain near Mt. Ephraim.

the north side of the hill of *G* .... Josh 24:30 — 1608
on the north side of the hill *G* .... Judg 2:9 — 1608
Hiddai of the brooks of *G* .... 2Sa 23:30 — 1608
Hurai of the brooks of *G*, Abiel .... 1Chr 11:32 — 1608

GABA (ga'-bah) See GEBA. A Levitical city in Benjamin.

and Ophni, and *G* .... Josh 18:24 — 1387
The children of Ramah and *G* .... Ezr 2:26 — 1387
The men of Ramah and *G*, six .... Neh 7:30 — 1387

GABBAI (gab'-bahee) A family of exiles.

And after him *G*, Sallai, nine .... Neh 11:8 — 1373

GABBATHA (gab'-ba-thah) Place where Pilate judged.

Pavement, but in the Hebrew, *G* .... Jn 19:13 — 1042

GABRIEL (ga'-bre-el) An angel.

of Ulai, which called, and said, *G* .... Dan 8:16 — 1403
in prayer, even the man *G* .... Dan 9:21 — 1403
answering said unto him, I am *G* .... Lk 1:19 — 1043
in the sixth month the angel *G* .... Lk 1:26 — 1043

GAD (gad)

1. A son of Jacob.

and she called his name *G* .... Gen 30:11 — 1410
Leah's handmaid; *G*, and Asher .... Gen 35:26 — 1410
And the sons of *G* .... Gen 46:16 — 1410
G, a troop shall overcome him .... Gen 49:19 — 1410
Dan, and Naphtali, *G*, and Asher .... Ex 1:4 — 1410
the children of *G* dwelt over .... 1Chr 5:11 — 1410

2. The tribe descended from Gad 1.

Of *G*; Eliasaph the son .... Num 1:14 — 1410
Of the children of *G*, by their .... Num 1:24 — 1410
of them, even of the tribe of *G* .... Num 1:25 — 1410
Then the tribe of *G* .... Num 2:14 — 1410
the captain of the sons of *G* .... Num 2:14 — 1410
prince of the children of *G* .... Num 7:42 — 1410

G was Eliasaph the son of Deuel .... Num 10:20 — 1410
Of the tribe of *G*, Geuel the son .... Num 13:15 — 1410
The children of *G* after their .... Num 26:15 — 1410
of *G* according to those that were .... Num 26:18 — 1410
the children of *G* had a very .... Num 32:1 — 1410
The children of *G* and the children .... Num 32:2 — 1410
Moses said unto the children of *G* .... Num 32:6 — 1410
And the children of *G* and the .... Num 32:25 — 1410
unto them, If the children of *G* .... Num 32:29 — 1410
And the children of *G* and the .... Num 32:31 — 1410
them, even to the children of *G* .... Num 32:33 — 1410
And the children of *G* built Dibon .... Num 32:34 — 1410
the tribe of the children of *G* .... Num 34:14 — 1410
Reuben, *G*, and Asher, and Zebulun, ... Deut 27:13 — 1410
of *G* he said, Blessed be he that .... Deut 33:20 — 1410
Blessed be he that enlargeth *G* .... Deut 33:20 — 1410
of Reuben, and the children of *G* .... Josh 4:12 — 1410
inheritance unto the tribe of *G* .... Josh 13:24 — 1410
of *G* according their families .... Josh 13:24 — 1410
of *G* after their families .... Josh 13:28 — 1410
and *G*, and Reuben, and half the .... Josh 18:7 — 1410
in Gilead out of the tribe of *G* .... Josh 20:8 — 1410
Reuben, and out of the tribe of *G* .... Josh 21:7 — 1410
And out of the tribe of *G*, Ramoth .... Josh 21:38 — 1410
of Reuben and the children of *G* .... Josh 22:9 — 1410
of Reuben and the children of *G* .... Josh 22:10 — 1410
of Reuben and the children of *G* .... Josh 22:11 — 1410
Reuben, and to the children of *G* .... Josh 22:13 — 1410
Reuben, and to the children of *G* .... Josh 22:15 — 1410
of Reuben and the children of *G* .... Josh 22:21 — 1410
of Reuben and children of *G* .... Josh 22:25 — 1410
of Reuben and the children of *G* .... Josh 22:30 — 1410
Reuben, and to the children of *G* .... Josh 22:31 — 1410
Reuben, and from the children of *G* .... Josh 22:32 — 1410
the children of Reuben and *G* dwelt ...... Josh 22:33 — 1410
the children of *G* called the .... Josh 22:34 — 1410
went over Jordan to the land of *G* .... 1Sa 13:7 — 1410
in the midst of the river of *G* .... 2Sa 24:5 — 1410
Joseph, and Benjamin, Naphtali, *G* .... 1Chr 2:2 — 1410
Reuben, and out of the tribe of *G* .... 1Chr 6:63 — 1410
And out of the tribe of *G* .... 1Chr 6:80 — 1410
These were of the sons of *G* .... 1Chr 12:14 — 1410
then doth their king inherit *G* .... Jer 49:1 — 1410
unto the west side, *G* a portion .... Eze 48:27 — 1410
And by the border of *G*, at the .... Eze 48:28 — 1410
one gate of *G*, one gate of Asher, ... Eze 48:34 — 1410
Of the tribe of *G* were sealed .... Rev 7:5 — 1045

3. A prophet who assisted David.

the prophet *G* said unto David,	1Sa 22:5	1410
the LORD came unto the prophet *G*	2Sa 24:11	1410
So *G* came to David, and told him,	2Sa 24:13	1410
And David said unto *G*, I am in a	2Sa 24:14	1410
G came that day to David, and said	2Sa 24:18	1410
according to the saying of *G*	2Sa 24:19	1410
And the LORD spake unto *G*, David's	1Chr 21:9	1410
So *G* came to David, and said unto	1Chr 21:11	1410
And David said unto *G*, I am in a	1Chr 21:13	1410
LORD commanded *G* to say to David	1Chr 21:18	1410
David went up at the saying of *G*	1Chr 21:19	1410
and in the book of *G* the seer	1Chr 29:29	1410
of *G* the king's seer, and Nathan	2Chr 29:25	1410

GADARENES (gad-a-renes') *Inhabitants of Gadara.*

sea, into the country of the *G*	Mk 5:1	1046
arrived at the country of the *G*	Lk 8:26	1046
the *G* round about besought him to	Lk 8:37	1046

GADDEST

Why *g* thou about so much to	Jer 2:36	235

GADDI (gad'-di) *One of the twelve spies.*

of Manasseh, *G* the son of Susi	Num 13:11	1426

GADDIEL (gad'-de-el) *One of the twelve spies.*

of Zebulun, *G* the son of Sodi	Num 13:10	1427

GADI (ga'-di) *Father of Menahem.*

the son of *G* went up from Tirzah	2Kin 15:14	1424
the son of *G* to reign over Israel	2Kin 15:17	1424

GADITE (gad'-ite) *See GADITES. A member of the tribe of Dan.*

of Nathan of Zobah, Bani the *G*	2Sa 23:36	1425

GADITES (gad'-ites)

I unto the Reubenites and to the *G*	Deut 3:12	1425
unto the *G* I gave from Gilead	Deut 3:16	1425
and Ramoth in Gilead, of the *G*	Deut 4:43	1425
unto the Reubenites, and to the *G*	Deut 29:8	1425
And to the Reubenites, and to the *G*	Josh 1:12	1425
unto the Reubenites, and the *G*	Josh 12:6	1425
the *G* have received their	Josh 13:8	1425
called the Reubenites, and the *G*	Josh 22:1	1425
all the land of Gilead, the *G*	2Kin 10:33	1425
The sons of Reuben, and the *G*	1Chr 5:18	1425
even the Reubenites, and the *G*	1Chr 5:26	1425
And of the *G* there separated	1Chr 12:8	1425
of the Reubenites, and the *G*	1Chr 12:37	1425
rulers over the Reubenites, the *G*	1Chr 26:32	1425

GAHAM (ga'-ham) *A son of Nahor.*

Reumah, she bare also Tebah, and *G*	Gen 22:24	1514

GAHAR (ga'-har) *A family of exiles.*

of Giddel, the children of *G*	Ezr 2:47	1515
of Giddel, the children of *G*	Neh 7:49	1515

GAHER See GAHAR.

GAIN

they took no *g* of money	Judg 5:19	1214
or is it *g* to him, that thou	Job 22:3	1214
of every one that is greedy of *g*	Prov 1:19	1214
the *g* thereof than fine gold	Prov 3:14	8393
He that is greedy of *g* troubleth	Prov 15:27	1214
unjust *g* increaseth his substance	Prov 28:8	8636
despiseth the *g* of oppressions	Is 33:15	1214
own way, every one for his *g*	Is 56:11	1214
dishonest *g* which thou hast made	Eze 22:13	1214
destroy souls, to get dishonest *g*	Eze 22:27	1214
that ye would *g* the time, because	Dan 2:8	2084
and shall divide the land for *g*	Dan 11:39	4242
consecrate their *g* unto the LORD	Mic 4:13	1214
if he shall *g* the whole world, and	Mt 16:26	2770
if he shall *g* the whole world, and	Mk 8:36	2770
if he *g* the whole world, and lose	Lk 9:25	2770
her masters much *g* by soothsaying	Acts 16:16	2039
brought no small *g* unto the	Acts 19:24	2039
unto all, that I might *g* the more	1Cor 9:19	2770
as a Jew, that I might *g* the Jews	1Cor 9:20	2770
that I might *g* them that are	1Cor 9:20	2770
that I might *g* them that are	1Cor 9:21	2770
as weak, that I might *g* the weak	1Cor 9:22	2770
Did I gain of you by any of	2Cor 12:17	4122
Did Titus make a *g* of you	2Cor 12:18	4122
to live is Christ, and to die is *g*	Phil 1:21	2771
But what things were *g* to me	Phil 3:7	2771
supposing that *g* is godliness	1Ti 6:5	4200
with contentment is great *g*	1Ti 6:6	4200
a year, and buy and sell, and get *g*	Jas 4:13	2770

GAINED

the hypocrite, though he hath *g*	Job 27:8	1214
thou hast greedily *g* of thy	Eze 22:12	1214

thee, thou hast *g* thy brother	Mt 18:15	2770
received two, he also *g* other two	Mt 25:17	2770
I have *g* beside them five talents	Mt 25:20	2770
I have *g* two other talents beside	Mt 25:22	2770
much every man had *g* by trading	Lk 19:15	*1281*
Lord, thy pound hath *g* ten pounds	Lk 19:16	*4333*
thy pound hath *g* five pounds	Lk 19:18	*4160*
to have *g* this harm and loss	Acts 27:21	2770

GAINS

that the hope of their *g* was gone	Acts 16:19	2039

GAINSAY

shall not be able to *g* nor resist	Lk 21:15	*471*

GAINSAYERS

to exhort and to convince the *g*	Titus 1:9	*483*

GAINSAYING

came I unto you without *g*	Acts 10:29	*369*
unto a disobedient and *g* people	Rom 10:21	*483*
and perished in the *g* of Core	Jude 11	*485*

GAIUS (gah'-yus)
1. A native of Macedonia.

and having caught *G* and Aristarchus	Acts 19:29	*1050*

2. A native of Derbe.

and *G* of Derbe, and Timotheus	Acts 20:4	*1050*

3. A native of Corinth.

G mine host, and of the whole	Rom 16:23	*1050*
none of you, but Crispus and *G*	1Cor 1:14	*1050*

4. Addressee of John's third epistle.

The elder unto the wellbeloved *G*	3Jn 1	*1050*

GALAL (ga'-lal)
1. Son of Jeduthun.

And Bakbakkar, Heresh, and *G*	1Chr 9:15	*1559*

2. A Levite exile.

the son of Shemaiah, the son of *G*	1Chr 9:16	*1559*
the son of Shammua, the son of *G*	Neh 11:17	*1559*

GALATIA (ga-la'-she-ah) *See GALATIANS. A Roman province in Asia Minor.*

Phrygia and the region of *G*	Acts 16:6	*1054*
and went over all the country of *G*	Acts 18:23	*1054*
given order to the churches of *G*	1Cor 16:1	*1053*
with me, unto the churches of *G*	Gal 1:2	*1053*
Crescens to *G*, Titus unto	2Ti 4:10	*1053*
scattered throughout Pontus, *G*	1Pet 1:1	*1053*

GALATIANS (ga-la'-she-uns) *Inhabitants of Galatia.*

O foolish *G*, who hath bewitched	Gal 3:1	*1052*
Unto the *G* written from Rome	Gal *s*	*1052*

GALBANUM

spices, stacte, and onycha, and *g*	Ex 30:34	2464

GALEED (ga'-le-ed) *See JAGAR-SAHADUTHA. A memorial mound of stones.*

but Jacob called it *G*	Gen 31:47	1567
was the name of it called *G*	Gen 31:48	1567

GALILAEAN (gal-i-le'-un) *See GALILAEANS. An inhabitant of Galilee.*

for thou art a *G*, and thy speech	Mk 14:70	*1057*
for he is a *G*	Lk 22:59	*1057*
he asked whether the man were a *G*	Lk 23:6	*1057*

GALILAEANS (gal-i-le-uns)

some that told him of the *G*	Lk 13:1	*1057*
Suppose ye that these *G* were	Lk 13:2	*1057*
were sinners above all the *G*	Lk 13:2	*1057*
the *G* received him, having seen	Jn 4:45	*1057*
are not all these which speak *G*	Acts 2:7	*1057*

GALILEE (gal'-i-lee) *See GALILAEAN. A district north of Samaria.*

Kedesh in *G* in mount Naphtali	Josh 20:7	1551
Kedesh in *G* with her suburbs, to	Josh 21:32	1551
twenty cities in the land of *G*	1Kin 9:11	1551
Kedesh, and Hazor, and Gilead, and *G*	2Kin 15:29	1551
Kedesh in *G* with her suburbs, and	1Chr 6:76	1551
Jordan, in *G* of the nations	Is 9:1	1551
turned aside into the parts of *G*	Mt 2:22	*1056*
Jesus from *G* to Jordan unto John	Mt 3:13	*1056*
into prison, he departed into *G*	Mt 4:12	*1056*
beyond Jordan, *G* of the Gentiles	Mt 4:15	*1056*
And Jesus, walking by the sea of *G*	Mt 4:18	*1056*
And Jesus went about all *G*	Mt 4:23	*1056*
great multitudes of people from *G*	Mt 4:25	*1056*
and came nigh unto the sea of *G*	Mt 15:29	*1056*
And while they abode in *G*, Jesus	Mt 17:22	*1056*
these sayings, he departed from *G*	Mt 19:1	*1056*
the prophet of Nazareth of *G*	Mt 21:11	*1056*
I will go before you into *G*	Mt 26:32	*1056*
Thou also wast with Jesus of *G*	Mt 26:69	*1056*
off, which followed Jesus from *G*	Mt 27:55	*1056*
he goeth before you into *G*	Mt 28:7	*1056*

GALL

GALLANT

GALLERIES

GALLERY

GALLEY

GALLIM (gal'-lim) *A city in Benjamin.*

GALLIO (gal'-le-o) *A Roman proconsul of Achaia.*

GALLOWS

GAMAD See GAMMADIMS.

GAMALIEL (gam-a'-le-el)
  1. A chief of Manasseh.
  2. A noted Rabbinic teacher.

GAMMAD See GAMMADIMS.

GAMMADIM See GAMMADIMS.

GAMMADIMS (gam'-ma-dims) *Defenders of Tyre.*

GAMUL (ga'-mul) See BETH-GAMUL. *A sanctuary servant in David's time.*

GAP

GAPED

GAPS

GARDEN

G

486

GARDENER

She, supposing him to be the *g*	Jn 20:15	*2780*

GARDENS

as *g* by the river's side, as the	Num 24:6	1593
I made me *g* and orchards, and I	Eccl 2:5	1593
A fountain of *g*, a well of living	Song 4:15	1588
beds of spices, to feed in the *g*	Song 6:2	1588
Thou that dwellest in the *g*	Song 8:13	1588
for the *g* that ye have chosen	Is 1:29	1593
that sacrificeth in *g*, and burneth	Is 65:3	1593
purify themselves in the *g* behind	Is 66:17	1593
and plant *g*, and eat the fruit of	Jer 29:5	1593
and plant *g*, and eat the fruit of	Jer 29:28	1593
when your *g* and your vineyards and	Amos 4:9	1593
they shall also make *g*, and eat	Amos 9:14	1593

GAREB (ga'-reb)

1. A "mighty man" of David.

Ira an Ithrite, *G* an Ithrite,	2Sa 23:38	1619
Ira the Ithrite, *G* the Ithrite,	1Chr 11:40	1619

2. A hill near Jerusalem.

over against it upon the hill *G*	Jer 31:39	1619

GARLANDS

g unto the gates, and would have	Acts 14:13	4725

GARLICK

leeks, and the onions, and the *g*	Num 11:5	7762

GARMENT

And Shem and Japheth took a *g*	Gen 9:23	8071
out red, all over like an hairy *g*	Gen 25:25	155
And she caught him by his *g*	Gen 39:12	899
and he left his *g* in her hand	Gen 39:12	899
he had left his *g* in her hand	Gen 39:13	899
cried, that he left his *g* with me	Gen 39:15	899
And she laid up his *g* by her	Gen 39:16	899
cried, that he left his *g* with me	Gen 39:18	899
priest shall put on his linen *g*	Lev 6:10	4055
of the blood thereof upon any *g*	Lev 6:27	899
The *g* also that the plague of	Lev 13:47	899
a woollen, or a linen *g*	Lev 13:47	899
be greenish or reddish in the *g*	Lev 13:49	899
if the plague be spread in the *g*	Lev 13:51	899
He shall therefore burn that *g*	Lev 13:52	899
the plague be not spread in the *g*	Lev 13:53	899
he shall rend it out of the *g*	Lev 13:56	899
And if it appear still in the *g*	Lev 13:57	899
And the *g*, either warp, or woof,	Lev 13:58	899
in a *g* of woollen or linen	Lev 13:59	899
And for the leprosy of a *g*	Lev 14:55	899
And every *g*, and every skin,	Lev 15:17	899
neither shall a *g* mingled of	Lev 19:19	899
shall a man put on a woman's *g*	Deut 22:5	8071
not wear a *g* of divers sorts,	Deut 22:11	8162
the spoils a goodly Babylonish *g*	Josh 7:21	155
of Zerah, and the silver, and the *g*	Josh 7:24	155
And they spread a *g*, and did cast	Judg 8:25	8071
she had a *g* of divers colours.	2Sa 13:18	3801
rent her *g* of divers colours that	2Sa 13:19	3801
Joab's *g* that he had put on was	2Sa 20:8	4055
he had clad himself with a new *g*	1Kin 11:29	8008
caught the new *g* that was on him	1Kin 11:30	8008
hasted, and took every man his *g*	2Kin 9:13	899
I heard this thing, I rent my *g*	Ezr 9:3	899
and having rent my *g* and my mantle,	Ezr 9:5	899
with a *g* of fine linen and purple	Est 8:15	8509
as a *g* that is moth eaten	Job 13:28	899
of my disease is my *g* changed	Job 30:18	3830
I made the cloud the *g* thereof	Job 38:9	3830
and they stand as a *g*	Job 38:14	3830
can discover the face of his *g*	Job 41:13	3830
I made sackcloth also my *g*	Ps 69:11	3830
violence covereth them as a *g*	Ps 73:6	7897
of them shall wax old like a *g*	Ps 102:26	899
thyself with light as with a *g*	Ps 104:2	8008
it with the deep as with a *g*	Ps 104:6	3830
with cursing like as with his *g*	Ps 109:18	4055
him as the *g* which covereth him	Ps 109:19	899
Take his *g* that is surety for a	Prov 20:16	899
taketh away a *g* in cold weather	Prov 25:20	899
Take his *g* that is surety for a	Prov 27:13	899
who hath bound the waters in a *g*	Prov 30:4	8071
lo, they all shall wax old as a *g*	Is 50:9	899
the earth shall wax old like a *g*	Is 51:6	899
moth shall eat them up like a *g*	Is 51:8	899
the *g* of praise for the spirit of	Is 61:3	4594
as a shepherd putteth on his *g*	Jer 43:12	899
hath covered the naked with a *g*	Eze 18:7	899
hath covered the naked with a *g*	Eze 18:16	899
whose *g* was white as snow, and the	Dan 7:9	3831
ye pull off the robe with the *g*	Mic 2:8	8008

holy flesh in the skirt of his *g*	Hag 2:12	899
they wear a rough *g* to deceive	Zec 13:4	155
one covereth violence with his *g*	Mal 2:16	3830
piece of new cloth unto an old *g*	Mt 9:16	*2440*
to fill it up taketh from the *g*	Mt 9:16	*2440*
him, and touched the hem of his *g*	Mt 9:20	*2440*
herself, If I may but touch his *g*	Mt 9:21	*2440*
might only touch the hem of his *g*	Mt 14:36	*2440*
man which had not on a wedding *g*	Mt 22:11	*1742*
in hither not having a wedding *g*	Mt 22:12	*1742*
a piece of new cloth on an old *g*	Mk 2:21	*2440*
press behind, and touched his *g*	Mk 5:27	*2440*
it were but the border of his *g*	Mk 6:56	*2440*
And he, casting away his *g*	Mk 10:50	*2440*
back again for to take up his *g*	Mk 13:16	*2440*
side, clothed in a long white *g*	Mk 16:5	*4749*
a piece of a new *g* upon an old	Lk 5:36	*2440*
and touched the border of his *g*	Lk 8:44	*2440*
hath no sword, let him sell his *g*	Lk 22:36	*2440*
Cast thy *g* about thee, and follow	Acts 12:8	*2440*
all shall wax old as doth a *g*	Heb 1:11	*2440*
hating even the *g* spotted by the	Jude 23	*5509*
clothed with a *g* down to the foot	Rev 1:13	*4158*

GARMENTS

and be clean, and change your *g*	Gen 35:2	8071
put her widow's *g* off from her	Gen 38:14	899
put on the *g* of her widowhood	Gen 38:19	899
he washed his *g* in wine, and his	Gen 49:11	3830
thou shalt make holy *g* for Aaron	Ex 28:2	899
make Aaron's *g* to consecrate him	Ex 28:3	899
these are the *g* which they shall	Ex 28:4	899
they shall make holy *g* for Aaron	Ex 28:4	899
And thou shalt take the *g*, and put	Ex 29:5	899
it upon Aaron, and upon his *g*	Ex 29:21	899
upon the *g* of his sons with him	Ex 29:21	899
and he shall be hallowed, and his *g*	Ex 29:21	899
his sons, and his sons' *g* with him	Ex 29:21	899
the holy *g* of Aaron shall be for	Ex 29:29	899
the holy *g* for Aaron the priest,	Ex 31:10	899
the *g* of his sons, to minister in	Ex 31:10	899
the holy *g* for Aaron the priest,	Ex 35:19	899
the *g* of his sons, to minister in	Ex 35:19	899
his service, and for the holy *g*	Ex 35:21	899
and made the holy *g* for Aaron	Ex 39:1	899
the holy *g* for Aaron the priest,	Ex 39:41	899
Aaron the priest, and his sons' *g*	Ex 39:41	899
shalt put upon Aaron the holy *g*	Ex 40:13	899
his *g*, and put on other *g*	Lev 6:11	899
and his sons with him, and the *g*	Lev 8:2	899
it upon Aaron, and upon his *g*	Lev 8:30	899
and upon his sons' *g* with him	Lev 8:30	899
and sanctified Aaron, and his *g*	Lev 8:30	899
his sons, and his sons' *g* with him	Lev 8:30	899
these are holy *g*	Lev 16:4	899
and shall put off the linen *g*	Lev 16:23	899
the holy place, and put on his *g*	Lev 16:24	899
linen clothes, even the holy *g*	Lev 16:32	899
is consecrated to put on the *g*	Lev 21:10	899
g throughout their generations	Num 15:38	899
And strip Aaron of his *g*, and put	Num 20:26	899
And Moses stripped Aaron of his *g*	Num 20:28	899
their feet, and old *g* upon them,	Josh 9:5	8008
and these our *g* and our shoes are	Josh 9:13	8008
sheets and thirty change of *g*	Judg 14:12	899
sheets and thirty change of *g*	Judg 14:13	899
gave change of *g* unto them which	Judg 14:19	899
and gave it to David, and his *g*	1Sa 18:4	4055
and cut off their *g* in the middle	2Sa 10:4	4063
the king arose, and tare his *g*	2Sa 13:31	899
silver, and vessels of gold, and *g*	1Kin 10:25	8008
of silver, and two changes of *g*	2Kin 5:22	899
two bags, with two changes of *g*	2Kin 5:23	899
to receive money, and to receive *g*	2Kin 5:26	899
and, lo, all the way was full of *g*	2Kin 7:15	899
And changed his prison *g*	2Kin 25:29	899
cut off their *g* in the midst hard	1Chr 19:4	4063
silver, and one hundred priests' *g*	Ezr 2:69	3801
five hundred and thirty priests' *g*	Neh 7:70	3801
and threescore and seven priests' *g*	Neh 7:72	3801
How thy *g* are warm, when he	Job 37:17	899
They part my *g* among them,	Ps 22:18	899
All thy *g* smell of myrrh, and	Ps 45:8	899
went down to the skirts of his *g*	Ps 133:2	4060
Let thy *g* be always white	Eccl 9:8	899
the smell of thy *g* is like the	Song 4:11	8008
noise, and *g* rolled in blood	Is 9:5	8071
put on thy beautiful *g*, O	Is 52:1	899
Their webs shall not become *g*	Is 59:6	899
he put on the *g* of vengeance for	Is 59:17	899
me with the *g* of salvation	Is 61:10	899

Edom, with dyed *g* from Bozrah .... Is 63:1   899
thy *g* like him that treadeth in .... Is 63:2   899
shall be sprinkled upon my *g* .... Is 63:3   899
were not afraid, nor rent their *g* .... Jer 36:24   899
And changed his prison *g* .... Jer 52:33   899
that men could not touch their *g* .... Lam 4:14   3830
of thy *g* thou didst take, and .... Eze 16:16   899
And tookest thy broidered *g* .... Eze 16:18   899
and put off their broidered *g* .... Eze 26:16   899
lay their *g* wherein they minister ...... Eze 42:14   899
and shall put on other *g*, and shall ... Eze 42:14   899
shall be clothed with linen *g* .... Eze 44:17   899
their *g* wherein they ministered .... Eze 44:19   899
and they shall put on other *g* .... Eze 44:19   899
sanctify the people with their *g* .... Eze 44:19   899
and their hats, and their other *g* .... Dan 3:21   3831
And rend your heart, and not your *g* ..... Joel 2:13   899
Joshua was clothed with filthy *g* .... Zec 3:3   899
Take away the filthy *g* from him .... Zec 3:4   899
his head, and clothed him with *g* .... Zec 3:5   899
spread their *g* in the way .... Mt 21:8   2440
and enlarge the borders of their *g* ... Mt 23:5   2440
crucified him, and parted his *g* .... Mt 27:35   2440
They parted my *g* among them .... Mt 27:35   2440
to Jesus, and cast their *g* on .... Mk 11:7   2440
And many spread their *g* in the way ...... Mk 11:8   2440
crucified him, they parted his *g* .... Mk 15:24   2440
they cast their *g* upon the colt .... Lk 19:35   2440
men stood by them in shining *g* .... Lk 24:4   2067
from supper, and laid aside his *g* .... Jn 13:4   2440
their feet, and had taken his *g* .... Jn 13:12   2440
had crucified Jesus, took his *g* .... Jn 19:23   2440
g which Dorcas made, while she .... Acts 9:39   2440
and your *g* are motheaten .... Jas 5:2   2440
which have not defiled their *g* .... Rev 3:4   2440
that watcheth, and keepeth his *g* .... Rev 16:15   2440

GARMITE (*gar'-mite*) A descendant of Judah.
Naham, the father of Keilah the *G* 1Chr 4:19   1636

GARNER
and gather his wheat into the *g* .... Mt 3:12   596
will gather the wheat into his *g* .... Lk 3:17   596

GARNERS
That our *g* may be full, affording .... Ps 144:13   4200
the *g* are laid desolate, the .... Joel 1:17   214

GARNISH
g* the sepulchres of the righteous .... Mt 23:29   2885

GARNISHED
he *g* the house with precious 2Chr 3:6   6823
his spirit he hath *g* the heavens .... Job 26:13   8235
he findeth it empty, swept, and *g* ...... Mt 12:44   2885
cometh, he findeth it swept and *g* ..... Lk 11:25   2885
g with all manner of precious .... Rev 21:19   2885

GARRISON
where is the *g* of the Philistines 1Sa 10:5   5333
Jonathan smote the *g* of the 1Sa 13:3   5333
smitten a *g* of the Philistines 1Sa 13:4   5333
the *g* of the Philistines went out 1Sa 13:23   4673
us go over to the Philistines' *g* 1Sa 14:1   4673
go over unto the Philistines' *g* 1Sa 14:4   4673
unto the *g* of these uncircumcised 1Sa 14:6   4673
unto the *g* of the Philistines 1Sa 14:11   4673
the men of the *g* answered 1Sa 14:12   4675
the *g*, and the spoilers, they also 1Sa 14:15   4673
the *g* of the Philistines was then 2Sa 23:14   4673
the Philistines' *g* was then at 1Chr 11:16   5333
city of the Damascenes with a *g* 2Cor 11:32   5432

GARRISONS
Then David put *g* in Syria of 2Sa 8:6   5333
And he put *g* in Edom 2Sa 8:14   5333
throughout all Edom put he *g* 2Sa 8:14   5333
Then David put *g* in 1Chr 18:6
And he put *g* in Edom 1Chr 18:13   5333
set *g* in the land of Judah, and in 2Chr 17:2   5333
thy strong *g* shall go down to the .... Eze 26:11   4676

GASHMU (*gash'-mu*) See GESHEM. A Samaritan in Nehemiah's time.
G saith it, that thou and the Jews .... Neh 6:6   1654

GAT
Abraham *g* up early in the morning .... Gen 19:27
cloud, and *g* him up into the mount .... Ex 24:18   5927
Moses *g* him into the camp, he and .... Num 11:30   622
g them up into the top of the .... Num 14:40   5927
So they *g* up from the tabernacle .... Num 16:27   5927
Abimelech *g* him up to mount .... Judg 9:48   5927
g them up to the top of the tower .... Judg 9:51   5927
rose up, and *g* him unto his place .... Judg 19:28   3212

g him up from Gilgal unto Gibeah 1Sa 13:15   5927
his men *g* them unto the hold 1Sa 24:22   5927
they *g* them away, and no man saw 1Sa 26:12   3212
g them away through the plain all 2Sa 4:7   3212
David *g* him a name when he 2Sa 8:13   6213
every man *g* him up upon his mule 2Sa 13:29   7392
g him home to his house, to his 2Sa 17:23   3212
the people *g* them by stealth that 2Sa 19:3   935
with clothes, but he *g* no heat 1Kin 1:1
the pains of hell *g* hold upon me .... Ps 116:3
I *g* me men singers and women .... Eccl 2:8   6213
We *g* our bread with the peril of .... Lam 5:9   935

GATAM (*ga'-tam*) A son of Eliphaz.
were Teman, Omar, Zepho, and *G* .... Gen 36:11   1609
Duke Korah, duke *G*, and duke .... Gen 36:16   1609
Teman, and Omar, Zephi, and *G* 1Chr 1:36   1609

GATE
and Lot sat in the *g* of Sodom .... Gen 19:1   8179
possess the *g* of his enemies .... Gen 22:17   8179
that went in at the *g* of his city .... Gen 23:10   8179
that went in at the *g* of his city .... Gen 23:18   8179
the *g* of those which hate them .... Gen 24:60   8179
God, and this is the *g* of heaven .... Gen 28:17   8179
son came unto the *g* of their city .... Gen 34:20   8179
went out of the *g* of his city .... Gen 34:24   8179
went out of the *g* of his city .... Gen 34:24   8179
of the *g* shall be fifteen cubits .... Ex 27:14
for the *g* of the court shall be .... Ex 27:16   8179
Moses stood in the *g* of the camp .... Ex 32:26   8179
out from *g* to *g* throughout the .... Ex 32:27   8179
side of the *g* were fifteen cubits .... Ex 38:14
for the other side of the court *g* .... Ex 38:15   8179
the hanging for the *g* of the .... Ex 38:18   8179
and the sockets of the court *g* .... Ex 38:31   8179
and the hanging for the court *g* .... Ex 39:40   8179
up the hanging at the court *g* .... Ex 40:8   8179
set up the hanging of the court *g* .... Ex 40:33   8179
the door of the *g* of the court .... Num 4:26   8179
city, and unto the *g* of his place .... Deut 21:19   8179
the elders of the city in the *g* .... Deut 22:15   8179
both out unto the *g* of that city .... Deut 22:24   8179
go up to the *g* unto the elders .... Deut 25:7   8179
the time of shutting of the *g* .... Josh 2:5   8179
were gone out, they shut the *g* .... Josh 2:7   8179
before the *g* even unto Shebarim .... Josh 7:5   8179
the entering of the *g* of the city .... Josh 8:29   8179
the entering of the *g* of the city .... Josh 20:4   8179
even unto the entering of the *g* .... Judg 9:35   8179
the entering of the *g* of the city .... Judg 9:40   8179
all night in the *g* of the city .... Judg 9:44   8179
the doors of the *g* of the city .... Judg 16:2   8179
stood by the entering of the *g* .... Judg 16:3   8179
stood in the entering of the *g* .... Judg 18:16   8179
Then went Boaz up to the *g* .... Judg 18:17   8179
and from the *g* of his place .... Ruth 4:1   8179
all the people that were in the *g* .... Ruth 4:10   8179
backward by the side of the *g* .... Ruth 4:11   8179
Saul drew near to Samuel in the *g* 1Sa 4:18   8179
scrabbled on the doors of the *g* 1Sa 9:18   8179
the *g* to speak with him quietly 1Sa 21:13   8179
array at the entering in of the *g* 2Sa 3:27   8179
even unto the entering of the *g* 2Sa 10:8   8179
and stood beside the way of the *g* 2Sa 11:23   8179
And the king stood by the *g* side 2Sa 15:2   8179
the roof over the *g* unto the wall 2Sa 18:4   8179
went up to the chamber over the *g* 2Sa 18:24   8179
the king arose, and sat in the *g* 2Sa 18:33   8179
the king doth sit in the *g* 2Sa 19:8   8179
of Beth-lehem, which is by the *g* 2Sa 19:8   8179
of Beth-lehem, that was by the *g* 2Sa 23:15   8179
when he came to the *g* of the city 2Sa 23:16   8179
the entrance of the *g* of Samaria 1Kin 17:10   6607
for a shekel, in the *g* of Samaria 1Kin 22:10   8179
men at the entering in of the *g* 2Kin 7:1   8179
to have the charge of the *g* 2Kin 7:3   8179
people trode upon him in the *g* 2Kin 7:17   8179
this time in the *g* of Samaria 2Kin 7:17   8179
people trode upon him in the *g* 2Kin 7:20   8179
And as the king entered in at the *g* 2Kin 9:31   8179
in of the *g* until the morning 2Kin 10:8   8179
part shall be at the *g* of Sur 2Kin 11:6   8179
part at the *g* behind the guard 2Kin 11:6   8179
came by the way of the *g* of the 2Kin 11:19   8179
g of Ephraim unto the corner 2Kin 14:13   8179
He built the higher *g* of the 2Kin 15:35   8179
g of Joshua the governor of the 2Kin 23:8   8179
left hand at the *g* of the city 2Kin 23:8   8179
way of the *g* between two walls 2Kin 25:4   8179
waited in the king's *g* eastward 1Chr 9:18   8179

Left column	Ref	Strong
of Beth-lehem, that is at the *g*	1Chr 11:17	8179
of Beth-lehem, that was by the *g*	1Chr 11:18	8179
in array before the *g* of the city	1Chr 19:9	6607
of their fathers, for every *g*	1Chr 26:13	8179
with the *g* Shallecheth, by the	1Chr 26:16	8179
also by their courses at every *g*	2Chr 8:14	8179
entering in of the *g* of Samaria	2Chr 18:9	8179
part at the *g* of the foundation	2Chr 23:5	8179
the horse *g* by the king's house	2Chr 23:15	8179
the high *g* into the king's house	2Chr 23:20	8179
set it without at the *g* of the	2Chr 24:8	8179
g of Ephraim to the corner *g*	2Chr 25:23	8179
corner *g*, and at the valley *g*	2Chr 26:9	8179
He built the high *g* of the house	2Chr 27:3	8179
the street of the *g* of the city	2Chr 32:6	8179
to the entering in at the fish *g*	2Chr 33:14	8179
and the porters waited at every *g*	2Chr 35:15	8179
by night by the *g* of the valley	Neh 2:13	8179
went on to the *g* of the fountain	Neh 2:14	8179
and entered by the *g* of the valley	Neh 2:15	8179
and they builded the sheep *g*	Neh 3:1	8179
But the fish *g* did the sons of	Neh 3:3	8179
Moreover the old *g* repaired	Neh 3:6	8179
The valley *g* repaired Hanun, and	Neh 3:13	8179
on the wall unto the dung *g*	Neh 3:13	8179
But the dung *g* repaired Malchiah	Neh 3:14	8179
But the *g* of the fountain	Neh 3:15	8179
the water *g* toward the east	Neh 3:26	8179
the horse *g* repaired the priests	Neh 3:28	8179
the keeper of the east *g*	Neh 3:29	8179
over against the *g* Miphkad	Neh 3:31	8179
sheep *g* repaired the goldsmiths	Neh 3:32	8179
that was before the water *g*	Neh 8:1	8179
that was before the water *g* from	Neh 8:3	8179
and in the street of the water *g*	Neh 8:16	8179
in the street of the *g* of Ephraim	Neh 8:16	8179
upon the wall toward the dung *g*	Neh 12:31	8179
And at the fountain *g*, which was	Neh 12:37	8179
even unto the water *g* eastward	Neh 12:37	8179
And from above the *g* of Ephraim	Neh 12:39	8179
the old *g*, and above the fish *g*	Neh 12:39	8179
of Meah, even unto the sheep *g*	Neh 12:39	8179
they stood still in the prison *g*	Neh 12:39	8179
then Mordecai sat in the king's *g*	Est 2:19	8179
Mordecai sat in the king's *g*	Est 2:21	8179
that were in the king's *g*	Est 3:2	8179
which were in the king's *g*	Est 3:3	8179
And came even before the king's *g*	Est 4:2	8179
king's *g* clothed with sackcloth	Est 4:2	8179
which was before the king's *g*	Est 4:6	8179
over against the *g* of the house	Est 5:1	6607
saw Mordecai in the king's *g*	Est 5:9	8179
the Jew sitting at the king's *g*	Est 5:13	8179
Jew, that sitteth at the king's *g*	Est 6:10	8179
came again to the king's *g*	Est 6:12	8179
and they are crushed in the *g*	Job 5:4	8179
out to the *g* through the city	Job 29:7	8179
when I saw my help in the *g*	Job 31:21	8179
sit in the *g* speak against me	Ps 69:12	8179
This *g* of the Lord, into which	Ps 118:20	8179
speak with the enemies in the *g*	Ps 127:5	8179
his *g* seeketh destruction	Prov 17:19	6607
oppress the afflicted in the *g*	Prov 22:22	8179
he openeth not his mouth in the *g*	Prov 24:7	8179
Heshbon, by the *g* of Bath-rabbim	Song 7:4	8179
Howl, O *g*; cry, O city	Is 14:31	8179
set themselves in array at the *g*	Is 22:7	8179
the *g* is smitten with destruction	Is 24:12	8179
that turn the battle to the *g*	Is 28:6	8179
for him that reproveth in the *g*	Is 29:21	8179
Stand in the *g* of the Lord's	Jer 7:2	8179
stand in the *g* of the children of	Jer 17:19	8179
is by the entry of the east *g*	Jer 19:2	8179
were in the high *g* of Benjamin	Jer 20:2	8179
of the new *g* of the Lord's house	Jer 26:10	8179
Hananeel unto the *g* of the corner	Jer 31:38	8179
of the horse *g* toward the east	Jer 31:40	8179
of the new *g* of the Lord's house	Jer 36:10	8179
when he was in the *g* of Benjamin	Jer 37:13	8179
then sitting in the *g* of Benjamin	Jer 38:7	8179
came in, and sat in the middle *g*	Jer 39:3	8179
by the *g* betwixt the two walls	Jer 39:4	8179
of the *g* between the two walls	Jer 52:7	8179
The elders have ceased from the *g*	Lam 5:14	8179
to the door of the inner *g*	Eze 8:3	8179
behold northward at the *g* of the	Eze 8:5	8179
g of the Lord's house which was	Eze 8:14	8179
came from the way of the higher *g*	Eze 9:2	8179
of the east *g* of the Lord's house	Eze 10:19	8179
the east *g* of the Lord's house	Eze 11:1	8179
behold at the door of the *g* five	Eze 11:1	8179

Right column	Ref	Strong
and he stood in the *g*	Eze 40:3	8179
Then came he unto the *g* which	Eze 40:6	8179
measured the threshold of the *g*	Eze 40:6	8179
and the other threshold of the *g*	Eze 40:6	
the threshold of the *g* by the	Eze 40:7	8179
of the *g* within was one reed	Eze 40:7	8179
also the porch of the *g* within	Eze 40:8	8179
measured he the porch of the *g*	Eze 40:9	8179
and the porch of the *g* was inward	Eze 40:9	8179
the little chambers of the *g*	Eze 40:10	8179
the breadth of the entry of the *g*	Eze 40:11	8179
and the length of the *g*, thirteen	Eze 40:11	8179
He measured then the *g* from the	Eze 40:13	8179
of the court round about the *g*	Eze 40:14	8179
from the face of the *g* of the	Eze 40:15	8179
of the inner *g* were fifty cubits	Eze 40:15	8179
posts within the *g* round about	Eze 40:16	8179
g unto the forefront of the inner	Eze 40:19	8179
the *g* of the outward court that	Eze 40:20	8179
after the measure of the first *g*	Eze 40:21	8179
g that looketh toward the east	Eze 40:22	8179
the *g* of the inner court was over	Eze 40:23	8179
against the *g* toward the north	Eze 40:23	8179
from *g* to *g* an hundred cubits	Eze 40:23	8179
behold a *g* toward the south	Eze 40:24	8179
there was a *g* in the inner court	Eze 40:27	8179
he measured from *g* to *g* toward	Eze 40:27	8179
to the inner court by the south *g*	Eze 40:28	8179
he measured the south *g* according	Eze 40:28	8179
he measured the *g* according to	Eze 40:32	8179
And he brought me to the north *g*	Eze 40:35	8179
in the porch of the *g* were two	Eze 40:39	8179
up to the entry of the north *g*	Eze 40:40	8179
which was at the porch of the *g*	Eze 40:40	8179
that side, by the side of the *g*	Eze 40:41	8179
without the inner *g* were the	Eze 40:44	8179
was at the side of the north *g*	Eze 40:44	8179
one at the side of the east *g*	Eze 40:44	8179
the breadth of the *g* was three	Eze 40:48	8179
g whose prospect is toward the	Eze 42:15	8179
Afterward he brought me to the *g*	Eze 43:1	8179
even the *g* that looketh toward	Eze 43:1	8179
the house by the way of the *g*	Eze 43:4	8179
g of the outward sanctuary which	Eze 44:1	8179
This *g* shall be shut, it shall	Eze 44:2	8179
by the way of the porch of that *g*	Eze 44:3	8179
of the north *g* before the house	Eze 44:4	8179
posts of the *g* of the inner court	Eze 45:19	8179
The *g* of the inner court that	Eze 46:1	8179
of the porch of that *g* without	Eze 46:2	8179
shall stand by the post of the *g*	Eze 46:2	8179
worship at the threshold of the *g*	Eze 46:2	8179
but the *g* shall not be shut until	Eze 46:2	8179
worship at the door of this *g*	Eze 46:3	8179
by the way of the porch of that *g*	Eze 46:8	8179
in by the way of the north *g* to	Eze 46:9	8179
go out by the way of the south *g*	Eze 46:9	8179
by the way of the south *g* shall	Eze 46:9	8179
forth by the way of the north *g*	Eze 46:9	8179
way of the *g* whereby he came in	Eze 46:9	8179
one shall then open him the *g*	Eze 46:12	8179
going forth one shall shut the *g*	Eze 46:12	8179
which was at the side of the *g*	Eze 46:19	8179
out of the way of the *g* northward	Eze 47:2	8179
utter *g* by the way that looketh	Eze 47:2	8179
one *g* of Reuben	Eze 48:31	8179
one *g* of Judah, one *g* of Levi	Eze 48:31	8179
one *g* of Joseph	Eze 48:32	8179
g of Benjamin, one *g* of Dan	Eze 48:32	8179
one *g* of Simeon	Eze 48:33	8179
of Issachar, one *g* of Zebulun	Eze 48:33	8179
one *g* of Gad	Eze 48:34	8179
g of Asher, one *g* of Naphtali	Eze 48:34	8179
Daniel sat in the *g* of the king	Dan 2:49	8651
hate him that rebuketh in the *g*	Amos 5:10	8179
poor in the *g* from their right	Amos 5:12	8179
and establish judgment in the *g*	Amos 5:15	8179
not have entered into the *g* of my	Obad 13	8179
is come unto the *g* of my people	Mic 1:9	8179
the Lord unto the *g* of Jerusalem	Mic 1:12	8179
up, and have passed through the *g*	Mic 2:13	8179
noise of a cry from the fish *g*	Zeph 1:10	8179
from Benjamin's *g* unto the place	Zec 14:10	8179
the first *g*, unto the corner *g*	Zec 14:10	8179
Enter ye in at the strait *g*	Mt 7:13	4439
for wide is the *g*, and broad is	Mt 7:13	4439
Because strait is the *g*, and	Mt 7:14	4439
he came nigh to the *g* of the city	Lk 7:12	4439
to enter in at the strait *g*	Lk 13:24	4439
Lazarus, which was laid at his *g*	Lk 16:20	4440
whom they laid daily at the *g* of	Acts 3:2	2374

at the Beautiful *g* of the temple	Acts 3:10	4439
house, and stood before the *g*	Acts 10:17	4440
they came unto the iron *g* that	Acts 12:10	4439
knocked at the door of the *g*	Acts 12:13	4440
she opened not the *g* for gladness	Acts 12:14	4440
told how Peter stood before the *g*	Acts 12:14	4440
own blood, suffered without the *g*	Heb 13:12	4439
every several *g* was of one pearl	Rev 21:21	

GATES

thy stranger that is within thy *g*	Ex 20:10	8179
were fenced with high walls, *g*	Deut 3:5	1817
thy stranger that is within thy *g*	Deut 5:14	8179
posts of thy house, and on thy *g*	Deut 6:9	8179
of thine house, and upon thy *g*	Deut 11:20	8179
the Levite that is within your *g*	Deut 12:12	8179
kill and eat flesh in all thy *g*	Deut 12:15	8179
thy *g* the tithe of thy corn	Deut 12:17	8179
the Levite that is within thy *g*	Deut 12:18	8179
thee, and thou shalt eat in thy *g*	Deut 12:21	8179
the stranger that is in thy *g*	Deut 14:21	8179
the Levite that is within thy *g*	Deut 14:27	8179
and shalt lay it up within thy *g*	Deut 14:28	8179
the widow, which are within thy *g*	Deut 14:29	8179
g in thy land which the LORD thy	Deut 15:7	8179
Thou shalt eat it within thy *g*	Deut 15:22	8179
the passover within any of thy *g*	Deut 16:5	8179
the Levite that is within thy *g*	Deut 16:11	8179
the widow, that are within thy *g*	Deut 16:14	8179
shalt thou make thee in all thy *g*	Deut 16:18	8179
within any of thy *g* which the	Deut 17:2	8179
that wicked thing, unto thy *g*	Deut 17:5	8179
of controversy within thy *g*	Deut 17:8	8179
any of thy *g* out of all Israel	Deut 18:6	8179
he shall choose in one of thy *g*	Deut 23:16	8179
that are in thy land within thy *g*	Deut 24:14	8179
that they may eat within thy *g*	Deut 26:12	8179
shall besiege thee in all thy *g*	Deut 28:52	8179
all thy *g* throughout all thy land	Deut 28:52	8179
shall distress thee in all thy *g*	Deut 28:55	8179
shall distress thee in thy *g*	Deut 28:57	8179
thy stranger that is within thy *g*	Deut 31:12	8179
son shall he set up the *g* of it	Josh 6:26	1817
then was war in the *g*	Judg 5:8	8179
of the LORD go down to the *g*	Judg 5:11	8179
the valley, and to the *g* of Ekron	1Sa 17:52	8179
entering into a town that hath *g*	1Sa 23:7	1817
And David sat between the two *g*	2Sa 18:24	8179
set up the *g* thereof in his	1Kin 16:34	1817
down the high places of the *g*	2Kin 23:8	8179
service, keepers of the *g* of the	1Chr 9:19	5592
porters in the *g* were two hundred	1Chr 9:22	5592
of the *g* of the house of the LORD	1Chr 9:23	8179
the nails for the doors of the *g*	1Chr 22:3	8179
fenced cities, with walls, *g*	2Chr 8:5	1817
about them walls, and towers, *g*	2Chr 14:7	1817
at the *g* of the house of the LORD	2Chr 23:19	8179
to praise in the *g* of the tents	2Chr 31:2	8179
the *g* thereof are burned with	Neh 1:3	8179
the *g* thereof are consumed with	Neh 2:3	8179
g of the palace which appertained	Neh 2:8	8179
the *g* thereof were consumed with	Neh 2:13	8179
the *g* thereof are burned with	Neh 2:17	8179
not set up the doors upon the *g*	Neh 6:1	8179
Let not the *g* of Jerusalem be	Neh 7:3	8179
and their brethren that kept the *g*	Neh 11:19	8179
ward at the thresholds of the *g*	Neh 12:25	8179
and purified the people, and the *g*	Neh 12:30	8179
that when the *g* of Jerusalem	Neh 13:19	8179
that the *g* should be shut	Neh 13:19	1817
of my servants set I at the *g*	Neh 13:19	8179
they should come and keep the *g*	Neh 13:22	8179
Have the *g* of death been opened	Job 38:17	8179
liftest me up from the *g* of death	Ps 9:13	8179
in the *g* of the daughter of Zion	Ps 9:14	8179
Lift up your heads, O ye *g*	Ps 24:7	8179
Lift up your heads, O ye *g*	Ps 24:9	8179
The LORD loveth the *g* of Zion	Ps 87:2	8179
Enter into his *g* with	Ps 100:4	8179
For he hath broken the *g* of brass	Ps 107:16	1817
draw near unto the *g* of death	Ps 107:18	8179
Open to me the *g* of righteousness	Ps 118:19	8179
Our feet shall stand within thy *g*	Ps 122:2	8179
strengthened the bars of thy *g*	Ps 147:13	8179
in the openings of the *g*	Prov 1:21	8179
She crieth at the *g*, at the entry	Prov 8:3	8179
me, watching daily at my *g*	Prov 8:34	1817
wicked at the *g* of the righteous	Prov 14:19	8179
Her husband is known in the *g*	Prov 31:23	8179
her own works praise her in the *g*	Prov 31:31	8179
at our *g* are all manner of	Song 7:13	6607

her *g* shall lament and mourn	Is 3:26	6607
may go into the *g* of the nobles	Is 13:2	6607
Open ye the *g*, that the righteous	Is 26:2	8179
I shall go to the *g* of the grave	Is 38:10	8179
open before him the two leaved *g*	Is 45:1	1817
and the *g* shall not be shut	Is 45:1	8179
break in pieces the *g* of brass	Is 45:2	1817
thy *g* of carbuncles, and all thy	Is 54:12	8179
Therefore thy *g* shall be open	Is 60:11	8179
walls Salvation, and thy *g* Praise	Is 60:18	8179
Go through, go through the *g*	Is 62:10	8179
entering of the *g* of Jerusalem	Jer 1:15	8179
in at these *g* to worship the LORD	Jer 7:2	8179
and the *g* thereof languish	Jer 14:2	8179
with a fan in the *g* of the land	Jer 15:7	8179
in all the *g* of Jerusalem	Jer 17:19	8179
that enter in by these *g*	Jer 17:20	8179
bring it in by the *g* of Jerusalem	Jer 17:21	8179
bring in no burden through the *g*	Jer 17:24	8179
into the *g* of this city kings	Jer 17:25	8179
even entering in at the *g* of	Jer 17:27	8179
I kindle a fire in the *g* thereof	Jer 17:27	8179
people that enter in by these *g*	Jer 22:2	8179
the *g* of this house kings sitting	Jer 22:4	8179
forth beyond the *g* of Jerusalem	Jer 22:19	8179
which have neither *g* nor bars	Jer 49:31	1817
her high *g* shall be burned with	Jer 51:58	8179
all her *g* are desolate	Lam 1:4	8179
Her *g* are sunk into the ground	Lam 2:9	8179
entered into the *g* of Jerusalem	Lam 4:12	8179
of the sword against all their *g*	Eze 21:12	8179
battering rams against the *g*	Eze 21:22	8179
that was the *g* of the people	Eze 26:2	1817
when he shall enter into thy *g*	Eze 26:10	8179
and having neither bars nor *g*	Eze 38:11	1817
g over against the length of the	Eze 40:18	8179
of the *g* was the lower pavement	Eze 40:18	8179
were by the posts of the *g*	Eze 40:38	8179
charge at the *g* of the house	Eze 44:11	8179
in at the *g* of the inner court	Eze 44:17	8179
in the *g* of the inner court	Eze 44:17	8179
the *g* of the city shall be after	Eze 48:31	8179
three *g* northward	Eze 48:31	8179
five hundred: and three *g*	Eze 48:32	8179
measures: and three *g*	Eze 48:33	8179
five hundred, with their three *g*	Eze 48:34	8179
and foreigners entered into his *g*	Obad 11	8179
The *g* of the rivers shall be	Nah 2:6	8179
the *g* of thy land shall be set	Nah 3:13	8179
of truth and peace in your *g*	Zec 8:16	8179
the *g* of hell shall not prevail	Mt 16:18	4439
And they watched the *g* day	Acts 9:24	4439
oxen and garlands unto the *g*	Acts 14:13	4440
great and high, and had twelve *g*	Rev 21:12	4440
at the twelve angels, and names	Rev 21:12	4440
On the east three *g*	Rev 21:13	4440
on the north three *g*	Rev 21:13	4440
on the south three *g*	Rev 21:13	4440
and on the west three *g*	Rev 21:13	4440
the *g* thereof, and the wall	Rev 21:15	4440
the twelve *g* were twelve pearls	Rev 21:21	4440
the *g* of it shall not be shut at	Rev 21:25	4440
in through the *g* into the city	Rev 22:14	4440

GATH (gath) See GATH-HEPHER, GATH-RIMMON, GITTITE,
MORESHETH-GATH. *A royal Philistine city.*

only in Gaza, in *G*, and in Ashdod,	Josh 11:22	1661
of Israel be carried about unto *G*	1Sa 5:8	1661
one, for Askelon one, for *G* one	1Sa 6:17	1661
to Israel, from Ekron even unto *G*	1Sa 7:14	1661
Philistines, named Goliath, of *G*	1Sa 17:4	1661
the champion, the Philistine of *G*	1Sa 17:23	1661
the way to Shaaraim, even unto *G*	1Sa 17:52	1661
afraid of Achish the king of *G*	1Sa 21:10	1661
the son of Maoch, king of *G*	1Sa 21:12	1661
And David dwelt with Achish at *G*	1Sa 27:2	1661
Saul that David was fled to *G*	1Sa 27:3	1661
alive, to bring tidings to *G*	1Sa 27:4	1661
Tell it not in *G*, publish it not	1Sa 27:11	1661
men which came after him from *G*	2Sa 1:20	1661
And there was yet a battle in *G*	2Sa 15:18	1661
four were born to the giant in *G*	2Sa 21:20	1661
Achish son of Maachah king of *G*	2Sa 21:22	1661
Behold, thy servants be in *G*	1Kin 2:39	1661
went to *G* to Achish to seek his	1Kin 2:39	1661
and brought his servants from *G*	1Kin 2:40	1661
had gone from Jerusalem to *G*	1Kin 2:40	1661
went up, and fought against *G*	2Kin 12:17	1661
whom the men of *G* that were born	1Chr 7:21	1661
drove away the inhabitants of *G*	1Chr 8:13	1661

G

and subdued them, and took *G*	1Chr 18:1	1661
And yet again there was war at *G*	1Chr 20:6	1661
were born unto the giant in *G*	1Chr 20:8	1661
And *G*, and Mareshah, and Ziph,	2Chr 11:8	1661
and brake down the wall of *G*	2Chr 26:6	1661
the Philistines took him in *G*	Ps 56:t	1661
then go down to *G* of the	Amos 6:2	1661
Declare ye it not at *G*, weep ye	Mic 1:10	1661

GATHER

eaten, and thou shalt *g* it to thee	Gen 6:21	622
said unto his brethren, *G* stones	Gen 31:46	3950
they shall *g* themselves together	Gen 34:30	622
let them *g* all the food of those	Gen 41:35	6908
G yourselves together, that I may	Gen 49:1	622
G yourselves together, and hear,	Gen 49:2	6908
g the elders of Israel together,	Ex 3:16	622
them go and *g* straw for themselves	Ex 5:7	7197
to *g* stubble instead of straw	Ex 5:12	7197
g thy cattle, and all that thou	Ex 9:19	5756
g a certain rate every day, that	Ex 16:4	3950
be twice as much as they *g* daily	Ex 16:5	3950
G of it every man according to	Ex 16:16	3950
Six days ye shall *g* it	Ex 16:26	3950
on the seventh day for to *g*	Ex 16:27	3950
shalt *g* in the fruits thereof	Ex 23:10	622
g thou all the congregation	Lev 8:3	6950
field, neither shalt thou *g* the	Lev 19:9	3950
neither shalt thou *g* every grape	Lev 19:10	3950
neither shalt thou *g* any gleaning	Lev 23:22	3950
and *g* in the fruit thereof	Lev 25:3	622
neither *g* the grapes of thy vine	Lev 25:5	1219
nor *g* the grapes in it of thy	Lev 25:11	1219
not sow, nor *g* in our increase	Lev 25:20	622
thou shalt *g* the whole assembly	Num 8:9	6950
shall *g* themselves unto thee	Num 10:4	3259
G unto me seventy men of the	Num 11:16	622
a man that is clean shall *g* up	Num 19:9	622
g thou the assembly together,	Num 20:8	6950
G the people together, and I will	Num 21:16	622
G me the people together, and I	Deut 4:10	6950
that thou mayest *g* in thy corn	Deut 11:14	622
thou shalt *g* the spoil of it	Deut 13:16	6908
shalt not *g* the grapes thereof	Deut 28:30	2490
field, and shalt *g* but little in	Deut 28:38	622
of the wine, nor *g* the grapes	Deut 28:39	103
g thee from all the nations	Deut 30:3	6908
will the LORD thy God *g* thee	Deut 30:4	6908
G the people together, men, and	Deut 31:12	6950
G unto me all the elders of your	Deut 31:28	6950
g after the reapers among the	Ruth 2:7	622
G all Israel to Mizpeh, and I will	1Sa 7:5	6908
will *g* all Israel unto my lord	2Sa 3:21	6908
Now therefore *g* the rest of the	2Sa 12:28	622
g to me all Israel unto mount	1Kin 18:19	6908
out into the field to *g* herbs	2Kin 4:39	3950
I will *g* thee unto thy fathers,	2Kin 22:20	622
that they may *g* themselves unto	1Chr 13:2	6908
g us together, and deliver us from	1Chr 16:35	6908
David commanded to *g* together the	1Chr 22:2	3664
g of all Israel money to repair	2Chr 24:5	6908
I will *g* thee to thy fathers, and	2Chr 34:28	622
that they should *g* themselves,	Ezr 10:7	6908
yet will I *g* them from thence, and	Neh 1:9	6908
heart to *g* them the nobles	Neh 7:5	6908
to *g* into them out of the fields	Neh 12:44	3664
that they may *g* together all the	Est 2:3	6908
g together all the Jews that are	Est 4:16	3664
city to *g* themselves together	Est 8:11	6950
or *g* together, then who can	Job 11:10	6950
they *g* the vintage of the wicked	Job 24:6	3953
if he *g* unto himself his spirit	Job 34:14	622
thy seed, and *g* it into thy barn	Job 39:12	622
G not my soul with sinners, nor	Ps 26:9	622
and knoweth not who shall *g* them	Ps 39:6	622
G my saints together unto me	Ps 50:5	622
They *g* themselves together, they	Ps 56:6	1481
They *g* themselves together	Ps 94:21	1413
they *g* themselves together, and	Ps 104:22	622
That thou givest them they *g*	Ps 104:28	3950
g us from among the heathen, to	Ps 106:47	6908
he shall *g* it for him that will	Prov 28:8	6908
sinner he giveth travail, to *g*	Eccl 2:26	622
a time to *g* stones together	Eccl 3:5	3664
in the gardens, and to *g* lilies	Song 6:2	3950
of Gebim *g* themselves to flee	Is 10:31	5756
g together the dispersed of Judah	Is 11:12	6908
and hatch, and *g* under her shadow	Is 34:15	1716
he shall *g* the lambs with his arm	Is 40:11	6908
the east, and *g* thee from the west	Is 43:5	6908
all these *g* themselves together,	Is 49:18	6908

with great mercies will I *g* thee	Is 54:7	6908
they shall surely *g* together	Is 54:15	1481
whosoever shall *g* together	Is 54:15	1481
Yet will I *g* others to him,	Is 56:8	6908
all they *g* themselves together,	Is 60:4	6908
g out the stones	Is 62:10	5619
come, that I will *g* all nations	Is 66:18	6908
g together, and say, Assemble	Jer 4:5	4390
g yourselves to flee out of the	Jer 6:1	5756
The children *g* wood, and the	Jer 7:18	3950
harvestman, and none shall *g* them	Jer 9:22	622
G up thy wares out of the land, O	Jer 10:17	622
I will *g* the remnant of my flock	Jer 23:3	6908
I will *g* you from all the nations	Jer 29:14	6908
g them from the coasts of the	Jer 31:8	6908
that scattered Israel will *g* him	Jer 31:10	6908
Behold, I will *g* them out of all	Jer 32:37	6908
g ye wine, and summer fruits, and	Jer 40:10	622
and none shall *g* up him that	Jer 49:5	6908
G ye together, and come against	Jer 49:14	6908
bright the arrows; *g* the shields	Jer 51:11	4390
I will even *g* you from the people	Eze 16:17	6908
therefore I will *g* all thy lovers	Eze 16:37	6908
I will even *g* them round about	Eze 16:37	6908
will *g* you out of the countries	Eze 20:34	6908
g you out of the countries	Eze 20:41	6908
therefore I will *g* you into the	Eze 22:19	6908
As they *g* silver, and brass, and	Eze 22:20	6910
so will I *g* you in mine anger and	Eze 22:20	6908
Yea, I will *g* you, and blow upon	Eze 22:21	3664
G the pieces thereof into it,	Eze 24:4	622
I *g* the Egyptians from the people	Eze 29:13	6908
g them from the countries, and	Eze 34:13	6908
g you out of all countries, and	Eze 36:24	6908
will *g* them on every side, and	Eze 37:21	6908
g yourselves on every side to my	Eze 39:17	622
sent to *g* together the princes	Dan 3:2	3673
the nations, now will I *g* them	Hos 8:10	6908
Egypt shall *g* them up, Memphis	Hos 9:6	6908
assembly, *g* the elders and all the	Joel 1:14	622
all faces shall *g* blackness	Joel 2:6	6908
G the people, sanctify the	Joel 2:16	622
g the children, and those that	Joel 2:16	622
I will also *g* all nations	Joel 3:2	6908
g yourselves together round about	Joel 3:11	6908
I will surely *g* the remnant of	Mic 2:12	6908
I will *g* her that is driven out,	Mic 4:6	6908
for he shall *g* them as the	Mic 4:12	6908
Now *g* thyself in troops, O	Mic 5:1	1413
the faces of them all *g* blackness	Nah 2:10	6908
they shall *g* the captivity as the	Hab 1:9	622
net, and *g* them in their drag	Hab 1:15	622
G yourselves together, yea,	Zeph 2:1	7197
g together, O nation not desired	Zeph 2:1	7197
determination is to *g* the nations	Zeph 3:8	622
I will *g* them that are sorrowful	Zeph 3:18	622
g her that was driven out	Zeph 3:19	6908
even in the time that I *g* you	Zeph 3:20	6908
I will hiss for them, and *g* them	Zec 10:8	6908
Egypt, and *g* them out of Assyria	Zec 10:10	6908
For I will *g* all nations against	Zec 14:2	622
g his wheat into the garner	Mt 3:12	4863
do they reap, nor *g* into barns	Mt 6:26	4863
Do men *g* grapes of thorns, or	Mt 7:16	4816
thou then that we go and *g* them up	Mt 13:28	4816
lest while ye *g* up the tares	Mt 13:29	4816
G ye together first the tares, and	Mt 13:30	4816
but *g* the wheat into my barn	Mt 13:30	4863
they shall *g* out of his kingdom	Mt 13:41	4816
they shall *g* together his elect	Mt 24:31	1996
g where I have not strawed	Mt 25:26	4863
shall *g* together his elect from	Mk 13:27	1996
will *g* the wheat into his garner	Lk 3:17	4863
For of thorns men do not *g* figs	Lk 6:44	4816
of a bramble bush *g* they grapes	Lk 6:44	5166
as a hen doth *g* her brood under	Lk 13:34	4863
G up the fragments that remain,	Jn 6:12	4863
but that also he should *g*	Jn 11:52	4863
men *g* them, and cast them into the	Jn 15:6	4863
g together in one all things in	Eph 1:10	346
g the clusters of the vine of the	Rev 14:18	5166
to *g* them to the battle of that	Rev 16:14	4863
g yourselves together unto the	Rev 19:17	4863
to *g* them together to battle	Rev 20:8	4863

GATHERED

be *g* together unto one place	Gen 1:9	6960
their substance that they had *g*	Gen 12:5	7408
and was *g* to his people	Gen 25:8	622
and was *g* unto his people	Gen 25:17	622
And thither were all the flocks *g*	Gen 29:3	622

the cattle should be *g* together	Gen 29:7	622
all the flocks be *g* together	Gen 29:8	622
Laban *g* together all the men of	Gen 29:22	622
was *g* unto his people, being old	Gen 35:29	622
he *g* up all the food of the seven	Gen 41:48	622
Joseph *g* corn as the sand of the	Gen 41:49	6651
Joseph *g* up all the money that	Gen 47:14	3950
I am to be *g* unto my people	Gen 49:29	622
he *g* up his feet into the bed, and	Gen 49:33	622
ghost, and was *g* unto his people	Gen 49:33	622
g together all the elders of the	Ex 4:29	622
they *g* them together upon heaps	Ex 8:14	6651
the waters were *g* together	Ex 15:8	6192
children of Israel did so, and *g*	Ex 16:17	3950
he that *g* much had nothing over,	Ex 16:18	
he that *g* little had no lack	Ex 16:18	
they *g* every man according to his	Ex 16:18	3950
they *g* it every morning, every	Ex 16:21	3950
day they *g* twice as much bread	Ex 16:22	3950
when thou hast *g* in thy labours	Ex 23:16	622
the people *g* themselves together	Ex 32:1	6950
all the sons of Levi *g* themselves	Ex 32:26	622
Moses *g* all the congregation of	Ex 35:1	6950
the assembly was *g* together unto	Lev 8:4	6950
when ye have *g* in the fruit of	Lev 23:39	622
when ye are *g* together within	Lev 26:25	622
congregation is to be *g* together	Num 10:7	6950
g it, and ground it in mills, or	Num 11:8	3950
of the sea be *g* together for them	Num 11:22	622
g the seventy men of the elders	Num 11:24	622
next day, and they *g* the quails	Num 11:32	622
that *g* least *g* ten homers	Num 11:32	622
that are *g* together against me	Num 14:35	3259
they found a man that *g* sticks	Num 15:32	7197
they *g* themselves together	Num 16:3	6950
all thy company are *g* together	Num 16:11	3259
Korah *g* all the congregation	Num 16:19	6950
congregation was *g* against Moses	Num 16:42	6950
they *g* themselves together	Num 20:2	6950
Aaron *g* the congregation together	Num 20:10	6950
Aaron shall be *g* unto his people	Num 20:24	622
Aaron shall be *g* unto his people,	Num 20:26	622
but Sihon *g* all his people	Num 21:23	622
g themselves together against the	Num 27:3	3259
also shalt be *g* unto thy people	Num 27:13	622
as Aaron thy brother was *g*	Num 27:13	622
shalt thou be *g* unto thy people	Num 31:2	622
that thou hast *g* in thy corn	Deut 16:13	622
goest up, and be *g* unto thy people	Deut 32:50	622
Hor, and was *g* unto his people	Deut 32:50	622
tribes of Israel were *g* together	Deut 33:5	622
That they *g* themselves together,	Josh 9:2	6908
g themselves together, and went up	Josh 10:5	622
are *g* together against us	Josh 10:6	6908
of the children of Israel	Josh 22:12	6950
Joshua *g* all the tribes of Israel	Josh 24:1	622
g their meat under my table	Judg 1:7	3950
were *g* unto their fathers	Judg 2:10	622
he *g* unto him the children of	Judg 3:13	622
Sisera *g* together all his	Judg 4:13	2199
of the east were *g* together	Judg 6:33	622
and Abi-ezer was *g* after him	Judg 6:34	2199
who also was *g* after him	Judg 6:35	2199
the men of Israel *g* themselves	Judg 7:23	6817
of Ephraim *g* themselves together	Judg 7:24	6817
all the men of Shechem *g* together	Judg 9:6	622
g their vineyards, and trode the	Judg 9:27	1219
tower of Shechem were *g* together	Judg 9:47	6908
children of Ammon were *g* together	Judg 10:17	6817
there were *g* vain men to Jephthah	Judg 11:3	3950
but Sihon *g* all his people	Judg 11:20	622
the men of Ephraim *g* themselves	Judg 12:1	6817
Then Jephthah *g* together all the	Judg 12:4	6908
g together for to offer a	Judg 16:23	6908
to Micah's house were *g* together	Judg 18:22	2199
was *g* together as one man	Judg 20:1	6950
of Israel were *g* against the city	Judg 20:11	622
But the children of Benjamin *g*	Judg 20:14	622
and *g* all the lords of the	1Sa 5:8	622
g together all the lords of the	1Sa 5:8	622
they *g* together to Mizpeh, and	1Sa 7:6	6908
Israel were *g* together to Mizpeh	1Sa 7:7	6908
of Israel *g* themselves together	1Sa 8:4	6908
the Philistines *g* themselves	1Sa 13:5	622
that the Philistines *g* themselves	1Sa 13:11	622
he *g* an host, and smote the	1Sa 14:48	6213
Saul *g* the people together, and	1Sa 15:4	8085
Now the Philistines *g* together	1Sa 17:1	622
were *g* together at Shochoh, which	1Sa 17:1	622
the men of Israel were *g* together	1Sa 17:2	622
And Jonathan's lad *g* up the arrows	1Sa 20:38	3950

g themselves unto him	1Sa 22:2	6908
the Israelites were *g* together	1Sa 25:1	6908
that the Philistines *g* their	1Sa 28:1	6908
the Philistines *g* themselves	1Sa 28:4	6908
Saul *g* all Israel together, and	1Sa 28:4	6908
Now the Philistines *g* together	1Sa 29:1	6908
the children of Benjamin *g*	2Sa 2:25	6908
when he had *g* all the people	2Sa 2:30	6908
David *g* together all the chosen	2Sa 6:1	3254
they *g* themselves together	2Sa 10:15	622
he *g* all Israel together, and	2Sa 10:17	622
David *g* all the people together,	2Sa 12:29	622
which cannot be *g* up again	2Sa 14:14	622
Israel be generally *g* unto thee	2Sa 17:11	622
and they were *g* together, and went	2Sa 20:14	7035
they *g* the bones of them that	2Sa 21:13	622
were there *g* together to battle	2Sa 23:9	622
the Philistines were *g* together	2Sa 23:11	622
Solomon *g* together chariots and	1Kin 10:26	622
he *g* men unto him, and became	1Kin 11:24	6908
g the prophets together unto	1Kin 18:20	6908
of Syria *g* all his host together	1Kin 20:1	6908
of Israel *g* the prophets together	1Kin 22:6	6908
they *g* all that were able to put	2Kin 3:21	6817
g thereof wild gourds his lap	2Kin 4:39	3950
king of Syria *g* all his host	2Kin 6:24	6908
Jehu *g* all the people together,	2Kin 10:18	6908
of the door have *g* of the people	2Kin 22:4	622
Thy servants have *g* the money	2Kin 22:9	5413
thou shalt be *g* into thy grave in	2Kin 22:20	622
they *g* unto him all the elders of	2Kin 23:1	622
Then all Israel *g* themselves to	1Chr 11:1	6908
were *g* together to battle	1Chr 11:13	622
So David *g* all Israel together,	1Chr 13:5	6950
David *g* all Israel together to	1Chr 15:3	6950
And the children of Ammon *g*	1Chr 19:7	622
he *g* all Israel, and passed over	1Chr 19:17	622
he *g* together all the princes of	1Chr 23:2	622
Solomon *g* chariots and horsemen	2Chr 1:14	622
he *g* of the house of Judah and	2Chr 11:1	6950
that were *g* together to Jerusalem	2Chr 12:5	622
there are *g* unto him vain men,	2Chr 13:7	6908
he *g* all Judah and Benjamin, and	2Chr 15:9	6908
So they *g* themselves together at	2Chr 15:10	6908
g together of prophets four	2Chr 18:5	6908
Judah *g* themselves together, to	2Chr 20:4	6908
g the Levites out of all the	2Chr 23:2	6908
he *g* together the priests and the	2Chr 24:5	6908
by day, and *g* money in abundance	2Chr 24:11	622
Moreover Amaziah *g* Judah together	2Chr 25:5	6908
Ahaz *g* together the vessels of	2Chr 28:24	622
g them together into the east	2Chr 29:4	622
they *g* their brethren, and	2Chr 29:15	622
g the rulers of the city, and went	2Chr 29:20	622
people *g* themselves together to	2Chr 30:3	622
So there was *g* much people	2Chr 32:4	622
g them together to him in the	2Chr 32:6	6908
had *g* of the hand of Manasseh	2Chr 34:9	622
they have *g* together the money	2Chr 34:17	5413
thou shalt be *g* to thy grave in	2Chr 34:28	622
g together all the elders of	2Chr 34:29	622
the people *g* themselves together	Ezr 3:1	622
I *g* together out of Israel chief	Ezr 7:28	6908
I *g* them together to the river	Ezr 8:15	6908
Benjamin *g* themselves together	Ezr 10:9	6908
all my servants were *g* thither	Neh 5:16	6908
all the people *g* themselves	Neh 8:1	622
on the second day were *g* together	Neh 8:13	622
the singers *g* themselves together	Neh 12:28	622
I *g* them together, and set them in	Neh 13:11	6908
when many maidens were *g* together	Est 2:8	6908
when the virgins were *g* together	Est 2:19	6908
The Jews *g* themselves together in	Est 9:2	6950
g themselves together on the	Est 9:15	6950
provinces *g* themselves together	Est 9:16	6950
they have *g* themselves together	Job 16:10	4390
lie down, but he shall not be *g*	Job 27:19	622
the nettles they were *g* together	Job 30:7	5596
and *g* themselves together	Ps 35:15	622
the abjects *g* themselves together	Ps 35:15	622
of the people are *g* together	Ps 47:9	622
the mighty are *g* against me	Ps 59:3	1481
When the people are *g* together	Ps 102:22	6908
g them out of the lands, from the	Ps 107:3	6908
are they *g* together for war	Ps 140:2	1481
and herbs of the mountains are *g*	Prov 27:25	622
who hath *g* the wind in his fists	Prov 30:4	622
I *g* me also silver and gold, and	Eccl 2:8	3664
I have *g* my myrrh with my spice	Song 5:1	717
g out the stones thereof, and	Is 5:2	
are left, have I *g* all the earth	Is 10:14	622

kingdoms of nations *g* together .... Is 13:4   622
ye *g* together the waters of the .... Is 22:9   6908
And they shall be *g* together .... Is 24:22   622
as prisoners are *g* in the pit .... Is 24:22   626
and ye shall be *g* one by one .... Is 27:12   3950
your spoil shall be *g* like the .... Is 33:4   622
shall the vultures also be *g* .... Is 34:15   6908
and his spirit it hath *g* them .... Is 34:16   6908
Let all the nations be *g* together .... Is 43:9   6908
let them all be *g* together .... Is 44:11   6908
to him, Though Israel be not *g* .... Is 49:5   622
beside those that are *g* unto him .... Is 56:8   6908
shall be *g* together unto thee .... Is 60:7   6908
they that have *g* it shall eat it .... Is 62:9   622
the nations shall be *g* unto it .... Jer 3:17   6960
they shall not be *g*, nor be .... Jer 8:2   622
shall not be lamented, neither *g* .... Jer 25:33   622
all the people were *g* against .... Jer 26:9   6950
g wine and summer fruits very much ..... Jer 40:12   622
that all the Jews which are *g* .... Jer 40:15   6908
When I shall have *g* the house of .... Eze 28:25   6908
not be brought together, nor *g* .... Eze 29:5   6908
is *g* out of many people, against .... Eze 38:8   6908
that are *g* out of the nations .... Eze 38:12   622
hast thou *g* thy company to take a .... Eze 38:13   6950
g them out of their enemies' .... Eze 39:27   6908
but I have *g* them unto their own .... Eze 39:28   3664
were *g* together unto the .... Dan 3:3   3673
being *g* together, saw these men, ... Dan 3:27   3673
children of Israel be *g* together .... Hos 1:11   6908
people shall be *g* against them .... Hos 10:10   622
for she *g* it of the hire of an .... Mic 1:7   6908
many nations are *g* against thee .... Mic 4:11   622
they have *g* the summer fruits .... Mic 7:1   622
earth be *g* together against it .... Zec 12:3   622
round about shall be *g* together .... Zec 14:14   622
when he had *g* all the chief .... Mt 2:4   4863
were *g* together unto him, so that .... Mt 13:2   4863
As therefore the tares are *g* .... Mt 13:40   4816
into the sea, and *g* of every kind .... Mt 13:47   4863
g the good into vessels, but cast .... Mt 13:48   4816
three are *g* together in my name .... Mt 18:20   4863
g together all as many as they .... Mt 22:10   4863
to silence, they were *g* together .... Mt 22:34   4863
the Pharisees were *g* together .... Mt 22:41   4863
I have *g* thy children together .... Mt 23:37   1996
will the eagles be *g* together .... Mt 24:28   4863
before him shall be *g* all nations .... Mt 25:32   4863
when they were *g* together .... Mt 27:17   4863
g unto him the whole band of .... Mt 27:27   4863
all the city was *g* together at .... Mk 1:33   1996
straightway many were *g* together .... Mk 2:2   4863
there was *g* unto him a great .... Mk 4:1   4863
side, much people *g* unto him .... Mk 5:21   4863
the apostles *g* themselves .... Mk 6:30   4863
when much people were *g* together .... Lk 8:4   4896
the people were *g* thick together .... Lk 11:29   1865
when there were *g* together an .... Lk 12:1   1996
I have *g* thy children together .... Lk 13:34   1996
the younger son *g* all together .... Lk 15:13   4863
will the eagles be *g* together .... Lk 17:37   4863
and found the eleven *g* together .... Lk 24:33   4867
Therefore they *g* them together .... Jn 6:13   4863
Then *g* the chief priests and the .... Jn 11:47   4863
were *g* together at Jerusalem .... Acts 4:6   4863
the rulers were *g* together .... Acts 4:26   4863
of Israel, were *g* together, ... Acts 4:27   4863
where many were *g* together .... Acts 12:12   4863
had *g* the church together, they .... Acts 14:27   4863
when they had *g* the multitude .... Acts 15:30   4863
g a company, and set all the city .... Acts 17:5   3792
where were *g* together .... Acts 20:8   4863
when Paul had *g* a bundle of .... Acts 28:3   4962
Christ, when ye are *g* together 1Cor 5:4   4863
He that had *g* much had nothing 2Cor 8:15
he that had *g* little had no lack 2Cor 8:15
g the vine of the earth, and cast .... Rev 14:19   5166
he *g* them together into a place .... Rev 16:16   4863
g together to make war against .... Rev 19:19   4863

GATHERER
herdman, and a *g* of sycomore fruit .... Amos 7:14   1103

GATHEREST
When thou *g* the grapes of thy .... Deut 24:21   1219

GATHERETH
he that *g* the ashes of the heifer .... Num 19:10   622
He *g* the waters of the sea .... Ps 33:7   3664
his heart *g* iniquity to itself .... Ps 41:6   6908
he *g* together the outcasts of .... Ps 147:2   3664
g her food in the harvest .... Prov 6:8   103

He that *g* in summer is a wise son .... Prov 10:5   103
but he that *g* by labour shall.................. Prov 13:11   6908
as one *g* eggs that are left, have .... Is 10:14   622
as when the harvestman *g* the corn .... Is 17:5   622
it shall be as he *g* the ears in .... Is 17:5   3950
The Lord GOD which *g* the outcasts ...... Is 56:8   6908
the mountains, and no man *g* them .... Nah 3:18   6908
but *g* unto him all nations, and............. Hab 2:5   622
he that *g* not with me scattereth .... Mt 12:30   4863
even as a hen *g* her chickens .... Mt 23:37   1996
he that *g* not with me scattereth .... Lk 11:23   4863
g fruit unto life eternal .... Jn 4:36   4863

GATHERING
the *g* together of the waters .... Gen 1:10   4723
him shall the *g* of the people be .... Gen 49:10   3349
they that found him *g* sticks .... Num 15:33   7197
widow woman was there *g* of sticks 1Kin 17:10   7197
I am *g* two sticks, that I may go 1Kin 17:12   7197
were three days in *g* of the spoil 2Chr 20:25   962
shall fail, the *g* shall not come .... Is 32:10   625
like the *g* of the caterpiller .... Is 33:4   625
g where thou hast not strawed .... Mt 25:24   4863
assuredly *g* that the Lord had .... Acts 16:10   4822
by our *g* together unto him, ... 2Th 2:1   1997

GATHERINGS
that there be no *g* when I come 1Cor 16:2   3048

GATH-HEPHER (*gath-he′-fer*) See GITTAH-HEPHER. *A town in Zebulun.*
the prophet, which was of *G* 2Kin 14:25   1662

GATH-RIMMON (*gath-rim′-mon*)
1. A Levitical town in Dan.
And Jehud, and Bene-berak, and *G* .... Josh 19:45   1667
2. A Levitical town in Manasseh.
her suburbs, *G* with her suburbs .... Josh 21:24   1667
suburbs, and *G* with her suburbs .... Josh 21:25   1667
suburbs, and *G* with her suburbs 1Chr 6:69   1667

GAVE
Adam *g* names to all cattle, and to .... Gen 2:20   7121
g also unto her husband with her .... Gen 3:6   5414
she *g* me of the tree, and I did .... Gen 3:12   5414
And he *g* him tithes of all .... Gen 14:20   5414
g her to her husband Abram to be .... Gen 16:3   5414
and good, and *g* it unto a young man .... Gen 18:7   5414
g them unto Abraham, and restored ...... Gen 20:14   5414
g it unto Hagar, putting it on .... Gen 21:14   5414
with water, and *g* the lad drink .... Gen 21:19
and oxen, and *g* them unto Abimelech ... Gen 21:27   5414
upon her hand, and *g* him drink .... Gen 24:18
g straw and provender for the .... Gen 24:32   5414
and raiment, and *g* them to Rebekah ..... Gen 24:53   5414
he *g* also to her brother and to .... Gen 24:53   5414
Abraham *g* all that he had unto .... Gen 25:5   5414
Abraham had, Abraham *g* gifts .... Gen 25:6   5414
Then Abraham *g* up the ghost .... Gen 25:8
he *g* up the ghost and died .... Gen 25:17   5414
Then Jacob *g* Esau bread and .... Gen 25:34   5414
she *g* the savoury meat and the .... Gen 27:17   5414
which God *g* unto Abraham .... Gen 28:4   5414
he blessed him he *g* him a charge .... Gen 28:6
Laban *g* unto his daughter Leah .... Gen 29:24   5414
he *g* him Rachel his daughter to .... Gen 29:28   5414
Laban *g* to Rachel his daughter .... Gen 29:29   5414
she *g* him Bilhah her handmaid to .... Gen 30:4   5414
her maid, and *g* her Jacob to wife .... Gen 30:9   5414
g them into the hand of his sons .... Gen 30:35   5414
they *g* unto Jacob all the strange .... Gen 35:4   5414
And the land which I *g* Abraham .... Gen 35:12   5414
Isaac *g* up the ghost, and died, and ...... Gen 35:29
he *g* it her, and came in unto her, ... Gen 38:18   5414
because that I *g* her not to .... Gen 38:26   5414
g him favour in the sight of the .... Gen 39:21   5414
I *g* the cup into Pharaoh's hand .... Gen 40:11   5414
he *g* the cup into Pharaoh's hand .... Gen 40:21   5414
he *g* him to wife Asenath the .... Gen 41:45   5414
g them water, and they washed .... Gen 43:24   5414
he *g* their asses provender .... Gen 43:24   5414
Joseph *g* them wagons, according .... Gen 45:21   5414
g them provision for the way .... Gen 45:21   5414
To all of them he *g* each man .... Gen 45:22   5414
but to Benjamin he *g* three .... Gen 45:22   5414
whom Laban *g* to Leah his daughter ..... Gen 46:18   5414
which Laban *g* unto Rachel his .... Gen 46:25   5414
g them a possession in the land .... Gen 47:11   5414
Joseph *g* them bread in exchange .... Gen 47:17   5414
portion which Pharaoh *g* them .... Gen 47:22   5414
he *g* Moses Zipporah his daughter .... Ex 2:21   5414
g them a charge unto the children .... Ex 6:13
the LORD *g* the people favour in .... Ex 11:3   5414

the LORD *g* the people favour in	Ex 12:36	5414
but it *g* light by night to these	Ex 14:20	
he *g* unto Moses, when he had made	Ex 31:18	5414
So they *g* it me	Ex 32:24	5414
he *g* them in commandment all that	Ex 34:32	
Moses *g* commandment, and they	Ex 36:6	
Moses *g* the money of them that	Num 3:51	5414
oxen, and *g* them unto the Levites	Num 7:6	5414
four oxen he *g* unto the sons of	Num 7:7	5414
eight oxen he *g* unto the sons of	Num 7:8	5414
unto the sons of Kohath he *g* none	Num 7:9	5414
g it unto the seventy elders	Num 11:25	5414
their princes *g* him a rod apiece	Num 17:6	5414
g him a charge, as the LORD	Num 27:23	
Moses *g* the tribute, which was	Num 31:41	5414
g them unto the Levites, which	Num 31:47	5414
Moses *g* unto them, even to this	Num 32:33	5414
g other names unto the cities	Num 32:38	7121
Moses *g* Gilead unto Machir the	Num 32:40	5414
which the LORD *g* unto them	Deut 2:12	5414
g I unto the Reubenites and to the	Deut 3:12	5414
g I unto the half tribe of	Deut 3:13	5414
And I *g* Gilead unto Machir	Deut 3:15	5414
unto the Gadites I *g* from Gilead	Deut 3:16	5414
that the LORD *g* me the two tables	Deut 9:11	5414
and the LORD *g* them unto me	Deut 10:4	5414
I *g* my daughter unto this man to	Deut 22:16	5414
g it for an inheritance unto the	Deut 29:8	5414
he *g* Joshua the son of Nun a	Deut 31:23	
Moses *g* you on this side Jordan	Josh 1:14	5414
g you on this side Jordan toward	Josh 1:15	5414
Joshua *g* it for an inheritance	Josh 11:23	5414
g it for a possession unto the	Josh 12:6	5414
which Joshua *g* unto the tribes of	Josh 12:7	5414
inheritance, which Moses *g* them	Josh 13:8	5414
the servant of the LORD *g* them	Josh 13:8	5414
of Levi he *g* none inheritance	Josh 13:14	5414
Moses *g* unto the tribe of the	Josh 13:15	5414
Moses *g* inheritance unto the	Josh 13:24	5414
Moses *g* inheritance unto the half	Josh 13:29	5414
Levi Moses *g* not any inheritance	Josh 13:33	5414
but unto the Levites he *g* none	Josh 14:3	5414
therefore they *g* no part unto the	Josh 14:4	5414
g unto Caleb the son of Jephunneh	Josh 14:13	5414
he *g* a part among the children of	Josh 15:13	5414
he *g* him Achsah his daughter to	Josh 15:17	5414
he *g* her the upper springs, and	Josh 15:19	5414
g them an inheritance among the	Josh 17:4	5414
the servant of the LORD *g* them	Josh 18:7	5414
the children of Israel *g* an	Josh 19:49	5414
g him the city which he asked	Josh 19:50	5414
the children of Israel *g* unto the	Josh 21:3	5414
the children of Israel *g* by lot	Josh 21:8	5414
they *g* out of the tribe of the	Josh 21:9	5414
they *g* them the city of Arba the	Josh 21:11	5414
g they to Caleb the son of	Josh 21:12	5414
Thus they *g* to the children of	Josh 21:13	5414
For they *g* them Shechem with her	Josh 21:21	5414
they *g* Golan in Bashan with her	Josh 21:27	
the LORD *g* unto Israel all the	Josh 21:43	5414
the LORD *g* them rest round about,	Josh 21:44	
g you on the other side Jordan	Josh 22:4	5414
g Joshua among their brethren on	Josh 22:7	5414
his seed, and *g* him Isaac	Josh 24:3	5414
I *g* unto Isaac Jacob and Esau	Josh 24:4	5414
I *g* unto Esau mount Seir, to	Josh 24:4	5414
I *g* them into your hand, that ye	Josh 24:8	5414
he *g* him Achsah his daughter to	Judg 1:13	5414
Caleb *g* her the upper springs and	Judg 1:15	5414
they *g* Hebron unto Caleb, as	Judg 1:20	5414
g their daughters to their sons,	Judg 3:6	5414
g him drink, and covered him	Judg 4:19	
He asked water, and she *g* him milk	Judg 5:25	5414
before you, and *g* you their land	Judg 6:9	5414
they *g* him threescore and ten	Judg 9:4	
and *g* them, and they did eat	Judg 14:9	5414
g change of garments unto them	Judg 14:19	5414
therefore I *g* her to thy	Judg 15:2	5414
g them to the founder, who made	Judg 17:4	5414
g provender unto the asses	Judg 19:21	
for the men of Israel *g* place to	Judg 20:36	5414
they *g* them wives which they had	Judg 21:14	5414
g to her that she had reserved	Ruth 2:18	5414
six measures of barley *g* he me	Ruth 3:17	5414
shoe, and *g* it to his neighbour	Ruth 4:7	5414
the LORD *g* her conception, and she	Ruth 4:13	5414
women her neighbours *g* it a name	Ruth 4:17	7121
he *g* to Peninnah his wife, and to	1Sa 1:4	5414
unto Hannah he *g* a worthy portion	1Sa 1:5	5414
g her son suck until she weaned	1Sa 1:23	5414
Bring the portion which I *g* thee	1Sa 9:23	5414

Samuel, God *g* him another heart	1Sa 10:9	
g it to David, and his garments,	1Sa 18:4	5414
they *g* them in full tale to the	1Sa 18:27	
Saul *g* him Michal his daughter to	1Sa 18:27	5414
Jonathan *g* his artillery unto his	1Sa 20:40	5414
So the priest *g* him hallowed	1Sa 21:6	5414
g him victuals, and *g* him the	1Sa 22:10	5414
Then Achish *g* him Ziklag that day	1Sa 27:6	5414
g him bread, and he did eat	1Sa 30:11	5414
they *g* him a piece of a cake of	1Sa 30:12	5414
I *g* thee thy master's house, and	2Sa 12:8	5414
g thee the house of Israel and of	2Sa 12:8	5414
king *g* all the captains charge	2Sa 18:5	
Joab *g* up the sum of the number	2Sa 24:9	5414
And God *g* Solomon wisdom and	1Kin 4:29	5414
So Hiram *g* Solomon cedar trees and	1Kin 5:10	5414
Solomon *g* Hiram twenty thousand	1Kin 5:11	5414
thus *g* Solomon to Hiram year by	1Kin 5:11	5414
the LORD *g* Solomon wisdom, as he	1Kin 5:12	5414
that then king Solomon *g* Hiram	1Kin 9:11	5414
she *g* the king an hundred and	1Kin 10:10	5414
queen of Sheba *g* to king Solomon	1Kin 10:10	5414
king Solomon *g* unto the queen of	1Kin 10:13	5414
Solomon *g* her of his royal bounty	1Kin 10:13	5414
which *g* him an house, and	1Kin 11:18	5414
him victuals, and *g* him land	1Kin 11:18	5414
so that he *g* him to wife the	1Kin 11:19	5414
old men's counsel that they *g* him	1Kin 12:13	3289
he *g* a sign the same day, saying,	1Kin 13:3	5414
the house of David, and *g* it thee	1Kin 14:8	5414
which he *g* to their fathers, and	1Kin 14:15	5414
g unto the people, and they did	1Kin 19:21	5414
And he *g* him his hand	2Kin 10:15	5414
upon him, and *g* him the testimony	2Kin 11:12	
they *g* the money, being told,	2Kin 12:11	5414
But they *g* that to the workmen,	2Kin 12:14	5414
the LORD *g* Israel a saviour, so	2Kin 13:5	5414
Menahem *g* Pul a thousand talents	2Kin 15:19	5414
his servant, and *g* him presents	2Kin 17:3	7725
Hezekiah *g* him all the silver	2Kin 18:15	5414
g it to the king of Assyria	2Kin 18:16	5414
the land which I *g* their fathers	2Kin 21:8	5414
Hilkiah *g* the book to Shaphan, and	2Kin 22:8	5414
Jehoiakim *g* the silver and the	2Kin 23:35	5414
and they *g* judgment upon him	2Kin 25:6	1696
Sheshan *g* his daughter to Jarha	1Chr 2:35	5414
they *g* them Hebron in the land of	1Chr 6:55	5414
they *g* to Caleb the son of	1Chr 6:56	5414
Aaron they *g* the cities of Judah	1Chr 6:57	5414
the children of Israel *g* to the	1Chr 6:64	5414
they *g* by lot out of the tribe of	1Chr 6:65	5414
they *g* unto them, of the cities	1Chr 6:67	5414
they *g* also Gezer with her	1Chr 6:67	
David *g* a commandment, and they	1Chr 14:12	
Joab *g* the sum of the number of	1Chr 21:5	5414
So David *g* to Ornan for the place	1Chr 21:25	5414
God *g* to Heman fourteen sons and	1Chr 25:5	5414
Then David *g* to Solomon his son	1Chr 28:11	5414
He *g* of gold by weight for things	1Chr 28:14	
by weight he *g* gold for the	1Chr 28:16	
for the golden basons he *g* gold	1Chr 28:17	
g for the service of the house of	1Chr 29:7	5414
g them to the treasure of the	1Chr 29:8	5414
she *g* the king an hundred and	2Chr 9:9	5414
the queen of Sheba *g* king Solomon	2Chr 9:9	5414
king Solomon *g* to the queen of	2Chr 9:12	5414
counsel which the old men *g* him	2Chr 10:8	3289
he *g* them victual in abundance	2Chr 11:23	5414
g the kingdom over Israel to	2Chr 13:5	5414
Then the men of Judah *g* a shout	2Chr 13:15	
the LORD *g* them rest round about	2Chr 15:15	
for his God *g* him rest round	2Chr 20:30	
their father *g* them great gifts	2Chr 21:3	5414
but the kingdom *g* he to Jehoram	2Chr 21:3	5414
g him the testimony, and made him	2Chr 23:11	
Jehoiada *g* it to such as did the	2Chr 24:12	5414
the Ammonites *g* gifts to Uzziah	2Chr 26:8	5414
the children of Ammon *g* him the	2Chr 27:5	5414
g them to eat and to drink, and	2Chr 28:15	
g it unto the king of Assyria	2Chr 28:21	5414
who therefore *g* them up to	2Chr 30:7	5414
the princes *g* to the congregation	2Chr 30:24	7311
unto him, and he *g* him a sign	2Chr 32:24	5414
they *g* it to the workmen that	2Chr 34:10	5414
artificers and builders *g* they it	2Chr 34:11	5414
Josiah *g* to the people, of the	2Chr 35:7	7311
his princes *g* willingly unto the	2Chr 35:8	7311
g unto the priests for the	2Chr 35:8	5414
g unto the Levites for passover	2Chr 35:9	7311
he *g* them all into his hand	2Chr 36:17	5414
They *g* after their ability unto	Ezr 2:69	5414

They *g* money also unto the masons	Ezr 3:7	5414
he *g* them into the hand of	Ezr 5:12	3052
Artaxerxes *g* unto Ezra the priest	Ezr 7:11	5414
they *g* their hands that they	Ezr 10:19	5414
the wine, and *g* it unto the king	Neh 2:1	5414
g them the king's letters	Neh 2:9	5414
That I my brother Hanani, and	Neh 7:2	
of the fathers *g* unto the work	Neh 7:70	5414
The Tirshatha *g* to the treasure a	Neh 7:70	5414
g to the treasure of the work	Neh 7:71	5414
g was twenty thousand drams of	Neh 7:72	5414
g the sense, and caused them to	Neh 8:8	7760
companies of them that *g* thanks	Neh 12:31	
g thanks went over against them	Neh 12:38	
that *g* thanks in the house of God	Neh 12:40	
g the portions of the singers and	Neh 12:47	5414
they *g* them drink in vessels of	Est 1:7	
he speedily *g* her her things for	Est 2:9	5414
g gifts, according to the state	Est 2:18	5414
g it unto Haman the son of	Est 3:10	5414
g him a commandment to Mordecai,	Est 4:5	
Also he *g* him the copy of the	Est 4:8	5414
g him commandment unto Mordecai	Est 4:10	
from Haman, and *g* it unto Mordecai	Est 8:2	5414
the LORD *g*, and the LORD hath	Job 1:21	5414
my servant, and he *g* me no answer	Job 19:16	
eye saw me, it *g* witness to me	Job 29:11	
Unto me men *g* ear, and waited, and	Job 29:21	
I *g* ear to your reasons, whilst	Job 32:11	
also the LORD *g* Job twice as much	Job 42:10	3254
every man also *g* him a piece of	Job 42:11	5414
their father *g* them inheritance	Job 42:15	5414
and the Highest *g* his voice	Ps 18:13	5414
The Lord *g* the word	Ps 68:11	5414
They *g* me also gall for my meat	Ps 69:21	5414
in my thirst they *g* me vinegar to	Ps 69:21	
and he *g* ear unto me	Ps 77:1	
g them drink as out of the great	Ps 78:15	
for he *g* them their own desire	Ps 78:29	935
He *g* also their increase unto the	Ps 78:46	5414
He *g* up their cattle also to the	Ps 78:48	5462
but *g* their life over to the	Ps 78:50	5462
He *g* his people over also unto	Ps 78:62	5462
So I *g* them up unto their own	Ps 81:12	7971
and the ordinance that he *g* them	Ps 99:7	5414
He *g* them hail for rain, and	Ps 105:32	5414
g them the lands of the heathen	Ps 105:44	5414
And he *g* them their request	Ps 106:15	5414
he *g* them into the hand of the	Ps 106:41	5414
g their land for an heritage, an	Ps 135:12	5414
g their land for an heritage	Ps 136:21	5414
When he *g* to the sea his decree,	Prov 8:29	7760
I *g* my heart to seek and search	Eccl 1:13	5414
I *g* my heart to know wisdom, and	Eccl 1:17	5414
shall return unto God who *g* it	Eccl 12:7	5414
he *g* good heed, and sought out, and	Eccl 12:9	
called him, but he *g* me no answer	Song 5:6	
g the nations before him, and made	Is 41:2	5414
he *g* them as the dust to his	Is 41:2	5414
Who *g* Jacob for a spoil, and	Is 42:24	5414
I *g* Egypt for thy ransom,	Is 43:3	5414
I *g* my back to the smiters, and my	Is 50:6	5414
the land that I *g* to your fathers	Jer 7:7	5414
unto the place which I *g* to you	Jer 7:14	5414
land that I *g* unto their fathers	Jer 16:15	5414
from thine heritage that I *g* thee	Jer 17:4	5414
you, and the city that I *g* you	Jer 23:39	5414
off the land that I *g* unto them	Jer 24:10	5414
land that I *g* to their fathers	Jer 30:3	5414
I *g* the evidence of the purchase	Jer 32:12	5414
g it to Baruch the scribe, the	Jer 36:32	5414
where he *g* judgment upon him	Jer 39:5	1696
g them vineyards and fields at the	Jer 39:10	5414
g charge concerning Jeremiah to	Jer 39:11	
of the guard *g* him victuals	Jer 40:5	5414
as I *g* Zedekiah king of Judah	Jer 44:30	5414
where he *g* judgment upon him	Jer 52:9	1696
mine elders *g* up the ghost in the	Lam 1:19	
My meat also which I *g* thee	Eze 16:19	5414
I *g* them my statutes, and shewed	Eze 20:11	5414
Moreover also I *g* them my	Eze 20:12	5414
Wherefore I *g* them also statutes	Eze 20:25	5414
the land that I *g* to your fathers	Eze 36:28	5414
g them into the hand of their	Eze 39:23	5414
the Lord *g* Jehoiakim king of	Dan 1:2	5414
the prince of the eunuchs *g* names	Dan 1:7	7760
for he *g* unto Daniel the name of	Dan 1:7	7760
and *g* them pulse	Dan 1:16	5414
God *g* them knowledge and skill in	Dan 1:17	
g him many great gifts, and made	Dan 2:48	3052
O thou king, the most high God *g*	Dan 5:18	3052

And for the majesty that he *g* him	Dan 5:19	3052
g thanks before his God, as he	Dan 6:10	
did not know that I *g* her corn	Hos 2:8	5414
I *g* thee a king in mine anger, and	Hos 13:11	5414
But ye *g* the Nazarites wine to	Amos 2:12	
I *g* them to him for the fear	Mal 2:5	5414
he *g* commandment to depart unto	Mt 8:18	2753
he *g* them power against unclean	Mt 10:1	1325
g the loaves to his disciples, and	Mt 14:19	1325
g thanks, and brake them	Mt 15:36	1325
g to his disciples, and the	Mt 15:36	1325
who *g* thee this authority	Mt 21:23	1325
unto one he *g* five talents, to	Mt 25:15	1325
I was an hungred, and ye *g* me meat	Mt 25:35	1325
I was thirsty, and ye *g* me drink	Mt 25:35	4222
or thirsty, and *g* thee drink	Mt 25:37	4222
an hungred, and ye *g* me no meat	Mt 25:42	1325
was thirsty, and ye *g* me no drink	Mt 25:42	4222
g it to the disciples, and said,	Mt 26:26	1325
g thanks, and *g* it to them,	Mt 26:27	1325
that betrayed him *g* them a sign	Mt 26:48	1325
g them for the potter's field, as	Mt 27:10	1325
They *g* him vinegar to drink	Mt 27:34	1325
it on a reed, and *g* him to drink	Mt 27:48	4222
they *g* large money unto the	Mt 28:12	1325
g also to them which were with	Mk 2:26	1325
And forthwith Jesus *g* them leave	Mk 5:13	2010
g them power over unclean spirits	Mk 6:7	1325
a charger, and *g* it to the damsel	Mk 6:28	1325
the damsel *g* it to her mother	Mk 6:28	1325
g them to his disciples to set	Mk 6:41	1325
g thanks, and brake	Mk 8:6	1325
g to his disciples to set before	Mk 8:6	1325
who *g* thee this authority to do	Mk 11:28	1325
g authority to his servants, and	Mk 13:34	1325
g to them, and said, Take, eat	Mk 14:22	1325
had given thanks, he *g* it to them	Mk 14:23	1325
they *g* him to drink wine mingled	Mk 15:23	1325
g him to drink, saying, Let alone	Mk 15:36	4222
a loud voice, and *g* up the ghost	Mk 15:37	
g up the ghost, he said, Truly	Mk 15:39	
he *g* the body to Joseph	Mk 15:45	1433
she coming in that instant *g*	Lk 2:38	437
he *g* it again to the minister, and	Lk 4:20	591
g also to them that were with him	Lk 6:4	1325
many that were blind he *g* sight	Lk 7:21	5483
g them power and authority over	Lk 9:1	1325
g to the disciples to set before	Lk 9:16	1325
g them to the host, and said unto	Lk 10:35	1325
and no man *g* unto him	Lk 15:16	1325
they saw it, *g* praise unto God	Lk 18:43	1325
or who is he that *g* thee this	Lk 20:2	1325
g thanks, and said, Take this, and	Lk 22:17	
g thanks, and brake it	Lk 22:19	
g unto them, saying, This is my	Lk 22:19	1325
Pilate *g* sentence that it should	Lk 23:24	
and the paps which never *g* suck	Lk 23:29	
said thus, he *g* up the ghost	Lk 23:46	
it, and brake, and *g* to them	Lk 24:30	1929
they *g* him a piece of a broiled	Lk 24:42	1929
to them *g* he power to become the	Jn 1:12	1325
that he *g* his only begotten Son,	Jn 3:16	1325
that Jacob *g* to his son Joseph	Jn 4:5	1325
which *g* us the well, and drank	Jn 4:12	1325
He *g* them bread from heaven to	Jn 6:31	1325
Moses *g* you not that bread from	Jn 6:32	1325
Moses therefore *g* unto you	Jn 7:22	1325
which *g* them me, is greater than	Jn 10:29	1325
he *g* me a commandment, what I	Jn 12:49	1325
he *g* it to Judas Iscariot, the	Jn 13:26	1325
as the Father *g* me commandment,	Jn 14:31	1781
which *g* counsel to the Jews, that	Jn 18:14	4823
But Jesus *g* him no answer	Jn 19:9	1325
bowed his head, and *g* up the ghost	Jn 19:30	3860
and Pilate *g* him leave	Jn 19:38	2010
And they *g* forth their lots	Acts 1:26	1325
as the Spirit *g* them utterance	Acts 2:4	1325
he *g* heed unto them, expecting to	Acts 3:5	1907
with great power *g* the apostles	Acts 4:33	591
fell down, and *g* up the ghost	Acts 5:5	
he *g* him none inheritance in it,	Acts 7:5	1325
And he *g* him the covenant of	Acts 7:8	1325
g him favour and wisdom in the	Acts 7:10	1325
g them up to worship the host of	Acts 7:42	3860
the people with one accord *g* heed	Acts 8:6	4337
To whom they all *g* heed, from the	Acts 8:10	4337
he *g* her his hand, and lifted her	Acts 9:41	1325
which *g* much alms to the people,	Acts 10:2	4160
Forasmuch then as God *g* them the	Acts 11:17	1325
And the people *g* a shout, saying,	Acts 12:22	
because he *g* not God the glory	Acts 12:23	1325

eaten of worms, and *g* up the ghost	Acts 12:23	
after that he *g* unto them judges	Acts 13:20	1325
God *g* unto them Saul the son of	Acts 13:21	1325
to whom also he *g* testimony	Acts 13:22	3140
which *g* testimony unto the word	Acts 14:3	3140
g us rain from heaven, and	Acts 14:17	1325
g audience to Barnabas and Paul,	Acts 15:12	
to whom we *g* no such commandment	Acts 15:24	1291
they *g* him audience unto this	Acts 22:22	
g commandment to his accusers	Acts 23:30	
I *g* my voice against them	Acts 26:10	2702
g him liberty to go unto his	Acts 27:3	2010
g thanks to God in presence of	Acts 27:35	
Wherefore God also *g* them up to	Rom 1:24	3860
For this cause God *g* them up unto	Rom 1:26	3860
God *g* them over to a reprobate	Rom 1:28	3860
even as the Lord *g* to every man	1Cor 3:5	1325
but God *g* the increase	1Cor 3:6	
but first *g* their own selves to	2Cor 8:5	1325
Who *g* himself for our sins, that	Gal 1:4	1325
To whom we *g* place by subjection,	Gal 2:5	1502
they *g* to me and Barnabas the	Gal 2:9	1325
who loved me, and *g* himself for me	Gal 2:20	3860
but God *g* it to Abraham by	Gal 3:18	5483
g him to be the head over all	Eph 1:22	1325
captive, and *g* gifts unto men	Eph 4:8	1325
And he *g* some, apostles	Eph 4:11	1325
the church, and *g* himself for it	Eph 5:25	3860
we *g* you by the Lord Jesus	1Th 4:2	1325
Who *g* himself a ransom for all,	1Ti 2:6	1325
Who *g* himself for us, that he	Titus 2:14	1325
Abraham *g* a tenth part of all	Heb 7:2	
Abraham *g* the tenth of the spoils	Heb 7:4	1325
of which no man *g* attendance at	Heb 7:13	4337
g commandment concerning his	Heb 11:22	
us, and we *g* them reverence	Heb 12:9	1788
again, and the heaven *g* rain	Jas 5:18	1325
up from the dead, and *g* him glory	1Pet 1:21	1325
another, as he *g* us commandment	1Jn 3:23	1325
the record that God *g* of his Son	1Jn 5:10	3140
when I *g* all diligence to write	Jude 3	4160
Christ, which God *g* unto him	Rev 1:1	1325
I *g* her space to repent of her	Rev 2:21	1325
g glory to the God of heaven	Rev 11:13	1325
the dragon *g* him his power, and	Rev 13:2	1325
which *g* power unto the beast	Rev 13:4	1325
one of the four beasts *g* unto the	Rev 15:7	1325
the sea *g* up the dead which were	Rev 20:13	1325

GAVEST

woman whom thou *g* to be with me	Gen 3:12	5414
which thou *g* unto their fathers	1Kin 8:34	5414
which thou *g* unto our fathers	1Kin 8:40	5414
which thou *g* unto their fathers,	1Kin 8:48	5414
the land which thou *g* to them	2Chr 6:25	5414
which thou *g* unto our fathers	2Chr 6:31	5414
which thou *g* unto their fathers,	2Chr 6:38	5414
g it to the seed of Abraham thy	2Chr 20:7	5414
g him the name of Abraham	Neh 9:7	7760
g them right judgments, and true	Neh 9:13	5414
g them bread from heaven for	Neh 9:15	5414
Thou *g* also thy good spirit to	Neh 9:20	5414
g them water for their thirst	Neh 9:20	5414
Moreover thou *g* them kingdoms	Neh 9:22	5414
g them into their hands, with	Neh 9:24	5414
mercies thou *g* them saviours	Neh 9:27	5414
therefore *g* thou them into the	Neh 9:30	5414
great goodness that thou *g* them	Neh 9:35	5414
fat land which thou *g* before them	Neh 9:35	5414
for the land that thou *g* unto our	Neh 9:36	5414
G thou the goodly wings unto the	Job 39:13	
thou *g* it him, even length of	Ps 21:4	5414
g him to be meat to the people	Ps 74:14	5414
thou *g* me no water for my feet	Lk 7:44	1325
Thou *g* me no kiss	Lk 7:45	1325
and yet thou never *g* me a kid	Lk 15:29	1325
Wherefore then *g* not thou my	Lk 19:23	1325
the work which thou *g* me to do	Jn 17:4	1325
which thou *g* me out of the world	Jn 17:6	1325
they were, and thou *g* them me	Jn 17:6	1325
them the words which thou *g* me	Jn 17:8	1325
those that thou *g* me I have kept	Jn 17:12	1325
which thou *g* me I have given them	Jn 17:22	1325
Of them which thou *g* me have I	Jn 18:9	1325

GAY

him that weareth the *g* clothing	Jas 2:3	2986

GAZA (ga'-zah) See AZZAH, GAZITES.
1. A royal Philistine city.

as thou comest to Gerar, unto *G*	Gen 10:19	5804
from Kadesh-barnea even unto *G*	Josh 10:41	5804

only in *G*, in Gath, and in Ashdod,	Josh 11:22	5804
G with her towns and her villages,	Josh 15:47	5804
Also Judah took *G* with the coast	Judg 1:18	5804
Then went Samson to *G*, and saw	Judg 16:1	5804
eyes, and brought him down to *G*	Judg 16:21	5804
for Ashdod one, for *G* one	1Sa 6:17	5804
the Philistines, even unto *G*	2Kin 18:8	5804
before that Pharaoh smote *G*	Jer 47:1	5804
Baldness is come upon *G*	Jer 47:5	5804
For three transgressions of *G*	Amos 1:6	5804
will send a fire on the wall of *G*	Amos 1:7	5804
For *G* shall be forsaken, and	Zeph 2:4	5804
G also shall see it, and be very	Zec 9:5	5804
and the king shall perish from *G*	Zec 9:5	5804
goeth down from Jerusalem unto *G*	Acts 8:26	1048

2. A city in Ephraim.

the earth, till thou come unto *G*	Judg 6:4	5804
also and the towns thereof, unto *G*	1Chr 7:28	5804

GAZATHITES (ga'-zath-ites) See GAZITES. *Inhabitants of Gaza.*

the *G*, and the Ashdothites, the	Josh 13:3	5841

GAZE

break through unto the LORD to *g*	Ex 19:21	7200

GAZER (ga'-zur) See GEZER. *A Canaanite city.*

from Geba until thou come to *G*	2Sa 5:25	1507
Philistines from Gibeon even to *G*	1Chr 14:16	1507

GAZEZ (ga'-zez) *A son of Caleb.*

bare Haran, and Moza, and *G*	1Chr 2:46	1495
and Haran begat *G*	1Chr 2:46	1495

GAZING

why stand ye *g* up into heaven	Acts 1:11	1689

GAZINGSTOCK

vile, and will set thee as a *g*	Nah 3:6	7210
were made a *g* both by reproaches	Heb 10:33	2301

GAZITES (ga'-zites) See GAZATHITES. *Inhabitants of Gaza.*

And it was told the *G*, saying,	Judg 16:2	5841

GAZZAM (gaz'-zam) *A family of exiles.*

of Nekoda, the children of *G*	Ezr 2:48	1502
The children of *G*, the children,	Neh 7:51	1502

GEBA (ghe'-bah) See GABA, GIBEAH, GIBEON. *A Levitical city in Benjamin.*

her suburbs, *G* with her suburbs,	Josh 21:17	1387
of the Philistines that was in *G*	1Sa 13:3	1387
from *G* until thou come to Gazer	2Sa 5:25	1387
Asa built with them *G* of Benjamin	1Kin 15:22	1387
from *G* to Beer-sheba, and brake	2Kin 23:8	1387
G with her suburbs, and Alemeth	1Chr 6:60	1387
fathers of the inhabitants of *G*	1Chr 8:6	1387
and he built therewith *G* and Mizpah	2Chr 16:6	1387
Benjamin from *G* dwelt at Michmash	Neh 11:31	1387
Gilgal, and out of the fields of *G*	Neh 12:29	1387
have taken up their lodging at *G*	Is 10:29	1387
G to Rimmon south of Jerusalem	Zec 14:10	1387

GEBAL (ghe'-bal) See GIBLITES.
1. An Edomite territory.

G, and Ammon, and Amalek	Ps 83:7	1381

2. A Phoenician trade city.

The ancients of *G* and the wise men	Eze 27:9	1381

GEBALITES See GIBLITES.

GEBER See EZION-GEBER.
1. Father of an officer of Solomon.

The son of *G*, in Ramoth-gilead	1Kin 4:13	1398

2. The son of Uri.

G the son of Uri was in the	1Kin 4:19	1398

GEBIM (ghe'-bim) *A city in Benjamin.*

the inhabitants of *G* gather	Is 10:31	1374

GEDALIAH (ghed-a-li'-ah)
1. Son of Ahikam.

them he made *G* the son of Ahikam	2Kin 25:22	1436
of Babylon had made *G* governor	2Kin 25:23	1436
there came to *G* to Mizpah	2Kin 25:23	1436
G sware to them, and to their men,	2Kin 25:24	1436
and ten men with him, and smote *G*	2Kin 25:25	1436
committed him unto *G* the son of	Jer 39:14	1436
Go back also to *G* the son of	Jer 40:5	1436
Then went Jeremiah unto *G* the son	Jer 40:6	1436
the king of Babylon had made *G*	Jer 40:7	1436
Then they came to *G* to Mizpah	Jer 40:8	1436
G the son of Ahikam the son of	Jer 40:9	1436
that he had set over them *G* the	Jer 40:11	1436
came to the land of Judah, to *G*	Jer 40:12	1436
the fields, came to *G* to Mizpah,	Jer 40:13	1436
But *G* the son of Ahikam believed	Jer 40:14	1436

G

spake to G in Mizpah secretly .... Jer 40:15   1436
But G the son of Ahikam said unto .... Jer 40:16   1436
came unto G the son of Ahikam to .... Jer 41:1   1436
smote the son of Ahikam the son .... Jer 41:2   1436
that were with him, even with G .... Jer 41:3   1436
second day after he had slain G .... Jer 41:4   1436
Come to G the son of Ahikam .... Jer 41:6   1436
whom he had slain because of G .... Jer 41:9   1436
committed to G the son of Ahikam ...... Jer 41:10   1436
he had slain G the son of Ahikam .... Jer 41:16   1436
had slain G the son of Ahikam .... Jer 41:18   1436
of the guard had left with G the .... Jer 43:6   1436
   2. A son of Jeduthun.
G, and Zeri, and Jeshaiah, ... 1Chr 25:3   1436
the second to G, who with his 1Chr 25:9   1436
   3. Priest who married a foreigner.
and Eliezer, and Jarib, and G .... Ezr 10:18   1436
   4. Grandfather of Zephaniah.
the son of Cushi, the son of G .... Zeph 1:1   1436
   5. A prince who had Jeremiah imprisoned.
G the son of Pashur, and Jucal the .... Jer 38:1   1436

GEDEON (ghed'-e-on) See GIDEON. *Greek form of*
   Gideon.
time would fail me to tell of G .... Heb 11:32   *1066*

GEDER (ghe'-dur) See BETH-GADER, GEDERITE, GEDOR. *A*
   Canaanite city.
the king of G, one .... Josh 12:13   1445

GEDERAH (ghed'-e-rah) See GEDERATHITE. *A city in*
   Judah.
And Sharaim, and Adithaim, and G .... Josh 15:36   1449

GEDERATHITE (ghed'-e-rath-ite) *An inhabitant of Ge-*
   derah.
and Johanan, and Josabad the G 1Chr 12:4   1452

GEDERITE (ghed'-e-rite) *An inhabitant of Geder.*
low plains was Baal-hanan the G 1Chr 27:28   1451

GEDEROTH (ghed'-e-roth) *A town in Judah.*
And G, Beth-dagon, and Naamah, and .. Josh 15:41   1450
Beth-shemesh, and Ajalon, and G 2Chr 28:18   1450

GEDEROTHAIM (ghed-e-ro-tha'-im) *A town in Judah.*
and Adithaim, and Gederah, and G .... Josh 15:36   1453

GEDOR (ghe'-dor) See GEDER.
   1. A city in Judah.
Halhul, Beth-zur, and G, ... Josh 15:58   1446
   2. Hometown of Jeroham.
the sons of Jeroham of G 1Chr 12:7   1446
   3. Son of Jehiel.
And G, and Ahio, and Zacher 1Chr 8:31   1446
And G, and Ahio, and Zechariah, and ... 1Chr 9:37   1446
   4. A descendant of Judah.
And Penuel the father of G 1Chr 4:4   1446
bare Jered the father of G 1Chr 4:18   1446
   5. A place in Judah.
And they went to the entrance of G 1Chr 4:39   1446

GE-HARASHIM See CHARASHIM.

GEHAZI (ghe-ha'-zi) *A servant of Elijah.*
he said to G his servant, Call 2Kin 4:12   1522
G answered, Verily she hath no 2Kin 4:14   1522
that he said to G his servant 2Kin 4:25   1522
but G came near to thrust her 2Kin 4:27   1522
Then he said to G, Gird up thy 2Kin 4:29   1522
G passed on before them, and laid 2Kin 4:31   1522
And he called G, and said, Call 2Kin 4:36   1522
But G, the servant of Elisha the 2Kin 5:20   1522
So G followed after Naaman 2Kin 5:21   1522
unto him, Whence comest thou, G 2Kin 5:25   1522
the king talked with G the 2Kin 8:4   1522
G said, My lord, O king, this is 2Kin 8:5   1522

GELILOTH (ghel'-il-oth) *Place on boundary of Benja-*
   min and Judah.
and went forth toward G, which is......... Josh 18:17   1553

GEMALLI (ghe-mal'-li) *One of the twelve spies.*
tribe of Dan, Ammiel the son of G .... Num 13:12   1582

GEMARIAH (ghem-a-ri'-ah)
   1. Son of Shaphan.
in the chamber of G the son of .... Jer 36:10   1587
When Michaiah the son of G .... Jer 36:11   1587
G the son of Shaphan, and Zedekiah ..... Jer 36:12   1587
G had made intercession to the .... Jer 36:25   1587
   2. Son of Hilkiah.
G the son of Hilkiah, (whom .... Jer 29:3   1587

GENDER
thy cattle g with a diverse kind .... Lev 19:19   7250
knowing that they do g strifes 2Ti 2:23   *1080*

GENDERED
frost of heaven, who hath g it .... Job 38:29   3205

GENDERETH
Their bull g, and faileth not..................... Job 21:10   5674
which g to bondage, which is Agar .... Gal 4:24   *1080*

GENEALOGIES
All these were reckoned by g in 1Chr 5:17   3187
in all by their g fourscore 1Chr 7:5   3187
were reckoned by their g twenty 1Chr 7:7   3187
So all Israel were reckoned by g............. 1Chr 9:1   3187
and of Iddo the seer concerning 2Chr 12:15   3187
reckoned by g among the Levites 2Chr 31:19   3187
give heed to fables and endless g 1Ti 1:4   *1076*
But avoid foolish questions, and g .... Titus 3:9   *1076*

GENEALOGY
their habitations, and their g 1Chr 4:33   3188
the g is not to be reckoned after 1Chr 5:1   3188
when the g of their generations 1Chr 5:7   3188
of them, after their g by their 1Chr 7:9   3188
the number throughout the g of 1Chr 7:40   3188
by their g in their villages 1Chr 9:22   3188
Beside their g of males, from 2Chr 31:16   3188
Both to the g of the priests by 2Chr 31:17   3188
to the g of all their little ones 2Chr 31:18   3188
those that were reckoned by g .... Ezr 2:62   3188
this is the g of them that went .... Ezr 8:1   3188
by g of the males an hundred .... Ezr 8:3   3188
that they might be reckoned by g.......... Neh 7:5   3188
I found a register of the g of .... Neh 7:5   3188
those that were reckoned by g .... Neh 7:64   3188

GENERAL
the g of the king's army was Joab 1Chr 27:34   8269
To the g assembly and church of .... Heb 12:23   *3831*

GENERALLY
Israel be g gathered unto thee 2Sa 17:11
There shall be lamentation g upon .... Jer 48:38   3605

GENERATION
righteous before me in this g .... Gen 7:1   1755
But in the fourth g they shall .... Gen 15:16   1755
Ephraim's children of the third g........... Gen 50:23
all his brethren, and all that g .... Ex 1:6   1755
with Amalek from g to g.......................... Ex 17:16   1755
fourth g of them that hate me .... Ex 20:5
unto the third and to the fourth g .... Ex 34:7   1755
unto the third and fourth g .... Num 14:18
forty years, until all the g .... Num 32:13   1755
of this evil g see that good land............. Deut 1:35   1755
until all the g of the men of war............ Deut 2:14   1755
fourth g of them that hate me, ... Deut 5:9
even to his tenth g shall he not .... Deut 23:2   1755
even to their tenth g shall they .... Deut 23:3   1755
of the LORD in their third g .... Deut 23:8   1755
So that the g to come of your .... Deut 29:22   1755
they are a perverse and crooked g .... Deut 32:5   1755
for they are a very froward g .... Deut 32:20   1755
also all that g were gathered .... Judg 2:10   1755
there arose another g after them........... Judg 2:10   1755
g shall sit on the throne of..................... 2Kin 10:30
of Israel unto the fourth g 2Kin 15:12   1755
and kept throughout every g .... Est 9:28   1755
them from this g for ever .... Ps 12:7   1755
God is in the g of the righteous .... Ps 14:5   1755
be accounted to the Lord for a g .... Ps 22:30   1755
This is the g of them that seek .... Ps 24:6   1755
ye may tell it to the g following .... Ps 48:13   1755
shall go to the g of his fathers............... Ps 49:19   1755
shewed thy strength unto this g .... Ps 71:18   1755
against the g of thy children .... Ps 73:15   1755
shewing to the g to come the .... Ps 78:4   1755
That the g to come might know .... Ps 78:6   1755
a stubborn and rebellious g.................... Ps 78:8   1755
a g that set not their heart..................... Ps 78:8   1755
long was I grieved with this g .... Ps 95:10   1755
be written for the g to come .... Ps 102:18   1755
in the g following let their name .... Ps 109:13   1755
the g of the upright shall be .... Ps 112:2   1755
One g shall praise thy works to .... Ps 145:4   1755
doth the crown endure to every g .... Prov 27:24   1755
There is a g that curseth their .... Prov 30:11   1755
There is a g that are pure in .... Prov 30:12   1755
There is a g, O how lofty are .... Prov 30:13   1755
There is a g, whose teeth are as .... Prov 30:14   1755
passeth away, and another g cometh ..... Eccl 1:4   1755
be dwelt in from g to g .... Is 13:20   1755
from g to g it shall lie............................. Is 34:10   1755
from g to g shall they .... Is 34:17   1755
my salvation from g to g......................... Is 51:8   1755
and who shall declare his g .... Is 53:8   1755

O g, see ye the word of the LORD	Jer 2:31	1755
and forsaken the g of his wrath	Jer 7:29	1755
be dwelt in from g to g	Jer 50:39	1755
thy throne from g to g	Lam 5:19	1755
dominion is from g to g	Dan 4:3	1859
kingdom is from g to g	Dan 4:34	1859
and their children another g	Joel 1:3	1755
and Jerusalem from g to g	Joel 3:20	1755
The book of the g of Jesus Christ	Mt 1:1	1078
O g of vipers, who hath warned	Mt 3:7	1081
whereunto shall I liken this g	Mt 11:16	1074
O g of vipers, how can ye, being	Mt 12:34	1081
adulterous g seeketh after a sign	Mt 12:39	1074
rise in judgment with this g	Mt 12:41	1074
up in the judgment with this g	Mt 12:42	1074
it be also unto this wicked g	Mt 12:45	1074
adulterous g seeketh after a sign	Mt 16:4	1074
said, O faithless and perverse g	Mt 17:17	1074
ye g of vipers, how can ye escape	Mt 23:33	1081
things shall come upon this g	Mt 23:36	1074
This g shall not pass, till all	Mt 24:34	1074
Why doth this g seek after a sign	Mk 8:12	1074
no sign be given unto this g	Mk 8:12	1074
in this adulterous and sinful g	Mk 8:38	1074
him, and saith, O faithless g	Mk 9:19	1074
that this g shall not pass, till	Mk 13:30	1074
fear him from g to g	Lk 1:50	1074
O g of vipers, who hath warned	Lk 3:7	1081
shall I liken the men of this g	Lk 7:31	1074
said, O faithless and perverse g	Lk 9:41	1074
began to say, This is an evil g	Lk 11:29	1074
also the Son of man be to this g	Lk 11:30	1074
judgment with the men of this g	Lk 11:31	1074
up in the judgment with this g	Lk 11:32	1074
world, may be required of this g	Lk 11:50	1074
It shall be required of this g	Lk 11:51	1074
g wiser than the children of	Lk 16:8	1074
things, and be rejected of this g	Lk 17:25	1074
This g shall not pass away, till	Lk 21:32	1074
yourselves from this untoward g	Acts 2:40	1074
and who shall declare his g	Acts 8:33	1074
his own g by the will of God	Acts 13:36	1074
I was grieved with that g	Heb 3:10	1074
But ye are a chosen g, a royal	1Pet 2:9	1085

GENERATIONS

These are the g of the heavens and	Gen 2:4	8435
This is the book of the g of Adam	Gen 5:1	8435
These are the g of Noah	Gen 6:9	8435
a just man and perfect in his g	Gen 6:9	8435
that is with you, for perpetual g	Gen 9:12	1755
Now these are the g of the sons	Gen 10:1	8435
the sons of Noah, after their g	Gen 10:32	8435
These are the g of Shem	Gen 11:10	8435
Now these are the g of Terah	Gen 11:27	8435
g for an everlasting covenant	Gen 17:7	1755
and thy seed after thee in their g	Gen 17:9	1755
you, every man child in your g	Gen 17:12	1755
Now these are the g of Ishmael	Gen 25:12	8435
their names, according to their g	Gen 25:13	8435
And these are the g of Isaac	Gen 25:19	8435
Now these are the g of Esau	Gen 36:1	8435
these are the g of Esau the	Gen 36:9	8435
These are the g of Jacob	Gen 37:2	8435
and this is my memorial unto all g	Ex 3:15	1755
sons of Levi according to their g	Ex 6:16	8435
of Levi according to their g	Ex 6:19	8435
to the LORD throughout your g	Ex 12:14	1755
your g by an ordinance for ever	Ex 12:17	1755
the children of Israel in their g	Ex 12:42	1755
omer of it to be kept for your g	Ex 16:32	1755
the LORD, to be kept for your g	Ex 16:33	1755
g on the behalf of the children	Ex 27:21	1755
g at the door of the tabernacle	Ex 29:42	1755
before the LORD throughout your g	Ex 30:8	1755
upon it throughout your g	Ex 30:10	1755
and to his seed throughout their g	Ex 30:21	1755
oil unto me throughout your g	Ex 30:31	1755
me and you throughout your g	Ex 31:13	1755
the sabbath throughout their g	Ex 31:16	1755
priesthood throughout their g	Ex 40:15	1755
g throughout all your dwellings	Lev 3:17	1755
be a statute for ever in your g	Lev 6:18	1755
for ever throughout your g	Lev 7:36	1755
for ever throughout your g	Lev 10:9	1755
ever unto them throughout their g	Lev 17:7	1755
in their g that hath any blemish	Lev 21:17	1755
be of all your seed among your g	Lev 22:3	1755
your g in all your dwellings	Lev 23:14	1755
your dwellings throughout your g	Lev 23:21	1755
your g in all your dwellings	Lev 23:31	1755

be a statute for ever in your g	Lev 23:41	1755
That your g may know that I made	Lev 23:43	1755
be a statute for ever in your g	Lev 24:3	1755
that bought it throughout his g	Lev 25:30	1755
Israel's eldest son, by their g	Num 1:20	8435
children of Simeon, by their g	Num 1:22	8435
the children of Gad, by their g	Num 1:24	8435
the children of Judah, by their g	Num 1:26	8435
children of Issachar, by their g	Num 1:28	8435
children of Zebulun, by their g	Num 1:30	8435
children of Ephraim, by their g	Num 1:32	8435
children of Manasseh, by their g	Num 1:34	8435
children of Benjamin, by their g	Num 1:36	8435
the children of Dan, by their g	Num 1:38	8435
the children of Asher, by their g	Num 1:40	8435
of Naphtali, throughout their g	Num 1:42	8435
These also are the g of Aaron	Num 3:1	8435
for ever throughout your g	Num 10:8	1755
whosoever be among you in your g	Num 15:14	1755
an ordinance for ever in your g	Num 15:15	1755
LORD an heave offering in your g	Num 15:21	1755
and henceforward among your g	Num 15:23	1755
their garments throughout their g	Num 15:38	1755
for ever throughout your g	Num 18:23	1755
your g in all your dwellings	Num 35:29	1755
his commandments to a thousand g	Deut 7:9	1755
old, consider the years of many g	Deut 32:7	1755
our g after us, that we might do	Josh 22:27	1755
to us or to our g in time to come	Josh 22:28	1755
Only that the g of the children	Judg 3:2	1755
Now these are the g of Pharez	Ruth 4:18	1755
These are their g	1Chr 1:29	8435
genealogy of their g was reckoned	1Chr 5:7	8435
valiant men of might in their g	1Chr 7:2	8435
And with them, by their g, after	1Chr 7:4	8435
after their genealogy by their g	1Chr 7:9	8435
heads of the fathers, by their g	1Chr 8:28	8435
brethren, according to their g	1Chr 9:9	8435
were chief throughout their g	1Chr 9:34	8435
he commanded to a thousand g	1Chr 16:15	1755
according to the g of his fathers	1Chr 26:31	8435
and his sons' sons, even four g	Job 42:16	1755
thoughts of his heart to all g	Ps 33:11	1755
name to be remembered in all g	Ps 45:17	1755
and their dwelling places to all g	Ps 49:11	1755
and his years as many g	Ps 61:6	1755
and moon endure, throughout all g	Ps 72:5	1755
shew forth thy praise to all g	Ps 79:13	1755
draw out thine anger to all g	Ps 85:5	1755
known thy faithfulness to all g	Ps 89:1	1755
and build up thy throne to all g	Ps 89:4	1755
been our dwelling place in all g	Ps 90:1	1755
and his truth endureth to all g	Ps 100:5	1755
and thy remembrance unto all g	Ps 102:12	1755
thy years are throughout all g	Ps 102:24	1755
he commanded to a thousand g	Ps 105:8	1755
unto all g for evermore	Ps 106:31	1755
Thy faithfulness is unto all g	Ps 119:90	1755
O LORD, throughout all g	Ps 135:13	1755
endureth throughout all g	Ps 145:13	1755
even thy God, O Zion, unto all g	Ps 146:10	1755
calling the g from the beginning	Is 41:4	1755
the ancient days, in the g of old	Is 51:9	1755
up the foundations of many g	Is 58:12	1755
excellency, a joy of many g	Is 60:15	1755
cities, the desolations of many g	Is 61:4	1755
it, even to the years of many g	Joel 2:2	1755
So all the g from Abraham to	Mt 1:17	1074
Abraham to David are fourteen g	Mt 1:17	1074
away into Babylon are fourteen g	Mt 1:17	1074
unto Christ are fourteen g	Mt 1:17	1074
from henceforth all g shall call	Lk 1:48	1074
hath been hid from ages and from g	Col 1:26	1074

GENNESARET (ghen-nes'-a-ret) See CHINNERETH. Same as Galilee.

they came into the land of G	Mt 14:34	1082
they came into the land of G	Mk 6:53	1082
of God, he stood by the lake of G	Lk 5:1	1082

GENTILE (jen'-tile) See GENTILES. A non-Jew.

the Jew first, and also of the G	Rom 2:9	1672
the Jew first, and also to the G	Rom 2:10	1672

GENTILES

of the G divided in their lands	Gen 10:5	1471
which dwelt in Harosheth of the G	Judg 4:2	1471
from Harosheth of the G unto the	Judg 4:13	1471
the host, unto Harosheth of the G	Judg 4:16	1471
to it shall the G seek	Is 11:10	1471
bring forth judgment to the G	Is 42:1	1471
the people, for a light of the G	Is 42:6	1471

G

give thee for a light to the *G*	Is 49:6	1471
I will lift up mine hand to the *G*	Is 49:22	1471
and thy seed shall inherit the *G*	Is 54:3	1471
the *G* shall come to thy light, and	Is 60:3	1471
the forces of the *G* shall come	Is 60:5	1471
unto thee the forces of the *G*	Is 60:11	1471
shalt also suck the milk of the *G*	Is 60:16	1471
ye shall eat the riches of the *G*	Is 61:6	1471
seed shall be known among the *G*	Is 61:9	1471
the *G* shall see thy righteousness	Is 62:2	1471
the glory of the *G* like a flowing	Is 66:12	1471
declare my glory among the *G*	Is 66:19	1471
destroyer of the *G* is on his way	Jer 4:7	1471
of the *G* that can cause rain	Jer 14:22	1471
the *G* shall come unto thee from	Jer 16:19	1471
the prophet against the *G*	Jer 46:1	1471
and her princes are among the *G*	Lam 2:9	1471
their defiled bread among the *G*	Eze 4:13	1471
the *G* as a vessel wherein is no	Hos 8:8	1471
Proclaim ye this among the *G*	Joel 3:9	1471
of Jacob shall be among the *G* in	Mic 5:8	1471
to cast out the horns of the *G*	Zec 1:21	1471
name shall be great among the *G*	Mal 1:11	1471
beyond Jordan, Galilee of the *G*	Mt 4:15	1484
all these things do the *G* seek	Mt 6:32	1484
Go not into the way of the *G*	Mt 10:5	1484
a testimony against them and the *G*	Mt 10:18	1484
he shall shew judgment to the *G*	Mt 12:18	1484
And in his name shall the *G* trust	Mt 12:21	1484
deliver him to the *G* to mock	Mt 20:19	1484
the *G* exercise dominion over them	Mt 20:25	1484
and shall deliver him to the *G*	Mk 10:33	1484
the *G* exercise lordship over them	Mk 10:42	1484
A light to lighten the *G*, and the	Lk 2:32	1484
he shall be delivered unto the *G*	Lk 18:32	1484
shall be trodden down of the *G*	Lk 21:24	1484
the times of the *G* be fulfilled	Lk 21:24	1484
The kings of the *G* exercise	Lk 22:25	1484
go unto the dispersed among the *G*	Jn 7:35	1672
the *G*, and teach the *G*	Jn 7:35	1672
and Pontius Pilate, with the *G*	Acts 4:27	1484
into the possession of the *G*	Acts 7:45	1484
me, to bear my name before the *G*	Acts 9:15	1484
because that on the *G* also was	Acts 10:45	1484
G had also received the word of	Acts 11:1	1484
Then hath God also to the *G*	Acts 11:18	1484
the *G* besought that these words	Acts 13:42	1484
life, lo, we turn to the *G*	Acts 13:46	1484
set thee to be a light of the *G*	Acts 13:47	1484
when the *G* heard this, they were	Acts 13:48	1484
unbelieving Jews stirred up the *G*	Acts 14:2	1484
was an assault made both of the *G*	Acts 14:5	1484
the door of faith unto the *G*	Acts 14:27	1484
declaring the conversion of the *G*	Acts 15:3	1484
that the *G* by my mouth should	Acts 15:7	1484
had wrought among the *G* by them	Acts 15:12	1484
God at the first did visit the *G*	Acts 15:14	1484
seek after the Lord, and all the *G*	Acts 15:17	1484
among the *G* are turned to God	Acts 15:19	1484
which are of the *G* in Antioch	Acts 15:23	1484
henceforth I will go unto the *G*	Acts 18:6	1484
him into the hands of the *G*	Acts 21:11	1484
among the *G* by his ministry	Acts 21:19	1484
are among the *G* to forsake Moses	Acts 21:21	1484
As touching the *G* which believe	Acts 21:25	1484
send thee far hence unto the *G*	Acts 22:21	1484
from the people, and from the *G*	Acts 26:17	1484
of Judaea, and then to the *G*	Acts 26:20	1484
unto the people, and to the *G*	Acts 28:28	1484
of God is sent unto the *G*	Acts 28:28	1484
you also, even as among other *G*	Rom 1:13	1484
For when the *G*, which have not	Rom 2:14	1484
among the *G* through you, as it is	Rom 2:24	1484
have before proved both Jews and *G*	Rom 3:9	1672
is he not also of the *G*	Rom 3:29	1484
Yes, of the *G* also	Rom 3:29	1484
the Jews only, but also of the *G*	Rom 9:24	1484
That the *G*, which followed not	Rom 9:30	1484
fall salvation is come unto the *G*	Rom 11:11	1484
of them the riches of the *G*	Rom 11:12	1484
For I speak to you *G*, inasmuch as	Rom 11:13	1484
as I am the apostle of the *G*	Rom 11:13	1484
the fulness of the *G* be come in	Rom 11:25	1484
that the *G* might glorify God for	Rom 15:9	1484
will confess to thee among the *G*	Rom 15:9	1484
And again he saith, Rejoice, ye *G*	Rom 15:10	1484
again, Praise the Lord, all ye *G*	Rom 15:11	1484
shall rise to reign over the *G*	Rom 15:12	1484
in him shall the *G* trust	Rom 15:12	1484
minister of Jesus Christ to the *G*	Rom 15:16	1484
up of the *G* might be acceptable	Rom 15:16	1484

by me, to make the *G* obedient	Rom 15:18	1484
For if the *G* have been made	Rom 15:27	1484
also all the churches of the *G*	Rom 16:4	1484
not so much as named among the *G*	1Cor 5:1	1484
the things which the *G* sacrifice	1Cor 10:20	1484
neither to the Jews, nor to the *G*	1Cor 10:32	1672
Ye know that ye were *G*, carried	1Cor 12:2	1484
one body, whether we be Jews or *G*	1Cor 12:13	1672
gospel which I preach among the *G*	Gal 2:2	1484
was mighty in me toward the *G*	Gal 2:8	1484
from James, he did eat with the *G*	Gal 2:12	1484
Jew, livest after the manner of *G*	Gal 2:14	1483
thou the *G* to live as do the Jews	Gal 2:14	1484
nature, and not sinners of the *G*	Gal 2:15	1484
on the *G* through Jesus Christ	Gal 3:14	1484
being in time past *G* in the flesh	Eph 2:11	1484
of Jesus Christ for you *G*	Eph 3:1	1484
That the *G* should be fellowheirs,	Eph 3:6	1484
the *G* the unsearchable riches of	Eph 3:8	1484
walk not as other *G* walk, in the	Eph 4:17	1484
glory of this mystery among the *G*	Col 1:27	1484
to the *G* that they might be saved	1Th 2:16	1484
even as the *G* which know not God	1Th 4:5	1484
a teacher of the *G* in faith	1Ti 2:7	1484
of angels, preached unto the *G*	1Ti 3:16	1484
an apostle, and a teacher of the *G*	2Ti 1:11	1484
and that all the *G* might hear	2Ti 4:17	1484
conversation honest among the *G*	1Pet 2:12	1484
to have wrought the will of the *G*	1Pet 4:3	1484
forth, taking nothing of the *G*	3Jn 7	1484
for it is given unto the *G*	Rev 11:2	1484

GENTLE

But we were *g* among you, even as	1Th 2:7	2261
but be *g* unto all men, apt to	2Ti 2:24	2261
no man, to be no brawlers, but *g*	Titus 3:2	1933
is first pure, then peaceable, *g*	Jas 3:17	1933
not only to the good and *g*	1Pet 2:18	1933

GENTLENESS

and thy *g* hath made me great	2Sa 22:36	6031
up, and thy *g* hath made me great	Ps 18:35	6038
g of Christ, who in presence am	2Cor 10:1	1932
joy, peace, longsuffering, *g*	Gal 5:22	5544

GENTLY

Deal *g* for my sake with the young	2Sa 18:5	3814
shall *g* lead those that are with	Is 40:11	

GENUBATH (ghen'-u-bath) Son of Hadad.

of Tahpenes bare him *G* his son	1Kin 11:20	1592
G was in Pharaoh's household	1Kin 11:20	1592

GERA (ghe'-rah) A son of Bela.

Belah, and Becher, and Ashbel, *G*	Gen 46:21	1617
up a deliverer, Ehud the son of *G*	Judg 3:15	1617
name was Shimei, the son of *G*	2Sa 16:5	1617
And Shimei the son of *G*, a	2Sa 19:16	1617
Shimei the son of *G* fell down	2Sa 19:18	1617
with thee Shimei the son of *G*	1Kin 2:8	1617
sons of Bela were, Addar, and *G*	1Chr 8:3	1617
And *G*, and Shephuphan, and Huram	1Chr 8:5	1617
And Naaman, and Ahiah, and *G*	1Chr 8:7	1617

GERAHS

(a shekel is twenty *g*	Ex 30:13	1626
twenty *g* shall be the shekel	Lev 27:25	1626
(the shekel is twenty *g*	Num 3:47	1626
the sanctuary, which is twenty *g*	Num 18:16	1626
And the shekel shall be twenty *g*	Eze 45:12	1626

GERAR (ghe'-rar) A city in Gaza.

from Sidon, as thou comest to *G*	Gen 10:19	1642
Kadesh and Shur, and sojourned in *G*	Gen 20:1	1642
and Abimelech king of *G* sent	Gen 20:2	1642
king of the Philistines unto *G*	Gen 26:1	1642
And Isaac dwelt in *G*	Gen 26:6	1642
his tent in the valley of *G*	Gen 26:17	1642
the herdmen of *G* did strive with	Gen 26:20	1642
Then Abimelech went to him from *G*	Gen 26:26	1642
were with him pursued them unto *G*	2Chr 14:13	1642
all the cities round about *G*	2Chr 14:14	1642

GERGESENES (ghur'-ghes-enes') Inhabitants of an area near Sea of Galilee.

side into the country of the *G*	Mt 8:28	1086

GERIZIM (gher'-iz-im) A mountain in central Palestine.

put the blessing upon mount *G*	Deut 11:29	1630
upon mount *G* to bless the people	Deut 27:12	1630
half of them over against mount *G*	Josh 8:33	1630
and stood in the top of mount *G*	Judg 9:7	1630

GERSHOM (ghur'-shom) See GERSHON.

1. Firstborn son of Moses.

a son, and he called his name G	Ex 2:22	1648
which the name of the one was G	Ex 18:3	1648
The sons of Moses were, G	1Chr 23:15	1648
Of the sons of G, Shebuel was the	1Chr 23:16	1648
And Shebuel the son of G, the son	1Chr 26:24	1648

2. A son of Levi.

G, Kohath, and Merari	1Chr 6:16	1648
be the names of the sons of G	1Chr 6:17	1648
Of G	1Chr 6:20	1648
The son of Jahath, the son of G	1Chr 6:43	1648
to the sons of G throughout their	1Chr 6:62	1648
Unto the sons of G were given out	1Chr 6:71	1648
Of the sons of G	1Chr 15:7	1648

3. A descendant of Phinehas.

of the sons of Phinehas; G	Ezr 8:2	1648

4. Father of Jonathan.

and Jonathan, the son of G	Judg 18:30	1648

GERSHON (ghur'-shon) See GERSHOM, GERSHONITE. A form of Gershom 2.

G, and Kohath, and Merari	Gen 46:11	1647
G, and Kohath, and Merari	Ex 6:16	1647
The sons of G	Ex 6:17	1647
G, and Kohath, and Merari	Num 3:17	1647
the sons of G by their families	Num 3:18	1647
Of G was the family of the	Num 3:21	1647
of G in the tabernacle of the	Num 3:25	1647
also the sum of the sons of G	Num 4:22	1647
of G in the tabernacle of the	Num 4:28	1647
were numbered of the sons of G	Num 4:38	1647
of the families of the sons of G	Num 4:41	1647
oxen he gave unto the sons of G	Num 7:7	1647
and the sons of G and the sons of	Num 10:17	1647
of G, the family of the	Num 26:57	1647
the children of G had by lot out	Josh 21:6	1647
And unto the children of G	Josh 21:27	1647
G, Kohath, and Merari	1Chr 6:1	1647
among the sons of Levi, namely, G	1Chr 23:6	1647

GERSHONITE (ghur'-shon-ites) See GERSHONITES. Descendant of Gershom 2.

the sons of the G Laadan, chief	1Chr 26:21	1649
fathers, even of Laadan the G	1Chr 26:21	1649
LORD, by the hand of Jehiel the G	1Chr 29:8	1649

GERSHONITES (ghur'-shon-ites)

these are the families of the G	Num 3:21	1649
The families of the G shall pitch	Num 3:23	1649
G shall be Eliasaph the son of	Num 3:24	1649
service of the families of the G	Num 4:24	1649
the service of the sons of the G	Num 4:27	1649
of Gershon, the family of the G	Num 26:57	1649
All the cities of the G according	Josh 21:33	1649
Of the G were, Laadan, and Shimei	1Chr 23:7	1649
and of the G	2Chr 29:12	1649

GERUTH See CHIMHAM.

GERUTH KIMHAM See CHIMHAM.

GESHAM (ghe'-sham) A son of Jahdai.

Regem, and Jotham, and G, and Pelet, ..	1Chr 2:47	1529

GESHAN See GESHAM.

GESHEM (ghe'-shem) See GASHMU. An opponent of Nehemiah.

G the Arabian, heard it, they	Neh 2:19	1654
G the Arabian, and the rest of our	Neh 6:1	1654
G sent unto me, saying, Come, let	Neh 6:2	1654

GESHUR (ghe'-shur) See GESHURITES. A kingdom in Bashan.

the daughter of Talmai king of G	2Sa 3:3	1650
the son of Ammihud, king of G	2Sa 13:37	1650
So Absalom fled, and went to G	2Sa 13:38	1650
So Joab arose and went to G	2Sa 14:23	1650
say, Wherefore am I come from G	2Sa 14:32	1650
a vow while I abode at G in Syria	2Sa 15:8	1650
And he took G, and Aram, with the	1Chr 2:23	1650
the daughter of Talmai king of G	1Chr 3:2	1650

GESHURI (ghesh'-u-ri) See GESHURITES.

1. Inhabitants of Geshur.

of Argob unto the coasts of G	Deut 3:14	1651

2. A people dwelling between Arabia and Philistia.

of the Philistines, and all G	Josh 13:2	1651

GESHURITES (gesh'-u-rites)

1. Inhabitants of Geshur.

Bashan, unto the border of the G	Josh 12:5	1651
And Gilead, and the border of the G	Josh 13:11	1651
of Israel expelled not the G	Josh 13:13	1651
but the G and the Maachathites	Josh 13:13	1651

2. Same as Geshuri 2.

his men went up, and invaded the G	1Sa 27:8	1651

GET

G thee out of thy country, and	Gen 12:1	3212
said, Up, g you out of this place	Gen 19:14	3318
g thee into the land of Moriah	Gen 22:2	3212
g thee out from this land, and	Gen 31:13	3318
saying, G me this damsel to wife	Gen 34:4	3947
g you possessions therein	Gen 34:10	
g you down thither, and buy for us	Gen 42:2	3381
g you up in peace unto your	Gen 44:17	5927
g you unto the land of Canaan	Gen 45:17	935
so g them up out of the land	Ex 1:10	5927
g you unto your burdens	Ex 5:4	3212
g you straw where ye can find it	Ex 5:11	3947
G thee unto Pharaoh in the	Ex 7:15	3212
G thee from me, take heed to	Ex 10:28	3212
G thee out, and all the people	Ex 11:8	3318
I will g me honour upon Pharaoh,	Ex 14:17	3513
g thee down, and thou shalt come	Ex 19:24	3381
said unto Moses, Go, g thee down	Ex 32:7	3381
he be poor, and cannot g so much	Lev 14:21	5381
pigeons, such as he is able to g	Lev 14:22	5381
young pigeons, such as he can g	Lev 14:30	5381
Even such as he is able to g	Lev 14:31	5381
whose hand is not able to g that	Lev 14:32	5381
beside that that his hand shall g	Num 6:21	5381
G you up this way southward, and	Num 13:17	5927
g you into the wilderness by the	Num 14:25	5265
saying, G you up from about the	Num 16:24	5927
G you up from among this	Num 16:45	7426
of Balak, G you into your land	Num 22:13	3212
thee, I will g me back again	Num 22:34	
G thee up into this mount Abarim,	Num 27:12	5927
g you over the brook Zered	Deut 2:13	5674
G thee up into the top of Pisgah,	Deut 3:27	5927
G you into your tents again	Deut 5:30	7725
giveth thee power to g wealth	Deut 8:18	6213
g thee down quickly from hence	Deut 9:12	3381
g thee up into the place which	Deut 17:8	5927
shall g up above thee very high	Deut 28:43	5927
G thee up into this mountain	Deut 32:49	5927
G you to the mountain, lest the	Josh 2:16	3212
LORD said unto Joshua, G thee up	Josh 7:10	6965
then g thee up to the wood	Josh 17:15	5927
g you unto your tents, and unto	Josh 22:4	3212
g thee down unto the host	Judg 7:9	3381
now therefore g her for me to	Judg 14:2	3947
unto his father, G her for me	Judg 14:3	3947
to morrow g you early on your way	Judg 19:9	
thee, and g thee down to the floor	Ruth 3:3	3381
Now therefore g you up	1Sa 9:13	5927
g you down from among the	1Sa 15:6	3381
in thine eyes, let me g away	1Sa 20:29	4422
g thee into the land of Judah	1Sa 22:5	935
David made haste to g away for	1Sa 23:26	3212
G you up to Carmel, and go to	1Sa 25:5	5927
lest he g him fenced cities, and	2Sa 20:6	4672
that my lord the king may g heat	1Kin 1:2	
g thee in unto king David, and say	1Kin 1:13	
G thee to Anathoth, unto thine	1Kin 2:26	3212
speed to g him up to his chariot	1Kin 12:18	5927
and g thee to Shiloh	1Kin 14:2	1980
g thee to thine own house	1Kin 14:12	3212
G thee hence, and turn thee	1Kin 17:3	3212
g thee to Zarephath, which	1Kin 17:9	3212
Ahab, G thee up, eat and drink	1Kin 18:41	5927
g thee down, that the rain stop	1Kin 18:44	3381
g thee to the prophets of thy	2Kin 3:13	3212
them alive, and g into the city	2Kin 7:12	935
speed to g him up to his chariot	2Chr 10:18	5927
So didst thou g thee a name	Neh 9:10	6213
thy precepts I g understanding	Ps 119:104	
G wisdom, g understanding	Prov 4:5	7069
therefore g wisdom	Prov 4:7	7069
all thy getting g understanding	Prov 4:7	7069
A wound and dishonour shall he g	Prov 6:33	4672
is it to g wisdom than gold	Prov 16:16	7069
to g understanding rather to be	Prov 16:16	7069
in the hand of a fool to g wisdom	Prov 17:16	7069
ways, and g a snare to thy soul	Prov 22:25	3947
A time to g, and a time to lose	Eccl 3:6	1245
I will g me to the mountain of	Song 4:6	3212
Let us g up early to the	Song 7:12	
g thee unto this treasurer, even	Is 22:15	935
G you out of the way, turn aside	Is 30:11	
shalt say unto it, G thee hence	Is 30:22	3318
g thee up into the high mountain	Is 40:9	5927
g thee into darkness, O daughter	Is 47:5	935

I will *g* me unto the great men,	Jer 5:5	3212
g thee a linen girdle, and put it	Jer 13:1	7069
g a potter's earthen bottle, and	Jer 19:1	7069
g up, ye horsemen, and stand forth	Jer 46:4	5927
Moab, that it may flee and *g* away	Jer 48:9	3318
g you far off, dwell deep, O ye	Jer 49:30	5110
g you up unto the wealthy nation,	Jer 49:31	5927
me about, that I cannot *g* out	Lam 3:7	3318
g thee unto the house of Israel,	Eze 3:4	935
g thee to them of the captivity,	Eze 3:11	935
said, *G* you far from the LORD	Eze 11:15	
souls, to *g* dishonest gain	Eze 22:27	1214
let the beasts *g* away from under	Dan 4:14	5111
come, *g* you down	Joel 3:13	3381
I will *g* them praise and fame in	Zeph 3:19	776
G you hence, walk to and fro	Zec 6:7	3212
unto him, *G* thee hence, Satan	Mt 4:10	5217
his disciples to *g* into a ship	Mt 14:22	1684
Peter, *G* thee behind me, Satan	Mt 16:23	5217
his disciples to *g* into the ship	Mk 6:45	1684
saying, *G* thee behind me, Satan	Mk 8:33	5217
unto him, *G* thee behind me, Satan	Lk 4:8	5217
about, and lodge, and *g* victuals	Lk 9:12	2147
G thee out, and depart hence	Lk 13:31	1831
G thee out of thy country, and	Acts 7:3	1831
g thee down, and go with them,	Acts 10:20	2597
g thee quickly out of Jerusalem	Acts 22:18	1831
first into the sea, and *g* to land	Acts 27:43	1826
Lest Satan should *g* an advantage	2Cor 2:11	4122
a year, and buy and sell, and *g* gain	Jas 4:13	

GETHER (ghe'-ther) A son of Aram.

Uz, and Hul, and *G*, and Mash	Gen 10:23	1666
Aram, and Uz, and Hul, and *G*	1Chr 1:17	1666

GETHSEMANE (gheth-sem'-a-ne) A garden near Jerusalem.

with them unto a place called *G*	Mt 26:36	1068
came to a place which was named *G*	Mk 14:32	1068

GETTETH

Whosoever *g* up to the gutter, and	2Sa 5:8	5060
the man that *g* understanding	Prov 3:13	6329
a scorner *g* to himself shame	Prov 9:7	3947
a wicked man *g* himself a blot	Prov 9:7	
heareth reproof *g* understanding	Prov 15:32	7069
heart of the prudent *g* knowledge	Prov 18:15	7069
He that *g* wisdom loveth his own	Prov 19:8	7069
so he that *g* riches, and not by	Jer 17:11	6213
he that *g* up out of the pit shall	Jer 48:44	5927

GETTING

had gotten, the cattle of his *g*	Gen 31:18	7075
with all thy *g* get understanding	Prov 4:7	7069
The *g* of treasures by a lying	Prov 21:6	6467

GEUEL (ghe-u'-el) A son of Machri.

tribe of Gad, *G* the son of Machi	Num 13:15	1345

GEZER (ghe'-zur) See GAZER, GEZRITES. A Canaanite
city.

Then Horam king of *G* came up to	Josh 10:33	1507
the king of *G*, one	Josh 12:12	1507
of Beth-horon the nether, and to *G*	Josh 16:3	1507
the Canaanites that dwelt in *G*	Josh 16:10	1507
and *G* with her suburbs,	Josh 21:21	1507
the Canaanites that dwelt in *G*	Judg 1:29	1507
Canaanites dwelt in *G* among them	Judg 1:29	1507
and Hazor, and Megiddo, and *G*	1Kin 9:15	1507
of Egypt had gone up, and taken *G*	1Kin 9:16	1507
And Solomon built *G*, and Beth-horon	1Kin 9:17	1507
they gave also *G* with her suburbs	1Chr 6:67	1507
Naaran, and westward *G*	1Chr 7:28	1507
war at *G* with the Philistines	1Chr 20:4	1507

GEZRITES (ghez'-rites) Inhabitants of Gezer.

invaded the Geshurites, and the *G*	1Sa 27:8	1511

GHOST

Then Abraham gave up the *g*	Gen 25:8	1478
and he gave up the *g* and died	Gen 25:17	1478
And Isaac gave up the *g*, and died,	Gen 35:29	1478
into the bed, and yielded up the *g*	Gen 49:33	1478
why did I not give up the *g* when	Job 3:11	1478
Oh that I had given up the *g*	Job 10:18	1478
be as the giving up of the *g*	Job 11:20	5315
my tongue, I shall give up the *g*	Job 13:19	1478
yea, man giveth up the *g*, and	Job 14:10	1478
she hath given up the *g*	Jer 15:9	5315
elders gave up the *g* in the city	Lam 1:19	1478
found with child of the Holy *G*	Mt 1:18	4151
conceived in her is of the Holy *G*	Mt 1:20	4151
shall baptize you with the Holy *G*	Mt 3:11	4151
G shall not be forgiven unto men	Mt 12:31	4151
speaketh against the Holy *G*	Mt 12:32	4151

a loud voice, yielded up the *g*	Mt 27:50	4151
and of the Son, and of the Holy *G*	Mt 28:19	4151
shall baptize you with the Holy *G*	Mk 1:8	4151
the Holy *G* hath never forgiveness	Mk 3:29	4151
David himself said by the Holy *G*	Mk 12:36	4151
not ye that speak, but the Holy *G*	Mk 13:11	4151
a loud voice, and gave up the *g*	Mk 15:37	1606
he so cried out, and gave up the *g*	Mk 15:39	1606
shall be filled with the Holy *G*	Lk 1:15	4151
The Holy *G* shall come upon thee,	Lk 1:35	4151
was filled with the Holy *G*	Lk 1:41	4151
was filled with the Holy *G*	Lk 1:67	4151
and the Holy *G* was upon him	Lk 2:25	4151
revealed unto him by the Holy *G*	Lk 2:26	4151
shall baptize you with the Holy *G*	Lk 3:16	4151
the Holy *G* descended in a bodily	Lk 3:22	4151
the Holy *G* returned from Jordan	Lk 4:1	4151
Holy *G* it shall not be forgiven	Lk 12:10	4151
For the Holy *G* shall teach you in	Lk 12:12	4151
said thus, he gave up the *g*	Lk 23:46	1606
which baptizeth with the Holy *G*	Jn 1:33	4151
for the Holy *G* was not yet given	Jn 7:39	4151
Comforter, which is the Holy *G*	Jn 14:26	4151
bowed his head, and gave up the *g*	Jn 19:30	4151
unto them, Receive ye the Holy *G*	Jn 20:22	4151
after that he through the Holy *G*	Acts 1:2	4151
the Holy *G* not many days hence	Acts 1:5	4151
that the Holy *G* is come upon you	Acts 1:8	4151
which the Holy *G* by the mouth of	Acts 1:16	4151
were all filled with the Holy *G*	Acts 2:4	4151
Father the promise of the Holy *G*	Acts 2:33	4151
receive the gift of the Holy *G*	Acts 2:38	4151
Peter, filled with the Holy *G*	Acts 4:8	4151
were all filled with the Holy *G*	Acts 4:31	4151
thine heart to lie to the Holy *G*	Acts 5:3	4151
words fell down, and gave up the *g*	Acts 5:5	1634
at his feet, and yielded up the *g*	Acts 5:10	1634
and so is also the Holy *G*, whom	Acts 5:32	4151
honest report, full of the Holy *G*	Acts 6:3	4151
full of faith and of the Holy *G*	Acts 6:5	4151
ye do always resist the Holy *G*	Acts 7:51	4151
But he, being full of the Holy *G*	Acts 7:55	4151
they might receive the Holy *G*	Acts 8:15	4151
them, and they received the Holy *G*	Acts 8:17	4151
hands the Holy *G* was given	Acts 8:18	4151
hands, he may receive the Holy *G*	Acts 8:19	4151
and be filled with the Holy *G*	Acts 9:17	4151
and in the comfort of the Holy *G*	Acts 9:31	4151
Jesus of Nazareth with the Holy *G*	Acts 10:38	4151
the Holy *G* fell on all them which	Acts 10:44	4151
poured out the gift of the Holy *G*	Acts 10:45	4151
received the Holy *G* as well as we	Acts 10:47	4151
the Holy *G* fell on them, as on us	Acts 11:15	4151
shall be baptized with the Holy *G*	Acts 11:16	4151
a good man, and full of the Holy *G*	Acts 11:24	4151
eaten of worms, and gave up the *g*	Acts 12:23	1634
Lord, and fasted, the Holy *G* said	Acts 13:2	4151
being sent forth by the Holy *G*	Acts 13:4	4151
Paul,) filled with the Holy *G*	Acts 13:9	4151
with joy, and with the Holy *G*	Acts 13:52	4151
witness, giving them the Holy *G*	Acts 15:8	4151
For it seemed good to the Holy *G*	Acts 15:28	4151
Holy *G* to preach the word in Asia	Acts 16:6	4151
the Holy *G* since ye believed	Acts 19:2	4151
heard whether there be any Holy *G*	Acts 19:2	4151
them, the Holy *G* came on them	Acts 19:6	4151
Save that the Holy *G* witnesseth	Acts 20:23	4151
Holy *G* hath made you overseers	Acts 20:28	4151
and said, Thus saith the Holy *G*	Acts 21:11	4151
Well spake the Holy *G* by Esaias	Acts 28:25	4151
the Holy *G* which is given unto us	Rom 5:5	4151
bearing me witness in the Holy *G*	Rom 9:1	4151
and peace, and joy in the Holy *G*	Rom 14:17	4151
through the power of the Holy *G*	Rom 15:13	4151
being sanctified by the Holy *G*	Rom 15:16	4151
but which the Holy *G* teacheth	1Cor 2:13	4151
of the Holy *G* which is in you	1Cor 6:19	4151
is the Lord, but by the Holy *G*	1Cor 12:3	4151
by kindness, by the Holy *G*	2Cor 6:6	4151
and the communion of the Holy *G*	2Cor 13:14	4151
also in power, and in the Holy *G*	1Th 1:5	4151
with joy of the Holy *G*	1Th 1:6	4151
the Holy *G* which dwelleth in us	2Ti 1:14	4151
and renewing of the Holy *G*	Titus 3:5	4151
miracles, and gifts of the Holy *G*	Heb 2:4	4151
Wherefore (as the Holy *G* saith	Heb 3:7	4151
were made partakers of the Holy *G*	Heb 6:4	4151
The Holy *G* this signifying, that	Heb 9:8	4151
Whereof the Holy *G* also is a	Heb 10:15	4151
the Holy *G* sent down from heaven	1Pet 1:12	4151
as they were moved by the Holy *G*	2Pet 1:21	4151

Father, the Word, and the Holy G............1Jn 5:7   4151
holy faith, praying in the Holy G............Jude 20   4151

GIAH (gi'-ah) *A place near the wilderness of Gibeon.*
that lieth before G by the way of 2Sa 2:24   1520

GIANT
which was of the sons of the g............2Sa 21:16   7497
which was of the sons of the g............2Sa 21:18   7497
and he also was born to the g............2Sa 21:20   7497
four were born to the g in Gath............2Sa 21:22   7497
that was of the children of the g............1Chr 20:4   7497
and he also was the son of the g............1Chr 20:6   7497
were born unto the g in Gath............1Chr 20:8   7497
he runneth upon me like a g............Job 16:14   1368

GIANTS
There were g in the earth in............Gen 6:4   5303
And there we saw the g............Num 13:33   5303
sons of Anak, which come of the g............Num 13:33   1368
Which also were accounted g............Deut 2:11   7497
also was accounted a land of g............Deut 2:20   7497
g dwelt therein in old time............Deut 2:20   7497
remained of the remnant of g............Deut 3:11   7497
which was called the land of g............Deut 3:13   7497
which was of the remnant of the g............Josh 12:4   7497
remained of the remnant of the g............Josh 13:12   7497
of the valley of the g northward............Josh 15:8   7497
of the Perizzites and of the g............Josh 17:15   7497
the valley of the g on the north............Josh 18:16   7497

GIBALITES See GIBLITES.

GIBBAR (gib'-bar) See GIBEON. *A family of exiles.*
The children of G, ninety and five............Ezr 2:20   1402

GIBBETHON (gib'-be-thon) *A town in Dan.*
And Eltekeh, and G, and Baalath,............Josh 19:44   1405
her suburbs, G with her suburbs,............Josh 21:23   1405
and Baasha smote him at G, which............1Kin 15:27   1405
and all Israel laid siege to G............1Kin 15:27   1405
people were encamped against G............1Kin 16:15   1405
And Omri went up from G, and all............1Kin 16:17   1405

GIBEA (gib'-e-ah) See GIBEAH. *Son of Sheva.*
of Machbenah, and the father of G............1Chr 2:49   1388

GIBEAH (gib'-e-ah) *A city in Judah.*
Cain, G, and Timnah............Josh 15:57   1390
we will pass over to G............Judg 19:12   1390
places to lodge all night, in G............Judg 19:13   1390
upon them when they were by G............Judg 19:14   1390
to go in and to lodge in G............Judg 19:15   1390
and he sojourned in G............Judg 19:16   1390
I came into G that belongeth to............Judg 20:4   1390
the men of G rose against me, and............Judg 20:5   1390
the thing which we will do to G............Judg 20:9   1390
when they come to G of Benjamin............Judg 20:10   1390
of Belial, which are in G............Judg 20:13   1390
together out of the cities unto G............Judg 20:14   1390
beside the inhabitants of G............Judg 20:15   1390
morning, and encamped against G............Judg 20:19   1390
array to fight against them at G............Judg 20:20   1390
of Benjamin came forth out of G............Judg 20:21   1390
them out of G the second day............Judg 20:25   1390
set liers in wait round about G............Judg 20:29   1390
put themselves in array against G............Judg 20:30   1390
and the other to G in the field............Judg 20:31   1390
even out of the meadows of G............Judg 20:33   1390
there came against G ten thousand............Judg 20:34   1390
wait which they had set beside G............Judg 20:36   1390
in wait hasted, and rushed upon G............Judg 20:37   1390
against G toward the sunrising............Judg 20:43   1390
And Saul also went home to G............1Sa 10:26   1390
came the messengers to G of Saul............1Sa 11:4   1390
with Jonathan in G of Benjamin............1Sa 13:2   1390
up from Gilgal unto G of Benjamin............1Sa 13:15   1390
with them, abode in G of Benjamin............1Sa 13:16   1390
in the uttermost part of G under............1Sa 14:2   1390
other southward over against G............1Sa 14:5   1390
of Saul in G of Benjamin looked............1Sa 14:16   1390
went up to his house to G of Saul............1Sa 15:34   1390
(now Saul abode in G under a tree............1Sa 22:6   1390
came up the Ziphites to Saul to G............1Sa 23:19   1390
the Ziphites come unto Saul to G............1Sa 26:1   1390
house of Abinadab that was in G............2Sa 6:3   1390
house of Abinadab which was at G............2Sa 6:4   1390
up unto the LORD in G of Saul............2Sa 21:6   1390
of G of the children of Benjamin............2Sa 23:29   1390
Ithai the son of Ribai of G............1Chr 11:31   1390
the daughter of Uriel of G............2Chr 13:2   1390
G of Saul is fled............Is 10:29   1390
Blow ye the cornet in G, and the............Hos 5:8   1390
themselves, as in the days of G............Hos 9:9   1390

hast sinned from the days of G............Hos 10:9   1390
the battle in G against the............Hos 10:9   1390

GIBEATH (gib'-e-ath) See GIBEAH, GIBEATHITE. *Same as Gibeah.*
and Jebusi, which is Jerusalem, G............Josh 18:28   1394

GIBEATH-HAARALOTH See FORESKINS.

GIBEATHITE (gib'-e-ath-ite) *An inhabitant of Gibeah.*
Joash, the sons of Shemaah the G............1Chr 12:3   1395

GIBEON (gib'-e-on) See GEBA, GIBEAH, GIBEONITE.
1. A Hivite city.
when the inhabitants of G heard............Josh 9:3   1391
Now their cities were G, and............Josh 9:17   1391
how the inhabitants of G had made............Josh 10:1   1391
because G was a great city, as............Josh 10:2   1391
and help me, that we may smite G............Josh 10:4   1391
their hosts, and encamped before G............Josh 10:5   1391
the men of G sent unto Joshua to............Josh 10:6   1391
them with a great slaughter at G............Josh 10:10   1391
Sun, stand thou still upon G............Josh 10:12   1391
country of Goshen, even unto G............Josh 10:41   1391
the Hivites the inhabitants of G............Josh 11:19   1391
2. A city in Benjamin.
G, and Ramah, and Beeroth,............Josh 18:25   1391
G with her suburbs, Geba with her............Josh 21:17   1391
Saul, went out from Mahanaim to G............2Sa 2:12   1391
and met together by the pool of G............2Sa 2:13   1391
Helkath-hazzurim, which is in G............2Sa 2:16   1391
by the way of the wilderness of G............2Sa 2:24   1391
brother Asahel at G in the battle............2Sa 3:30   1391
at the great stone which is in G............2Sa 20:8   1391
the king went to G to sacrifice............1Kin 3:4   1391
In G the LORD appeared to Solomon............1Kin 3:5   1391
as he had appeared unto him at G............1Kin 9:2   1391
at G dwelt the father of Gibeon............1Chr 8:29   1391
in G dwelt the father of Gibeon,............1Chr 9:35   1391
Philistines from G even to Gazer............1Chr 14:16   1391
in the high place that was at G............1Chr 16:39   1391
season in the high place at G............1Chr 21:29   1391
to the high place that was at G............2Chr 1:3   1391
place that was at G to Jerusalem............2Chr 1:13   1391
the Meronothite, the men of G............Neh 3:7   1391
The children of G, ninety and five............Neh 7:25   1391
be wroth as in the valley of G............Is 28:21   1391
Azur the prophet, which was of G............Jer 28:1   1391
by the great waters that are in G............Jer 41:12   1391
whom he had brought again from G............Jer 41:16   1391

GIBEONITE (gib'-e-on-ite) See GIBEONITES. *An inhabitant of Gibeon.*
And Ismaiah the G, a mighty man............1Chr 12:4   1393
unto them repaired Melatiah the G............Neh 3:7   1393

GIBEONITES (gib'-e-on-ites)
house, because he slew the G............2Sa 21:1   1393
And the king called the G, and said............2Sa 21:2   1393
(now the G were not of the............2Sa 21:2   1393
Wherefore David said unto the G............2Sa 21:3   1393
the G said unto him, We will have............2Sa 21:4   1393
them into the hands of the G............2Sa 21:9   1393

GIBLITES (gib'-lites) *Inhabitants of Gebal.*
And the land of the G, and all............Josh 13:5   1382

GIDDALTI (ghid-dal'-ti) *A son of Heman.*
Hananiah, Hanani, Eliathah, G............1Chr 25:4   1437
The two and twentieth to G............1Chr 25:29   1437

GIDDEL (ghid'-del)
1. A family of exiles.
The children of G, the children............Ezr 2:47   1435
of Hanan, the children of G............Neh 7:49   1435
2. Servants of Solomon.
of Darkon, the children of G............Ezr 2:56   1435
of Darkon, the children of G............Neh 7:58   1435

GIDEON (ghid'-e-on) See GEDEON, JERUBBAAL. *A judge of Israel.*
his son G threshed wheat by the............Judg 6:11   1439
G said unto him, Oh my Lord, if............Judg 6:13   1439
G went in, and made ready a kid,............Judg 6:19   1439
when G perceived that he was an............Judg 6:22   1439
LORD, G said, Alas, O Lord GOD............Judg 6:22   1439
Then G built an altar there unto............Judg 6:24   1439
Then G took ten men of his............Judg 6:27   1439
G the son of Joash hath done this............Judg 6:29   1439
Spirit of the LORD came upon G............Judg 6:34   1439
G said unto God, If thou wilt............Judg 6:36   1439
G said unto God, Let not thine............Judg 6:39   1439
Then Jerubbaal, who is G, and all............Judg 7:1   1439
And the LORD said unto G, The............Judg 7:2   1439
And the LORD said unto G, The............Judg 7:4   1439
and the LORD said unto G, Every............Judg 7:5   1439

G

And the LORD said unto G, By the .... Judg 7:7 1439
when G was come, behold, there .... Judg 7:13 1439
the sword of G the son of Joash .... Judg 7:14 1439
when G heard the telling of the .... Judg 7:15 1439
The sword of the LORD, and of G .... Judg 7:18 1439
So G, and the hundred men that .... Judg 7:19 1439
The sword of the LORD, and of G .... Judg 7:20 1439
G sent messengers throughout all .... Judg 7:24 1439
Zeeb to G on the other side .... Judg 7:25 1439
G came to Jordan, and passed over, ... Judg 8:4 1439
G said, Therefore when the LORD .... Judg 8:7 1439
G went up by the way of them that .... Judg 8:11 1439
G the son of Joash returned from .... Judg 8:13 1439
G arose, and slew Zebah and .... Judg 8:21 1439
the men of Israel said unto G .... Judg 8:22 1439
G said unto them, I will not rule .... Judg 8:23 1439
G said unto them, I would desire .... Judg 8:24 1439
G made an ephod thereof, and put .... Judg 8:27 1439
which thing became a snare unto G ...... Judg 8:27 1439
forty years in the days of G .... Judg 8:28 1439
G had threescore and ten sons of .... Judg 8:30 1439
G the son of Joash died in a good .... Judg 8:32 1439
to pass, as soon as G was dead .... Judg 8:33 1439
the house of Jerubbaal, namely, G .... Judg 8:35 1439

GIDEONI (ghid-e-o'-ni) *A Benjamite who counted the
people.*
Abidan the son of G .... Num 1:11 1441
shall be Abidan the son of G .... Num 2:22 1441
the ninth day Abidan the son of G .... Num 7:60 1441
offering of Abidan the son of G .... Num 7:65 1441
Benjamin was Abidan the son of G .... Num 10:24 1441

GIDOM (ghi'-dom) *A place near Bethel.*
and pursued hard after them unto G ..... Judg 20:45 1440

GIER
and the pelican, and the g eagle, ... Lev 11:18 7360
the g eagle, and the cormorant, ... Deut 14:17 7360

GIFT
Ask me never so much dowry and g .... Gen 34:12 4976
And thou shalt take no g .... Ex 23:8 7810
for the g blindeth the wise, and .... Ex 23:8 7810
given the Levites as a g to Aaron .... Num 8:19 4979
are given as a g for the LORD .... Num 18:6 4979
office unto you as a service of g .... Num 18:7 4979
the heave offering of their g .... Num 18:11 4976
respect persons, neither take a g .... Deut 16:19 7810
for a g doth blind the eyes of .... Deut 16:19 7810
or hath he given us any g 2Sa 19:42 5379
of Tyre shall be there with a g .... Ps 45:12 4503
A g is as a precious stone in the .... Prov 17:8 7810
A wicked man taketh a g out of .... Prov 17:23 7810
A man's g maketh room for him, and ...... Prov 18:16 4976
A g in secret pacifieth anger .... Prov 21:14 4976
of a false g is like clouds .... Prov 25:14 4991
his labour, it is the g of God .... Eccl 3:13 4991
this is the g of God .... Eccl 5:19 4991
and a g destroyeth the heart .... Eccl 7:7 4979
give a g unto any of his sons .... Eze 46:16 4979
But if he give a g of his .... Eze 46:17 4979
if thou bring thy g to the altar .... Mt 5:23 1435
Leave there thy g before the .... Mt 5:24 1435
and then come and offer thy g .... Mt 5:24 1435
offer the g that Moses commanded, ... Mt 8:4 1435
father or his mother, It is a g .... Mt 15:5 1435
sweareth by the g that is upon it .... Mt 23:18 1435
for whether is greater, the g .... Mt 23:19 1435
the altar that sanctifieth the g .... Mt 23:19 1435
It is Corban, that is to say, a g .... Mk 7:11 1435
her, If thou knewest the g of God .... Jn 4:10 1431
receive the g of the Holy Ghost .... Acts 2:38 1431
thou hast thought that the g of .... Acts 8:20 1431
out the g of the Holy Ghost .... Acts 10:45 1431
them the like g as he did unto us .... Acts 11:17 1431
impart unto you some spiritual g .... Rom 1:11 5486
offence, so also is the free g .... Rom 5:15 5486
the g by grace, which is by one .... Rom 5:15 1431
by one that sinned, so is the g .... Rom 5:16 1434
but the free g is of many .... Rom 5:16 5486
of the g of righteousness shall .... Rom 5:17 1431
the free g came upon all men unto .... Rom 5:18 1434
but the g of God is eternal life .... Rom 6:23 5486
So that ye come behind in no g 1Cor 1:7 5486
man hath his proper g of God 1Cor 7:7 5486
though I have the g of prophecy 1Cor 13:2
that for the g bestowed upon us 2Cor 1:11 5486
that we would receive the g 2Cor 8:4 5485
be unto God for his unspeakable g 2Cor 9:15 1431
it is the g of God .... Eph 2:8 1435
according to the g of the grace .... Eph 3:7 1431
to the measure of the g of Christ .... Eph 4:7 1431

Not because I desire a g .... Phil 4:17 1390
Neglect not the g that is in the 1Ti 4:14 5486
that thou stir up the g of God 2Ti 1:6 5486
and have tasted of the heavenly g .... Heb 6:4 1431
good g and every perfect g .... Jas 1:17 1394
As every man hath received the g 1Pet 4:10 5486

GIFTS
which Abraham had, Abraham gave g .. Gen 25:6 4979
shall hallow in all their holy g .... Ex 28:38 4979
of the LORD, and beside your g .... Lev 23:38 4979
Out of all your g ye shall offer .... Num 18:29 4979
David's servants, and brought g 2Sa 8:2 4503
servants to David, and brought g 2Sa 8:6 4503
David's servants, and brought g 1Chr 18:2 4503
David's servants, and brought g 1Chr 18:6 4503
of persons, nor taking of g 2Chr 19:7 7810
gave them great g of silver 2Chr 21:3 4979
And the Ammonites gave g to Uzziah .. 2Chr 26:8 4503
many brought g unto the LORD to 2Chr 32:23 4503
to the provinces, and gave g .... Est 2:18 4864
one to another, and g to the poor .... Est 9:22 4979
thou hast received g for men .... Ps 68:18 4979
of Sheba and Seba shall offer g .... Ps 72:10 814
though thou givest many g .... Prov 6:35 7810
but he that hateth g shall live .... Prov 15:27 4979
is a friend to him that giveth g .... Prov 19:6 4976
that receiveth g overthroweth it .... Prov 29:4 8641
every one loveth g, and followeth .... Is 1:23 7810
They give g to all whores .... Eze 16:33 5078
givest thy g to all thy lovers .... Eze 16:33 5083
And I polluted them in their own g ...... Eze 20:26 4979
For when ye offer your g, when ye ...... Eze 20:31 4979
my holy name no more with your g ...... Eze 20:39 4979
have they taken g to shed blood .... Eze 22:12 7810
thereof, ye shall receive of me g .... Dan 2:6 4978
man, and gave him many great g .... Dan 2:48 4978
Let thy g be to thyself, and give .... Dan 5:17 4978
they presented unto him g .... Mt 2:11 1435
to give good g unto your children .... Mt 7:11 1435
to give good g unto your children .... Lk 11:13 1390
casting their g into the treasury .... Lk 21:1 1435
adorned with goodly stones and g .... Lk 21:5 334
For the g and calling of God are .... Rom 11:29 5486
Having then g differing according .... Rom 12:6 5486
Now concerning spiritual g 1Cor 12:1
Now there are diversities of g 1Cor 12:4 5486
to another the g of healing by 1Cor 12:9 5486
then g of healings, helps, ... 1Cor 12:28 5486
Have all the g of healing 1Cor 12:30 5486
But covet earnestly the best g 1Cor 12:31 5486
charity, and desire spiritual g 1Cor 14:1
as ye are zealous of spiritual g 1Cor 14:12
captive, and gave g unto men .... Eph 4:8 1390
g of the Holy Ghost, according to .... Heb 2:4 3311
to God, that he may offer both g .... Heb 5:1 1435
priest is ordained to offer g .... Heb 8:3 1435
that offer g according to the law .... Heb 8:4 1435
in which were offered both g .... Heb 9:9 1435
God testifying of his g .... Heb 11:4 1435
shall send g one to another .... Rev 11:10 1435

GIHON (ghi'-hon)
  1. *A river in the Garden of Eden.*
the name of the second river is G .... Gen 2:13 1521
  2. *A place near Jerusalem.*
own mule, and bring him down to G 1Kin 1:33 1521
David's mule, and brought him to G 1Kin 1:38 1521
have anointed him king in G 1Kin 1:45 1521
the upper watercourse of G 2Chr 32:30 1521
of David, on the west side of G 2Chr 33:14 1521

GILALAI (ghil'-a-lahee) *A priest who dedicated the
wall.*
Shemaiah, and Azareel, Milalai, G .... Neh 12:36 1562

GILBOA (ghil-bo'-ah)
  1. *A district in Manasseh.*
together, and they pitched in G 1Sa 28:4 1533
Philistines had slain Saul in G 2Sa 21:12 1533
  2. *A mountain near the valley Jezreel.*
and fell down slain in mount G 1Sa 31:1 1533
his three sons fallen in mount G 1Sa 31:8 1533
I happened by chance upon mount G 2Sa 1:6 1533
Ye mountains of G, let there be 2Sa 1:21 1533
and fell down slain in mount G 1Chr 10:1 1533
and his sons fallen in mount G 1Chr 10:8 1533

GILEAD (ghil'-e-ad) See GILEADITE, GILEAD'S, JABESH-
  GILEAD, RAMOTH-GILEAD.
  1. *District east of the Jordan River.*
of Ishmeelites came from G with .... Gen 37:25 1568
land of Jazer, and the land of G .... Num 32:1 1568

shall be there in the cities of *G*	Num 32:26	1568
the land of *G* for a possession	Num 32:29	1568
the son of Manasseh went to *G*	Num 32:39	1568
Moses gave *G* unto Machir the son	Num 32:40	1568
that is by the river, even unto *G*	Deut 2:36	1568
the cities of the plain, and all *G*	Deut 3:10	1568
And the rest of *G*, and all Bashan,	Deut 3:13	1568
And I gave *G* unto Machir	Deut 3:15	1568
unto the Gadites I gave from *G*	Deut 3:16	1568
and Ramoth in *G*, of the Gadites	Deut 4:43	1568
LORD shewed him all the land of *G*	Deut 34:1	1568
of the river, and from half *G*	Josh 12:2	1568
and the Maachathites, and half *G*	Josh 12:5	1568
And *G*, and the border of the	Josh 13:11	1568
was Jazer, and all the cities of *G*	Josh 13:25	1568
And half *G*, and Ashtaroth, and Edrei	Josh 13:31	1568
a man of war, therefore he had *G*	Josh 17:1	1568
to Manasseh, beside the land of *G*	Josh 17:5	1568
Manasseh's sons had the land of *G*	Josh 17:6	1568
Ramoth in *G* out of the tribe of	Josh 20:8	1568
Ramoth in *G* with her suburbs, to	Josh 21:38	1568
to go unto the country of *G*	Josh 22:9	1568
of Manasseh, into the land of *G*	Josh 22:13	1568
of Manasseh, unto the land of *G*	Josh 22:15	1568
of Gad, out of the land of *G*	Josh 22:32	1568
G abode beyond Jordan	Judg 5:17	1568
day, which are in the land of *G*	Judg 10:4	1568
of the Amorites, which is in *G*	Judg 10:8	1568
together, and encamped in *G*	Judg 10:17	1568
princes of *G* said one to another,	Judg 10:18	1568
over all the inhabitants of *G*	Judg 10:18	1568
the elders of *G* went to fetch	Judg 11:5	1568
said unto the elders of *G*	Judg 11:7	1568
the elders of *G* said unto	Judg 11:8	1568
over all the inhabitants of *G*	Judg 11:8	1568
said unto the elders of *G*	Judg 11:9	1568
the elders of *G* said unto	Judg 11:10	1568
went with the elders of *G*	Judg 11:11	1568
Jephthah, and he passed over *G*	Judg 11:29	1568
and passed over *G*	Judg 11:29	1568
from Mizpeh of *G* he passed over	Judg 11:29	1568
together all the men of *G*	Judg 12:4	1568
the men of *G* smote Ephraim,	Judg 12:4	1568
that the men of *G* said unto him	Judg 12:5	1568
buried in one of the cities of *G*	Judg 12:7	1568
to Beer-sheba, with the land of *G*	Judg 20:1	1568
Jordan to the land of Gad and *G*	1Sa 13:7	1568
And made him king over *G*, and over	2Sa 2:9	1568
Absalom pitched in the land of *G*	2Sa 17:26	1568
Then they came to *G*, and to the	2Sa 24:6	1568
son of Manasseh, which are in *G*	1Kin 4:13	1568
of Uri was in the country of *G*	1Kin 4:19	1568
who was of the inhabitants of *G*	1Kin 17:1	1568
Know ye that Ramoth in *G* is ours	1Kin 22:3	1568
eastward, all the land of *G*	2Kin 10:33	1568
is by the river Arnon, even *G*	2Kin 10:33	1568
and Kedesh, and Hazor, and *G*	2Kin 15:29	1568
and twenty cities in the land of *G*	1Chr 2:22	1568
were multiplied in the land of *G*	1Chr 5:9	1568
throughout all the east land of *G*	1Chr 5:10	1568
And they dwelt in *G* in Bashan	1Chr 5:16	1568
Ramoth in *G* with her suburbs, and	1Chr 6:80	1568
men of valour at Jazer of *G*	1Chr 26:31	1568
the half tribe of Manasseh in *G*	1Chr 27:21	1568
G is mine, and Manasseh is mine	Ps 60:7	1568
G is mine	Ps 108:8	1568
flock of goats that appear from *G*	Song 6:5	1568
Is there no balm in *G*	Jer 8:22	1568
Thou art *G* unto me, and the head	Jer 22:6	1568
Go up into *G*, and take balm, O	Jer 46:11	1568
satisfied upon mount Ephraim and *G*	Jer 50:19	1568
and from Damascus, and from *G*	Eze 47:18	1568
G is a city of them that work	Hos 6:8	1568
Is there iniquity in *G*	Hos 12:11	1568
because they have threshed *G* with	Amos 1:3	1568
the women with child of *G*	Amos 1:13	1568
and Benjamin shall possess *G*	Obad 19	1568
let them feed in Bashan and *G*	Mic 7:14	1568
bring them into the land of *G*	Zec 10:10	1568

2. A mountain range in Gilead 1.

set his face toward the mount *G*	Gen 31:21	1568
they overtook him in the mount *G*	Gen 31:23	1568
pitched in the mount of *G*	Gen 31:25	1568
the river Arnon, and half mount *G*	Deut 3:12	1568
and depart early from mount *G*	Judg 7:3	1568
goats, that appear from mount *G*	Song 4:1	1568

3. Son of Machir.

and Machir begat *G*	Num 26:29	1568
of *G* come the family of the	Num 26:29	1568
These are the sons of *G*	Num 26:30	1568
the son of Hepher, the son of *G*	Num 27:1	1568

the families of the children of *G*	Num 36:1	1568
of Manasseh, the father of *G*	Josh 17:1	1568
the son of Hepher, the son of *G*	Josh 17:3	1568
of Machir the father of *G*	1Chr 2:21	1568
sons of Machir the father of *G*	1Chr 2:23	1568
bare Machir the father of *G*	1Chr 7:14	1568
These were the sons of *G*, the son	1Chr 7:17	1568

4. Father of Jephthah.

and *G* begat Jephthah	Judg 11:1	1568

5. A chief of Gad.

the son of Jaroah, the son of *G*	1Chr 5:14	1568

GILEADITE (*ghil'-e-ad-ite*) See GILEADITES. *A descendant of Gilead.*

And after him arose Jair, a *G*	Judg 10:3	1569
Now Jephthah the *G* was a mighty	Judg 11:1	1569
the *G* four days in a year	Judg 11:40	1569
Then died Jephthah the *G*, and was	Judg 12:7	1569
and Barzillai the *G* of Rogelim	2Sa 17:27	1569
Barzillai the *G* came down from	2Sa 19:31	1569
unto the sons of Barzillai the *G*	1Kin 2:7	1569
the daughters of Barzillai the *G*	Ezr 2:61	1569
of Barzillai the *G* to wife	Neh 7:63	1569

GILEADITES (*ghil'-e-ad-ites*)

Gilead come the family of the *G*	Num 26:29	1569
Ye *G* are fugitives of Ephraim	Judg 12:4	1569
the *G* took the passages of Jordan	Judg 12:5	1569
and with him fifty men of the *G*	2Kin 15:25	1569

GILEAD'S (*ghil'-e-ads*) *Refers to Gilead 4.*

And *G* wife bare him sons	Judg 11:2	1568

GILGAL (*ghil'-gal*)

1. A place near Jericho.

in the champaign over against *G*	Deut 11:30	1537
the first month, and encamped in *G*	Josh 4:19	1537
of Jordan, did Joshua pitch in *G*	Josh 4:20	1537
place is called *G* unto this day	Josh 5:9	1537
children of Israel encamped in *G*	Josh 5:10	1537
sent unto Joshua to the camp to *G*	Josh 10:6	1537
So Joshua ascended from *G*	Josh 10:7	1537
and went up from *G* all night	Josh 10:9	1537
with him, unto the camp to *G*	Josh 10:15	1537
with him, unto the camp to *G*	Josh 10:43	1537
of Judah came unto Joshua in *G*	Josh 14:6	1537
and so northward, looking toward *G*	Josh 15:7	1537
the LORD came up from *G* to Bochim	Judg 2:1	1537
from the quarries that were by *G*	Judg 3:19	1537
year in circuit to Beth-el, and *G*	1Sa 7:16	
thou shalt go down before me to *G*	1Sa 10:8	
people, Come, and let us go to *G*	1Sa 11:14	1537
And all the people went to *G*	1Sa 11:15	1537
Saul king before the LORD in *G*	1Sa 11:15	1537
called together after Saul to *G*	1Sa 13:4	1537
As for Saul, he was yet in *G*	1Sa 13:7	1537
but Samuel came not to *G*	1Sa 13:8	1537
will come down now upon me to *G*	1Sa 13:12	1537
gat him up from *G* unto Gibeah of	1Sa 13:15	1537
and passed on, and gone down to *G*	1Sa 15:12	1537
unto the LORD thy God in *G*	1Sa 15:21	1537
in pieces before the LORD in *G*	1Sa 15:33	1537
And Judah came to *G*, to go to meet	2Sa 19:15	1537
Then the king went on to *G*	2Sa 19:40	1537
Also from the house of *G*, and out	Neh 12:29	1537
and come not ye unto *G*, neither go	Hos 4:15	1537
All their wickedness is in *G*	Hos 9:15	1537
they sacrifice bullocks in *G*	Hos 12:11	1537
at *G* multiply transgression	Amos 4:4	1537
not Beth-el, nor enter into *G*	Amos 5:5	1537
for *G* shall surely go into	Amos 5:5	1537
answered him from Shittim unto *G*	Mic 6:5	1537

2. A city between Dor and Tirsa.

the king of the nations of *G*	Josh 12:23	1537

3. A city north of Joppa.

went to Joshua unto the camp at *G*	Josh 9:6	1537

4. A place south of Ebal and Gerizim.

Elijah went with Elisha from *G*	2Kin 2:1	1537
And Elisha came again to *G*	2Kin 4:38	1537

GILO See GILOH.

GILOH (*ghi'-loh*) See GILONITE. *A town in Judah.*

And Goshen, and Holon, and *G*	Josh 15:51	1542
from his city, even from *G*	2Sa 15:12	1542

GILONITE (*ghi'-lo-nite*) *An inhabitant of Giloh.*

Absalom sent for Ahithophel the *G*	2Sa 15:12	1526
Eliam the son of Ahithophel the *G*	2Sa 23:34	1526

GIMZO (*ghim'-zo*) *A city in Judah.*

G also and the villages thereof	2Chr 28:18	1579

GIN

The *g* shall take him by the heel,	Job 18:9	6341
the houses of Israel, for a *g*	Is 8:14	6341
the earth, where no *g* is for him	Amos 3:5	4170

GINATH (ghi´-nath) *Father of Tibni.*

followed Tibni the son of *G*	1Kin 16:21	1527
that followed Tibni the son of *G*	1Kin 16:22	1527

GINNETHO (ghin´-ne-tho) See GINNETHON. *A priest who renewed the covenant.*

Iddo, *G*, Abijah,	Neh 12:4	1599

GINNETHOI See GINNETHO.

GINNETHON (ghin´-ne-thon) See GINNETHO. *Same as Ginnetho.*

Daniel, *G*, Baruch,	Neh 10:6	1599
of *G*, Meshullam	Neh 12:16	1599

GINS

they have set *g* for me	Ps 140:5	4170
the *g* of the workers of iniquity	Ps 141:9	4170

GIRD

g him with the curious girdle of	Ex 29:5	640
thou shalt *g* them with girdles,	Ex 29:9	2296
he did *g* it under his raiment	Judg 3:16	2296
G ye on every man his sword	1Sa 25:13	2296
g you with sackcloth, and mourn	2Sa 3:31	2296
G up thy loins, and take my staff	2Kin 4:29	2296
G up thy loins, and take this box	2Kin 9:1	2296
G up now thy loins like a man	Job 38:3	247
G up thy loins now like a man	Job 40:7	247
G thy sword upon thy thigh, O	Ps 45:3	2296
g yourselves, and ye shall be	Is 8:9	247
g yourselves, and ye shall be	Is 8:9	247
shall *g* themselves with sackcloth	Is 15:3	2296
g sackcloth upon your loins	Is 32:11	2290
Thou therefore *g* up thy loins	Jer 1:17	2296
For this *g* you with sackcloth,	Jer 4:8	2296
g thee with sackcloth, and wallow	Jer 6:26	2296
of Rabbah, *g* you with sackcloth	Jer 49:3	2296
They shall also *g* themselves with	Eze 7:18	2296
g them with sackcloth, and they	Eze 27:31	2296
they shall not *g* themselves with	Eze 44:18	2296
G yourselves, and lament, ye	Joel 1:13	2296
unto you, that he shall *g* himself	Lk 12:37	4024
g thyself, and serve me, till I	Lk 17:8	4024
hands, and another shall *g* thee	Jn 21:18	2224
G thyself, and bind on thy sandals	Acts 12:8	2224
Wherefore *g* up the loins of your	1Pet 1:13	328

GIRDED

with your loins *g*, your shoes on	Ex 12:11	2296
g him with the girdle, and clothed	Lev 8:7	2296
he *g* him with the curious girdle	Lev 8:7	2296
g them with girdles, and put	Lev 8:13	2296
shall be *g* with a linen girdle,	Lev 16:4	2296
when ye had *g* on every man his	Deut 1:41	2296
that stumbled are *g* with strength	1Sa 2:4	247
a child, *g* with a linen ephod	1Sa 2:18	2296
David *g* his sword upon his armour	1Sa 17:39	2296
they *g* on every man his sword	1Sa 25:13	2296
David also *g* on his sword	1Sa 25:13	2296
David was *g* with a linen ephod	2Sa 6:14	2296
that he had put on was *g* unto him	2Sa 20:8	2296
he being *g* with a new sword,	2Sa 21:16	2296
For thou hast *g* me with strength	2Sa 22:40	247
he *g* up his loins, and ran before	1Kin 18:46	8151
So they *g* sackcloth on their	1Kin 20:32	2296
one had his sword *g* by his side	Neh 4:18	631
For thou hast *g* me with strength	Ps 18:39	247
sackcloth, and *g* me with gladness	Ps 30:11	247
being *g* with power	Ps 65:6	247
wherewith he hath *g* himself	Ps 93:1	247
wherewith he is *g* continually	Ps 109:19	2296
I *g* thee, though thou hast not	Is 45:5	247
they have *g* themselves with	Lam 2:10	2296
I *g* thee about with fine linen,	Eze 16:10	2280
G with girdles upon their loins,	Eze 23:15	2289
whose loins were *g* with fine gold	Dan 10:5	2296
Lament like a virgin *g* with	Joel 1:8	2296
Let your loins be g about	Lk 12:35	4024
and took a towel, and *g* himself	Jn 13:4	1241
with the towel wherewith he was *g*	Jn 13:5	1241
breasts *g* with golden girdles	Rev 15:6	4024

GIRDEDST

thou *g* thyself, and walkedst	Jn 21:18	2224

GIRDETH

Let not him that *g* on his harness	1Kin 20:11	2296
g their loins with a girdle	Job 12:18	631

It is God that *g* me with strength	Ps 18:32	247
She *g* her loins with strength, and	Prov 31:17	2296

GIRDING

of a stomacher a *g* of sackcloth	Is 3:24	4228
baldness, and to *g* with sackcloth	Is 22:12	2296

GIRDLE

a broidered coat, a mitre, and a *g*	Ex 28:4	73
the curious *g* of the ephod, which	Ex 28:8	2805
above the curious *g* of the ephod	Ex 28:27	2805
above the curious *g* of the ephod	Ex 28:28	2805
shalt make the *g* of needlework	Ex 28:39	73
with the curious *g* of the ephod	Ex 29:5	2805
the curious *g* of his ephod, that	Ex 39:5	2805
above the curious *g* of the ephod	Ex 39:20	2805
above the curious *g* of the ephod	Ex 39:21	2805
a *g* of fine twined linen, and blue	Ex 39:29	73
coat, and girded him with the *g*	Lev 8:7	73
with the curious *g* of the ephod	Lev 8:7	2805
and shall be girded with a linen *g*	Lev 16:4	73
sword, and to his bow, and to his *g*	1Sa 18:4	2290
ten shekels of silver, and a *g*	2Sa 18:11	2290
upon it a *g* with a sword fastened	2Sa 20:8	2290
his *g* that was about his loins	1Kin 2:5	2290
girt with a *g* of leather about	2Kin 1:8	232
and girdeth their loins with a *g*	Job 12:18	232
for a *g* wherewith he is girded	Ps 109:19	4206
and instead of a *g* a rent	Is 3:24	2290
neither shall the *g* of their	Is 5:27	232
shall be the *g* of his loins	Is 11:5	232
faithfulness the *g* of his reins	Is 11:5	232
and strengthen him with thy *g*	Is 22:21	73
unto me, Go and get thee a linen *g*	Jer 13:1	232
So I got a *g* according to the	Jer 13:2	232
Take the *g* that thou hast got,	Jer 13:4	232
take the *g* from thence, which I	Jer 13:6	232
took the *g* from the place where I	Jer 13:7	232
behold, the *g* was marred, it was	Jer 13:7	232
them, shall even be as this *g*	Jer 13:10	232
For as the *g* cleaveth to the	Jer 13:11	232
a leathern *g* about his loins	Mt 3:4	2223
with a *g* of a skin about his	Mk 1:6	2223
come unto us, he took Paul's *g*	Acts 21:11	2223
bind the man that owneth this *g*	Acts 21:11	2223
about the paps with a golden *g*	Rev 1:13	2223

GIRDLES

and thou shalt make for them *g*	Ex 28:40	73
And thou shalt gird them with *g*	Ex 29:9	73
upon them, and girded them with *g*	Lev 8:13	73
delivereth *g* unto the merchant	Prov 31:24	2289
Girded with *g* upon their loins,	Eze 23:15	232
breasts girded with golden *g*	Rev 15:6	2223

GIRGASHITE (ghur´-gash-ite) See GIRGASHITES, GIRGA-SITE. *A Canaanitish tribe.*

also, and the Amorite, and the *G*	1Chr 1:14	1622

GIRGASHITES (ghur´-gash-ites)

and the Canaanites, and the *G*	Gen 15:21	1622
thee, the Hittites, and the *G*	Deut 7:1	1622
and the Perizzites, and the *G*	Josh 3:10	1622
and the Hittites, and the *G*	Josh 24:11	1622
and the Jebusites, and the *G*	Neh 9:8	1622

GIRGASITE (ghur´-ga-site) See GIRGASHITE. *Same as Girgashite.*

and the Amorite, and the *G*	Gen 10:16	1622

GIRL

sold a *g* for wine, that they	Joel 3:3	3207

GIRLS

g playing in the streets thereof	Zec 8:5	3207

GIRT

g with a girdle of leather about	2Kin 1:8	247
he *g* his fisher's coat unto him,	Jn 21:7	1241
your loins *g* about with truth	Eph 6:14	4024
g about the paps with a golden	Rev 1:13	4024

GIRZITES See GEZRITES.

GISHPA See GISPA.

GISPA (ghis´-pah) *An overseer of the Nethinim.*

G were over the Nethinims	Neh 11:21	1658

GISPHA See GISPA.

GITTAH-HEPHER (ghit´-tah-he´-fer) See GATH-HEPHER. *A town in Zebulun.*

passeth on along on the east to *G*	Josh 19:13	1662

GITTAIM (ghit-ta´-im)

1. A city of refuge.

And the Beerothites fled to *G*	2Sa 4:3	1664

2. *A Benjamite city.*
Hazor, Ramah, *G*, ...Neh 11:33   1664

GITTITE (*ghit´-tite*) See GITTITES, GITTITH. *An inhabitant of Gath.*
into the house of Obed-edom the *G* 2Sa 6:10   1663
of Obed-edom the *G* three months..........2Sa 6:11   1663
Then said the king to Ittai the *G* 2Sa 15:19   1663
Ittai the *G* passed over, and all 2Sa 15:22   1663
under the hand of Ittai the *G* 2Sa 18:2   1663
slew the brother of Goliath the *G* 2Sa 21:19   1663
into the house of Obed-edom the *G* 1Chr 13:13   1663
the brother of Goliath the *G*...................1Chr 20:5   1663

GITTITES
the Eshkalonites, the *G*, and the ....Josh 13:3   1663
all the Pelethites, and all the *G*...............2Sa 15:18   1663

GITTITH (*ghit´-tith*) *A musical instrument.*
To the chief Musician upon *G* ....Ps 8:t   1665
To the chief Musician upon *G* ....Ps 81:t   1665
To the chief Musician upon *G* ....Ps 84:t   1665

GIVE
heaven to *g* light upon the earth ....Gen 1:15
heaven to *g* light upon the earth ....Gen 1:17
Unto thy seed will I *g* this land ....Gen 12:7   5414
thou seest, to thee will I *g* it ....Gen 13:15   5414
for I will *g* it unto thee ....Gen 13:17   5414
G me the persons, and take the ....Gen 14:21   5414
Lord GOD, what wilt thou *g* me ....Gen 15:2   5414
to *g* thee this land to inherit it ....Gen 15:7   5414
I will *g* unto thee, and to thy.................Gen 17:8   5414
her, and *g* thee a son also of her ....Gen 17:16   5414
g me a possession of a ....Gen 23:4   5414
That he may *g* me the cave of ....Gen 23:9   5414
g it me for a possession of a ....Gen 23:9   5414
the field *g* I thee, and the cave ....Gen 23:11   5414
cave that is therein; I *g* it thee ....Gen 23:11   5414
the sons of my people *g* I it thee ....Gen 23:11   5414
saying, But if thou wilt *g* it ....Gen 23:13   5414
I will *g* thee money for the field ....Gen 23:13   5414
Unto thy seed will I *g* this land............Gen 24:7   5414
I will *g* thy camels drink also ....Gen 24:14
if they *g* not thee one, thou ....Gen 24:41   5414
G me, I pray thee, a little water ....Gen 24:43
I will *g* thy camels drink also ....Gen 24:46
I will *g* all these countries, and............Gen 26:3   5414
will *g* unto thy seed all these ....Gen 26:4   5414
Therefore God *g* thee of the dew ....Gen 27:28   5414
g thee the blessing of Abraham, ...Gen 28:4   5414
thou liest, to thee will I *g* it ....Gen 28:13   5414
will *g* me bread to eat, and ....Gen 28:20   5414
of all that thou shalt *g* me I ....Gen 28:22   5414
will surely *g* the tenth unto thee ....Gen 28:22
It is better that I *g* her to thee ....Gen 29:19   5414
I should *g* her to another man ....Gen 29:19   5414
G me my wife, for my days are ....Gen 29:21   3051
to *g* the younger before the ....Gen 29:26   5414
we will *g* thee this also for the ....Gen 29:27   5414
G me children, or else I die ....Gen 30:1   3051
G me, I pray thee, of thy son's ....Gen 30:14   5414
G me my wives and my children, for......Gen 30:26   5414
me thy wages, and I will *g* it ....Gen 30:28   5414
And he said, What shall I *g* thee ....Gen 30:31   5414
Thou shalt not *g* me any thing...............Gen 30:31   5414
I pray you *g* him to wife ....Gen 34:8   5414
g your daughters unto us, and take.......Gen 34:9   5414
ye shall say unto me I will *g* ....Gen 34:11   5414
I will *g* according as ye shall ....Gen 34:12   5414
but *g* me the damsel to wife ....Gen 34:12   5414
to *g* our sister to one that is ....Gen 34:14   5414
Then will we *g* our daughters unto ....Gen 34:16   5414
let us *g* them our daughters ....Gen 34:21   5414
and Isaac, to thee I will *g* it ....Gen 35:12   5414
seed after thee will I *g* the land ....Gen 35:12   5414
he should *g* seed to his brother ....Gen 38:9   5414
And she said, What wilt thou *g* me ....Gen 38:16   5414
Wilt thou *g* me a pledge, till ....Gen 38:17   5414
said, What pledge shall I *g* thee ....Gen 38:18   5414
God shall *g* Pharaoh an answer of ....Gen 41:16
to *g* them provision for the way ....Gen 42:25   5414
to *g* his ass provender in the inn ....Gen 42:27   5414
God Almighty *g* you mercy before ....Gen 43:14   5414
I will *g* you the good of the land ....Gen 45:18   5414
unto Joseph, and said, *G* us bread.........Gen 47:15   3051
And Joseph said, *G* your cattle ....Gen 47:16   3051
I will *g* you for your cattle, if................Gen 47:16   5414
g us seed, that we may live, and ....Gen 47:19   5414
that ye shall *g* the fifth part ....Gen 47:24   5414
will *g* this land to thy seed ....Gen 48:4   5414
me, and I will *g* thee thy wages ....Ex 2:9   5414
I will *g* this people favour in ....Ex 3:21   5414

Ye shall no more *g* the people ....Ex 5:7
Pharaoh, I will not *g* you straw ....Ex 5:10   5414
to *g* them the land of Canaan, the.........Ex 6:4   5414
I did swear to *g* it to Abraham ....Ex 6:8   5414
I will *g* it you for an heritage.................Ex 6:8   5414
Thou must *g* us also sacrifices and ....Ex 10:25   5414
land which the LORD will *g* you ....Ex 12:25   5414
sware unto thy fathers to *g* thee ....Ex 13:5   5414
thy fathers, and shall *g* it thee, ...Ex 13:11   5414
a pillar of fire, to *g* them light ....Ex 13:21
wilt *g* ear to his commandments, ...Ex 15:26
when the LORD shall *g* you in the ....Ex 16:8   5414
G us water that we may drink ....Ex 17:2   5414
I will *g* thee counsel, and God ....Ex 18:19
then thou shalt *g* life for life ....Ex 21:23   5414
then he shall *g* for the ransom of ....Ex 21:30   5414
he shall *g* unto their master ....Ex 21:32   5414
g money unto the owner of them, ...Ex 21:34   7725
utterly refuse to *g* her unto him ....Ex 22:17   5414
of thy sons shalt thou *g* unto me............Ex 22:29   5414
the eighth day thou shalt *g* it me ....Ex 22:30   5414
I will *g* thee tables of stone, and ....Ex 24:12   5414
testimony which I shall *g* thee ....Ex 25:16   5414
the testimony that I shall *g* thee ....Ex 25:21   5414
of all things which I will *g* thee ....Ex 25:22   5414
that they may *g* light over ....Ex 25:37
then shall they *g* every man a ....Ex 30:12   5414
This they shall *g*, every one that ....Ex 30:13   5414
shall *g* an offering unto the LORD ....Ex 30:14   5414
The rich shall not *g* more ....Ex 30:15
the poor shall not *g* less than ....Ex 30:15
when they *g* an offering unto the ....Ex 30:15   5414
spoken of will I *g* unto your seed ....Ex 32:13   5414
saying, Unto thy seed will I *g* it ....Ex 33:1   5414
with thee, and I will *g* thee rest ....Ex 33:14
thereto, and *g* it unto the priest ....Lev 5:16   5414
and *g* it unto him to whom it ....Lev 6:5   5414
the right shoulder shall ye *g*..................Lev 7:32   5414
which I *g* to you for a possession ....Lev 14:34   5414
and *g* them unto the priest ....Lev 15:14   5414
I will *g* it unto you to possess ....Lev 20:24   5414
shall *g* it unto the priest with ....Lev 22:14   5414
into the land which I *g* unto you ....Lev 23:10   5414
which ye *g* unto the LORD ....Lev 23:38   5414
come into the land which I *g* you ....Lev 25:2   5414
Thou shalt not *g* him thy money ....Lev 25:37   5414
to *g* you the land of Canaan, and ....Lev 25:38   5414
he shall *g* again the price of his ....Lev 25:51   7725
unto his years shall he *g* him ....Lev 25:52   7725
Then I will *g* you rain in due ....Lev 26:4   5414
I will *g* peace in the land, and ye.........Lev 26:6   5414
he shall *g* thine estimation in...............Lev 27:23   5414
thou shalt *g* the Levites unto ....Num 3:9   5414
And thou shalt *g* the money ....Num 3:48   5414
g it unto him against whom he ....Num 5:7   5414
upon thee, and *g* thee peace ....Num 6:26   7760
thou shalt *g* them unto the ....Num 7:5   5414
the seven lamps shall *g* light................Num 8:2
the LORD said, I will *g* you ....Num 10:29   5414
Who shall *g* us flesh to eat ....Num 11:4
flesh to *g* unto all this people ....Num 11:13   5414
G us flesh, that we may eat ....Num 11:13   5414
Who shall *g* us flesh to eat ....Num 11:18
the LORD will *g* you flesh ....Num 11:18   5414
I will *g* them flesh, that they ....Num 11:21   5414
which I *g* unto the children of ....Num 13:2   5414
us into this land, and *g* it us ....Num 14:8   5414
habitations, which I *g* unto you, ...Num 15:2   5414
first of your dough ye shall *g* ....Num 15:21   5414
ye shall *g* thereof the LORD's ....Num 18:28   5414
ye shall *g* her unto Eleazar the ....Num 19:3   5414
it shall *g* forth his water, and ....Num 20:8   5414
so thou shalt *g* the congregation ....Num 20:8
Thus Edom refused to *g* Israel ....Num 20:21   5414
together, and I will *g* them water ....Num 21:16   5414
to *g* me leave to go with you ....Num 22:13   5414
If Balak would *g* me his house ....Num 22:18   5414
If Balak would *g* me his house ....Num 24:13   5414
I *g* unto him my covenant of peace ....Num 25:12   5414
To many thou shalt *g* the more ....Num 26:54
to few thou shalt *g* the less ....Num 26:54
G unto us therefore a possession ....Num 27:4   5414
thou shalt surely *g* them a ....Num 27:7   5414
then ye shall *g* his inheritance ....Num 27:9   5414
then ye shall *g* his inheritance ....Num 27:10   5414
then ye shall *g* his inheritance ....Num 27:11   5414
g him a charge in their sight ....Num 27:19
g it unto Eleazar the priest, for.............Num 31:29   5414
g them unto the Levites, which ....Num 31:30   5414
then ye shall *g* them the land of ....Num 32:29   5414
ye shall *g* the more inheritance..............Num 33:54

ye shall *g* the less inheritance	Num 33:54	
to *g* unto the nine tribes	Num 34:13	5414
that they *g* unto the Levites of	Num 35:2	5414
ye shall *g* also unto the Levites	Num 35:2	5414
which ye shall *g* unto the Levites	Num 35:4	5414
g unto the Levites there shall be	Num 35:6	5414
g to the Levites be forty	Num 35:7	5414
them shall ye *g* with their	Num 35:7	
the cities which ye shall *g* shall	Num 35:8	5414
that have many ye shall *g* many	Num 35:8	
them that have few ye shall *g* few	Num 35:8	
every one shall *g* of his cities	Num 35:8	5414
g six cities shall ye have for	Num 35:13	5414
Ye shall *g* three cities on this	Num 35:14	5414
shall ye *g* in the land of Canaan	Num 35:14	5414
The LORD commanded my lord to *g*	Num 36:2	5414
was commanded by the LORD to *g*	Num 36:2	5414
to *g* unto them and to their seed	Deut 1:8	5414
the LORD our God doth *g* unto us	Deut 1:20	5414
which the LORD our God doth *g* us	Deut 1:25	5414
which I sware to *g* unto your	Deut 1:35	5414
to him will I *g* the land that he	Deut 1:36	5414
thither, and unto them will I *g* it	Deut 1:39	5414
to your voice, nor *g* ear unto you	Deut 1:45	
for I will not *g* you of their	Deut 2:5	5414
for I will not *g* thee of their	Deut 2:9	5414
for I will not *g* thee of the land	Deut 2:19	5414
g me water for money, that I may	Deut 2:28	5414
Behold, I have begun to *g* Sihon	Deut 2:31	5414
to *g* thee their land for an	Deut 4:38	5414
land which I *g* them to possess it	Deut 5:31	5414
to *g* thee great and goodly cities,	Deut 6:10	5414
to *g* us the land which he sware	Deut 6:23	5414
thou shalt not *g* unto his son	Deut 7:3	5414
sware unto thy fathers to *g* thee	Deut 7:13	5414
unto their fathers to *g* unto them	Deut 10:11	5414
unto your fathers to *g* unto them	Deut 11:9	5414
That I will *g* you the rain of	Deut 11:14	5414
sware unto your fathers to *g* them	Deut 11:21	5414
thou shalt *g* it unto the stranger	Deut 14:21	5414
Thou shalt surely *g* him, and thine	Deut 15:10	5414
thee thou shalt *g* unto him	Deut 15:14	5414
which thou shalt *g* unto the LORD	Deut 16:10	5414
Every man shall *g* as he is able	Deut 16:17	
they shall *g* unto the priest the	Deut 18:3	5414
of thy sheep, shalt thou *g* him	Deut 18:4	5414
g thee all the land which he	Deut 19:8	5414
he promised to *g* unto thy fathers	Deut 19:8	5414
doth *g* thee for an inheritance	Deut 20:16	5414
g occasions of speech against her	Deut 22:14	7760
g them unto the father of the	Deut 22:19	5414
g unto the damsel's father fifty	Deut 22:29	5414
to *g* up thine enemies before thee	Deut 23:14	5414
g it in her hand, and send her out	Deut 24:1	5414
his day thou shalt *g* him his hire	Deut 24:15	5414
Forty stripes he may *g* him	Deut 25:3	
unto our fathers for to *g* us	Deut 26:3	5414
sware unto thy fathers to *g* thee	Deut 28:11	5414
the heaven to *g* the rain unto thy	Deut 28:12	5414
So that he will not *g* to any of	Deut 28:55	5414
but the LORD shall *g* thee there a	Deut 28:65	5414
to Isaac, and to Jacob, to *g* them	Deut 30:20	5414
the LORD shall *g* them up before	Deut 31:5	5414
unto their fathers to *g* them	Deut 31:7	5414
that I may *g* him a charge	Deut 31:14	
G ear, O ye heavens, and I will	Deut 32:1	
which I *g* unto the children of	Deut 32:49	5414
which I *g* the children of Israel	Deut 32:52	5414
I will *g* it unto thy seed	Deut 34:4	5414
the land which I do *g* to them	Josh 1:2	5414
unto their fathers to *g* them	Josh 1:6	5414
house, and *g* me a true token	Josh 2:12	5414
their fathers that he would *g* us	Josh 5:6	5414
Joshua said unto Achan, My son, *g*	Josh 7:19	7760
for I will *g* it into thine hand	Josh 8:18	5414
Moses to *g* you all the land	Josh 9:24	5414
Now therefore *g* me this mountain,	Josh 14:12	5414
to him will I *g* Achsah my	Josh 15:16	5414
Who answered, *G* me a blessing	Josh 15:19	5414
g me also springs of water	Josh 15:19	5414
to *g* us an inheritance among our	Josh 17:4	5414
G out from among you three men	Josh 18:4	3051
g him a place, that he may dwell	Josh 20:4	5414
Moses to *g* us cities to dwell in	Josh 21:2	5414
he sware to *g* unto their fathers	Josh 21:43	5414
to him will I *g* Achsah my	Judg 1:12	5414
said unto him, *G* me a blessing	Judg 1:15	3051
g me also springs of water	Judg 1:15	5414
G me, I pray thee, a little water	Judg 4:19	5414
g ear, O ye princes	Judg 5:3	
thee are too many for me to *g* the	Judg 7:2	5414

said unto the men of Succoth, *G*	Judg 8:5	5414
that we should *g* bread unto thine	Judg 8:6	5414
that we should *g* bread unto thy	Judg 8:15	5414
that ye would *g* me every man the	Judg 8:24	5414
We will willingly *g* them	Judg 8:25	5414
then I will *g* you thirty sheets	Judg 14:12	5414
then shall ye *g* me thirty sheets	Judg 14:13	5414
we will *g* thee every one of us	Judg 16:5	5414
I will *g* thee ten shekels of	Judg 17:10	5414
g here your advice and counsel	Judg 20:7	3051
There shall not any of us *g* his	Judg 21:1	5414
by the LORD that we will not *g*	Judg 21:7	5414
Howbeit we may not *g* them wives	Judg 21:18	5414
for ye did not *g* unto them at	Judg 21:22	5414
shall *g* thee of this young woman	Ruth 4:12	5414
but wilt *g* unto thine handmaid a	1Sa 1:11	5414
then I will *g* him unto the LORD	1Sa 1:11	5414
he shall *g* strength unto his king	1Sa 2:10	5414
G flesh to roast for the priest	1Sa 2:15	5414
but thou shalt *g* it me now	1Sa 2:16	5414
The LORD *g* thee seed of this	1Sa 2:20	7760
did I *g* unto the house of thy	1Sa 2:28	5414
wealth which God shall *g* Israel	1Sa 2:32	3190
ye shall *g* glory unto the God of	1Sa 6:5	5414
said, *G* us a king to judge us	1Sa 8:6	5414
them, and *g* them to his servants	1Sa 8:14	5414
g to his officers, and to his	1Sa 8:15	5414
that will I *g* to the man of God,	1Sa 9:8	5414
g thee two loaves of bread	1Sa 10:4	5414
G us seven days' respite, that we	1Sa 11:3	
God of Israel, *G* a perfect lot	1Sa 14:41	3051
g me a man, that we may fight	1Sa 17:10	5414
will *g* him his daughter, and make	1Sa 17:25	5414
I will *g* thy flesh unto the fowls	1Sa 17:44	5414
I will *g* the carcases of the host	1Sa 17:46	5414
he will *g* you into our hands	1Sa 17:47	5414
her will I *g* thee to wife	1Sa 18:17	5414
I will *g* him her, that she may be	1Sa 18:21	5414
g me five loaves of bread in mine	1Sa 21:3	5414
none like that; *g* it me	1Sa 21:9	5414
will the son of Jesse *g* every one	1Sa 22:7	5414
g, I pray thee, whatsoever cometh	1Sa 25:8	5414
g it unto men, whom I know not	1Sa 25:11	5414
let them *g* me a place in some	1Sa 27:5	5414
we will not *g* them ought of the	1Sa 30:22	5414
g them unto thy neighbour, and he	2Sa 12:11	5414
g me meat, and dress the meat in	2Sa 13:5	1262
I will *g* charge concerning thee	2Sa 14:8	
G counsel among you what we shall	2Sa 16:20	3051
And the king said, I will *g* them	2Sa 21:6	5414
I will *g* thanks unto thee	2Sa 22:50	
Oh that one would *g* me drink of	2Sa 23:15	
as a king, *g* unto the king	2Sa 24:23	5414
g thee counsel, that thou mayest	1Kin 1:12	
that he *g* me Abishag the	1Kin 2:17	5414
God said, Ask what I shall *g* thee	1Kin 3:5	5414
G therefore thy servant an	1Kin 3:9	5414
in the morning to *g* my child suck	1Kin 3:21	5414
g half to the one, and half to the	1Kin 3:25	5414
g her the living child, and in no	1Kin 3:26	5414
G her the living child, and in no	1Kin 3:27	5414
unto thee will I *g* hire for thy	1Kin 5:6	5414
to *g* him according to his	1Kin 8:32	5414
g rain upon thy land, which thou	1Kin 8:36	5414
g to every man according to his	1Kin 8:39	5414
g them compassion before them who	1Kin 8:50	5414
thee, and will *g* it to thy servant	1Kin 11:11	5414
but will *g* one tribe to thy son	1Kin 11:13	5414
will *g* ten tribes to thee	1Kin 11:31	5414
will *g* it unto thee, even ten	1Kin 11:35	5414
unto his son will I *g* one tribe	1Kin 11:36	5414
David, and will *g* Israel unto thee	1Kin 11:38	5414
What counsel *g* ye that we may	1Kin 12:9	
and I will *g* thee a reward	1Kin 13:7	5414
If thou wilt *g* me half thine	1Kin 13:8	5414
he shall *g* Israel up because of	1Kin 14:16	5414
his God *g* him a lamp in Jerusalem	1Kin 15:4	5414
And he said unto her, *G* me thy son	1Kin 17:19	5414
them therefore *g* us two bullocks	1Kin 18:23	5414
G me thy vineyard, that I may	1Kin 21:2	5414
I will *g* thee for it a better	1Kin 21:2	5414
I will *g* thee the worth of it in	1Kin 21:2	5414
that I should *g* the inheritance	1Kin 21:3	5414
I will not *g* thee the inheritance	1Kin 21:4	5414
G me thy vineyard for money	1Kin 21:6	5414
I will *g* thee another vineyard	1Kin 21:6	5414
I will not *g* thee my vineyard	1Kin 21:6	5414
I will *g* thee the vineyard of	1Kin 21:7	5414
he refused to *g* thee for money	1Kin 21:15	5414
G unto the people, that they may	2Kin 4:42	5414
G the people, that they may eat	2Kin 4:43	5414

g them, I pray thee, a talent of..............	2Kin 5:22	5414
G thy son, that we may eat him to	2Kin 6:28	5414
G thy son, that we may eat him	2Kin 6:29	5414
him to *g* him alway a light	2Kin 8:19	5414
If it be, *g* me thine hand	2Kin 10:15	5414
the priest *g* king David's spears	2Kin 11:10	5414
G thy daughter to my son to wife	2Kin 14:9	5414
to *g* to the king of Assyria	2Kin 15:20	5414
g pledges to my lord the king of	2Kin 18:23	
let them *g* it to the doers of the	2Kin 22:5	5414
but he taxed the land to *g* the	2Kin 23:35	5414
to *g* it unto Pharaoh-nechoh	2Kin 23:35	5414
Oh that one would *g* me drink of	1Chr 11:17	
G thanks unto the LORD, call upon	1Chr 16:8	
Unto thee will I *g* the land of..........	1Chr 16:18	5414
G unto the LORD, ye kindreds of	1Chr 16:28	3051
g unto the LORD glory and strength.....	1Chr 16:28	3051
G unto the LORD the glory due	1Chr 16:29	3051
O *g* thanks unto the LORD	1Chr 16:34	
that we may *g* thanks to thy holy	1Chr 16:35	
to *g* thanks unto the LORD, because	1Chr 16:41	
I *g* thee the oxen also for burnt........	1Chr 21:23	5414
meat offering; I *g* it all	1Chr 21:23	5414
I will *g* him rest from all his........	1Chr 22:9	
be Solomon, and I will *g* peace	1Chr 22:9	
Only the LORD *g* thee wisdom	1Chr 22:12	5414
g thee charge concerning Israel, ...	1Chr 22:12	
to *g* thanks and to praise the LORD	1Chr 25:3	
great, and to *g* strength unto all......	1Chr 29:12	
g unto Solomon my son a perfect	1Chr 29:19	
unto him, Ask what I shall *g* thee......	2Chr 1:7	5414
G me now wisdom and knowledge,......	2Chr 1:10	5414
I will *g* thee riches, and wealth,........	2Chr 1:12	5414
I will *g* to thy servants, the............	2Chr 2:10	5414
What counsel *g* ye me to return	2Chr 10:6	
What advice *g* ye that we may	2Chr 10:9	
he promised to *g* a light to him........	2Chr 21:7	5414
but they would not *g* ear..............	2Chr 24:19	
The LORD is able to *g* thee much........	2Chr 25:9	5414
G thy daughter to my son to wife	2Chr 25:18	5414
was to *g* them one heart to do the	2Chr 30:12	5414
g to the congregation a thousand	2Chr 30:24	7311
to *g* thanks, and to praise in the	2Chr 31:2	
to *g* the portion of the priests........	2Chr 31:4	5414
to *g* to their brethren by courses	2Chr 31:15	5414
to *g* portions to all the males	2Chr 31:19	5414
to *g* over yourselves to die by........	2Chr 32:11	5414
that they might *g* according to	2Chr 35:12	5414
G ye now commandment to cause	Ezr 4:21	7761
to *g* us a nail in his holy place,..........	Ezr 9:8	5414
g us a little reviving in our..............	Ezr 9:8	5414
to *g* us a reviving, to set up the	Ezr 9:9	5414
to *g* us a wall in Judah and in............	Ezr 9:9	5414
Now therefore *g* not your................	Ezr 9:12	5414
that he may *g* me timber to make	Neh 2:8	5414
g them for a prey in the land of	Neh 4:4	5414
to *g* the land of the Canaanites	Neh 9:8	5414
and the Girgashites, to *g* it	Neh 9:8	5414
to *g* them light in the way	Neh 9:12	
which thou hadst sworn to *g* them	Neh 9:15	5414
yet would they not *g* ear	Neh 9:30	
that we would not *g* our daughters	Neh 10:30	5414
to *g* thanks, according to the	Neh 12:24	
Ye shall not *g* your daughters	Neh 13:25	5414
let the king *g* her royal estate	Est 1:19	5414
all the wives shall *g* to their..........	Est 1:20	5414
g the house of Haman the Jews'........	Est 8:1	5414
a man hath will *g* for his life............	Job 2:4	5414
why did I not *g* up the ghost when	Job 3:11	1478
G a reward for me of your	Job 6:22	
my tongue, I shall *g* up the ghost	Job 13:19	1478
neither let me *g* flattering	Job 32:21	1478
I know not to *g* flattering titles	Job 32:22	
g ear unto me, ye that have	Job 34:2	
I shall *g* thee the heathen for	Ps 2:8	5415
G ear to my words, O LORD..............	Ps 5:1	
the grave who shall *g* thee thanks	Ps 6:5	
g ear unto my prayer, that goeth	Ps 17:1	
will I *g* thanks unto thee	Ps 18:49	
G them according to their deeds, ...	Ps 28:4	5414
g them after the work of their	Ps 28:4	5414
G unto the LORD, O ye mighty, ...	Ps 29:1	3051
g unto the LORD glory and strength.....	Ps 29:1	3051
G unto the LORD the glory due	Ps 29:2	3051
The LORD will *g* strength unto his........	Ps 29:11	5414
g thanks at the remembrance of............	Ps 30:4	
I will *g* thanks unto thee for............	Ps 30:12	
I will *g* thanks in the great	Ps 35:18	
he shall *g* thee the desires of............	Ps 37:4	
O LORD, and *g* ear unto my cry	Ps 39:12	5414
g ear, all ye inhabitants of the	Ps 49:1	

nor *g* to God a ransom for him	Ps 49:7	5414
else would I *g* it	Ps 51:16	5414
g ear to the words of my mouth	Ps 54:2	
G ear to my prayer, O God	Ps 55:1	
I will sing and *g* praise	Ps 57:7	
G us help from trouble	Ps 60:11	3051
G the king thy judgments, O God, ...	Ps 72:1	5414
O God, do we *g*	Ps 75:1	
unto thee do we *g* thanks	Ps 75:1	
G ear, O my people, to my law	Ps 78:1	
can he *g* bread also	Ps 78:20	
will *g* thee thanks for ever	Ps 79:13	5414
G ear, O Shepherd of Israel, thou	Ps 80:1	
g ear, O God of Jacob	Ps 84:8	
the LORD will *g* grace and glory	Ps 84:11	5414
the LORD shall *g* that which is..........	Ps 85:12	5414
G ear, O LORD, unto my prayer	Ps 86:6	
g thy strength unto thy servant, ...	Ps 86:16	5414
For he shall *g* his angels charge	Ps 91:11	
thing to *g* thanks unto the LORD	Ps 92:1	
That thou mayest *g* him rest from	Ps 94:13	
G unto the LORD, O ye kindreds of	Ps 96:7	3051
g unto the LORD glory and strength.....	Ps 96:7	3051
G unto the LORD the glory due	Ps 96:8	3051
g thanks at the remembrance of	Ps 97:12	
They *g* drink to every beast of	Ps 104:11	
that thou mayest *g* them their	Ps 104:27	5414
O *g* thanks unto the LORD	Ps 105:1	
Unto thee will I *g* the land of............	Ps 105:11	5414
fire to *g* light in the night	Ps 105:39	
O *g* thanks unto the LORD	Ps 106:1	
to *g* thanks unto thy holy name, ...	Ps 106:47	
O *g* thanks unto the LORD, for he	Ps 107:1	
g praise, even with my glory	Ps 108:1	
G us help from trouble	Ps 108:12	3051
but I *g* myself unto prayer	Ps 109:4	
that he may *g* them the heritage	Ps 111:6	5441
us, but unto thy name *g* glory	Ps 115:1	
O *g* thanks unto the LORD	Ps 118:1	
O *g* thanks unto the LORD	Ps 118:1	
G me understanding, and I shall	Ps 118:29	
At midnight I will rise to *g*	Ps 119:34	
g me understanding, that I may	Ps 119:62	
g me understanding, that I may	Ps 119:73	
g me understanding, and I shall	Ps 119:125	
g me understanding according to	Ps 119:144	
to *g* thanks unto the name of the	Ps 119:169	
I will not *g* sleep to mine eyes, ...	Ps 122:4	
O *g* thanks unto the LORD	Ps 132:4	5414
O *g* thanks unto the God of gods	Ps 136:1	
O *g* thanks to the Lord of lords..........	Ps 136:2	
O *g* thanks unto the God of heaven	Ps 136:3	
shall *g* thanks unto thy name	Ps 136:26	
g ear unto my voice, when I cry	Ps 140:13	
g ear to my supplications	Ps 141:1	
To *g* subtilty to the simple, to	Ps 143:1	
come again, and to morrow I will *g*......	Prov 1:4	5414
For I *g* you good doctrine,..............	Prov 3:28	5414
She shall *g* to thine head an	Prov 4:2	5414
Lest thou *g* thine honour unto	Prov 4:9	5414
G not sleep to thine eyes, nor	Prov 5:9	5414
he shall *g* all the substance of..........	Prov 6:4	5414
G instruction to a wise man, and	Prov 6:31	5414
g me thine heart, and let thine	Prov 9:9	5414
be hungry, *g* him bread to eat	Prov 23:26	5414
be thirsty, *g* him water to drink	Prov 25:21	
The rod and reproof *g* wisdom	Prov 25:21	
thy son, and he shall *g* thee rest........	Prov 29:15	5414
he shall *g* delight unto thy soul	Prov 29:17	
g me neither poverty nor riches	Prov 29:17	5414
two daughters, crying, *G, g*..............	Prov 30:8	5414
two daughters, crying, *G, g*..............	Prov 30:15	3051
G not thy strength unto women, ...	Prov 30:15	3051
G strong drink unto him that is	Prov 31:3	5414
G her of the fruit of her hands	Prov 31:6	5414
mine heart to *g* myself unto wine	Prov 31:31	5414
that he may *g* to him that is good	Eccl 2:3	4900
than to *g* the sacrifice of fools	Eccl 2:26	5414
G a portion to seven, and also to	Eccl 5:1	5414
the tender grape *g* a good smell	Eccl 11:2	5414
there will I *g* thee my loves	Song 2:13	5414
The mandrakes *g* a smell, and at	Song 7:12	5414
if a man would *g* all the	Song 7:13	5414
O heavens, and *g* ear, O earth	Song 8:7	5414
g ear unto the law of our God, ye	Is 1:2	
I will *g* children to be their..............	Is 1:10	
Lord himself shall *g* you a sign..........	Is 3:4	5414
of milk that they shall *g*	Is 7:14	5414
g ear, all ye of far countries............	Is 7:22	6213
of my wrath will I *g* him a charge	Is 8:9	
thereof shall not *g* their light	Is 10:6	
	Is 13:10	

shall *g* thee rest from thy sorrow .... Is 14:3
the Egyptians will I *g* over into .... Is 19:4 | 5534
G ye ear, and hear my voice .... Is 28:23
though the Lord *g* you the bread .... Is 30:20 | 5414
Then shall he *g* the rain of thy .... Is 30:23 | 5414
g ear unto my speech .... Is 32:9
Now therefore *g* pledges, I pray .... Is 36:8
I will *g* thee two thousand horses .... Is 36:8 | 5414
I will *g* to Jerusalem one that .... Is 41:27 | 5414
g thee for a covenant of the .... Is 42:6 | 5414
my glory will I not *g* to another .... Is 42:8 | 5414
Let them *g* glory unto the LORD, ... Is 42:12 | 7760
Who among you will *g* ear to this .... Is 42:23
therefore will I *g* men for thee .... Is 43:4 | 5414
I will say to the north, *G* up .... Is 43:6 | 5414
because I *g* waters in the .... Is 43:20 | 5414
to *g* drink to my people, my .... Is 43:20
I will *g* thee the treasures of .... Is 45:3 | 5414
I will not *g* my glory unto .... Is 48:11 | 5414
I will also *g* thee for a light to .... Is 49:6 | 5414
g thee for a covenant of the .... Is 49:8 | 5414
place to me that I may dwell................. Is 49:20 | 5066
g ear unto me, O my nation .... Is 51:4
that it may *g* seed to the sower, ... Is 55:10 | 5414
unto them will I *g* in mine house .... Is 56:5 | 5414
I will *g* them an everlasting name .... Is 56:5 | 5414
shall the moon *g* light unto thee .... Is 60:19
to *g* unto them beauty for ashes, ... Is 61:3 | 5414
g him no rest, till he establish, ... Is 62:7 | 5414
Surely I will no more *g* thy corn .... Is 62:8 | 5414
I will *g* you pastors according to .... Jer 3:15 | 5414
g thee a pleasant land, a goodly .... Jer 3:19 | 5414
now also will I *g* sentence .... Jer 4:12 | 1696
g out their voice against the .... Jer 4:16 | 5414
g warning, that they may hear .... Jer 6:10
Therefore will I *g* their wives .... Jer 8:10 | 5414
g them water of gall to drink .... Jer 9:15
to *g* them a land flowing with .... Jer 11:5 | 5414
Hear ye, and *g* ear .... Jer 13:15
G glory to the LORD your God, ... Jer 13:16 | 5414
but I will *g* you assured peace in .... Jer 14:13 | 5414
or can the heavens *g* showers .... Jer 14:22 | 5414
thy treasures will I *g* to the .... Jer 15:13 | 5414
neither shall men *g* them the cup .... Jer 16:7
I will *g* thy substance and all thy .... Jer 17:3 | 5414
even to *g* every man according to .... Jer 17:10 | 5414
let us not *g* heed to any of his .... Jer 18:18
G heed to me, O LORD, and hearken ...... Jer 18:19
their carcases will I *g* to be .... Jer 19:7 | 5414
I will *g* all Judah into the hand .... Jer 20:4 | 5414
of the kings of Judah will I *g* .... Jer 20:5 | 5414
I will *g* thee into the hand of .... Jer 22:25 | 5414
I will *g* them an heart to know me .... Jer 24:7 | 5414
So will I *g* Zedekiah the king of .... Jer 24:8 | 5414
he shall *g* a shout, as they that............ Jer 25:30
he will *g* them that are wicked to .... Jer 25:31 | 5414
that they should not *g* him into .... Jer 26:24 | 5414
g your daughters to husbands, ... Jer 29:6 | 5414
of evil, to *g* you an expected end .... Jer 29:11 | 5414
upon thee will I *g* for a prey .... Jer 30:16 | 5414
I will *g* this city into the hand .... Jer 32:3 | 5414
to *g* every one according to his .... Jer 32:19 | 5414
swear to their fathers to *g* them .... Jer 32:22 | 5414
I will *g* this city into the hand .... Jer 32:28 | 5414
I will *g* them one heart, and one .... Jer 32:39 | 5414
I will *g* this city into the hand .... Jer 34:2 | 5414
I will *g* the men that have .... Jer 34:18 | 5414
I will even *g* them into the hand .... Jer 34:20 | 5414
his princes will I *g* into the .... Jer 34:21 | 5414
chambers, and *g* them wine to drink ..... Jer 35:2
that they should *g* him daily a .... Jer 37:21 | 5414
if I *g* thee counsel, wilt thou .... Jer 38:15
neither shall I *g* thee into the .... Jer 38:16 | 5414
I will *g* Pharaoh-hophra king of .... Jer 44:30 | 5414
but thy life will I *g* unto thee .... Jer 45:5 | 5414
G wings unto Moab, that it may .... Jer 48:9 | 5414
that he may *g* rest to the land, ... Jer 50:34
g thyself no rest .... Lam 2:18 | 5414
G them sorrow of heart, thy curse......... Lam 3:65 | 5414
they *g* suck to their young ones .... Lam 4:3
thy mouth, and eat that I *g* thee .... Eze 2:8 | 5414
with this roll that I *g* thee .... Eze 3:3 | 5414
mouth, and *g* them warning from me ..... Eze 3:17
I will *g* it into the hands of the .... Eze 7:21 | 5414
g wicked counsel in this city .... Eze 11:2
I will *g* you the land of Israel .... Eze 11:17 | 5414
I will *g* them one heart, and I............... Eze 11:19 | 5414
will *g* them an heart of flesh .... Eze 11:19 | 5414
so will I *g* the inhabitants of .... Eze 15:6 | 5414
They *g* gifts to all whores .... Eze 16:33 | 5414
which thou didst *g* unto them .... Eze 16:36 | 5414

I will *g* thee blood in fury and............. Eze 16:38 | 5414
I will also *g* thee into their .... Eze 16:39 | 5414
thou also shalt *g* no hire any .... Eze 16:41 | 5414
I will *g* them unto thee for .... Eze 16:61 | 5414
that they might *g* him horses .... Eze 17:15 | 5414
up mine hand to *g* it to them .... Eze 20:28 | 5414
mine hand to *g* it to your fathers .... Eze 20:42 | 5414
to *g* it into the hand of the .... Eze 21:11 | 5414
and I will *g* it him .... Eze 21:27 | 5414
therefore will I *g* her cup into .... Eze 23:31 | 5414
will *g* them to be removed and .... Eze 23:46 | 5414
will *g* them in possession, that .... Eze 25:10 | 5414
I will *g* the land of Egypt unto .... Eze 29:19 | 5414
I will *g* thee the opening of the .... Eze 29:21 | 5414
and the moon shall not *g* her light .... Eze 32:7
g again that he had robbed, walk .... Eze 33:15 | 7999
is in the open field will I *g* to .... Eze 33:27 | 5414
A new heart also will I *g* you .... Eze 36:26 | 5414
I will *g* you an heart of flesh .... Eze 36:26 | 5414
I will *g* thee unto the ravenous .... Eze 39:4 | 5414
that I will *g* unto Gog a place .... Eze 39:11 | 5414
thou shalt *g* to the priests the .... Eze 43:19 | 5414
ye shall *g* them no possession in .... Eze 44:28 | 5414
ye shall also *g* unto the priest .... Eze 44:30 | 5414
they *g* to the house of Israel .... Eze 45:8 | 5414
ye shall *g* the sixth part of an .... Eze 45:13
the people of the land shall *g* ...... Eze 45:16 | 1961,413
part to *g* burnt offerings .... Eze 45:17
lambs as he shall be able to *g* .... Eze 46:5 | 4991
to the lambs as he is able to *g* .... Eze 46:11 | 4991
If the prince *g* a gift unto any .... Eze 46:16 | 5414
But if he *g* a gift of his .... Eze 46:17 | 5414
but he shall *g* his sons .... Eze 46:18
hand to *g* it unto your fathers .... Eze 47:14 | 5414
there shall ye *g* him his .... Eze 47:23 | 5414
let them *g* us pulse to eat, and .... Dan 1:12 | 5415
the king that he would *g* him time .... Dan 2:16 | 5415
and *g* thy rewards to another .... Dan 5:17 | 3052
might *g* accounts unto them .... Dan 6:2 | 3052
to *g* both the sanctuary and the .... Dan 8:13 | 5414
am now come forth to *g* thee skill .... Dan 9:22
he shall *g* him the daughter of .... Dan 11:17 | 5414
to whom they shall not *g* the .... Dan 11:21 | 5414
that *g* me my bread and my water, ... Hos 2:5 | 5414
I will *g* her her vineyards from .... Hos 2:15 | 5414
rulers with shame do love, *G* ye .... Hos 4:18 | 3051
g ye ear, O house of the king .... Hos 5:1
G them, O LORD .... Hos 9:14 | 5414
what wilt thou *g* .... Hos 9:14 | 5414
g them a miscarrying womb and dry ..... Hos 9:14 | 5414
How shall I *g* thee up, Ephraim .... Hos 11:8 | 5414
saidst, *G* me a king and princes .... Hos 13:10 | 5414
g ear, all ye inhabitants of the .... Joel 1:2
g not thine heritage to reproach, ... Joel 2:17 | 5414
Therefore shalt thou *g* presents .... Mic 1:14 | 5414
Therefore will he *g* them up .... Mic 5:3 | 5414
shall I *g* my firstborn for my .... Mic 6:7 | 5414
will I *g* up to the sword .... Mic 6:14 | 5414
and in this place will I *g* peace .... Hag 2:9 | 5414
I will *g* thee places to walk .... Zec 3:7 | 5414
the vine shall *g* her fruit .... Zec 8:12 | 5414
the ground shall *g* her increase .... Zec 8:12 | 5414
and the heavens shall *g* their dew .... Zec 8:12 | 5414
g them showers of rain, to every .... Zec 10:1 | 5414
If ye think good, *g* me my price .... Zec 11:12 | 3051
to *g* glory unto my name, saith .... Mal 2:2 | 5414
He shall *g* his angels charge .... Mt 4:6
All these things will I *g* thee .... Mt 4:9 | 1325
let him *g* her a writing of .... Mt 5:31 | 1325
G to him that asketh thee, and .... Mt 5:42 | 1325
G us this day our daily bread .... Mt 6:11 | 1325
G not that which is holy unto the.......... Mt 7:6 | 1325
ask bread, will he *g* him a stone .... Mt 7:9 | 1929
a fish, will he *g* him a serpent .... Mt 7:10 | 1929
know how to *g* good gifts unto .... Mt 7:11 | 1325
g good things to them that ask .... Mt 7:11 | 1325
He said unto them, *G* place .... Mt 9:24 | 402
freely ye have received, freely *g* .... Mt 10:8 | 1325
whosoever shall *g* to drink unto .... Mt 10:42 | 4222
heavy laden, and I will *g* you rest .... Mt 11:28
they shall *g* account thereof in .... Mt 12:36 | 591
he promised with an oath to *g* her .... Mt 14:7 | 1325
G me here John Baptist's head in .... Mt 14:8 | 1325
g ye them to eat .... Mt 14:16 | 1325
I will *g* unto thee the keys of .... Mt 16:19 | 1325
or what shall a man *g* in exchange .... Mt 16:26 | 1325
g unto them for me and thee .... Mt 17:27 | 1325
to *g* a writing of divorcement .... Mt 19:7 | 1325
g to the poor, and thou shalt have .... Mt 19:21 | 1325
whatsoever is right I will *g* you............. Mt 20:4
g them their hire, beginning from .... Mt 20:8 | 591

I will *g* unto this last, even as	Mt 20:14	1325
and on my left, is not mine to *g*	Mt 20:23	1325
to *g* his life a ransom for many	Mt 20:28	1325
Is it lawful to *g* tribute unto	Mt 22:17	1325
to them that *g* suck in those days	Mt 24:19	
and the moon shall not *g* her light	Mt 24:29	1325
to *g* them meat in due season	Mt 24:45	1325
unto the wise, *G* us of your oil	Mt 25:8	1325
g it unto him which hath ten	Mt 25:28	1325
said unto them, What will ye *g* me	Mt 26:15	1325
he shall presently *g* me more than	Mt 26:53	3936
thou wilt, and I will *g* it thee	Mk 6:22	1325
I will *g* it thee, unto the half	Mk 6:23	1325
saying, I will that thou *g* me by	Mk 6:25	1325
said unto them, *G* ye them to eat	Mk 6:37	1325
of bread, and *g* them to eat	Mk 6:37	1325
Or what shall a man *g* in exchange	Mk 8:37	1325
For whosoever shall *g* you a cup	Mk 9:41	4222
g to the poor, and thou shalt have	Mk 10:21	1325
on my left hand is not mine to *g*	Mk 10:40	1325
to *g* his life a ransom for many	Mk 10:45	1325
will *g* the vineyard unto others	Mk 12:9	1325
Is it lawful to *g* tribute to	Mk 12:14	1325
Shall we *g*, or shall we not *g*	Mk 12:15	1325
to them that *g* suck in those days	Mk 13:17	
and the moon shall not *g* her light	Mk 13:24	1325
glad, and promised to *g* him money	Mk 14:11	1325
the Lord God shall *g* unto him the	Lk 1:32	1325
To *g* knowledge of salvation unto	Lk 1:77	1325
To *g* light to them that sit in	Lk 1:79	2014
him, All this power will I *g* thee	Lk 4:6	1325
and to whomsoever I will I *g* it	Lk 4:6	1325
He shall *g* his angels charge over	Lk 4:10	
G to every man that asketh of	Lk 6:30	1325
G, and it shall be given unto you	Lk 6:38	1325
shall men *g* into your bosom	Lk 6:38	1325
and he commanded to *g* her meat	Lk 8:55	1325
said unto them, *G* ye them to eat	Lk 9:13	1325
and drinking such things as they *g*	Lk 10:7	3844
I *g* unto you power to tread on	Lk 10:19	1325
G us day by day our daily bread	Lk 11:3	1325
I cannot rise and *g* thee	Lk 11:7	1325
g him, because he is his friend	Lk 11:8	1325
g him as many as he needeth	Lk 11:8	1325
a father, will he *g* him a stone	Lk 11:11	1929
he for a fish *g* him a serpent	Lk 11:11	1929
know how to *g* good gifts unto	Lk 11:13	1325
g the Holy Spirit to them that	Lk 11:13	1325
of a candle doth *g* thee light	Lk 11:36	5461
But rather *g* alms of such things	Lk 11:41	1325
pleasure to *g* you the kingdom	Lk 12:32	1325
Sell that ye have, and *g* alms	Lk 12:33	1325
to *g* them their portion of meat	Lk 12:42	1325
I am come to *g* peace on earth	Lk 12:51	1325
g diligence that thou mayest be	Lk 12:58	1325
and say to thee, *G* this man place	Lk 14:9	1325
g me the portion of goods that	Lk 15:12	1325
g an account of thy stewardship	Lk 16:2	591
who shall *g* you that which is	Lk 16:12	1325
that returned to *g* glory to God	Lk 17:18	1325
I *g* tithes of all that I possess	Lk 18:12	1325
half of my goods I *g* to the poor	Lk 19:8	1325
g it to him that hath ten pounds	Lk 19:24	1325
that they should *g* him of the	Lk 20:10	1325
shall *g* the vineyard to others	Lk 20:16	1325
for us to *g* tribute unto Caesar	Lk 20:22	1325
For I will *g* you a mouth and	Lk 21:15	1325
child, and to them that *g* suck	Lk 21:23	
and covenanted to *g* him money	Lk 22:5	1325
forbidding to *g* tribute to Caesar	Lk 23:2	1325
that we may *g* an answer to them	Jn 1:22	1325
saith unto her, *G* me to drink	Jn 4:7	1325
that saith to thee, *G* me to drink	Jn 4:10	1325
I shall *g* him shall never thirst	Jn 4:14	1325
but the water that I shall *g* him	Jn 4:14	1325
g me this water, that I thirst	Jn 4:15	1325
the Son of man shall *g* unto you	Jn 6:27	1325
Lord, evermore *g* us this bread	Jn 6:34	1325
bread that I will *g* is my flesh	Jn 6:51	1325
which I will *g* for the life of	Jn 6:51	1325
How can this man *g* us his flesh	Jn 6:52	1325
Did not Moses *g* you the law	Jn 7:19	1325
said unto him, *G* God the praise	Jn 9:24	1325
I *g* unto them eternal life	Jn 10:28	1325
ask of God, God will *g* it thee	Jn 11:22	1325
He it is, to whom I shall *g* a sop	Jn 13:26	1929
that he should *g* something to the	Jn 13:29	1325
A new commandment I *g* unto you	Jn 13:34	1325
he shall *g* you another Comforter,	Jn 14:16	1325
with you, my peace I *g* unto you	Jn 14:27	1325
as the world giveth, *g* I unto you	Jn 14:27	1325

in my name, he may *g* it you	Jn 15:16	1325
in my name, he will *g* it you	Jn 16:23	1325
that he should *g* eternal life to	Jn 17:2	1325
but such as I have *g* I thee	Acts 3:6	1325
for to *g* repentance to Israel, and	Acts 5:31	1325
But we will *g* ourselves	Acts 6:4	4342
g it to him for a possession	Acts 7:5	1325
the lively oracles to *g* unto us	Acts 7:38	1325
G me also this power, that on	Acts 8:19	1325
To him *g* all the prophets witness	Acts 10:43	
and ye that fear God, *g* audience	Acts 13:16	
I will *g* you the sure mercies of	Acts 13:34	1325
g an account of this concourse	Acts 19:40	591
to *g* you an inheritance among all	Acts 20:32	1325
more blessed to *g* than to receive	Acts 20:35	1325
him also freely *g* us all things	Rom 8:32	5483
but rather *g* place unto wrath	Rom 12:19	1325
if he thirst, *g* him drink	Rom 12:20	4222
shall *g* account of himself to God	Rom 14:12	1325
unto whom not only I *g* thanks	Rom 16:4	
that ye may *g* yourselves to	1Cor 7:5	4980
yet I *g* my judgment, as one that	1Cor 7:25	1325
of for that for which I *g* thanks	1Cor 10:30	
G none offence, neither to the	1Cor 10:32	1096
Wherefore I *g* you to understand,	1Cor 12:3	
though I *g* my body to be burned,	1Cor 13:3	3860
except they *g* a distinction in	1Cor 14:7	1325
the trumpet give an uncertain sound	1Cor 14:8	1325
to *g* the light of the knowledge	2Cor 4:6	
but *g* you occasion to glory on	2Cor 5:12	4222
And herein I *g* my advice	2Cor 8:10	1325
in his heart, so let him *g*	2Cor 9:7	
Cease not to *g* thanks for you,	Eph 1:16	
may *g* unto you the spirit of	Eph 1:17	1325
Neither *g* place to the devil	Eph 4:27	1325
may have to *g* to him that needeth	Eph 4:28	3330
and Christ shall *g* thee light	Eph 5:14	
We *g* thanks to God and the Father	Col 1:3	
g unto your servants that which	Col 4:1	3930
We *g* thanks to God always for you	1Th 1:16	
In every thing *g* thanks	1Th 5:18	
But we are bound to *g* thanks,	2Th 2:13	
g you peace always by all means	2Th 3:16	1325
Neither *g* heed to fables and	1Ti 1:4	
g attendance to reading, to	1Ti 4:13	
g thyself wholly to them	1Ti 4:15	2468
And these things *g* in charge	1Ti 5:7	
g none occasion to the adversary	1Ti 5:14	1325
I *g* thee charge in the sight of	1Ti 6:13	
The Lord *g* mercy unto the house	2Ti 1:16	1325
the Lord *g* thee understanding in	2Ti 2:7	1325
will *g* them repentance to the	2Ti 2:25	1325
judge, shall *g* me at that day	2Ti 4:8	591
Therefore we ought to *g* the more	Heb 2:1	
as they that must *g* account	Heb 13:17	591
notwithstanding ye *g* them not	Jas 2:16	1325
be ready always to *g* an answer to	1Pet 3:15	
Who shall *g* account to him that	1Pet 4:5	591
g diligence to make your calling	2Pet 1:10	
he shall *g* him life for them that	1Jn 5:16	1325
I *g* to eat of the tree of life	Rev 2:7	1325
I will *g* thee a crown of life	Rev 2:10	1325
I *g* to eat of the hidden manna	Rev 2:17	1325
will *g* him a white stone, and in	Rev 2:17	1325
I will *g* unto every one of you	Rev 2:23	1325
to him will I *g* power over the	Rev 2:26	1325
I will *g* him the morning star	Rev 2:28	1325
And when those beasts *g* glory	Rev 4:9	1325
unto him, *G* me the little book	Rev 10:9	1325
I will *g* power unto my two	Rev 11:3	1325
We *g* thee thanks, O Lord God	Rev 11:17	
that thou shouldest *g* reward unto	Rev 11:18	1325
he had power to *g* life unto the	Rev 13:15	1325
Fear God, and *g* glory to him	Rev 14:7	1325
they repented not to *g* him glory	Rev 16:9	1325
to *g* unto her the cup of the wine	Rev 16:19	1325
shall *g* their power and strength	Rev 17:13	1239
g their kingdom unto the beast,	Rev 17:17	1325
so much torment and sorrow *g* her	Rev 18:7	1325
and rejoice, and *g* honour to him	Rev 19:7	1325
I will *g* unto him that is athirst	Rev 21:6	1325
to *g* every man according as his	Rev 22:12	591

GIVEN See APPENDIX.

GIVER
so with the *g* of usury to him	Is 24:2	
for God loveth a cheerful *g*	2Cor 9:7	1395

GIVEST
brother, and thou *g* him nought	Deut 15:9	5414
be grieved when thou *g* unto him	Deut 15:10	5414

G

be righteous, what *g* thou him	Job 35:7	5414
Thou *g* thy mouth to evil, and thy	Ps 50:19	7971
g them tears to drink in great	Ps 80:5	
That thou *g* them they gather	Ps 104:28	5414
thou *g* them their meat in due	Ps 145:15	5414
content, though thou *g* many gifts	Prov 6:35	
thou *g* him not warning, nor	Eze 3:18	
but thou *g* thy gifts to all thy	Eze 16:33	5414
and in that thou *g* a reward	Eze 16:34	5414
For thou verily *g* thanks well	1Cor 14:17	

GIVETH See APPENDIX.

GIVING

And when she had done *g* him drink	Gen 24:19	
in *g* him food and raiment	Deut 10:18	5414
by *g* him a double portion of all	Deut 21:17	5414
his people in *g* them bread	Ruth 1:6	5414
in *g* food for my household	1Kin 5:9	5414
by *g* him according to his	2Chr 6:23	5414
and *g* thanks unto the LORD	Ezr 3:11	
shall be as the *g* up of the ghost	Job 11:20	4646
g in marriage, until the day that	Mt 24:38	
face at his feet, *g* him thanks	Lk 17:16	
g out that himself was some great	Acts 8:9	3004
g them the Holy Ghost, even as he	Acts 15:8	1325
strong in faith, *g* glory to God	Rom 4:20	
the *g* of the law, and the service	Rom 9:4	3548
even things without life *g* sound	1Cor 14:7	1325
say Amen at thy *g* of thanks	1Cor 14:16	
G no offence in any thing, that	2Cor 6:3	1325
but rather *g* of thanks	Eph 5:4	
G thanks always for all things	Eph 5:20	
with me as concerning *g* and	Phil 4:15	1394
G thanks unto the Father, which	Col 1:12	
g thanks to God and the Father by	Col 3:17	
g of thanks, be made for all men	1Ti 2:1	
g heed to seducing spirits, and	1Ti 4:1	
Not *g* heed to Jewish fables, and	Titus 1:14	
of our lips *g* thanks to his name	Heb 13:15	
g honour unto the wife, as unto	1Pet 3:7	632
g all diligence, add to your	2Pet 1:5	3923
g themselves over to fornication,	Jude 7	

GIZONITE *(ghi'-zo-nite) A bodyguard of David.*

The sons of Hashem the *G*,	1Chr 11:34	1493

GLAD

he will be *g* in his heart	Ex 4:14	8056
And the priest's heart was *g*	Judg 18:20	8190
and they were *g*	1Sa 11:9	8056
g of heart for all the goodness	1Kin 8:66	2896
Let the heavens be *g*, and let the	1Chr 16:31	8056
people away into their tents, *g*	2Chr 7:10	8056
that day joyful and with a *g* heart	Est 5:9	2896
city of Shushan rejoiced and was *g*	Est 8:15	8056
rejoice exceedingly, and are *g*	Job 3:22	7797
The righteous see it, and are *g*	Job 22:19	8056
I will be *g* and rejoice in thee	Ps 9:2	8056
rejoice, and Israel shall be *g*	Ps 14:7	8056
Therefore my heart is *g*, and my	Ps 16:9	8056
exceeding *g* with thy countenance	Ps 21:6	2302
I will be *g* and rejoice in thy	Ps 31:7	1523
Be *g* in the LORD, and rejoice, ye	Ps 32:11	8056
shall hear thereof, and be *g*	Ps 34:2	8056
Let them shout for joy, and be *g*	Ps 35:27	8056
seek thee rejoice and be *g* in thee	Ps 40:16	8056
whereby they have made thee *g*	Ps 45:8	8056
shall make *g* the city of God	Ps 46:4	8056
let the daughters of Judah be *g*	Ps 48:11	1528
rejoice, and Israel shall be *g*	Ps 53:6	8056
righteous shall be *g* in the LORD	Ps 64:10	8056
O let the nations be *g* and sing	Ps 67:4	8056
But let the righteous be *g*	Ps 68:3	8056
humble shall see this, and be *g*	Ps 69:32	8056
seek thee rejoice and be *g* in thee	Ps 70:4	8056
may rejoice and be *g* all our days	Ps 90:14	8056
Make us *g* according to the days	Ps 90:15	8056
hast made me *g* through thy work	Ps 92:4	8056
rejoice, and let the earth be *g*	Ps 96:11	1523
multitude of isles be *g* thereof	Ps 97:1	8056
Zion heard, and was *g*	Ps 97:8	8056
that maketh *g* the heart of man	Ps 104:15	8056
I will be *g* in the LORD	Ps 104:34	8056
Egypt was *g* when they departed	Ps 105:38	8056
Then are they *g* because they be	Ps 107:30	8056
we will rejoice and be *g* in it	Ps 118:24	8056
thee will be *g* when they see me	Ps 119:74	8056
I was *g* when they said unto me,	Ps 122:1	8056
whereof we are *g*	Ps 126:3	8056
A wise son maketh a *g* father	Prov 10:1	8056
but a good word maketh it *g*	Prov 12:25	8056
A wise son maketh a *g* father	Prov 15:20	8056

he that is *g* at calamities shall	Prov 17:5	8056
father and thy mother shall be *g*	Prov 23:25	8056
heart be *g* when he stumbleth	Prov 24:17	1523
son, be wise, and make my heart *g*	Prov 27:11	8056
we will be *g* and rejoice in thee,	Song 1:4	1528
have waited for him, we will be *g*	Is 25:9	1528
place shall be *g* for them	Is 35:1	7996
And Hezekiah was *g* of them	Is 39:2	8056
But be ye *g* and rejoice for ever	Is 65:18	7796
be *g* with her, all ye that love	Is 66:10	1528
making him very *g*	Jer 20:15	8056
were with him, then they were *g*	Jer 41:13	8056
Because ye were *g*, because ye	Jer 50:11	8056
they are *g* that thou hast done it	Lam 1:21	7796
Rejoice and be *g*, O daughter of	Lam 4:21	8056
was the king exceeding *g* for him	Dan 6:23	2868
They make the king *g* with their	Hos 7:3	8056
be *g* and rejoice	Joel 2:21	1523
Be *g* then, ye children of Zion,	Joel 2:23	1523
was exceeding *g* of the gourd	Jonah 4:6	8056
therefore they rejoice and are *g*	Hab 1:15	1523
be *g* and rejoice with all the	Zeph 3:14	8056
children shall see it, and be *g*	Zec 10:7	8056
Rejoice, and be exceeding *g*	Mt 5:12	21
when they heard it, they were *g*	Mk 14:11	5463
and to shew thee these *g* tidings	Lk 1:19	2097
shewing the *g* tidings of the	Lk 8:1	2097
we should make merry, and be *g*	Lk 15:32	5463
And they were *g*, and covenanted to	Lk 22:5	5463
saw Jesus, he was exceeding *g*	Lk 23:8	5463
and he saw it, and was *g*	Jn 8:56	5463
I am *g* for your sakes that I was	Jn 11:15	5463
Then were the disciples *g*	Jn 20:20	5463
heart rejoice, and my tongue was *g*	Acts 2:26	21
had seen the grace of God, was *g*	Acts 11:23	5463
And we declare unto you *g* tidings	Acts 13:32	2097
Gentiles heard this, they were *g*	Acts 13:48	5463
bring *g* tidings of good things	Rom 10:15	2097
I am *g* therefore on your behalf	Rom 16:19	5463
I am *g* of the coming of Stephanas	1Cor 16:17	5463
who is he then that maketh me *g*	2Cor 2:2	2165
For we are *g*, when we are weak,	2Cor 13:9	5463
ye may be *g* also with exceeding	1Pet 4:13	5463
Let us be *g* and rejoice, and give	Rev 19:7	5463

GLADLY

did many things, and heard him *g*	Mk 6:20	2234
And the common people heard him *g*	Mk 12:37	2234
the people *g* received him	Lk 8:40	
Then they that *g* received his	Acts 2:41	780
the brethren received us *g*	Acts 21:17	780
For ye suffer fools *g*, seeing ye	2Cor 11:19	2234
Most *g* therefore will I rather	2Cor 12:9	2236
And I will very *g* spend and be	2Cor 12:15	2236

GLADNESS

Also in the day of your *g*	Num 10:10	8057
and with *g* of heart, for the	Deut 28:47	2898
into the city of David with *g*	2Sa 6:12	8057
strength and *g* are in his place	1Chr 16:27	2304
the LORD on that day with great *g*	1Chr 29:22	8057
And they sang praises with *g*	2Chr 29:30	8057
bread seven days with great *g*	2Chr 30:21	8057
they kept other seven days with *g*	2Chr 30:23	8057
And there was very great *g*	Neh 8:17	8057
to keep the dedication with *g*	Neh 12:27	8057
The Jews had light, and *g*, and joy,	Est 8:16	8057
came, the Jews had joy and *g*	Est 8:17	8342
and made it a day of feasting and *g*	Est 9:17	8057
and made it a day of feasting and *g*	Est 9:18	8057
day of the month Adar a day of *g*	Est 9:19	8057
Thou hast put *g* in my heart	Ps 4:7	8057
my sackcloth, and girded me with *g*	Ps 30:11	8057
the oil of *g* above thy fellows	Ps 45:7	8342
With *g* and rejoicing shall they be	Ps 45:15	8057
Make me to hear joy and *g*	Ps 51:8	8057
g for the upright in heart	Ps 97:11	8057
Serve the LORD with *g*	Ps 100:2	8057
with joy, and his chosen with *g*	Ps 105:43	7440
rejoice in the *g* of thy nation	Ps 106:5	8057
hope of the righteous shall be *g*	Prov 10:28	8057
in the day of the *g* of his heart	Song 3:11	8057
g is taken away, and joy out of	Is 16:10	8057
And behold joy and *g*, slaying oxen,	Is 22:13	8057
g of heart, as when one goeth	Is 30:29	8057
they shall obtain joy and *g*	Is 35:10	8057
g shall be found therein,	Is 51:3	8057
they shall obtain *g* and joy	Is 51:11	8057
voice of mirth, and the voice of *g*	Jer 7:34	8057
voice of mirth, and the voice of *g*	Jer 16:9	8057
voice of mirth, and the voice of *g*	Jer 25:10	8057
Sing with *g* for Jacob, and shout	Jer 31:7	8057

voice of joy, and the voice of *g* ....Jer 33:11   8057
g is taken from the plentiful ....Jer 48:33   8057
g from the house of our God ....Joel 1:16   1524
be to the house of Judah joy and *g* ....Zec 8:19   8057
immediately receive it with *g* ....Mk 4:16   5479
And thou shalt have joy and *g* ....Lk 1:14   20
house, did eat their meat with *g* ....Acts 2:46   20
she opened not the gate for *g* ....Acts 12:14   5479
filling our hearts with food and *g* ....Acts 14:17   2167
therefore in the Lord with all *g* ....Phil 2:29   5479
the oil of *g* above thy fellows ....Heb 1:9   20

GLASS
strong, and as a molten looking *g* ....Job 37:18   7209
For now we see through a *g* 1Cor 13:12   2072
as in a *g* the glory of the Lord................2Cor 3:18   2734
beholding his natural face in a *g* ....Jas 1:23   2072
was a sea of *g* like unto crystal ....Rev 4:6   5193
were a sea of *g* mingled with fire ....Rev 15:2   5193
his name, stand on the sea of *g* ....Rev 15:2   5193
was pure gold, like unto clear *g* ....Rev 21:18   5194
gold, as it were transparent *g* ....Rev 21:21   5194

GLASSES
The *g*, and the fine linen, and the ....Is 3:23   1549

GLEAN
And thou shalt not *g* thy vineyard ....Lev 19:10   5953
thou shalt not *g* it afterward ....Deut 24:21   5953
g ears of corn after him in whose ....Ruth 2:2   3950
And she said, I pray you, let me *g* ....Ruth 2:7   3950
Go not to *g* in another field, ...Ruth 2:8   3950
And when she was risen up to *g* ....Ruth 2:15   3950
Let her *g* even among the sheaves, ...Ruth 2:15   3950
leave them, that she may *g* them ....Ruth 2:16   3950
g unto the end of barley harvest ....Ruth 2:23   3950
They shall throughly *g* the ....Jer 6:9   5953

GLEANED
they *g* of them in the highways ....Judg 20:45   5953
g in the field after the reapers ....Ruth 2:3   3950
So she *g* in the field until even, ...Ruth 2:17   3950
even, and beat out that she had *g* ....Ruth 2:17   3950
mother in law saw what she had *g* ....Ruth 2:18   3950
her, Where hast thou *g* to day ....Ruth 2:19   3950

GLEANING
thou gather any *g* of thy harvest ....Lev 23:22   3951
Is not the *g* of the grapes of ....Judg 8:2   5955
Yet *g* grapes shall be left in it, ...Is 17:6   5955
as the *g* grapes when the vintage..........Is 24:13   5955
they will not leave some *g* grapes ....Jer 49:9   5955

GLEANINGS
thou gather the *g* of thy harvest ....Lev 19:9   3951

GLEDE
And the *g*, and the kite, and the ....Deut 14:13   7201

GLISTERING
g stones, and of divers colours, ...1Chr 29:2   6320
and his raiment was white and *g* ....Lk 9:29   1823

GLITTER
it is furbished that it may *g* ....Eze 21:10   1300

GLITTERING
If I whet my *g* sword, and mine ....Deut 32:41   1300
the *g* sword cometh out of his ....Job 20:25   1300
the *g* spear and the shield......................Job 39:23   3851
to consume because of the *g* ....Eze 21:28   1300
the bright sword and the *g* spear ....Nah 3:3   1300
and at the shining of thy *g* spear ....Hab 3:11   1300

GLOOMINESS
A day of darkness and of *g* ....Joel 2:2   653
a day of darkness and *g*, a day of..........Zeph 1:15   653

GLORIEST
Wherefore *g* thou in the valleys, ...Jer 49:4   1984

GLORIETH
But let him that *g* glory in this ....Jer 9:24   1984
as it is written, He that *g*.......................1Cor 1:31   2744
But he that *g*, let him glory in 2Cor 10:17   2744

GLORIFIED
before all the people I will be *g*..............Lev 10:3   3513
thou art *g* ....Is 26:15   3513
Jacob, and *g* himself in Israel ....Is 44:23   6286
O Israel, in whom I will be *g* ....Is 49:3   6286
for he hath *g* thee..................................Is 55:5   6286
of Israel, because he hath *g* thee ....Is 60:9   6286
work of my hands, that I may be *g*..........Is 60:21   6286
of the Lord, that he might be *g* ....Is 61:3   6286
sake, said, Let the Lord be *g* ....Is 66:5   3513
I will be *g* in the midst of thee ....Eze 28:22   3513
renown the day that I shall be *g* ....Eze 39:13   3513

are all thy ways, hast thou not *g* ....Dan 5:23   1922
pleasure in it, and I will be *g* ....Hag 1:8   3513
g God, which had given such power ......Mt 9:8   1392
and they *g* the God of Israel ....Mt 15:31   1392
g God, saying, We never saw it on ....Mk 2:12   1392
their synagogues, being *g* of all............Lk 4:15   1392
were all amazed, and they *g* God ....Lk 5:26   1392
and they *g* God, saying, That a ....Lk 7:16   1392
she was made straight, and *g* God ....Lk 13:13   1392
back, and with a loud voice *g* God ....Lk 17:15   1392
he *g* God, saying, Certainly this ....Lk 23:47   1392
because that Jesus was not yet *g* ....Jn 7:39   1392
the Son of God might be *g* thereby ......Jn 11:4   1392
but when Jesus was *g*, then ....Jn 12:16   1392
that the Son of man should be *g* ....Jn 12:23   1392
heaven, saying, I have both *g* it ....Jn 12:28   1392
said, Now is the Son of man *g* ....Jn 13:31   1392
man *g*, and God is *g* in him ....Jn 13:31   1392
If God be *g* in him, God shall ....Jn 13:32   1392
the Father may be *g* in the Son ....Jn 14:13   1392
Herein is my Father *g*, that ye ....Jn 15:8   1392
I have *g* thee on the earth ....Jn 17:4   1392
and I am *g* in them ....Jn 17:10   1392
our fathers, hath *g* his Son Jesus ....Acts 3:13   1392
for all men *g* God for that which ....Acts 4:21   1392
g God, saying, Then hath God also ....Acts 11:18   1392
glad, and *g* the word of the Lord ....Acts 13:48   1392
they *g* the Lord, and said unto him ......Acts 21:20   1392
they *g* him not as God, neither ....Rom 1:21   1392
that we may be also *g* together ....Rom 8:17   4888
whom he justified, them he also *g* ....Rom 8:30   1392
And they *g* God in me ....Gal 1:24   1392
shall come to be *g* in his saints...........2Th 1:10   1740
Lord Jesus Christ may be *g* in you 2Th 1:12   1740
may have free course, and be *g* 2Th 3:1   1392
So also Christ *g* not himself to ....Heb 5:5   1392
may be *g* through Jesus Christ 1Pet 4:11   1392
of, but on your part he is *g* 1Pet 4:14   1392
How much she hath *g* herself ....Rev 18:7   1392

GLORIFIETH
Whoso offereth praise *g* me ....Ps 50:23   3513

GLORIFY
all ye the seed of Jacob, *g* him..............Ps 22:23   3513
deliver thee, and thou shalt *g* me..........Ps 50:15   3513
and shall *g* thy name ....Ps 86:9   3513
I will *g* thy name for evermore ....Ps 86:12   3513
Wherefore *g* ye the Lord in the ....Is 24:15   3513
shall the strong people *g* thee ....Is 25:3   3513
I will *g* the house of my glory.................Is 60:7   6286
I will also *g* them, and they shall............Jer 30:19   3513
g your Father which is in heaven ....Mt 5:16   1392
Father, *g* thy name ....Jn 12:28   1392
glorified it, and will *g* it again................Jn 12:28   1392
God shall also *g* him in himself..........Jn 13:32   1392
and shall straightway *g* him ....Jn 13:32   1392
He shall *g* me ....Jn 16:14   1392
the hour is come; *g* thy Son ....Jn 17:1   1392
that thy Son also may *g* thee ....Jn 17:1   1392
g* thou me with thine own self ....Jn 17:5   1392
by what death he should *g* God ....Jn 21:19   1392
with one mind and one mouth *g* God ....Rom 15:6   1392
might *g* God for his mercy ....Rom 15:9   1392
therefore *g* God in your body, and 1Cor 6:20   1392
they *g* God for your professed...............2Cor 9:13   1392
g God in the day of visitation................1Pet 2:12   1392
but let him *g* God on this behalf............1Pet 4:16   1392
fear thee, O Lord, and *g* thy name ....Rev 15:4   1392

GLORIFYING
And the shepherds returned, *g*..............Lk 2:20   1392
departed to his own house, *g* God ....Lk 5:25   1392
his sight, and followed him, *g* God.........Lk 18:43   1392

GLORIOUS
O Lord, is become *g* in power ....Ex 15:6   142
g in holiness, fearful in praises ....Ex 15:11   142
that thou mayest fear this *g* ....Deut 28:58   3513
How *g* was the king of Israel!.................2Sa 6:20   3513
thank thee, and praise thy *g* name 1Chr 29:13   8597
and blessed be thy *g* name, which ....Neh 9:5   3519
the riches of his *g* kingdom ....Est 1:4   3519
king's daughter is all *g* within ....Ps 45:13   3520
make his praise *g*...................................Ps 66:2   3519
And blessed be his *g* name for ever ....Ps 72:19   3519
Thou art more *g* and excellent than ....Ps 76:4   215
G things are spoken of thee, O ....Ps 87:3   3513
His work is honourable and *g* ....Ps 111:3   1926
I will speak of the *g* honour of ....Ps 145:5   3519
the *g* majesty of his kingdom ....Ps 145:12   3519
of the Lord be beautiful and *g*...............Is 4:2   3519
and his rest shall be *g*...........................Is 11:10   3519

he shall be for a *g* throne to his	Is 22:23	3519
whose *g* beauty is a fading flower	Is 28:1	6643
the *g* beauty, which is on the	Is 28:4	6643
cause his *g* voice to be heard	Is 30:30	1935
But there the *g* LORD will be unto	Is 33:21	117
yet shall I be *g* in the eyes of	Is 49:5	3513
will make the place of my feet *g*	Is 60:13	3513
this that is *g* in his apparel,	Is 63:1	1921
hand of Moses with his *g* arm	Is 63:12	8597
people, to make thyself a *g* name	Is 63:14	8597
A *g* high throne from the	Jer 17:12	3519
made very *g* in the midst of the	Eze 27:25	3519
and he shall stand in the *g* land	Dan 11:16	6643
shall enter also into the *g* land	Dan 11:41	6643
the seas in the *g* holy mountain	Dan 11:45	6643
g things that were done by him	Lk 13:17	1741
g liberty of the children of God	Rom 8:21	1391
and engraven in stones, was *g*	2Cor 3:7	1722,1391
of the spirit be rather *g*	2Cor 3:8	1722,1391
g had no glory in this respect	2Cor 3:10	1392
if that which is done away was *g*	2Cor 3:11	1223,1391
more that which remaineth is *g*	2Cor 3:11	1722,1391
light of the *g* gospel of Christ	2Cor 4:4	1391
present it to himself a *g* church	Eph 5:27	1741
be fashioned like unto his *g* body	Phil 3:21	1391
might, according to his *g* power	Col 1:11	1391
According to the *g* gospel of the	1Ti 1:11	1391
the *g* appearing of the great God	Titus 2:13	1391

GLORIOUSLY

the LORD, for he hath triumphed *g*	Ex 15:1	
the LORD, for he hath triumphed *g*	Ex 15:21	
and before his ancients *g*	Is 24:23	3519

GLORY

hath he gotten all this *g*	Gen 31:1	3519
my father of all my *g* in Egypt	Gen 45:13	3519
said unto Pharaoh, *G* over me	Ex 8:9	6286
ye shall see the *g* of the LORD	Ex 16:7	3519
the *g* of the LORD appeared in the	Ex 16:10	3519
the *g* of the LORD abode upon	Ex 24:16	3519
the sight of the *g* of the LORD	Ex 24:17	3519
for Aaron thy brother for *g*	Ex 28:2	3519
shalt thou make for them, for *g*	Ex 28:40	3519
shall be sanctified by my *g*	Ex 29:43	3519
I beseech thee, shew me thy *g*	Ex 33:18	3519
while my *g* passeth by, that I	Ex 33:22	3519
the *g* of the LORD filled the	Ex 40:34	3519
the *g* of the LORD filled the	Ex 40:35	3519
the *g* of the LORD shall appear	Lev 9:6	3519
the *g* of the LORD appeared unto	Lev 9:23	3519
the *g* of the LORD appeared in the	Num 14:10	3519
be filled with the *g* of the LORD	Num 14:21	3519
those men which have seen my *g*	Num 14:22	3519
the *g* of the LORD appeared unto	Num 16:19	3519
the *g* of the LORD appeared	Num 16:42	3519
the *g* of the LORD appeared unto	Num 20:6	3519
LORD our God hath shewed us his *g*	Deut 5:24	3519
His *g* is like the firstling of	Deut 33:17	1926
g to the LORD God of Israel, and	Josh 7:19	3519
make them inherit the throne of *g*	1Sa 2:8	3519
The *g* is departed from Israel	1Sa 4:21	3519
The *g* is departed from Israel	1Sa 4:22	3519
ye shall give *g* unto the God of	1Sa 6:5	3519
for the *g* of the LORD had filled	1Kin 8:11	3519
g of this, and tarry at home	2Kin 14:10	3513
G ye in his holy name	1Chr 16:10	1984
Declare his *g* among the heathen	1Chr 16:24	3519
G and honour are in his presence	1Chr 16:27	1935
the people, give unto the LORD *g*	1Chr 16:28	3519
the LORD the *g* due unto his name	1Chr 16:29	3519
thy holy name, and *g* in thy praise	1Chr 16:35	7623
of *g* throughout all countries	1Chr 22:5	8597
greatness, and the power, and the *g*	1Chr 29:11	8597
for the *g* of the LORD had filled	2Chr 5:14	3519
the *g* of the LORD filled the	2Chr 7:1	3519
because the *g* of the LORD had	2Chr 7:2	3519
the *g* of the LORD upon the house,	2Chr 7:3	3519
told them of the *g* of his riches	Est 5:11	3519
He hath stripped me of my *g*	Job 19:9	3519
My *g* was fresh in me, and my bow	Job 29:20	3519
the *g* of his nostrils is terrible	Job 39:20	1935
and array thyself with *g* and beauty	Job 40:10	1935
my *g*, and the lifter up of mine	Ps 3:3	3519
long will ye turn my *g* into shame	Ps 4:2	3519
who hast set thy *g* above the	Ps 8:1	1935
and hast crowned him with *g*	Ps 8:5	3519
heart is glad, and my *g* rejoiceth	Ps 16:9	3519
The heavens declare the *g* of God	Ps 19:1	3519
His *g* is great in thy salvation	Ps 21:5	3519
the King of *g* shall come in	Ps 24:7	3519
Who is this King of *g*	Ps 24:8	3519

the King of *g* shall come in	Ps 24:9	3519
Who is this King of *g*	Ps 24:10	3519
of hosts, he is the King of *g*	Ps 24:10	3519
O ye mighty, give unto the LORD *g*	Ps 29:1	3519
the LORD the *g* due unto his name	Ps 29:2	3519
the God of *g* thundereth	Ps 29:3	3519
doth every one speak of his *g*	Ps 29:9	3519
To the end that my *g* may sing	Ps 30:12	3519
thigh, O most mighty, with thy *g*	Ps 45:3	1935
when the *g* of his house is	Ps 49:16	3519
his *g* shall not descend after him	Ps 49:17	3519
let thy *g* be above all the earth	Ps 57:5	3519
Awake up, my *g*	Ps 57:8	3519
let thy *g* be above all the earth	Ps 57:11	3519
In God is my salvation and my *g*	Ps 62:7	3519
To see thy power and thy *g*	Ps 63:2	3519
one that sweareth by him shall *g*	Ps 63:11	1984
all the upright in heart shall *g*	Ps 64:10	1984
whole earth be filled with his *g*	Ps 72:19	3519
and afterward receive me to *g*	Ps 73:24	3519
his *g* into the enemy's hand	Ps 78:61	8597
salvation, for the *g* of thy name	Ps 79:9	3519
the LORD will give grace and *g*	Ps 84:11	3519
that *g* may dwell in our land	Ps 85:9	3519
For thou art the *g* of their	Ps 89:17	8597
Thou hast made his *g* to cease	Ps 89:44	2892
thy *g* unto their children	Ps 90:16	1926
Declare his *g* among the heathen	Ps 96:3	3519
the people, give unto the LORD *g*	Ps 96:7	3519
the LORD the *g* due unto his name	Ps 96:8	3519
and all the people see his *g*	Ps 97:6	3519
all the kings of the earth thy *g*	Ps 102:15	3519
up Zion, he shall appear in his *g*	Ps 102:16	3519
The *g* of the LORD shall endure	Ps 104:31	3519
G ye in his holy name	Ps 105:3	1984
nation, that I may *g* with thine	Ps 106:5	1984
Thus they changed their *g* into	Ps 106:20	3519
and give praise, even with my *g*	Ps 108:1	3519
thy *g* above all the earth	Ps 108:5	3519
and his *g* above the heavens	Ps 113:4	3519
unto us, but unto thy name give *g*	Ps 115:1	3519
for great is the *g* of the LORD	Ps 138:5	3519
speak of the *g* of thy kingdom	Ps 145:11	3519
his *g* is above the earth and	Ps 148:13	1935
Let the saints be joyful in *g*	Ps 149:5	3519
The wise shall inherit *g*	Prov 3:35	3519
a crown of *g* shall she deliver to	Prov 4:9	8597
The hoary head is a crown of *g*	Prov 16:31	8597
the *g* of children are their	Prov 17:6	8597
it is his *g* to pass over a	Prov 19:11	8597
The *g* of young men is their	Prov 20:29	8597
It is the *g* of God to conceal a	Prov 25:2	3519
search their own *g* is not *g*	Prov 25:27	3519
men do rejoice, there is great *g*	Prov 28:12	8597
LORD, and for the *g* of his majesty	Is 2:10	1926
for the *g* of his majesty, when he	Is 2:19	1926
for the *g* of his majesty, when he	Is 2:21	1926
to provoke the eyes of his *g*	Is 3:8	3519
for upon all the *g* shall be a	Is 4:5	3519
and their *g*, and their multitude,	Is 5:14	1926
the whole earth is full of his *g*	Is 6:3	3519
the king of Assyria, and all his *g*	Is 8:7	3519
and where will ye leave your *g*	Is 10:3	3519
and the *g* of his high looks	Is 10:12	8597
under his *g* he shall kindle a	Is 10:16	3519
shall consume the *g* of his forest	Is 10:18	3519
the *g* of kingdoms, the beauty of	Is 13:19	6643
even all of them, lie in *g*	Is 14:18	3519
the *g* of Moab shall be contemned,	Is 16:14	3519
they shall be as the *g* of the	Is 17:3	3519
that the *g* of Jacob shall be made	Is 17:4	3519
expectation, and of Egypt their *g*	Is 20:5	8597
all the *g* of Kedar shall fail	Is 21:16	3519
thy *g* shall be the shame of thy	Is 22:18	3519
all the *g* of his father's house	Is 22:24	3519
it, to stain the pride of all *g*	Is 23:9	6643
songs, even *g* to the righteous	Is 24:16	6643
LORD of hosts shall be for a crown of *g*	Is 28:5	6643
the *g* of Lebanon shall be given	Is 35:2	3519
they shall see the *g* of the LORD	Is 35:2	3519
the *g* of the LORD shall be	Is 40:5	3519
shalt *g* in the Holy One of Israel	Is 41:16	1984
my *g* will I not give to another,	Is 42:8	3519
Let them give *g* unto the LORD	Is 42:12	3519
for I have created him for my *g*	Is 43:7	3519
Israel be justified, and shall *g*	Is 45:25	1984
salvation in Zion for Israel my *g*	Is 46:13	8597
I will not give my *g* unto another	Is 48:11	3519
the *g* of the LORD shall be thy	Is 58:8	3519
his *g* from the rising of the sun	Is 59:19	3519
the *g* of the LORD is risen upon	Is 60:1	3519

Left column			Right column		

his *g* shall be seen upon thee................. Is 60:2 — 3519
I will glorify the house of my *g* .... Is 60:7 — 8597
The *g* of Lebanon shall come unto .... Is 60:13 — 3519
light, and thy God thy *g* .... Is 60:19 — 8597
in their *g* shall ye boast....................... Is 61:6 — 3519
righteousness, and all kings thy *g* .... Is 62:2 — 3519
of *g* in the hand of the LORD .... Is 62:3 — 8597
of thy holiness and of thy *g* .... Is 63:15 — 8597
with the abundance of her *g*.................. Is 66:11 — 3519
the *g* of the Gentiles like a .... Is 66:12 — 3519
and they shall come, and see my *g*......... Is 66:18 — 3519
my fame, neither have seen my *g* .... Is 66:19 — 3519
declare my *g* among the Gentiles .... Is 66:19 — 3519
my people have changed their *g* .... Jer 2:11 — 3519
in him, and in him shall they *g*............... Jer 4:2 — 1984
not the wise man *g* in his wisdom .... Jer 9:23 — 1984
let the mighty man *g* in his might .... Jer 9:23 — 1984
not the rich man *g* in his riches .... Jer 9:23 — 1984
let him that glorieth *g* in this .... Jer 9:24 — 1984
name, and for a praise, and for a *g*........ Jer 13:11 — 8597
Give *g* to the LORD your God,................. Jer 13:16 — 3519
down, even the crown of your *g*............. Jer 13:18 — 8597
not disgrace the throne of thy *g*............. Jer 14:21 — 3519
Ah lord! or, Ah his *g*!............................ Jer 22:18 — 1935
Dibon, come down from thy *g* .... Jer 48:18 — 3519
the likeness of the *g* of the LORD .... Eze 1:28 — 3519
Blessed be the *g* of the LORD from .... Eze 3:12 — 3519
the *g* of the LORD stood there, as .... Eze 3:23 — 3519
as the *g* which I saw by the river .... Eze 3:23 — 3519
the *g* of the God of Israel was .... Eze 8:4 — 3519
the *g* of the God of Israel was .... Eze 9:3 — 3519
Then the *g* of the LORD went up .... Eze 10:4 — 3519
of the brightness of the LORD's *g* .... Eze 10:4 — 3519
Then the *g* of the LORD departed .... Eze 10:18 — 3519
the *g* of the God of Israel was .... Eze 10:19 — 3519
the *g* of the God of Israel was .... Eze 11:22 — 3519
the *g* of the LORD went up from .... Eze 11:23 — 3519
which is the *g* of all lands...................... Eze 20:6 — 6643
which is the *g* of all lands...................... Eze 20:15 — 3519
strength, the joy of their *g* .... Eze 24:25 — 8597
frontiers, the *g* of the country, ... Eze 25:9 — 6643
I shall set *g* in the land of the .... Eze 26:20 — 6643
To whom art thou thus like in *g* .... Eze 31:18 — 3519
I will set my *g* among the heathen .... Eze 39:21 — 3519
the *g* of the God of Israel came .... Eze 43:2 — 3519
and the earth shined with his *g* .... Eze 43:2 — 3519
the *g* of the LORD came into the .... Eze 43:4 — 3519
the *g* of the LORD filled the .... Eze 43:5 — 3519
the *g* of the LORD filled the .... Eze 44:4 — 3519
kingdom, power, and strength, and *g*...... Dan 2:37 — 3367
for the *g* of my kingdom, mine .... Dan 4:36 — 3367
father a kingdom and majesty, and *g*..... Dan 5:18 — 3367
and they took his *g* from him .... Dan 5:20 — 3367
was given him dominion, and *g* .... Dan 7:14 — 3367
of taxes in the *g* of the kingdom .... Dan 11:20 — 1925
acknowledge and increase with *g* .... Dan 11:39 — 3519
will I change their *g* into shame .... Hos 4:7 — 3519
their *g* shall fly away like a .... Hos 9:11 — 3519
rejoiced on it, for the *g* thereof............. Hos 10:5 — 3519
come unto Adullam the *g* of Israel .... Mic 1:15 — 3519
have ye taken away my *g* for ever .... Mic 2:9 — 1926
g out of all the pleasant.......................... Nah 2:9 — 3519
knowledge of the *g* of the LORD .... Hab 2:14 — 3519
Thou art filled with shame for *g* .... Hab 2:16 — 3519
spewing shall be on thy *g*...................... Hab 2:16 — 3519
His *g* covered the heavens, and the .... Hab 3:3 — 1935
saw this house in her first *g* .... Hag 2:3 — 3519
and I will fill this house with *g* .... Hag 2:7 — 3519
The *g* of this latter house shall .... Hag 2:9 — 3519
will be the *g* in the midst of her .... Zec 2:5 — 3519
After the *g* hath he sent me unto .... Zec 2:8 — 3519
and he shall bear the *g*, and shall .... Zec 6:13 — 1935
for their *g* is spoiled............................. Zec 11:3 — 155
that the *g* of the house of David............ Zec 12:7 — 8597
the *g* of the inhabitants of .... Zec 12:7 — 8597
to give *g* unto my name, saith the .... Mal 2:2 — 3519
of the world, and the *g* of them .... Mt 4:8 — 1391
that they may have *g* of men .... Mt 6:2 — 1392
kingdom, and the power, and the *g* ...... Mt 6:13 — 1391
his *g* was not arrayed like one of .... Mt 6:29 — 1391
Son of man coming in the *g* of .... Mt 16:27 — 1391
shall sit in the throne of his *g* .... Mt 19:28 — 1391
of heaven with power and great *g* .... Mt 24:30 — 1391
Son of man shall come in his *g* .... Mt 25:31 — 1391
he sit upon the throne of his *g*............ Mt 25:31 — 1391
when he cometh in the *g* of his .... Mk 8:38 — 1391
other on thy left hand, in thy *g*.............. Mk 10:37 — 1391
the clouds with great power and *g* .... Mk 13:26 — 1391
the *g* of the Lord shone round .... Lk 2:9 — 1391
G to God in the highest, and on .... Lk 2:14 — 1391
the *g* of thy people Israel....................... Lk 2:32 — 1391

I give thee, and the *g* of them .... Lk 4:6 — 1391
when he shall come in his own *g* .... Lk 9:26 — 1391
Who appeared in *g*, and spake of .... Lk 9:31 — 1391
they were awake, they saw his *g*........... Lk 9:32 — 1391
that Solomon in all his *g* was not .... Lk 12:27 — 1391
that returned to give *g* to God .... Lk 17:18 — 1391
in heaven, and *g* in the highest .... Lk 19:38 — 1391
in a cloud with power and great *g* .... Lk 21:27 — 1391
things, and to enter into his *g* .... Lk 24:26 — 1391
among us, (and we beheld his *g* .... Jn 1:14 — 1391
the *g* as of the only begotten of............. Jn 1:14 — 1391
and manifested forth his *g* .... Jn 2:11 — 1391
of himself seeketh his own *g* .... Jn 7:18 — 1391
that seeketh his *g* that sent him .... Jn 7:18 — 1391
And I seek not mine own *g* .... Jn 8:50 — 1391
unto death, but for the *g* of God .... Jn 11:4 — 1391
thou shouldest see the *g* of God .... Jn 11:40 — 1391
said Esaias, when he saw his *g* .... Jn 12:41 — 1391
g which I had with thee before .... Jn 17:5 — 1391
the *g* which thou gavest me I have .... Jn 17:22 — 1391
that they may behold my *g* .... Jn 17:24 — 1391
The God of *g* appeared unto our .... Acts 7:2 — 1391
into heaven, and saw the *g* of God .... Acts 7:55 — 1391
because he gave not God the *g*.............. Acts 12:23 — 1391
not see for the *g* of that light................. Acts 22:11 — 1391
And changed the *g* of the .... Rom 1:23 — 1391
in well doing seek for *g* and .... Rom 2:7 — 1391
But *g*, honour, and peace, to every........ Rom 2:10 — 1391
through my lie unto his *g* .... Rom 3:7 — 1391
and come short of the *g* of God .... Rom 3:23 — 1391
by works, he hath whereof to *g*.............. Rom 4:2 — 2745
strong in faith, giving *g* to God .... Rom 4:20 — 1391
rejoice in hope of the *g* of God .... Rom 5:2 — 1391
but we *g* in tribulations also .... Rom 5:3 — 2744
the dead by the *g* of the Father .... Rom 6:4 — 1391
g which shall be revealed in us .... Rom 8:18 — 1391
pertaineth the adoption, and the *g* .... Rom 9:4 — 1391
of his *g* on the vessels of mercy .... Rom 9:23 — 1391
he had afore prepared unto *g* .... Rom 9:23 — 1391
to whom be *g* for ever .... Rom 11:36 — 1391
also received us to the *g* of God .... Rom 15:7 — 1391
g through Jesus Christ in those .... Rom 15:17 — 2746
be *g* through Jesus Christ for .... Rom 16:27 — 1391
no flesh should *g* in his presence .... 1Cor 1:29 — 2744
glorieth, let him *g* in the Lord .... 1Cor 1:31 — 2744
before the world unto our *g* .... 1Cor 2:7 — 1391
not have crucified the Lord of *g* .... 1Cor 2:8 — 1391
Therefore let no man *g* in men .... 1Cor 3:21 — 2744
didst receive it, why dost thou *g* .... 1Cor 4:7 — 2744
gospel, I have nothing to *g* of................. 1Cor 9:16 — 2745
ye do, do all to the *g* of God .... 1Cor 10:31 — 1391
as he is the image and *g* of God .... 1Cor 11:7 — 1391
but the woman is the *g* of the man .... 1Cor 11:7 — 1391
have long hair, it is a *g* to her .... 1Cor 11:15 — 1391
but the *g* of the celestial is one .... 1Cor 15:40 — 1391
the *g* of the terrestrial is........................ 1Cor 15:40 — 1391
There is one *g* of the sun .... 1Cor 15:41 — 1391
another *g* of the moon .... 1Cor 15:41 — 1391
and another *g* of the stars .... 1Cor 15:41 — 1391
differeth from another star in *g* .... 1Cor 15:41 — 1391
it is raised in *g*...................................... 1Cor 15:43 — 1391
him Amen, unto the *g* of God by us........ 2Cor 1:20 — 1391
for the *g* of his countenance .... 2Cor 3:7 — 1391
which *g* was to be done away .... 2Cor 3:7 — 1391
ministration of condemnation be *g*........ 2Cor 3:9 — 1391
of righteousness exceed in *g* .... 2Cor 3:9 — 1391
glorious had no *g* in this respect........... 2Cor 3:10 — 1392
by reason of the *g* that excelleth........... 2Cor 3:10 — 1391
as in a glass the *g* of the Lord .... 2Cor 3:18 — 1391
the same image from *g* to *g* .... 2Cor 3:18 — 1391
the *g* of God in the face of Jesus .... 2Cor 4:6 — 1391
of many redound to the *g* of God .... 2Cor 4:15 — 1391
exceeding and eternal weight of *g*......... 2Cor 4:17 — 1391
you occasion to *g* on our behalf .... 2Cor 5:12 — 2745
answer them which *g* in appearance...... 2Cor 5:12 — 2744
by us to the *g* of the same Lord .... 2Cor 8:19 — 1391
the churches, and the *g* of Christ .... 2Cor 8:23 — 1391
glorieth, let him *g* in the Lord .... 2Cor 10:17 — 2744
that wherein they *g*, they may be .... 2Cor 11:12 — 2744
g after the flesh, I will *g* also .... 2Cor 11:18 — 2744
If I must needs *g*, I will *g* .... 2Cor 11:30 — 2744
expedient for me doubtless to *g* .... 2Cor 12:1 — 2744
Of such an one will I *g*........................... 2Cor 12:5 — 2744
yet of myself I will not *g* .... 2Cor 12:5 — 2744
For though I would desire to *g* .... 2Cor 12:6 — 2744
will I rather *g* in my infirmities.............. 2Cor 12:9 — 2744
To whom be *g* for ever and ever .... Gal 1:5 — 1391
Let us not be desirous of vain *g*............ Gal 5:26 — 2755
that they may *g* in your flesh .... Gal 6:13 — 2744
But God forbid that I should *g* .... Gal 6:14 — 2744
the praise of the *g* of his grace .... Eph 1:6 — 1391

G

should be to the praise of his *g*	Eph 1:12	1391
unto the praise of his *g*	Eph 1:14	1391
Jesus Christ, the Father of *g*	Eph 1:17	1391
what the riches of the *g* of his	Eph 1:18	1391
for you, which is your *g*	Eph 3:13	1391
according to the riches of his *g*	Eph 3:16	1391
Unto him be *g* in the church by	Eph 3:21	1391
are by Jesus Christ, unto the *g*	Phil 1:11	1391
to the *g* of God the Father	Phil 2:11	1391
whose *g* is in their shame, who	Phil 3:19	1391
his riches in *g* by Christ Jesus	Phil 4:19	1391
God and our Father be *g* for ever	Phil 4:20	1391
the *g* of this mystery among the	Col 1:27	1391
is Christ in you, the hope of *g*	Col 1:27	1391
ye also appear with him in *g*	Col 3:4	1391
Nor of men sought we *g*, neither	1Th 2:6	1391
called you unto his kingdom and *g*	1Th 2:12	1391
For ye are our *g* and joy	1Th 2:20	1391
So that we ourselves *g* in you in	2Th 1:4	2744
Lord, and from the *g* of his power	2Th 1:9	1391
to the obtaining of the *g* of our	2Th 2:14	1391
be honour and *g* for ever and ever	1Ti 1:17	1391
in the world, received up into *g*	1Ti 3:16	1391
is in Christ Jesus with eternal *g*	2Ti 2:10	1391
to whom be *g* for ever and ever	2Ti 4:18	1391
Who being the brightness of his *g*	Heb 1:3	1391
thou crownedst him with *g*	Heb 2:7	1391
of death, crowned with *g* and	Heb 2:9	1391
in bringing many sons unto *g*	Heb 2:10	1391
worthy of more *g* than Moses	Heb 3:3	1391
of *g* shadowing the mercyseat	Heb 9:5	1391
to whom be *g* for ever and ever	Heb 13:21	1391
Lord Jesus Christ, the Lord of *g*	Jas 2:1	1391
g not, and lie not against the	Jas 3:14	2620
g at the appearing of Jesus	1Pet 1:7	1391
with joy unspeakable and full of *g*	1Pet 1:8	1392
and the *g* that should follow	1Pet 1:11	1391
up from the dead, and gave him *g*	1Pet 1:21	1391
all the *g* of man as the flower of	1Pet 1:24	1391
For what *g* is it, if, when ye be	1Pet 2:20	2811
when his *g* shall be revealed, ye	1Pet 4:13	1391
for the spirit of *g* and of God	1Pet 4:14	1391
of the *g* that shall be revealed	1Pet 5:1	1391
a crown of *g* that fadeth not away	1Pet 5:4	1391
his eternal *g* by Christ Jesus	1Pet 5:10	1391
To him be *g* and dominion for ever	1Pet 5:11	1391
of him that hath called us to *g*	2Pet 1:3	1391
from God the Father honour and *g*	2Pet 1:17	1391
voice to him from the excellent *g*	2Pet 1:17	1391
To him be *g* both now and for ever	2Pet 3:18	1391
of his *g* with exceeding joy	Jude 24	1391
only wise God our Saviour, be *g*	Jude 25	1391
to him be *g* and dominion for ever	Rev 1:6	1391
And when those beasts give *g*	Rev 4:9	1391
art worthy, O Lord, to receive *g*	Rev 4:11	1391
and strength, and honour, and *g*	Rev 5:12	1391
saying, Blessing, and honour, and *g*	Rev 5:13	1391
Blessing, and *g*, and wisdom, and	Rev 7:12	1391
gave *g* to the God of heaven	Rev 11:13	1391
voice, Fear God, and give *g* to him	Rev 14:7	1391
with smoke from the *g* of God	Rev 15:8	1391
they repented not to give him *g*	Rev 16:9	1391
earth was lightened with his *g*	Rev 18:1	1391
Salvation, and *g*, and honour, and	Rev 19:1	1391
Having the *g* of God	Rev 21:11	1391
for the *g* of God did lighten it,	Rev 21:23	1391
of the earth do bring their *g*	Rev 21:24	1391
And they shall bring the *g*	Rev 21:26	1391

GLORYING

Your *g* is not good	1Cor 5:6	2745
any man should make my *g* void	1Cor 9:15	2745
toward you, great is my *g* of you	2Cor 7:4	2746
I am become a fool in *g*	2Cor 12:11	2744

GLUTTON

he is a *g*, and a drunkard	Deut 21:20	2151
the *g* shall come to poverty	Prov 23:21	2151

GLUTTONOUS

and they say, Behold a man *g*	Mt 11:19	5314
and ye say, Behold a *g* man	Lk 7:34	5314

GNASH

he shall *g* with his teeth, and	Ps 112:10	2786
they hiss and *g* the teeth	Lam 2:16	2786

GNASHED

they *g* upon me with their teeth	Ps 35:16	2786
they *g* on him with their teeth	Acts 7:54	1031

GNASHETH

he *g* upon me with his teeth	Job 16:9	2786
g upon him with his teeth	Ps 37:12	2786
g with his teeth, and pineth away	Mk 9:18	5149

GNASHING

shall be weeping and *g* of teeth	Mt 8:12	1030
shall be wailing and *g* of teeth	Mt 13:42	1030
shall be wailing and *g* of teeth	Mt 13:50	1030
shall be weeping and *g* of teeth	Mt 22:13	1030
shall be weeping and *g* of teeth	Mt 24:51	1030
shall be weeping and *g* of teeth	Mt 25:30	1030
g of teeth, when ye shall see	Lk 13:28	1030

GNAT

blind guides, which strain at a *g*	Mt 23:24	2971

GNAW

they *g* not the bones till the	Zeph 3:3	1633

GNAWED

they *g* their tongues for pain,	Rev 16:10	3145

GO See APPENDIX.

GOAD

six hundred men with an ox *g*	Judg 3:31	4451

GOADS

for the axes, and to sharpen the *g*	1Sa 13:21	1861
The words of the wise are as *g*	Eccl 12:11	1861

GOAH See GOATH.

GOAT

a she *g* of three years old, and a	Gen 15:9	5795
And if his offering be a *g*	Lev 3:12	5795
his hand upon the head of the *g*	Lev 4:24	8163
fat, of ox, or of sheep, or of *g*	Lev 7:23	5795
people's offering, and took the *g*	Lev 9:15	8163
sought the *g* of the sin offering	Lev 10:16	8163
Aaron shall bring the *g* upon	Lev 16:9	8163
But the *g*, on which the lot fell	Lev 16:10	8163
he kill the *g* of the sin offering	Lev 16:15	8163
bullock, and of the blood of the *g*	Lev 16:18	8163
altar, he shall bring the live *g*	Lev 16:20	8163
hands upon the head of the live *g*	Lev 16:21	8163
them upon the head of the *g*	Lev 16:21	8163
the *g* shall bear upon him all	Lev 16:22	8163
let go the *g* in the wilderness	Lev 16:22	8163
he that let go the *g* for the	Lev 16:26	8163
the *g* for the sin offering, whose	Lev 16:27	8163
that killeth an ox, or lamb, or *g*	Lev 17:3	5795
a bullock, or a sheep, or a *g*	Lev 22:27	5795
then he shall bring a she *g* of	Num 15:27	5795
a sheep, or the firstling of a *g*	Num 18:17	5795
one *g* for a sin offering, to make	Num 28:22	8163
And one *g* for a sin offering	Num 29:22	8163
And one *g* for a sin offering	Num 29:28	8163
And one *g* for a sin offering	Num 29:31	8163
And one *g* for a sin offering	Num 29:34	8163
And one *g* for a sin offering	Num 29:38	8163
the ox, the sheep, and the *g*	Deut 14:4	5795
and the fallow deer, and the wild *g*	Deut 14:5	689
an he *g* also	Prov 30:31	8495
every day a *g* for a sin offering	Eze 43:25	8163
an he *g* came from the west on the	Dan 8:5	5795
the *g* had a notable horn between	Dan 8:5	6842
the he *g* waxed very great	Dan 8:8	6842
the rough *g* is the king of Grecia	Dan 8:21	6842

GOATH (go'-ath) A place near Jerusalem.

and shall compass about to *G*	Jer 31:39	1601

GOATS

thence two good kids of the *g*	Gen 27:9	5795
the kids of the *g* upon his hands	Gen 27:16	5795
spotted and speckled among the *g*	Gen 30:32	5795
speckled and spotted among the *g*	Gen 30:33	5795
the he *g* that were ringstraked	Gen 30:35	8495
all the she *g* that were speckled	Gen 30:35	5795
thy she *g* have not cast their	Gen 31:38	5795
Two hundred she *g*	Gen 32:14	5795
and twenty he *g*	Gen 32:14	8495
coat, and killed a kid of the *g*	Gen 37:31	5795
out from the sheep, or from the *g*	Ex 12:5	5795
namely, of the sheep, or of the *g*	Lev 1:10	5795
his offering, a kid of the *g*	Lev 4:23	5795
his offering, a kid of the *g*	Lev 4:28	5795
flock, a lamb or a kid of the *g*	Lev 5:6	5795
a kid of the *g* for a sin offering	Lev 9:3	5795
kids of the *g* for a sin offering	Lev 16:5	5795
And he shall take the two *g*	Lev 16:7	8163
shall cast lots upon the two *g*	Lev 16:8	8163
beeves, of the sheep, or of the *g*	Lev 22:19	5795
kid of the *g* for a sin offering	Lev 23:19	5795

One kid of the *g* for a sin...........................Num 7:16   5795
two oxen, five rams, five he *g*...............Num 7:17   6260
One kid of the *g* for a sin...........................Num 7:22   5795
two oxen, five rams, five he *g*...............Num 7:23   6260
One kid of the *g* for a sin...........................Num 7:28   5795
two oxen, five rams, five he *g*...............Num 7:29   6260
One kid of the *g* for a sin...........................Num 7:34   5795
two oxen, five rams, five he *g*...............Num 7:35   6260
One kid of the *g* for a sin...........................Num 7:40   5795
two oxen, five rams, five he *g*...............Num 7:41   6260
One kid of the *g* for a sin...........................Num 7:46   5795
two oxen, five rams, five he *g*...............Num 7:47   6260
One kid of the *g* for a sin...........................Num 7:52   5795
two oxen, five rams, five he *g*...............Num 7:53   6260
One kid of the *g* for a sin...........................Num 7:58   5795
two oxen, five rams, five he *g*...............Num 7:59   6260
One kid of the *g* for a sin...........................Num 7:64   5795
two oxen, five rams, five he *g*...............Num 7:65   6260
One kid of the *g* for a sin...........................Num 7:70   5795
two oxen, five rams, five he *g*...............Num 7:71   6260
One kid of the *g* for a sin...........................Num 7:76   5795
two oxen, five rams, five he *g*...............Num 7:77   6260
One kid of the *g* for a sin...........................Num 7:82   5795
two oxen, five rams, five he *g*...............Num 7:83   6260
the kids of the *g* for sin.........................Num 7:87   5795
the rams sixty, the he *g* sixty.............Num 7:88   6260
one kid of the *g* for a sin....................Num 15:24   5795
one kid of the *g* for a sin....................Num 28:15   5795
And one kid of the *g*, to make an...........Num 28:30   5795
one kid of the *g* for a sin......................Num 29:5   5795
One kid of the *g* for a sin....................Num 29:11   5795
one kid of the *g* for a sin....................Num 29:16   5795
one kid of the *g* for a sin....................Num 29:19   5795
one kid of the *g* for a sin....................Num 29:25   5795
rams of the breed of Bashan, and *g*.......Deut 32:14   6260
men upon the rocks of the wild *g*..........1Sa 24:2   3277
thousand sheep, and a thousand *g*.........1Sa 25:2   5795
thousand and seven hundred he *g*..........2Chr 17:11   8495
and seven lambs, and seven he *g*...........2Chr 29:21   5795
they brought forth the he *g* for............2Chr 29:23   8163
for all Israel, twelve he *g*.......................Ezr 6:17   5795
twelve he *g* for a sin offering................Ezr 8:35   6842
wild *g* of the rock bring forth..................Job 39:1   3277
nor he *g* out of thy folds..........................Ps 50:9   6260
of bulls, or drink the blood of *g*.............Ps 50:13   6260
I will offer bullocks with *g*.....................Ps 66:15   6260
hills are a refuge for the wild *g*.............Ps 104:18   3277
the *g* are the price of the field.............Prov 27:26   6260
thy hair is as a flock of *g*.......................Song 4:1   5795
of *g* that appear from Gilead.................Song 6:5   5795
bullocks, or of lambs, or of he *g*.............Is 1:11   6260
and with the blood of lambs and *g*.........Is 34:6   6260
be as the he *g* before the flocks...........Jer 50:8   6260
slaughter, like rams with he *g*...............Jer 51:40   6260
with thee in lambs, and rams, and *g*.....Eze 27:21   6260
between the rams and the he *g*..............Eze 34:17   6260
earth, of rams, of lambs, and of *g*..........Eze 39:18   6260
the *g* without blemish for a sin............Eze 43:22   5795
a kid of the *g* daily for a sin.................Eze 45:23   5795
shepherds, and I punished the *g*............Zec 10:3   6260
divideth his sheep from the *g*..............Mt 25:32   2056
right hand, but the *g* on the left.........Mt 25:33   2055
Neither by the blood of *g*.......................Heb 9:12   5131
For if the blood of bulls and of *g*...........Heb 9:13   5131
took the blood of calves and of *g*..........Heb 9:19   5131
of *g* should take away sins.....................Heb 10:4   5131

GOATS'

and fine linen, and *g* hair,.....................Ex 25:4   5795
thou shalt make curtains of *g*................Ex 26:7   5795
and fine linen, and *g* hair,.....................Ex 35:6   5795
g hair, and red skins of rams, and.........Ex 35:23   5795
them up in wisdom spun *g* hair..............Ex 35:26   5795
he made curtains of *g* hair for...............Ex 36:14   5795
of skins, and all work of *g* hair............Num 31:20   5795
put a pillow of *g* hair for his.................1Sa 19:13   5795
with a pillow of *g* hair for his...............1Sa 19:16   5795
thou shalt have *g* milk enough for.........Prov 27:27   5795

GOATSKINS

about in sheepskins and *g*.............Heb 11:37   122,1192

GOB (gob) *A place where David battled the Philistines.*
battle with the Philistines at *G*...........2Sa 21:18   1359
battle in *G* with the Philistines...........2Sa 21:19   1359

GOBLET

Thy navel is like a round *g*....................Song 7:2   101

GOD (god) See GODDESS, GODHEAD, GOD'S, GODS, GOD-
WARD.

    *1. Creator and Ruler of the world, Israel, and the
    church.*
In the beginning *G* created the..............Gen 1:1   430
the Spirit of *G* moved upon the..............Gen 1:2   430
G said, Let there be light......................Gen 1:3   430
G saw the light, that it was good...........Gen 1:4   430
G divided the light from the..................Gen 1:4   430
G called the light Day, and the..............Gen 1:5   430
G said, Let there be a firmament...........Gen 1:6   430
G made the firmament, and divided........Gen 1:7   430
G called the firmament Heaven..............Gen 1:8   430
G said, Let the waters under the...........Gen 1:9   430
G called the dry land Earth..................Gen 1:10   430
and *G* saw that it was good...................Gen 1:10   430
G said, Let the earth bring forth..........Gen 1:11   430
and *G* saw that it was good...................Gen 1:12   430
G said, Let there be lights in...............Gen 1:14   430
And *G* made two great lights.................Gen 1:16   430
G set them in the firmament of..............Gen 1:17   430
and *G* saw that it was good...................Gen 1:18   430
G said, Let the waters bring.................Gen 1:20   430
G created great whales, and every........Gen 1:21   430
and *G* saw that it was good...................Gen 1:21   430
G blessed them, saying, Be...................Gen 1:22   430
G said, Let the earth bring forth..........Gen 1:24   430
G made the beast of the earth...............Gen 1:25   430
and *G* saw that it was good...................Gen 1:25   430
G said, Let us make man in our..............Gen 1:26   430
So *G* created man in his own image........Gen 1:27   430
in the image of *G* created he him...........Gen 1:27   430
G blessed them, and *G* said unto..........Gen 1:28   430
G said unto them, Be fruitful, and.........Gen 1:28   430
G said, Behold, I have given you............Gen 1:29   430
G saw every thing that he had...............Gen 1:31   430
on the seventh day *G* ended his..............Gen 2:2   430
G blessed the seventh day, and..............Gen 2:3   430
from all his work which *G* created..........Gen 2:3   430
that the LORD *G* made the earth.............Gen 2:4   430
for the LORD *G* had not caused to...........Gen 2:5   430
the LORD *G* formed man of the dust........Gen 2:7   430
the LORD *G* planted a garden................Gen 2:8   430
LORD *G* to grow every tree that is..........Gen 2:9   430
the LORD *G* took the man, and put..........Gen 2:15   430
the LORD *G* commanded the man,............Gen 2:16   430
And the LORD *G* said, It is not...............Gen 2:18   430
out of the ground the LORD *G*................Gen 2:19   430
the LORD *G* caused a deep sleep to.........Gen 2:21   430
which the LORD *G* had taken from...........Gen 2:22   430
field which the LORD *G* had made...........Gen 3:1   430
unto the woman, Yea, hath *G* said..........Gen 3:1   430
G hath said, Ye shall not eat of.............Gen 3:3   430
For *G* doth know that in the day............Gen 3:5   430
heard the voice of the LORD *G*...............Gen 3:8   430
from the presence of the LORD *G*...........Gen 3:8   430
the LORD *G* called unto Adam, and.........Gen 3:9   430
the LORD *G* said unto the woman,...........Gen 3:13   430
the LORD *G* said unto the serpent,..........Gen 3:14   430
the LORD *G* make coats of skins.............Gen 3:21   430
And the LORD *G* said, Behold, the...........Gen 3:22   430
Therefore the LORD *G* sent him..............Gen 3:23   430
For *G*, said she, hath appointed.............Gen 4:25   430
In the day that *G* created man...............Gen 5:1   430
in the likeness of *G* made he him...........Gen 5:1   430
Enoch walked with *G* after he...............Gen 5:22   430
And Enoch walked with *G*......................Gen 5:24   430
for *G* took him....................................Gen 5:24   430
That the sons of *G* saw the...................Gen 6:2   430
when the sons of *G* came in unto............Gen 6:4   430
G saw that the wickedness of man.........Gen 6:5   3068
and Noah walked with *G*.......................Gen 6:9   430
earth also was corrupt before *G*............Gen 6:11   430
G looked upon the earth, and,...............Gen 6:12   430
G said unto Noah, The end of all...........Gen 6:13   430
to all that *G* commanded him.................Gen 6:22   430
female, as *G* had commanded Noah........Gen 7:9   430
all flesh, as *G* had commanded him.........Gen 7:16   430
G remembered Noah, and every..............Gen 8:1   430
G made a wind to pass over the.............Gen 8:1   430
G spake unto Noah, saying,...................Gen 8:15   430
G blessed Noah and his sons, and..........Gen 9:1   430
for in the image of *G* made he man.........Gen 9:6   430
G spake unto Noah, and to his sons,.......Gen 9:8   430
G said, This is the token of the.............Gen 9:12   430
everlasting covenant between *G*............Gen 9:16   430
G said unto Noah, This is the................Gen 9:17   430
Blessed be the LORD *G* of Shem.............Gen 9:26   430
G shall enlarge Japheth, and he............Gen 9:27   430
was the priest of the most high *G*..........Gen 14:18   410
be Abram of the most high *G*.................Gen 14:19   410

G

And blessed be the most high *G*	Gen 14:20	410
unto the Lord, the most high *G*	Gen 14:22	410
And Abram said, Lord *G*, what wilt	Gen 15:2	3069
And he said, Lord *G*, whereby shall	Gen 15:8	3069
spake unto her, Thou *G* seest me	Gen 16:13	410
unto him, I am the Almighty *G*	Gen 17:1	410
G talked with him, saying,	Gen 17:3	430
to be a *G* unto thee, and to thy	Gen 17:7	430
and I will be their *G*	Gen 17:8	430
G said unto Abraham, Thou shalt	Gen 17:9	430
G said unto Abraham, As for Sarai	Gen 17:15	430
And Abraham said unto *G*, O that	Gen 17:18	430
G said, Sarah thy wife shall bear	Gen 17:19	430
him, and *G* went up from Abraham	Gen 17:22	430
day, as *G* had said unto him	Gen 17:23	430
when *G* destroyed the cities of	Gen 19:29	430
that *G* remembered Abraham, and	Gen 19:29	430
But *G* came to Abimelech in a	Gen 20:3	430
G said unto him in a dream, Yea,	Gen 20:6	430
Surely the fear of *G* is not in	Gen 20:11	430
when *G* caused me to wander from	Gen 20:13	430
So Abraham prayed unto *G*	Gen 20:17	430
G healed Abimelech, and his wife,	Gen 20:17	430
time of which *G* had spoken to him	Gen 21:2	430
days old, as *G* had commanded him	Gen 21:4	430
G hath made me to laugh, so that	Gen 21:6	430
G said unto Abraham, Let it not	Gen 21:12	430
G heard the voice of the lad	Gen 21:17	430
the angel of *G* called to Hagar	Gen 21:17	430
for *G* hath heard the voice of the	Gen 21:17	430
G opened her eyes, and she saw a	Gen 21:19	430
And *G* was with the lad	Gen 21:20	430
G is with thee in all that thou	Gen 21:22	430
G that thou wilt not deal falsely	Gen 21:23	430
of the Lord, the everlasting *G*	Gen 21:33	410
that *G* did tempt Abraham, and said	Gen 22:1	430
the place of which *G* had told him	Gen 22:3	430
G will provide himself a lamb for	Gen 22:8	430
the place which *G* had told him of	Gen 22:9	430
now I know that thou fearest *G*	Gen 22:12	430
the *G* of heaven	Gen 24:3	430
the *G* of the earth	Gen 24:3	430
The Lord *G* of heaven, which took	Gen 24:7	430
O Lord *G* of my master Abraham, I	Gen 24:12	430
Blessed be the Lord *G* of my	Gen 24:27	430
O Lord *G* of my master Abraham, if	Gen 24:42	430
blessed the Lord *G* of my master	Gen 24:48	430
that *G* blessed his son Isaac	Gen 25:11	430
I am the *G* of Abraham thy father	Gen 26:24	430
the Lord thy *G* brought it to me	Gen 27:20	430
Therefore *G* give thee of the dew	Gen 27:28	430
G Almighty bless thee, and make	Gen 28:3	410
which *G* gave unto Abraham	Gen 28:4	430
behold the angels of *G* ascending	Gen 28:12	430
I am the Lord *G* of Abraham thy	Gen 28:13	430
thy father, and the *G* of Isaac	Gen 28:13	430
is none other but the house of *G*	Gen 28:17	430
If *G* will be with me, and will	Gen 28:20	430
then shall the Lord be my *G*	Gen 28:21	430
G hath judged me, and hath also	Gen 30:6	430
G hearkened unto Leah, and she	Gen 30:17	430
G hath given me my hire, because	Gen 30:18	430
G hath endued me with a good	Gen 30:20	430
G remembered Rachel	Gen 30:22	430
G hearkened to her, and opened her	Gen 30:22	430
G hath taken away my reproach	Gen 30:23	430
but the *G* of my father hath been	Gen 31:5	430
but *G* suffered him not to hurt me	Gen 31:7	430
Thus *G* hath taken away the cattle	Gen 31:9	430
the angel of *G* spake unto me in a	Gen 31:11	430
I am the *G* of Beth-el, where thou	Gen 31:13	410
For all the riches which *G* hath	Gen 31:16	430
whatsoever *G* hath said unto thee,	Gen 31:16	430
G came to Laban the Syrian in a	Gen 31:24	430
but the *G* of your father spake	Gen 31:29	430
Except the *G* of my father	Gen 31:42	430
the *G* of Abraham, and the fear of	Gen 31:42	430
G hath seen mine affliction and	Gen 31:42	430
G is witness betwixt me and thee	Gen 31:50	430
The *G* of Abraham	Gen 31:53	430
the *G* of Nahor	Gen 31:53	430
the *G* of their father, judge	Gen 31:53	430
way, and the angels of *G* met him	Gen 32:1	430
O *G* of my father Abraham	Gen 32:9	430
G of my father Isaac, the Lord	Gen 32:9	430
a prince hast thou power with *G*	Gen 32:28	430
for I have seen *G* face to face	Gen 32:30	430
The children which *G* hath	Gen 33:5	430
though I had seen the face of *G*	Gen 33:10	430
because *G* hath dealt graciously	Gen 33:11	430
G said unto Jacob, Arise, go up	Gen 35:1	430
and make there an altar unto *G*	Gen 35:1	410
I will make there an altar unto *G*	Gen 35:3	410
the terror of *G* was upon the	Gen 35:5	430
because there *G* appeared unto him	Gen 35:7	430
G appeared unto Jacob again, when	Gen 35:9	430
G said unto him, Thy name is	Gen 35:10	430
And *G* said unto him	Gen 35:11	430
I am *G* Almighty	Gen 35:11	410
G went up from him in the place	Gen 35:13	430
the place where *G* spake with him	Gen 35:15	430
wickedness, and sin against *G*	Gen 39:9	430
not interpretations belong to *G*	Gen 40:8	430
G shall give Pharaoh an answer of	Gen 41:16	430
G hath shewed Pharaoh what he is	Gen 41:25	430
What *G* is about to do he sheweth	Gen 41:28	430
the thing is established by *G*	Gen 41:32	430
G will shortly bring it to pass	Gen 41:32	430
a man in whom the Spirit of *G* is	Gen 41:38	430
Forasmuch as *G* hath shewed thee	Gen 41:39	430
For *G*, said he, hath made me	Gen 41:51	430
For *G* hath caused me to be	Gen 41:52	430
for I fear *G*	Gen 42:18	430
is this that *G* hath done unto us	Gen 42:28	430
G Almighty give you mercy before	Gen 43:14	410
your *G*, and the *G* of your father	Gen 43:23	430
G be gracious unto thee, my son	Gen 43:29	430
G forbid that thy servants should	Gen 44:7	430
G hath found out the iniquity of	Gen 44:16	430
G forbid that I should do so	Gen 44:17	410
for *G* did send me before you to	Gen 45:5	430
G sent me before you to preserve	Gen 45:7	430
you that sent me hither, but *G*	Gen 45:8	430
G hath made me lord of all Egypt	Gen 45:9	430
unto the *G* of his father Isaac	Gen 46:1	430
G spake unto Israel in the	Gen 46:2	430
I am *G*, the *G* of thy father	Gen 46:3	430
G Almighty appeared unto me at	Gen 48:3	410
whom *G* hath given me in this	Gen 48:9	430
G hath shewed me also thy seed	Gen 48:11	430
And he blessed Joseph, and said, *G*	Gen 48:15	430
the *G* which fed me all my life	Gen 48:15	430
G make thee as Ephraim and as	Gen 48:20	430
but *G* shall be with you, and bring	Gen 48:21	430
hands of the mighty *G* of Jacob	Gen 49:24	430
Even by the *G* of thy father, who	Gen 49:25	410
servants of the *G* of thy father	Gen 50:17	430
for am I in the place of *G*	Gen 50:19	430
but *G* meant it unto good, to	Gen 50:20	430
G will surely visit you, and bring	Gen 50:24	430
G will surely visit you, and ye	Gen 50:25	430
But the midwives feared *G*	Ex 1:17	430
Therefore *G* dealt well with the	Ex 1:20	430
because the midwives feared *G*	Ex 1:21	430
their cry came up unto *G* by	Ex 2:23	430
G heard their groaning	Ex 2:24	430
G remembered his covenant with	Ex 2:24	430
G looked upon the children of	Ex 2:25	430
and *G* had respect unto them	Ex 2:25	430
and came to the mountain of *G*	Ex 3:1	430
G called unto him out of the	Ex 3:4	430
I am the *G* of thy father	Ex 3:6	430
the *G* of Abraham	Ex 3:6	430
G of Isaac, and the *G* of Jacob	Ex 3:6	430
for he was afraid to look upon *G*	Ex 3:6	430
And Moses said unto *G*, Who am I,	Ex 3:11	430
ye shall serve *G* upon this	Ex 3:12	430
And Moses said unto *G*, Behold,	Ex 3:13	430
The *G* of your fathers hath sent	Ex 3:13	430
G said unto Moses, I AM THAT I AM	Ex 3:14	430
G said moreover unto Moses, Thus	Ex 3:15	430
The Lord *G* of your fathers	Ex 3:15	430
the *G* of Abraham	Ex 3:15	430
the *G* of Isaac	Ex 3:15	430
the *G* of Jacob	Ex 3:15	430
The Lord *G* of your fathers	Ex 3:16	430
the *G* of Abraham, of Isaac, and of	Ex 3:16	430
The Lord *G* of the Hebrews hath	Ex 3:18	430
may sacrifice to the Lord our *G*	Ex 3:18	430
that the Lord *G* of their fathers	Ex 4:5	430
the *G* of Abraham	Ex 4:5	430
the *G* of Isaac	Ex 4:5	430
the *G* of Jacob	Ex 4:5	430
thou shalt be to him instead of *G*	Ex 4:16	430
took the rod of *G* in his hand	Ex 4:20	430
and met him in the mount of *G*	Ex 4:27	430
Thus saith the Lord *G* of Israel	Ex 5:1	430
The *G* of the Hebrews hath met	Ex 5:3	430
and sacrifice unto the Lord our *G*	Ex 5:3	430
Let us go and sacrifice to our *G*	Ex 5:8	430
G spake unto Moses, and said unto	Ex 6:2	430
Jacob, by the name of *G* Almighty	Ex 6:3	410

a people, and I will be to you a *G*	Ex 6:7	430
know that I am the Lord your *G*	Ex 6:7	430
The Lord *G* of the Hebrews hath	Ex 7:16	430
is none like unto the Lord our *G*	Ex 8:10	430
Pharaoh, This is the finger of *G*	Ex 8:19	430
sacrifice to your *G* in the land	Ex 8:25	430
the Egyptians to the Lord our *G*	Ex 8:26	430
and sacrifice to the Lord our *G*	Ex 8:27	430
the Lord your *G* in the wilderness	Ex 8:28	430
saith the Lord *G* of the Hebrews	Ex 9:1	430
saith the Lord *G* of the Hebrews	Ex 9:13	430
ye will not yet fear the Lord *G*	Ex 9:30	430
saith the Lord *G* of the Hebrews	Ex 10:3	430
they may serve the Lord their *G*	Ex 10:7	430
them, Go, serve the Lord your *G*	Ex 10:8	430
sinned against the Lord your *G*	Ex 10:16	430
once, and intreat the Lord your *G*	Ex 10:17	430
may sacrifice unto the Lord our *G*	Ex 10:25	430
we take to serve the Lord our *G*	Ex 10:26	430
that *G* led them not through the	Ex 13:17	430
for *G* said, Lest peradventure the	Ex 13:17	430
But *G* led the people about,	Ex 13:18	430
saying, *G* will surely visit you	Ex 13:19	430
And the angel of *G*, which went	Ex 14:19	430
he is my *G*, and I will prepare him	Ex 15:2	410
my father's *G*, and I will exalt	Ex 15:2	430
to the voice of the Lord thy *G*	Ex 15:26	430
Would to *G* we had died by the	Ex 16:3	430
know that I am the Lord your *G*	Ex 16:12	430
with the rod of *G* in mine hand	Ex 17:9	430
heard of all that *G* had done for	Ex 18:1	430
for the *G* of my father, said he,	Ex 18:4	430
he encamped at the mount of *G*	Ex 18:5	430
offering and sacrifices for *G*	Ex 18:12	430
Moses' father in law before *G*	Ex 18:12	430
come unto me to enquire of *G*	Ex 18:15	430
make them know the statutes of *G*	Ex 18:16	430
counsel, and *G* shall be with thee	Ex 18:19	430
mayest bring the causes unto *G*	Ex 18:19	430
people able men, such as fear *G*	Ex 18:21	430
G command thee so, then thou	Ex 18:23	430
And Moses went up unto *G*, and the	Ex 19:3	430
out of the camp to meet with *G*	Ex 19:17	430
G answered him by a voice	Ex 19:19	430
G spake all these words, saying,	Ex 20:1	430
I am the Lord thy *G*, which have	Ex 20:2	430
I the Lord thy *G* am a jealous	Ex 20:5	430
I the Lord thy *G* am a jealous *G*	Ex 20:5	410
name of the Lord thy *G* in vain	Ex 20:7	430
is the sabbath of the Lord thy *G*	Ex 20:10	430
which the Lord thy *G* giveth thee	Ex 20:12	430
but let not *G* speak with us, lest	Ex 20:19	430
for *G* is come to prove you, and	Ex 20:20	430
the thick darkness where *G* was	Ex 20:21	430
but *G* deliver him into his hand	Ex 21:13	430
shall appear before the Lord *G*	Ex 23:17	3068
into the house of the Lord thy *G*	Ex 23:19	430
And ye shall serve the Lord your *G*	Ex 23:25	430
And they saw the *G* of Israel	Ex 24:10	430
also they saw *G*, and did eat and	Ex 24:11	430
Moses went up into the mount of *G*	Ex 24:13	430
of Israel, and will be their *G*	Ex 29:45	430
know that I am the Lord their *G*	Ex 29:46	430
I am the Lord their *G*	Ex 29:46	430
filled him with the spirit of *G*	Ex 31:3	430
written with the finger of *G*	Ex 31:18	430
And Moses besought the Lord his *G*	Ex 32:11	430
And the tables were the work of *G*	Ex 32:16	430
the writing was the writing of *G*	Ex 32:16	430
Thus saith the Lord *G* of Israel	Ex 32:27	430
proclaimed, The Lord, The Lord *G*	Ex 34:6	410
name is Jealous, is a jealous *G*	Ex 34:14	410
children appear before the Lord *G*	Ex 34:23	3068
the *G* of Israel	Ex 34:23	430
the Lord thy *G* thrice in the year	Ex 34:24	430
unto the house of the Lord thy *G*	Ex 34:26	430
filled him with the spirit of *G*	Ex 35:31	430
thy *G* to be lacking from thy meat	Lev 2:13	430
commandments of the Lord his *G*	Lev 4:22	430
G hath given it you to bear the	Lev 10:17	430
For I am the Lord your *G*	Lev 11:44	430
the land of Egypt, to be your *G*	Lev 11:45	430
unto them, I am the Lord your *G*	Lev 18:2	430
I am the Lord your *G*	Lev 18:4	430
thou profane the name of thy *G*	Lev 18:21	430
I am the Lord your *G*	Lev 18:30	430
for I the Lord your *G* am holy	Lev 19:2	430
I am the Lord your *G*	Lev 19:3	430
I am the Lord your *G*	Lev 19:4	430
I am the Lord your *G*	Lev 19:10	430
thou profane the name of thy *G*	Lev 19:12	430
the blind, but shalt fear thy *G*	Lev 19:14	430
I am the Lord your *G*	Lev 19:25	430
I am the Lord your *G*	Lev 19:31	430
of the old man, and fear thy *G*	Lev 19:32	430
I am the Lord your *G*	Lev 19:34	430
I am the Lord your *G*, which	Lev 19:36	430
for I am the Lord your *G*	Lev 20:7	430
I am the Lord your *G*, which have	Lev 20:24	430
They shall be holy unto their *G*	Lev 21:6	430
not profane the name of their *G*	Lev 21:6	430
by fire, and the bread of their *G*	Lev 21:6	430
for he is holy unto his *G*	Lev 21:7	430
he offereth the bread of thy *G*	Lev 21:8	430
profane the sanctuary of his *G*	Lev 21:12	430
oil of his *G* is upon him	Lev 21:12	430
to offer the bread of his *G*	Lev 21:17	430
nigh to offer the bread of his *G*	Lev 21:21	430
He shall eat the bread of his *G*	Lev 21:22	430
bread of your *G* of any of these	Lev 22:25	430
the land of Egypt, to be your *G*	Lev 22:33	430
brought an offering unto your *G*	Lev 23:14	430
I am the Lord your *G*	Lev 23:22	430
for you before the Lord your *G*	Lev 23:28	430
before the Lord your *G* seven days	Lev 23:40	430
I am the Lord your *G*	Lev 23:43	430
curseth his *G* shall bear his sin	Lev 24:15	430
for I am the Lord your *G*	Lev 24:22	430
but thou shalt fear thy *G*	Lev 25:17	430
for I am the Lord your *G*	Lev 25:17	430
but fear thy *G*	Lev 25:36	430
I am the Lord your *G*, which	Lev 25:38	430
land of Canaan, and to be your *G*	Lev 25:38	430
but shalt fear thy *G*	Lev 25:43	430
I am the Lord your *G*	Lev 25:55	430
for I am the Lord your *G*	Lev 26:1	430
walk among you, and will be your *G*	Lev 26:12	430
I am the Lord your *G*, which	Lev 26:13	430
for I am the Lord their *G*	Lev 26:44	430
heathen, that I might be their *G*	Lev 26:45	430
of his *G* is upon his head	Num 6:7	430
remembered before the Lord your *G*	Num 10:9	430
you for a memorial before your *G*	Num 10:10	430
I am the Lord your *G*	Num 10:10	430
would *G* that all the Lord's	Num 11:29	
Lord, saying, Heal her now, O *G*	Num 12:13	410
Would *G* that we had died in the	Num 14:2	
or would *G* we had died in this	Num 14:2	
and be holy unto your *G*	Num 15:40	430
I am the Lord your *G*, which	Num 15:41	430
the land of Egypt, to be your *G*	Num 15:41	430
I am the Lord your *G*	Num 15:41	430
that the *G* of Israel hath	Num 16:9	430
upon their faces, and said, O *G*	Num 16:22	410
the *G* of the spirits of all flesh	Num 16:22	430
Would *G* that we had died when our	Num 20:3	
And the people spake against *G*	Num 21:5	430
G came unto Balaam, and said, What	Num 22:9	430
And Balaam said unto *G*, Balak the	Num 22:10	430
G said unto Balaam, Thou shalt	Num 22:12	430
beyond the word of the Lord my *G*	Num 22:18	430
G came unto Balaam at night, and	Num 22:20	430
the word that *G* putteth in my	Num 22:38	430
And *G* met Balaam	Num 23:4	430
I curse, whom *G* hath not cursed	Num 23:8	410
G is not a man, that he should	Num 23:19	410
the Lord his *G* is with him	Num 23:21	430
G brought them out of Egypt	Num 23:22	410
and of Israel, What hath *G* wrought	Num 23:23	410
peradventure it will please *G*	Num 23:27	430
and the spirit of *G* came upon him	Num 24:2	430
said, which heard the words of *G*	Num 24:4	410
G brought him forth out of Egypt	Num 24:8	410
said, which heard the words of *G*	Num 24:16	410
who shall live when *G* doeth this	Num 24:23	410
because he was zealous for his *G*	Num 25:13	430
the *G* of the spirits of all flesh	Num 27:16	430
The Lord our *G* spake unto us in	Deut 1:6	430
The Lord your *G* hath multiplied	Deut 1:10	430
(The Lord *G* of your fathers make	Deut 1:11	430
as the Lord our *G* commanded us	Deut 1:19	430
the Lord our *G* doth give unto us	Deut 1:20	430
the Lord thy *G* hath set the land	Deut 1:21	430
as the Lord *G* of thy fathers hath	Deut 1:21	430
which the Lord our *G* doth give us	Deut 1:25	430
commandment of the Lord your *G*	Deut 1:26	430
The Lord your *G* which goeth	Deut 1:30	430
how that the Lord thy *G* bare thee	Deut 1:31	430
did not believe the Lord your *G*	Deut 1:32	430
that the Lord our *G* commanded us	Deut 1:41	430
For the Lord thy *G* hath blessed	Deut 2:7	430
Lord thy *G* hath been with thee	Deut 2:7	430

G

which the Lord our G giveth us	Deut 2:29	430
for the Lord thy G hardened his	Deut 2:30	430
the Lord our G delivered him	Deut 2:33	430
the Lord our G delivered all unto	Deut 2:36	430
the Lord our G forbad us	Deut 2:37	430
So the Lord our G delivered into	Deut 3:3	430
The Lord your G hath given you	Deut 3:18	430
the land which the Lord your G	Deut 3:20	430
seen all that the Lord your G	Deut 3:21	430
for the Lord your G he shall	Deut 3:22	430
O Lord G, thou hast begun to shew	Deut 3:24	3069
for what G is there in heaven or	Deut 3:24	410
Lord G of your fathers giveth you	Deut 4:1	430
Lord your G which I command you	Deut 4:2	430
the Lord thy G hath destroyed	Deut 4:3	430
did cleave unto the Lord your G	Deut 4:4	430
as the Lord my G commanded me	Deut 4:5	430
who hath G so nigh unto them	Deut 4:7	430
as the Lord our G is in all	Deut 4:7	430
before the Lord thy G in Horeb	Deut 4:10	430
which the Lord thy G hath divided	Deut 4:19	430
which the Lord thy G giveth thee	Deut 4:21	430
the covenant of the Lord your G	Deut 4:23	430
which the Lord thy G hath	Deut 4:23	430
For the Lord thy G is a consuming	Deut 4:24	430
consuming fire, even a jealous G	Deut 4:24	410
in the sight of the Lord thy G	Deut 4:25	430
thou shalt seek the Lord thy G	Deut 4:29	430
if thou turn to the Lord thy G	Deut 4:30	430
the Lord thy G is a merciful G	Deut 4:31	430
the Lord thy G is a merciful G	Deut 4:31	410
since the day that G created man	Deut 4:32	430
of G speaking out of the midst of	Deut 4:33	430
Or hath G assayed to go and take	Deut 4:34	430
to all that the Lord your G did	Deut 4:34	430
know that the Lord he is G	Deut 4:35	430
the Lord he is G in heaven above	Deut 4:39	430
which the Lord thy G giveth thee	Deut 4:40	430
The Lord our G made a covenant	Deut 5:2	430
I am the Lord thy G, which	Deut 5:6	430
I the Lord thy G am a jealous G	Deut 5:9	430
I the Lord thy G am a jealous G	Deut 5:9	410
name of the Lord thy G in vain	Deut 5:11	430
as the Lord thy G hath commanded	Deut 5:12	430
is the sabbath of the Lord thy G	Deut 5:14	430
that the Lord thy G brought thee	Deut 5:15	430
therefore the Lord thy G	Deut 5:15	430
as the Lord thy G hath commanded	Deut 5:16	430
which the Lord thy G giveth thee	Deut 5:16	430
the Lord our G hath shewed us his	Deut 5:24	430
day that G doth talk with man	Deut 5:24	430
voice of the Lord our G any more	Deut 5:25	430
G speaking out of the midst of	Deut 5:26	430
all that the Lord our G shall say	Deut 5:27	430
Lord our G shall speak unto thee	Deut 5:27	430
Lord your G hath commanded you	Deut 5:32	430
Lord your G hath commanded you	Deut 5:33	430
which the Lord your G commanded	Deut 6:1	430
thou mightest fear the Lord thy G	Deut 6:2	430
as the Lord G of thy fathers hath	Deut 6:3	430
The Lord our G is one Lord	Deut 6:4	430
Lord thy G with all thine heart	Deut 6:5	430
when the Lord thy G shall have	Deut 6:10	430
Thou shalt fear the Lord thy G	Deut 6:13	430
(For the Lord thy G is a jealous	Deut 6:15	430
G among you) lest the anger of	Deut 6:15	410
thy G be kindled against thee	Deut 6:15	430
shall not tempt the Lord your G	Deut 6:16	430
commandments of the Lord your G	Deut 6:17	430
the Lord our G hath commanded you	Deut 6:20	430
statutes, to fear the Lord our G	Deut 6:24	430
before the Lord our G, as he hath	Deut 6:25	430
When the Lord thy G shall bring	Deut 7:1	430
when the Lord thy G shall deliver	Deut 7:2	430
holy people unto the Lord thy G	Deut 7:6	430
the Lord thy G hath chosen thee	Deut 7:6	430
that the Lord thy G, he is G	Deut 7:9	430
the faithful G, which keepeth covenant	Deut 7:9	410
that the Lord thy G shall keep	Deut 7:12	430
the Lord thy G shall deliver thee	Deut 7:16	430
the Lord thy G did unto Pharaoh	Deut 7:18	430
the Lord thy G brought thee out	Deut 7:19	430
so shall the Lord thy G do unto	Deut 7:19	430
Moreover the Lord thy G will send	Deut 7:20	430
for the Lord thy G is among you	Deut 7:21	430
a mighty G and terrible	Deut 7:21	410
the Lord thy G will put out those	Deut 7:22	430
But the Lord thy G shall deliver	Deut 7:23	430
an abomination to the Lord thy G	Deut 7:25	430
G led thee these forty years in	Deut 8:2	430
so the Lord thy G chasteneth thee	Deut 8:5	430
commandments of the Lord thy G	Deut 8:6	430
For the Lord thy G bringeth thee	Deut 8:7	430
thou shalt bless the Lord thy G	Deut 8:10	430
thou forget not the Lord thy G	Deut 8:11	430
up, and thou forget the Lord thy G	Deut 8:14	430
shalt remember the Lord thy G	Deut 8:18	430
do at all forget the Lord thy G	Deut 8:19	430
unto the voice of the Lord your G	Deut 8:20	430
that the Lord thy G is he which	Deut 9:3	430
after that the Lord thy G hath	Deut 9:4	430
of these nations the Lord thy G	Deut 9:5	430
that the Lord thy G giveth thee	Deut 9:6	430
thy G to wrath in the wilderness	Deut 9:7	430
written with the finger of G	Deut 9:10	430
sinned against the Lord your G	Deut 9:16	430
commandment of the Lord your G	Deut 9:23	430
unto the Lord, and said, O Lord G	Deut 9:26	3069
as the Lord thy G promised him	Deut 10:9	430
the Lord thy G require of thee	Deut 10:12	430
but to fear the Lord thy G	Deut 10:12	430
the Lord thy G with all thy heart	Deut 10:12	430
of heavens is the Lord's thy G	Deut 10:14	430
the Lord your G is G of gods	Deut 10:17	430
gods, and Lord of lords, a great G	Deut 10:17	410
Thou shalt fear the Lord thy G	Deut 10:20	430
He is thy praise, and he is thy G	Deut 10:21	430
now the Lord thy G hath made thee	Deut 10:22	430
thou shalt love the Lord thy G	Deut 11:1	430
chastisement of the Lord your G	Deut 11:2	430
which the Lord thy G careth for	Deut 11:12	430
the Lord thy G are always upon it	Deut 11:12	430
this day, to love the Lord your G	Deut 11:13	430
do them, to love the Lord your G	Deut 11:22	430
for the Lord your G shall lay the	Deut 11:25	430
commandments of the Lord your G	Deut 11:27	430
commandments of the Lord your G	Deut 11:28	430
when the Lord thy G hath brought	Deut 11:29	430
which the Lord your G giveth you	Deut 11:31	430
which the Lord G of thy fathers	Deut 12:1	430
not do so unto the Lord your G	Deut 12:4	430
G shall choose out of all your	Deut 12:5	430
shall eat before the Lord your G	Deut 12:7	430
the Lord thy G hath blessed thee	Deut 12:7	430
which the Lord your G giveth you	Deut 12:9	430
Lord your G giveth you to inherit	Deut 12:10	430
G shall choose to cause his name	Deut 12:11	430
rejoice before the Lord your G	Deut 12:12	430
thy G which he hath given thee	Deut 12:15	430
eat them before the Lord thy G in	Deut 12:18	430
which the Lord thy G shall choose	Deut 12:18	430
rejoice before the Lord thy G	Deut 12:18	430
When the Lord thy G shall enlarge	Deut 12:20	430
thy G hath chosen to put his name	Deut 12:21	430
upon the altar of the Lord thy G	Deut 12:27	430
upon the altar of the Lord thy G	Deut 12:27	430
in the sight of the Lord thy G	Deut 12:28	430
When the Lord thy G shall cut off	Deut 12:29	430
not do so unto the Lord thy G	Deut 12:31	430
for the Lord your G proveth you	Deut 13:3	430
Lord your G with all your heart	Deut 13:3	430
shall walk after the Lord your G	Deut 13:4	430
you away from the Lord your G	Deut 13:5	430
thy G commanded thee to walk in	Deut 13:5	430
thee away from the Lord thy G	Deut 13:10	430
which the Lord thy G hath given	Deut 13:12	430
every whit, for the Lord thy G	Deut 13:16	430
to the voice of the Lord thy G	Deut 13:18	430
in the eyes of the Lord thy G	Deut 13:18	430
the children of the Lord your G	Deut 14:1	430
holy people unto the Lord thy G	Deut 14:2	430
holy people unto the Lord thy G	Deut 14:21	430
shalt eat before the Lord thy G	Deut 14:23	430
to fear the Lord thy G always	Deut 14:23	430
which the Lord thy G shall choose	Deut 14:24	430
the Lord thy G hath blessed thee	Deut 14:24	430
which the Lord thy G shall choose	Deut 14:25	430
eat there before the Lord thy G	Deut 14:26	430
that the Lord thy G may bless	Deut 14:29	430
G giveth thee for an inheritance	Deut 15:4	430
unto the voice of the Lord thy G	Deut 15:5	430
For the Lord thy G blesseth thee	Deut 15:6	430
which the Lord thy G giveth thee	Deut 15:7	430
thy G shall bless thee in all thy	Deut 15:10	430
G hath blessed thee thou shalt	Deut 15:14	430
the Lord thy G redeemed thee	Deut 15:15	430
the Lord thy G shall bless thee	Deut 15:18	430
sanctify unto the Lord thy G	Deut 15:19	430
eat it before the Lord thy G year	Deut 15:20	430
sacrifice it unto the Lord thy G	Deut 15:21	430
the passover unto the Lord thy G	Deut 16:1	430
the month of Abib the Lord thy G	Deut 16:1	430

the passover unto the LORD thy *G* .... Deut 16:2   430
which the LORD thy *G* giveth thee .... Deut 16:5   430
G shall choose to place his name .... Deut 16:6   430
which the LORD thy *G* shall choose .... Deut 16:7   430
solemn assembly to the LORD thy *G* ...... Deut 16:8   430
of weeks unto the LORD thy *G* with .... Deut 16:10   430
shalt give unto the LORD thy *G* .... Deut 16:10   430
the LORD thy *G* hath blessed thee.......... Deut 16:10   430
rejoice before the LORD thy *G*................. Deut 16:11   430
G hath chosen to place his name ...... Deut 16:11   430
thy *G* in the place which the LORD ...... Deut 16:15   430
because the LORD thy *G* shall .... Deut 16:15   430
appear before the LORD thy *G* in .... Deut 16:16   430
thy *G* which he hath given thee .... Deut 16:17   430
which the LORD thy *G* giveth thee .... Deut 16:18   430
which the LORD thy *G* giveth thee .... Deut 16:20   430
unto the altar of the LORD thy *G* .... Deut 16:21   430
which the LORD thy *G* hateth .... Deut 16:22   430
unto the LORD thy *G* any bullock .... Deut 17:1   430
abomination unto the LORD thy *G* .... Deut 17:1   430
which the LORD thy *G* giveth thee .... Deut 17:2   430
in the sight of the LORD thy *G* .... Deut 17:2   430
which the LORD thy *G* shall choose .... Deut 17:8   430
there before the LORD thy *G* .... Deut 17:12   430
which the LORD thy *G* giveth thee .... Deut 17:14   430
whom the LORD thy *G* shall choose .... Deut 17:15   430
may learn to fear the LORD his *G* .... Deut 17:19   430
For the LORD thy *G* hath chosen .... Deut 18:5   430
in the name of the LORD his *G* .... Deut 18:7   430
which the LORD thy *G* giveth thee .... Deut 18:9   430
G doth drive them out from before .... Deut 18:12   430
be perfect with the LORD thy *G* .... Deut 18:13   430
the LORD thy *G* hath not suffered .... Deut 18:14   430
The LORD thy *G* will raise up unto .... Deut 18:15   430
thy *G* in Horeb in the day of the .... Deut 18:16   430
again the voice of the LORD my *G* .... Deut 18:16   430
When the LORD thy *G* hath cut off .... Deut 19:1   430
land the LORD thy *G* giveth thee .... Deut 19:1   430
which the LORD thy *G* giveth thee .... Deut 19:2   430
which the LORD thy *G* giveth thee .... Deut 19:3   430
if the LORD thy *G* enlarge thy.................. Deut 19:8   430
this day, to love the LORD thy *G* .... Deut 19:9   430
which the LORD thy *G* giveth thee .... Deut 19:10   430
thy *G* giveth thee to possess it................ Deut 19:14   430
for the LORD thy *G* is with thee .... Deut 20:1   430
For the LORD your *G* is he that............... Deut 20:4   430
And when the LORD thy *G* hath .... Deut 20:13   430
the LORD thy *G* hath given thee .... Deut 20:14   430
which the LORD thy *G* doth give.............. Deut 20:16   430
as the LORD thy *G* hath commanded ..... Deut 20:17   430
ye sin against the LORD your *G* .... Deut 20:18   430
thy *G* giveth thee to possess it .... Deut 21:1   430
for them the LORD thy *G* hath .... Deut 21:5   430
the LORD thy *G* hath delivered .... Deut 21:10   430
that is hanged is accursed of *G*.............. Deut 21:23   430
which the LORD thy *G* giveth thee .... Deut 21:23   430
abomination unto the LORD thy *G* .... Deut 22:5   430
Nevertheless the LORD thy *G* would ...... Deut 23:5   430
but the LORD thy *G* turned the .... Deut 23:5   430
because the LORD thy *G* loved thee .... Deut 23:5   430
For the LORD thy *G* walketh in the......... Deut 23:14   430
of the LORD thy *G* for any vow .... Deut 23:18   430
abomination unto the LORD thy *G* .... Deut 23:18   430
that the LORD thy *G* may bless.............. Deut 23:20   430
vow a vow unto the LORD thy *G*.............. Deut 23:21   430
for the LORD thy *G* will surely .... Deut 23:21   430
hast vowed unto the LORD thy *G*............ Deut 23:23   430
which the LORD thy *G* giveth thee .... Deut 24:4   430
thy *G* did unto Miriam by the way .... Deut 24:9   430
unto thee before the LORD thy *G* .... Deut 24:13   430
the LORD thy *G* redeemed thee .... Deut 24:18   430
that the LORD thy *G* may bless .... Deut 24:19   430
which the LORD thy *G* giveth thee .... Deut 25:15   430
abomination unto the LORD thy *G* .... Deut 25:16   430
and he feared not *G*................................ Deut 25:18   430
when the LORD thy *G* hath given .... Deut 25:19   430
G giveth thee for an inheritance............. Deut 25:19   430
the land which the LORD thy *G* .... Deut 26:1   430
that the LORD thy *G* giveth thee .... Deut 26:2   430
the place which the LORD thy *G*............. Deut 26:2   430
this day unto the LORD thy *G* .... Deut 26:3   430
the altar of the LORD thy *G*................... Deut 26:4   430
and say before the LORD thy *G*.............. Deut 26:5   430
unto the LORD *G* of our fathers............... Deut 26:7   430
set it before the LORD thy *G* .... Deut 26:10   430
and worship before the LORD thy *G* .... Deut 26:10   430
LORD thy *G* hath given unto thee............ Deut 26:11   430
shalt say before the LORD thy *G*............ Deut 26:13   430
to the voice of the LORD my *G*................ Deut 26:14   430
This day the LORD thy *G* hath .... Deut 26:16   430
the LORD this day to be thy *G*................ Deut 26:17   430

holy people unto the LORD thy *G*............ Deut 26:19   430
which the LORD thy *G* giveth thee .... Deut 27:2   430
which the LORD thy *G* giveth thee .... Deut 27:3   430
as the LORD *G* of thy fathers hath.......... Deut 27:3   430
an altar unto the LORD thy *G* .... Deut 27:5   430
of the LORD thy *G* of whole stones.......... Deut 27:6   430
thereon unto the LORD thy *G* .... Deut 27:6   430
and rejoice before the LORD thy *G* .... Deut 27:7   430
the people of the LORD thy *G*.................. Deut 27:9   430
obey the voice of the LORD thy *G* .... Deut 27:10   430
unto the voice of the LORD thy *G* .... Deut 28:1   430
that the LORD thy *G* will set thee .... Deut 28:1   430
unto the voice of the LORD thy *G* .... Deut 28:2   430
which the LORD thy *G* giveth thee .... Deut 28:8   430
commandments of the LORD thy *G* .... Deut 28:9   430
commandments of the LORD thy *G* .... Deut 28:13   430
unto the voice of the LORD thy *G* .... Deut 28:15   430
unto the voice of the LORD thy *G* .... Deut 28:45   430
the LORD thy *G* with joyfulness .... Deut 28:47   430
the LORD thy *G* hath given thee .... Deut 28:52   430
the LORD thy *G* hath given thee .... Deut 28:53   430
and fearful name, THE LORD THY *G* .... Deut 28:58   430
obey the voice of the LORD thy *G* .... Deut 28:62   430
shalt say, Would *G* it were even .... Deut 28:67
say, Would *G* it were morning .... Deut 28:67
know that I am the LORD your *G*............. Deut 29:6   430
all of you before the LORD your *G* .... Deut 29:10   430
into covenant with the LORD thy *G* .... Deut 29:12   430
which the LORD thy *G* maketh with .... Deut 29:12   430
and that he may be unto thee a *G*........... Deut 29:13   430
us this day before the LORD our *G* .... Deut 29:15   430
away this day from the LORD our *G* .... Deut 29:18   430
of the LORD *G* of their fathers .... Deut 29:25   430
things belong unto the LORD our *G*........ Deut 29:29   430
the LORD thy *G* hath driven thee .... Deut 30:1   430
shalt return unto the LORD thy *G*........... Deut 30:2   430
That then the LORD thy *G* will............... Deut 30:3   430
LORD thy *G* hath scattered thee .... Deut 30:3   430
will the LORD thy *G* gather thee .... Deut 30:4   430
the LORD thy *G* will bring thee .... Deut 30:5   430
the LORD thy *G* will circumcise .... Deut 30:6   430
LORD thy *G* with all thine heart .... Deut 30:6   430
the LORD thy *G* will put all these .... Deut 30:7   430
the LORD thy *G* will make thee .... Deut 30:9   430
unto the voice of the LORD thy *G* .... Deut 30:10   430
LORD thy *G* with all thine heart .... Deut 30:10   430
this day to love the LORD thy *G*............. Deut 30:16   430
the LORD thy *G* shall bless thee .... Deut 30:16   430
thou mayest love the LORD thy *G* .... Deut 30:20   430
The LORD thy *G*, he will go over .... Deut 31:3   430
for the LORD thy *G*, he it is that .... Deut 31:6   430
thy *G* in the place which he shall .... Deut 31:11   430
learn, and fear the LORD your *G* .... Deut 31:12   430
and learn to fear the LORD your *G* .... Deut 31:13   430
because our *G* is not among us............... Deut 31:17   430
the covenant of the LORD your *G*........... Deut 31:26   430
ascribe ye greatness unto our *G*............. Deut 32:3   430
a *G* of truth and without iniquity, ... Deut 32:4   410
then he forsook *G* which made him........ Deut 32:15   433
sacrificed unto devils, not to *G*.............. Deut 32:17   433
hast forgotten *G* that formed thee .... Deut 32:18   410
jealousy with that which is not *G* .... Deut 32:21   410
wherewith Moses the man of *G*............... Deut 33:1   430
none like unto the *G* of Jeshurun .... Deut 33:26   430
The eternal *G* is thy refuge, and............ Deut 33:27   430
for the LORD thy *G* is with thee .... Josh 1:9   430
which the LORD your *G* giveth you .... Josh 1:11   430
The LORD your *G* hath given you .... Josh 1:13   430
which the LORD your *G* giveth them ...... Josh 1:15   430
only the LORD thy *G* be with thee .... Josh 1:17   430
for the LORD your *G*, he is *G* in............. Josh 2:11   430
the covenant of the LORD your *G* .... Josh 3:3   430
hear the words of the LORD your *G*........ Josh 3:9   430
that the living *G* is among you................ Josh 3:10   410
your *G* into the midst of Jordan .... Josh 4:5   430
For the LORD your *G* dried up the .... Josh 4:23   430
as the LORD your *G* did to the Red .... Josh 4:23   430
fear the LORD your *G* for ever................. Josh 4:24   430
And Joshua said, Alas, O LORD *G*........... Josh 7:7   3069
would to *G* we had been content, ... Josh 7:7
thus saith the LORD *G* of Israel.............. Josh 7:13   430
glory to the LORD *G* of Israel .... Josh 7:19   430
against the LORD *G* of Israel .... Josh 7:20   430
for the LORD your *G* will deliver .... Josh 8:7   430
LORD *G* of Israel in mount Ebal .... Josh 8:30   430
of the name of the LORD thy *G* .... Josh 9:9   430
unto them by the LORD *G* of Israel......... Josh 9:18   430
unto them by the LORD *G* of Israel .... Josh 9:19   430
of water for the house of my *G* .... Josh 9:23   430
how that the LORD thy *G* commanded ... Josh 9:24   430
for the LORD your *G* hath......................... Josh 10:19   430

G

as the LORD G of Israel commanded	Josh 10:40	430
because the LORD G of Israel	Josh 10:42	430
LORD G of Israel made by fire are	Josh 13:14	430
the LORD G of Israel was their	Josh 13:33	430
Moses the man of G concerning me	Josh 14:6	430
I wholly followed the LORD my G	Josh 14:8	430
wholly followed the LORD my G	Josh 14:9	430
followed the LORD G of Israel	Josh 14:14	430
which the LORD G of your fathers	Josh 18:3	430
you here before the LORD our G	Josh 18:6	430
commandment of the LORD your G	Josh 22:3	430
now the LORD your G hath given	Josh 22:4	430
you, to love the LORD your G	Josh 22:5	430
committed against the G of Israel	Josh 22:16	430
the altar of the LORD our G	Josh 22:19	430
The LORD G of gods, the LORD G	Josh 22:22	410
to do with the LORD G of Israel	Josh 22:24	430
G forbid that we should rebel	Josh 22:29	
the altar of the LORD our G that	Josh 22:29	430
the children of Israel blessed G	Josh 22:33	430
between us that the LORD is G	Josh 22:34	430
your G hath done unto all these	Josh 23:3	430
for the LORD your G is he that	Josh 23:3	430
And the LORD your G, he shall	Josh 23:5	430
as the LORD your G hath promised	Josh 23:5	430
But cleave unto the LORD your G	Josh 23:8	430
for the LORD your G, he it is	Josh 23:10	430
that ye love the LORD your G	Josh 23:11	430
G will no more drive out any of	Josh 23:13	430
the LORD your G hath given you	Josh 23:13	430
LORD your G spake concerning you	Josh 23:15	430
the LORD your G promised you	Josh 23:15	430
the LORD your G hath given you	Josh 23:15	430
the covenant of the LORD your G	Josh 23:16	430
presented themselves before G	Josh 24:1	430
Thus saith the LORD G of Israel	Josh 24:2	430
G forbid that we should forsake	Josh 24:16	
For the LORD our G, he it is that	Josh 24:17	430
for he is our G	Josh 24:18	430
for he is an holy G	Josh 24:19	430
he is a jealous G	Josh 24:19	410
heart unto the LORD G of Israel	Josh 24:23	430
The LORD our G will we serve, and	Josh 24:24	430
words in the book of the law of G	Josh 24:26	430
unto you, lest ye deny your G	Josh 24:27	430
have done, so G hath requited me	Judg 1:7	430
the LORD G of their fathers	Judg 2:12	430
LORD, and forgat the LORD their G	Judg 3:7	430
I have a message from G unto thee	Judg 3:20	430
Hath not the LORD G of Israel	Judg 4:6	430
So G subdued on that day Jabin	Judg 4:23	430
praise to the LORD G of Israel	Judg 5:3	430
from before the LORD G of Israel	Judg 5:5	430
Thus saith the LORD G of Israel	Judg 6:8	430
unto you, I am the LORD your G	Judg 6:10	430
the angel of G said unto him,	Judg 6:20	430
LORD, Gideon said, Alas, O LORD G	Judg 6:22	3069
thy G upon the top of this rock	Judg 6:26	430
And Gideon said unto G, If thou	Judg 6:36	430
And Gideon said unto G, Let not	Judg 6:39	430
And G did so that night	Judg 6:40	430
his hand hath G delivered Midian	Judg 7:14	430
G hath delivered into your hands	Judg 8:3	430
remembered not the LORD their G	Judg 8:34	430
that G may hearken unto you	Judg 9:7	430
wherewith by me they honour G	Judg 9:9	430
I leave my wine, which cheereth G	Judg 9:13	430
Then G sent an evil spirit	Judg 9:23	430
would to G this people were under	Judg 9:29	
Thus G rendered the wickedness of	Judg 9:56	430
did G render upon their heads	Judg 9:57	430
because we have forsaken our G	Judg 10:10	430
the LORD G of Israel delivered	Judg 11:21	430
So now the LORD G of Israel hath	Judg 11:23	430
So whomsoever the LORD our G	Judg 11:24	430
a Nazarite unto G from the womb	Judg 13:5	430
A man of G came unto me, and his	Judg 13:6	430
the countenance of an angel of G	Judg 13:6	430
child shall be a Nazarite to G	Judg 13:7	430
let the man of G which thou didst	Judg 13:8	430
G hearkened to the voice of	Judg 13:9	430
the angel of G came again unto	Judg 13:9	430
die, because we have seen G	Judg 13:22	430
But G clave an hollow place that	Judg 15:19	430
unto G from my mother's womb	Judg 16:17	430
unto the LORD, and said, O Lord G	Judg 16:28	3069
I pray thee, only this once, O G	Judg 16:28	430
Ask counsel, we pray thee, of G	Judg 18:5	430
for G hath given it into your	Judg 18:10	430
that the house of G was in Shiloh	Judg 18:31	430
the assembly of the people of G	Judg 20:2	430

and went up to the house of G	Judg 20:18	1008
and asked counsel of G	Judg 20:18	1008
up, and came unto the house of G	Judg 20:26	1008
of G was there in those days	Judg 20:27	430
one goeth up to the house of G	Judg 20:31	1008
the people came to the house of G	Judg 21:2	1008
and abode there till even before G	Judg 21:2	430
O LORD G of Israel, why is this	Judg 21:3	430
thee of the LORD G of Israel	Ruth 2:12	430
the G of Israel grant thee thy	1Sa 1:17	430
is there any rock like our G	1Sa 2:2	430
for the LORD is a G of knowledge	1Sa 2:3	410
And there came a man of G unto Eli	1Sa 2:27	430
the LORD G of Israel saith	1Sa 2:30	430
wealth which G shall give Israel	1Sa 2:32	
ere the lamp of G went out in the	1Sa 3:3	430
the LORD, where the ark of G was	1Sa 3:3	430
G do so to thee, and more also, if	1Sa 3:17	430
with the ark of the covenant of G	1Sa 4:4	430
said, G is come into the camp	1Sa 4:7	430
And the ark of G was taken	1Sa 4:11	430
heart trembled for the ark of G	1Sa 4:13	430
dead, and the ark of G is taken	1Sa 4:17	430
he made mention of the ark of G	1Sa 4:18	430
that the ark of G was taken	1Sa 4:19	430
because the ark of G was taken	1Sa 4:21	430
for the ark of G is taken	1Sa 4:22	430
the Philistines took the ark of G	1Sa 5:1	430
the Philistines took the ark of G	1Sa 5:2	430
The ark of the G of Israel shall	1Sa 5:7	430
with the ark of the G of Israel	1Sa 5:8	430
Let the ark of the G of Israel be	1Sa 5:8	430
of the G of Israel about thither	1Sa 5:8	430
they sent the ark of G to Ekron	1Sa 5:10	430
as the ark of G came to Ekron	1Sa 5:10	430
the ark of the G of Israel to us	1Sa 5:10	430
away the ark of the G of Israel	1Sa 5:11	430
the hand of G was very heavy	1Sa 5:11	430
away the ark of the G of Israel	1Sa 6:3	430
give glory unto the G of Israel	1Sa 6:5	430
to stand before this holy LORD G	1Sa 6:20	430
to cry unto the LORD our G for us	1Sa 7:8	430
there is in this city a man of G	1Sa 9:6	430
present to bring to the man of G	1Sa 9:7	430
that will I give to the man of G	1Sa 9:8	430
when a man went to enquire of G	1Sa 9:9	430
the city where the man of G was	1Sa 9:10	430
I may shew thee the word of G	1Sa 9:27	430
men going up to G to Beth-el	1Sa 10:3	430
thou shalt come to the hill of G	1Sa 10:5	430
for G is with thee	1Sa 10:7	430
Samuel, G gave him another heart	1Sa 10:9	430
and the Spirit of G came upon him	1Sa 10:10	430
Thus saith the LORD G of Israel	1Sa 10:18	430
ye have this day rejected your G	1Sa 10:19	430
shouted, and said, G save the king	1Sa 10:24	
men, whose hearts G had touched	1Sa 10:26	430
the Spirit of G came upon Saul,	1Sa 11:6	430
when they forgat the LORD their G	1Sa 12:9	430
the LORD your G was your king	1Sa 12:12	430
following the LORD your G	1Sa 12:14	430
thy servants unto the LORD thy G	1Sa 12:19	430
G forbid that I should sin	1Sa 12:23	
the commandment of the LORD thy G	1Sa 13:13	430
Ahiah, Bring hither the ark of G	1Sa 14:18	430
For the ark of G was at that time	1Sa 14:18	430
Let us draw near hither unto G	1Sa 14:36	430
And Saul asked counsel of G	1Sa 14:37	430
said unto the LORD G of Israel	1Sa 14:41	430
answered, G do so and more also	1Sa 14:44	430
G forbid: as the LORD liveth	1Sa 14:45	
he hath wrought with G this day	1Sa 14:45	430
to sacrifice unto the LORD thy G	1Sa 15:15	430
unto the LORD thy G in Gilgal	1Sa 15:21	430
that I may worship the LORD thy G	1Sa 15:30	430
evil spirit from G troubleth thee	1Sa 16:15	430
evil spirit from G is upon thee	1Sa 16:16	430
evil spirit from G was upon Saul	1Sa 16:23	430
defy the armies of the living G	1Sa 17:26	430
defied the armies of the living G	1Sa 17:36	430
the G of the armies of Israel,	1Sa 17:45	430
know that there is a G in Israel	1Sa 17:46	430
evil spirit from G came upon Saul	1Sa 18:10	430
the Spirit of G was upon the	1Sa 19:20	430
the Spirit of G was upon him also	1Sa 19:23	430
And he said unto him, G forbid	1Sa 20:2	
O LORD G of Israel, when I have	1Sa 20:12	430
till I know what G will do for me	1Sa 22:3	430
and hast enquired of G for him	1Sa 22:13	430
begin to enquire of G for him	1Sa 22:15	430
G hath delivered him into mine	1Sa 23:7	430

O Lord *G* of Israel, thy servant	1Sa 23:10	430
O Lord *G* of Israel, I beseech	1Sa 23:11	430
but *G* delivered him not into his	1Sa 23:14	430
and strengthened his hand in *G*	1Sa 23:16	430
more also do *G* unto the enemies	1Sa 25:22	430
of life with the Lord thy *G*	1Sa 25:29	430
Blessed be the Lord *G* of Israel	1Sa 25:32	430
as the Lord *G* of Israel liveth,	1Sa 25:34	430
G hath delivered thine enemy into	1Sa 26:8	430
G is departed from me, and	1Sa 28:15	430
in my sight, as an angel of *G*	1Sa 29:9	430
himself in the Lord his *G*	1Sa 30:6	430
And he said, Swear unto me by *G*	1Sa 30:15	430
As the Lord, unless thou hadst	2Sa 2:27	430
So do *G* to Abner, and more also,	2Sa 3:9	430
sware, saying, So do *G* to me	2Sa 3:35	430
the Lord *G* of hosts was with him	2Sa 5:10	430
bring up from thence the ark of *G*	2Sa 6:2	430
set the ark of *G* upon a new cart	2Sa 6:3	430
Gibeah, accompanying the ark of *G*	2Sa 6:4	430
forth his hand to the ark of *G*	2Sa 6:6	430
G smote him there for his error	2Sa 6:7	430
and there he died by the ark of *G*	2Sa 6:7	430
unto him, because of the ark of *G*	2Sa 6:12	430
brought up the ark of *G* from the	2Sa 6:12	430
but the ark of *G* dwelleth within	2Sa 7:2	430
and he said, Who am I, O Lord *G*	2Sa 7:18	3069
thing in thy sight, O Lord *G*	2Sa 7:19	3069
this the manner of man, O Lord *G*	2Sa 7:19	3069
for thou, Lord *G*, knowest thy	2Sa 7:20	3069
thou art great, O Lord *G*	2Sa 7:22	430
is there any *G* beside thee	2Sa 7:22	430
whom *G* went to redeem for a	2Sa 7:23	430
and thou, Lord, art become their *G*	2Sa 7:24	430
And now, O Lord *G*, the word that	2Sa 7:25	430
of hosts is the *G* over Israel	2Sa 7:26	430
G of Israel, hast revealed to thy	2Sa 7:27	430
And now, O Lord *G*	2Sa 7:28	3069
thou art that *G*	2Sa 7:28	430
for thou, O Lord *G*, hast spoken	2Sa 7:29	3069
shew the kindness of *G* unto him	2Sa 9:3	430
and for the cities of our *G*	2Sa 10:12	430
Thus saith the Lord *G* of Israel	2Sa 12:7	430
besought *G* for the child	2Sa 12:16	430
Who can tell whether *G* will be	2Sa 12:22	3068
the king remember the Lord thy *G*	2Sa 14:11	430
a thing against the people of *G*	2Sa 14:13	430
neither doth *G* respect any person	2Sa 14:14	430
out of the inheritance of *G*	2Sa 14:16	430
for as an angel of *G*, so is my	2Sa 14:17	430
the Lord thy *G* will be with thee	2Sa 14:17	430
to the wisdom of an angel of *G*	2Sa 14:20	430
the ark of the covenant of *G*	2Sa 15:24	430
and they set down the ark of *G*	2Sa 15:24	430
back the ark of *G* into the city	2Sa 15:25	430
the ark of *G* again to Jerusalem	2Sa 15:29	430
the mount, where he worshipped *G*	2Sa 15:32	430
G save the king, *G* save the	2Sa 16:16	
had enquired at the oracle of *G*	2Sa 16:23	430
said, Blessed be the Lord thy *G*	2Sa 18:28	430
would *G* I had died for thee, O	2Sa 18:33	
G do so to me, and more also, if	2Sa 19:13	430
lord the king is as an angel of *G*	2Sa 19:27	430
after that *G* was intreated for	2Sa 21:14	430
The *G* of my rock	2Sa 22:3	430
upon the Lord, and cried to my *G*	2Sa 22:7	430
not wickedly departed from my *G*	2Sa 22:22	430
by my *G* have I leaped over a wall	2Sa 22:30	430
As for *G*, his way is perfect	2Sa 22:31	410
For who is *G*, save the Lord	2Sa 22:32	410
and who is a rock, save our *G*	2Sa 22:32	430
G is my strength and power	2Sa 22:33	410
exalted be the *G* of the rock of	2Sa 22:47	430
It is *G* that avengeth me, and that	2Sa 22:48	410
the anointed of the *G* of Jacob	2Sa 23:1	430
The *G* of Israel said, the Rock of	2Sa 23:3	430
be just, ruling in the fear of *G*	2Sa 23:3	430
my house be not so with *G*	2Sa 23:5	410
Now the Lord thy *G* add unto the	2Sa 24:3	430
king, The Lord thy *G* accept thee	2Sa 24:23	430
my *G* of that which doth cost me	2Sa 24:24	430
Lord thy *G* unto thine handmaid	1Ki 1:17	430
him, and say, *G* save king Adonijah	1Ki 1:25	
unto thee by the Lord *G* of Israel	1Ki 1:30	430
and say, *G* save king Solomon	1Ki 1:34	
the Lord *G* of my lord the king	1Ki 1:36	430
people said, *G* save king Solomon	1Ki 1:39	
G make the name of Solomon better	1Ki 1:47	430
Blessed be the Lord *G* of Israel	1Ki 1:48	430
keep the charge of the Lord thy *G*	1Ki 2:3	430
G do so to me, and more also, if	1Ki 2:23	430

the Lord *G* before David my father	1Ki 2:26	3069
G said, Ask what I shall give	1Ki 3:5	430
And now, O Lord my *G*, thou hast	1Ki 3:7	430
G said unto him, Because thou	1Ki 3:11	430
that the wisdom of *G* was in him	1Ki 3:28	430
And *G* gave Solomon wisdom and	1Ki 4:29	430
G for the wars which were about	1Ki 5:3	430
But now the Lord my *G* hath given	1Ki 5:4	430
unto the name of the Lord my *G*	1Ki 5:5	430
Blessed be the Lord *G* of Israel	1Ki 8:15	430
the name of the Lord *G* of Israel	1Ki 8:17	430
the name of the Lord *G* of Israel	1Ki 8:20	
Lord *G* of Israel, there is no *G*	1Ki 8:23	430
Lord *G* of Israel, keep with thy	1Ki 8:25	430
O *G* of Israel, let thy word, I	1Ki 8:26	430
But will *G* indeed dwell on the	1Ki 8:27	430
to his supplication, O Lord my *G*	1Ki 8:28	430
fathers out of Egypt, O Lord *G*	1Ki 8:53	3069
The Lord our *G* be with us	1Ki 8:57	430
be nigh unto the Lord our *G* day	1Ki 8:59	430
earth may know that the Lord is *G*	1Ki 8:60	430
be perfect with the Lord our *G*	1Ki 8:61	430
of Egypt, before the Lord our *G*	1Ki 8:65	430
they forsook the Lord their *G*	1Ki 9:9	430
Blessed be the Lord thy *G*	1Ki 10:9	430
which *G* had put in his heart	1Ki 10:24	430
not perfect with the Lord his *G*	1Ki 11:4	430
turned from the Lord *G* of Israel	1Ki 11:9	430
And *G* stirred him up another	1Ki 11:23	430
the *G* of Israel, Behold, I will	1Ki 11:31	430
But the word of *G* came unto	1Ki 12:22	430
came unto Shemaiah the man of *G*	1Ki 12:22	430
there came a man of *G* out of	1Ki 13:1	430
heard the saying of the man of *G*	1Ki 13:4	430
of *G* had given by the word of the	1Ki 13:5	430
and said unto the man of *G*	1Ki 13:6	430
now the face of the Lord thy *G*	1Ki 13:6	430
the man of *G* besought the Lord,	1Ki 13:6	430
the king said unto the man of *G*	1Ki 13:7	430
the man of *G* said unto the king,	1Ki 13:8	430
of *G* had done that day in Beth-el	1Ki 13:11	430
seen what way the man of *G* went	1Ki 13:12	430
And went after the man of *G*	1Ki 13:14	430
Art thou the man of *G* that camest	1Ki 13:14	430
the man of *G* that came from Judah	1Ki 13:21	430
the Lord thy *G* commanded thee	1Ki 13:21	430
he said, It is the man of *G*	1Ki 13:26	430
up the carcase of the man of *G*	1Ki 13:29	430
wherein the man of *G* is buried	1Ki 13:31	430
Thus saith the Lord *G* of Israel	1Ki 14:7	430
Lord *G* of Israel in the house of	1Ki 14:13	430
not perfect with the Lord his *G*	1Ki 15:3	430
G give him a lamp in Jerusalem	1Ki 15:4	430
the Lord *G* of Israel to anger	1Ki 15:30	430
in provoking the Lord *G* of Israel	1Ki 16:13	430
to provoke the Lord *G* of Israel	1Ki 16:26	430
did more to provoke the Lord *G* of	1Ki 16:33	430
As the Lord *G* of Israel liveth,	1Ki 17:1	430
said, As the Lord thy *G* liveth	1Ki 17:12	430
thus saith the Lord *G* of Israel	1Ki 17:14	430
to do with thee, O thou man of *G*	1Ki 17:18	430
the Lord, and said, O Lord my *G*	1Ki 17:20	430
the Lord, and said, O Lord my *G*	1Ki 17:21	430
I know that thou art a man of *G*	1Ki 17:24	430
As the Lord thy *G* liveth, there	1Ki 18:10	430
if the Lord be *G*, follow him	1Ki 18:21	430
the *G* that answereth by fire, let	1Ki 18:24	430
answereth by fire, let him be *G*	1Ki 18:24	430
Lord *G* of Abraham, Isaac, and of	1Ki 18:36	430
day that thou art *G* in Israel	1Ki 18:36	430
may know that thou art the Lord *G*	1Ki 18:37	430
they said, The Lord, he is the *G*	1Ki 18:39	430
the Lord, he is the *G*	1Ki 18:39	430
nights unto Horeb the mount of *G*	1Ki 19:8	430
jealous for the Lord *G* of hosts	1Ki 19:10	430
jealous for the Lord *G* of hosts	1Ki 19:14	430
And there came a man of *G*, and	1Ki 20:28	430
The Lord is *G* of the hills	1Ki 20:28	430
but he is not *G* of the valleys,	1Ki 20:28	430
saying, Thou didst blaspheme *G*	1Ki 21:10	430
saying, Naboth did blaspheme *G*	1Ki 21:13	430
to anger the Lord *G* of Israel	1Ki 22:53	430
there is not a *G* in Israel	2Ki 1:3	430
there is not a *G* in Israel	2Ki 1:6	430
he spake unto him, Thou man of *G*	2Ki 1:9	430
of fifty, If I be a man of *G*	2Ki 1:10	430
and said unto him, O man of *G*	2Ki 1:11	430
unto them, If I be a man of *G*	2Ki 1:12	430
the fire of *G* came down from	2Ki 1:12	430
him, and said unto him, O man of *G*	2Ki 1:13	430
no *G* in Israel to enquire of his	2Ki 1:16	430

G

Where is the Lord G of Elijah	2Kin 2:14	430
she came and told the man of G	2Kin 4:7	430
that this is an holy man of G	2Kin 4:9	430
said, Nay, my lord, thou man of G	2Kin 4:16	430
him on the bed of the man of G	2Kin 4:21	430
that I may run to the man of G	2Kin 4:22	430
unto the man of G to mount Carmel	2Kin 4:25	430
when the man of G saw her afar	2Kin 4:25	430
came to the man of G to the hill	2Kin 4:27	430
And the man of G said, Let her	2Kin 4:27	430
out, and said, O thou man of G	2Kin 4:40	430
brought the man of G bread of the	2Kin 4:42	430
Would G my lord were with the	2Kin 5:3	
rent his clothes, and said, Am I G	2Kin 5:7	430
when Elisha the man of G had	2Kin 5:8	430
on the name of the Lord his	2Kin 5:11	430
to the saying of the man of G	2Kin 5:14	430
And he returned to the man of G	2Kin 5:15	430
there is no G in all the earth	2Kin 5:15	430
servant of Elisha the man of G	2Kin 5:20	430
And the man of G said, Where fell	2Kin 6:6	430
the man of G sent unto the king	2Kin 6:9	430
place which the man of G told him	2Kin 6:10	430
of the man of G was risen early	2Kin 6:15	430
G do so and more also to me, if	2Kin 6:31	430
king leaned answered the man of G	2Kin 7:2	430
he died, as the man of G had said	2Kin 7:17	430
man of G had spoken to the king	2Kin 7:18	430
that lord answered the man of G	2Kin 7:19	430
after the saying of the man of G	2Kin 8:2	430
the servant of the man of G	2Kin 8:4	430
The man of G is come hither	2Kin 8:7	430
hand, and go, meet the man of G	2Kin 8:8	430
and the man of G wept	2Kin 8:11	430
Thus saith the Lord G of Israel	2Kin 9:6	430
G of Israel with all his heart	2Kin 10:31	430
hands, and said, G save the king	2Kin 11:12	
the man of G was wroth with him,	2Kin 13:19	430
the word of the Lord G of Israel	2Kin 14:25	430
in the sight of the Lord his G	2Kin 15:2	430
sinned against the Lord their G	2Kin 17:7	430
right against the Lord their G	2Kin 17:9	430
not believe in the Lord their G	2Kin 17:14	430
commandments of the Lord their G	2Kin 17:16	430
commandments of the Lord their G	2Kin 17:19	430
the manner of the G of the land	2Kin 17:26	430
the manner of the G of the land	2Kin 17:26	430
the manner of the G of the land	2Kin 17:27	430
But the Lord your G ye shall fear	2Kin 17:39	430
trusted in the Lord G of Israel	2Kin 18:5	430
not the voice of the Lord their G	2Kin 18:12	430
me, We trust in the Lord our G	2Kin 18:22	430
It may be the Lord thy G will	2Kin 19:4	430
sent to reproach the living G	2Kin 19:4	430
which the Lord thy G hath heard	2Kin 19:4	430
Let not thy G in whom thou	2Kin 19:10	430
O Lord G of Israel, which	2Kin 19:15	430
the cherubims, thou art the G	2Kin 19:15	430
sent him to reproach the living G	2Kin 19:16	430
Now therefore, O Lord our G	2Kin 19:19	430
may know that thou art the Lord G	2Kin 19:19	430
Thus saith the Lord G of Israel	2Kin 19:20	430
the G of David thy father, I have	2Kin 20:5	430
thus saith the Lord G of Israel	2Kin 21:12	430
forsook the Lord G of his fathers	2Kin 21:22	430
Thus saith the Lord G of Israel	2Kin 22:15	430
Thus saith the Lord G of Israel	2Kin 22:18	430
which the man of G proclaimed	2Kin 23:16	430
is the sepulchre of the man of G	2Kin 23:17	430
the passover unto the Lord your G	2Kin 23:21	430
Jabez called on the G of Israel	1Chr 4:10	430
G granted that which he	1Chr 4:10	430
for they cried to G in the battle	1Chr 5:20	430
slain, because the war was of G	1Chr 5:22	430
against the G of their fathers	1Chr 5:25	430
whom G destroyed before them	1Chr 5:25	430
the G of Israel stirred up the	1Chr 5:26	430
the tabernacle of the house of G	1Chr 6:48	430
the servant of G had commanded	1Chr 6:49	430
the ruler of the house of G	1Chr 9:11	430
of the service of the house of G	1Chr 9:13	430
and treasuries of the house of G	1Chr 9:26	430
lodged round about the house of G	1Chr 9:27	430
the Lord thy G said unto thee,	1Chr 11:2	430
My G forbid it me, that I should	1Chr 11:19	430
the G of our fathers look thereon	1Chr 12:17	430
for thy G helpeth thee	1Chr 12:18	430
a great host, like the host of G	1Chr 12:22	430
and that it be of the Lord our G	1Chr 13:2	430
again the ark of our G to us	1Chr 13:3	430
the ark of G from Kirjath-jearim	1Chr 13:5	430

up thence the ark of G the Lord	1Chr 13:6	430
they carried the ark of G in a	1Chr 13:7	430
before G with all their might	1Chr 13:8	430
and there he died before G	1Chr 13:10	430
And David was afraid of G that day	1Chr 13:12	430
I bring the ark of G home to me	1Chr 13:12	430
the ark of G remained with the	1Chr 13:14	430
And David enquired of G, saying,	1Chr 14:10	430
G hath broken in upon mine	1Chr 14:11	430
David enquired again of G	1Chr 14:14	430
G said unto him, Go not up after	1Chr 14:14	430
for G is gone forth before thee	1Chr 14:15	430
therefore did as G commanded him	1Chr 14:16	430
prepared a place for the ark of G	1Chr 15:1	430
the ark of G but the Levites	1Chr 15:2	430
Lord chosen to carry the ark of G	1Chr 15:2	430
bring up the ark of the Lord G of	1Chr 15:12	430
the Lord our G made a breach upon	1Chr 15:13	430
the ark of the Lord G of Israel	1Chr 15:14	430
G upon their shoulders with the	1Chr 15:15	430
the trumpets before the ark of G	1Chr 15:24	430
when G helped the Levites that	1Chr 15:26	430
So they brought the ark of G	1Chr 16:1	430
and peace offerings before G	1Chr 16:1	430
and praise the Lord G of Israel	1Chr 16:4	430
the ark of the covenant of G	1Chr 16:6	430
He is the Lord our G	1Chr 16:14	430
O G of our salvation, and gather	1Chr 16:35	430
be the Lord G of Israel for ever	1Chr 16:36	430
and with musical instruments of G	1Chr 16:42	430
for G is with thee	1Chr 17:2	430
that the word of G came to Nathan	1Chr 17:3	430
Lord, and said, Who am I, O Lord G	1Chr 17:16	430
a small thing in thine eyes, O G	1Chr 17:17	430
of a man of high degree, O Lord G	1Chr 17:17	430
is there any G beside thee	1Chr 17:20	430
whom G went to redeem to be his	1Chr 17:21	430
and thou, Lord, becamest their G	1Chr 17:22	430
G of Israel, even a G to Israel	1Chr 17:24	430
For thou, O my G, hast told thy	1Chr 17:25	430
And now, Lord, thou art G, and hast	1Chr 17:26	430
and for the cities of our G	1Chr 19:13	430
G was displeased with this thing	1Chr 21:7	430
And David said unto G, I have	1Chr 21:8	430
G sent an angel unto Jerusalem to	1Chr 21:15	430
And David said unto G, Is it not I	1Chr 21:17	430
hand, I pray thee, O Lord my G	1Chr 21:17	430
not go before it to enquire of G	1Chr 21:30	430
This is the house of the Lord G	1Chr 22:1	430
stones to build the house of G	1Chr 22:2	430
an house for the Lord G of Israel	1Chr 22:6	430
unto the name of the Lord my G	1Chr 22:7	430
build the house of the Lord thy G	1Chr 22:11	430
keep the law of the Lord thy G	1Chr 22:12	430
Is not the Lord your G with you	1Chr 22:18	430
your soul to seek the Lord your G	1Chr 22:19	430
ye the sanctuary of the Lord G	1Chr 22:19	430
Lord, and the holy vessels of G	1Chr 22:19	430
Now concerning Moses the man of G	1Chr 23:14	430
The Lord G of Israel hath given	1Chr 23:25	430
of the service of the house of G	1Chr 23:28	430
and governors of the house of G	1Chr 24:5	430
as the Lord G of Israel had	1Chr 24:19	430
the king's seer in the words of G	1Chr 25:5	430
G gave to Heman fourteen sons and	1Chr 25:5	430
for the service of the house of G	1Chr 25:6	430
for G blessed him	1Chr 26:5	430
the treasures of the house of G	1Chr 26:20	430
for every matter pertaining to G	1Chr 26:32	430
and for the footstool of our G	1Chr 28:2	430
But G said unto me, Thou shalt	1Chr 28:3	430
Howbeit the Lord G of Israel	1Chr 28:4	430
Lord, and in the audience of our G	1Chr 28:8	430
commandments of the Lord your G	1Chr 28:8	430
know thou the G of thy father	1Chr 28:9	430
the treasuries of the house of G	1Chr 28:12	430
for the Lord G, even my G	1Chr 28:20	430
all the service of the house of G	1Chr 28:21	430
whom alone G hath chosen, is yet	1Chr 29:1	430
not for man, but for the Lord G	1Chr 29:1	430
my might for the house of my G	1Chr 29:2	430
my affection to the house of my G	1Chr 29:3	430
I have given to the house of my G	1Chr 29:3	430
G of gold five thousand talents	1Chr 29:7	430
Lord G of Israel our father, for	1Chr 29:10	430
Now therefore, our G, we thank	1Chr 29:13	430
O Lord our G, all this store that	1Chr 29:16	430
I know also, my G, that thou	1Chr 29:17	430
O Lord G of Abraham, Isaac, and of	1Chr 29:18	430
Now bless the Lord your G	1Chr 29:20	430
the Lord G of their fathers	1Chr 29:20	430

and the LORD his *G* was with him 2Chr 1:1   430
of the congregation of *G*, which 2Chr 1:3   430
But the ark of *G* had David 2Chr 1:4   430
In that night did *G* appear unto 2Chr 1:7   430
And Solomon said unto *G*, Thou hast 2Chr 1:8   430
Now, O LORD *G*, let thy promise............. 2Chr 1:9   430
G said to Solomon, Because this 2Chr 1:11   430
to the name of the LORD my *G* 2Chr 2:4   430
solemn feasts of the LORD our *G* 2Chr 2:4   430
for great is our *G* above all gods 2Chr 2:5   430
Blessed be the LORD *G* of Israel............. 2Chr 2:12   430
the building of the house of *G* 2Chr 3:3   430
king Solomon for the house of *G* 2Chr 4:11   430
that were for the house of *G* 2Chr 4:19   430
the treasures of the house of *G* 2Chr 5:1   430
LORD had filled the house of *G* 2Chr 5:14   430
Blessed be the LORD *G* of Israel............. 2Chr 6:4   430
the name of the LORD *G* of Israel 2Chr 6:7   430
the name of the LORD *G* of Israel 2Chr 6:10   430
O LORD *G* of Israel 2Chr 6:14   430
there is no *G* like thee in the 2Chr 6:14   430
O LORD *G* of Israel, keep with thy 2Chr 6:16   430
O LORD *G* of Israel, let thy word 2Chr 6:17   430
But will *G* in very deed dwell 2Chr 6:18   430
to his supplication, O LORD my *G* 2Chr 6:19   430
Now, my *G*, let, I beseech thee, ... 2Chr 6:40   430
Now therefore arise, O LORD *G* 2Chr 6:41   430
let thy priests, O LORD *G* 2Chr 6:41   430
O LORD *G*, turn not away the face 2Chr 6:42   430
people dedicated the house of *G* 2Chr 7:5   430
the LORD *G* of their fathers 2Chr 7:22   430
had David the man of *G* commanded 2Chr 8:14   430
Blessed be the LORD thy *G* 2Chr 9:8   430
to be king for the LORD thy *G* 2Chr 9:8   430
because thy *G* loved Israel, to 2Chr 9:8   430
that *G* had put in his heart 2Chr 9:23   430
for the cause was of *G*, that the 2Chr 10:15   430
came to Shemaiah the man of *G* 2Chr 11:2   430
G of Israel came to Jerusalem 2Chr 11:16   430
unto the LORD *G* of their fathers 2Chr 11:16   430
ye not to know that the LORD *G* of 2Chr 13:5   430
But as for us, the LORD is our *G* 2Chr 13:10   430
keep the charge of the LORD our *G* 2Chr 13:11   430
G himself is with us for our 2Chr 13:12   430
the LORD *G* of your fathers 2Chr 13:12   430
that *G* smote Jeroboam and all.............. 2Chr 13:15   430
G delivered them into their hand 2Chr 13:16   430
upon the LORD *G* of their fathers 2Chr 13:18   430
in the eyes of the LORD his *G* 2Chr 14:2   430
seek the LORD *G* of their fathers 2Chr 14:4   430
we have sought the LORD our *G* 2Chr 14:7   430
And Asa cried unto the LORD his *G* 2Chr 14:11   430
help us, O LORD our *G* 2Chr 14:11   430
O LORD, thou art our *G* 2Chr 14:11   430
the Spirit of *G* came upon Azariah 2Chr 15:1   430
hath been without the true *G*................. 2Chr 15:3   430
turn unto the LORD *G* of Israel.............. 2Chr 15:4   430
for *G* did vex them with all................... 2Chr 15:6   430
that the LORD his *G* was with him 2Chr 15:9   430
a covenant to seek the LORD *G* of 2Chr 15:12   430
would not seek the LORD *G* of 2Chr 15:13   430
he brought into the house of *G* 2Chr 15:18   430
and not relied on the LORD thy *G*........... 2Chr 16:7   430
to the LORD *G* of his father 2Chr 17:4   430
for *G* will deliver it into the 2Chr 18:5   430
LORD liveth, even what my *G* saith........ 2Chr 18:13   430
G moved them to depart from him 2Chr 18:31   430
prepared thine heart to seek *G*.............. 2Chr 19:3   430
unto the LORD *G* of their fathers 2Chr 19:4   430
no iniquity with the LORD our *G* 2Chr 19:7   430
O LORD *G* of our fathers......................... 2Chr 20:6   430
art not thou *G* in heaven 2Chr 20:6   430
Art not thou our *G*, who didst 2Chr 20:7   430
O our *G*, wilt thou not judge them 2Chr 20:12   430
stood up to praise the LORD *G* of 2Chr 20:19   430
Believe in the LORD your *G*.................... 2Chr 20:20   430
the fear of *G* was on all the 2Chr 20:29   430
for his *G* gave him rest round 2Chr 20:30   430
unto the *G* of their fathers 2Chr 20:33   430
the LORD *G* of his fathers 2Chr 21:10   430
the LORD *G* of David thy father 2Chr 21:12   430
was of *G* by coming to Joram 2Chr 22:7   430
hid in the house of *G* six years 2Chr 22:12   430
with the king in the house of *G*............. 2Chr 23:3   430
which were in the house of *G* 2Chr 23:9   430
him, and said, *G* save the king.............. 2Chr 23:11   430
house of your *G* from year to year........ 2Chr 24:5   430
had broken up the house of *G*............... 2Chr 24:7   430
of *G* laid upon Israel in the 2Chr 24:9   430
set the house of *G* in his state.............. 2Chr 24:13   430
good in Israel, both toward *G* 2Chr 24:16   430

of the LORD *G* of their fathers................ 2Chr 24:18   430
the Spirit of *G* came upon 2Chr 24:20   430
and said unto them, Thus saith *G* 2Chr 24:20   430
the LORD *G* of their fathers 2Chr 24:24   430
the repairing of the house of *G* 2Chr 24:27   430
But there came a man of *G* to him 2Chr 25:7   430
G shall make thee fall before the........... 2Chr 25:8   430
for *G* hath power to help, and to 2Chr 25:8   430
And Amaziah said to the man of *G*........ 2Chr 25:9   430
And the man of *G* answered, The 2Chr 25:9   430
I know that *G* hath determined to 2Chr 25:16   430
for it came of *G*, that he might.............. 2Chr 25:20   430
in the house of *G* with Obed-edom 2Chr 25:24   430
he sought *G* in the days of.................... 2Chr 26:5   430
understanding in the visions of *G*.......... 2Chr 26:5   430
the LORD, *G* made him to prosper.......... 2Chr 26:5   430
And *G* helped him against the............... 2Chr 26:7   430
against the LORD his *G*, and went 2Chr 26:16   430
for thine honour from the LORD *G*.......... 2Chr 26:18   430
his ways before the LORD his *G*.............. 2Chr 27:6   430
Wherefore the LORD his *G* 2Chr 28:5   430
the LORD *G* of their fathers 2Chr 28:6   430
because the LORD *G* of your 2Chr 28:9   430
you, sins against the LORD your *G*.......... 2Chr 28:10   430
the vessels of the house of *G* 2Chr 28:24   430
the vessels of the house of *G* 2Chr 28:24   430
anger the LORD *G* of his fathers 2Chr 28:25   430
of the LORD *G* of your fathers 2Chr 29:5   430
in the eyes of the LORD our *G* 2Chr 29:6   430
holy place unto the *G* of Israel.............. 2Chr 29:7   430
with the LORD *G* of Israel...................... 2Chr 29:10   430
that *G* had prepared the people 2Chr 29:36   430
unto the LORD *G* of Israel...................... 2Chr 30:1   430
the LORD *G* of Israel at Jerusalem 2Chr 30:5   430
again unto the LORD *G* of Abraham 2Chr 30:6   430
the LORD *G* of their fathers 2Chr 30:7   430
and serve the LORD your *G*, that 2Chr 30:8   430
for the LORD your *G* is gracious 2Chr 30:9   430
Also in Judah the hand of *G* was 2Chr 30:12   430
to the law of Moses the man of *G*.......... 2Chr 30:16   430
prepareth his heart to seek *G*................ 2Chr 30:19   430
the LORD *G* of his fathers, though 2Chr 30:19   430
to the LORD *G* of their fathers 2Chr 30:22   430
consecrated unto the LORD their *G*......... 2Chr 31:6   430
the ruler of the house of *G*.................... 2Chr 31:13   430
over the freewill offerings of *G* 2Chr 31:14   430
and truth before the LORD his *G* 2Chr 31:20   430
in the service of the house of *G* 2Chr 31:21   430
the commandments, to seek his *G* 2Chr 31:21   430
us is the LORD our *G* to help us............. 2Chr 32:8   430
The LORD our *G* shall deliver us 2Chr 32:11   430
that your *G* should be able to 2Chr 32:14   430
how much less shall your *G* 2Chr 32:15   430
spake yet more against the LORD *G* 2Chr 32:16   430
to rail on the LORD *G* of Israel............... 2Chr 32:17   430
so shall not the *G* of Hezekiah............... 2Chr 32:17   430
spake against the *G* of Jerusalem 2Chr 32:19   430
for *G* had given him substance 2Chr 32:29   430
G left him, to try him, that he 2Chr 32:31   430
he had made, in the house of *G* 2Chr 33:7   430
of which *G* had said to David and 2Chr 33:7   430
he besought the LORD his *G* 2Chr 33:12   430
before the *G* of his fathers 2Chr 33:12   430
knew that the LORD he was *G* 2Chr 33:13   430
to serve the LORD *G* of Israel................. 2Chr 33:16   430
yet unto the LORD their *G* only 2Chr 33:17   430
and his prayer unto his *G*..................... 2Chr 33:18   430
the name of the LORD *G* of Israel........... 2Chr 33:18   430
how *G* was intreated of him, and.......... 2Chr 33:19   430
after the *G* of David his father 2Chr 34:3   430
the house of the LORD his *G* 2Chr 34:8   430
was brought into the house of *G* 2Chr 34:9   430
Thus saith the LORD *G* of Israel............. 2Chr 34:23   430
Thus saith the LORD *G* of Israel............. 2Chr 34:26   430
didst humble thyself before *G* 2Chr 34:27   430
according to the covenant of *G* 2Chr 34:32   430
the *G* of their fathers............................ 2Chr 34:32   430
even to serve the LORD their *G*.............. 2Chr 34:33   430
the LORD, the *G* of their fathers 2Chr 34:33   430
serve now the LORD your *G* 2Chr 35:3   430
Jehiel, rulers of the house of *G*.............. 2Chr 35:8   430
for *G* commanded me to make haste 2Chr 35:21   430
forbear thee from meddling with *G*........ 2Chr 35:21   430
of Necho from the mouth of *G* 2Chr 35:22   430
in the sight of the LORD his *G*............... 2Chr 36:5   430
in the sight of the LORD his *G*............... 2Chr 36:12   430
who had made him swear by *G* 2Chr 36:13   430
turning unto the LORD *G* of Israel.......... 2Chr 36:13   430
the LORD *G* of their fathers sent 2Chr 36:15   430
they mocked the messengers of *G* 2Chr 36:16   430
all the vessels of the house of *G* 2Chr 36:18   430

G

And they burnt the house of *G*	2Chr 36:19	430
the LORD *G* of heaven given me	2Chr 36:23	430
The LORD his *G* be with him	2Chr 36:23	430
The LORD *G* of heaven hath given	Ezr 1:2	430
his *G* be with him, and let him go	Ezr 1:3	430
LORD *G* of Israel, (he is the *G*	Ezr 1:3	430
house of *G* that is in Jerusalem	Ezr 1:4	430
them whose spirit *G* had raised	Ezr 1:5	430
of *G* to set it up in his place	Ezr 2:68	430
the altar of the *G* of Israel	Ezr 3:2	430
in the law of Moses the man of *G*	Ezr 3:2	430
unto the house of *G* at Jerusalem	Ezr 3:8	430
the workmen in the house of *G*	Ezr 3:9	430
temple unto the LORD *G* of Israel	Ezr 4:1	430
for we seek your *G*, as ye do	Ezr 4:2	430
us to build an house unto our *G*	Ezr 4:3	430
build unto the LORD *G* of Israel	Ezr 4:3	430
house of *G* which is at Jerusalem	Ezr 4:24	426
in the name of the *G* of Israel	Ezr 5:1	426
house of *G* which is at Jerusalem	Ezr 5:2	426
the prophets of *G* helping them	Ezr 5:2	426
But the eye of their *G* was upon	Ezr 5:5	426
to the house of the great *G*	Ezr 5:8	426
the servants of the *G* of heaven	Ezr 5:11	426
the *G* of heaven unto wrath	Ezr 5:12	426
a decree to build this house of *G*	Ezr 5:13	426
gold and silver of the house of *G*	Ezr 5:14	426
let the house of *G* be builded in	Ezr 5:15	426
house of *G* which is in Jerusalem	Ezr 5:16	426
this house of *G* at Jerusalem	Ezr 5:17	426
the house of *G* at Jerusalem	Ezr 6:3	426
silver vessels of the house of *G*	Ezr 6:5	426
and place them in the house of *G*	Ezr 6:5	426
the work of this house of *G* alone	Ezr 6:7	426
this house of *G* in his place	Ezr 6:7	426
the building of this house of *G*	Ezr 6:8	426
offerings unto the *G* of heaven	Ezr 6:9	426
savours unto the *G* of heaven	Ezr 6:10	426
the *G* that hath caused his name	Ezr 6:12	426
house of *G* which is at Jerusalem	Ezr 6:12	426
commandment of the *G* of Israel	Ezr 6:14	426
of this house of *G* with joy	Ezr 6:16	426
house of *G* an hundred bullocks	Ezr 6:17	426
courses, for the service of *G*	Ezr 6:18	426
to seek the LORD *G* of Israel	Ezr 6:21	430
the house of *G*, the *G* of Israel	Ezr 6:22	430
which the LORD *G* of Israel had	Ezr 7:6	430
hand of the LORD his *G* upon him	Ezr 7:6	430
the good hand of his *G* upon him	Ezr 7:9	430
of the law of the *G* of heaven	Ezr 7:12	426
of thy *G* which is in thine hand	Ezr 7:14	426
offered unto the *G* of Israel	Ezr 7:15	426
of their *G* which is in Jerusalem	Ezr 7:16	426
of your *G* which is in Jerusalem	Ezr 7:17	426
that do after the will of your *G*	Ezr 7:18	426
the service of the house of thy *G*	Ezr 7:19	426
thou before the *G* of Jerusalem	Ezr 7:19	426
be needful for the house of thy *G*	Ezr 7:20	426
of the law of the *G* of heaven	Ezr 7:21	426
is commanded by the *G* of heaven	Ezr 7:23	426
for the house of the *G* of heaven	Ezr 7:23	426
or ministers of this house of *G*	Ezr 7:24	426
Ezra, after the wisdom of thy *G*	Ezr 7:25	426
such as know the laws of thy *G*	Ezr 7:25	426
will not do the law of thy *G*	Ezr 7:26	426
be the LORD *G* of our fathers	Ezr 7:27	430
hand of the LORD my *G* was upon me	Ezr 7:28	430
ministers for the house of our *G*	Ezr 8:17	430
by the good hand of our *G* upon us	Ezr 8:18	430
afflict ourselves before our *G*	Ezr 8:21	430
The hand of our *G* is upon all	Ezr 8:22	430
fasted and besought our *G* for this	Ezr 8:23	430
offering of the house of our *G*	Ezr 8:25	430
unto the LORD *G* of your fathers	Ezr 8:28	430
Jerusalem unto the house of our *G*	Ezr 8:30	430
and the hand of our *G* was upon us	Ezr 8:31	430
weighed in the house of our *G* by	Ezr 8:33	430
offerings unto the *G* of Israel	Ezr 8:35	430
the people, and the house of *G*	Ezr 8:36	430
at the words of the *G* of Israel	Ezr 9:4	430
out my hands unto the LORD my *G*	Ezr 9:5	430
And said, O my *G*, I am ashamed and	Ezr 9:6	430
to lift up my face to thee, my *G*	Ezr 9:6	430
been shewed from the LORD our *G*	Ezr 9:8	430
that our *G* may lighten our eyes,	Ezr 9:8	430
yet our *G* hath not forsaken us in	Ezr 9:9	430
to set up the house of our *G*	Ezr 9:9	430
And now, O our *G*, what shall we	Ezr 9:10	430
seeing that thou our *G* hast	Ezr 9:13	430
O LORD *G* of Israel, thou art	Ezr 9:15	430
down before the house of *G*	Ezr 10:1	430

We have trespassed against our *G*	Ezr 10:2	430
our *G* to put away all the wives	Ezr 10:3	430
at the commandment of our *G*	Ezr 10:3	430
up from before the house of *G*	Ezr 10:6	430
in the street of the house of *G*	Ezr 10:9	430
unto the LORD *G* of your fathers	Ezr 10:11	430
until the fierce wrath of our *G*	Ezr 10:14	430
and prayed before the *G* of heaven	Neh 1:4	430
O LORD *G* of heaven	Neh 1:5	430
the great and terrible *G*	Neh 1:5	410
So I prayed to the *G* of heaven	Neh 2:4	430
to the good hand of my *G* upon me	Neh 2:8	430
my *G* had put in my heart to do at	Neh 2:12	430
of my *G* which was good upon me	Neh 2:18	430
The *G* of heaven, he will prosper	Neh 2:20	430
Hear, O our *G*	Neh 4:4	430
we made our prayer unto our *G*	Neh 4:9	430
G had brought their counsel to	Neh 4:15	430
our *G* shall fight for us	Neh 4:20	430
G because of the reproach of the	Neh 5:9	430
So *G* shake out every man from his	Neh 5:13	430
not I, because of the fear of *G*	Neh 5:15	430
Think upon me, my *G*, for good,	Neh 5:19	430
Now therefore, O *G*, strengthen my	Neh 6:9	430
meet together in the house of *G*	Neh 6:10	430
perceived that *G* had not sent him	Neh 6:12	430
My *G*, think thou upon Tobiah and	Neh 6:14	430
this work was wrought of our *G*	Neh 6:16	430
man, and feared *G* above many	Neh 7:2	430
my *G* put into mine heart to	Neh 7:5	430
blessed the LORD, the great *G*	Neh 8:6	430
book in the law of *G* distinctly	Neh 8:8	430
day is holy unto the LORD your *G*	Neh 8:9	430
in the courts of the house of *G*	Neh 8:16	430
read in the book of the law of *G*	Neh 8:18	430
G one fourth part of the day	Neh 9:3	430
and worshipped the LORD their *G*	Neh 9:3	430
loud voice unto the LORD their *G*	Neh 9:4	430
and bless the LORD your *G* for ever	Neh 9:5	430
Thou art the LORD the *G*, who	Neh 9:7	430
but thou art a *G* ready to pardon,	Neh 9:17	433
This is thy *G* that brought thee	Neh 9:18	430
thou art a gracious and merciful *G*	Neh 9:31	410
Now therefore, our *G*, the great,	Neh 9:32	430
the mighty, and the terrible *G*	Neh 9:32	410
of the lands unto the law of *G*	Neh 10:28	430
given by Moses the servant of *G*	Neh 10:29	430
the service of the house of our *G*	Neh 10:32	430
the work of the house of our *G*	Neh 10:33	430
bring it into the house of our *G*	Neh 10:34	430
upon the altar of the LORD our *G*	Neh 10:34	430
to bring to the house of our *G*	Neh 10:36	430
minister in the house of our *G*	Neh 10:36	430
chambers of the house of our *G*	Neh 10:37	430
tithes unto the house of our *G*	Neh 10:38	430
not forsake the house of our *G*	Neh 10:39	430
was the ruler of the house of *G*	Neh 11:11	430
business of the house of *G*	Neh 11:16	430
the business of the house of *G*	Neh 11:22	430
commandment of David the man of *G*	Neh 12:24	430
instruments of David the man of *G*	Neh 12:36	430
gave thanks in the house of *G*	Neh 12:40	430
for *G* had made them rejoice with	Neh 12:43	430
porters kept the ward of their *G*	Neh 12:45	430
of praise and thanksgiving unto *G*	Neh 12:46	430
the congregation of *G* for ever	Neh 13:1	430
howbeit our *G* turned the curse	Neh 13:2	430
the chamber of the house of our *G*	Neh 13:4	430
in the courts of the house of *G*	Neh 13:7	430
the vessels of the house of *G*	Neh 13:9	430
Why is the house of *G* forsaken	Neh 13:11	430
Remember me, O my *G*, concerning	Neh 13:14	430
I have done for the house of my *G*	Neh 13:14	430
did not our *G* bring all this evil	Neh 13:18	430
Remember me, O my *G*, concerning	Neh 13:22	430
hair, and made them swear by *G*	Neh 13:25	430
him, who was beloved of his *G*	Neh 13:26	430
G made him king over all Israel	Neh 13:26	430
our *G* in marrying strange wives	Neh 13:27	430
Remember them, O my *G*, because	Neh 13:29	430
Remember me, O my *G*, for good,	Neh 13:31	430
and upright, and one that feared *G*	Job 1:1	430
and cursed *G* in their hearts.	Job 1:5	430
of *G* came to present themselves	Job 1:6	430
upright man, one that feareth *G*	Job 1:8	430
said, Doth Job fear *G* for nought	Job 1:9	430
The fire of *G* is fallen from	Job 1:16	430
not, nor charged *G* foolishly	Job 1:22	430
of *G* came to present themselves	Job 2:1	430
upright man, one that feareth *G*	Job 2:3	430
curse *G*, and die	Job 2:9	430

we receive good at the hand of G .... Job 2:10	430
let not G regard it from above, ... Job 3:4	433
is hid, and whom G hath hedged in... Job 3:23	433
By the blast of G they perish .... Job 4:9	433
mortal man be more just than G .... Job 4:17	433
I would seek unto G .... Job 5:8	410
unto G would I commit my cause .... Job 5:8	430
is the man whom G correcteth .... Job 5:17	433
the terrors of G do set .... Job 6:4	433
that G would grant me the thing .... Job 6:8	433
it would please G to destroy me .... Job 6:9	433
Doth G pervert judgment .... Job 8:3	410
thou wouldest seek unto G betimes .... Job 8:5	410
the paths of all that forget G .... Job 8:13	410
G will not cast away a perfect .... Job 8:20	410
but how should man be just with G.... Job 9:2	410
If G will not withdraw his anger, ... Job 9:13	433
I will say unto G, Do not condemn .... Job 10:2	433
But oh that G would speak .... Job 11:5	433
Know therefore that G exacteth of........ Job 11:6	433
thou by searching find out G .... Job 11:7	410
his neighbour, who calleth upon G .... Job 12:4	433
and they that provoke G are secure ... Job 12:6	433
into whose hand G bringeth .... Job 12:6	410
and I desire to reason with G .... Job 13:3	433
Will ye speak wickedly for G .... Job 13:7	410
will ye contend for G .... Job 13:8	410
and restraineth prayer before G .... Job 15:4	410
Hast thou heard the secret of G .... Job 15:8	433
consolations of G small with thee .... Job 15:11	410
thou turnest thy spirit against G........ Job 15:13	410
stretcheth out his hand against G....... Job 15:25	410
G hath delivered me to the .... Job 16:11	410
mine eye poureth out tears unto G........ Job 16:20	433
one might plead for a man with G .... Job 16:21	433
place of him that knoweth not G .... Job 18:21	410
Know now that G hath overthrown .... Job 19:6	433
for the hand of G hath touched me ...... Job 19:21	433
Why do ye persecute me as G .... Job 19:22	410
yet in my flesh shall I see G .... Job 19:26	433
G shall cast them out of his .... Job 20:15	410
G shall cast the fury of his.............. Job 20:23	
portion of a wicked man from G .... Job 20:29	430
heritage appointed unto him by G......... Job 20:29	410
neither is the rod of G upon them......... Job 21:9	433
Therefore they say unto G .... Job 21:14	410
G distributeth sorrows in his .... Job 21:17	
G layeth up his iniquity for his .... Job 21:19	433
Shall any teach G knowledge .... Job 21:22	410
Can a man be profitable unto G......... Job 22:2	410
Is not G in the height of heaven........... Job 22:12	433
And thou sayest, How doth G know ..... Job 22:13	410
Which said unto G, Depart from us ..... Job 22:17	410
and shalt lift up thy face unto G......... Job 22:26	433
For G maketh my heart soft, and .... Job 23:16	410
yet G layeth not folly to them .... Job 24:12	433
then can man be justified with G .... Job 25:4	410
As G liveth, who hath taken away .... Job 27:2	410
the spirit of G is in my nostrils .... Job 27:3	433
G forbid that I should justify .... Job 27:5	
when G taketh away his soul .... Job 27:8	433
Will G hear his cry when trouble .... Job 27:9	401
will he always call upon G .... Job 27:10	433
I will teach you by the hand of G......... Job 27:11	410
portion of a wicked man with G .... Job 27:13	410
For G shall cast upon him, and not .... Job 27:22	
G understandeth the way thereof,......... Job 28:23	430
in the days when G preserved me .... Job 29:2	433
when the secret of G was upon my .... Job 29:4	433
portion of G is there from above .... Job 31:2	433
that G may know mine integrity............ Job 31:6	433
then shall I do when G riseth up .... Job 31:14	410
from G was a terror to me..................... Job 31:23	410
have denied the G that is above .... Job 31:28	410
justified himself rather than G .... Job 32:2	430
G thrusteth him down, not man .... Job 32:13	410
The spirit of G hath made me .... Job 33:4	410
that G is greater than man .... Job 33:12	433
For G speaketh once, yea twice, ... Job 33:14	410
He shall pray unto G, and he will .... Job 33:26	433
worketh G oftentimes with man .... Job 33:29	410
G hath taken away my judgment .... Job 34:5	410
he should delight himself with G .... Job 34:9	430
far be it from G, that he should.............. Job 34:10	410
surely G will not do wickedly,............... Job 34:12	410
should enter into judgment with G ...... Job 34:23	410
it is meet to be said unto G .... Job 34:31	410
multiplieth his words against G........... Job 34:37	410
none saith, Where is G my maker .... Job 35:10	433
Surely G will not hear vanity, ... Job 35:13	410
G is mighty, and despiseth not any ...... Job 36:5	410

Behold, G exalteth by his power............. Job 36:22	410
G is great, and we know him not,....... Job 36:26	410
G thundereth marvellously with .... Job 37:5	410
By the breath of G frost is given .... Job 37:10	410
consider the wondrous works of G ...... Job 37:14	410
thou know when G disposed them........ Job 37:15	433
with G is terrible majesty................... Job 37:22	433
all the sons of G shouted for joy .... Job 38:7	430
when his young ones cry unto G .... Job 38:41	430
Because G hath deprived her of............. Job 39:17	433
he that reproveth G, let him .... Job 40:2	433
Hast thou an arm like G...................... Job 40:9	410
He is the chief of the ways of G.......... Job 40:19	410
There is no help for him in G .... Ps 3:2	430
save me, O my G.................................. Ps 3:7	430
I call, O G of my righteousness .... Ps 4:1	430
voice of my cry, my King, and my G ..... Ps 5:2	430
For thou art not a G that hath .... Ps 5:4	410
Destroy thou them, O G .... Ps 5:10	430
O lord my G, in thee do I put my.......... Ps 7:1	430
O LORD my G, if I have done this .... Ps 7:3	430
the righteous G trieth the hearts .... Ps 7:9	430
My defence is of G, which saveth .... Ps 7:10	430
G judgeth the righteous .... Ps 7:11	430
G is angry with the wicked every .... Ps 7:11	410
and all the nations that forget G .... Ps 9:17	430
will not seek after G .... Ps 10:4	
G is not in all his thoughts .... Ps 10:4	430
in his heart, G hath forgotten .... Ps 10:11	410
O G, lift up thine hand........................ Ps 10:12	410
doth the wicked contemn G .... Ps 10:13	430
Consider and hear me, O LORD my G..... Ps 13:3	430
said in his heart, There is no G............. Ps 14:1	430
that did understand, and seek G .... Ps 14:2	430
for G is in the generation of the .... Ps 14:5	430
Preserve me, O G .... Ps 16:1	410
thee, for thou wilt hear me, O G .... Ps 17:6	430
my G, my strength, in whom I will .... Ps 18:2	410
upon the LORD, and cried unto my G ..... Ps 18:6	430
not wickedly departed from my G .... Ps 18:21	430
the LORD my G will enlighten my .... Ps 18:28	430
by my G have I leaped over a wall .... Ps 18:29	430
As for G, his way is perfect .... Ps 18:30	410
For who is G save the LORD.................. Ps 18:31	433
or who is a rock save our G .... Ps 18:31	430
It is G that girdeth me with................. Ps 18:32	410
let the G of my salvation be .... Ps 18:46	430
It is G that avengeth me, and............. Ps 18:47	410
heavens declare the glory of G .... Ps 19:1	410
the name of the G of Jacob defend .... Ps 20:1	430
in the name of our G we will set .... Ps 20:5	430
the name of the LORD our G.................. Ps 20:7	430
My G, my G, why hast thou .... Ps 22:1	410
O my G, I cry in the daytime, but .... Ps 22:2	430
thou art my G from my mother's .... Ps 22:10	410
from the G of his salvation .... Ps 24:5	430
O my G, I trust in thee .... Ps 25:2	430
thou art the G of my salvation .... Ps 25:5	430
Redeem Israel, O G, out of all .... Ps 25:22	430
forsake me, O G of my salvation .... Ps 27:9	430
the G of glory thundereth .... Ps 29:3	410
O LORD my G, I cried unto thee,........... Ps 30:2	430
O LORD my G, I will give thanks............ Ps 30:12	430
redeemed me, O LORD G of truth.......... Ps 31:5	410
I said, Thou art my G .... Ps 31:14	430
is the nation whose G is the LORD .... Ps 33:12	430
even unto my cause, my G .... Ps 35:23	430
Judge me, O LORD my G, according ...... Ps 35:24	430
is no fear of G before his eyes .... Ps 36:1	430
is thy lovingkindness, O G................... Ps 36:7	430
The law of his G is in his heart .... Ps 37:31	430
thou wilt hear, O Lord my G .... Ps 38:15	430
O my G, be not far from me .... Ps 38:21	430
my mouth, even praise unto our G .... Ps 40:3	430
Many, O LORD my G, are thy................. Ps 40:5	430
I delight to do thy will, O my G .... Ps 40:8	430
make no tarrying, O my G .... Ps 40:17	430
Blessed be the LORD G of Israel............. Ps 41:13	430
panteth my soul after thee, O G .... Ps 42:1	430
My soul thirsteth for G........................ Ps 42:2	430
for the living G .... Ps 42:2	410
shall I come and appear before G .... Ps 42:2	430
say unto me, Where is thy G .... Ps 42:3	430
went with them to the house of G .... Ps 42:4	430
hope thou in G..................................... Ps 42:5	430
O my G, my soul is cast down .... Ps 42:6	430
my prayer unto the G of my life .... Ps 42:8	430
I will say unto G my rock .... Ps 42:9	410
say daily unto me, Where is thy G .... Ps 42:10	430
hope thou in G..................................... Ps 42:11	430
health of my countenance, and my G..... Ps 42:11	430

G

Judge me, O *G*, and plead my cause	Ps 43:1	430
For thou art the *G* of my strength	Ps 43:2	430
will I go unto the altar of *G*	Ps 43:4	430
of *G*, unto my exceeding joy	Ps 43:4	410
will I praise thee, O *G* my *G*	Ps 43:4	430
hope in *G*: for I shall yet praise	Ps 43:5	430
health of my countenance, and my *G*	Ps 43:5	430
We have heard with our ears, O *G*	Ps 44:1	430
Thou art my King, O *G*	Ps 44:4	430
In *G* we boast all the day long,	Ps 44:8	430
have forgotten the name of our *G*	Ps 44:20	430
Shall not *G* search this out	Ps 44:21	430
therefore *G* hath blessed thee for	Ps 45:2	430
Thy throne, O *G*, is for ever and	Ps 45:6	430
therefore *G*, thy *G*, hath	Ps 45:7	430
G is our refuge and strength, a	Ps 46:1	430
shall make glad the city of *G*	Ps 46:4	430
G is in the midst of her	Ps 46:5	430
G shall help her, and that right	Ps 46:5	430
the *G* of Jacob is our refuge	Ps 46:7	430
Be still, and know that I am *G*	Ps 46:10	430
the *G* of Jacob is our refuge	Ps 46:11	430
shout unto *G* with the voice of	Ps 47:1	430
G is gone up with a shout, the	Ps 47:5	430
Sing praises to *G*, sing praises	Ps 47:6	430
For *G* is the King of all the	Ps 47:7	430
G reigneth over the heathen	Ps 47:8	430
G sitteth upon the throne of his	Ps 47:8	430
the people of the *G* of Abraham	Ps 47:9	430
of the earth belong unto *G*	Ps 47:9	430
be praised in the city of our *G*	Ps 48:1	430
G is known in her palaces for a	Ps 48:3	430
of hosts, in the city of our *G*	Ps 48:8	430
G will establish it for ever	Ps 48:8	430
of thy lovingkindness, O *G*	Ps 48:9	430
According to thy name, O *G*	Ps 48:10	430
For this *G* is our *G* for ever	Ps 48:14	430
nor give to *G* a ransom for him	Ps 49:7	430
But *G* will redeem my soul from	Ps 49:15	430
The mighty *G*, even the LORD, hath	Ps 50:1	430
of beauty, *G* hath shined	Ps 50:2	430
Our *G* shall come, and shall not	Ps 50:3	430
for *G* is judge himself	Ps 50:6	430
I am *G*, even thy *G*	Ps 50:7	430
Offer unto *G* thanksgiving	Ps 50:14	430
But unto the wicked *G* saith	Ps 50:16	430
consider this, ye that forget *G*	Ps 50:22	433
will I shew the salvation of *G*	Ps 50:23	430
Have mercy upon me, O *G*,	Ps 51:1	430
Create in me a clean heart, O *G*	Ps 51:10	430
O *G*, thou *G* of my salvation	Ps 51:14	430
The sacrifices of *G* are a broken	Ps 51:17	430
a broken and a contrite heart, O *G*	Ps 51:17	410
the goodness of *G* endureth	Ps 52:1	430
G shall likewise destroy thee for	Ps 52:5	410
man that made not *G* his strength	Ps 52:7	430
olive tree in the house of *G*	Ps 52:8	430
trust in the mercy of *G* for ever	Ps 52:8	430
said in his heart, There is no *G*	Ps 53:1	430
G looked down from heaven upon	Ps 53:2	430
did understand, that did seek *G*	Ps 53:2	430
they have not called upon *G*	Ps 53:4	430
for *G* hath scattered the bones of	Ps 53:5	430
because *G* hath despised them	Ps 53:5	430
When *G* bringeth back the	Ps 53:6	430
Save me, O *G*, by thy name, and	Ps 54:1	430
Hear my prayer, O *G*	Ps 54:2	430
they have not set *G* before them	Ps 54:3	430
Behold, *G* is mine helper	Ps 54:4	430
Give ear to my prayer, O *G*	Ps 55:1	430
unto the house of *G* in company	Ps 55:14	430
As for me, I will call upon *G*	Ps 55:16	430
G shall hear, and afflict them,	Ps 55:19	410
therefore they fear not *G*	Ps 55:19	430
But thou, O *G*, shalt bring them	Ps 55:23	430
Be merciful unto me, O *G*,	Ps 56:1	430
In *G* I will praise his word	Ps 56:4	430
in *G* I have put my trust	Ps 56:4	430
anger cast down the people, O *G*	Ps 56:7	430
for *G* is for me	Ps 56:9	430
In *G* will I praise his word	Ps 56:10	430
In *G* have I put my trust	Ps 56:11	430
Thy vows are upon me, O *G*	Ps 56:12	430
that I may walk before *G* in the	Ps 56:13	430
Be merciful unto me, O *G*, be	Ps 57:1	430
I will cry unto *G* most high	Ps 57:2	410
unto *G* that performeth all things	Ps 57:2	430
G shall send forth his mercy and	Ps 57:3	430
Be thou exalted, O *G*, above the	Ps 57:5	430
My heart is fixed, O *G*, my heart	Ps 57:7	430
Be thou exalted, O *G*, above the	Ps 57:11	430
Break their teeth, O *G*, in their	Ps 58:6	430
verily he is a *G* that judgeth in	Ps 58:11	430
me from mine enemies, O my *G*	Ps 59:1	430
O LORD *G* of hosts, the *G* of	Ps 59:5	430
for *G* is my defence	Ps 59:9	430
The *G* of my mercy shall prevent	Ps 59:10	430
G shall let me see my desire upon	Ps 59:10	430
let them know that *G* ruleth in	Ps 59:13	430
for *G* is my defence, and the *G*	Ps 59:17	430
O *G*, thou hast cast us off, thou	Ps 60:1	430
G hath spoken in his holiness	Ps 60:6	430
Wilt not thou, O *G*, which hadst	Ps 60:10	430
and thou, O *G*, which didst not go	Ps 60:10	430
Through *G* we shall do valiantly	Ps 60:12	430
Hear my cry, O *G*	Ps 61:1	430
For thou, O *G*, hast heard my vows	Ps 61:5	430
He shall abide before *G* for ever	Ps 61:7	430
Truly my soul waiteth upon *G*	Ps 62:1	430
My soul, wait thou only upon *G*	Ps 62:5	430
In *G* is my salvation and my glory	Ps 62:7	430
strength, and my refuge, is in *G*	Ps 62:7	430
G is a refuge for us	Ps 62:8	430
G hath spoken once	Ps 62:11	430
that power belongeth unto *G*	Ps 62:11	430
O *g*, thou art	Ps 63:1	410
thou art my *G*	Ps 63:1	430
But the king shall rejoice in *G*	Ps 63:11	430
Hear my voice, O *G*, in my prayer	Ps 64:1	430
But *G* shall shoot at them with an	Ps 64:7	430
and shall declare the work of *G*	Ps 64:9	430
waiteth for thee, O *G* in Sion	Ps 65:1	430
answer us, O *G* of our salvation	Ps 65:5	430
enrichest it with the river of *G*	Ps 65:9	430
Make a joyful noise unto *G*	Ps 66:1	430
Say unto *G*, How terrible art thou	Ps 66:3	430
Come and see the works of *G*	Ps 66:5	430
O bless our *G*, ye people, and make	Ps 66:8	430
For thou, O *G*, hast proved us	Ps 66:10	430
Come and hear, all ye that fear *G*	Ps 66:16	430
But verily *G* hath heard me	Ps 66:19	430
Blessed be *G*, which hath not	Ps 66:20	430
G be merciful unto us, and bless	Ps 67:1	430
Let the people praise thee, O *G*	Ps 67:3	430
Let the people praise thee, O *G*	Ps 67:5	430
and *G*, even our own *G*, shall	Ps 67:6	430
G shall bless us	Ps 67:7	430
Let *G* arise, let his enemies be	Ps 68:1	430
perish at the presence of *G*	Ps 68:2	430
let them rejoice before *G*	Ps 68:3	430
Sing unto *G*, sing praises to his	Ps 68:4	430
is *G* in his holy habitation	Ps 68:5	430
G setteth the solitary in	Ps 68:6	430
O *G*, when thou wentest forth	Ps 68:7	430
also dropped at the presence of *G*	Ps 68:8	430
presence of *G*, the *G* of Israel	Ps 68:8	430
Thou, O *G*, didst send a plentiful	Ps 68:9	430
thou, O *G*, hast prepared of thy	Ps 68:10	430
The hill of *G* is as the hill of	Ps 68:15	430
hill which *G* desireth to dwell in	Ps 68:16	430
The chariots of *G* are twenty	Ps 68:17	430
that the LORD *G* might dwell among	Ps 68:18	430
even the *G* of our salvation	Ps 68:19	410
is our *G* is the *G* of salvation	Ps 68:20	410
unto *G* the Lord belong the issues	Ps 68:20	3069
But *G* shall wound the head of his	Ps 68:21	430
They have seen thy goings, O *G*	Ps 68:24	430
even the goings of my *G*, my King,	Ps 68:24	410
Bless ye *G* in the congregations,	Ps 68:26	430
Thy *G* hath commanded thy strength	Ps 68:28	430
strengthen, O *G*, that which thou	Ps 68:28	430
soon stretch out her hands unto *G*	Ps 68:31	430
Sing unto *G*, ye kingdoms of the	Ps 68:32	430
Ascribe ye strength unto *G*	Ps 68:34	430
O *G*, thou art terrible out of thy	Ps 68:35	430
the *G* of Israel is he that giveth	Ps 68:35	410
Blessed be *G*	Ps 68:35	430
Save me, O *G*	Ps 69:1	430
eyes fail while I wait for my *G*	Ps 69:3	430
O *G*, thou knowest my foolishness	Ps 69:5	430
O Lord *G* of hosts, be ashamed for	Ps 69:6	3069
for my sake, O *G* of Israel	Ps 69:6	430
O *G*, in the multitude of thy	Ps 69:13	430
let thy salvation, O *G*, set me up	Ps 69:29	430
praise the name of *G* with a song	Ps 69:30	430
your heart shall live that seek *G*	Ps 69:32	430
For *G* will save Zion, and will	Ps 69:35	430
Make haste, O *G*, to deliver me	Ps 70:1	430
continually, Let *G* be magnified	Ps 70:4	430
make haste unto me, O *G*,	Ps 70:5	430
Deliver me, O my *G*, out of the	Ps 71:4	430
For thou art my hope, O Lord *G*	Ps 71:5	3069

Saying, *G* hath forsaken him	Ps 71:11	430
O *G*, be not far from me	Ps 71:12	430
O my *G*, make haste for my help	Ps 71:12	430
go in the strength of the Lord *G*	Ps 71:16	3069
O *G*, thou hast taught me from my	Ps 71:17	430
when I am old and greyheaded, O *G*	Ps 71:18	430
Thy righteousness also, O *G*	Ps 71:19	430
O *G*, who is like unto thee	Ps 71:19	430
psaltery, even thy truth, O my *G*	Ps 71:22	430
Give the king thy judgments, O *G*	Ps 72:1	430
Blessed be the Lord *G*	Ps 72:18	430
the *G* of Israel, who only doeth	Ps 72:18	430
Truly *G* is good to Israel, even	Ps 73:1	430
And they say, How doth *G* know	Ps 73:11	4010
I went into the sanctuary of *G*	Ps 73:17	410
but *G* is the strength of my heart	Ps 73:26	430
is good for me to draw near to *G*	Ps 73:28	430
I have put my trust in the Lord *G*	Ps 73:28	3069
O *G*, why hast thou cast us off	Ps 74:1	430
the synagogues of *G* in the land	Ps 74:8	410
O *G*, how long shall the adversary	Ps 74:10	430
For *G* is my King of old, working	Ps 74:12	430
Arise, O *G*, plead thine own cause	Ps 74:22	430
Unto thee, O *G*, do we give thanks	Ps 75:1	430
But *G* is the judge	Ps 75:7	430
sing praises to the *G* of Jacob	Ps 75:9	430
In Judah is *G* known	Ps 76:1	430
O *G* of Jacob, both the chariot and	Ps 76:6	430
When *G* arose to judgment, to save	Ps 76:9	430
Vow, and pay unto the Lord your *G*	Ps 76:11	430
I cried unto *G* with my voice	Ps 77:1	430
even unto *G* with my voice	Ps 77:1	430
I remembered *G*, and was troubled	Ps 77:3	430
Hath *G* forgotten to be gracious	Ps 77:9	410
Thy way, O *G*, is in the sanctuary	Ps 77:13	430
who is so great a *G*	Ps 77:13	410
as our *G*	Ps 77:13	430
Thou art the *G* that doest wonders	Ps 77:14	410
The waters saw thee, O *G*, the	Ps 77:16	430
they might set their hope in *G*	Ps 78:7	430
and not forget the works of *G*	Ps 78:7	410
spirit was not stedfast with *G*	Ps 78:8	410
They kept not the covenant of *G*	Ps 78:10	430
they tempted *G* in their heart by	Ps 78:18	410
Yea, they spake against *G*	Ps 78:19	430
Can *G* furnish a table in the	Ps 78:19	410
Because they believed not in *G*	Ps 78:22	430
The wrath of *G* came upon them, and	Ps 78:31	430
and enquired early after *G*	Ps 78:34	410
remembered that *G* was their rock	Ps 78:35	430
the high *G* their redeemer	Ps 78:35	410
they turned back and tempted *G*	Ps 78:41	410
and provoked the most high *G*	Ps 78:56	430
When *G* heard this, he was wroth,	Ps 78:59	430
O *g*, the heathen are come into	Ps 79:1	430
O *G* of our salvation, for the	Ps 79:9	430
the heathen say, Where is their *G*	Ps 79:10	430
Turn us again, O *G*, and cause thy	Ps 80:3	430
O Lord *G* of hosts, how long wilt	Ps 80:4	430
O *G* of hosts, and cause thy face	Ps 80:14	430
we beseech thee, O *G* of hosts	Ps 80:14	430
O Lord *G* of hosts, cause thy face	Ps 80:19	430
Sing aloud unto *G* our strength	Ps 81:1	430
joyful noise unto the *G* of Jacob	Ps 81:1	430
and a law of the *G* of Jacob	Ps 81:4	430
I am the Lord thy *G*, which	Ps 81:10	430
G standeth in the congregation of	Ps 82:1	430
Arise, O *G*, judge the earth	Ps 82:8	430
Keep not thou silence, O *G*	Ps 83:1	430
thy peace, and be not still, O *G*	Ps 83:1	410
the houses of *G* in possession	Ps 83:12	430
O my *G*, make them like a wheel	Ps 83:13	430
flesh crieth out for the living *G*	Ps 84:2	410
O Lord of hosts, my King, and my *G*	Ps 84:3	430
them in Zion appeareth before *G*	Ps 84:7	430
O Lord *G* of hosts, hear my prayer	Ps 84:8	430
give ear, O *G* of Jacob	Ps 84:8	430
O *G* our shield, and look upon the	Ps 84:9	430
a doorkeeper in the house of my *G*	Ps 84:10	430
For the Lord *G* is a sun and shield	Ps 84:11	430
O *G* of our salvation, and cause	Ps 85:4	430
I will hear what the Lord will	Ps 85:8	410
O thou my *G*, save thy servant	Ps 86:2	430
thou art *G* alone	Ps 86:10	430
I will praise thee, O Lord my *G*	Ps 86:12	430
O *G*, the proud are risen against	Ps 86:14	430
art a *G* full of compassion, and	Ps 86:15	410
are spoken of thee, O city of *G*	Ps 87:3	430
O lord *G* of my salvation, I have	Ps 88:1	430
G is greatly to be feared in the	Ps 89:7	410
O Lord *G* of hosts, who is a	Ps 89:8	430

unto me, Thou art my father, my *G*	Ps 89:26	410
A Prayer of Moses, the man of *G*	Ps 90:t	430
to everlasting, thou art *G*	Ps 90:2	410
of the Lord our *G* be upon us	Ps 90:17	430
refuge and my fortress: my *G*	Ps 91:2	430
flourish in the courts of our *G*	Ps 92:13	430
O Lord *G*, to whom vengeance	Ps 94:1	410
O *G*, to whom vengeance belongeth,	Ps 94:1	410
neither shall the *G* of Jacob	Ps 94:7	430
my *G* is the rock of my refuge	Ps 94:22	430
the Lord our *G* shall cut them off	Ps 94:23	430
For the Lord is a great *G*	Ps 95:3	410
For he is our *G*	Ps 95:7	430
have seen the salvation of our *G*	Ps 98:3	430
Exalt ye the Lord our *G*, and	Ps 99:5	430
answeredst them, O Lord our *G*	Ps 99:8	430
thou wast a *G* that forgavest them	Ps 99:8	410
Exalt the Lord our *G*, and worship	Ps 99:9	430
for the Lord our *G* is holy	Ps 99:9	430
Know ye that the Lord he is *G*	Ps 100:3	430
I said, O my *G*, take me not away	Ps 102:24	410
O Lord my *G*, thou art very great	Ps 104:1	430
prey, and seek their meat from *G*	Ps 104:21	410
to my *G* while I have my being	Ps 104:33	430
He is the Lord our *G*	Ps 105:7	430
and tempted *G* in the desert	Ps 106:14	410
They forgat *G* their saviour	Ps 106:21	410
Save us, O Lord our *G*, and gather	Ps 106:47	430
Blessed be the Lord *G* of Israel	Ps 106:48	430
rebelled against the words of *G*	Ps 107:11	410
O *G*, my heart is fixed	Ps 108:1	430
Be thou exalted, O *G*, above the	Ps 108:5	430
G hath spoken in his holiness	Ps 108:7	430
Wilt not thou, O *G*, who hast cast	Ps 108:11	430
and wilt not thou, O *G*, go forth	Ps 108:11	430
Through *G* we shall do valiantly	Ps 108:13	430
not thy peace, O *G* of my praise	Ps 109:1	430
O *G* the Lord, for thy name's sake	Ps 109:21	3069
Help me, O Lord my *G*	Ps 109:26	430
Who is like unto the Lord our *G*	Ps 113:5	430
at the presence of the *G* of Jacob	Ps 114:7	433
heathen say, Where is now their *G*	Ps 115:2	430
But our *G* is in the heavens	Ps 115:3	430
yea, our *G* is merciful	Ps 116:5	430
G is the Lord, which hath shewed	Ps 118:27	410
Thou art my *G*, and I will praise	Ps 118:28	410
thou art my *G*, I will exalt thee	Ps 118:28	430
keep the commandments of my *G*	Ps 119:115	430
Lord our *G* I will seek thy good	Ps 122:9	430
our eyes wait upon the Lord our *G*	Ps 123:2	430
vowed unto the mighty *G* of Jacob	Ps 132:2	430
for the mighty *G* of Jacob	Ps 132:5	
the courts of the house of our *G*	Ps 135:2	
O give thanks unto the *G* of gods	Ps 136:2	430
give thanks unto the *G* of heaven	Ps 136:26	410
are thy thoughts unto me, O *G*	Ps 139:17	410
thou wilt slay the wicked, O *G*	Ps 139:19	433
Search me, O *G*, and know my heart	Ps 139:23	410
said unto the Lord, Thou art my *G*	Ps 140:6	410
O *G* the Lord, the strength of my	Ps 140:7	
eyes are unto thee, O *G* the Lord	Ps 141:8	3069
for thou art my *G*	Ps 143:10	430
sing a new song unto thee, O *G*	Ps 144:9	430
that people, whose *G* is the Lord	Ps 144:15	430
I will extol thee, my *G*, O king	Ps 145:1	430
unto my *G* while I have any being	Ps 146:2	430
hath the *G* of Jacob for his help	Ps 146:5	410
whose hope is in the Lord his *G*	Ps 146:5	430
shall reign for ever, even thy *G*	Ps 146:10	430
good to sing praises unto our *G*	Ps 147:1	430
praise upon the harp unto our *G*	Ps 147:7	430
praise thy *G*, O Zion	Ps 147:12	430
praises of *G* be in their mouth	Ps 149:6	410
Praise *G* in his sanctuary	Ps 150:1	410
Lord, and find the knowledge of *G*	Prov 2:5	430
forgetteth the covenant of her *G*	Prov 2:17	430
understanding in the sight of *G*	Prov 3:4	430
but *G* overthroweth the wicked for	Prov 21:12	
the glory of *G* to conceal a thing	Prov 25:2	430
The great *G* that formed all	Prov 26:10	
Every word of *G* is pure	Prov 30:5	433
and take the name of my *G* in vain	Prov 30:9	430
this sore travail hath *G* given to	Eccl 1:13	430
that it was from the hand of *G*	Eccl 2:24	430
For *G* giveth to a man that is	Eccl 2:26	
give to him that is good before *G*	Eccl 2:26	430
which *G* hath given to the sons of	Eccl 3:10	430
G maketh from the beginning to	Eccl 3:11	430
his labour, it is the gift of *G*	Eccl 3:13	430
I know that, whatsoever *G* doeth	Eccl 3:14	430
G doeth it, that men should fear	Eccl 3:14	430

not the voice of the LORD their G	Jer 7:28	430
for the LORD our G hath put us to	Jer 8:14	430
LORD of hosts, the G of Israel	Jer 9:15	430
the true G, he is the living G	Jer 10:10	430
Thus saith the LORD G of Israel	Jer 11:3	430
be my people, and I will be your G	Jer 11:4	430
Thus saith the LORD G of Israel	Jer 13:12	430
Give glory to the LORD your G	Jer 13:16	430
Then said I, Ah, Lord G	Jer 14:13	3069
art not thou he, O LORD our G	Jer 14:22	430
by thy name, O LORD G of hosts	Jer 15:16	430
LORD of hosts, the G of Israel	Jer 16:9	430
committed against the LORD our G	Jer 16:10	430
LORD of hosts, the G of Israel	Jer 19:3	430
LORD of hosts, the G of Israel	Jer 19:15	430
Thus saith the LORD G of Israel	Jer 21:4	430
the covenant of the LORD their G	Jer 22:9	430
G of Israel against the pastors	Jer 23:2	430
Am I a G at hand, saith the LORD,	Jer 23:23	430
and not a G afar off	Jer 23:23	430
the words of the living G	Jer 23:36	430
of the LORD of hosts our G	Jer 23:36	430
saith the LORD, the G of Israel	Jer 24:5	430
my people, and I will be their G	Jer 24:7	430
the LORD G of Israel unto me	Jer 25:15	430
LORD of hosts, the G of Israel	Jer 25:27	430
obey the voice of the LORD your G	Jer 26:13	430
us in the name of the LORD our G	Jer 26:16	430
LORD of hosts, the G of Israel	Jer 27:4	430
the G of Israel, concerning the	Jer 27:21	430
the G of Israel, saying, I have	Jer 28:2	430
LORD of hosts, the G of Israel	Jer 28:14	430
the G of Israel, unto all that	Jer 29:4	430
LORD of hosts, the G of Israel	Jer 29:8	430
the G of Israel, of Ahab the son	Jer 29:21	430
the G of Israel, saying, Because	Jer 29:25	430
speaketh the LORD G of Israel	Jer 30:2	430
they shall serve the LORD their G	Jer 30:9	430
be my people, and I will be your G	Jer 30:22	430
will I be the G of all the	Jer 31:1	430
go up to Zion unto the LORD our G	Jer 31:6	430
for thou art the LORD my G	Jer 31:18	430
LORD of hosts, the G of Israel	Jer 31:23	430
and will be their G, and they shall	Jer 31:33	430
LORD of hosts, the G of Israel	Jer 32:14	430
LORD of hosts, the G of Israel	Jer 32:15	430
Ah Lord G!	Jer 32:17	3069
the Great, the Mighty G, the LORD	Jer 32:18	410
thou hast said unto me, O Lord G	Jer 32:25	3069
I am the LORD, the G of all flesh	Jer 32:27	430
the G of Israel, concerning this	Jer 32:36	430
my people, and I will be their G	Jer 32:38	430
the G of Israel, concerning the	Jer 33:4	430
saith the LORD, the G of Israel	Jer 34:2	430
saith the LORD, the G of Israel	Jer 34:13	430
the son of Igdaliah, a man of G	Jer 35:4	430
LORD of hosts, the G of Israel	Jer 35:13	430
G of hosts, the G of Israel	Jer 35:17	430
LORD of hosts, the G of Israel	Jer 35:18	430
LORD of hosts, the G of Israel	Jer 35:19	430
now unto the LORD our G for us	Jer 37:3	430
saith the LORD, the G of Israel	Jer 37:7	430
the G of hosts, the G of Israel	Jer 38:17	430
LORD of hosts, the G of Israel	Jer 39:16	430
The LORD thy G hath pronounced	Jer 40:2	430
pray for us unto the LORD thy G	Jer 42:2	430
That the LORD thy G may shew us	Jer 42:3	430
your G according to your words	Jer 42:4	430
LORD thy G shall send thee to us	Jer 42:5	430
obey the voice of the LORD our G	Jer 42:6	430
obey the voice of the LORD our G	Jer 42:6	430
the G of Israel, unto whom ye	Jer 42:9	430
obey the voice of the LORD your G	Jer 42:13	430
LORD of hosts, the G of Israel	Jer 42:15	430
LORD of hosts, the G of Israel	Jer 42:18	430
ye sent me unto the LORD your G	Jer 42:20	430
Pray for us unto the LORD our G	Jer 42:20	430
all that the LORD our G shall say	Jer 42:20	430
the voice of the LORD your G	Jer 42:21	430
all the words of the LORD their G	Jer 43:1	430
LORD their G had sent him to them	Jer 43:1	430
the LORD our G hath not sent thee	Jer 43:2	430
LORD of hosts, the G of Israel	Jer 43:10	430
LORD of hosts, the G of Israel	Jer 44:2	430
the G of hosts, the G of Israel	Jer 44:7	430
LORD of hosts, the G of Israel	Jer 44:11	430
of hosts, the G of Israel, saying,	Jer 44:25	430
Egypt, saying, The Lord G liveth	Jer 44:26	3069
the G of Israel, unto thee, O	Jer 45:2	430
is the day of the Lord G of hosts	Jer 46:10	3069
for the Lord G of hosts hath a	Jer 46:10	3069
of hosts, the G of Israel, saith	Jer 46:25	430
LORD of hosts, the G of Israel	Jer 48:1	430
thee, saith the Lord G of hosts	Jer 49:5	3069
go, and seek the LORD their G	Jer 50:4	430
LORD of hosts, the G of Israel	Jer 50:18	430
G of hosts in the land of the	Jer 50:25	3069
the vengeance of the LORD our G	Jer 50:28	430
proud, saith the Lord G of hosts	Jer 50:31	3069
As G overthrew Sodom and Gomorrah	Jer 50:40	430
been forsaken, nor Judah of his G	Jer 51:5	430
Zion the work of the LORD our G	Jer 51:10	430
LORD of hosts, the G of Israel	Jer 51:33	430
for the LORD G of recompences	Jer 51:56	410
our hands unto G in the heavens	Lam 3:41	410
opened, and I saw visions of G	Eze 1:1	430
unto them, Thus saith the Lord G	Eze 2:4	3069
tell thee, Thus saith the Lord G	Eze 3:11	3069
unto them, Thus saith the Lord G	Eze 3:27	3069
Then said I, Ah Lord G	Eze 4:14	3069
Thus saith the Lord G	Eze 5:5	3069
Therefore thus saith the Lord G	Eze 5:7	3069
Therefore thus saith the Lord G	Eze 5:8	3069
as I live, saith the Lord G	Eze 5:11	3069
hear the word of the Lord G	Eze 6:3	3069
saith the Lord G to the mountains	Eze 6:3	3069
Thus saith the Lord G	Eze 6:11	3069
thus saith the Lord G unto the	Eze 7:2	3069
Thus saith the Lord G	Eze 7:5	3069
of the Lord G fell there upon me	Eze 8:1	3069
in the visions of G to Jerusalem	Eze 8:3	430
the glory of the G of Israel was	Eze 8:4	430
the glory of the G of Israel was	Eze 9:3	430
and cried, and said, Ah Lord G	Eze 9:8	3069
the Almighty G when he speaketh	Eze 10:5	410
the glory of the G of Israel was	Eze 10:19	430
the G of Israel by the river of	Eze 10:20	430
Therefore thus saith the Lord G	Eze 11:7	3069
sword upon you, saith the Lord G	Eze 11:8	3069
a loud voice, and said, Ah Lord G	Eze 11:13	3069
say, Thus saith the Lord G	Eze 11:16	3069
say, Thus saith the Lord G	Eze 11:17	3069
my people, and I will be their G	Eze 11:20	430
their own heads, saith the Lord G	Eze 11:21	3069
the glory of the G of Israel was	Eze 11:22	430
by the Spirit of G into Chaldea	Eze 11:24	430
unto them, Thus saith the Lord G	Eze 12:10	3069
Thus saith the Lord G of the	Eze 12:19	3069
therefore, Thus saith the Lord G	Eze 12:23	3069
will perform it, saith the Lord G	Eze 12:25	3069
unto them, Thus saith the Lord G	Eze 12:28	3069
shall be done, saith the Lord G	Eze 12:28	3069
Thus saith the Lord G	Eze 13:3	3069
Therefore thus saith the Lord G	Eze 13:8	3069
am against you, saith the Lord G	Eze 13:8	3069
shall know that I am the Lord G	Eze 13:9	3069
Therefore thus saith the Lord G	Eze 13:13	3069
is no peace, saith the Lord G	Eze 13:16	3069
And say, Thus saith the Lord G	Eze 13:18	3069
Wherefore thus saith the Lord G	Eze 13:20	3069
unto them, Thus saith the Lord G	Eze 14:4	3069
of Israel, Thus saith the Lord G	Eze 14:6	3069
be my people, and I may be their G	Eze 14:11	430
saith the Lord G	Eze 14:11	3069
righteousness, saith the Lord G	Eze 14:14	3069
it, as I live, saith the Lord G	Eze 14:16	3069
it, as I live, saith the Lord G	Eze 14:18	3069
it, as I live, saith the Lord G	Eze 14:20	3069
For thus saith the Lord G	Eze 14:21	3069
have done in it, saith the Lord G	Eze 14:23	3069
Therefore thus saith the Lord G	Eze 15:6	3069
a trespass, saith the Lord G	Eze 15:8	3069
saith the Lord G unto Jerusalem	Eze 16:3	3069
with thee, saith the Lord G	Eze 16:8	3069
put upon thee, saith the Lord G	Eze 16:14	3069
and thus it was, saith the Lord G	Eze 16:19	3069
saith the Lord G	Eze 16:23	3069
is thine heart, saith the Lord G	Eze 16:30	3069
Thus saith the Lord G	Eze 16:36	3069
upon thine head, saith the Lord G	Eze 16:43	3069
As I live, saith the Lord G	Eze 16:48	3069
For thus saith the Lord G	Eze 16:59	3069
thou hast done, saith the Lord G	Eze 16:63	3069
And say, Thus saith the Lord G	Eze 17:3	3069
Say thou, Thus saith the Lord G	Eze 17:9	3069
As I live, saith the Lord G	Eze 17:16	3069
Therefore thus saith the Lord G	Eze 17:19	3069
Thus saith the Lord G	Eze 17:22	3069
As I live, saith the Lord G	Eze 18:3	3069
surely live, saith the Lord G	Eze 18:9	3069
saith the Lord G	Eze 18:23	3069
to his ways, saith the Lord G	Eze 18:30	3069

G

him that dieth, saith the Lord *G*	Eze 18:32	3069
unto them, Thus saith the Lord *G*	Eze 20:3	3069
As I live, saith the Lord *G*	Eze 20:3	3069
unto them, Thus saith the Lord *G*	Eze 20:5	3069
saying, I am the Lord your *G*	Eze 20:5	430
I am the Lord your *G*	Eze 20:7	430
I am the Lord your *G*	Eze 20:19	430
know that I am the Lord your *G*	Eze 20:20	430
unto them, Thus saith the Lord *G*	Eze 20:27	3069
of Israel, Thus saith the Lord *G*	Eze 20:30	3069
As I live, saith the Lord *G*	Eze 20:31	3069
As I live, saith the Lord *G*	Eze 20:33	3069
plead with you, saith the Lord *G*	Eze 20:36	3069
of Israel, thus saith the Lord *G*	Eze 20:39	3069
of Israel, saith the Lord *G*	Eze 20:40	3069
house of Israel, saith the Lord *G*	Eze 20:44	3069
Thus saith the Lord *G*	Eze 20:47	3069
Then said I, Ah Lord *G*	Eze 20:49	3069
brought to pass, saith the Lord *G*	Eze 21:7	3069
be no more, saith the Lord *G*	Eze 21:13	3069
Therefore thus saith the Lord *G*	Eze 21:24	3069
Thus saith the Lord *G*	Eze 21:26	3069
Thus saith the Lord *G* concerning	Eze 21:28	3069
say thou, Thus saith the Lord *G*	Eze 22:3	3069
forgotten me, saith the Lord *G*	Eze 22:12	3069
Therefore thus saith the Lord *G*	Eze 22:19	3069
saying, Thus saith the Lord *G*	Eze 22:28	3069
their heads, saith the Lord *G*	Eze 22:31	3069
O Aholibah, thus saith the Lord *G*	Eze 23:22	3069
For thus saith the Lord *G*	Eze 23:28	3069
Thus saith the Lord *G*	Eze 23:32	3069
have spoken it, saith the Lord *G*	Eze 23:34	3069
Therefore thus saith the Lord *G*	Eze 23:35	3069
For thus saith the Lord *G*	Eze 23:46	3069
shall know that I am the Lord *G*	Eze 23:49	3069
unto them, Thus saith the Lord *G*	Eze 24:3	3069
Wherefore thus saith the Lord *G*	Eze 24:6	3069
Therefore thus saith the Lord *G*	Eze 24:9	3069
they judge thee, saith the Lord *G*	Eze 24:14	3069
of Israel, Thus saith the Lord *G*	Eze 24:21	3069
shall know that I am the Lord *G*	Eze 24:24	3069
Hear the word of the Lord *G*	Eze 25:3	3069
Thus saith the Lord *G*	Eze 25:3	3069
For thus saith the Lord *G*	Eze 25:6	3069
Thus saith the Lord *G*	Eze 25:8	3069
Thus saith the Lord *G*	Eze 25:12	3069
Therefore thus saith the Lord *G*	Eze 25:13	3069
my vengeance, saith the Lord *G*	Eze 25:14	3069
Thus saith the Lord *G*	Eze 25:15	3069
Therefore thus saith the Lord *G*	Eze 25:16	3069
Therefore thus saith the Lord *G*	Eze 26:3	3069
have spoken it, saith the Lord *G*	Eze 26:5	3069
For thus saith the Lord *G*	Eze 26:7	3069
have spoken it, saith the Lord *G*	Eze 26:14	3069
Thus saith the Lord *G* to Tyrus	Eze 26:15	3069
For thus saith the Lord *G*	Eze 26:19	3069
be found again, saith the Lord *G*	Eze 26:21	3069
many isles, Thus saith the Lord *G*	Eze 27:3	3069
of Tyrus, Thus saith the Lord *G*	Eze 28:2	3069
up, and thou hast said, I am a *G*	Eze 28:2	410
I sit in the seat of *G*	Eze 28:2	430
yet thou art a man, and not *G*	Eze 28:2	410
set thine heart as the heart of *G*	Eze 28:2	430
Therefore thus saith the Lord *G*	Eze 28:6	3069
set thine heart as the heart of *G*	Eze 28:6	430
him that slayeth thee, I am *G*	Eze 28:9	430
but thou shalt be a man, and no *G*	Eze 28:9	410
have spoken it, saith the Lord *G*	Eze 28:10	3069
unto him, Thus saith the Lord *G*	Eze 28:12	3069
hast been in Eden the garden of *G*	Eze 28:13	430
wast upon the holy mountain of *G*	Eze 28:14	430
profane out of the mountain of *G*	Eze 28:16	430
And say, Thus saith the Lord *G*	Eze 28:22	3069
shall know that I am the Lord *G*	Eze 28:24	3069
Thus saith the Lord *G*	Eze 28:25	3069
know that I am the Lord their *G*	Eze 28:26	430
and say, Thus saith the Lord *G*	Eze 29:3	3069
Therefore thus saith the Lord *G*	Eze 29:8	3069
Yet thus saith the Lord *G*	Eze 29:13	3069
shall know that I am the Lord *G*	Eze 29:16	3069
Therefore thus saith the Lord *G*	Eze 29:19	3069
wrought for me, saith the Lord *G*	Eze 29:20	3069
and say, Thus saith the Lord *G*	Eze 30:2	3069
it by the sword, saith the Lord *G*	Eze 30:6	3069
Thus saith the Lord *G*	Eze 30:10	3069
Thus saith the Lord *G*	Eze 30:13	3069
Therefore thus saith the Lord *G*	Eze 30:22	3069
garden of *G* could not hide him	Eze 31:8	430
nor any tree in the garden of *G*	Eze 31:8	430
that were in the garden of *G*	Eze 31:9	430
Therefore thus saith the Lord *G*	Eze 31:10	3069
Thus saith the Lord *G*	Eze 31:15	430
his multitude, saith the Lord *G*	Eze 31:18	3069
Thus saith the Lord *G*	Eze 32:3	3069
upon thy land, saith the Lord *G*	Eze 32:8	3069
For thus saith the Lord *G*	Eze 32:11	3069
to run like oil, saith the Lord *G*	Eze 32:14	3069
her multitude, saith the Lord *G*	Eze 32:16	3069
by the sword, saith the Lord *G*	Eze 32:31	3069
his multitude, saith the Lord *G*	Eze 32:32	3069
them, As I live, saith the Lord *G*	Eze 33:11	3069
unto them, Thus saith the Lord *G*	Eze 33:25	3069
unto them, Thus saith the Lord *G*	Eze 33:27	3069
the Lord *G* unto the shepherds	Eze 34:2	3069
As I live saith the Lord *G*	Eze 34:8	3069
Thus saith the Lord *G*	Eze 34:10	3069
For thus saith the Lord *G*	Eze 34:11	3069
to lie down, saith the Lord *G*	Eze 34:15	3069
O my flock, thus saith the Lord *G*	Eze 34:17	3069
thus saith the Lord *G* unto them	Eze 34:20	3069
And I the Lord will be their *G*	Eze 34:24	430
I the Lord their *G* am with them	Eze 34:30	430
are my people, saith the Lord *G*	Eze 34:30	3069
pasture, are men, and I am your *G*	Eze 34:31	430
saith the Lord *G*	Eze 34:31	3069
unto it, Thus saith the Lord *G*	Eze 35:3	3069
as I live, saith the Lord *G*	Eze 35:6	3069
as I live, saith the Lord *G*	Eze 35:11	3069
Thus saith the Lord *G*	Eze 35:14	3069
Thus saith the Lord *G*	Eze 36:2	3069
and say, Thus saith the Lord *G*	Eze 36:3	3069
hear the word of the Lord *G*	Eze 36:4	3069
saith the Lord *G* to the mountains	Eze 36:4	3069
Therefore thus saith the Lord *G*	Eze 36:5	3069
valleys, Thus saith the Lord *G*	Eze 36:6	3069
Therefore thus saith the Lord *G*	Eze 36:7	3069
Thus saith the Lord *G*	Eze 36:13	3069
any more, saith the Lord *G*	Eze 36:14	3069
fall any more, saith the Lord *G*	Eze 36:15	3069
of Israel, Thus saith the Lord *G*	Eze 36:22	3069
I am the Lord, saith the Lord *G*	Eze 36:23	3069
be my people, and I will be your *G*	Eze 36:28	430
sakes do I this, saith the Lord *G*	Eze 36:32	3069
Thus saith the Lord *G*	Eze 36:33	3069
Thus saith the Lord *G*	Eze 36:37	3069
And I answered, O Lord *G*, thou	Eze 37:3	3069
saith the Lord *G* unto these bones	Eze 37:5	3069
the wind, Thus saith the Lord *G*	Eze 37:9	3069
unto them, Thus saith the Lord *G*	Eze 37:12	3069
unto them, Thus saith the Lord *G*	Eze 37:19	3069
unto them, Thus saith the Lord *G*	Eze 37:21	3069
my people, and I will be their *G*	Eze 37:23	430
yea, I will be their *G*, and they	Eze 37:27	430
And say, Thus saith the Lord *G*	Eze 38:3	3069
Thus saith the Lord *G*	Eze 38:10	3069
unto Gog, Thus saith the Lord *G*	Eze 38:14	3069
Thus saith the Lord *G*	Eze 38:17	3069
land of Israel, saith the Lord *G*	Eze 38:18	3069
my mountains, saith the Lord *G*	Eze 38:21	3069
and say, Thus saith the Lord *G*	Eze 39:1	3069
have spoken it, saith the Lord *G*	Eze 39:5	3069
and it is done, saith the Lord *G*	Eze 39:8	3069
robbed them, saith the Lord *G*	Eze 39:10	3069
be glorified, saith the Lord *G*	Eze 39:13	3069
son of man, thus saith the Lord *G*	Eze 39:17	3069
all men of war, saith the Lord *G*	Eze 39:20	3069
am the Lord their *G* from that day	Eze 39:22	430
Therefore thus saith the Lord *G*	Eze 39:25	3069
know that I am the Lord their *G*	Eze 39:28	430
house of Israel, saith the Lord *G*	Eze 39:29	3069
In the visions of *G* brought he me	Eze 40:2	430
the glory of the *G* of Israel came	Eze 43:2	430
Son of man, thus saith the Lord *G*	Eze 43:18	3069
unto me, saith the Lord *G*	Eze 43:19	3069
will accept you, saith the Lord *G*	Eze 43:27	3069
the *G* of Israel, hath entered in	Eze 44:2	430
of Israel, Thus saith the Lord *G*	Eze 44:6	3069
Thus saith the Lord *G*	Eze 44:9	3069
against them, saith the Lord *G*	Eze 44:12	3069
and the blood, saith the Lord *G*	Eze 44:15	3069
sin offering, saith the Lord *G*	Eze 44:27	3069
Thus saith the Lord *G*	Eze 45:9	3069
from my people, saith the Lord *G*	Eze 45:9	3069
for them, saith the Lord *G*	Eze 45:15	3069
Thus saith the Lord *G*	Eze 45:18	3069
Thus saith the Lord *G*	Eze 46:1	3069
Thus saith the Lord *G*	Eze 46:16	3069
Thus saith the Lord *G*	Eze 47:13	3069
his inheritance, saith the Lord *G*	Eze 47:23	3069
their portions, saith the Lord *G*	Eze 48:29	3069
of the vessels of the house of *G*	Dan 1:2	430
Now *G* had brought Daniel into	Dan 1:9	430

G gave them knowledge and skill in	Dan 1:17	430
the *G* of heaven concerning this	Dan 2:18	426
Daniel blessed the *G* of heaven	Dan 2:19	426
Blessed be the name of *G* for ever	Dan 2:20	426
O thou *G* of my fathers, who hast	Dan 2:23	426
But there is a *G* in heaven that	Dan 2:28	426
for the *G* of heaven hath given	Dan 2:37	426
the *G* of heaven set up a kingdom	Dan 2:44	426
the great *G* hath made known to	Dan 2:45	426
is, that your *G* is a *G* of gods	Dan 2:47	426
who is that *G* that shall deliver	Dan 3:15	426
our *G* whom we serve is able to	Dan 3:17	426
the fourth is like the Son of *G*	Dan 3:25	426
ye servants of the most high *G*	Dan 3:26	426
Blessed be the *G* of Shadrach	Dan 3:28	426
except their own *G*	Dan 3:28	426
amiss against the *G* of Shadrach	Dan 3:29	426
because there is no other *G* that	Dan 3:29	426
wonders that the high *G* hath	Dan 4:2	426
house of *G* which was at Jerusalem	Dan 5:3	426
O thou king, the most high *G* gave	Dan 5:18	426
G ruled in the kingdom of men	Dan 5:21	426
the *G* in whose hand thy breath is	Dan 5:23	426
G hath numbered thy kingdom, and	Dan 5:26	426
him concerning the law of his *G*	Dan 6:5	426
of any *G* or man for thirty days	Dan 6:7	426
and gave thanks before his *G*	Dan 6:10	426
making supplication before his *G*	Dan 6:11	426
any *G* or man within thirty days	Dan 6:12	426
Daniel, Thy *G* whom thou servest	Dan 6:16	426
of the living *G*, is thy *G*	Dan 6:20	426
My *G* hath sent his angel, and hath	Dan 6:22	426
him, because he believed in his *G*	Dan 6:23	426
and fear before the *G* of Daniel	Dan 6:26	426
for he is the living *G*, and	Dan 6:26	426
And I set my face unto the Lord *G*	Dan 9:3	430
And I prayed unto the Lord my *G*	Dan 9:4	430
O Lord, the great and dreadful *G*	Dan 9:4	410
To the Lord our *G* belong mercies	Dan 9:9	430
the voice of the Lord our *G*	Dan 9:10	430
the law of Moses the servant of *G*	Dan 9:11	430
our prayer before the Lord our *G*	Dan 9:13	430
for the Lord our *G* is righteous	Dan 9:14	430
And now, O Lord our *G*, that hast	Dan 9:15	430
Now therefore, O our *G*, hear the	Dan 9:17	430
O my *G*, incline thine ear, and	Dan 9:18	430
not, for thine own sake, O my *G*	Dan 9:19	430
G for the holy mountain of my *G*	Dan 9:20	430
to chasten thyself before thy *G*	Dan 10:12	430
do know their *G* shall be strong	Dan 11:32	430
things against the *G* of gods	Dan 11:36	410
he regard the *G* of his fathers	Dan 11:37	430
shall he honour the *G* of forces	Dan 11:38	433
G said unto him, Call her name	Hos 1:6	
save them by the Lord their *G*	Hos 1:7	430
Then said *G*, Call his name	Hos 1:9	
people, and I will not be your *G*	Hos 1:9	
Ye are the sons of the living *G*	Hos 1:10	410
and they shall say, Thou art my *G*	Hos 2:23	430
return, and seek the Lord their *G*	Hos 3:5	430
nor knowledge of *G* in the land	Hos 4:1	430
hast forgotten the law of thy *G*	Hos 4:6	430
gone a whoring from under their *G*	Hos 4:12	430
their doings to turn unto their *G*	Hos 5:4	430
the knowledge of *G* more than	Hos 6:6	430
do not return to the Lord their *G*	Hos 7:10	430
Israel shall cry unto me, My *G*	Hos 8:2	430
therefore it is not *G*	Hos 8:6	430
hast gone a whoring from thy *G*	Hos 9:1	430
watchman of Ephraim was with my *G*	Hos 9:8	430
and hatred in the house of his *G*	Hos 9:8	430
My *G* will cast them away, because	Hos 9:17	430
for I am *G*, and not man	Hos 11:9	410
but Judah yet ruleth with *G*	Hos 11:12	430
his strength he had power with *G*	Hos 12:3	430
Even the Lord *G* of hosts	Hos 12:5	430
Therefore turn thou to thy *G*	Hos 12:6	430
and wait on thy *G* continually	Hos 12:6	430
I that am the Lord thy *G* from the	Hos 12:9	430
Yet I am the Lord thy *G* from the	Hos 13:4	430
she hath rebelled against her *G*	Hos 13:16	430
return unto the Lord thy *G*	Hos 14:1	430
sackcloth, ye ministers of my *G*	Joel 1:13	430
from the house of your *G*	Joel 1:13	430
into the house of the Lord your *G*	Joel 1:14	430
gladness from the house of our *G*	Joel 1:16	430
and turn unto the Lord your *G*	Joel 2:13	430
offering unto the Lord your *G*	Joel 2:14	430
the people, Where is their *G*	Joel 2:17	430
and rejoice in the Lord your *G*	Joel 2:23	430
the name of the Lord your *G*	Joel 2:26	430

and that I am the Lord your *G*	Joel 2:27	430
the Lord your *G* dwelling in Zion	Joel 3:17	430
shall perish, saith the Lord *G*	Amos 1:8	3069
Surely the Lord *G* will do nothing	Amos 3:7	3069
the Lord *G* hath spoken, who can	Amos 3:8	3069
Therefore thus saith the Lord *G*	Amos 3:11	3069
house of Jacob, saith the Lord *G*	Amos 3:13	3069
the *G* of hosts	Amos 3:13	430
The Lord *G* hath sworn by his	Amos 4:2	3069
of Israel, saith the Lord *G*	Amos 4:5	3069
as *G* overthrew Sodom and Gomorrah,	Amos 4:11	430
unto thee, prepare to meet thy *G*	Amos 4:12	430
The *G* of hosts, is his name	Amos 4:13	430
For thus saith the Lord *G*	Amos 5:3	3069
the *G* of hosts, shall be with you	Amos 5:14	430
it may be that the Lord *G* of	Amos 5:15	430
the *G* of hosts, the Lord, saith	Amos 5:16	430
whose name is The *G* of hosts	Amos 5:27	430
The Lord *G* hath sworn by himself,	Amos 6:8	3069
saith the Lord the *G* of hosts	Amos 6:8	430
saith the Lord the *G* of hosts	Amos 6:14	430
hath the Lord *G* shewed unto me	Amos 7:1	3069
the land, then I said, O Lord *G*	Amos 7:2	3069
hath the Lord *G* shewed unto me	Amos 7:4	3069
the Lord *G* called to contend by	Amos 7:4	3069
Then said I, O Lord *G*, cease, I	Amos 7:5	3069
shall not be, saith the Lord *G*	Amos 7:6	3069
hath the Lord *G* shewed unto me	Amos 8:1	3069
in that day, saith the Lord *G*	Amos 8:3	3069
in that day, saith the Lord *G*	Amos 8:9	3069
the days come, saith the Lord *G*	Amos 8:11	3069
the Lord *G* of hosts is that	Amos 9:5	3069
the eyes of the Lord *G* are upon	Amos 9:8	3069
given them, saith the Lord thy *G*	Amos 9:15	430
saith the Lord *G* concerning Edom	Obad 1	3069
arise, call upon thy *G*	Jonah 1:6	430
if so be that *G* will think upon	Jonah 1:6	430
the *G* of heaven, which hath made	Jonah 1:9	430
his *G* out of the fish's belly	Jonah 2:1	430
life from corruption, O Lord my *G*	Jonah 2:6	430
the people of Nineveh believed *G*	Jonah 3:5	430
sackcloth, and cry mightily unto *G*	Jonah 3:8	430
Who can tell if *G* will turn	Jonah 3:9	430
G saw their works, that they	Jonah 3:10	430
G repented of the evil, that he	Jonah 3:10	430
I knew that thou art a gracious *G*	Jonah 4:2	410
the Lord *G* prepared a gourd, and	Jonah 4:6	430
But *G* prepared a worm when the	Jonah 4:7	430
that *G* prepared a vehement east	Jonah 4:8	430
G said to Jonah, Doest thou well	Jonah 4:9	430
let the Lord *G* be witness against	Mic 1:2	3069
for there is no answer of *G*	Mic 3:7	430
and to the house of the *G* of Jacob	Mic 4:2	430
name of the Lord our *G* for ever	Mic 4:5	430
of the name of the Lord his *G*	Mic 5:4	430
and bow myself before the high *G*	Mic 6:6	430
and to walk humbly with thy *G*	Mic 6:8	430
wait for the *G* of my salvation	Mic 7:7	430
my *G* will hear me	Mic 7:7	430
unto me, Where is the Lord thy *G*	Mic 7:10	430
shall be afraid of the Lord our *G*	Mic 7:17	430
Who is a *G* like unto thee, that	Mic 7:18	410
G is jealous, and the Lord	Nah 1:2	410
not from everlasting, O Lord my *G*	Hab 1:12	430
and, O mighty *G*, thou hast	Hab 1:12	6697
G came from Teman, and the Holy	Hab 3:3	433
will joy in the *G* of my salvation	Hab 3:18	430
The Lord *G* is my strength, and he	Hab 3:19	136
at the presence of the Lord *G*	Zeph 1:7	3069
the Lord their *G* shall visit them	Zeph 2:7	430
the *G* of Israel, Surely Moab	Zeph 2:9	430
she drew not near to her *G*	Zeph 3:2	430
The Lord thy *G* in the midst of	Zeph 3:17	430
the voice of the Lord their *G*	Hag 1:12	430
as the Lord their *G* had sent him	Hag 1:12	430
of the Lord of hosts, their *G*	Hag 1:14	430
obey the voice of the Lord your *G*	Zec 6:15	430
sent unto the house of *G* Sherezer	Zec 7:2	1008
my people, and I will be their *G*	Zec 8:8	430
we have heard that *G* is with you	Zec 8:23	430
even he, shall be for our *G*	Zec 9:7	430
the Lord *G* shall blow the trumpet	Zec 9:14	3069
the Lord their *G* shall save them	Zec 9:16	430
for I am the Lord their *G*	Zec 10:6	430
Thus saith the Lord my *G*	Zec 11:4	430
in the Lord of hosts their *G*	Zec 12:5	430
the house of David shall be as *G*	Zec 12:8	430
they shall say, The Lord is my *G*	Zec 13:9	430
and the Lord my *G* shall come	Zec 14:5	430
beseech *G* that he will be	Mal 1:9	410
hath not one *G* created us	Mal 2:10	410

G

shall I liken the kingdom of *G*..........Lk 13:20	2316	
the prophets, in the kingdom of *G*..........Lk 13:28	2316	
sit down in the kingdom of *G*..........Lk 13:29	2316	
eat bread in the kingdom of *G*..........Lk 14:15	2316	
the presence of the angels of *G*..........Lk 15:10	2316	
Ye cannot serve *G* and mammon..........Lk 16:13	2316	
but *G* knoweth your hearts..........Lk 16:15	2316	
is abomination in the sight of *G*..........Lk 16:15	2316	
time the kingdom of *G* is preached..........Lk 16:16	2316	
and with a loud voice glorified *G*..........Lk 17:15	2316	
that returned to give glory to *G*..........Lk 17:18	2316	
when the kingdom of *G* should come..........Lk 17:20	2316	
The kingdom of *G* cometh not with..........Lk 17:20	2316	
the kingdom of *G* is within you..........Lk 17:21	2316	
city a judge, which feared not *G*..........Lk 18:2	2316	
himself, Though I fear not *G*..........Lk 18:4	2316	
shall not *G* avenge his own elect,..........Lk 18:7	2316	
and prayed thus with himself, *G*..........Lk 18:11	2316	
G be merciful to me a sinner..........Lk 18:13	2316	
for of such is the kingdom of *G*..........Lk 18:16	2316	
not receive the kingdom of *G* as a..........Lk 18:17	2316	
is good, save one, that is, *G*..........Lk 18:19	2316	
enter into the kingdom of *G*..........Lk 18:24	2316	
to enter into the kingdom of *G*..........Lk 18:25	2316	
with men are possible with *G*..........Lk 18:27	2316	
and followed him, glorifying *G*..........Lk 18:43	2316	
they saw it, gave praise unto *G*..........Lk 18:43	2316	
of *G* should immediately appear..........Lk 19:11	2316	
praise *G* with a loud voice for..........Lk 19:37	2316	
heard it, they said, *G* forbid..........Lk 20:16	3361,1096	
but teachest the way of *G* truly..........Lk 20:21	2316	
unto *G* the things which be God's..........Lk 20:25	2316	
and are the children of *G*, being..........Lk 20:36	2316	
calleth the Lord the *G* of Abraham..........Lk 20:37	2316	
G of Isaac, and the *G* of Jacob..........Lk 20:37	2316	
For he is not a *G* of the dead..........Lk 20:38	2316	
cast in unto the offerings of *G*..........Lk 21:4	2316	
the kingdom of *G* is nigh at hand..........Lk 21:31	2316	
be fulfilled in the kingdom of *G*..........Lk 22:16	2316	
until the kingdom of *G* shall come..........Lk 22:18	2316	
the right hand of the power of *G*..........Lk 22:69	2316	
all, Art thou then the Son of *G*..........Lk 22:70	2316	
if he be Christ, the chosen of *G*..........Lk 23:35	2316	
him, saying, Dost not thou fear *G*..........Lk 23:40	2316	
saw what was done, he glorified *G*..........Lk 23:47	2316	
waited for the kingdom of *G*..........Lk 23:51	2316	
mighty in deed and word before *G*..........Lk 24:19	2316	
temple, praising and blessing *G*..........Lk 24:53	2316	
was with *G*, and the Word was *G*..........Jn 1:1	2316	
same was in the beginning with *G*..........Jn 1:2	2316	
There was a man sent from *G*..........Jn 1:6	2316	
he power to become the sons of *G*..........Jn 1:12	2316	
nor of the will of man, but of *G*..........Jn 1:13	2316	
No man hath seen *G* at any time..........Jn 1:18	2316	
and saith, Behold the Lamb of *G*..........Jn 1:29	2316	
record that this is the Son of *G*..........Jn 1:34	2316	
he saith, Behold the Lamb of *G*..........Jn 1:36	2316	
him, Rabbi, thou art the Son of *G*..........Jn 1:49	2316	
and the angels of *G* ascending..........Jn 1:51	2316	
thou art a teacher come from *G*..........Jn 3:2	2316	
thou doest, except *G* be with him..........Jn 3:2	2316	
he cannot see the kingdom of *G*..........Jn 3:3	2316	
enter into the kingdom of *G*..........Jn 3:5	2316	
For *G* so loved the world, that he..........Jn 3:16	2316	
For *G* sent not his Son into the..........Jn 3:17	2316	
of the only begotten Son of *G*..........Jn 3:18	2316	
that they are wrought in *G*..........Jn 3:21	2316	
set to his seal that *G* is true..........Jn 3:33	2316	
For he whom *G* hath sent speaketh..........Jn 3:34	2316	
hath sent speaketh the words of *G*..........Jn 3:34	2316	
for *G* giveth not the Spirit by..........Jn 3:34	2316	
but the wrath of *G* abideth on him..........Jn 3:36	2316	
If thou knewest the gift of *G*..........Jn 4:10	2316	
G is a Spirit..........Jn 4:24	2316	
said also that *G* was his Father..........Jn 5:18	2316	
making himself equal with *G*..........Jn 5:18	2316	
hear the voice of the Son of *G*..........Jn 5:25	2316	
ye have not the love of *G* in you..........Jn 5:42	2316	
honour that cometh from *G* only..........Jn 5:44	2316	
for him hath *G* the Father sealed..........Jn 6:27	2316	
that we might work the works of *G*..........Jn 6:28	2316	
unto them, This is the work of *G*..........Jn 6:29	2316	
For the bread of *G* is he which..........Jn 6:33	2316	
And they shall be all taught of *G*..........Jn 6:45	2316	
the Father, save he which is of *G*..........Jn 6:46	2316	
Christ, the Son of the living *G*..........Jn 6:69	2316	
the doctrine, whether it be of *G*..........Jn 7:17	2316	
truth, which I have heard of *G*..........Jn 8:40	2316	
we have one Father, even *G*..........Jn 8:41	2316	
If *G* were your Father, ye would..........Jn 8:42	2316	
I proceeded forth and came from *G*..........Jn 8:42	2316	

He that is of *G* heareth God's..........Jn 8:47	2316	
them not, because ye are not of *G*..........Jn 8:47	2316	
of whom ye say, that he is your *G*..........Jn 8:54	2316	
but that the works of *G* should be..........Jn 9:3	2316	
Pharisees, This man is not of *G*..........Jn 9:16	2316	
said unto him, Give *G* the praise..........Jn 9:24	2316	
We know that *G* spake unto Moses..........Jn 9:29	2316	
Now we know that *G* heareth not..........Jn 9:31	2316	
if any man be a worshipper of *G*..........Jn 9:31	2316	
If this man were not of *G*..........Jn 9:33	2318	
Dost thou believe on the Son of *G*..........Jn 9:35	2316	
being a man, makest thyself *G*..........Jn 10:33	2316	
unto whom the word of *G* came..........Jn 10:35	2316	
because I said, I am the Son of *G*..........Jn 10:36	2316	
death, but for the glory of *G*..........Jn 11:4	2316	
that the Son of *G* might be..........Jn 11:4	2316	
ask of *G*, *G* will give it thee..........Jn 11:22	2316	
thou art the Christ, the Son of *G*..........Jn 11:27	2316	
thou shouldest see the glory of *G*..........Jn 11:40	2316	
of *G* that were scattered abroad..........Jn 11:52	2316	
of men more than the praise of *G*..........Jn 12:43	2316	
was come from *G*, and went to *G*..........Jn 13:3	2316	
and *G* is glorified in him..........Jn 13:31	2316	
If *G* be glorified in him..........Jn 13:32	2316	
G shall also glorify him..........Jn 13:32	2316	
ye believe in *G*, believe also in..........Jn 14:1	2316	
think that he doeth *G* service..........Jn 16:2	2316	
believed that I came out from *G*..........Jn 16:27	2316	
that thou camest forth from *G*..........Jn 16:30	2316	
might know thee the only true *G*..........Jn 17:3	2316	
he made himself the Son of *G*..........Jn 19:7	2316	
and to my *G*, and your *G*..........Jn 20:17	2316	
and said unto him, My Lord and my *G*..........Jn 20:28	2316	
Jesus is the Christ, the Son of *G*..........Jn 20:31	2316	
by what death he should glorify *G*..........Jn 21:19	2316	
pertaining to the kingdom of *G*..........Acts 1:3	2316	
tongues the wonderful works of *G*..........Acts 2:11	2316	
to pass in the last days, saith *G*..........Acts 2:17	2316	
a man approved of *G* among you by..........Acts 2:22	2316	
which *G* did by him in the midst..........Acts 2:22	2316	
counsel and foreknowledge of *G*..........Acts 2:23	2316	
Whom *G* hath raised up, having..........Acts 2:24	2316	
knowing that *G* had sworn with an..........Acts 2:30	2316	
This Jesus hath *G* raised up..........Acts 2:32	2316	
by the right hand of *G* exalted..........Acts 2:33	2316	
that *G* hath made that same Jesus,..........Acts 2:36	2316	
many as the Lord our *G* shall call..........Acts 2:39	2316	
Praising *G*, and having favour with..........Acts 2:47	2316	
and leaping, and praising *G*..........Acts 3:8	2316	
saw him walking and praising *G*..........Acts 3:9	2316	
The *G* of Abraham, and of Isaac, and..........Acts 3:13	2316	
the *G* of our fathers, hath..........Acts 3:13	2316	
whom *G* hath raised from the dead..........Acts 3:15	2316	
which *G* before had shewed by the..........Acts 3:18	2316	
which *G* hath spoken by the mouth..........Acts 3:21	2316	
your *G* raise up unto you of your..........Acts 3:22	2316	
which *G* made with our fathers..........Acts 3:25	2316	
Unto you first *G*, having raised..........Acts 3:26	2316	
whom *G* raised from the dead, even..........Acts 4:10	2316	
it be right in the sight of *G* to..........Acts 4:19	2316	
hearken unto you more than unto *G*..........Acts 4:19	2316	
for all men glorified *G* for that..........Acts 4:21	2316	
their voice to *G* with one accord..........Acts 4:24	2316	
and said, Lord, thou art *G*..........Acts 4:24	2316	
spake the word of *G* with boldness..........Acts 4:31	2316	
not lied unto men, but unto *G*..........Acts 5:4	2316	
ought to obey *G* rather than men..........Acts 5:29	2316	
The *G* of our fathers raised up..........Acts 5:30	2316	
Him hath *G* exalted with his right..........Acts 5:31	2316	
whom *G* hath given to them that..........Acts 5:32	2316	
But if it be of *G*, ye cannot..........Acts 5:39	2316	
be found even to fight against *G*..........Acts 5:39	2314	
we should leave the word of *G*..........Acts 6:2	2316	
And the word of *G* increased..........Acts 6:7	2316	
words against Moses, and against *G*..........Acts 6:11	2316	
The *G* of glory appeared unto our..........Acts 7:2	2316	
G spake on this wise, That his..........Acts 7:6	2316	
in bondage will I judge, said *G*..........Acts 7:7	2316	
but *G* was with him,..........Acts 7:9	2316	
which *G* had sworn to Abraham, the..........Acts 7:17	2316	
G by his hand would deliver them..........Acts 7:25	2316	
I am the *G* of thy fathers..........Acts 7:32	2316	
the *G* of Abraham..........Acts 7:32	2316	
G of Isaac, and the *G* of Jacob..........Acts 7:32	2316	
the same did *G* send to be a ruler..........Acts 7:35	2316	
your *G* raise up unto you of your..........Acts 7:37	2316	
Then *G* turned, and gave them up to..........Acts 7:42	2316	
whom *G* drave out before the face..........Acts 7:45	2316	
Who found favour before *G*..........Acts 7:46	2316	
a tabernacle for the *G* of Jacob..........Acts 7:46	2316	
heaven, and saw the glory of *G*..........Acts 7:55	2316	

G

standing on the right hand of *G*	Acts 7:55	2316
standing on the right hand of *G*	Acts 7:56	2316
stoned Stephen, calling upon *G*	Acts 7:59	
This man is the great power of *G*	Acts 8:10	2316
concerning the kingdom of *G*	Acts 8:12	2316
had received the word of *G*	Acts 8:14	2316
of *G* may be purchased with money	Acts 8:20	2316
is not right in the sight of *G*	Acts 8:21	2316
of this thy wickedness, and pray *G*	Acts 8:22	2316
that Jesus Christ is the Son of *G*	Acts 8:37	2316
that he is the Son of *G*	Acts 9:20	2316
one that feared *G* with all his	Acts 10:2	2316
the people, and prayed to *G* alway	Acts 10:2	2316
an angel of *G* coming in to him	Acts 10:3	2316
come up for a memorial before *G*	Acts 10:4	2316
What *G* hath cleansed, that call	Acts 10:15	2316
a just man, and one that feareth *G*	Acts 10:22	2316
was warned from *G* by an holy	Acts 10:22	
but *G* hath shewed me that I	Acts 10:28	2316
in remembrance in the sight of *G*	Acts 10:31	2316
are we all here present before *G*	Acts 10:33	2316
that are commanded thee of *G*	Acts 10:33	2316
that *G* is no respecter of persons	Acts 10:34	2316
The word which *G* sent unto the	Acts 10:36	
How *G* anointed Jesus of Nazareth	Acts 10:38	2316
for *G* was with him	Acts 10:38	2316
Him *G* raised up the third day, and	Acts 10:40	2316
unto witnesses chosen before of *G*	Acts 10:41	2316
of *G* to be the Judge of quick	Acts 10:42	2316
speak with tongues, and magnify *G*	Acts 10:46	2316
had also received the word of *G*	Acts 11:1	2316
What *G* hath cleansed, that call	Acts 11:9	2316
Forasmuch then as *G* gave them the	Acts 11:17	2316
was I, that I could withstand *G*	Acts 11:17	2316
held their peace, and glorified *G*	Acts 11:18	2316
Then hath *G* also to the Gentiles	Acts 11:18	2316
came, and had seen the grace of *G*	Acts 11:23	2316
of the church unto *G* for him	Acts 12:5	2316
because he gave not *G* the glory	Acts 12:23	2316
But the word of *G* grew and	Acts 12:24	2316
they preached the word of *G* in	Acts 13:5	2316
and desired to hear the word of *G*	Acts 13:7	2316
Men of Israel, and ye that fear *G*	Acts 13:16	2316
The *G* of this people of Israel	Acts 13:17	2316
G gave unto them Saul the son of	Acts 13:21	2316
Of this man's seed hath *G*	Acts 13:23	2316
and whosoever among you feareth *G*	Acts 13:26	2316
But *G* raised him from the dead	Acts 13:30	2316
G hath fulfilled the same unto us	Acts 13:33	2316
own generation by the will of *G*	Acts 13:36	2316
whom *G* raised again, saw no	Acts 13:37	2316
to continue in the grace of *G*	Acts 13:43	2316
together to hear the word of *G*	Acts 13:44	2316
G should first have been spoken	Acts 13:46	2316
these vanities unto the living *G*	Acts 14:15	2316
enter into the kingdom of *G*	Acts 14:22	2316
of *G* for the work which they	Acts 14:26	2316
all that *G* had done with them	Acts 14:27	2316
things that *G* had done with them	Acts 15:4	2316
while ago *G* made choice among us	Acts 15:7	2316
And *G*, which knoweth the hearts,	Acts 15:8	2316
Now therefore why tempt ye *G*	Acts 15:10	2316
wonders *G* had wrought among the	Acts 15:12	2316
Simeon hath declared how *G* at the	Acts 15:14	2316
Known unto *G* are all his works	Acts 15:18	2316
the Gentiles are turned to *G*	Acts 15:19	2316
the brethren unto the grace of *G*	Acts 15:40	2316
of Thyatira, which worshipped *G*	Acts 16:14	2316
the servants of the most high *G*	Acts 16:17	2316
prayed, and sang praises unto *G*	Acts 16:25	2316
believing in *G* with all his house	Acts 16:34	2316
G was preached of Paul at Berea	Acts 17:13	2316
inscription, TO THE UNKNOWN *G*	Acts 17:23	2316
G that made the world and all	Acts 17:24	2316
then as we are the offspring of *G*	Acts 17:29	2316
of this ignorance *G* winked at	Acts 17:30	2316
Justus, one that worshipped *G*	Acts 18:7	2316
teaching the word of *G* among them	Acts 18:11	2316
to worship *G* contrary to the law	Acts 18:13	2316
return again unto you, if *G* will	Acts 18:21	2316
him the way of *G* more perfectly	Acts 18:26	2316
concerning the kingdom of *G*	Acts 19:8	2316
G wrought special miracles by the	Acts 19:11	2316
G So mightily grew the word of *G*	Acts 19:20	2962
the Greeks, repentance toward *G*	Acts 20:21	2316
the gospel of the grace of *G*	Acts 20:24	2316
gone preaching the kingdom of *G*	Acts 20:25	2316
unto you all the counsel of *G*	Acts 20:27	2316
to feed the church of *G*, which	Acts 20:28	2316
now, brethren, I commend you to *G*	Acts 20:32	2316
particularly what things *G* had	Acts 21:19	2316

fathers, and was zealous toward *G*	Acts 22:3	2316
The *G* of our fathers hath chosen	Acts 22:14	2316
before *G* until this day	Acts 23:1	2316
G shall smite thee, thou whited	Acts 23:3	2316
him, let us not fight against *G*	Acts 23:9	2313
so worship I the *G* of my fathers	Acts 24:14	2316
And have hope toward *G*, which they	Acts 24:15	2316
void of offence toward *G*, and	Acts 24:16	2316
made of *G* unto our fathers	Acts 26:6	2316
tribes, instantly serving *G* day	Acts 26:7	
that *G* should raise the dead	Acts 26:8	2316
and from the power of Satan unto *G*	Acts 26:18	2316
they should repent and turn to *G*	Acts 26:20	2316
therefore obtained help of *G*	Acts 26:22	2316
And Paul said, I would to *G*	Acts 26:29	2316
by me this night the angel of *G*	Acts 27:23	2316
G hath given thee all them that	Acts 27:24	2316
for I believe *G*, that it shall be	Acts 27:25	2316
gave thanks to *G* in presence of	Acts 27:35	2316
whom when Paul saw, he thanked *G*	Acts 28:15	2316
and testified the kingdom of *G*	Acts 28:23	2316
that the salvation of *G* is sent	Acts 28:28	2316
Preaching the kingdom of *G*	Acts 28:31	2316
separated unto the gospel of *G*	Rom 1:1	2316
to be the Son of *G* with power	Rom 1:4	2316
all that be in Rome, beloved of *G*	Rom 1:7	2316
to you and peace from *G* our Father	Rom 1:7	2316
I thank my *G* through Jesus Christ	Rom 1:8	2316
For *G* is my witness, whom I serve	Rom 1:9	2316
by the will of *G* to come unto you	Rom 1:10	2316
for it is the power of *G* unto	Rom 1:16	2316
of *G* revealed from faith to faith	Rom 1:17	2316
For the wrath of *G* is revealed	Rom 1:18	2316
be known of *G* is manifest in them	Rom 1:19	2316
for *G* hath shewed it unto them	Rom 1:19	2316
Because that, when they knew *G*	Rom 1:21	2316
they glorified him not as *G*	Rom 1:21	2316
G into an image made like to	Rom 1:23	2316
Wherefore *G* also gave them up to	Rom 1:24	2316
changed the truth of *G* into a lie	Rom 1:25	2316
For this cause *G* gave them up	Rom 1:26	2316
to retain *G* in their knowledge	Rom 1:28	2316
G gave them over to a reprobate	Rom 1:28	2316
Backbiters, haters of *G*	Rom 1:30	2319
Who knowing the judgment of *G*	Rom 1:32	2316
G is according to truth against	Rom 2:2	2316
shalt escape the judgment of *G*	Rom 2:3	2316
of *G* leadeth thee to repentance	Rom 2:4	2316
of the righteous judgment of *G*	Rom 2:5	2316
is no respect of persons with *G*	Rom 2:11	2316
of the law are just before *G*	Rom 2:13	2316
In the day when *G* shall judge the	Rom 2:16	2316
the law, and makest thy boast of *G*	Rom 2:17	2316
the law dishonourest thou *G*	Rom 2:23	2316
For the name of *G* is blasphemed	Rom 2:24	2316
praise is not of men, but of *G*	Rom 2:29	2316
were committed the oracles of *G*	Rom 3:2	2316
the faith of *G* without effect	Rom 3:3	2316
G forbid: yea	Rom 3:4	3361,1096
let *G* be true, but every man a	Rom 3:4	2316
commend the righteousness of *G*	Rom 3:5	2316
Is *G* unrighteous who taketh	Rom 3:5	2316
G forbid: for then how	Rom 3:6	3361,1096
then how shall *G* judge the world	Rom 3:6	2316
For if the truth of *G* hath more	Rom 3:7	2316
is none that seeketh after *G*	Rom 3:11	2316
is no fear of *G* before their eyes	Rom 3:18	2316
world may become guilty before *G*	Rom 3:19	2316
But now the righteousness of *G*	Rom 3:21	2316
Even the righteousness of *G* which	Rom 3:22	2316
and come short of the glory of *G*	Rom 3:23	2316
Whom *G* hath set forth to be a	Rom 3:25	2316
through the forbearance of *G*	Rom 3:25	2316
Is he the *G* of the Jews only	Rom 3:29	2316
Seeing it is one *G*, which shall	Rom 3:30	2316
G forbid: yea, we establish	Rom 3:31	3361,1096
but not before *G*	Rom 4:2	2316
Abraham believed *G*, and it was	Rom 4:3	2316
of the man, unto whom *G* imputeth	Rom 4:6	2316
him whom he believed, even *G*	Rom 4:17	2316
the promise of *G* through unbelief	Rom 4:20	2316
in faith, giving glory to *G*	Rom 4:20	2316
we have peace with *G* through our	Rom 5:1	2316
rejoice in hope of the glory of *G*	Rom 5:2	2316
because the love of *G* is shed	Rom 5:5	2316
But *G* commendeth his love toward	Rom 5:8	2316
we were reconciled to *G* by the	Rom 5:10	2316
but we also joy in *G* through our	Rom 5:11	2316
be dead, much more the grace of *G*	Rom 5:15	2316
G forbid. How shall we	Rom 6:2	3361,1096
that he liveth, he liveth unto *G*	Rom 6:10	2316

but alive unto *G* through Jesus............... Rom 6:11   *2316*
but yield yourselves unto *G*..................... Rom 6:13   *2316*
of righteousness unto *G*........................... Rom 6:13   *2316*
but under grace? *G* forbid .... Rom 6:15   *3361,1096*
But *G* be thanked, that ye were .... Rom 6:17   *2316*
from sin, and become servants to *G*... Rom 6:22   *2316*
but the gift of *G* is eternal life............. Rom 6:23   *2316*
should bring forth fruit unto *G* .... Rom 7:4   *2316*
Is the law sin? *G* forbid.................... Rom 7:7   *3361,1096*
made death unto me? *G* forbid .... Rom 7:13   *3361,1096*
the law of *G* after the inward man......... Rom 7:22   *2316*
I thank *G* through Jesus Christ............. Rom 7:25   *2316*
mind I myself serve the law of *G*......... Rom 7:25   *2316*
G sending his own Son in the .... Rom 8:3   *2316*
carnal mind is enmity against *G*........... Rom 8:7   *2316*
it is not subject to the law of *G*........... Rom 8:7   *2316*
are in the flesh cannot please *G*......... Rom 8:8   *2316*
that the Spirit of *G* dwell in you........... Rom 8:9   *2316*
as are led by the Spirit of *G*.............. Rom 8:14   *2316*
they are the sons of *G*....................... Rom 8:14   *2316*
that we are the children of *G*............ Rom 8:16   *2316*
heirs of *G*, and joint-heirs with .... Rom 8:17   *2316*
manifestation of the sons of *G*............. Rom 8:19   *2316*
liberty of the children of *G* .... Rom 8:21   *2316*
saints according to the will of *G*......... Rom 8:27   *2316*
for good to them that love *G*.............. Rom 8:28   *2316*
If *G* be for us, who can be .... Rom 8:31   *2316*
It is *G* that justifieth .... Rom 8:33   *2316*
is even at the right hand of *G*............. Rom 8:34   *2316*
to separate us from the love of *G*...... Rom 8:39   *2316*
of the law, and the service of *G*........... Rom 9:4   *2316*
is over all, *G* blessed for ever .... Rom 9:5   *2316*
word of *G* hath taken none effect ...... Rom 9:6   *2316*
these are not the children of *G* .... Rom 9:8   *2316*
that the purpose of *G* according........... Rom 9:11   *2316*
Is there unrighteousness with *G*?......... Rom 9:14   *2316*
G forbid... Rom 9:14   *3361,1096*
but of *G* that sheweth mercy .... Rom 9:16   *2316*
art thou that repliest against *G*........... Rom 9:20   *2316*
What if *G*, willing to shew his............. Rom 9:22   *2316*
the children of the living *G*................... Rom 9:26   *2316*
prayer to *G* for Israel is, that .... Rom 10:1   *2316*
record that they have a zeal of *G* ...... Rom 10:2   *2316*
unto the righteousness of *G*................. Rom 10:3   *2316*
believe in thine heart that *G*................. Rom 10:9   *2316*
and hearing by the word of *G*............ Rom 10:17   *2316*
Hath *G* cast away his people............... Rom 11:1   *2316*
cast away his people? *G* forbid....... Rom 11:1   *3361,1096*
G hath not cast away his people............ Rom 11:2   *2316*
intercession to *G* against Israel.............. Rom 11:2   *2316*
saith the answer of *G* unto him............. Rom 11:4   *2316*
G hath given them the spirit of........... Rom 11:8   *2316*
that they should fall? *G* forbid....... Rom 11:11   *3361,1096*
For if *G* spared not the natural............. Rom 11:21   *2316*
the goodness and severity of *G*........... Rom 11:22   *2316*
for *G* is able to graff them in .... Rom 11:23   *2316*
gifts and calling of *G* are without....... Rom 11:29   *2316*
in times past have not believed *G*...... Rom 11:30   *2316*
For *G* hath concluded them all in .... Rom 11:32   *2316*
of the wisdom and knowledge of *G*....... Rom 11:33   *2316*
brethren, by the mercies of *G*................. Rom 12:1   *2316*
holy, acceptable unto *G*, which .... Rom 12:1   *2316*
acceptable, and perfect, will of *G*......... Rom 12:2   *2316*
according as *G* hath dealt to .... Rom 12:3   *2316*
For there is no power but of *G*............. Rom 13:1   *2316*
powers that be are ordained of *G*......... Rom 13:1   *2316*
resisteth the ordinance of *G*................. Rom 13:2   *2316*
minister of *G* to thee for good............. Rom 13:4   *2316*
for he is the minister of *G*................... Rom 13:4   *2316*
for *G* hath received him .... Rom 14:3   *2316*
for *G* is able to make him stand .... Rom 14:4   *2316*
the Lord, for he giveth *G* thanks........... Rom 14:6   *2316*
he eateth not, and giveth *G* thanks...... Rom 14:6   *2316*
every tongue shall confess to *G* .... Rom 14:11   *2316*
give account of himself to *G*................. Rom 14:12   *2316*
For the kingdom of *G* is not meat .... Rom 14:17   *2316*
serveth Christ is acceptable to *G*......... Rom 14:18   *2316*
meat destroy not the work of *G*............. Rom 14:20   *2316*
have it to thyself before *G*................... Rom 14:22   *2316*
Now the *G* of patience and .... Rom 15:5   *2316*
one mind and one mouth glorify *G* .... Rom 15:6   *2316*
received us to the glory of *G*................. Rom 15:7   *2316*
circumcision for the truth of *G* .... Rom 15:8   *2316*
might glorify *G* for his mercy .... Rom 15:9   *2316*
Now the *G* of hope fill you with .... Rom 15:13   *2316*
grace that is given to me of *G*............. Rom 15:15   *2316*
ministering the gospel of *G*................. Rom 15:16   *2316*
those things which pertain to *G*........... Rom 15:17   *2316*
by the power of the Spirit of *G*........... Rom 15:19   *2316*
me in your prayers to *G* for me .... Rom 15:30   *2316*
you with joy by the will of *G*............... Rom 15:32   *2316*

Now the *G* of peace be with you .... Rom 15:33   *2316*
the *G* of peace shall bruise Satan .... Rom 16:20   *2316*
commandment of the everlasting *G*....... Rom 16:26   *2316*
To *G* only wise, be glory through........... Rom 16:27   *2316*
Christ through the will of *G* 1Cor 1:1   *2316*
Unto the church of *G* which is at 1Cor 1:2   *2316*
from *G* our Father, and from the 1Cor 1:3   *2316*
I thank my *G* always on your............... 1Cor 1:4   *2316*
for the grace of *G* which is given......... 1Cor 1:4   *2316*
G is faithful, by whom ye were............... 1Cor 1:9   *2316*
I thank *G* that I baptized none of........... 1Cor 1:14   *2316*
are saved it is the power of *G* 1Cor 1:18   *2316*
hath not *G* made foolish the................. 1Cor 1:20   *2316*
that in the wisdom of *G*....................... 1Cor 1:21   *2316*
the world by wisdom knew not *G*........... 1Cor 1:21   *2316*
it pleased *G* by the foolishness 1Cor 1:21   *2316*
power of *G*, and the wisdom of *G*......... 1Cor 1:24   *2316*
of *G* is wiser than men........................ 1Cor 1:25   *2316*
the weakness of *G* is stronger 1Cor 1:25   *2316*
But *G* hath chosen the foolish.............. 1Cor 1:27   *2316*
G hath chosen the weak things of 1Cor 1:27   *2316*
hath *G* chosen, yea, and things........... 1Cor 1:28   *2316*
who of *G* is made unto us wisdom, ... 1Cor 1:30   *2316*
unto you the testimony of *G*................. 1Cor 2:1   *2316*
of men, but in the power of *G*............... 1Cor 2:5   *2316*
the wisdom of *G* in a mystery............... 1Cor 2:7   *2316*
which *G* ordained before the world......... 1Cor 2:7   *2316*
the things which *G* hath prepared 1Cor 2:9   *2316*
But *G* hath revealed them unto us 1Cor 2:10   *2316*
things, yea, the deep things of *G*......... 1Cor 2:10   *2316*
so the things of *G* knoweth no man 1Cor 2:11   *2316*
but the Spirit of *G*............................. 1Cor 2:11   *2316*
but the spirit which is of *G*................... 1Cor 2:12   *2316*
that are freely given to us of *G*........... 1Cor 2:12   *2316*
not the things of the Spirit of *G*........... 1Cor 2:14   *2316*
but *G* gave the increase....................... 1Cor 3:6   *2316*
but *G* that giveth the increase 1Cor 3:7   *2316*
we are labourers together with *G*........... 1Cor 3:9   *2316*
grace of *G* which is given unto me 1Cor 3:10   *2316*
not that ye are the temple of *G*........... 1Cor 3:16   *2316*
the Spirit of *G* dwelleth in you 1Cor 3:16   *2316*
If any man defile the temple of *G* 1Cor 3:17   *2316*
him shall *G* destroy............................. 1Cor 3:17   *2316*
for the temple of *G* is holy 1Cor 3:17   *2316*
this world is foolishness with *G*............. 1Cor 3:19   *2316*
and stewards of the mysteries of *G*....... 1Cor 4:1   *2316*
shall every man have praise of *G*........... 1Cor 4:5   *2316*
I would to *G* ye did reign, that............... 1Cor 4:8   *2316*
For I think that *G* hath set forth 1Cor 4:9   *2316*
the kingdom of *G* is not in word............. 1Cor 4:20   *2316*
them that are without *G* judgeth 1Cor 5:13   *2316*
not inherit the kingdom of *G*................. 1Cor 6:9   *2316*
shall inherit the kingdom of *G* 1Cor 6:10   *2316*
Jesus, and by the Spirit of our *G*......... 1Cor 6:11   *2316*
but *G* shall destroy both it and............. 1Cor 6:13   *2316*
G hath both raised up the Lord, ... 1Cor 6:14   *2316*
members of an harlot? *G* forbid 1Cor 6:15   *3361,1096*
is in you, which ye have of *G*............... 1Cor 6:19   *2316*
therefore glorify *G* in your body........... 1Cor 6:20   *2316*
man hath his proper gift of *G* 1Cor 7:7   *2316*
but *G* hath called us to peace............... 1Cor 7:15   *2316*
But as *G* hath distributed to................. 1Cor 7:17   *2316*
keeping of the commandments of *G*....... 1Cor 7:19   *2316*
is called, therein abide with *G*............... 1Cor 7:24   *2316*
also that I have the Spirit of *G*............. 1Cor 7:40   *2316*
But if any man love *G*, the same 1Cor 8:3   *2316*
there is none other *G* but one 1Cor 8:4   *2316*
But to us there is but one *G*................. 1Cor 8:6   *2316*
But meat commendeth us not to *G*......... 1Cor 8:8   *2316*
Doth *G* take care for oxen................... 1Cor 9:9   *2316*
law, (being not without law to *G* 1Cor 9:21   *2316*
of them *G* was not well pleased 1Cor 10:5   *2316*
but *G* is faithful, who will not............... 1Cor 10:13   *2316*
sacrifice to devils, and not to *G*........... 1Cor 10:20   *2316*
ye do, do all to the glory of *G*............. 1Cor 10:31   *2316*
Gentiles, nor to the church of *G*........... 1Cor 10:32   *2316*
and the head of Christ is *G*................... 1Cor 11:3   *2316*
as he is the image and glory of *G*......... 1Cor 11:7   *2316*
but all things of *G*............................. 1Cor 11:12   *2316*
a woman pray unto *G* uncovered............. 1Cor 11:13   *2316*
custom, neither the churches of *G* 1Cor 11:16   *2316*
or despise ye the church of *G*............... 1Cor 11:22   *2316*
of *G* calleth Jesus accursed................. 1Cor 12:3   *2316*
but it is the same *G* which................... 1Cor 12:6   *2316*
But now hath *G* set the members 1Cor 12:18   *2316*
but *G* hath tempered the body............... 1Cor 12:24   *2316*
G hath set some in the church, ... 1Cor 12:28   *2316*
speaketh not unto men, but unto *G*....... 1Cor 14:2   *2316*
I thank my *G*, I speak with 1Cor 14:18   *2316*
on his face he will worship *G*............... 1Cor 14:25   *2316*
report that *G* is in you of a.................. 1Cor 14:25   *2316*

let him speak to himself, and to G	1Cor 14:28	2316
For G is not the author of	1Cor 14:33	2316
came the word of G out from you	1Cor 14:36	2316
I persecuted the church of G	1Cor 15:9	2316
by the grace of G I am what I am	1Cor 15:10	2316
but the grace of G which was with	1Cor 15:10	2316
we are found false witnesses of G	1Cor 15:15	2316
of G that he raised up Christ	1Cor 15:15	2316
delivered up the kingdom to G	1Cor 15:24	2316
him, that G may be all in all	1Cor 15:28	2316
some have not the knowledge of G	1Cor 15:34	2316
But G giveth it a body as it hath	1Cor 15:38	2316
cannot inherit the kingdom of G	1Cor 15:50	2316
But thanks be to G, which giveth	1Cor 15:57	2316
as G hath prospered him, that	1Cor 16:2	
of Jesus Christ by the will of	2Cor 1:1	2316
unto the church of G which is at	2Cor 1:1	2316
to you and peace from G our Father	2Cor 1:2	2316
Blessed be G, even the Father of	2Cor 1:3	2316
mercies, and the G of all comfort	2Cor 1:3	2316
we ourselves are comforted of G	2Cor 1:4	2316
but in G which raiseth the dead	2Cor 1:9	2316
wisdom, but by the grace of G	2Cor 1:12	2316
But as G is true, our word toward	2Cor 1:18	2316
For the Son of G, Jesus Christ,	2Cor 1:19	2316
the promises of G in him are yea	2Cor 1:20	2316
Amen, unto the glory of G by us	2Cor 1:20	2316
Christ, and hath anointed us, is G	2Cor 1:21	2316
Moreover I call G for a record	2Cor 1:23	2316
Now thanks be unto G, which	2Cor 2:14	2316
For we are unto G a sweet savour	2Cor 2:15	2316
many, which corrupt the word of G	2Cor 2:17	2316
but as of sincerity, but as of G	2Cor 2:17	2316
in the sight of G speak we in	2Cor 2:17	2316
with the Spirit of the living G	2Cor 3:3	2316
but our sufficiency is of G	2Cor 3:5	2316
the word of G deceitfully	2Cor 4:2	2316
conscience in the sight of G	2Cor 4:2	2316
of Christ, who is the image of G	2Cor 4:4	2316
For G, who commanded the light to	2Cor 4:6	2316
of G in the face of Jesus Christ	2Cor 4:6	2316
of the power may be of G, and not	2Cor 4:7	2316
of many redound to the glory of G	2Cor 4:15	2316
we have a building of G, an	2Cor 5:1	2316
us for the selfsame thing is G	2Cor 5:5	2316
but we are made manifest unto G	2Cor 5:11	2316
be beside ourselves, it is to G	2Cor 5:13	2316
And all things are of G, who hath	2Cor 5:18	2316
that G was in Christ, reconciling	2Cor 5:19	2316
as though G did beseech you by us	2Cor 5:20	2316
stead, be ye reconciled to G	2Cor 5:20	2316
the righteousness of G in him	2Cor 5:21	2316
not the grace of G in vain	2Cor 6:1	2316
ourselves as the ministers of G	2Cor 6:4	2316
word of truth, by the power of G	2Cor 6:7	2316
hath the temple of G with idols	2Cor 6:16	2316
ye are the temple of the living G	2Cor 6:16	2316
as G hath said, I will dwell in	2Cor 6:16	2316
and I will be their G, and they	2Cor 6:16	2316
holiness in the fear of G	2Cor 7:1	2316
Nevertheless G, that comforteth	2Cor 7:6	2316
sight of G might appear unto you	2Cor 7:12	2316
of G bestowed on the churches of	2Cor 8:1	2316
Lord, and unto us by the will of G	2Cor 8:5	2316
But thanks be to G, which put the	2Cor 8:16	2316
for G loveth a cheerful giver	2Cor 9:7	2316
G is able to make all grace	2Cor 9:8	2316
through us thanksgiving to G	2Cor 9:11	2316
also by many thanksgivings unto G	2Cor 9:12	2316
G for your professed subjection	2Cor 9:13	2316
the exceeding grace of G in you	2Cor 9:14	2316
Thanks be unto G for his	2Cor 9:15	2316
but mighty through G to the	2Cor 10:4	2316
itself against the knowledge of G	2Cor 10:5	2316
which G hath distributed to us	2Cor 10:13	2316
Would to G ye could bear with me	2Cor 11:1	2316
to you the gospel of G freely	2Cor 11:7	2316
I love you not? G knoweth	2Cor 11:11	2316
The G and Father of our Lord Jesus	2Cor 11:31	2316
body, I cannot tell: G knoweth	2Cor 12:2	2316
I cannot tell: G knoweth	2Cor 12:3	2316
we speak before G in Christ	2Cor 12:19	2316
my G will humble me among you, and	2Cor 12:21	2316
yet he liveth by the power of G	2Cor 13:4	2316
him by the power of G toward you	2Cor 13:4	2316
Now I pray to G that ye do no	2Cor 13:7	2316
the G of love and peace shall be	2Cor 13:11	2316
Jesus Christ, and the love of G	2Cor 13:14	2316
G the Father, who raised him from	Gal 1:1	2316
to you and peace from G the Father	Gal 1:3	2316
world, according to the will of G	Gal 1:4	2316

For do I now persuade men, or G	Gal 1:10	2316
I persecuted the church of G	Gal 1:13	2316
But when it pleased G, who	Gal 1:15	2316
write unto you, behold, before G	Gal 1:20	2316
And they glorified G in me	Gal 1:24	2316
G accepteth no man's person	Gal 2:6	2316
minister of sin? G forbid	Gal 2:17	3361,1096
the law, that I might live unto G	Gal 2:19	2316
live by the faith of the Son of G	Gal 2:20	2316
I do not frustrate the grace of G	Gal 2:21	2316
Even as Abraham believed G	Gal 3:6	2316
foreseeing that G would justify	Gal 3:8	2316
by the law in the sight of G	Gal 3:11	2316
confirmed before of G in Christ	Gal 3:17	2316
but G gave it to Abraham by	Gal 3:18	2316
a mediator of one, but G is one	Gal 3:20	2316
then against the promises of G	Gal 3:21	2316
G forbid for if there had	Gal 3:21	3361,1096
of G by faith in Christ Jesus	Gal 3:26	2316
G sent forth his Son, made of a	Gal 4:4	2316
G hath sent forth the Spirit of	Gal 4:6	2316
then an heir of G through Christ	Gal 4:7	2316
Howbeit then, when ye knew not G	Gal 4:8	2316
now, after that ye have known G	Gal 4:9	2316
or rather are known of G	Gal 4:9	2316
but received me as an angel of G	Gal 4:14	2316
not inherit the kingdom of G	Gal 5:21	2316
G is not mocked	Gal 6:7	2316
But G forbid that I should glory,	Gal 6:14	3361,1096
and mercy, and upon the Israel of G	Gal 6:16	2316
of Jesus Christ by the will of G	Eph 1:1	2316
from G our Father, and from the	Eph 1:2	2316
Blessed be the G and Father of our	Eph 1:3	2316
That the G of our Lord Jesus	Eph 1:17	2316
But G, who is rich in mercy, for	Eph 2:4	2316
it is the gift of G	Eph 2:8	2316
which G hath before ordained that	Eph 2:10	2316
hope, and without G in the world	Eph 2:12	112
unto G in one body by the cross	Eph 2:16	2316
saints, and of the household of G	Eph 2:19	2316
of G through the Spirit	Eph 2:22	2316
dispensation of the grace of G	Eph 3:2	2316
to the gift of the grace of G	Eph 3:7	2316
of the world hath been hid in G	Eph 3:9	2316
church the manifold wisdom of G	Eph 3:10	2316
filled with all the fulness of G	Eph 3:19	2316
One G and Father of all, who is	Eph 4:6	2316
of the knowledge of the Son of G	Eph 4:13	2316
alienated from the life of G	Eph 4:18	2316
which after G is created in	Eph 4:24	2316
grieve not the holy Spirit of G	Eph 4:30	2316
even as G for Christ's sake hath	Eph 4:32	2316
Be ye therefore followers of G	Eph 5:1	2316
and a sacrifice to G for a	Eph 5:2	2316
in the kingdom of Christ and of G	Eph 5:5	2316
wrath of G upon the children of	Eph 5:6	2316
always for all things unto G	Eph 5:20	2316
one to another in the fear of G	Eph 5:21	2316
the will of G from the heart	Eph 6:6	2316
Put on the whole armour of G	Eph 6:11	2316
unto you the whole armour of G	Eph 6:13	2316
Spirit, which is the word of G	Eph 6:17	2316
from G the Father and the Lord	Eph 6:23	2316
from G our Father, and from the	Phil 1:2	2316
I thank my G upon every	Phil 1:3	2316
For G is my record, how greatly I	Phil 1:8	2316
unto the glory and praise of G	Phil 1:11	2316
to you of salvation, and that of G	Phil 1:28	2316
Who, being in the form of G	Phil 2:6	2316
it not robbery to be equal with G	Phil 2:6	2316
Wherefore G also hath highly	Phil 2:9	2316
to the glory of G the Father	Phil 2:11	2316
For it is G which worketh in you	Phil 2:13	2316
and harmless, the sons of G	Phil 2:15	2316
but G had mercy on him	Phil 2:27	2316
which worship G in the spirit	Phil 3:3	2316
which is of G by faith	Phil 3:9	2316
high calling of G in Christ Jesus	Phil 3:14	2316
G shall reveal even this unto you	Phil 3:15	2316
whose G is their belly, and whose	Phil 3:19	2316
requests be made known unto G	Phil 4:6	2316
And the peace of G, which passeth	Phil 4:7	2316
the G of peace shall be with you	Phil 4:9	2316
acceptable, wellpleasing to G	Phil 4:18	2316
But my G shall supply all your	Phil 4:19	2316
Now unto G and our Father be glory	Phil 4:20	2316
of Jesus Christ by the will of G	Col 1:1	2316
from G our Father and the Lord	Col 1:2	2316
We give thanks to G and the Father	Col 1:3	2316
and knew the grace of G in truth	Col 1:6	2316
increasing in the knowledge of G	Col 1:10	2316

is the image of the invisible *G*	Col 1:15	2316
to the dispensation of *G* which is	Col 1:25	2316
for you, to fulfil the word of *G*	Col 1:25	2316
To whom *G* would make known what	Col 1:27	2316
of the mystery of, *G*, and of the	Col 2:2	2316
the faith of the operation of *G*	Col 2:12	2316
increaseth with the increase of *G*	Col 2:19	2316
sitteth on the right hand of *G*	Col 3:1	2316
your life is hid with Christ in *G*	Col 3:3	2316
of *G* cometh on the children of	Col 3:6	2316
on therefore, as the elect of *G*	Col 3:12	2316
let the peace of *G* rule in your	Col 3:15	2316
Lord Jesus, giving thanks to *G*	Col 3:17	2316
in singleness of heart, fearing *G*	Col 3:22	2316
that *G* would open unto us a door	Col 4:3	2316
workers unto the kingdom of *G*	Col 4:11	2316
and complete in all the will of *G*	Col 4:12	2316
which is in *G* the Father and in	1Th 1:1	2316
from *G* our Father, and the Lord	1Th 1:1	2316
We give thanks to *G* always for	1Th 1:2	2316
Jesus Christ, in the sight of *G*	1Th 1:3	2316
beloved, your election of *G*	1Th 1:4	2316
how ye turned to *G* from idols to	1Th 1:9	2316
to serve the living and true *G*	1Th 1:9	2316
we were bold in our *G* to speak	1Th 2:2	2316
gospel of *G* with much contention	1Th 2:2	2316
But as we were allowed of *G* to be	1Th 2:4	2316
not as pleasing men, but *G*	1Th 2:4	2316
cloke of covetousness; *G* is witness	1Th 2:5	2316
you, not the gospel of *G* only	1Th 2:8	2316
preached unto you the gospel of *G*	1Th 2:9	2316
G also, how holily and justly and	1Th 2:10	2316
That ye would walk worthy of *G*	1Th 2:12	2316
also thank we *G* without ceasing	1Th 2:13	2316
word of *G* which ye heard of us	1Th 2:13	2316
as it is in truth, the word of *G*	1Th 2:13	2316
followers of the churches of *G*	1Th 2:14	2316
and they please not *G*, and are	1Th 2:15	2316
our brother, and minister of *G*	1Th 3:2	2316
can we render to *G* again for you	1Th 3:9	2316
joy for your sakes before our *G*	1Th 3:9	2316
Now *G* himself and our Father, and	1Th 3:11	2316
unblameable in holiness before *G*	1Th 3:13	2316
ye ought to walk and to please *G*	1Th 4:1	2316
For this is the will of *G*	1Th 4:3	2316
as the Gentiles which know not *G*	1Th 4:5	2316
For *G* hath not called us unto	1Th 4:7	2316
despiseth not man, but *G*	1Th 4:8	2316
taught of *G* to love one another	1Th 4:9	2316
in Jesus will *G* bring with him	1Th 4:14	2312
archangel, and the trump of *G*	1Th 4:16	2316
For *G* hath not appointed us to	1Th 5:9	2316
for this is the will of *G* in	1Th 5:18	2316
the very *G* of peace sanctify you	1Th 5:23	2316
I pray *G* your whole spirit and	1Th 5:23	2316
the Thessalonians in *G* our Father	2Th 1:1	
from *G* our Father and the Lord	2Th 1:2	2316
bound to thank *G* always for you	2Th 1:3	2316
churches of *G* for your patience	2Th 1:4	2316
of the righteous judgment of *G*	2Th 1:5	2316
worthy of the kingdom of *G*	2Th 1:5	2316
G to recompense tribulation to	2Th 1:6	2316
vengeance on them that know not *G*	2Th 1:8	2316
that our *G* would count you worthy	2Th 1:11	2316
according to the grace of our *G*	2Th 1:12	2316
above all that is called *G*	2Th 2:4	2316
as *G* sitteth in the temple of *G*	2Th 2:4	2316
shewing himself that he is *G*	2Th 2:4	2316
for this cause *G* shall send them	2Th 2:11	2316
to give thanks alway to *G* for you	2Th 2:13	2316
because *G* hath from the beginning	2Th 2:13	2316
Lord Jesus Christ himself, and *G*	2Th 2:16	2316
your hearts into the love of *G*	2Th 3:5	2316
the commandment of *G* our Saviour	1Ti 1:1	2316
from *G* our Father and Jesus Christ	1Ti 1:2	2316
glorious gospel of the blessed *G*	1Ti 1:11	2316
invisible, the only wise *G*	1Ti 1:17	2316
in the sight of *G* our Saviour	1Ti 2:3	2316
For there is one *G*	1Ti 2:5	2316
and one mediator between *G*	1Ti 2:5	2316
he take care of the church of *G*	1Ti 3:5	2316
behave thyself in the house of *G*	1Ti 3:15	2316
is the church of the living *G*	1Ti 3:15	2316
G was manifest in the flesh,	1Ti 3:16	2316
which *G* hath created to be	1Ti 4:3	2316
For every creature of *G* is good	1Ti 4:4	2316
it is sanctified by the word of *G*	1Ti 4:5	2316
because we trust in the living *G*	1Ti 4:10	2316
is good and acceptable before *G*	1Ti 5:4	2316
and desolate, trusteth in *G*	1Ti 5:5	2316
I charge thee before *G*, and the	1Ti 5:21	2316
of all honour, that the name of *G*	1Ti 6:1	2316
But thou, O man of *G*, flee these	1Ti 6:11	2316
thee charge in the sight of *G*	1Ti 6:13	2316
riches, but in the living *G*	1Ti 6:17	2316
of Jesus Christ by the will of *G*	2Ti 1:1	2316
from *G* the Father and Christ Jesus	2Ti 1:2	2316
I thank *G*, whom I serve from my	2Ti 1:3	2316
that thou stir up the gift of *G*	2Ti 1:6	2316
For *G* hath not given us the	2Ti 1:7	2316
according to the power of *G*	2Ti 1:8	2316
but the word of *G* is not bound	2Ti 2:9	2316
to shew thyself approved unto *G*	2Ti 2:15	2316
the foundation of *G* standeth sure	2Ti 2:19	2316
if *G* peradventure will give them	2Ti 2:25	2316
pleasures more than lovers of *G*	2Ti 3:4	2316
is given by inspiration of *G*	2Ti 3:16	5377
That the man of *G* may be perfect	2Ti 3:17	2315
I charge thee therefore before *G*	2Ti 4:1	2316
I pray *G* that it may not be laid	2Ti 4:16	2316
Paul, a servant of *G*, and an	Titus 1:1	
In hope of eternal life, which *G*	Titus 1:2	2316
the commandment of *G* our Saviour	Titus 1:3	2316
from *G* the Father and the Lord	Titus 1:4	2316
be blameless, as the steward of *G*	Titus 1:7	2316
They profess that they know *G*	Titus 1:16	2316
that the word of *G* be not	Titus 2:5	2316
of *G* our Saviour in all things	Titus 2:10	2316
For the grace of *G* that bringeth	Titus 2:11	2316
glorious appearing of the great *G*	Titus 2:13	2316
love of *G* our Saviour toward man	Titus 3:4	2316
they which have believed in *G*	Titus 3:8	2316
from *G* our Father and the Lord	Philem 3	2316
I thank my *G*, making mention of	Philem 4	2316
G, who at sundry times and in	Heb 1:1	2316
all the angels of *G* worship him	Heb 1:6	2316
the Son he saith, Thy throne, O *G*	Heb 1:8	2316
therefore *G*, even thy *G*	Heb 1:9	2316
G also bearing them witness, both	Heb 2:4	2316
that he by the grace of *G* should	Heb 2:9	2316
children which *G* hath given me	Heb 2:13	2316
priest in things pertaining to *G*	Heb 2:17	2316
but he that built all things is *G*	Heb 3:4	2316
in departing from the living *G*	Heb 3:12	2316
G did rest the seventh day from	Heb 4:4	2316
a rest to the people of *G*	Heb 4:9	2316
his own works, as *G* did from his	Heb 4:10	2316
For the word of *G* is quick	Heb 4:12	2316
the heavens, Jesus the Son of *G*	Heb 4:14	2316
for men in things pertaining to *G*	Heb 5:1	2316
but he that is called of *G*	Heb 5:4	2316
Called of *G* an high priest after	Heb 5:10	2316
principles of the oracles of *G*	Heb 5:12	2316
dead works, and of faith toward *G*	Heb 6:1	2316
And this will we do, if *G* permit	Heb 6:3	2316
And have tasted the good word of *G*	Heb 6:5	2316
to themselves the Son of *G* afresh	Heb 6:6	2316
receiveth blessing from *G*	Heb 6:7	2316
For *G* is not unrighteous to	Heb 6:10	2316
For when *G* made promise to	Heb 6:13	2316
Wherein *G*, willing more	Heb 6:17	2316
it was impossible for *G* to lie	Heb 6:18	2316
Salem, priest of the most high *G*	Heb 7:1	2316
but made like unto the Son of *G*	Heb 7:3	2316
by the which we draw nigh unto *G*	Heb 7:19	2316
uttermost that come unto *G* by him	Heb 7:25	2316
as Moses was admonished of *G* when	Heb 8:5	5537
and I will be to them a *G*, and they	Heb 8:10	2316
accomplishing the service of *G*	Heb 9:6	
offered himself without spot to *G*	Heb 9:14	2316
dead works to serve the living *G*	Heb 9:14	2316
which *G* hath enjoined unto you	Heb 9:20	2316
in the presence of *G* for us	Heb 9:24	2316
of me,) to do thy will, O *G*	Heb 10:7	2316
Lo, I come to do thy will, O *G*	Heb 10:9	2316
sat down on the right hand of *G*	Heb 10:12	2316
high priest over the house of *G*	Heb 10:21	2316
trodden under foot the Son of *G*	Heb 10:29	2316
into the hands of the living *G*	Heb 10:31	2316
after ye have done the will of *G*	Heb 10:36	2316
were framed by the word of *G*	Heb 11:3	2316
By faith Abel offered unto *G* a	Heb 11:4	2316
G testifying of his gifts	Heb 11:4	2316
because *G* had translated him	Heb 11:5	2316
this testimony, that he pleased *G*	Heb 11:5	2316
for he that cometh to *G* must	Heb 11:6	2316
being warned of *G* of things not	Heb 11:7	
whose builder and maker is *G*	Heb 11:10	2316
wherefore *G* is not ashamed to	Heb 11:16	2316
not ashamed to be called their *G*	Heb 11:16	2316
Accounting that *G* was able to	Heb 11:19	2316
affliction with the people of *G*	Heb 11:25	2316

G having provided some better	Heb 11:40	2316
the right hand of the throne of G	Heb 12:2	2316
G dealeth with you as with sons	Heb 12:7	2316
any man fail of the grace of G	Heb 12:15	2316
and unto the city of the living G	Heb 12:22	2316
to G the Judge of all, and to the	Heb 12:23	2316
whereby we may serve G acceptably	Heb 12:28	2316
For our G is a consuming fire	Heb 12:29	2316
and adulterers G will judge	Heb 13:4	2316
spoken unto you the word of G	Heb 13:7	2316
of praise to G continually	Heb 13:15	2316
such sacrifices G is well pleased	Heb 13:16	2316
Now the G of peace, that brought	Heb 13:20	2316
James, a servant of G and of the	Jas 1:1	2316
you lack wisdom, let him ask of G	Jas 1:5	2316
he is tempted, I am tempted of G	Jas 1:13	2316
for G cannot be tempted with evil	Jas 1:13	2316
not the righteousness of G	Jas 1:20	2316
religion and undefiled before G	Jas 1:27	2316
Hath not G chosen the poor of	Jas 2:5	2316
believest that there is one G	Jas 2:19	2316
which saith, Abraham believed G	Jas 2:23	2316
and he was called the Friend of G	Jas 2:23	2316
Therewith bless we G, even the	Jas 3:9	2316
made after the similitude of G	Jas 3:9	2316
of the world is enmity with G	Jas 4:4	2316
of the world is the enemy of G	Jas 4:4	2316
G resisteth the proud, but giveth	Jas 4:6	2316
Submit yourselves therefore to G	Jas 4:7	2316
Draw nigh to G, and he will draw	Jas 4:8	2316
the foreknowledge of G the Father	1Pet 1:2	2316
Blessed be the G and Father of our	1Pet 1:3	2316
of G through faith unto salvation	1Pet 1:5	2316
Who by him do believe in G	1Pet 1:21	2316
your faith and hope might be in G	1Pet 1:21	2316
incorruptible, by the word of G	1Pet 1:23	2316
indeed of men, but chosen of G	1Pet 2:4	2316
acceptable to G by Jesus Christ	1Pet 2:5	2316
but are now the people of G	1Pet 2:10	2316
behold, glorify G in the day of	1Pet 2:12	2316
For so is the will of G, that	1Pet 2:15	2316
but as the servants of G	1Pet 2:16	2316
Fear G. Honour the king.	1Pet 2:17	2316
conscience toward G endure grief.	1Pet 2:19	2316
this is acceptable with G	1Pet 2:20	2316
in the sight of G of great price.	1Pet 3:4	2316
holy women also, who trusted in G	1Pet 3:5	2316
the Lord G in your hearts.	1Pet 3:15	2316
is better, if the will of G be so	1Pet 3:17	2316
that he might bring us to G	1Pet 3:18	2316
of G waited in the days of Noah	1Pet 3:20	2316
of a good conscience toward G	1Pet 3:21	2316
and is on the right hand of G	1Pet 3:22	2316
of men, but to the will of G	1Pet 4:2	2316
live according to G in the spirit	1Pet 4:6	2316
of the manifold grace of G	1Pet 4:10	2316
let him speak as the oracles of G	1Pet 4:11	2316
as of the ability which G giveth	1Pet 4:11	2316
that G in all things may be	1Pet 4:11	2316
of glory and of G resteth upon you	1Pet 4:14	2316
let him glorify G on this behalf	1Pet 4:16	2316
must begin at the house of G	1Pet 4:17	2316
that obey not the gospel of G	1Pet 4:17	2316
of G commit the keeping of their	1Pet 4:19	2316
Feed the flock of G which is	1Pet 5:2	2316
for G resisteth the proud, and	1Pet 5:5	2316
under the mighty hand of G	1Pet 5:6	2316
But the G of all grace, who hath	1Pet 5:10	2316
true grace of G wherein ye stand	1Pet 5:12	2316
us through the righteousness of G	2Pet 1:1	2316
you through the knowledge of G	2Pet 1:2	2316
received from G the Father honour	2Pet 1:17	2316
but holy men of G spake as they	2Pet 1:21	2316
For if G spared not the angels	2Pet 2:4	2316
that by the word of G the heavens	2Pet 3:5	2316
unto the coming of the day of G	2Pet 3:12	2316
that G is light, and in him is no	1Jn 1:5	2316
verily is the love of G perfected	1Jn 2:5	2316
the word of G abideth in you, and	1Jn 2:14	2316
the will of G abideth for ever	1Jn 2:17	2316
we should be called the sons of G	1Jn 3:1	2316
Beloved, now are we the sons of G	1Jn 3:2	2316
the Son of G was manifested	1Jn 3:8	2316
is born of G doth not commit sin	1Jn 3:9	2316
sin, because he is born of G	1Jn 3:9	2316
the children of G are manifest	1Jn 3:10	2316
not righteousness is not of G	1Jn 3:10	2316
Hereby perceive we the love of G	1Jn 3:16	
how dwelleth the love of G in him	1Jn 3:17	2316
G is greater than our heart, and	1Jn 3:20	2316
then have we confidence toward G	1Jn 3:21	2316

the spirits whether they are of G	1Jn 4:1	2316
Hereby know ye the Spirit of G	1Jn 4:2	2316
is come in the flesh is of G	1Jn 4:2	2316
is come in the flesh is not of G	1Jn 4:3	2316
Ye are of G, little children, and	1Jn 4:4	2316
We are of G	1Jn 4:6	2316
he that knoweth G heareth us	1Jn 4:6	2316
that is not of G heareth not us	1Jn 4:6	2316
for love is of G	1Jn 4:7	2316
is born of G, and knoweth G	1Jn 4:7	2316
He that loveth not knoweth not G	1Jn 4:8	2316
for G is love	1Jn 4:8	2316
the love of G toward us, because	1Jn 4:9	2316
because that G sent his only	1Jn 4:9	2316
is love, not that we loved G	1Jn 4:10	2316
if G so loved us, we ought also	1Jn 4:11	2316
No man hath seen G at any time	1Jn 4:12	2316
G dwelleth in us, and his love is	1Jn 4:12	2316
that Jesus is the Son of G	1Jn 4:15	2316
G dwelleth in him, and he in G	1Jn 4:15	2316
the love that G hath to us	1Jn 4:16	2316
G is love	1Jn 4:16	2316
love dwelleth in G, and G in him	1Jn 4:16	2316
If a man say, I love G, and hateth	1Jn 4:20	2316
how can he love G whom he hath	1Jn 4:20	2316
That he who loveth G love his	1Jn 4:21	2316
Jesus is the Christ is born of G	1Jn 5:1	2316
children of G, when we love G	1Jn 5:2	2316
For this is the love of G	1Jn 5:3	2316
is born of G overcometh the world	1Jn 5:4	2316
that Jesus is the Son of G	1Jn 5:5	2316
men, the witness of G is greater	1Jn 5:9	2316
for this is the witness of G	1Jn 5:9	2316
of G hath the witness in himself	1Jn 5:10	2316
not G hath made him a liar	1Jn 5:10	2316
the record that G gave of his Son	1Jn 5:10	2316
that G hath given to us eternal	1Jn 5:11	2316
not the Son of G hath not life	1Jn 5:12	2316
on the name of the Son of G	1Jn 5:13	2316
on the name of the Son of G	1Jn 5:13	2316
is born of G sinneth not	1Jn 5:18	2316
is begotten of G keepeth himself	1Jn 5:18	2316
And we know that we are of G	1Jn 5:19	2316
we know that the Son of G is come	1Jn 5:20	2316
This is the true G, and eternal	1Jn 5:20	2316
from G the Father, and from the	2Jn 3	2316
doctrine of Christ, hath not G	2Jn 9	2316
house, neither bid him G speed	2Jn 10	2316
For he that biddeth him G speed	2Jn 11	2316
He that doeth good is of G	3Jn 11	
that doeth evil hath not seen G	3Jn 11	2316
are sanctified by G the Father	Jude 1	2316
of our G into lasciviousness	Jude 4	2316
and denying the only Lord G	Jude 4	2316
Keep yourselves in the love of G	Jude 21	2316
To the only wise G our Saviour	Jude 25	2316
which G gave unto him, to shew	Rev 1:1	2316
Who bare record of the word of G	Rev 1:2	2316
made us kings and priests unto G	Rev 1:6	2316
called Patmos, for the word of G	Rev 1:9	2316
in the midst of the paradise of G	Rev 2:7	2316
These things saith the Son of G	Rev 2:18	2316
that hath the seven Spirits of G	Rev 3:1	2316
found thy works perfect before G	Rev 3:2	2316
a pillar in the temple of my G	Rev 3:12	2316
write upon him the name of my G	Rev 3:12	2316
and the name of the city of my G	Rev 3:12	2316
down out of heaven from my G	Rev 3:12	2316
beginning of the creation of G	Rev 3:14	2316
which are the seven Spirits of G	Rev 4:5	2316
Lord G Almighty, which was, and is	Rev 4:8	2316
G sent forth into all the earth	Rev 5:6	2316
hast redeemed us to G by thy	Rev 5:9	2316
And hast made us unto our G kings	Rev 5:10	2316
that were slain for the word of G	Rev 6:9	2316
having the seal of the living G	Rev 7:2	2316
of our G in their foreheads	Rev 7:3	2316
Salvation to our G which sitteth	Rev 7:10	2316
on their faces, and worshipped G	Rev 7:11	2316
and might, be unto our G for ever	Rev 7:12	2316
are they before the throne of G	Rev 7:15	2316
G shall wipe away all tears from	Rev 7:17	2316
seven angels which stood before G	Rev 8:2	2316
ascended up before G out of the	Rev 8:4	2316
the seal of G in their foreheads	Rev 9:4	2316
golden altar which is before G	Rev 9:13	2316
the mystery of G should be	Rev 10:7	2316
Rise, and measure the temple of G	Rev 11:1	2316
before the G of the earth	Rev 11:4	2316
of life from G entered into them	Rev 11:11	2316
and gave glory to the G of heaven	Rev 11:13	2316

which sat before *G* on their seats	Rev 11:16	2316
upon their faces, and worshipped *G*	Rev 11:16	2316
O Lord *G* Almighty, which art, and	Rev 11:17	2316
the temple of *G* was opened in	Rev 11:19	2316
and her child was caught up unto *G*	Rev 12:5	2316
she hath a place prepared of *G*	Rev 12:6	2316
strength, and the kingdom of our *G*	Rev 12:10	2316
accused them before our *G* day	Rev 12:10	2316
which keep the commandments of *G*	Rev 12:17	2316
his mouth in blasphemy against *G*	Rev 13:6	2316
men, being the firstfruits unto *G*	Rev 14:4	2316
fault before the throne of *G*	Rev 14:5	2316
Saying with a loud voice, Fear *G*	Rev 14:7	2316
of the wine of the wrath of *G*	Rev 14:10	2316
that keep the commandments of *G*	Rev 14:12	2316
great winepress of the wrath of *G*	Rev 14:19	2316
them is filled up the wrath of *G*	Rev 15:1	2316
of glass, having the harps of *G*	Rev 15:2	2316
song of Moses the servant of *G*	Rev 15:3	2316
are thy works, Lord *G* Almighty	Rev 15:3	2316
vials full of the wrath of *G*	Rev 15:7	2316
with smoke from the glory of *G*	Rev 15:8	2316
of the wrath of *G* upon the earth	Rev 16:1	2316
Even so, Lord *G* Almighty, true and	Rev 16:7	2316
heat, and blasphemed the name of *G*	Rev 16:9	2316
blasphemed the *G* of heaven	Rev 16:11	2316
of that great day of *G* Almighty	Rev 16:14	2316
came in remembrance before *G*	Rev 16:19	2316
men blasphemed *G* because of the	Rev 16:21	2316
For *G* hath put in their hearts to	Rev 17:17	2316
the words of *G* shall be fulfilled	Rev 17:17	2316
G hath remembered her iniquities	Rev 18:5	2316
is the Lord *G* who judgeth her	Rev 18:8	2316
for *G* hath avenged you on her	Rev 18:20	2316
and power, unto the Lord our *G*	Rev 19:1	2316
worshipped *G* that sat on the	Rev 19:4	2316
the throne, saying, Praise our *G*	Rev 19:5	2316
for the Lord *G* omnipotent	Rev 19:6	2316
These are the true sayings of *G*	Rev 19:9	2316
worship *G*	Rev 19:10	2316
his name is called The Word of *G*	Rev 19:13	2316
fierceness and wrath of Almighty *G*	Rev 19:15	2316
unto the supper of the great *G*	Rev 19:17	2316
of Jesus, and for the word of *G*	Rev 20:4	2316
but they shall be priests of *G*	Rev 20:6	2316
came down from *G* out of heaven	Rev 20:9	2316
small and great, stand before *G*	Rev 20:12	2316
coming down from *G* out of heaven	Rev 21:2	2316
the tabernacle of *G* is with men	Rev 21:3	2316
G himself shall be with them	Rev 21:3	2316
and be their *G*	Rev 21:3	2316
G shall wipe away all tears from	Rev 21:4	2316
and I will be his *G*, and he shall	Rev 21:7	2316
descending out of heaven from *G*	Rev 21:10	2316
Having the glory of *G*	Rev 21:11	2316
for the Lord *G* Almighty and the	Rev 21:22	2316
for the glory of *G* did lighten it	Rev 21:23	2316
proceeding out of the throne of *G*	Rev 22:1	2316
but the throne of *G* and of the	Rev 22:3	2316
for the Lord *G* giveth them light	Rev 22:5	2316
the Lord *G* of the holy prophets	Rev 22:6	2316
worship *G*	Rev 22:9	2316
G shall add unto him the plagues	Rev 22:18	2316
G shall take away his part out of	Rev 22:19	2316

2. *Any deity other than God 1.*

I have made thee a *g* to Pharaoh	Ex 7:1	430
He that sacrificeth unto any *g*	Ex 22:20	430
For thou shalt worship no other *g*	Ex 34:14	410
there was no strange *g* with him	Deut 32:12	410
am he, and there is no *g* with me	Deut 32:39	430
if he be a *g*, let him plead for	Judg 6:31	430
and made Baal-berith their *g*	Judg 8:33	430
and went into the house of their *g*	Judg 9:27	430
hold of the house of the *g* Berith	Judg 9:46	410
thy *g* giveth thee to possess	Judg 11:24	430
sacrifice unto Dagon their *g*	Judg 16:23	430
Our *g* hath delivered Samson our	Judg 16:23	430
saw him, they praised their *g*	Judg 16:24	430
Our *g* hath delivered into our	Judg 16:24	430
sore upon us, and upon Dagon our *g*	1Sa 5:7	430
Chemosh the *g* of the Moabites, and	1Kin 11:33	430
Milcom the *g* of the children of	1Kin 11:33	430
for he is a *g*	1Kin 18:27	430
the *g* of Ekron whether I shall	2Kin 1:2	430
of Baal-zebub the *g* of Ekron	2Kin 1:3	430
of Baal-zebub the *g* of Ekron	2Kin 1:6	430
of Baal-zebub the *g* of Ekron	2Kin 1:16	430
in the house of Nisroch his *g*	2Kin 19:37	430
for no *g* of any nation or kingdom	2Chr 32:15	433
was come into the house of his *g*	2Chr 32:21	430
that hasten after another *g*	Ps 16:4	

out our hands to a strange *g*	Ps 44:20	410
shall no strange *g* be in thee	Ps 81:9	410
shalt thou worship any strange *g*	Ps 81:9	410
there was no strange *g* among you	Is 43:12	
Who hath formed a *g*, or molten a	Is 44:10	410
yea, he maketh a *g*, and	Is 44:15	410
the residue thereof he maketh a *g*	Is 44:17	410
for thou art my *g*	Is 44:17	410
pray unto a *g* that cannot save	Is 45:20	410
and he maketh it a *g*	Is 46:6	410
of Shinar to the house of his *g*	Dan 1:2	430
into the treasure house of his *g*	Dan 1:2	430
might not serve nor worship any *g*	Dan 3:28	426
according to the name of my *g*	Dan 4:8	426
and magnify himself above every *g*	Dan 11:36	410
desire of women, nor regard any *g*	Dan 11:37	433
a *g* whom his fathers knew not	Dan 11:38	433
strong holds with a strange *g*	Dan 11:39	433
and thou shalt know no *g* but me	Hos 13:4	430
condemned in the house of their *g*	Amos 2:8	430
your images, the star of your *g*	Amos 5:26	430
the sin of Samaria, and say, Thy *g*	Amos 8:14	430
and cried every man unto his *g*	Jonah 1:5	430
every one in the name of his *g*	Mic 4:5	430
this his power unto his *g*	Hab 1:11	430
the daughter of a strange *g*	Mal 2:11	410
and the star of your *g* Remphan	Acts 7:43	2316
saying, It is the voice of a *g*	Acts 12:22	2316
minds, and said that he was a *g*	Acts 28:6	2316
In whom the *g* of this world hath	2Cor 4:4	2316

GODDESS

Ashtoreth the *g* of the Zidonians	1Kin 11:5	430
Ashtoreth the *g* of the Zidonians	1Kin 11:33	430
great *g* Diana should be despised	Acts 19:27	2299
a worshipper of the great *g* Diana	Acts 19:35	2299
nor yet blasphemers of your *g*	Acts 19:37	2299

GODHEAD *That which is divine.*

that the *G* is like unto gold	Acts 17:29	2304
made, even his eternal power and *G*	Rom 1:20	2305
all the fulness of the *G* bodily	Col 2:9	2320

GODLINESS

quiet and peaceable life in all *g*	1Ti 2:2	2150
professing *g*) with good works	1Ti 2:10	2317
great is the mystery of *g*	1Ti 3:16	2150
and exercise thyself rather unto *g*	1Ti 4:7	2150
but *g* is profitable unto all	1Ti 4:8	2150
doctrine which is according to *g*	1Ti 6:3	2150
truth, supposing that gain is *g*	1Ti 6:5	2150
But *g* with contentment is great	1Ti 6:6	2150
and follow after righteousness, *g*	1Ti 6:11	2150
Having a form of *g*, but denying	2Ti 3:5	2150
of the truth which is after *g*	Titus 1:1	2150
that pertain unto life and *g*	2Pet 1:3	2150
and to patience *g*	2Pet 1:6	2150
And to *g* brotherly kindness	2Pet 1:7	2150
be in all holy conversation and *g*	2Pet 3:11	2150

GODLY

apart him that is *g* for himself	Ps 4:3	2623
for the *g* man ceaseth	Ps 12:1	2623
this shall every one that is *g*	Ps 32:6	2623
That he might seek a *g* seed	Mal 2:15	430
g sincerity, not with fleshly	2Cor 1:12	2316
were made sorry after a *g* manner	2Cor 7:9	2596,2316
For *g* sorrow worketh repentance	2Cor 7:10	2596,2316
that ye sorrowed after a *g* sort	2Cor 7:11	2596,2316
jealous over you with *g* jealousy	2Cor 11:2	2316
rather than *g* edifying which is	1Ti 1:4	2316
all that will live *g* in Christ	2Ti 3:12	2153
live soberly, righteously, and *g*	Titus 2:12	2153
with reverence and *g* fear	Heb 12:28	
deliver the *g* out of temptations	2Pet 2:9	2152
on their journey after a *g* sort	3Jn 6	516,2316

GOD'S *Refers to God 1.*

for a pillar, shall be *G* house	Gen 28:22	430
and he said, Am I in *G* stead	Gen 30:2	430
saw them, he said, This is *G* host	Gen 32:2	430
G anger was kindled because he	Num 22:22	430
for the judgment is *G*	Deut 1:17	430
the battle is not yours, but *G*	2Chr 20:15	430
and into an oath, to walk in *G* law	Neh 10:29	430
according to thy wish in *G* stead	Job 33:6	410
My righteousness is more than *G*	Job 35:2	410
I have yet to speak on *G* behalf	Job 36:2	433
for it is *G* throne	Mt 5:34	2316
and unto God the things that are *G*	Mt 22:21	2316
and to God the things that are *G*	Mk 12:17	2316
for the kingdom of *G* sake	Lk 18:29	2316
and unto God the things which be *G*	Lk 20:25	2316

He that is of God heareth *G* words	Jn 8:47	2316
said, Revilest thou *G* high priest	Acts 23:4	2316
thing to the charge of *G* elect	Rom 8:33	2316
being ignorant of *G* righteousness	Rom 10:3	2316
for they are *G* ministers,	Rom 13:6	2316
ye are *G* husbandry, ye are *G*	1Cor 3:9	2316
and Christ is *G*	1Cor 3:23	2316
and in your spirit, which are *G*	1Cor 6:20	2316
according to the faith of *G* elect	Titus 1:1	2316
as being lords over *G* heritage	1Pet 5:3	2316

GODS *Refers to God 2.*

be opened, and ye shall be as *g*	Gen 3:5	430
wherefore hast thou stolen my *g*	Gen 31:30	430
whomsoever thou findest thy *g*	Gen 31:32	430
the strange *g* that are among you	Gen 35:2	430
g which were in their hand	Gen 35:4	430
against all the *g* of Egypt I will	Ex 12:12	430
unto thee, O Lord, among the *g*	Ex 15:11	410
the Lord is greater than all *g*	Ex 18:11	430
shalt have no other *g* before me	Ex 20:3	430
not make with me *g* of silver	Ex 20:23	430
shall ye make unto you *g* of gold	Ex 20:23	430
Thou shalt not revile the *g*	Ex 22:28	430
no mention of the name of other *g*	Ex 23:13	430
shalt not bow down to their *g*	Ex 23:24	430
with them, nor with their *g*	Ex 23:32	430
for if thou serve their *g*	Ex 23:33	430
and said unto him, Up, make us *g*	Ex 32:1	430
and they said, These be thy *g*	Ex 32:4	430
and said, These be thy *g*, O	Ex 32:8	430
For they said unto me, Make us *g*	Ex 32:23	430
sin, and have made them *g* of gold	Ex 32:31	430
they go a whoring after their *g*	Ex 34:15	430
and do sacrifice unto their *g*	Ex 34:15	430
go a whoring after their *g*	Ex 34:16	430
sons go a whoring after their *g*	Ex 34:16	430
Thou shalt make thee no molten *g*	Ex 34:17	430
nor make to yourselves molten *g*	Lev 19:4	430
unto the sacrifices of their *g*	Num 25:2	430
did eat, and bowed down to their *g*	Num 25:2	430
upon their *g* also the Lord	Num 33:4	430
And there ye shall serve *g*	Deut 4:28	430
shalt have none other *g* before me	Deut 5:7	430
Ye shall not go after other *g*	Deut 6:14	430
of the *g* of the people which are	Deut 6:14	430
me, that they may serve other *g*	Deut 7:4	430
neither shalt thou serve their *g*	Deut 7:16	430
their *g* shall ye burn with fire	Deut 7:25	430
thy God, and walk after other *g*	Deut 8:19	430
For the Lord your God is God of *g*	Deut 10:17	430
ye turn aside, and serve other *g*	Deut 11:16	430
you this day, to go after other *g*	Deut 11:28	430
ye shall possess served their *g*	Deut 12:2	430
down the graven images of their *g*	Deut 12:3	430
thou enquire not after their *g*	Deut 12:30	430
did these nations serve their *g*	Deut 12:30	430
have they done unto their *g*	Deut 12:31	430
have burnt in the fire to their *g*	Deut 12:31	430
saying, Let us go after other *g*	Deut 13:2	430
Let us go and serve other *g*	Deut 13:6	430
of the *g* of the people which are	Deut 13:7	430
Let us go and serve other *g*	Deut 13:13	430
And hath gone and served other *g*	Deut 17:3	430
speak in the name of other *g*	Deut 18:20	430
which they have done unto their *g*	Deut 20:18	430
to go after other *g* to serve them	Deut 28:14	430
and there shalt thou serve other *g*	Deut 28:36	430
and there thou shalt serve other *g*	Deut 28:64	430
serve the *g* of these nations	Deut 29:18	430
For they went and served other *g*	Deut 29:26	430
g whom they knew not, and whom he	Deut 29:26	430
be drawn away, and worship other *g*	Deut 30:17	430
go a whoring after the *g* of the	Deut 31:16	430
that they are turned unto other *g*	Deut 31:18	430
then will they turn unto other *g*	Deut 31:20	430
him to jealousy with strange *g*	Deut 32:16	430
to *g* whom they knew not	Deut 32:17	430
to new *g* that came newly up, whom	Deut 32:17	430
he shall say, Where are their *g*	Deut 32:37	430
God of *g*, the Lord God of *g*	Josh 22:22	430
mention of the names of their *g*	Josh 23:7	430
and have gone and served other *g*	Josh 23:16	430
and they served other *g*	Josh 24:2	430
put away the *g* which your fathers	Josh 24:14	430
whether the *g* which your fathers	Josh 24:15	430
or the *g* of the Amorites, in	Josh 24:15	430
the Lord, to serve other *g*	Josh 24:20	430
the Lord, and serve strange *g*	Josh 24:23	430
the strange *g* which are among you	Josh 24:23	430
their *g* shall be a snare unto you	Judg 2:3	430

of Egypt, and followed other *g*	Judg 2:12	430
of the *g* of the people that were	Judg 2:12	430
they went a whoring after other *g*	Judg 2:17	430
following other *g* to serve them	Judg 2:19	430
to their sons, and served their *g*	Judg 3:6	430
They chose new *g*	Judg 5:8	430
fear not the *g* of the Amorites,	Judg 6:10	430
the *g* of Syria	Judg 10:6	430
the *g* of Zidon	Judg 10:6	430
the *g* of Moab	Judg 10:6	430
the *g* of the children of Ammon	Judg 10:6	430
the *g* of the Philistines, and	Judg 10:6	430
forsaken me, and served other *g*	Judg 10:13	430
cry unto the *g* which ye have	Judg 10:14	430
the strange *g* from among them	Judg 10:16	430
the man Micah had an house of *g*	Judg 17:5	430
have taken away my *g* which I made	Judg 18:24	430
unto her people, and unto her *g*	Ruth 1:15	430
out of the hand of these mighty *G*	1Sa 4:8	430
these are the *G* that smote the	1Sa 4:8	430
from off you, and from off your *g*	1Sa 6:5	430
then put away the strange *g*	1Sa 7:3	430
forsaken him, and served other *g*	1Sa 8:8	430
Philistine cursed David by his *g*	1Sa 17:43	430
Lord, saying, Go, serve other *g*	1Sa 26:19	430
I saw *g* ascending out of the	1Sa 28:13	430
from the nations and their *g*	2Sa 7:23	430
you, but go and serve other *g*	1Kin 9:6	430
and have taken hold upon other *g*	1Kin 9:9	430
away your heart after their *g*	1Kin 11:2	430
away his heart after other *g*	1Kin 11:4	430
and sacrificed unto their *g*	1Kin 11:8	430
he should not go after other *g*	1Kin 11:10	430
behold thy *g*, O Israel, which	1Kin 12:28	430
hast gone and made thee other *g*	1Kin 14:9	430
And call ye on the name of your *g*	1Kin 18:24	430
and call on the name of your *g*	1Kin 18:25	430
saying, So let the *g* do to me	1Kin 19:2	430
The *g* do so unto me, and more also	1Kin 20:10	430
Their *g* are *g* of the hills	1Kin 20:23	430
Their *g* are *g* of the hills	1Kin 20:23	430
nor sacrifice unto other *g*	2Kin 5:17	430
of Egypt, and had feared other *g*	2Kin 17:7	430
every nation made *g* of their own	2Kin 17:29	430
Anammelech, the *g* of Sepharvaim	2Kin 17:31	430
the Lord, and served their own *g*	2Kin 17:33	430
saying, Ye shall not fear other *g*	2Kin 17:35	430
and ye shall not fear other *g*	2Kin 17:37	430
neither shall ye fear other *g*	2Kin 17:38	430
Hath any of the *g* of the nations	2Kin 18:33	430
Where are the *g* of Hamath	2Kin 18:34	430
where are the *g* of Sepharvaim	2Kin 18:34	430
among all the *g* of the countries	2Kin 18:35	430
Have the *g* of the nations	2Kin 19:12	430
have cast their *g* into the fire	2Kin 19:18	430
for they were no *g*, but the work	2Kin 19:18	430
have burned incense unto other *g*	2Kin 22:17	430
went a whoring after the *g* of the	1Chr 5:25	430
armour in the house of their *g*	1Chr 10:10	430
when they had left their *g* there	1Chr 14:12	430
also is to be feared above all *g*	1Chr 16:25	430
For all the *g* of the people are	1Chr 16:26	430
for great is our God above all *g*	2Chr 2:5	430
you, and shall go and serve other *g*	2Chr 7:19	430
of Egypt, and laid hold on other *g*	2Chr 7:22	430
which Jeroboam made you for *g*	2Chr 13:8	430
be a priest of them that are no *g*	2Chr 13:9	430
away the altars of the strange *g*	2Chr 14:3	430
that he brought the *g* of the	2Chr 25:14	430
Seir, and set them up to be his *g*	2Chr 25:14	430
sought after the *g* of the people	2Chr 25:15	430
they sought after the *g* of Edom	2Chr 25:20	430
sacrificed unto the *g* of Damascus	2Chr 28:23	430
Because the *g* of the kings of	2Chr 28:23	430
to burn incense unto other *g*	2Chr 28:25	430
were the *g* of the nations of	2Chr 32:13	430
the *g* of those nations that my	2Chr 32:14	430
As the *g* of the nations of other	2Chr 32:17	430
as against the *g* of the people of	2Chr 32:19	430
And he took away the strange *g*	2Chr 33:15	430
have burned incense unto other *g*	2Chr 34:25	430
put them in the house of his *g*	Ezr 1:7	430
he judgeth among the *g*	Ps 82:1	430
I have said, Ye are *g*	Ps 82:6	430
Among the *g* there is none like	Ps 86:8	430
God, and a great King above all *g*	Ps 95:3	430
he is to be feared above all *g*	Ps 96:4	430
For all the *g* of the nations are	Ps 96:5	430
worship him, all ye *g*	Ps 97:7	430
thou art exalted far above all *g*	Ps 97:9	430
and that our Lord is above all *g*	Ps 135:5	430

O give thanks unto the God of *g*	Ps 136:2	430
before the *g* will I sing praise	Ps 138:1	430
all the graven images of her *g* he	Is 21:9	430
Hath any of the *g* of the nations	Is 36:18	430
Where are the *g* of Hamath	Is 36:19	430
where are the *g* of Sepharvaim	Is 36:19	430
among all the *g* of these lands	Is 36:20	430
Have the *g* of the nations	Is 37:12	430
have cast their *g* into the fire	Is 37:19	430
for they were no *g*, but the work	Is 37:19	430
that we may know that ye are *g*	Is 41:23	430
the molten images, Ye are our *g*	Is 42:17	430
have burned incense unto other *g*	Jer 1:16	430
their *g*, which are yet no *g*	Jer 2:11	430
But where are thy *g* that thou	Jer 2:28	430
number of thy cities are thy *g*	Jer 2:28	430
and sworn by them that are no *g*	Jer 5:7	430
and served strange *g* in your land	Jer 5:19	430
walk after other *g* to your hurt	Jer 7:6	430
after other *g* whom ye know not	Jer 7:9	430
out drink offerings unto other *g*	Jer 7:18	430
The *g* that have not made the	Jer 10:11	426
went after other *g* to serve them	Jer 11:10	430
cry unto the *g* unto whom they	Jer 11:12	430
number of thy cities were thy *g*	Jer 11:13	430
heart, and walk after other *g*	Jer 13:10	430
and have walked after other *g*	Jer 16:11	430
there shall ye serve other *g* day	Jer 16:13	430
Shall a man make *g* unto himself	Jer 16:20	430
and they are no *g*	Jer 16:20	430
burned incense in it unto other *g*	Jer 19:4	430
out drink offerings unto other *g*	Jer 19:13	430
their God, and worshipped other *g*	Jer 22:9	430
not after other *g* to serve them	Jer 25:6	430
out drink offerings unto other *g*	Jer 32:29	430
not after other *g* to serve them	Jer 35:15	430
in the houses of the *g* of Egypt	Jer 43:12	430
the houses of the *g* of the	Jer 43:13	430
burn incense, and to serve other *g*	Jer 44:3	430
to burn no incense unto other *g*	Jer 44:5	430
unto other *g* in the land of Egypt	Jer 44:8	430
had burned incense unto other *g*	Jer 44:15	430
Pharaoh, and Egypt, with their *g*	Jer 46:25	430
him that burneth incense to his *g*	Jer 48:35	430
it before the king, except the *g*	Dan 2:11	426
is, that your God is a God of *g*	Dan 2:47	426
they serve not thy *g*, nor worship	Dan 3:12	426
Abed-nego, do not ye serve my *g*	Dan 3:14	426
that we will not serve thy *g*	Dan 3:18	426
whom is the spirit of the holy *g*	Dan 4:8	426
spirit of the holy *g* is in thee	Dan 4:9	426
spirit of the holy *g* is in thee	Dan 4:18	426
wine, and praised the *g* of gold	Dan 5:4	426
whom is the spirit of the holy *g*	Dan 5:11	426
wisdom, like the wisdom of the *g*	Dan 5:11	426
the spirit of the *g* is in thee	Dan 5:14	426
thou hast praised the *g* of silver	Dan 5:23	426
carry captives into Egypt their *g*	Dan 11:8	430
things against the God of *g*	Dan 11:36	410
of Israel, who look to other *g*	Hos 3:1	430
work of our hands, Ye are our *g*	Hos 14:3	430
out of the house of thy *g* will I	Nah 1:14	430
famish all the *g* of the earth	Zeph 2:11	430
in your law, I said, Ye are *g*	Jn 10:34	2316
If he called them *g*, unto whom	Jn 10:35	2316
Make us *g* to go before us	Acts 7:40	2316
The *g* are come down to us in the	Acts 14:11	2316
to be a setter forth of strange *g*	Acts 17:18	1140
people, saying that they be no *g*	Acts 19:26	2316
though there be that are called *g*	1Cor 8:5	2316
or in earth, (as there be many	1Cor 8:5	2316
them which by nature are no *g*	Gal 4:8	2316

GOD-WARD

Be thou for the people to *G*	Ex 18:19	4136,430
trust have we through Christ to *G*	2Cor 3:4	4314,2316
your faith to *G* is spread abroad	1Th 1:8	4314,2316

GOEST See APPENDIX.

GOETH See APPENDIX.

GOG See HAMON-GOG, MAGOG.
  1. Son of Shemariah.

G his son, Shimei his son,	1Chr 5:4	1463

  2. A prince of Scythia.

of man, set thy face against *G*	Eze 38:2	1463
Behold, I am against thee, O *G*	Eze 38:3	1463
of man, prophesy and say unto *G*	Eze 38:14	1463
shall be sanctified in thee, O *G*	Eze 38:16	1463
to pass at the same time when *G*	Eze 38:18	1463
son of man, prophesy against *G*	Eze 39:1	1463
Behold, I am against thee, O *G*	Eze 39:1	1463

that I will give unto *G* a place	Eze 39:11	1463
and there shall they bury *G*	Eze 39:11	1463
the four quarters of the earth, *G*	Rev 20:8	*1136*

GOIIM See NATIONS

GOING See APPENDIX.

GOINGS See APPENDIX.

GOLAN *(go'-lan) A Levitical city in Manasseh.*

G in Bashan, of the Manassites	Deut 4:43	1474
G in Bashan out of the tribe of	Josh 20:8	1474
gave *G* in Bashan with her suburbs	Josh 21:27	1474
G in Bashan with her suburbs, and	1Chr 6:71	1474

GOLD

land of Havilah, where there is *g*	Gen 2:11	2091
the *g* of that land is good	Gen 2:12	2091
in cattle, in silver, and in *g*	Gen 13:2	2091
hands of ten shekels weight of *g*	Gen 24:22	2091
flocks, and herds, and silver, and *g*	Gen 24:35	2091
jewels of silver, and jewels of *g*	Gen 24:53	2091
put a *g* chain about his neck	Gen 41:42	2091
of thy lord's house silver or *g*	Gen 44:8	2091
jewels of silver, and jewels of *g*	Ex 3:22	2091
jewels of silver, and jewels of *g*	Ex 11:2	2091
jewels of silver, and jewels of *g*	Ex 12:35	2091
shall ye make unto you gods of *g*	Ex 20:23	2091
g, and silver, and brass	Ex 25:3	2091
thou shalt overlay it with pure *g*	Ex 25:11	2091
upon it a crown of *g* round about	Ex 25:11	2091
shalt cast four rings of *g* for it	Ex 25:12	2091
wood, and overlay them with *g*	Ex 25:13	2091
shalt make a mercy seat of pure *g*	Ex 25:17	2091
shalt make two cherubims of *g*	Ex 25:18	2091
thou shalt overlay it with pure *g*	Ex 25:24	2091
thereto a crown of *g* round about	Ex 25:24	2091
shalt make for it four rings of *g*	Ex 25:26	2091
wood, and overlay them with *g*	Ex 25:28	2091
of pure *g* shalt thou make them	Ex 25:29	2091
make a candlestick of pure *g*	Ex 25:31	2091
be one beaten work of pure *g*	Ex 25:36	2091
thereof, shall be of pure *g*	Ex 25:38	2091
talent of pure *g* shall he make it	Ex 25:39	2091
thou shalt make fifty taches of *g*	Ex 26:6	2091
shalt overlay the boards with *g*	Ex 26:29	2091
make their rings of *g* for places	Ex 26:29	2091
shalt overlay the bars with *g*	Ex 26:29	2091
of shittim wood overlaid with *g*	Ex 26:32	2091
their hooks shall be of *g*	Ex 26:32	2091
wood, and overlay them with *g*	Ex 26:37	2091
and their hooks shall be of *g*	Ex 26:37	2091
And they shall take *g*, and blue, and	Ex 28:5	2091
And they shall make the ephod of *g*	Ex 28:6	2091
even of *g*, of blue, and purple, and	Ex 28:8	2091
them to be set in ouches of *g*	Ex 28:11	2091
And thou shalt make ouches of *g*	Ex 28:13	2091
two chains of pure *g* at the ends	Ex 28:14	2091
of *g*, of blue, and of purple, and	Ex 28:15	2091
be set in *g* in their inclosings	Ex 28:20	2091
ends of wreathen work of pure *g*	Ex 28:22	2091
the breastplate two rings of *g*	Ex 28:23	2091
g in the two rings which are on	Ex 28:24	2091
And thou shalt make two rings of *g*	Ex 28:26	2091
other rings of *g* thou shalt make	Ex 28:27	2091
bells of *g* between them round	Ex 28:33	2091
thou shalt make a plate of pure *g*	Ex 28:36	2091
thou shalt overlay it with pure *g*	Ex 30:3	2091
unto it a crown of *g* round about	Ex 30:3	2091
wood, and overlay them with *g*	Ex 30:5	2091
cunning works, to work in *g*	Ex 31:4	2091
unto them, Whosoever hath any *g*	Ex 32:24	2091
sin, and have made them gods of *g*	Ex 32:31	2091
g, and silver, and brass,	Ex 35:5	2091
and tablets, all jewels of *g*	Ex 35:22	2091
an offering of *g* unto the LORD	Ex 35:22	2091
curious works, to work in *g*	Ex 35:32	2091
And he made fifty taches of *g*	Ex 36:13	2091
And he overlaid the boards with *g*	Ex 36:34	2091
made their rings of *g* to be	Ex 36:34	2091
bars, and overlaid the bars with *g*	Ex 36:34	2091
wood, and overlaid them with *g*	Ex 36:36	2091
their hooks were of *g*	Ex 36:36	2091
chapiters and their fillets with *g*	Ex 36:38	2091
he overlaid it with pure *g* within	Ex 37:2	2091
made a crown of *g* to it round	Ex 37:2	2091
And he cast for it four rings of *g*	Ex 37:3	2091
wood, and overlaid them with *g*	Ex 37:4	2091
he made the mercy seat of pure *g*	Ex 37:6	2091
And he made two cherubims of *g*	Ex 37:7	2091
And he overlaid it with pure *g*	Ex 37:11	2091
a crown of *g* round about	Ex 37:11	2091

G

made a crown of *g* for the border	Ex 37:12	2091
And he cast for it four rings of *g*	Ex 37:13	2091
wood, and overlaid them with *g*	Ex 37:15	2091
covers to cover withal, of pure *g*	Ex 37:16	2091
he made the candlestick of pure *g*	Ex 37:17	2091
it was one beaten work of pure *g*	Ex 37:22	2091
and his snuffdishes, of pure *g*	Ex 37:23	2091
Of a talent of pure *g* made he it	Ex 37:24	2091
And he overlaid it with pure *g*	Ex 37:26	2091
unto it a crown of *g* round about	Ex 37:26	2091
he made two rings of *g* for it	Ex 37:27	2091
wood, and overlaid them with *g*	Ex 37:28	2091
All the *g* that was occupied for	Ex 38:24	2091
even the *g* of the offering, was	Ex 38:24	2091
And he made the ephod of *g*	Ex 39:2	2091
did beat the *g* into thin plates	Ex 39:3	2091
of *g*, blue, and purple, and scarlet	Ex 39:5	2091
stones inclosed in ouches of *g*	Ex 39:6	2091
of *g*, blue, and purple, and scarlet	Ex 39:8	2091
ouches of *g* in their inclosings	Ex 39:13	2091
ends, of wreathen work of pure *g*	Ex 39:15	2091
And they made two ouches of *g*	Ex 39:16	2091
ouches of *g*, and two *g* rings	Ex 39:16	2091
put the two wreathen chains of *g*	Ex 39:17	2091
And they made two rings of *g*	Ex 39:19	2091
And they made bells of pure *g*	Ex 39:25	2091
plate of the holy crown of pure *g*	Ex 39:30	2091
thou shalt set the altar of *g* for	Ex 40:5	2091
One spoon of ten shekels of *g*	Num 7:14	2091
One spoon of *g* of ten shekels,	Num 7:20	2091
silver bowls, twelve spoons of *g*	Num 7:84	2091
all the *g* of the spoons was an	Num 7:86	2091
the candlestick was of beaten *g*	Num 8:4	2091
me his house full of silver and *g*	Num 22:18	2091
me his house full of silver and *g*	Num 24:13	2091
Only the *g*, and the silver, the	Num 31:22	2091
man hath gotten, of jewels of *g*	Num 31:50	2091
the priest took the *g* of them	Num 31:51	2091
all the *g* of the offering that	Num 31:52	2091
Eleazar the priest took the *g* of	Num 31:54	2091
the silver or *g* that is on them	Deut 7:25	2091
thy *g* is multiplied, and all that	Deut 8:13	2091
multiply to himself silver and *g*	Deut 17:17	2091
idols, wood and stone, silver and *g*	Deut 29:17	2091
But all the silver, and *g*, and	Josh 6:19	2091
only the silver, and the *g*	Josh 6:24	2091
a wedge of *g* of fifty shekels	Josh 7:21	2091
and the garment, and the wedge of *g*	Josh 7:24	2091
cattle, with silver, and with *g*	Josh 22:8	2091
and seven hundred shekels of *g*	Judg 8:26	2091
and put the jewels of *g*, which ye	1Sa 6:8	2091
and the coffer with the mice of *g*	1Sa 6:11	2091
it, wherein the jewels of *g* were	1Sa 6:15	2091
ornaments of *g* upon your apparel	2Sa 1:24	2091
David took the shields of *g* that	2Sa 8:7	2091
of silver, and vessels of *g*	2Sa 8:10	2091
g that he had dedicated of all	2Sa 8:11	2091
of *g* with the precious stones	2Sa 12:30	2091
will have no silver nor *g* of Saul	2Sa 21:4	2091
and he overlaid it with pure *g*	1Kin 6:20	2091
the house within with pure *g*	1Kin 6:21	2091
the chains of *g* before the oracle	1Kin 6:21	2091
and he overlaid it with *g*	1Kin 6:21	2091
whole house he overlaid with *g*	1Kin 6:22	2091
by the oracle he overlaid with *g*	1Kin 6:22	2091
he overlaid the cherubims with *g*	1Kin 6:28	2091
of the house he overlaid with *g*	1Kin 6:30	2091
flowers, and overlaid them with *g*	1Kin 6:32	2091
spread *g* upon the cherubims, and	1Kin 6:32	2091
covered them with *g* fitted upon	1Kin 6:35	2091
altar of *g*, and the table of *g*	1Kin 7:48	2091
And the candlesticks of pure *g*	1Kin 7:49	2091
and the lamps, and the tongs of *g*	1Kin 7:49	2091
spoons, and the censers of pure *g*	1Kin 7:50	2091
and the hinges of *g*, both for the	1Kin 7:50	2091
even the house, and the *g*	1Kin 7:51	2091
trees and fir trees, and with *g*	1Kin 9:11	2091
to the king sixscore talents of *g*	1Kin 9:14	2091
Ophir, and fetched from thence *g*	1Kin 9:28	2091
that bare spices, and very much *g*	1Kin 10:2	2091
an hundred and twenty talents of *g*	1Kin 10:10	2091
Hiram, that brought *g* from Ophir	1Kin 10:11	2091
Now the weight of *g* that came to	1Kin 10:14	2091
threescore and six talents of *g*	1Kin 10:14	2091
two hundred targets of beaten *g*	1Kin 10:16	2091
shekels of *g* went to one target	1Kin 10:16	2091
three hundred shields of beaten *g*	1Kin 10:17	2091
three pound of *g* went to one	1Kin 10:17	2091
and overlaid it with the best *g*	1Kin 10:18	2091
drinking vessels were of *g*	1Kin 10:21	2091
forest of Lebanon were of pure *g*	1Kin 10:21	2091
the navy of Tharshish, bringing *g*	1Kin 10:22	2091
of silver, and vessels of *g*	1Kin 10:25	2091
counsel, and made two calves of *g*	1Kin 12:28	2091
of *g* which Solomon had made	1Kin 14:26	2091
house of the LORD, silver, and *g*	1Kin 15:15	2091
the *g* that were left in the	1Kin 15:18	2091
thee a present of silver and *g*	1Kin 15:19	2091
Thy silver and thy *g* is mine	1Kin 20:3	2091
deliver me thy silver, and thy *g*	1Kin 20:5	2091
and for my silver, and for my *g*	1Kin 20:7	2091
of Tharshish to go to Ophir for *g*	1Kin 22:48	2091
and six thousand pieces of *g*	2Kin 5:5	2091
and carried thence silver, and *g*	2Kin 7:8	2091
trumpets, any vessels of *g*	2Kin 12:13	2091
all the *g* that was found in the	2Kin 12:18	2091
And he took all the *g* and silver,	2Kin 14:14	2091
g that was found in the house of	2Kin 16:8	2091
of silver and thirty talents of *g*	2Kin 18:14	2091
time did Hezekiah cut off the *g*	2Kin 18:16	
things, the silver, and the *g*	2Kin 20:13	2091
of silver, and a talent of *g*	2Kin 23:33	2091
the silver and the *g* to Pharaoh	2Kin 23:35	2091
the *g* of the people of the land,	2Kin 23:35	2091
of *g* which Solomon king of Israel	2Kin 24:13	2091
such things as were of *g*, in *g*	2Kin 25:15	2091
David took the shields of *g* that	1Chr 18:7	2091
him all manner of vessels of *g*	1Chr 18:10	2091
the *g* that he brought from all	1Chr 18:11	2091
found it to weigh a talent of *g*	1Chr 20:2	2091
hundred shekels of *g* by weight	1Chr 21:25	2091
an hundred thousand talents of *g*	1Chr 22:14	2091
Of the *g*, the silver, and the	1Chr 22:16	2091
of *g* by weight for things of *g*	1Chr 28:14	2091
weight for the candlesticks of *g*	1Chr 28:15	2091
and for their lamps of *g*	1Chr 28:15	2091
by weight he gave *g* for the	1Chr 28:16	2091
Also pure *g* for the fleshhooks,	1Chr 28:17	2091
gave *g* by weight for every bason	1Chr 28:17	
of incense refined by weight	1Chr 28:18	2091
g for the pattern of the chariot	1Chr 28:18	2091
g for things to be made of *g*	1Chr 29:2	2091
of mine own proper good, of *g*	1Chr 29:3	2091
Even three thousand talents of *g*	1Chr 29:4	2091
of the *g* of Ophir, and seven	1Chr 29:4	2091
The *g* for things of *g*, and the	1Chr 29:5	2091
of God of *g* five thousand talents	1Chr 29:7	2091
g at Jerusalem as plenteous as	2Chr 1:15	2091
a man cunning to work in *g*	2Chr 2:7	2091
man of Tyre, skilful to work in *g*	2Chr 2:14	2091
he overlaid it within with pure *g*	2Chr 3:4	2091
which he overlaid with fine *g*	2Chr 3:5	2091
and the *g* was *g* of Parvaim	2Chr 3:6	2091
and the doors thereof, with *g*	2Chr 3:7	2091
and he overlaid it with fine *g*	2Chr 3:8	2091
the nails was fifty shekels of *g*	2Chr 3:9	2091
the upper chambers with *g*	2Chr 3:9	2091
work, and overlaid them with *g*	2Chr 3:10	2091
of *g* according to their form	2Chr 4:7	2091
And he made an hundred basons of *g*	2Chr 4:8	2091
before the oracle, of pure *g*	2Chr 4:20	2091
he of *g*, and that perfect *g*	2Chr 4:21	2091
spoons, and the censers, of pure *g*	2Chr 4:22	2091
house of the temple, were of *g*	2Chr 4:22	2091
and the silver, and the *g*, and all	2Chr 5:1	2091
hundred and fifty talents of *g*	2Chr 8:18	2091
g in abundance, and precious	2Chr 9:1	2091
an hundred and twenty talents of *g*	2Chr 9:9	2091
which brought *g* from Ophir	2Chr 9:10	2091
Now the weight of *g* that came to	2Chr 9:13	2091
and threescore and six talents of *g*	2Chr 9:13	2091
of the country brought *g* and	2Chr 9:14	2091
two hundred targets of beaten *g*	2Chr 9:15	2091
of beaten *g* went to one target	2Chr 9:15	2091
shields made he of beaten *g*	2Chr 9:16	2091
shekels of *g* went to one shield	2Chr 9:16	2091
ivory, and overlaid it with pure *g*	2Chr 9:17	2091
the throne, with a footstool of *g*	2Chr 9:18	2091
vessels of king Solomon were of *g*	2Chr 9:20	2091
forest of Lebanon were of pure *g*	2Chr 9:20	2091
the ships of Tarshish bringing *g*	2Chr 9:21	2091
of silver, and vessels of *g*	2Chr 9:24	2091
of *g* which Solomon had made	2Chr 12:9	2091
the candlestick of *g* with the	2Chr 13:11	2091
had dedicated, silver, and *g*	2Chr 15:18	2091
g out of the treasures of the	2Chr 16:2	2091
I have sent thee silver and *g*	2Chr 16:3	2091
great gifts of silver, and of *g*	2Chr 21:3	2091
and spoons, and vessels of *g*	2Chr 24:14	2091
And he took all the *g* and the	2Chr 25:24	2091
treasuries for silver, and for *g*	2Chr 32:27	2091
of silver and a talent of *g*	2Chr 36:3	2091

help him with silver, and with *g*	Ezr 1:4	2091
with vessels of silver, with *g*	Ezr 1:6	2091
thirty chargers of *g*, a thousand	Ezr 1:9	2091
Thirty basons of *g*, silver basons	Ezr 1:10	2091
All the vessels of *g* and of silver	Ezr 1:11	2091
and one thousand drams of *g*	Ezr 2:69	2091
And the vessels also of *g* and	Ezr 5:14	1722
And to carry the silver and *g*	Ezr 7:15	1722
g that thou canst find in all the	Ezr 7:16	1722
the rest of the silver and the *g*	Ezr 7:18	1722
unto them the silver, and the *g*	Ezr 8:25	2091
and of *g* an hundred talents	Ezr 8:26	2091
Also twenty basons of *g*, of a	Ezr 8:27	2091
of fine copper, precious as *g*	Ezr 8:27	2091
the *g* are a freewill offering	Ezr 8:28	2091
weight of the silver, and the *g*	Ezr 8:30	2091
day was the silver and the *g*	Ezr 8:33	2091
treasure a thousand drams of *g*	Neh 7:70	2091
work twenty thousand drams of *g*	Neh 7:71	2091
was twenty thousand drams of *g*	Neh 7:72	2091
the beds were of *g* and silver,	Est 1:6	2091
gave them drink in vessels of *g*	Est 1:7	2091
white, and with a great crown of *g*	Est 8:15	2091
Or with princes that had *g*	Job 3:15	2091
Then shalt thou lay up *g* as dust	Job 22:24	1220
the *g* of Ophir as the stones of	Job 22:24	1220
tried me, I shall come forth as *g*	Job 23:10	2091
a place for *g* where they fine it	Job 28:1	2091
and it hath dust of *g*	Job 28:6	2091
It cannot be gotten for *g*	Job 28:15	5458
be valued with the *g* of Ophir	Job 28:16	3800
The *g* and the crystal cannot equal	Job 28:17	2091
shall not be for jewels of fine *g*	Job 28:17	6337
shall it be valued with pure *g*	Job 28:19	3800
If I have made *g* my hope	Job 31:24	2091
or have said to the fine *g*	Job 31:24	3800
no, not *g*, nor all the forces of	Job 36:19	1222
and every one an earring of *g*	Job 42:11	2091
to be desired are they than *g*	Ps 19:10	2091
yea, than much fine *g*	Ps 19:10	6337
a crown of pure *g* on his head	Ps 21:3	6337
did stand the queen in *g* of Ophir	Ps 45:9	3800
her clothing is of wrought *g*	Ps 45:13	2091
and her feathers with yellow *g*	Ps 68:13	2742
shall be given of the *g* of Sheba	Ps 72:15	2091
them forth also with silver and *g*	Ps 105:37	2091
Their idols are silver and *g*	Ps 115:4	2091
unto me than thousands of *g*	Ps 119:72	2091
I love thy commandments above *g*	Ps 119:127	2091
yea, above fine *g*	Ps 119:127	6337
of the heathen are silver and *g*	Ps 135:15	2091
and the gain thereof than fine *g*	Prov 3:14	2742
and knowledge rather than choice *g*	Prov 8:10	2742
My fruit is better than *g*	Prov 8:19	2742
yea, than fine *g*	Prov 8:19	6337
As a jewel of *g* in a swine's	Prov 11:22	2091
better is it to get wisdom than *g*	Prov 16:16	2742
for silver, and the furnace for *g*	Prov 17:3	2091
There is *g*, and a multitude of	Prov 20:15	2091
favour rather than silver and *g*	Prov 22:1	2091
apples of *g* in pictures of silver	Prov 25:11	2091
As an earring of *g*, and an	Prov 25:12	2091
of *g*, and an ornament of fine *g*	Prov 25:12	3800
for silver, and the furnace for *g*	Prov 27:21	2091
I gathered me also silver and *g*	Eccl 2:8	2091
jewels, thy neck with chains of *g*	Song 1:10	
borders of *g* with studs of silver	Song 1:11	2091
silver, the bottom thereof of *g*	Song 3:10	2091
His head is as the most fine *g*	Song 5:11	6337
His hands are as *g* rings set with	Song 5:14	2091
set upon sockets of fine *g*	Song 5:15	6337
land also is full of silver and *g*	Is 2:7	2091
of silver, and his idols of *g*	Is 2:20	2091
a man more precious than fine *g*	Is 13:12	6337
and as for *g*, they shall not	Is 13:17	2091
of thy molten images of *g*	Is 30:22	2091
of silver, and his idols of *g*	Is 31:7	2091
things, the silver, and the *g*	Is 39:2	2091
spreadeth it over with *g*, and	Is 40:19	2091
They lavish *g* out of the bag, and	Is 46:6	2091
they shall bring *g* and incense	Is 60:6	2091
their *g* with them, unto the name	Is 60:9	2091
For brass I will bring *g*, and for	Is 60:17	2091
deckest thee with ornaments of *g*	Jer 4:30	2091
deck it with silver and with *g*	Jer 10:4	2091
g from Uphaz, the work of the	Jer 10:9	2091
that which was of *g* in *g*	Jer 52:19	2091
How is the *g* become dim	Lam 4:1	2091
how is the most fine *g* changed	Lam 4:1	3800
of Zion, comparable to fine *g*	Lam 4:2	6337
and their *g* shall be removed	Eze 7:19	2091

their *g* shall not be able to	Eze 7:19	2091
Thus wast thou decked with *g*	Eze 16:13	2091
taken thy fair jewels of my *g*	Eze 16:17	2091
and with all precious stones, and *g*	Eze 27:22	2091
thee riches, and hast gotten *g*	Eze 28:4	2091
emerald, and the carbuncle, and *g*	Eze 28:13	2091
to carry away silver and *g*	Eze 38:13	2091
This image's head was of fine *g*	Dan 2:32	1722
the brass, the silver, and the *g*	Dan 2:35	1722
Thou art this head of *g*	Dan 2:38	1722
the clay, the silver, and the *g*	Dan 2:45	1722
the king made an image of *g*	Dan 3:1	1722
wine, and praised the gods of *g*	Dan 5:4	1722
have a chain of *g* about his neck	Dan 5:7	1722
have a chain of *g* about thy neck	Dan 5:16	1722
praised the gods of silver, and *g*	Dan 5:23	1722
put a chain of *g* about his neck	Dan 5:29	1722
were girded with fine *g* of Uphaz	Dan 10:5	3800
vessels of silver and of *g*	Dan 11:8	2091
knew not shall he honour with *g*	Dan 11:38	2091
power over the treasures of *g*	Dan 11:43	2091
and multiplied her silver and *g*	Hos 2:8	2091
their *g* have they made them idols	Hos 8:4	2091
ye have taken my silver and my *g*	Joel 3:5	2091
of silver, take the spoil of *g*	Nah 2:9	2091
Behold, it is laid over with *g*	Hab 2:19	2091
g shall be able to deliver them	Zeph 1:18	2091
the *g* is mine, saith the LORD of	Hag 2:8	2091
and behold a candlestick all of *g*	Zec 4:2	2091
Then take silver and *g*, and make	Zec 6:11	2091
fine *g* as the mire of the streets	Zec 9:3	2742
and will try them as *g* is tried	Zec 13:9	2091
shall be gathered together, *g*	Zec 14:14	2091
sons of Levi, and purge them as *g*	Mal 3:3	2091
g, and frankincense, and myrrh	Mt 2:11	5557
Provide neither *g*, nor silver,	Mt 10:9	5557
swear by the *g* of the temple	Mt 23:16	5557
for whether is greater, the *g*	Mt 23:17	5557
the temple that sanctifieth the *g*	Mt 23:17	5557
said, Silver and *g* have I none	Acts 3:6	5553
that the Godhead is like unto *g*	Acts 17:29	5557
coveted no man's silver, or *g*	Acts 20:33	5557
man build upon this foundation *g*	1Cor 3:12	5557
not with broided hair, or *g*	1Ti 2:9	5557
there are not only vessels of *g*	2Ti 2:20	5552
overlaid round about with *g*	Heb 9:4	5553
your assembly a man with a *g* ring	Jas 2:2	5554
Your *g* and silver is cankered	Jas 5:3	5557
precious than of *g* that perisheth	1Pet 1:7	5553
things, as silver and *g*, from your	1Pet 1:18	5553
the hair, and of wearing of *g*	1Pet 3:3	5553
to buy of me *g* tried in the fire	Rev 3:18	5553
had on their heads crowns of *g*	Rev 4:4	5552
were as it were crowns like *g*	Rev 9:7	5557
not worship devils, and idols of *g*	Rev 9:20	5552
scarlet colour, and decked with *g*	Rev 17:4	5557
The merchandise of *g*, and silver,	Rev 18:12	5557
and scarlet, and decked with *g*	Rev 18:16	5557
and the city was pure *g*, like unto	Rev 21:18	5553
the street of the city was pure *g*	Rev 21:21	5553

GOLDEN

that the man took a *g* earring of	Gen 24:22	2091
thou shalt make a *g* crown to the	Ex 25:25	2091
A *g* bell and a pomegranate	Ex 28:34	2091
a *g* bell and a pomegranate, upon	Ex 28:34	2091
two *g* rings shalt thou make to it	Ex 30:4	2091
them, Break off the *g* earrings	Ex 32:2	2091
g earrings which were in their	Ex 32:3	2091
And they made two other *g* rings	Ex 39:20	2091
the *g* altar, and the anointing oil	Ex 39:38	2091
he put the *g* altar in the tent of	Ex 40:26	2091
forefront, did he put the *g* plate	Lev 8:9	2091
upon the *g* altar they shall	Num 4:11	2091
One *g* spoon of ten shekels, full	Num 7:26	2091
One *g* spoon of ten shekels, full	Num 7:32	2091
One *g* spoon of ten shekels, full	Num 7:38	2091
One *g* spoon of ten shekels, full	Num 7:44	2091
One *g* spoon of ten shekels, full	Num 7:50	2091
One *g* spoon of ten shekels, full	Num 7:56	2091
One *g* spoon of ten shekels, full	Num 7:62	2091
One *g* spoon of ten shekels, full	Num 7:68	2091
One *g* spoon of ten shekels, full	Num 7:74	2091
One *g* spoon of ten shekels, full	Num 7:80	2091
The *g* spoons were twelve, full of	Num 7:86	2091
(For they had *g* earrings, because	Judg 8:24	2091
the weight of the *g* earrings that	Judg 8:26	2091
g emerods, and five *g* mice	1Sa 6:4	2091
these are the *g* emerods which the	1Sa 6:17	2091
the *g* mice, according to the	1Sa 6:18	2091
the *g* calves that were in Beth-el	2Kin 10:29	2091

G

for the *g* basons he gave gold by 1Chr 28:17	2091
the *g* altar also, and the tables 2Chr 4:19	2091
and there are with you *g* calves.............. 2Chr 13:8	2091
And also let the *g* and silver .... Ezr 6:5	1722
king shall hold out the *g* sceptre .... Est 4:11	2091
g sceptre that was in his hand................ Est 5:2	2091
out the *g* sceptre toward Esther .... Est 8:4	2091
or the *g* bowl be broken, or the.............. Eccl 12:6	2091
a man than the *g* wedge of Ophir.......... Is 13:12	3800
the *g* city ceased .... Is 14:4	4062
Babylon hath been a *g* cup in the .... Jer 51:7	2091
down and worship the *g* image that .... Dan 3:5	1722
worshipped the *g* image that .... Dan 3:7	1722
fall down and worship the *g* image .... Dan 3:10	1722
nor worship the *g* image which.............. Dan 3:12	1722
nor worship the *g* image which I .... Dan 3:14	1722
nor worship the *g* image which............... Dan 3:18	1722
wine, commanded to bring the *g* .... Dan 5:2	1722
Then they brought the *g* vessels .... Dan 5:3	1722
g pipes empty the *g* oil out.................... Zec 4:12	2091
Which had the *g* censer, and the .... Heb 9:4	5552
wherein was the *g* pot that had .... Heb 9:4	5552
I saw seven *g* candlesticks .... Rev 1:12	5552
about the paps with a *g* girdle................ Rev 1:13	5552
hand, and the seven *g* candlesticks .... Rev 1:20	5552
midst of the seven *g* candlesticks......... Rev 2:1	5552
g vials full of odours, which are............. Rev 5:8	5552
at the altar, having a *g* censer .... Rev 8:3	5552
the *g* altar which was before the............ Rev 8:3	5552
the *g* altar which is before God.............. Rev 9:13	5552
man, having on his head a *g* crown .... Rev 14:14	5552
breasts girded with *g* girdles .... Rev 15:6	5552
unto the seven angels seven *g* .... Rev 15:7	5552
having a *g* cup in her hand full............... Rev 17:4	5552
had a *g* reed to measure the city.......... Rev 21:15	5552

GOLDSMITH

the *g* spreadeth it over with gold .... Is 40:19	6884
So the carpenter encouraged the *g* .... Is 41:7	6884
in the balance, and hire a *g* .... Is 46:6	6884

GOLDSMITH'S

the *g* son unto the place of the.............. Neh 3:31	6885

GOLDSMITHS

the son of Harhaiah, of the *g* .... Neh 3:8	6884
the sheep gate repaired the *g* .... Neh 3:32	6884

GOLGOTHA (gol'-go-thah) See CALVARY. *Hill where Jesus was crucified.*

were come unto a place called *G* .... Mt 27:33	*1115*
they bring him unto the place *G* .... Mk 15:22	*1115*
which is called in the Hebrew *G* .... Jn 19:17	*1115*

GOLIATH (go-li'-ath) *Philistine warrior killed by David.*

camp of the Philistines, named *G* 1Sa 17:4	1555
G by name, out of the armies of 1Sa 17:23	1555
The sword of *G* the Philistine, ... 1Sa 21:9	1555
him the sword of *G* the Philistine 1Sa 22:10	1555
slew the brother of *G* the Gittite 2Sa 21:19	1555
the brother of *G* the Gittite........................ 1Chr 20:5	1555

GOMER (go'-mer)
1. Son of Japheth.

G, and Magog, and Madai, and Javan, .. Gen 10:2	1586
And the sons of *G*.................................... Gen 10:3	1586
G, and Magog, and Madai, and Javan, .. 1Chr 1:5	1586
And the sons of *G*.................................... 1Chr 1:6	1586

2. Descendants of Gomer 1.

G, and all his bands .... Eze 38:6	1586

3. Wife of Hosea.

took *G* the daughter of Diblaim .... Hos 1:3	1586

GOMORRAH (go-mor'-rah) See GOMORRHA. *City destroyed by God.*

as thou goest, unto Sodom, and *G* .... Gen 10:19	6017
the LORD destroyed Sodom and *G* .... Gen 13:10	6017
Sodom, and with Birsha king of *G*.......... Gen 14:2	6017
king of Sodom, and the king of *G* .... Gen 14:8	6017
of Sodom and *G* fled, and fell there .... Gen 14:10	6017
took all the goods of Sodom and *G* .... Gen 14:11	6017
G is great, and because their sin .... Gen 18:20	6017
upon *G* brimstone and fire from the....... Gen 19:24	6017
And he looked toward Sodom and *G* ...... Gen 19:28	6017
like the overthrow of Sodom, and *G* ...... Deut 29:23	6017
of Sodom, and of the fields of *G* .... Deut 32:32	6017
we should have been like unto *G* .... Is 1:9	6017
law of our God, ye people of *G*............... Is 1:10	6017
as when God overthrew Sodom and *G*.... Is 13:19	6017
and the inhabitants thereof as *G* .... Jer 23:14	6017
As in the overthrow of Sodom and *G* ..... Jer 49:18	6017
As God overthrew Sodom and *G* .... Jer 50:40	6017
you, as God overthrew Sodom and *G* ..... Amos 4:11	6017

and the children of Ammon as *G* .... Zeph 2:9	6017
G into ashes condemned them with 2Pet 2:6	*1116*

GOMORRHA (go-mor'-rah) See GOMORRAH. *Greek form of Gomorrah.*

G in the day of judgment, than .... Mt 10:15	*1116*
G in the day of judgment, than .... Mk 6:11	*1116*
Sodoma, and been made like unto *G* ..... Rom 9:29	*1116*
Even as Sodom and *G*, and the cities ..... Jude 7	*1116*

GONE See APPENDIX.

GOOD See APPENDIX.

GOODLIER

of Israel a *g* person than he 1Sa 9:2	2896

GOODLIEST

your *g* young men, and your asses, ... 1Sa 8:16	2896
also and thy children, even the *g* 1Kin 20:3	2896

GOODLINESS

all the *g* thereof is as the........................ Is 40:6	2617

GOODLY See APPENDIX.

GOODMAN

For the *g* is not at home, he is .... Prov 7:19	376
against the *g* of the house...................... Mt 20:11	*3611*
that if the *g* of the house had............... Mt 24:43	*3611*
in, say ye to the *g* of the house .... Mk 14:14	*3611*
that if the *g* of the house had............... Lk 12:39	*3611*
shall say unto the *g* of the house .... Lk 22:11	*3611*

GOODNESS See APPENDIX.

GOODNESS'

remember thou me for thy *g* sake .... Ps 25:7	2898

GOODS

And they took all the *g* of Sodom .... Gen 14:11	7399
son, who dwelt in Sodom, and his *g*........ Gen 14:12	7399
And he brought back all the *g* .... Gen 14:16	7399
again his brother Lot, and his *g* .... Gen 14:16	7399
persons, and take the *g* to thyself.......... Gen 14:21	7399
for all the *g* of his master were.............. Gen 24:10	2898
all his *g* which he had gotten, ... Gen 31:18	7399
took their cattle, and their *g* .... Gen 46:6	7399
his hand unto his neighbour's *g*.............. Ex 22:8	4399
his hand unto his neighbour's *g* .... Ex 22:11	4399
unto Korah, and all their *g*..................... Num 16:32	7399
all their flocks, and all their *g*................ Num 31:9	2428
for their cattle, and for their *g* .... Num 35:3	7399
shall make thee plenteous in *g* .... Deut 28:11	2896
and thy wives, and all thy *g* 2Chr 21:14	7399
silver, and with gold, and with *g* .... Ezr 1:4	7399
of silver, with gold, with *g* .... Ezr 1:6	7399
that of the king's *g*, even of the .... Ezr 6:8	5232
or to confiscation of *g*, or to .... Ezr 7:26	5232
and possessed houses full of all *g* .... Neh 9:25	2898
his hands shall restore their *g* .... Job 20:10	202
shall no man look for his *g* .... Job 20:21	2898
his *g* shall flow away in the day .... Job 20:28	
When *g* increase, they are .... Eccl 5:11	2896
which have gotten cattle and *g*............... Eze 38:12	7075
and gold, to take away cattle and *g*....... Eze 38:13	7075
Therefore their *g* shall become a .... Zeph 1:13	2428
man's house, and spoil his *g* .... Mt 12:29	4632
make him ruler over all his *g*............... Mt 24:47	5224
and delivered unto them his *g*............... Mt 25:14	5224
man's house, and spoil his *g* .... Mk 3:27	4632
away thy *g* ask them not again .... Lk 6:30	4674
his palace, his *g* are in peace................. Lk 11:21	5224
I bestow all my fruits and my *g* .... Lk 12:18	*18*
thou hast much *g* laid up for many .... Lk 12:19	*18*
portion of *g* that falleth to me .... Lk 15:12	3776
unto him that he had wasted his *g* .... Lk 16:1	5224
the half of my *g* I give to the.................. Lk 19:8	5224
And sold their possessions and *g*............ Acts 2:45	5223
bestow all my *g* to feed the poor 1Cor 13:3	5224
joyfully the spoiling of your *g* .... Heb 10:34	5224
I am rich, and increased with *g*............. Rev 3:17	*4147*

GOPHER

Make thee an ark of *g* wood .... Gen 6:14	1613

GORE

If an ox *g* a man or a woman, that........ Ex 21:28	5055

GORED

Whether he have *g* a son....................... Ex 21:31	5055
or have *g* a daughter, according............ Ex 21:31	5055

GORGEOUS

him, and arrayed him in a *g* robe.......... Lk 23:11	*2986*

GORGEOUSLY

captains and rulers clothed most *g* .... Eze 23:12	4358
they which are *g* apparelled.................. Lk 7:25	*1741*

GOSHEN (go'-shen)

1. A district of Egypt.

thou shalt dwell in the land of *G*	Gen 45:10	1657
Joseph, to direct his face unto *G*	Gen 46:28	1657
and they came into the land of *G*	Gen 46:28	1657
to meet Israel his father, to *G*	Gen 46:29	1657
ye may dwell in the land of *G*	Gen 46:34	1657
behold, they are in the land of *G*	Gen 47:1	1657
servants dwell in the land of *G*	Gen 47:4	1657
in the land of *G* let them dwell	Gen 47:6	1657
of Egypt, in the country of *G*	Gen 47:27	1657
herds, they left in the land of *G*	Gen 50:8	1657
sever in that day the land of *G*	Ex 8:22	1657
Only in the land of *G*, where the	Ex 9:26	1657

2. A district in southern Palestine.

Gaza, and all the country of *G*	Josh 10:41	1657
country, and all the land of *G*	Josh 11:16	1657

3. A town in Judea.

And *G*, and Holon, and Giloh	Josh 15:51	1657

GOSPEL

preaching the *g* of the kingdom,	Mt 4:23	2098
preaching the *g* of the kingdom,	Mt 9:35	2098
poor have the *g* preached to them	Mt 11:5	2097
this *g* of the kingdom shall be	Mt 24:14	2098
Wheresoever this *g* shall be	Mt 26:13	2098
of the *g* of Jesus Christ, the Son	Mk 1:1	2098
preaching the *g* of the kingdom of	Mk 1:14	2098
repent ye, and believe the *g*.	Mk 1:15	2098
the *g* must first be published	Mk 13:10	2098
Wheresoever this *g* shall be	Mk 14:9	2098
preach the *g* to every creature	Mk 16:15	2098
me to preach the *g* to the poor	Lk 4:18	2097
to the poor the *g* is preached	Lk 7:22	2097
the towns, preaching the *g*	Lk 9:6	2097
in the temple, and preached the *g*	Lk 20:1	2097
preached the *g* in many villages	Acts 8:25	2097
And there they preached the *g*	Acts 14:7	2097
had preached the *g* to that city	Acts 14:21	2097
should hear the word of the *g*	Acts 15:7	2098
us for to preach the *g* unto them	Acts 16:10	2097
to testify the *g* of the grace of	Acts 20:24	2098
separated unto the *g* of God	Rom 1:1	2098
my spirit in the *g* of his Son	Rom 1:9	2098
I am ready to preach the *g* to you	Rom 1:15	2097
am not ashamed of the *g* of Christ	Rom 1:16	2098
by Jesus Christ according to my *g*	Rom 2:16	2098
them that preach the *g* of peace	Rom 10:15	2097
they have not all obeyed the *g*	Rom 10:16	2098
As concerning the *g*, they are	Rom 11:28	2098
ministering the *g* of God.	Rom 15:16	2098
fully preached the *g* of Christ	Rom 15:19	2098
so have I strived to preach the *g*	Rom 15:20	2097
the blessing of the *g* of Christ	Rom 15:29	2098
to stablish you according to my *g*	Rom 16:25	2098
to baptize, but to preach the *g*	1Cor 1:17	2097
I have begotten you through the *g*	1Cor 4:15	2098
we should hinder the *g* of Christ	1Cor 9:12	2098
the *g* should live of the	1Cor 9:14	2098
For though I preach the *g*	1Cor 9:16	2097
is unto me, if I preach not the *g*	1Cor 9:16	2097
of the *g* is committed unto me	1Cor 9:17	
Verily that, when I preach the *g*	1Cor 9:18	2097
I may make the *g* of Christ	1Cor 9:18	2098
I abuse not my power in the *g*	1Cor 9:18	2098
I declare unto you the *g* which I	1Cor 15:1	2098
to Troas to preach Christ's *g*	2Cor 2:12	2098
But if our *g* be hid, it is hid to	2Cor 4:3	2098
light of the glorious *g* of Christ	2Cor 4:4	2098
brother, whose praise is in the *g*	2Cor 8:18	2098
subjection into the *g* of Christ	2Cor 9:13	2098
also in preaching the *g* of Christ	2Cor 10:14	2098
To preach the *g* in the regions	2Cor 10:16	2097
have not received, or another *g*	2Cor 11:4	2098
to you the *g* of God freely	2Cor 11:7	2098
grace of Christ unto another *g*	Gal 1:6	2098
and would pervert the *g* of Christ	Gal 1:7	2098
preach any other *g* unto you than	Gal 1:8	2097
g unto you than that ye have	Gal 1:9	2097
that the *g* which was preached of	Gal 1:11	2098
that which I preach among the	Gal 2:2	2098
that the truth of the *g* might	Gal 2:5	2098
when they saw that the *g* of the	Gal 2:7	2098
as the *g* of the circumcision was	Gal 2:7	
according to the truth of the *g*	Gal 2:14	2098
before the *g* unto Abraham	Gal 3:8	4283
the *g* unto you at the first	Gal 4:13	2097
of truth, the *g* of your salvation	Eph 1:13	2098
of his promise in Christ by the *g*	Eph 3:6	2098
the preparation of the *g* of peace	Eph 6:15	2098
make known the mystery of the *g*	Eph 6:19	2098
For your fellowship in the *g* from	Phil 1:5	2098
defence and comfirmation of the *g*	Phil 1:7	2098
unto the furtherance of the *g*	Phil 1:12	2098
I am set for the defence of the *g*	Phil 1:17	2098
be as it becometh the *g* of Christ	Phil 1:27	2098
together for the faith of the *g*	Phil 1:27	2098
he hath served with me in the *g*	Phil 2:22	2098
which laboured with me in the *g*	Phil 4:3	2098
that in the beginning of the *g*	Phil 4:15	2098
in the word of the truth of the *g*	Col 1:5	2098
moved away from the hope of the *g*	Col 1:23	2098
For our *g* came not unto you in	1Th 1:5	2098
the *g* of God with much contention	1Th 2:2	2098
God to be put in trust with the *g*	1Th 2:4	2098
not the *g* of God only, but also	1Th 2:8	2098
we preached unto you the *g* of God	1Th 2:9	2098
fellowlabourer in the *g* of Christ	1Th 3:2	2098
that obey not the *g* of our Lord	2Th 1:8	2098
Whereunto he called you by our *g*	2Th 2:14	2098
the glorious *g* of the blessed God	1Ti 1:11	2098
of the afflictions of the *g*	2Ti 1:8	2098
to light through the *g*	2Ti 1:10	2098
from the dead according to my *g*	2Ti 2:8	2098
unto me in the bonds of the *g*	Philem 13	2098
For unto us was the *g* preached	Heb 4:2	2097
g unto you with the Holy Ghost	1Pet 1:12	2097
by the *g* is preached unto you	1Pet 1:25	2097
For for this cause was the *g*	1Pet 4:6	2097
them that obey not the *g* of God	1Pet 4:17	2098
having the everlasting *g* to	Rev 14:6	2098

GOSPEL'S

his life for my sake and the *g*	Mk 8:35	2098
or lands, for my sake, and the *g*	Mk 10:29	2098
And this I do for the *g* sake	1Cor 9:23	2098

GOT

which he had *g* in the land of	Gen 36:6	7408
her hand, and fled, and *g* him out	Gen 39:12	3318
with me, and fled, and *g* him out	Gen 39:15	3318
For they *g* not the land in	Ps 44:3	3423
I *g* me servants and maidens, and	Eccl 2:7	7069
So I *g* a girdle according to the	Jer 13:2	7069
Take the girdle that thou hast *g*	Jer 13:4	7069

GOTTEN See APPENDIX.

GOURD

And the LORD God prepared a *g*	Jonah 4:6	7021
Jonah was exceeding glad of the *g*	Jonah 4:6	7021
it smote the *g* that it withered	Jonah 4:7	7021
thou well to be angry for the *g*	Jonah 4:9	7021
LORD, Thou hast had pity on the *g*	Jonah 4:10	7021

GOURDS

thereof wild *g* his lap full	2Kin 4:39	6498

GOVERN

Dost thou now *g* the kingdom of	1Kin 21:7	6213
Shall even he that hateth right *g*	Job 34:17	2280
and *g* the nations upon earth	Ps 67:4	5148

GOVERNMENT

the *g* shall be upon his shoulder	Is 9:6	4951
Of the increase of his *g* and peace	Is 9:7	4951
I will commit thy *g* into his hand	Is 22:21	4475
lust of uncleanness, and despise *g*	2Pet 2:10	2963

GOVERNMENTS

then gifts of healings, helps, *g*	1Cor 12:28	2941

GOVERNOR

And Joseph was the *g* over the land	Gen 42:6	7989
he is *g* over all the land of	Gen 45:26	4910
which was the *g* of his house	1Kin 18:3	5921
back unto Amon the *g* of the city	1Kin 22:26	8269
gate of Joshua the *g* of the city	2Kin 23:8	8269
of Babylon had made Gedaliah *g*	2Kin 25:23	6485
unto the LORD to be the chief *g*	1Chr 29:22	5057
to every *g* in all Israel, the	2Chr 1:2	5387
back to Amon the *g* of the city	2Chr 18:25	8269
Azrikam the *g* of the house, and	2Chr 28:7	5057
and Maaseiah the *g* of the city	2Chr 34:8	8269
g on this side the river, and	Ezr 5:3	6347
g on this side the river, and	Ezr 5:6	6347
Sheshbazzar, whom he had made *g*	Ezr 5:14	6347
Tatnai, *g* beyond the river,	Ezr 6:6	6347
let the *g* of the Jews and the	Ezr 6:7	6347
g on this side the river,	Ezr 6:13	6347
of the *g* on this side the river	Neh 3:7	6346
be their *g* in the land of Judah	Neh 5:14	6346
have not eaten the bread of the *g*	Neh 5:14	6346
required not I the bread of the *g*	Neh 5:18	6346
and in the days of Nehemiah the *g*	Neh 12:26	6346
he is the *g* among the nations	Ps 22:28	4910

G

who was also chief *g* in the house .... Jer 20:1   5057
their *g* shall proceed from the .... Jer 30:21   4910
made *g* over the cities of Judah .... Jer 40:5   6485
the son of Ahikam *g* in the land .... Jer 40:7   6485
Babylon had made *g* over the land .... Jer 41:2   6485
of Babylon made *g* in the land .... Jer 41:18   6485
g of Judah, and to Joshua the son .... Hag 1:1   6346
g of Judah, and the spirit of .... Hag 1:14   6346
g of Judah, and to Joshua the son .... Hag 2:2   6346
g of Judah, saying, I will shake .... Hag 2:21   6346
and he shall be as a *g* in Judah .... Zec 9:7   441
offer it now unto thy *g* .... Mal 1:8   6346
for out of thee shall come a *G* .... Mt 2:6   2233
him to Pontius Pilate the *g* .... Mt 27:2   2232
And Jesus stood before the *g* .... Mt 27:11   2232
the *g* asked him, saying, Art thou .... Mt 27:11   2232
that the *g* marvelled greatly .... Mt 27:14   2232
Now at that feast the *g* was wont .... Mt 27:15   2232
The *g* answered and said unto them, ... Mt 27:21   2232
the *g* said, Why, what evil hath .... Mt 27:23   2232
Then the soldiers of the *g* took .... Mt 27:27   2232
made when Cyrenius was *g* of Syria .... Lk 2:2   2230
Pontius Pilate being *g* of Judaea .... Lk 3:1   2230
the power and authority of the *g* .... Lk 20:20   2230
and bear unto the *g* of the feast .... Jn 2:8   755
the *g* of the feast called the .... Jn 2:9   755
and he made him *g* over Egypt .... Acts 7:10   2233
bring him safe unto Felix the *g* .... Acts 23:24   2232
g Felix sendeth greeting .... Acts 23:26   2232
and delivered the epistle to the *g* .... Acts 23:33   2232
when the *g* had read the letter, ... Acts 23:34   2232
who informed the *g* against Paul .... Acts 24:1   2232
after that the *g* had beckoned .... Acts 24:10   2232
the king rose up, and the *g* .... Acts 26:30   2232
In Damascus the *g* under Aretas 2Cor 11:32   1481
helm, whithersoever the *g* listeth .... Jas 3:4   2116

GOVERNOR'S
And if this come to the *g* ears .... Mt 28:14   2232

GOVERNORS
heart is toward the *g* of Israel .... Judg 5:9   2710
out of Machir came down *g* .... Judg 5:14   2710
and of the *g* of the country 1Kin 10:15   6346
for the *g* of the sanctuary, and 1Chr 24:5   8269
g of the house of God, were of 1Chr 24:5   8269
g of the country brought gold and 2Chr 9:14   6346
the *g* of the people, and all the 2Chr 23:20   4910
to the *g* on this side the river .... Ezr 8:36   6346
me to the *g* beyond the river .... Neh 2:7   6346
I came to the *g* beyond the river .... Neh 2:9   6346
But the former *g* that had been .... Neh 5:15   6346
to the *g* that were over every .... Est 3:12   6346
chief of the *g* over all the wise .... Dan 2:48   5461
together the princes, the *g* .... Dan 3:2   5461
Then the princes, the *g*, and .... Dan 3:3   5461
And the princes, *g*, and captains, ... Dan 3:27   5461
presidents of the kingdom, the *g* .... Dan 6:7   5461
the *g* of Judah shall say in their .... Zec 12:5   441
In that day will I make the *g* of .... Zec 12:6   441
And ye shall be brought before *g* .... Mt 10:18   2232
g until the time appointed of the .... Gal 4:2   3623
Or unto *g*, as unto them that are 1Pet 2:14   2232

GOYIM See NATIONS

GOZAN (go'-zan) *An Assyrian city.*
and in Habor by the river of *G* 2Kin 17:6   1470
and in Habor by the river of *G* 2Kin 18:11   1470
as *G*, and Haran, and Rezeph, and the .. 2Kin 19:12   1470
Habor, and Hara, and to the river *G* 1Chr 5:26   1470
my fathers have destroyed, as *G* .... Is 37:12   1470

GRACE
But Noah found *g* in the eyes of .... Gen 6:8   2580
servant hath found *g* in thy sight .... Gen 19:19   2580
that I may find *g* in thy sight .... Gen 32:5   2580
These are to find *g* in the sight .... Gen 33:8   2580
now I have found *g* in thy sight, ... Gen 33:10   2580
let me find *g* in the sight of my .... Gen 33:15   2580
Let me find *g* in your eyes, and .... Gen 34:11   2580
And Joseph found *g* in his sight .... Gen 39:4   2580
let us find *g* in the sight of my .... Gen 47:25   2580
now I have found *g* in thy sight .... Gen 47:29   2580
now I have found *g* in your eyes .... Gen 50:4   2580
hast also found *g* in my sight .... Ex 33:12   2580
if I have found *g* in thy sight .... Ex 33:13   2580
that I may find *g* in thy sight .... Ex 33:13   2580
people have found *g* in thy sight .... Ex 33:16   2580
for thou hast found *g* in my sight .... Ex 33:17   2580
now I have found *g* in thy sight .... Ex 34:9   2580
if we have found *g* in thy sight .... Num 32:5   2580
now I have found *g* in thy sight .... Judg 6:17   2580

him in whose sight I shall find *g* .... Ruth 2:2   2580
Why have I found *g* in thine eyes .... Ruth 2:10   2580
handmaid find *g* in thy sight 1Sa 1:18   2580
that I have found *g* in thine eyes 1Sa 20:3   2580
I have now found *g* in thine eyes 1Sa 27:5   2580
that I have found *g* in thy sight 2Sa 14:22   2580
that I may find *g* in thy sight 2Sa 16:4   2580
now for a little space a *g* hath .... Ezr 9:8   8467
all the women, and she obtained *g* .... Est 2:17   2580
g is poured into thy lips .... Ps 45:2   2580
the LORD will give *g* and glory .... Ps 84:11   2580
be an ornament of *g* unto thy head .... Prov 1:9   2580
unto thy soul, and *g* to thy neck .... Prov 3:22   2580
but he giveth *g* unto the lowly .... Prov 3:34   2580
to thine head an ornament of *g* .... Prov 4:9   2580
for the *g* of his lips the king .... Prov 22:11   2580
sword found *g* in the wilderness .... Jer 31:2   2580
crying, *G*, *g* unto it .... Zec 4:7   2580
of Jerusalem, the spirit of *g* .... Zec 12:10   2580
the *g* of God was upon him .... Lk 2:40   5485
of the Father,) full of *g* .... Jn 1:14   5485
all we received, and *g* for *g* .... Jn 1:16   5485
the law was given by Moses, but *g* .... Jn 1:17   5485
great *g* was upon them all .... Acts 4:33   5485
he came, and had seen the *g* of God .... Acts 11:23   5485
them to continue in the *g* of God .... Acts 13:43   5485
testimony unto the word of his *g* .... Acts 14:3   5485
had been recommended to the *g* of ...... Acts 14:26   5485
the *g* of the Lord Jesus Christ we .... Acts 15:11   5485
by the brethren unto the *g* of God .... Acts 15:40   5485
much which had believed through *g* ...... Acts 18:27   5485
the gospel of the *g* of God .... Acts 20:24   5485
to God, and to the word of his *g* .... Acts 20:32   5485
By whom we have received *g* .... Rom 1:5   5485
G to you and peace from God our .... Rom 1:7   5485
Being justified freely by his *g* .... Rom 3:24   5485
is the reward not reckoned of *g* .... Rom 4:4   5485
of faith, that it might be by *g* .... Rom 4:16   5485
into this *g* wherein we stand .... Rom 5:2   5485
g of God, and the gift by *g* .... Rom 5:15   5485
they which receive abundance of *g* .... Rom 5:17   5485
abounded, *g* did much more abound ...... Rom 5:20   5485
even so might *g* reign through .... Rom 5:21   5485
in sin, that *g* may abound .... Rom 6:1   5485
not under the law, but under *g* .... Rom 6:14   5485
not under the law, but under *g* .... Rom 6:15   5485
according to the election of *g* .... Rom 11:5   5485
And if by *g*, then is it no more of .... Rom 11:6   5485
otherwise *g* is no more *g* .... Rom 11:6   5485
be of works, then is it no more *g* .... Rom 11:6   5485
through the *g* given unto me, to .... Rom 12:3   5485
to the *g* that is given to us .... Rom 12:6   5485
because of the *g* that is given to .... Rom 15:15   5485
The *g* of our Lord Jesus Christ be .... Rom 16:20   5485
The *g* of our Lord Jesus Christ be .... Rom 16:24   5485
G be unto you, and peace, from God 1Cor 1:3   5485
for the *g* of God which is given 1Cor 1:4   5485
According to the *g* of God which 1Cor 3:10   5485
For if I by *g* be a partaker, why 1Cor 10:30   5485
But by the *g* of God I am what I 1Cor 15:10   5485
his *g* which was bestowed upon me 1Cor 15:10   5485
but the *g* of God which was with 1Cor 15:10   5485
The *g* of our Lord Jesus Christ be 1Cor 16:23   5485
G be to you and peace from God our 2Cor 1:2   5485
wisdom, but by the *g* of God 2Cor 1:12   5485
that the abundant *g* might through 2Cor 4:15   5485
receive not the *g* of God in vain 2Cor 6:1   5485
we do you to wit of the *g* of God 2Cor 8:1   5485
finish in you the same *g* also 2Cor 8:6   5485
see that ye abound in this *g* also 2Cor 8:7   5485
For ye know the *g* of our Lord 2Cor 8:9   5485
to travel with us with this *g* 2Cor 8:19   5485
to make all *g* abound toward you 2Cor 9:8   5485
for the exceeding *g* of God in you 2Cor 9:14   5485
My *g* is sufficient for thee 2Cor 12:9   5485
The *g* of the Lord Jesus Christ, ... 2Cor 13:14   5485
G be to you and peace from God the .... Gal 1:3   5485
him that called you into the *g* of .... Gal 1:6   5485
womb, and called me by his *g* .... Gal 1:15   5485
perceived the *g* that was given .... Gal 2:9   5485
I do not frustrate the *g* of God .... Gal 2:21   5485
ye are fallen from *g* .... Gal 5:4   5485
the *g* of our Lord Jesus Christ be .... Gal 6:18   5485
G be to you, and peace, from God .... Eph 1:2   5485
the praise of the glory of his *g* .... Eph 1:6   5485
according to the riches of his *g* .... Eph 1:7   5485
with Christ, (by *g* ye are saved .... Eph 2:5   5485
his *g* in his kindness toward us .... Eph 2:7   5485
For by *g* are ye saved through .... Eph 2:8   5485
of the dispensation of the *g* of .... Eph 3:2   5485
the *g* of God given unto me by the .... Eph 3:7   5485

of all saints, is this g given....................Eph 3:8   5485
unto every one of us is given g...............Eph 4:7   5485
may minister g unto the hearers ....Eph 4:29   5485
G be with all them that love our ....Eph 6:24   5485
G be unto you, and peace, from God.....Phil 1:2   5485
ye all are partakers of my g....................Phil 1:7   5485
The g of our Lord Jesus Christ be ....Phil 4:23   5485
G be unto you, and peace, from God.....Col 1:2   5485
knew the g of God in truth.....................Col 1:6   5485
singing with g in your hearts to.............Col 3:16   5485
Let your speech be alway with g ....Col 4:6   5485
G be with you ....Col 4:18   5485
G be unto you, and peace, from God.....1Th 1:1   5485
The g of our Lord Jesus Christ be 1Th 5:28   5485
G unto you, and peace, from God...........2Th 1:2   5485
according to the g of our God 2Th 1:12   5485
and good hope through g, ...2Th 2:16   5485
The g of our Lord Jesus Christ be 2Th 3:18   5485
G, mercy, and peace, from God our 1Ti 1:2   5485
the g of our Lord was exceeding 1Ti 1:14   5485
G be with thee 1Ti 6:21   5485
G, mercy, and peace, from God the 2Ti 1:2   5485
according to his own purpose and g 2Ti 1:9   5485
be strong in the g that is in 2Ti 2:1   5485
G be with you 2Ti 4:22   5485
G, mercy, and peace, from God the ....Titus 1:4   5485
For the g of God that bringeth ....Titus 2:11   5485
That being justified by his g ....Titus 3:7   5485
G be with you all ....Titus 3:15   5485
G to you, and peace, from God our ....Philem 3   5485
The g of our Lord Jesus Christ be ....Philem 25   5485
that he by the g of God should...............Heb 2:9   5485
come boldly unto the throne of g ....Heb 4:16   5485
find g to help in time of need ....Heb 4:16   5485
done despite unto the Spirit of g ....Heb 10:29   5485
lest any man fail of the g of God ....Heb 12:15   5485
cannot be moved, let us have g..............Heb 12:28   5485
the heart be established with g ....Heb 13:9   5485
G be with you all ....Heb 13:25   5485
the g of the fashion of it ....Jas 1:11   2143
But he giveth more g ....Jas 4:6   5485
but giveth g unto the humble ....Jas 4:6   5485
G unto you, and peace, be 1Pet 1:2   5485
who prophesied of the g that 1Pet 1:10   5485
hope to the end for the g that is 1Pet 1:13   5485
heirs together of the g of life 1Pet 3:7   5485
stewards of the manifold g of God 1Pet 4:10   5485
proud, and giveth g to the humble 1Pet 5:5   5485
But the God of all g, who hath................1Pet 5:10   5485
that this is the true g of God..................1Pet 5:12   5485
G and peace be multiplied unto you.......2Pet 1:2   5485
But grow in g, and in the........................2Pet 3:18   5485
G be with you, mercy, and peace, ...2Jn 3   5485
turning the g of our God into ....Jude 4   5485
G be unto you, and peace, from him ......Rev 1:4   5485
The g of our Lord Jesus Christ be ....Rev 22:21   5485

GRACIOUS

God be g unto thee, my son ....Gen 43:29   2603
for I am g ....Ex 22:27   2587
be g to whom I will be g ....Ex 33:19   2603
Lord, The Lord God, merciful and g.....Ex 34:6   2587
upon thee, and be g unto thee ....Num 6:25   2603
tell whether God will be g to me 2Sa 12:22   2603
And the Lord was g unto them...............2Kin 13:23   2603
for the Lord your God is g 2Chr 30:9   2587
thou art a God ready to pardon, g ....Neh 9:17   2587
for thou art a g and merciful God ....Neh 9:31   2587
Then he is g unto him, and saith, ...Job 33:24   2603
Hath God forgotten to be g ....Ps 77:9   2589
a God full of compassion, and g ....Ps 86:15   2587
The Lord is merciful and g ....Ps 103:8   2587
the Lord is g and full of..........................Ps 111:4   2587
he is g, and full of compassion, ...Ps 112:4   2587
G is the Lord, and righteous...................Ps 116:5   2587
The Lord is g, and full of........................Ps 145:8   2587
A g woman retaineth honour ....Prov 11:16   2580
words of a wise man's mouth are g ....Eccl 10:12   2580
wait, that he may be g unto you ....Is 30:18   2603
he will be very g unto thee at ....Is 30:19   2603
O Lord, be g unto us ....Is 33:2   2603
how g shalt thou be when pangs ....Jer 22:23   2603
for he is g and merciful, slow to ....Joel 2:13   2587
be g unto the remnant of Joseph ....Amos 5:15   2587
for I knew that thou art a g God ....Jonah 4:2   2587
God that he will be g unto us.................Mal 1:9   2603
wondered at the g words which ....Lk 4:22   5485
ye have tasted that the Lord is g 1Pet 2:3   5543

GRACIOUSLY

God hath g given thy servant ....Gen 33:5   2603
because God hath dealt g with me ....Gen 33:11   2603

and grant me thy law g ....Ps 119:29   2603
all iniquity, and receive us g ....Hos 14:2   2896

GRAFF

God is able to g them in again ....Rom 11:23   *1461*

GRAFFED

wert g in among them, and with ....Rom 11:17   *1461*
broken off, that I might be g in ....Rom 11:19   *1461*
still in unbelief, shall be g in ....Rom 11:23   *1461*
wert g contrary to nature into a ....Rom 11:24   *1461*
be g into their own olive tree ....Rom 11:24   *1461*

GRAIN

the least g fall upon the earth ....Amos 9:9   6872
is like to a g of mustard seed..................Mt 13:31   *2848*
have faith as a g of mustard seed..........Mt 17:20   *2848*
It is like a g of mustard seed, ...Mk 4:31   *2848*
It is like a g of mustard seed, ...Lk 13:19   *2848*
had faith as a g of mustard seed...........Lk 17:6   *2848*
body that shall be, but bare g................1Cor 15:37   *2848*
of wheat, or of some other g 1Cor 15:37

GRANDMOTHER

which dwelt first in thy g Lois................2Ti 1:5   *3125*

GRANT

shall g a redemption for the land ....Lev 25:24   5414
The Lord g you that ye may find ....Ruth 1:9   5414
the God of Israel g thee thy 1Sa 1:17   5414
to Ornan, G me the place of this 1Chr 21:22   5414
thou shalt g it me for the full 1Chr 21:22   5414
them, but I will g them some..................2Chr 12:7   5414
according to the g that they had ....Ezr 3:7   7558
g him mercy in the sight of this ....Neh 1:11   5414
please the king to g my petition ....Est 5:8   5414
that God would g me the thing................Job 6:8   5414
G thee according to thine own................Ps 20:4   5414
O Lord, and g us thy salvation...............Ps 85:7   5414
and g me thy law graciously ....Ps 119:29
G not, O Lord, the desires of the ....Ps 140:8   5414
G that these my two sons may sit, ...Mt 20:21   2036
G unto us that we may sit, one on ....Mk 10:37   1325
That he would g unto us, that we, ...Lk 1:74   1325
g unto thy servants, that with ....Acts 4:29   1325
and consolation g you to be ....Rom 15:5   1325
That he would g you, according to..........Eph 3:16   1325
The Lord g unto him that he may 2Ti 1:18   1325
I g to sit with me in my throne ....Rev 3:21   1325

GRANTED

God g him that which he requested 1Chr 4:10   935
and knowledge is g unto thee 2Chr 1:12   5414
the king g him all his request,...............Ezr 7:6   5414
And the king g me, according to............Neh 2:8   5414
and it shall be g thee ....Est 5:6   5414
and it shall be g thee ....Est 7:2   5414
Wherein the king g the Jews which........Est 8:11   5414
and it shall be g thee ....Est 9:12   5414
let it be g to the Jews which are ....Est 9:13   5414
Thou hast g me life and favour, and ......Job 10:12   6213
of the righteous shall be g......................Prov 10:24   5414
a murderer to be g unto you...................Acts 3:14   *5483*
Gentiles g repentance unto life ....Acts 11:18   1325
g signs and wonders to be done by ....Acts 14:3   1325
to her was g that she should be ....Rev 19:8   1325

GRAPE

gather every g of thy vineyard ....Lev 19:10   6528
drink the pure blood of the g ....Deut 32:14   6025
off his unripe g as the vine.....................Job 15:33   1154
the tender g give a good smell................Song 2:13   5563
whether the tender g appear...................Song 7:12   5563
the sour g is ripening in the...................Is 18:5   1155
The fathers have eaten a sour g ....Jer 31:29   1155
every man that eateth the sour g ....Jer 31:30   1155

GRAPEGATHERER

hand as a g into the baskets...................Jer 6:9   1219

GRAPEGATHERERS

If g come to thee, would they not ....Jer 49:9   1219
if the g came to thee, would they ....Obad 5   1219

GRAPEGLEANINGS

fruits, as the g of the vintage ....Mic 7:1   5955

GRAPES

thereof brought forth ripe g ....Gen 40:10   6025
and I took the g, and pressed them ....Gen 40:11   6025
and his clothes in the blood of g.............Gen 49:11   6025
neither gather the g of thy vine..............Lev 25:5   6025
nor gather the g of it thy ....Lev 25:11   6025
liquor of g, nor eat moist g ....Num 6:3   6025
was the time of the firstripe g................Num 13:20   6025
a branch with one cluster of g ....Num 13:23   6025

G

because of the cluster of *g* which	Num 13:24	
then thou mayest eat *g* thy fill	Deut 23:24	6025
gatherest the *g* of thy vineyard	Deut 24:21	
and shalt not gather the *g* thereof	Deut 28:30	
of the wine, nor gather the *g*	Deut 28:39	
their *g* are *g* of gall	Deut 32:32	6025
the *g* of Ephraim better than the	Judg 8:2	
their vineyards, and trode the *g*	Judg 9:27	
as also wine, *g*, and figs, and all	Neh 13:15	6025
for our vines have tender *g*	Song 2:15	5563
and thy breasts to clusters of *g*	Song 7:7	
that it should bring forth *g*	Is 5:2	6025
and it brought forth wild *g*	Is 5:2	891
that it should bring forth *g*	Is 5:4	6025
brought it forth wild *g*	Is 5:4	891
Yet gleaning *g* shall be left in	Is 17:6	
as the gleaning *g* when the	Is 24:13	
there shall be no *g* on the vine	Jer 8:13	6025
a shout, as they that tread the *g*	Jer 25:30	
they not leave some gleaning *g*	Jer 49:9	
The fathers have eaten sour *g*	Eze 18:2	1154
Israel like *g* in the wilderness	Hos 9:10	6025
the treader of *g* him that soweth	Amos 9:13	6025
thee, would they not leave some *g*	Obad 5	
Do men gather *g* of thorns	Mt 7:16	*4718*
of a bramble bush gather they *g*	Lk 6:44	*4718*
for her *g* are fully ripe	Rev 14:18	*4718*

GRASS

said, Let the earth bring forth *g*	Gen 1:11	1877
And the earth brought forth *g*	Gen 1:12	1877
ox licketh up the *g* of the field	Num 22:4	3418
I will send *g* in thy fields for	Deut 11:15	6212
nor any *g* groweth therein, like	Deut 29:23	6212
and as the showers upon the *g*	Deut 32:2	6212
as the tender *g* springing out of	2Sa 23:4	1877
we may find *g* to save the horses	1Kin 18:5	2682
they were as the *g* of the field	2Kin 19:26	6212
as the *g* on the house tops, and as	2Kin 19:26	2682
offspring as the *g* of the earth	Job 5:25	6212
the wild ass bray when he hath *g*	Job 6:5	1877
he eateth *g* as an ox	Job 40:15	2682
shall soon be cut down like the *g*	Ps 37:2	2682
down like rain upon the mown *g*	Ps 72:6	
flourish like *g* of the earth	Ps 72:16	6212
they are like *g* which groweth up	Ps 90:5	2682
When the wicked spring as the *g*	Ps 92:7	6212
is smitten, and withered like *g*	Ps 102:4	6212
and I am withered like *g*	Ps 102:11	6212
As for man, his days are as *g*	Ps 103:15	2682
He causeth the *g* to grow for the	Ps 104:14	2682
similitude of an ox that eateth *g*	Ps 106:20	6212
be as the *g* upon the housetops	Ps 129:6	2682
who maketh *g* to grow upon the	Ps 147:8	2682
his favour is as dew upon the *g*	Prov 19:12	6212
the tender *g* sheweth itself, and	Prov 27:25	1877
the *g* faileth, there is no green	Is 15:6	1877
shall be *g* with reeds and rushes	Is 35:7	2682
they were as the *g* of the field	Is 37:27	6212
as the *g* on the housetops, and as	Is 37:27	2682
All flesh is *g*, and all the	Is 40:6	2682
The *g* withereth, the flower	Is 40:7	2682
surely the people is *g*	Is 40:7	2682
The *g* withereth, the flower	Is 40:8	2682
shall spring up as among the *g*	Is 44:4	2682
of man which shall be made as *g*	Is 51:12	2682
it, because there was no *g*	Jer 14:5	1758
did fail, because there was no *g*	Jer 14:6	6212
are grown fat as the heifer at *g*	Jer 50:11	1877
in the tender *g* of the field	Dan 4:15	1883
the beasts in the *g* of the earth	Dan 4:15	6211
in the tender *g* of the field	Dan 4:23	1883
shall make thee to eat *g* as oxen	Dan 4:25	6211
shall make thee to eat *g* as oxen	Dan 4:32	6211
from men, and did eat *g* as oxen	Dan 4:33	6211
they fed him with *g* like oxen	Dan 5:21	6211
end of eating the *g* of the land	Amos 7:2	6212
LORD, as the showers upon the *g*	Mic 5:7	6212
rain, to every one *g* in the field	Zec 10:1	6212
God so clothe the *g* of the field	Mt 6:30	5528
multitude to sit down on the *g*	Mt 14:19	5528
by companies upon the green *g*	Mk 6:39	5528
If then God so clothe the *g*	Lk 12:28	5528
Now there was much *g* in the place	Jn 6:10	5528
of the *g* he shall pass away	Jas 1:10	5528
heat, but it withereth the *g*	Jas 1:11	5528
For all flesh is as *g*, and all the	1Pet 1:24	5528
glory of man as the flower of *g*	1Pet 1:24	5528
The *g* withereth, and the flower	1Pet 1:24	5528
up, and all green *g* was burnt up	Rev 8:7	5528
not hurt the *g* of the earth	Rev 9:4	5528

GRASSHOPPER

his kind, and the *g* after his kind	Lev 11:22	2284
Canst thou make him afraid as a *g*	Job 39:20	697
the *g* shall be a burden, and	Eccl 12:5	2284

GRASSHOPPERS

and we were in our own sight as *g*	Num 13:33	2284
they came as *g* for multitude	Judg 6:5	697
the valley like *g* for multitude	Judg 7:12	697
the inhabitants thereof are as *g*	Is 40:22	2284
because they are more than the *g*	Jer 46:23	697
he formed *g* in the beginning of	Amos 7:1	1462
and thy captains as the great *g*	Nah 3:17	1462

GRATE

for it a *g* of network of brass	Ex 27:4	4345
burnt offering, with his brasen *g*	Ex 35:16	4345
g of network under the compass	Ex 38:4	4345
the four ends of the *g* of brass	Ex 38:5	4345
altar, and the brasen *g* for it	Ex 38:30	4345
his *g* of brass, his staves, and	Ex 39:39	4345

GRAVE

And Jacob set a pillar upon her *g*	Gen 35:20	6900
of Rachel's *g* unto this day	Gen 35:20	6900
into the *g* unto my son mourning	Gen 37:35	7585
gray hairs with sorrow to the *g*	Gen 42:38	7585
gray hairs with sorrow to the *g*	Gen 44:29	7585
our father with sorrow to the *g*	Gen 44:31	7585
in my *g* which I have digged for	Gen 50:5	6913
g on them the names of the	Ex 28:9	6605
g upon it, like the engravings of	Ex 28:36	6605
body, or a bone of a man, or a *g*	Num 19:16	6913
or one slain, or one dead, or a *g*	Num 19:18	6913
he bringeth down to the *g*	1Sa 2:6	7585
voice, and wept at the *g* of Abner	2Sa 3:32	6913
be buried by the *g* of my father	2Sa 19:37	6913
head go down to the *g* in peace	1Kin 2:6	7585
thou down to the *g* with blood	1Kin 2:9	7585
he laid his carcase in his own *g*	1Kin 13:30	6913
of Jeroboam shall come to the *g*	1Kin 14:13	6913
be gathered into thy *g* in peace	2Kin 22:20	6913
that can skill to *g* with the	2Chr 2:7	6603
also to *g* any manner of graving	2Chr 2:14	6605
be gathered to thy *g* in peace	2Chr 34:28	6913
glad, when they can find the *g*	Job 3:22	6913
shalt come to thy *g* in a full age	Job 5:26	6913
to the *g* shall come up no more	Job 7:9	7585
carried from the womb to the *g*	Job 10:19	6913
thou wouldest hide me in the *g*	Job 14:13	7585
If I wait, the *g* is mine house	Job 17:13	7585
and in a moment go down to the *g*	Job 21:13	7585
Yet shall he be brought to the *g*	Job 21:32	6913
so doth the *g* those which have	Job 24:19	7585
not stretch out his hand to the *g*	Job 30:24	1164
his soul draweth near unto the *g*	Job 33:22	7845
in the *g* who shall give thee	Ps 6:5	7585
brought up my soul from the *g*	Ps 30:3	7585
and let them be silent in the *g*	Ps 31:17	7585
Like sheep they are laid in the *g*	Ps 49:14	7585
in the *g* from their dwelling	Ps 49:14	7585
my soul from the power of the *g*	Ps 49:15	7585
my life draweth nigh unto the *g*	Ps 88:3	7585
like the slain that lie in the *g*	Ps 88:5	6913
be declared in the *g*	Ps 88:11	6913
his soul from the hand of the *g*	Ps 89:48	7585
us swallow them up alive as the *g*	Prov 1:12	7585
The *g*; and the barren	Prov 30:16	7585
knowledge, nor wisdom, in the *g*	Eccl 9:10	7585
jealousy is cruel as the *g*	Song 8:6	7585
Thy pomp is brought down to the *g*	Is 14:11	7585
thy *g* like an abominable branch	Is 14:19	6913
I shall go to the gates of the *g*	Is 38:10	7585
For the *g* cannot praise thee	Is 38:18	7585
he made his *g* with the wicked, and	Is 53:9	6913
my mother might have been my *g*	Jer 20:17	6913
down to the *g* I caused a mourning	Eze 31:15	7585
her company is round about her *g*	Eze 32:23	6900
her multitude round about her *g*	Eze 32:24	6900
them from the power of the *g*	Hos 13:14	7585
O *g*, I will be thy destruction	Hos 13:14	7585
I will make thy *g*	Nah 1:14	6913
lain in the *g* four days already	Jn 11:17	*3419*
goeth unto the *g* to weep there	Jn 11:31	*3419*
in himself cometh to the *g*	Jn 11:38	*3419*
he called Lazarus out of his *g*	Jn 12:17	*3419*
O *g*, where is thy victory	1Cor 15:55	*86*
Likewise must the deacons be *g*	1Ti 3:8	*4586*
Even so must their wives be *g*	1Ti 3:11	*4586*
That the aged men be sober, *g*	Titus 2:2	*4586*

GRAVECLOTHES

forth, bound hand and foot with *g*	Jn 11:44	*2750*

GRAVED

he g cherubims, lions, and palm	1Kin 7:36	6605
and g cherubims on the walls	2Chr 3:7	6605

GRAVEL

his mouth shall be filled with g	Prov 20:17	2687
of thy bowels like the g thereof	Is 48:19	4579
broken my teeth with g stones	Lam 3:16	2687

GRAVEN

not make unto thee any g image	Ex 20:4	6459
writing of God, g upon the tables	Ex 32:16	2801
inclosed in ouches of gold, g	Ex 39:6	6605
of gold, g, as signets are g	Ex 39:6	6605
make you no idols nor g image	Lev 26:1	6459
yourselves, and make you a g image	Deut 4:16	6459
with you, and make you a g image	Deut 4:23	6459
yourselves, and make a g image	Deut 4:25	6459
shalt not make thee any g image	Deut 5:8	6459
burn their g images with fire	Deut 7:5	6456
The g images of their gods shall	Deut 7:25	6456
down the g images of their gods	Deut 12:3	6456
that maketh any g or molten image	Deut 27:15	6459
for my son, to make a g image	Judg 17:3	6459
who made thereof a g image	Judg 17:4	6459
a g image, and a molten image	Judg 18:14	6459
in thither, and took the g image	Judg 18:17	6459
the g image, and went in the midst	Judg 18:20	6459
of Dan set up the g image	Judg 18:30	6459
they set them up Micah's g image	Judg 18:31	6459
LORD, and served their g images	2Kin 17:41	6456
he set a g image of the grove	2Kin 21:7	6459
g images, before he was humbled	2Chr 33:19	6456
had beaten the g images into	2Chr 34:7	6456
That they were g with an iron pen	Job 19:24	2672
to jealousy with their g images	Ps 78:58	6456
be all they that serve g images	Ps 97:7	6459
whose g images did excel them of	Is 10:10	6456
all the g images of her gods he	Is 21:9	6456
of thy g images of silver	Is 30:22	6456
The workman melteth a g image	Is 40:19	6459
workman to prepare a g image	Is 40:20	6459
neither my praise to g images	Is 42:8	6456
ashamed, that trust in g images	Is 42:17	6459
They that make a g image are all	Is 44:9	6459
or molten a g image that is	Is 44:10	6459
he maketh it a g image, and	Is 44:15	6459
he maketh a god, even his g image	Is 44:17	6459
set up the wood of their g image	Is 45:20	6459
my g image, and my molten image,	Is 48:5	6459
I have g thee upon the palms of	Is 49:16	2710
me to anger with their g images	Jer 8:19	6456
is confounded by the g image	Jer 10:14	6459
it is upon the table of their	Jer 17:1	2790
for it is the land of g images	Jer 50:38	6456
is confounded by the g image	Jer 51:17	6459
upon the g images of Babylon	Jer 51:47	6456
do judgment upon her g images	Jer 51:52	6456
and burned incense to g images	Hos 11:2	6456
all the g images thereof shall be	Mic 1:7	6456
Thy g images also will I cut off,	Mic 5:13	6456
gods will I cut off the g image	Nah 1:14	6459
What profiteth the g image that	Hab 2:18	6459
that the maker thereof hath g it	Hab 2:18	6458
stone, g by art and man's device	Acts 17:29	5480

GRAVE'S

are scattered at the g mouth	Ps 141:7	7585

GRAVES

Because there were no g in Egypt	Ex 14:11	6913
the powder thereof upon the g of	2Kin 23:6	6913
strowed it upon the g of them	2Chr 34:4	6913
extinct, the g are ready for me	Job 17:1	6913
Which remain among the g, and	Is 65:4	6913
of Jerusalem, out of their g	Jer 8:1	6913
into the g of the common people	Jer 26:23	6913
his g are about him	Eze 32:22	6913
Whose g are set in the sides of	Eze 32:23	6913
her g are round about him	Eze 32:25	6913
her g are round about him	Eze 32:26	6913
O my people, I will open your g	Eze 37:12	6913
you to come up out of your g	Eze 37:12	6913
LORD, when I have opened your g	Eze 37:13	6913
and brought you up out of your g	Eze 37:13	6913
Gog a place there of g in Israel	Eze 39:11	6913
And the g were opened	Mt 27:52	3419
came out of the g after his	Mt 27:53	3419
for ye are as g which appear not,	Lk 11:44	3419
are in the g shall hear his voice	Jn 5:28	3419

their dead bodies to be put in g	Rev 11:9	3418

GRAVETH

that g an habitation for himself	Is 22:16	2710

GRAVING

and fashioned it with a g tool	Ex 32:4	2747
also to grave any manner of g	2Chr 2:14	6603
I will engrave the g thereof	Zec 3:9	6603

GRAVINGS

of it were g with their borders	1Kin 7:31	4734

GRAVITY

children in subjection with all g	1Ti 3:4	4587
doctrine shewing uncorruptness, g	Titus 2:7	4587

GRAY

then shall ye bring down my g	Gen 42:38	7872
ye shall bring down my g hairs	Gen 44:29	7872
servants shall bring down the g	Gen 44:31	7872
also with the man of g hairs	Deut 32:25	7872
g hairs are here and there upon	Hos 7:9	7872

GRAYHEADED

and I am old and g	1Sa 12:2	7867
With us are both the g and very	Job 15:10	7867

GREASE

Their heart is as fat as g	Ps 119:70	2459

G

GREAT

And God made two g lights	Gen 1:16	1419
And God created g whales, and every	Gen 1:21	1419
of man was g in the earth	Gen 6:5	7227
fountains of the g deep broken up	Gen 7:11	7227
the same is a g city	Gen 10:12	1419
And I will make of thee a g nation	Gen 12:2	1419
bless thee, and make thy name g	Gen 12:2	1431
his house with g plagues because	Gen 12:17	1419
for their substance was g	Gen 13:6	7227
shield, and thy exceeding g reward	Gen 15:1	7235
an horror of g darkness fell upon	Gen 15:12	1419
they come out with g substance	Gen 15:14	1419
river of Egypt unto the g river	Gen 15:18	1419
and I will make him a g nation	Gen 17:20	1419
Abraham shall surely become a g	Gen 18:18	1419
the cry of Sodom and Gomorrah is g	Gen 18:20	7227
with blindness, both small and g	Gen 19:11	1419
the cry of them is waxen g before	Gen 19:13	1431
on me and on my kingdom a g sin	Gen 20:9	1419
Abraham made a g feast the same	Gen 21:8	1419
for I will make him a g nation	Gen 21:18	1419
and he is become g	Gen 24:35	1431
And the man waxed g, and went	Gen 26:13	1431
and grew until he became very g	Gen 26:13	1431
of herds, and g store of servants	Gen 26:14	7227
of his father, he cried with a g	Gen 27:34	1419
a g stone was upon the well's	Gen 29:2	1419
With g wrestlings have I wrestled	Gen 30:8	430
then can I do this g wickedness	Gen 39:9	1419
there come seven years of g	Gen 41:29	1419
your lives by a g deliverance	Gen 45:7	1419
there make of thee a g nation	Gen 46:3	1419
a people, and he also shall be g	Gen 48:19	1431
and it was a very g company	Gen 50:9	3515
and there they mourned with a g	Gen 50:10	1419
turn aside, and see this g sight	Ex 3:3	1419
out arm, and with g judgments	Ex 6:6	1419
the land of Egypt by g judgments	Ex 7:4	1419
was very g in the land of Egypt	Ex 11:3	1419
there shall be a g cry throughout	Ex 11:6	1419
out from Pharaoh in a g anger	Ex 11:8	2750
there was a g cry in Egypt	Ex 12:30	1419
Israel saw that g work which the	Ex 14:31	1419
that every g matter they shall	Ex 18:22	1419
upon the g toe of their right	Ex 29:20	
and I will make of thee a g nation	Ex 32:10	1419
of the land of Egypt with g power	Ex 32:11	1419
hast brought so g a sin upon them	Ex 32:21	1419
people, Ye have sinned a g sin	Ex 32:30	1419
this people have sinned a g sin	Ex 32:31	1419
upon the g toe of his right foot	Lev 8:23	
upon the g toes of their right	Lev 8:24	
and the cormorant, and the g owl	Lev 11:17	3244
upon the g toe of his right foot	Lev 14:14	
upon the g toe of his right foot,	Lev 14:17	
upon the g toe of his right foot	Lev 14:25	
upon the g toe of his right foot,	Lev 14:28	
the people with a very g plague	Num 11:33	7227
the cities are walled, and very g	Num 13:28	1419
saw in it are men of a g stature	Num 13:32	
let the power of my LORD be g	Num 14:17	1431
of g mercy, forgiving iniquity and	Num 14:18	7227

promote thee unto very g honour	Num 22:17	
people shall rise up as a g lion	Num 23:24	3833
down as a lion, and as a g lion	Num 24:9	3833
to promote thee unto g honour	Num 24:11	
had a very g multitude of cattle	Num 32:1	6099
even have the g sea for a border	Num 34:6	1419
from the g sea ye shall point out	Num 34:7	1419
and unto Lebanon, unto the g river	Deut 1:7	1419
hear the small as well as the g	Deut 1:17	1419
Horeb, we went through all that g	Deut 1:19	1419
the cities are g and walled up to	Deut 1:28	1419
walking through this g wilderness	Deut 2:7	1419
therein in times past, a people g	Deut 2:10	1419
A people g, and many, and tall, as	Deut 2:21	1419
beside unwalled towns a g many	Deut 3:5	3966
Surely this g nation is a wise and	Deut 4:6	1419
For what nation is there so g	Deut 4:7	1419
And what nation is there so g	Deut 4:8	1419
any such thing as this g thing is	Deut 4:32	1419
by g terrors, according to all	Deut 4:34	1419
earth he shewed thee his g fire	Deut 4:36	1419
thick darkness, with a g voice	Deut 5:22	1419
for this g fire will consume us	Deut 5:25	1419
and to Jacob, to give thee g	Deut 6:10	1419
LORD shewed signs and wonders, g	Deut 6:22	1419
The g temptations which thine	Deut 7:19	1419
Who led thee through that g	Deut 8:15	1419
mightier than thyself, cities g	Deut 9:1	1419
A people g and tall, the children	Deut 9:2	1419
a g God, a mighty, and a terrible	Deut 10:17	1419
that hath done for thee these g	Deut 10:21	1419
g acts of the LORD which he did	Deut 11:7	1419
The little owl, and the g owl	Deut 14:16	3244
let me see this g fire any more	Deut 18:16	1419
in thy bag divers weights, a g	Deut 25:13	1419
thine house divers measures, a g	Deut 25:14	1419
few, and became there a nation, g	Deut 26:5	1419
with g terribleness, and with	Deut 26:8	1419
thou shalt set thee up g stones	Deut 27:2	1419
even g plagues, and of long	Deut 28:59	1419
The g temptations which thine	Deut 29:3	1419
the signs, and those g miracles	Deut 29:3	1419
meaneth the heat of this g anger	Deut 29:24	1419
in g indignation, and cast them	Deut 29:28	1419
in all the g terror which Moses	Deut 34:12	1419
Lebanon even unto the g river	Josh 1:4	1419
unto the g sea toward the going	Josh 1:4	1419
people shall shout with a g shout	Josh 6:5	1419
the people shouted with a g shout	Josh 6:20	1419
what wilt thou do unto thy g name	Josh 7:9	1419
they raised over him a g heap of	Josh 7:26	1419
raise thereon a g heap of stones	Josh 8:29	1419
of the g sea over against Lebanon	Josh 9:1	1419
because Gibeon was a g city	Josh 10:2	1419
slew them with a g slaughter at	Josh 10:10	1419
that the LORD cast down g stones	Josh 10:11	1419
Roll g stones upon the mouth of	Josh 10:18	1419
them with a very g slaughter	Josh 10:20	1419
laid g stones in the cave's mouth	Josh 10:27	1419
them, and chased them unto g Zidon	Josh 11:8	7227
there, and that the cities were g	Josh 14:12	1419
which Arba was a g man among the	Josh 14:15	1419
the west border was to the g sea	Josh 15:12	1419
the river of Egypt, and the g sea	Josh 15:47	1419
inherit, seeing I am a g people	Josh 17:14	7227
them, If thou be a g people	Josh 17:15	7227
saying, Thou art a g people	Josh 17:17	7227
and hast g power	Josh 17:17	1419
and Kanah, even unto g Zidon	Josh 19:28	7227
by Jordan, a g altar to see to	Josh 22:10	1419
off, even unto the g sea westward	Josh 23:4	1419
out from before you g nations	Josh 23:9	1419
which did those g signs in our	Josh 24:17	1419
the law of God, and took a g stone	Josh 24:26	1419
cut off his thumbs and his g toes	Judg 1:6	
their g toes cut off, gathered	Judg 1:7	
seen all the g works of the LORD	Judg 2:7	1419
there were g thoughts of heart	Judg 5:15	1419
there were g searchings of heart	Judg 5:16	1419
with a very g slaughter	Judg 11:33	1419
my people were at g strife with	Judg 12:2	3699
hip and thigh with a g slaughter	Judg 15:8	1419
and said, Thou hast given this g	Judg 15:18	1419
see wherein his g strength lieth	Judg 16:5	1419
wherein thy g strength lieth, and	Judg 16:6	1419
me wherein thy g strength lieth	Judg 16:15	1419
them together for to offer a g	Judg 16:23	1419
that they should make a g flame	Judg 20:38	7235
For they had made a g oath	Judg 21:5	1419
men was very g before the LORD	1Sa 2:17	1419

all Israel shouted with a g shout	1Sa 4:5	1419
this g shout in the camp of the	1Sa 4:6	1419
and there was a very g slaughter	1Sa 4:10	1419
and there hath been also a g	1Sa 4:17	1419
city with a very g destruction	1Sa 5:9	1419
men of the city, both small and g	1Sa 5:9	1419
then he hath done us this g evil	1Sa 6:9	1419
there, where there was a g stone	1Sa 6:14	1419
were, and put them on the g stone	1Sa 6:15	1419
even unto the g stone of Abel	1Sa 6:18	1419
of the people with a g slaughter	1Sa 6:19	1419
a g thunder on that day upon the	1Sa 7:10	1419
stand and see this g thing	1Sa 12:16	1419
and see that your wickedness is g	1Sa 12:17	7227
his people for his g name's sake	1Sa 12:22	1419
for consider how g things he hath	1Sa 12:24	1431
so it was a very g trembling	1Sa 14:15	430
there was a very g discomfiture	1Sa 14:20	1419
roll a g stone unto me this day	1Sa 14:33	1419
this g salvation in Israel	1Sa 14:45	1419
Hath the LORD as g delight in	1Sa 15:22	1419
will enrich him with g riches	1Sa 17:25	1419
the LORD wrought a g salvation	1Sa 19:5	1419
and slew them with a g slaughter	1Sa 19:8	1419
came to a g well that is in Sechu	1Sa 19:22	1419
will do nothing either g or small	1Sa 20:2	1419
and smote them with a g slaughter	1Sa 23:5	1419
and the man was very g, and he had	1Sa 25:2	1419
a g space being between them	1Sa 26:13	7227
thou shalt both do g things	1Sa 26:25	
either g or small, but carried	1Sa 30:2	1419
because of all the g spoil that	1Sa 30:16	1419
to them, neither small nor g	1Sa 30:19	1419
brought in a g spoil with them	2Sa 3:22	7227
a g man fallen this day in Israel	2Sa 3:38	1419
And David went on, and grew g	2Sa 5:10	1419
sight, and have made thee a g name	2Sa 7:9	1419
the g men that are in the earth	2Sa 7:9	1419
house for a g while to come	2Sa 7:19	7350
hast thou done all these g things	2Sa 7:21	1420
Wherefore thou art g, O LORD God	2Sa 7:22	1431
a name, and to do for you g things	2Sa 7:23	1420
by this deed thou hast given g	2Sa 12:14	5006
spoil of the city in g abundance	2Sa 12:30	3966
there was there a g slaughter	2Sa 18:7	1419
under the thick boughs of a g oak	2Sa 18:9	1419
cast him into a g pit in the wood	2Sa 18:17	1419
laid a very g heap of stones upon	2Sa 18:17	1419
me thy servant, I saw a g tumult	2Sa 18:29	1419
for he was a very g man	2Sa 19:32	1419
When they were at the g stone	2Sa 20:8	1419
where was a man of g stature	2Sa 21:20	
and thy gentleness hath made me g	2Sa 22:36	7235
LORD wrought a g victory that day	2Sa 23:10	1419
and the LORD wrought a g victory	2Sa 23:12	1419
said unto Gad, I am in a g strait	2Sa 24:14	3966
for his mercies are g	2Sa 24:14	7227
pipes, and rejoiced with g joy	1Kin 1:40	1419
for that was the g high place	1Kin 3:4	1419
servant David my father g mercy	1Kin 3:6	1419
hast kept for him this g kindness	1Kin 3:6	1419
a g people, that cannot be	1Kin 3:8	7227
to judge this thy so g a people	1Kin 3:9	3515
threescore g cities with walls and	1Kin 4:13	1419
a wise son over this g people	1Kin 5:7	7227
and they brought g stones	1Kin 5:17	1419
on the outside toward the g court	1Kin 7:9	1419
even g stones, stones of ten	1Kin 7:10	1419
the g court round about was with	1Kin 7:12	1419
For they shall hear of thy g name	1Kin 8:42	1419
a g congregation, from the	1Kin 8:65	1419
to Jerusalem with a very g train	1Kin 10:2	3515
gold, and of spices very g store	1Kin 10:10	7235
Ophir g plenty of almug trees	1Kin 10:11	3966
the king made a g throne of ivory	1Kin 10:18	1419
Hadad found g favour in the sight	1Kin 11:19	3966
as g as would contain two	1Kin 18:32	1004
and wind, and there was a g rain	1Kin 18:45	1419
the journey is too g for thee	1Kin 19:7	7227
the LORD passed by, and a g	1Kin 19:11	1419
thou seen all this g multitude	1Kin 20:13	1419
the Syrians with a g slaughter	1Kin 20:21	1419
will I deliver all this g	1Kin 20:28	1419
Fight neither with small nor g	1Kin 22:31	1419
there was g indignation against	2Kin 3:27	1419
to Shunem, where was a g woman	2Kin 4:8	1419
his servant, Set on the g pot	2Kin 4:38	1419
was a g man with his master, and	2Kin 5:1	1419
had bid thee do some g thing	2Kin 5:13	1419
horses, and chariots, and a g host	2Kin 6:14	3515

he prepared *g* provision for them	2Kin 6:23	1419
there was a *g* famine in Samaria	2Kin 6:25	1419
even the noise of a *g* host	2Kin 7:6	1419
all the *g* things that Elisha hath	2Kin 8:4	1419
that he should do this *g* thing	2Kin 8:13	1419
were with the *g* men of the city,	2Kin 10:6	1419
Ahab in Jezreel, and all his *g* men	2Kin 10:11	1419
for I have a *g* sacrifice to do to	2Kin 10:19	1419
Upon the *g* altar burn the morning	2Kin 16:15	1419
LORD, and made them sin a *g* sin	2Kin 17:21	1419
of the land of Egypt with *g* power	2Kin 17:36	1419
with a *g* host against Jerusalem	2Kin 18:17	3515
Hezekiah, Thus saith the *g* king	2Kin 18:19	1419
Hear the word of the *g* king	2Kin 18:28	1419
for *g* is the wrath of the LORD	2Kin 22:13	1419
all the people, both small and *g*	2Kin 23:2	1419
the fierceness of his *g* wrath	2Kin 23:26	1419
every *g* man's house burnt he with	2Kin 25:9	1419
all the people, both small and *g*	2Kin 25:26	1419
saved them by a *g* deliverance	1Chr 11:14	1419
an Egyptian, a man of *g* stature	1Chr 11:23	
help him, until it was a *g* host	1Chr 12:22	1419
For *g* is the LORD, and greatly to	1Chr 16:25	1419
the *g* men that are in the earth	1Chr 17:8	1419
house for a *g* while to come	1Chr 17:17	7350
making known all these *g* things	1Chr 17:19	1420
where was a man of *g* stature	1Chr 20:6	
said unto Gad, I am in a *g* strait	1Chr 21:13	3966
for very *g* are his mercies	1Chr 21:13	7227
abundantly, and hast made *g* wars	1Chr 22:8	1419
ward, as well the small as the *g*	1Chr 25:8	1419
lots, as well the small as the *g*	1Chr 26:13	1419
young and tender, and the work is *g*	1Chr 29:1	1419
the king also rejoiced with *g* joy	1Chr 29:9	1419
and in thine hand it is to make *g*	1Chr 29:12	1431
LORD on that day with *g* gladness	1Chr 29:22	1419
Thou hast shewed *g* mercy unto	2Chr 1:8	1419
this thy people, that is so *g*	2Chr 1:10	1419
And the house which I build is *g*	2Chr 2:5	1419
for *g* is our God above all gods	2Chr 2:5	1419
to build shall be wonderful *g*	2Chr 2:9	1419
the *g* court, and doors for the	2Chr 4:9	1419
all these vessels in *g* abundance	2Chr 4:18	3966
far country for thy *g* name's sake	2Chr 6:32	1419
a very *g* congregation, from the	2Chr 7:8	1419
Jerusalem, with a very *g* company	2Chr 9:1	3515
of gold, and of spices *g* abundance	2Chr 9:9	3966
the king made a *g* throne of ivory	2Chr 9:17	1419
ye be a *g* multitude, and there are	2Chr 13:8	7227
slew them with a *g* slaughter	2Chr 13:17	7227
but *g* vexations were upon all the	2Chr 15:5	7227
put to death, whether small or *g*	2Chr 15:13	1419
until his disease was exceeding *g*	2Chr 16:12	
made a very *g* burning for him	2Chr 16:14	1419
Jehoshaphat waxed *g* exceedingly	2Chr 17:12	1432
Fight ye not with small or *g*	2Chr 18:30	1419
There cometh a *g* multitude	2Chr 20:2	1419
we have no might against this *g*	2Chr 20:12	7227
by reason of this *g* multitude	2Chr 20:15	7227
gave them *g* gifts of silver	2Chr 21:3	7227
with a *g* plague will the LORD	2Chr 21:14	1419
thou shalt have *g* sickness by	2Chr 21:15	7227
a very *g* host into their hand	2Chr 24:24	7230
(for they left him in *g* diseases	2Chr 24:25	1419
and they returned home in *g* anger	2Chr 25:10	2750
shoot arrows and *g* stones withal	2Chr 26:15	1419
carried away a *g* multitude of	2Chr 28:5	1419
who smote him with a *g* slaughter	2Chr 28:5	1419
for our trespass is *g*, and there	2Chr 28:13	7227
month, a very *g* congregation	2Chr 30:13	7230
bread seven days with *g* gladness	2Chr 30:21	1419
a *g* number of priests sanctified	2Chr 30:24	7230
So there was *g* joy in Jerusalem	2Chr 30:26	1419
which is left is this *g* store	2Chr 31:10	
as well to the *g* as to the small	2Chr 31:15	1419
and raised it up a very *g* height	2Chr 33:14	
for *g* is the wrath of the LORD	2Chr 34:21	1419
the Levites, and all the people, *g*	2Chr 34:30	1419
vessels of the house of God, *g*	2Chr 36:18	1419
the people shouted with a *g* shout	Ezr 3:11	1419
rest of the nations whom the *g*	Ezr 4:10	7229
Judea, to the house of the *g* God	Ezr 5:8	7229
which is builded with *g* stones	Ezr 5:8	1560
which a *g* king of Israel builded	Ezr 5:11	7229
With three rows of *g* stones	Ezr 6:4	1560
in a *g* trespass unto this day	Ezr 9:7	1419
for our trespass, seeing that	Ezr 9:13	1419
a very *g* congregation of men	Ezr 10:1	7227
of this matter, and for the *g* rain	Ezr 10:9	

the province are in *g* affliction	Neh 1:3	1419
thee, O LORD God of heaven, the *g*	Neh 1:5	1419
thou hast redeemed by thy *g* power	Neh 1:10	1419
over against the *g* tower that	Neh 3:27	1419
took *g* indignation, and mocked the	Neh 4:1	7235
remember the LORD, which is *g*	Neh 4:14	1419
rest of the people, The work is *g*	Neh 4:19	7235
there was a *g* cry of the people	Neh 5:1	1419
I set a *g* assembly against them	Neh 5:7	1419
them, saying, I am doing a *g* work	Neh 6:3	1419
Now the city was large and *g*	Neh 7:4	1419
Ezra blessed the LORD, the *g* God	Neh 8:6	1419
send portions, and to make *g* mirth	Neh 8:12	1419
And there was very *g* gladness	Neh 8:17	1419
of *g* kindness, and forsookest them	Neh 9:17	7227
had wrought *g* provocations	Neh 9:18	1419
themselves in thy *g* goodness	Neh 9:25	1419
and they wrought *g* provocations	Neh 9:26	1419
Nevertheless for thy *g* mercies'	Neh 9:31	7227
Now therefore, our God, the *g*	Neh 9:32	1419
in thy *g* goodness that thou	Neh 9:35	7227
pleasure, and we are in *g* distress	Neh 9:37	1419
the son of one of the *g* men	Neh 11:14	1419
appointed two *g* companies of them	Neh 12:31	1419
day they offered *g* sacrifices	Neh 12:43	1419
had made them rejoice with *g* joy	Neh 12:43	1419
had prepared for him a *g* chamber	Neh 13:5	1419
unto you to do all this *g* evil	Neh 13:27	1419
Shushan the palace, both unto *g*	Est 1:5	1419
all his empire, (for it is *g*	Est 1:20	7227
their husbands honour, both to *g*	Est 1:20	1419
Then the king made a *g* feast unto	Est 2:18	1419
there was *g* mourning among the	Est 4:3	1419
with a *g* crown of gold, and with a	Est 8:15	1419
For Mordecai was *g* in the king's	Est 9:4	1419
g among the Jews, and accepted of	Est 10:3	1419
she asses, and a very *g* household	Job 1:3	7227
there came a *g* wind from the	Job 1:19	1419
saw that his grief was very *g*	Job 2:13	1431
The small and *g* are there	Job 3:19	1419
Which doeth *g* things and	Job 5:9	1419
also that thy seed shall be *g*	Job 5:25	7227
Which doeth *g* things past finding	Job 9:10	1419
Is not thy wickedness *g*	Job 22:5	7227
plead against me with his *g* power	Job 23:6	7227
By the *g* force of my disease is	Job 30:18	7227
rejoiced because my wealth was *g*	Job 31:25	7227
Did I fear a *g* multitude, or did	Job 31:34	7227
G men are not always wise	Job 32:9	7227
he knoweth it not in *g* extremity	Job 35:15	3966
then a *g* ransom cannot deliver	Job 36:18	7227
Behold, God is *g*, and we know him	Job 36:26	7689
g things doeth he, which we	Job 37:5	1419
to the *g* rain of his strength	Job 37:6	4306
the number of thy days is *g*	Job 38:21	7227
him, because his strength is *g*	Job 39:11	7227
There were they in *g* fear	Ps 14:5	6343
and thy gentleness hath made me *g*	Ps 18:35	7235
G deliverance giveth he to his	Ps 18:50	1431
keeping of them there is *g* reward	Ps 19:11	7227
innocent from the *g* transgression	Ps 19:13	7227
His glory is *g* in thy salvation	Ps 21:5	1419
be of thee in the *g* congregation	Ps 22:25	7227
mine iniquity; for it is *g*	Ps 25:11	7227
Oh how *g* is thy goodness, which	Ps 31:19	7227
surely in the floods of *g* waters	Ps 32:6	7227
he deliver any by his *g* strength	Ps 33:17	7230
thee thanks in the *g* congregation	Ps 35:18	7227
is like the *g* mountains	Ps 36:6	410
thy judgments are a *g* deep	Ps 36:6	7227
I have seen the wicked in *g* power	Ps 37:35	
in the *g* congregation	Ps 40:9	7227
thy truth from the *g* congregation	Ps 40:10	7227
he is a *g* King over all the earth	Ps 47:2	1419
G is the LORD, and greatly to be	Ps 48:1	1419
the north, the city of the *g* King	Ps 48:2	7227
There were they in *g* fear	Ps 53:5	
thy mercy is *g* unto the heavens	Ps 57:10	1419
break out the *g* teeth of the	Ps 58:6	4459
g was the company of those that	Ps 68:11	7227
very high, who hast done *g* things	Ps 71:19	1419
Thou, who hast shewed me *g*	Ps 71:20	7229
his name is *g* in Israel	Ps 76:1	1419
who is so *g* a God as our God	Ps 77:13	1419
sea, and thy path in the *g* waters	Ps 77:19	7227
them drink as out of the *g* depths	Ps 78:15	7227
From following the ewes with *g*	Ps 78:71	
them tears to drink in *g* measure	Ps 80:5	7991
For thou art *g*, and doest wondrous	Ps 86:10	1419
For *g* is thy mercy toward me	Ps 86:13	1419

G

O Lord, how *g* are thy works	Ps 92:5	1431
For the Lord is a *g* God	Ps 95:3	1419
and a *g* King above all gods	Ps 95:3	1419
For the Lord is *g*, and greatly to	Ps 96:4	1419
The Lord is *g* in Zion	Ps 99:2	1419
Let them praise thy *g* and terrible	Ps 99:3	1419
so *g* is his mercy toward them	Ps 103:11	1396
O Lord my God, thou art very *g*	Ps 104:1	1431
So is this *g* and wide sea, wherein	Ps 104:25	1419
both small and *g* beasts	Ps 104:25	1419
which had done *g* things in Egypt	Ps 106:21	1419
that do business in *g* waters	Ps 107:23	7227
For thy mercy is *g* above the	Ps 108:4	1419
The works of the Lord are *g*	Ps 111:2	1419
fear the Lord, both small and *g*	Ps 115:13	1419
merciful kindness is *g* toward us	Ps 117:2	1396
G are thy tender mercies, O Lord	Ps 119:156	7227
word, as one that findeth *g* spoil	Ps 119:162	7227
G peace have they which love thy	Ps 119:165	7227
Lord hath done *g* things for them	Ps 126:2	1431
Lord hath done *g* things for us	Ps 126:3	1431
do I exercise myself in *g* matters	Ps 131:1	1419
For I know that the Lord is *g*	Ps 135:5	1419
Who smote *g* nations, and slew	Ps 135:10	7227
To him who alone doeth *g* wonders	Ps 136:4	1419
To him that made *g* lights	Ps 136:7	1419
To him which smote *g* kings	Ps 136:17	1419
for *g* is the glory of the Lord	Ps 138:5	1419
How *g* is the sum of them	Ps 139:17	6105
me, and deliver me out of *g* waters	Ps 144:7	7227
G is the Lord, and greatly to be	Ps 145:3	1419
the memory of thy *g* goodness	Ps 145:7	7227
slow to anger, and of *g* mercy	Ps 145:8	1419
G is our Lord, and of *g* power	Ps 147:5	1419
G is our Lord, and of *g* power	Ps 147:5	7227
himself poor, yet hath *g* riches	Prov 13:7	7227
to wrath is of *g* understanding	Prov 14:29	7227
fear of the Lord than *g* treasure	Prov 15:16	7227
than *g* revenues without right	Prov 16:8	7230
brother to him that is a *g* waster	Prov 18:9	1167
him, and bringeth him before *g* men	Prov 18:16	1419
A man of *g* wrath shall suffer	Prov 19:19	
rather to be chosen than *g* riches	Prov 22:1	7227
stand not in the place of *g* men	Prov 25:6	1419
The *g* God that formed all things	Prov 26:10	7227
men do rejoice, there is *g* glory	Prov 28:12	7227
is also a *g* oppressor	Prov 28:16	7227
saying, Lo, I am come to *g* estate	Eccl 1:16	1431
my heart had *g* experience of	Eccl 1:16	7235
I made me *g* works	Eccl 2:4	1431
also I had *g* possessions of *g*	Eccl 2:7	7235
also I had *g* possessions of *g*	Eccl 2:7	1241
So I was *g*, and increased more	Eccl 2:9	1431
This also is vanity and a *g* evil	Eccl 2:21	7227
the misery of man is *g* upon him	Eccl 8:6	7227
the sun, and it seemed *g* unto me	Eccl 9:13	1419
there came a *g* king against it,	Eccl 9:14	1419
built bulwarks against it	Eccl 9:14	1419
for yielding pacifieth *g* offences	Eccl 10:4	1419
Folly is set in *g* dignity	Eccl 10:6	7227
under his shadow with *g* delight	Song 2:3	
the *g* man humbleth himself	Is 2:9	
houses shall be desolate, even *g*	Is 5:9	1419
there be a *g* forsaking in the	Is 6:12	7227
said unto me, Take thee a *g* roll	Is 8:1	1419
in darkness have seen a *g* light	Is 9:2	1419
for *g* is the Holy One of Israel	Is 12:6	1419
mountains, like as of a *g* people	Is 13:4	7227
with all that *g* multitude	Is 16:14	7227
a *g* one, and he shall deliver them	Is 19:20	7227
by *g* waters the seed of Sihor,	Is 23:3	7227
day the Lord with his sore and *g*	Is 27:1	1419
that the trumpet shall be blown	Is 27:13	1419
g noise, with storm and tempest,	Is 29:6	1419
in the day of the *g* slaughter	Is 30:25	7227
as the shadow of a *g* rock in a	Is 32:2	3515
is the prey of a *g* spoil divided	Is 33:23	4766
a *g* slaughter in the land of	Is 34:6	1419
There shall the *g* owl make her	Is 34:15	7091
unto king Hezekiah with a *g* army	Is 36:2	3515
Hezekiah, Thus saith the *g* king	Is 36:4	1419
Hear ye the words of the *g* king	Is 36:13	1419
for peace I had *g* bitterness	Is 38:17	
for the *g* abundance of thine	Is 47:9	3966
the sea, the waters of the *g* deep	Is 51:10	7227
I divide him a portion with the *g*	Is 53:12	7227
but with *g* mercies will I gather	Is 54:7	1419
g shall be the peace of thy	Is 54:13	7227
the *g* goodness toward the house	Is 63:7	7227
the north, and a *g* destruction	Jer 4:6	1419

I will get me unto the *g* men	Jer 5:5	1419
therefore they are become *g*	Jer 5:27	1431
of the north, and *g* destruction	Jer 6:1	1419
a *g* nation shall be raised from	Jer 6:22	1419
thou art *g*, and thy name is *g*	Jer 10:6	1419
g, and thy name is *g* in might	Jer 10:6	1419
a *g* commotion out of the north	Jer 10:22	1419
with the noise of a *g* tumult he	Jer 11:16	1419
and the *g* pride of Jerusalem	Jer 13:9	7227
people is broken with a *g* breach	Jer 14:17	1419
Both the *g* and the small shall die	Jer 16:6	1419
all this *g* evil against us	Jer 16:10	1419
her womb to be always a *g* with me	Jer 20:17	2030
anger, and in fury, and in *g* wrath	Jer 21:5	1419
they shall die of a *g* pestilence	Jer 21:6	1419
Lord done thus unto this *g* city	Jer 22:8	1419
g kings shall serve themselves of	Jer 25:14	1419
a *g* whirlwind shall be raised up	Jer 25:32	1419
Thus might we procure *g* evil	Jer 26:19	1419
upon the ground, by my *g* power	Jer 27:5	1419
g kings shall serve themselves of	Jer 27:7	1419
against *g* kingdoms, of war, and of	Jer 28:8	1419
for that day is *g*, so that none	Jer 30:7	1419
a *g* company shall return thither	Jer 31:8	1419
and the earth by thy *g* power	Jer 32:17	1419
the *G*, the Mighty God, the Lord	Jer 32:18	1419
G in counsel, and mighty in work	Jer 32:19	1419
out arm, and with *g* terror	Jer 32:21	1419
and in my fury, and in *g* wrath	Jer 32:37	1419
all this *g* evil upon this people	Jer 32:42	1419
will answer thee, and shew thee *g*	Jer 33:3	1419
for *g* is the anger and the fury	Jer 36:7	1419
found him by the *g* waters that	Jer 41:12	7227
Take *g* stones in thine hand, and	Jer 43:9	1419
ye this *g* evil against your souls	Jer 44:7	1419
a *g* multitude, even all the	Jer 44:15	1419
Behold, I have sworn by my *g* name	Jer 44:26	1419
seekest thou *g* things for thyself	Jer 45:5	1419
spoiling and *g* destruction	Jer 48:3	1419
g nations from the north country	Jer 50:9	1419
in the land, and of *g* destruction	Jer 50:22	1419
a *g* nation, and many kings shall	Jer 50:41	1419
g destruction from the land of	Jer 51:54	1419
destroyed out of her the *g* voice	Jer 51:55	1419
her waves do roar like *g* waters	Jer 51:55	7227
and all the houses of the *g* men	Jer 52:13	1419
she that was *g* among the nations,	Lam 1:1	7227
and because of *g* servitude	Lam 1:3	7230
for thy breach is *g* like the sea	Lam 2:13	1419
g is thy faithfulness	Lam 3:23	7227
a *g* cloud, and a fire infolding	Eze 1:4	1419
wings, like the noise of *g* waters	Eze 1:24	7227
behind me a voice of a *g* rushing	Eze 3:12	1419
them, and a noise of a *g* rushing	Eze 3:13	1419
even the *g* abominations that the	Eze 8:6	1419
of Israel and Judah is exceeding *g*	Eze 9:9	1419
O *g* hailstones, shall fall	Eze 13:11	417
g hailstones in my fury to	Eze 13:13	417
and thou hast increased and waxen *g*	Eze 16:7	1431
thy neighbours, *g* of flesh	Eze 16:26	1432
A *g* eagle with *g* wings,	Eze 17:3	1419
he placed it by *g* waters, and set	Eze 17:5	7227
another *g* eagle with *g* wings	Eze 17:7	1419
in a good soil by *g* waters	Eze 17:8	7227
even without *g* power or many	Eze 17:9	1419
g company make for him in the war	Eze 17:17	7227
sword of the *g* men that are slain	Eze 21:14	1419
g lords and renowned, all of them	Eze 23:23	7991
even make the pile for fire *g*	Eze 24:9	1431
her *g* scum went not forth out of	Eze 24:12	7227
I will execute *g* vengeance upon	Eze 25:17	1419
g waters shall cover thee	Eze 26:19	7227
have brought thee into *g* waters	Eze 27:26	7227
By thy *g* wisdom and by thy	Eze 28:5	7230
the *g* dragon that lieth in the	Eze 29:3	1419
serve a *g* service against Tyrus	Eze 29:18	1419
g pain shall be in Ethiopia, when	Eze 30:4	
g pain shall come upon them, as	Eze 30:9	
Sin shall have *g* pain, and No	Eze 30:16	2342
The waters made him *g*, the deep	Eze 31:4	1431
his shadow dwelt all *g* nations	Eze 31:6	7227
for his root was by *g* waters	Eze 31:7	7227
and the *g* waters were stayed	Eze 31:15	7227
thereof from beside the *g* waters	Eze 32:13	7227
And I will sanctify my *g* name	Eze 36:23	1419
their feet, an exceeding *g* army	Eze 37:10	1419
even a *g* company with bucklers and	Eze 38:4	7227
and goods, to take a *g* spoil	Eze 38:13	1419
a *g* company, and a mighty army	Eze 38:15	1419
in that day there shall be a *g*	Eze 38:19	1419

g hailstones, fire, and brimstone	Eze 38:22	417
even a g sacrifice upon the	Eze 39:17	1419
were a full reed of six g cubits	Eze 41:8	679
be a very g multitude of fish	Eze 47:9	7227
kinds, as the fish of the g sea	Eze 47:10	1419
the north side, from the g sea	Eze 47:15	1419
in Kadesh, the river to the g sea	Eze 47:19	1419
be the g sea from the border	Eze 47:20	1419
and to the river toward the g sea	Eze 48:28	1419
me gifts and rewards and g honour	Dan 2:6	7690
king, sawest, and behold a g image	Dan 2:31	7690
This g image, whose brightness	Dan 2:31	7229
the image became a g mountain	Dan 2:35	7229
the g God hath made known to the	Dan 2:45	7229
Then the king made Daniel a g man	Dan 2:48	7236
and gave him many g gifts	Dan 2:48	7260
How g are his signs	Dan 4:3	7260
and the height thereof was g	Dan 4:10	7260
and said, Is not this g Babylon	Dan 4:30	7690
a g feast to a thousand of his	Dan 5:1	7227
the heaven strove upon the g sea	Dan 7:2	7227
four g beasts came up from the	Dan 7:3	7229
and it had g iron teeth	Dan 7:7	7260
man, and a mouth speaking g things	Dan 7:8	7260
the g words which the horn spake	Dan 7:11	7260
These g beasts, which are four,	Dan 7:17	7260
a mouth that spake very g things	Dan 7:20	7260
he shall speak g words against	Dan 7:25	
to his will, and became g	Dan 8:4	1431
the he goat waxed very g	Dan 8:8	1431
was strong, the g horn was broken	Dan 8:8	1419
horn, which waxed exceeding g	Dan 8:9	1431
And it waxed g, even to the host	Dan 8:10	1431
the g horn that is between his	Dan 8:21	1419
and said, O Lord, the g and	Dan 9:4	1419
us, by bringing upon us a g evil	Dan 9:12	1419
but for thy g mercies	Dan 9:18	7227
I was by the side of the g river	Dan 10:4	1419
but a g quaking fell upon them,	Dan 10:7	1419
left alone, and saw this g vision	Dan 10:8	1419
that shall rule with g dominion	Dan 11:3	7227
dominion shall be a g dominion	Dan 11:5	7227
assemble a multitude of g forces	Dan 11:10	7227
he shall set forth a g multitude	Dan 11:11	7227
after certain years with a g army	Dan 11:13	1419
king of the south with a g army	Dan 11:25	1419
up to battle with a very g	Dan 11:25	1419
into his land with g riches	Dan 11:28	1419
go forth with g fury to destroy	Dan 11:44	1419
the g prince which standeth for	Dan 12:1	1419
land hath committed g whoredom	Hos 1:2	
for g shall be the day of Jezreel	Hos 1:11	1419
to him the g things of my law	Hos 8:12	7239
thine iniquity, and the g hatred	Hos 9:7	7227
you because of your g wickedness	Hos 10:15	7451
in the land of g drought	Hos 13:5	8514
hath the cheek teeth of a g lion	Joel 1:6	3833
a g people and a strong	Joel 2:2	7227
for his camp is very g	Joel 2:11	7227
for the day of the LORD is g	Joel 2:11	1419
of g kindness, and repenteth him	Joel 2:13	7227
up, because he hath done g things	Joel 2:20	1431
for the LORD will do g things	Joel 2:21	1431
my g army which I sent among you	Joel 2:25	1419
the moon into blood, before the g	Joel 2:31	1419
for their wickedness is g	Joel 3:13	7227
behold the g tumults in the midst	Amos 3:9	7227
the g houses shall have an end,	Amos 3:15	1419
from thence go ye to Hamath the g	Amos 6:2	7227
he will smite the g house with	Amos 6:11	1419
fire, and it devoured the g deep	Amos 7:4	7227
the ephah small, and the shekel g	Amos 8:5	1431
Arise, go to Nineveh, that g city	Jonah 1:2	1419
sent out a g wind into the sea	Jonah 1:4	1419
sake this g tempest is upon you	Jonah 1:12	1419
a g fish to swallow up Jonah	Jonah 1:17	1419
go unto Nineveh, that g city	Jonah 3:2	1419
g city of three days' journey	Jonah 3:3	1419
of g kindness, and repentest thee	Jonah 4:2	7227
not I spare Nineveh, that g city	Jonah 4:11	1419
they shall make g noise by reason	Mic 2:12	
for now shall he be g unto the	Mic 5:4	1431
and the g man, he uttereth his	Mic 7:3	1419
g in power, and will not at all	Nah 1:3	1431
slain, and a g number of carcases	Nah 3:3	3514
all her g men were bound in	Nah 3:10	1419
captains as the g grasshoppers	Nah 3:17	1462
through the heap of g waters	Hab 3:15	7227
a g crashing from the hills	Zeph 1:10	1419

The g day of the LORD is near, it	Zeph 1:14	1419
and for Zion with a g jealousy	Zec 1:14	1419
Who art thou, O g mountain	Zec 4:7	1419
therefore came a g wrath from the	Zec 7:12	1419
jealous for Zion with g jealousy	Zec 8:2	1419
I was jealous for her with g fury	Zec 8:2	1419
For how g is his goodness	Zec 9:17	
and how g is his beauty	Zec 9:17	
be a g mourning in Jerusalem	Zec 12:11	1431
and there shall be a very g valley	Zec 14:4	1419
that a g tumult from the LORD	Zec 14:13	7227
and apparel, in g abundance	Zec 14:14	3966
shall be g among the Gentiles	Mal 1:11	1419
name shall be g among the heathen	Mal 1:11	1419
for I am a g King, saith the LORD	Mal 1:14	1419
before the coming of the g	Mal 4:5	1419
rejoiced with exceeding g joy	Mt 2:10	3173
g mourning, Rachel weeping for	Mt 2:18	4183
which sat in darkness saw g light	Mt 4:16	3173
there followed him g multitudes	Mt 4:25	4183
for g is your reward in heaven	Mt 5:12	4183
called g in the kingdom of heaven	Mt 5:19	3173
for it is the city of the g King	Mt 5:35	3173
darkness, how g is that darkness	Mt 6:23	4214
and g was the fall of it	Mt 7:27	3173
g multitudes followed him	Mt 8:1	4183
you, I have not found so g faith	Mt 8:10	5118
Now when Jesus saw g multitudes	Mt 8:18	4183
there arose a g tempest in the	Mt 8:24	3173
and there was a g calm	Mt 8:26	3173
g multitudes followed him, and he	Mt 12:15	4183
g multitudes were gathered	Mt 13:2	4183
he had found one pearl of g price	Mt 13:46	4186
saw a g multitude, and was moved	Mt 14:14	4183
unto her, O woman, g is thy faith	Mt 15:28	3173
g multitudes came unto him,	Mt 15:30	4183
as to fill so g a multitude	Mt 15:33	5118
g multitudes followed him	Mt 19:2	4183
for he had g possessions	Mt 19:22	4183
them, and they that are g exercise	Mt 20:25	3171
but whosoever will be g among you	Mt 20:26	3173
a g multitude followed him	Mt 20:29	4183
a very g multitude spread their	Mt 21:8	4118
which is the g commandment in the	Mt 22:36	3173
is the first and g commandment	Mt 22:38	3173
For then shall be g tribulation	Mt 24:21	3173
prophets, and shall shew g signs	Mt 24:24	3173
of heaven with power and g glory	Mt 24:30	4183
with a g sound of a trumpet	Mt 24:31	3173
with him a g multitude with	Mt 26:47	4183
he rolled a g stone to the door	Mt 27:60	3173
behold, there was a g earthquake	Mt 28:2	3173
the sepulchre with fear and g joy	Mt 28:8	3173
rising up a g while before day,	Mk 1:35	3029
a g multitude from Galilee	Mk 3:7	4183
a g multitude, when they had	Mk 3:8	4183
had heard what g things he did	Mk 3:8	3745
gathered unto him a g multitude	Mk 4:1	4183
herbs, and shooteth out g branches	Mk 4:32	3173
And there arose a g storm of wind	Mk 4:37	3173
ceased, and there was a g calm	Mk 4:39	3173
a g herd of swine feeding	Mk 5:11	3173
tell them how g things the Lord	Mk 5:19	3745
to publish in Decapolis how g	Mk 5:20	3745
astonished with a g astonishment	Mk 5:42	3173
so much the more a g deal they	Mk 7:36	3123
days the multitude being very g	Mk 8:1	3827
he saw a g multitude about them,	Mk 9:14	4183
for he had g possessions	Mk 10:22	4183
their g ones exercise authority	Mk 10:42	3173
but whosoever will be g among you	Mk 10:43	3173
a g number of people, blind	Mk 10:46	2425
but he cried the more a g deal	Mk 10:48	4183
him, Seest thou these g buildings	Mk 13:2	3173
coming in the clouds with g power	Mk 13:26	4183
with him a g multitude with	Mk 14:43	4183
for it was very g	Mk 16:4	3173
For he shall be g in the sight of	Lk 1:15	3173
He shall be g, and shall be called	Lk 1:32	3173
mighty hath done to me g things	Lk 1:49	3167
Lord had shewed g mercy upon her	Lk 1:58	3170
espoused wife, being g with child	Lk 2:5	
I bring you good tidings of g joy	Lk 2:10	3173
she was of a g age, and had lived	Lk 2:36	4183
when g famine was throughout all	Lk 4:25	3173
mother was taken with a g fever	Lk 4:38	3173
they inclosed a g multitude of	Lk 5:6	4183
g multitudes came together to	Lk 5:15	4183
Levi made him a g feast in his	Lk 5:29	3173
and there was a g company of	Lk 5:29	4183
a g multitude of people out of	Lk 6:17	4183

G

your reward is *g* in heaven	Lk 6:23	4183
and your reward shall be *g*	Lk 6:35	4183
and the ruin of that house was *g*	Lk 6:49	3173
you, I have not found so *g* faith	Lk 7:9	5118
That a *g* prophet is risen up	Lk 7:16	3173
for they were taken with *g* fear	Lk 8:37	3173
shew how *g* things God hath done	Lk 8:39	3745
throughout the whole city how *g*	Lk 8:39	3745
you all, the same shall be *g*	Lk 9:48	3173
unto them, The harvest truly is *g*	Lk 10:2	4183
they had a *g* while ago repented,	Lk 10:13	3819
and it grew, and waxed a *g* tree	Lk 13:19	3173
A certain man made a *g* supper	Lk 14:16	3173
there went *g* multitudes with him	Lk 14:25	4183
the other is yet a *g* way off	Lk 14:32	
But when he was yet a *g* way off	Lk 15:20	3112
us and you there is a *g* gulf fixed	Lk 16:26	3173
g earthquakes shall be in divers	Lk 21:11	3173
g signs shall there be from	Lk 21:11	3173
for there shall be *g* distress in	Lk 21:23	3173
in a cloud with power and *g* glory	Lk 21:27	4183
his sweat was as it were *g* drops	Lk 22:44	
him a *g* company of people	Lk 23:27	4183
returned to Jerusalem with *g* joy	Lk 24:52	3173
In these lay a *g* multitude of	Jn 5:3	4183
a *g* multitude followed him,	Jn 6:2	4183
saw a *g* company come unto him, he	Jn 6:5	4183
by reason of a *g* wind that blew	Jn 6:18	3173
that *g* day of the feast, Jesus	Jn 7:37	3173
the net to land full of *g* fishes	Jn 21:11	3173
moon into blood, before that *g*	Acts 2:20	3173
with *g* power gave the apostles	Acts 4:33	3173
g grace was upon them all	Acts 4:33	3173
g fear came on all them that	Acts 5:5	3173
g fear came upon all the church,	Acts 5:11	3173
a *g* company of the priests were	Acts 6:7	4183
did *g* wonders and miracles among	Acts 6:8	3173
Egypt and Chanaan, and *g* affliction	Acts 7:11	3173
at that time there was a *g*	Acts 8:1	3173
made *g* lamentation over him	Acts 8:2	3173
there was *g* joy in that city	Acts 8:8	3173
out that himself was some *g* one	Acts 8:9	3173
This man is the *g* power of God	Acts 8:10	3173
an eunuch of *g* authority under	Acts 8:27	
For I will shew him how *g* things	Acts 9:16	3745
as it had been a *g* sheet knit at	Acts 10:11	3173
descend, as it had been a *g* sheet	Acts 11:5	3173
a *g* number believed, and turned	Acts 11:21	4183
g dearth throughout all the world	Acts 11:28	3173
that a *g* multitude both of the	Acts 14:1	4183
they caused *g* joy unto all the	Acts 15:3	3173
suddenly there was a *g* earthquake	Acts 16:26	3173
the devout Greeks a *g* multitude	Acts 17:4	4183
of the *g* goddess Diana should be	Acts 19:27	3173
G is Diana of the Ephesians	Acts 19:28	3173
G is Diana of the Ephesians	Acts 19:34	3173
worshipper of the *g* goddess Diana	Acts 19:35	3173
when there was made a *g* silence	Acts 21:40	4183
heaven a *g* light round about me	Acts 22:6	2425
With a *g* sum obtained I this	Acts 22:28	4183
And there arose a *g* cry	Acts 23:9	3173
when there arose a *g* dissension	Acts 23:10	4183
bound ourselves under a *g* curse	Acts 23:14	
that by thee we enjoy *g* quietness	Acts 24:2	4183
with *g* violence took him away out	Acts 24:7	4183
was come, and Bernice, with *g* pomp	Acts 25:23	4183
witnessing both to small and *g*	Acts 26:22	3173
after they had looked a *g* while	Acts 28:6	4183
had *g* reasoning among themselves	Acts 28:29	3173
That I have *g* heaviness and	Rom 9:2	3173
having a *g* desire these many	Rom 15:23	1974
is it a *g* thing if we shall reap	1Cor 9:11	3173
For a *g* door and effectual is	1Cor 16:9	3173
delivered us from so *g* a death	2Cor 1:10	5082
we use *g* plainness of speech	2Cor 3:12	4183
G is my boldness of speech toward	2Cor 7:4	4183
you, *g* is my glorying of you	2Cor 7:4	4183
How that in a *g* trial of	2Cor 8:2	4183
upon the *g* confidence which I	2Cor 8:22	4183
Therefore it is no *g* thing if his	2Cor 11:15	3173
for his *g* love wherewith he loved	Eph 2:4	4183
This is a *g* mystery	Eph 5:32	3173
what *g* conflict I have for you	Col 2:1	2245
that he hath a *g* zeal for you	Col 4:13	4183
to see your face with *g* desire	1Th 2:17	4183
g boldness in the faith which is	1Ti 3:13	4183
without controversy is the	1Ti 3:16	3173
with contentment is *g* gain	1Ti 6:6	3173
But in a *g* house there are not	2Ti 2:20	3173
glorious appearing of the *g* God	Titus 2:13	3173

For we have *g* joy and consolation	Philem 7	4183
if we neglect so *g* salvation	Heb 2:3	5082
then that we have a *g* high priest	Heb 4:14	3173
Now consider how *g* this man was	Heb 7:4	4080
ye endured a *g* fight of	Heb 10:32	4183
which hath *g* recompence of reward	Heb 10:35	3173
with so *g* a cloud of witnesses	Heb 12:1	5118
that *g* shepherd of the sheep,	Heb 13:20	3173
ships, which though they be so *g*	Jas 3:4	5082
member, and boasteth *g* things	Jas 3:5	3166
how *g* a matter a little fire	Jas 3:5	2245
is in the sight of God of *g* price	1Pet 3:4	4185
are given unto us exceeding *g*	2Pet 1:4	3176
For when they speak *g* swelling	2Pet 2:18	5246
shall pass away with a *g* noise	2Pet 3:10	3173
unto the judgment of the *g* day	Jude 6	3173
mouth speaketh *g* swelling words	Jude 16	5246
day, and heard behind me a *g* voice	Rev 1:10	3173
with her into *g* tribulation	Rev 2:22	3173
was given unto him a *g* sword	Rev 6:4	3173
and, lo, there was a *g* earthquake	Rev 6:12	3173
kings of the earth, and the *g* men	Rev 6:15	3175
For the *g* day of his wrath is	Rev 6:17	3173
a *g* multitude, which no man could	Rev 7:9	4183
which came out of *g* tribulation	Rev 7:14	3173
as it were a *g* mountain burning	Rev 8:8	3173
there fell a *g* star from heaven,	Rev 8:10	3173
pit, as the smoke of a *g* furnace	Rev 9:2	3173
bound in the *g* river Euphrates	Rev 9:14	3173
lie in the street of the *g* city	Rev 11:8	3173
g fear fell upon them which saw	Rev 11:11	3173
they heard a *g* voice from heaven	Rev 11:12	3173
hour was there a *g* earthquake	Rev 11:13	3173
there were *g* voices in heaven,	Rev 11:15	3173
hast taken to thee thy *g* power	Rev 11:17	3173
that fear thy name, small and *g*	Rev 11:18	3173
and an earthquake, and *g* hail	Rev 11:19	3173
appeared a *g* wonder in heaven	Rev 12:1	3173
behold a *g* red dragon, having	Rev 12:3	3173
the *g* dragon was cast out, that	Rev 12:9	3173
down unto you, having *g* wrath	Rev 12:12	3173
were given two wings of a *g* eagle	Rev 12:14	3173
and his seat, and *g* authority	Rev 13:2	3173
him a mouth speaking *g* things	Rev 13:5	3173
And he doeth *g* wonders, so that he	Rev 13:13	3173
he causeth all, both small and *g*	Rev 13:16	3173
and as the voice of a *g* thunder	Rev 14:2	3173
is fallen, is fallen, that *g* city	Rev 14:8	3173
cast it into the *g* winepress of	Rev 14:19	3173
I saw another sign in heaven, *g*	Rev 15:1	3173
the song of the Lamb, saying, *G*	Rev 15:3	3173
I heard a *g* voice out of the	Rev 16:1	3173
And men were scorched with *g* heat	Rev 16:9	3173
vial upon the *g* river Euphrates	Rev 16:12	3173
of that *g* day of God Almighty	Rev 16:14	3173
there came a *g* voice out of the	Rev 16:17	3173
and there was a *g* earthquake	Rev 16:18	3173
so mighty an earthquake, and so *g*	Rev 16:18	3173
the *g* city was divided into three	Rev 16:19	3173
g Babylon came in remembrance	Rev 16:19	3173
upon men a *g* hail out of heaven	Rev 16:21	3173
plague thereof was exceeding *g*	Rev 16:21	3173
g whore that sitteth upon many	Rev 17:1	3173
written, MYSTERY, BABYLON THE *G*	Rev 17:5	3173
her, I wondered with *g* admiration	Rev 17:6	3173
which thou sawest is that *g* city	Rev 17:18	3173
down from heaven, having *g* power	Rev 18:1	3173
saying, Babylon the *g* is fallen	Rev 18:2	3173
alas that *g* city Babylon, that	Rev 18:10	3173
And saying, Alas, alas that *g* city	Rev 18:16	3173
For in one hour so *g* riches is	Rev 18:17	5118
city is like unto this *g* city	Rev 18:18	4183
saying, Alas, alas that *g* city	Rev 18:19	3173
up a stone like a *g* millstone	Rev 18:21	3173
g city Babylon be thrown down	Rev 18:21	3173
were the *g* men of the earth	Rev 18:23	3175
after these things I heard a *g*	Rev 19:1	3173
for he hath judged the *g* whore	Rev 19:2	3173
ye that fear him, both small and *g*	Rev 19:5	3173
were the voice of a *g* multitude	Rev 19:6	4185
unto the supper of the *g* God	Rev 19:17	3173
free and bond, both small and *g*	Rev 19:18	3173
pit and a *g* chain in his hand	Rev 20:1	3173
I saw a *g* white throne, and him	Rev 20:11	3173
And I saw the dead, small and *g*	Rev 20:12	3173
I heard a *g* voice out of heaven	Rev 21:3	3173
me away in the spirit to a *g*	Rev 21:10	3173
and shewed me that *g* city	Rev 21:10	3173
And had a wall *g* and high, and had	Rev 21:12	3173

GREATER See APPENDIX.

GREATEST See APPENDIX.

GREATLY See APPENDIX.

GREATNESS See APPENDIX.

GREAVES
he had *g* of brass upon his legs, ...1Sa 17:6 4697

GRECIA See GRECIANS, GREECE. *Latin form of Greece.*
the rough goat is the king of *G* ....Dan 8:21 3120
lo, the prince of *G* shall come.................Dan 10:20 3120
up all against the realm of *G*...................Dan 11:2 3120

GRECIANS See GREEKS.
1. Inhabitants of Greece.
Jerusalem have ye sold unto the *G* ....Joel 3:6 3125
2. Hellenistic Jews.
of the *G* against the Hebrews ....Acts 6:1 1675
Jesus, and disputed against the *G* ....Acts 9:29 1675
come to Antioch, spake unto the *G*..........Acts 11:20 1675

GREECE See GRECIA. *Peninsula south of the Balkans.*
O Zion, against thy sons, O *G*.................Zec 9:13 3120
much exhortation, he came into *G* ....Acts 20:2 1671

GREEDILY
He coveteth *g* all the day long................Prov 21:26 8378
thou hast *g* gained of thy ....Eze 22:12
ran *g* after the error of Balaam ....Jude 11 1632

GREEDINESS
to work all uncleanness with *g* ....Eph 4:19 4124

GREEDY
as a lion that is *g* of his prey..................Ps 17:12 3700
of every one that is *g* of gain.................Prov 1:19 1214
He that is *g* of gain troubleth................Prov 15:27 1214
they are *g* dogs which can never ....Is 56:11 5794,5315
no striker, not *g* of filthy lucre 1Ti 3:3 866
much wine, not *g* of filthy lucre 1Ti 3:8 146

GREEK See GREEKS.
1. A native of Greece.
written over him in letters of *G*..............Lk 23:38 1673
and it was written in Hebrew, and *G*......Jn 19:20 1676
but his father was a *G* ....Acts 16:1 1672
knew all that his father was a *G* ....Acts 16:3 1672
the Jew first, and also to the *G* ....Rom 1:16 1672
between the Jew and the *G* ....Rom 10:12 1672
Titus, who was with me, being a *G*........Gal 2:3 1672
There is neither Jew nor *G* ....Gal 3:28 1672
Where there is neither *G* nor Jew ....Col 3:11 1672
2. A language.
Who said, Canst thou speak *G* ....Acts 21:37 1676
but in the *G* tongue hath his name........Rev 9:11 1673
3. A female.
The woman was a *G*, a ....Mk 7:26 1674

GREEKS See GRECIANS. *Plural of Greek 1.*
there were certain *G* among them ....Jn 12:20 1672
Jews and also of the *G* believed.............Acts 14:1 1672
of the devout *G* a great multitude ....Acts 17:4 1672
of honourable women which were *G* ....Acts 17:12 1674
and persuaded the Jews and the *G* ....Acts 18:4 1672
Then all the *G* took Sosthenes ....Acts 18:17 1672
of the Lord Jesus, both Jews and *G*........Acts 19:10 1672
G also dwelling at Ephesus ....Acts 19:17 1672
to the Jews, and also to the *G* ....Acts 20:21 1672
further brought *G* also into the ....Acts 21:28 1672
I am debtor both to the *G* ....Rom 1:14 1672
sign, and the *G* seek after wisdom 1Cor 1:22 1672
and unto the *G* foolishness....................1Cor 1:23 1672
which are called, both Jews and *G*..........1Cor 1:24 1672

GREEN
have given every *g* herb for meat ....Gen 1:30 3418
even as the *g* herb have I given ....Gen 9:3 3418
Jacob took him rods of *g* poplar ....Gen 30:37 3892
not any *g* thing in the trees...................Ex 10:15 3418
offering of thy firstfruits *g*....................Lev 2:14
nor *g* ears, until the selfsame................Lev 23:14
the hills, and under every *g* tree ....Deut 12:2 7488
If they bind me with seven *g* ....Judg 16:7 3892
brought up to her seven *g* withs ....Judg 16:8 3892
high hill, and under every *g* tree 1Kin 14:23 7488
the hills, and under every *g* tree 2Kin 16:4 7488
high hill, and under every *g* tree............2Kin 17:10 7488
of the field, and as the *g* herb 2Kin 19:26 3410
the hills, and under every *g* tree 2Chr 28:4 7488
Where were white, *g*, and blue, ...Est 1:6 3768
He is *g* before the sun, and his...............Job 8:16 7373
and his branch shall not be *g* ....Job 15:32 7488
he searcheth after every *g* thing ....Job 39:8 3387

---

me to lie down in *g* pastures ....Ps 23:2 1877
grass, and wither as the *g* herb ....Ps 37:2 3418
himself like a *g* bay tree.......................Ps 37:35 7488
But I am like a *g* olive tree in ....Ps 52:8 7488
also our bed is *g*.................................Song 1:16 7488
fig tree putteth forth her *g* figs ....Song 2:13 6291
faileth, there is no *g* thing ....Is 15:6 3418
of the field, and as the *g* herb ....Is 37:27 3419
with idols under every *g* tree ....Is 57:5 7488
under every *g* tree thou wanderest ....Jer 2:20 7488
mountain and under every *g* tree ....Jer 3:6 7488
the strangers under every *g* tree ....Jer 3:13 7488
A *g* olive tree, fair, and of ....Jer 11:16 7488
their groves by the *g* trees upon ....Jer 17:2 7488
cometh, but her leaf shall be *g*...............Jer 17:8 7488
mountains, and under every *g* tree ....Eze 6:13 7488
tree, have dried up the *g* trees...............Eze 17:24 3892
shall devour every *g* tree in thee ....Eze 20:47 3892
I am like a *g* fir tree............................Hos 14:8 7488
by companies upon the *g* grass ....Mk 6:39 5515
they do these things in a *g* tree............Lk 23:31 5200
up, and all *g* grass was burnt up ....Rev 8:7 5515
of the earth, neither any *g* thing ....Rev 9:4 5515

GREENISH
if the plague be *g* or reddish in ....Lev 13:49 3422
g or reddish, which in sight are.............Lev 14:37 3422

GREENNESS
Whilst it is yet in his *g* ....Job 8:12 3

GREET
go to Nabal, and *g* him...................1Sa 25:5 7592,7965
G Priscilla and Aquila my helpers ....Rom 16:3 782
Likewise *g* the church that is in ....Rom 16:5
G Mary, who bestowed much labour ....Rom 16:6 782
G Amplias my beloved in the Lord ....Rom 16:8 782
G them that be of the household............Rom 16:11 782
All the brethren *g* you 1Cor 16:20 782
G ye one another with an holy 1Cor 16:20 782
G one another with an holy kiss 2Cor 13:12 782
brethren which are with me *g* you ....Phil 4:21 782
physician, and Demas, *g* you ....Col 4:14 782
G all the brethren with an holy 1Th 5:26 782
G them that love us in the faith ....Titus 3:15 782
G ye one another with a kiss of 1Pet 5:14 782
of thy elect sister *g* thee 2Jn 13 782
G the friends by name 3Jn 14 782

GREETETH
Eubulus *g* thee, and Pudens, and............2Ti 4:21 782

GREETING
brethren send *g* unto the brethren ....Acts 15:23 5463
governor Felix sendeth *g*.....................Acts 23:26 5463
which are scattered abroad, *g* ....Jas 1:1 5463

GREETINGS
g in the markets, and to be called .... Mt 23:7 783
synagogues, and *g* in the markets.....Lk 11:43 783
love *g* in the markets, and the..............Lk 20:46 783

GREW
herb of the field before it *g* ....Gen 2:5 6779
that which *g* upon the ground ....Gen 19:25 6780
And the child *g*, and was weaned ....Gen 21:8 1431
and he *g*, and dwelt in the ....Gen 21:20 1431
And the boys *g* ....Gen 25:27 1431
g until he became very great ....Gen 26:13 1432
had possessions therein, and *g* ....Gen 47:27 6509
the more they multiplied and *g* ....Ex 1:12 6555
And the child *g*, and she brought............Ex 2:10 1431
and his wife's sons *g* up, and they ....Judg 11:2 1431
and the child *g*, and the LORD ....Judg 13:24 1431
child Samuel *g* before the LORD 1Sa 2:21 1431
And the child Samuel *g* on, and was ..1Sa 2:26 1432
And Samuel *g*, and the LORD was with ..1Sa 3:19 1431
g great, and the LORD God of hosts 2Sa 5:10
it *g* up together with him, and 2Sa 12:3 1431
And it *g*, and became a spreading..........Eze 17:6 6779
wither in the furrows where it *g* ....Eze 17:10 6780
The tree *g*, and was strong, and the ......Dan 4:11 7236
tree that thou sawest, which *g* ....Dan 4:20 7236
among thorns, and the thorns *g* up......Mk 4:7 305
bettered, but rather *g* worse..................Mk 5:26 2064
And the child *g*, and waxed strong ....Lk 1:80 837
And the child *g*, and waxed strong ....Lk 2:40 837
and it *g*, and waxed a great tree ....Lk 13:19 837
sworn to Abraham, the people *g*............Acts 7:17 837
But the word of God *g* and ....Acts 12:24 837
So mightily *g* the word of God and........Acts 19:20 837

G

GREY
beauty of old men is the *g* head .... Prov 20:29   7872

GREYHEADED
Now also when I am old and *g* .... Ps 71:18   7872

GREYHOUND
A *g*; an he goat also; and a .... Prov 30:31   2223,4975

GRIEF
Which were a *g* of mind unto Isaac .... Gen 26:35   4786
and *g* have I spoken hitherto................. 1Sa 1:16   3708
That this shall be no *g* unto thee 1Sa 25:31   6330
know his own sore and his own *g* 2Chr 6:29   4341
saw that his *g* was very great .... Job 2:13   3511
O that my *g* were throughly .... Job 6:2   3708
of my lips should assuage your *g* .... Job 16:5   4834
I speak, my *g* is not asswaged .... Job 16:6   3511
Mine eye is consumed because of *g* .... Ps 6:7   3708
mine eye is consumed with *g* .... Ps 31:9   3708
For my life is spent with *g* .... Ps 31:10   3015
they talk to the *g* of those whom .... Ps 69:26   4341
foolish son is a *g* to his father .... Prov 17:25   3708
For in much wisdom is much *g* .... Eccl 1:18   3708
are sorrows, and his travail *g* .... Eccl 2:23   3708
shall be a heap in the day of *g* .... Is 17:11   2470
of sorrows, and acquainted with *g* .... Is 53:3   2483
he hath put him to *g* .... Is 53:10   2470
before me continually is *g* .... Jer 6:7   2483
but I said, Truly this is a *g* .... Jer 10:19   2483
LORD hath added *g* to my sorrow .... Jer 45:3   3015
But though he cause *g*, yet will .... Lam 3:32   3013
head, to deliver him from his *g* .... Jonah 4:6   7451
But if any have caused *g*, he hath 2Cor 2:5   *3076*
may do it with joy, and not with *g* .... Heb 13:17   *4727*
conscience toward God endure *g* 1Pet 2:19   *3077*

GRIEFS
Surely he hath borne our *g* .... Is 53:4   2483

GRIEVANCE
iniquity, and cause me to behold *g* .... Hab 1:3   5999

GRIEVE
thine eyes, and to *g* thine heart 1Sa 2:33   109
from evil, that it may not *g* me 1Chr 4:10   6087
and *g* him in the desert .... Ps 78:40   6087
nor *g* the children of men .... Lam 3:33   3013
g not the holy Spirit of God, ... Eph 4:30   *3076*

GRIEVED
earth, and it *g* him at his heart .... Gen 6:6   6087
and the men were *g*, and they were .... Gen 34:7   6087
Now therefore be not *g*, nor angry......... Gen 45:5   6087
The archers have sorely *g* him .... Gen 49:23   4843
they were *g* because of the .... Ex 1:12   6973
thine heart shall not be *g* when .... Deut 15:10   7489
his soul was *g* for the misery of .... Judg 10:16   7114
and why is thy heart *g*........................ 1Sa 1:8   7489
And it *g* Samuel 1Sa 15:11   2734
Jonathan know this, lest he be *g* 1Sa 20:3   6087
for he was *g* for David, because 1Sa 20:34   6087
the soul of all the people was *g* 1Sa 30:6   4784
how the king was *g* for his son 2Sa 19:2   6087
it *g* them exceedingly that there .... Neh 2:10   7489
neither be *g* .... Neh 8:11   6087
And it *g* me sore .... Neh 13:8   7489
Then was the queen exceedingly *g* .... Est 4:4   2342
commune with thee, wilt thou be *g*......... Job 4:2   3811
was not my soul *g* for the poor .... Job 30:25   5701
Thus my heart was *g*, and I was........... Ps 73:21   2556
long was I *g* with this generation .... Ps 95:10   6962
The wicked shall see it, and be *g*.......... Ps 112:10   3707
the transgressors, and was *g* .... Ps 119:158   6962
am not I *g* with those that rise .... Ps 139:21   6962
g in spirit, and a wife of youth, ... Is 54:6   6087
therefore thou wast not *g* .... Is 57:10   2470
them, but they have not *g* .... Jer 5:3   2342
I Daniel was *g* in my spirit in .... Dan 7:15   3735
therefore he shall be *g*, and .... Dan 11:30   3512
but they are not *g* for the .... Amos 6:6   2470
being *g* for the hardness of their .... Mk 3:5   *4818*
at that saying, and went away *g* .... Mk 10:22   *3076*
Peter was *g* because he said unto .... Jn 21:17   *3076*
Being *g* that they taught the .... Acts 4:2   *1278*
But Paul, being *g*, turned and said .... Acts 16:18   *1278*
if thy brother be *g* with thy meat.......... Rom 14:15   *3076*
not that ye should be *g*, but that........... 2Cor 2:4   *3076*
caused grief, he hath not *g* me 2Cor 2:5   *3076*
Wherefore I was *g* with that .... Heb 3:10   *4360*
with whom was he *g* forty years .... Heb 3:17   *4360*

GRIEVETH
for it *g* me much for your sakes .... Ruth 1:13   4843
it *g* him to bring it again to his............ Prov 26:15   3811

GRIEVING
nor any *g* thorn of all that are .... Eze 28:24   3510

GRIEVOUS
for the famine was *g* in the land .... Gen 12:10   3515
and because their sin is very *g* .... Gen 18:20   3513
the thing was very *g* in Abraham's .... Gen 21:11   7489
Let it not be *g* in thy sight .... Gen 21:12   7489
for it shall be very *g* .... Gen 41:31   3515
This is a *g* mourning to the .... Gen 50:11   3515
there came a *g* swarm of flies .... Ex 8:24   3515
there shall be a very *g* murrain .... Ex 9:3   3515
cause it to rain a very *g* hail .... Ex 9:18   3515
mingled with the hail, very *g* .... Ex 9:24   3515
very *g* were they .... Ex 10:14   3515
which cursed me with a *g* curse in........ 1Kin 2:8   4834
Thy father made our yoke *g* 1Kin 12:4   7185
thou the *g* service of thy father 1Kin 12:4   7186
Thy father made our yoke *g* 2Chr 10:4   7185
ease thou somewhat the *g* 2Chr 10:4   7186
His ways are always *g* .... Ps 10:5   2342
which speak *g* things proudly and........ Ps 31:18   6277
but *g* words stir up anger .... Prov 15:1   6089
Correction is *g* unto him that............... Prov 15:10   7451
under the sun is *g* unto me.................. Eccl 2:17   7451
his life shall be *g* unto him .... Is 15:4   3415
A *g* vision is declared unto me.............. Is 21:2   7186
They are all *g* revolters, walking.......... Jer 6:28   5493
my wound is *g* .... Jer 10:19   2470
great breach, with a very *g* blow .... Jer 14:17   2470
They shall die of *g* deaths .... Jer 16:4   8463
forth in fury, even a *g* whirlwind .... Jer 23:19   2342
is incurable, and thy wound is *g* .... Jer 30:12   2470
thy wound is *g* .... Nah 3:19   2470
g* to be borne, and lay them on .... Mt 23:4   *1418*
men with burdens *g* to be borne .... Lk 11:46   *1418*
shall *g* wolves enter in among you .... Acts 20:29   *926*
g complaints against Paul, which .... Acts 25:7   *926*
to you, to me indeed is not *g* .... Phil 3:1   *3636*
seemeth to be joyous, but *g*................. Heb 12:11   *3077*
and his commandments are not *g* 1Jn 5:3   *926*
g sore upon the men which had the .... Rev 16:2   *4190*

GRIEVOUSLY
afterward did more *g* afflict her .... Is 9:1   3513
it shall fall *g* upon the head of .... Jer 23:19   2342
Jerusalem hath *g* sinned .... Lam 1:8   2399
for I have *g* rebelled .... Lam 1:20   4784
against me by trespassing *g* .... Eze 14:13   4604
sick of the palsy, *g* tormented .... Mt 8:6   *1171*
my daughter is *g* vexed with a .... Mt 15:22   *2560*

GRIEVOUSNESS
that write *g* which they have................ Is 10:1   5999
bent bow, and from the *g* of war .... Is 21:15   3514

GRIND
he did *g* in the prison house .... Judg 16:21   2912
Then let my wife *g* unto another............ Job 31:10   2912
and *g* the faces of the poor.................. Is 3:15   2912
Take the millstones, and *g* meal........... Is 47:2   2912
They took the young men to *g* .... Lam 5:13   2911
fall, it will *g* him to powder .... Mt 21:44   *3039*
fall, it will *g* him to powder .... Lk 20:18   *3039*

GRINDERS
the *g* cease because they are few,.......... Eccl 12:3   2912

GRINDING
when the sound of the *g* is low .... Eccl 12:4   2913
Two women shall be *g* at the mill...... Mt 24:41   *229*
Two women shall be *g* together.......... Lk 17:35   *229*

GRISLED
were ringstraked, speckled, and *g* .... Gen 31:10   1261
are ringstraked, speckled, and *g* .... Gen 31:12   1261
and in the fourth chariot *g* .... Zec 6:3   1261
the *g* go forth toward the south .... Zec 6:6   1261

GROAN
Men *g* from out of the city, and............ Job 24:12   5008
all her land the wounded shall *g*........... Jer 51:52   602
he shall *g* before him with the .... Eze 30:24   5008
How do the beasts *g* .... Joel 1:18   584
we ourselves *g* within ourselves .... Rom 8:23   *4727*
For in this we *g*, earnestly 2Cor 5:2   *4727*
that are in this tabernacle do *g* 2Cor 5:4   *4727*

GROANED
he *g* in the spirit, and was .... Jn 11:33   *1690*

GROANETH
we know that the whole creation *g* .... Rom 8:22   *4959*

GROANING
And God heard their *g*, and God .... Ex 2:24   5009

I have also heard the *g* of the	Ex 6:5	5009
my stroke is heavier than my *g*	Job 23:2	585
I am weary with my *g*	Ps 6:6	585
my *g* is not hid from thee	Ps 38:9	585
my *g* my bones cleave to my skin	Ps 102:5	585
To hear the *g* of the prisoner	Ps 102:20	603
Jesus therefore again *g* in	Jn 11:38	1690
in Egypt, and I have heard their *g*	Acts 7:34	4726

GROANINGS

of their *g* by reason of them that	Judg 2:18	5009
the *g* of a deadly wounded man	Eze 30:24	5009
us with *g* which cannot be uttered	Rom 8:26	4726

GROPE

And thou shalt *g* at noonday	Deut 28:29	4959
g in the noonday as in the night	Job 5:14	4959
They *g* in the dark without light,	Job 12:25	4959
We *g* for the wall like the blind,	Is 59:10	1659
we *g* as if we had no eyes	Is 59:10	1659

GROPETH

as the blind *g* in darkness	Deut 28:29	4959

GROSS

earth, and *g* darkness the people	Is 60:2	6205
of death, and make it *g* darkness	Jer 13:16	6205
this people's heart is waxed *g*	Mt 13:15	3975
heart of this people is waxed *g*	Acts 28:27	3975

GROUND

there was not a man to till the *g*	Gen 2:5	127
watered the whole face of the *g*	Gen 2:6	127
formed man of the dust of the *g*	Gen 2:7	127
out of the *g* made the LORD God to	Gen 2:9	127
out of the *g* the LORD God formed	Gen 2:19	127
cursed is the *g* for thy sake	Gen 3:17	127
till thou return unto the *g*	Gen 3:19	127
to till the *g* from whence he was	Gen 3:23	127
but Cain was a tiller of the *g*	Gen 4:2	127
the *g* an offering unto the LORD	Gen 4:3	127
blood crieth unto me from the *g*	Gen 4:10	127
When thou tillest the *g*, it shall	Gen 4:12	127
because of the *g* which the LORD	Gen 5:29	127
which was upon the face of the *g*	Gen 7:23	127
abated from off the face of the *g*	Gen 8:8	127
behold, the face of the *g* was dry	Gen 8:13	127
the *g* any more for man's sake,	Gen 8:21	127
and bowed himself toward the *g*	Gen 18:2	776
with his face toward the *g*	Gen 19:1	776
and that which grew upon the *g*	Gen 19:25	127
himself to the *g* seven times	Gen 33:3	776
wife, that he spilled it on the *g*	Gen 38:9	776
down every man his sack to the *g*	Gen 44:11	776
and they fell before him on the *g*	Gen 44:14	776
whereon thou standest is holy *g*	Ex 3:5	127
And he said, Cast it on the *g*	Ex 4:3	776
And he cast it on the *g*, and it	Ex 4:3	776
also the *g* whereon they are	Ex 8:21	127
and the fire ran along upon the *g*	Ex 9:23	776
of Israel shall go on dry *g*	Ex 14:16	
midst of the sea upon the dry *g*	Ex 14:22	
small as the hoar frost on the *g*	Ex 16:14	776
g it to powder, and strawed it	Ex 32:20	2912
thing that creepeth on the *g*	Lev 20:25	127
g it in mills, or beat it in a	Num 11:8	2912
that the *g* clave asunder that was	Num 16:31	127
any thing that creepeth on the *g*	Deut 4:18	127
g it very small, even until it	Deut 9:21	2912
shalt pour it upon the *g* as water	Deut 15:23	776
the way in any tree, or on the *g*	Deut 22:6	776
thy body, and the fruit of thy *g*	Deut 28:4	127
cattle, and in the fruit of thy *g*	Deut 28:11	127
foot upon the *g* for delicateness	Deut 28:56	776
on dry *g* in the midst of Jordan	Josh 3:17	
Israelites passed over on dry *g*	Josh 3:17	
in a parcel of *g* which Jacob	Josh 24:32	7704
and fastened it into the *g*	Judg 4:21	776
upon all the *g* let there be dew	Judg 6:39	
and there was dew on all the *g*	Judg 6:40	776
and fell on their faces to the *g*	Judg 13:20	776
destroyed down to the *g* of the	Judg 20:21	776
destroyed down to the *g* of the	Judg 20:25	776
face, and bowed herself to the *g*	Ruth 2:10	776
none of his words fall to the *g*	1Sa 3:19	776
the *g* before the ark of the LORD	1Sa 5:4	776
and will set them to ear his *g*	1Sa 8:12	2758
and there was honey upon the *g*	1Sa 14:25	7704
and calves, and slew them on the *g*	1Sa 14:32	776
hair of his head fall to the *g*	1Sa 14:45	776
son of Jesse liveth upon the *g*	1Sa 20:31	127
and fell on his face to the *g*	1Sa 20:41	776

face, and bowed herself to the *g*	1Sa 25:23	776
stuck in the *g* at his bolster	1Sa 26:7	776
he stooped with his face to the *g*	1Sa 28:14	776
should I smite thee to the *g*	2Sa 2:22	776
line, casting them down to the *g*	2Sa 8:2	776
she fell on her face to the *g*	2Sa 14:4	776
and are as water spilt on the *g*	2Sa 14:14	776
And Joab fell to the *g* on his face	2Sa 14:22	776
his face to the *g* before the king	2Sa 14:33	776
him as the dew falleth on the *g*	2Sa 17:12	127
mouth, and spread *g* corn thereon	2Sa 17:19	7383
thou not smite him there to the *g*	2Sa 18:11	776
and shed out his bowels to the *g*	2Sa 20:10	776
was a piece of *g* full of lentiles	2Sa 23:11	7704
he stood in the midst of the *g*	2Sa 23:12	2513
the king on his face upon the *g*	2Sa 24:20	776
the king with his face to the *g*	1Kin 1:23	776
in the clay *g* between Succoth and	1Kin 7:46	127
that they two went over on dry *g*	2Kin 2:8	
themselves to the *g* before him	2Kin 2:15	776
water is naught, and the *g* barren	2Kin 2:19	776
feet, and bowed herself to the *g*	2Kin 4:37	776
and cast him into the plat of *g*	2Kin 9:26	
king of Israel, Smite upon the *g*	2Kin 13:18	776
was a parcel of *g* full of barley	1Chr 11:13	7704
to David with his face to the *g*	1Chr 21:21	776
the *g* was Ezri the son of Chelub	1Chr 27:26	127
in the clay *g* between Succoth and	2Chr 4:17	127
faces to the *g* upon the pavement	2Chr 7:3	776
his head with his face to the *g*	2Chr 20:18	776
LORD with their faces to the *g*	Neh 8:6	776
to bring the firstfruits of our *g*	Neh 10:35	127
tithes of our *g* unto the Levites	Neh 10:37	127
his head, and fell down upon the *g*	Job 1:20	776
with him upon the *g* seven days	Job 2:13	776
doth trouble spring out of the *g*	Job 5:6	127
and the stock thereof die in the *g*	Job 14:8	6083
he poureth out my gall upon the *g*	Job 16:13	776
snare is laid for him in the *g*	Job 18:10	776
satisfy the desolate and waste *g*	Job 38:27	
swalloweth the *g* with fierceness	Job 39:24	776
place of thy name to the *g*	Ps 74:7	776
his crown by casting it to the *g*	Ps 89:39	776
and cast his throne down to the *g*	Ps 89:44	776
and devoured the fruit of their *g*	Ps 105:35	127
and the watersprings into dry *g*	Ps 107:33	
water, and dry *g* into watersprings	Ps 107:35	127
smitten my life down to the *g*	Ps 143:3	776
casteth the wicked down to the *g*	Ps 147:6	776
desolate shall sit upon the *g*	Is 3:26	776
how art thou cut down to the *g*	Is 14:12	776
gods he hath broken unto the *g*	Is 21:9	776
down, lay low, and bring to the *g*	Is 25:12	776
he layeth it low, even to the *g*	Is 26:5	776
open and break the clods of his *g*	Is 28:24	127
down, and shalt speak out of the *g*	Is 29:4	776
a familiar spirit, out of the *g*	Is 29:4	776
that thou shalt sow the *g* withal	Is 30:23	127
the *g* shall eat clean provender	Is 30:24	127
the parched *g* shall become a pool	Is 35:7	
thirsty, and floods upon the dry *g*	Is 44:3	
daughter of Babylon, sit on the *g*	Is 47:1	776
thou hast laid thy body as the *g*	Is 51:23	776
and as a root out of a dry *g*	Is 53:2	776
Jerusalem, Break up your fallow *g*	Jer 4:3	
field, and upon the fruit of the *g*	Jer 7:20	127
they are black unto the *g*	Jer 14:2	776
Because the *g* is chapt, for there	Jer 14:4	127
they shall be dung upon the *g*	Jer 25:33	127
and the beast that are upon the *g*	Jer 27:5	776
hath brought them down to the *g*	Lam 2:2	776
Her gates are sunk into the *g*	Lam 2:9	776
daughter of Zion sit upon the *g*	Lam 2:10	776
hang down their heads to the *g*	Lam 2:10	776
old lie on the *g* in the streets	Lam 2:21	776
thy face, that thou see not the *g*	Eze 12:6	776
he see not the *g* with his eyes	Eze 12:12	776
morter, and bring it down to the *g*	Eze 13:14	776
fury, she was cast down to the *g*	Eze 19:12	776
wilderness, in a dry and thirsty *g*	Eze 19:13	776
she poured it not upon the *g*	Eze 24:7	776
garrisons shall go down to the *g*	Eze 26:11	776
they shall sit upon the *g*	Eze 26:16	776
I will cast thee to the *g*	Eze 28:17	776
and every wall shall fall to the *g*	Eze 38:20	776
from the *g* up to the windows, and	Eze 41:16	776
From the *g* unto above the door	Eze 41:20	776
and the middlemost from the *g*	Eze 42:6	776
from the bottom upon the *g* even	Eze 43:14	776
whole earth, and touched not the *g*	Dan 8:5	776

G

but he cast him down to the *g*	Dan 8:7	776
the host and of the stars to the *g*	Dan 8:10	776
it cast down the truth to the *g*	Dan 8:12	776
sleep on my face toward the *g*	Dan 8:18	776
my face, and my face toward the *g*	Dan 10:9	776
me, I set my face toward the *g*	Dan 10:15	776
with the creeping things of the *g*	Hos 2:18	127
break up your fallow *g*	Hos 10:12	
be cut off, and fall to the *g*	Amos 3:14	776
Who shall bring me down to the *g*	Obad 3	776
that which the *g* bringeth forth	Hag 1:11	127
the *g* shall give her increase, and	Zec 8:12	776
not destroy the fruits of your *g*	Mal 3:11	127
fall on the *g* without your Father	Mt 10:29	1093
But other fell into good *g*	Mt 13:8	1093
***g* is he that heareth the word**	Mt 13:23	1093
multitude to sit down on the *g*	Mt 15:35	1093
And some fell on stony *g*, where it	Mk 4:5	
And other fell on good *g*, and did	Mk 4:8	1093
which are sown on stony *g*	Mk 4:16	
are they which are sown on good *g*	Mk 4:20	1093
a man should cast seed into the *g*	Mk 4:26	1093
the people to sit down on the *g*	Mk 8:6	1093
and he fell on the *g*, and wallowed	Mk 9:20	1093
a little, and fell on the *g*	Mk 14:35	1093
And other fell on good *g*, and	Lk 8:8	1093
But that on the good *g* are they	Lk 8:15	1093
The *g* of a certain rich man	Lk 12:16	5561
why cumbereth it the *g*	Lk 13:7	1093
him, I have bought a piece of *g*	Lk 14:18	68
And shall lay thee even with the *g*	Lk 19:44	1474
of blood falling down to the *g*	Lk 22:44	1093
near to the parcel of *g* that	Jn 4:5	5564
and with his finger wrote on the *g*	Jn 8:6	1093
stooped down, and wrote on the *g*	Jn 8:8	1093
had thus spoken, he spat on the *g*	Jn 9:6	5476
a corn of wheat fall into the *g*	Jn 12:24	1093
went backward, and fell to the *g*	Jn 18:6	5476
where thou standest is holy *g*	Acts 7:33	1093
And I fell unto the *g*, and heard a	Acts 22:7	1475
God, the pillar and *g* of the truth	1Ti 3:15	1477

GROUNDED

where the *g* staff shall pass	Is 30:32	4145
ye, being rooted and *g* in love,	Eph 3:17	2311
If ye continue in the faith *g*	Col 1:23	2311

GROVE

Abraham planted a *g* in Beer-sheba	Gen 21:33	815
a *g* of any trees near unto the	Deut 16:21	842
cut down the *g* that is by it	Judg 6:25	842
the *g* which thou shalt cut down	Judg 6:26	842
the *g* was cut down that was by it	Judg 6:28	842
cut down the *g* that was by it	Judg 6:30	842
she had made an idol in a *g*	1Kin 15:13	842
And Ahab made a *g*	1Kin 16:33	842
remained the *g* also in Samaria	2Kin 13:6	842
even two calves, and made a *g*	2Kin 17:16	842
up altars for Baal, and made a *g*	2Kin 21:3	842
he set a graven image of the *g*	2Kin 21:7	842
were made for Baal, and for the *g*	2Kin 23:4	842
he brought out the *g* from the	2Kin 23:6	842
the women wove hangings for the *g*	2Kin 23:7	842
small to powder, and burned the *g*	2Kin 23:15	842
she had made an idol in a *g*	2Chr 15:16	842

GROVES

their images, and cut down their *g*	Ex 34:13	842
their images, and cut down their *g*	Deut 7:5	842
and burn their *g* with fire	Deut 12:3	842
God, and served Baalim and the *g*	Judg 3:7	842
because they have made their *g*	1Kin 14:15	842
them high places, and images, and *g*	1Kin 14:23	842
prophets of the *g* four hundred	1Kin 18:19	842
g in every high hill, and under	2Kin 17:10	842
the images, and cut down the *g*	2Kin 18:4	842
the images, and cut down the *g*	2Kin 23:14	842
the images, and cut down the *g*	2Chr 14:3	842
the high places and *g* out of Judah	2Chr 17:6	842
taken away the *g* out of the land	2Chr 19:3	842
God of their fathers, and served *g*	2Chr 24:18	842
in pieces, and cut down the *g*	2Chr 31:1	842
up altars for Baalim, and made *g*	2Chr 33:3	842
he built high places, and set up *g*	2Chr 33:19	842
from the high places, and the *g*	2Chr 34:3	842
and the *g*, and the carved images,	2Chr 34:4	842
broken down the altars and the *g*	2Chr 34:7	842
fingers have made, either the *g*	Is 17:8	842
that are beaten in sunder, the *g*	Is 27:9	842
their *g* by the green trees upon	Jer 17:2	842
I will pluck up thy *g* out of the	Mic 5:14	842

GROW

g every tree that is pleasant to	Gen 2:9	6779
let them *g* into a multitude in	Gen 48:16	1711
locks of the hair of his head *g*	Num 6:5	1431
to *g* again after he was shaven	Judg 16:22	6779
although he make it not to *g*	2Sa 23:5	6779
such things as *g* of themselves	2Kin 19:29	5599
why should damage *g* to the hurt	Ezr 4:22	7680
Can the rush *g* up without mire	Job 8:11	1342
can the flag *g* without water	Job 8:11	6779
out of the earth shall others *g*	Job 8:19	6779
g out of the dust of the earth	Job 14:19	5599
Let thistles *g* instead of wheat,	Job 31:40	3318
good liking, they *g* up with corn	Job 39:4	7235
he shall *g* like a cedar in	Ps 92:12	7685
the grass to *g* for the cattle	Ps 104:14	6779
grass to *g* upon the mountains	Ps 147:8	6779
nor how the bones do *g* in the	Eccl 11:5	
a Branch shall *g* out of his roots	Is 11:1	6509
shalt thou make thy plant to *g*	Is 17:11	7735
For he shall *g* up before him as a	Is 53:2	5927
they *g*, yea, they bring forth	Jer 12:2	3212
righteousness to *g* up unto David	Jer 33:15	6779
nor suffer their locks to *g* long	Eze 44:20	7971
shall *g* all trees for meat, whose	Eze 47:12	5927
he shall *g* as the lily, and cast	Hos 14:5	6524
as the corn, and *g* as the vine	Hos 14:7	6524
not laboured, neither madest it *g*	Jonah 4:10	1431
he shall *g* up out of his place,	Zec 6:12	6779
g up as calves of the stall	Mal 4:2	6335
lilies of the field, how they *g*	Mt 6:28	837
Let both *g* together until the	Mt 13:30	4886
unto it, Let no fruit *g* on thee	Mt 21:19	1096
and *g* up, he knoweth not how	Mk 4:27	3373
Consider the lilies how they *g*	Lk 12:27	837
of them whereunto this would *g*	Acts 5:24	1096
may *g* up into him in all things,	Eph 4:15	837
the word, that ye may *g* thereby	1Pet 2:2	837
But *g* in grace, and in the	2Pet 3:18	837

GROWETH

which *g* for you out of the field	Ex 10:5	6779
freckled spot that *g* in the skin	Lev 13:39	6524
That which *g* of its own accord of	Lev 25:5	5599
reap that which *g* of itself in it	Lev 25:11	5599
beareth, nor any grass *g* therein	Deut 29:23	5927
the day *g* to an end, lodge here,	Judg 19:9	2583
When the dust *g* into hardness	Job 38:38	3332
they are like grass which *g* up	Ps 90:5	2498
morning it flourisheth, and *g* up	Ps 90:6	2498
which withereth afore it *g* up	Ps 129:6	8025
eat this year such as *g* of itself	Is 37:30	5599
But when it is sown, it *g* up	Mk 4:32	305
building fitly framed together *g*	Eph 2:21	837
that your faith *g* exceedingly	2Th 1:3	5232

GROWN

house, till Shelah my son be *g*	Gen 38:11	1431
for she saw that Shelah was *g*	Gen 38:14	1431
in those days, when Moses was *g*	Ex 2:11	1431
for they were not *g* up	Ex 9:32	648
there is black hair *g* up therein	Lev 13:37	6779
art waxen fat, thou art *g* thick	Deut 32:15	
tarry for them till they were *g*	Ruth 1:13	1431
at Jericho until your beards be *g*	2Sa 10:5	6779
young men that were *g* up with him	1Kin 12:8	1431
the young men that were *g* up with	1Kin 12:10	1431
And when the child was *g*, it fell	2Kin 4:18	1431
as corn blasted before it be *g* up	2Kin 19:26	6965
at Jericho until your beards be *g*	1Chr 19:5	6779
our trespass is *g* up unto the	Ezr 9:6	1431
be as plants *g* up in their youth	Ps 144:12	1431
it was all *g* over with thorns, and	Prov 24:31	5927
as corn blasted before it be *g* up	Is 37:27	6965
because ye are *g* fat as the	Jer 50:11	6335
are fashioned, and thine hair is *g*	Eze 16:7	6779
It is thou, O king, that art *g*	Dan 4:22	7236
for thy greatness is *g*, and	Dan 4:22	7236
till his hairs were *g* like	Dan 4:33	7236
but when it is *g*, it is the	Mt 13:32	837

GROWTH

the shooting up of the latter *g*	Amos 7:1	3954
it was the latter *g* after the	Amos 7:1	3954

GRUDGE

nor bear any *g* against the	Lev 19:18	5201
g if they be not satisfied	Ps 59:15	3885
G not one against another,	Jas 5:9	4727

GRUDGING

one to another without *g* 1Pet 4:9   *1112*

GRUDGINGLY

not *g*, or of necessity 2Cor 9:7   *1537,3077*

GUARD

of Pharaoh's, and captain of the *g* ....Gen 37:36 2876
of Pharaoh, captain of the *g* ....Gen 39:1 2876
the house of the captain of the *g* ....Gen 40:3 2876
the captain of the *g* charged ....Gen 40:4 2876
servant to the captain of the *g* ....Gen 41:12 2876
And David set him over his *g* 2Sa 23:23 4928
the hands of the chief of the *g* 1Kin 14:27 7323
that the *g* bare them, and brought 1Kin 14:28 7323
them back into the *g* chamber 1Kin 14:28 7323
offering, that Jehu said to the *g* 2Kin 10:25 7323
and the *g* and the captains cast 2Kin 10:25 7323
with the captains and the *g* 2Kin 11:4 7323
part at the gate behind the *g* 2Kin 11:6 7323
the *g* stood, every man with his 2Kin 11:11 7323
Athaliah heard the noise of the *g* 2Kin 11:13 7323
and the captains, and the *g* 2Kin 11:19 7323
gate of the *g* to the king's house 2Kin 11:19 7323
Nebuzar-adan, captain of the *g* 2Kin 25:8 2876
were with the captain of the *g* 2Kin 25:10 2876
the captain of the *g* carry away 2Kin 25:11 2876
But the captain of the *g* left of 2Kin 25:12 2876
the captain of the *g* took away 2Kin 25:15 2876
the captain of the *g* took Seraiah 2Kin 25:18 2876
captain of the *g* took these 2Kin 25:20 2876
and David set him over his *g* 1Chr 11:25 4928
the hands of the chief of the *g* 2Chr 12:10 7323
the *g* came and fetched them, and 2Chr 12:11 7323
them again into the *g* chamber 2Chr 12:11 7323
the night they may be a *g* to us ....Neh 4:22 4929
men of the *g* which followed me ....Neh 4:23 4929
the *g* carried away captive into ....Jer 39:9 2876
g left of the poor of the people ....Jer 39:10 2876
Nebuzar-adan the captain of the *g* ....Jer 39:11 2876
the captain of the *g* sent ....Jer 39:13 2876
the *g* had let him go from Ramah ....Jer 40:1 2876
captain of the *g* took Jeremiah ....Jer 40:2 2876
of the *g* gave him victuals ....Jer 40:5 2876
g had committed to Gedaliah the ....Jer 41:10 2876
g had left with Gedaliah the son ....Jer 43:6 2876
Nebuzar-adan, captain of the *g* ....Jer 52:12 2876
were with the captain of the *g* ....Jer 52:14 2876
g carried away captive certain of ....Jer 52:15 2876
g left certain of the poor of the ....Jer 52:16 2876
took the captain of the *g* away ....Jer 52:19 2876
the captain of the *g* took Seraiah ....Jer 52:24 2876
the captain of the *g* took them ....Jer 52:26 2876
the *g* carried away captive of the ....Jer 52:30 2876
thee, and be thou a *g* unto them ....Eze 38:7 4929
the captain of the king's *g* ....Dan 2:14 2877
prisoners to the captain of the *g* ....Acts 28:16 4759

GUARD'S

in the captain of the *g* house ....Gen 41:10 2876

GUDGODAH (gud-go'-dah) See Hor-hagidgad. *A wilderness encampment of Israel.*

From thence they journeyed unto *G* ....Deut 10:7 1412
from *G* to Jotbath, a land of ....Deut 10:7 1412

GUEST

That he was gone to be *g* with a ....Lk 19:7 *2647*

GUESTCHAMBER

The Master saith, Where is the *g* ...Mk 14:14 *2646*
saith unto thee, Where is the *g* ....Lk 22:11 *2646*

GUESTS

all the *g* that were with him 1Kin 1:41 7121
all the *g* that were with Adonijah 1Kin 1:49 7121
that her *g* are in the depths of ....Prov 9:18 7121
a sacrifice, he hath bid his *g* ....Zeph 1:7 7121
the wedding was furnished with *g* ....Mt 22:10 *345*
the king came in to see the *g* ....Mt 22:11 *345*

GUIDE

or canst thou *g* Arcturus with his ....Job 38:32 5148
The meek will he *g* in judgment ....Ps 25:9 1869
thy name's sake lead me, and *g* me ....Ps 31:3 5095
I will *g* thee with mine eye ....Ps 32:8 3289
he will be our *g* even unto death ....Ps 48:14 5090
was thou, a man mine equal, my *g* ....Ps 55:13 441
Thou shalt *g* me with thy counsel, ...Ps 73:24 5148
he will *g* his affairs with ....Ps 112:5 3557
forsaketh the *g* of her youth ....Prov 2:17 441
Which having no *g*, overseer, or ....Prov 6:7 7101
of the upright shall *g* them ....Prov 11:3 5148

wise, and *g* thine heart in the way ....Prov 23:19 833
springs of water shall he *g* them ....Is 49:10 5095
There is none to *g* her among all ....Is 51:18 5095
the Lord shall *g* thee continually ....Is 58:11 5148
thou art the *g* of my youth ....Jer 3:4 441
put ye not confidence in a *g* ....Mic 7:5 441
to *g* our feet into the way of ....Lk 1:79 *2720*
he will *g* you into all truth ....Jn 16:13 *3594*
which was *g* to them that took ....Acts 1:16 *3595*
I, except some man should *g* me ....Acts 8:31 *3594*
thou thyself art a *g* of the blind ....Rom 2:19 *3595*
g the house, give none occasion 1Ti 5:14 *3616*

GUIDED

thou hast *g* them in thy strength ....Ex 15:13 5095
other, and *g* them on every side 2Chr 32:22 5095
I have *g* her from my mother's ....Job 31:18 5148
g them in the wilderness like a ....Ps 78:52 5090
g them by the skilfulness of his ....Ps 78:72 5148

GUIDES

Woe unto you, ye blind *g*, which ....Mt 23:16 *3595*
Ye blind *g*, which strain at a ....Mt 23:24 *3595*

GUIDING

head, *g* his hands wittingly ....Gen 48:14 7919

GUILE

his neighbour, to slay him with *g* ....Ex 21:14 6195
and in whose spirit there is no *g* ....Ps 32:2 7423
evil, and thy lips from speaking *g* ....Ps 34:13 4820
g depart not from her streets ....Ps 55:11 4820
Israelite indeed, in whom is no *g* ....Jn 1:47 *1388*
being crafty, I caught you with *g* 2Cor 12:16 *1388*
nor of uncleanness, nor in *g* 1Th 2:3 *1388*
laying aside all malice, and all *g* 1Pet 2:1 *1388*
neither was *g* found in his mouth 1Pet 2:22 *1388*
and his lips that they speak no *g* 1Pet 3:10 *1388*
And in their mouth was found no *g* ....Rev 14:5 *1388*

GUILT

but thou shalt put away the *g* of ....Deut 19:13
So shalt thou put away the *g* of ....Deut 21:9

GUILTINESS

shouldest have brought *g* upon us ....Gen 26:10 817

GUILTLESS

g that taketh his name in vain ....Ex 20:7 5352
shall the man be *g* from iniquity ....Num 5:31 5352
be *g* before the Lord, and before ....Num 32:22 5355
g that taketh his name in vain ....Deut 5:11 5352
be upon his head, and we will be *g* ....Josh 2:19 5355
the Lord's anointed, and be *g* 1Sa 26:9 5352
my kingdom are *g* before the Lord 2Sa 3:28 5355
and the king and his throne be *g* 2Sa 14:9 5355
Now therefore hold him not *g* 1Kin 2:9 5352
ye would not have condemned the *g* ......Mt 12:7 *338*

GUILTY

We are verily *g* concerning our ....Gen 42:21 816
that by no means clear the *g* ....Ex 34:7
should not be done, and are *g* ....Lev 4:13 816
which should not be done, and is *g* ....Lev 4:22 816
ought not to be done, and be *g* ....Lev 4:27 816
he also shall be unclean, and *g* ....Lev 5:2 816
knoweth of it, then he shall be *g* ....Lev 5:3 816
he shall be *g* in one of these ....Lev 5:4 816
when he shall be *g* in one of ....Lev 5:5 816
he wist it not, yet is he *g* ....Lev 5:17 816
because he hath sinned, and is *g* ....Lev 6:4 816
the Lord, and that person be *g* ....Num 5:6 816
and by no means clearing the *g* ....Num 14:18
he shall not be *g* of blood ....Num 35:27
a murderer, which is *g* of death ....Num 35:31 7563
at this time, that ye should be *g* ....Judg 21:22 816
and being *g*, they offered a ram of ....Ezr 10:19 816
he curse thee, and thou be found *g* ....Prov 30:10 816
Thou art become *g* in thy blood ....Eze 22:4 816
them, and hold themselves not *g* ....Zec 11:5 816
the gift that is upon it, he is *g* ....Mt 23:18 *3784*
and said, He is *g* of death ....Mt 26:66 *1777*
condemned him to be *g* of death ....Mk 14:64 *1777*
the world may become *g* before God ....Rom 3:19 *5267*
shall be *g* of the body and blood 1Cor 11:27 *1777*
in one point, he is *g* of all ....Jas 2:10 *1777*

GULF

and you there is a great *g* fixed ....Lk 16:26 *5490*

GUNI (gu'-ni) See Gunites.
1. A son of Naphtali.

Jahzeel, and *G*, and Jezer, and ....Gen 46:24 1476
of *G*, the family of the Gunites ....Num 26:48 1476
Jahziel, and *G*, and Jezer, and 1Chr 7:13 1476

2. Father of Abdiel.
the son of Abdiel, the son of G 1Chr 5:15   1476

GUNITES (gu'-nites) *Descendants of Guni 1.*
of Guni, the family of the G .... Num 26:48   1477

GUR (gur) *See* GUR-BAAL. *A hill near Ibleam.*
they did so at the going up to G 2Kin 9:27   1483

GUR-BAAL (gur-ba'-al) *Place in western Arabia.*
the Arabians that dwelt in G 2Chr 26:7   1485

GUSH
our eyelids g out with waters .... Jer 9:18   5140

GUSHED
till the blood g out upon them 1Kin 18:28   8210
the rock, that the waters g out .... Ps 78:20   2100
the rock, and the waters g out .... Ps 105:41   2100
rock also, and the waters g out .... Is 48:21   2100
midst, and all his bowels g out .... Acts 1:18   *1632*

GUTTER
Whosoever getteth up to the g 2Sa 5:8   6794

GUTTERS
g in the watering troughs when .... Gen 30:38   7298
the eyes of the cattle in the g .... Gen 30:41   7298

H

HA
saith among the trumpets, H, h .... Job 39:25   1889

HAAHASHTARI (ha-a-hash'-te-ri) *A son of Naarah.*
and Hepher, and Temeni, and H 1Chr 4:6   326

HABAIAH (hab-ah'-yah) *A family of exiles.*
the children of H, the children .... Ezr 2:61   2252
the children of H, the children .... Neh 7:63   2252

HABAKKUK (hab'-ak-kuk) *A prophet of Judah.*
The burden which H the prophet .... Hab 1:1   2265
A prayer of H the prophet upon .... Hab 3:1   2265

HABAZINIAH (hab-az-in-i'-ah) *Head of a Rechabite family.*
the son of Jeremiah, the son of H .... Jer 35:3   2262

HABAZZINIAH *See* HABAZINIAH.

HABERGEON
it, as it were the hole of an h .... Ex 28:32   8473
of the robe, as the hole of an h .... Ex 39:23   8473
the spear, the dart, nor the h .... Job 41:26   8302

HABERGEONS
and spears, and helmets, and h 2Chr 26:14   8302
shields, and the bows, and the h .... Neh 4:16   8302

HABITABLE
Rejoicing in the h part of his .... Prov 8:31   8398

HABITATION
God, and I will prepare him an h .... Ex 15:2   5115
in thy strength unto thy holy h .... Ex 15:13   5116
without the camp shall his h be .... Lev 13:46   4186
even unto his h shall ye seek .... Deut 12:5   7933
Look down from thy holy h .... Deut 26:15   4583
which I have commanded in my h 1Sa 2:29   4583
thou shalt see an enemy in my h 1Sa 2:32   4583
and shew me both it, and his h 2Sa 15:25   5116
have built an house of h for thee 2Chr 6:2   2073
faces from the h of the LORD 2Chr 29:6   4908
Israel, whose h is in Jerusalem, ... Ezr 7:15   4907
but suddenly I cursed his h .... Job 5:3   5116
and thou shalt visit thy h .... Job 5:24   5116
make the h of thy righteousness .... Job 8:6   5116
shall be scattered upon his h .... Job 18:15   5116
I have loved the h of thy house .... Ps 26:8   4583
From the place of his h he .... Ps 33:14   3427
the widows, is God in his holy h .... Ps 68:5   4583
Let their h be desolate .... Ps 69:25   2918
Be thou my strong h, whereunto I .... Ps 71:3   4583
judgment are the h of thy throne .... Ps 89:14   4349
refuge, even the most High, thy h .... Ps 91:9   4583
judgment are the h of his throne .... Ps 97:2   4349
fowls of the heaven have their h .... Ps 104:12   7931
that they might go to a city of h .... Ps 107:7   4186
they may prepare a city for h .... Ps 107:36   4186
an h for the mighty God of Jacob .... Ps 132:5   4908
he hath desired it for his h .... Ps 132:13   4186
but he blesseth the h of the just .... Prov 3:33   5116
that graveth an h for himself in .... Is 22:16   4908
the h forsaken, and left like a .... Is 27:10   5116
shall dwell in a peaceable h .... Is 32:18   5116
shall see Jerusalem a quiet h .... Is 33:20   5116
and it shall be an h of dragons .... Is 34:13   5116
in the h of dragons, where each .... Is 35:7   5116
behold from the h of thy holiness .... Is 63:15   2073
Thine h is in the midst of deceit .... Jer 9:6   3427
him, and have made his h desolate ..... Jer 10:25   5116
utter his voice from his holy h .... Jer 25:30   4583
he shall mightily roar upon his h .... Jer 25:30   5116
O h of justice, and mountain of .... Jer 31:23   5116
shall be an h of shepherds .... Jer 33:12   5116
and dwelt in the h of Chimham .... Jer 41:17   1628
against the h of the strong .... Jer 49:19   5116
the h of justice, even the LORD, ... Jer 50:7   5116

will bring Israel again to his h .... Jer 50:19   5116
Jordan unto the h of the strong .... Jer 50:44   5116
make their h desolate with them .... Jer 50:45   5116
Pathros, into the land of their h .... Eze 29:14   4351
fowls of the heaven had their h .... Dan 4:21   7932
of the rock, whose h is high .... Obad 3   3427
and moon stood still in their h .... Hab 3:11   2073
he is raised up out of his holy h .... Zec 2:13   4583
Let his h be desolate, and let no .... Acts 1:20   *1886*
and the bounds of their h .... Acts 17:26   2733
an h of God through the Spirit .... Eph 2:22   2732
estate, but left their own h .... Jude 6   *3613*
and is become the h of devils .... Rev 18:2   2732

HABITATIONS
according to their h in the land .... Gen 36:43   4186
of cruelty are in their h .... Gen 49:5   4380
in all your h shall ye eat .... Ex 12:20   4186
your h upon the sabbath day .... Ex 35:3   4186
Ye shall bring out of your h two .... Lev 23:17   4186
be come into the land of your h .... Num 15:2   4186
These were their h, and their 1Chr 4:33   4186
the h that were found there, and 1Chr 4:41   4583
h were, Beth-el and the towns 1Chr 7:28   4186
are full of the h of cruelty .... Ps 74:20   4999
their camp, round about their h .... Ps 78:28   4908
forth the curtains of thine h .... Is 54:2   4908
for the h of the wilderness a .... Jer 9:10   4999
or who shall enter into our h .... Jer 21:13   4585
the peaceable h are cut down .... Jer 25:37   4999
make their h desolate with them .... Jer 49:20   5116
swallowed up all the h of Jacob .... Lam 2:2   4999
toward Diblath, in all their h .... Eze 6:14   4186
the h of the shepherds shall .... Amos 1:2   4999
receive you into everlasting h ...... Lk 16:9   *4638*

HABOR (ha'-bor) *A Mesopotamian district.*
in H by the river of Gozan, and in 2Kin 17:6   2249
in H by the river of Gozan, and in 2Kin 18:11   2249
and brought them unto Halah, and H 1Chr 5:26   2249

HACALIAH *See* HACHILAH.

HACHALIAH (hak-a-li'-ah) *Father of Nehemiah.*
words of Nehemiah the son of H .... Neh 1:1   2446
the Tirshatha, the son of H .... Neh 10:1   2446

HACHILAH (hak'-i-lah) *A hill in Judah.*
in the wood, in the hill of H 1Sa 23:19   2444
hide himself in the hill of H 1Sa 26:1   2444
And Saul pitched in the hill of H 1Sa 26:3   2444

HACHMONI (hak'-mo-ni) *See* HACHMONITE. *Father of Jehiel.*
Jehiel the son of H was with the 1Chr 27:32   *2453*

HACHMONITE (hak'-mo-nite) *See* TACHMONITE. *A descendant of Hachmoni.*
Jashobeam, a H, the chief of the 1Chr 11:11   2453

HAD *See* APPENDIX.

HADAD (ha'-dad) *See* BEN-HADAD, HADADRIMMON, HADAR.
1. A son of Bedad.
H the son of Bedad, who smote .... Gen 36:35   1908
H died, and Samlah of Masrekah .... Gen 36:36   1908
H the son of Bedad, which smote 1Chr 1:46   1908
when H was dead, Samlah of 1Chr 1:47   1908
2. A royal Edomite.
unto Solomon, H the Edomite 1Kin 11:14   1908
That H fled, he and certain 1Kin 11:17   1908
H being yet a little child 1Kin 11:17   1908
H found great favour in the sight 1Kin 11:19   1908
when H heard in Egypt that David 1Kin 11:21   1908
H said to Pharaoh, Let me depart, ... 1Kin 11:21   1908
beside the mischief that H did 1Kin 11:25   1908

3. *A son of Ishmael.*
Mishma, and Dumah, Massa, *H* 1Chr 1:30   2301
4. *An early king of Edom.*
was dead, *H* reigned in his stead 1Chr 1:50   1908
H died also 1Chr 1:51   1908

HADADEZER (had-a-de'-zer) See HADAREZER. *King of Zobah.*
David smote also *H*, the son of 2Sa 8:3   1909
came to succour *H* king of Zobah...........2Sa 8:5   1909
that were on the servants of *H* 2Sa 8:7   1909
and from Berothai, cities of *H* 2Sa 8:8   1909
had smitten all the host of *H* 2Sa 8:9   1909
because he had fought against *H* 2Sa 8:10   1909
for *H* had wars with Toi 2Sa 8:10   1909
of Amalek, and of the spoil of *H* 2Sa 8:12   1909
from his lord *H* king of Zobah................1Kin 11:23   1909

HADADRIMMON (ha'-dad-rim'-mon) *A place in the valley of Megiddo.*
as the mourning of *H* in the ....Zec 12:11   1910

HADAR (ha'-dar) See HADAD.
1. *A son of Ishmael.*
H, and Tema, Jetur, Naphish, and..........Gen 25:15   1924
2. *An early king of Edom.*
died, and *H* reigned in his stead............Gen 36:39   1924

HADAREZER (had-a-re'-zer) See HADADEZER. *Another name for Hadadezer.*
H sent, and brought out the 2Sa 10:16   1928
of the host of *H* went before them...........2Sa 10:16   1928
to *H* saw that they were smitten..............2Sa 10:19   1928
David smote *H* king of Zobah unto 1Chr 18:3   1928
came to help *H* king of Zobah.................1Chr 18:5   1928
that were on the servants of *H*................1Chr 18:7   1928
and from Chun, cities of *H* 1Chr 18:8   1928
all the host of *H* king of Zobah 1Chr 18:9   1928
because he had fought against *H* 1Chr 18:10   1928
for *H* had war with Tou............................1Chr 18:10   1928
of the host of *H* went before them 1Chr 19:16   1928
when the servants of *H* saw that 1Chr 19:19   1928

HADASHAH (had'-a-shah) *A town in Judah.*
Zenan, and *H*, and Migdal-gad,.............Josh 15:37   2322

HADASSAH (ha-das'-sah) See ESTHER. *Another name for Esther.*
And he brought up *H*, that is, ...Est 2:7   1919

HADATTAH (ha-dat'-tah) See HAZOR-HADATTAH. *Another name for Hazor.*
And Hazor, *H*, and Kerioth, and.............Josh 15:25   2675

HADES See HELL.

HADID (ha'-did) *A city in Benjamin.*
The children of Lod, *H*, and Ono, ...Ezr 2:33   2307
The children of Lod, *H*, and Ono, ...Neh 7:37   2307
H, Zeboim, Neballat, ...Neh 11:34   2307

HADLAI (had'-la-i) *Father of Amasa.*
of Shallum, and Amasa the son of *H*......2Chr 28:12   2311

HADORAM (ha-do'-ram) See ADORAM.
1. *A son of Joktan.*
And *H*, and Uzal, and Diklah,................Gen 10:27   1913
H also, and Uzal, and Diklah,................1Chr 1:21   1913
2. *A son of Tou.*
He sent *H* his son to king David, ...1Chr 18:10   1913
3. *An officer of Rehoboam.*
Then king Rehoboam sent *H* that..........2Chr 10:18   1913

HADRACH (ha'-drak) *A district in Syria.*
word of the LORD in the land of *H* ....Zec 9:1   2317

HADST
little which thou *h* before I came ....Gen 30:30
surely thou *h* sent me away now ....Gen 31:42
that thou *h* utterly hated her ....Judg 15:2
thee, except thou *h* hasted 1Sa 25:34
God liveth, unless thou *h* spoken 2Sa 2:27
then thou smitten Syria till.......................2Kin 13:19
Syria till thou *h* consumed it 2Kin 13:19
with us till thou *h* consumed us ....Ezr 9:14
which thou *h* sworn to give them ....Neh 9:15
concerning which thou *h* promised ....Neh 9:23
because thou *h* a favour unto them........Ps 44:3
thou, O God, which *h* cast us off ....Ps 60:10
or ever thou *h* formed the earth ....Ps 90:2
thou *h* removed it far unto all ....Is 26:15
O that thou *h* hearkened to my ....Is 48:18
thou *h* a whore's forehead, thou ....Jer 3:3
For thou *h* cast me into the deep, ...Jonah 2:3
Saying, If thou *h* known, even ....Lk 19:42
if thou *h* been here, my brother ....Jn 11:21
if thou *h* been here, my brother ....Jn 11:32

as if thou *h* not received it 1Cor 4:7
neither *h* pleasure therein ....Heb 10:8

HA-ELEPH See ELEPH.

HAFT
the *h* also went in after the ....Judg 3:22   5325

HAGAB (ha'-gab) See HAGABA. *A family of exiles.*
The children of *H*, the children ....Ezr 2:46   2285

HAGABA (hag'-a-bah) *Same as Hagab.*
of Lebana, the children of *H*....................Neh 7:48   2286

HAGABAH (hag'-a-bah) See HAGABA. *Same as Hagaba.*
of Lebanah, the children of *H* ....Ezr 2:45   2286

HAGAR (ha'-gar) *Sarah's handmaid.*
an Egyptian, whose name was *H* ....Gen 16:1   1904
wife took *H* her maid the Egyptian ....Gen 16:3   1904
And he went in unto *H*, and she..............Gen 16:4   1904
And he said, *H*, Sarai's maid,.................Gen 16:8   1904
And *H* bare Abram a son ....Gen 16:15   1904
his son's name, which *H* bare ....Gen 16:15   1904
when *H* bare Ishmael to Abram ....Gen 16:16   1904
saw the son of *H* the Egyptian ....Gen 21:9   1904
of water, and gave it unto *H* ....Gen 21:14   1904
of God called to *H* out of heaven ....Gen 21:17   1904
unto her, What aileth thee, *H* ....Gen 21:17   1904
whom *H* the Egyptian, Sarah's ....Gen 25:12   1904

HAGARENES (haga-renes') See HAGARITES. *A people east of the Jordan.*
of Moab, and the *H*.................................Ps 83:6   1905

HAGARITES (hag'-a-rites) *Same as Hagarenes.*
of Saul they made war with the *H* 1Chr 5:10   1905
And they made war with the *H*.................1Chr 5:19   1905
the *H* were delivered into their 1Chr 5:20   1905

HAGERITE (hag'-e-rite) See HAGARITES, HAGGERI. *Family of David's herdsmen.*
over the flocks was Jaziz the *H* 1Chr 27:31   1905

HAGGAI (hag'-ga-i) *A prophet.*
H the prophet, and Zechariah the ....Ezr 5:1   2292
the prophesying of *H* the prophet ....Ezr 6:14   2292
came the word of the LORD by *H*..............Hag 1:1   2292
word of the LORD by *H* the prophet ....Hag 1:3   2292
and the words of *H* the prophet ....Hag 1:12   2292
Then spake *H* the LORD's messenger ......Hag 1:13   2292
word of the LORD by *H* the prophet *H*......Hag 2:1   2292
word of the LORD by *H* the prophet ....Hag 2:10   2292
Then said *H*, If one that is ....Hag 2:13   2292
Then answered *H*, and said, So is..........Hag 2:14   2292
the LORD came unto *H* in the four ....Hag 2:20   2292

HAGGEDOLIM See Neh 12:14.

HAGGERI (hag'-gher-i) See HAGERITE. *Father of Mibhar.*
of Nathan, Mibhar the son of *H* 1Chr 11:38   1905

HAGGI (hag'-ghi) See HAGGITES. *A son of Gad.*
Ziphion, and *H*, Shuni, and Ezbon,........Gen 46:16   2291
of *H*, the family of the Haggites ....Num 26:15   2291

HAGGIAH (hag-ghi'-ah) *A descendant of Merari.*
H his son, Asaiah his son 1Chr 6:30   2293

HAGGITES (hag'-ghites) See HAGGI. *Descendants of Haggi.*
of Haggi, the family of the *H* ....Num 26:15   2291

HAGGITH (hag'-ghith) *A wife of David.*
the fourth, Adonijah the son of *H*............2Sa 3:4   2294
the son of *H* exalted himself....................1Kin 1:5   2294
Adonijah the son of *H* doth reign 1Kin 1:11   2294
Adonijah the son of *H* came to................1Kin 2:13   2294
the fourth, Adonijah the son of *H* 1Chr 3:2   2294

HAGRI See HAGGERI.

HAGRITE See HAGERITE.

HAGRITES See HAGARITES.

HAI (ha'-i) See AI. *A form of Ai.*
on the west, and *H* on the east ....Gen 12:8   5857
beginning, between Beth-el and *H* ....Gen 13:3   5857

HAIL
it to rain a very grievous *h*......................Ex 9:18   1259
the *h* shall come down upon them, ...Ex 9:19   1259
that there may be *h* in all the ....Ex 9:22   1259
and the LORD sent thunder and *h* ....Ex 9:23   1259
the LORD rained *h* upon the land...........Ex 9:23   1259
h, and fire mingled with the *h* ....Ex 9:24   1259
the *h* smote throughout all the ....Ex 9:25   1259
the *h* smote every herb of the ....Ex 9:25   1259
of Israel were, was there no *h* ....Ex 9:26   1259
no more mighty thunderings and *h* ....Ex 9:28   1259
neither shall there be any more *h*...........Ex 9:29   1259

H

h ceased, and the rain was not	Ex 9:33	1259
saw that the rain and the *h*	Ex 9:34	1259
remaineth unto you from the *h*	Ex 10:5	1259
even all that the *h* hath left	Ex 10:12	1259
of the trees which the *h* had left	Ex 10:15	1259
thou seen the treasures of the *h*	Job 38:22	1259
h stones and coals of fire	Ps 18:12	1259
h stones and coals of fire	Ps 18:13	1259
He destroyed their vines with *h*	Ps 78:47	1259
up their cattle also to the *h*	Ps 78:48	1259
He gave them *h* for rain, and	Ps 105:32	1259
Fire, and *h*; snow, and vapours	Ps 148:8	1259
one, which as a tempest of *h*	Is 28:2	1259
the *h* shall sweep away the refuge	Is 28:17	1259
When it shall *h*, coming down on	Is 32:19	1258
with *h* in all the labours of your	Hag 2:17	1259
he came to Jesus, and said, *H*	Mt 26:49	5463
him, and mocked him, saying, *H*	Mt 27:29	5463
Jesus met them, saying, All *h*	Mt 28:9	5463
And began to salute him, *H*	Mk 15:18	5463
came in unto her, and said, *H*	Lk 1:28	5463
And said, *H*, King of the Jews	Jn 19:3	5463
sounded, and there followed *h*	Rev 8:7	5464
and an earthquake, and great *h*	Rev 11:19	5464
upon men a great *h* out of heaven	Rev 16:21	5464
because of the plague of the *h*	Rev 16:21	5464

HAILSTONES

h than they whom the children of	Josh 10:11	68,1259
scattering, and tempest, and *h*	Is 30:30	68,1259
and ye, O great *h*, shall fall	Eze 13:11	68,417
great *h* in my fury to consume it	Eze 13:13	68,417
and overflowing rain, and great *h*	Eze 38:22	68,417

HAIR

and fine linen, and goats' *h*	Ex 25:4	
h to be a covering upon the	Ex 26:7	
and fine linen, and goats' *h*	Ex 35:6	
and fine linen, and goats' *h*	Ex 35:23	
them up in wisdom spun goats' *h*	Ex 35:26	
of goats' *h* for the tent over the	Ex 36:14	
when the *h* in the plague is	Lev 13:3	8181
the *h* thereof be not turned white	Lev 13:4	8181
and it have turned the *h* white	Lev 13:10	8181
the *h* thereof be turned white	Lev 13:20	8181
if the *h* in the bright spot be	Lev 13:25	8181
there be no white *h* in the bright	Lev 13:26	8181
and there be in it a yellow thin *h*	Lev 13:30	8181
and that there is no black *h* in it	Lev 13:31	8181
and there be in it no yellow *h*	Lev 13:32	8181
shall not seek for yellow *h*	Lev 13:36	8181
there is black *h* grown up therein	Lev 13:37	8181
the man whose *h* is fallen off his	Lev 13:40	4803
he that hath his *h* fallen off	Lev 13:41	4803
clothes, and shave off all his *h*	Lev 14:8	8181
shave all his *h* off his head	Lev 14:9	8181
even all his *h* he shall shave off	Lev 14:9	8181
locks of the *h* of his head grow	Num 6:5	8181
shall take the *h* of the head of	Num 6:18	8181
after the *h* of his separation is	Num 6:19	
of skins, and all work of goats' *h*	Num 31:20	
Howbeit the *h* of his head began	Judg 16:22	8181
sling stones at an *h* breadth	Judg 20:16	8185
there not one *h* of his head	1Sa 14:45	8185
of goats' *h* for his bolster	1Sa 19:13	
of goats' *h* for his bolster	1Sa 19:16	
there shall not one *h* of thy son	2Sa 14:11	8185
because the *h* was heavy on him,	2Sa 14:26	
he weighed the *h* of his head	2Sa 14:26	8181
there shall not an *h* of him fall	1Kin 1:52	8185
and plucked off the *h* of my head	Ezr 9:3	8181
of them, and plucked off their *h*	Neh 13:25	
the *h* of my flesh stood up	Job 4:15	8185
thy *h* is as a flock of goats,	Song 4:1	8181
thy *h* is as a flock of goats that	Song 6:5	8181
the *h* of thine head like purple	Song 7:5	1803
and instead of well set *h* baldness	Is 3:24	4748
the head, and the *h* of the feet	Is 7:20	8181
to them that plucked off the *h*	Is 50:6	
Cut off thine *h*, O Jerusalem, and	Jer 7:29	5145
to weigh, and divide the *h*	Eze 5:1	
thine *h* is grown, whereas thou	Eze 16:7	8181
nor was an *h* of their head singed	Dan 3:27	8177
the *h* of his head like the pure	Dan 7:9	8177
John had his raiment of camel's *h*	Mt 3:4	2359
not make one *h* white or black	Mt 5:36	2359
John was clothed with camel's *h*	Mk 1:6	2359
not an *h* of your head perish	Lk 21:18	2359
and wiped his feet with her *h*	Jn 11:2	2359
and wiped his feet with her *h*	Jn 12:3	2359
for there shall not an *h* fall	Acts 27:34	2359
you, that, if a man have long *h*	1Cor 11:14	2863

But if a woman have long *h*	1Cor 11:15	2863
for her *h* is given her for a	1Cor 11:15	2864
not with broided *h*, or gold, or	1Ti 2:9	4117
adorning of plaiting the *h*	1Pet 3:3	2359
became black as sackcloth of *h*	Rev 6:12	5155
they had *h* as the *h* of women,	Rev 9:8	2359

HAIRS

gray *h* with sorrow to the grave	Gen 42:38	
gray *h* with sorrow to the grave	Gen 44:29	
shall bring down the gray *h* of	Gen 44:31	
there be no white *h* therein	Lev 13:21	8181
also with the man of gray *h*	Deut 32:25	
are more than the *h* of mine head	Ps 40:12	8185
are more than the *h* of mine head	Ps 69:4	8185
even to hoar *h* will I carry you	Is 46:4	
till his *h* were grown like	Dan 4:33	8177
gray *h* are here and there upon him	Hos 7:9	
But the very *h* of your head are	Mt 10:30	2359
wipe them with the *h* of her head	Lk 7:38	2359
wiped them with the *h* of her head	Lk 7:44	2359
But even the very *h* of your head	Lk 12:7	2359
his *h* were white like wool, as	Rev 1:14	2359

HAIRY

red, all over like an *h* garment	Gen 25:25	8181
Esau my brother is a *h* man	Gen 27:11	8163
him not, because his hands were *h*	Gen 27:23	8163
answered him, He was an *h* man	2Kin 1:8	1167,8181
the *h* scalp of such an one as	Ps 68:21	8181

HAKELDAMA See ACELDAMA.

HAKKATAN (hak'-ka-tan) *A family of exiles.*

Johanan the son of *H*, and with him	Ezr 8:12	6997

HAKKOZ (hak'-koz) See Koz. *A sanctuary servant.*

The seventh to *H*, the eighth to	1Chr 24:10	6976

HAKUPHA (ha-ku'-fah) *A family of exiles.*

of Bakbuk, the children of *H*	Ezr 2:51	2709
of Bakbuk, the children of *H*	Neh 7:53	2709

HALAH (ha'-lah) *An Assyrian district.*

into Assyria, and placed them in *H*	2Kin 17:6	2477
unto Assyria, and put them in *H*	2Kin 18:11	2477
Manasseh, and brought them unto *H*	1Chr 5:26	2477

HALAK (ha'-lak) *A mountain in southern Canaan.*

Even from the mount *H*, that goeth	Josh 11:17	2510
of Lebanon even unto the mount *H*	Josh 12:7	2510

HALE

lest he *h* thee to the judge, and	Lk 12:58	2694

HALF

earring of *h* a shekel weight	Gen 24:22	1235
Moses took *h* of the blood, and put	Ex 24:6	2677
h of the blood he sprinkled on	Ex 24:6	2677
a *h* shall be the length thereof,	Ex 25:10	2677
a *h* the breadth thereof	Ex 25:10	2677
a cubit and a *h* the height thereof	Ex 25:10	2677
a *h* shall be the length thereof,	Ex 25:17	2677
cubit and a *h* the breadth thereof	Ex 25:17	2677
a cubit and a *h* the height thereof	Ex 25:23	2677
the *h* curtain that remaineth,	Ex 26:12	2677
a *h* shall be the breadth of one	Ex 26:16	2677
h a shekel after the shekel of	Ex 30:13	4276
an *h* shekel shall be the	Ex 30:13	4276
not give less than a *h* shekel	Ex 30:15	4276
and of sweet cinnamon *h* so much	Ex 30:23	4276
of a board one cubit and a *h*	Ex 36:21	2677
a *h* was the length of it, and a	Ex 37:1	2677
a *h* the breadth of it	Ex 37:1	2677
a cubit and a *h* the height of it	Ex 37:1	2677
a *h* was the length thereof, and	Ex 37:6	2677
cubit and a *h* the breadth thereof	Ex 37:6	2677
a cubit and a *h* the height thereof	Ex 37:10	2677
h a shekel, after the shekel of	Ex 38:26	4276
h of it in the morning, and *h*	Lev 6:20	4276
of whom the flesh is *h* consumed	Num 12:12	2677
mingled with *h* an hin of oil	Num 15:9	2677
a drink offering *h* an hin of wine	Num 15:10	2677
h an hin of wine unto a bullock	Num 28:14	2677
Take it of their *h*, and give it	Num 31:29	4276
And of the children of Israel's *h*	Num 31:30	4276
And the *h*, which was the portion	Num 31:36	4276
And of the children of Israel's *h*	Num 31:42	4275
(Now the *h* that pertained unto	Num 31:43	4275
of the children of Israel's *h*	Num 31:47	4276
unto *h* the tribe of Manasseh the	Num 32:33	2677
nine tribes, and to the *h* tribe	Num 34:13	2677
h the tribe of Manasseh have	Num 34:14	2677
the *h* tribe have received their	Num 34:15	2677
h mount Gilead, and the cities	Deut 3:12	2677
gave I unto the *h* tribe of	Deut 3:13	2677

unto the river Arnon *h* the valley	Deut 3:16	8432
to the *h* tribe of Manasseh	Deut 29:8	2677
to *h* the tribe of Manasseh, spake	Josh 1:12	2677
h the tribe of Manasseh, passed	Josh 4:12	2677
h of them over against mount	Josh 8:33	2677
h of them over against mount Ebal	Josh 8:33	2677
from *h* Gilead, even unto the	Josh 12:2	2677
h Gilead, the border of Sihon	Josh 12:5	2677
and the *h* tribe of Manasseh	Josh 12:6	2677
and the *h* tribe of Manasseh	Josh 13:7	2677
h the land of the children of	Josh 13:25	2677
unto the *h* tribe of Manasseh	Josh 13:29	2677
of the *h* tribe of the children of	Josh 13:29	2677
h Gilead, and Ashtaroth, and Edrei,	Josh 13:31	2677
even to the one *h* of the children	Josh 13:31	2677
nine tribes, and for the *h* tribe	Josh 14:2	2677
an *h* tribe on the other side	Josh 14:3	2677
h the tribe of Manasseh, have	Josh 18:7	2677
out of the *h* tribe of Manasseh.	Josh 21:5	2677
out of the *h* tribe of Manasseh in	Josh 21:6	2677
out of the *h* tribe of Manasseh,	Josh 21:25	4276
out of the other *h* tribe of	Josh 21:27	2677
and the *h* tribe of Manasseh,	Josh 22:1	2677
Now to the one *h* of the tribe of	Josh 22:7	2677
but the other *h* thereof gave	Josh 22:7	2677
the *h* tribe of Manasseh returned	Josh 22:9	2677
the *h* tribe of Manasseh built	Josh 22:10	2677
the *h* tribe of Manasseh have	Josh 22:11	2677
to the *h* tribe of Manasseh, into	Josh 22:13	2677
to the *h* tribe of Manasseh, unto	Josh 22:15	2677
the *h* tribe of Manasseh answered	Josh 22:21	2677
as it were an *h* acre of land	1Sa 14:14	2677
off the one *h* of their beards	2Sa 10:4	2677
neither if *h* of us die, will they	2Sa 18:3	2677
also *h* the people of Israel	2Sa 19:40	2677
give *h* to the one, and *h* to the	1Kin 3:25	2677
work of the base, a cubit and an *h*	1Kin 7:31	2677
a wheel was a cubit and a cubit	1Kin 7:32	2677
a round compass of *h* a cubit high	1Kin 7:35	2677
and, behold, the *h* was not told me	1Kin 10:7	2677
thou wilt give me *h* thine house	1Kin 13:8	2677
captain of *h* his chariots,	1Kin 16:9	4276
h of the people followed Tibni	1Kin 16:21	2677
and *h* followed Omri	1Kin 16:21	2677
Haroeh, and *h* of the Manahethites	1Chr 2:52	2677
h of the Manahethites, the	1Chr 2:54	2677
h the tribe of Manasseh, of	1Chr 5:18	2677
the children of the *h* tribe of	1Chr 5:23	2677
the *h* tribe of Manasseh, and	1Chr 5:26	2677
cities given out of the *h* tribe	1Chr 6:61	2677
out of the *h* tribe of Manasseh.	1Chr 6:61	4276
out of the *h* tribe of Manasseh	1Chr 6:70	4276
family of the *h* tribe of Manasseh	1Chr 6:71	2677
of the *h* tribe of Manasseh	1Chr 12:31	2677
of the *h* tribe of Manasseh, with	1Chr 12:37	2677
the *h* tribe of Manasseh, for	1Chr 26:32	2677
of the *h* tribe of Manasseh, Joel	1Chr 27:20	2677
Of the *h* tribe of Manasseh in	1Chr 27:21	2677
the one *h* of the greatness of thy	2Chr 9:6	2677
the ruler of the *h* part of	Neh 3:9	2677
the ruler of the *h* part of	Neh 3:12	2677
ruler of the *h* part of Beth-zur	Neh 3:16	2677
the ruler of the *h* part of Keilah	Neh 3:17	2677
the ruler of the *h* part of Keilah	Neh 3:18	2677
together unto the *h* thereof	Neh 4:6	2677
that the *h* of my servants wrought	Neh 4:16	2677
the other *h* of them held both the	Neh 4:16	2677
h of them held the spears from	Neh 4:21	2677
h of the princes of Judah,	Neh 12:32	2677
the *h* of the people upon the wall	Neh 12:38	2677
the *h* of the rulers with me	Neh 12:40	2677
their children spake *h* in the	Neh 13:24	2677
thee to the *h* of the kingdom	Est 5:3	2677
even to the *h* of the kingdom it	Est 5:6	2677
even to the *h* of the kingdom	Est 7:2	2677
shall not live out *h* their days	Ps 55:23	2673
Samaria committed *h* of thy sins	Eze 16:51	2677
an *h* long, and a cubit and an *h*	Eze 40:42	2677
about it shall be *h* a cubit	Eze 43:17	2677
be for a time, times, and an *h*	Dan 12:7	2677
barley, and an *h* homer of barley	Hos 3:2	2677
h of the city shall go forth into	Zec 14:2	2677
h of the mountain shall remove	Zec 14:4	2677
and *h* of it toward the south	Zec 14:4	2677
h of them toward the former sea	Zec 14:8	2677
h of them toward the hinder sea	Zec 14:8	2677
it thee, unto the *h* of my kingdom	Mk 6:23	2255
and departed, leaving him *h* dead	Lk 10:30	2253
the *h* of my goods I give to the	Lk 19:8	2255
about the space of *h* an hour	Rev 8:1	2256
dead bodies three days and an *h*	Rev 11:9	2255

an *h* the Spirit of life from God	Rev 11:11	2255
h a time, from the face of the	Rev 12:14	2255

HALHUL (hal'-hul) *A city in Judah.*

H, Beth-zur, and Gedor,	Josh 15:58	2478

HALI (ha'-li) *A town in Asher.*

And their border was Helkath, and *H*	Josh 19:25	2482

HALING

h men and women committed them to	Acts 8:3	4951

HALL

took Jesus into the common *h*	Mt 27:27	4232
soldiers led him away into the *h*	Mk 15:16	833
a fire in the midst of the *h*	Lk 22:55	833
Caiaphas unto the *h* of judgment	Jn 18:28	4232
went not into the judgment *h*	Jn 18:28	4232
entered into the judgment *h* again	Jn 18:33	4232
And went again into the judgment *h*	Jn 19:9	4232
to be kept in Herod's judgment *h*	Acts 23:35	4232

HALLOHESH (hal-lo'-hesh) See HALOHESH. *Father of Shallum.*

H, Pileha, Shobek,	Neh 10:24	3873

HALLOW

shall *h* in all their holy gifts	Ex 28:38	6942
thou shalt do unto them to *h* them	Ex 29:1	6942
that is therein, and shalt *h* it	Ex 40:9	6942
h it from the uncleanness of	Lev 16:19	6942
those things which they *h* unto me	Lev 22:2	6942
of Israel *h* unto the LORD	Lev 22:3	6942
I am the LORD which *h* you	Lev 22:32	6942
ye shall *h* the fiftieth year, and	Lev 25:10	6942
shall *h* his head that same day	Num 6:11	6942
The same day did the king the *h*	1Kin 8:64	6942
but *h* ye the sabbath day, as I	Jer 17:22	6942
but *h* the sabbath day, to do no	Jer 17:24	6942
unto me to *h* the sabbath day	Jer 17:27	6942
And *h* my sabbaths	Eze 20:20	6942
and they shall *h* my sabbaths	Eze 44:24	6942

HALLOWED

blessed the sabbath day, and *h* it	Ex 20:11	6942
and he shall be *h*, and his garments	Ex 29:21	6942
she shall touch no *h* thing	Lev 12:4	6944
profaned the *h* thing of the LORD	Lev 19:8	6944
but I will be *h* among the	Lev 22:32	6942
in the land of Egypt I *h* unto me	Num 3:13	6942
every man's *h* things shall be his	Num 5:10	6944
for they are *h*	Num 16:37	6942
the LORD, therefore they are *h*	Num 16:38	6942
the *h* things of the children of	Num 18:8	6944
even the *h* part thereof out of it	Num 18:29	4720
I have brought away the *h* things	Deut 26:13	6944
mine hand, but there is *h* bread	1Sa 21:4	6944
So the priest gave him *h* bread	1Sa 21:6	6944
I have *h* this house, which thou	1Kin 9:3	6942
house, which I have *h* for my name	1Kin 9:7	6942
all the *h* things that Jehoshaphat	2Kin 12:18	6944
dedicated, and his own *h* things	2Kin 12:18	6944
Moreover Solomon *h* the middle of	2Chr 7:7	6942
LORD which he had *h* in Jerusalem	2Chr 36:14	6942
art in heaven, *H* be thy name	Mt 6:9	37
art in heaven, *H* be thy name	Lk 11:2	37

HALOHESH (ha-lo'-hesh) See HALOHESH. *Same as Hallohesh.*

him repaired Shallum the son of *H*	Neh 3:12	3873

HALT

How long *h* ye between two	1Kin 18:21	6452
For I am ready to *h*, and my sorrow	Ps 38:17	6761
to enter into life *h* or maimed	Mt 18:8	5560
for thee to enter *h* into life	Mk 9:45	5560
the poor, and the maimed, and the *h*	Lk 14:21	5560
of impotent folk, of blind, *h*	Jn 5:3	5560

HALTED

upon him, and he *h* upon his thigh	Gen 32:31	6761
I will make her that *h* a remnant	Mic 4:7	6761

HALTETH

LORD, will I assemble her that *h*	Mic 4:6	6761
and I will save her that *h*	Zeph 3:19	6761

HALTING

All my familiars watched for my *h*	Jer 20:10	6761

HAM (ham)

1. A son of Noah.

and Noah begat Shem, *H*, and Japheth	Gen 5:32	2526
And Noah begat three sons, Shem, *H*	Gen 6:10	2526
day entered Noah, and Shem, and *H*	Gen 7:13	2526
forth of the ark, were Shem, and *H*	Gen 9:18	2526
H is the father of Canaan	Gen 9:18	2526
And *H*, the father of Canaan, saw	Gen 9:22	2526

H

of the sons of Noah, Shem, *H* .... Gen 10:1   2526
And the sons of *H* .... Gen 10:6   2526
These are the sons of *H*, after .... Gen 10:20   2526
Karnaim, and the Zuzims in *H* .... Gen 14:5   1990
Noah, Shem, *H*, and Japheth 1Chr 1:4   2526
The sons of *H* 1Chr 1:8   2526
   2. *Descendants and land of Ham.*
for they of *H* had dwelt there of 1Chr 4:40   2526
strength in the tabernacles of *H* .... Ps 78:51   2526
Jacob sojourned in the land of *H* ..... Ps 105:23   2526
them, and wonders in the land of *H* .. Ps 105:27   2526
Wondrous works in the land of *H* ...... Ps 106:22   2526

HAMAN (ha'-man) See HAMAN'S. *Prime minister under*
   King Ahasuerus.
H the son of Hammedatha the .... Est 3:1   2001
gate, bowed, and reverenced *H* .... Est 3:2   2001
not unto them, that they told *H* .... Est 3:4   2001
when *H* saw that Mordecai bowed .... Est 3:5   2001
then was *H* full of wrath .... Est 3:5   2001
wherefore *H* sought to destroy all .... Est 3:6   2001
before *H* from day to day, and from ...... Est 3:7   2001
H said unto king Ahasuerus, There ..... Est 3:8   2001
gave it unto *H* the son of .... Est 3:10   2001
And the king said unto *H*, The .... Est 3:11   2001
H had commanded unto the king's .... Est 3:12   2001
the king and *H* sat down to drink .... Est 3:15   2001
that *H* had promised to pay to the .... Est 4:7   2001
H come this day unto the banquet .... Est 5:4   2001
Cause *H* to make haste, that he .... Est 5:5   2001
H came to the banquet that Esther .... Est 5:5   2001
H come to the banquet that I .... Est 5:8   2001
Then went *H* forth that day joyful .... Est 5:9   2001
but when *H* saw Mordecai in the .... Est 5:9   2001
Nevertheless *H* refrained himself .... Est 5:10   2001
H told them of the glory of his .... Est 5:11   2001
H said moreover, Yea, Esther the .... Est 5:12   2001
And the thing pleased *H* .... Est 5:14   2001
Now *H* was come into the outward .... Est 6:4   2001
Behold, *H* standeth in the court .... Est 6:5   2001
So *H* came in .... Est 6:6   2001
Now *H* thought in his heart, To .... Est 6:6   2001
H answered the king, For the man .... Est 6:7   2001
Then the king said to *H*, Make .... Est 6:10   2001
Then took *H* the apparel and the .... Est 6:11   2001
But *H* hasted to his house .... Est 6:12   2001
H told Zeresh his wife and all his .... Est 6:13   2001
hasted to bring *H* unto the .... Est 6:14   2001
H came to banquet with Esther the ...... Est 7:1   2001
and enemy is this wicked *H* .... Est 7:6   2001
Then was *H* afraid before the king .... Est 7:6   2001
H stood up to make request for .... Est 7:7   2001
H was fallen upon the bed whereon ...... Est 7:8   2001
which *H* had made for Mordecai, ... Est 7:9   2001
king, standeth in the house of *H* .... Est 7:9   2001
So they hanged *H* on the gallows .... Est 7:10   2001
Ahasuerus give the house of *H* the ...... Est 8:1   2001
ring, which he had taken from *H* .... Est 8:2   2001
set Mordecai over the house of *H* .... Est 8:2   2001
the mischief of *H* the Agagite .... Est 8:3   2001
by *H* the son of Hammedatha the .... Est 8:5   2001
have given Esther the house of *H* .... Est 8:7   2001
The ten sons of *H* the son of .... Est 9:10   2001
the palace, and the ten sons of *H* .... Est 9:12   2001
Because *H* the son of Hammedatha, ... Est 9:24   2001

HAMAN'S (ha'-mans)
king's mouth, they covered *H* face .... Est 7:8   2001
let *H* ten sons be hanged upon the .... Est 9:13   2001
and they hanged *H* ten sons .... Est 9:14   2001

HAMATH (ha'-math) See HAMATHITE, HAMATH-ZOBAH,
   HEMATH. *A capital of Syria.*
Zin unto Rehob, as men come to *H* .... Num 13:21   2574
border unto the entrance of *H* .... Num 34:8   2574
Hermon unto the entering into *H* .... Josh 13:5   2574
unto the entering in of *H* .... Judg 3:3   2574
When Toi king of *H* heard that 2Sa 8:9   2574
in of *H* unto the river of Egypt 1Kin 8:65   2574
of *H* unto the sea of the plain 2Kin 14:25   2574
how he recovered Damascus, and *H* 2Kin 14:28   2574
Cuthah, and from Ava, and from *H* 2Kin 17:24   2574
the men of *H* made Ashima, ... 2Kin 17:30   2574
Where are the gods of *H*, and of 2Kin 18:34   2574
Where is the king of *H*, and the 2Kin 19:13   2574
bands at Riblah in the land of *H* 2Kin 23:33   2574
them at Riblah in the land of *H* 2Kin 25:21   2574
Hadarezer king of Zobah unto *H* 1Chr 18:3   2574
Now when Toi king of *H* heard how 1Chr 18:9   2574
in of *H* unto the river of Egypt 2Chr 7:8   2574
store cities, which he built in *H* 2Chr 8:4   2574
is not *H* as Arpad .... Is 10:9   2574

Elam, and from Shinar, and from *H* .... Is 11:11   2574
Where are the gods of *H* and Arphad ... Is 36:19   2574
Where is the king of *H*, and the .... Is 37:13   2574
to Riblah in the land of *H* .... Jer 39:5   2574
H is confounded, and Arpad .... Jer 49:23   2574
to Riblah in the land of *H* .... Jer 52:9   2574
death in Riblah in the land of *H* .... Jer 52:27   2574
H, Berothah, Sibraim, which is .... Eze 47:16   2574
of Damascus and the border of *H* .... Eze 47:16   2574
northward, and the border of *H* .... Eze 47:17   2574
till a man come over against *H* .... Eze 47:20   2574
way of Hethlon, as one goeth to *H* ...... Eze 48:1   2574
northward, to the coast of *H* .... Eze 48:1   2574
from thence go ye to *H* the great .... Amos 6:2   2579
H also shall border thereby .... Zec 9:2   2574

HAMATHITE
and the Zemarite, and the *H* .... Gen 10:18   2577
and the Zemarite, and the *H* 1Chr 1:16   2577

HAMATH-ZOBAH (ha'-math-zo'-bah) *Full name of Ha-*
   math.
And Solomon went to *H*, and 2Chr 8:3   2578

HAMITES See HAM.

HAMMATH (ham'-math) *A city in Naphtali.*
cities are Ziddim, Zer, and *H* .... Josh 19:35   2575

HAMMEDATHA (ham-med'a-thah) *Father of Haman.*
Haman the son of *H* the Agagite .... Est 3:1   4099
Haman the son of *H* the Agagite .... Est 3:10   4099
by Haman the son of *H* the Agagite .... Est 8:5   4099
ten sons of Haman the son of *H* .... Est 9:10   4099
Because Haman the son of *H* .... Est 9:24   4099

HAMMELECH (ham'-me-lek) *Father of Jerahmeel.*
commanded Jerahmeel the son of *H* ..... Jer 36:26   4429
dungeon of Malchiah the son of *H* .... Jer 38:6   4429

HAMMER
took an *h* in her hand, and went .... Judg 4:21   4718
her right hand to the workmen's *h* .... Judg 5:26   1989
with the *h* she smote Sisera, she .... Judg 5:26
so that there was neither *h* nor 1Kin 6:7   4717
the *h* him that smote the anvil .... Is 41:7   6360
like a *h* that breaketh the rock .... Jer 23:29   6360
How is the *h* of the whole earth .... Jer 50:23   6360

HAMMERS
thereof at once with axes and *h* .... Ps 74:6   3597
coals, and fashioneth it with *h* .... Is 44:12   4717
fasten it with nails and with *h* .... Jer 10:4   4717

HAMMOLEKETH (ham-mol'-e-keth) *Daughter of Ma-*
   chir.
And his sister *H* bare Ishod 1Chr 7:18   4447

HAMMON (ham'-mon)
   1. *A city in Asher.*
And Hebron, and Rehob, and *H* .... Josh 19:28   2540
   2. *A city in Naphtali.*
H with her suburbs, and Kirjathaim 1Chr 6:76   2540

HAMMOTH-DOR (ham'-moth-dor') *Same as Ham-*
   mon 2.
H with her suburbs, and Kartan .... Josh 21:32   2576

HAMMUEL See HAMUEL.

HAMONAH (ha-mo'-nah) *Place where Gog is buried.*
the name of the city shall be *H* .... Eze 39:16   1997

HAMON-GOG (ha'-mon-gog) *Same as Hamonah.*
shall call it The valley of *H* .... Eze 39:11   1996
have buried it in the valley of *H* .... Eze 39:15   1996

HAMOR (ha'-mor) See EMMOR, HAMOR'S. *Father of She-*
   chem.
at the hand of the children of *H* .... Gen 33:19   2544
Shechem the son of *H* the Hivite .... Gen 34:2   2544
Shechem spake unto his father *H* .... Gen 34:4   2544
H the father of Shechem went out .... Gen 34:6   2544
H communed with them, saying, The ..... Gen 34:8   2544
H his father deceitfully, and said .... Gen 34:13   2544
And their words pleased *H*, and .... Gen 34:18   2544
And *H* and Shechem his son came unto Gen 34:20   2544
And unto *H* and unto Shechem his son.. Gen 34:24   2544
And they slew *H* and Shechem his son .. Gen 34:26   2544
Jacob bought of the sons of *H* the .... Josh 24:32   2544
serve the men of *H* the father of .... Judg 9:28   2544

HAMOR'S (ha'-mors)
pleased Hamor, and Shechem *H* son ...... Gen 34:18   2544

HAMRAN See AMRAN.

HAMUEL (ha-mu'-el) *Son of Mishma.*
H his son, Zacchur his son, ... 1Chr 4:26   2536

HAMUL (ha'-mul) See HAMULITES. *A son of Pharez.*
sons of Pharez were Hezron and H .... Gen 46:12   2538
of H, the family of the Hamulites .... Num 26:21   2538
Hezron, and H. 1Chr 2:5   2538

HAMULITES (ha'-mu-lites) *Descendants of Hamul.*
of Hamul, the family of the H .... Num 26:21   2539

HAMUTAL (ha-mu'-tal) *Mother of King Jehoahaz.*
And his mother's name was H 2Kin 23:31   2537
And his mother's name was H 2Kin 24:18   2537
his mother's name was H the .... Jer 52:1   2537

HANAMEAL See HANAMEEL.

HANAMEEL (ha-nam'-e-el) *Son of Shallum.*
H the son of Shallum thine uncle .... Jer 32:7   2601
So H mine uncle's son came to me .... Jer 32:8   2601
the field of H my uncle's son .... Jer 32:9   2601
in the sight of H mine uncle's .... Jer 32:12   2601

HANAMEL See HANAMEEL.

HANAN (ha'-nan) See BAAL-HANAN, BEN-HANAN, ELON-
BETH-HANAN.
   1. A son of Shashak.
And Abdon, and Zichri, and H 1Chr 8:23   2605
   2. A son of Azel.
and Sheariah, and Obadiah, and H 1Chr 8:38   2605
and Sheariah, and Obadiah, and H 1Chr 9:44   2605
   3. A "mighty man" of David.
H the son of Maachah, and 1Chr 11:43   2605
   4. Family of exiles.
of Shalmai, the children of H .... Ezr 2:46   2605
The children of H, the children .... Neh 7:49   2605
   5. A priest who assisted Ezra.
Kelita, Azariah, Jozabad, H .... Neh 8:7   2605
   6. A Levite who renewed the covenant.
Hodijah, Kelita, Pelaiah, H .... Neh 10:10   2605
next to them was H the son of .... Neh 13:13   2605
   7. A chief who renewed the covenant.
Pelatiah, H, Anaiah, ... Neh 10:22   2605
   8. Another chief who renewed the covenant.
And Ahijah, H, Anan, ... Neh 10:26   2605
   9. Son of Igdaliah.
into the chamber of the sons of H .... Jer 35:4   2605

HANANEAL See HANANEEL.

HANANEEL (ha-nan'-e-el) *A tower on Jerusalem's wall.*
it, unto the tower of H .... Neh 3:1   2606
the fish gate, and the tower of H .... Neh 12:39   2606
of H unto the gate of the corner .... Jer 31:38   2606
from the tower of H unto the .... Zec 14:10   2606

HANANEL See HANANEEL.

HANANI (ha-na'-ni)
   1. A son of Heman.
Shebuel, and Jerimoth, Hananiah, H 1Chr 25:4   2607
The eighteenth to H, he, his sons 1Chr 25:25   2607
   2. A prophet.
at that time H the seer came to 2Chr 16:7   2607
   3. Father of Jehu.
Jehu the son of H against Baasha 1Kin 16:1   2607
of H came the word of the LORD 1Kin 16:7   2607
Jehu the son of H the seer went 2Chr 19:2   2607
in the book of Jehu the son of H 2Chr 20:34   2607
   4. Married a foreigner in exile.
of Immer; H, and Zebadiah .... Ezr 10:20   2607
   5. Brother of Nehemiah.
That H, one of my brethren, came, ... Neh 1:2   2607
That I gave my brother H, and .... Neh 7:2   2607
   6. A priest.
Maai, Nethaneel, and Judah, H .... Neh 12:36   2607

HANANIAH (han-a-ni'-ah) See SHADRACH.
   1. A son of Heman.
Uzziel, Shebuel, and Jerimoth, H 1Chr 25:4   2608
The sixteenth to H, he, his sons, ... 1Chr 25:23   2608
Meraiah; of Jeremiah, H .... Neh 12:12   2608
Hear now, H; The LORD hath .... Jer 28:15   2608
   2. A captain of King Uzziah.
the ruler, under the hand of H 2Chr 26:11   2608
   3. Father of Zedekiah.
Shaphan, and Zedekiah the son of H ..... Jer 36:12   2608
   4. A false prophet.
that H the son of Azur the .... Jer 28:1   2608
H in the presence of the priests .... Jer 28:5   2608
Then H the prophet took the yoke .... Jer 28:10   2608
H spake in the presence of all .... Jer 28:11   2608
after that H the prophet had .... Jer 28:12   2608
Go and tell H, saying, Thus saith .... Jer 28:13   2608
Jeremiah unto H the prophet .... Jer 28:15   2608
So H the prophet died the same .... Jer 28:17   2608

   5. Grandfather of Irijah.
son of Shelemiah, the son of H .... Jer 37:13   2608
   6. Son of Shashak.
And H, and Elam, and Antothijah, ... 1Chr 8:24   2608
   7. Hebrew form of Shadrach.
the children of Judah, Daniel, H .... Dan 1:6   2608
and to H, of Shadrach .... Dan 1:7   2608
eunuchs had set over Daniel, H .... Dan 1:11   2608
all was found none like Daniel, H .... Dan 1:19   2608
and made the thing known to H .... Dan 2:17   2608
   8. A son of Zerubbabel.
Meshullam, and H, and Shelomith 1Chr 3:19   2608
And the sons of H, ... 1Chr 3:21   2608
   9. Married a foreigner in exile.
Jehohanan, H, Zabbai, and Athlai .... Ezr 10:28   2608
   10. A rebuilder of Jerusalem's wall.
repaired H the son of one of the .... Neh 3:8   2608
   11. Another rebuilder of Jerusalem's wall.
After him repaired H the son of .... Neh 3:30   2608
   12. A palace servant of Nehemiah.
H the ruler of the palace, charge .... Neh 7:2   2608
   13. An Israelite who renewed the covenant.
Hoshea, H, Hashub, ... Neh 10:23   2608
   14. A priest.
Elioenai, Zechariah, and H .... Neh 12:41   2608

HAND See APPENDIX.

HANDBREADTH
a border of an h round about.................. Ex 37:12   2948
And the thickness of it was an h 2Chr 4:5   2947
thou hast made my days as an h .... Ps 39:5   2947

HANDED
him while he is weary and weak h 2Sa 17:2   3027

HANDFUL
his h of the flour thereof .... Lev 2:2   4393,7062
the priest shall take his h of it .... Lev 5:12   4393,7062
And he shall take of it his h .... Lev 6:15   7062
offering, and took an h thereof........ Lev 9:17   4390,3709
shall take an h of the offering .... Num 5:26   7061
but an h of meal in a barrel, and 1Kin 17:12   4390,3709
There shall be an h of corn in .... Ps 72:16   6451
Better is an h with quietness, ... Eccl 4:6   4390,3709
as the h after the harvestman, and .... Jer 9:22   5995

HANDFULS
the earth brought forth by h .... Gen 41:47   7062
Take to you h of ashes of the.......... Ex 9:8   4393,2651
some of the h of purpose for her .... Ruth 2:16   6653
of Samaria shall suffice for h 1Kin 20:10   8168
among my people for h of barley .... Eze 13:19   8168

HANDKERCHIEFS
brought unto the sick h or aprons .... Acts 19:12   *4676*

HANDLE
father of all such as h the harp.............. Gen 4:21   8610
they that h the pen of the writer............ Judg 5:14   4900
the battle, that could h shield 1Chr 12:8   6186
forth to war, that could h spear 2Chr 25:5   270
They have hands, but they h not .... Ps 115:7   4184
they that h the law knew me not .... Jer 2:8   8610
and the Libyans, that h the shield .... Jer 46:9   8610
and the Lydians, that h and bend.......... Jer 46:9   8610
And all that h the oar, the .... Eze 27:29   8610
h me, and see .... Lk 24:39   *5584*
taste not; h not .... Col 2:21   *2345*

HANDLED
to be furbished, that it may be h .... Eze 21:11   8610,3709
and sent him away shamefully h .... Mk 12:4   *821*
looked upon, and our hands have h 1Jn 1:1   *5584*

HANDLES
myrrh, upon the h of the lock .... Song 5:5   3709

HANDLETH
He that h a matter wisely shall .... Prov 16:20   5921
him that h the sickle in the time .... Jer 50:16   8610
shall he stand that h the bow .... Amos 2:15   8610

HANDLING
and shields, all of them h swords .... Eze 38:4   8610
nor h the word of God deceitfully 2Cor 4:2   *1389*

HANDMAID
and she had an h, an Egyptian, ... Gen 16:1   8198
Hagar the Egyptian, Sarah's h .... Gen 25:12   8198
Leah Zilpah his maid for an h .... Gen 29:24   8198
Bilhah his h to be her maid.................... Gen 29:29   8198
she gave him Bilhah her h to wife .... Gen 30:4   8198
And the sons of Bilhah, Rachel's h ...... Gen 35:25   8198
And the sons of Zilpah, Leah's h .... Gen 35:26   8198
ass may rest, and the son of thy h .... Ex 23:12   519
and wine also for me, and for thy h ...... Judg 19:19   519

H

hast spoken friendly unto thine *h*	Ruth 2:13	8198
she answered, I am Ruth thine *h*	Ruth 3:9	519
therefore thy skirt over thine *h*	Ruth 3:9	519
look on the affliction of thine *h*	1Sa 1:11	519
me, and not forget thine *h*	1Sa 1:11	519
give unto thine *h* a man child	1Sa 1:11	519
Count not thine *h* for a daughter	1Sa 1:16	519
Let thine *h* find grace in thy	1Sa 1:18	8198
and let thine *h*, I pray thee,	1Sa 25:24	519
and hear the words of thine *h*	1Sa 25:24	519
but I thine *h* saw not the young	1Sa 25:25	519
thine *h* hath brought unto my lord	1Sa 25:27	8198
forgive the trespass of thine *h*	1Sa 25:28	519
my lord, then remember thine *h*	1Sa 25:31	519
let thine *h* be a servant to wash	1Sa 25:41	519
thine *h* hath obeyed thy voice, and	1Sa 28:21	8198
also unto the voice of thine *h*	1Sa 28:22	8198
thy *h* had two sons, and they two	2Sa 14:6	8198
family is risen against thine *h*	2Sa 14:7	8198
Then the woman said, Let thine *h*	2Sa 14:12	8198
thy *h* said, I will now speak unto	2Sa 14:15	8198
will perform the request of his *h*	2Sa 14:15	519
to deliver his *h* out of the hand	2Sa 14:16	519
Then thine *h* said, The word of my	2Sa 14:17	8198
words in the mouth of thine *h*	2Sa 14:19	8198
him, Hear the words of thine *h*	2Sa 20:17	519
lord, O king, swear unto thine *h*	1Kin 1:13	519
by the LORD thy God unto thine *h*	1Kin 1:17	519
beside me, while thine *h* slept	1Kin 3:20	519
Thine *h* hath not any thing in the	2Kin 4:2	8198
of God, do not lie unto thine *h*	2Kin 4:16	8198
and save the son of thine *h*	Ps 86:16	519
servant, and the son of thine *h*	Ps 116:16	519
an *h* that is heir to her mistress	Prov 30:23	8198
his servant, and every man his *h*	Jer 34:16	8198
said, Behold the *h* of the Lord	Lk 1:38	1399

HANDMAIDEN
regarded the low estate of his *h*	Lk 1:48	1399

HANDMAIDENS
Then the *h* came near, they and	Gen 33:6	8198
I be not like unto one of thine *h*	Ruth 2:13	8198
on my *h* I will pour out in those	Acts 2:18	1399

HANDMAIDS
and unto Rachel, and unto the two *h*	Gen 33:1	8198
And he put the *h* and their children	Gen 33:2	8198
the eyes of the *h* of his servants	2Sa 6:20	519
of the LORD for servants and *h*	Is 14:2	8198
and caused the servants and the *h*	Jer 34:11	8198
subjection for servants and for *h*	Jer 34:11	8198
be unto you for servants and for *h*	Jer 34:16	8198
upon the *h* in those days will I	Joel 2:29	8198

HANDS See APPENDIX.

HANDSTAVES
bows and the arrows, and the *h*	Eze 39:9	4731,3027

HANDWRITING
Blotting out the *h* of ordinances	Col 2:14	5498

HANDYWORK
and the firmament sheweth his *h*	Ps 19:1	4639,3027

HANES (ha'-nees) See TAHPANES. *A place in Egypt.*
and his ambassadors came to *H*	Is 30:4	2609

HANG
thee, and shall *h* thee on a tree	Gen 40:19	8518
shall *h* over the backside of the	Ex 26:12	5628
it shall *h* over the sides of the	Ex 26:13	5628
thou shalt *h* it upon four pillars	Ex 26:32	5414
thou shalt *h* up the vail under	Ex 26:33	5414
h up the hanging at the court	Ex 40:8	5414
h them up before the LORD against	Num 25:4	3363
to death, and thou *h* him on a tree	Deut 21:22	8518
thy life shall *h* in doubt before	Deut 28:66	8511
we will *h* them up unto the LORD	2Sa 21:6	3363
to speak unto the king to *h*	Est 6:4	8518
Then the king said, *H* him thereon	Est 7:9	8518
whereon there *h* a thousand	Song 4:4	8518
they shall *h* upon him all the	Is 22:24	8518
the virgins of Jerusalem *h* down	Lam 2:10	3381
pin of it to *h* any vessel thereon	Eze 15:3	8518
two commandments *h* all the law	Mt 22:40	2910
the venomous beast *h* on his hand	Acts 28:4	2910
lift up the hands which *h* down	Heb 12:12	3935

HANGED
But he *h* the chief baker	Gen 40:22	8518
unto mine office, and him he *h*	Gen 41:13	8518
(for he that is *h* is accursed of	Deut 21:23	8518
the king of Ai he *h* on a tree	Josh 8:29	8518
them, and *h* them on five trees	Josh 10:26	8518

h them up over the pool in Hebron	2Sa 4:12	8518
h himself, and died, and was buried	2Sa 17:23	2614
Behold, I saw Absalom *h* in an oak	2Sa 18:10	8518
they *h* them in the hill before	2Sa 21:9	3363
where the Philistines had *h* them	2Sa 21:12	8511
the bones of them that were *h*	2Sa 21:13	3363
set up, let him be *h* thereon	Ezr 6:11	4223
they were both *h* on a tree	Est 2:23	8518
that Mordecai may be *h* thereon	Est 5:14	8518
So they *h* Haman on the gallows	Est 7:10	8518
him they have *h* upon the gallows,	Est 8:7	8518
ten sons be *h* upon the gallows	Est 9:13	8518
and they *h* Haman's ten sons	Est 9:14	8518
sons should be *h* on the gallows	Est 9:25	8518
We *h* our harps upon the willows	Ps 137:2	8518
Princes are *h* up by their hand	Lam 5:12	8518
they *h* the shield and helmet in	Eze 27:10	8518
they *h* their shields upon thy	Eze 27:11	8518
a millstone were *h* about his neck	Mt 18:6	2910
and departed, and went and *h* himself	Mt 27:5	519
a millstone were *h* about his neck	Mk 9:42	4029
a millstone were *h* about his neck	Lk 17:2	4029
which were *h* railed on him	Lk 23:39	2910
whom ye slew and *h* on a tree	Acts 5:30	2910
whom they slew and *h* on a tree	Acts 10:39	2910

HANGETH
and *h* the earth upon nothing	Job 26:7	8518
is every one that *h* on a tree	Gal 3:13	2910

HANGING
thou shalt make an *h* for the door	Ex 26:36	4539
thou shalt make for the *h* five	Ex 26:37	4539
shall be an *h* of twenty cubits	Ex 27:16	4539
the *h* for the door at the	Ex 35:15	4539
the *h* for the door of the court,	Ex 35:17	4539
he made an *h* for the tabernacle	Ex 36:37	4539
the *h* for the gate of the court	Ex 38:18	4539
the *h* for the tabernacle door,	Ex 39:38	4539
the *h* for the court gate, his	Ex 39:40	4539
put the *h* of the door to the	Ex 40:5	4539
hang up the *h* at the court gate	Ex 40:8	4539
he set up the *h* at the door of	Ex 40:28	4539
set up the *h* of the court gate	Ex 40:33	4539
the *h* for the door of the	Num 3:25	4539
wherewith they minister, and the *h*	Num 3:31	4539
the *h* for the door of the	Num 4:25	4539
the *h* for the door of the gate of	Num 4:26	4539
they were *h* upon the trees until	Josh 10:26	8518

HANGINGS
be *h* for the court of fine twined	Ex 27:9	7050
be *h* of an hundred cubits long	Ex 27:11	7050
side shall be *h* of fifty cubits	Ex 27:12	7050
The *h* of one side of the gate	Ex 27:14	7050
side shall be *h* fifteen cubits	Ex 27:15	7050
The *h* of the court, his pillars,	Ex 35:17	7050
the *h* of the court were of fine	Ex 38:9	7050
side the *h* were an hundred cubits.	Ex 38:11	
west side were *h* of fifty cubits	Ex 38:12	7050
The *h* of the one side of the gate	Ex 38:14	7050
hand, were *h* of fifteen cubits	Ex 38:15	7050
All the *h* of the court round.	Ex 38:16	7050
answerable to the *h* of the court	Ex 38:18	7050
The *h* of the court, his pillars,	Ex 39:40	7050
the *h* of the court, and the	Num 3:26	7050
the *h* of the court, and the	Num 4:26	7050
the women wove *h* for the grove	2Kin 23:7	1004
were white, green, and blue, *h*	Est 1:6	

HANIEL (ha'-ne-el) See HANNIEL. *A son of Ulla.*
Arah, and *H*, and Rezia	1Chr 7:39	2592

HANNAH (han'-nah) *Mother of Samuel.*
the name of the one was *H*	1Sa 1:2	2584
children, but *H* had no children	1Sa 1:2	2584
But unto *H* he gave a worthy	1Sa 1:5	2584
for he loved *H*	1Sa 1:5	2584
Elkanah her husband to her, *H*	1Sa 1:8	2584
So *H* rose up after they had eaten	1Sa 1:9	2584
Now *H*, she spake in her heart	1Sa 1:13	2584
H answered and said, No, my lord,	1Sa 1:15	2584
and Elkanah knew *H* his wife	1Sa 1:19	2584
come about after *H* had conceived	1Sa 1:20	2584
But *H* went not up	1Sa 1:22	2584
H prayed, and said, My heart	1Sa 2:1	2584
And the LORD visited *H*, so that	1Sa 2:21	2584

HANNATHON (han'-na-thon) *A city in Zebulun.*
it on the north side to *H*	Josh 19:14	2615

HANNIEL (han'-ne-el) See HANIEL. *A prince of Manasseh.*
of Manasseh, *H* the son of Ephod	Num 34:23	2592

HANOCH (ha'-nok) See HANOCHITES, HENOCH.
1. A son of Midian.
Ephah, and Epher, and H, and Abidah, ..Gen 25:4   2585
2. A son of Reuben.
H, and Phallu, and Hezron, and Carmi ..Gen 46:9   2585
H, and Pallu, Hezron, and Carmi .... Ex 6:14   2585
H, of whom cometh the family of .... Num 26:5   2585
the firstborn of Israel were, H 1Chr 5:3   2585

HANOCHITES (ha'-nok-ites) Descendants of Hanoch 2.
whom cometh the family of the H .... Num 26:5   2599

HANUN (ha'-nun)
1. A king of Ammon.
H his son reigned in his stead 2Sa 10:1   2586
kindness unto H the son of Nahash 2Sa 10:2   2586
of Ammon said unto H their lord 2Sa 10:3   2586
Wherefore H took David's servants 2Sa 10:4   2586
kindness unto H the son of Nahash 1Chr 19:2   2586
of the children of Ammon to H 1Chr 19:2   2586
the children of Ammon said to H 1Chr 19:3   2586
Wherefore H took David's servants 1Chr 19:4   2586
themselves odious to David, H 1Chr 19:6   2586
2. A son of Zalaph.
H the sixth son of Zalaph, ... Neh 3:30   2586
3. A rebuilder of Jerusalem's wall.
The valley gate repaired H .... Neh 3:13   2586

HAP
her h was to light on a part of .... Ruth 2:3   4745

HAPHRAIM (haf-ra'-im) A city in Issachar.
And H, and Shihon, and Anaharath, ... Josh 19:19   2663

HAPLY
if h the people had eaten freely 1Sa 14:30   3863
if h he might find any thing .... Mk 11:13   686
Lest h, after he hath laid the .... Lk 14:29   3379
lest h ye be moved even to fight .... Acts 5:39   3379
if h they might feel after him, ... Acts 17:27   686
Lest h if they of Macedonia come 2Cor 9:4   3381

HAPPEN See APPENDIX.

HAPPENED See APPENDIX.

HAPPENETH
also that one event h to them all .... Eccl 2:14   7136
As it h to the fool .... Eccl 2:15   4745
so it h even to me .... Eccl 2:15   7136
unto whom it h according to the .... Eccl 8:14   5060
to whom it h according to the .... Eccl 8:14   5060
but time and chance h to them all .... Eccl 9:11   7136

HAPPIER
But she is h if she so abide, ... 1Cor 7:40   3107

HAPPIZZEZ See APHSES.

HAPPY
H am I, for the daughters will .... Gen 30:13   837
H art thou, O Israel .... Deut 33:29   835
H are thy men, are these 1Kin 10:8   835
H are thy men, and h are these 2Chr 9:7   835
h is the man whom God correcteth .... Job 5:17   835
H is the man that hath his quiver .... Ps 127:5   835
h shalt thou be, and it shall be .... Ps 128:2   835
h shall he be, that rewardeth .... Ps 137:8   835
H shall he be, that taketh and .... Ps 137:9   835
H is that people, that is in such .... Ps 144:15   835
h is that people, whose God is .... Ps 144:15   835
H is he that hath the God of .... Ps 146:5   835
H is the man that findeth wisdom .... Prov 3:13   835
h is every one that retaineth her .... Prov 3:18   833
hath mercy on the poor, h is he .... Prov 14:21   835
trusteth in the LORD, h is he .... Prov 16:20   835
H is the man that feareth alway .... Prov 28:14   835
he that keepeth the law, h is he .... Prov 29:18   835
wherefore are all they h that .... Jer 12:1   7951
And now we call the proud h .... Mal 3:15   833
things, h are ye if ye do them .... Jn 13:17   3107
I think myself h, king Agrippa, ... Acts 26:2   3107
H is he that condemneth not .... Rom 14:22   3107
we count them h which endure .... Jas 5:11   3106
for righteousness' sake, h are ye 1Pet 3:14   3107
for the name of Christ, h are ye 1Pet 4:14   3107

HARA (ha'-rah) An Assyrian province.
them unto Halah, and Habor, and H 1Chr 5:26   2024

HARADAH (har'-a-dah) A Hebrew encampment in the wilderness.
mount Shapher, and encamped in H ...... Num 33:24   2732
And they removed from H, and .... Num 33:25   2732

HARAN (ha'-ran) See BETH-HARAN, CHARRAN.
1. A son of Terah.
and begat Abram, Nahor, and H .... Gen 11:26   2309
Terah begat Abram, Nahor, and H .... Gen 11:27   2309
and H begat Lot .... Gen 11:27   2309
H died before his father Terah in .... Gen 11:28   2309
wife, Milcah, the daughter of H .... Gen 11:29   2309
and Lot the son of H his son's son .... Gen 11:31   2309
2. A Levite.
Shelomith, and Haziel, and H 1Chr 23:9   2039
3. A son of Caleb.
Ephah, Caleb's concubine, bare H 1Chr 2:46   2771
and H begat Gazez 1Chr 2:46   2771
4. A city in northern Mesopotamia.
and they came unto H, and dwelt .... Gen 11:31   2771
and Terah died in H .... Gen 11:32   2771
old when he departed out of H .... Gen 12:4   2771
souls that they had gotten in H .... Gen 12:5   2771
thou to Laban my brother to H .... Gen 27:43   2771
from Beer-sheba, and went toward H .... Gen 28:10   2771
And they said, Of H are we .... Gen 29:4   2771
as Gozan, and H, and Rezeph, and the .. 2Kin 19:12   2771
have destroyed, as Gozan, and H .... Is 37:12   2771
H, and Canneh, and Eden, the .... Eze 27:23   2771

HARARITE (har'-a-rite) Native of the hill country of Judah.
was Shammah the son of Agee the H 2Sa 23:11   2043
Shammah the H, Ahiam the son of 2Sa 23:33   2043
Ahiam the son of Sharar the H 2Sa 23:33   2043
Jonathan the son of Shage the H 1Chr 11:34   2043
Ahiam the son of Sacar the H 1Chr 11:35   2043

HARBONA (har-bo'-nah) See HARBONAH. A servant of King Ahasuerus.
he commanded Mehuman, Biztha, H ..... Est 1:10   2726

HARBONAH (har-bo'-nah) See HARBONA. Same as Harbona.
And H, one of the chamberlains, ... Est 7:9   2726

HARD
Is any thing too h for the LORD .... Gen 18:14   6381
travailed, and she had h labour .... Gen 35:16   7185
to pass, when she was in h labour .... Gen 35:17   7185
their lives bitter with h bondage .... Ex 1:14   7186
the h causes they brought unto .... Ex 18:26   7186
he take off h by the backbone .... Lev 3:9   5980
the cause that is too h for you .... Deut 1:17   7185
It shall not seem h unto thee .... Deut 15:18   7185
matter too h for thee in judgment .... Deut 17:8   6381
us, and laid upon us h bondage .... Deut 26:6   7186
went h unto the door of the tower .... Judg 9:52   5066
pursued h after them unto Gidom, ... Judg 20:45
even they also followed h after 1Sa 14:22   1692
Philistines followed h upon Saul 1Sa 31:2   1692
and horsemen followed h after him 2Sa 1:6   1692
sons of Zeruiah be too h for me 2Sa 3:39   7186
Amnon thought it h for him to do 2Sa 13:2   6381
to prove him with h questions 1Kin 10:1   2420
h by the palace of Ahab king of 1Kin 21:1   681
said, Thou hast asked a h thing 2Kin 2:10   7185
Philistines followed h after Saul 1Chr 10:2   5221
in the midst h by their buttocks 1Chr 19:4
with h questions at Jerusalem 2Chr 9:1   2420
as h as a piece of the nether .... Job 41:24   3332
hast shewed thy people h things .... Ps 60:3   7186
My soul followeth h after thee .... Ps 63:8   1692
Thy wrath lieth h upon me .... Ps 88:7   5564
they utter and speak h things .... Ps 94:4   6277
but the way of transgressors is h .... Prov 13:15   386
from the h bondage wherein thou .... Is 14:3   7186
there is nothing too h for thee .... Jer 32:17   6381
is there any thing too h for me .... Jer 32:27   6381
of an h language, but to the .... Eze 3:5   3515
of an h language, whose words .... Eze 3:6   3515
dreams, and shewing of h sentences ..... Dan 5:12   280
rowed h to bring it to the land .... Jonah 1:13
knew thee that thou art an h man .... Mt 25:24   4642
how h is it for them that trust .... Mk 10:24   1422
this, said, This is an h saying .... Jn 6:60   4642
it is h for thee to kick against .... Acts 9:5   4642
house joined h to the synagogue .... Acts 18:7   4927
it is h for thee to kick against .... Acts 26:14   4642
h to be uttered, seeing ye are .... Heb 5:11   1421
some things h to be understood 2Pet 3:16   1425
of all their h speeches which .... Jude 15   4642

HARDEN
but I will h his heart, that he .... Ex 4:21   2388
I will h Pharaoh's heart, and .... Ex 7:3   7185
I will h Pharaoh's heart, that he .... Ex 14:4   2388
I will h the hearts of the .... Ex 14:17   2388

H

thou shalt not *h* thine heart	Deut 15:7	533
was of the LORD to *h* their hearts	Josh 11:20	2388
then do ye *h* your hearts, as the	1Sa 6:6	5513
I would *h* myself in sorrow	Job 6:10	5539
H not your heart, as in the	Ps 95:8	7185
H not your hearts, as in the	Heb 3:8	4645
h not your hearts, as in the	Heb 3:15	4645
hear his voice, *h* not your hearts	Heb 4:7	4645

HARDENED

he *h* Pharaoh's heart, that he	Ex 7:13	2388
unto Moses, Pharaoh's heart is *h*	Ex 7:14	3515
and Pharaoh's heart was *h*, neither	Ex 7:22	2388
he *h* his heart, and hearkened not	Ex 8:15	3515
and Pharaoh's heart was *h*, and he	Ex 8:19	2388
Pharaoh *h* his heart at this time	Ex 8:32	3513
And the heart of Pharaoh was *h*	Ex 9:7	3515
the LORD *h* the heart of Pharaoh	Ex 9:12	2388
h his heart, he and his servants	Ex 9:34	3513
And the heart of Pharaoh was *h*	Ex 9:35	2388
for I have *h* his heart, and the	Ex 10:1	3513
But the LORD *h* Pharaoh's heart	Ex 10:20	2388
But the LORD *h* Pharaoh's heart	Ex 10:27	2388
the LORD *h* Pharaoh's heart, so	Ex 11:10	2388
the LORD *h* the heart of Pharaoh	Ex 14:8	2388
for the LORD thy God *h* his spirit	Deut 2:30	7185
and Pharaoh *h* their hearts	1Sa 6:6	3513
but *h* their necks, like to the	2Kin 17:14	7185
h his heart from turning unto the	2Chr 36:13	553
h their necks, and hearkened not	Neh 9:16	7185
but *h* their necks, and in their	Neh 9:17	7185
h their neck, and would not hear	Neh 9:29	7185
who hath *h* himself against him	Job 9:4	7185
She is *h* against her young ones	Job 39:16	7188
h our heart from thy fear	Is 63:17	7188
their ear, but *h* their neck	Jer 7:26	7185
because they have *h* their necks	Jer 19:15	7185
lifted up, and his mind *h* in pride	Dan 5:20	8631
for their heart was *h*	Mk 6:52	4456
have ye your heart yet *h*	Mk 8:17	4456
their eyes, and *h* their heart	Jn 12:40	4456
But when divers were *h*, and	Acts 19:9	4645
lest any of you be *h* through the	Heb 3:13	4645

HARDENETH

A wicked man *h* his face	Prov 21:29	5810
but he that *h* his heart shall	Prov 28:14	7185
being often reproved *h* his neck	Prov 29:1	7185
have mercy, and whom he will he *h*	Rom 9:18	4645

HARDER

A brother offended is *h* to be won	Prov 18:19	
made their faces *h* than a rock	Jer 5:3	2388
As an adamant *h* than flint have I	Eze 3:9	2389

HARDHEARTED

Israel are impudent and *h*	Eze 3:7	7186,3820

HARDLY

And when Sarai dealt *h* with her	Gen 16:6	6031
when Pharaoh would *h* let us go	Ex 13:15	7185
through it, *h* bestead and hungry	Is 8:21	7185
That a rich man shall *h* **enter**	Mt 19:23	1423
How *h* **shall they that have riches**	Mk 10:23	1423
bruising him *h* departeth from him	Lk 9:39	3425
How *h* shall they that have riches	Lk 18:24	1423
h passing it, came unto a place	Acts 27:8	3433

HARDNESS

When the dust groweth into *h*	Job 38:38	4165
Moses because of the *h* **of your**	Mt 19:8	4641
grieved for the *h* of their hearts	Mk 3:5	4457
For the *h* **of your heart he wrote**	Mk 10:5	4641
h of heart, because they believed	Mk 16:14	4641
But after thy *h* and impenitent	Rom 2:5	4643
Thou therefore endure *h*, as a	2Ti 2:3	2553

HARE

And the *h*, because he cheweth the	Lev 11:6	768
as the camel, and the *h*, and the	Deut 14:7	768

HAREPH (ha'-ref) *A son of Caleb.*

H the father of Beth-gader	1Chr 2:51	2780

HARETH (ha'-reth) *Forest land in Judah.*

came into the forest of *H*	1Sa 22:5	2802

HARHAIAH (har-ha-i'-ah) *Father of Uzziel.*

him repaired Uzziel the son of *H*	Neh 3:8	2736

HARHAS (har'-has) See HASRAH. *Grandfather of Shallum.*

the son of Tikvah, the son of *H*	2Kin 22:14	2745

HARHUR (har'-hur) *A family in exile.*

of Hakupha, the children of *H*	Ezr 2:51	2744
of Hakupha, the children of *H*	Neh 7:53	2744

HARIM (ha'-rim)

1. A priest.

The third to *H*, the fourth to	1Chr 24:8	2766
The children of *H*, a thousand and	Ezr 2:39	2766
And of the sons of *H*	Ezr 10:21	2766
Malchijah the son of *H*, and Hashub	Neh 3:11	2766
The children of *H*, a thousand and	Neh 7:42	2766
Of *H*, Adna; of Meraioth	Neh 12:15	2766

2. A family in exile.

The children of *H*, three hundred	Ezr 2:32	2766
The children of *H*, three hundred	Neh 7:35	2766

3. Married a foreigner in exile.

And of the sons of *H*	Ezr 10:31	2766

4. An Israelite who renewed the covenant.

H, Meremoth, Obadiah	Neh 10:5	2766

5. A family who renewed the covenant.

Malluch, *H*, Baanah	Neh 10:27	2766

HARIPH (ha'-rif) See JORAH.

1. A family of exiles.

The children of *H*, an hundred and	Neh 7:24	2756

2. A family who renewed the covenant.

H, Anathoth, Nebai	Neh 10:19	2756

HARLOT

deal with our sister as with an *h*	Gen 34:31	2181
her, he thought her to be an *h*	Gen 38:15	2181
place, saying, Where is the *h*	Gen 38:21	6948
There was no *h* in this place	Gen 38:21	6948
that there was no *h* in this place	Gen 38:22	6948
daughter in law hath played the *h*	Gen 38:24	2181
woman, or profane, or an *h*	Lev 21:14	2181
only Rahab the *h* shall live	Josh 6:17	2181
And Joshua saved Rahab the *h* alive	Josh 6:25	2181
valour, and he was the son of an *h*	Judg 11:1	2181
Samson to Gaza, and saw there an *h*	Judg 16:1	2181
a woman with the attire of an *h*	Prov 7:10	2181
is the faithful city become an *h*	Is 1:21	2181
years shall Tyre sing as an *h*	Is 23:15	2181
thou *h* that hast been forgotten	Is 23:16	2181
thou wanderest, playing the *h*	Jer 2:20	2181
played the *h* with many lovers	Jer 3:1	2181
tree, and there hath played the *h*	Jer 3:6	2181
but went and played the *h* also	Jer 3:8	2181
playedst the *h* because of thy	Eze 16:15	2181
and playedst the *h* thereupon	Eze 16:16	2181
thou hast played the *h* with them	Eze 16:28	2181
and hast not been as an *h*, in that	Eze 16:31	2181
Wherefore, O *h*, hear the word of	Eze 16:35	2181
thee to cease from playing the *h*	Eze 16:41	2181
played the *h* when she was mine	Eze 23:5	2181
played the *h* in the land of Egypt	Eze 23:19	2181
unto a woman that playeth the *h*	Eze 23:44	2181
their mother hath played the *h*	Hos 2:5	2181
thou shalt not play the *h*	Hos 3:3	2181
Though thou, Israel, play the *h*	Hos 4:15	2181
and have given a boy for an *h*	Joel 3:3	2181
wife shall be an *h* in the city	Amos 7:17	2181
gathered it of the hire of an *h*	Mic 1:7	2181
shall return to the hire of an *h*	Mic 1:7	2181
whoredoms of the wellfavoured *h*	Nah 3:4	2181
and make them the members of an *h*	1Cor 6:15	4204
is joined to an *h* is one body	1Cor 6:16	4204
By faith the *h* Rahab perished not	Heb 11:31	4204
Rahab the *h* justified by works	Jas 2:25	4204

HARLOT'S

went, and came into an *h* house	Josh 2:1	2181
the country, Go into the *h* house	Josh 6:22	2181

HARLOTS

came there two women, that were *h*	1Kin 3:16	2181
with *h* spendeth his substance	Prov 29:3	2181
whores, and they sacrifice with *h*	Hos 4:14	6948
the *h* **go into the kingdom of God**	Mt 21:31	4204
publicans and the *h* **believed him**	Mt 21:32	4204
hath devoured thy living with *h*	Lk 15:30	4204
THE GREAT, THE MOTHER OF *H*	Rev 17:5	4204

HARLOTS'

by troops in the *h* houses	Jer 5:7	2181

HARM

and this pillar unto me, for *h*	Gen 31:52	7451
he shall make amends for the *h*	Lev 5:16	2398
his enemies, neither sought his *h*	Num 35:23	7451
for I will no more do thee *h*	1Sa 26:21	7489
do us more *h* than did Absalom	2Sa 20:6	3415
And there was no *h* in the pot	2Kin 4:41	1697,7451
anointed, and do my prophets no *h*	1Chr 16:22	7489
anointed, and do my prophets no *h*	Ps 105:15	7489
cause, if he have done thee no *h*	Prov 3:30	7451
look well to him, and do him no *h*	Jer 39:12	7451
voice, saying, Do thyself no *h*	Acts 16:28	2556

Crete, and to have gained this *h* .... Acts 27:21	5196	
beast into the fire, and felt no *h* .... Acts 28:5	2556	
saw no *h* come to him, they.................... Acts 28:6	824	
shewed or spake any *h* of thee .... Acts 28:21	4190	
And who is he that will *h* you 1Pet 3:13	2559	

HAR-MAGEDON See ARMAGEDDON.

HARMLESS
wise as serpents, and *h* as doves ...... Mt 10:16   *185*
That ye may be blameless and *h* .... Phil 2:15   *185*
priest became us, who is holy, *h* .... Heb 7:26   *172*

HARNEPHER (har-ne´-fur) *A son of Zophah.*
Suah, and *H*, and Shual, and Beri, and.. 1Chr 7:36   2774

HARNESS
on his *h* boast himself as he that 1Kin 20:11
between the joints of the *h* 1Kin 22:34   8302
and vessels of gold, and raiment, *h* 2Chr 9:24   5402
between the joints of the *h* 2Chr 18:33   8302
H the horses .... Jer 46:4   631

HARNESSED
up *h* out of the land of Egypt .... Ex 13:18   2571

HAROD (ha´-rod) See HARODITE. *A spring of water.*
and pitched beside the well of *H* .... Judg 7:1   5878

HARODITE (ha-ro´-dite) See HARORITE. *Family name of two of David's "mighty men."*
Shammah the *H*, Elika the *H*................. 2Sa 23:25   2733

HAROEH (ha-ro´-eh) See REAIAH. *A son of Shobal.*
H, and half of the Manahethites 1Chr 2:52   7204

HARORITE (ha´-ro-rite) *Family name of a "mighty man."*
Shammoth the *H*, Helez the 1Chr 11:27   2033

HAROSHETH (har-o-sheth) *A city in Galilee.*
which dwelt in *H* of the Gentiles .... Judg 4:2   2800
from *H* of the Gentiles unto the .... Judg 4:13   2800
the host, unto *H* of the Gentiles .... Judg 4:16   2800

HARP
of all such as handle the *h* .... Gen 4:21   3658
songs, with tabret, and with *h* .... Gen 31:27   3658
and a tabret, and a pipe, and a *h* 1Sa 10:5   3658
who is a cunning player on an *h* 1Sa 16:16   3658
upon Saul, that David took an *h* 1Sa 16:23   3658
Jeduthun, who prophesied with a *h* 1Chr 25:3   3658
They take the timbrel and *h*................... Job 21:12   3658
My *h* also is turned to mourning,........... Job 30:31   3658
Praise the LORD with *h* .... Ps 33:2   3658
upon the *h* will I praise thee, O .... Ps 43:4   3658
open my dark saying upon the *h*............. Ps 49:4   3658
awake, psaltery and *h*............................ Ps 57:8   3658
unto thee will I sing with the *h*............... Ps 71:22   3658
the pleasant *h* with the psaltery .... Ps 81:2   3658
upon the *h* with a solemn sound .... Ps 92:3   3658
Sing unto the LORD with the *h* .... Ps 98:5   3658
with the *h*, and the voice of a .... Ps 98:5   3658
Awake, psaltery and *h* .... Ps 108:2   3658
praise upon the *h* unto our God .... Ps 147:7   3658
unto him with the timbrel and *h*............. Ps 149:3   3658
praise him with the psaltery and *h* .... Ps 150:3   3658
And the *h*, and the viol, the tabret .... Is 5:12   3658
shall sound like an *h* for Moab .... Is 16:11   3658
Take an *h*, go about the city,.................. Is 23:16   3658
endeth, the joy of the *h* ceaseth .... Is 24:8   3658
the sound of the cornet, flute, *h* .... Dan 3:5   7030
the sound of the cornet, flute, *h* .... Dan 3:7   7030
the sound of the cornet, flute, *h* .... Dan 3:10   7030
the sound of the cornet, flute, *h* .... Dan 3:15   7030
giving sound, whether pipe or *h* 1Cor 14:7   2788

HARPED
it be known what is piped or *h* 1Cor 14:7   2789

HARPERS
I heard the voice of *h* harping .... Rev 14:2   2790
And the voice of *h*, and musicians,........ Rev 18:22   2790

HARPING
of harpers *h* with their harps.................. Rev 14:2   2789

HARPS
made of fir wood, even on *h*................... 2Sa 6:5   3658
h also and psalteries for singers 1Kin 10:12   3658
might, and with singing, and with *h* 1Chr 13:8   3658
of musick, psalteries and *h* 1Chr 15:16   3658
with *h* on the Sheminith to excel 1Chr 15:21   3658
a noise with psalteries and *h* 1Chr 15:28   3658
Jeiel with psalteries and with *h* 1Chr 16:5   3658
who should prophesy with *h* 1Chr 25:1   3658
with cymbals, psalteries, and *h* 1Chr 25:6   3658
having cymbals and psalteries and *h*...... 2Chr 5:12   3658
and to the king's palace, and *h*.............. 2Chr 9:11   3658

to Jerusalem with psalteries and *h* 2Chr 20:28	3658	
with psalteries, and with *h*................... 2Chr 29:25	3658	
cymbals, psalteries, and with *h* .... Neh 12:27	3658	
We hanged our *h* upon the willows .... Ps 137:2	3658	
it shall be with tabrets and *h*............... Is 30:32	3658	
the sound of thy *h* shall be no .... Eze 26:13	3658	
Lamb, having every one of them *h* .... Rev 5:8	2788	
of harpers harping with their *h* .... Rev 14:2	2788	
sea of glass, having the *h* of God .... Rev 15:2	2788	

HARROW
or will he *h* the valleys after .... Job 39:10   7702

HARROWS
under *h* of iron, and under axes of.......... 2Sa 12:31   2757
with *h* of iron, and with axes 1Chr 20:3   2757

HARSHA (har´-shah) *A family of exiles.*
of Mehida, the children of *H*................... Ezr 2:52   2797
of Mehida, the children of *H*................... Neh 7:54   2797

HART
as of the roebuck, and as of the *h* .... Deut 12:15   354
the *h* is eaten, so thou shalt eat .... Deut 12:22   354
The *h*, and the roebuck, and the .... Deut 14:5   354
as the roebuck, and as the *h* .... Deut 15:22   354
As the *h* panteth after the water .... Ps 42:1   354
is like a roe or a young *h* .... Song 2:9   354
h upon the mountains of Bether .... Song 2:17   354
like to a roe or to a young *h* .... Song 8:14   354
shall the lame man leap as an *h* .... Is 35:6   354

HARTS
and an hundred sheep, beside *h* 1Kin 4:23   354
like *h* that find no pasture .... Lam 1:6   354

HARUM (ha´-rum) *Father of Aharhel.*
families of Aharhel the son of *H* 1Chr 4:8   2037

HARUMAPH (ha-ru´-maf) *Father of Jedaiah.*
repaired Jedaiah the son of *H*................. Neh 3:10   2739

HARUPHITE (ha´-ru-fite) *A Korhite soldier.*
and Shemariah, and Shephatiah the *H*.. 1Chr 12:5   2741

HARUZ (ha´-ruz) *Father of Meshullemeth.*
the daughter of *H* of Jotbah 2Kin 21:19   2743

HARVEST
earth remaineth, seedtime and *h* .... Gen 8:22   7105
went in the days of wheat *h* .... Gen 30:14   7105
shall neither be earing nor *h* .... Gen 45:6   7105
And the feast of *h*, the .... Ex 23:16   7105
time and in *h* thou shalt rest.................. Ex 34:21   7105
of the firstfruits of wheat *h* .... Ex 34:22   7105
when ye reap the *h* of your land .... Lev 19:9   7105
gather the gleanings of thy *h*.................. Lev 19:9   7105
you, and shall reap the *h* thereof .... Lev 23:10   7105
of your *h* unto the priest........................ Lev 23:10   7105
when ye reap the *h* of your land .... Lev 23:22   7105
thou gather any gleaning of thy *h* .... Lev 23:22   7105
of thy *h* thou shalt not reap .... Lev 25:5   7105
cuttest down thine *h* in thy field .... Deut 24:19   7105
all his banks all the time of *h* .... Josh 3:15   7105
after, in the time of wheat *h* .... Judg 15:1   7105
in the beginning of barley *h* .... Ruth 1:22   7105
until they have ended all my *h* .... Ruth 2:21   7105
of barley *h* and of wheat *h* .... Ruth 2:23   7105
their wheat *h* in the valley 1Sa 6:13   7105
ear his ground, and to reap his *h* 1Sa 8:12   7105
Is it not wheat *h* to day 1Sa 12:17   7105
put to death in the days of *h*.................. 2Sa 21:9   7105
in the beginning of barley *h*................... 2Sa 21:9   7105
from the beginning of *h* until 2Sa 21:10   7105
came to David in the time of *h* 2Sa 23:13   7105
Whose *h* the hungry eateth up, and ,..... Job 5:5   7105
and gathereth her food in the *h* .... Prov 6:8   7105
but he that sleepeth in *h* is a .... Prov 10:5   7105
therefore shall he beg in *h* .... Prov 20:4   7105
the cold of snow in the time of *h* .... Prov 25:13   7105
snow in summer, and as rain in *h* .... Prov 26:1   7105
thee according to the joy in *h* .... Is 9:3   7105
fruits and for thy *h* is fallen .... Is 16:9   7105
but the *h* shall be a heap in the............. Is 17:11   7105
a cloud of dew in the heat of *h* .... Is 18:4   7105
For afore the *h*, when the bud is .... Is 18:5   7105
the *h* of the river, is her .... Is 23:3   7105
And they shall eat up thine *h* .... Jer 5:17   7105
us the appointed weeks of the *h* .... Jer 5:24   7105
The *h* is past, the summer is .... Jer 8:20   7105
the sickle in the time of *h* .... Jer 50:16   7105
and the time of her *h* shall come .... Jer 51:33   7105
Judah, he hath set an *h* for thee .... Hos 6:11   7105
because the *h* of the field is .... Joel 1:11   7105
in the sickle, for the *h* is ripe .... Joel 3:13   7105
were yet three months to the *h* .... Amos 4:7   7105

H

The *h* truly is plenteous, but the	Mt 9:37	2326
ye therefore the Lord of the *h*	Mt 9:38	2326
send forth labourers into his *h*	Mt 9:38	2326
both grow together until the *h*	Mt 13:30	2326
in the time of *h* I will say to	Mt 13:30	2326
the *h* is the end of the world	Mt 13:39	2326
the sickle, because the *h* is come	Mk 4:29	2326
The *h* truly is great, but the	Lk 10:2	2326
ye therefore the Lord of the *h*	Lk 10:2	2326
send forth labourers into his *h*	Lk 10:2	2326
yet four months, and then cometh *h*	Jn 4:35	2326
for they are white already to *h*	Jn 4:35	2326
for the *h* of the earth is ripe	Rev 14:15	2326

HARVESTMAN

as when the *h* gathereth the corn	Is 17:5	7105
and as the handful into the *h*	Jer 9:22	7114

HASADIAH (has-a-di'-ah) *A son of Zerubbabel.*

and Ohel, and Berechiah, and *H*	1Chr 3:20	2619

HASENUAH (has-e-nu'-ah) See SENUAH. *Father of Hod-aviah.*

the son of Hodaviah, the son of *H*	1Chr 9:7	5574

HASHABIAH (hash-a-bi'-ah)
1. Son of Amaziah.

The son of *H*, the son of Amaziah,	1Chr 6:45	2811

2. A Merarite Levite.

the son of Azrikam, the son of *H*	1Chr 9:14	2811

3. A son of Jeduthun.

Gedaliah, and Zeri, and Jeshaiah, *H*	1Chr 25:3	2811
The twelfth to *H*, he, his sons,	1Chr 25:19	2811

4. A descendant of Hebron.

And of the Hebronites, *H* and his	1Chr 26:30	2811

5. Son of Kemuel.

the Levites, the son of Kemuel	1Chr 27:17	2811

6. A Levite chief.

and Nethaneel, his brethren, and *H*	2Chr 35:9	2811

7. A Levite in exile.

And *H*, and with him Jeshaiah of the	Ezr 8:19	2811

8. A chief priest.

of the priests, Sherebiah, *H*	Ezr 8:24	2811

9. A rebuilder of Jerusalem's wall.

Next unto him repaired *H*, the	Neh 3:17	2811

10. A Levite who renewed the covenant.

Micha, Rehob, *H*,	Neh 10:11	2811

11. Son of Bunni.

the son of Azrikam, the son of *H*	Neh 11:15	2811

12. Another Levite.

the son of Bani, the son of *H*	Neh 11:22	2811

13. A priest in Joiakim's time.

Of Hilkiah, *H*,	Neh 12:21	2811

14. A chief Levite.

H, Sherebiah, and Jeshua the son	Neh 12:24	2811

HASHABNAH (hash-ab'-nah) *A clan leader who renewed the covenant.*

Rehum, *H*, Maaseiah,	Neh 10:25	2812

HASHABNEIAH See HASHABNIAH.

HASHABNIAH (hash-ab-ni'-ah)
1. Father of Hattush.

him repaired Hattush the son of *H*	Neh 3:10	2813

2. A Levite.

Jeshua, and Kadmiel, Bani, *H*	Neh 9:5	2813

HASHBADANA (hash-bad'-a-nah) *A priest.*

and Malchiah, and Hashum, and *H*	Neh 8:4	2806

HASHBADDANAH See HASHBADANA.

HASHEM (ha'-shem) *Father of several "mighty men."*

The sons of *H* the Gizonite,	1Chr 11:34	2044

HASHMONAH (hash-mo'-nah) *A Hebrew encampment in the wilderness.*

from Mithcah, and pitched in *H*	Num 33:29	2832
And they departed from *H*, and	Num 33:30	2832

HASHUB (ha'-shub) See HASSHUB.
1. Father of Shemaiah.

Shemaiah the son of *H*, the son of	Neh 11:15	2815

2. Son of Pahath-moab.

H the son of Pahath-moab,	Neh 3:11	2815

3. A rebuilder of Jerusalem's wall.

H over against their house	Neh 3:23	2815

4. A clan leader who renewed the covenant.

Hoshea, Hananiah, *H*,	Neh 10:23	2815

HASHUBAH (hash-u'-bah) *A son of Zerubbabel.*

And *H*, and Ohel, and Berechiah, and	1Chr 3:20	2807

HASHUM (ha'-shum)
1. A family of exiles.

The children of *H*, two hundred	Ezr 2:19	2828
Of the sons of *H*	Ezr 10:33	2828
The children of *H*, three hundred	Neh 7:22	2828

2. A priest.

and Mishael, and Malchiah, and *H*	Neh 8:4	2828

3. A clan leader who renewed the covenant.

Hodijah, *H*, Bezai,	Neh 10:18	2828

HASHUPHA (hash-u'-fah) See HASUPHA. *A family of exiles.*

of Ziha, the children of *H*	Neh 7:46	2817

HASRAH (has'-rah) See HARHAS. *Same as Harhas.*

the son of Tikvath, the son of *H*	2Chr 34:22	2641

HASSENAAH (has-se-na'-ah) See SENAAH. *Father of some rebuilders of Jerusalem's wall.*

fish gate did the sons of *H* build	Neh 3:3	5570

HASSENUAH See SENUAH.

HASSHUB (hash'-ub) See HASHUB. *Father of She-maiah.*

Shemaiah the son of *H*, the son of	1Chr 9:14	2815

HASSPHERETH See SOPHERETH.

HAST See APPENDIX.

HASTE

H thee, escape thither	Gen 19:22	4116
And she made *h*, and let down her	Gen 24:46	4116
And Joseph made *h*	Gen 43:30	4116
H ye, and go up to my father, and	Gen 45:9	4116
and ye shall *h* and bring down my	Gen 45:13	4116
called for Moses and Aaron in *h*	Ex 10:16	4116
and ye shall eat it in *h*	Ex 12:11	2649
send them out of the land in *h*	Ex 12:33	4116
And Moses made *h*, and bowed his	Ex 34:8	4116
out of the land of Egypt in *h*	Deut 16:3	2649
that shall come upon them make *h*	Deut 32:35	2363
What ye have seen me do, make *h*	Judg 9:48	4116
And the woman made *h*, and ran, and	Judg 13:10	4116
make *h* now, for he came to day to	1Sa 9:12	4116
after the lad, Make speed, *h*	1Sa 20:38	2363
the king's business required *h*	1Sa 21:8	5169
David made *h* to get away for fear	1Sa 23:26	2648
Saul, saying, *H* thee, and come	1Sa 23:27	4116
Then Abigail made *h*, and took two	1Sa 25:18	2648
to pass, as she made *h* to flee	2Sa 4:4	2648
Syrians had cast away in their *h*	2Kin 7:15	2648
for God commanded me to make *h*	2Chr 35:21	926
they went up in *h* to Jerusalem	Ezr 4:23	924
king said, Cause Haman to make *h*	Est 5:5	4116
the king said to Haman, Make *h*	Est 6:10	4116
to answer, and for this I make *h*	Job 20:2	2363
O my strength, *h* thee to help me	Ps 22:19	2363
For I said in my *h*, I am cut off	Ps 31:22	2648
Make *h* to help me, O Lord my	Ps 38:22	2363
O LORD, make *h* to help me	Ps 40:13	2363
Make *h*, O God, to deliver me	Ps 70:1	
to help me, O LORD	Ps 70:1	2363
make *h* unto me, O God	Ps 70:5	2363
O my God, make *h* for my help	Ps 71:12	2439
I said in my *h*, All men are liars	Ps 116:11	2648
I made *h*, and delayed not to keep	Ps 119:60	2363
make *h* unto me	Ps 141:1	2363
to evil, and make *h* to shed blood	Prov 1:16	4116
but he that maketh *h* to be rich	Prov 28:20	213
Make *h*, my beloved, and be thou	Song 8:14	1272
that believeth shall not make *h*	Is 28:16	2363
Thy children shall make *h*	Is 49:17	4116
For ye shall not go out with *h*	Is 52:12	2649
they *h* to shed innocent	Is 59:7	4116
And let them make *h*, and take up a	Jer 9:18	4116
in Daniel before the king in *h*	Dan 2:25	927
was astonied, and rose up in *h*	Dan 3:24	927
went in *h* unto the den of lions	Dan 6:19	927
they shall make *h* to the wall	Nah 2:5	4116
straightway with *h* unto the king	Mk 6:25	4710
went into the hill country with *h*	Lk 1:39	4710
And they came with *h*, and found	Lk 2:16	4692
said unto him, Zacchaeus, make *h*	Lk 19:5	4692
And he made *h*, and came down, and	Lk 19:6	4692
And saw him saying unto me, Make *h*	Acts 22:18	4692

HASTED

and he *h* to dress it	Gen 18:7	4116
and she *h*, and let down her pitcher	Gen 24:18	4116
And she *h*, and emptied her pitcher	Gen 24:20	4116
And the taskmasters *h* them	Ex 5:13	213
and the people *h* and passed over	Josh 4:10	4116
king of Ai saw it, that they *h*	Josh 8:14	4116
into the city, and took it, and *h*	Josh 8:19	4116
h not to go down about a whole	Josh 10:13	213
And the liers in wait *h*, and rushed	Judg 20:37	2363
nigh to meet David, that David *h*	1Sa 17:48	4116
And when Abigail saw David, she *h*	1Sa 25:23	4116

HASTEN (continued)

hurting thee, except thou hadst *h* .... 1Sa 25:34 — 4116
And Abigail *h*, and arose, and rode .... 1Sa 25:42 — 4116
and she *h*, and killed it, and took .... 1Sa 28:24 — 4116
which was of Bahurim, *h* and came ...... 2Sa 19:16 — 4116
And he *h*, and took the ashes away .... 1Kin 20:41 — 4116
Then they *h*, and took every man .... 2Kin 9:13 — 4116
himself *h* also to go out, because .... 2Chr 26:20 — 1765
But Haman *h* to his house mourning .... Est 6:12 — 1765
h to bring Haman unto the banquet ...... Est 6:14 — 926
or if my foot hath *h* to deceit .... Job 31:5 — 2363
they were troubled, and *h* away .... Ps 48:5 — 2648
voice of thy thunder they *h* away .... Ps 104:7 — 2648
for he *h*, if it were possible for .... Acts 20:16 — *4692*

HASTEN
H hither Micaiah the son of Imlah .... 1Kin 22:9 — 4116
year, and see that ye *h* the matter .... 2Chr 24:5 — 4116
that *h* after another god .... Ps 16:4 — 4116
I would *h* my escape from the .... Ps 55:8 — 2363
eat, or who else can *h* hereunto .... Eccl 2:25 — 2363
h his work, that we may see it .... Is 5:19 — 2363
I the LORD will *h* it in his time .... Is 60:22 — 2363
for I will *h* my word to perform .... Jer 1:12 — 8245

HASTENED
Abraham *h* into the tent unto .... Gen 18:6 — 4116
arose, then the angels *h* Lot .... Gen 19:15 — 213
Howbeit the Levites *h* it not .... 2Chr 24:5 — 4116
being *h* by the king's commandment .... Est 3:15 — 1765
mules and camels went out, being *h* .... Est 8:14 — 926
I have not *h* from being a pastor .... Jer 17:16 — 213

HASTENETH
The captive exile *h* that he may .... Is 51:14 — 4116

HASTETH
as the eagle that *h* to the prey .... Job 9:26 — 2907
he drinketh up a river, and *h* not .... Job 40:23 — 2648
as a bird *h* to the snare, and .... Prov 7:23 — 4116
he that *h* with his feet sinneth .... Prov 19:2 — 213
He that *h* to be rich hath an evil .... Prov 28:22 — 926
h to his place where he arose .... Eccl 1:5 — 7602
to come, and his affliction *h* fast .... Jer 48:16 — 4116
fly as the eagle that *h* to eat .... Hab 1:8 — 2363
h greatly, even the voice of the .... Zeph 1:14 — 4116

HASTILY
they brought him *h* out of the .... Gen 41:14 — 7323
without driving them out *h* .... Judg 2:23 — 4118
Then he called *h* unto the young .... Judg 9:54 — 4120
And the man came in *h*, and told Eli ..... 1Sa 4:14 — 4116
come from him, and did *h* catch it .... 1Kin 20:33 — 4116
may be gotten *h* at the beginning .... Prov 20:21 — 926
Go not forth *h* to strive, lest .... Prov 25:8 — 4118
they saw Mary, that she rose up *h* .... Jn 11:31 — *5030*

HASTING
judgment, and *h* righteousness .... Is 16:5 — 4106
h unto the coming of the day of .... 2Pet 3:12 — *4692*

HASTY
but he that is *h* of spirit .... Prov 14:29 — 7116
every one that is *h* only to want .... Prov 21:5 — 213
thou a man that is *h* in his words .... Prov 29:20 — 213
let not thine heart be *h* to utter .... Eccl 5:2 — 4116
Be not *h* in thy spirit to be .... Eccl 7:9 — 926
Be not *h* to go out of his sight .... Eccl 8:3 — 926
as the *h* fruit before the summer .... Is 28:4 — 1061
is the decree so *h* from the king .... Dan 2:15 — 2685
h nation, which shall march .... Hab 1:6 — 4116

HASUPHA (has·u´·fah) A family of exiles.
of Ziha, the children of *H* .... Ezr 2:43 — 2817

HATACH (ha´-tak) A servant of King Ahasuerus.
Then called Esther for *H*, one of .... Est 4:5 — 2047
So *H* went forth to Mordecai unto .... Est 4:6 — 2047
H came and told Esther the words .... Est 4:9 — 2047
Again Esther spake unto *H* .... Est 4:10 — 2047

HATCH
owl make her nest, and lay, and *h* .... Is 34:15 — 1234
They as cockatrice' eggs, and weave .... Is 59:5 — 1234

HATCHETH
sitteth on eggs, and *h* them not .... Jer 17:11 — 3205

HATE
the gate of those which *h* them .... Gen 24:60 — 8130
come ye to me, seeing ye *h* me .... Gen 26:27 — 8130
Joseph will peradventure *h* us .... Gen 50:15 — 7852
generation of them that *h* me .... Ex 20:5 — 8130
Thou shalt not *h* thy brother in .... Lev 19:17 — 8130
they that *h* you shall reign over .... Lev 26:17 — 8130
let them that *h* thee flee before .... Num 10:35 — 8130
generation of them that *h* me .... Deut 5:9 — 8130
them that *h* him to their face .... Deut 7:10 — 8130

them upon all them that *h* thee .... Deut 7:15 — 8130
But if any man *h* his neighbour .... Deut 19:11 — 8130
and go in unto her, and *h* her, ... Deut 22:13 — 8130
And if the latter husband *h* her .... Deut 24:3 — 8130
enemies, and on them that *h* thee .... Deut 30:7 — 8130
and will reward them that *h* me .... Deut 32:41 — 8130
him, and of them that *h* him .... Deut 33:11 — 8130
elders of Gilead, Did not ye *h* me .... Judg 11:7 — 8130
him, and said, Thou dost but *h* me .... Judg 14:16 — 8130
I might destroy them that *h* me .... 2Sa 22:41 — 8130
but I *h* him .... 1Kin 22:8 — 8130
but I *h* him .... 2Chr 18:7 — 8130
and love them that *h* the LORD .... 2Chr 19:2 — 8130
They that *h* thee shall be clothed .... Job 8:22 — 8130
which I suffer of them that *h* me .... Ps 9:13 — 8130
I might destroy them that *h* me .... Ps 18:40 — 8130
shall find out those that *h* thee .... Ps 21:8 — 8130
they *h* me with cruel hatred .... Ps 25:19 — 8130
they that *h* the righteous shall .... Ps 34:21 — 8130
the eye that *h* me without a cause .... Ps 35:19 — 8130
they that *h* me wrongfully are .... Ps 38:19 — 8130
All that *h* me whisper together .... Ps 41:7 — 8130
they which *h* us spoil for .... Ps 44:10 — 8130
upon me, and in wrath they *h* me .... Ps 55:3 — 7852
let them also that *h* him flee .... Ps 68:1 — 8130
They that *h* me without a cause .... Ps 69:4 — 8130
be delivered from them that *h* me .... Ps 69:14 — 8130
they that *h* thee have lifted up .... Ps 83:2 — 8130
that they which *h* me may see it .... Ps 86:17 — 8130
face, and plague them that *h* him .... Ps 89:23 — 8130
Ye that love the LORD, *h* evil .... Ps 97:10 — 8130
I *h* the work of them that turn .... Ps 101:3 — 8130
their heart to *h* his people .... Ps 105:25 — 8130
see my desire upon them that *h* me ...... Ps 118:7 — 8130
therefore I *h* every false way .... Ps 119:104 — 8130
I *h* vain thoughts .... Ps 119:113 — 8130
and I *h* every false way .... Ps 119:128 — 8130
I *h* and abhor lying .... Ps 119:163 — 8130
and turned back that *h* Zion .... Ps 129:5 — 8130
I *h* them, O LORD, that *h* thee .... Ps 139:21 — 8130
I *h* them with perfect hatred .... Ps 139:22 — 8130
scorning, and fools *h* knowledge .... Prov 1:22 — 8130
These six things doth the LORD *h* .... Prov 6:16 — 8130
The fear of the LORD is to *h* evil .... Prov 8:13 — 8130
way, and the froward mouth, do I *h* ...... Prov 8:13 — 8130
all they that *h* me love death .... Prov 8:36 — 8130
not a scorner, lest he *h* thee .... Prov 9:8 — 8130
the brethren of the poor do *h* him .... Prov 19:7 — 8130
he be weary of thee, and so *h* thee .... Prov 25:17 — 8130
The bloodthirsty *h* the upright .... Prov 29:10 — 8130
A time to love, and a time to *h* .... Eccl 3:8 — 8130
I *h* robbery for burnt offering .... Is 61:8 — 8130
this abominable thing that I *h* .... Jer 44:4 — 8130
unto the will of them that *h* thee .... Eze 16:27 — 8130
the dream to them that *h* thee .... Dan 4:19 — 8131
They *h* him that rebuketh in the .... Amos 5:10 — 8130
H the evil, and love the good, and .... Amos 5:15 — 8130
I *h*, I despise your feast days, ... Amos 5:21 — 8130
of Jacob, and *h* his palaces .... Amos 6:8 — 8130
Who *h* the good, and love the evil .... Mic 3:2 — 8130
for all these are things that I *h* .... Zec 8:17 — 8130
thy neighbour, and *h* thine enemy ..... Mt 5:43 — *3404*
you, do good to them that *h* you .... Mt 5:44 — *3404*
for either he will *h* the one .... Mt 6:24 — *3404*
another, and shall *h* one another .... Mt 24:10 — *3404*
and from the hand of all that *h* us .... Lk 1:71 — *3404*
are ye, when men shall *h* you .... Lk 6:22 — *3404*
do good to them which *h* you .... Lk 6:27 — *3404*
***h* not his father, and mother, and** .... Lk 14:26 — *3404*
for either he will *h* the one .... Lk 16:13 — *3404*
The world cannot *h* you .... Jn 7:7 — *3404*
If the world *h* you, ye know that .... Jn 15:18 — *3404*
but what I *h*, that do I .... Rom 7:15 — *3404*
my brethren, if the world *h* you .... 1Jn 3:13 — *3404*
the Nicolaitanes, which I also *h* .... Rev 2:6 — *3404*
the Nicolaitanes, which I *h* .... Rev 2:15 — *3404*
beast, these shall *h* the whore .... Rev 17:16 — *3404*

HATED
Esau *h* Jacob because of the .... Gen 27:41 — 7852
when the LORD saw that Leah was *h* ..... Gen 29:31 — 8130
the LORD hath heard that I was *h* .... Gen 29:33 — 8130
than all his brethren, they *h* him .... Gen 37:4 — 8130
and they *h* him yet the more .... Gen 37:5 — 8130
they *h* him yet the more for his .... Gen 37:8 — 8130
him, and shot at him, and *h* him .... Gen 49:23 — 7852
and said, Because the LORD *h* us .... Deut 1:27 — 8135
and *h* him not in times past .... Deut 4:42 — 8130
them, and because he *h* them .... Deut 9:28 — 8135
whom he *h* not in time past .... Deut 19:4 — 8130
inasmuch as he *h* him not in time .... Deut 19:6 — 8130

H

wives, one beloved, and another *h*	Deut 21:15	8130
both the beloved and the *h*	Deut 21:15	8130
firstborn son be hers that was *h*	Deut 21:15	8146
firstborn before the son of the *h*	Deut 21:16	8130
son of the *h* for the firstborn	Deut 21:17	8130
and *h* him not beforetime	Josh 20:5	8130
that thou hadst utterly *h* her	Judg 15:2	8130
that are *h* of David's soul, he	2Sa 5:8	8130
Then Amnon *h* her exceedingly	2Sa 13:15	8130
h her was greater than the love	2Sa 13:15	8130
for Absalom *h* Amnon, because he	2Sa 13:22	8130
enemy, and from them that *h* me	2Sa 22:18	8130
had rule over them that *h* them	Est 9:1	8130
they would unto those that *h* them	Est 9:5	8130
the destruction of him that *h* me	Job 31:29	8130
enemy, and from them which *h* me	Ps 18:17	8130
I have *h* the congregation of	Ps 26:5	8130
I have *h* them that regard lying	Ps 31:6	8130
hast put them to shame that *h* us	Ps 44:7	8130
neither was it he that *h* me that	Ps 55:12	8130
from the hand of him that *h* them	Ps 106:10	8130
they that *h* them ruled over them	Ps 106:41	8130
For that they *h* knowledge	Prov 1:29	8130
How have I *h* instruction, and my	Prov 5:12	8130
and a man of wicked devices is *h*	Prov 14:17	8130
The poor is *h* even of his own	Prov 14:20	8130
Therefore I *h* life	Eccl 2:17	8130
I *h* all my labour which I had	Eccl 2:18	8130
thou hast been forsaken and *h*	Is 60:15	8130
Your brethren that *h* you, that	Is 66:5	8130
therefore have I *h* it	Jer 12:8	8130
with all them that thou hast *h*	Eze 16:37	8130
sith thou hast not *h* blood	Eze 35:6	8130
for there I *h* them	Hos 9:15	8130
I *h* Esau, and laid his mountains	Mal 1:3	8130
ye shall be *h* of all men for my	Mt 10:22	3404
ye shall be *h* of all nations for	Mt 24:9	3404
ye shall be *h* of all men for my	Mk 13:13	3404
But his citizens *h* him, and sent a	Lk 19:14	3404
ye shall be *h* of all men for my	Lk 21:17	3404
ye know that it *h* me before it	Jn 15:18	3404
me before it *h* you	Jn 15:18	
seen and *h* both me and my Father	Jn 15:24	3404
They *h* me without a cause	Jn 15:25	3404
and the world hath *h* them, because	Jn 17:14	3404
have I loved, but Esau have I *h*	Rom 9:13	3404
no man ever yet *h* his own flesh	Eph 5:29	3404
righteousness, and *h* iniquity	Heb 1:9	3404

HATEFUL
his iniquity be found to be *h*	Ps 36:2	8130
living in malice and envy, *h*	Titus 3:3	4767
a cage of every unclean and *h* bird	Rev 18:2	3404

HATEFULLY
And they shall deal with thee *h*	Eze 23:29	8135

HATERS
The *h* of the LORD should have	Ps 81:15	8130
h of God, despiteful, proud,	Rom 1:30	2319

HATEST
thine enemies, and *h* thy friends	2Sa 19:6	8130
thou *h* all workers of iniquity	Ps 5:5	8130
righteousness, and *h* wickedness	Ps 45:7	8130
Seeing thou *h* instruction	Ps 50:17	8130
into the hand of them whom thou *h*	Eze 23:28	8130
that thou *h* the deeds of the	Rev 2:6	3404

HATETH
h thee lying under his burden	Ex 23:5	8130
not be slack to him that *h* him	Deut 7:10	8130
to the LORD, which he *h*, have	Deut 12:31	8130
which the LORD thy God *h*	Deut 16:22	8130
this man to wife, and he *h* her	Deut 22:16	8130
teareth me in his wrath, who *h* me	Job 16:9	7852
Shall even he that *h* right govern	Job 34:17	8130
that loveth violence his soul *h*	Ps 11:5	8130
long dwelt with him that *h* peace	Ps 120:6	8130
he that *h* suretiship is sure	Prov 11:15	8130
but he that *h* reproof is brutish	Prov 12:1	8130
A righteous man *h* lying	Prov 13:5	8130
He that spareth his rod *h* his son	Prov 13:24	8130
he that *h* reproof shall die	Prov 15:10	8130
but he that *h* gifts shall live	Prov 15:27	8130
He that *h* dissembleth with his	Prov 26:24	8130
A lying tongue *h* those that are	Prov 26:28	8130
but he that *h* covetousness shall	Prov 28:16	8130
with a thief *h* his own soul	Prov 29:24	8130
your appointed feasts my soul *h*	Is 1:14	8130
saith that he *h* putting away	Mal 2:16	8130
one that doeth evil *h* the light	Jn 3:20	3404
but me it *h*, because I testify of	Jn 7:7	3404

he that *h* his life in this world	Jn 12:25	3404
world, therefore the world *h* you	Jn 15:19	3404
He that *h* me *h* my Father	Jn 15:23	3404
h his brother, is in darkness	1Jn 2:9	3404
But he that *h* his brother is in	1Jn 2:11	3404
Whosoever *h* his brother is a	1Jn 3:15	3404
h his brother, he is a liar	1Jn 4:20	3404

HATH See APPENDIX.

HATHACH See HATACH.

HATHATH (ha'-thath) *Son of Othniel.*
sons of Othniel; H	1Chr 4:13	2867

HATING
God, men of truth, *h* covetousness	Ex 18:21	8130
envy, hateful, and *h* one another	Titus 3:3	3404
h even the garment spotted by the	Jude 23	3404

HATIPHA (hat'-if-ah) *A family of exiles.*
of Neziah, the children of H	Ezr 2:54	2412
of Neziah, the children of H	Neh 7:56	2412

HATITA (hat'-it-ah) *A family of exiles.*
of Akkub, the children of H	Ezr 2:42	2410
of Akkub, the children of H	Neh 7:45	2410

HATRED
But if he thrust him of *h*	Num 35:20	8135
so that the *h* wherewith he hated	2Sa 13:15	8135
and they hate me with cruel *h*	Ps 25:19	8135
me about also with words of *h*	Ps 109:3	8135
evil for good, and *h* for my love	Ps 109:5	8135
I hate them with perfect *h*	Ps 139:22	8135
H stirreth up strifes	Prov 10:12	8135
He that hideth *h* with lying lips,	Prov 10:18	8135
than a stalled ox and *h* therewith	Prov 15:17	8135
Whose *h* is covered by deceit, his	Prov 26:26	8135
or *h* by all that is before them	Eccl 9:1	8135
Also their love, and their *h*	Eccl 9:6	8135
to destroy it for the old *h*	Eze 25:15	342
thou hast had a perpetual *h*	Eze 35:5	8135
used out of thy *h* against them	Eze 35:11	8135
of thine iniquity, and the great *h*	Hos 9:7	4895
h in the house of his God	Hos 9:8	4895
Idolatry, witchcraft, *h*, variance	Gal 5:20	2189

HATS
coats, their hosen, and their *h*	Dan 3:21	3737

HATTIL (hat'-til) *A family of exiles.*
of Shephatiah, the children of H	Ezr 2:57	2411
of Shephatiah, the children of H	Neh 7:59	2411

HATTUSH (hat'-tush)
1. A son of Shemaiah.
H, and Igeal, and Bariah, and	1Chr 3:22	2407
the sons of David; H	Ezr 8:2	2407

3. A priest.
Amariah, Malluch, H,	Neh 12:2	2407

4. A rebuilder of Jerusalem's wall.
repaired H the son of Hashabniah	Neh 3:10	2407

5. Renewed the covenant.
H, Shebaniah, Malluch,	Neh 10:4	2407

HAUGHTILY
neither shall ye go *h*	Mic 2:3	7317

HAUGHTINESS
the *h* of men shall be bowed down,	Is 2:11	7312
the *h* of men shall be made low	Is 2:17	7312
lay low the *h* of the terrible	Is 13:11	1346
even of his *h*, and his pride, and	Is 16:6	1346
his pride, and the *h* of his heart	Jer 48:29	7312

HAUGHTY
but thine eyes are upon the *h*	2Sa 22:28	7311
Lord, my heart is not *h*, nor mine	Ps 131:1	1361
an *h* spirit before a fall	Prov 16:18	1363
destruction the heart of man is *h*	Prov 18:12	1361
h scorner is his name, who	Prov 21:24	3093
the daughters of Zion are *h*	Is 3:16	1361
down, and the *h* shall be humbled	Is 10:33	1364
the *h* people of the earth do	Is 24:4	4791
And they were *h*, and committed	Eze 16:50	1361
thou shalt no more be *h* because	Zeph 3:11	1361

HAUNT
and see his place where his *h* is	1Sa 23:22	7272
himself and his men were wont to *h*	1Sa 30:31	1980
terror to be on all that *h* it	Eze 26:17	3427

HAURAN (hau'-ran) *A province south of Damascus.*
which is by the coast of H	Eze 47:16	2362
east side ye shall measure from H	Eze 47:18	2362

HAVE See APPENDIX.

HAVEN

shall dwell at the *h* of the sea	Gen 49:13	2348
and he shall be for an *h* of ships	Gen 49:13	2348
them unto their desired *h*.	Ps 107:30	4231
because the *h* was not commodious	Acts 27:12	3040
which is an *h* of Crete, and lieth	Acts 27:12	3040

HAVENS

place which is called The fair *h*	Acts 27:8	2568

HAVILAH (hav'-il-ah)
1. A son of Cush.

and *H*, and Sabtah, and Raamah,	Gen 10:7	2341
Seba, and *H*, and Sabta, and Raamah,	1Chr 1:9	2341

2. A son of Joktan.

And Ophir, and *H*, and Jobab	Gen 10:29	2341
And Ophir, and *H*, and Jobab	1Chr 1:23	2341

3. A land west of Ural.

compasseth the whole land of *H*	Gen 2:11	2341

4. A district east of Amalek.

And they dwelt from *H* unto Shur	Gen 25:18	2341
from *H* until thou comest to Shur	1Sa 15:7	2341

HAVING See APPENDIX.

HAVOCK

he made *h* of the church, entering	Acts 8:3	3075

HAVOTH-JAIR (ha'-voth-ja'-ir) See BASHAN-HAVOTH.
Villages in Gilead.

towns thereof, and called them *H*	Num 32:41	2334
which are called *H* unto this day	Judg 10:4	2334

HAWK

And the owl, and the night *h*	Lev 11:16	8464
cuckow, and the *h* after his kind,	Lev 11:16	5322
And the owl, and the night *h*	Deut 14:15	8464
cuckow, and the *h* after his kind,	Deut 14:15	5322
Doth the *h* fly by thy wisdom, and	Job 39:26	5322

HAY

The *h* appeareth, and the tender	Prov 27:25	2682
for the *h* is withered away, the	Is 15:6	2682
silver, precious stones, wood, *h*	1Cor 3:12	5528

HAZAEL (ha'-za-el) A king of Syria.

anoint *H* to be king over Syria	1Kin 19:15	2371
the sword of *H* shall Jehu slay	1Kin 19:17	2371
And the king said unto *H*, Take a	2Kin 8:8	2371
So *H* went to meet him, and took a	2Kin 8:9	2371
H said, Why weepeth my lord	2Kin 8:12	2371
H said, But what, is thy servant	2Kin 8:13	2371
and *H* reigned in his stead.	2Kin 8:15	2371
H king of Syria in Ramoth-gilead	2Kin 8:28	2371
he fought against *H* king of Syria	2Kin 8:29	2371
because of *H* king of Syria	2Kin 9:14	2371
he fought with *H* king of Syria	2Kin 9:15	2371
H smote them in all the coasts of	2Kin 10:32	2371
Then *H* king of Syria went up, and	2Kin 12:17	2371
H set his face to go up to	2Kin 12:17	2371
sent it to *H* king of Syria	2Kin 12:18	2371
into the hand of *H* king of Syria	2Kin 13:3	2371
hand of Ben-hadad the son of *H*	2Kin 13:3	2371
But *H* king of Syria oppressed	2Kin 13:22	2371
So *H* king of Syria died	2Kin 13:24	2371
Ben-hadad the son of *H* the cities	2Kin 13:25	2371
king of Israel to war against *H*	2Chr 22:5	2371
he fought with *H* king of Syria	2Chr 22:6	2371
send a fire into the house of *H*	Amos 1:4	2371

HAZAIAH (ha-za-i'-ah) Son of Adaiah.

the son of Colhozeh, the son of *H*	Neh 11:5	2382

HAZAR-ADDAR (ha'-zar-ad'-dar) See ADDAR. A place in southern Palestine.

and shall go on to *H*, and pass on	Num 34:4	2692

HAZARDED

Men that have *h* their lives for	Acts 15:26	3860

HAZAR-ENAN (ha'-zar-e'-nan) A village in north-eastern Palestine.

goings out of it shall be at *H*	Num 34:9	2704
east border from *H* to Shepham	Num 34:10	2704
border from the sea shall be *H*	Eze 47:17	2703
as one goeth to Hamath, *H*	Eze 48:1	2704

HAZAR-GADDAH (ha'-zar-gad'-dah) A town in Judah.

And *H*, and Heshmon, and Beth-palet,	Josh 15:27	2693

HAZAR-HATTICON (ha'-zar-hat'-ti-con) A place in Hauran.

H, which is by the coast of	Eze 47:16	2694

HAZARMAVETH (ha-zar-ma'-veth) A son of Joktan.

begat Almodad, and Sheleph, and *H*	Gen 10:26	2700
begat Almodad, and Sheleph, and *H*	1Chr 1:20	2700

HAZAR-SHUAL (ha'-zar-shoo'-al) A town in Judah.

And *H*, and Beer-sheba, and	Josh 15:28	2705
And *H*, and Balah, and Azem,	Josh 19:3	2705
at Beer-sheba, and Moladah, and *H*	1Chr 4:28	2705
And at *H*, and at Beer-sheba, and in	Neh 11:27	2705

HAZAR-SUSAH (ha'-zar-soo'-sah) See HAZAR-SUSIM. A city in Judah.

Ziklag, and Beth-marcaboth, and *H*	Josh 19:5	2701

HAZAR-SUSIM (ha'-zar-soo'-sim) See HAZAR-SUSAH. Same as Hazar-susah.

And at Beth-marcaboth, and *H*	1Chr 4:31	2702

HAZAZON-TAMAR (haz'-a-zon-ta'-mar) See HAZEZON-TAMAR. A name for En-gedi.

and, behold, they be in *H*, which	2Chr 20:2	2688

HAZEL

rods of green poplar, and of the *h*	Gen 30:37	3869

HAZELELPONI (haz-el-el-po'-ni) Sister of the sons of Etam.

and the name of their sister was *H*	1Chr 4:3	6753

HAZER-HATTICON See HAZAR-HATTICON.

HAZERIM (haz'-e-rim) A district near Gaza.

And the Avims which dwelt in *H*	Deut 2:23	2699

HAZEROTH (haz'-e-roth) A Hebrew encampment in the wilderness.

from Kibroth-hattaavah unto *H*	Num 11:35	2698
and abode at *H*	Num 11:35	2698
the people removed from *H*	Num 12:16	2698
and encamped at *H*	Num 33:17	2698
And they departed from *H*, and	Num 33:18	2698
Paran, and Tophel, and Laban, and *H*	Deut 1:1	2698

HAZEZON-TAMAR (haz'-e-zon-ta'-mar) See EN-GEDI, HAZAZON-TAMAR. Same as Hazazon-tamar.

the Amorites, that dwelt in *H*	Gen 14:7	2688

HAZIEL (ha'-ze-el) A Levite.

Shelomith, and *H*, and Haran, three	1Chr 23:9	2381

HAZO (ha'-zo) A son of Nahor.

And Chesed, and *H*, and Pildash, and	Gen 22:22	2375

HAZOBEBAH See HAZELELPONI.

HAZOR (ha'-zor) See BAAL-HAZOR, EN-HAZOR, HEZRON.
1. A fortified city in Naphtali.

when Jabin king of *H* had heard	Josh 11:1	2674
that time turned back, and took *H*	Josh 11:10	2674
for *H* beforetime was the head of	Josh 11:10	2674
and he burnt *H* with fire	Josh 11:11	2674
burned none of them, save *H* only	Josh 11:13	2674
the king of *H*, one	Josh 12:19	2674
And Adamah, and Ramah, and *H*	Josh 19:36	2674
king of Canaan, that reigned in *H*	Judg 4:2	2674
peace between Jabin the king of *H*	Judg 4:17	2674
Sisera, captain of the host of *H*	1Sa 12:9	2674
and the wall of Jerusalem, and *H*	1Kin 9:15	2674
H, Ramah, Gittaim,	Neh 11:33	2674

2. A city in Judah.

And Kedesh, and *H*, and Ithnan,	Josh 15:23	2674
and Janoah, and Kedesh, and *H*	2Kin 15:29	2674

3. Another town in Judah.

And *H*, Hadattah, and Kerioth, and	Josh 15:25	2675
and Kerioth, and Hezron, which is *H*	Josh 15:25	2674

4. Where the Benjamites lived after the Exile.

and concerning the kingdoms of *H*	Jer 49:28	2674

5. An area in eastern Arabia.

dwell deep, O ye inhabitants of *H*	Jer 49:30	2674
H shall be a dwelling for dragons	Jer 49:33	2674

HAZZELELPONI See HAZELELPONI.

HE (hay) See APPENDIX. A Hebrew letter.

HEAD

it shall bruise thy *h*, and thou	Gen 3:15	7218
And the man bowed down his *h*	Gen 24:26	
And I bowed down my *h*, and	Gen 24:48	
shall Pharaoh lift up thine *h*	Gen 40:13	7218
I had three white baskets on my *h*	Gen 40:16	7218
them out of the basket upon my *h*	Gen 40:17	7218
lift up thy *h* from off thee	Gen 40:19	7218
he lifted up the *h* of the chief	Gen 40:20	7218
bowed himself upon the bed's *h*	Gen 47:31	7218
hand, and laid it upon Ephraim's *h*	Gen 48:14	7218
his left hand upon Manasseh's *h*	Gen 48:14	7218
right hand upon the *h* of Ephraim	Gen 48:17	7218
Ephraim's *h* unto Manasseh's *h*	Gen 48:17	7218
put thy right hand upon his *h*	Gen 48:18	7218
they shall be on the *h* of Joseph	Gen 49:26	7218
on the crown of the *h* of him that	Gen 49:26	6936
his *h* with his legs, and with the	Ex 12:9	7218
And the people bowed the *h*	Ex 12:27	

above the *h* of it unto one ring	Ex 26:24	7218
shalt put the mitre upon his *h*	Ex 29:6	7218
oil, and pour it upon his *h*	Ex 29:7	7218
hands upon the *h* of the bullock	Ex 29:10	7218
their hands upon the *h* of the ram	Ex 29:15	7218
unto his pieces, and unto his *h*	Ex 29:17	7218
their hands upon the *h* of the ram	Ex 29:19	7218
bowed his *h* toward the earth, and	Ex 34:8	
coupled together at the *h* thereof	Ex 36:29	7218
upon the *h* of the burnt offering	Lev 1:4	7218
sons, shall lay the parts, the *h*	Lev 1:8	7218
it into his pieces, with his *h*	Lev 1:12	7218
the altar, and wring off his *h*	Lev 1:15	7218
hand upon the *h* of his offering	Lev 3:2	7218
hand upon the *h* of his offering	Lev 3:8	7218
lay his hand upon the *h* of it	Lev 3:13	7218
lay his hand upon the bullock's *h*	Lev 4:4	7218
and all his flesh, with his *h*	Lev 4:11	7218
h of the bullock before the LORD	Lev 4:15	7218
his hand upon the *h* of the goat	Lev 4:24	7218
upon the *h* of the sin offering	Lev 4:29	7218
upon the *h* of the sin offering	Lev 4:33	7218
and wring off his *h* from his neck	Lev 5:8	7218
And he put the mitre upon his *h*	Lev 8:9	7218
the anointing oil upon Aaron's *h*	Lev 8:12	7218
the *h* of the bullock for the sin	Lev 8:14	7218
their hands upon the *h* of the ram	Lev 8:18	7218
and Moses burnt the *h*, and the	Lev 8:20	7218
their hands upon the *h* of the ram	Lev 8:22	7218
with the pieces thereof, and the *h*	Lev 9:13	7218
from his *h* even to his foot	Lev 13:12	7218
a plague upon the *h* or the beard	Lev 13:29	7218
a leprosy upon the *h* or beard	Lev 13:30	7218
whose hair is fallen off his *h*	Lev 13:40	7218
the part of his *h* toward his face	Lev 13:41	7218
And if there be in the bald *h*	Lev 13:42	
a leprosy sprung up in his bald *h*	Lev 13:42	
be white reddish in his bald *h*	Lev 13:43	
his plague is in his *h*	Lev 13:44	7218
his *h* bare, and he shall put a	Lev 13:45	7218
shave all his hair off his *h*	Lev 14:9	7218
hand he shall pour upon the *h* of	Lev 14:18	7218
hand he shall put upon the *h* of	Lev 14:29	7218
hands upon the *h* of the live goat	Lev 16:21	7218
them upon the *h* of the goat	Lev 16:21	7218
shalt rise up before the hoary *h*	Lev 19:32	
not make baldness upon their *h*	Lev 21:5	7218
upon whose *h* the anointing oil	Lev 21:10	7218
garments, shall not uncover his *h*	Lev 21:10	7218
him lay their hands upon his *h*	Lev 24:14	7218
every one *h* of the house of his	Num 1:4	7218
LORD, and uncover the woman's *h*	Num 5:18	7218
shall no razor come upon his *h*	Num 6:5	7218
locks of the hair of his *h* grow	Num 6:5	7218
of his God is upon his *h*	Num 6:7	7218
defiled the *h* of his consecration	Num 6:9	7218
then he shall shave his *h* in the	Num 6:9	7218
shall hallow his *h* that same day	Num 6:11	7218
the Nazarite shall shave the *h* of	Num 6:18	7218
hair of the *h* of his separation	Num 6:18	7218
for one rod shall be for the *h* of	Num 17:3	7218
and he bowed down his *h*, and fell	Num 22:31	
he was *h* over a people, and of a	Num 25:15	7218
the *h* slippeth from the helve, and	Deut 19:5	1270
and she shall shave her *h*, and pare	Deut 21:12	7218
And the LORD shall make thee the *h*	Deut 28:13	7218
that is over thy *h* shall be brass	Deut 28:23	7218
of thy foot unto the top of thy *h*	Deut 28:35	6936
he shall be the *h*, and thou shalt	Deut 28:44	7218
come upon the *h* of Joseph	Deut 33:16	7218
upon the top of the *h* of him that	Deut 33:16	6936
the arm with the crown of the *h*	Deut 33:20	6936
his blood shall be upon his *h*	Josh 2:19	7218
his blood shall be on our *h*	Josh 2:19	7218
was the *h* of all those kingdoms	Josh 11:10	7218
each one was an *h* of the house of	Josh 22:14	7218
smote Sisera, she smote off his *h*	Judg 5:26	7218
of a millstone upon Abimelech's *h*	Judg 9:53	7218
he shall be *h* over all the	Judg 10:18	7218
be our *h* over all the inhabitants	Judg 11:8	7218
them before me, shall I be your *h*	Judg 11:9	7218
Gilead, and the people made him *h*	Judg 11:11	7218
and no razor shall come on his *h*	Judg 13:5	7218
seven locks of my *h* with the web	Judg 16:13	7218
hath not come a razor upon mine *h*	Judg 16:17	7218
off the seven locks of his *h*	Judg 16:19	7218
Howbeit the hair of his *h* began	Judg 16:22	7218
shall no razor come upon his *h*	1Sa 1:11	7218
rent, and with earth upon his *h*	1Sa 4:12	7218
the *h* of Dagon and both the palms	1Sa 5:4	7218
of oil, and poured it upon his *h*	1Sa 10:1	7218

hair of his *h* fall to the ground	1Sa 14:45	7218
wast thou not made the *h* of the	1Sa 15:17	7218
had an helmet of brass upon his *h*	1Sa 17:5	7218
his spear's *h* weighed six hundred	1Sa 17:7	3852
put an helmet of brass upon his *h*	1Sa 17:38	7218
thee, and take thine *h* from thee	1Sa 17:46	7218
him, and cut off his *h* therewith	1Sa 17:51	7218
And David took the *h* of the	1Sa 17:54	7218
him before Saul the *h* of the	1Sa 17:57	7218
of Nabal upon his own *h*	1Sa 25:39	7218
thee keeper of mine *h* for ever	1Sa 28:2	7218
And they cut off his *h*, and	1Sa 31:9	7218
clothes rent, and earth upon his *h*	2Sa 1:2	7218
the crown that was upon his *h*	2Sa 1:10	7218
unto him, Thy blood be upon thy *h*	2Sa 1:16	7218
every one his fellow by the *h*	2Sa 2:16	7218
and said, Am I a dog's *h*, which	2Sa 3:8	7218
Let it rest on the *h* of Joab	2Sa 3:29	7218
and beheaded him, and took his *h*	2Sa 4:7	7218
they brought the *h* of Ish-bosheth	2Sa 4:8	7218
Behold the *h* of Ish-bosheth	2Sa 4:8	7218
they took the *h* of Ish-bosheth	2Sa 4:12	7218
their king's crown from off his *h*	2Sa 12:30	7218
and it was set on David's *h*	2Sa 12:30	7218
And Tamar put ashes on her *h*	2Sa 13:19	7218
on her, and laid her hand on her *h*	2Sa 13:19	7218
his *h* there was no blemish in him	2Sa 14:25	6936
And when he polled his *h*, (for it	2Sa 14:26	7218
he weighed the hair of his *h* at	2Sa 14:26	7218
he went up, and had his *h* covered	2Sa 15:30	7218
with him covered every man his *h*	2Sa 15:30	7218
coat rent, and earth upon his *h*	2Sa 15:32	7218
I pray thee, and take off his *h*	2Sa 16:9	7218
his *h* caught hold of the oak, and	2Sa 18:9	7218
his *h* shall be thrown to thee	2Sa 20:21	7218
they cut off the *h* of Sheba the	2Sa 20:22	7218
kept me to be *h* of the heathen	2Sa 22:44	7218
let not his hoar *h* go down to the	1Kin 2:6	
but his hoar *h* bring thou down to	1Kin 2:9	
return his blood upon his own *h*	1Kin 2:32	7218
return upon the *h* of Joab	1Kin 2:33	7218
upon the *h* of his seed for ever	1Kin 2:33	7218
blood shall be upon thine own *h*	1Kin 2:37	7218
thy wickedness upon thine own *h*	1Kin 2:44	7218
to bring his way upon his *h*	1Kin 8:32	7218
and a cruse of water at his *h*	1Kin 19:6	4763
away thy master from thy *h* to day	2Kin 2:3	7218
away thy master from thy *h* to day	2Kin 2:5	7218
said unto him, Go up, thou bald *h*	2Kin 2:23	
go up, thou bald *h*	2Kin 2:23	
unto his father, My *h*, my *h*	2Kin 4:19	7218
the ax *h* fell into the water	2Kin 6:5	1270
until an ass's *h* was sold for	2Kin 6:25	7218
if the *h* of Elisha the son of	2Kin 6:31	7218
hath sent to take away mine *h*	2Kin 6:32	7218
box of oil, and pour it on his *h*	2Kin 9:3	7218
and he poured the oil on his *h*	2Kin 9:6	7218
painted her face, and tired her *h*	2Kin 9:30	7218
hath shaken her *h* at thee	2Kin 19:21	7218
began to reign did lift up the *h*	2Kin 25:27	7218
had stripped him, they took his *h*	1Chr 10:9	7218
fastened his *h* in the temple of	1Chr 10:10	1538
of their king from off his *h*	1Chr 20:2	7218
and it was set upon David's *h*	1Chr 20:2	7218
thou art exalted as *h* above all	1Chr 29:11	7218
his way upon his own *h*	2Chr 6:23	7218
Jehoshaphat bowed his *h* with his	2Chr 20:18	
and plucked off the hair of my *h*	Ezr 9:3	7218
are increased over our *h*, and our	Ezr 9:6	7218
their reproach upon their own *h*	Neh 4:4	7218
he set the royal crown upon her *h*	Est 2:17	7218
royal which is set upon his *h*	Est 6:8	7218
mourning, and having his *h* covered	Est 6:12	7218
should return upon his own *h*	Est 9:25	7218
rent his mantle, and shaved his *h*	Job 1:20	7218
yet will I not lift up my *h*	Job 10:15	7218
you, and shake mine *h* at you	Job 16:4	7218
and taken the crown from my *h*	Job 19:9	7218
his *h* reach unto the clouds	Job 20:6	7218
When his candle shined upon my *h*	Job 29:3	7218
or his *h* with fish spears	Job 41:7	7218
glory, and the lifter up of mine *h*	Ps 3:3	7218
shall return upon his own *h*	Ps 7:16	7218
hast made me the *h* of the heathen	Ps 18:43	7218
a crown of pure gold on his *h*	Ps 21:3	7218
out the lip, they shake the *h*	Ps 22:7	7218
thou anointest my *h* with oil	Ps 23:5	7218
now shall mine *h* be lifted up	Ps 27:6	7218
iniquities are gone over mine *h*	Ps 38:4	7218
are more than the hairs of mine *h*	Ps 40:12	7218
shaking of the *h* among the people	Ps 44:14	7218

also is the strength of mine *h*	Ps 60:7	7218
shall wound the *h* of his enemies	Ps 68:21	7218
are more than the hairs of mine *h*	Ps 69:4	7218
hate thee have lifted up the *h*	Ps 83:2	7218
also is the strength of mine *h*	Ps 108:8	7218
therefore shall he lift up the *h*	Ps 110:7	7218
become the *h* stone of the corner	Ps 118:22	7218
the precious ointment upon the *h*	Ps 133:2	7218
covered my *h* in the day of battle	Ps 140:7	7218
As for the *h* of those that	Ps 140:9	7218
oil, which shall not break my *h*	Ps 141:5	7218
an ornament of grace unto thy *h*	Prov 1:9	7218
to thine *h* an ornament of grace	Prov 4:9	7218
are upon the *h* of the just	Prov 10:6	7218
upon the *h* of him that selleth it	Prov 11:26	7218
The hoary *h* is a crown of glory,	Prov 16:31	
beauty of old men is the grey *h*	Prov 20:29	
heap coals of fire upon his *h*	Prov 25:22	7218
The wise man's eyes are in his *h*	Eccl 2:14	7218
let thy *h* lack no ointment	Eccl 9:8	7218
His left hand is under my *h*	Song 2:6	7218
for my *h* is filled with dew, and	Song 5:2	7218
His *h* is as the most fine gold,	Song 5:11	7218
Thine *h* upon thee is like Carmel,	Song 7:5	7218
the hair of thine *h* like purple	Song 7:5	7218
left hand should be under my *h*	Song 8:3	7218
the whole *h* is sick, and the whole	Is 1:5	7218
the *h* there is no soundness in it	Is 1:6	7218
of the *h* of the daughters of Zion	Is 3:17	6936
For the *h* of Syria is Damascus,	Is 7:8	7218
the *h* of Damascus is Rezin	Is 7:8	7218
the *h* of Ephraim is Samaria, and	Is 7:9	7218
the *h* of Samaria is Remaliah's	Is 7:9	7218
by the king of Assyria, the *h*	Is 7:20	7218
LORD will cut off from Israel *h*	Is 9:14	7218
and honourable, he is the *h*	Is 9:15	7218
for Egypt, which the *h* or tail	Is 19:15	7218
which are on the *h* of the fat	Is 28:1	7218
which is on the *h* of the fat	Is 28:4	7218
hath shaken her *h* at thee	Is 37:22	7218
joy shall be upon their *h*	Is 51:11	7218
they lie at the *h* of all the	Is 51:20	7218
it to bow down his *h* as a bulrush	Is 58:5	7218
an helmet of salvation upon his *h*	Is 59:17	7218
have broken the crown of thy *h*	Jer 2:16	6936
him, and thine hands upon thine *h*	Jer 2:37	7218
Oh that my *h* were waters, and mine	Jer 9:1	7218
shall be astonished, and wag his *h*	Jer 18:16	7218
unto me, and the *h* of Lebanon	Jer 22:6	7218
upon the *h* of the wicked	Jer 23:19	7218
pain upon the *h* of the wicked	Jer 30:23	7218
For every *h* shall be bald, and	Jer 48:37	7218
the crown of the *h* of the	Jer 48:45	6936
the *h* of Jehoiachin king of Judah	Jer 52:31	7218
wag their *h* at the daughter of	Lam 2:15	7218
Waters flowed over mine *h*	Lam 3:54	7218
The crown is fallen from our *h*	Lam 5:16	7218
and cause it to pass upon thine *h*	Eze 5:1	7218
and took me by a lock of mine *h*	Eze 8:3	7218
recompense their way upon their *h*	Eze 9:10	7218
firmament that was above the *h* of	Eze 10:1	7218
the *h* looked they followed it	Eze 10:11	7218
make kerchiefs upon the *h* of	Eze 13:18	7218
and a beautiful crown upon thine *h*	Eze 16:12	7218
high place at every *h* of the way	Eze 16:25	7218
place in the *h* of every way	Eze 16:31	7218
recompense thy way upon thine *h*	Eze 16:43	7218
will I recompense upon his own *h*	Eze 17:19	7218
choose it at the *h* of the way to	Eze 21:19	7218
at the *h* of the two ways, to use	Eze 21:21	7218
the tire of thine *h* upon thee	Eze 24:17	
every *h* was made bald, and every	Eze 29:18	7218
his blood shall be upon his own *h*	Eze 33:4	7218
was a door in the *h* of the way	Eze 42:12	7218
make me endanger my *h* to the king	Dan 1:10	7218
the visions of thy *h* upon thy bed	Dan 2:28	7217
This image's *h* was of fine gold,	Dan 2:32	7217
Thou art this *h* of gold	Dan 2:38	7217
nor was an hair of their *h* singed	Dan 3:27	7217
the visions of my *h* troubled me	Dan 4:5	7217
the visions of mine *h* in my bed	Dan 4:10	7217
the visions of my *h* upon my bed	Dan 4:13	7217
and visions of his *h* upon his bed	Dan 7:1	7217
the hair of his *h* like the pure	Dan 7:9	7217
the visions of my *h* troubled me	Dan 7:15	7217
the ten horns that were in his *h*	Dan 7:20	7217
and appoint themselves one *h*	Hos 1:11	7218
your recompence upon your own *h*	Joel 3:4	7218
your recompence upon your own *h*	Joel 3:7	7218
of the earth on the *h* of the poor	Amos 2:7	7218
loins, and baldness upon every *h*	Amos 8:10	7218

and cut them in the *h*, all of them	Amos 9:1	7218
shall return upon thine own *h*	Obad 15	7218
the weeds were wrapped about my *h*	Jonah 2:5	7218
it might be a shadow over his *h*	Jonah 4:6	7218
the sun beat upon the *h* of Jonah	Jonah 4:8	7218
and the LORD on the *h* of them	Mic 2:13	7218
thou woundedst the *h* out of the	Hab 3:13	7218
his staves the *h* of his villages	Hab 3:14	7218
so that no man did lift up his *h*	Zec 1:21	7218
them set a fair mitre upon his *h*	Zec 3:5	7218
they set a fair mitre upon his *h*	Zec 3:5	7218
set them upon the *h* of Joshua the	Zec 6:11	7218
Neither shalt thou swear by thy *h*	Mt 5:36	2776
when thou fastest, anoint thine *h*	Mt 6:17	2776
man hath not where to lay his *h*	Mt 8:20	2776
hairs of your *h* are all numbered	Mt 10:30	2776
John Baptist's *h* in a charger,	Mt 14:8	2776
his *h* was brought in a charger,	Mt 14:11	2776
is become the *h* of the corner	Mt 21:42	2776
ointment, and poured it on his *h*	Mt 26:7	2776
of thorns, they put it upon his *h*	Mt 27:29	2776
the reed, and smote him on the *h*	Mt 27:30	2776
set up over his *h* his accusation	Mt 27:37	2776
The *h* of John the Baptist	Mk 6:24	2776
charger the *h* of John the Baptist	Mk 6:25	2776
and commanded his *h* to be brought	Mk 6:27	2776
brought his *h* in a charger, and	Mk 6:28	2776
stones, and wounded him in the *h*	Mk 12:4	2775
is become the *h* of the corner	Mk 12:10	2776
the box, and poured it on his *h*	Mk 14:3	2776
of thorns, and put it about his *h*	Mk 15:17	
smote him on the *h* with a reed	Mk 15:19	2776
wipe them with the hairs of her *h*	Lk 7:38	2776
them with the hairs of her *h*	Lk 7:44	2776
My *h* with oil thou didst not	Lk 7:46	2776
man hath not where to lay his *h*	Lk 9:58	2776
hairs of your *h* are all numbered	Lk 12:7	2776
is become the *h* of the corner	Lk 20:17	2776
not an hair of your *h* perish	Lk 21:18	2776
only, but also my hands and my *h*	Jn 13:9	2776
of thorns, and put it on his *h*	Jn 19:2	2776
and he bowed his *h*, and gave up the	Jn 19:30	2776
the napkin, that was about his *h*	Jn 20:7	2776
white sitting, the one at the *h*	Jn 20:12	2776
is become the *h* of the corner	Acts 4:11	2776
having shorn his *h* in Cenchrea	Acts 18:18	2776
fall from the *h* of any of you	Acts 27:34	2776
shalt heap coals of fire on his *h*	Rom 12:20	2776
that the *h* of every man is Christ	1Cor 11:3	2776
the *h* of the woman is the man	1Cor 11:3	2776
and the *h* of Christ is God	1Cor 11:3	2776
prophesying, having his *h* covered	1Cor 11:4	2776
h uncovered dishonoureth her *h*	1Cor 11:5	2776
indeed ought not to cover his *h*	1Cor 11:7	2776
on her *h* because of the angels	1Cor 11:10	2776
nor again the *h* to the feet	1Cor 12:21	2776
gave him to be the *h* over all	Eph 1:22	2776
him in all things, which is the *h*	Eph 4:15	2776
the husband is the *h* of the wife	Eph 5:23	2776
as Christ is the *h* of the church	Eph 5:23	2776
he is the *h* of the body, the	Col 1:18	2776
in him, which is the *h* of all	Col 2:10	2776
And not holding the *H*, from which	Col 2:19	2776
same is made the *h* of the corner	1Pet 2:7	2776
His *h* and his hairs were white	Rev 1:14	2776
and a rainbow was upon his *h*	Rev 10:1	2776
upon her *h* a crown of twelve	Rev 12:1	2776
having on his *h* a golden crown,	Rev 14:14	2776
on his *h* were many crowns	Rev 19:12	2776

HEADBANDS

ornaments of the legs, and the *h*	Is 3:20	7196

HEADLONG

of the froward is carried *h*	Job 5:13	
that they might cast him down *h*	Lk 4:29	2630
and falling *h*, he burst asunder in	Acts 1:18	4248

HEADS

was parted, and became into four *h*	Gen 2:10	7218
And they bowed down their *h*	Gen 43:28	
then they bowed their *h* and	Ex 4:31	
These be the *h* of their fathers'	Ex 6:14	7218
these are the *h* of the fathers of	Ex 6:25	7218
made them *h* over the people,	Ex 18:25	7218
his sons, Uncover not your *h*	Lev 10:6	7218
not round the corners of your *h*	Lev 19:27	7218
fathers, of thousands in Israel	Num 1:16	7218
h of the house of their fathers,	Num 7:2	7218
hands upon the *h* of the bullocks	Num 8:12	7218
which are *h* of the thousands of	Num 10:4	7218
all those men were *h* of the	Num 13:3	7218
Take all the *h* of the people, and	Num 25:4	7218

H

Moses spake unto the *h* of the .... Num 30:1 7218
and known, and made them *h* over you . Deut 1:15 7218
even all the *h* of your tribes, and .... Deut 5:23 7218
when the *h* of the people and the .... Deut 33:5 7218
he came with the *h* of the people .... Deut 33:21 7218
Israel, and put dust upon their *h* .... Josh 7:6 7218
the *h* of the fathers of the .... Josh 14:1 7218
the *h* of the fathers of the .... Josh 19:51 7218
Then came near the *h* of the .... Josh 21:1 7218
unto the *h* of the fathers of the .... Josh 21:1 7218
said unto the *h* of the thousands .... Josh 22:21 7218
h of the thousands of Israel .... Josh 22:30 7218
for their elders, and for their *h* .... Josh 23:2 7218
elders of Israel, and for their *h* .... Josh 24:1 7218
Midian, and brought the *h* of Oreb .... Judg 7:25 7218
they lifted up their *h* no more .... Judg 8:28 7218
did God render upon their *h* .... Judg 9:57 7218
it not be with the *h* of these men 1Sa 29:4 7218
all the *h* of the tribes, the 1Kin 8:1 7218
on our loins, and ropes upon our *h* 1Kin 20:31 7218
loins, and put ropes on their *h* 1Kin 20:32 7218
take ye the *h* of the men your 2Kin 10:6 7218
put their *h* in baskets, and sent 2Kin 10:7 7218
brought the *h* of the king's sons 2Kin 10:8 7218
these were the *h* of the house of 1Chr 5:24 7218
h of the house of their fathers 1Chr 5:24 7218
h of their father's house, to wit 1Chr 7:2 7218
h of the house of their fathers, ... 1Chr 7:7 7218
h of the house of their fathers, ... 1Chr 7:9 7218
by the *h* of their fathers, mighty 1Chr 7:11 7218
h of their father's house, choice 1Chr 7:40 7218
these are the *h* of the fathers of 1Chr 8:6 7218
were his sons, *h* of the fathers. 1Chr 8:10 7218
who were *h* of the fathers of the 1Chr 8:13 7218
These were the *h* of the fathers, by 1Chr 8:28 7218
h of the house of their fathers, ... 1Chr 9:13 7218
Saul to the jeopardy of our *h* 1Chr 12:19 7218
the *h* of them were two hundred 1Chr 12:32
fathers, and bowed down their *h* 1Chr 29:20
put them on the *h* of the pillars 2Chr 3:16 7218
all the *h* of the tribes, the 2Chr 5:2 7218
Then certain of the *h* of the 2Chr 28:12
gladness, and they bowed their *h* 2Chr 29:30
and they bowed their *h*, and .... Neh 8:6
dust upon their *h* toward heaven .... Job 2:12 7218
Lift up your *h*, O ye gates .... Ps 24:7 7218
Lift up your *h*, O ye gates .... Ps 24:9 7218
caused men to ride over our *h* .... Ps 66:12 7218
thou brakest the *h* of the dragons .... Ps 74:13 7218
Thou brakest the *h* of leviathan .... Ps 74:14 7218
upon me they shaked their *h* .... Ps 109:25 7218
he shall wound the *h* over many .... Ps 110:6 7218
on all their *h* shall be baldness, ... Is 15:2 7218
and everlasting joy upon their *h* .... Is 35:10 7218
and confounded, and covered their *h* .... Jer 14:3 7218
ashamed, and they covered their *h* .... Jer 14:4 7218
have cast up dust upon their *h* .... Lam 2:10 7218
hang down their *h* to the ground .... Lam 2:10 7218
of the firmament upon the *h* of .... Eze 1:22 7218
forth over their *h* above .... Eze 1:22 7218
firmament that was over their *h* .... Eze 1:25 7218
h was the likeness of a throne .... Eze 1:26 7218
and baldness upon all their *h* .... Eze 7:18 7218
their way upon their own *h* .... Eze 11:21 7218
have I recompensed upon their *h* .... Eze 22:31 7218
in dyed attire upon their *h* .... Eze 23:15 7218
and beautiful crowns upon their *h* .... Eze 23:42 7218
your tires shall be upon your *h* .... Eze 24:23 7218
shall cast up dust upon their *h* .... Eze 27:30 7218
laid their swords under their *h* .... Eze 32:27 7218
have linen bonnets upon their *h* .... Eze 44:18 7218
Neither shall they shave their *h* .... Eze 44:20 7218
they shall only poll their *h* .... Eze 44:20 7218
the beast had also four *h* .... Dan 7:6 7217
O *h* of Jacob, and ye princes of .... Mic 3:1 7218
ye *h* of the house of Jacob, and .... Mic 3:9 7218
The *h* thereof judge for reward, ... Mic 3:11 7218
by reviled him, wagging their *h* .... Mt 27:39 2776
by railed on him, wagging their *h* .... Mk 15:29 2776
then look up, and lift up your *h* .... Lk 21:28 2776
Your blood be upon your own *h* .... Acts 18:6 2776
them, that they may shave their *h* .... Acts 21:24 2776
had on their *h* crowns of gold .... Rev 4:4 2776
on their *h* were as it were crowns .... Rev 9:7 2776
the *h* of the horses were as the .... Rev 9:17 2776
the horses were as the *h* of lions .... Rev 9:17 2776
were like unto serpents, and had *h* .... Rev 9:19 2776
great red dragon, having seven *h* .... Rev 12:3 2776
horns, and seven crowns upon his *h* ..... Rev 13:1 2776
up out of the sea, having seven *h* .... Rev 13:1 2776
upon his *h* the name of blasphemy .... Rev 13:1 2776

I saw one of his *h* as it were .... Rev 13:3 2776
of blasphemy, having seven *h* .... Rev 17:3 2776
her, which hath the seven *h* .... Rev 17:7 2776
The seven *h* are seven mountains, ... Rev 17:9 2776
And they cast dust on their *h* .... Rev 18:19 2776

HEADSTONE
the *h* thereof with shoutings .... Zec 4:7 68,7222

HEADY
Traitors, *h*, highminded, lovers 2Ti 3:4 4312

HEAL
H her now, O God, I beseech thee .... Num 12:13 7495
I wound, and I *h* .... Deut 32:39 7495
behold, I will *h* thee 2Kin 20:5 7495
the sign that the LORD will *h* me 2Kin 20:8 7495
their sin, and will *h* their land 2Chr 7:14 7495
O LORD, *h* me .... Ps 6:2 7495
h my soul .... Ps 41:4 7495
h the breaches thereof .... Ps 60:2 7495
A time to kill, and a time to *h* .... Eccl 3:3 7495
he shall smite and *h* it .... Is 19:22 7495
of them, and shall *h* them .... Is 19:22 7495
have seen his ways, and will *h* him .... Is 57:18 7495
and I will *h* him .... Is 57:19 7495
I will *h* your backslidings .... Jer 3:22 7495
H me, O LORD, and I shall be .... Jer 17:14 7495
I will *h* thee of thy wounds, ... Jer 30:17 7495
who can *h* thee? .... Lam 2:13 7495
yet could he not *h* you, nor cure .... Hos 5:13 7495
for he hath torn, and he will *h* us .... Hos 6:1 7495
I will *h* their backsliding, I .... Hos 14:4 7495
nor *h* that that is broken, nor .... Zec 11:16 7495
unto him, I will come and *h* him .... Mt 8:7 2323
to *h* all manner of sickness and .... Mt 10:1 2323
H the sick, cleanse the lepers, ... Mt 10:8 2323
Is it lawful to *h* on the sabbath .... Mt 12:10 2323
be converted, and I should *h* them .... Mt 13:15 2390
whether he would *h* him on the .... Mk 3:2 2323
And to have power to *h* sicknesses......... Mk 3:15 2323
sent me to *h* the brokenhearted .... Lk 4:18 2390
proverb, Physician, *h* thyself .... Lk 4:23 2323
of the Lord was present to *h* them .... Lk 5:17 2390
whether he would *h* on the sabbath ...... Lk 6:7 2323
he would come and *h* his servant .... Lk 7:3 1295
kingdom of God, and to *h* the sick .... Lk 9:2 2390
h the sick that are therein, and .... Lk 10:9 2323
Is it lawful to *h* on the sabbath .... Lk 14:3 2323
he would come down, and *h* his son ...... Jn 4:47 2390
be converted, and I should *h* them .... Jn 12:40 2390
stretching forth thine hand to *h* .... Acts 4:30 2392
be converted, and I should *h* them .... Acts 28:27 2392

HEALED
God *h* Abimelech, and his wife, and ...... Gen 20:17 7495
cause him to be thoroughly *h* .... Ex 21:19 7495
skin thereof, was a boil, and is *h* .... Lev 13:18 7495
the scall is *h*, he is clean .... Lev 13:37 7495
of leprosy be *h* in the leper .... Lev 14:3 7495
clean, because the plague is *h* .... Lev 14:48 7495
itch, whereof thou canst not be *h* .... Deut 28:27 7495
a sore botch that cannot be *h* .... Deut 28:35 7495
then ye shall be *h*, and it shall 1Sa 6:3 7495
the LORD, I have *h* these waters 2Kin 2:21 7495
the waters were *h* unto this day 2Kin 2:22 7495
king Joram went back to be *h* in 2Kin 8:29 7495
king Joram was returned to be *h* 2Kin 9:15 7495
he returned to be *h* in Jezreel 2Chr 22:6 7495
to Hezekiah, and *h* the people 2Chr 30:20 7495
unto thee, and thou hast *h* me .... Ps 30:2 7495
h them, and delivered them from .... Ps 107:20 7495
their heart, and convert, and be *h* .... Is 6:10 7495
and with his stripes we are *h* .... Is 53:5 7495
They have *h* also the hurt of the .... Jer 6:14 7495
For they have *h* the hurt of the .... Jer 8:11 7495
incurable, which refuseth to be *h* .... Jer 15:18 7495
*H*eal me, O LORD, and I shall be *h* .... Jer 17:14 7495
her pain, if so be she may be *h* .... Jer 51:8 7495
h Babylon, but she is not *h* .... Jer 51:9 7495
it shall not be bound up to be *h* ...... Eze 30:21 5414,7499
neither have ye *h* that which was .... Eze 34:4 7495
the sea, the waters shall be *h* .... Eze 47:8 7495
for they shall be *h* .... Eze 47:9 7495
marishes thereof shall not be *h* .... Eze 47:11 7495
When I would have *h* Israel .... Hos 7:1 7495
but they knew not that I *h* them .... Hos 11:3 7495
and he *h* them .... Mt 4:24 2323
only, and my servant shall be *h* .... Mt 8:8 2390
his servant was *h* in the selfsame .... Mt 8:13 2390
his word, and *h* all that were sick.......... Mt 8:16 2323
followed him, and he *h* them all .... Mt 12:15 2323
he *h* him, insomuch that the blind .... Mt 12:22 2323

toward them, and he *h* their sick	Mt 14:14	2323
and he *h* them	Mt 15:30	2323
and he *h* them there	Mt 19:2	2323
and he *h* them	Mt 21:14	2323
he *h* many that were sick of	Mk 1:34	2323
For he had *h* many	Mk 3:10	2323
hands on her, that she may be *h*	Mk 5:23	4982
that she was *h* of that plague	Mk 5:29	2390
upon a few sick folk, and *h* them	Mk 6:5	2323
many that were sick, and *h* them	Mk 6:13	2323
on every one of them, and *h* them	Lk 4:40	2323
hear, and to be *h* by him of their	Lk 5:15	2323
to be *h* of their diseases	Lk 6:17	2390
and they were *h*	Lk 6:18	2323
virtue out of him, and *h* them all	Lk 6:19	2390
a word, and my servant shall be *h*	Lk 7:7	2390
which had been *h* of evil spirits	Lk 8:2	2390
was possessed of the devils was *h*	Lk 8:36	4982
neither could be *h* of any	Lk 8:43	2323
him, and how she was *h* immediately	Lk 8:47	2390
h them that had need of healing	Lk 9:11	2390
h the child, and delivered him	Lk 9:42	2390
Jesus had *h* on the sabbath day	Lk 13:14	2323
in them therefore come and be *h*	Lk 13:14	2323
took him, and *h* him, and let him go	Lk 14:4	2323
them, when he saw that he was *h*	Lk 17:15	2390
And he touched his ear, and *h* him	Lk 22:51	2390
he that was *h* wist not who was	Jn 5:13	2390
lame man which was *h* held Peter	Acts 3:11	2390
which was *h* standing with them	Acts 4:14	2323
and they were *h* every one	Acts 5:16	2323
and that were lame, were *h*	Acts 8:7	2323
that he had faith to be *h*	Acts 14:9	4982
laid his hands on him, and *h* him	Acts 28:8	2390
in the island, came, and were *h*	Acts 28:9	2323
but let it rather be *h*	Heb 12:13	2390
one for another, that ye may be *h*	Jas 5:16	2390
by whose stripes ye were *h*	1Pet 2:24	2390
and his deadly wound was *h*	Rev 13:3	2323
beast, whose deadly wound was *h*	Rev 13:12	2323

HEALER

swear, saying, I will not be an *h*	Is 3:7	2280

HEALETH

for I am the LORD that *h* thee	Ex 15:26	7495
who *h* all thy diseases	Ps 103:3	7495
He *h* the broken in heart, and	Ps 147:3	7495
h the stroke of their wound	Is 30:26	7495

HEALING

us, and there is no *h* for us	Jer 14:19	4832
and for the time of *h*, and behold	Jer 14:19	4832
thou hast no *h* medicines	Jer 30:13	8585
There is no *h* of thy bruise	Nah 3:19	3545
arise with *h* in his wings	Mal 4:2	4832
h all manner of sickness and all	Mt 4:23	2323
h every sickness and every disease	Mt 9:35	2323
the gospel, and *h* every where	Lk 9:6	2323
and healed them that had need of *h*	Lk 9:11	2322
whom this miracle of *h* was shewed	Acts 4:22	2392
h all that were oppressed of the	Acts 10:38	2390
the gifts of *h* by the same Spirit	1Cor 12:9	2386
Have all the gifts of *h*	1Cor 12:30	2386
were for the *h* of the nations	Rev 22:2	2322

HEALINGS

that miracles, then gifts of *h*	1Cor 12:28	2386

HEALTH

servant our father is in good *h*	Gen 43:28	7965
Joab said to Amasa, Art thou in *h*	2Sa 20:9	7965
who is the *h* of my countenance,	Ps 42:11	3444
who is the *h* of my countenance,	Ps 43:5	3444
thy saving *h* among all nations	Ps 67:2	
It shall be *h* to thy navel, and	Prov 3:8	7500
them, and *h* to all their flesh	Prov 4:22	4832
but the tongue of the wise is *h*	Prov 12:18	4832
but a faithful ambassador is *h*	Prov 13:17	4832
to the soul, and to the bones	Prov 16:24	4832
thine *h* shall spring forth	Is 58:8	724
and for a time of *h*, and behold	Jer 8:15	4832
why then is not the *h* of the	Jer 8:22	724
For I will restore *h* unto thee	Jer 30:17	724
Behold, I will bring it *h*	Jer 33:6	724
for this is for your *h*	Acts 27:34	4491
thou mayest prosper and be in *h*	3Jn 2	5198

HEAP

and they took stones, and made an *h*	Gen 31:46	1530
and they did eat there upon the *h*	Gen 31:46	1530
This *h* is a witness between me and	Gen 31:48	1530
said to Jacob, Behold this *h*	Gen 31:51	1530
This *h* be witness, and this pillar	Gen 31:52	1530

will not pass over this *h* to thee	Gen 31:52	1530
thou shalt not pass over this *h*	Gen 31:52	1530
the floods stood upright as an *h*	Ex 15:8	5067
and it shall be an *h* for ever	Deut 13:16	8510
I will *h* mischiefs upon them	Deut 32:23	5595
and they shall stand upon an *h*	Josh 3:13	5067
rose up upon an *h* very far from	Josh 3:16	5067
a great *h* of stones unto this day	Josh 7:26	1530
Ai, and made it an *h* for ever	Josh 8:28	8510
raise thereon a great *h* of stones	Josh 8:29	1530
down at the end of the *h* of corn	Ruth 3:7	6194
laid a very great *h* of stones	2Sa 18:17	1530
His roots are wrapped about the *h*	Job 8:17	1530
I could *h* up words against you,	Job 16:4	2266
Though he *h* up silver as the dust	Job 27:16	6651
hypocrites in heart *h* up wrath	Job 36:13	7760
of the sea together as an *h*	Ps 33:7	5067
made the waters to stand as an *h*	Ps 78:13	5067
For thou shalt *h* coals of fire	Prov 25:22	2846
travail, to gather and to *h* up	Eccl 2:26	3664
thy belly is like an *h* of wheat	Song 7:2	6194
city, and it shall be a ruinous *h*	Is 17:1	4596
shall be a *h* in the day of grief	Is 17:11	5067
For thou hast made of a city an *h*	Is 25:2	1530
shall be builded upon her own *h*	Jer 30:18	8510
and it shall be a desolate *h*	Jer 49:2	8510
H on wood, kindle the fire,	Eze 24:10	7235
make Samaria as an *h* of the field	Mic 1:6	5856
for they shall *h* dust, and take it	Hab 1:10	6651
through the *h* of great waters	Hab 3:15	2563
came to an *h* of twenty measures	Hag 2:16	6194
shalt *h* coals of fire on his head	Rom 12:20	*4987*
they *h* to themselves teachers	2Ti 4:3	2002

HEAPED

h up silver as the dust, and fine	Zec 9:3	6651
Ye have *h* treasure together for	Jas 5:3	*2343*

HEAPETH

he *h* up riches, and knoweth not	Ps 39:6	6651
nations, and *h* unto him all people	Hab 2:5	6908

HEAPS

gathered them together upon *h*	Ex 8:14	2563
h upon *h*, with the jaw of an	Judg 15:16	2565
Lay ye them in two *h* at the	2Kin 10:8	6632
fenced cities into ruinous *h*	2Kin 19:25	1530
LORD their God, and laid them by *h*	2Chr 31:6	6194
to lay the foundation of the *h*	2Chr 31:7	6194
and the princes came and saw the *h*	2Chr 31:8	6194
and the Levites concerning the *h*	2Chr 31:9	6194
revive the stones out of the *h* of	Neh 4:2	6194
which are ready to become *h*	Job 15:28	1530
they have laid Jerusalem on *h*	Ps 79:1	5856
defenced cities into ruinous *h*	Is 37:26	1530
And I will make Jerusalem *h*	Jer 9:11	1530
and Jerusalem shall become *h*	Jer 26:18	5856
up waymarks, make thee high *h*	Jer 31:21	8564
cast her up as *h*, and destroy her	Jer 50:26	6194
And Babylon shall become *h*	Jer 51:37	1530
their altars are as *h* in the	Hos 12:11	1530
and Jerusalem shall become *h*	Mic 3:12	5856

HEAR

wives, Adah and Zillah, *H* my voice	Gen 4:23	8085
so that all that *h* will laugh	Gen 21:6	8085
H us, my lord	Gen 23:6	8085
h me, and intreat for me to Ephron	Gen 23:8	8085
Nay, my lord, *h* me	Gen 23:11	8085
wilt give it, I pray thee, *h* me	Gen 23:13	8085
And he said unto them, *H*, I pray	Gen 37:6	8085
he besought us, and we would not *h*	Gen 42:21	8085
and ye would not *h*	Gen 42:22	8085
Gather yourselves together, and *h*	Gen 49:2	8085
how then shall Pharaoh *h* me	Ex 6:12	8085
hitherto thou wouldest not *h*	Ex 7:16	8085
The people shall *h*, and be afraid	Ex 15:14	8085
that the people may *h* when I	Ex 19:9	8085
Speak thou with us, and we will *h*	Ex 20:19	8085
me, I will surely *h* their cry	Ex 22:23	8085
he crieth unto me, that I will *h*	Ex 22:27	8085
noise of them that sing do I *h*	Ex 32:18	8085
h the voice of swearing, and is a	Lev 5:1	8085
I will *h* what the LORD will	Num 9:8	8085
And he said, *H* now my words	Num 12:6	8085
Then the Egyptians shall *h* it	Num 14:13	8085
And Moses said unto Korah, *H*	Num 16:8	8085
said unto them, *H* now, ye rebels	Num 20:10	8085
and said, Rise up, Balak, and *h*	Num 23:18	8085
And her father *h* her vow, and her	Num 30:4	8085
H the causes between your	Deut 1:16	8085
but ye shall *h* the small as well	Deut 1:17	8085
bring it unto me, and I will *h* it	Deut 1:17	8085

and ye would not *h*, but rebelled	Deut 1:43	8085
who shall *h* report of thee, and	Deut 2:25	8085
for your sakes, and would not *h* me	Deut 3:26	8085
which shall *h* all these statutes,	Deut 4:6	8085
and I will make them *h* my words	Deut 4:10	8085
stone, which neither see, nor *h*	Deut 4:28	8085
Did ever people *h* the voice of	Deut 4:33	8085
he made thee to *h* his voice	Deut 4:36	8085
all Israel, and said unto them, *H*	Deut 5:1	8085
if we *h* the voice of the LORD our	Deut 5:25	8085
h all that the LORD our God shall	Deut 5:27	8085
and we will *h* it, and do it	Deut 5:27	8085
H therefore, O Israel, and observe	Deut 6:3	8085
H, O Israel	Deut 6:4	8085
H, O Israel	Deut 9:1	8085
h all these words which I command	Deut 12:28	8085
And all Israel shall *h*, and fear,	Deut 13:11	8085
If thou shalt *h* say in one of thy	Deut 13:12	8085
And all the people shall *h*	Deut 17:13	8085
Let me not *h* again the voice of	Deut 18:16	8085
And those which remain shall *h*	Deut 19:20	8085
And shall say unto them, *H*	Deut 20:3	8085
and all Israel shall *h*, and fear	Deut 21:21	8085
and eyes to see, and ears to *h*	Deut 29:4	8085
it unto us, that we may *h* it	Deut 30:12	8085
it unto us, that we may *h* it	Deut 30:13	8085
away, so that thou wilt not *h*	Deut 30:17	8085
within thy gates, that they may *h*	Deut 31:12	8085
have not known any thing, may *h*	Deut 31:13	8085
and *h*, O earth, the words of my	Deut 32:1	8085
and he said, *H*, LORD, the voice of	Deut 33:7	8085
h the words of the LORD your God	Josh 3:9	8085
when ye *h* the sound of the	Josh 6:5	8085
of the land shall *h* of it	Josh 7:9	8085
H, O ye kings	Judg 5:3	8085
to *h* the bleatings of the flocks	Judg 5:16	8085
thou shalt *h* what they say	Judg 7:11	8085
thy riddle, that we may *h* it	Judg 14:13	8085
for I *h* of your evil dealings by	1Sa 2:23	8085
for it is no good report that I *h*	1Sa 2:24	8085
LORD will not *h* you in that day	1Sa 8:18	6030
land, saying, Let the Hebrews *h*	1Sa 13:3	8085
the lowing of the oxen which I *h*	1Sa 15:14	8085
if Saul *h* it, he will kill me	1Sa 16:2	8085
about him, *H* now, ye Benjamites	1Sa 22:7	8085
H now, thou son of Ahitub	1Sa 22:12	8085
h the words of thine handmaid	1Sa 25:24	8085
let my lord the king *h* the words	1Sa 26:19	8085
For the king will *h*, to deliver	2Sa 14:16	8085
man deputed of the king to *h* thee	2Sa 15:3	8085
As soon as ye *h* the sound of the	2Sa 15:10	8085
shalt *h* out of the king's house	2Sa 15:35	8085
unto me every thing that ye can *h*	2Sa 15:36	8085
all Israel shall *h* that thou art	2Sa 16:21	8085
let us *h* likewise what he saith	2Sa 17:5	8085
can I *h* any more the voice of	2Sa 19:35	8085
woman out of the city, *H*, *h*	2Sa 20:16	8085
H the words of thine handmaid	2Sa 20:17	8085
And he answered, I do *h*	2Sa 20:17	8085
he did *h* my voice out of his	2Sa 22:7	8085
as soon as they *h*, they shall be	2Sa 22:45	8085
people to *h* the wisdom of Solomon	1Kin 4:34	8085
h thou in heaven thy dwelling	1Kin 8:30	8085
Then *h* thou in heaven, and do, and	1Kin 8:32	8085
Then *h* thou in heaven, and forgive	1Kin 8:34	8085
Then *h* thou in heaven, and forgive	1Kin 8:36	8085
Then *h* thou in heaven thy	1Kin 8:39	8085
(For they shall *h* of thy great	1Kin 8:42	8085
H thou in heaven thy dwelling	1Kin 8:43	8085
Then *h* thou in heaven their	1Kin 8:45	8085
Then *h* thou their prayer and their	1Kin 8:49	8085
before thee, and that *h* thy wisdom	1Kin 10:8	8085
to *h* his wisdom, which God had	1Kin 10:24	8085
until noon, saying, O Baal, *h* us	1Kin 18:26	6030
H me, O LORD, *h* me, that this	1Kin 18:37	6030
H thou therefore the word of the	1Kin 22:19	8085
H ye the word of the LORD	2Kin 7:1	8085
Syrians to *h* a noise of chariots	2Kin 7:6	8085
But Amaziah would not *h*	2Kin 14:11	8085
Notwithstanding they would not *h*	2Kin 17:14	8085
commanded, and would not *h* them	2Kin 18:12	8085
H the word of the great king, the	2Kin 18:28	8085
h all the words of Rab-shakeh	2Kin 19:4	8085
upon him, and he shall *h* a rumour	2Kin 19:7	8085
LORD, bow down thine ear, and *h*	2Kin 19:16	8085
h the words of Sennacherib, which	2Kin 19:16	8085
Hezekiah, *H* the word of the LORD	2Kin 20:16	8085
when thou shalt *h* a sound of	1Chr 14:15	8085
H me, my brethren, and my people	1Chr 28:2	8085
h thou from thy dwelling place,	2Chr 6:21	8085
Then *h* thou from heaven, and do,	2Chr 6:23	8085

Then *h* thou from the heavens, and	2Chr 6:25	8085
Then *h* thou from heaven, and	2Chr 6:27	8085
Then *h* thou from heaven thy	2Chr 6:30	8085
Then *h* thou from the heavens, and	2Chr 6:33	8085
Then *h* thou from the heavens	2Chr 6:35	8085
Then *h* thou from the heavens,	2Chr 6:39	8085
then will I *h* from heaven	2Chr 7:14	8085
before thee, and *h* thy wisdom	2Chr 9:7	8085
to *h* his wisdom, that God had put	2Chr 9:23	8085
H me, thou Jeroboam, and all	2Chr 13:4	8085
H ye me, Asa, and all Judah and	2Chr 15:2	8085
Therefore *h* the word of the LORD	2Chr 18:18	8085
our affliction, then thou wilt *h*	2Chr 20:9	8085
H me, O Judah, and ye inhabitants	2Chr 20:20	8085
But Amaziah would not *h*	2Chr 25:20	8085
Now *h* me therefore, and deliver	2Chr 28:11	8085
H me, ye Levites, sanctify now	2Chr 29:5	8085
that thou mayest *h* the prayer of	Neh 1:6	8085
H, O our God	Neh 4:4	8085
ye *h* the sound of the trumpet	Neh 4:20	8085
women, and all that could *h* with	Neh 8:2	8085
their neck, and would not *h*	Neh 9:29	8085
they *h* not the voice of the	Job 3:18	8085
h it, and know thou it for thy	Job 5:27	8085
H now my reasoning, and hearken to	Job 13:6	8085
H diligently my speech, and my	Job 13:17	8085
I will shew thee, *h* me	Job 15:17	8085
H diligently my speech, and let	Job 21:2	8085
unto him, and he shall *h* thee	Job 22:27	8085
Will God *h* his cry when trouble	Job 27:9	8085
unto thee, and thou dost not *h* me	Job 30:20	6030
Oh that one would *h* me	Job 31:35	8085
h my speeches, and hearken to all	Job 33:1	8085
H my words, O ye wise men	Job 34:2	8085
thou hast understanding, *h* this	Job 34:16	8085
Surely God will not *h* vanity	Job 35:13	8085
H attentively the noise of his	Job 37:2	8085
H, I beseech thee, and I will	Job 42:4	8085
H me when I call, O God of my	Ps 4:1	6030
mercy upon me, and *h* my prayer	Ps 4:1	8085
the LORD will *h* when I call unto	Ps 4:3	8085
voice shalt thou *h* in the morning	Ps 5:3	8085
thou wilt cause thine ear to *h*	Ps 10:17	7181
Consider and *h* me, O LORD my God	Ps 13:3	6030
H the right, O LORD, attend unto	Ps 17:1	8085
upon thee, for thou wilt *h* me	Ps 17:6	6030
thine ear unto me, and *h* my speech	Ps 17:6	8085
As soon as they *h* of me	Ps 18:44	8085
The LORD *h* thee in the day of	Ps 20:1	6030
he will *h* him from his holy	Ps 20:6	6030
let the king *h* us when we call	Ps 20:9	6030
H, O LORD, when I cry with my	Ps 27:7	8085
H the voice of my supplications	Ps 28:2	8085
H, O LORD, and have mercy upon me	Ps 30:10	8085
the humble shall *h* thereof	Ps 34:2	8085
thou wilt *h*, O Lord my God	Ps 38:15	6030
H me, lest otherwise they should	Ps 38:16	8085
H my prayer, O LORD, and give ear	Ps 39:12	8085
H this, all ye people	Ps 49:1	8085
H, O my people, and I will speak	Ps 50:7	8085
Make me to *h* joy and gladness	Ps 51:8	8085
H my prayer, O God	Ps 54:2	8085
Attend unto me, and *h* me	Ps 55:2	6030
and he shall *h* my voice	Ps 55:17	8085
God shall *h*, and afflict them,	Ps 55:19	8085
for who, say they, doth *h*	Ps 59:7	8085
save with thy right hand, and *h* me	Ps 60:5	6030
H my cry, O God	Ps 61:1	8085
H my voice, O God, in my prayer	Ps 64:1	8085
Come and *h*, all ye that fear God,	Ps 66:16	8085
my heart, the Lord will not *h* me	Ps 66:18	8085
the multitude of thy mercy *h* me	Ps 69:13	6030
H me, O LORD	Ps 69:16	6030
h me speedily	Ps 69:17	6030
H, O my people, and I will testify	Ps 81:8	8085
O LORD God of hosts, *h* my prayer	Ps 84:8	8085
I will *h* what God the LORD will	Ps 85:8	8085
Bow down thine ear, O LORD, *h* me	Ps 86:1	6030
mine ears shall *h* my desire of	Ps 92:11	8085
planted the ear, shall he not *h*	Ps 94:9	8085
To day if ye will *h* his voice	Ps 95:7	8085
H my prayer, O LORD, and let my	Ps 102:1	8085
To *h* the groaning of the prisoner	Ps 102:20	8085
They have ears, but they *h* not	Ps 115:6	8085
h me, O LORD	Ps 119:145	6030
H my voice according unto thy	Ps 119:149	8085
Lord, *h* my voice	Ps 130:2	8085
They have ears, but they *h* not	Ps 135:17	238
when they *h* the words of thy	Ps 138:4	8085
h the voice of my supplications,	Ps 140:6	238
places, they shall *h* my words	Ps 141:6	8085

H my prayer, O LORD, give ear to	Ps 143:1	8085
H me speedily, O LORD	Ps 143:7	6030
Cause me to *h* thy lovingkindness	Ps 143:8	8085
he also will *h* their cry, and will	Ps 145:19	8085
A wise man will *h*, and will	Prov 1:5	8085
h the instruction of thy father,	Prov 1:8	8085
H, ye children, the instruction	Prov 4:1	8085
H, O my son, and receive my	Prov 4:10	8085
H me now therefore, O ye children	Prov 5:7	8085
H; for I will speak	Prov 8:6	8085
H instruction, and be wise, and	Prov 8:33	8085
H counsel, and receive instruction	Prov 19:20	8085
to *h* the instruction that causeth	Prov 19:27	8085
h the words of the wise, and apply	Prov 22:17	8085
H thou, my son, and be wise, and	Prov 23:19	8085
of God, and be more ready to *h*	Eccl 5:1	8085
It is better to *h* the rebuke of	Eccl 7:5	8085
for a man to *h* the song of fools	Eccl 7:5	8085
lest thou *h* thy servant curse	Eccl 7:21	8085
Let us *h* the conclusion of the	Eccl 12:13	8085
countenance, let me *h* thy voice	Song 2:14	8085
cause me to *h* it	Song 8:13	8085
H, O heavens, and give ear, O	Is 1:2	8085
H the word of the LORD, ye rulers	Is 1:10	8085
make many prayers, I will not *h*	Is 1:15	8085
H ye indeed, but understand not	Is 6:9	8085
h with their ears, and understand	Is 6:10	8085
H ye now, O house of David	Is 7:13	8085
when he bloweth a trumpet, *h* ye	Is 18:3	8085
yet they would not *h*	Is 28:12	8085
Wherefore *h* the word of the LORD,	Is 28:14	8085
Give ye ear, and *h* my voice	Is 28:23	8085
hearken, and *h* my speech	Is 28:23	8085
the deaf *h* the words of the book	Is 29:18	8085
will not *h* the law of the LORD	Is 30:9	8085
when he shall *h* it, he will	Is 30:19	8085
thine ears shall *h* a word behind	Is 30:21	8085
ears of them that *h* shall hearken	Is 32:3	8085
h my voice, ye careless daughters	Is 32:9	8085
H, ye that are far off, what I	Is 33:13	8085
Come near, ye nations, to *h*	Is 34:1	8085
let the earth *h*, and all that is	Is 34:1	8085
H ye the words of the great king,	Is 36:13	8085
God will *h* the words of Rabshakeh	Is 37:4	8085
upon him, and he shall *h* a rumour	Is 37:7	8085
Incline thine ear, O LORD, and *h*	Is 37:17	8085
h all the words of Sennacherib,	Is 37:17	8085
H the word of the LORD of hosts	Is 39:5	8085
thirst, I the LORD will *h* them	Is 41:17	6030
H, ye deaf	Is 42:18	8085
hearken and *h* for the time to come	Is 42:23	8085
or let them *h*, and say, It is	Is 43:9	8085
Yet now *h*, O Jacob my servant	Is 44:1	8085
Therefore *h* now this, thou that	Is 47:8	8085
H ye this, O house of Jacob,	Is 48:1	8085
All ye, assemble yourselves, and *h*	Is 48:14	8085
Come ye near unto me, *h* ye this	Is 48:16	8085
mine ear to *h* as the learned	Is 50:4	8085
Therefore *h* now this, thou	Is 51:21	8085
h, and your soul shall live	Is 55:3	8085
his ear heavy, that it cannot *h*	Is 59:1	8085
face from you, that he will not *h*	Is 59:2	8085
when I spake, ye did not *h*	Is 65:12	8085
they are yet speaking, I will *h*	Is 65:24	8085
when I spake, they did not *h*	Is 66:4	8085
H the word of the LORD, ye that	Is 66:5	8085
H ye the word of the LORD, O	Jer 2:4	8085
h the sound of the trumpet	Jer 4:21	8085
H now this, O foolish people, and	Jer 5:21	8085
which have ears, and *h* not	Jer 5:21	8085
and give warning, that they may *h*	Jer 6:10	8085
Therefore *h*, ye nations, and know,	Jer 6:18	8085
H, O earth	Jer 6:19	8085
H the word of the LORD, all ye of	Jer 7:2	8085
for I will not *h* thee	Jer 7:16	8085
neither can men *h* the voice of	Jer 9:10	8085
Yet *h* the word of the LORD, O ye	Jer 9:20	8085
H ye the word which the LORD	Jer 10:1	8085
H ye the words of this covenant,	Jer 11:2	8085
H ye the words of this covenant,	Jer 11:6	8085
which refused to *h* my words	Jer 11:10	8085
for I will not *h* them in the time	Jer 11:14	8085
which refuse to *h* my words	Jer 13:10	8085
but they would not *h*	Jer 13:11	8085
H ye, and give ear	Jer 13:15	8085
But if ye will not *h* it, my soul	Jer 13:17	8085
they fast, I will not *h* their cry	Jer 14:12	8085
H ye the word of the LORD, ye	Jer 17:20	8085
neck stiff, that they might not *h*	Jer 17:23	8085
I will cause thee to *h* my words	Jer 18:2	8085
H ye the word of the LORD, O	Jer 19:3	8085

that they might not *h* my words	Jer 19:15	8085
let him *h* the cry in the morning,	Jer 20:16	8085
H ye the word of the LORD	Jer 21:11	8085
H the word of the LORD, O king of	Jer 22:2	8085
But if ye will not *h* these words	Jer 22:5	8085
but thou saidst, I will not *h*	Jer 22:21	8085
earth, *h* the word of the LORD	Jer 22:29	8085
caused my people to *h* my words	Jer 23:22	8085
nor inclined your ear to *h*	Jer 25:4	8085
Nevertheless *h* thou now this word	Jer 28:7	8085
the prophet, *H* now, Hananiah	Jer 28:15	8085
but ye would not *h*, saith	Jer 29:19	8085
H ye therefore the word of the	Jer 29:20	8085
H the word of the LORD, O ye	Jer 31:10	8085
which shall *h* all the good that I	Jer 33:9	8085
Yet *h* the word of the LORD, O	Jer 34:4	8085
h all the evil which I purpose to	Jer 36:3	8085
but he would not *h* them	Jer 36:25	8085
Therefore *h* now, I pray thee, O	Jer 37:20	8085
But if the princes *h* that I have	Jer 38:25	8085
nor *h* the sound of the trumpet,	Jer 42:14	8085
now therefore *h* the word of the	Jer 42:15	8085
H the word of the LORD, all Judah	Jer 44:24	8085
Therefore *h* ye the word of the	Jer 44:26	8085
Therefore *h* the counsel of the	Jer 49:20	8085
Therefore *h* ye the counsel of the	Jer 50:45	8085
h, I pray you, all people, and	Lam 1:18	8085
And they, whether they will *h*	Eze 2:5	8085
unto them, whether they will *h*	Eze 2:7	8085
of man, *h* what I say unto thee	Eze 2:8	8085
thine heart, and *h* with thine ears	Eze 3:10	8085
whether they will *h*, or whether	Eze 3:11	8085
therefore *h* the word at my mouth,	Eze 3:17	8085
He that heareth, let him *h*	Eze 3:27	8085
h the word of the Lord GOD	Eze 6:3	8085
loud voice, yet will I not *h* them	Eze 8:18	8085
they have ears to *h*, and *h* not	Eze 12:2	8085
H ye the word of the LORD	Eze 13:2	8085
to my people that *h* your lies	Eze 13:19	8085
O harlot, *h* the word of the LORD	Eze 16:35	8085
H now, O house of Israel	Eze 18:25	8085
the south, *H* the word of the LORD	Eze 20:47	8085
to cause thee to *h* it with thine	Eze 24:26	2045
H the word of the Lord GOD	Eze 25:3	8085
thou shalt *h* the word at my mouth	Eze 33:7	8085
h what is the word that cometh	Eze 33:30	8085
they *h* thy words, but they will	Eze 33:31	8085
for they *h* thy words, but they do	Eze 33:32	8085
shepherds, *h* the word of the LORD	Eze 34:7	8085
shepherds, *h* the word of the LORD	Eze 34:9	8085
of Israel, *h* the word of the LORD	Eze 36:1	8085
h the word of the Lord GOD	Eze 36:4	8085
men to *h* in thee the shame of the	Eze 36:15	8085
dry bones, *h* the word of the LORD	Eze 37:4	8085
h with thine ears, and set thine	Eze 40:4	8085
h with thine ears all that I say	Eze 44:5	8085
That at what time ye *h* the sound	Dan 3:5	8086
shall *h* the sound of the cornet	Dan 3:10	8086
time ye *h* the sound of the cornet	Dan 3:15	8086
and stone, which see not, nor *h*	Dan 5:23	8086
h the prayer of thy servant, and	Dan 9:17	8085
O my God, incline thine ear, and *h*	Dan 9:18	8085
O Lord, *h*; O Lord	Dan 9:19	8085
to pass in that day, I will *h*	Hos 2:21	6030
I will *h* the heavens	Hos 2:21	6030
and they shall *h* the earth	Hos 2:21	6030
And the earth shall *h* the corn	Hos 2:22	6030
and they shall *h* Jezreel	Hos 2:22	6030
H the word of the LORD, ye	Hos 4:1	8085
H ye this, O priests	Hos 5:1	8085
H this, ye old men, and give ear,	Joel 1:2	8085
H this word that the LORD hath	Amos 3:1	8085
H ye, and testify in the house of	Amos 3:13	8085
H this word, ye kine of Bashan,	Amos 4:1	8085
H ye this word which I take up	Amos 5:1	8085
for I will not *h* the melody of	Amos 5:23	8085
Now therefore *h* thou the word of	Amos 7:16	8085
H this, O ye that swallow up the	Amos 8:4	8085
H, all ye people	Mic 1:2	8085
And I said, *H*, I pray you, O heads	Mic 3:1	8085
the LORD, but he will not *h* them	Mic 3:4	6030
H this, I pray you, ye heads of	Mic 3:9	8085
H ye now what the LORD saith	Mic 6:1	8085
and let the hills *h* thy voice	Mic 6:1	8085
H ye, O mountains, the LORD's	Mic 6:2	8085
h ye the rod, and who hath	Mic 6:9	8085
my God will *h* me	Mic 7:7	8085
all that *h* the bruit of thee	Nah 3:19	8085
shall I cry, and thou wilt not *h*	Hab 1:2	8085
but they did not *h*, nor hearken	Zec 1:4	8085
H now, O Joshua the high priest,	Zec 3:8	8085

Should ye not *h* the words which	Zec 7:7	
ears, that they should not *h*	Zec 7:11	8085
stone, lest they should *h* the law	Zec 7:12	8085
as he cried, and they would not *h*	Zec 7:13	8085
so they cried, and I would not *h*	Zec 7:13	8085
ye that *h* in these days these	Zec 8:9	8085
LORD their God, and will *h* them	Zec 10:6	6030
call on my name, and I will *h* them	Zec 13:9	6030
If ye will not *h*, and if ye will	Mal 2:2	8085
nor *h* your words, when ye depart	Mt 10:14	191
what ye *h* in the ear, that preach	Mt 10:27	191
again those things which ye do *h*	Mt 11:4	191
are cleansed, and the deaf *h*	Mt 11:5	191
that hath ears to *h*, let him *h*	Mt 11:15	191
neither shall any man *h* his voice	Mt 12:19	191
earth to *h* the wisdom of Solomon	Mt 12:42	191
Who hath ears to *h*, let him *h*	Mt 13:9	191
and hearing they *h* not, neither do	Mt 13:13	191
saith, By hearing ye shall *h*	Mt 13:14	191
***h* with their ears, and should**	Mt 13:15	191
and your ears, for they *h*	Mt 13:16	191
to *h* those things which ye *h*	Mt 13:17	191
***H* ye therefore the parable of the**	Mt 13:18	191
Who hath ears to *h*, let him *h*	Mt 13:43	191
multitude, and said unto them, *H*	Mt 15:10	191
h ye him	Mt 17:5	191
if he shall *h* thee, thou hast	Mt 18:15	191
But if he will not *h* thee	Mt 18:16	191
And if he shall neglect to *h* them	Mt 18:17	3878
but if he neglect to *h* the church	Mt 18:17	3878
***H* another parable**	Mt 21:33	191
And ye shall *h* of wars and rumours	Mt 24:6	191
that hath ears to *h*, let him *h*	Mk 4:9	191
and hearing they may *h*, and not	Mk 4:12	191
such as *h* the word,	Mk 4:18	191
such as *h* the word, and receive it	Mk 4:20	191
man have ears to *h*, let him *h*	Mk 4:23	191
unto them, Take heed what ye *h*	Mk 4:24	191
unto you that *h* shall more be	Mk 4:24	191
them, as they were able to *h* it	Mk 4:33	191
shall not receive you, nor *h* you	Mk 6:11	191
man have ears to *h*, let him *h*	Mk 7:16	191
he maketh both the deaf to *h*	Mk 7:37	191
and having ears, *h* ye not	Mk 8:18	191
h him	Mk 9:7	191
of all the commandments is, *H*	Mk 12:29	191
And when ye shall *h* of wars	Mk 13:7	191
upon him to *h* the word of God	Lk 5:1	191
multitudes came together to *h*	Lk 5:15	191
and Sidon, which came to *h* him	Lk 6:17	191
But I say unto you which *h*	Lk 6:27	191
lepers are cleansed, the deaf *h*	Lk 7:22	191
that hath ears to *h*, let him *h*	Lk 8:8	191
by the way side are they that *h*	Lk 8:12	191
rock are they, which, when they *h*	Lk 8:13	191
Take heed therefore how ye *h*	Lk 8:18	191
are these which *h* the word of God	Lk 8:21	191
is this, of whom I *h* such things	Lk 9:9	191
h him	Lk 9:35	191
to *h* those things which ye *h*,	Lk 10:24	191
are they that *h* the word of God	Lk 11:28	191
earth to *h* the wisdom of Solomon	Lk 11:31	191
that hath ears to *h*, let him *h*	Lk 14:35	191
publicans and sinners for to *h* him	Lk 15:1	191
How is it that I *h* this of thee	Lk 16:2	191
let them *h* them	Lk 16:29	191
If they *h* not Moses and the	Lk 16:31	191
***H* what the unjust judge saith**	Lk 18:6	191
were very attentive to *h* him	Lk 19:48	191
But when ye shall *h* of wars	Lk 21:9	191
him in the temple, for to *h* him	Lk 21:38	191
when the dead shall *h* the voice	Jn 5:25	191
and they that *h* shall live	Jn 5:25	191
in the graves shall *h* his voice	Jn 5:28	191
as I *h*, I judge	Jn 5:30	191
who can *h* it?	Jn 6:60	191
judge any man, before it *h* him	Jn 7:51	191
even because ye cannot *h* my word	Jn 8:43	191
ye therefore *h* them not, because	Jn 8:47	191
told you already, and ye did not *h*	Jn 9:27	191
wherefore would ye *h* it again	Jn 9:27	191
and the sheep *h* his voice	Jn 10:3	191
but the sheep did not *h* them	Jn 10:8	191
bring, and they shall *h* my voice	Jn 10:16	191
why *h* ye him?	Jn 10:20	191
My sheep *h* my voice, and I know	Jn 10:27	191
And if any man *h* my words, and	Jn 12:47	191
the word which ye *h* is not mine	Jn 14:24	191
but whatsoever he shall *h*	Jn 16:13	191
how *h* we every man in our own	Acts 2:8	191
we do *h* them speak in our tongues	Acts 2:11	191

Ye men of Israel, *h* these words	Acts 2:22	191
forth this, which ye now see and *h*	Acts 2:33	191
him shall ye *h* in all things	Acts 3:22	191
which will not *h* that prophet	Acts 3:23	191
him shall ye *h*.	Acts 7:37	191
his house, and to *h* words of thee	Acts 10:22	191
God, to *h* all things that are	Acts 10:33	191
desired to *h* the word of God	Acts 13:7	191
together to *h* the word of God	Acts 13:44	191
should *h* the word of the gospel	Acts 15:7	191
to tell, or to *h* some new thing	Acts 17:21	191
We will *h* thee again of this	Acts 17:32	191
Moreover ye see and *h*, that not	Acts 19:26	191
for they will *h* that thou art	Acts 21:22	191
h ye my defence which I make now	Acts 22:1	191
shouldest *h* the voice of his	Acts 22:14	191
I will *h* thee, said he, when	Acts 23:35	1251
h us of thy clemency a few words	Acts 24:4	191
I would also *h* the man myself	Acts 25:22	191
morrow, said he, thou shalt *h* him	Acts 25:22	191
I beseech thee to *h* me patiently	Acts 26:3	191
but also all that *h* me this day	Acts 26:29	191
But we desire to *h* of thee what	Acts 28:22	191
and say, Hearing ye shall *h*	Acts 28:26	191
h with their ears, and understand	Acts 28:27	191
Gentiles, and that they will *h* it	Acts 28:28	191
how shall they *h* without a	Rom 10:14	191
and ears that they should not *h*	Rom 11:8	191
I *h* that there be divisions among	1Cor 11:18	191
for all that will they not *h* me	1Cor 14:21	1522
the law, do ye not *h* the law	Gal 4:21	191
I may *h* of your affairs, that ye	Phil 1:27	191
saw in me, and now *h* to be in me	Phil 1:30	191
For we *h* that there are some	2Th 3:11	191
save thyself, and them that *h* thee	1Ti 4:16	191
and that all the Gentiles might *h*	2Ti 4:17	191
To day if ye will *h* his voice	Heb 3:7	191
To day if ye will *h* his voice	Heb 3:15	191
To day if ye will *h* his voice	Heb 4:7	191
let every man be swift to *h*	Jas 1:19	191
And if we know that he *h* us	1Jn 5:15	191
I have no greater joy than to *h*	3Jn 4	191
they that *h* the words of this	Rev 1:3	191
let him *h* what the Spirit saith	Rev 2:7	191
let him *h* what the Spirit saith	Rev 2:11	191
let him *h* what the Spirit saith	Rev 2:17	191
let him *h* what the Spirit saith	Rev 2:29	191
let him *h* what the Spirit saith	Rev 3:6	191
let him *h* what the Spirit saith	Rev 3:13	191
if any man *h* my voice, and open	Rev 3:20	191
let him *h* what the Spirit saith	Rev 3:22	191
which neither can see, nor *h*	Rev 9:20	191
If any man have an ear, let him *h*	Rev 13:9	191

HEARD

they *h* the voice of the LORD God	Gen 3:8	8085
I *h* thy voice in the garden, and I	Gen 3:10	8085
when Abram *h* that his brother was	Gen 14:14	8085
the LORD hath *h* thy affliction	Gen 16:11	8085
And as for Ishmael, I have *h* thee	Gen 17:20	8085
Sarah *h* it in the tent door,	Gen 18:10	8085
God *h* the voice of the lad	Gen 21:17	8085
for God hath *h* the voice of the	Gen 21:17	8085
tell me, neither yet *h* I of it	Gen 21:26	8085
when he *h* the words of Rebekah	Gen 24:30	8085
Abraham's servant *h* their words	Gen 24:52	8085
Rebekah *h* when Isaac spake to	Gen 27:5	8085
I *h* thy father speak unto Esau	Gen 27:6	8085
when Esau *h* the words of his	Gen 27:34	8085
when Laban *h* the tidings of Jacob	Gen 29:13	8085
the LORD hath *h* that I was hated	Gen 29:33	8085
me, and hath also *h* my voice	Gen 30:6	8085
he *h* the words of Laban's sons,	Gen 31:1	8085
Jacob *h* that he had defiled Dinah	Gen 34:5	8085
out of the field when they *h* it	Gen 34:7	8085
and Israel *h* it	Gen 35:22	8085
for I *h* them say, Let us go to	Gen 37:17	8085
And Reuben *h* it, and he delivered	Gen 37:21	8085
when he *h* that I lifted up my	Gen 39:15	8085
when his master *h* the words of	Gen 39:19	8085
I have *h* say of thee, that thou	Gen 41:15	8085
I have *h* that there is corn in	Gen 42:2	8085
for they *h* that they should eat	Gen 43:25	8085
and the house of Pharaoh *h*	Gen 45:2	8085
thereof was *h* in Pharaoh's house	Gen 45:16	8085
Now when Pharaoh *h* this thing	Ex 2:15	8085
God *h* their groaning, and God	Ex 2:24	8085
have *h* their cry by reason of	Ex 3:7	8085
when they *h* that the LORD had	Ex 4:31	8085
I have also *h* the groaning of the	Ex 6:5	8085
for he hath *h* your murmurings	Ex 16:9	8085

I have *h* the murmurings of the	Ex 16:12	8085
h of all that God had done for	Ex 18:1	8085
let it be *h* out of thy mouth	Ex 23:13	8085
his sound shall be *h* when he	Ex 28:35	8085
when Joshua *h* the noise of the	Ex 32:17	8085
when the people *h* these evil	Ex 33:4	8085
And when Moses *h* that, he was	Lev 10:20	8085
let all that *h* him lay their	Lev 24:14	8085
then he *h* the voice of one	Num 7:89	8085
and the LORD *h* it	Num 11:1	8085
Then Moses *h* the people weep	Num 11:10	8085
And the LORD *h* it	Num 12:2	8085
for they have *h* that thou LORD	Num 14:14	8085
h the fame of thee will speak	Num 14:15	8085
I have *h* the murmurings of the	Num 14:27	8085
And when Moses *h* it, he fell upon	Num 16:4	8085
he *h* our voice, and sent an angel,	Num 20:16	8085
h tell that Israel came by the	Num 21:1	8085
when Balak *h* that Balaam was come	Num 22:36	8085
which *h* the words of God, which	Num 24:4	8085
which *h* the words of God, and knew	Num 24:16	8085
And her husband *h* it, and held his	Num 30:7	8085
at her in the day that he *h* it	Num 30:7	8085
her on the day that he *h* it	Num 30:8	8085
And her husband *h* it, and held his	Num 30:11	8085
them void on the day he *h* them	Num 30:12	8085
at her in the day that he *h* them	Num 30:14	8085
void after that he hath *h* them	Num 30:15	8085
h of the coming of the children	Num 33:40	8085
the LORD *h* the voice of your	Deut 1:34	8085
ye *h* the voice of the words, but	Deut 4:12	8085
only ye *h* a voice	Deut 4:12	8085
thing is, or hath been *h* like it	Deut 4:32	8085
midst of the fire, as thou hast *h*	Deut 4:33	8085
when ye *h* the voice out of the	Deut 5:23	8085
we have *h* his voice out of the	Deut 5:24	8085
that hath *h* the voice of the	Deut 5:26	8085
the LORD *h* the voice of your	Deut 5:28	8085
I have *h* the voice of the words	Deut 5:28	8085
and of whom thou hast *h* say	Deut 9:2	8085
told thee, and thou hast *h* of it	Deut 17:4	8085
the LORD *h* our voice, and looked	Deut 26:7	8085
For we have *h* how the LORD dried	Josh 2:10	8085
as soon as we had *h* these things	Josh 2:11	8085
h that the LORD had dried up the	Josh 5:1	8085
when the people *h* the sound of	Josh 6:20	8085
and the Jebusite, *h* thereof	Josh 9:1	8085
h what Joshua had done unto	Josh 9:3	8085
for we have *h* the fame of him, and	Josh 9:9	8085
that they *h* that they were their	Josh 9:16	8085
king of Jerusalem had *h* how	Josh 10:1	8085
king of Hazor had *h* those things	Josh 11:1	8085
And the children of Israel *h* say	Josh 22:11	8085
the children of Israel *h* of it	Josh 22:12	8085
h the words that the children of	Josh 22:30	8085
for it hath *h* all the words of	Josh 24:27	8085
when Gideon *h* the telling of the	Judg 7:15	8085
Zebul the ruler of the city *h* the	Judg 9:30	8085
of the tower of Shechem *h* that	Judg 9:46	8085
Let not thy voice be *h* among us	Judg 18:25	8085
h that the children of Israel	Judg 20:3	8085
for she had *h* in the country of	Ruth 1:6	8085
moved, but her voice was not *h*	1Sa 1:13	8085
h all that his sons did unto all	1Sa 2:22	8085
when the Philistines *h* the noise	1Sa 4:6	8085
when Eli *h* the noise of the	1Sa 4:14	8085
when she *h* the tidings that the	1Sa 4:19	8085
when the Philistines *h* that the	1Sa 7:7	8085
when the children of Israel *h* it	1Sa 7:7	8085
and the LORD *h* him	1Sa 7:9	6030
Samuel *h* all the words of the	1Sa 8:21	8085
upon Saul when he *h* those tidings	1Sa 11:6	8085
Geba, and the Philistines *h* of it	1Sa 13:3	8085
all Israel *h* say that Saul had	1Sa 13:4	8085
when they *h* that the Philistines	1Sa 14:22	8085
But Jonathan *h* not when his	1Sa 14:27	8085
all Israel *h* those words of the	1Sa 17:11	8085
and David *h* them	1Sa 17:23	8085
Eliab his eldest brother *h* when	1Sa 17:28	8085
words were *h* which David spake	1Sa 17:31	8085
and all his father's house *h* it	1Sa 22:1	8085
When Saul *h* that David was	1Sa 22:6	8085
thy servant hath certainly *h* that	1Sa 23:10	8085
come down, as thy servant hath *h*	1Sa 23:11	8085
And when Saul *h* that, he pursued	1Sa 23:25	8085
David *h* in the wilderness that	1Sa 25:4	8085
now I have *h* that thou hast	1Sa 25:7	8085
when David *h* that Nabal was dead,	1Sa 25:39	8085
inhabitants of Jabesh-gilead *h* of	1Sa 31:11	8085
And afterward when David *h* it	2Sa 3:28	8085
when Saul's son *h* that Abner was	2Sa 4:1	8085

But when the Philistines *h* that	2Sa 5:17	8085
and David *h* of it, and went down to	2Sa 5:17	8085
all that we have *h* with our ears	2Sa 7:22	8085
When Toi king of Hamath *h* that	2Sa 8:9	8085
And when David *h* of it, he sent	2Sa 10:7	8085
when the wife of Uriah *h* that	2Sa 11:26	8085
king David *h* of all these things	2Sa 13:21	8085
all the people *h* when the king	2Sa 18:5	8085
for the people *h* say that day how	2Sa 19:2	8085
Hast thou not *h* that Adonijah the	1Kin 1:11	8085
h it as they had made an end of	1Kin 1:41	8085
when Joab *h* the sound of the	1Kin 1:41	8085
This is the noise that ye have *h*	1Kin 1:45	8085
The word that I have *h* is good	1Kin 2:42	8085
all Israel *h* of the judgment	1Kin 3:28	8085
which had *h* of his wisdom	1Kin 4:34	8085
for he had *h* that they had	1Kin 5:1	8085
when Hiram *h* the words of Solomon	1Kin 5:7	8085
any tool of iron *h* in the house	1Kin 6:7	8085
I have *h* thy prayer and thy	1Kin 9:3	8085
of Sheba *h* of the fame of Solomon	1Kin 10:1	8085
It was a true report that I *h* in	1Kin 10:6	8085
exceedeth the fame which I *h*	1Kin 10:7	8085
when Hadad *h* in Egypt that David	1Kin 11:21	8085
h of it, (for he was fled from	1Kin 12:2	8085
when all Israel *h* that Jeroboam	1Kin 12:20	8085
when king Jeroboam *h* the saying	1Kin 13:4	8085
him back from the way *h* thereof	1Kin 13:26	8085
when Ahijah *h* the sound of her	1Kin 14:6	8085
to pass, when Baasha *h* thereof	1Kin 15:21	8085
people that were encamped *h* say	1Kin 16:16	8085
the LORD *h* the voice of Elijah	1Kin 17:22	8085
And it was so, when Elijah *h* it	1Kin 19:13	8085
when Ben-hadad *h* this message	1Kin 20:12	8085
we have *h* that the kings of the	1Kin 20:31	8085
when Jezebel *h* that Naboth was	1Kin 21:15	8085
when Ahab *h* that Naboth was dead,	1Kin 21:16	8085
when Ahab *h* those words, that he	1Kin 21:27	8085
when all the Moabites *h* that the	2Kin 3:21	8085
had *h* that the king of Israel had	2Kin 5:8	8085
when the king *h* the words of the	2Kin 6:30	8085
come to Jezreel, Jezebel *h* of it	2Kin 9:30	8085
when Athaliah *h* the noise of the	2Kin 11:13	8085
to pass, when king Hezekiah *h* it	2Kin 19:1	8085
which the LORD thy God hath *h*	2Kin 19:4	8085
of the words which thou hast *h*	2Kin 19:6	8085
for he had *h* that he was departed	2Kin 19:8	8085
when he *h* say of Tirhakah king of	2Kin 19:9	8085
thou hast *h* what the kings of	2Kin 19:11	8085
king of Assyria I have *h*	2Kin 19:20	8085
Hast thou not *h* long ago how I	2Kin 19:25	8085
I have *h* thy prayer, I have seen	2Kin 20:5	8085
for he had *h* that Hezekiah had	2Kin 20:12	8085
when the king *h* the words of	2Kin 22:11	8085
the words which thou hast *h*	2Kin 22:18	8085
I also have *h* thee, saith the	2Kin 22:19	8085
h that the king of Babylon had	2Kin 25:23	8085
when all Jabesh-gilead *h* all that	1Chr 10:11	8085
when the Philistines *h* that David	1Chr 14:8	8085
And David *h* of it, and went out	1Chr 14:8	8085
all that we have *h* with our ears	1Chr 17:20	8085
Now when Tou king of Hamath *h* how	1Chr 18:9	8085
And when David *h* of it, he sent	1Chr 19:8	8085
one sound to be *h* in praising	2Chr 5:13	8085
I have *h* thy prayer, and have	2Chr 7:12	8085
of Sheba *h* of the fame of Solomon	2Chr 9:1	8085
It was a true report which I *h* in	2Chr 9:5	8085
thou exceedest the fame that I *h*	2Chr 9:6	8085
h it, that Jeroboam returned out	2Chr 10:2	8085
when Asa *h* these words, and the	2Chr 15:8	8085
it came to pass, when Baasha *h* it	2Chr 16:5	8085
when they had *h* that the LORD	2Chr 20:29	8085
Now when Athaliah *h* the noise of	2Chr 23:12	8085
and their voice was *h,* and their	2Chr 30:27	8085
h his supplication, and brought	2Chr 33:13	8085
when the king had *h* the words of	2Chr 34:19	8085
the words which thou hast *h*	2Chr 34:26	8085
I have even *h* thee also, saith	2Chr 34:27	8085
and the noise was *h* afar off	Ezr 3:13	8085
Benjamin *h* that the children of	Ezr 4:1	8085
when I *h* this thing, I rent my	Ezr 9:3	8085
when I *h* these words, that I sat	Neh 1:4	8085
h of it, it grieved them	Neh 2:10	8085
h it, they laughed us to scorn,	Neh 2:19	8085
that when Sanballat *h* that we	Neh 4:1	8085
h that the walls of Jerusalem	Neh 4:7	8085
when our enemies *h* that it was	Neh 4:15	8085
was very angry when I *h* their cry	Neh 5:6	8085
h that I had builded the wall, and	Neh 6:1	8085
when all our enemies *h* thereof	Neh 6:16	8085
when they *h* the words of the law	Neh 8:9	8085

of Jerusalem was *h* even afar off	Neh 12:43	8085
to pass, when they had *h* the law	Neh 13:3	8085
which have *h* of the deed of the	Est 1:18	8085
commandment and his decree was *h*	Est 2:8	8085
Now when Job's three friends *h* of	Job 2:11	8085
silence, and I *h* a voice, saying,	Job 4:16	8085
seen all this, mine ear hath *h*	Job 13:1	8085
Hast thou *h* the secret of God	Job 15:8	8085
I have *h* many such things	Job 16:2	8085
cry out of wrong, but I am not *h*	Job 19:7	6030
I have *h* the check of my reproach	Job 20:3	8085
how little a portion is *h* of him	Job 26:14	8085
We have *h* the fame thereof with	Job 28:22	8085
When the ear *h* me, then it	Job 29:11	8085
I have *h* the voice of thy words,	Job 33:8	8085
not stay them when his voice is *h*	Job 37:4	8085
I have *h* of thee by the hearing	Job 42:5	8085
he *h* me out of his holy hill	Ps 3:4	6030
for the Lord hath *h* the voice of	Ps 6:8	8085
The Lord hath *h* my supplication	Ps 6:9	8085
thou hast *h* the desire of the	Ps 10:17	8085
he *h* my voice out of his temple,	Ps 18:6	8085
where their voice is not *h*	Ps 19:3	8085
for thou hast *h* me from the horns	Ps 22:21	6030
but when he cried unto him, he *h*	Ps 22:24	8085
because he hath *h* the voice of my	Ps 28:6	8085
For I have *h* the slander of many	Ps 31:13	8085
I sought the Lord, and he *h* me	Ps 34:4	6030
poor man cried, and the Lord *h* him	Ps 34:6	8085
But I, as a deaf man, *h* not	Ps 38:13	8085
he inclined unto me, and *h* my cry	Ps 40:1	8085
We have *h* with our ears, O God,	Ps 44:1	8085
As we have *h*, so have we seen in	Ps 48:8	8085
For thou, O God, hast *h* my vows	Ps 61:5	8085
twice have I *h* this	Ps 62:11	8085
the voice of his praise to be *h*	Ps 66:8	8085
But verily God hath *h* me	Ps 66:19	8085
judgment to be *h* from heaven	Ps 76:8	8085
Which we have *h* and known, and our	Ps 78:3	8085
Therefore the Lord *h* this	Ps 78:21	8085
When God *h* this, he was wroth, and	Ps 78:59	8085
where I *h* a language that I	Ps 81:5	8085
Zion *h*, and was glad	Ps 97:8	8085
affliction, when he *h* their cry	Ps 106:44	8085
Lord, because he hath *h* my voice	Ps 116:1	8085
for thou hast *h* me, and art become	Ps 118:21	6030
I cried unto the Lord, and he *h* me	Ps 120:1	6030
Lo, we *h* of it at Ephratah	Ps 132:6	8085
cry himself, but shall not be *h*	Prov 21:13	6030
despised, and his words are not *h*	Eccl 9:16	8085
The words of wise men are *h* in	Eccl 9:17	8085
of the turtle is *h* in our land	Song 2:12	8085
Also I *h* the voice of the Lord,	Is 6:8	8085
cause it to be *h* unto Laish	Is 10:30	7181
voice shall be *h* even unto Jahaz	Is 15:4	8085
We have *h* of the pride of Moab	Is 16:6	8085
that which I have *h* of the Lord	Is 21:10	8085
part of the earth have we *h* songs	Is 24:16	8085
for I have *h* from the Lord God of	Is 28:22	8085
cause his glorious voice to be *h*	Is 30:30	8085
to pass, when king Hezekiah *h* it	Is 37:1	8085
which the Lord thy God hath *h*	Is 37:4	8085
of the words that thou hast *h*	Is 37:6	8085
for he had *h* that he was departed	Is 37:8	8085
he *h* say concerning Tirhakah king	Is 37:9	8085
And when he *h* it, he sent	Is 37:9	8085
thou hast *h* what the kings of	Is 37:11	8085
Hast thou not *h* long ago, how I	Is 37:26	8085
I have *h* thy prayer, I have seen	Is 38:5	8085
for he had *h* that he had been	Is 39:1	8085
have ye not *h*?	Is 40:21	8085
hast thou not *h*, that the	Is 40:28	8085
his voice to be *h* in the street	Is 42:2	8085
Thou hast *h*, see all this	Is 48:6	8085
an acceptable time have I *h* thee	Is 49:8	6030
had not *h* shall they consider	Is 52:15	8085
make your voice to be *h* on high	Is 58:4	8085
shall no more be *h* in thy land	Is 60:18	8085
of the world men have not *h*	Is 64:4	8085
weeping shall be no more *h* in her	Is 65:19	8085
Who hath *h* such a thing	Is 66:8	8085
afar off, that have not *h* my fame	Is 66:19	8085
A voice was *h* upon the high	Jer 3:21	8085
my peace, because thou hast *h*	Jer 4:19	8085
For I have *h* a voice as of a	Jer 4:31	8085
violence and spoil is *h* in her	Jer 6:7	8085
We have *h* the fame thereof	Jer 6:24	8085
early and speaking, but ye *h* not	Jer 7:13	8085
I hearkened and *h*, but they spake	Jer 8:6	8085
of his horses was *h* from Dan	Jer 8:16	8085
voice of wailing is *h* out of Zion	Jer 9:19	8085
heathen, who hath *h* such things	Jer 18:13	8085
Let a cry be *h* from their houses,	Jer 18:22	8085
h that Jeremiah prophesied these	Jer 20:1	8085
For I *h* the defaming of many,	Jer 20:10	8085
and hath perceived and *h* his word	Jer 23:18	8085
who hath marked his word, and *h* it	Jer 23:18	8085
I have *h* what the prophets said,	Jer 23:25	8085
Because ye have not *h* my words	Jer 25:8	8085
of the flock, shall be *h*	Jer 25:36	8085
all the people *h* Jeremiah	Jer 26:7	8085
princes of Judah *h* these things	Jer 26:10	8085
as ye have *h* with your ears	Jer 26:11	8085
city all the words that ye have *h*	Jer 26:12	8085
h his words, the king sought to	Jer 26:21	8085
but when Urijah *h* it, he was	Jer 26:21	8085
We have *h* a voice of trembling,	Jer 30:5	8085
A voice was *h* in Ramah,	Jer 31:15	8085
I have surely *h* Ephraim bemoaning	Jer 31:18	8085
there shall be *h* in this place	Jer 33:10	8085
h that every one should let his	Jer 34:10	8085
unto them, but they have not *h*	Jer 35:17	8085
had *h* out of the book all the	Jer 36:11	8085
them all the words that he had *h*	Jer 36:13	8085
when they had *h* all the words	Jer 36:16	8085
servants that *h* all these words	Jer 36:24	8085
Jerusalem *h* tidings of them	Jer 37:5	8085
h the words that Jeremiah had	Jer 38:1	8085
h that they had put Jeremiah in	Jer 38:7	8085
h that the king of Babylon had	Jer 40:7	8085
h that the king of Babylon had	Jer 40:11	8085
h of all the evil that Ishmael	Jer 41:11	8085
said unto them, I have *h* you	Jer 42:4	8085
The nations have *h* of thy shame	Jer 46:12	8085
ones have caused a cry to be *h*	Jer 48:4	8085
have *h* a cry of destruction	Jer 48:5	8085
We have *h* the pride of Moab, (he	Jer 48:29	8085
be *h* in Rabbah of the Ammonites	Jer 49:2	8085
I have *h* a rumour from the Lord,	Jer 49:14	8085
thereof was *h* in the Red sea	Jer 49:21	8085
for they have *h* evil tidings	Jer 49:23	8085
Babylon hath *h* the report of them	Jer 50:43	8085
the cry is *h* among the nations	Jer 50:46	8085
that shall be *h* in the land	Jer 51:46	8085
because we have *h* reproach	Jer 51:51	8085
They have *h* that I sigh	Lam 1:21	8085
mine enemies have *h* of my trouble	Lam 1:21	8085
Thou hast *h* my voice	Lam 3:56	8085
Thou hast *h* their reproach, O	Lam 3:61	8085
I *h* the noise of their wings,	Eze 1:24	8085
I *h* a voice of one that spake	Eze 1:28	8085
that I *h* him that spake unto me	Eze 2:2	8085
I *h* behind me a voice of a great	Eze 3:12	8085
I *h* also the noise of the wings	Eze 3:13	8085
was *h* even to the outer court	Eze 10:5	8085
The nations also *h* of him	Eze 19:4	8085
his voice should no more be *h*	Eze 19:9	8085
of thy harps shall be no more *h*	Eze 26:13	8085
their voice to be *h* against thee	Eze 27:30	8085
He *h* the sound of the trumpet, and	Eze 33:5	8085
that I have *h* all thy blasphemies	Eze 35:12	8085
I have *h* them	Eze 35:13	8085
I *h* him speaking unto me out of	Eze 43:6	8085
when all the people *h* the sound	Dan 3:7	8086
I have even *h* of thee, that the	Dan 5:14	8086
I have *h* of thee, that thou canst	Dan 5:16	8086
when he *h* these words, was sore	Dan 6:14	8086
Then I *h* one saint speaking, and	Dan 8:13	8085
I *h* a man's voice between the	Dan 8:16	8085
Yet *h* I the voice of his words	Dan 10:9	8085
when I *h* the voice of his words,	Dan 10:9	8085
before thy God, thy words were *h*	Dan 10:12	8085
I *h* the man clothed in linen,	Dan 12:7	8085
And I *h*, but I understood not	Dan 12:8	8085
as their congregation hath *h*	Hos 7:12	8085
I have *h* him, and observed him	Hos 14:8	6030
We have *h* a rumour from the Lord,	Obad 1	8085
unto the Lord, and he *h* me	Jonah 2:2	6030
heathen, such as they have not *h*	Mic 5:15	8085
thy messengers shall no more be *h*	Nah 2:13	8085
I have *h* thy speech, and was	Hab 3:2	8085
When I *h*, my belly trembled	Hab 3:16	8085
I have *h* the reproach of Moab, and	Zeph 2:8	8085
for we have *h* that God is with	Zec 8:23	8085
h it, and a book of remembrance	Mal 3:16	8085
Herod the king had *h* these things	Mt 2:3	*191*
When they had *h* the king, they	Mt 2:9	*191*
In Rama was there a voice *h*	Mt 2:18	*191*
But when he *h* that Archelaus did	Mt 2:22	*191*
Now when Jesus had *h* that John	Mt 4:12	*191*
Ye have *h* that it was said by	Mt 5:21	*191*
Ye have *h* that it was said by	Mt 5:27	*191*

ye have *h* that it hath been said	Mt 5:33	*191*
Ye have *h* that it hath been said,	Mt 5:38	*191*
Ye have *h* that it hath been said,	Mt 5:43	*191*
be *h* for their much speaking	Mt 6:7	*1522*
When Jesus *h* it, he marvelled, and	Mt 8:10	*191*
But when Jesus *h* that, he said	Mt 9:12	*191*
Now when John had *h* in the prison	Mt 11:2	*191*
But when the Pharisees *h* it	Mt 12:24	*191*
which ye hear, and have not *h* them	Mt 13:17	*191*
tetrarch *h* of the fame of Jesus	Mt 14:1	*191*
When Jesus *h* of it, he departed	Mt 14:13	*191*
and when the people had *h* thereof	Mt 14:13	*191*
after they *h* this saying	Mt 15:12	*191*
And when the disciples *h* it	Mt 17:6	*191*
when the young man *h* that saying	Mt 19:22	*191*
When his disciples *h* it, they	Mt 19:25	*191*
And when the ten *h* it, they were	Mt 20:24	*191*
when they *h* that Jesus passed by,	Mt 20:30	*191*
and Pharisees had *h* his parables	Mt 21:45	*191*
But when the king *h* thereof	Mt 22:7	*191*
When they had *h* these words	Mt 22:22	*191*
And when the multitude *h* this	Mt 22:33	*191*
But when the Pharisees had *h* that	Mt 22:34	*191*
now ye have *h* his blasphemy	Mt 26:65	*191*
stood there, when they *h* that	Mt 27:47	*191*
When Jesus *h* it, he saith unto	Mk 2:17	*191*
when they had *h* what great things	Mk 3:8	*191*
And when his friends *h* of it	Mk 3:21	*191*
but when they have *h*, Satan	Mk 4:15	*191*
who, when they have *h* the word	Mk 4:16	*191*
When she had *h* of Jesus, came in	Mk 5:27	*191*
As soon as Jesus *h* the word that	Mk 5:36	*191*
And king Herod *h* of him	Mk 6:14	*191*
But when Herod *h* thereof, he said	Mk 6:16	*191*
and when he *h* him, he did many	Mk 6:20	*191*
did many things, and *h* him gladly	Mk 6:20	*191*
And when his disciples *h* of it	Mk 6:29	*191*
were sick, where they *h* he was	Mk 6:55	*191*
h of him, and came and fell at his	Mk 7:25	*191*
And when the ten *h* it, they began	Mk 10:41	*191*
when he *h* that it was Jesus of	Mk 10:47	*191*
And his disciples *h* it	Mk 11:14	*191*
the scribes and chief priests *h* it	Mk 11:18	*191*
having *h* them reasoning together,	Mk 12:28	*191*
And the common people *h* him gladly	Mk 12:37	*191*
And when they *h* it, they were glad	Mk 14:11	*191*
We *h* him say, I will destroy this	Mk 14:58	*191*
Ye have *h* the blasphemy	Mk 14:64	*191*
stood by, when they *h* it said	Mk 15:35	*191*
when they had *h* that he was alive	Mk 16:11	*191*
for thy prayer is *h*	Lk 1:13	*1522*
when Elisabeth *h* the salutation	Lk 1:41	*191*
her cousins *h* how the Lord had	Lk 1:58	*191*
all they that *h* them laid them up	Lk 1:66	*191*
all they that *h* it wondered at	Lk 2:18	*191*
all the things that they had *h*	Lk 2:20	*191*
all that *h* him were astonished at	Lk 2:47	*191*
we have *h* done in Capernaum	Lk 4:23	*191*
when they *h* these things, were	Lk 4:28	*191*
when he *h* of Jesus, he sent unto	Lk 7:3	*191*
When Jesus *h* these things, he	Lk 7:9	*191*
what things ye have seen and *h*	Lk 7:22	*191*
And all the people that *h* him	Lk 7:29	*191*
are they, which, when they have *h*	Lk 8:14	*191*
having *h* the word, keep it, and	Lk 8:15	*191*
But when Jesus *h* it, he answered	Lk 8:50	*191*
Now Herod the tetrarch *h* of all	Lk 9:7	*191*
which ye hear, and have not *h* them	Lk 10:24	*191*
sat at Jesus' feet, and *h* his word	Lk 10:39	*191*
darkness shall be *h* in the light	Lk 12:3	*191*
at meat with him *h* these things	Lk 14:15	*191*
the house, he *h* musick and dancing	Lk 15:25	*191*
were covetous, *h* all these things	Lk 16:14	*191*
Now when Jesus *h* these things	Lk 18:22	*191*
And when he *h* this, he was very	Lk 18:23	*191*
And they that *h* it said, Who then	Lk 18:26	*191*
as they *h* these things, he added	Lk 19:11	*191*
And when they *h* it, they said, God	Lk 20:16	*191*
ourselves have *h* of his own mouth	Lk 22:71	*191*
When Pilate *h* of Galilee, he	Lk 23:6	*191*
because he had *h* many things of	Lk 23:8	*191*
And the two disciples *h* him speak	Jn 1:37	*191*
One of the two which *h* John speak	Jn 1:40	*191*
And what he hath seen and *h*	Jn 3:32	*191*
Pharisees had *h* that Jesus made	Jn 4:1	*191*
for we have *h* him ourselves, and	Jn 4:42	*191*
When he *h* that Jesus was come out	Jn 4:47	*191*
Ye have neither *h* his voice at	Jn 5:37	*191*
Every man therefore that hath *h*	Jn 6:45	*191*
disciples, when they had *h* this	Jn 6:60	*191*
The Pharisees *h* that the people	Jn 7:32	*191*
when they *h* this saying, said, Of	Jn 7:40	*191*
ground, as though he *h* them not	Jn 8:6	
And they which *h* it, being	Jn 8:9	*191*
things which I have *h* of him	Jn 8:26	*191*
the truth, which I have *h* of God	Jn 8:40	*191*
the world began was it not *h* that	Jn 9:32	*191*
Jesus *h* that they had cast him	Jn 9:35	*191*
which were with him *h* these words	Jn 9:40	*191*
When Jesus *h* that, he said, This	Jn 11:4	*191*
When he had *h* therefore that he	Jn 11:6	*191*
as soon as she *h* that Jesus was	Jn 11:20	*191*
As soon as she *h* that, she arose	Jn 11:29	*191*
I thank thee that thou hast *h* me	Jn 11:41	*191*
when they *h* that Jesus was coming	Jn 12:12	*191*
for that they *h* that he had done	Jn 12:18	*191*
h it, said that it thundered	Jn 12:29	*191*
We have *h* out of the law that	Jn 12:34	*191*
Ye have *h* how I said unto you, I	Jn 14:28	*191*
for all things that I have *h* of	Jn 15:15	*191*
ask them which *h* me, what I have	Jn 18:21	*191*
Pilate therefore *h* that saying	Jn 19:8	*191*
Pilate therefore *h* that saying	Jn 19:13	*191*
Peter *h* that it was the Lord	Jn 21:7	*191*
which, saith he, ye have *h* of me	Acts 1:4	*191*
because that every man *h* them	Acts 2:6	*191*
Now when they *h* this, they were	Acts 2:37	*191*
of them which *h* the word believed	Acts 4:4	*191*
things which we have seen and *h*	Acts 4:20	*191*
And when they *h* that, they lifted	Acts 4:24	*191*
on all them that *h* these things	Acts 5:5	*191*
and upon as many as *h* these things	Acts 5:11	*191*
And when they *h* that, they entered	Acts 5:21	*191*
the chief priests *h* these things	Acts 5:24	*191*
When they *h* that, they were cut	Acts 5:33	*191*
We have *h* him speak blasphemous	Acts 6:11	*191*
For we have *h* him say, that this	Acts 6:14	*191*
But when Jacob *h* that there was	Acts 7:12	*191*
I have *h* their groaning, and am	Acts 7:34	*191*
When they *h* these things, they	Acts 7:54	*191*
which were at Jerusalem *h* that	Acts 8:14	*191*
h him read the prophet Esaias, and	Acts 8:30	*191*
h a voice saying unto him, Saul,	Acts 9:4	*191*
I have *h* by many of this man, how	Acts 9:13	*191*
But all that *h* him were amazed,	Acts 9:21	*191*
the disciples had *h* that Peter	Acts 9:38	*191*
said, Cornelius, thy prayer is *h*	Acts 10:31	*1522*
fell on all them which *h* the word	Acts 10:44	*191*
For they *h* them speak with	Acts 10:46	*191*
h that the Gentiles had also	Acts 11:1	*191*
I *h* a voice saying unto me, Arise	Acts 11:7	*191*
When they *h* these things, they	Acts 11:18	*191*
And when the Gentiles *h* this	Acts 13:48	*191*
The same *h* Paul speak	Acts 14:9	*191*
h of, they rent their clothes, and	Acts 14:14	*191*
Forasmuch as we have *h*, that	Acts 15:24	*191*
which worshipped God, *h* us	Acts 16:14	*191*
and the prisoners *h* them	Acts 16:25	*1874*
when they *h* that they were Romans	Acts 16:38	*191*
city, when they *h* these things	Acts 17:8	*191*
when they *h* of the resurrection	Acts 17:32	*191*
when Aquila and Priscilla had *h*	Acts 18:26	*191*
We have not so much as *h* whether	Acts 19:2	*191*
When they *h* this, they were	Acts 19:5	*191*
Asia *h* the word of the Lord Jesus	Acts 19:10	*191*
when they *h* these sayings, they	Acts 19:28	*191*
when we *h* these things, both we,	Acts 21:12	*191*
And when they *h* it, they glorified	Acts 21:20	*191*
when they *h* that he spake in the	Acts 22:2	*191*
***h* a voice saying unto me, Saul,**	Acts 22:7	*191*
but they *h* not the voice of him	Acts 22:9	*191*
men of what thou hast seen and *h*	Acts 22:15	*191*
When the centurion *h* that	Acts 22:26	*191*
son *h* of their lying in wait	Acts 23:16	*191*
when Felix *h* these things, having	Acts 24:22	*191*
h him concerning the faith in	Acts 24:24	*191*
I *h* a voice speaking unto me, and	Acts 26:14	*191*
thence, when the brethren *h* of us	Acts 28:15	*191*
in him of whom they have not *h*	Rom 10:14	*191*
But I say, Have they not *h*	Rom 10:18	*191*
that have not *h* shall understand	Rom 15:21	*191*
Eye hath not seen, nor ear *h*	1Cor 2:9	*191*
I have *h* thee in a time accepted,	2Cor 6:2	*1873*
h unspeakable words, which it is	2Cor 12:4	*191*
For ye have *h* of my conversation	Gal 1:13	*191*
But they had *h* only, That he	Gal 1:23	*191*
after that ye *h* the word of truth	Eph 1:13	*191*
after I *h* of your faith in the	Eph 1:15	*191*
If ye have *h* of the dispensation	Eph 3:2	*191*
If so be that ye have *h* him	Eph 4:21	*191*
because that ye had *h* that he had	Phil 2:26	*191*
both learned, and received, and *h*	Phil 4:9	*191*

Since we *h* of your faith in	Col 1:4	191
whereof ye *h* before in the word	Col 1:5	4257
in you, since the day ye *h* of it	Col 1:6	191
we also, since the day we *h* it	Col 1:9	191
of the gospel, which ye have *h*	Col 1:23	191
the word of God which ye *h* of us	1Th 2:13	189
words, which thou hast *h* of me	2Ti 1:13	191
the things that thou hast *h* of me	2Ti 2:2	191
to the things which we have *h*	Heb 2:1	191
unto us by them that *h* him	Heb 2:3	191
For some, when they had *h*	Heb 3:16	191
with faith in them that *h* it	Heb 4:2	191
death, and was *h* in that he feared	Heb 5:7	1522
which voice they that *h* intreated	Heb 12:19	191
Ye have *h* of the patience of Job,	Jas 5:11	191
voice which came from heaven we *h*	2Pet 1:18	191
the beginning, which we have *h*	1Jn 1:1	191
h declare we unto you, that ye	1Jn 1:3	191
message which we have *h* of him	1Jn 1:5	191
ye have *h* from the beginning	1Jn 2:7	191
as ye have *h* that antichrist	1Jn 2:18	191
in you, which ye have *h* from the	1Jn 2:24	191
If that which ye have *h* from the	1Jn 2:24	191
that ye *h* from the beginning	1Jn 3:11	191
whereof ye have *h* that it should	1Jn 4:3	191
as ye have *h* from the beginning,	2Jn 6	191
h behind me a great voice, as of	Rev 1:10	191
how thou hast received and *h*	Rev 3:3	191
the first voice which I *h* was as	Rev 4:1	191
I *h* the voice of many angels	Rev 5:11	191
h I saying, Blessing, and honour,	Rev 5:13	191
opened one of the seals, and I *h*	Rev 6:1	191
I *h* the second beast say, Come and	Rev 6:3	191
I *h* the third beast say, Come and	Rev 6:5	191
I *h* a voice in the midst of the	Rev 6:6	191
I *h* the voice of the fourth beast	Rev 6:7	191
I *h* the number of them which were	Rev 7:4	191
h an angel flying through the	Rev 8:13	191
I *h* a voice from the four horns	Rev 9:13	191
and I *h* the number of them	Rev 9:16	191
I *h* a voice from heaven saying	Rev 10:4	191
the voice which I *h* from heaven	Rev 10:8	191
they *h* a great voice from heaven	Rev 11:12	191
I *h* a loud voice saying in heaven	Rev 12:10	191
I *h* a voice from heaven, as the	Rev 14:2	191
I *h* the voice of harpers harping	Rev 14:2	191
I *h* a voice from heaven saying	Rev 14:13	191
I *h* a great voice out of the	Rev 16:1	191
I *h* the angel of the waters say,	Rev 16:5	191
I *h* another out of the altar say,	Rev 16:7	191
I *h* another voice from heaven,	Rev 18:4	191
shall be *h* no more at all in thee	Rev 18:22	191
shall be *h* no more at all in thee	Rev 18:22	191
of the bride shall be *h* no more	Rev 18:23	191
after these things I *h* a great	Rev 19:1	191
I *h* as it were the voice of a	Rev 19:6	191
I *h* a great voice out of heaven	Rev 21:3	191
John saw these things, and *h* them	Rev 22:8	191
And when I had *h* and seen, I fell	Rev 22:8	191

HEARDEST

thou *h* his words out of the midst	Deut 4:36	8085
for thou *h* in that day how the	Josh 14:12	8085
when thou *h* what I spake against	2Kin 22:19	8085
when thou *h* his words against	2Chr 34:27	8085
h their cry by the Red sea	Neh 9:9	8085
thee, thou *h* them from heaven	Neh 9:27	8085
thee, thou *h* them from heaven	Neh 9:28	8085
nevertheless thou *h* the voice of	Ps 31:22	8085
declared my ways, and thou *h* me	Ps 119:26	6030
the day when thou *h* them not	Is 48:7	8085
Yea, thou *h* not	Is 48:8	8085
hell cried I, and thou *h* my voice	Jonah 2:2	8085

HEARER

For if any be a *h* of the word	Jas 1:23	202
he being not a forgetful *h*	Jas 1:25	202

HEARERS

(For not the *h* of the law are	Rom 2:13	202
it may minister grace unto the *h*	Eph 4:29	191
but to the subverting of the *h*	2Ti 2:14	191
not *h* only, deceiving your own	Jas 1:22	202

HEAREST

Ruth, *H* thou not, my daughter	Ruth 2:8	8085
Wherefore *h* thou men's words,	1Sa 24:9	8085
when thou *h* the sound of a going	2Sa 5:24	8085
and when thou *h*, forgive	1Kin 8:30	8085
and when thou *h*, forgive	2Chr 6:21	8085
in the daytime, but thou *h* not	Ps 22:2	6030
O thou that *h* prayer, unto thee	Ps 65:2	8085
unto him, *H* thou what these say	Mt 21:16	191

H thou not how many things they	Mt 27:13	191
thou *h* the sound thereof, but	Jn 3:8	191
And I knew that thou *h* me always	Jn 11:42	191

HEARETH

for that he *h* your murmurings	Ex 16:7	8085
for that the LORD *h* your	Ex 16:8	8085
disallow her in the day that he *h*	Num 30:5	8085
when he *h* the words of this curse	Deut 29:19	8085
for thy servant *h*	1Sa 3:9	8085
for thy servant *h*	1Sa 3:10	8085
every one that *h* it shall tingle	1Sa 3:11	8085
that whosoever *h* it will say	2Sa 17:9	8085
and Judah, that whosoever *h* of it	2Kin 21:12	8085
he *h* the cry of the afflicted	Job 34:28	8085
The righteous cry, and the LORD *h*	Ps 34:17	8085
Thus I was as a man that *h* not	Ps 38:14	8085
For the LORD *h* the poor, and	Ps 69:33	8085
Blessed is the man that *h* me	Prov 8:34	8085
A wise son *h* his father's	Prov 13:1	8085
but a scorner *h* not rebuke	Prov 13:1	8085
but the poor *h* not rebuke	Prov 13:8	8085
but he *h* the prayer of the	Prov 15:29	8085
The ear that *h* the reproof of	Prov 15:31	8085
but he that *h* reproof getteth	Prov 15:32	8085
answereth a matter before he *h* it	Prov 18:13	8085
but the man that *h* speaketh	Prov 21:28	8085
Lest he that *h* it put thee to	Prov 25:10	8085
he *h* cursing, and bewrayeth it not	Prov 29:24	8085
there is none that *h* your words	Is 41:26	8085
opening the ears, but he *h* not	Is 42:20	8085
this place, the which whosoever *h*	Jer 19:3	8085
He that *h*, let him hear	Eze 3:27	8085
Then whosoever *h* the sound of the	Eze 33:4	8085
Therefore whosoever *h* these	Mt 7:24	191
every one that *h* these sayings of	Mt 7:26	191
When any one *h* the word of the	Mt 13:19	191
the same is he that *h* the word	Mt 13:20	191
the thorns is he that *h* the word	Mt 13:22	191
good ground is he that *h* the word	Mt 13:23	191
h my sayings, and doeth them, I	Lk 6:47	191
But he that *h*, and doeth not, is	Lk 6:49	191
He that *h* you me	Lk 10:16	191
h him, rejoiceth greatly because	Jn 3:29	191
I say unto you, He that *h* my word	Jn 5:24	191
He that is of God *h* God's words	Jn 8:47	191
we know that God *h* not sinners	Jn 9:31	191
God, and doeth his will, him he *h*	Jn 9:31	191
that is of the truth *h* my voice	Jn 18:37	191
me to be, or that he *h* of me	2Cor 12:6	191
of the world, and the world *h* them	1Jn 4:5	191
he that knoweth God *h* us	1Jn 4:6	191
he that is not of God *h* not us	1Jn 4:6	191
according to his will, he *h* us	1Jn 5:14	191
And let him that *h* say, Come	Rev 22:17	191
h the words of the prophecy of	Rev 22:18	191

HEARING

law before all Israel in their *h*	Deut 31:11	241
for in our *h* the king charged	2Sa 18:12	241
there was neither voice, nor *h*	2Kin 4:31	7182
Surely thou hast spoken in mine *h*	Job 33:8	241
heard of thee by the *h* of the ear	Job 42:5	8088
The *h* ear, and the seeing eye, the	Prov 20:12	8085
away his ear from the law	Prov 28:9	8085
seeing, nor the ear filled with *h*	Eccl 1:8	8085
reprove after the *h* of his ears	Is 11:3	4926
I was bowed down at the *h* of it	Is 21:3	8085
stoppeth his ears from *h* of blood	Is 33:15	8085
to the others he said in mine *h*	Eze 9:5	241
it was cried unto them in my *h*	Eze 10:13	241
but of *h* the words of the LORD	Amos 8:11	8085
***h* they hear not, neither do they**	Mt 13:13	191
By *h* ye shall hear, and shall not	Mt 13:14	189
and their ears are dull of *h*	Mt 13:15	191
and *h* they may hear, and not	Mk 4:12	191
many *h* him were astonished,	Mk 6:2	191
midst of the doctors, both *h* them	Lk 2:46	191
***h* they might not understand**	Lk 8:10	191
h the multitude pass by, he asked	Lk 18:36	191
Ananias *h* these words fell down,	Acts 5:5	191
things which Philip spake, *h*	Acts 8:6	191
a voice, but seeing no man	Acts 9:7	191
of the Corinthians *h* believed	Acts 18:8	191
reserved unto the *h* of Augustus	Acts 25:21	1233
was entered into the place of *h*	Acts 25:23	201
H ye shall hear, and shall not	Acts 28:26	189
and their ears are dull of *h*	Acts 28:27	191
So then faith cometh by *h*	Rom 10:17	189
and *h* by the word of God	Rom 10:17	189
were an eye, where were the *h*	1Cor 12:17	189
If the whole were *h*, where were	1Cor 12:17	189

of the law, or by the *h* of faith .... Gal 3:2   *189*
of the law, or by the *h* of faith .... Gal 3:5   *189*
H of thy love and faith, which .... Philem 5   *191*
uttered, seeing ye are dull of *h* .... Heb 5:11   *189*
among them, in seeing and *h* 2Pet 2:8   *189*

HEARKEN

wives of Lamech, *h* unto my speech ...... Gen 4:23   238
said unto thee, *h* unto her voice .... Gen 21:12   8085
My lord, *h* unto me .... Gen 23:15   8085
But if ye will not *h* unto us .... Gen 34:17   8085
h unto Israel your father .... Gen 49:2   8085
they shall *h* to thy voice .... Ex 3:18   8085
believe me, nor *h* unto my voice .... Ex 4:1   8085
neither *h* to the voice of the .... Ex 4:8   8085
neither *h* unto thy voice, that .... Ex 4:9   8085
and how shall Pharaoh *h* unto me ...... Ex 6:30   8085
But Pharaoh shall not *h* unto you ...... Ex 7:4   8085
neither did he *h* unto them .... Ex 7:22   8085
Pharaoh shall not *h* unto you .... Ex 11:9   8085
If thou wilt diligently *h* to the .... Ex 15:26   8085
H now unto my voice, I will give .... Ex 18:19   8085
But if ye will not *h* unto me .... Lev 26:14   8085
not yet for all this *h* unto me .... Lev 26:18   8085
unto me, and will not *h* unto me .... Lev 26:21   8085
will not for all this *h* unto me .... Lev 26:27   8085
h unto me, thou son of Zippor .... Num 23:18   238
Now therefore *h*, O Israel, unto ...... Deut 1:45   8085
if ye *h* to these judgments, and .... Deut 4:1   8085
if ye shall *h* diligently unto my .... Deut 7:12   8085
Thou shalt not *h* unto the words .... Deut 11:13   8085
consent unto him, nor *h* unto him ...... Deut 13:3   8085
When thou shalt *h* to the voice of ...... Deut 13:8   8085
Only if thou carefully *h* unto the ...... Deut 13:18   8085
will not *h* unto the priest that .... Deut 15:5   8085
unto him ye shall *h* .... Deut 17:12   8085
that whosoever will not *h* unto my ...... Deut 18:15   8085
him, will not *h* unto them .... Deut 18:19   8085
thy God would not *h* unto Balaam ...... Deut 21:18   8085
judgments, and to *h* unto his voice ...... Deut 23:5   8085
Israel, saying, Take heed, and *h* .... Deut 26:17   8085
if thou shalt *h* diligently unto .... Deut 27:9   8085
if thou shalt *h* unto the voice of .... Deut 28:1   8085
if that thou *h* unto the .... Deut 28:2   8085
if thou wilt not *h* unto the voice .... Deut 28:13   8085
If thou shalt *h* unto the voice of .... Deut 28:15   8085
things, so will we *h* unto thee .... Deut 30:10   8085
will not *h* thy words in all .... Josh 1:17   8085
But I would not *h* unto Balaam ...... Josh 1:18   8085
would not *h* unto their judges .... Josh 24:10   8085
to know whether they would *h* unto ...... Judg 2:17   8085
H unto me, ye men of Shechem, unto ...... Judg 3:4   8085
that God may *h* unto you .... Judg 9:7   8085
king of Edom would not *h* thereto ...... Judg 9:7   8085
But the men would not *h* to him ...... Judg 11:17   8085
h to the voice of their brethren ...... Judg 19:25   8085
H unto the voice of the people in ...... Judg 20:13   8085
Now therefore *h* unto their voice 1Sa 8:7   8085
H unto their voice, and make them 1Sa 8:9   8085
now therefore *h* thou unto the 1Sa 8:22   8085
to *h* than the fat of rams 1Sa 15:1   8085
h thou also unto the voice of 1Sa 15:22   7181
For who will *h* unto you in this 1Sa 28:22   8085
he would not *h* unto our voice 1Sa 30:24   8085
he would not *h* unto her voice 2Sa 12:18   8085
But he would not *h* unto her 2Sa 13:14   8085
to *h* unto the cry and to the 2Sa 13:16   8085
that thou mayest *h* unto the 1Kin 8:28   8085
h thou to the supplication of thy 1Kin 8:29   8085
to *h* unto them in all that they 1Kin 8:30   8085
if thou wilt *h* unto all that I 1Kin 8:52   8085
H not unto him, nor consent 1Kin 11:38   8085
And he said, *H*, O people, every 1Kin 20:8   8085
if ye will *h* unto my voice, take 1Kin 22:28   8085
Howbeit they did not *h*, but they 2Kin 10:6   8085
H not to Hezekiah 2Kin 17:40   8085
h not unto Hezekiah, when he 2Kin 18:31   8085
to *h* unto the cry and the prayer 2Kin 18:32   8085
to *h* unto the prayer which thy 2Chr 6:19   8085
H therefore unto the.................. 2Chr 6:20   8085
the king would not *h* unto them 2Chr 6:21   8085
And he said, *H*, all ye people 2Chr 10:16   8085
he said, *H* ye, all Judah, and ye 2Chr 18:27   8085
but they would not *h* 2Chr 20:15   7181
Shall we then *h* unto you to do 2Chr 33:10   7181
h to the pleadings of my lips ...... Neh 13:27   8085
Therefore I said, *H* to me .... Job 13:6   7181
my speeches, and *h* to all my words ...... Job 32:10   8085
Mark well, O Job, *h* unto me .... Job 33:1   238
If not, *h* unto me.......................... Job 33:31   8085
     Job 33:33   8085

Therefore *h* unto me, ye men of ...... Job 34:10   8085
h to the voice of my words .... Job 34:16   238
me, and let a wise man *h* unto me ...... Job 34:34   8085
H unto this, O Job .... Job 37:14   238
H unto the voice of my cry, my .... Ps 5:2   7181
Come, ye children, *h* unto me .... Ps 34:11   8085
H, O daughter, and consider, and ...... Ps 45:10   8085
Which will not *h* to the voice of ...... Ps 58:5   8085
O Israel, if thou wilt *h* unto me ...... Ps 81:8   8085
my people would not *h* to my voice ...... Ps 81:11   8085
H unto me now therefore, O ye ...... Prov 7:24   8085
Now therefore *h* unto me, O ye ...... Prov 8:32   8085
H unto thy father that begat thee ...... Prov 23:22   8085
If a ruler *h* to lies, all his .... Prov 29:12   7181
the companions *h* to thy voice ...... Song 8:13   7181
h, and hear my speech .... Is 28:23   7181
ears of them that hear shall *h* .... Is 32:3   7181
and *h*, ye people .... Is 34:1   7181
H not to Hezekiah .... Is 36:16   8085
who will *h* and hear for the time ...... Is 42:23   7181
H unto me, O house of Jacob, and ...... Is 46:3   8085
H unto me, ye stouthearted, that ...... Is 46:12   8085
H unto me, O Jacob and Israel, my ...... Is 48:12   8085
and *h*, ye people, from far .... Is 49:1   7181
H to me, ye that follow after .... Is 51:1   8085
H unto me, my people .... Is 51:4   7181
H unto me, ye that know .... Is 51:7   8085
h diligently unto me, and eat ye ...... Is 55:2   8085
uncircumcised, and they cannot *h* ...... Jer 6:10   7181
H to the sound of the trumpet ...... Jer 6:17   7181
But they said, We will not *h* .... Jer 6:17   7181
but they will not *h* to thee .... Jer 7:27   7181
unto me, I will not *h* unto them ...... Jer 11:11   8085
that they may not *h* unto me ...... Jer 16:12   8085
pass, if ye diligently *h* unto me ...... Jer 17:24   8085
But if ye will not *h* unto me to ...... Jer 17:27   8085
h to the voice of them that .... Jer 18:19   7181
H not unto the words of the .... Jer 23:16   8085
If so be they will *h*, and turn .... Jer 26:3   8085
If ye will not *h* to me, to walk ...... Jer 26:4   8085
To *h* to the words of my servants ...... Jer 26:5   8085
Therefore *h* not ye to your .... Jer 27:9   8085
Therefore *h* not unto the words of ...... Jer 27:14   8085
H not to the words of your .... Jer 27:16   8085
H not unto them .... Jer 27:17   8085
neither *h* to your dreams which ye ...... Jer 29:8   8085
unto me, and I will *h* unto you ...... Jer 29:12   8085
instruction to *h* to my words .... Jer 35:13   8085
did *h* unto the words of the LORD ...... Jer 37:2   8085
counsel, wilt thou not *h* unto me ...... Jer 38:15   8085
the LORD, we will not *h* unto thee ...... Jer 44:16   8085
of Israel will not *h* unto thee .... Eze 3:7   8085
for they will not *h* unto me .... Eze 3:7   8085
me, and would not *h* unto me ...... Eze 20:8   8085
also, if ye will not *h* unto me ...... Eze 20:39   8085
O Lord, *h* and do .... Dan 9:19   7181
and *h*, ye house of Israel .... Hos 5:1   7181
because they did not *h* unto him ...... Hos 9:17   8085
h, O earth, and all that therein ...... Mic 1:2   7181
nor *h* unto me, saith the LORD ...... Zec 1:4   7181
But they refused to *h*, and pulled ...... Zec 7:11   7181
H, Behold, there went .... Mk 4:3   *191*
H unto me every one of you, and ...... Mk 7:14   *191*
known unto you, and *h* to my words ...... Acts 2:14   *1801*
to *h* unto you more than unto God ...... Acts 4:19   *191*
Men, brethren, and fathers, *h* ...... Acts 7:2   *191*
of the gate, a damsel came to *h* ...... Acts 12:13   *5219*
Men and brethren, *h* unto me ...... Acts 15:13   *191*
H, my beloved brethren, Hath not ...... Jas 2:5   *191*

HEARKENED

Because thou hast *h* unto the .... Gen 3:17   8085
Abram *h* to the voice of Sarai .... Gen 16:2   8085
And Abraham *h* unto Ephron ...... Gen 23:16   8085
God *h* unto Leah, and she conceived ...... Gen 30:17   8085
God *h* to her, and opened her womb ...... Gen 30:22   8085
unto Shechem his son *h* all that ...... Gen 34:24   8085
that he *h* not unto her, to lie by ...... Gen 39:10   8085
but they *h* not unto Moses for ...... Ex 6:9   8085
of Israel have not *h* unto me ...... Ex 6:12   8085
heart, that he *h* not unto them ...... Ex 7:13   8085
his heart, and *h* not unto them ...... Ex 8:15   8085
hardened, and he *h* not unto them ...... Ex 8:19   8085
of Pharaoh, and he *h* not unto them ...... Ex 9:12   8085
they *h* not unto Moses .... Ex 16:20   8085
So Moses *h* to the voice of his ...... Ex 18:24   8085
times, and have not *h* to my voice ...... Num 14:22   8085
the LORD *h* to the voice of Israel ...... Num 21:3   8085
But the LORD *h* unto me at that ...... Deut 9:19   8085
him not, nor *h* to his voice .... Deut 9:23   8085
the LORD *h* unto me at that time ...... Deut 10:10   8085

h unto observers of times, and	Deut 18:14	8085
but I have *h* to the voice of the	Deut 26:14	8085
the children of Israel *h* unto him	Deut 34:9	8085
According as we *h* unto Moses in	Josh 1:17	8085
that the LORD *h* unto the voice of	Josh 10:14	8085
and have not *h* unto my voice	Judg 2:20	8085
king of the children of Ammon *h*	Judg 11:28	8085
God *h* to the voice of Manoah	Judg 13:9	8085
Notwithstanding they *h* not unto	1Sa 2:25	8085
I have *h* unto your voice in all	1Sa 12:1	8085
Saul *h* unto the voice of Jonathan	1Sa 19:6	8085
I have *h* to thy voice, and have	1Sa 25:35	8085
have *h* unto thy words which thou	1Sa 28:21	8085
and he *h* unto their voice	1Sa 28:23	8085
Wherefore the king *h* not unto the	1Kin 12:15	8085
saw that the king *h* not unto them	1Kin 12:16	8085
They *h* therefore to the word of	1Kin 12:24	8085
So Ben-hadad *h* unto king Asa, and	1Kin 15:20	8085
he *h* unto their voice, and did so	1Kin 20:25	8085
the LORD, and the LORD *h* unto him	2Kin 13:4	8085
And the king of Assyria *h* unto him	2Kin 16:9	8085
Hezekiah *h* unto them, and shewed	2Kin 20:13	8085
But they *h* not	2Kin 21:9	8085
not *h* unto the words of this book	2Kin 22:13	8085
So the king *h* not unto the people	2Chr 10:15	8085
Ben-hadad *h* unto king Asa, and	2Chr 16:4	8085
Then the king *h* unto them	2Chr 24:17	8085
hast not *h* unto my counsel	2Chr 25:16	8085
the LORD *h* to Hezekiah, and healed	2Chr 30:20	8085
h not unto the words of Necho	2Chr 35:22	8085
h not to thy commandments,	Neh 9:16	8085
h not unto thy commandments, but	Neh 9:29	8085
nor *h* unto thy commandments and	Neh 9:34	7181
he *h* not unto them, that they	Est 3:4	8085
that he had *h* unto my voice	Job 9:16	238
Oh that my people had *h* unto me	Ps 81:13	8085
h not unto the voice of the LORD	Ps 106:25	8085
he *h* diligently with much heed	Is 21:7	7181
O that thou hadst *h* to my	Is 48:18	7181
they have not *h* unto my words	Jer 6:19	7181
But they *h* not, nor inclined	Jer 7:24	8085
Yet they *h* not unto me, nor	Jer 7:26	8085
I *h* and heard, but they spake not	Jer 8:6	8085
but ye have not *h*	Jer 25:3	8085
but ye have not *h*, nor inclined	Jer 25:4	8085
Yet ye have not *h* unto me	Jer 25:7	8085
sending them, but ye have not *h*	Jer 26:5	8085
they have not *h* to my words	Jer 29:19	8085
yet they have not *h* to receive	Jer 32:33	8085
but your fathers *h* not unto me	Jer 34:14	8085
Ye have not *h* unto me, in	Jer 34:17	8085
but ye *h* not unto me	Jer 35:14	8085
inclined your ear, nor *h* unto me	Jer 35:15	8085
this people hath not *h* unto me	Jer 35:16	8085
but they *h* not	Jer 36:31	8085
But he *h* not to him	Jer 37:14	8085
But they *h* not, nor inclined	Jer 44:5	8085
them, they would have *h* unto thee	Eze 3:6	8085
Neither have we *h* unto thy	Dan 9:6	8085
and the LORD *h*, and heard it, and a	Mal 3:16	7181
Sirs, ye should have *h* unto me	Acts 27:21	3980

HEARKENEDST

because thou *h* not unto the voice	Deut 28:45	8085

HEARKENETH

But whoso *h* unto me shall dwell	Prov 1:33	8085
but he that *h* unto counsel is	Prov 12:15	8085

HEARKENING

h unto the voice of his word	Ps 103:20	8085

HEART

of the thoughts of his *h* was only	Gen 6:5	3820
earth, and it grieved him at his *h*	Gen 6:6	3820
and the LORD said in his *h*	Gen 8:21	3820
of man's *h* is evil from his youth	Gen 8:21	3820
and laughed, and said in his *h*	Gen 17:17	3820
in the integrity of my *h* and	Gen 20:5	3824
this in the integrity of thy *h*	Gen 20:6	3824
I had done speaking in mine *h*	Gen 24:45	3820
and Esau said in his *h*, The days	Gen 27:41	3820
their *h* failed them, and they were	Gen 42:28	3820
And Jacob's *h* fainted, for he	Gen 45:26	3820
thee, he will be glad in his *h*	Ex 4:14	3820
but I will harden his *h*, that he	Ex 4:21	3820
And I will harden Pharaoh's *h*	Ex 7:3	3820
And he hardened Pharaoh's *h*	Ex 7:13	3820
Pharaoh's *h* is hardened, he	Ex 7:14	3820
Pharaoh's *h* was hardened, neither	Ex 7:22	3820
did he set his *h* to this also	Ex 7:23	3820
was respite, he hardened his *h*	Ex 8:15	3820
Pharaoh's *h* was hardened, and he	Ex 8:19	3820

hardened his *h* at this time also	Ex 8:32	3820
the *h* of Pharaoh was hardened, and	Ex 9:7	3820
LORD hardened the *h* of Pharaoh	Ex 9:12	3820
send all my plagues upon thine *h*	Ex 9:14	3820
yet more, and hardened his *h*	Ex 9:34	3820
the *h* of Pharaoh was hardened,	Ex 9:35	3820
for I have hardened his *h*	Ex 10:1	3820
the *h* of his servants, that I	Ex 10:1	3820
But the LORD hardened Pharaoh's *h*	Ex 10:20	3820
But the LORD hardened Pharaoh's *h*	Ex 10:27	3820
and the LORD hardened Pharaoh's *h*	Ex 11:10	3820
And I will harden Pharaoh's *h*	Ex 14:4	3820
the *h* of Pharaoh and of his	Ex 14:5	3824
the LORD hardened the *h* of	Ex 14:8	3820
congealed in the *h* of the sea	Ex 15:8	3820
for ye know the *h* of a stranger	Ex 23:9	5315
his *h* ye shall take my offering	Ex 25:2	3820
of judgment upon his *h*, when he	Ex 28:29	3820
and they shall be upon Aaron's *h*	Ex 28:30	3820
his *h* before the LORD continually	Ex 28:30	3820
whosoever is of a willing *h*	Ex 35:5	3820
every one whose *h* stirred him up	Ex 35:21	3820
all the women whose *h* stirred	Ex 35:26	3820
whose *h* made them willing to	Ex 35:29	3820
put in his *h* that he may teach	Ex 35:34	3820
hath he filled with wisdom of *h*	Ex 35:35	3820
in whose *h* the LORD had put	Ex 36:2	3820
even every one whose *h* stirred	Ex 36:2	3820
not hate thy brother in thine *h*	Lev 19:17	3824
the eyes, and cause sorrow of *h*	Lev 26:16	5315
that ye seek not after your own *h*	Num 15:39	3824
wherefore discourage ye the *h* of	Num 32:7	3820
they discouraged the *h* of the	Num 32:9	3820
brethren have discouraged our *h*	Deut 1:28	3824
made his *h* obstinate, that he	Deut 2:30	3824
thy *h* all the days of thy life	Deut 4:9	3824
if thou seek him with all thy *h*	Deut 4:29	3824
day, and consider it in thine *h*	Deut 4:39	3824
that there were such an *h* in them	Deut 5:29	3824
the LORD thy God with all thine *h*	Deut 6:5	3824
this day, shall be in thine *h*	Deut 6:6	3824
If thou shalt say in thine *h*	Deut 7:17	3824
thee, to know what was in thine *h*	Deut 8:2	3824
shalt also consider in thine *h*	Deut 8:5	3824
Then thine *h* be lifted up, and	Deut 8:14	3824
And thou say in thine *h*, My power	Deut 8:17	3824
Speak not thou in thine *h*	Deut 9:4	3824
or for the uprightness of thine *h*	Deut 9:5	3824
the LORD thy God with all thy *h*	Deut 10:12	3824
therefore the foreskin of your *h*	Deut 10:16	3824
and to serve him with all your *h*	Deut 11:13	3824
that your *h* be not deceived, and	Deut 11:16	3824
lay up these my words in your *h*	Deut 11:18	3824
the LORD your God with all your *h*	Deut 13:3	3824
thou shalt not harden thine *h*	Deut 15:7	3824
be not a thought in thy wicked *h*	Deut 15:9	3824
thine *h* shall not be grieved when	Deut 15:10	3824
himself, that his *h* turn not away	Deut 17:17	3824
That his *h* be not lifted up above	Deut 17:20	3824
And if thou say in thine *h*	Deut 18:21	3824
the slayer, while his *h* is hot	Deut 19:6	3824
h faint as well as his *h*	Deut 20:8	3824
is poor, and setteth his *h* upon it	Deut 24:15	5315
keep and do them with all thine *h*	Deut 26:16	3824
blindness, and astonishment of *h*	Deut 28:28	3824
joyfulness, and with gladness of *h*	Deut 28:47	3824
give thee there a trembling *h*	Deut 28:65	3820
for the fear of thine *h* wherewith	Deut 28:67	3824
not given you an *h* to perceive	Deut 29:4	3820
whose *h* turneth away this day	Deut 29:18	3824
that he bless himself in his *h*	Deut 29:19	3824
walk in the imagination of mine *h*	Deut 29:19	3824
and thy children, with all thine *h*	Deut 30:2	3824
thy God will circumcise thine *h*	Deut 30:6	3824
the *h* of thy seed, to love the	Deut 30:6	3824
the LORD thy God with all thine *h*	Deut 30:6	3824
the LORD thy God with all thine *h*	Deut 30:10	3824
thee, in thy mouth, and in thy *h*	Deut 30:14	3824
But if thine *h* turn away, so that	Deut 30:17	3824
passed over, that their *h* melted	Josh 5:1	3824
word again as it was in mine *h*	Josh 14:7	3824
me made the *h* of the people melt	Josh 14:8	3820
and to serve him with all your *h*	Josh 22:5	3824
incline your *h* unto the LORD God	Josh 24:23	3824
My *h* is toward the governors of	Judg 5:9	3820
there were great thoughts of *h*	Judg 5:15	3820
there were great searchings of *h*	Judg 5:16	3820
when thine *h* is not with me	Judg 16:15	3820
That he told her all his *h*	Judg 16:17	3820
that he had told her all his *h*	Judg 16:18	3820
for he hath shewed me all his *h*	Judg 16:18	3820

And the priest's *h* was glad	Judg 18:20	3820
Comfort thine *h* with a morsel of	Judg 19:5	3820
night, and let thine *h* be merry	Judg 19:6	3820
father said, Comfort thine *h*	Judg 19:8	3824
that thine *h* may be merry	Judg 19:9	3824
his *h* was merry, he went to lie	Ruth 3:7	3820
and why is thy *h* grieved	1Sa 1:8	3824
Now Hannah, she spake in her *h*	1Sa 1:13	3820
My *h* rejoiceth in the LORD, mine	1Sa 2:1	3820
thine eyes, and to grieve thine *h*	1Sa 2:33	5315
to that which is in mine *h*	1Sa 2:35	3824
for his *h* trembled for the ark of	1Sa 4:13	3820
tell thee all that is in thine *h*	1Sa 9:19	3824
Samuel, God gave him another *h*	1Sa 10:9	3820
serve the LORD with all your *h*	1Sa 12:20	3824
him in truth with all your *h*	1Sa 12:24	3824
sought him a man after his own *h*	1Sa 13:14	3824
him, Do all that is in thine *h*	1Sa 14:7	3824
I am with thee according to thy *h*	1Sa 14:7	3824
but the LORD looketh on the *h*	1Sa 16:7	3824
and the naughtiness of thine *h*	1Sa 17:28	3824
Let no man's *h* fail because of	1Sa 17:32	3820
laid up these words in his *h*	1Sa 21:12	3824
that David's *h* smote him	1Sa 24:5	3820
nor offence of *h* unto my lord	1Sa 25:31	3820
Nabal's *h* was merry within him	1Sa 25:36	3820
that his *h* died within him, and he	1Sa 25:37	3820
And David said in his *h*, I shall	1Sa 27:1	3820
afraid, and his *h* greatly trembled	1Sa 28:5	3820
over all that thine *h* desireth	2Sa 3:21	5315
and she despised him in her *h*	2Sa 6:16	3820
Go, do all that is in thine *h*	2Sa 7:3	3824
sake, and according to thine own *h*	2Sa 7:21	3820
h to pray this prayer unto thee	2Sa 7:27	3820
when Amnon's *h* is merry with wine	2Sa 13:28	3820
the king take the thing to his *h*	2Sa 13:33	3820
the king's *h* was toward Absalom	2Sa 14:1	3820
whose *h* is as the *h* of a lion	2Sa 17:10	3820
them through the *h* of Absalom	2Sa 18:14	3820
he bowed the *h* of all the men of	2Sa 19:14	3824
Judah, even as the *h* of one man	2Sa 19:14	
the king should take it to his *h*	2Sa 19:19	3820
David's *h* smote him after that he	2Sa 24:10	3820
me in truth with all their *h*	1Kin 2:4	3824
which thine *h* is privy to	1Kin 2:44	3824
and in uprightness of *h* with thee	1Kin 3:6	3824
h to judge thy people, that I may	1Kin 3:9	3820
thee a wise and an understanding *h*	1Kin 3:12	3820
exceeding much, and largeness of *h*	1Kin 4:29	3820
it was in the *h* of David my	1Kin 8:17	3824
Whereas it was in thine *h* to	1Kin 8:18	3824
didst well that it was in thine *h*	1Kin 8:18	3824
walk before thee with all their *h*	1Kin 8:23	3824
every man the plague of his own *h*	1Kin 8:38	3824
to his ways, whose *h* thou knowest	1Kin 8:39	3824
return unto thee with all their *h*	1Kin 8:48	3824
Let your *h* therefore be perfect	1Kin 8:61	3824
glad of *h* for all the goodness	1Kin 8:66	3824
mine *h* shall be there perpetually	1Kin 9:3	3824
father walked, in integrity of *h*	1Kin 9:4	3824
with him of all that was in her *h*	1Kin 10:2	3824
which God had put in his *h*	1Kin 10:24	3820
turn away your *h* after their gods	1Kin 11:2	3824
and his wives turned away his *h*	1Kin 11:3	3820
away his *h* after other gods	1Kin 11:4	3824
his *h* was not perfect with the	1Kin 11:4	3824
as was the *h* of David his father	1Kin 11:4	3824
because his *h* was turned from the	1Kin 11:9	3824
And Jeroboam said in his *h*	1Kin 12:26	3824
then shall the *h* of this people	1Kin 12:27	3820
which he had devised of his own *h*	1Kin 12:33	3820
and who followed me with all his *h*	1Kin 14:8	3824
his *h* was not perfect with the	1Kin 15:3	3824
as the *h* of David his father	1Kin 15:3	3824
nevertheless Asa's *h* was perfect	1Kin 15:14	3824
hast turned their *h* back again	1Kin 18:37	3824
bread, and let thine *h* be merry	1Kin 21:7	3820
him, Went not mine *h* with thee	2Kin 5:26	3820
Therefore the *h* of the king of	2Kin 6:11	3820
and the arrow went out at his *h*	2Kin 9:24	3820
and said to him, Is thine *h* right	2Kin 10:15	3824
as my *h* is with thy *h*	2Kin 10:15	3824
to all that was in mine *h*	2Kin 10:30	3824
LORD God of Israel with all his *h*	2Kin 10:31	3824
that cometh into any man's *h* to	2Kin 12:4	3820
thine *h* hath lifted thee up	2Kin 14:10	3820
thee in truth and with a perfect *h*	2Kin 20:3	3824
Because thine *h* was tender	2Kin 22:19	3824
and his statutes with all their *h*	2Kin 23:3	3820
turned to the LORD with all his *h*	2Kin 23:25	3824
mine *h* shall be knit unto you	1Chr 12:17	3824

they were not of double *h*	1Chr 12:33	3820
came with a perfect *h* to Hebron	1Chr 12:38	3820
were of one *h* to make David king	1Chr 12:38	3824
and she despised him in her *h*	1Chr 15:29	3820
let the *h* of them rejoice that	1Chr 16:10	3820
David, Do all that is in thine *h*	1Chr 17:2	3824
sake, and according to thine own *h*	1Chr 17:19	3820
in his *h* to pray before thee	1Chr 17:25	
Now set your *h* and your soul to	1Chr 22:19	3824
I had in mine *h* to build an house	1Chr 28:2	3824
and serve him with a perfect *h*	1Chr 28:9	3820
because with perfect *h* they	1Chr 28:9	3824
my God, that thou triest the *h*	1Chr 29:17	3824
in the uprightness of mine *h* I	1Chr 29:17	3824
thoughts of the *h* of thy people	1Chr 29:18	3824
and prepare their *h* unto thee	1Chr 29:18	3824
unto Solomon my son a perfect *h*	1Chr 29:19	3824
Because this was in thine *h*	2Chr 1:11	3824
Now it was in the *h* of David my	2Chr 6:7	3824
Forasmuch as it was in thine *h* to	2Chr 6:8	3824
well in that it was in thine *h*	2Chr 6:8	3824
his ways, whose *h* thou knowest	2Chr 6:30	3824
return to thee with all their *h*	2Chr 6:38	3824
merry in *h* for the goodness that	2Chr 7:10	3820
h to make in the house of the	2Chr 7:11	3820
mine *h* shall be there perpetually	2Chr 7:16	3820
with him of all that was in her *h*	2Chr 9:1	3824
wisdom, that God had put in his *h*	2Chr 9:23	3820
not his *h* to seek the LORD	2Chr 12:14	3820
of their fathers with all their *h*	2Chr 15:12	3824
they had sworn with all their *h*	2Chr 15:15	3824
nevertheless the *h* of Asa was	2Chr 15:17	3824
whose *h* is perfect toward him	2Chr 16:9	3824
his *h* was lifted up in the ways	2Chr 17:6	3820
hast prepared thine *h* to seek God	2Chr 19:3	3824
faithfully, and with a perfect *h*	2Chr 19:9	3824
sought the LORD with all his *h*	2Chr 22:9	3824
LORD, but not with a perfect *h*	2Chr 25:2	3824
thine *h* lifteth thee up to boast	2Chr 25:19	3820
his *h* was lifted up to his	2Chr 26:16	3820
Now it is in mine *h* to make a	2Chr 29:10	3824
were of a free *h* burnt offerings	2Chr 29:31	3820
Levites were more upright in *h* to	2Chr 29:34	3824
of God was to give them one *h* to	2Chr 30:12	3820
That prepareth his *h* to seek God	2Chr 30:19	3824
his God, he did it with all his *h*	2Chr 31:21	3824
for his *h* was lifted up	2Chr 32:25	3820
himself for the pride of his *h*	2Chr 32:26	3820
might know all that was in his *h*	2Chr 32:31	3824
Because thine *h* was tender	2Chr 34:27	3824
and his statutes, with all his *h*	2Chr 34:31	3824
hardened his *h* from turning unto	2Chr 36:13	3820
turned the *h* of the king of	Ezr 6:22	3820
For Ezra had prepared his *h* to	Ezr 7:10	3824
a thing as this in the king's *h*	Ezr 7:27	3820
is nothing else but sorrow of *h*	Neh 2:2	3820
put in my *h* to do at Jerusalem	Neh 2:12	3820
feignest them out of thine own *h*	Neh 6:8	3820
my God put into mine *h* to gather	Neh 7:5	3820
foundest his *h* faithful before	Neh 9:8	3824
when the *h* of the king was merry	Est 1:10	3820
that day joyful and with a glad *h*	Est 5:9	3820
Now Haman thought in his *h*	Est 6:6	3820
durst presume in his *h* to do so	Est 7:5	3820
shouldest set thine *h* upon him	Job 7:17	3820
and utter words out of their *h*	Job 8:10	3820
He is wise in *h*, and mighty in	Job 9:4	3824
things hast thou hid in thine *h*	Job 10:13	3824
If thou prepare thine *h*, and	Job 11:13	3824
He taketh away the *h* of the chief	Job 12:24	3820
Why doth thine *h* carry thee away	Job 15:12	3820
hid their *h* from understanding	Job 17:4	3820
off, even the thoughts of my *h*	Job 17:11	3824
and lay up his words in thine *h*	Job 22:22	3824
For God maketh my *h* soft, and the	Job 23:16	3820
my *h* shall not reproach me so	Job 27:6	3824
the widow's *h* to sing for joy	Job 29:13	3820
mine *h* walked after mine eyes, and	Job 31:7	3820
If mine *h* have been deceived by a	Job 31:9	3820
my *h* hath been secretly enticed,	Job 31:27	3820
be of the uprightness of my *h*	Job 33:3	3820
If he set his *h* upon man, if he	Job 34:14	3820
the hypocrites in *h* heap up wrath	Job 36:13	3820
At this also my *h* trembleth	Job 37:1	3820
not any that are wise of *h*	Job 37:24	3820
hath given understanding to the *h*	Job 38:36	7907
His *h* is as firm as a stone	Job 41:24	3820
with your own *h* upon your bed	Ps 4:4	3824
Thou hast put gladness in my *h*	Ps 4:7	3820
which saveth the upright in *h*	Ps 7:10	3820
thee, O LORD, with my whole *h*	Ps 9:1	3820

He hath said in his *h*, I shall	Ps 10:6	3820
He hath said in his *h*, God hath	Ps 10:11	3820
he hath said in his *h*, Thou wilt	Ps 10:13	3820
thou wilt prepare their *h*	Ps 10:17	3820
privily shoot at the upright in *h*	Ps 11:2	3820
and with a double *h* do they speak	Ps 12:2	3820
soul, having sorrow in my *h* daily	Ps 13:2	3824
my *h* shall rejoice in thy	Ps 13:5	3820
The fool hath said in his	Ps 14:1	3820
and speaketh the truth in his *h*	Ps 15:2	3824
Therefore my *h* is glad, and my	Ps 16:9	3820
Thou hast proved mine *h*	Ps 17:3	3820
LORD are right, rejoicing the *h*	Ps 19:8	3820
mouth, and the meditation of my *h*	Ps 19:14	3820
thee according to thine own *h*	Ps 20:4	3824
my *h* is like wax	Ps 22:14	3820
your *h* shall live for ever	Ps 22:26	3824
hath clean hands, and a pure *h*	Ps 24:4	3824
The troubles of my *h* are enlarged	Ps 25:17	3824
try my reins and my *h*	Ps 26:2	3820
against me, my *h* shall not fear	Ps 27:3	3820
my *h* said unto thee, Thy face,	Ps 27:8	3820
and he shall strengthen thine *h*	Ps 27:14	3820
my *h* trusted in him, and I am	Ps 28:7	3820
therefore my *h* greatly rejoiceth	Ps 28:7	3820
and he shall strengthen your *h*	Ps 31:24	3824
joy, all ye that are upright in *h*	Ps 32:11	3820
of his *h* to all generations	Ps 33:11	3820
For our *h* shall rejoice in him,	Ps 33:21	3820
unto them that are of a broken *h*	Ps 34:18	3820
of the wicked saith within my *h*	Ps 36:1	3820
righteousness to the upright in *h*	Ps 36:10	3820
give thee the desires of thine *h*	Ps 37:4	3820
shall enter into their own *h*	Ps 37:15	3820
The law of his God is in his *h*	Ps 37:31	3820
of the disquietness of my *h*	Ps 38:8	3820
My *h* panteth, my strength faileth	Ps 38:10	3820
My *h* was hot within me	Ps 39:3	3820
yea, thy law is within my *h*	Ps 40:8	4578
hid thy righteousness within my *h*	Ps 40:10	3820
therefore my *h* faileth me	Ps 40:12	3820
his *h* gathereth iniquity to	Ps 41:6	3820
Our *h* is not turned back, neither	Ps 44:18	3820
he knoweth the secrets of the *h*	Ps 44:21	3820
My *h* is inditing a good matter	Ps 45:1	3820
in the *h* of the king's enemies	Ps 45:5	3820
the meditation of my *h* shall be	Ps 49:3	3820
Create in me a clean *h*, O God	Ps 51:10	3820
a broken and a contrite *h*, O God,	Ps 51:17	3820
The fool hath said in his *h*	Ps 53:1	3820
My *h* is sore pained within me	Ps 55:4	3820
than butter, but war was in his *h*	Ps 55:21	3820
My *h* is fixed, O God, my *h* is	Ps 57:7	3820
Yea, in *h* ye work wickedness	Ps 58:2	3820
thee, when my *h* is overwhelmed	Ps 61:2	3824
pour out your *h* before him	Ps 62:8	3824
set not your *h* upon them	Ps 62:10	3820
of every one of them, and the *h*	Ps 64:6	3820
all the upright in *h* shall glory	Ps 64:10	3820
If I regard iniquity in my *h*	Ps 66:18	3820
Reproach hath broken my *h*	Ps 69:20	3820
your *h* shall live that seek God	Ps 69:32	3824
even to such as are of a clean *h*	Ps 73:1	3824
they have more than *h* could wish	Ps 73:7	3824
I have cleansed my *h* in vain	Ps 73:13	3824
Thus my *h* was grieved, and I was	Ps 73:21	3824
My flesh and my *h* faileth	Ps 73:26	3824
but God is the strength of my *h*	Ps 73:26	3824
I commune with mine own *h*	Ps 77:6	3824
that set not their *h* aright	Ps 78:8	3820
they tempted God in their *h* by	Ps 78:18	3824
For their *h* was not right with	Ps 78:37	3820
to the integrity of his *h*	Ps 78:72	3824
my *h* and my flesh crieth out for	Ps 84:2	3820
in whose *h* are the ways of them	Ps 84:5	3824
unite my *h* to fear thy name	Ps 86:11	3824
O Lord my God, with all my *h*	Ps 86:12	3824
the upright in *h* shall follow it	Ps 94:15	3820
Harden not your *h*, as in the	Ps 95:8	3824
a people that do err in their *h*	Ps 95:10	3824
and gladness for the upright in *h*	Ps 97:11	3820
within my house with a perfect *h*	Ps 101:2	3824
A froward *h* shall depart from me	Ps 101:4	3820
a proud *h* will not I suffer	Ps 101:5	3824
My *h* is smitten, and withered like	Ps 102:4	3820
that maketh glad the *h* of man	Ps 104:15	3824
bread which strengtheneth man's *h*	Ps 104:15	3824
let the *h* of them rejoice that	Ps 105:3	3820
He turned their *h* to hate his	Ps 105:25	3820
brought down their *h* with labour	Ps 107:12	3820
O God, my *h* is fixed	Ps 108:1	3820

might even slay the broken in *h*	Ps 109:16	3824
my *h* is wounded within me	Ps 109:22	3820
praise the LORD with my whole *h*	Ps 111:1	3824
his *h* is fixed, trusting in the	Ps 112:7	3820
His *h* is established, he shall	Ps 112:8	3820
and that seek him with the whole *h*	Ps 119:2	3820
praise thee with uprightness of *h*	Ps 119:7	3824
With my whole *h* have I sought	Ps 119:10	3820
Thy word have I hid in mine *h*	Ps 119:11	3820
when thou shalt enlarge my *h*	Ps 119:32	3820
shall observe it with my whole *h*	Ps 119:34	3820
Incline my *h* unto thy testimonies	Ps 119:36	3820
thy favour with my whole *h*	Ps 119:58	3820
keep thy precepts with my whole *h*	Ps 119:69	3820
Their *h* is as fat as grease	Ps 119:70	3820
Let my *h* be sound in thy statutes	Ps 119:80	3820
they are the rejoicing of my *h*	Ps 119:111	3820
I have inclined mine *h* to perform	Ps 119:112	3820
I cried with my whole *h*	Ps 119:145	3820
but my *h* standeth in awe of thy	Ps 119:161	3820
my *h* is not haughty, nor mine	Ps 131:1	3820
will praise thee with my whole *h*	Ps 138:1	3820
Search me, O God, and know my *h*	Ps 139:23	3824
imagine mischiefs in their *h*	Ps 140:2	3820
Incline not my *h* to any evil	Ps 141:4	3820
my *h* within me is desolate	Ps 143:4	3820
He healeth the broken in *h*	Ps 147:3	3820
apply thine *h* to understanding	Prov 2:2	3820
When wisdom entereth into thine *h*	Prov 2:10	3820
but let thine *h* keep my	Prov 3:1	3820
them upon the table of thine *h*	Prov 3:3	3820
in the LORD with all thine *h*	Prov 3:5	3820
Let thine *h* retain my words	Prov 4:4	3820
keep them in the midst of thine *h*	Prov 4:21	3824
Keep thy *h* with all diligence	Prov 4:23	3820
and my *h* despised reproof	Prov 5:12	3820
Frowardness is in his *h*, he	Prov 6:14	3820
An *h* that deviseth wicked	Prov 6:18	3820
them continually upon thine *h*	Prov 6:21	3820
not after her beauty in thine *h*	Prov 6:25	3824
them upon the table of thine *h*	Prov 7:3	3820
of an harlot, and subtil of *h*	Prov 7:10	3820
Let not thine *h* decline to her	Prov 7:25	3820
be ye of an understanding *h*	Prov 8:5	3820
The wise in *h* will receive	Prov 10:8	3820
the *h* of the wicked is little	Prov 10:20	3820
They that are of a froward *h* are	Prov 11:20	3820
shall be servant to the wise of *h*	Prov 11:29	3820
of a perverse *h* shall be despised	Prov 12:8	3820
Deceit is in the *h* of them that	Prov 12:20	3820
but the *h* of fools proclaimeth	Prov 12:23	3820
Heaviness in the *h* of man maketh	Prov 12:25	3820
Hope deferred maketh the *h* sick	Prov 13:12	3820
The *h* knoweth his own bitterness	Prov 14:10	3820
in laughter the *h* is sorrowful	Prov 14:13	3820
The backslider in *h* shall be	Prov 14:14	3820
A sound *h* is the life of the	Prov 14:30	3820
Wisdom resteth in the *h* of him	Prov 14:33	3820
but the *h* of the foolish doeth	Prov 15:7	3820
A merry *h* maketh a cheerful	Prov 15:13	3820
of the *h* the spirit is broken	Prov 15:13	3820
The *h* of him that hath	Prov 15:14	3820
a merry *h* hath a continual feast	Prov 15:15	3820
The *h* of the righteous studieth	Prov 15:28	3820
light of the eyes rejoiceth the *h*	Prov 15:30	3820
The preparations of the *h* in man	Prov 16:1	3820
Every one that is proud in *h* is	Prov 16:5	3820
A man's *h* deviseth his way	Prov 16:9	3820
The wise in *h* shall be called	Prov 16:21	3820
The *h* of the wise teacheth his	Prov 16:23	3820
wisdom, seeing he hath no *h* to it	Prov 17:16	3820
hath a froward *h* findeth no good	Prov 17:20	3820
A merry *h* doeth good like a	Prov 17:22	3820
but that his *h* may discover	Prov 18:2	3820
the *h* of man is haughty	Prov 18:12	3820
The *h* of the prudent getteth	Prov 18:15	3820
his *h* fretteth against the LORD	Prov 19:3	3820
are many devices in a man's *h*	Prov 19:21	3820
Counsel in the *h* of man is like	Prov 20:5	3820
can say, I have made my *h* clean	Prov 20:9	3820
The king's *h* is in the hand of	Prov 21:1	3820
An high look, and a proud *h*	Prov 21:4	3820
He that loveth pureness of *h*	Prov 22:11	3820
is bound in the *h* of a child	Prov 22:15	3820
apply thine *h* unto my knowledge	Prov 22:17	3820
For as he thinketh in his *h*	Prov 23:7	5315
but his *h* is not with thee	Prov 23:7	3820
Apply thine *h* unto instruction,	Prov 23:12	3820
My son, if thine *h* be wise	Prov 23:15	3820
my *h* shall rejoice, even mine	Prov 23:15	3820
Let not thine *h* envy sinners	Prov 23:17	3820

wise, and guide thine *h* in the way	Prov 23:19	3820
My son, give me thine *h*, and let	Prov 23:26	3820
thine *h* shall utter perverse	Prov 23:33	3820
For their *h* studieth destruction,	Prov 24:2	3820
that pondereth the *h* consider it	Prov 24:12	3826
let not thine *h* be glad when he	Prov 24:17	3820
the *h* of kings is unsearchable	Prov 25:3	3820
that singeth songs to an heavy *h*	Prov 25:20	3820
a wicked *h* are like a potsherd	Prov 26:23	3820
are seven abominations in his *h*	Prov 26:25	3820
Ointment and perfume rejoice the *h*	Prov 27:9	3820
son, be wise, and make my *h* glad	Prov 27:11	3820
to face, so the *h* of man to man	Prov 27:19	3820
his *h* shall fall into mischief	Prov 28:14	3820
of a proud *h* stirreth up strife	Prov 28:25	5315
trusteth in his own *h* is a fool	Prov 28:26	3820
The *h* of her husband doth safely	Prov 31:11	3820
And I gave my *h* to seek and search	Eccl 1:13	3820
I communed with mine own *h*	Eccl 1:16	3820
my *h* had great experience of	Eccl 1:16	3820
I gave my *h* to know wisdom, and to	Eccl 1:17	3820
I said in mine *h*, Go to now, I	Eccl 2:1	3820
I sought in mine *h* to give myself	Eccl 2:3	3820
acquainting mine *h* with wisdom	Eccl 2:3	3820
I withheld not my *h* from any joy	Eccl 2:10	3820
for my *h* rejoiced in all my	Eccl 2:10	3820
Then said I in my *h*, As it	Eccl 2:15	3820
Then I said in my *h*, that this	Eccl 2:15	3820
I went about to cause my *h* to	Eccl 2:20	3820
and of the vexation of his *h*	Eccl 2:22	3820
his *h* taketh not rest in the	Eccl 2:23	3820
he hath set the world in their *h*	Eccl 3:11	3820
I said in mine *h*, God shall judge	Eccl 3:17	3820
I said in mine *h* concerning the	Eccl 3:18	3820
let not thine *h* be hasty to utter	Eccl 5:2	3820
answereth him in the joy of his *h*	Eccl 5:20	3820
the living will lay it to his *h*	Eccl 7:2	3820
countenance the *h* is made better	Eccl 7:3	3820
The *h* of the wise is in the house	Eccl 7:4	3820
but the *h* of fools is in the	Eccl 7:4	3820
and a gift destroyeth the *h*	Eccl 7:7	3820
own *h* knoweth that thyself	Eccl 7:22	3820
I applied mine *h* to know, and to	Eccl 7:25	3820
whose *h* is snares and nets, and her	Eccl 7:26	3820
a wise man's *h* discerneth both	Eccl 8:5	3820
applied my *h* unto every work that	Eccl 8:9	3820
therefore the *h* of the sons of	Eccl 8:11	3820
I applied mine *h* to know wisdom	Eccl 8:16	3820
in my *h* even to declare all this	Eccl 9:1	3820
also the *h* of the sons of men is	Eccl 9:3	3824
is in their *h* while they live	Eccl 9:3	3820
and drink thy wine with a merry *h*	Eccl 9:7	3820
A wise man's *h* is at his right	Eccl 10:2	3820
but a fool's *h* at his left	Eccl 10:2	3820
let thy *h* cheer thee in the days	Eccl 11:9	3820
and walk in the ways of thine *h*	Eccl 11:9	3820
remove sorrow from thy *h*, and put	Eccl 11:10	3820
the day of the gladness of his *h*	Song 3:11	3820
Thou hast ravished my *h*, my	Song 4:9	3823
thou hast ravished my *h* with one	Song 4:9	3823
I sleep, but my *h* waketh	Song 5:2	3820
Set me as a seal upon thine *h*	Song 8:6	3820
is sick, and the whole *h* faint	Is 1:5	3824
Make the *h* of this people fat, and	Is 6:10	3820
ears, and understand with their *h*	Is 6:10	3824
his *h* was moved, and the *h* of	Is 7:2	3824
in the pride and stoutness of *h*	Is 9:9	3824
so, neither doth his *h* think so	Is 10:7	3824
but it is in his *h* to destroy	Is 10:7	3824
stout *h* of the king of Assyria	Is 10:12	3824
and every man's *h* shall melt	Is 13:7	3824
For thou hast said in thine *h*	Is 14:13	3824
My *h* shall cry out for Moab	Is 15:5	3820
the *h* of Egypt shall melt in the	Is 19:1	3824
My *h* panted, fearfulness	Is 21:4	3824
have removed their *h* far from me	Is 29:13	3820
and gladness of *h*, as when one	Is 30:29	3824
The *h* also of the rash shall	Is 32:4	3824
his *h* will work iniquity, to	Is 32:6	3820
Thine *h* shall meditate terror	Is 33:18	3820
to them that are of a fearful *h*	Is 35:4	3820
thee in truth and with a perfect *h*	Is 38:3	3820
him, yet he laid it not to *h*	Is 42:25	3820
And none considereth in his *h*	Is 44:19	3820
a deceived *h* hath turned him	Is 44:20	3820
not lay these things to thy *h*	Is 47:7	3820
that sayest in thine *h*, I am, and	Is 47:8	3824
and thou hast said in thine *h*	Is 47:10	3820
Then shalt thou say in thine *h*	Is 49:21	3824
the people in whose *h* is my law	Is 51:7	3820
and no man layeth it to *h*	Is 57:1	3820
me, nor laid it to thy *h*	Is 57:11	3820
to revive the *h* of the contrite	Is 57:15	3820
on frowardly in the way of his *h*	Is 57:17	3820
uttering from the *h* words of	Is 59:13	3820
thine *h* shall fear, and be	Is 60:5	3824
the day of vengeance is in mine *h*	Is 63:4	3820
hardened our *h* from thy fear	Is 63:17	3820
servants shall sing for joy of *h*	Is 65:14	3820
but ye shall cry for sorrow of *h*	Is 65:14	3820
your *h* shall rejoice, and your	Is 66:14	3820
turned unto me with her whole *h*	Jer 3:10	3820
you pastors according to mine *h*	Jer 3:15	3820
the imagination of their evil *h*	Jer 3:17	3820
take away the foreskins of your *h*	Jer 4:4	3824
that the *h* of the king shall	Jer 4:9	3820
perish, and the *h* of the princes	Jer 4:9	3820
wash thine *h* from wickedness,	Jer 4:14	3820
because it reacheth unto thine *h*	Jer 4:18	3820
I am pained at my very *h*	Jer 4:19	3820
my *h* maketh a noise in me	Jer 4:19	3820
a revolting and a rebellious *h*	Jer 5:23	3820
Neither say they in their *h*	Jer 5:24	3824
the imagination of their evil *h*	Jer 7:24	3820
not, neither came it into my *h*	Jer 7:31	3820
sorrow, and my *h* is faint in me	Jer 8:18	3820
but in *h* he layeth his wait	Jer 9:8	7130
the imagination of their own *h*	Jer 9:14	3820
Israel are uncircumcised in the *h*	Jer 9:26	3820
the imagination of their evil *h*	Jer 11:8	3820
that triest the reins and the *h*	Jer 11:20	3820
me, and tried mine *h* toward thee	Jer 12:3	3820
because no man layeth it to *h*	Jer 12:11	3820
in the imagination of their *h*	Jer 13:10	3820
And if thou say in thine *h*	Jer 13:22	3824
nought, and the deceit of their *h*	Jer 14:14	3820
me the joy and rejoicing of mine *h*	Jer 15:16	3824
the imagination of his evil *h*	Jer 16:12	3820
graven upon the table of their *h*	Jer 17:1	3820
whose *h* departeth from the LORD	Jer 17:5	3820
The *h* is deceitful above all	Jer 17:9	3820
I the LORD search the *h*, I try	Jer 17:10	3820
do the imagination of his own *h*	Jer 18:12	3820
But his word was in mine *h* as a	Jer 20:9	3820
and seest the reins and the *h*	Jer 20:12	3820
thine *h* are not but for thy	Jer 22:17	3820
Mine *h* within me is broken	Jer 23:9	3820
speak a vision of their own *h*	Jer 23:16	3820
the imagination of his own *h*	Jer 23:17	3820
performed the thoughts of his *h*	Jer 23:20	3820
h of the prophets that prophesy	Jer 23:26	3820
of the deceit of their own *h*	Jer 23:26	3820
I will give them an *h* to know me	Jer 24:7	3820
return unto me with their whole *h*	Jer 24:7	3820
search for me with all your *h*	Jer 29:13	3824
engaged his *h* to approach unto me	Jer 30:21	3820
performed the intents of his *h*	Jer 30:24	3820
set thine *h* toward the highway,	Jer 31:21	3820
And I will give them one *h*	Jer 32:39	3820
land assuredly with my whole *h*	Jer 32:41	3820
and the haughtiness of his *h*	Jer 48:29	3820
mine *h* shall mourn for the men of	Jer 48:31	3820
Therefore mine *h* shall sound for	Jer 48:36	3820
mine *h* shall sound like pipes for	Jer 48:36	3820
as the *h* of a woman in her pangs	Jer 48:41	3820
thee, and the pride of thine *h*	Jer 49:16	3820
at that day shall the *h* of the	Jer 49:22	3820
as the *h* of a woman in her pangs	Jer 49:22	3820
And lest your *h* faint, and ye fear	Jer 51:46	3824
mine *h* is turned within me	Lam 1:20	3820
sighs are many, and my *h* is faint	Lam 1:22	3820
Their *h* cried unto the Lord, O	Lam 2:18	3820
h like water before the face of	Lam 2:19	3820
Let us lift up our *h* with our	Lam 3:41	3824
Mine eye affecteth mine *h* because	Lam 3:51	5315
Give them sorrow of *h*, thy curse	Lam 3:65	3820
The joy of our *h* is ceased	Lam 5:15	3820
For this our *h* is faint	Lam 5:17	3820
unto thee receive in thine *h*	Eze 3:10	3824
I am broken with their whorish *h*	Eze 6:9	3820
And I will give them one *h*	Eze 11:19	3820
the stony *h* out of their flesh	Eze 11:19	3820
and will give them an *h* of flesh	Eze 11:19	3820
But as for them whose *h* walketh	Eze 11:21	3820
the *h* of their detestable things	Eze 11:21	3820
which prophesy out of their own *h*	Eze 13:17	3820
made the *h* of the righteous sad	Eze 13:22	3820
set up their idols in their *h*	Eze 14:3	3820
setteth up his idols in his *h*	Eze 14:4	3820
house of Israel in their own *h*	Eze 14:5	3820
and setteth up his idols in his *h*	Eze 14:7	3820
How weak is thine *h*, saith the	Eze 16:30	3826

H

and make you a new *h* and a new	Eze 18:31	3820
for their *h* went after their	Eze 20:16	3820
every *h* shall melt, and all hands	Eze 21:7	3820
gates, that their *h* may faint	Eze 21:15	3820
Can thine *h* endure, or can thine	Eze 22:14	3820
rejoiced in *h* with all thy	Eze 25:6	5315
vengeance with a despiteful *h*	Eze 25:15	5315
for thee with bitterness of *h*	Eze 27:31	5315
Because thine *h* is lifted up	Eze 28:2	3820
set thine *h* as the *h* of God	Eze 28:2	3820
thine *h* is lifted up because of	Eze 28:5	3824
set thine *h* as the *h* of God	Eze 28:6	3820
Thine *h* was lifted up because of	Eze 28:17	3820
his *h* is lifted up in his height	Eze 31:10	3824
but their *h* goeth after their	Eze 33:31	3820
with the joy of all their *h*	Eze 36:5	3824
A new *h* also will I give you, and	Eze 36:26	3820
the stony *h* out of your flesh	Eze 36:26	3820
and I will give you an *h* of flesh	Eze 36:26	3820
set thine *h* upon all that I shall	Eze 40:4	3820
strangers, uncircumcised in *h*	Eze 44:7	3820
No stranger, uncircumcised in *h*	Eze 44:9	3820
in his *h* that he would not defile	Dan 1:8	3820
know the thoughts of thy *h*	Dan 2:30	3825
Let his *h* be changed from man's,	Dan 4:16	3825
let a beast's *h* be given unto him	Dan 4:16	3825
But when his *h* was lifted up, and	Dan 5:20	3825
his *h* was made like the beasts,	Dan 5:21	3825
hast not humbled thine *h*	Dan 5:22	3825
set his *h* on Daniel to deliver	Dan 6:14	1079
a man's *h* was given to it	Dan 7:4	3825
but I kept the matter in my *h*	Dan 7:28	3821
he shall magnify himself in his *h*	Dan 8:25	3824
didst set thine *h* to understand	Dan 10:12	3820
his *h* shall be lifted up	Dan 11:12	3824
his *h* shall be against the holy	Dan 11:28	3824
they set their *h* on their	Hos 4:8	5315
wine and new wine take away the *h*	Hos 4:11	3820
made ready their *h* like an oven	Hos 7:6	3820
is like a silly dove without *h*	Hos 7:11	3820
not cried unto me with their *h*	Hos 7:14	3820
Their *h* is divided	Hos 10:2	3820
mine *h* is turned within me, my	Hos 11:8	3820
filled, and their *h* was exalted	Hos 13:6	3820
and will rend the caul of their *h*	Hos 13:8	3824
ye even to me with all your *h*	Joel 2:12	3824
And rend your *h*, and not your	Joel 2:13	3820
of thine *h* hath deceived thee	Obad 3	3820
that saith in his *h*, Who shall	Obad 3	3820
the *h* melteth, and the knees smite	Nah 2:10	3820
that say in their *h*, The LORD	Zeph 1:12	3824
carelessly, that said in her *h*	Zeph 2:15	3824
be glad and rejoice with all the *h*	Zeph 3:14	3820
against his brother in your *h*	Zec 7:10	3824
their *h* shall rejoice as through	Zec 10:7	3820
their *h* shall rejoice in the LORD	Zec 10:7	3820
of Judah shall say in their *h*	Zec 12:5	3820
and if ye will not lay it to *h*	Mal 2:2	3820
because ye do not lay it to *h*	Mal 2:2	3820
he shall turn the *h* of the	Mal 4:6	3820
the *h* of the children to their	Mal 4:6	3820
Blessed are the pure in *h*	Mt 5:8	2588
with her already in his *h*	Mt 5:28	2588
is, there will your *h* be also	Mt 6:21	2588
for I am meek and lowly in *h*	Mt 11:29	2588
of the *h* the mouth speaketh	Mt 12:34	2588
the *h* bringeth forth good things	Mt 12:35	2588
nights in the *h* of the earth	Mt 12:40	2588
this people's *h* is waxed gross	Mt 13:15	2588
and should understand with their *h*	Mt 13:15	2588
away that which was sown in his *h*	Mt 13:19	2588
but their *h* is far from me	Mt 15:8	2588
the mouth come forth from the *h*	Mt 15:18	2588
For out of the *h* proceed evil	Mt 15:19	2588
the Lord thy God with all thy *h*	Mt 22:37	2588
evil servant shall say in his *h*	Mt 24:48	2588
for their *h* was hardened	Mk 6:52	2588
but their *h* is far from me	Mk 7:6	2588
it entereth not into his *h*	Mk 7:19	2588
from within, out of the *h* of men	Mk 7:21	2588
have ye your *h* yet hardened	Mk 8:17	2588
For the hardness of your *h* he	Mk 10:5	4641
and shall not doubt in his *h*	Mk 11:23	2588
the Lord thy God with all thy *h*	Mk 12:30	2588
And to love him with all the *h*	Mk 12:33	2588
their unbelief and hardness of *h*	Mk 16:14	4641
things, and pondered them in her *h*	Lk 2:19	2588
kept all these sayings in her *h*	Lk 2:51	2588
***h* bringeth forth that which is**	Lk 6:45	2588
***h* bringeth forth that which is**	Lk 6:45	2588
of the *h* his mouth speaketh	Lk 6:45	2588

which in an honest and good *h*	Lk 8:15	2588
perceiving the thought of their *h*	Lk 9:47	2588
the Lord thy God with all thy *h*	Lk 10:27	2588
is, there will your *h* be also	Lk 12:34	2588
and if that servant say in his *h*	Lk 12:45	2588
slow of *h* to believe all that the	Lk 24:25	2588
Did not our *h* burn within us,	Lk 24:32	2588
their eyes, and hardened their *h*	Jn 12:40	2588
eyes, nor understand with their *h*	Jn 12:40	2588
put into the heart of Judas Iscariot	Jn 13:2	2588
Let not your *h* be troubled	Jn 14:1	2588
Let not your *h* be troubled	Jn 14:27	2588
you, sorrow hath filled your *h*	Jn 16:6	2588
your *h* shall rejoice, and your joy	Jn 16:22	2588
Therefore did my *h* rejoice	Acts 2:26	2588
they were pricked in their *h*	Acts 2:37	2588
with gladness and singleness of *h*	Acts 2:46	2588
them that believed were of one *h*	Acts 4:32	2588
thine *h* to lie to the Holy Ghost	Acts 5:3	2588
conceived this thing in thine *h*	Acts 5:4	2588
that, they were cut to the *h*	Acts 5:33	
it came into his *h* to visit his	Acts 7:23	2588
stiffnecked and uncircumcised in *h*	Acts 7:51	2588
things, they were cut to the *h*	Acts 7:54	2588
for thy *h* is not right in the	Acts 8:21	2588
of thine *h* may be forgiven thee	Acts 8:22	2588
thou believest with all thine *h*	Acts 8:37	2588
that with purpose of *h* they would	Acts 11:23	2588
of Jesse, a man after mine own *h*	Acts 13:22	2588
whose *h* the Lord opened, that she	Acts 16:14	2588
ye to weep and to break mine *h*	Acts 21:13	2588
For the *h* of this people is waxed	Acts 28:27	2588
ears, and understand with their *h*	Acts 28:27	2588
and their foolish *h* was darkened	Rom 1:21	2588
impenitent *h* treasurest up unto	Rom 2:5	2588
and circumcision is that of the *h*	Rom 2:29	2588
but ye have obeyed from the *h*	Rom 6:17	2588
and continual sorrow in my *h*	Rom 9:2	2588
on this wise, Say not in thine *h*	Rom 10:6	2588
even in thy mouth, and in thy *h*	Rom 10:8	2588
shalt believe in thine *h* that God	Rom 10:9	2588
For with the *h* man believeth unto	Rom 10:10	2588
have entered into the *h* of man	1Cor 2:9	2588
that standeth stedfast in his *h*	1Cor 7:37	2588
hath so decreed in his *h* that he	1Cor 7:37	2588
secrets of his *h* made manifest	1Cor 14:25	2588
anguish of *h* I wrote unto you	2Cor 2:4	2588
but in fleshly tables of the *h*	2Cor 3:3	2588
is read, the vail is upon their *h*	2Cor 3:15	2588
glory in appearance, and not in *h*	2Cor 5:12	2588
open unto you, our *h* is enlarged	2Cor 6:11	2588
care into the *h* of Titus for you	2Cor 8:16	2588
as he purposeth in his *h*, so let	2Cor 9:7	2588
of the blindness of their *h*	Eph 4:18	2588
melody in your *h* to the Lord	Eph 5:19	2588
in singleness of your *h*, as unto	Eph 6:5	2588
doing the will of God from the *h*	Eph 6:6	5590
all, because I have you in my *h*	Phil 1:7	2588
but in singleness of *h*, fearing	Col 3:22	2588
short time in presence, not in *h*	1Th 2:17	2588
is charity out of a pure *h*	1Ti 1:5	2588
call on the Lord out of a pure *h*	2Ti 2:22	2588
They do alway err in their *h*	Heb 3:10	2588
any of you an evil *h* of unbelief	Heb 3:12	2588
the thoughts and intents of the *h*	Heb 4:12	2588
true *h* in full assurance of faith	Heb 10:22	2588
the *h* be established with grace	Heb 13:9	2588
tongue, but deceiveth his own *h*	Jas 1:26	2588
another with a pure *h* fervently	1Pet 1:22	2588
let it be the hidden man of the *h*	1Pet 3:4	2588
an *h* they have exercised with	2Pet 2:14	2588
For if our *h* condemn	1Jn 3:20	2588
God is greater than our *h*	1Jn 3:20	2588
if our *h* condemn us not, then	1Jn 3:21	2588
for she saith in her *h*, I sit a	Rev 18:7	2588

HEARTED

speak unto all that are wise *h*	Ex 28:3	3820
that are wise *h* I have put wisdom	Ex 31:6	3820
every wise *h* among you shall come	Ex 35:10	3820
women, as many as were willing *h*	Ex 35:22	3820
wise *h* did spin with their hands	Ex 35:25	3820
and Aholiab, and every wise *h* man	Ex 36:1	3820
and Aholiab, and every wise *h* man	Ex 36:2	3820
every wise *h* man among them that	Ex 36:8	3820

HEARTH

it, and make cakes upon the *h*	Gen 18:6	
and my bones are burned as an *h*	Ps 102:3	4168
a sherd to take fire from the *h*	Is 30:14	3344
fire on the *h* burning before him	Jer 36:22	254
into the fire that was on the *h*	Jer 36:23	254

in the fire that was on the *h*	Jer 36:23	254
like an *h* of fire among the wood	Zec 12:6	3595

HEARTILY

And whatsoever ye do, do it *h*	Col 3:23	*1537,5590*

HEART'S

wicked boasteth of his *h* desire	Ps 10:3	5315
Thou hast given him his *h* desire	Ps 21:2	3820
my *h* desire and prayer to God for	Rom 10:1	2588

HEARTS

of bread, and comfort ye your *h*	Gen 18:5	3820
harden the *h* of the Egyptians	Ex 14:17	3820
in the *h* of all that are wise	Ex 31:6	3820
send a faintness into their *h* in	Lev 26:36	3824
their uncircumcised *h* be humbled	Lev 26:41	3824
let not your *h* faint, fear not	Deut 20:3	3824
Set your *h* unto all the words	Deut 32:46	3824
our *h* did melt, neither did there	Josh 2:11	3824
wherefore the *h* of the people	Josh 7:5	3824
was of the LORD to harden their *h*	Josh 11:20	3820
and ye know in all your *h* and in	Josh 23:14	3824
their *h* inclined to follow	Judg 9:3	3820
to pass, when their *h* were merry	Judg 16:25	3820
as they were making their *h* merry	Judg 19:22	3820
then do ye harden your *h*, as the	1Sa 6:6	3824
and Pharaoh hardened their *h*	1Sa 6:6	3820
unto the LORD with all your *h*	1Sa 7:3	3824
prepare your *h* unto the LORD, and	1Sa 7:3	3824
of men, whose *h* God had touched	1Sa 10:26	3820
stole the *h* of the men of Israel	2Sa 15:6	3820
The *h* of the men of Israel are	2Sa 15:13	3820
knowest the *h* of all the children	1Kin 8:39	3824
he may incline our *h* unto him	1Kin 8:58	3824
for the LORD searcheth all *h*	1Chr 28:9	3824
walk before thee with all their *h*	2Chr 6:14	3820
the *h* of the children of men	2Chr 6:30	3824
of Israel such as set their *h* to	2Chr 11:16	3824
h unto the God of their fathers	2Chr 20:33	3824
sinned, and cursed God in their *h*	Job 1:5	3824
the righteous God trieth the *h*	Ps 7:9	3826
but mischief is in their *h*	Ps 28:3	3824
He fashioneth their *h* alike	Ps 33:15	3820
Let them not say in their *h*	Ps 35:25	3820
They said in their *h*, Let us	Ps 74:8	3820
we may apply our *h* unto wisdom	Ps 90:12	3824
them that are upright in their *h*	Ps 125:4	3826
then the *h* of the children of men	Prov 15:11	3826
but the LORD trieth the *h*	Prov 17:3	3826
but the LORD pondereth the *h*	Prov 21:2	3826
unto those that be of heavy *h*	Prov 31:6	5315
and their *h*, that they cannot	Is 44:18	3826
parts, and write it in their *h*	Jer 31:33	3820
but I will put my fear in their *h*	Jer 32:40	3824
For ye dissembled in your *h*	Jer 42:20	5315
the mighty men's *h* in Moab at	Jer 48:41	3820
that prophesy out of their own *h*	Eze 13:2	3820
also vex the *h* of many people	Eze 32:9	3820
both these kings' *h* shall be to	Dan 11:27	3824
their *h* that I remember all their	Hos 7:2	3824
they made their *h* as an adamant	Zec 7:12	3820
in your *h* against his neighbour	Zec 8:17	3820
Wherefore think ye evil in your *h*	Mt 9:4	2588
if ye from your *h* forgive not	Mt 18:35	2588
***h* suffered you to put away your**	Mt 19:8	4641
there, and reasoning in their *h*	Mk 2:6	2588
reason ye these things in your *h*	Mk 2:8	2588
for the hardness of their *h*	Mk 3:5	2588
the word that was sown in their *h*	Mk 4:15	2588
to turn the *h* of the fathers to	Lk 1:17	2588
in the imagination of their *h*	Lk 1:51	2588
them laid them up in their *h*	Lk 1:66	2588
of many *h* may be revealed	Lk 2:35	2588
all men mused in their *h* of John	Lk 3:15	2588
them, What reason ye in your *h*	Lk 5:22	2588
away the word out of their *h*	Lk 8:12	2588
but God knoweth your *h*	Lk 16:15	2588
Settle it therefore in your *h*	Lk 21:14	2588
Men's *h* failing them for fear, and	Lk 21:26	674
lest at any time your *h* be	Lk 21:34	2588
why do thoughts arise in your *h*	Lk 24:38	2588
which knowest the *h* of all men	Acts 1:24	2589
in their *h* turned back again into	Acts 7:39	2588
seasons, filling our *h* with food	Acts 14:17	2588
And God, which knoweth the *h*	Acts 15:8	2588
them, purifying their *h* by faith	Acts 15:9	2588
through the lusts of their own *h*	Rom 1:24	2588
of the law written in their *h*	Rom 2:15	2588
our *h* by the Holy Ghost which is	Rom 5:5	2588
he that searcheth the *h* knoweth	Rom 8:27	2588
deceive the *h* of the simple	Rom 16:18	2588

manifest the counsels of the *h*	1Cor 4:5	2588
earnest of the Spirit in our *h*	2Cor 1:22	2588
are our epistle written in our *h*	2Cor 3:2	2588
of darkness, hath shined in our *h*	2Cor 4:6	2588
that ye are in our *h* to die	2Cor 7:3	2588
the Spirit of his Son into your *h*	Gal 4:6	2588
may dwell in your *h* by faith	Eph 3:17	2588
and that he might comfort your *h*	Eph 6:22	2588
understanding, shall keep your *h*	Phil 4:7	2588
That their *h* might be comforted,	Col 2:2	2588
the peace of God rule in your *h*	Col 3:15	2588
with grace in your *h* to the Lord	Col 3:16	2588
your estate, and comfort your *h*	Col 4:8	2588
men, but God, which trieth our *h*	1Th 2:4	2588
h unblameable in holiness before	1Th 3:13	2588
Comfort your *h*, and stablish you	2Th 2:17	2588
your *h* into the love of God	2Th 3:5	2588
Harden not your *h*, as in the	Heb 3:8	2588
hear his voice, harden not your *h*	Heb 3:15	2588
hear his voice, harden not your *h*	Heb 4:7	2588
mind, and write them in their *h*	Heb 8:10	2588
I will put my laws into their *h*	Heb 10:16	2588
having our *h* sprinkled from an	Heb 10:22	2588
envying and strife in your *h*	Jas 3:14	2588
and purify your *h*, ye double	Jas 4:8	2588
ye have nourished your *h*, as in a	Jas 5:5	2588
ye also patient; stablish your *h*	Jas 5:8	2588
sanctify the Lord God in your *h*	1Pet 3:15	2588
and the day star arise in your *h*	2Pet 1:19	2588
and shall assure our *h* before him	1Jn 3:19	2588
he which searcheth the reins and *h*	Rev 2:23	2588
put in their *h* to fulfil his will	Rev 17:17	2588

HEARTS'

them up unto their own *h* lust	Ps 81:12	3820

HEARTY

of a man's friend by *h* counsel	Prov 27:9	5315

HEAT

seedtime and harvest, and cold and *h*	Gen 8:22	2527
the tent door in the *h* of the day	Gen 18:1	2527
what meaneth the *h* of this great	Deut 29:24	2750
and devoured with burning *h*	Deut 32:24	7565
Ammonites until the *h* of the day	1Sa 11:11	2527
came about the *h* of the day to	2Sa 4:5	2527
him with clothes, but he gat no *h*	1Kin 1:1	3179
that my lord the king may get *h*	1Kin 1:2	2552
h consume the snow waters	Job 24:19	2527
me, and my bones are burned with *h*	Job 30:30	2721
is nothing hid from the *h* thereof	Ps 19:6	2535
lie together, then they have *h*	Eccl 4:11	2552
shadow in the daytime from the *h*	Is 4:6	2721
place like a clear *h* upon herbs	Is 18:4	2527
cloud of dew in the *h* of harvest	Is 18:4	2527
the storm, a shadow from the *h*	Is 25:4	2721
as the *h* in a dry place	Is 25:5	2721
even the *h* with the shadow of a	Is 25:5	2721
neither shall the *h* nor sun smite	Is 49:10	8273
and shall not see when *h* cometh	Jer 17:8	2527
be cast out in the day to the *h*	Jer 36:30	2721
In their *h* I will make their	Jer 51:39	2527
bitterness, in the *h* of my spirit	Eze 3:14	2534
commanded that they should *h* the	Dan 3:19	228
borne the burden and *h* of the day	Mt 20:12	2742
blow, ye say, There will be *h*	Lk 12:55	2742
there came a viper out of the *h*	Acts 28:3	2329
no sooner risen with a burning *h*	Jas 1:11	2742
shall melt with fervent *h*	2Pet 3:10	2741
shall melt with fervent *h*	2Pet 3:12	2741
the sun light on them, nor any *h*	Rev 7:16	2738
And men were scorched with great *h*	Rev 16:9	2738

HEATED

more than it was wont to be *h*	Dan 3:19	228
as an oven *h* by the baker, who	Hos 7:4	1197

HEATH

shall be like the *h* in the desert	Jer 17:6	6176
be like the *h* in the wilderness	Jer 48:6	6176

HEATHEN

shall be of the *h* that are round	Lev 25:44	1471
And I will scatter you among the *h*	Lev 26:33	1471
And ye shall perish among the *h*	Lev 26:38	1471
of Egypt in the sight of the *h*	Lev 26:45	1471
be left few in number among the *h*	Deut 4:27	1471
hast kept me to be head of the *h*	2Sa 22:44	1471
unto thee, O LORD, among the *h*	2Sa 22:50	1471
to the abominations of the *h*	2Kin 16:3	1471
walked in the statutes of the *h*	2Kin 17:8	1471
as did the *h* whom the LORD	2Kin 17:11	1471
went after the *h* that were round	2Kin 17:15	1471
after the abominations of the *h*	2Kin 21:2	1471

Declare his glory among the *h*	1Chr 16:24	1471
and deliver us from the *h*	1Chr 16:35	1471
over all the kingdoms of the *h*	2Chr 20:6	1471
the *h* whom the LORD had cast out	2Chr 28:3	1471
unto the abominations of the *h*	2Chr 33:2	1471
to err, and to do worse than the *h*	2Chr 33:9	1471
all the abominations of the *h*	2Chr 36:14	1471
filthiness of the *h* of the land	Ezr 6:21	1471
Jews, which were sold unto the *h*	Neh 5:8	1471
the reproach of the *h* our enemies	Neh 5:9	1471
among the *h* that are about us	Neh 5:17	1471
It is reported among the *h*	Neh 6:6	1471
all the *h* that were about us saw	Neh 6:16	1471
Why do the *h* rage, and the people	Ps 2:1	1471
thee the *h* for thine inheritance	Ps 2:8	1471
Thou hast rebuked the *h*, thou	Ps 9:5	1471
The *h* are sunk down in the pit	Ps 9:15	1471
let the *h* be judged in thy sight	Ps 9:19	1471
the *h* are perished out of his	Ps 10:16	1471
hast made me the head of the *h*	Ps 18:43	1471
unto thee, O LORD, among the *h*	Ps 18:49	1471
the counsel of the *h* to nought	Ps 33:10	1471
drive out the *h* with thy hand	Ps 44:2	1471
and hast scattered us among the *h*	Ps 44:11	1471
makest us a byword among the *h*	Ps 44:14	1471
The *h* raged, the kingdoms were	Ps 46:6	1471
I will be exalted among the *h*	Ps 46:10	1471
God reigneth over the *h*	Ps 47:8	1471
Israel, awake to visit all the *h*	Ps 59:5	1471
shalt have all the *h* in derision	Ps 59:8	1471
He cast out the *h* also before	Ps 78:55	1471
the *h* are come into thine	Ps 79:1	1471
the *h* that have not known thee	Ps 79:6	1471
Wherefore should the *h* say	Ps 79:10	1471
let him be known among the *h* in	Ps 79:10	1471
thou hast cast out the *h*, and	Ps 80:8	1471
He that chastiseth the *h*, shall	Ps 94:10	1471
Declare his glory among the *h*	Ps 96:3	1471
Say among the *h* that the LORD	Ps 96:10	1471
shewed in the sight of the *h*	Ps 98:2	1471
So the *h* shall fear the name of	Ps 102:15	1471
And gave them the lands of the *h*	Ps 105:44	1471
But were mingled among the *h*	Ps 106:35	1471
gave them into the hand of the *h*	Ps 106:41	1471
and gather us from among the *h*	Ps 106:47	1471
He shall judge among the *h*	Ps 110:6	1471
give them the heritage of the *h*	Ps 111:6	1471
Wherefore should the *h* say	Ps 115:2	1471
then said they among the *h*	Ps 126:2	1471
The idols of the *h* are silver	Ps 135:15	1471
To execute vengeance upon the *h*	Ps 149:7	1471
the lords of the *h* have broken	Is 16:8	1471
scatter them also among the *h*	Jer 9:16	1471
LORD, Learn not the way of the *h*	Jer 10:2	1471
for the *h* are dismayed at them	Jer 10:2	1471
upon the *h* that know thee not	Jer 10:25	1471
Ask ye now among the *h*, who hath	Jer 18:13	1471
an ambassador is sent unto the *h*	Jer 49:14	1471
will make thee small among the *h*	Jer 49:15	1471
she dwelleth among the *h*, she	Lam 1:3	1471
the *h* entered into her sanctuary	Lam 1:10	1471
wandered, they said among the *h*	Lam 4:15	1471
shadow we shall live among the *h*	Lam 4:20	1471
I will bring the worst of the *h*	Eze 7:24	1471
of the *h* that are round about you	Eze 11:12	1471
cast them far off among the *h*	Eze 11:16	1471
among the *h* whither they come	Eze 12:16	1471
forth among the *h* for thy beauty	Eze 16:14	1471
not be polluted before the *h*	Eze 20:9	1471
not be polluted before the *h*	Eze 20:14	1471
be polluted in the sight of the *h*	Eze 20:22	1471
I would scatter them among the *h*	Eze 20:23	1471
that ye say, We will be as the *h*	Eze 20:32	1471
be sanctified in you before the *h*	Eze 20:41	1471
I made thee a reproach unto the *h*	Eze 22:4	1471
I will scatter thee among the *h*	Eze 22:15	1471
in thyself in the sight of the *h*	Eze 22:16	1471
hast gone a whoring after the *h*	Eze 23:30	1471
deliver thee for a spoil to the *h*	Eze 25:7	1471
of Judah is like unto all the *h*	Eze 25:8	1471
in them in the sight of the *h*	Eze 28:25	1471
it shall be the time of the *h*	Eze 30:3	1471
hand of the mighty one of the *h*	Eze 31:11	1471
his shadow in the midst of the *h*	Eze 31:17	1471
shall no more be a prey to the *h*	Eze 34:28	1471
bear the shame of the *h* any more	Eze 34:29	1471
unto the residue of the *h*	Eze 36:3	1471
of the *h* that are round about	Eze 36:4	1471
against the residue of the *h*	Eze 36:5	1471
ye have borne the shame of the *h*	Eze 36:6	1471
Surely the *h* that are about you,	Eze 36:7	1471

thee the shame of the *h* any more	Eze 36:15	1471
And I scattered them among the *h*	Eze 36:19	1471
And when they entered unto the *h*	Eze 36:20	1471
Israel had profaned among the *h*	Eze 36:21	1471
ye have profaned among the *h*	Eze 36:22	1471
which was profaned among the *h*	Eze 36:23	1471
the *h* shall know that I am the	Eze 36:23	1471
I will take you from among the *h*	Eze 36:24	1471
reproach of famine among the *h*	Eze 36:30	1471
Then the *h* that are left round	Eze 36:36	1471
of Israel from among the *h*	Eze 37:21	1471
the *h* shall know that I the LORD	Eze 37:28	1471
that the *h* may know me, when I	Eze 38:16	1471
the *h* shall know that I am the	Eze 39:7	1471
I will set my glory among the *h*	Eze 39:21	1471
all the *h* shall see my judgment	Eze 39:21	1471
the *h* shall know that the house	Eze 39:23	1471
be led into captivity among the *h*	Eze 39:28	1471
that the *h* should rule over them	Joel 2:17	1471
make you a reproach among the *h*	Joel 2:19	1471
yourselves, and come, all ye *h*	Joel 3:11	1471
Let the *h* be wakened, and come up	Joel 3:12	1471
to judge all the *h* round about	Joel 3:12	1471
remnant of Edom, and of all the *h*	Amos 9:12	1471
an ambassador is sent among the *h*	Obad 1	1471
have made thee small among the *h*	Obad 2	1471
the LORD is near upon all the *h*	Obad 15	1471
so shall all the *h* drink	Obad 16	1471
in anger and fury upon the *h*	Mic 5:15	1471
Behold ye among the *h*, and regard,	Hab 1:5	1471
thou didst thresh the *h* in anger	Hab 3:12	1471
even all the isles of the *h*	Zeph 2:11	1471
strength of the kingdoms of the *h*	Hag 2:22	1471
with the *h* that are at ease	Zec 1:15	1471
as ye were a curse among the *h*	Zec 8:13	1471
he shall speak peace unto the *h*	Zec 9:10	1471
the wealth of all the *h* round	Zec 14:14	1471
the LORD will smite the *h* that	Zec 14:18	1471
name shall be great among the *h*	Mal 1:11	1471
my name is dreadful among the *h*	Mal 1:14	1471
not vain repetitions, as the *h* do	Mt 6:7	*1482*
let him be unto thee as an *h* man	Mt 18:17	*1482*
hast said, Why did the *h* rage	Acts 4:25	*1484*
countrymen, in perils by the *h*	2Cor 11:26	*1484*
I might preach him among the *h*	Gal 1:16	*1484*
that we should go unto the *h*	Gal 2:9	*1484*
would justify the *h* through faith	Gal 3:8	*1484*

HEAVE

and the shoulder of the *h* offering	Ex 29:27	8641
for it is an *h* offering	Ex 29:28	8641
it shall be an *h* offering from	Ex 29:28	8641
even their *h* offering unto the	Ex 29:28	8641
for an *h* offering unto the LORD	Lev 7:14	8641
h offering of the sacrifices of	Lev 7:32	8641
the *h* shoulder have I taken of	Lev 7:34	8641
h shoulder shall ye eat in a	Lev 10:14	8641
The *h* shoulder and the wave breast	Lev 10:15	8641
the wave breast and *h* shoulder	Num 6:20	8641
ye shall offer up an *h* offering	Num 15:19	8641
of your dough for an *h* offering	Num 15:20	8641
as ye do the *h* offering of the	Num 15:20	8641
threshingfloor, so shall ye *h* it	Num 15:20	7311
an *h* offering in your generations	Num 15:21	8641
h offerings of all the hallowed	Num 18:8	8641
the *h* offering of their gift,	Num 18:11	8641
All the *h* offerings of the holy	Num 18:19	8641
as an *h* offering unto the LORD	Num 18:24	8641
then ye shall offer up an *h*	Num 18:26	8641
this your *h* offering shall be	Num 18:27	8641
Thus ye also shall offer an *h*	Num 18:28	8641
h offering to Aaron the priest	Num 18:28	8641
every *h* offering of the LORD	Num 18:29	8641
for an *h* offering of the LORD	Num 31:29	8641
which was the LORD's *h* offering	Num 31:41	8641
h offerings of your hand, and your	Deut 12:6	8641
the *h* offering of your hand, and	Deut 12:11	8641
or *h* offering of thine hand	Deut 12:17	8641

HEAVED

which is waved, and which is *h* up	Ex 29:27	7311
When ye have *h* the best thereof	Num 18:30	7311
when ye have *h* from it the best	Num 18:32	7311

HEAVEN

the beginning God created the *h*	Gen 1:1	8064
And God called the firmament *H*	Gen 1:8	8064
Let the waters under the *h* be	Gen 1:9	8064
the *h* to divide the day from the	Gen 1:14	8064
h to give light upon the earth	Gen 1:15	8064
h to give light upon the earth	Gen 1:17	8064
earth in the open firmament of *h*	Gen 1:20	8064

the breath of life, from under *h*............... Gen 6:17   8064
and the windows of *h* were opened........ Gen 7:11   8064
that were under the whole *h* .... Gen 7:19   8064
things, and the fowl of the *h* .... Gen 7:23   8064
and the windows of *h* were stopped ...... Gen 8:2   8064
the rain from *h* was restrained............... Gen 8:2   8064
tower, whose top may reach unto *h* .... Gen 11:4   8064
the most high God, possessor of *h* .... Gen 14:19   8064
most high God, the possessor of *h* .... Gen 14:22   8064
and said, Look now toward *h* .... Gen 15:5   8064
and fire from the LORD out of *h* .... Gen 19:24   8064
of God called to Hagar out of *h* .... Gen 21:17   8064
the LORD called unto him out of *h* .... Gen 22:11   8064
Abraham out of *h* the second time .... Gen 22:15   8064
thy seed as the stars of *h* .... Gen 22:17   8064
swear by the LORD, the God of *h* .... Gen 24:3   8064
The LORD God of *h*, which took me .... Gen 24:7   8064
to multiply as the stars of *h* .... Gen 26:4   8064
God give thee of the dew of *h* .... Gen 27:28   8064
and of the dew of *h* from above .... Gen 27:39   8064
and the top of it reached to *h* .... Gen 28:12   8064
of God, and this is the gate of *h* .... Gen 28:17   8064
thee with blessings of *h* above............... Gen 49:25   8064
the *h* in the sight of Pharaoh .... Ex 9:8   8064
and Moses sprinkled it up toward *h* ..... Ex 9:10   8064
Stretch forth thine hand toward *h* .... Ex 9:22   8064
stretched forth his rod toward *h*............ Ex 9:23   8064
Stretch out thine hand toward *h* .... Ex 10:21   8064
stretched forth his hand toward *h* .... Ex 10:22   8064
I will rain bread from *h* for you .... Ex 16:4   8064
of Amalek from under *h* .... Ex 17:14   8064
of any thing that is in *h* above............... Ex 20:4   8064
For in six days the LORD made *h*.......... Ex 20:11   8064
I have talked with you from *h* .... Ex 20:22   8064
the body of *h* in his clearness .... Ex 24:10   8064
for in six days the LORD made *h* .... Ex 31:17   8064
your seed as the stars of *h* .... Ex 32:13   8064
and I will make your *h* as iron .... Lev 26:19   8064
as the stars of *h* for multitude................ Deut 1:10   8064
are great and walled up to *h* .... Deut 1:28   8064
that are under the whole *h*.................... Deut 2:25   8064
God is there in *h* or in earth .... Deut 3:24   8064
with fire unto the midst of *h* .... Deut 4:11   8064
thou lift up thine eyes unto *h* .... Deut 4:19   8064
the stars, even all the host of *h*............ Deut 4:19   8064
all nations under the whole *h* .... Deut 4:19   8064
I call *h* and earth to witness................ Deut 4:26   8064
the one side of *h* unto the other .... Deut 4:32   8064
Out of *h* he made thee to hear his .... Deut 4:36   8064
the LORD he is God in *h* above.............. Deut 4:39   8064
of any thing that is in *h* above............... Deut 5:8   8064
destroy their name from under *h* .... Deut 7:24   8064
cities great and fenced up to *h* .... Deut 9:1   8064
blot out their name from under *h* .... Deut 9:14   8064
Behold, the *h* and the *h* of .... Deut 10:14   8064
as the stars of *h* for multitude................ Deut 10:22   8064
drinketh water of the rain of *h*............ Deut 11:11   8064
against you, and he shut up the *h* .... Deut 11:17   8064
as the days of *h* upon the earth............ Deut 11:21   8064
or moon, or any of the host of *h* .... Deut 17:3   8064
of Amalek from under *h* .... Deut 25:19   8064
from thy holy habitation, from *h* .... Deut 26:15   8064
the *h* to give the rain unto thy .... Deut 28:12   8064
thy *h* that is over thy head shall .... Deut 28:23   8064
from *h* shall it come down upon .... Deut 28:24   8064
as the stars of *h* for multitude................ Deut 28:62   8064
blot out his name from under *h* .... Deut 29:20   8064
out unto the outmost parts of *h* .... Deut 30:4   8064
It is not in *h*, that thou .... Deut 30:12   8064
say, Who shall go up for us to *h* .... Deut 30:12   8064
I call *h* and earth to record this .... Deut 30:19   8064
words in their ears, and call *h* .... Deut 31:28   8064
For I lift up my hand to *h* .... Deut 32:40   8064
for the precious things of *h* .... Deut 33:13   8064
who rideth upon the *h* in thy help .... Deut 33:26   8064
your God, he is God in *h* above .... Josh 2:11   8064
of the city ascended up to *h* .... Josh 8:20   8064
from *h* upon them unto Azekah .... Josh 10:11   8064
sun stood still in the midst of *h* .... Josh 10:13   8064
They fought from *h* .... Judg 5:20   8064
up toward *h* from off the altar .... Judg 13:20   8064
of the city ascended up to *h* .... Judg 20:40   8064
out of *h* shall he thunder upon.............. 1Sa 2:10   8064
the cry of the city went up to *h*............ 1Sa 5:12   8064
and he was taken up between the *h* 2Sa 18:9   8064
water dropped upon them out of *h* 2Sa 21:10   8064
the foundations of *h* moved 2Sa 22:8   8064
The LORD thundered from *h* 2Sa 22:14   8064
spread forth his hands toward *h* 1Kin 8:22   8064
in *h* above, or on earth beneath, ... 1Kin 8:23   8064
behold, the *h* and *h* of........................ 1Kin 8:27   8064

hear thou in *h* thy dwelling place 1Kin 8:30   8064
Then hear thou in *h*, and do, and 1Kin 8:32   8064
Then hear thou in *h*, and forgive 1Kin 8:34   8064
When *h* is shut up, and there is no 1Kin 8:35   8064
Then hear thou in *h*, and forgive 1Kin 8:36   8064
Then hear thou in *h* thy dwelling 1Kin 8:39   8064
Hear thou in *h* thy dwelling place 1Kin 8:43   8064
Then hear thou in *h* their prayer 1Kin 8:45   8064
in *h* thy dwelling place, and.................. 1Kin 8:49   8064
with his hands spread up to *h* 1Kin 8:54   8064
that the *h* was black with clouds 1Kin 18:45   8064
all the host of *h* standing by him 1Kin 22:19   8064
then let fire come down from *h*.............. 2Kin 1:10   8064
And there came down fire from *h* 2Kin 1:10   8064
of God, let fire come down from *h* 2Kin 1:12   8064
the fire of God came down from *h* 2Kin 1:12   8064
there came fire down from *h*.................. 2Kin 1:14   8064
up Elijah into *h* by a whirlwind 2Kin 2:1   8064
went up by a whirlwind into *h* 2Kin 2:11   8064
the LORD would make windows in *h* 2Kin 7:2   8064
the LORD should make windows in *h* 2Kin 7:19   8064
the name of Israel from under *h* 2Kin 14:27   8064
and worshipped all the host of *h* 2Kin 17:16   8064
thou hast made *h* and earth.................. 2Kin 19:15   8064
and worshipped all the host of *h* 2Kin 21:3   8064
altars for all the host of *h* in 2Kin 21:5   8064
grove, and for all the host of *h* 2Kin 23:4   8064
planets, and to all the host of *h* 2Kin 23:5   8064
stand between the earth and the *h* 1Chr 21:16   8064
he answered him from *h* by fire.............. 1Chr 21:26   8064
for all that is in the *h* and in.................. 1Chr 29:11   8064
build him an house, seeing the *h* 2Chr 2:6   8064
h of heavens cannot contain him............ 2Chr 2:6   8064
LORD God of Israel, that made *h* 2Chr 2:12   8064
spread forth his hands toward *h* 2Chr 6:13   8064
is no God like thee in the *h* 2Chr 6:14   8064
behold, *h* and the *h* of........................ 2Chr 6:18   8064
thy dwelling place, even from *h* 2Chr 6:21   8064
Then hear thou from *h*, and do, and...... 2Chr 6:23   8064
When the *h* is shut up, and there 2Chr 6:26   8064
Then hear thou from *h*, and forgive 2Chr 6:27   8064
thou from *h* thy dwelling place 2Chr 6:30   8064
the fire came down from *h* 2Chr 7:1   8064
If I shut up *h* that there be no 2Chr 7:13   8064
then will I hear from *h*, and will............ 2Chr 7:14   8064
all the host of *h* standing on his 2Chr 18:18   8064
fathers, art not thou God in *h* 2Chr 20:6   8064
in a rage that reacheth up unto *h* 2Chr 28:9   8064
holy dwelling place, even unto *h* 2Chr 30:27   8064
son of Amoz, prayed and cried to *h* 2Chr 32:20   8064
and worshipped all the host of *h* 2Chr 33:3   8064
altars for all the host of *h* in 2Chr 33:5   8064
hath the LORD God of *h* given me.......... 2Chr 36:23   8064
The LORD God of *h* hath given me .... Ezr 1:2   8064
are the servants of the God of *h* .... Ezr 5:11   8065
provoked the God of *h* unto wrath .... Ezr 5:12   8065
burnt offerings of the God of *h* .... Ezr 6:9   8065
sweet savours unto the God of *h* .... Ezr 6:10   8065
scribe of the law of the God of *h*.......... Ezr 7:12   8065
scribe of the law of the God of *h*.......... Ezr 7:21   8065
is commanded by the God of *h* .... Ezr 7:23   8065
for the house of the God of *h* .... Ezr 7:23   8065
and prayed before the God of *h* .... Neh 1:4   8064
I beseech thee, O LORD God of *h* .... Neh 1:5   8064
unto the uttermost part of the *h* .... Neh 1:9   8064
So I prayed to the God of *h* .... Neh 2:4   8064
and said unto them, The God of *h* .... Neh 2:20   8064
thou hast made *h*, the *h* of.................. Neh 9:6   8064
the host of *h* worshippeth thee .... Neh 9:6   8064
and spakest with them from *h* .... Neh 9:13   8064
bread from *h* for their hunger .... Neh 9:15   8064
thou as the stars of *h*, and .... Neh 9:23   8064
thee, thou heardest them from *h* .... Neh 9:27   8064
thee, thou heardest them from *h* .... Neh 9:28   8064
The fire of God is fallen from *h*.............. Job 1:16   8064
dust upon their heads toward *h* .... Job 2:12   8064
It is as high as *h* .... Job 11:8   8064
now, behold, my witness is in *h*............ Job 16:19   8064
The *h* shall reveal his iniquity .... Job 20:27   8064
Is not God in the height of *h* .... Job 22:12   8064
and he walketh in the circuit of *h* .... Job 22:14   8064
The pillars of *h* tremble, and are .... Job 26:11   8064
earth, and seeth under the whole *h* ...... Job 28:24   8064
us wiser than the fowls of *h* .... Job 35:11   8064
He directeth it under the whole *h* .... Job 37:3   8064
and the hoary frost of *h*, who hath .... Job 38:29   8064
Knowest thou the ordinances of *h* .... Job 38:33   8064
or who can stay the bottles of *h* .... Job 38:37   8064
is under the whole *h* is mine .... Job 41:11   8064
temple, the LORD's throne is in *h* .... Ps 11:4   8064
from *h* upon the children of men .... Ps 14:2   8064

H

forth is from the end of the *h*	Ps 19:6	8064
he will hear him from his holy *h*	Ps 20:6	8064
The LORD looketh from *h*	Ps 33:13	8064
God looked down from *h* upon the	Ps 53:2	8064
He shall send from *h*, and save me	Ps 57:3	8064
Let the *h* and earth praise him,	Ps 69:34	8064
Whom have I in *h* but thee	Ps 73:25	8064
cause judgment to be heard from *h*	Ps 76:8	8064
voice of thy thunder was in the *h*	Ps 77:18	1534
above, and opened the doors of *h*	Ps 78:23	8064
had given them of the corn of *h*	Ps 78:24	8064
an east wind to blow in the *h*	Ps 78:26	8064
be meat unto the fowls of the *h*	Ps 79:2	8064
look down from *h*, and behold, and	Ps 80:14	8064
shall look down from *h*	Ps 85:11	8064
For who in the *h* can be compared	Ps 89:6	7834
and his throne as the days of *h*	Ps 89:29	8064
and as a faithful witness in *h*	Ps 89:37	7834
from *h* did the LORD behold the	Ps 102:19	8064
For as the *h* is high above the	Ps 103:11	8064
of the *h* have their habitation	Ps 104:12	8064
them with the bread of *h*	Ps 105:40	8064
They mount up to the *h*, they go	Ps 107:26	8064
behold the things that are in *h*	Ps 113:6	8064
blessed of the LORD which made *h*	Ps 115:15	8064
The *h*, even the heavens, are the	Ps 115:16	8064
O LORD, thy word is settled in *h*	Ps 119:89	8064
from the LORD, which made *h*	Ps 121:2	8064
the name of the LORD, who made *h*	Ps 124:8	8064
The LORD that made *h* and earth	Ps 134:3	8064
LORD pleased, that did he in *h*	Ps 135:6	8064
O give thanks unto the God of *h*	Ps 136:26	8064
If I ascend up into *h*, thou art	Ps 139:8	8064
Which made *h*, and earth, the sea,	Ps 146:6	8064
Who covereth the *h* with clouds	Ps 147:8	8064
his glory is above the earth and *h*	Ps 148:13	8064
fly away as an eagle toward *h*	Prov 23:5	8064
The *h* for height, and the earth	Prov 25:3	8064
Who hath ascended up into *h*	Prov 30:4	8064
all things that are done under *h*	Eccl 1:13	8064
the *h* all the days of their life	Eccl 2:3	8064
time to every purpose under the *h*	Eccl 3:1	8064
for God is in *h*, and thou upon	Eccl 5:2	8064
a far country, from the end of *h*	Is 13:5	8064
For the stars of *h* and the	Is 13:10	8064
How art thou fallen from *h*	Is 14:12	8064
thine heart, I will ascend into *h*	Is 14:13	8064
all the host of *h* shall be	Is 34:4	8064
For my sword shall be bathed in *h*	Is 34:5	8064
thou hast made *h* and earth	Is 37:16	8064
meted out *h* with the span, and	Is 40:12	8064
cometh down, and the snow from *h*	Is 55:10	8064
Look down from *h*, and behold from	Is 63:15	8064
The *h* is my throne, and the earth	Is 66:1	8064
to make cakes to the queen of *h*	Jer 7:18	8064
be meat for the fowls of the *h*	Jer 7:33	8064
and the moon, and all the host of *h*	Jer 8:2	8064
the stork in the *h* knoweth her	Jer 8:7	8064
be not dismayed at the signs of *h*	Jer 10:2	8064
to tear, and the fowls of the *h*	Jer 15:3	8064
shall be meat for the fowls of *h*	Jer 16:4	8064
to be meat for the fowls of the *h*	Jer 19:7	8064
incense unto all the host of *h*	Jer 19:13	8064
Do not I fill *h* and earth	Jer 23:24	8064
If *h* above can be measured, and	Jer 31:37	8064
behold, thou hast made the *h*	Jer 32:17	8064
As the host of *h* cannot be	Jer 33:22	8064
not appointed the ordinances of *h*	Jer 33:25	8064
for meat unto the fowls of the *h*	Jer 34:20	8064
burn incense unto the queen of *h*	Jer 44:17	8064
to burn incense to the queen of *h*	Jer 44:18	8064
burned incense to the queen of *h*	Jer 44:19	8064
to burn incense to the queen of *h*	Jer 44:25	8064
winds from the four quarters of *h*	Jer 49:36	8064
for her judgment reacheth unto *h*	Jer 51:9	8064
out the *h* by his understanding	Jer 51:15	8064
Then the *h* and the earth, and all	Jer 51:48	8064
Babylon should mount up to *h*	Jer 51:53	8064
cast down from *h* unto the earth	Lam 2:1	8064
LORD look down, and behold from *h*	Lam 3:50	8064
swifter than the eagles of the *h*	Lam 4:19	8064
me up between the earth and the *h*	Eze 8:3	8064
field and to the fowls of the *h*	Eze 29:5	8064
All the fowls of *h* made their	Eze 31:6	8064
all the fowls of the *h* remain	Eze 31:13	8064
of the *h* to remain upon thee	Eze 32:4	8064
put thee *h*, I will cover the *h*	Eze 32:7	8064
All the bright lights of *h* will I	Eze 32:8	8064
of the sea, and the fowls of the *h*	Eze 38:20	8064
God of *h* concerning this secret	Dan 2:18	8065
Then Daniel blessed the God of *h*	Dan 2:19	8065

But there is a God in *h* that	Dan 2:28	8065
for the God of *h* hath given thee	Dan 2:37	8065
the fowls of the *h* hath he given	Dan 2:38	8065
the God of *h* set up a kingdom	Dan 2:44	8065
the height thereof reached unto *h*	Dan 4:11	8065
the fowls of the *h* dwelt in the	Dan 4:12	8065
and an holy one came down from *h*	Dan 4:13	8065
let it be wet with the dew of *h*	Dan 4:15	8065
whose height reached unto the *h*	Dan 4:20	8065
of the *h* had their habitation	Dan 4:21	8065
is grown, and reacheth unto *h*	Dan 4:22	8065
and an holy one coming down from *h*	Dan 4:23	8065
let it be wet with the dew of *h*	Dan 4:23	8065
shall wet thee with the dew of *h*	Dan 4:25	8065
mouth, there fell a voice from *h*	Dan 4:31	8065
body was wet with the dew of *h*	Dan 4:33	8065
lifted up mine eyes unto *h*	Dan 4:34	8065
to his will in the army of *h*	Dan 4:35	8065
and extol and honour the King of *h*	Dan 4:37	8065
body was wet with the dew of *h*	Dan 5:21	8065
up thyself against the Lord of *h*	Dan 5:23	8065
he worketh signs and wonders in *h*	Dan 6:27	8065
the four winds of the *h* strove	Dan 7:2	8065
of man came with the clouds of *h*	Dan 7:13	8065
of the kingdom under the whole *h*	Dan 7:27	8065
ones toward the four winds of *h*	Dan 8:8	8064
great, even to the host of *h*	Dan 8:10	8064
for under the whole *h* hath not	Dan 9:12	8064
toward the four winds of *h*	Dan 11:4	8064
hand and his left hand unto *h*	Dan 12:7	8064
the field, and with the fowls of *h*	Hos 2:18	8064
the field, and with the fowls of *h*	Hos 4:3	8064
them down as the fowls of the *h*	Hos 7:12	8064
though they climb up to *h*	Amos 9:2	8064
buildeth his stories in the *h*	Amos 9:6	8064
and I fear the LORD, the God of *h*	Jonah 1:9	8064
merchants above the stars of *h*	Nah 3:16	8064
I will consume the fowls of the *h*	Zeph 1:3	8064
the host of *h* upon the housetops	Zeph 1:5	8064
Therefore the *h* over you is	Hag 1:10	8064
abroad as the four winds of the *h*	Zec 2:6	8064
ephah between the earth and the *h*	Zec 5:9	8064
not open you the windows of *h*	Mal 3:10	8064
for the kingdom of *h* is at hand	Mt 3:2	3772
And lo a voice from *h*, saying	Mt 3:17	3772
for the kingdom of *h* is at hand	Mt 4:17	3772
for theirs is the kingdom of *h*	Mt 5:3	3772
for theirs is the kingdom of *h*	Mt 5:10	3772
for great is your reward in *h*	Mt 5:12	3772
glorify your Father which is in *h*	Mt 5:16	3772
For verily I say unto you, Till *h*	Mt 5:18	3772
the least in the kingdom of *h*	Mt 5:19	3772
called great in the kingdom of *h*	Mt 5:19	3772
case enter into the kingdom of *h*	Mt 5:20	3772
Swear not at all; neither by *h*	Mt 5:34	3772
of your Father which is in *h*	Mt 5:45	3772
Father which is in *h* is perfect	Mt 5:48	3772
of your Father which is in *h*	Mt 6:1	3772
Our Father which art in *h*	Mt 6:9	3772
be done in earth, as it is in *h*	Mt 6:10	3772
up for yourselves treasures in *h*	Mt 6:20	3772
h give good things to them that	Mt 7:11	3772
shall enter into the kingdom of *h*	Mt 7:21	3772
will of my Father which is in *h*	Mt 7:21	3772
and Jacob, in the kingdom of *h*	Mt 8:11	3772
The kingdom of *h* is at hand	Mt 10:7	3772
before my Father which is in *h*	Mt 10:32	3772
before my Father which is in *h*	Mt 10:33	3772
kingdom of *h* is greater than he	Mt 11:11	3772
kingdom of *h* suffereth violence	Mt 11:12	3772
which art exalted unto *h*	Mt 11:23	3772
I thank thee, O Father, Lord of *h*	Mt 11:25	3772
will of my Father which is in *h*	Mt 12:50	3772
the mysteries of the kingdom of *h*	Mt 13:11	3772
The kingdom of *h* is likened unto	Mt 13:24	3772
The kingdom of *h* is like to a	Mt 13:31	3772
The kingdom of *h* is like unto	Mt 13:33	3772
the kingdom of *h* is like unto	Mt 13:44	3772
the kingdom of *h* is like unto a	Mt 13:45	3772
the kingdom of *h* is like unto a	Mt 13:47	3772
h is like unto a man that is an	Mt 13:52	3772
two fishes, and looking up to *h*	Mt 14:19	3772
he would shew them a sign from *h*	Mt 16:1	3772
thee, but my Father which is in *h*	Mt 16:17	3772
thee the keys of the kingdom of *h*	Mt 16:19	3772
bind on earth shall be bound in *h*	Mt 16:19	3772
on earth shall be loosed in *h*	Mt 16:19	3772
the greatest in the kingdom of *h*	Mt 18:1	3772
not enter into the kingdom of *h*	Mt 18:3	3772
is greatest in the kingdom of *h*	Mt 18:4	3772
That in *h* their angels do always	Mt 18:10	3772

face of my Father which is in *h*	Mt 18:10	3772
will of your Father which is in *h*	Mt 18:14	3772
bind on earth shall be bound in *h*	Mt 18:18	3772
on earth shall be loosed in *h*	Mt 18:18	3772
them of my Father which is in *h*	Mt 18:19	3772
of *h* likened unto a certain king	Mt 18:23	3772
for of such is the kingdom of *h*	Mt 19:14	3772
and thou shalt have treasure in *h*	Mt 19:21	3772
enter into the kingdom of *h*	Mt 19:23	3772
For the kingdom of *h* is like unto	Mt 20:1	3772
from *h*, or of men	Mt 21:25	3772
saying, If we shall say, From *h*	Mt 21:25	3772
The kingdom of *h* is like unto a	Mt 22:2	3772
but are as the angels of God in *h*	Mt 22:30	3772
one is your Father, which is in *h*	Mt 23:9	3772
up the kingdom of *h* against men	Mt 23:13	3772
And he that shall swear by *h*	Mt 23:22	3772
and the stars shall fall from *h*	Mt 24:29	3772
the sign of the Son of man in *h*	Mt 24:30	3772
in the clouds of *h* with power	Mt 24:30	3772
from one end of *h* to the other	Mt 24:31	3772
H and earth shall pass away, but	Mt 24:35	3772
no man, no, not the angels of *h*	Mt 24:36	3772
Then shall the kingdom of *h* be	Mt 25:1	3772
For the kingdom of *h* is as a man	Mt 25:14	
and coming in the clouds of *h*	Mt 26:64	3772
of the Lord descended from *h*	Mt 28:2	3772
All power is given unto me in *h*	Mt 28:18	3772
And there came a voice from *h*	Mk 1:11	3772
the two fishes, he looked up to *h*	Mk 6:41	3772
And looking up to *h*, he sighed, and	Mk 7:34	3772
him, seeking of him a sign from *h*	Mk 8:11	3772
and thou shalt have treasure in *h*	Mk 10:21	3772
your Father also which is in *h*	Mk 11:25	3772
is in *h* forgive your trespasses	Mk 11:26	3772
baptism of John, was it from *h*	Mk 11:30	3772
saying, If we shall say, From *h*	Mk 11:31	3772
are as the angels which are in *h*	Mk 12:25	3772
And the stars of *h* shall fall	Mk 13:25	3772
that are in *h* shall be shaken	Mk 13:25	3772
earth to the uttermost part of *h*	Mk 13:27	3772
H and earth shall pass away	Mk 13:31	3772
no, not the angels which are in *h*	Mk 13:32	3772
and coming in the clouds of *h*	Mk 14:62	3772
them, he was received up into *h*	Mk 16:19	3772
were gone away from them into *h*	Lk 2:15	3772
and praying, the *h* was opened	Lk 3:21	3772
upon him, and a voice came from *h*	Lk 3:22	3772
when the *h* was shut up three	Lk 4:25	3772
behold, your reward is great in *h*	Lk 6:23	3772
two fishes, and looking up to *h*	Lk 9:16	3772
command fire to come down from *h*	Lk 9:54	3772
Capernaum, which art exalted to *h*	Lk 10:15	3772
Satan as lightning fall from *h*	Lk 10:18	3772
your names are written in *h*	Lk 10:20	3772
I thank thee, O Father, Lord of *h*	Lk 10:21	3772
say, Our Father which art in *h*	Lk 11:2	3772
Thy will be done, as in *h*	Lk 11:2	3772
him, sought of him a sign from *h*	Lk 11:16	3772
that likewise joy shall be in *h*	Lk 15:7	3772
Father, I have sinned against *h*	Lk 15:18	3772
Father, I have sinned against *h*	Lk 15:21	3772
And it is easier for *h* and earth to	Lk 16:17	3772
out of the one part under *h*	Lk 17:24	3772
unto the other part under *h*	Lk 17:24	3772
rained fire and brimstone from *h*	Lk 17:29	3772
up so much as his eyes unto *h*	Lk 18:13	3772
and thou shalt have treasure in *h*	Lk 18:22	3772
peace in *h*, and glory in the	Lk 19:38	3772
baptism of John, was it from *h*	Lk 20:4	3772
saying, If we shall say, From *h*	Lk 20:5	3772
great signs shall there be from *h*	Lk 21:11	3772
the powers of *h* shall be shaken	Lk 21:26	3772
H and earth shall pass away	Lk 21:33	3772
appeared an angel unto him from *h*	Lk 22:43	3772
from them, and carried up into *h*	Lk 24:51	3772
descending from *h* like a dove	Jn 1:32	3772
Hereafter ye shall see *h* open	Jn 1:51	3772
And no man hath ascended up to *h*	Jn 3:13	3772
but he that came down from *h*	Jn 3:13	3772
even the Son of man which is in *h*	Jn 3:13	3772
except it be given him from *h*	Jn 3:27	3772
that cometh from *h* is above all	Jn 3:31	3772
He gave them bread from *h* to eat	Jn 6:31	3772
gave you not that bread from *h*	Jn 6:32	3772
giveth you the true bread from *h*	Jn 6:32	3772
is he which cometh down from *h*	Jn 6:33	3772
For I came down from *h*, not to do	Jn 6:38	3772
the bread which came down from *h*	Jn 6:41	3772
that he saith, I came down from *h*	Jn 6:42	3772
bread which cometh down from *h*	Jn 6:50	3772

bread which came down from *h*	Jn 6:51	3772
that bread which came down from *h*	Jn 6:58	3772
Then came there a voice from *h*	Jn 12:28	3772
Jesus, and lifted up his eyes to *h*	Jn 17:1	3772
stedfastly toward *h* as he went up	Acts 1:10	3772
why stand ye gazing up into *h*	Acts 1:11	3772
which is taken up from you into *h*	Acts 1:11	3772
as ye have seen him go into *h*	Acts 1:11	3772
there came a sound from *h* as of a	Acts 2:2	3772
men, out of every nation under *h*	Acts 2:5	3772
And I will shew wonders in *h* above	Acts 2:19	3772
Whom the *h* must receive until the	Acts 3:21	3772
name under *h* given among men	Acts 4:12	3772
thou art God, which hast made *h*	Acts 4:24	3772
them up to worship the host of *h*	Acts 7:42	3772
H is my throne, and earth is my	Acts 7:49	3772
looked up stedfastly into *h*	Acts 7:55	3772
round about him a light from *h*	Acts 9:3	3772
saw *h* opened, and a certain vessel	Acts 10:11	3772
was received up again into *h*	Acts 10:16	3772
let down from *h* by four corners	Acts 11:5	3772
voice answered me again from *h*	Acts 11:9	3772
and all were drawn up again into *h*	Acts 11:10	3772
unto the living God, which made *h*	Acts 14:15	3772
did good, and gave us rain from *h*	Acts 14:17	3771
seeing that he is Lord of *h*	Acts 17:24	3772
suddenly there shone from *h* a	Acts 22:6	3772
I saw in the way a light from *h*	Acts 26:13	3771
from *h* against all ungodliness	Rom 1:18	3772
heart, Who shall ascend into *h*	Rom 10:6	3772
whether in *h* or in earth, (as	1Cor 8:5	3772
the second man is the Lord from *h*	1Cor 15:47	3772
with our house which is from *h*	2Cor 5:2	3772
an one caught up to the third *h*	2Cor 12:2	3772
But though we, or an angel from *h*	Gal 1:8	3772
in Christ, both which are in *h*	Eph 1:10	3772
Of whom the whole family in *h*	Eph 3:15	3772
that your Master also is in *h*	Eph 6:9	3772
knee should bow, of things in *h*	Phil 2:10	2032
For our conversation is in *h*	Phil 3:20	3772
which is laid up for you in *h*	Col 1:5	3772
all things created, that are in *h*	Col 1:16	3772
things in earth, or things in *h*	Col 1:20	3772
every creature which is under *h*	Col 1:23	3772
that ye also have a Master in *h*	Col 4:1	3772
And to wait for his Son from *h*	1Th 1:10	3772
shall descend from *h* with a shout	1Th 4:16	3772
from *h* with his mighty angels	2Th 1:7	3772
but into *h* itself, now to appear	Heb 9:24	3772
that ye have in *h* a better	Heb 10:34	3772
firstborn, which are written in *h*	Heb 12:23	3772
from him that speaketh from *h*	Heb 12:25	3772
not the earth only, but also *h*	Heb 12:26	3772
brethren, swear not, neither by *h*	Jas 5:12	3772
the *h* gave rain, and the earth	Jas 5:18	3772
not away, reserved in *h* for you	1Pet 1:4	3772
the Holy Ghost sent down from *h*	1Pet 1:12	3772
Who is gone into *h*, and is on the	1Pet 3:22	3772
voice which came from *h* we heard	2Pet 1:18	3772
are three that bear record in *h*	1Jn 5:7	3772
cometh down out of *h* from my God	Rev 3:12	3772
behold, a door was opened in *h*	Rev 4:1	3772
and, behold, a throne was set in *h*	Rev 4:2	3772
And no man in *h*, nor in earth	Rev 5:3	3772
And every creature which is in *h*	Rev 5:13	3772
the stars of *h* fell unto the	Rev 6:13	3772
the *h* departed as a scroll when	Rev 6:14	3772
there was silence in *h* about the	Rev 8:1	3772
and there fell a great star from *h*	Rev 8:10	3772
flying through the midst of *h*	Rev 8:13	3321
a star fall from *h* unto the earth	Rev 9:1	3772
mighty angel come down from *h*	Rev 10:1	3772
a voice from *h* saying unto me	Rev 10:4	3772
the earth lifted up his hand to *h*	Rev 10:5	3772
for ever and ever, who created *h*	Rev 10:6	3772
heard from *h* spake unto me again	Rev 10:8	3772
These have power to shut *h*	Rev 11:6	3772
voice from *h* saying unto them	Rev 11:12	3772
they ascended up to *h* in a cloud	Rev 11:12	3772
and gave glory to the God of *h*	Rev 11:13	3772
and there were great voices in *h*	Rev 11:15	3772
the temple of God was opened in *h*	Rev 11:19	3772
appeared a great wonder in *h*	Rev 12:1	3772
appeared another wonder in *h*	Rev 12:3	3772
the third part of the stars of *h*	Rev 12:4	3772
And there was war in *h*	Rev 12:7	3772
their place found any more in *h*	Rev 12:8	3772
I heard a loud voice saying in *h*	Rev 12:10	3772
and them that dwell in *h*	Rev 13:6	3772
h on the earth in the sight of	Rev 13:13	3772
And I heard a voice from *h*	Rev 14:2	3772

angel fly in the midst of *h* .... Rev 14:6 — *3321*
and worship him that made *h* .... Rev 14:7 — *3772*
a voice from *h* saying unto me................ Rev 14:13 — *3772*
out of the temple which is in *h*................ Rev 14:17 — *3772*
And I saw another sign in *h*...................... Rev 15:1 — *3772*
of the testimony in *h* was opened .... Rev 15:5 — *3772*
blasphemed the God of *h* because .... Rev 16:11 — *3772*
voice out of the temple of *h*..................... Rev 16:17 — *3772*
upon men a great hail out of *h* .... Rev 16:21 — *3772*
another angel come down from *h* .... Rev 18:1 — *3772*
And I heard another voice from *h* .... Rev 18:4 — *3772*
For her sins have reached unto *h* .... Rev 18:5 — *3772*
Rejoice over her, thou *h*, and ye .... Rev 18:20 — *3772*
a great voice of much people in *h*........... Rev 19:1 — *3772*
I saw *h* opened, and behold a white ...... Rev 19:11 — *3772*
the armies which were in *h*...................... Rev 19:14 — *3772*
fowls that fly in the midst of *h* .... Rev 19:17 — *3321*
I saw an angel come down from *h*.......... Rev 20:1 — *3772*
fire came down from God out of *h*........... Rev 20:9 — *3772*
face the earth and the *h* fled away ...... Rev 20:11 — *3772*
And I saw a new *h* and a new earth ...... Rev 21:1 — *3772*
for the first *h* and the first .... Rev 21:1 — *3772*
coming down from God out of *h* .... Rev 21:2 — *3772*
a great voice out of *h* saying................... Rev 21:3 — *3772*
descending out of *h* from God............... Rev 21:10 — *3772*

HEAVENLY
your *h* Father will also forgive............. Mt 6:14 — *3770*
yet your *h* Father feedeth them .... Mt 6:26 — *3770*
for your *h* Father knoweth that .... Mt 6:32 — *3770*
which my *h* Father hath not .... Mt 15:13 — *3770*
So likewise shall my *h* Father do .... Mt 18:35 — *2032*
of the *h* host praising God .... Lk 2:13 — *2032*
much more shall your *h* Father .... Lk 11:13 — *1537,3772*
if I tell you of *h* things .... Jn 3:12 — *2032*
not disobedient unto the *h* vision .... Acts 26:19 — *3770*
and as is the *h*, such are they .... 1Cor 15:48 — *2032*
such are they also that are *h* .... 1Cor 15:48 — *2032*
also bear the image of the *h*............... 1Cor 15:49 — *2032*
blessings in *h* places in Christ................ Eph 1:3 — *2032*
own right hand in the *h* places .... Eph 1:20 — *2032*
in *h* places in Christ Jesus..................... Eph 2:6 — *2032*
powers in *h* might be known .... Eph 3:10 — *2032*
preserve me unto his *h* kingdom .... 2Ti 4:18 — *2032*
partakers of the *h* calling....................... Heb 3:1 — *2032*
and have tasted of the *h* gift................... Heb 6:4 — *2032*
the example and shadow of *h* things ...... Heb 8:5 — *2032*
but the *h* things themselves with .... Heb 9:23 — *2032*
a better country, that is, an *h* .... Heb 11:16 — *2032*
the *h* Jerusalem, and to an .... Heb 12:22 — *2032*

HEAVEN'S
eunuchs for the kingdom of *h* sake....... Mt 19:12 — *3772*

HEAVENS
Thus the *h* and the earth were .... Gen 2:1 — *8064*
are the generations of the *h* .... Gen 2:4 — *8064*
LORD God made the earth and the *h*...... Gen 2:4 — *8064*
the heaven of *h* is the LORD's thy .... Deut 10:14 — *8064*
Give ear, O ye *h*, and I will speak .... Deut 32:1 — *8064*
also his *h* shall drop down dew .... Deut 33:28 — *8064*
the *h* dropped, the clouds also .... Judg 5:4 — *8064*
He bowed the *h* also, and came down .... 2Sa 22:10 — *8064*
heaven of *h* cannot contain thee............ 1Kin 8:27 — *8064*
but the LORD made the *h* .... 1Chr 16:26 — *8064*
Let the *h* be glad, and let the .... 1Chr 16:31 — *8064*
Israel like to the stars of the *h*............... 1Chr 27:23 — *8064*
heaven of *h* cannot contain him .... 2Chr 2:6 — *8064*
the heaven of *h* cannot contain............... 2Chr 6:18 — *8064*
Then hear thou from the *h* .... 2Chr 6:25 — *8064*
Then hear thou from the *h* .... 2Chr 6:33 — *8064*
hear thou from the *h* their prayer .... 2Chr 6:35 — *8064*
Then hear thou from the *h* .... 2Chr 6:39 — *8064*
trespass is grown up unto the *h* .... Ezr 9:6 — *8064*
hast made heaven, the heaven of *h* .... Neh 9:6 — *8064*
Which alone spreadeth out the *h* .... Job 9:8 — *8064*
till the *h* be no more, they shall .... Job 14:12 — *8064*
the *h* are not clean in his sight.............. Job 15:15 — *8064*
his excellency mount up to the *h* .... Job 20:6 — *8064*
spirit he hath garnished the *h* .... Job 26:13 — *8064*
Look unto the *h*, and see .... Job 35:5 — *8064*
that sitteth in the *h* shall laugh .... Ps 2:4 — *8064*
hast set thy glory above the *h* .... Ps 8:1 — *8064*
When I consider thy *h*, the work .... Ps 8:3 — *8064*
He bowed the *h* also, and came down.... Ps 18:9 — *8064*
The LORD also thundered in the *h* .... Ps 18:13 — *8064*
The *h* declare the glory of God .... Ps 19:1 — *8064*
word of the LORD were the *h* made .... Ps 33:6 — *8064*
Thy mercy, O LORD, is in the *h* .... Ps 36:5 — *8064*
He shall call to the *h* from above .... Ps 50:4 — *8064*
And the *h* shall declare his .... Ps 50:6 — *8064*
thou exalted, O God, above the *h* .... Ps 57:5 — *8064*
For thy mercy is great unto the *h* .... Ps 57:10 — *8064*

thou exalted, O God, above the *h* .... Ps 57:11 — *8064*
rideth upon the *h* by his name JAH .... Ps 68:4 — *6160*
the *h* also dropped at the .... Ps 68:8 — *8064*
that rideth upon the *h* of *h*.................... Ps 68:33 — *8064*
set their mouth against the *h* .... Ps 73:9 — *8064*
thou establish in the very *h* .... Ps 89:2 — *8064*
the *h* shall praise thy wonders, O........... Ps 89:5 — *8064*
The *h* are thine, the earth also .... Ps 89:11 — *8064*
but the LORD made the *h*........................ Ps 96:5 — *8064*
Let the *h* rejoice, and let the .... Ps 96:11 — *8064*
The *h* declare his righteousness,............ Ps 97:6 — *8064*
the *h* are the work of thy hands .... Ps 102:25 — *8064*
hath prepared his throne in the *h* .... Ps 103:19 — *8064*
out the *h* like a curtain........................... Ps 104:2 — *8064*
thy mercy is great above the *h* .... Ps 108:4 — *8064*
thou exalted, O God, above the *h* .... Ps 108:5 — *8064*
nations, and his glory above the *h* .... Ps 113:4 — *8064*
But our God is in the *h*........................... Ps 115:3 — *8064*
The heaven, even the *h*, are the .... Ps 115:16 — *8064*
O thou that dwellest in the *h* .... Ps 123:1 — *8064*
To him that by wisdom made the *h* .... Ps 136:5 — *8064*
Bow thy *h*, O LORD, and come down .... Ps 144:5 — *8064*
Praise ye the LORD from the *h* .... Ps 148:1 — *8064*
Praise him, ye *h* of *h*............................ Ps 148:4 — *8064*
and ye waters that be above the *h* .... Ps 148:4 — *8064*
hath he established the *h*........................ Prov 3:19 — *8064*
When he prepared the *h*, I was .... Prov 8:27 — *8064*
Hear, O *h*, and give ear, O earth............. Is 1:2 — *8064*
is darkened in the *h* thereof................... Is 5:30 — *6183*
Therefore I will shake the *h* .... Is 13:13 — *8064*
the *h* shall be rolled together as .... Is 34:4 — *8064*
stretcheth out the *h* as a curtain............ Is 40:22 — *8064*
the LORD, he that created the *h* .... Is 42:5 — *8064*
Sing, O ye *h* .... Is 44:23 — *8064*
that stretcheth forth the *h* alone............ Is 44:24 — *8064*
Drop down, ye *h*, from above, and.......... Is 45:8 — *8064*
hands, have stretched out the *h* .... Is 45:12 — *8064*
saith the LORD that created the *h* .... Is 45:18 — *8064*
my right hand hath spanned the *h* .... Is 48:13 — *8064*
Sing, O *h*... Is 49:13 — *8064*
I clothe the *h* with blackness, and.......... Is 50:3 — *8064*
Lift up your eyes to the *h* .... Is 51:6 — *8064*
for the *h* shall vanish away like .... Is 51:6 — *8064*
that hath stretched forth the *h* .... Is 51:13 — *8064*
mine hand, that I may plant the *h*........... Is 51:16 — *8064*
For as the *h* are higher than the .... Is 55:9 — *8064*
Oh that thou wouldest rend the *h*........... Is 64:1 — *8064*
For, behold, I create new *h*.................... Is 65:17 — *8064*
For as the new *h* and the new earth ...... Is 66:22 — *8064*
Be astonished, O ye *h*, at this,............... Jer 2:12 — *8064*
and the *h*, and they had no light .... Jer 4:23 — *8064*
all the birds of the *h* were fled .... Jer 4:25 — *8064*
mourn, and the *h* above be black .... Jer 4:28 — *8064*
both the fowl of the *h* and the................ Jer 9:10 — *8064*
The gods that have not made the *h*....... Jer 10:11 — *8065*
the earth, and from under these *h*......... Jer 10:11 — *8065*
out the *h* by his discretion..................... Jer 10:12 — *8064*
is a multitude of waters in the *h* .... Jer 10:13 — *8064*
or can the *h* give showers .... Jer 14:22 — *8064*
is a multitude of waters in the *h* .... Jer 51:16 — *8064*
with our hands unto God in the *h* .... Lam 3:41 — *8064*
from under the *h* of the LORD................. Lam 3:66 — *8064*
that the *h* were opened, and I saw .... Eze 1:1 — *8064*
have known that the *h* do rule............... Dan 4:26 — *8065*
saith the LORD, I will hear the *h* .... Hos 2:21 — *8064*
the *h* shall tremble................................ Joel 2:10 — *8064*
And I will shew wonders in the *h*........... Joel 2:30 — *8064*
and the *h* and the earth shall shake ...... Joel 3:16 — *8064*
His glory covered the *h*, and the............ Hab 3:3 — *8064*
while, and I will shake the *h* .... Hag 2:6 — *8064*
Judah, saying, I will shake the *h* .... Hag 2:21 — *8064*
are the four spirits of the *h* .... Zec 6:5 — *8064*
the *h* shall give their dew .... Zec 8:12 — *8064*
which stretcheth forth the *h* .... Zec 12:1 — *8064*
the *h* were opened unto him, and he ..... Mt 3:16 — *3772*
powers of the *h* shall be shaken .... Mt 24:29 — *3772*
of the water, he saw the *h* opened.......... Mk 1:10 — *3772*
in the *h* that faileth not....................... Lk 12:33 — *3772*
David is not ascended into the *h* .... Acts 2:34 — *3772*
said, Behold, I see the *h* opened .... Acts 7:56 — *3772*
made with hands, eternal in the *h* .... 2Cor 5:1 — *3772*
that ascended up far above all *h*............ Eph 4:10 — *3772*
the *h* are the works of thine .... Heb 1:10 — *3772*
priest, that is passed into the *h* .... Heb 4:14 — *3772*
and made higher than the *h* .... Heb 7:26 — *3772*
throne of the Majesty in the *h* .... Heb 8:1 — *3772*
h should be purified with these .... Heb 9:23 — *3772*
the word of God the *h* were of old.......... 2Pet 3:5 — *3772*
But the *h* and the earth, which are .... 2Pet 3:7 — *3772*
in the which the *h* shall pass .... 2Pet 3:10 — *3772*
wherein the *h* being on fire shall............ 2Pet 3:12 — *3772*

to his promise, look for new *h* 2Pet 3:13   3772
Therefore rejoice, ye *h*, and ye .... Rev 12:12   3772

HEAVIER
For now it would be *h* than the .... Job 6:3   3513
my stroke is *h* than my groaning .... Job 23:2   3513
fool's wrath is *h* than them both .... Prov 27:3   3513

HEAVILY
wheels, that they drave them *h* .... Ex 14:25   3517
I bowed down *h*, as one that .... Ps 35:14   6957
hast thou very *h* laid thy yoke .... Is 47:6   3513

HEAVINESS
sacrifice I arose up from my *h* .... Ezr 9:5   8589
complaint, I will leave off my *h* .... Job 9:27   6440
and I am full of *h* .... Ps 69:20   5136
My soul melteth for *h* .... Ps 119:28   8424
son is the *h* of his mother .... Prov 10:1   8424
H in the heart of man maketh it .... Prov 12:25   1674
and the end of that mirth is *h* .... Prov 14:13   8424
Ariel, and there shall be *h* .... Is 29:2   8386
of praise for the spirit of *h* .... Is 61:3   3544
That I have great *h* and continual .... Rom 9:2   3077
would not come again to you in *h* 2Cor 2:1   3077
after you all, and was full of *h* .... Phil 2:26   85
to mourning, and your joy to *h* .... Jas 4:9   2726
ye are in *h* through manifold 1Pet 1:6   3076

HEAVY
But Moses' hands were *h* .... Ex 17:12   3515
for this thing is too *h* for thee .... Ex 18:18   3515
alone, because it is too *h* for me .... Num 11:14   3515
for he was an old man, and *h* 1Sa 4:18   3513
LORD was *h* upon them of Ashdod 1Sa 5:6   3513
the hand of God was very *h* there 1Sa 5:11   3513
because the hair was *h* on him 2Sa 14:26   3513
his *h* yoke which he put upon us, ... 1Kin 12:4   3515
Thy father made our yoke *h* 1Kin 12:10   3513
father did lade you with a *h* yoke 1Kin 12:11   3515
My father made your yoke *h* 1Kin 12:14   3513
I am sent to thee with *h* tidings 1Kin 14:6   7186
of Israel went to his house *h* 1Kin 20:43   5620
And Ahab came into his house *h* 1Kin 21:4   5620
his *h* yoke that he put upon us, ... 2Chr 10:4   3515
Thy father made our yoke *h* 2Chr 10:10   3513
my father put a *h* yoke upon you 2Chr 10:11   3515
My father made your yoke *h* 2Chr 10:14   3513
bondage was *h* upon this people .... Neh 5:18   3513
shall my hand be *h* upon thee .... Job 33:7   3513
and night thy hand was *h* upon me .... Ps 32:4   3513
as an *h* burden they are too *h* .... Ps 38:4   3515
burden they are too *h* for me .... Ps 38:4   3513
that singeth songs to an *h* heart .... Prov 25:20   7451
A stone is *h*, and the sand weighty .... Prov 27:3   3514
unto those that be of *h* hearts .... Prov 31:6   4751
people fat, and make their ears *h* .... Is 6:10   3513
thereof shall be *h* upon it .... Is 24:20   3513
anger, and the burden thereof is *h* .... Is 30:27   3514
your carriages were *h* loaden .... Is 46:1
wickedness, to undo the *h* burdens .... Is 58:6   4133
neither his ear *h*, that it cannot .... Is 59:1   3513
he hath made my chain *h* .... Lam 3:7   3513
are *h* laden, and I will give you .... Mt 11:28
For they bind *h* burdens and .... Mt 23:4   926
began to be sorrowful and very *h* .... Mt 26:37   85
for their eyes were *h* .... Mt 26:43   916
be sore amazed, and to be very *h* .... Mk 14:33   85
again, (for their eyes were *h* .... Mk 14:40   916
were with him were *h* with sleep .... Lk 9:32   916

HEBER (*he'-bur*) See EBER, HEBER'S, HEBERITES.
1. A son of Beriah.
H, and Malchiel.................................... Gen 46:17   2268
of *H*, the family of the Heberites .... Num 26:45   2268
H, and Malchiel, who is the father 1Chr 7:31   2268
H begat Japhlet, and Shomer, and 1Chr 7:32   2268
of Phalec, which was the son of *H* .... Lk 3:35   1443
2. Husband of Jael.
Now *H* the Kenite, which was of .... Judg 4:11   2268
of Jael the wife of *H* the Kenite .... Judg 4:17   2268
and the house of *H* the Kenite .... Judg 4:17   2268
Jael the wife of *H* the Kenite be .... Judg 5:24   2268
3. A son of Ezra.
H the father of Socho, and..................... 1Chr 4:18   2268
4. A son of Elpaal.
and Meshullam, and Hezeki, and *H* 1Chr 8:17   2268
5. A head of a Gadite family.
and Jorai, and Jachan, and Zia, and *H* .. 1Chr 5:13   5677
6. A son of Shashak.
And Ishpan, and *H*, and Eliel, ... 1Chr 8:22   5677

HEBERITES (*he'-bur-ites*) Descendants of Heber.
of Heber, the family of the *H*................... Num 26:45   2277

HEBER'S (*he'-burs*) Refers to Heber 2.
Then Jael *H* wife took a nail of.............. Judg 4:21   2268

HEBREW (*he'-broo*) See HEBREWESS, HEBREWS.
1. Descendants of Jacob.
had escaped, and told Abram the *H*....... Gen 14:13   5680
in an *H* unto us to mock us .... Gen 39:14   5680
The *H* servant, which thou hast .... Gen 39:17   5680
there with us a young man, an *H* .... Gen 41:12   5680
of Egypt spake to the *H* midwives .... Ex 1:15   5680
of a midwife to the *H* women .... Ex 1:16   5680
Because the *H* women are not as .... Ex 1:19   5680
to thee a nurse of the *H* women .... Ex 2:7   5680
he spied an Egyptian smiting an *H*........ Ex 2:11   5680
If thou buy an *H* servant, six .... Ex 21:2   5680
an *H* man, or an *H* woman, be .... Deut 15:12   5680
being an *H* or an Hebrewess, go .... Jer 34:9   5680
ye go every man his brother an *H* .... Jer 34:14   5680
And he said unto them, I am an *H* .... Jonah 1:9   5680
of Benjamin, an *H* of the Hebrews .... Phil 3:5   1446
2. A language.
letters of Greek, and Latin, and *H* .... Lk 23:38   1444
called in the *H* tongue Bethesda .... Jn 5:2   1447
called the Pavement, but in the *H* .... Jn 19:13   1447
which is called in the *H* Golgotha .... Jn 19:17   1447
and it was written in *H*, and Greek, ... Jn 19:20   1447
spake unto them in the *H* tongue .... Acts 21:40   1446
he spake in the *H* tongue to them .... Acts 22:2   1446
me, and saying in the *H* tongue .... Acts 26:14   1446
name in the *H* tongue is Abaddon .... Rev 9:11   1447
called in the *H* tongue Armageddon ...... Rev 16:16   1447

HEBREWESS (*he'-broo-ess*)
being an Hebrew or an *H*, go free .... Jer 34:9   5680

HEBREWS (*he'-brooz*) See HEBREWS'
away out of the land of the *H* .... Gen 40:15   5680
might not eat bread with the *H* .... Gen 43:32   5680
two men of the *H* strove together .... Ex 2:13   5680
God of the *H* hath met with us .... Ex 3:18   5680
The God of the *H* hath met with us .... Ex 5:3   5680
The LORD God of the *H* hath met .... Ex 7:16   5680
Thus saith the LORD God of the *H* .... Ex 9:1   5680
Thus saith the LORD God of the *H* .... Ex 9:13   5680
Thus saith the LORD God of the *H* .... Ex 10:3   5680
great shout in the camp of the *H* 1Sa 4:6   5680
ye be not servants unto the *H* 1Sa 4:9   5680
the land, saying, Let the *H* hear 1Sa 13:3   5680
some of the *H* went over Jordan to 1Sa 13:7   5680
Lest the *H* make them swords or 1Sa 13:19   5680
the *H* come forth out of the holes 1Sa 14:11   5680
Moreover the *H* that were with the 1Sa 14:21   5680
Philistines, What do these *H* here 1Sa 29:3   5680
of the Grecians against the *H*............... Acts 6:1   1445
Are they *H* 2Cor 11:22   1445
of Benjamin, an Hebrew of the *H*........... Phil 3:5   1445
Written to the *H* from Italy by .... Heb s

HEBREWS' (*he'-brooz*)
This is one of the *H* children .... Ex 2:6   5680

HEBRON (*he'-brun*) See HEBRONITES.
1. A city in Asher.
And *H*, and Rehob, and Hammon, and... Josh 19:28   2275
2. A city in Judah.
the plain of Mamre, which is in *H* .... Gen 13:18   2275
the same is *H* in the land of .... Gen 23:2   2275
the same is *H* in the land of .... Gen 23:19   2275
the city of Arbah, which is *H*................. Gen 35:27   2275
he sent him out of the vale of *H* .... Gen 37:14   2275
by the south, and came unto *H*............. Num 13:22   2275
(Now *H* was built seven years .... Num 13:22   2275
sent unto Hoham king of *H* .... Josh 10:3   2275
king of Jerusalem, the king of *H*........... Josh 10:5   2275
king of Jerusalem, the king of *H*........... Josh 10:23   2275
and all Israel with him, unto *H* .... Josh 10:36   2275
as he had done to *H*, so he did to .... Josh 10:39   2275
from the mountains, from *H* .... Josh 11:21   2275
the king of *H*, one .... Josh 12:10   2275
of Jephunneh *H* for an inheritance .... Josh 14:13   2275
H therefore became the .... Josh 14:14   2275
And the name of *H* before was .... Josh 14:15   2275
father of Anak, which city is *H* .... Josh 15:13   2275
and Kirjath-arba, which is *H*................. Josh 15:54   2275
and Kirjath-arba, which is *H*................. Josh 20:7   2275
father of Anak, which city is *H* .... Josh 21:11   2275
the priest *H* with her suburbs .... Josh 21:13   2275
the Canaanites that dwelt in *H*............. Judg 1:10   2275
(now the name of *H* before was .... Judg 1:10   2275
they gave *H* unto Caleb, as Moses .... Judg 1:20   2275
top of an hill that is before *H* .... Judg 16:3   2275
And to them which were in *H* 1Sa 30:31   2275
And he said, Unto *H* 2Sa 2:1   2275
and they dwelt in the cities of *H* 2Sa 2:3   2275

in _H_ over the house of Judah was 2Sa 2:11   2275
they came to _H_ at break of day 2Sa 2:32   2275
And unto David were sons born in _H_ 2Sa 3:2   2275
These were born to David in _H_ 2Sa 3:5   2275
speak in the ears of David in _H_ 2Sa 3:19   2275
So Abner came to David to _H_ 2Sa 3:20   2275
but Abner was not with David in _H_ 2Sa 3:22   2275
And when Abner was returned to _H_ 2Sa 3:27   2275
And they buried Abner in _H_ 2Sa 3:32   2275
heard that Abner was dead in _H_ 2Sa 4:1   2275
of Ish-bosheth unto David to _H_ 2Sa 4:8   2275
hanged them up over the pool in _H_ 2Sa 4:12   2275
it in the sepulchre of Abner in _H_ 2Sa 4:12   2275
tribes of Israel to David unto _H_ 2Sa 5:1   2275
of Israel came to the king to _H_ 2Sa 5:3   2275
with them in _H_ before the LORD 2Sa 5:3   2275
In _H_ he reigned over Judah seven 2Sa 5:5   2275
after he was come from _H_ 2Sa 5:13   2275
I have vowed unto the LORD, in _H_ 2Sa 15:7   2275
So he arose, and went to _H_ 2Sa 15:9   2275
shall say, Absalom reigneth in _H_ 2Sa 15:10   2275
seven years reigned he in _H_ 1Kin 2:11   2275
which were born unto him in _H_ 1Chr 3:1   2275
Amram, Izhar, and _H_, and Uzziel 1Chr 6:2   2275
they gave them _H_ in the land of 1Chr 6:55   2275
the cities of Judah, namely, ... 1Chr 6:57   2275
themselves to David unto _H_ 1Chr 11:1   2275
elders of Israel to the king to _H_ 1Chr 11:3   2275
with them in _H_ before the LORD 1Chr 11:3   2275
to the war, and came to David to _H_ 1Chr 12:23   2275
came with a perfect heart to _H_ 1Chr 12:38   2275
seven years reigned he in _H_ 1Chr 29:27   2275
And Zorah, and Aijalon, and _H_ 2Chr 11:10   2275

    3. A son of Kohath.

Amram, and Izhar, and _H_, and Uzziel .... Ex 6:18   2275
Amram, and Izehar, _H_, and Uzziel .... Num 3:19   2275
These six were born unto him in _H_ 1Chr 3:4   2275
were, Amram, and Izhar, and _H_ 1Chr 6:18   2275
Amram, Izhar, _H_, and Uzziel, four 1Chr 23:12   2275
Of the sons of _H_ 1Chr 23:19   2275
And the sons of _H_ 1Chr 24:23   2275

    4. A son of Mareshah.

sons of Mareshah the father of _H_ 1Chr 2:42   2275
And the sons of _H_ 1Chr 2:43   2275
Of the sons of _H_ 1Chr 15:9   2275

HEBRONITES _(he'-brun-ites) Descendants of Hebron 3._
and the family of the _H_, and the .... Num 3:27   2276
the Libnites, the family of the _H_ .... Num 26:58   2276
and the Izharites, the _H_, and the 1Chr 26:23   2276
And of the _H_, Hashabiah and his 1Chr 26:30   2276
Among the _H_ was Jerijah the chief 1Chr 26:31   2276
even among the _H_, according to the 1Chr 26:31   2276

HEDGE
Hast not thou made an _h_ about him ...... Job 1:10   7753
slothful man is as an _h_ of thorns .... Prov 15:19   4881
and whoso breaketh an _h_, a serpent ...... Eccl 10:8   1447
I will take away the _h_ thereof .... Is 5:5   4881
neither made up the _h_ for the .... Eze 13:5   1447
them, that should make up the _h_ .... Eze 22:30   1447
I will _h_ up thy way with thorns, ... Hos 2:6   7753
upright is sharper than a thorn _h_ .... Mic 7:4   4534
set an _h_ about it, and digged a .... Mk 12:1   _5418_

HEDGED
way is hid, and whom God hath _h_ in...... Job 3:23   5526
He hath _h_ me about, that I cannot........ Lam 3:7   1443
_h_ it round about, and digged a....... Mt 21:33   _5418,4060_

HEDGES
that dwelt among plants and _h_ 1Chr 4:23   1448
hast thou then broken down her _h_......... Ps 80:12   1447
Thou hast broken down all his _h_ .... Ps 89:40   1448
lament, and run to and fro by the _h_ .... Jer 49:3   1448
camp in the _h_ in the cold day.............. Nah 3:17   1448
Go out into the highways and _h_ .... Lk 14:23   _5418_

HEED
Take _h_ that thou speak not to .... Gen 31:24   8104
Take thou _h_ that thou speak not............ Gen 31:29   8104
take _h_ to yourselves, that ye go .... Ex 10:28   8104
Take _h_ to yourselves, that ye go .... Ex 19:12   8104
Take _h_ to thyself, lest thou make......... Ex 34:12   8104
Must I not take _h_ to speak that............ Num 23:12   8104
take ye good _h_ unto yourselves .... Deut 2:4   8104
Only take _h_ to thyself, and keep .... Deut 4:9   8104
therefore good _h_ unto yourselves .... Deut 4:15   8104
Take _h_ unto yourselves, lest ye .... Deut 4:23   8104
Take _h_ to yourselves, that your .... Deut 11:16   8104
Take _h_ to thyself that thou offer .... Deut 12:13   8104
Take _h_ to thyself that thou .... Deut 12:19   8104
Take _h_ to thyself that thou be .... Deut 12:30   8104
Take _h_ in the plague of leprosy, ... Deut 24:8   8104

unto all Israel, saying, Take _h_ .... Deut 27:9   5535
But take diligent _h_ to do the .... Josh 22:5   8104
Take good _h_ therefore unto .... Josh 23:11   8104
take _h_ to thyself until the 1Sa 19:2   8104
But Amasa took no _h_ to the sword........ 2Sa 20:10   8104
thy children take _h_ to their way 1Kin 2:4   8104
thy children take _h_ to their way 1Kin 8:25   8104
But Jehu took no _h_ to walk in the 2Kin 10:31   8104
if thou takest _h_ to fulfil the 1Chr 22:13   8104
Take _h_ now 1Chr 28:10   7200
yet so that thy children take _h_............... 2Chr 6:16   8104
to the judges, Take _h_ what ye do 2Chr 19:6   7200
take _h_ and do it 2Chr 19:7   8104
so that they will take _h_ to do 2Chr 33:8   8104
Take _h_ now that ye fail not to do .... Ezr 4:22   2095
Take _h_, regard not iniquity................... Job 36:21   8104
I said, I will take _h_ to my ways .... Ps 39:1   8104
by taking _h_ thereto according to .... Ps 119:9   8104
doer giveth _h_ to false lips .... Prov 17:4   7181
Also take no _h_ unto all words .... Eccl 7:21   5414,3820
yea, he gave good _h_, and sought .... Eccl 12:9   238
And say unto him, Take _h_, and be .... Is 7:4   8104
hearkened diligently with much _h_ .... Is 21:7   7182
Take ye _h_ every one of his .... Jer 9:4   8104
Take _h_ to yourselves, and bear no .... Jer 17:21   8104
let us not give _h_ to any of his .... Jer 18:18   7181
Give _h_ to me, O LORD, and hearken .... Jer 18:19   7181
left off to take _h_ to the LORD .... Hos 4:10   8104
Therefore take _h_ to your spirit .... Mal 2:15   8104
therefore take _h_ to your spirit .... Mal 2:16   8104
Take _h_ that ye do not your alms .... Mt 6:1   _4337_
Then Jesus said unto them, Take _h_ ..... Mt 16:6   _3708_
Take _h_ that ye despise not one of .... Mt 18:10   _3708_
Take _h_ that no man deceive you .... Mt 24:4   _991_
unto them, Take _h_ what ye hear .... Mk 4:24   _991_
he charged them, saying, Take _h_ .... Mk 8:15   _3708_
Take _h_ lest any man deceive you .... Mk 13:5   _991_
But take _h_ to yourselves .... Mk 13:9   _991_
But take ye _h_ .... Mk 13:23   _991_
Take ye _h_, watch and pray .... Mk 13:33   _991_
Take _h_ therefore how ye hear .... Lk 8:18   _991_
Take _h_ therefore that the light .... Lk 11:35   _4648_
And he said unto them, Take _h_ .... Lk 12:15   _3708_
Take _h_ to yourselves .... Lk 17:3   _4337_
Take _h_ that ye be not deceived .... Lk 21:8   _991_
take _h_ to yourselves, lest at any .... Lk 21:34   _4337_
he gave _h_ unto them, expecting to .... Acts 3:5   _1907_
take _h_ to yourselves what ye .... Acts 5:35   _4337_
_h_ unto those things which Philip............ Acts 8:6   _4337_
To whom they all gave _h_, from the .... Acts 8:10   _4337_
Take _h_ therefore unto yourselves, ... Acts 20:28   _4337_
saying, Take _h_ what thou doest .... Acts 22:26   _3708_
take _h_ lest he also spare not................. Rom 11:21
But let every man take _h_ how he........... 1Cor 3:10   _991_
But take _h_ lest by any means this .... 1Cor 8:9   _991_
he standeth take _h_ lest he fall............... 1Cor 10:12   _991_
take _h_ that ye be not consumed .... Gal 5:15   _991_
Take _h_ to the ministry which thou .... Col 4:17   _991_
Neither give _h_ to fables and .... 1Ti 1:4   _4337_
giving _h_ to seducing spirits, and .... 1Ti 4:1   _4337_
Take _h_ unto thyself, and unto the .... 1Ti 4:16   _1907_
Not giving _h_ to Jewish fables, and .... Titus 1:14   _4337_
_h_ to the things which we have .... Heb 2:1   _4337_
Take _h_, brethren, lest there be .... Heb 3:12   _991_
ye do well that ye take _h_ .... 2Pet 1:19   _433_

HEEL
head, and thou shalt bruise his _h_ .... Gen 3:15   6119
and his hand took hold on Esau's _h_....... Gen 25:26   6119
The gin shall take him by the _h_............. Job 18:9   6119
hath lifted up his _h_ against me .... Ps 41:9   6119
his brother by the _h_ in the womb........... Hos 12:3   6117
hath lifted up his _h_ against me .... Jn 13:18   _4418_

HEELS
the path, that biteth the horse _h_ .... Gen 49:17   6119
a print upon the _h_ of my feet .... Job 13:27   8328
of my _h_ shall compass me about .... Ps 49:5   6120
discovered, and thy _h_ made bare .... Jer 13:22   6119

HEGAI _(he'-gahee) See_ HEGE. _Servant of King Ahasu-_
    erus.
the palace, to the custody of _H_ .... Est 2:8   1896
king's house, to the custody of _H_ .... Est 2:8   1896
but what _H_ the king's chamberlain .... Est 2:15   1896

HEGE _(he'-ghe) See_ HEGAI. _Same as Hegai._
unto the custody of _H_ the king's .... Est 2:3   1896

HEIFER
Take me an _h_ of three years old, ... Gen 15:9   5697
bring thee a red _h_ without spot .... Num 19:2   6510
one shall burn the _h_ in his sight .... Num 19:5   6510
the midst of the burning of the _h_ .... Num 19:6   6510

gather up the ashes of the *h* .... Num 19:9   6510
of the *h* shall wash his clothes .... Num 19:10   6510
burnt *h* of purification for sin .... Num 19:17
of that city shall take an *h* .... Deut 21:3   5697
down the *h* unto a rough valley .... Deut 21:4   5697
h that is beheaded in the valley .... Deut 21:6   5697
If ye had not plowed with my *h* .... Judg 14:18   5697
Take an *h* with thee, and say, I am 1Sa 16:2   5697
Zoar, an *h* of three years old .... Is 15:5   5697
Egypt is like a very fair *h* .... Jer 46:20   5697
as an *h* of three years old .... Jer 48:34   5697
are grown fat as the *h* at grass .... Jer 50:11   5697
slideth back as a backsliding *h* .... Hos 4:16   6510
Ephraim is as an *h* that is taught .... Hos 10:11   5697
the ashes of an *h* sprinkling the .... Heb 9:13   *1151*

HEIFER'S
shall strike off the *h* neck there .... Deut 21:4   5697

HEIGHT
the *h* of it thirty cubits........................ Gen 6:15   6967
a cubit and a half the *h* thereof .... Ex 25:10   6967
a cubit and a half the *h* thereof .... Ex 25:23   6967
the *h* thereof shall be three .... Ex 27:1   6967
the *h* five cubits of fine twined.............. Ex 27:18   6967
two cubits shall be the *h* thereof.......... Ex 30:2   6967
and a cubit and a half the *h* of it .... Ex 37:1   6967
a cubit and a half the *h* thereof .... Ex 37:10   6967
and two cubits was the *h* of it .... Ex 37:25   6967
and three cubits the *h* thereof.............. Ex 38:1   6967
the *h* in the breadth were five .... Ex 38:18   6967
or on the *h* of his stature 1Sa 16:7   1364
whose *h* was six cubits and a span 1Sa 17:4   1363
the *h* thereof thirty cubits 1Kin 6:2   6967
and twenty cubits in the *h* thereof.......... 1Kin 6:20   6967
The *h* of the one cherub was ten 1Kin 6:26   6967
the *h* thereof thirty cubits, upon 1Kin 7:2   6967
the *h* of the one chapiter was 1Kin 7:16   6967
the *h* of the other chapiter was 1Kin 7:16   6967
about, and his *h* was five cubits 1Kin 7:23   6967
and three cubits the *h* of it 1Kin 7:27   6967
the *h* of a wheel was a cubit and 1Kin 7:32   6967
come up to the *h* of the mountains 2Kin 19:23   4791
The *h* of the one pillar was 2Kin 25:17   6967
the *h* of the chapiter three.................... 2Kin 25:17   6967
the *h* was an hundred and twenty 2Chr 3:4   1363
and ten cubits the *h* thereof 2Chr 4:1   6967
and five cubits the *h* thereof 2Chr 4:2   6967
and raised it up a very great *h* 2Chr 33:14   1361
the *h* thereof threescore cubits, ... Ezr 6:3   7312
Is not God in the *h* of heaven.................. Job 22:12   1363
behold the *h* of the stars, how .... Job 22:12   7218
down from the *h* of his sanctuary.......... Ps 102:19   4791
The heaven for *h*, and the earth .... Prov 25:3   7312
in the depth, or in the *h* above.............. Is 7:11   1361
come up to the *h* of the mountains .... Is 37:24   4791
enter into the *h* of his border .... Is 37:24   4791
come and sing in the *h* of Zion.............. Jer 31:12   4791
that holdest the *h* of the hill .... Jer 49:16   4791
fortify the *h* of her strength.................. Jer 51:53   4791
the *h* of one pillar was eighteen.............. Jer 52:21   6967
the *h* of one chapiter was five .... Jer 52:22   6967
In the mountain of the *h* of .... Eze 17:23   4791
she appeared in her *h* with the.............. Eze 19:11   1363
the mountain of the *h* of Israel .... Eze 20:40   4791
Therefore his *h* was exalted above .... Eze 31:5   6967
thou hast lifted up thyself in *h* .... Eze 31:10   6967
his heart is lifted up in his *h* .... Eze 31:10   1363
exalt themselves for their *h*.................... Eze 31:14   6967
their trees stand up in their *h*................ Eze 31:14   1363
and fill the valleys with thy *h* .... Eze 32:5   7419
and the *h*, one reed .... Eze 40:5   6967
I saw also the *h* of the house .... Eze 41:8   1364
whose *h* was threescore cubits, and .... Dan 3:1   7314
earth, and the *h* thereof was great .... Dan 4:10   7314
the *h* thereof reached unto heaven .... Dan 4:11   7314
whose *h* reached unto the heaven, ... Dan 4:20   7314
whose *h* was like the *h* of .... Amos 2:9   1363
was like the *h* of the cedars .... Amos 2:9   1363
Nor *h*, nor depth, nor any other .... Rom 8:39   *5313*
and length, and depth, and *h* .... Eph 3:18   *5311*
breadth and the *h* of it are equal .... Rev 21:16   *5311*

HEIGHTS
praise him in the *h* .... Ps 148:1   4791
ascend above the *h* of the clouds .... Is 14:14   1116

HEINOUS
For this is an *h* crime.............................. Job 31:11   2154

HEIR
one born in my house is mine *h* .... Gen 15:3   3423
saying, This shall not be thine *h* .... Gen 15:4   3423

thine own bowels shall be thine *h* .... Gen 15:4   3423
shall not be *h* with my son...................... Gen 21:10   3423
and we will destroy the *h* also 2Sa 14:7   3423
that is *h* to her mistress .... Prov 30:23   3423
hath he no *h*?...................................... Jer 49:1   3423
then shall Israel be *h* unto them .... Jer 49:2   3423
Yet will I bring an *h* unto thee .... Mic 1:15   3423
among themselves, This is the *h* .... Mt 21:38   *2818*
among themselves, This is the *h* .... Mk 12:7   *2818*
themselves, saying, This is the *h* ...... Lk 20:14   *2818*
he should be the *h* of the world.............. Rom 4:13   *2818*
Now I say, That the *h*, as long as .... Gal 4:1   *2818*
then an *h* of God through Christ.......... Gal 4:7   *2818*
of the bondwoman shall not be *h*.......... Gal 4:30   *2816*
he hath appointed *h* of all things .... Heb 1:2   *2818*
became *h* of the righteousness .... Heb 11:7   *2818*

HEIRS
be heir unto them that were his *h* .... Jer 49:2   3423
if they which are of the law be *h* .... Rom 4:14   *2818*
And if children, then *h*.......................... Rom 8:17   *2818*
h of God, and joint-heirs with .... Rom 8:17   *2818*
h according to the promise .... Gal 3:29   *2818*
we should be made *h* according to .... Titus 3:7   *2818*
them who shall be *h* of salvation.......... Heb 1:14   *2816*
abundantly to shew unto the *h* of .... Heb 6:17   *2818*
the *h* with him of the same .... Heb 11:9   *4789*
h of the kingdom which he hath .... Jas 2:5   *2818*
as being *h* together of the grace............ 1Pet 3:7   *4789*

HELAH *(he'-lah) A wife of Asher.*
father of Tekoa had two wives, H............ 1Chr 4:5   2458
And the sons of *H* were, Zereth, and 1Chr 4:7   2458

HELAM *(he'-lam) A place east of the Jordan.*
and they came to H.................................. 2Sa 10:16   2431
passed over Jordan, and came to H 2Sa 10:17   2431

HELBAH *(hel'-bah) A town in Asher.*
of Ahlab, nor of Achzib, nor of H .... Judg 1:31   2462

HELBON *(hel'-bon) A city near Damascus.*
in the wine of H, and white wool .... Eze 27:18   2463

HELD
man wondering at her *h* his peace .... Gen 24:21   2790
Jacob *h* his peace until they were .... Gen 34:5   2790
he *h* up his father's hand, to.................. Gen 48:17   8557
when Moses *h* up his hand, that............ Ex 17:11   7311
the loops *h* one curtain to .... Ex 36:12   6901
And Aaron *h* his peace.......................... Lev 10:3   1826
h his peace at her in the day .... Num 30:7   2790
h his peace at her, and disallowed .... Num 30:11   2790
because he *h* his peace at her in .... Num 30:14   2790
h the lamps in their left hands, ... Judg 7:20   2388
the lad that *h* him by the hand .... Judg 16:26   2388
And when she *h* it, he measured six ...... Ruth 3:15   270
But he *h* his peace 1Sa 10:27   2790
he *h* a feast in his house, like 1Sa 25:36
for Joab *h* back the people.................... 2Sa 18:16   2820
And at that time Solomon *h* a feast 1Kin 8:65   6213
But the people *h* their peace.................. 2Kin 18:36   2790
and *h* three thousand baths.................... 2Chr 4:5   3557
half of them *h* both the spears .... Neh 4:16   2388
and with the other hand *h* a weapon ...... Neh 4:17   2388
half of them *h* the spears from .... Neh 4:21   2388
Then *h* they their peace, and found........ Neh 5:8   2790
the king *h* out to Esther the .... Est 5:2   3447
I had *h* my tongue, although the .... Est 7:4   2790
Then the king *h* out the golden .... Est 8:4   3447
My foot hath *h* his steps, his way .... Job 23:11   270
The nobles *h* their peace, and .... Job 29:10   2244
whose mouth must be *h* in with bit .... Ps 32:9   1102
I *h* my peace, even from good................ Ps 39:2   2814
thy mercy, O Lᴏʀᴅ, *h* me up.................. Ps 94:18   5582
I *h* him, and would not let him go, ... Song 3:4   270
the king is *h* in the galleries .... Song 7:5   631
But they *h* their peace, and.................... Is 36:21   2790
have not I *h* my peace even of old .... Is 57:11   2814
took them captives *h* them fast .... Jer 50:33   2388
when he *h* up his right hand and .... Dan 12:7   7311
h a council against him, how they .... Mt 12:14   2983
But Jesus *h* his peace .... Mt 26:63   4623
h him by the feet, and worshipped .... Mt 28:9   2902
But they *h* their peace .... Mk 3:4   4623
But they *h* their peace .... Mk 9:34   4623
But he *h* his peace, and answered .... Mk 14:61   4623
the morning the chief priests *h* a.......... Mk 15:1   4160
And they *h* their peace .... Lk 14:4   2270
at his answer, and *h* their peace .... Lk 20:26   4601
the men that *h* Jesus mocked him, ... Lk 22:63   4912
lame man which was healed *h* Peter ...... Acts 3:11   2902
they *h* their peace, and glorified............ Acts 11:18   2270
part *h* with the Jews, and part .... Acts 14:4   2258

And after they had *h* their peace .... Acts 15:13   4601
that being dead wherein we were *h* .... Rom 7:6   2722
and for the testimony which they *h* .... Rev 6:9   2192

HELDAI (hel'-dahee) See HELED, HELEM.
   1. A sanctuary servant.
month was *H* the Netophathite 1Chr 27:15   2469
   2. An honored exile.
them of the captivity, even of *H* .... Zec 6:10   2469

HELEB (he'-leb) See HELED. A "mighty man" of David.
H the son of Baanah, a 2Sa 23:29   2460

HELECH See HELEK.

HELED (he'-led) See HELEB, HELDAI. Same as Heleb.
H the son of Baanah the 1Chr 11:30   2466

HELEK (he'-lek) See HELEKITES. A son of Gilead.
of *H*, the family of the Helekites .... Num 26:30   2507
Abiezer, and for the children of *H* .... Josh 17:2   2507

HELEKITES (he'-lek-ites) Descendants of Helek.
of Helek, the family of the *H* .... Num 26:30   2516

HELEM (he'-lem)
   1. A descendant of Asher.
And the sons of his brother *H* 1Chr 7:35   2494
   2. Same as Heldai.
And the crowns shall be to *H* .... Zec 6:14   2494

HELEPH (he'-lef) A town in Naphtali.
And their coast was from *H* .... Josh 19:33   2501

HELEZ (he'-lez)
   1. A "mighty man" of David.
H the Paltite, Ira the son of 2Sa 23:26   2503
the Harorite, *H* the Pelonite, ... 1Chr 11:27   2503
seventh month was *H* the Pelonite 1Chr 27:10   2503
   2. A son of Azariah.
And Azariah begat *H*, and Helez 1Chr 2:39   2503
begat Helez, and *H* begat Eleasah, ... 1Chr 2:39   2503

HELI (he'-li) See ELI. Father of Joseph; ancestor of Jesus.
of Joseph, which was the son of *H* .... Lk 3:23   2242

HELKAI (hel'-kahee) A priest.
Adna; of Meraioth, *H* .... Neh 12:15   2517

HELKATH (hel'-kath) See HELKATH-HAZZURIM, HUKOK.
   A town in Asher.
And their border was *H*, and Hali, ... Josh 19:25   2520
H with her suburbs, and Rehob with ...... Josh 21:31   2520

HELKATH-HAZZURIM (hel'-kath-haz'zu-rim) A plain
   near the pool of Gibeon.
wherefore that place was called *H* 2Sa 2:16   2521

HELL
and shall burn unto the lowest *h* .... Deut 32:22   7585
The sorrows of *h* compassed me 2Sa 22:6   7585
deeper than *h* .... Job 11:8   7585
H is naked before him, and .... Job 26:6   7585
The wicked shall be turned into *h* .... Ps 9:17   7585
thou wilt not leave my soul in *h* .... Ps 16:10   7585
The sorrows of *h* compassed me .... Ps 18:5   7585
and let them go down quick into *h* .... Ps 55:15   7585
my soul from the lowest *h* .... Ps 86:13   7585
the pains of *h* gat hold upon me .... Ps 116:3   7585
if I make my bed in *h*, behold, ... Ps 139:8   7585
her steps take hold on *h* .... Prov 5:5   7585
Her house is the way to *h* .... Prov 7:27   7585
Her guests are in the depths of *h* .... Prov 9:18   7585
H and destruction are before the .... Prov 15:11   7585
that he may depart from *h* beneath .... Prov 15:24   7585
and shalt deliver his soul from *h* .... Prov 23:14   7585
H and destruction are never full .... Prov 27:20   7585
Therefore *h* hath enlarged herself .... Is 5:14   7585
H from beneath is moved for thee .... Is 14:9   7585
thou shalt be brought down to *h* .... Is 14:15   7585
with *h* are we at agreement .... Is 28:15   7585
agreement with *h* shall not stand .... Is 28:18   7585
didst debase thyself even unto *h* .... Is 57:9   7585
when I cast him down to *h* with .... Eze 31:16   7585
They also went down into *h* with .... Eze 31:17   7585
of *h* with them that help him .... Eze 32:21   7585
which are gone down to *h* with .... Eze 32:27   7585
Though they dig into *h*, thence .... Amos 9:2   7585
out of the belly of *h* cried I .... Jonah 2:2   7585
who enlargeth his desire as *h* .... Hab 2:5   7585
shall be in danger of *h* fire. .... Mt 5:22   1067
whole body should be cast into *h* .... Mt 5:29   1067
whole body should be cast into *h* .... Mt 5:30   1067
to destroy both soul and body in *h* .... Mt 10:28   1067
shalt be brought down to *h* .... Mt 11:23   86
the gates of *h* shall not prevail .... Mt 16:18   86
two eyes to be cast into *h* fire .... Mt 18:9   1067
the child of *h* than yourselves .... Mt 23:15   1067

can ye escape the damnation of *h* .... Mt 23:33   1067
having two hands to go into *h* .... Mk 9:43   1067
having two feet to be cast into *h* .... Mk 9:45   1067
two eyes to be cast into *h* fire .... Mk 9:47   1067
heaven, shalt be thrust down to *h* .... Lk 10:15   86
killed hath power to cast into *h* .... Lk 12:5   1067
in *h* he lift up his eyes, being .... Lk 16:23   86
thou wilt not leave my soul in *h* .... Acts 2:27   86
that his soul was not left in *h* .... Acts 2:31   86
and it is set on fire of *h* .... Jas 3:6   1067
sinned, but cast them down to *h* 2Pet 2:4   5020
and have the keys of *h* and of death ...... Rev 1:18   86
was Death, and *H* followed with him ...... Rev 6:8   86
h delivered up the dead which .... Rev 20:13   86
h were cast into the lake of fire .... Rev 20:14   86

HELLENISTS See GRECIANS.

HELM
turned about with a very small *h* .... Jas 3:4   4079

HELMET
he had an *h* of brass upon his 1Sa 17:5   3553
he put an *h* of brass upon his 1Sa 17:38   6959
an *h* of salvation upon his head .... Is 59:17   3553
and shield and *h* round about .... Eze 23:24   6959
hanged the shield and *h* in thee .... Eze 27:10   3553
all of them with shield and *h* .... Eze 38:5   3553
take the *h* of salvation, and the .... Eph 6:17   4030
and for an *h*, the hope of 1Th 5:8   4030

HELMETS
the host shields, and spears, and *h* 2Chr 26:14   3553
and stand forth with your *h* .... Jer 46:4   3553

HELON (he'-lon) Father of Eliab.
Eliab the son of *H* .... Num 1:9   2497
Eliab the son of *H* shall be .... Num 2:7   2497
the third day Eliab the son of *H* .... Num 7:24   2497
offering of Eliab the son of *H* .... Num 7:29   2497
of Zebulun was Eliab the son of *H* .... Num 10:16   2497

HELP
I will make him an *h* meet for him .... Gen 2:18   5828
was not found an *h* meet for him .... Gen 2:20   5828
of thy father, who shall *h* thee .... Gen 49:25   5826
of my father, said he, was mine *h* .... Ex 18:4   5828
and wouldest forbear to *h* him .... Ex 23:5   5800
thou shalt surely *h* with him .... Ex 23:5   5800
thou shalt surely *h* him to lift .... Deut 22:4   6965
h you, and be your protection .... Deut 32:38   5826
be thou an *h* to him from his .... Deut 33:7   5828
rideth upon the heaven in thy *h* .... Deut 33:26   5828
by the LORD, the shield of thy *h* .... Deut 33:29   5828
mighty men of valour, and *h* them .... Josh 1:14   5826
h me, that we may smite Gibeon .... Josh 10:4   5826
us quickly, and save us, and *h* us .... Josh 10:6   5826
of Gezer came up to *h* Lachish .... Josh 10:33   5826
came not to the *h* of the LORD .... Judg 5:23   5833
to the *h* of the LORD against the .... Judg 5:23   5833
the sun be hot, ye shall have *h* 1Sa 11:9   8668
for me, then thou shalt *h* me 2Sa 10:11   3447
thee, then I will come and *h* thee 2Sa 10:11   3467
So the Syrians feared to *h* the 2Sa 10:19   3467
and did obeisance, and said, *H* 2Sa 14:4   3467
cried a woman unto him, saying, *H*........ 2Kin 6:26   3467
h thee, whence shall I *h* thee 2Kin 6:27   3467
be come peaceably unto me to *h* me 1Chr 12:17   5826
day there came to David to *h* him 1Chr 12:22   5826
came to *h* Hadarezer king of Zobah 1Chr 18:5   5826
for me, then thou shalt *h* me 1Chr 19:12   8668
for thee, then I will *h* thee 1Chr 19:12   3467
neither would the Syrians *h* the 1Chr 19:19   3467
of Israel to *h* Solomon his son 1Chr 22:17   5826
it is nothing with thee to *h* 2Chr 14:11   5826
h us, O LORD our God 2Chr 14:11   5826
Shouldest thou *h* the ungodly 2Chr 19:2   5826
together, to ask *h* of the LORD 2Chr 20:4
then thou wilt hear and *h* 2Chr 20:9   3467
for God hath power to *h*, and to 2Chr 25:8   5826
to *h* the king against the enemy 2Chr 26:13   5826
the kings of Assyria to *h* him 2Chr 28:16   5826
gods of the kings of Syria *h* them 2Chr 28:23   5826
to them, that they may *h* me 2Chr 28:23   5826
brethren the Levites did *h* them 2Chr 29:34   2388
and they did *h* him 2Chr 32:3   5826
us is the LORD our God to *h* us 2Chr 32:8   5826
of his place *h* them with silver .... Ezr 1:4   5375
horsemen to *h* us against the .... Ezr 8:22   5826
Is not my *h* in me .... Job 6:13   5833
neither will he *h* the evil doers .... Job 8:20   2388
and him that had none to *h* him .... Job 29:12   5826
when I saw my *h* in the gate .... Job 31:21   5833
There is no *h* for him in God .... Ps 3:2   3444

H, LORD; for the godly	Ps 12:1	3467
Send thee *h* from the sanctuary,	Ps 20:2	5828
for there is none to *h*	Ps 22:11	5826
O my strength, haste thee to *h* me	Ps 22:19	5833
thou hast been my *h*	Ps 27:9	5833
he is our *h* and our shield	Ps 33:20	5828
buckler, and stand up for mine *h*	Ps 35:2	5833
And the LORD shall *h* them, and	Ps 37:40	5826
Make haste to *h* me, O Lord my	Ps 38:22	5833
O LORD, make haste to *h* me	Ps 40:13	5833
thou art my *h* and my deliverer	Ps 40:17	5833
him for the *h* of his countenance	Ps 42:5	3444
Arise for our *h*, and redeem us for	Ps 44:26	5833
a very present *h* in trouble	Ps 46:1	5833
God shall *h* her, and that right	Ps 46:5	5826
awake to my *h*, and behold	Ps 59:4	7125
Give us *h* from trouble	Ps 60:11	5833
for vain is the *h* of man	Ps 60:11	8668
Because thou hast been my *h*	Ps 63:7	5833
make haste to *h* me, O LORD	Ps 70:1	5833
thou art my *h* and my deliverer	Ps 70:5	5828
O my God, make haste for my *h*	Ps 71:12	5833
H us, O God of our salvation, for	Ps 79:9	5826
I have laid *h* upon one that is	Ps 89:19	5828
Unless the LORD had been my *h*	Ps 94:17	5833
fell down, and there was none to *h*	Ps 107:12	5826
Give us *h* from trouble	Ps 108:12	5833
for vain is the *h* of man	Ps 108:12	8668
H me, O LORD my God	Ps 109:26	5826
he is their *h* and their shield	Ps 115:9	5828
he is their *h* and their shield	Ps 115:10	5828
he is their *h* and their shield	Ps 115:11	5828
my part with them that *h* me	Ps 118:7	5826
h thou me	Ps 119:86	5826
Let thine hand *h* me	Ps 119:173	5826
and let thy judgments *h* me	Ps 119:175	5826
hills, from whence cometh my *h*	Ps 121:1	5828
My *h* cometh from the LORD, which	Ps 121:2	5828
Our *h* is in the name of the LORD,	Ps 124:8	5828
son of man, in whom there is no *h*	Ps 146:3	8668
hath the God of Jacob for his *h*	Ps 146:5	5828
he hath not another to *h* him up	Eccl 4:10	6965
to whom will ye flee for *h*	Is 10:3	5833
whither we flee for *h* to be	Is 20:6	5833
nor be an *h* nor profit, but a	Is 30:5	5828
For the Egyptians shall *h* in vain	Is 30:7	5826
them that go down to Egypt for *h*	Is 31:1	5833
against the *h* of them that work	Is 31:2	5833
yea, I will *h* thee	Is 41:10	5826
I will *h* thee	Is 41:13	5826
I will *h* thee, saith the LORD, and	Is 41:14	5826
from the womb, which will *h* thee	Is 44:2	5826
For the Lord GOD will *h* me	Is 50:7	5826
Behold, the Lord GOD will *h* me	Is 50:9	5826
I looked, and there was none to *h*	Is 63:5	5826
which is come forth to *h* you	Jer 37:7	5833
of the enemy, and none did *h* her	Lam 1:7	5826
eyes as yet failed for our vain *h*	Lam 4:17	5833
all that are about him to *h* him	Eze 12:14	5828
of hell with them that *h* him	Eze 32:21	5826
the chief princes, came to *h* me	Dan 10:13	5826
shall be holpen with a little *h*	Dan 11:34	5828
to his end, and none shall *h* him	Dan 11:45	5826
but in me is thine *h*	Hos 13:9	5828
him, saying, Lord, *h* me	Mt 15:25	997
have compassion on us, and *h* us	Mk 9:22	997
h thou mine unbelief	Mk 9:24	997
that they should come and *h* them	Lk 5:7	4815
bid her therefore that she *h* me	Lk 10:40	4878
Come over into Macedonia, and *h* us	Acts 16:9	997
Crying out, Men of Israel, *h*	Acts 21:28	997
therefore obtained *h* of God	Acts 26:22	1947
h those women which laboured with	Phil 4:3	4815
find grace to *h* in time of need	Heb 4:16	996

HELPED

h them, and watered their flock	Ex 2:17	3467
Hitherto hath the LORD *h* us	1Sa 7:12	5826
and they following Adonijah *h* him	1Kin 1:7	5826
thirty and two kings that *h* him	1Kin 20:16	5826
they were *h* against them, and the	1Chr 5:20	5826
but they *h* them not	1Chr 12:19	5826
they *h* David against the band of	1Chr 12:21	5826
when God *h* the Levites that bare	1Chr 15:26	5826
cried out, and the LORD *h* him	2Chr 18:31	5826
every one to destroy another	2Chr 20:23	5826
God *h* him against the Philistines	2Chr 26:7	5826
for he was marvellously *h*	2Chr 26:15	5826
but he *h* him not	2Chr 28:21	5826
and Shabbethai the Levite *h* them	Ezr 10:15	5826
officers of the king, *h* the Jews	Est 9:3	5375

How hast thou *h* him that is	Job 26:2	5826
heart trusted in him, and I am *h*	Ps 28:7	5826
I was brought low, and he *h* me	Ps 116:6	3467
but the LORD *h* me	Ps 118:13	5826
They *h* every one his neighbour	Is 41:6	5826
a day of salvation have I *h* thee	Is 49:8	5826
they *h* forward the affliction	Zec 1:15	5826
h them much which had believed	Acts 18:27	4820
And the earth *h* the woman, and the	Rev 12:16	997

HELPER

any left, nor any *h* for Israel	2Kin 14:26	5826
my calamity, they have no *h*	Job 30:13	5826
thou art the *h* of the fatherless	Ps 10:14	5826
LORD, be thou my *h*	Ps 30:10	5826
Behold, God is mine *h*	Ps 54:4	5826
poor also, and him that hath no *h*	Ps 72:12	5826
Zidon every *h* that remaineth	Jer 47:4	5826
our *h* in Christ, and Stachys my	Rom 16:9	4904
may boldly say, The Lord is my *h*	Heb 13:6	998

HELPERS

the mighty men, *h* of the war	1Chr 12:1	5826
unto thee, and peace be to thine *h*	1Chr 12:18	5826
the proud *h* do stoop under him	Job 9:13	5826
when all her *h* shall be destroyed	Eze 30:8	5826
Put and Lubim were thy *h*	Nah 3:9	5833
Aquila my *h* in Christ Jesus	Rom 16:3	4904
your faith, but are *h* of your joy	2Cor 1:24	4904

HELPETH

for thy God *h* thee	1Chr 12:18	5826
hand, both he that *h* shall fall	Is 31:3	5826
the Spirit also *h* our infirmities	Rom 8:26	4878
and to every one that *h* with us	1Cor 16:16	4903

HELPING

were the prophets of God *h* them	Ezr 5:2	5582
why art thou so far from *h* me	Ps 22:1	3467
Ye also *h* together by prayer for	2Cor 1:11	4943

HELPS

they had taken up, they used *h*	Acts 27:17	996
then gifts of healings, *h*	1Cor 12:28	484

HELVE

and the head slippeth from the *h*	Deut 19:5	6086

HEM

beneath upon the *h* of it thou	Ex 28:33	7757
round about the *h* thereof	Ex 28:33	7757
upon the *h* of the robe round	Ex 28:34	7757
upon the *h* of the robe, round	Ex 39:25	7757
round about the *h* of the robe to	Ex 39:26	7757
touched the *h* of his garment	Mt 9:20	2899
only touch the *h* of his garment	Mt 14:36	2899

HEMAM (he'-mam) See HOMAM. *A son of Lotan.*

children of Lotan were Hori and *H*	Gen 36:22	1967

HEMAN (he'-man)

1. A son of Zerah.

than Ethan the Ezrahite, and *H*	1Kin 4:31	1968
Zimri, and Ethan, and *H*, and Calcol,	1Chr 2:6	1968
Of *H*: the sons of *H*	1Chr 25:4	1968

2. A son of Joel.

H a singer, the son of Joel, the	1Chr 6:33	1968
appointed *H* the son of Joel	1Chr 15:17	1968
So the singers, *H*, Asaph, and	1Chr 15:19	1968
And with them *H* and Jeduthun, and	1Chr 16:41	1968
And with them *H* and Jeduthun with	1Chr 16:42	1968
of the sons of Asaph, and of *H*	1Chr 25:1	1968
All these were the sons of *H* the	1Chr 25:5	1968
God gave to *H* fourteen sons and	1Chr 25:5	1968
order to Asaph, Jeduthun, and *H*	1Chr 25:6	1968
all of them of Asaph, of *H*	2Chr 5:12	1968
And of the sons of *H*	2Chr 29:14	1968
of David, and Asaph, and *H*, and	2Chr 35:15	1968
Maschil of *H* the Ezrahite	Ps 88:t	1968

HEMATH (he'-math) See HAMATH.

1. Same as Hamath.

Egypt even unto the entering of *H*	1Chr 13:5	2574
in of *H* unto the river of the	Amos 6:14	2574

2. Father of the Kenites and Rechabites.

are the Kenites that came of *H*	1Chr 2:55	2574

HEMDAN (hem'-dan) See AMRAM. *Son of Dishon.*

H, and Eshban, and Ithran, and	Gen 36:26	2533

HEMLOCK

as *h* in the furrows of the field	Hos 10:4	7219
the fruit of righteousness into *h*	Amos 6:12	3939

HEMS

they made upon the *h* of the robe	Ex 39:24	7757

H

HEN (hen) A son of Zephaniah.

to *H* the son of Zephaniah, for a	Zec 6:14	2581
even as a *h* gathereth her	Mt 23:37	3733
as a *h* doth gather her brood	Lk 13:34	3733

HENA (he'-nah) A city on the Euphrates.

are the gods of Sepharvaim, *H*	2Kin 18:34	2012
of the city of Sepharvaim, of *H*	2Kin 19:13	2012
king of the city of Sepharvaim, *H*	Is 37:13	2012

HENADAD (hen'-a-dad) A Levite.

the sons of *H*, with their sons and	Ezr 3:9	2582
brethren, Bavai the son of *H*	Neh 3:18	2582
Binnui the son of *H* another piece	Neh 3:24	2582
Azaniah, Binnui of the sons of *H*	Neh 10:9	2582

HENCE

the man said, They are departed *h*	Gen 37:17	2088
Pharaoh ye shall not go forth *h*	Gen 42:15	2088
ye shall carry up my bones from *h*	Gen 50:25	2088
afterwards he will let you go *h*	Ex 11:1	2088
thrust you out *h* altogether	Ex 11:1	2088
carry up my bones away *h* with you	Ex 13:19	2088
unto Moses, Depart, and go up *h*	Ex 33:1	2088
go not with me, carry us not up *h*	Ex 33:15	2088
get thee down quickly from *h*	Deut 9:12	2088
Take you *h* out of the midst of	Josh 4:3	2088
Depart not *h*, I pray thee, until	Judg 6:18	2088
another field, neither go from *h*	Ruth 2:8	2088
Get thee *h*, and turn thee eastward	1Kin 17:3	2088
recover strength, before I go *h*	Ps 39:13	2088
shalt say unto it, Get thee *h*	Is 30:22	3318
Take from *h* thirty men with thee,	Jer 38:10	2088
and he said, Get you *h*, walk to and	Zec 6:7	3212
saith Jesus unto him, Get thee *h*	Mt 4:10	5217
Remove *h* to yonder place	Mt 17:20	1782
of God, cast thyself down from *h*	Lk 4:9	1782
him, Get thee out, and depart *h*	Lk 13:31	1782
would pass from *h* to you cannot	Lk 16:26	1782
sold doves, Take these things *h*	Jn 2:16	1782
therefore said unto him, Depart *h*	Jn 7:3	1782
Arise, let us go *h*	Jn 14:31	1782
but now is my kingdom not from *h*	Jn 18:36	1782
Sir, if thou have borne him *h*	Jn 20:15	1782
the Holy Ghost not many days *h*	Acts 1:5	3226,5025
send thee far *h* unto the Gentiles	Acts 22:21	1821
come they not *h*, even of your	Jas 4:1	1782

HENCEFORTH

it shall not *h* yield unto thee	Gen 4:12	3254
must the children of Israel *h*	Num 18:22	5750
Ye shall *h* return no more that	Deut 17:16	3254
shall *h* commit no more any such	Deut 19:20	3254
I also will not *h* drive out any	Judg 2:21	3254
for thy servant will *h* offer	2Kin 5:17	5750
therefore from *h* thou shalt have	2Chr 16:9	6258
his people from *h* even for ever	Ps 125:2	6258
Israel hope in the Lord from *h*	Ps 131:3	6258
with justice from *h* even for ever	Is 9:7	6258
for *h* there shall no more come	Is 52:1	6258
seed, saith the Lord, from *h*	Is 59:21	3254
thou shalt no more *h* bereave them	Eze 36:12	
over them in mount Zion from *h*	Mic 4:7	
unto you, Ye shall not see me *h*	Mt 23:39	575,737
I will not drink *h* of this fruit	Mt 26:29	575,737
from *h* all generations shall call	Lk 1:48	3568
from *h* thou shalt catch men	Lk 5:10	3568
For from *h* there shall be five in	Lk 12:52	3568
from *h* ye know him, and have seen	Jn 14:7	737
H I call you not servants	Jn 15:15	3765
that they speak *h* to no man in	Acts 4:17	3371
from *h* I will go unto the	Acts 18:6	3568
that *h* we should not serve sin	Rom 6:6	3371
should not *h* live unto themselves	2Cor 5:15	3371
h know we no man after	2Cor 5:16	575,3588,3568
yet now *h* know we him no more	2Cor 5:16	2089
From *h* let no man trouble me	Gal 6:17	3063
That we *h* be no more children,	Eph 4:14	3063
that ye *h* walk not as other	Eph 4:17	3371
H there is laid up for me a crown	2Ti 4:8	3063
From *h* expecting till his enemies	Heb 10:13	3063
dead which die in the Lord from *h*	Rev 14:13	534

HENCEFORWARD

and *h* among your generations	Num 15:23	1973
no fruit grow on thee *h* for ever	Mt 21:19	3371

HENNA See Camphire.

HENOCH (he'-nok) See Enoch. Same as Enoch.

H, Methuselah, Lamech,	1Chr 1:3	2585
Ephah, and Epher, and *H*, and Abida,	1Chr 1:33	2585

HEPHER (he'-fer) See Gath-hepher, Hepherites.

1. A son of Gilead.

and of *H*, the family of the	Num 26:32	2660
the son of *H* had no sons, but	Num 26:33	2660
of Zelophehad, the son of *H*	Num 27:1	2660
Shechem, and for the children of *H*	Josh 17:2	2660
But Zelophehad, the son of *H*	Josh 17:3	2660

2. A son of Naarah.

And Naarah bare him Ahuzam, and *H*..	1Chr 4:6	2660

3. A mighty man of David.

H the Mecherathite, Ahijah the	1Chr 11:36	2660

4. A Canaanite city.

the king of *H*, one	Josh 12:17	2660
Sochoh, and all the land of *H*	1Kin 4:10	2660

HEPHERITES (he'-fer-ites) Descendants of Hepher 1.

and of Hepher, the family of the *H*	Num 26:32	2662

HEPHZI-BAH (hef'-zi-bah)

1. Wife of King Hezekiah.

And his mother's name was *H*	2Kin 21:1	2657

2. A symbolic name for Jerusalem.

but thou shalt be called *H*	Is 62:4	2657

HER See APPENDIX.

HERALD

Then an *h* cried aloud, To you it	Dan 3:4	3744

HERB

the *h* yielding seed, and the fruit	Gen 1:11	6212
h yielding seed after his kind,	Gen 1:12	6212
given you every *h* bearing seed	Gen 1:29	6212
have given every green *h* for meat	Gen 1:30	6212
every *h* of the field before it	Gen 2:5	6212
thou shalt eat the *h* of the field	Gen 3:18	6212
even as the green *h* have I given	Gen 9:3	6212
upon every *h* of the field,	Ex 9:22	6212
hail smote every *h* of the field	Ex 9:25	6212
eat every *h* of the land, even all	Ex 10:12	6212
they did eat every *h* of the land	Ex 10:15	6212
the small rain upon the tender *h*	Deut 32:2	1877
of the field, and as the green *h*	2Kin 19:26	1877
it withereth before any other *h*	Job 8:12	2682
of the tender *h* to spring forth	Job 38:27	1877
grass, and wither as the green *h*	Ps 37:2	1877
and *h* for the service of man	Ps 104:14	6212
of the field, and as the green *h*	Is 37:27	1877
bones shall flourish like an *h*	Is 66:14	1877

HERBS

or in the *h* of the field, through	Ex 10:15	6212
with bitter *h* they shall eat it	Ex 12:8	
with unleavened bread and bitter *h*	Num 9:11	
with thy foot, as a garden of *h*	Deut 11:10	3419
I may have it for a garden of *h*	1Kin 21:2	3419
out into the field to gather *h*	2Kin 4:39	219
eat up all the *h* in their land	Ps 105:35	6212
is a dinner of *h* where love is	Prov 15:17	3419
h of the mountains are gathered	Prov 27:25	6212
place like a clear heat upon *h*	Is 18:4	216
for thy dew is as the dew of *h*	Is 26:19	219
and hills, and dry up all their *h*	Is 42:15	6212
the *h* of every field wither, for	Jer 12:4	6212
grown, it is the greatest among *h*	Mt 13:32	3001
and becometh greater than all *h*	Mk 4:32	3001
mint and rue and all manner of *h*	Lk 11:42	3001
another, who is weak, eateth *h*	Rom 14:2	3001
bringeth forth *h* meet for them by	Heb 6:7	1008

HERD

And Abraham ran unto the *h*	Gen 18:7	1241
of the cattle, even of the *h*	Lev 1:2	1241
be a burnt sacrifice of the *h*	Lev 1:3	1241
offering, if he offer it of the *h*	Lev 3:1	1241
And concerning the tithe of the *h*	Lev 27:32	1241
savour unto the Lord, of the *h*	Num 15:3	1241
then thou shalt kill of thy *h*	Deut 12:21	1241
males that come of thy *h* and of	Deut 15:19	1241
thy God, of the flock and the *h*	Deut 16:2	1241
came after the *h* out of the field	1Sa 11:5	1241
of his own flock and of his own *h*	2Sa 12:4	1241
young of the flock and of the *h*	Jer 31:12	1241
h nor flock, taste any thing	Jonah 3:7	1241
there shall be no *h* in the stalls	Hab 3:17	1241
them an *h* of many swine feeding	Mt 8:30	34
us to go away into the *h* of swine	Mt 8:31	34
they went into the *h* of swine	Mt 8:32	34
behold, the whole *h* of swine ran	Mt 8:32	34
a great *h* of swine feeding	Mk 5:11	34
the *h* ran violently down a steep	Mk 5:13	34
there was there an *h* of many	Lk 8:32	34
the *h* ran violently down a steep	Lk 8:33	34

HERDMAN
but I was an *h*, and a gatherer of .... Amos 7:14   951

HERDMEN
between the *h* of Abram's cattle .... Gen 13:7   7462
cattle and the *h* of Lot's cattle .... Gen 13:7   7462
and between my *h* and thy *h* .... Gen 13:8   7462
the *h* of Gerar did strive with .... Gen 26:20   7462
Gerar did strive with Isaac's *h* .... Gen 26:20   7462
the chiefest of the *h* that 1Sa 21:7   7462
who was among the *h* of Tekoa............... Amos 1:1   5349

HERDS
went with Abram, had flocks, and *h* ...... Gen 13:5   1241
and he hath given him flocks, and *h* ...... Gen 24:35   1241
of flocks, and possession of *h*.................. Gen 26:14   1241
was with him, and the flocks, and *h*...... Gen 32:7   1241
and *h* with young are with me .... Gen 33:13   1241
children, and thy flocks, and thy *h* .... Gen 45:10   1241
brought their flocks, and their *h* .... Gen 46:32   1241
and their flocks, and their *h* .... Gen 47:1   1241
and for the cattle of the *h*...................... Gen 47:17   1241
my lord also hath our *h* of cattle .... Gen 47:18   4735
ones, and their flocks, and their *h* .... Gen 50:8   1241
flocks and with our *h* will we go............ Ex 10:9   1241
your flocks and your *h* be stayed .... Ex 10:24   1241
Also take your flocks and your *h*........... Ex 12:32   1241
and flocks, and *h*, even very much .... Ex 12:38   1241
nor *h* feed before that mount .... Ex 34:3   1241
the *h* be slain for them, to...................... Num 11:22   1241
And when thy *h* and thy flocks .... Deut 8:13   1241
and the firstlings of your *h* .... Deut 12:6   1241
of thy *h* or of thy flock, nor any .... Deut 12:17   1241
oil, and the firstlings of thy *h*................. Deut 14:23   1241
took all the flocks and the *h* 1Sa 30:20   1241
had exceeding many flocks and *h* 2Sa 12:2   1241
over the *h* that fed in Sharon was 1Chr 27:29   1241
over the *h* that were in the 1Chr 27:29   1241
of flocks and *h* in abundance 2Chr 32:29   1241
law, and the firstlings of our *h* .... Neh 10:36   1241
thy flocks, and look well to thy *h* .... Prov 27:23   5739
a place for the *h* to lie down in .... Is 65:10   1241
their flocks and their *h*, their .... Jer 3:24   1241
eat up thy flocks and thine *h* .... Jer 5:17   1241
with their *h* to seek the LORD................. Hos 5:6   1241
the *h* of cattle are perplexed, ... Joel 1:18   5739

HERE See APPENDIX.

HEREAFTER See APPENDIX.

HEREBY
H ye shall be proved .... Gen 42:15   2063
H shall I know that ye are true .... Gen 42:33   2063
H ye shall know that the LORD................ Num 16:28   2063
H ye shall know that the living............... Josh 3:10   2063
yet am I not *h* justified 1Cor 4:4   1722,5129
h we do know that we know him, if 1Jn 2:3   1722,5129
h know we that we are in him 1Jn 3:16   1722,5129
H perceive we the love of God,........ 1Jn 3:16   1722,5129
h we know that we are of the 1Jn 3:19   1722,5129
h we know that he abideth in us,.... 1Jn 3:24   1722,5129
H know ye the Spirit of God............ 1Jn 4:2   1722,5129
H know we the spirit of truth, and.. 1Jn 4:6   1537,5124
H know we that we dwell in him, ... 1Jn 4:13   1722,5129

HEREIN
Only *h* will the men consent unto .... Gen 34:22   2063
H thou hast done foolishly 2Chr 16:9   5921,2063
h is that saying true, One soweth .. Jn 4:37   1722,5129
Why *h* is a marvellous thing, that.. Jn 9:30   1722,5129
H is my Father glorified, that ye .... Jn 15:8   1722,5129
h do I exercise myself, to have .... Acts 24:16   1722,5129
And *h* I give my advice 2Cor 8:10   1722,5129
H is love, not that we loved God, ... 1Jn 4:10   1722,5129
H is our love made perfect, that 1Jn 4:17   1722,5129

HEREOF
the fame *h* went abroad into all.............. Mt 9:26   3778
And by reason *h* he ought, as for .... Heb 5:3   5026

HERES (he'-res) See KIR-HERES, TIMMATH-HERES. A mountain in Judah.
would dwell in mount *H* in Aijalon.......... Judg 1:35   2776

HERESH (he'-resh) A Levite.
And Bakbakkar, *H*, and Galal, and 1Chr 9:15   2792

HERESIES
there must be also *h* among you 1Cor 11:19   139
wrath, strife, seditions, *h* .... Gal 5:20   139
privily shall bring in damnable *h* 2Pet 2:1   139

HERESY
after the way which they call *h*............... Acts 24:14   139

HERETH See HARETH.

HERETICK
man that is an *h* after the first .... Titus 3:10   141

HERETOFORE
I am not eloquent, neither *h*.................... Ex 4:10   8543
people straw to make brick, as *h* .... Ex 5:7   8543
the bricks, which they did make *h* .... Ex 5:8   8543
both yesterday and to day, as *h* .... Ex 5:14   8543
for ye have not passed this way *h* .... Josh 3:4   8543
a people which thou knewest not *h* .... Ruth 2:11   8543
hath not been such a thing *h*.................. 1Sa 4:7   865
write to them which *h* have sinned 2Cor 13:2   4258

HEREUNTO
can eat, or who else can hasten *h*.......... Eccl 2:25
For even *h* were ye called 1Pet 2:21   1519,5124

HEREWITH
and yet thou wast not satisfied *h* .... Eze 16:29   2063
in mine house, and prove me now *h* .... Mal 3:10   2063

HERITAGE
and I will give it you for an *h*.................. Ex 6:8   4181
the *h* appointed unto him by God .... Job 20:29   5159
the *h* of oppressors, which they .... Job 27:13   5159
yea, I have a goodly *h* .... Ps 16:6   5159
thou hast given me the *h* of those .... Ps 61:5   3425
O LORD, and afflict thine *h*...................... Ps 94:5   5159
give them the *h* of the heathen .... Ps 111:6   5159
have I taken as an *h* for ever .... Ps 119:111   5157
Lo, children are an *h* of the LORD .... Ps 127:3   5159
And gave their land for an *h*................... Ps 135:12   5159
an *h* unto Israel his people .... Ps 135:12   5159
And gave their land for an *h* .... Ps 136:21   5159
Even an *h* unto Israel his servant .... Ps 136:22   5159
This is the *h* of the servants of............... Is 54:17   5159
feed thee with the *h* of Jacob thy .... Is 58:14   5159
made mine *h* an abomination................. Jer 2:7   5159
a goodly *h* of the hosts of .... Jer 3:19   5159
mine house, I have left mine *h* .... Jer 12:7   5159
Mine *h* is unto me as a lion in .... Jer 12:8   5159
Mine *h* is unto me as a speckled .... Jer 12:9   5159
them again, every man to his *h*.............. Jer 12:15   5159
from thine *h* that I gave thee .... Jer 17:4   5159
O ye destroyers of mine *h* .... Jer 50:11   5159
and give not thine *h* to reproach .... Joel 2:17   5159
for my people and for my *h* Israel.......... Joel 3:2   5159
and his house, even a man and his *h* ..... Mic 2:2   5159
thy rod, the flock of thine *h*.................... Mic 7:14   5159
of the remnant of his *h* .... Mic 7:18   5159
his *h* waste for the dragons of .... Mal 1:3   5159
as being lords over God's *h* 1Pet 5:3   2819

HERITAGES
cause to inherit the desolate *h* .... Is 49:8   5159

HERMAS (her'-mas) A Christian acquaintance of Paul.
Salute Asyncritus, Phlegon, *H* .... Rom 16:14   2057

HERMES (her'-mees) A Christian acquaintance of Paul.
Phlegon, Hermas, Patrobas, *H* .... Rom 16:14   2060

HERMOGENES (her-mog'-e-nees) A false Christian teacher.
of whom are Phygellus and *H* 2Ti 1:15   2061

HERMON
the river of Arnon unto mount *H* .... Deut 3:8   2768
(Which *H* the Sidonians call .... Deut 3:9   2768
even unto mount Sion which is *H* .... Deut 4:48   2768
to the Hivite under *H* in the land........... Josh 11:3   2768
valley of Lebanon under mount *H*........... Josh 11:17   2768
from the river Arnon unto mount *H* .... Josh 12:1   2768
And reigned in mount *H*, and in .... Josh 12:5   2768
from Baal-gad under mount *H* unto .... Josh 13:5   2768
and Maachathites, and all mount *H*....... Josh 13:11   2768
and Senir, and unto mount *H* 1Chr 5:23   2768
H shall rejoice in thy name .... Ps 89:12   2768
As the dew of *H*, and as the dew .... Ps 133:3   2768
from the top of Shenir and *H* .... Song 4:8   2768

HERMONITES (her'-mon-ites) See HERMON. Inhabitants of Mt. Hermon.
the land of Jordan, and of the *H* .... Ps 42:6   2769

HEROD (her'-od) See HERODIANS, HEROD'S.
1. Herod the Great.
Judaea in the days of *H* the king .... Mt 2:1   2264
When *H* the king had heard these .... Mt 2:3   2264
Then *H*, when he had privily.................... Mt 2:7   2264
that they should not return to *H*............ Mt 2:12   2264
for *H* will seek the young child .... Mt 2:13   2264
And was there until the death of *H* .... Mt 2:15   2264
Then *H*, when he saw that he was .... Mt 2:16   2264
But when *H* was dead, behold, an .... Mt 2:19   2264
in the room of his father *H* .... Mt 2:22   2264

H

There was in the days of *H* .... Lk 1:5   2264
No, nor yet *H*: for I sent .... Lk 23:15   2264
    2. Herod Antipas.
At that time *H* the tetrarch heard .... Mt 14:1   2264
For *H* had laid hold on John, and .... Mt 14:3   2264
danced before them, and pleased *H* ...... Mt 14:6   2264
And king *H* heard of him .... Mk 6:14   2264
But when *H* heard thereof, he said .... Mk 6:16   2264
For *H* himself had sent forth and........... Mk 6:17   2264
For John had said unto *H*, It is............... Mk 6:18   2264
For *H* feared John, knowing that .... Mk 6:20   2264
that *H* on his birthday made a .... Mk 6:21   2264
came in, and danced, and pleased *H* ...... Mk 6:22   2264
Pharisees, and of the leaven of *H* ...... Mk 8:15   2264
H being tetrarch of Galilee, and .... Lk 3:1   2264
But *H* the tetrarch, being .... Lk 3:19   2264
all the evils which *H* had done................ Lk 3:19   2264
Now *H* the tetrarch heard of all .... Lk 9:7   2264
H said, John have I beheaded .... Lk 9:9   2264
for *H* will kill thee .... Lk 13:31   2264
jurisdiction, he sent him to *H*.............. Lk 23:7   2264
And when *H* saw Jesus, he was .... Lk 23:8   2264
H with his men of war set him at .... Lk 23:11   2264
H were made friends together............... Lk 23:12   2264
whom thou hast anointed, both *H* .... Acts 4:27   2264
brought up with *H* the tetrarch .... Acts 13:1   2264
    3. Herod Agrippa I.
Now about that time *H* the king .... Acts 12:1   2264
when *H* would have brought him .... Acts 12:6   2264
delivered me out of the hand of *H* .... Acts 12:11   2264
when *H* had sought for him, and .... Acts 12:19   2264
H was highly displeased with them .... Acts 12:20   2264
And upon a set day *H*, arrayed in .... Acts 12:21   2264

HERODIANS (he-ro'-de-uns) *Hellenizing Jews.*
him their disciples with the *H*................ Mt 22:16   2265
counsel him against him .... Mk 3:6   2265
of the Pharisees and of the *H*............... Mk 12:13   2265

HERODIAS (he-ro'-de-as) See HERODIAS'. *Grand-daughter of Herod 1.*
the daughter of *H* danced before .... Mt 14:6   2266
Therefore *H* had a quarrel against......... Mk 6:19   2266
daughter of the said *H* came in............. Mk 6:22   2266
for *H* his brother Philip's wife .... Lk 3:19   2266

HERODIAS' (he-ro'-de-as)
and put him in prison for *H* sake .... Mt 14:3   2266
and bound him in prison for *H* sake....... Mk 6:17   2266

HERODION (he-ro'-de-on) *A relative of Paul.*
Salute *H* my kinsman............................ Rom 16:11   2267

HEROD'S (her'-ods)
    1. Refers to Herod 2.
But when *H* birthday was kept, the .... Mt 14:6   2264
the wife of Chuza *H* steward .... Lk 8:3   2264
he belonged unto *H* jurisdiction............. Lk 23:7   2264
    2. Refers to Herod 3.
him to be kept in *H* judgment hall......... Acts 23:35   2264

HERON
the *h* after her kind, and the .... Lev 11:19   601
the *h* after her kind, and the .... Deut 14:18   601

HERS See APPENDIX.

HERSELF See APPENDIX.

HESED (he'-sed) See JUSHAB-HESED. *Father of an officer of Solomon.*
The son of *H*, in Aruboth 1Kin 4:10   2618

HESHBON (hesh'-bon) *A Levitical city in Reuben and Gad.*
the cities of the Amorites, in *H* .... Num 21:25   2809
For *H* was the city of Sihon the............. Num 21:26   2809
in proverbs say, Come into *H* .... Num 21:27   2809
For there is a fire gone out of *H* .... Num 21:28   2809
H is perished even unto Dibon, and .... Num 21:30   2809
of the Amorites, which dwelt at *H* .... Num 21:34   2809
Dibon, and Jazer, and Nimrah, and *H*.... Num 32:3   2809
And the children of Reuben built *H* .... Num 32:37   2809
of the Amorites, which dwelt in *H*......... Deut 1:4   2809
hand Sihon the Amorite, king of *H* .... Deut 2:24   2809
king of *H* with words of peace .... Deut 2:26   2809
But Sihon king of *H* would not let......... Deut 2:30   2809
of the Amorites, which dwelt at *H* .... Deut 3:2   2809
as we did unto Sihon king of *H* .... Deut 3:6   2809
of the Amorites, who dwelt at *H* .... Deut 4:46   2809
this place, Sihon the king of *H* .... Deut 29:7   2809
beyond Jordan, to Sihon king of *H* .... Josh 9:10   2809
of the Amorites, who dwelt in *H* .... Josh 12:2   2809
the border of Sihon king of *H*............... Josh 12:5   2809
the Amorites, which reigned in *H* .... Josh 13:10   2809
H, and all her cities that are in............... Josh 13:17   2809

the Amorites, which reigned in *H* .... Josh 13:21   2809
from *H* unto Ramath-mizpeh, and......... Josh 13:26   2809
of the kingdom of Sihon king of *H* .... Josh 13:27   2809
H with her suburbs, Jazer with .... Josh 21:39   2809
of the Amorites, the king of *H* .... Judg 11:19   2809
While Israel dwelt in *H* and her .... Judg 11:26   2809
H with her suburbs, and Jazer with 1Chr 6:81   2809
and the land of the king of *H* .... Neh 9:22   2809
eyes like the fishpools in *H* .... Song 7:4   2809
And *H* shall cry, and Elealeh .... Is 15:4   2809
For the fields of *H* languish .... Is 16:8   2809
water thee with my tears, O *H*.............. Is 16:9   2809
in *H* they have devised evil .... Jer 48:2   2809
From the cry of *H* even unto .... Jer 48:34   2809
shadow of *H* because of the force .... Jer 48:45   2809
a fire shall come forth out of *H* .... Jer 48:45   2809
Howl, O *H*, for Ai is spoiled.................. Jer 49:3   2809

HESHMON (hesh'-mon) See AZMON. *A town in Judah.*
And Hazar-gaddah, and *H*, and.............. Josh 15:27   2829

HESLI See ESLI.

HETH (heth) *Son of Canaan.*
begat Sidon his firstborn, and *H* .... Gen 10:15   2845
dead, and spake unto the sons of *H* ...... Gen 23:3   2845
the children of *H* answered .... Gen 23:5   2845
land, even to the children of *H* .... Gen 23:7   2845
dwelt among the children of *H* .... Gen 23:10   2845
the audience of the children of *H* .... Gen 23:10   2845
in the audience of the sons of *H* .... Gen 23:16   2845
the presence of the children of *H* .... Gen 23:18   2845
a buryingplace by the sons of *H* .... Gen 23:20   2845
purchased of the sons of *H* .... Gen 25:10   2845
because of the daughters of *H* .... Gen 27:46   2845
take a wife of the daughters of *H*.......... Gen 27:46   2845
was from the children of *H*.................... Gen 49:32   2845
begat Zidon his firstborn, and *H* 1Chr 1:13   2845

HETHLON (heth'-lon) *A place in northern Palestine.*
from the great sea, the way of *H* .... Eze 47:15   2855
end to the coast of the way of *H* .... Eze 48:1   2855

HEW
H thee two tables of stone like.............. Ex 34:1   6458
H thee two tables of stone like.............. Deut 10:1   6458
ye shall *h* down the graven images .... Deut 12:3   1438
wood with his neighbour to *h* wood ...... Deut 19:5   2404
command thou that they *h* me cedar 1Kin 5:6   3772
h timber like unto the Sidonians 1Kin 5:6   3772
and Hiram's builders did *h* them........... 1Kin 5:18   6458
he set masons to *h* wrought stones 1Chr 22:2   2672
thousand to *h* in the mountain 2Chr 2:2   2672
H ye down trees, and cast a mount .... Jer 6:6   3772
H down the tree, and cut off his .... Dan 4:14   1414
H the tree down, and destroy it .... Dan 4:23   1414

HEWED
he *h* two tables of stone like................. Ex 34:4   6458
h two tables of stone like unto .... Deut 10:3   6458
h them in pieces, and sent them 1Sa 11:7   5408
Samuel *h* Agag in pieces before 1Sa 15:33   8158
h stones, to lay the foundation 1Kin 5:17   1496
court with three rows of *h* stone 1Kin 6:36   1496
to the measures of *h* stones 1Kin 7:9   1496
after the measures of *h* stones 1Kin 7:11   1496
was with three rows of *h* stones 1Kin 7:12   1496
h stone to repair the breaches of 2Kin 12:12   4274
that thou hast *h* thee out a .... Is 22:16   2672
h them out cisterns, broken .... Jer 2:13   2672
Therefore have I *h* them by the .... Hos 6:5   2672

HEWER
from the *h* of thy wood unto the .... Deut 29:11   2404

HEWERS
but let them be *h* of wood .... Josh 9:21   2404
h of wood and drawers of water for ...... Josh 9:23   2404
made them that day *h* of wood .... Josh 9:27   2404
thousand *h* in the mountains 1Kin 5:15   2672
h of stone, and to buy timber and.......... 2Kin 12:12   2672
workmen with thee in abundance, *h* 1Chr 22:15   2672
the *h* that cut timber, twenty................ 2Chr 2:10   2404
thousand to be *h* in the mountain 2Chr 2:18   2672
her with axes, as *h* of wood .... Jer 46:22   2404

HEWETH
against him that *h* therewith .... Is 10:15   2672
as he that *h* him out an sepulchre .... Is 22:16   2672
He *h* him down cedars, and taketh .... Is 44:14   3772

HEWN
shalt not build it of *h* stone .... Ex 20:25   1496
h stone to repair the house 2Kin 22:6   4274
gave they it, to buy *h* stone 2Chr 34:11   4274
she hath *h* out her seven pillars .... Prov 9:1   2672

but we will build with *h* stones	Is 9:10	1496
ones of stature shall be *h* down	Is 10:33	1438
Lebanon is ashamed and *h* down	Is 33:9	7060
unto the rock whence ye are *h*	Is 51:1	2672
inclosed my ways with *h* stone	Lam 3:9	1496
the four tables were of *h* stone	Eze 40:42	1496
ye have built houses of *h* stone	Amos 5:11	1496
not forth good fruit is *h* down	Mt 3:10	1581
not forth good fruit is *h* down	**Mt 7:19**	*1581*
which he had *h* out in the rock	Mt 27:60	2998
which was *h* out of a rock	Mk 15:46	2998
not forth good fruit is *h* down	Lk 3:9	*1581*
a sepulchre that was *h* in stone	Lk 23:53	2991

HEZEKI (hez'-e-ki) *A Benjamite.*
And Zebadiah, and Meshullam, and *H*	1Chr 8:17	2395

HEZEKIAH (hez-e-ki'-ah) See EZEKIAS, HIZKIAH.
1. Son of King Ahaz.
H his son reigned in his stead	2Kin 16:20	2396
that *H* the son of Ahaz king of	2Kin 18:1	2396
pass in the fourth year of king *H*	2Kin 18:9	2396
even in the sixth year of *H*	2Kin 18:10	2396
in the fourteenth year of king *H*	2Kin 18:13	2396
H king of Judah sent to the king	2Kin 18:14	2396
H king of Judah three hundred	2Kin 18:14	2396
H gave him all the silver that	2Kin 18:15	2396
At that time did *H* cut off the	2Kin 18:16	2396
from the pillars which *H* king of	2Kin 18:16	2396
king *H* with a great host against	2Kin 18:17	2396
said unto them, Speak ye now to *H*	2Kin 18:19	2396
whose altars *H* hath taken away	2Kin 18:22	2396
the king, Let not *H* deceive you	2Kin 18:29	2396
Neither let *H* make you trust in	2Kin 18:30	2396
Hearken not to *H*	2Kin 18:31	2396
and hearken not unto *H*, when he	2Kin 18:32	2396
to *H* with their clothes rent, and	2Kin 18:37	2396
to pass, when king *H* heard it	2Kin 19:1	2396
they said unto him, Thus saith *H*	2Kin 19:3	2396
servants of king *H* came to Isaiah	2Kin 19:5	2396
he sent messengers again unto *H*	2Kin 19:9	2396
shall ye speak to *H* king of Judah	2Kin 19:10	2396
H received the letter of the hand	2Kin 19:14	2396
H went up into the house of the	2Kin 19:14	2396
H prayed before the LORD, and said	2Kin 19:15	2396
Isaiah the son of Amoz sent to *H*	2Kin 19:20	2396
those days was *H* sick unto death	2Kin 20:1	2396
And *H* wept sore	2Kin 20:3	2396
tell *H* the captain of my people,	2Kin 20:5	2396
H said unto Isaiah, What shall be	2Kin 20:8	2396
H answered, It is a light thing	2Kin 20:10	2396
sent letters and a present unto *H*	2Kin 20:12	2396
he had heard that *H* had been sick	2Kin 20:12	2396
H hearkened unto them, and shewed	2Kin 20:13	2396
dominion, that *H* shewed them not	2Kin 20:13	2396
Isaiah the prophet unto king *H*	2Kin 20:14	2396
H said, They are come from a far	2Kin 20:14	2396
H answered, All the things that	2Kin 20:15	2396
And Isaiah said unto *H*, Hear the	2Kin 20:16	2396
Then said *H* unto Isaiah, Good is	2Kin 20:19	2396
And the rest of the acts of *H*	2Kin 20:20	2396
And *H* slept with his fathers	2Kin 20:21	2396
which *H* his father had destroyed	2Kin 21:3	2396
H his son, Manasseh his son,	1Chr 3:13	2396
in the days of *H* king of Judah	1Chr 4:41	2396
H his son reigned in his stead	2Chr 28:27	2396
H began to reign when he was five	2Chr 29:1	2396
Then they went in to *H* the king	2Chr 29:18	2396
Then the king rose early, and	2Chr 29:20	2396
H commanded to offer the burnt	2Chr 29:27	2396
Moreover the king and the	2Chr 29:30	2396
Then *H* answered and said, Now ye	2Chr 29:31	2396
H rejoiced, and all the people,	2Chr 29:36	2396
H sent to all Israel and Judah, and	2Chr 30:1	2396
But *H* prayed for them, saying,	2Chr 30:18	2396
And the LORD hearkened to *H*	2Chr 30:20	2396
H spake comfortably unto all the	2Chr 30:22	2396
For *H* king of Judah did give to	2Chr 30:24	2396
H appointed the courses of	2Chr 31:2	2396
And when *H* and the princes came and	2Chr 31:8	2396
Then *H* questioned with the	2Chr 31:9	2396
Then *H* commanded to prepare	2Chr 31:11	2396
at the commandment of *H* the king	2Chr 31:13	2396
thus did *H* throughout all Judah,	2Chr 31:20	2396
when *H* saw that Sennacherib was	2Chr 32:2	2396
upon the words of *H* king of Judah	2Chr 32:8	2396
unto *H* king of Judah, and unto	2Chr 32:9	2396
Doth not *H* persuade you to give	2Chr 32:11	2396
Hath not the same *H* taken away	2Chr 32:12	2396
therefore let not *H* deceive you	2Chr 32:15	2396
God, and against his servant *H*	2Chr 32:16	2396
so shall not the God of *H* deliver	2Chr 32:17	2396

And for this cause *H* the king	2Chr 32:20	2396
Thus the LORD saved *H* and the	2Chr 32:22	2396
presents to *H* king of Judah	2Chr 32:23	2396
In those days *H* was sick to the	2Chr 32:24	2396
But *H* rendered not again	2Chr 32:25	2396
Notwithstanding *H* humbled himself	2Chr 32:26	2396
not upon them in the days of *H*	2Chr 32:26	2396
H had exceeding much riches and	2Chr 32:27	2396
This same *H* also stopped the	2Chr 32:30	2396
H prospered in all his works	2Chr 32:30	2396
Now the rest of the acts of *H*	2Chr 32:32	2396
H slept with his fathers, and they	2Chr 32:33	2396
His father had broken down	2Chr 33:3	2396
which the men of *H* king of Judah	Prov 25:1	2396
of Uzziah, Jotham, Ahaz, and *H*	Is 1:1	2396
in the fourteenth year of king *H*	Is 36:1	2396
unto king *H* with a great army	Is 36:2	2396
said unto them, Say ye now to *H*	Is 36:4	2396
whose altars *H* hath taken away,	Is 36:7	2396
the king, Let not *H* deceive you	Is 36:14	2396
Neither let *H* make you trust in	Is 36:15	2396
Hearken not to *H*	Is 36:16	2396
Beware lest *H* persuade you,	Is 36:18	2396
to *H* with their clothes rent, and	Is 36:22	2396
to pass, when king *H* heard it	Is 37:1	2396
they said unto him, Thus saith *H*	Is 37:3	2396
servants of king *H* came to Isaiah	Is 37:5	2396
heard it, he sent messengers to *H*	Is 37:9	2396
shall ye speak to *H* king of Judah	Is 37:10	2396
H received the letter from the	Is 37:14	2396
H went up unto the house of the	Is 37:14	2396
H prayed unto the LORD, saying,	Is 37:15	2396
the son of Amoz sent unto *H*	Is 37:21	2396
those days was *H* sick unto death	Is 38:1	2396
Then *H* turned his face toward the	Is 38:2	2396
And *H* wept sore	Is 38:3	2396
Go, and say to *H*, Thus saith the	Is 38:5	2396
The writing of *H* king of Judah	Is 38:9	2396
H also had said, What is the sign	Is 38:22	2396
sent letters and a present to *H*	Is 39:1	2396
H was glad of them, and shewed	Is 39:2	2396
dominion, that *H* shewed them not	Is 39:2	2396
Isaiah the prophet unto king *H*	Is 39:3	2396
H said, They are come from a far	Is 39:3	2396
H answered, All that is in mine	Is 39:4	2396
Then said Isaiah to *H*, Hear the	Is 39:5	2396
Then said *H* to Isaiah, Good is	Is 39:8	2396
the son of *H* king of Judah	Jer 15:4	2396
in the days of *H* king of Judah	Jer 26:18	2396
Did *H* king of Judah and all Judah	Jer 26:19	2396
of Uzziah, Jotham, Ahaz, and *H*	Hos 1:1	2396
in the days of Jotham, Ahaz, and *H*	Mic 1:1	2396

2. A son of Neariah.
Elioenai, and *H*, and Azrikam, three	1Chr 3:23	2396

3. A family of exiles.
The children of Ater of *H*	Ezr 2:16	2396
The children of Ater of *H*	Neh 7:21	2396

HEZION (he'-zi-on) *Grandfather of King Benhadad of Syria.*
the son of Tabrimon, the son of *H*	1Kin 15:18	2383

HEZIR (he'-zir)
1. A sanctuary servant.
The seventeenth to *H*, the	1Chr 24:15	2387

2. An Israelite who renewed the covenant.
Magpiash, Meshullam, *H*,	Neh 10:20	2387

HEZRAI (hez'-rahee) See HEZRO. *A mighty man of David.*
H the Carmelite, Paarai the	2Sa 23:35	2695

HEZRO (hez'-ro) See HEZRAI. *Same as Hezrai.*
H the Carmelite, Naarai the son	1Chr 11:37	2695

HEZRON (hez'-ron) See HAZOR, HEZRONITES, HEZBON'S.
1. Son of Pharez.
And the sons of Pharez were *H*	Gen 46:12	2696
Of *H*, the family of the	Num 26:6	2696
of *H*, the family of the	Num 26:21	2696
Pharez begat *H*,	Ruth 4:18	2696
H begat Ram, and Ram begat	Ruth 4:19	2696
of Pharez; *H*, and Hamul	1Chr 2:5	2696
The sons also of *H*, that were	1Chr 2:9	2696
Caleb the son of *H* begat children	1Chr 2:18	2696
afterward *H* went in to the	1Chr 2:21	2696
And after that *H* was dead in	1Chr 2:25	2696
Jerahmeel the firstborn of *H* were	1Chr 2:25	2696
Pharez, *H*, and Carmi, and Hur, and	1Chr 4:1	2696

2. A son of Reuben.
and Phallu, and *H*, and Carmi	Gen 46:9	2696
Hanoch, and Pallu, *H*, and Carmi	Ex 6:14	2696
Israel were, Hanoch, and Pallu, *H*	1Chr 5:3	2696

H

3. *A town in Judah.*
and passed along to *H*, and went up ...... Josh 15:3   2696
Hazor, Hadattah, and Kerioth, and *H* ....Josh 15:25   2696

HEZRONITES *(hez'-ron-ites) Descendants of Hezron 2.*
Of Hezron, the family of the *H* .... Num 26:6   2697
of Hezron, the family of the *H* .... Num 26:21   2697

HEZRON'S *(hez'-ronz) Refers to Hezron 2.*
then Abiah *H* wife bare him Ashur 1Chr 2:24   2696

HID
his wife *h* themselves from the .... Gen 3:8   2244
and I *h* myself .... Gen 3:10   2244
and from thy face shall I be *h* .... Gen 4:14   5641
Jacob *h* them under the oak which .... Gen 35:4   2934
child, she *h* him three months .... Ex 2:2   6845
Egyptian, and *h* him in the sand .... Ex 2:12   2934
And Moses *h* his face .... Ex 3:6   5641
the thing be *h* from the eyes of .... Lev 4:13   5956
withal, and it be *h* from him .... Lev 5:3   5956
with an oath, and it be *h* from him ...... Lev 5:4   5956
it be *h* from the eyes of her .... Num 5:13   5956
and of treasures *h* in the sand .... Deut 33:19   2934
h them, and said thus, There came .... Josh 2:4   6845
h them with the stalks of flax, ... Josh 2:6   2934
because she *h* the messengers that .... Josh 6:17   2244
because she *h* the messengers, ... Josh 6:25   2244
they are *h* in the earth in .... Josh 7:21   2934
it was *h* in his tent, and the .... Josh 7:22   2934
h themselves in a cave at .... Josh 10:16   2244
are found *h* in a cave at Makkedah .... Josh 10:17   2244
the cave wherein they had been *h* .... Josh 10:27   2244
for he *h* himself .... Judg 9:5   2244
every whit, and *h* nothing from him 1Sa 3:18   3582
he hath *h* himself among the stuff 1Sa 10:22   2244
holes where they had *h* themselves 1Sa 14:11   2244
had *h* themselves in mount Ephraim 1Sa 14:22   2244
So David *h* himself in the field 1Sa 20:24   5641
he is *h* now in some pit, or in 2Sa 17:9   2244
is no matter *h* from the king 2Sa 18:13   3582
was not any thing *h* from the king 1Kin 10:3   5956
h them by fifty in a cave, and fed 1Kin 18:4   2244
how I *h* an hundred men of the 1Kin 18:13   2244
and the LORD hath *h* it from me 2Kin 4:27   5956
and she hath *h* her son 2Kin 6:29   2244
gold, and raiment, and went and *h* it.... 2Kin 7:8   2934
thence also, and went and *h* it 2Kin 7:8   2934
and they *h* him, even him and his 2Kin 11:2   5641
he was with her *h* in the house of 2Kin 11:3   2244
four sons with him *h* themselves 1Chr 21:20   2244
there was nothing *h* from Solomon 2Chr 9:2   5956
him, (for he was *h* in Samaria 2Chr 22:9   2244
h him from Athaliah, so that she 2Chr 22:11   5641
he was with them *h* in the house 2Chr 22:12   2244
nor *h* sorrow from mine eyes .... Job 3:10   5641
for it more than for *h* treasures .... Job 3:21   4301
given to a man whose way is *h* .... Job 3:23   5641
Thou shalt be *h* from the scourge .... Job 5:21   2244
the ice, and wherein the snow is *h* .... Job 6:16   5956
things hast thou *h* in thine heart .... Job 10:13   6845
their fathers, and have not *h* it .... Job 15:18   3582
For thou hast *h* their heart from .... Job 17:4   6845
shall be *h* in his secret places .... Job 20:26   2244
the thing that is *h* bringeth he .... Job 28:11   8587
Seeing it is *h* from the eyes of .... Job 28:21   5956
young men saw me, and *h* themselves ... Job 29:8   2244
The waters are *h* as with a stone, ... Job 38:30   2244
in the net which they *h* is their .... Ps 9:15   2934
thou fillest with thy *h* treasure .... Ps 17:14   6845
there is nothing *h* from the heat .... Ps 19:6   5641
neither hath he *h* his face from .... Ps 22:24   5641
and mine iniquity have I not *h* .... Ps 32:5   3680
they *h* for me their net in a pit .... Ps 35:7   2934
net that he hath *h* catch himself .... Ps 35:8   2934
and my groaning is not *h* from thee....... Ps 38:9   5641
I have not *h* thy righteousness .... Ps 40:10   3680
I would have *h* myself from him .... Ps 55:12   5641
and my sins are not *h* from thee .... Ps 69:5   3582
Thy word have I *h* in mine heart .... Ps 119:11   6845
My substance was not *h* from thee .... Ps 139:15   3582
The proud have *h* a snare for me .... Ps 140:5   2934
for her as for *h* treasures .... Prov 2:4   4301
falsehood have we *h* ourselves .... Is 28:15   5641
of their prudent men shall be *h* .... Is 29:14   5641
My way is *h* from the LORD, and my ...... Is 40:27   5641
they are *h* in prison houses .... Is 42:22   2244
shadow of his hand hath he *h* me.......... Is 49:2   2244
in his quiver hath he *h* me .... Is 49:2   5641
I *h* not my face from shame and .... Is 50:6   5641
we *h* as it were our faces from .... Is 53:3   5641
In a little wrath I *h* my face .... Is 54:8   5641

I *h* me, and was wroth, and he went ...... Is 57:17   5641
your sins have *h* his face from .... Is 59:2   5641
for thou hast *h* thy face from us, ... Is 64:7   5641
because they are *h* from mine eyes .... Is 65:16   5641
h it by Euphrates, as the LORD .... Jer 13:5   2934
from the place where I had *h* it .... Jer 13:7   2934
they are not *h* from my face.................... Jer 16:17   5641
their iniquity *h* from mine eyes.............. Jer 16:17   6845
take me, and *h* snares for my feet .... Jer 18:22   2934
I have *h* my face from this city .... Jer 33:5   5641
but the LORD *h* them .... Jer 36:26   5641
upon these stones that I have *h* .... Jer 43:10   2934
have *h* their eyes from my .... Eze 22:26   5956
therefore *h* I my face from them, ... Eze 39:23   5641
unto them, and *h* my face from them .... Eze 39:24   5641
and Israel is not *h* from me .... Hos 5:3   3582
his sin is *h* .... Hos 13:12   6845
shall be *h* from mine eyes .... Hos 13:14   5956
though they be *h* from my sight in .... Amos 9:3   5641
thou shalt be *h*, thou also shalt .... Nah 3:11   5956
it may be ye shall be *h* in the .... Zeph 2:3   5641
is set on an hill cannot be *h* .... Mt 5:14   2928
and *h*, that shall not be known .... Mt 10:26   2927
because thou hast *h* these things .... Mt 11:25   *613*
***h* in three measures of meal, till** .... Mt 13:33   *1470*
like unto treasure *h* in a field .... Mt 13:44   2928
the earth, and *h* his lord's money .... Mt 25:18   *613*
***h* thy talent in the earth** .... Mt 25:25   2928
For there is nothing *h*, which .... Mk 4:22   2927
but he could not be *h* .... Mk 7:24   2990
h herself five months, saying, ... Lk 1:24   4032
neither any thing *h*, that shall .... Lk 8:17   *614*
the woman saw that she was not *h* .... Lk 8:47   2990
it was *h* from them, that they .... Lk 9:45   3871
that thou hast *h* these things .... Lk 10:21   *613*
neither *h*, that shall not be .... Lk 12:2   2927
***h* in three measures of meal, till** .... Lk 13:21   *1470*
and this saying was *h* from them .... Lk 18:34   2928
now they are *h* from thine eyes .... Lk 19:42   2928
but Jesus *h* himself, and went out .... Jn 8:59   2928
But if our gospel be *h*, it is *h* 2Cor 4:3   2572
of the world hath been *h* in God .... Eph 3:9   *613*
which hath been *h* from ages .... Col 1:26   *613*
In whom are *h* all the treasures .... Col 2:3   *614*
your life is *h* with Christ in God .... Col 3:3   2928
that are otherwise cannot be *h* 1Ti 5:25   2928
was *h* three months of his parents .... Heb 11:23   2928
h themselves in the dens and in .... Rev 6:15   2928

HIDDAI *(hid'-dahee) See HURAI. A mighty man of David.*
H of the brooks of Gaash, ... 2Sa 23:30   1914

HIDDEKEL *(hid'-de-kel) A name for the Tigris River.*
the name of the third river is *H* .... Gen 2:14   2313
of the great river, which is *H* .... Dan 10:4   2313

HIDDEN
things, and if it be *h* from him .... Lev 5:2   5956
this day, it is not *h* from thee .... Deut 30:11   6381
Or as an *h* untimely birth I had .... Job 3:16   2934
of years is *h* to the oppressor................ Job 15:20   6845
times are not *h* from the Almighty .... Job 24:1   6845
in the *h* part thou shalt make me .... Ps 51:6   5640
and consulted against thy *h* ones........... Ps 83:3   6845
when the wicked rise, a man is *h* .... Prov 28:12   2664
h riches of secret places, that .... Is 45:3   4301
even *h* things, and thou didst not .... Is 48:6   5341
how are his *h* things sought up .... Obad 6   4710
of these things are *h* from him .... Acts 26:26   2990
in a mystery, even the *h* wisdom 1Cor 2:7   *613*
to light the *h* things of darkness........... 1Cor 4:5   2927
the *h* things of dishonesty 2Cor 4:2   2927
let it be the *h* man of the heart............ 1Pet 3:4   2927
will I give to eat of the *h* manna .... Rev 2:17   2928

HIDE
Shall I *h* from Abraham that thing .... Gen 18:17   3680
We will not *h* it from my lord, ... Gen 47:18   3582
when she could not longer *h* him .... Ex 2:3   6845
But the bullock, and his *h* .... Lev 8:17   5785
the *h* he burnt with fire without............ Lev 9:11   5785
ways *h* their eyes from the man .... Lev 20:4   5956
h themselves from thee, be .... Deut 7:20   5641
go astray, and *h* thyself from them ...... Deut 22:1   5956
thou mayest not *h* thyself .... Deut 22:3   5956
the way, and *h* thyself from them .... Deut 22:4   5956
I will *h* my face from them, and .... Deut 31:17   5641
I will surely *h* my face in that .... Deut 31:18   5641
I will *h* my face from them, I .... Deut 32:20   5641
h yourselves there three days, ... Josh 2:16   2247
h it not from me .... Josh 7:19   3582
to *h* it from the Midianites .... Judg 6:11   5127

I pray thee *h* it not from me	1Sa 3:17	3582
if thou *h* any thing from me of	1Sa 3:17	3582
people did *h* themselves in caves	1Sa 13:6	2244
in a secret place, and *h* thyself	1Sa 19:2	2244
my father is this thing from me	1Sa 20:2	5641
that I may *h* myself in the field	1Sa 20:5	5641
h thyself when the business was	1Sa 20:19	5641
Doth not David *h* himself with us	1Sa 23:19	5641
Doth not David *h* himself in the	1Sa 26:1	5641
H not from me, I pray thee, the	2Sa 14:18	3582
h thyself by the brook Cherith,	1Kin 17:3	5641
an inner chamber to *h* thyself	1Kin 22:25	2247
camp to *h* themselves in the field	2Kin 7:12	2247
an inner chamber to *h* thyself	2Chr 18:24	2244
then I will not *h* myself from	Job 13:20	5641
thou wouldest *h* me in the grave	Job 14:13	6845
though he *h* it under his tongue	Job 20:12	3582
the earth *h* themselves together	Job 24:4	2244
his purpose, and *h* pride from man	Job 33:17	3680
of iniquity may *h* themselves	Job 34:22	5641
H them in the dust together	Job 40:13	2934
long wilt thou *h* thy face from me	Ps 13:1	5641
h me under the shadow of thy	Ps 17:8	5641
he shall *h* me in his pavilion	Ps 27:5	6845
of his tabernacle shall he *h* me	Ps 27:5	5641
H not thy face far from me	Ps 27:9	5641
thou didst *h* thy face, and I was	Ps 30:7	5641
Thou shalt *h* them in the secret	Ps 31:20	5641
H thy face from my sins, and blot	Ps 51:9	5641
Doth not David *h* himself with us	Ps 54:*t*	5641
and *h* not thyself from my	Ps 55:1	5956
they *h* themselves, they mark my	Ps 56:6	6845
H me from the secret counsel of	Ps 64:2	5641
h not thy face from thy servant	Ps 69:17	5641
We will not *h* them from their	Ps 78:4	3582
wilt thou *h* thyself for ever	Ps 89:46	5641
H not thy face from me in the day	Ps 102:2	5641
h not thy commandments from me	Ps 119:19	5641
h not thy face from me, lest I be	Ps 143:7	5641
I flee unto thee to *h* me	Ps 143:9	3680
h my commandments with thee	Prov 2:1	6845
the wicked rise, men *h* themselves	Prov 28:28	5641
I will *h* mine eyes from you	Is 1:15	5956
h thee in the dust, for fear of	Is 2:10	2934
their sin as Sodom, they *h* it not	Is 3:9	3582
h the outcasts	Is 16:3	5641
h thyself as it were for a little	Is 26:20	2247
to *h* their counsel from the LORD	Is 29:15	5641
that thou *h* not thyself from	Is 58:7	5956
h it there in a hole of the rock	Jer 13:4	2934
which I commanded thee to *h* there	Jer 13:6	2934
Can any *h* himself in secret	Jer 23:24	5641
Go, *h* thee, thou and Jeremiah	Jer 36:19	5641
h nothing from me	Jer 38:14	3582
h it not from us, and we will not	Jer 38:25	3582
h them in the clay in the	Jer 43:9	2934
he shall not be able to *h* himself	Jer 49:10	2247
h not thine ear at my breathing,	Lam 3:56	5956
secret that they can *h* from thee	Eze 28:3	6004
the garden of God could not *h* him	Eze 31:8	6004
Neither will I *h* my face any more	Eze 39:29	5641
so that they fled to *h* themselves	Dan 10:7	2244
though they *h* themselves in the	Amos 9:3	2244
he will even *h* his face from them	Mic 3:4	5641
and did *h* himself from them	Jn 12:36	2928
shall *h* a multitude of sins	Jas 5:20	2572
h us from the face of him that	Rev 6:16	2928

HIDEST

Wherefore *h* thou thy face, and	Job 13:24	5641
why *h* thou thyself in times of	Ps 10:1	5956
Wherefore *h* thou thy face, and	Ps 44:24	5641
why *h* thou thy face from me	Ps 88:14	5641
Thou *h* thy face, they are	Ps 104:29	5641
thou art a God that *h* thyself	Is 45:15	5641

HIDETH

lurking places where he *h* himself	1Sa 23:23	2244
he *h* himself on the right hand,	Job 23:9	5848
when he *h* his face, who then can	Job 34:29	5641
Who is he that *h* counsel without	Job 42:3	5956
he *h* his face	Ps 10:11	5641
the darkness *h* not from thee	Ps 139:12	2821
He that *h* hatred with lying lips,	Prov 10:18	3680
A slothful man *h* his hand in his	Prov 19:24	2934
foreseeth the evil, and *h* himself,	Prov 22:3	5641
The slothful *h* his hand in his	Prov 26:15	2934
foreseeth the evil, and *h* himself,	Prov 27:12	5641
Whosoever *h* her the wind,	Prov 27:16	6845
but he that *h* his eyes shall have	Prov 28:27	5956
that *h* his face from the house of	Is 8:17	5641
which when a man hath found, he *h*.	Mt 13:44	2928

HIDING

by *h* mine iniquity in my bosom	Job 31:33	2934
Thou art my *h* place	Ps 32:7	5643
Thou art my *h* place and my shield	Ps 119:114	5643
waters shall overflow the *h* place	Is 28:17	5643
be as an *h* place from the wind	Is 32:2	4224
and there was the *h* of his power	Hab 3:4	2253

HIEL (*hi*'-*el*) *A Bethelite*.

In his days did *H* the Beth-elite	1Kin 16:34	2419

HIERAPOLIS (*hi-e-rap'-o-lis*) *A city in Phrygia*.

are in Laodicea, and them in *H*	Col 4:13	2404

HIGGAION (*hig-gah'-yon*) *A musical notation*.

work of his own hands. *H*.	Ps 9:16	1902

HIGH See APPENDIX.

HIGHER

and his king shall be *h* than Agag	Num 24:7	7311
upward he was *h* than any of the	1Sa 9:2	1364
he was *h* than any of the people	1Sa 10:23	1361
He built the *h* gate of the house	2Kin 15:35	5945
the wall, and on the *h* places	Neh 4:13	6706
the clouds which are *h* than thou	Job 35:5	1361
me to the rock that is *h* than I	Ps 61:2	7311
h than the kings of the earth	Ps 89:27	5945
for he that is *h* than the highest	Eccl 5:8	1364
and there be *h* than they	Eccl 5:8	1364
the heavens are *h* than the earth	Is 55:9	1361
so are my ways *h* than your ways	Is 55:9	1361
the scribe, in the *h* court	Jer 36:10	5945
came from the way of the *h* gate	Eze 9:2	5945
the galleries were *h* than these	Eze 42:5	3201
this shall be the *h* place of the	Eze 43:13	1354
but one was *h* than the other	Dan 8:3	1364
and the *h* came up last	Dan 8:3	1364
say unto thee, Friend, go up *h*	Lk 14:10	511
soul be subject unto the *h* powers	Rom 13:1	5242
and made *h* than the heavens	Heb 7:26	5308

HIGHEST

heavens, and the *H* gave his voice	Ps 18:13	5945
the *h* himself shall establish her	Ps 87:5	5945
nor the *h* part of the dust of the	Prov 8:26	7218
upon the *h* places of the city	Prov 9:3	4791
is higher than the *h* regardeth	Eccl 5:8	1364
took the *h* branch of the cedar	Eze 17:3	6788
I will also take of the *h* branch	Eze 17:22	6788
chamber to the *h* by the midst	Eze 41:7	5945
Hosanna in the *h*	Mt 21:9	5310
Hosanna in the *h*	Mk 11:10	5310
shall be called the Son of the *H*	Lk 1:32	5310
thee, and the power of the *H* shall	Lk 1:35	5310
be called the prophet of the *H*	Lk 1:76	5310
Glory to God in the *h*, and on	Lk 2:14	5310
ye shall be the children of the *H*	Lk 6:35	5310
sit not down in the *h* room	Lk 14:8	4411
in heaven, and glory in the *h*	Lk 19:38	5310
the *h* seats in the synagogue, and	Lk 20:46	4410

HIGHLY

Hail, thou that art *h* favoured	Lk 1:28	
for that which is *h* esteemed	Lk 16:15	5308
Herod was *h* displeased with them	Acts 12:20	2371
more than he ought to think	Rom 12:3	5252
God also hath *h* exalted him	Phil 2:9	5251
to esteem them very *h* in love for	1Th 5:13	1537,4053

HIGHMINDED

Be not *h*, but fear	Rom 11:20	5309
in this world, that they be not *h*	1Ti 6:17	5309
Traitors, heady, *h*, lovers of	2Ti 3:4	5187

HIGHNESS

by reason of his *h* I could not	Job 31:23	7613
even them that rejoice in my *h*	Is 13:3	1346

HIGHWAY

on the east side of the *h* that	Judg 21:19	4546
Beth-shemesh, and went along the *h*	1Sa 6:12	4546
in blood in the midst of the *h*	2Sa 20:12	4546
Amasa out of the *h* into the field	2Sa 20:12	4546
When he was removed out of the *h*	2Sa 20:13	4546
which is in the *h* of the fuller's	2Kin 18:17	4546
The *h* of the upright is to depart	Prov 16:17	4546
in the *h* of the fuller's field	Is 7:3	4546
there shall be an *h* for the	Is 11:16	4546
be a *h* out of Egypt to Assyria	Is 19:23	4546
an *h* shall be there, and a way, and	Is 35:8	4547
in the *h* of the fuller's field	Is 36:2	4546
in the desert a *h* for our God	Is 40:3	4546
set thine heart toward the *h*	Jer 31:21	4546
sat by the *h* side begging	Mk 10:46	3598

HIGHWAYS

the *h* were unoccupied, and the	Judg 5:6	734
kill, as at other times, in the *h*	Judg 20:31	4546
them from the city unto the *h*	Judg 20:32	4546
them in the *h* five thousand men	Judg 20:45	4546
The *h* lie waste, the wayfaring	Is 33:8	4546
a way, and my *h* shall be exalted	Is 49:11	4546
cast up, cast up the *h*	Is 62:10	4546
and they shall say in all the *h*	Amos 5:16	2351
Go ye therefore into the *h*	Mt 22:9	1327,3598
servants went out into the *h*	Mt 22:10	3598
the servant, Go out into the *h*	Lk 14:23	3598

HILEN (hi'-len) See HOLON. *A Levitical city in Judah.*

H with her suburbs, Debir with	1Chr 6:58	2432

HILKIAH (hil-ki'-ah) See HELKAI, HILKIAH'S.

1. Father of Eliakim.

out to them Eliakim the son of *H*	2Kin 18:18	2518
Then said Eliakim the son of *H*	2Kin 18:26	2518
Then came Eliakim the son of *H*	2Kin 18:37	2518
And Shallum begat *H*	1Chr 6:13	2518
and *H* begat Azariah	1Chr 6:13	2518
Of *H*, Hashabiah; of Jedaiah	Neh 12:21	2518
my servant Eliakim the son of *H*	Is 22:20	2518
Then came Eliakim, the son of *H*	Is 36:22	2518

2. A High Priest.

Go up to *H* the high priest, that	2Kin 22:4	2518
H the high priest said unto	2Kin 22:8	2518
H gave the book to Shaphan, and he	2Kin 22:8	2518
H the priest hath delivered me a	2Kin 22:10	2518
the king commanded *H* the priest	2Kin 22:12	2518
So *H* the priest, and Ahikam, and	2Kin 22:14	2518
king commanded *H* the high priest	2Kin 23:4	2518
H the priest found in the house	2Kin 23:24	2518
And Azariah the son of *H*, the son	1Chr 9:11	2518
they came to *H* the high priest	2Chr 34:9	2518
H the priest found a book of the	2Chr 34:14	2518
H answered and said to Shaphan the	2Chr 34:15	2518
H delivered the book to Shaphan	2Chr 34:15	2518
H the priest hath given me a book	2Chr 34:18	2518
And the king commanded *H*, and	2Chr 34:20	2518
And *H*, and they that the king had	2Chr 34:22	2518
H and Zechariah and Jehiel, rulers	2Chr 35:8	2518
the son of Azariah, the son of *H*	Ezr 7:1	2518
Shaphan, and Gemariah the son of *H*	Jer 29:3	2518

3. A descendant of Merari.

the son of Amaziah, the son of *H*	1Chr 6:45	2518

4. A son of Hosah.

H the second, Tebaliah the third,	1Chr 26:11	2518

5. A priest who assisted Ezra.

Anaiah, and Urijah, and *H*	Neh 8:4	2518
Seraiah the son of *H*, the son of	Neh 11:11	2518
Sallu, Amok, *H*, Jedaiah	Neh 12:7	2518

6. Father of Jeremiah.

words of Jeremiah the son of *H*	Jer 1:1	2518

HILKIAH'S (hil-ki'-ahs) Refers to Hilkiah 1.

H son, which was over the house,	Is 36:3	2518

HILL

the *h* with the rod of God in mine	Ex 17:9	1389
Hur went up to the top of the *h*	Ex 17:10	1389
and builded an altar under the *h*	Ex 24:4	2022
presumed to go up unto the *h* top	Num 14:44	2022
Canaanites which dwelt in that *h*	Num 14:45	2022
ye were ready to go up into the *h*	Deut 1:41	2022
went presumptuously up into the *h*	Deut 1:43	2022
Israel at the *h* of the foreskins	Josh 5:3	1389
the *h* country from Lebanon unto	Josh 13:6	2022
was drawn from the top of the *h*	Josh 15:9	2022
The *h* is not enough for us	Josh 17:16	2022
near the *h* that lieth on the	Josh 18:13	2022
from the *h* that lieth before	Josh 18:14	2022
in the *h* country of Judah, with	Josh 21:11	2022
the north side of the *h* of Gaash	Josh 24:30	2022
they buried him in a *h* that	Josh 24:33	1389
on the north side of the *h* Gaash	Judg 2:9	2022
by the *h* of Moreh, in the valley	Judg 7:1	1389
top of an *h* that is before Hebron	Judg 16:3	2022
the house of Abinadab in the *h*	1Sa 7:1	1389
as they went up the *h* to the city	1Sa 9:11	4608
thou shalt come to the *h* of God	1Sa 10:5	1389
when they came thither to the *h*	1Sa 10:10	1389
in the *h* of Hachilah, which is on	1Sa 23:19	1389
came down by the covert of the *h*	1Sa 25:20	2022
hide himself in the *h* of Hachilah	1Sa 26:1	1389
Saul pitched in the *h* of Hachilah	1Sa 26:3	1389
stood on the top of an *h* afar off	1Sa 26:13	2022
they were come to the *h* of Ammah	2Sa 2:24	1389
and stood on the top of an *h*	2Sa 2:25	1389
the way of the *h* side behind him	2Sa 13:34	2022
a little past the top of the *h*	2Sa 16:1	

them in the *h* before the LORD	2Sa 21:9	2022
in the *h* that is before Jerusalem	1Kin 11:7	2022
and groves, on every high *h*	1Kin 14:23	1389
he bought the *h* Samaria of Shemer	1Kin 16:24	2022
of silver, and built on the *h*	1Kin 16:24	2022
name of Shemer, owner of the *h*	1Kin 16:24	2022
behold, he sat on the top of an *h*	2Kin 1:9	2022
came to the man of God to the *h*	2Kin 4:27	2022
images and groves in every high *h*	2Kin 17:10	1389
my king upon my holy *h* of Zion	Ps 2:6	2022
and he heard me out of his holy *h*	Ps 3:4	2022
who shall dwell in thy holy *h*	Ps 15:1	2022
ascend into the *h* of the LORD	Ps 24:3	2022
the Hermonites, from the *h* Mizar	Ps 42:6	2022
let them bring me unto thy holy *h*	Ps 43:3	2022
h of God is as the *h* of Bashan	Ps 68:15	2022
an high *h* as the *h* of Bashan	Ps 68:15	2022
this is the *h* which God desireth	Ps 68:16	2022
our God, and worship at his holy *h*	Ps 99:9	2022
and to the *h* of frankincense	Song 4:6	1389
a vineyard in a very fruitful *h*	Is 5:1	7161
of Zion, the *h* of Jerusalem	Is 10:32	1389
mountain, and as an ensign on an *h*	Is 30:17	1389
mountain, and upon every high *h*	Is 30:25	1389
mount Zion, and for the *h* thereof	Is 31:4	1389
mountain and *h* shall be made low	Is 40:4	1389
when upon every high *h* and under	Jer 2:20	1389
every mountain, and from every *h*	Jer 16:16	1389
over against it upon the *h* Gareb	Jer 31:39	1389
that holdest the height of the *h*	Jer 49:16	1389
they have gone from mountain to *h*	Jer 50:6	1389
their altars, upon every high *h*	Eze 6:13	1389
them, then they saw every high *h*	Eze 20:28	1389
mountains, and upon every high *h*	Eze 34:6	1389
round about my *h* a blessing	Eze 34:26	1389
that is set on an *h* cannot be hid	Mt 5:14	3735
went into the *h* country with	Lk 1:39	3714
all the *h* country of Judaea	Lk 1:65	3714
and *h* shall be brought low	Lk 3:5	1015
h whereon their city was built	Lk 4:29	3735
they were come down from the *h*	Lk 9:37	3735
stood in the midst of Mars' *h*	Acts 17:22	697

HILLEL (hil'-lel) *Father of Abdon.*

And after him Abdon the son of *H*	Judg 12:13	1985
And Abdon the son of *H* the	Judg 12:15	1985

HILL'S

on the *h* side over against him	2Sa 16:13	2022

HILLS

and all the high *h*, that were	Gen 7:19	2022
utmost bound of the everlasting *h*	Gen 49:26	1389
him, and from the *h* I behold him	Num 23:9	1389
thereunto, in the plain, in the *h*	Deut 1:7	2022
that spring out of valleys and *h*	Deut 8:7	2022
out of whose *h* thou mayest dig	Deut 8:9	2042
go to possess it, is a land of *h*	Deut 11:11	2022
the high mountains, and upon the *h*	Deut 12:2	1389
precious things of the lasting *h*	Deut 33:15	1389
on this side Jordan, in the *h*	Josh 9:1	2022
smote all the country of the *h*	Josh 10:40	2022
Joshua took all that land, the *h*	Josh 11:16	2022
him, Their gods are gods of the *h*	1Kin 20:23	2022
said, The LORD is God of the *h*	1Kin 20:28	2022
all Israel scattered upon the *h*	1Kin 22:17	2022
in the high places, and on the *h*	2Kin 16:4	1389
in the high places, and on the *h*	2Chr 28:4	1389
or wast thou made before the *h*	Job 15:7	2022
foundations also of the *h* moved	Ps 18:7	2022
and the cattle upon a thousand *h*	Ps 50:10	2042
the little *h* rejoice on every	Ps 65:12	1389
Why leap ye, ye high *h*	Ps 68:16	2022
to the people, and the little *h*	Ps 72:3	1389
The *h* were covered with the	Ps 80:10	2022
the strength of the *h* is his also	Ps 95:4	2022
The *h* melted like wax at the	Ps 97:5	2022
let the *h* be joyful together	Ps 98:8	2022
valleys, which run among the *h*	Ps 104:10	2022
He watereth the *h* from his	Ps 104:13	2022
The high *h* are a refuge for the	Ps 104:18	2022
he toucheth the *h*, and they smoke	Ps 104:32	2022
rams, and the little *h* like lambs	Ps 114:4	1389
and ye little *h*, like lambs	Ps 114:6	1389
will lift up mine eyes unto the *h*	Ps 121:1	2022
Mountains, and all *h*	Ps 148:9	2022
before the *h* was I brought forth	Prov 8:25	1389
mountains, skipping upon the *h*	Song 2:8	1389
and shall be exalted above the *h*	Is 2:2	1389
upon all the *h* that are lifted up	Is 2:14	1389
the *h* did tremble, and their	Is 5:25	2022
on all *h* that shall be digged	Is 7:25	2022

in scales, and the *h* in a balance	Is 40:12	1389
and shalt make the *h* as chaff	Is 41:15	1389
I will make waste mountains and *h*	Is 42:15	1389
shall depart, and the *h* be removed	Is 54:10	1389
the *h* shall break forth before	Is 55:12	1389
and blasphemed me upon the *h*	Is 65:7	1389
is salvation hoped for from the *h*	Jer 3:23	1389
and all the *h* moved lightly	Jer 4:24	1389
on the *h* in the fields	Jer 13:27	1389
the green trees upon the high *h*	Jer 17:2	1389
GOD to the mountains, and to the *h*	Eze 6:3	1389
in thy *h*, and in thy valleys, and	Eze 35:8	1389
GOD to the mountains, and to the *h*	Eze 36:4	1389
unto the mountains, and to the *h*	Eze 36:6	1389
and burn incense upon the *h*	Hos 4:13	1389
and to the *h*, Fall on us	Hos 10:8	1389
the *h* shall flow with milk, and	Joel 3:18	1389
wine, and all the *h* shall melt	Amos 9:13	1389
it shall be exalted above the *h*	Mic 4:1	1389
and let the *h* hear thy voice	Mic 6:1	1389
the *h* melt, and the earth is	Nah 1:5	1389
the perpetual *h* did bow	Hab 3:6	1389
and a great crashing from the *h*	Zeph 1:10	1389
and to the *h*, Cover us	Lk 23:30	*1015*

HIM See APPENDIX.

HIMSELF See APPENDIX.

HIN

fourth part of an *h* of beaten oil	Ex 29:40	1969
the fourth part of an *h* of wine	Ex 29:40	1969
sanctuary, and of oil olive an *h*	Ex 30:24	1969
a just ephah, and a just *h*	Lev 19:36	1969
of wine, the fourth part of a *h*	Lev 23:13	1969
the fourth part of an *h* of oil	Num 15:4	1969
the fourth part of an *h* of wine	Num 15:5	1969
the third part of an *h* of oil	Num 15:6	1969
the third part of an *h* of wine	Num 15:7	1969
mingled with half an *h* of oil	Num 15:9	1969
drink offering half an *h* of wine	Num 15:10	1969
fourth part of an *h* of beaten oil	Num 28:5	1969
part of an *h* for the one lamb	Num 28:7	1969
half an *h* of wine unto a bullock	Num 28:14	1969
the third part of an *h* unto a ram	Num 28:14	1969
a fourth part of an *h* unto a lamb	Num 28:14	1969
measure, the sixth part of an *h*	Eze 4:11	1969
ram, and an *h* of oil for an ephah	Eze 45:24	1969
give, and an *h* of oil to an ephah	Eze 46:5	1969
unto, and an *h* of oil to an ephah	Eze 46:7	1969
give, and an *h* of oil to an ephah	Eze 46:11	1969
and the third part of an *h* of oil	Eze 46:14	1969

HIND

Naphtali is a *h* let loose	Gen 49:21	355
Let her be as the loving *h*	Prov 5:19	365
the *h* also calved in the field,	Jer 14:5	365

HINDER

H me not, seeing the LORD hath	Gen 24:56	309
h thee from coming unto me	Num 22:16	4513
wherefore Abner with the *h* end of	2Sa 2:23	310
all their *h* parts were inward	1Kin 7:25	268
all their *h* parts were inward	2Chr 4:4	268
against Jerusalem, and to *h* it	Neh 4:8	6213,8442
he taketh away, who can *h* him	Job 9:12	7725
together, then who can *h* him	Job 11:10	7725
smote his enemies in the *h* parts	Ps 78:66	268
his *h* part toward the utmost sea	Joel 2:20	5490
and half of them toward the *h* sea	Zec 14:8	314
he was in the *h* part of the ship,	Mk 4:38	4403
what doth *h* me to be baptized	Acts 8:36	2967
the *h* part was broken with	Acts 27:41	4403
lest we should *h* the gospel of	1Cor 9:12	5100,1464,1325
who did *h* you that ye should not	Gal 5:7	348

HINDERED

these men, that they be not *h*	Ezr 6:8	989
them that were entering in ye *h*	Lk 11:52	2967
been much *h* from coming to you	Rom 15:22	1465
but Satan *h* us	1Th 2:18	1465
that your prayers be not *h*	1Pet 3:7	1581

HINDERETH

anger, is persecuted, and none *h*	Is 14:6	2820

HINDERMOST

after, and Rachel and Joseph *h*	Gen 33:2	314
the *h* of the nations shall be a	Jer 50:12	319

HINDMOST

They shall go *h* with their	Num 2:31	314
the way, and smote the *h* of thee	Deut 25:18	2179
enemies, and smite the *h* of them	Josh 10:19	2179

HINDS

thou mark when the *h* do calve	Job 39:1	355
of the LORD maketh the *h* to calve	Ps 29:9	355
by the *h* of the field, that ye	Song 2:7	355
by the *h* of the field, that ye	Song 3:5	355

HINDS'

He maketh my feet like *h* feet	2Sa 22:34	355
He maketh my feet like *h* feet	Ps 18:33	355
he will make my feet like *h* feet	Hab 3:19	355

HINGES

the *h* of gold, both for the doors	1Kin 7:50	6596
As the door turneth upon his *h*	Prov 26:14	6735

HINNOM (hin'·nom) *A valley near Jerusalem.*

of *H* unto the south side of the	Josh 15:8	2011
before the valley of *H* westward	Josh 15:8	2011
before the valley of the son of *H*	Josh 18:16	2011
and descended to the valley of *H*	Josh 18:16	2011
the valley of the children of *H*	2Kin 23:10	2011
in the valley of the son of *H*	2Chr 28:3	2011
in the valley of the son of *H*	2Chr 33:6	2011
Beer-sheba unto the valley of *H*	Neh 11:30	2011
is in the valley of the son of *H*	Jer 7:31	2011
nor the valley of the son of *H*	Jer 7:32	2011
unto the valley of the son of *H*	Jer 19:2	2011
nor The valley of the son of *H*	Jer 19:6	2011
are in the valley of the son of *H*	Jer 32:35	2011

HIP

And he smote them *h* and thigh with	Judg 15:8	7785

HIRAH (hi'·rah) *A friend of Judah.*

Adullamite, whose name was *H*	Gen 38:1	2437
his friend *H* the Adullamite	Gen 38:12	2437

HIRAM (hi'·ram) See HIRAM'S, HURAM.
  1. A king of Tyre.

H king of Tyre sent messengers to	2Sa 5:11	2438
H king of Tyre sent his servants	1Kin 5:1	2438
for *H* was ever a lover of David	1Kin 5:1	2438
And Solomon sent to *H*, saying,	1Kin 5:2	2438
when *H* heard the words of Solomon	1Kin 5:7	2438
H sent to Solomon, saying, I have	1Kin 5:8	2438
So *H* gave Solomon cedar trees and	1Kin 5:10	2438
Solomon gave *H* twenty thousand	1Kin 5:11	2438
gave Solomon to *H* year by year	1Kin 5:11	2438
and there was peace between *H*	1Kin 5:12	2438
(Now *H* the king of Tyre had	1Kin 9:11	2438
H twenty cities in the land of	1Kin 9:11	2438
H came out from Tyre to see the	1Kin 9:12	2438
H sent to the king sixscore	1Kin 9:14	2438
H sent in the navy his servants,	1Kin 9:27	2438
And the navy also of *H*, that	1Kin 10:11	2438
of Tharshish with the navy of *H*	1Kin 10:22	2438
Now *H* king of Tyre sent	1Chr 14:1	2438
  2. An architect.

sent and fetched *H* out of Tyre	1Kin 7:13	2438
H made the lavers, and the shovels	1Kin 7:40	2438
So *H* made an end of doing all the	1Kin 7:40	2438
which *H* made to king Solomon for	1Kin 7:45	2438

HIRAM'S (hi'·rams) *Refers to Hiram 1.*

H builders did hew them, and the	1Kin 5:18	2438

HIRE

Leah said, God hath given me my *h*	Gen 30:18	7939
and of such shall be my *h*	Gen 30:32	7939
come for my *h* before thy face	Gen 30:33	7939
The ringstraked shall be thy *h*	Gen 31:8	7939
an hired thing, it came for his *h*	Ex 22:15	7939
shalt not bring the *h* of a whore	Deut 23:18	868
his day thou shalt give him his *h*	Deut 24:15	7939
unto thee will I give *h* for thy	1Kin 5:6	7939
of silver to *h* them chariots	1Chr 19:6	7936
Tyre, and she shall turn to her *h*	Is 23:17	868
her *h* shall be holiness to the	Is 23:18	868
in the balance, and *h* a goldsmith	Is 46:6	7936
harlot, in that thou scornest *h*	Eze 16:31	868
also shalt give no *h* any more	Eze 16:41	868
gathered it of the *h* of an harlot	Mic 1:7	868
return to the *h* of an harlot	Mic 1:7	868
the priests thereof teach for *h*	Mic 3:11	4242
h for man, nor any *h* for beast	Zec 8:10	7939
to *h* labourers into his vineyard	Mt 20:1	3409
labourers, and give them their *h*	Mt 20:8	3408
the labourer is worthy of his *h*	Lk 10:7	3408
the *h* of the labourers who have	Jas 5:4	3408

HIRED

for surely I have *h* thee with my	Gen 30:16	7936
an *h* servant shall not eat	Ex 12:45	7916
if it be an *h* thing, it came for	Ex 22:15	7916
the wages of him that is *h* shall	Lev 19:13	7916

or an *h* servant, shall not eat of	Lev 22:10	7916
thy maid, and for thy *h* servant	Lev 25:6	7916
But as an *h* servant, and as a	Lev 25:40	7916
according to the time of an *h*	Lev 25:50	7916
as a yearly *h* servant shall he be	Lev 25:53	7916
worth a double *h* servant to thee	Deut 15:18	7916
because they *h* against thee	Deut 23:4	7936
oppress an *h* servant that is poor	Deut 24:14	7916
wherewith Abimelech *h* vain	Judg 9:4	7936
Micah with me, and hath *h* me	Judg 18:4	7936
have *h* out themselves for bread	1Sa 2:5	7936
h the Syrians of Beth-rehob, and	2Sa 10:6	7936
the king of Israel hath *h* against	2Kin 7:6	7936
So they *h* thirty and two thousand	1Chr 19:7	7936
h masons and carpenters to repair	2Chr 24:12	7936
He *h* also an hundred thousand	2Chr 25:6	7936
h counsellors against them, to	Ezr 4:5	7936
for Tobiah and Sanballat had *h* him	Neh 6:12	7936
Therefore was he *h*, that I should	Neh 6:13	7936
but *h* Balaam against them, that	Neh 13:2	7936
Lord shave with a razor that is *h*	Is 7:20	7917
Also her *h* men are in the midst	Jer 46:21	7916
Ephraim hath *h* lovers	Hos 8:9	8566
though they have *h* among the	Hos 8:10	8566
him, Because no man hath *h* us	Mt 20:7	3409
were *h* about the eleventh hour	Mt 20:9	
in the ship with the *h* servants	Mk 1:20	3411
How many *h* servants of my	Lk 15:17	3407
make me as one of thy *h* servants	Lk 15:19	3407
whole years in his own *h* house	Acts 28:30	3410

HIRELING

days also like the days of a *h*	Job 7:1	7916
as a *h* looketh for the reward of	Job 7:2	7916
till he shall accomplish, as an *h*	Job 14:6	7916
three years, as the years of an *h*	Is 16:14	7916
according to the years of an *h*	Is 21:16	7916
that oppress the *h* in his wages	Mal 3:5	7916
But he that is an *h*, and not the	Jn 10:12	3411
h* fleeth, because he is an *h	Jn 10:13	3411

HIRES

all the *h* thereof shall be burned	Mic 1:7	868

HIREST

h them, that they may come unto	Eze 16:33	7806

HIS See APPENDIX.

HISS

shall be astonished, and shall *h*	1Kin 9:8	8319
shall *h* him out of his place	Job 27:23	8319
will *h* unto them from the end of	Is 5:26	8319
that the Lord shall *h* for the fly	Is 7:18	8319
h because of all the plagues	Jer 19:8	8319
shall *h* at all the plagues	Jer 49:17	8319
and *h* at all her plagues	Jer 50:13	8319
they *h* and wag their head at the	Lam 2:15	8319
they *h* and gnash the teeth	Lam 2:16	8319
among the people shall *h* at thee	Eze 27:36	8319
one that passeth by her shall *h*	Zeph 2:15	8319
I will *h* for them, and gather them	Zec 10:8	8319

HISSING

trouble, to astonishment, and to *h*	2Chr 29:8	8322
land desolate, and a perpetual *h*	Jer 18:16	8292
make this city desolate, and an *h*	Jer 19:8	8322
them an astonishment, and an *h*	Jer 25:9	8322
desolation, an astonishment, an *h*	Jer 25:18	8322
and an astonishment, and an *h*	Jer 29:18	8322
dragons, an astonishment, and an *h*	Jer 51:37	8322
and the inhabitants thereof an *h*	Mic 6:16	8322

HIT

Saul, and the archers *h* him	1Sa 31:3	4672
Saul, and the archers *h* him	1Chr 10:3	4672

HITHER

they shall come *h* again	Gen 15:16	2008
your youngest brother come *h*	Gen 42:15	
yourselves, that ye sold me *h*	Gen 45:5	
now it was not you that sent me *h*	Gen 45:8	
haste and bring down my father *h*	Gen 45:13	
And he said, Draw not nigh *h*	Ex 3:5	1988
there came men in *h* to night of	Josh 2:2	
the children of Israel, Come *h*	Josh 3:9	5066
and bring the description *h* to me	Josh 18:6	
Gazites, saying, Samson is come *h*	Judg 16:2	
said unto him, Who brought thee *h*	Judg 18:3	1988
We will not turn aside *h* into the	Judg 19:12	
unto her, At mealtime come thou *h*	Ruth 2:14	1988
Bring *h* a burnt offering to me,	1Sa 13:9	5066
Ahiah, Bring *h* the ark of God	1Sa 14:18	5066
Bring me *h* every man his ox, and	1Sa 14:34	5066
Let us draw near *h* unto God	1Sa 14:36	1988

And Saul said, Draw ye near *h*	1Sa 14:38	1988
Bring ye *h* to me Agag the king of	1Sa 15:32	5066
will not sit down till he come *h*	1Sa 16:11	6311
he said, Why camest thou down *h*	1Sa 17:28	
the priest, Bring *h* the ephod	1Sa 23:9	5066
I pray thee, bring me *h* the ephod	1Sa 30:7	5066
have brought them *h* unto my lord	2Sa 1:10	
lame, thou shalt not come in *h*	2Sa 5:6	
I sent unto thee, saying, Come *h*	2Sa 14:32	
pray you, unto Joab, Come near *h*	2Sa 20:16	
Hasten *h* Micaiah the son of Imlah	1Kin 22:9	
waters, and they were divided *h*	2Kin 2:8	
smitten the waters, they parted *h*	2Kin 2:14	
saying, The man of God is come *h*	2Kin 8:7	2008
to David, Thou shalt not come *h*	1Chr 11:5	
shall not bring in the captives *h*	2Chr 28:13	
of Assur, which brought us up *h*	Ezr 4:2	
Therefore his people return *h*	Ps 73:10	1988
bring *h* the timbrel, the pleasant	Ps 81:2	
is simple, let him turn in *h*	Prov 9:4	
is simple, let him turn in *h*	Prov 9:16	
it be said unto thee, Come up *h*	Prov 25:7	
But draw near *h*, ye sons of the	Is 57:3	
them unto thee art thou brought *h*	Eze 40:4	
high God, come forth, and come *h*	Dan 3:26	
art thou come *h* to torment us	Mt 8:29	5602
He said, Bring them *h* to me	Mt 14:18	5602
bring him *h* to me	Mt 17:17	5602
how camest thou in *h* not having a	Mt 22:12	5602
and straightway he will send him *h*	Mk 11:3	5602
Bring thy son *h*	Lk 9:41	5602
the city, and bring in *h* the poor	Lk 14:21	5602
bring *h* the fatted calf, and kill	Lk 15:23	
I should reign over them, bring *h*	Lk 19:27	5602
loose him, and bring him *h*	Lk 19:30	
not, neither come *h* to draw	Jn 4:15	1759
Go, call thy husband, and come *h*	Jn 4:16	1759
him, Rabbi, when camest thou *h*	Jn 6:25	5602
Reach *h* thy finger, and behold my	Jn 20:27	5602
reach *h* thy hand, and thrust it	Jn 20:27	5602
came *h* for that intent, that he	Acts 9:21	5602
call *h* Simon, whose surname is	Acts 10:32	3333
world upside down are come *h* also	Acts 17:6	1759
For ye have brought *h* these men	Acts 19:37	
Therefore, when they were come *h*	Acts 25:17	1759
which said, Come up *h*, and I will	Rev 4:1	5602
saying unto them, Come up *h*	Rev 11:12	5602
with me, saying unto me, Come *h*	Rev 17:1	1204
and talked with me, saying, Come *h*	Rev 21:9	1204

HITHERTO

behold, *h* thou wouldest not hear	Ex 7:16	5704,3541
as the Lord hath blessed me *h*	Josh 17:14	5704,3541
H thou hast mocked me, and told	Judg 16:13	5704,2008
and grief have I spoken *h*	1Sa 1:16	5704,2008
H hath the Lord helped us	1Sa 7:12	5704,2008
that thou hast brought me *h*	2Sa 7:18	1988
have been thy father's servant *h*	2Sa 15:34	227
Who *h* waited in the king's gate	1Chr 9:18	5704,2008
for *h* the greatest part of them	1Chr 12:29	5704,2008
that thou hast brought me *h*	1Chr 17:16	1988
H shalt thou come, but no further	Job 38:11	5704,6311
h have I declared thy wondrous	Ps 71:17	5704,2008
terrible from their beginning *h*	Is 18:2	1973
terrible from their beginning *h*	Is 18:7	1973
H is the end of the matter	Dan 7:28	5705,3542
them, My Father worketh *h*	Jn 5:17	2193,737
***H* have ye asked nothing in my**	Jn 16:24	2193,737
to come unto you, (but was let *h*	Rom 1:13	891,1204
for *h* ye were not able to bear it	1Cor 3:2	3768

HITTITE (hit'-tite) See HITTITES. *A descendant of Heth.*

Ephron the *H* answered Abraham in	Gen 23:10	2850
of Ephron the son of Zohar the *H*	Gen 25:9	2850
the daughter of Beeri the *H*	Gen 26:34	2850
the daughter of Elon the *H*	Gen 26:34	2850
Adah the daughter of Elon the *H*	Gen 36:2	2850
is in the field of Ephron the *H*	Gen 49:29	2850
the *H* for a possession of a	Gen 49:30	2850
of a buryingplace of Ephron the *H*	Gen 50:13	2850
Hivite, the Canaanite, and the *H*	Ex 23:28	2850
Canaanite, the Amorite, and the *H*	Ex 33:2	2850
and the Canaanite, and the *H*	Ex 34:11	2850
sea over against Lebanon, and the *H*	Josh 9:1	2850
west, and to the Amorite, and the *H*	Josh 11:3	2850
David and said to Ahimelech the *H*	1Sa 26:6	2850
of Eliam, the wife of Uriah the *H*	2Sa 11:3	2850
Joab, saying, Send me Uriah the *H*	2Sa 11:6	2850
and Uriah the *H* died also	2Sa 11:17	2850
servant Uriah the *H* is dead also	2Sa 11:21	2850
servant Uriah the *H* is dead also	2Sa 11:24	2850
killed Uriah the *H* with the sword	2Sa 12:9	2850

of Uriah the *H* to be thy wife	2Sa 12:10	2850
Uriah the *H:* thirty and seven	2Sa 23:39	2850
only in the matter of Uriah the *H*	1Kin 15:5	2850
Uriah the *H,* Zabad the son of	1Chr 11:41	2850
an Amorite, and thy mother an *H*	Eze 16:3	2850
your mother was an *H,* and your	Eze 16:45	2850

HITTITES (hit'-tites)

And the *H,* and the Perizzites, and	Gen 15:20	2850
place of the Canaanites, and the *H*	Ex 3:8	2850
land of the Canaanites, and the *H*	Ex 3:17	2850
land of the Canaanites, and the *H*	Ex 13:5	2850
in unto the Amorites, and the *H*	Ex 23:23	2850
and the *H,* and the Jebusites, and	Num 13:29	2850
many nations before thee, the *H*	Deut 7:1	2850
namely, the *H,* and the Amorites,	Deut 20:17	2850
Euphrates, all the land of the *H*	Josh 1:4	2850
you the Canaanites, and the *H*	Josh 3:10	2850
the *H,* the Amorites, and the	Josh 12:8	2850
and the Canaanites, and the *H*	Josh 24:11	2850
man went into the land of the *H*	Judg 1:26	2850
dwelt among the Canaanites, *H*	Judg 3:5	2850
that were left of the Amorites, *H*	1Kin 9:20	2850
and so for all the kings of the *H*	1Kin 10:29	2850
Edomites, Zidonians, and *H*	1Kin 11:1	2850
against us the kings of the *H*	2Kin 7:6	2850
horses for all the kings of the *H*	2Chr 1:17	2850
people that were left of the *H*	2Chr 8:7	2850
even of the Canaanites, the *H*	Ezr 9:1	2850
the land of the Canaanites, the *H*	Neh 9:8	2850

HIVITE (hi'-vite) *A descendant of Canaan.*

And the *H,* and the Arkite, and the	Gen 10:17	2340
Shechem the son of Hamor the *H*	Gen 34:2	2340
Anah the daughter of Zibeon the *H*	Gen 36:2	2340
thee, which shall drive out the *H*	Ex 23:28	2340
Hittite, and the Perizzite, the *H*	Ex 33:2	2340
and the Perizzite, and the *H*	Ex 34:11	2340
Canaanite, the Perizzite, the *H*	Josh 9:1	2340
to the *H* under Hermon in the land	Josh 11:3	2340
And the *H,* and the Arkite, and the	1Chr 1:15	2340

HIVITES (hi'-vites)

and the Perizzites, and the *H*	Ex 3:8	2340
and the Perizzites, and the *H*	Ex 3:17	2340
and the Amorites, and the *H*	Ex 13:5	2340
and the Canaanites, the *H*	Ex 23:23	2340
and the Perizzites, and the *H*	Deut 7:1	2340
and the Perizzites, the *H*	Deut 20:17	2340
and the Hittites, and the *H*	Josh 3:10	2340
the men of Israel said unto the *H*	Josh 9:7	2340
save the *H* the inhabitants of	Josh 11:19	2340
Canaanites, the Perizzites, the *H*	Josh 12:8	2340
and the Girgashites, the *H*	Josh 24:11	2340
the *H* that dwelt in mount Lebanon	Judg 3:3	2340
and Amorites, and Perizzites, and *H*	Judg 3:5	2340
and to all the cities of the *H*	2Sa 24:7	2340
Amorites, Hittites, Perizzites, *H*	1Kin 9:20	2340
and the Perizzites, and the *H*	2Chr 8:7	2340

HIZKI See HEZEKI.

HIZKIAH (hiz-ki'-ah) *See* HEZEKIAH, HIZKIJAH. *An ancestor of Zephaniah.*

the son of Amariah, the son of *H*	Zeph 1:1	2396

HIZKIJAH (hiz-ki'-jah) *See* HIZKIAH. *An Israelite who renewed the covenant.*

Ater, *H,* Azzur,	Neh 10:17	2396

HO

unto whom he said, *H,* such a one	Ruth 4:1	1945
H, every one that thirsteth, come	Is 55:1	1945
H, h, come forth, and flee from	Zec 2:6	1945

HOAR

as small as the *h* frost on the	Ex 16:14	3713
let not his *h* head go down to the	1Kin 2:6	7872
but his *h* head bring thou down to	1Kin 2:9	7872
scattereth the *h* frost like ashes	Ps 147:16	3713
even to *h* hairs will I carry you	Is 46:4	7872

HOARY

shalt rise up before the *h* head	Lev 19:32	7872
the *h* frost of heaven, who hath	Job 38:29	3713
one would think the deep to be *h*	Job 41:32	7872
The *h* head is a crown of glory,	Prov 16:31	7872

HOBAB (ho'-bab) *See* JETHRO. *Another name for Jethro.*

And Moses said unto *H,* the son of	Num 10:29	2246
of *H* the father in law of Moses	Judg 4:11	2246

HOBAH (ho'-bah) *Place where Abraham pursued the five kings.*

them, and pursued them unto *H*	Gen 14:15	2327

HOBAIAH See HABAIAH.

HOD (hod) *A son of Zophah.*

Bezer, and *H,* and Shamma, and	1Chr 7:37	1963

HODAIAH (ho-da-i'-ah) *See* HODAVIAH. *A royal descendant of Judah.*

And the sons of Elioenai were, *H*	1Chr 3:24	1939

HODAVIAH (ho-da-vi'-ah) *See* HODAIAH, HODEVAH.
1. *A chief of Manasseh.*

and Azriel, and Jeremiah, and *H*	1Chr 5:24	1938

2. *Son of Hassenuah.*

son of Meshullam, the son of *H*	1Chr 9:7	1938

3. *A family of exiles.*

and Kadmiel, of the children of *H*	Ezr 2:40	1938

HODESH (ho'-desh) *Wife of Shaharaim.*

And he begat of *H* his wife	1Chr 8:9	2321

HODEVAH (ho-de'-vah) *See* HODAVIAH. *A family of exiles.*

Kadmiel, and of the children of *H*	Neh 7:43	1937

HODIAH (ho-di'-ah) *See* HODIJAH. *A wife of Mered.*

of his wife *H* the sister of Naham	1Chr 4:19	1940

HODIJAH (ho-di'-jah) *See* HODIAH.
1. *A Levite.*

Jamin, Akkub, Shabbethai, *H*	Neh 8:7	1940
Bani, Hashabniah, Sherebiah, *H*	Neh 9:5	1940
And their brethren, Shebaniah, *H*	Neh 10:10	1940
H, Bani, Beninu	Neh 10:13	1940

2. *A leader of the people.*

H, Hashum, Bezai,	Neh 10:18	1940

HOGLAH (hog'-lah) *See* BETH-HOGLAH. *A daughter of Zelophehad.*

were Mahlah, and Noah, *H,* Milcah,	Num 26:33	2295
Mahlah, Noah, and *H,* and Milcah,	Num 27:1	2295
For Mahlah, Tirzah, and *H,* and	Num 36:11	2295
his daughters, Mahlah, and Noah, *H*	Josh 17:3	2295

HOHAM (ho'-ham) *An Amorite king.*

sent unto *H* king of Hebron	Josh 10:3	1944

HOISED

h up the mainsail to the wind, and	Acts 27:40	*1869*

HOLD

the men laid *h* upon his hand, and	Gen 19:16	2388
the lad, and *h* him in thine hand	Gen 21:18	2388
his hand took *h* on Esau's heel	Gen 25:26	270
that they may *h* a feast unto me	Ex 5:1	
them go, and wilt *h* them still,	Ex 9:2	2388
for we must *h* a feast unto the	Ex 10:9	
for you, and ye shall *h* your peace	Ex 14:14	2790
sorrow shall take *h* on the	Ex 15:14	270
trembling shall take *h* upon them	Ex 15:15	270
for the LORD will not *h* him	Ex 20:7	
loops may take *h* one of another	Ex 26:5	6901
father shall *h* his peace at her	Num 30:4	2790
h his peace at her from day to	Num 30:14	2790
for the LORD will not *h* him	Deut 5:11	
father and his mother lay *h* on him	Deut 21:19	8610
lay *h* on her, and lie with her, and	Deut 22:28	8610
and mine hand take *h* on judgment	Deut 32:41	270
they entered into an *h* of the	Judg 9:46	6877
Abimelech, and put them to the *h*	Judg 9:49	6877
set the *h* on fire upon them	Judg 9:49	6877
Samson took *h* of the two middle	Judg 16:29	3943
H thy peace, lay thine hand upon	Judg 18:19	2790
laid *h* on his concubine, and	Judg 19:29	2388
that thou hast upon thee, and *h* it	Ruth 3:15	270
he laid *h* upon the skirt of his	1Sa 15:27	2388
the while that David was in the *h*	1Sa 22:4	4686
unto David, Abide not in the *h*	1Sa 22:5	4686
and his men gat them up unto the *h*	1Sa 24:22	4686
Then David took *h* on his clothes	2Sa 1:11	2388
lay thee *h* on one of the young	2Sa 2:21	270
how then should I *h* up my face to	2Sa 2:22	5375
good tidings, I took *h* of him	2Sa 4:10	270
David took the strong *h* of Zion	2Sa 5:7	4686
of it, and went down to the *h*	2Sa 5:17	4686
the ark of God, and took *h* of it	2Sa 6:6	270
unto him to eat, he took *h* of her	2Sa 13:11	2388
but *h* now thy peace, my sister	2Sa 13:20	2790
and his head caught *h* of the oak	2Sa 18:9	2388
And David was then in an *h*	2Sa 23:14	4686
And came to the strong *h* of Tyre	2Sa 24:7	4013
caught *h* on the horns of the	1Kin 1:50	2388
he hath caught *h* on the horns of	1Kin 1:51	270
Now therefore *h* him not guiltless	1Kin 2:9	
caught *h* on the horns of the	1Kin 2:28	2388
have taken *h* upon other gods, and	1Kin 9:9	2388
the altar, saying, Lay *h* on him	1Kin 13:4	8610
h ye your peace	2Kin 2:3	2814
h ye your peace	2Kin 2:5	2814

H

he took *h* of his own clothes, and	2Kin 2:12	2388
door, and *h* him fast at the door	2Kin 6:32	3905
good tidings, and we *h* our peace	2Kin 7:9	2814
And David was then in the *h*	1Chr 11:16	4686
h to the wilderness men of might	1Chr 12:8	4679
and Judah to the *h* unto David	1Chr 12:16	4679
put forth his hand to *h* the ark	1Chr 13:9	270
and laid *h* on other gods, and	2Chr 7:22	2388
H your peace, for the day is holy	Neh 8:11	2013
shall *h* out the golden sceptre	Est 4:11	3447
Teach me, and I will *h* my tongue	Job 6:24	2790
he shall *h* it fast, but it shall	Job 8:15	2388
that thou wilt not *h* me innocent	Job 9:28	
thy lies make men *h* their peace	Job 11:3	2790
ye would altogether *h* your peace	Job 13:5	2790
H your peace, let me alone, that	Job 13:13	2790
if I *h* my tongue, I shall give up	Job 13:19	2790
righteous also shall *h* on his way	Job 17:9	270
and trembling taketh *h* on my flesh	Job 21:6	270
My righteousness I *h* fast	Job 27:6	2388
Terrors take *h* on him as waters,	Job 27:20	5381
affliction have taken *h* upon me	Job 30:16	270
h thy peace, and I will speak	Job 33:31	2790
h thy peace, and I shall teach	Job 33:33	2790
and justice take *h* on thee	Job 36:17	8551
That it might take *h* of the ends	Job 38:13	270
him that layeth at him cannot *h*	Job 41:26	6965
H up my goings in thy paths, that	Ps 17:5	8551
Take *h* of shield and buckler, and	Ps 35:2	2388
h not thy peace at my tears	Ps 39:12	2790
iniquities have taken *h* upon me	Ps 40:12	5381
Fear took *h* upon them there, and	Ps 48:6	270
thy wrathful anger take *h* of them	Ps 69:24	5381
h not thy peace, and be not still,	Ps 83:1	2790
H not thy peace, O God of my	Ps 109:1	2790
the pains of hell gat *h* upon me	Ps 116:3	4672
Horror hath taken *h* upon me	Ps 119:53	270
H thou me up, and I shall be safe	Ps 119:117	5582
and anguish have taken *h* on me	Ps 119:143	4672
me, and thy right hand shall *h* me	Ps 139:10	270
neither take they *h* of the paths	Prov 2:19	5381
life to them that lay *h* upon her	Prov 3:18	2388
Take fast *h* of instruction	Prov 4:13	2388
her steps take *h* on hell	Prov 5:5	8551
spider take *h* with her hands	Prov 30:28	8610
and her hands *h* the distaff	Prov 31:19	8551
to lay *h* on folly, till I might	Eccl 2:3	270
thou shouldest take *h* of this	Eccl 7:18	270
They all *h* swords, being expert	Song 3:8	270
I will take *h* of the boughs	Song 7:8	270
When a man shall take *h* of his	Is 3:6	8610
women shall take *h* of one man	Is 4:1	2388
lay *h* of the prey, and shall carry	Is 5:29	270
and sorrows shall take *h* of them	Is 13:8	270
pangs have taken *h* upon me	Is 21:3	270
Or let him take *h* of my strength	Is 27:5	2388
over to his strong *h* for fear	Is 31:9	5553
thy God will *h* thy right hand	Is 41:13	2388
will *h* thine hand, and will keep	Is 42:6	2388
son of man that layeth *h* on it	Is 56:2	2388
me, and take *h* of my covenant	Is 56:4	2388
it, and taketh *h* of my covenant	Is 56:6	2388
Zion's sake will I not *h* my peace	Is 62:1	2814
which shall never *h* their peace	Is 62:6	2814
up himself to take *h* of thee	Is 64:7	2388
wilt thou *h* thy peace, and afflict	Is 64:12	2814
cisterns, that can *h* no water	Jer 2:13	3557
I cannot *h* my peace, because thou	Jer 4:19	2790
They shall lay *h* on bow and spear	Jer 6:23	2388
anguish hath taken *h* of us	Jer 6:24	2388
they *h* fast deceit, they refuse	Jer 8:5	2388
astonishment hath taken *h* on me	Jer 8:21	2388
They shall *h* the bow and the lance	Jer 50:42	2388
anguish took *h* of him, and pangs	Jer 50:43	2388
When they took *h* of thee by thy	Eze 29:7	8610
to make it strong to *h* the sword	Eze 30:21	8610
about, that they might have *h*	Eze 41:6	270
but they had not *h* in the wall of	Eze 41:6	270
Then shall he say, *H* thy tongue	Amos 6:10	2013
the strong *h* of the daughter of	Mic 4:8	6076
and thou shalt take *h*, but shalt	Mic 6:14	5253
a strong *h* in the day of trouble	Nah 1:7	4581
they shall deride every strong *h*	Hab 1:10	4013
H thy peace at the presence of	Zeph 1:7	
they not take *h* of your fathers	Zec 1:5	5381
that ten men shall take *h* out of	Zec 8:23	2388
even shall take *h* of the skirt of	Zec 8:23	2388
did build herself a strong *h*	Zec 9:3	4692
Turn you to the strong *h*, ye	Zec 9:12	1225
them, and *h* themselves not guilty	Zec 11:5	816
they shall lay *h* every one on the	Zec 14:13	2388

or else he will *h* to the one	Mt 6:24	472
day, will he not lay *h* on it	Mt 12:11	2902
For Herod had laid *h* on John	Mt 14:3	2902
because they should *h* their peace	Mt 20:31	4623
for all *h* John as a prophet	Mt 21:26	2192
same is he: *h* him fast	Mt 26:48	2902
the temple, and ye laid no *h* on me	Mt 26:55	2902
they that had laid *h* on Jesus led	Mt 26:57	2902
H thy peace, and come out of him	Mk 1:25	5392
it, they went out to lay *h* on him	Mk 3:21	2902
laid *h* upon John, and bound him in	Mk 6:17	2902
be, which they have received to *h*	Mk 7:4	2902
ye *h* the tradition of men, as the	Mk 7:8	2902
him that he should *h* his peace	Mk 10:48	4623
And they sought to lay *h* on him	Mk 12:12	2902
and the young men laid *h* on him	Mk 14:51	2902
H thy peace, and come out of him	Lk 4:35	5392
or else he will *h* to the one	Lk 16:13	472
him, that he should *h* his peace	Lk 18:39	4623
if these should *h* their peace	Lk 19:40	4623
they might take *h* of his words	Lk 20:20	1949
they could not take *h* of his	Lk 20:26	1949
they laid *h* upon one Simon, a	Lk 23:26	1949
put them in *h* unto the next day	Acts 4:3	5084
with the hand to *h* their peace	Acts 12:17	4601
but speak, and *h* not thy peace	Acts 18:9	4623
of men, who *h* the truth in	Rom 1:18	2722
by, let the first *h* his peace	1Cor 14:30	4601
and *h* such in reputation	Phil 2:29	2192
h fast that which is good	1Th 5:21	2722
h the traditions which ye have	2Th 2:15	2902
lay *h* on eternal life, whereunto	1Ti 6:12	1949
they may lay *h* on eternal life	1Ti 6:19	1949
H fast the form of sound words,	2Ti 1:13	2192
if we *h* fast the confidence and	Heb 3:6	2722
if we *h* the beginning of our	Heb 3:14	2722
let us *h* fast our profession	Heb 4:14	2902
lay *h* upon the hope set before us	Heb 6:18	2902
Let us *h* fast the profession of	Heb 10:23	2722
that *h* the doctrine of Balaam	Rev 2:14	2902
them that *h* the doctrine of the	Rev 2:15	2902
have already *h* fast till I come	Rev 2:25	2902
and heard, and *h* fast, and repent	Rev 3:3	5083
h that fast which thou hast, that	Rev 3:11	2902
the *h* of every foul spirit, and a	Rev 18:2	5438
he laid *h* on the dragon, that old	Rev 20:2	2902

HOLDEN

Surely there was not *h* such a	2Kin 23:22	6213
was *h* to the LORD in Jerusalem	2Kin 23:23	6213
be *h* in cords of affliction	Job 36:8	3920
and thy right hand hath *h* me up	Ps 18:35	5582
have I been *h* up from the womb	Ps 71:6	5564
thou hast *h* me by my right hand	Ps 73:23	270
he shall be *h* with the cords of	Prov 5:22	8551
I have long time *h* my peace	Is 42:14	2814
Cyrus, whose right hand I have *h*	Is 45:1	2388
But their eyes were *h* that they	Lk 24:16	2902
that he should be *h* of it	Acts 2:24	2902
Yea, he shall be *h* up	Rom 14:4	

HOLDEST

h thy peace at this time, then	Est 4:14	2790
thy face, and *h* me for thine enemy	Job 13:24	2803
Thou *h* mine eyes waking	Ps 77:4	270
that *h* the height of the hill	Jer 49:16	8610
h thy tongue when the wicked	Hab 1:13	2790
thou *h* fast my name, and hast not	Rev 2:13	2902

HOLDETH

still he *h* fast his integrity,	Job 2:3	2388
He *h* back the face of his throne,	Job 26:9	270
Which *h* our soul in life, and	Ps 66:9	7760
man of understanding *h* his peace	Prov 11:12	2790
when he *h* his peace, is counted	Prov 17:28	2790
there is none that *h* with me in	Dan 10:21	2388
him that *h* the sceptre from the	Amos 1:5	8551
him that *h* the sceptre from	Amos 1:8	8551
These things saith he that *h* the	Rev 2:1	2902

HOLDING

his hands from *h* of bribes	Is 33:15	8551
I am weary with *h* in	Jer 6:11	3557
h the tradition of the elders	Mk 7:3	2902
H forth the word of life	Phil 2:16	1907
not *h* the Head, from which all	Col 2:19	2902
H faith, and a good conscience	1Ti 1:19	2192
H the mystery of the faith in a	1Ti 3:9	2192
H fast the faithful word as he	Titus 1:9	472
h the four winds of the earth,	Rev 7:1	2902

HOLDS

whether in tents, or in strong *h* .... Num 13:19   4013
mountains, and caves, and strong *h* .... Judg 6:2   4679
in the wilderness in strong *h* 1Sa 23:14   4679
with us in strong *h* in the wood 1Sa 23:19   4679
and dwelt in strong *h* at En-gedi 1Sa 23:29   4679
their strong *h* wilt thou set on 2Kin 8:12   4013
And he fortified his strong *h* 2Chr 11:11   4694
hast brought his strong *h* to ruin .... Ps 89:40   4013
to destroy the strong *h* thereof .... Is 23:11   4581
and he shall destroy thy strong *h* .... Jer 48:18   4013
the strong *h* are surprised, and .... Jer 48:41   4679
they have remained in their *h* .... Jer 51:30   4679
strong *h* of the daughter of Judah .... Lam 2:2   4013
he hath destroyed his strong *h* .... Lam 2:5   4013
they brought him into *h*, that his .... Eze 19:9   4686
his devices against the strong *h* .... Dan 11:24   4013
most strong *h* with a strange god .... Dan 11:39   4013
and throw down all thy strong *h* .... Mic 5:11   4013
All thy strong *h* shall be like .... Nah 3:12   4013
the siege, fortify thy strong *h* .... Nah 3:14   4013
to the pulling down of strong *h* 2Cor 10:4   4013

HOLE

shall be an *h* in the top of it .... Ex 28:32   6310
work round about the *h* of it .... Ex 28:32   6310
as it were the *h* of an habergeon, ... Ex 28:32   6310
there was an *h* in the midst of .... Ex 39:23   6310
as the *h* of an habergeon, with a .... Ex 39:23   6310
with a band round about the *h* .... Ex 39:23   6310
bored a *h* in the lid of it, and 2Kin 12:9   2356
in his hand by the *h* of the door .... Song 5:4   2356
shall play on the *h* of the asp .... Is 11:8   2356
to the *h* of the pit whence ye are .... Is 51:1   4718
hide it there in a *h* of the rock .... Jer 13:4   5357
I looked, behold a *h* in the wall .... Eze 8:7   2356

HOLE'S

nest in the sides of the *h* mouth .... Jer 48:28   6354

HOLES

h where they had hid themselves 1Sa 14:11   2356
shall go into the *h* of the rocks .... Is 2:19   4631
in the *h* of the rocks, and upon .... Is 7:19   5357
they are all of them snared in *h* .... Is 42:22   2356
out of the *h* of the rocks .... Jer 16:16   5357
their *h* like worms of the earth .... Mic 7:17   4526
and filled his *h* with prey .... Nah 2:12   2356
wages to put it into a bag with *h* .... Hag 1:6   5344
shall consume away in their *h* .... Zec 14:12   2356
saith unto him, The foxes have *h* .... Mt 8:20   5454
Jesus said unto him, Foxes have *h* ..... Lk 9:58   5454

HOLIER

for I am *h* than thou .... Is 65:5   6942

HOLIEST

which is called the *H* of all .... Heb 9:3   *39*
that the way into the *h* of all .... Heb 9:8   *39*
into the *h* by the blood of Jesus .... Heb 10:19   *39*

HOLILY

are witnesses, and God also, how *h* 1Th 2:10   *3743*

HOLINESS

Who is like thee, glorious in *h* .... Ex 15:11   6944
of a signet, *H* TO THE LORD .... Ex 28:36   6944
of a signet, *H* TO THE LORD .... Ex 39:30   6944
the LORD in the beauty of *h* 1Chr 16:29   6944
should praise the beauty of *h* 2Chr 20:21   6944
they sanctified themselves in *h* 2Chr 31:18   6944
the LORD in the beauty of *h* .... Ps 29:2   6944
at the remembrance of his *h* .... Ps 30:4   6944
sitteth upon the throne of his *h* .... Ps 47:8   6944
our God, in the mountain of his *h* .... Ps 48:1   6944
God hath spoken in his *h* .... Ps 60:6   6944
Once have I sworn by my *h* that I .... Ps 89:35   6944
h becometh thine house, O LORD, ... Ps 93:5   6944
the LORD in the beauty of *h* .... Ps 96:9   6944
at the remembrance of his *h* .... Ps 97:12   6944
God hath spoken in his *h* .... Ps 108:7   6944
in the beauties of *h* from the .... Ps 110:3   6944
her hire shall be *h* to the LORD .... Is 23:18   6944
it shall be called The way of *h* .... Is 35:8   6944
drink it in the courts of my *h* .... Is 62:9   6944
from the habitation of thy *h* .... Is 63:15   6944
The people of thy *h* have .... Is 63:18   6944
Israel was *h* unto the LORD, and .... Jer 2:3   6944
and because of the words of his *h* .... Jer 23:9   6944
of justice, and mountain of *h* .... Jer 31:23   6944
The Lord GOD hath sworn by his *h* .... Amos 4:2   6944
deliverance, and there shall be *h* .... Obad 17   6944
of the horses, *H* UNTO THE LORD .... Zec 14:20   6944
in Judah shall be *h* unto the LORD .... Zec 14:21   6944

---

the *h* of the LORD which he loved .... Mal 2:11   6944
In *h* and righteousness before him, ... Lk 1:75   *3742*
or *h* we had made this man to walk ...... Acts 3:12   *2150*
according to the spirit of *h* .... Rom 1:4   *42*
servants to righteousness unto *h* .... Rom 6:19   *38*
to God, ye have your fruit unto *h* .... Rom 6:22   *38*
perfecting *h* in the fear of God 2Cor 7:1   *42*
in righteousness and true *h* .... Eph 4:24   *3742*
unblameable in *h* before God 1Th 3:13   *42*
us unto uncleanness, but unto *h* 1Th 4:7   *38*
and charity and *h* with sobriety 1Ti 2:15   *38*
be in behaviour as becometh *h* .... Titus 2:3   *2412*
we might be partakers of his *h* .... Heb 12:10   *41*
Follow peace with all men, and *h* .... Heb 12:14   *38*

HOLLOW

he touched the *h* of his thigh .... Gen 32:25   3709
the *h* of Jacob's thigh was out of .... Gen 32:25   3709
which is upon the *h* of the thigh .... Gen 32:32   3709
because he touched the *h* of .... Gen 32:32   3709
H with boards shalt thou make it .... Ex 27:8   5014
he made the altar *h* with boards .... Ex 38:7   5014
walls of the house with *h* strakes .... Lev 14:37   8258
But God clave an *h* place that was .... Judg 15:19   4388
the waters in the *h* of his hand .... Is 40:12   8168
was four fingers: it was *h* .... Jer 52:21   5014

HOLON (ho'-lon) See HILEN.

1. A Levitical city in Judah.
And Goshen, and *H*, and Giloh .... Josh 15:51   2473
H with her suburbs, and Debir with ...... Josh 21:15   2473
   2. A Moabite city.
upon *H*, and upon Jahazah, and upon ... Jer 48:21   2473

HOLPEN

they have *h* the children of Lot .... Ps 83:8   2220
because thou, LORD, hast *h* me .... Ps 86:17   5826
he that is *h* shall fall down, and .... Is 31:3   5826
they shall be *h* with a little .... Dan 11:34   5826
He hath *h* his servant Israel, in .... Lk 1:54   *482*

HOLY

whereon thou standest is *h* ground .... Ex 3:5   6944
there shall be an *h* convocation .... Ex 12:16   6944
shall be an *h* convocation to you .... Ex 12:16   6944
strength unto thy *h* habitation .... Ex 15:13   6944
of the *h* sabbath unto the LORD .... Ex 16:23   6944
of priests, and an *h* nation .... Ex 19:6   6918
the sabbath day, to keep it *h* .... Ex 20:8   6942
And ye shall be *h* men unto me .... Ex 22:31   6944
the *h* place and the most *h* .... Ex 26:33   6944
the testimony in the most *h* place .... Ex 26:34   6944
thou shalt make *h* garments for .... Ex 28:2   6944
they shall make *h* garments for .... Ex 28:4   6944
when he goeth in unto the *h* place .... Ex 28:29   6944
unto the *h* place before the LORD .... Ex 28:35   6944
bear the iniquity of the *h* things .... Ex 28:38   6944
shall hallow in all their *h* gifts .... Ex 28:38   6944
altar to minister in the *h* place .... Ex 28:43   6944
put the *h* crown upon the mitre .... Ex 29:6   6944
the *h* garments of Aaron shall be .... Ex 29:29   6944
to minister in the *h* place .... Ex 29:30   6944
seethe his flesh in the *h* place .... Ex 29:31   6918
eat thereof, because they are *h* .... Ex 29:33   6944
not be eaten, because it is *h* .... Ex 29:34   6944
and it shall be an altar most *h* .... Ex 29:37   6944
toucheth the altar shall be *h* .... Ex 29:37   6944
it is most *h* unto the LORD .... Ex 30:10   6944
make it an oil of *h* ointment .... Ex 30:25   6944
it shall be an *h* anointing oil .... Ex 30:25   6944
them, that they may be most *h* .... Ex 30:29   6944
toucheth them shall be *h* .... Ex 30:29   6942
This shall be an *h* anointing oil .... Ex 30:31   6944
it is *h*, and it shall be *h* unto .... Ex 30:32   6944
tempered together, pure and *h* .... Ex 30:35   6944
it shall be unto you most *h* .... Ex 30:36   6944
shall be unto thee *h* for the LORD .... Ex 30:37   6944
the *h* garments for Aaron the .... Ex 31:10   6944
and sweet incense for the *h* place .... Ex 31:11   6944
for it is *h* unto you .... Ex 31:14   6944
sabbath of rest, *h* to the LORD .... Ex 31:15   6944
there shall be to you an *h* day .... Ex 35:2   6944
to do service in the *h* place .... Ex 35:19   6944
the *h* garments for Aaron the .... Ex 35:19   6944
service, and for the *h* garments .... Ex 35:21   6944
he made the *h* anointing oil, and .... Ex 37:29   6944
in all the work of the *h* place .... Ex 38:24   6944
to do service in the *h* place .... Ex 39:1   6944
made the *h* garments for Aaron .... Ex 39:1   6944
plate of the *h* crown of pure gold .... Ex 39:30   6944
to do service in the *h* place .... Ex 39:41   6944
the *h* garments for Aaron the .... Ex 39:41   6944
and it shall be *h* .... Ex 40:9   6944

and it shall be an altar most *h*	Ex 40:10	6944
put upon Aaron the *h* garments	Ex 40:13	6944
it is a thing most *h* of the	Lev 2:3	6944
it is a thing most *h* of the	Lev 2:10	6944
in the *h* things of the LORD	Lev 5:15	6944
that he hath done in the *h* thing	Lev 5:16	6944
shall it be eaten in the *h* place	Lev 6:16	6918
it is most *h*, as is the sin	Lev 6:17	6944
one that toucheth them shall be *h*	Lev 6:18	6942
it is most *h*	Lev 6:25	6944
in the *h* place shall it be eaten,	Lev 6:26	6918
the flesh thereof shall be *h*	Lev 6:27	6942
it was sprinkled in the *h* place	Lev 6:27	6918
it is most *h*	Lev 6:29	6944
reconcile withal in the *h* place	Lev 6:30	6944
it is most *h*	Lev 7:1	6944
it shall be eaten in the *h* place	Lev 7:6	6918
it is most *h*	Lev 7:6	6944
put the golden plate, the *h* crown	Lev 8:9	6944
ye may put difference between *h*	Lev 10:10	6944
for it is most *h*	Lev 10:12	6944
And ye shall eat it in the *h* place	Lev 10:13	6918
h place, seeing it is most *h*	Lev 10:17	6944
not brought in within the *h* place	Lev 10:18	6944
have eaten it in the *h* place	Lev 10:18	6944
yourselves, and ye shall be *h*	Lev 11:44	6918
for I am *h*	Lev 11:44	6918
therefore be *h*, for I am *h*	Lev 11:45	6918
burnt offering, in the *h* place	Lev 14:13	6944
it is most *h*	Lev 14:13	6944
h place within the vail before	Lev 16:2	6944
shall Aaron come into the *h* place	Lev 16:3	6944
He shall put on the *h* linen coat	Lev 16:4	6944
these are *h* garments	Lev 16:4	6944
make an atonement for the *h* place	Lev 16:16	6944
make an atonement in the *h* place	Lev 16:17	6944
an end of reconciling the *h* place	Lev 16:20	6944
on when he went into the *h* place	Lev 16:23	6944
flesh with water in the *h* place	Lev 16:24	6918
to make atonement in the *h* place	Lev 16:27	6944
clothes, even the *h* garments	Lev 16:32	6944
an atonement for the *h* sanctuary	Lev 16:33	6944
and say unto them, Ye shall be *h*	Lev 19:2	6918
for I the LORD your God am *h*	Lev 19:2	6918
be *h* to praise the LORD withal	Lev 19:24	6944
and to profane my *h* name	Lev 20:3	6944
yourselves therefore, and be ye *h*	Lev 20:7	6918
And ye shall be *h* unto me	Lev 20:26	6918
for I the LORD am *h*, and have	Lev 20:26	6918
They shall be *h* unto their God,	Lev 21:6	6918
therefore they shall be *h*	Lev 21:6	6944
for he is *h* unto his God	Lev 21:7	6918
he shall be *h* unto thee	Lev 21:8	6918
LORD, which sanctify you, am *h*	Lev 21:8	6918
of the most *h*, and of the *h*	Lev 21:22	6944
the *h* things of the children of	Lev 22:2	6944
that they profane not my *h* name	Lev 22:2	6944
that goeth unto the *h* things	Lev 22:3	6944
he shall not eat of the *h* things	Lev 22:4	6944
and shall not eat of the *h* things	Lev 22:6	6944
afterward eat of the *h* things	Lev 22:7	6944
no stranger eat of the *h* thing	Lev 22:10	6944
shall not eat of the *h* thing	Lev 22:10	6944
of an offering of the *h* things	Lev 22:12	6944
eat of the *h* thing unwittingly	Lev 22:14	6944
unto the priest with the *h* thing	Lev 22:14	6944
the *h* things of the children of	Lev 22:15	6944
when they eat their *h* things	Lev 22:16	6944
shall ye profane my *h* name	Lev 22:32	6944
proclaim to be *h* convocations	Lev 23:2	6944
sabbath of rest, an *h* convocation	Lev 23:3	6944
even *h* convocations, which ye	Lev 23:4	6944
ye shall have an *h* convocation	Lev 23:7	6944
seventh day is an *h* convocation	Lev 23:8	6944
they shall be *h* to the LORD for	Lev 23:20	6944
that it may be an *h* convocation	Lev 23:21	6944
of trumpets, an *h* convocation	Lev 23:24	6944
it shall be an *h* convocation unto	Lev 23:27	6944
day shall be an *h* convocation	Lev 23:35	6944
be an *h* convocation unto you	Lev 23:36	6944
proclaim to be *h* convocations	Lev 23:37	6944
they shall eat it in the *h* place	Lev 24:9	6918
for it is most *h* unto him of the	Lev 24:9	6944
it shall be *h* unto you	Lev 25:12	6944
of such unto the LORD shall be *h*	Lev 27:9	6944
the exchange thereof shall be *h*	Lev 27:10	6944
his house to be *h* unto the LORD	Lev 27:14	6944
shall be *h* unto the LORD, as a	Lev 27:21	6944
as a *h* thing unto the LORD	Lev 27:23	6944
thing is most *h* unto the LORD	Lev 27:28	6944
it is *h* unto the LORD	Lev 27:30	6944

tenth shall be *h* unto the LORD	Lev 27:32	6944
and the change thereof shall be *h*	Lev 27:33	6944
about the most *h* things	Num 4:4	6944
they shall not touch any *h* thing	Num 4:15	6944
approach unto the most *h* things	Num 4:19	6944
see when the *h* things are covered	Num 4:20	6944
the *h* things of the children of	Num 5:9	6944
the priest shall take *h* water in	Num 5:17	6918
unto the LORD, he shall be *h*	Num 6:5	6918
separation he is *h* unto the LORD	Num 6:8	6918
this is *h* for the priest, with	Num 6:20	6918
and be *h* unto your God	Num 15:40	6918
seeing all the congregation are *h*	Num 16:3	6918
shew who are his, and who is *h*	Num 16:5	6918
LORD doth choose, he shall be *h*	Num 16:7	6918
be thine of the most *h* things	Num 18:9	6944
unto me, shall be most *h* for thee	Num 18:9	6944
In the most *h* place shalt thou	Num 18:10	6944
it shall be *h* unto thee	Num 18:10	6944
they are *h*	Num 18:17	6944
heave offerings of the *h* things	Num 18:19	6944
the *h* things of the children of	Num 18:32	6944
in the *h* place shalt thou cause	Num 28:7	6944
day shall be an *h* convocation	Num 28:18	6944
ye shall have an *h* convocation	Num 28:25	6944
ye shall have an *h* convocation	Num 28:26	6944
ye shall have an *h* convocation	Num 29:1	6944
seventh month an *h* convocation	Num 29:7	6944
ye shall have an *h* convocation	Num 29:12	6944
with the *h* instruments, and the	Num 31:6	6944
which was anointed with the *h* oil	Num 35:25	6944
For thou art an *h* people unto the	Deut 7:6	6918
Only thy *h* things which thou hast	Deut 12:26	6944
For thou art an *h* people unto the	Deut 14:2	6918
for thou art an *h* people unto the	Deut 14:21	6944
therefore shall thy camp be *h*	Deut 23:14	6918
Look down from thy *h* habitation	Deut 26:15	6944
that thou mayest be an *h* people	Deut 26:19	6918
thee an *h* people unto himself	Deut 28:9	6918
and thy Urim be with thy *h* one	Deut 33:8	2623
place whereon thou standest is *h*	Josh 5:15	6944
for he is an *h* God	Josh 24:19	6918
There is none *h* as the LORD	1Sa 2:2	6918
to stand before this *h* LORD God	1Sa 6:20	6918
vessels of the young men are *h*	1Sa 21:5	6944
oracle, even for the most *h* place	1Kin 6:16	6944
the inner house, the most *h* place	1Kin 7:50	6944
all the *h* vessels that were in	1Kin 8:4	6944
of the house, to the most *h* place	1Kin 8:6	6944
in the *h* place before the oracle	1Kin 8:8	6944
were come out of the *h* place	1Kin 8:10	6944
that this is an *h* man of God	2Kin 4:9	6918
even against the *H* One of Israel	2Kin 19:22	6918
all the work of the place most *h*	1Chr 6:49	6944
Glory ye in his *h* name	1Chr 16:10	6944
we may give thanks to thy *h* name	1Chr 16:35	6944
the *h* vessels of God, into the	1Chr 22:19	6944
should sanctify the most *h* things	1Chr 23:13	6944
in the purifying of all *h* things	1Chr 23:28	6944
and the charge of the *h* things	1Chr 23:32	6944
I have prepared for the *h* house	1Chr 29:3	6944
thine *h* name cometh of thine hand	1Chr 29:16	6944
And he made the most *h* house	2Chr 3:8	6944
in the most *h* house he made two	2Chr 3:10	6944
thereof for the most *h* place	2Chr 4:22	6944
all the *h* vessels that were in	2Chr 5:5	6944
the house, into the most *h* place	2Chr 5:7	6944
were come out of the *h* place	2Chr 5:11	6944
Israel, because the places are *h*	2Chr 8:11	6944
they shall go in, for they are *h*	2Chr 23:6	6944
the filthiness out of the *h* place	2Chr 29:5	6944
h place unto the God of Israel	2Chr 29:7	6944
came up to his *h* dwelling place	2Chr 30:27	6944
the tithe of *h* things which were	2Chr 31:6	6944
of the LORD, and the most *h* things	2Chr 31:14	6944
which were *h* unto the LORD	2Chr 35:3	6918
Put the *h* ark in the house which	2Chr 35:3	6944
stand in the *h* place according to	2Chr 35:5	6944
but the other *h* offerings sod	2Chr 35:13	6944
not eat of the most *h* things	Ezr 2:63	6944
unto them, Ye are *h* unto the LORD	Ezr 8:28	6944
the vessels are *h* also	Ezr 8:28	6944
so that the *h* seed have mingled	Ezr 9:2	6944
to give us a nail in his *h* place	Ezr 9:8	6944
not eat of the most *h* things	Neh 7:65	6944
This day is *h* unto the LORD your	Neh 8:9	6918
for this day is *h* unto our Lord	Neh 8:10	6918
Hold your peace, for the day is *h*	Neh 8:11	6918
known unto them thy *h* sabbath	Neh 9:14	6944
on the sabbath, or on the *h* day	Neh 10:31	6944
set feasts, and for the *h* things	Neh 10:33	6944

to dwell in Jerusalem the *h* city	Neh 11:1	6944
All the Levites in the *h* city	Neh 11:18	6944
they sanctified *h* things unto the	Neh 12:47	
concealed the words of the *H* One	Job 6:10	6918
my king upon my *h* hill of Zion	Ps 2:6	6944
and he heard me out of his *h* hill	Ps 3:4	6944
I worship toward thy *h* temple	Ps 5:7	6944
The LORD is in his *h* temple	Ps 11:4	6944
who shall dwell in thy *h* hill	Ps 15:1	6944
thine *H* One to see corruption	Ps 16:10	2623
he will hear him from his *h*	Ps 20:6	6944
But thou art *h*, O thou that	Ps 22:3	6918
or who shall stand in his *h* place	Ps 24:3	6944
up my hands toward thy *h* oracle	Ps 28:2	6944
we have trusted in his *h* name	Ps 33:21	6944
let them bring me unto thy *h* hill	Ps 43:3	6944
the *h* place of the tabernacles of	Ps 46:4	6918
take not thy *h* spirit from me	Ps 51:11	6944
thy house, even of thy *h* temple	Ps 65:4	6918
is God in his *h* habitation	Ps 68:5	6944
them, as in Sinai, in the *h* place	Ps 68:17	6944
art terrible out of thy *h* places	Ps 68:35	4720
the harp, O thou *H* One of Israel	Ps 71:22	6918
limited the *H* One of Israel	Ps 78:41	6918
thy *h* temple have they defiled	Ps 79:1	6944
for I am *h*	Ps 86:2	2623
foundation is in the *h* mountains	Ps 87:1	6944
the *H* One of Israel is our king	Ps 89:18	6918
spakest in vision to thy *h* one	Ps 89:19	2623
with my *h* oil have I anointed him	Ps 89:20	6944
his right hand, and his *h* arm	Ps 98:1	6944
for it is *h*	Ps 99:3	6918
for he is *h*	Ps 99:5	6918
our God, and worship at his *h* hill	Ps 99:9	6944
for the LORD our God is *h*	Ps 99:9	6918
is within me, bless his *h* name	Ps 103:1	6944
Glory ye in his *h* name	Ps 105:3	6944
For he remembered his *h* promise	Ps 105:42	6944
to give thanks unto thy *h* name	Ps 106:47	6944
h and reverend is his name	Ps 111:9	6918
will worship toward thy *h* temple	Ps 138:2	6944
his ways, and in all his works	Ps 145:17	2623
flesh bless his *h* name for ever	Ps 145:21	6944
of the *h* is understanding	Prov 9:10	6918
man who devoureth that which is *h*	Prov 20:25	6944
nor have the knowledge of the *h*	Prov 30:3	6918
and gone from the place of the *h*	Eccl 8:10	6918
they have provoked the *H* One of	Is 1:4	6918
in Jerusalem, shall be called *h*	Is 4:3	6918
God that is *h* shall be sanctified	Is 5:16	6918
let the counsel of the *H* One of	Is 5:19	6918
the word of the *H* One of Israel	Is 5:24	6918
another, and said, *H, h, h*	Is 6:3	6918
so the *h* seed shall be the	Is 6:13	6944
a fire, and his *H* One for a flame	Is 10:17	6918
the *H* One of Israel, in truth	Is 10:20	6918
nor destroy in all my *h* mountain	Is 11:9	6944
for great is the *H* One of Israel	Is 12:6	6918
respect to the *H* One of Israel	Is 17:7	6918
LORD in the *h* mount at Jerusalem	Is 27:13	6944
rejoice in the *H* One of Israel	Is 29:19	6918
and sanctify the *H* One of Jacob	Is 29:23	6918
cause the *H* One of Israel to	Is 30:11	6918
thus saith the *H* One of Israel	Is 30:12	6918
the Lord GOD, the *H* One of Israel	Is 30:15	6918
night when a *h* solemnity is kept	Is 30:29	6942
look not unto the *H* One of Israel	Is 31:1	6918
even against the *H* One of Israel	Is 37:23	6918
I be equal? saith the *H* One	Is 40:25	6918
thy redeemer, the *H* One of Israel	Is 41:14	6918
glory in the *H* One of Israel	Is 41:16	6918
the *H* One of Israel hath created	Is 41:20	6918
the *H* One of Israel, thy Saviour	Is 43:3	6918
redeemer, the *H* One of Israel	Is 43:14	6918
I am the LORD, your *H* One	Is 43:15	6918
the *H* One of Israel, and his Maker	Is 45:11	6918
is his name, the *H* One of Israel	Is 47:4	6918
call themselves of the *h* city	Is 48:2	6944
thy Redeemer, the *H* One of Israel	Is 48:17	6918
Redeemer of Israel, and his *H* One	Is 49:7	6918
the *H* One of Israel, and he shall	Is 49:7	6918
garments, O Jerusalem, the *h* city	Is 52:1	6944
his *h* arm in the eyes of all the	Is 52:10	6944
thy Redeemer the *H* One of Israel	Is 54:5	6918
God, and for the *H* One of Israel	Is 55:5	6918
will I bring to my *h* mountain	Is 56:7	6944
and shall inherit my *h* mountain	Is 57:13	6944
eternity, whose name is *H*	Is 57:15	6918
h place, with him also that is of	Is 57:15	6918
doing thy pleasure on my *h* day	Is 58:13	6944
the *h* of the LORD, honourable	Is 58:13	6918

to the *H* One of Israel, because	Is 60:9	6918
The Zion of the *H* One of Israel	Is 60:14	6918
The *h* people, The redeemed of the	Is 62:12	6944
rebelled, and vexed his *h* Spirit	Is 63:10	6944
that put his *h* Spirit within him	Is 63:11	6944
Thy *h* cities are a wilderness,	Is 64:10	6944
Our *h* and our beautiful house,	Is 64:11	6944
LORD, that forget my *h* mountain	Is 65:11	6944
nor destroy in all my *h* mountain	Is 65:25	6944
to my *h* mountain Jerusalem, saith	Is 66:20	6944
the *h* flesh is passed from thee	Jer 11:15	6944
his voice from his *h* habitation	Jer 25:30	6944
east, shall be *h* unto the LORD	Jer 31:40	6944
against the *H* One of Israel	Jer 50:29	6944
sin against the *H* One of Israel	Jer 51:5	6918
their *h* places shall be defiled	Eze 7:24	6942
but pollute ye my *h* name no more	Eze 20:39	6944
For in mine *h* mountain, in the	Eze 20:40	6944
oblations, with all your *h* things	Eze 20:40	
drop thy word toward the *h* places	Eze 21:2	4720
Thou hast despised mine *h* things	Eze 22:8	6944
and have profaned mine *h* things	Eze 22:26	6944
put no difference between the *h*	Eze 22:26	6944
wast upon the *h* mountain of God	Eze 28:14	6944
went, they profaned my *h* name	Eze 36:20	6944
But I had pity for mine *h* name	Eze 36:21	6944
but for mine *h* name's sake	Eze 36:22	6944
As the *h* flock, as the flock of	Eze 36:38	6944
So will I make my *h* name known in	Eze 39:7	6944
them pollute my *h* name any more	Eze 39:7	6944
am the LORD, the *H* One in Israel	Eze 39:7	6918
and will be jealous for my *h* name	Eze 39:25	6944
unto me, This is the most *h* place	Eze 41:4	6944
they be *h* chambers, where the	Eze 42:13	6944
LORD shall eat the most *h* things	Eze 42:13	6944
shall they lay the most *h* things	Eze 42:13	6944
for the place is *h*	Eze 42:13	6918
the *h* place into the utter court	Eze 42:14	6944
for they are *h*	Eze 42:14	
my *h* name, shall the house of	Eze 43:7	6944
they have even defiled my *h* name	Eze 43:8	6944
round about shall be most *h*	Eze 43:12	6944
kept the charge of mine *h* things	Eze 44:8	6944
h things, in the most *h* place	Eze 44:13	6944
and lay them in the *h* chambers	Eze 44:19	6944
the difference between the *h*	Eze 44:23	6944
LORD, an *h* portion of the land	Eze 45:1	6944
This shall be *h* in all the	Eze 45:1	6944
the sanctuary and the most *h* place	Eze 45:3	6944
The *h* portion of the land shall	Eze 45:4	6944
an *h* place for the sanctuary	Eze 45:4	4720
the oblation of the *h* portion	Eze 45:6	6944
of the oblation of the *h* portion	Eze 45:7	6944
the oblation of the *h* portion	Eze 45:7	6944
into the *h* chambers of the	Eze 46:19	6944
priests, shall be this *h* oblation	Eze 48:10	6944
h by the border of the Levites	Eze 48:12	6944
for it is *h* unto the LORD	Eze 48:14	6944
against the oblation of the *h*	Eze 48:18	6944
the oblation of the *h* portion	Eze 48:18	6944
ye shall offer the *h* oblation	Eze 48:20	6944
and on the other of the *h* oblation	Eze 48:21	6944
and it shall be the *h* oblation	Eze 48:21	6944
whom is the spirit of the *h* gods	Dan 4:8	6922
spirit of the *h* gods is in thee	Dan 4:9	6922
an *h* one came down from heaven	Dan 4:13	6922
demand by the word of the *h* ones	Dan 4:17	6922
spirit of the *h* gods is in thee	Dan 4:18	6922
an *h* one coming down from heaven,	Dan 4:23	6922
whom is the spirit of the *h* gods	Dan 5:11	6922
the mighty and the *h* people	Dan 8:24	6918
city Jerusalem, thy *h* mountain	Dan 9:16	6944
God for the *h* mountain of my God	Dan 9:20	6944
thy people and upon thy *h* city	Dan 9:24	6944
prophecy, and to anoint the most *H*	Dan 9:24	6944
shall be against the *h* covenant	Dan 11:28	6944
against the *h* covenant	Dan 11:30	6944
them that forsake the *h* covenant	Dan 11:30	6944
seas in the glorious *h* mountain	Dan 11:45	6944
scatter the power of the *h* people	Dan 12:7	6944
the *H* One in the midst of thee	Hos 11:9	6918
sound an alarm in my *h* mountain	Joel 2:1	6944
dwelling in Zion, my *h* mountain	Joel 3:17	6944
then shall Jerusalem be *h*	Joel 3:17	6944
same maid, to profane my *h* name	Amos 2:7	6944
ye have drunk upon my *h* mountain	Obad 16	6944
look again toward thy *h* temple	Jonah 2:4	6944
in unto thee, into thine *h* temple	Jonah 2:7	6944
you, the Lord from his *h* temple	Mic 1:2	6944
O LORD my God, mine *H* One	Hab 1:12	6918
But the LORD is in his *h* temple	Hab 2:20	6944

the *H* One from mount Paran	Hab 3:3	6918
haughty because of my *h* mountain	Zeph 3:11	6944
If one bear *h* flesh in the skirt	Hag 2:12	6944
oil, or any meat, shall it be *h*	Hag 2:12	6942
Judah his portion in the *h* land	Zec 2:12	6944
raised up out of his *h* habitation	Zec 2:13	6944
the LORD of hosts the *h* mountain	Zec 8:3	6944
found with child of the *H* Ghost	Mt 1:18	40
in her is of the *H* Ghost	Mt 1:20	40
baptize you with the *H* Ghost	Mt 3:11	40
taketh him up into the *h* city	Mt 4:5	40
not that which is *h* unto the dogs	Mt 7:6	40
the *H* Ghost shall not be forgiven	Mt 12:31	
speaketh against the *H* Ghost	Mt 12:32	40
the prophet, stand in the *h* place	Mt 24:15	40
all the *h* angels with him, then	Mt 25:31	40
and went into the *h* city, and	Mt 27:53	40
and of the Son, and of the *H* Ghost	Mt 28:19	40
baptize you with the *H* Ghost	Mk 1:8	40
who thou art, the *H* One of God	Mk 1:24	40
shall blaspheme against the *H*.	Mk 3:29	40
that he was a just man and an *h*	Mk 6:20	40
of his Father with the *h* angels	Mk 8:38	40
David himself said by the *H* Ghost	Mk 12:36	40
ye that speak, but the *H* Ghost	Mk 13:11	40
shall be filled with the *H* Ghost	Lk 1:15	40
The *H* Ghost shall come upon thee,	Lk 1:35	40
therefore also that *h* thing which	Lk 1:35	40
was filled with the *H* Ghost	Lk 1:41	40
and *h* is his name	Lk 1:49	40
was filled with the *H* Ghost	Lk 1:67	40
by the mouth of his *h* prophets	Lk 1:70	40
and to remember his *h* covenant	Lk 1:72	40
shall be called *h* to the Lord	Lk 2:23	40
and the *H* Ghost was upon him	Lk 2:25	40
revealed unto him by the *H* Ghost	Lk 2:26	40
baptize you with the *H* Ghost	Lk 3:16	40
the *H* Ghost descended in a bodily	Lk 3:22	40
Jesus being full of the *H* Ghost	Lk 4:1	40
the *H* One of God	Lk 4:34	40
his Father's, and of the *h* angels	Lk 9:26	40
the *H* Spirit to them that ask him	Lk 11:13	40
that blasphemeth against the *H*.	Lk 12:10	40
For the *H* Ghost shall teach you	Lk 12:12	40
which baptizeth with the *H* Ghost	Jn 1:33	40
for the *H* Ghost was not yet given	Jn 7:39	40
Comforter, which is the *H* Ghost	Jn 14:26	40
H Father, keep through thine own	Jn 17:11	40
unto them, Receive ye the *H* Ghost	Jn 20:22	40
after that he through the *H* Ghost	Acts 1:2	40
the *H* Ghost not many days hence	Acts 1:5	40
after that the *H* Ghost is come	Acts 1:8	40
which the *H* Ghost by the mouth of	Acts 1:16	40
were all filled with the *H* Ghost	Acts 2:4	40
thine *H* One to see corruption	Acts 2:27	3741
Father the promise of the *H* Ghost	Acts 2:33	40
receive the gift of the *H* Ghost	Acts 2:38	40
But ye denied the *H* One and the	Acts 3:14	40
h prophets since the world began	Acts 3:21	40
Peter, filled with the *H* Ghost	Acts 4:8	40
a truth against thy *h* child Jesus	Acts 4:27	40
by the name of thy *h* child Jesus	Acts 4:30	40
were all filled with the *H* Ghost	Acts 4:31	40
thine heart to lie to the *H* Ghost	Acts 5:3	40
and so is also the *H* Ghost	Acts 5:32	40
report, full of the *H* Ghost	Acts 6:3	40
full of faith and of the *H* Ghost	Acts 6:5	40
words against this *h* place	Acts 6:13	40
where thou standest is *h* ground	Acts 7:33	40
ye do always resist the *H* Ghost	Acts 7:51	40
But he, being full of the *H* Ghost	Acts 7:55	40
they might receive the *H* Ghost	Acts 8:15	40
and they received the *H* Ghost	Acts 8:17	40
hands the *H* Ghost was given	Acts 8:18	40
hands, he may receive the *H* Ghost	Acts 8:19	40
and be filled with the *H* Ghost	Acts 9:17	40
and in the comfort of the *H* Ghost	Acts 9:31	40
was warned from God by an *h* angel	Acts 10:22	40
of Nazareth with the *H* Ghost	Acts 10:38	40
the *H* Ghost fell on all them	Acts 10:44	40
out the gift of the *H* Ghost	Acts 10:45	40
the *H* Ghost as well as we	Acts 10:47	40
the *H* Ghost fell on them, as on	Acts 11:15	40
be baptized with the *H* Ghost	Acts 11:16	40
good man, and full of the *H* Ghost	Acts 11:24	40
the *H* Ghost said, Separate me	Acts 13:2	40
being sent forth by the *H* Ghost	Acts 13:4	40
Paul,) filled with the *H* Ghost	Acts 13:9	40
thine *H* One to see corruption	Acts 13:35	3741
with joy, and with the *H* Ghost	Acts 13:52	40
witness, giving them the *H* Ghost	Acts 15:8	40

For it seemed good to the *H* Ghost	Acts 15:28	40
were forbidden of the *H* Ghost to	Acts 16:6	40
Have ye received the *H* Ghost	Acts 19:2	40
whether there be any *H* Ghost	Acts 19:2	40
them, the *H* Ghost came on them	Acts 19:6	40
Save that the *H* Ghost witnesseth	Acts 20:23	40
over the which the *H* Ghost hath	Acts 20:28	40
and said, Thus saith the *H* Ghost	Acts 21:11	40
and hath polluted this *h* place	Acts 21:28	40
Well spake the *H* Ghost by Esaias	Acts 28:25	40
his prophets in the *h* scriptures	Rom 1:2	40
abroad in our hearts by the *H*	Rom 5:5	40
law is *h*, and the commandment *h*	Rom 7:12	40
bearing me witness in the *H* Ghost	Rom 9:1	40
be *h*, the lump is also *h*	Rom 11:16	40
and if the root be *h*, so are the	Rom 11:16	40
your bodies a living sacrifice, *h*	Rom 12:1	40
and peace, and joy in the *H* Ghost	Rom 14:17	40
through the power of the *H* Ghost	Rom 15:13	40
being sanctified by the *H* Ghost	Rom 15:16	40
Salute one another with an *h* kiss	Rom 16:16	40
but which the *H* Ghost teacheth	1Cor 2:13	40
for the temple of God is *h*	1Cor 3:17	40
of the *H* Ghost which is in you	1Cor 6:19	40
but now are they *h*	1Cor 7:14	40
that she may be *h* both in body	1Cor 7:34	40
h things live of the things of	1Cor 9:13	2413
is the Lord, but by the *H* Ghost	1Cor 12:3	40
ye one another with an *h* kiss	1Cor 16:20	40
by kindness, by the *H* Ghost	2Cor 6:6	40
Greet one another with an *h* kiss	2Cor 13:12	40
and the communion of the *H* Ghost	2Cor 13:14	40
of the world, that we should be *h*	Eph 1:4	40
with that *h* Spirit of promise	Eph 1:13	40
unto an *h* temple in the Lord	Eph 2:21	40
now revealed unto his *h* apostles	Eph 3:5	40
And grieve not the *h* Spirit of God	Eph 4:30	40
but that it should be *h* and	Eph 5:27	40
through death, to present you *h*	Col 1:22	40
therefore, as the elect of God, *h*	Col 3:12	40
also in power, and in the *H* Ghost	1Th 1:5	40
with joy of the *H* Ghost	1Th 1:6	40
also given unto us his *h* Spirit	1Th 4:8	40
all the brethren with an *h* kiss	1Th 5:26	40
be read unto all the *h* brethren	1Th 5:27	40
every where, lifting up *h* hands	1Ti 2:8	3741
and called us with an *h* calling	2Ti 1:9	40
the *H* Ghost which dwelleth in us	2Ti 1:14	40
thou hast known the *h* scriptures	2Ti 3:15	2413
lover of good men, sober, just, *h*	Titus 1:8	3741
and renewing of the *H* Ghost	Titus 3:5	40
miracles, and gifts of the *H* Ghost	Heb 2:4	40
h brethren, partakers of the	Heb 3:1	40
Wherefore (as the *H* Ghost saith	Heb 3:7	40
made partakers of the *H* Ghost	Heb 6:4	40
high priest became us, who is *h*	Heb 7:26	3741
The *H* Ghost this signifying, that	Heb 9:8	40
entered in once into the *h* place	Heb 9:12	39
into the *h* places made with hands	Heb 9:24	39
high priest entereth into the *h*	Heb 9:25	39
Whereof the *H* Ghost also is a	Heb 10:15	40
the *H* Ghost sent down from heaven	1Pet 1:12	40
as he which hath called you is *h*	1Pet 1:15	40
so be ye *h* in all manner of	1Pet 1:15	40
Be ye *h*; for I am *h*	1Pet 1:16	40
an *h* priesthood, to offer up	1Pet 2:5	40
an *h* nation, a peculiar people	1Pet 2:9	40
in the old time the *h* women also	1Pet 3:5	40
we were with him in the *h* mount	2Pet 1:18	40
but *h* men of God spake as they	2Pet 1:21	40
as they were moved by the *H* Ghost	2Pet 1:21	40
to turn from the *h* commandment	2Pet 2:21	40
spoken before by the *h* prophets	2Pet 3:2	40
ye to be in all *h* conversation	2Pet 3:11	40
ye have an unction from the *H* One	1Jn 2:20	40
Father, the Word, and the *H* Ghost	1Jn 5:7	40
yourselves on your most *h* faith	Jude 20	40
praying in the *H* Ghost	Jude 20	40
These things saith he that is *h*	Rev 3:7	40
and night, saying, *H*, *h*, *h*	Rev 4:8	40
saying, How long, O Lord, *h*	Rev 6:10	40
the *h* city shall they tread under	Rev 11:2	40
in the presence of the *h* angels	Rev 14:10	40
for thou only art *h*	Rev 15:4	3741
ye *h* apostles and prophets	Rev 18:20	40
h is he that hath part in the	Rev 20:6	40
And I John saw the *h* city, new	Rev 21:2	40
the *h* Jerusalem, descending out	Rev 21:10	40
the Lord God of the *h* prophets	Rev 22:6	40
that is *h*, let him be *h* still	Rev 22:11	37
of life, and out of the *h* city	Rev 22:19	40

HOLYDAY

with a multitude that kept *h*	Ps 42:4	2287
ir. drink, or in respect of an *h*	Col 2:16	1859

HOMAM (ho'-mam) See HEMAM. *A son of Lotan.*

of Lotan; Hori, and *H*	1Chr 1:39	1950

HOME

by her, until his lord came *h*	Gen 39:16	1004
of his house, Bring these men *h*	Gen 43:16	1004
And when Joseph came *h*, they	Gen 43:26	1004
field, and shall not be brought *h*	Ex 9:19	1004
mother, whether she be born at *h*	Lev 18:9	1004
shalt bring her *h* to thine house	Deut 21:12	8432
he shall be free at *h* one year	Deut 24:5	1004
father's household, *h* unto thee	Josh 2:18	1004
If ye bring me *h* again to fight	Judg 11:9	7725
your way, that thou mayest go *h*	Judg 19:9	168
hath brought me *h* again empty	Ruth 1:21	7725
And they went unto their own *h*	1Sa 2:20	4725
and bring their calves *h* from them	1Sa 6:7	1004
and shut up their calves at *h*	1Sa 6:10	1004
And Saul also went to Gibeah	1Sa 10:26	1004
no more *h* to his father's house	1Sa 18:2	7725
And Saul went *h*	1Sa 24:22	1004
Then David sent *h* to Tamar	2Sa 13:7	1004
not fetch *h* again his banished	2Sa 14:13	7725
gat him *h* to his house, to his	2Sa 17:23	1004
in Lebanon, and two months at *h*	1Kin 5:14	1004
Come *h* with me, and refresh	1Kin 13:7	1004
Come *h* with me, and eat bread	1Kin 13:15	1004
glory of this, and tarry at *h*	2Kin 14:10	1004
I bring the ark of God *h* to me	1Chr 13:12	
So David brought not the ark *h* to	1Chr 13:13	
him out of Ephraim, to go *h* again	2Chr 25:10	4725
they returned *h* in great anger	2Chr 25:10	4725
abide now at *h*	2Chr 25:19	1004
and when he came *h*, he sent and	Est 5:10	1004
that he will bring *h* thy seed	Job 39:12	7725
tarried at *h* divided the spoil	Ps 68:12	1004
For the goodman is not at *h*	Prov 7:19	1004
will come *h* at the day appointed	Prov 7:20	1004
because man goeth to his long *h*	Eccl 12:5	1004
that he should carry him *h*	Jer 39:14	1004
bereaveth, at *h* there is as death	Lam 1:20	1004
a proud man, neither keepeth at *h*	Hab 2:5	5115
and when ye brought it *h*, I did	Hag 1:9	1004
lieth at *h* sick of the palsy	Mt 8:6	3614
Go *h* to thy friends, and tell them	Mk 5:19	3624
which are at *h* at my house	Lk 9:61	
And when he cometh *h*, he calleth	Lk 15:6	3624
disciple took her unto his own *h*	Jn 19:27	
went away again unto their own *h*	Jn 20:10	1438
and they returned *h* again	Acts 21:6	2398
any man hunger, let him eat at *h*	1Cor 11:34	3624
let them ask their husbands at *h*	1Cor 14:35	3624
whilst we are at *h* in the body	2Cor 5:6	1736
learn first to shew piety at *h*	1Ti 5:4	2398
be discreet, chaste, keepers at *h*	Titus 2:5	3626

HOMEBORN

One law shall be to him that is *h*	Ex 12:49	249
is he a *h* slave?	Jer 2:14	1004

HOMER

a *h* of barley seed shall be	Lev 27:16	2563
the seed of an *h* shall yield an	Is 5:10	2563
contain the tenth part of an *h*	Eze 45:11	2563
the ephah the tenth part of an *h*	Eze 45:11	2563
thereof shall be after the *h*	Eze 45:11	2563
part of an ephah of an *h* of wheat	Eze 45:13	2563
of an ephah of an *h* of barley	Eze 45:13	2563
which is an *h* of ten baths	Eze 45:14	2563
for ten baths are an *h*	Eze 45:14	2563
an *h* of barley, and an half *h*	Hos 3:2	2563

HOMERS

gathered least gathered ten *h*	Num 11:32	2563

HONEST

ground are they, which in an *h*	Lk 8:15	2570
among you seven men of *h* report	Acts 6:3	
Provide things in the sight of	Rom 12:17	2570
Providing for *h* things, not only	2Cor 8:21	2570
that ye should do that which is *h*	2Cor 13:7	2570
are true, whatsoever things are *h*	Phil 4:8	4586
conversation *h* among the Gentiles	1Pet 2:12	2570

HONESTLY

Let us walk *h*, as in the day	Rom 13:13	2156
That ye may walk *h* toward them	1Th 4:12	2156
in all things willing to live *h*	Heb 13:18	2573

HONESTY

life in all godliness and *h*	1Ti 2:2	4587

HONEY

a little balm, and a little *h*	Gen 43:11	1706
a land flowing with milk and *h*	Ex 3:8	1706
a land flowing with milk and *h*	Ex 3:17	1706
a land flowing with milk and *h*	Ex 13:5	1706
of it was like wafers made with *h*	Ex 16:31	1706
a land flowing with milk and *h*	Ex 33:3	1706
shall burn no leaven, nor any *h*	Lev 2:11	1706
land that floweth with milk and	Lev 20:24	1706
surely it floweth with milk and *h*	Num 13:27	1706
land which floweth with milk and *h*	Num 14:8	1706
land that floweth with milk and *h*	Num 16:13	1706
land that floweth with milk and *h*	Num 16:14	1706
land that floweth with milk and *h*	Deut 6:3	1706
a land of oil olive, and *h*	Deut 8:8	1706
land that floweth with milk and *h*	Deut 11:9	1706
land that floweth with milk and *h*	Deut 26:9	1706
land that floweth with milk and *h*	Deut 26:15	1706
land that floweth with milk and *h*	Deut 27:3	1706
that floweth with milk and *h*	Deut 31:20	1706
him to suck *h* out of the rock	Deut 32:13	1706
land that floweth with milk and *h*	Josh 5:6	1706
h in the carcase of the lion	Judg 14:8	1706
h out of the carcase of the lion	Judg 14:9	1706
went down, What is sweeter than *h*	Judg 14:18	1706
there was *h* upon the ground	1Sa 14:25	1706
the wood, behold, the *h* dropped	1Sa 14:26	1706
I tasted a little of this *h*	1Sa 14:29	1706
I did but taste a little *h* with	1Sa 14:43	1706
And *h*, and butter, and sheep, and	2Sa 17:29	1706
and cracknels, and a cruse of *h*	1Kin 14:3	1706
a land of oil olive and of *h*	2Kin 18:32	1706
of corn, wine, and oil, and *h*	2Chr 31:5	1706
the floods, the brooks of *h*	Job 20:17	1706
sweeter also than *h* and the	Ps 19:10	1706
with *h* out of the rock should I	Ps 81:16	1706
yea, sweeter than *h* to my mouth	Ps 119:103	1706
My son, eat thou *h*, because it is	Prov 24:13	1706
Hast thou found *h*?	Prov 25:16	1706
It is not good to eat much *h*	Prov 25:27	1706
h and milk are under thy tongue	Song 4:11	1706
have eaten my honeycomb with my *h*	Song 5:1	1706
h shall he eat, that he may know	Is 7:15	1706
h shall every one eat that is	Is 7:22	1706
a land flowing with milk and *h*	Jer 11:5	1706
a land flowing with milk and *h*	Jer 32:22	1706
and of barley, and of oil, and of *h*	Jer 41:8	1706
in my mouth as *h* for sweetness	Eze 3:3	1706
thou didst eat fine flour, and *h*	Eze 16:13	1706
thee, fine flour, and oil, and *h*	Eze 16:19	1706
for them, flowing with milk and *h*	Eze 20:6	1706
them, flowing with milk and *h*	Eze 20:15	1706
wheat of Minnith, and Pannag, and *h*	Eze 27:17	1706
and his meat was locusts and wild *h*	Mt 3:4	3192
and he did eat locusts and wild *h*	Mk 1:6	3192
shall be in thy mouth sweet as *h*	Rev 10:9	3192
and it was in my mouth sweet as *h*	Rev 10:10	3192

HONEYCOMB

in his hand, and dipped it in an *h*	1Sa 14:27	3295,1706
sweeter also than honey and the *h*	Ps 19:10	5317,6688
of a strange woman drop as an *h*	Prov 5:3	5317
Pleasant words are as an *h*	Prov 16:24	6688,1706
and the *h*, which is sweet to thy	Prov 24:13	5317
The full soul loatheth an *h*	Prov 27:7	5317
lips, O my spouse, drop as the *h*	Song 4:11	5317
I have eaten my *h* with my honey	Song 5:1	3293
of a broiled fish, and of an *h*	Lk 24:42	3193,2781

HONOUR

unto their assembly, mine *h*	Gen 49:6	3519
and I will get me *h* upon Pharaoh	Ex 14:17	3513
I have gotten me *h* upon Pharaoh	Ex 14:18	3513
H thy father and thy mother	Ex 20:12	3513
nor *h* the person of the mighty	Lev 19:15	1921
h the face of the old man, and	Lev 19:32	1921
promote thee unto very great *h*	Num 22:17	3513
able indeed to promote thee to *h*	Num 22:37	3513
to promote thee unto great *h*	Num 24:11	3513
LORD hath kept thee back from *h*	Num 24:11	3519
put some of thine *h* upon him	Num 27:20	1935
H thy father and thy mother, as	Deut 5:16	3513
in praise, and in name, and in *h*	Deut 26:19	8597
takest shall not be for thine *h*	Judg 4:9	8597
wherewith by me they *h* God	Judg 9:9	3513
come to pass we may do thee *h*	Judg 13:17	3513
for them that *h* me I will *h*	1Sa 2:30	3513
yet *h* me now, I pray thee, before	1Sa 15:30	3513
of, of them shall I be had in *h*	2Sa 6:22	3513
thou that David doth *h* thy father	2Sa 10:3	3513
hast not asked, both riches, and *h*	1Kin 3:13	3519
Glory and *h* are in his presence	1Chr 16:27	1926

to thee for the *h* of thy servant	1Chr 17:18	3519
thou that David doth *h* thy father	1Chr 19:3	3513
h come of thee, and thou reignest	1Chr 29:12	3519
age, full of days, riches, and *h*	1Chr 29:28	3519
not asked riches, wealth, or *h*	2Chr 1:11	3519
give thee riches, and wealth, and *h*	2Chr 1:12	3519
he had riches and *h* in abundance	2Chr 17:5	3519
h in abundance, and joined	2Chr 18:1	3519
be for thine *h* from the LORD God	2Chr 26:18	3519
had exceeding much riches and *h*	2Chr 32:27	3519
Jerusalem did him *h* at his death	2Chr 32:33	3519
the *h* of his excellent majesty	Est 1:4	3366
shall give to their husbands *h*	Est 1:20	3366
And the king said, What *h* and	Est 6:3	3366
man whom the king delighteth to *h*	Est 6:6	3366
to do *h* more than to myself	Est 6:6	3366
man whom the king delighteth to *h*	Est 6:7	3366
whom the king delighteth to *h*	Est 6:9	3366
man whom the king delighteth to *h*	Est 6:9	3366
man whom the king delighteth to *h*	Est 6:11	3366
light, and gladness, and joy, and *h*	Est 8:16	3366
His sons come to *h*, and he knoweth	Job 14:21	3513
earth, and lay mine *h* in the dust	Ps 7:5	3519
hast crowned him with glory and *h*	Ps 8:5	1926
h and majesty hast thou laid upon	Ps 21:5	1935
the place where thine *h* dwelleth	Ps 26:8	3519
man being in *h* abideth not	Ps 49:12	3366
Man that is in *h*, and	Ps 49:20	3366
Sing forth the *h* of his name	Ps 66:2	3519
praise and with thy *h* all the day	Ps 71:8	8597
I will deliver him, and *h* him	Ps 91:15	3515
H and majesty are before him	Ps 96:6	1935
thou art clothed with *h* and	Ps 104:1	1935
his horn shall be exalted with *h*	Ps 112:9	3519
of the glorious *h* of thy majesty	Ps 145:5	1926
this *h* have all his saints	Ps 149:9	1926
H the LORD with thy substance, and	Prov 3:9	3513
and in her left hand riches and *h*	Prov 3:16	3519
she shall bring thee to *h*	Prov 4:8	3513
thou give thine *h* unto others	Prov 5:9	1935
Riches and *h* are with me	Prov 8:18	3519
A gracious woman retaineth *h*	Prov 11:16	3519
of people is the king's *h*	Prov 14:28	1927
and before *h* is humility	Prov 15:33	3519
and before *h* is humility	Prov 18:12	3519
It is an *h* for a man to cease	Prov 20:3	3519
findeth life, righteousness, and *h*	Prov 21:21	3519
fear of the LORD are riches, and *h*	Prov 22:4	3519
but the *h* of kings is to search	Prov 25:2	3519
so *h* is not seemly for a fool	Prov 26:1	3519
so is he that giveth *h* to a fool	Prov 26:8	3519
but *h* shall uphold the humble in	Prov 29:23	3519
Strength and *h* are her clothing	Prov 31:25	1926
hath given riches, wealth, and *h*	Eccl 6:2	3519
is in reputation for wisdom and *h*	Eccl 10:1	3519
mouth, and with their lips do *h* me	Is 29:13	3513
The beast of the field shall *h* me	Is 43:20	3513
and shalt *h* him, not doing thine	Is 58:13	3513
an *h* before all the nations of	Jer 33:9	8597
of me gifts and rewards and great *h*	Dan 2:6	3367
power, and for the *h* of my majesty	Dan 4:30	3367
the glory of my kingdom, mine *h*	Dan 4:36	1923
h the King of heaven, all whose	Dan 4:37	1922
and majesty, and glory, and *h*	Dan 5:18	1923
not give the *h* of the kingdom	Dan 11:21	1935
shall he *h* the God of forces	Dan 11:38	3513
knew not shall he *h* with gold	Dan 11:38	3513
I be a father, where is mine *h*	Mal 1:6	3519
them, A prophet is not without *h*	Mt 13:57	820
saying, *H* thy father and mother	Mt 15:4	5091
***h* not his father or his mother,**	Mt 15:6	5091
***H* thy father and thy mother**	Mt 19:19	5091
them, A prophet is not without *h*	Mk 6:4	820
***H* thy father and thy mother**	Mk 7:10	5091
not, *H* thy father and mother	Mk 10:19	5091
***H* thy father and thy mother**	Lk 18:20	5091
hath no *h* in his own country	Jn 4:44	5092
That all men should *h* the Son	Jn 5:23	5091
even as they *h* the Father	Jn 5:23	5091
I receive not *h* from men	Jn 5:41	1391
which receive *h* one of another,	Jn 5:44	1391
seek not the *h* that cometh from	Jn 5:44	1391
but I *h* my Father, and ye do	Jn 8:49	5091
I *h* myself, my *h* is nothing	Jn 8:54	1391
serve me, him will my Father *h*	Jn 12:26	5091
in well doing seek for glory and *h*	Rom 2:7	5092
But glory, *h*, and peace, to every	Rom 2:10	5092
lump to make one vessel unto *h*	Rom 9:21	5092
in *h* preferring one another	Rom 12:10	5092
to whom fear; *h* to whom *h*	Rom 13:7	5092
these we bestow more abundant *h*	1Cor 12:23	5092

h to that part which lacked	1Cor 12:24	5092
By *h* and dishonour, by evil report	2Cor 6:8	1391
H thy father and mother	Eph 6:2	5091
not in any *h* to the satisfying of	Col 2:23	5092
his vessel in sanctification and *h*	1Th 4:4	5092
the only wise God, be *h* and glory	1Ti 1:17	5092
H widows that are widows indeed	1Ti 5:3	5091
be counted worthy of double *h*	1Ti 5:17	5092
their own masters worthy of all *h*	1Ti 6:1	5092
to whom be *h* and power everlasting	1Ti 6:16	5092
and some to *h*, and some to	2Ti 2:20	5092
he shall be a vessel unto *h*	2Ti 2:21	5092
crownedst him with glory and *h*	Heb 2:7	5092
of death, crowned with glory and *h*	Heb 2:9	5092
house hath more *h* than the house	Heb 3:3	5092
no man taketh this *h* unto himself	Heb 5:4	5092
might be found unto praise and *h*	1Pet 1:7	5092
H all men	1Pet 2:17	5091
H the king	1Pet 2:17	5091
giving *h* unto the wife, as unto	1Pet 3:7	5092
he received from God the Father *h*	2Pet 1:17	5092
when those beasts give glory and *h*	Rev 4:9	5092
O Lord, to receive glory and *h*	Rev 4:11	5092
and wisdom, and strength, and *h*	Rev 5:12	5092
heard I saying, Blessing, and *h*	Rev 5:13	5092
and wisdom, and thanksgiving, and *h*	Rev 7:12	5092
Salvation, and glory, and *h*	Rev 19:1	5092
glad and rejoice, and give *h* to him	Rev 19:7	1391
do bring their glory and *h* into it	Rev 21:24	5092
glory and *h* of the nations into it	Rev 21:26	5092

HONOURABLE

he was more *h* than all the house	Gen 34:19	3513
more, and more *h* than they	Num 22:15	3513
a man of God, and he is an *h* man	1Sa 9:6	3513
bidding, and is *h* in thine house	1Sa 22:14	3513
Was he not most *h* of three	2Sa 23:19	3513
He was more *h* than the thirty,	2Sa 23:23	3513
great man with his master, and *h*	2Kin 5:1	5375,6440
Jabez was more *h* than his	1Chr 4:9	3513
he was more *h* than the two	1Chr 11:21	3513
he was *h* among the thirty, but	1Chr 11:25	3513
and the *h* man dwelt in it	Job 22:8	5375,6440
daughters were among thy *h* women	Ps 45:9	3368
His work is *h* and glorious	Ps 111:3	1935
captain of fifty, and the *h* man	Is 3:3	5375,6440
and the base against the *h*	Is 3:5	3519
their *h* men are famished, and	Is 5:13	3519
The ancient and *h*, he is the head	Is 9:15	5375,6440
are the *h* of the earth	Is 23:8	1935
contempt all the *h* of the earth	Is 23:9	3513
magnify the law, and make it *h*	Is 42:21	142
in my sight, thou hast been *h*	Is 43:4	3513
delight, the holy of the LORD, *h*	Is 58:13	3513
and they cast lots for her *h* men	Nah 3:10	3513
an *h* counsellor, which also	Mk 15:43	2158
lest a more *h* man than thou be	Lk 14:8	1784
h women, and the chief men of the	Acts 13:50	2158
also of *h* women which were Greeks	Acts 17:12	2158
ye are *h*, but we are despised	1Cor 4:10	1741
body, which we think to be less *h*	1Cor 12:23	820
Marriage is *h* in all, and the bed	Heb 13:4	5093

HONOURED

I will be *h* upon Pharaoh, and upon	Ex 14:4	3513
that regardeth reproof shall be *h*	Prov 13:18	3513
waiteth on his master shall be *h*	Prov 27:18	3513
neither hast thou *h* me with thy	Is 43:23	3513
all that *h* her despise her,	Lam 1:8	3513
the faces of elders were not *h*	Lam 5:12	1921
h him that liveth for ever, whose	Dan 4:34	1922
Who also *h* us with many honours	Acts 28:10	5092
or one member be *h*, all the	1Cor 12:26	1392

HONOUREST

h thy sons above me, to make	1Sa 2:29	3513

HONOURETH

but he *h* them that fear the LORD	Ps 15:4	3513
is better than he that *h* himself	Prov 12:9	3513
but he that *h* him hath mercy on	Prov 14:31	3513
A son *h* his father, and a servant	Mal 1:6	3513
mouth, and *h* me with their lips	Mt 15:8	5091
This people *h* me with their lips,	Mk 7:6	5091
He that *h* not the Son *h* not	Jn 5:23	5091
it is my Father that *h* me	Jn 8:54	1392

HONOURS

Who also honoured us with many *h*	Acts 28:10	5091

HOODS

and the fine linen, and the *h*	Is 3:23	6797

HOOF

shall not an *h* be left behind	Ex 10:26	6541
Whatsoever parteth the *h*, and is	Lev 11:3	6541
cud, or of them that divide the *h*	Lev 11:4	6541
the cud, but divideth not the *h*	Lev 11:4	6541
the cud, but divideth not the *h*	Lev 11:5	6541
the cud, but divideth not the *h*	Lev 11:6	6541
the swine, though he divide the *h*	Lev 11:7	6541
every beast which divideth the *h*	Lev 11:26	6541
And every beast that parteth the *h*	Deut 14:6	6541
of them that divide the cloven *h*	Deut 14:7	6541
the cud, but divideth not the *h*	Deut 14:7	6541
swine, because it divideth the *h*	Deut 14:8	6541

HOOFS

or bullock that hath horns and *h*	Ps 69:31	6536
their horses' *h* shall be counted	Is 5:28	6541
of the *h* of his strong horses	Jer 47:3	6541
With the *h* of his horses shall he	Eze 26:11	6541
nor the *h* of beasts trouble them	Eze 32:13	6541
iron, and I will make thy *h* brass	Mic 4:13	6541

HOOK

I will put my *h* in thy nose	2Kin 19:28	2397
thou draw out leviathan with an *h*	Job 41:1	100
Canst thou put an *h* into his nose	Job 41:2	2443
will I put my *h* in thy nose	Is 37:29	2397
go thou to the sea, and cast an *h*	Mt 17:27	44

HOOKS

their *h* shall be of gold, upon	Ex 26:32	2053
gold, and their *h* shall be of gold	Ex 26:37	2053
the *h* of the pillars and their	Ex 27:10	2053
the *h* of the pillars and their	Ex 27:11	2053
their *h* shall be of silver, and	Ex 27:17	2053
their *h* were of gold	Ex 36:36	2053
five pillars of it with their *h*	Ex 36:38	2053
the *h* of the pillars and their	Ex 38:10	2053
the *h* of the pillars and their	Ex 38:11	2053
the *h* of the pillars and their	Ex 38:12	2053
the *h* of the pillars and their	Ex 38:17	2053
their *h* of silver, and the	Ex 38:19	2053
shekels he made *h* for the pillars	Ex 38:28	2053
But I will put *h* in thy jaws	Eze 29:4	2397
put *h* into thy jaws, and I will	Eze 38:4	2397
And within were *h*, an hand broad,	Eze 40:43	8240
that he will take you away with *h*	Amos 4:2	6793

HOPE

If I should say, I have *h*	Ruth 1:12	8615
yet now there is *h* in Israel	Ezr 10:2	4723
thy fear, thy confidence, thy *h*	Job 4:6	8615
So the poor hath *h*, and iniquity	Job 5:16	8615
is my strength, that I should *h*	Job 6:11	3176
shuttle, and are spent without *h*	Job 7:6	8615
and the hypocrite's *h* shall perish	Job 8:13	8615
Whose *h* shall be cut off, and	Job 8:14	3689
be secure, because there is *h*	Job 11:18	8615
their *h* shall be as the giving up	Job 11:20	8615
For there is *h* of a tree, if it	Job 14:7	8615
and thou destroyest the *h* of man	Job 14:19	8615
And where is now my *h*	Job 17:15	8615
as for my *h*, who shall see it	Job 17:15	8615
mine *h* hath he removed like a	Job 19:10	8615
For what is the *h* of the	Job 27:8	8615
If I have made gold my *h*, or have	Job 31:24	3689
Behold, the *h* of him is in vain	Job 41:9	8431
my flesh also shall rest in *h*	Ps 16:9	983
thou didst make me *h* when I was	Ps 22:9	982
heart, all ye that *h* in the LORD	Ps 31:24	3176
upon them that *h* in his mercy	Ps 33:18	3176
us, according as we *h* in thee	Ps 33:22	3176
For in thee, O LORD, do I *h*	Ps 38:15	3176
my *h* is in thee	Ps 39:7	8431
h thou in God	Ps 42:5	3176
h thou in God	Ps 42:11	3176
h in God	Ps 43:5	3176
For thou art my *h*, O Lord GOD	Ps 71:5	8615
But I will *h* continually, and will	Ps 71:14	3176
they might set their *h* in God	Ps 78:7	3689
which thou hast caused me to *h*	Ps 119:49	3176
but I *h* in thy word	Ps 119:81	3176
I *h* in thy word	Ps 119:114	3176
and let me not be ashamed of my *h*	Ps 119:116	7664
doth wait, and in his word do I *h*	Ps 130:5	3176
Let Israel *h* in the LORD	Ps 130:7	3176
Let Israel *h* in the LORD from	Ps 131:3	3176
whose *h* is in the LORD his God	Ps 146:5	7664
him, in those that *h* in his mercy	Ps 147:11	3176
The *h* of the righteous shall be	Prov 10:28	8431
the *h* of unjust men perisheth	Prov 11:7	8431
H deferred maketh the heart sick,	Prov 13:12	8431
the righteous hath *h* in his death	Prov 14:32	2620

Chasten thy son while there is *h*	Prov 19:18	8615
there is more *h* of a fool than of	Prov 26:12	8615
there is more *h* of a fool than of	Prov 29:20	8615
to all the living there is *h*	Eccl 9:4	986
the pit cannot *h* for thy truth	Is 38:18	7663
saidst thou not, There is no *h*	Is 57:10	2976
but thou saidst, There is no *h*	Jer 2:25	2976
O the *h* of Israel, the saviour	Jer 14:8	4723
the LORD, and whose the LORD is	Jer 17:7	4009
the *h* of Israel, all that forsake	Jer 17:13	4723
thou art my *h* in the day of evil	Jer 17:17	4268
And they said, There is no *h*	Jer 18:12	2976
there is *h* in thine end, saith	Jer 31:17	8615
the LORD, the *h* of their fathers	Jer 50:7	4723
my *h* is perished from the LORD	Lam 3:18	8431
to my mind, therefore have I *h*	Lam 3:21	3176
therefore will I *h* in him	Lam 3:24	3176
is good that a man should both *h*	Lam 3:26	2342
if so be there may be *h*	Lam 3:29	8615
they have made others to *h* that	Eze 13:6	3176
her *h* was lost, then she took	Eze 19:5	8615
bones are dried, and our *h* is lost	Eze 37:11	8615
valley of Achor for a door of *h*	Hos 2:15	8615
LORD will be the *h* of his people	Joel 3:16	4268
strong hold, ye prisoners of *h*	Zec 9:12	8615
to them of whom ye *h* to receive	Lk 6:34	*1679*
also my flesh shall rest in *h*	Acts 2:26	*1680*
the *h* of their gains was gone	Acts 16:19	*1680*
of the *h* and resurrection of the	Acts 23:6	*1680*
have *h* toward God, which they	Acts 24:15	*1680*
am judged for the *h* of the	Acts 26:6	*1680*
God day and night, *h* to come	Acts 26:7	*1679*
all *h* that we should be saved was	Acts 27:20	*1680*
because that for the *h* of Israel	Acts 28:20	*1680*
Who against *h* believed in *h*,	Rom 4:18	*1680*
Who against *h* believed in *h*	Rom 4:18	*1680*
rejoice in *h* of the glory of God	Rom 5:2	*1680*
experience; and experience, *h*	Rom 5:4	*1680*
And *h* maketh not ashamed	Rom 5:5	*1680*
who hath subjected the same in *h*	Rom 8:20	*1680*
For we are saved by *h*	Rom 8:24	*1680*
but *h* that is seen is not *h*	Rom 8:24	*1680*
man seeth, why doth he yet *h* for	Rom 8:24	*1679*
But if we *h* for that we see not,	Rom 8:25	*1679*
Rejoicing in *h*	Rom 12:12	*1680*
of the scriptures might have *h*	Rom 15:4	*1680*
Now the God of *h* fill you with	Rom 15:13	*1680*
that ye may abound in *h*, through	Rom 15:13	*1680*
he that ploweth should plow in *h*	1Cor 9:10	*1680*
that he that thresheth in *h*	1Cor 9:10	*1680*
h should be partaker of his *h*	1Cor 9:10	*1680*
And now abideth faith, *h*, charity,	1Cor 13:13	*1680*
life only we have *h* in Christ	1Cor 15:19	*1679*
our *h* of you is stedfast, knowing	2Cor 1:7	*1680*
Seeing then that we have such *h*	2Cor 3:12	*1680*
but having *h*, when your faith is	2Cor 10:15	*1680*
the *h* of righteousness by faith	Gal 5:5	*1680*
know what is the *h* of his calling	Eph 1:18	*1680*
covenants of promise, having no *h*	Eph 2:12	*1680*
called in one *h* of your calling	Eph 4:4	*1680*
to my earnest expectation and my *h*	Phil 1:20	*1680*
Him therefore I *h* to send	Phil 2:23	*1679*
For the *h* which is laid up for	Col 1:5	*1680*
away from the *h* of the gospel	Col 1:23	*1680*
is Christ in you, the *h* of glory	Col 1:27	*1680*
patience of *h* in our Lord Jesus	1Th 1:3	*1680*
For what is our *h*, or joy, or	1Th 2:19	*1680*
even as others which have no *h*	1Th 4:13	*1680*
for an helmet, the *h* of salvation	1Th 5:8	*1680*
and good *h* through grace,	2Th 2:16	*1680*
Lord Jesus Christ, which is our *h*	1Ti 1:1	*1680*
In *h* of eternal life, which God,	Titus 1:2	*1680*
Looking for that blessed *h*	Titus 2:13	*1680*
to the *h* of eternal life	Titus 3:7	*1680*
of the *h* firm unto the end	Heb 3:6	*1680*
full assurance of *h* unto the end	Heb 6:11	*1680*
lay hold upon the *h* set before us	Heb 6:18	*1680*
Which *h* we have as an anchor of	Heb 6:19	*1680*
the bringing in of a better *h* did	Heb 7:19	*1680*
h by the resurrection of Jesus	1Pet 1:3	*1680*
h to the end for the grace that	1Pet 1:13	*1679*
your faith and *h* might be in God	1Pet 1:21	*1680*
h that is in you with meekness	1Pet 3:15	*1680*
this *h* in him purifieth himself	1Jn 3:3	*1680*

HOPED

Jews *h* to have power over them	Est 9:1	7663
confounded because they had *h*	Job 6:20	982
for I have *h* in thy judgments	Ps 119:43	3176
because I have *h* in thy word	Ps 119:74	3176
I *h* in thy word	Ps 119:147	3176

H

I have *h* for thy salvation, and .... Ps 119:166   7663
is salvation *h* for from the hills .... Jer 3:23
he *h* to have seen some miracle .... Lk 23:8   *1679*
He *h* also that money should have .... Acts 24:26   *1679*
And this they did, not as we *h* 2Cor 8:5   *1679*
is the substance of things *h* for .... Heb 11:1   *1679*

HOPE'S
For which *h* sake, king Agrippa, I .... Acts 26:7   *1679*

HOPETH
    h all things, endureth all things 1Cor 13:7   *1679*

HOPHNI (hof'-ni) *A son of Eli.*
And the two sons of Eli, *H* 1Sa 1:3   2652
come upon thy two sons, on *H* 1Sa 2:34   2652
and the two sons of Eli, *H* 1Sa 4:4   2652
and the two sons of Eli, *H* 1Sa 4:11   2652
people, and thy two sons also, *H* 1Sa 4:17   2652

HOPING
    and lend, *h* for nothing again .... Lk 6:35   *560*
    h to come unto thee shortly 1Ti 3:14   *1679*

HOR (hor) *See* Hor-hagidgad.
    1. *A mountain in Moab.*
from Kadesh, and came unto mount *H* .. Num 20:22   2023
unto Moses and Aaron in mount *H* .... Num 20:23   2023
and bring them up unto mount *H* .... Num 20:25   2023
mount *H* in the sight of all the .... Num 20:27   2023
mount *H* by the way of the Red sea .... Num 21:4   2023
Kadesh, and pitched in mount *H* .... Num 33:37   2023
the priest went up into mount *H* .... Num 33:38   2023
years old when he died in mount *H* ...... Num 33:39   2023
And they departed from mount *H* .... Num 33:41   2023
Aaron thy brother died in mount *H* .... Deut 32:50   2023
    2. *A hill in northern Israel.*
shall point out for you mount *H* .... Num 34:7   2023
From mount *H* ye shall point out .... Num 34:8   2023

HORAM (ho'-ram) *A Canaanite king.*
Then *H* king of Gezer came up to .... Josh 10:33   2036

HOREB (ho'-reb) *See* Sinai. *A mountain range in Sinai.*
to the mountain of God, even to *H* .... Ex 3:1   2722
thee there upon the rock in *H* .... Ex 17:6   2722
of their ornaments by the mount *H* .... Ex 33:6   2722
H by the way of mount Seir unto .... Deut 1:2   2722
Lord our God spake unto us in *H* .... Deut 1:6   2722
And when we departed from *H* .... Deut 1:19   2722
before the Lord thy God in *H* .... Deut 4:10   2722
in *H* out of the midst of the fire .... Deut 4:15   2722
God made a covenant with us in *H* .... Deut 5:2   2722
Also in *H* ye provoked the Lord to .... Deut 9:8   2722
of the Lord thy God in *H* in the .... Deut 18:16   2722
which he made with them in *H* .... Deut 29:1   2722
stone, which Moses put there at *H* 1Kin 8:9   2722
nights unto *H* the mount of God 1Kin 19:8   2722
which Moses put therein at *H* 2Chr 5:10   2722
They made a calf in *H*, and..................... Ps 106:19   2722
unto him in *H* for all Israel .... Mal 4:4   2722

HOREM (ho'-rem) *A city in Naphtali.*
And Iron, and Migdal-el, *H*, and .... Josh 19:38   2765

HORESH *See* Ziph.

HOR-HAGIDGAD (hor-hag-id'-gad) *An encampment of Israel in the wilderness.*
Bene-jaakan, and encamped at *H* .... Num 33:32   2735
And they went from *H*, and pitched .... Num 33:33   2735

HORI (ho'-ri) *See* Horite.
    1. *Son of Lotan.*
And the children of Lotan were *H* .... Gen 36:22   2753
are the dukes that came of *H* .... Gen 36:30   2753
H, and Homam 1Chr 1:39   2753
    2. *Father of Shapat.*
of Simeon, Shaphat the son of *H* .... Num 13:5   2753

HORIMS (ho'-rims) *See* Horites. *Inhabitants of Mt. Seir.*
The *H* also dwelt in Seir .... Deut 2:12   2752
destroyed the *H* from before them .... Deut 2:22   2752

HORITE (ho'-rite) *See* Hori, Horites. *An inhabitant of Mt. Seir.*
These are the sons of Seir the *H* .... Gen 36:20   2752

HORITES (ho'-rites) *See* Horims. *Same as Horims.*
the *H* in their mount Seir, unto .... Gen 14:6   2752
these are the dukes of the *H* .... Gen 36:21   2752
are the dukes that came of the *H* .... Gen 36:29   2752

HORMAH (hor'-mah) *See* Zephath. *A Canaanite royal town.*
and discomfited them, even unto *H* .... Num 14:45   2767
he called the name of the place *H* .... Num 21:3   2767
you in Seir, even unto *H*......................... Deut 1:44   2767

The king of *H*, one.................................. Josh 12:14   2767
And Eltolad, and Chesil, and *H*.............. Josh 15:30   2767
And Eltolad, and Bethul, and *H* .... Josh 19:4   2767
the name of the city was called *H* .... Judg 1:17   2767
And to them which were in *H* 1Sa 30:30   2767
And at Bethuel, and at *H*, and at........... 1Chr 4:30   2767

HORN
to push with his *h* in time past.............. Ex 21:29
a long blast with the ram's *h* .... Josh 6:5   7161
mine *h* is exalted in the Lord................. 1Sa 2:1   7161
exalt the *h* of his anointed...................... 1Sa 2:10   7161
fill thine *h* with oil, and go, I................. 1Sa 16:1   7161
Then Samuel took the *h* of oil 1Sa 16:13   7161
the *h* of my salvation, my high 2Sa 22:3   7161
Zadok the priest took an *h* of oil 1Kin 1:39   7161
words of God, to lift up the *h* 1Chr 25:5   7161
skin, and defiled my *h* in the dust .... Job 16:15   7161
the *h* of my salvation, and my high........ Ps 18:2   7161
to the wicked, Lift not up the *h*............. Ps 75:4   7161
Lift not up your *h* on high .... Ps 75:5   7161
thy favour our *h* shall be exalted .... Ps 89:17   7161
in my name shall his *h* be exalted .... Ps 89:24   7161
But my *h* shalt thou exalt like .... Ps 92:10   7161
exalt like the *h* of an unicorn .... Ps 92:10   7161
his *h* shall be exalted with .... Ps 112:9   7161
will I make the *h* of David to bud .... Ps 132:17   7161
also exalteth the *h* of his people .... Ps 148:14   7161
The *h* of Moab is cut off, and his .... Jer 48:25   7161
fierce anger all the *h* of Israel .... Lam 2:3   7161
he hath set up the *h* of thine .... Lam 2:17   7161
In that day will I cause the *h* of............. Eze 29:21   7161
up among them another little *h* .... Dan 7:8   7162
in this *h* were eyes like the eyes .... Dan 7:8   7162
the great words which the *h* spake .... Dan 7:11   7162
even of that *h* that had eyes, and .... Dan 7:20   7162
the same *h* made war with the .... Dan 7:21   7162
had a notable *h* between his eyes .... Dan 8:5   7161
strong, the great *h* was broken .... Dan 8:8   7161
one of them came forth a little *h* .... Dan 8:9   7161
the great *h* that is between his .... Dan 8:21   7161
for I will make thine *h* iron .... Mic 4:13   7161
which lifted up their *h* over the .... Zec 1:21   7161
hath raised up an *h* of salvation .... Lk 1:69   *2768*

HORNET
God will send the *h* among them............ Deut 7:20   6880
And I sent the *h* before you.................... Josh 24:12   6880

HORNETS
And I will send *h* before thee .... Ex 23:28   6880

HORNS
ram caught in a thicket by his *h* .... Gen 22:13   7161
thou shalt make the *h* of it upon .... Ex 27:2   7161
his *h* shall be of the same .... Ex 27:2   7161
put it upon the *h* of the altar .... Ex 29:12   7161
the *h* thereof shall be of the .... Ex 30:2   7161
round about, and the *h* thereof .... Ex 30:3   7161
make an atonement upon the *h* of.......... Ex 30:10   7161
the *h* thereof were of the same............... Ex 37:25   7161
round about, and the *h* of it .... Ex 37:26   7161
he made the *h* thereof on the four .... Ex 38:2   7161
the *h* thereof were of the same.............. Ex 38:2   7161
h of the altar of sweet incense .... Lev 4:7   7161
h of the altar which is before .... Lev 4:18   7161
put it upon the *h* of the altar of .... Lev 4:25   7161
put it upon the *h* of the altar of .... Lev 4:30   7161
put it upon the *h* of the altar of .... Lev 4:34   7161
put it upon the *h* of the altar .... Lev 8:15   7161
and put it upon the *h* of the altar .... Lev 9:9   7161
put it upon the *h* of the altar .... Lev 16:18   7161
h are like the *h* of unicorns .... Deut 33:17   7161
the ark seven trumpets of rams' *h* .... Josh 6:4   3104
h before the ark of the Lord .... Josh 6:6   3104
rams' *h* passed on before the Lord .... Josh 6:8
h before the ark of the Lord went .... Josh 6:13   3104
caught hold on the *h* of the altar 1Kin 1:50   7161
caught hold on the *h* of the altar 1Kin 1:51   7161
caught hold on the *h* of the altar 1Kin 2:28   7161
of Chenaanah made him *h* of iron 1Kin 22:11   7161
Chenaanah had made him *h* of iron 2Chr 18:10   7161
me from the *h* of the unicorns .... Ps 22:21   7161
than an ox or bullock that hath *h* .... Ps 69:31   7160
All the *h* of the wicked also will .... Ps 75:10   7161
but the *h* of the righteous shall.............. Ps 75:10   7161
even unto the *h* of the altar .... Ps 118:27   7161
upon the *h* of your altars....................... Jer 17:1   7161
thee for a present *h* of ivory................... Eze 27:15   7161
all the diseased with your *h*................... Eze 34:21   7161
altar and upward shall be four *h* .... Eze 43:15   7161
and put it on the four *h* of it.................. Eze 43:20   7161
and it had ten *h*..................................... Dan 7:7   7162

I considered the *h*, and, behold,	Dan 7:8	7162
first *h* plucked up by the roots	Dan 7:8	7162
of the ten *h* that were in his	Dan 7:20	7162
the ten *h* out of this kingdom are	Dan 7:24	7162
the river a ram which had two *h*	Dan 8:3	7161
and the two *h* were high	Dan 8:3	7161
he came to the ram that had two *h*	Dan 8:6	7161
smote the ram, and brake his two *h*	Dan 8:7	7161
two *h* are the kings of Media	Dan 8:20	7161
the *h* of the altar shall be cut	Amos 3:14	7161
taken to us *h* by our own strength	Amos 6:13	7161
he had *h* coming out of his hand	Hab 3:4	7161
eyes, and saw, and behold four *h*	Zec 1:18	7161
These are the *h* which have	Zec 1:19	7161
These are the *h* which have	Zec 1:21	7161
to cast out the *h* of the Gentiles	Zec 1:21	7161
it had been slain, having seven *h*	Rev 5:6	2768
h of the golden altar which is	Rev 9:13	2768
having seven heads and ten *h*	Rev 12:3	2768
sea, having seven heads and ten *h*	Rev 13:1	2768
upon his *h* ten crowns, and upon	Rev 13:1	2768
he had two *h* like a lamb, and he	Rev 13:11	2768
having seven heads and ten *h*	Rev 17:3	2768
hath the seven heads and ten *h*	Rev 17:7	2768
the ten *h* which thou sawest are	Rev 17:12	2768
the ten *h* which thou sawest upon	Rev 17:16	2768

HORONAIM (*hor·o·na'-im*) See HOLON. *A Moabite city.*

for in the way of *H* they shall	Is 15:5	2773
A voice of crying shall be from *H*	Jer 48:3	2773
for in the going down of *H* the	Jer 48:5	2773
voice, from Zoar even unto *H*	Jer 48:34	2773

HORONITE (*ho'-ron-ite*) *A native of Horonaim.*

When Sanballat the *H*, and Tobiah	Neh 2:10	2772
But when Sanballat the *H*, and	Neh 2:19	2772
was son in law to Sanballat the *H*	Neh 13:28	2772

HORRIBLE

and brimstone, and an *h* tempest	Ps 11:6	2152
me up also out of an *h* pit	Ps 40:2	7588
h thing is committed in the land	Jer 5:30	8186
Israel hath done a very *h* thing	Jer 18:13	8186
prophets of Jerusalem an *h* thing	Jer 23:14	8186
I have seen an *h* thing in the	Hos 6:10	8186

HORRIBLY

be *h* afraid, be ye very desolate,	Jer 2:12	8175
kings shall be *h* afraid for thee	Eze 32:10	8178

HORROR

an *h* of great darkness fell upon	Gen 15:12	367
upon me, and *h* hath overwhelmed me	Ps 55:5	6427
H hath taken hold upon me because	Ps 119:53	2152
sackcloth, and *h* shall cover them	Eze 7:18	6427

HORSE

the path, that biteth the *h* heels	Gen 49:17	5483
the *h* and his rider hath he thrown	Ex 15:1	5483
For the *h* of Pharaoh went in with	Ex 15:19	5483
the *h* and his rider hath he thrown	Ex 15:21	5483
an *h* for an hundred and fifty	1Kin 10:29	5483
escaped on an *h* with the horsemen	1Kin 20:20	5483
h for *h*, and chariot for	1Kin 20:25	5483
that thou hast lost, *h* for *h*	1Kin 20:25	5483
an *h* for an hundred and fifty	2Chr 1:17	5483
of the *h* gate by the king's house	2Chr 23:15	5483
From above the *h* gate repaired	Neh 3:28	5483
the *h* that the king rideth upon,	Est 6:8	5483
h be delivered to the hand of one	Est 6:9	5483
and take the apparel and the *h*	Est 6:10	5483
took Haman the apparel and the *h*	Est 6:11	5483
on high, she scorneth the *h*	Job 39:18	5483
Hath thou given the *h* strength	Job 39:19	5483
Be ye not as the *h*, or as the	Ps 32:9	5483
An *h* is a vain thing for safety	Ps 33:17	5483
h are cast into a dead sleep	Ps 76:6	5483
not in the strength of the *h*	Ps 147:10	5483
The *h* is prepared against the day	Prov 21:31	5483
A whip for the *h*, a bridle for	Prov 26:3	5483
bringeth forth the chariot and *h*	Is 43:17	5483
as an *h* in the wilderness, that	Is 63:13	5483
as the *h* rusheth into the battle	Jer 8:6	5483
of the *h* gate toward the east	Jer 31:40	5483
thee will I break in pieces the *h*	Jer 51:21	5483
that rideth the *h* deliver himself	Amos 2:15	5483
behold a man riding upon a red *h*	Zec 1:8	5483
the *h* from Jerusalem, and the	Zec 9:10	5483
as his goodly *h* in the battle	Zec 10:3	5483
smite every *h* with astonishment	Zec 12:4	5483
will smite every *h* of the people	Zec 12:4	5483
so shall be the plague of the *h*	Zec 14:15	5483
And I saw, and behold a white *h*	Rev 6:2	2462
went out another *h* that was red	Rev 6:4	2462

And I beheld, and lo a black *h*	Rev 6:5	2462
And I looked, and behold a pale *h*	Rev 6:8	2462
even unto the *h* bridles, by the	Rev 14:20	2462
opened, and behold a white *h*	Rev 19:11	2462
war against him that sat on the *h*	Rev 19:19	2462
sword of him that sat upon the *h*	Rev 19:21	2462

HORSEBACK

there went one on *h* to meet him	2Kin 9:18	7392,5483
Then he sent out a second on *h*	2Kin 9:19	7392,5483
bring him on *h* through the street	Est 6:9	7392
brought him on *h* through the	Est 6:11	7392
and sent letters by posts on *h*	Est 8:10	5483

HORSEHOOFS

Then were the *h* broken by the	Judg 5:22	6119,5483

HORSELEACH

The *h* hath two daughters, crying,	Prov 30:15	5936

HORSEMAN

And Joram said, Take an *h*, and send	2Kin 9:17	7395
The *h* lifteth up both the bright	Nah 3:3	6571

HORSEMEN

up with him both chariots and *h*	Gen 50:9	6571
and chariots of Pharaoh, and his *h*	Ex 14:9	6571
upon his chariots, and upon his *h*	Ex 14:17	6571
upon his chariots, and upon his *h*	Ex 14:18	6571
horses, his chariots, and his *h*	Ex 14:23	6571
their chariots, and their *h*	Ex 14:26	6571
and covered the chariots, and the *h*	Ex 14:28	6571
with his *h* into the sea, and the	Ex 15:19	6571
chariots and *h* unto the Red sea	Josh 24:6	6571
for his chariots, and to be his *h*	1Sa 8:11	6571
chariots, and six thousand *h*	1Sa 13:5	6571
h followed hard after him	2Sa 1:6	6571
chariots, and seven hundred *h*	2Sa 8:4	6571
the Syrians, and forty thousand *h*	2Sa 10:18	6571
and he prepared him chariots and *h*	1Kin 1:5	6571
chariots, and twelve thousand *h*	1Kin 4:26	6571
his chariots, and cities for his *h*	1Kin 9:19	6571
rulers of his chariots, and his *h*	1Kin 9:22	6571
gathered together chariots and *h*	1Kin 10:26	6571
chariots, and twelve thousand *h*	1Kin 10:26	6571
escaped on an horse with the *h*	1Kin 20:20	6571
of Israel, and the *h* thereof	2Kin 2:12	6571
people to Jehoahaz but fifty *h*	2Kin 13:7	6571
of Israel, and the *h* thereof	2Kin 13:14	6571
on Egypt for chariots and for *h*	2Kin 18:24	6571
chariots, and seven thousand *h*	1Chr 18:4	6571
h out of Mesopotamia, and out of	1Chr 19:6	6571
And Solomon gathered chariots and *h*	2Chr 1:14	6571
chariots, and twelve thousand *h*	2Chr 1:14	6571
cities, and the cities of the *h*	2Chr 8:6	6571
and captains of his chariots and *h*	2Chr 8:9	6571
and chariots, and twelve thousand *h*	2Chr 9:25	6571
and threescore thousand *h*	2Chr 12:3	6571
with very many chariots and *h*	2Chr 16:8	6571
h to help us against the enemy in	Ezr 8:22	6571
captains of the army and *h* with me	Neh 2:9	6571
saw a chariot with a couple of *h*	Is 21:7	6571
of men, with a couple of *h*	Is 21:9	6571
quiver with chariots of men and *h*	Is 22:6	6571
the *h* shall set themselves in	Is 22:7	6571
cart, nor bruise it with his *h*	Is 28:28	6571
and in *h*, because they are very	Is 31:1	6571
on Egypt for chariots and for *h*	Is 36:9	6571
shall flee for the noise of the *h*	Jer 4:29	6571
and get up, ye *h*, and stand forth	Jer 46:4	6571
young men, *h* riding upon horses	Eze 23:6	6571
h riding upon horses, all of them	Eze 23:12	6571
and with chariots, and with *h*	Eze 26:7	6571
shall shake at the noise of the *h*	Eze 26:10	6571
in thy fairs with horses and *h*	Eze 27:14	6571
and all thine army, horses and *h*	Eze 38:4	6571
with chariots, and with *h*	Dan 11:40	6571
by battle, by horses, nor by *h*	Hos 1:7	6571
and as *h*, so shall they run	Joel 2:4	6571
their *h* shall spread themselves,	Hab 1:8	6571
their *h* shall come from far	Hab 1:8	6571
h threescore and ten, and spearmen	Acts 23:23	2460
they left the *h* to go with him	Acts 23:32	2460
the *h* were two hundred thousand	Rev 9:16	2461

HORSES

gave them bread in exchange for *h*	Gen 47:17	5483
which is in the field, upon the *h*	Ex 9:3	5483
pursued after them, all the *h*	Ex 14:9	5483
of the sea, even all Pharaoh's *h*	Ex 14:23	5483
the army of Egypt, unto their *h*	Deut 11:4	5483
shall not multiply *h* to himself	Deut 17:16	5483
the end that he should multiply *h*	Deut 17:16	5483
against thine enemies, and seest *h*	Deut 20:1	5483

sea shore in multitude, with *h*	Josh 11:4	5483
thou shalt hough their *h*, and burn	Josh 11:6	5483
he houghed their *h*, and burnt	Josh 11:9	5483
David houghed all the chariot *h*	2Sa 8:4	
prepared him chariots and *h*	2Sa 15:1	5483
stalls of *h* for his chariots	1Kin 4:26	5483
Barley also and straw for the *h*	1Kin 4:28	5483
garments, and armour, and spices, *h*	1Kin 10:25	5483
Solomon had *h* brought out of	1Kin 10:28	5483
we may find grass to save the *h*	1Kin 18:5	5483
and two kings with him, and *h*	1Kin 20:1	5483
Israel went out, and smote the *h*	1Kin 20:21	5483
as thy people, my *h* as thy *h*	1Kin 22:4	5483
h of fire, and parted them both	2Kin 2:11	5483
thy people, and my *h* as thy *h*	2Kin 3:7	5483
So Naaman came with his *h*	2Kin 5:9	5483
Therefore sent he thither *h*	2Kin 6:14	5483
compassed the city both with *h*	2Kin 6:15	5483
the mountain was full of *h*	2Kin 6:17	5483
of chariots, and a noise of *h*	2Kin 7:6	5483
and left their tents, and their *h*	2Kin 7:7	5483
but *h* tied, and asses tied, and the	2Kin 7:10	5483
thee, five of the *h* that remain	2Kin 7:13	5483
They took therefore two chariot *h*	2Kin 7:14	5483
on the wall, and on the *h*	2Kin 9:33	5483
there are with you chariots and *h*	2Kin 10:2	5483
the *h* came into the king's house	2Kin 11:16	5483
And they brought him on *h*	2Kin 14:20	5483
will deliver thee two thousand *h*	2Kin 18:23	5483
he took away the *h* that the kings	2Kin 23:11	5483
also houghed all the chariot *h*	1Chr 18:4	5483
Solomon had *h* brought out of	2Chr 1:16	5483
so brought they out *h* for all the	2Chr 1:17	5483
and raiment, harness, and spices, *h*	2Chr 9:24	5483
had four thousand stalls for *h*	2Chr 9:25	5483
unto Solomon *h* out of Egypt	2Chr 9:28	5483
And they brought him upon	2Chr 25:28	5483
Their *h* were seven hundred thirty	Ezr 2:66	5483
Their *h*, seven hundred thirty and	Neh 7:68	5483
trust in chariots, and some in *h*	Ps 20:7	5483
I have seen servants upon *h*	Eccl 10:7	5483
to a company of *h* in Pharaoh's	Song 1:9	5484
their land is also full of *h*	Is 2:7	5483
for we will flee upon *h*	Is 30:16	5483
and stay on *h*, and trust in	Is 31:1	5483
and their *h* flesh, and not spirit	Is 31:3	5483
I will give thee two thousand *h*	Is 36:8	5483
LORD out of all nations upon *h*	Is 66:20	5483
his *h* are swifter than eagles	Jer 4:13	5483
They were as fed *h* in the morning	Jer 5:8	5483
and they ride upon *h*, set in array	Jer 6:23	5483
of his *h* was heard from Dan	Jer 8:16	5483
how canst thou contend with *h*	Jer 12:5	5483
David, riding in chariots and on *h*	Jer 17:25	5483
David, riding in chariots and on *h*	Jer 22:4	5483
Harness the *h*	Jer 46:4	5483
Come up, ye *h*	Jer 46:9	5483
of the hoofs of his strong *h*	Jer 47:3	5483
A sword is upon their *h*, and upon	Jer 50:37	5483
sea, and they shall ride upon *h*	Jer 50:42	5483
cause the *h* to come up as the	Jer 51:27	5483
Egypt, that they might give him *h*	Eze 17:15	5483
young men, horsemen riding upon *h*	Eze 23:6	5483
horsemen riding upon *h*, all of	Eze 23:12	5483
issue is like the issue of *h*	Eze 23:20	5483
all of them riding upon *h*	Eze 23:23	5483
of kings, from the north, with *h*	Eze 26:7	5483
his *h* their dust shall cover thee	Eze 26:10	5483
With the hoofs of his *h* shall he	Eze 26:11	5483
traded in thy fairs with *h*	Eze 27:14	5483
thee forth, and all thine army, *h*	Eze 38:4	5483
thee, all of them riding upon *h*	Eze 38:15	5483
be filled at my table with *h*	Eze 39:20	5483
nor by sword, nor by battle, by *h*	Hos 1:7	5483
we will not ride upon *h*	Hos 14:3	5483
of them is as the appearance of *h*	Joel 2:4	5483
sword, and have taken away your *h*	Amos 4:10	5483
Shall *h* run upon the rock	Amos 6:12	5483
that I will cut off thy *h* out of	Mic 5:10	5483
the wheels, and of the prancing *h*	Nah 3:2	5483
Their *h* also are swifter than the	Hab 1:8	5483
that thou didst ride upon thine *h*	Hab 3:8	5483
walk through the sea with thine *h*	Hab 3:15	5483
and the *h* and their riders shall	Hag 2:22	5483
and behind him were there red *h*	Zec 1:8	5483
In the first chariot were red *h*	Zec 6:2	5483
and in the second chariot black *h*	Zec 6:2	5483
And in the third chariot white *h*	Zec 6:3	5483
fourth chariot grisled and bay *h*	Zec 6:3	5483
The black *h* which are therein go	Zec 6:6	5483
them, and the riders on *h* shall be	Zec 10:5	5483

there be upon the bells of the *h*	Zec 14:20	5483
like unto *h* prepared unto battle	Rev 9:7	2462
of many *h* running to battle	Rev 9:9	2462
And thus I saw the *h* in the vision	Rev 9:17	2462
the heads of the *h* were as the	Rev 9:17	2462
wheat, and beasts, and sheep, and *h*	Rev 18:13	2462
heaven followed him upon white *h*	Rev 19:14	2462
of mighty men, and the flesh of *h*	Rev 19:18	2462

HORSES'
their *h* hoofs shall be counted	Is 5:28	5483
we put bits in the *h* mouths	Jas 3:3	2462

HOSAH (ho'-sah)
1. A city in Asher.
and the coast turneth to H	Josh 19:29	2621
2. A Levite.		
of Jeduthun and H to be porters	1Chr 16:38	2621
Also H, of the children of Merari	1Chr 26:10	2621
brethren of H were thirteen	1Chr 26:11	2621
H the lot came forth westward,	1Chr 26:16	2621

HOSANNA
saying, H to the son of David	Mt 21:9	5614
H in the highest	Mt 21:9	5614
and saying, H to the son of David	Mt 21:15	5614
that followed, cried, saying, H	Mk 11:9	5614
H in the highest	Mk 11:10	5614
forth to meet him, and cried, H	Jn 12:13	5614

HOSEA (ho-se'-ah) See HOSHEA, OSEE, OSHEA. *A prophet.*
word of the LORD that came unto H	Hos 1:1	1954
of the word of the LORD by H	Hos 1:2	1954
And the LORD said to H, Go, take	Hos 1:2	1954

HOSEN
bound in their coats, their *h*	Dan 3:21	6361

HOSHAIAH (ho-sha-i'-ah)
1. Helped dedicate the wall.
And after them went H, and half of	Neh 12:32	1955
2. Father of Jezaniah.		
Kareah, and Jezaniah the son of H	Jer 42:1	1955
Then spake Azariah the son of H	Jer 43:2	1955

HOSHAMA (ho-sha'-mah) *Father of Jeconiah.*
Pedaiah, and Shenazar, Jecamiah, H	1Chr 3:18	1953

HOSHEA (ho-she'-ah) See HOSEA.
1. Original name of Joshua.
people, he, and H the son of Nun	Deut 32:44	1954
2. An Ephramite ruler.		
of Ephraim, H the son of Azariah	1Chr 27:20	1954
3. Last king of Israel.		
And H the son of Elah made a	2Kin 15:30	1954
H the son of Elah to reign in	2Kin 17:1	1954
H became his servant, and gave him	2Kin 17:3	1954
of Assyria found conspiracy in H	2Kin 17:4	1954
In the ninth year of H the king	2Kin 17:6	1954
of H son of Elah king of Israel	2Kin 18:1	1954
of H son of Elah king of Israel	2Kin 18:9	1954
ninth year of H king of Israel	2Kin 18:10	1954
4. An Israelite who renewed the covenant.		
H, Hananiah, Hashub,	Neh 10:23	1954

HOSPITALITY
given to *h*	Rom 12:13	5381
of good behaviour, given to *h*	1Ti 3:2	5382
But a lover of *h*, a lover of good	Titus 1:8	5382
Use *h* one to another without	1Pet 4:9	5382

HOST
finished, and all the *h* of them	Gen 2:1	6635
of his *h* spake unto Abraham	Gen 21:22	6635
the chief captain of his *h*	Gen 21:32	6635
them, he said, This is God's *h*	Gen 32:2	4264
upon Pharaoh, and upon all his *h*	Ex 14:4	2428
upon Pharaoh, and upon all his *h*	Ex 14:17	2428
h of the Egyptians through the	Ex 14:24	4264
troubled the *h* of the Egyptians,	Ex 14:24	4264
all the *h* of Pharaoh that came	Ex 14:28	2428
his *h* hath he cast into the sea	Ex 15:4	2428
the dew lay round about the *h*	Ex 16:13	4264
And his *h*, and those that were	Num 2:4	6635
And his *h*, and those that were	Num 2:6	6635
And his *h*, and those that were	Num 2:8	6635
And his *h*, and those that were	Num 2:11	6635
And his *h*, and those that were	Num 2:13	6635
And his *h*, and those that were	Num 2:15	6635
And his *h*, and those that were	Num 2:19	6635
And his *h*, and those that were	Num 2:21	6635
And his *h*, and those that were	Num 2:23	6635
And his *h*, and those that were	Num 2:26	6635
And his *h*, and those that were	Num 2:28	6635
And his *h*, and those that were	Num 2:30	6635

old, all that enter into the *h*	Num 4:3	6635
over his *h* was Nahshon the son of	Num 10:14	
over the *h* of the tribe of the	Num 10:15	6635
over the *h* of the tribe of the	Num 10:16	6635
over his *h* was Elizur the son of	Num 10:18	6635
over the *h* of the tribe of the	Num 10:19	6635
over the *h* of the tribe of the	Num 10:20	6635
over his *h* was Elishama the son	Num 10:22	6635
over the *h* of the tribe of the	Num 10:23	6635
over the *h* of the tribe of the	Num 10:24	6635
over his *h* was Ahiezer the son of	Num 10:25	6635
over the *h* of the tribe of the	Num 10:26	6635
over the *h* of the tribe of the	Num 10:27	6635
wroth with the officers of the *h*	Num 31:14	2428
were over thousands of the *h*	Num 31:48	6635
were wasted out from among the *h*	Deut 2:14	4264
to destroy them from among the *h*	Deut 2:15	4264
stars, even all the *h* of heaven	Deut 4:19	6635
moon, or any of the *h* of heaven	Deut 17:3	6635
When the *h* goeth forth against	Deut 23:9	4264
Pass through the *h*, and command	Josh 1:11	4264
the officers went through the *h*	Josh 3:2	4264
but as captain of the *h* of the	Josh 5:14	6635
of the LORD's *h* said unto Joshua	Josh 5:15	6635
even all the *h* that was on the	Josh 8:13	4264
to Joshua to the *h* at Shiloh	Josh 18:9	4264
the captain of whose *h* was Sisera	Judg 4:2	6635
and all his chariots, and all his *h*	Judg 4:15	4264
the chariots, and after the *h*	Judg 4:16	4264
all the *h* of Sisera fell upon the	Judg 4:16	4264
so that the *h* of the Midianites	Judg 7:1	4264
the *h* of Midian was beneath him	Judg 7:8	4264
Arise, get thee down unto the *h*	Judg 7:9	4264
Phurah thy servant down to the *h*	Judg 7:10	4264
to go down unto the *h*	Judg 7:11	4264
the armed men that were in the *h*	Judg 7:11	4264
tumbled into the *h* of Midian	Judg 7:13	4264
delivered Midian, and all the *h*	Judg 7:14	4264
and returned into the *h* of Israel	Judg 7:15	4264
into your hand the *h* of Midian	Judg 7:15	4264
and all the *h* ran, and cried, and	Judg 7:21	4264
fellow, even throughout all the *h*	Judg 7:22	4264
the *h* fled to Beth-shittah in	Judg 7:22	4264
Nobah and Jogbehah, and smote the *h*	Judg 8:11	4264
for the *h* was secure	Judg 8:11	4264
and discomfited all the *h*	Judg 8:12	4264
of the *h* in the morning watch	1Sa 11:11	4264
Sisera, captain of the *h* of Hazor	1Sa 12:9	6635
And there was trembling in the *h*	1Sa 14:15	4264
the *h* of the Philistines went on	1Sa 14:19	4264
And he gathered an *h*, and smote the	1Sa 14:48	2428
of the captain of his *h* was Abner	1Sa 14:50	6635
as the *h* was going forth to the	1Sa 17:20	2428
the *h* of the Philistines this day	1Sa 17:46	4264
unto Abner, the captain of the *h*	1Sa 17:55	6635
son of Ner, the captain of his *h*	1Sa 26:5	6635
when Saul the *h* of the	1Sa 28:5	4264
h of Israel into the hand of the	1Sa 28:19	4264
me in the *h* is good in my sight	1Sa 29:6	4264
son of Ner, captain of Saul's *h*	2Sa 2:8	6635
all the *h* that was with him were	2Sa 3:23	6635
to smite the *h* of the Philistines	2Sa 5:24	6635
smitten all the *h* of Hadadezer	2Sa 8:9	2428
the son of Zeruiah was over the *h*	2Sa 8:16	6635
all the *h* of the mighty men	2Sa 10:7	6635
Shobach the captain of the *h* of	2Sa 10:16	6635
Shobach the captain of their *h*	2Sa 10:18	6635
captain of the *h* instead of Joab	2Sa 17:25	6635
h before me continually in the	2Sa 19:13	6635
Joab was over all the *h* of Israel	2Sa 20:23	6635
through the *h* of the Philistines	2Sa 23:16	4264
said to Joab the captain of the *h*	2Sa 24:2	2428
and against the captains of the *h*	2Sa 24:4	2428
the captains of the *h* went out	2Sa 24:4	2428
and Joab the captain of the *h*	1Kin 1:19	6635
sons, and the captains of the *h*	1Kin 1:25	6635
Ner, captain of the *h* of Israel	1Kin 2:32	6635
Jether, captain of the *h* of Judah	1Kin 2:32	6635
Jehoiada in his room over the *h*	1Kin 2:35	6635
son of Jehoiada was over the *h*	1Kin 4:4	6635
Joab the captain of the *h* was	1Kin 11:15	6635
the captain of the *h* was dead	1Kin 11:21	6635
made Omri, the captain of the *h*	1Kin 16:16	6635
Syria gathered all his *h* together	1Kin 20:1	2428
all the *h* of heaven standing by	1Kin 22:19	6635
hand, and carry me out of the *h*	1Kin 22:34	4264
a proclamation throughout the *h*	1Kin 22:36	4264
and there was no water for the *h*	2Kin 3:9	4264
king, or to the captain of the *h*	2Kin 5:1	6635
captain of the *h* of the king of	2Kin 5:1	6635
horses, and chariots, and a great *h*	2Kin 6:14	2428
an *h* compassed the city both with	2Kin 6:15	2428
king of Syria gathered all his *h*	2Kin 6:24	
us fall unto the *h* of the Syrians	2Kin 7:4	4264
For the LORD had made the *h* of	2Kin 7:6	4264
even the noise of a great *h*	2Kin 7:6	2428
sent after the *h* of the Syrians	2Kin 7:14	4264
captains of the *h* were sitting	2Kin 9:5	2428
hundreds, the officers of the *h*	2Kin 11:15	2428
and worshipped all the *h* of heaven	2Kin 17:16	6635
with a great *h* against Jerusalem	2Kin 18:17	2426
and worshipped all the *h* of heaven	2Kin 21:3	6635
he built altars for all the *h* of	2Kin 21:5	6635
grove, and for all the *h* of heaven	2Kin 23:4	6635
and to all the *h* of heaven	2Kin 23:5	6635
of Babylon came, he, and all his *h*	2Kin 25:1	2428
and the principal scribe of the *h*	2Kin 25:19	6635
being over the *h* of the LORD	1Chr 14:9	4264
the *h* of the Philistines encamped	1Chr 11:15	4264
through the *h* of the Philistines	1Chr 11:18	4264
sons of Gad, captains of the *h*	1Chr 12:14	6635
valour, and were captains in the *h*	1Chr 12:21	6635
a great *h*, like the *h* of God	1Chr 12:22	4264
to smite the *h* of the Philistines	1Chr 14:15	4264
and they smote the *h* of the	1Chr 14:16	4264
the *h* of Hadarezer king of Zobah	1Chr 18:9	2428
the son of Zeruiah was over the *h*	1Chr 18:15	6635
all the *h* of the mighty men	1Chr 19:8	6635
Shophach the captain of the *h* of	1Chr 19:16	6635
Shophach the captain of the *h*	1Chr 19:18	6635
the captains of the *h* separated	1Chr 25:1	6635
and the captains of the *h*	1Chr 26:26	6635
of the *h* for the first month	1Chr 27:3	6635
The third captain of the *h* for	1Chr 27:5	6635
with an *h* of a thousand thousand	2Chr 14:9	2428
before the LORD, and before his *h*	2Chr 14:13	4264
therefore is the *h* of the king of	2Chr 16:7	2428
Ethiopians and the Lubims a huge *h*	2Chr 16:8	2428
all the *h* of heaven standing on	2Chr 18:18	6635
thou mayest carry me out of the *h*	2Chr 18:33	6635
hundreds that were set over the *h*	2Chr 23:14	2428
that the *h* of Syria came up	2Chr 24:23	2428
a very great *h* into their hand	2Chr 24:24	2428
Uzziah had an *h* of fighting men	2Chr 26:11	2428
them throughout all the *h* shields	2Chr 26:14	6635
before the *h* that came to Samaria	2Chr 28:9	6635
and worshipped all the *h* of heaven	2Chr 33:3	6635
he built altars for all the *h* of	2Chr 33:5	6635
of the *h* of the king of Assyria	2Chr 33:11	6635
of heavens, with all their *h*	Neh 9:6	6635
the *h* of heaven worshippeth thee	Neh 9:6	6635
Though an *h* should encamp against	Ps 27:3	4264
all the *h* of them by the breath	Ps 33:6	6635
saved by the multitude of an *h*	Ps 33:16	2428
Pharaoh and his *h* in the Red sea	Ps 136:15	2428
mustereth the *h* of the battle	Is 13:4	6635
h of the high ones that are on	Is 24:21	6635
all the *h* of heaven shall be	Is 34:4	6635
all their *h* shall fall down, as	Is 34:4	6635
bringeth out their *h* by number	Is 40:26	6635
all their *h* have I commanded	Is 45:12	6635
all the *h* of heaven, whom they	Jer 8:2	6635
incense unto all the *h* of heaven	Jer 19:13	6635
As the *h* of heaven cannot be	Jer 33:22	6635
destroy ye utterly all her *h*	Jer 51:3	6635
and the principal scribe of the *h*	Jer 52:25	6635
of speech, as the noise of an *h*	Eze 1:24	4264
great, even to the *h* of heaven	Dan 8:10	6635
and it cast down some of the *h*	Dan 8:10	6635
even to the prince of the *h*	Dan 8:11	6635
an *h* was given him against the	Dan 8:12	6635
the *h* to be trodden under foot	Dan 8:13	6635
the captivity of this *h* of the	Obad 20	2426
them that worship the *h* of heaven	Zeph 1:5	6635
of the heavenly *h* praising God	Lk 2:13	4756
two pence, and gave them to the *h*	Lk 10:35	*3830*
up to worship the *h* of heaven	Acts 7:42	*4756*
Gaius mine *h*, and of the whole	Rom 16:23	*3581*

HOSTAGES

of the king's house, and *h*	2Kin 14:14	1121,8594
the *h* also, and returned to	2Chr 25:24	1121,8594

HOSTS

that all the *h* of the LORD went	Ex 12:41	6635
own standard, throughout their *h*	Num 1:52	6635
their *h* were six hundred thousand	Num 2:32	6635
all the camps throughout their *h*	Num 10:25	6635
and went up, they and all their *h*	Josh 10:5	6635
they and all their *h* with them	Josh 11:4	4264
their *h* with them, about fifteen	Judg 8:10	4264
the *h* of the children of the east	Judg 8:10	4264
unto the LORD of *h* in Shiloh	1Sa 1:3	6635

vowed a vow, and said, O LORD of h 1Sa 1:11	6635
of the covenant of the LORD of h 1Sa 4:4	6635
Thus saith the LORD of h, I 1Sa 15:2	6635
thee in the name of the LORD of h 1Sa 17:45	6635
and the LORD God of h was with him 2Sa 5:10	6635
of h that dwelleth between the 2Sa 6:2	6635
in the name of the LORD of h 2Sa 6:18	6635
David, Thus saith the LORD of h 2Sa 7:8	6635
The LORD of h is the God over 2Sa 7:26	6635
For thou, O LORD of h, God of 2Sa 7:27	6635
two captains of the h of Israel 1Kin 2:5	6635
sent the captains of the h which 1Kin 15:20	2428
said, As the LORD of h liveth 1Kin 18:15	6635
jealous for the LORD God of h 1Kin 19:10	6635
jealous for the LORD God of h 1Kin 19:14	6635
said, As the LORD of h liveth 2Kin 3:14	6635
of the LORD of h shall do this 2Kin 19:31	
for the LORD of h was with him 1Chr 11:9	6635
David, Thus saith the LORD of h 1Chr 17:7	6635
The LORD of h is the God of.................. 1Chr 17:24	6635
The LORD of h, he is the King of............ Ps 24:10	6635
The LORD of h is with us...................... Ps 46:7	6635
The LORD of h is with us...................... Ps 46:11	6635
seen in the city of the LORD of h .... Ps 48:8	6635
Thou therefore, O LORD God of h.......... Ps 59:5	6635
wait on thee, O Lord GOD of h .... Ps 69:6	6635
O LORD God of h, how long wilt .... Ps 80:4	6635
Turn us again, O God of h .... Ps 80:7	6635
we beseech thee, O God of h .... Ps 80:14	6635
Turn us again, O LORD God of h .... Ps 80:19	6635
are thy tabernacles, O LORD of h .... Ps 84:1	6635
even thine altars, O LORD of h .... Ps 84:3	6635
O LORD God of h, hear my prayer .... Ps 84:8	6635
O LORD of h, blessed is the man .... Ps 84:12	6635
O LORD God of h, who is a strong.......... Ps 89:8	6635
Bless ye the LORD, all ye his h .... Ps 103:21	6635
thou, O God, go forth with our h .... Ps 108:11	6635
praise ye him, all his h .... Ps 148:2	6635
Except the LORD of h had left................ Is 1:9	6635
saith the Lord, the LORD of h .... Is 1:24	6635
For the day of the LORD of h .... Is 2:12	6635
behold, the Lord, the LORD of h .... Is 3:1	6635
saith the Lord GOD of h .... Is 3:15	6635
LORD of h is the house of Israel .... Is 5:7	6635
In mine ears said the LORD of h............. Is 5:9	6635
But the LORD of h shall be.................... Is 5:16	6635
away the law of the LORD of h .... Is 5:24	6635
holy, holy, is the LORD of h .... Is 6:3	6635
have seen the King, the LORD of h .... Is 6:5	6635
Sanctify the LORD of h himself.............. Is 8:13	6635
in Israel from the LORD of h .... Is 8:18	6635
the LORD of h will perform this .... Is 9:7	6635
do they seek the LORD of h .... Is 9:13	6635
LORD of h is the land darkened .... Is 9:19	6635
shall the Lord, the Lord of h .... Is 10:16	6635
For the Lord GOD of h shall make .... Is 10:23	6635
thus saith the LORD God of h .... Is 10:24	6635
the LORD of h shall stir up a .... Is 10:26	6635
Behold, the Lord, the LORD of h............. Is 10:33	6635
the LORD of h mustereth the host .... Is 13:4	6635
in the wrath of the LORD of h .... Is 13:13	6635
against them, saith the LORD of h .... Is 14:22	6635
destruction, saith the LORD of h .... Is 14:23	6635
The LORD of h hath sworn, saying, ... Is 14:24	6635
For the LORD of h hath purposed........... Is 14:27	6635
of Israel, saith the LORD of h................ Is 17:3	6635
LORD of h of a people scattered .... Is 18:7	6635
of the name of the LORD of h .... Is 18:7	6635
saith the Lord, the LORD of h .... Is 19:4	6635
of h hath purposed upon Egypt............. Is 19:12	6635
of the hand of the LORD of h .... Is 19:16	6635
of the counsel of the LORD of h .... Is 19:17	6635
Canaan, and swear to the LORD of h ..... Is 19:18	6635
LORD of h in the land of Egypt .... Is 19:20	6635
Whom the LORD of h shall bless .... Is 19:25	6635
I have heard of the LORD of h............... Is 21:10	6635
God of h in the valley of vision .... Is 22:5	6635
the Lord GOD of h call to weeping .... Is 22:12	6635
in mine ears by the LORD of h .... Is 22:14	6635
ye die, saith the Lord GOD of h .... Is 22:14	6635
Thus saith the Lord GOD of h................ Is 22:15	6635
In that day, saith the LORD of h .... Is 22:25	6635
The LORD of h hath purposed it, ... Is 23:9	6635
when the LORD of h shall reign in.......... Is 24:23	6635
h make unto all people a feast of .... Is 25:6	6635
LORD of h be for a crown of glory .... Is 28:5	6635
the Lord GOD of h a consumption........... Is 28:22	6635
cometh forth from the LORD of h .... Is 28:29	6635
of the LORD of h with thunder .... Is 29:6	6635
so shall the LORD of h come down .... Is 31:4	6635
the LORD of h defend Jerusalem............ Is 31:5	6635

O LORD of h, God of Israel, that............. Is 37:16	6635
of the LORD of h shall do this .... Is 37:32	6635
Hear the word of the LORD of h .... Is 39:5	6635
and his redeemer the LORD of h .... Is 44:6	6635
nor reward, saith the LORD of h .... Is 45:13	6635
the LORD of h is his name..................... Is 47:4	6635
The LORD of h is his name .... Is 48:2	6635
The LORD of h is his name .... Is 51:15	6635
the LORD of h is his name .... Is 54:5	6635
in thee, saith the Lord GOD of h .... Jer 2:19	6635
heritage of the h of nations .... Jer 3:19	6635
thus saith the LORD God of h .... Jer 5:14	6635
For thus hath the LORD of h said .... Jer 6:6	6635
Thus saith the LORD of h, They .... Jer 6:9	6635
Thus saith the LORD of h, the God .... Jer 7:3	6635
Thus saith the LORD of h, the God .... Jer 7:21	6635
driven them, saith the LORD of h .... Jer 8:3	6635
thus saith the LORD of h, Behold, ... Jer 9:7	6635
thus saith the LORD of h, the God .... Jer 9:15	6635
Thus saith the LORD of h, ... Jer 9:17	6635
The LORD of h is his name..................... Jer 10:16	6635
For the LORD of h, that planted .... Jer 11:17	6635
But, O LORD of h, that judgest .... Jer 11:20	6635
thus saith the LORD of h, Behold, ... Jer 11:22	6635
by my name, O LORD God of h .... Jer 15:16	6635
For thus saith the LORD of h.................. Jer 16:9	6635
Thus saith the LORD of h, the God .... Jer 19:3	6635
them, Thus saith the LORD of h .... Jer 19:11	6635
Thus saith the LORD of h, the God .... Jer 19:15	6635
But, O LORD of h, that triest the .... Jer 20:12	6635
thus saith the LORD of h .... Jer 23:15	6635
Thus saith the LORD of h, Hearken .... Jer 23:16	6635
God, of the LORD of h our God .... Jer 23:36	6635
thus saith the LORD of h .... Jer 25:8	6635
them, Thus saith the LORD of h .... Jer 25:27	6635
them, Thus saith the LORD of h .... Jer 25:28	6635
of the earth, saith the LORD of h .... Jer 25:29	6635
Thus saith the LORD of h, Behold, ... Jer 25:32	6635
saying, Thus saith the LORD of h .... Jer 26:18	6635
masters, Thus saith the LORD of h .... Jer 27:4	6635
intercession to the LORD of h................. Jer 27:18	6635
LORD of h concerning the pillars............. Jer 27:19	6635
Yea, thus saith the LORD of h .... Jer 27:21	6635
Thus speaketh the LORD of h .... Jer 28:2	6635
For thus saith the LORD of h.................. Jer 28:14	6635
Thus saith the LORD of h, the God .... Jer 29:4	6635
For thus saith the LORD of h.................. Jer 29:8	6635
Thus saith the LORD of h .... Jer 29:17	6635
Thus saith the LORD of h, the God .... Jer 29:21	6635
Thus speaketh the LORD of h .... Jer 29:25	6635
in that day, saith the LORD of h .... Jer 30:8	6635
Thus saith the LORD of h, the God .... Jer 31:23	6635
The LORD of h is his name .... Jer 31:35	6635
Thus saith the LORD of h, the God .... Jer 32:14	6635
For thus saith the LORD of h.................. Jer 32:15	6635
the Mighty God, the LORD of h .... Jer 32:18	6635
shall say, Praise the LORD of h .... Jer 33:11	6635
Thus saith the LORD of h .... Jer 33:12	6635
Thus saith the LORD of h, the God .... Jer 35:13	6635
thus saith the LORD God of h .... Jer 35:17	6635
Thus saith the LORD of h .... Jer 35:18	6635
thus saith the LORD of h, the God .... Jer 35:19	6635
Thus saith the LORD, the God of h .... Jer 38:17	6635
saying, Thus saith the LORD of h .... Jer 39:16	6635
Thus saith the LORD of h, the God .... Jer 42:15	6635
For thus saith the LORD of h.................. Jer 42:18	6635
them, Thus saith the LORD of h .... Jer 43:10	6635
Thus saith the LORD of h, the God .... Jer 44:2	6635
thus saith the LORD, the God of h .... Jer 44:7	6635
thus saith the LORD of h, the God .... Jer 44:11	6635
Thus saith the LORD of h, the God .... Jer 44:25	6635
is the day of the Lord GOD of h .... Jer 46:10	6635
for the Lord GOD of h hath a................. Jer 46:10	6635
King, whose name is the LORD of h .... Jer 46:18	6635
The LORD of h, the God of Israel............ Jer 46:25	6635
Moab thus saith the LORD of h .... Jer 48:1	6635
King, whose name is the LORD of h .... Jer 48:15	6635
thee, saith the Lord GOD of h .... Jer 49:5	6635
Edom, thus saith the LORD of h .... Jer 49:7	6635
in that day, saith the LORD of h .... Jer 49:26	6635
Thus saith the LORD of h .... Jer 49:35	6635
thus saith the LORD of h, the God .... Jer 50:18	6635
of h in the land of the Chaldeans .... Jer 50:25	6635
proud, saith the Lord GOD of h .... Jer 50:31	6635
Thus saith the LORD of h .... Jer 50:33	6635
the LORD of h is his name .... Jer 50:34	6635
of his God, of the LORD of h.................. Jer 51:5	6635
The LORD of h hath sworn by .... Jer 51:14	6635
the LORD of h is his name .... Jer 51:19	6635
For thus saith the LORD of h.................. Jer 51:33	6635
King, whose name is the LORD of h .... Jer 51:57	6635

Thus saith the LORD of *h*	Jer 51:58	6635
Even the LORD God of *h*	Hos 12:5	6635
saith the Lord GOD, the God of *h*	Amos 3:13	6635
the earth, The LORD, The God of *h*	Amos 4:13	6635
and so the LORD, the God of *h*	Amos 5:14	6635
of *h* will be gracious unto the	Amos 5:15	6635
Therefore the LORD, the God of *h*	Amos 5:16	6635
LORD, whose name is The God of *h*	Amos 5:27	6635
saith the LORD the God of *h*	Amos 6:8	6635
saith the LORD the God of *h*	Amos 6:14	6635
the Lord GOD of *h* is he that	Amos 9:5	6635
of the LORD of *h* hath spoken it	Mic 4:4	6635
against thee, saith the LORD of *h*	Nah 2:13	6635
against thee, saith the LORD of *h*	Nah 3:5	6635
is it not of the LORD of *h* that	Hab 2:13	6635
as I live, saith the LORD of *h*	Zeph 2:9	6635
the people of the LORD of *h*	Zeph 2:10	6635
Thus speaketh the LORD of *h*	Hag 1:2	6635
thus saith the LORD of *h*	Hag 1:5	6635
Thus saith the LORD of *h*	Hag 1:7	6635
saith the LORD of *h*	Hag 1:9	6635
in the house of the LORD of *h*	Hag 1:14	6635
am I with you, saith the LORD of *h*	Hag 2:4	6635
For thus saith the LORD of *h*	Hag 2:6	6635
with glory, saith the LORD of *h*	Hag 2:7	6635
gold is mine, saith the LORD of *h*	Hag 2:8	6635
the former, saith the LORD of *h*	Hag 2:9	6635
I give peace, saith the LORD of *h*	Hag 2:9	6635
Thus saith the LORD of *h*	Hag 2:11	6635
In that day, saith the LORD of *h*	Hag 2:23	6635
chosen thee, saith the LORD of *h*	Hag 2:23	6635
them, Thus saith the LORD of *h*	Zec 1:3	6635
ye unto me, saith the LORD of *h*	Zec 1:3	6635
unto you, saith the LORD of *h*	Zec 1:3	6635
saying, Thus saith the LORD of *h*	Zec 1:4	6635
Like as the LORD of *h* thought to	Zec 1:6	6635
answered and said, O LORD of *h*	Zec 1:12	6635
saying, Thus saith the LORD of *h*	Zec 1:14	6635
built in it, saith the LORD of *h*	Zec 1:16	6635
saying, Thus saith the LORD of *h*	Zec 1:17	6635
For thus saith the LORD of *h*	Zec 2:8	6635
that the LORD of *h* hath sent me	Zec 2:9	6635
LORD of *h* hath sent me unto thee	Zec 2:11	6635
Thus saith the LORD of *h*	Zec 3:7	6635
thereof, saith the LORD of *h*	Zec 3:9	6635
In that day, saith the LORD of *h*	Zec 3:10	6635
by my spirit, saith the LORD of *h*	Zec 4:6	6635
LORD of *h* hath sent me unto you	Zec 4:9	6635
it forth, saith the LORD of *h*	Zec 5:4	6635
Thus speaketh the LORD of *h*	Zec 6:12	6635
LORD of *h* hath sent me unto you	Zec 6:15	6635
in the house of the LORD of *h*	Zec 7:3	6635
the word of the LORD of *h* unto me	Zec 7:4	6635
Thus speaketh the LORD of *h*	Zec 7:9	6635
the words which the LORD of *h*	Zec 7:12	6635
a great wrath from the LORD of *h*	Zec 7:12	6635
not hear, saith the LORD of *h*	Zec 7:13	6635
word of the LORD of *h* came to me	Zec 8:1	6635
Thus saith the LORD of *h*	Zec 8:2	6635
the LORD of *h* the holy mountain	Zec 8:3	6635
Thus saith the LORD of *h*	Zec 8:4	6635
Thus saith the LORD of *h*	Zec 8:6	6635
saith the LORD of *h*	Zec 8:6	6635
Thus saith the LORD of *h*	Zec 8:7	6635
Thus saith the LORD of *h*	Zec 8:9	6635
house of the LORD of *h* was laid	Zec 8:9	6635
former days, saith the LORD of *h*	Zec 8:11	6635
For thus saith the LORD of *h*	Zec 8:14	6635
me to wrath, saith the LORD of *h*	Zec 8:14	6635
of the LORD of *h* came unto me	Zec 8:18	6635
Thus saith the LORD of *h*	Zec 8:19	6635
Thus saith the LORD of *h*	Zec 8:20	6635
LORD, and to seek the LORD of *h*	Zec 8:21	6635
seek the LORD of *h* in Jerusalem	Zec 8:22	6635
Thus saith the LORD of *h*	Zec 8:23	6635
The LORD of *h* shall defend them	Zec 9:15	6635
for the LORD of *h* hath visited	Zec 10:3	6635
in the LORD of *h* their God	Zec 12:5	6635
in that day, saith the LORD of *h*	Zec 13:2	6635
is my fellow, saith the LORD of *h*	Zec 13:7	6635
worship the King, the LORD of *h*	Zec 14:16	6635
worship the King, the LORD of *h*	Zec 14:17	6635
be holiness unto the LORD of *h*	Zec 14:21	6635
in the house of the LORD of *h*	Zec 14:21	6635
thus saith the LORD of *h*, They	Mal 1:4	6635
saith the LORD of *h* unto you	Mal 1:6	6635
saith the LORD of *h*	Mal 1:8	6635
saith the LORD of *h*	Mal 1:9	6635
in you, saith the LORD of *h*	Mal 1:10	6635
the heathen, saith the LORD of *h*	Mal 1:11	6635
at it, saith the LORD of *h*	Mal 1:13	6635

a great King, saith the LORD of *h*	Mal 1:14	6635
unto my name, saith the LORD of *h*	Mal 2:2	6635
be with Levi, saith the LORD of *h*	Mal 2:4	6635
is the messenger of the LORD of *h*	Mal 2:7	6635
of Levi, saith the LORD of *h*	Mal 2:8	6635
an offering unto the LORD of *h*	Mal 2:12	6635
his garment, saith the LORD of *h*	Mal 2:16	6635
shall come, saith the LORD of *h*	Mal 3:1	6635
fear not me, saith the LORD of *h*	Mal 3:5	6635
unto you, saith the LORD of *h*	Mal 3:7	6635
now herewith, saith the LORD of *h*	Mal 3:10	6635
in the field, saith the LORD of *h*	Mal 3:11	6635
land, saith the LORD of *h*	Mal 3:12	6635
mournfully before the LORD of *h*	Mal 3:14	6635
be mine, saith the LORD of *h*	Mal 3:17	6635
burn them up, saith the LORD of *h*	Mal 4:1	6635
do this, saith the LORD of *h*	Mal 4:3	6635

HOT

and when the sun waxed *h*, it	Ex 16:21	2552
And my wrath shall wax *h*, and I	Ex 22:24	2734
my wrath may wax *h* against them	Ex 32:10	2734
wrath wax *h* against thy people	Ex 32:11	2734
and Moses' anger waxed *h*, and he	Ex 32:19	2734
not the anger of my lord wax *h*	Ex 32:22	2734
skin whereof there is a *h* burning	Lev 13:24	784
h displeasure, wherewith the LORD	Deut 9:19	2534
the slayer, while his heart is *h*	Deut 19:6	3179
This our bread we took *h* for our	Josh 9:12	2525
of the LORD was *h* against Israel	Judg 2:14	2734
of the LORD was *h* against Israel	Judg 2:20	2734
of the LORD was *h* against Israel	Judg 3:8	2734
not thine anger be *h* against me	Judg 6:39	2734
of the LORD was *h* against Israel	Judg 10:7	2734
morrow, by that time the sun be *h*	1Sa 11:9	2527
to put *h* bread in the day when it	1Sa 21:6	2527
be opened until the sun be *h*	Neh 7:3	2527
when it is *h*, they are consumed	Job 6:17	2527
chasten me in thy *h* displeasure	Ps 6:1	2534
chasten me in thy *h* displeasure	Ps 38:1	2534
My heart was *h* within me	Ps 39:3	2552
and their flocks to *h* thunderbolts	Ps 78:48	7565
Can one go upon *h* coals, and his	Prov 6:28	
that the brass of it may be *h*	Eze 24:11	3179
and the furnace exceeding *h*	Dan 3:22	228
They are all *h* as an oven	Hos 7:7	2552
conscience seared with a *h* iron	1Ti 4:2	2743
that thou art neither cold nor *h*	Rev 3:15	2200
I would thou wert cold or *h*	Rev 3:15	2200
lukewarm, and neither cold nor *h*	Rev 3:16	2200

HOTHAM (ho'-tham) See HOTHAN. *A son of Heber.*

begat Japhlet, and Shomer, and *H*	1Chr 7:32	2369

HOTHAN (ho'-than) See HOTHAM. *Father of Shama and Jehiel.*

Jehiel the sons of *H* the Aroerite	1Chr 11:44	2369

HOTHIR (ho'-thir) *A son of Heman.*

Joshbekashah, Mallothi, *H*	1Chr 25:4	1956
The one and twentieth to *H*	1Chr 25:28	1956

HOTLY

thou hast so *h* pursued after me	Gen 31:36	1814

HOTTEST

in the forefront of the *h* battle	2Sa 11:15	2389

HOUGH

thou shalt *h* their horses, and	Josh 11:6	6131

HOUGHED

he *h* their horses, and burnt their	Josh 11:9	6131
David *h* all the chariot horses,	2Sa 8:4	6131
David also *h* all the chariot	1Chr 18:4	6131

HOUR

worshippeth shall the same *h* be	Dan 3:6	8160
ye shall be cast the same *h* into	Dan 3:15	8160
was astonied for one *h*, and his	Dan 4:19	8160
The same *h* was the thing	Dan 4:33	8160
In the same *h* came forth fingers	Dan 5:5	8160
was healed in the selfsame *h*	Mt 8:13	5610
woman was made whole from that *h*	Mt 9:22	5610
that same *h* what ye shall speak	Mt 10:19	5610
was made whole from that very *h*	Mt 15:28	5610
child was cured from that very *h*	Mt 17:18	5610
And he went out about the third *h*	Mt 20:3	5610
out about the sixth and ninth *h*	Mt 20:5	5610
about the eleventh *h* he went out	Mt 20:6	5610
were hired about the eleventh *h*	Mt 20:9	5610
These last have wrought but one *h*	Mt 20:12	5610
***h* knoweth no man, no, not the**	Mt 24:36	5610
not what *h* your Lord doth come	Mt 24:42	5610
for in such an *h* as ye think not	Mt 24:44	5610

H

in an *h* that he is not aware of,	Mt 24:50	5610
h wherein the Son of man cometh	Mt 25:13	5610
could ye not watch with me one *h*	Mt 26:40	5610
the *h* is at hand, and the Son of	Mt 26:45	5610
In that same *h* said Jesus to the	Mt 26:55	5610
Now from the sixth *h* there was	Mt 27:45	5610
all the land unto the ninth *h*	Mt 27:45	5610
about the ninth *h* Jesus cried	Mt 27:46	5610
shall be given you in that *h*	Mk 13:11	5610
that *h* knoweth no man, no, not	Mk 13:32	5610
the *h* might pass from him	Mk 14:35	5610
couldest not thou watch one *h*	Mk 14:37	5610
it is enough, the *h* is come	Mk 14:41	5610
And it was the third *h*, and they	Mk 15:25	5610
And when the sixth *h* was come	Mk 15:33	5610
the whole land until the ninth *h*	Mk 15:33	5610
at the ninth *h* Jesus cried with a	Mk 15:34	5610
in that same *h* he cured many of	Lk 7:21	5610
In that *h* Jesus rejoiced in	Lk 10:21	5610
the same *h* what ye ought to say	Lk 12:12	5610
known what *h* the thief would come	Lk 12:39	5610
cometh at an *h* when ye think not	Lk 12:40	5610
at an *h* when he is not aware, and	Lk 12:46	5610
the scribes the same *h* sought to	Lk 20:19	5610
And when the *h* was come, he sat	Lk 22:14	5610
but this is your *h*, and the power	Lk 22:53	5610
about the space of one *h* after	Lk 22:59	5610
And it was about the sixth *h*	Lk 23:44	5610
all the earth until the ninth *h*	Lk 23:44	5610
And they rose up the same *h*	Lk 24:33	5610
for it was about the tenth *h*	Jn 1:39	5610
mine *h* is not yet come	Jn 2:4	5610
and it was about the sixth *h*	Jn 4:6	5610
the *h* cometh, when ye shall	Jn 4:21	5610
But the *h* cometh, and now is, when	Jn 4:23	5610
them the *h* when he began to amend	Jn 4:52	5610
the seventh *h* the fever left him	Jn 4:52	5610
knew that it was at the same *h*	Jn 4:53	5610
The *h* is coming, and now is, when	Jn 5:25	5610
for the *h* is coming, in the which	Jn 5:28	5610
because his *h* was not yet come	Jn 7:30	5610
for his *h* was not yet come	Jn 8:20	5610
The *h* is come, that the Son of	Jn 12:23	5610
Father, save me from this *h*	Jn 12:27	5610
for this cause came I unto this *h*	Jn 12:27	5610
when Jesus knew that his *h* was	Jn 13:1	5610
sorrow, because her *h* is come	Jn 16:21	5610
the *h* cometh, yea, is now come,	Jn 16:32	5610
and said, Father, the *h* is come	Jn 17:1	5610
passover, and about the sixth *h*	Jn 19:14	5610
from that *h* that disciple took	Jn 19:27	5610
it is but the third *h* of the day	Acts 2:15	5610
h of prayer, being the ninth *h*	Acts 3:1	
evidently about the ninth *h* of	Acts 10:3	5610
to pray about the sixth *h*	Acts 10:9	5610
ago I was fasting until this *h*	Acts 10:30	5610
at the ninth *h* I prayed in my	Acts 10:30	5610
And he came out the same *h*	Acts 16:18	5610
took them the same *h* of the night	Acts 16:33	5610
the same *h* I looked up upon him	Acts 22:13	5610
at the third *h* of the night	Acts 23:23	5610
this present *h* we both hunger	1Cor 4:11	5610
of the idol unto this *h* eat it as	1Cor 8:7	734
why stand we in jeopardy every *h*	1Cor 15:30	5610
by subjection, no, not for an *h*	Gal 2:5	5610
know what *h* I will come upon thee	Rev 3:3	5610
thee from the *h* of temptation	Rev 3:10	5610
about the space of half an *h*	Rev 8:1	2256
which were prepared for an *h*	Rev 9:15	5610
the same *h* was there a great	Rev 11:13	5610
for the *h* his judgment is come	Rev 14:7	5610
as kings one *h* with the beast	Rev 17:12	5610
for in one *h* is thy judgment come	Rev 18:10	5610
For in one *h* so great riches is	Rev 18:17	5610
for in one *h* is she made desolate	Rev 18:19	5610

HOURS

Are there not twelve *h* in the day	Jn 11:9	5610
about the space of three *h* after	Acts 5:7	5610
the space of two *h* cried out	Acts 19:34	5610

HOUSE

thou and all thy *h* into the ark	Gen 7:1	1004
kindred, and from thy father's *h*	Gen 12:1	1004
woman was taken into Pharaoh's *h*	Gen 12:15	1004
his *h* with great plagues because	Gen 12:17	1004
servants, born in his own *h*	Gen 14:14	1004
the steward of my *h* is this	Gen 15:2	1004
lo, one born in my *h* is mine heir	Gen 15:3	1004
he that is born in the *h*	Gen 17:12	1004
He that is born in thy *h*, and he	Gen 17:13	1004
and all that were born in his *h*	Gen 17:23	1004

male among the men of Abraham's *h*	Gen 17:23	1004
men of his *h*, born in the *h*	Gen 17:27	1004
I pray you, into your servant's *h*	Gen 19:2	1004
unto him, and entered into his *h*	Gen 19:3	1004
of Sodom, compassed the *h* round	Gen 19:4	1004
and pulled Lot into the *h* to them	Gen 19:10	1004
the door of the *h* with blindness	Gen 19:11	1004
me to wander from my father's *h*	Gen 20:13	1004
the wombs of the *h* of Abimelech	Gen 20:18	1004
unto his eldest servant of his *h*	Gen 24:2	1004
which took me from my father's *h*	Gen 24:7	1004
thy father's *h* for us to lodge in	Gen 24:23	1004
the LORD led me to the *h* of my	Gen 24:27	1004
of her mother's *h* these things	Gen 24:28	1004
for I have prepared the *h*	Gen 24:31	1004
And the man came into the *h*	Gen 24:32	1004
thou shalt go unto my father's *h*	Gen 24:38	1004
my kindred, and of my father's *h*	Gen 24:40	1004
which were in her *h*	Gen 27:15	1004
to the *h* of Bethuel thy mother's	Gen 28:2	1004
is none other but the *h* of God	Gen 28:17	1004
again to my father's *h* in peace	Gen 28:21	1004
for a pillar, shall be God's *h*	Gen 28:22	1004
him, and brought him to his *h*	Gen 29:13	1004
I provide for mine own *h* also	Gen 30:30	1004
for us in our father's *h*	Gen 31:14	1004
longedst after thy father's *h*	Gen 31:30	1004
have I been twenty years in thy *h*	Gen 31:41	1004
to Succoth, and built him an *h*	Gen 33:17	1004
than all the *h* of his father	Gen 34:19	1004
and took Dinah out of Shechem's *h*	Gen 34:26	1004
even all that was in the *h*	Gen 34:29	1004
I shall be destroyed, I and my *h*	Gen 34:30	1004
and all the persons of his *h*	Gen 36:6	1004
Remain a widow at thy father's *h*	Gen 38:11	1004
went and dwelt in her father's *h*	Gen 38:11	1004
he was in the *h* of his master the	Gen 39:2	1004
he made him overseer over his *h*	Gen 39:4	1004
he had made him overseer in his *h*	Gen 39:5	1004
Egyptian's *h* for Joseph's sake	Gen 39:5	1004
was upon all that he had in the *h*	Gen 39:5	1004
not what is with me in the *h*	Gen 39:8	1004
is none greater in this *h* than I	Gen 39:9	1004
into the *h* to do his business	Gen 39:11	1004
of the men of the *h* there within	Gen 39:11	1004
she called unto the men of her *h*	Gen 39:14	1004
he put them in ward in the *h* of	Gen 40:3	1004
him in the ward of his lord's *h*	Gen 40:7	1004
and bring me out of this *h*	Gen 40:14	1004
in the captain of the guard's *h*	Gen 41:10	1004
Thou shalt be over my *h*, and	Gen 41:40	1004
all my toil, and all my father's *h*	Gen 41:51	1004
be bound in the *h* of your prison	Gen 42:19	1004
he said to the ruler of his *h*	Gen 43:16	1004
brought the men into Joseph's *h*	Gen 43:17	1004
they were brought into Joseph's *h*	Gen 43:18	1004
near to the steward of Joseph's *h*	Gen 43:19	1004
with him at the door of the *h*	Gen 43:19	1004
brought the men into Joseph's *h*	Gen 43:24	1004
was in their hand into the *h*	Gen 43:26	1004
he commanded the steward of his *h*	Gen 44:1	1004
of thy lord's *h* silver or gold	Gen 44:8	1004
his brethren came to Joseph's *h*	Gen 44:14	1004
and the *h* of Pharaoh heard	Gen 45:2	1004
to Pharaoh, and lord of all his *h*	Gen 45:8	1004
thereof was heard in Pharaoh's *h*	Gen 45:16	1004
all the souls of the *h* of Jacob	Gen 46:27	1004
brethren, and unto his father's *h*	Gen 46:31	1004
My brethren, and my father's *h*	Gen 46:31	1004
the money into Pharaoh's *h*	Gen 47:14	1004
spake unto the *h* of Pharaoh	Gen 50:4	1004
of Pharaoh, the elders of his *h*	Gen 50:7	1004
all the *h* of Joseph, and his	Gen 50:8	1004
his brethren, and his father's *h*	Gen 50:8	1004
in Egypt, he, and his father's *h*	Gen 50:22	1004
there went a man of the *h* of Levi	Ex 2:1	1004
of her that sojourneth in her *h*	Ex 3:22	1004
Pharaoh turned and went into his *h*	Ex 7:23	1004
shall go up and come into thine *h*	Ex 8:3	1004
into the *h* of thy servants, and	Ex 8:3	1004
of flies into the *h* of Pharaoh	Ex 8:24	1004
to the *h* of their fathers	Ex 12:3	1004
of their fathers, a lamb for an *h*	Ex 12:3	1004
his neighbour next unto his *h*	Ex 12:4	1004
door of his *h* until the morning	Ex 12:22	1004
for there was not a *h* where there	Ex 12:30	1004
In one *h* shall it be eaten	Ex 12:46	1004
of the flesh abroad out of the *h*	Ex 12:46	1004
Egypt, out of the *h* of bondage	Ex 13:3	1004
from Egypt, from the *h* of bondage	Ex 13:14	1004
the *h* of Israel called the name	Ex 16:31	1004

shalt thou say to the *h* of Jacob	Ex 19:3	1004
of Egypt, out of the *h* of bondage	Ex 20:2	1004
shalt not covet thy neighbour's *h*	Ex 20:17	1004
it be stolen out of the man's *h*	Ex 22:7	1004
then the master of the *h* shall be	Ex 22:8	1004
into the *h* of the Lord thy God	Ex 23:19	1004
unto the *h* of the Lord thy God	Ex 34:26	1004
the sight of all the *h* of Israel	Ex 40:38	1004
brethren, the whole *h* of Israel	Lev 10:6	1004
h of the land of your possession	Lev 14:34	1004
he that owneth the *h* shall come	Lev 14:35	1004
is as it were a plague in the *h*	Lev 14:35	1004
command that they empty the *h*	Lev 14:36	1004
is in the *h* be not made unclean	Lev 14:36	1004
priest shall go in to see the *h*	Lev 14:36	1004
of the *h* with hollow strakes	Lev 14:37	1004
of the *h* to the door of the *h*	Lev 14:38	1004
and shut up the *h* seven days	Lev 14:38	1004
he shall cause the *h* to be	Lev 14:39	1004
be spread in the walls of the *h*	Lev 14:39	1004
he shall cause the *h* to be	Lev 14:41	1004
morter, and shall plaister the *h*	Lev 14:42	1004
come again, and break out in the *h*	Lev 14:43	1004
and after he hath scraped the *h*	Lev 14:43	1004
if the plague be spread in the *h*	Lev 14:44	1004
it is a fretting leprosy in the *h*	Lev 14:44	1004
And he shall break down the *h*	Lev 14:45	1004
and all the morter of the *h*	Lev 14:45	1004
h all the while that it is shut	Lev 14:46	1004
he that lieth in the *h* shall wash	Lev 14:47	1004
he that eateth in the *h* shall	Lev 14:47	1004
plague hath not spread in the *h*	Lev 14:48	1004
after the *h* was plaistered	Lev 14:48	1004
shall pronounce the *h* clean	Lev 14:48	1004
take to cleanse the *h* two birds	Lev 14:49	1004
and sprinkle the *h* seven times	Lev 14:51	1004
he shall cleanse the *h* with the	Lev 14:52	1004
and make an atonement for the *h*	Lev 14:53	1004
leprosy of a garment, and of a *h*	Lev 14:55	1004
for himself, and for his *h*	Lev 16:6	1004
for himself, and for his *h*	Lev 16:11	1004
there be of the *h* of Israel	Lev 17:3	1004
man there be of the *h* of Israel	Lev 17:8	1004
man there be of the *h* of Israel	Lev 17:10	1004
it, and he that is born in his *h*	Lev 22:11	1004
is returned unto her father's *h*	Lev 22:13	1004
he be of the *h* of Israel, or of	Lev 22:18	1004
a dwelling *h* in a walled city	Lev 25:29	1004
then the *h* that is in the walled	Lev 25:30	1004
then the *h* that was sold, and the	Lev 25:33	1004
his *h* to be holy unto the Lord	Lev 27:14	1004
sanctified it will redeem his *h*	Lev 27:15	1004
by the *h* of their fathers, with	Num 1:2	1004
one head of the *h* of his fathers	Num 1:4	1004
by the *h* of their fathers,	Num 1:18	1004
by the *h* of their fathers,	Num 1:20	1004
by the *h* of their fathers, those	Num 1:22	1004
by the *h* of their fathers,	Num 1:24	1004
by the *h* of their fathers,	Num 1:26	1004
by the *h* of their fathers,	Num 1:28	1004
by the *h* of their fathers,	Num 1:30	1004
by the *h* of their fathers,	Num 1:32	1004
by the *h* of their fathers,	Num 1:34	1004
by the *h* of their fathers,	Num 1:36	1004
by the *h* of their fathers,	Num 1:38	1004
by the *h* of their fathers,	Num 1:40	1004
by the *h* of their fathers,	Num 1:42	1004
one was for the *h* of his fathers	Num 1:44	1004
by the *h* of their fathers, from	Num 1:45	1004
the ensign of their father's *h*	Num 2:2	1004
Israel by the *h* of their fathers	Num 2:32	1004
to the *h* of their fathers	Num 2:34	1004
Levi after the *h* of their fathers	Num 3:15	1004
to the *h* of their fathers	Num 3:20	1004
the chief of the *h* of the father	Num 3:24	1004
the chief of the *h* of the father	Num 3:30	1004
the chief of the *h* of the father	Num 3:35	1004
by the *h* of their fathers	Num 4:2	1004
by the *h* of their fathers	Num 4:29	1004
after the *h* of their fathers,	Num 4:34	1004
by the *h* of their fathers,	Num 4:38	1004
by the *h* of their fathers, were	Num 4:40	1004
by the *h* of their fathers,	Num 4:42	1004
after the *h* of their fathers,	Num 4:46	1004
heads of the *h* of their fathers,	Num 7:2	1004
so, who is faithful in all mine *h*	Num 12:7	1004
to the *h* of their fathers	Num 17:2	1004
h of their fathers twelve rods	Num 17:2	1004
head of the *h* of their fathers	Num 17:3	1004
for the *h* of Levi was budded	Num 17:8	1004
thy father's *h* with thee shall	Num 18:1	1004
is clean in thy *h* shall eat of it	Num 18:11	1004

clean in thine *h* shall eat of it	Num 18:13	1004
days, even all the *h* of Israel	Num 20:29	1004
give me his *h* full of silver	Num 22:18	1004
give me his *h* full of silver	Num 24:13	1004
a prince of a chief *h* among the	Num 25:14	1004
people, and of a chief *h* in Midian	Num 25:15	1004
throughout their fathers' *h*	Num 26:2	1004
in her father's *h* in her youth	Num 30:3	1004
if she vowed in her husband's *h*	Num 30:10	1004
in her youth in her father's *h*	Num 30:16	1004
to the *h* of their fathers	Num 34:14	1004
to the *h* of their fathers	Num 34:14	1004
of Egypt, from the *h* of bondage	Deut 5:6	1004
thou covet thy neighbour's *h*	Deut 5:21	1004
them when thou sittest in thine *h*	Deut 6:7	1004
them upon the posts of thy *h*	Deut 6:9	1004
of Egypt, from the *h* of bondage	Deut 6:12	1004
you out of the *h* of bondmen	Deut 7:8	1004
bring an abomination into thine *h*	Deut 7:26	1004
of Egypt, from the *h* of bondage	Deut 8:14	1004
them when thou sittest in thine *h*	Deut 11:19	1004
upon the door posts of thine *h*	Deut 11:20	1004
you out of the *h* of bondage	Deut 13:5	1004
of Egypt, from the *h* of bondage	Deut 13:10	1004
because he loveth thee and thine *h*	Deut 15:16	1004
is there that hath built a new *h*	Deut 20:5	1004
let him go and return to his *h*	Deut 20:5	1004
him also go and return unto his *h*	Deut 20:6	1004
let him go and return unto his *h*	Deut 20:7	1004
let him go and return unto his *h*	Deut 20:8	1004
shalt bring her home to thine *h*	Deut 21:12	1004
her, and shall remain in thine *h*	Deut 21:13	1004
shalt bring it unto thine own *h*	Deut 22:2	1004
When thou buildest a new *h*	Deut 22:8	1004
thou bring not blood upon thine *h*	Deut 22:8	1004
to the door of her father's *h*	Deut 22:21	1004
play the whore in her father's *h*	Deut 22:21	1004
into the *h* of the Lord thy God	Deut 23:18	1004
hand, and send her out of his *h*	Deut 24:1	1004
when she is departed out of his *h*	Deut 24:2	1004
hand, and sendeth her out of his *h*	Deut 24:3	1004
go into his *h* to fetch his pledge	Deut 24:10	1004
will not build up his brother's *h*	Deut 25:9	1004
The *h* of him that hath his shoe	Deut 25:10	1004
have in thine *h* divers measures	Deut 25:14	1004
given unto thee, and unto thine *h*	Deut 26:11	1004
the hallowed things out of mine *h*	Deut 26:13	1004
thou shalt build an *h*, and thou	Deut 28:30	1004
went, and came into an harlot's *h*	Josh 2:1	1004
which are entered into thine *h*	Josh 2:3	1004
them up to the roof of the *h*	Josh 2:6	1004
shew kindness unto my father's *h*	Josh 2:12	1004
for her *h* was upon the town wall,	Josh 2:15	1004
doors of thy *h* into the street	Josh 2:19	1004
shall be with thee in the *h*	Josh 2:19	1004
and all that are with her in the *h*	Josh 6:17	1004
country, Go into the harlot's *h*	Josh 6:22	1004
the treasury of the *h* of the Lord	Josh 6:24	1004
of water for the *h* of my God	Josh 9:23	1004
Joshua spake unto the *h* of Joseph	Josh 17:17	1004
the *h* of Joseph shall abide in	Josh 18:5	1004
his own city, and unto his own *h*	Josh 20:6	1004
had spoken unto the *h* of Israel	Josh 21:45	1004
princes, of each chief *h* a prince	Josh 22:14	1004
the *h* of their fathers among the	Josh 22:14	1004
but as for me and my *h*, we will	Josh 24:15	1004
from the *h* of bondage, and which	Josh 24:17	1004
the *h* of Joseph, they also went	Judg 1:22	1004
the *h* of Joseph sent to descry	Judg 1:23	1004
hand of the *h* of Joseph prevailed	Judg 1:35	1004
the *h* of Heber the Kenite	Judg 4:17	1004
you forth out of the *h* of bondage	Judg 6:8	1004
I am the least in my father's *h*	Judg 6:15	1004
a snare unto Gideon, and to his *h*	Judg 8:27	1004
Joash went and dwelt in his own *h*	Judg 8:29	1004
kindness to the *h* of Jerubbaal	Judg 8:35	1004
of the *h* of his mother's father	Judg 9:1	1004
out of the *h* of Baal-berith	Judg 9:4	1004
unto his father's *h* at Ophrah	Judg 9:5	1004
all the *h* of Millo, and went, and	Judg 9:6	1004
well with Jerubbaal and his *h*	Judg 9:16	1004
up against my father's *h* this day	Judg 9:18	1004
Jerubbaal and with his *h* this day	Judg 9:19	1004
men of Shechem, and the *h* of Millo	Judg 9:20	1004
Shechem, and from the *h* of Millo	Judg 9:20	1004
and went into the *h* of their god	Judg 9:27	1004
hold of the *h* of the god Berith	Judg 9:46	1004
and against the *h* of Ephraim	Judg 10:9	1004
not inherit in our father's *h*	Judg 11:2	1004
and expel me out of my father's *h*	Judg 11:7	1004
of the doors of my *h* to meet me	Judg 11:31	1004

came to Mizpeh unto his *h*	Judg 11:34	1004
we will burn thine *h* upon thee	Judg 12:1	1004
thee and thy father's *h* with fire	Judg 14:15	1004
and he went up to his father's *h*	Judg 14:19	1004
and he did grind in the prison *h*	Judg 16:21	1004
for Samson out of the prison *h*	Judg 16:25	1004
pillars whereupon the *h* standeth	Judg 16:26	1004
Now the *h* was full of men and	Judg 16:27	1004
pillars upon which the *h* stood	Judg 16:29	1004
the *h* fell upon the lords, and	Judg 16:30	1004
all the *h* of his father came down	Judg 16:31	1004
and they were in the *h* of Micah	Judg 17:4	1004
And the man Micah had an *h* of gods	Judg 17:5	1004
mount Ephraim to the *h* of Micah	Judg 17:8	1004
priest, and was in the *h* of Micah	Judg 17:12	1004
to the *h* of Micah, they lodged	Judg 18:2	1004
When they were by the *h* of Micah	Judg 18:3	1004
and came unto the *h* of Micah	Judg 18:13	1004
came to the *h* of the young man	Judg 18:15	1004
Levite, even unto the *h* of Micah	Judg 18:15	1004
And these went into Micah's *h*	Judg 18:18	1004
be a priest unto the *h* of one man	Judg 18:19	1004
a good way from the *h* of Micah	Judg 18:22	1004
Micah's *h* were gathered together	Judg 18:22	1004
he turned and went back unto his *h*	Judg 18:26	1004
that the *h* of God was in Shiloh	Judg 18:31	1004
father's *h* to Beth-lehem-judah	Judg 19:2	1004
brought him into her father's *h*	Judg 19:3	1004
took them into his *h* to lodging	Judg 19:15	1004
am now going to the *h* of the LORD	Judg 19:18	1004
is no man that receiveth me to *h*	Judg 19:18	1004
So he brought him into his *h*	Judg 19:21	1004
beset the *h* round about, and beat	Judg 19:22	1004
and spake to the master of the *h*	Judg 19:22	1004
the man that came into thine *h*	Judg 19:22	1004
And the man, the master of the *h*	Judg 19:23	1004
that this man is come into mine *h*	Judg 19:23	1004
of the man's *h* where her lord was	Judg 19:26	1004
and opened the doors of the *h*	Judg 19:27	1004
fallen down at the door of the *h*	Judg 19:27	1004
And when he was come into his *h*	Judg 19:29	1004
beset the *h* round about upon me	Judg 20:5	1004
will we any of us turn into his *h*	Judg 20:8	1004
arose, and went up to the *h* of God	Judg 20:18	1008
up, and came unto the *h* of God	Judg 20:26	1008
one goeth up to the *h* of God	Judg 20:31	1008
the people came to the *h* of God	Judg 21:2	1008
Go, return each to her mother's *h*	Ruth 1:8	1004
of you in the *h* of her husband	Ruth 1:9	1004
she tarried a little in the *h*	Ruth 2:7	1004
is come into thine *h* like Rachel	Ruth 4:11	1004
two did build the *h* of Israel	Ruth 4:11	1004
thy *h* be like the *h* of Pharez	Ruth 4:12	1004
she went up to the *h* of the LORD	1Sa 1:7	1004
and came to their *h* to Ramah	1Sa 1:19	1004
And the man Elkanah, and all his *h*	1Sa 1:21	1004
brought him unto the *h* of the	1Sa 1:24	1004
And Elkanah went to Ramah to his *h*	1Sa 2:11	1004
appear unto the *h* of thy father	1Sa 2:27	1004
they were in Egypt in Pharaoh's *h*	1Sa 2:27	1004
did I give unto the *h* of thy	1Sa 2:28	1004
saith, I said indeed that thy *h*	1Sa 2:30	1004
the *h* of thy father, should walk	1Sa 2:30	1004
arm, and the arm of thy father's *h*	1Sa 2:31	1004
not be an old man in thine *h*	1Sa 2:31	1004
be an old man in thine *h* for ever	1Sa 2:32	1004
all the increase of thine *h* shall	1Sa 2:33	1004
and I will build him a sure *h*	1Sa 2:35	1004
is left in thine *h* shall come	1Sa 2:36	1004
I have spoken concerning his *h*	1Sa 3:12	1004
told him that I will judge his *h*	1Sa 3:13	1004
I have sworn unto the *h* of Eli	1Sa 3:14	1004
Eli's *h* shall not be purged with	1Sa 3:14	1004
the doors of the *h* of the LORD	1Sa 3:15	1004
brought it into the *h* of Dagon	1Sa 5:2	1004
nor any that come into Dagon's *h*	1Sa 5:5	1004
brought it into the *h* of Abinadab	1Sa 7:1	1004
all the *h* of Israel lamented	1Sa 7:2	1004
spake unto all the *h* of Israel	1Sa 7:3	1004
for there was his *h*	1Sa 7:17	1004
pray thee, where the seer's *h* is	1Sa 9:18	1004
on thee, and on all thy father's *h*	1Sa 9:20	1004
with Saul upon the top of the *h*	1Sa 9:25	
called Saul to the top of the *h*	1Sa 9:26	
people away, every man to his *h*	1Sa 10:25	1004
up to his *h* to Gibeah of Saul	1Sa 15:34	1004
his father's *h* free in Israel	1Sa 17:25	1004
go no more home to his father's *h*	1Sa 18:2	1004
prophesied in the midst of the *h*	1Sa 18:10	1004
as he sat in his *h* with his	1Sa 19:9	1004
sent messengers unto David's *h*	1Sa 19:11	1004

thy kindness from my *h* for ever	1Sa 20:15	1004
a covenant with the *h* of David	1Sa 20:16	1004
shall this fellow come into my *h*	1Sa 21:15	1004
and all his father's *h* heard it	1Sa 22:1	1004
of Ahitub, and all his father's *h*	1Sa 22:11	1004
and is honourable in thine *h*	1Sa 22:14	1004
nor to all the *h* of my father	1Sa 22:15	1004
thou, and all thy father's *h*	1Sa 22:16	1004
all the persons of thy father's *h*	1Sa 22:22	1004
wood, and Jonathan went to his *h*	1Sa 23:18	1004
my name out of my father's *h*	1Sa 24:21	1004
and buried him in his *h* at Ramah	1Sa 25:1	1004
and he was of the *h* of Caleb	1Sa 25:3	1004
to thee, and peace be to thine *h*	1Sa 25:6	1004
certainly make my lord a sure *h*	1Sa 25:28	1004
her, Go up in peace to thine *h*	1Sa 25:35	1004
behold, he held a feast in his *h*	1Sa 25:36	1004
the woman had a fat calf in the *h*	1Sa 28:24	1004
it in the *h* of their idols	1Sa 31:9	1004
his armour in the *h* of Ashtaroth	1Sa 31:10	1004
the LORD, and for the *h* of Israel	2Sa 1:12	1004
David king over the *h* of Judah	2Sa 2:4	1004
also the *h* of Judah have anointed	2Sa 2:7	1004
But the *h* of Judah followed David	2Sa 2:10	1004
the *h* of Judah was seven years	2Sa 2:11	1004
h of Saul and the *h* of David	2Sa 3:1	1004
the *h* of Saul waxed weaker and	2Sa 3:1	1004
was war between the *h* of Saul	2Sa 3:6	1004
the *h* of David, that Abner made	2Sa 3:6	1004
himself strong for the *h* of Saul	2Sa 3:6	1004
day unto the *h* of Saul thy father	2Sa 3:8	1004
the kingdom from the *h* of Saul	2Sa 3:10	1004
good to the whole *h* of Benjamin	2Sa 3:19	1004
of Joab, and on all his father's *h*	2Sa 3:29	1004
let there not fail from the *h* of	2Sa 3:29	1004
the day to the *h* of Ish-bosheth	2Sa 4:5	1004
thither into the midst of the *h*	2Sa 4:6	1004
For when they came into the *h*	2Sa 4:7	1004
person in his own *h* upon his bed	2Sa 4:11	1004
lame shall not come into the *h*	2Sa 5:8	1004
and they built David an *h*	2Sa 5:11	1004
brought it out of the *h* of	2Sa 6:3	1004
they brought it out of the *h* of	2Sa 6:4	1004
all the *h* of Israel played before	2Sa 6:5	1004
the *h* of Obed-edom the Gittite	2Sa 6:10	1004
of the LORD continued in the *h* of	2Sa 6:11	1004
hath blessed the *h* of Obed-edom	2Sa 6:12	1004
up the ark of God from the *h* of	2Sa 6:12	1004
all the *h* of Israel brought up	2Sa 6:15	1004
departed every one to his *h*	2Sa 6:19	1004
thy father, and before all his *h*	2Sa 6:21	1004
pass, when the king sat in his *h*	2Sa 7:1	1004
See now, I dwell in an *h* of cedar	2Sa 7:2	1004
build me an *h* for me to dwell in	2Sa 7:5	1004
h since the time that I brought	2Sa 7:6	1004
Why build ye not me an *h* of cedar	2Sa 7:7	1004
thee that he will make thee an *h*	2Sa 7:11	1004
He shall build an *h* for my name	2Sa 7:13	1004
And thine *h* and thy kingdom shall	2Sa 7:16	1004
and what is my *h*, that thou hast	2Sa 7:18	1004
h for a great while to come	2Sa 7:19	1004
thy servant, and concerning his *h*	2Sa 7:25	1004
let the *h* of thy servant David be	2Sa 7:26	1004
saying, I will build thee an *h*	2Sa 7:27	1004
to bless the *h* of thy servant	2Sa 7:29	1004
with thy blessing let the *h* of	2Sa 7:29	1004
any that is left of the *h* of Saul	2Sa 9:1	1004
there was of the *h* of Saul a	2Sa 9:2	1004
not yet any of the *h* of Saul	2Sa 9:3	1004
Behold, he is in the *h* of Machir	2Sa 9:4	1004
him out of the *h* of Machir	2Sa 9:5	1004
pertained to Saul and to all his *h*	2Sa 9:9	1004
all that dwelt in the *h* of Ziba	2Sa 9:12	1004
upon the roof of the king's *h*	2Sa 11:2	1004
and she returned unto her *h*	2Sa 11:4	1004
said to Uriah, Go down to thy *h*	2Sa 11:8	1004
departed out of the king's *h*	2Sa 11:8	1004
h with all the servants of his	2Sa 11:9	1004
lord, and went not down to his *h*	2Sa 11:9	1004
Uriah went not down unto his *h*	2Sa 11:10	1004
thou not go down unto thine *h*	2Sa 11:10	1004
shall I then go into mine *h*	2Sa 11:11	1004
lord, but went not down to his *h*	2Sa 11:13	1004
sent and fetched her to his *h*	2Sa 11:27	1004
And I gave thee thy master's *h*	2Sa 12:8	1004
and gave thee the *h* of Israel	2Sa 12:8	1004
shall never depart from thine *h*	2Sa 12:10	1004
against thee out of thine own *h*	2Sa 12:11	1004
And Nathan departed unto his *h*	2Sa 12:15	1004
And the elders of his *h* arose	2Sa 12:17	1004
and came into the *h* of the LORD	2Sa 12:20	1004

then he came to his own *h*	2Sa 12:20	1004
Go now to thy brother Amnon's *h*	2Sa 13:7	1004
went to her brother Amnon's *h*	2Sa 13:8	1004
in her brother Absalom's *h*	2Sa 13:20	1004
unto the woman, Go to thine *h*	2Sa 14:8	1004
be on me, and on my father's *h*	2Sa 14:9	1004
said, Let him turn to his own *h*	2Sa 14:24	1004
So Absalom returned to his own *h*	2Sa 14:24	1004
and came to Absalom unto his *h*	2Sa 14:31	1004
were concubines, to keep the *h*	2Sa 15:16	1004
shalt hear out of the king's *h*	2Sa 15:35	1004
Today shall the *h* of Israel	2Sa 16:3	1004
of the family of the *h* of Saul	2Sa 16:5	1004
all the blood of the *h* of Saul	2Sa 16:8	1004
which he hath left to keep the *h*	2Sa 16:21	1004
a tent upon the top of the *h*	2Sa 16:22	1004
and came to a man's *h* in Bahurim	2Sa 17:18	1004
came to the woman to the *h*	2Sa 17:20	1004
arose, and gat him home to his *h*	2Sa 17:23	1004
Joab came into the *h* to the king	2Sa 19:5	1004
to bring the king back to his *h*	2Sa 19:11	1004
come to the king, even to his *h*	2Sa 19:11	1004
Ziba the servant of the *h* of Saul	2Sa 19:17	1004
the first this day of all the *h*	2Sa 19:20	1004
For all of my father's *h* were but	2Sa 19:28	1004
again in peace unto his own *h*	2Sa 19:30	1004
David came to his *h* at Jerusalem	2Sa 20:3	1004
whom he had left to keep the *h*	2Sa 20:3	1004
is for Saul, and for his bloody *h*	2Sa 21:1	1004
nor gold of Saul, nor of the *h*	2Sa 21:4	1004
Although my *h* be not so with God	2Sa 23:5	1004
me, and against my father's *h*	2Sa 24:17	1004
said unto him, Go to thine *h*	1Kin 1:53	1004
father, and who hath made me an *h*	1Kin 2:24	1004
concerning the *h* of Eli in Shiloh	1Kin 2:27	1004
me, and from the *h* of my father	1Kin 2:31	1004
and upon his seed, and upon his *h*	1Kin 2:33	1004
in his own *h* in the wilderness	1Kin 2:34	1004
him, Build thee an *h* in Jerusalem	1Kin 2:36	1004
made an end of building his own *h*	1Kin 3:1	1004
the *h* of the Lord, and the wall of	1Kin 3:1	1004
because there was no *h* built unto	1Kin 3:2	1004
I and this woman dwell in one *h*	1Kin 3:17	1004
of a child with her in the *h*	1Kin 3:17	1004
was no stranger with us in the *h*	1Kin 3:18	1004
save we two in the *h*	1Kin 3:18	1004
my father could not build an *h*	1Kin 5:3	1004
I purpose to build an *h* unto the	1Kin 5:5	1004
he shall build an *h* unto my name	1Kin 5:5	1004
to lay the foundation of the *h*	1Kin 5:17	1004
timber and stones to build the *h*	1Kin 5:18	1004
began to build the *h* of the Lord	1Kin 6:1	1004
the *h* which king Solomon built	1Kin 6:2	1004
porch before the temple of the *h*	1Kin 6:3	1004
according to the breadth of the *h*	1Kin 6:3	1004
the breadth thereof before the *h*	1Kin 6:3	1004
for the *h* he made windows of	1Kin 6:4	1004
against the wall of the *h* he	1Kin 6:5	1004
the walls of the *h* round about	1Kin 6:5	1004
h he made narrowed rests round	1Kin 6:6	1004
be fastened in the walls of the *h*	1Kin 6:6	1004
And the *h*, when it was in building	1Kin 6:7	1004
any tool of iron heard in the *h*	1Kin 6:7	1004
was in the right side of the *h*	1Kin 6:8	1004
So he built the *h*, and finished it	1Kin 6:9	1004
and covered the *h* with beams	1Kin 6:9	1004
built chambers against all the *h*	1Kin 6:10	1004
they rested on the *h* with timber	1Kin 6:10	1004
Concerning this *h* which thou art	1Kin 6:12	1004
So Solomon built the *h*, and	1Kin 6:14	1004
he built the walls of the *h*	1Kin 6:15	1004
of cedar, both the floor of the *h*	1Kin 6:15	1004
floor of the *h* with planks of fir	1Kin 6:15	1004
cubits on the sides of the *h*	1Kin 6:16	1004
And the *h*, that is, the temple	1Kin 6:17	1004
the cedar of the *h* within was	1Kin 6:18	1004
he prepared in the *h* within	1Kin 6:19	1004
the *h* within with pure gold	1Kin 6:21	1004
the whole *h* he overlaid with gold	1Kin 6:22	1004
until he had finished all the *h*	1Kin 6:22	1004
the cherubims within the inner *h*	1Kin 6:27	1004
one another in the midst of the *h*	1Kin 6:27	1004
he carved all the walls of the *h*	1Kin 6:29	1004
the floor of the *h* he overlaid	1Kin 6:30	1004
of the *h* of the Lord laid	1Kin 6:37	1004
was the *h* finished throughout all	1Kin 6:38	1004
building his own *h* thirteen years	1Kin 7:1	1004
and he finished all his *h*	1Kin 7:1	1004
He built also the *h* of the forest	1Kin 7:2	1004
his *h* where he dwelt had another	1Kin 7:8	1004
Solomon made also an *h* for	1Kin 7:8	1004
inner court of the *h* of the Lord	1Kin 7:12	1004
and for the porch of the *h*	1Kin 7:12	1004
bases on the right side of the *h*	1Kin 7:39	1004
and five on the left side of the *h*	1Kin 7:39	1004
sea on the right side of the *h*	1Kin 7:39	1004
Solomon for the *h* of the Lord	1Kin 7:40	1004
Solomon for the *h* of the Lord	1Kin 7:45	1004
pertained unto the *h* of the Lord	1Kin 7:48	1004
both for the doors of the inner *h*	1Kin 7:50	1004
place, and for the doors of the *h*	1Kin 7:50	1004
made for the *h* of the Lord	1Kin 7:51	1004
treasures of the *h* of the Lord	1Kin 7:51	1004
place, into the oracle of the *h*	1Kin 8:6	1004
cloud filled the *h* of the Lord	1Kin 8:10	1004
Lord had filled the *h* of the Lord	1Kin 8:11	1004
built thee an *h* to dwell in	1Kin 8:13	1004
tribes of Israel to build an *h*	1Kin 8:16	1004
of David my father to build an *h*	1Kin 8:17	1004
heart to build an *h* unto my name	1Kin 8:18	1004
thou shalt not build the *h*	1Kin 8:19	1004
he shall build the *h* unto my name	1Kin 8:19	1004
have built an *h* for the name of	1Kin 8:20	1004
how much less this *h* that I have	1Kin 8:27	1004
may be open toward this *h* night	1Kin 8:29	1004
come before thine altar in this *h*	1Kin 8:31	1004
supplication unto thee in this *h*	1Kin 8:33	1004
forth his hands toward this *h*	1Kin 8:38	1004
shall come and pray toward this *h*	1Kin 8:42	1004
and that they may know that this *h*	1Kin 8:43	1004
toward the *h* that I have built	1Kin 8:44	1004
the *h* which I have built for thy	1Kin 8:48	1004
dedicated the *h* of the Lord	1Kin 8:63	1004
that was before the *h* of the Lord	1Kin 8:64	1004
the building of the *h* of the Lord	1Kin 9:1	1004
of the Lord, and the king's *h*	1Kin 9:1	1004
I have hallowed this *h*, which	1Kin 9:3	1004
and this *h*, which I have hallowed	1Kin 9:7	1004
And at this *h*, which is high,	1Kin 9:8	1004
thus unto this land, and to this *h*	1Kin 9:8	1004
the *h* of the Lord, and the king's	1Kin 9:10	1004
of the Lord, and the king's *h*	1Kin 9:10	1004
h of the Lord, and his own *h*	1Kin 9:15	1004
of the city of David unto her *h*	1Kin 9:24	1004
So he finished the *h*	1Kin 9:25	1004
and the *h* that he had built,	1Kin 10:4	1004
he went up unto the *h* of the Lord	1Kin 10:5	1004
pillars for the *h* of the Lord	1Kin 10:12	1004
of the Lord, and for the king's *h*	1Kin 10:12	1004
in the *h* of the forest of Lebanon	1Kin 10:17	1004
all the vessels of the *h* of the	1Kin 10:21	1004
which gave him an *h*, and appointed	1Kin 11:18	1004
Tahpenes weaned in Pharaoh's *h*	1Kin 11:20	1004
all the charge of the *h* of Joseph	1Kin 11:28	1004
with thee, and build thee a sure *h*	1Kin 11:38	1004
now see to thine own *h*, David	1Kin 12:16	1004
the *h* of David unto this day	1Kin 12:19	1004
none that followed the *h* of David	1Kin 12:20	1004
he assembled all the *h* of Judah	1Kin 12:21	1004
to fight against the *h* of Israel	1Kin 12:21	1004
Judah, and unto all the *h* of Judah	1Kin 12:23	1004
return every man to his *h*	1Kin 12:24	1004
kingdom return to the *h* of David	1Kin 12:26	1004
in the *h* of the Lord at Jerusalem	1Kin 12:27	1004
he made an *h* of high places, and	1Kin 12:31	1004
shall be born unto the *h* of David	1Kin 13:2	1004
If thou wilt give me half thine *h*	1Kin 13:8	1004
him back with thee into thine *h*	1Kin 13:18	1004
him, and did eat bread in his *h*	1Kin 13:19	1004
became sin unto the *h* of Jeroboam	1Kin 13:34	1004
and came to the *h* of Ahijah	1Kin 14:4	1004
kingdom away from the *h* of David	1Kin 14:8	1004
bring evil upon the *h* of Jeroboam	1Kin 14:10	1004
the remnant of the *h* of Jeroboam	1Kin 14:10	1004
get thee to thine own *h*	1Kin 14:12	1004
of Israel into the *h* of Jeroboam	1Kin 14:13	1004
off the *h* of Jeroboam that day	1Kin 14:14	1004
treasures of the *h* of the Lord	1Kin 14:26	1004
and the treasures of the king's *h*	1Kin 14:26	1004
kept the door of the king's *h*	1Kin 14:27	1004
king went into the *h* of the Lord	1Kin 14:28	1004
into the *h* of the Lord, silver,	1Kin 15:15	1004
treasures of the *h* of the Lord	1Kin 15:18	1004
and the treasures of the king's *h*	1Kin 15:18	1004
of the *h* of Issachar, conspired	1Kin 15:27	1004
he smote all the *h* of Jeroboam	1Kin 15:29	1004
Baasha, and the posterity of his *h*	1Kin 16:3	1004
thy *h* like the *h* of Jeroboam	1Kin 16:3	1004
against Baasha, and against his *h*	1Kin 16:7	1004
in being like the *h* of Jeroboam	1Kin 16:7	1004
drinking himself drunk in the *h*	1Kin 16:9	1004
Arza steward of his *h* in Tirzah	1Kin 16:9	1004

H

that he slew all the *h* of Baasha	1Kin 16:11	1004
Zimri destroy all the *h* of Baasha	1Kin 16:12	1004
into the palace of the king's *h*	1Kin 16:18	1004
burnt the king's *h* over him with	1Kin 16:18	1004
altar for Baal in the *h* of Baal	1Kin 16:32	1004
and she, and he, and her *h*, did eat	1Kin 17:15	1004
the woman, the mistress of the *h*	1Kin 17:17	1004
out of the chamber into the *h*	1Kin 17:23	1004
which was the governor of his *h*	1Kin 18:3	1004
but thou, and thy father's *h*	1Kin 18:18	1004
and they shall search thine *h*	1Kin 20:6	1004
heard that the kings of the *h* of	1Kin 20:31	1004
of Israel went to his *h* heavy	1Kin 20:43	1004
because it is near unto my *h*	1Kin 21:2	1004
And Ahab came into his *h* heavy	1Kin 21:4	1004
will make thine *h* like the *h*	1Kin 21:22	1004
h of Jeroboam the son of Nebat	1Kin 21:22	1004
like the *h* of Baasha the son of	1Kin 21:22	1004
will I bring the evil upon his *h*	1Kin 21:29	1004
every man to his *h* in peace	1Kin 22:17	1004
the ivory *h* which he made, and all	1Kin 22:39	1004
tell me, what hast thou in the *h*	2Kin 4:2	1004
hath not any thing in the *h*	2Kin 4:2	1004
when Elisha was come into the *h*	2Kin 4:32	1004
returned, and walked in the *h* to	2Kin 4:35	1004
at the door of the *h* of Elisha	2Kin 5:9	1004
the *h* of Rimmon to worship there	2Kin 5:18	1004
I bow myself in the *h* of Rimmon	2Kin 5:18	1004
down myself in the *h* of Rimmon	2Kin 5:18	1004
hand, and bestowed them in the *h*	2Kin 5:24	1004
But Elisha sat in his *h*, and the	2Kin 6:32	1004
told it to the king's *h* within	2Kin 7:11	1004
to cry unto the king for her *h*	2Kin 8:3	1004
life, cried unto the king for her *h*	2Kin 8:5	1004
of Israel, as did the *h* of Ahab	2Kin 8:18	1004
in the way of the *h* of Ahab	2Kin 8:27	1004
of the Lord, as did the *h* of Ahab	2Kin 8:27	1004
the son in law of the *h* of Ahab	2Kin 8:27	1004
And he arose, and went into the *h*	2Kin 9:6	1004
smite the *h* of Ahab thy master	2Kin 9:7	1004
For the whole *h* of Ahab shall	2Kin 9:8	1004
I will make the *h* of Ahab like	2Kin 9:9	1004
h of Jeroboam the son of Nebat	2Kin 9:9	1004
like the *h* of Baasha the son of	2Kin 9:9	1004
fled by the way of the garden *h*	2Kin 9:27	1004
and fight for your master's *h*	2Kin 10:3	1004
And he that was over the *h*	2Kin 10:5	1004
spake concerning the *h* of Ahab	2Kin 10:10	1004
of the *h* of Ahab in Jezreel	2Kin 10:11	1004
was at the shearing *h* in the way	2Kin 10:12	1004
them at the pit of the shearing *h*	2Kin 10:14	1004
And they came into the *h* of Baal	2Kin 10:21	1004
the *h* of Baal was full from one	2Kin 10:21	1004
son of Rechab, into the *h* of Baal	2Kin 10:23	1004
went to the city of the *h* of Baal	2Kin 10:25	1004
the images out of the *h* of Baal	2Kin 10:26	1004
Baal, and brake down the *h* of Baal	2Kin 10:27	1004
made it a draught *h* unto this day	2Kin 10:27	
hast done unto the *h* of Ahab	2Kin 10:30	1004
in the *h* of the Lord six years	2Kin 11:3	1004
to him into the *h* of the Lord	2Kin 11:4	1004
oath of them in the *h* of the Lord	2Kin 11:4	1004
of the watch of the king's *h*	2Kin 11:5	1004
shall ye keep the watch of the *h*	2Kin 11:6	1004
the *h* of the Lord about the king	2Kin 11:7	1004
not be slain in the *h* of the Lord	2Kin 11:15	1004
the horses came into the king's *h*	2Kin 11:16	1004
the land went into the *h* of Baal	2Kin 11:18	1004
officers over the *h* of the Lord	2Kin 11:18	1004
the king from the *h* of the Lord	2Kin 11:19	1004
gate of the guard to the king's *h*	2Kin 11:19	1004
the sword beside the king's *h*	2Kin 11:20	1004
is brought into the *h* of the Lord	2Kin 12:4	1004
to bring into the *h* of the Lord	2Kin 12:4	1004
them repair the breaches of the *h*	2Kin 12:5	1004
repaired the breaches of the *h*	2Kin 12:6	1004
ye not the breaches of the *h*	2Kin 12:7	1004
it for the breaches of the *h*	2Kin 12:7	1004
to repair the breaches of the *h*	2Kin 12:8	1004
one cometh into the *h* of the Lord	2Kin 12:9	1004
brought into the *h* of the Lord	2Kin 12:9	1004
was found in the *h* of the Lord	2Kin 12:10	1004
oversight of the *h* of the Lord	2Kin 12:11	1004
wrought upon the *h* of the Lord	2Kin 12:11	1004
the breaches of the *h* of the Lord	2Kin 12:12	1004
laid out for the *h* to repair it	2Kin 12:12	1004
the *h* of the Lord bowls of silver	2Kin 12:13	1004
brought into the *h* of the Lord	2Kin 12:13	1004
therewith the *h* of the Lord	2Kin 12:14	1004
brought into the *h* of the Lord	2Kin 12:16	1004
treasures of the *h* of the Lord	2Kin 12:18	1004
of the Lord, and in the king's *h*	2Kin 12:18	1004
and slew Joash in the *h* of Millo	2Kin 12:20	1004
the sins of the *h* of Jeroboam	2Kin 13:6	1004
were found in the *h* of the Lord	2Kin 14:14	1004
in the treasures of the king's *h*	2Kin 14:14	1004
death, and dwelt in a several *h*	2Kin 15:5	1004
the king's son was over the *h*	2Kin 15:5	1004
in the palace of the king's *h*	2Kin 15:25	1004
higher gate of the *h* of the Lord	2Kin 15:35	1004
was found in the *h* of the Lord	2Kin 16:8	1004
in the treasures of the king's *h*	2Kin 16:8	1004
Lord, from the forefront of the *h*	2Kin 16:14	1004
the *h* of the Lord, and put it on	2Kin 16:14	1004
that they had built in the *h*	2Kin 16:18	1004
turned he from the *h* of the Lord	2Kin 16:18	1004
rent Israel from the *h* of David	2Kin 17:21	1004
was found in the *h* of the Lord	2Kin 18:15	1004
in the treasures of the king's *h*	2Kin 18:15	1004
and went into the *h* of the Lord	2Kin 19:1	1004
went up into the *h* of the Lord	2Kin 19:14	1004
herb, as the grass on the *h* tops	2Kin 19:26	
h of Judah shall yet again take	2Kin 19:30	1004
in the *h* of Nisroch his god	2Kin 19:37	1004
the Lord, Set thine *h* in order	2Kin 20:1	1004
go up unto the *h* of the Lord	2Kin 20:5	1004
the *h* of the Lord the third day	2Kin 20:8	1004
shewed them all the *h* of his	2Kin 20:13	1004
all the *h* of his armour, and all	2Kin 20:13	1004
there was nothing in his *h*	2Kin 20:13	1004
What have they seen in thine *h*	2Kin 20:15	1004
that are in mine *h* have they seen	2Kin 20:15	1004
come, that all that is in thine *h*	2Kin 20:17	1004
built altars in the *h* of the Lord	2Kin 21:4	1004
two courts of the *h* of the Lord	2Kin 21:5	1004
grove that he had made in the *h*	2Kin 21:7	1004
and to Solomon his son, In this *h*	2Kin 21:7	1004
and the plummet of the *h* of Ahab	2Kin 21:13	1004
buried in the garden of his own *h*	2Kin 21:18	1004
and slew the king in his own *h*	2Kin 21:23	1004
to the *h* of the Lord, saying	2Kin 22:3	1004
is brought into the *h* of the Lord	2Kin 22:4	1004
oversight of the *h* of the Lord	2Kin 22:5	1004
which is in the *h* of the Lord	2Kin 22:5	1004
to repair the breaches of the *h*	2Kin 22:5	1004
and hewn stone to repair the *h*	2Kin 22:6	1004
of the law in the *h* of the Lord	2Kin 22:8	1004
the money that was found in the *h*	2Kin 22:9	1004
oversight of the *h* of the Lord	2Kin 22:9	1004
went up into the *h* of the Lord	2Kin 23:2	1004
was found in the *h* of the Lord	2Kin 23:2	1004
the grove from the *h* of the Lord	2Kin 23:6	1004
that were by the *h* of the Lord	2Kin 23:7	1004
entering in of the *h* of the Lord	2Kin 23:11	1004
two courts of the *h* of the Lord	2Kin 23:12	1004
priest found in the *h* of the Lord	2Kin 23:24	1004
the *h* of which I said, My name	2Kin 23:27	1004
treasures of the *h* of the Lord	2Kin 24:13	1004
and the treasures of the king's *h*	2Kin 24:13	1004
And he burnt the *h* of the Lord	2Kin 25:9	1004
of the Lord, and the king's *h*	2Kin 25:9	1004
every great man's *h* burnt he with	2Kin 25:9	1004
that were in the *h* of the Lord	2Kin 25:13	1004
sea that was in the *h* of the Lord	2Kin 25:13	1004
had made for the *h* of the Lord	2Kin 25:16	1004
the *h* of Joab, and half of the	1Chr 2:54	5854
the father of the *h* of Rechab	1Chr 2:55	1004
the families of the *h* of them	1Chr 4:21	1004
fine linen, of the *h* of Ashbea,	1Chr 4:21	1004
the *h* of their fathers increased	1Chr 4:38	1004
of the *h* of their fathers were	1Chr 5:13	1004
chief of the *h* of their fathers	1Chr 5:15	1004
heads of the *h* of their fathers	1Chr 5:24	1004
heads of the *h* of their fathers	1Chr 5:24	1004
of song in the *h* of the Lord	1Chr 6:31	1004
the *h* of the Lord in Jerusalem	1Chr 6:32	1004
of the tabernacle of the *h* of God	1Chr 6:48	1004
heads of their father's *h*	1Chr 7:2	1004
after the *h* of their fathers,	1Chr 7:4	1004
heads of the *h* of their fathers,	1Chr 7:7	1004
heads of the *h* of their fathers,	1Chr 7:9	1004
because it went evil with his *h*	1Chr 7:23	1004
Asher, heads of their father's *h*	1Chr 7:40	1004
fathers in the *h* of their fathers	1Chr 9:9	1004
Ahitub, the ruler of the *h* of God	1Chr 9:11	1004
heads of the *h* of their fathers,	1Chr 9:13	1004
of the service of the *h* of God	1Chr 9:13	1004
of the *h* of his father, the	1Chr 9:19	1004
of the gates of the *h* of the Lord	1Chr 9:23	1004
the *h* of the tabernacle, by wards	1Chr 9:23	1004
and treasuries of the *h* of God	1Chr 9:26	1004
lodged round about the *h* of God	1Chr 9:27	1004

sons, and all his *h* died together	1Chr 10:6	1004
his armour in the *h* of their gods	1Chr 10:10	1004
and of his father's *h* twenty	1Chr 12:28	1004
kept the ward of the *h* of Saul	1Chr 12:29	1004
throughout the *h* of their fathers	1Chr 12:30	1004
new cart out of the *h* of Abinadab	1Chr 13:7	1004
the *h* of Obed-edom the Gittite	1Chr 13:13	1004
Obed-edom in his *h* three months	1Chr 13:14	1004
Lord blessed the *h* of Obed-edom	1Chr 13:14	1004
and carpenters, to build him an *h*	1Chr 14:1	1004
of the *h* of Obed-edom with joy	1Chr 15:25	1004
departed every man to his *h*	1Chr 16:43	1004
and David returned to bless his *h*	1Chr 16:43	1004
to pass, as David sat in his *h*	1Chr 17:1	1004
Lo, I dwell in an *h* of cedars	1Chr 17:1	1004
not build me an *h* to dwell in	1Chr 17:4	1004
For I have not dwelt in an *h*	1Chr 17:5	1004
ye not built me an *h* of cedars	1Chr 17:6	1004
the Lord will build thee an *h*	1Chr 17:10	1004
He shall build me an *h*, and I will	1Chr 17:12	1004
But I will settle him in mine *h*	1Chr 17:14	1004
I, O Lord God, and what is mine *h*	1Chr 17:16	1004
h for a great while to come	1Chr 17:17	1004
concerning his *h* be established	1Chr 17:23	1004
let the *h* of David thy servant be	1Chr 17:24	1004
that thou wilt build him an *h*	1Chr 17:25	1004
to bless the *h* of thy servant	1Chr 17:27	1004
be on me, and on my father's *h*	1Chr 21:17	1004
This is the *h* of the Lord God, and	1Chr 22:1	1004
stones to build the *h* of God	1Chr 22:2	1004
the *h* that is to be builded for	1Chr 22:5	1004
charged him to build an *h* for the	1Chr 22:6	1004
an *h* unto the name of the Lord my	1Chr 22:7	1004
shalt not build an *h* unto my name	1Chr 22:8	1004
He shall build an *h* for my name	1Chr 22:10	1004
build the *h* of the Lord thy God,	1Chr 22:11	1004
h of the Lord an hundred thousand	1Chr 22:14	1004
into the *h* that is to be built to	1Chr 22:19	1004
the work of the *h* of the Lord	1Chr 23:4	1004
according to their father's *h*	1Chr 23:11	1004
Levi after the *h* of their fathers	1Chr 23:24	1004
the service of the *h* of the Lord	1Chr 23:24	1004
the service of the *h* of the Lord	1Chr 23:28	1004
of the service of the *h* of God	1Chr 23:28	1004
the service of the *h* of the Lord	1Chr 23:32	1004
men of the *h* of their fathers	1Chr 24:4	1004
to the *h* of their fathers	1Chr 24:4	1004
and governors of the *h* of God	1Chr 24:5	1004
to come into the *h* of the Lord	1Chr 24:19	1004
after the *h* of their fathers	1Chr 24:30	1004
for song in the *h* of the Lord	1Chr 25:6	1004
for the service of the *h* of God	1Chr 25:6	1004
throughout the *h* of their father	1Chr 26:6	1004
to minister in the *h* of the Lord	1Chr 26:12	1004
to the *h* of their fathers	1Chr 26:13	1004
and to his sons the *h* of Asuppim	1Chr 26:15	1004
the treasures of the *h* of God	1Chr 26:20	1004
treasures of the *h* of the Lord	1Chr 26:22	1004
to maintain the *h* of the Lord	1Chr 26:27	1004
an *h* of rest for the ark of the	1Chr 28:2	1004
shalt not build an *h* for my name	1Chr 28:3	1004
h of my father to be king over	1Chr 28:4	1004
h of Judah, the *h* of my father	1Chr 28:4	1004
thy son, he shall build my *h*	1Chr 28:6	1004
to build an *h* for the sanctuary	1Chr 28:10	1004
the courts of the *h* of the Lord	1Chr 28:12	1004
of the treasuries of the *h* of God	1Chr 28:12	1004
the service of the *h* of the Lord	1Chr 28:13	1004
of service in the *h* of the Lord	1Chr 28:13	1004
the service of the *h* of the Lord	1Chr 28:20	1004
all the service of the *h* of God	1Chr 28:21	1004
with all my might for the *h* of my	1Chr 29:2	1004
my affection to the *h* of my God	1Chr 29:3	1004
I have given to the *h* of my God	1Chr 29:3	1004
I have prepared for the holy *h*	1Chr 29:3	1004
gave for the service of the *h* of	1Chr 29:7	1004
the treasure of the *h* of God	1Chr 29:8	1004
h for thine holy name cometh of	1Chr 29:16	1004
an *h* for the name of the Lord	2Chr 2:1	1004
the Lord, and an *h* for his kingdom	2Chr 2:1	1004
build him an *h* to dwell therein	2Chr 2:3	1004
I build an *h* to the name of the	2Chr 2:4	1004
the *h* which I build is great	2Chr 2:5	1004
But who is able to build him an *h*	2Chr 2:6	1004
that I should build him an *h*	2Chr 2:6	1004
for the *h* which I am about to	2Chr 2:9	1004
might build an *h* for the Lord	2Chr 2:12	1004
and an *h* for his kingdom	2Chr 2:12	1004
the *h* of the Lord at Jerusalem in	2Chr 3:1	1004
for the building of the *h* of God	2Chr 3:3	1004
that was in the front of the *h*	2Chr 3:4	

according to the breadth of the *h*	2Chr 3:4	1004
the greater *h* he cieled with fir	2Chr 3:5	1004
he garnished the *h* with precious	2Chr 3:6	1004
He overlaid also the *h*, the beams	2Chr 3:7	1004
And he made the most holy *h*	2Chr 3:8	1004
according to the breadth of the *h*	2Chr 3:8	1004
in the most holy *h* he made two	2Chr 3:10	1004
reaching to the wall of the *h*	2Chr 3:11	1004
reaching to the wall of the *h*	2Chr 3:12	1004
the *h* two pillars of thirty	2Chr 3:15	1004
for king Solomon for the *h* of God	2Chr 4:11	1004
the *h* of the Lord of bright brass	2Chr 4:16	1004
that were for the *h* of God	2Chr 4:19	1004
and the entry of the *h*, the inner	2Chr 4:22	1004
the doors of the *h* of the temple	2Chr 4:22	1004
the *h* of the Lord was finished	2Chr 5:1	1004
the treasures of the *h* of God	2Chr 5:1	1004
his place, to the oracle of the *h*	2Chr 5:7	1004
that then the *h* was filled with a	2Chr 5:13	1004
a cloud, even the *h* of the Lord	2Chr 5:13	1004
the Lord had filled the *h* of God	2Chr 5:14	1004
But I have built an *h* of	2Chr 6:2	1004
tribes of Israel to build an *h* in	2Chr 6:5	1004
of David my father to build an *h*	2Chr 6:7	1004
heart to build an *h* for my name	2Chr 6:8	1004
thou shalt not build the *h*	2Chr 6:9	1004
he shall build the *h* for my name	2Chr 6:9	1004
have built the *h* for the name of	2Chr 6:10	1004
less this *h* which I have built	2Chr 6:18	1004
eyes may be open upon this *h* day	2Chr 6:20	1004
come before thine altar in this *h*	2Chr 6:22	1004
before thee in this *h*	2Chr 6:24	1004
spread forth his hands in this *h*	2Chr 6:29	1004
if they come and pray in this *h*	2Chr 6:32	1004
may know that this *h* which I have	2Chr 6:33	1004
the *h* which I have built for thy	2Chr 6:34	1004
toward the *h* which I have built	2Chr 6:38	1004
glory of the Lord filled the *h*	2Chr 7:1	1004
not enter into the *h* of the Lord	2Chr 7:2	1004
the Lord had filled the Lord's *h*	2Chr 7:2	1004
the glory of the Lord upon the *h*	2Chr 7:3	1004
the people dedicated the *h* of God	2Chr 7:5	1004
that was before the *h* of the Lord	2Chr 7:7	1004
finished the *h* of the Lord	2Chr 7:11	1004
of the Lord, and the king's *h*	2Chr 7:11	1004
to make in the *h* of the Lord	2Chr 7:11	1004
of the Lord, and in his own *h*	2Chr 7:11	1004
to myself for an *h* of sacrifice	2Chr 7:12	1004
I chosen and sanctified this *h*	2Chr 7:16	1004
and this *h*, which I have	2Chr 7:20	1004
And this *h*, which is high, shall	2Chr 7:21	1004
unto this land, and unto this *h*	2Chr 7:21	1004
h of the Lord, and his own *h*	2Chr 8:1	1004
the *h* that he had built for her	2Chr 8:11	1004
in the *h* of David king of Israel	2Chr 8:11	1004
foundation of the *h* of the Lord	2Chr 8:16	1004
So the *h* of the Lord was	2Chr 8:16	1004
and the *h* that he had built,	2Chr 9:3	1004
he went up into the *h* of the Lord	2Chr 9:4	1004
terraces to the *h* of the Lord	2Chr 9:11	1004
in the *h* of the forest of Lebanon	2Chr 9:16	1004
all the vessels of the *h* of the	2Chr 9:20	1004
and now, David, see to thine own *h*	2Chr 10:16	1004
the *h* of David unto this day	2Chr 10:19	1004
he gathered of the *h* of Judah	2Chr 11:1	1004
return every man to his *h*	2Chr 11:4	1004
treasures of the *h* of the Lord	2Chr 12:9	1004
and the treasures of the king's *h*	2Chr 12:9	1004
kept the entrance of the king's *h*	2Chr 12:10	1004
entered into the *h* of the Lord	2Chr 12:11	1004
he brought into the *h* of God the	2Chr 15:18	1004
treasures of the *h* of the Lord	2Chr 16:2	1004
of the Lord and of the king's *h*	2Chr 16:2	1004
seer, and put him in a prison *h*	2Chr 16:10	1004
to the *h* of their fathers	2Chr 17:14	1004
every man to his *h* in peace	2Chr 18:16	1004
to his *h* in peace to Jerusalem	2Chr 19:1	1004
the ruler of the *h* of Judah	2Chr 19:11	1004
in the *h* of the Lord, before the	2Chr 20:5	1004
or famine, we stand before this *h*	2Chr 20:9	1004
(for thy name is in this *h*	2Chr 20:9	1004
trumpets unto the *h* of the Lord	2Chr 20:28	1004
Israel, like as did the *h* of Ahab	2Chr 21:6	1004
would not destroy the *h* of David	2Chr 21:7	1004
to the whoredoms of the *h* of Ahab	2Chr 21:13	1004
thy brethren of thy father's *h*	2Chr 21:13	1004
that was found in the king's *h*	2Chr 21:17	1004
in the ways of the *h* of Ahab	2Chr 22:3	1004
of the Lord like the *h* of Ahab	2Chr 22:4	1004
anointed to cut off the *h* of Ahab	2Chr 22:7	1004
judgment upon the *h* of Ahab	2Chr 22:8	1004

H

So the *h* of Ahaziah had no power 2Chr 22:9   1004
the seed royal of the *h* of Judah 2Chr 22:10   1004
hid in the *h* of God six years................... 2Chr 22:12   1004
with the king in the *h* of God 2Chr 23:3   1004
part shall be at the king's *h* 2Chr 23:5   1004
the courts of the *h* of the LORD 2Chr 23:5   1004
none come into the *h* of the LORD 2Chr 23:6   1004
whosoever else cometh into the *h* 2Chr 23:7   1004
which were in the *h* of God 2Chr 23:9   1004
the people into the *h* of the LORD 2Chr 23:12   1004
Slay her not in the *h* of the LORD 2Chr 23:14   1004
of the horse gate by the king's *h*............ 2Chr 23:15   1004
the people went to the *h* of Baal 2Chr 23:17   1004
appointed the offices of the *h* of 2Chr 23:18   1004
distributed in the *h* of the LORD 2Chr 23:18   1004
at the gates of the *h* of the LORD 2Chr 23:19   1004
the king from the *h* of the LORD 2Chr 23:20   1004
the high gate into the king's *h* 2Chr 23:20   1004
to repair the *h* of the LORD 2Chr 24:4   1004
h of your God from year to year 2Chr 24:5   1004
woman, had broken up the *h* of God 2Chr 24:7   1004
the *h* of the LORD did they bestow 2Chr 24:7   1004
at the gate of the *h* of the LORD 2Chr 24:8   1004
the service of the *h* of the LORD 2Chr 24:12   1004
to repair the *h* of the LORD 2Chr 24:12   1004
brass to mend the *h* of the LORD 2Chr 24:12   1004
they set the *h* of God in his 2Chr 24:13   1004
vessels for the *h* of the LORD 2Chr 24:14   1004
offered burnt offerings in the *h* 2Chr 24:14   1004
both toward God, and toward his *h*........ 2Chr 24:16   1004
they left the *h* of the LORD God 2Chr 24:18   1004
in the court of the *h* of the LORD 2Chr 24:21   1004
and the repairing of the *h* of God 2Chr 24:27   1004
in the *h* of God with Obed-edom 2Chr 25:24   1004
and the treasures of the king's *h* 2Chr 25:24   1004
the priests in the *h* of the LORD 2Chr 26:19   1004
death, and dwelt in a several *h* 2Chr 26:21   1004
cut off from the *h* of the LORD 2Chr 26:21   1004
his son was over the king's *h* 2Chr 26:21   1004
high gate of the *h* of the LORD 2Chr 27:3   1004
and Azrikam the governor of the *h* 2Chr 28:7   1004
portion out of the *h* of the LORD 2Chr 28:21   1004
out of the *h* of the king, and of............... 2Chr 28:21   1004
the vessels of the *h* of God 2Chr 28:24   1004
the vessels of the *h* of God 2Chr 28:24   1004
up the doors of the *h* of the LORD 2Chr 28:24   1004
the doors of the *h* of the LORD 2Chr 29:3   1004
sanctify the *h* of the LORD God of 2Chr 29:5   1004
to cleanse the *h* of the LORD.................. 2Chr 29:15   1004
inner part of the *h* of the LORD 2Chr 29:16   1004
the court of the *h* of the LORD 2Chr 29:16   1004
so they sanctified the *h* of the 2Chr 29:17   1004
cleansed all the *h* of the LORD 2Chr 29:18   1004
and went up to the *h* of the LORD 2Chr 29:20   1004
in the *h* of the LORD with cymbals 2Chr 29:25   1004
offerings into the *h* of the LORD............. 2Chr 29:31   1004
So the service of the *h* of the 2Chr 29:35   1004
to the *h* of the LORD at Jerusalem........... 2Chr 30:1   1004
offerings into the *h* of the LORD............. 2Chr 30:15   1004
of the *h* of Zadok answered him 2Chr 31:10   1004
offerings into the *h* of the LORD............. 2Chr 31:10   1004
chambers in the *h* of the LORD 2Chr 31:11   1004
Azariah the ruler of the *h* of God 2Chr 31:13   1004
entereth into the *h* of the LORD 2Chr 31:16   1004
priests by the *h* of their fathers 2Chr 31:17   1004
in the service of the *h* of God 2Chr 31:21   1004
he was come into the *h* of his god 2Chr 32:21   1004
built altars in the *h* of the LORD 2Chr 33:4   1004
two courts of the *h* of the LORD 2Chr 33:5   1004
he had made, in the *h* of God 2Chr 33:7   1004
and to Solomon his son, In this *h* 2Chr 33:7   1004
the idol out of the *h* of the LORD 2Chr 33:15   1004
in the mount of the *h* of the LORD 2Chr 33:15   1004
and they buried him in his own *h*............ 2Chr 33:20   1004
him, and slew him in his own *h* 2Chr 33:24   1004
he had purged the land, and the *h* 2Chr 34:8   1004
to repair the *h* of the LORD his 2Chr 34:8   1004
was brought into the *h* of God 2Chr 34:9   1004
oversight of the *h* of the LORD 2Chr 34:10   1004
that wrought in the *h* of the LORD 2Chr 34:10   1004
LORD, to repair and amend the *h* 2Chr 34:10   1004
brought into the *h* of the LORD 2Chr 34:14   1004
of the law in the *h* of the LORD 2Chr 34:15   1004
was found in the *h* of the LORD 2Chr 34:17   1004
went up into the *h* of the LORD 2Chr 34:30   1004
was found in the *h* of the LORD 2Chr 34:30   1004
the service of the *h* of the LORD 2Chr 35:2   1004
Put the holy ark in the *h* which 2Chr 35:3   1004
and Jehiel, rulers of the *h* of God 2Chr 35:8   1004
but against the *h* wherewith I................ 2Chr 35:21   1004
of the *h* of the LORD to Babylon 2Chr 36:7   1004

vessels of the *h* of the LORD.................... 2Chr 36:10   1004
polluted the *h* of the LORD which 2Chr 36:14   1004
sword in the *h* of their sanctuary 2Chr 36:17   1004
all the vessels of the *h* of God................ 2Chr 36:18   1004
treasures of the *h* of the LORD 2Chr 36:18   1004
And they burnt the *h* of God 2Chr 36:19   1004
me to build him an *h* in Jerusalem......... 2Chr 36:23   1004
me to build him an *h* at Jerusalem........ Ezr 1:2   1004
build the *h* of the LORD God of .... Ezr 1:3   1004
the *h* of God that is in Jerusalem .... Ezr 1:4   1004
to go up to build the *h* of the.................. Ezr 1:5   1004
the vessels of the *h* of the LORD .... Ezr 1:7   1004
had put them in the *h* of his gods .... Ezr 1:7   1004
of the *h* of Jeshua, nine hundred .... Ezr 2:36   1004
could not shew their father's *h* .... Ezr 2:59   1004
when they came to the *h* of the .... Ezr 2:68   1004
offered freely for the *h* of God................ Ezr 2:68   1004
unto the *h* of God at Jerusalem .... Ezr 3:8   1004
the work of the *h* of the LORD .... Ezr 3:8   1004
the workmen in the *h* of the LORD .... Ezr 3:9   1004
of the *h* of the LORD was laid................... Ezr 3:11   1004
men, that had seen the first *h*................. Ezr 3:12   1004
this *h* was laid before their eyes .... Ezr 3:12   1004
us to build an *h* unto our God .... Ezr 4:3   1004
Then ceased the work of the *h* of .... Ezr 4:24   1005
began to build the *h* of God which .... Ezr 5:2   1005
commanded you to build this *h* .... Ezr 5:3   1005
to the *h* of the great God, which............ Ezr 5:8   1005
Who commanded you to build this *h* ..... Ezr 5:9   1005
build the *h* that was builded .... Ezr 5:11   1005
Chaldean, who destroyed this *h* .... Ezr 5:12   1005
a decree to build this *h* of God .... Ezr 5:13   1005
of gold and silver of the *h* of God........... Ezr 5:14   1005
let the *h* of God be builded in .... Ezr 5:15   1005
laid the foundation of the *h* of .... Ezr 5:16   1005
made in the king's treasure *h* .... Ezr 5:17   1005
build this *h* of God at Jerusalem .... Ezr 5:17   1005
was made in the *h* of the rolls................ Ezr 6:1   1005
the *h* of God at Jerusalem .... Ezr 6:3   1005
Let the *h* be builded, the place .... Ezr 6:3   1005
be given out of the king's *h* .... Ezr 6:4   1004
and silver vessels of the *h* of God.......... Ezr 6:5   1005
and place them in the *h* of God .... Ezr 6:5   1005
the work of this *h* of God alone.............. Ezr 6:7   1005
build this *h* of God in his place .... Ezr 6:7   1005
for the building of this *h* of God............. Ezr 6:8   1005
timber be pulled down from his *h* .... Ezr 6:11   1005
let his *h* be made a dunghill for .... Ezr 6:11   1005
to destroy this *h* of God which is........... Ezr 6:12   1005
this *h* was finished on the third .... Ezr 6:15   1005
of this *h* of God with joy .... Ezr 6:16   1005
at the dedication of this *h* of .... Ezr 6:17   1005
hands in the work of the *h* of God .... Ezr 6:22   1004
the *h* of their God which is in .... Ezr 7:16   1005
of the *h* of your God which is in .... Ezr 7:17   1005
the service of the *h* of thy God............... Ezr 7:19   1005
be needful for the *h* of thy God.............. Ezr 7:20   1005
it out of the king's treasure *h*................ Ezr 7:20   1005
for the *h* of the God of heaven .... Ezr 7:23   1005
or ministers of this *h* of God .... Ezr 7:24   1005
to beautify the *h* of the LORD .... Ezr 7:27   1004
us ministers for the *h* of our God .... Ezr 8:17   1004
the offering of the *h* of our God .... Ezr 8:25   1004
the chambers of the *h* of the LORD .... Ezr 8:29   1004
Jerusalem unto the *h* of our God............ Ezr 8:30   1004
the *h* of our God by the hand of............. Ezr 8:33   1004
the people, and the *h* of God.................. Ezr 8:36   1004
to set up the *h* of our God .... Ezr 9:9   1004
himself down before the *h* of God.......... Ezr 10:1   1004
rose up from before the *h* of God........... Ezr 10:6   1004
sat in the street of the *h* of God............. Ezr 10:9   1004
after the *h* of their fathers, and............. Ezr 10:16   1004
I and my father's *h* have sinned .... Neh 1:6   1004
palace which appertained to the *h*......... Neh 2:8   1004
for the *h* that I shall enter into .... Neh 2:8   1004
Harumaph, even over against his *h* .... Neh 3:10   1004
made, and unto the *h* of the mighty....... Neh 3:16   1004
the *h* of Eliashib the high priest .... Neh 3:20   1004
from the door of the *h* of........................ Neh 3:21   1004
to the end of the *h* of Eliashib .... Neh 3:21   1004
and Hashub over against their *h*............ Neh 3:23   1004
the son of Ananiah by his *h* .... Neh 3:23   1004
from the *h* of Azariah unto the............... Neh 3:24   1004
lieth out from the king's high *h* .... Neh 3:25   1004
every one over against his *h* .... Neh 3:28   1004
son of Immer over against his *h* .... Neh 3:29   1004
were behind all the *h* of Judah .... Neh 4:16   1004
shake out every man from his *h* .... Neh 5:13   1004
Afterward I came unto the *h* of .... Neh 6:10   1004
us meet together in the *h* of God............ Neh 6:10   1004
one to be over against his *h* .... Neh 7:3   1004

of the *h* of Jeshua, nine hundred .... Neh 7:39
could not shew their father's *h* .... Neh 7:61   1004
every one upon the roof of his *h* .... Neh 8:16   1004
and in the courts of the *h* of God .... Neh 8:16
the service of the *h* of our God .... Neh 10:32   1004
all the work of the *h* of our God .... Neh 10:33   1004
to bring it into the *h* of our God .... Neh 10:34   1004
by year, unto the *h* of the LORD .... Neh 10:35   1004
to bring to the *h* of our God .... Neh 10:36   1004
that minister in the *h* of our God .... Neh 10:36   1004
the chambers of the *h* of our God .... Neh 10:37   1004
the tithes unto the *h* of our God .... Neh 10:38   1004
the chambers, into the treasure *h* .... Neh 10:38   1004
will not forsake the *h* of our God .... Neh 10:39   1004
was the ruler of the *h* of God .... Neh 11:11   1004
that did the work of the *h* were .... Neh 11:12   1004
outward business of the *h* of God .... Neh 11:16   1004
over the business of the *h* of God .... Neh 11:22   1004
Also from the *h* of Gilgal .... Neh 12:29   1004
of the wall, above the *h* of David .... Neh 12:37   1004
that gave thanks in the *h* of God .... Neh 12:40   1004
the chamber of the *h* of our God .... Neh 13:4   1004
in the courts of the *h* of God .... Neh 13:7   1004
again the vessels of the *h* of God .... Neh 13:9   1004
Why is the *h* of God forsaken .... Neh 13:11   1004
I have done for the *h* of my God .... Neh 13:14   1004
to all the officers of his *h* .... Est 1:8   1004
royal *h* which belonged to king .... Est 1:9   1004
man should bear rule in his own *h* .... Est 1:22   1004
to the *h* of the women, unto the .... Est 2:3   1004
brought also unto the king's *h* .... Est 2:8   1004
be given her, out of the king's *h* .... Est 2:9   1004
best place of the *h* of the women .... Est 2:9   1004
before the court of the women's *h* .... Est 2:11   1004
h of the women unto the king's .... Est 2:13   1004
of the women unto the king's *h* .... Est 2:13   1004
into the second *h* of the women .... Est 2:14   1004
his *h* royal in the tenth month .... Est 2:16   1004
thou shalt escape in the king's *h* .... Est 4:13   1004
thy father's *h* shall be destroyed .... Est 4:14   1004
the inner court of the king's *h* .... Est 5:1   1004
h, over against the king's *h* .... Est 5:1   1004
his royal throne in the royal *h* .... Est 5:1   1004
over against the gate of the *h* .... Est 5:1   1004
the outward court of the king's *h* .... Est 6:4   1004
Haman hasted to his *h* mourning .... Est 6:12   1004
the queen also before me in the *h* .... Est 7:8   1004
king, standeth in the *h* of Haman .... Est 7:9   1004
h of Haman the Jews' enemy unto .... Est 8:1   1004
set Mordecai over the *h* of Haman .... Est 8:2   1004
have given Esther the *h* of Haman .... Est 8:7   1004
was great in the king's *h* .... Est 9:4   1004
hedge about him, and about his *h* .... Job 1:10   1004
wine in their eldest brother's *h* .... Job 1:13   1004
wine in their eldest brother's *h* .... Job 1:18   1004
smote the four corners of the *h* .... Job 1:19   1004
He shall return no more to his *h* .... Job 7:10   1004
He shall lean upon his *h*, but it .... Job 8:15   1004
If I wait, the grave is mine *h* .... Job 17:13   1004
They that dwell in mine *h* .... Job 19:15   1004
away an *h* which he builded not .... Job 20:19   1004
increase of his *h* shall depart .... Job 20:28   1004
hath he in his *h* after him .... Job 21:21   1004
Where is the *h* of the prince .... Job 21:28   1004
He buildeth his *h* as a moth .... Job 27:18   1004
to the *h* appointed for all living .... Job 30:23   1004
know the paths to the *h* thereof .... Job 38:20   1004
Whose *h* I have made the .... Job 39:6   1004
did eat bread with him in his *h* .... Job 42:11   1004
I will come into thy *h* in the .... Ps 5:7   1004
I will dwell in the *h* of the LORD .... Ps 23:6   1004
loved the habitation of thy *h* .... Ps 26:8   1004
that I may dwell in the *h* of the .... Ps 27:4   1004
the dedication of the *h* of David .... Ps 30:*t*   1004
for an *h* of defence to save me .... Ps 31:2   1004
with the fatness of thy *h* .... Ps 36:8   1004
I went with them to the *h* of God .... Ps 42:4   1004
own people, and thy father's *h* .... Ps 45:10   1004
the glory of his *h* is increased .... Ps 49:16   1004
will take no bullock out of thy *h* .... Ps 50:9   1004
is come to the *h* of Ahimelech .... Ps 52:*t*   1004
green olive tree in the *h* of God .... Ps 52:8   1004
walked unto the *h* of God in .... Ps 55:14   1004
and they watched the *h* to kill him .... Ps 59:*t*   1004
with the goodness of thy *h* .... Ps 65:4   1004
I will go into thy *h* with burnt .... Ps 66:13   1004
zeal of thine *h* hath eaten me up .... Ps 69:9   1004
Yea, the sparrow hath found an *h* .... Ps 84:3   1004
are they that dwell in thy *h* .... Ps 84:4   1004
a doorkeeper in the *h* of my God .... Ps 84:10   1004
Those that be planted in the *h* of .... Ps 92:13   1004

holiness becometh thine *h* .... Ps 93:5   1004
his truth toward the *h* of Israel .... Ps 98:3   1004
within my *h* with a perfect heart .... Ps 101:2   1004
shall not dwell within my *h* .... Ps 101:7   1004
as a sparrow alone upon the *h* top .... Ps 102:7
stork, the fir trees are her *h* .... Ps 104:17   1004
He made him lord of his *h* .... Ps 105:21   1004
and riches shall be in his *h* .... Ps 112:3   1004
maketh the barren woman to keep *h* .... Ps 113:9   1004
the *h* of Jacob from a people of .... Ps 114:1   1004
O *h* of Aaron, trust in the LORD .... Ps 115:10   1004
he will bless the *h* of Israel .... Ps 115:12   1004
he will bless the *h* of Aaron .... Ps 115:12   1004
In the courts of the LORD's *h* .... Ps 116:19   1004
Let the *h* of Aaron now say, that .... Ps 118:3   1004
you out of the *h* of the LORD .... Ps 118:26   1004
songs in the *h* of my pilgrimage .... Ps 119:54   1004
Let us go into the *h* of the LORD .... Ps 122:1   1004
the thrones of the *h* of David .... Ps 122:5   1004
Because of the *h* of the LORD our .... Ps 122:9   1004
Except the LORD build the *h* .... Ps 127:1   1004
vine by the sides of thine *h* .... Ps 128:3   1004
come into the tabernacle of my *h* .... Ps 132:3   1004
night stand in the *h* of the LORD .... Ps 134:1   1004
that stand in the *h* of the LORD .... Ps 135:2   1004
in the courts of the *h* of our God .... Ps 135:2   1004
Bless the LORD, O *h* of Israel .... Ps 135:19   1004
bless the LORD, O *h* of Aaron .... Ps 135:19   1004
Bless the LORD, O *h* of Levi .... Ps 135:20   1004
For her *h* inclineth unto death .... Prov 2:18   1004
LORD is in the *h* of the wicked .... Prov 3:33   1004
come not nigh the door of her *h* .... Prov 5:8   1004
labours be in the *h* of a stranger .... Prov 5:10   1004
give all the substance of his *h* .... Prov 6:31   1004
For at the window of my *h* I .... Prov 7:6   1004
and he went the way to her *h* .... Prov 7:8   1004
her feet abide not in her *h* .... Prov 7:11   1004
Her *h* is the way to hell, going .... Prov 7:27   1004
Wisdom hath builded her *h* .... Prov 9:1   1004
she sitteth at the door of her *h* .... Prov 9:14   1004
his own *h* shall inherit the wind .... Prov 11:29   1004
but the *h* of the righteous shall .... Prov 12:7   1004
Every wise woman buildeth her *h* .... Prov 14:1   1004
The *h* of the wicked shall be .... Prov 14:11   1004
In the *h* of the righteous is much .... Prov 15:6   1004
will destroy the *h* of the proud .... Prov 15:25   1004
of gain troubleth his own *h* .... Prov 15:27   1004
than an *h* full of sacrifices with .... Prov 17:1   1004
evil shall not depart from his *h* .... Prov 17:13   1004
H and riches are the inheritance .... Prov 19:14   1004
a brawling woman and in a wide *h* .... Prov 21:9   1004
considereth the *h* of the wicked .... Prov 21:12   1004
Through wisdom is an *h* builded .... Prov 24:3   1004
and afterwards build thine *h* .... Prov 24:27   1004
thy foot from thy neighbour's *h* .... Prov 25:17   1004
a brawling woman and in a wide *h* .... Prov 25:24   1004
h in the day of thy calamity .... Prov 27:10   1004
and had servants born in my *h* .... Eccl 2:7   1004
when thou goest to the *h* of God .... Eccl 5:1   1004
better to go to the *h* of mourning .... Eccl 7:2   1004
than to go to the *h* of feasting .... Eccl 7:2   1004
the wise is in the *h* of mourning .... Eccl 7:4   1004
of fools is in the *h* of mirth .... Eccl 7:4   1004
the hands the *h* droppeth through .... Eccl 10:18   1004
keepers of the *h* shall tremble .... Eccl 12:3   1004
The beams of our *h* are cedar .... Song 1:17   1004
He brought me to the banqueting *h* .... Song 2:4   1004
brought him into my mother's *h* .... Song 3:4   1004
and bring thee into my mother's *h* .... Song 8:2   1004
the substance of his *h* for love .... Song 8:7   1004
h shall be established in the top .... Is 2:2   1004
to the *h* of the God of Jacob .... Is 2:3   1004
O *h* of Jacob, come ye, and let us .... Is 2:5   1004
thy people the *h* of Jacob .... Is 2:6   1004
brother of the *h* of his father .... Is 3:6   1004
for in my *h* is neither bread nor .... Is 3:7   1004
LORD of hosts is the *h* of Israel .... Is 5:7   1004
unto them that join *h* to *h* .... Is 5:8   1004
the *h* was filled with smoke .... Is 6:4   1004
And it was told the *h* of David .... Is 7:2   1004
said, Hear ye now, O *h* of David .... Is 7:13   1004
people, and upon thy father's *h* .... Is 7:17   1004
his face from the *h* of Jacob .... Is 8:17   1004
as are escaped of the *h* of Jacob .... Is 10:20   1004
shall cleave to the *h* of Jacob .... Is 14:1   1004
the *h* of Israel shall possess .... Is 14:2   1004
opened not the *h* of his prisoners .... Is 14:17   1004
in glory, every one in his own *h* .... Is 14:18   1004
the armour of the *h* of the forest .... Is 22:8   1004
unto Shebna, which is over the *h* .... Is 22:15   1004
be the shame of thy lord's *h* .... Is 22:18   1004

Jerusalem, and to the h of Judah	Is 22:21	1004
the key of the h of David will I	Is 22:22	1004
glorious throne to his father's h	Is 22:23	1004
all the glory of his father's h	Is 22:24	1004
laid waste, so that there is no h	Is 23:1	1004
every h is shut up, that no man	Is 24:10	1004
concerning the h of Jacob	Is 29:22	1004
against the h of the evildoers	Is 31:2	1004
son, which was over the h	Is 36:3	1004
and went into the h of the LORD	Is 37:1	1004
went up unto the h of the LORD	Is 37:14	1004
h of Judah shall again take root	Is 37:31	1004
in the h of Nisroch his god	Is 37:38	1004
the LORD, Set thine h in order	Is 38:1	1004
of our life in the h of the LORD	Is 38:20	1004
shall go up to the h of the LORD	Is 38:22	1004
shewed them the h of his precious	Is 39:2	1004
all the h of his armour, and all	Is 39:2	1004
there was nothing in his h	Is 39:2	1004
What have they seen in thine h	Is 39:4	1004
that is in mine h have they seen	Is 39:4	1004
come, that all that is in thine h	Is 39:6	1004
in darkness out of the prison h	Is 42:7	1004
that it may remain in the h	Is 44:13	1004
O h of Jacob, and all the remnant	Is 46:3	1004
the remnant of the h of Israel	Is 46:3	1004
O h of Jacob, which are called by	Is 48:1	1004
unto them will I give in mine h	Is 56:5	1004
them joyful in my h of prayer	Is 56:7	1004
for mine h shall be called an	Is 56:7	1004
an h of prayer for all people	Is 56:7	1004
the h of Jacob their sins	Is 58:1	1004
poor that are cast out to thy h	Is 58:7	1004
I will glorify the h of my glory	Is 60:7	1004
goodness toward the h of Israel	Is 63:7	1004
Our holy and our beautiful h	Is 64:11	1004
where is the h that ye build unto	Is 66:1	1004
vessel into the h of the LORD	Is 66:20	1004
O h of Jacob, and all the families	Jer 2:4	1004
the families of the h of Israel	Jer 2:4	1004
so is the h of Israel ashamed	Jer 2:26	1004
In those days the h of Judah	Jer 3:18	1004
shall walk with the h of Israel	Jer 3:18	1004
O h of Israel, saith the LORD	Jer 3:20	1004
h of Israel and the h of Judah	Jer 5:11	1004
O h of Israel, saith the LORD	Jer 5:15	1004
Declare this in the h of Jacob	Jer 5:20	1004
Stand in the gate of the LORD's h	Jer 7:2	1004
come and stand before me in this h	Jer 7:10	1004
Is this h, which is called by my	Jer 7:11	1004
Therefore will I do unto this h	Jer 7:14	1004
the h which is called by my name	Jer 7:30	1004
and all the h of Israel are	Jer 9:26	1004
speaketh unto you, O h of Israel	Jer 10:1	1004
h of Israel and the h of Judah	Jer 11:10	1004
hath my beloved to do in mine h	Jer 11:15	1004
for the evil of the h of Israel	Jer 11:17	1004
Of the h of Judah, which they	Jer 11:17	1004
the h of thy father, even they	Jer 12:6	1004
I have forsaken mine h, I have	Jer 12:7	1004
pluck out the h of Judah from	Jer 12:14	1004
unto me the whole h of Israel	Jer 13:11	1004
of Israel and the whole h of Judah	Jer 13:11	1004
Enter not into the h of mourning	Jer 16:5	1004
also go into the h of feasting	Jer 16:8	1004
of praise, unto the h of the LORD	Jer 17:26	1004
and go down to the potter's h	Jer 18:2	1004
I went down to the potter's h	Jer 18:3	1004
O h of Israel, cannot I do with	Jer 18:6	1004
ye in mine hand, O h of Israel	Jer 18:6	1004
in the court of the LORD's h	Jer 19:14	1004
governor in the h of the LORD	Jer 20:1	1004
which was by the h of the LORD	Jer 20:2	1004
thine h shall go into captivity	Jer 20:6	1004
touching the h of the king of	Jer 21:11	1004
O h of David, thus saith the LORD	Jer 21:12	1004
Go down to the h of the king of	Jer 22:1	1004
h kings sitting upon the throne	Jer 22:4	1004
that this h shall become a	Jer 22:5	1004
LORD unto the king's h of Judah	Jer 22:6	1004
buildeth his h by unrighteousness	Jer 22:13	1004
saith, I will build me a wide h	Jer 22:14	1004
which led the seed of the h of	Jer 23:8	1004
in my h have I found their	Jer 23:11	1004
even punish that man and his h	Jer 23:34	1004
in the court of the LORD's h	Jer 26:2	1004
come to worship in the LORD's h	Jer 26:2	1004
will I make this h like Shiloh	Jer 26:6	1004
these words in the h of the LORD	Jer 26:7	1004
This h shall be like Shiloh, and	Jer 26:9	1004
Jeremiah in the h of the LORD	Jer 26:9	1004

h unto the h of the LORD	Jer 26:10	1004
of the new gate of the LORD's h	Jer 26:10	1004
me to prophesy against this h	Jer 26:12	1004
the mountain of the h as the high	Jer 26:18	1004
the vessels of the LORD's h shall	Jer 27:16	1004
are left in the h of the LORD	Jer 27:18	1004
in the h of the king of Judah, and	Jer 27:18	1004
that remain in the h of the LORD	Jer 27:21	1004
in the h of the king of Judah and	Jer 27:21	1004
unto me in the h of the LORD	Jer 28:1	1004
all the vessels of the LORD's h	Jer 28:3	1004
that stood in the h of the LORD	Jer 28:5	1004
again the vessels of the LORD's h	Jer 28:6	1004
be officers in the h of the LORD	Jer 29:26	1004
that I will sow the h of Israel	Jer 31:27	1004
the h of Judah with the seed of	Jer 31:27	1004
new covenant with the h of Israel	Jer 31:31	1004
and with the h of Judah	Jer 31:31	1004
I will make with the h of Israel	Jer 31:33	1004
was in the king of Judah's h	Jer 32:2	1004
set their abominations in the h	Jer 32:34	1004
of praise into the h of the LORD	Jer 33:11	1004
promised unto the h of Israel	Jer 33:14	1004
of Israel and to the h of Judah	Jer 33:14	1004
the throne of the h of Israel	Jer 33:17	1004
of Egypt, out of the h of bondmen	Jer 34:13	1004
the h which is called by my name	Jer 34:15	1004
Go unto the h of the Rechabites,	Jer 35:2	1004
bring them into the h of the LORD	Jer 35:2	1004
the whole h of the Rechabites	Jer 35:3	1004
them into the h of the LORD	Jer 35:4	1004
I set before the sons of the h of	Jer 35:5	1004
Neither shall ye build h, nor sow	Jer 35:7	1004
said unto the h of the Rechabites	Jer 35:18	1004
It may be that the h of Judah	Jer 36:3	1004
cannot go into the h of the LORD	Jer 36:5	1004
the LORD's h upon the fasting day	Jer 36:6	1004
words of the LORD in the LORD's h	Jer 36:8	1004
of Jeremiah in the h of the LORD	Jer 36:10	1004
of the new gate of the LORD's h	Jer 36:10	1004
he went down into the king's h	Jer 36:12	1004
in the h of Jonathan the scribe	Jer 37:15	1004
king asked him secretly in his h	Jer 37:17	1004
to the h of Jonathan the scribe	Jer 37:20	1004
eunuchs which was in the king's h	Jer 38:7	1004
went forth out of the king's h	Jer 38:8	1004
went into the h of the king under	Jer 38:11	1004
that is in the h of the LORD	Jer 38:14	1004
and thou shalt live, and thine h	Jer 38:17	1004
h shall be brought forth to the	Jer 38:22	1004
me to return to Jonathan's h	Jer 38:26	1004
the Chaldeans burned the king's h	Jer 39:8	1004
bring them to the h of the LORD	Jer 41:5	1004
entry of Pharaoh's h in Tahpanhes	Jer 43:9	1004
as the h of Israel was ashamed of	Jer 48:13	1004
the sanctuaries of the LORD's h	Jer 51:51	1004
h of the LORD, and the king's h	Jer 52:13	1004
h of the LORD, and the king's h	Jer 52:17	1004
that were in the h of the LORD	Jer 52:17	1004
sea that was in the h of the LORD	Jer 52:20	1004
had made in the h of the LORD	Lam 2:7	1004
made a noise in the h of the LORD	Lam 2:7	1004
(for they are a rebellious h	Eze 2:5	1004
though they be a rebellious h	Eze 2:6	
rebellious like that rebellious h	Eze 2:8	1004
and go speak unto the h of Israel	Eze 3:1	1004
go, get thee unto the h of Israel	Eze 3:4	1004
language, but to the h of Israel	Eze 3:5	1004
But the h of Israel will not	Eze 3:7	1004
for all the h of Israel are	Eze 3:7	1004
though they be a rebellious h	Eze 3:9	1004
a watchman unto the h of Israel	Eze 3:17	1004
Go, shut thyself within thine h	Eze 3:24	1004
for they are a rebellious h	Eze 3:26	1004
for they are a rebellious h	Eze 3:27	1004
be a sign to the h of Israel	Eze 4:3	1004
of the h of Israel upon it	Eze 4:4	1004
the iniquity of the h of Israel	Eze 4:5	1004
of the h of Judah forty days	Eze 4:6	1004
forth into all the h of Israel	Eze 5:4	1004
abominations of the h of Israel	Eze 6:11	1004
of the month, as I sat in mine h	Eze 8:1	1004
the h of Israel committeth here	Eze 8:6	1004
all the idols of the h of Israel	Eze 8:10	1004
the ancients of the h of Israel	Eze 8:11	1004
of the h of Israel do in the dark	Eze 8:12	1004
h which was toward the north	Eze 8:14	1004
of the h of the LORD's h	Eze 8:16	1004
the inner court of the LORD's h	Eze 8:16	1004
Is it a light thing to the h of	Eze 8:17	1004
he was, to the threshold of the h	Eze 9:3	1004
men which were before the h	Eze 9:6	1004
he said unto them, Defile the h	Eze 9:7	1004

The iniquity of the *h* of Israel	Eze 9:9	1004
stood on the right side of the *h*	Eze 10:3	1004
stood over the threshold of the *h*	Eze 10:4	1004
the *h* was filled with the cloud,	Eze 10:4	1004
from off the threshold of the *h*	Eze 10:18	1004
of the east gate of the LORD's *h*	Eze 10:19	1004
the east gate of the LORD's *h*	Eze 11:1	1004
Thus have ye said, O *h* of Israel	Eze 11:5	1004
all the *h* of Israel wholly, are	Eze 11:15	1004
in the midst of a rebellious *h*	Eze 12:2	1004
for they are a rebellious *h*	Eze 12:2	1004
though they be a rebellious *h*	Eze 12:3	1004
for a sign unto the *h* of Israel	Eze 12:6	1004
h of Israel, the rebellious *h*	Eze 12:9	1004
all the *h* of Israel that are	Eze 12:10	1004
divination within the *h* of Israel	Eze 12:24	1004
for in your days, O rebellious *h*	Eze 12:25	1004
they of the *h* of Israel say, The	Eze 12:27	1004
the *h* of Israel to stand in the	Eze 13:5	1004
in the writing of the *h* of Israel	Eze 13:9	1004
Every man of the *h* of Israel that	Eze 14:4	1004
That I may take the *h* of Israel	Eze 14:5	1004
say unto the *h* of Israel, Thus	Eze 14:6	1004
For every one of the *h* of Israel	Eze 14:7	1004
That the *h* of Israel may go no	Eze 14:11	1004
a parable unto the *h* of Israel	Eze 17:2	1004
Say now to the rebellious *h*	Eze 17:12	1004
to the idols of the *h* of Israel	Eze 18:6	1004
to the idols of the *h* of Israel	Eze 18:15	1004
Hear now, O *h* of Israel	Eze 18:25	1004
Yet saith the *h* of Israel	Eze 18:29	1004
O *h* of Israel, are not my ways	Eze 18:29	1004
you, O *h* of Israel, every one	Eze 18:30	1004
why will ye die, O *h* of Israel	Eze 18:31	1004
unto the seed of the *h* of Jacob	Eze 20:5	1004
But the *h* of Israel rebelled	Eze 20:13	1004
man, speak unto the *h* of Israel	Eze 20:27	1004
say unto the *h* of Israel, Thus	Eze 20:30	1004
enquired of by you, O *h* of Israel	Eze 20:31	1004
O *h* of Israel, thus saith the	Eze 20:39	1004
there shall all the *h* of Israel	Eze 20:40	1004
O ye *h* of Israel, saith the Lord	Eze 20:44	1004
the *h* of Israel is to me become	Eze 22:18	1004
they done in the midst of mine *h*	Eze 23:39	1004
a parable unto the rebellious *h*	Eze 24:3	1004
Speak unto the *h* of Israel	Eze 24:21	1004
and against the *h* of Judah	Eze 25:3	1004
the *h* of Judah is like unto all	Eze 25:8	1004
Edom hath dealt against the *h* of	Eze 25:12	1004
They of the *h* of Togarmah traded	Eze 27:14	1004
brier unto the *h* of Israel	Eze 28:24	1004
When I shall have gathered the *h*	Eze 28:25	1004
staff of reed to the *h* of Israel	Eze 29:6	1004
the confidence of the *h* of Israel	Eze 29:16	1004
of the *h* of Israel to bud forth	Eze 29:21	1004
a watchman unto the *h* of Israel	Eze 33:7	1004
man, speak unto the *h* of Israel	Eze 33:10	1004
why will ye die, O *h* of Israel	Eze 33:11	1004
O ye *h* of Israel, I will judge	Eze 33:20	1004
even the *h* of Israel, are my	Eze 34:30	1004
inheritance of the *h* of Israel	Eze 35:15	1004
all the *h* of Israel, even all of	Eze 36:10	1004
when the *h* of Israel dwelt in	Eze 36:17	1004
which the *h* of Israel had	Eze 36:21	1004
say unto the *h* of Israel, Thus	Eze 36:22	1004
O *h* of Israel, but for mine holy	Eze 36:22	1004
for your own ways, O *h* of Israel	Eze 36:32	1004
be enquired of by the *h* of Israel	Eze 36:37	1004
bones are the whole *h* of Israel	Eze 37:11	1004
for all the *h* of Israel his	Eze 37:16	1004
the *h* of Togarmah of the north	Eze 38:6	1004
seven months shall the *h* of	Eze 39:12	1004
So the *h* of Israel shall know	Eze 39:22	1004
h of Israel went into captivity	Eze 39:23	1004
mercy upon the whole *h* of Israel	Eze 39:25	1004
my spirit upon the *h* of Israel	Eze 39:29	1004
thou seest to the *h* of Israel	Eze 40:4	1004
the outside of the *h* round about	Eze 40:5	1004
keepers of the charge of the *h*	Eze 40:45	1004
the altar that was before the *h*	Eze 40:47	1004
brought me to the porch of the *h*	Eze 40:48	1004
he measured the wall of the *h*	Eze 41:5	1004
round about the *h* on every side	Eze 41:5	1004
the *h* for the side chambers round	Eze 41:6	1004
had not hold in the wall of the *h*	Eze 41:6	1004
for the winding about of the *h*	Eze 41:7	1004
still upward round about the *h*	Eze 41:7	1004
breadth of the *h* was still upward	Eze 41:7	1004
the height of the *h* round about	Eze 41:8	1004
round about the *h* on every side	Eze 41:10	1004
So he measured the *h*, an hundred	Eze 41:13	1004

the breadth of the face of the *h*	Eze 41:14	1004
the door, even unto the inner *h*	Eze 41:17	1004
through all the *h* round about	Eze 41:19	1004
upon the side chambers of the *h*	Eze 41:26	1004
an end of measuring the inner *h*	Eze 42:15	1004
h by the way of the gate whose	Eze 43:4	1004
glory of the LORD filled the *h*	Eze 43:5	1004
him speaking unto me out of the *h*	Eze 43:6	1004
shall the *h* of Israel no more	Eze 43:7	1004
shew the *h* to the *h* of Israel	Eze 43:10	1004
done, shew them the form of the *h*	Eze 43:11	1004
This is the law of the *h*	Eze 43:12	1004
Behold, this is the law of the *h*	Eze 43:12	1004
in the appointed place of the *h*	Eze 43:21	1004
of the north gate before the *h*	Eze 44:4	1004
the LORD filled the *h* of the LORD	Eze 44:4	1004
ordinances of the *h* of the LORD	Eze 44:5	1004
well the entering in of the *h*	Eze 44:5	1004
even to the *h* of Israel, Thus	Eze 44:6	1004
O ye *h* of Israel, let it suffice	Eze 44:6	1004
to pollute it, even my *h*	Eze 44:7	1004
charge at the gates of the *h*	Eze 44:11	1004
h, and ministering to the *h*	Eze 44:11	1004
caused the *h* of Israel to fall	Eze 44:12	1004
keepers of the charge of the *h*	Eze 44:14	1004
of the seed of the *h* of Israel	Eze 44:22	1004
the blessing to rest in thine *h*	Eze 44:30	1004
Levites, the ministers of the *h*	Eze 45:5	1004
be for the whole *h* of Israel	Eze 45:6	1004
h of Israel according to their	Eze 45:8	1004
solemnities of the *h* of Israel	Eze 45:17	1004
for the *h* of Israel	Eze 45:17	1004
and put it upon the posts of the *h*	Eze 45:19	1004
so shall ye reconcile the *h*	Eze 45:20	1004
where the ministers of the *h*	Eze 46:24	1004
me again unto the door of the *h*	Eze 47:1	1004
the threshold of the *h* eastward	Eze 47:1	1004
of the *h* stood toward the east	Eze 47:1	1004
from the right side of the *h*	Eze 47:1	1004
the sanctuary of the *h* shall be	Eze 48:21	1004
of the vessels of the *h* of God	Dan 1:2	1004
of Shinar to the *h* of his god	Dan 1:2	1004
into the treasure *h* of his god	Dan 1:2	1004
Then Daniel went to his *h*	Dan 2:17	1005
was at rest in mine *h*, and	Dan 4:4	1005
that I have built for the *h* of	Dan 4:30	1005
h of God which was at Jerusalem	Dan 5:3	1005
lords, came into the banquet *h*	Dan 5:10	1005
the vessels of his *h* before thee	Dan 5:23	1005
was signed, he went into his *h*	Dan 6:10	1005
of Jezreel upon the *h* of Jehu	Hos 1:4	1004
the kingdom of the *h* of Israel	Hos 1:4	1004
have mercy upon the *h* of Israel	Hos 1:6	1004
have mercy upon the *h* of Judah	Hos 1:7	1004
and hearken, ye *h* of Israel	Hos 5:1	1004
and give ye ear, O *h* of the king	Hos 5:1	1004
to the *h* of Judah as rottenness	Hos 5:12	1004
as a young lion to the *h* of Judah	Hos 5:14	1004
horrible thing in the *h* of Israel	Hos 6:10	1004
eagle against the *h* of the LORD	Hos 8:1	1004
not come into the *h* of the LORD	Hos 9:4	1004
and hatred in the *h* of his God	Hos 9:8	1004
I will drive them out of mine *h*	Hos 9:15	1004
the *h* of Israel with deceit	Hos 11:12	1004
is cut off from the *h* of the LORD	Joel 1:9	1004
withholden from the *h* of your God	Joel 1:13	1004
into the *h* of the LORD your God	Joel 1:14	1004
and gladness from the *h* of our God	Joel 1:16	1004
come forth of the *h* of the LORD	Joel 3:18	1004
send a fire into the *h* of Hazael	Amos 1:4	1004
the sceptre from the *h* of Eden	Amos 1:5	1004
condemned in the *h* of their god	Amos 2:8	1004
ye, and testify in the *h* of Jacob	Amos 3:13	1004
winter *h* with the summer *h*	Amos 3:15	1004
even a lamentation, O *h* of Israel	Amos 5:1	1004
leave ten, to the *h* of Israel	Amos 5:3	1004
the LORD unto the *h* of Israel	Amos 5:4	1004
out like fire in the *h* of Joseph	Amos 5:6	1004
or went into the *h*, and leaned his	Amos 5:19	1004
forty years, O *h* of Israel	Amos 5:25	1004
to whom the *h* of Israel came	Amos 6:1	1004
if there remain ten men in one *h*	Amos 6:9	1004
bring out the bones out of the *h*	Amos 6:10	1004
him that is by the sides of the *h*	Amos 6:10	1004
smite the great *h* with breaches	Amos 6:11	1004
and the little *h* with clefts	Amos 6:11	1004
O *h* of Israel, saith the LORD the	Amos 6:14	1004
I will rise against the *h* of	Amos 7:9	1004
in the midst of the *h* of Israel	Amos 7:10	1004
thy word against the *h* of Isaac	Amos 7:16	1004
utterly destroy the *h* of Jacob	Amos 9:8	1004

H

I will sift the *h* of Israel among	Amos 9:9	1004
the *h* of Jacob shall possess	Obad 17	1004
the *h* of Jacob shall be a fire,	Obad 18	1004
the *h* of Joseph a flame, and the	Obad 18	1004
the *h* of Esau for stubble, and	Obad 18	1004
be any remaining of the *h* of Esau	Obad 18	1004
for the sins of the *h* of Israel	Mic 1:5	1004
in the *h* of Aphrah roll thyself	Mic 1:10	1035
so they oppress a man and his *h*	Mic 2:2	1004
that art named the *h* of Jacob	Mic 2:7	1004
and ye princes of the *h* of Israel	Mic 3:1	1004
you, ye heads of the *h* of Jacob	Mic 3:9	1004
and princes of the *h* of Israel	Mic 3:9	1004
the mountain of the *h* as the high	Mic 3:12	1004
of the *h* of the LORD shall be	Mic 4:1	1004
to the *h* of the God of Jacob	Mic 4:2	1004
thee out of the *h* of servants	Mic 6:4	1004
wickedness in the *h* of the wicked	Mic 6:10	1004
and all the works of the *h* of Ahab	Mic 6:16	1004
enemies are the men of his own *h*	Mic 7:6	1004
out of the *h* of thy gods will I	Nah 1:14	1004
an evil covetousness to his *h*	Hab 2:9	1004
thy *h* by cutting off many people	Hab 2:10	1004
head out of the *h* of the wicked	Hab 3:13	1004
for the remnant of the *h* of Judah	Zeph 2:7	1004
that the LORD's *h* should be built	Hag 1:2	1004
houses, and this *h* lie waste	Hag 1:4	1004
and bring wood, and build the *h*	Hag 1:8	1004
Because of mine *h* that is waste	Hag 1:9	1004
ye run every man unto his own *h*	Hag 1:9	1004
did work in the *h* of the LORD of	Hag 1:14	1004
saw this *h* in her first glory	Hag 2:3	1004
and I will fill this *h* with glory	Hag 2:7	1004
The glory of this latter *h* shall	Hag 2:9	1004
my *h* shall be built in it, saith	Zec 1:16	1004
then thou shalt also judge my *h*	Zec 3:7	1004
laid the foundation of this *h*	Zec 4:9	1004
enter into the *h* of the thief	Zec 5:4	1004
into the *h* of him that sweareth	Zec 5:4	1004
remain in the midst of his *h*	Zec 5:4	1004
To build it an *h* in the land of	Zec 5:11	1004
go into the *h* of Josiah the son	Zec 6:10	1004
sent unto the *h* of God Sherezer	Zec 7:2	1008
in the *h* of the LORD of hosts	Zec 7:3	1004
h of the LORD of hosts was laid	Zec 8:9	1004
O *h* of Judah, and *h* of Israel	Zec 8:13	1004
Jerusalem and to the *h* of Judah	Zec 8:15	1004
shall be to the *h* of Judah joy	Zec 8:19	1004
about mine *h* because of the army	Zec 9:8	1004
visited his flock the *h* of Judah	Zec 10:3	1004
I will strengthen the *h* of Judah	Zec 10:6	1004
and I will save the *h* of Joseph	Zec 10:6	1004
the potter in the *h* of the LORD	Zec 11:13	1004
mine eyes upon the *h* of Judah	Zec 12:4	1004
that the glory of the *h* of David	Zec 12:7	1004
the *h* of David shall be as God,	Zec 12:8	1004
I will pour upon the *h* of David	Zec 12:10	1004
family of the *h* of David apart	Zec 12:12	1004
family of the *h* of Nathan apart	Zec 12:12	1004
The family of the *h* of Levi apart	Zec 12:13	1004
fountain opened to the *h* of David	Zec 13:1	1004
wounded in the *h* of my friends	Zec 13:6	1004
the pots in the LORD's *h* shall be	Zec 14:20	1004
in the *h* of the LORD of hosts	Zec 14:21	1004
that there may be meat in mine *h*	Mal 3:10	1004
And when they were come into the *h*	Mt 2:11	*3614*
light unto all that are in the *h*	Mt 5:15	*3614*
which built his *h* upon a rock	Mt 7:24	*3614*
winds blew, and beat upon that *h*	Mt 7:25	*3614*
which built his *h* upon the sand	Mt 7:26	*3614*
winds blew, and beat upon that *h*	Mt 7:27	*3614*
Jesus was come into Peter's *h*	Mt 8:14	*3614*
up thy bed, and go unto thine *h*	Mt 9:6	*3624*
And he arose, and departed to his *h*	Mt 9:7	*3624*
as Jesus sat at meat in the *h*	Mt 9:10	*3614*
Jesus came into the ruler's *h*	Mt 9:23	*3614*
And when he was come into the *h*	Mt 9:28	*3614*
the lost sheep of the *h* of Israel	Mt 10:6	*3624*
And when ye come into an *h*	Mt 10:12	*3614*
if the *h* be worthy, let your	Mt 10:13	*3614*
ye depart out of that *h* or city	Mt 10:14	*3614*
the master of the *h* Beelzebub	Mt 10:25	*3617*
How he entered into the *h* of God	Mt 12:4	*3624*
every city or *h* divided against	Mt 12:25	*3614*
one enter into a strong man's *h*	Mt 12:29	*3614*
and then he will spoil his *h*	Mt 12:29	*3614*
I will return into my *h* from	Mt 12:44	*3624*
same day went Jesus out of the *h*	Mt 13:1	*3614*
away, and went into the *h*	Mt 13:36	*3614*
his own country, and in his own *h*	Mt 13:57	*3614*
the lost sheep of the *h* of Israel	Mt 15:24	*3624*
And when he was come into the *h*	Mt 17:25	*3614*
against the goodman of the *h*	Mt 20:11	*3617*
My *h* shall be called the *h* of	Mt 21:13	*3624*
your *h* is left unto you desolate	Mt 23:38	*3624*
to take any thing out of his *h*	Mt 24:17	*3614*
that if the goodman of the *h* had	Mt 24:43	*3617*
suffered his *h* to be broken up	Mt 24:43	*3614*
in the *h* of Simon the leper,	Mt 26:6	*3614*
at thy *h* with my disciples	Mt 26:18	
they entered into the *h* of Simon	Mk 1:29	*3614*
was noised that he was in the *h*	Mk 2:1	*3624*
bed, and go thy way into thine *h*	Mk 2:11	*3624*
as Jesus sat at meat in his *h*	Mk 2:15	*3614*
How he went into the *h* of God in	Mk 2:26	*3624*
and they went into an *h*	Mk 3:19	*3624*
if a *h* be divided against itself,	Mk 3:25	*3614*
that *h* cannot stand	Mk 3:25	*3614*
can enter into a strong man's *h*	Mk 3:27	*3614*
and then he will spoil his *h*	Mk 3:27	*3614*
synagogue's *h* certain which said	Mk 5:35	
he cometh to the *h* of the ruler	Mk 5:38	*3624*
his own kin, and in his own *h*	Mk 6:4	*3614*
place soever ye enter into a *h*	Mk 6:10	*3614*
into the *h* from the people	Mk 7:17	*3624*
and Sidon, and entered into an *h*	Mk 7:24	*3614*
And when she was come to her *h*	Mk 7:30	*3624*
And he sent him away to his *h*	Mk 8:26	*3624*
And when he was come into the *h*	Mk 9:28	*3624*
being in the *h* he asked them,	Mk 9:33	*3614*
in the *h* his disciples asked him	Mk 10:10	*3614*
There is no man that hath left *h*	Mk 10:29	*3614*
My *h* shall be called of all	Mk 11:17	*3624*
of all nations the *h* of prayer	Mk 11:17	*3624*
housetop not go down into the *h*	Mk 13:15	*3614*
to take any thing out of his *h*	Mk 13:15	*3614*
a far journey, who left his *h*	Mk 13:34	*3614*
when the master of the *h* cometh	Mk 13:35	*3614*
in the *h* of Simon the leper	Mk 14:3	*3614*
say ye to the goodman of the *h*	Mk 14:14	*3617*
he departed to his own *h*	Lk 1:23	*3624*
was Joseph, of the *h* of David	Lk 1:27	*3624*
over the *h* of Jacob for ever	Lk 1:33	*3624*
entered into the *h* of Zacharias	Lk 1:40	*3624*
months, and returned to her own *h*	Lk 1:56	*3624*
us in the *h* of his servant David	Lk 1:69	*3624*
(because he was of the *h* and	Lk 2:4	*3624*
and entered into Simon's *h*	Lk 4:38	*3614*
up thy couch, and go into thine *h*	Lk 5:24	*3624*
he lay, and departed to his own *h*	Lk 5:25	*3624*
him a great feast in his own *h*	Lk 5:29	*3614*
How he went into the *h* of God	Lk 6:4	*3624*
He is like a man which built an *h*	Lk 6:48	*3614*
beat vehemently upon that *h*	Lk 6:48	*3614*
built an *h* upon the earth	Lk 6:49	*3614*
and the ruin of that *h* was great	Lk 6:49	*3614*
he was now not far from the *h*	Lk 7:6	*3614*
were sent, returning to the *h*	Lk 7:10	*3624*
And he went into the Pharisee's *h*	Lk 7:36	*3614*
sat at meat in the Pharisee's *h*	Lk 7:37	*3614*
I entered into thine *h*, thou	Lk 7:44	*3614*
clothes, neither abode in any *h*	Lk 8:27	*3614*
Return to thine own *h*, and shew	Lk 8:39	*3624*
him that he would come into his *h*	Lk 8:41	*3624*
the ruler of the synagogue's *h*	Lk 8:49	
And when he came into the *h*	Lk 8:51	*3614*
whatsoever *h* ye enter into, there	Lk 9:4	*3614*
which are at home at my *h*	Lk 9:61	*3624*
And into whatsoever *h* ye enter	Lk 10:5	*3614*
first say, Peace be to this *h*	Lk 10:5	*3624*
And in the same *h* remain, eating	Lk 10:7	*3614*
Go not from *h* to *h*	Lk 10:7	*3614*
Martha received him into her *h*	Lk 10:38	*3624*
***h* divided against a *h* falleth**	Lk 11:17	*3624*
unto my *h* whence I came out	Lk 11:24	*3624*
that if the goodman of the *h* had	Lk 12:39	*3617*
his *h* to be broken through	Lk 12:39	*3624*
shall be five in one *h* divided	Lk 12:52	*3624*
the master of the *h* is risen up	Lk 13:25	*3617*
your *h* is left unto you desolate	Lk 13:35	*3624*
as he went into the *h* of one of	Lk 14:1	*3624*
Then the master of the *h* being	Lk 14:21	*3617*
come in, that my *h* may be filled	Lk 14:23	*3624*
light a candle, and sweep the *h*	Lk 15:8	*3614*
as he came and drew nigh to the *h*	Lk 15:25	*3614*
send him to my father's *h*	Lk 16:27	*3624*
housetop, and his stuff in the *h*	Lk 17:31	*3614*
this man went down to his *h*	Lk 18:14	*3624*
There is no man that hath left *h*	Lk 18:29	*3614*
for to day I must abide at thy *h*	Lk 19:5	*3624*
day is salvation come to this *h*	Lk 19:9	*3624*
My *h* is the *h* of prayer	Lk 19:46	*3624*

follow him into the *h* where he	Lk 22:10	3614
say unto the goodman of the *h*	Lk 22:11	3614
him into the high priest's *h*	Lk 22:54	3624
h an *h* of merchandise	Jn 2:16	3624
zeal of thine *h* hath eaten me up	Jn 2:17	3624
himself believed, and his whole *h*	Jn 4:53	3614
And every man went unto his own *h*	Jn 7:53	3624
abideth not in the *h* for ever	Jn 8:35	3614
but Mary sat still in the *h*	Jn 11:20	3624
then which were with her in the *h*	Jn 11:31	3614
the *h* was filled with the odour	Jn 12:3	3614
In my Father's *h* are many	Jn 14:2	3614
it filled all the *h* where they	Acts 2:2	3624
Therefore let all the *h* of Israel	Acts 2:36	3624
and breaking bread from *h* to *h*	Acts 2:46	3624
in the temple, and in every *h*	Acts 5:42	3624
governor over Egypt and all his *h*	Acts 7:10	3624
up in his father's *h* three months	Acts 7:20	3624
O ye *h* of Israel, have ye offered	Acts 7:42	3624
But Solomon built him an *h*	Acts 7:47	3624
what *h* will ye build me	Acts 7:49	3624
the church, entering into every *h*	Acts 8:3	3624
enquire in the *h* of Judas for one	Acts 9:11	3614
his way, and entered into the *h*	Acts 9:17	3624
that feared God with all his *h*	Acts 10:2	3624
whose *h* is by the sea side	Acts 10:6	3614
had made enquiry for Simon's *h*	Acts 10:17	3614
angel to send for thee into his *h*	Acts 10:22	3624
the ninth hour I prayed in my *h*	Acts 10:30	3624
he is lodged in the *h* of one	Acts 10:32	3614
come unto the *h* where I was	Acts 11:11	3614
and we entered into the man's *h*	Acts 11:12	3624
how he had seen an angel in his *h*	Acts 11:13	3624
thou and all thy *h* shall be saved	Acts 11:14	3624
he came to the *h* of Mary the	Acts 12:12	3614
to the Lord, come into my *h*	Acts 16:15	3624
and thou shalt be saved, and thy *h*	Acts 16:31	3624
and to all that were in his *h*	Acts 16:32	3614
he had brought them into his *h*	Acts 16:34	3624
believing in God with all his *h*	Acts 16:34	3832
and entered into the *h* of Lydia	Acts 16:40	
and assaulted the *h* of Jason	Acts 17:5	3614
and entered into a certain man's *h*	Acts 18:7	3614
whose *h* joined hard to the	Acts 18:7	3614
on the Lord with all his *h*	Acts 18:8	3624
they fled out of that *h* naked	Acts 19:16	3624
publickly, and from *h* to *h*	Acts 20:20	3624
we entered into the *h* of Philip	Acts 21:8	3624
whole years in his own hired *h*	Acts 28:30	
the church that is in their *h*	Rom 16:5	3624
them which are of the *h* of Chloe	1Cor 1:11	
(ye know the *h* of Stephanas	1Cor 16:15	3614
the church that is in their *h*	1Cor 16:19	3624
earthly *h* of this tabernacle were	2Cor 5:1	3614
an *h* not made with hands, eternal	2Cor 5:1	3614
with our *h* which is from heaven	2Cor 5:2	3613
and the church which is in his *h*	Col 4:15	3624
One that ruleth well his own *h*	1Ti 3:4	3624
know not how to rule his own *h*	1Ti 3:5	3624
to behave thyself in the *h* of God	1Ti 3:15	3624
specially for those of his own *h*	1Ti 5:8	3609
wandering about from *h* to *h*	1Ti 5:13	3614
marry, bear children, guide the *h*	1Ti 5:14	3616
mercy unto the *h* of Onesiphorus	2Ti 1:16	3624
But in a great *h* there are not	2Ti 2:20	3614
and to the church in thy *h*	Philem 2	3624
Moses was faithful in all his *h*	Heb 3:2	3624
h hath more honour than the *h*	Heb 3:3	3624
For every *h* is builded by some	Heb 3:4	3624
verily was faithful in all his *h*	Heb 3:5	3624
Christ as a son over his own *h*	Heb 3:6	3624
whose *h* are we, if we hold fast	Heb 3:6	3624
new covenant with the *h* of Israel	Heb 8:8	3624
of Israel and with the *h* of Judah	Heb 8:8	3624
that I will make with the *h* of	Heb 8:10	3624
an high priest over the *h* of God	Heb 10:21	3624
an ark to the saving of his *h*	Heb 11:7	3624
are built up a spiritual *h*	1Pet 2:5	3624
must begin at the *h* of God	1Pet 4:17	3624
receive him not into your *h*	2Jn 10	3614

HOUSEHOLD

his *h* after him, and they shall	Gen 18:19	1004
thou found of all thy *h* stuff	Gen 31:37	1004
Then Jacob said unto his *h*	Gen 35:2	1004
lest thou, and thy *h*, and all that	Gen 45:11	1004
brethren, and all his father's *h*	Gen 47:12	1004
man and his *h* came with Jacob	Ex 1:1	1004
if the *h* be too little for the	Ex 12:4	1004
for himself, and for his *h*	Lev 16:17	1004
upon Pharaoh, and upon all his *h*	Deut 6:22	1004

shalt rejoice, thou, and thine *h*	Deut 14:26	1004
LORD shall choose, thou and thy *h*	Deut 15:20	1004
brethren, and all thy father's *h*	Josh 2:18	1004
harlot alive, and her father's *h*	Josh 6:25	1004
the *h* which the LORD shall take	Josh 7:14	1004
And he brought his *h* man by man	Josh 7:18	1004
because he feared his father's *h*	Judg 6:27	1004
thy life, with the lives of thy *h*	Judg 18:25	1004
our master, and against all his *h*	1Sa 25:17	1004
and his men, every man with his *h*	1Sa 27:3	1004
bring up, every man with his *h*	2Sa 2:3	1004
blessed Obed-edom, and all his *h*	2Sa 6:11	1004
David returned to bless his *h*	2Sa 6:20	1004
forth, and all his *h* after him	2Sa 15:16	1004
be for the king's *h* to ride on	2Sa 16:2	1004
put his *h* in order, and hanged	2Sa 17:23	1004
boat to carry over the king's *h*	2Sa 19:18	1004
have brought the king, and his *h*	2Sa 19:41	1004
And Ahishar was over the *h*	1Kin 4:6	1004
victuals for the king and his *h*	1Kin 4:7	1004
desire, in giving food for my *h*	1Kin 5:9	1004
of wheat for food to his *h*	1Kin 5:11	1004
h among the sons of Pharaoh	1Kin 11:20	1004
we may go and tell the king's *h*	2Kin 7:9	1004
Arise, and go thou and thine *h*	2Kin 8:1	1004
and she went with her *h*, and	2Kin 8:2	1004
of Hilkiah, which was over the *h*	2Kin 18:18	1004
of Hilkiah, which was over the *h*	2Kin 18:37	1004
Eliakim, which was over the *h*	2Kin 19:2	1004
one principal *h* being taken for	1Chr 24:6	1004
the *h* stuff of Tobiah out of the	Neh 13:8	1004
she asses, and a very great *h*	Job 1:3	5657
thy food, for the food of thy *h*	Prov 27:27	1004
night, and giveth meat to her *h*	Prov 31:15	1004
not afraid of the snow for her *h*	Prov 31:21	1004
for all her *h* are clothed with	Prov 31:21	1004
looketh well to the ways of her *h*	Prov 31:27	1004
of Hilkiah, that was over the *h*	Is 36:22	1004
sent Eliakim, who was over the *h*	Is 37:2	1004
shall they call them of his *h*	Mt 10:25	3615
foes shall be they of his own *h*	Mt 10:36	3615
lord hath made ruler over his *h*	Mt 24:45	2322
lord shall make ruler over his *h*	Lk 12:42	2322
he called two of his *h* servants	Acts 10:7	3610
when she was baptized, and her *h*	Acts 16:15	3624
them which are of Aristobulus' *h*	Rom 16:10	
that be of the *h* of Narcissus	Rom 16:11	
baptized also the *h* of Stephanas	1Cor 1:16	3624
them who are of the *h* of faith	Gal 6:10	3609
the saints, and of the *h* of God	Eph 2:19	3609
they that are of Caesar's *h*	Phil 4:22	3614
Aquila, and the *h* of Onesiphorus	2Ti 4:19	3624

HOUSEHOLDER

So the servants of the *h* came	Mt 13:27	3617
is like unto a man that is an *h*	Mt 13:52	3617
is like unto a man that is an *h*	Mt 20:1	3617
There was a certain *h*, which	Mt 21:33	3617

HOUSEHOLDS

food for the famine of your *h*	Gen 42:33	1004
And take your father and your *h*	Gen 45:18	1004
your food, and for them of your *h*	Gen 47:24	1004
it in every place, ye and your *h*	Num 18:31	1004
and swallowed them up, and their *h*	Deut 11:6	1004
put your hand unto, ye and your *h*	Deut 12:7	1004
LORD shall take shall come by *h*	Josh 7:14	1004

HOUSES

corn for the famine of your *h*	Gen 42:19	1004
feared God, that he made them *h*	Ex 1:21	1004
be the heads of their fathers' *h*	Ex 6:14	1004
the frogs from thee and thy *h*	Ex 8:9	1004
depart from thee, and from thy *h*	Ex 8:11	1004
and the frogs died out of the *h*	Ex 8:13	1004
and upon thy people, and into thy *h*	Ex 8:21	1004
the *h* of the Egyptians shall be	Ex 8:21	1004
Pharaoh, and into his servants' *h*	Ex 8:24	1004
and his cattle flee into the *h*	Ex 9:20	1004
And they shall fill thy *h*	Ex 10:6	1004
the *h* of all thy servants	Ex 10:6	1004
the *h* of all the Egyptians	Ex 10:6	1004
on the upper door post of the *h*	Ex 12:7	1004
a token upon the *h* where ye are	Ex 12:13	1004
put away leaven out of your *h*	Ex 12:15	1004
be no leaven found in your *h*	Ex 12:19	1004
come in unto your *h* to smite you	Ex 12:23	1004
who passed over the *h* of the	Ex 12:27	1004
the Egyptians, and delivered our *h*	Ex 12:27	1004
But the *h* of the villages which	Lev 25:31	1004
the *h* of the cities of their	Lev 25:32	1004
for the *h* of the cities of the	Lev 25:33	1004

H

throughout the *h* of their fathers	Num 4:22	1004
and swallowed them up, and their *h*	Num 16:32	1004
according to their fathers' *h*	Num 17:6	1004
We will not return unto our *h*	Num 32:18	1004
h full of all good things, which	Deut 6:11	1004
art full, and hast built goodly *h*	Deut 8:12	1004
in their cities, and in their *h*	Deut 19:1	1004
for our provision out of our *h* on	Josh 9:12	1004
that there is in these *h* an ephod	Judg 18:14	1004
the men that were in the *h* near	Judg 18:22	1004
when Solomon had built the two *h*	1Kin 9:10	1004
against all the *h* of the high	1Kin 13:32	1004
house, and the *h* of thy servants	1Kin 20:6	1004
put them in the *h* of the high	2Kin 17:29	1004
them in the *h* of the high places	2Kin 17:32	1004
brake down the *h* of the sodomites	2Kin 23:7	1004
all the *h* also of the high places	2Kin 23:19	1004
all the *h* of Israel, and every	2Kin 25:9	1004
David made him *h* in the city of	1Chr 15:1	1004
of the *h* thereof, and of the	1Chr 28:11	1004
overlay the walls of the *h* withal	1Chr 29:4	1004
to the *h* of their fathers	2Chr 25:5	1004
to floor the *h* which the kings of	2Chr 34:11	1004
by the *h* of your fathers, after	2Chr 35:4	1004
daughters, your wives, and your *h*	Neh 4:14	1004
our lands, vineyards, and *h*	Neh 5:3	1004
their oliveyards, and their *h*	Neh 5:11	1004
and the *h* were not builded	Neh 7:4	
possessed *h* full of all goods,	Neh 9:25	1004
after the *h* of our fathers, at	Neh 10:34	1004
sons went and feasted in their *h*	Job 1:4	1004
who filled their *h* with silver	Job 3:15	1004
in them that dwell in *h* of clay	Job 4:19	1004
in *h* which no man inhabiteth,	Job 15:28	1004
Their *h* are safe from fear,	Job 21:9	1004
filled their *h* with good things	Job 22:18	1004
In the dark they dig through *h*	Job 24:16	1004
that their *h* shall continue for	Ps 49:11	1004
the *h* of God in possession	Ps 83:12	4999
we shall fill our *h* with spoil	Prov 1:13	1004
make they their *h* in the rocks	Prov 30:26	1004
I builded me *h*	Eccl 2:4	1004
spoil of the poor is in your *h*	Is 3:14	1004
Of a truth many *h* shall be	Is 5:9	1004
the *h* without man, and the land be	Is 6:11	1004
offence to both the *h* of Israel	Is 8:14	1004
their *h* shall be spoiled, and	Is 13:16	1004
their *h* shall be full of doleful	Is 13:21	1004
shall cry in their desolate *h*	Is 13:22	490
on the tops of their *h*, and in	Is 15:3	
have numbered the *h* of Jerusalem	Is 22:10	1004
the *h* have ye broken down to	Is 22:10	1004
upon all the *h* of joy in the	Is 32:13	1004
and they are hid in prison *h*	Is 42:22	1004
And they shall build *h*, and inhabit	Is 65:21	1004
by troops in the harlots' *h*	Jer 5:7	1004
so are their *h* full of deceit	Jer 5:27	1004
their *h* shall be turned unto	Jer 6:12	1004
out of your *h* on the sabbath day	Jer 17:22	1004
Let a cry be heard from their *h*	Jer 18:22	1004
the *h* of Jerusalem	Jer 19:13	1004
the *h* of the kings of Judah,	Jer 19:13	1004
because of all the *h* upon whose	Jer 19:13	1004
Build ye *h*, and dwell in them	Jer 29:5	1004
build ye *h*, and dwell in them	Jer 29:28	1004
H and fields and vineyards shall be	Jer 32:15	1004
this city, and burn it with the *h*	Jer 32:29	1004
concerning the *h* of this city	Jer 33:4	1004
concerning the *h* of the kings of	Jer 33:4	1004
Nor to build *h* for us to dwell in	Jer 35:9	1004
the *h* of the people, with fire,	Jer 39:8	1004
in the *h* of the gods of Egypt	Jer 43:12	1004
and the *h* of the gods of the	Jer 43:13	1004
all the *h* of Jerusalem, and all	Jer 52:13	1004
all the *h* of the great men,	Jer 52:13	1004
to strangers, our *h* to aliens	Lam 5:2	1004
and they shall possess their *h*	Eze 7:24	1004
let us build *h*	Eze 11:3	1004
they shall burn thine *h* with fire	Eze 16:41	1004
and burn up their *h* with fire	Eze 23:47	1004
walls, and destroy thy pleasant *h*	Eze 26:12	1004
safely therein, and shall build *h*	Eze 28:26	1004
walls and in the doors of the *h*	Eze 33:30	1004
it shall be a place for their *h*	Eze 45:4	1004
your *h* shall be made a dunghill	Dan 2:5	1005
their *h* shall be made a dunghill	Dan 3:29	1005
and I will place them in their *h*	Hos 11:11	1004
they shall climb upon the *h*	Joel 2:9	1004
the *h* of ivory shall perish, and	Amos 3:15	1004
the great *h* shall have an end,	Amos 3:15	1004
ye have built *h* of hewn stone	Amos 5:11	1004

the *h* of Achzib shall be a lie to	Mic 1:14	1004
and *h*, and take them away	Mic 2:2	1004
ye cast out from their pleasant *h*	Mic 2:9	1004
their masters' *h* with violence	Zeph 1:9	1004
a booty, and their *h* a desolation	Zeph 1:13	1004
they shall also build *h*, but not	Zeph 1:13	1004
in the *h* of Ashkelon shall they	Zeph 2:7	1004
O ye, to dwell in your cieled *h*	Hag 1:4	1004
the *h* rifled, and the women	Zec 14:2	1004
soft clothing are in kings' *h*	Mt 11:8	3624
And every one that hath forsaken *h*	Mt 19:29	3614
for ye devour widows' *h*, and for a	Mt 23:14	3614
them away fasting to their own *h*	Mk 8:3	3624
hundredfold now in this time, *h*	Mk 10:30	3614
Which devour widows' *h*, and for a	Mk 12:40	3614
they may receive me into their *h*	Lk 16:4	3624
Which devour widows' *h*, and for a	Lk 20:47	3614
of lands or *h* sold them, and	Acts 4:34	3614
have ye not *h* to eat and to drink	1Cor 11:22	3614
children and their own *h* well	1Ti 3:12	3624
sort are they which creep into *h*	2Ti 3:6	3614
be stopped, who subvert whole *h*	Titus 1:11	3624

HOUSETOP

to dwell in a corner of the *h*	Prov 21:9	1406
to dwell in the corner of the *h*	Prov 25:24	1406
Let him which is on the *h* not	Mt 24:17	1430
let him that is on the *h* not go	Mk 13:15	1430
multitude, they went upon the *h*	Lk 5:19	1430
day, he which shall be upon the *h*	Lk 17:31	1430
Peter went up upon the *h* to pray	Acts 10:9	1430

HOUSETOPS

them be as the grass upon the *h*	Ps 129:6	1406
thou art wholly gone up to the *h*	Is 22:1	1406
green herb, as the grass on the *h*	Is 37:27	1406
generally upon all the *h* of Moab	Jer 48:38	1406
the host of heaven upon the *h*	Zeph 1:5	1406
ear, that preach ye upon the *h*	Mt 10:27	1430
shall be proclaimed upon the *h*	Lk 12:3	1430

HOW See APPENDIX.

HOWBEIT

H Sisera fled away on his feet to	Judg 4:17	
H the king of the children of	Judg 11:28	
H the hair of his head began to	Judg 16:22	
h the name of the city was Laish	Judg 18:29	199
H we may not give them wives of	Judg 21:18	
h there is a kinsman nearer than	Ruth 3:12	
h yet protest solemnly unto them,	1Sa 8:9	389
H he refused to turn aside	2Sa 2:23	
H, because by this deed thou hast	2Sa 12:14	657
H he would not hearken unto her	2Sa 13:14	
h he would not go, but blessed	2Sa 13:25	
h he attained not unto the first	2Sa 23:19	
h the kingdom is turned about, and	1Kin 2:15	
H I believed not the words, until	1Kin 10:7	
H I will not rend away all the	1Kin 11:13	7535
h let me go in any wise	1Kin 11:22	
H I will not take the whole	1Kin 11:34	
h the slingers went about it, and	2Kin 3:25	
h the LORD hath shewed me that he	2Kin 8:10	
H from the sins of Jeroboam the	2Kin 10:29	
H there were not made for the	2Kin 12:13	
H the high places were not taken	2Kin 14:4	
H the high places were not	2Kin 15:35	
H every nation made gods of their	2Kin 17:29	
H they did not hearken, but they	2Kin 17:40	
H there was no reckoning made	2Kin 22:7	
h he attained not to the first	1Chr 11:21	
H the LORD God of Israel chose me	1Chr 28:4	
H I believed not their words,	2Chr 9:6	
h the king of Israel stayed	2Chr 18:34	
H the high places were not taken	2Chr 20:33	
H the LORD would not destroy the	2Chr 21:7	
H they buried him in the city of	2Chr 21:20	
H the Levites hastened it not	2Chr 24:5	
h he entered not into the temple	2Chr 27:2	
H in the business of the	2Chr 32:31	3651
H thou art just in all that is	Neh 9:33	
h our God turned the curse into a	Neh 13:2	
H he will not stretch out his	Job 30:24	
H he meaneth not so, neither doth	Is 10:7	
H I sent unto you all my servants	Jer 44:4	
***H* this kind goeth not out but by**	Mt 17:21	
H Jesus suffered him not, but	Mk 5:19	
***H* in vain do they worship me,**	Mk 7:7	
(*H* there came other boats from	Jn 6:23	1161
H no man spake openly of him for	Jn 7:13	3305
H we know this man whence he is	Jn 7:27	235
H Jesus spake of his death	Jn 11:13	
***H* when he, the Spirit of truth,**	Jn 16:13	

H many of them which heard the	Acts 4:4	
H the most High dwelleth not in	Acts 7:48	235
H, as the disciples stood round	Acts 14:20	
H certain men clave unto him, and	Acts 17:34	
H we must be cast upon a certain	Acts 27:26	
H they looked when he should have	Acts 28:6	
H we speak wisdom among them that	1Cor 2:6	
H there is not in every man that	1Cor 8:7	235
h in the spirit he speaketh	1Cor 14:2	
h in malice be ye children, but	1Cor 14:20	235
H that was not first which is	1Cor 15:46	235
H whereinsoever any is bold,	2Cor 11:21	
H then, when ye knew not God, ye	Gal 4:8	235
H for this cause I obtained mercy	1Ti 1:16	235
h not all that came out of Egypt	Heb 3:16	235

HOWL

H ye; for the day of the Lord	Is 13:6	3213
H, O gate	Is 14:31	3213
Moab shall *h* over Nebo, and over	Is 15:2	3213
their streets, every one shall *h*	Is 15:3	3213
h for Moab, every one shall *h*	Is 16:7	3213
H, ye ships of Tarshish	Is 23:1	3213
h, ye inhabitants of the isle	Is 23:6	3213
H, ye ships of Tarshish	Is 23:14	3213
rule over them make them to *h*	Is 52:5	3213
shall *h* for vexation of spirit	Is 65:14	3213
you with sackcloth, lament and *h*	Jer 4:8	3213
H, ye shepherds, and cry	Jer 25:34	3213
inhabitants of the land shall *h*	Jer 47:2	3213
h and cry; tell ye it	Jer 48:20	3213
Therefore will I *h* for Moab	Jer 48:31	3213
They shall *h*, saying, How is it	Jer 48:39	3213
H, O Heshbon, for Ai is spoiled	Jer 49:3	3213
h for her; take balm	Jer 51:8	3213
Cry and *h*, son of man	Eze 21:12	3213
H ye, Woe worth the day	Eze 30:2	3213
and *h*, all ye drinkers of wine,	Joel 1:5	3213
h, O ye vinedressers, for the	Joel 1:11	3213
h, ye ministers of the altar	Joel 1:13	3213
Therefore I will wail and *h*	Mic 1:8	3213
H, ye inhabitants of Maktesh, for	Zeph 1:11	3213
H, fir tree; for the cedar	Zec 11:2	3213
h, O ye oaks of Bashan	Zec 11:2	3213
h for your miseries that shall	Jas 5:1	*3649*

HOWLED

when they *h* upon their beds	Hos 7:14	3213

HOWLING

and in the waste *h* wilderness	Deut 32:10	3214
the *h* thereof unto Eglaim, and the	Is 15:8	3213
the *h* thereof unto Beer-elim	Is 15:8	3213
an *h* of the principal of the	Jer 25:36	3213
an *h* from the second, and a great	Zeph 1:10	3213
a voice of the *h* of the shepherds	Zec 11:3	3213

HOWLINGS

the temple shall be *h* in that day	Amos 8:3	3213

HOWSOEVER

h let all thy wants lie upon me	Judg 19:20	7535
of Zadok yet again to Joab, But *h*	2Sa 18:22	1961,4101
But *h*, said he, let me run	2Sa 18:23	
not be cut off, *h* I punished them	Zeph 3:7	3605,834

HOZAI See Seers.

HUBBAH See Juhubbah.

HUGE

Ethiopians and the Lubims a *h* host	2Chr 16:8	7230

HUKKOK (huk'-kok) See Helkath, Hukok. *A place in Naphtali.*

and goeth out from thence to *H*	Josh 19:34	2712

HUKOK (hu'-kok) See Hukkok. *A city in Asher.*

H with her suburbs, and Rehob with	1Chr 6:75	2712

HUL (hul) *A son of Aram.*

Uz, and *H*, and Gether, and Mash	Gen 10:23	2343
and Lud, and Aram, and Uz, and *H*	1Chr 1:17	2343

HULDAH (hul'-dah) *A prophetess.*

went unto *H* the prophetess, the	2Kin 22:14	2468
went to *H* the prophetess, the	2Chr 34:22	2468

HUMBLE

refuse to *h* thyself before me	Ex 10:3	6031
to *h* thee, and to prove thee, to	Deut 8:2	6031
knew not, that he might *h* thee	Deut 8:16	6031
h ye them, and do with them what	Judg 19:24	6031
shall *h* themselves, and pray, and	2Chr 7:14	3665
thou didst *h* thyself before God,	2Chr 34:27	3665
and he shall save the *h* person	Job 22:29	7807,5869
forgetteth not the cry of the *h*	Ps 9:12	6041
forget not the *h*	Ps 10:12	6041

hast heard the desire of the *h*	Ps 10:17	6041
the *h* shall hear thereof, and be	Ps 34:2	6041
The *h* shall see this, and be glad	Ps 69:32	6041
h thyself, and make sure thy	Prov 6:3	7511
be of an *h* spirit with the lowly	Prov 16:19	8213
shall uphold the *h* in spirit	Prov 29:23	8217
that is of a contrite and *h* spirit	Is 57:15	8217
to revive the spirit of the *h*	Is 57:15	8217
the queen, *H* yourselves, sit down	Jer 13:18	8213
Whosoever therefore shall *h*	Mt 18:4	*5013*
he that shall *h* himself shall be	Mt 23:12	*5013*
my God will *h* me among you, and	2Cor 12:21	*5013*
but giveth grace unto the *h*	Jas 4:6	*5011*
H yourselves in the sight of the	Jas 4:10	*5013*
proud, and giveth grace to the *h*	1Pet 5:5	*5011*
H yourselves therefore under the	1Pet 5:6	*5013*

HUMBLED

their uncircumcised hearts be *h*	Lev 26:41	3665
he *h* thee, and suffered thee to	Deut 8:3	6031
of her, because thou hast *h* her	Deut 21:14	6031
because he hath *h* his neighbour's	Deut 22:24	6031
because he hath *h* her, he may not	Deut 22:29	6031
thou hast *h* thyself before the	2Kin 22:19	3665
Israel and the king *h* themselves	2Chr 12:6	3665
Lord saw that they *h* themselves	2Chr 12:7	3665
saying, They have *h* themselves	2Chr 12:7	3665
And when he *h* himself, the wrath	2Chr 12:12	3665
and of Zebulun *h* themselves	2Chr 30:11	3665
Notwithstanding Hezekiah *h*	2Chr 32:26	3665
h himself greatly before the God	2Chr 33:12	3665
and graven images, before he was *h*	2Chr 33:19	3665
h not himself before the Lord, as	2Chr 33:23	3665
Manasseh his father had *h* himself	2Chr 33:23	3665
h not himself before Jeremiah the	2Chr 36:12	3665
I *h* my soul with fasting	Ps 35:13	6031
The lofty looks of man shall be *h*	Is 2:11	8213
and the mighty man shall be *h*	Is 5:15	8213
the eyes of the lofty shall be *h*	Is 5:15	8213
down, and the haughty shall be *h*	Is 10:33	8213
They are not *h* even unto this day	Jer 44:10	1792
in remembrance, and is *h* in me	Lam 3:20	7743
in thee have they *h* her that was	Eze 22:10	6031
another in thee hath *h* his sister	Eze 22:11	6031
hast not *h* thine heart, though	Dan 5:22	8214
he *h* himself, and became obedient	Phil 2:8	*5013*

HUMBLEDST

h thyself before me, and didst	2Chr 34:27	3665

HUMBLENESS

kindness, *h* of mind, meekness,	Col 3:12	*5012*

HUMBLETH

thou how Ahab *h* himself before me	1Kin 21:29	3665
because he *h* himself before me, I	1Kin 21:29	3665
h himself, that the poor may fall	Ps 10:10	7817
Who *h* himself to behold the	Ps 113:6	8213
down, and the great man *h* himself	Is 2:9	8213
he that *h* himself shall be	Lk 14:11	*5013*
he that *h* himself shall be	Lk 18:14	*5013*

HUMBLY

I *h* beseech thee that I may find	2Sa 16:4	7812
mercy, and to walk *h* with thy God	Mic 6:8	6800

HUMILIATION

In his *h* his judgment was taken	Acts 8:33	*5014*

HUMILITY

and before honour is *h*	Prov 15:33	6038
and before honour is *h*	Prov 18:12	6038
By *h* and the fear of the Lord are	Prov 22:4	6038
the Lord with all *h* of mind	Acts 20:19	*5012*
of your reward in a voluntary *h*	Col 2:18	*5012*
of wisdom in will worship, and *h*	Col 2:23	*5012*
to another, and be clothed with *h*	1Pet 5:5	*5012*

HUMTAH (hum'-tah) *A city in Judah.*

And *H*, and Kirjath-arba, which is	Josh 15:54	2457

HUNDRED See APPENDIX.

HUNDREDFOLD

received in the same year an *h*	Gen 26:12	3967,8180
how many soever they be, an *h*	2Sa 24:3	
and brought forth fruit, some an *h*	Mt 13:8	*1540*
and bringeth forth, some an *h*	Mt 13:23	*1540*
name's sake, shall receive an *h*	Mt 19:29	*1542*
receive an *h* now in this time	Mk 10:30	*1542*
and sprang up, and bare fruit an *h*	Lk 8:8	*1542*

HUNDREDS

of thousands, and rulers of *h*	Ex 18:21	3967
rulers of thousands, rulers of *h*	Ex 18:25	3967
thousands, and captains over *h*	Num 31:14	3967

H

of thousands, and captains of h	Num 31:48	3967
and of the captains of h, was	Num 31:52	3967
the captains of thousands and of h	Num 31:54	3967
thousands, and captains over h	Deut 1:15	3967
of thousands, and captains of h	1Sa 22:7	3967
of the Philistines passed on by h	1Sa 29:2	3967
and captains of h over them	2Sa 18:1	3967
and all the people came out by h	2Sa 18:4	3967
sent and fetched the rulers over h	2Kin 11:4	3967
the captains over the h did	2Kin 11:9	3967
to the captains over h did the	2Kin 11:10	3967
commanded the captains of the h	2Kin 11:15	3967
And he took the rulers over h	2Kin 11:19	3967
the captains of thousands and h	1Chr 13:1	3967
the captains over thousands and h	1Chr 26:26	3967
and captains of thousands and h	1Chr 27:1	3967
thousands, and captains over the h	1Chr 28:1	3967
the captains of thousands and of h	1Chr 29:6	3967
the captains of thousands and of h	2Chr 1:2	3967
and took the captains of h	2Chr 23:1	3967
to the captains of h spears	2Chr 23:9	3967
of h that were set over the host	2Chr 23:14	3967
And he took the captains of h	2Chr 23:20	3967
thousands, and captains over h	2Chr 25:5	3967
And they sat down in ranks, by h	Mk 6:40	*1540*

HUNDREDTH

In the six h year of Noah's life,	Gen 7:11	3967
And it came to pass in the six h	Gen 8:13	3967
also the h part of the money, and	Neh 5:11	3967

HUNGER

kill this whole assembly with h	Ex 16:3	7457
thee, and suffered thee to h	Deut 8:3	7456
shall send against thee, in h	Deut 28:48	7457
They shall be burnt with h	Deut 32:24	7457
bread from heaven for their h	Neh 9:15	7457
young lions do lack, and suffer h	Ps 34:10	7456
and an idle soul shall suffer h	Prov 19:15	7456
They shall not h nor thirst	Is 49:10	7456
he is like to die for h in the	Jer 38:9	7457
the trumpet, nor have h of bread	Jer 42:14	7456
that faint for h in the top of	Lam 2:19	7457
than they that be slain with h	Lam 4:9	7456
more consumed with h in the land	Eze 34:29	7457
Blessed are they which do h	Mt 5:6	*3983*
Blessed are ye that h now	Lk 6:21	*3983*
for ye shall h	Lk 6:25	*3983*
and to spare, and I perish with h	Lk 15:17	*3042*
that cometh to me shall never h	Jn 6:35	*3983*
Therefore if thine enemy h	Rom 12:20	*3983*
unto this present hour we both h	1Cor 4:11	*3983*
And if any man h, let him eat at	1Cor 11:34	*3983*
in watchings often, in h	2Cor 11:27	*3042*
to kill with sword, and with h	Rev 6:8	*3042*
They shall h no more, neither	Rev 7:16	*3983*

HUNGERBITTEN

His strength shall be h, and	Job 18:12	7457

HUNGERED

he returned into the city, he h	Mt 21:18	*3983*
they were ended, he afterward h	Lk 4:2	*3983*

HUNGRED

nights, he was afterward an h	Mt 4:2	*3983*
and his disciples were an h	Mt 12:1	*3983*
what David did, when he was an h	Mt 12:3	*3983*
For I was an h, and ye gave me	Mt 25:35	*3983*
Lord, when saw we thee an h	Mt 25:37	*3983*
For I was an h, and ye gave me no	Mt 25:42	*3983*
Lord, when saw we thee an h	Mt 25:44	*3983*
when he had need, and was an h	Mk 2:25	*3983*
David did, when himself was an h	Lk 6:3	*3983*

HUNGRY

and they that were h ceased	1Sa 2:5	7456
for they said, The people is h	2Sa 17:29	7456
They know that we be h	2Kin 7:12	7456
Whose harvest the h eateth up	Job 5:5	7456
hast withholden bread from the h	Job 22:7	7456
take away the sheaf from the h	Job 24:10	7456
If I were h, I would not tell	Ps 50:12	7456
H and thirsty, their soul fainted	Ps 107:5	7456
filleth the h soul with goodness	Ps 107:9	7456
And there he maketh the h to dwell	Ps 107:36	7456
which giveth food to the h	Ps 146:7	7456
to satisfy his soul when he is h	Prov 6:30	7456
If thine enemy be h, give him	Prov 25:21	7456
but to the h soul every bitter	Prov 27:7	7456
through it, hardly bestead and h	Is 8:21	7456
pass, that when they shall be h	Is 8:21	7456
snatch on the right hand, and be h	Is 9:20	7456
even be as when an h man dreameth	Is 29:8	7456

to make empty the soul of the h	Is 32:6	7456
yea, he is h, and his strength	Is 44:12	7456
it not to deal thy bread to the h	Is 58:7	7456
thou draw out thy soul to the h	Is 58:10	7456
shall eat, but ye shall be h	Is 65:13	7456
hath given his bread to the h	Eze 18:7	7456
but hath given his bread to the h	Eze 18:16	7456
were come from Bethany, he was h	Mk 11:12	*3983*
filled the h with good things	Lk 1:53	*3983*
And he became very h, and would	Acts 10:10	*4361*
and one is h, and another is	1Cor 11:21	*3983*
both to be full and to be h	Phil 4:12	*3983*

HUNT

to the field to h for venison	Gen 27:5	6679
as when one doth h a partridge in	1Sa 26:20	7291
Wilt thou h the prey for the lion	Job 38:39	6679
evil shall h the violent man to	Ps 140:11	6679
the adulteress will h for the	Prov 6:26	6679
they shall h them from every	Jer 16:16	6679
They h our steps, that we cannot	Lam 4:18	6679
head of every stature to h souls	Eze 13:18	6679
Will ye h the souls of my people,	Eze 13:18	6679
wherewith ye there h the souls to	Eze 13:20	6679
souls that ye h to make them fly	Eze 13:20	6679
they h every man his brother with	Mic 7:2	6679

HUNTED

be no more in your hand to be h	Eze 13:21	4686

HUNTER

He was a mighty h before the LORD	Gen 10:9	6718
the mighty h before the LORD	Gen 10:9	6718
and Esau was a cunning h, a man of	Gen 25:27	6718
as a roe from the hand of the h	Prov 6:5	6718

HUNTERS

and after will I send for many h	Jer 16:16	6719

HUNTEST

yet thou h my soul to take it	1Sa 24:11	6658
Thou h me as a fierce lion	Job 10:16	6679

HUNTETH

that sojourn among you, which h	Lev 17:13	6679

HUNTING

his brother came in from his h	Gen 27:30	6718
not that which he took in h	Prov 12:27	6718

HUPHAM (hu'-fam) See HUPPIM, HUPHAMITES. *A son of Benjamin.*

of H, the family of the	Num 26:39	2349

HUPHAMITES (hu'-fam-ites) *Descendants of Hupham.*

of Hupham, the family of the H	Num 26:39	2350

HUPPAH (hup'-pah) *A priest.*

The thirteenth to H, the	1Chr 24:13	2647

HUPPIM (hup'-pim) See HUPHAM. *Head of a Benjamite family.*

Ehi, and Rosh, Muppim, and H	Gen 46:21	2650
Shuppim also, and H, the children	1Chr 7:12	2650
took to wife the sister of H	1Chr 7:15	2650

HUPPITES See HUPPIM.

HUR (hur)
1. *Assisted Moses at Rephidim.*

H went up to the top of the hill	Ex 17:10	2354
H stayed up his hands, the one on	Ex 17:12	2354
behold, Aaron and H are with you	Ex 24:14	2354

2. *A son of Caleb.*

the son of Uri, the son of H	Ex 31:2	2354
the son of Uri, the son of H	Ex 35:30	2354
the son of Uri, the son of H	Ex 38:22	2354
him Ephrath, which bare him H	1Chr 2:19	2354
H begat Uri, and Uri begat	1Chr 2:20	2354
the son of Uri, the son of H	2Chr 1:5	2354

3. *A Midianite king.*

Evi, and Rekem, and Zur, and H	Num 31:8	2354
Evi, and Rekem, and Zur, and H	Josh 13:21	2354

4. *An officer of Solomon.*

The son of H, in mount Ephraim	1Kin 4:8	2354

5. *Father of Caleb.*

the sons of Caleb the son of H	1Chr 2:50	2354
These are the sons of H, the	1Chr 4:4	2354

6. *A descendant of Judah.*

Pharez, Hezron, and Carmi, and H	1Chr 4:1	2354

7. *A rebuilder of Jerusalem's wall.*

repaired Rephaiah the son of H	Neh 3:9	2354

HURAI (hu'-rahee) See HIDDAI. *A mighty man of David.*

H of the brooks of Gaash, Abiel	1Chr 11:32	2360

HURAM (hu'-ram) See HIRAM.
1. *Son of Bela.*

And Gera, and Shephuphan, and H	1Chr 8:5	2361

2. *Same as Hiram 1.*

Solomon sent to *H* the king of	2Chr 2:3	2361
Then *H* the king of Tyre answered	2Chr 2:11	2438
H said moreover, Blessed be the	2Chr 2:12	2361
understanding, of *H* my father's,	2Chr 2:13	2438
That the cities which *H* had	2Chr 8:2	2438
H sent him by the hands of his	2Chr 8:18	2438
And the servants also of *H*	2Chr 9:10	2438
Tarshish with the servants of *H*	2Chr 9:21	2438

3. *Same as Hiram 2.*

H made the pots, and the shovels,	2Chr 4:11	2361
H finished the work that he was	2Chr 4:11	2361
did *H* his father make to king	2Chr 4:16	2361

HURAM-ABI See HURAM.

HURI *(hu'-ri) Father of Abihail.*

children of Abihail the son of *H*	1Chr 5:14	2359

HURL

or *h* at him by laying of wait,	Num 35:20	7993

HURLETH

as a storm *h* him out of his place	Job 27:21	8175

HURLING

hand and the left in *h* stones	1Chr 12:2	

HURT

wounding, and a young man to my *h*	Gen 4:23	2250
That thou wilt do us no *h*	Gen 26:29	7451
but God suffered him not to *h* me	Gen 31:7	7489
the power of my hand to do you *h*	Gen 31:29	7451
h a woman with child, so that her	Ex 21:22	5062
And if one man's ox *h* another's	Ex 21:35	5062
and it die, or be *h*, or driven	Ex 22:10	7665
of his neighbour, and it be *h*	Ex 22:14	7665
neither have I *h* one of them	Num 16:15	7489
then he will turn and do you *h*	Josh 24:20	7489
there is peace to thee, and no *h*	1Sa 20:21	1697
Behold, David seeketh thy *h*	1Sa 24:9	7451
we *h* them not, neither was there	1Sa 25:7	3637
good unto us, and we were not *h*	1Sa 25:15	3637
rise against thee to do thee *h*	2Sa 18:32	7451
shouldest thou meddle to thy *h*?	2Kin 14:10	7451
shouldest thou meddle to thine *h*	2Chr 25:19	7451
damage grow to the *h* of the kings	Ezr 4:22	5142
hand on such as sought their *h*	Est 9:2	7451
may *h* a man as thou art	Job 35:8	
He that sweareth to his own *h*	Ps 15:4	7489
to confusion that devise my *h*	Ps 35:4	7451
together that rejoice at mine *h*	Ps 35:26	7451
they that seek my *h* speak	Ps 38:12	7451
against me do they devise my *h*	Ps 41:7	7451
to confusion, that desire my *h*	Ps 70:2	7451
and dishonour that seek my *h*	Ps 71:13	7451
unto shame, that seek my *h*	Ps 71:24	7451
Whose feet they *h* with fetters	Ps 105:18	6031
for the owners thereof to their *h*	Eccl 5:13	7451
ruleth over another to his own *h*	Eccl 8:9	7451
stones shall be *h* therewith	Eccl 10:9	6087
They shall not *h* nor destroy in	Is 11:9	7489
lest any *h* it, I will keep it	Is 27:3	6485
They shall not *h* nor destroy in	Is 65:25	7489
They have healed also the *h* of	Jer 6:14	7667
walk after other gods to your *h*	Jer 7:6	7451
For they have healed the *h* of the	Jer 8:11	7667
For the *h* of the daughter of my	Jer 8:21	7667
the daughter of my people am I *h*	Jer 8:21	7665
Woe is me for my *h*	Jer 10:19	7667
kingdoms of the earth for their *h*	Jer 24:9	7451
and I will do you no *h*	Jer 25:6	7489
works of your hands to your own *h*	Jer 25:7	7451
welfare of this people, but the *h*	Jer 38:4	7451
of the fire, and they have no *h*	Dan 3:25	2257
mouths, that they have not *h* me	Dan 6:22	2255
thee, O king, have I done no *h*	Dan 6:22	2248
no manner of *h* was found upon him	Dan 6:23	2257
deadly thing, it shall not *h* them	Mk 16:18	*984*
he came out of him, and *h* him not	Lk 4:35	*984*
nothing shall by any means *h* you	Lk 10:19	*91*
man shall set on thee to *h* thee	Acts 18:10	2559
that this voyage will be with *h*	Acts 27:10	5196
not be *h* of the second death	Rev 2:11	*91*
see him *h* not the oil and the	Rev 6:6	*91*
whom it was given to *h* the earth	Rev 7:2	*91*
H not the earth, neither the sea,	Rev 7:3	*91*
not *h* the grass of the earth	Rev 9:4	*91*
power was to *h* men five months	Rev 9:10	*91*
had heads, and with them they do *h*	Rev 9:19	*91*
And if any man will *h* them	Rev 11:5	*91*
and if any man will *h* them	Rev 11:5	*91*

HURTFUL

h unto kings and provinces, and	Ezr 4:15	5142
his servant from the *h* sword	Ps 144:10	7451
h lusts, which drown men in	1Ti 6:9	*983*

HURTING

hath kept me back from *h* thee	1Sa 25:34	7489

HUSBAND

and gave also unto her *h* with her	Gen 3:6	376
and thy desire shall be to thy *h*	Gen 3:16	376
gave her to her *h* Abram to be his	Gen 16:3	376
now therefore my *h* will love me	Gen 29:32	376
time will my *h* be joined unto me	Gen 29:34	376
matter that thou hast taken my *h*	Gen 30:15	376
I have given my maiden to my *h*	Gen 30:18	376
now will my *h* dwell with me,	Gen 30:20	376
Surely a bloody *h* art thou to me	Ex 4:25	2860
she said, A bloody *h* thou art	Ex 4:26	2860
the woman's *h* will lay upon him	Ex 21:22	1167
is a bondmaid, betrothed to an *h*	Lev 19:20	376
unto him, which hath had no *h*	Lev 21:3	376
take a woman put away from her *h*	Lev 21:7	376
it be hid from the eyes of her *h*	Num 5:13	376
with another instead of thy *h*	Num 5:19	376
aside to another instead of thy *h*	Num 5:20	376
lain with thee beside thine *h*	Num 5:20	376
have done trespass against her *h*	Num 5:27	376
aside to another instead of her *h*	Num 5:29	376
And if she had at all an *h*	Num 30:6	376
her *h* heard it, and held his peace	Num 30:7	376
But if her *h* disallowed her on	Num 30:8	376
her *h* heard it, and held his peace	Num 30:11	376
But if her *h* hath utterly made	Num 30:12	376
her *h* hath made them void	Num 30:12	376
her *h* may establish it	Num 30:13	376
or her *h* may make it void	Num 30:13	376
But if her *h* altogether hold his	Num 30:14	376
shalt go in unto her, and be her *h*	Deut 21:13	1167
with a woman married to an *h*	Deut 22:22	1167
a virgin be betrothed unto an *h*	Deut 22:23	376
And if the latter *h* hate her	Deut 24:3	376
or if the latter *h* die, which	Deut 24:3	376
Her former *h*, which sent her away	Deut 24:4	1167
her *h* out of the hand of him that	Deut 25:11	376
be evil toward the *h* of her bosom	Deut 28:56	376
Then the woman came and told her *h*	Judg 13:6	376
but Manoah her *h* was not with her	Judg 13:9	376
haste, and ran, and shewed her *h*	Judg 13:10	376
unto Samson's wife, Entice thy *h*	Judg 14:15	376
her *h* arose, and went after her,	Judg 19:3	376
the *h* of the woman that was slain	Judg 20:4	376
And Elimelech Naomi's *h* died	Ruth 1:3	376
was left of her two sons and her *h*	Ruth 1:5	376
each of you in the house of her *h*	Ruth 1:9	376
for I am too old to have an *h*	Ruth 1:12	376
I should have an *h* also to night	Ruth 1:12	376
in law since the death of thine *h*	Ruth 2:11	376
Then said Elkanah her *h* to her	1Sa 1:8	376
for she said unto her *h*, I will	1Sa 1:22	376
Elkanah her *h* said unto her, Do	1Sa 1:23	376
when she came up with her *h* to	1Sa 2:19	376
her *h* were dead, she bowed	1Sa 4:19	376
of her father in law and her *h*	1Sa 4:21	376
But she told not her *h* Nabal	1Sa 25:19	376
sent, and took her from her *h*	2Sa 3:15	376
her *h* went with her along weeping	2Sa 3:16	376
heard that Uriah her *h* was dead	2Sa 11:26	376
she mourned for her *h*	2Sa 11:26	1167
a widow woman, and mine *h* is dead	2Sa 14:5	376
shall not leave to my *h* neither	2Sa 14:7	376
saying, Thy servant my *h* is dead	2Kin 4:1	376
And she said unto her *h*, Behold	2Kin 4:9	376
hath no child, and her *h* is old	2Kin 4:14	376
And she called unto her *h*, and said	2Kin 4:22	376
is it well with thy *h*	2Kin 4:26	376
woman is a crown to her *h*	Prov 12:4	1167
The heart of her *h* doth safely	Prov 31:11	1167
Her *h* is known in the gates, when	Prov 31:23	1167
her *h* also, and he praiseth her	Prov 31:28	1167
For thy Maker is thine *h*	Is 54:5	1167
departeth from her *h*, so have ye	Jer 3:20	1167
for even the *h* with the wife	Jer 6:11	376
although I was an *h* unto them	Jer 31:32	1167
taketh strangers instead of her *h*	Eze 16:32	376
daughter, that lotheth her *h*	Eze 16:45	376
or for sister that hath had no *h*	Eze 44:25	376
not my wife, neither am I her *h*	Hos 2:2	376
I will go and return to my first *h*	Hos 2:7	376
sackcloth for the *h* of her youth	Joel 1:8	1167
Jacob begat Joseph the *h* of Mary	Mt 1:16	435

Then Joseph her *h*, being a just	Mt 1:19	435
if a woman shall put away her *h*	Mk 10:12	435
had lived with an *h* seven years	Lk 2:36	435
from her *h* committeth adultery	Lk 16:18	435
saith unto her, Go, call thy *h*	Jn 4:16	435
answered and said, I have no *h*	Jn 4:17	435
Thou hast well said, I have no *h*	Jn 4:17	435
whom thou now hast is not thy *h*	Jn 4:18	435
have buried thy *h* are at the door	Acts 5:9	435
her forth, buried her by her *h*	Acts 5:10	435
an *h* is bound by the law to her	Rom 7:2	5220
law to her *h* so long as he liveth	Rom 7:2	435
but if the *h* be dead, she is	Rom 7:2	435
is loosed from the law of her *h*	Rom 7:2	435
So then if, while her *h* liveth	Rom 7:3	435
but if her *h* be dead, she is free	Rom 7:3	435
and let every woman have her own *h*	1Cor 7:2	435
Let the *h* render unto the wife	1Cor 7:3	435
likewise also the wife unto the *h*	1Cor 7:3	435
power of her own body, but the *h*	1Cor 7:4	435
likewise also the *h* hath not	1Cor 7:4	435
not the wife depart from her *h*	1Cor 7:10	435
or be reconciled to her *h*	1Cor 7:11	435
let not the *h* put away his wife	1Cor 7:11	435
hath an *h* that believeth not	1Cor 7:13	435
For the unbelieving *h* is	1Cor 7:14	435
wife is sanctified by the *h*	1Cor 7:14	435
whether thou shalt save thy *h*	1Cor 7:16	435
world, how she may please her *h*	1Cor 7:34	435
the law as long as her *h* liveth	1Cor 7:39	435
but if her *h* be dead, she is at	1Cor 7:39	435
for I have espoused you to one *h*	2Cor 11:2	435
children than she which hath a *h*	Gal 4:27	435
For the *h* is the head of the wife	Eph 5:23	435
wife see that she reverence her *h*	Eph 5:33	435
the *h* of one wife, vigilant,	1Ti 3:2	435
the *h* of one wife, having	Titus 1:6	435
as a bride adorned for her *h*	Rev 21:2	435

HUSBANDMAN

Noah began to be an *h*, and he	Gen 9:20	376,127
thee will I break in pieces the *h*	Jer 51:23	406
they shall call the *h* to mourning	Amos 5:16	406
say, I am no prophet, I am an *h*	Zec 13:5	5647
true vine, and my Father is the *h*	Jn 15:1	1092
The *h* that laboureth must be	2Ti 2:6	1092
the *h* waiteth for the precious	Jas 5:7	1092

HUSBANDMEN

the land to be vinedressers and *h*	2Kin 25:12	1461
h also, and vine dressers in the	2Chr 26:10	406
the cities thereof together, *h*	Jer 31:24	406
land for vinedressers and for *h*	Jer 52:16	3009
Be ye ashamed, O ye *h*	Joel 1:11	406
built a tower, and let it out to *h*	Mt 21:33	1092
he sent his servants to the *h*	Mt 21:34	1092
the *h* took his servants, and beat	Mt 21:35	1092
But when the *h* saw the son	Mt 21:38	1092
what will he do unto those *h*	Mt 21:40	1092
let out his vineyard unto other *h*	Mt 21:41	1092
built a tower, and let it out to *h*	Mk 12:1	1092
season he sent to the *h* a servant	Mk 12:2	1092
***h* of the fruit of the vineyard**	Mk 12:2	1092
But those *h* said among themselves	Mk 12:7	1092
he will come and destroy the *h*	Mk 12:9	1092
a vineyard, and let it forth to *h*	Lk 20:9	1092
season he sent a servant to the *h*	Lk 20:10	1092
but the *h* beat him, and sent him	Lk 20:10	1092
But when the *h* saw him, they	Lk 20:14	1092
He shall come and destroy these *h*	Lk 20:16	1092

HUSBANDRY

for he loved *h*	2Chr 26:10	127
ye are God's *h*, ye are God's	1Cor 3:9	1091

HUSBAND'S

And if she vowed in her *h* house	Num 30:10	376
her *h* brother shall go in unto	Deut 25:5	2993
the duty of an *h* brother unto her	Deut 25:5	2992
My *h* brother refuseth to raise up	Deut 25:7	2993
perform the duty of my *h* brother	Deut 25:7	2992
And Naomi had a kinsman of her *h*	Ruth 2:1	376

HUSBANDS

my womb, that they may be your *h*	Ruth 1:11	582
ye stay for them from having *h*	Ruth 1:13	376
despise their *h* in their eyes	Est 1:17	1167
shall give to their *h* honour	Est 1:20	1167
sons, and give your daughters to *h*	Jer 29:6	582
thy sisters, which lothed their *h*	Eze 16:45	582
For thou hast had five *h*	Jn 4:18	435
let them ask their *h* at home	1Cor 14:35	435
submit yourselves unto your own *h*	Eph 5:22	435

be to their own *h* in every thing	Eph 5:24	435
H, love your wives, even as	Eph 5:25	435
submit yourselves unto your own *h*	Col 3:18	435
H, love your wives, and be not	Col 3:19	435
the deacons be the *h* of one wife	1Ti 3:12	435
to be sober, to love their *h*	Titus 2:4	5362
good, obedient to their own *h*	Titus 2:5	435
be in subjection to your own *h*	1Pet 3:1	435
in subjection unto their own *h*	1Pet 3:5	435
Likewise, ye *h*, dwell with them	1Pet 3:7	435

HUSHAH *(hu'-shah)* See HUSHATHITE, SHUAH. *A son of Ezer.*

of Gedor, and Ezer the father of *H*	1Chr 4:4	2364

HUSHAI *(hu'-shahee) Friend and advisor of David.*

H the Archite came to meet him	2Sa 15:32	2365
So *H* David's friend came into the	2Sa 15:37	2365
when *H* the Archite, David's	2Sa 16:16	2365
that *H* said unto Absalom, God	2Sa 16:16	2365
And Absalom said to *H*, Is this thy	2Sa 16:17	2365
And *H* said unto Absalom, Nay	2Sa 16:18	2365
Call now *H* the Archite also, and	2Sa 17:5	2365
when *H* was come to Absalom,	2Sa 17:6	2365
H said unto Absalom, The counsel	2Sa 17:7	2365
For, said *H*, thou knowest thy	2Sa 17:8	2365
The counsel of *H* the Archite is	2Sa 17:14	2365
Then said *H* unto Zadok and to	2Sa 17:15	2365
Baanah the son of *H* was in Asher	1Kin 4:16	2365
H the Archite was the king's	1Chr 27:33	2365

HUSHAM *(hu'-sham) A king of Edom.*

H of the land of Temani reigned	Gen 36:34	2367
H died, and Hadad the son of Bedad	Gen 36:35	2367
H of the land of the Temanites	1Chr 1:45	2367
when *H* was dead, Hadad the son of	1Chr 1:46	2367

HUSHATHITE *(hu'-shath-ite) A descendant of Hushah.*

then Sibbechai the *H* slew Saph	2Sa 21:18	2843
the Anethothite, Mebunnai the *H*	2Sa 23:27	2843
Sibbecai the *H*, Ilai the Ahohite,	1Chr 11:29	2843
time Sibbechai the *H* slew Sippai	1Chr 20:4	2843
eighth month was Sibbecai the *H*	1Chr 27:11	2843

HUSHIM *(hu'-shim)* See SHUHAM.

1. A son of Dan.

the sons of Dan; *H*	Gen 46:23	2366

2. Son of Aher.

Huppim, the children of Ir, and *H*	1Chr 7:12	2366

3. A wife of Shaharaim.

H and Baara were his wives	1Chr 8:8	2366
of *H* he begat Abitub, and Elpaal	1Chr 8:11	2366

HUSHITES See HUSHIM.

HUSK

from the kernels even to the *h*	Num 6:4	2085
ears of corn in the *h* thereof	2Kin 4:42	6861

HUSKS

with the *h* that the swine did eat	Lk 15:16	2769

HUZ *(huz) A son of Nabor.*

H his firstborn, and Buz his	Gen 22:21	5780

HUZZAB *(huz'-zab) A region in Assyria.*

H shall be led away captive, she	Nah 2:7	5324

HYMENAEUS *(hy-men-e'-us) A false Christian teacher.*

Of whom is *H* and Alexander	1Ti 1:20	5211
of whom is *H* and Philetus	2Ti 2:17	5211

HYMN

And when they had sung an *h*	Mt 26:30	5214
And when they had sung an *h*	Mk 14:26	

HYMNS

to yourselves in psalms and *h*	Eph 5:19	5215
one another in psalms and *h*	Col 3:16	5215

HYPOCRISIES

all malice, and all guile, and *h*	1Pet 2:1	5272

HYPOCRISY

will work iniquity, to practise *h*	Is 32:6	2612
men, but within ye are full of *h*	Mt 23:28	5272
But he, knowing their *h*, said	Mk 12:15	5272
of the Pharisees, which is *h*	Lk 12:1	5272
Speaking lies in *h*	1Ti 4:2	5272
without partiality, and without *h*	Jas 3:17	505

HYPOCRITE

for an *h* shall not come before	Job 13:16	2611
stir up himself against the *h*	Job 17:8	2611
the joy of the *h* but for a moment	Job 20:5	2611
For what is the hope of the *h*	Job 27:8	2611
That the *h* reign not, lest the	Job 34:30	120,2611
An *h* with his mouth destroyeth	Prov 11:9	2611
for every one is an *h* and an	Is 9:17	2611
Thou *h*, first cast out the beam	Mt 7:5	5275

Thou *h*, cast out first the beam	Lk 6:42	5273
answered him, and said, Thou *h*	Lk 13:15	5273

HYPOCRITE'S
and the *h* hope shall perish	Job 8:13	2611

HYPOCRITES
of *h* shall be desolate, and fire	Job 15:34	2611
But the *h* in heart heap up wrath	Job 36:13	2611
fearfulness hath surprised the *h*	Is 33:14	120,2611
as the *h* do in the synagogues and	Mt 6:2	5273
thou shalt not be as the *h* are	Mt 6:5	5273
when ye fast, be not, as the *h*	Mt 6:16	5273
Ye *h*, well did Esaias prophesy of	Mt 15:7	5273
O ye *h*, ye can discern the face	Mt 16:3	5273
and said, Why tempt ye me, ye *h*	Mt 22:18	5273
unto you, scribes and Pharisees, *h*	Mt 23:13	5273
unto you, scribes and Pharisees, *h*	Mt 23:14	5273
unto you, scribes and Pharisees, *h*	Mt 23:15	5273
unto you, scribes and Pharisees, *h*	Mt 23:23	5273
unto you, scribes and Pharisees, *h*	Mt 23:25	5273
unto you, scribes and Pharisees, *h*	Mt 23:27	5273

unto you, scribes and Pharisees, *h*	Mt 23:29	5273
him his portion with the *h*	Mt 24:51	5273
hath Esaias prophesied of you *h*	Mk 7:6	5273
unto you, scribes and Pharisees, *h*	Lk 11:44	5273
Ye *h*, ye can discern the face of	Lk 12:56	5273

HYPOCRITICAL
With *h* mockers in feasts, they	Ps 35:16	2611
will send him against an *h* nation	Is 10:6	2611

HYSSOP
And ye shall take a bunch of *h*	Ex 12:22	231
and cedar wood, and scarlet, and *h*	Lev 14:4	231
wood, and the scarlet, and the *h*	Lev 14:6	231
and cedar wood, and scarlet, and *h*	Lev 14:49	231
take the cedar wood, and the *h*	Lev 14:51	231
the cedar wood, and with the *h*	Lev 14:52	231
shall take cedar wood, and *h*	Num 19:6	231
And a clean person shall take *h*	Num 19:18	231
is in Lebanon even unto the *h*	1Kin 4:33	231
Purge me with *h*, and I shall be	Ps 51:7	231
with vinegar, and put it upon *h*	Jn 19:29	5301
with water, and scarlet wool, and *h*	Heb 9:19	5301

I

I See APPENDIX.

IBHAR (ib'-har) *A son of David.*
I also, and Elishua, and Nepheg, and	2Sa 5:15	2984
I also, and Elishama, and Eliphelet	1Chr 3:6	2984
And *I*, and Elishua, and Elpalet	1Chr 14:5	2984

IBLEAM (ib'-le-am) *A city in Asher.*
Beth-shean and her towns, and *I*	Josh 17:11	2991
towns, nor the inhabitants of *I*	Judg 1:27	2991
going up to Gur, which is by *I*	2Kin 9:27	2991

IBNEIAH (ib-ne-i'-ah) *A son of Jeroham.*
I the son of Jeroham, and Elah the	1Chr 9:8	2997

IBNIJAH (ib-ni'-jah) *A family of exiles.*
the son of Reuel, the son of *I*	1Chr 9:8	2998

IBRI (ib'-ri) *A descendant of Levi.*
Beno, and Shoham, and Zaccur, and *I*	1Chr 24:27	5681

IBSAM See JIBSAM.

IBZAN (ib'-zan) *A judge of Israel.*
after him *I* of Beth-lehem judged	Judg 12:8	78
Then died *I*, and was buried at	Judg 12:10	78

ICE
are blackish by reason of the *i*	Job 6:16	7140
Out of whose womb came the *i*	Job 38:29	7140
casteth forth his *i* like morsels	Ps 147:17	7140

I-CHABOD (ik'-a-bod) See I-CHABOD'S. *Son of Phinehas.*
And she named the child *I*, saying,	1Sa 4:21	350

ICHABOD See I-CHABOD.

I-CHABOD'S (ik'-a-bods)
I brother, the son of Phinehas	1Sa 14:3	350

ICONIUM (i-co'-ne-um) *A city in Asia Minor.*
feet against them, and came unto *I*	Acts 13:51	2430
And it came to pass in *I*, that	Acts 14:1	2430
certain Jews from Antioch and *I*	Acts 14:19	2430
returned again to Lystra, and *I*	Acts 14:21	2430
brethren that were at Lystra and *I*	Acts 16:2	2430
came unto me at Antioch, at *I*	2Ti 3:11	2430

IDALAH (id'-a-lah) *A town in Zebulun.*
and Nahallal, and Shimron, and *I*	Josh 19:15	3030

IDBASH (id'-bash) *A son of Abi-etam.*
Jezreel, and Ishma, and *I*	1Chr 4:3	3031

IDDO (id'-do)
1. Father of Ahinadab.
the son of *I* had Mahanaim	1Kin 4:14	5714
2. A descendant of Gershom.
I his son, Zerah his son,	1Chr 6:21	5714
3. A son of Zechariah.
in Gilead, *I* the son of Zechariah	1Chr 27:21	3035
4. A seer.
in the visions of *I* the seer	2Chr 9:29	3260
and of *I* the seer concerning	2Chr 12:15	5714
in the story of the prophet *I*	2Chr 13:22	5714
5. An ancestor of Zechariah.
and Zechariah the son of *I*	Ezr 5:1	5714
prophet and Zechariah the son of *I*	Ezr 6:14	5714
the son of *I* the prophet, saying,	Zec 1:1	5714
the son of *I* the prophet, saying,	Zec 1:7	5714

6. A Nethinim chief in exile.
I the chief at the place Casiphia	Ezr 8:17	112
them what they should say unto *I*	Ezr 8:17	112
7. A priest.
I, Ginnetho, Abijah,	Neh 12:4	5714
Of *I*, Zechariah	Neh 12:16	5714

IDLE
for they be *i*	Ex 5:8	7504
he said, Ye are *i*, ye are *i*	Ex 5:17	7504
an *i* soul shall suffer hunger	Prov 19:15	7423
That every *i* word that men shall	Mt 12:36	692
standing *i* in the marketplace	Mt 20:3	692
out, and found others standing *i*	Mt 20:6	692
Why stand ye here all the day *i*	Mt 20:6	692
words seemed to them as *i* tales	Lk 24:11	3026
And withal they learn to be *i*	1Ti 5:13	692
and not only *i*, but tattlers also	1Ti 5:13	692

IDLENESS
and eateth not the bread of *i*	Prov 31:27	6104
through *i* of the hands the house	Eccl 10:18	8220
and abundance of *i* was in her	Eze 16:49	8252

IDOL
she had made an *i* in a grove	1Kin 15:13	4656
and Asa destroyed her *i*, and burnt	1Kin 15:13	4656
she had made an *i* in a grove	2Chr 15:16	4656
and Asa cut down her *i*, and stamped	2Chr 15:16	4656
the *i* which he had made, in the	2Chr 33:7	5566
the *i* out of the house of the	2Chr 33:15	5566
Mine *i* hath done them, and my	Is 48:5	6090
incense, as if he blessed an *i*	Is 66:3	205
man Coniah a despised broken *i*	Jer 22:28	6089
Woe to the *i* shepherd that	Zec 11:17	457
and offered sacrifice unto the *i*	Acts 7:41	1497
we know that an *i* is nothing in	1Cor 8:4	1497
the *i* unto this hour eat it as a	1Cor 8:7	1497
it as a thing offered unto an *i*	1Cor 8:7	1494
that the *i* is any thing, or that	1Cor 10:19	1497

IDOLATER
fornicator, or covetous, or an *i*	1Cor 5:11	1496
nor covetous man, who is an *i*	Eph 5:5	1496

IDOLATERS
or extortioners, or with *i*	1Cor 5:10	1496
neither fornicators, nor *i*	1Cor 6:9	1496
Neither be ye *i*, as were some of	1Cor 10:7	1496
whoremongers, and sorcerers, and *i*	Rev 21:8	1496
whoremongers, and murderers, and *i*	Rev 22:15	1496

IDOLATRIES
banquetings, and abominable *i*	1Pet 4:3	1495

IDOLATROUS
And he put down the *i* priests	2Kin 23:5	3649

IDOLATRY
stubbornness is as iniquity and *i*	1Sa 15:23	8655
he saw the city wholly given to *i*	Acts 17:16	2712
my dearly beloved, flee from *i*	1Cor 10:14	1495
I, witchcraft, hatred, variance,	Gal 5:20	1495
and covetousness, which is *i*	Col 3:5	1495

IDOL'S
sit at meat in the *i* temple	1Cor 8:10	1493

IDOLS

Turn ye not unto *i*, nor make to	Lev 19:4	457
make you no *i* nor graven image	Lev 26:1	457
upon the carcases of your *i*	Lev 26:30	1544
their abominations, and their *i*	Deut 29:17	1544
it in the house of their *i*	1Sa 31:9	6091
removed all the *i* that his	1Kin 15:12	1544
very abominably in following *i*	1Kin 21:26	1544
For they served *i*, whereof the	2Kin 17:12	1544
made Judah also to sin with his *i*	2Kin 21:11	1544
served the *i* that his father	2Kin 21:21	1544
wizards, and the images, and the *i*	2Kin 23:24	1544
to carry tidings unto their *i*	1Chr 10:9	6091
all the gods of the people are *i*	1Chr 16:26	457
put away the abominable *i* out of	2Chr 15:8	8251
fathers, and served groves and *i*	2Chr 24:18	6091
cut down all the *i* throughout all	2Chr 34:7	2553
all the gods of the nations are *i*	Ps 96:5	457
that boast themselves of *i*	Ps 97:7	457
And they served their *i*	Ps 106:36	6091
sacrificed unto the *i* of Canaan	Ps 106:38	6091
Their *i* are silver and gold, the	Ps 115:4	6091
The *i* of the heathen are silver	Ps 135:15	6091
Their land also is full of *i*	Is 2:8	457
the *i* he shall utterly abolish	Is 2:18	457
a man shall cast his *i* of silver	Is 2:20	457
his *i* of gold, which they made	Is 2:20	457
hath found the kingdoms of the *i*	Is 10:10	457
I have done unto Samaria and her *i*	Is 10:11	457
so do to Jerusalem and her *i*	Is 10:11	6091
the *i* of Egypt shall be moved at	Is 19:1	457
and they shall seek to the *i*	Is 19:3	457
shall cast away his *i* of silver	Is 31:7	457
his *i* of gold, which your own	Is 31:7	457
together that are makers of *i*	Is 45:16	6736
their *i* were upon the beasts, and	Is 46:1	6091
with *i* under every green tree	Is 57:5	410
her *i* are confounded, her images	Jer 50:2	6091
and they are mad upon their *i*	Jer 50:38	367
down your slain men before your *i*	Eze 6:4	1544
children of Israel before their *i*	Eze 6:5	1544
your *i* may be broken and cease, and	Eze 6:6	1544
which go a whoring after their *i*	Eze 6:9	1544
their *i* round about their altars	Eze 6:13	1544
offer sweet savour to all their *i*	Eze 6:13	1544
all the *i* of the house of Israel	Eze 8:10	1544
set up their *i* in their heart	Eze 14:3	1544
setteth up his *i* in his heart	Eze 14:4	1544
to the multitude of his *i*	Eze 14:4	1544
estranged from me through their *i*	Eze 14:5	1544
and turn yourselves from your *i*	Eze 14:6	1544
and setteth up his *i* in his heart	Eze 14:7	1544
lovers, and with all the *i* of thy	Eze 16:36	1544
to the *i* of the house of Israel	Eze 18:6	1544
hath lifted up his eyes to the *i*	Eze 18:12	1544
to the *i* of the house of Israel	Eze 18:15	1544
yourselves with the *i* of Egypt	Eze 20:7	1544
did they forsake the *i* of Egypt	Eze 20:8	1544
their heart went after their *i*	Eze 20:16	1544
defile yourselves with their *i*	Eze 20:18	1544
eyes were after their fathers' *i*	Eze 20:24	1544
yourselves with all your *i*	Eze 20:31	1544
Go ye, serve ye every one his *i*	Eze 20:39	1544
with your gifts, and with your *i*	Eze 20:39	1544
maketh against herself to	Eze 22:3	1544
in thine *i* which thou hast made	Eze 22:4	1544
with all their *i* she defiled	Eze 23:7	1544
thou art polluted with their *i*	Eze 23:30	1544
with their *i* have they committed	Eze 23:37	1544
slain their children to their *i*	Eze 23:39	1544
ye shall bear the sins of your *i*	Eze 23:49	1544
I will also destroy the *i*	Eze 30:13	1544
lift up your eyes toward your *i*	Eze 33:25	1544
for their *i* wherewith they had	Eze 36:18	1544
filthiness, and from all your *i*	Eze 36:25	1544
themselves any more with their *i*	Eze 37:23	1544
astray away from me after their *i*	Eze 44:10	1544
unto them before their *i*, and	Eze 44:12	1544
Ephraim is joined to *i*	Hos 4:17	6091
their gold have they made them *i*	Hos 8:4	6091
and *i* according to their own	Hos 13:2	6091
What have I to do any more with *i*	Hos 14:8	6091
all the *i* thereof will I lay	Mic 1:7	6091
trusteth therein, to make dumb *i*	Hab 2:18	457
For the *i* have spoken vanity, and	Zec 10:2	8655
names of the *i* out of the land	Zec 13:2	6091
they abstain from pollutions of *i*	Acts 15:20	1497
abstain from meats offered to *i*	Acts 15:29	1494
from things offered to *i*, and from	Acts 21:25	1494
thou that abhorrest *i*, dost thou	Rom 2:22	1497
as touching things offered unto *i*	1Cor 8:1	1494

are offered in sacrifice unto *i*	1Cor 8:4	1494
things which are offered to *i*	1Cor 8:10	1494
in sacrifice to *i* is any thing	1Cor 10:19	1494
is offered in sacrifice unto *i*	1Cor 10:28	1494
carried away unto these dumb *i*	1Cor 12:2	1497
hath the temple of God with *i*	2Cor 6:16	1497
to God from *i* to serve the living	1Th 1:9	1497
children, keep yourselves from *i*	1Jn 5:21	1497
to eat things sacrificed unto *i*	Rev 2:14	1494
to eat things sacrificed unto *i*	Rev 2:20	1494
i of gold, and silver, and brass,	Rev 9:20	1497

IDUMAEA (i-doo-me'-ah) See IDUMEA. *Greek form of* Edom.

And from Jerusalem, and from *I*	Mk 3:8	2401

IDUMEA (i-doo-me'-ah) See EDOM, IDUMAEA. *Same as* Edom.

behold, it shall come down upon *I*	Is 34:5	123
great slaughter in the land of *I*	Is 34:6	123
desolate, O mount Seir, and all *I*	Eze 35:15	123
of the heathen, and against all *I*	Eze 36:5	123

IEZERITES See JEEZERITES.

IF See APPENDIX.

IGAL (i'-gal) See IGEAL.
    1. One of the twelve spies.

of Issachar, *I* the son of Joseph	Num 13:7	3008

    2. A "mighty man" of David.

I the son of Nathan of Zobah,	2Sa 23:36	3008

IGDALIAH (ig-da-li'-ah) *Father of Hanan.*

the sons of Hanan, the of God	Jer 35:4	3012

IGEAL (ig'-e-al) See IGAL. *A royal descendant of Judah.*

Hattush, and *I*, and Bariah, and	1Chr 3:22	3008

IGNOMINY

also contempt, and with *i* reproach	Prov 18:3	7036

IGNORANCE

If a soul shall sin through *i*	Lev 4:2	7684
of Israel sin through *i*, and the	Lev 4:13	7686
done somewhat through *i* against	Lev 4:22	7684
the common people sin through *i*	Lev 4:27	7684
a trespass, and sin through *i*	Lev 5:15	7684
concerning his *i* wherein he erred	Lev 5:18	7684
if ought be committed by *i*	Num 15:24	7684
for it is *i*	Num 15:25	7684
before the LORD, for their *i*	Num 15:25	7684
seeing all the people were in *i*	Num 15:26	7684
And if any soul sin through *i*	Num 15:27	7684
he sinneth by *i* before the LORD	Num 15:28	7684
for him that sinneth through *i*	Num 15:29	7684
I wot that through *i* ye did it	Acts 3:17	52
the times of this *i* God winked at	Acts 17:30	52
God through the *i* that is in them	Eph 4:18	52
to the former lusts in your *i*	1Pet 1:14	52
to silence the *i* of foolish men	1Pet 2:15	56

IGNORANT

So foolish was I, and *i*	Ps 73:22	3808,3045
they are all *i*, they are all dumb	Is 56:10	3808,3045
father, though Abraham be *i* of us	Is 63:16	3808,3045
and *i* men, they marvelled	Acts 4:13	2399
Now I would not have you *i*	Rom 1:13	50
For they being *i* of God's	Rom 10:3	50
ye should be *i* of this mystery	Rom 11:25	50
I would not that ye should be *i*	1Cor 10:1	50
brethren, I would not have you *i*	1Cor 12:1	50
any man be *i*, let him be *i*	1Cor 14:38	50
have you *i* of our trouble which	2Cor 1:8	50
for we are not *i* of his devices	2Cor 2:11	50
But I would not have you to be *i*	1Th 4:13	50
Who can have compassion on the *i*	Heb 5:2	50
For this they willingly are *i* of	2Pet 3:5	2990
be not *i* of this one thing, that	2Pet 3:8	2990

IGNORANTLY

for the soul that sinneth *i*	Num 15:28	7683
Whoso killeth his neighbour *i*	Deut 19:4	1097,1847
Whom therefore ye *i* worship	Acts 17:23	50
because I did it *i* in unbelief	1Ti 1:13	50

IIM (i'-im) See IJE-ABARIM.
    1. A Hebrew encampment in the wilderness.

And they departed from *I*, and	Num 33:45	5864

    2. A town in Judah.

Baalah, and *I*, and Azem,	Josh 15:29	5864

IJE-ABARIM (i'-je-ab'-a-rim) See IIM. *Same as* Iim 1.

from Oboth, and pitched at *I*	Num 21:11	5863
from Oboth, and pitched in *I*	Num 33:44	5863

IJON (i'-jon) *A town in Naphtali.*
the cities of Israel, and smote I.............1Kin 15:20 5859
king of Assyria, and took I.......................2Kin 15:29 5859
and they smote I, and Dan, and 2Chr 16:4 5859

IKKESH (ik'-kesh) *Father of Ira.*
Ira the son of I the Tekoite 2Sa 23:26 6142
Ira the son of I the Tekoite 1Chr 11:28 6142
was Ira the son of I the Tekoite..............1Chr 27:9 6142

ILAI (i'-lahee) See ZALMON. *A "mighty man" of David.*
the Hushathite, I the Ahohite,.................1Chr 11:29 5866

ILL
i favoured and leanfleshed ....Gen 41:3 7451
the i favoured and leanfleshed ....Gen 41:4 7451
very i favoured and leanfleshed,............Gen 41:19 7451
the i favoured kine did eat up ....Gen 41:20 7451
but they were still i favoured ....Gen 41:21 7451
i favoured kine that came up ....Gen 41:27 7451
Wherefore dealt ye so i with me ....Gen 43:6 7489
or blind, or have any i blemish ....Deut 15:21 7451
it shall go i with him that is....................Job 20:26 3415
so that it went i with Moses for ....Ps 106:32 3415
it shall be i with him............................Is 3:11 7451
but if it seem i unto thee to ....Jer 40:4 7489
his i savour shall come up,.....................Joel 2:20 6709
themselves i in their doings ....Mic 3:4 7489
Love worketh no i to his ....Rom 13:10 2556

ILLUMINATED
days, in which, after ye were i ....Heb 10:32 5461

ILLYRICUM (il-lir'-ic-um) *A Roman Adriatic province.*
Jerusalem, and round about unto I ......Rom 15:19 2437

IMAGE
said, Let us make man in our i ....Gen 1:26 6754
So God created man in his own i..........Gen 1:27 6754
in the i of God created he him ....Gen 1:27 6754
in his own likeness, after his i ....Gen 5:3 6754
for in the i of God made he man ....Gen 9:6 6754
not make unto thee any graven i...........Ex 20:4
make you no idols nor graven i.............Lev 26:1
neither rear you up a standing i ....Lev 26:1 6676
up any i of stone in your land ....Lev 26:1 4906
and make you a graven i, the ....Deut 4:16
with you, and make you a graven i ....Deut 4:23
yourselves, and make a graven i ....Deut 4:25
shalt not make thee any graven i ....Deut 5:8
they have made them a molten i ....Deut 9:12
shalt thou set thee up any i ....Deut 16:22 4676
maketh any graven or molten i..............Deut 27:15
make a graven i and a molten i ....Judg 17:3
a graven i and a molten i ....Judg 17:4
and a graven i, and a molten i ....Judg 18:14
in thither, and took the graven i ....Judg 18:17
and the teraphim, and the molten i ....Judg 18:17
house, and fetched the carved i ....Judg 18:18
and the teraphim, and the molten i ....Judg 18:18
and the teraphim, and the graven i ....Judg 18:20
of Dan set up the graven i ....Judg 18:30
they set them up Micah's graven i ....Judg 18:31
And Michal took an i, and laid it 1Sa 19:13 8655
behold, there was an i in the bed...........1Sa 19:16 8655
for he put away the i of Baal 2Kin 3:2 4676
And they brake down the i of Baal........2Kin 10:27 4676
he set a graven i of the grove 2Kin 21:7
he made two cherubims of i work 2Chr 3:10 6816
And he set a carved i, the idol 2Chr 33:7
an i was before mine eyes, there...........Job 4:16 8544
thou shalt despise their i ....Ps 73:20 6754
Horeb, and worshipped the molten i .....Ps 106:19
The workman melteth a graven i ....Is 40:19
workman to prepare a graven i ....Is 40:20
a graven i are all of them vanity ....Is 44:9
or molten a graven i that is ....Is 44:10
he maketh it a graven i, and..................Is 44:15
maketh a god, even his graven i ....Is 44:17
set up the wood of their graven i ....Is 45:20
hath done them, and my graven i ....Is 48:5
my graven i, and my molten i ....Is 48:5
is confounded by the graven i ....Jer 10:14 6459
for his molten i is falsehood ....Jer 10:14
is confounded by the graven i ....Jer 51:17 6459
for his molten i is falsehood ....Jer 51:17
was the seat of the i of jealousy............Eze 8:3 5566
this i of jealousy in the entry ....Eze 8:5 5566
king, sawest, and behold a great i ....Dan 2:31 6755
This great i, whose brightness...............Dan 2:31 6755
which smote the i upon his feet ....Dan 2:34 6755
the i became a great mountain................Dan 2:35 6755
the king made an i of gold ....Dan 3:1 6755
i which Nebuchadnezzar the king ....Dan 3:2 6755

unto the dedication of the i that ....Dan 3:3 6755
they stood before the i that ....Dan 3:3 6755
worship the golden i that ....Dan 3:5 6755
worshipped the golden i that ....Dan 3:7 6755
fall down and worship the golden i.........Dan 3:10 6755
golden i which thou hast set up ....Dan 3:12 6755
the golden i which I have set up ....Dan 3:14 6755
worship the i which I have made...........Dan 3:15 6755
golden i which thou hast set up ....Dan 3:18 6755
a sacrifice, and without an i ....Hos 3:4 6755
gods will I cut off the graven i ....Nah 1:14
the graven i and the molten i ....Nah 1:14
What profiteth the graven i that ....Hab 2:18
the molten i, and a teacher of ....Hab 2:18
saith unto them, Whose is this i ....Mt 22:20 1504
saith unto them, Whose is this i ....Mk 12:16 1504
Whose i and superscription hath it ....Lk 20:24 1504
of the i which fell down from..................Acts 19:35
an i made like to corruptible man..........Rom 1:23 1504
be conformed to the i of his Son ....Rom 8:29 1504
bowed the knee to the i of Baal ....Rom 11:4
head, forasmuch as he is the i 1Cor 11:7 1504
we have borne the i of the earthy 1Cor 15:49 1504
also bear the i of the heavenly..............1Cor 15:49 1504
the same i from glory to glory 2Cor 3:18 1504
of Christ, who is the i of God 2Cor 4:4 1504
Who is the i of the invisible God ....Col 1:15 1504
the i of him that created him ....Col 3:10 1504
the express i of his person, and ....Heb 1:3 5481
not the very i of the things, can.............Heb 10:1 1504
should make an i to the beast ....Rev 13:14 1504
give life unto the i of the beast ....Rev 13:15 1504
that the i of the beast should ....Rev 13:15 1504
i of the beast should be killed................Rev 13:15 1504
man worship the beast and his i ....Rev 14:9 1504
who worship the beast and his i ....Rev 14:11 1504
over the beast, and over his i ....Rev 15:2 1504
upon them which worshipped his i ....Rev 16:2 1504
and them that worshipped his i ....Rev 19:20 1504
the beast, neither his i, neither ....Rev 20:4 1504

IMAGERY
man in the chambers of his i ....Eze 8:12 4906

IMAGE'S
This i head was of fine gold, his ....Dan 2:32 6755

IMAGES
Rachel had stolen the i that were ....Gen 31:19 8655
Now Rachel had taken the i....................Gen 31:34 8655
he searched, but found not the i.............Gen 31:35 8655
them, and quite break down their i ....Ex 23:24 4676
their altars, break their i ....Ex 34:13 4676
high places, and cut down your i ....Lev 26:30 2553
and destroy all their molten i.................Num 33:52
altars, and break down their i ....Deut 7:5 4676
and burn their graven i with fire ....Deut 7:5
The graven i of their gods shall.............Deut 7:25
down the graven i of their gods ....Deut 12:3
ye shall make i of your emerods............1Sa 6:5 6754
i of your mice that mar the land............1Sa 6:5 6754
of gold and the i of their emerods..........1Sa 6:11 6754
And there they left their i 2Sa 5:21 6091
made thee other gods, and molten i 1Kin 14:9
also built them high places, and i 1Kin 14:23 4676
they brought forth the i out of 2Kin 10:26 4676
his i brake they in pieces.......................2Kin 11:18 6754
And they set them up and groves 2Kin 17:10 4676
their God, and made them molten i 2Kin 17:16
LORD, and served their graven i............2Kin 17:41
the high places, and brake the i 2Kin 18:4 4676
And he brake in pieces the i 2Kin 23:14 4676
spirits, and the wizards, and the 2Kin 23:24 8655
high places, and brake down the i 2Chr 14:3 4676
of Judah the high places and the i 2Chr 14:5
his i in pieces, and slew Mattan 2Chr 23:17 6754
and made also molten i for Baalim 2Chr 28:2
Judah, and brake the i in pieces............2Chr 31:1 4676
and set up groves and graven i 2Chr 33:19
i which Manasseh his father had 2Chr 33:22
carved i, and the molten i 2Chr 34:3
and the i, that were on high above 2Chr 34:4 2553
carved i, and the molten i 2Chr 34:4
beaten the graven i into powder 2Chr 34:7 6456
to jealousy with their graven i ....Ps 78:58 6456
be all they that serve graven i ....Ps 97:7
whose graven i did excel them of ....Is 10:10
made, either the groves, or the i ....Is 17:8 2553
all the graven i of her gods he ....Is 21:9
groves and i shall not stand up ....Is 27:9 2553
of thy graven i of silver.........................Is 30:22
ornament of thy molten i of gold ....Is 30:22

I

their molten *i* are wind and...................Is 41:29
neither my praise to graven *i*..................Is 42:8
ashamed, that trust in graven *i*.............Is 42:17
i, that say to the molten *i*...................Is 42:17
me to anger with their graven *i*.............Jer 8:19
break also the *i* of Beth-shemesh...........Jer 43:13   4676
her *i* are broken in pieces..................Jer 50:2   1544
for it is the land of graven *i*................Jer 50:38
upon the graven *i* of Babylon...............Jer 51:47
do judgment upon her graven *i*.............Jer 51:52
and your *i* shall be broken.................Eze 6:4   2553
your *i* may be cut down, and your.........Eze 6:6   2553
but they made the *i* of them.................Eze 7:20   6754
and madest to thyself *i* of men.............Eze 16:17   6754
bright, he consulted with *i*................Eze 21:21   8655
the *i* of the Chaldeans portrayed........Eze 23:14   6754
I will cause their *i* to cease out..............Eze 30:13   457
his land they have made goodly *i*..........Hos 10:1   4676
altars, he shall spoil their *i*...............Hos 10:2   4676
and burned incense to graven *i*.............Hos 11:2
them molten *i* of their silver...............Hos 13:2
of your Moloch and Chiun your *i*...........Amos 5:26   6754
all the graven *i* thereof shall be..........Mic 1:7
Thy graven *i* also will I cut off,............Mic 5:13   4676
thy standing *i* out of the midst..............Mic 5:13

IMAGINATION
that every *i* of the thoughts of..........Gen 6:5   3336
for the *i* of man's heart is evil.............Gen 8:21   3336
I walk in the *i* of mine heart...............Deut 29:19   8307
for I know their *i* which they go.........Deut 31:21   3336
keep this for ever in the *i* of............1Chr 29:18   3336
after the *i* of their evil heart..............Jer 3:17   8307
in the *i* of their evil heart, and..............Jer 7:24   8307
after the *i* of their own heart...............Jer 9:14   8307
one in the *i* of their evil heart..............Jer 11:8   8307
walk in the *i* of their heart...............Jer 13:10   8307
one after the *i* of his evil heart............Jer 16:12   8307
one do the *i* of his evil heart.............Jer 18:12   8307
after the *i* of his own heart...............Jer 23:17   8307
proud in the *i* of their hearts.............Lk 1:51   1271

IMAGINATIONS
all the *i* of the thoughts..........1Chr 28:9   3336
An heart that deviseth wicked *i*...........Prov 6:18   4284
and all their *i* against me............Lam 3:60   4284
O LORD, and all their *i* against me.......Lam 3:61   4284
but became vain in their *i*...............Rom 1:21   1261
Casting down *i*, and every high.............2Cor 10:5   3053

IMAGINE
Do ye *i* to reprove words, and the..........Job 6:26   2803
which ye wrongfully *i* against me.........Job 21:27   2554
the people *i* a vain thing..................Ps 2:1   1897
i deceits all the day long.................Ps 38:12   1897
How long will ye *i* mischief?...............Ps 62:3   2050
Which *i* mischiefs in their heart.........Ps 140:2   2803
in the heart of them that *i* evil..........Prov 12:20   2790
yet do they *i* mischief against me.........Hos 7:15   2803
What do ye *i* against the LORD..............Nah 1:9   2803
let none of you *i* evil against...............Zec 7:10   2803
let none of you *i* evil in your...............Zec 8:17   2803
rage, and the people *i* vain things.........Acts 4:25   3191

IMAGINED
them, which they have *i* to do.............Gen 11:6   2161
in the devices that they have *i*............Ps 10:2   2803
they *i* a mischievous device,...............Ps 21:11   2803

IMAGINETH
that *i* evil against the LORD, a.............Nah 1:11   2803

IMLA (im'-lah) See IMLAH. *Father of Michaiah.*
the same is Micaiah the son of *I*............2Chr 18:7   3229
quickly Micaiah the son of *I*...............2Chr 18:8   3229

IMLAH (im'-lah) See IMLA. *Same as Imla.*
yet one man, Micaiah the son of *I*..........1Kin 22:8   3229
hither Micaiah the son of *I*................1Kin 22:9   3229

IMMANUEL (im-man'-u-el) See EMMANUEL. *A Messianic name.*
a son, and shall call his name *I*............Is 7:14   6005
fill the breadth of thy land, O *I*...........Is 8:8   6005

IMMEDIATELY
they *i* left the ship and their...............Mt 4:22   2112
i his leprosy was cleansed...............Mt 8:3   2112
i Jesus stretched forth his hand,...........Mt 14:31   2112
i their eyes received sight, and...........Mt 20:34   2112
I after the tribulation of those.............Mt 24:29   2112
And *i* the cock crew..........................Mt 26:74   2112
i the spirit driveth him into the...........Mk 1:12   2117
And *i* his fame spread abroad.............Mk 1:28   2117
i the fever left her, and she...............Mk 1:31   2112

i the leprosy departed from him, ...Mk 1:42   *2112*
i when Jesus perceived in his ....Mk 2:8   *2112*
i he arose, took up the bed, and ....Mk 2:12   *2112*
i* it sprang up, because it had no ....Mk 4:5   *2112*
they have heard, Satan cometh *i* ....Mk 4:15   *2112*
i* receive it with gladness ....Mk 4:16   *2112*
word's sake, *i* they are offended ....Mk 4:17   *2112*
i he putteth in the sickle, ...Mk 4:29   *2112*
i there met him out of the tombs ....Mk 5:2   *2112*
i knowing in himself that virtue ....Mk 5:30   *2112*
i the king sent an executioner, ...Mk 6:27   *2112*
i he talked with them, and saith...........Mk 6:50   *2112*
i he received his sight, and ....Mk 10:52   *2112*
And *i*, while he yet spake, cometh ....Mk 14:43   *2112*
And his mouth was opened *i*................Lk 1:64   *3916*
i she arose and ministered unto ....Lk 4:39   *2112*
i the leprosy departed from him ....Lk 5:13   *2112*
i he rose up before them, and took ....Lk 5:25   *3916*
did beat vehemently, and *i* it fell ....Lk 6:49   *2112*
i her issue of blood stanched ....Lk 8:44   *3916*
him, and how she was healed *i*............Lk 8:47   *3916*
they may open unto him *i* ....Lk 12:36   *2112*
i she was made straight, and............Lk 13:13   *3916*
i he received his sight, and ....Lk 18:43   *3916*
kingdom of God should *i* appear ....Lk 19:11   *3916*
peace, the stones would *i* cry out ....Lk 19:40   *2112*
And *i*, while he yet spake, the...............Lk 22:60   *3916*
i the man was made whole, and took.....Jn 5:9   *2112*
i the ship was at the land...................Jn 6:21   *2112*
received the sop went *i* out ....Jn 13:30   *2112*
and *i* the cock crew ....Jn 18:27   *2112*
forth, and entered into a ship *i* ....Jn 21:3   *2117*
i his feet and ancle bones ....Acts 3:7   *3916*
i there fell from his eyes as it ....Acts 9:18   *2112*
And he arose *i* ....Acts 9:34   *2112*
I therefore I sent to thee ....Acts 10:33   *1824*
i there were three men already............Acts 11:11   *1824*
i the angel of the Lord smote him ....Acts 12:23   *2112*
i there fell on him a mist and a ....Acts 13:11   *3916*
i we endeavoured to go into ....Acts 16:10   *2112*
i all the doors were opened, and...........Acts 16:26   *3916*
the brethren *i* sent away Paul and.........Acts 17:10   *2112*
then *i* the brethren sent away ....Acts 17:14   *2112*
Who *i* took soldiers and centurions........Acts 21:32   *1824*
i I conferred not with flesh and ....Gal 1:16   *2112*
And *i* I was in the spirit....................Rev 4:2   *2112*

IMMER (im'-mur)
1. Father of Meshillemeth.
son of Meshillemith, the son of *I*...........1Chr 9:12   564
The children of *I*, a thousand ....Ezr 2:37   564
And of the sons of *I* ....Ezr 10:20   564
The children of *I*, a thousand ....Neh 7:40   564
son of Meshillemoth, the son of *I*...........Neh 11:13   564
2. A sanctuary servant.
to Bilgah, the sixteenth to *I*...............1Chr 24:14   564
3. An exile.
Tel-harsa, Cherub, Addan, and *I* ....Ezr 2:59   564
Tel-haresha, Cherub, Addon, and *I* ....Neh 7:61   564
4. Father of Zadok.
son of *I* over against his house ....Neh 3:29   564
5. A priest.
Pashur the son of *I* the priest...............Jer 20:1   564

IMMORTAL
Now unto the King eternal, *i*...................1Ti 1:17   862

IMMORTALITY
seek for glory and honour and *i*.............Rom 2:7   861
and this mortal must put on *i* 1Cor 15:53   110
this mortal shall have put on *i*.............1Cor 15:54   110
Who only hath *i*, dwelling in the...........1Ti 6:16   110
i to light through the gospel 2Ti 1:10   861

IMMUTABILITY
of promise the *i* of his counsel ....Heb 6:17   276

IMMUTABLE
That by two *i* things, in which it ....Heb 6:18   276

IMNA (im'-nah) See IMNAH, JIMNA. *A son of Helem.*
Zophah, and *I*, and Shelesh, and Amal... 1Chr 7:35   3234

IMNAH (im'-nah) See IMNA, JIMNAH.
1. Son of Asher.
I, and Isuah, and Ishuai, and Beriah...... 1Chr 7:30   3232
2. Father of Kore.
And Kore the son of *I* the Levite 2Chr 31:14   3232

IMPART
let him *i* to him that hath none...............Lk 3:11   3330
that I may *i* unto you some ....Rom 1:11   3330

IMPARTED
wisdom, neither hath he *i* to her ....Job 39:17   2505
were willing to have *i* unto you 1Th 2:8   3330

IMPEDIMENT
deaf, and had an *i* in his speech............ Mk 7:32 — 3424

IMPENITENT
i heart treasurest up unto..................... Rom 2:5 — 279

IMPERIOUS
the work of an *i* whorish woman .... Eze 16:30 — 7986

IMPLACABLE
without natural affection, *i* .... Rom 1:31 — 786

IMPLEAD
let them *i* one another .... Acts 19:38 — 1458

IMPORTUNITY
yet because of his *i* he will rise............. Lk 11:8 — 335

IMPOSE
it shall not be lawful to *i* toll .... Ezr 7:24 — 7412

IMPOSED
i on them until the time of..................... Heb 9:10 — 1942

IMPOSSIBLE
and nothing shall be *i* unto you........... Mt 17:20 — 101
unto them, With men this is *i*............... Mt 19:26 — 102
upon them saith, With men it is *i*........ Mk 10:27 — 102
For with God nothing shall be *i*............. Lk 1:37 — 101
It is *i* but that offences will............... Lk 17:1 — 418
The things which are *i* with men .... Lk 18:27 — 102
For it is *i* for those who were................. Heb 6:4 — 102
in which it was *i* for God to lie............... Heb 6:18 — 102
faith it is *i* to please him........................ Heb 11:6 — 102

IMPOTENT
lay a great multitude of *i* folk................ Jn 5:3 — 770
The *i* man answered him, Sir, I............... Jn 5:7 — 770
the good deed done to the *i* man .... Acts 4:9 — 772
i in his feet, being a cripple.................... Acts 14:8 — 102

IMPOVERISH
they shall *i* thy fenced cities,................ Jer 5:17 — 7567

IMPOVERISHED
Israel was greatly *i* because of .... Judg 6:6 — 1809
He that is so *i* that he hath no............... Is 40:20 — 5533
Whereas Edom saith, We are *i*.............. Mal 1:4 — 7567

IMPRISONED
I said, Lord, they know that I *i* .... Acts 22:19 — 5439

IMPRISONMENT
to confiscation of goods, or to *i*............. Ezr 7:26 — 613
yea, moreover of bonds and *i* .... Heb 11:36 — 5438

IMPRISONMENTS
In stripes, in *i*, in tumults, in.................. 2Cor 6:5 — 5438

IMPUDENT
with an *i* face said unto him, ... Prov 7:13 — 5810
For they are *i* children and............. Eze 2:4 — 7186,6440
for all the house of Israel are *i* .... Eze 3:7 — 2389,4696

IMPUTE
let not the king *i* any thing unto........... 1Sa 22:15 — 7760
Let not my lord *i* iniquity unto............... 2Sa 19:19 — 2803
to whom the Lord will not *i* sin............. Rom 4:8 — 3049

IMPUTED
neither shall it be *i* unto him.................. Lev 7:18 — 2803
blood shall be *i* unto that man .... Lev 17:4 — 2803
might be *i* unto them also .... Rom 4:11 — 3049
therefore it was *i* to him.......................... Rom 4:22 — 3049
sake alone, that it was *i* to him.............. Rom 4:23 — 3049
us also, to whom it shall be *i* .... Rom 4:24 — 3049
but sin is not *i* when there is no............. Rom 5:13 — 1677
God, and it was *i* unto him for............... Jas 2:23 — 3049

IMPUTETH
unto whom the Lord *i* not iniquity .... Ps 32:2 — 2803
unto whom God *i* righteousness .... Rom 4:6 — 3049

IMPUTING
i this his power unto his god.................. Hab 1:11
not *i* their trespasses unto them............ 2Cor 5:19 — 3049

IMRAH *(im'-rah)* A chief of Asher.
and Shual, and Beri, and I, ... 1Chr 7:36 — 3236

IMRI *(im'-ri)*
1. Son of Bani.
the son of Omri, the son of I .... 1Chr 9:4 — 556
2. Father of Zaccur.
them builded Zaccur the son of I........... Neh 3:2 — 556

IN See APPENDIX.

INASMUCH See APPENDIX.

INCENSE
for anointing oil, and for sweet *i* .... Ex 25:6 — 7004
make an altar to burn *i* upon .... Ex 30:1 — 7004

thereon sweet *i* every morning................ Ex 30:7 — 7004
lamps, he shall burn *i* upon it .... Ex 30:7
at even, he shall burn *i* upon it .... Ex 30:8 — 6999
a perpetual *i* before the Lord .... Ex 30:8 — 7004
shall offer no strange *i* thereon.............. Ex 30:9 — 7004
and his vessels, and the altar of *i*.......... Ex 30:27 — 7004
his furniture, and the altar of *i* .... Ex 31:8 — 7004
sweet *i* for the holy place .... Ex 31:11 — 7004
anointing oil, and for the sweet *i* .... Ex 35:8 — 7004
the *i* altar, and his staves, and .... Ex 35:15 — 7004
the anointing oil, and the sweet *i* .... Ex 35:15 — 7004
anointing oil, and for the sweet *i* .... Ex 35:28 — 7004
he made the *i* altar of shittim .... Ex 37:25 — 7004
the pure *i* of sweet spices, ... Ex 37:29 — 7004
the anointing oil, and the sweet *i* .... Ex 39:38 — 7004
set the altar of gold for the *i* .... Ex 40:5 — 7004
And he burnt sweet *i* thereon................. Ex 40:27 — 7004
altar of sweet *i* before the Lord .... Lev 4:7 — 7004
put *i* thereon, and offered strange .... Lev 10:1 — 7004
full of sweet *i* beaten small .... Lev 16:12 — 7004
he shall put the *i* upon the fire .... Lev 16:13 — 7004
that the cloud of the *i* may cover .... Lev 16:13 — 7004
oil for the light, and the sweet *i* .... Num 4:16 — 7004
of ten shekels of gold, full of *i* .... Num 7:14 — 7004
of gold of ten shekels, full of *i* .... Num 7:20 — 7004
spoon of ten shekels, full of *i*................. Num 7:26 — 7004
spoon of ten shekels, full of *i*................. Num 7:32 — 7004
spoon of ten shekels, full of *i*................. Num 7:38 — 7004
spoon of ten shekels, full of *i*................. Num 7:44 — 7004
spoon of ten shekels, full of *i*................. Num 7:50 — 7004
spoon of ten shekels, full of *i*................. Num 7:56 — 7004
spoon of ten shekels, full of *i*................. Num 7:62 — 7004
spoon of ten shekels, full of *i*................. Num 7:68 — 7004
spoon of ten shekels, full of *i*................. Num 7:74 — 7004
spoon of ten shekels, full of *i*................. Num 7:80 — 7004
spoons were twelve, full of *i* .... Num 7:86 — 7004
put *i* in them before the Lord to............. Num 16:7 — 7004
put *i* in them, and bring ye before......... Num 16:17 — 7004
laid *i* thereon, and stood in the .... Num 16:18 — 7004
and fifty men that offered *i* .... Num 16:35 — 7004
near to offer *i* before the Lord .... Num 16:40 — 7004
from off the altar, and put on *i*.............. Num 16:46 — 7004
and he put on *i*, and made an................ Num 16:47 — 7004
they shall put *i* before thee .... Deut 33:10 — 7004
offer upon mine altar, to burn *i* .... 1Sa 2:28 — 7004
and burnt *i* in high places .... 1Kin 3:3 — 6999
he burnt *i* upon the altar that .... 1Kin 9:25 — 6999
his strange wives, which burnt *i*............. 1Kin 11:8 — 6999
upon the altar, and burnt *i* .... 1Kin 12:33 — 6999
stood by the altar to burn *i* .... 1Kin 13:1 — 6999
high places that burn *i* upon thee .... 1Kin 13:2 — 6999
burnt *i* yet in the high places................. 1Kin 22:43 — 6999
burnt *i* in the high places .... 2Kin 12:3 — 6999
burnt *i* on the high places .... 2Kin 14:4 — 6999
burnt *i* still on the high places .... 2Kin 15:4 — 6999
burned *i* still in the high places .... 2Kin 15:35 — 6999
burnt *i* in the high places, and on .... 2Kin 16:4 — 6999
there they burnt *i* in all the................... 2Kin 17:11 — 6999
of Israel did burn *i* to it .... 2Kin 18:4 — 6999
have burned *i* unto other gods,.............. 2Kin 22:17 — 6999
burn *i* in the high places in the .... 2Kin 23:5 — 6999
them also that burned *i* unto Baal .... 2Kin 23:5 — 6999
where the priests had burned *i*............... 2Kin 23:8 — 6999
offering, and on the altar of *i* .... 1Chr 6:49 — 7004
to burn *i* before the Lord, to .... 1Chr 23:13 — 6999
for the altar of *i* refined gold .... 1Chr 28:18 — 7004
and to burn before him sweet *i* .... 2Chr 2:4 — 7004
burnt sacrifices and sweet *i* .... 2Chr 13:11 — 7004
them, and burned *i* unto them .... 2Chr 25:14 — 6999
burn *i* upon the altar of *i*...................... 2Chr 26:16 — 6999
to burn *i* unto the Lord, but to .... 2Chr 26:18 — 6999
that are consecrated to burn *i* .... 2Chr 26:18 — 6999
a censer in his hand to burn *i* .... 2Chr 26:19 — 6999
the Lord, from beside the *i* altar .... 2Chr 26:19 — 7004
Moreover he burnt *i* in the valley .... 2Chr 28:3 — 6999
burnt *i* in the high places, and on .... 2Chr 28:4 — 6999
places to burn *i* unto other gods........... 2Chr 28:25 — 6999
have not burned *i* nor offered .... 2Chr 29:7 — 7004
minister unto him, and burn *i*................. 2Chr 29:11 — 6999
the altars for *i* took they away .... 2Chr 30:14 — 6999
one altar, and burn *i* upon it .... 2Chr 32:12 — 6999
have burned *i* unto other gods,.............. 2Chr 34:25 — 6999
of fatlings, with the *i* of rams .... Ps 66:15 — 7004
be set forth before thee as *i* .... Ps 141:2 — 7004
i is an abomination unto me .... Is 1:13 — 7004
offering, nor wearied thee with *i*............. Is 43:23 — 3828
they shall bring gold and *i* .... Is 60:6 — 3828
burneth *i* upon altars of brick .... Is 65:3 — 6999
which have burned *i* upon the .... Is 65:7 — 6999
he that burneth *i*, as if he .... Is 66:3 — 3828
have burned *i* unto other gods, and ...... Jer 1:16 — 6999

cometh there to me *i* from Sheba	Jer 6:20	3828
burn *i* unto Baal, and walk after	Jer 7:9	6999
the gods unto whom they offer *i*	Jer 11:12	6999
even altars to burn *i* unto Baal	Jer 11:13	6999
to anger in offering *i* unto Baal	Jer 11:17	6999
and meat offerings, and, *i*, and	Jer 17:26	3828
me, they have burned *i* to vanity	Jer 18:15	6999
have burned *i* in it unto other	Jer 19:4	6999
i unto all the host of heaven	Jer 19:13	6999
they have offered *i* unto Baal	Jer 32:29	6999
i in their hand, to bring them to	Jer 41:5	3828
in that they went to burn *i*	Jer 44:3	6999
to burn no *i* unto other gods	Jer 44:5	6999
burning *i* unto other gods in the	Jer 44:8	6999
had burned *i* unto other gods	Jer 44:15	6999
to burn *i* unto the queen of	Jer 44:17	6999
to burn *i* to the queen of heaven	Jer 44:18	6999
when we burned *i* to the queen of	Jer 44:19	6999
The *i* that ye burned in the	Jer 44:21	7002
Because ye have burned *i*, and	Jer 44:23	6999
to burn *i* to the queen of heaven,	Jer 44:25	6999
and him that burneth *i* to his gods	Jer 48:35	6999
and a thick cloud of *i* went up	Eze 8:11	7004
mine oil and mine *i* before them	Eze 16:18	7004
whereupon thou hast set mine *i*	Eze 23:41	7004
wherein she burned *i* to them	Hos 2:13	6999
burn *i* upon the hills, under oaks	Hos 4:13	6999
burned *i* to graven images	Hos 11:2	6999
net, and burn *i* unto their drag	Hab 1:16	6999
in every place *i* shall be offered	Mal 1:11	6999
his lot was to burn *i* when he	Lk 1:9	2370
praying without at the time of *i*	Lk 1:10	2368
the right side of the altar of *i*	Lk 1:11	2368
there was given unto him much *i*	Rev 8:3	2368
And the smoke of the *i*, which came	Rev 8:4	2368

INCENSED

all they that were *i* against thee	Is 41:11	2734
all that are *i* against him shall	Is 45:24	2734

INCLINE

i your heart unto the Lord God of	Josh 24:23	5186
That he may *i* our hearts unto him	1Kin 8:58	5186
i thine ear unto me, and hear my	Ps 17:6	5186
and consider, and *i* thine ear	Ps 45:10	5186
I will *i* mine ear to a parable	Ps 49:4	5186
i thine ear unto me, and save me	Ps 71:2	5186
i your ears to the words of my	Ps 78:1	5186
i thine ear unto my cry	Ps 88:2	5186
i thine ear unto me	Ps 102:2	5186
I my heart unto thy testimonies,	Ps 119:36	5186
I not my heart to any evil thing,	Ps 141:4	5186
So that thou *i* thine ear unto	Prov 2:2	7181
i thine ear unto my sayings	Prov 4:20	5186
I thine ear, O Lord, and hear	Is 37:17	5186
I your ear, and come unto me	Is 55:3	5186
O my God, *i* thine ear, and hear	Dan 9:18	5186

INCLINED

and their hearts *i* to follow	Judg 9:3	5186
he *i* unto me, and heard my cry	Ps 40:1	5186
Because he hath *i* his ear unto me	Ps 116:2	5186
I have *i* mine heart to perform	Ps 119:112	5186
nor *i* mine ear to them that	Prov 5:13	5186
nor *i* their ear, but walked in	Jer 7:24	5186
nor *i* their ear, but hardened	Jer 7:26	5186
nor *i* their ear, but walked every	Jer 11:8	5186
neither *i* their ear, but made	Jer 17:23	5186
hearkened, nor *i* your ear to hear	Jer 25:4	5186
not unto me, neither *i* their ear	Jer 34:14	5186
but ye have not *i* your ear	Jer 35:15	5186
nor *i* their ear to turn from	Jer 44:5	5186

INCLINETH

For her house *i* unto death	Prov 2:18	7743

INCLOSE

we will *i* her with boards of	Song 8:9	6696

INCLOSED

onyx stones *i* in ouches of gold	Ex 39:6	4142
they were *i* in ouches of gold in	Ex 39:13	4142
Thus they *i* the Benjamites round	Judg 20:43	3803
They are *i* in their own fat	Ps 17:10	5462
assembly of the wicked have *i* me	Ps 22:16	5362
A garden *i* is my sister, my	Song 4:12	5274
He hath *i* my ways with hewn stone	Lam 3:9	1443
they *i* a great multitude of	Lk 5:6	4788

INCLOSINGS

shall be set in gold in their *i*	Ex 28:20	4396
in ouches of gold in their *i*	Ex 39:13	4396

INCONTINENCY

Satan tempt you not for your *i*	1Cor 7:5	192

INCONTINENT

trucebreakers, false accusers, *i*	2Ti 3:3	193

INCORRUPTIBLE

but we an *i*	1Cor 9:25	862
and the dead shall be raised *i*	1Cor 15:52	862
To an inheritance *i*, and undefiled	1Pet 1:4	862
not of corruptible seed, but of *i*	1Pet 1:23	862

INCORRUPTION

it is raised in *i*	1Cor 15:42	861
neither doth corruption inherit *i*	1Cor 15:50	861
this corruptible must put on *i*	1Cor 15:53	861
corruptible shall have put on *i*	1Cor 15:54	861

INCREASE

And it shall come to pass in the *i*	Gen 47:24	8393
may yield unto you the *i* thereof	Lev 19:25	8393
shall all the *i* thereof be meat	Lev 25:7	8393
ye shall eat the *i* thereof out of	Lev 25:12	8393
thou shalt *i* the price thereof	Lev 25:16	7235
not sow, nor gather in our *i*	Lev 25:20	8393
Take thou no usury of him, or *i*	Lev 25:36	8635
nor lend him thy victuals for *i*	Lev 25:37	4768
and the land shall yield her *i*	Lev 26:4	2981
your land shall not yield her *i*	Lev 26:20	2981
as the *i* of the threshingfloor	Num 18:30	8393
as the *i* of the winepress	Num 18:30	8393
an *i* of sinful men, to augment	Num 32:14	8635
thee, and that ye may *i* mightily	Deut 6:3	7235
the *i* of thy kine, and the flocks	Deut 7:13	7698
beasts of the field *i* upon thee	Deut 7:22	7235
truly tithe all the *i* of thy seed	Deut 14:22	8393
tithe of thine *i* the same year	Deut 14:28	8393
shall bless thee in all thine *i*	Deut 16:15	8393
tithes of thine *i* the third year	Deut 26:12	8393
the *i* of thy kine, and the flocks	Deut 28:4	7698
the *i* of thy kine, and the flocks	Deut 28:18	7698
or the *i* of thy kine, or flocks	Deut 28:51	7698
he might eat the *i* of the fields	Deut 32:13	8570
consume the earth with her *i*	Deut 32:22	2981
and destroyed the *i* of the earth	Judg 6:4	2981
I thine army, and come out	Judg 9:29	7235
all the *i* of thine house shall	1Sa 2:33	4768
the Lord had said he would *i*	1Chr 27:23	7235
over the *i* of the vineyards for	1Chr 27:27	
of all the *i* of the field	2Chr 31:5	8393
also for the *i* of corn, and wine,	2Chr 32:28	8393
to *i* the trespass of Israel	Ezr 10:10	3254
it yieldeth much *i* unto the kings	Neh 9:37	8393
thy latter end should greatly *i*	Job 8:7	7685
The *i* of his house shall depart,	Job 20:28	2981
and would root out all mine *i*	Job 31:12	8393
dost not *i* thy wealth by their	Ps 44:12	7235
if riches *i*, set not your heart	Ps 62:10	5107
Then shall the earth yield her *i*	Ps 67:6	2981
Thou shalt *i* my greatness, and	Ps 71:21	7235
they *i* in riches	Ps 73:12	7685
He gave also their *i* unto the	Ps 78:46	2981
and our land shall yield her *i*	Ps 85:12	2981
which may yield fruits of *i*	Ps 107:37	8393
The Lord shall *i* you more	Ps 115:14	3254
man will hear, and will *i* learning	Prov 1:5	3254
the firstfruits of all thine *i*	Prov 3:9	8393
man, and he will *i* in learning	Prov 9:9	3254
that gathereth by labour shall *i*	Prov 13:11	7235
but much *i* is by the strength of	Prov 14:4	8393
with the *i* of his lips shall he	Prov 18:20	8393
the poor to *i* his riches, and he	Prov 22:16	7235
when they perish, the righteous *i*	Prov 28:28	7235
he that loveth abundance with *i*	Eccl 5:10	8393
When goods *i*, they are increased	Eccl 5:11	7235
be many things that *i* vanity	Eccl 6:11	7235
Of the *i* of his government and	Is 9:7	4768
The meek also shall *i* their joy	Is 29:19	3254
and bread of the *i* of the earth	Is 30:23	8393
didst *i* thy perfumes, and didst	Is 57:9	7235
Lord, and the firstfruits of his *i*	Jer 2:3	8393
and they shall be fruitful and *i*	Jer 23:3	7235
I will *i* the famine upon you, and	Eze 5:16	3254
usury, neither hath taken any *i*	Eze 18:8	8635
forth upon usury, and hath taken *i*	Eze 18:13	8635
hath not received usury nor *i*	Eze 18:17	8635
thou hast taken usury and *i*	Eze 22:12	8635
and the earth shall yield her *i*	Eze 34:27	2981
and they shall *i* and bring fruit.	Eze 36:11	7235
call for the corn, and will *i* it	Eze 36:29	7235
the *i* of the field, that ye shall	Eze 36:30	8570
I will *i* them with men like a	Eze 36:37	7235
the *i* thereof shall be for food	Eze 48:18	8393
shall acknowledge and *i* with glory	Dan 11:39	7235
commit whoredom, and shall not *i*	Hos 4:10	6555

and the ground shall give her *i* .... Zec 8:12 — 2981
they shall *i* as they have .... Zec 10:8 — 7235
said unto the Lord, *I* our faith .... Lk 17:5 — 4369
He must *i*, but I must decrease .... Jn 3:30 — 837
but God gave the *i* .... 1Cor 3:6 — 837
but God that giveth the *i* .... 1Cor 3:7 — 837
sown, and *i* the fruits of your .... 2Cor 9:10 — 837
maketh *i* of the body unto the .... Eph 4:16 — 838
increaseth with the *i* of God .... Col 2:19 — 838
And the Lord make you to *i* .... 1Th 3:12 — 4121
you, brethren, that ye *i* more .... 1Th 4:10 — 4052
for they will *i* unto more .... 2Ti 2:16 — 4298

INCREASED
and the waters *i*, and bare up the .... Gen 7:17 — 7235
were *i* greatly upon the earth .... Gen 7:18 — 7235
it is now *i* unto a multitude .... Gen 30:30 — 6555
the man *i* exceedingly, and had .... Gen 30:43 — 6555
i abundantly, and multiplied, and .... Ex 1:7 — 8317
from before thee, until thou be *i* .... Ex 23:30 — 6509
of the Philistines went on and *i* .... 1Sa 14:19 — 7227
for the people *i* continually with .... 2Sa 15:12 — 7227
And the battle *i* that day .... 1Kin 22:35 — 5927
house of their fathers *i* greatly .... 1Chr 4:38 — 6555
they *i* from Bashan unto .... 1Chr 5:23 — 7235
And the battle *i* that day .... 2Chr 18:34 — 5927
iniquities are *i* over our head .... Ezr 9:6 — 7235
and his substance is *i* in the land .... Job 1:10 — 6555
how are they that trouble me .... Ps 3:1 — 7231
that their corn and their wine *i* .... Ps 4:7 — 7231
when the glory of his house is *i* .... Ps 49:16 — 7235
And he *i* his people greatly .... Ps 105:24 — 6509
the years of thy life shall be *i* .... Prov 9:11 — 3254
i more than all that were before .... Eccl 2:9 — 3254
they are *i* that eat them .... Eccl 5:11 — 7231
the nation, and not *i* the joy .... Is 9:3 — 1431
Thou hast *i* the nation, O Lord, ... Is 26:15 — 3254
thou hast *i* the nation .... Is 26:15 — 3254
alone, and blessed him, and *i* him .... Is 51:2 — 7235
i in the land, in those days, ... Jer 3:16 — 6509
many, and their backslidings are *i* .... Jer 5:6 — 6105
Their widows are *i* to me above .... Jer 15:8 — 6105
that ye may be *i* there, and not .... Jer 29:6 — 7235
because thy sins were *i* .... Jer 30:14 — 6105
because thy sins were *i*, I have .... Jer 30:15 — 6105
hath *i* in the daughter of Judah .... Lam 2:5 — 7235
bud of the field, and thou hast *i* .... Eze 16:7 — 7235
hast *i* thy whoredoms, to provoke .... Eze 16:26 — 7235
And that she *i* her whoredoms .... Eze 23:14 — 3254
traffick hast thou *i* thy riches .... Eze 28:5 — 7235
so *i* from the lowest chamber to .... Eze 41:7 — 5927
and fro, and knowledge shall be *i* .... Dan 12:4 — 7235
As they were *i*, so they sinned .... Hos 4:7 — 7230
of his fruit he hath *i* the altars .... Hos 10:1 — 7235
fig trees and your olive trees *i* .... Amos 4:9 — 7235
shall increase as they have *i* .... Zec 10:8 — 7235
yield fruit that sprang up and *i* .... Mk 4:8 — 837
Jesus *i* in wisdom and stature, and ...... Lk 2:52 — 4298
And the word of God *i* .... Acts 6:7 — 837
But Saul *i* the more in strength, ... Acts 9:22 — 1743
the faith, and *i* in number daily .... Acts 16:5 — 4052
having hope, when your faith is *i* .... 2Cor 10:15 — 837
i* with goods, and have need of .... Rev 3:17 — 4147

INCREASEST
i thine indignation upon me .... Job 10:17 — 7235

INCREASETH
For it *i*. Thou huntest me .... Job 10:16 — 1342
He *i* the nations, and destroyeth .... Job 12:23 — 7679
up against thee *i* continually .... Ps 74:23 — 5927
is that scattereth, and yet *i* .... Prov 11:24 — 3254
sweetness of the lips *i* learning .... Prov 16:21 — 3254
i the transgressors among men .... Prov 23:28 — 3254
a man of knowledge *i* strength .... Prov 24:5 — 553
unjust gain *i* his substance, he .... Prov 28:8 — 7235
are multiplied, transgression *i* .... Prov 29:16 — 7235
he that *i* knowledge *i* sorrow .... Eccl 1:18 — 3254
that have no might he *i* strength .... Is 40:29 — 7235
he daily *i* lies and desolation. .... Hos 12:1 — 7235
Woe to him that *i* that which is .... Hab 2:6 — 7235
i with the increase of God .... Col 2:19 — 837

INCREASING
i in the knowledge of God .... Col 1:10 — 837

INCREDIBLE
it be thought a thing *i* with you .... Acts 26:8 — 571

INCURABLE
in his bowels with an *i* disease .... 2Chr 21:18 — 369,4832
my wound is *i* without .... Job 34:6 — 605
my pain perpetual, and my wound *i* ...... Jer 15:18 — 605
saith the Lord, Thy bruise is *i* .... Jer 30:12 — 605

thy sorrow is *i* for the multitude .... Jer 30:15 — 605
For her wound is *i* .... Mic 1:9 — 605

INDEBTED
forgive every one that is *i* to us .... Lk 11:4 — 3784

INDEED See APPENDIX.

INDIA *(in'-de-ah) Eastern boundary of the Persian Empire.*
reigned from *I* even unto Ethiopia .... Est 1:1 — 1912
which are from *I* unto Ethiopia .... Est 8:9 — 1912

INDIGNATION
anger, and in wrath, and in great *i* .... Deut 29:28 — 7110
there was great *i* against Israel .... 2Kin 3:27 — 7110
he was wroth, and took great *i* .... Neh 4:1 — 3707
he was full of *i* against Mordecai .... Est 5:9 — 2534
me, and increasest thine *i* upon me ...... Job 10:17 — 3708
Pour out thine *i* upon them .... Ps 69:24 — 2195
of his anger, wrath, and *i* .... Ps 78:49 — 2195
Because of thine *i* and thy wrath .... Ps 102:10 — 2195
the staff in their hand is mine *i* .... Is 10:5 — 2195
the *i* shall cease, and mine anger .... Is 10:25 — 2195
the Lord, and the weapons of his *i* .... Is 13:5 — 2195
moment, until the *i* be overpast .... Is 26:20 — 2195
his lips are full of *i*, and his .... Is 30:27 — 2195
with the *i* of his anger, and with .... Is 30:30 — 2197
For the *i* of the Lord is upon all .... Is 34:2 — 7110
and his *i* toward his enemies .... Is 66:14 — 2194
shall not be able to abide his *i* .... Jer 10:10 — 2195
for thou hast filled me with *i* .... Jer 15:17 — 2195
forth the weapons of his *i* .... Jer 50:25 — 2195
hath despised in the *i* of his .... Lam 2:6 — 2195
I will pour out mine *i* upon thee .... Eze 21:31 — 2195
nor rained upon in the day of *i* .... Eze 22:24 — 2195
I poured out mine *i* upon them .... Eze 22:31 — 2195
shall be in the last end of the *i* .... Dan 8:19 — 2195
have *i* against the holy covenant .... Dan 11:30 — 2194
till the *i* be accomplished .... Dan 11:36 — 2195
I will bear the *i* of the Lord .... Mic 7:9 — 2197
Who can stand before his *i* .... Nah 1:6 — 2195
didst march through the land in *i* .... Hab 3:12 — 2195
to pour upon them mine *i* .... Zeph 3:8 — 2195
thou hast had *i* these threescore .... Zec 1:12 — 2194
whom the Lord hath *i* for ever .... Mal 1:4 — 2194
they were moved with *i* against .... Mt 20:24 — 23
his disciples saw it, they had *i* .... Mt 26:8 — 23
some that had *i* within themselves .... Mk 14:4 — 23
of the synagogue answered with *i* .... Lk 13:14 — 23
Sadducees,) and were filled with *i* .... Acts 5:17 — 2205
but obey unrighteousness, *i* .... Rom 2:8 — 2372
of yourselves, yea, what *i* .... 2Cor 7:11 — 24
for of judgment and fiery *i* .... Heb 10:27 — 2205
mixture into the cup of his *i* .... Rev 14:10 — 3709

INDITING
My heart is *i* a good matter .... Ps 45:1 — 7370

INDUSTRIOUS
the young man that he was *i* .... 1Kin 11:28 — 6213,4399

INEXCUSABLE
Therefore thou art *i*, O man, ... Rom 2:1 — 379

INFALLIBLE
his passion by many *i* proofs .... Acts 1:3

INFAMOUS
shall mock thee, which art *i* .... Eze 22:5 — 2931,8034

INFAMY
shame, and thine *i* turn not away .... Prov 25:10 — 1681
and are an *i* of the people .... Eze 36:3 — 1681

INFANT
but slay both man and woman, *i* .... 1Sa 15:3 — 5768
be no more thence an *i* of days .... Is 65:20 — 5764

INFANTS
as *i* which never saw light .... Job 3:16 — 5768
their *i* shall be dashed in pieces .... Hos 13:16 — 5768
And they brought unto him also *i* .... Lk 18:15 — 1025

INFERIOR
I am not *i* to you .... Job 12:3 — 5307
I am not *i* unto you .... Job 13:2 — 5307
arise another kingdom *i* to thee .... Dan 2:39 — 772
ye were *i* to other churches .... 2Cor 12:13 — 2274

INFIDEL
hath he that believeth with an *i* .... 2Cor 6:15 — 571
the faith, and is worse than an *i* .... 1Ti 5:8 — 571

INFINITE
and thine iniquities *i* .... Job 22:5 — 369,7093
his understanding is *i* .... Ps 147:5 — 369,4557
were her strength, and it was *i* .... Nah 3:9 — 369,7093

INFIRMITIES

saying, Himself took our *i*	Mt 8:17	769
and to be healed by him of their *i*	Lk 5:15	769
hour he cured many of their *i*	Lk 7:21	3554
been healed of evil spirits and *i*	Lk 8:2	769
the Spirit also helpeth our *i*	Rom 8:26	769
ought to bear the *i* of the weak	Rom 15:1	771
the things which concern mine *i*	2Cor 11:30	769
I will not glory, but in mine *i*	2Cor 12:5	769
will I rather glory in my *i*	2Cor 12:9	769
Therefore I take pleasure in *i*	2Cor 12:10	769
stomach's sake and thine often *i*	1Ti 5:23	769
touched with the feeling of our *i*	Heb 4:15	769

INFIRMITY

for her *i* shall she be unclean	Lev 12:2	1738
And I said, This is my *i*	Ps 77:10	2470
of a man will sustain his *i*	Prov 18:14	4245
had a spirit of *i* eighteen years	Lk 13:11	769
thou art loosed from thine *i*	Lk 13:12	769
was there, which had an *i* thirty	Jn 5:5	769
because of the *i* of your flesh	Rom 6:19	769
Ye know how through *i* of the	Gal 4:13	769
himself also is compassed with *i*	Heb 5:2	769
men high priests which have *i*	Heb 7:28	769

INFLAME

until night, till wine *i* them	Is 5:11	1814

INFLAMMATION

for it is an *i* of the burning	Lev 13:28	6867
and with a fever, and with an *i*	Deut 28:22	1816

INFLICTED

punishment, which was *i* of many	2Cor 2:6	

INFLUENCES

thou bind the sweet *i* of Pleiades	Job 38:31	4575

INFOLDING

a great cloud, and a fire *i* itself	Eze 1:4	3947

INFORM

according to all that they *i* thee	Deut 17:10	3384

INFORMED

And he *i* me, and talked with me, and	Dan 9:22	995
And they are *i* of thee, that thou	Acts 21:21	2727
they were *i* concerning thee	Acts 21:24	2727
who the governor against Paul	Acts 24:1	1718
of the Jews *i* him against Paul	Acts 25:2	1718
and the elders of the Jews *i* me	Acts 25:15	1718

INGATHERING

and the feast of *i*, which is in	Ex 23:16	614
the feast of *i* at the year's end	Ex 34:22	614

INHABIT

the land which ye shall *i*	Num 35:34	3427
the wicked shall not *i* the earth	Prov 10:30	7931
the villages that Kedar doth *i*	Is 42:11	3427
shall build houses, and *i* them	Is 65:21	3427
shall not build, and another *i*	Is 65:22	3427
but shall *i* the parched places in	Jer 17:6	7931
Thou daughter that dost *i* Dibon	Jer 48:18	3427
they that *i* those wastes of the	Eze 33:24	3427
build the waste cities, and *i* them	Amos 9:14	3427
also build houses, but not *i* them	Zeph 1:13	3427

INHABITANT

The flood breaketh out from the *i*	Job 28:4	1481
even great and fair, without *i*	Is 5:9	3427
the cities be wasted without *i*	Is 6:11	3427
the *i* of Samaria, that say in the	Is 9:9	3427
Cry out and shout, thou *i* of Zion	Is 12:6	3427
the *i* of this isle shall say in	Is 20:6	3427
are upon thee, O *i* of the earth	Is 24:17	3427
the *i* shall not say, I am sick	Is 33:24	7934
his cities are burned without *i*	Jer 2:15	3427
shall be laid waste, without an *i*	Jer 4:7	3427
of Judah desolate, without an *i*	Jer 9:11	3427
of the land, O *i* of the fortress	Jer 10:17	3427
O *i* of the valley, and rock of the	Jer 21:13	3427
O *i* of Lebanon, that makest thy	Jer 22:23	3427
shall be desolate without an *i*	Jer 26:9	3427
without man, and without *i*	Jer 33:10	3427
Judah a desolation without an *i*	Jer 34:22	3427
and a curse, without an *i*	Jer 44:22	3427
be waste and desolate without an *i*	Jer 46:19	3427
O *i* of Aroer, stand by the way,	Jer 48:19	3427
O *i* of Moab, saith the LORD	Jer 48:43	3427
Babylon a desolation without an *i*	Jer 51:29	3427
Babylon, shall the *i* of Zion say	Jer 51:35	3427
and an hissing, without an *i*	Jer 51:37	3427
cut off the *i* from the plain of	Amos 1:5	3427
I will cut off the *i* from Ashdod	Amos 1:8	3427

thou *i* of Saphir, having thy	Mic 1:11	3427
the *i* of Zaanan came not forth in	Mic 1:11	3427
For the *i* of Maroth waited	Mic 1:12	3427
O thou *i* of Lachish, bind the	Mic 1:13	3427
heir unto thee, O *i* of Mareshah	Mic 1:15	3427
thee, that there shall be no *i*	Zeph 2:5	3427
is no man, that there is none *i*	Zeph 3:6	3427

INHABITANTS

all the *i* of the cities, and that	Gen 19:25	3427
to stink among the *i* of the land	Gen 34:30	3427
when the *i* of the land, the	Gen 50:11	3427
take hold on the *i* of Palestina	Ex 15:14	3427
all the *i* of Canaan shall melt	Ex 15:15	3427
for I will deliver the *i* of the	Ex 23:31	3427
thou make a covenant with the *i*	Ex 34:12	3427
a covenant with the *i* of the land	Ex 34:15	3427
land itself vomiteth out her *i*	Lev 18:25	3427
the land unto all the *i* thereof	Lev 25:10	3427
land that eateth up the *i* thereof	Num 13:32	3427
tell it to the *i* of this land	Num 14:14	3427
because of the *i* of the land	Num 32:17	3427
the *i* of the land from before you	Num 33:52	3427
dispossess the *i* of the land	Num 33:53	
the *i* of the land from before you	Num 33:55	3427
withdrawn the *i* of their city	Deut 13:13	3427
Thou shalt surely smite the *i* of	Deut 13:15	3427
that all the *i* of the land faint	Josh 2:9	3427
for even all the *i* of the country	Josh 2:24	3427
all the *i* of the land shall hear	Josh 7:9	3427
all the *i* of Ai in the field	Josh 8:24	3427
utterly destroyed all the *i* of Ai	Josh 8:26	3427
when the *i* of Gibeon heard what	Josh 9:3	3427
all the *i* of our country spake to	Josh 9:11	3427
to destroy all the *i* of the land	Josh 9:24	3427
how the *i* of Gibeon had made	Josh 10:1	3427
save the Hivites the *i* of Gibeon	Josh 11:19	3427
All the *i* of the hill country	Josh 13:6	3427
went up thence to the *i* of Debir	Josh 15:15	3427
the Jebusites the *i* of Jerusalem	Josh 15:63	3427
hand unto the *i* of En-tappuah	Josh 17:7	3427
the *i* of Dor and her towns	Josh 17:11	3427
the *i* of En-dor and her towns, and	Josh 17:11	3427
the *i* of Taanach and her towns, and	Josh 17:11	3427
the *i* of Megiddo and her towns,	Josh 17:11	3427
drive out the *i* of those cities	Josh 17:12	3427
he went against the *i* of Debir	Judg 1:11	3427
drave out the *i* of the mountain	Judg 1:19	3427
not drive out the *i* of the valley	Judg 1:19	3427
drive out the *i* of Beth-shean	Judg 1:27	3427
and her towns, nor the *i* of Dor	Judg 1:27	3427
nor the *i* of Ibleam and her towns,	Judg 1:27	3427
nor the *i* of Megiddo and her towns	Judg 1:27	3427
Zebulun drive out the *i* of Kitron	Judg 1:30	3427
nor the *i* of Nahalol	Judg 1:30	3427
Asher drive out the *i* of Accho	Judg 1:31	3427
nor the *i* of Zidon, nor of Ahlab,	Judg 1:31	3427
the Canaanites, the *i* of the land	Judg 1:32	3427
drive out the *i* of Beth-shemesh	Judg 1:33	3427
nor the *i* of Beth-anath	Judg 1:33	3427
the Canaanites, the *i* of the land	Judg 1:33	3427
the *i* of Beth-shemesh and of	Judg 1:33	3427
no league with the *i* of this land	Judg 2:2	3427
The *i* of the villages ceased,	Judg 5:7	
the *i* of his villages in Israel	Judg 5:11	
curse ye bitterly the *i* thereof	Judg 5:23	3427
be head over all the *i* of Gilead	Judg 10:18	3427
our head over all the *i* of Gilead	Judg 11:8	3427
Amorites, the *i* of that country	Judg 11:21	3427
sword, beside the *i* of Gibeah	Judg 20:15	3427
of the *i* of Jabesh-gilead there	Judg 21:9	3427
smite the *i* of Jabesh-gilead with	Judg 21:10	3427
they found among the *i* of	Judg 21:12	3427
thee, saying, Buy it before the *i*	Ruth 4:4	3427
to the *i* of Kirjath-jearim	1Sa 6:21	3427
So David saved the *i* of Keilah	1Sa 23:5	3427
were of old the *i* of the land	1Sa 27:8	3427
when the *i* of Jabesh-gilead heard	1Sa 31:11	3427
the Jebusites, the *i* of the land	2Sa 5:6	3427
who was of the *i* of Gilead	1Kin 17:1	8453
nobles who were the *i* in his city	1Kin 21:11	3427
Therefore their *i* were of small	2Kin 19:26	3427
this place, and upon the *i* thereof	2Kin 22:16	3427
place, and against the *i* thereof	2Kin 22:19	3427
all the *i* of Jerusalem with him,	2Kin 23:2	3427
of the fathers of the *i* of Geba	1Chr 8:6	3427
the fathers of the *i* of Aijalon	1Chr 8:13	3427
who drove away the *i* of Gath	1Chr 8:13	3427
Now the first *i* that dwelt in	1Chr 9:2	3427
Jebusites were, the *i* of the land	1Chr 11:4	3427
the *i* of Jebus said to David,	1Chr 11:5	3427

for he hath given the *i* of the	1Chr 22:18	3427
upon all the *i* of the countries	2Chr 15:5	3427
who didst drive out the *i* of this	2Chr 20:7	3427
ye *i* of Jerusalem, and thou king	2Chr 20:15	3427
the *i* of Jerusalem fell before	2Chr 20:18	3427
me, O Judah, and ye *i* of Jerusalem	2Chr 20:20	3427
up against the *i* of mount Seir	2Chr 20:23	3427
had made an end of the *i* of Seir	2Chr 20:23	3427
caused the *i* of Jerusalem to	2Chr 21:11	3427
the *i* of Jerusalem to go a	2Chr 21:13	3427
the *i* of Jerusalem made Ahaziah	2Chr 22:1	3427
the *i* of Jerusalem from the hand	2Chr 32:22	3427
the *i* of Jerusalem, so that the	2Chr 32:26	3427
the *i* of Jerusalem did him honour	2Chr 32:33	3427
the *i* of Jerusalem to err, and to	2Chr 33:9	3427
this place, and upon the *i* thereof	2Chr 34:24	3427
place, and against the *i* thereof	2Chr 34:27	3427
place, and upon the *i* of the same	2Chr 34:28	3427
the *i* of Jerusalem, and the	2Chr 34:30	3427
the *i* of Jerusalem did according	2Chr 34:32	3427
present, and the *i* of Jerusalem	2Chr 35:18	3427
accusation against the *i* of Judah	Ezr 4:6	3427
Hanun, and the *i* of Zanoah	Neh 3:13	3427
watches of the *i* of Jerusalem	Neh 7:3	3427
before them the *i* of the land	Neh 9:24	3427
the waters, and the *i* thereof	Job 26:5	7934
let all the *i* of the world stand	Ps 33:8	3427
upon all the *i* of the earth	Ps 33:14	3427
give ear, all ye *i* of the world	Ps 49:1	3427
all the *i* thereof are dissolved	Ps 75:3	3427
Philistines with the *i* of Tyre	Ps 83:7	3427
O *i* of Jerusalem, and men of Judah	Is 5:3	3427
for a snare to the *i* of Jerusalem	Is 8:14	3427
put down the *i* like a valiant man	Is 10:13	3427
the *i* of Gebim gather themselves	Is 10:31	3427
All ye *i* of the world, and	Is 18:3	3427
The *i* of the land of Tema brought	Is 21:14	3427
be a father to the *i* of Jerusalem	Is 22:21	3427
Be still, ye *i* of the isle	Is 23:2	3427
howl, ye *i* of the isle	Is 23:6	3427
scattereth abroad the *i* thereof	Is 24:1	3427
is defiled under the *i* thereof	Is 24:5	3427
therefore the *i* of the earth are	Is 24:6	3427
the *i* of the world will learn	Is 26:9	3427
neither have the *i* of the world	Is 26:18	3427
out of his place to punish the *i*	Is 26:21	3427
Therefore their *i* were of small	Is 37:27	3427
no more with the *i* of the world	Is 38:11	3427
the *i* thereof are as grasshoppers	Is 40:22	3427
the isles, and the *i* thereof	Is 42:10	3427
let the *i* of the rock sing, let	Is 42:11	3427
be too narrow by reason of the *i*	Is 49:19	3427
forth upon all the *i* of the land	Jer 1:14	3427
ye men of Judah and *i* of Jerusalem	Jer 4:4	3427
my hand upon the *i* of the land	Jer 6:12	3427
the bones of the *i* of Jerusalem	Jer 8:1	3427
I will sling out the *i* of the	Jer 10:18	3427
Judah, and to the *i* of Jerusalem	Jer 11:2	3427
and among the *i* of Jerusalem	Jer 11:9	3427
i of Jerusalem go, and cry unto	Jer 11:12	3427
will fill all the *i* of this land	Jer 13:13	3427
all the *i* of Jerusalem, with	Jer 13:13	3427
all the *i* of Jerusalem, that	Jer 17:20	3427
of Judah, and the *i* of Jerusalem	Jer 17:25	3427
to the *i* of Jerusalem, saying,	Jer 18:11	3427
kings of Judah, and *i* of Jerusalem	Jer 19:3	3427
to the *i* thereof, and even make	Jer 19:12	3427
I will smite the *i* of this city	Jer 21:6	3427
the *i* thereof as Gomorrah	Jer 23:14	3427
to all the *i* of Jerusalem, saying	Jer 25:2	3427
land, and against the *i* thereof	Jer 25:9	3427
sword upon all the *i* of the earth	Jer 25:29	3427
against all the *i* of the earth	Jer 25:30	3427
this city, and upon the *i* thereof	Jer 26:15	3427
of Judah, and the *i* of Jerusalem	Jer 32:32	3427
the *i* of Jerusalem, Will ye not	Jer 35:13	3427
upon all the *i* of Jerusalem all	Jer 35:17	3427
upon the *i* of Jerusalem, and upon	Jer 36:31	3427
forth upon the *i* of Jerusalem	Jer 42:18	3427
destroy the city and the *i* thereof	Jer 46:8	3427
all the *i* of the land shall howl	Jer 47:2	3427
back, dwell deep, O *i* of Dedan	Jer 49:8	3427
purposed against the *i* of Teman	Jer 49:20	3427
O ye *i* of Hazor, saith the LORD	Jer 49:30	3427
it, and against the *i* of Pekod	Jer 50:21	3427
and disquiet the *i* of Babylon	Jer 50:34	3427
upon the *i* of Babylon, and upon	Jer 50:35	3427
he spake against the *i* of Babylon	Jer 51:12	3427
to all the *i* of Chaldea all their	Jer 51:24	3427
and my blood upon the *i* of Chaldea	Jer 51:35	3427
all the *i* of the world, would not	Lam 4:12	3427
whom the *i* of Jerusalem have said	Eze 11:15	3427
Lord GOD of the *i* of Jerusalem	Eze 12:19	3427
so will I give the *i* of Jerusalem	Eze 15:6	3427
strong in the sea, she and her *i*	Eze 26:17	3427
The *i* of Zidon and Arvad were thy	Eze 27:8	3427
All the *i* of the isles shall be	Eze 27:35	3427
all the *i* of Egypt shall know	Eze 29:6	3427
all the *i* of the earth are	Dan 4:35	1753
and among the *i* of the earth	Dan 4:35	1753
to the *i* of Jerusalem, and unto	Dan 9:7	3427
with the *i* of the land, because	Hos 4:1	3427
The *i* of Samaria shall fear	Hos 10:5	7934
and give ear, all ye *i* of the land	Joel 1:2	3427
all the *i* of the land into the	Joel 1:14	3427
let all the *i* of the land tremble	Joel 2:1	3427
the *i* thereof have spoken lies,	Mic 6:12	3427
and the *i* thereof an hissing	Mic 6:16	3427
and upon all the *i* of Jerusalem	Zeph 1:4	3427
ye *i* of Maktesh, for all the	Zeph 1:11	3427
Woe unto the *i* of the sea coast,	Zeph 2:5	3427
people, and the *i* of many cities	Zec 8:20	3427
the *i* of one city shall go to	Zec 8:21	3427
no more pity the *i* of the land	Zec 11:6	3427
The *i* of Jerusalem shall be my	Zec 12:5	3427
the glory of the *i* of Jerusalem	Zec 12:7	3427
LORD defend the *i* of Jerusalem	Zec 12:8	3427
upon the *i* of Jerusalem, the	Zec 12:10	3427
to the *i* of Jerusalem for sin and	Zec 13:1	3427
the *i* of the earth have been made	Rev 17:2	2730

INHABITED

Seir the Horite, who *i* the land	Gen 36:20	3427
until they came to a land *i*	Ex 16:35	3427
iniquities unto a land not *i*	Lev 16:22	1509
the Canaanites that *i* Zephath	Judg 1:17	3427
the Jebusites that *i* Jerusalem	Judg 1:21	3427
eastward he *i* unto the entering	1Chr 5:9	3427
It shall never be *i*, neither	Is 13:20	3427
to Jerusalem, Thou shalt be *i*	Is 44:26	3427
not in vain, he formed it to be *i*	Is 45:18	3427
make the desolate cities to be *i*	Is 54:3	3427
make thee desolate, a land not *i*	Jer 6:8	3427
in a salt land and not *i*	Jer 17:6	3427
and cities which are not *i*	Jer 22:6	3427
and afterward it shall be *i*	Jer 46:26	7931
of the LORD it shall not be *i*	Jer 50:13	3427
and it shall be no more *i* for ever	Jer 50:39	3427
that are *i* shall be laid waste	Eze 12:20	3427
that wast *i* of seafaring men, the	Eze 26:17	3427
like the cities that are not *i*	Eze 26:19	3427
to the pit, that thou be not *i*	Eze 26:20	3427
neither shall it be *i* forty years	Eze 29:11	3427
in all the *i* places of the	Eze 34:13	4186
and the cities shall be *i*, and the	Eze 36:10	3427
are become fenced, and are *i*	Eze 36:35	3427
desolate places that are now *i*	Eze 38:12	3427
Jerusalem shall be *i* as towns	Zec 2:4	3427
prophets, when Jerusalem was *i*	Zec 7:7	3427
when men *i* the south and the plain	Zec 7:7	3427
Gaza, and Ashkelon shall not be *i*	Zec 9:5	3427
Jerusalem shall be *i* again in her	Zec 12:6	3427
i in her place, from Benjamin's	Zec 14:10	3427
but Jerusalem shall be safely *i*	Zec 14:11	3427

INHABITERS

to the *i* of the earth by reason	Rev 8:13	2730
Woe to the *i* of the earth and of	Rev 12:12	2730

INHABITEST

O thou that *i* the praises of	Ps 22:3	3427

INHABITETH

and in houses which no man *i*	Job 15:28	3427
high and lofty One that *i* eternity	Is 57:15	7931

INHABITING

to the people *i* the wilderness	Ps 74:14	6728

INHERIT

to give thee this land to *i* it	Gen 15:7	3423
shall I know that I shall *i* it	Gen 15:8	3423
that thou mayest *i* the land	Gen 28:4	3423
thou be increased, and *i* the land	Ex 23:30	5157
seed, and they shall *i* it for ever	Ex 32:13	5157
Ye shall *i* their land, and I will	Lev 20:24	3423
to *i* them for a possession	Lev 25:46	3423
I have given to the Levites to *i*	Num 18:24	5159
of their fathers they shall *i*	Num 26:55	5157
For we will not *i* with them on	Num 32:19	5157
tribes of your fathers ye shall *i*	Num 33:54	5157
the land which ye shall *i* by lot	Num 34:13	5157
for he shall cause Israel to *i* it	Deut 1:38	5157
that thou mayest *i* his land	Deut 2:31	3423
he shall cause them to *i* the land	Deut 3:28	5157

the Lord your God giveth you to *i*	Deut 12:10	5157
i the land which the Lord thy God	Deut 16:20	3423
the Lord thy God giveth thee to *i*	Deut 19:3	5157
which thou shalt *i* in the land	Deut 19:14	5157
his sons to *i* that which he hath	Deut 21:16	5157
and thou shalt cause them to *i* it	Deut 31:7	5157
but one lot and one portion to *i*	Josh 17:14	5159
Thou shalt not *i* in our father's	Judg 11:2	5157
to make them *i* the throne of	1Sa 2:8	5157
which thou hast given us to *i*	2Chr 20:11	3423
and his seed shall *i* the earth	Ps 25:13	3423
the Lord, they shall *i* the earth	Ps 37:9	3423
But the meek shall *i* the earth	Ps 37:11	3423
blessed of him shall *i* the earth	Ps 37:22	3423
The righteous shall *i* the land	Ps 37:29	3423
he shall exalt thee to *i* the land	Ps 37:34	3423
also of his servants shall *i* it	Ps 69:36	5157
for thou shalt *i* all nations	Ps 82:8	5157
The wise shall *i* glory	Prov 3:35	5157
those that love me to *i* substance	Prov 8:21	5157
his own house shall *i* the wind	Prov 11:29	5157
The simple *i* folly	Prov 14:18	5157
to cause to *i* the desolate	Is 49:8	5157
and thy seed shall *i* the Gentiles	Is 54:3	3423
land, and shall *i* my holy mountain	Is 57:13	3423
they shall *i* the land for ever,	Is 60:21	3423
and mine elect shall *i* it, and my	Is 65:9	3423
fields to them that shall *i* them	Jer 8:10	3423
have caused my people Israel to *i*	Jer 12:14	5157
why then doth their king *i* Gad	Jer 49:1	3423
whereby ye shall *i* the land	Eze 47:13	5157
And ye shall *i* it, one as well as	Eze 47:14	3423
the Lord shall *i* Judah his	Zec 2:12	5157
for they shall *i* the earth	Mt 5:5	2816
and shall *i* everlasting life	Mt 19:29	2816
***i* the kingdom prepared for you**	Mt 25:34	2816
I do that I may *i* eternal life	Mk 10:17	2816
what shall I do to *i* eternal life	Lk 10:25	2816
what shall I do to *i* eternal life	Lk 18:18	2816
shall not *i* the kingdom of God	1Cor 6:9	2816
shall *i* the kingdom of God	1Cor 6:10	2816
blood cannot *i* the kingdom of God	1Cor 15:50	2816
doth corruption *i* incorruption	1Cor 15:50	2816
shall not *i* the kingdom of God	Gal 5:21	2816
faith and patience *i* the promises	Heb 6:12	2816
that ye should *i* a blessing	1Pet 3:9	2816
overcometh shall *i* all things	Rev 21:7	2816

INHERITANCE

Is there yet any portion or *i* for	Gen 31:14	5159
name of their brethren in their *i*	Gen 48:6	5159
them in the mountain of thine *i*	Ex 15:17	5159
our sin, and take us for thine *i*	Ex 34:9	5157
ye shall take them as an *i* for	Lev 25:46	5157
and honey, or given us *i* of fields	Num 16:14	5159
shalt have no *i* in their land	Num 18:20	5157
thine *i* among the children of	Num 18:20	5159
all the tenth in Israel for an *i*	Num 18:21	5159
children of Israel they have no *i*	Num 18:23	5159
of Israel they shall have no *i*	Num 18:24	5159
given you from them for your *i*	Num 18:26	5159
an *i* according to the number of	Num 26:53	5159
many thou shalt give the more *i*	Num 26:54	5159
to few thou shalt give the less *i*	Num 26:54	5159
to every one shall his *i* be given	Num 26:54	5159
because there was no *i* given them	Num 26:62	5159
give them a possession of an *i*	Num 27:7	5159
thou shalt cause the *i* of their	Num 27:7	5159
then ye shall cause his *i* to pass	Num 27:8	5159
give his *i* unto his brethren	Num 27:9	5159
then ye shall give his *i* unto his	Num 27:10	5159
then ye shall give his *i* unto his	Num 27:11	5159
have inherited every man his *i*	Num 32:18	5159
because our *i* is fallen to us on	Num 32:19	5159
that the possession of our *i* on	Num 32:32	5159
lot for an *i* among their families	Num 33:54	5157
the more ye shall give the more *i*	Num 33:54	5159
fewer ye shall give the less *i*	Num 33:54	5159
every man's *i* shall be in the	Num 33:54	
that shall fall unto you for an *i*	Num 34:2	5159
fathers, have received their *i*	Num 34:14	
of Manasseh have received their *i*	Num 34:14	5159
their *i* on this side Jordan near	Num 34:15	5159
tribe, to divide the land by *i*	Num 34:18	5157
Lord commanded to divide the *i*	Num 34:29	5157
give unto the Levites for *i* of	Num 35:2	5159
to his *i* which he inheriteth	Num 35:8	5159
an *i* by lot to the children of	Num 36:2	5159
by the Lord to give the *i* of	Num 36:2	5159
then shall their *i* be taken from	Num 36:3	5159
taken from the *i* of our fathers	Num 36:3	5159

shall be put to the *i* of the	Num 36:3	5159
it be taken from the lot of our *i*	Num 36:3	5159
i be put unto the *i* of	Num 36:4	5159
so shall their *i* be taken away	Num 36:4	5159
be taken away from the *i* of the	Num 36:4	5159
So shall not the *i* of the	Num 36:7	5159
shall keep himself to the *i* of	Num 36:7	5159
that possesseth an *i* in any tribe	Num 36:8	5159
every man the *i* of his fathers	Num 36:8	5159
Neither shall the *i* remove from	Num 36:9	5159
shall keep himself to his own *i*	Num 36:9	5159
their *i* remained in the tribe of	Num 36:12	5159
to be unto him a people of *i*	Deut 4:20	5159
Lord thy God giveth thee for an *i*	Deut 4:21	5159
to give thee their land for an *i*	Deut 4:38	5159
destroy not thy people and thine *i*	Deut 9:26	5159
they are thy people and thine *i*	Deut 9:29	5159
no part nor *i* with his brethren	Deut 10:9	5159
the Lord is his *i*, according as	Deut 10:9	5159
yet come to the rest and to the *i*	Deut 12:9	5159
as he hath no part nor *i* with you	Deut 12:12	5159
he hath no part nor *i* with thee	Deut 14:27	5159
he hath no part nor *i* with thee	Deut 14:29	5159
thee for an *i* to possess it	Deut 15:4	5159
have no part nor *i* with Israel	Deut 18:1	5159
the Lord made by fire, and his *i*	Deut 18:1	5159
have no *i* among their brethren	Deut 18:2	5159
the Lord is their *i*, as he hath	Deut 18:2	5159
Lord thy God giveth thee for an *i*	Deut 19:10	5159
of old time have set in thine *i*	Deut 19:14	5159
thy God doth give thee for an *i*	Deut 20:16	5159
Lord thy God giveth thee for an *i*	Deut 21:23	5159
Lord thy God giveth thee for an *i*	Deut 24:4	5159
thee for an *i* to possess it	Deut 25:19	5159
Lord thy God giveth thee for an *i*	Deut 26:1	5159
gave it for an *i* unto the	Deut 29:8	5159
divided to the nations their *i*	Deut 32:8	5157
Jacob is the lot of his *i*	Deut 32:9	5159
even the *i* of the congregation of	Deut 33:4	4181
thou divide for an *i* the land	Josh 1:6	5157
Joshua gave it for an *i* unto	Josh 11:23	5159
lot unto the Israelites for an *i*	Josh 13:6	5159
for an *i* unto the nine tribes	Josh 13:7	5159
the Gadites have received their *i*	Josh 13:8	5159
the tribe of Levi he gave none *i*	Josh 13:14	5159
Israel made by fire are their *i*	Josh 13:14	5159
i according to their families	Josh 13:15	
This was the *i* of the children of	Josh 13:23	5159
Moses gave *i* unto the tribe of	Josh 13:24	
This is the *i* of the children of	Josh 13:28	5159
Moses gave *i* unto the half tribe	Josh 13:29	
for *i* in the plains of Moab	Josh 13:32	5157
of Levi Moses gave not any *i*	Josh 13:33	5159
Lord God of Israel was their *i*	Josh 13:33	5159
Israel, distributed for *i* to them	Josh 14:1	5157
By lot was their *i*, as the Lord	Josh 14:2	5159
had given the *i* of two tribes	Josh 14:3	5159
Levites he gave none *i* among them	Josh 14:3	5159
have trodden shall be thine *i*	Josh 14:9	5159
son of Jephunneh Hebron for an *i*	Josh 14:13	5159
Hebron therefore became the *i* of	Josh 14:14	5159
This is the *i* of the tribe of the	Josh 15:20	5159
Manasseh and Ephraim, took their *i*	Josh 16:4	5157
of their *i* on the east side was	Josh 16:5	5159
This is the *i* of the tribe of the	Josh 16:8	5159
of Ephraim were among the *i* of	Josh 16:9	5159
give us an *i* among our brethren	Josh 17:4	5159
an *i* among the brethren of their	Josh 17:4	5159
Manasseh had an *i* among his sons	Josh 17:6	5157
had not yet received their *i*	Josh 18:2	5159
it according to the *i* of them	Josh 18:4	5159
priesthood of the Lord is their *i*	Josh 18:7	5159
have received their *i* beyond	Josh 18:7	5159
This was the *i* of the children of	Josh 18:20	5159
This is the *i* of the children of	Josh 18:28	5159
and their *i* was within the	Josh 19:1	5159
the *i* of the children of Judah	Josh 19:1	5159
And they had in their *i* Beer-sheba	Josh 19:2	5159
This is the *i* of the tribe of	Josh 19:8	5159
the *i* of the children of Simeon	Josh 19:9	5159
i within the *i* of them	Josh 19:9	5159
border of their *i* was unto Sarid	Josh 19:10	5159
This is the *i* of the children of	Josh 19:16	5159
This is the *i* of the tribe of the	Josh 19:23	5159
This is the *i* of the tribe of the	Josh 19:31	5159
This is the *i* of the tribe of the	Josh 19:39	5159
And the coast of their *i* was Zorah	Josh 19:41	5159
This is the *i* of the tribe of the	Josh 19:48	5159
the land for *i* by their coasts	Josh 19:49	5157
i to Joshua the son of Nun among	Josh 19:49	5159
divided for an *i* by lot in Shiloh	Josh 19:51	5157

unto the Levites out of their *i*	Josh 21:3	5159
to be an *i* for your tribes, from	Josh 23:4	5159
depart, every man unto his *i*	Josh 24:28	5159
border of his *i* in Timnath-serah	Josh 24:30	5159
it became the *i* of the children	Josh 24:32	5159
unto his *i* to possess the land	Judg 2:6	5159
border of his *i* in Timnath-heres	Judg 2:9	5159
sought them an *i* to dwell in	Judg 18:1	5159
for unto that day all their *i* had	Judg 18:1	5159
the country of the *i* of Israel	Judg 20:6	5159
There must be an *i* for them that	Judg 21:17	3425
went and returned unto their *i*	Judg 21:23	5159
from thence every man to his *i*	Judg 21:24	5159
the name of the dead upon his *i*	Ruth 4:5	5159
for myself, lest I mar mine own *i*	Ruth 4:6	5159
the name of the dead upon his *i*	Ruth 4:10	5159
thee to be captain over his *i*	1Sa 10:1	5159
from abiding in the *i* of the Lord	1Sa 26:19	5159
son together out of the *i* of God	2Sa 14:16	5159
neither have we *i* in the son of	2Sa 20:1	5159
thou swallow up the *i* of the Lord	2Sa 20:19	5159
ye may bless the *i* of the Lord	2Sa 21:3	5159
hast given to thy people for an *i*	1Kin 8:36	5159
they be thy people, and thine *i*	1Kin 8:51	5159
of the earth, to be thine *i*	1Kin 8:53	5159
neither have we *i* in the son of	1Kin 12:16	5159
that I should give the *i* of my	1Kin 21:3	5159
not give thee the *i* of my fathers	1Kin 21:4	5159
forsake the remnant of mine *i*	2Kin 21:14	5159
land of Canaan, the lot of your *i*	1Chr 16:18	5159
leave it for an *i* for your	1Chr 28:8	5157
given unto thy people for an *i*	2Chr 6:27	5159
we have none *i* in the son of	2Chr 10:16	5159
leave it for an *i* to your	Ezr 9:12	3423
of Judah, every one in his *i*	Neh 11:20	5159
what *i* of the Almighty from on	Job 31:2	5159
gave them *i* among their brethren	Job 42:15	5159
give thee the heathen for thine *i*	Ps 2:8	5159
The Lord is the portion of mine *i*	Ps 16:5	2506
Save thy people, and bless thine *i*	Ps 28:9	5159
whom he hath chosen for his own *i*	Ps 33:12	5159
their *i* shall be for ever	Ps 37:18	5159
He shall choose our *i* for us	Ps 47:4	5159
thou didst confirm thine *i*	Ps 68:9	5159
the rod of thine *i*, which thou	Ps 74:2	5159
and divided them an *i* by line	Ps 78:55	5159
and was wroth with his *i*	Ps 78:62	5159
Jacob his people, and Israel his *i*	Ps 78:71	5159
the heathen are come into thine *i*	Ps 79:1	5159
neither will he forsake his *i*	Ps 94:14	5159
land of Canaan, the lot of your *i*	Ps 105:11	5159
that I may glory with thine *i*	Ps 106:5	5159
that he abhorred his own *i*	Ps 106:40	5159
A good man leaveth an *i* to his	Prov 13:22	5157
part of the *i* among the brethren	Prov 17:2	5159
and riches are the *i* of fathers	Prov 19:14	5159
An *i* may be gotten hastily at the	Prov 20:21	5159
Wisdom is good with an *i*	Eccl 7:11	5159
of my hands, and Israel mine *i*	Is 19:25	5159
my people, I have polluted mine *i*	Is 47:6	5159
sake, the tribes of thine *i*	Is 63:17	5159
given for an *i* unto your fathers	Jer 3:18	5157
and Israel is the rod of his *i*	Jer 10:16	5159
that touch the *i* which I have	Jer 12:14	5159
they have filled mine *i* with the	Jer 16:18	5159
for the right of *i* is thine	Jer 32:8	3425
and Israel is the rod of his *i*	Jer 51:19	5159
Our *i* is turned to strangers, our	Lam 5:2	5159
thou shalt take thine *i* in	Eze 22:16	2490
the land is given us for *i*	Eze 33:24	4181
at the *i* of the house of Israel	Eze 35:15	5159
thee, and thou shalt be their *i*	Eze 36:12	5159
And it shall be unto them for an *i*	Eze 44:28	5159
I am their *i*	Eze 44:28	5159
divide by lot the land for *i*	Eze 45:1	5159
the *i* thereof shall be his sons'	Eze 46:16	5159
it shall be their possession by *i*	Eze 46:16	5159
of his *i* to one of his servants	Eze 46:17	5159
but his *i* shall be his sons' for	Eze 46:17	5159
of the people's *i* by oppression	Eze 46:18	5159
sons *i* out of his own possession	Eze 46:18	5157
land shall fall unto you for *i*	Eze 47:14	5159
it by lot for an *i* unto you	Eze 47:22	5159
they shall have *i* with you among	Eze 47:22	5159
there shall ye give him his *i*	Eze 47:23	5159
unto the tribes of Israel for *i*	Eze 48:29	5159
him, and let us seize on his *i*	Mt 21:38	2817
kill him, and the *i* shall be ours	Mk 12:7	2817
that he divide the *i* with me	Lk 12:13	2817
kill him, that the *i* may be ours	Lk 20:14	2817
And he gave him none *i* in it	Acts 7:5	2817

to give you an *i* among all them	Acts 20:32	2817
***i* among them which are sanctified**	Acts 26:18	2819
For if the *i* be of the law, it is	Gal 3:18	2817
whom also we have obtained an *i*	Eph 1:11	2820
our *i* until the redemption of the	Eph 1:14	2817
the glory of his *i* in the saints	Eph 1:18	2817
hath any *i* in the kingdom of	Eph 5:5	2817
of the *i* of the saints in light	Col 1:12	2819
shall receive the reward of the *i*	Col 3:24	2817
as he hath by *i* obtained a more	Heb 1:4	2820
receive the promise of eternal *i*	Heb 9:15	2817
he should after receive for an *i*	Heb 11:8	2817
To an *i* incorruptible, and	1Pet 1:4	2817

INHERITANCES
These are the *i*, which Eleazar	Josh 19:51	5159

INHERITED
have *i* every man his inheritance	Num 32:18	5157
of Israel *i* in the land of Canaan	Josh 14:1	5157
they *i* the labour of the people	Ps 105:44	3423
Surely our fathers have *i* lies	Jer 16:19	5157
Abraham was one, and he *i* the land	Eze 33:24	3423
when he would have *i* the blessing	Heb 12:17	2816

INHERITETH
to his inheritance which he *i*	Num 35:8	5157

INHERITOR
out of Judah an *i* of my mountains	Is 65:9	3423

INIQUITIES
confess over him all the *i* of the	Lev 16:21	5771
their *i* unto a land not inhabited	Lev 16:22	5771
also in the *i* of their fathers	Lev 26:39	5771
for a year, shall ye bear your *i*	Num 14:34	5771
for our *i* are increased over our	Ezr 9:6	5771
and for our *i* have we, our kings,	Ezr 9:7	5771
us less than our *i* deserve	Ezr 9:13	5771
sins, and the *i* of their fathers	Neh 9:2	5771
How many are mine *i* and sins	Job 13:23	5771
me to possess the *i* of my youth	Job 13:26	5771
and thine *i* infinite	Job 22:5	5771
For mine *i* are gone over mine	Ps 38:4	5771
mine *i* have taken hold upon me,	Ps 40:12	5771
my sins, and blot out all mine *i*	Ps 51:9	5771
They search out *i*	Ps 64:6	5766
I prevail against me	Ps 65:3	1647,5771
remember not against us former *i*	Ps 79:8	5771
Thou hast set our *i* before thee	Ps 90:8	5771
Who forgiveth all thine *i*	Ps 103:3	5771
rewarded us according to our *i*	Ps 103:10	5771
and because of their *i*, are	Ps 107:17	5771
If thou, Lord, shouldest mark *i*	Ps 130:3	5771
redeem Israel from all his *i*	Ps 130:8	5771
His own *i* shall take the wicked	Prov 5:22	5771
thou hast wearied me with thine *i*	Is 43:24	5771
Behold, for your *i* have ye sold	Is 50:1	5771
he was bruised for our *i*	Is 53:5	5771
for he shall bear their *i*	Is 53:11	5771
But your *i* have separated between	Is 59:2	5771
and as for our *i*, we know them	Is 59:12	5771
and our *i*, like the wind, have	Is 64:6	5771
consumed us, because of our *i*	Is 64:7	5771
Your *i*, and the *i* of your	Is 65:7	5771
Your *i* have turned away these	Jer 5:25	5771
to the *i* of their forefathers	Jer 11:10	5771
though our *i* testify against us,	Jer 14:7	5771
and I will pardon all their *i*	Jer 33:8	5771
the *i* of her priests, that have	Lam 4:13	5771
and we have borne their *i*	Lam 5:7	5771
but ye shall pine away for your *i*	Eze 24:23	5771
by the multitude of thine *i*	Eze 28:18	5771
but their *i* shall be upon their	Eze 32:27	5771
in your own sight for your *i*	Eze 36:31	5771
i I will also cause you to dwell	Eze 36:33	5771
they may be ashamed of their *i*	Eze 43:10	5771
thine *i* by shewing mercy to the	Dan 4:27	5758
that we might turn from our *i*	Dan 9:13	5771
for the *i* of our fathers,	Dan 9:16	5771
I will punish you for all your *i*	Amos 3:2	5771
he will subdue our *i*	Mic 7:19	5771
away every one of you from his *i*	Acts 3:26	4189
are they whose *i* are forgiven	Rom 4:7	458
their *i* will I remember no more	Heb 8:12	458
i will I remember no more	Heb 10:17	458
and God hath remembered her *i*	Rev 18:5	92

INIQUITY
for the *i* of the Amorites is not	Gen 15:16	5771
be consumed in the *i* of the city	Gen 19:15	5771
found out the *i* of thy servants	Gen 44:16	5771
visiting the *i* of the fathers	Ex 20:5	5771
may bear the *i* of the holy things	Ex 28:38	5771

that they bear not *i*, and die	Ex 28:43	5771
mercy for thousands, forgiving *i*	Ex 34:7	5771
visiting the *i* of the fathers	Ex 34:7	5771
and pardon our *i* and our sin, and	Ex 34:9	5771
it, then he shall bear his *i*	Lev 5:1	5771
is he guilty, and shall bear his *i*	Lev 5:17	5771
eateth of it shall bear his *i*	Lev 7:18	5771
to bear the *i* of the congregation	Lev 10:17	5771
then he shall bear his *i*	Lev 17:16	5771
I do visit the *i* thereof upon it	Lev 18:25	5771
that eateth it shall bear his *i*	Lev 19:8	5771
he shall bear his *i*	Lev 20:17	5771
they shall bear their *i*	Lev 20:19	5771
them to bear the *i* of trespass	Lev 22:16	5771
in their *i* in your enemies' lands	Lev 26:39	5771
If they shall confess their *i*	Lev 26:40	5771
the *i* of their fathers, with	Lev 26:40	5771
of the punishment of their *i*	Lev 26:41	5771
of the punishment of their *i*	Lev 26:43	5771
bringing *i* to remembrance	Num 5:15	5771
shall the man be guiltless from *i*	Num 5:31	5771
and this woman shall bear her *i*	Num 5:31	5771
and of great mercy, forgiving *i*	Num 14:18	5771
visiting the *i* of the fathers	Num 14:18	5771
the *i* of this people according	Num 14:19	5771
his *i* shall be upon him	Num 15:31	5771
shall bear the *i* of the sanctuary	Num 18:1	5771
bear the *i* of your priesthood	Num 18:1	5771
and they shall bear the *i*	Num 18:23	5771
He hath not beheld *i* in Jacob	Num 23:21	205
then he shall bear her *i*	Num 30:15	5771
visiting the *i* of the fathers	Deut 5:9	5771
rise up against a man for any *i*	Deut 19:15	5771
a God of truth and without *i*	Deut 32:4	5766
Is the *i* of Peor too little for	Josh 22:17	5771
man perished not alone in his *i*	Josh 22:20	5771
ever for the *i* which he knoweth	1Sa 3:13	5771
that the *i* of Eli's house shall	1Sa 3:14	5771
and stubbornness is as *i* and	1Sa 15:23	205
what is mine *i*?	1Sa 20:1	5771
if there be in me *i*, slay me	1Sa 20:8	5771
my lord, upon me let this *i* be	1Sa 25:24	5771
If he commit *i*, I will chasten	2Sa 7:14	5753
the *i* be on me, and on my father's	2Sa 14:9	5771
and if there be any *i* in me	2Sa 14:32	5771
Let not my lord impute *i* unto me	2Sa 19:19	5771
and have kept myself from mine *i*	2Sa 22:24	5771
take away the *i* of thy servant	2Sa 24:10	5771
do away the *i* of thy servant	1Chr 21:8	5771
for there is no *i* with the Lord	2Chr 19:7	5766
And cover not their *i*, and let not	Neh 4:5	5771
as I have seen, they that plow *i*	Job 4:8	205
hope, and *i* stoppeth her mouth	Job 5:16	5766
I pray you, let it not be *i*	Job 6:29	5766
Is there *i* in my tongue	Job 6:30	5766
and take away mine *i*	Job 7:21	5771
That thou enquirest after mine *i*	Job 10:6	5771
wilt not acquit me from mine *i*	Job 10:14	5771
thee less than thine *i* deserveth	Job 11:6	5771
If *i* be in thine hand, put it far	Job 11:14	205
a bag, and thou sewest up mine *i*	Job 14:17	5771
For thy mouth uttereth thine *i*	Job 15:5	5771
man, which drinketh *i* like water	Job 15:16	5766
The heaven shall reveal his *i*	Job 20:27	5771
layeth up his *i* for his children	Job 21:19	205
thou shalt put away *i* far from	Job 22:23	5766
punishment to the workers of *i*	Job 31:3	205
it is an *i* to be punished by the	Job 31:11	5771
This also were an *i* to be	Job 31:28	5771
by hiding mine *i* in my bosom	Job 31:33	5771
neither is there *i* in me	Job 33:9	5771
in company with the workers of *i*	Job 34:8	205
Almighty, that he should commit *i*	Job 34:10	5766
workers of *i* may hide themselves	Job 34:22	205
if I have done *i*, I will do no	Job 34:32	5766
that they return from *i*	Job 36:10	205
Take heed, regard not *i*	Job 36:21	205
who can say, Thou hast wrought *i*	Job 36:23	5766
thou hatest all workers of *i*	Ps 5:5	205
from me, all ye workers of *i*	Ps 6:8	205
if there be *i* in my hands	Ps 7:3	5766
Behold, he travaileth with *i*	Ps 7:14	205
all the workers of *i* no knowledge	Ps 14:4	205
him, and I kept myself from mine *i*	Ps 18:23	5771
sake, O Lord, pardon mine *i*	Ps 25:11	5771
wicked, and with the workers of *i*	Ps 28:3	205
faileth because of mine *i*	Ps 31:10	5771
unto whom the Lord imputeth not *i*	Ps 32:2	5771
thee, and mine *i* have I not hid	Ps 32:5	5771
and thou forgavest the *i* of my sin	Ps 32:5	5771
until his *i* be found to be	Ps 36:2	5771

The words of his mouth are *i*	Ps 36:3	205
There are the workers of *i* fallen	Ps 36:12	205
envious against the workers of *i*	Ps 37:1	5766
For I will declare mine *i*	Ps 38:18	5771
rebukes dost correct man for *i*	Ps 39:11	5771
his heart gathereth *i* to itself	Ps 41:6	205
when the *i* of my heels shall	Ps 49:5	5771
Wash me throughly from mine *i*	Ps 51:2	5771
Behold, I was shapen in *i*	Ps 51:5	5771
they, and have done abominable *i*	Ps 53:1	5766
the workers of *i* no knowledge	Ps 53:4	205
for they cast *i* upon me, and in	Ps 55:3	205
Shall they escape by *i*	Ps 56:7	205
Deliver me from the workers of *i*	Ps 59:2	205
insurrection of the workers of *i*	Ps 64:2	205
If I regard *i* in my heart	Ps 66:18	205
Add *i* unto their *i*	Ps 69:27	5771
of compassion, forgave their *i*	Ps 78:38	5771
hast forgiven the *i* of thy people	Ps 85:2	5771
the rod, and their *i* with stripes	Ps 89:32	5771
all the workers of *i* do flourish	Ps 92:7	205
workers of *i* shall be scattered	Ps 92:9	205
the workers of *i* boast themselves	Ps 94:4	205
for me against the workers of *i*	Ps 94:16	205
Shall the throne of *i* have	Ps 94:20	1942
shall bring upon them their own *i*	Ps 94:23	205
our fathers, we have committed *i*	Ps 106:6	5753
and were brought low for their *i*	Ps 106:43	5771
all *i* shall stop her mouth	Ps 107:42	5766
Let the *i* of his fathers be	Ps 109:14	5771
They also do no *i*	Ps 119:3	5766
let not any *i* have dominion over	Ps 119:133	205
put forth their hands unto *i*	Ps 125:3	5766
them forth with the workers of *i*	Ps 125:5	205
wicked works with men that work *i*	Ps 141:4	205
and the gins of the workers of *i*	Ps 141:9	205
shall be to the workers of *i*	Prov 10:29	205
By mercy and truth *i* is purged	Prov 16:6	5771
mouth of the wicked devoureth *i*	Prov 19:28	205
shall be to the workers of *i*	Prov 21:15	205
He that soweth *i* shall reap	Prov 22:8	205
righteousness, that *i* was there	Eccl 3:16	7562
nation, a people laden with *i*	Is 1:4	5771
it is *i*, even the solemn meeting	Is 1:13	205
that draw *i* with cords of vanity	Is 5:18	5771
thine *i* is taken away, and thy sin	Is 6:7	5771
evil, and the wicked for their *i*	Is 13:11	5771
for the *i* of their fathers	Is 14:21	5771
Surely this *i* shall not be purged	Is 22:14	5771
of the earth for their *i*	Is 26:21	5771
shall the *i* of Jacob be purged	Is 27:9	5771
all that watch for *i* are cut off	Is 29:20	205
Therefore this *i* shall be to you	Is 30:13	5771
the help of them that work *i*	Is 31:2	205
villany, and his heart will work *i*	Is 32:6	205
therein shall be forgiven their *i*	Is 33:24	5771
that her *i* is pardoned	Is 40:2	5771
hath laid on him the *i* of us all	Is 53:6	5771
For the *i* of his covetousness was	Is 57:17	5771
blood, and your fingers with *i*	Is 59:3	5771
mischief, and bring forth *i*	Is 59:4	205
their works are works of *i*	Is 59:6	205
their thoughts are thoughts of *i*	Is 59:7	205
Lord, neither remember *i* for ever	Is 64:9	5771
What *i* have your fathers found in	Jer 2:5	5766
yet thine *i* is marked before me,	Jer 2:22	5771
Only acknowledge thine *i*, that	Jer 3:13	5771
and weary themselves to commit *i*	Jer 9:5	5753
thine *i* are thy skirts discovered	Jer 13:22	5771
he will now remember their *i*	Jer 14:10	5771
and the *i* of our fathers	Jer 14:20	5771
or what is our *i*	Jer 16:10	5771
neither is their *i* hid from mine	Jer 16:17	5771
first I will recompense their *i*	Jer 16:18	5771
forgive not their *i*, neither blot	Jer 18:23	5771
saith the Lord, for their *i*	Jer 25:12	5771
one, for the multitude of thine *i*	Jer 30:14	5771
for the multitude of thine *i*	Jer 30:15	5771
every one shall die for his own *i*	Jer 31:30	5771
for I will forgive their *i*	Jer 31:34	5771
recompensest the *i* of the fathers	Jer 32:18	5771
cleanse them from all their *i*	Jer 33:8	5771
that I may forgive their *i*	Jer 36:3	5771
seed and his servants for their *i*	Jer 36:31	5771
the *i* of Israel shall be sought	Jer 50:20	5771
be not cut off in her *i*	Jer 51:6	5771
they have not discovered thine *i*	Lam 2:14	5771
For the punishment of the *i* of	Lam 4:6	5771
of thine *i* is accomplished	Lam 4:22	5771
he will visit thine *i*, O daughter	Lam 4:22	5771
wicked man shall die in his *i*	Eze 3:18	5771

wicked way, he shall die in his *i*	Eze 3:19	5771
his righteousness, and commit *i*	Eze 3:20	5766
lay the *i* of the house of Israel	Eze 4:4	5771
upon it thou shalt bear their *i*	Eze 4:4	5771
upon thee the years of their *i*	Eze 4:5	5771
bear the *i* of the house of Israel	Eze 4:5	5771
thou shalt bear the *i* of the	Eze 4:6	5771
and consume away for their *i*	Eze 4:17	5771
himself in the *i* of his life	Eze 7:13	5771
mourning, every one for his *i*	Eze 7:16	5771
is the stumblingblock of their *i*	Eze 7:19	5771
The *i* of the house of Israel and	Eze 9:9	5771
of their *i* before their face	Eze 14:3	5771
of his *i* before his face, and	Eze 14:4	5771
of his *i* before his face, and	Eze 14:7	5771
bear the punishment of their *i*	Eze 14:10	5771
this was the *i* of thy sister	Eze 16:49	5771
hath withdrawn his hand from *i*	Eze 18:8	5766
not die for the *i* of his father	Eze 18:17	5771
lo, even he shall die in his *i*	Eze 18:18	5771
the son bear the *i* of the father	Eze 18:19	5771
not bear the *i* of the father	Eze 18:20	5771
the father bear the *i* of the son	Eze 18:20	5771
righteousness, and committeth *i*	Eze 18:24	5766
righteousness, and committeth *i*	Eze 18:26	5766
for his *i* that he hath done shall	Eze 18:26	5766
so *i* shall not be your ruin	Eze 18:30	5771
he will call to remembrance the *i*	Eze 21:23	5771
have made your *i* to be remembered	Eze 21:24	5771
when *i* shall have an end,	Eze 21:25	5771
when their *i* shall have an end	Eze 21:29	5771
created, till *i* was found in thee	Eze 28:15	5766
by the *i* of thy traffick	Eze 28:18	5766
bringeth their *i* to remembrance	Eze 29:16	5771
them, he is taken away in his *i*	Eze 33:6	5771
wicked man shall die in his *i*	Eze 33:8	5771
his way, he shall die in his *i*	Eze 33:9	
own righteousness, and commit *i*	Eze 33:13	5766
but for his *i* that he hath	Eze 33:13	5766
of life, without committing *i*	Eze 33:15	5766
righteousness, and committeth *i*	Eze 33:18	5766
the time that their *i* had an end	Eze 35:5	5771
went into captivity for their *i*	Eze 39:23	5771
they shall even bear their *i*	Eze 44:10	5771
house of Israel to fall into *i*	Eze 44:12	5771
God, and they shall bear their *i*	Eze 44:12	5771
have sinned, and have committed *i*	Dan 9:5	5753
and to make reconciliation for *i*	Dan 9:24	5771
they set their heart on their *i*	Hos 4:8	5771
Israel and Ephraim fall in their *i*	Hos 5:5	5771
is a city of them that work *i*	Hos 6:8	205
then the *i* of Ephraim was	Hos 7:1	5771
now will he remember their *i*	Hos 8:13	5771
mad, for the multitude of thine *i*	Hos 9:7	5771
he will remember their *i*, he will	Hos 9:9	5771
of *i* did not overtake them	Hos 10:9	5932
wickedness, ye have reaped *i*	Hos 10:13	5766
find none *i* in me that were sin	Hos 12:8	5771
Is there *i* in Gilead	Hos 12:11	205
The *i* of Ephraim is bound up	Hos 13:12	5771
for thou hast fallen by thine *i*	Hos 14:1	5771
say unto him, Take away all *i*	Hos 14:2	5771
Woe to them that devise *i*	Mic 2:1	205
with blood, and Jerusalem with *i*	Mic 3:10	5766
like unto thee, that pardoneth *i*	Mic 7:18	5771
Why dost thou shew me *i*, and cause	Hab 1:3	205
evil, and canst not look on *i*	Hab 1:13	5999
blood, and stablisheth a city by *i*	Hab 2:12	5766
he will not do *i*	Zeph 3:5	5766
remnant of Israel shall not do *i*	Zeph 3:13	5766
caused *i* to pass from thee	Zec 3:4	5771
I will remove the *i* of that land	Zec 3:9	5771
i was not found in his lips	Mal 2:6	5766
and did turn many away from *i*	Mal 2:6	5771
depart from me, ye that work *i*	Mt 7:23	*458*
that offend, and them which do *i*	Mt 13:41	*458*
ye are full of hypocrisy and *i*	Mt 23:28	*458*
because *i* shall abound, the love	Mt 24:12	*458*
from me, all ye workers of *i*	Lk 13:27	*93*
a field with the reward of *i*	Acts 1:18	*93*
bitterness, and in the bond of *i*	Acts 8:23	*93*
uncleanness and to *i* unto *i*	Rom 6:19	*458*
Rejoiceth not in *i*, but rejoiceth	1Cor 13:6	*93*
mystery of *i* doth already work	2Th 2:7	*458*
the name of Christ depart from *i*	2Ti 2:19	*93*
he might redeem us from all *i*	Titus 2:14	*458*
loved righteousness, and hated *i*	Heb 1:9	*458*
tongue is a fire, a world of *i*	Jas 3:6	*93*
But was rebuked for his *i*	2Pet 2:16	*3892*

INJURED

ye have not *i* me at all	Gal 4:12	*91*

INJURIOUS

blasphemer, and a persecutor, and *i*	1Ti 1:13	*5197*

INJUSTICE

Not for any *i* in mine hands	Job 16:17	2555

INK

I wrote them with *i* in the book	Jer 36:18	1773
by us, written not with *i*	2Cor 3:3	*3188*
I would not write with paper and *i*	2Jn 12	*3188*
to write, but I will not with *i*	3Jn 13	*3188*

INKHORN

with a writer's *i* by his side	Eze 9:2	7083
had the writer's *i* by his side	Eze 9:3	7083
which had the *i* by his side	Eze 9:11	7083

INN

give his ass provender in the *i*	Gen 42:27	4411
to pass, when we came to the *i*	Gen 43:21	4411
came to pass by the way in the *i*	Ex 4:24	4411
was no room for them in the *i*	Lk 2:7	*2646*
own beast, and brought him to an *i*	Lk 10:34	*3829*

INNER

the cherubims within the *i* house	1Kin 6:27	6442
he built the *i* court with three	1Kin 6:36	6442
both for the *i* court of the house	1Kin 7:12	6442
both for the doors of the *i* house	1Kin 7:50	6442
into the city, into an *i* chamber	1Kin 20:30	2315
into an *i* chamber to hide thyself	1Kin 22:25	2315
and carry him to an *i* chamber	2Kin 9:2	2315
of the *i* parlours thereof, and of	1Chr 28:11	6442
the *i* doors thereof for the most	2Chr 4:22	6442
into an *i* chamber to hide thyself	2Chr 18:24	2315
the priests went into the *i* part	2Chr 29:16	6441
unto the king into the *i* court	Est 4:11	6442
stood in the *i* court of the	Est 5:1	6442
to the door of the *i* gate	Eze 8:3	6442
he brought me into the *i* court of	Eze 8:16	6442
and the cloud filled the *i* court	Eze 10:3	6442
of the *i* gate were fifty cubits	Eze 40:15	6442
forefront of the *i* court without	Eze 40:19	6442
the gate of the *i* court was over	Eze 40:23	6442
in the *i* court toward the south	Eze 40:27	6442
he brought me to the *i* court by	Eze 40:28	6442
into the *i* court toward the east	Eze 40:32	6442
without the *i* gate were the	Eze 40:44	6442
of the singers in the *i* court	Eze 40:44	6442
hundred cubits, with the *i* temple	Eze 41:15	6442
the door, even unto the *i* house	Eze 41:17	6442
cubits which were for the *i* court	Eze 42:3	6442
an end of measuring the *i* house	Eze 42:15	6442
and brought me into the *i* court	Eze 43:5	6442
in at the gates of the *i* court	Eze 44:17	6442
in the gates of the *i* court	Eze 44:17	6442
when they enter into the *i* court	Eze 44:21	6442
the sanctuary, unto the *i* court	Eze 44:27	6442
posts of the gate of the *i* court	Eze 45:19	6442
The gate of the *i* court that	Eze 46:1	6442
thrust them into the *i* prison	Acts 16:24	*2082*
might by his Spirit in the *i* man	Eph 3:16	*2080*

INNERMOST

into the *i* parts of the belly	Prov 18:8	2315
into the *i* parts of the belly	Prov 26:22	2315

INNOCENCY

i of my hands have I done this	Gen 20:5	5356
I will wash mine hands in *i*	Ps 26:6	5356
in vain, and washed my hands in *i*	Ps 73:13	5356
as before him *i* was found in me	Dan 6:22	2136
will it be ere they attain to *i*	Hos 8:5	5356

INNOCENT

and the *i* and righteous slay thou	Ex 23:7	5355
That *i* blood be not shed in thy	Deut 19:10	5355
the guilt of *i* blood from Israel	Deut 19:13	5355
lay not *i* blood unto thy people	Deut 21:8	5355
guilt of *i* blood from among you	Deut 21:9	5355
taketh reward to slay an *i* person	Deut 27:25	5355
wilt thou sin against *i* blood	1Sa 19:5	5355
thou mayest take away the *i* blood	1Kin 2:31	2600
Manasseh shed *i* blood very much	2Kin 21:16	5355
also for the *i* blood that he shed	2Kin 24:4	5355
he filled Jerusalem with *i* blood	2Kin 24:4	5355
thee, who ever perished, being *i*	Job 4:7	5355
will laugh at the trial of the *i*	Job 9:23	5355
know that thou wilt not hold me *i*	Job 9:28	5352
the *i* shall stir up himself	Job 17:8	5355
the *i* laugh them to scorn	Job 22:19	5355
shall deliver the island of the *i*	Job 22:30	5355

the *i* shall divide the silver .... Job 27:17   5355
without transgression, I am *i* .... Job 33:9   2643
places doth he murder the *i* .... Ps 10:8   5355
nor taketh reward against the *i* .... Ps 15:5   5355
I shall be *i* from the great .... Ps 19:13   5352
righteous, and condemn the *i* blood ...... Ps 94:21   5355
shed *i* blood, even the blood of .... Ps 106:38   5355
privily for the *i* without cause .... Prov 1:11   5355
and hands that shed *i* blood .... Prov 6:17   5355
toucheth her shall not be *i* .... Prov 6:29   5352
haste to be rich shall not be *i* .... Prov 28:20   5352
they make haste to shed *i* blood .... Is 59:7   5355
Yet thou sayest, Because I am *i* .... Jer 2:35   5352
shed not *i* blood in this place, ... Jer 7:6   5355
neither shed *i* blood in this .... Jer 22:3   5355
and for to shed *i* blood, and for .... Jer 22:17   5355
bring *i* blood upon yourselves .... Jer 26:15   5355
have shed *i* blood in their land .... Joel 3:19   5355
life, and lay not upon us *i* blood .... Jonah 1:14   5355
that I have betrayed the *i* blood .... Mt 27:4   121
I am *i* of the blood of this just .... Mt 27:24   121

INNOCENTS
blood of the souls of the poor *i* .... Jer 2:34   5355
this place with the blood of *i* .... Jer 19:4   5355

INNUMERABLE
him, as there are *i* before him .... Job 21:33   369,4557
For *i* evils have compassed me .... Ps 40:12   369,4557
wherein are things creeping *i* .... Ps 104:25   369,4557
than the grasshoppers, and are *i* .... Jer 46:23   369,4557
together an *i* multitude of people .... Lk 12:1   3461
sand which is by the sea shore *i* .... Heb 11:12   382
to an *i* company of angels, ... Heb 12:22   3461

INORDINATE
corrupt in her *i* love than she .... Eze 23:11   5691
i affection, evil concupiscence, ... Col 3:5   3806

INQUISITION
the judges shall make diligent *i* .... Deut 19:18   1875
when *i* was made of the matter, it .... Est 2:23   1245
When he maketh *i* for blood .... Ps 9:12   1875

INSCRIPTION
I found an altar with this *i* .... Acts 17:23   1924

INSIDE See APPENDIX.

INSOMUCH See APPENDIX.

INSPIRATION
the *i* of the Almighty giveth them .... Job 32:8   5397
scripture is given by *i* of God 2Ti 3:16   2315

INSTANT
yea, it shall be at an *i* suddenly .... Is 29:5   6621
breaking cometh suddenly at an *i* .... Is 30:13   6621
At what *i* I shall speak .... Jer 18:7   7281
And at what *i* I shall speak .... Jer 18:9   7281
she coming in that *i* gave thanks .... Lk 2:38   5610
they were *i* with loud voices, ... Lk 23:23   1945
continuing *i* in prayer .... Rom 12:12   4342
be *i* in season, out of season 2Ti 4:2   2186

INSTANTLY
to Jesus, they besought him *i* .... Lk 7:4   4705
i serving God day and night, hope . Acts 26:7   1722,1616

INSTEAD See APPENDIX.

INSTRUCT
his voice, that he might *i* thee .... Deut 4:36   3256
also thy good spirit to *i* them .... Neh 9:20   7919
with the Almighty *i* him .... Job 40:2   3250
my reins also *i* me in the night .... Ps 16:7   3256
I will *i* thee and teach thee in .... Ps 32:8   7919
my mother's house, who would *i* me ...... Song 8:2   3925
For his God doth *i* him to .... Is 28:26   3256
among the people shall *i* many .... Dan 11:33   995
of the Lord, that he may *i* him 1Cor 2:16   4822

INSTRUCTED
he *i* him, he kept him as the .... Deut 32:10   995
wherein Jehoiada the priest *i* him 2Kin 12:2   3384
he *i* about the song, because he 1Chr 15:22   3256
were *i* in the songs of the LORD 1Chr 25:7   3925
i for the building of the house 2Chr 3:3   3245
Behold, thou hast *i* many, and thou .... Job 4:3   3256
be *i*, ye judges of the earth .... Ps 2:10   3256
mine ear to them that *i* me .... Prov 5:13   3925
and when the wise is *i*, he .... Prov 21:11   7919
i me that I should not walk in .... Is 8:11   3256
took he counsel, and who *i* him .... Is 40:14   995
Be thou *i*, O Jerusalem, lest my .... Jer 6:8   3256
and after that I was *i*, I smote .... Jer 31:19   3045
i unto the kingdom of heaven is .... Mt 13:52   3100
being before *i* of her mother, ... Mt 14:8   4264

things, wherein thou hast been *i* .... Lk 1:4   2727
This man was *i* in the way of the .... Acts 18:25   2727
excellent, being *i* out of the law .... Rom 2:18   2727
all things I am *i* both to be full .... Phil 4:12   3453

INSTRUCTER
an *i* of every artificer in brass .... Gen 4:22   3913

INSTRUCTERS
ye have ten thousand *i* in Christ 1Cor 4:15   3807

INSTRUCTING
In meekness *i* those that oppose 2Ti 2:25   3811

INSTRUCTION
ears of men, and sealeth their *i* .... Job 33:16   4561
Seeing thou hatest *i*, and castest .... Ps 50:17   4148
To know wisdom and *i* .... Prov 1:2   4148
To receive the *i* of wisdom .... Prov 1:3   4148
but fools despise wisdom and *i* .... Prov 1:7   4148
hear the *i* of thy father, and .... Prov 1:8   4148
the *i* of a father, and attend to .... Prov 4:1   4148
Take fast hold of *i* .... Prov 4:13   4148
And say, How have I hated *i* .... Prov 5:12   4148
He shall die without *i* .... Prov 5:23   4148
reproofs of *i* are the way of life .... Prov 6:23   4148
Receive my *i*, and not silver .... Prov 8:10   4148
Hear *i*, and be wise, and refuse it not .... Prov 8:33   4148
Give *i* to a wise man, and he will .... Prov 9:9
in the way of life that keepeth *i* .... Prov 10:17   4148
Whoso loveth *i* loveth knowledge .... Prov 12:1   4148
A wise son heareth his father's *i* .... Prov 13:1   4148
shall be to him that refuseth *i* .... Prov 13:18   4148
A fool despiseth his father's *i* .... Prov 15:5   4148
He that refuseth *i* despiseth his .... Prov 15:32   4148
of the LORD is the *i* of wisdom .... Prov 15:33   4148
but the *i* of fools is folly .... Prov 16:22   4148
Hear counsel, and receive *i* .... Prov 19:20   4148
to hear the *i* that causeth to err .... Prov 19:27   4148
Apply thine heart unto *i*, and .... Prov 23:12   4148
also wisdom, and *i*, and .... Prov 23:23   4148
I looked upon it, and received *i* .... Prov 24:32   4148
might not hear, nor receive *i* .... Jer 17:23   4148
have not hearkened to receive .... Jer 32:33   4148
Will ye not receive *i* to hearken .... Jer 35:13   4148
be a reproach and a taunt, an *i* .... Eze 5:15   4148
wilt fear me, thou wilt receive *i* .... Zeph 3:7   4148
for *i* in righteousness 2Ti 3:16   3809

INSTRUCTOR
An *i* of the foolish, a teacher of .... Rom 2:20   3810

INSTRUMENT
if he smite him with an *i* of iron .... Num 35:16   3627
psaltery and an *i* of ten strings .... Ps 33:2
Upon an *i* of ten strings, and upon .... Ps 92:3
an *i* of ten strings will I sing .... Ps 144:9
not threshed with a threshing *i* .... Is 28:27
sharp threshing *i* having teeth .... Is 41:15
bringeth forth an *i* for his work .... Is 54:16   3627
voice, and can play well on an *i* .... Eze 33:32

INSTRUMENTS
i of cruelty are in their .... Gen 49:5   3627
the pattern of all the *i* thereof .... Ex 25:9   3627
they shall keep all the *i* of the .... Num 3:8   3627
shall take all the *i* of ministry .... Num 4:12   3627
all the *i* of their service, and .... Num 4:26   3627
and their cords, with all their *i* .... Num 4:32   3627
by name ye shall reckon the *i* of .... Num 4:32   3627
it, and all the *i* thereof, both .... Num 7:1   3627
to the war, with the holy *i* .... Num 31:6   3627
harvest, and to make his *i* of war 1Sa 8:12   3627
and *i* of his chariots 1Sa 8:12   3627
with joy, and with *i* of musick 1Sa 18:6   7991
all manner of *i* made of fir wood 2Sa 6:5
burnt sacrifice, and threshing *i* 2Sa 24:22
other *i* of the oxen for wood 2Sa 24:22   3627
flesh with the *i* of the oxen 1Kin 19:21   3627
all the *i* of the sanctuary, and 1Chr 9:29   3627
expert in war, with all *i* of war 1Chr 12:33   3627
with all manner of *i* of war for 1Chr 12:37   3627
be the singers with *i* of musick 1Chr 15:16   3627
a sound, and with musical *i* of God 1Chr 16:42   3627
and the threshing *i* for wood 1Chr 21:23
the LORD with the *i* which I made 1Chr 23:5   3627
for all *i* of all manner of 1Chr 28:14   3627
for all *i* of silver by weight 1Chr 28:14   3627
for all *i* of every kind of 1Chr 28:14   3627
and the fleshhooks, and all their *i* 2Chr 4:16   3627
silver, and the gold, and all the *i* 2Chr 5:1   3627
i of musick, and praised the LORD 2Chr 5:13   3627
also with *i* of musick of the LORD 2Chr 7:6   3627
also the singers with *i* of musick 2Chr 23:13   3627

INTO See APPENDIX.

INTREAT
i for me to Ephron the son of	Gen 23:8	6293
I the LORD, that he may take away	Ex 8:8	6279
when shall *I* for thee, and for	Ex 8:9	6279
very far away: *i* for me	Ex 8:28	6279
I will *i* the LORD that the swarms	Ex 8:29	6279
I the LORD (for it is enough)	Ex 9:28	6279
i the LORD your God, that he may	Ex 10:17	6279
I me not to leave thee, or to	Ruth 1:16	6293
the LORD, who shall *i* for him	1Sa 2:25	6419
I now the face of the LORD thy	1Kin 13:6	2470
the people shall *i* thy favour	Ps 45:12	2470
Many will *i* the favour of the	Prov 19:6	2470
Being defamed, we	1Cor 4:13	3870
I *i* thee also, true yokefellow,	Phil 4:3	2065
an elder, but *i* him as a father	1Ti 5:1	3870

INTREATED
Isaac *i* the LORD for his wife,	Gen 25:21	6279
and the LORD was *i* of him, and	Gen 25:21	6279
out from Pharaoh, and *i* the LORD	Ex 8:30	6279
out from Pharaoh, and *i* the LORD	Ex 10:18	6279
Then Manoah *i* the LORD, and said,	Judg 13:8	6279
after that God was *i* for the land	2Sa 21:14	6279
So the LORD was *i* for the land	2Sa 24:25	6279
the battle, and he was *i* of them	1Chr 5:20	6279
and he was *i* of him, and heard his	2Chr 33:13	6279
also, and how God was *i* of him	2Chr 33:19	6279
and he was *i* of us	Ezr 8:23	6279
I *i* him with my mouth	Job 19:16	2603
though I *i* for the children's	Job 19:17	2589
I *i* thy favour with my whole	Ps 119:58	2470
LORD, and he shall be *i* of them	Is 19:22	6279
came his father out, and *i* him	Lk 15:28	3870
i that the word should not be	Heb 12:19	3862
gentle, and easy to be *i*, full of	Jas 3:17	2138

INTREATIES
The poor useth *i*	Prov 18:23	8469

INTREATY
Praying us with much *i* that we	2Cor 8:4	3874

INTRUDING
i into those things which he hath	Col 2:18	1687

INVADE
thou wouldest not let Israel *i*	2Chr 20:10	935
he will *i* them with his troops	Hab 3:16	1464

INVADED
the Philistines have *i* the land	1Sa 23:27	6584
i the Geshurites, and the Gezrites	1Sa 27:8	6584
the Amalekites had *i* the south	1Sa 30:1	6584
the bands of the Moabites *i* the	2Kin 13:20	935
The Philistines also had *i* the	2Chr 28:18	6584

INVASION
We made an *i* upon the south of	1Sa 30:14	6584

INVENT
i to themselves instruments of	Amos 6:5	2803

INVENTED
i by cunning men, to be on the	2Chr 26:15	2803

INVENTIONS
thou tookest vengeance of their *i*	Ps 99:8	5949
him to anger with their *i*	Ps 106:29	4611
went a whoring with their own *i*	Ps 106:39	4611
and find out knowledge of witty *i*	Prov 8:12	4209
but they have sought out many *i*	Eccl 7:29	2810

INVENTORS
i of evil things, disobedient to	Rom 1:30	2182

INVISIBLE
For the *i* things of him from the	Rom 1:20	517
Who is the image of the *i* God	Col 1:15	517
that are in earth, visible and *i*	Col 1:16	517
the King eternal, immortal, *i*	1Ti 1:17	517
endured, as seeing him who is *i*	Heb 11:27	517

INVITED
since I said, I have *i* the people	1Sa 9:24	7121
Absalom *i* all the king's sons	2Sa 13:23	7121
to morrow am I *i* unto her also	Est 5:12	7121

INWARD
is in the side of the ephod *i*	Ex 28:26	1004
was on the side of the ephod *i*	Ex 39:19	1004
it is fret *i*, whether it be bare	Lev 13:55	
built round about from Millo and *i*	2Sa 5:9	1004
and all their hinder parts were *i*	1Kin 7:25	1004
their feet, and their faces were *i*	2Chr 4:4	1004
and all their hinder parts were *i*	2Chr 4:4	1004
All my *i* friends abhorred me	Job 19:19	5475

hath put wisdom in the *i* parts	Job 38:36	2910
their *i* part is very wickedness	Ps 5:9	7130
Their *i* thought is, that their	Ps 49:11	7130
desirest truth in the *i* parts	Ps 51:6	2910
both the *i* thought of every one	Ps 64:6	7130
searching all the *i* parts of the	Prov 20:27	2315
so do stripes the *i* parts of the	Prov 20:30	2315
mine *i* parts for Kir-haresh	Is 16:11	7130
will put my law in their *i* parts	Jer 31:33	7130
and the porch of the gate was *i*	Eze 40:9	1004
and windows were round about *i*	Eze 40:16	6441
Then went he *i*, and measured the	Eze 41:3	6441
a walk of ten cubits breadth *i*	Eze 42:4	6442
but your *i* part is full of	Lk 11:39	2081
in the law of God after the *i* man	Rom 7:22	2080
yet the *i* man is renewed day by	2Cor 4:16	2081
his *i* affection is more abundant	2Cor 7:15	4698

INWARDLY
their mouth, but they curse *i*	Ps 62:4	7130
but *i* they are ravening wolves	Mt 7:15	2081
But he is a Jew, which is one *i*	Rom 2:29	1722,2927

INWARDS
all the fat that covereth the *i*	Ex 29:13	7130
in pieces, and wash the *i* of him	Ex 29:17	7130
and the fat that covereth the *i*	Ex 29:22	7130
But his *i* and his legs shall he	Lev 1:9	7130
But he shall wash the *i* and the	Lev 1:13	7130
the fat that covereth the *i*	Lev 3:3	7130
and all the fat that is upon the *i*	Lev 3:3	7130
and the fat that covereth the *i*	Lev 3:9	7130
and all the fat that is upon the *i*	Lev 3:9	7130
the fat that covereth the *i*	Lev 3:14	7130
and all the fat that is upon the *i*	Lev 3:14	7130
the fat that covereth the *i*	Lev 4:8	7130
and all the fat that is upon the *i*	Lev 4:8	7130
head, and with his legs, and his *i*	Lev 4:11	7130
and the fat that covereth the *i*	Lev 7:3	7130
all the fat that was upon the *i*	Lev 8:16	7130
And he washed the *i* and the legs in	Lev 8:21	7130
all the fat that was upon the *i*	Lev 8:25	7130
And he did wash the *i* and the legs,	Lev 9:14	7130
and that which covereth the *i*	Lev 9:19	

IOB See JOB.

IPHEDEIAH (if-e-di'-ah) A son of Shashak.
And *I*, and Penuel, the sons of	1Chr 8:25	3301

IPHTAH See JIPHTAH.

IPHTAH EL See JIPHTHAH-EL.

IR (ur) See IR-NAHASH, IR-SHEMESH. *Father of Machir.*
and Huppim, the children of *I*	1Chr 7:12	5893

IRA (i'-rah)
1. An officer of David.
I also the Jairite was a chief	2Sa 20:26	5896

2. A mighty man of David.
I the son of Ikkesh the Tekoite,	2Sa 23:26	5896
I an Ithrite, Gareb an Ithrite,	2Sa 23:38	5896
I the son of Ikkesh the Tekoite,	1Chr 11:28	5896
I the Ithrite, Gareb the Ithrite,	1Chr 11:40	5896
I the son of Ikkesh the Tekoite	1Chr 27:9	5896

IRAD (i'-rad) Son of Enoch.
And unto Enoch was born *I*	Gen 4:18	5897
and *I* begat Mehujael	Gen 4:18	5897

IRAM (i'-ram) An Edomite leader.
Duke Magdiel, duke *I*	Gen 36:43	5902
Duke Magdiel, duke *I*	1Chr 1:54	5902

IRI (i'-ri) A son of Bela.
and Uzziel, and Jerimoth, and *I*	1Chr 7:7	5901

IRIJAH (i-ri'-jah) A captain of the guard.
ward was there, whose name was *I*	Jer 37:13	3376
so *I* took Jeremiah, and brought	Jer 37:14	3376

IR-NAHASH (ur-na'-hash) A descendant of Chelub.
and Tehinnah the father of *I*	1Chr 4:12	5904

IRON (i'-ron) A city in Naphtali.
And *I*, and Migdal-el, Horem, and	Josh 19:38	3375
of every artificer in brass and *i*	Gen 4:22	1270
and I will make your heaven as *i*	Lev 26:19	1270
and the silver, the brass, the *i*	Num 31:22	1270
smite him with an instrument of *i*	Num 35:16	1270
his bedstead was a bedstead of *i*	Deut 3:11	1270
you forth out of the *i* furnace	Deut 4:20	1270
a land whose stones are *i*	Deut 8:9	1270
not lift up any *i* tool upon them	Deut 27:5	1270
that is under thee shall be *i*	Deut 28:23	1270
put a yoke of *i* upon thy neck	Deut 28:48	1270
Thy shoes shall be *i* and brass	Deut 33:25	1270

and gold, and vessels of brass and *i*	Josh 6:19	1270
and the vessels of brass and of *i*	Josh 6:24	1270
which no man hath lift up any *i*	Josh 8:31	1270
of the valley have chariots of *i*	Josh 17:16	1270
though they have *i* chariots	Josh 17:18	1270
gold, and with brass, and with *i*	Josh 22:8	1270
because they had chariots of *i*	Judg 1:19	1270
he had nine hundred chariots of *i*	Judg 4:3	1270
even nine hundred chariots of *i*	Judg 4:13	1270
weighed six hundred shekels of *i*	1Sa 17:7	1270
of iron, and under axes of *i*	2Sa 12:31	1270
touch them must be fenced with *i*	2Sa 23:7	1270
any tool of *i* heard in the house	1Kin 6:7	1270
the midst of the furnace of *i*	1Kin 8:51	1270
of Chenaanah made him horns of *i*	1Kin 22:11	1270
and the *i* did swim	2Kin 6:6	1270
with saws, and with harrows of *i*	1Chr 20:3	1270
David prepared *i* in abundance for	1Chr 22:3	1270
and of brass and *i* without weight	1Chr 22:14	1270
silver, and the brass, and the *i*	1Chr 22:16	1270
the *i* for things of iron, and wood	1Chr 29:2	1270
brass, the iron for things of *i*	1Chr 29:2	1270
one hundred thousand talents of *i*	1Chr 29:7	1270
in silver, and in brass, and in *i*	2Chr 2:7	1270
and in silver, in brass, in *i*	2Chr 2:14	1270
Chenaanah had made him horns of *i*	2Chr 18:10	1270
Lord, and also such as wrought *i*	2Chr 24:12	1270
they were graven with an *i* pen	Job 19:24	1270
He shall flee from the *i* weapon	Job 20:24	1270
I is taken out of the earth, and	Job 28:2	1270
his bones are like bars of *i*	Job 40:18	1270
He esteemeth *i* as straw, and brass	Job 41:27	1270
shalt break them with a rod of *i*	Ps 2:9	1270
he was laid in *i*	Ps 105:18	1270
being bound in affliction and *i*	Ps 107:10	1270
and cut the bars of *i* in sunder	Ps 107:16	1270
and their nobles with fetters of *i*	Ps 149:8	1270
I sharpeneth iron	Prov 27:17	1270
Iron sharpeneth *i*	Prov 27:17	1270
If the *i* be blunt, and he do not	Eccl 10:10	1270
the thickets of the forest with *i*	Is 10:34	1270
and cut in sunder the bars of *i*	Is 45:2	1270
and thy neck is an *i* sinew	Is 48:4	1270
for *i* I will bring silver, and for	Is 60:17	1270
for wood brass, and for stones *i*	Is 60:17	1270
an *i* pillar, and brasen walls	Jer 1:18	1270
they are brass and *i*	Jer 6:28	1270
land of Egypt, from the *i* furnace	Jer 11:4	1270
Shall *i* break the northern iron	Jer 15:12	1270
Shall iron break the northern *i*	Jer 15:12	1270
Judah is written with a pen of *i*	Jer 17:1	1270
shalt make for them yokes of *i*	Jer 28:13	1270
I have put a yoke of *i* upon the	Jer 28:14	1270
take thou unto thee an *i* pan	Eze 4:3	1270
it for a wall of *i* between thee	Eze 4:3	1270
all they are brass, and tin, and *i*	Eze 22:18	1270
gather silver, and brass, and *i*	Eze 22:20	1270
with silver, *i*, tin, and lead,	Eze 27:12	1270
bright *i*, cassia, and calamus,	Eze 27:19	1270
legs of iron, his feet part of *i*	Dan 2:33	6523
upon his feet that were of *i*	Dan 2:34	6523
Then was the *i*, the clay, the	Dan 2:35	6523
kingdom shall be strong as *i*	Dan 2:40	6523
forasmuch as *i* breaketh in pieces	Dan 2:40	6523
as *i* that breaketh all these,	Dan 2:40	6523
of potters' clay, and part of *i*	Dan 2:41	6523
be in it of the strength of the *i*	Dan 2:41	6523
sawest the *i* mixed with miry clay	Dan 2:41	6523
toes of the feet were part of *i*	Dan 2:42	6523
whereas thou sawest *i* mixed with	Dan 2:43	6523
even as *i* is not mixed with clay	Dan 2:43	6523
and that it brake in pieces the *i*	Dan 2:45	6523
the earth, even with a band of *i*	Dan 4:15	6523
the earth, even with a band of *i*	Dan 4:23	6523
and of silver, of brass, of *i*	Dan 5:4	6523
of silver, and gold, of brass, *i*	Dan 5:23	6523
and it had great *i* teeth	Dan 7:7	6523
dreadful, whose teeth were of *i*	Dan 7:19	6523
with threshing instruments of *i*	Amos 1:3	1270
for I will make thine horn *i*	Mic 4:13	1270
they came unto the *i* gate that	Acts 12:10	4603
conscience seared with a hot *i*	1Ti 4:2	
shall rule them with a rod of *i*	Rev 2:27	4603
as it were breastplates of *i*	Rev 9:9	4603
rule all nations with a rod of *i*	Rev 12:5	4603
precious wood, and of brass, and *i*	Rev 18:12	4604
shall rule them with a rod of *i*	Rev 19:15	4603

IRONS

thou fill his skin with barbed *i*	Job 41:7	7905

IRPEEL *(ur'-pe-el) A city in Benjamin.*

And Rekem, and *I*, and Taralah,	Josh 18:27	3416

IR-SHEMESH *(ur-she'-mesh) A city in Dan.*

was Zorah, and Eshtaol, and *I*	Josh 19:41	5905

IRU *(i'-ru) A son of Caleb.*

I, Elah, and Naam	1Chr 4:15	5902

IS See APPENDIX.

ISAAC *(i'-za-ak)* See Isaac's. *Son of Abraham and Sarah.*

and thou shalt call his name *I*	Gen 17:19	3327
covenant will I establish with *I*	Gen 17:21	3327
him, whom Sarah bare to him, *I*	Gen 21:3	3327
his son *I* being eight days old	Gen 21:4	3327
when his son *I* was born unto him	Gen 21:5	3327
the same day that *I* was weaned	Gen 21:8	3327
be heir with my son, even with *I*	Gen 21:10	3327
for in *I* shall thy seed be called	Gen 21:12	3327
now thy son, thine only son *I*	Gen 22:2	3327
I his son, and clave the wood for	Gen 22:3	3327
and laid it upon *I* his son	Gen 22:6	3327
I spake unto Abraham his father,	Gen 22:7	3327
bound *I* his son, and laid him on	Gen 22:9	3327
and take a wife unto my son *I*	Gen 24:4	3327
hast appointed for thy servant *I*	Gen 24:14	3327
I came from the way of the well	Gen 24:62	3327
I went out to meditate in the	Gen 24:63	3327
up her eyes, and when she saw *I*	Gen 24:64	3327
the servant told *I* all things	Gen 24:66	3327
I brought her into his mother	Gen 24:67	3327
I was comforted after his	Gen 24:67	3327
gave all that he had unto *I*	Gen 25:5	3327
and sent them away from *I* his son	Gen 25:6	3327
And his sons *I* and Ishmael buried	Gen 25:9	3327
that God blessed his son *I*	Gen 25:11	3327
I dwelt by the well Lahai-roi	Gen 25:11	3327
And these are the generations of *I*	Gen 25:19	3327
Abraham begat *I*	Gen 25:19	3327
I was forty years old when he	Gen 25:20	3327
I intreated the Lord for his wife	Gen 25:21	3327
I was threescore years old when	Gen 25:26	3327
I loved Esau, because he did eat	Gen 25:28	3327
I went unto Abimelech king of the	Gen 26:1	3327
And *I* dwelt in Gerar	Gen 26:6	3327
I was sporting with Rebekah his	Gen 26:8	3327
And Abimelech called *I*, and said,	Gen 26:9	3327
I said unto him, Because I said,	Gen 26:9	3327
Then *I* sowed in that land, and	Gen 26:12	3327
And Abimelech said unto *I*, Go from	Gen 26:16	3327
I departed thence, and pitched his	Gen 26:17	3327
I digged again the wells of water	Gen 26:18	3327
I said unto them, Wherefore come	Gen 26:27	3327
I sent them away, and they	Gen 26:31	3327
Which were a grief of mind unto *I*	Gen 26:35	3327
came to pass, that when *I* was old	Gen 27:1	3327
Rebekah heard when *I* spake to	Gen 27:5	3327
I said unto his son, How is it	Gen 27:20	3327
I said unto Jacob, Come near, I	Gen 27:21	3327
Jacob went near unto *I* his father	Gen 27:22	3327
his father *I* said unto him, Come	Gen 27:26	3327
as soon as *I* had made an end of	Gen 27:30	3327
from the presence of *I* his father	Gen 27:30	3327
I his father said unto him, Who	Gen 27:32	3327
I trembled very exceedingly, and	Gen 27:33	3327
I answered and said unto Esau,	Gen 27:37	3327
I his father answered and said	Gen 27:39	3327
And Rebekah said to *I*, I am weary	Gen 27:46	3327
I called Jacob, and blessed him,	Gen 28:1	3327
And *I* sent away Jacob	Gen 28:5	3327
Esau saw that *I* had blessed Jacob	Gen 28:6	3327
Canaan pleased not *I* his father	Gen 28:8	3327
thy father, and the God of *I*	Gen 28:13	3327
for to go to *I* his father in the	Gen 31:18	3327
God of Abraham, and the fear of *I*	Gen 31:42	3327
sware by the fear of his father *I*	Gen 31:53	3327
Abraham, and God of my father *I*	Gen 32:9	3327
land which I gave Abraham and *I*	Gen 35:12	3327
Jacob came unto *I* his father unto	Gen 35:27	3327
where Abraham and *I* sojourned	Gen 35:27	3327
the days of *I* were an hundred and	Gen 35:28	3327
I gave up the ghost, and died, and	Gen 35:29	3327
unto the God of his father *I*	Gen 46:1	3327
I did walk, the God which fed me	Gen 48:15	3327
name of my fathers Abraham and *I*	Gen 48:16	3327
there they buried *I* and Rebekah	Gen 49:31	3327
which he sware to Abraham, to *I*	Gen 50:24	3327
his covenant with Abraham, with *I*	Ex 2:24	3327
the God of Abraham, the God of *I*	Ex 3:6	3327
the God of Abraham, the God of *I*	Ex 3:15	3327
fathers, the God of Abraham, of *I*	Ex 3:16	3327

the God of Abraham, the God of *I*	Ex 4:5	3327
I appeared unto Abraham, unto *I*	Ex 6:3	3327
swear to give it to Abraham, to *I*	Ex 6:8	3327
Remember Abraham, *I*, and Israel,	Ex 32:13	3327
which I sware unto Abraham, to *I*	Ex 33:1	3327
Jacob, and also my covenant with *I*	Lev 26:42	3327
I sware unto Abraham, unto *I*	Num 32:11	3327
unto your fathers, Abraham, *I*	Deut 1:8	3327
thy fathers, to Abraham, to *I*	Deut 6:10	3327
unto thy fathers, Abraham, *I*	Deut 9:5	3327
Remember thy servants, Abraham, *I*	Deut 9:27	3327
thy fathers, to Abraham, to *I*	Deut 29:13	3327
thy fathers, to Abraham, to *I*	Deut 30:20	3327
I sware unto Abraham, unto *I*	Deut 34:4	3327
his seed, and gave him *I*	Josh 24:3	3327
And I gave unto *I* Jacob and Esau	Josh 24:4	3327
and said, LORD God of Abraham, *I*	1Kin 18:36	3327
of his covenant with Abraham, *I*	2Kin 13:23	3327
I, and Ishmael	1Chr 1:28	3327
And Abraham begat *I*	1Chr 1:34	3327
The sons of *I*	1Chr 1:34	3327
Abraham, and of his oath unto *I*	1Chr 16:16	3327
O LORD God of Abraham, *I*, and of	1Chr 29:18	3327
unto the LORD God of Abraham, *I*	2Chr 30:6	3327
with Abraham, and his oath unto *I*	Ps 105:9	3446
over the seed of Abraham, *I*	Jer 33:26	3446
places of *I* shall be desolate	Amos 7:9	3446
thy word against the house of *I*	Amos 7:16	3446
Abraham begat *I*	Mt 1:2	2664
and *I* begat Jacob	Mt 1:2	2664
shall sit down with Abraham, and *I*	Mt 8:11	2664
God of Abraham, and the God of *I*	Mt 22:32	2664
God of Abraham, and the God of *I*	Mk 12:26	2664
of Jacob, which was the son of *I*	Lk 3:34	2664
when ye shall see Abraham, and *I*	Lk 13:28	2664
God of Abraham, and the God of *I*	Lk 20:37	2664
The God of Abraham, and of *I*	Acts 3:13	2664
and so Abraham begat *I*	Acts 7:8	2664
and *I* begat Jacob	Acts 7:8	2664
God of Abraham, and the God of *I*	Acts 7:32	2664
In *I* shall thy seed be called	Rom 9:7	2664
by one, even by our father *I*	Rom 9:10	2664
as *I* was, are the children of	Gal 4:28	2664
dwelling in tabernacles with *I*	Heb 11:9	2664
when he was tried, offered up *I*	Heb 11:17	2664
That in *I* shall thy seed be	Heb 11:18	2664
By faith *I* blessed Jacob and Esau	Heb 11:20	2664
when he had offered *I* his son	Jas 2:21	2664

ISAAC'S *(i'-za-aks)*

I servants digged in the valley,	Gen 26:19	3327
Gerar did strive with *I* herdmen	Gen 26:20	3327
there *I* servants digged a well	Gen 26:25	3327
that *I* servants came, and told him	Gen 26:32	3327

ISAIAH *(i-za'-yah)* See ESAIAS. *A prophet.*

to *I* the prophet the son of Amoz	2Kin 19:2	3470
of king Hezekiah came to *I*	2Kin 19:5	3470
I said unto them, Thus shall ye	2Kin 19:6	3470
Then *I* the son of Amoz sent to	2Kin 19:20	3470
the prophet *I* the son of Amoz	2Kin 20:1	3470
afore *I* was gone out into the	2Kin 20:4	3470
I said, Take a lump of figs	2Kin 20:7	3470
And Hezekiah said unto *I*, What	2Kin 20:8	3470
I said, This sign shalt thou have	2Kin 20:9	3470
I the prophet cried unto the LORD	2Kin 20:11	3470
Then came *I* the prophet unto king	2Kin 20:14	3470
I said unto Hezekiah, Hear the	2Kin 20:16	3470
Then said Hezekiah unto *I*	2Kin 20:19	3470
did *I* the prophet, the son of	2Chr 26:22	3470
the prophet *I* the son of Amoz,	2Chr 32:20	3470
in the vision of *I* the prophet	2Chr 32:32	3470
The vision of *I* the son of Amoz,	Is 1:1	3470
The word that *I* the son of Amoz	Is 2:1	3470
Then said the LORD unto *I*	Is 7:3	3470
which *I* the son of Amoz did see	Is 13:1	3470
the LORD by *I* the son of Amoz	Is 20:2	3470
as my servant *I* hath walked naked	Is 20:3	3470
unto *I* the prophet the son of	Is 37:2	3470
of king Hezekiah came to *I*	Is 37:5	3470
I said unto them, Thus shall ye	Is 37:6	3470
Then *I* the son of Amoz sent unto	Is 37:21	3470
I the prophet the son of Amoz	Is 38:1	3470
came the word of the LORD to *I*	Is 38:4	3470
For *I* had said, Let them take a	Is 38:21	3470
Then came *I* the prophet unto king	Is 39:3	3470
Then said *I* to Hezekiah, Hear the	Is 39:5	3470
Then said Hezekiah to *I*, Good is	Is 39:8	3470

ISCAH *(is'-cah)* See SARAH. *A daughter of Haran.*

of Milcah, and the father of *I*	Gen 11:29	3252

ISCARIOT *(is-car'-e-ot)* See JUDAS. *Disciple who betrayed Jesus.*

Simon the Canaanite, and Judas *I*	Mt 10:4	2469
one of the twelve, called Judas *I*	Mt 26:14	2469
And Judas *I*, which also betrayed	Mk 3:19	2469
And Judas *I*, one of the twelve,	Mk 14:10	2469
the brother of James, and Judas *I*	Lk 6:16	2469
Satan into Judas surnamed *I*	Lk 22:3	2469
spake of Judas *I* the son of Simon	Jn 6:71	2469
one of his disciples, Judas *I*	Jn 12:4	2469
now put into the heart of Judas *I*	Jn 13:2	2469
the sop, he gave it to Judas *I*	Jn 13:26	2469
Judas saith unto him, not *I*	Jn 14:22	2469

ISHBAH *(ish'-bah)* *Father of Eshtemoa.*

and *I* the father of Eshtemoa	1Chr 4:17	3431

ISHBAK *(ish'-bak)* *A son of Abraham.*

and Medan, and Midian, and *I*	Gen 25:2	3435
and Medan, and Midian, and *I*	1Chr 1:32	3435

ISHBI-BENOB *(ish'-bi-be'-nob)* *A Philistine giant.*

And *I*, which was of the sons of	2Sa 21:16	3430

ISH-BOSHETH *(ish-bo'-sheth)* See ESH-BAAL. *Son of Saul.*

took *I* the son of Saul, and	2Sa 2:8	378
I Saul's son was forty years old	2Sa 2:10	378
the servants of *I* the son of Saul	2Sa 2:12	378
pertained to *I* the son of Saul	2Sa 2:15	378
i said to Abner, Wherefore hast	2Sa 3:7	
very wroth for the words of *I*	2Sa 3:8	378
sent messengers to *I* Saul's son	2Sa 3:14	378
I sent, and took her from her	2Sa 3:15	378
heat of the day to the house of *I*	2Sa 4:5	378
head of *I* unto David to Hebron	2Sa 4:8	378
Behold the head of *I* the son of	2Sa 4:8	378
But they took the head of *I*	2Sa 4:12	378

ISHI *(i'-shi)*
  1. A descendant of Pharez.

sons of Appaim; *I*	1Chr 2:31	3469
And the sons of *I*	1Chr 2:31	3469
  2. A descendant of Judah.
| And the sons of *I* were, Zoheth, and | 1Chr 4:20 | 3469 |
  3. A Simeonite.
| and Uzziel, the sons of *I* | 1Chr 4:42 | 3469 |
  4. A chief of Manasseh.
| their fathers, even Epher, and *I* | 1Chr 5:24 | 3469 |
  5. A symbolic name for Israel.
| LORD, that thou shalt call me *I* | Hos 2:16 | 376 |

ISHIAH *(i-shi'-ah)* See ISHIJAH, ISSHIAH. *A son of Izrahiah.*

Michael, and Obadiah, and Joel, *I*	1Chr 7:3	3449

ISHIJAH *(i-shi'-jah)* See ISHIAH, JESIAH. *Married a foreigner in exile.*

Eliezer, *I*, Malchiah, Shemaiah,	Ezr 10:31	3449

ISHMA *(ish'-mah)* *A descendant of Caleb.*

Jezreel, and *I*, and Idbash	1Chr 4:3	3457

ISHMAEL *(ish'-ma-el)* See ISHMAELITE, ISHMAEL'S.
  1. Son of Abraham and Hagar.

a son, and shalt call his name *I*	Gen 16:11	3458
son's name, which Hagar bare, *I*	Gen 16:15	3458
old, when Hagar bare *I* to Abram	Gen 16:16	3458
O that *I* might live before thee	Gen 17:18	3458
And as for *I*, I have heard thee	Gen 17:20	3458
And Abraham took *I* his son	Gen 17:23	3458
I his son was thirteen years old,	Gen 17:25	3458
Abraham circumcised, and *I* his son	Gen 17:26	3458
I buried him in the cave of	Gen 25:9	3458
these are the generations of *I*	Gen 25:12	3458
are the names of the sons of *I*	Gen 25:13	3458
the firstborn of *I*, Nebajoth	Gen 25:13	3458
These are the sons of *I*, and these	Gen 25:16	3458
are the years of the life of *I*	Gen 25:17	3458
Then went Esau unto *I*, and took	Gen 28:9	3458
the daughter of *I* Abraham's son	Gen 28:9	3458
Isaac, and *I*	1Chr 1:28	3458
The firstborn of *I*, Nebaioth	1Chr 1:29	3458
These are the sons of *I*	1Chr 1:31	3458
  2. A ruler of Judah.
| and Zebadiah the son of *I*, the | 2Chr 19:11 | 3458 |
  3. Son of Azel.
| are these, Azrikam, Bocheru, and *I* | 1Chr 8:38 | 3458 |
| are these, Azrikam, Bocheru, and *I* | 1Chr 9:44 | 3458 |
  4. A captain who aided Joash.
| *I* the son of Jehohanan, and | 2Chr 23:1 | 3458 |
  5. Married a foreigner in exile.
| Elioenai, Maaseiah, *I*, Nethaneel, | Ezr 10:22 | 3458 |
  6. The son of Nethaniah.
| even *I* the son of Nethaniah, and | 2Kin 25:23 | 3458 |
| that *I* the son of Nethaniah, the | 2Kin 25:25 | 3458 |

even *I* the son of Nethaniah, and	Jer 40:8	3458
I the son of Nethaniah to slay	Jer 40:14	3458
thee, and I will slay *I* the son of	Jer 40:15	3458
for thou speakest falsely of *I*	Jer 40:16	3458
that *I* the son of Nethaniah the	Jer 41:1	3458
Then arose *I* the son of Nethaniah	Jer 41:2	3458
I also slew all the Jews that	Jer 41:3	3458
I the son of Nethaniah went forth	Jer 41:6	3458
that *I* the son of Nethaniah slew	Jer 41:7	3458
found among them that said unto *I*	Jer 41:8	3458
Now the pit wherein *I* had cast	Jer 41:9	3458
I the son of Nethaniah filled it	Jer 41:9	3458
Then *I* carried away captive all	Jer 41:10	3458
I the son of Nethaniah carried	Jer 41:10	3458
heard of all the evil that *I* the	Jer 41:11	3458
went to fight with *I* the son of	Jer 41:12	3458
I saw Johanan the son of Kareah	Jer 41:13	3458
So all the people that *I* had	Jer 41:14	3458
But *I* the son of Nethaniah	Jer 41:15	3458
from *I* the son of Nethaniah	Jer 41:16	3458
because *I* the son of Nethaniah	Jer 41:18	3458

ISHMAELITE *(ish'-ma-el-ite) Descendants of Ishmael 1.*
the camels also was Obil the *I*	1Chr 27:30	3458

ISHMAELITES *(ish'-ma-el-lites)* See ISHMEELITES.
earrings, because they were *I*	Judg 8:24	3459
The tabernacles of Edom, and the *I*	Ps 83:6	3459

ISHMAEL'S *(ish'-ma-els) Refers to Ishmael 1.*
And Bashemath *I* daughter, sister	Gen 36:3	3458

ISHMAIAH *(ish-ma-i'-ah)* See ISMAIAH. *A prince of Zebulun.*
Of Zebulun, *I* the son of Obadiah	1Chr 27:19	3460

ISHMEELITE *(ish'-me-el-ite)* See ISHMAELITE, ISHMEELITES. *Same as Ishmaelite.*
father of Amasa was Jether the *I*	1Chr 2:17	3459

ISHMEELITES *(ish'-me-el-ites)* See ISHMAELITES.
a company of *I* came from Gilead	Gen 37:25	3459
Come, and let us sell him to the *I*	Gen 37:27	3459
sold Joseph to the *I* for twenty	Gen 37:28	3459
bought him of the hands of the *I*	Gen 39:1	3459

ISHMERAI *(ish'-me-rahee) A chief of Benjamin.*
I also, and Jezliah, and Jobab, the	1Chr 8:18	3461

ISHOD *(i'-shod) A son of Hammoleketh.*
And his sister Hammoleketh bare *I*	1Chr 7:18	379

ISHPAH See ISPAH.

ISHPAN *(ish'-pan) A son of Shashak.*
And *I*, and Heber, and Eliel,	1Chr 8:22	3473

ISH-TOB *(ish'-tob) A district of Aram.*
men, and of *I* twelve thousand men	2Sa 10:6	382
of Zoba, and of Rehob, and *I*	2Sa 10:8	382

ISHUAH *(ish'-u-ah)* See ISUAH. *A son of Asher.*
Jimnah, and *I*, and Isui, and Beriah,	Gen 46:17	3438

ISHUAI
Imnah, and Isuah, and *I*, and Beriah,	1Chr 7:30	3440

ISHUI *(ish'-u-i)* See ISHUAI, JESUI. *A son of Saul.*
sons of Saul were Jonathan, and *I*	1Sa 14:49	3440

ISLAND
deliver the *i* of the innocent	Job 22:30	336
with the wild beasts of the *i*	Is 34:14	338
certain *i* which is called Clauda	Acts 27:16	3519
we must be cast upon a certain *i*	Acts 27:26	3520
knew that the *i* was called Melita	Acts 28:1	3520
of the chief man of the *i*	Acts 28:7	3520
also, which had diseases in the *i*	Acts 28:9	3520
i were moved out of their places	Rev 6:14	3520
every *i* fled away, and the	Rev 16:20	3520

ISLANDS
Hamath, and from the *i* of the sea	Is 11:11	339
the wild beasts of the *i* shall	Is 13:22	338
Keep silence before me, O *i*	Is 41:1	339
and declare his praise in the *i*	Is 42:12	339
and I will make the rivers *i*	Is 42:15	339
to the *i* he will repay recompence	Is 59:18	339
beasts of the *i* shall dwell there	Jer 50:39	339

ISLE
of this *i* shall say in that day	Is 20:6	339
Be still, ye inhabitants of the *i*	Is 23:2	339
howl, ye inhabitants of the *i*	Is 23:6	339
gone through the *i* unto Paphos	Acts 13:6	3520
which had wintered in the *i*	Acts 28:11	3520
was in the *i* that is called	Rev 1:9	3520

ISLES
By these were the *i* of the	Gen 10:5	339
land, and upon the *i* of the sea	Est 10:1	339

of the *i* shall bring presents	Ps 72:10	339
multitude of *i* be glad thereof	Ps 97:1	339
God of Israel in the *i* of the sea	Is 24:15	339
he taketh up the *i* as a very	Is 40:15	339
The *i* saw it, and feared	Is 41:5	339
the *i* shall wait for his law	Is 42:4	339
the *i*, and the inhabitants thereof	Is 42:10	339
Listen, O *i*, unto me	Is 49:1	339
the *i* shall wait upon me, and on	Is 51:5	339
Surely the *i* shall wait for me,	Is 60:9	339
to the *i* afar off, that have not	Is 66:19	339
For pass over the *i* of Chittim	Jer 2:10	339
the kings of the *i* which are	Jer 25:22	339
and declare it in the *i* afar off	Jer 31:10	339
Shall not the *i* shake at the	Eze 26:15	339
Now shall the *i* tremble in the	Eze 26:18	339
the *i* that are in the sea shall	Eze 26:18	339
merchant of the people for many *i*	Eze 27:3	339
brought out of the *i* of Chittim	Eze 27:6	339
purple from the *i* of Elishah was	Eze 27:7	339
many *i* were the merchandise of	Eze 27:15	339
All the inhabitants of the *i*	Eze 27:35	339
that dwell carelessly in the *i*	Eze 39:6	339
shall he turn his face unto the *i*	Dan 11:18	339
even all the *i* of the heathen	Zeph 2:11	339

ISMACHIAH *(is-ma-ki'-ah) A temple servant.*
and Jozabad, and Eliel, and *I*	2Chr 31:13	3253

ISMAIAH *(is-ma-i'-ah)* See ISHMAIAH. *A warrior in David's army.*
I the Gibeonite, a mighty man	1Chr 12:4	3460

ISPAH *(is'-pah) A son of Beriah.*
And Michael, and *I*, and Joha, the	1Chr 8:16	3472

ISRAEL *(iz'-ra-el)* See EL-ELOHE-ISRAEL, ISRAELITE, ISRAEL'S, JACOB, JESHURUN.
1. Name given to Jacob.
be called no more Jacob, but *I*	Gen 32:28	3478
Jacob, but *I* shall be thy name	Gen 35:10	3478
and he called his name *I*	Gen 35:10	3478
I journeyed, and spread his tent	Gen 35:21	3478
when *I* dwelt in that land, that	Gen 35:22	3478
and *I* heard it	Gen 35:22	3478
Now *I* loved Joseph more than all	Gen 37:3	3478
I said unto Joseph, Do not thy	Gen 37:13	3478
the sons of *I* came to buy corn	Gen 42:5	3478
I said, Wherefore dealt ye so ill	Gen 43:6	3478
And Judah said unto *I* his father	Gen 43:8	3478
their father *I* said unto them, If	Gen 43:11	3478
And the children of *I* did so	Gen 45:21	3478
And *I* said, It is enough	Gen 45:28	3478
I took his journey with all that	Gen 46:1	3478
God spake unto *I* in the visions	Gen 46:2	3478
the sons of *I* carried Jacob their	Gen 46:5	3478
the names of the children of *I*	Gen 46:8	3478
and went up to meet *I* his father	Gen 46:29	3478
I said unto Joseph, Now let me	Gen 46:30	3478
I dwelt in the land of Egypt, in	Gen 47:27	3478
time drew nigh that *I* must die	Gen 47:29	3478
I bowed himself upon the bed's	Gen 47:31	3478
I strengthened himself, and sat	Gen 48:2	3478
I beheld Joseph's sons, and said,	Gen 48:8	3478
Now the eyes of *I* were dim for	Gen 48:10	3478
I said unto Joseph, I had not	Gen 48:11	3478
I stretched out his right hand,	Gen 48:14	3478
saying, In thee shall *I* bless	Gen 48:20	3478
I said unto Joseph, Behold, I die	Gen 48:21	3478
and hearken unto *I* your father	Gen 49:2	3478
and the physicians embalmed *I*	Gen 50:2	3478
the names of the children of *I*	Ex 1:1	3478
the children of *I* were fruitful	Ex 1:7	3478
sons of Reuben the firstborn of *I*	Ex 6:14	3478
Remember Abraham, Isaac, and *I*.	Ex 32:13	3478
Reuben, the eldest son of *I*	Num 26:5	3478
their father, who was born unto *I*	Judg 18:29	3478
came, saying, *I* shall be thy name	1Kin 18:31	3478
God of Abraham, Isaac, and of *I*	1Kin 18:36	3478
of Jacob, whom he named *I*	2Kin 17:34	3478
The sons of Isaac; Esau and *I*	1Chr 1:34	3478
These are the sons of *I*	1Chr 2:1	3478
sons of Reuben the firstborn of *I*	1Chr 5:1	3478
the sons of Joseph the son of *I*	1Chr 5:1	3478
of Reuben the firstborn of *I* were	1Chr 5:3	3478
the son of Levi, the son of *I*	1Chr 6:38	3478
children of Joseph the son of *I*	1Chr 7:29	3478
be thou, LORD God of *I* our father	1Chr 29:10	3478
God of Abraham, Isaac, and of *I*	1Chr 29:18	3478
LORD God of Abraham, Isaac, and *I*	2Chr 30:6	3478
the son of Levi, the son of *I*	Ezr 8:18	3478

I

2. People descended from Jacob.

Therefore the children of *I* eat	Gen 32:32	3478
I in lying with Jacob's daughter	Gen 34:7	3478
any king over the children of *I*	Gen 36:31	3478
in Jacob, and scatter them in *I*	Gen 49:7	3478
people, as one of the tribes of *I*	Gen 49:16	3478
is the shepherd, the stone of *I*	Gen 49:24	3478
these are the twelve tribes of *I*	Gen 49:28	3478
took an oath of the children of *I*	Gen 50:25	3478
of the children of *I* are more	Ex 1:9	3478
because of the children of *I*	Ex 1:12	3478
of *I* to serve with rigour	Ex 1:13	3478
the children of *I* sighed by	Ex 2:23	3478
God looked upon the children of *I*	Ex 2:25	3478
the children of *I* is come unto me	Ex 3:9	3478
the children of *I* out of Egypt	Ex 3:10	3478
the children of *I* out of Egypt	Ex 3:11	3478
I come unto the children of *I*	Ex 3:13	3478
thou say unto the children of *I*	Ex 3:14	3478
thou say unto the children of *I*	Ex 3:15	3478
gather the elders of *I* together	Ex 3:16	3478
come, thou and the elders of *I*	Ex 3:18	3478
I is my son, even my firstborn	Ex 4:22	3478
the elders of the children of *I*	Ex 4:29	3478
had visited the children of *I*	Ex 4:31	3478
Thus saith the LORD God of *I*	Ex 5:1	3478
should obey his voice to let *I* go	Ex 5:2	3478
the LORD, neither will I let *I* go	Ex 5:2	3478
the officers of the children of *I*	Ex 5:14	3478
of the children of *I* came	Ex 5:15	3478
I did see that they were in evil	Ex 5:19	3478
the groaning of the children of *I*	Ex 6:5	3478
say unto the children of *I*	Ex 6:6	3478
spake so unto the children of *I*	Ex 6:9	3478
children of *I* go out of his land	Ex 6:11	3478
the children of *I* have not	Ex 6:12	3478
a charge unto the children of *I*	Ex 6:13	3478
of *I* out of the land of Egypt	Ex 6:13	3478
of *I* from the land of Egypt	Ex 6:26	3478
out the children of *I* from Egypt	Ex 6:27	3478
the children of *I* out of his land	Ex 7:2	3478
and my people the children of *I*	Ex 7:4	3478
the children of *I* from among them	Ex 7:5	3478
sever between the cattle of *I*	Ex 9:4	3478
all that is the children's of *I*	Ex 9:4	3478
of the children of *I* died not one	Ex 9:6	3478
where the children of *I* were	Ex 9:26	3478
would he let the children of *I* go	Ex 9:35	3478
not let the children of *I* go	Ex 10:20	3478
but all the children of *I* had	Ex 10:23	3478
against any of the children of *I*	Ex 11:7	3478
between the Egyptians and *I*	Ex 11:7	3478
children of *I* go out of his land	Ex 11:10	3478
ye unto all the congregation of *I*	Ex 12:3	3478
of *I* shall kill it in the evening	Ex 12:6	3478
that soul shall be cut off from *I*	Ex 12:15	3478
off from the congregation of *I*	Ex 12:19	3478
called for all the elders of *I*	Ex 12:21	3478
of the children of *I* in Egypt	Ex 12:27	3478
And the children of *I* went away	Ex 12:28	3478
both ye and the children of *I*	Ex 12:31	3478
the children of *I* did according	Ex 12:35	3478
the children of *I* journeyed from	Ex 12:37	3478
sojourning of the children of *I*	Ex 12:40	3478
of *I* in their generations	Ex 12:42	3478
congregation of *I* shall keep it	Ex 12:47	3478
Thus did all the children of *I*	Ex 12:50	3478
of *I* out of the land of Egypt by	Ex 12:51	3478
the womb among the children of *I*	Ex 13:2	3478
the children of *I* went up	Ex 13:18	3478
straitly sworn the children of *I*	Ex 13:19	3478
Speak unto the children of *I*	Ex 14:2	3478
will say of the children of *I*	Ex 14:3	3478
that we have let *I* go from	Ex 14:5	3478
pursued after the children of *I*	Ex 14:8	3478
the children of *I* went out with	Ex 14:8	3478
the children of *I* lifted up their	Ex 14:10	3478
the children of *I* cried out unto	Ex 14:10	3478
speak unto the children of *I*	Ex 14:15	3478
the children of *I* shall go on dry	Ex 14:16	3478
which went before the camp of *I*	Ex 14:19	3478
of the Egyptians and the camp of *I*	Ex 14:20	3478
the children of *I* went into the	Ex 14:22	3478
Let us flee from the face of *I*	Ex 14:25	3478
But the children of *I* walked upon	Ex 14:29	3478
Thus the LORD saved *I* that day	Ex 14:30	3478
I saw the Egyptians dead upon the	Ex 14:30	3478
I saw that great work which the	Ex 14:31	3478
the children of *I* this song unto	Ex 15:1	3478
but the children of *I* went on dry	Ex 15:19	3478
Moses brought *I* from the Red sea	Ex 15:22	3478
I came unto the wilderness of Sin	Ex 16:1	3478
of *I* murmured against Moses	Ex 16:2	3478
the children of *I* said unto them	Ex 16:3	3478
said unto all the children of *I*	Ex 16:6	3478
congregation of the children of *I*	Ex 16:9	3478
congregation of the children of *I*	Ex 16:10	3478
murmurings of the children of *I*	Ex 16:12	3478
And when the children of *I* saw it	Ex 16:15	3478
And the children of *I* did so	Ex 16:17	3478
the house of *I* called the name	Ex 16:31	3478
the children of *I* did eat manna	Ex 16:35	3478
I journeyed from the wilderness	Ex 17:1	3478
take with thee of the elders of *I*	Ex 17:5	3478
in the sight of the elders of *I*	Ex 17:6	3478
the chiding of the children of *I*	Ex 17:7	3478
and fought with *I* in Rephidim	Ex 17:8	3478
up his hand, that *I* prevailed	Ex 17:11	3478
for *I* his people, and that the	Ex 18:1	3478
LORD had brought *I* out of Egypt	Ex 18:1	3478
which the LORD had done to *I*	Ex 18:9	3478
came, and all the elders of *I*	Ex 18:12	3478
Moses chose able men out of all *I*	Ex 18:25	3478
when the children of *I* were gone	Ex 19:1	3478
there *I* camped before the mount	Ex 19:2	3478
Jacob, and tell the children of *I*	Ex 19:3	3478
speak unto the children of *I*	Ex 19:6	3478
shalt say unto the children of *I*	Ex 20:22	3478
and seventy of the elders of *I*	Ex 24:1	3478
to the twelve tribes of *I*	Ex 24:4	3478
young men of the children of *I*	Ex 24:5	3478
and seventy of the elders of *I*	Ex 24:9	3478
And they saw the God of *I*	Ex 24:10	3478
of *I* he laid not his hand	Ex 24:11	3478
in the eyes of the children of *I*	Ex 24:17	3478
Speak unto the children of *I*	Ex 25:2	3478
unto the children of *I*	Ex 25:22	3478
shalt command the children of *I*	Ex 27:20	3478
the behalf of the children of *I*	Ex 27:21	3478
him, from among the children of *I*	Ex 28:1	3478
the names of the children of *I*	Ex 28:9	3478
the names of the children of *I*	Ex 28:11	3478
memorial unto the children of *I*	Ex 28:12	3478
the names of the children of *I*	Ex 28:21	3478
the names of the children of *I* in	Ex 28:29	3478
I upon his heart before the LORD	Ex 28:30	3478
which the children of *I* shall	Ex 28:38	3478
for ever from the children of *I*	Ex 29:28	3478
offering from the children of *I*	Ex 29:28	3478
will meet with the children of *I*	Ex 29:43	3478
dwell among the children of *I*	Ex 29:45	3478
children of *I* after their number	Ex 30:12	3478
money of the children of *I*	Ex 30:16	3478
the children of *I* before the LORD	Ex 30:16	3478
speak unto the children of *I*	Ex 30:31	3478
thou also unto the children of *I*	Ex 31:13	3478
of *I* shall keep the sabbath	Ex 31:16	3478
me and the children of *I* for ever	Ex 31:17	3478
they said, These be thy gods, O *I*	Ex 32:4	3478
and said, These be thy gods, O *I*	Ex 32:8	3478
the children of *I* drink of it	Ex 32:20	3478
Thus saith the LORD God of *I*	Ex 32:27	3478
Moses, Say unto the children of *I*	Ex 33:5	3478
the children of *I* stripped	Ex 33:6	3478
before the Lord GOD, the God of *I*	Ex 34:23	3478
a covenant with thee and with *I*	Ex 34:27	3478
all the children of *I* saw Moses	Ex 34:30	3478
all the children of *I* came nigh	Ex 34:32	3478
spake unto the children of *I* that	Ex 34:34	3478
the children of *I* saw the face of	Ex 34:35	3478
of the children of *I* together	Ex 35:1	3478
congregation of the children of *I*	Ex 35:4	3478
I departed from the presence of	Ex 35:20	3478
The children of *I* brought a	Ex 35:29	3478
Moses said unto the children of *I*	Ex 35:30	3478
which the children of *I* had	Ex 36:3	3478
the names of the children of *I*	Ex 39:6	3478
a memorial to the children of *I*	Ex 39:7	3478
to the names of the children of *I*	Ex 39:14	3478
the children of *I* did according	Ex 39:32	3478
children of *I* made all the work	Ex 39:42	3478
the children of *I* went onward in	Ex 40:36	3478
the sight of all the house of *I*	Ex 40:38	3478
Speak unto the children of *I*	Lev 1:2	3478
Speak unto the children of *I*	Lev 4:2	3478
of *I* sin through ignorance	Lev 4:13	3478
Speak unto the children of *I*	Lev 7:23	3478
Speak unto the children of *I*	Lev 7:29	3478
of *I* from off the sacrifices of	Lev 7:34	3478
ever from among the children of *I*	Lev 7:34	3478
given them of the children of *I*	Lev 7:36	3478
he commanded the children of *I* to	Lev 7:38	3478

and his sons, and the elders of *I*	Lev 9:1	3478
children of *I* thou shalt speak	Lev 9:3	3478
brethren, the whole house of *I*	Lev 10:6	3478
ye may teach the children of *I*	Lev 10:11	3478
offerings of the children of *I*	Lev 10:14	3478
Speak unto the children of *I*	Lev 11:2	3478
Speak unto the children of *I*	Lev 12:2	3478
Speak unto the children of *I*	Lev 15:2	3478
of *I* from their uncleanness	Lev 15:31	3478
I two kids of the goats for a sin	Lev 16:5	3478
uncleanness of the children of *I*	Lev 16:16	3478
and for all the congregation of *I*	Lev 16:17	3478
uncleanness of the children of *I*	Lev 16:19	3478
iniquities of the children of *I*	Lev 16:21	3478
atonement for the children of *I*	Lev 16:34	3478
and unto all the children of *I*	Lev 17:2	3478
soever there be of the house of *I*	Lev 17:3	3478
of *I* may bring their sacrifices	Lev 17:5	3478
man there be of the house of *I*	Lev 17:8	3478
man there be of the house of *I*	Lev 17:10	3478
I said unto the children of *I*	Lev 17:12	3478
man there be of the children of *I*	Lev 17:13	3478
I said unto the children of *I*	Lev 17:14	3478
Speak unto the children of *I*	Lev 18:2	3478
congregation of the children of *I*	Lev 19:2	3478
shalt say to the children of *I*	Lev 20:2	3478
he be of the children of *I*	Lev 20:2	3478
the strangers that sojourn in *I*	Lev 20:2	3478
and unto all the children of *I*	Lev 21:24	3478
holy things of the children of *I*	Lev 22:2	3478
of *I* hallow unto the LORD	Lev 22:3	3478
holy things of the children of *I*	Lev 22:15	3478
and unto all the children of *I*	Lev 22:18	3478
he be of the house of *I*	Lev 22:18	3478
or of the strangers in *I*	Lev 22:18	3478
hallowed among the children of *I*	Lev 22:32	3478
Speak unto the children of *I*	Lev 23:2	3478
Speak unto the children of *I*	Lev 23:10	3478
Speak unto the children of *I*	Lev 23:24	3478
Speak unto the children of *I*	Lev 23:34	3478
children of *I* to dwell in booths	Lev 23:43	3478
of *I* the feasts of the LORD	Lev 23:44	3478
Command the children of *I*	Lev 24:2	3478
of *I* by an everlasting covenant	Lev 24:8	3478
went out among the children of *I*	Lev 24:10	3481
a man of *I* strove together in the	Lev 24:10	3478
speak unto the children of *I*	Lev 24:15	3478
Moses spake to the children of *I*	Lev 24:23	3478
the children of *I* did as the LORD	Lev 24:23	3478
Speak unto the children of *I*	Lev 25:2	3478
among the children of *I*	Lev 25:33	3478
your brethren the children of *I*	Lev 25:46	3478
me the children of *I* are servants	Lev 25:55	3478
the children of *I* in mount Sinai	Lev 26:46	3478
Speak unto the children of *I*	Lev 27:2	3478
the children of *I* in mount Sinai	Lev 27:34	3478
congregation of the children of *I*	Num 1:2	3478
are able to go forth to war in *I*	Num 1:3	3478
fathers, heads of thousands in *I*	Num 1:16	3478
numbered, and the princes of *I*	Num 1:44	3478
numbered of the children of *I*	Num 1:45	3478
were able to go forth to war in *I*	Num 1:45	3478
of them among the children of *I*	Num 1:49	3478
the children of *I* shall pitch	Num 1:52	3478
congregation of the children of *I*	Num 1:53	3478
the children of *I* did according	Num 1:54	3478
Every man of the children of *I*	Num 2:2	3478
numbered of the children of *I* by	Num 2:32	3478
numbered among the children of *I*	Num 2:33	3478
the children of *I* did according	Num 2:34	3478
the charge of the children of *I*	Num 3:8	3478
unto him out of the children of *I*	Num 3:9	3478
from among the children of *I*	Num 3:12	3478
matrix among the children of *I*	Num 3:12	3478
unto me all the firstborn in *I*	Num 3:13	3478
the charge of the children of *I*	Num 3:38	3478
children of *I* from a month old	Num 3:40	3478
firstborn among the children of *I*	Num 3:41	3478
the cattle of the children of *I*	Num 3:41	3478
firstborn among the children of *I*	Num 3:42	3478
firstborn among the children of *I*	Num 3:45	3478
firstborn of the children of *I*	Num 3:46	3478
children of *I* took he the money	Num 3:50	3478
Aaron and the chief of *I* numbered	Num 4:46	3478
Command the children of *I*	Num 5:2	3478
And the children of *I* did so	Num 5:4	3478
Moses, so did the children of *I*	Num 5:4	3478
Speak unto the children of *I*	Num 5:6	3478
holy things of the children of *I*	Num 5:9	3478
Speak unto the children of *I*	Num 5:12	3478
Speak unto the children of *I*	Num 6:2	3478
ye shall bless the children of *I*	Num 6:23	3478
my name upon the children of *I*	Num 6:27	3478
That the princes of *I*, heads of	Num 7:2	3478
was anointed, by the princes of *I*	Num 7:84	3478
from among the children of *I*	Num 8:6	3478
of the children of *I* together	Num 8:9	3478
the children of *I* shall put their	Num 8:10	3478
an offering of the children of *I*	Num 8:11	3478
from among the children of *I*	Num 8:14	3478
me from among the children of *I*	Num 8:16	3478
of all the children of *I*, have I	Num 8:16	3478
of the children of *I* are mine	Num 8:17	3478
firstborn of the children of *I*	Num 8:18	3478
sons from among the children of *I*	Num 8:19	3478
of *I* in the tabernacle of the	Num 8:19	3478
atonement for the children of *I*	Num 8:19	3478
no plague among the children of *I*	Num 8:19	3478
when the children of *I* come nigh	Num 8:19	3478
congregation of the children of *I*	Num 8:20	3478
did the children of *I* unto them	Num 8:20	3478
Let the children of *I* also keep	Num 9:2	3478
spake unto the children of *I*	Num 9:4	3478
Moses, so did the children of *I*	Num 9:5	3478
season among the children of *I*	Num 9:7	3478
Speak unto the children of *I*	Num 9:10	3478
that the children of *I* journeyed	Num 9:17	3478
children of *I* pitched their tents	Num 9:17	3478
LORD the children of *I* journeyed	Num 9:18	3478
then the children of *I* kept the	Num 9:19	3478
the children of *I* abode in their	Num 9:22	3478
are heads of the thousands of *I*	Num 10:4	3478
the children of *I* took their	Num 10:12	3478
of *I* according to their armies	Num 10:28	3478
hath spoken good concerning *I*	Num 10:29	3478
unto the many thousands of *I*	Num 10:36	3478
the children of *I* also wept again	Num 11:4	3478
me seventy men of the elders of *I*	Num 11:16	3478
the camp, he and the elders of *I*	Num 11:30	3478
I give unto the children of *I*	Num 13:2	3478
were heads of the children of *I*	Num 13:3	3478
of *I* cut down from thence	Num 13:24	3478
congregation of the children of *I*	Num 13:26	3478
searched unto the children of *I*	Num 13:32	3478
all the children of *I* murmured	Num 14:2	3478
congregation of the children of *I*	Num 14:5	3478
the company of the children of *I*	Num 14:7	3478
before all the children of *I*	Num 14:10	3478
murmurings of the children of *I*	Num 14:27	3478
unto all the children of *I*	Num 14:39	3478
Speak unto the children of *I*	Num 15:2	3478
Speak unto the children of *I*	Num 15:18	3478
congregation of the children of *I*	Num 15:25	3478
congregation of the children of *I*	Num 15:26	3478
is born among the children of *I*	Num 15:29	3478
while the children of *I* were in	Num 15:32	3478
Speak unto the children of *I*	Num 15:38	3478
with certain of the children of *I*	Num 16:2	3478
that the God of *I* hath separated	Num 16:9	3478
you from the congregation of *I*	Num 16:9	3478
and the elders of *I* followed him	Num 16:25	3478
all *I* that were round about them	Num 16:34	3478
be a sign unto the children of *I*	Num 16:38	3478
a memorial unto the children of *I*	Num 16:40	3478
of *I* murmured against Moses	Num 16:41	3478
Speak unto the children of *I*	Num 17:2	3478
murmurings of the children of *I*	Num 17:5	3478
spake unto the children of *I*	Num 17:6	3478
LORD unto all the children of *I*	Num 17:9	3478
the children of *I* spake unto	Num 17:12	3478
any more upon the children of *I*	Num 18:5	3478
from among the children of *I*	Num 18:6	3478
things of the children of *I*	Num 18:8	3478
offerings of the children of *I*	Num 18:11	3478
thing devoted in *I* shall be thine	Num 18:14	3478
children of *I* offer unto the LORD	Num 18:19	3478
among the children of *I*	Num 18:20	3478
the tenth in *I* for an inheritance	Num 18:21	3478
of *I* henceforth come nigh the	Num 18:22	3478
of *I* they have no inheritance	Num 18:23	3478
the tithes of the children of *I*	Num 18:24	3478
Among the children of *I* they	Num 18:24	3478
I the tithes which I have given	Num 18:26	3478
ye receive of the children of *I*	Num 18:28	3478
holy things of the children of *I*	Num 18:32	3478
Speak unto the children of *I*	Num 19:2	3478
of *I* for a water of separation	Num 19:9	3478
shall be unto the children of *I*	Num 19:10	3478
that soul shall be cut off from *I*	Num 19:13	3478
Then came the children of *I*	Num 20:1	3478
in the eyes of the children of *I*	Num 20:12	3478
of *I* strove with the LORD	Num 20:13	3478

of Edom, Thus saith thy brother *I*	Num 20:14	3478
the children of *I* said unto him	Num 20:19	3478
Thus Edom refused to give *I*	Num 20:21	3478
wherefore *I* turned away from him	Num 20:21	3478
And the children of *I*, even the	Num 20:22	3478
have given unto the children of *I*	Num 20:24	3478
days, even all the house of *I*	Num 20:29	3478
heard tell that *I* came by the way	Num 21:1	3478
then he fought against *I*, and took	Num 21:1	3478
I vowed a vow unto the LORD, and	Num 21:2	3478
LORD hearkened to the voice of *I*	Num 21:3	3478
and much people of *I* died	Num 21:6	3478
And the children of *I* set forward	Num 21:10	3478
Then *I* sang this song, Spring up,	Num 21:17	3478
I sent messengers unto Sihon king	Num 21:21	3478
Sihon would not suffer *I* to pass	Num 21:23	3478
went out against *I* into the	Num 21:23	3478
to Jahaz, and fought against *I*	Num 21:23	3478
I smote him with the edge of the	Num 21:24	3478
And *I* took all these cities	Num 21:25	3478
I dwelt in all the cities of the	Num 21:25	3478
Thus *I* dwelt in the land of the	Num 21:31	3478
And the children of *I* set forward	Num 22:1	3478
that *I* had done to the Amorites	Num 22:2	3478
because of the children of *I*	Num 22:3	3478
curse me Jacob, and come, defy *I*	Num 23:7	3478
number of the fourth part of *I*	Num 23:10	3478
hath he seen perverseness in *I*	Num 23:21	3478
is there any divination against *I*	Num 23:23	3478
it shall be said of Jacob and of *I*	Num 23:23	3478
it pleased the LORD to bless *I*	Num 24:1	3478
he saw *I* abiding in his tents	Num 24:2	3478
O Jacob, and thy tabernacles, O *I*	Num 24:5	3478
and a Sceptre shall rise out of *I*	Num 24:17	3478
and *I* shall do valiantly	Num 24:18	3478
I abode in Shittim, and the people	Num 25:1	3478
I joined himself unto Baal-peor	Num 25:3	3478
of the LORD was kindled against *I*	Num 25:3	3478
LORD may be turned away from *I*	Num 25:4	3478
Moses said unto the judges of *I*	Num 25:5	3478
one of the children of *I* came	Num 25:6	3478
congregation of the children of *I*	Num 25:6	3478
after the man of *I* into the tent	Num 25:8	3478
of them through, the man of *I*	Num 25:8	3478
was stayed from the children of *I*	Num 25:8	3478
wrath away from the children of *I*	Num 25:11	3478
the children of *I* in my jealousy	Num 25:11	3478
atonement for the children of *I*	Num 25:13	3478
congregation of the children of *I*	Num 26:2	3478
that are able to go to war in *I*	Num 26:2	3478
Moses and the children of *I*	Num 26:4	3478
the numbered of the children of *I*	Num 26:51	3478
numbered among the children of *I*	Num 26:62	3478
them among the children of *I*	Num 26:62	3478
who numbered the children of *I* in	Num 26:62	3478
of *I* in the wilderness of Sinai	Num 26:64	3478
speak unto the children of *I*	Num 27:8	3478
of *I* a statute of judgment	Num 27:11	3478
have given unto the children of *I*	Num 27:12	3478
the children of *I* may be obedient	Num 27:20	3478
and all the children of *I* with him	Num 27:21	3478
Command the children of *I*	Num 28:2	3478
Moses told the children of *I*	Num 29:40	3478
concerning the children of *I*	Num 30:1	3478
children of *I* of the Midianites	Num 31:2	3478
throughout all the tribes of *I*	Num 31:4	3478
out of the thousands of *I*	Num 31:5	3478
the children of *I* took all the	Num 31:9	3478
congregation of the children of *I*	Num 31:12	3478
these caused the children of *I*	Num 31:16	3478
the children of *I* before the LORD	Num 31:54	3478
before the congregation of *I*	Num 32:4	3478
I from going over into the land	Num 32:7	3478
the heart of the children of *I*	Num 32:9	3478
anger was kindled against *I*	Num 32:13	3478
fierce anger of the LORD toward *I*	Num 32:14	3478
armed before the children of *I*	Num 32:17	3478
until the children of *I* have	Num 32:18	3478
before the LORD, and before *I*	Num 32:22	3478
the tribes of the children of *I*	Num 32:28	3478
the journeys of the children of *I*	Num 33:1	3478
the passover the children of *I*	Num 33:3	3478
the children of *I* removed from	Num 33:5	3478
year after the children of *I* were	Num 33:38	3478
the coming of the children of *I*	Num 33:40	3478
Speak unto the children of *I*	Num 33:51	3478
Command the children of *I*	Num 34:2	3478
Moses commanded the children of *I*	Num 34:13	3478
unto the children of *I* in the	Num 34:29	3478
Command the children of *I*	Num 35:2	3478
possession of the children of *I*	Num 35:8	3478
Speak unto the children of *I*	Num 35:10	3478
both for the children of *I*	Num 35:15	3478
dwell among the children of *I*	Num 35:34	3478
fathers of the children of *I*	Num 36:1	3478
by lot to the children of *I*	Num 36:2	3478
other tribes of the children of *I*	Num 36:3	3478
of the children of *I* shall be	Num 36:4	3478
of *I* according to the word of the	Num 36:5	3478
of *I* remove from tribe to tribe	Num 36:7	3478
of *I* shall keep himself to the	Num 36:7	3478
in any tribe of the children of *I*	Num 36:8	3478
that the children of *I* may enjoy	Num 36:8	3478
I shall keep himself to his own	Num 36:9	3478
of Moses unto the children of *I*	Num 36:13	3478
all *I* on this side Jordan in the	Deut 1:1	3478
spake unto the children of *I*	Deut 1:3	3478
he shall cause *I* to inherit it	Deut 1:38	3478
as *I* did unto the land of his	Deut 2:12	3478
your brethren the children of *I*	Deut 3:18	3478
Now therefore hearken, O *I*	Deut 4:1	3478
set before the children of *I*	Deut 4:44	3478
spake unto the children of *I*	Deut 4:45	3478
Moses and the children of *I* smote	Deut 4:46	3478
And Moses called all *I*	Deut 5:1	3478
and said unto them, Hear, O *I*	Deut 5:1	3478
Hear therefore, O *I*, and observe	Deut 6:3	3478
Hear, O *I*: The LORD our God	Deut 6:4	3478
Hear, O *I*: Thou art to pass	Deut 9:1	3478
the children of *I* took their	Deut 10:6	3478
And now, *I*, what doth the LORD thy	Deut 10:12	3478
possession, in the midst of all *I*	Deut 11:6	3478
all *I* shall hear, and fear, and	Deut 13:11	3478
such abomination is wrought in *I*	Deut 17:4	3478
shalt put away the evil from *I*	Deut 17:12	3478
his children, in the midst of *I*	Deut 17:20	3478
no part nor inheritance with *I*	Deut 18:1	3478
any of thy gates out of all *I*	Deut 18:6	3478
guilt of innocent blood from *I*	Deut 19:13	3478
And shall say unto them, Hear, O *I*	Deut 20:3	3478
O LORD, unto thy people *I*	Deut 21:8	3478
all *I* shall hear, and fear	Deut 21:21	3478
an evil name upon a virgin of *I*	Deut 22:19	3478
she hath wrought folly in *I*	Deut 22:21	3478
shalt thou put away evil from *I*	Deut 22:22	3478
be no whore of the daughters of *I*	Deut 23:17	3478
nor a sodomite of the sons of *I*	Deut 23:17	3478
his brethren of the children of *I*	Deut 24:7	3478
that his name be not put out of *I*	Deut 25:6	3478
up unto his brother a name in *I*	Deut 25:7	3478
And his name shall be called in *I*	Deut 25:10	3478
heaven, and bless thy people *I*	Deut 26:15	3478
elders of *I* commanded the people	Deut 27:1	3478
the Levites spake unto all *I*	Deut 27:9	3478
Take heed, and hearken, O *I*	Deut 27:9	3478
the men of *I* with a loud voice	Deut 27:14	3478
children of *I* in the land of Moab	Deut 29:1	3478
And Moses called unto all *I*	Deut 29:2	3478
officers, with all the men of *I*	Deut 29:10	3478
evil out of all the tribes of *I*	Deut 29:21	3478
and spake these words unto all *I*	Deut 31:1	3478
unto him in the sight of all *I*	Deut 31:7	3478
LORD, and unto all the elders of *I*	Deut 31:9	3478
When all *I* is come to appear	Deut 31:11	3478
law before all *I* in their hearing	Deut 31:11	3478
and teach it the children of *I*	Deut 31:19	3478
for me against the children of *I*	Deut 31:19	3478
and taught it the children of *I*	Deut 31:22	3478
of *I* into the land which I sware	Deut 31:23	3478
of *I* the words of this song	Deut 31:30	3478
the number of the children of *I*	Deut 32:8	3478
speaking all these words to all *I*	Deut 32:45	3478
children of *I* for a possession	Deut 32:49	3478
me among the children of *I* at the	Deut 32:51	3478
in the midst of the children of *I*	Deut 32:51	3478
which I give the children of *I*	Deut 32:52	3478
children of *I* before his death	Deut 33:1	3478
the tribes of *I* were gathered	Deut 33:5	3478
Jacob thy judgments, and *I* thy law	Deut 33:10	3478
the LORD, and his judgments with *I*	Deut 33:21	3478
I then shall dwell in safety	Deut 33:28	3478
Happy art thou, O *I*	Deut 33:29	3478
the children of *I* wept for Moses	Deut 34:8	3478
the children of *I* hearkened unto	Deut 34:9	3478
since in *I* like unto Moses	Deut 34:10	3478
shewed in the sight of all *I*	Deut 34:12	3478
them, even to the children of *I*	Josh 1:2	3478
of *I* to search out the country	Josh 2:2	3478
he and all the children of *I*	Josh 3:1	3478
thee in the sight of all *I*	Josh 3:7	3478
said unto the children of *I*	Josh 3:9	3478
twelve men out of the tribes of *I*	Josh 3:12	3478

had prepared of the children of *I*	Josh 4:4	3478
the tribes of the children of *I*	Josh 4:5	3478
unto the children of *I* for ever	Josh 4:7	3478
the children of *I* did so as	Josh 4:8	3478
the tribes of the children of *I*	Josh 4:8	3478
armed before the children of *I*	Josh 4:12	3478
Joshua in the sight of all *I*	Josh 4:14	3478
he spake unto the children of *I*	Josh 4:21	3478
I came over this Jordan on dry	Josh 4:22	3478
from before the children of *I*	Josh 5:1	3478
because of the children of *I*	Josh 5:1	3478
the children of *I* the second time	Josh 5:2	3478
circumcised the children of *I* at	Josh 5:3	3478
For the children of *I* walked	Josh 5:6	3478
the children of *I* encamped in	Josh 5:10	3478
the children of *I* manna any more	Josh 5:12	3478
up because of the children of *I*	Josh 6:1	3478
and make the camp of *I* a curse	Josh 6:18	3478
left them without the camp of *I*	Josh 6:23	3478
she dwelleth in *I* even unto this	Josh 6:25	3478
But the children of *I* committed a	Josh 7:1	3478
kindled against the children of *I*	Josh 7:1	3478
eventide, he and the elders of *I*	Josh 7:6	3478
when *I* turneth their backs before	Josh 7:8	3478
I hath sinned, and they have also	Josh 7:11	3478
Therefore the children of *I* could	Josh 7:12	3478
for thus saith the LORD God of *I*	Josh 7:13	3478
thing in the midst of thee, O *I*	Josh 7:13	3478
he hath wrought folly in *I*	Josh 7:15	3478
brought *I* by their tribes	Josh 7:16	3478
thee, glory to the LORD God of *I*	Josh 7:19	3478
sinned against the LORD God of *I*	Josh 7:20	3478
and unto all the children of *I*	Josh 7:23	3478
all *I* with him, took Achan the	Josh 7:24	3478
all *I* stoned him with stones, and	Josh 7:25	3478
and went up, he and the elders of *I*	Josh 8:10	3478
city went out against *I* to battle	Josh 8:14	3478
all *I* made as if they were beaten	Josh 8:15	3478
that went not out after *I*	Josh 8:17	3478
the city open, and pursued after *I*	Josh 8:17	3478
all *I* saw that the ambush had	Josh 8:21	3478
so they were in the midst of *I*	Josh 8:22	3478
when *I* had made an end of slaying	Josh 8:24	3478
the spoil of that city *I* took for	Josh 8:27	3478
the LORD God of *I* in mount Ebal	Josh 8:30	3478
LORD commanded the children of *I*	Josh 8:31	3478
the presence of the children of *I*	Josh 8:32	3478
And all *I*, and their elders, and	Josh 8:33	3478
they should bless the people of *I*	Josh 8:33	3478
before all the congregation of *I*	Josh 8:35	3478
to fight with Joshua and with *I*	Josh 9:2	3478
said unto him, and to the men of *I*	Josh 9:6	3478
the men of *I* said unto the	Josh 9:7	3478
And the children of *I* journeyed	Josh 9:17	3478
the children of *I* smote them not	Josh 9:18	3478
unto them by the LORD God of *I*	Josh 9:18	3478
unto them by the LORD God of *I*	Josh 9:19	3478
of the hand of the children of *I*	Josh 9:26	3478
of Gibeon had made peace with *I*	Josh 10:1	3478
Joshua and with the children of *I*	Josh 10:4	3478
LORD discomfited them before *I*	Josh 10:10	3478
pass, as they fled from before *I*	Josh 10:11	3478
children of *I* slew with the sword	Josh 10:11	3478
Amorites before the children of *I*	Josh 10:12	3478
and he said in the sight of *I*	Josh 10:12	3478
for the LORD fought for *I*	Josh 10:14	3478
all *I* with him, unto the camp to	Josh 10:15	3478
the children of *I* had made an end	Josh 10:20	3478
against any of the children of *I*	Josh 10:21	3478
called for all the men of *I*	Josh 10:24	3478
all *I* with him, unto Libnah, and	Josh 10:29	3478
king thereof, into the hand of *I*	Josh 10:30	3478
all *I* with him, unto Lachish, and	Josh 10:31	3478
Lachish into the hand of *I*	Josh 10:32	3478
unto Eglon, and all *I* with him	Josh 10:34	3478
all *I* with him, unto Hebron	Josh 10:36	3478
and all *I* with him, to Debir	Josh 10:38	3478
as the LORD God commanded	Josh 10:40	3478
LORD God of *I* fought for Israel	Josh 10:42	3478
LORD God of Israel fought for *I*	Josh 10:42	3478
all *I* with him, unto the camp to	Josh 10:43	3478
of Merom, to fight against *I*	Josh 11:5	3478
them up all slain before *I*	Josh 11:6	3478
delivered them into the hand of *I*	Josh 11:8	3478
I burned none of them, save Hazor	Josh 11:13	3478
the children of *I* took for a prey	Josh 11:14	3478
the plain, and the mountain of *I*	Josh 11:16	3478
made peace with the children of *I*	Josh 11:19	3478
should come against *I* in battle	Josh 11:20	3478
and from all the mountains of *I*	Josh 11:21	3478
in the land of the children of *I*	Josh 11:22	3478

I according to their divisions by	Josh 11:23	3478
which the children of *I* smote	Josh 12:1	3478
LORD and the children of *I* smite	Josh 12:6	3478
the children of *I* smote on this	Josh 12:7	3478
I for a possession according to	Josh 12:7	3478
out from before the children of *I*	Josh 13:6	3478
of *I* expelled not the Geshurites	Josh 13:13	3478
God of *I* made by fire are their	Josh 13:14	3478
did the children of *I* slay with	Josh 13:22	3478
the LORD God of *I* was their	Josh 13:33	3478
I inherited in the land of Canaan	Josh 14:1	3478
the tribes of the children of *I*	Josh 14:1	3478
Moses, so the children of *I* did	Josh 14:5	3478
while the children of *I* wandered	Josh 14:10	3478
wholly followed the LORD God of *I*	Josh 14:14	3478
children of *I* were waxen strong	Josh 17:13	3478
of *I* assembled together at Shiloh	Josh 18:1	3478
the children of *I* seven tribes	Josh 18:2	3478
said unto the children of *I*	Josh 18:3	3478
of *I* according to their divisions	Josh 18:10	3478
the children of *I* gave an	Josh 19:49	3478
the tribes of the children of *I*	Josh 19:51	3478
Speak to the children of *I*	Josh 20:2	3478
for all the children of *I*	Josh 20:9	3478
the tribes of the children of *I*	Josh 21:1	3478
the children of *I* gave unto the	Josh 21:3	3478
the children of *I* gave by lot	Josh 21:8	3478
of the children of *I* were forty	Josh 21:41	3478
the LORD gave unto *I* all the land	Josh 21:43	3478
had spoken unto the house of *I*	Josh 21:45	3478
the children of *I* out of Shiloh	Josh 22:9	3478
And the children of *I* heard say	Josh 22:11	3478
the passage of the children of *I*	Josh 22:11	3478
the children of *I* heard of it	Josh 22:12	3478
I gathered themselves together at	Josh 22:12	3478
the children of *I* sent unto the	Josh 22:13	3478
throughout all the tribes of *I*	Josh 22:14	3478
fathers among the thousands of *I*	Josh 22:14	3478
committed against the God of *I*	Josh 22:16	3478
with the whole congregation of *I*	Josh 22:18	3478
fell on all the congregation of *I*	Josh 22:20	3478
the heads of the thousands of *I*	Josh 22:21	3478
he knoweth, and *I* he shall know	Josh 22:22	3478
ye to do with the LORD God of *I*	Josh 22:24	3478
of *I* which were with him, heard	Josh 22:30	3478
of *I* out of the hand of the LORD	Josh 22:31	3478
of Canaan, to the children of *I*	Josh 22:32	3478
thing pleased the children of *I*	Josh 22:33	3478
and the children of *I* blessed God	Josh 22:33	3478
I from all their enemies round	Josh 23:1	3478
And Joshua called for all *I*	Josh 23:2	3478
all the tribes of *I* to Shechem	Josh 24:1	3478
and called for the elders of *I*	Josh 24:1	3478
Thus saith the LORD God of *I*	Josh 24:2	3478
Moab, arose and warred against *I*	Josh 24:9	3478
your heart unto the LORD God of *I*	Josh 24:23	3478
I served the LORD all the days of	Josh 24:31	3478
the LORD, that he had done for *I*	Josh 24:31	3478
which the children of *I* brought	Josh 24:32	3478
the children of *I* asked the LORD	Judg 1:1	3478
when *I* was strong, that they put	Judg 1:28	3478
words unto all the children of *I*	Judg 2:4	3478
the children of *I* went every man	Judg 2:6	3478
of the LORD, that he did for *I*	Judg 2:7	3478
the works which he had done for *I*	Judg 2:10	3478
the children of *I* did evil in the	Judg 2:11	3478
of the LORD was hot against *I*	Judg 2:14	3478
of the LORD was hot against *I*	Judg 2:20	3478
That through them I may prove *I*	Judg 2:22	3478
the LORD left, to prove *I* by them	Judg 3:1	3478
even as many of *I* as had not	Judg 3:1	3478
of the children of *I* might know	Judg 3:2	
And they were to prove *I* by them	Judg 3:4	
the children of *I* dwelt among the	Judg 3:5	
the children of *I* did evil in the	Judg 3:7	
of the LORD was hot against *I*	Judg 3:8	
and the children of *I* served	Judg 3:8	
children of *I* cried unto the LORD	Judg 3:9	
a deliverer to the children of *I*	Judg 3:9	
came upon him, and he judged *I*	Judg 3:10	
the children of *I* did evil again	Judg 3:12	
Eglon the king of Moab against *I*	Judg 3:12	
and Amalek, and went and smote *I*	Judg 3:13	
So the children of *I* served Eglon	Judg 3:14	
children of *I* cried unto the LORD	Judg 3:15	
by him the children of *I* sent a	Judg 3:15	
the children of *I* went down with	Judg 3:27	
that day under the hand of *I*	Judg 3:30	
and he also delivered *I*	Judg 3:31	
the children of *I* again did evil	Judg 4:1	3478
the children of *I* cried unto the	Judg 4:3	3478

oppressed the children of *I*	Judg 4:3	3478
she judged *I* at that time	Judg 4:4	3478
the children of *I* came up to her	Judg 4:5	3478
not the LORD God of *I* commanded	Judg 4:6	3478
Canaan before the children of *I*	Judg 4:23	3478
of the children of *I* prospered	Judg 4:24	3478
ye the LORD for the avenging of *I*	Judg 5:2	3478
sing praise to the LORD God of *I*	Judg 5:3	3478
from before the LORD God of *I*	Judg 5:5	3478
villages ceased, they ceased in *I*	Judg 5:7	3478
arose, that I arose a mother in *I*	Judg 5:7	3478
seen among forty thousand in *I*	Judg 5:8	3478
is toward the governors of *I*	Judg 5:9	3478
inhabitants of his villages in *I*	Judg 5:11	3478
the children of *I* did evil in the	Judg 6:1	3478
of Midian prevailed against *I*	Judg 6:2	3478
the Midianites the children of *I*	Judg 6:2	3478
when *I* had sown, that the	Judg 6:3	3478
Gaza, and left no sustenance for *I*	Judg 6:4	3478
I was greatly impoverished	Judg 6:6	3478
the children of *I* cried unto the	Judg 6:6	3478
when the children of *I* cried unto	Judg 6:7	3478
a prophet unto the children of *I*	Judg 6:8	3478
Thus saith the LORD God of *I*	Judg 6:8	3478
thou shalt save *I* from the hand	Judg 6:14	3478
my Lord, wherewith shall I save *I*	Judg 6:15	3478
If thou wilt save *I* by mine hand	Judg 6:36	3478
thou wilt save *I* by mine hand	Judg 6:37	3478
lest *I* vaunt themselves against	Judg 7:2	3478
rest of *I* every man unto his tent	Judg 7:8	3478
the son of Joash, a man of *I*	Judg 7:14	3478
and returned into the host of *I*	Judg 7:15	3478
the men of *I* gathered themselves	Judg 7:23	3478
Then the men of *I* said unto	Judg 8:22	3478
all *I* went thither a whoring	Judg 8:27	3478
subdued before the children of *I*	Judg 8:28	3478
the children of *I* turned again	Judg 8:33	3478
the children of *I* remembered not	Judg 8:34	3478
which he had shewed unto *I*	Judg 8:35	3478
had reigned three years over *I*	Judg 9:22	3478
when the men of *I* saw that	Judg 9:55	3478
to defend *I* Tola the son of Puah	Judg 10:1	3478
And he judged *I* twenty and three	Judg 10:2	3478
a Gileadite, and judged *I* twenty	Judg 10:3	3478
the children of *I* did evil again	Judg 10:6	3478
of the LORD was hot against *I*	Judg 10:7	3478
and oppressed the children of *I*	Judg 10:8	3478
all the children of *I* that were	Judg 10:8	3478
so that *I* was sore distressed	Judg 10:9	3478
the children of *I* cried unto the	Judg 10:10	3478
LORD said unto the children of *I*	Judg 10:11	3478
the children of *I* said unto the	Judg 10:15	3478
was grieved for the misery of *I*	Judg 10:16	3478
the children of *I* assembled	Judg 10:17	3478
of Ammon made war against *I*	Judg 11:4	3478
of Ammon made war against *I*	Judg 11:5	3478
Because *I* took away my land, when	Judg 11:13	3478
I took not away the land of Moab	Judg 11:15	3478
But when *I* came up from Egypt, and	Judg 11:16	3478
Then *I* sent messengers unto the	Judg 11:17	3478
and *I* abode in Kadesh	Judg 11:17	3478
I sent messengers unto Sihon king	Judg 11:19	3478
I said unto him, Let us pass, we	Judg 11:19	3478
But Sihon trusted not *I* to pass	Judg 11:20	3478
in Jahaz, and fought against *I*	Judg 11:20	3478
the LORD God of *I* delivered Sihon	Judg 11:21	3478
all his people into the hand of *I*	Judg 11:21	3478
so *I* possessed all the land of	Judg 11:21	3478
So now the LORD God of *I* hath	Judg 11:23	3478
Amorites from before his people *I*	Judg 11:23	3478
did he ever strive against *I*	Judg 11:25	3478
While *I* dwelt in Heshbon and her	Judg 11:26	3478
day between the children of *I*	Judg 11:27	3478
subdued before the children of *I*	Judg 11:33	3478
And it was a custom in *I*,	Judg 11:39	3478
That the daughters of *I* went	Judg 11:40	3478
And Jephthah judged *I* six years	Judg 12:7	3478
him Ibzan of Beth-lehem judged *I*	Judg 12:8	3478
And he judged *I* seven years	Judg 12:9	3478
him Elon, a Zebulonite, judged *I*	Judg 12:11	3478
and he judged *I* ten years	Judg 12:11	3478
Hillel, a Pirathonite, judged *I*	Judg 12:13	3478
and he judged *I* eight years	Judg 12:14	3478
the children of *I* did evil again	Judg 13:1	3478
deliver *I* out of the hand of the	Judg 13:5	3478
Philistines had dominion over *I*	Judg 14:4	3478
he judged *I* in the days of the	Judg 15:20	3478
And he judged *I* twenty years	Judg 16:31	3478
those days there was no king in *I*	Judg 17:6	3478
those days there was no king in *I*	Judg 18:1	3478
unto them among the tribes of *I*	Judg 18:1	3478
unto a tribe and a family in *I*	Judg 18:19	3478
days, when there was no king in *I*	Judg 19:1	3478
that is not of the children of *I*	Judg 19:12	3478
sent her into all the coasts of *I*	Judg 19:29	3478
of *I* came up out of the land of	Judg 19:30	3478
all the children of *I* went out	Judg 20:1	3478
even of all the tribes of *I*	Judg 20:2	3478
of *I* were gone up to Mizpeh	Judg 20:3	3478
Then said the children of *I*	Judg 20:3	3478
country of the inheritance of *I*	Judg 20:6	3478
committed lewdness and folly in *I*	Judg 20:6	3478
Behold, ye are all children of *I*	Judg 20:7	3478
throughout all the tribes of *I*	Judg 20:10	3478
folly that they have wrought in *I*	Judg 20:10	3478
So all the men of *I* were gathered	Judg 20:11	3478
the tribes of *I* sent men through	Judg 20:12	3478
to death, and put away evil from *I*	Judg 20:13	3478
their brethren the children of *I*	Judg 20:13	3478
battle against the children of *I*	Judg 20:14	3478
And the men of *I*, beside Benjamin,	Judg 20:17	3478
And the children of *I* arose	Judg 20:18	3478
the children of *I* rose up in the	Judg 20:19	3478
the men of *I* went out to battle	Judg 20:20	3478
the men of *I* put themselves in	Judg 20:20	3478
men of *I* encouraged themselves	Judg 20:22	3478
(And the children of *I* went up	Judg 20:23	3478
the children of *I* came near	Judg 20:24	3478
of *I* again eighteen thousand men	Judg 20:25	3478
Then all the children of *I*	Judg 20:26	3478
the children of *I* enquired of the	Judg 20:27	3478
I set liers in wait round about	Judg 20:29	3478
the children of *I* went up against	Judg 20:30	3478
the field, about thirty men of *I*	Judg 20:31	3478
But the children of *I* said	Judg 20:32	3478
all the men of *I* rose up out of	Judg 20:33	3478
the liers in wait of *I* came forth	Judg 20:33	3478
thousand chosen men out of all *I*	Judg 20:34	3478
the LORD smote Benjamin before *I*	Judg 20:35	3478
the children of *I* destroyed of	Judg 20:35	3478
for the men of *I* gave place to	Judg 20:36	3478
sign between the men of *I*	Judg 20:38	3478
when the men of *I* retired in the	Judg 20:39	3478
kill of the men of *I* about thirty	Judg 20:39	3478
And when the men of *I* turned again	Judg 20:41	3478
their backs before the men of *I*	Judg 20:42	3478
the men of *I* turned again upon	Judg 20:48	3478
Now the men of *I* had sworn in	Judg 21:1	3478
And said, O LORD God of *I*	Judg 21:3	3478
why is this come to pass in *I*	Judg 21:3	3478
be to day one tribe lacking in *I*	Judg 21:3	3478
And the children of *I* said	Judg 21:5	3478
of *I* that came not up with the	Judg 21:5	3478
the children of *I* repented them	Judg 21:6	3478
one tribe cut off from *I* this day	Judg 21:6	3478
I that came not up to Mizpeh to	Judg 21:8	3478
made a breach in the tribes of *I*	Judg 21:15	3478
a tribe be not destroyed out of *I*	Judg 21:17	3478
for the children of *I* have sworn	Judg 21:18	3478
the children of *I* departed thence	Judg 21:24	3478
those days there was no king in *I*	Judg 21:25	3478
given thee of the LORD God of *I*	Ruth 2:12	3478
time in *I* concerning redeeming	Ruth 4:7	3478
and this was a testimony in *I*	Ruth 4:7	3478
two did build the house of *I*	Ruth 4:11	3478
that his name may be famous in *I*	Ruth 4:14	3478
the God of *I* grant thee thy	1Sa 1:17	3478
all that his sons did unto all *I*	1Sa 2:22	3478
the tribes of *I* to be my priest	1Sa 2:28	3478
made by fire of the children of *I*	1Sa 2:28	3478
all the offerings of *I* my people	1Sa 2:29	3478
Wherefore the LORD God of *I* saith	1Sa 2:30	3478
the wealth which God shall give *I*	1Sa 2:32	3478
Behold, I will do a thing in *I*	1Sa 3:11	3478
all *I* from Dan even to Beer-sheba	1Sa 3:20	3478
the word of Samuel came to all *I*	1Sa 4:1	3478
Now *I* went out against the	1Sa 4:1	3478
put themselves in array against *I*	1Sa 4:2	3478
battle, *I* was smitten before the	1Sa 4:2	3478
the camp, the elders of *I* said	1Sa 4:3	3478
all *I* shouted with a great shout,	1Sa 4:5	3478
I was smitten, and they fled every	1Sa 4:10	3478
for there fell of *I* thirty	1Sa 4:10	3478
I is fled before the Philistines,	1Sa 4:17	3478
And he had judged *I* forty years	1Sa 4:18	3478
The glory is departed from *I*	1Sa 4:21	3478
The glory is departed from *I*	1Sa 4:22	3478
The ark of the God of *I* shall not	1Sa 5:7	3478
do with the ark of the God of *I*	1Sa 5:8	3478
Let the ark of the God of *I* be	1Sa 5:8	3478
ark of the God of *I* about thither	1Sa 5:8	3478
the ark of the God of *I* to us	1Sa 5:10	3478

Send away the ark of the God of *I*	1Sa 5:11	3478
send away the ark of the God of *I*	1Sa 6:3	3478
give glory unto the God of *I*	1Sa 6:5	3478
all the house of *I* lamented after	1Sa 7:2	3478
spake unto all the house of *I*	1Sa 7:3	3478
children of *I* did put away Baalim	1Sa 7:4	3478
said, Gather all *I* to Mizpeh	1Sa 7:5	3478
the children of *I* in Mizpeh	1Sa 7:6	3478
of *I* were gathered together to	1Sa 7:7	3478
the Philistines went up against *I*	1Sa 7:7	3478
when the children of *I* heard it	1Sa 7:7	3478
the children of *I* said to Samuel	1Sa 7:8	3478
Samuel cried unto the LORD for *I*	1Sa 7:9	3478
drew near to battle against *I*	1Sa 7:10	3478
and they were smitten before *I*	1Sa 7:10	3478
the men of *I* went out of Mizpeh,	1Sa 7:11	3478
came no more into the coast of *I*	1Sa 7:13	3478
from *I* were restored to Israel	1Sa 7:14	3478
the coasts thereof did *I* deliver	1Sa 7:14	3478
And there was peace between *I*	1Sa 7:14	3478
Samuel judged *I* all the days of	1Sa 7:15	3478
judged *I* in all those places	1Sa 7:16	3478
and there he judged *I*	1Sa 7:17	3478
he made his sons judges over *I*	1Sa 8:1	3478
Then all the elders of *I* gathered	1Sa 8:4	3478
And Samuel said unto the men of *I*	1Sa 8:22	3478
of *I* a goodlier person than he	1Sa 9:2	3478
(Beforetime in *I*, when a man went	1Sa 9:9	3478
to be captain over my people *I*	1Sa 9:16	3478
And on whom is all the desire of *I*	1Sa 9:20	3478
the smallest of the tribes of *I*	1Sa 9:21	3478
And said unto the children of *I*	1Sa 10:18	3478
Thus saith the LORD God of *I*	1Sa 10:18	3478
I brought up *I* out of Egypt	1Sa 10:18	3478
all the tribes of *I* to come near	1Sa 10:20	3478
lay it for a reproach upon all *I*	1Sa 11:2	3478
unto all the coasts of *I*	1Sa 11:3	3478
of *I* by the hands of messengers	1Sa 11:7	3478
the children of *I* were three	1Sa 11:8	3478
LORD hath wrought salvation in *I*	1Sa 11:13	3478
all the men of *I* rejoiced greatly	1Sa 11:15	3478
And Samuel said unto all *I*	1Sa 12:1	3478
he had reigned two years over *I*	1Sa 13:1	3478
chose him three thousand men of *I*	1Sa 13:2	3478
all *I* heard say that Saul had	1Sa 13:4	3478
and that *I* also was had in	1Sa 13:4	3478
together to fight with *I*, thirty	1Sa 13:5	3478
When the men of *I* saw that they	1Sa 13:6	3478
thy kingdom upon *I* for ever	1Sa 13:13	3478
throughout all the land of *I*	1Sa 13:19	3478
delivered them into the hand of *I*	1Sa 14:12	3478
that time with the children of *I*	1Sa 14:18	3478
Likewise all the men of *I* which	1Sa 14:22	3478
So the LORD saved *I* that day	1Sa 14:23	3478
the men of *I* were distressed that	1Sa 14:24	3478
deliver them into the hand of *I*	1Sa 14:37	3478
the LORD liveth, which saveth *I*	1Sa 14:39	3478
Then said he unto all *I*, Be ye on	1Sa 14:40	3478
Saul said unto the LORD God of *I*	1Sa 14:41	3478
wrought this great salvation in *I*	1Sa 14:45	3478
So Saul took the kingdom over *I*	1Sa 14:47	3478
delivered *I* out of the hands of	1Sa 14:48	3478
be king over his people, over *I*	1Sa 15:1	3478
that which Amalek did to *I*	1Sa 15:2	3478
kindness to all the children of *I*	1Sa 15:6	3478
made the head of the tribes of *I*	1Sa 15:17	3478
LORD anointed thee king over *I*	1Sa 15:17	3478
thee from being king over *I*	1Sa 15:26	3478
kingdom of *I* from thee this day	1Sa 15:28	3478
also the Strength of *I* will not	1Sa 15:29	3478
elders of my people, and before *I*	1Sa 15:30	3478
that he had made Saul king over *I*	1Sa 15:35	3478
rejected him from reigning over *I*	1Sa 16:1	3478
the men of *I* were gathered	1Sa 17:2	3478
I stood on a mountain on the	1Sa 17:3	3478
and cried unto the armies of *I*	1Sa 17:8	3478
I defy the armies of *I* this day	1Sa 17:10	3478
all *I* heard those words of the	1Sa 17:11	3478
and they, and all the men of *I*	1Sa 17:19	3478
For *I* and the Philistines had put	1Sa 17:21	3478
And all the men of *I*, when they	1Sa 17:24	3478
And the men of *I* said, Have ye	1Sa 17:25	3478
surely to defy *I* is he come up	1Sa 17:25	3478
make his father's house free in *I*	1Sa 17:25	3478
taketh away the reproach from *I*	1Sa 17:26	3478
hosts, the God of the armies of *I*	1Sa 17:45	3478
may know that there is a God in *I*	1Sa 17:46	3478
And the men of *I* and of Judah arose	1Sa 17:52	3478
the children of *I* returned from	1Sa 17:53	3478
women came out of all cities of *I*	1Sa 18:6	3478
But all *I* and Judah loved David,	1Sa 18:16	3478
life, or my father's family in *I*	1Sa 18:18	3478
a great salvation for all *I*	1Sa 19:5	3478
said unto David, O LORD God of *I*	1Sa 20:12	3478
Then said David, O LORD God of *I*	1Sa 23:10	3478
O LORD God of *I*, I beseech thee,	1Sa 23:11	3478
and thou shalt be king over *I*	1Sa 23:17	3478
thousand chosen men out of all *I*	1Sa 24:2	3478
whom is the king of *I* come out	1Sa 24:14	3478
that the kingdom of *I* shall be	1Sa 24:20	3478
have appointed thee ruler over *I*	1Sa 25:30	3478
Blessed be the LORD God of *I*	1Sa 25:32	3478
deed, as the LORD God of *I* liveth	1Sa 25:34	3478
thousand chosen men of *I* with him	1Sa 26:2	3478
and who is like to thee in *I*	1Sa 26:15	3478
for the king of *I* is come out to	1Sa 26:20	3478
me any more in any coast of *I*	1Sa 27:1	3478
his people *I* utterly to abhor him	1Sa 27:12	3478
for warfare, to fight with *I*	1Sa 28:1	3478
all *I* had lamented him, and buried	1Sa 28:3	3478
and Saul gathered all *I* together	1Sa 28:4	3478
the LORD will also deliver *I* with	1Sa 28:19	3478
host of *I* into the hand of the	1Sa 28:19	3478
the servant of Saul the king of *I*	1Sa 29:3	3478
an ordinance for *I* unto this day	1Sa 30:25	3478
the Philistines fought against *I*	1Sa 31:1	3478
the men of *I* fled from before the	1Sa 31:1	3478
when the men of *I* that were on	1Sa 31:7	3478
saw that the men of *I* fled	1Sa 31:7	3478
Out of the camp of *I* am I escaped	2Sa 1:3	3478
the LORD, and for the house of *I*	2Sa 1:12	3478
The beauty of *I* is slain upon thy	2Sa 1:19	3478
Ye daughters of *I*, weep over Saul	2Sa 1:24	3478
and over Benjamin, and over all *I*	2Sa 2:9	3478
old when he began to reign over *I*	2Sa 2:10	3478
Abner was beaten, and the men of *I*	2Sa 2:17	3478
still, and pursued after *I* no more	2Sa 2:28	3478
set up the throne of David over *I*	2Sa 3:10	3478
to bring about all *I* unto thee	2Sa 3:12	3478
with the elders of *I*, saying, Ye	2Sa 3:17	3478
people *I* out of the hand of the	2Sa 3:18	3478
Hebron all that seemed good to *I*	2Sa 3:19	3478
will gather all *I* unto my lord	2Sa 3:21	3478
all *I* understood that day that it	2Sa 3:37	3478
a great man fallen this day in *I*	2Sa 3:38	3478
tribes of *I* to David unto Hebron	2Sa 5:1	3478
leddest out and broughtest in *I*	2Sa 5:2	3478
thee, Thou shalt feed my people *I*	2Sa 5:2	3478
and thou shalt be a captain over *I*	2Sa 5:2	3478
So all the elders of *I* came to	2Sa 5:3	3478
they anointed David king over *I*	2Sa 5:3	3478
thirty and three years over all *I*	2Sa 5:5	3478
had established him king over *I*	2Sa 5:12	3478
had anointed David king over *I*	2Sa 5:17	3478
together all the chosen men of *I*	2Sa 6:1	3478
all the house of *I* played before	2Sa 6:5	3478
all the house of *I* brought up the	2Sa 6:15	3478
among the whole multitude of *I*	2Sa 6:19	3478
glorious was the king of *I* today	2Sa 6:20	3478
the people of the LORD, over *I*	2Sa 6:21	3478
up the children of *I* out of Egypt	2Sa 7:6	3478
I spake I a word with any of the	2Sa 7:7	3478
word with any of the tribes of *I*	2Sa 7:7	3478
I commanded to feed my people *I*	2Sa 7:7	3478
be ruler over my people, over *I*	2Sa 7:8	3478
appoint a place for my people *I*	2Sa 7:10	3478
judges to be over my people *I*	2Sa 7:11	3478
is like thy people, even like *I*	2Sa 7:23	3478
I to be a people unto thee for	2Sa 7:24	3478
LORD of hosts is the God over *I*	2Sa 7:26	3478
thou, O LORD of hosts, God of *I*	2Sa 7:27	3478
And David reigned over all *I*	2Sa 8:15	3478
chose of all the choice men of *I*	2Sa 10:9	3478
that they were smitten before *I*	2Sa 10:15	3478
David, he gathered all *I* together	2Sa 10:17	3478
And the Syrians fled before *I*	2Sa 10:18	3478
that they were smitten before *I*	2Sa 10:19	3478
Israel, they made peace with *I*	2Sa 10:19	3478
his servants with him, and all *I*	2Sa 11:1	3478
said unto David, The ark, and *I*	2Sa 11:11	3478
Thus saith the LORD God of *I*	2Sa 12:7	3478
I anointed thee king over *I*	2Sa 12:7	3478
and gave thee the house of *I*	2Sa 12:8	3478
I will do this thing before all *I*	2Sa 12:12	3478
such thing ought to be done in *I*	2Sa 13:12	3478
shalt be as one of the fools in *I*	2Sa 13:13	3478
But in all *I* there was none to be	2Sa 14:25	3478
is of one of the tribes of *I*	2Sa 15:2	3478
all *I* that came to the king for	2Sa 15:6	3478
stole the hearts of the men of *I*	2Sa 15:6	3478
throughout all the tribes of *I*	2Sa 15:10	3478
of the men of *I* are after Absalom	2Sa 15:13	3478

Today shall the house of *I*	2Sa 16:3	3478
and all the people the men of *I*	2Sa 16:15	3478
this people, and all the men of *I*	2Sa 16:18	3478
all *I* shall hear that thou art	2Sa 16:21	3478
concubines in the sight of all *I*	2Sa 16:22	3478
well, and all the elders of *I*	2Sa 17:4	3478
for all *I* knoweth that thy father	2Sa 17:10	3478
Therefore I counsel that all *I* be	2Sa 17:11	3478
then shall all *I* bring ropes to	2Sa 17:13	3478
Absalom and all the men of *I* said	2Sa 17:14	3478
Absalom and the elders of *I*	2Sa 17:15	3478
he and all the men of *I* with him	2Sa 17:24	3478
So *I* and Absalom pitched in the	2Sa 17:26	3478
went out into the field against *I*	2Sa 18:6	3478
Where the people of *I* were slain	2Sa 18:7	3478
returned from pursuing after *I*	2Sa 18:16	3478
all *I* fled every one to his tent	2Sa 18:17	3478
for *I* had fled every man to his	2Sa 19:8	3478
throughout all the tribes of *I*	2Sa 19:9	3478
of all *I* is come to the king	2Sa 19:11	3478
man be put to death this day in *I*	2Sa 19:22	3478
that I am this day king over *I*	2Sa 19:22	3478
and also half the people of *I*	2Sa 19:40	3478
all the men of *I* came to the king	2Sa 19:41	3478
of Judah answered the men of *I*	2Sa 19:42	3478
the men of *I* answered the men of	2Sa 19:43	3478
than the words of the men of *I*	2Sa 19:43	3478
every man to his tents, O *I*	2Sa 20:1	3478
So every man of *I* went up from	2Sa 20:2	3478
all the tribes of *I* unto Abel	2Sa 20:14	3478
are peaceable and faithful in *I*	2Sa 20:19	3478
destroy a city and a mother in *I*	2Sa 20:19	3478
Joab was over all the host of *I*	2Sa 20:23	3478
were not of the children of *I*	2Sa 21:2	3478
the children of *I* had sworn unto	2Sa 21:2	3478
in his zeal to the children of *I*	2Sa 21:2	3478
us shalt thou kill any man in *I*	2Sa 21:4	3478
in any of the coasts of *I*	2Sa 21:5	3478
had yet war again with *I*	2Sa 21:15	3478
thou quench not the light of *I*	2Sa 21:17	3478
And when he defied *I*, Jonathan the	2Sa 21:21	3478
Jacob, and the sweet psalmist of *I*	2Sa 23:1	3478
The God of *I* said, the Rock of	2Sa 23:3	3478
said, the Rock of *I* spake to me	2Sa 23:3	3478
the men of *I* were gone away	2Sa 23:9	3478
of the LORD was kindled against *I*	2Sa 24:1	3478
against them to say, Go, number *I*	2Sa 24:1	3478
now through all the tribes of *I*	2Sa 24:2	3478
king, to number the people of *I*	2Sa 24:4	3478
there were in *I* eight hundred	2Sa 24:9	3478
I from the morning even to the	2Sa 24:15	3478
and the plague was stayed from *I*	2Sa 24:25	3478
throughout all the coasts of *I*	1Kin 1:3	3478
the eyes of all *I* are upon thee	1Kin 1:20	3478
unto thee by the LORD God of *I*	1Kin 1:30	3478
anoint him there king over *I*	1Kin 1:34	3478
appointed him to be ruler over *I*	1Kin 1:35	3478
Blessed be the LORD God of *I*	1Kin 1:48	3478
said he) a man on the throne of *I*	1Kin 2:4	3478
two captains of the hosts of *I*	1Kin 2:5	3478
reigned over *I* were forty years	1Kin 2:11	3478
that all *I* set their faces on me,	1Kin 2:15	3478
of Ner, captain of the host of *I*	1Kin 2:32	3478
all *I* heard of the judgment which	1Kin 3:28	3478
king Solomon was king over all *I*	1Kin 4:1	3478
had twelve officers over all *I*	1Kin 4:7	3478
raised a levy out of all *I*	1Kin 5:13	3478
year after the children of *I* were	1Kin 6:1	3478
year of Solomon's reign over *I*	1Kin 6:1	3478
dwell among the children of *I*	1Kin 6:13	3478
and will not forsake my people *I*	1Kin 6:13	3478
Solomon assembled the elders of *I*	1Kin 8:1	3478
the fathers of the children of *I*	1Kin 8:1	3478
all the men of *I* assembled	1Kin 8:2	3478
And all the elders of *I* came	1Kin 8:3	3478
and all the congregation of *I*	1Kin 8:5	3478
a covenant with the children of *I*	1Kin 8:9	3478
blessed all the congregation of *I*	1Kin 8:14	3478
all the congregation of *I* stood	1Kin 8:14	3478
Blessed be the LORD God of *I*	1Kin 8:15	3478
forth my people *I* out of Egypt	1Kin 8:16	3478
the tribes of *I* to build an house	1Kin 8:16	3478
David to be over my people *I*	1Kin 8:16	3478
for the name of the LORD God of *I*	1Kin 8:17	3478
father, and sit on the throne of *I*	1Kin 8:20	3478
for the name of the LORD God of *I*	1Kin 8:20	3478
of all the congregation of *I*	1Kin 8:22	3478
And he said, LORD God of *I*	1Kin 8:23	3478
Therefore now, LORD God of *I*	1Kin 8:25	3478
sight to sit on the throne of *I*	1Kin 8:25	3478
And now, O God of *I*, let thy word,	1Kin 8:26	3478
thy servant, and of thy people *I*	1Kin 8:30	3478
When thy people *I* be smitten down	1Kin 8:33	3478
forgive the sin of thy people *I*	1Kin 8:34	3478
thy servants, and of thy people *I*	1Kin 8:36	3478
any man, or by all thy people *I*	1Kin 8:38	3478
that is not of thy people *I*	1Kin 8:41	3478
to fear thee, as do thy people *I*	1Kin 8:43	3478
the supplication of thy people *I*	1Kin 8:52	3478
of *I* with a loud voice, saying,	1Kin 8:55	3478
hath given rest unto his people *I*	1Kin 8:56	3478
of his people *I* at all times	1Kin 8:59	3478
all *I* with him, offered sacrifice	1Kin 8:62	3478
all the children of *I* dedicated	1Kin 8:63	3478
feast, and all *I* with him, a great	1Kin 8:65	3478
his servant, and for *I* his people	1Kin 8:66	3478
of thy kingdom upon *I* for ever	1Kin 9:5	3478
thee a man upon the throne of *I*	1Kin 9:5	3478
Then will I cut off *I* out of the	1Kin 9:7	3478
I shall be a proverb and a byword	1Kin 9:7	3478
were not of the children of *I*	1Kin 9:20	3478
whom the children of *I* also were	1Kin 9:21	3478
But of the children of *I* did	1Kin 9:22	3478
to set thee on the throne of *I*	1Kin 10:9	3478
because the LORD loved *I* for ever	1Kin 10:9	3478
LORD said unto the children of *I*	1Kin 11:2	3478
was turned from the LORD God of *I*	1Kin 11:9	3478
did Joab remain there with all *I*	1Kin 11:16	3478
he was an adversary to *I* all the	1Kin 11:25	3478
and he abhorred *I*, and reigned over	1Kin 11:25	3478
thus saith the LORD, the God of *I*	1Kin 11:31	3478
chosen out of all the tribes of *I*	1Kin 11:32	3478
desireth, and shalt be king over *I*	1Kin 11:37	3478
David, and will give *I* unto thee	1Kin 11:38	3478
over all *I* was forty years	1Kin 11:42	3478
for all *I* were come to Shechem to	1Kin 12:1	3478
and all the congregation of *I* came	1Kin 12:3	3478
So when all *I* saw that the king	1Kin 12:16	3478
to your tents, O *I*	1Kin 12:16	3478
So *I* departed unto their tents	1Kin 12:16	3478
But as for the children of *I*	1Kin 12:17	3478
Thus saith the LORD God of *I*	1Kin 14:7	3478
made thee prince over my people *I*	1Kin 14:7	3478
choose out of all the tribes of *I*	1Kin 14:21	3478
cast out before the children of *I*	1Kin 14:24	3478
sin wherewith he made *I* to sin	1Kin 15:34	3478
I to anger than all the kings of	1Kin 16:33	3478
Ahab, As the LORD God of *I* liveth	1Kin 17:1	3478
For thus saith the LORD God of *I*	1Kin 17:14	3478
this day that thou art God in *I*	1Kin 18:36	3478
to anger the LORD God of *I*	1Kin 22:53	3478
my father, the chariot of *I*	2Kin 2:12	3478
him, Thus saith the LORD God of *I*	2Kin 9:6	3478
LORD God of *I* with all his heart	2Kin 10:31	3478
He restored the coast of *I* from	2Kin 14:25	3478
to the word of the LORD God of *I*	2Kin 14:25	3478
of *I* did burn incense to it	2Kin 18:4	3478
He trusted in the LORD God of *I*	2Kin 18:5	3478
LORD, and said, O LORD God of *I*	2Kin 19:15	3478
Thus saith the LORD God of *I*	2Kin 19:20	3478
even against the Holy One of *I*	2Kin 19:22	3478
cast out before the children of *I*	2Kin 21:2	3478
a grove, as did Ahab king of *I*	2Kin 21:3	3478
chosen out of all tribes of *I*	2Kin 21:7	3478
I move any more out of the land	2Kin 21:8	3478
before the children of *I*	2Kin 21:9	3478
thus saith the LORD God of *I*	2Kin 21:12	3478
Thus saith the LORD God of *I*	2Kin 22:15	3478
him, Thus saith the LORD God of *I*	2Kin 22:18	3478
which Solomon the king of *I* had	2Kin 23:13	3478
days of the judges that judged *I*	2Kin 23:22	3478
I had made in the temple of the	2Kin 24:13	3478
reigned over the children of *I*	1Chr 1:43	3478
Achar, the troubler of *I*, who	1Chr 2:7	3478
And Jabez called on the God of *I*	1Chr 4:10	3478
the God of *I* stirred up the	1Chr 5:26	3478
and to make an atonement for *I*	1Chr 6:49	3478
the children of *I* gave to the	1Chr 6:64	3478
So all *I* were reckoned by	1Chr 9:1	3478
the Philistines fought against *I*	1Chr 10:1	3478
the men of *I* fled from before the	1Chr 10:1	3478
when all the men of *I* that were	1Chr 10:7	3478
Then all *I* gathered themselves to	1Chr 11:1	3478
leddest out and broughtest in *I*	1Chr 11:2	3478
thee, Thou shalt feed my people *I*	1Chr 11:2	3478
shalt be ruler over my people *I*	1Chr 11:2	3478
elders of *I* to the king to Hebron	1Chr 11:3	3478
they anointed David king over *I*	1Chr 11:3	3478
all *I* went to Jerusalem, which is	1Chr 11:4	3478
him in his kingdom, and with all *I*	1Chr 11:10	3478
the word of the LORD concerning *I*	1Chr 11:10	3478
times, to know what *I* ought to do	1Chr 12:32	3478

to make David king over all *I*	1Chr 12:38	3478
all the rest also of *I* were of	1Chr 12:38	3478
for there was joy in *I*	1Chr 12:40	3478
unto all the congregation of *I*	1Chr 13:2	3478
are left in all the land of *I*	1Chr 13:2	3478
So David gathered all *I* together	1Chr 13:5	3478
And David went up, and all *I*	1Chr 13:6	3478
all *I* played before God with all	1Chr 13:8	3478
had confirmed him king over *I*	1Chr 14:2	3478
on high, because of his people *I*	1Chr 14:2	3478
was anointed king over all *I*	1Chr 14:8	3478
David gathered all *I* together to	1Chr 15:3	3478
of *I* unto the place that I have	1Chr 15:12	3478
up the ark of the LORD God of *I*	1Chr 15:14	3478
So David, and the elders of *I*	1Chr 15:25	3478
Thus all *I* brought up the ark of	1Chr 15:28	3478
And he dealt to every one of *I*	1Chr 16:3	3478
thank and praise the LORD God of *I*	1Chr 16:4	3478
O ye seed of *I* his servant	1Chr 16:13	3478
to *I* for an everlasting covenant,	1Chr 16:17	3478
be the LORD God of *I* for ever	1Chr 16:36	3478
of the LORD, which he commanded *I*	1Chr 16:40	3478
that I brought up *I* unto this day	1Chr 17:5	3478
I have walked with all *I*, spake I	1Chr 17:6	3478
a word to any of the judges of *I*	1Chr 17:6	3478
be ruler over my people *I*	1Chr 17:7	3478
ordain a place for my people *I*	1Chr 17:9	3478
judges to be over my people *I*	1Chr 17:10	3478
in the earth is like thy people *I*	1Chr 17:21	3478
For thy people *I* didst thou make	1Chr 17:22	3478
God of Israel, even a God to *I*	1Chr 17:24	3478
So David reigned over all *I*	1Chr 18:14	3478
chose out of all the choice of *I*	1Chr 19:10	3478
were put to the worse before *I*	1Chr 19:16	3478
and he gathered all *I*, and passed	1Chr 19:17	3478
But the Syrians fled before *I*	1Chr 19:18	3478
were put to the worse before *I*	1Chr 19:19	3478
But when he defied *I*, Jonathan	1Chr 20:7	3478
And Satan stood up against *I*	1Chr 21:1	3478
and provoked David to number *I*	1Chr 21:1	3478
number *I* from Beer-sheba even to	1Chr 21:2	3478
he be a cause of trespass to *I*	1Chr 21:3	3478
and went throughout all *I*	1Chr 21:4	3478
all they of *I* were a thousand	1Chr 21:5	3478
therefore he smote *I*	1Chr 21:7	3478
throughout all the coasts of *I*	1Chr 21:12	3478
the LORD sent pestilence upon *I*	1Chr 21:14	3478
there fell of *I* seventy thousand	1Chr 21:14	3478
Then David and the elders of *I*	1Chr 21:16	3478
altar of the burnt offering for *I*	1Chr 22:1	3478
that were in the land of *I*	1Chr 22:2	3478
an house for the LORD God of *I*	1Chr 22:6	3478
and quietness unto *I* in his days	1Chr 22:9	3478
of his kingdom over *I* for ever	1Chr 22:10	3478
and give thee charge concerning *I*	1Chr 22:12	3478
charged Moses with concerning *I*	1Chr 22:13	3478
of *I* to help Solomon his son	1Chr 22:17	3478
made Solomon his son king over *I*	1Chr 23:1	3478
together all the princes of *I*	1Chr 23:2	3478
The LORD God of *I* hath given rest	1Chr 23:25	3478
LORD God of *I* had commanded him	1Chr 24:19	3478
for the outward business over *I*	1Chr 26:29	3478
were officers among them of *I* on	1Chr 26:30	3478
children of *I* after their number	1Chr 27:1	3478
Furthermore over the tribes of *I*	1Chr 27:16	3478
the princes of the tribes of *I*	1Chr 27:22	3478
I like to the stars of the	1Chr 27:23	3478
there fell wrath for it against *I*	1Chr 27:24	3478
assembled all the princes of *I*	1Chr 28:1	3478
Howbeit the LORD God of *I* chose	1Chr 28:4	3478
father to be king over *I* for ever	1Chr 28:4	3478
me to make me king over all *I*	1Chr 28:4	3478
of the kingdom of the LORD over *I*	1Chr 28:5	3478
in the sight of all *I* the	1Chr 28:8	3478
and princes of the tribes of *I*	1Chr 29:6	3478
sacrifices in abundance for all *I*	1Chr 29:21	3478
and all *I* obeyed him	1Chr 29:23	3478
exceedingly in the sight of all *I*	1Chr 29:25	3478
been on any king before him in *I*	1Chr 29:25	3478
son of Jesse reigned over all *I*	1Chr 29:26	3478
he reigned over *I* was forty years	1Chr 29:27	3478
that went over him, and over *I*	1Chr 29:30	3478
Then Solomon spake unto all *I*	2Chr 1:2	3478
and to every governor in all *I*	2Chr 1:2	3478
congregation, and reigned over *I*	2Chr 1:13	3478
is an ordinance for ever to *I*	2Chr 2:4	3478
Blessed be the LORD God of *I*	2Chr 2:12	3478
that were in the land of *I*	2Chr 2:17	3478
Solomon assembled the elders of *I*	2Chr 5:2	3478
the fathers of the children of *I*	2Chr 5:2	3478
Wherefore all the men of *I*	2Chr 5:3	3478
And all the elders of *I* came	2Chr 5:4	3478
all the congregation of *I* that	2Chr 5:6	3478
a covenant with the children of *I*	2Chr 5:10	3478
the whole congregation of *I*	2Chr 6:3	3478
all the congregation of *I* stood	2Chr 6:3	3478
Blessed be the LORD God of *I*	2Chr 6:4	3478
tribes of *I* to build an house in	2Chr 6:5	3478
to be a ruler over my people *I*	2Chr 6:5	3478
David to be over my people *I*	2Chr 6:6	3478
for the name of the LORD God of *I*	2Chr 6:7	3478
and am set on the throne of *I*	2Chr 6:10	3478
for the name of the LORD God of *I*	2Chr 6:10	3478
he made with the children of *I*	2Chr 6:11	3478
of all the congregation of *I*	2Chr 6:12	3478
before all the congregation of *I*	2Chr 6:13	3478
And said, O LORD God of *I*, there	2Chr 6:14	3478
Now therefore, O LORD God of *I*	2Chr 6:16	3478
sight to sit upon the throne of *I*	2Chr 6:16	3478
Now then, O LORD God of *I*	2Chr 6:17	3478
thy servant, and of thy people *I*	2Chr 6:21	3478
if thy people *I* be put to the	2Chr 6:24	3478
forgive the sin of thy people *I*	2Chr 6:25	3478
thy servants, and of thy people *I*	2Chr 6:27	3478
any man, or of all thy people *I*	2Chr 6:29	3478
which is not of thy people *I*	2Chr 6:32	3478
fear thee, as doth thy people *I*	2Chr 6:33	3478
when all the children of *I* saw	2Chr 7:3	3478
before them, and all *I* stood	2Chr 7:6	3478
all *I* with him, a very great	2Chr 7:8	3478
and to Solomon, and to *I* his people	2Chr 7:10	3478
fail thee a man to be ruler in *I*	2Chr 7:18	3478
the children of *I* to dwell there	2Chr 8:2	3478
Jebusites, which were not of *I*	2Chr 8:7	3478
the children of *I* consumed not	2Chr 8:8	3478
But of the children of *I* did	2Chr 8:9	3478
in the house of David king of *I*	2Chr 8:11	3478
because thy God loved *I*, to	2Chr 9:8	3478
Jerusalem over all *I* forty years	2Chr 9:30	3478
were all *I* come to make him king	2Chr 10:1	3478
all *I* came and spake to Rehoboam,	2Chr 10:3	3478
when all *I* saw that the king	2Chr 10:16	3478
every man to your tents, O *I*	2Chr 10:16	3478
So all *I* went to their tents	2Chr 10:16	3478
But as for the children of *I* that	2Chr 10:17	3478
to all *I* in Judah and Benjamin,	2Chr 11:3	3478
LORD God of *I* came to Jerusalem	2Chr 11:16	3478
of the LORD, and all *I* with him	2Chr 12:1	3478
Whereupon the princes of *I*	2Chr 12:6	3478
chosen out of all the tribes of *I*	2Chr 12:13	3478
to know that the LORD God of *I*	2Chr 13:5	3478
kingdom over *I* to David for ever	2Chr 13:5	3478
Now for a long season *I* hath been	2Chr 15:3	3478
did turn unto the LORD God of *I*	2Chr 15:4	3478
God of *I* should be put to death	2Chr 15:13	3478
of the chief of the fathers of *I*	2Chr 19:8	3478
of this land before thy people *I*	2Chr 20:7	3478
thou wouldest not let *I* invade	2Chr 20:10	3478
of *I* with a loud voice on high	2Chr 20:19	3478
fought against the enemies of *I*	2Chr 20:29	3478
and the chief of the fathers of *I*	2Chr 23:2	3478
gather of all *I* money to repair	2Chr 24:5	3478
LORD, and of the congregation of *I*	2Chr 24:6	3478
God laid upon *I* in the wilderness	2Chr 24:9	3478
because he had done good in *I*	2Chr 24:16	3478
cast out before the children of *I*	2Chr 28:3	3478
were the ruin of him, and of all *I*	2Chr 28:23	3478
book of the kings of Judah and *I*	2Chr 28:26	3478
the sepulchres of the kings of *I*	2Chr 28:27	3478
the holy place unto the God of *I*	2Chr 29:7	3478
a covenant with the LORD God of *I*	2Chr 29:10	3478
to make an atonement for all *I*	2Chr 29:24	3478
offering should be made for all *I*	2Chr 29:24	3478
ordained by David king of *I*	2Chr 29:27	3478
And Hezekiah sent to all *I*	2Chr 30:1	3478
passover unto the LORD God of *I*	2Chr 30:1	3478
proclamation throughout all *I*	2Chr 30:5	3478
the LORD God of *I* at Jerusalem	2Chr 30:5	3478
king, saying, Ye children of *I*	2Chr 30:6	3478
the son of David king of *I* there	2Chr 30:26	3478
all *I* that were present went out	2Chr 31:1	3478
all the children of *I* returned	2Chr 31:1	3478
the children of *I* brought in	2Chr 31:5	3478
blessed the LORD, and his people *I*	2Chr 31:8	3478
to rail on the LORD God of *I*	2Chr 32:17	3478
cast out before the children of *I*	2Chr 33:2	3478
chosen before all the tribes of *I*	2Chr 33:7	3478
of *I* from out of the land which I	2Chr 33:8	3478
before the children of *I*	2Chr 33:9	3478
Judah to serve the LORD God of *I*	2Chr 33:16	3478
in the name of the LORD God of *I*	2Chr 33:18	3478
in the book of the kings of *I*	2Chr 33:18	3478

I

throughout all the land of *I*	2Chr 34:7	3478
Thus saith the Lord God of *I*	2Chr 34:23	3478
Thus saith the Lord God of *I*	2Chr 34:26	3478
pertained to the children of *I*	2Chr 34:33	3478
that were present in *I* to serve	2Chr 34:33	3478
the Levites that taught all *I*	2Chr 35:3	3478
son of David king of *I* did build	2Chr 35:3	3478
Lord your God, and his people *I*	2Chr 35:3	3478
to the writing of David king of *I*	2Chr 35:4	3478
the children of *I* that were	2Chr 35:17	3478
in *I* from the days of Samuel the	2Chr 35:18	3478
and made them an ordinance in *I*	2Chr 35:25	3478
turning unto the Lord God of *I*	2Chr 36:13	3478
the house of the Lord God of *I*	Ezr 1:3	3478
of the men of the people of *I*	Ezr 2:2	3478
seed, whether they were of *I*	Ezr 2:59	3478
cities, and all *I* in their cities	Ezr 2:70	3478
the children of *I* were in the	Ezr 3:1	3478
builded the altar of the God of *I*	Ezr 3:2	3478
the ordinance of David king of *I*	Ezr 3:10	3478
mercy endureth for ever toward *I*	Ezr 3:11	3478
the temple unto the Lord God of *I*	Ezr 4:1	3478
of the chief of the fathers of *I*	Ezr 4:3	3478
will build unto the Lord God of *I*	Ezr 4:3	3478
in the name of the God of *I*	Ezr 5:1	3479
which a great king of *I* builded	Ezr 5:11	3479
the commandment of the God of *I*	Ezr 6:14	3479
And the children of *I*, the priests	Ezr 6:16	3479
and for a sin offering for all *I*	Ezr 6:17	3479
to the number of the tribes of *I*	Ezr 6:17	3479
And the children of *I*, which were	Ezr 6:21	3478
land, to seek the Lord God of *I*	Ezr 6:21	3478
of the house of God, the God of *I*	Ezr 6:22	3478
which the Lord God of *I* had given	Ezr 7:6	3478
went up some of the children of *I*	Ezr 7:7	3478
do it, and to teach in *I* statutes	Ezr 7:10	3478
the Lord, and of his statutes to *I*	Ezr 7:11	3478
that all they of the people of *I*	Ezr 7:13	3479
freely offered unto the God of *I*	Ezr 7:15	3479
of *I* chief men to go up with me	Ezr 7:28	3478
all *I* there present, had offered	Ezr 8:25	3478
and chief of the fathers of *I*	Ezr 8:29	3478
burnt offerings unto the God of *I*	Ezr 8:35	3478
twelve bullocks for all *I*	Ezr 8:35	3478
to me, saying, The people of *I*	Ezr 9:1	3478
at the words of the God of *I*	Ezr 9:4	3478
O Lord God of *I*, thou art	Ezr 9:15	3478
of *I* a very great congregation of	Ezr 10:1	3478
hope in *I* concerning this thing	Ezr 10:2	3478
priests, the Levites, and all *I*	Ezr 10:5	3478
to increase the trespass of *I*	Ezr 10:10	3478
Moreover of *I*: of the sons of	Ezr 10:25	3478
the children of *I* thy servants	Neh 1:6	3478
the sins of the children of *I*	Neh 1:6	3478
the welfare of the children of *I*	Neh 2:10	3478
men of the people of *I* was this	Neh 7:7	3478
seed, whether they were of *I*	Neh 7:61	3478
and the Nethinims, and all *I*	Neh 7:73	3478
the children of *I* were in their	Neh 7:73	3478
which the Lord had commanded to *I*	Neh 8:1	3478
that the children of *I* should	Neh 8:14	3478
had not the children of *I* done so	Neh 8:17	3478
of *I* were assembled with fasting	Neh 9:1	3478
And the seed of *I* separated	Neh 9:2	3478
to make an atonement for *I*	Neh 10:33	3478
For the children of *I* and the	Neh 10:39	3478
in their cities, to wit, *I*	Neh 11:3	3478
And the residue of *I*, of the	Neh 11:20	3478
all *I* in the days of Zerubbabel,	Neh 12:47	3478
not the children of *I* with bread	Neh 13:2	3478
from *I* all the mixed multitude	Neh 13:3	3478
upon *I* by profaning the sabbath	Neh 13:18	3478
king of *I* sin by these things	Neh 13:26	3478
and God made him king over all *I*	Neh 13:26	3478
of *I* were come out of Zion	Ps 14:7	3478
shall rejoice, and *I* shall be glad	Ps 14:7	3478
that inhabitest the praises of *I*	Ps 22:3	3478
and fear him, all ye the seed of *I*	Ps 22:23	3478
Redeem *I*, O God, out of all his	Ps 25:22	3478
Lord God of *I* from everlasting	Ps 41:13	3478
O *I*, and I will testify against	Ps 50:7	3478
of *I* were come out of Zion	Ps 53:6	3478
shall rejoice, and *I* shall be glad	Ps 53:6	3478
O Lord God of hosts, the God of *I*	Ps 59:5	3478
the presence of God, the God of *I*	Ps 68:8	3478
the Lord, from the fountain of *I*	Ps 68:26	3478
his excellency is over *I*, and his	Ps 68:34	3478
the God of *I* is he that giveth	Ps 68:35	3478
for my sake, O God of *I*	Ps 69:6	3478
the harp, O thou Holy One of *I*	Ps 71:22	3478
be the Lord God, the God of *I*	Ps 72:18	3478
Truly God is good to *I*, even to	Ps 73:1	3478
his name is great in *I*	Ps 76:1	3478
in Jacob, and appointed a law in *I*	Ps 78:5	3478
and anger also came up against *I*	Ps 78:21	3478
and smote down the chosen men of *I*	Ps 78:31	3478
God, and limited the Holy One of *I*	Ps 78:41	3478
made the tribes of *I* to dwell in	Ps 78:55	3478
was wroth, and greatly abhorred *I*	Ps 78:59	3478
his people, and *I* his inheritance	Ps 78:71	3478
Give ear, O Shepherd of *I*	Ps 80:1	3478
For this was a statute for *I*	Ps 81:4	3478
O *I*, if thou wilt hearken unto me	Ps 81:8	3478
and *I* would none of me	Ps 81:11	3478
me, and *I* had walked in my ways	Ps 81:13	3478
that the name of *I* may be no more	Ps 83:4	3478
and the Holy One of *I* is our king	Ps 89:18	3478
his truth toward the house of *I*	Ps 98:3	3478
his acts unto the children of *I*	Ps 103:7	3478
to *I* for an everlasting covenant	Ps 105:10	3478
I also came into Egypt	Ps 105:23	3478
Blessed be the Lord God of *I* from	Ps 106:48	3478
When *I* went out of Egypt, the	Ps 114:1	3478
his sanctuary, and *I* his dominion	Ps 114:2	3478
O *I*, trust thou in the Lord	Ps 115:9	3478
he will bless the house of *I*	Ps 115:12	3478
Let *I* now say, that his mercy	Ps 118:2	3478
he that keepeth *I* shall neither	Ps 121:4	3478
the Lord, unto the testimony of *I*	Ps 122:4	3478
was on our side, now may *I* say	Ps 124:1	3478
but peace shall be upon *I*	Ps 125:5	3478
children, and peace upon *I*	Ps 128:6	3478
me from my youth, may *I* now say	Ps 129:1	3478
Let *I* hope in the Lord	Ps 130:7	3478
he shall redeem *I* from all his	Ps 130:8	3478
Let *I* hope in the Lord from	Ps 131:3	3478
I for his peculiar treasure	Ps 135:4	3478
an heritage unto *I* his people	Ps 135:12	3478
Bless the Lord, O house of *I*	Ps 135:19	3478
brought out *I* from among them	Ps 136:11	3478
made *I* to pass through the midst	Ps 136:14	3478
an heritage unto *I* his servant	Ps 136:22	3478
together the outcasts of *I*	Ps 147:2	3478
statutes and his judgments unto *I*	Ps 147:19	3478
even of the children of *I*	Ps 148:14	3478
Let *I* rejoice in him that made	Ps 149:2	3478
the son of David, king of *I*	Prov 1:1	3478
was king over *I* in Jerusalem	Eccl 1:12	3478
are about it, the valiant of *I*	Song 3:7	3478
but *I* doth not know, my people	Is 1:3	3478
the Holy One of *I* unto anger	Is 1:4	3478
of hosts, the mighty One of *I*	Is 1:24	3478
for them that are escaped of *I*	Is 4:2	3478
Lord of hosts is the house of *I*	Is 5:7	3478
of the Holy One of *I* draw nigh	Is 5:19	3478
the word of the Holy One of *I*	Is 5:24	3478
offence to both the houses of *I*	Is 8:14	3478
for wonders in *I* from the Lord of	Is 8:18	3478
Jacob, and it hath lighted upon *I*	Is 9:8	3478
shall devour *I* with open mouth	Is 9:12	3478
the Lord will cut off from *I* head	Is 9:14	3478
the light of *I* shall be for a	Is 10:17	3478
that day, that the remnant of *I*	Is 10:20	3478
upon the Lord, the Holy One of *I*	Is 10:20	3478
For though thy people *I* be as the	Is 10:22	3478
shall assemble the outcasts of *I*	Is 11:12	3478
like as it was to *I* in the day	Is 11:16	3478
One of *I* in the midst of thee	Is 12:6	3478
on Jacob, and will yet choose *I*	Is 14:1	3478
the house of *I* shall possess them	Is 14:2	3478
as the glory of the children of *I*	Is 17:3	3478
thereof, saith the Lord God of *I*	Is 17:6	3478
have respect to the Holy One of *I*	Is 17:7	3478
left because of the children of *I*	Is 17:9	3478
In that day shall *I* be the third	Is 19:24	3478
my hands, and *I* mine inheritance	Is 19:25	3478
the Lord of hosts, the God of *I*	Is 21:10	3478
the Lord God of *I* hath spoken it	Is 21:17	3478
God of *I* in the isles of the sea	Is 24:15	3478
I shall blossom and bud, and fill	Is 27:6	3478
one by one, O ye children of *I*	Is 27:12	3478
rejoice in the Holy One of *I*	Is 29:19	3478
Jacob, and shall fear the God of *I*	Is 29:23	3478
cause the Holy One of *I* to cease	Is 30:11	3478
thus saith the Holy One of *I*	Is 30:12	3478
the Lord God, the Holy One of *I*	Is 30:15	3478
the Lord, to the mighty One of *I*	Is 30:29	3478
look not unto the Holy One of *I*	Is 31:1	3478
of *I* have deeply revolted	Is 31:6	3478
O Lord of hosts, God of *I*	Is 37:16	3478
Thus saith the Lord God of *I*	Is 37:21	3478
even against the Holy One of *I*	Is 37:23	3478

thou, O Jacob, and speakest, O *I*	Is 40:27	3478
But thou, *I*, art my servant,	Is 41:8	3478
thou worm Jacob, and ye men of *I*	Is 41:14	3478
thy redeemer, the Holy One of *I*	Is 41:14	3478
shalt glory in the Holy One of *I*	Is 41:16	3478
I the God of *I* will not forsake	Is 41:17	3478
the Holy One of *I* hath created it	Is 41:20	3478
for a spoil, and *I* to the robbers	Is 42:24	3478
and he that formed thee, O *I*	Is 43:1	3478
LORD thy God, the Holy One of *I*	Is 43:3	3478
your redeemer, the Holy One of *I*	Is 43:14	3478
your Holy One, the creator of *I*	Is 43:15	3478
thou hast been weary of me, O *I*	Is 43:22	3478
to the curse, and *I* to reproaches	Is 43:28	3478
and *I*, whom I have chosen	Is 44:1	3478
surname himself by the name of *I*	Is 44:5	3478
Thus saith the LORD the King of *I*	Is 44:6	3478
Remember these, O Jacob and *I*	Is 44:21	3478
O *I*, thou shalt not be forgotten	Is 44:21	3478
Jacob, and glorified himself in *I*	Is 44:23	3478
thee by thy name, am the God of *I*	Is 45:3	3478
I mine elect, I have even called	Is 45:4	3478
saith the LORD, the Holy One of *I*	Is 45:11	3478
that hidest thyself, O God of *I*	Is 45:15	3478
But *I* shall be saved in the LORD	Is 45:17	3478
all the seed of *I* be justified	Is 45:25	3478
all the remnant of the house of *I*	Is 46:3	3478
salvation in Zion for *I* my glory	Is 46:13	3478
is his name, the Holy One of *I*	Is 47:4	3478
which are called by the name of *I*	Is 48:1	3478
and make mention of the God of *I*	Is 48:1	3478
stay themselves upon the God of *I*	Is 48:2	3478
Hearken unto me, O Jacob and *I*	Is 48:12	3478
thy Redeemer, the Holy One of *I*	Is 48:17	3478
unto me, Thou art my servant, O *I*	Is 49:3	3478
Though *I* be not gathered, yet	Is 49:5	3478
and to restore the preserved of *I*	Is 49:6	3478
saith the LORD, the Redeemer of *I*	Is 49:7	3478
is faithful, and the Holy One of *I*	Is 49:7	3478
the God of *I* will be your	Is 52:12	3478
and thy Redeemer the Holy One of *I*	Is 54:5	3478
thy God, and for the Holy One of *I*	Is 55:5	3478
gathereth the outcasts of *I* saith	Is 56:8	3478
thy God, and to the Holy One of *I*	Is 60:9	3478
The Zion of the Holy One of *I*	Is 60:14	3478
goodness toward the house of *I*	Is 63:7	3478
of us, and *I* acknowledge us not	Is 63:16	3478
as the children of *I* bring an	Is 66:20	3478
I was holiness unto the LORD, and	Jer 2:3	3478
the families of the house of *I*	Jer 2:4	3478
Is *I* a servant?	Jer 2:14	3478
with me, O house of *I*, saith the	Jer 3:20	3478
of the children of *I*	Jer 3:21	3478
our God is the salvation of *I*	Jer 3:23	3478
If thou wilt return, O *I*, saith	Jer 4:1	3478
upon you from far, O house of *I*	Jer 5:15	3478
glean the remnant of *I* as a vine	Jer 6:9	3478
the LORD of hosts, the God of *I*	Jer 7:3	3478
for the wickedness of my people *I*	Jer 7:12	3478
the LORD of hosts, the God of *I*	Jer 7:21	3478
the LORD of hosts, the God of *I*	Jer 9:15	3478
speaketh unto you, O house of *I*	Jer 10:1	3478
I is the rod of his inheritance	Jer 10:16	3478
Thus saith the LORD God of *I*	Jer 11:3	3478
caused my people *I* to inherit	Jer 12:14	3478
unto me the whole house of *I*	Jer 13:11	3478
Thus saith the LORD God of *I*	Jer 13:12	3478
O the hope of *I*, the saviour	Jer 14:8	3478
the LORD of hosts, the God of *I*	Jer 16:9	3478
of *I* out of the land of Egypt	Jer 16:14	3478
of *I* from the land of the north	Jer 16:15	3478
O LORD, the hope of *I*, all that	Jer 17:13	3478
O house of *I*, cannot I do with	Jer 18:6	3478
are ye in mine hand, O house of *I*	Jer 18:6	3478
the virgin of *I* hath done a very	Jer 18:13	3478
the LORD of hosts, the God of *I*	Jer 19:3	3478
the LORD of hosts, the God of *I*	Jer 19:15	3478
Thus saith the LORD God of *I*	Jer 21:4	3478
thus saith the LORD God of *I*	Jer 23:2	3478
of *I* out of the land of Egypt	Jer 23:7	3478
of *I* out of the north country	Jer 23:8	3478
and caused my people *I* to err	Jer 23:13	3478
Thus saith the LORD, the God of *I*	Jer 24:5	3478
saith the LORD God of *I* unto me	Jer 25:15	3478
the LORD of hosts, the God of *I*	Jer 25:27	3478
the LORD of hosts, the God of *I*	Jer 27:4	3478
the LORD of hosts, the God of *I*	Jer 27:21	3478
the LORD of hosts, the God of *I*	Jer 28:2	3478
the LORD of hosts, the God of *I*	Jer 28:14	3478
the LORD of hosts, the God of *I*	Jer 29:4	3478
the LORD of hosts, the God of *I*	Jer 29:8	3478
the LORD of hosts, the God of *I*	Jer 29:21	3478
they have committed villany in *I*	Jer 29:23	3478
the LORD of hosts, the God of *I*	Jer 29:25	3478
Thus speaketh the LORD God of *I*	Jer 30:2	3478
the captivity of my people *I*	Jer 30:3	3478
that the LORD spake concerning *I*	Jer 30:4	3478
neither be dismayed, O *I*	Jer 30:10	3478
the God of all the families of *I*	Jer 31:1	3478
even *I*, when I went to cause him	Jer 31:2	3478
shalt be built, O virgin of *I*	Jer 31:4	3478
save thy people, the remnant of *I*	Jer 31:7	3478
for I am a father to *I*, and	Jer 31:9	3478
that scattered *I* will gather him	Jer 31:10	3478
turn again, O virgin of *I*	Jer 31:21	3478
the LORD of hosts, the God of *I*	Jer 31:23	3478
I will make with the house of *I*	Jer 31:33	3478
then the seed of *I* also shall	Jer 31:36	3478
of *I* for all that they have done	Jer 31:37	3478
the LORD of hosts, the God of *I*	Jer 32:14	3478
the LORD of hosts, the God of *I*	Jer 32:15	3478
even unto this day, and in *I*	Jer 32:20	3478
I out of the land of Egypt with	Jer 32:21	3478
for the children of *I* have only	Jer 32:30	3478
thus saith the LORD, the God of *I*	Jer 32:36	3478
thus saith the LORD, the God of *I*	Jer 33:4	3478
and the captivity of *I* to return	Jer 33:7	3478
have promised unto the house of *I*	Jer 33:14	3478
upon the throne of the house of *I*	Jer 33:17	3478
Thus saith the LORD, the God of *I*	Jer 34:2	3478
Thus saith the LORD, the God of *I*	Jer 34:13	3478
the LORD of hosts, the God of *I*	Jer 35:13	3478
LORD God of hosts, the God of *I*	Jer 35:17	3478
the LORD of hosts, the God of *I*	Jer 35:18	3478
the LORD of hosts, the God of *I*	Jer 35:19	3478
I have spoken unto thee against *I*	Jer 36:2	3478
Thus saith the LORD, the God of *I*	Jer 37:7	3478
the God of hosts, the God of *I*	Jer 38:17	3478
the LORD of hosts, the God of *I*	Jer 39:16	3478
Thus saith the LORD, the God of *I*	Jer 42:9	3478
the LORD of hosts, the God of *I*	Jer 42:15	3478
the LORD of hosts, the God of *I*	Jer 42:18	3478
the LORD of hosts, the God of *I*	Jer 43:10	3478
the LORD of hosts, the God of *I*	Jer 44:2	3478
the God of hosts, the God of *I*	Jer 44:7	3478
the LORD of hosts, the God of *I*	Jer 44:11	3478
the LORD of hosts, the God of *I*	Jer 44:25	3478
Thus saith the LORD, the God of *I*	Jer 45:2	3478
The LORD of hosts, the God of *I*	Jer 46:25	3478
Jacob, and be not dismayed, O *I*	Jer 46:27	3478
the LORD of hosts, the God of *I*	Jer 48:1	3478
For was not *I* a derision unto	Jer 48:27	3478
Hath *I* no sons?	Jer 49:1	3478
then shall *I* be heir unto them	Jer 49:2	3478
the children of *I* shall come	Jer 50:4	3478
I is a scattered sheep	Jer 50:17	3478
the LORD of hosts, the God of *I*	Jer 50:18	3478
I will bring *I* again to his	Jer 50:19	3478
the iniquity of *I* shall be sought	Jer 50:20	3478
LORD, against the Holy One of *I*	Jer 50:29	3478
For *I* hath not been forsaken, nor	Jer 51:5	3478
sin against the Holy One of *I*	Jer 51:5	3478
I is the rod of his inheritance	Jer 51:19	3478
the LORD of hosts, the God of *I*	Jer 51:33	3478
caused the slain of *I* to fall	Jer 51:49	3478
unto the earth the beauty of *I*	Lam 2:1	3478
fierce anger all the horn of *I*	Lam 2:3	3478
he hath swallowed up *I*, he hath	Lam 2:5	3478
I send thee to the children of *I*	Eze 2:3	3478
and go speak unto the house of *I*	Eze 3:1	3478
go, get thee unto the house of *I*	Eze 3:4	3478
language, but to the house of *I*	Eze 3:5	3478
But the house of *I* will not	Eze 3:7	3478
all the house of *I* are impudent	Eze 3:7	3478
a watchman unto the house of *I*	Eze 3:17	3478
shall be a sign to the house of *I*	Eze 4:3	3478
I eat their defiled bread among	Eze 4:13	3478
forth into all the house of *I*	Eze 5:4	3478
face toward the mountains of *I*	Eze 6:2	3478
And say, Ye mountains of *I*	Eze 6:3	3478
children of *I* before their idols	Eze 6:5	3478
abominations of the house of *I*	Eze 6:11	3478
the Lord GOD unto the land of *I*	Eze 7:2	3478
glory of the God of *I* was there	Eze 8:4	3478
the house of *I* committeth here	Eze 8:6	3478
all the idols of the house of *I*	Eze 8:10	3478
of the ancients of the house of *I*	Eze 8:11	3478
of the house of *I* do in the dark	Eze 8:12	3478
the glory of the God of *I* was	Eze 9:3	3478
I in thy pouring out of thy fury	Eze 9:8	3478
the God of *I* was over them above	Eze 10:19	3478
God of *I* by the river of Chebar	Eze 10:20	3478

I

Thus have ye said, O house of *I*	Eze 11:5	3478
will judge you in the border of *I*	Eze 11:10	3478
will judge you in the border of *I*	Eze 11:11	3478
a full end of the remnant of *I*	Eze 11:13	3478
and all the house of *I* wholly	Eze 11:15	3478
and I will give you the land of *I*	Eze 11:17	3478
the God of *I* was over them above	Eze 11:22	3478
for a sign unto the house of *I*	Eze 12:6	3478
of man, hath not the house of *I*	Eze 12:9	3478
all the house of *I* that are among	Eze 12:10	3478
of Jerusalem, and of the land of *I*	Eze 12:19	3478
that ye have in the land of *I*	Eze 12:22	3478
no more use it as a proverb in *I*	Eze 12:23	3478
divination within the house of *I*	Eze 12:24	3478
they of the house of *I* say	Eze 12:27	3478
the prophets of *I* that prophesy	Eze 13:2	3478
O *I*, thy prophets are like the	Eze 13:4	3478
I to stand in the battle in the	Eze 13:5	3478
in the writing of the house of *I*	Eze 13:9	3478
they enter into the land of *I*	Eze 13:9	3478
the prophets of *I* which prophesy	Eze 13:16	3478
of the elders of *I* unto me	Eze 14:1	3478
Every man of the house of *I* that	Eze 14:4	3478
the house of *I* in their own heart	Eze 14:5	3478
Therefore say unto the house of *I*	Eze 14:6	3478
For every one of the house of *I*	Eze 14:7	3478
the stranger that sojourneth in *I*	Eze 14:7	3478
him from the midst of my people *I*	Eze 14:9	3478
That the house of *I* may go no	Eze 14:11	3478
a parable unto the house of *I*	Eze 17:2	3478
the height of *I* will I plant it	Eze 17:23	3478
proverb concerning the land of *I*	Eze 18:2	3478
any more to use this proverb in *I*	Eze 18:3	3478
to the idols of the house of *I*	Eze 18:6	3478
to the idols of the house of *I*	Eze 18:15	3478
Hear now, O house of *I*	Eze 18:25	3478
Yet saith the house of *I*, The way	Eze 18:29	3478
O house of *I*, are not my ways	Eze 18:29	3478
I will judge you, O house of *I*	Eze 18:30	3478
for why will ye die, O house of *I*	Eze 18:31	3478
lamentation for the princes of *I*	Eze 19:1	3478
be heard upon the mountains of *I*	Eze 19:9	3478
of *I* came to enquire of the LORD	Eze 20:1	3478
man, speak unto the elders of *I*	Eze 20:3	3478
In the day when I chose *I*	Eze 20:5	3478
But the house of *I* rebelled	Eze 20:13	3478
of man, speak unto the house of *I*	Eze 20:27	3478
Wherefore say unto the house of *I*	Eze 20:30	3478
enquired of by you, O house of *I*	Eze 20:31	3478
not enter into the land of *I*	Eze 20:38	3478
As for you, O house of *I*, thus	Eze 20:39	3478
the mountain of the height of *I*	Eze 20:40	3478
there shall all the house of *I*	Eze 20:40	3478
bring you into the land of *I*	Eze 20:42	3478
corrupt doings, O ye house of *I*	Eze 20:44	3478
and prophesy against the land of *I*	Eze 21:2	3478
And say to the land of *I*, Thus	Eze 21:3	3478
be upon all the princes of *I*	Eze 21:12	3478
thou, profane wicked prince of *I*	Eze 21:25	3478
Behold, the princes of *I*, every	Eze 22:6	3478
the house of *I* is to me become	Eze 22:18	3478
Speak unto the house of *I*	Eze 24:21	3478
and against the land of *I*, when it	Eze 25:3	3478
thy despite against the land of *I*	Eze 25:6	3478
Edom by the hand of my people *I*	Eze 25:14	3478
brier unto the house of *I*	Eze 28:24	3478
have gathered the house of *I* from	Eze 28:25	3478
a staff of reed to the house of *I*	Eze 29:6	3478
the confidence of the house of *I*	Eze 29:16	3478
of the house of *I* to bud forth	Eze 29:21	3478
a watchman unto the house of *I*	Eze 33:7	3478
of man, speak unto the house of *I*	Eze 33:10	3478
for why will ye die, O house of *I*	Eze 33:11	3478
O ye house of *I*, I will judge you	Eze 33:20	3478
wastes of the land of *I* speak	Eze 33:24	3478
the mountains of *I* shall be	Eze 33:28	3478
against the shepherds of *I*	Eze 34:2	3478
of *I* that do feed themselves	Eze 34:2	3478
the mountains of *I* by the rivers	Eze 34:13	3478
of *I* shall their fold be	Eze 34:14	3478
they feed upon the mountains of *I*	Eze 34:14	3478
and that they, even the house of *I*	Eze 34:30	3478
of *I* by the force of the sword in	Eze 35:5	3478
spoken against the mountains of *I*	Eze 35:12	3478
the inheritance of the house of *I*	Eze 35:15	3478
prophesy unto the mountains of *I*	Eze 36:1	3478
and say, Ye mountains of *I*	Eze 36:1	3478
Therefore, ye mountains of *I*	Eze 36:4	3478
concerning the land of *I*, and say	Eze 36:6	3478
But ye, O mountains of *I*, ye	Eze 36:8	3478
your fruit to my people of *I*	Eze 36:8	3478
men upon you, all the house of *I*	Eze 36:10	3478
walk upon you, even my people *I*	Eze 36:12	3478
when the house of *I* dwelt in	Eze 36:17	3478
which the house of *I* had profaned	Eze 36:21	3478
Therefore say unto the house of *I*	Eze 36:22	3478
this for your sakes, O house of *I*	Eze 36:22	3478
for your own ways, O house of *I*	Eze 36:32	3478
be enquired of by the house of *I*	Eze 36:37	3478
bones are the whole house of *I*	Eze 37:11	3478
and bring you into the land of *I*	Eze 37:12	3478
all the house of *I* his companions	Eze 37:16	3478
and the tribes of *I* his fellows	Eze 37:19	3478
of *I* from among the heathen	Eze 37:21	3478
the land upon the mountains of *I*	Eze 37:22	3478
that I the LORD do sanctify *I*	Eze 37:28	3478
against the mountains of *I*	Eze 38:8	3478
my people of *I* dwelleth safely	Eze 38:14	3478
come up against my people of *I*	Eze 38:16	3478
by my servants the prophets of *I*	Eze 38:17	3478
shall come against the land of *I*	Eze 38:18	3478
a great shaking in the land of *I*	Eze 38:19	3478
thee upon the mountains of *I*	Eze 39:2	3478
fall upon the mountains of *I*	Eze 39:4	3478
known in the midst of my people *I*	Eze 39:7	3478
I am the LORD, the Holy One in *I*	Eze 39:7	3478
in the cities of *I* shall go forth	Eze 39:9	3478
Gog a place there of graves in *I*	Eze 39:11	3478
the house of *I* be burying of them	Eze 39:12	3478
sacrifice upon the mountains of *I*	Eze 39:17	3478
So the house of *I* shall know that	Eze 39:22	3478
shall know that the house of *I*	Eze 39:23	3478
mercy upon the whole house of *I*	Eze 39:25	3478
out my spirit upon the house of *I*	Eze 39:29	3478
brought he me into the land of *I*	Eze 40:2	3478
that thou seest to the house of *I*	Eze 40:4	3478
the glory of the God of *I* came	Eze 43:2	3478
of the children of *I* for ever	Eze 43:7	3478
the house of *I* no more defile	Eze 43:7	3478
shew the house to the house of *I*	Eze 43:10	3478
because the LORD, the God of *I*	Eze 44:2	3478
even to the house of *I*, Thus	Eze 44:6	3478
O ye house of *I*, let it suffice	Eze 44:6	3478
that is among the children of *I*	Eze 44:9	3478
when *I* went astray, which went	Eze 44:10	3478
caused the house of *I* to fall	Eze 44:12	3478
of the seed of the house of *I*	Eze 44:22	3478
give them no possession in *I*	Eze 44:28	3478
thing in *I* shall be their's	Eze 44:29	3478
shall be for the whole house of *I*	Eze 45:6	3478
land shall be his possession in *I*	Eze 45:8	3478
of *I* according to their tribes	Eze 45:8	3478
it suffice you, O princes of *I*	Eze 45:9	3478
out of the fat pastures of *I*	Eze 45:15	3478
this oblation for the prince in *I*	Eze 45:16	3478
all solemnities of the house of *I*	Eze 45:17	3478
reconciliation for the house of *I*	Eze 45:17	3478
to the twelve tribes of *I*	Eze 47:13	3478
and from the land of *I* by Jordan	Eze 47:18	3478
you according to the tribes of *I*	Eze 47:21	3478
country among the children of *I*	Eze 47:22	3478
with you among the tribes of *I*	Eze 47:22	3478
the children of *I* went astray	Eze 48:11	3478
it out of all the tribes of *I*	Eze 48:19	3478
the tribes of *I* for inheritance	Eze 48:29	3478
the names of the tribes of *I*	Eze 48:31	3478
certain of the children of *I*	Dan 1:3	3478
of Jerusalem, and unto all *I*	Dan 9:7	3478
all *I* have transgressed thy law,	Dan 9:11	3478
my sin and the sin of my people *I*	Dan 9:20	3478
the son of Joash, king of *I*	Hos 1:1	3478
the kingdom of the house of *I*	Hos 1:4	3478
bow of *I* in the valley of Jezreel	Hos 1:5	3478
have mercy upon the house of *I*	Hos 1:6	3478
the number of the children of *I*	Hos 1:10	3478
the children of *I* be gathered	Hos 1:11	3478
the LORD toward the children of *I*	Hos 3:1	3478
For the children of *I* shall abide	Hos 3:4	3478
shall the children of *I* return	Hos 3:5	3478
of the LORD, ye children of *I*	Hos 4:1	3478
Though thou, *I*, play the harlot,	Hos 4:15	3478
For *I* slideth back as a	Hos 4:16	3478
and hearken, ye house of *I*	Hos 5:1	3478
Ephraim, and *I* is not hid from me	Hos 5:3	3478
whoredom, and *I* is defiled	Hos 5:3	3478
the pride of *I* doth testify to	Hos 5:5	3478
therefore shall *I* and Ephraim fall	Hos 5:5	3478
among the tribes of *I* have I made	Hos 5:9	3478
horrible thing in the house of *I*	Hos 6:10	3478
whoredom of Ephraim, *I* is defiled	Hos 6:10	3478
When I would have healed *I*	Hos 7:1	3478
the pride of *I* testifieth to his	Hos 7:10	3478

I shall cry unto me, My God, we	Hos 8:2	3478
I hath cast off the thing that is	Hos 8:3	3478
For from *I* was it also	Hos 8:6	3478
I is swallowed up	Hos 8:8	3478
For *I* hath forgotten his Maker,	Hos 8:14	3478
Rejoice not, O *I*, for joy, as	Hos 9:1	3478
I shall know it	Hos 9:7	3478
I found *I* like grapes in the	Hos 9:10	3478
I is an empty vine, he bringeth	Hos 10:1	3478
I shall be ashamed of his own	Hos 10:6	3478
places also of Aven, the sin of *I*	Hos 10:8	3478
O *I*, thou hast sinned from the	Hos 10:9	3478
the king of *I* utterly be cut off	Hos 10:15	3478
When *I* was a child, then I loved	Hos 11:1	3478
how shall I deliver thee, *I*	Hos 11:8	3478
and the house of *I* with deceit	Hos 11:12	3478
I served for a wife, and for a	Hos 12:12	3478
the LORD brought *I* out of Egypt	Hos 12:13	3478
he exalted himself in *I*	Hos 13:1	3478
O *I*, thou hast destroyed thyself	Hos 13:9	3478
O *I*, return unto the LORD thy God	Hos 14:1	3478
I will be as the dew unto *I*	Hos 14:5	3478
know that I am in the midst of *I*	Joel 2:27	3478
my people and for my heritage *I*	Joel 3:2	3478
the strength of the children of *I*	Joel 3:16	3478
which he saw concerning *I* in the	Amos 1:1	3478
the son of Joash king of *I*	Amos 1:1	3478
For three transgressions of *I*	Amos 2:6	3478
not even thus, O ye children of *I*	Amos 2:11	3478
against you, O children of *I*	Amos 3:1	3478
so shall the children of *I* be	Amos 3:12	3478
visit the transgressions of *I*	Amos 3:14	3478
liketh you, O ye children of *I*	Amos 4:5	3478
thus will I do unto thee, O *I*	Amos 4:12	3478
prepare to meet thy God, O *I*	Amos 4:12	3478
even a lamentation, O house of *I*	Amos 5:1	3478
The virgin of *I* is fallen	Amos 5:2	3478
leave ten, to the house of *I*	Amos 5:3	3478
the LORD unto the house of *I*	Amos 5:4	3478
forty years, O house of *I*	Amos 5:25	3478
to whom the house of *I* came	Amos 6:1	3478
you a nation, O house of *I*	Amos 6:14	3478
in the midst of my people *I*	Amos 7:8	3478
the sanctuaries of *I* shall be	Amos 7:9	3478
sent to Jeroboam king of *I*	Amos 7:10	3478
in the midst of the house of *I*	Amos 7:10	3478
I shall surely be led away	Amos 7:11	3478
me, Go, prophesy unto my people *I*	Amos 7:15	3478
sayest, Prophesy not against *I*	Amos 7:16	3478
I shall surely go into captivity	Amos 7:17	3478
end is come upon my people of *I*	Amos 8:2	3478
unto me, O children of *I*	Amos 9:7	3478
Have not I brought up *I* out of	Amos 9:7	3478
the house of *I* among all nations	Amos 9:9	3478
the captivity of my people of *I*	Amos 9:14	3478
of *I* shall possess that of the	Obad 20	3478
and for the sins of the house of *I*	Mic 1:5	3478
of *I* were found in thee	Mic 1:13	3478
shall be a lie to the kings of *I*	Mic 1:14	3478
come unto Adullam the glory of *I*	Mic 1:15	3478
surely gather the remnant of *I*	Mic 2:12	3478
and ye princes of the house of *I*	Mic 3:1	3478
transgression, and to *I* his sin	Mic 3:8	3478
and princes of the house of *I*	Mic 3:9	3478
of *I* with a rod upon the cheek	Mic 5:1	3478
unto me that is to be ruler in *I*	Mic 5:2	3478
return unto the children of *I*	Mic 5:3	3478
people, and he will plead with *I*	Mic 6:2	3478
of Jacob, as the excellency of *I*	Nah 2:2	3478
the LORD of hosts, the God of *I*	Zeph 2:9	3478
The remnant of *I* shall not do	Zeph 3:13	3478
shout, O *I*	Zeph 3:14	3478
the king of *I*, even the LORD, is	Zeph 3:15	3478
of man, as of all the tribes of *I*	Zec 9:1	3478
of the word of the LORD for *I*	Zec 12:1	3478
word of the LORD to *I* by Malachi	Mal 1:1	3478
be magnified from the border of *I*	Mal 1:5	3478
For the LORD, the God of *I*	Mal 2:16	3478
unto him in Horeb for all *I*	Mal 4:4	3478
that shall rule my people *I*	Mt 2:6	2474
mother, and go into the land of *I*	Mt 2:20	2474
and came into the land of *I*	Mt 2:21	2474
so great faith, no, not in *I*	Mt 8:10	2474
saying, It was never so seen in *I*	Mt 9:33	2474
the lost sheep of the house of *I*	Mt 10:6	2474
have gone over the cities of *I*	Mt 10:23	2474
the lost sheep of the house of *I*	Mt 15:24	2474
and they glorified the God of *I*	Mt 15:31	2474
judging the twelve tribes of *I*	Mt 19:28	2474
of the children of *I* did value	Mt 27:9	2474
If he be the King of *I*, let him	Mt 27:42	2474

the commandments is, Hear, O *I*	Mk 12:29	2474
Let Christ the King of *I* descend	Mk 15:32	2474
many of the children of *I* shall	Lk 1:16	2474
He hath holpen his servant *I*	Lk 1:54	2474
Blessed be the Lord God of *I*	Lk 1:68	2474
the day of his shewing unto *I*	Lk 1:80	2474
waiting for the consolation of *I*	Lk 2:25	2474
and the glory of thy people *I*	Lk 2:32	2474
fall and rising again of many in *I*	Lk 2:34	2474
many widows were in *I* in the days	Lk 4:25	2474
many lepers were in *I* in the time	Lk 4:27	2474
so great faith, no, not in *I*	Lk 7:9	2474
judging the twelve tribes of *I*	Lk 22:30	2474
he which should have redeemed *I*	Lk 24:21	2474
he should be made manifest to *I*	Jn 1:31	2474
thou art the King of *I*	Jn 1:49	2474
unto him, Art thou a master of *I*	Jn 3:10	2474
Blessed is the King of *I* that	Jn 12:13	2474
restore again the kingdom to *I*	Acts 1:6	2474
Ye men of *I*, hear these words	Acts 2:22	2475
all the house of *I* know assuredly	Acts 2:36	2474
unto the people, Ye men of *I*	Acts 3:12	2475
of the people, and elders of *I*	Acts 4:8	2474
all, and to all the people of *I*	Acts 4:10	2474
the Gentiles, and the people of *I*	Acts 4:27	2474
the senate of the children of *I*	Acts 5:21	2474
for to give repentance to *I*	Acts 5:31	2474
And said unto them, Ye men of *I*	Acts 5:35	2475
his brethren the children of *I*	Acts 7:23	2474
which said unto the children of *I*	Acts 7:37	2474
of the prophets, O ye house of *I*	Acts 7:42	2474
and kings, and the children of *I*	Acts 9:15	2474
God sent unto the children of *I*	Acts 10:36	2474
with his hand said, Men of *I*	Acts 13:16	2475
people of *I* chose our fathers	Acts 13:17	2474
promise raised unto *I* a Saviour	Acts 13:23	2474
repentance to all the people of *I*	Acts 13:24	2474
Crying out, Men of *I*, help	Acts 21:28	2475
of *I* I am bound with this chain	Acts 28:20	2474
For they are not all *I*, which are	Rom 9:6	2474
not all Israel, which are of *I*	Rom 9:6	2474
Esaias also crieth concerning *I*	Rom 9:27	2474
of *I* be as the sand of the sea	Rom 9:27	2474
But *I*, which followed after the	Rom 9:31	2474
desire and prayer to God for *I* is	Rom 10:1	2474
But I say, Did not *I* know	Rom 10:19	2474
But to *I* he saith, All day long I	Rom 10:21	2474
intercession to God against *I*	Rom 11:2	2474
I hath not obtained that which he	Rom 11:7	2474
in part is happened to *I*, until	Rom 11:25	2474
And so all *I* shall be saved	Rom 11:26	2474
Behold *I* after the flesh	1Cor 10:18	2474
so that the children of *I* could	2Cor 3:7	2474
that the children of *I* could not	2Cor 3:13	2474
and mercy, and upon the *I* of God	Gal 6:16	2474
aliens from the commonwealth of *I*	Eph 2:12	2474
the eighth day, of the stock of *I*	Phil 3:5	2474
new covenant with the house of *I*	Heb 8:8	2474
the house of *I* after those days	Heb 8:10	2474
departing of the children of *I*	Heb 11:22	2474
before the children of *I*, to eat	Rev 2:14	2474
the tribes of the children of *I*	Rev 7:4	2474
tribes of the children of *I*	Rev 21:12	2474
3. The ten northern tribes.		
I were many, as the sand which is	1Kin 4:20	3478
I dwelt safely, every man under	1Kin 4:25	3478
all *I* stoned him with stones,	1Kin 12:18	3478
So *I* rebelled against the house	1Kin 12:19	3478
when all *I* heard that Jeroboam	1Kin 12:20	3478
and made him king over all *I*	1Kin 12:20	3478
to fight against the house of *I*	1Kin 12:21	3478
your brethren the children of *I*	1Kin 12:24	3478
behold thy gods, O *I*, which	1Kin 12:28	3478
a feast unto the children of *I*	1Kin 12:33	3478
him that is shut up and left in *I*	1Kin 14:10	3478
all *I* shall mourn for him, and	1Kin 14:13	3478
God of *I* in the house of Jeroboam	1Kin 14:13	3478
shall raise him up a king over *I*	1Kin 14:14	3478
For the LORD shall smite *I*	1Kin 14:15	3478
he shall root up *I* out of this	1Kin 14:15	3478
he shall give *I* up because of the	1Kin 14:16	3478
who did sin, and who made *I* to sin	1Kin 14:16	3478
all I mourned for him, according	1Kin 14:18	3478
the chronicles of the kings of *I*	1Kin 14:19	3478
king of *I* reigned Asa over Judah	1Kin 15:9	3478
Baasha king of *I* all their days	1Kin 15:16	3478
Baasha king of *I* went up against	1Kin 15:17	3478
thy league with Baasha king of *I*	1Kin 15:19	3478
he had against the cities of *I*	1Kin 15:20	3478
I in the second year of Asa king	1Kin 15:25	3478
and reigned over *I* two years	1Kin 15:25	3478

the chronicles of the kings of *I*	2Kin 15:15	3478
the son of Gadi to reign over *I*	2Kin 15:17	3478
son of Nebat, who made *I* to sin	2Kin 15:18	3478
And Menahem exacted the money of *I*	2Kin 15:20	3478
the chronicles of the kings of *I*	2Kin 15:21	3478
began to reign over *I* in Samaria	2Kin 15:23	3478
son of Nebat, who made *I* to sin	2Kin 15:24	3478
the chronicles of the kings of *I*	2Kin 15:26	3478
began to reign over *I* in Samaria	2Kin 15:27	3478
son of Nebat, who made *I* to sin	2Kin 15:28	3478
of *I* came Tiglath-pileser king of	2Kin 15:29	3478
the chronicles of the kings of *I*	2Kin 15:31	3478
the son of Remaliah king of *I*	2Kin 15:32	3478
in the way of the kings of *I*	2Kin 16:3	3478
out from before the children of *I*	2Kin 16:3	3478
of *I* came up to Jerusalem to war	2Kin 16:5	3478
out of the hand of the king of *I*	2Kin 16:7	3478
in Samaria over *I* nine years	2Kin 17:1	3478
kings of *I* that were before him	2Kin 17:2	3478
carried *I* away into Assyria, and	2Kin 17:6	3478
that the children of *I* had sinned	2Kin 17:7	3478
out from before the children of *I*	2Kin 17:8	3478
and of the kings of *I*	2Kin 17:8	3478
the children of *I* did secretly	2Kin 17:9	3478
Yet the LORD testified against *I*	2Kin 17:13	3478
the LORD was very angry with *I*	2Kin 17:18	3478
the statutes of *I* which they made	2Kin 17:19	3478
LORD rejected all the seed of *I*	2Kin 17:20	3478
For he rent *I* from the house of	2Kin 17:21	3478
Jeroboam drave *I* from following	2Kin 17:21	3478
For the children of *I* walked in	2Kin 17:22	3478
LORD removed *I* out of his sight	2Kin 17:23	3478
So was *I* carried away out of	2Kin 17:23	3478
instead of the children of *I*	2Kin 17:24	3478
of Hoshea son of Elah king of *I*	2Kin 18:1	3478
of Hoshea son of Elah king of *I*	2Kin 18:9	3478
ninth year of Hoshea king of *I*	2Kin 18:10	3478
did carry away *I* unto Assyria	2Kin 18:11	3478
son of Nebat, who made *I* to sin	2Kin 23:15	3478
which the kings of *I* had made to	2Kin 23:19	3478
in all the days of the kings of *I*	2Kin 23:22	3478
of my sight, as I have removed *I*	2Kin 23:27	3478
in the days of Jeroboam king of *I*	1Chr 5:17	3478
in the book of the kings of *I*	1Chr 9:1	3478
the children of *I* stoned him with	2Chr 10:18	3478
I rebelled against the house of	2Chr 10:19	3478
were warriors, to fight against *I*	2Chr 11:1	3478
all *I* resorted to him out of all	2Chr 11:13	3478
of *I* such as set their hearts to	2Chr 11:16	3478
Hear me, thou Jeroboam, and all *I*	2Chr 13:4	3478
O children of *I*, fight ye not	2Chr 13:12	3478
all *I* before Abijah and Judah	2Chr 13:15	3478
the children of *I* fled before	2Chr 13:16	3478
so there fell down slain of *I*	2Chr 13:17	3478
Thus the children of *I* were	2Chr 13:18	3478
fell to him out of *I* in abundance	2Chr 15:9	3478
were not taken away out of *I*	2Chr 15:17	3478
king of *I* came up against Judah	2Chr 16:1	3478
thy league with Baasha king of *I*	2Chr 16:3	3478
armies against the cities of *I*	2Chr 16:4	3478
book of the kings of Judah and *I*	2Chr 16:11	3478
and strengthened himself against *I*	2Chr 17:1	3478
and not after the doings of *I*	2Chr 17:4	3478
And Ahab king of *I* said unto	2Chr 18:3	3478
said unto the king of *I*, Enquire	2Chr 18:4	3478
Therefore the king of *I* gathered	2Chr 18:5	3478
And the king of *I* said unto	2Chr 18:7	3478
the king of *I* called for one of	2Chr 18:8	3478
And the king of *I* and Jehoshaphat	2Chr 18:9	3478
I did see all *I* scattered upon	2Chr 18:16	3478
the king of *I* said to Jehoshaphat	2Chr 18:17	3478
Who shall entice Ahab king of *I*	2Chr 18:19	3478
Then the king of *I* said, Take ye	2Chr 18:25	3478
So the king of *I* and Jehoshaphat	2Chr 18:28	3478
And the king of *I* said unto	2Chr 18:29	3478
So the king of *I* disguised	2Chr 18:29	3478
save only with the king of *I*	2Chr 18:30	3478
they said, It is the king of *I*	2Chr 18:31	3478
that it was not the king of *I*	2Chr 18:32	3478
smote the king of *I* between the	2Chr 18:33	3478
howbeit the king of *I* stayed	2Chr 18:34	3478
in the book of the kings of *I*	2Chr 20:34	3478
himself with Ahaziah king of *I*	2Chr 20:35	3478
the sons of Jehoshaphat king of *I*	2Chr 21:2	3478
divers also of the princes of *I*	2Chr 21:4	3478
in the way of the kings of *I*	2Chr 21:6	3478
in the way of the kings of *I*	2Chr 21:13	3478
I to war against Hazael king of	2Chr 22:5	3478
of *I* for an hundred talents of	2Chr 25:6	3478
not the army of *I* go with thee	2Chr 25:7	3478
for the LORD is not with *I*	2Chr 25:7	3478
I have given to the army of *I*	2Chr 25:9	3478
the son of Jehu, king of *I*	2Chr 25:17	3478
Joash king of *I* sent to Amaziah	2Chr 25:18	3478
So Joash the king of *I* went up	2Chr 25:21	3478
was put to the worse before *I*	2Chr 25:22	3478
Joash the king of *I* took Amaziah	2Chr 25:23	3478
Jehoahaz king of *I* fifteen years	2Chr 25:25	3478
book of the kings of Judah and *I*	2Chr 25:26	3478
in the book of the kings of *I*	2Chr 27:7	3478
in the ways of the kings of *I*	2Chr 28:2	3478
into the hand of the king of *I*	2Chr 28:5	3478
the children of *I* carried away	2Chr 28:8	3478
there is fierce wrath against *I*	2Chr 28:13	3478
low because of Ahaz king of *I*	2Chr 28:19	3478
and his princes throughout all *I*	2Chr 30:6	3478
the children of *I* that were	2Chr 30:21	3478
congregation that came out of *I*	2Chr 30:25	3478
that came out of the land of *I*	2Chr 30:25	3478
And concerning the children of *I*	2Chr 31:6	3478
book of the kings of Judah and *I*	2Chr 32:32	3478
and of all the remnant of *I*	2Chr 34:9	3478
and for them that are left in *I*	2Chr 34:21	3478
neither did all the kings of *I*	2Chr 35:18	3478
I that were present, and the	2Chr 35:18	3478
in the book of the kings of *I*	2Chr 35:27	3478
in the book of the kings of *I*	2Chr 36:8	3478
the son of Remaliah, king of *I*	Is 7:1	3478
so is the house of *I* ashamed	Jer 2:26	3478
Have I been a wilderness unto *I*	Jer 2:31	3478
which backsliding *I* hath done	Jer 3:6	3478
I committed adultery I had put	Jer 3:8	3478
The backsliding *I* hath justified	Jer 3:11	3478
say, Return, thou backsliding *I*	Jer 3:12	3478
shall walk with the house of *I*	Jer 3:18	3478
For the house of *I* and the house	Jer 5:11	3478
and all the house of *I* are	Jer 9:26	3478
the house of *I* and the house of	Jer 11:10	3478
for the evil of the house of *I*	Jer 11:17	3478
be saved, and *I* shall dwell safely	Jer 23:6	3478
that I will sow the house of *I*	Jer 31:27	3478
new covenant with the house of *I*	Jer 31:31	3478
For the children of *I* and the	Jer 32:30	3478
all the evil of the children of *I*	Jer 32:32	3478
made for fear of Baasha king of *I*	Jer 41:9	3478
as the house of *I* was ashamed of	Jer 48:13	3478
The children of *I* and the children	Jer 50:33	3478
of the house of *I* upon it	Eze 4:4	3478
the iniquity of the house of *I*	Eze 4:5	3478
The iniquity of the house of *I*	Eze 9:9	3478
Judah, and the land of *I*, they	Eze 27:17	3478
the children of *I* his companions	Eze 37:16	3478
children of *I* went astray from me	Eze 44:15	3478
which have scattered Judah, *I*	Zec 1:19	3478
O house of Judah, and house of *I*	Zec 8:13	3478
brotherhood between Judah and *I*	Zec 11:14	3478
an abomination is committed in *I*	Mal 2:11	3478

ISRAELITE (*iz'-ra-el-ite*) See ISRAELITES, ISRAELITISH.
   A member of Israel 3.

the name of the *I* that was slain	Num 25:14	1121,3478
son, whose name was Ithra an *I*	2Sa 17:25	3481
saith of him, Behold an *I* indeed	Jn 1:47	2475
For I also am an *I*, of the seed	Rom 11:1	2475

ISRAELITES (*iz'-ra-el-ites*)

one of the cattle of the *I* dead	Ex 9:7	3478
all that are *I* born shall dwell	Lev 23:42	3478
all the *I* passed over on dry	Josh 3:17	3478
that all the *I* returned unto Ai,	Josh 8:24	3478
lot unto the *I* for an inheritance	Josh 13:6	3478
dwell among the *I* until this day	Josh 13:13	3478
ground of the *I* that day twenty	Judg 20:21	3478
unto all the *I* that came thither	1Sa 2:14	3478
But all the *I* went down to the	1Sa 13:20	3478
be with the *I* that were with Saul	1Sa 14:21	3478
all the *I* were gathered together,	1Sa 25:1	3478
the *I* pitched by a fountain which	1Sa 29:1	3478
and all the *I* were troubled	2Sa 4:1	3478
the *I* rose up and smote the	2Kin 3:24	3478
of the *I* that are consumed	2Kin 7:13	3478
in their cities were, the *I*	1Chr 9:2	3478
Who are *I*	Rom 9:4	2475
Are they *I*	2Cor 11:22	2475

ISRAELITISH

And the son of an *I* woman, whose	Lev 24:10	3482
and this son of the *I* woman	Lev 24:10	3482
the *I* woman's son blasphemed the	Lev 24:11	3482

ISRAEL'S (iz'-ra-els)
1. Refers to Israel 1.
his right hand toward *I* left hand .... Gen 48:13   3478
his left hand toward *I* right hand .... Gen 48:13   3478
of Reuben, *I* eldest son, by their .... Num 1:20   3478
2. Refers to Israel 2.
and to the Egyptians for *I* sake .... Ex 18:8   3478
And of the children of *I* half .... Num 31:30   3478
And of the children of *I* half .... Num 31:42   3478
Even of the children of *I* half .... Num 31:47   3478
blood unto thy people of *I* charge .... Deut 21:8   3478
his kingdom for his people *I* sake 2Sa 5:12   3478
3. Refers to Israel 3.
the king of *I* servants answered 2Kin 3:11   3478

ISSACHAR (is'-sa-kar)
1. A son of Jacob.
and she called his name *I* .... Gen 30:18   3485
Simeon, and Levi, and Judah, and *I* .... Gen 35:23   3485
And the sons of *I* .... Gen 46:13   3485
I is a strong ass couching down............. Gen 49:14   3485
I, Zebulun, and Benjamin, ... Ex 1:3   3485
Reuben, Simeon, Levi, and Judah, *I* 1Chr 2:1   3485
Now the sons of *I* were, Tola, and 1Chr 7:1   3485
2. Descendants of Issachar 1.
Of *I* .... Num 1:8   3485
Of the children of *I*, by their.................... Num 1:28   3485
of them, even of the tribe of *I* .... Num 1:29   3485
unto him shall be the tribe of *I* .... Num 2:5   3485
be captain of the children of *I*................. Num 2:5   3485
the son of Zuar, prince of *I* .... Num 7:18   3485
I was Nethaneel the son of Zuar .... Num 10:15   3485
Of the tribe of *I*, Igal the son .... Num 13:7   3485
Of the sons of *I* after their .... Num 26:23   3485
These are the families of *I*...................... Num 26:25   3485
of the tribe of the children of *I* .... Num 34:26   3485
Simeon, and Levi, and Judah, and *I* .... Deut 27:12   3485
and, *I*, in thy tents.................................. Deut 33:18   3485
on the north, and in *I* on the east .... Josh 17:10   3485
And Manasseh had in *I* and in Asher .... Josh 17:11   3485
And the fourth lot came out to *I* .... Josh 19:17   3485
for the children of *I* according .... Josh 19:17   3485
of *I* according to their families............... Josh 19:23   3485
of the families of the tribe of *I*................ Josh 21:6   3485
And out of the tribe of *I*, Kishon .... Josh 21:28   3485
the princes of *I* were with .... Judg 5:15   3485
even *I*, and also Barak .... Judg 5:15   3485
Puah, the son of Dodo, a man of *I* .... Judg 10:1   3485
the son of Paruah, in *I* 1Kin 4:17   3485
son of Ahijah, of the house of *I* 1Kin 15:27   3485
families out of the tribe of *I*.................... 1Chr 6:62   3485
And out of the tribe of *I*.......................... 1Chr 6:72   3485
of *I* were valiant men of might 1Chr 7:5   3485
And of the children of *I*, which............... 1Chr 12:32   3485
that were nigh them, even unto *I* 1Chr 12:40   3485
of *I*, Omri the son of Michael 1Chr 27:18   3485
many of Ephraim, and Manasseh, *I* 2Chr 30:18   3485
unto the west side, *I* a portion .... Eze 48:25   3485
And by the border of *I*, from the .... Eze 48:25   3485
one gate of Simeon, one gate of *I*........... Eze 48:33   3485
Of the tribe of *I* were sealed .... Rev 7:7   2466
3. A porter of the tabernacle.
I the seventh, Peulthai the 1Chr 26:5   3485

ISSHIAH (is-shi'-ah) See ISAIAH, JESIAH.
1. A descendant of Moses.
sons of Rehabiah, the first was *I* 1Chr 24:21   3449
2. A Levite.
The brother of Michah was *I*................... 1Chr 24:25   3449
of the sons of *I* 1Chr 24:25

ISSHIJAH See ISHIJAH.

ISSHOD See ISHOD.

ISSUE
And thy *i*, which thou begettest.............. Gen 48:6   4138
cleansed from the *i* of her blood .... Lev 12:7   4726
hath a running *i* out of his flesh .... Lev 15:2   2100
because of his *i* he is unclean .... Lev 15:2   2101
shall be his uncleanness in his *i* .... Lev 15:3   2101
whether his flesh run with his *i* .... Lev 15:3   2101
his flesh be stopped from his *i*............... Lev 15:3   2101
whereon he lieth that hath the *i* .... Lev 15:4   2100
hath the *i* shall wash his clothes .... Lev 15:6   2100
hath the *i* shall wash his clothes .... Lev 15:7   2100
if he that hath the *i* spit upon .... Lev 15:8   2100
that hath the *i* shall be unclean .... Lev 15:9   2100
he toucheth that hath the *i*..................... Lev 15:11   2100
that he toucheth which hath the *i* .... Lev 15:12   2100
when he that hath an *i* is........................ Lev 15:13   2100
an *i* is cleansed of his *i* .... Lev 15:13   2101
for him before the LORD for his *i* .... Lev 15:15   2101

And if a woman have an *i* .... Lev 15:19   2100
her *i* in her flesh be, she...................... Lev 15:19   2101
if a woman have an *i* of her blood .... Lev 15:25   2100
all the days of the *i* of her...................... Lev 15:25   2101
she lieth all the days of her *i* .... Lev 15:26   2101
But if she be cleansed of her *i* .... Lev 15:28   2101
LORD for the *i* for her uncleanness .... Lev 15:30   2101
is the law of him that hath an *i* .... Lev 15:32   2100
flowers, and of him that hath an *i* .... Lev 15:33   2100
is a leper, or hath a running *i* .... Lev 22:4   2100
and every one that hath an *i*................... Num 5:2   2100
house of Joab one that hath an *i* 2Sa 3:29   2100
thy sons that shall *i* from thee 2Kin 20:18   3318
house, the offspring and the *i* .... Is 22:24   6849
thy sons that shall *i* from thee .... Is 39:7   3318
i is like the *i* of horses........................... Eze 23:20   2231
These waters *i* out toward the................ Eze 47:8   3318
with an *i* of blood twelve years............... Mt 9:20   *131*
a wife, deceased, and, having no *i* .... Mt 22:25   *4690*
which had an *i* of blood twelve .... Mk 5:25   *4511*
a woman having an *i* of blood .... Lk 8:43   *4511*
immediately her *i* of blood .... Lk 8:44   *4511*

ISSUED
the other *i* out of the city........................ Josh 8:22   3318
as if it had *i* out of the womb .... Job 38:8   3318
waters *i* out from under the..................... Eze 47:1   3318
they they *i* out of the sanctuary............. Eze 47:12   3318
A fiery stream *i* and came forth .... Dan 7:10   5047
and out of their mouths *i* fire................. Rev 9:17   *1607*
which *i* out of their mouths .... Rev 9:18   *1607*

ISSUES
the Lord belong the *i* from death .... Ps 68:20   8444
for out of it are the *i* of life .... Prov 4:23   8444

ISUAH (is'-u-ah) See ISHUAH. *A son of Asher.*
Imnah, and *I*, and Ishuai, and Beriah ... 1Chr 7:30   3440

ISUI (is'-u-i) See ISHUI. *A son of Asher.*
Jimnah, and Ishuah, and *I*, and............. Gen 46:17   3440

IT See APPENDIX.

ITALIAN (it-al'-yan)
of the band called the *I* band .... Acts 10:1   2483

ITALY (it'-a-lee) *Homeland of most Roman citizens.*
in Pontus, lately come from *I*................... Acts 18:2   2482
that we should sail into *I* .... Acts 27:1   2482
ship of Alexandria sailing into *I* .... Acts 27:6   2482
They of *I* salute you .... Heb 13:24   2482
to the Hebrews from *I* by Timothy .... Heb s

ITCH
and with the scab, and with the *i* .... Deut 28:27   2775

ITCHING
teachers, having *i* ears 2Ti 4:3   2833

ITHAI (ith'-a-i) See ITTAI. *A mighty man of David.*
I the son of Ribai of Gibeah, ... 1Chr 11:31   863

ITHAMAR (ith'-a-mar) *A son of Aaron.*
Nadab, and Abihu, Eleazar, and *I* .... Ex 6:23   385
Nadab and Abihu, Eleazar and *I*........... Ex 28:1   385
of the Levites, by the hand of *I* .... Ex 38:21   385
Aaron, and unto Eleazar and unto *I* ...... Lev 10:6   385
Aaron, and unto Eleazar and unto *I* .... Lev 10:12   385
and he was angry with Eleazar and *I* .... Lev 10:16   385
and Abihu, Eleazar, and *I* .... Num 3:2   385
I ministered in the priest's .... Num 3:4   385
shall be under the hand of *I* the............. Num 4:28   385
under the hand of *I* the son of .... Num 4:33   385
under the hand of *I* the son of .... Num 7:8   385
Nadab, and Abihu, Eleazar, and *I* .... Num 26:60   385
Nadab, and Abihu, Eleazar, and *I* 1Chr 6:3   385
Nadab, and Abihu, Eleazar, and *I* 1Chr 24:1   385
I executed the priest's office 1Chr 24:2   385
and Ahimelech of the sons of *I* 1Chr 24:3   385
of Eleazar than of the sons of *I*............... 1Chr 24:4   385
eight among the sons of *I* 1Chr 24:4   385
of Eleazar, and of the sons of *I* 1Chr 24:5   385
for Eleazar, and one taken for *I* 1Chr 24:6   385
of the sons of *I* .... Ezr 8:2   385

ITHIEL (ith'-e-el)
1. Son of Jesaiah.
the son of Maaseiah, the son of *I*........... Neh 11:7   384
2. Person mentioned in Proverbs.
the man spake unto *I*, even unto .... Prov 30:1   384
spake unto Ithiel, even unto *I* .... Prov 30:1   384

ITHLAH See JETHLAH.

ITHMAH (ith'-mah) *A mighty man of David.*
sons of Elnaam, and *I* the Moabite, ... 1Chr 11:46   3495

ITHNAN (ith'-nan) *A town in Judah.*		
And Kedesh, and Hazor, and *I* .... Josh 15:23	3497	
ITHRA (ith'-rah) See JETHER. *Father of Amasa.*		
whose name was *I* an Israelite 2Sa 17:25	3501	
ITHRAN (ith'-ran)		
1. A son of Dishon.		
Hemdan, and Eshban, and *I*, and .... Gen 36:26	3506	
Amram, and Eshban, and *I*, and		
Cheran 1Chr 1:41	3506	
2. A son of Zophah.		
Hod, and Shamma, and Shilshah, and *I* 1Chr 7:37	3506	
ITHREAM (ith'-re-am) *A son of David.*		
And the sixth, *I*, by Eglah David's 2Sa 3:5	3507	
the sixth, *I* by Eglah his wife 1Chr 3:3	3507	
ITHRITE (ith'-rite) See ITHRITES. *A descendant of Jether.*		
Ira an *I*, Gareb an *I*, ... 2Sa 23:38	3505	
Ira an *I*, Gareb an *I* 2Sa 23:38	3505	
Ira the *I*, Gareb the *I*, ... 1Chr 11:40	3505	
Ira the *I*, Gareb the *I* 1Chr 11:40	3505	
ITHRITES (ith'-rites)		
the *I*, and the Puhites, and the 1Chr 2:53	3505	
ITS See APPENDIX.		
ITSELF See APPENDIX.		
ITTAH-KAZIN (it'-tah-ka'-zin) *A city in Zebulun.*		
the east to Gittah-hepher, to *I* .... Josh 19:13	6278	
ITTAI (it'-ta-i) See ITHAI.		
1. A Philistine in David's army.		
said the king to *I* the Gittite 2Sa 15:19	863	
I answered the king, and said, As 2Sa 15:21	863	
And David said to *I*, Go and pass 2Sa 15:22	863	
I the Gittite passed over, and all 2Sa 15:22	863	
under the hand of *I* the Gittite 2Sa 18:2	863	
commanded Joab and Abishai and *I* 2Sa 18:5	863	
king charged thee and Abishai and *I* 2Sa 18:12	863	
2. A mighty man of David.		
I the son of Ribai out of Gibeah 2Sa 23:29	863	
ITURAEA (i-tu-re'-ah) *A province near Mt. Hermon.*		
his brother Philip tetrarch of *I* .... Lk 3:1	2434	
IVAH (i'-vah) See AHAVA, AVA. *A Mesopotamian district.*		
gods of Sepharvaim, Hena, and *I* 2Kin 18:34	5755	
city of Sepharvaim, of Hena, and *I* 2Kin 19:13	5755	
city of Sepharvaim, Hena, and *I* .... Is 37:13	5755	

IVORY		
the king made a great throne of *i* 1Kin 10:18	8127	
bringing gold, and silver, *i* 1Kin 10:22	8143	
the *i* house which he made, and all 1Kin 22:39	8127	
the king made a great throne of *i* 2Chr 9:17	8127	
bringing gold, and silver, *i* 2Chr 9:21	8143	
and cassia, out of the *i* palaces .... Ps 45:8	8127	
his belly is as bright *i* overlaid .... Song 5:14	8127	
Thy neck is as a tower of *i* .... Song 7:4	8127	
have made thy benches of *i* .... Eze 27:6	8127	
thee for a present horns of *i* .... Eze 27:15	8127	
and the houses of *i* shall perish .... Amos 3:15	8127	
That lie upon beds of *i*, and .... Amos 6:4	8127	
wood, and all manner vessels of *i* .... Rev 18:12	*1661*	
IZEHAR (iz'-e-har) See IZEHARITES, IZHAR. *A son of Kohath.*		
Amram, and *I*, Hebron, and Uzziel .... Num 3:19	3324	
IZEHARITES (iz'-e-har-ites) See IZHARITE. *Descendants of Izehar.*		
Amramites, and the family of the *I* .... Num 3:27	3325	
IZHAR (iz'-har) See IZEHAB, IZEHARITES. *Same as Izehar.*		
Amram, and *I*, and Hebron, and Uzziel . Ex 6:18	3324	
And the sons of *I* .... Ex 6:21	3324	
Now Korah, the son of *I*, the son .... Num 16:1	3324	
Amram, *I*, and Hebron, and Uzziel 1Chr 6:2	3324	
sons of Kohath were, Amram, and *I* 1Chr 6:18	3324	
The son of *I*, the son of Kohath, ... 1Chr 6:38	3324	
Amram, *I*, Hebron, and Uzziel, four 1Chr 23:12	3324	
Of the sons of *I* 1Chr 23:18	3324	
IZHARITES (iz'-har-ites) See IZEHARITES. *Same as Izeharites.*		
Of the *I*; Shelomoth 1Chr 24:22	3325	
Of the Amramites, and the *I* 1Chr 26:23	3325	
Of the *I*, Chenaniah and his sons 1Chr 26:29	3325	
IZLIAH See JEZLIAH.		
IZRAHIAH (iz-ra-hi'-ah) See JEZRAHIAH. *Grandson of Tola.*		
the sons of Uzzi; *I* 1Chr 7:3	3156	
and the sons of *I* 1Chr 7:3	3156	
IZRAHITE (iz'-ra-hite) See EZRAHITE. *Family name of Shamhuth.*		
fifth month was Shamhuth the *I* 1Chr 27:8	3155	
IZRI (iz'-ri) See ZERI. *A sanctuary servant.*		
The fourth to *I*, he, his sons, and 1Chr 25:11	3342	
IZZIAH See JEZIAH.		

J

JAAKAN (ja'-a-kan) See AKAN, BENE-JAAKAN. *A son of Ezer.*		
of the children of *J* to Mosera .... Deut 10:6	3292	
JAAKOBAH (ja-ak'-o-bah) *A descendant of Simeon.*		
And Elioenai, and *J*, and Jeshohaiah, ... 1Chr 4:36	3291	
JAALA (ja'-a-lah) See JAALAH. *A family of exiles.*		
The children of *J*, the children .... Neh 7:58	3279	
JAALAH (ja'-a-lah) See JAALA. *Same as Jaala.*		
The children of *J*, the children .... Ezr 2:56	3279	
JAALAM (ja'-a-lam) *A son of Esau.*		
And Aholibamah bare Jeush, and *J* .... Gen 36:5	3281	
and she bare to Esau Jeush, and *J* .... Gen 36:14	3281	
duke Jeush, duke *J*, duke Korah .... Gen 36:18	3281	
Eliphaz, Reuel, and Jeush, and *J* 1Chr 1:35	3281	
JAANAI (ja'-a-nahee) *A Gadite.*		
chief, and Shapham the next, and *J* 1Chr 5:12	3285	
JAAR See WOOD.		
JAARE-OREGIM (ja'-a-re-or'-eg-im) See JAIR. *Father of Elhanan.*		
where Elhanan the son of *J* 2Sa 21:19	3296	
JAASAU (ja-a'-saw) *Married a foreigner in exile.*		
Mattaniah, Mattenai, and *J* .... Ezr 10:37	3299	
JAASIEL (ja-a'-se-el) *A son of Abner.*		
of Benjamin, *J* the son of Abner 1Chr 27:21	3300	
JAASU See JAASAU.		
JAAZANIAH (ja-az-a-ni'-ah) See JEZANIAH.		
1. A son of a Maachathite.		
J the son of a Maachathite, they 2Kin 25:23	2970	
2. A chief Rechabite.		
Then I took *J* the son of Jeremiah .... Jer 35:3	2970	
3. Son of Shaphan.		
them stood *J* the son of Shaphan .... Eze 8:11	2970	

4. Son of Azur.		
whom I saw *J* the son of Azur .... Eze 11:1	2970	
JAAZER (ja-a'-zer) See JAZER. *A city in Gilead.*		
And Moses sent to spy out *J* .... Num 21:32	3270	
And Atroth, Shophan, and *J*, and .... Num 32:35	3270	
JAAZIAH (ja-a-zi'-ah) *A descendant of Merari.*		
the sons of *J*; Beno 1Chr 24:26	3269	
The sons of Merari by *J* 1Chr 24:27	3269	
JA-AZIEL See BEN.		
JAAZIEL (ja-a'-ze-el) See AZIEL. *A priest.*		
degree, Zechariah, Ben, and *J* 1Chr 15:18	3268	
JABAL (ja'-bal) *A son of Adah.*		
And Adah bare *J* .... Gen 4:20	2989	
JABBOK (jab'-bok) *A brook in Bashan.*		
sons, and passed over the ford *J* .... Gen 32:22	2999	
his land from Arnon unto *J* .... Num 21:24	2999	
nor unto any place of the river *J* .... Deut 2:37	2999	
the border even unto the river *J* .... Deut 3:16	2999	
Gilead, even unto the river *J* .... Josh 12:2	2999	
of Egypt, from Arnon even unto *J* .... Judg 11:13	2999	
Amorites, from Arnon even unto *J* .... Judg 11:22	2999	
JABESH (ja'-besh) See JABESH-GILEAD.		
1. A city in Gad.		
all the men of *J* said unto Nahash 1Sa 11:1	3003	
And the elders of *J* said unto him 1Sa 11:3	3003	
him the tidings of the men of *J* 1Sa 11:5	3003	
came and shewed it to the men of *J* 1Sa 11:9	3003	
Therefore the men of *J* said 1Sa 11:10	3003	
wall of Beth-shan, and came to *J* 1Sa 31:12	3003	
and buried them under a tree at *J* 1Sa 31:13	3003	
of his sons, and brought them to *J* 1Chr 10:12	3003	
their bones under the oak in *J* 1Chr 10:12	3003	

2. Father of Shallum.
Shallum the son of J conspired 2Kin 15:10   3003
Shallum the son of J began to 2Kin 15:13   3003
Shallum the son of J in Samaria 2Kin 15:14   3003

JABESH-GILEAD *(ja'-besh-ghil'-e-ad) Same as Jabesh 1.*
the camp from J to the assembly .... Judg 21:8   3003,1568
of the inhabitants of J there .... Judg 21:9   3003,1568
smite the inhabitants of J with...... Judg 21:10   3003,1568
of J four hundred young virgins ...... Judg 21:12   3003,1568
had saved alive of the women of J .. Judg 21:14   3003,1568
came up, and encamped against J . 1Sa 11:1   3003,1568
shall ye say unto the men of J......... 1Sa 11:9   3003,1568
of J heard of that which the 1Sa 31:11   3003,1568
That the men of J were they that ... 2Sa 2:4   3003,1568
sent messengers unto the men of J . 2Sa 2:5   3003,1568
his son from the men of J 2Sa 21:12   3003,1568
when all J heard all that the 1Chr 10:11   3003,1568

JABEZ *(ja'-bez)*
1. A city in Judah.
of the scribes which dwelt at J 1Chr 2:55   3258
2. Head of a family of Judah.
J was more honourable than he 1Chr 4:9   3258
and his mother called his name J 1Chr 4:9   3258
J called on the God of Israel, ... 1Chr 4:10   3258

JABIN *(ja'-bin) See* JABIN'S.
1. A king of Hazor.
when J king of Hazor had heard .... Josh 11:1   2985
2. Another king of Hazor.
into the hand of J king of Canaan .... Judg 4:2   2985
peace between J the king of Hazor .... Judg 4:17   2985
So God subdued on that day J the .... Judg 4:23   2985
prevailed against J the king of .... Judg 4:24   2985
had destroyed J king of Canaan............ Judg 4:24   2985
as to Sisera, as to J, at the .... Ps 83:9   2985

JABIN'S
Sisera, the captain of J army .... Judg 4:7   2985

JABNEEL *(jab'-ne-el) See* JABNEH.
1. A city in Judah.
mount Baalah, and went out unto J........ Josh 15:11   2995
2. A city in Naphtali.
Zaanannim, and Adami, Nekeb, and J...Josh 19:33   2995

JABNEH *(jab'-neh) See* JABNEEL. *A Philistine city.*
wall of Gath, and the wall of J 2Chr 26:6   2996

JACAN *See* JACHAN.

JACHAN *(ja'-kan) See* AKAN. *Head of a Gadite family.*
and Sheba, and Jorai, and J 1Chr 5:13   3275

JACHIN *(ja'-kin) See* JACHINITES, JARIB.
1. A son of Simeon.
Jemuel, and Jamin, and Ohad, and J ..... Gen 46:10   3199
Jemuel, and Jamin, and Ohad, and J ..... Ex 6:15   3199
of J, the family of the .... Num 26:12   3199
2. A pillar of Solomon's Temple.
and called the name thereof J................. 1Kin 7:21   3199
name of that on the right hand J 2Chr 3:17   3199
3. A family of exiles.
Jedaiah, and Jehoiarib, and J 1Chr 9:10   3199
Jedaiah the son of Joiarib, J.................... Neh 11:10   3199
4. A sanctuary servant.
The one and twentieth to J 1Chr 24:17   3199

JACHINITES *(ja'-kin-ites) Descendants of Jachin 1.*
of Jachin, the family of the J .... Num 26:12   3200

JACINTH
breastplates of fire, and of j .... Rev 9:17   5191
the eleventh, a j .... Rev 21:20   5192

JACOB *(ja'-cub) See* ISRAEL, JACOB'S, JAMES.
1. Son of Isaac and Rebekah.
and his name was called J .... Gen 25:26   3290
J was a plain man, dwelling in................ Gen 25:27   3290
but Rebekah loved J .... Gen 25:28   3290
And J sod pottage .... Gen 25:29   3290
And Esau said to J, Feed me, I .... Gen 25:30   3290
J said, Sell me this day thy .... Gen 25:31   3290
J said, Swear to me this day .... Gen 25:33   3290
and he sold his birthright unto J .... Gen 25:33   3290
Then J gave Esau bread and pottage ..... Gen 25:34   3290
And Rebekah spake unto J her son .... Gen 27:6   3290
J said to Rebekah his mother, ... Gen 27:11   3290
put them upon J her younger son .... Gen 27:15   3290
into the hand of J her younger son .... Gen 27:17   3290
J said unto his father, I am Esau............ Gen 27:19   3290
And Isaac said unto J, Come near,......... Gen 27:21   3290
J went near unto Isaac his father .... Gen 27:22   3290
had made an end of blessing J................ Gen 27:30   3290
J was yet scarce gone out from .... Gen 27:30   3290
said, Is not he rightly named J .... Gen 27:36   3290

Esau hated J because of the.................... Gen 27:41   3290
then will I slay my brother J .... Gen 27:41   3290
called J her younger son, and said......... Gen 27:42   3290
if J take a wife of the daughters............. Gen 27:46   3290
And Isaac called J, and blessed him ..... Gen 28:1   3290
And Isaac sent away J............................. Gen 28:5   3290
Esau saw that Isaac had blessed J......... Gen 28:6   3290
that J obeyed his father and his .... Gen 28:7   3290
J went out from Beer-sheba, and .... Gen 28:10   3290
J awaked out of his sleep, and he .... Gen 28:16   3290
J rose up early in the morning,.............. Gen 28:18   3290
J vowed a vow, saying, If God .... Gen 28:20   3290
Then J went on his journey, and............ Gen 29:1   3290
J said unto them, My brethren,.............. Gen 29:4   3290
when J saw Rachel the daughter of .... Gen 29:10   3290
that J went near, and rolled the .... Gen 29:10   3290
J kissed Rachel, and lifted up his .... Gen 29:11   3290
J told Rachel that he was her .... Gen 29:12   3290
the tidings of J his sister's son .... Gen 29:13   3290
And Laban said to J, Because .... Gen 29:15   3290
And J loved Rachel................................... Gen 29:18   3290
J served seven years for Rachel.............. Gen 29:20   3290
J said unto Laban, Give me my .... Gen 29:21   3290
J did so, and fulfilled her week .... Gen 29:28   3290
saw that she bare J no children .... Gen 30:1   3290
and said unto J, Give me children,......... Gen 30:1   3290
and J went in unto her .... Gen 30:4   3290
Bilhah conceived, and bare J a son .... Gen 30:5   3290
again, and bare J a second son .... Gen 30:7   3290
her maid, and gave her J to wife .... Gen 30:9   3290
Zilpah Leah's maid bare J a son............ Gen 30:10   3290
Leah's maid bare J a second son .... Gen 30:12   3290
J came out of the field in the .... Gen 30:16   3290
and bare J the fifth son .... Gen 30:17   3290
again, and bare J the sixth son .... Gen 30:19   3290
that J said unto Laban, Send me .... Gen 30:25   3290
J said, Thou shalt not give me .... Gen 30:31   3290
journey betwixt himself and J .... Gen 30:36   3290
J fed the rest of Laban's flocks .... Gen 30:36   3290
J took him rods of green poplar, ... Gen 30:37   3290
J did separate the lambs, and set .... Gen 30:40   3290
that J laid the rods before the .... Gen 30:41   3290
J hath taken away all that was .... Gen 31:1   3290
J beheld the countenance of Laban .... Gen 31:2   3290
And the LORD said unto J, Return .... Gen 31:3   3290
J sent and called Rachel and Leah........ Gen 31:4   3290
unto me in a dream, saying, ... Gen 31:11   3290
Then J rose up, and set his sons............ Gen 31:17   3290
J stole away unawares to Laban .... Gen 31:20   3290
on the third day that J was fled .... Gen 31:22   3290
speak not to J either good or bad........... Gen 31:24   3290
Then J overtook J .... Gen 31:25   3290
Now J had pitched his tent in the .... Gen 31:25   3290
And Laban said to J, What hast .... Gen 31:26   3290
speak not to J either good or bad........... Gen 31:29   3290
J answered and said to Laban, ... Gen 31:31   3290
For J knew not that Rachel was .... Gen 31:32   3290
J was wroth, and chode with Laban .... Gen 31:36   3290
J answered and said to Laban, What..... Gen 31:36   3290
And Laban answered and said unto J .... Gen 31:43   3290
J took a stone, and set it up for............. Gen 31:45   3290
J said unto his brethren, Gather .... Gen 31:46   3290
but J called it Galeed............................... Gen 31:47   3290
And Laban said to J, Behold this .... Gen 31:51   3290
J sware by the fear of his father............. Gen 31:53   3290
Then J offered sacrifice upon the .... Gen 31:54   3290
J went on his way, and the angels.......... Gen 32:1   3290
when J saw them, he said, This is.......... Gen 32:2   3290
J sent messengers before him to .... Gen 32:3   3290
Thy servant J saith thus, I have .... Gen 32:4   3290
And the messengers returned to J.......... Gen 32:6   3290
Then J was greatly afraid and .... Gen 32:7   3290
J said, O God of my father .... Gen 32:9   3290
thy servant J is behind us .... Gen 32:20   3290
And J was left alone .... Gen 32:24   3290
And he said, J... Gen 32:27   3290
name shall be called no more J .... Gen 32:28   3290
J asked him, and said, Tell me, I .... Gen 32:29   3290
J called the name of the place .... Gen 32:30   3290
J lifted up his eyes, and looked, ... Gen 33:1   3290
J said, Nay, I pray thee, if now .... Gen 33:10   3290
J journeyed to Succoth, and built .... Gen 33:17   3290
J came to Shalem, a city of .... Gen 33:18   3290
of Leah, which she bare unto J .... Gen 34:1   3290
unto Dinah the daughter of J .... Gen 34:3   3290
J heard that he had defiled Dinah......... Gen 34:5   3290
J held his peace until they were .... Gen 34:5   3290
out unto J to commune with him .... Gen 34:6   3290
the sons of J came out of the.................. Gen 34:7   3290
the sons of J answered Shechem and ..... Gen 34:13   3290
sore, that two of the sons of J................. Gen 34:25   3290

The sons of *J* came upon the slain	Gen 34:27	3290
J said to Simeon and Levi, Ye have	Gen 34:30	3290
And God said unto *J*, Arise, go up	Gen 35:1	3290
Then *J* said unto his household,	Gen 35:2	3290
they gave unto *J* all the strange	Gen 35:4	3290
J hid them under the oak which	Gen 35:4	3290
not pursue after the sons of *J*	Gen 35:5	3290
So *J* came to Luz, which is in the	Gen 35:6	3290
And God appeared unto *J* again	Gen 35:9	3290
God said unto him, Thy name is *J*	Gen 35:10	3290
shall not be called any more *J*	Gen 35:10	3290
J set up a pillar in the place	Gen 35:14	3290
J called the name of the place	Gen 35:15	3290
J set a pillar upon her grave	Gen 35:20	3290
Now the sons of *J* were twelve	Gen 35:22	3290
these are the sons of *J*, which	Gen 35:26	3290
J came unto Isaac his father unto	Gen 35:27	3290
and his sons Esau and *J* buried him	Gen 35:29	3290
from the face of his brother *J*	Gen 36:6	3290
J dwelt in the land wherein his	Gen 37:1	3290
These are the generations of *J*	Gen 37:2	3290
J rent his clothes, and put	Gen 37:34	3290
Now when *J* saw that there was	Gen 42:1	3290
J said unto his sons, Why do ye	Gen 42:1	3290
J sent not with his brethren	Gen 42:4	3290
they came unto *J* their father	Gen 42:29	3290
J their father said unto them, Me	Gen 42:36	3290
of Canaan unto *J* their father	Gen 45:25	3290
the spirit of *J* their father	Gen 45:27	3290
of the night, and said, *J*, *J*	Gen 46:2	3290
J rose up from Beer-sheba	Gen 46:5	3290
of Israel carried *J* their father	Gen 46:5	3290
of Canaan, and came into Egypt, *J*	Gen 46:6	3290
Israel, which came into Egypt, *J*	Gen 46:8	3290
she bare unto *J* in Padan-aram	Gen 46:15	3290
and these she bare unto *J*	Gen 46:18	3290
of Rachel, which were born to *J*	Gen 46:22	3290
and she bare these unto *J*	Gen 46:25	3290
souls that came with *J* into Egypt	Gen 46:26	3290
all the souls of the house of *J*	Gen 46:27	3290
And Joseph brought in *J* his father	Gen 47:7	3290
and *J* blessed Pharaoh	Gen 47:7	3290
And Pharaoh said unto *J*, How old	Gen 47:8	3290
J said unto Pharaoh, The days of	Gen 47:9	3290
J blessed Pharaoh, and went out	Gen 47:10	3290
J lived in the land of Egypt	Gen 47:28	3290
so the whole age of *J* was an	Gen 47:28	3290
And one told *J*, and said, Behold,	Gen 48:2	3290
J said unto Joseph, God Almighty	Gen 48:3	3290
J called unto his sons, and said,	Gen 49:1	3290
together, and hear, ye sons of *J*	Gen 49:2	3290
I will divide them in *J*, and	Gen 49:7	3290
the hands of the mighty God of *J*	Gen 49:24	3290
when *J* had made an end of	Gen 49:33	3290
to Abraham, to Isaac, and to *J*	Gen 50:24	3290
man and his household came with *J*	Ex 1:1	3290
the loins of *J* were seventy souls	Ex 1:5	3290
Abraham, with Isaac, and with *J*	Ex 2:24	3290
the God of Isaac, and the God of *J*	Ex 3:6	3290
the God of Isaac, and the God of *J*	Ex 3:15	3290
God of Abraham, of Isaac, and of *J*	Ex 3:16	3290
the God of Isaac, and the God of *J*	Ex 4:5	3290
Abraham, unto Isaac, and unto *J*	Ex 6:3	3290
it to Abraham, to Isaac, and to *J*	Ex 6:8	3290
shalt thou say to the house of *J*	Ex 19:3	3290
unto Abraham, to Isaac, and to *J*	Ex 33:1	3290
I remember my covenant with *J*	Lev 26:42	3290
Abraham, unto Isaac, and unto *J*	Num 32:11	3290
fathers, Abraham, Isaac, and *J*	Deut 1:8	3290
to Abraham, to Isaac, and to *J*	Deut 6:10	3290
thy fathers, Abraham, Isaac, and *J*	Deut 9:5	3290
servants, Abraham, Isaac, and *J*	Deut 9:27	3290
to Abraham, to Isaac, and to *J*	Deut 29:13	3290
to Abraham, to Isaac, and to *J*	Deut 30:20	3290
Abraham, unto Isaac, and unto *J*	Deut 34:4	3290
And I gave unto Isaac *J* and Esau	Josh 24:4	3290
but *J* and his children went down	Josh 24:4	3290
in a parcel of ground which *J*	Josh 24:32	3290
When *J* was come into Egypt, and	1Sa 12:8	3290
with Abraham, Isaac, and *J*	2Kin 13:23	3290
yet I loved *J*,	Mal 1:2	3290
and Isaac begat *J*	Mt 1:2	2384
J begat Judas and his brethren	Mt 1:2	2384
down with Abraham, and Isaac, and *J*.	Mt 8:11	2384
the God of Isaac, and the God of *J*	Mt 22:32	2384
the God of Isaac, and the God of *J*	Mk 12:26	2384
over the house of *J* for ever	Lk 1:33	2384
Which was the son of *J*, which was	Lk 3:34	2384
shall see Abraham, and Isaac, and *J*	Lk 13:28	2384
the God of Isaac, and the God of *J*	Lk 20:37	2384
that *J* gave to his son Joseph	Jn 4:5	2384
thou greater than our father *J*	Jn 4:12	2384
of Abraham, and of Isaac, and of *J*	Acts 3:13	2384
and Isaac begat *J*	Acts 7:8	2384
J begat the twelve patriarchs	Acts 7:8	2384
But when *J* heard that there was	Acts 7:12	2384
and called his father *J* to him	Acts 7:14	2384
So *J* went down into Egypt, and	Acts 7:15	2384
the God of Isaac, and the God of *J*	Acts 7:32	2384
a tabernacle for the God of *J*	Acts 7:46	2384
J have I loved, but Esau have I	Rom 9:13	2384
turn away ungodliness from *J*	Rom 11:26	2384
in tabernacles with Isaac and *J*	Heb 11:9	2384
By faith Isaac blessed *J* and Esau	Heb 11:20	2384
By faith *J*, when he was a dying,	Heb 11:21	2384

2. *Father of Joseph; ancestor of Jesus.*

and Matthan begat *J*	Mt 1:15	2384
J begat Joseph the husband of	Mt 1:16	2384

3. *Descendants of Jacob.*

east, saying, Come, curse me *J*	Num 23:7	3290
Who can count the dust of *J*	Num 23:10	3290
He hath not beheld iniquity in *J*	Num 23:21	3290
there is no enchantment against *J*	Num 23:23	3290
this time it shall be said of *J*	Num 23:23	3290
How goodly are thy tents, O *J*	Num 24:5	3290
there shall come a Star out of *J*	Num 24:17	3290
Out of *J* shall come he that shall	Num 24:19	3290
J is the lot of his inheritance	Deut 32:9	3290
of the congregation of *J*	Deut 33:4	3290
They shall teach *J* thy judgments	Deut 33:10	3290
the fountain of *J* shall be upon a	Deut 33:28	3290
the anointed of the God of *J*	2Sa 23:1	3290
of the tribes of the sons of *J*	1Kin 18:31	3290
LORD commanded the children of *J*	2Kin 17:34	3290
his servant, ye children of *J*	1Chr 16:13	3290
confirmed the same to *J* for a law	1Chr 16:17	3290
J shall rejoice, and Israel shall	Ps 14:7	3290
name of the God of *J* defend thee	Ps 20:1	3290
all ye the seed of *J*, glorify him	Ps 22:23	3290
seek him, that seek thy face, O *J*	Ps 24:6	3290
command deliverances for *J*	Ps 44:4	3290
the God of *J* is our refuge	Ps 46:7	3290
the God of *J* is our refuge	Ps 46:11	3290
the excellency of *J* whom he loved	Ps 47:4	3290
J shall rejoice, and Israel shall	Ps 53:6	3290
in *J* unto the ends of the earth	Ps 59:13	3290
will sing praises to the God of *J*	Ps 75:9	3290
At thy rebuke, O God of *J*	Ps 76:6	3290
thy people, the sons of *J*	Ps 77:15	3290
he established a testimony in *J*	Ps 78:5	3290
so a fire was kindled against *J*	Ps 78:21	3290
brought him to feed *J* his people	Ps 78:71	3290
For they have devoured *J*, and laid	Ps 79:7	3290
a joyful noise unto the God of *J*	Ps 81:1	3290
Israel, and a law of the God of *J*	Ps 81:4	3290
give ear, O God of *J*	Ps 84:8	3290
brought back the captivity of *J*	Ps 85:1	3290
more than all the dwellings of *J*	Ps 87:2	3290
shall the God of *J* regard it	Ps 94:7	3290
judgment and righteousness in *J*	Ps 99:4	3290
ye children of *J* his chosen	Ps 105:6	3290
the same unto *J* for a law	Ps 105:10	3290
J sojourned in the land of Ham	Ps 105:23	3290
the house of *J* from a people of	Ps 114:1	3290
at the presence of the God of *J*	Ps 114:7	3290
and vowed unto the mighty God of *J*	Ps 132:2	3290
for the mighty God of *J*	Ps 132:5	3290
LORD hath chosen *J* unto himself	Ps 135:4	3290
hath the God of *J* for his help	Ps 146:5	3290
He sheweth his word unto *J*	Ps 147:19	3290
to the house of the God of *J*	Is 2:3	3290
O house of *J*, come ye, and let us	Is 2:5	3290
thy people the house of *J*	Is 2:6	3290
his face from the house of *J*	Is 8:17	3290
The Lord sent a word into *J*	Is 9:8	3290
as are escaped of the house of *J*	Is 10:20	3290
return, even the remnant of *J*	Is 10:21	3290
For the LORD will have mercy on *J*	Is 14:1	3290
shall cleave to the house of *J*	Is 14:1	3290
that the glory of *J* shall be made	Is 17:4	3290
them that come of *J* to take root	Is 27:6	3290
shall the iniquity of *J* be purged	Is 27:9	3290
concerning the house of *J*	Is 29:22	3290
J shall not now be ashamed,	Is 29:22	3290
and sanctify the Holy One of *J*	Is 29:23	3290
Why sayest thou, O *J*, and speakest	Is 40:27	3290
J whom I have chosen, the seed of	Is 41:8	3290
Fear not, thou worm *J*, and ye men	Is 41:14	3290
reasons, saith the King of *J*	Is 41:21	3290
Who gave *J* for a spoil, and Israel	Is 42:24	3290
the LORD that created thee, O *J*	Is 43:1	3290
thou hast not called upon me, O *J*	Is 43:22	3290

J

have given *J* to the curse, and	Is 43:28	3290
Yet now hear, O *J* my servant	Is 44:1	3290
Fear not, O *J*, my servant	Is 44:2	3290
call himself by the name of *J*	Is 44:5	3290
Remember these, O *J* and Israel	Is 44:21	3290
for the LORD hath redeemed *J*	Is 44:23	3290
For *J* my servant's sake, and	Is 45:4	3290
I said not unto the seed of *J*	Is 45:19	3290
Hearken unto me, O house of *J*	Is 46:3	3290
Hear ye this, O house of *J*	Is 48:1	3290
Hearken unto me, O *J* and Israel,	Is 48:12	3290
LORD hath redeemed his servant *J*	Is 48:20	3290
to bring *J* again to him, Though	Is 49:5	3290
to raise up the tribes of *J*	Is 49:6	3290
thy Redeemer, the mighty One of *J*	Is 49:26	3290
and the house of *J* their sins	Is 58:1	3290
with the heritage of *J* thy father	Is 58:14	3290
that turn from transgression in *J*	Is 59:20	3290
thy Redeemer, the mighty One of *J*	Is 60:16	3290
will bring forth a seed out of *J*	Is 65:9	3290
word of the LORD, O house of *J*	Jer 2:4	3290
Declare this in the house of *J*	Jer 5:20	3290
The portion of *J* is not like them	Jer 10:16	3290
for they have eaten up *J*, and	Jer 10:25	3290
fear thou not, O my servant *J*	Jer 30:10	3290
J shall return, and shall be in	Jer 30:10	3290
Sing with gladness for *J*, and	Jer 31:7	3290
For the LORD hath redeemed *J*	Jer 31:11	3290
will I cast away the seed of *J*	Jer 33:26	3290
the seed of Abraham, Isaac, and *J*	Jer 33:26	3290
But fear not thou, O my servant *J*	Jer 46:27	3290
J shall return, and be in rest and	Jer 46:27	3290
O *J* my servant, saith the LORD	Jer 46:28	3290
The portion of *J* is not like them	Jer 51:19	3290
LORD hath commanded concerning *J*	Lam 1:17	3290
up all the habitations of *J*	Lam 2:2	3290
he burned against *J* like a	Lam 2:3	3290
unto the seed of the house of *J*	Eze 20:5	3290
that I have given to my servant *J*	Eze 28:25	3290
I have given unto *J* my servant	Eze 37:25	3290
I bring again the captivity of *J*	Eze 39:25	3290
plow, and *J* shall break his clods	Hos 10:11	3290
will punish *J* according to his	Hos 12:2	3290
J fled into the country of Syria,	Hos 12:12	3290
ye, and testify in the house of *J*	Amos 3:13	3290
I abhor the excellency of *J*	Amos 6:8	3290
by whom shall *J* arise	Amos 7:2	3290
by whom shall *J* arise	Amos 7:5	3290
hath sworn by the excellency of *J*	Amos 8:7	3290
utterly destroy the house of *J*	Amos 9:8	3290
brother *J* shame shall cover thee	Obad 10	3290
the house of *J* shall possess	Obad 17	3290
the house of *J* shall be a fire,	Obad 18	3290
transgression of *J* is all this	Mic 1:5	3290
What is the transgression of *J*	Mic 1:5	3290
that art named the house of *J*	Mic 2:7	3290
I will surely assemble, O *J*	Mic 2:12	3290
Hear, I pray you, O heads of *J*	Mic 3:1	3290
of might, to declare unto *J* his	Mic 3:8	3290
you, ye heads of the house of *J*	Mic 3:9	3290
and to the house of the God of *J*	Mic 4:2	3290
the remnant of *J* shall be in the	Mic 5:7	3290
the remnant of *J* shall be among	Mic 5:8	3290
Thou wilt perform the truth to *J*	Mic 7:20	3290
turned away the excellency of *J*	Nah 2:2	3290
out of the tabernacles of *J*	Mal 2:12	3290
ye sons of *J* are not consumed	Mal 3:6	3290

JACOB'S (*ja'-cubs*)
1. Refers to Jacob 1.

and said, The voice is *J* voice	Gen 27:22	3290
Syrian, the brother of Rebekah, *J*	Gen 28:5	3290
J anger was kindled against	Gen 30:2	3290
were Laban's, and the stronger *J*	Gen 30:42	3290
And Laban went into *J* tent	Gen 31:33	3290
shalt say, They be thy servant *J*	Gen 32:18	3290
the hollow of *J* thigh was out of	Gen 32:25	3290
he touched the hollow of *J* thigh	Gen 32:32	3290
Israel in lying with *J* daughter	Gen 34:7	3290
he had delight in *J* daughter	Gen 34:19	3290
J firstborn, and Simeon, and Levi,	Gen 35:23	3290
J heart fainted, for he believed	Gen 45:26	3290
Reuben, *J* firstborn	Gen 46:8	3290
The sons of Rachel *J* wife	Gen 46:19	3290
besides *J* sons' wives, all the	Gen 46:26	3290
Was not Esau *J* brother	Mal 1:2	3290
Now *J* well was there	Jn 4:6	2384

2. Refers to Jacob 3.

is even the time of *J* trouble	Jer 30:7	3290
rain the captivity of *J* tents	Jer 30:18	3290

JADA (*ja'-dah*) *A grandson of Jerahmeel.*

sons of Onam were, Shammai, and *J*	1Chr 2:28	3047
the sons of *J* the brother of	1Chr 2:32	3047

JADAH See JARAH.

JADAI See JADAU.

JADAU (*ja'-daw*) *Married a foreigner in exile.*

Mattithiah, Zabad, Zebina, *J*	Ezr 10:43	3035

JADDAI See JADAU.

JADDUA (*jad'-du-ah*)
1. A Levite.

Meshezabeel, Zadok, *J*,	Neh 10:21	3037

2. A priest.

Jonathan, and Jonathan begat *J*	Neh 12:11	3037
Joiada, and Johanan, and *J*	Neh 12:22	3037

JADON (*ja'-don*) *A repairer of Jerusalem's wall.*

J the Meronothite, the men of	Neh 3:7	3036

JAEL (*ja'-el*) *The wife of Heber.*

of *J* the wife of Heber the Kenite	Judg 4:17	3278
J went out to meet Sisera, and	Judg 4:18	3278
Then *J* Heber's wife took a nail	Judg 4:21	3278
J came out to meet him, and said	Judg 4:22	3278
son of Anath, in the days of *J*	Judg 5:6	3278
Blessed above women shall *J* be	Judg 5:24	3278

JAGUR (*ja'-gur*) *A town in Judah.*

were Kabzeel, and Eder, and *J*	Josh 15:21	3017

JAH (*jah*) See JEHOVAH. *A shortened form of Jehovah.*

upon the heavens by his name *J*	Ps 68:4	3050

JAHALALEEL See JAHLEEL.

JAHATH (*ja'-hath*)
1. A descendant of Shobal.

Reaiah the son of Shobal begat *J*	1Chr 4:2	3189
and *J* begat Ahumai, and Lahad	1Chr 4:2	3189

2. A descendant of Gershom.

J his son, Zimmah his son,	1Chr 6:20	3189
The son of *J*, the son of Gershom,	1Chr 6:43	3189

3. Another descendant of Gershom.

And the sons of Shimei were, *J*	1Chr 23:10	3189
J was the chief, and Zizah the	1Chr 23:11	3189

4. A descendant of Kohath.

of the sons of Shelomoth; *J*	1Chr 24:22	3189

5. A descendant of Merari.

and the overseers of them were *J*	2Chr 34:12	3189

JAHAZ (*ja'-haz*) See JAHAZA, JAHAZAH, JAHZAH. *A Levitical city in Reuben.*

and he came to *J*, and fought	Num 21:23	3096
and all his people, to fight at *J*	Deut 2:32	3096
people together, and pitched in *J*	Judg 11:20	3096
voice shall be heard even unto *J*	Is 15:4	3096
even unto Elealeh, and even unto *J*	Jer 48:34	3096

JAHAZA (*ja-ha'-zah*) See JAHAZ. *Same as Jahaz.*

And *J*, and Kedemoth, and Mephaath,	Josh 13:18	3096

JAHAZAH (*ja-ha'-zah*) See JAHAZ. *Same as Jahaz.*

suburbs, and *J* with her suburbs,	Josh 21:36	3096
upon Holon, and upon *J*, and upon	Jer 48:21	3096

JAHAZIAH (*ja-ha-zi'-ah*) *Son of Tikvah.*

J the son of Tikvah were employed	Ezr 10:15	3167

JAHAZIEL (*ja-ha'-ze-el*)
1. A captain in David's army.

Jeremiah, and *J*, and Johanan, and	1Chr 12:4	3166

2. A priest.

J the priests with trumpets	1Chr 16:6	3166

3. A son of Hebron.

J the third, and Jekameam the	1Chr 23:19	3166
J the third, Jekameam the fourth	1Chr 24:23	3166

4. A Levite.

Then upon *J* the son of Zechariah,	2Chr 20:14	3166

5. A family of exiles.

the son of *J*, and with him three	Ezr 8:5	3166

JAHDAI (*jah'-dahee*) *A descendant of Caleb.*

And the sons of *J*	1Chr 2:47	3056

JAHDIEL (*jah'-de-el*) *Head of a family of Manasseh.*

and Jeremiah, and Hodaviah, and *J*	1Chr 5:24	3164

JAHDO (*jah'-do*) *Son of Buz.*

son of Jeshishai, the son of *J*	1Chr 5:14	3163

JAHLEEL (*jah'-le-el*) See JAHLEELITES. *A son of Zebulun.*

Sered, and Elon, and *J*	Gen 46:14	3177
of *J*, the family of the	Num 26:26	3177

JAHLEELITES (*jah'-le-el-ites*) *Descendants of Jahleel.*

of Jahleel, the family of the *J*	Num 26:26	3178

JAHMAI (jah'-mahee) A son of Tola.		
and Rephaiah, and Jeriel, and J............ 1Chr 7:2	3181	

JAHZAH (jah'-zah) See JAHAZ. A Levitical city in Reuben.
suburbs, and J with her suburbs, ... 1Chr 6:78 3096

JAHZEEL (jah'-ze-el) See JAHZEELITES, JAHZIEL. A son of Naphtali.
J, and Guni, and Jezer, and Shillem........ Gen 46:24 3183
of J, the family of the .... Num 26:48 3183

JAHZEELITES (jah'-ze-el-ites) Descendants of Jahzeel.
of Jahzeel, the family of the J................. Num 26:48 3184

JAHZEIAH See JAHAZIAH.

JAHZERAH (jah'-ze-rah) See AHAZAI. The son of Meshullam.
the son of Adiel, the son of J.................. 1Chr 9:12 3170

JAHZIEL (jah'-ze-el) See JAHZEEL. Same as Jahzeel.
J, and Guni, and Jezer, and Shallum, ... 1Chr 7:13 3185

JAILER
charging the j to keep them .... Acts 16:23 1200

JAIR (ja'-ur) See HAVOTH-JAIR, JAARE-OREGIM, JAIRITE.
1. A descendant of Judah and Manasseh.
J the son of Manasseh went and............. Num 32:41 2971
J the son of Manasseh took all .... Deut 3:14 2971
towns of J the son of Manasseh 1Kin 4:13 2971
And Segub begat J, who had three........ 1Chr 2:22 2971
2. A judge.
And after him arose J, a Gileadite.......... Judg 10:3 2971
J died, and was buried in Camon .... Judg 10:5 2971
3. A district in Bashan.
of Bashan, and all the towns of J........... Josh 13:30 2971
and Aram, with the towns of J 1Chr 2:23 2971
4. Father of Mordecai.
name was Mordecai, the son of J........... Est 2:5 2971
5. Father of Elhanan.
Elhanan the son of J slew Lahmi 1Chr 20:5 2971

JAIRITE (ja'-ur-ite) A descendant of Jair 1.
Ira also the J was a chief ruler 2Sa 20:26 2972

JAIRUS (ja-i'-rus) A ruler of a synagogue.
of the synagogue, J by name.................. Mk 5:22 2383
behold, there came a man named J....... Lk 8:41 2383

JAKAN (ja'-kan) See AKAN, JAAKAN. A son of Ezer.
Bilhan, and Zavan, and J......................... 1Chr 1:42 3292

JAKEH (ja'-keh) Father of Agur.
The words of Agur the son of J .... Prov 30:1 3348

JAKIM (ja'-kim)
1. Son of Shimhi.
And J, and Zichri, and Zabdi,.................. 1Chr 8:19 3356
2. A sanctuary servant.
to Eliashib, the twelfth to J 1Chr 24:12 3356

JAKIN See JACHINITES.

JAKINITE See JACHINITES.

JALAM See JAALAM.

JALON (ja'-lon) A son of Ezra.
Jether, and Mered, and Epher, and J....... 1Chr 4:17 3210

JAMBRES (jam'-brees) An opponent of Moses.
J withstood Moses, so do these 2Ti 3:8 2387

JAMES (james) See JACOB.
1. Son of Zebedee.
J the son of Zebedee, and John his .... Mt 4:21 2385
J the son of Zebedee, and John his .... Mt 10:2 2385
six days Jesus taketh Peter, J................ Mt 17:1 2385
he saw J the son of Zebedee, and .... Mk 1:19 2385
house of Simon and Andrew, with J........ Mk 1:29 2385
And J the son of..................................... Mk 3:17 2385
and John the brother of J .... Mk 3:17 2385
J, and John the brother of J .... Mk 5:37 2385
Jesus taketh with him Peter, and J .... Mk 9:2 2385
And J and John, the sons of Zebedee ..... Mk 10:35 2385
to be much displeased with J.................. Mk 10:41 2385
against the temple, Peter and J............... Mk 13:3 2385
And he taketh with him Peter and J........ Mk 14:33 2385
And so was also J, and John, the .... Lk 5:10 2385
Peter, and Andrew his brother, J .... Lk 6:14 2385
no man to go in, save Peter, and J .... Lk 8:51 2385
he took Peter and John and J .... Lk 9:28 2385
And when his disciples J and John .... Lk 9:54 2385
where abode both Peter, and J .... Acts 1:13 2385
he killed J the brother of John .... Acts 12:2 2385
2. Son of Alphaeus.
J the son of Alphaeus, and..................... Mt 10:3 2385
J the son of Alphaeus, and..................... Mk 3:18 2385

J the son of Alphaeus, and Simon .... Lk 6:15 2385
J the son of Alphaeus, and Simon .... Acts 1:13 2385
3. Brother of Jesus.
and his brethren, J, and Joses, and .... Mt 13:55 2385
and Mary the mother of J and Joses ...... Mt 27:56 2385
the son of Mary, the brother of J............. Mk 6:3 2385
and Mary the mother of J the less .... Mk 15:40 2385
and Mary the mother of J, and............... Mk 16:1 2385
And Judas the brother of J..................... Lk 6:16 2385
Joanna, and Mary the mother of J .... Lk 24:10 2385
and Judas the brother of J..................... Acts 1:13 2385
said, Go shew these things unto J .... Acts 12:17 2385
J answered, saying, Men and .... Acts 15:13 2385
Paul went in with us unto J .... Acts 21:18 2385
After that, he was seen of J 1Cor 15:7 2385
save J the Lord's brother .... Gal 1:19 2385
And when J, Cephas, and John, who...... Gal 2:9 2385
before that certain came from J............. Gal 2:12 2385
J, a servant of God and of the .... Jas 1:1 2385
of Jesus Christ, and brother of J............. Jude 1 2385

JAMIN (ja'-min) See JAMINITES.
1. A son of Simeon.
Jemuel, and J, and Ohad, and Jachin, ... Gen 46:10 3226
Jemuel, and J, and Ohad, and Jachin, ... Ex 6:15 3226
of J, the family of the Jaminites .... Num 26:12 3226
sons of Simeon were, Nemuel, and J 1Chr 4:24 3226
2. A descendant of Hezron.
of Jerahmeel were, Maaz, and J.............. 1Chr 2:27 3226
3. A priest.
Jeshua, and Bani, and Sherebiah, J........ Neh 8:7 3226

JAMINITES (ja'-min-ites) Descendants of Jamin.
of Jamin, the family of the J .... Num 26:12 3228

JAMLECH (jam'-lek) A royal descendant of Simeon.
And Meshobab, and J, and Joshah the ... 1Chr 4:34 3230

JANAI See JAANAI.

JANGLING
have turned aside unto vain j 1Ti 1:6 3150

JANIM See JANUM.

JANNA (jan'-nah) Father of Melchi; ancestor of Jesus.
of Melchi, which was the son of J .... Lk 3:24 2388

JANNAI See JANNA.

JANNES (jan'-nees) An opponent of Moses.
Now as J and Jambres withstood 2Ti 3:8 2389

JANOAH (ja-no'-ah) See JANOHAH. A city in Naphtali.
Ijon, and Abel-beth-maachah, and J 2Kin 15:29 3239

JANOHAH (ja-no'-hah) See JANOAH. A city between Ephraim and Manasseh.
and passed by it on the east to J .... Josh 16:6 3239
And it went down from J to Ataroth .... Josh 16:7 3239

JANUM (ja'-num) A city in Judah.
J, and Beth-tappuah, and Aphekah......... Josh 15:53 3241

JAPHETH (ja'-feth) A son of Noah.
and Noah begat Shem, Ham, and J........ Gen 5:32 3315
begat three sons, Shem, Ham, and J...... Gen 6:10 3315
Noah, and Shem, and Ham, and J .... Gen 7:13 3315
the ark, were Shem, and Ham, and J ..... Gen 9:18 3315
J took a garment, and laid it upon.......... Gen 9:23 3315
God shall enlarge J, and he shall........... Gen 9:27 3315
the sons of Noah, Shem, Ham, and J..... Gen 10:1 3315
The sons of J; Gomer .... Gen 10:2 3315
Eber, the brother of J the elder .... Gen 10:21 3315
Noah, Shem, Ham, and J........................ 1Chr 1:4 3315
The sons of J; Gomer 1Chr 1:5 3315

JAPHIA (ja-fi'-ah)
1. An Amorite king.
unto J king of Lachish, and unto............ Josh 10:3 3309
2. A town in Zebulun.
out to Daberath, and goeth up to J .... Josh 19:12 3309
3. A son of David.
also, and Elishua, and Nepheg, and J..... 2Sa 5:15 3309
And Nogah, and Nepheg, and J 1Chr 3:7 3309
And Nogah, and Nepheg, and J 1Chr 14:6 3309

JAPHLET (jaf'-let) See JAPHLETI. A grandson of Beriah.
And Heber begat J, and Shomer, and...... 1Chr 7:32 3310
And the sons of J.................................... 1Chr 7:33 3310
These are the children of J 1Chr 7:33 3310

JAPHLETI (jaf'-let-i) See JAPHLET. A landmark in Ephraim.
down westward to the coast of J............. Josh 16:3 3311

JAPHLETITES See JAPHLETI.

JAPHO (ja'-fo) See JOPPA. A city in Dan.
Rakkon, with the border before J............ Josh 19:46 3305

J

JARAH (ja'-rah) See JEHOADAH. *A son of Ahaz.*
And Ahaz begat J .... 1Chr 9:42　3294
J begat Alemeth, and Azmaveth, and .... 1Chr 9:42　3294

JAREB (ja'-reb) *An Assyrian king.*
the Assyrian, and sent to king J .... Hos 5:13　3377
Assyria for a present to king J .... Hos 10:6　3377

JARED (ja'-red) See JERED.
　1. *A descendant of Seth.*
sixty and five years, and begat J .... Gen 5:15　3382
after he begat J eight hundred................ Gen 5:16　3382
J lived an hundred sixty and two .... Gen 5:18　3382
J lived after he begat Enoch .... Gen 5:19　3382
all the days of J were nine .... Gen 5:20　3382
　2. *Father of Enoch; ancestor of Jesus.*
of Enoch, which was the son of J .... Lk 3:37　2391

JARESIAH (ja-re-si'-ah) *A descendant of Benjamin.*
And J, and Eliah, and Zichri, the .... 1Chr 8:27　3298

JARHA (jar'-hah) *An Egyptian servant.*
an Egyptian, whose name was J .... 1Chr 2:34　3398
daughter to J his servant to wife............. 1Chr 2:35　3398

JARIB (ja'-rib) See JACHIN.
　1. *A son of Simeon.*
Simeon were, Nemuel, and Jamin, J .... 1Chr 4:24　3402
　2. *A family of exiles.*
and for Elnathan, and for J .... Ezr 8:16　3402
　3. *Married a foreigner.*
Maaseiah, and Eliezer, and J .... Ezr 10:18　3402

JARMUTH (jar'-muth) See REMETH.
　1. *A city in Judah.*
Hebron, and unto Piram king of J........... Josh 10:3　3412
the king of Hebron, the king of J............. Josh 10:5　3412
the king of Hebron, the king of J............. Josh 10:23　3412
The king of J, one .... Josh 12:11　3412
J, and Adullam, Socoh, and Azekah, ... Josh 15:35　3412
J with her suburbs, En-gannim .... Josh 21:29　3412
En-rimmon, and at Zareah, and at J ...... Neh 11:29　3412

JAROAH (ja-ro'-ah) *A descendant of Gad.*
the son of Huri, the son of J .... 1Chr 5:14　3386

JASHAR See JASHER.

JASHEN (ja'-shen) See HASHEM. *Father of several "mighty men" of David.*
the Shaalbonite, of the sons of J .... 2Sa 23:32　3464

JASHER (ja'-shur) *A book of songs.*
not this written in the book of J.............. Josh 10:13　3477
it is written in the book of J .... 2Sa 1:18　3477

JASHOBEAM (jash-o'-be-am)
　1. *A "mighty man" of David.*
J, a Hachmonite, the chief of the .... 1Chr 11:11　3434
month was J the son of Zabdiel .... 1Chr 27:2　3434
　2. *Another "mighty man" of David.*
and Azareel, and Joezer, and J .... 1Chr 12:6　3434

JASHUB (ja'-shub) See JASHUBI-LEHEM, JOB, JASHUB-ITES, SHEAR-JASHUB.
　1. *A son of Issachar.*
Of J, the family of the............................. Num 26:24　3437
Issachar were, Tola, and Puah, J .... 1Chr 7:1　3437
　2. *Married a foreigner in exile.*
Meshullam, Malluch, and Adaiah, J .... Ezr 10:29　3437

JASHUBI-LAHEM See JASHUBI-LEHEM.

JASHUBI-LEHEM (jash'-u-bi-le'-hem) *A descendant of Shelah.*
had the dominion in Moab, and J .... 1Chr 4:22　3433

JASHUBITES (jash'-u-bites) *Descendants of Jashub.*
Of Jashub, the family of the J .... Num 26:24　3432

JASIEL (ja'-se-el) *A "mighty man" of David.*
and Obed, and J the Mesobaite .... 1Chr 11:47　3300

JASON (ja'-sun)
　1. *A Christian in Thessalonica.*
and assaulted the house of J .... Acts 17:5　2394
they found them not, they drew J............ Acts 17:6　2394
Whom J hath received:............................ Acts 17:7　2394
when they had taken security of J .... Acts 17:9　2394
　2. *A relative of Paul.*
my workfellow, and Lucius, and J .... Rom 16:21　2394

JASPER
row a beryl, and an onyx, and a j .... Ex 28:20　3471
row, a beryl, an onyx, and a j .... Ex 39:13　3471
the beryl, the onyx, and the j .... Eze 28:13　3471
sat was to look upon like a j .... Rev 4:3　2393
precious, even like a j stone .... Rev 21:11　2393
of the wall of it was of j.......................... Rev 21:18　2393
The first foundation was j....................... Rev 21:19　2393

JATHNIEL (jath'-ne-el) *A son of Meshelemiah.*
Zebadiah the third, J the fourth,............. 1Chr 26:2　3496

JATTIR (jat'-tur) *A Levitical city in Judah.*
And in the mountains, Shamir, and J ..... Josh 15:48　3492
J with her suburbs, and Eshtemoa .... Josh 21:14　3492
and to them which were in J .... 1Sa 30:27　3492
and Libnah with her suburbs, and J....... 1Chr 6:57　3492

JAVAN (ja'-van)
　1. *A son of Joktan.*
Gomer, and Magog, and Madai, and J.... Gen 10:2　3120
And the sons of J..................................... Gen 10:4　3120
Gomer, and Magog, and Madai, and J.... 1Chr 1:5　3120
And the sons of J..................................... 1Chr 1:7　3120
　2. *Descendants of Javan 1.*
that draw the bow, to Tubal, and J.......... Is 66:19　3120
　3. *A city in southern Arabia.*
J, Tubal, and Meshech, they were .... Eze 27:13　3120
J going to and fro occupied in thy .... Eze 27:19　3120

JAVELIN
and took a j in his hand.......................... Num 25:7　7420
there was a j in Saul's hand .... 1Sa 18:10　2595
And Saul cast the j .... 1Sa 18:11　2595
his house with his j in his hand .... 1Sa 19:9　2595
David even to the wall with the j .... 1Sa 19:10　2595
he smote the j into the wall .... 1Sa 19:10　2595
Saul cast a j at him to smite him .... 1Sa 20:33　2595

JAW
with the j of an ass have I slain .... Judg 15:16　3895
an hollow place that was in the j .... Judg 15:19　3895
or bore his j through with a .... Job 41:2　3895
their j teeth as knives, to........................ Prov 30:14　4973

JAWBONE
And he found a new j of an ass.............. Judg 15:15　3895
With the j of an ass, heaps upon .... Judg 15:16　3895
cast away the j out of his hand .... Judg 15:17　3895

JAWS
I brake the j of the wicked, and............. Job 29:17　4973
and my tongue cleaveth to my j .... Ps 22:15　4455
a bridle in the j of the people .... Is 30:28　3895
But I will put hooks in thy j .... Eze 29:4　3895
back, and put hooks into thy j .... Eze 38:4　3895
that take off the yoke on their j .... Hos 11:4　3895

JAZER (ja'-zur) See JAAZER. *A Levitical city in Gad.*
and when they saw the land of J............. Num 32:1　3270
Ataroth, and Dibon, and and................... Num 32:3　3270
And their coast was J, and all the .... Josh 13:25　3270
her suburbs, J with her suburbs.............. Josh 21:39　3270
of the river of Gad, and toward J .... 2Sa 24:5　3270
suburbs, and J with her suburbs .... 1Chr 6:81　3270
men of valour at J of Gilead .... 1Chr 26:31　3270
they are come even unto J .... Is 16:8　3270
weeping of J the vine of Sibmah .... Is 16:9　3270
for thee with the weeping of J .... Jer 48:32　3270
they reach even to the sea of J............... Jer 48:32　3270

JAZIZ (ja'-ziz) *Overseer of David's flocks.*
the flocks was J the Hagerite .... 1Chr 27:31　3151

JEALOUS
for I the LORD thy God am a j God .... Ex 20:5　7067
whose name is J, is a God .... Ex 34:14　7065
he be j of his wife, and she be .... Num 5:14　7065
he be j of his wife, and she be .... Num 5:14　7065
he be j over his wife, and shall............... Num 5:30　7065
is a consuming fire, even a j God .... Deut 4:24　7067
for I the LORD thy God am a j God .... Deut 5:9　7067
(For the LORD thy God is a j God .... Deut 6:15　7067
he is a j God .... Josh 24:19　7072
I have been very j for the LORD .... 1Kin 19:10　7065
I have been very j for the LORD .... 1Kin 19:14　7065
will be j for my holy name .... Eze 39:25　7065
will the LORD be j for his land .... Joel 2:18　7065
God is j, and the LORD revengeth........... Nah 1:2　7072
I am j for Jerusalem and for Zion .... Zec 1:14　7065
I was j for Zion with great .... Zec 8:2　7065
I was j for her with great fury................ Zec 8:2　7065
For I am j over you with godly .... 2Cor 11:2　2206

JEALOUSIES
This is the law of j, when a wife............. Num 5:29　7068

JEALOUSY
And the spirit of j come upon him .... Num 5:14　7068
if the spirit of j come upon him .... Num 5:14　7068
for it is an offering of j .... Num 5:15　7068
hands, which is the j offering .... Num 5:18　7068
the j offering out of the woman's .... Num 5:25　7068
the spirit of j cometh upon him .... Num 5:30　7068
the children of Israel in my j .... Num 25:11　7068

his *j* shall smoke against that	Deut 29:20	7068
him to *j* with strange gods	Deut 32:16	7065
They have moved me to *j* with that	Deut 32:21	7065
I will move them to *j* with those	Deut 32:21	7065
they provoked him to *j* with their	1Kin 14:22	7065
moved him to *j* with their graven	Ps 78:58	7065
shall thy *j* burn like fire	Ps 79:5	7068
For *j* is the rage of a man	Prov 6:34	7068
j is cruel as the grave	Song 8:6	7068
he shall stir up *j* like a man of	Is 42:13	7068
of *j*, which provoketh to *j*	Eze 8:3	7069
this image of *j* in the entry	Eze 8:5	7068
will give thee blood in fury and *j*	Eze 16:38	7068
my *j* shall depart from thee, and I	Eze 16:42	7068
And I will set my *j* against thee	Eze 23:25	7068
Surely in the fire of my *j* have I	Eze 36:5	7068
Behold, I have spoken in my *j*	Eze 36:6	7068
For in my *j* and in the fire of my	Eze 38:19	7068
be devoured by the fire of his *j*	Zeph 1:18	7068
be devoured with the fire of my *j*	Zeph 3:8	7068
and for Zion with a great *j*	Zec 1:14	7068
was jealous for Zion with great *j*	Zec 8:2	7068
I will provoke you to *j* by them	Rom 10:19	
for to provoke them to *j*	Rom 11:11	
Do we provoke the Lord to *j*	1Cor 10:22	
am jealous over you with godly *j*	2Cor 11:2	2205

JEARIM (je'-a-rim) See Kirjath-jearim. *A mountain in Judah.*

along unto the side of mount *J*	Josh 15:10	3297

JEATERAI (je-at'-e-rahee) *A descendant of Gershom.*

his son, Zerah his son, *J* his son	1Chr 6:21	2979

JEATHERAI See Jeaterai.

JEBERECHIAH (je-ber'-e-ki'ah) *Father of Zechariah.*

priest, and Zechariah the son of *J*	Is 8:2	3000

JEBEREKIAH See Jeberechiah.

JEBUS (je'-bus) See Jebusi, Jebusite, Jerusalem. *Original name of Jerusalem.*

departed, and came over against *J*	Judg 19:10	2982
And when they were by *J*, the day	Judg 19:11	2982
went to Jerusalem, which is *J*	1Chr 11:4	2982
inhabitants of *J* said to David	1Chr 11:5	2982

JEBUSI (jeb'-u-si) See Jebusite. *Same as Jebus.*

to the side of *J* on the south	Josh 18:16	2983
And Zelah, Eleph, and *J*, which is	Josh 18:28	2983

JEBUSITE (jeb'-u-site) See Jebusites. *Descendant of Canaan.*

And the *J*, and the Amorite, and the	Gen 10:16	2983
Perizzite, the Hivite, and the *J*	Ex 33:2	2983
and the Hivite, and the *J*	Ex 34:11	2983
Perizzite, the Hivite, and the *J*	Josh 9:1	2983
the *J* in the mountains, and to the	Josh 11:3	2983
unto the south side of the *J*	Josh 15:8	2983
threshingplace of Araunah the *J*	2Sa 24:16	2983
threshingfloor of Araunah the *J*	2Sa 24:18	2983
The *J* also, and the Amorite, and	1Chr 1:14	2983
the threshingfloor of Ornan the *J*	1Chr 21:15	2983
the threshingfloor of Ornan the *J*	1Chr 21:18	2983
the threshingfloor of Ornan the *J*	1Chr 21:28	2983
the threshingfloor of Ornan the *J*	2Chr 3:1	2983
in Judah, and Ekron as a *J*	Zec 9:7	2983

JEBUSITES (jeb'-u-sites)

and the Girgashites, and the *J*	Gen 15:21	2983
and the Hivites, and the *J*	Ex 3:8	2983
and the Hivites, and the *J*	Ex 3:17	2983
and the Hivites, and the *J*	Ex 13:5	2983
Canaanites, the Hivites, and the *J*	Ex 23:23	2983
and the Hittites, and the *J*	Num 13:29	2983
and the Hivites, and the *J*	Deut 7:1	2983
Perizzites, the Hivites, and the *J*	Deut 20:17	2983
and the Amorites, and the *J*	Josh 3:10	2983
Perizzites, the Hivites, and the *J*	Josh 12:8	2983
As for the *J* the inhabitants of	Josh 15:63	2983
but the *J* dwell with the children	Josh 15:63	2983
the Hivites, and the *J*	Josh 24:11	2983
the *J* that inhabited Jerusalem	Judg 1:21	2983
but the *J* dwell with the children	Judg 1:21	2983
and Perizzites, and Hivites, and *J*	Judg 3:5	2983
turn in into this city of the *J*	Judg 19:11	2983
men went to Jerusalem unto the *J*	2Sa 5:6	2983
to the gutter, and smiteth the *J*	2Sa 5:8	2983
Perizzites, Hivites, and *J*	1Kin 9:20	2983
where the *J* were, the inhabitants	1Chr 11:4	2983
the *J* first shall be chief	1Chr 11:6	2983
and the Hivites, and the *J*	2Chr 8:7	2983
Hittites, the Perizzites, the *J*	Ezr 9:1	2983
and the Perizzites, and the *J*	Neh 9:8	2983

JECAMIAH (jek-a-mi'ah) See Jekamiah. *A son of Jeconiah.*

also, and Pedaiah, and Shenazar, *J*	1Chr 3:18	3359

JECHILIAH See Jecholiah.

JECHOLIAH (jek-o-li'-ah) See Jecoliah. *Mother of Uzziah.*

mother's name was *J* of Jerusalem	2Kin 15:2	3203

JECHONIAS (jek-o-ni'-as) See Jeconiah. *Greek form of Jeconiah.*

And Josias begat *J* and his brethren	Mt 1:11	2423
to Babylon, *J* begat Salathiel	Mt 1:12	2423

JECOLIAH (jek-o-li'-ah) See Jecholiah. *Same as Jecholiah.*

name also was *J* of Jerusalem	2Chr 26:3	3203

JECONIAH (jek-o-ni'-ah) See Coniah, Jechonias, Jehoiachin. *A king of Judah.*

J his son, Zedekiah his son	1Chr 3:16	3204
And the sons of *J*	1Chr 3:17	3204
carried away with *J* king of Judah	Est 2:6	3204
had carried away captive *J* the	Jer 24:1	3204
J the son of Jehoiakim king of	Jer 27:20	3204
J the son of Jehoiakim king of	Jer 28:4	3204
(After that *J* the king, and the	Jer 29:2	3204

JEDAIAH (jed-a-i'-ah)
1. *A descendant of Simeon.*

the son of Allon, the son of *J*	1Chr 4:37	3042

2. *A rebuilder of Jerusalem's wall.*

repaired *J* the son of Harumaph	Neh 3:10	3042

3. *A priest in Jerusalem.*

J, and Jehoiarib, and Jachin	1Chr 9:10	3048
to Jehoiarib, the second to *J*	1Chr 24:7	3048
the children of *J*, of the house	Ezr 2:36	3048
the children of *J*, of the house	Neh 7:39	3048

4. *A family of exiles.*

J the son of Joiarib, Jachin	Neh 11:10	3048
Shemaiah, and Joiarib, *J*,	Neh 12:6	3048
Mattenai; of *J* Uzzi	Neh 12:19	3048
of Heldai, of Tobijah, and of *J*	Zec 6:10	3048
to Helem, and to Tobijah, and to *J*	Zec 6:14	3048

5. *A priest.*

Sallu, Amok, Hilkiah, *J*	Neh 12:7	3048
of *J*, Nethaneel	Neh 12:21	3048

JEDIAEL (jed-e-a'-el)
1. *A son of Benjamin.*

Bela, and Becher, and *J*, three	1Chr 7:6	3043
The sons also of *J*	1Chr 7:10	3043
All these the sons of *J*, by the	1Chr 7:11	3043

2. *A "mighty man" of David.*

J the son of Shimri, and Joha his	1Chr 11:45	3043

3. *A warrior in David's army.*

Manasseh, Adnah, and Jozabad, and *J*	1Chr 12:20	3043

4. *Son of Meshelemiah.*

J the second, Zebadiah the third,	1Chr 26:2	3043

JEDIDAH (je-di'-dah) *Mother of King Josiah.*

And his mother's name was *J*	2Kin 22:1	3040

JEDIDIAH (jed-id-i'-ah) *Another name for Solomon.*

and he called his name *J*, because	2Sa 12:25	3041

JEDUTHUN (jed'-u-thun) *A Levite.*

the son of Galal, the son of *J*	1Chr 9:16	3038
Obed-edom also the son of *J*	1Chr 16:38	3038
And with them Heman and *J*, and the	1Chr 16:41	3038
J with trumpets and cymbals for	1Chr 16:42	3038
the sons of *J* were porters	1Chr 16:42	3038
of Asaph, and of Heman, and of *J*	1Chr 25:1	3038
Of *J*: the sons of *J*	1Chr 25:3	3038
under the hands of their father *J*	1Chr 25:3	3038
to the king's order to Asaph, *J*	1Chr 25:6	3038
of them of Asaph, of Heman, of *J*	2Chr 5:12	3038
and of the sons of *J*	2Chr 29:14	3038
and Heman, and *J* the king's seer	2Chr 35:15	3038
the son of Galal, the son of *J*	Neh 11:17	3038
To the chief Musician, even to *J*	Ps 39:*t*	3038
To the chief Musician, to *J*	Ps 62:*t*	3038
To the chief Musician, to *J*	Ps 77:*t*	3038

JEEZER (je-e'-zur) See Abiezer, Jeezerites. *A son of Gilead.*

of *J*, the family of the	Num 26:30	372

JEEZERITES (je-e'-zur-ites) *Descendants of Jeezer.*

of Jeezer, the family of the *J*	Num 26:30	373

JEGAR-SAHADUTHA

And Laban called it *J*	Gen 31:47	3026

JEHALELEEL (je-hal-e'-le-el) See Jehalelel. *A descendant of Judah.*

And the sons of *J*	1Chr 4:16	3094

J

JEHALELEL (je-hal'-e-lel) See JEHALELEEL. *A descendant of Merari.*
of Abdi, and Azariah the son of J 2Chr 29:12   3094

JEHALLELEL See JEHALELEL.

JEHDEIAH (jeh-di'-ah)
    1. A sanctuary servant.
the sons of Shubael; J 1Chr 24:20   3165
    2. A herdsman of David.
the asses was J the Meronothite 1Chr 27:30   3165

JEHEZEKEL (je-hez'-e-kel) See EZEKIEL. *A sanctuary servant.*
to Pethahiah, the twentieth to J 1Chr 24:16   3168

JEHEZEL See JEHEZEKEL.

JEHIAH (je-hi'-ah) See JEHIEL. *A priest.*
J were doorkeepers for the ark 1Chr 15:24   3174

JEHIEL (je-hi'-el) See JEHIAH, JEIEL, JEHIELI.
    1. A Levite.
and Jaaziel, and Shemiramoth, and J ... 1Chr 15:18   3171
and Aziel, and Shemiramoth, and J 1Chr 15:20   3171
Jeiel, and Shemiramoth, and J 1Chr 16:5   3171
    2. A Gershonite.
the chief was J, and Zetham, and 1Chr 23:8   3171
by the hand of J the Gershonite 1Chr 29:8   3171
    3. A friend of David's son.
J the son of Hachmoni was with 1Chr 27:32   3171
    4. Son of King Jehoshaphat.
of Jehoshaphat, Azariah, and J............... 2Chr 21:2   3171
    5. A son of Heman.
sons of Heman; J, and Shimei 2Chr 29:14   3171
    6. A Levite in Hezekiah's time.
And J, and Azaziah, and Nahath, and ... 2Chr 31:13   3171
    7. A chief priest.
Hilkiah and Zechariah and J 2Chr 35:8   3171
    8. A family of exiles.
Obadiah the son of J, and with him .... Ezr 8:9   3171
    9. The father of Shechaniah.
And Shechaniah the son of J.................. Ezr 10:2   3171
    10. A son of Harim.
and Elijah, and Shemaiah, and J .... Ezr 10:21   3171
    11. A man of Elam's family who married a foreigner.
Mattaniah, Zechariah, and J................... Ezr 10:26   3171
    12. Father of Gibeon.
dwelt the father of Gibeon, J 1Chr 9:35   3273
    13. A "mighty man" of David.
J the sons of Hothan the Aroerite 1Chr 11:44   3273

JEHIELI (je-hi'-el-i) See JEHIEL. *A sanctuary servant.*
of Laadan the Gershonite, were J 1Chr 26:21   3172
The sons of J; Zetham, and 1Chr 26:22   3172

JEHIELITES See JEHIEL.

JEHIZKIAH (je-hiz-ki'-ah) See HEZEKIAH. *A son of Shallum.*
J the son of Shallum, and Amasa 2Chr 28:12   3169

JEHOADAH (je-ho'-a-dah) See JARAH. *Son of Ahaz.*
And Ahaz begat J 1Chr 8:36   3085
J begat Alemeth, and Azmaveth, and 1Chr 8:36   3085

JEHOADDAH See JEHOADAH.

JEHOADDAN (je-ho-ad'-dan) *Mother of King Amaziah.*
mother's name was J of Jerusalem 2Kin 14:2   3086
mother's name was J of Jerusalem 2Chr 25:1   3086

JEHOADDIN See JEHOADDAN.

JEHOAHAZ (je-ho'-a-haz) See AHAZIAH, JOAHAZ, SHALLUM.
    1. Son of King Jehu.
J his son reigned in his stead................. 2Kin 10:35   3059
son of Ahaziah king of Judah J.............. 2Kin 13:1   3059
J besought the LORD, and the LORD 2Kin 13:4   3059
people to J but fifty horsemen................. 2Kin 13:7   3059
Now the rest of the acts of J.................... 2Kin 13:8   3059
And J slept with his fathers 2Kin 13:9   3059
Judah began Jehoash the son of J 2Kin 13:10   3059
Israel all the days of J............................. 2Kin 13:22   3059
Jehoash the son of J took again.............. 2Kin 13:25   3059
the hand of J his father by war 2Kin 13:25   3059
J king of Israel reigned Amaziah 2Kin 14:1   3099
the son of J son of Jehu, king of 2Kin 14:8   3059
the death of Jehoash son of J.................. 2Kin 14:17   3059
and sent to Joash, the son of J................ 2Chr 25:17   3059
of J king of Israel fifteen years 2Chr 25:25   3059
    2. Son of King Josiah.
the land took J the son of Josiah 2Kin 23:30   3059
J was twenty and three years old 2Kin 23:31   3059
name to Jehoiakim, and took J away 2Kin 23:34   3059
J was twenty and three years old 2Chr 36:2   3059
Necho took J his brother, and................. 2Chr 36:4   3059

    3. A son of King Jehoram.
was never a son left him, save J 2Chr 21:17   3059
the son of Joash, the son of J 2Chr 25:23   3059

JEHOASH (je-ho'-ash) See JOASH.
    1. A king of Judah.
Seven years old was J when he 2Kin 11:21   3060
year of Jehu J began to reign.................. 2Kin 12:1   3060
J did that which was right in the 2Kin 12:2   3060
J said to the priests, All the 2Kin 12:4   3060
twentieth year of king J the.................... 2Kin 12:6   3060
Then king J called for Jehoiada.............. 2Kin 12:7   3060
J king of Judah took all the 2Kin 12:18   3060
the son of J the son of Ahaziah, ... 2Kin 14:13   3060
    2. A king of Israel.
J the son of Jehoahaz to reign 2Kin 13:10   3060
J the son of Jehoahaz took again........... 2Kin 13:25   3060
Then Amaziah sent messengers to J 2Kin 14:8   3060
J the king of Israel sent to 2Kin 14:9   3060
Therefore J king of Israel went 2Kin 14:11   3060
J king of Israel took Amaziah................. 2Kin 14:13   3060
of the acts of J which he did 2Kin 14:15   3060
J slept with his fathers, and was 2Kin 14:16   3060
J son of Jehoahaz king of Israel 2Kin 14:17   3060

JEHOHANAN (je-ho'-ha-nan)
    1. A sanctuary servant.
J the sixth, Elioenai the seventh 1Chr 26:3   3076
    2. A chief captain.
And next to him was J the captain 2Chr 17:15   3076
    3. Father of Ishmael.
Jeroham, and Ishmael the son of J 2Chr 23:1   3076
    4. Married a foreigner in exile.
J, Hananiah, Zabbai, and Athlai............. Ezr 10:28   3076
    5. A priest in exile.
Meshullam; of Amariah, J....................... Neh 12:13   3076
    6. A priest who dedicated the wall.
and Eleazar, and Uzzi, and J .... Neh 12:42   3076

JEHOIACHIN (je-hoy'-a-kin) See CONIAH, JECONIAH, JECONIAS, JEHOIACHIN'S. *A king of Judah.*
J his son reigned in his stead.................. 2Kin 24:6   3078
J was eighteen years old when he 2Kin 24:8   3078
J the king of Judah went out to 2Kin 24:12   3078
And he carried away J to Babylon 2Kin 24:15   3078
the captivity of J king of Judah 2Kin 25:27   3078
of J king of Judah out of prison 2Kin 25:27   3078
J his son reigned in his stead................. 2Chr 36:8   3078
J was eight years old when he 2Chr 36:9   3078
the captivity of J king of Judah .... Jer 52:31   3078
up the head of J king of Judah .... Jer 52:31   3078

JEHOIACHIN'S (je-hoy'-a-kins)
fifth year of king J captivity................... Eze 1:2   3112

JEHOIADA (je-hoy'-a-dah) See BERECHIAS, JOIADA.
    1. Father of Benaiah.
Benaiah the son of J was over................. 2Sa 8:18   3111
Benaiah the son of J was over the 2Sa 20:23   3111
And Benaiah the son of J, the son 2Sa 23:20   3111
things did Benaiah the son of J.............. 2Sa 23:22   3111
priest, and Benaiah the son of J 1Kin 1:8   3111
priest, and Benaiah the son of J 1Kin 1:26   3111
prophet, and Benaiah the son of J 1Kin 1:32   3111
the son of J answered the king............... 1Kin 1:36   3111
prophet, and Benaiah the son of J 1Kin 1:38   3111
prophet, and Benaiah the son of J 1Kin 1:44   3111
the hand of Benaiah the son of J 1Kin 2:25   3111
Solomon sent Benaiah the son of J 1Kin 2:29   3111
So Benaiah the son of J went up............ 1Kin 2:34   3111
of J in his room over the host 1Kin 2:35   3111
commanded Benaiah the son of J........... 1Kin 2:46   3111
the son of J was over the host 1Kin 4:4   3111
Benaiah the son of J, the son of 1Chr 11:22   3111
things did Benaiah the son of J.............. 1Chr 11:24   3111
Benaiah the son of J was over the 1Chr 18:17   3111
month was Benaiah the son of J 1Chr 27:5   3111
    2. A high priest.
And the seventh year J sent 2Kin 11:4   3111
that J the priest commanded 2Kin 11:9   3111
sabbath, and came to J the priest 2Kin 11:9   3111
But J the priest commanded the............. 2Kin 11:15   3111
J made a covenant between the.............. 2Kin 11:17   3111
J the priest instructed him 2Kin 12:2   3111
Jehoash called for J the priest 2Kin 12:7   3111
But J the priest took a chest, and 2Kin 12:9   3111
Jehoram, the wife of J the priest 2Chr 22:11   3111
And in the seventh year J....................... 2Chr 23:1   3111
that J the priest had commanded 2Chr 23:8   3111
for J the priest dismissed not................. 2Chr 23:8   3111
Moreover J the priest delivered 2Chr 23:9   3111
And J and his sons anointed him, and ... 2Chr 23:11   3111
Then J the priest brought out the 2Chr 23:14   3111

J made a covenant between him, and 2Chr 23:16   3111
Also *J* appointed the offices of 2Chr 23:18   3111
LORD all the days of *J* the priest............. 2Chr 24:2   3111
And *J* took for him two wives................. 2Chr 24:3   3111
the king called for *J* the chief................. 2Chr 24:6   3111
J gave it to such as did the work 2Chr 24:12   3111
of the money before the king and *J*........ 2Chr 24:14   3111
continually all the days of *J*.................... 2Chr 24:14   3111
But *J* waxed old, and was full of 2Chr 24:15   3111
Now after the death of *J* came the.......... 2Chr 24:17   3111
Zechariah the son of *J* the priest............ 2Chr 24:20   3111
not the kindness which *J* his 2Chr 24:22   3111
blood of the sons of *J* the priest 2Chr 24:25   3111
    3. A captain in David's army.
J was the leader of the Aaronites 1Chr 12:27   3111
    4. Son of Benaiah.
was *J* the son of Benaiah, and................. 1Chr 27:34   3111
    5. A rebuilder of Jerusalem's wall.
gate repaired *J* the son of Paseah........... Neh 3:6   3111
    6. A pre-exilic priest.
in the stead of *J* the priest...................... Jer 29:26   3111

JEHOIAKIM *(je-hoy'-a-kim)* See ELIAKIM, JOIAKIM.
    A king of Judah.
father, and turned his name to *J* 2Kin 23:34   3079
J gave the silver and the gold to 2Kin 23:35   3079
J was twenty and five years old 2Kin 23:36   3079
J became his servant three years 2Kin 24:1   3079
Now the rest of the acts of *J*.................... 2Kin 24:5   3079
So *J* slept with his fathers 2Kin 24:6   3079
according to all that *J* had done 2Kin 24:19   3079
firstborn Johanan, the second *J*.............. 1Chr 3:15   3079
And the sons of *J*.................................... 1Chr 3:16   3079
and turned his name to *J* 2Chr 36:4   3079
J was twenty and five years old 2Chr 36:5   3079
Now the rest of the acts of *J*.................... 2Chr 36:8   3079
It came also in the days of the .... Jer 1:3   3079
thus saith the LORD concerning *J*............ Jer 22:18   3079
though Coniah the son of *J* king .... Jer 22:24   3079
the son of *J* king of Judah...................... Jer 24:1   3079
of Judah in the fourth year of *J*............... Jer 25:1   3079
the beginning of the reign of *J* .... Jer 26:1   3079
when *J* the king, with all his .... Jer 26:21   3079
J the king sent men into Egypt, ... Jer 26:22   3079
and brought him unto *J* the king .... Jer 26:23   3079
the beginning of the reign of *J* .... Jer 27:1   3079
captive Jeconiah the son of *J* .... Jer 27:20   3079
the son of *J* king of Judah...................... Jer 28:4   3079
from the LORD in the days of *J* .... Jer 35:1   3079
to pass in the fourth year of *J*................. Jer 36:1   3079
to pass in the fifth year of *J* .... Jer 36:9   3079
which *J* the king of Judah hath............... Jer 36:28   3079
thou shalt say to *J* king of Judah .... Jer 36:29   3079
saith the LORD of *J* king of Judah .... Jer 36:30   3079
J king of Judah had burned in the .... Jer 36:32   3079
instead of Coniah the son of *J*................. Jer 37:1   3079
in the fourth year of *J* the son .... Jer 45:1   3079
smote in the fourth year of *J* the .... Jer 46:2   3079
according to all that *J* had done .... Jer 52:2   3079
the reign of *J* king of Judah came .... Dan 1:1   3079
the Lord gave *J* king of Judah................. Dan 1:2   3079

JEHOIARIB *(je-hoy'-a-rib)* See JOIARIB.
    1. A priest.
Jedaiah, and, *J*, and Jachin, ... 1Chr 9:10   3080
    2. A sanctuary servant.
Now the first lot came forth to *J* 1Chr 24:7   3080

JEHONADAB *(je-hon'-a-dab)* See JONADAB. *A son of*
    Rechab.
he lighted on *J* the son of Rechab........... 2Kin 10:15   3082
And *J* answered, It is............................... 2Kin 10:15   3082
J the son of Rechab, into the 2Kin 10:23   3082

JEHONATHAN *(je-hon'-a-than)* See JONATHAN.
    1. A storehouse servant.
castles, was *J* the son of Uzziah 1Chr 27:25   3083
    2. A Levite teacher.
and Asahel, and Shemiramoth, and *J* 2Chr 17:8   3083
    3. A priest
of Shemaiah, *J*.. Neh 12:18   3083

JEHORAM *(je-ho'-ram)* See HADORAM, JORAM.
    1. A king of Judah.
J his son reigned in his stead................. 1Kin 22:50   3088
J the son of Jehoshaphat king of............ 2Kin 1:17   3088
J the son of Jehoshaphat king of............ 2Kin 8:16   3088
of *J* king of Judah begin to reign 2Kin 8:25   3088
Ahaziah the son of *J* king of 2Kin 8:29   3088
things that Jehoshaphat, and *J*............... 2Kin 12:18   3088
J his son reigned in his stead.................. 2Chr 21:1   3088
but the kingdom gave he to *J* 2Chr 21:3   3088
Now when *J* was risen up to the 2Chr 21:4   3088

J was thirty and two years old 2Chr 21:5   3088
Then *J* went forth with his...................... 2Chr 21:9   3088
the LORD stirred up against *J* the 2Chr 21:16   3088
son of *J* king of Judah reigned 2Chr 22:1   3088
Azariah the son of *J* king of 2Chr 22:6   3088
the daughter of king *J*, the wife 2Chr 22:11   3088
    2. A son of Ahab.
J reigned in his stead in the................... 2Kin 1:17   3088
Now *J* the son of Ahab began to............. 2Kin 3:1   3088
king *J* went out of Samaria the 2Kin 3:6   3088
smote *J* between his arms, and the 2Kin 9:24   3088
went with *J* the son of Ahab king 2Chr 22:5   3088
see *J* the son of Ahab at Jezreel 2Chr 22:6   3088
he went out with *J* against Jehu 2Chr 22:7   3088
    3. A priest.
and with them Elishama and *J* 2Chr 17:8   3088

JEHOSHABEATH *(je-ho-shab'-e-ath)* See JEHOSHEBA.
    A daughter of King Jehoram.
But *J*, the daughter of the king,.............. 2Chr 22:11   3090
So *J*, the daughter of king 2Chr 22:11   3090

JEHOSHAPHAT *(je-hosh'-a-fat)* See JOSAPHAT,
    JOSHAPHAT.
    1. David's recorder.
J the son of Ahilud was recorder............. 2Sa 8:16   3092
J the son of Ahilud was recorder............. 2Sa 20:24   3092
J the son of Ahilud, the recorder 1Kin 4:3   3092
J the son of Ahilud, recorder 1Chr 18:15   3092
    2. An officer of Solomon.
J the son of Paruah, in Issachar 1Kin 4:17   3092
    3. A king of Judah.
J his son reigned in his stead................. 1Kin 15:24   3092
that *J* the king of Judah came................ 1Kin 22:2   3092
And he said unto *J*, Wilt thou go............ 1Kin 22:4   3092
J said to the king of Israel, I 1Kin 22:4   3092
J said unto the king of Israel,................. 1Kin 22:5   3092
J said, Is there not here a 1Kin 22:7   3092
And the king of Israel said unto *J* 1Kin 22:8   3092
J said, Let not the king say so................ 1Kin 22:8   3092
J the king of Judah sat each on 1Kin 22:10   3092
And the king of Israel said unto *J* 1Kin 22:18   3092
J the king of Judah went up to 1Kin 22:29   3092
And the king of Israel said unto *J* 1Kin 22:30   3092
captains of the chariots saw *J*................ 1Kin 22:32   3092
and *J* cried out....................................... 1Kin 22:32   3092
J the son of Asa began to reign 1Kin 22:41   3092
J was thirty and five years old 1Kin 22:42   3092
J made peace with the king of 1Kin 22:44   3092
Now the rest of the acts of *J*................... 1Kin 22:45   3092
J made ships of Tharshish to go 1Kin 22:48   3092
Ahaziah the son of Ahab unto *J* 1Kin 22:49   3092
But *J* would not....................................... 1Kin 22:49   3092
J slept with his fathers, and was 1Kin 22:50   3092
year of *J* king of Judah, and 1Kin 22:51   3092
the son of *J* king of Judah...................... 2Kin 1:17   3092
year of *J* king of Judah, and 2Kin 3:1   3092
sent to *J* the king of Judah,.................... 2Kin 3:7   3092
But *J* said, Is there not here a 2Kin 3:11   3092
J said, The word of the LORD is 2Kin 3:12   3092
So the king of Israel and *J* 2Kin 3:12   3092
presence of *J* the king of Judah 2Kin 3:14   3092
J being then king of Judah,.................... 2Kin 8:16   3092
Jehoram the son of *J* king of 2Kin 8:16   3092
all the hallowed things that *J*................. 2Kin 12:18   3092
his son, Asa his son, *J* his son,.............. 1Chr 3:10   3092
J his son reigned in his stead,................ 2Chr 17:1   3092
And the LORD was with *J*, because.......... 2Chr 17:3   3092
all Judah brought to *J* presents 2Chr 17:5   3092
that they made no war against *J* 2Chr 17:10   3092
Philistines brought *J* presents 2Chr 17:11   3092
J waxed great exceedingly 2Chr 17:12   3092
Now *J* had riches and honour in 2Chr 18:1   3092
Israel said unto *J* king of Judah............. 2Chr 18:3   3092
J said unto the king of Israel,................. 2Chr 18:4   3092
But *J* said, Is there not here a 2Chr 18:6   3092
And the king of Israel said unto *J* 2Chr 18:7   3092
J said, Let not the king say so................ 2Chr 18:7   3092
J king of Judah sat either of 2Chr 18:9   3092
And the king of Israel said to *J*.............. 2Chr 18:17   3092
J the king of Judah went up to 2Chr 18:28   3092
And the king of Israel said unto *J* 2Chr 18:29   3092
captains of the chariots saw *J*................ 2Chr 18:31   3092
but *J* cried out, and the LORD................. 2Chr 18:31   3092
J the king of Judah returned to 2Chr 19:1   3092
to meet him, and said to king *J*.............. 2Chr 19:2   3092
And *J* dwelt at Jerusalem 2Chr 19:4   3092
did *J* set of the Levites, and of............... 2Chr 19:8   3092
came against *J* to battle 2Chr 20:1   3092
Then there came some that told *J* 2Chr 20:2   3092
J feared, and set himself to seek 2Chr 20:3   3092
J stood in the congregation of 2Chr 20:5   3092

J

of Jerusalem, and thou king *J* 2Chr 20:15 3092
J bowed his head with his face to 2Chr 20:18 3092
J stood and said, Hear me, O Judah....... 2Chr 20:20 3092
And when *J* and his people came to 2Chr 20:25 3092
J in the forefront of them, to go............ 2Chr 20:27 3092
So the realm of *J* was quiet..................... 2Chr 20:30 3092
And *J* reigned over Judah...................... 2Chr 20:31 3092
Now the rest of the acts of *J*................... 2Chr 20:34 3092
after this did *J* king of Judah 2Chr 20:35 3092
of Mareshah prophesied against *J* 2Chr 20:37 3092
Now *J* slept with his fathers, and 2Chr 21:1 3092
And he had brethren the sons of *J*.......... 2Chr 21:2 3092
were the sons of *J* king of Israel 2Chr 21:2 3092
in the ways of *J* thy father 2Chr 21:12 3092
said they, he is the son of *J* 2Chr 22:9 3092
   4. Father of Jehu.
the son of *J* the son of Nimshi................ 2Kin 9:2 3092
So Jehu the son of *J* the son of............. 2Kin 9:14 3092
   5. A priest.
And Shebaniah, and *J*, and Nethaneel, .. 1Chr 15:24 3046
   6. A valley near Jerusalem.
them down into the valley of *J* .... Joel 3:2 3092
and come up to the valley of *J* .... Joel 3:12 3092

JEHOSHEBA *(je-hosh'-e-bah)* See JEHOSHABEATH. *Same as Jehoshabeath.*
But *J*, the daughter of king Joram........... 2Kin 11:2 3089

JEHOSHUA *(je-hosh'-u-ah)* See JEHOSHUAH, JOSHUA. *Same as Joshua, son of Nun.*
called Oshea the son of Nun *J* .... Num 13:16 3091

JEHOSHUAH *(je-hosh'-u-ah)* Same as Joshua, son of Nun.
Non his son, *J* his son 1Chr 7:27 3091

JEHOVAH *(je-ho'-vah)* See GOD, JAH, JEHOVAH-JIREH, JEHOVAH-NISSI, JEHOVAH-SHALOM, LORD. *A name for God.*
but by my name *J* was I not known........ Ex 6:3 3068
that thou, whose name alone is *J*............ Ps 83:18 3068
for the LORD *J* is my strength and .... Is 12:2 3068
for in the LORD *J* is everlasting................ Is 26:4 3068

JEHOVAH-JIREH *(je-ho'-vah-ji'-reh)* Mt. Moriah.
called the name of that place *J*............... Gen 22:14 3070

JEHOVAH-NISSI *(je-ho'-vah-nis'-si)* An altar built by Moses.
altar, and called the name of it *J* .... Ex 17:15 3071

JEHOVAH-SHALOM *(je-ho'-vah-sha'-lom)* An altar built by Gideon.
unto the LORD, and called it *J* .... Judg 6:24 3073

JEHOZABAD *(je-hoz'-a-bad)* See JOZABAD.
   1. Son of Shomer.
J the son of Shomer, his servants 2Kin 12:21 3075
J the son of Shimrith a Moabitess 2Chr 24:26 3075
   2. A son of Obed-edom.
J the second, Joah the third, and 1Chr 26:4 3075
   3. A general of Jehoshaphat.
And next him was *J*, and with him an 2Chr 17:18 3075

JEHOZADAK *(je-hoz'-a-dak)* Great-grandson of Hilkiah.
begat Seraiah, and Seraiah begat *J*........ 1Chr 6:14 3087
J went into captivity, when the.............. 1Chr 6:15 3087

JEHU *(je-hu)*
   1. A son of Hanani.
to *J* the son of Hanani against 1Kin 16:1 3058
J the son of Hanani came the word 1Kin 16:7 3058
against Baasha by *J* the prophet 1Kin 16:12 3058
J the son of Hanani the seer went 2Chr 19:2 3058
the book of *J* the son of Hanani 2Chr 20:34 3058
   2. A king of Israel.
J the son of Nimshi shalt thou 1Kin 19:16 3058
the sword of Hazael shall *J* slay 1Kin 19:17 3058
the sword of *J* shall Elisha slay 1Kin 19:17 3058
look out there *J* the son of 2Kin 9:2 3058
J said, Unto which of all us 2Kin 9:5 3058
Then *J* came forth to the servants 2Kin 9:11 3058
with trumpets, saying, *J* is king 2Kin 9:13 3058
So *J* the son of Jehoshaphat the 2Kin 9:14 3058
J said, If it be your minds, then............ 2Kin 9:15 3058
So *J* rode in a chariot, and went 2Kin 9:16 3058
spied the company of *J* as he came 2Kin 9:17 3058
J said, What hast thou to do with......... 2Kin 9:18 3058
J answered, What hast thou to do 2Kin 9:19 3058
driving of *J* the son of Nimshi.............. 2Kin 9:20 3058
and they went out against *J* 2Kin 9:21 3058
it came to pass, when Joram saw *J* 2Kin 9:22 3058
that he said, Is it peace, *J*.................... 2Kin 9:22 3058
J drew a bow with his full 2Kin 9:24 3058
Then said *J* to Bidkar his captain 2Kin 9:25 3058
J followed after him, and said,.............. 2Kin 9:27 3058

when *J* was come to Jezreel, ... 2Kin 9:30 3058
as *J* entered in at the gate, she 2Kin 9:31 3058
J wrote letters, and sent to 2Kin 10:1 3058
up of the children, sent to *J* 2Kin 10:5 3058
So *J* slew all that remained of................ 2Kin 10:11 3058
J met with the brethren of 2Kin 10:13 3058
J gathered all the people 2Kin 10:18 3058
but *J* shall serve him much 2Kin 10:18 3058
But *J* did it in subtilty, to the 2Kin 10:19 3058
J said, Proclaim a solemn 2Kin 10:20 3058
J sent through all Israel 2Kin 10:21 3058
J went, and Jehonadab the son of 2Kin 10:23 3058
J appointed fourscore men without 2Kin 10:24 3058
that *J* said to the guard and to 2Kin 10:25 3058
Thus *J* destroyed Baal out of 2Kin 10:28 3058
J departed not from after them,............. 2Kin 10:29 3058
And the LORD said unto *J*, Because......... 2Kin 10:30 3058
But *J* took no heed to walk in the 2Kin 10:31 3058
Now the rest of the acts of *J*.................. 2Kin 10:34 3058
And *J* slept with his fathers 2Kin 10:35 3058
the time that *J* reigned over 2Kin 10:36 3058
year of *J* Jehoash began to reign 2Kin 12:1 3058
of Judah Jehoahaz the son of *J* 2Kin 13:1 3058
the son of Jehoahaz son of *J* 2Kin 14:8 3058
of the LORD which he spake unto *J* 2Kin 15:12 3058
against *J* the son of Nimshi 2Chr 22:7 3058
when *J* was executing judgment 2Chr 22:8 3058
in Samaria,) and brought him to *J* 2Chr 22:9 3058
the son of Jehoahaz, the son of *J* 2Chr 25:17 3058
of Jezreel upon the house of *J* .... Hos 1:4 3058
   3. A son of Obed.
begat Jehu, and *J* begat Azariah,........... 1Chr 2:38 3058
   4. A son of Josibiah.
J the son of Josibiah, the son of 1Chr 4:35 3058
   5. A warrior in David's army.
and Berachah, and *J* the Antothite, ... 1Chr 12:3 3058

JEHUBBAH *(je-hub'-bah)* A descendant of Shamer.
Ahi, and Rohgah, *J*, and Aram............... 1Chr 7:34 3160

JEHUCAL *(je-hu'-kal)* See JUCAL. A son of Shelemiah.
king sent *J* the son of Shelemiah .... Jer 37:3 3081

JEHUD *(je'-hud)* A city in Dan.
And *J*, and Bene-berak, and.................... Josh 19:45 3055

JEHUDI *(je-hu'-di)* Son of Nethaniah.
sent *J* the son of Nethaniah .... Jer 36:14 3065
So the king sent *J* to fetch the................ Jer 36:21 3065
J read it in the ears of the king.............. Jer 36:21 3065
that when *J* had read three or .... Jer 36:23 3065

JEHUDIJAH *(je-hu-di'-jah)* See HODIAH. A descendant of Judah.
his wife *J* bare Jered the father.............. 1Chr 4:18 3057

JEHUSH *(je'-hush)* See JEUSH. A descendant of King Saul.
J the second, and Eliphelet the 1Chr 8:39 3266

JEIEL *(je-i'-el)* See JEHIEL, JEUEL.
   1. A chief Reubenite.
was reckoned, were the chief, *J*.............. 1Chr 5:7 3273
   2. A Levite gatekeeper.
and Mikneiah, and Obed-edom, and *J* ... 1Chr 15:18 3273
and Mikneiah, and Obed-edom, and *J* ... 1Chr 15:21 3273
and next to him Zechariah, *J*.................. 1Chr 16:5 3273
J with psalteries and with harps............. 1Chr 16:5 3273
   3. A Levite of the Asaph family.
the son of Benaiah, the son of *J* 2Chr 20:14 3273
   4. A scribe.
by the hand of *J* the scribe 2Chr 26:11 3273
   5. A Levite in Hezekiah's time.
Shimri, and *J*: and of the sons 2Chr 29:13 3273
   6. A chief Levite.
his brethren, and Hashabiah and *J* 2Chr 35:9 3273
   7. An exile.
names these, Eliphelet, *J*...................... Ezr 8:13 3273
   8. Married a foreigner in exile.
J, Mattithiah, Zabad, Zebina, ... Ezr 10:43 3273

JEKABZEEL *(je-kab'-ze-el)* See KABZEEL. A city in Judah.
in the villages thereof, and at *J*.............. Neh 11:25 3343

JEKAMEAM *(je-kam'-e-am)* Son of Hebron.
the third, and *J* the fourth 1Chr 23:19 3360
Jahaziel the third, *J* the fourth............... 1Chr 24:23 3360

JEKAMIAH *(jek-a-mi'-ah)* See JECAMIAH. A descendant of Shallum.
And Shallum begat *J* 1Chr 2:41 3359
and *J* begat Elishama 1Chr 2:41 3359

JEKUTHIEL *(je-ku'-the-el)* A descendant of Ezra.
Socho, and *J* the father of Zanoah 1Chr 4:18 3354

JEMIMA *(je-mi'-mah) A daughter of Job.*
called the name of the first, J .... Job 42:14   3224

JEMIMAH See JEMIMA.

JEMUEL *(je-mu'-el)* See NEMUEL. *A son of Simeon.*
J, and Jamin, and Ohad, and Jachin, ... Gen 46:10   3223
J, and Jamin, and Ohad, and Jachin, ... Ex 6:15   3223

JEOPARDED
Naphtali were a people that *j* .... Judg 5:18   2778

JEOPARDY
men that went in *j* of their lives 2Sa 23:17
that have put their lives in *j* 1Chr 11:19
for with the *j* of their lives 1Chr 11:19
master Saul to the *j* of our heads 1Chr 12:19
filled with water, and were in *j* .... Lk 8:23   2793
And why stand we in *j* every hour 1Cor 15:30   2793

JEPHTHAE *(jef-thah-e)* See JEPHTHAH. *Same as Jephthah.*
of Barak, and of Samson, and of J .... Heb 11:32   2422

JEPHTHAH *(jef-thah)* See JEPHTHAE, JIPHTHAH-EL.
A judge.
Now J the Gileadite was a mighty .... Judg 11:1   3316
and Gilead begat J .... Judg 11:1   3316
grew up, and they thrust out J .... Judg 11:2   3316
Then J fled from his brethren, and .... Judg 11:3   3316
there were gathered vain men to J .... Judg 11:3   3316
to fetch J out of the land of Tob .... Judg 11:5   3316
And they said unto J, Come, and be .... Judg 11:6   3316
J said unto the elders of Gilead, ... Judg 11:7   3316
the elders of Gilead said unto J .... Judg 11:8   3316
J said unto the elders of Gilead, ... Judg 11:9   3316
the elders of Gilead said unto J .... Judg 11:10   3316
Then J went with the elders of .... Judg 11:11   3316
J uttered all his words before .... Judg 11:11   3316
J sent messengers unto the king .... Judg 11:12   3316
answered unto the messengers of J .... Judg 11:13   3316
J sent messengers again unto the .... Judg 11:14   3316
And said unto him, Thus saith J .... Judg 11:15   3316
the words of J which he sent him .... Judg 11:28   3316
Spirit of the LORD came upon J .... Judg 11:29   3316
J vowed a vow unto the LORD, and .... Judg 11:30   3316
So J passed over unto the .... Judg 11:32   3316
J came to Mizpeh unto his house, ... Judg 11:34   3316
to lament the daughter of J the .... Judg 11:40   3316
and went northward, and said unto J ..... Judg 12:1   3316
J said unto them, I and my people .... Judg 12:2   3316
Then J gathered together all the .... Judg 12:4   3316
J judged Israel six years .... Judg 12:7   3316
Then died J the Gileadite, and was .... Judg 12:7   3316
sent Jerubbaal, and Bedan, and J 1Sa 12:11   3316

JEPHUNNEH *(je-fun'-neh)*
1. Father of Caleb.
of Judah, Caleb the son of J .... Num 13:6   3312
son of Nun, and Caleb the son of J .... Num 14:6   3312
therein, save Caleb the son of J .... Num 14:30   3312
son of Nun, and Caleb the son of J .... Num 14:38   3312
of them, save Caleb the son of J .... Num 26:65   3312
Caleb the son of J the Kenezite .... Num 32:12   3312
of Judah, Caleb the son of J .... Num 34:19   3312
Save Caleb the son of J .... Deut 1:36   3312
Caleb the son of J the Kenezite .... Josh 14:6   3312
of J Hebron for an inheritance .... Josh 14:13   3312
of J the Kenezite unto this day .... Josh 14:14   3312
unto Caleb the son of J he gave a .... Josh 15:13   3312
the son of J for his possession .... Josh 21:12   3312
And the sons of Caleb the son of J 1Chr 4:15   3312
they gave to Caleb the son of J 1Chr 6:56   3312
2. Head of an Asherite family.
J, and Pispah, and Ara 1Chr 7:38   3312

JERAH *(je'-rah) A son of Joktan.*
and Sheleph, and Hazarmaveth, and J .. Gen 10:26   3392
and Sheleph, and Hazarmaveth, and J .. 1Chr 1:20   3392

JERAHMEEL *(je-rah'-me-el)* See JERAHMEELITES.
1. A son of Hezron.
J, and Ram, and Chelubai 1Chr 2:9   3396
the sons of J the firstborn of 1Chr 2:25   3396
J had also another wife, whose 1Chr 2:26   3396
of Ram the firstborn of J were 1Chr 2:27   3396
These were the sons of J 1Chr 2:33   3396
of Caleb the brother of J were 1Chr 2:42   3396
2. A son of Kish.
the son of Kish was J 1Chr 24:29   3396
3. An officer of Jehoiakim.
commanded J the son of Hammelech ..... Jer 36:26   3396

JERAHMEELITES *(je-rah'-me-el-ites) Descendants of Jerahmeel.*
and against the south of the J 1Sa 27:10   3397
which were in the cities of the J 1Sa 30:29   3397

JERED *(je'-red)* See JARED.
1. A descendant of Seth.
Kenan, Mahalaleel, J, ... 1Chr 1:2   3382
2. A descendant of Ezra.
bare J the father of Gedor 1Chr 4:18   3382

JEREMAI *(jer'-e-mahee) Married a foreigner in exile.*
Mattathah, Zabad, Eliphelet, J .... Ezr 10:33   3413

JEREMIAH *(jer-e-mi'-ah)* See JEREMIAH'S, JEREMIAS, JEREMY.
1. Father of Hamutal.
the daughter of J of Libnah 2Kin 23:31   3414
the daughter of J of Libnah 2Kin 24:18   3414
the daughter of J of Libnah .... Jer 52:1   3414
2. Head of a Manassite family.
Ishi, and Eliel, and Azriel, and J 1Chr 5:24   3414
3. A warrior in David's army.
and J, and Jahaziel, and Johanan, and .. 1Chr 12:4   3414
4. A Gadite warrior.
the fourth, J the fifth, ... 1Chr 12:10   3414
5. Another Gadite warrior.
J the tenth, Machbanai the 1Chr 12:13   3414
6. A prophet.
And J lamented for Josiah 2Chr 35:25   3414
humbled not himself before J the 2Chr 36:12   3414
of the LORD by the mouth of J 2Chr 36:21   3414
mouth of J might be accomplished 2Chr 36:22   3414
the mouth of J might be fulfilled............. Ezr 1:1   3414
The words of J the son of Hilkiah .... Jer 1:1   3414
the LORD came unto me, saying, J .... Jer 1:11   3414
word that came to J from the LORD .... Jer 7:1   3414
word that came to J from the LORD .... Jer 11:1   3414
came to J concerning the dearth .... Jer 14:1   3414
which came to J from the LORD............... Jer 18:1   3414
let us devise devices against J .... Jer 18:18   3414
Then came J from Tophet, whither.......... Jer 19:14   3414
heard that J prophesied these................. Jer 20:1   3414
Then Pashur smote J the prophet .... Jer 20:2   3414
brought forth J out of the stocks............ Jer 20:3   3414
Then said J unto him, The LORD .... Jer 20:3   3414
which came unto J from the LORD .... Jer 21:1   3414
Then said J unto them, Thus shall .... Jer 21:3   3414
LORD unto me, What seest thou, J .... Jer 24:3   3414
The word that came to J .... Jer 25:1   3414
The which J the prophet spake .... Jer 25:2   3414
which J hath prophesied against .... Jer 25:13   3414
all the people when J speaking .... Jer 26:7   3414
when J had made an end of .... Jer 26:8   3414
J in the house of the LORD .... Jer 26:9   3414
Then spake J unto all the princes........... Jer 26:12   3414
according to all the words of J................. Jer 26:20   3414
the son of Shaphan was with J .... Jer 26:24   3414
this word unto J from the LORD.............. Jer 27:1   3414
Then the prophet J said unto the .... Jer 28:5   3414
Even the prophet J said, Amen .... Jer 28:6   3414
the prophet J went his way .... Jer 28:11   3414
the LORD came unto the prophet .... Jer 28:12   3414
off the neck of the prophet J................... Jer 28:12   3414
Then said the prophet J unto .... Jer 28:15   3414
the words of the letter that J .... Jer 29:1   3414
thou not reproved J of Anathoth .... Jer 29:27   3414
in the ears of the prophet .... Jer 29:29   3414
came the word of the LORD unto J .... Jer 29:30   3414
word that came to J from the LORD .... Jer 30:1   3414
The word that came to J from the .... Jer 32:1   3414
J the prophet was shut up in the............ Jer 32:2   3414
J said, The word of the LORD came .... Jer 32:6   3414
came the word of the LORD unto J .... Jer 32:26   3414
LORD came unto J the second time .... Jer 33:1   3414
the word of the LORD came unto J .... Jer 33:19   3414
the word of the LORD came to J.............. Jer 33:23   3414
which came unto J from the LORD .... Jer 34:1   3414
Then J the prophet spake all .... Jer 34:6   3414
that came unto J from the LORD .... Jer 34:8   3414
the LORD came to J from the LORD .... Jer 34:12   3414
The word which came unto J from.......... Jer 35:1   3414
I took Jaazaniah the son of J .... Jer 35:3   3414
came the word of the LORD unto J .... Jer 35:12   3414
J said unto the house of the .... Jer 35:18   3414
word came unto J from the LORD .... Jer 36:1   3414
Then J called Baruch the son of.............. Jer 36:4   3414
of J all the words of the LORD .... Jer 36:4   3414
J commanded Baruch, saying, I am .... Jer 36:5   3414
that J the prophet commanded him .... Jer 36:8   3414
of J in the house of the LORD .... Jer 36:10   3414
Baruch, Go, hide thee, thou and J.......... Jer 36:19   3414

the scribe and J the prophet	Jer 36:26	3414
the word of the LORD came to J	Jer 36:27	3414
Baruch wrote at the mouth of J	Jer 36:27	3414
Then took J another roll, and gave	Jer 36:32	3414
J all the words of the book which	Jer 36:32	3414
which he spake by the prophet J	Jer 37:2	3414
the priest to the prophet J	Jer 37:3	3414
Now J came in and went out among	Jer 37:4	3414
of the LORD unto the prophet J	Jer 37:6	3414
Then J went forth out of	Jer 37:12	3414
he took J the prophet, saying,	Jer 37:13	3414
Then said J, It is false	Jer 37:14	3414
so Irijah took J, and brought him	Jer 37:14	3414
the princes were wroth with J	Jer 37:15	3414
When J was entered into the	Jer 37:16	3414
J had remained there many days	Jer 37:16	3414
And J said, There is	Jer 37:17	3414
Moreover J said unto king	Jer 37:18	3414
that they should commit J into	Jer 37:21	3414
Thus J remained in the court of	Jer 37:21	3414
heard the words that J had spoken	Jer 38:1	3414
Then took they J, and cast him	Jer 38:6	3414
and they let down J with cords	Jer 38:6	3414
so J sunk in the mire	Jer 38:6	3414
they had put J in the dungeon	Jer 38:7	3414
they have done to J the prophet	Jer 38:9	3414
take up J the prophet out of the	Jer 38:10	3414
by cords into the dungeon to J	Jer 38:11	3414
the Ethiopian said unto J	Jer 38:12	3414
And J did so	Jer 38:12	3414
So they drew up J with cords	Jer 38:13	3414
J remained in the court of the	Jer 38:13	3414
took J the prophet unto him into	Jer 38:14	3414
and the king said unto J, I will	Jer 38:14	3414
Then J said unto Zedekiah, If I	Jer 38:15	3414
the king sware secretly unto J	Jer 38:16	3414
Then said J unto Zedekiah, Thus	Jer 38:17	3414
And Zedekiah the king said unto J	Jer 38:19	3414
But J said, They shall not	Jer 38:20	3414
Then said Zedekiah unto J	Jer 38:24	3414
Then came all the princes unto J	Jer 38:27	3414
So J abode in the court of the	Jer 38:28	3414
J to Nebuzar-adan the captain of	Jer 39:11	3414
took J out of the court of the	Jer 39:14	3414
the word of the LORD came unto J	Jer 39:15	3414
word that came to J from the LORD	Jer 40:1	3414
the captain of the guard took J	Jer 40:2	3414
Then went J unto Gedaliah the son	Jer 40:6	3414
said unto J the prophet, Let, we	Jer 42:2	3414
Then J the prophet said unto them	Jer 42:4	3414
Then they said to J, The LORD be	Jer 42:5	3414
the word of the LORD came unto J	Jer 42:7	3414
that when J had made an end of	Jer 43:1	3414
all the proud men, saying unto J	Jer 43:2	3414
J the prophet, and Baruch the son	Jer 43:6	3414
of the LORD unto J in Tahpanhes	Jer 43:8	3414
The word that came to J	Jer 44:1	3414
of Egypt, in Pathros, answered J	Jer 44:15	3414
Then J said unto all the people,	Jer 44:20	3414
Moreover J said unto all the	Jer 44:24	3414
The word that J the prophet spake	Jer 45:1	3414
words in a book at the mouth of J	Jer 45:1	3414
came to J the prophet against the	Jer 46:1	3414
the LORD spake to J the prophet	Jer 46:13	3414
came to J the prophet against the	Jer 47:1	3414
word of the LORD that came to J	Jer 49:34	3414
of the Chaldeans by J the prophet	Jer 50:1	3414
The word which J the prophet	Jer 51:59	3414
So J wrote in a book all the evil	Jer 51:60	3414
J said to Seraiah, When thou	Jer 51:61	3414
Thus far are the words of J	Jer 51:64	3414
of the LORD came to J the prophet	Dan 9:2	3414
7. A priest.		
Seraiah, Azariah, J,	Neh 10:2	3414
Seraiah, J, Ezra,	Neh 12:1	3414
of J, Hananiah	Neh 12:12	3414
and Benjamin, and Shemaiah, and J	Neh 12:34	3414

JEREMIAH'S (jer-e-mi'-ahz) Refers to Jeremiah 6.

yoke from off the prophet J neck	Jer 28:10	3414

JEREMIAS (jer-e-mi'-as) See JEREMIAH. Greek form of Jeremiah.

and others, J, or one of the	Mt 16:14	2408

JEREMOTH (jer'-e-moth) See JERIMOTH.

1. A son of Beriah.

And Ahio, Shashak, and J,	1Chr 8:14	3406

2. A son of Elam.

and Jehiel, and Abdi, and J	Ezr 10:26	3406

3. Another who married a foreigner in exile.

Eliashib, Mattaniah, and J	Ezr 10:27	3406

4. A son of Mushi.

Mahli, and Eder, and J, three	1Chr 23:23	3406

5. A sanctuary servant.

The fifteenth to J, he, his sons,	1Chr 25:22	3406

JEREMY (jer'-e-mee) See JEREMIAH. Latin form of Jeremiah.

which was spoken by J the prophet	Mt 2:17	2408
which was spoken by J the prophet	Mt 27:9	2408

JERIAH (je-ri'-ah) See JERIJAH. A descendant of Hebron.

J the first, Amariah the second,	1Chr 23:19	3404
J the first, Amariah the second,	1Chr 24:23	3404

JERIBAI (jer'-ib-ahee) A "mighty man" of David.

Eliel the Mahavite, and J, and	1Chr 11:46	3403

JERICHO (jer'-ik-o) A city in Benjamin.

of Moab on this side Jordan by J	Num 22:1	3405
plains of Moab by Jordan near J	Num 26:3	3405
plains of Moab by Jordan near J	Num 26:63	3405
Moab, which are by Jordan near J	Num 31:12	3405
plains of Moab by Jordan near J	Num 33:48	3405
plains of Moab by Jordan, near J	Num 33:50	3405
this side Jordan near J eastward	Num 34:15	3405
plains of Moab by Jordan near J	Num 35:1	3405
plains of Moab by Jordan near J	Num 36:13	3405
of Moab, that is over against J	Deut 32:49	3405
of Pisgah, that is over against J	Deut 34:1	3405
and the plain of the valley of J	Deut 34:3	3405
saying, Go view the land, even J	Josh 2:1	3405
And it was told the king of J	Josh 2:2	3405
the king of J sent unto Rahab	Josh 2:3	3405
passed over right against J	Josh 3:16	3405
unto battle, to the plains of J	Josh 4:13	3405
Gilgal, in the east border of J	Josh 4:19	3405
month at even in the plains of J	Josh 5:10	3405
to pass, when Joshua was by J	Josh 5:13	3405
Now J was straitly shut up	Josh 6:1	3405
I have given into thine hand J	Josh 6:2	3405
which Joshua sent to spy out J	Josh 6:25	3405
riseth up and buildeth this city J	Josh 6:26	3405
And Joshua sent men from J to Ai	Josh 7:2	3405
and her king as thou didst unto J	Josh 8:2	3405
heard what Joshua had done unto J	Josh 9:3	3405
as he had done to J and her king,	Josh 10:1	3405
as he did unto the king of J	Josh 10:28	3405
as he did unto the king of J	Josh 10:30	3405
The king of J, one	Josh 12:9	3405
on the other side Jordan, by J	Josh 13:32	3405
of Joseph fell from Jordan by J	Josh 16:1	3405
unto the water of J on the east	Josh 16:1	3405
from J throughout mount Beth-el	Josh 16:1	3405
and to Naarath, and came to J	Josh 16:7	3405
the side of J on the north side	Josh 18:12	3405
to their families were J, and	Josh 18:21	3405
other side Jordan by J eastward	Josh 20:8	3405
went over Jordan, and came unto J	Josh 24:11	3405
the men of J fought against you,	Josh 24:11	3405
Tarry at J until your beards be	2Sa 10:5	3405
did Hiel the Beth-elite build J	1Kin 16:34	3405
for the LORD hath sent me to J	2Kin 2:4	3405
So they came to J	2Kin 2:4	3405
that were at J came to Elisha	2Kin 2:5	3405
which were to view at J saw him	2Kin 2:15	3405
to him, (for he tarried at J	2Kin 2:18	3405
overtook him in the plains of J	2Kin 25:5	3405
And on the other side Jordan by J	1Chr 6:78	3405
Tarry at J until your beards be	1Chr 19:5	3405
upon asses, and brought them to J	2Chr 28:15	3405
The children of J, three hundred	Ezr 2:34	3405
unto him builded the men of J	Neh 3:2	3405
The children of J, three hundred	Neh 7:36	3405
Zedekiah in the plains of J	Jer 39:5	3405
Zedekiah in the plains of J	Jer 52:8	3405
And as they departed from J	Mt 20:29	2410
And they came to J	Mk 10:46	2410
as he went out of J with his	Mk 10:46	2410
man went down from Jerusalem to J	Lk 10:30	2410
that as he was come nigh unto J	Lk 18:35	2410
Jesus entered and passed through J	Lk 19:1	2410
By faith the walls of J fell down	Heb 11:30	2410

JERIEL (je-ri'-el) A son of Tola.

Uzzi, and Rephaiah, and J, and	1Chr 7:2	3400

JERIJAH (je-ri'-jah) Same as Jeriah.

the Hebronites was J the chief	1Chr 26:31	3404

JERIMOTH (jer'-im-oth) See JERIMOTH.

1. A son of Bela.

Ezbon, and Uzzi, and Uzziel, and J	1Chr 7:7	3406

2. A son of Becher.

and Elioenai, and Omri, and J	1Chr 7:8	3406

3. A warrior in David's army.
Eluzai, and J, and Bealiah, and 1Chr 12:5   3406
   4. A son of Mushi.
Mahli, and Eder, and J.............................1Chr 24:30   3406
   5. A sanctuary servant.
Mattaniah, Uzziel, Shebuel, and J..........1Chr 25:4   3406
   6. A Naphtalite ruler.
of Naphtali, J the son of Azriel................1Chr 27:19   3406
   7. A son of David.
of J the son of David to wife 2Chr 11:18   3406
   8. A Temple servant.
and Nahath, and Asahel, and J 2Chr 31:13   3406

JERIOTH *(je'-re-oth) A wife of Caleb.*
of Azubah his wife, and of J....................1Chr 2:18   3408

JEROBOAM *(jer-o-bo'-am)* See Jeroboam's.
   1. A king of Israel.
J the son of Nebat, an Ephrathite 1Kin 11:26   3379
the man J was a mighty man of 1Kin 11:28   3379
time when J went out of Jerusalem 1Kin 11:29   3379
And he said to J, Take thee ten 1Kin 11:31   3379
sought therefore to kill J 1Kin 11:40   3379
J arose, and fled into Egypt, unto...........1Kin 11:40   3379
when J the son of Nebat, who was 1Kin 12:2   3379
king Solomon, and J dwelt in Egypt 1Kin 12:2   3379
And J and all the congregation of...........1Kin 12:3   3379
So J and all the people came to 1Kin 12:12   3379
Shilonite unto J the son of Nebat............1Kin 12:15   3379
heard that J was come again 1Kin 12:20   3379
Then J built Shechem in mount 1Kin 12:25   3379
J said in his heart, Now shall...................1Kin 12:26   3379
J ordained a feast in the eighth 1Kin 12:32   3379
J stood by the altar to burn.......................1Kin 13:1   3379
when king J heard the saying of 1Kin 13:4   3379
After this thing J returned not 1Kin 13:33   3379
became sin unto the house of J..............1Kin 13:34   3379
Abijah the son of J fell sick......................1Kin 14:1   3379
J said to his wife, Arise, I pray...............1Kin 14:2   3379
be not known to be the wife of J 1Kin 14:2   3379
the wife of J cometh to ask a 1Kin 14:5   3379
he said, Come in, thou wife of J 1Kin 14:6   3379
Go, tell J, Thus saith the Lord...............1Kin 14:7   3379
bring evil upon the house of J 1Kin 14:10   3379
will cut off from J him that.......................1Kin 14:10   3379
the remnant of the house of J 1Kin 14:10   3379
Him that dieth of J in the city 1Kin 14:11   3379
for he only of J shall come to..................1Kin 14:13   3379
God of Israel in the house of J 1Kin 14:13   3379
cut off the house of J that day 1Kin 14:14   3379
up because of the sins of J 1Kin 14:16   3379
And the rest of the acts of J 1Kin 14:19   3379
the days which J reigned were two 1Kin 14:20   3379
Rehoboam and J all their days 1Kin 14:30   3379
in the eighteenth year of king J 1Kin 15:1   3379
J all the days of his life 1Kin 15:6   3379
there was war between Abijam and J.....1Kin 15:7   3379
in the twentieth year of J king 1Kin 15:9   3379
Nadab the son of J began to reign 1Kin 15:25   3379
that he smote all the house of J 1Kin 15:29   3379
he left not to J any that 1Kin 15:29   3379
of the sins of J which he sinned 1Kin 15:30   3379
Lord, and walked in the way of J 1Kin 15:34   3379
thou hast walked in the way of J 1Kin 16:2   3379
the house of J the son of Nebat 1Kin 16:3   3379
in being like the house of J.....................1Kin 16:7   3379
Lord, in walking in the way of J 1Kin 16:19   3379
all the way of J the son of Nebat 1Kin 16:26   3379
in the sins of J the son of Nebat.............1Kin 16:31   3379
the house of J the son of Nebat 1Kin 21:22   3379
in the way of J the son of Nebat, ...1Kin 22:52   3379
the sins of J the son of Nebat 2Kin 3:3   3379
the house of J the son of Nebat 2Kin 9:9   3379
the sins of J the son of Nebat 2Kin 10:29   3379
departed not from the sins of J 2Kin 10:31   3379
the sins of J the son of Nebat 2Kin 13:2   3379
from the sins of the house of J 2Kin 13:6   3379
the sins of J the son of Nebat 2Kin 13:11   3379
the sins of J the son of Nebat 2Kin 14:24   3379
the sins of J the son of Nebat 2Kin 15:9   3379
the sins of J the son of Nebat 2Kin 15:18   3379
the sins of J the son of Nebat 2Kin 15:24   3379
the sins of J the son of Nebat 2Kin 15:28   3379
they made J the son of Nebat king 2Kin 17:21   3379
J drave Israel from following the 2Kin 17:21   3379
in all the sins of J which he did 2Kin 17:22   3379
place which J the son of Nebat 2Chr 23:15   3379
seer against J the son of Nebat 2Chr 9:29   3379
when J the son of Nebat, who was.........2Chr 10:2   3379
that J returned out of Egypt 2Chr 10:2   3379
So J and all Israel came and spake 2Chr 10:3   3379
So J and all the people came to 2Chr 10:12   3379

Shilonite to J the son of Nebat 2Chr 10:15   3379
and returned from going against J.........2Chr 11:4   3379
for J and his sons had cast them 2Chr 11:14   3379
between Rehoboam and J continually ...2Chr 12:15   3379
king J began Abijah to reign over 2Chr 13:1   3379
there was war between Abijah and J.....2Chr 13:2   3379
J also set the battle in array 2Chr 13:3   3379
Ephraim, and said, Hear me, thou J 2Chr 13:4   3379
Yet J the son of Nebat, the......................2Chr 13:6   3379
which J made you for gods....................2Chr 13:8   3379
But J caused an ambushment to 2Chr 13:13   3379
it came to pass, that God smote J 2Chr 13:15   3379
And Abijah pursued after J.....................2Chr 13:19   3379
Neither did J recover strength 2Chr 13:20   3379
   2. Another king of Israel, son of Jehoash.
and J sat upon his throne.......................2Kin 13:13   3379
J his son reigned in his stead.................2Kin 14:16   3379
the son of Joash king of Judah J............2Kin 14:23   3379
by the hand of J the son of Joash 2Kin 14:27   3379
Now the rest of the acts of J..................2Kin 14:28   3379
J slept with his fathers, even 2Kin 14:29   3379
seventh year of J king of Israel 2Kin 15:1   3379
of J reign over Israel in Samaria 2Kin 15:8   3379
in the days of J king of Israel 1Chr 5:17   3379
in the days of J the son of Joash ....Hos 1:1   3379
in the days of J the son of Joash ....Amos 1:1   3379
the house of J with the sword ....Amos 7:9   3379
Beth-el sent to J king of Israel ....Amos 7:10   3379
J shall die by the sword, and ....Amos 7:11   3379

JEROBOAM'S *(jer-o-bo'-ams) Refers to Jeroboam 1.*
J wife did so, and arose, and went 1Kin 14:4   3379
J wife arose, and departed, and.............1Kin 14:17   3379

JEROHAM *(je-ro'-ham)*
   1. Grandfather of Samuel.
name was Elkanah, the son of J 1Sa 1:1   3395
J his son, Elkanah his son 1Chr 6:27   3395
The son of Elkanah, the son of J............1Chr 6:34   3395
   2. Head of a Benjamite family.
Eliah, and Zichri, the sons of J...............1Chr 8:27   3395
   3. A descendant of Benjamin.
And Ibneiah the son of J, and Elah........1Chr 9:8   3395
   4. A family of exiles.
And Adaiah the son of J, the son 1Chr 9:12   3395
and Adaiah the son of J, the son ....Neh 11:12   3395
   5. A warrior in David's army.
Zebadiah, the sons of J of Gedor 1Chr 12:7   3395
   6. Father of Azareel.
Of Dan, Azareel the son of J 1Chr 27:22   3395
   7. Father of Azariah.
of hundreds, Azariah the son of J...........2Chr 23:1   3395

JERUBBAAL *(je-rub'-ba-al)* See Gideon, Jerubbesheth.
   Another name for Gideon.
on that day he called him J ....Judg 6:32   3378
Then J, who is Gideon, and all the ....Judg 7:1   3378
J the son of Joash went and dwelt ....Judg 8:29   3378
they kindness to the house of J ....Judg 8:35   3378
Abimelech the son of J went to...............Judg 9:1   3378
either that all the sons of J ....Judg 9:2   3378
slew his brethren the sons of J ....Judg 9:5   3378
the youngest son of J was left ....Judg 9:5   3378
and if ye have dealt well with J...............Judg 9:16   3378
dealt truly and sincerely with J...............Judg 9:19   3378
and ten sons of J might come ....Judg 9:24   3378
is not he the son of J ....Judg 9:28   3378
the curse of Jotham the son of J ....Judg 9:57   3378
And the Lord sent J, and Bedan, and.....1Sa 12:11   3378

JERUBBESHETH *(je-rub'-be-sheth)* See Jerubbaal.
   Another name for Gideon.
Who smote Abimelech the son of J.........2Sa 11:21   3380

JERUEL *(je-ru'-el) A wilderness in Judah.*
brook, before the wilderness of J............2Chr 20:16   3385

JERUSALEM *(je-ru'-sa-lem)* See Jerusalem's, Salem.
   City where the Temple was located.
when Adoni-zedek king of J had ....Josh 10:1   3389
Wherefore Adoni-zedek king of J............Josh 10:3   3389
of the Amorites, the king of J ....Josh 10:5   3389
out of the cave, the king of J ....Josh 10:23   3389
The king of J, one ....Josh 12:10   3389
Jebusite; the same is J ....Josh 15:8   3389
Jebusites the inhabitants of J ....Josh 15:63   3389
of Judah at J unto this day.....................Josh 15:63   3389
Eleph, and Jebusi, which is J ....Josh 18:28   3389
And they brought him to J, and ....Judg 1:7   3389
of Judah had fought against J ....Judg 1:8   3389
the Jebusites that inhabited J ....Judg 1:21   3389
of Benjamin in J unto this day ....Judg 1:21   3389
over against Jebus, which is J ....Judg 19:10   3389
Philistine, and brought it to J.................1Sa 17:54   3389

in *J* he reigned thirty and three 2Sa 5:5   3389
his men went to *J* unto the 2Sa 5:6   3389
more concubines and wives out of *J* 2Sa 5:13   3389
that were born unto him in *J* 2Sa 5:14   3389
Hadadezer, and brought them to *J* 2Sa 8:7   3389
So Mephibosheth dwelt in *J* 2Sa 9:13   3389
children of Ammon, and came to *J* 2Sa 10:14   3389
But David tarried still at *J* 2Sa 11:1   3389
So Uriah abode in *J* that day 2Sa 11:12   3389
and all the people returned unto *J* 2Sa 12:31   3389
Geshur, and brought Absalom to *J* 2Sa 14:23   3389
Absalom dwelt two full years in *J* 2Sa 14:28   3389
shall bring me again indeed to *J* 2Sa 15:8   3389
went two hundred men out of *J* 2Sa 15:11   3389
servants that were with him at *J* 2Sa 15:14   3389
carried the ark of God again to *J* 2Sa 15:29   3389
the city, and Absalom came into *J* 2Sa 15:37   3389
the king, Behold, he abideth at *J* 2Sa 16:3   3389
the men of Israel, came to *J* 2Sa 16:15   3389
not find them, they returned to *J* 2Sa 17:20   3389
my lord the king went out of *J* 2Sa 19:19   3389
he was come to *J* to meet the king 2Sa 19:25   3389
and I will feed thee with me in *J* 2Sa 19:33   3389
should go up with the king unto *J* 2Sa 19:34   3389
their king, from Jordan even to *J* 2Sa 20:2   3389
And David came to his house at *J* 2Sa 20:3   3389
and they went out of *J*, to pursue 2Sa 20:7   3389
Joab returned to *J* unto the king 2Sa 20:22   3389
they came to *J* at the end of nine 2Sa 24:8   3389
out his hand unto *J* to destroy it 2Sa 24:16   3389
and three years reigned he in *J* 1Kin 2:11   3389
him, Build thee an house in *J* 1Kin 2:36   3389
And Shimei dwelt in *J* many days 1Kin 2:38   3389
Shimei had gone from *J* to Gath 1Kin 2:41   3389
and the wall of *J* round about 1Kin 3:1   3389
And he came to *J*, and stood before 1Kin 3:15   3389
of Israel, unto king Solomon in *J* 1Kin 8:1   3389
house, and Millo, and the wall of *J* 1Kin 9:15   3389
Solomon desired to build in *J* 1Kin 9:19   3389
she came to *J* with a very great 1Kin 10:2   3389
chariots, and with the king at *J* 1Kin 10:26   3389
made silver to be in *J* as stones 1Kin 10:27   3389
in the hill that is before *J* 1Kin 11:7   3389
time when Jeroboam went out of *J* 1Kin 11:29   3389
have a light alway before me in *J* 1Kin 11:36   3389
time that Solomon reigned in *J* 1Kin 11:42   3389
up to his chariot, to flee to *J* 1Kin 12:18   3389
And when Rehoboam was come to *J* 1Kin 12:21   3389
in the house of the LORD at *J* 1Kin 12:27   3389
is too much for you to go up to *J* 1Kin 12:28   3389
he reigned seventeen years in *J* 1Kin 14:21   3389
king of Egypt came up against *J* 1Kin 14:25   3389
Three years reigned he in *J* 1Kin 15:2   3389
LORD his God give him a lamp in *J* 1Kin 15:4   3389
son after him, and to establish *J* 1Kin 15:4   3389
and one years reigned he in *J* 1Kin 15:10   3389
reigned twenty and five years in *J* 1Kin 22:42   3389
and he reigned eight years in *J* 2Kin 8:17   3389
and he reigned one year in *J* 2Kin 8:26   3389
carried him in a chariot to *J* 2Kin 9:28   3389
and forty years reigned he in *J* 2Kin 12:1   3389
Hazael set his face to go up to *J* 2Kin 12:17   3389
and he went away from *J* 2Kin 12:18   3389
reigned twenty and nine years in *J* 2Kin 14:2   3389
mother's name was Jehoaddan of *J* 2Kin 14:2   3389
at Beth-shemesh, and came to *J* 2Kin 14:13   3389
brake down the wall of *J* from the 2Kin 14:13   3389
a conspiracy against him in *J* 2Kin 14:19   3389
he was buried at *J* with his 2Kin 14:20   3389
reigned two and fifty years in *J* 2Kin 15:2   3389
mother's name was Jecholiah of *J* 2Kin 15:2   3389
and he reigned sixteen years in *J* 2Kin 15:33   3389
and reigned sixteen years in *J* 2Kin 16:2   3389
of Israel came up to *J* to war 2Kin 16:5   3389
reigned twenty and nine years in *J* 2Kin 18:2   3389
with a great host against *J* 2Kin 18:17   3389
And they went up and came to *J* 2Kin 18:17   3389
away, and hath said to Judah and *J* 2Kin 18:22   3389
worship before this altar in *J* 2Kin 18:22   3389
should deliver *J* out of mine hand 2Kin 18:35   3389
J shall not be delivered into the 2Kin 19:10   3389
the daughter of *J* hath shaken her 2Kin 19:21   3389
For out of *J* shall go forth a 2Kin 19:31   3389
reigned fifty and five years in *J* 2Kin 21:1   3389
said, In *J* will I put my name 2Kin 21:4   3389
his son, In this house, and in *J* 2Kin 21:7   3389
I am bringing such evil upon *J* 2Kin 21:12   3389
over *J* the line of Samaria 2Kin 21:13   3389
I will wipe *J* as a man wipeth a 2Kin 21:13   3389
till he had filled *J* from one end 2Kin 21:16   3389
and he reigned two years in *J* 2Kin 21:19   3389

reigned thirty and one years in *J* 2Kin 22:1   3389
now she dwelt in *J* in the college 2Kin 22:14   3389
all the elders of Judah and of *J* 2Kin 23:1   3389
all the inhabitants of *J* with him 2Kin 23:2   3389
he burned them without *J* in the 2Kin 23:4   3389
and in the places round about *J* 2Kin 23:5   3389
the house of the LORD, without *J* 2Kin 23:6   3389
up to the altar of the LORD in *J* 2Kin 23:9   3389
high places that were before *J* 2Kin 23:13   3389
bones upon them, and returned to *J* 2Kin 23:20   3389
was holden to the LORD in *J* 2Kin 23:23   3389
in the land of Judah and in *J* 2Kin 23:24   3389
this city *J* which I have chosen 2Kin 23:27   3389
from Megiddo, and brought him to *J* 2Kin 23:30   3389
and he reigned three months in *J* 2Kin 23:31   3389
that he might not reign in *J* 2Kin 23:33   3389
and he reigned eleven years in *J* 2Kin 23:36   3389
for he filled *J* with innocent 2Kin 24:4   3389
and he reigned in *J* three months 2Kin 24:8   3389
the daughter of Elnathan of *J* 2Kin 24:8   3389
king of Babylon came up against *J* 2Kin 24:10   3389
And he carried away all *J*, and all 2Kin 24:14   3389
into captivity from *J* to Babylon 2Kin 24:15   3389
and he reigned eleven years in *J* 2Kin 24:18   3389
of the LORD it came to pass in *J* 2Kin 24:20   3389
he, and all his host, against *J* 2Kin 25:1   3389
of the king of Babylon, unto *J* 2Kin 25:8   3389
house, and all the houses of *J* 2Kin 25:9   3389
down the walls of *J* round about 2Kin 25:10   3389
in *J* he reigned thirty and three 1Chr 3:4   3389
And these were born unto him in *J* 1Chr 3:5   3389
temple that Solomon built in *J* 1Chr 6:10   3389
J by the hand of Nebuchadnezzar 1Chr 6:15   3389
built the house of the LORD in *J* 1Chr 6:32   3389
These dwelt in *J* 1Chr 8:28   3389
dwelt with their brethren in *J* 1Chr 8:32   3389
in *J* dwelt of the children of 1Chr 9:3   3389
these dwelt at *J* 1Chr 9:34   3389
dwelt with their brethren at *J* 1Chr 9:38   3389
And David and all Israel went to *J* 1Chr 11:4   3389
And David took more wives at *J* 1Chr 14:3   3389
of his children which he had in *J* 1Chr 14:4   3389
gathered all Israel together to *J* 1Chr 15:3   3389
Hadarezer, and brought them to *J* 1Chr 18:7   3389
Then Joab came to *J* 1Chr 19:15   3389
But David tarried at *J* 1Chr 20:1   3389
and all the people returned to *J* 1Chr 20:3   3389
all Israel, and came to *J* 1Chr 21:4   3389
an angel unto *J* to destroy it 1Chr 21:15   3389
in his hand stretched out over *J* 1Chr 21:16   3389
that they may dwell in *J* for ever 1Chr 23:25   3389
with all the valiant men, unto *J* 1Chr 28:1   3389
and three years reigned he in *J* 1Chr 29:27   3389
he had pitched a tent for it at *J* 2Chr 1:4   3389
place that was at Gibeon to *J* 2Chr 1:13   3389
cities, and with the king at *J* 2Chr 1:14   3389
gold at *J* as plenteous as stones 2Chr 1:15   3389
that are with me in Judah and in *J* 2Chr 2:7   3389
and thou shalt carry it up to *J* 2Chr 2:16   3389
of the LORD at *J* in mount Moriah 2Chr 3:1   3389
of the children of Israel, unto *J* 2Chr 5:2   3389
But I have chosen *J*, that my name 2Chr 6:6   3389
Solomon desired to build in *J* 2Chr 8:6   3389
Solomon with hard questions at *J* 2Chr 9:1   3389
cities, and with the king at *J* 2Chr 9:25   3389
king made silver in *J* as stones 2Chr 9:27   3389
Solomon reigned in *J* over all 2Chr 9:30   3389
up to his chariot, to flee to *J* 2Chr 10:18   3389
And when Rehoboam was come to *J* 2Chr 11:1   3389
And Rehoboam dwelt in *J*, and built 2Chr 11:5   3389
possession, and came to Judah and *J* 2Chr 11:14   3389
the LORD God of Israel came to *J* 2Chr 11:16   3389
king of Egypt came up against *J* 2Chr 12:2   3389
pertained to Judah, and came to *J* 2Chr 12:4   3389
together to *J* because of Shishak 2Chr 12:5   3389
out upon *J* by the hand of Shishak 2Chr 12:7   3389
king of Egypt came up against *J* 2Chr 12:9   3389
strengthened himself in *J* 2Chr 12:13   3389
he reigned seventeen years in *J* 2Chr 12:13   3389
He reigned three years in *J* 2Chr 13:2   3389
in abundance, and returned to *J* 2Chr 14:15   3389
together at *J* in the third month 2Chr 15:10   3389
mighty men of valour, were in *J* 2Chr 17:13   3389
to his house in peace to *J* 2Chr 19:1   3389
And Jehoshaphat dwelt at *J* 2Chr 19:4   3389
Moreover in *J* did Jehoshaphat set 2Chr 19:8   3389
when they returned to *J* 2Chr 19:8   3389
in the congregation of Judah and *J* 2Chr 20:5   3389
all Judah, and ye inhabitants of *J* 2Chr 20:15   3389
the LORD with you, O Judah and *J* 2Chr 20:17   3389
the inhabitants of *J* fell before 2Chr 20:18   3389

O Judah, and ye inhabitants of *J*	2Chr 20:20	3389
returned, every man of Judah and *J*	2Chr 20:27	3389
them, to go again to *J* with joy	2Chr 20:27	3389
they came to *J* with psalteries and	2Chr 20:28	3389
reigned twenty and five years in *J*	2Chr 20:31	3389
and he reigned eight years in *J*	2Chr 21:5	3389
of *J* to commit fornication	2Chr 21:11	3389
inhabitants of *J* to go a whoring	2Chr 21:13	3389
and he reigned in *J* eight years	2Chr 21:20	3389
the inhabitants of *J* made Ahaziah	2Chr 22:1	3389
and he reigned one year in *J*	2Chr 22:2	3389
of Israel, and they came to *J*	2Chr 23:2	3389
and he reigned forty years in *J*	2Chr 24:1	3389
Judah and out of *J* the collection,	2Chr 24:6	3389
a proclamation through Judah and *J*	2Chr 24:9	3389
J for this their trespass	2Chr 24:18	3389
and they came to Judah and *J*	2Chr 24:23	3389
reigned twenty and nine years in *J*	2Chr 25:1	3389
mother's name was Jehoaddan of *J*	2Chr 25:1	3389
Beth-shemesh, and brought him to *J*	2Chr 25:23	3389
brake down the wall of *J* from the	2Chr 25:23	3389
a conspiracy against him in *J*	2Chr 25:27	3389
reigned fifty and two years in *J*	2Chr 26:3	3389
name also was Jecoliah of *J*	2Chr 26:3	3389
towers in *J* at the corner gate	2Chr 26:9	3389
And he made in *J* engines, invented	2Chr 26:15	3389
and he reigned sixteen years in *J*	2Chr 27:1	3389
and reigned sixteen years in *J*	2Chr 27:8	3389
and he reigned sixteen years in *J*	2Chr 28:1	3389
J for bondmen and bondwomen unto	2Chr 28:10	3389
him altars in every corner of *J*	2Chr 28:24	3389
buried him in the city, even in *J*	2Chr 28:27	3389
reigned nine and twenty years in *J*	2Chr 29:1	3389
of the LORD was upon Judah and *J*	2Chr 29:8	3389
to the house of the LORD at *J*	2Chr 30:1	3389
and all the congregation in *J*	2Chr 30:2	3389
gathered themselves together to *J*	2Chr 30:3	3389
unto the LORD God of Israel at *J*	2Chr 30:5	3389
humbled themselves, and came to *J*	2Chr 30:11	3389
there assembled at *J* much people	2Chr 30:13	3389
away the altars that were in *J*	2Chr 30:14	3389
at *J* kept the feast of unleavened	2Chr 30:21	3389
So there was great joy in *J*	2Chr 30:26	3389
there was not the like in *J*	2Chr 30:26	3389
the people that dwelt in *J* to	2Chr 31:4	3389
was purposed to fight against *J*	2Chr 32:2	3389
of Assyria send his servants to *J*	2Chr 32:9	3389
and unto all Judah that were at *J*	2Chr 32:9	3389
that ye abide in the siege in *J*	2Chr 32:10	3389
altars, and commanded Judah and *J*	2Chr 32:12	3389
people of *J* that were on the wall	2Chr 32:18	3389
they spake against the God of *J*	2Chr 32:19	3389
the inhabitants of *J* from the	2Chr 32:22	3389
brought gifts unto the LORD to *J*	2Chr 32:23	3389
upon him, and upon Judah and *J*	2Chr 32:25	3389
both he and the inhabitants of *J*	2Chr 32:26	3389
the inhabitants of *J* did him	2Chr 32:33	3389
reigned fifty and five years in *J*	2Chr 33:1	3389
In *J* shall my name be for ever	2Chr 33:4	3389
his son, In this house, and in *J*	2Chr 33:7	3389
and the inhabitants of *J* to err	2Chr 33:9	3389
him again to *J* into his kingdom	2Chr 33:13	3389
of the house of the LORD, and in *J*	2Chr 33:15	3389
reign, and reigned two years in *J*	2Chr 33:21	3389
to reign, and he reigned in *J* one	2Chr 34:1	3389
J from the high places, and the	2Chr 34:3	3389
altars, and cleansed Judah and *J*	2Chr 34:5	3389
land of Israel, he returned to *J*	2Chr 34:7	3389
and they returned to *J*	2Chr 34:9	3389
now she dwelt in *J* in the college	2Chr 34:22	3389
all the elders of Judah and *J*	2Chr 34:29	3389
of Judah, and the inhabitants of *J*	2Chr 34:30	3389
caused all that were present in *J*	2Chr 34:32	3389
And the inhabitants of *J* did	2Chr 34:32	3389
a passover unto the LORD in *J*	2Chr 35:1	3389
present, and the inhabitants of *J*	2Chr 35:18	3389
and they brought him to *J*, and he	2Chr 35:24	3389
all Judah and *J* mourned for Josiah	2Chr 35:24	3389
king in his father's stead in *J*	2Chr 36:1	3389
and he reigned three months in *J*	2Chr 36:2	3389
king of Egypt put him down at *J*	2Chr 36:3	3389
his brother king over Judah and *J*	2Chr 36:4	3389
and he reigned eleven years in *J*	2Chr 36:5	3389
three months and ten days in *J*	2Chr 36:9	3389
his brother king over Judah and *J*	2Chr 36:10	3389
and reigned eleven years in *J*	2Chr 36:11	3389
LORD which he had hallowed in *J*	2Chr 36:14	3389
God, and brake down the wall of *J*	2Chr 36:19	3389
me to build him an house in *J*	2Chr 36:23	3389
me to build him an house at *J*	Ezr 1:2	3389
with him, and let him go up to *J*	Ezr 1:3	3389
(he is the God,) which is in *J*	Ezr 1:3	3389
for the house of the LORD that is in *J*	Ezr 1:4	3389
house of the LORD which is in *J*	Ezr 1:5	3389
had brought forth out of *J*	Ezr 1:7	3389
brought up from Babylon unto *J*	Ezr 1:11	3389
Babylon, and came again unto *J*	Ezr 2:1	3389
house of the LORD which is at *J*	Ezr 2:68	3389
together as one man to *J*	Ezr 3:1	3389
coming unto the house of God at *J*	Ezr 3:8	3389
come out of the captivity unto *J*	Ezr 3:8	3389
the inhabitants of Judah and *J*	Ezr 4:6	3389
scribe wrote a letter against *J*	Ezr 4:8	3390
from thee to us are come unto *J*	Ezr 4:12	3390
been mighty kings also over *J*	Ezr 4:20	3390
up in haste to *J* unto the Jews	Ezr 4:23	3390
of the house of God which is at *J*	Ezr 4:24	3390
J in the name of the God of	Ezr 5:1	3390
the house of God which is at *J*	Ezr 5:2	3390
out of the temple that was in *J*	Ezr 5:14	3390
them into the temple that is in *J*	Ezr 5:15	3390
of the house of God which is in *J*	Ezr 5:16	3390
to build this house of God at *J*	Ezr 5:17	3390
concerning the house of God at *J*	Ezr 6:3	3390
out of the temple which is at *J*	Ezr 6:5	3390
unto the temple which is at *J*	Ezr 6:5	3390
of the priests which are at *J*	Ezr 6:9	3390
this house of God which is at *J*	Ezr 6:12	3390
the service of God, which is at *J*	Ezr 6:18	3390
porters, and the Nethinims, unto *J*	Ezr 7:7	3389
he came to *J* in the fifth month,	Ezr 7:8	3389
of the fifth month came he to *J*	Ezr 7:9	3389
their own freewill to go up to *J*	Ezr 7:13	3390
to enquire concerning Judah and *J*	Ezr 7:14	3390
Israel, whose habitation is in *J*	Ezr 7:15	3390
house of their God which is in *J*	Ezr 7:16	3390
house of your God which is in *J*	Ezr 7:17	3390
deliver thou before the God of *J*	Ezr 7:19	3390
house of the LORD which is in *J*	Ezr 7:27	3390
of the fathers of Israel, at *J*	Ezr 8:29	3389
to bring them to *J* unto the house	Ezr 8:30	3389
of the first month, to go unto *J*	Ezr 8:31	3389
And we came to *J*, and abode there	Ezr 8:32	3389
give us a wall in Judah and in *J*	Ezr 9:9	3389
J unto all the children of the	Ezr 10:7	3389
gather themselves together unto *J*	Ezr 10:7	3389
together unto *J* within three days	Ezr 10:9	3389
of the captivity, and concerning *J*	Neh 1:2	3389
the wall of *J* also is broken down	Neh 1:3	3389
So I came to *J*, and was there	Neh 2:11	3389
had put in my heart to do at *J*	Neh 2:12	3389
port, and viewed the walls of *J*	Neh 2:13	3389
how *J* lieth waste, and the gates	Neh 2:17	3389
and let us build up the wall of *J*	Neh 2:17	3389
nor right, nor memorial, in *J*	Neh 2:20	3389
they fortified *J* unto the broad	Neh 3:8	3389
the ruler of the half part of *J*	Neh 3:9	3389
the ruler of the half part of *J*	Neh 3:12	3389
that the walls of *J* were made up	Neh 4:7	3389
to come and to fight against *J*	Neh 4:8	3389
with his servant lodge within *J*	Neh 4:22	3389
prophets to preach of thee at *J*	Neh 6:7	3389
of the palace, charge over *J*	Neh 7:2	3389
Let not the gates of *J* be opened	Neh 7:3	3389
watches of the inhabitants of *J*	Neh 7:3	3389
carried away, and came again to *J*	Neh 7:6	3389
in all their cities, and in *J*	Neh 8:15	3389
rulers of the people dwelt at *J*	Neh 11:1	3389
ten to dwell in *J* the holy city	Neh 11:1	3389
offered themselves to dwell at *J*	Neh 11:2	3389
of the province that dwelt in *J*	Neh 11:3	3389
at *J* dwelt certain of the	Neh 11:4	3389
at *J* were four hundred threescore	Neh 11:6	3389
at *J* was Uzzi the son of Bani	Neh 11:22	3389
the dedication of the wall of *J*	Neh 12:27	3389
their places, to bring them to *J*	Neh 12:27	3389
the plain country round about *J*	Neh 12:28	3389
them villages round about *J*	Neh 12:29	3389
so that the joy of *J* was heard	Neh 12:43	3389
in all this time was not I at *J*	Neh 13:6	3389
And I came to *J*, and understood of	Neh 13:7	3389
brought into *J* on the sabbath day	Neh 13:15	3389
the children of Judah, and in *J*	Neh 13:16	3389
that when the gates of *J* began to	Neh 13:19	3389
lodged without *J* once or twice	Neh 13:20	3389
J with the captivity which had	Est 2:6	3389
build thou the walls of *J*	Ps 51:18	3389
Because of thy temple at *J* shall	Ps 68:29	3389
they have laid *J* on heaps	Ps 79:1	3389
shed like water round about *J*	Ps 79:3	3389
LORD in Zion, and his praise in *J*	Ps 102:21	3389
house, in the midst of thee, O *J*	Ps 116:19	3389

shall stand within thy gates, O J	Ps 122:2	3389
J is builded as a city that is	Ps 122:3	3389
Pray for the peace of J	Ps 122:6	3389
the mountains are round about J	Ps 125:2	3389
of J all the days of thy life	Ps 128:5	3389
out of Zion, which dwelleth at J	Ps 135:21	3389
If I forget thee, O J, let my	Ps 137:5	3389
if I prefer not J above my chief	Ps 137:6	3389
children of Edom in the day of J	Ps 137:7	3389
The LORD doth build up J	Ps 147:2	3389
Praise the LORD, O J	Ps 147:12	3389
the son of David, king in J	Eccl 1:1	3389
was king over Israel in J	Eccl 1:12	3389
that have been before me in J	Eccl 1:16	3389
all that were in J before me	Eccl 2:7	3389
than all that were before me in J	Eccl 2:9	3389
but comely, O ye daughters of J	Song 1:5	3389
I charge you, O ye daughters of J	Song 2:7	3389
I charge you, O ye daughters of J	Song 3:5	3389
with love, for the daughters of J	Song 3:10	3389
I charge you, O daughters of J	Song 5:8	3389
is my friend, O daughters of J	Song 5:16	3389
O my love, as Tirzah, comely as J	Song 6:4	3389
I charge you, O daughters of J	Song 8:4	3389
J in the days of Uzziah, Jotham,	Is 1:1	3389
of Amoz saw concerning Judah and J	Is 2:1	3389
and the word of the LORD from J	Is 2:3	3389
of hosts, doth take away from J	Is 3:1	3389
For J is ruined, and Judah is	Is 3:8	3389
Zion, and he that remaineth in J	Is 4:3	3389
is written among the living in J	Is 4:3	3389
J from the midst thereof by the	Is 4:4	3389
And now, O inhabitants of J	Is 5:3	3389
went up toward J to war against	Is 7:1	3389
a snare to the inhabitants of J	Is 8:14	3389
graven images did excel them of J	Is 10:10	3389
Samaria and her idols, so do to J	Is 10:11	3389
work upon mount Zion and on J	Is 10:12	3389
daughter of Zion, the hill of J	Is 10:32	3389
ye have numbered the houses of J	Is 22:10	3389
a father to the inhabitants of J	Is 22:21	3389
reign in mount Zion, and in J	Is 24:23	3389
the LORD in the holy mount at J	Is 27:13	3389
rule this people which is in J	Is 28:14	3389
people shall dwell in Zion at J	Is 30:19	3389
will the LORD of hosts defend J	Is 31:5	3389
is in Zion, and his furnace in J	Is 31:9	3389
shall see J a quiet habitation	Is 33:20	3389
sent Rabshakeh from Lachish to J	Is 36:2	3389
away, and said to Judah and to J	Is 36:7	3389
should deliver J out of my hand	Is 36:20	3389
J shall not be given into the	Is 37:10	3389
the daughter of J hath shaken her	Is 37:22	3389
For out of J shall go forth a	Is 37:32	3389
Speak ye comfortably to J	Is 40:2	3389
O J, that bringest good tidings,	Is 40:9	3389
I will give to J one that	Is 41:27	3389
that saith to J, Thou shalt be	Is 44:26	3389
even saying to J, Thou shalt be	Is 44:28	3389
Awake, awake, stand up, O J	Is 51:17	3389
on thy beautiful garments, O J	Is 52:1	3389
arise, and sit down, O J	Is 52:2	3389
together, ye waste places of J	Is 52:9	3389
his people, he hath redeemed J	Is 52:9	3389
set watchmen upon thy walls, O J	Is 62:6	3389
till he make J a praise in the	Is 62:7	3389
is a wilderness, J a desolation	Is 64:10	3389
I create J a rejoicing, and her	Is 65:18	3389
And I will rejoice in J, and joy in	Is 65:19	3389
Rejoice ye with J, and be glad,	Is 66:10	3389
and ye shall be comforted in J	Is 66:13	3389
beasts, to my holy mountain J	Is 66:20	3389
unto the carrying away of J	Jer 1:3	3389
at the entering of the gates of J	Jer 1:15	3389
Go and cry in the ears of J	Jer 2:2	3389
call J the throne of the LORD	Jer 3:17	3389
it, to the name of the LORD, to J	Jer 3:17	3389
the LORD to the men of Judah and J	Jer 4:3	3389
men of Judah and inhabitants of J	Jer 4:4	3389
ye in Judah, and publish in J	Jer 4:5	3389
greatly deceived this people and J	Jer 4:10	3389
it be said to this people and to J	Jer 4:11	3389
O J, wash thine heart from	Jer 4:14	3389
behold, publish against J	Jer 4:16	3389
and fro through the streets of J	Jer 5:1	3389
to flee out of the midst of J	Jer 6:1	3389
trees, and cast a mount against J	Jer 6:6	3389
Be thou instructed, O J, lest my	Jer 6:8	3389
of Judah and in the streets of J	Jer 7:17	3389
Cut off thine hair, O J, and cast	Jer 7:29	3389
Judah, and from the streets of J	Jer 7:34	3389

the bones of the inhabitants of J	Jer 8:1	3389
Why then is this people of J	Jer 8:5	3389
And I will make J heaps, and a den	Jer 9:11	3389
Judah, and to the inhabitants of J	Jer 11:2	3389
of Judah, and in the streets of J	Jer 11:6	3389
and among the inhabitants of J	Jer 11:9	3389
of Judah and inhabitants of J go	Jer 11:12	3389
J have ye set up altars to that	Jer 11:13	3389
of Judah, and the great pride of J	Jer 13:9	3389
and all the inhabitants of J	Jer 13:13	3389
Woe unto thee, O J	Jer 13:27	3389
and the cry of J is gone up	Jer 14:2	3389
of J because of the famine	Jer 14:16	3389
Judah, for that which he did in J	Jer 15:4	3389
shall have pity upon thee, O J	Jer 15:5	3389
go out, and in all the gates of J	Jer 17:19	3389
and all the inhabitants of J	Jer 17:20	3389
nor bring it in by the gates of J	Jer 17:21	3389
of Judah, and the inhabitants of J	Jer 17:25	3389
Judah, and from the places about J	Jer 17:26	3389
the gates of J on the sabbath day	Jer 17:27	3389
it shall devour the palaces of J	Jer 17:27	3389
Judah, and to the inhabitants of J	Jer 18:11	3389
of Judah, and inhabitants of J	Jer 19:3	3389
of Judah and J in this place	Jer 19:7	3389
And the houses of J, and the houses	Jer 19:13	3389
cast forth beyond the gates of J	Jer 22:19	3389
prophets of J an horrible thing	Jer 23:14	3389
for from the prophets of J is	Jer 23:15	3389
the carpenters and smiths, from J	Jer 24:1	3389
his princes, and the residue of J	Jer 24:8	3389
and to all the inhabitants of J	Jer 25:2	3389
To wit, J, and the cities of Judah	Jer 25:18	3389
J shall become heaps, and the	Jer 26:18	3389
to J unto Zedekiah king of Judah	Jer 27:3	3389
of the king of Judah, and at J	Jer 27:18	3389
king of Judah from J to Babylon	Jer 27:20	3389
and all the nobles of Judah and J	Jer 27:20	3389
of the king of Judah and of J	Jer 27:21	3389
J unto the residue of the elders	Jer 29:1	3389
away captive from J to Babylon	Jer 29:1	3389
the princes of Judah and J	Jer 29:2	3389
the smiths, were departed from J	Jer 29:2	3389
carried away from J unto Babylon	Jer 29:4	3389
I have sent from J to Babylon	Jer 29:20	3389
unto all the people that are at J	Jer 29:25	3389
king of Babylon's army besieged J	Jer 32:2	3389
of Judah, and the inhabitants of J	Jer 32:32	3389
and in the places about J	Jer 32:44	3389
of Judah, and in the streets of J	Jer 33:10	3389
and in the places about J	Jer 33:13	3389
be saved, and J shall dwell safely	Jer 33:16	3389
all the people, fought against J	Jer 34:1	3389
unto Zedekiah king of Judah in J	Jer 34:6	3389
Babylon's army fought against J	Jer 34:7	3389
all the people which were at J	Jer 34:8	3389
of Judah, and the princes of J	Jer 34:19	3389
let us go to J for fear of the	Jer 35:11	3389
so we dwell at J	Jer 35:11	3389
of Judah and the inhabitants of J	Jer 35:13	3389
of J all the evil that I have	Jer 35:17	3389
the LORD to all the people in J	Jer 36:9	3389
from the cities of Judah unto J	Jer 36:9	3389
and upon the inhabitants of J	Jer 36:31	3389
besieged J heard tidings of them	Jer 37:5	3389
of them, they departed from J	Jer 37:5	3389
from J for fear of Pharaoh's army	Jer 37:11	3389
J to go into the land of Benjamin	Jer 37:12	3389
until the day that J was taken	Jer 38:28	3389
and he was there when J was taken	Jer 38:28	3389
Babylon and all his army against J	Jer 39:1	3389
and brake down the walls of J	Jer 39:8	3389
were carried away captive of J	Jer 40:1	3389
forth upon the inhabitants of J	Jer 42:18	3389
evil that I have brought upon J	Jer 44:2	3389
of Judah and in the streets of J	Jer 44:6	3389
of Judah, and in the streets of J	Jer 44:9	3389
of Egypt, as I have punished J	Jer 44:13	3389
of Judah, and in the streets of J	Jer 44:17	3389
of Judah, and in the streets of J	Jer 44:21	3389
of Chaldea, shall J say	Jer 51:35	3389
let J come into your mind	Jer 51:50	3389
and he reigned eleven years in J	Jer 52:1	3389
of the LORD it came to pass in J	Jer 52:3	3389
he and all his army, against J	Jer 52:4	3389
the king of Babylon, into J	Jer 52:12	3389
and all the houses of J, and all	Jer 52:13	3389
all the walls of J round about	Jer 52:14	3389
from J eight hundred thirty	Jer 52:29	3389
J remembered in the days of her	Lam 1:7	3389
J hath grievously sinned	Lam 1:8	3389

J is as a menstruous woman among	Lam 1:17	3389
the virgins of *J* hang down their	Lam 2:10	3389
I liken to thee, O daughter of *J*	Lam 2:13	3389
their head at the daughter of *J*	Lam 2:15	3389
have entered into the gates of *J*	Lam 4:12	3389
pourtray upon it the city, even *J*	Eze 4:1	3389
thy face toward the siege of *J*	Eze 4:7	3389
break the staff of bread in *J*	Eze 4:16	3389
This is *J*	Eze 5:5	3389
me in the visions of God to *J*	Eze 8:3	3389
the city, through the midst of *J*	Eze 9:4	3389
pouring out of thy fury upon *J*	Eze 9:8	3389
the inhabitants of *J* have said	Eze 11:15	3389
burden concerneth the prince in *J*	Eze 12:10	3389
Lord GOD of the inhabitants of *J*	Eze 12:19	3389
which prophesy concerning *J*	Eze 13:16	3389
my four sore judgments upon *J*	Eze 14:21	3389
evil that I have brought upon *J*	Eze 14:22	3389
will I give the inhabitants of *J*	Eze 15:6	3389
cause *J* to know her abominations,	Eze 16:2	3389
Thus saith the Lord GOD unto *J*	Eze 16:3	3389
the king of Babylon is come to *J*	Eze 17:12	3389
Son of man, set thy face toward *J*	Eze 21:2	3389
to Judah in *J* the defenced	Eze 21:20	3389
hand was the divination for *J*	Eze 21:22	3389
gather you into the midst of *J*	Eze 22:19	3389
Samaria is Aholah, and *J* Aholibah	Eze 23:4	3389
himself against *J* this same day	Eze 24:2	3389
that Tyrus hath said against *J*	Eze 26:2	3389
had escaped out of *J* came unto me	Eze 33:21	3389
as the flock of *J* in her solemn	Eze 36:38	3389
king of Babylon unto *J*, and	Dan 1:1	3389
out of the temple which was in *J*	Dan 5:2	3390
the house of God which was at *J*	Dan 5:3	3390
open in his chamber toward *J*	Dan 6:10	3390
years in the desolations of *J*	Dan 9:2	3389
Judah, and to the inhabitants of *J*	Dan 9:7	3389
done as hath been done upon *J*	Dan 9:12	3389
be turned away from thy city *J*	Dan 9:16	3389
the iniquities of our fathers, *J*	Dan 9:16	3389
to build *J* unto the Messiah the	Dan 9:25	3389
in *J* shall be deliverance, as the	Joel 2:32	3389
again the captivity of Judah and *J*	Joel 3:1	3389
the children of *J* have ye sold	Joel 3:6	3389
Zion, and utter his voice from *J*	Joel 3:16	3389
then shall *J* be holy, and there	Joel 3:17	3389
J from generation to generation	Joel 3:20	3389
Zion, and utter his voice from *J*	Amos 1:2	3389
it shall devour the palaces of *J*	Amos 2:5	3389
his gates, and cast lots upon *J*	Obad 11	3389
and the captivity of *J*, which is	Obad 20	3389
he saw concerning Samaria and *J*	Mic 1:1	3389
are they not *J*?	Mic 1:5	3389
the gate of my people, even to *J*	Mic 1:9	3389
from the LORD unto the gate of *J*	Mic 1:12	3389
with blood, and *J* with iniquity	Mic 3:10	3389
J shall become heaps, and the	Mic 3:12	3389
and the word of the LORD from *J*	Mic 4:2	3389
shall come to the daughter of *J*	Mic 4:8	3389
and upon all the inhabitants of *J*	Zeph 1:4	3389
that I will search *J* with candles	Zeph 1:12	3389
all the heart, O daughter of *J*	Zeph 3:14	3389
In that day it shall be said to *J*	Zeph 3:16	3389
wilt thou not have mercy on *J*	Zec 1:12	3389
I am jealous for *J* and for Zion	Zec 1:14	3389
I am returned to *J* with mercies	Zec 1:16	3389
shall be stretched forth upon *J*	Zec 1:16	3389
Zion, and shall yet choose *J*	Zec 1:17	3389
scattered Judah, Israel, and *J*	Zec 1:19	3389
And he said unto me, To measure *J*	Zec 2:2	3389
J shall be inhabited as towns	Zec 2:4	3389
land, and shall choose *J* again	Zec 2:12	3389
that hath chosen *J* rebuke thee	Zec 3:2	3389
when *J* was inhabited and in	Zec 7:7	3389
and will dwell in the midst of *J*	Zec 8:3	3389
J shall be called a city of truth	Zec 8:3	3389
women dwell in the streets of *J*	Zec 8:4	3389
shall dwell in the midst of *J*	Zec 8:8	3389
in these days to do well unto *J*	Zec 8:15	3389
to seek the LORD of hosts in *J*	Zec 8:22	3389
shout, O daughter of *J*	Zec 9:9	3389
from Ephraim, and the horse from *J*	Zec 9:10	3389
I will make *J* a cup of trembling	Zec 12:2	3389
both against Judah and against *J*	Zec 12:2	3389
in that day will I make *J* a	Zec 12:3	3389
The inhabitants of *J* shall be my	Zec 12:5	3389
J shall be inhabited again in her	Zec 12:6	3389
again in her own place, even in *J*	Zec 12:6	3389
of *J* do not magnify themselves	Zec 12:7	3389
LORD defend the inhabitants of *J*	Zec 12:8	3389
the nations that come against *J*	Zec 12:9	3389
and upon the inhabitants of *J*	Zec 12:10	3389
there be a great mourning in *J*	Zec 12:11	3389
to the inhabitants of *J* for sin	Zec 13:1	3389
all nations against *J* to battle	Zec 14:2	3389
which is before *J* on the east	Zec 14:4	3389
living waters shall go out from *J*	Zec 14:8	3389
from Geba to Rimmon south of *J*	Zec 14:10	3389
but *J* shall be safely inhabited	Zec 14:11	3389
people that have fought against *J*	Zec 14:12	3389
And Judah also shall fight at *J*	Zec 14:14	3389
J shall even go up from year to	Zec 14:16	3389
earth unto *J* to worship the King	Zec 14:17	3389
Yea, every pot in *J* and in Judah	Zec 14:21	3389
is committed in Israel and in *J*	Mal 2:11	3389
J be pleasant unto the LORD, as	Mal 3:4	3389
came wise men from the east to *J*	Mt 2:1	*2414*
was troubled, and all *J* with him	Mt 2:3	*2414*
Then went out to him *J*, and all	Mt 3:5	*2414*
and from Decapolis, and from *J*	Mt 4:25	*2414*
neither by *J*; for it is the city	Mt 5:35	*2414*
and Pharisees, which were of *J*	Mt 15:1	*2414*
how that he must go unto *J*	Mt 16:21	*2414*
Jesus going up to *J* took the	Mt 20:17	*2414*
Behold, we go up to *J*	Mt 20:18	*2414*
And when they drew nigh unto *J*	Mt 21:1	*2414*
And when he was come into *J*	Mt 21:10	*2414*
O *J*, *J*, thou that killest	Mt 23:37	*2419*
the land of Judaea, and they of *J*	Mk 1:5	*2414*
And from *J*, and from Idumaea, and	Mk 3:8	*2414*
which came down from *J* said	Mk 3:22	*2414*
of the scribes, which came from *J*	Mk 7:1	*2414*
were in the way going up to *J*	Mk 10:32	*2414*
Saying, Behold, we go up to *J*	Mk 10:33	*2414*
And when they came nigh to *J*	Mk 11:1	*2419*
And Jesus entered into *J*, and into	Mk 11:11	*2414*
And they come to *J*	Mk 11:15	*2414*
And they come again to *J*	Mk 11:27	*2414*
which came up with him unto *J*	Mk 15:41	*2414*
they brought him to *J*, to	Lk 2:22	*2414*
And, behold, there was a man in *J*	Lk 2:25	*2419*
that looked for redemption in *J*	Lk 2:38	*2419*
Now his parents went to *J* every	Lk 2:41	*2419*
they went up to *J* after the	Lk 2:42	*2414*
child Jesus tarried behind in *J*	Lk 2:43	*2419*
not, they turned back again to *J*	Lk 2:45	*2419*
And he brought him to *J*, and set	Lk 4:9	*2419*
town of Galilee, and Judaea, and *J*	Lk 5:17	*2419*
of people out of all Judaea and *J*	Lk 6:17	*2419*
which he should accomplish at *J*	Lk 9:31	*2419*
set his face to go to *J*,	Lk 9:51	*2419*
was as though he would go to *J*	Lk 9:53	*2419*
man went down from *J* to Jericho	Lk 10:30	*2419*
above all men that dwelt in *J*	Lk 13:4	*2419*
teaching, and journeying toward *J*	Lk 13:22	*2419*
be that a prophet perish out of *J*	Lk 13:33	*2419*
O *J*, *J*, which killest the	Lk 13:34	*2419*
it came to pass, as he went to *J*	Lk 17:11	*2419*
unto them, Behold, we go up to *J*	Lk 18:31	*2414*
parable, because he was nigh to *J*	Lk 19:11	*2419*
he went before, ascending up to *J*	Lk 19:28	*2414*
when ye shall see *J* compassed	Lk 21:20	*2419*
***J* shall be trodden down of the**	Lk 21:24	*2419*
also was at *J* at that time	Lk 23:7	*2414*
unto them said, Daughters of *J*	Lk 23:28	*2419*
which was from *J* about threescore	Lk 24:13	*2419*
Art thou only a stranger in *J*	Lk 24:18	*2419*
the same hour, and returned to *J*	Lk 24:33	*2419*
among all nations, beginning at *J*	Lk 24:47	*2419*
but tarry ye in the city of *J*	Lk 24:49	*2419*
returned to *J* with great joy	Lk 24:52	*2419*
and Levites from *J* to ask him	Jn 1:19	*2414*
at hand, and Jesus went up to *J*	Jn 2:13	*2414*
when he was in *J* at the passover	Jn 2:23	*2414*
that in *J* is the place where men	Jn 4:20	*2414*
in this mountain, nor yet at *J*	Jn 4:21	*2414*
that he did at *J* at the feast	Jn 4:45	*2414*
and Jesus went up to *J*	Jn 5:1	*2414*
Now there is at *J* by the sheep	Jn 5:2	*2414*
Then said some of them of *J*	Jn 7:25	*2414*
it was at *J* the feast of the	Jn 10:22	*2414*
Now Bethany was nigh unto *J*	Jn 11:18	*2414*
up to *J* before the passover	Jn 11:55	*2414*
heard that Jesus was coming to *J*	Jn 12:12	*2414*
they should not depart from *J*	Acts 1:4	*2414*
be witnesses unto me both in *J*	Acts 1:8	*2419*
Then returned they unto *J* from	Acts 1:12	*2419*
which is from *J* a sabbath day's	Acts 1:12	*2419*
known unto all the dwellers at *J*	Acts 1:19	*2419*
And there were dwelling at *J* Jews	Acts 2:5	*2419*
Judaea, and all ye that dwell at *J*	Acts 2:14	*2419*
were gathered together at *J*	Acts 4:6	*2419*

to all them that dwell in *J*	Acts 4:16	2419
of the cities round about unto *J*	Acts 5:16	2419
ye have filled *J* with your	Acts 5:28	2419
disciples multiplied in *J* greatly	Acts 6:7	2419
against the church which was at *J*	Acts 8:1	2414
J heard that Samaria had received	Acts 8:14	2414
word of the Lord, returned to *J*	Acts 8:25	2419
that goeth down from *J* unto Gaza	Acts 8:26	2419
had come to *J* for to worship,	Acts 8:27	2419
he might bring them bound unto *J*	Acts 9:2	2419
he hath done to thy saints at *J*	Acts 9:13	2419
which called on this name in *J*	Acts 9:21	2419
And when Saul was come to *J*	Acts 9:26	2419
them coming in and going out at *J*	Acts 9:28	2419
in the land of the Jews, and in *J*	Acts 10:39	2419
And when Peter was come up to *J*	Acts 11:2	2414
ears of the church which was in *J*	Acts 11:22	2414
came prophets from *J* unto Antioch	Acts 11:27	2414
Barnabas and Saul returned from *J*	Acts 12:25	2419
departing from them returned to *J*	Acts 13:13	2414
For they that dwell at *J*, and	Acts 13:27	2419
up with him from Galilee to *J*	Acts 13:31	2419
should go up to *J* unto the	Acts 15:2	2419
And when they were come to *J*	Acts 15:4	2419
and elders which were at *J*	Acts 16:4	2419
keep this feast that cometh in *J*	Acts 18:21	2414
Macedonia and Achaia, to go to *J*	Acts 19:21	2414
to be at *J* the day of Pentecost	Acts 20:16	2414
I go bound in the spirit unto *J*	Acts 20:22	2419
that he should not go up to *J*	Acts 21:4	2419
So shall the Jews at *J* bind the	Acts 21:11	2419
besought him not to go up to *J*	Acts 21:12	2419
but also to die at *J* for the name	Acts 21:13	2419
up our carriages, and went up to *J*	Acts 21:15	2419
And when we were come to *J*	Acts 21:17	2414
that all *J* was in an uproar	Acts 21:31	2419
which were there bound unto *J*	Acts 22:5	2419
that, when I was come again to *J*	Acts 22:17	2419
and get thee quickly out of *J*	Acts 22:18	2419
as thou hast testified of me in *J*	Acts 23:11	2419
I went up to *J* for to worship	Acts 24:11	2419
he ascended from Caesarea to *J*	Acts 25:1	2414
that he would send for him to *J*	Acts 25:3	2419
down from *J* stood round about	Acts 25:7	2414
and said, Wilt thou go up to *J*	Acts 25:9	2414
About whom, when I was at *J*	Acts 25:15	2419
him whether he would go to *J*	Acts 25:20	2419
have dealt with me, both at *J*	Acts 25:24	2414
first among mine own nation at *J*	Acts 26:4	2414
Which thing I also did in *J*	Acts 26:10	2414
unto them of Damascus, and at *J*	Acts 26:20	2414
J into the hands of the Romans	Acts 28:17	2414
so that from *J*, and round about	Rom 15:19	2419
But now I go unto *J* to minister	Rom 15:25	2419
the poor saints which are at *J*	Rom 15:26	2419
my service which I have for *J* may	Rom 15:31	2419
to bring your liberality unto *J*	1Cor 16:3	2419
Neither went I up to *J* to them	Gal 1:17	2414
years I went up to *J* to see Peter	Gal 1:18	2414
went up again to *J* with Barnabas	Gal 2:1	2414
and answereth to *J* which now is	Gal 4:25	2419
But *J* which is above is free,	Gal 4:26	2419
of the living God, the heavenly *J*	Heb 12:22	2419
city of my God, which is new *J*	Rev 3:12	2419
I John saw the holy city, new *J*	Rev 21:2	2419
me that great city, the holy *J*	Rev 21:10	2419

JERUSALEM'S (*je-ru'-sa-lems*)

for *J* sake which I have chosen	1Kin 11:13	3389
for *J* sake, the city which I have	1Kin 11:32	3389
for *J* sake I will not rest, until	Is 62:1	3389

JERUSHA (*je-ru'-shah*) See Jerushah. *Mother of King Jotham of Judah.*

And his mother's name was *J*	2Kin 15:33	3388

JERUSHAH (*je-ru'-shah*) See Jerusha. *Same as Jerusha.*

His mother's name also was *J*	2Chr 27:1	3388

JESAIAH (*jes-a-i'-ah*) See Isaiah, Jeshaiah.
   1. Grandson of Zerubbabel.

Hananiah; Pelatiah, and *J*	1Chr 3:21	3470

   2. A family of exiles.

the son of Ithiel, the son of *J*	Neh 11:7	3470

JESHAIAH (*jesh-a-i'-ah*) See Jesaiah.
   1. A sanctuary servant.

Gedaliah, and Zeri, and *J*,	1Chr 25:3	3740
The eighth to *J*, he, his sons, and	1Chr 25:15	3740

   2. A grandson of Eliezer.

J his son, and Joram his son, and	1Chr 26:25	3740

   3. An Elamite exile.

J the son of Athaliah, and with	Ezr 8:7	3740

   4. A Merarite exile.

with him *J* of the sons of Merari,	Ezr 8:19	3740

JESHANAH (*je-sha'-nah*) *A city near Bethel.*

J with the towns thereof, and	2Chr 13:19	3466

JESHARELAH (*je-shar'-e-lah*) See Asarelah. *A sanctuary servant.*

The seventh to *J*, he, his sons,	1Chr 25:14	3480

JESHEBEAB (*je-sheb'-e-ab*) *A sanctuary servant.*

to Huppah, the fourteenth to *J*	1Chr 24:13	3434

JESHER (*je'-shur*) *A son of Caleb.*

J, and Shobab, and Ardon	1Chr 2:18	3475

JESHIMON (*jesh'-im-on*)
   1. A place in the Sinai.

of Pisgah, which looketh toward *J*	Num 21:20	3452
of Peor, that looketh toward *J*	Num 23:28	3452

   2. A place in the wilderness of Judah.

which is on the south of *J*	1Sa 23:19	3452
in the plain on the south of *J*	1Sa 23:24	3452
of Hachilah, which is before *J*	1Sa 26:1	3452
of Hachilah, which is before *J*	1Sa 26:3	3452

JESHISHAI (*jesh'-i-shahee*) *Ancestor of a Gadite family.*

the son of Michael, the son of *J*	1Chr 5:14	3454

JESHOHAIAH (*je-sho-ha-i'-ah*) *A descendant of Simeon.*

And Elioenai, and Jaakobah, and *J*	1Chr 4:36	3439

JESHUA (*jesh'-u-ah*) See Jeshuah, Joshua.
   1. A sanctuary servant.

of Jedaiah, of the house of *J*	Ezr 2:36	3442
of Jedaiah, of the house of *J*	Neh 7:39	3442

   2. A Levite in Hezekiah's time.

The ninth to *J*, the tenth to	1Chr 24:11	3442
him were Eden, and Miniamin, and *J*	2Chr 31:15	3442
the children of *J* and Kadmiel, of	Ezr 2:40	3442
the children of *J*, of Kadmiel, and	Neh 7:43	3442

   3. A priest in exile.

J, Nehemiah, Seraiah, Reelaiah,	Ezr 2:2	3442
Then stood up *J* the son of	Ezr 3:2	3442
J the son of Jozadak, and the	Ezr 3:8	3442
Then stood *J* with his sons and his	Ezr 3:9	3442
But Zerubbabel, and *J*, and the rest	Ezr 4:3	3442
J the son of Jozadak, and began to	Ezr 5:2	3443
of the sons of *J* the son of	Ezr 10:18	3442
Who came with Zerubbabel, *J*	Neh 7:7	3442
the son of Shealtiel, and *J*	Neh 12:1	3442
their brethren in the days of *J*	Neh 12:7	3442
J begat Joiakim, Joiakim also	Neh 12:10	3442
the days of Joiakim the son of *J*	Neh 12:26	3442

   4. Father of Jozabad.

them was Jozabad the son of *J*	Ezr 8:33	3443

   5. A family of exiles.

Pahath-moab, of the children of *J*	Ezr 2:6	3442
Pahath-moab, of the children of *J*	Neh 7:11	3442

   6. Father of Ezer.

to him repaired Ezer the son of *J*	Neh 3:19	3442

   7. A priest who assisted Ezra.

Also *J*, and Bani, and Sherebiah,	Neh 8:7	3442
the stairs, of the Levites, *J*	Neh 9:4	3442
Then the Levites, *J*, and Kadmiel,	Neh 9:5	3442
J, Binnui, Kadmiel, Sherebiah,	Neh 12:8	3442
J the son of Kadmiel, with their	Neh 12:24	3442

   8. Same as Joshua, son of Nun.

for since the days of *J* the son	Neh 8:17	3442

   9. A Levite who renewed the covenant.

both *J* the son of Azaniah, Binnui	Neh 10:9	3442

   10. A city in Benjamin.

And at *J*, and at Moladah, and at	Neh 11:26	3442

JESHURUN (*jesh'-u-run*) *Another name for the people Israel.*

But *J* waxed fat, and kicked	Deut 32:15	3484
And he was king in *J*, when the	Deut 33:5	3484
is none like unto the God of *J*	Deut 33:26	3484

JESIAH (*je-si'-ah*) See Ishiah.
   1. A warrior in David's army.

Elkanah, and *J*, and Azareel, and	1Chr 12:6	3449

   2. A descendant of Uzziel.

Micah the first, and *J* the second	1Chr 23:20	3449

JESIMIEL (*je-sim'-e-el*) *A descendant of Simeon.*

and Asaiah, and Adiel, and *J*	1Chr 4:36	3450

JESSE (*jes'-se*) *Father of David.*

he is the father of *J*, the father	Ruth 4:17	3448
begat *J*, and *J* begat David	Ruth 4:22	3448
send thee to *J* the Beth-lehemite	1Sa 16:1	3448
call *J* to the sacrifice, and I	1Sa 16:3	3448

And he sanctified *J* and his sons,	1Sa 16:5	3448
Then *J* called Abinadab, and made	1Sa 16:8	3448
Then *J* made Shammah to pass by	1Sa 16:9	3448
J made seven of his sons to pass	1Sa 16:10	3448
And Samuel said unto *J*, The LORD	1Sa 16:10	3448
And Samuel said unto *J*, Are here	1Sa 16:11	3448
And Samuel said unto *J*, Send and	1Sa 16:11	3448
seen a son of *J* the Beth-lehemite	1Sa 16:18	3448
Saul sent messengers unto *J*	1Sa 16:19	3448
J took an ass laden with bread,	1Sa 16:20	3448
And Saul sent to *J*, saying, Let	1Sa 16:22	3448
whose name was *J*; and he had	1Sa 17:12	3448
the three eldest sons of *J* went	1Sa 17:13	3448
J said unto David his son, Take	1Sa 17:17	3448
and went, as *J* had commanded him	1Sa 17:20	3448
thy servant *J* the Beth-lehemite	1Sa 17:58	3448
cometh not the son of *J* to meat	1Sa 20:27	3448
son of *J* to thine own confusion	1Sa 20:30	3448
son of *J* liveth upon the ground	1Sa 20:31	3448
will the son of *J* give every one	1Sa 22:7	3448
made a league with the son of *J*	1Sa 22:8	3448
I saw the son of *J* coming to Nob	1Sa 22:9	3448
against me, thou and the son of *J*	1Sa 22:13	3448
and who is the son of *J*	1Sa 25:10	3448
we inheritance in the son of *J*	2Sa 20:1	3448
David the son of *J* said, and the	2Sa 23:1	3448
we inheritance in the son of *J*	1Kin 12:16	3448
Boaz begat Obed, and Obed begat *J*	1Chr 2:12	3448
J begat his firstborn Eliab, and	1Chr 2:13	3448
kingdom over David the son of *J*	1Chr 10:14	3448
and on thy side, thou son of *J*	1Chr 12:18	3448
Thus David the son of *J* reigned	1Chr 29:26	3448
none inheritance in the son of *J*	2Chr 10:16	3448
daughter of Eliab the son of *J*	2Chr 11:18	3448
of David the son of *J* are ended	Ps 72:20	3448
forth a rod out of the stem of *J*	Is 11:1	3448
day there shall be a root of *J*	Is 11:10	3448
and Obed begat *J*	Mt 1:5	2421
And *J* begat David the king	Mt 1:6	2421
Which was the son of *J*, which was	Lk 3:32	2421
I have found David the son of *J*	Acts 13:22	2421
saith, There shall be a root of *J*	Rom 15:12	2421

JESSHIAH See JESIAH.

JESTING
nor foolish talking, nor *j*	Eph 5:4	2160

JESUI (*jes'-u-i*) See ISHUI, JESUITES. *A descendant of Asher.*
of *J*, the family of the Jesuites	Num 26:44	3440

JESUITES (*jes'-u-ites*) *Descendants of Jesui.*
of Jesui, the family of the *J*	Num 26:44	3441

JESURUN (*jes'-u-run*) See JESHURUN. *Same as Jeshurun.*
and thou, *J*, whom I have chosen	Is 44:2	3484

JESUS (*je'-zus*) See BAR-JESUS, CHRIST, JESUS', JOSHUA, JUSTUS.

  1. The Christ.
of the generation of *J* Christ	Mt 1:1	2424
of Mary, of whom was born *J*	Mt 1:16	2424
Now the birth of *J* Christ was on	Mt 1:18	2424
and thou shalt call his name *J*	Mt 1:21	2424
and he called his name *J*	Mt 1:25	2424
Now when *J* was born in Bethlehem	Mt 2:1	2424
Then cometh *J* from Galilee to	Mt 3:13	2424
J answering said unto him, Suffer	Mt 3:15	2424
And *J*, when he was baptized, went	Mt 3:16	2424
Then was *J* led up of the spirit	Mt 4:1	2424
J said unto him, It is written	Mt 4:7	2424
Then saith *J* unto him, Get thee	Mt 4:10	2424
Now when *J* had heard that John	Mt 4:12	2424
From that time *J* began to preach,	Mt 4:17	2424
And *J*, walking by the sea of	Mt 4:18	2424
J went about all Galilee,	Mt 4:23	2424
when *J* had ended these sayings,	Mt 7:28	2424
J put forth his hand, and touched	Mt 8:3	2424
J saith unto him, See thou tell	Mt 8:4	2424
when *J* was entered into Capernaum	Mt 8:5	2424
J saith unto him, I will come and	Mt 8:7	2424
When *J* heard it, he marvelled, and	Mt 8:10	2424
J said unto the centurion, Go thy	Mt 8:13	2424
when *J* was come into Peter's	Mt 8:14	2424
Now when *J* saw great multitudes	Mt 8:18	2424
J saith unto him, The foxes have	Mt 8:20	2424
But *J* said unto him, Follow me	Mt 8:22	2424
What have we to do with thee, *J*	Mt 8:29	2424
the whole city came out to meet *J*	Mt 8:34	2424
J seeing their faith said unto	Mt 9:2	2424
J knowing their thoughts said,	Mt 9:4	2424
as *J* passed forth from thence, he	Mt 9:9	2424
as *J* sat at meat in the house,	Mt 9:10	2424
But when *J* heard that, he said	Mt 9:12	2424
J said unto them, Can the	Mt 9:15	2424
J arose, and followed him, and so	Mt 9:19	2424
But *J* turned him about, and when	Mt 9:22	2424
when *J* came into the ruler's	Mt 9:23	2424
when *J* departed thence, two blind	Mt 9:27	2424
J saith unto them, Believe ye	Mt 9:28	2424
J straitly charged them, saying,	Mt 9:30	2424
J went about all the cities and	Mt 9:35	2424
These twelve *J* sent forth	Mt 10:5	2424
when *J* had made an end of	Mt 11:1	2424
J answered and said unto them, Go	Mt 11:4	2424
departed, *J* began to say unto the	Mt 11:7	2424
At that time *J* answered and said,	Mt 11:25	2424
At that time *J* went on the	Mt 12:1	2424
But when *J* knew it, he withdrew	Mt 12:15	2424
J knew their thoughts, and said	Mt 12:25	2424
same day went *J* out of the house	Mt 13:1	2424
All these things spake *J* unto the	Mt 13:34	2424
Then *J* sent the multitude away,	Mt 13:36	2424
J saith unto them, Have ye	Mt 13:51	2424
that when *J* had finished these	Mt 13:53	2424
But *J* said unto them, A prophet	Mt 13:57	2424
tetrarch heard of the fame of *J*	Mt 14:1	2424
and buried it, and went and told *J*	Mt 14:12	2424
When *J* heard of it, he departed	Mt 14:13	2424
J went forth, and saw a great	Mt 14:14	2424
But *J* said unto them, They need	Mt 14:16	2424
straightway *J* constrained his	Mt 14:22	2424
of the night *J* went unto them	Mt 14:25	2424
But straightway *J* spake unto them	Mt 14:27	2424
walked on the water, to go to *J*	Mt 14:29	2424
immediately *J* stretched forth his	Mt 14:31	2424
Then came to *J* scribes and	Mt 15:1	2424
J said, Are ye also yet without	Mt 15:16	2424
Then *J* went thence, and departed	Mt 15:21	2424
Then *J* answered and said unto her,	Mt 15:28	2424
J departed from thence, and came	Mt 15:29	2424
Then *J* called his disciples unto	Mt 15:32	2424
J saith unto them, How many	Mt 15:34	2424
Then *J* said unto them, Take heed	Mt 16:6	2424
Which when *J* perceived, he said	Mt 16:8	2424
When *J* came into the coasts of	Mt 16:13	2424
J answered and said unto him,	Mt 16:17	2424
no man that he was *J* the Christ	Mt 16:20	2424
J to shew unto his disciples	Mt 16:21	2424
Then said *J* unto his disciples,	Mt 16:24	2424
And after six days *J* taketh Peter	Mt 17:1	2424
answered Peter, and said unto *J*	Mt 17:4	2424
J came and touched them, and said,	Mt 17:7	2424
they saw no man, save *J* only	Mt 17:8	2424
J charged them, saying, Tell the	Mt 17:9	2424
J answered and said unto them,	Mt 17:11	2424
Then *J* answered and said, O	Mt 17:17	2424
And *J* rebuked the devil	Mt 17:18	2424
came the disciples to *J* apart	Mt 17:19	2424
J said unto them, Because of your	Mt 17:20	2424
J said unto them, The Son of man	Mt 17:22	2424
J prevented him, saying, What	Mt 17:25	2424
J saith unto him, Then are the	Mt 17:26	2424
time came the disciples unto *J*	Mt 18:1	2424
J called a little child unto him,	Mt 18:2	2424
J saith unto him, I say not unto	Mt 18:22	2424
that when *J* had finished these	Mt 19:1	2424
But *J* said, Suffer little	Mt 19:14	2424
J said, Thou shalt do no murder,	Mt 19:18	2424
J said unto him, If thou wilt be	Mt 19:21	2424
Then said *J* unto his disciples,	Mt 19:23	2424
But *J* beheld them, and said unto	Mt 19:26	2424
J said unto them, Verily I say	Mt 19:28	2424
J going up to Jerusalem took the	Mt 20:17	2424
But *J* answered and said, Ye know	Mt 20:22	2424
But *J* called them unto him, and	Mt 20:25	2424
when they heard that *J* passed by	Mt 20:30	2424
J stood still, and called them, and	Mt 20:32	2424
So *J* had compassion on them, and	Mt 20:34	2424
then sent *J* two disciples,	Mt 21:1	2424
went, and did as *J* commanded them,	Mt 21:6	2424
This is *J* the prophet of Nazareth	Mt 21:11	2424
J went into the temple of God, and	Mt 21:12	2424
And *J* saith unto them, Yea	Mt 21:16	2424
J answered and said unto them,	Mt 21:21	2424
J answered and said unto them, I	Mt 21:24	2424
And they answered *J*, and said, We	Mt 21:27	2424
J saith unto them, Verily I say	Mt 21:31	2424
J saith unto them, Did ye never	Mt 21:42	2424
J answered and spake unto them	Mt 22:1	2424
But *J* perceived their wickedness,	Mt 22:18	2424
J answered and said unto them, Ye	Mt 22:29	2424
J said unto him, Thou shalt love	Mt 22:37	2424

J

gathered together, *J* asked them,	Mt 22:41	2424
Then spake *J* to the multitude, and	Mt 23:1	2424
J went out, and departed from the	Mt 24:1	2424
J said unto them, See ye not all	Mt 24:2	2424
J answered and said unto them,	Mt 24:4	2424
when *J* had finished all these	Mt 26:1	2424
they might take *J* by subtilty	Mt 26:4	2424
Now when *J* was in Bethany, in the	Mt 26:6	2424
When *J* understood it, he said	Mt 26:10	2424
bread the disciples came to *J*	Mt 26:17	2424
did as *J* had appointed them	Mt 26:19	2424
J took bread, and blessed it, and	Mt 26:26	2424
Then saith *J* unto them, All ye	Mt 26:31	2424
J said unto him, Verily I say	Mt 26:34	2424
Then cometh *J* with them unto a	Mt 26:36	2424
And forthwith he came to *J*	Mt 26:49	2424
And J said unto him, Friend,	Mt 26:50	2424
came they, and laid hands on *J*	Mt 26:50	2424
with *J* stretched out his hand	Mt 26:51	2424
Then said J unto him, Put up	Mt 26:52	2424
hour said *J* to the multitudes	Mt 26:55	2424
they that had laid hold on *J* led	Mt 26:57	2424
sought false witness against *J*	Mt 26:59	2424
But *J* held his peace	Mt 26:63	2424
J saith unto him, Thou hast said	Mt 26:64	2424
Thou also wast with *J* of Galilee	Mt 26:69	2424
was also with *J* of Nazareth	Mt 26:71	2424
And Peter remembered the word of *J*	Mt 26:75	2424
against *J* to put him to death	Mt 27:1	2424
J stood before the governor	Mt 27:11	2424
J said unto him, Thou sayest	Mt 27:11	2424
or *J* which is called Christ	Mt 27:17	2424
should ask Barabbas, and destroy *J*	Mt 27:20	2424
with *J* which is called Christ	Mt 27:22	2424
and when he had scourged *J*	Mt 27:26	2424
took *J* into the common hall	Mt 27:27	2424
THIS IS *J* THE KING OF THE JEWS	Mt 27:37	2424
about the ninth hour *J* cried with	Mt 27:46	2424
J, when he had cried again with a	Mt 27:50	2424
that were with him, watching *J*	Mt 27:54	2424
which followed *J* from Galilee	Mt 27:55	2424
Pilate, and begged the body of *J*	Mt 27:58	2424
for I know that ye seek *J*	Mt 28:5	2424
J met them, saying, All hail	Mt 28:9	2424
Then said J unto them, Be not	Mt 28:10	2424
where *J* had appointed them	Mt 28:16	2424
J came and spake unto them, saying	Mt 28:18	2424
of the gospel of *J* Christ	Mk 1:1	2424
that *J* came from Nazareth of	Mk 1:9	2424
J came into Galilee, preaching	Mk 1:14	2424
J said unto them, Come ye after	Mk 1:17	2424
do with thee, thou *J* of Nazareth	Mk 1:24	2424
J rebuked him, saying, Hold thy	Mk 1:25	2424
And *J*, moved with compassion, put	Mk 1:41	2424
insomuch that *J* could no more	Mk 1:45	2424
When *J* saw their faith, he said	Mk 2:5	2424
immediately when *J* perceived in	Mk 2:8	2424
as *J* sat at meat in his house,	Mk 2:15	2424
sinners sat also together with *J*	Mk 2:15	2424
When *J* heard it, he saith unto	Mk 2:17	2424
J said unto them, Can the	Mk 2:19	2424
But *J* withdrew himself with his	Mk 3:7	2424
But when he saw *J* afar off	Mk 5:6	2424
What have I to do with thee, *J*	Mk 5:7	2424
forthwith *J* gave them leave	Mk 5:13	2424
And they come to *J*, and see him	Mk 5:15	2424
Howbeit *J* suffered him not, but	Mk 5:19	2424
great things *J* had done for him	Mk 5:20	2424
when *J* was passed over again by	Mk 5:21	2424
And *J* went with him	Mk 5:24	2424
When she had heard of *J*, came in	Mk 5:27	2424
And *J*, immediately knowing in	Mk 5:30	2424
As soon as *J* heard the word that	Mk 5:36	2424
But J said unto them, A prophet	Mk 6:4	2424
themselves together with *J*	Mk 6:30	2424
And *J*, when he came out, saw much	Mk 6:34	2424
But J said unto her, Let the	Mk 7:27	2424
J called his disciples unto him,	Mk 8:1	2424
when *J* knew it, he saith unto	Mk 8:17	2424
J went out, and his disciples,	Mk 8:27	2424
after six days *J* taketh with him	Mk 9:2	2424
and they were talking with *J*	Mk 9:4	2424
And Peter answered and said to *J*	Mk 9:5	2424
save *J* only with themselves	Mk 9:8	2424
J said unto him, If thou canst	Mk 9:23	2424
When *J* saw that the people came	Mk 9:25	2424
But *J* took him by the hand, and	Mk 9:27	2424
But J said, Forbid him not.	Mk 9:39	2424
J answered and said unto them, For	Mk 10:5	2424
But when *J* saw it, he was much	Mk 10:14	2424
J said unto him, Why callest thou	Mk 10:18	2424

Then *J* beholding him loved him,	Mk 10:21	2424
J looked round about, and saith	Mk 10:23	2424
But *J* answereth again, and saith	Mk 10:24	2424
J looking upon them saith, With	Mk 10:27	2424
J answered and said, Verily I say	Mk 10:29	2424
and *J* went before them	Mk 10:32	2424
But J said unto them, Ye know not	Mk 10:38	2424
J said unto them, Ye shall indeed	Mk 10:39	2424
But *J* called them to him, and	Mk 10:42	2424
heard that it was *J* of Nazareth	Mk 10:47	2424
he began to cry out, and say, *J*	Mk 10:47	2424
J stood still, and commanded him	Mk 10:49	2424
his garment, rose, and came to *J*	Mk 10:50	2424
J answered and said unto him, What	Mk 10:51	2424
J said unto him, Go thy way	Mk 10:52	2424
sight, and followed *J* in the way	Mk 10:52	2424
unto them even as *J* had commanded	Mk 11:6	2424
And they brought the colt to *J*	Mk 11:7	2424
J entered into Jerusalem, and into	Mk 11:11	2424
J answered and said unto it, No	Mk 11:14	2424
J went into the temple, and began	Mk 11:15	2424
J answering saith unto them, Have	Mk 11:22	2424
J answered and said unto them, I	Mk 11:29	2424
And they answered and said unto *J*	Mk 11:33	2424
J answering saith unto them,	Mk 11:33	2424
J answering said unto them,	Mk 12:17	2424
J answering said unto them, Do ye	Mk 12:24	2424
J answered him, The first of all	Mk 12:29	2424
when *J* saw that he answered	Mk 12:34	2424
J answered and said, while he	Mk 12:35	2424
J sat over against the treasury,	Mk 12:41	2424
J answering said unto him, Seest	Mk 13:2	2424
J answering them began to say,	Mk 13:5	2424
And *J* said, Let her alone	Mk 14:6	2424
J said, Verily I say unto you,	Mk 14:18	2424
J took bread, and blessed, and	Mk 14:22	2424
J saith unto them, All ye shall	Mk 14:27	2424
J saith unto him, Verily I say	Mk 14:30	2424
J answered and said unto them, Are	Mk 14:48	2424
they led *J* away to the high	Mk 14:53	2424
against *J* to put him to death	Mk 14:55	2424
stood up in the midst, and asked *J*	Mk 14:60	2424
And J said, I am.	Mk 14:62	2424
thou also wast with *J* of Nazareth	Mk 14:67	2424
the word that *J* said unto him	Mk 14:72	2424
and the whole council, and bound *J*	Mk 15:1	2424
But *J* yet answered nothing	Mk 15:5	2424
unto them, and delivered *J*	Mk 15:15	2424
at the ninth hour *J* cried with a	Mk 15:34	2424
J cried with a loud voice, and	Mk 15:37	2424
Pilate, and craved the body of *J*	Mk 15:43	2424
Ye seek *J* of Nazareth, which was	Mk 16:6	2424
Now when *J* was risen early the	Mk 16:9	2424
a son, and shalt call his name *J*	Lk 1:31	2424
the child, his name was called *J*	Lk 2:21	2424
parents brought in the child *J*	Lk 2:27	2424
the child *J* tarried behind in	Lk 2:43	2424
J increased in wisdom and stature,	Lk 2:52	2424
that *J* also being baptized, and	Lk 3:21	2424
J himself began to be about	Lk 3:23	2424
J being full of the Holy Ghost	Lk 4:1	2424
J answered him, saying, It is	Lk 4:4	2424
J answered and said unto him, Get	Lk 4:8	2424
J answering said unto him, It is	Lk 4:12	2424
J returned in the power of the	Lk 4:14	2424
do with thee, thou *J* of Nazareth	Lk 4:34	2424
J rebuked him, saying, Hold thy	Lk 4:35	2424
J said unto Simon, Fear not	Lk 5:10	2424
who seeing *J* fell on his face, and	Lk 5:12	2424
his couch into the midst before *J*	Lk 5:19	2424
But when *J* perceived their	Lk 5:22	2424
J answering said unto them, They	Lk 5:31	2424
J answering them said, Have ye	Lk 6:3	2424
Then said J unto them, I will ask	Lk 6:9	2424
another what they might do to *J*	Lk 6:11	2424
And when he heard of *J*, he sent	Lk 7:3	2424
And when they came to *J*, they	Lk 7:4	2424
Then *J* went with them	Lk 7:6	2424
When *J* heard these things, he	Lk 7:9	2424
of his disciples sent them to *J*	Lk 7:19	2424
Then *J* answering said unto them,	Lk 7:22	2424
when she knew that *J* sat at meat	Lk 7:37	2424
J answering said unto him, Simon,	Lk 7:40	2424
When he saw *J*, he cried out, and	Lk 8:28	2424
What have I to do with thee, *J*	Lk 8:28	2424
J asked him, saying, What is thy	Lk 8:30	2424
and came to *J*, and found the man,	Lk 8:35	2424
sitting at the feet of *J*	Lk 8:35	2424
but *J* sent him away, saying,	Lk 8:38	2424
great things *J* had done unto him	Lk 8:39	2424
when *J* was returned, the people	Lk 8:40	2424

And *J* said, Who touched me	Lk 8:45	2424
J said, Somebody hath touched me	Lk 8:46	2424
But when *J* heard it, he answered	Lk 8:50	2424
from him, Peter said unto *J*	Lk 9:33	2424
voice was past, *J* was found alone	Lk 9:36	2424
J answering said, O faithless and	Lk 9:41	2424
J rebuked the unclean spirit, and	Lk 9:42	2424
one at all things which *J* did	Lk 9:43	2424
And *J*, perceiving the thought of	Lk 9:47	2424
J said unto him, Forbid him not	Lk 9:50	2424
J said unto him, Foxes have holes	Lk 9:58	2424
J said unto him, Let the dead	Lk 9:60	2424
J said unto him, No man, having	Lk 9:62	2424
In that hour *J* rejoiced in spirit	Lk 10:21	2424
to justify himself, said unto *J*	Lk 10:29	2424
J answering said, A certain man	Lk 10:30	2424
Then said *J* unto him, Go, and do	Lk 10:37	2424
J answered and said unto her,	Lk 10:41	2424
J answering said unto them,	Lk 13:2	2424
when *J* saw her, he called her to	Lk 13:12	2424
because that *J* had healed on the	Lk 13:14	2424
J answering spake unto the	Lk 14:3	2424
up their voices, and said, *J*	Lk 17:13	2424
J answering said, Were there not	Lk 17:17	2424
But *J* called them unto him, and	Lk 18:16	2424
J said unto him, Why callest thou	Lk 18:19	2424
Now when *J* heard these things, he	Lk 18:22	2424
when *J* saw that he was very	Lk 18:24	2424
that *J* of Nazareth passeth by	Lk 18:37	2424
And he cried, saying, *J*, thou son	Lk 18:38	2424
J stood, and commanded him to be	Lk 18:40	2424
J said unto him, Receive thy	Lk 18:42	2424
J entered and passed through	Lk 19:1	
And he sought to see *J* who he was	Lk 19:3	2424
when *J* came to the place, he	Lk 19:5	2424
J said unto him, This day is	Lk 19:9	2424
And they brought him to *J*	Lk 19:35	2424
the colt, and they set *J* thereon	Lk 19:35	2424
J said unto them, Neither tell I	Lk 20:8	2424
J answering said unto them, The	Lk 20:34	2424
and drew near unto *J* to kiss him	Lk 22:47	2424
But *J* said unto him, Judas,	Lk 22:48	2424
J answered and said, Suffer ye	Lk 22:51	2424
Then *J* said unto the chief	Lk 22:52	2424
And the men that held *J* mocked him	Lk 22:63	2424
And when Herod saw *J*, he was	Lk 23:8	2424
therefore, willing to release *J*	Lk 23:20	2424
but he delivered *J* to their will	Lk 23:25	2424
that he might bear it after *J*	Lk 23:26	2424
But *J* turning unto them said,	Lk 23:28	2424
Then said *J*, Father, forgive them	Lk 23:34	2424
And he said unto *J*, Lord, remember	Lk 23:42	2424
J said unto him, Verily I say	Lk 23:43	2424
when *J* had cried with a loud	Lk 23:46	2424
Pilate, and begged the body of *J*	Lk 23:52	2424
found not the body of the Lord *J*	Lk 24:3	2424
J himself drew near, and went with	Lk 24:15	2424
Concerning *J* of Nazareth, which	Lk 24:19	2424
J himself stood in the midst of	Lk 24:36	2424
grace and truth came by *J* Christ	Jn 1:17	2424
day John seeth *J* coming unto him	Jn 1:29	2424
And looking upon *J* as he walked	Jn 1:36	2424
him speak, and they followed *J*	Jn 1:37	2424
Then *J* turned, and saw them	Jn 1:38	2424
And he brought him to *J*	Jn 1:42	2424
when *J* beheld him, he said, Thou	Jn 1:42	2424
The day following *J* would go	Jn 1:43	2424
J of Nazareth, the son of Joseph	Jn 1:45	2424
J saw Nathanael coming to him, and	Jn 1:47	2424
J answered and said unto him,	Jn 1:48	2424
J answered and said unto him,	Jn 1:50	2424
and the mother of *J* was there	Jn 2:1	2424
both *J* was called, and his	Jn 2:2	2424
the mother of *J* saith unto him,	Jn 2:3	2424
J saith unto her, Woman, what	Jn 2:4	2424
J saith unto them, Fill the	Jn 2:7	2424
miracles did *J* in Cana of Galilee	Jn 2:11	2424
hand, and *J* went up to Jerusalem	Jn 2:13	2424
J answered and said unto them,	Jn 2:19	2424
and the word which *J* had said	Jn 2:22	2424
But *J* did not commit himself unto	Jn 2:24	2424
The same came to *J* by night	Jn 3:2	2424
J answered and said unto him,	Jn 3:3	2424
J answered, Verily, verily, I say	Jn 3:5	2424
J answered and said unto him, Art	Jn 3:10	2424
After these things came *J*	Jn 3:22	2424
Pharisees had heard that *J* made	Jn 4:1	2424
(Though *J* himself baptized not,	Jn 4:2	2424
J therefore, being wearied with	Jn 4:6	2424
J saith unto her, Give me to	Jn 4:7	2424
J answered and said unto her, If	Jn 4:10	2424
J answered and said unto her,	Jn 4:13	2424
J saith unto her, Go, call thy	Jn 4:16	2424
J said unto her, Thou hast well	Jn 4:17	2424
J saith unto her, Woman, believe	Jn 4:21	2424
J saith unto her, I that speak	Jn 4:26	2424
J saith unto them, My meat is to	Jn 4:34	2424
For *J* himself testified, that a	Jn 4:44	2424
So *J* came again into Cana of	Jn 4:46	2424
When he heard that *J* was come out	Jn 4:47	2424
Then said *J* unto him, Except ye	Jn 4:48	2424
J saith unto him, Go thy way	Jn 4:50	2424
word that *J* had spoken unto him,	Jn 4:50	2424
in the which *J* said unto him, Thy	Jn 4:53	2424
the second miracle that *J* did	Jn 4:54	2424
and *J* went up to Jerusalem	Jn 5:1	2424
When *J* saw him lie, and knew that	Jn 5:6	2424
J saith unto him, Rise, take up	Jn 5:8	2424
for *J* had conveyed himself away,	Jn 5:13	2424
Afterward *J* findeth him in the	Jn 5:14	2424
and told the Jews that it was *J*	Jn 5:15	2424
did the Jews persecute *J*, and	Jn 5:16	2424
But *J* answered them, My Father	Jn 5:17	2424
Then answered *J* and said unto them	Jn 5:19	2424
After these things *J* went over	Jn 6:1	2424
J went up into a mountain, and	Jn 6:3	2424
When *J* then lifted up his eyes,	Jn 6:5	2424
J said, Make the men sit down	Jn 6:10	2424
And *J* took the loaves	Jn 6:11	2424
had seen the miracle that *J* did	Jn 6:14	2424
When *J* therefore perceived that	Jn 6:15	2424
dark, and *J* was not come to them	Jn 6:17	2424
they see *J* walking on the sea, and	Jn 6:19	2424
and that *J* went not with his	Jn 6:22	2424
saw that *J* was not there, neither	Jn 6:24	2424
came to Capernaum, seeking for *J*	Jn 6:24	2424
J answered them and said, Verily,	Jn 6:26	2424
J answered and said unto them,	Jn 6:29	2424
Then *J* said unto them, Verily,	Jn 6:32	2424
J said unto them, I am the bread	Jn 6:35	2424
And they said, Is not this *J*	Jn 6:42	2424
J therefore answered and said unto	Jn 6:43	2424
Then *J* said unto them, Verily,	Jn 6:53	2424
When *J* knew in himself that his	Jn 6:61	2424
For *J* knew from the beginning who	Jn 6:64	2424
Then said *J* unto the twelve, Will	Jn 6:67	2424
J answered them, Have not I	Jn 6:70	2424
these things *J* walked in Galilee	Jn 7:1	2424
Then *J* said unto them, My time is	Jn 7:6	2424
feast *J* went up into the temple	Jn 7:14	2424
J answered them, and said, My	Jn 7:16	2424
J answered and said unto them, I	Jn 7:21	2424
Then cried *J* in the temple as he	Jn 7:28	2424
Then said *J* unto them, Yet a	Jn 7:33	2424
J stood and cried, saying, If any	Jn 7:37	2424
because that *J* was not yet	Jn 7:39	2424
them, (he that came to *J* by night	Jn 7:50	846
J went unto the mount of Olives	Jn 8:1	2424
But *J* stooped down, and with his	Jn 8:6	2424
J was left alone, and the woman	Jn 8:9	2424
When *J* had lifted up himself, and	Jn 8:10	2424
J said unto her, Neither do I	Jn 8:11	2424
Then spake *J* again unto them,	Jn 8:12	2424
J answered and said unto them,	Jn 8:14	2424
J answered, Ye neither know me,	Jn 8:19	2424
words spake *J* in the treasury	Jn 8:20	2424
Then said *J* again unto them, I go	Jn 8:21	2424
J saith unto them, Even the same	Jn 8:25	2424
Then said *J* unto them, When ye	Jn 8:28	2424
Then said *J* to those Jews which	Jn 8:31	2424
J answered them, Verily, verily,	Jn 8:34	2424
J saith unto them, If ye were	Jn 8:39	2424
J said unto them, If God were	Jn 8:42	2424
J answered, I have not a devil,	Jn 8:49	2424
J answered, If I honour myself,	Jn 8:54	2424
J said unto them, Verily, verily,	Jn 8:58	2424
but *J* hid himself, and went out of	Jn 8:59	2424
as *J* passed by, he saw a man	Jn 9:1	
J answered, Neither hath this man	Jn 9:3	2424
A man that is called *J* made clay	Jn 9:11	2424
sabbath day when *J* made the clay	Jn 9:14	2424
J heard that they had cast him	Jn 9:35	2424
J said unto him, Thou hast both	Jn 9:37	2424
J said, For judgment I am come	Jn 9:39	2424
J said unto them, If ye were	Jn 9:41	2424
This parable spake *J* unto them	Jn 10:6	2424
Then said *J* unto them again,	Jn 10:7	2424
J walked in the temple in	Jn 10:23	2424
J answered them, I told you, and	Jn 10:25	2424
J answered them, Many good works	Jn 10:32	2424
J answered them, Is it not	Jn 10:34	2424
When *J* heard that, he said, This	Jn 11:4	2424

J

Now *J* loved Martha, and her sister	Jn 11:5	2424
J answered, Are there not twelve	Jn 11:9	2424
Howbeit *J* spake of his death	Jn 11:13	2424
Then said *J* unto them plainly,	Jn 11:14	2424
Then when *J* came, he found that	Jn 11:17	2424
as she heard that *J* was coming	Jn 11:20	2424
Then said Martha unto *J*, Lord, if	Jn 11:21	2424
J saith unto her, Thy brother	Jn 11:23	2424
J said unto her, I am the	Jn 11:25	2424
Now *J* was not yet come into the	Jn 11:30	2424
when Mary was come where *J* was	Jn 11:32	2424
When *J* therefore saw her weeping,	Jn 11:33	2424
J wept	Jn 11:35	2424
J therefore again groaning in	Jn 11:38	2424
J said, Take ye away the stone	Jn 11:39	2424
J saith unto her, Said I not unto	Jn 11:40	2424
J lifted up his eyes, and said,	Jn 11:41	2424
J saith unto them, Loose him, and	Jn 11:44	2424
had seen the things which *J* did	Jn 11:45	2424
told them what things *J* had done	Jn 11:46	2424
he prophesied that *J* should die	Jn 11:51	2424
J therefore walked no more openly	Jn 11:54	2424
Then sought they for *J*, and spake	Jn 11:56	2424
Then *J* six days before the	Jn 12:1	2424
costly, and anointed the feet of *J*	Jn 12:3	2424
Then said *J*, Let her alone	Jn 12:7	2424
Jews went away, and believed on *J*	Jn 12:11	2424
when they heard that *J* was coming	Jn 12:12	2424
And *J*, when he had found a young	Jn 12:14	2424
but when *J* was glorified, then	Jn 12:16	2424
him, saying, Sir, we would see *J*	Jn 12:21	2424
and again Andrew and Philip tell *J*	Jn 12:22	2424
J answered them, saying, The hour	Jn 12:23	2424
J answered and said, This voice	Jn 12:30	2424
Then *J* said unto them, Yet a	Jn 12:35	2424
These things spake *J*, and departed	Jn 12:36	2424
J cried and said, He that	Jn 12:44	2424
when *J* knew that his hour was	Jn 13:1	2424
J knowing that the Father had	Jn 13:3	2424
J answered and said unto him, What	Jn 13:7	2424
J answered him, If I wash thee	Jn 13:8	2424
J saith to him, He that is washed	Jn 13:10	2424
When *J* had thus said, he was	Jn 13:21	2424
of his disciples, whom *J* loved	Jn 13:23	2424
J answered, He it is, to whom I	Jn 13:26	2424
Then said *J* unto him, That thou	Jn 13:27	2424
that *J* had said unto him, Buy	Jn 13:29	2424
J said, Now is the Son of man	Jn 13:31	2424
J answered him, Whither I go,	Jn 13:36	2424
J answered him, Wilt thou lay	Jn 13:38	2424
J saith unto him, I am the way,	Jn 14:6	2424
J saith unto him, Have I been so	Jn 14:9	2424
J answered and said unto him, If a	Jn 14:23	2424
Now *J* knew that they were	Jn 16:19	2424
J answered them, Do ye now	Jn 16:31	2424
These words spake *J*, and lifted up	Jn 17:1	2424
J Christ, whom thou hast sent	Jn 17:3	2424
When *J* had spoken these words, he	Jn 18:1	2424
for *J* ofttimes resorted thither	Jn 18:2	2424
J therefore, knowing all things	Jn 18:4	2424
They answered him, *J* of Nazareth	Jn 18:5	2424
J saith unto them, I am he	Jn 18:5	2424
And they said, *J* of Nazareth	Jn 18:7	2424
J answered, I have told you that	Jn 18:8	2424
Then said *J* unto Peter, Put up	Jn 18:11	2424
and officers of the Jews took *J*	Jn 18:12	2424
And Simon Peter followed *J*	Jn 18:15	2424
went in with *J* into the palace of	Jn 18:15	2424
then asked *J* of his disciples	Jn 18:19	2424
J answered him, I spake openly to	Jn 18:20	2424
J with the palm of his hand	Jn 18:22	2424
J answered him, If I have spoken	Jn 18:23	2424
Then led they *J* from Caiaphas	Jn 18:28	2424
saying of *J* might be fulfilled	Jn 18:32	2424
judgment hall again, and called *J*	Jn 18:33	2424
J answered him, Sayest thou this	Jn 18:34	2424
J answered, My kingdom is not of	Jn 18:36	2424
J answered, Thou sayest that I am	Jn 18:37	2424
Then Pilate therefore took *J*	Jn 19:1	2424
Then came *J* forth, wearing the	Jn 19:5	2424
judgment hall, and saith unto *J*	Jn 19:9	2424
But *J* gave him no answer	Jn 19:9	2424
J answered, Thou couldest have no	Jn 19:11	2424
that saying, he brought *J* forth	Jn 19:13	2424
And they took *J*, and led him away	Jn 19:16	2424
side one, and *J* in the midst	Jn 19:18	2424
J OF NAZARETH THE KING OF THE	Jn 19:19	2424
for the place where *J* was	Jn 19:20	2424
when they had crucified *J*	Jn 19:23	2424
by the cross of *J* his mother	Jn 19:25	2424
When *J* therefore saw his mother,	Jn 19:26	2424

J knowing that all things were	Jn 19:28	2424
When *J* therefore had received the	Jn 19:30	2424
But when they came to *J*, and saw	Jn 19:33	2424
Arimathaea, being a disciple of *J*	Jn 19:38	2424
he might take away the body of *J*	Jn 19:38	2424
therefore, and took the body of *J*	Jn 19:38	2424
at the first came to *J* by night	Jn 19:39	2424
Then took they the body of *J*	Jn 19:40	2424
There laid they *J* therefore	Jn 19:42	2424
whom *J* loved, and saith unto them,	Jn 20:2	2424
where the body of *J* had lain	Jn 20:12	2424
saw *J* standing, and knew not that	Jn 20:14	2424
and knew not that it was *J*	Jn 20:14	2424
J saith unto her, Woman, why	Jn 20:15	2424
J saith unto her, Mary	Jn 20:16	2424
J saith unto her, Touch me not	Jn 20:17	2424
for fear of the Jews	Jn 20:19	2424
Then said *J* to them again, Peace	Jn 20:21	2424
was not with them when *J* came	Jn 20:24	2424
then came *J*, the doors being shut	Jn 20:26	2424
J saith unto him, Thomas, because	Jn 20:29	2424
did *J* in the presence of his	Jn 20:30	2424
believe that *J* is the Christ	Jn 20:31	2424
After these things *J* shewed	Jn 21:1	2424
now come, *J* stood on the shore	Jn 21:4	2424
disciples knew not that it was *J*	Jn 21:4	2424
Then *J* saith unto them, Children,	Jn 21:5	2424
whom *J* loved saith unto Peter	Jn 21:7	2424
J saith unto them, Bring of the	Jn 21:10	2424
J saith unto them, Come and dine	Jn 21:12	2424
J then cometh, and taketh bread,	Jn 21:13	2424
J shewed himself to his disciples	Jn 21:14	2424
J saith to Simon Peter, Simon,	Jn 21:15	2424
J saith unto him, Feed my sheep	Jn 21:17	2424
disciple whom *J* loved following	Jn 21:20	2424
Peter seeing him saith to *J*	Jn 21:21	2424
J saith unto him, If I will that	Jn 21:22	2424
yet *J* said not unto him, He shall	Jn 21:23	2424
many other things which *J* did	Jn 21:25	2424
of all that *J* began both to do and	Acts 1:1	2424
this same *J*, which is taken up	Acts 1:11	2424
women, and Mary the mother of *J*	Acts 1:14	2424
was guide to them that took *J*	Acts 1:16	2424
the time that the Lord *J* went in	Acts 1:21	2424
J of Nazareth, a man approved of	Acts 2:22	2424
This *J* hath God raised up,	Acts 2:32	2424
that God hath made that same *J*	Acts 2:36	2424
of *J* Christ for the remission of	Acts 2:38	2424
In the name of *J* Christ of	Acts 3:6	2424
fathers, hath glorified his Son *J*	Acts 3:13	2424
And he shall send *J* Christ	Acts 3:20	2424
God, having raised up his Son *J*	Acts 3:26	2424
people, and preached through *J* the	Acts 4:2	2424
the name of *J* Christ of Nazareth	Acts 4:10	2424
them, that they had been with *J*	Acts 4:13	2424
at all nor teach in the name of *J*	Acts 4:18	2424
a truth against thy holy child *J*	Acts 4:27	2424
by the name of thy holy child *J*	Acts 4:30	2424
of the resurrection of the Lord *J*	Acts 4:33	2424
God of our fathers raised up *J*	Acts 5:30	2424
should not speak in the name of *J*	Acts 5:40	2424
not to teach and preach *J* Christ	Acts 5:42	2424
that this *J* of Nazareth shall	Acts 6:14	2424
with *J* into the possession of the	Acts 7:45	2424
J standing on the right hand of	Acts 7:55	2424
upon God, and saying, Lord *J*	Acts 7:59	2424
of God, and the name of *J* Christ	Acts 8:12	2424
in the name of the Lord *J*	Acts 8:16	2424
scripture, and preached unto him *J*	Acts 8:35	2424
I believe that *J* Christ is the	Acts 8:37	2424
I am *J* whom thou persecutest	Acts 9:5	2424
Brother Saul, the Lord, even *J*	Acts 9:17	2424
at Damascus in the name of *J*	Acts 9:27	2424
boldly in the name of the Lord *J*	Acts 9:29	2424
J Christ maketh thee whole	Acts 9:34	2424
preaching peace by *J* Christ	Acts 10:36	2424
How God anointed *J* of Nazareth	Acts 10:38	2424
who believed on the Lord *J* Christ	Acts 11:17	2424
Grecians, preaching the Lord *J*	Acts 11:20	2424
raised unto Israel a Saviour, *J*	Acts 13:23	2424
in that he hath raised up *J* again	Acts 13:33	2424
Lord *J* Christ we shall be saved	Acts 15:11	2424
for the name of our Lord *J* Christ	Acts 15:26	2424
of *J* Christ to come out of her	Acts 16:18	2424
Believe on the Lord *J* Christ	Acts 16:31	2424
and that this *J*, whom I preach	Acts 17:3	2424
that there is another king, one *J*	Acts 17:7	2424
because he preached unto them *J*	Acts 17:18	2424
to the Jews that *J* was Christ	Acts 18:5	2424
the scriptures that *J* was Christ	Acts 18:28	2424
after him, that is, on Christ *J*	Acts 19:4	2424

in the name of the Lord J	Acts 19:5	2424
Asia heard the word of the Lord J	Acts 19:10	2424
spirits the name of the Lord J	Acts 19:13	2424
We adjure you by J whom Paul	Acts 19:13	2424
and said, J I know, and Paul I know	Acts 19:15	2424
name of the Lord J was magnified	Acts 19:17	2424
and faith toward our Lord J Christ	Acts 20:21	2424
I have received of the Lord J	Acts 20:24	2424
remember the words of the Lord J	Acts 20:35	2424
for the name of the Lord J	Acts 21:13	2424
I am J of Nazareth, whom thou	Acts 22:8	2424
own superstition, and of one J	Acts 25:19	2424
to the name of J of Nazareth	Acts 26:9	2424
I am J whom thou persecutest	Acts 26:15	2424
God, persuading them concerning J	Acts 28:23	2424
which concern the Lord J Christ	Acts 28:31	2424
Paul, a servant of J Christ	Rom 1:1	2424
his Son J Christ our Lord	Rom 1:3	2424
ye also the called of J Christ	Rom 1:6	2424
our Father, and the Lord J Christ	Rom 1:7	2424
God through J Christ for you all	Rom 1:8	2424
judge the secrets of men by J	Rom 2:16	2424
is by faith of J Christ unto all	Rom 3:22	2424
redemption that is in Christ J	Rom 3:24	2424
of him which believeth in J	Rom 3:26	2424
up J our Lord from the dead	Rom 4:24	2424
God through our Lord J Christ	Rom 5:1	2424
in God through our Lord J Christ	Rom 5:11	2424
J Christ, hath abounded unto many	Rom 5:15	2424
reign in life by one, J Christ	Rom 5:17	2424
eternal life by J Christ our Lord	Rom 5:21	2424
of us as were baptized into J	Rom 6:3	2424
God through J Christ our Lord	Rom 6:11	2424
life through J Christ our Lord	Rom 6:23	2424
God through J Christ our Lord	Rom 7:25	2424
to them which are in Christ J	Rom 8:1	2424
the Spirit of life in Christ J	Rom 8:2	2424
up J from the dead dwell in you	Rom 8:11	2424
which is in Christ J our Lord	Rom 8:39	2424
confess with thy mouth the Lord J	Rom 10:9	2424
But put ye on the Lord J Christ	Rom 13:14	2424
and am persuaded by the Lord J	Rom 14:14	2424
another according to Christ J	Rom 15:5	2424
the Father of our Lord J Christ	Rom 15:6	2424
Now I say that J Christ was a	Rom 15:8	2424
of J Christ to the Gentiles	Rom 15:16	2424
whereof I may glory through J	Rom 15:17	2424
for the Lord J Christ's sake, and	Rom 15:30	2424
and Aquila my helpers in Christ J	Rom 16:3	2424
such serve not our Lord J Christ	Rom 16:18	2424
of our Lord J Christ be with you	Rom 16:20	2424
The grace of our Lord J Christ be	Rom 16:24	2424
and the preaching of J Christ	Rom 16:25	2424
glory through J Christ for ever	Rom 16:27	2424
called to be an apostle of J	1Cor 1:1	2424
that are sanctified in Christ J	1Cor 1:2	2424
the name of J Christ our Lord	1Cor 1:2	2424
Father, and from the Lord J Christ	1Cor 1:3	2424
which is given you by J Christ	1Cor 1:4	2424
the coming of our Lord J Christ	1Cor 1:7	2424
in the day of our Lord J Christ	1Cor 1:8	2424
of his Son J Christ our Lord	1Cor 1:9	2424
by the name of our Lord J Christ	1Cor 1:10	2424
But of him are ye in Christ J	1Cor 1:30	2424
save J Christ, and him crucified	1Cor 2:2	2424
that is laid, which is J Christ	1Cor 3:11	2424
for in Christ J I have begotten	1Cor 4:15	2424
In the name of our Lord J Christ	1Cor 5:4	2424
the power of our Lord J Christ	1Cor 5:4	2424
be saved in the day of the Lord J	1Cor 5:5	2424
in the name of the Lord J	1Cor 6:11	2424
and one Lord J Christ, by whom are	1Cor 8:6	2424
have I not seen J Christ our Lord	1Cor 9:1	2424
That the Lord J the same night in	1Cor 11:23	2424
Spirit of God calleth J accursed	1Cor 12:3	2424
no man can say that J is the Lord	1Cor 12:3	2424
which I have in Christ J our Lord	1Cor 15:31	2424
victory through our Lord J Christ	1Cor 15:57	2424
man love not the Lord J Christ	1Cor 16:22	2424
of our Lord J Christ be with you	1Cor 16:23	2424
love be with you all in Christ J	1Cor 16:24	2424
an apostle of J Christ by the	2Cor 1:1	2424
Father, and from the Lord J Christ	2Cor 1:2	2424
the Father of our Lord J Christ	2Cor 1:3	2424
are ours in the day of the Lord J	2Cor 1:14	2424
J Christ, who was preached among	2Cor 1:19	2424
ourselves, but Christ J the Lord	2Cor 4:5	2424
of God in the face of J Christ	2Cor 4:6	2424
the body the dying of the Lord J	2Cor 4:10	2424
that the life also of J might be	2Cor 4:10	2424
that the life also of J might be	2Cor 4:11	2424

he which raised up the Lord J	2Cor 4:14	2424
shall raise up us also by J	2Cor 4:14	2424
us to himself by J Christ	2Cor 5:18	2424
the grace of our Lord J Christ	2Cor 8:9	2424
that cometh preacheth another J	2Cor 11:4	2424
and Father of our Lord J Christ	2Cor 11:31	2424
how that J Christ is in you,	2Cor 13:5	2424
The grace of the Lord J Christ	2Cor 13:14	2424
neither by man, but by J Christ	Gal 1:1	2424
Father, and from our Lord J Christ	Gal 1:3	2424
but by the revelation of J Christ	Gal 1:12	2424
liberty which we have in Christ J	Gal 2:4	2424
law, but by the faith of J Christ	Gal 2:16	2424
even we have believed in J Christ	Gal 2:16	2424
before whose eyes J Christ hath	Gal 3:1	2424
on the Gentiles through Christ J	Gal 3:14	2424
that the promise by faith of J	Gal 3:22	2424
of God by faith in Christ J	Gal 3:26	2424
for ye are all one in Christ J	Gal 3:28	2424
an angel of God, even as Christ J	Gal 4:14	2424
For in J Christ neither	Gal 5:6	2424
in the cross of our Lord J Christ	Gal 6:14	2424
For in Christ J neither	Gal 6:15	2424
my body the marks of the Lord J	Gal 6:17	2424
the grace of our Lord J Christ be	Gal 6:18	2424
an apostle of J Christ by the	Eph 1:1	2424
and to the faithful in Christ J	Eph 1:1	2424
Father, and from the Lord J Christ	Eph 1:2	2424
and Father of our Lord J Christ	Eph 1:3	2424
children by J Christ to himself	Eph 1:5	2424
heard of your faith in the Lord J	Eph 1:15	2424
That the God of our Lord J Christ	Eph 1:17	2424
in heavenly places in Christ J	Eph 2:6	2424
toward us through Christ J	Eph 2:7	2424
in Christ J unto good works	Eph 2:10	2424
But now in Christ J ye who	Eph 2:13	2424
J Christ himself being the chief	Eph 2:20	2424
the prisoner of J Christ for you	Eph 3:1	2424
created all things by J Christ	Eph 3:9	2424
he purposed in Christ J our Lord	Eph 3:11	2424
the Father of our Lord J Christ	Eph 3:14	2424
by Christ J throughout all ages	Eph 3:21	2424
by him, as the truth is in J	Eph 4:21	2424
in the name of our Lord J Christ	Eph 5:20	2424
the Father and the Lord J Christ	Eph 6:23	2424
our Lord J Christ in sincerity	Eph 6:24	2424
the servants of Christ	Phil 1:1	2424
in Christ J which are at Philippi	Phil 1:1	2424
Father, and from the Lord J Christ	Phil 1:2	2424
it until the day of J Christ	Phil 1:6	2424
you all in the bowels of J Christ	Phil 1:8	2424
which are by J Christ, unto the	Phil 1:11	2424
supply of the Spirit of J Christ	Phil 1:19	2424
may be more abundant in J Christ	Phil 1:26	2424
you, which was also in Christ J	Phil 2:5	2424
That at the name of J every knee	Phil 2:10	2424
confess that J Christ is Lord	Phil 2:11	2424
But I trust in the Lord J to send	Phil 2:19	2424
the things which are J Christ's	Phil 2:21	2424
spirit, and rejoice in Christ J	Phil 3:3	2424
the knowledge of Christ J my Lord	Phil 3:8	2424
also I am apprehended of Christ J	Phil 3:12	2424
high calling of God in Christ J	Phil 3:14	2424
the Saviour, the Lord J Christ	Phil 3:20	2424
hearts and minds through Christ J	Phil 4:7	2424
his riches in glory by Christ J	Phil 4:19	2424
Salute every saint in Christ J	Phil 4:21	2424
The grace of our Lord J Christ be	Phil 4:23	2424
an apostle of J Christ by the	Col 1:1	2424
our Father and the Lord J Christ	Col 1:2	2424
the Father of our Lord J Christ	Col 1:3	2424
heard of your faith in Christ J	Col 1:4	2424
every man perfect in Christ J	Col 1:28	2424
received Christ J the Lord	Col 2:6	2424
do all in the name of the Lord J	Col 3:17	2424
Father and in the Lord J Christ	1Th 1:1	2424
our Father, and the Lord J Christ	1Th 1:1	2424
of hope in our Lord J Christ	1Th 1:3	2424
he raised from the dead, even J	1Th 1:10	2424
which in Judaea are in Christ J	1Th 2:14	2424
Who both killed the Lord J	1Th 2:15	2424
our Lord J Christ at his coming	1Th 2:19	2424
our Father, and our Lord J Christ	1Th 3:11	2424
at the coming of our Lord J	1Th 3:13	2424
and exhort you by the Lord J	1Th 4:1	2424
we gave you by the Lord J	1Th 4:2	2424
For if we believe that J died	1Th 4:14	2424
in J will God bring with him	1Th 4:14	2424
salvation by our Lord J Christ	1Th 5:9	2424
of God in Christ J concerning you	1Th 5:18	2424
the coming of our Lord J Christ	1Th 5:23	2424

J

of our Lord *J* Christ be with you	1Th 5:28	2424
our Father and the Lord *J* Christ	2Th 1:1	2424
our Father and the Lord *J* Christ	2Th 1:2	2424
when the Lord *J* shall be revealed	2Th 1:7	2424
the gospel of our Lord *J* Christ	2Th 1:8	2424
That the name of our Lord *J*	2Th 1:12	2424
of our God and the Lord *J* Christ	2Th 1:12	2424
the coming of our Lord *J* Christ	2Th 2:1	2424
of the glory of our Lord *J* Christ	2Th 2:14	2424
Now our Lord *J* Christ himself, and	2Th 2:16	2424
in the name of our Lord *J* Christ	2Th 3:6	2424
and exhort by our Lord *J* Christ	2Th 3:12	2424
The grace of our Lord *J* Christ be	2Th 3:18	2424
an apostle of *J* Christ by the	1Ti 1:1	2424
Lord *J* Christ, which is our hope	1Ti 1:1	2424
our Father and *J* Christ our Lord	1Ti 1:2	2424
And I thank Christ *J* our Lord	1Ti 1:12	2424
and love which is in Christ *J*	1Ti 1:14	2424
that Christ *J* came into the world	1Ti 1:15	2424
that in me first *J* Christ might	1Ti 1:16	2424
God and men, the man Christ *J*	1Ti 2:5	2424
in the faith which is in Christ *J*	1Ti 3:13	2424
be a good minister of *J* Christ	1Ti 4:6	2424
before God, and the Lord *J* Christ	1Ti 5:21	2424
the words of our Lord *J* Christ	1Ti 6:3	2424
all things, and before Christ *J*	1Ti 6:13	2424
appearing of our Lord *J* Christ	1Ti 6:14	2424
an apostle of *J* Christ by the	2Ti 1:1	2424
of life which is in Christ *J*	2Ti 1:1	2424
the Father and Christ *J* our Lord	2Ti 1:2	2424
Christ *J* before the world began	2Ti 1:9	2424
appearing of our Saviour *J* Christ	2Ti 1:10	2424
and love which is in Christ *J*	2Ti 1:13	2424
in the grace that is in Christ *J*	2Ti 2:1	2424
as a good soldier of *J* Christ	2Ti 2:3	2424
Remember that *J* Christ of the	2Ti 2:8	2424
is in Christ *J* with eternal glory	2Ti 2:10	2424
Christ *J* shall suffer persecution	2Ti 3:12	2424
faith which is in Christ *J*	2Ti 3:15	2424
before God, and the Lord *J* Christ	2Ti 4:1	2424
The Lord *J* Christ be with thy	2Ti 4:22	2424
of God, and an apostle of *J* Christ	Titus 1:1	2424
the Lord *J* Christ our Saviour	Titus 1:4	2424
great God and our Saviour *J* Christ	Titus 2:13	2424
through *J* Christ our Saviour	Titus 3:6	2424
Paul, a prisoner of *J* Christ	Philem 1	2424
our Father and the Lord *J* Christ	Philem 3	2424
which thou hast toward the Lord *J*	Philem 5	2424
thing which is in you in Christ *J*	Philem 6	2424
now also a prisoner of *J* Christ	Philem 9	2424
my fellowprisoner in Christ *J*	Philem 23	2424
The grace of our Lord *J* Christ be	Philem 25	2424
But we see *J*, who was made a	Heb 2:9	2424
of our profession, Christ *J*	Heb 3:1	2424
J the Son of God, let us hold	Heb 4:14	2424
is for us entered, even *J*	Heb 6:20	2424
By so much was *J* made a surety of	Heb 7:22	2424
the body of *J* Christ once for all	Heb 10:10	2424
the holiest by the blood of *J*	Heb 10:19	2424
Looking unto *J* the author	Heb 12:2	2424
to *J* the mediator of the new	Heb 12:24	2424
J Christ the same yesterday, and	Heb 13:8	2424
Wherefore *J* also, that he might	Heb 13:12	2424
again from the dead our Lord *J*	Heb 13:20	2424
in his sight, through *J* Christ	Heb 13:21	2424
of God and of the Lord *J* Christ	Jas 1:1	2424
the faith of our Lord *J* Christ	Jas 2:1	2424
Peter, an apostle of *J* Christ	1Pet 1:1	2424
of the blood of *J* Christ	1Pet 1:2	2424
and Father of our Lord *J* Christ	1Pet 1:3	2424
of *J* Christ from the dead	1Pet 1:3	2424
at the appearing of *J* Christ	1Pet 1:7	2424
you at the revelation of *J* Christ	1Pet 1:13	2424
acceptable to God by *J* Christ	1Pet 2:5	2424
by the resurrection of *J* Christ	1Pet 3:21	2424
may be glorified through *J* Christ	1Pet 4:11	2424
his eternal glory by *J* Christ	1Pet 5:10	2424
with you all that are in Christ *J*	1Pet 5:14	2424
servant and an apostle of *J* Christ	2Pet 1:1	2424
of God and our Saviour *J* Christ	2Pet 1:1	2424
of God, and of *J* our Lord,	2Pet 1:2	2424
knowledge of our Lord *J* Christ	2Pet 1:8	2424
of our Lord and Saviour *J* Christ	2Pet 1:11	2424
even as our Lord *J* Christ hath	2Pet 1:14	2424
and coming of our Lord *J* Christ	2Pet 1:16	2424
of the Lord and Saviour *J* Christ	2Pet 2:20	2424
of our Lord and Saviour *J* Christ	2Pet 3:18	2424
Father, and with his Son *J* Christ	1Jn 1:3	2424
the blood of *J* Christ his Son	1Jn 1:7	2424
Father, *J* Christ the righteous	1Jn 2:1	2424
that denieth that *J* is the Christ	1Jn 2:22	2424

on the name of his Son *J* Christ	1Jn 3:23	2424
spirit that confesseth that *J*	1Jn 4:2	2424
J Christ is come in the flesh is	1Jn 4:3	2424
confess that *J* is the Son of God	1Jn 4:15	2424
Whosoever believeth that *J* is the	1Jn 5:1	2424
that *J* is the Son of God	1Jn 5:5	2424
by water and blood, even *J* Christ	1Jn 5:6	2424
is true, even in his Son *J* Christ	1Jn 5:20	2424
Father, and from the Lord *J* Christ	2Jn 3	2424
who confess not that *J* Christ is	2Jn 7	2424
Jude, the servant of *J* Christ	Jude 1	2424
Father, and preserved in *J* Christ	Jude 1	2424
Lord God, and our Lord *J* Christ	Jude 4	2424
the apostles of our Lord *J* Christ	Jude 17	2424
Lord *J* Christ unto eternal life	Jude 21	2424
The Revelation of *J* Christ	Rev 1:1	2424
and of the testimony of *J* Christ	Rev 1:2	2424
from *J* Christ, who is the	Rev 1:5	2424
kingdom and patience of *J* Christ	Rev 1:9	2424
and for the testimony of *J*	Rev 1:9	2424
and have the testimony of *J* Christ	Rev 12:17	2424
of God, and the faith of *J*	Rev 14:12	2424
the blood of the martyrs of *J*	Rev 17:6	2424
that have the testimony of *J*	Rev 19:10	2424
for the testimony of *J* is the	Rev 19:10	2424
beheaded for the witness of *J*	Rev 20:4	2424
I *J* have sent mine angel to	Rev 22:16	2424
Even so, come, Lord *J*	Rev 22:20	2424
The grace of our Lord *J* Christ be	Rev 22:21	2424

2. Joshua, son of Nun.

For if *J* had given them rest,	Heb 4:8	2424

3. Justus, a Roman Christian.

And *J*, which is called Justus, who	Col 4:11	2424

JESUS' *(je'-zus) Refers to the Christ.*

and cast them down at *J* feet	Mt 15:30	2424
who also himself was *J* disciple	Mt 27:57	2424
saw it, he fell down at *J* knees	Lk 5:8	2424
and he fell down at *J* feet	Lk 8:41	2424
Mary, which also sat at *J* feet	Lk 10:39	2424
and they came not for *J* sake only	Jn 12:9	2424
Now there was leaning on *J* bosom	Jn 13:23	2424
He then lying on *J* breast saith	Jn 13:25	2424
your servants for *J* sake	2Cor 4:5	2424
delivered unto death for *J* sake	2Cor 4:11	2424

JETHER *(je'-thur)* See HOBAB, ITHRA, ITHRITES, JETHRO, RAGUEL.

1. A son of Gideon.

he said unto *J* his firstborn, Up,	Judg 8:20	3500

2. Father of Amasa.

Ner, and unto Amasa the son of *J*	1Kin 2:5	3500
of Israel, and Amasa the son of *J*	1Kin 2:32	3500
of Amasa was *J* the Ishmeelite	1Chr 2:17	3500

3. A son of Jerahmeel.

J, and Jonathan	1Chr 2:32	3500
and *J* died without children	1Chr 2:32	3500

4. A son of Ezra.

And the sons of Ezra were, *J*	1Chr 4:17	3500

5. A descendant of Asher.

And the sons of *J*	1Chr 7:38	3500

JETHETH *(je'-theth) A prince of Edom.*

duke Timnah, duke Alvah, duke *J*	Gen 36:40	3509
duke Timnah, duke Aliah, duke *J*	1Chr 1:51	3509

JETHLAH *(jeth'-lah) A city in Dan.*

And Shaalabbin, and Ajalon, and *J*	Josh 19:42	3494

JETHRO *(je'-thro)* See JETHER. *Father-in-law of Moses.*

the flock of *J* his father in law	Ex 3:1	3503
returned to *J* his father in law,	Ex 4:18	3503
J said to Moses, Go in peace	Ex 4:18	3503
When *J*, the priest of Midian,	Ex 18:1	3503
Then *J*, Moses' father in law,	Ex 18:2	3503
And *J*, Moses' father in law, came	Ex 18:5	3503
father in law *J* am come unto thee	Ex 18:6	3503
J rejoiced for all the goodness	Ex 18:9	3503
J said, Blessed be the LORD, who	Ex 18:10	3503
And *J*, Moses' father in law, took	Ex 18:12	3503

JETUR *(je'-tur)*

1. A son of Ishmael.

Hadar, and Tema, *J*, Naphish, and	Gen 25:15	3195
J, Naphish, and Kedemah	1Chr 1:31	3195

2. Descendants of Jetur.

war with the Hagarites, with *J*	1Chr 5:19	3195

JEUEL *(je-u'-el)* See JEIEL. *A descendant of Zerah.*

J, and their brethren, six hundred	1Chr 9:6	3262

JEUSH *(je'-ush)* See JEHUSH.

1. A son of Esau.

And Aholibamah bare *J*, and Jaalam,	Gen 36:5	3266
and she bare to Esau *J*, and Jaalam,	Gen 36:14	3266

duke *J*, duke Jaalam, duke Korah .... Gen 36:18   3266
Eliphaz, Reuel, and *J*, and Jaalam, ... 1Chr 1:35   3266
    2. *Grandson of Jediael.*
J, and Benjamin, and Ehud, and 1Chr 7:10   3266
    3. *A sanctuary servant.*
Shimei were, Jahath, Zina, and *J* 1Chr 23:10   3266
but *J* and Beriah had not many sons 1Chr 23:11   3266
    4. *A son of Rehoboam.*
J, and Shamariah, and Zaham................ 2Chr 11:19   3266

JEUZ *(je'-uz) Son of Shaharaim.*
And *J*, and Shachia, and Mirma 1Chr 8:10   3263

JEW *(jew)* See JEWESS, JEWISH, JEWS. *Post-exilic term*
    for the Israelites.
the palace there was a certain *J* .... Est 2:5   3064
he had told them that he was a *J* .... Est 3:4   3064
the *J* sitting at the king's gate .... Est 5:13   3064
and do even so to Mordecai the *J* .... Est 6:10   3064
the queen and to Mordecai the *J* .... Est 8:7   3064
of Abihail, and Mordecai the *J* .... Est 9:29   3064
according as Mordecai the *J* .... Est 9:31   3064
For Mordecai the *J* was next unto .... Est 10:3   3064
them, to wit, of a *J* his brother .... Jer 34:9   3064
of the skirt of him that is a *J* .... Zec 8:23   3064
How is it that thou, being a *J* .... Jn 4:9   2453
Pilate answered, Am I a *J* .... Jn 18:35   2453
a man that is a *J* to keep company .... Acts 10:28   2453
sorcerer, a false prophet, a *J* .... Acts 13:6   2453
And found a certain *J* named Aquila ...... Acts 18:2   2453
a certain *J* named Apollos, born .... Acts 18:24   2453
were seven sons of one Sceva, a *J* .... Acts 19:14   2453
when they knew that he was a *J* .... Acts 19:34   2453
I am a man which am a *J* of Tarsus .... Acts 21:39   2453
I am verily a man which am a *J* .... Acts 22:3   2453
to the *J* first, and also to the .... Rom 1:16   2453
that doeth evil, of the *J* first .... Rom 2:9   2453
that worketh good, to the *J* first .... Rom 2:10   2453
Behold, thou art called a *J* .... Rom 2:17   2453
For he is not a *J*, which is one .... Rom 2:28   2453
But he is a *J*, which is one .... Rom 2:29   2453
What advantage then hath the *J* .... Rom 3:1   2453
is no difference between the *J* .... Rom 10:12   2453
And unto the Jews I became as a *J* 1Cor 9:20   2453
them all, If thou, being a *J* .... Gal 2:14   2453
There is neither *J* nor Greek.................... Gal 3:28   2453
there is neither Greek nor *J* .... Col 3:11   2453

JEWEL
As a *j* of gold in a swine's snout .... Prov 11:22   5141
of knowledge are a precious *j* .... Prov 20:15   3627
I put a *j* on thy forehead, and .... Eze 16:12   5141

JEWELS
servant brought forth *j* of silver .... Gen 24:53   3627
j of gold, and raiment, and gave .... Gen 24:53   3627
j of silver, and *j* of gold, ... Ex 3:22   3627
j of silver, and *j* of gold .... Ex 11:2   3627
of the Egyptians *j* of silver .... Ex 12:35   3627
and *j* of gold, and raiment .... Ex 12:35   3627
rings, and tablets, all *j* of gold................ Ex 35:22   3627
gotten, of *j* of gold, chains, and .... Num 31:50   3627
gold of them, even all wrought *j*.............. Num 31:51   3627
and put the *j* of gold, which ye 1Sa 6:8   3627
wherein the *j* of gold were, and 1Sa 6:15   3627
the dead bodies, and precious *j* 2Chr 20:25   3627
and for all manner of pleasant *j* 2Chr 32:27   3627
shall not be for *j* of fine gold.................. Job 28:17   3627
cheeks are comely with rows of *j* .... Song 1:10
joints of thy thighs are like *j* .... Song 7:1   2484
The rings, and nose *j*,............................. Is 3:21   5141
bride adorneth herself with her *j* .... Is 61:10   3627
also taken thy fair *j* of my gold .... Eze 16:17   3627
clothes, and shall take thy fair *j* .... Eze 16:39   3627
clothes, and take away thy fair *j* .... Eze 23:26   3627
with her earrings and her *j* .... Hos 2:13   2484
in that day when I make up my *j* .... Mal 3:17   5459

JEWESS *(jew'-ess) A female Jew.*
of a certain woman, which was a *J* .... Acts 16:1   2453
his wife Drusilla, which was a *J* .... Acts 24:24   2453

JEWISH *(jew'-ish) Of or relating to the Jews.*
Not giving heed to *J* fables..................... Titus 1:14   2451

JEWRY *(jew'-ree)* See JUDEA. *Of or relating to the Jews.*
king my father brought out of *J* .... Dan 5:13   3061
people, teaching throughout all *J* .... Lk 23:5   2449
for he would not walk in *J* .... Jn 7:1   2449

JEWS *(jews)* See JEWS'.
Syria, and drave the *J* from Elath 2Kin 16:6   3064
Gedaliah, that he died, and the *J* 2Kin 25:25   3064
that the *J* which came up from .... Ezr 4:12   3062
in haste to Jerusalem unto the *J*............ Ezr 4:23   3062

unto the *J* that were in Judah .... Ezr 5:1   3062
God was upon the elders of the *J* .... Ezr 5:5   3062
let the governor of the *J* .... Ezr 6:7   3062
the elders of the *J* build this .... Ezr 6:7   3062
J for the building of this house .... Ezr 6:8   3062
And the elders of the *J* builded.............. Ezr 6:14   3062
concerning the *J* that had escaped........ Neh 1:2   3064
had I as yet told it to the *J* .... Neh 2:16   3064
indignation, and mocked the *J* .... Neh 4:1   3064
and said, What do these feeble *J* .... Neh 4:2   3064
that when the *J* which dwelt by .... Neh 4:12   3064
against their brethren the *J* .... Neh 5:1   3064
have redeemed our brethren the *J* .... Neh 5:8   3064
an hundred and fifty of the *J*.................. Neh 5:17   3064
that thou and the *J* think to rebel........... Neh 6:6   3064
In those days also saw I *J* that .... Neh 13:23   3064
J that were throughout the whole .... Est 3:6   3064
and to cause to perish, all *J* .... Est 3:13   3064
was great mourning among the *J* .... Est 4:3   3064
the king's treasuries for the *J* .... Est 4:7   3064
king's house, more than all the *J* .... Est 4:13   3064
arise to the *J* from another place............. Est 4:14   3064
gather together all the *J* that .... Est 4:16   3064
Mordecai be of the seed of the *J* .... Est 6:13   3064
that he had devised against the *J* .... Est 8:3   3064
the *J* which are in all the king's .... Est 8:5   3064
he laid his hand upon the *J* .... Est 8:7   3064
Write ye also for the *J*, as it .... Est 8:8   3064
Mordecai commanded unto the *J* .... Est 8:9   3064
to the *J* according to their .... Est 8:9   3064
the *J* which were in every city to .... Est 8:11   3064
that the *J* should be ready....................... Est 8:13   3064
The *J* had light, and gladness, and .... Est 8:16   3064
the *J* had joy and gladness, a................. Est 8:17   3064
the people of the land became *J* .... Est 8:17   3054
the fear of the *J* fell upon them .... Est 8:17   3064
J hoped to have power over them .... Est 9:1   3064
that the *J* had rule over them .... Est 9:1   3064
The *J* gathered themselves .... Est 9:2   3064
of the king, helped the *J* .... Est 9:3   3064
Thus the *J* smote all their....................... Est 9:5   3064
in Shushan the palace the *J* slew .... Est 9:6   3064
of Hammedatha, the enemy of the *J* ...... Est 9:10   3064
The *J* have slain and destroyed .... Est 9:12   3064
let it be granted to the *J* which .... Est 9:13   3064
For the *J* that were in Shushan .... Est 9:15   3064
But the other *J* that were in the .... Est 9:16   3064
But the *J* that were at Shushan .... Est 9:18   3064
Therefore the *J* of the villages................ Est 9:19   3064
sent letters unto all the *J* that .... Est 9:20   3064
As the days wherein the *J* rested............ Est 9:22   3064
the *J* undertook to do as they had .... Est 9:23   3064
Agagite, the enemy of all the *J* .... Est 9:24   3064
against the *J* to destroy them .... Est 9:24   3064
which he devised against the *J*............... Est 9:25   3064
The *J* ordained, and took upon them ...... Est 9:27   3064
should not fail from among the *J* .... Est 9:28   3064
sent the letters unto all the *J* .... Est 9:30   3064
Ahasuerus, and great among the *J*........ Est 10:3   3064
before all the *J* that sat in the .... Jer 32:12   3064
I am afraid of the *J* that are .... Jer 38:19   3064
when all the *J* that were in Moab .... Jer 40:11   3064
Even all the *J* returned out of .... Jer 40:12   3064
that all the *J* which are gathered .... Jer 40:15   3064
slew all the *J* that were with him .... Jer 41:3   3064
the *J* which dwell in the land of .... Jer 44:1   3064
the seventh year three thousand *J* .... Jer 52:28   3064
of the *J* seven hundred forty .... Jer 52:30   3064
came near, and accused the *J* .... Dan 3:8   3064
There are certain *J* whom thou .... Dan 3:12   3064
is he that is born King of the *J*............... Mt 2:2   2453
Art thou the King of the *J* .... Mt 27:11   2453
him, saying, Hail, King of the *J* .... Mt 27:29   2453
THIS IS JESUS THE KING OF THE *J* .. Mt 27:37   2453
among *J* until this day .... Mt 28:15   2453
For the Pharisees, and all the *J* .... Mk 7:3   2453
him, Art thou the King of the *J* .... Mk 15:2   2453
unto you the King of the *J* .... Mk 15:9   2453
whom ye call the King of the *J* .... Mk 15:12   2453
salute him, Hail, King of the *J* .... Mk 15:18   2453
written over, THE KING OF THE *J* .... Mk 15:26   2453
sent unto him the elders of the *J* .... Lk 7:3   2453
Art thou the King of the *J* .... Lk 23:3   2453
If thou be the king of the *J* .... Lk 23:37   2453
THIS IS THE KING OF THE *J* .... Lk 23:38   2453
of Arimathaea, a city of the *J*................. Lk 23:51   2453
when the *J* sent priests and..................... Jn 1:19   2453
manner of the purifying of the *J* .... Jn 2:6   2453
Then answered the *J* and said unto .... Jn 2:18   2453
Then said the *J*, Forty and six .... Jn 2:20   2453
named Nicodemus, a ruler of the *J*......... Jn 3:1   2453

J

and the *J* about purifying .... Jn 3:25   2453
for the *J* have no dealings with .... Jn 4:9   2453
for salvation is of the *J* .... Jn 4:22   2453
this there was a feast of the *J* .... Jn 5:1   2453
The *J* therefore said unto him .... Jn 5:10   2453
told the *J* that it was Jesus, ... Jn 5:15   2453
did the *J* persecute Jesus .... Jn 5:16   2453
Therefore the *J* sought the more .... Jn 5:18   2453
And the passover, a feast of the *J* .... Jn 6:4   2453
The *J* then murmured at him, ... Jn 6:41   2453
The *J* therefore strove among .... Jn 6:52   2453
because the *J* sought to kill him .... Jn 7:1   2453
Then the *J* sought him at the .... Jn 7:11   2453
openly of him for fear of the *J* .... Jn 7:13   2453
the *J* marvelled, saying, How .... Jn 7:15   2453
Then said the *J* among themselves, ... Jn 7:35   2453
Then said the *J*, Will he kill .... Jn 8:22   2453
to those *J* which believed on him .... Jn 8:31   2453
Then answered the *J*, and said unto .... Jn 8:48   2453
Then said the *J* unto him, Now we .... Jn 8:52   2453
Then said the *J* unto him, Thou .... Jn 8:57   2453
But the *J* did not believe .... Jn 9:18   2453
because they feared the *J* .... Jn 9:22   2453
for the *J* had agreed already, ... Jn 9:22   2453
among the *J* for these sayings .... Jn 10:19   2453
Then came the *J* round about him, ... Jn 10:24   2453
Then the *J* took up stones again .... Jn 10:31   2453
The *J* answered him, saying, For a .... Jn 10:33   2453
the *J* of late sought to stone .... Jn 11:8   2453
many of the *J* came to Martha and .... Jn 11:19   2453
The *J* then which were with her in .... Jn 11:31   2453
the *J* also weeping which came .... Jn 11:33   2453
Then said the *J*, Behold how he .... Jn 11:36   2453
Then many of the *J* which came to .... Jn 11:45   2453
walked no more openly among the *J* .... Jn 11:54   2453
Much people of the *J* therefore .... Jn 12:9   2453
of him many of the *J* went away .... Jn 12:11   2453
and as I said unto the *J*, Whither ..... Jn 13:33   2453
and officers of the *J* took Jesus .... Jn 18:12   2453
he, which gave counsel to the *J* .... Jn 18:14   2453
whither the *J* always resort .... Jn 18:20   2453
The *J* therefore said unto him, It .... Jn 18:31   2453
him, Art thou the King of the *J* .... Jn 18:33   2453
should not be delivered to the *J* ..... Jn 18:36   2453
he went out again unto the *J* .... Jn 18:38   2453
unto you the King of the *J* .... Jn 18:39   2453
And said, Hail, King of the *J* .... Jn 19:3   2453
The *J* answered him, We have a law ..... Jn 19:7   2453
but the *J* cried out, saying, If .... Jn 19:12   2453
and he saith unto the *J*, Behold .... Jn 19:14   2453
OF NAZARETH THE KING OF THE *J* .. Jn 19:19   2453
title then read many of the *J* .... Jn 19:20   2453
chief priests of the *J* to Pilate .... Jn 19:21   2453
Write not, The King of the *J* .... Jn 19:21   2453
that he said, I am King of the *J* .... Jn 19:21   2453
The *J* therefore, because it was .... Jn 19:31   2453
but secretly for fear of the *J* .... Jn 19:38   2453
as the manner of the *J* is to bury ..... Jn 19:40   2453
were assembled for fear of the *J* ..... Jn 20:19   2453
were dwelling at Jerusalem *J* .... Acts 2:5   2453
Cyrene, and strangers of Rome, *J* .... Acts 2:10   2453
confounded the *J* which dwelt at ...... Acts 9:22   2453
the *J* took counsel to kill him .... Acts 9:23   2453
among all the nation of the *J* .... Acts 10:22   2453
he did both in the land of the *J* ..... Acts 10:39   2453
word to none but unto the *J* only ... Acts 11:19   2453
because he saw it pleased the *J* ..... Acts 12:3   2453
of the people of the *J* .... Acts 12:11   2453
of God in the synagogues of the *J* .. Acts 13:5   2453
when the *J* were gone out of the .... Acts 13:42   2453
was broken up, many of the *J* ...... Acts 13:43   2453
But when the *J* saw the multitudes ... Acts 13:45   2453
But the *J* stirred up the devout ..... Acts 13:50   2453
into the synagogue of the *J* .... Acts 14:1   2453
a great multitude both of the *J* ..... Acts 14:1   2453
But the unbelieving *J* stirred up .... Acts 14:2   2453
and part held with the *J*, and part .. Acts 14:4   2453
also of the *J* with their rulers, ... Acts 14:5   2453
thither certain *J* from Antioch ..... Acts 14:19   2453
J which were in those quarters ..... Acts 16:3   2453
saying, These men, being *J* .... Acts 16:20   2453
where was a synagogue of the *J* ... Acts 17:1   2453
But the *J* which believed not, ... Acts 17:5   2453
went into the synagogue of the *J* .. Acts 17:10   2453
But when the *J* of Thessalonica .... Acts 17:13   2453
he in the synagogue with the *J* .... Acts 17:17   2453
all *J* to depart from Rome .... Acts 18:2   2453
every sabbath, and persuaded the *J* ... Acts 18:4   2453
testified to the *J* that Jesus was .... Acts 18:5   2453
the *J* made insurrection with one ... Acts 18:12   2453
his mouth, Gallio said unto the *J* ... Acts 18:14   2453

wrong or wicked lewdness, O ye *J* ...... Acts 18:14   2453
synagogue, and reasoned with the *J* ..... Acts 18:19   2453
For he mightily convinced the *J* .... Acts 18:28   2453
word of the Lord Jesus, both *J* .... Acts 19:10   2453
Then certain of the vagabond *J* .... Acts 19:13   2453
And this was known to all the *J* .... Acts 19:17   2453
the *J* putting him forward .... Acts 19:33   2453
when the *J* laid wait for him, as ...... Acts 20:3   2453
me by the lying in wait of the *J* .... Acts 20:19   2453
Testifying both to the *J*, and also ..... Acts 20:21   2453
So shall the *J* at Jerusalem bind ...... Acts 21:11   2453
how many thousands of *J* there are .... Acts 21:20   2453
that thou teachest all the *J* .... Acts 21:21   2453
the *J* which were of Asia, when .... Acts 21:27   2453
of all the *J* which dwelt there .... Acts 22:12   2453
wherefore he was accused of the *J* .... Acts 22:30   2453
certain of the *J* banded together, ... Acts 23:12   2453
The *J* have agreed to desire thee ...... Acts 23:20   2453
This man was taken of the *J* .... Acts 23:27   2453
that the *J* laid wait for the man ...... Acts 23:30   2453
all the *J* throughout the world .... Acts 24:5   2453
the *J* also assented, saying that ...... Acts 24:9   2453
Whereupon certain *J* from Asia ...... Acts 24:18   2453
willing to shew the *J* a pleasure ..... Acts 24:27   2453
the chief of the *J* informed him ..... Acts 25:2   2453
the *J* which came down from .... Acts 25:7   2453
Neither against the law of the *J* ..... Acts 25:8   2453
willing to do the *J* a pleasure .... Acts 25:9   2453
to the *J* have I done no wrong, as ... Acts 25:10   2453
the elders of the *J* informed me ..... Acts 25:15   2453
of the *J* have dealt with me .... Acts 25:24   2453
whereof I am accused of the *J* ...... Acts 26:2   2453
questions which are among the *J* ... Acts 26:3   2453
at Jerusalem, know all the *J* .... Acts 26:4   2453
Agrippa, I am accused of the *J* ..... Acts 26:7   2453
For these causes the *J* caught me ... Acts 26:21   2453
the chief of the *J* together .... Acts 28:17   2453
But when the *J* spake against it, ... Acts 28:19   2453
the *J* departed, and had great ...... Acts 28:29   2453
for we have before proved both *J* ... Rom 3:9   2453
Is he the God of the *J* only .... Rom 3:29   2453
he hath called, not of the *J* only ... Rom 9:24   2453
For the *J* require a sign, and the 1Cor 1:22   2453
unto the *J* a stumblingblock, and ... 1Cor 1:23   2453
them which are called, both *J* 1Cor 1:24   2453
unto the *J* I became as a Jew, ... 1Cor 9:20   2453
as a Jew, that I might gain the *J* ... 1Cor 9:20   2453
none offence, neither to the *J* 1Cor 10:32   2453
body, whether we be *J* or Gentiles .. 1Cor 12:13   2453
Of the *J* five times received I 2Cor 11:24   2453
the other *J* dissembled likewise .... Gal 2:13   2453
of Gentiles, and not as do the *J* .... Gal 2:14   2452
the Gentiles to live as do the *J* .... Gal 2:14   2450
We who are *J* by nature, and not ... Gal 2:15   2453
even as they have of the *J* 1Th 2:14   2453
of them which say they are *J* ..... Rev 2:9   2453
of Satan, which say they are *J* ... Rev 3:9   2453

JEWS' *(jews)*
talk not with us in the *J* 2Kin 18:26   3066
a loud voice in the *J* language 2Kin 18:28   3066
the *J* speech unto the people of 2Chr 32:18   3066
could not speak in the *J* language .... Neh 13:24   3066
the Agagite, the *J* enemy .... Est 3:10   3064
the *J* enemy unto Esther the queen .... Est 8:1   3064
speak not to us in the *J* language .... Is 36:11   3064
a loud voice in the *J* language .... Is 36:13   3064
the *J* passover was at hand, and .... Jn 2:13   2453
Now the *J* feast of tabernacles .... Jn 7:2   2453
the *J* passover was nigh at hand .... Jn 11:55   2453
because of the *J* preparation day .... Jn 19:42   2453
in time past in the *J* religion .... Gal 1:13   2454
profited in the *J* religion above .... Gal 1:14   2454

JEZANIAH *(jez-a-ni'-ah)* See JAAZANIAH. *A Jewish captain.*
J the son of a Maachathite, they .... Jer 40:8   3153
J the son of Hoshaiah, and all the .... Jer 42:1   3153

JEZEBEL *(jez'-e-bel)* See JEZEBEL'S. *Wife of King Ahab.*
that he took to wife the *J* 1Kin 16:31   348
when *J* cut off the prophets of 1Kin 18:4   348
told my lord what I did when *J* 1Kin 18:13   348
Ahab told *J* all that Elijah had 1Kin 19:1   348
Then *J* sent a messenger unto 1Kin 19:2   348
But *J* his wife came to him, and 1Kin 21:5   348
J his wife said unto him, Dost 1Kin 21:7   348
did as *J* had sent unto them, and 1Kin 21:11   348
Then they sent to *J*, saying, ... 1Kin 21:14   348
when *J* heard that Naboth was 1Kin 21:15   348
that *J* said to Ahab, Arise, take 1Kin 21:15   348
of *J* also spake the LORD, saying, ... 1Kin 21:23   348

The dogs shall eat *J* by the wall	1Kin 21:23	348
whom *J* his wife stirred up	1Kin 21:25	348
of the LORD, at the hand of *J*	2Kin 9:7	348
the dogs shall eat *J* in the	2Kin 9:10	348
as the whoredoms of thy mother *J*	2Kin 9:22	348
come to Jezreel, *J* heard of it	2Kin 9:30	348
shall dogs eat the flesh of *J*	2Kin 9:36	348
the carcase of *J* shall be as dung	2Kin 9:37	348
they shall not say, This is *J*	2Kin 9:37	348
thou sufferest that woman *J*	Rev 2:20	2403

JEZEBEL'S *(jez'-e-bels)*
hundred, which eat at *J* table	1Kin 18:19	348

JEZER *(je'-zur)* See JEZERITES. *A son of Naphtali.*
Jahzeel, and Guni, and *J*, and	Gen 46:24	3337
Of *J*, the family of the Jezerites	Num 26:49	3337
Jahziel, and Guni, and *J*, and	1Chr 7:13	3337

JEZERITES *(je'-zur-ites)* Descendants of Jezer.
Of Jezer, the family of the	Num 26:49	3339

JEZIAH *(je-zi'-ah)* Married a foreigner in exile.
Ramiah, and *J*, and Malchiah, and	Ezr 10:25	3150

JEZIEL *(je'-ze-el)* A warrior in David's army.
and *J*, and Pelet, the sons of	1Chr 12:3	3149

JEZLIAH *(jez-li'-ah)* A son of Elpaal.
Ishmerai also, and *J*, and Jobab,	1Chr 8:18	3152

JEZOAR *(je-zo'-ar)* See ZOAR. A son of Helah.
sons of Helah were, Zereth, and *J*	1Chr 4:7	3328

JEZRAHIAH *(jez-ra-hi'-ah)* See IZRAHIAH. A priest.
sang loud, with *J* their overseer	Neh 12:42	3156

JEZREEL *(jez'-re-el)* See JEZREELITE.
1. A city in Judah.
And *J*, and Jokdeam, and Zanoah,	Josh 15:56	3157
and pitched in the valley of *J*	Judg 6:33	3157
David also took Ahinoam of *J*	1Sa 25:43	3157
by a fountain which is in *J*	1Sa 29:1	3157
And the Philistines went up to *J*	1Sa 29:11	3157
2. A city in Issachar.
And their border was toward	Josh 19:18	3157
and over the Ashurites, and over *J*	2Sa 2:9	3157
came of Saul and Jonathan out of *J*	2Sa 4:4	3157
which is by Zartanah beneath *J*	1Kin 4:12	3157
And Ahab rode, and went to *J*	1Kin 18:45	3157
before Ahab to the entrance of *J*	1Kin 18:46	3157
had a vineyard, which was in *J*	1Kin 21:1	3157
eat Jezebel by the wall of *J*	1Kin 21:23	3157
J of the wounds which the Syrians	2Kin 8:29	3157
to see Joram the son of Ahab in *J*	2Kin 8:29	3157
eat Jezebel in the portion of *J*	2Kin 9:10	3157
was returned to be healed in *J* of	2Kin 9:15	3157
of the city to go to tell it in *J*	2Kin 9:15	3157
rode in a chariot, and went to *J*	2Kin 9:16	3157
a watchman on the tower in *J*	2Kin 9:17	3157
And when Jehu was come to *J*	2Kin 9:30	3157
In the portion of *J* shall dogs	2Kin 9:36	3157
of the field in the portion of *J*	2Kin 9:37	3157
to Samaria, unto the rulers of *J*	2Kin 10:1	3157
come to me to *J* by to morrow this	2Kin 10:6	3157
in baskets, and sent him them to *J*	2Kin 10:7	3157
of the house of Ahab in *J*	2Kin 10:11	3157
in *J* because of the wounds which	2Chr 22:6	3157
see Jehoram the son of Ahab at *J*	2Chr 22:6	3157
3. A plain.
they who are of the valley of *J*	Josh 17:16	3157
bow of Israel in the valley of *J*	Hos 1:5	3157
and they shall hear *J*	Hos 2:22	3157
4. A descendant of Etam.
J, and Ishma, and Idbash	1Chr 4:3	3157
5. Symbolic name for Hosea's eldest son.
said unto him, Call his name *J*	Hos 1:4	3157
blood of *J* upon the house of Jehu	Hos 1:4	3157
for great shall be the day of *J*	Hos 1:11	3157

JEZREELITE *(jez'-re-el-ite)* See JEZREELITESS. An inhabitant of Jezreel.
that Naboth the *J* had a vineyard	1Kin 21:1	3158
Naboth the *J* had spoken to him	1Kin 21:4	3158
Because I spake unto Naboth the *J*	1Kin 21:6	3158
thee the vineyard of Naboth the *J*	1Kin 21:7	3158
of the vineyard of Naboth the *J*	1Kin 21:15	3158
to the vineyard of Naboth the *J*	1Kin 21:16	3158
in the portion of Naboth the *J*	2Kin 9:21	3158
of the field of Naboth the *J*	2Kin 9:25	3158

JEZREELITESS *(jez'-re-el-i-tess)* A female Jezreelite.
with his two wives, Ahinoam the *J*	1Sa 27:3	3159
taken captives, Ahinoam the *J*	1Sa 30:5	3159
his two wives also, Ahinoam the *J*	2Sa 2:2	3159

was Amnon, of Ahinoam the *J*	2Sa 3:2	3159
firstborn Amnon, of Ahinoam the *J*	1Chr 3:1	3159

JIBSAM *(jib'-sam)* A son of Tola.
and Jeriel, and Jahmai, and *J*	1Chr 7:2	3005

JIDLAPH *(jid'-laf)* A son of Nahor.
Chesed, and Hazo, and Pildash, and *J*	Gen 22:22	3044

JIMNA *(jim'-nah)* See IMNA, JIMNAH, JIMNITES. A son of Asher.
of *J*, the family of the Jimnites	Num 26:44	3232

JIMNAH *(jim'-nah)* See JIMNA. Same as Jimna.
J, and Ishuah, and Isui, and Beriah,	Gen 46:17	3232

JIMNITES *(jim'-nites)* Descendants of Jimna.
of Jimna, the family of the *J*	Num 26:44	3232

JIPHTAH *(jif'-tah)* See JEPHTHAH, JIPHTHAH-EL. A city in Judah.
And *J*, and Ashnah, and Nezib,	Josh 15:43	3316

JIPHTHAH-EL *(jif-thah-el)* A valley in Zebulun.
thereof are in the valley of *J*	Josh 19:14	3317
to the valley of *J* toward the	Josh 19:27	3317

JOAB *(jo'-ab)* See ATAROTH, HOUSE, JOAB'S.
1. Commander of David's army.
the son of Zeruiah, brother to *J*	1Sa 26:6	3097
J the son of Zeruiah, and the	2Sa 2:13	3097
And Abner said to *J*, Let the young	2Sa 2:14	3097
And *J* said, Let them arise	2Sa 2:14	3097
three sons of Zeruiah there, *J*	2Sa 2:18	3097
hold up my face to *J* thy brother	2Sa 2:22	3097
J also and Abishai pursued after	2Sa 2:24	3097
Then Abner called to *J*, and said,	2Sa 2:26	3097
J said, As God liveth, unless	2Sa 2:27	3097
So *J* blew a trumpet, and all the	2Sa 2:28	3097
J returned from following Abner	2Sa 2:30	3097
And *J* and his men went all night,	2Sa 2:32	3097
J came from pursuing a troop, and	2Sa 3:22	3097
When *J* and all the host that was	2Sa 3:23	3097
with him were come, they told *J*	2Sa 3:23	3097
Then *J* came to the king, and said,	2Sa 3:24	3097
when *J* was come out from David,	2Sa 3:26	3097
J took him aside in the gate to	2Sa 3:27	3097
Let it rest on the head of *J*	2Sa 3:29	3097
house of *J* one that hath an issue	2Sa 3:29	3097
So *J* and Abishai his brother slew	2Sa 3:30	3097
And David said to *J*, and to all the	2Sa 3:31	3097
J the son of Zeruiah was over the	2Sa 8:16	3097
when David heard of it, he sent *J*	2Sa 10:7	3097
When *J* saw that the front of the	2Sa 10:9	3097
J drew nigh, and the people that	2Sa 10:13	3097
So *J* returned from the children	2Sa 10:14	3097
to battle, that David sent *J*	2Sa 11:1	3097
And David sent to *J*, saying, Send	2Sa 11:6	3097
And *J* sent Uriah to David	2Sa 11:6	3097
David demanded of him how *J* did	2Sa 11:7	3097
and my lord *J*, and the servants of	2Sa 11:11	3097
that David wrote a letter to *J*	2Sa 11:14	3097
when *J* observed the city, that he	2Sa 11:16	3097
city went out, and fought with *J*	2Sa 11:17	3097
Then *J* sent and told David all the	2Sa 11:18	3097
David all that *J* had sent him for	2Sa 11:22	3097
Thus shalt thou say unto *J*	2Sa 11:25	3097
J fought against Rabbah of the	2Sa 12:26	3097
J sent messengers to David, and	2Sa 12:27	3097
Now *J* the son of Zeruiah	2Sa 14:1	3097
J sent to Tekoah, and fetched	2Sa 14:2	3097
So *J* put the words in her mouth,	2Sa 14:3	3097
Is not the hand of *J* with thee in	2Sa 14:19	3097
for thy servant *J*, he bade me, and	2Sa 14:19	3097
thy servant *J* done this thing	2Sa 14:20	3097
And the king said unto *J*, Behold	2Sa 14:21	3097
J fell to the ground on his face,	2Sa 14:22	3097
J said, Today thy servant knoweth	2Sa 14:22	3097
So *J* arose and went to Geshur, and	2Sa 14:23	3097
Therefore Absalom sent for *J*	2Sa 14:29	3097
Then *J* arose, and came to Absalom	2Sa 14:31	3097
And Absalom answered *J*, Behold, I	2Sa 14:32	3097
So *J* came to the king, and told	2Sa 14:33	3097
captain of the host instead of *J*	2Sa 17:25	3097
of the people under the hand of *J*	2Sa 18:2	3097
And the king commanded *J* and	2Sa 18:5	3097
a certain man saw it, and told *J*	2Sa 18:10	3097
J said unto the man that told him	2Sa 18:11	3097
And the man said unto *J*, Though I	2Sa 18:12	3097
Then said *J*, I may not tarry thus	2Sa 18:14	3097
J blew the trumpet, and the people	2Sa 18:16	3097
for *J* held back the people	2Sa 18:16	3097
J said unto him, Thou shalt not	2Sa 18:20	3097
Then said *J* to Cushi, Go tell the	2Sa 18:21	3097
And Cushi bowed himself unto *J*	2Sa 18:21	3097

J

the son of Zadok yet again to *J*	2Sa 18:22	3097
J said, Wherefore wilt thou run,	2Sa 18:22	3097
When *J* sent the king's servant,	2Sa 18:29	3097
And it was told *J*, Behold, the	2Sa 19:1	3097
J came into the house to the king	2Sa 19:5	3097
me continually in the room of *J*	2Sa 19:13	3097
J said to Amasa, Art thou in	2Sa 20:9	3097
J took Amasa, by the beard with	2Sa 20:9	3097
So *J* and Abishai his brother	2Sa 20:10	3097
him, and said, He that favoureth *J*	2Sa 20:11	3097
is for David, let him go after *J*	2Sa 20:11	3097
all the people went on after *J*	2Sa 20:13	3097
were with *J* battered the wall	2Sa 20:15	3097
say, I pray you, unto *J*, Come	2Sa 20:16	3097
her, the woman said, Art thou *J*	2Sa 20:17	3097
J answered and said, Far be it,	2Sa 20:20	3097
And the woman said unto *J*, Behold,	2Sa 20:21	3097
of Bichri, and cast it out to *J*	2Sa 20:22	3097
J returned to Jerusalem unto the	2Sa 20:22	3097
Now *J* was over all the host of	2Sa 20:23	3097
And Abishai, the brother of *J*	2Sa 23:18	3097
of *J* was one of the thirty	2Sa 23:24	3097
armourbearer to *J* the son of	2Sa 23:37	3097
For the king said to *J* the	2Sa 24:2	3097
J said unto the king, Now the	2Sa 24:3	3097
king's word prevailed against *J*	2Sa 24:4	3097
And *J* and the captains of the host	2Sa 24:4	3097
J gave up the sum of the number	2Sa 24:9	3097
he conferred with *J* the son of	1Kin 1:7	3097
J the captain of the host	1Kin 1:19	3097
when *J* heard the sound of the	1Kin 1:41	3097
J the son of Zeruiah did to me	1Kin 2:5	3097
and for *J* the son of Zeruiah	1Kin 2:22	3097
Then tidings came to *J*	1Kin 2:28	3097
for *J* had turned after Adonijah,	1Kin 2:28	3097
J fled unto the tabernacle of the	1Kin 2:28	3097
it was told king Solomon that *J*	1Kin 2:29	3097
word again, saying, Thus said *J*	1Kin 2:30	3097
the innocent blood, which *J* shed	1Kin 2:31	3097
return upon the head of *J*	1Kin 2:33	3097
J the captain of the host was	1Kin 11:15	3097
(For six months did *J* remain	1Kin 11:16	3097
that *J* the captain of the host	1Kin 11:21	3097
Abishai, and *J*, and Asahel, three	1Chr 2:16	3097
So *J* the son of Zeruiah went	1Chr 11:6	3097
J repaired the rest of the city	1Chr 11:8	3097
And Abishai the brother of *J*	1Chr 11:20	3097
were, Asahel the brother of *J*	1Chr 11:26	3097
of *J* the son of Zeruiah,	1Chr 11:39	3097
J the son of Zeruiah was over the	1Chr 18:15	3097
when David heard of it, he sent *J*	1Chr 19:8	3097
Now when *J* saw that the battle	1Chr 19:10	3097
So *J* and the people that were with	1Chr 19:14	3097
Then *J* came to Jerusalem	1Chr 19:15	3097
J led forth the power of the army	1Chr 20:1	3097
J smote Rabbah, and destroyed it	1Chr 20:1	3097
And David said to *J* and to the	1Chr 21:2	3097
J answered, The LORD make his	1Chr 21:3	3097
king's word prevailed against *J*	1Chr 21:4	3097
Wherefore *J* departed, and went	1Chr 21:4	3097
J gave the sum of the number of	1Chr 21:5	3097
king's word was abominable to *J*	1Chr 21:6	3097
J the son of Zeruiah, had	1Chr 26:28	3097
month was Asahel the brother of *J*	1Chr 27:7	3097
J the son of Zeruiah began to	1Chr 27:24	3097
general of the king's army was *J*	1Chr 27:34	3097
when *J* returned, and smote of Edom	Ps 60:t	3097

2. A descendant of Caleb.

Ataroth, the house of *J*, and half	1Chr 2:54	5854

3. A grandson of Kenaz.

and Seraiah begat *J*, the father of	1Chr 4:14	3097

4. A family of exiles with Zerubbabel.

of the children of Jeshua and *J*	Ezr 2:6	3097
of the children of Jeshua and *J*	Neh 7:11	3097

5. A family of exiles with Ezra.

Of the sons of *J*	Ezr 8:9	3097

JOAB'S (jo′-abs) *Refers to Joab 1.*

J field is near mine, and he hath	2Sa 14:30	3097
sister to Zeruiah *J* mother	2Sa 17:25	3097
J brother, and a third part under	2Sa 18:2	3097
bare *J* armour compassed about	2Sa 18:15	3097
And there went out after him *J* men	2Sa 20:7	3097
J garment that he had put on was	2Sa 20:8	3097
to the sword that was in *J* hand	2Sa 20:10	3097
one of *J* men stood by him, and	2Sa 20:11	3097

JOAH (jo′-ah) *See* ETHAN.

1. A son of Asaph.

J the son of Asaph the recorder	2Kin 18:18	3098
son of Hilkiah, and Shebna, and *J*	2Kin 18:26	3098
J the son of Asaph the recorder,	2Kin 18:37	3098

house, and Shebna the scribe, and *J*	Is 36:3	3098
J unto Rabshakeh, Speak, I pray	Is 36:11	3098
and Shebna the scribe, and *J*	Is 36:22	3098

2. A descendant of Gershom.

J his son, Iddo his son, Zerah	1Chr 6:21	3098
J the son of Zimmah	2Chr 29:12	3098
and Eden the son of *J*	2Chr 29:12	3098

3. A sanctuary servant.

J the third, and Sacar the fourth,	1Chr 26:4	3098

4. A Levite.

J the son of Joahaz the recorder	2Chr 34:8	3098

JOAHAZ (jo′-a-haz) *See* JEHOAHAZ. *Father of Joah.*

and Joah the son of *J* the recorder	2Chr 34:8	3098

JOANAN *See* JOANNA.

JOANNA (jo-an′-nah)

1. A female disciple.

J the wife of Chuza Herod's	Lk 8:3	2489
It was Mary Magdalene, and *J*	Lk 24:10	2489

2. An ancestor of Jesus.

Which was the son of *J*, which was	Lk 3:27	2489

JOASH (jo′-ash) *See* JEHOASH.

1. A son of Becher.

Zemira, and *J*, and Eliezer, and	1Chr 7:8	3135

2. A sanctuary servant.

and over the cellars of oil was *J*	1Chr 27:28	3135

3. Father of Gideon.

pertained unto *J* the Abi-ezrite	Judg 6:11	3101
Gideon the son of *J* hath done	Judg 6:29	3101
the men of the city said unto *J*	Judg 6:30	3101
J said unto all that stood	Judg 6:31	3101
the sword of Gideon the son of *J*	Judg 7:14	3101
Gideon the son of *J* returned from	Judg 8:13	3101
And Jerubbaal the son of *J* went	Judg 8:29	3101
Gideon the son of *J* died in a	Judg 8:32	3101
in the sepulchre of *J* his father	Judg 8:32	3101

4. A son of King Ahab.

the city, and to *J* the king's son	1Kin 22:26	3101
the city, and to *J* the king's son	2Chr 18:25	3101

5. A son of King Ahaziah.

took *J* the son of Ahaziah, and	2Kin 11:2	3101
And the rest of the acts of *J*	2Kin 12:19	3101
slew *J* in the house of Millo,	2Kin 12:20	3101
twentieth year of *J* the son of	2Kin 13:1	3101
seventh year of *J* king of Judah	2Kin 13:10	3101
the son of *J* king of Judah	2Kin 14:1	3101
to all things as *J* his father did	2Kin 14:3	3101
Amaziah the son of *J* king of	2Kin 14:17	3101
year of Amaziah the son of *J* king	2Kin 14:23	3101
son, Ahaziah his son, *J* his son,	1Chr 3:11	3101
took *J* the son of Ahaziah, and	2Chr 22:11	3101
J was seven years old when he	2Chr 24:1	3101
J did that which was right in the	2Chr 24:2	3101
that *J* was minded to repair the	2Chr 24:4	3101
Thus *J* the king remembered not	2Chr 24:22	3101
they executed judgment against *J*	2Chr 24:24	3101
king of Judah, the son of *J*	2Chr 25:23	3101
Amaziah the son of *J* king of	2Chr 25:25	3101

6. A king of Israel.

J his son reigned in his stead	2Kin 13:9	3101
And the rest of the acts of *J*	2Kin 13:12	3101
And *J* slept with his fathers	2Kin 13:13	3101
J was buried in Samaria with the	2Kin 13:13	3101
J the king of Israel came down	2Kin 13:14	3101
Three times did *J* beat him	2Kin 13:25	3101
In the second year of *J* son of	2Kin 14:1	3101
of Judah Jeroboam the son of *J*	2Kin 14:23	3101
the hand of Jeroboam the son of *J*	2Kin 14:27	3101
Judah took advice, and sent to *J*	2Chr 25:17	3101
J king of Israel sent to Amaziah	2Chr 25:18	3101
So *J* the king of Israel went up	2Chr 25:21	3101
J the king of Israel took Amaziah	2Chr 25:23	3101
J son of Jehoahaz king of Israel	2Chr 25:25	3101
the days of Jeroboam the son of *J*	Hos 1:1	3101
the son of *J* king of Israel	Amos 1:1	3101

7. A descendant of Shelah.

and the men of Chozeba, and *J*	1Chr 4:22	3101

8. A captain in David's army.

The chief was Ahiezer, then *J*	1Chr 12:3	3101

JOATHAM (jo′-a-tham) *See* JOTHAM. *Ancestor of Joseph, husband of Mary.*

And Ozias begat *J*	Mt 1:9	2488
and *J* begat Achaz	Mt 1:9	2488

JOAZCAR *See* JOZACHAR.

JOB (jobe) *See* JASHUB, JOB'S.

1. A descendant of Issachar.

Tola, and Phuvah, and *J*, and Shimron	Gen 46:13	3102

2. A righteous sufferer.
the land of Uz, whose name was *J* ... Job 1:1 347
were gone about, that *J* sent ... Job 1:5 347
for *J* said, It may be that my ... Job 1:5 347
Thus did *J* continually ... Job 1:5 347
Hast thou considered my servant *J* ... Job 1:8 347
Doth *J* fear God for nought ... Job 1:9 347
And there came a messenger unto *J* ... Job 1:14 347
Then *J* arose, and rent his mantle, ... Job 1:20 347
In all this *J* sinned not, nor ... Job 1:22 347
Hast thou considered my servant *J* ... Job 2:3 347
smote *J* with sore boils from the ... Job 2:7 347
this did not *J* sin with his lips ... Job 2:10 347
After this opened *J* his mouth ... Job 3:1 347
And *J* spake, and said, ... Job 3:2 347
But *J* answered and said, ... Job 6:1 347
Then *J* answered and said, ... Job 9:1 347
And *J* answered and said, ... Job 12:1 347
Then *J* answered and said, ... Job 16:1 347
Then *J* answered and said, ... Job 19:1 347
But *J* answered and said, ... Job 21:1 347
Then *J* answered and said, ... Job 23:1 347
But *J* answered and said, ... Job 26:1 347
Moreover *J* continued his parable, ... Job 27:1 347
Moreover *J* continued his parable, ... Job 29:1 347
The words of *J* are ended ... Job 31:40 347
three men ceased to answer *J* ... Job 32:1 347
against *J* was his wrath kindled, ... Job 32:2 347
no answer, and yet had condemned *J* ... Job 32:3 347
had waited till *J* had spoken ... Job 32:4 347
was none of you that convinced *J* ... Job 32:12 347
Wherefore, *J*, I pray thee, hear ... Job 33:1 347
Mark well, O *J*, hearken unto me ... Job 33:31 347
For *J* hath said, I am righteous ... Job 34:5 347
What man is like *J*, who drinketh ... Job 34:7 347
J hath spoken without knowledge, ... Job 34:35 347
My desire is that *J* may be tried ... Job 34:36 347
Therefore doth *J* open his mouth ... Job 35:16 347
Hearken unto this, O *J* ... Job 37:14 347
answered *J* out of the whirlwind ... Job 38:1 347
Moreover the LORD answered *J* ... Job 40:1 347
Then *J* answered the LORD, and said ... Job 40:3 347
LORD unto *J* out of the whirlwind ... Job 40:6 347
Then *J* answered the LORD, and said ... Job 42:1 347
had spoken these words unto *J* ... Job 42:7 347
is right, as my servant *J* hath ... Job 42:7 347
seven rams, and go to my servant *J* ... Job 42:8 347
my servant *J* shall pray for you ... Job 42:8 347
which is right, like my servant *J* ... Job 42:8 347
the LORD also accepted *J* ... Job 42:9 347
LORD turned the captivity of *J* ... Job 42:10 347
also the LORD gave *J* twice as ... Job 42:10 347
end of *J* more than his beginning ... Job 42:12 347
so fair as the daughters of *J* ... Job 42:15 347
After this lived *J* an hundred ... Job 42:16 347
So *J* died, being old and full of ... Job 42:17 347
three men, Noah, Daniel, and *J* ... Eze 14:14 347
Though Noah, Daniel, and *J* ... Eze 14:20 347
have heard of the patience of *J* ... Jas 5:11 *2492*

JOBAB *(jo'-bab)*
1. A son of Joktan.
And Ophir, and Havilah, and *J* ... Gen 10:29 3103
And Ophir, and Havilah, and *J* ... 1Chr 1:23 3103
2. A king of Edom.
J the son of Zerah of Bozrah ... Gen 36:33 3103
J died, and Husham of the land of ... Gen 36:34 3103
J the son of Zerah of Bozrah ... 1Chr 1:44 3103
when *J* was dead, Husham of the ... 1Chr 1:45 3103
3. A Canaanite king.
that he sent to *J* king of Madon ... Josh 11:1 3103
4. A son of Shaharaim.
And he begat of Hodesh his wife, *J* ... 1Chr 8:9 3103
5. A son of Elpaal.
Ishmerai also, and Jezliah, and *J* ... 1Chr 8:18 3103

JOB'S *(jobes) Refers to Job 2.*
Now when *J* three friends heard of ... Job 2:11 347

JOCHEBED *(jok'-e-bed) Wife of Amram.*
Amram took him *J* his father's ... Ex 6:20 3115
And the name of Amram's wife was *J* ... Num 26:59 3115

JODA See JUDA.

JOED *(jo'-ed) A son of Pedaiah.*
son of Meshullam, the son of *J* ... Neh 11:7 3133

JOEL *(jo'-el)*
1. A son of Samuel.
the name of his firstborn was *J* ... 1Sa 8:2 3100
Heman a singer, the son of *J* ... 1Chr 6:33 3100
appointed Heman the son of *J* ... 1Chr 15:17 3100
2. A Simeonite.
And *J*, and Jehu the son of Josibiah ... 1Chr 4:35 3100
3. Father of Shemaiah.
The sons of *J* ... 1Chr 5:4 3100
the son of Shema, the son of *J* ... 1Chr 5:8 3100
4. A chief Gadite.
J the chief, and Shapham the next, ... 1Chr 5:12 3100
5. A Kohathite.
The son of Elkanah, the son of *J* ... 1Chr 6:36 3100
6. A descendant of Tola.
Michael, and Obadiah, and *J* ... 1Chr 7:3 3100
7. A "mighty man" of David.
J the brother of Nathan, Mibhar ... 1Chr 11:38 3100
8. A Gershomite.
J the chief, and his brethren an ... 1Chr 15:7 3100
Levites, for Uriel, Asaiah, and *J* ... 1Chr 15:11 3100
chief was Jehiel, and Zetham, and *J* ... 1Chr 23:8 3100
9. A treasurer of the Temple.
J his brother, which were over ... 1Chr 26:22 3100
10. A prince of Manasseh.
of Manasseh, *J* the son of Pedaiah ... 1Chr 27:20 3100
11. A Kohathite who cleansed the Temple.
J the son of Azariah, of the sons ... 2Chr 29:12 3100
12. Married a foreigner in exile.
Zabad, Zebina, Jadau, and *J* ... Ezr 10:43 3100
13. An overseer of the Benjamites.
J the son of Zichri was their ... Neh 11:9 3100
14. A prophet.
that came to *J* the son of Pethuel ... Joel 1:1 3100
which was spoken by the prophet *J* ... Acts 2:16 *2493*

JOELAH *(jo-e'-lah) A member of David's band.*
And *J*, and Zebadiah, the sons of ... 1Chr 12:7 3132

JOEZER *(jo-e'-zer) A warrior in David's army.*
and Jesiah, and Azareel, and *J* ... 1Chr 12:6 3134

JOGBEHAH *(jog'-be-hah) A place in Gad.*
Atroth, Shophan, and Jaazer, and *J* ... Num 32:35 3011
tents on the east of Nobah and *J* ... Judg 8:11 3011

JOGLI *(jog'-li) A Danite prince.*
of Dan, Bukki the son of *J* ... Num 34:22 3020

JOHA *(jo'-hah)*
1. Son of Beriah.
And Michael, and Ispah, and *J* ... 1Chr 8:16 3109
2. A "mighty man" of David.
J his brother, the Tizite, ... 1Chr 11:45 3109

JOHANAN *(jo-ha'-nan)* See JEHOHANAN, JOHN.
1. A son of Kareah.
J the son of Careah, and Seraiah ... 2Kin 25:23 3110
the son of Nethaniah, and *J* ... Jer 40:8 3110
Moreover *J* the son of Kareah, and ... Jer 40:13 3110
Then *J* the son of Kareah spake to ... Jer 40:15 3110
said unto *J* the son of Kareah ... Jer 40:16 3110
But when *J* the son of Kareah, and ... Jer 41:11 3110
Ishmael saw *J* the son of Kareah ... Jer 41:13 3110
went unto *J* the son of Kareah ... Jer 41:14 3110
escaped from *J* with eight men ... Jer 41:15 3110
Then took *J* the son of Kareah, and ... Jer 41:16 3110
J the son of Kareah, and Jezaniah ... Jer 42:1 3110
Then called he *J* the son of ... Jer 42:8 3110
J the son of Kareah, and all the ... Jer 43:2 3110
So *J* the son of Kareah, and all ... Jer 43:4 3110
But *J* the son of Kareah, and all ... Jer 43:5 3110
2. A son of King Josiah.
of Josiah were, the firstborn *J* ... 1Chr 3:15 3110
3. A son of Elioenai.
and Pelaiah, and Akkub, and *J* ... 1Chr 3:24 3110
4. A grandson of Ahimaaz.
begat Azariah, and Azariah begat *J* ... 1Chr 6:9 3110
J begat Azariah, (he it is that ... 1Chr 6:10 3110
5. A warrior in David's army.
and Jeremiah, and Jahaziel, and *J* ... 1Chr 12:4 3110
6. A Gadite warrior in David's army.
J the eighth, Elzabad the ninth, ... 1Chr 12:12 3110
7. An Ephraimite.
of Ephraim, Azariah the son of *J* ... 2Chr 28:12 3076
8. An exile with Ezra.
J the son of Hakkatan, and with ... Ezr 8:12 3110
9. A priest in exile with Ezra.
chamber of *J* the son of Eliashib ... Ezr 10:6 3076
10. A son of Tobiah.
his son *J* had taken the daughter ... Neh 6:18 3076
11. A priest in exile with Zerubbabel.
days of Eliashib, Joiada, and *J* ... Neh 12:22 3110
the days of *J* the son of Eliashib ... Neh 12:23 3110

JOHN *(jon)* See BAPTIST, JEHOHANAN, JOHN'S, MARK.
1. The Baptizer.
In those days came *J* the Baptist ... Mt 3:1 *2491*
the same *J* had his raiment of ... Mt 3:4 *2491*

from Galilee to Jordan unto *J* .... Mt 3:13   2491
But *J* forbad him, saying, I have .... Mt 3:14   2491
heard that *J* was cast into prison .... Mt 4:12   2491
came to him the disciples of *J* .... Mt 9:14   2491
Now when *J* had heard in the .... Mt 11:2   2491
shew *J* again those things which ...... Mt 11:4   2491
unto the multitudes concerning *J* .... Mt 11:7   2491
a greater than *J* the Baptist .... Mt 11:11   2491
from the days of *J* the Baptist .... Mt 11:12   2491
and the law prophesied until *J* .... Mt 11:13   2491
For *J* came neither eating nor .... Mt 11:18   2491
servants, This is *J* the Baptist .... Mt 14:2   2491
For Herod had laid hold on *J* .... Mt 14:3   2491
For *J* said unto him, It is not .... Mt 14:4   2491
Give me here *J* Baptist's head in .... Mt 14:8   2491
sent, and beheaded *J* in the prison .... Mt 14:10   2491
say that thou art *J* the Baptist .... Mt 16:14   2491
spake unto them of the Baptist .... Mt 17:13   2491
The baptism of *J*, whence was it ...... Mt 21:25   2491
for all hold *J* as a prophet .... Mt 21:26   2491
For *J* came unto you in the way of ...... Mt 21:32   2491
J did baptize in the wilderness, ... Mk 1:4   2491
J was clothed with camel's hair, ... Mk 1:6   2491
and was baptized of *J* in Jordan .... Mk 1:9   2491
Now after that *J* was put in .... Mk 1:14   2491
And the disciples of *J* and of the .... Mk 2:18   2491
him, Why do the disciples of *J* .... Mk 2:18   2491
That *J* the Baptist was risen from .... Mk 6:14   2491
heard thereof, he said, It is *J* .... Mk 6:16   2491
sent forth and laid hold upon *J* .... Mk 6:17   2491
For *J* had said unto Herod, It is .... Mk 6:18   2491
For Herod feared *J*, knowing that .... Mk 6:20   2491
said, The head of *J* the Baptist .... Mk 6:24   2491
charger the head of *J* the Baptist .... Mk 6:25   2491
And they answered, The Baptist .... Mk 8:28   2491
The baptism of *J*, was it from .... Mk 11:30   2491
for all men counted *J*, that he .... Mk 11:32   2491
and thou shalt call his name *J* .... Lk 1:13   2491
but he shall be called *J* .... Lk 1:60   2491
and wrote, saying, His name is *J* .... Lk 1:63   2491
the word of God came unto *J* the .... Lk 3:2   2491
men mused in their hearts of *J* .... Lk 3:15   2491
J answered, saying unto them all, ... Lk 3:16   2491
all, that he shut up *J* in prison .... Lk 3:20   2491
do the disciples of *J* fast often .... Lk 5:33   2491
the disciples of *J* shewed him of .... Lk 7:18   2491
J calling unto him two of his .... Lk 7:19   2491
J Baptist hath sent us unto thee, ... Lk 7:20   2491
tell *J* what things ye have seen .... Lk 7:22   2491
the messengers of *J* were departed .... Lk 7:24   2491
unto the people concerning *J* .... Lk 7:24   2491
prophet than *J* the Baptist .... Lk 7:28   2491
baptized with the baptism of *J* .... Lk 7:29   2491
For *J* the Baptist came neither .... Lk 7:33   2491
that *J* was risen from the dead .... Lk 9:7   2491
And Herod said, *J* have I beheaded ...... Lk 9:9   2491
answering said, *J* the Baptist .... Lk 9:19   2491
as *J* also taught his disciples .... Lk 11:1   2491
law and the prophets were until *J* ..... Lk 16:16   2491
The baptism of *J*, was it from .... Lk 20:4   2491
be persuaded that *J* was a prophet .... Lk 20:6   2491
sent from God, whose name was *J* .... Jn 1:6   2491
J bare witness of him, and cried, ... Jn 1:15   2491
And this is the record of *J* .... Jn 1:19   2491
J answered them, saying, I .... Jn 1:26   2491
Jordan, where *J* was baptizing .... Jn 1:28   2491
The next day *J* seeth Jesus coming .... Jn 1:29   2491
J bare record, saying, I saw the .... Jn 1:32   2491
Again the next day after *J* stood .... Jn 1:35   2491
of the two which heard *J* speak .... Jn 1:40   2491
J also was baptizing in Aenon .... Jn 3:23   2491
For *J* was not yet cast into .... Jn 3:24   2491
And they came unto *J*, and said unto ..... Jn 3:26   2491
J answered and said, A man can .... Jn 3:27   2491
and baptized more disciples than *J*, ... Jn 4:1   2491
Ye sent unto *J*, and he bare .... Jn 5:33   2491
greater witness than that of *J* .... Jn 5:36   2491
place where *J* at first baptized .... Jn 10:40   2491
him, and said, *J* did no miracle .... Jn 10:41   2491
but all things that *J* spake of .... Jn 10:41   2491
For *J* truly baptized with water .... Acts 1:5   2491
Beginning from the baptism of *J* .... Acts 1:22   2491
the baptism which *J* preached .... Acts 10:37   2491
J indeed baptized with water .... Acts 11:16   2491
When *J* had first preached before .... Acts 13:24   2491
as *J* fulfilled his course, he .... Acts 13:25   2491
knowing only the baptism of *J* .... Acts 18:25   2491
J verily baptized with the .... Acts 19:4   2491
    2. Son of Zebedee.
J his brother, in a ship with .... Mt 4:21   2491
son of Zebedee, and *J* his brother .... Mt 10:2   2491

J his brother, and bringeth them .... Mt 17:1   2491
J his brother, who also were in .... Mk 1:19   2491
Simon and Andrew, with James and *J*... Mk 1:29   2491
and *J* the brother of James .... Mk 3:17   2491
James, and *J* the brother of James .... Mk 5:37   2491
with him Peter, and James, and *J* .... Mk 9:2   2491
J answered him, saying, Master, ... Mk 9:38   2491
And James and *J*, the sons of .... Mk 10:35   2491
much displeased with James and *J* .... Mk 10:41   2491
the temple, Peter and James and *J* .... Mk 13:3   2491
with him Peter and James and *J* .... Mk 14:33   2491
And so was also James, and *J* .... Lk 5:10   2491
and Andrew his brother, James and *J*.... Lk 6:14   2491
go in, save Peter, and James, and *J*...... Lk 8:51   2491
these sayings, he took Peter and *J* .... Lk 9:28   2491
J answered and said, Master, we .... Lk 9:49   2491
J saw this, they said, Lord, wilt .... Lk 9:54   2491
And he sent Peter and *J*, saying, Go ..... Lk 22:8   2491
abode both Peter, and James, and *J* ...... Acts 1:13   2491
J went up together into the .... Acts 3:1   2491
J about to go into the temple .... Acts 3:3   2491
his eyes upon him with *J*, said, ... Acts 3:4   2491
which was healed held Peter and *J* .... Acts 3:11   2491
saw the boldness of Peter and *J* .... Acts 4:13   2491
J answered and said unto them, ... Acts 4:19   2491
they sent unto them Peter and *J* .... Acts 8:14   2491
the brother of *J* with the sword .... Acts 12:2   2491
And when James, Cephas, and *J* .... Gal 2:9   2491
by his angel unto his servant *J* .... Rev 1:1   2491
J to the seven churches which are .... Rev 1:4   2491
I *J*, who also am your brother, and .... Rev 1:9   2491
I *J* saw the holy city, new .... Rev 21:2   2491
I *J* saw these things, and heard .... Rev 22:8   2491
    3. A relative of Annas the priest.
high priest, and Caiaphas, and *J* .... Acts 4:6   2491
    4. Surnamed Mark.
the house of Mary the mother of *J* .... Acts 12:12   2491
ministry, and took with them *J* .... Acts 12:25   2491
they had also *J* to their minister .... Acts 13:5   2491
J departing from them returned to .... Acts 13:13   2491
determined to take with them *J* .... Acts 15:37   2491

JOHN'S *(jonz) Refers to John 1.*
between some of *J* disciples .... Jn 3:25   2491
And they said, Unto *J* baptism .... Acts 19:3   2491

JOIADA *(joy'-a-dah)* See JEHOIADA. *A priest with*
    Zerubbabel.
Eliashib, and Eliashib begat *J* .... Neh 12:10   3111
J begat Jonathan, and Jonathan .... Neh 12:11   3111
in the days of Eliashib, of *J* .... Neh 12:22   3111
And one of the sons of *J*, the son .... Neh 13:28   3111

JOIAKIM *(joy'-a-kim)* See JEHOIAKIM. *Another priest*
    with Zerubbabel.
And Jeshua begat *J* .... Neh 12:10   3113
J also begat Eliashib .... Neh 12:10   3113
And in the days of *J* were priests.......... Neh 12:12   3113
the days of *J* the son of Jeshua .... Neh 12:26   3113

JOIARIB *(joy'-a-rib)* See JEHOIARIB.
    1. A messenger for Ezra.
also for *J*, and for Elnathan, men........... Ezr 8:16   3114
    2. A descendant of Perez.
the son of Adaiah, the son of *J* .... Neh 11:5   3114
    3. Father of Jedaiah.
Jedaiah the son of *J*, Jachin................. Neh 11:10   3114
Shemaiah, and *J*, Jedaiah, ... Neh 12:6   3114
And of *J*, Mattenai .... Neh 12:19   3114

JOIN
they *j* also unto our enemies, and .... Ex 1:10   3254
j himself with Ahaziah king of.............. 2Chr 20:35   2266
j in affinity with the people of .... Ezr 9:14   2859
Though hand *j* in hand, the wicked .... Prov 11:21
though hand *j* in hand, he shall .... Prov 16:5
unto them that *j* house to house .... Is 5:8   5060
him, and *j* his enemies together .... Is 9:11   5526
that *j* themselves to the LORD, to .... Is 56:6   3867
let us *j* ourselves to the LORD in .... Jer 50:5   3867
j them one to another into one .... Eze 37:17   7126
they shall *j* themselves together .... Dan 11:6   2266
durst no man *j* himself to them .... Acts 5:13   2853
j thyself to this chariot .... Acts 8:29   2853
he assayed to *j* himself to the .... Acts 9:26   2853

JOINED
All these were *j* together in the .... Gen 14:3   2266
they *j* battle with them in the .... Gen 14:8   6186
time will my husband be *j* unto me .... Gen 29:34   3867
j at the two edges thereof .... Ex 28:7   2266
and so it shall be *j* together .... Ex 28:7   2266
that they may be *j* unto thee .... Num 18:2   3867
And they shall be *j* unto thee .... Num 18:4   3867

JOINING (continued)

Israel *j* himself unto Baal-peor	Num 25:3	6775
men that were *j* unto Baal-peor	Num 25:5	6775
and when they *j* battle, Israel was	1Sa 4:2	5208
of the wheels were *j* to the base	1Kin 7:32	
the seventh day the battle was *j*	1Kin 20:29	7126
and *j* affinity with Ahab	2Chr 18:1	2859
he *j* himself with him to make	2Chr 20:36	2266
Because thou hast *j* thyself with	2Chr 20:37	2266
thereof, and *j* the foundations	Ezr 4:12	2338
all the wall was *j* together unto	Neh 4:6	7194
upon all such as *j* themselves	Est 9:27	3867
let it not be *j* unto the days of	Job 3:6	2302
They are *j* one to another, they	Job 41:17	1692
of his flesh are *j* together	Job 41:23	1692
Assur also is *j* with them	Ps 83:8	2266
They *j* themselves also unto	Ps 106:28	6775
For to him that is *j* to all the	Eccl 9:4	977
every one that is *j* unto them	Is 13:15	5595
strangers shall be *j* with them	Is 14:1	3867
Thou shalt not be *j* with them in	Is 14:20	3161
that hath *j* himself to the Lord,	Is 56:3	3867
Their wings were *j* one to another	Eze 1:9	2266
every one were *j* one to another	Eze 1:11	2266
courts *j* of forty cubits long	Eze 46:22	7000
Ephraim is *j* to idols	Hos 4:17	2266
many nations shall be *j* to the	Zec 2:11	3867
therefore God hath *j* together	Mt 19:6	4801
therefore God hath *j* together	Mk 10:9	4801
***j* himself to a citizen of that**	Lk 15:15	2853
about four hundred, *j* themselves	Acts 5:36	4347
whose house *j* hard to the	Acts 18:7	4927
but that ye be perfectly *j*	1Cor 1:10	2675
is *j* to an harlot is one body	1Cor 6:16	2853
But he that is *j* unto the Lord is	1Cor 6:17	2853
the whole body fitly *j* together	Eph 4:16	4883
shall be *j* unto his wife, and they	Eph 5:31	4347

JOINING

j to the wing of the other cherub	2Chr 3:12	1692

JOININGS

doors of the gates, and for the *j*	1Chr 22:3	4226

JOINT

of Jacob's thigh was out of *j*	Gen 32:25	3363
and all my bones are out of *j*	Ps 22:14	6504
broken tooth, and a foot out of *j*	Prov 25:19	4154
by that which every *j* supplieth	Eph 4:16	860

JOINT-HEIRS

heirs of God, and *j* with Christ	Rom 8:17	4789

JOINTS

between the *j* of the harness	1Kin 22:34	1694
between the *j* of the harness	2Chr 18:33	1694
the *j* of thy thighs are like	Song 7:1	2542
so that the *j* of his loins were	Dan 5:6	7001
from which all the body by *j*	Col 2:19	860
of soul and spirit, and of the *j*	Heb 4:12	719

JOKDEAM (jok'-de-am) *A city in Judah.*

And Jezreel, and *J*, and Zanoah,	Josh 15:56	3347

JOKIM (jo'-kim) *A descendant of Shelah.*

And *J*, and the men of Chozeba, and	1Chr 4:22	3137

JOKMEAM (jok'-me-am) See JOKNEAM. *A Levitical city in Ephraim.*

J with her suburbs, and Beth-horon	1Chr 6:68	3361

JOKNEAM (jok'-ne-am) See JOKMEAM, KIBZAIM.
  1. A Levitical city in Zebulun.

the king of *J* of Carmel, one	Josh 12:22	3362
to the river that is before *J*	Josh 19:11	3362
J with her suburbs, and Kartah	Josh 21:34	3362

  2. A Levitical city in Ephraim.

unto the place that is beyond *J*	1Kin 4:12	3362

JOKSHAN (jok'-shan) *A son of Abraham.*

And she bare him Zimran, and *J*	Gen 25:2	3370
And *J* begat Sheba, and Dedan	Gen 25:3	3370
she bare Zimran, and *J*, and Medan,	1Chr 1:32	3370
And the sons of *J*	1Chr 1:32	3370

JOKTAN (jok'-tan) *A son of Eber.*

and his brother's name was *J*	Gen 10:25	3355
J begat Almodad, and Sheleph, and	Gen 10:26	3355
all these were the sons of *J*	Gen 10:29	3355
and his brother's name was *J*	1Chr 1:19	3355
J begat Almodad, and Sheleph, and	1Chr 1:20	3355
All these were the sons of *J*	1Chr 1:23	3355

JOKTHEEL (jok'-the-el) See SELAH.
  1. A city in Judah.

And Dilean, and Mizpeh, and *J*	Josh 15:38	3371

  2. Another name for Petra in Edom.

the name of it *J* unto this day	2Kin 14:7	3371

JONA (jo'-nah) See BAR-JONA, JONAH, JONAS. *Greek form of Jonah.*

said, Thou art Simon the son of *J*	Jn 1:42	2495

JONADAB (jon'-a-dab) See JEHONADAB.
  1. A son of Shimeah.

had a friend, whose name was *J*	2Sa 13:3	3122
and *J* was a very subtil man	2Sa 13:3	3122
J said unto him, Lay thee down on	2Sa 13:5	3122
And *J*, the son of Shimeah David's	2Sa 13:32	3122
J said unto the king, Behold, the	2Sa 13:35	3122

  2. A son of Rechab.

for *J* the son of Rechab our	Jer 35:6	3122
have we obeyed the voice of *J* the	Jer 35:8	3082
that *J* our father commanded us	Jer 35:10	3122
The words of *J* the son of Rechab,	Jer 35:14	3082
Because the sons of *J* the son of	Jer 35:16	3082
the commandment of *J* your father	Jer 35:18	3082
J the son of Rechab shall not	Jer 35:19	3122

JONAH (jo'-nah) See JONA, JONAS. *A prophet.*

by the hand of his servant *J*	2Kin 14:25	3124
came unto *J* the son of Amittai	Jonah 1:1	3124
But *J* rose up to flee unto	Jonah 1:3	3124
But *J* was gone down into the	Jonah 1:5	3124
cast lots, and the lot fell upon *J*	Jonah 1:7	3124
So they took up *J*, and cast him	Jonah 1:15	3124
a great fish to swallow up *J*	Jonah 1:17	3124
J was in the belly of the fish	Jonah 1:17	3124
Then *J* prayed unto the Lord his	Jonah 2:1	3124
it vomited out *J* upon the dry	Jonah 2:10	3124
Lord came unto *J* the second time	Jonah 3:1	3124
So *J* arose, and went unto Nineveh,	Jonah 3:3	3124
J began to enter into the city a	Jonah 3:4	3124
But it displeased *J* exceedingly	Jonah 4:1	3124
So *J* went out of the city, and sat	Jonah 4:5	3124
and made it to come up over *J*	Jonah 4:6	3124
So *J* was exceeding glad of the	Jonah 4:6	3124
the sun beat upon the head of *J*	Jonah 4:8	3124
And God said to *J*, Doest thou well	Jonah 4:9	3124

JONAM See JONAN.

JONAN (jo'-nan) *Ancestor of Joseph, husband of Mary.*

of Joseph, which was the son of *J*	Lk 3:30	2494

JONAS (jo'-nas) See JONA, JONAH.
  1. Same as Jonah.

it, but the sign of the prophet *J*	Mt 12:39	2495
For as *J* was three days and three	Mt 12:40	2495
repented at the preaching of *J*	Mt 12:41	2495
behold, a greater than *J* is here	Mt 12:41	2495
it, but the sign of the prophet *J*	Mt 16:4	2495
it, but the sign of the prophet *J*	Lk 11:29	2495
For as *J* was a sign unto the	Lk 11:30	2495
repented at the preaching of *J*	Lk 11:32	2495
behold, a greater than *J* is here	Lk 11:32	2495

  2. Father of Peter.

to Simon Peter, Simon, son of *J*	Jn 21:15	2495
the second time, Simon, son of *J*	Jn 21:16	2495
the third time, Simon, son of *J*	Jn 21:17	2495

JONATHAN (jon'-a-than) See JEHONATHAN, JONATHAN'S.
  1. A Levite.

and *J*, the son of Gershom, the son	Judg 18:30	3129

  2. Son of Saul.

a thousand were with *J* in Gibeah	1Sa 13:2	3129
J smote the garrison of the	1Sa 13:3	3129
J his son, and the people that	1Sa 13:16	3129
people that were with Saul and *J*	1Sa 13:22	3129
with *J* his son was there found	1Sa 13:22	3129
that *J* the son of Saul said unto	1Sa 14:1	3129
people knew not that *J* was gone	1Sa 14:3	3129
by which *J* sought to go over unto	1Sa 14:4	3129
J said to the young man that bare	1Sa 14:6	3083
Then said *J*, Behold, we will pass	1Sa 14:8	3083
men of the garrison answered *J*	1Sa 14:12	3129
J said unto his armourbearer,	1Sa 14:12	3129
J climbed up upon his hands and	1Sa 14:13	3129
and they fell before *J*	1Sa 14:13	3129
And that first slaughter, which *J*	1Sa 14:14	3129
when they had numbered, behold, *J*	1Sa 14:17	3129
that were with Saul and *J*	1Sa 14:21	3129
But *J* heard not when his father	1Sa 14:27	3129
Then said *J*, My father hath	1Sa 14:29	3129
Israel, though it be in *J* my son	1Sa 14:39	3129
J my son will be on the other	1Sa 14:40	3129
And Saul and *J* were taken	1Sa 14:41	3129
Cast lots between me and *J* my son	1Sa 14:42	3129
And *J* was taken	1Sa 14:42	3129
Then Saul said to *J*, Tell me what	1Sa 14:43	3129
J told him, and said, I did but	1Sa 14:43	3129
for thou shalt surely die, *J*	1Sa 14:44	3129

said unto Saul, Shall J die 1Sa 14:45   3129
So the people rescued J, that he 1Sa 14:45   3129
Now the sons of Saul were J 1Sa 14:49   3129
that the soul of J was knit with 1Sa 18:1   3083
J loved him as his own soul.................... 1Sa 18:1   3083
Then J and David made a covenant, ... 1Sa 18:3   3083
J stripped himself of the robe 1Sa 18:4   3083
And Saul spake to J his son 1Sa 19:1   3129
But J Saul's son delighted much 1Sa 19:2   3083
J told David, saying, Saul my 1Sa 19:2   3083
J spake good of David unto Saul 1Sa 19:4   3083
hearkened unto the voice of J 1Sa 19:6   3083
J called David, and Jonathan 1Sa 19:7   3083
J shewed him all those things 1Sa 19:7   3083
J brought David to Saul, and he 1Sa 19:7   3083
Ramah, and came and said before J 1Sa 20:1   3083
Let not J know this, lest he be 1Sa 20:3   3083
Then said J unto David, ... 1Sa 20:4   3083
And David said unto J, Behold, to 1Sa 20:5   3083
J said, Far be it from thee....................... 1Sa 20:9   3083
Then said David to J, Who shall 1Sa 20:10   3083
J said unto David, Come, and let 1Sa 20:11   3083
J said unto David, O LORD God of......... 1Sa 20:12   3083
The LORD do so and much more to J 1Sa 20:13   3083
So J made a covenant with the............... 1Sa 20:16   3083
J caused David to swear again, ... 1Sa 20:17   3083
Then J said to David, To morrow 1Sa 20:18   3083
J arose, and Abner sat by Saul's............ 1Sa 20:25   3083
and Saul said unto J his son 1Sa 20:27   3083
J answered Saul his father, and 1Sa 20:28   3083
anger was kindled against J 1Sa 20:30   3083
J answered Saul his father, and 1Sa 20:32   3083
whereby J knew that it was 1Sa 20:33   3083
So J arose from the table in 1Sa 20:34   3083
that J went out into the field at 1Sa 20:35   3083
of the arrow which J had shot................. 1Sa 20:37   3083
J cried after the lad, and said, ... 1Sa 20:37   3083
J cried after the lad, Make speed 1Sa 20:38   3083
only J and David knew the matter 1Sa 20:39   3083
J gave his artillery unto his lad 1Sa 20:40   3083
J said to David, Go in peace, ... 1Sa 20:42   3083
and J went into the city 1Sa 20:42   3083
J Saul's son arose, and went to 1Sa 23:16   3083
the wood, and J went to his house 1Sa 23:18   3083
and the Philistines slew J 1Sa 31:2   3083
Saul and J his son are dead also 2Sa 1:4   3083
that Saul and J his son be dead............. 2Sa 1:5   3083
for J his son, and for the people 2Sa 1:12   3083
over Saul and over J his son 2Sa 1:17   3083
the bow of J turned not back, and 2Sa 1:22   3083
J were lovely and pleasant in 2Sa 1:23   3083
O J, thou wast slain in thine.................. 2Sa 1:25   3083
distressed for thee, my brother J 2Sa 1:26   3083
And J, Saul's son, had a son that 2Sa 4:4   3083
J out of Jezreel, and his nurse 2Sa 4:4   3083
J hath yet a son, which is lame.............. 2Sa 9:3   3083
when Mephibosheth, the son of J.......... 2Sa 9:6   3083
kindness for J thy father's sake............. 2Sa 9:7   3083
the son of J the son of Saul.................... 2Sa 21:7   3083
David and J the son of Saul 2Sa 21:7   3083
the bones of J his son from the 2Sa 21:12   3083
of Saul and the bones of J his son 2Sa 21:13   3083
J his son buried they in the 2Sa 21:14   3083
Kish begat Saul, and Saul begat J 1Chr 8:33   3083
the son of J was Merib-baal.................... 1Chr 8:34   3083
and Saul begat J, and Malchi-shua,....... 1Chr 9:39   3083
the son of J was Merib-baal 1Chr 9:40   3083
and the Philistines slew J 1Chr 10:2   3129
   3. A son of Abiathar.
thy son, and J the son of Abiathar 2Sa 15:27   3083
Zadok's son, and J Abiathar's son 2Sa 15:36   3083
Now J and Ahimaaz stayed by 2Sa 17:17   3083
they said, Where is Ahimaaz and J 2Sa 17:20   3083
J the son of Abiathar the priest 1Kin 1:42   3129
J answered and said to Adonijah, ... 1Kin 1:43   3129
   4. A son of Shimea.
J the son of Shimeah the brother 2Sa 21:21   3083
J the son of Shimea David's 1Chr 20:7   3083
   5. A "mighty man" of David.
of the sons of Jashen, J.......................... 2Sa 23:32   3083
J the son of Shage the Hararite, ... 1Chr 11:34   3129
   6. A son of Jada.
Shammai; Jether, and J........................... 1Chr 2:32   3129
And the sons of J 1Chr 2:33   3129
   7. An uncle of David.
Also J David's uncle was a 1Chr 27:32   3083
   8. A family of exiles.
Ebed the son of J, and with him............. Ezr 8:6   3083
   9. Son of Asahel.
Only J the son of Asahel and .... Ezr 10:15   3083

   10. A descendant of Jeshua.
And Joiada begat J .... Neh 12:11   3083
and J begat Jaddua................................. Neh 12:11   3083
   11. A priest descended from Melicu.
Of Melicu, J... Neh 12:14   3083
   12. A priest descended from Shemaiah.
namely, Zechariah the son of J .... Neh 12:35   3083
   13. A scribe.
in the house of J the scribe.................... Jer 37:15   3083
to the house of J the scribe.................... Jer 37:20   3083
   14. A son of Kareah.
J the sons of Kareah, and Seraiah.......... Jer 40:8   3129

JONATHAN'S (jon'-a-thans) Refers to Jonathan 2.
J lad gathered up the arrows, and.......... 1Sa 20:38   3129
may shew him kindness for J sake 2Sa 9:1   3129
not cause me to return to J house .... Jer 38:26   3129

JONATH-ELEM-RECHOKIM (jo'-nath-e'-lem-re-ko'-kim)
   A musical notation.
To the chief Musician upon J.................. Ps 56:t   3128

JOPPA (jop'-pah) A seaport in Dan.
it to thee in flotes by sea to J 2Chr 2:16   3305
from Lebanon to the sea of J.................. Ezr 3:7   3305
of the LORD, and went down to J .... Jonah 1:3   3305
Now there was at J a certain .... Acts 9:36   2445
forasmuch as Lydda was nigh to J .... Acts 9:38   2445
And it was known throughout all J......... Acts 9:42   2445
days in J with one Simon a tanner .... Acts 9:43   2445
And now send men to J, and call for....... Acts 10:5   2445
unto them, he sent them to J .... Acts 10:8   2445
brethren from J accompanied him .... Acts 10:23   2445
Send therefore to J, and call .... Acts 10:32   2445
I was in the city of J praying.................. Acts 11:5   2445
and said unto him, Send men to J .... Acts 11:13   2445

JORAH (jo'-rah) See HARIPH. A family of exiles.
The children of J, an hundred and .... Ezr 2:18   3139

JORAI (jo'-rahee) Head of a Gadite family.
and Meshullam, and Sheba, and J.......... 1Chr 5:13   3140

JORAM (jo'-ram) See JEHORAM.
   1. A son of Toi.
Then Toi sent J his son unto king 2Sa 8:10   3141
J brought with him vessels of 2Sa 8:10   3141
   2. Same as Jehoram.
So J went over to Zair, and all............... 2Kin 8:21   3141
And the rest of the acts of J 2Kin 8:23   3141
J slept with his fathers, and was............ 2Kin 8:24   3141
Jehosheba, the daughter of king J 2Kin 11:2   3141
J his son, Ahaziah his son, Joash 1Chr 3:11   3141
and Josaphat begat J .... Mt 1:8   2496
and J begat Ozias .... Mt 1:8   2496
   3. A son of Ahab.
in the fifth year of J the son of 2Kin 8:16   3141
In the twelfth year of J the son 2Kin 8:25   3141
he went with J the son of Ahab to 2Kin 8:28   3141
and the Syrians wounded J 2Kin 8:28   3141
king J went back to be healed in 2Kin 8:29   3141
see J the son of Ahab in Jezreel 2Kin 8:29   3141
son of Nimshi conspired against J 2Kin 9:14   3141
(Now J had kept Ramoth-gilead, he 2Kin 9:14   3141
But king J was returned to be................ 2Kin 9:15   3188
for J lay there 2Kin 9:16   3141
of Judah was come down to see J 2Kin 9:16   3141
J said, Take an horseman, and send...... 2Kin 9:17   3188
And J said, Make ready 2Kin 9:21   3188
J king of Israel and Ahaziah king 2Kin 9:21   3188
when J saw Jehu, that he said, Is 2Kin 9:22   3188
J turned his hands, and fled, and 2Kin 9:23   3188
in the eleventh year of J the son 2Kin 9:29   3188
and the Syrians smote J 2Chr 22:5   3141
Ahaziah was of God by coming to J....... 2Chr 22:7   3141
   4. A descendant of Eliezer.
J his son, and Zichri his son, and 1Chr 26:25   3141

JORDAN (jor'-dan) A river that runs from the Sea of
      Galilee to the Dead Sea.
and beheld all the plain of J .... Gen 13:10   3383
Lot chose him all the plain of J.............. Gen 13:11   3383
my staff I passed over this J .... Gen 32:10   3383
of Atad, which is beyond J...................... Gen 50:10   3383
Abel-mizraim, which is beyond J .... Gen 50:11   3383
by the sea, and by the coast of J............ Num 13:29   3383
of Moab on this side J by Jericho .... Num 22:1   3383
plains of Moab by J near Jericho .... Num 26:3   3383
plains of Moab by J near Jericho .... Num 26:63   3383
Moab, which are by J near Jericho .... Num 31:12   3383
and bring us not over J .... Num 32:5   3383
with them on yonder side J.................... Num 32:19   3383
to us on this side J eastward .... Num 32:19   3383
you armed over J before the LORD .... Num 32:21   3383

Reuben will pass with you over J	Num 32:29	3383
on this side J may be ours	Num 32:32	3383
plains of Moab by J near Jericho	Num 33:48	3383
And they pitched by J, from	Num 33:49	3383
Moses in the plains of Moab by	Num 33:50	3383
over J into the land of Canaan	Num 33:51	3383
And the border shall go down to J	Num 34:12	3383
this side J near Jericho eastward	Num 34:15	3383
plains of Moab by J near Jericho	Num 35:1	3383
When ye be come over J into the	Num 35:10	3383
give three cities on this side J	Num 35:14	3383
plains of Moab by J near Jericho	Num 36:13	3383
on this side J in the wilderness	Deut 1:1	3383
On this side J, in the land of	Deut 1:5	3383
until I shall pass over J into	Deut 2:29	3383
the land that was on this side J	Deut 3:8	3383
The plain also, and J, and the	Deut 3:17	3383
your God given them beyond J	Deut 3:20	3383
the good land that is beyond J	Deut 3:25	3383
for thou shalt not go over this J	Deut 3:27	3383
sware that I should not go over J	Deut 4:21	3383
this land, I must not go over J	Deut 4:22	3383
ye go over J to possess it	Deut 4:26	3383
this side J toward the sunrising	Deut 4:41	3383
On this side J, in the valley	Deut 4:46	3383
this side J toward the sunrising	Deut 4:47	3383
the plain on this side J eastward	Deut 4:49	3383
Thou art to pass over J this day	Deut 9:1	3383
Are they not on the other side J	Deut 11:30	3383
For ye shall pass over J to go in	Deut 11:31	3383
But when ye go over J, and dwell	Deut 12:10	3383
J unto the land which the LORD	Deut 27:2	3383
shall be when ye be gone over J	Deut 27:4	3383
people, when ye are come over J	Deut 27:12	3383
over J to go to possess it	Deut 30:18	3383
me, Thou shalt not go over this J	Deut 31:2	3383
ye go over J to possess it	Deut 31:13	3383
ye go over J to possess it	Deut 32:47	3383
therefore arise, go over this J	Josh 1:2	3383
days ye shall pass over this J	Josh 1:11	3383
Moses gave you on this side J	Josh 1:14	3383
this side J toward the sunrising	Josh 1:15	3383
them the way to J unto the fords	Josh 2:7	3383
that were on the other side J	Josh 2:10	3383
from Shittim, and came to J	Josh 3:1	3383
to the brink of the water of J	Josh 3:8	3383
J, ye shall stand still in J	Josh 3:8	3383
passeth over before you into J	Josh 3:11	3383
shall rest in the waters of J	Josh 3:13	3383
that the waters of J shall be cut	Josh 3:13	3383
from their tents, to pass over J	Josh 3:14	3383
bare the ark were come unto J	Josh 3:15	3383
(for J overfloweth all his banks	Josh 3:15	3383
on dry ground in the midst of J	Josh 3:17	3383
people were passed clean over J	Josh 3:17	3383
people were clean passed over J	Josh 4:1	3383
you hence out of the midst of J	Josh 4:3	3383
LORD your God into the midst of J	Josh 4:5	3383
That the waters of J were cut off	Josh 4:7	3383
when it passed over J	Josh 4:7	3383
the waters of J were cut off	Josh 4:7	3383
stones out of the midst of J	Josh 4:8	3383
twelve stones in the midst of J	Josh 4:9	3383
the ark stood in the midst of J	Josh 4:10	3383
that they come up out of J	Josh 4:16	3383
saying, Come ye up out of J	Josh 4:17	3383
come up out of the midst of J	Josh 4:18	3383
that the waters of J returned	Josh 4:18	3383
the people came up out of J on	Josh 4:19	3383
stones, which they took out of J	Josh 4:20	3383
came over this J on dry land	Josh 4:22	3383
the waters of J from before you	Josh 4:23	3383
were on the side of J westward	Josh 5:1	3383
of J from before the children of	Josh 5:1	3383
at all brought this people over J	Josh 7:7	3383
and dwelt on the other side J	Josh 7:7	3383
kings which were on this side J	Josh 9:1	3383
the Amorites, that were beyond J	Josh 9:10	3383
J toward the rising of the sun	Josh 12:1	3383
smote on this side J on the west	Josh 12:7	3383
beyond J eastward, even as Moses	Josh 13:8	3383
of the children of Reuben was J	Josh 13:23	3383
of Sihon king of Heshbon, J	Josh 13:27	3383
on the other side J eastward	Josh 13:27	3383
of Moab, on the other side J	Josh 13:32	3383
an half tribe on the other side J	Josh 14:3	3383
salt sea, even unto the end of J	Josh 15:5	3383
sea at the uttermost part of J	Josh 15:5	3383
of Joseph fell from J by Jericho	Josh 16:1	3383
came to Jericho, and went out at J	Josh 16:7	3383
which were on the other side J	Josh 17:5	3383
inheritance beyond J on the east	Josh 18:7	3383
on the north side was from J	Josh 18:12	3383
salt sea at the south end of J	Josh 18:19	3383
J was the border of it on the	Josh 18:20	3383
of their border were at J	Josh 19:22	3383
the outgoings thereof were at J	Josh 19:33	3383
to Judah upon J toward the	Josh 19:34	3383
on the other side J by Jericho	Josh 20:8	3383
LORD gave you on the other side J	Josh 22:4	3383
brethren on this side J westward	Josh 22:7	3383
they came unto the borders of J	Josh 22:10	3383
built there an altar by J	Josh 22:10	3383
of Canaan, in the borders of J	Josh 22:11	3383
hath made J a border between us	Josh 22:25	3383
for your tribes, from J, with all	Josh 23:4	3383
which dwelt on the other side of J	Josh 24:8	3383
And ye went over J, and came unto	Josh 24:11	3383
took the fords of J toward Moab	Judg 3:28	3383
Gilead abode beyond J	Judg 5:17	3383
the waters unto Beth-barah and J	Judg 7:24	3383
the waters unto Beth-barah and J	Judg 7:24	3383
to Gideon on the other side J	Judg 7:25	3383
And Gideon came to J, and passed	Judg 8:4	3383
J in the land of the Amorites	Judg 10:8	3383
J to fight also against Judah	Judg 10:9	3383
Arnon even unto Jabbok, and unto J	Judg 11:13	3383
from the wilderness even unto J	Judg 11:22	3383
of J before the Ephraimites	Judg 12:5	3383
and slew him at the passages of J	Judg 12:6	3383
went over J to the land of Gad	1Sa 13:7	3383
that were on the other side J	1Sa 31:7	3383
the plain, and passed over J	2Sa 2:29	3383
Israel together, and passed over J	2Sa 10:17	3383
with him, and they passed over J	2Sa 17:22	3383
of them that was not gone over J	2Sa 17:22	3383
And Absalom passed over J, he and	2Sa 17:24	3383
the king returned, and came to J	2Sa 19:15	3383
king, to conduct the king over J	2Sa 19:15	3383
they went over J before the king	2Sa 19:17	3383
the king, as he was come over J	2Sa 19:18	3383
went over J with the king	2Sa 19:31	3383
to conduct him over J	2Sa 19:31	3383
a little way over J with the king	2Sa 19:36	3383
And all the people went over J	2Sa 19:39	3383
all David's men with him, over J	2Sa 19:41	3383
king, from J even to Jerusalem	2Sa 20:2	3383
And they passed over J, and pitched	2Sa 24:5	3383
but he came down to meet me at J	1Kin 2:8	3383
In the plain of J did the king	1Kin 7:46	3383
brook Cherith, that is before J	1Kin 17:3	3383
brook Cherith, that is before J	1Kin 17:5	3383
for the LORD hath sent me to J	2Kin 2:6	3383
and they two stood by J	2Kin 2:7	3383
back, and stood by the bank of J	2Kin 2:13	3383
wash in J seven times, and thy	2Kin 5:10	3383
dipped himself seven times in J	2Kin 5:14	3383
Let us go, we pray thee, unto J	2Kin 6:2	3383
And when they came to J, they cut	2Kin 6:4	3383
And they went after them unto J	2Kin 7:15	3383
From J eastward, all the land of	2Kin 10:33	3383
And on the other side J by Jericho	1Chr 6:78	3383
on the east side of J	1Chr 6:78	3383
went over J in the first month	1Chr 12:15	3383
And on the other side of J	1Chr 12:37	3383
all Israel, and passed over J	1Chr 19:17	3383
them of Israel on this side J	1Chr 26:30	3383
In the plain of J did the king	2Chr 4:17	3383
he can draw up J into his mouth	Job 40:23	3383
remember thee from the land of J	Ps 42:6	3383
J was driven back	Ps 114:3	3383
thou J, that thou wast driven	Ps 114:5	3383
by the way of the sea, beyond J	Is 9:1	3383
wilt thou do in the swelling of J	Jer 12:5	3383
a lion from the swelling of J	Jer 49:19	3383
of J unto the habitation of the	Jer 50:44	3383
and from the land of Israel by J	Eze 47:18	3383
for the pride of J is spoiled	Zec 11:3	3383
and all the region round about J	Mt 3:5	2446
And were baptized of him in J	Mt 3:6	2446
Jesus from Galilee to J unto John	Mt 3:13	2446
by the way of the sea, beyond J	Mt 4:15	2446
and from Judaea, and from beyond J	Mt 4:25	2446
the coasts of Judaea beyond J	Mt 19:1	2446
baptized of him in the river of J	Mk 1:5	2446
and was baptized of John in J	Mk 1:9	2446
and from Idumaea, and from beyond J	Mk 3:8	2446
Judaea by the farther side of J	Mk 10:1	2446
came into all the country about J	Lk 3:3	2446
of the Holy Ghost returned from J	Lk 4:1	2446
were done in Bethabara beyond J	Jn 1:28	2446

J

he that was with thee beyond *J*	Jn 3:26	2446
went away again beyond *J* into the	Jn 10:40	2446

JORIM *(jo'-rim) Son of Matthat; ancestor of Jesus.*

Eliezer, which was the son of *J*	Lk 3:29	2497

JORKEAM See JORKOAM.

JORKOAM *(jor'-ko-am) A descendant of Hebron.*

begat Raham, the father of *J*	1Chr 2:44	3421

JOSABAD *(jos'-a-bad)* See JOZABAD. *A warrior in David's army.*

and Johanan, and *J* the Gederathite,	1Chr 12:4	3107

JOSAPHAT *(jos'-a-fat)* See JEHOSHAPHAT. *Son of Asa; ancestor of Jesus.*

And Asa begat *J*	Mt 1:8	2498
and *J* begat Joram	Mt 1:8	2498

JOSE *(jo'-ze)* See JOSES. *Son of Eliezer; ancestor of Jesus.*

Which was the son of *J*, which was	Lk 3:29	2499

JOSECH See JOSEPH.

JOSEDECH *(jos'-e-dek)* See JOZADAK. *Father of Joshua, the priest.*

Judah, and to Joshua the son of *J*	Hag 1:1	3087
Shealtiel, and Joshua the son of *J*	Hag 1:12	3087
the spirit of Joshua the son of *J*	Hag 1:14	3087
Judah, and to Joshua the son of *J*	Hag 2:2	3087
and be strong, O Joshua, son of *J*	Hag 2:4	3087
the head of Joshua the son of *J*	Zec 6:11	3087

JOSEPH *(jo'-zef)* See BARSABAS, JOSEPH'S.
1. *Son of Jacob and Rachel.*

And she called his name *J*	Gen 30:24	3130
to pass, when Rachel had born *J*	Gen 30:25	3130
after, and Rachel and *J* hindermost	Gen 33:2	3130
and after came *J* near and Rachel,	Gen 33:7	3130
sons of Rachel; *J*, and Benjamin	Gen 35:24	3130
J, being seventeen years old, was	Gen 37:2	3130
J brought unto his father their	Gen 37:2	3130
Now Israel loved *J* more than all	Gen 37:3	3130
J dreamed a dream, and he told it	Gen 37:5	3130
And Israel said unto *J*, Do not thy	Gen 37:13	3130
J went after his brethren, and	Gen 37:17	3130
when *J* was come unto his brethren	Gen 37:23	3130
they stript *J* out of his coat	Gen 37:23	3130
lifted up *J* out of the pit, and	Gen 37:28	3130
sold *J* to the Ishmeelites for	Gen 37:28	3130
and they brought *J* into Egypt	Gen 37:28	3130
and, behold, *J* was not in the pit	Gen 37:29	3130
J is without doubt rent in pieces	Gen 37:33	3130
J was brought down to Egypt	Gen 39:1	3130
And the LORD was with *J*, and he was	Gen 39:2	3130
J found grace in his sight, and he	Gen 39:4	3130
J was a goodly person, and well	Gen 39:6	3130
wife cast her eyes upon *J*	Gen 39:7	3130
as she spake to *J* day by day	Gen 39:10	3130
that *J* went into the house to do	Gen 39:11	3130
But the LORD was with *J*, and	Gen 39:21	3130
the place where *J* was bound	Gen 40:3	3130
of the guard charged *J* with them	Gen 40:4	3130
J came in unto them in the	Gen 40:6	3130
And *J* said unto them, Do not	Gen 40:8	3130
chief butler told his dream to *J*	Gen 40:9	3130
J said unto him, This is the	Gen 40:12	3130
was good, he said unto *J*, I also	Gen 40:16	3130
J answered and said, This is the	Gen 40:18	3130
as *J* had interpreted to them	Gen 40:22	3130
not the chief butler remember *J*	Gen 40:23	3130
Then Pharaoh sent and called *J*	Gen 41:14	3130
And Pharaoh said unto *J*, I have	Gen 41:15	3130
J answered Pharaoh, saying, It is	Gen 41:16	3130
And Pharaoh said unto *J*, In my	Gen 41:17	3130
J said unto Pharaoh, The dream of	Gen 41:25	3130
And Pharaoh said unto *J*, Forasmuch	Gen 41:39	3130
And Pharaoh said unto *J*, See, I	Gen 41:41	3130
And Pharaoh said unto *J*, I am	Gen 41:44	3130
J went out over all the land of	Gen 41:45	3130
J was thirty years old when he	Gen 41:46	3130
J went out from the presence of	Gen 41:46	3130
J gathered corn as the sand of	Gen 41:49	3130
unto *J* were born two sons before	Gen 41:50	3130
And *J* called the name of the	Gen 41:51	3130
to come, according as *J* had said	Gen 41:54	3130
unto all the Egyptians, Go unto *J*	Gen 41:55	3130
J opened all the storehouses, and	Gen 41:56	3130
into Egypt to *J* for to buy corn	Gen 41:57	3130
J was the governor over the land,	Gen 42:6	3130
J saw his brethren, and he knew	Gen 42:7	3130
J knew his brethren, but they	Gen 42:8	3130
J remembered the dreams which he	Gen 42:9	3130

J said unto them, That is it that	Gen 42:14	3130
J said unto them the third day,	Gen 42:18	3130
knew not that *J* understood them	Gen 42:23	3130
Then *J* commanded to fill their	Gen 42:25	3130
J is not, and Simeon is not, and ye	Gen 42:36	3130
down to Egypt, and stood before *J*	Gen 43:15	3130
when *J* saw Benjamin with them, he	Gen 43:16	3130
And the man did as *J* bade	Gen 43:17	3130
present against *J* came at noon	Gen 43:25	3130
when *J* came home, they brought	Gen 43:26	3130
And *J* made haste	Gen 43:30	3130
to the word that *J* had spoken	Gen 44:2	3130
J said unto his steward, Up,	Gen 44:4	3130
J said unto them, What deed is	Gen 44:15	3130
Then *J* could not refrain himself	Gen 45:1	3130
while *J* made himself known unto	Gen 45:1	3130
J said unto his brethren	Gen 45:3	3130
I am *J*; doth my father yet	Gen 45:3	3130
J said unto his brethren, Come	Gen 45:4	3130
I am *J* your brother, whom ye sold	Gen 45:4	3130
unto him, Thus saith thy son *J*	Gen 45:9	3130
And Pharaoh said unto *J*, Say unto	Gen 45:17	3130
J gave them wagons, according to	Gen 45:21	3130
J is yet alive, and he is governor	Gen 45:26	3130
they told him all the words of *J*	Gen 45:27	3130
which *J* had sent to carry him	Gen 45:27	3130
J my son is yet alive	Gen 45:28	3130
J shall put his hand upon thine	Gen 46:4	3130
Jacob's wife; *J*, and Benjamin	Gen 46:19	3130
unto *J* in the land of Egypt were	Gen 46:20	3130
And the sons of *J*, which were born	Gen 46:27	3130
he sent Judah before him unto *J*	Gen 46:28	3130
J made ready his chariot, and went	Gen 46:29	3130
And Israel said unto *J*, Now let me	Gen 46:30	3130
J said unto his brethren, and unto	Gen 46:31	3130
Then *J* came and told Pharaoh, and	Gen 47:1	3130
And Pharaoh spake unto *J*, saying,	Gen 47:5	3130
J brought in Jacob his father, and	Gen 47:7	3130
J placed his father and his	Gen 47:11	3130
J nourished his father, and his	Gen 47:12	3130
J gathered up all the money that	Gen 47:14	3130
and *J* brought the money into	Gen 47:14	3130
all the Egyptians came unto *J*	Gen 47:15	3130
And *J* said, Give your cattle	Gen 47:16	3130
they brought their cattle unto *J*	Gen 47:17	3130
J gave them bread in exchange for	Gen 47:17	3130
J bought all the land of Egypt	Gen 47:20	3130
Then *J* said unto the people,	Gen 47:23	3130
J made it a law over the land of	Gen 47:26	3130
and he called his son *J*, and said	Gen 47:29	3130
these things, that one told *J*	Gen 48:1	3130
thy son *J* cometh unto thee	Gen 48:2	3130
And Jacob said unto *J*, God	Gen 48:3	3130
J said unto his father, They are	Gen 48:9	3130
And Israel said unto *J*, I had not	Gen 48:11	3130
J brought them out from between	Gen 48:12	3130
J took them both, Ephraim in his	Gen 48:13	3130
And he blessed *J*, and said, God,	Gen 48:15	3130
when *J* saw that his father laid	Gen 48:17	3130
J said unto his father, Not so,	Gen 48:18	3130
And Israel said unto *J*, Behold, I	Gen 48:21	3130
J is a fruitful bough, even a	Gen 49:22	3130
they shall be on the head of *J*	Gen 49:26	3130
J fell upon his father's face, and	Gen 50:1	3130
J commanded his servants the	Gen 50:2	3130
J spake unto the house of Pharaoh	Gen 50:4	3130
J went up to bury his father	Gen 50:7	3130
And all the house of *J*, and his	Gen 50:8	3130
J returned into Egypt, he, and his	Gen 50:14	3130
J will peradventure hate us, and	Gen 50:15	3130
And they sent a messenger unto *J*	Gen 50:16	3130
So shall ye say unto *J*, Forgive,	Gen 50:17	3130
J wept when they spake unto him	Gen 50:17	3130
J said unto them, Fear not	Gen 50:19	3130
J dwelt in Egypt, he, and his	Gen 50:22	3130
J lived an hundred and ten years	Gen 50:22	3130
J saw Ephraim's children of the	Gen 50:23	3130
J said unto his brethren, I die	Gen 50:24	3130
J took an oath of the children of	Gen 50:25	3130
So *J* died, being an hundred and	Gen 50:26	3130
for *J* was in Egypt already	Ex 1:5	3130
J died, and all his brethren, and	Ex 1:6	3130
king over Egypt, which knew not *J*	Ex 1:8	3130
took the bones of *J* with him	Ex 13:19	3130
families of Manasseh the son of *J*	Num 26:1	3130
tribe of Manasseh the son of *J*	Num 32:33	3130
The prince of the children of *J*	Num 34:23	3130
the sons of Manasseh the son of *J*	Num 36:12	3130
Levi, and Judah, and Issachar, and *J*	Deut 27:12	3130
the children of *J* were two tribes	Josh 14:4	3130
the lot of the children of *J* fell	Josh 16:1	3130

So the children of *J*, Manasseh and .... Josh 16:4   3130
for he was the firstborn of *J* .... Josh 17:1   3130
the son of *J* by their families .... Josh 17:2   3130
the children of *J* spake unto .... Josh 17:14   3130
And the children of *J* said........................ Josh 17:16   3130
And the bones of *J*, which the .... Josh 24:32   3130
Dan, *J*, and Benjamin, Naphtali, ... 1Chr 2:2   3130
He sent a man before them, even *J*......... Ps 105:17   3130
that Jacob gave to his son *J* .... Jn 4:5   2501
with envy, sold *J* into Egypt..................... Acts 7:9   2501
at the second time *J* was made .... Acts 7:13   2501
Then sent *J*, and called his father .... Acts 7:14   2501
king arose, which knew not *J* .... Acts 7:18   2501
dying, blessed both the sons of *J* .... Heb 11:21   2501
By faith *J*, when he died, made .... Heb 11:22   2501
   2. Descendants of Joseph 1.
Of the children of *J*................................. Num 1:10   3130
Of the children of *J*, namely, of .... Num 1:32   3130
Of the tribe of *J*, namely, of the .... Num 13:11   3130
The sons of *J* after their.......................... Num 26:28   3130
sons of *J* after their families .... Num 26:37   3130
of the families of the sons of *J* .... Num 36:1   3130
of the sons of *J* hath said well .... Num 36:5   3130
of *J* he said, Blessed of the LORD .... Deut 33:13   3130
blessing come upon the head of *J*........... Deut 33:16   3130
Joshua spake unto the house of *J*........... Josh 17:17   3130
the house of *J* shall abide in .... Josh 18:5   3130
of Judah and the children of *J* .... Josh 18:11   3130
inheritance of the children of *J*.............. Josh 24:32   3130
And the house of *J*, they also went......... Judg 1:22   3130
the house of *J* sent to descry .... Judg 1:23   3130
hand of the house of *J* prevailed .... Judg 1:35   3130
this day of all the house of *J* to 2Sa 19:20   3130
all the charge of the house of *J* 1Kin 11:28   3130
the sons of *J* the son of Israel................. 1Chr 5:1   3130
children of *J* the son of Israel................. 1Chr 7:29   3130
people, the sons of Jacob and *J* .... Ps 77:15   3130
he refused the tabernacle of *J*................ Ps 78:67   3130
thou that leadest *J* like a flock............... Ps 80:1   3130
he ordained in *J* for a testimony .... Ps 81:5   3084
stick, and write upon it, For *J*................. Eze 37:16   3130
I will take the stick of *J* .... Eze 37:19   3130
J shall have two portions .... Eze 47:13   3130
and one gate of *J*, one gate of .... Eze 48:32   3130
out like fire in the house of *J* .... Amos 5:6   3130
be gracious unto the remnant of *J*......... Amos 5:15   3130
grieved for the affliction of *J* .... Amos 6:6   3130
a fire, and the house of *J* a flame .... Obad 18   3130
and I will save the house of *J* .... Zec 10:6   3130
Of the tribe of *J* were sealed .... Rev 7:8   2501
   3. A spy sent to the Promised Land.
of Issachar, Igal the son of *J*.................. Num 13:7   3130
   4. A son of Asaph.
Zaccur, and *J*, and Nethaniah, and......... 1Chr 25:2   3130
lot came forth for Asaph to *J* 1Chr 25:9   3130
   5. Married a foreigner in exile.
Shallum, Amariah, and *J*........................ Ezr 10:42   3130
   6. A priest.
Jonathan; of Shebaniah, *J* .... Neh 12:14   3130
   7. Husband of Mary, the mother of Jesus.
Jacob begat *J* the husband of Mary .... Mt 1:16   2501
his mother Mary was espoused to *J*....... Mt 1:18   2501
Then *J* her husband, being a just .... Mt 1:19   2501
unto him in a dream, saying, ... *J* .... Mt 1:20   2501
Then *J* being raised from sleep............... Mt 1:24   2501
Lord appeareth to *J* in a dream.............. Mt 2:13   2501
in a dream to *J* in Egypt,........................ Mt 2:19   2501
to a man whose name was *J*.................... Lk 1:27   2501
J also went up from Galilee, out .... Lk 2:4   2501
with haste, and found Mary, and *J* .... Lk 2:16   2501
And *J* and his mother marvelled at .... Lk 2:33   2501
and *J* and his mother knew not of it ...... Lk 2:43   2501
(as was supposed) the son of *J* .... Lk 3:23   2501
Jesus of Nazareth, the son of *J* .... Jn 1:45   2501
Is not this Jesus, the son of *J* .... Jn 6:42   2501
   8. A disciple of Jesus.
a rich man of Arimathaea, named *J* ...... Mt 27:57   2501
when *J* had taken the body, he............... Mt 27:59   2501
J of Arimathaea, an honourable .... Mk 15:43   2501
centurion, he gave the body to *J* .... Mk 15:45   2501
behold, there was a man named *J* .... Lk 23:50   2501
after this *J* of Arimathaea, being........... Jn 19:38   2501
   9. Son of Mattathias; ancestor of Jesus.
of Janna, which was the son of *J* .... Lk 3:24   2501
   10. Son of Juda; ancestor of Jesus.
of Semei, which was the son of *J* .... Lk 3:26   2501
   11. Son of Jonan; ancestor of Jesus.
of Juda, which was the son of *J*............. Lk 3:30   2501
   12. A nominee for Judas' apostleship.
J called Barsabas, who was .... Acts 1:23   2501

JOSEPH'S *(jo'-zefs)*
   1. Refers to Joseph 1.
And they took *J* coat, and killed a .... Gen 37:31   3130
the Egyptian's house for *J* sake .... Gen 39:5   3130
he left all that he had in *J* hand............. Gen 39:6   3130
J master took him, and put him............. Gen 39:20   3130
of the prison committed to *J* hand......... Gen 39:22   3130
his hand, and put it upon *J* hand........... Gen 41:42   3130
And Pharaoh called *J* name .... Gen 41:45   3130
J ten brethren went down to buy .... Gen 42:3   3130
J brother, Jacob sent not with .... Gen 42:4   3130
J brethren came, and bowed down .... Gen 42:6   3130
man brought the men into *J* house .... Gen 43:17   3130
they were brought into *J* house .... Gen 43:18   3130
near to the steward of *J* house .... Gen 43:19   3130
man brought the men into *J* house .... Gen 43:24   3130
and his brethren came to *J* house .... Gen 44:14   3130
saying, *J* brethren are come .... Gen 45:16   3130
And Israel beheld *J* sons, and said, ... Gen 48:8   3130
when *J* brethren saw that their............... Gen 50:15   3130
were brought up upon *J* knees .... Gen 50:23   3130
but the birthright was *J*.......................... 1Chr 5:2   3130
J kindred was made known unto .... Acts 7:13   2501
   2. Refers to Joseph 7.
And they said, Is not this *J* son .... Lk 4:22   2501

JOSES *(jo'-zez)* See JOSE.
   1. A brother of Jesus.
and his brethren, James, and *J* .... Mt 13:55   2500
Mary, the brother of James, and *J* .... Mk 6:3   2500
   2. Brother of James the younger.
and Mary the mother of James and *J* .... Mt 27:56   2500
mother of James the less and of *J* .... Mk 15:40   2500
Mary the mother of *J* beheld where .... Mk 15:47   2500
   3. Same as Barnabas.
And *J*, who by the apostles was .... Acts 4:36   2500

JOSHAH *(jo'-shah)* *A descendant of Simeon.*
Jamlech, and *J* the son of Amaziah, ... 1Chr 4:34   3144

JOSHAPHAT *(josh'-a-fat)* See JEHOSHAPHAT, JOSAPHAT.
   A "mighty man" of David.
of Maachah, and *J* the Mithnite, ... 1Chr 11:43   3146

JOSHAVIAH *(josh-a-vi'-ah)* *A "mighty man" of David.*
the Mahavite, and Jeribai, and *J*............. 1Chr 11:46   3145

JOSHBEKASHAH *(josh-bek'-a-shah)* *A sanctuary servant.*
Giddalti, and Romamti-ezer, *J* 1Chr 25:4   3436
The seventeenth to *J*, he, his.................. 1Chr 25:24   3436

JOSHEB-BASSHEBETH See ADINO.

JOSHUA *(josh'-u-ah)* See HOSEA, HOSHEA, JEHOSHUAH, JESHUA, JESHUAH, JESUS, OSEA, OSHEA.
   1. Son of Nun.
And Moses said unto *J*, Choose us .... Ex 17:9   3091
So *J* did as Moses had said to him .... Ex 17:10   3091
J discomfited Amalek and his .... Ex 17:13   3091
and rehearse it in the ears of *J* .... Ex 17:14   3091
Moses rose up, and his minister *J* .... Ex 24:13   3091
when *J* heard the noise of the .... Ex 32:17   3091
but his servant, *J* the son of Nun .... Ex 33:11   3091
J the son of Nun, the servant of .... Num 11:28   3091
J the son of Nun, and Caleb the............. Num 14:6   3091
of Jephunneh, and *J* the son of Nun ...... Num 14:30   3091
But *J* the son of Nun, and Caleb .... Num 14:38   3091
of Jephunneh, and *J* the son of Nun ...... Num 26:65   3091
Take thee *J* the son of Nun, a man .... Num 27:18   3091
and he took *J*, and set him before .... Num 27:22   3091
the Kenezite, and *J* the son of Nun .... Num 32:12   3091
J the son of Nun, and the chief .... Num 32:28   3091
the priest, and *J* the son of Nun............. Num 34:17   3091
But *J* the son of Nun, which .... Deut 1:38   3091
I commanded *J* at that time, ... Deut 3:21   3091
But charge *J*, and encourage him, ... Deut 3:28   3091
and *J*, he shall go over before .... Deut 31:3   3091
And Moses called unto *J*, and said .... Deut 31:7   3091
call *J*, and present yourselves in .... Deut 31:14   3091
J went, and presented themselves .... Deut 31:14   3091
he gave the son of Nun a charge .... Deut 31:23   3091
J the son of Nun was full of the .... Deut 34:9   3091
LORD spake unto *J* the son of Nun .... Josh 1:1   3091
Then *J* commanded the officers of .... Josh 1:10   3091
the tribe of Manasseh, spake *J* .... Josh 1:12   3091
And they answered *J*, saying, All .... Josh 1:16   3091
J the son of Nun sent out of .... Josh 2:1   3091
came to the son of Nun, and told .... Josh 2:23   3091
And they said unto *J*, Truly the .... Josh 2:24   3091
J rose early in the morning .... Josh 3:1   3091
J said unto the people, Sanctify .... Josh 3:5   3091
J spake unto the priests, saying,............. Josh 3:6   3091
And the LORD said unto *J*, This day .... Josh 3:7   3091
J said unto the children of .... Josh 3:9   3091

J said, Hereby ye shall know that	Josh 3:10	3091
that the LORD spake unto *J*	Josh 4:1	3091
Then *J* called the twelve men,	Josh 4:4	3091
J said unto them, Pass over	Josh 4:5	3091
of Israel did so as *J* commanded	Josh 4:8	3091
Jordan, as the LORD spake unto *J*	Josh 4:8	3091
J set up twelve stones in the	Josh 4:9	3091
that the LORD commanded *J* to	Josh 4:10	3091
to all that Moses commanded *J*	Josh 4:10	3091
J in the sight of all Israel	Josh 4:14	3091
And the LORD spake unto *J*, saying,	Josh 4:15	3091
J therefore commanded the priests	Josh 4:17	3091
of Jordan, did *J* pitch in Gilgal	Josh 4:20	3091
At that time the LORD said unto *J*	Josh 5:2	3091
J made him sharp knives, and	Josh 5:3	3091
is the cause why *J* did circumcise	Josh 5:4	3091
their stead, them *J* circumcised	Josh 5:7	3091
And the LORD said unto *J*, This day	Josh 5:9	3091
when *J* was by Jericho, that he	Josh 5:13	3091
J went unto him, and said unto him	Josh 5:13	3091
J fell on his face to the earth,	Josh 5:14	3091
of the LORD's host said unto *J*	Josh 5:15	3091
And *J* did so	Josh 5:15	3091
And the LORD said unto *J*, See, I	Josh 6:2	3091
J the son of Nun called the	Josh 6:6	3091
when *J* had spoken unto the people	Josh 6:8	3091
J had commanded the people,	Josh 6:10	3091
J rose early in the morning, and	Josh 6:12	3091
J said unto the people, Shout	Josh 6:16	3091
But *J* had said unto the two men	Josh 6:22	3091
J saved Rahab the harlot alive,	Josh 6:25	3091
which *J* sent to spy out Jericho	Josh 6:25	3091
J adjured them at that time,	Josh 6:26	3091
So the LORD was with *J*.	Josh 6:27	3091
J sent men from Jericho to Ai,	Josh 7:2	3091
And they returned to *J*, and said	Josh 7:3	3091
J rent his clothes, and fell to	Josh 7:6	3091
J said, Alas, O Lord GOD,	Josh 7:7	3091
And the LORD said unto *J*, Get thee	Josh 7:10	3091
So *J* rose up early in the morning	Josh 7:16	3091
J said unto Achan, My son, give,	Josh 7:19	3091
And Achan answered *J*, and said,	Josh 7:20	3091
So *J* sent messengers, and they ran	Josh 7:22	3091
the tent, and brought them unto *J*	Josh 7:23	3091
And *J*, and all Israel with him,	Josh 7:24	3091
J said, Why hast thou troubled us	Josh 7:25	3091
And the LORD said unto *J*, Fear not	Josh 8:1	3091
So *J* arose, and all the people of	Josh 8:3	3091
J chose out thirty thousand	Josh 8:3	3091
J therefore sent them forth	Josh 8:9	3091
but *J* lodged that night among the	Josh 8:9	3091
J rose up early in the morning,	Josh 8:10	3091
J went that night into the midst	Josh 8:13	3091
And *J* and all Israel made as if	Josh 8:15	3091
and they pursued after *J*, and were	Josh 8:16	3091
And the LORD said unto *J*, Stretch	Josh 8:18	3091
J stretched out the spear that he	Josh 8:18	3091
And when *J* and all Israel saw that	Josh 8:21	3091
took alive, and brought him to *J*	Josh 8:23	3091
For *J* drew not his hand back,	Josh 8:26	3091
of the LORD which he commanded *J*	Josh 8:27	3091
J burnt Ai, and made it an heap	Josh 8:28	3091
J commanded that they should take	Josh 8:29	3091
Then *J* built an altar unto the	Josh 8:30	3091
which *J* read not before all the	Josh 8:35	3091
together, to fight with *J*.	Josh 9:2	3091
of Gibeon heard what *J* had done	Josh 9:3	3091
they went to *J* unto the camp at	Josh 9:6	3091
And they said unto *J*, We are thy	Josh 9:8	3091
J said unto them, Who are ye	Josh 9:8	3091
J made peace with them, and made a	Josh 9:15	3091
J called for them, and he spake	Josh 9:22	3091
And they answered *J*, and said,	Josh 9:24	3091
J made them that day hewers of	Josh 9:27	3091
had heard how *J* had taken Ai	Josh 10:1	3091
for it hath made peace with *J*	Josh 10:4	3091
sent unto *J* to the camp to Gilgal	Josh 10:6	3091
So *J* ascended from Gilgal, he, and	Josh 10:7	3091
And the LORD said unto *J*, Fear	Josh 10:8	3091
J therefore came unto them	Josh 10:9	3091
Then spake *J* to the LORD in the	Josh 10:12	3091
J returned, and all Israel with	Josh 10:15	3091
And it was told *J*, saying, The	Josh 10:17	3091
J said, Roll great stones upon	Josh 10:18	3091
And it came to pass, when *J*	Josh 10:20	3091
camp to *J* at Makkedah in peace	Josh 10:21	3091
Then said *J*, Open the mouth of	Josh 10:22	3091
brought out those kings unto *J*	Josh 10:24	3091
that *J* called for all the men of	Josh 10:24	3091
J said unto them, Fear not, nor	Josh 10:25	3091
afterward *J* smote them, and slew	Josh 10:26	3091
that *J* commanded, and they took	Josh 10:27	3091
that day *J* took Makkedah, and	Josh 10:28	3091
Then *J* passed from Makkedah, and	Josh 10:29	3091
J passed from Libnah, and all	Josh 10:31	3091
J smote him and his people, until	Josh 10:33	3091
from Lachish *J* passed unto Eglon,	Josh 10:34	3091
J went up from Eglon, and all	Josh 10:36	3091
J returned, and all Israel with	Josh 10:38	3091
So *J* smote all the country of the	Josh 10:40	3091
J smote them from Kadesh-barnea	Josh 10:41	3091
their land did *J* take at one time	Josh 10:42	3091
J returned, and all Israel with	Josh 10:43	3091
And the LORD said unto *J*, Be not	Josh 11:6	3091
So *J* came, and all the people of	Josh 11:7	3091
J did unto them as the LORD bade	Josh 11:9	3091
J at that time turned back, and	Josh 11:10	3091
did *J* take, and smote them with	Josh 11:12	3091
that did *J* burn	Josh 11:13	3091
Moses command *J*, and so did *J*	Josh 11:15	3091
So *J* took all that land, the	Josh 11:16	3091
J made war a long time with all	Josh 11:18	3091
And at that time came *J*, and cut	Josh 11:21	3091
J destroyed them utterly with	Josh 11:21	3091
So *J* took the whole land,	Josh 11:23	3091
J gave it for an inheritance unto	Josh 11:23	3091
the kings of the country which *J*	Josh 12:7	3091
which *J* gave unto the tribes of	Josh 12:7	3091
Now *J* was old and stricken in	Josh 13:1	3091
J the son of Nun, and the heads of	Josh 14:1	3091
of Judah came unto *J* in Gilgal	Josh 14:6	3091
J blessed him, and gave unto Caleb	Josh 14:13	3091
the commandment of the LORD to *J*	Josh 15:13	3091
before *J* the son of Nun, and	Josh 17:4	3091
children of Joseph spake unto *J*	Josh 17:14	3091
J answered them, If thou be a	Josh 17:15	3091
J spake unto the house of Joseph,	Josh 17:17	3091
J said unto the children of	Josh 18:3	3091
J charged them that went to	Josh 18:8	3091
came again to *J* to the host at	Josh 18:9	3091
J cast lots for them in Shiloh	Josh 18:10	3091
there *J* divided the land unto the	Josh 18:10	3091
to *J* the son of Nun among them	Josh 19:49	3091
J the son of Nun, and the heads of	Josh 19:51	3091
The LORD also spake unto *J*	Josh 20:1	3091
unto *J* the son of Nun, and unto	Josh 21:1	3091
Then *J* called the Reubenites, and	Josh 22:1	3091
So *J* blessed them, and sent them	Josh 22:6	3091
the other half thereof gave *J*	Josh 22:7	3091
when *J* sent them away also unto	Josh 22:7	3091
that *J* waxed old and stricken in	Josh 23:1	3091
J called for all Israel, and for	Josh 23:2	3091
J gathered all the tribes of	Josh 24:1	3091
J said unto all the people, Thus	Josh 24:2	3091
J said unto the people, Ye cannot	Josh 24:19	3091
And the people said unto *J*	Josh 24:21	3091
J said unto the people, Ye are	Josh 24:22	3091
And the people said unto *J*	Josh 24:24	3091
So *J* made a covenant with the	Josh 24:25	3091
J wrote these words in the book	Josh 24:26	3091
J said unto all the people,	Josh 24:27	3091
So *J* let the people depart, every	Josh 24:28	3091
that *J* the son of Nun, the	Josh 24:29	3091
served the LORD all the days of *J*	Josh 24:31	3091
of the elders that overlived *J*	Josh 24:31	3091
the death of *J* it came to pass	Judg 1:1	3091
when *J* had let the people go, the	Judg 2:6	3091
served the LORD all the days of *J*	Judg 2:7	3091
of the elders that outlived *J*	Judg 2:7	3091
J the son of Nun, the servant of	Judg 2:8	3091
nations which *J* left when he died	Judg 2:21	3091
he them into the hand of *J*	Judg 2:23	3091
he spake by *J* the son of Nun	1Kin 16:34	3091
2. A Bethshemite.		
the cart came into the field of *J*	1Sa 6:14	3091
unto this day in the field of *J*.	1Sa 6:18	3091
3. A governor of Jerusalem.		
of *J* the governor of the city	2Kin 23:8	3091
4. A High Priest.		
to *J* the son of Josedech, the	Hag 1:1	3091
J the son of Josedech, the high	Hag 1:12	3091
the spirit of *J* the son of	Hag 1:14	3091
to *J* the son of Josedech, the	Hag 2:2	3091
and be strong, O *J*, son of	Hag 2:4	3091
he shewed me *J* the high priest	Zec 3:1	3091
Now *J* was clothed with filthy	Zec 3:3	3091
of the LORD protested unto *J*	Zec 3:6	3091
O *J* the high priest, thou, and thy	Zec 3:8	3091
stone that I have laid before *J*	Zec 3:9	3091
the head of *J* the son of Josedech	Zec 6:11	3091

JOSIAH (jo-si'-ah) See JOSIAS.
1. A king of Judah.

the house of David, J by name	1Kin 13:2	2977
made J his son king in his stead	2Kin 21:24	2977
J his son reigned in his stead	2Kin 21:26	2977
J was eight years old when he	2Kin 22:1	2977
in the eighteenth year of king J	2Kin 22:3	2977
as J turned himself, he spied the	2Kin 23:16	2977
J took away, and did to them	2Kin 23:19	2977
in the eighteenth year of king J	2Kin 23:23	2977
did J put away, that he might	2Kin 23:24	2977
Now the rest of the acts of J	2Kin 23:28	2977
and king J went against him	2Kin 23:29	2977
land took Jehoahaz the son of J	2Kin 23:30	2977
made Eliakim the son of J king in	2Kin 23:34	2977
king in the room of J his father	2Kin 23:34	2977
Amon his son, J his son	1Chr 3:14	2977
And the sons of J were, the	1Chr 3:15	2977
made J his son king in his stead	2Chr 33:25	2977
J was eight years old when he	2Chr 34:1	2977
J took away all the abominations	2Chr 34:33	2977
Moreover J kept a passover unto	2Chr 35:1	2977
J gave to the people, of the	2Chr 35:7	2977
to the commandment of king J	2Chr 35:16	2977
keep such a passover as J kept	2Chr 35:18	2977
reign of J was this passover kept	2Chr 35:19	2977
when J had prepared the temple,	2Chr 35:20	2977
and J went out against him	2Chr 35:20	2977
Nevertheless J would not turn his	2Chr 35:22	2977
And the archers shot at king J	2Chr 35:23	2977
Judah and Jerusalem mourned for J	2Chr 35:24	2977
And Jeremiah lamented for J	2Chr 35:25	2977
the singing women spake of J in	2Chr 35:25	2977
Now the rest of the acts of J	2Chr 35:26	2977
land took Jehoahaz the son of J	2Chr 36:1	2977
J the son of Amon king of Judah	Jer 1:2	2977
the son of J king of Judah	Jer 1:3	2977
the son of J king of Judah	Jer 1:3	2977
unto me in the days of J the king	Jer 3:6	2977
the son of J king of Judah	Jer 22:11	2977
reigned instead of J his father	Jer 22:11	2977
the son of J king of Judah	Jer 22:18	2977
the son of J king of Judah	Jer 25:1	2977
From the thirteenth year of J the	Jer 25:3	2977
of J king of Judah came this word	Jer 26:1	2977
of J king of Judah came this word	Jer 27:1	2977
the son of J king of Judah	Jer 35:1	2977
the son of J king of Judah	Jer 36:1	2977
unto thee, from the days of J	Jer 36:2	2977
the son of J king of Judah	Jer 36:9	2977
king Zedekiah the son of J	Jer 37:1	2977
the son of J king of Judah	Jer 45:1	2977
the son of J king of Judah	Jer 46:2	2977
in the days of J the son of Amon,	Zeph 1:1	2977

2. A son of Zephaniah.

house of J the son of Zephaniah	Zec 6:10	2977

JOSIAS (jo-si'-as) See JOSIAH. *Son of Amon; ancestor of Jesus.*

and Amon begat J	Mt 1:10	2502
J begat Jechonias and his brethren	Mt 1:11	2502

JOSIBIAH (jos-ib-i'-ah) *A Simeonite.*

And Joel, and Jehu the son of J	1Chr 4:35	3143

JOSIPHIAH (jos-if-i'-ah) *A family of exiles.*

the son of J, and with him an	Ezr 8:10	3131

JOT

one j or one tittle shall in no	Mt 5:18	2503

JOTBAH (jot'-bah) *A place near Hebron.*

the daughter of Haruz of J	2Kin 21:19	3192

JOTBATH (jot'-bath) See JOTBATHAH. *An encampment during the Exodus.*

and from Gudgodah to J, a land of	Deut 10:7	3193

JOTBATHAH (jot'-ba-thah) See JOTBATH. *Same as Jotbath.*

Hor-hagidgad, and pitched in J	Num 33:33	3193
And they removed from J, and	Num 33:34	3193

JOTHAM (jo'-tham) See JOATHAM.
1. A son of Gideon.

notwithstanding yet J the	Judg 9:5	3147
And when they told it to J	Judg 9:7	3147
J ran away, and fled, and went to	Judg 9:21	3147
curse of J the son of Jerubbaal	Judg 9:57	3147

2. Father of King Ahaz.

J the king's son was over the	2Kin 15:5	3147
J his son reigned in his stead	2Kin 15:7	3147
year of J the son of Uzziah	2Kin 15:30	3147
Remaliah king of Israel began J	2Kin 15:32	3147
Now the rest of the acts of J	2Kin 15:36	3147

J slept with his fathers, and was	2Kin 15:38	3147
of J king of Judah began to reign	2Kin 16:1	3147
son, Azariah his son, J his son,	1Chr 3:12	3147
in the days of J king of Judah	1Chr 5:17	3147
J his son was over the king's	2Chr 26:21	3147
J his son reigned in his stead	2Chr 26:23	3147
J was twenty and five years old	2Chr 27:1	3147
So J became mighty, because he	2Chr 27:6	3147
Now the rest of the acts of J	2Chr 27:7	3147
J slept with his fathers, and they	2Chr 27:9	3147
in the days of Uzziah, J, Ahaz,	Is 1:1	3147
in the days of Ahaz the son of J	Is 7:1	3147
Beeri, in the days of Uzziah, J	Hos 1:1	3147
the Morasthite in the days of J	Mic 1:1	3147

3. A descendant of Caleb.

Regem, and J, and Gesham, and Pelet, ..	1Chr 2:47	3147

JOURNEY

had made his j prosperous or not	Gen 24:21	1870
Jacob went on his j, and came	Gen 29:1	5575,7272
set three days' j betwixt himself	Gen 30:36	1870
pursued after him seven days' j	Gen 31:23	1870
And he said, Let us take our j	Gen 33:12	5265
Israel took his j with all that	Gen 46:1	5265
three days' j into the wilderness	Ex 3:18	1870
three days' j into the desert, and	Ex 5:3	1870
three days' j into the wilderness	Ex 8:27	1870
And they took their j from Succoth	Ex 13:20	5265
And they took their j from Elim	Ex 16:1	5265
dead body, or be in a j afar off	Num 9:10	1870
that is clean, and is not in a j	Num 9:13	1870
the south side shall take their j	Num 10:6	5265
they first took their j according	Num 10:13	5265
mount of the LORD three days' j	Num 10:33	1870
before them in the three days' j	Num 10:33	1870
as it were a day's j on this side	Num 11:31	1870
were a day's j on the other side	Num 11:31	1870
went three days' j in the	Num 33:8	1870
they took their j out of the	Num 33:12	5265
(There are eleven days' j from	Deut 1:2	
Turn you, and take your j, and go	Deut 1:7	5265
take your j into the wilderness	Deut 1:40	5265
took our j into the wilderness by	Deut 2:1	5265
Rise ye up, take your j, and pass	Deut 2:24	5265
children of Israel took their j	Deut 10:6	5265
take thy j before the people,	Deut 10:11	4550
Take victuals with you for the j	Josh 9:11	1870
old by reason of the very long j	Josh 9:13	1870
notwithstanding if that thou	Judg 4:9	1870
And the LORD sent thee on a j	1Sa 15:18	1870
Uriah, Camest thou not from thy j	2Sa 11:10	1870
he is pursuing, or he is in a j	1Kin 18:27	1870
a day's j into the wilderness	1Kin 19:4	1870
because the j is too great for	1Kin 19:7	1870
a compass of seven days' j	2Kin 3:9	1870
Then Solomon came from his j to	2Chr 1:13	
him,) For how long shall thy j be	Neh 2:6	4109
not at home, he is gone a long j	Prov 7:19	1870
great city of three days' j	Jonah 3:3	4109
to enter into the city a day's j	Jonah 3:4	4109
Nor scrip for your j, neither two	Mt 10:10	3598
and straightway took his j	Mt 25:15	589
should take nothing for their j	Mk 6:8	3598
of man is as a man taking a far j	Mk 13:34	590
in the company, went a day's j	Lk 2:44	3598
them, Take nothing for your j	Lk 9:3	3598
of mine in his j is come to me	Lk 11:6	3598
took his j into a far country, and	Lk 15:13	589
being wearied with his j	Jn 4:6	3597
from Jerusalem a sabbath day's j	Acts 1:12	3598
morrow, as they went on their j	Acts 10:9	3596
to pass, that, as I made my j	Acts 22:6	4198
I might have a prosperous j by	Rom 1:10	2137
Whensoever I take my j into Spain	Rom 15:24	4198
for I trust to see you in my j	Rom 15:24	1279
me on my j whithersoever I go	1Cor 16:6	
and Apollos on their j diligently	Titus 3:13	
on their j after a godly sort	3Jn 6	

JOURNEYED

as they j from the east, that	Gen 11:2	5265
And Abram j, going on still toward	Gen 12:9	5265
and Lot j east	Gen 13:11	5265
Abraham j from thence toward the	Gen 20:1	5265
Jacob j to Succoth, and built him	Gen 33:17	5265
And they j and the terror	Gen 35:5	5265
And they j from Beth-el	Gen 35:16	5265
And Israel j, and spread his tent	Gen 35:21	5265
the children of Israel j from	Ex 12:37	5265
of the children of Israel j from	Ex 17:1	5265
then they j not till the day that	Ex 40:37	5265
that the children of Israel j	Num 9:17	5265

the LORD the children of Israel *j*............ Num 9:18 5265
the charge of the LORD, and *j* not........... Num 9:19 5265
commandment of the LORD they *j* .... Num 9:20 5265
up in the morning, then they *j*.................. Num 9:21 5265
the cloud was taken up, they *j*................. Num 9:21 5265
abode in their tents, and *j* not................ Num 9:22 5265
but when it was taken up, they *j*............ Num 9:22 5265
commandment of the LORD they *j* .... Num 9:23 5265
And the people *j* from .... Num 11:35 5265
the people *j* not till Miriam was.............. Num 12:15 5265
j from Kadesh, and came unto mount .... Num 20:22 5265
they *j* from mount Hor by the way .... Num 21:4 5265
they *j* from Oboth, and pitched at .... Num 21:11 5265
they *j* from Rissah, and pitched in.......... Num 33:22 5265
From thence they *j* unto Gudgodah .... Deut 10:7 5265
And the children of Israel *j*..................... Josh 9:17 5265
to the house of Micah, as he *j* .... Judg 17:8 6213,1870
But a certain Samaritan, as he *j*....... Lk 10:33 3593
And as he *j*, he came near Damascus .... Acts 9:3 4198
the men which *j* with him stood............ Acts 9:7 4922
about me and them which *j* with me ...... Acts 26:13 4198

JOURNEYING

and for the *j* of the camps...................... Num 10:2 4550
We are *j* unto the place of which .... Num 10:29 5265
teaching, and *j* toward Jerusalem ... Lk 13:22 4197,4160

JOURNEYINGS

Thus were the *j* of the children.............. Num 10:28 4550
In *j* often, in perils of waters,.................. 2Cor 11:26 3597

JOURNEYS

he went on his *j* from the south.............. Gen 13:3 4550
wilderness of Sin, after their *j* .... Ex 17:1 4550
Israel went onward in all their *j*............. Ex 40:36 4550
of Israel, throughout all their *j*.............. Ex 40:38 4550
shall blow an alarm for their *j* .... Num 10:6 4550
children of Israel took their *j* .... Num 10:12 4550
These are the *j* of the children .... Num 33:1 4550
goings out according to their *j*............... Num 33:2 4550
these are their *j* according to................. Num 33:2 4550

JOY

king Saul, with tabrets, with *j*,.............. 1Sa 18:6 8057
pipes, and rejoiced with great *j* 1Kin 1:40 8057
for there was *j* in Israel.......................... 1Chr 12:40 8057
by lifting up the voice with *j* 1Chr 15:16 8057
of the house of Obed-edom with *j* 1Chr 15:25 8057
king also rejoiced with great *j* 1Chr 29:9 8057
now have I seen with *j* thy people........... 1Chr 29:17 8057
to go again to Jerusalem with *j*.............. 2Chr 20:27 8057
So there was great *j* in Jerusalem 2Chr 30:26 8057
and many shouted aloud for *j* .... Ezr 3:12 8057
the noise of the shout of *j* from .... Ezr 3:13 8057
of this house of God with *j* .... Ezr 6:16 2305
bread seven days with *j*.......................... Ezr 6:22 8057
for the *j* of the LORD is your .... Neh 8:10 2304
made them rejoice with great *j* .... Neh 12:43 8057
so that the *j* of Jerusalem was .... Neh 12:43 8057
Jews had light, and gladness, and *j*....... Est 8:16 8342
his decree came, the Jews had *j* .... Est 8:17 8057
turned unto them from sorrow to *j*......... Est 9:22 8057
make them days of feasting and *j* .... Est 9:22 8057
Behold, this is the *j* of his way .... Job 8:19 4885
the *j* of the hypocrite but for a .... Job 20:5 8057
the widow's heart to sing for *j* .... Job 29:13 7442
and he shall see his face with *j*............... Job 33:26 8643
all the sons of God shouted for *j* .... Job 38:7
is turned into *j* before him .... Job 41:22
let them ever shout for *j* .... Ps 5:11
in thy presence is fulness of *j*................. Ps 16:11 8057
The king shall *j* in thy strength,............. Ps 21:1 8055
in his tabernacle sacrifices of *j*.............. Ps 27:6 8643
but *j* cometh in the morning.................... Ps 30:5 7440
and shout for *j*, all ye that are .... Ps 32:11
Let them shout for *j*, and be glad,.......... Ps 35:27
house of God, with the voice of *j* .... Ps 42:4 7440
of God, unto God my exceeding *j* .... Ps 43:4 1524
the *j* of the whole earth, is .... Ps 48:2 4885
Make me to hear *j* and gladness .... Ps 51:8 8342
unto me the *j* of thy salvation .... Ps 51:12 8342
they shout for *j*, they also sing .... Ps 65:13
the nations be glad and sing for *j*........... Ps 67:4
brought forth his people with *j* .... Ps 105:43 8342
that sow in tears shall reap in *j*............... Ps 126:5 7440
and let thy saints shout for *j* .... Ps 132:9 7442
saints shall shout aloud for *j* .... Ps 132:16 7442
not Jerusalem above my chief *j* .... Ps 137:6 8057
to the counsellors of peace is *j*............... Prov 12:20 8057
doth not intermeddle with his *j*.............. Prov 14:10 8057
Folly is *j* to him that is .... Prov 15:21 8057
A man hath *j* by the answer of his .... Prov 15:23 8057
and the father of a fool hath no *j* .... Prov 17:21 8056

It is *j* to the just to do.............................. Prov 21:15 8057
a wise child shall have *j* of him............... Prov 23:24 8056
withheld not my heart from any *j*........... Eccl 2:10 8057
sight wisdom, and knowledge, and *j*....... Eccl 2:26 8057
him in the *j* of his heart .... Eccl 5:20 8057
Go thy way, eat thy bread with *j* .... Eccl 9:7 8057
nation, and not increased the *j* .... Is 9:3 8057
they *j* before thee according to .... Is 9:3 8055
according to the *j* in harvest .... Is 9:3 8055
have no *j* in their young men.................. Is 9:17 8055
Therefore with *j* shall ye draw............... Is 12:3 8342
j out of the plentiful field .... Is 16:10 1524
And behold *j* and gladness, slaying .... Is 22:13 8342
the *j* of the harp ceaseth .... Is 24:8 4885
all *j* is darkened, the mirth of................. Is 24:11 8057
increase their *j* in the LORD..................... Is 29:19 8057
houses of *j* in the joyous city .... Is 32:13 4885
a *j* of wild asses, a pasture of .... Is 32:14 4885
and rejoice even with *j* and .... Is 35:2 1525
everlasting *j* upon their heads .... Is 35:10 8057
they shall obtain *j* and gladness, ... Is 35:10 8057
j and gladness shall be found .... Is 51:3 8342
everlasting *j* shall be upon their .... Is 51:11 8057
they shall obtain gladness and *j* .... Is 51:11 8057
Break forth into *j*, sing together............. Is 52:9
For ye shall go out with *j*........................ Is 55:12 8057
a *j* of many generations .... Is 60:15 4885
the oil of *j* for mourning, the .... Is 61:3 8342
everlasting *j* shall be unto them .... Is 61:7 8057
shall sing for *j* of heart .... Is 65:14 2898
a rejoicing, and her people a *j*................. Is 65:18 4885
in Jerusalem, and *j* in my people .... Is 65:19 7796
but he shall appear to your *j*.................. Is 66:5 8057
rejoice for *j* with her, all ye .... Is 66:10 4885
and thy word was unto me the *j* .... Jer 15:16 8342
I will turn their mourning into *j*............. Jer 31:13 8342
And it shall be to me a name of *j* .... Jer 33:9 8342
The voice of *j*, and the voice of............... Jer 33:11 8342
of him, thou skippedst for *j* .... Jer 48:27
And *j* and gladness is taken from........... Jer 48:33 8057
praise not left, the city of my *j* .... Jer 49:25 4885
beauty, The *j* of the whole earth .... Lam 2:15 4885
The *j* of our heart is ceased..................... Lam 5:15 4885
the *j* of their glory, the desire .... Eze 24:25 4885
with the *j* of all their heart .... Eze 36:5 8057
Rejoice not, O Israel, for *j*...................... Hos 9:1 1524
because *j* is withered away from............ Joel 1:12 8342
cut off before our eyes, yea, *j* .... Joel 1:16 8057
I will *j* in the God of my.......................... Hab 3:18 1523
he will rejoice over thee with *j* .... Zeph 3:17 8057
he will *j* over thee with singing .... Zeph 3:17 1523
shall be to the house of Judah *j* .... Zec 8:19 8342
rejoiced with exceeding great *j*.............. Mt 2:10 5479
word, and anon with *j* **receiveth it** .... Mt 13:20 5479
for *j* **thereof goeth and selleth** .... Mt 13:44 5479
enter thou into the *j* **of thy lord** .... Mt 25:21 5479
enter thou into the *j* **of thy lord** .... Mt 25:23 5479
sepulchre with fear and great *j*.............. Mt 28:8 5479
And thou shalt have *j* and gladness ...... Lk 1:14 5479
the babe leaped in my womb for *j*.......... Lk 1:44 20
bring you good tidings of great *j* .... Lk 2:10 5479
ye in that day, and leap for *j*.................. Lk 6:23
hear, receive the word with *j*............... Lk 8:13 5479
the seventy returned again with *j* .... Lk 10:17 5479
that likewise *j* **shall be in** .... Lk 15:7 5479
there is *j* **in the presence of the** .... Lk 15:10 5479
while they yet believed not for *j* .... Lk 24:41 5479
to Jerusalem with great *j* .... Lk 24:52 5479
this my *j* therefore is fulfilled .... Jn 3:29 5479
that my *j* **might remain in you, and** ...... Jn 15:11 5479
that your *j* **might be full** .... Jn 15:11 5479
sorrow shall be turned into *j* .... Jn 16:20 5479
for *j* **that a man is born into the** .... Jn 16:21 5479
your *j* **no man taketh from you**.............. Jn 16:22 5479
receive, that your *j* **may be full** .... Jn 16:24 5479
have my *j* **fulfilled in themselves**.......... Jn 17:13 5479
me full of *j* with thy countenance .... Acts 2:28 2167
And there was great *j* in that city .... Acts 8:8 5479
the disciples were filled with *j*............... Acts 13:52 5479
they caused great *j* unto all the .... Acts 15:3 5479
I might finish my course with *j*............... Acts 20:24 5479
but we also *j* in God through our............ Rom 5:11 2744
and peace, and *j* in the Holy Ghost .... Rom 14:17 5479
God of hope fill you with all *j* .... Rom 15:13 5479
you with *j* by the will of God .... Rom 15:32 5479
faith, but are helpers of your *j*............... 2Cor 1:24 5479
that my *j* is the *j* of you all 2Cor 2:3 5479
that my *j* is the *j* of you all 2Cor 2:3
more joyed we for the *j* of Titus............. 2Cor 7:13 5479
the abundance of their *j* and their 2Cor 8:2 5479
fruit of the Spirit is love, *j* .... Gal 5:22 5479

for you all making request with *j*	Phil 1:4	5479
your furtherance and *j* of faith	Phil 1:25	5479
Fulfil ye my *j*, that ye be	Phil 2:2	5479
and service of your faith, I *j*	Phil 2:17	5468
For the same cause also do ye *j*	Phil 2:18	5468
beloved and longed for, my *j*	Phil 4:1	5479
with *j* of the Holy Ghost	1Th 1:6	5479
For what is our hope, or *j*	1Th 2:19	5479
For ye are our glory and *j*	1Th 2:20	5479
for all the *j* wherewith we *j*	1Th 3:9	5479
for all the *j* wherewith we *j*	1Th 3:9	5468
that I may be filled with *j*	2Ti 1:4	5479
For we have great *j* and	Philem 7	5485
let me have *j* of thee in the Lord	Philem 20	3685
who for the *j* that was set before	Heb 12:2	5479
that they may do it with *j*	Heb 13:17	5479
count it all *j* when ye fall into	Jas 1:2	5479
mourning, and your *j* to heaviness	Jas 4:9	5479
ye rejoice with *j* unspeakable	1Pet 1:8	5479
may be glad also with exceeding *j*	1Pet 4:13	21
unto you, that your *j* may be full	1Jn 1:4	5479
to face, that our *j* may be full	2Jn 12	5479
I have no greater *j* than to hear	3Jn 4	5479
of his glory with exceeding *j*	Jude 24	20

JOYED
exceedingly the more *j* we for the	2Cor 7:13	5463

JOYFUL
king, and went unto their tents *j*	1Kin 8:66	8056
for the LORD had made them *j*	Ezr 6:22	8055
Then went Haman forth that day *j*	Est 5:9	8056
let no *j* voice come therein	Job 3:7	7445
that love thy name be *j* in thee	Ps 5:11	5970
And my soul shall be *j* in the LORD	Ps 35:9	1523
shall praise thee with *j* lips	Ps 63:5	7445
Make a *j* noise unto God, all ye	Ps 66:1	
make a *j* noise unto the God of	Ps 81:1	
the people that know the *j* sound	Ps 89:15	8643
let us make a *j* noise to the rock	Ps 95:1	
make a *j* noise unto him with	Ps 95:2	
Let the field be *j*, and all that	Ps 96:12	5937
Make a *j* noise unto the LORD, all	Ps 98:4	
make a *j* noise before the LORD	Ps 98:6	
let the hills be *j* together	Ps 98:8	7442
Make a *j* noise unto the LORD, all	Ps 100:1	
to be a *j* mother of children	Ps 113:9	8056
of Zion be *j* in their King	Ps 149:2	1523
Let the saints be *j* in glory	Ps 149:5	5937
In the day of prosperity be *j*	Eccl 7:14	2896
and be *j*, O earth	Is 49:13	1523
make them *j* in my house of prayer	Is 56:7	8055
my soul shall be *j* in my God	Is 61:10	1523
I am exceeding *j* in all our	2Cor 7:4	5479

JOYFULLY
Live *j* with the wife whom thou	Eccl 9:9	2416
and came down, and received him *j*	Lk 19:6	5463
took *j* the spoiling of your goods	Heb 10:34	3326,5479

JOYFULNESS
not the LORD thy God with *j*	Deut 28:47	8057
patience and longsuffering with *j*	Col 1:11	5479

JOYING
am I with you in the spirit, *j*	Col 2:5	5463

JOYOUS
a tumultuous city, a *j* city	Is 22:2	5947
Is this your *j* city, whose	Is 23:7	5947
the houses of joy in thy *j* city	Is 32:13	5947
for the present seemeth to be *j*	Heb 12:11	5479

JOZABAD *(joz'-a-bad)*
1. Another warrior in David's army.
to him of Manasseh, Adnah, and *J*	1Chr 12:20	3107
and Jediael, and Michael, and *J*	1Chr 12:20	3107
2. A Chief Levite in Josiah's time.
and Asahel, and Jerimoth, and *J*	2Chr 31:13	3107
3. An exile with Ezra.
and Hashabiah and Jeiel and *J*	2Chr 35:9	3107
4. A priest.
with them was *J* the son of Jeshua	Ezr 8:33	3107
5. A Levite.
Maaseiah, Ishmael, Nethaneel, *J*	Ezr 10:22	3107
6. A priest who helped Ezra.
J, and Shimei, and Kelaiah, (the	Ezr 10:23	3107
7. A chief Levite in exile.
Maaseiah, Kelita, Azariah, *J*	Neh 8:7	3107
8. A chief Levite in exile.
And Shabbethai and *J*, of the chief	Neh 11:16	3107

JOZACHAR *(joz'-a-kar)* See ZABAD. *Son of Shimeath.*
For *J* the son of Shimeath, and	2Kin 12:21	3108

JOZADAK *(joz'-a-dak)* See JEHOZADAK, JOSEDECH.
A priest with Zerubbabel.
Then stood up Jeshua the son of *J*	Ezr 3:2	3136
Shealtiel, and Jeshua the son of *J*	Ezr 3:8	3136
Shealtiel, and Jeshua the son of *J*	Ezr 5:2	3136
the sons of Jeshua the son of *J*	Ezr 10:18	3136
the son of Jeshua, the son of *J*	Neh 12:26	3136

JUBAL *(ju'-bal)* *Son of Adah.*
And his brother's name was *J*	Gen 4:21	3106

JUBILE
j to sound on the tenth day of	Lev 25:9	8643
it shall be a *j* unto you	Lev 25:10	3104
A *j* shall that fiftieth year be	Lev 25:11	3104
For it is the *j*	Lev 25:12	3104
In the year of this *j* ye shall	Lev 25:13	3104
the number of years after the *j*	Lev 25:15	3104
bought it until the year of *j*	Lev 25:28	3104
in the *j* it shall go out, and he	Lev 25:28	3104
it shall not go out in the *j*	Lev 25:30	3104
and they shall go out in the *j*	Lev 25:31	3104
shall go out in the year of *j*	Lev 25:33	3104
serve thee unto the year of *j*	Lev 25:40	3104
sold to him unto the year of *j*	Lev 25:50	3104
but few years unto the year of *j*	Lev 25:52	3104
he shall go out in the year of *j*	Lev 25:54	3104
his field from the year of *j*	Lev 27:17	3104
he sanctify his field after the *j*	Lev 27:18	3104
even unto the year of the *j*	Lev 27:18	3104
field, when it goeth out in the *j*	Lev 27:21	3104
even unto the year of the *j*	Lev 27:23	3104
In the year of the *j* the field	Lev 27:24	3104
when the *j* of the children of	Num 36:4	3104

JUCAL *(ju'-kal)* See JEHUCAL. *An enemy of Jeremiah.*
J the son of Shelemiah, and Pashur	Jer 38:1	3116

JUDA *(ju'-dah)* See JUDAH.
1. Greek form of Judah, the tribe.
thou Bethlehem, in the land of *J*	Mt 2:6	2455
the least among the princes of *J*	Mt 2:6	2455
with haste, into a city of *J*	Lk 1:39	2448
that our Lord sprang out of *J*	Heb 7:14	2455
the Lion of the tribe of *J*	Rev 5:5	2455
Of the tribe of *J* were sealed	Rev 7:5	2455
2. A brother of Jesus.
of James, and Joses, and of *J*	Mk 6:3	2455
3. Son of Jacob; an ancestor of Jesus.
of Phares, which was the son of *J*	Lk 3:33	2455

JUDAEA *A Roman province.*
J in the days of Herod the king	Mt 2:1	2449
said unto him, In Bethlehem of *J*	Mt 2:5	2449
that Archelaus did reign in *J* in	Mt 2:22	2499
preaching in the wilderness of *J*	Mt 3:1	2449
out to him Jerusalem, and all *J*	Mt 3:5	2449
and from Jerusalem, and from *J*	Mt 4:25	2449
the coasts of *J* beyond Jordan	Mt 19:1	2449
be in *J* flee into the mountains	Mt 24:16	2449
out unto him all the land of *J*	Mk 1:5	2449
Galilee followed him, and from *J*	Mk 3:7	2449
cometh into the coasts of *J* by	Mk 10:1	2449
be in *J* flee to the mountains	Mk 13:14	2449
the days of Herod, the king of *J*	Lk 1:5	2449
all the hill country of *J*	Lk 1:65	2449
of the city of Nazareth, into *J*	Lk 2:4	2449
Pilate being governor of *J*	Lk 3:1	2449
of every town of Galilee, and *J*	Lk 5:17	2449
multitude of people out of all *J*	Lk 6:17	2449
him went forth throughout all *J*	Lk 7:17	2449
are in *J* flee to the mountains	Lk 21:21	2449
his disciples into the land of *J*	Jn 3:22	2449
He left *J*, and departed again into	Jn 4:3	2449
was come out of *J* into Galilee	Jn 4:47	2449
he was come out of *J* into Galilee	Jn 4:54	2449
him, Depart hence, and go into *J*	Jn 7:3	2449
disciples, Let us go into *J* again	Jn 11:7	2449
me both in Jerusalem, and in all *J*	Acts 1:8	2449
dwellers in Mesopotamia, and in *J*	Acts 2:9	2449
and said unto them, Ye men of *J*	Acts 2:14	2453
throughout the regions of *J*	Acts 8:1	2449
churches rest throughout all *J*	Acts 9:31	2449
was published throughout all *J*	Acts 10:37	2449
brethren that were in *J* heard	Acts 11:1	2449
the brethren which dwelt in *J*	Acts 11:29	2449
he went down from *J* to Caesarea	Acts 12:19	2449
down from *J* taught the brethren	Acts 15:1	2449
down from *J* a certain prophet	Acts 21:10	2449
and throughout all the coasts of *J*	Acts 26:20	2449
letters out of *J* concerning thee	Acts 28:21	2449
them that do not believe in *J*	Rom 15:31	2449
to be brought on my way toward *J*	2Cor 1:16	2449

of *J* which were in Christ	Gal 1:22	*2449*
which in *J* are in Christ Jesus	1Th 2:14	*2449*

JUDAH (*ju'-dah*) See BETHLEHEM-JUDAH, JUDA, JUDAH'S, JUDAS, JUDEA, JUDE.

1. Son of Jacob and Leah.

therefore she called his name *J*	Gen 29:35	3063
and Simeon, and Levi, and *J*	Gen 35:23	3063
J said unto his brethren, What	Gen 37:26	3063
that *J* went down from his	Gen 38:1	3063
J saw there a daughter of a	Gen 38:2	3063
And *J* took a wife for Er his	Gen 38:6	3063
J said unto Onan, Go in unto thy	Gen 38:8	3063
Then said *J* to Tamar his daughter	Gen 38:11	3063
J was comforted, and went up unto	Gen 38:12	3063
When *J* saw her, he thought her to	Gen 38:15	3063
J sent the kid by the hand of his	Gen 38:20	3063
And he returned to *J*, and said, I	Gen 38:22	3063
J said, Let her take it to her,	Gen 38:23	3063
months after, that it was told *J*	Gen 38:24	3063
J said, Bring her forth, and let	Gen 38:24	3063
J acknowledged them, and said, She	Gen 38:26	3063
J spake unto him, saying, The man	Gen 43:3	3063
J said unto Israel his father,	Gen 43:8	3063
And *J* and his brethren came to	Gen 44:14	3063
J said, What shall we say unto my	Gen 44:16	3063
Then *J* came near unto him, and	Gen 44:18	3063
And the sons of *J*	Gen 46:12	3063
he sent *J* before him unto Joseph,	Gen 46:28	3063
J, thou art he whom thy brethren	Gen 49:8	3063
J is a lion's whelp	Gen 49:9	3063
Reuben, Simeon, Levi, and *J*	Ex 1:2	3063
The sons of *J* were Er and Onan	Num 26:19	3063
of Pharez, whom Tamar bare unto *J*	Ruth 4:12	3063
Reuben, Simeon, Levi, and *J*	1Chr 2:1	3063
The sons of *J*; Er, and	1Chr 2:3	3063
And Er, the firstborn of *J*	1Chr 2:3	3063
All the sons of *J* were five	1Chr 2:4	3063
prince of the children of *J*	1Chr 2:10	3063
The sons of *J*; Pharez	1Chr 4:1	3063
sons of Shelah the son of *J* were	1Chr 4:21	3063
like to the children of *J*	1Chr 4:27	3063
For *J* prevailed above his	1Chr 5:2	3063
children of Pharez the son of *J*	1Chr 9:4	3063
children of Zerah the son of *J*	Neh 11:24	3063

2. The tribe and its land.

sceptre shall not depart from *J*	Gen 49:10	3063
the son of Hur, of the tribe of *J*	Ex 31:2	3063
the son of Hur, of the tribe of *J*	Ex 35:30	3063
the son of Hur, of the tribe of *J*	Ex 38:22	3063
Of *J*; Nashon the son	Num 1:7	3063
Of the children of *J*, by their	Num 1:26	3063
of them, even of the tribe of *J*	Num 1:27	3063
J pitch throughout their armies	Num 2:3	3063
be captain of the children of *J*	Num 2:3	3063
of *J* were an hundred thousand	Num 2:9	3063
of Amminadab, of the tribe of *J*	Num 7:12	3063
of *J* according to their armies	Num 10:14	3063
Of the tribe of *J*, Caleb the son	Num 13:6	3063
the sons of *J* after their	Num 26:20	3063
These are the families of *J*	Num 26:22	3063
Of the tribe of *J*, Caleb the son	Num 34:19	3063
Simeon, and Levi, and *J*, and	Deut 27:12	3063
And this is the blessing of *J*	Deut 33:7	3063
said, Hear, LORD, the voice of *J*	Deut 33:7	3063
and Manasseh, and all the land of *J*	Deut 34:2	3063
son of Zerah, of the tribe of *J*	Josh 7:1	3063
and the tribe of *J* was taken	Josh 7:16	3063
And he brought the family of *J*	Josh 7:17	3063
son of Zerah, of the tribe of *J*	Josh 7:18	3063
and from all the mountains of *J*	Josh 11:21	3063
Then the children of *J* came unto	Josh 14:6	3063
children of *J* by their families	Josh 15:1	3063
J round about according to their	Josh 15:12	3063
a part among the children of *J*	Josh 15:13	3063
of *J* according to their families	Josh 15:20	3063
of *J* toward the coast of Edom	Josh 15:21	3063
the children of *J* could not drive	Josh 15:63	3063
of *J* at Jerusalem unto this day	Josh 15:63	3063
J shall abide in their coast on	Josh 18:5	3063
forth between the children of *J*	Josh 18:11	3063
a city of the children of *J*	Josh 18:14	3063
inheritance of the children of *J*	Josh 19:1	3063
of *J* was the inheritance of the	Josh 19:9	3063
of *J* was too much for them	Josh 19:9	3063
to *J* upon Jordan toward the	Josh 19:34	3063
is Hebron, in the mountain of *J*	Josh 20:7	3063
had by lot out of the tribe of *J*	Josh 21:4	3063
of the tribe of the children of *J*	Josh 21:9	3063
Hebron, in the hill country of *J*	Josh 21:11	3063
And the LORD said, *J* shall go up	Judg 1:2	3063

J said unto Simeon his brother,	Judg 1:3	3063
And *J* went up	Judg 1:4	3063
Now the children of *J* had fought	Judg 1:8	3063
afterward the children of *J* went	Judg 1:9	3063
J went against the Canaanites	Judg 1:10	3063
of *J* into the wilderness of Judah	Judg 1:16	3063
of Judah into the wilderness of *J*	Judg 1:16	3063
J went with Simeon his brother,	Judg 1:17	3063
Also *J* took Gaza with the coast	Judg 1:18	3063
And the LORD was with *J*	Judg 1:19	3063
Jordan to fight also against *J*	Judg 10:9	3063
went up, and pitched in *J*, and	Judg 15:9	3063
And the men of *J* said, Why are ye	Judg 15:10	3063
Then three thousand men of *J* went	Judg 15:11	3063
of the family of *J*, who was a	Judg 17:7	3063
pitched in Kirjath-jearim, in *J*	Judg 18:12	3063
LORD said, *J* shall go up first	Judg 20:18	3063
way to return unto the land of *J*	Ruth 1:7	3063
the men of *J* thirty thousand	1Sa 11:8	3063
footmen, and ten thousand men of *J*	1Sa 15:4	3063
at Shochoh, which belongeth to *J*	1Sa 17:1	3063
of *J* arose, and shouted, and	1Sa 17:52	3063
J loved David, because he went	1Sa 18:16	3063
and get thee into the land of *J*	1Sa 22:5	3063
Behold, we be afraid here in *J*	1Sa 23:3	3063
throughout all the thousands of *J*	1Sa 23:23	3063
unto the kings of *J* unto this day	1Sa 27:6	3063
said, Against the south of *J*	1Sa 27:10	3063
the coast which belongeth to *J*	1Sa 30:14	3063
and out of the land of *J*	1Sa 30:16	3063
of the spoil unto the elders of *J*	1Sa 30:26	3063
children of *J* the use of the bow	2Sa 1:18	3063
go up into any of the cities of *J*	2Sa 2:1	3063
And the men of *J* came, and there	2Sa 2:4	3063
David king over the house of *J*	2Sa 2:4	3063
also the house of *J* have anointed	2Sa 2:7	3063
But the house of *J* followed David	2Sa 2:10	3063
the house of *J* was seven years	2Sa 2:11	3063
which against *J* do shew kindness	2Sa 3:8	3063
of David over Israel and over *J*	2Sa 3:10	3063
he reigned over *J* seven years	2Sa 5:5	3063
three years over all Israel and *J*	2Sa 5:5	3063
were with him from Baale of *J*	2Sa 6:2	3063
David, The ark, and Israel, and *J*	2Sa 11:11	3063
thee the house of Israel and of *J*	2Sa 12:8	3063
Speak unto the elders of *J*	2Sa 19:11	3063
the heart of all the men of *J*	2Sa 19:14	3063
J came to Gilgal, to go to meet	2Sa 19:15	3063
the men of *J* to meet king David	2Sa 19:16	3063
all the people of *J* conducted the	2Sa 19:40	3063
the men of *J* stolen thee away	2Sa 19:41	3063
all the men of *J* answered the men	2Sa 19:42	3063
of Israel answered the men of *J*	2Sa 19:43	3063
the words of the men of *J* were	2Sa 19:43	3063
but the men of *J* clave unto their	2Sa 20:2	3063
me the men of *J* within three days	2Sa 20:4	3063
went to assemble the men of *J*	2Sa 20:5	3063
to the children of Israel and *J*	2Sa 21:2	3063
to say, Go, number Israel and *J*	2Sa 24:1	3063
they went out to the south of *J*	2Sa 24:7	3063
the men of *J* were five hundred	2Sa 24:9	3063
all the men of *J* the king's	1Kin 1:9	3063
to be ruler over Israel and over *J*	1Kin 1:35	3063
Jether, captain of the host of *J*	1Kin 2:32	3063
J and Israel were many, as the	1Kin 4:20	3063
And *J* and Israel dwelt safely,	1Kin 4:25	3063
gave them Hebron in the land of *J*	1Chr 6:55	3063
Aaron they gave the cities of *J*	1Chr 6:57	3063
of the tribe of the children of *J*	1Chr 6:65	3063
dwelt of the children of *J*	1Chr 9:3	3063
and *J* to the hold unto David	1Chr 12:16	3063
The children of *J* that bare	1Chr 12:24	3063
which belonged to *J*, to bring up	1Chr 13:6	3063
Of *J*, Elihu, one of the brethren	1Chr 27:18	3063
he hath chosen *J* to be the ruler	1Chr 28:4	3063
and of the house of *J*, the house	1Chr 28:4	3063
cunning men that are with me in *J*	2Chr 2:7	3063
such seen before in the land of *J*	2Chr 9:11	3063
house at Jerusalem, which is in *J*	Ezr 1:2	3063
go up to Jerusalem, which is in *J*	Ezr 1:3	3063
up the chief of the fathers of *J*	Ezr 1:5	3063
unto Sheshbazzar, the prince of *J*	Ezr 1:8	3063
the hands of the people of *J*	Ezr 4:4	3063
against the inhabitants of *J*	Ezr 4:6	3063
unto the Jews that were in *J*	Ezr 5:1	3061
to enquire concerning *J* and	Ezr 7:14	3061
and to give us a wall in *J*	Ezr 9:9	3063
made proclamation throughout *J*	Ezr 10:7	3063
Then all the men of *J* and Benjamin	Ezr 10:9	3063
came, he and certain men of *J*	Neh 1:2	3063
that thou wouldest send me unto *J*	Neh 2:5	3063

convey me over till I come into *J*	Neh 2:7	3063
J said, The strength of the	Neh 4:10	3063
were behind all the house of *J*	Neh 4:16	3063
their governor in the land of *J*	Neh 5:14	3063
saying, There is a king in *J*	Neh 6:7	3063
in those days the nobles of *J*	Neh 6:17	3063
were many in *J* sworn unto him	Neh 6:18	3063
came again to Jerusalem and to *J*	Neh 7:6	3063
but in the cities of *J* dwelt	Neh 11:3	3063
certain of the children of *J*	Neh 11:4	3063
Of the children of *J*	Neh 11:4	3063
were in all the cities of *J*	Neh 11:20	3063
of *J* dwelt at Kirjath-arba	Neh 11:25	3063
the Levites were divisions in *J*	Neh 11:36	3063
up the princes of *J* upon the wall	Neh 12:31	3063
and half of the princes of *J*	Neh 12:32	3063
for *J* rejoiced for the priests and	Neh 12:44	3063
Then brought all *J* the tithe of	Neh 13:12	3063
In those days saw I in *J* some	Neh 13:15	3063
sabbath unto the children of *J*	Neh 13:16	3063
I contended with the nobles of *J*	Neh 13:17	3063
away with Jeconiah king of *J*	Est 2:6	3063
let the daughters of *J* be glad	Ps 48:11	3063
J is my lawgiver	Ps 60:7	3063
he was in the wilderness of *J*	Ps 63:*t*	3063
their ruler, the princes of *J*	Ps 68:27	3063
and will build the cities of *J*	Ps 69:35	3063
In *J* is God known	Ps 76:1	3063
But chose the tribe of *J*, the	Ps 78:68	3063
the daughters of *J* rejoiced	Ps 97:8	3063
J is my lawgiver	Ps 108:8	3063
J was his sanctuary, and Israel	Ps 114:2	3063
of Israel and with the house of *J*	Heb 8:8	*2455*

3. The southern kingdom after the revolt of the ten northern tribes.

which dwelt in the cities of *J*	1Kin 12:17	3063
of David, but the tribe of *J* only	1Kin 12:20	3063
he assembled all the house of *J*	1Kin 12:21	3063
the son of Solomon, king of *J*	1Kin 12:23	3063
Judah, and unto all the house of *J*	1Kin 12:23	3063
even unto Rehoboam king of *J*	1Kin 12:27	3063
and go again to Rehoboam king of *J*	1Kin 12:27	3063
like unto the feast that is in *J*	1Kin 12:32	3063
of *J* by the word of the LORD unto	1Kin 13:1	3063
of God went, which came from *J*	1Kin 13:12	3063
the man of God that camest from *J*	1Kin 13:14	3063
the man of God that came from *J*	1Kin 13:21	3063
the son of Solomon reigned in *J*	1Kin 14:21	3063
J did evil in the sight of the	1Kin 14:22	3063
the chronicles of the kings of *J*	1Kin 14:29	3063
of Nebat reigned Abijam over *J*	1Kin 15:1	3063
the chronicles of the kings of *J*	1Kin 15:7	3063
king of Israel reigned Asa over *J*	1Kin 15:9	3063
king of Israel went up against *J*	1Kin 15:17	3063
out or come in to Asa king of *J*	1Kin 15:17	3063
a proclamation throughout all *J*	1Kin 15:22	3063
the chronicles of the kings of *J*	1Kin 15:23	3063
the second year of Asa king of *J*	1Kin 15:25	3063
Asa king of *J* did Baasha slay him	1Kin 15:28	3063
the third year of Asa king of *J*	1Kin 15:33	3063
sixth year of Asa king of *J* began	1Kin 16:8	3063
and seventh year of Asa king of *J*	1Kin 16:10	3063
seventh year of Asa king of *J* did	1Kin 16:15	3063
first year of Asa king of *J* began	1Kin 16:23	3063
eighth year of Asa king of *J*	1Kin 16:29	3063
Beer-sheba, which belongeth to *J*	1Kin 19:3	3063
that Jehoshaphat the king of *J*	1Kin 22:2	3063
king of *J* sat each on his throne	1Kin 22:10	3063
Jehoshaphat the king of *J* went up	1Kin 22:29	3063
son of Asa began to reign over *J*	1Kin 22:41	3063
the chronicles of the kings of *J*	1Kin 22:45	3063
year of Jehoshaphat king of *J*	1Kin 22:51	3063
the son of Jehoshaphat king of *J*	2Kin 1:17	3063
year of Jehoshaphat king of *J*	2Kin 3:1	3063
sent to Jehoshaphat the king of *J*	2Kin 3:7	3063
of Israel went, and the king of *J*	2Kin 3:9	3063
of Jehoshaphat the king of *J*	2Kin 3:14	3063
Jehoshaphat being then king of *J*	2Kin 8:16	3063
king of *J* began to reign	2Kin 8:16	3063
J for David his servant's sake	2Kin 8:19	3063
revolted from under the hand of *J*	2Kin 8:20	3063
under the hand of *J* unto this day	2Kin 8:22	3063
the chronicles of the kings of *J*	2Kin 8:23	3063
Jehoram king of *J* begin to reign	2Kin 8:25	3063
the son of Jehoram king of *J* went	2Kin 8:29	3063
Ahaziah king of *J* was come down	2Kin 9:16	3063
and Ahaziah king of *J* went out	2Kin 9:21	3063
Ahaziah the king of *J* saw this	2Kin 9:27	3063
began Ahaziah to reign over *J*	2Kin 9:29	3063
the brethren of Ahaziah king of *J*	2Kin 10:13	3063
Jehoash king of *J* took all the	2Kin 12:18	3063
Ahaziah, his fathers, kings of *J*	2Kin 12:18	3063
the chronicles of the kings of *J*	2Kin 12:19	3063
the son of Ahaziah king of *J*	2Kin 13:1	3063
of *J* began Jehoash the son of	2Kin 13:10	3063
fought against Amaziah king of *J*	2Kin 13:12	3063
the son of Joash king of *J*	2Kin 14:1	3063
Israel sent to Amaziah king of *J*	2Kin 14:9	3063
fall, even thou, and *J* with thee	2Kin 14:10	3063
Amaziah king of *J* looked one	2Kin 14:11	3063
which belongeth to *J*	2Kin 14:11	3063
J was put to the worse before	2Kin 14:12	3063
of Israel took Amaziah king of *J*	2Kin 14:13	3063
he fought with Amaziah king of *J*	2Kin 14:15	3063
of *J* lived after the death of	2Kin 14:17	3063
the chronicles of the kings of *J*	2Kin 14:18	3063
all the people of *J* took Azariah	2Kin 14:21	3063
built Elath, and restored it to *J*	2Kin 14:22	3063
the son of Joash king of *J*	2Kin 14:23	3063
and Hamath, which belonged to *J*	2Kin 14:28	3063
son of Amaziah king of *J* to reign	2Kin 15:1	3063
the chronicles of the kings of *J*	2Kin 15:6	3063
of *J* did Zachariah the son of	2Kin 15:8	3063
year of Uzziah king of *J*	2Kin 15:13	3063
year of Azariah king of *J* began	2Kin 15:17	3063
year of Azariah king of *J*	2Kin 15:23	3063
year of Azariah king of *J* Pekah	2Kin 15:27	3063
son of Uzziah king of *J* to reign	2Kin 15:32	3063
the chronicles of the kings of *J*	2Kin 15:36	3063
against *J* Rezin the king of Syria	2Kin 15:37	3063
Jotham king of *J* began to reign	2Kin 16:1	3063
the chronicles of the kings of *J*	2Kin 16:19	3063
twelfth year of Ahaz king of *J*	2Kin 17:1	3063
against Israel, and against *J*	2Kin 17:13	3063
none left but the tribe of *J* only	2Kin 17:18	3063
Also *J* kept not the commandments	2Kin 17:19	3063
of Ahaz king of *J* began to reign	2Kin 18:1	3063
like him among all the kings of *J*	2Kin 18:5	3063
all the fenced cities of *J*	2Kin 18:13	3063
Hezekiah king of *J* sent to the	2Kin 18:14	3063
J three hundred talents of silver	2Kin 18:14	3063
Hezekiah king of *J* had overlaid	2Kin 18:16	3063
taken away, and hath said to *J*	2Kin 18:22	3063
ye speak to Hezekiah king of *J*	2Kin 19:10	3063
of *J* shall yet again take root	2Kin 19:30	3063
the chronicles of the kings of *J*	2Kin 20:20	3063
Because Manasseh king of *J* hath	2Kin 21:11	3063
hath made *J* also to sin with his	2Kin 21:11	3063
such evil upon Jerusalem and *J*	2Kin 21:12	3063
sin wherewith he made *J* to sin	2Kin 21:16	3063
the chronicles of the kings of *J*	2Kin 21:17	3063
the chronicles of the kings of *J*	2Kin 21:25	3063
and for the people, and for all *J*	2Kin 22:13	3063
which the king of *J* hath read	2Kin 22:16	3063
But to the king of *J* which sent	2Kin 22:18	3063
unto him all the elders of *J*	2Kin 23:1	3063
of the LORD, and all the men of *J*	2Kin 23:2	3063
whom the kings of *J* had ordained	2Kin 23:5	3063
high places in the cities of *J*	2Kin 23:5	3063
priests out of the cities of *J*	2Kin 23:8	3063
kings of *J* had given to the sun	2Kin 23:11	3063
which the kings of *J* had made	2Kin 23:12	3063
the man of God, which came from *J*	2Kin 23:17	3063
of Israel, nor of the kings of *J*	2Kin 23:22	3063
that were spied in the land of *J*	2Kin 23:24	3063
his anger was kindled against *J*	2Kin 23:26	3063
I will remove *J* also out of my	2Kin 23:27	3063
the chronicles of the kings of *J*	2Kin 23:28	3063
sent them against *J* to destroy it	2Kin 24:2	3063
of the LORD came this upon *J*	2Kin 24:3	3063
the chronicles of the kings of *J*	2Kin 24:5	3063
Jehoiachin the king of *J* went out	2Kin 24:12	3063
it came to pass in Jerusalem and *J*	2Kin 24:20	3063
So *J* was carried away out of	2Kin 25:21	3063
that remained in the land of *J*	2Kin 25:22	3063
captivity of Jehoiachin king of *J*	2Kin 25:27	3063
king of *J* out of prison	2Kin 25:27	3063
in the days of Hezekiah king of *J*	1Chr 4:41	3063
in the days of Jotham king of *J*	1Chr 5:17	3063
when the LORD carried away *J*	1Chr 6:15	3063
book of the kings of Israel and *J*	1Chr 9:1	3063
J was four hundred threescore and	1Chr 21:5	3063
that dwelt in the cities of *J*	2Chr 10:17	3063
he gathered of the house of *J*	2Chr 11:1	3063
the son of Solomon, king of *J*	2Chr 11:3	3063
of Judah, and to all Israel in *J*	2Chr 11:3	3063
and built cities for defence in *J*	2Chr 11:5	3063
and Hebron, which are in *J*	2Chr 11:10	3063
them exceeding strong, having *J*	2Chr 11:12	3063
and their possession, and came to *J*	2Chr 11:14	3063
strengthened the kingdom of *J*	2Chr 11:17	3063
throughout all the countries of *J*	2Chr 11:23	3063

cities which pertained to *J*	2Chr 12:4	3063
Rehoboam, and to the princes of *J*	2Chr 12:5	3063
also in *J* things went well	2Chr 12:12	3063
began Abijah to reign over *J*	2Chr 13:1	3063
so they were before *J*, and the	2Chr 13:13	3063
when *J* looked back, behold, the	2Chr 13:14	3063
Then the men of *J* gave a shout	2Chr 13:15	3063
and as the men of *J* shouted	2Chr 13:15	3063
and all Israel before Abijah and *J*	2Chr 13:15	3063
children of Israel fled before *J*	2Chr 13:16	3063
and the children of *J* prevailed	2Chr 13:18	3063
commanded *J* to seek the LORD God	2Chr 14:4	3063
the cities of *J* the high places	2Chr 14:5	3063
And he built fenced cities in *J*	2Chr 14:6	3063
Therefore he said unto *J*, Let us	2Chr 14:7	3063
out of *J* three hundred thousand	2Chr 14:8	3063
before Asa, and before *J*	2Chr 14:12	3063
him, Hear ye me, Asa, and all *J*	2Chr 15:2	3063
idols out of all the land of *J*	2Chr 15:8	3063
And he gathered all *J* and Benjamin,	2Chr 15:9	3063
all *J* rejoiced at the oath	2Chr 15:15	3063
king of Israel came up against *J*	2Chr 16:1	3063
out or come in to Asa king of *J*	2Chr 16:1	3063
Then Asa the king took all *J*	2Chr 16:6	3063
the seer came to Asa king of *J*	2Chr 16:7	3063
in the book of the kings of *J*	2Chr 16:11	3063
in all the fenced cities of *J*	2Chr 17:2	3063
and set garrisons in the land of *J*	2Chr 17:2	3063
all *J* brought to Jehoshaphat	2Chr 17:5	3063
high places and groves out of *J*	2Chr 17:6	3063
to teach in the cities of *J*	2Chr 17:7	3063
And they taught in *J*, and had the	2Chr 17:9	3063
throughout all the cities of *J*	2Chr 17:10	3063
the lands were round about *J*	2Chr 17:10	3063
and he built in *J* castles, and	2Chr 17:12	3063
much business in the cities of *J*	2Chr 17:13	3063
Of *J*, the captains of thousands	2Chr 17:14	3063
fenced cities throughout all *J*	2Chr 17:19	3063
said unto Jehoshaphat king of *J*	2Chr 18:3	3063
Jehoshaphat king of *J* sat either	2Chr 18:9	3063
Jehoshaphat the king of *J* went up	2Chr 18:28	3063
Jehoshaphat the king of *J*	2Chr 19:1	3063
all the fenced cities of *J*	2Chr 19:5	3063
the ruler of the house of *J*	2Chr 19:11	3063
a fast throughout all *J*	2Chr 20:3	3063
J gathered themselves together,	2Chr 20:4	3063
of *J* they came to seek the LORD	2Chr 20:4	3063
stood in the congregation of *J*	2Chr 20:5	3063
all *J* stood before the LORD, with	2Chr 20:13	3063
And he said, Hearken ye, all *J*	2Chr 20:15	3063
of the LORD with you, O *J*	2Chr 20:17	3063
and all *J* and the inhabitants of	2Chr 20:18	3063
stood and said, Hear me, O *J*	2Chr 20:20	3063
Seir, which were come against *J*	2Chr 20:22	3063
when *J* came toward the watch	2Chr 20:24	3063
they returned, every man of *J*	2Chr 20:27	3063
And Jehoshaphat reigned over *J*	2Chr 20:31	3063
this did Jehoshaphat king of *J*	2Chr 20:35	3063
things, with fenced cities in *J*	2Chr 21:3	3063
from under the dominion of *J*	2Chr 21:8	3063
under the hand of *J* unto this day	2Chr 21:10	3063
high places in the mountains of *J*	2Chr 21:11	3063
and compelled *J* thereto	2Chr 21:11	3063
nor in the ways of Asa king of *J*	2Chr 21:12	3063
kings of Israel, and hast made *J*	2Chr 21:13	3063
And they came up into *J*, and brake	2Chr 21:17	3063
son of Jehoram king of *J* reigned	2Chr 22:1	3063
the son of Jehoram king of *J* went	2Chr 22:6	3063
Ahab, and found the princes of *J*	2Chr 22:8	3063
the seed royal of the house of *J*	2Chr 22:10	3063
And they went about in *J*, and	2Chr 23:2	3063
out of all the cities of *J*	2Chr 23:2	3063
all *J* did according to all things	2Chr 23:8	3063
them, Go out unto the cities of *J*	2Chr 24:5	3063
the Levites to bring in out of *J*	2Chr 24:6	3063
made a proclamation through *J*	2Chr 24:9	3063
of Jehoiada came the princes of *J*	2Chr 24:17	3063
and wrath came upon *J* and Jerusalem	2Chr 24:18	3063
and they came to *J* and Jerusalem,	2Chr 24:23	3063
Amaziah gathered *J* together	2Chr 25:5	3063
their fathers, throughout all *J*	2Chr 25:5	3063
was greatly kindled against *J*	2Chr 25:10	3063
children of *J* carry away captive	2Chr 25:12	3063
battle, fell upon the cities of *J*	2Chr 25:13	3063
Amaziah king of *J* took advice	2Chr 25:17	3063
Israel sent to Amaziah king of *J*	2Chr 25:18	3063
fall, even thou, and *J* with thee	2Chr 25:19	3063
both he and Amaziah king of *J*	2Chr 25:21	3063
which belongeth to *J*	2Chr 25:21	3063
J was put to the worse before	2Chr 25:22	3063
of Israel took Amaziah king of *J*	2Chr 25:23	3063

the son of Joash king of *J* lived	2Chr 25:25	3063
in the book of the kings of *J*	2Chr 25:26	3063
with his fathers in the city of *J*	2Chr 25:28	3063
all the people of *J* took Uzziah	2Chr 26:1	3063
built Eloth, and restored it to *J*	2Chr 26:2	3063
cities in the mountains of *J*	2Chr 27:4	3063
book of the kings of Israel and *J*	2Chr 27:7	3063
of Remaliah slew in *J* an hundred	2Chr 28:6	3063
of your fathers was wroth with *J*	2Chr 28:9	3063
to keep under the children of *J*	2Chr 28:10	3063
Edomites had come and smitten *J*	2Chr 28:17	3063
low country, and of the south of *J*	2Chr 28:18	3063
For the LORD brought *J* low	2Chr 28:19	3063
for he made *J* naked, and	2Chr 28:19	3063
in every several city of *J* he	2Chr 28:25	3063
in the book of the kings of *J*	2Chr 28:26	3063
the wrath of the LORD was upon *J*	2Chr 29:8	3063
and for the sanctuary, and for *J*	2Chr 29:21	3063
Hezekiah sent to all Israel and *J*	2Chr 30:1	3063
throughout all Israel and *J*	2Chr 30:6	3063
Also in *J* the hand of God was to	2Chr 30:12	3063
For Hezekiah king of *J* did give	2Chr 30:24	3063
And all the congregation of *J*	2Chr 30:25	3063
of Israel, and that dwelt in *J*	2Chr 30:25	3063
went out to the cities of *J*	2Chr 31:1	3063
places and the altars out of all *J*	2Chr 31:1	3063
the children of Israel and *J*	2Chr 31:6	3063
that dwelt in the cities of *J*	2Chr 31:6	3063
did Hezekiah throughout all *J*	2Chr 31:20	3063
Assyria came, and entered into *J*	2Chr 32:1	3063
the words of Hezekiah king of *J*	2Chr 32:8	3063
him,) unto Hezekiah king of *J*	2Chr 32:9	3063
unto all *J* that were at Jerusalem	2Chr 32:9	3063
and his altars, and commanded *J*	2Chr 32:12	3063
and presents to Hezekiah king of *J*	2Chr 32:23	3063
was wrath upon him, and upon *J*	2Chr 32:25	3063
and in the book of the kings of *J*	2Chr 32:32	3063
and all *J* and the inhabitants of	2Chr 32:33	3063
So Manasseh made *J* and the	2Chr 33:9	3063
war in all the fenced cities of *J*	2Chr 33:14	3063
commanded *J* to serve the LORD God	2Chr 33:16	3063
twelfth year he began to purge *J*	2Chr 34:3	3063
upon their altars, and cleansed *J*	2Chr 34:5	3063
remnant of Israel, and of all *J*	2Chr 34:9	3063
the kings of *J* had destroyed	2Chr 34:11	3063
that are left in Israel and in *J*	2Chr 34:21	3063
have read before the king of *J*	2Chr 34:24	3063
And as for the king of *J*, who sent	2Chr 34:26	3063
together and the elders of *J*	2Chr 34:29	3063
of the LORD, and all the men of *J*	2Chr 34:30	3063
priests, and the Levites, and all *J*	2Chr 35:18	3063
I to do with thee, thou king of *J*	2Chr 35:21	3063
And all *J* and Jerusalem mourned for	2Chr 35:24	3063
book of the kings of Israel and *J*	2Chr 35:27	3063
Eliakim his brother king over *J*	2Chr 36:4	3063
book of the kings of Israel and *J*	2Chr 36:8	3063
Zedekiah his brother king over *J*	2Chr 36:10	3063
house in Jerusalem, which is in *J*	2Chr 36:23	3063
and came again unto Jerusalem and *J*	Ezr 2:1	3063
Now when the adversaries of *J*	Ezr 4:1	3063
of Hezekiah king of *J* copied out	Prov 25:1	3063
Amoz, which he saw concerning *J*	Is 1:1	3063
Ahaz, and Hezekiah, kings of *J*	Is 1:1	3063
the son of Amoz saw concerning *J*	Is 2:1	3063
from *J* the stay and the staff, the	Is 3:1	3063
is ruined, and *J* is fallen	Is 3:8	3063
of Jerusalem, and men of *J*	Is 5:3	3063
the men of *J* his pleasant plant	Is 5:7	3063
the son of Uzziah, king of *J*	Is 7:1	3063
Let us go up against *J*, and vex it	Is 7:6	3063
day that Ephraim departed from *J*	Is 7:17	3063
And he shall pass through *J*	Is 8:8	3063
they together shall be against *J*	Is 9:21	3063
together the dispersed of *J* from	Is 11:12	3063
adversaries of *J* shall be cut off	Is 11:13	3063
Ephraim shall not envy *J*, and	Is 11:13	3063
Judah, and *J* shall not vex Ephraim	Is 11:13	3063
the land of *J* shall be a terror	Is 19:17	3063
he discovered the covering of *J*	Is 22:8	3063
Jerusalem, and to the house of *J*	Is 22:21	3063
song be sung in the land of *J*	Is 26:1	3063
all the defenced cities of *J*	Is 36:1	3063
hath taken away, and said to *J*	Is 36:7	3063
ye speak to Hezekiah king of *J*	Is 37:10	3063
J shall again take root downward	Is 37:31	3063
The writing of Hezekiah king of *J*	Is 38:9	3063
say unto the cities of *J*, Behold	Is 40:9	3063
and to the cities of *J*, Ye shall	Is 44:26	3063
come forth out of the waters of *J*	Is 48:1	3063
out of *J* an inheritor of my	Is 65:9	3063
Josiah the son of Amon king of *J*	Jer 1:2	3063

the son of Josiah king of *J*	Jer 1:3	3063
the son of Josiah king of *J*	Jer 1:3	3063
and against all the cities of *J*	Jer 1:15	3063
land, against the kings of *J*	Jer 1:18	3063
of thy cities are thy gods, O *J*	Jer 2:28	3063
her treacherous sister *J* saw it	Jer 3:7	3063
treacherous sister *J* feared not	Jer 3:8	3063
J hath not turned unto me with	Jer 3:10	3063
herself more than treacherous *J*	Jer 3:11	3063
In those days the house of *J*	Jer 3:18	3063
saith the LORD to the men of *J*	Jer 4:3	3063
of your heart, ye men of *J*	Jer 4:4	3063
Declare ye in *J*, and publish in	Jer 4:5	3063
voice against the cities of *J*	Jer 4:16	3063
the house of *J* have dealt very	Jer 5:11	3063
of Jacob, and publish it in	Jer 5:20	3063
the word of the LORD, all ye of *J*	Jer 7:2	3063
what they do in the cities of *J*	Jer 7:17	3063
For the children of *J* have done	Jer 7:30	3063
to cease from the cities of *J*	Jer 7:34	3063
out the bones of the kings of *J*	Jer 8:1	3063
make the cities of *J* desolate	Jer 9:11	3063
Egypt, and, *J*, and Edom, and the	Jer 9:26	3063
to make the cities of *J* desolate	Jer 10:22	3063
and speak unto the men of *J*	Jer 11:2	3063
these words in the cities of *J*	Jer 11:6	3063
is found among the men of *J*	Jer 11:9	3063
the house of *J* have broken my	Jer 11:10	3063
Then shall the cities of *J*	Jer 11:12	3063
of thy cities were thy gods, O *J*	Jer 11:13	3063
of Israel and of the house of *J*	Jer 11:17	3063
the house of *J* from among them	Jer 12:14	3063
manner will I mar the pride of *J*	Jer 13:9	3063
of Israel and the whole house of *J*	Jer 13:11	3063
J shall be carried away captive	Jer 13:19	3063
J mourneth, and the gates thereof	Jer 14:2	3063
Hast thou utterly rejected *J*	Jer 14:19	3063
the son of Hezekiah king of *J*	Jer 15:4	3063
The sin of *J* is written with a	Jer 17:1	3063
whereby the kings of *J* come in	Jer 17:19	3063
word of the LORD, ye kings of *J*	Jer 17:20	3063
LORD, ye kings of Judah, and all *J*	Jer 17:20	3063
and their princes, the men of *J*	Jer 17:25	3063
shall come from the cities of *J*	Jer 17:26	3063
go to, speak to the men of *J*	Jer 18:11	3063
word of the LORD, O kings of *J*	Jer 19:3	3063
have known, nor the kings of *J*	Jer 19:4	3063
I will make void the counsel of *J*	Jer 19:7	3063
and the houses of the kings of *J*	Jer 19:13	3063
I will give all *J* into the hand	Jer 20:4	3063
of *J* will I give into the hand of	Jer 20:5	3063
I will deliver Zedekiah king of *J*	Jer 21:7	3063
the house of the king of *J*	Jer 21:11	3063
to the house of the king of *J*	Jer 22:1	3063
the word of the LORD, O king of *J*	Jer 22:2	3063
LORD unto the king's house of *J*	Jer 22:6	3063
the son of Josiah king of *J*	Jer 22:11	3063
the son of Josiah king of *J*	Jer 22:18	3063
the son of Jehoiakim king of *J*	Jer 22:24	3063
of David, and ruling any more in *J*	Jer 22:30	3063
In his days *J* shall be saved, and	Jer 23:6	3063
the son of Jehoiakim king of *J*	Jer 24:1	3063
and the princes of *J*	Jer 24:1	3063
are carried away captive of *J*	Jer 24:5	3063
I give Zedekiah the king of *J*	Jer 24:8	3063
concerning all the people of *J* in	Jer 25:1	3063
the son of Josiah king of *J*	Jer 25:1	3063
spake unto all the people of *J*	Jer 25:2	3063
Josiah the son of Amon king of *J*	Jer 25:3	3063
Jerusalem, and the cities of *J*	Jer 25:18	3063
the son of Josiah king of *J* came	Jer 26:1	3063
and speak unto all the cities of *J*	Jer 26:2	3063
princes of *J* heard these things	Jer 26:10	3063
in the days of Hezekiah king of *J*	Jer 26:18	3063
and spake to all the people of *J*	Jer 26:18	3063
Did Hezekiah king of *J* and all	Jer 26:19	3063
all *J* put him at all to death	Jer 26:19	3063
the son of Josiah king of *J* came	Jer 27:1	3063
Jerusalem unto Zedekiah king of *J*	Jer 27:3	3063
of *J* according to all these words	Jer 27:12	3063
and in the house of the king of *J*	Jer 27:18	3063
of *J* from Jerusalem to Babylon	Jer 27:20	3063
and all the nobles of *J*	Jer 27:20	3063
and in the house of the king of *J*	Jer 27:21	3063
the reign of Zedekiah king of *J*	Jer 28:1	3063
the son of Jehoiakim king of *J*	Jer 28:4	3063
Judah, with all the captives of *J*	Jer 28:4	3063
and the eunuchs, the princes of *J*	Jer 29:2	3063
king of *J* sent unto Babylon to	Jer 29:3	3063
of *J* which are in Babylon	Jer 29:22	3063
of my people Israel and *J*, saith	Jer 30:3	3063
concerning Israel and concerning *J*	Jer 30:4	3063
use this speech in the land of *J*	Jer 31:23	3063
And there shall dwell in *J* itself	Jer 31:24	3063
the house of *J* with the seed of	Jer 31:27	3063
of Israel, and with the house of *J*	Jer 31:31	3063
tenth year of Zedekiah king of *J*	Jer 32:1	3063
king of *J* had shut him up	Jer 32:3	3063
Zedekiah king of *J* shall not	Jer 32:4	3063
the children of *J* have only done	Jer 32:30	3063
of Israel and of the children of *J*	Jer 32:32	3063
their prophets, and the men of *J*	Jer 32:32	3063
abomination, to cause *J* to sin	Jer 32:35	3063
Jerusalem, and in the cities of *J*	Jer 32:44	3063
the houses of the kings of *J*	Jer 33:4	3063
I will cause the captivity of *J*	Jer 33:7	3063
beast, even in the cities of *J*	Jer 33:10	3063
Jerusalem, and in the cities of *J*	Jer 33:13	3063
of Israel and to the house of *J*	Jer 33:14	3063
In those days shall *J* be saved	Jer 33:16	3063
Go and speak to Zedekiah king of *J*	Jer 34:2	3063
of the LORD, O Zedekiah king of *J*	Jer 34:4	3063
Zedekiah king of *J* in Jerusalem	Jer 34:6	3063
the cities of *J* that were left	Jer 34:7	3063
remained of the cities of *J*	Jer 34:7	3063
The princes of *J*, and the princes	Jer 34:19	3063
And Zedekiah king of *J* and his	Jer 34:21	3063
of *J* a desolation without an	Jer 34:22	3063
the son of Josiah king of *J*	Jer 35:1	3063
Go and tell the men of *J* and the	Jer 35:13	3063
Behold, I will bring upon *J*	Jer 35:17	3063
the son of Josiah king of *J*	Jer 36:1	3063
thee against Israel, and against *J*	Jer 36:2	3063
It may be that the house of *J*	Jer 36:3	3063
read them in the ears of all *J*	Jer 36:6	3063
the son of Josiah king of *J*	Jer 36:9	3063
the cities of *J* unto Jerusalem	Jer 36:9	3063
the king of *J* hath burned	Jer 36:28	3063
shalt say to Jehoiakim king of *J*	Jer 36:29	3063
the LORD of Jehoiakim king of *J*	Jer 36:30	3063
Jerusalem, and upon the men of *J*	Jer 36:31	3063
king of *J* had burned in the fire	Jer 36:32	3063
made king in the land of *J*	Jer 37:1	3063
shall ye say to the king of *J*	Jer 37:7	3063
ninth year of Zedekiah king of *J*	Jer 39:1	3063
Zedekiah the king of *J* saw them	Jer 39:4	3063
Babylon slew all the nobles of *J*	Jer 39:6	3063
had nothing, in the land of *J*	Jer 39:10	3063
away captive of Jerusalem and *J*	Jer 40:1	3063
governor over the cities of *J*	Jer 40:5	3063
Babylon had left a remnant of *J*	Jer 40:11	3063
driven, and came to the land of *J*	Jer 40:12	3063
and the remnant in *J* perish	Jer 40:15	3063
word of the LORD, ye remnant of *J*	Jer 42:15	3063
concerning you, O ye remnant of *J*	Jer 42:19	3063
LORD, to dwell in the land of *J*	Jer 43:4	3063
forces, took all the remnant of *J*	Jer 43:5	3063
driven, to dwell in the land of *J*	Jer 43:5	3063
in the sight of the men of *J*	Jer 43:9	3064
and upon all the cities of *J*	Jer 44:2	3063
and was kindled in the cities of *J*	Jer 44:6	3063
child and suckling, out of *J*	Jer 44:7	3063
the wickedness of the kings of *J*	Jer 44:9	3063
have committed in the land of *J*	Jer 44:9	3063
you for evil, and to cut off all *J*	Jer 44:11	3063
And I will take the remnant of *J*	Jer 44:12	3063
So that none of the remnant of *J*	Jer 44:14	3063
should return into the land of *J*	Jer 44:14	3063
our princes, in the cities of *J*	Jer 44:17	3063
that ye burned in the cities of *J*	Jer 44:21	3063
all *J* that are in the land of	Jer 44:24	3063
all *J* that dwell in the land of	Jer 44:26	3063
man of *J* in all the land of Egypt	Jer 44:26	3063
all the men of *J* that are in the	Jer 44:27	3063
land of Egypt into the land of *J*	Jer 44:28	3063
and all the remnant of *J*	Jer 44:28	3063
as I gave Zedekiah king of *J* into	Jer 44:30	3063
the son of Josiah king of *J*	Jer 45:1	3063
the son of Josiah king of *J*	Jer 46:2	3063
the reign of Zedekiah king of *J*	Jer 49:34	3063
and the children of *J* together	Jer 50:4	3063
and the sins of *J*, and they shall	Jer 50:20	3063
the children of *J* were oppressed	Jer 50:33	3063
nor *J* of his God, of the LORD of	Jer 51:5	3063
went with Zedekiah the king of *J*	Jer 51:59	3063
it came to pass in Jerusalem and *J*	Jer 52:3	3063
all the princes of *J* in Riblah	Jer 52:10	3063
Thus *J* was carried away captive	Jer 52:27	3063
captivity of Jehoiakim king of *J*	Jer 52:31	3063
the head of Jehoiachin king of *J*	Jer 52:31	3063
J is gone into captivity because	Lam 1:3	3063
the virgin, the daughter of *J*	Lam 1:15	3063

J

strong holds of the daughter of *J*	Lam 2:2	3063
in the daughter of *J* mourning	Lam 2:5	3063
and the maids in the cities of *J*	Lam 5:11	3063
of the house of *J* forty days	Eze 4:6	3063
and the elders of *J* sat before me	Eze 8:1	3063
house of *J* that they commit the	Eze 8:17	3063
J is exceeding great, and the land	Eze 9:9	3063
to *J* in Jerusalem the defenced	Eze 21:20	3063
and against the house of *J*	Eze 25:3	3063
the house of *J* is like unto all	Eze 25:8	3063
house of *J* by taking vengeance	Eze 25:12	3063
J, and the land of Israel, they	Eze 27:17	3063
stick, and write upon it, For *J*	Eze 37:16	3063
him, even with the stick of *J*	Eze 37:19	3063
the west side, a portion for *J*	Eze 48:7	3063
And by the border of *J*, from the	Eze 48:8	3063
prince's, between the border of *J*	Eze 48:22	3063
one gate of Reuben, one gate of *J*	Eze 48:31	3063
of *J* came Nebuchadnezzar king of	Dan 1:1	3063
Jehoiakim king of *J* into his hand	Dan 1:2	3063
these were the children of *J*	Dan 1:6	3063
found a man of the captives of *J*	Dan 2:25	3061
children of the captivity of *J*	Dan 5:13	3061
children of the captivity of *J*	Dan 6:13	3061
to the men of *J*, and to the	Dan 9:7	3063
Ahaz, and Hezekiah, kings of *J*	Hos 1:1	3063
have mercy upon the house of *J*	Hos 1:7	3063
Then shall the children of *J*	Hos 1:11	3063
the harlot, yet let not *J* offend	Hos 4:15	3063
J also shall fall with them	Hos 5:5	3063
The princes of *J* were like them	Hos 5:10	3063
to the house of *J* as rottenness	Hos 5:12	3063
J saw his wound, then went	Hos 5:13	3063
as a young lion to the house of *J*	Hos 5:14	3063
O *J*, what shall I do unto thee	Hos 6:4	3063
Also, O *J*, he hath set an harvest	Hos 6:11	3063
J hath multiplied fenced cities	Hos 8:14	3063
J shall plow, and Jacob shall	Hos 10:11	3063
but *J* yet ruleth with God, and is	Hos 11:12	3063
hath also a controversy with *J*	Hos 12:2	3063
bring again the captivity of *J*	Joel 3:1	3063
The children also of *J* and the	Joel 3:6	3063
the hand of the children of *J*	Joel 3:8	3063
all the rivers of *J* shall flow	Joel 3:18	3063
against the children of *J*	Joel 3:19	3063
But *J* shall dwell for ever, and	Joel 3:20	3063
in the days of Uzziah king of *J*	Amos 1:1	3063
For three transgressions of *J*	Amos 2:4	3063
But I will send a fire upon *J*	Amos 2:5	3063
flee thee away into the land of *J*	Amos 7:12	3063
rejoiced over the children of *J*	Obad 12	3063
Ahaz, and Hezekiah, kings of *J*	Mic 1:1	3063
and what are the high places of *J*	Mic 1:5	3063
for it is come unto *J*	Mic 1:9	3063
little among the thousands of *J*	Mic 5:2	3063
O *J*, keep thy solemn feasts,	Nah 1:15	3063
Josiah the son of Amon, king of *J*	Zeph 1:1	3063
also stretch out mine hand upon *J*	Zeph 1:4	3063
for the remnant of the house of *J*	Zeph 2:7	3063
son of Shealtiel, governor of *J*	Hag 1:1	3063
son of Shealtiel, governor of *J*	Hag 1:14	3063
son of Shealtiel, governor of *J*	Hag 2:2	3063
to Zerubbabel, governor of *J*	Hag 2:21	3063
Jerusalem and on the cities of *J*	Zec 1:12	3063
the horns which have scattered *J*	Zec 1:19	3063
the horns which have scattered *J*	Zec 1:21	3063
over the land of *J* to scatter it	Zec 1:21	3063
the LORD shall inherit *J* his	Zec 2:12	3063
among the heathen, O house of *J*	Zec 8:13	3063
Jerusalem and to the house of *J*	Zec 8:15	3063
shall be to the house of *J* joy	Zec 8:19	3063
and he shall be as a governor in *J*	Zec 9:7	3063
When I have bent *J* for me	Zec 9:13	3063
visited his flock the house of *J*	Zec 10:3	3063
I will strengthen the house of *J*	Zec 10:6	3063
break the brotherhood between *J*	Zec 11:14	3063
be in the siege both against *J*	Zec 12:2	3063
mine eyes upon the house of *J*	Zec 12:4	3063
the governors of *J* shall say in	Zec 12:5	3063
of *J* like an hearth of fire among	Zec 12:6	3063
shall save the tents of *J* first	Zec 12:7	3063
not magnify themselves against *J*	Zec 12:7	3063
in the days of Uzziah king of *J*	Zec 14:5	3063
J also shall fight at Jerusalem	Zec 14:14	3063
in *J* shall be holiness unto the	Zec 14:21	3063
J hath dealt treacherously, and an	Mal 2:11	3063
for *J* hath profaned the holiness	Mal 2:11	3063
Then shall the offering of *J*	Mal 3:4	3063
4. A Levite.		
and his sons, the sons of *J*	Ezr 3:9	3063

5. A Levite who married a foreigner.

the same is Kelita,) Pethahiah, *J*	Ezr 10:23	3063

6. An overseer.

J the son of Senuah was second	Neh 11:9	3063

7. A Levite with Zerubbabel.

Binnui, Kadmiel, Sherebiah, *J*	Neh 12:8	3063

8. An exile.

J, and Benjamin, and Shemaiah, and	Neh 12:34	3063

9. A musician in exile.

Gilalai, Maai, Nethaneel, and *J*	Neh 12:36	3063

JUDAH'S (ju'-dahs)
    1. Refers to Judah 1.

J firstborn, was wicked in the	Gen 38:7	3063
the daughter of Shuah *J* wife died	Gen 38:12	3063
which was in the king of *J* house	Jer 32:2	3063
that are left in the king of *J*	Jer 38:22	3063

JUDAISM See JEWS, PROSELYTES.

JUDAS (ju'-das) See BARSABAS, ISCARIOT, JUDAH, JUDE, LEBBAEUS, THADDAEUS.
    1. Betrayer of Jesus.

J Iscariot, who also betrayed him	Mt 10:4	2455
called *J* Iscariot, went unto the	Mt 26:14	2455
Then *J*, which betrayed him,	Mt 26:25	2455
And while he yet spake, lo, *J*	Mt 26:47	2455
Then *J*, which had betrayeth him,	Mt 27:3	2455
J Iscariot, which also betrayed	Mk 3:19	2455
J Iscariot, one of the twelve,	Mk 14:10	2455
while he yet spake, cometh *J*	Mk 14:43	2455
J Iscariot, which also was the	Lk 6:16	2455
Satan into *J* surnamed Iscariot	Lk 22:3	2455
and he that was called *J*, one of	Lk 22:47	2455
But Jesus said unto him, *J*	Lk 22:48	2455
He spake of *J* Iscariot the son of	Jn 6:71	2455
J Iscariot, Simon's son, which	Jn 12:4	2455
put into the heart of *J* Iscariot	Jn 13:2	2455
the sop, he gave it to *J* Iscariot	Jn 13:26	2455
because *J* had the bag, that Jesus	Jn 13:29	2455
J also, which betrayed him, knew	Jn 18:2	2455
J then, having received a band of	Jn 18:3	2455
J also, which betrayed him, stood	Jn 18:5	2455
David spake before concerning *J*	Acts 1:16	2455
from which *J* by transgression	Acts 1:25	2455

    2. A brother of Jesus.

James, and Joses, and Simon, and *J*	Mt 13:55	2455

    3. A disciple of Jesus.

J the brother of James, and Judas	Lk 6:16	2455
J saith unto him, not Iscariot,	Jn 14:22	2455
and *J* the brother of James	Acts 1:13	2455

    4. A seditious Galilean.

After this man rose up *J* of	Acts 5:37	2455

    5. Lodged Paul in Damascus.

house of *J* **for one called Saul**	Acts 9:11	2455

    6. Surnamed Barsabas.

J surnamed Barsabas, and Silas,	Acts 15:22	2455
We have sent therefore *J* and Silas	Acts 15:27	2455
And *J* and Silas, being prophets	Acts 15:32	2455

    7. A Greek form of Joseph.

and Jacob begat *J* and his brethren	Mt 1:2	2455
J begat Phares and Zara of Thamar	Mt 1:3	2455

JUDE (jood) See JUDAS. *A brother of Jesus.*

J, the servant of Jesus Christ,	Jude 1	2455

JUDEA (ju-de'-ah) See JEWRY, JUDAH. *Southern portion of Israel.*

we went into the province of *J*	Ezr 5:8	3061

JUDGE

whom they shall serve, will I *j*	Gen 15:14	1777
the LORD *j* between me and thee	Gen 16:5	8199
Shall not the *J* of all the earth	Gen 18:25	8199
sojourn, and he will needs be a *j*	Gen 19:9	8199
that they may *j* betwixt us both	Gen 31:37	3198
God of their father, *j* betwixt us	Gen 31:53	8199
Dan shall *j* his people, as one of	Gen 49:16	1777
made thee a prince and a *j* over us	Ex 2:14	8199
The LORD look upon you, and *j*	Ex 5:21	8199
that Moses sat to *j* the people	Ex 18:13	8199
I *j* between one and another, and I	Ex 18:16	8199
let them *j* the people at all	Ex 18:22	8199
every small matter they shall *j*	Ex 18:22	8199
shalt thou *j* thy neighbour	Lev 19:15	8199
shall *j* between the slayer	Num 35:24	8199
j righteously between every man	Deut 1:16	8199
they shall *j* the people with just	Deut 16:18	8199
unto the *j* that shall be in those	Deut 17:9	8199
the LORD thy God, or unto the *j*	Deut 17:12	8199
that the judges may *j* them	Deut 25:1	8199
that the *j* shall cause him to lie	Deut 25:2	8199
For the LORD shall *j* his people	Deut 32:36	1777
then the LORD was with the *j*	Judg 2:18	8199

enemies all the days of the *j*	Judg 2:18	8199
came to pass, when the *j* was dead	Judg 2:19	8199
the LORD the *J* be *j* this day	Judg 11:27	8199
the LORD shall *j* the ends of the	1Sa 2:10	1777
another, the *j* shall *j* him	1Sa 2:25	430
will *j* his house for ever for the	1Sa 3:13	8199
now make us a king to *j* us like	1Sa 8:5	8199
they said, Give us a king to *j* us	1Sa 8:6	8199
and that our king may *j* us	1Sa 8:20	8199
The LORD *j* between me and thee, and	1Sa 24:12	8199
The LORD therefore be *j*	1Sa 24:15	1784
j between me and thee, and see, and	1Sa 24:15	8199
Oh that I were made *j* in the land	2Sa 15:4	8199
heart to *j* thy people, that I may	1Kin 3:9	8199
for who is able to *j* this thy so	1Kin 3:9	8199
for the throne where he might *j*	1Kin 7:7	8199
j thy servants, condemning the	1Kin 8:32	8199
because he cometh to *j* the earth	1Chr 16:33	8199
for who can *j* this thy people,	2Chr 1:10	8199
that thou mayest *j* my people	2Chr 1:11	8199
j thy servants, by requiting the	2Chr 6:23	8199
for ye *j* not for man, but for the	2Chr 19:6	8199
O our God, wilt thou not *j* them	2Chr 20:12	8199
which may *j* all the people that	Ezr 7:25	
I would make supplication to my *j*	Job 9:15	8199
can he *j* through the dark cloud	Job 22:13	8199
I be delivered for ever from my *j*	Job 23:7	8199
iniquity to be punished by the *j*	Job 31:28	6416
The LORD shall *j* the people	Ps 7:8	1777
j me, O LORD, according to my	Ps 7:8	8199
And he shall *j* the world in	Ps 9:8	8199
To *j* the fatherless and the	Ps 10:18	8199
J me, O LORD	Ps 26:1	8199
J me, O LORD my God, according to	Ps 35:24	8199
J me, O God, and plead my cause	Ps 43:1	8199
earth, that he may *j* his people	Ps 50:4	1777
for God is *j* himself	Ps 50:6	8199
thy name, and *j* me by thy strength	Ps 54:1	1777
do ye *j* uprightly, O ye sons of	Ps 58:1	8199
for thou shalt *j* the people	Ps 67:4	8199
a *j* of the widows, is God in his	Ps 68:5	1781
He shall *j* thy people with	Ps 72:2	1777
He shall *j* the poor of the people	Ps 72:4	8199
congregation I will *j* uprightly	Ps 75:2	8199
But God is the *j*	Ps 75:7	8199
How long will ye *j* unjustly	Ps 82:2	8199
Arise, O God, *j* the earth	Ps 82:8	8199
up thyself, thou *j* of the earth	Ps 94:2	8199
he shall *j* the people righteously	Ps 96:10	1777
for he cometh to *j* the earth	Ps 96:13	8199
he shall *j* the world with	Ps 96:13	8199
for he cometh to *j* the earth	Ps 98:9	8199
shall he *j* the world, and the	Ps 98:9	8199
He shall *j* among the heathen, he	Ps 110:6	1777
For the LORD will *j* his people	Ps 135:14	1777
j righteously, and plead the cause	Prov 31:9	8199
God shall *j* the righteous and the	Eccl 3:17	8199
j the fatherless, plead for the	Is 1:17	8199
they *j* not the fatherless,	Is 1:23	8199
he shall *j* among the nations, and	Is 2:4	8199
man, and the man of war, the *j*	Is 3:2	8199
and standeth to *j* the people	Is 3:13	1777
of Jerusalem, and men of Judah, *j*	Is 5:3	8199
he shall not *j* after the sight of	Is 11:3	8199
righteousness shall he *j* the poor	Is 11:4	8199
For the LORD is our *j*, the LORD	Is 33:22	8199
and mine arms shall *j* the people	Is 51:5	8199
they *j* not the cause, the cause	Jer 5:28	1777
right of the needy do they not *j*	Jer 5:28	8199
j thou my cause	Lam 3:59	8199
will *j* thee according to thy ways	Eze 7:3	8199
I will *j* thee according to thy	Eze 7:8	8199
to their deserts will I *j* them	Eze 7:27	8199
I will *j* you in the border of	Eze 11:10	8199
but I will *j* you in the border of	Eze 11:11	8199
And I will *j* thee, as women that	Eze 16:38	8199
Therefore I will *j* you, O house	Eze 18:30	8199
Wilt thou *j* them, son of man,	Eze 20:4	8199
son of man, wilt thou *j* them	Eze 20:4	8199
I will *j* thee in the place where	Eze 21:30	8199
Now, thou son of man, wilt thou *j*	Eze 22:2	8199
wilt thou *j* the bloody city	Eze 22:2	8199
they shall *j* thee according to	Eze 23:24	8199
Son of man, wilt thou *j* Aholah	Eze 23:36	8199
they shall *j* them after the	Eze 23:45	8199
to thy doings, shall they *j* thee	Eze 24:14	8199
I will *j* you every one after his	Eze 33:20	8199
I *j* between cattle and cattle,	Eze 34:17	8199
will *j* between the fat cattle and	Eze 34:20	8199
I will *j* between cattle and cattle	Eze 34:22	8199
they shall *j* it according to my	Eze 44:24	8199
for there will I sit to *j* all the	Joel 3:12	8199
I will cut off the *j* from the	Amos 2:3	8199
mount Zion to *j* the mount of Esau	Obad 21	8199
The heads thereof *j* for reward	Mic 3:11	8199
he shall *j* among many people, and	Mic 4:3	8199
they shall smite the *j* of Israel	Mic 5:1	8199
the *j* asketh for a reward	Mic 7:3	8199
then thou shalt also *j* my house	Zec 3:7	1777
adversary deliver thee to the *j*	Mt 5:25	2923
the *j* deliver thee to the officer	Mt 5:25	2923
***J* not, that ye be not judged**	Mt 7:1	2919
For with what judgment ye *j*	Mt 7:2	2919
***J* not, and ye shall not be judged**	Lk 6:37	2919
who made me a *j* or a divider over	Lk 12:14	1348
yourselves *j* ye not what is right	Lk 12:57	2919
lest he hale thee to the *j*	Lk 12:58	2923
the *j* deliver thee to the officer	Lk 12:58	2923
Saying, There was in a city a *j*	Lk 18:2	2923
Hear what the unjust *j* saith	Lk 18:6	2923
of thine own mouth will I *j* thee	Lk 19:22	2919
as I hear, I *j*	Jn 5:30	2919
***J* not according to the appearance**	Jn 7:24	2919
but *j* righteous judgment	Jn 7:24	2919
Doth our law *j* any man, before it	Jn 7:51	2919
Ye *j* after the flesh	Jn 8:15	2919
I *j* no man	Jn 8:15	2919
And yet if I *j*, my judgment is	Jn 8:16	2919
many things to say and to *j* of you	Jn 8:26	2919
and believe not, I *j* him not	Jn 12:47	2919
for I came not to *j* the world	Jn 12:47	2919
the same shall *j* him in the last	Jn 12:48	2919
j him according to your law	Jn 18:31	2919
unto you more than unto God, *j* ye	Acts 4:19	2919
they shall be in bondage will I *j*	Acts 7:7	2919
made thee a ruler and a *j* over us	Acts 7:27	1348
Who made thee a ruler and a *j*	Acts 7:35	1348
of God to be the *J* of quick	Acts 10:42	2923
you, and *j* yourselves unworthy of	Acts 13:46	2919
in the which he will *j* the world	Acts 17:31	2919
I will be no *j* of such matters	Acts 18:15	2923
thou to *j* me after the law	Acts 23:3	2919
many years a *j* unto this nation	Acts 24:10	2923
In the day when God shall *j* the	Rom 2:16	2919
j thee, who by the letter and	Rom 2:27	2919
then how shall God *j* the world	Rom 3:6	2919
eateth not *j* him that eateth	Rom 14:3	2919
But why dost thou *j* thy brother	Rom 14:10	2919
therefore *j* one another any more	Rom 14:13	2919
but *j* this rather, that no man	Rom 14:13	2919
yea, I *j* not mine own self	1Cor 4:3	350
Therefore *j* nothing before the	1Cor 4:5	2919
For what have I to do to *j* them	1Cor 5:12	2919
do not ye *j* them that are within	1Cor 5:12	2919
that the saints shall *j* the world	1Cor 6:2	2919
are ye unworthy to *j* the smallest	1Cor 6:2	2922
ye not that we shall *j* angels	1Cor 6:3	2919
set them to *j* who are least	1Cor 6:4	
be able to *j* between his brethren	1Cor 6:5	1252
j ye what I say	1Cor 10:15	2919
***J* in yourselves**	1Cor 11:13	2919
For if we would *j* ourselves	1Cor 11:31	1252
two or three, and let the other *j*	1Cor 14:29	1252
because we thus *j*, that if one	2Cor 5:14	2919
no man therefore *j* you in meat	Col 2:16	2919
Christ, who shall *j* the quick	2Ti 4:1	2919
which the Lord, the righteous *j*	2Ti 4:8	2923
The Lord shall *j* his people	Heb 10:30	2919
in heaven, and to God the *J* of all	Heb 12:23	2923
and adulterers God will *j*	Heb 13:4	2919
but if thou *j* the law, thou art	Jas 4:11	2919
not a doer of the law, but a *j*	Jas 4:11	2923
the *j* standeth before the door	Jas 5:9	2923
him that is ready to *j* the quick	1Pet 4:5	2919
holy and true, dost thou not *j*	Rev 6:10	2919
and in righteousness he doth *j*	Rev 19:11	2919

JUDGED

And Rachel said, God hath *j* me	Gen 30:6	1777
they *j* the people at all seasons	Ex 18:26	8199
small matter they *j* themselves	Ex 18:26	8199
he *j* Israel, and went out to war	Judg 3:10	8199
she *j* Israel at that time	Judg 4:4	8199
he *j* Israel twenty and three years	Judg 10:2	8199
j Israel twenty and two years	Judg 10:3	8199
Jephthah *j* Israel six years	Judg 12:7	8199
him Ibzan of Beth-lehem *j* Israel	Judg 12:8	8199
And he *j* Israel seven years	Judg 12:9	8199
him Elon, a Zebulonite, *j* Israel	Judg 12:11	8199
and he *j* Israel ten years	Judg 12:11	8199
Hillel, a Pirathonite, *j* Israel	Judg 12:13	8199
and he *j* Israel eight years	Judg 12:14	8199

J

he j Israel in the days of the	Judg 15:20	8199
And he j Israel twenty years	Judg 16:31	8199
he had j Israel forty years	1Sa 4:18	8199
Samuel j the children of Israel	1Sa 7:6	8199
Samuel j Israel all the days of	1Sa 7:15	8199
j Israel in all those places	1Sa 7:16	8199
and there he j Israel	1Sa 7:17	8199
the judgment which the king had j	1Kin 3:28	8199
days of the judges that j Israel	2Kin 23:22	8199
let the heathen be j in thy sight	Ps 9:19	8199
nor condemn him when he is j	Ps 37:33	8199
When he shall be j, let him be	Ps 109:7	8199
He j the cause of the poor and	Jer 22:16	1777
break wedlock and shed blood are j	Eze 16:38	4941
which hast j thy sisters, bear	Eze 16:52	6419
the wounded shall be j in the	Eze 28:23	5307
among them, when I have j thee	Eze 35:11	8199
to their doings I j them	Eze 36:19	8199
and against our judges that j us	Dan 9:12	8199
Judge not, that ye be not j	Mt 7:1	2919
judgment ye judge, ye shall be j	Mt 7:2	2919
Judge not, and ye shall not be j	Lk 6:37	2919
unto him, Thou hast rightly j	Lk 7:43	2919
the prince of this world is j	Jn 16:11	2919
If ye have j me to be faithful to	Acts 16:15	2919
would have j according to our law	Acts 24:6	2919
there be j of these things before	Acts 25:9	2919
seat, where I ought to be j	Acts 25:10	2919
there be j of these matters	Acts 25:20	2919
am j for the hope of the promise	Acts 26:6	2919
in the law shall be j by the law	Rom 2:12	2919
mightest overcome when thou art j	Rom 3:4	2919
why yet am I also j as a sinner	Rom 3:7	2919
yet he himself is j of no man	1Cor 2:15	350
thing that I should be j of you	1Cor 4:3	350
have j already, as though I were	1Cor 5:3	2919
and if the world shall be j by you	1Cor 6:2	2919
for why is my liberty j of	1Cor 10:29	2919
ourselves, we should not be j	1Cor 11:31	2919
But when we are j, we are	1Cor 11:32	2919
convinced of all, he is j of all	1Cor 14:24	350
because she j him faithful who	Heb 11:11	2233
shall be j by the law of liberty	Jas 2:12	2919
that they might be j according to	1Pet 4:6	2919
the dead, that they should be j	Rev 11:18	2919
be, because thou hast j thus	Rev 16:5	2919
for he hath j the great whore,	Rev 19:2	2919
the dead were j out of those	Rev 20:12	2919
they were j every man according	Rev 20:13	2919

JUDGES

master shall bring him unto the j	Ex 21:6	430
he shall pay as the j determine	Ex 21:22	6414
house shall be brought unto the j	Ex 22:8	430
parties shall come before the j	Ex 22:9	430
whom the j shall condemn, he	Ex 22:9	430
Moses said unto the j of Israel	Num 25:5	8199
And I charged your j at that time	Deut 1:16	8199
J and officers shalt thou make	Deut 16:18	8199
LORD, before the priests and the j	Deut 19:17	8199
the j shall make diligent	Deut 19:18	8199
thy j shall come forth, and they	Deut 21:2	8199
that the j may judge them	Deut 25:1	8199
our enemies themselves being j	Deut 32:31	6414
elders, and officers, and their j	Josh 8:33	8199
for their heads, and for their j	Josh 23:2	8199
for their heads, and for their j	Josh 24:1	8199
Nevertheless the LORD raised up j	Judg 2:16	8199
would not hearken unto their j	Judg 2:17	8199
And when the LORD raised them up j	Judg 2:18	8199
pass in the days when the j ruled	Ruth 1:1	8199
he made his sons j over Israel	1Sa 8:1	8199
they were j in Beer-sheba	1Sa 8:2	8199
j to be over my people Israel	2Sa 7:11	8199
days of the judges that j Israel	2Kin 23:22	8199
a word to any of the j of Israel	1Chr 17:6	8199
j to be over my people Israel	1Chr 17:10	8199
six thousand were officers and j	1Chr 23:4	8199
over Israel, for officers and j	1Chr 26:29	8199
and of hundreds, and to the j	2Chr 1:2	8199
he set j in the land throughout	2Chr 19:5	8199
And said to the j, Take heed what	2Chr 19:6	8199
thine hand, set magistrates and j	Ezr 7:25	1782
the j thereof, until the fierce	Ezr 10:14	8199
the faces of the j thereof	Job 9:24	8199
spoiled, and maketh the j fools	Job 12:17	8199
iniquity to be punished by the j	Job 31:11	6414
be instructed, ye j of the earth	Ps 2:10	8199
When their j are overthrown in	Ps 141:6	8199
princes, and all j of the earth	Ps 148:11	8199
even all the j of the earth	Prov 8:16	8199

restore thy j as at the first	Is 1:26	8199
he maketh the j of the earth as	Is 40:23	8199
governors, and the captains, the j	Dan 3:2	148
the governors, and captains, the j	Dan 3:3	148
against our j that judged us, by	Dan 9:12	8199
an oven, and have devoured their j	Hos 7:7	8199
thy j of whom thou saidst, Give	Hos 13:10	8199
her j are evening wolves	Zeph 3:3	8199
therefore they shall be your j	Mt 12:27	2923
therefore shall they be your j	Lk 11:19	2923
after that he gave unto them j	Acts 13:20	2923
are become j of evil thoughts	Jas 2:4	2923

JUDGEST

speakest, and be clear when thou j	Ps 51:4	8199
that j righteously, that triest	Jer 11:20	8199
O man, whosoever thou art that j	Rom 2:1	2919
for wherein thou j another	Rom 2:1	2919
for thou that j doest the same	Rom 2:1	2919
that j them which do such things,	Rom 2:3	2919
Who art thou that j another man's	Rom 14:4	2919
who art thou that j another	Jas 4:12	2919

JUDGETH

seeing he j those that are high	Job 21:22	8199
For by them j he the people	Job 36:31	1777
God j the righteous, and God is	Ps 7:11	8199
he is a God that j in the earth	Ps 58:11	8199
he j among the gods	Ps 82:1	8199
king that faithfully j the poor	Prov 29:14	8199
For the Father j no man, but hath	Jn 5:22	2919
there is one that seeketh and j	Jn 8:50	2919
not my words, hath one that j him	Jn 12:48	2919
he that is spiritual j all things	1Cor 2:15	350
but he that j me is the Lord	1Cor 4:4	2919
But them that are without God j	1Cor 5:13	2919
j his brother, speaketh evil of	Jas 4:11	2919
evil of the law, and j the law	Jas 4:11	2919
j according to every man's work	1Pet 1:17	2919
himself to him that j righteously	1Pet 2:23	2919
strong is the Lord God who j her	Rev 18:8	2919

JUDGING

house, j the people of the land	2Kin 15:5	8199
house, j the people of the land	2Chr 26:21	8199
thou satest in the throne j right	Ps 9:4	8199
in the tabernacle of David, j	Is 16:5	8199
j the twelve tribes of Israel	Mt 19:28	2919
sit on thrones j the twelve	Lk 22:30	2919

JUDGMENT

of the LORD, to do justice and j	Gen 18:19	4941
gods of Egypt I will execute j	Ex 12:12	8201
according to this j shall it be	Ex 21:31	4941
to decline after many to wrest j	Ex 23:2	4941
the j of thy poor in his cause	Ex 23:6	4941
of j with cunning work	Ex 28:15	4941
breastplate of j upon his heart	Ex 28:29	4941
in the breastplate of j the Urim	Ex 28:30	4941
Aaron shall bear the j of the	Ex 28:30	4941
shall do no unrighteousness in j	Lev 19:15	4941
shall do no unrighteousness in j	Lev 19:35	4941
children of Israel a statute of j	Num 27:11	4941
the j of Urim before the LORD	Num 27:21	4941
before the congregation in j	Num 35:12	4941
of j unto you throughout your	Num 35:29	4941
Ye shall not respect persons in j	Deut 1:17	4941
for the j is God's	Deut 1:17	4941
execute the j of the fatherless	Deut 10:18	4941
judge the people with just j	Deut 16:18	4941
Thou shalt not wrest j	Deut 16:19	4941
a matter too hard for thee in j	Deut 17:8	4941
shall shew thee the sentence of j	Deut 17:9	4941
according to the j which they	Deut 17:11	4941
not pervert the j of the stranger	Deut 24:17	4941
between men, and they come unto j	Deut 25:1	4941
perverteth the j of the stranger	Deut 27:19	4941
for all his ways are j	Deut 32:4	4941
and mine hand shall hold on j	Deut 32:41	4941
before the congregation for j	Josh 20:6	4941
of Israel came up to her for j	Judg 4:5	4941
on white asses, ye that sit in j	Judg 5:10	4055
and took bribes, and perverted j	1Sa 8:3	4941
and David executed j and justice	2Sa 8:15	4941
came to the king for j, then	2Sa 15:2	4941
that came to the king for j	2Sa 15:6	4941
understanding to discern j	1Kin 3:11	4941
all Israel heard of the j which	1Kin 3:28	4941
wisdom of God was in him, to do j	1Kin 3:28	4941
might judge, even the porch of j	1Kin 7:7	4941
made he the king, to do j	1Kin 10:9	4941
said unto him, So shall thy j be	1Kin 20:40	4941
and they gave j upon him	2Kin 25:6	4941

over all Israel, and executed *j*	1Chr 18:14	4941
he thee king over them, to do *j*	2Chr 9:8	4941
LORD, who is with you in the *j*	2Chr 19:6	
for the *j* of the LORD, and for	2Chr 19:8	4941
cometh upon us, as the sword, *j*	2Chr 20:9	8196
j upon the house of Ahab, and	2Chr 22:8	8199
So they executed *j* against Joash	2Chr 24:24	8201
let *j* be executed speedily upon	Ezr 7:26	1780
toward all that knew law and *j*	Est 1:13	1779
Doth God pervert *j*?	Job 8:3	4941
and if of *j*, who shall set me a	Job 9:19	4941
and we should come together in *j*	Job 9:32	4941
and bringest me into *j* with thee	Job 14:3	4941
I cry aloud, but there is no *j*	Job 19:7	4941
that ye may know there is a *j*	Job 19:29	1779
will he enter with thee into *j*	Job 22:4	4941
liveth, who hath taken away my *j*	Job 27:2	4941
my *j* was as a robe and a diadem	Job 29:14	4941
neither do the aged understand *j*	Job 32:9	4941
Let us choose to us *j*	Job 34:4	4941
and God hath taken away my *j*	Job 34:5	4941
will the Almighty pervert *j*	Job 34:12	4941
he should enter into *j* with God	Job 34:23	4941
not see him, yet *j* is before him	Job 35:14	1779
fulfilled the *j* of the wicked	Job 36:17	1779
j and justice take hold on thee	Job 36:17	1779
he is excellent in power, and in *j*	Job 37:23	4941
Wilt thou also disannul my *j*	Job 40:8	4941
ungodly shall not stand in the *j*	Ps 1:5	4941
awake for me to the *j* that thou	Ps 7:6	4941
he hath prepared his throne for *j*	Ps 9:7	4941
he shall minister *j* to the people	Ps 9:8	1777
known by the *j* which he executeth	Ps 9:16	4941
The meek will he guide in *j*	Ps 25:9	4941
He loveth righteousness and *j*	Ps 33:5	4941
Stir up thyself, and awake to my *j*	Ps 35:23	4941
light, and thy *j* as the noonday	Ps 37:6	4941
For the LORD loveth *j*, and	Ps 37:28	4941
and his tongue talketh of *j*	Ps 37:30	4941
righteousness and thy poor with *j*	Ps 72:2	4941
Thou didst cause *j* to be heard	Ps 76:8	1779
When God arose to *j*, to save all	Ps 76:9	4941
j are the habitation of thy	Ps 89:14	4941
But *j* shall return unto	Ps 94:15	4941
j are the habitation of his	Ps 97:2	4941
The king's strength also loveth *j*	Ps 99:4	4941
equity, thou executest *j* and	Ps 99:4	4941
I will sing of mercy and *j*	Ps 101:1	4941
j for all that are oppressed	Ps 103:6	4941
Blessed are they that keep *j*	Ps 106:3	4941
stood up Phinehas, and executed *j*	Ps 106:30	6419
of his hands are verity and *j*	Ps 111:7	4941
Teach me good *j* and knowledge	Ps 119:66	2940
when wilt thou execute *j* on them	Ps 119:84	4941
I have done *j* and justice	Ps 119:121	4941
quicken me according to thy *j*	Ps 119:149	4941
For there are set thrones of *j*	Ps 122:5	4941
enter not into *j* with thy servant	Ps 143:2	4941
Which executeth *j* for the	Ps 146:7	4941
execute upon them the *j* written	Ps 149:9	4941
of wisdom, justice, and, *j*, and	Prov 1:3	4941
He keepeth the paths of *j*	Prov 2:8	4941
understand righteousness, and *j*	Prov 2:9	4941
in the midst of the paths of *j*	Prov 8:20	4941
that is destroyed for want of *j*	Prov 13:23	4941
his mouth transgresseth not in *j*	Prov 16:10	4941
bosom to pervert the ways of *j*	Prov 17:23	4941
to overthrow the righteous in *j*	Prov 18:5	4941
An ungodly witness scorneth *j*	Prov 19:28	4941
j scattereth away all evil with	Prov 20:8	1779
j is more acceptable to the LORD	Prov 21:3	4941
because they refuse to do *j*	Prov 21:7	4941
It is joy to the just to do *j*	Prov 21:15	4941
to have respect of persons in *j*	Prov 24:23	4941
Evil men understand not *j*	Prov 28:5	4941
The king by *j* establisheth the	Prov 29:4	4941
but every man's *j* cometh from the	Prov 29:26	4941
pervert the *j* of any of the	Prov 31:5	1779
saw under the sun the place of *j*	Eccl 3:16	4941
poor, and violent perverting of *j*	Eccl 5:8	4941
heart discerneth both time and *j*	Eccl 8:5	4941
every purpose there is time and *j*	Eccl 8:6	4941
things God will bring thee into *j*	Eccl 11:9	4941
God shall bring every work into *j*	Eccl 12:14	4941
seek *j*, relieve the oppressed,	Is 1:17	4941
it was full of *j*	Is 1:21	4941
Zion shall be redeemed with *j*	Is 1:27	4941
The LORD will enter into *j* with	Is 3:14	4941
midst thereof by the spirit of *j*	Is 4:4	4941
and he looked for *j*, but behold	Is 5:7	4941
of hosts shall be exalted in *j*	Is 5:16	4941

it, and to establish it with *j*	Is 9:7	4941
To turn aside the needy from *j*	Is 10:2	1779
Take counsel, execute *j*	Is 16:3	6415
of David, judging, and seeking *j*	Is 16:5	4941
j to him that sitteth in *j*	Is 28:6	4941
err in vision, they stumble in *j*	Is 28:7	6417
J also will I lay to the line, and	Is 28:17	4941
for the LORD is a God of *j*	Is 30:18	4941
and princes shall rule in *j*	Is 32:1	4941
Then *j* shall dwell in the	Is 32:16	4941
he hath filled Zion with *j*	Is 33:5	4941
upon the people of my curse, to *j*	Is 34:5	4941
and taught him in the path of *j*	Is 40:14	4941
my *j* is passed over from my God	Is 40:27	4941
let us come near together to *j*	Is 41:1	4941
bring forth *j* to the Gentiles	Is 42:1	4941
he shall bring forth *j* unto truth	Is 42:3	4941
till he have set *j* in the earth	Is 42:4	4941
yet surely my *j* is with the LORD,	Is 49:4	4941
I will make my *j* to rest for a	Is 51:4	4941
was taken from prison and from *j*	Is 53:8	4941
thee in *j* thou shalt condemn	Is 54:17	4941
Thus saith the LORD, Keep ye *j*	Is 56:1	4941
there is no *j* in their goings	Is 59:8	4941
Therefore is *j* far from us	Is 59:9	4941
we look for *j*, but there is none	Is 59:11	4941
j is turned away backward, and	Is 59:14	4941
him that there was no *j*	Is 59:15	4941
For I the LORD love *j*, I hate	Is 61:8	4941
The LORD liveth, in truth, in *j*	Jer 4:2	4941
if there be any that executeth *j*	Jer 5:1	4941
the LORD, nor the *j* of their God	Jer 5:4	4941
the LORD, and the *j* of their God	Jer 5:5	4941
throughly execute *j* between a man	Jer 7:5	4941
people know not the *j* of the LORD	Jer 8:7	4941
which exercise lovingkindness, *j*	Jer 9:24	4941
O LORD, correct me, but with *j*	Jer 10:24	4941
Execute *j* in the morning, and	Jer 21:12	4941
Execute ye *j* and righteousness, and	Jer 22:3	4941
thy father eat and drink, and do *j*	Jer 22:15	4941
and prosper, and shall execute *j*	Jer 23:5	4941
and he shall execute *j* and	Jer 33:15	4941
Hamath, where he gave *j* upon him	Jer 39:5	4941
j is come upon the plain country	Jer 48:21	4941
Thus far is the *j* of Moab	Jer 48:47	4941
they whose *j* was not to drink of	Jer 49:12	4941
for her *j* reacheth unto heaven,	Jer 51:9	4941
that I will do *j* upon the graven	Jer 51:47	6485
that I will do *j* upon her graven	Jer 51:52	6485
where he gave *j* upon him	Jer 52:9	4941
hath executed true *j* between man	Eze 18:8	4941
for they had executed *j* upon her	Eze 23:10	8196
I will set *j* before them, and they	Eze 23:24	4941
I will feed them with *j*	Eze 34:16	4941
see my *j* that I have executed	Eze 39:21	4941
controversy they shall stand in *j*	Eze 44:24	8199
violence and spoil, and execute *j*	Eze 45:9	4941
works are truth, and his ways *j*	Dan 4:37	1780
the *j* was set, and the books were	Dan 7:10	1780
j was given to the saints of the	Dan 7:22	1780
But the *j* shall sit, and they	Dan 7:26	1780
unto me in righteousness, and in *j*	Hos 2:19	4941
for *j* is toward you, because ye	Hos 5:1	4941
is oppressed and broken in *j*	Hos 5:11	4941
thus *j* springeth up as hemlock in	Hos 10:4	4941
keep mercy and *j*, and wait on thy	Hos 12:6	4941
Ye who turn *j* to wormwood	Amos 5:7	4941
good, and establish *j* in the gate	Amos 5:15	4941
But let *j* run down as waters, and	Amos 5:24	4941
for ye have turned *j* into gall	Amos 6:12	4941
Is it not for you to know *j*	Mic 3:1	4941
the spirit of the LORD, and of *j*	Mic 3:8	4941
the house of Israel, that abhor *j*	Mic 3:9	4941
my cause, and execute *j* for me	Mic 7:9	4941
slacked, and *j* doth never go forth	Hab 1:4	4941
therefore wrong *j* proceedeth	Hab 1:4	4941
their *j* and their dignity shall	Hab 1:7	4941
thou hast ordained them for *j*	Hab 1:12	4941
earth, which have wrought his *j*	Zeph 2:3	4941
doth he bring his *j* to light	Zeph 3:5	4941
of hosts, saying, Execute true *j*	Zec 7:9	4941
execute the *j* of truth and peace	Zec 8:16	4941
or, Where is the God of *j*	Mal 2:17	4941
And I will come near to you to *j*	Mal 3:5	4941
kill shall be in danger of the *j*	Mt 5:21	2920
cause shall be in danger of the *j*	Mt 5:22	2920
For with what *j* ye judge, ye	Mt 7:2	2917
Sodom and Gomorrha in the day of *j*	Mt 10:15	2920
for Tyre and Sidon at the day of *j*	Mt 11:22	2920
the land of Sodom in the day of *j*	Mt 11:24	2920
he shall shew *j* to the Gentiles	Mt 12:18	2920

J

till he send forth *j* unto victory	Mt 12:20	2920
account thereof in the day of *j*	Mt 12:36	2920
rise in *j* with this generation	Mt 12:41	2920
up in the *j* with this generation	Mt 12:42	2920
weightier matters of the law, *j*	Mt 23:23	2920
he was set down on the *j* seat	Mt 27:19	968
Sodom and Gomorrha in the day of *j*	Mk 6:11	2920
for Tyre and Sidon at the *j*	Lk 10:14	2920
the south shall rise up in the *j*	Lk 11:31	2920
up in the *j* with this generation	Lk 11:32	2920
manner of herbs, and pass over *j*	Lk 11:42	2920
hath committed all *j* unto the Son	Jn 5:22	2920
him authority to execute *j* also	Jn 5:27	2920
and my *j* is just	Jn 5:30	2920
appearance, but judge righteous *j*	Jn 7:24	2920
And yet if I judge, my *j* is true	Jn 8:16	2920
For *j* I am come into this world,	Jn 9:39	2917
Now is the *j* of this world	Jn 12:31	2920
sin, and of righteousness, and of *j*	Jn 16:8	2920
Of *j*, because the prince of this	Jn 16:11	2920
from Caiaphas unto the hall of *j*	Jn 18:28	4232
went not into the *j* hall, lest	Jn 18:28	4232
entered into the *j* hall again	Jn 18:33	4232
And went again into the *j* hall	Jn 19:9	4232
sat down in the *j* seat in a place	Jn 19:13	968
humiliation his *j* was taken away	Acts 8:33	2920
and brought him to the *j* seat	Acts 18:12	968
And he drave them from the *j* seat	Acts 18:16	968
and beat him before the *j* seat	Acts 18:17	968
him to be kept in Herod's *j* hall	Acts 23:35	4232
j to come, Felix trembled, and	Acts 24:25	2917
the *j* seat commanded Paul to be	Acts 25:6	968
Paul, I stand at Caesar's *j* seat	Acts 25:10	968
desiring to have *j* against him	Acts 25:15	1349
on the morrow I sat on the *j* seat	Acts 25:17	968
Who knowing the *j* of God, that	Rom 1:32	1345
But we are sure that the *j* of God	Rom 2:2	2917
thou shalt escape the *j* of God	Rom 2:3	2917
of the righteous *j* of God	Rom 2:5	1341
for the *j* was by one to	Rom 5:16	2917
of one *j* came upon all men to	Rom 5:18	
stand before the *j* seat of Christ	Rom 14:10	968
in the same mind and in the same *j*	1Cor 1:10	1106
be judged of you, or of man's *j*	1Cor 4:3	2250
yet I give my *j*, as one that hath	1Cor 7:25	1106
if she so abide, after my *j*	1Cor 7:40	1106
before the *j* seat of Christ	2Cor 5:10	968
troubleth you shall bear his *j*	Gal 5:10	2917
and more in knowledge and in all *j*	Phil 1:9	144
token of the righteous *j* of God	2Th 1:5	2920
beforehand, going before to *j*	1Ti 5:24	2920
of the dead, and of eternal *j*	Heb 6:2	2917
once to die, but after this the *j*	Heb 9:27	2920
certain fearful looking for of *j*	Heb 10:27	2920
and draw you before the *j* seats	Jas 2:6	2922
For he shall have *j* without mercy	Jas 2:13	2920
and mercy rejoiceth against *j*	Jas 2:13	2920
For the time is come that *j* must	1Pet 4:17	2917
whose *j* now of a long time	2Pet 2:3	2917
darkness, to be reserved unto *j*	2Pet 2:4	2920
unto the day of *j* to be punished	2Pet 2:9	2920
unto fire against the day of *j*	2Pet 3:7	2920
may have boldness in the day of *j*	1Jn 4:17	2920
unto the *j* of the great day	Jude 6	2920
To execute *j* upon all, and to	Jude 15	2920
for the hour of his *j* is come	Rev 14:7	2920
I will shew unto thee the *j* of	Rev 17:1	2917
for in one hour is thy *j* come	Rev 18:10	2920
them, and *j* was given unto them	Rev 20:4	2917

JUDGMENTS

out arm, and with great *j*	Ex 6:6	8201
of the land of Egypt by great *j*	Ex 7:4	8201
Now these are the *j* which thou	Ex 21:1	4941
words of the LORD, and all the *j*	Ex 24:3	4941
Ye shall do my *j*, and keep mine	Lev 18:4	4941
keep my statutes, and my *j*	Lev 18:5	4941
keep my statutes and my *j*, and	Lev 18:26	4941
all my statutes, and all my *j*	Lev 19:37	4941
keep all my statutes, and all my *j*	Lev 20:22	4941
do my statutes, and keep my *j*	Lev 25:18	4941
or if your soul abhor my *j*	Lev 26:15	4941
even because they despised my *j*	Lev 26:43	4941
These are the statutes and *j*	Lev 26:46	4941
gods also the LORD executed *j*	Num 33:4	8201
of blood according to these *j*	Num 35:24	4941
are the commandments and the *j*	Num 36:13	4941
unto the statutes and unto the *j*	Deut 4:1	4941
I have taught you statutes and *j*	Deut 4:5	4941
j so righteous as all this law,	Deut 4:8	4941
time to teach you statutes and *j*	Deut 4:14	4941
and the statutes, and the *j*	Deut 4:45	4941
j which I speak in your ears this	Deut 5:1	4941
and the statutes, and the *j*	Deut 5:31	4941
the statutes, and the *j*, which	Deut 6:1	4941
and the statutes, and the *j*	Deut 6:20	4941
and the statutes, and the *j*	Deut 7:11	4941
to pass, if ye hearken to these *j*	Deut 7:12	4941
his commandments, and his *j*	Deut 8:11	4941
charge, and his statutes, and his *j*	Deut 11:1	4941
j which I set before you this day	Deut 11:32	4941
These are the statutes and *j*	Deut 12:1	4941
thee to do these statutes and *j*	Deut 26:16	4941
and his commandments, and his *j*	Deut 26:17	4941
and his statutes and his *j*, that	Deut 30:16	4941
They shall teach Jacob thy *j*	Deut 33:10	4941
of the LORD, and his *j* with Israel	Deut 33:21	4941
For all his *j* were before me	2Sa 22:23	4941
and his commandments, and his *j*	1Kin 2:3	4941
in my statutes, and execute my *j*	1Kin 6:12	4941
and his statutes, and his *j*	1Kin 8:58	4941
and wilt keep my statutes and my *j*	1Kin 9:4	4941
and to keep my statutes and my *j*	1Kin 11:33	4941
wonders, and the *j* of his mouth	1Chr 16:12	4941
his *j* are in all the earth	1Chr 16:14	4941
j which the LORD charged Moses	1Chr 22:13	4941
to do my commandments and my *j*	1Chr 28:7	4941
shalt observe my statutes and my *j*	2Chr 7:17	4941
law and commandment, statutes and *j*	2Chr 19:10	4941
to teach in Israel statutes and *j*	Ezr 7:10	4941
nor the statutes, nor the *j*	Neh 1:7	4941
heaven, and gavest them right *j*	Neh 9:13	4941
but sinned against thy *j*	Neh 9:29	4941
of the LORD our Lord, and his *j*	Neh 10:29	4941
thy *j* are far above out of his	Ps 10:5	4941
For all his *j* were before me, and	Ps 18:22	4941
the *j* of the LORD are true and	Ps 19:9	4941
thy *j* are a great deep	Ps 36:6	4941
Judah be glad, because of thy *j*	Ps 48:11	4941
Give the king thy *j*, O God, and	Ps 72:1	4941
my law, and walk not in my *j*	Ps 89:30	4941
Judah rejoiced because of thy *j*	Ps 97:8	4941
wonders, and the *j* of his mouth	Ps 105:5	4941
his *j* are in all the earth	Ps 105:7	4941
have learned thy righteous *j*	Ps 119:7	4941
I declared all the *j* of thy mouth	Ps 119:13	4941
it hath unto thy *j* at all times	Ps 119:20	4941
thy *j* have I laid before me	Ps 119:30	4941
for thy *j* are good	Ps 119:39	4941
for I have hoped in thy *j*	Ps 119:43	4941
I remembered thy *j* of old	Ps 119:52	4941
thee because of thy righteous *j*	Ps 119:62	4941
that thy *j* are right, and that	Ps 119:75	4941
I have not departed from thy *j*	Ps 119:102	4941
that I will keep thy righteous *j*	Ps 119:106	4941
mouth, O LORD, and teach me thy *j*	Ps 119:108	4941
and I am afraid of thy *j*	Ps 119:120	4941
O LORD, and upright are thy *j*	Ps 119:137	4941
quicken me according to thy *j*	Ps 119:156	4941
thy righteous *j* endureth for ever	Ps 119:160	4941
thee because of thy righteous *j*	Ps 119:164	4941
and let thy *j* help me	Ps 119:175	4941
his statutes and his *j* unto Israel	Ps 147:19	4941
and as for his *j*, they have not	Ps 147:20	4941
J are prepared for scorners, and	Prov 19:29	8201
Yea, in the way of thy *j*, O LORD,	Is 26:8	4941
for when thy *j* are in the earth,	Is 26:9	4941
I will utter my *j* against them	Jer 1:16	4941
let me talk with thee of thy *j*	Jer 12:1	4941
she hath changed my *j* into	Eze 5:6	4941
for they have refused my *j*	Eze 5:6	4941
statutes, neither have kept my *j*	Eze 5:7	4941
have done according to the *j* of	Eze 5:7	4941
will execute *j* in the midst of	Eze 5:8	4941
and I will execute *j* in thee	Eze 5:10	8201
shall execute *j* in thee in anger	Eze 5:15	8201
and will execute *j* among you	Eze 11:9	8201
statutes, neither executed my *j*	Eze 11:12	4941
my four sore *j* upon Jerusalem	Eze 14:21	8201
execute *j* upon thee in the sight	Eze 16:41	8201
in my statutes, and hath kept my *j*	Eze 18:9	4941
nor increase, hath executed my *j*	Eze 18:17	4941
my statutes, and shewed them my *j*	Eze 20:11	4941
statutes, and they despised my *j*	Eze 20:13	4941
Because they despised my *j*	Eze 20:16	4941
fathers, neither observe their *j*	Eze 20:18	4941
walk in my statutes, and keep my *j*	Eze 20:19	4941
neither kept my *j* to do them	Eze 20:21	4941
they had not executed my *j*	Eze 20:24	4941
j whereby they should not live	Eze 20:25	4941
judge thee according to their *j*	Eze 23:24	4941
And I will execute *j* upon Moab	Eze 25:11	8201

I shall have executed *j* in her	Eze 28:22	8201
when I have executed *j* upon all	Eze 28:26	8201
in Zoan, and will execute *j* in No	Eze 30:14	8201
Tl.us will I execute *j* in Egypt	Eze 30:19	8201
statutes, and ye shall keep my *j*	Eze 36:27	4941
they shall also walk in my *j*	Eze 37:24	4941
shall judge it according to my *j*	Eze 44:24	4941
from thy precepts and from thy *j*	Dan 9:5	4941
thy *j* are as the light that goeth	Hos 6:5	4941
The LORD hath taken away thy *j*	Zeph 3:15	4941
Israel, with the statutes and *j*	Mal 4:4	4941
how unsearchable are his *j*	Rom 11:33	2917
If then ye have *j* of things	1Cor 6:4	2922
for thy *j* are made manifest	Rev 15:4	1345
true and righteous are thy *j*	Rev 16:7	2920
For true and righteous are his *j*	Rev 19:2	2920

JUDITH *(ju'-dith) A wife of Esau.*

wife *J* the daughter of Beeri from	Gen 26:34	3067

JUICE

wine of the *j* of my pomegranate	Song 8:2	6071

JULIA *(ju'-le-ah) A Christian acquaintance of Paul.*

Salute Philologus, and *J*, Nereus,	Rom 16:15	2456

JULIUS *(ju'-le-us) A Roman centurion.*

other prisoners unto one named *J*	Acts 27:1	2457
J courteously entreated Paul, and	Acts 27:3	2457

JUMPING

horses, and of the *j* chariots	Nah 3:2	7540

JUNIA *(ju'-ne-ah) A Christian acquaintance of Paul.*

Salute Andronicus and *J*, my	Rom 16:7	2458

JUNIPER

came and sat down under a *j* tree	1Kin 19:4	7574
as he lay and slept under a *j* tree	1Kin 19:5	7574
bushes, and *j* roots for their meat	Job 30:4	7574
of the mighty, with coals of *j*	Ps 120:4	7574

JUPITER *(ju'-pit-ur) Chief god of the Romans.*

And they called Barnabas, *J*	Acts 14:12	2203
Then the priest of *J*, which was	Acts 14:13	2203
the image which fell down from *J*	Acts 19:35	1356

JURISDICTION

that he belonged unto Herod's *j*	Lk 23:7	1849

JUSHAB-HESED *(ju'-shab-he'-sed) A son of Zerubbabel.*

and Berechiah, and Hasadiah, *J*	1Chr 3:20	3142

JUST

Noah was a *j* man and perfect in	Gen 6:9	6662
J balances, *j* weights	Lev 19:36	6664
a *j* ephah, and a *j* hin, shall	Lev 19:36	6664
judge the people with *j* judgment	Deut 16:18	6664
is altogether *j* shalt thou follow	Deut 16:20	6664
j weight, a perfect and	Deut 25:15	6664
j measure shalt thou have	Deut 25:15	6664
of truth and without iniquity, *j*	Deut 32:4	6662
He that ruleth over men must be *j*	2Sa 23:3	6662
Howbeit thou art *j* in all that is	Neh 9:33	6662
mortal man be more *j* than God	Job 4:17	6663
but how should man be *j* with God	Job 9:2	6663
the *j* upright man is laughed to	Job 12:4	6662
but the *j* shall put it on, and the	Job 27:17	6662
Behold, in this thou art not *j*	Job 33:12	6663
thou condemn him that is most *j*	Job 34:17	6662
but establish the *j*	Ps 7:9	6662
The wicked plotteth against the *j*	Ps 37:12	6662
blesseth the habitation of the *j*	Prov 3:33	6662
But the path of the *j* is as the	Prov 4:18	6662
teach a *j* man, and he will	Prov 9:9	6662
are upon the head of the *j*	Prov 10:6	6662
The memory of the *j* is blessed	Prov 10:7	6662
The tongue of the *j* is as choice	Prov 10:20	6662
The mouth of the *j* bringeth forth	Prov 10:31	6662
but a *j* weight is his delight	Prov 11:1	8003
shall the *j* be delivered	Prov 11:9	6662
but the *j* shall come out of	Prov 12:13	6662
shall no evil happen to the *j*	Prov 12:21	6662
the sinner is laid up for the *j*	Prov 13:22	6662
A *j* weight and balance are the	Prov 16:11	4941
and he that condemneth the *j*	Prov 17:15	6662
Also to punish the *j* is not good	Prov 17:26	6662
first in his own cause seemeth *j*	Prov 18:17	6662
The *j* man walketh in his	Prov 20:7	6662
It is joy to the *j* to do judgment	Prov 21:15	6662
For a *j* man falleth seven times,	Prov 24:16	6662
but the *j* seek his soul	Prov 29:10	3477
man is an abomination to the *j*	Prov 29:27	6662
there is a *j* man that perisheth	Eccl 7:15	6662
there is not a *j* man upon earth	Eccl 7:20	6662

that there be *j* men, unto whom it	Eccl 8:14	6662
The way of the *j* is uprightness	Is 26:7	6662
dost weigh the path of the *j*	Is 26:7	6662
turn aside the *j* for a thing of	Is 29:21	6662
a *j* God and a Saviour	Is 45:21	6662
of the *j* in the midst of her	Lam 4:13	6662
But if a man be *j*, and do that	Eze 18:5	6662
he is *j*, he shall surely live,	Eze 18:9	6662
Ye shall have *j* balances, and a	Eze 45:10	6664
a *j* ephah, and a *j* bath	Eze 45:10	6664
and the *j* shall walk in them	Hos 14:9	6662
they afflict the *j*, they take a	Amos 5:12	6662
but the *j* shall live by his faith	Hab 2:4	6662
The *j* LORD is in the midst	Zeph 3:5	6662
he is *j*, and having salvation.	Zec 9:9	6662
Joseph her husband, being a *j* man	Mt 1:19	1342
good, and sendeth rain on the *j*	Mt 5:45	1342
sever the wicked from among the *j*	Mt 13:49	1342
nothing to do with that *j* man	Mt 27:19	1342
of the blood of this *j* person	Mt 27:24	1342
John, knowing that he was a *j* man	Mk 6:20	1342
to the wisdom of the *j*	Lk 1:17	1342
and the same man was *j* and devout,	Lk 2:25	1342
at the resurrection of the *j*	Lk 14:14	1342
nine *j* persons, which need no	Lk 15:7	1342
should feign themselves *j* men	Lk 20:20	1342
and he was a good man, and a *j*	Lk 23:50	1342
and my judgment is *j*	Jn 5:30	1342
ye denied the Holy One and the *J*	Acts 3:14	1342
before of the coming of the *J* One	Acts 7:52	1342
a *j* man, and one that feareth God,	Acts 10:22	1342
know his will, and see that *J* One	Acts 22:14	1342
of the dead, both of the *j*	Acts 24:15	1342
The *j* shall live by faith	Rom 1:17	1342
of the law are *j* before God	Rom 2:13	1342
whose damnation is *j*	Rom 3:8	1738
that he might be *j*, and the	Rom 3:26	1342
and the commandment holy, and *j*	Rom 7:12	1342
The *j* shall live by faith	Gal 3:11	1342
honest, whatsoever things are *j*	Phil 4:8	1342
your servants that which is *j*	Col 4:1	1342
a lover of good men, sober, *j*	Titus 1:8	1342
received a *j* recompence of reward	Heb 2:2	1738
Now the *j* shall live by faith	Heb 10:38	1342
the spirits of *j* men made perfect	Heb 12:23	1342
Ye have condemned and killed the *j*	Jas 5:6	1342
the *j* for the unjust, that he	1Pet 3:18	1342
And delivered *j* Lot, vexed with	2Pet 2:7	1342
j to forgive us our sins, and to	1Jn 1:9	1342
j and true are thy ways, thou King	Rev 15:3	1342

JUSTICE

keep the way of the LORD, to do *j*	Gen 18:19	6666
he executed the *j* of the LORD	Deut 33:21	6666
judgment and *j* unto all his people	2Sa 8:15	6666
come unto me, and I would do him *j*	2Sa 15:4	6663
he thee king, to do judgment and *j*	1Kin 10:9	6666
and *j* among all his people	1Chr 18:14	6666
over them, to do judgment and *j*	2Chr 9:8	6666
or doth the Almighty pervert *j*	Job 8:3	6664
judgment and *j* take hold on thee	Job 36:17	4941
and in judgment, and in plenty of *j*	Job 37:23	6666
do *j* to the afflicted and needy	Ps 82:3	6663
J and judgment are the habitation	Ps 89:14	6666
I have done judgment and *j*	Ps 119:121	6664
the instruction of wisdom, *j*	Prov 1:3	6664
kings reign, and princes decree *j*	Prov 8:15	6664
To do *j* and judgment is more	Prov 21:3	6666
j in a province, marvel not at	Eccl 5:8	6664
with *j* from henceforth even for	Is 9:7	6666
LORD, Keep ye judgment, and do *j*	Is 56:1	6666
ask of me the ordinances of *j*	Is 58:2	6664
None calleth for *j*, nor any	Is 59:4	6666
us, neither doth *j* overtake us	Is 59:9	6666
backward, and *j* standeth afar off	Is 59:14	6666
eat and drink, and do judgment and *j*	Jer 22:15	6666
judgment and *j* in the earth	Jer 23:5	6666
bless thee, O habitation of *j*	Jer 31:23	6664
the LORD, the habitation of *j*	Jer 50:7	6664
spoil, and execute judgment and *j*	Eze 45:9	6666

JUSTIFICATION

and was raised again for our *j*	Rom 4:25	1347
gift is of many offences unto *j*	Rom 5:16	1345
came upon all men unto *j* of life	Rom 5:18	1347

JUSTIFIED

and should a man full of talk be *j*	Job 11:2	6663
I know that I shall be *j*	Job 13:18	6663
How then can man be *j* with God	Job 25:4	6663

J

because he *j* himself rather than	Job 32:2	6663
mightest be *j* when thou speakest	Ps 51:4	6663
sight shall no man living be *j*	Ps 143:2	6663
witnesses, that they may be *j*	Is 43:9	6663
thou, that thou mayest be *j*	Is 43:26	6663
shall all the seed of Israel be *j*	Is 45:25	6663
The backsliding Israel hath *j*	Jer 3:11	6663
hast *j* thy sisters in a little	Eze 16:51	6663
in that thou hast *j* thy sisters	Eze 16:52	6663
But wisdom is *j* of her children	Mt 11:19	1344
For by thy words thou shalt be *j*	Mt 12:37	1344
j God, being baptized with the	Lk 7:29	1344
But wisdom is *j* of all her	Lk 7:35	1344
his house *j* rather than the other	Lk 18:14	1344
believe are *j* from all things	Acts 13:39	1344
not be *j* by the law of Moses	Acts 13:39	1344
the doers of the law shall be *j*	Rom 2:13	1344
thou mightest be *j* in thy sayings	Rom 3:4	1344
shall no flesh be *j* in his sight	Rom 3:20	1344
Being *j* freely by his grace	Rom 3:24	1344
we conclude that a man is *j* by	Rom 3:28	1344
For if Abraham were *j* by works	Rom 4:2	1344
Therefore being *j* by faith	Rom 5:1	1344
being now *j* by his blood, we	Rom 5:9	1344
and whom he called, them he also *j*	Rom 8:30	1344
and whom he *j*, them he also	Rom 8:30	1344
yet am I not hereby *j*	1Cor 4:4	1344
but ye are *j* in the name of the	1Cor 6:11	1344
is not *j* by the works of the law	Gal 2:16	1344
that we might be *j* by the faith	Gal 2:16	1344
of the law shall no flesh be *j*	Gal 2:16	1344
while we seek to be *j* by Christ	Gal 2:17	1344
But that no man is *j* by the law	Gal 3:11	1344
that we might be *j* by faith	Gal 3:24	1344
whosoever of you are *j* by the law	Gal 5:4	1344
j in the Spirit, seen of angels,	1Ti 3:16	1344
That being *j* by his grace, we	Titus 3:7	1344
not Abraham our father *j* by works	Jas 2:21	1344
then how that by works a man is *j*	Jas 2:24	1344
not Rahab the harlot *j* by works	Jas 2:25	1344

JUSTIFIER

the *j* of him which believeth in	Rom 3:26	1344

JUSTIFIETH

He that *j* the wicked, and he that	Prov 17:15	6663
He is near that *j* me	Is 50:8	6663
on him that *j* the ungodly	Rom 4:5	1344
It is God that *j*	Rom 8:33	1344

JUSTIFY

for I will not *j* the wicked	Ex 23:7	6663
then they shall *j* the righteous	Deut 25:1	6663
If I *j* myself, mine own mouth	Job 9:20	6663
God forbid that I should *j* you	Job 27:5	6663
speak, for I desire to *j* thee	Job 33:32	6663
Which *j* the wicked for reward, and	Is 5:23	6663
shall my righteous servant *j* many	Is 53:11	6663
But he, willing to *j* himself	Lk 10:29	1344
Ye are they which *j* yourselves	Lk 16:15	1344
which shall *j* the circumcision by	Rom 3:30	1344
would *j* the heathen through faith	Gal 3:8	1344

JUSTIFYING

j the righteous, to give him	1Kin 8:32	6663
by *j* the righteous, by giving him	2Chr 6:23	6663

JUSTLE

they shall *j* one against another	Nah 2:4	8264

JUSTLY

LORD require of thee, but to do *j*	Mic 6:8	4941
And we indeed *j*; for we receive	Lk 23:41	1346
and God also, how holily and *j*	1Th 2:10	1346

JUSTUS (*jus'-tus*) See BARSABAS, JESUS.
 1. *Surname for Barsabas.*

Barsabas, who was surnamed *J*	Acts 1:23	2459

 2. *A Corinthian Christian.*

a certain man's house, named *J*	Acts 18:7	2459

 3. *A Christian acquaintance of Paul.*

And Jesus, which is called *J*	Col 4:11	2459

JUTTAH (*jut'-tah*) *A city in Judah.*

Maon, Carmel, and Ziph, and *J*	Josh 15:55	3194
and *J* with her suburbs, and	Josh 21:16	3194

K

KABZEEL (*kab'-ze-el*) See JEKABZEEL. *A city in Judah.*

coast of Edom southward were *K*	Josh 15:21	6909
the son of a valiant man, of *K*	2Sa 23:20	6909
the son of a valiant man of *K*	1Chr 11:22	6909

KADESH (*ka'-desh*) See EN-MISHPAT, KADESH-BARNEA,
 KEDESH. *A place in the wilderness, south of Judah.*

and came to Enmishpat, which is *K*	Gen 14:7	6946
behold, it is between *K* and Bered	Gen 16:14	6946
country, and dwelled between *K*	Gen 20:1	6946
the wilderness of Paran, to *K*	Num 13:26	6946
and the people abode in *K*	Num 20:1	6946
from *K* unto the king of Edom	Num 20:14	6946
and, behold, we are in *K*, a city	Num 20:16	6946
congregation, journeyed from *K*	Num 20:22	6946
in *K* in the wilderness of Zin	Num 27:14	6946
the wilderness of Zin, which is *K*	Num 33:36	6946
And they removed from *K*, and	Num 33:37	6946
So ye abode in *K* many days	Deut 1:46	6946
unto the Red sea, and came to *K*	Judg 11:16	6946
and Israel abode in *K*	Judg 11:17	6946
LORD shaketh the wilderness of *K*	Ps 29:8	6946
even to the waters of strife in *K*	Eze 47:19	6946
unto the waters of strife in *K*	Eze 48:28	6946

KADESH-BARNEA (*ka'-desh-bar'-ne-ah*) See KADESH.
 Same as Kadesh.

sent them from *K* to see the land	Num 32:8	6947
shall be from the south to *K*	Num 34:4	6947
by the way of mount Seir unto *K*	Deut 1:2	6947
and we came to *K*	Deut 1:19	6947
the space in which we came from *K*	Deut 2:14	6947
when the LORD sent you from *K*	Deut 9:23	6947
smote them from *K* even unto Gaza	Josh 10:41	6947
of God concerning me and thee in *K*	Josh 14:6	6947
me from *K* to espy out the land	Josh 14:7	6947
up on the south side unto *K*	Josh 15:3	6947

KADMIEL (*kad'-me-el*)
 1. *An exile.*

the children of Jeshua and *K*	Ezr 2:40	6934
the children of Jeshua, of *K*	Neh 7:43	6934

 2. *A rebuilder of the Temple.*

with his sons and his brethren, *K*	Ezr 3:9	6934

 3. *A Levite with Nehemiah.*

the Levites, Jeshua, and Bani, *K*	Neh 9:4	6934
Then the Levites, Jeshua, and *K*	Neh 9:5	6934
Binnui of the sons of Henadad, *K*	Neh 10:9	6934
Jeshua, Binnui, *K*, Sherebiah,	Neh 12:8	6934
Sherebiah, and Jeshua the son of *K*	Neh 12:24	6934

KADMONITES (*kad'-mo-nites*) *A Phoenician tribe.*

and the Kenizzites, and the *K*	Gen 15:19	6935

KAIN See CAIN.

KAIWAN See CHIUN.

KALLAI (*kal'-la-i*) *A priest.*

Of Sallai, *K*; of Amok	Neh 12:20	7040

KAMON See CAMON.

KANAH (*ka'-nah*)
 1. *A brook between Ephraim and Manasseh.*

Tappuah westward unto the river *K*	Josh 16:8	7071
coast descended unto the river *K*	Josh 17:9	7071

 2. *A city in Asher.*

and Rehob, and Hammon, and *K*	Josh 19:28	7071

KAREAH (*ka'-re-ah*) See CAREAH. *A captain of the
 Jews.*

Johanan and Jonathan the sons of *K*	Jer 40:8	7143
Moreover Johanan the son of *K*	Jer 40:13	7143
Then Johanan the son of *K* spake	Jer 40:15	7143
said unto Johanan the son of *K*	Jer 40:16	7143
But when Johanan the son of *K*	Jer 41:11	7143
Ishmael saw Johanan the son of *K*	Jer 41:13	7143
and went unto Johanan the son of *K*	Jer 41:14	7143
Then took Johanan the son of *K*	Jer 41:16	7143
forces, and Johanan the son of *K*	Jer 42:1	7143
called he Johanan the son of *K*	Jer 42:8	7143
Hoshaiah, and Johanan the son of *K*	Jer 43:2	7143
So Johanan the son of *K*, and all	Jer 43:4	7143
But Johanan the son of *K*, and all	Jer 43:5	7143

KARKA See KARKAA.

KARKAA (*kar'-ka-ah*) *A city in Judah.*

Adar, and fetched a compass to *K*	Josh 15:3	7173

KARKOR (*kar'-kor*) *A Gadite city.*

Now Zebah and Zalmunna were in *K*	Judg 8:10	7174

KARNAIM (kar'-na-im) See ASHTEROTH. *A city in Og.*
smote the Rephaims in Ashteroth *K* ......Gen 14:5

KARTAH (kar'-tah) See KATTATH. *A Levitical city in Zebulun.*
suburbs, and *K* with her suburbs, ...Josh 21:34   7177

KARTAN (kar'-tan) See KIRJATHAIM. *A Levitical city in Naphtali.*
suburbs, and *K* with her suburbs ....Josh 21:32   7178

KATTATH (kat'-tath) See KARTAH, KITRON. *A city in Zebulun.*
And *K*, and Nahallal, and Shimron, ...Josh 19:15   7005

KEBAR See CHEBAR.

KEDAR (ke'-dar)
  1. A son of Ishmael.
and *K*, and Adbeel, and Mibsam, ...Gen 25:13   6938
then *K*, and Adbeel, and Mibsam, ...1Chr 1:29   6938
  2. The tribe.
that I dwell in the tents of *K* ....Ps 120:5   6938
of Jerusalem, as the tents of *K* ....Song 1:5   6938
and all the glory of *K* shall fail ....Is 21:16   6938
mighty men of the children of *K* ....Is 21:17   6938
the villages that *K* doth inhabit.............Is 42:11   6938
All the flocks of *K* shall be ....Is 60:7   6938
and send unto *K*, and consider..........Jer 2:10   6938
Concerning *K*, and concerning the ....Jer 49:28   6938
Arise ye, go up to *K*, and spoil..............Jer 49:28   6938
Arabia, and all the princes of *K* ....Eze 27:21   6938

KEDEMAH (ked'-e-mah) *A son of Ishmael.*
and Tema, Jetur, Naphish, and *K*...........Gen 25:15   6929
Jetur, Naphish, and *K* 1Chr 1:31   6929

KEDEMOTH (ked'-e-moth)
  1. A wilderness in Reuben.
out of the wilderness of *K* unto ....Deut 2:26   6932
  2. A Levitical city in Reuben.
And Jahaza, and *K*, and Mephaath.......Josh 13:18   6932
K with her suburbs, and Mephaath........Josh 21:37   6932
K also with her suburbs, and 1Chr 6:79   6932

KEDESH (ke'-desh) See KADESH, KEDESH-NAPHTALI, KISHION.
  1. A Canaanite city.
The king of *K*, one ....Josh 12:22   6943
And *K*, and Edrei, and En-hazor, ...Josh 19:37   6943
  2. A city of refuge in Naphtali.
they appointed *K* in Galilee in ....Josh 20:7   6943
K in Galilee with her suburbs, to...........Josh 21:32   6943
arose, and went with Barak to *K* ....Judg 4:9   6943
called Zebulun and Naphtali to *K* ....Judg 4:10   6943
plain of Zaanaim, which is by *K*.............Judg 4:11   6943
and Janoah, and *K*, and Hazor, and......2Kin 15:29   6943
K in Galilee with her suburbs, and......1Chr 6:76   6943
  3. A Levitical city in Issachar.
K with her suburbs, Daberath with........1Chr 6:72   6943
  4. A city in Judah.
And *K*, and Hazor, and Ithnan, ...Josh 15:23   6943

KEDESH-NAPHTALI (ke'-desh-naf-ta-li) *Same as Kedesh 2.*
Barak the son of Abinoam out of *K* Judg 4:6   6943,5321

KEDOLAOMER See CHEDORLAOMER.

KEEP
of Eden to dress it and to *k* it.................Gen 2:15   8104
to *k* the way of the tree of life ....Gen 3:24   8104
to *k* them alive with thee.........................Gen 6:19   8104
come unto thee, to *k* them alive.............Gen 6:20   8104
to *k* seed alive upon the face of ....Gen 7:3
Abraham, Thou shalt *k* my covenant ......Gen 17:9   8104
is my covenant, which ye shall *k* ....Gen 17:10   8104
they shall *k* the way of the LORD,..........Gen 18:19   8104
will *k* thee in all places whither ....Gen 28:15   8104
will *k* me in this way that I go, ...Gen 28:20   8104
I will again feed and *k* thy flock ....Gen 30:31   8104
k that thou hast unto thyself...................Gen 33:9   1961
let them *k* food in the cities....................Gen 41:35   8104
whom the Egyptians *k* in bondage ....Ex 6:5
ye shall *k* it up until the ....Ex 12:6   4931
ye shall *k* it a feast to the LORD ....Ex 12:14   2287
ye shall *k* it a feast by an ....Ex 12:14   2287
that ye shall *k* this service ....Ex 12:25   8104
congregation of Israel shall *k* it ....Ex 12:47   6213
will *k* the passover to the LORD,.............Ex 12:48   6213
and then let him come near and *k* it ......Ex 12:48   6213
that thou shalt *k* this service in ....Ex 13:5   5647
Thou shalt therefore *k* this ....Ex 13:10   8104
k all his statutes, I will put ....Ex 15:26   8104
refuse ye to *k* my commandments ....Ex 16:28   8104
k my covenant, then ye shall be a ....Ex 19:5   8104

love me, and *k* my commandments ....Ex 20:6   8104
the sabbath day, to *k* it holy ....Ex 20:8   6942
his neighbour money or stuff to *k*..........Ex 22:7   8104
or a sheep, or any beast, to *k*.................Ex 22:10   8104
K thee far from a false matter ....Ex 23:7   7368
Three times thou shalt *k* a feast ....Ex 23:14   2287
Thou shalt *k* the feast of.........................Ex 23:15   8104
to *k* thee in the way, and to bring ....Ex 23:20   8104
Verily my sabbaths ye shall *k* ....Ex 31:13   8104
Ye shall *k* the sabbath therefore ....Ex 31:14   8104
of Israel shall *k* the sabbath ....Ex 31:16   8104
of unleavened bread shalt thou *k* ....Ex 34:18   8104
that which was delivered him to *k* ....Lev 6:2
that which was delivered him to *k* ....Lev 6:4   6485
k the charge of the LORD, that ye.........Lev 8:35   8104
k mine ordinances, to walk ....Lev 18:4   8104
Ye shall therefore *k* my statutes ....Lev 18:5   8104
Ye shall therefore *k* my statutes ....Lev 18:26   8104
shall ye *k* mine ordinance ....Lev 18:30   8104
and his father, and *k* my sabbaths........Lev 19:3   8104
Ye shall *k* my statutes ....Lev 19:19   8104
Ye shall *k* my sabbaths, and ....Lev 19:30   8104
ye shall *k* my statutes, and do ....Lev 20:8   8104
shall therefore *k* all my statutes ....Lev 20:22   8104
shall therefore *k* mine ordinance ....Lev 22:9   8104
shall ye *k* my commandments ....Lev 22:31   8104
ye shall *k* a feast unto the LORD ....Lev 23:39   2287
ye shall *k* it a feast unto the..................Lev 23:41   2287
then shall the land *k* a sabbath ....Lev 25:2
k my judgments, and do them ....Lev 25:18   8104
Ye shall *k* my sabbaths, and ....Lev 26:2   8104
k my commandments, and do them ......Lev 26:3   8104
the Levites shall *k* the charge of............Num 1:53   8104
And they shall *k* his charge ....Num 3:7   8104
they shall *k* all the instruments ....Num 3:8   8104
k the charge of the sanctuary ....Num 3:32   8104
The LORD bless thee, and *k* thee ....Num 6:24   8104
to *k* the charge, and shall do no ....Num 8:26   8104
k the passover at his appointed.............Num 9:2   6213
ye shall *k* it in his appointed.................Num 9:3   6213
ceremonies thereof, shall ye *k* it ....Num 9:3   6213
that they should *k* the passover ....Num 9:4   6213
that they could not *k* the ....Num 9:6   6213
yet he shall *k* the passover unto............Num 9:10   6213
month at even they shall *k* it ....Num 9:11   6213
of the passover they shall *k* it ....Num 9:12   6213
and forbeareth to *k* the passover...........Num 9:13   6213
will *k* the passover unto the LORD ....Num 9:14   6213
And they shall *k* thy charge...................Num 18:3   8104
k the charge of the tabernacle of...........Num 18:4   8104
ye shall *k* the charge of the...................Num 18:5   8104
thy sons with them shall *k* your.............Num 18:7   8104
ye shall *k* a feast unto the LORD ....Num 29:12   2287
with him, *k* alive for yourselves.............Num 31:18
which *k* the charge of the ....Num 31:30   8104
k himself to the inheritance of...............Num 36:7   1692
k himself to his own inheritance ....Num 36:9   1692
that ye may *k* the commandments of .....Deut 4:2   8104
K therefore and do them.........................Deut 4:6   8104
k thy soul diligently, lest thou ....Deut 4:9   8104
Thou shalt *k* therefore his.......................Deut 4:40   8104
day, that ye may learn them, and *k*........Deut 5:1   8104
that love me and *k* my commandments .Deut 5:10   8104
K the sabbath day to sanctify it,............Deut 5:12   8104
thee to *k* the sabbath day.......................Deut 5:15   6213
k all my commandments always,............Deut 5:29   8104
to *k* all his statutes and his ....Deut 6:2   8104
Ye shall diligently *k* the ....Deut 6:17   8104
because he would *k* the oath which........Deut 7:8   8104
k his commandments to a thousand ......Deut 7:9   8104
therefore *k* the commandments ....Deut 7:11   8104
hearken to these judgments, and *k*........Deut 7:12   8104
shall *k* unto thee the covenant ....Deut 7:12   8104
thou wouldest *k* his commandments ......Deut 8:2   8104
Therefore thou shalt *k* the ....Deut 8:6   8104
To *k* the commandments of the LORD ......Deut 10:13   8104
k his charge, and his statutes, and.......Deut 11:1   8104
Therefore shall ye *k* all the ....Deut 11:8   8104
For if ye shall diligently *k* all.................Deut 11:22   8104
k his commandments, and obey his ......Deut 13:4   8104
to *k* all his commandments which I ....Deut 13:18   8104
k the passover unto the LORD thy ....Deut 16:1   6213
thou shalt *k* the feast of weeks ....Deut 16:10   6213
Seven days shalt thou *k* a solemn ....Deut 16:15   2287
to *k* all the words of this law and ....Deut 17:19   8104
If thou shalt *k* all these ....Deut 19:9   8104
then *k* thee from every wicked................Deut 23:9   8104
gone out of thy lips thou shalt *k* ....Deut 23:23   8104
thou shalt therefore *k* and do them ....Deut 26:16   8104
to *k* his statutes, and his ....Deut 26:17   8104
that thou shouldest *k* all his ....Deut 26:18   8104

K all the commandments which I	Deut 27:1	8104
if thou shalt *k* the commandments	Deut 28:9	8104
to *k* his commandments and his	Deut 28:45	8104
K therefore the words of this	Deut 29:9	8104
to *k* his commandments and his	Deut 30:10	8104
to *k* his commandments and his	Deut 30:16	8104
in any wise *k* yourselves from the	Josh 6:18	8104
and set men by it for to *k* them	Josh 10:18	8104
to *k* his commandments, and to	Josh 22:5	8104
ye therefore very courageous to *k*	Josh 23:6	8104
whether they will *k* the way of	Judg 2:22	8104
as their fathers did *k* it	Judg 2:22	8104
who said, *K* silence	Judg 3:19	
Thou shalt *k* fast by my young men	Ruth 2:21	1692
He will *k* the feet of his saints,	1Sa 2:9	8104
his son to *k* the ark of the Lord	1Sa 7:1	8104
and with one full line to *k* alive	2Sa 8:2	
were concubines, to *k* the house	2Sa 15:16	8104
which he hath left to *k* the house	2Sa 16:21	8104
I have no son to *k* my name in	2Sa 18:18	
whom he had left to *k* the house	2Sa 20:3	8104
k the charge of the Lord thy God,	1Kin 2:3	8104
to *k* his statutes, and his	1Kin 2:3	8104
my ways, to *k* my statutes and my	1Kin 3:14	8104
k all my commandments to walk in	1Kin 6:12	8104
k with my servant David my	1Kin 8:25	8104
to *k* his commandments, and his	1Kin 8:58	8104
to *k* his commandments, as at this	1Kin 8:61	8104
thee, and wilt *k* my statutes and my	1Kin 9:4	8104
will not *k* my commandments and my	1Kin 9:6	8104
to *k* my statutes and my judgments,	1Kin 11:33	
my sight, to *k* my statutes and my	1Kin 11:38	8104
man unto me, and said, *K* this man	1Kin 20:39	8104
so shall ye *k* the watch of the	2Kin 11:6	8104
even they shall *k* the watch of	2Kin 11:7	8104
k my commandments and my statutes,	2Kin 17:13	8104
to *k* his commandments and his	2Kin 23:3	8104
K the passover unto the Lord your	2Kin 23:21	6213
that thou wouldest *k* me from evil	1Chr 4:10	6213
thousand, which could *k* rank	1Chr 12:33	5737
men of war, that could *k* rank	1Chr 12:38	5737
that thou mayest *k* the law of the	1Chr 22:12	8104
that they should *k* the charge of	1Chr 23:32	8104
and in the audience of our God, *k*	1Chr 28:8	8104
fathers, *k* this for ever in the	1Chr 29:18	8104
to *k* thy commandments, thy	1Chr 29:19	8104
k with thy servant David my	2Chr 6:16	8104
for we *k* the charge of the Lord	2Chr 13:11	8104
no power to *k* still the kingdom	2Chr 22:9	6113
shall *k* the watch of the Lord	2Chr 23:6	8104
now ye purpose to *k* under the	2Chr 28:10	3533
to *k* the passover unto the Lord	2Chr 30:1	6213
to *k* the passover in the second	2Chr 30:2	6213
they could not *k* it at that time	2Chr 30:3	6213
that they should come to *k* the	2Chr 30:5	6213
at Jerusalem much people to *k* the	2Chr 30:13	6213
counsel to *k* other seven days	2Chr 30:23	6213
to *k* his commandments, and his	2Chr 34:31	8104
to *k* the passover, and to offer	2Chr 35:16	6213
did all the kings of Israel *k*	2Chr 35:18	6213
k them, until ye weigh them	Ezr 8:29	8104
k my commandments, and do them	Neh 1:9	8104
to *k* the dedication with gladness	Neh 12:27	6213
k the gates, to sanctify the	Neh 13:22	8104
neither will they *k* the king's laws	Est 3:8	6213
that they should *k* the fourteenth	Est 9:21	6213
that they would *k* these two days	Est 9:27	6213
that thou wouldest *k* me secret	Job 14:13	
but *k* it still within his mouth	Job 20:13	4513
Thou shalt *k* them, O Lord, thou	Ps 12:7	8104
K me as the apple of the eye	Ps 17:8	8104
K back thy servant also from	Ps 19:13	2820
none can *k* alive his own soul	Ps 22:29	
truth unto such as *k* his covenant	Ps 25:10	5341
O *k* my soul, and deliver me	Ps 25:20	8104
thou shalt *k* them secretly in a	Ps 31:20	
to *k* them alive in famine	Ps 33:19	
K thy tongue from evil, and thy	Ps 34:13	5341
k not silence	Ps 35:22	
k his way, and he shall exalt thee	Ps 37:34	8104
I will *k* my mouth with a bridle,	Ps 39:1	8104
will preserve him, and *k* him alive	Ps 41:2	
come, and shall not *k* silence	Ps 50:3	
of God, but *k* his commandments	Ps 78:7	5341
K not thou silence, O God	Ps 83:1	
My mercy will I *k* for him for	Ps 89:28	8104
and *k* not my commandments	Ps 89:31	8104
to *k* thee in all thy ways	Ps 91:11	8104
neither will he *k* his anger for	Ps 103:9	5201
To such as *k* his covenant, and to	Ps 103:18	8104
his statutes, and *k* his laws	Ps 105:45	5341

Blessed are they that *k* judgment	Ps 106:3	8104
the barren woman to *k* house	Ps 113:9	
are they that *k* his testimonies	Ps 119:2	5341
us to *k* thy precepts diligently	Ps 119:4	8104
were directed to *k* thy statutes	Ps 119:5	8104
I will *k* thy statutes	Ps 119:8	8104
that I may live, and *k* thy word	Ps 119:17	8104
I shall *k* it unto the end	Ps 119:33	5341
and I shall *k* thy law	Ps 119:34	5341
So shall I *k* thy law continually	Ps 119:44	8104
said that I would *k* thy words	Ps 119:57	8104
delayed not to *k* thy commandments	Ps 119:60	8104
and of them that *k* thy precepts	Ps 119:63	8104
but I will *k* thy precepts with my	Ps 119:69	5341
so shall I *k* the testimony of thy	Ps 119:88	8104
because I *k* thy precepts	Ps 119:100	5341
evil way, that I might *k* thy word	Ps 119:101	8104
that I will *k* thy righteous	Ps 119:106	8104
for I will *k* the commandments of	Ps 119:115	5341
therefore doth my soul *k* them	Ps 119:129	5341
so will I *k* thy precepts	Ps 119:134	5341
eyes, because they *k* not thy law	Ps 119:136	8104
I will *k* thy statutes	Ps 119:145	8104
I shall *k* thy testimonies	Ps 119:146	8104
except the Lord *k* the city	Ps 127:1	8104
thy children will *k* my covenant	Ps 132:12	8104
K me, O Lord, from the hands of	Ps 140:4	8104
K the door of my lips	Ps 141:3	5341
K me from the snares which they	Ps 141:9	8104
thee, understanding shall *k* thee	Prov 2:11	5341
k the paths of the righteous	Prov 2:20	8104
let thine heart *k* my commandments	Prov 3:1	5341
k sound wisdom and discretion	Prov 3:21	5341
shall *k* thy foot from being taken	Prov 3:26	8104
k my commandments, and live	Prov 4:4	8104
love her, and she shall *k* thee	Prov 4:6	5341
let her not go: *k* her	Prov 4:13	5341
k them in the midst of thine	Prov 4:21	8104
K thy heart with all diligence	Prov 4:23	5341
and that thy lips may *k* knowledge	Prov 5:2	5341
k thy father's commandment, and	Prov 6:20	5341
thou sleepest, it shall *k* thee	Prov 6:22	8104
To *k* thee from the evil woman,	Prov 6:24	8104
My son, *k* my words, and lay up my	Prov 7:1	8104
K my commandments, and live	Prov 7:2	8104
That they may *k* thee from the	Prov 7:5	8104
blessed are they that *k* my ways	Prov 8:32	8104
he that doth *k* his soul shall be	Prov 22:5	8104
thing if thou *k* them within thee	Prov 22:18	8104
but such as *k* the law contend	Prov 28:4	8104
a time to *k*, and a time to cast	Eccl 3:6	8104
a time to *k* silence, and a time to	Eccl 3:7	
K thy foot when thou goest to the	Eccl 5:1	8104
I counsel thee to *k* the king's	Eccl 8:2	8104
Fear God, and *k* his commandments	Eccl 12:13	8104
those that *k* the fruit thereof	Song 8:12	5201
Thou wilt *k* him in perfect peace,	Is 26:3	5341
I the Lord do *k* it	Is 27:3	5341
hurt it, I will *k* it night and day	Is 27:3	5341
K silence before me, O islands	Is 41:1	
hold thine hand, and will *k* thee	Is 42:6	5341
and to the south, *K* not back	Is 43:6	3607
K ye judgment, and do justice	Is 56:1	8104
the eunuchs that *k* my sabbaths	Is 56:4	8104
of the Lord, *k* not silence,	Is 62:6	
I will not *k* silence, but will	Is 65:6	
will he *k* it to the end	Jer 3:5	8104
I will not *k* anger for ever	Jer 3:12	5201
k him, as a shepherd doth his	Jer 31:10	8104
I will *k* nothing back from you	Jer 42:4	4513
sit upon the ground, and *k* silence	Lam 2:10	
k mine ordinances, and do them	Eze 11:20	8104
k all my statutes, and do that	Eze 18:21	8104
k my judgments, and do them	Eze 20:19	8104
ye shall *k* my judgments, and do	Eze 36:27	8104
that they may *k* the whole form	Eze 43:11	8104
me, and they shall *k* my charge	Eze 44:16	8104
and they shall *k* my laws and my	Eze 44:24	8104
to them that *k* his commandments	Dan 9:4	8104
k mercy and judgment, and wait on	Hos 12:6	8104
shall *k* silence in that time	Amos 5:13	
k the doors of thy mouth from her	Mic 7:5	8104
k thy solemn feasts, perform thy	Nah 1:15	2287
k the munition, watch the way,	Nah 2:1	5341
let all the earth *k* silence	Hab 2:20	
ways, and if thou wilt *k* my charge	Zec 3:7	8104
house, and shalt also *k* my courts	Zec 3:7	8104
me to *k* cattle from my youth	Zec 13:5	7069
to *k* the feast of tabernacles	Zec 14:16	2287
up to *k* the feast of tabernacles	Zec 14:18	2287
up to *k* the feast of tabernacles	Zec 14:19	2287

priest's lips should *k* knowledge	Mal 2:7	2287
into life, *k* the commandments	Mt 19:17	5083
I will *k* the passover at thy	Mt 26:18	4160
that ye may *k* your own tradition	Mk 7:9	5083
charge over thee, to *k* thee	Lk 4:10	1314
k it, and bring forth fruit with	Lk 8:15	2722
hear the word of God, and *k* it	Lk 11:28	5442
and *k* thee in on every side,	Lk 19:43	4912
If a man *k* my saying, he shall	Jn 8:51	5083
If a man *k* my saying, he shall	Jn 8:52	5083
but I know him, and *k* his saying	Jn 8:55	5083
shall *k* it unto life eternal	Jn 12:25	5442
If ye love me, *k* my commandments	Jn 14:15	5083
a man love me, he will *k* my words	Jn 14:23	5083
If ye *k* my commandments, ye shall	Jn 15:10	5083
my saying, they will *k* yours also	Jn 15:20	5083
k through thine own name those	Jn 17:11	5083
shouldest *k* them from the evil	Jn 17:15	5083
to *k* back part of the price of	Acts 5:3	3557
a man that is a Jew to *k* company	Acts 10:28	2853
quaternions of soldiers to *k* him	Acts 12:4	5442
them to *k* the law of Moses	Acts 15:5	5083
must be circumcised, and *k* the law	Acts 15:24	5083
from which if ye *k* yourselves	Acts 15:29	1301
them the decrees for to *k*	Acts 16:4	5442
the jailer to *k* them safely	Acts 16:23	5083
I must by all means *k* this feast	Acts 18:21	4160
save only that they *k* themselves	Acts 21:25	5442
commanded a centurion to *k* Paul	Acts 24:23	5083
profiteth, if thou *k* the law	Rom 2:25	4238
k the righteousness of the law	Rom 2:26	5442
Therefore let us *k* the feast	1Cor 5:8	1858
written unto you not to *k* company	1Cor 5:11	4874
heart that he will *k* his virgin	1Cor 7:37	5083
But I *k* under my body, and bring	1Cor 9:27	5299
k the ordinances, as I delivered	1Cor 11:2	2722
let him *k* silence in the church	1Cor 14:28	4601
Let your women *k* silence in the	1Cor 14:34	4601
if ye *k* in memory what I preached	1Cor 15:2	2722
unto you, and so will I *k* myself	2Cor 11:9	5083
who are circumcised *k* the law	Gal 6:13	5442
Endeavouring to *k* the unity of	Eph 4:3	5083
shall *k* your hearts and minds	Phil 4:7	5432
stablish you, and *k* you from evil	2Th 3:3	5442
k thyself pure	1Ti 5:22	5083
That thou *k* this commandment	1Ti 6:14	5083
k that which is committed to thy	1Ti 6:20	5442
to *k* that which I have committed	2Ti 1:12	5442
thee *k* by the Holy Ghost which	2Ti 1:14	5442
to *k* himself unspotted from the	Jas 1:27	5083
whosoever shall *k* the whole law	Jas 2:10	5083
him, if we *k* his commandments	1Jn 2:3	5083
because we *k* his commandments, and	1Jn 3:22	5083
love God, and *k* his commandments	1Jn 5:2	5083
that we *k* his commandments	1Jn 5:3	5083
children, *k* yourselves from idols	1Jn 5:21	5442
K yourselves in the love of God,	Jude 21	5083
is able to *k* you from falling	Jude 24	5442
k those things which are written	Rev 1:3	5083
I also will *k* thee from the hour	Rev 3:10	5083
which *k* the commandments of God,	Rev 12:17	5083
here are they that *k* the	Rev 14:12	5083
of them which *k* the sayings of	Rev 22:9	5083

KEEPER

And Abel was a *k* of sheep, but	Gen 4:2	7462
Am I my brother's *k*	Gen 4:9	8104
the sight of the *k* of the prison	Gen 39:21	8269
the *k* of the prison committed to	Gen 39:22	8269
The *k* of the prison looked not to	Gen 39:23	8269
and left the sheep with a *k*	1Sa 17:20	8104
the hand of the *k* of the carriage	1Sa 17:22	8104
make thee *k* of mine head for ever	1Sa 28:2	8104
son of Harhas, *k* of the wardrobe	2Kin 22:14	8104
son of Hasrah, *k* of the wardrobe	2Chr 34:22	8104
Asaph the *k* of the king's forest	Neh 2:8	8104
the *k* of the east gate	Neh 3:29	8104
chamberlain, *k* of the women	Est 2:3	8104
custody of Hegai, *k* of the women	Est 2:8	8104
the *k* of the women, appointed	Est 2:15	8104
and as a booth that the *k* maketh	Job 27:18	5341
The LORD is thy *k*	Ps 121:5	8104
made me the *k* of the vineyards	Song 1:6	5201
son of Shallum, the *k* of the door	Jer 35:4	8104
the *k* of the prison awaking out	Acts 16:27	1200
the *k* of the prison told this	Acts 16:36	1200

KEEPERS

be *k* of the watch of the king's	2Kin 11:5	8104
which the *k* of the door have	2Kin 22:4	8104
the *k* of the door, to bring forth	2Kin 23:4	8104
and the three *k* of the door	2Kin 25:18	8104

k of the gates of the tabernacle	1Chr 9:19	8104
of the LORD, were *k* of the entry	1Chr 9:19	8104
the *k* of the door, who sought to	Est 6:2	8104
In the day when the *k* of the	Eccl 12:3	8104
the *k* of the walls took away my	Song 5:7	8104
he let out the vineyard unto *k*	Song 8:11	5201
As *k* of a field, are they against	Jer 4:17	8104
and the three *k* of the door	Jer 52:24	8104
the *k* of the charge of the house	Eze 40:45	8104
the *k* of the charge of the altar	Eze 40:46	8104
but ye have set *k* of my charge in	Eze 44:8	8104
But I will make them *k* of the	Eze 44:14	8104
for fear of him the *k* did shake	Mt 28:4	5083
the *k* standing without before the	Acts 5:23	5441
the *k* before the door kept the	Acts 12:6	5441
found him not, he examined the *k*	Acts 12:19	5441
k at home, good, obedient to	Titus 2:5	3626

KEEPEST

who *k* covenant and mercy with thy	1Kin 8:23	8104
which *k* covenant, and shewest	2Chr 6:14	8104
who *k* covenant and mercy, let not	Neh 9:32	8104
walkest orderly, and *k* the law	Acts 21:24	5442

KEEPETH

and he die not, but *k* his bed	Ex 21:18	5307
which *k* covenant and mercy with	Deut 7:9	8104
and, behold, he *k* the sheep	1Sa 16:11	7462
that *k* covenant and mercy for them	Neh 1:5	8104
He *k* back his soul from the pit,	Job 33:18	2820
He *k* all his bones	Ps 34:20	8104
he that *k* thee will not slumber	Ps 121:3	8104
he that *k* Israel neither	Ps 121:4	8104
which *k* truth for ever	Ps 146:6	8104
He *k* the paths of judgment, and	Prov 2:8	5341
way of life that *k* instruction	Prov 10:17	8104
He that *k* his mouth *k* his	Prov 13:3	5341
that *k* his mouth *k* his life	Prov 13:3	8104
Righteousness *k* him that is	Prov 13:6	5341
he that *k* his way preserveth his	Prov 16:17	5341
he that *k* understanding shall	Prov 19:8	8104
He that *k* the commandment *k*	Prov 19:16	8104
Whoso *k* his mouth and his tongue	Prov 21:23	8104
his tongue *k* his soul from	Prov 21:23	8104
he that *k* thy soul, doth not he	Prov 24:12	5341
Whoso *k* the fig tree shall eat	Prov 27:18	5341
Whoso *k* the law is a wise son	Prov 28:7	5341
but he that *k* company with	Prov 29:3	
but a wise man *k* it in till	Prov 29:11	7623
but he that *k* the law, happy is	Prov 29:18	8104
Whoso *k* the commandment shall	Eccl 8:5	8104
which *k* the truth may enter in	Is 26:2	8104
that *k* the sabbath from polluting	Is 56:2	8104
k his hand from doing any evil	Is 56:2	8104
every one that *k* the sabbath from	Is 56:6	8104
cursed be he that *k* back his	Jer 48:10	4513
k silence, because he hath borne	Lam 3:28	
is a proud man, neither *k* at home	Hab 2:5	
a strong man armed *k* his palace	Lk 11:21	5442
law, and yet none of you *k* the law	Jn 7:19	4160
because he *k* not the sabbath day	Jn 9:16	5083
k them, he it is that loveth me	Jn 14:21	5083
loveth me not *k* not my sayings	Jn 14:24	5083
k not his commandments, is a liar	1Jn 2:4	5083
But whoso *k* his word, in him	1Jn 2:5	5083
he that *k* his commandments	1Jn 3:24	5083
that is begotten of God *k* himself	1Jn 5:18	5083
k my works unto the end, to him	Rev 2:26	5083
k his garments, lest he walk	Rev 16:15	5083
blessed is he that *k* the sayings	Rev 22:7	5083

KEEPING

K mercy for thousands, forgiving	Ex 34:7	5341
k the charge of the sanctuary for	Num 3:28	8104
k the charge of the sanctuary for	Num 3:38	8104
in not *k* his commandments, and his	Deut 8:11	8104
we were with them *k* the sheep	1Sa 25:16	7462
were porters *k* the ward at the	Neh 12:25	8104
in *k* of them there is great	Ps 19:11	8104
but that by *k* of his covenant it	Eze 17:14	8104
k the covenant and mercy to them	Dan 9:4	8104
k watch over their flock by night	Lk 2:8	5442
but the *k* of the commandments of	1Cor 7:19	5084
k of their souls to him in well	1Pet 4:19	

KEHELATHAH (ke-hel'-a-thah) *An Israelite encampment in the wilderness.*

from Rissah, and pitched in *K*	Num 33:22	6954
And they went from *K*, and pitched	Num 33:23	6954

K

KEILAH (ki'-lah)
1. A city in Judah.
And K, and Achzib, and Mareshah .... Josh 15:44   7084
the Philistines fight against K 1Sa 23:1   7084
smite the Philistines, and save K 1Sa 23:2   7084
to K against the armies of the 1Sa 23:3   7084
him and said, Arise, go down to K 1Sa 23:4   7084
So David and his men went to K 1Sa 23:5   7084
David saved the inhabitants of K 1Sa 23:5   7084
of Ahimelech fled to David to K 1Sa 23:6   7084
Saul that David was come to K 1Sa 23:7   7084
together to war, to go down to K 1Sa 23:8   7084
that Saul seeketh to come to K............... 1Sa 23:10   7084
Will the men of K deliver me up............. 1Sa 23:11   7084
Will the men of K deliver me 1Sa 23:12   7084
arose and departed out of K 1Sa 23:13   7084
that David was escaped from K 1Sa 23:13   7084
the ruler of the half part of K................. Neh 3:17   7084
the ruler of the half part of K................. Neh 3:18   7084
2. A descendant of Caleb.
the father of K the Garmite..................... 1Chr 4:19   7084

KELAIAH (kel-ah'-yah) See KELITA. *Married a foreigner in exile.*
Jozabad, and Shimei, and K, (the .... Ezr 10:23   7041

KELAL See CHELAL.

KELITA (kel'-i-tah) See KELAIAH.
1. Married a foreigner in exile.
and Kelaiah, (the same is K .... Ezr 10:23   7042
2. A priest who assisted Ezra.
Shabbethai, Hodijah, Maaseiah, K......... Neh 8:7   7042
3. A Levite who renewed the covenant.
brethren, Shebaniah, Hodijah, K .... Neh 10:10   7042

KELUB See CHELUB.

KELUHI See CHELLUH.

KEMUEL (kem-u'-el)
1. A son of Nahor.
brother, and K the father of Aram, ... Gen 22:21   7055
2. An Ephraimite prince.
of Ephraim, K the son of Shiphtan .... Num 34:24   7055
3. Father of Hashabiah.
Levites, Hashabiah the son of K 1Chr 27:17   7055

KENAANAH See CHENAANAH.

KENAN (ke'-nan) See CAINAN. *Son of Enosh.*
K, Mahalaleel, Jered, ... 1Chr 1:2   7018

KENANI See CHENANI.

KENANIAH See CHENANIAH.

KENATH (ke'-nath) See NOBAH. *A city in Bashan.*
And Nobah went and took K, and the .... Num 32:42   7079
towns of Jair, from them, with K 1Chr 2:23   7079

KENAZ (ke'-naz) See KENEZITE.
1. A son of Eliphaz.
Omar, Zepho, and Gatam, and K .... Gen 36:11   7073
duke Omar, duke Zepho, duke K............. Gen 36:15   7073
and Omar, Zephi, and Gatam, K............. 1Chr 1:36   7073
2. A duke of Edom.
Duke K, duke Teman, duke Mibzar, ... Gen 36:42   7073
Duke K, duke Teman, duke Mibzar, ... 1Chr 1:53   7073
3. Brother of Caleb.
And Othniel the son of K, the .... Josh 15:17   7073
And Othniel the son of K, Caleb's.......... Judg 1:13   7073
them, even Othniel the son of K .... Judg 3:9   7073
And Othniel the son of K died .... Judg 3:11   7073
And the sons of K................................... 1Chr 4:13   7073
4. A grandson of Caleb.
and the sons of Elah, even K.................. 1Chr 4:15   7073

KENEZITE (ken'-e-zite) See KENIZZITES. *Descendants of Jephunneh.*
Caleb the son of Jephunneh the K .... Num 32:12   7074
of Jephunneh the K said unto him .... Josh 14:6   7074
of Jephunneh the K unto this day .... Josh 14:14   7074

KENITE (ken'-ite) See KENITES. *A member of a Canaanite tribe.*
the K shall be wasted, until .... Num 24:22   7014
And the children of the K, Moses'........... Judg 1:16   7017
Now Heber the K, which was of the .... Judg 4:11   7014
of Jael the wife of Heber the K............... Judg 4:17   7017
Hazor and the house of Heber the K ...... Judg 4:17   7017
Jael the wife of Heber the K be.............. Judg 5:24   7017

KENITES (ken'-ites) See MIDIANITES.
The K, and the Kenizzites, and the......... Gen 15:19   7017
And he looked on the K, and took up ..... Num 24:21   7017
had severed himself from the K.............. Judg 4:11   7017
And Saul said unto the K, Go, ... 1Sa 15:6   7017
So the K departed from among the 1Sa 15:6   7017

and against the south of the K 1Sa 27:10   7017
which were in the cities of the K............. 1Sa 30:29   7017
These are the K that came of.................. 1Chr 2:55   7017

KENIZZITE See KENIZZITES.

KENIZZITES (ken'-iz-zites) See KENEZITE. *A Canaanite tribe in Abraham's time.*
The Kenites, and the K, and the .... Gen 15:19   7074

KENNIZZITE See KENIZZITES.

KEPHER AMMONI See CHEPHAR-HAAMMONAI.

KEPHIRAH See CHEPHIRAH.

KEPT
k my charge, my commandments, my ... Gen 26:5   8104
father's sheep: for she k them .... Gen 29:9   7462
neither hath he k back any thing .... Gen 39:9   2820
and ye shall be k in prison .... Gen 42:16   631
Now Moses k the flock of Jethro............ Ex 3:1   7462
for you to be k until the morning .... Ex 16:23   4931
it to be k for your generations................ Ex 16:32   4931
to be k for your generations .... Ex 16:33   4931
up before the Testimony, to be k .... Ex 16:34   4931
owner, and he hath not k him in .... Ex 21:29   8104
and his owner hath not k him in............. Ex 21:36   8104
be k close, and she be defiled, and .... Num 5:13   5641
they k the passover on the .... Num 9:5   6213
wherefore are we k back, that we .... Num 9:7   1639
Israel k the charge of the LORD.............. Num 9:19   8104
they k the charge of the LORD, at........... Num 9:23   8104
to be k for a token against the................ Num 17:10   4931
place, and it shall be k for the .... Num 19:9   4931
the LORD hath k thee back from .... Num 24:11   4513
which k the charge of the .... Num 31:47   8104
he k him as the apple of his eye .... Deut 32:10   5341
thy word, and k thy covenant................. Deut 33:9   5341
k the passover on the fourteenth .... Josh 5:10   6213
behold, the LORD hath k me alive .... Josh 14:10
Ye have k all that Moses the .... Josh 22:2   8104
but k the charge of the .... Josh 22:3   8104
So she k fast by the maidens of .... Ruth 2:23   1692
it been k for these since I said................ 1Sa 9:24   8104
thou hast not k the commandment 1Sa 13:13   8104
because thou hast not k that 1Sa 13:14   8104
Thy servant k his father's sheep, ... 1Sa 17:34   7462
if the young men have k 1Sa 21:4   8104
Of a truth women have been k from 1Sa 21:5   6113
Surely in vain have I k all that 1Sa 25:21   8104
which hast k me this day from 1Sa 25:33   3607
which hast k me back from hurting........ 1Sa 25:34   4513
hath k his servant from evil 1Sa 25:39   2820
hast thou not k thy lord the king 1Sa 26:15   8104
because ye have not k your master 1Sa 26:16   8104
the young man that k the watch............. 2Sa 13:34
For I have k the ways of the LORD 2Sa 22:22   8104
have k myself from mine iniquity 2Sa 22:24   8104
thou hast k me to be head of the 2Sa 22:44   8104
thou not k the oath of the LORD 1Kin 2:43   8104
thou hast k for him this great 1Kin 3:6   8104
Who hast k with thy servant David 1Kin 8:24   8104
but he k not that which the LORD 1Kin 11:10   8104
and thou hast not k my covenant 1Kin 11:11   8104
because he k my commandments and ... 1Kin 11:34   8104
hast not k the commandment which 1Kin 13:21   8104
who k my commandments, and who 1Kin 14:8   8104
which k the door of the king's 1Kin 14:27   8104
(Now Joram had k Ramoth-gilead 2Kin 9:14   8104
the priests that k the door put 2Kin 12:9   8104
Also Judah k not the commandments 2Kin 17:19   8104
but k his commandments, which the...... 2Kin 18:6   8104
word of the LORD, which he k not 1Chr 10:13   8104
while he yet k himself close 1Chr 12:1   6113
k the ward of the house of Saul 1Chr 12:29
Thou which hast k with thy 2Chr 6:15   8104
Solomon k the feast seven days 2Chr 7:8   6213
for they k the dedication of the 2Chr 7:9   6213
that k the entrance of the king's 2Chr 12:10   8104
k the feast of unleavened bread 2Chr 30:21   6213
they k other seven days with.................. 2Chr 30:23   6213
which the Levites that k the 2Chr 34:9   6213
have not k the word of the LORD 2Chr 34:21   8104
Moreover Josiah k a passover unto 2Chr 35:1   6213
k the passover at that time 2Chr 35:17   6213
that k in Israel from the days of 2Chr 35:18   6213
keep such a passover as Josiah k 2Chr 35:18   6213
of Josiah was this passover k.................. 2Chr 35:19   6213
as she lay desolate she k sabbath 2Chr 36:21   7673
They k also the feast of .... Ezr 3:4   6213
k the dedication of this house of .... Ezr 6:16   5648
captivity k the passover upon the .... Ezr 6:19   6213
k the feast of unleavened bread.............. Ezr 6:22   6213

have not *k* the commandments, nor	Neh 1:7	8104
they *k* the feast seven days	Neh 8:18	6213
k thy law, nor hearkened unto thy	Neh 9:34	6213
their brethren that *k* the gates	Neh 11:19	8104
the porters *k* the ward of their	Neh 12:45	8104
which *k* the concubines..........................	Est 2:14	8104
Teresh, of those which *k* the door	Est 2:21	8104
k throughout every generation, ...	Est 9:28	6213
held his steps, his way have I *k*..............	Job 23:11	8104
k close from the fowls of the air..............	Job 28:21	5641
and *k* silence at my counsel....................	Job 29:21	
that I *k* silence, and went not out	Job 31:34	
I have *k* me from the paths of the............	Ps 17:4	8104
For I have *k* the ways of the LORD..........	Ps 18:21	8104
I *k* myself from mine iniquity	Ps 18:23	8104
thou hast *k* me alive, that I	Ps 30:3	
When I *k* silence, my bones waxed	Ps 32:3	2790
with a multitude that *k* holyday	Ps 42:4	2287
hast thou done, and I *k* silence	Ps 50:21	2790
They *k* not the covenant of God, ...	Ps 78:10	8104
God, and *k* not his testimonies	Ps 78:56	8104
they *k* his testimonies, and the	Ps 99:7	8104
for I have *k* thy testimonies	Ps 119:22	5341
in the night, and have *k* thy law	Ps 119:55	8104
I had, because I *k* thy precepts...............	Ps 119:56	5341
but now have I *k* thy word......................	Ps 119:67	8104
because they *k* not thy word	Ps 119:158	8104
My soul hath *k* thy testimonies	Ps 119:167	8104
I have *k* thy precepts and thy	Ps 119:168	8104
eyes desired I *k* not from them	Eccl 2:10	680
riches *k* for the owners thereof...............	Eccl 5:13	8104
mine own vineyard have I not *k*..............	Song 1:6	5201
night when a holy solemnity is *k*	Is 30:29	6942
forsaken me, and have not *k* my law	Jer 16:11	8104
k all his precepts, and done	Jer 35:18	8104
neither have *k* my judgments	Eze 5:7	6213
hath *k* my judgments, to deal	Eze 18:9	8104
hath *k* all my statutes, and hath	Eze 18:19	8104
neither *k* my judgments to do them	Eze 20:21	8104
ye have not *k* the charge of mine............	Eze 44:8	8104
that *k* the charge of my sanctuary	Eze 44:15	8104
which have *k* my charge, which.............	Eze 48:11	8104
and whom he would he *k* alive...............	Dan 5:19	
but I *k* the matter in my heart	Dan 7:28	5202
a wife, and for a wife he *k* sheep	Hos 12:12	8104
and he *k* his wrath for ever	Amos 1:11	8104
have not *k* my commandments, and	Amos 2:4	8104
For the statutes of Omri are *k*	Mic 6:16	8104
as ye have not *k* my ways, but	Mal 2:9	8104
ordinances, and have not *k* them...........	Mal 3:7	8104
it that we have *k* his ordinance..............	Mal 3:14	8104
And they that *k* them fled, and went	Mt 8:33	1006
utter things which have been *k*	Mt 13:35	
But when Herod's birthday was *k*..........	Mt 14:6	71
things have I *k* from my youth up	Mt 19:20	5442
neither was any thing *k* secret	Mk 4:22	1096
And they *k* that saying with	Mk 9:10	2902
But Mary *k* all these things, and	Lk 2:19	4933
but his mother *k* all these......................	Lk 2:51	1301
he was *k* bound with chains and in	Lk 8:29	5442
they *k* it close, and told no man	Lk 9:36	4601
these have I *k* from my youth up	Lk 18:21	5442
which I have *k* laid up in a	Lk 19:20	2192
but thou hast *k* the good wine	Jn 2:10	5083
day of my burying hath she *k* this.........	Jn 12:7	5083
even as I have *k* my Father's	Jn 15:10	5083
if they have *k* my saying, they	Jn 15:20	5083
and they have *k* thy word.......................	Jn 17:6	5083
the world, I *k* them in thy name.............	Jn 17:12	5083
that thou gavest me I have *k*	Jn 17:12	5442
and spake unto her that *k* the door........	Jn 18:16	2377
damsel that *k* the door unto Peter	Jn 18:17	2377
k back part of the price, his	Acts 5:2	3557
of angels, and have not *k* it	Acts 7:53	5442
which had *k* his bed eight years,...........	Acts 9:33	2621
Peter therefore was *k* in prison	Acts 12:5	5083
before the door the prison	Acts 12:6	5083
Then all the multitude *k* silence............	Acts 15:12	4601
how I *k* back nothing that was	Acts 20:20	5288
to them, they *k* the more silence	Acts 22:2	3930
k the raiment of them that slew.............	Acts 22:20	5442
he commanded him to be *k* in	Acts 23:35	5442
that Paul should be *k* at Caesarea	Acts 25:4	5083
I commanded him to be *k* till I	Acts 25:21	5083
k them from their purpose	Acts 27:43	2967
himself with a soldier that *k* him...........	Acts 28:16	5442
which was *k* secret since the..................	Rom 16:25	
in all things I have *k* myself..................	2Cor 11:9	5083
governor under Aretas the king *k*...........	2Cor 11:32	5432
we were *k* under the law, shut up	Gal 3:23	5432
my course, I have *k* the faith	2Ti 4:7	5083

Through faith he *k* the passover	Heb 11:28	4160
which is of you *k* back by fraud..............	Jas 5:4	650
Who are *k* by the power of God...............	1Pet 1:5	5432
by the same word are *k* in store	2Pet 3:7	2343
the angels which *k* not their	Jude 6	5083
hast *k* my word, and hast not	Rev 3:8	5083
Because thou hast *k* the word of	Rev 3:10	5083

KERAN See CHERAN.

KERCHIEFS

make *k* upon the head of every...............	Eze 13:18	4556
Your *k* also will I tear, and	Eze 13:21	4556

KEREN-HAPPUCH (ke'-ren-hap'-puk) A daughter of Job.

and the name of the third, *K*..................	Job 42:14	7163

KERETHITE See CHERETHITES.

KERETHITES See CHERETHITES.

KERIOTH (ke'-re-oth) See ISCARIOT, KIRIOTH.
    1. A city in Judah.

And Hazor, Hadattah, and *K*, and	Josh 15:25	7152

    2. A city in Moab.

And upon *K*, and upon Bozrah, and.......	Jer 48:24	7152
K is taken, and the strong holds	Jer 48:41	7152

KERIOTH HEZRON See KERIOTH.

KERITH See CHERITH.

KERNELS

from the *k* even to the husk	Num 6:4	2785

KEROS (ke'-ros) A family of exiles.

The children of *K*, the children................	Ezr 2:44	7026
The children of *K*, the children................	Neh 7:47	7026

KERUB See CHERUB.

KESALON See CHESALON.

KESED See CHESED.

KESIL See CHESIL.

KESULLOTH See CHESULLOTH.

KETTLE

he struck it into the pan, or *k*	1Sa 2:14	1731

KETURAH (ket-u'-rah) A wife of Abraham.

took a wife, and her name was *K*	Gen 25:1	6989
All these were the children of *K*.............	Gen 25:4	6989
Now the sons of *K*, Abraham's................	1Chr 1:32	6989
All these are the sons of *K*	1Chr 1:33	6989

KEY

therefore they took a *k*, and	Judg 3:25	4668
the *k* of the house of David will	Is 22:22	4668
taken away the *k* of knowledge	Lk 11:52	2807
true, he that hath the *k* of David...........	Rev 3:7	2807
to him was given the *k* of the	Rev 9:1	2807
having the *k* of the bottomless	Rev 20:1	2807

KEYS

the *k* of the kingdom of heaven	Mt 16:19	2807
and have the *k* of hell and of death	Rev 1:18	2807

KEZIA (ke-zi'-ah) A daughter of Job.

and the name of the second, *K*	Job 42:14	7103

KEZIAH See KEZIA.

KEZIB See CHEZIB.

KEZIZ (ke'-ziz) A valley in Benjamin.

Beth-hoglah, and the valley of *K*............	Josh 18:21	7104

KIBROTH-HATTAAVAH (kib'-roth-hat-ta'-a-vah) A Hebrew encampment in the wilderness.

called the name of that place *K*..............	Num 11:34	6914
journeyed from *K* unto Hazeroth	Num 11:35	6914
desert of Sinai, and pitched at *K*............	Num 33:16	6914
And they departed from *K*, and	Num 33:17	6914
at Taberah, and at Massah, and at *K* ...	Deut 9:22	6914

KIBZAIM (kib-za'-im) See JOKMEAM. A Levitical city in Ephraim.

K with her suburbs, and Beth-horon	Josh 21:22	6911

KICK

Wherefore *k* ye at my sacrifice and	1Sa 2:29	1163
for thee to *k* against the pricks	Acts 9:5	2979
for thee to *k* against the pricks	Acts 26:14	2979

KICKED

But Jeshurun waxed fat, and *k*	Deut 32:15	1163

KID

killed a *k* of the goats, and....................	Gen 37:31	8163
will send thee a *k* from the flock	Gen 38:17	1423
Judah sent the *k* by the hand of	Gen 38:20	1423
behold, I sent this *k*, and thou	Gen 38:23	1423

K

seethe a *k* in his mother's milk	Ex 23:19	1423
seethe a *k* in his mother's milk	Ex 34:26	1423
a *k* of the goats, a male without	Lev 4:23	8163
a *k* of the goats, a female	Lev 4:28	8166
a lamb or a *k* of the goats, for a	Lev 5:6	8166
Take ye a *k* of the goats for a	Lev 9:3	8163
Then ye shall sacrifice one *k* of	Lev 23:19	8163
One *k* of the goats for a sin	Num 7:16	8163
One *k* of the goats for a sin	Num 7:22	8163
One *k* of the goats for a sin	Num 7:28	8163
One *k* of the goats for a sin	Num 7:34	8163
One *k* of the goats for a sin	Num 7:40	8163
One *k* of the goats for a sin	Num 7:46	8163
One *k* of the goats for a sin	Num 7:52	8163
One *k* of the goats for a sin	Num 7:58	8163
One *k* of the goats for a sin	Num 7:64	8163
One *k* of the goats for a sin	Num 7:70	8163
One *k* of the goats for a sin	Num 7:76	8163
One *k* of the goats for a sin	Num 7:82	8163
one ram, or for a lamb, or a *k*	Num 15:11	5795
one *k* of the goats for a sin	Num 15:24	8163
one *k* of the goats for a sin	Num 28:15	8163
one *k* of the goats, to make an	Num 28:30	8163
one *k* of the goats for a sin	Num 29:5	8163
One *k* of the goats for a sin	Num 29:11	8163
one *k* of the goats for a sin	Num 29:16	8163
one *k* of the goats for a sin	Num 29:19	8163
one *k* of the goats for a sin	Num 29:25	8163
seethe a *k* in his mother's milk	Deut 14:21	1423
went in, and made ready a *k*	Judg 6:19	1423,5795
have made ready a *k* for thee	Judg 13:15	1423,5795
So Manoah took a *k* with a meat	Judg 13:19	1423,5795
him as he would have rent a *k*	Judg 14:6	1423
Samson visited his wife with a *k*	Judg 15:1	1423,5795
and a bottle of wine, and a *k*	1Sa 16:20	1423,5795
leopard shall lie down with the *k*	Is 11:6	1423
a *k* of the goats without blemish	Eze 43:22	8163
a *k* of the goats daily for a sin	Eze 45:23	8163
and yet thou never gavest me a *k*	Lk 15:29	*2056*

KIDNEYS

is above the liver, and the two *k*	Ex 29:13	3629
above the liver, and the two *k*	Ex 29:22	3629
And the two *k*, and the fat that is	Lev 3:4	3629
caul above the liver, with the *k*	Lev 3:4	3629
And the two *k*, and the fat that is	Lev 3:10	3629
caul above the liver, with the *k*	Lev 3:10	3629
And the two *k*, and the fat that is	Lev 3:15	3629
caul above the liver, with the *k*	Lev 3:15	3629
And the two *k*, and the fat that is	Lev 4:9	3629
caul above the liver, with the *k*	Lev 4:9	3629
And the two *k*, and the fat that is	Lev 7:4	3629
is above the liver, with the *k*	Lev 7:4	3629
above the liver, and the two *k*	Lev 8:16	3629
above the liver, and the two *k*	Lev 8:25	3629
But the fat, and the *k*, and the	Lev 9:10	3629
covereth the inwards, and the *k*	Lev 9:19	3629
goats, with the fat of *k* of wheat	Deut 32:14	3629
with the fat of the *k* of rams	Is 34:6	3629

KIDRON (kid'-ron) *A brook near Jerusalem.*

himself passed over the brook *K*	2Sa 15:23	6939
out, and passest over the brook *K*	1Kin 2:37	6939
idol, and burnt it by the brook *K*	1Kin 15:13	6939
Jerusalem in the fields of *K*	2Kin 23:4	6939
Jerusalem, unto the brook *K*	2Kin 23:6	6939
and burned it at the brook *K*	2Kin 23:6	6939
the dust of them into the brook *K*	2Kin 23:12	6939
it, and burnt it at the brook *K*	2Chr 15:16	6939
it out abroad into the brook *K*	2Chr 29:16	6939
and cast them into the brook *K*	2Chr 30:14	6939
the fields unto the brook of *K*	Jer 31:40	6939

KIDS

thence two good *k* of the goats	Gen 27:9	1423
she put the skins of the *k* of the	Gen 27:16	1423
of the children of Israel two *k*	Lev 16:5	8163
the *k* of the goats for sin	Num 7:87	8163
to Beth-el, one carrying three *k*	1Sa 10:3	1423
them like two little flocks of *k*	1Kin 20:27	5795
people, of the flock, lambs and *k*	2Chr 35:7	
feed thy *k* beside the shepherds'	Song 1:8	1423

KILEAB See CHILEAB.

KILION See CHILION.

KILION'S See CHILION'S.

KILL

lest any finding him should *k* him	Gen 4:15	5221
and they will *k* me, but they will	Gen 12:12	2026
the place should *k* me for Rebekah	Gen 26:7	2026
himself, purposing to *k* thee	Gen 27:42	2026

and said, Let us not *k* him	Gen 37:21	5221
it be a son, then ye shall *k* him	Ex 1:16	4191
intendest thou to *k* me, as thou	Ex 2:14	2026
LORD met him, and sought to *k* him	Ex 4:24	4191
Israel shall *k* it in the evening	Ex 12:6	7819
your families, and the passover	Ex 12:21	7819
to *k* this whole assembly with	Ex 16:3	4191
us up out of Egypt, to *k* us	Ex 17:3	4191
Thou shalt not *k*	Ex 20:13	7523
or a sheep, and *k* it, or sell it	Ex 22:1	2873
I will *k* you with the sword	Ex 22:24	2026
thou shalt *k* the bullock before	Ex 29:11	7819
Then shalt thou *k* the ram	Ex 29:20	7819
he shall *k* the bullock before the	Lev 1:5	7819
he shall *k* it on the side of the	Lev 1:11	7819
and *k* it at the door of the	Lev 3:2	7819
k it before the tabernacle of the	Lev 3:8	7819
k it before the tabernacle of the	Lev 3:13	7819
k the bullock before the LORD	Lev 4:4	7819
k it in the place where they *k*	Lev 4:24	7819
where they *k* the burnt offering	Lev 4:33	7819
In the place where they *k* the	Lev 7:2	7819
they *k* the trespass offering	Lev 7:2	7819
where he shall *k* the sin offering	Lev 14:13	7819
he shall *k* the burnt offering	Lev 14:19	7819
he shall *k* the lamb of the	Lev 14:25	7819
he shall *k* the one of the birds	Lev 14:50	7819
shall *k* the bullock of the sin	Lev 16:11	7819
Then shall he *k* the goat of the	Lev 16:15	7819
seed unto Molech, and *k* him not	Lev 20:4	4191
thereto, thou shalt *k* the woman	Lev 20:16	2026
be cow or ewe, ye shall not *k* it	Lev 22:28	7819
k me, I pray thee, out of hand	Num 11:15	2026
Now if thou shalt *k* all this	Num 14:15	4191
to *k* us in the wilderness, except	Num 16:13	4191
mine hand, for now would I *k* thee	Num 22:29	2026
Now therefore *k* every male among	Num 31:17	2026
k every woman that hath known man	Num 31:17	2026
revenger of blood *k* the slayer	Num 35:27	7523
which should *k* his neighbour	Deut 4:42	7523
Thou shalt not *k*	Deut 5:17	7523
Notwithstanding thou mayest *k*	Deut 12:15	2076
then thou shalt *k* of thy herd	Deut 12:21	2076
But thou shalt surely *k* him	Deut 13:9	2026
I *k*, and I make alive	Deut 32:39	4191
If the LORD were pleased to *k* us	Judg 13:23	4191
but surely we will not *k* thee	Judg 15:13	2026
when it is day, we shall *k* him	Judg 16:2	2026
to smite of the people, and *k*	Judg 20:31	2491
k of the men of Israel about	Judg 20:39	2491
if Saul hear it, he will *k* me	1Sa 16:2	2026
able to fight with me, and to *k* me	1Sa 17:9	5221
k him, then shall ye be our	1Sa 17:9	5221
that they should *k* David	1Sa 19:1	4191
Saul my father seeketh to *k* thee	1Sa 19:2	4191
why should I *k* thee	1Sa 19:17	4191
and some bade me *k* thee	1Sa 24:10	2026
God, that thou wilt neither *k* me	1Sa 30:15	4191
then *k* him, fear not	2Sa 13:28	4191
his brother, that we may *k* him	2Sa 14:7	4191
any iniquity in me, let him *k* me	2Sa 14:32	4191
us shalt thou *k* any man in Israel	2Sa 21:4	4191
sought therefore to *k* Jeroboam	1Kin 11:40	4191
king of Judah, and they shall *k* me	1Kin 12:27	2026
clothes, and said, Am I God, to *k*	2Kin 5:7	4191
and if they *k* us, we shall but die	2Kin 7:4	4191
followeth her *k* with the sword	2Kin 11:15	4191
So *k* the passover, and sanctify	2Chr 35:6	7819
provinces, to destroy, to *k*	Est 3:13	2026
they watched the house to *k* him	Ps 59:*t*	4191
A time to *k*, and a time to heal	Eccl 3:3	2026
I will *k* thy root with famine, and	Is 14:30	4191
let them *k* sacrifices	Is 29:1	5362
the wool, ye *k* them that are fed	Eze 34:3	2076
of old time, Thou shalt not *k*	Mt 5:21	*5407*
whosoever shall *k* shall be in	Mt 5:21	*5407*
And fear not them which *k* the body	Mt 10:28	*615*
but are not able to *k* the soul	Mt 10:28	*615*
And they shall *k* him, and the third	Mt 17:23	*615*
come, let us *k* him, and let us	Mt 21:38	*615*
and some of them ye shall *k*	Mt 23:34	*615*
to be afflicted, and shall *k* you	Mt 24:9	*615*
take Jesus by subtilty, and *k* him	Mt 26:4	*615*
to save life, or to *k*	Mk 3:4	*615*
hands of men, and they shall *k* him	Mk 9:31	*615*
Do not commit adultery, Do not *k*	Mk 10:19	*5407*
spit upon him, and shall *k* him	Mk 10:34	*615*
come, let us *k* him, and the	Mk 12:7	*615*
afraid of them that *k* the body	Lk 12:4	*615*
for Herod will *k* thee	Lk 13:31	*615*
hither the fatted calf, and *k* it	Lk 15:23	*2380*

Do not commit adultery, Do not *k*	Lk 18:20	5407
come, let us *k* him, that the	Lk 20:14	615
sought how they might *k* him	Lk 22:2	337
the Jews sought the more to *k* him	Jn 5:18	615
because the Jews sought to *k* him	Jn 7:1	615
Why go ye about to *k* me	Jn 7:19	615
who goeth about to *k* thee	Jn 7:20	615
not this he, whom they seek to *k*	Jn 7:25	615
said the Jews, Will he *k* himself	Jn 8:22	615
but ye seek to *k* me, because my	Jn 8:37	615
But now ye seek to *k* me, a man	Jn 8:40	615
not, but for to steal, and to *k*	Jn 10:10	2380
Wilt thou *k* me, as thou diddest	Acts 7:28	337
the Jews took counsel to *k* him	Acts 9:23	337
the gates day and night to *k* him	Acts 9:24	337
Rise, Peter; *k*, and eat	Acts 10:13	2380
And as they went about to *k* him	Acts 21:31	615
he come near, are ready to *k* him	Acts 23:15	337
laying wait in the way to *k* him	Acts 25:3	337
the temple, and went about to *k* me	Acts 26:21	1315
counsel was to *k* the prisoners	Acts 27:42	615
commit adultery, Thou shalt not *k*	Rom 13:9	5407
adultery, said also, Do not *k*	Jas 2:11	5407
commit no adultery, yet if thou *k*	Jas 2:11	5407
ye *k*, and desire to have, and	Jas 4:2	5407
I will *k* her children with death	Rev 2:23	615
and that they should *k* one another	Rev 6:4	4969
to *k* with sword, and with hunger,	Rev 6:8	615
given that they should not *k* them	Rev 9:5	615
and shall overcome them, and *k* them	Rev 11:7	615

KILLED

k a kid of the goats, and dipped	Gen 37:31	7819
that he hath *k* a man or a woman	Ex 21:29	4191
shall be *k* before the LORD	Lev 4:15	7819
is *k* shall the sin offering be	Lev 6:25	7819
sin offering be *k* before the LORD	Lev 6:25	7819
And he *k* it; and Moses	Lev 8:19	7819
that one of the birds be *k* in an	Lev 14:5	7819
that was *k* over the running water	Lev 14:6	7819
Ye have *k* the people of the LORD	Num 16:41	4191
whosoever hath *k* any person	Num 31:19	2026
k thee not, know thou and see that	1Sa 24:11	2026
that I have *k* for my shearers	1Sa 25:11	2873
k it, and took flour, and kneaded	1Sa 28:24	2076
thou hast *k* Uriah the Hittite	2Sa 12:9	5221
and smote the Philistine, and *k* him	2Sa 21:17	4191
and because he *k* him	1Kin 16:7	5221
k him, in the twenty and seventh	1Kin 16:10	4191
Thus saith the LORD, Hast thou *k*	1Kin 21:19	7523
he *k* him, and reigned in his room	2Kin 15:25	4191
k Shophach the captain of the	1Chr 19:18	4191
Ahab *k* sheep and oxen for him in	2Chr 18:2	3076
that had *k* the king his father	2Chr 25:3	5221
So they *k* the bullocks, and the	2Chr 29:22	7819
when they had *k* the rams	2Chr 29:22	7819
they *k* also the lambs, and they	2Chr 29:22	7819
And the priests *k* them, and they	2Chr 29:24	7819
Then they *k* the passover on the	2Chr 30:15	7819
they *k* the passover on the	2Chr 35:1	7819
they *k* the passover, and the	2Chr 35:1	7819
k the passover for all the	Ezr 6:20	7819
sake are we *k* all the day long	Ps 44:22	2026
She hath *k* her beasts	Prov 9:2	2873
thou hast *k*, and not pitied	Lam 2:21	2873
chief priests and scribes, and be *k*	Mt 16:21	615
k another, and stoned another	Mt 21:35	615
my oxen and my fatlings are *k*	Mt 22:4	2380
of them which *k* the prophets	Mt 23:31	5407
against him, and would have *k* him	Mk 6:19	615
priests, and scribes, and be *k*	Mk 8:31	615
and after that he is *k*, he shall	Mk 9:31	615
and him they *k*, and many others	Mk 12:5	615
k him, and cast him out of the	Mk 12:8	615
when they *k* the passover, his	Mk 14:12	2380
prophets, and your fathers *k* them	Lk 11:47	615
for they indeed *k* them, and ye	Lk 11:48	615
which after he hath *k* hath power	Lk 12:5	615
thy father hath *k* the fatted calf	Lk 15:27	2380
thou hast *k* for him the fatted	Lk 15:30	2380
him out of the vineyard, and *k* him	Lk 20:15	615
when the passover must be *k*	Lk 22:7	2380
k the Prince of life, whom God	Acts 3:15	615
he *k* James the brother of John	Acts 12:2	337
sword, and would have *k* himself	Acts 16:27	337
nor drink till they had *k* Paul	Acts 23:12	615
nor drink till they have *k* him	Acts 23:21	337
and should have been *k* of them	Acts 23:27	615
sake we are *k* all the day long	Rom 8:36	2289
they have *k* thy prophets, and	Rom 11:3	615
as chastened, and not *k*	2Cor 6:9	2289

Who both *k* the Lord Jesus, and	1Th 2:15	615
Ye have condemned and *k* the just	Jas 5:6	5407
that should be *k* as they were	Rev 6:11	615
three was the third part of men *k*	Rev 9:18	615
k by these plagues yet repented	Rev 9:20	615
them, he must in this manner be *k*	Rev 11:5	615
sword must be *k* with the sword	Rev 13:10	615
image of the beast should be *k*	Rev 13:15	615

KILLEDST

kill me, as thou *k* the Egyptian	Ex 2:14	2026
me into thine hand, thou *k* me not	1Sa 24:18	2026

KILLEST

thou that *k* the prophets, and	Mt 23:37	615
which *k* the prophets, and stonest	Lk 13:34	615

KILLETH

that *k* an ox, or lamb, or goat,	Lev 17:3	7819
or that *k* it out of the camp,	Lev 17:3	7819
he that *k* any man shall surely be	Lev 24:17	5221
he that *k* a beast shall make it	Lev 24:18	5221
And he that *k* a beast, he shall	Lev 24:21	5221
and he that *k* a man, he shall be	Lev 24:21	5221
which *k* any person at unawares	Num 35:11	5221
that every one that *k* any person	Num 35:15	5221
Whoso *k* any person, the murderer	Num 35:30	5221
Whoso *k* his neighbour ignorantly,	Deut 19:4	5221
slayer that *k* any person unawares	Josh 20:3	5221
that whosoever *k* any person at	Josh 20:9	5221
The LORD *k*, and maketh alive	1Sa 2:6	4191
shall be, that the man who *k* him	1Sa 17:25	5221
to the man that *k* this Philistine	1Sa 17:26	5221
it be done to the man that *k* him	1Sa 17:27	5221
For wrath *k* the foolish man, and	Job 5:2	2026
rising with the light *k* the poor	Job 24:14	6991
The desire of the slothful *k* him	Prov 21:25	4191
He that *k* an ox is as if he slew	Is 66:3	7819
that whosoever *k* you will think	Jn 16:2	615
for the letter *k*, but the spirit	2Cor 3:6	615
he that *k* with the sword must be	Rev 13:10	615

KILLING

him in the *k* of his brethren	Judg 9:24	2026
Levites had the charge of the *k*	2Chr 30:17	7821
k sheep, eating flesh, and	Is 22:13	7819
By swearing, and lying, and *k*	Hos 4:2	7523
beating some, and *k* some	Mk 12:5	615

KILMAD See CHILMAD.

KIMHAM See CHIMHAM.

KIN

to any that is near of *k* to him	Lev 18:6	1320
for he uncovereth his near *k*	Lev 20:19	7607
But for his *k*, that is near unto	Lev 21:2	7607
if any of his *k* come to redeem it	Lev 25:25	7138
or any that is nigh of *k* unto him	Lev 25:49	1320
her, The man is near of *k* unto us	Ruth 2:20	
the king is near of *k* to us	2Sa 19:42	
own country, and among his own *k*	Mk 6:4	4773

KINAH *(ki'-nah) A city in Judah.*

And K, and Dimonah, and Adadah,	Josh 15:22	7016

KIND

tree yielding fruit after his *k*	Gen 1:11	4327
and herb yielding seed after his *k*	Gen 1:12	4327
seed was in itself, after his *k*	Gen 1:12	4327
forth abundantly, after their *k*	Gen 1:21	4327
and every winged fowl after his *k*	Gen 1:21	4327
the living creature after his *k*	Gen 1:24	4327
and beast of the earth after his *k*	Gen 1:24	4327
his *k*, and cattle after their *k*	Gen 1:25	4327
upon the earth after his *k*	Gen 1:25	4327
Of fowls after their *k*	Gen 6:20	4327
and of cattle after their *k*	Gen 6:20	4327
thing of the earth after his *k*	Gen 6:20	4327
They, and every beast after his *k*	Gen 7:14	4327
and all the cattle after their *k*	Gen 7:14	4327
upon the earth after his *k*	Gen 7:14	4327
and every fowl after his *k*	Gen 7:14	4327
vulture, and the kite after his *k*	Lev 11:14	4327
Every raven after his *k*	Lev 11:15	4327
cuckow, and the hawk after his *k*	Lev 11:16	4327
the stork, the heron after her *k*	Lev 11:19	4327
the locust after his *k*	Lev 11:22	4327
and the bald locust after his *k*	Lev 11:22	4327
and the beetle after his *k*	Lev 11:22	4327
and the grasshopper after his *k*	Lev 11:22	4327
and the tortoise after his *k*	Lev 11:29	4327
cattle gender with a diverse *k*	Lev 19:19	
kite, and the vulture after his *k*	Deut 14:13	4327
And every raven after his *k*	Deut 14:14	4327

K

cuckow, and the hawk after his *k*	Deut 14:15	4327
stork, and the heron after her *k*	Deut 14:18	4327
instruments of every *k* of service	1Chr 28:14	
If thou be *k* to this people, and	2Chr 10:7	2896
sellers of all *k* of ware lodged	Neh 13:20	
trees in them of all *k* of fruits	Eccl 2:5	
the multitude of all *k* of riches	Eze 27:12	
the sea, and gathered of every *k*	Mt 13:47	*1085*
Howbeit this *k* goeth not out but	Mt 17:21	*1085*
This *k* can come forth by nothing,	Mk 9:29	*1085*
for he is *k* unto the unthankful	Lk 6:35	*5543*
Charity suffereth long, and is *k*	1Cor 13:4	*5541*
there is one *k* of flesh of men	1Cor 15:39	
And be ye *k* one to another,	Eph 4:32	*5543*
truth, that we should be a *k* of	Jas 1:18	*5100*
For every *k* of beasts, and of	Jas 3:7	*5449*

KINDLE

Ye shall *k* no fire throughout	Ex 35:3	1197
is a contentious man to *k* strife	Prov 26:21	2787
shall *k* in the thickets of the	Is 9:18	3341
under his glory he shall *k* a	Is 10:16	3344
a stream of brimstone, doth *k* it	Is 30:33	1197
shall the flame *k* upon thee	Is 43:2	1197
Behold, all ye that *k* a fire	Is 50:11	6919
wood, and the fathers *k* the fire	Jer 7:18	1197
then will I *k* a fire in the gates	Jer 17:27	3341
I will *k* a fire in the forest	Jer 21:14	3341
to *k* meat offerings, and to do	Jer 33:18	6999
I will *k* a fire in the houses of	Jer 43:12	3341
I will *k* a fire in the wall of	Jer 49:27	3341
I will *k* a fire in his cities, and	Jer 50:32	3341
I will *k* a fire in thee, and it	Eze 20:47	3341
k the fire, consume the flesh, and	Eze 24:10	1814
But I will *k* a fire in the wall	Amos 1:14	3341
stubble, and they shall *k* in them	Obad 18	1814
neither do ye *k* fire on mine	Mal 1:10	215

KINDLED

anger was *k* against Rachel	Gen 30:2	2734
that his wrath was *k*	Gen 39:19	2734
of the LORD was *k* against Moses	Ex 4:14	2734
he that *k* the fire shall surely	Ex 22:6	1197
the burning which the LORD hath *k*	Lev 10:6	8313
and his anger was *k*	Num 11:1	2734
anger of the LORD was *k* greatly	Num 11:10	2734
the LORD was *k* against the people	Num 11:33	2734
of the LORD was *k* against them	Num 12:9	2734
God's anger was *k* because he went	Num 22:22	2734
and Balaam's anger was *k*, and he	Num 22:27	2734
anger was *k* against Balaam	Num 24:10	2734
of the LORD was *k* against Israel	Num 25:3	2734
LORD's anger was *k* the same time	Num 32:10	2734
LORD's anger was *k* against Israel	Num 32:13	
LORD thy God be *k* against thee	Deut 6:15	2734
of the LORD be *k* against you	Deut 7:4	2734
the LORD's wrath be *k* against you	Deut 11:17	2734
the LORD was *k* against this land	Deut 29:27	2734
Then my anger shall be *k* against	Deut 31:17	2734
For a fire is *k* in mine anger	Deut 32:22	6919
the anger of the LORD was *k*	Josh 7:1	2734
of the LORD be *k* against you	Josh 23:16	2734
the son of Ebed, was *k*, and he went up	Judg 9:30	2734
And his anger was *k*, and he went up	Judg 14:19	2734
and his anger was *k* greatly	1Sa 11:6	2734
Eliab's anger was *k* against David	1Sa 17:28	2734
anger was *k* against Jonathan	1Sa 20:30	2734
of the LORD was *k* against Uzzah	2Sa 6:7	2734
was greatly *k* against the man	2Sa 12:5	2734
coals were *k* by it	2Sa 22:9	1197
before him were coals of fire *k*	2Sa 22:13	1197
of the LORD was *k* against Israel	2Sa 24:1	2734
of the LORD was *k* against Israel	2Kin 13:3	2734
of the LORD that is *k* against us	2Kin 22:13	3341
shall be *k* against this place	2Kin 22:17	3341
his anger was *k* against Judah	2Kin 23:26	2734
of the LORD was *k* against Uzza	1Chr 13:10	2734
anger was greatly *k* against Judah	2Chr 25:10	2734
of the LORD was *k* against Amaziah	2Chr 25:15	2734
He hath also *k* his wrath against	Job 19:11	2734
Then was *k* the wrath of Elihu the	Job 32:2	2734
against Job was his wrath *k*	Job 32:2	2734
his three friends was his wrath *k*	Job 32:3	2734
three men, then his wrath was *k*	Job 32:5	2734
My wrath is *k* against thee, and	Job 42:7	2734
when his wrath is *k* but a little	Ps 2:12	1197
coals were *k* by it	Ps 18:8	1197
so a fire was *k* against Jacob	Ps 78:21	5400
a fire was *k* in their company	Ps 106:18	1197
of the LORD *k* against his people	Ps 106:40	2734
when their wrath was *k* against us	Ps 124:3	2734
of the LORD against his people	Is 5:25	2734

and in the sparks that ye have *k*	Is 50:11	1197
tumult he hath *k* fire upon it	Jer 11:16	3341
for a fire is *k* in mine anger	Jer 15:14	6919
for ye have *k* a fire in mine	Jer 17:4	6919
was *k* in the cities of Judah and	Jer 44:6	1197
hath *k* a fire in Zion, and it hath	Lam 4:11	3341
see that I the LORD have *k* it	Eze 20:48	1197
mine anger is *k* against them	Hos 8:5	2734
me, my repentings are *k* together	Hos 11:8	3648
Mine anger was *k* against the	Zec 10:3	2734
what will I, if it be already *k*	Lk 12:49	*381*
when they had *k* a fire in the	Lk 22:55	*681*
for they *k* a fire, and received us	Acts 28:2	*381*

KINDLETH

His breath *k* coals, and a flame	Job 41:21	3857
yea, he *k* it, and baketh bread	Is 44:15	5400
great a matter a little fire *k*	Jas 3:5	*381*

KINDLY

And now if ye will deal *k* and truly	Gen 24:49	2617
and spake *k* unto the damsel	Gen 34:3	5921,3820
hand under my thigh, and deal *k*	Gen 47:29	2617
them, and spake *k* unto them	Gen 50:21	5921,3820
us the land, that we will deal *k*	Josh 2:14	2617
the LORD deal *k* with you, as ye	Ruth 1:8	2617
shalt deal *k* with thy servant	1Sa 20:8	2617
And he spake *k* to him, and set his	2Kin 25:28	2896
spake *k* unto him, and set his	Jer 52:32	2896
Be *k* affectioned one to another	Rom 12:10	*5387*

KINDNESS

This is thy *k* which thou shalt	Gen 20:13	2617
but according to the *k* that I	Gen 21:23	2617
shew *k* unto my master Abraham	Gen 24:12	2617
thou hast shewed *k* unto my master	Gen 24:14	2617
be well with thee, and shew *k*	Gen 40:14	2617
LORD, since I have shewed you *k*	Josh 2:12	2617
shew *k* unto my father's house	Josh 2:12	2617
Neither shewed they *k* to the	Judg 8:35	2617
not left off his *k* to the living	Ruth 2:20	2617
for thou hast shewed more *k* in	Ruth 3:10	2617
for ye shewed *k* to all the	1Sa 15:6	2617
I live shew me the *k* of the LORD	1Sa 20:14	2617
off thy *k* from my house for ever	1Sa 20:15	2617
have shewed this *k* unto your lord	2Sa 2:5	2617
And now the LORD shew *k* and truth	2Sa 2:6	2617
and I also will requite you this *k*	2Sa 2:6	2896
which against Judah do shew *k*	2Sa 3:8	2617
shew him *k* for Jonathan's sake	2Sa 9:1	2617
I may shew the *k* of God unto him	2Sa 9:3	2617
for I will surely shew thee *k* for	2Sa 9:7	2617
I will shew *k* unto Hanun the son	2Sa 10:2	2617
as his father shewed *k* unto me	2Sa 10:2	2617
Is this thy *k* to thy friend	2Sa 16:17	2617
But shew *k* unto the sons of	1Kin 2:7	2617
hast kept for him this great *k*	1Kin 3:6	2617
I will shew *k* unto Hanun the son	1Chr 19:2	2617
because his father shewed *k* to me	1Chr 19:2	2617
the king remembered not the *k*	2Chr 24:22	2617
slow to anger, and of great *k*	Neh 9:17	2617
him, and she obtained *k* of him	Est 2:9	2617
his marvellous *k* in a strong city	Ps 31:21	2617
For his merciful *k* is great	Ps 117:2	2617
thy merciful *k* be for my comfort,	Ps 119:76	2617
it shall be a *k*	Ps 141:5	2617
The desire of a man is his *k*	Prov 19:22	2617
and in her tongue is the law of *k*	Prov 31:26	2617
but with everlasting *k* will I	Is 54:8	2617
but my *k* shall not depart from	Is 54:10	2617
the *k* of thy youth, the love of	Jer 2:2	2617
slow to anger, and of great *k*	Joel 2:13	2617
slow to anger, and of great *k*	Jonah 4:2	2617
people shewed us no little *k*	Acts 28:2	5363
knowledge, by longsuffering, by *k*	2Cor 6:6	5544
riches of his grace in his *k*	Eph 2:7	5544
and beloved, bowels of mercies, *k*	Col 3:12	5544
But after that the *k* and love of	Titus 3:4	5544
And to godliness brotherly *k*	2Pet 1:7	5360
and to brotherly *k* charity	2Pet 1:7	5360

KINDRED

out of thy country, and from thy *k*	Gen 12:1	4138
go unto my country, and to my *k*	Gen 24:4	4138
house, and from the land of my *k*	Gen 24:7	4138
my father's house, and to my *k*	Gen 24:38	4940
take a wife for my son of my *k*	Gen 24:40	4940
my oath, when thou comest to my *k*	Gen 24:41	4940
land of thy fathers, and to thy *k*	Gen 31:3	4138
and return unto the land of thy *k*	Gen 31:13	4138
unto thy country, and to thy *k*	Gen 32:9	4138
of our state, and of our *k*	Gen 43:7	4138
to mine own land, and to my *k*	Num 10:30	4138

and they brought out all her *k* .... Josh 6:23   4940
who was of the *k* of Elimelech................ Ruth 2:3   4940
And now is not Boaz of our *k* .... Ruth 3:2   4130
the *k* of Saul, three thousand 1Chr 12:29   250
not shewed her people nor her *k* .... Est 2:10   4138
yet shewed her *k* nor her people .... Est 2:20   4138
to see the destruction of my *k* .... Est 8:6   4138
the Buzite, of the *k* of Ram .... Job 32:2   4940
thy brethren, the men of thy *k* .... Eze 11:15   1353
There is none of thy *k* that is .... Lk 1:61   4772
were of the *k* of the high priest .... Acts 4:6   1085
out of thy country, and from thy *k* .... Acts 7:3   4772
Joseph's *k* was made known unto .... Acts 7:13   1085
father Jacob to him, and all his *k* .... Acts 7:14   4772
same dealt subtilly with our *k* .... Acts 7:19   1085
God by thy blood out of every *k*............ Rev 5:9   5443
earth, and to every nation, and *k* .... Rev 14:6   5443

KINDREDS

ye *k* of the people, give unto the 1Chr 16:28   4940
all the *k* of the nations shall.................. Ps 22:27   4940
O ye *k* of the people, give unto .... Ps 96:7   4940
all the *k* of the earth be blessed .... Acts 3:25   3965
all *k* of the earth shall wail .... Rev 1:7   5443
number, of all nations, and *k* .... Rev 7:9   5443
And they of the people and *k* .... Rev 11:9   5443
and power was given him over all *k* .... Rev 13:7   5443

KINDS

upon the earth, after their *k* .... Gen 8:19   4940
divers *k* of spices prepared by 2Chr 16:14   2177
I will appoint over them four *k* .... Jer 15:3   4940
shall be according to their *k* .... Eze 47:10   4327
all *k* of musick, ye fall down and .... Dan 3:5   2177
all *k* of musick, all the people, ... Dan 3:7   2177
all *k* of musick, shall fall down .... Dan 3:10   2177
all *k* of musick, ye fall down and .... Dan 3:15   2177
to another divers *k* of tongues 1Cor 12:10   1085
so many *k* of voices in the world,.......... 1Cor 14:10   1085

KINE

camels with their colts, forty *k* .... Gen 32:15   6510
the river seven well favoured *k* .... Gen 41:2   6510
seven other *k* came up after them .... Gen 41:3   6510
stood by the other *k* upon the .... Gen 41:3   6510
leanfleshed *k* did eat up the.................. Gen 41:4   6510
the seven well favoured and fat *k* .... Gen 41:4   6510
came up out of the river seven *k* .... Gen 41:18   6510
seven other *k* came up after them, ... Gen 41:19   6510
the ill favoured *k* did eat up the .... Gen 41:20   6510
did eat up the first seven fat *k* .... Gen 41:20   6510
The seven good *k* are seven years .... Gen 41:26   6510
ill favoured *k* that came up after .... Gen 41:27   6510
thine oil, the increase of thy *k* .... Deut 7:13   504
thy cattle, the increase of thy *k* .... Deut 28:4   504
thy land, the increase of thy *k* .... Deut 28:18   504
or oil, or the increase of thy *k* .... Deut 28:51   504
Butter of *k*, and milk of sheep, ... Deut 32:14   1241
a new cart, and take two milch *k* 1Sa 6:7   6510
tie the *k* to the cart, and bring............. 1Sa 6:7   6510
and took two milch *k*, and tied them...... 1Sa 6:10   6510
the *k* took the straight way to 1Sa 6:12   6510
offered the *k* a burnt offering 1Sa 6:14   6510
butter, and sheep, and cheese of *k* 2Sa 17:29   1241
ye *k* of Bashan, that are in the .... Amos 4:1   6510

KING

the days of Amraphel *k* of Shinar.......... Gen 14:1   4428
Arioch *k* of Ellasar, Chedorlaomer .... Gen 14:1   4428
Ellasar, Chedorlaomer *k* of Elam .... Gen 14:1   4428
of Elam, and Tidal *k* of nations............. Gen 14:1   4428
made war with Bera *k* of Sodom .... Gen 14:2   4428
and with Birsha *k* of Gomorrah .... Gen 14:2   4428
Shinab *k* of Admah .... Gen 14:2   4428
Shemeber *k* of Zeboiim .... Gen 14:2   4428
the *k* of Bela, which is Zoar .... Gen 14:2   4428
And there went out the *k* of Sodom .... Gen 14:8   4428
the *k* of Gomorrah .... Gen 14:8   4428
the *k* of Admah .... Gen 14:8   4428
the *k* of Zeboiim .... Gen 14:8   4428
the *k* of Bela (the same is Zoar .... Gen 14:8   4428
With Chedorlaomer the *k* of Elam .... Gen 14:9   4428
and with Tidal *k* of nations .... Gen 14:9   4428
Amraphel *k* of Shinar, and Arioch......... Gen 14:9   4428
of Shinar, and Arioch *k* of Ellasar .... Gen 14:9   4428
the *k* of Sodom went out to meet .... Gen 14:17   4428
Melchizedek *k* of Salem brought .... Gen 14:18   4428
the *k* of Sodom said unto Abram, ... Gen 14:21   4428
And Abram said to the *k* of Sodom .... Gen 14:22   4428
Abimelech *k* of Gerar sent, and .... Gen 20:2   4428
Isaac went unto Abimelech *k* of............. Gen 26:1   4428
time, that Abimelech *k* of the .... Gen 26:8   4428
before there reigned any *k* over .... Gen 36:31   4428

that the butler of the *k* of Egypt .... Gen 40:1   4428
their lord the *k* of Egypt .... Gen 40:1   4428
and the baker of the *k* of Egypt .... Gen 40:5   4428
stood before Pharaoh *k* of Egypt .... Gen 41:46   4428
there arose up a new *k* over Egypt.......... Ex 1:8   4428
the *k* of Egypt spake to the .... Ex 1:15   4428
did not as the *k* of Egypt .... Ex 1:17   4428
the *k* of Egypt called for the .... Ex 1:18   4428
of time, that the *k* of Egypt died .... Ex 2:23   4428
of Israel, unto the *k* of Egypt .... Ex 3:18   4428
I am sure that the *k* of Egypt .... Ex 3:19   4428
the *k* of Egypt said unto them,............... Ex 5:4   4428
in, speak unto Pharaoh *k* of Egypt......... Ex 6:11   4428
and unto Pharaoh *k* of Egypt .... Ex 6:13   4428
which spake to Pharaoh *k* of Egypt .... Ex 6:27   4428
speak thou unto Pharaoh *k* of................ Ex 6:29   4428
it was told the *k* of Egypt that................ Ex 14:5   4428
the heart of Pharaoh *k* of Egypt .... Ex 14:8   4428
from Kadesh unto the *k* of Edom .... Num 20:14   4428
when *k* Arad the Canaanite, which......... Num 21:1   4428
unto Sihon *k* of the Amorites .... Num 21:21   4428
of Sihon the *k* of the Amorites .... Num 21:26   4428
against the former *k* of Moab .... Num 21:26   4428
unto Sihon *k* of the Amorites .... Num 21:29   4428
Og the *k* of Bashan went out .... Num 21:33   4428
unto Sihon *k* of the Amorites .... Num 21:34   4428
Balak the son of Zippor was *k* of .... Num 22:4   4428
k of Moab, hath sent unto me, ... Num 22:10   4428
Balak the *k* of Moab hath brought .... Num 23:7   4428
and the shout of a *k* is among them .... Num 23:21   4428
his *k* shall be higher than Agag, ... Num 24:7   4428
of Sihon *k* of the Amorites...................... Num 32:33   4428
and the kingdom of Og *k* of Bashan........ Num 32:33   4428
k Arad the Canaanite, which dwelt .... Num 33:40   4428
slain Sihon the *k* of the Amorites .... Deut 1:4   4428
Og the *k* of Bashan, which dwelt .... Deut 1:4   4428
k of Heshbon, and his land.................... Deut 2:24   4428
of Kedemoth unto Sihon *k* of................. Deut 2:26   4428
But Sihon *k* of Heshbon would not .... Deut 2:30   4428
Og the *k* of Bashan came out .... Deut 3:1   4428
unto Sihon *k* of the Amorites .... Deut 3:2   4428
the *k* of Bashan, and all his .... Deut 3:3   4428
as we did unto Sihon *k* of Heshbon .... Deut 3:6   4428
For only Og *k* of Bashan remained........ Deut 3:11   4428
land of Sihon *k* of the Amorites .... Deut 4:46   4428
and the land of Og *k* of Bashan............. Deut 4:47   4428
the hand of Pharaoh *k* of Egypt............. Deut 7:8   4428
Egypt unto Pharaoh the *k* of Egypt........ Deut 11:3   4428
shalt say, I will set a *k* over me............. Deut 17:14   4428
in any wise set him *k* over thee .... Deut 17:15   4428
shalt thou set *k* over thee .... Deut 17:15   4428
thy *k* which thou shalt set over .... Deut 28:36   4428
Sihon the *k* of Heshbon .... Deut 29:7   4428
Og the *k* of Bashan, came out .... Deut 29:7   4428
he was *k* in Jeshurun, when the............. Deut 33:5   4428
And it was told the *k* of Jericho............. Josh 2:2   4428
the *k* of Jericho sent unto Rahab, ... Josh 2:3   4428
the *k* thereof, and the mighty men.......... Josh 6:2   4428
given into thy hand the *k* of Ai.............. Josh 8:1   4428
her *k* as thou didst unto Jericho............ Josh 8:2   4428
thou didst unto Jericho and her *k* .... Josh 8:2   4428
when the *k* of Ai saw it, that .... Josh 8:14   4428
the *k* of Ai they took alive, and .... Josh 8:23   4428
the *k* of Ai he hanged on a tree .... Josh 8:29   4428
to Sihon *k* of Heshbon .... Josh 9:10   4428
to Og *k* of Bashan, which was at .... Josh 9:10   4428
when Adoni-zedek *k* of Jerusalem .... Josh 10:1   4428
he had done to Jericho and her *k* .... Josh 10:1   4428
so he had done to Ai and her *k* .... Josh 10:1   4428
Wherefore Adoni-zedek *k* of .... Josh 10:3   4428
sent unto Hoham *k* of Hebron .... Josh 10:3   4428
and unto Piram *k* of Jarmuth .... Josh 10:3   4428
and unto Japhia *k* of Lachish................. Josh 10:3   4428
and unto Debir *k* of Eglon .... Josh 10:3   4428
the *k* of Jerusalem .... Josh 10:5   4428
the *k* of Hebron .... Josh 10:5   4428
the *k* of Jarmuth .... Josh 10:5   4428
the *k* of Lachish .... Josh 10:5   4428
the *k* of Eglon, gathered .... Josh 10:5   4428
the *k* of Jerusalem .... Josh 10:23   4428
the *k* of Hebron .... Josh 10:23   4428
the *k* of Jarmuth .... Josh 10:23   4428
the *k* of Lachish .... Josh 10:23   4428
and the *k* of Eglon .... Josh 10:23   4428
and the *k* thereof he utterly................... Josh 10:28   4428
he did to the *k* of Makkedah as he .... Josh 10:28   4428
as he did unto the *k* of Jericho .... Josh 10:28   4428
the *k* thereof, into the hand of .... Josh 10:30   4428
but did unto the *k* thereof as he .... Josh 10:30   4428
as he did unto the *k* of Jericho .... Josh 10:30   4428
Then Horam *k* of Gezer came up to .... Josh 10:33   4428

K

the *k* thereof, and all the cities	Josh 10:37	4428
the *k* thereof, and all the cities	Josh 10:39	4428
did to Debir, and to the *k* thereof	Josh 10:39	4428
done also to Libnah, and to her *k*	Josh 10:39	4428
when Jabin *k* of Hazor had heard	Josh 11:1	4428
that he sent to Jobab *k* of Madon	Josh 11:1	4428
to the *k* of Shimron	Josh 11:1	4428
and to the *k* of Achshaph	Josh 11:1	4428
smote the *k* thereof with the	Josh 11:10	4428
Sihon *k* of the Amorites, who	Josh 12:2	4428
And the coast of Og *k* of Bashan	Josh 12:4	4428
the border of Sihon *k* of Heshbon	Josh 12:5	4428
The *k* of Jericho, one	Josh 12:9	4428
the *k* of Ai, which is beside	Josh 12:9	4428
The *k* of Jerusalem, one	Josh 12:10	4428
the *k* of Hebron, one	Josh 12:10	4428
The *k* of Jarmuth, one	Josh 12:11	4428
the *k* of Lachish, one	Josh 12:11	4428
The *k* of Eglon, one	Josh 12:12	4428
the *k* of Gezer, one	Josh 12:12	4428
The *k* of Debir, one	Josh 12:13	4428
the *k* of Geder, one	Josh 12:13	4428
The *k* of Hormah, one	Josh 12:14	4428
the *k* of Arad, one	Josh 12:14	4428
The *k* of Libnah, one	Josh 12:15	4428
the *k* of Adullam, one	Josh 12:15	4428
The *k* of Makkedah, one	Josh 12:16	4428
the *k* of Beth-el, one	Josh 12:16	4428
The *k* of Tappuah, one	Josh 12:17	4428
the *k* of Hepher, one	Josh 12:17	4428
The *k* of Aphek, one	Josh 12:18	4428
the *k* of Lasharon, one	Josh 12:18	4428
The *k* of Madon, one	Josh 12:19	4428
the *k* of Hazor, one	Josh 12:19	4428
The *k* of Shimron-meron, one	Josh 12:20	4428
the *k* of Achshaph, one	Josh 12:20	4428
The *k* of Taanach, one	Josh 12:21	4428
the *k* of Megiddo, one	Josh 12:21	4428
The *k* of Kedesh, one	Josh 12:22	4428
the *k* of Jokneam of Carmel, one	Josh 12:22	4428
The *k* of Dor in the coast of Dor,	Josh 12:23	4428
the *k* of the nations of Gilgal,	Josh 12:23	4428
The *k* of Tirzah, one	Josh 12:24	4428
cities of Sihon *k* of the Amorites	Josh 13:10	4428
of Sihon *k* of the Amorites	Josh 13:21	4428
the kingdom of Sihon *k* of Heshbon	Josh 13:27	4428
all the kingdom of Og *k* of Bashan	Josh 13:30	4428
k of Moab, arose and warred	Josh 24:9	4428
k of Mesopotamia	Judg 3:8	4428
k of Mesopotamia into his hand	Judg 3:10	4428
the *k* of Moab against Israel	Judg 3:12	4428
the *k* of Moab eighteen years	Judg 3:14	4428
present to Eglon the *k* of Moab	Judg 3:15	4428
the present unto Eglon *k* of Moab	Judg 3:17	4428
a secret errand unto thee, O *k*	Judg 3:19	4428
the hand of Jabin *k* of Canaan	Judg 4:2	4428
between Jabin the *k* of Hazor	Judg 4:17	4428
k of Canaan before the children	Judg 4:23	4428
against Jabin the *k* of Canaan	Judg 4:24	4428
had destroyed Jabin *k* of Canaan	Judg 4:24	4428
one resembled the children of a *k*	Judg 8:18	4428
and went, and made Abimelech *k*	Judg 9:6	4428
on a time to anoint a *k* over them	Judg 9:8	4428
in truth ye anoint me *k* over you	Judg 9:15	4428
in that ye have made Abimelech *k*	Judg 9:16	4427
k over the men of Shechem,	Judg 9:18	4427
the *k* of the children of Ammon	Judg 11:12	4428
the *k* of the children of Ammon	Judg 11:13	4428
the *k* of the children of Ammon	Judg 11:14	4428
messengers unto the *k* of Edom	Judg 11:17	4428
but the *k* of Edom would not	Judg 11:17	4428
they sent unto the *k* of Moab	Judg 11:17	4428
unto Sihon *k* of the Amorites	Judg 11:19	4428
of the Amorites, the *k* of Heshbon	Judg 11:19	4428
the son of Zippor, *k* of Moab	Judg 11:25	4428
Howbeit the *k* of the children of	Judg 11:28	4428
days there was no *k* in Israel	Judg 17:6	4428
days there was no *k* in Israel	Judg 18:1	4428
when there was no *k* in Israel	Judg 19:1	4428
days there was no *k* in Israel	Judg 21:25	4428
he shall give strength unto his *k*	1Sa 2:10	4428
now make us a *k* to judge us like	1Sa 8:5	4428
said, Give us a *k* to judge us	1Sa 8:6	4428
the *k* that shall reign over them	1Sa 8:9	4428
the people that asked of him a *k*	1Sa 8:10	4428
the *k* that shall reign over you	1Sa 8:11	4428
k which ye shall have chosen you	1Sa 8:18	4428
but we will have a *k* over us	1Sa 8:19	4428
that our *k* may judge us, and go	1Sa 8:20	4428
their voice, and make them a *k*	1Sa 8:22	4428
him, Nay, but set a *k* over us	1Sa 10:19	4428
shouted, and said, God save the *k*	1Sa 10:24	4428
there they made Saul *k* before the	1Sa 11:15	4427
me, and have made a *k* over you	1Sa 12:1	4428
behold, the *k* walketh before you	1Sa 12:2	4428
and into the hand of the *k* of Moab	1Sa 12:9	4428
when ye saw that Nahash the *k* of	1Sa 12:12	4428
but a *k* shall reign over us	1Sa 12:12	4428
when the LORD your God was your *k*	1Sa 12:12	4428
behold the *k* whom ye have chosen	1Sa 12:13	4428
the LORD hath set a *k* over you	1Sa 12:13	4428
also the *k* that reigneth over you	1Sa 12:14	4428
of the LORD, in asking you a *k*	1Sa 12:17	4428
our sins this evil, to ask us a *k*	1Sa 12:19	4428
be consumed, both ye and your *k*	1Sa 12:25	4428
thee to be *k* over his people	1Sa 15:1	4428
he took Agag the *k* of the	1Sa 15:8	4428
that I have set up Saul to be *k*	1Sa 15:11	4428
LORD anointed thee *k* over Israel	1Sa 15:17	4428
have brought Agag the *k* of Amalek	1Sa 15:20	4428
also rejected thee from being *k*	1Sa 15:23	4428
thee from being *k* over Israel	1Sa 15:26	4428
me Agag the *k* of the Amalekites	1Sa 15:32	4428
he had made Saul *k* over Israel	1Sa 15:35	4427
provided me a *k* among his sons	1Sa 16:1	4428
the *k* will enrich him with great	1Sa 17:25	4428
said, As thy soul liveth, O *k*	1Sa 17:55	4428
the *k* said, Enquire thou whose	1Sa 17:56	4428
and dancing, to meet *k* Saul	1Sa 18:6	4428
I should be son in law to the *k*	1Sa 18:18	4428
the *k* hath delight in thee, and	1Sa 18:22	4428
The *k* desireth not any dowry, but	1Sa 18:25	4428
gave them in full tale to the *k*	1Sa 18:27	4428
Let not the *k* sin against his	1Sa 19:4	4428
fail to sit with the *k* at meat	1Sa 20:5	4428
the *k* sat him down to eat meat	1Sa 20:24	4428
the *k* sat upon his seat, as at	1Sa 20:25	4428
The *k* hath commanded me a	1Sa 21:2	4428
and went to Achish the *k* of Gath	1Sa 21:10	4428
not this David the *k* of the land	1Sa 21:11	4428
afraid of Achish the *k* of Gath	1Sa 21:12	4428
and he said unto the *k* of Moab	1Sa 22:3	4428
brought them before the *k* of Moab	1Sa 22:4	4428
Then the *k* sent to call Ahimelech	1Sa 22:11	4428
and they came all of them to the *k*	1Sa 22:11	4428
Then Ahimelech answered the *k*	1Sa 22:14	4428
let not the *k* impute any thing	1Sa 22:15	4428
the *k* said, Thou shalt surely die	1Sa 22:16	4428
the *k* said unto the footmen that	1Sa 22:17	4428
But the servants of the *k* would	1Sa 22:17	4428
the *k* said to Doeg, Turn thou, and	1Sa 22:18	4428
and thou shalt be *k* over Israel	1Sa 23:17	4427
Now therefore, O *k*, come down	1Sa 23:20	4428
after Saul, saying, My lord the *k*	1Sa 24:8	4428
After whom is the *k* of Israel	1Sa 24:14	4428
well that thou shalt surely be *k*	1Sa 24:20	4428
his house, like the feast of a *k*	1Sa 25:36	4428
Who art thou that criest to the *k*	1Sa 26:14	4428
hast thou not kept thy lord the *k*	1Sa 26:15	4428
in to destroy the *k* thy lord	1Sa 26:15	4428
It is my voice, my lord, O *k*	1Sa 26:17	4428
let my lord the *k* hear the words	1Sa 26:19	4428
for the *k* of Israel is come out	1Sa 26:20	4428
the son of Maoch, *k* of Gath	1Sa 27:2	4428
the *k* said unto her, Be not	1Sa 28:13	4428
servant of Saul the *k* of Israel	1Sa 29:3	4428
the enemies of my lord the *k*	1Sa 29:8	4428
David *k* over the house of Judah	2Sa 2:4	4428
have anointed me *k* over them	2Sa 2:7	4428
made him *k* over Gilead, and over	2Sa 2:9	4427
the time that David was *k* in	2Sa 2:11	4428
daughter of Talmai *k* of Geshur	2Sa 3:3	4428
in times past to be *k* over you	2Sa 3:17	4428
all Israel unto my lord the *k*	2Sa 3:21	4428
the son of Ner came to the *k*	2Sa 3:23	4428
Then Joab came to the *k*, and said,	2Sa 3:24	4428
k David himself followed the bier	2Sa 3:31	4428
the *k* lifted up his voice, and	2Sa 3:32	4428
the *k* lamented over Abner, and	2Sa 3:33	4428
as whatsoever the *k* did pleased	2Sa 3:36	4428
k to slay Abner the son of Ner	2Sa 3:37	4428
the *k* said unto his servants,	2Sa 3:38	4428
this day weak, though anointed *k*	2Sa 3:39	4428
David to Hebron, and said to the *k*	2Sa 4:8	4428
my lord the *k* this day of Saul	2Sa 4:8	4428
past, when Saul was *k* over us	2Sa 5:2	4428
of Israel came to the *k* to Hebron	2Sa 5:3	4428
k David made a league with them	2Sa 5:3	4428
they anointed David *k* over Israel	2Sa 5:3	4428
And the *k* and his men went to	2Sa 5:6	4428
Hiram *k* of Tyre sent messengers	2Sa 5:11	4428
had established him *k* over Israel	2Sa 5:12	4428

had anointed David *k* over Israel	2Sa 5:17	4428
And it was told *k* David, saying,	2Sa 6:12	4428
saw *k* David leaping and dancing	2Sa 6:16	4428
was the *k* of Israel today	2Sa 6:20	4428
when the *k* sat in his house, and	2Sa 7:1	4428
That the *k* said unto Nathan the	2Sa 7:2	4428
And Nathan said to the *k*, Go, do	2Sa 7:3	4428
Then went *k* David in, and sat	2Sa 7:18	4428
k of Zobah, as he went to recover	2Sa 8:3	4428
to succour Hadadezer *k* of Zobah	2Sa 8:5	4428
k David took exceeding much brass	2Sa 8:8	4428
When Toi *k* of Hamath heard that	2Sa 8:9	4428
sent Joram his son unto *k* David	2Sa 8:10	4428
Which also *k* David did dedicate	2Sa 8:11	4428
son of Rehob, *k* of Zobah	2Sa 8:12	4428
the *k* said unto him, Art thou	2Sa 9:2	4428
the *k* said, is there not yet any	2Sa 9:3	4428
And Ziba said unto the *k*, Jonathan	2Sa 9:3	4428
the *k* said unto him, Where is he	2Sa 9:4	4428
And Ziba said unto the *k*, Behold,	2Sa 9:4	4428
Then *k* David sent, and fetched him	2Sa 9:5	4428
Then the *k* called to Ziba, Saul's	2Sa 9:9	4428
Then said Ziba unto the *k*	2Sa 9:11	4428
to all that my lord the *k* hath	2Sa 9:11	4428
As for Mephibosheth, said the *k*	2Sa 9:11	4428
that the *k* of the children of	2Sa 10:1	4428
the *k* said, Tarry at Jericho	2Sa 10:5	4428
of *k* Maacah a thousand men, and of	2Sa 10:6	4428
him a mess of meat from the *k*	2Sa 11:8	4428
the matters of the war unto the *k*	2Sa 11:19	4428
I anointed thee *k* over Israel	2Sa 12:7	4428
when the *k* was come to see him,	2Sa 13:6	4428
to see him, Amnon said unto the *k*	2Sa 13:6	4428
I pray thee, speak unto the *k*	2Sa 13:13	4428
But when *k* David heard of all	2Sa 13:21	4428
And Absalom came to the *k*, and said	2Sa 13:24	4428
let the *k*, I beseech thee, and his	2Sa 13:24	4428
the *k* said to Absalom, Nay, my	2Sa 13:25	4428
the *k* said unto him, Why should	2Sa 13:26	4428
Then the *k* arose, and tare his	2Sa 13:31	4428
the *k* take the thing to his heart	2Sa 13:33	4428
And Jonadab said unto the *k*	2Sa 13:35	4428
the *k* also and all his servants	2Sa 13:36	4428
the son of Ammihud, *k* of Geshur	2Sa 13:37	4428
the soul of *k* David longed to go	2Sa 13:39	4428
And come to the *k*, and speak on	2Sa 14:3	4428
woman of Tekoah spake to the *k*	2Sa 14:4	4428
did obeisance, and said, Help, O *k*	2Sa 14:4	4428
the *k* said unto her, What aileth	2Sa 14:5	4428
the *k* said unto the woman, Go to	2Sa 14:8	4428
said unto the *k*, My lord, O *k*	2Sa 14:9	4428
and the *k* and his throne be	2Sa 14:9	4428
the *k* said, Whosoever saith ought	2Sa 14:10	4428
let the *k* remember the LORD thy	2Sa 14:11	4428
speak one word unto my lord the *k*	2Sa 14:12	4428
for the *k* doth speak this thing	2Sa 14:13	4428
in that the *k* doth not fetch home	2Sa 14:13	4428
of this thing unto my lord the *k*	2Sa 14:15	4428
said, I will now speak unto the *k*	2Sa 14:15	4428
it may be that the *k* will perform	2Sa 14:15	4428
For the *k* will hear, to deliver	2Sa 14:16	4428
The word of my lord the *k* shall	2Sa 14:17	4428
is my lord the *k* to discern good	2Sa 14:17	4428
Then the *k* answered and said unto	2Sa 14:18	4428
said, Let my lord the *k* now speak	2Sa 14:18	4428
the *k* said, Is not the hand of	2Sa 14:19	4428
As thy soul liveth, my lord the *k*	2Sa 14:19	4428
that my lord the *k* hath spoken	2Sa 14:19	4428
the *k* said unto Joab, Behold now,	2Sa 14:21	4428
bowed himself, and thanked the *k*	2Sa 14:22	4428
grace in thy sight, my lord, O *k*	2Sa 14:22	4428
in that the *k* hath fulfilled the	2Sa 14:22	4428
the *k* said, Let him turn to his	2Sa 14:24	4428
Joab, to have sent him to the *k*	2Sa 14:29	4428
that I may send thee to the *k*	2Sa 14:32	4428
So Joab came to the *k*, and told	2Sa 14:33	4428
for Absalom, he came to the *k*	2Sa 14:33	4428
face to the ground before the *k*	2Sa 14:33	4428
and the *k* kissed Absalom	2Sa 14:33	4428
came to the *k* for judgment	2Sa 15:2	4428
man deputed of the *k* to hear thee	2Sa 15:3	4428
that came to the *k* for judgment	2Sa 15:6	4428
that Absalom said unto the *k*	2Sa 15:7	4428
the *k* said unto him, Go in peace	2Sa 15:9	4428
king's servants said unto the *k*	2Sa 15:15	4428
my lord the *k* shall appoint	2Sa 15:15	4428
the *k* went forth, and all his	2Sa 15:16	4428
the *k* left ten women, which were	2Sa 15:16	4428
the *k* went forth, and all the	2Sa 15:18	4428
from Gath, passed on before the *k*	2Sa 15:18	4428
Then said the *k* to Ittai the	2Sa 15:19	4428
to thy place, and abide with the *k*	2Sa 15:19	4428
And Ittai answered the *k*, and said,	2Sa 15:21	4428
and as my lord the *k* liveth	2Sa 15:21	4428
what place my lord the *k* shall be	2Sa 15:21	4428
the *k* also himself passed over	2Sa 15:23	4428
the *k* said unto Zadok, Carry back	2Sa 15:25	4428
The *k* said also unto Zadok the	2Sa 15:27	4428
I will be thy servant, O *k*	2Sa 15:34	4428
the *k* said unto Ziba, What	2Sa 16:2	4428
the *k* said, And where is thy	2Sa 16:3	4428
And Ziba said unto the *k*, Behold,	2Sa 16:3	4428
Then said the *k* to Ziba, Behold,	2Sa 16:4	4428
grace in thy sight, my lord, O *k*	2Sa 16:4	4428
when *k* David came to Bahurim,	2Sa 16:5	4428
and at all the servants of *k* David	2Sa 16:6	4428
the son of Zeruiah unto the *k*	2Sa 16:9	4428
this dead dog curse my lord the *k*	2Sa 16:9	4428
the *k* said, What have I to do	2Sa 16:10	4428
And he, and all the people that	2Sa 16:14	4428
God save the *k*, God save the *k*	2Sa 16:16	4428
and I will smite the *k* only	2Sa 17:2	4428
lest the *k* be swallowed up, and	2Sa 17:16	4428
and they went and told *k* David	2Sa 17:17	4428
told *k* David, and said unto David,	2Sa 17:21	4428
the *k* said unto the people, I	2Sa 18:2	4428
the *k* said unto them, What	2Sa 18:4	4428
the *k* stood by the gate side, and	2Sa 18:4	4428
the *k* commanded Joab and Abishai	2Sa 18:5	4428
k gave all the captains charge	2Sa 18:5	4428
in our hearing the *k* charged thee	2Sa 18:12	4428
there is no matter hid from the *k*	2Sa 18:13	4428
me now run, and bear the *k* tidings	2Sa 18:19	4428
Go tell the *k* what thou hast seen	2Sa 18:21	4428
the watchman cried, and told the *k*	2Sa 18:25	4428
the *k* said, If he be alone, there	2Sa 18:25	4428
the *k* said, He also bringeth	2Sa 18:26	4428
the *k* said, He is a good man, and	2Sa 18:27	4428
called, and said unto the *k*	2Sa 18:28	4428
earth upon his face before the *k*	2Sa 18:28	4428
their hand against my lord the *k*	2Sa 18:28	4428
the *k* said, Is the young man	2Sa 18:29	4428
the *k* said unto him, Turn aside,	2Sa 18:30	4428
said, Tidings, my lord the *k*	2Sa 18:31	4428
the *k* said unto Cushi, Is the	2Sa 18:32	4428
The enemies of my lord the *k*	2Sa 18:32	4428
the *k* was much moved, and went up	2Sa 18:33	4428
the *k* weepeth and mourneth for	2Sa 19:1	4428
how the *k* was grieved for his son	2Sa 19:2	4428
But the *k* covered his face, and	2Sa 19:4	4428
the *k* cried with a loud voice, O	2Sa 19:4	4428
Joab came into the house to the *k*	2Sa 19:5	4428
Then the *k* arose, and sat in the	2Sa 19:8	4428
the *k* doth sit in the gate	2Sa 19:8	4428
all the people came before the *k*	2Sa 19:8	4428
The *k* saved us out of the hand of	2Sa 19:9	4428
not a word of bringing the *k* back	2Sa 19:10	4428
k David sent to Zadok and to	2Sa 19:11	4428
to bring the *k* back to his house	2Sa 19:11	4428
of all Israel is come to the *k*	2Sa 19:11	4428
ye the last to bring back the *k*	2Sa 19:12	4428
they sent this word unto the *k*	2Sa 19:14	4428
So the *k* returned, and came to	2Sa 19:15	4428
to Gilgal, to go to meet the *k*	2Sa 19:15	4428
to conduct the *k* over Jordan	2Sa 19:15	4428
the men of Judah to meet *k* David	2Sa 19:16	4428
went over Jordan before the *k*	2Sa 19:17	4428
of Gera fell down before the *k*	2Sa 19:18	4428
And said unto the *k*, Let not my	2Sa 19:19	4428
lord the *k* went out of Jerusalem	2Sa 19:19	4428
that the *k* should take it to his	2Sa 19:19	4428
to go down to meet my lord the *k*	2Sa 19:20	4428
that I am this day *k* over Israel	2Sa 19:22	4428
Therefore the *k* said unto Shimei,	2Sa 19:23	4428
And he sware unto him	2Sa 19:23	4428
of Saul came down to meet the *k*	2Sa 19:24	4428
from the day the *k* departed until	2Sa 19:24	4428
come to Jerusalem to meet the *k*	2Sa 19:25	4428
that the *k* said unto him,	2Sa 19:25	4428
And he answered, My lord, O *k*	2Sa 19:26	4428
may ride thereon, and go to the *k*	2Sa 19:26	4428
thy servant unto my lord the *k*	2Sa 19:27	4428
but my lord the *k* is as an angel	2Sa 19:27	4428
but dead men before my lord the *k*	2Sa 19:28	4428
I yet to cry any more unto the *k*	2Sa 19:28	4428
the *k* said unto him, Why speakest	2Sa 19:29	4428
And Mephibosheth said unto the *k*	2Sa 19:30	4428
forasmuch as my lord the *k* is	2Sa 19:30	4428
and went over Jordan with the *k*	2Sa 19:31	4428
and he had provided the *k* of	2Sa 19:32	4428
the *k* said unto Barzillai, Come	2Sa 19:33	4428
And Barzillai said unto the *k*	2Sa 19:34	4428

K

go up with the *k* unto Jerusalem	2Sa 19:34	4428
yet a burden unto my lord the *k*	2Sa 19:35	4428
little way over Jordan with the *k*	2Sa 19:36	4428
why should the *k* recompense it me	2Sa 19:36	4428
him go over with my lord the *k*	2Sa 19:37	4428
the *k* answered, Chimham shall go	2Sa 19:38	4428
when the *k* was come over	2Sa 19:39	4428
the *k* kissed Barzillai, and	2Sa 19:39	4428
Then the *k* went on to Gilgal, and	2Sa 19:40	4428
people of Judah conducted the *k*	2Sa 19:40	4428
to the *k*, and said unto the *k*	2Sa 19:41	4428
thee away, and have brought the *k*	2Sa 19:41	4428
Because the *k* is near of kin to	2Sa 19:42	4428
said, We have ten parts in the *k*	2Sa 19:43	4428
first had in bringing back our *k*	2Sa 19:43	4428
men of Judah clave unto their *k*	2Sa 20:2	4428
the *k* took the ten women his	2Sa 20:3	4428
Then said the *k* to Amasa,	2Sa 20:4	4428
lifted up his hand against the *k*	2Sa 20:21	4428
returned to Jerusalem unto the *k*	2Sa 20:22	4428
the *k* called the Gibeonites, and	2Sa 21:2	4428
And they answered the *k*, The man	2Sa 21:5	4428
the *k* said, I will give them	2Sa 21:6	4428
But the *k* spared Mephibosheth,	2Sa 21:7	4428
But the *k* took the two sons of	2Sa 21:8	4428
all that the *k* commanded	2Sa 21:14	4428
the tower of salvation for his *k*	2Sa 22:51	4428
For the *k* said to Joab the	2Sa 24:2	4428
And Joab said unto the *k*, Now the	2Sa 24:3	4428
eyes of my lord the *k* may see it	2Sa 24:3	4428
lord the *k* delight in this thing	2Sa 24:3	4428
out from the presence of the *k*	2Sa 24:4	4428
number of the people unto the *k*	2Sa 24:9	4428
And Araunah looked, and saw the *k*	2Sa 24:20	4428
bowed himself before the *k* on his	2Sa 24:20	4428
my lord the *k* come to his servant	2Sa 24:21	4428
David, Let my lord the *k* take	2Sa 24:22	4428
as a *k*, give unto the *k*	2Sa 24:23	4428
And Araunah said unto the *k*	2Sa 24:23	4428
the *k* said unto Araunah, Nay	2Sa 24:23	4428
Now *k* David was old and stricken	1Kin 1:1	4428
for my lord the *k* a young virgin	1Kin 1:2	4428
and let her stand before the *k*	1Kin 1:2	4428
that my lord the *k* may get heat	1Kin 1:2	4428
and brought her to the *k*	1Kin 1:3	4428
was very fair, and cherished the *k*	1Kin 1:4	4428
but the *k* knew her not	1Kin 1:4	4428
himself, saying, I will be *k*	1Kin 1:5	4427
Go and get thee in unto *k* David	1Kin 1:13	4428
him, Didst not thou, my lord, O *k*	1Kin 1:13	4428
thou yet talkest there with the *k*	1Kin 1:14	4428
in unto the *k* into the chamber	1Kin 1:15	4428
and the *k* was very old	1Kin 1:15	4428
Shunammite ministered unto the *k*	1Kin 1:15	4428
and did obeisance unto the *k*	1Kin 1:16	4428
the *k* said, What wouldest thou	1Kin 1:16	4428
and now, my lord the *k*, thou	1Kin 1:18	4428
hath called all the sons of the *k*	1Kin 1:19	4428
And thou, my lord, O *k*, the eyes	1Kin 1:20	4428
throne of my lord the *k* after him	1Kin 1:20	4428
when my lord the *k* shall sleep	1Kin 1:21	4428
while she yet talked with the *k*	1Kin 1:22	4428
And they told the *k*, saying,	1Kin 1:23	4428
when he was come in before the *k*	1Kin 1:23	4428
the *k* with his face to the ground	1Kin 1:23	4428
And Nathan said, My lord, O *k*	1Kin 1:24	4428
him, and say, God save *k* Adonijah	1Kin 1:25	4428
this thing done by my lord the *k*	1Kin 1:27	4428
throne of my lord the *k* after him	1Kin 1:27	4428
Then *k* David answered and said,	1Kin 1:28	4428
presence, and stood before the *k*	1Kin 1:28	4428
the *k* sware, and said, As the LORD	1Kin 1:29	4428
earth, and did reverence to the *k*	1Kin 1:31	4428
Let my lord *k* David live for ever	1Kin 1:31	4428
k David said, Call me Zadok the	1Kin 1:32	4428
And they came before the *k*	1Kin 1:32	4428
The *k* also said unto them, Take	1Kin 1:33	4428
anoint him there *k* over Israel	1Kin 1:34	4428
and say, God save *k* Solomon	1Kin 1:34	4428
for he shall be *k* in my stead.	1Kin 1:35	4427
son of Jehoiada answered the *k*	1Kin 1:36	4428
God of my lord the *k* say so too	1Kin 1:36	4428
LORD hath been with my lord the *k*	1Kin 1:37	4428
the throne of my lord *k* David	1Kin 1:37	4428
to ride upon *k* David's mule	1Kin 1:38	4428
people said, God save *k* Solomon	1Kin 1:39	4428
k David made Solomon *k*	1Kin 1:43	4427
the *k* hath sent with him Zadok	1Kin 1:44	4428
have anointed him *k* in Gihon	1Kin 1:45	4428
came to bless our lord *k* David	1Kin 1:47	4428
the *k* bowed himself upon the bed	1Kin 1:47	4428
And also thus said the *k*, Blessed	1Kin 1:48	4428
Adonijah feareth *k* Solomon	1Kin 1:51	4428
Let *k* Solomon swear unto me to	1Kin 1:51	4428
So *k* Solomon sent, and they	1Kin 1:53	4428
and bowed himself to *k* Solomon	1Kin 1:53	4428
I pray thee, unto Solomon the *k*	1Kin 2:17	4428
I will speak for thee unto the *k*	1Kin 2:18	4428
therefore went unto *k* Solomon	1Kin 2:19	4428
the *k* rose up to meet her, and	1Kin 2:19	4428
the *k* said unto her, Ask on, my	1Kin 2:20	4428
k Solomon answered and said unto	1Kin 2:22	4428
Then *k* Solomon sware by the LORD,	1Kin 2:23	4428
k Solomon sent by the hand of	1Kin 2:25	4428
Abiathar the priest said the *k*	1Kin 2:26	4428
it was told *k* Solomon that Joab	1Kin 2:29	4428
said unto him, Thus saith the *k*	1Kin 2:30	4428
Benaiah brought the *k* word again	1Kin 2:30	4428
the *k* said unto him, Do as he	1Kin 2:31	4428
the *k* put Benaiah the son of	1Kin 2:35	4428
Zadok the priest did the *k* put in	1Kin 2:35	4428
the *k* sent and called for Shimei,	1Kin 2:36	4428
And Shimei said unto the *k*	1Kin 2:38	4428
as my lord the *k* hath said	1Kin 2:38	4428
Achish son of Maachah *k* of Gath	1Kin 2:39	4428
the *k* sent and called for Shimei,	1Kin 2:42	4428
The *k* said moreover to Shimei,	1Kin 2:44	4428
k Solomon shall be blessed, and	1Kin 2:45	4428
So the *k* commanded Benaiah the	1Kin 2:46	4428
affinity with Pharaoh *k* of Egypt	1Kin 3:1	4428
the *k* went to Gibeon to sacrifice	1Kin 3:4	4428
k instead of David my father.	1Kin 3:7	4427
that were harlots, unto the *k*	1Kin 3:16	4428
Thus they spake before the *k*	1Kin 3:22	4428
Then said the *k*, The one saith,	1Kin 3:23	4428
the *k* said, Bring me a sword	1Kin 3:24	4428
they brought a sword before the *k*	1Kin 3:24	4428
the *k* said, Divide the living	1Kin 3:25	4428
the living child was unto the *k*	1Kin 3:26	4428
Then the *k* answered and said, Give	1Kin 3:27	4428
judgment which the *k* had judged	1Kin 3:28	4428
and they feared the *k*	1Kin 3:28	4428
So *k* Solomon was *k* over all	1Kin 4:1	4428
which provided victuals for the *k*	1Kin 4:7	4428
of Sihon *k* of the Amorites	1Kin 4:19	4428
and of Og *k* of Bashan	1Kin 4:19	4428
provided victual for *k* Solomon	1Kin 4:27	4428
that came unto *k* Solomon's table	1Kin 4:27	4428
Hiram *k* of Tyre sent his servants	1Kin 5:1	4428
him *k* in the room of his father	1Kin 5:1	4428
k Solomon raised a levy out of	1Kin 5:13	4428
the *k* commanded, and they brought	1Kin 5:17	4428
the house which *k* Solomon built	1Kin 6:2	4428
k Solomon sent and fetched Hiram	1Kin 7:13	4428
And he came to *k* Solomon, and	1Kin 7:14	4428
k Solomon for the house of the	1Kin 7:40	4428
which Hiram made to *k* Solomon for	1Kin 7:45	4428
of Jordan did the *k* cast them	1Kin 7:46	4428
k Solomon made for the house of	1Kin 7:51	4428
unto *k* Solomon in Jerusalem, that	1Kin 8:1	4428
assembled themselves unto *k*	1Kin 8:2	4428
And *k* Solomon, and all the	1Kin 8:5	4428
the *k* turned his face about, and	1Kin 8:14	4428
And the *k*, and all Israel with him,	1Kin 8:62	4428
So the *k* and all the children of	1Kin 8:63	4428
The same day did the *k* hallow the	1Kin 8:64	4428
and they blessed the *k*, and went	1Kin 8:66	4428
(Now Hiram the *k* of Tyre had	1Kin 9:11	4428
that then *k* Solomon gave Hiram	1Kin 9:11	4428
Hiram sent to the *k* sixscore	1Kin 9:14	4428
the levy which *k* Solomon raised	1Kin 9:15	4428
For Pharaoh *k* of Egypt had gone	1Kin 9:16	4428
k Solomon made a navy of ships in	1Kin 9:26	4428
and brought it to *k* Solomon	1Kin 9:28	4428
was not any thing hid from the *k*	1Kin 10:3	4428
And she said to the *k*, It was a	1Kin 10:6	4428
ever, therefore made he thee *k*	1Kin 10:9	4428
And she gave the *k* an hundred	1Kin 10:10	4428
queen of Sheba gave to *k* Solomon	1Kin 10:10	4428
the *k* made of the almug trees	1Kin 10:12	4428
k Solomon gave unto the queen of	1Kin 10:13	4428
k Solomon made two hundred	1Kin 10:16	4428
the *k* put them in the house of	1Kin 10:17	4428
Moreover the *k* made a great	1Kin 10:18	4428
all *k* Solomon's drinking vessels	1Kin 10:21	4428
For the *k* had at sea a navy of	1Kin 10:22	4428
So *k* Solomon exceeded all the	1Kin 10:23	4428
and with the *k* at Jerusalem	1Kin 10:26	4428
the *k* made silver to be in	1Kin 10:27	4428
But *k* Solomon loved many strange	1Kin 11:1	4428
to Egypt, unto Pharaoh *k* of Egypt	1Kin 11:18	4428
his lord Hadadezer *k* of Zobah	1Kin 11:23	4428

K

So the *k* appointed unto her a	2Kin 8:6	4428
Ben-hadad the *k* of Syria was sick	2Kin 8:7	4428
the *k* said unto Hazael, Take a	2Kin 8:8	4428
Thy son Ben-hadad *k* of Syria hath	2Kin 8:9	4428
that thou shalt be *k* over Syria	2Kin 8:13	4428
Joram the son of Ahab *k* of Israel	2Kin 8:16	4428
Jehoshaphat being then *k* of Judah	2Kin 8:16	4428
k of Judah began to reign	2Kin 8:16	4428
and made a *k* over themselves	2Kin 8:20	4428
k of Israel did Ahaziah the son	2Kin 8:25	4428
Jehoram *k* of Judah begin to reign	2Kin 8:25	4428
the daughter of Omri *k* of Israel	2Kin 8:26	4428
k of Syria in Ramoth-gilead	2Kin 8:28	4428
k Joram went back to be healed in	2Kin 8:29	4428
fought against Hazael *k* of Syria	2Kin 8:29	4428
Ahaziah the son of Jehoram *k* of	2Kin 8:29	4428
have anointed thee *k* over Israel	2Kin 9:3	4428
I have anointed thee *k* over the	2Kin 9:6	4428
have anointed thee *k* over Israel	2Kin 9:12	4428
with trumpets, saying, Jehu is *k*	2Kin 9:13	4427
because of Hazael *k* of Syria	2Kin 9:14	4428
But *k* Joram was returned to be	2Kin 9:15	4428
he fought with Hazael *k* of Syria	2Kin 9:15	4428
Ahaziah *k* of Judah was come down	2Kin 9:16	4428
him, and said, Thus saith the *k*	2Kin 9:18	4428
them, and said, Thus saith the *k*	2Kin 9:19	4428
Joram *k* of Israel and Ahaziah *k*	2Kin 9:21	4428
Ahaziah the *k* of Judah saw this	2Kin 9:27	4428
we will not make any *k*	2Kin 10:5	4427
brethren of Ahaziah *k* of Judah	2Kin 10:13	4428
to salute the children of the *k*	2Kin 10:13	4428
the daughter of *k* Joram, sister	2Kin 11:2	4428
the house of the LORD about the *k*	2Kin 11:7	4428
shall compass the *k* round about	2Kin 11:8	4428
be ye with the *k* as he goeth out	2Kin 11:8	4428
the priest give David's spears	2Kin 11:10	4428
in his hand, round about the *k*	2Kin 11:11	4428
and they made him *k*, and anointed	2Kin 11:12	4427
hands, and said, God save the *k*	2Kin 11:12	4428
the *k* stood by a pillar, as the	2Kin 11:14	4428
and the trumpeters by the *k*	2Kin 11:14	4428
between the LORD and the *k*	2Kin 11:17	4428
between the *k* also and the people	2Kin 11:17	4428
they brought down the *k* from the	2Kin 11:19	4428
twentieth year of *k* Jehoash the	2Kin 12:6	4428
Then *k* Jehoash called for	2Kin 12:7	4428
Then Hazael *k* of Syria went up,	2Kin 12:17	4428
Jehoash *k* of Judah took all the	2Kin 12:18	4428
and sent it to Hazael *k* of Syria	2Kin 12:18	4428
of Joash the son of Ahaziah *k* of	2Kin 13:1	4428
the hand of Hazael *k* of Syria	2Kin 13:3	4428
because the *k* of Syria oppressed	2Kin 13:4	4428
for the *k* of Syria had destroyed	2Kin 13:7	4428
seventh year of Joash *k* of Judah	2Kin 13:10	4428
fought against Amaziah *k* of Judah	2Kin 13:12	4428
Joash the *k* of Israel came down	2Kin 13:14	4428
And he said to the *k* of Israel	2Kin 13:16	4428
And he said unto the *k* of Israel	2Kin 13:18	4428
But Hazael *k* of Syria oppressed	2Kin 13:22	4428
So Hazael *k* of Syria died	2Kin 13:24	4428
k of Israel reigned Amaziah the	2Kin 14:1	4428
the son of Joash *k* of Judah	2Kin 14:1	4428
which had slain the *k* his father	2Kin 14:5	4428
k of Israel, saying, Come, let us	2Kin 14:8	4428
Jehoash the *k* of Israel sent to	2Kin 14:9	4428
Israel sent to Amaziah *k* of Judah	2Kin 14:9	4428
Jehoash *k* of Israel went up	2Kin 14:11	4428
Amaziah *k* of Judah looked one	2Kin 14:11	4428
Jehoash *k* of Israel took Amaziah	2Kin 14:13	4428
of Israel took Amaziah *k* of Judah	2Kin 14:13	4428
he fought with Amaziah *k* of Judah	2Kin 14:15	4428
Amaziah the son of Joash *k* of	2Kin 14:17	4428
k of Israel fifteen years	2Kin 14:17	4428
made him *k* instead of his father	2Kin 14:21	4427
after that the *k* slept with his	2Kin 14:22	4428
of Amaziah the son of Joash *k* of	2Kin 14:23	4428
k of Israel began to reign in	2Kin 14:23	4428
seventh year of Jeroboam *k* of	2Kin 15:1	4428
of Amaziah *k* of Judah to reign	2Kin 15:1	4428
And the LORD smote the *k*, so that	2Kin 15:5	4428
eighth year of Azariah *k* of Judah	2Kin 15:8	4428
year of Uzziah *k* of Judah	2Kin 15:13	4428
thirtieth year of Azariah *k* of	2Kin 15:13	4428
Pul the *k* of Assyria came against	2Kin 15:19	4428
to give to the *k* of Assyria	2Kin 15:20	4428
So the *k* of Assyria turned back,	2Kin 15:20	4428
k of Judah Pekahiah the son of	2Kin 15:23	4428
fiftieth year of Azariah *k* of	2Kin 15:27	4428
In the days of Pekah *k* of Israel	2Kin 15:29	4428
came Tiglath-pileser *k* of Assyria	2Kin 15:29	4428
of Pekah the son of Remaliah *k* of	2Kin 15:32	4428
son of Uzziah *k* of Judah to reign	2Kin 15:32	4428
Judah Rezin *k* of Syria	2Kin 15:37	4428
Jotham *k* of Judah began to reign	2Kin 16:1	4428
Then Rezin *k* of Syria and Pekah	2Kin 16:5	4428
Pekah son of Remaliah *k* of Israel	2Kin 16:5	4428
At that time Rezin *k* of Syria	2Kin 16:6	4428
to Tiglath-pileser *k* of Assyria	2Kin 16:7	4428
out of the hand of the *k* of Syria	2Kin 16:7	4428
of the hand of the *k* of Israel	2Kin 16:7	4428
for a present to the *k* of Assyria	2Kin 16:8	4428
the *k* of Assyria hearkened unto	2Kin 16:9	4428
for the *k* of Assyria went up	2Kin 16:9	4428
k Ahaz went to Damascus to meet	2Kin 16:10	4428
meet Tiglath-pileser *k* of Assyria	2Kin 16:10	4428
k Ahaz sent to Urijah the priest	2Kin 16:10	4428
k Ahaz had sent from Damascus	2Kin 16:11	4428
against *k* Ahaz came from Damascus	2Kin 16:11	4428
when the *k* was come from Damascus	2Kin 16:12	4428
the *k* saw the altar	2Kin 16:12	4428
the *k* approached to the altar, and	2Kin 16:12	4428
k Ahaz commanded Urijah the	2Kin 16:15	4428
to all that *k* Ahaz commanded	2Kin 16:16	4428
k Ahaz cut off the borders of the	2Kin 16:17	4428
of the LORD for the *k* of Assyria	2Kin 16:18	4428
In the twelfth year of Ahaz *k* of	2Kin 17:1	4428
came up Shalmaneser *k* of Assyria	2Kin 17:3	4428
the *k* of Assyria found conspiracy	2Kin 17:4	4428
sent messengers to So *k* of Egypt	2Kin 17:4	4428
no present to the *k* of Assyria	2Kin 17:4	4428
therefore the *k* of Assyria shut	2Kin 17:4	4428
Then the *k* of Assyria came up	2Kin 17:5	4428
the *k* of Assyria took Samaria	2Kin 17:6	4428
the hand of Pharaoh *k* of Egypt	2Kin 17:7	4428
made Jeroboam the son of Nebat *k*	2Kin 17:21	4427
the *k* of Assyria brought men from	2Kin 17:24	4428
they spake to the *k* of Assyria	2Kin 17:26	4428
Then the *k* of Assyria commanded,	2Kin 17:27	4428
of Hoshea son of Elah *k* of Israel	2Kin 18:1	4428
of Ahaz *k* of Judah began to reign	2Kin 18:1	4428
rebelled against the *k* of Assyria	2Kin 18:7	4428
in the fourth year of *k* Hezekiah	2Kin 18:9	4428
of Hoshea son of Elah *k* of Israel	2Kin 18:9	4428
that Shalmaneser *k* of Assyria	2Kin 18:9	4428
ninth year of Hoshea *k* of Israel	2Kin 18:10	4428
the *k* of Assyria did carry away	2Kin 18:11	4428
k Hezekiah did Sennacherib *k*	2Kin 18:13	4428
Hezekiah *k* of Judah sent to the	2Kin 18:14	4428
to the *k* of Assyria to Lachish	2Kin 18:14	4428
the *k* of Assyria appointed unto	2Kin 18:14	4428
k of Judah three hundred talents	2Kin 18:14	4428
Hezekiah *k* of Judah had overlaid	2Kin 18:16	4428
and gave it to the *k* of Assyria	2Kin 18:16	4428
the *k* of Assyria sent Tartan and	2Kin 18:17	4428
to *k* Hezekiah with a great host	2Kin 18:17	4428
And when they had called to the *k*	2Kin 18:18	4428
Hezekiah, Thus saith the great *k*	2Kin 18:19	4428
the *k* of Assyria, What confidence	2Kin 18:19	4428
so is Pharaoh *k* of Egypt unto all	2Kin 18:21	4428
to my lord the *k* of Assyria	2Kin 18:23	4428
the great *k*, the *k* of Assyria	2Kin 18:28	4428
Thus saith the *k*, Let not	2Kin 18:29	4428
into the hand of the *k* of Assyria	2Kin 18:30	4428
for thus saith the *k* of Assyria	2Kin 18:31	4428
of the hand of the *k* of Assyria	2Kin 18:33	4428
when *k* Hezekiah heard it, that he	2Kin 19:1	4428
whom the *k* of Assyria his master	2Kin 19:4	4428
So the servants of *k* Hezekiah	2Kin 19:5	4428
k of Assyria have blasphemed me	2Kin 19:6	4428
found the *k* of Assyria warring	2Kin 19:8	4428
say of Tirhakah *k* of Ethiopia	2Kin 19:9	4428
ye speak to Hezekiah *k* of Judah	2Kin 19:10	4428
into the hand of the *k* of Assyria	2Kin 19:10	4428
Where is the *k* of Hamath	2Kin 19:13	4428
the *k* of Arpad	2Kin 19:13	4428
the *k* of the city of Sepharvaim,	2Kin 19:13	4428
k of Assyria I have heard	2Kin 19:20	4428
LORD concerning the *k* of Assyria	2Kin 19:32	4428
So Sennacherib *k* of Assyria	2Kin 19:36	4428
of the hand of the *k* of Assyria	2Kin 20:6	4428
k of Babylon, sent letters and a	2Kin 20:12	4428
the prophet unto *k* Hezekiah	2Kin 20:14	4428
in the palace of the *k* of Babylon	2Kin 20:18	4428
a grove, as did Ahab *k* of Israel	2Kin 21:3	4428
Because Manasseh *k* of Judah hath	2Kin 21:11	4428
slew the *k* in his own house	2Kin 21:23	4428
that had conspired against *k* Amon	2Kin 21:24	4428
Josiah his son in his stead	2Kin 21:24	4427
the eighteenth year of *k* Josiah	2Kin 22:3	4428
that the *k* sent Shaphan the son	2Kin 22:3	4428
Shaphan the scribe came to the *k*	2Kin 22:9	4428
and brought the *k* word again	2Kin 22:9	4428

Shaphan the scribe shewed the *k*	2Kin 22:10	4428
And Shaphan read it before the *k*	2Kin 22:10	4428
when the *k* had heard the words of	2Kin 22:11	4428
the *k* commanded Hilkiah the	2Kin 22:12	4428
which the *k* of Judah hath read	2Kin 22:16	4428
But to the *k* of Judah which sent	2Kin 22:18	4428
And they brought the *k* word again	2Kin 22:20	4428
the *k* sent, and they gathered unto	2Kin 23:1	4428
the *k* went up into the house of	2Kin 23:2	4428
the *k* stood by a pillar, and made	2Kin 23:3	4428
the *k* commanded Hilkiah the high	2Kin 23:4	4428
did the *k* beat down, and brake	2Kin 23:12	4428
which Solomon the *k* of Israel had	2Kin 23:13	4428
of Ammon, did the *k* defile	2Kin 23:13	4428
the *k* commanded all the people,	2Kin 23:21	4428
the eighteenth year of *k* Josiah	2Kin 23:23	4428
him was there no *k* before him	2Kin 23:25	4428
In his days Pharaoh-nechoh *k* of	2Kin 23:29	4428
the *k* of Assyria to the river	2Kin 23:29	4428
k Josiah went against him	2Kin 23:29	4428
made him *k* in his father's stead	2Kin 23:30	4427
k in the room of Josiah his	2Kin 23:34	4427
k of Babylon came up, and	2Kin 24:1	4428
the *k* of Egypt came not again any	2Kin 24:7	4428
for the *k* of Babylon had taken	2Kin 24:7	4428
that pertained to the *k* of Egypt	2Kin 24:7	4428
k of Babylon came up against	2Kin 24:10	4428
Nebuchadnezzar *k* of Babylon came	2Kin 24:11	4428
Jehoiachin the *k* of Judah went	2Kin 24:12	4428
went out to the *k* of Babylon	2Kin 24:12	4428
the *k* of Babylon took him in the	2Kin 24:12	4428
k of Israel had made in the	2Kin 24:13	4428
even them the *k* of Babylon	2Kin 24:16	4428
the *k* of Babylon made Mattaniah	2Kin 24:17	4428
father's brother *k* in his stead	2Kin 24:17	4427
rebelled against the *k* of Babylon	2Kin 24:20	4428
Nebuchadnezzar *k* of Babylon came	2Kin 25:1	4428
the eleventh year of *k* Zedekiah	2Kin 25:2	4428
the *k* went the way toward the	2Kin 25:4	
the Chaldees pursued after the *k*	2Kin 25:5	4428
So they took the *k*, and brought	2Kin 25:6	4428
up to the *k* of Babylon to Riblah	2Kin 25:6	4428
k Nebuchadnezzar *k* of Babylon	2Kin 25:8	4428
a servant of the *k* of Babylon	2Kin 25:8	4428
fell away to the *k* of Babylon	2Kin 25:11	4428
brought them to the *k* of Babylon	2Kin 25:20	4428
the *k* of Babylon smote them, and	2Kin 25:21	4428
k of Babylon had left, even over	2Kin 25:22	4428
heard that the *k* of Babylon had	2Kin 25:23	4428
land, and serve the *k* of Babylon	2Kin 25:24	4428
of Jehoiachin *k* of Judah, in the	2Kin 25:27	4428
that Evil-merodach *k* of Babylon	2Kin 25:27	4428
k of Judah out of prison	2Kin 25:27	4428
allowance given him of the *k*	2Kin 25:30	4428
k reigned over the children of	1Chr 1:43	4428
daughter of Talmai *k* of Geshur	1Chr 3:2	4428
dwelt with the *k* for his work	1Chr 4:23	4428
the days of Hezekiah *k* of Judah	1Chr 4:41	4428
whom Tilgath-pilneser *k* of	1Chr 5:6	4428
in the days of Jotham *k* of Judah	1Chr 5:17	4428
the days of Jeroboam *k* of Israel	1Chr 5:17	4428
up the spirit of Pul *k* of Assyria	1Chr 5:26	4428
of Tilgath-pilneser *k* of Assyria	1Chr 5:26	4428
time past, even when Saul was *k*	1Chr 11:2	4428
of Israel to the *k* to Hebron	1Chr 11:3	4428
they anointed David *k* over Israel	1Chr 11:3	4428
and with all Israel, to make him *k*	1Chr 11:10	4427
by name, to come and make David *k*	1Chr 12:31	4427
to make David *k* over all Israel	1Chr 12:38	4427
were of one heart to make David *k*	1Chr 12:38	4427
Now Hiram *k* of Tyre sent	1Chr 14:1	4428
had confirmed him *k* over Israel	1Chr 14:2	4428
was anointed *k* over all Israel	1Chr 14:8	4428
at a window saw *k* David dancing	1Chr 15:29	4428
And David the *k* came and sat before	1Chr 17:16	4428
Hadarezer *k* of Zobah unto Hamath	1Chr 18:3	4428
came to help Hadarezer *k* of Zobah	1Chr 18:5	4428
Now when Tou *k* of Hamath heard	1Chr 18:9	4428
the host of Hadarezer *k* of Zobah	1Chr 18:9	4428
sent Hadoram his son to *k* David	1Chr 18:10	4428
Them also *k* David dedicated unto	1Chr 18:11	4428
of David were chief about the *k*	1Chr 18:17	4428
that Nahash the *k* of the children	1Chr 19:1	4428
the *k* said, Tarry at Jericho	1Chr 19:5	4428
the *k* of Maachah and his people	1Chr 19:7	4428
of their *k* from off his head	1Chr 20:2	4428
but, my lord the *k*, are they not	1Chr 21:3	4428
let my lord the *k* do that which	1Chr 21:23	4428
k David said to Ornan, Nay	1Chr 21:24	4428
Solomon his son *k* over Israel	1Chr 23:1	4427
Levites, wrote them before the *k*	1Chr 24:6	4428

in the presence of David the *k*	1Chr 24:31	4428
according to the order of the *k*	1Chr 25:2	4428
things, which David the *k*	1Chr 26:26	4428
LORD, and in the service of the *k*	1Chr 26:30	4428
whom *k* David made rulers over the	1Chr 26:32	4428
to God, and affairs of the *k*	1Chr 26:32	4428
k in any matter of the courses	1Chr 27:1	4428
of the Chronicles of *k* David	1Chr 27:24	4428
the substance which was *k* David's	1Chr 27:31	4428
ministered to the *k* by course	1Chr 28:1	4428
substance and possession of the *k*	1Chr 28:1	4428
Then David the *k* stood up upon	1Chr 28:2	4428
to be *k* over Israel for ever	1Chr 28:4	4428
me to make me *k* over all Israel	1Chr 28:4	4427
Furthermore David the *k* said unto	1Chr 29:1	4428
David the *k* also rejoiced with	1Chr 29:9	4428
and worshipped the LORD, and the *k*	1Chr 29:20	4428
son of David *k* the second time	1Chr 29:22	4428
as *k* instead of David his father	1Chr 29:23	4428
all the sons likewise of *k* David	1Chr 29:24	4428
themselves unto Solomon the *k*	1Chr 29:24	4428
on any *k* before him in Israel	1Chr 29:25	4428
Now the acts of David the *k*	1Chr 29:29	4428
for thou hast made me *k* over a	2Chr 1:9	4427
over whom I have made thee *k*	2Chr 1:11	4427
and with the *k* at Jerusalem	2Chr 1:14	4428
the *k* made silver and gold at	2Chr 1:15	4428
sent to Huram the *k* of Tyre	2Chr 2:3	4428
Then Huram the *k* of Tyre answered	2Chr 2:11	4428
he hath made thee *k* over them	2Chr 2:11	4427
given to David the *k* a wise son	2Chr 2:12	4428
k Solomon for the house of God	2Chr 4:11	4428
to *k* Solomon for the house of the	2Chr 4:16	4428
of Jordan did the *k* cast them	2Chr 4:17	4428
k in the feast which was in the	2Chr 5:3	4428
Also *k* Solomon, and all the	2Chr 5:6	4428
the *k* turned his face, and blessed	2Chr 6:3	4428
Then the *k* and all the people	2Chr 7:4	4428
k Solomon offered a sacrifice of	2Chr 7:5	4428
so the *k* and all the people	2Chr 7:5	4428
which David the *k* had made to	2Chr 7:6	4428
the chief of Solomon's officers	2Chr 8:10	4428
in the house of David of Israel	2Chr 8:11	4428
of the *k* unto the priests	2Chr 8:15	4428
and brought them to *k* Solomon	2Chr 8:18	4428
And she said to the *k*, It was a	2Chr 9:5	4428
to be *k* for the LORD thy God	2Chr 9:8	4428
made he thee *k* over them, to do	2Chr 9:8	4428
And she gave the *k* an hundred	2Chr 9:9	4428
the queen of Sheba gave *k* Solomon	2Chr 9:9	4428
the *k* made of the algum trees	2Chr 9:11	4428
k Solomon gave to the queen of	2Chr 9:12	4428
which she had brought unto the *k*	2Chr 9:12	4428
k Solomon made two hundred	2Chr 9:15	4428
the *k* put them in the house of	2Chr 9:16	4428
Moreover the *k* made a great	2Chr 9:17	4428
vessels of *k* Solomon were of gold	2Chr 9:20	4428
k Solomon passed all the kings of	2Chr 9:22	4428
and with the *k* at Jerusalem	2Chr 9:25	4428
the *k* made silver in Jerusalem as	2Chr 9:27	4428
all Israel come to make him *k*	2Chr 10:1	4427
the presence of Solomon the *k*	2Chr 10:2	4428
k Rehoboam took counsel with the	2Chr 10:6	4428
on the third day, as the *k* bade	2Chr 10:12	4428
the *k* answered them roughly	2Chr 10:13	4428
k Rehoboam forsook the counsel of	2Chr 10:13	4428
So the *k* hearkened not unto the	2Chr 10:15	4428
the *k* would not hearken unto them	2Chr 10:16	4428
the people answered the *k*	2Chr 10:16	4428
Then *k* Rehoboam sent Hadoram that	2Chr 10:18	4428
But *k* Rehoboam made speed to get	2Chr 10:18	4428
k of Judah, and to all Israel in	2Chr 11:3	4428
for he thought to make him *k*	2Chr 11:22	4427
that in the fifth year of *k*	2Chr 12:2	4428
k of Egypt came up against	2Chr 12:2	4428
and the *k* humbled themselves	2Chr 12:6	4428
So Shishak *k* of Egypt came up	2Chr 12:9	4428
Instead of which *k* Rehoboam made	2Chr 12:10	4428
when the *k* entered into the house	2Chr 12:11	4428
So *k* Rehoboam strengthened	2Chr 12:13	4428
Now in the eighteenth year of *k*	2Chr 13:1	4428
Maachah the mother of Asa the *k*	2Chr 15:16	4428
k of Israel came up against Judah	2Chr 16:1	4428
out or come in to Asa *k* of Judah	2Chr 16:1	4428
and sent to Ben-hadad *k* of Syria	2Chr 16:2	4428
league with Baasha *k* of Israel	2Chr 16:3	4428
And Ben-hadad hearkened unto *k* Asa	2Chr 16:4	4428
Then Asa the *k* took all Judah	2Chr 16:6	4428
the seer came to Asa *k* of Judah	2Chr 16:7	4428
hast relied on the *k* of Syria	2Chr 16:7	4428
therefore is the host of the *k* of	2Chr 16:7	4428

K

These waited on the *k* 2Chr 17:19 4428
beside those whom the *k* put in 2Chr 17:19 4428
Ahab *k* of Israel said unto 2Chr 18:3 4428
said unto Jehoshaphat *k* of Judah 2Chr 18:3 4428
said unto the *k* of Israel...........................2Chr 18:4 4428
Therefore the *k* of Israel 2Chr 18:5 4428
the *k* of Israel said unto...........................2Chr 18:7 4428
said, Let not the *k* say so..........................2Chr 18:7 4428
the *k* of Israel called for one of 2Chr 18:8 4428
the *k* of Israel and Jehoshaphat 2Chr 18:9 4428
Jehoshaphat *k* of Judah sat either 2Chr 18:9 4428
deliver it into the hand of the *k* 2Chr 18:11 4428
good to the *k* with one assent 2Chr 18:12 4428
And when he was come to the *k* 2Chr 18:14 4428
the *k* said unto him, Micaiah, ...2Chr 18:14 4428
the *k* said to him, How many times 2Chr 18:15 4428
And the *k* of Israel said to 2Chr 18:17 4428
Who shall entice Ahab *k* of Israel.........2Chr 18:19 4428
Then the *k* of Israel said, Take................2Chr 18:25 4428
And say, Thus saith the *k*, Put...............2Chr 18:25 4428
So the *k* of Israel and Jehoshaphat 2Chr 18:28 4428
Jehoshaphat the *k* of Judah went 2Chr 18:28 4428
the *k* of Israel said unto.........................2Chr 18:29 4428
So the *k* of Israel disguised...................2Chr 18:29 4428
Now the *k* of Syria had commanded......2Chr 18:30 4428
save only with the *k* of Israel 2Chr 18:30 4428
they said, It is the *k* of Israel 2Chr 18:31 4428
that it was not the *k* of Israel.................2Chr 18:32 4428
smote the *k* of Israel between the..........2Chr 18:33 4428
howbeit the *k* of Israel stayed 2Chr 18:34 4428
Jehoshaphat *k* of Judah 2Chr 19:1 4428
said to *k* Jehoshaphat, Shouldest 2Chr 19:2 4428
thou *k* Jehoshaphat, Thus saith 2Chr 19:2 4428
k of Judah join himself with 2Chr 20:35 4428
himself with Ahaziah *k* of Israel 2Chr 20:35 4428
sons of Jehoshaphat *k* of Israel.............2Chr 21:2 4428
of Judah, and made themselves a *k* 2Chr 21:8 4428
nor in the ways of Asa *k* of Judah 2Chr 21:12 4427
his youngest son *k* in his stead 2Chr 22:1 4428
son of Jehoram *k* of Judah reigned.........2Chr 22:1 4428
with Jehoram the son of Ahab *k* of.........2Chr 22:5 4428
k of Syria at Ramoth-gilead 2Chr 22:5 4428
he fought with Hazael *k* of Syria 2Chr 22:6 4428
k of Judah went down to see 2Chr 22:6 4428
the daughter of the *k*, took 2Chr 22:11 4428
the daughter of *k* Jehoram 2Chr 22:11 4428
with the *k* in the house of God...............2Chr 23:3 4428
shall compass the *k* round about 2Chr 23:7 4428
ye with the *k* when he cometh in 2Chr 23:7 4428
shields, that had been *k* David's 2Chr 23:9 4428
the temple, by the *k* round about 2Chr 23:10 4428
him the testimony, and made him *k* 2Chr 23:11 4427
him, and said, God save the *k*................2Chr 23:11 4428
people running and praising the *k* 2Chr 23:12 4428
the *k* stood at his pillar at the 2Chr 23:13 4428
princes and the trumpets by the *k* 2Chr 23:13 4428
all the people, and between the *k* 2Chr 23:16 4428
brought down the *k* from the house.......2Chr 23:20 4428
set the *k* upon the throne of the.............2Chr 23:20 4428
the *k* called for Jehoiada the 2Chr 24:6 4428
And the *k* and Jehoiada gave it to 2Chr 24:12 4428
rest of the money before the *k*................2Chr 24:14 4428
Judah, and made obeisance to the *k* 2Chr 24:17 4428
Then the *k* hearkened unto them............2Chr 24:17 4428
at the commandment of the *k* in 2Chr 24:21 4428
Thus Joash the *k* remembered not 2Chr 24:22 4428
of them unto the *k* of Damascus.............2Chr 24:23 4428
that had killed the *k* his father 2Chr 25:3 4428
a man of God to him, saying, O *k* 2Chr 25:7 4428
that the *k* said unto him, Art 2Chr 25:16 4428
Then Amaziah *k* of Judah took...............2Chr 25:17 4428
k of Israel, saying, Come, let us 2Chr 25:17 4428
Joash *k* of Israel sent to Amaziah 2Chr 25:18 4428
Israel sent to Amaziah *k* of Judah 2Chr 25:18 4428
So Joash the *k* of Israel went up 2Chr 25:21 4428
both he and Amaziah *k* of Judah, at......2Chr 25:21 4428
Joash the *k* of Israel took 2Chr 25:23 4428
of Israel took Amaziah *k* of Judah 2Chr 25:23 4428
Amaziah the son of Joash *k* of...............2Chr 25:25 4428
k of Israel fifteen years..........................2Chr 25:25 4428
made him *k* in the room of his...............2Chr 26:1 4427
after that the *k* slept with his.................2Chr 26:2 4428
to help the *k* against the enemy 2Chr 26:13 4428
And they withstood Uzziah the *k* 2Chr 26:18 4428
Uzziah the *k* was a leper unto the 2Chr 26:21 4428
also with the *k* of the Ammonites 2Chr 27:5 4428
into the hand of the *k* of Syria 2Chr 28:5 4428
into the hand of the *k* of Israel 2Chr 28:5 4428
and Elkanah that was next to the *k* 2Chr 28:7 4428
At that time did *k* Ahaz send unto 2Chr 28:16 4428
low because of Ahaz *k* of Israel..............2Chr 28:19 4428

Tilgath-pilneser *k* of Assyria 2Chr 28:20 4428
and out of the house of the *k*.................2Chr 28:21 4428
and gave it unto the *k* of Assyria 2Chr 28:21 4428
this is that *k* Ahaz 2Chr 28:22 4428
to the commandment of the *k* 2Chr 29:15 4428
they went in to Hezekiah the *k* 2Chr 29:18 4428
which *k* Ahaz in his reign did 2Chr 29:19 4428
Then Hezekiah the *k* rose early..............2Chr 29:20 4428
for the sin offering before the *k*.............2Chr 29:23 4428
for the *k* commanded that the 2Chr 29:24 4428
ordained by David *k* of Israel 2Chr 29:27 4428
made an end of offering, the *k* 2Chr 29:29 4428
Moreover Hezekiah the *k* and the 2Chr 29:30 4428
For the *k* had taken counsel, and 2Chr 30:2 4428
And the thing pleased the *k*...................2Chr 30:4 4428
went with the letters from the *k* 2Chr 30:6 4428
to the commandment of the *k* 2Chr 30:6 4428
to do the commandment of the *k* 2Chr 30:12 4428
For Hezekiah *k* of Judah did give 2Chr 30:24 4428
k of Israel there was not the 2Chr 30:26 4428
the commandment of Hezekiah the *k* 2Chr 31:13 4428
Sennacherib *k* of Assyria came, and......2Chr 32:1 4428
nor dismayed for the *k* of Assyria 2Chr 32:7 4428
the words of Hezekiah *k* of Judah 2Chr 32:8 4428
After this did Sennacherib *k* of..............2Chr 32:9 4428
him,) unto Hezekiah *k* of Judah 2Chr 32:9 4428
saith Sennacherib *k* of Assyria...............2Chr 32:10 4428
of the hand of the *k* of Assyria 2Chr 32:11 4428
And for this cause Hezekiah the *k* 2Chr 32:20 4428
in the camp of the *k* of Assyria 2Chr 32:21 4428
of Sennacherib the *k* of Assyria.............2Chr 32:22 4428
presents to Hezekiah *k* of Judah 2Chr 32:23 4428
of the host of the *k* of Assyria 2Chr 33:11 4428
that had conspired against *k* Amon 2Chr 33:25 4428
Josiah his son *k* in his stead 2Chr 33:25 4427
Shaphan carried the book to the *k*..........2Chr 34:16 4428
brought the *k* word back again,.............2Chr 34:16 4428
Shaphan the scribe told the *k* 2Chr 34:18 4428
And Shaphan read it before the *k* 2Chr 34:18 4428
when the *k* had heard the words of........2Chr 34:19 4428
the *k* commanded Hilkiah, and 2Chr 34:20 4428
and they that the *k* had appointed 2Chr 34:22 4428
have read before the *k* of Judah 2Chr 34:24 4428
And as for the *k* of Judah, who 2Chr 34:26 4428
So they brought the *k* word again 2Chr 34:28 4428
Then the *k* sent and gathered 2Chr 34:29 4428
the *k* went up into the house of 2Chr 34:30 4428
the *k* stood in his place, and made 2Chr 34:31 4428
of David *k* of Israel did build..................2Chr 35:3 4428
the writing of David *k* of Israel..............2Chr 35:4 4428
to the commandment of *k* Josiah 2Chr 35:16 4428
Necho *k* of Egypt came up to fight 2Chr 35:20 4428
to do with thee, thou *k* of Judah 2Chr 35:21 4428
And the archers shot at *k* Josiah 2Chr 35:23 4428
the *k* said to his servants, Have 2Chr 35:23 4428
made him *k* in his father's stead 2Chr 36:1 4427
the *k* of Egypt put him down at 2Chr 36:3 4428
the *k* of Egypt made Eliakim his 2Chr 36:4 4428
Eliakim his brother *k* over Judah 2Chr 36:4 4427
up Nebuchadnezzar *k* of Babylon 2Chr 36:6 4428
k Nebuchadnezzar sent, and brought 2Chr 36:10 4428
Zedekiah his brother *k* over Judah 2Chr 36:10 4427
rebelled against *k* Nebuchadnezzar.......2Chr 36:13 4428
upon them the *k* of the Chaldees 2Chr 36:17 4428
LORD, and the treasures of the *k*............2Chr 36:18 4428
first year of Cyrus *k* of Persia 2Chr 36:22 4428
the spirit of Cyrus *k* of Persia 2Chr 36:22 4428
Thus saith Cyrus *k* of Persia..................2Chr 36:23 4428
first year of Cyrus *k* of Persia ....Ezr 1:1 4428
the spirit of Cyrus *k* of Persia ....Ezr 1:1 4428
Thus saith Cyrus *k* of Persia ....Ezr 1:2 4428
Also Cyrus the *k* brought forth...............Ezr 1:7 4428
Even those did Cyrus *k* of Persia...........Ezr 1:8 4428
whom Nebuchadnezzar the *k* of ....Ezr 2:1 4428
they had of Cyrus *k* of Persia ....Ezr 3:7 4428
ordinance of David *k* of Israel................Ezr 3:10 4428
days of Esar-haddon *k* of Assur ....Ezr 4:2 4428
as *k* Cyrus the *k* of Persia ....Ezr 4:3 4428
all the days of Cyrus *k* of Persia ....Ezr 4:5 4428
the reign of Darius *k* of Persia ....Ezr 4:5 4428
unto Artaxerxes *k* of Persia ....Ezr 4:7 4428
to Artaxerxes the *k* in this sort...............Ezr 4:8 4430
him, even unto Artaxerxes the *k* ....Ezr 4:11 4430
Be it known unto the *k*, that the ....Ezr 4:12 4430
Be it known now unto the *k* ....Ezr 4:13 4430
have we sent and certified the *k* ....Ezr 4:14 4430
We certify the *k* that, if this ....Ezr 4:16 4430
Then sent the *k* an answer unto ....Ezr 4:17 4430
Now when the copy of *k* ....Ezr 4:23 4430
the reign of Darius *k* of Persia ....Ezr 4:24 4430
the river, sent unto Darius the *k* ....Ezr 5:6 4430

Unto Darius the *k*, all peace	Ezr 5:7	4430	according to the state of the *k*	Est 2:18	4428
Be it known unto the *k*, that we	Ezr 5:8	4430	to lay hand on the *k* Ahasuerus	Est 2:21	4428
which a great *k* of Israel builded	Ezr 5:11	4430	Esther certified the *k* thereof in	Est 2:22	4428
Nebuchadnezzar the *k* of Babylon	Ezr 5:12	4430	of the chronicles before the *k*	Est 2:23	4428
k of Babylon the same *k* Cyrus	Ezr 5:13	4430	After these things did *k*	Est 3:1	4428
those did Cyrus the *k* take out of	Ezr 5:14	4430	for the *k* had so commanded	Est 3:2	4428
if it seem good to the *k*	Ezr 5:17	4430	the twelfth year of *k* Ahasuerus	Est 3:7	4428
k to build this house of God at	Ezr 5:17	4430	And Haman said unto *k* Ahasuerus	Est 3:8	4428
let the *k* send his pleasure to us	Ezr 5:17	4430	If it please the *k*, let it be	Est 3:9	4428
Then Darius the *k* made a decree	Ezr 6:1	4430	the *k* took his ring from his hand	Est 3:10	4428
the *k* the same Cyrus the *k*	Ezr 6:3	4430	the *k* said unto Haman, The silver	Est 3:11	4428
and pray for the life of the *k*	Ezr 6:10	4430	in the name of *k* Ahasuerus was it	Est 3:12	4428
that which Darius the *k* had sent	Ezr 6:13	4430	And the *k* and Haman sat down to	Est 3:15	4428
Darius, and Artaxerxes *k* of Persia	Ezr 6:14	4430	that she should go in unto the *k*	Est 4:8	4428
year of the reign of Darius the *k*	Ezr 6:15	4430	shall come unto the *k* into the	Est 4:11	4428
of the *k* of Assyria unto them	Ezr 6:22	4430	except such to whom the *k* shall	Est 4:11	4428
reign of Artaxerxes *k* of Persia	Ezr 7:1	4428	in unto the *k* these thirty days	Est 4:11	4428
the *k* granted him all his request	Ezr 7:6	4428	and so will I go in unto the *k*	Est 4:16	4428
seventh year of Artaxerxes the *k*	Ezr 7:7	4428	the *k* sat upon his royal throne	Est 5:1	4428
was in the seventh year of the *k*	Ezr 7:8	4428	when the *k* saw Esther the queen	Est 5:2	4428
k Artaxerxes gave unto Ezra the	Ezr 7:11	4428	the *k* held out to Esther the	Est 5:2	4428
k of kings, unto Ezra the priest,	Ezr 7:12	4430	Then said the *k* unto her, What	Est 5:3	4428
as thou art sent of the *k*	Ezr 7:14	4430	good unto the *k*, let the *k*	Est 5:4	4428
the silver and gold, which the *k*	Ezr 7:15	4430	Then the *k* said, Cause Haman to	Est 5:5	4428
And I, even I Artaxerxes the *k*	Ezr 7:21	4430	So the *k* and Haman came to the	Est 5:5	4428
wrath against the realm of the *k*	Ezr 7:23	4430	the *k* said unto Esther at the	Est 5:6	4428
of thy God, and the law of the *k*	Ezr 7:26	4430	favour in the sight of the *k*	Est 5:8	4428
mercy unto me before the *k*	Ezr 7:28	4428	if it please the *k* to grant my	Est 5:8	4428
in the reign of Artaxerxes the *k*	Ezr 8:1	4428	to perform my request, let the *k*	Est 5:8	4428
of the *k* a band of soldiers	Ezr 8:22	4428	do to morrow as the *k* hath said	Est 5:8	4428
because we had spoken unto the *k*	Ezr 8:22	4428	wherein the *k* had promoted him	Est 5:11	4428
the house of our God, which the *k*	Ezr 8:25	4428	the princes and servants of the *k*	Est 5:11	4428
year of Artaxerxes the *k*, that	Neh 2:1	4428	*k* unto the banquet that she had	Est 5:12	4428
the wine, and gave it unto the *k*	Neh 2:1	4428	invited unto her also with the *k*	Est 5:12	4428
Wherefore the *k* said unto me	Neh 2:2	4428	the *k* that Mordecai may be hanged	Est 5:14	4428
the *k*, Let the *k* live for ever	Neh 2:3	4428	with the *k* unto the banquet	Est 5:14	4428
Then the *k* said unto me, For what	Neh 2:4	4428	that night could not the *k* sleep	Est 6:1	4428
unto the *k*, If it please the *k*	Neh 2:5	4428	and they were read before the *k*	Est 6:1	4428
the *k* said unto her, (the queen	Neh 2:6	4428	to lay hand on the *k* Ahasuerus	Est 6:2	4428
So it pleased the *k* to send me	Neh 2:6	4428	the *k* said, What honour and	Est 6:3	4428
unto the *k*, If it please the *k*	Neh 2:7	4428	the *k* said, Who is in the court	Est 6:4	4428
the *k* granted me, according to	Neh 2:8	4428	to speak unto the *k* to hang	Est 6:4	4428
Now the *k* had sent captains of	Neh 2:9	4428	the *k* said, Let him come in	Est 6:5	4428
will ye rebel against the *k*	Neh 2:19	4428	the *k* said unto him, What shall	Est 6:6	4428
year of Artaxerxes the *k*, that is	Neh 5:14	4428	whom the *k* delighteth to honour	Est 6:6	4428
wall, that thou mayest be their *k*	Neh 6:6	4428	To whom would the *k* delight to do	Est 6:6	4428
saying, There is a *k* in Judah	Neh 6:7	4428	And Haman answered the *k*, For the	Est 6:7	4428
to the *k* according to these words	Neh 6:7	4428	whom the *k* delighteth to honour	Est 6:7	4428
whom Nebuchadnezzar the *k* of	Neh 7:6	4428	brought which the *k* useth to wear	Est 6:8	4428
and the land of the *k* of Heshbon	Neh 9:22	4428	the horse that the *k* rideth upon	Est 6:8	4428
and the land of Og *k* of Bashan	Neh 9:22	4428	whom the *k* delighteth to honour	Est 6:9	4428
k of Babylon came I unto the *k*	Neh 13:6	4428	whom the *k* delighteth to honour	Est 6:9	4428
days obtained I leave of the *k*	Neh 13:6	4428	Then the *k* said to Haman, Make	Est 6:10	4428
Did not Solomon *k* of Israel sin	Neh 13:26	4428	whom the *k* delighteth to honour	Est 6:11	4428
nations was there no *k* like him	Neh 13:26	4428	So the *k* and Haman came to banquet	Est 7:1	4428
God made him *k* over all Israel	Neh 13:26	4428	the *k* said again unto Esther on	Est 7:2	4428
when the *k* Ahasuerus sat on the	Est 1:2	4428	O *k*, and if it please the *k*	Est 7:3	4428
the *k* made a feast unto all the	Est 1:5	4428	Then the *k* Ahasuerus answered and	Est 7:5	4428
according to the state of the *k*	Est 1:7	4428	Haman was afraid before the *k*	Est 7:6	4428
for so the *k* had appointed to all	Est 1:8	4428	the *k* arising from the banquet of	Est 7:7	4428
which belonged to *k* Ahasuerus	Est 1:9	4428	determined against him by the *k*	Est 7:7	4428
of the *k* was merry with wine	Est 1:10	4428	Then the *k* returned out of the	Est 7:8	4428
the presence of Ahasuerus the *k*	Est 1:10	4428	Then said the *k*, Will he force	Est 7:8	4428
before the *k* with the crown royal	Est 1:11	4428	chamberlains, said before the *k*	Est 7:9	4428
therefore was the *k* very wroth	Est 1:12	4428	who had spoken good for the *k*	Est 7:9	4428
Then the *k* said to the wise men,	Est 1:13	4428	Then the *k* said, Hang him thereon	Est 7:9	4428
the commandment of the *k*	Est 1:15	4428	On that day did the *k* Ahasuerus	Est 8:1	4428
And Memucan answered before the *k*	Est 1:16	4428	And Mordecai came before the *k*	Est 8:1	4428
hath not done wrong to the *k* only	Est 1:16	4428	the *k* took off his ring, which he	Est 8:2	4428
the provinces of the *k* Ahasuerus	Est 1:16	4428	spake yet again before the *k*	Est 8:3	4428
The *k* Ahasuerus commanded Vashti	Est 1:17	4428	Then the *k* held out the golden	Est 8:4	4428
If it please the *k*, let there go	Est 1:19	4428	arose, and stood before the *k*	Est 8:4	4428
come no more before *k* Ahasuerus	Est 1:19	4428	And said, If it please the *k*	Est 8:5	4428
let the *k* give her royal estate	Est 1:19	4428	the thing seem right before the *k*	Est 8:5	4428
And the saying pleased the *k*	Est 1:21	4428	Then the *k* Ahasuerus said unto	Est 8:7	4428
the *k* did according to the word	Est 1:21	4428	he wrote in the *k* Ahasuerus' name	Est 8:10	4428
when the wrath of *k* Ahasuerus was	Est 2:1	4428	Wherein the *k* granted the Jews	Est 8:11	4428
young virgins sought for the *k*	Est 2:2	4428	all the provinces of *k* Ahasuerus	Est 8:12	4428
let the *k* appoint officers in all	Est 2:3	4428	of the *k* in royal apparel of blue	Est 8:15	4428
the *k* be queen instead of Vashti	Est 2:4	4428	the provinces of the *k* Ahasuerus	Est 9:2	4428
And the thing pleased the *k*	Est 2:4	4428	deputies, and officers of the *k*	Est 9:3	4428
away with Jeconiah *k* of Judah	Est 2:6	4428	palace was brought before the *k*	Est 9:11	4428
whom Nebuchadnezzar the *k* of	Est 2:6	4428	the *k* said unto Esther the queen,	Est 9:12	4428
was come to go in to *k* Ahasuerus	Est 2:12	4428	said Esther, If it please the *k*	Est 9:13	4428
thus came every maiden unto the *k*	Est 2:13	4428	the *k* commanded it so to be done	Est 9:14	4428
she came in unto the *k* no more	Est 2:14	4428	the provinces of the *k* Ahasuerus	Est 9:20	4428
except the *k* delighted in her, and	Est 2:14	4428	But when Esther came before the *k*	Est 9:25	4428
was come to go in unto the *k*	Est 2:15	4428	the *k* Ahasuerus laid a tribute	Est 10:1	4428
So Esther was taken unto *k*	Est 2:16	4428	whereunto the *k* advanced him	Est 10:2	4428
the *k* loved Esther above all the	Est 2:17	4428	the Jew was next unto *k* Ahasuerus	Est 10:3	4428
Then the *k* made a great feast	Est 2:18	4428	as a *k* ready to the battle	Job 15:24	4428

K

bring him to the *k* of terrors	Job 18:14	4428
dwelt as a *k* in the army, as one	Job 29:25	4428
Is it fit to say to a *k*, Thou art	Job 34:18	4428
he is a *k* over all the children	Job 41:34	4428
Yet have I set my *k* upon my holy	Ps 2:6	4428
unto the voice of my cry, my *K*	Ps 5:2	4428
The LORD is *K* for ever and ever	Ps 10:16	4428
deliverance giveth he to his *k*	Ps 18:50	4428
let the *k* hear us when we call	Ps 20:9	4428
The *k* shall joy in thy strength,	Ps 21:1	4428
For the *k* trusteth in the LORD,	Ps 21:7	4428
the *K* of glory shall come in	Ps 24:7	4428
Who is this *K* of glory	Ps 24:8	4428
the *K* of glory shall come in	Ps 24:9	4428
Who is this *K* of glory	Ps 24:10	4428
of hosts, he is the *K* of glory	Ps 24:10	4428
yea, the LORD sitteth *K* for ever	Ps 29:10	4428
There is no *k* saved by the	Ps 33:16	4428
Thou art my *K*, O God	Ps 44:4	4428
which I have made touching the *k*	Ps 45:1	4428
So shall the *k* greatly desire thy	Ps 45:11	4428
the *k* in raiment of needlework	Ps 45:14	4428
he is a great *K* over all the	Ps 47:2	4428
sing praises unto our *K*, sing	Ps 47:6	4428
For God is the *K* of all the earth	Ps 47:7	4428
north, the city of the great *K*	Ps 48:2	4428
But the *k* shall rejoice in God	Ps 63:11	4428
even the goings of my God, my *K*	Ps 68:24	4428
Give the *k* thy judgments, O God,	Ps 72:1	4428
For God is my *K* of old, working	Ps 74:12	4428
altars, O LORD of hosts, my *K*	Ps 84:3	4428
the Holy One of Israel is our *k*	Ps 89:18	4428
God, and a great *K* above all gods	Ps 95:3	4428
noise before the LORD, the *K*	Ps 98:6	4428
The *k* sent and loosed him	Ps 105:20	4428
Sihon *k* of the Amorites	Ps 135:11	4428
Og *k* of Bashan, and all the	Ps 135:11	4428
Sihon *k* of the Amorites	Ps 136:19	4428
And Og the *k* of Bashan	Ps 136:20	4428
I will extol thee, my God, O *k*	Ps 145:1	4428
of Zion be joyful in their *K*	Ps 149:2	4428
the son of David, *k* of Israel	Prov 1:1	4428
sentence is in the lips of the *k*	Prov 16:10	4428
The wrath of a *k* is as messengers	Prov 16:14	4428
The fear of a *k* is as the roaring	Prov 20:2	4428
A *k* that sitteth in the throne of	Prov 20:8	4428
A wise *k* scattereth the wicked,	Prov 20:26	4428
Mercy and truth preserve the *k*	Prov 20:28	4428
lips the *k* shall be his friend	Prov 22:11	4428
son, fear thou the LORD and the *k*	Prov 24:21	4428
of Hezekiah *k* of Judah copied out	Prov 25:1	4428
away the wicked from before the *k*	Prov 25:5	4428
thyself in the presence of the *k*	Prov 25:6	4428
The *k* by judgment establisheth	Prov 29:4	4428
The *k* that faithfully judgeth the	Prov 29:14	4428
The locusts have no *k*, yet go	Prov 30:27	4428
and a *k*, against whom there is no	Prov 30:31	4428
The words of *k* Lemuel, the	Prov 31:1	4428
the son of David, *k* in Jerusalem	Eccl 1:1	4428
I the Preacher was *k* over Israel	Eccl 1:12	4428
man do that cometh after the *k*	Eccl 2:12	4428
child than an old and foolish *k*	Eccl 4:13	4428
the *k* himself is served by the	Eccl 5:9	4428
Where the word of a *k* is, there	Eccl 8:4	4428
there came a great *k* against it	Eccl 9:14	4428
when thy *k* is a child, and thy	Eccl 10:16	4428
when thy *k* is the son of nobles,	Eccl 10:17	4428
Curse not the *k*, no not in thy	Eccl 10:20	4428
the *k* hath brought me into his	Song 1:4	4428
While the *k* sitteth at his table,	Song 1:12	4428
K Solomon made himself a chariot	Song 3:9	4428
behold *k* Solomon with the crown	Song 3:11	4428
the *k* is held in the galleries	Song 7:5	4428
In the year that *k* Uzziah died I	Is 6:1	4428
for mine eyes have seen the *K*	Is 6:5	4428
k of Judah, that Rezin the *k*	Is 7:1	4428
Judah, that Rezin *k* of Syria	Is 7:1	4428
k of Israel, went up toward	Is 7:1	4428
set a *k* in the midst of it, even	Is 7:6	4428
even the *k* of Assyria	Is 7:17	4428
by the *k* of Assyria, the head, and	Is 7:20	4428
away before the *k* of Assyria	Is 8:4	4428
even the *k* of Assyria, and all his	Is 8:7	4428
fret themselves, and curse their *k*	Is 8:21	4428
stout heart of the *k* of Assyria	Is 10:12	4428
proverb against the *k* of Babylon	Is 14:4	4428
In the year that *k* Ahaz died was	Is 14:28	4428
a fierce *k* shall rule over them,	Is 19:4	4428
(when Sargon the *k* of Assyria	Is 20:1	4428
So shall the *k* of Assyria lead	Is 20:4	4428
delivered from the *k* of Assyria	Is 20:6	4428
according to the days of one *k*	Is 23:15	4428
yea, for the *k* it is prepared	Is 30:33	4428
a *k* shall reign in righteousness,	Is 32:1	4428
shall see the *k* in his beauty	Is 33:17	4428
our lawgiver, the LORD is our *k*	Is 33:22	4428
the fourteenth year of *k* Hezekiah	Is 36:1	4428
that Sennacherib *k* of Assyria	Is 36:1	4428
the *k* of Assyria sent Rabshakeh	Is 36:2	4428
unto *k* Hezekiah with a great army	Is 36:2	4428
Hezekiah, Thus saith the great *k*	Is 36:4	4428
the *k* of Assyria, What confidence	Is 36:4	4428
so is Pharaoh *k* of Egypt to all	Is 36:6	4428
to my master the *k* of Assyria	Is 36:8	4428
the great *k*, the *k* of Assyria	Is 36:13	4428
Thus saith the *k*, Let not	Is 36:14	4428
into the hand of the *k* of Assyria	Is 36:15	4428
for thus saith the *k* of Assyria	Is 36:16	4428
of the hand of the *k* of Assyria	Is 36:18	4428
when *k* Hezekiah heard it, that he	Is 37:1	4428
whom the *k* of Assyria his master	Is 37:4	4428
So the servants of *k* Hezekiah	Is 37:5	4428
k of Assyria have blasphemed me	Is 37:6	4428
found the *k* of Assyria warring	Is 37:8	4428
concerning Tirhakah *k* of Ethiopia	Is 37:9	4428
ye speak to Hezekiah *k* of Judah	Is 37:10	4428
into the hand of the *k* of Assyria	Is 37:10	4428
Where is the *k* of Hamath	Is 37:13	4428
the *k* of Arphad	Is 37:13	4428
the *k* of the city of Sepharvaim,	Is 37:13	4428
against Sennacherib *k* of Assyria	Is 37:21	4428
LORD concerning the *k* of Assyria	Is 37:33	4428
So Sennacherib *k* of Assyria	Is 37:37	4428
of the hand of the *k* of Assyria	Is 38:6	4428
writing of Hezekiah *k* of Judah	Is 38:9	4428
k of Babylon, sent letters and a	Is 39:1	4428
the prophet unto *k* Hezekiah	Is 39:3	4428
in the palace of the *k* of Babylon	Is 39:7	4428
reasons, saith the *K* of Jacob	Is 41:21	4428
the creator of Israel, your *K*	Is 43:15	4428
saith the LORD the *K* of Israel	Is 44:6	4428
wentest to the *k* with ointment	Is 57:9	4428
Josiah the son of Amon *k* of Judah	Jer 1:2	4428
the son of Josiah *k* of Judah	Jer 1:3	4428
the son of Josiah *k* of Judah	Jer 1:3	4428
me in the days of Josiah the *k*	Jer 3:6	4428
the heart of the *k* shall perish	Jer 4:9	4428
is not her *k* in her	Jer 8:19	4428
not fear thee, O *K* of nations	Jer 10:7	4428
living God, and an everlasting *k*	Jer 10:10	4428
Say unto the *k* and to the queen,	Jer 13:18	4428
the son of Hezekiah *k* of Judah	Jer 15:4	4428
into the hand of the *k* of Babylon	Jer 20:4	4428
when *k* Zedekiah sent unto him	Jer 21:1	4428
for Nebuchadrezzar *k* of Babylon	Jer 21:2	4428
ye fight against the *k* of Babylon	Jer 21:4	4428
will deliver Zedekiah *k* of Judah	Jer 21:7	4428
of Nebuchadrezzar *k* of Babylon	Jer 21:7	4428
into the hand of the *k* of Babylon	Jer 21:10	4428
the house of the *k* of Judah	Jer 21:11	4428
to the house of the *k* of Judah	Jer 22:1	4428
O *k* of Judah, that sittest upon	Jer 22:2	4428
the son of Josiah *k* of Judah	Jer 22:11	4428
the son of Josiah *k* of Judah	Jer 22:18	4428
Coniah the son of Jehoiakim *k* of	Jer 22:24	4428
of Nebuchadrezzar *k* of Babylon	Jer 22:25	4428
a *K* shall reign and prosper, and	Jer 23:5	4428
after that Nebuchadrezzar *k* of	Jer 24:1	4428
the son of Jehoiakim *k* of Judah	Jer 24:1	4428
I give Zedekiah the *k* of Judah	Jer 24:8	4428
the son of Josiah *k* of Judah	Jer 25:1	4428
of Nebuchadrezzar *k* of Babylon	Jer 25:1	4428
Josiah the son of Amon *k* of Judah	Jer 25:3	4428
Nebuchadrezzar *k* of Babylon	Jer 25:9	4428
the *k* of Babylon seventy years	Jer 25:11	4428
I will punish the *k* of Babylon	Jer 25:12	4428
Pharaoh *k* of Egypt, and his	Jer 25:19	4428
the *k* of Sheshach shall drink	Jer 25:26	4428
k of Judah came this word from	Jer 26:1	4428
the days of Hezekiah *k* of Judah	Jer 26:18	4428
Did Hezekiah *k* of Judah and all	Jer 26:19	4428
And when Jehoiakim the *k*, with all	Jer 26:21	4428
the *k* sought to put him to death	Jer 26:21	4428
Jehoiakim the *k* sent men into	Jer 26:22	4428
brought him unto Jehoiakim the *k*	Jer 26:23	4428
k of Judah came this word unto	Jer 27:1	4428
And send them to the *k* of Edom	Jer 27:3	4428
to the *k* of Moab	Jer 27:3	4428
to the *k* of the Ammonites	Jer 27:3	4428
to the *k* of Tyrus	Jer 27:3	4428
to the *k* of Zidon	Jer 27:3	4428
unto Zedekiah *k* of Judah	Jer 27:3	4428

Nebuchadnezzar the *k* of Babylon	Jer 27:6	4428
Nebuchadnezzar the *k* of Babylon	Jer 27:8	4428
the yoke of the *k* of Babylon	Jer 27:8	4428
shall not serve the *k* of Babylon	Jer 27:9	4428
the yoke of the *k* of Babylon	Jer 27:11	4428
I spake also to Zedekiah *k* of	Jer 27:12	4428
the yoke of the *k* of Babylon	Jer 27:12	4428
will not serve the *k* of Babylon	Jer 27:13	4428
shall not serve the *k* of Babylon	Jer 27:14	4428
serve the *k* of Babylon, and live	Jer 27:17	4428
and in the house of the *k* of Judah	Jer 27:18	4428
k of Babylon took not, when he	Jer 27:20	4428
k of Judah from Jerusalem to	Jer 27:20	4428
and in the house of the *k* of Judah	Jer 27:21	4428
the reign of Zedekiah *k* of Judah	Jer 28:1	4428
the yoke of the *k* of Babylon	Jer 28:2	4428
that Nebuchadnezzar *k* of Babylon	Jer 28:3	4428
the son of Jehoiakim *k* of Judah	Jer 28:4	4428
the yoke of the *k* of Babylon	Jer 28:4	4428
the yoke of Nebuchadnezzar *k* of	Jer 28:11	4428
serve Nebuchadnezzar *k* of Babylon	Jer 28:14	4428
(After that Jeconiah the *k*	Jer 29:2	4428
(whom Zedekiah *k* of Judah sent	Jer 29:3	4428
k of Babylon) saying,	Jer 29:3	4428
k that sitteth upon the throne of	Jer 29:16	4428
of Nebuchadrezzar *k* of Babylon	Jer 29:21	4428
whom the *k* of Babylon roasted in	Jer 29:22	4428
LORD their God, and David their *k*	Jer 30:9	4428
tenth year of Zedekiah *k* of Judah	Jer 32:1	4428
For then the *k* of Babylon's army	Jer 32:2	4428
was in the *k* of Judah's house	Jer 32:2	4428
For Zedekiah *k* of Judah had shut	Jer 32:3	4428
into the hand of the *k* of Babylon	Jer 32:3	4428
Zedekiah *k* of Judah shall not	Jer 32:4	4428
into the hand of the *k* of Babylon	Jer 32:4	4428
of Nebuchadnezzar *k* of Babylon	Jer 32:28	4428
of the *k* of Babylon by the sword	Jer 32:36	4428
when Nebuchadnezzar *k* of Babylon	Jer 34:1	4428
and speak to Zedekiah *k* of Judah	Jer 34:2	4428
into the hand of the *k* of Babylon	Jer 34:2	4428
the eyes of the *k* of Babylon	Jer 34:3	4428
the LORD, O Zedekiah *k* of Judah	Jer 34:4	4428
Zedekiah *k* of Judah in Jerusalem	Jer 34:6	4428
When the *k* of Babylon's army	Jer 34:7	4428
after that the *k* Zedekiah had	Jer 34:8	4428
And Zedekiah *k* of Judah and his	Jer 34:21	4428
hand of the *k* of Babylon's army	Jer 34:21	4428
the son of Josiah *k* of Judah	Jer 35:1	4428
when Nebuchadnezzar *k* of Babylon	Jer 35:11	4428
the son of Josiah *k* of Judah	Jer 36:1	4428
the son of Josiah *k* of Judah	Jer 36:9	4428
tell the *k* of all these words	Jer 36:16	4428
went in to the *k* into the court	Jer 36:20	4428
the words in the ears of the *k*	Jer 36:20	4428
So the *k* sent Jehudi to fetch the	Jer 36:21	4428
read it in the ears of the *k*	Jer 36:21	4428
princes which stood beside the *k*	Jer 36:21	4428
Now the *k* sat in the winterhouse	Jer 36:22	4428
their garments, neither the *k*	Jer 36:24	4428
had made intercession to the *k*	Jer 36:25	4428
But the *k* commanded Jerahmeel the	Jer 36:26	4428
after that the *k* had burned the	Jer 36:27	4428
which Jehoiakim the *k* of Judah	Jer 36:28	4428
shalt say to Jehoiakim *k* of Judah	Jer 36:29	4428
The *k* of Babylon shall certainly	Jer 36:29	4428
the LORD of Jehoiakim *k* of Judah	Jer 36:30	4428
of the book which Jehoiakim *k* of	Jer 36:32	4428
k Zedekiah the son of Josiah	Jer 37:1	4428
whom Nebuchadnezzar *k* of Babylon	Jer 37:1	4428
made *k* in the land of Judah	Jer 37:1	4428
Zedekiah the *k* sent Jehucal the	Jer 37:3	4428
shall ye say to the *k* of Judah	Jer 37:7	4428
Then Zedekiah the *k* sent, and took	Jer 37:17	4428
the *k* asked him secretly in his	Jer 37:17	4428
into the hand of the *k* of Babylon	Jer 37:17	4428
Jeremiah said unto *k* Zedekiah	Jer 37:18	4428
The *k* of Babylon shall not come	Jer 37:19	4428
now, I pray thee, O my lord the *k*	Jer 37:20	4428
Then Zedekiah the *k* commanded	Jer 37:21	4428
hand of the *k* of Babylon's army	Jer 38:3	4428
the princes said unto the *k*	Jer 38:4	4428
Then Zedekiah the *k* said, Behold,	Jer 38:5	4428
for the *k* is not he that can do	Jer 38:5	4428
the *k* then sitting in the gate of	Jer 38:7	4428
king's house, and spake to the *k*	Jer 38:8	4428
My lord the *k*, these men have	Jer 38:9	4428
Then the *k* commanded Ebed-melech	Jer 38:10	4428
house of the *k* under the treasury	Jer 38:11	4428
Then Zedekiah the *k* sent, and took	Jer 38:14	4428
the *k* said unto Jeremiah, I will	Jer 38:14	4428
So Zedekiah the *k* sware secretly	Jer 38:16	4428
unto the *k* of Babylon's princes	Jer 38:17	4428
to the *k* of Babylon's princes	Jer 38:18	4428
Zedekiah the *k* said unto Jeremiah	Jer 38:19	4428
the *k* of Judah's house shall be	Jer 38:22	4428
to the *k* of Babylon's princes	Jer 38:22	4428
by the hand of the *k* of Babylon	Jer 38:23	4428
what thou hast said unto the *k*	Jer 38:25	4428
also what the *k* said unto thee	Jer 38:25	4428
my supplication before the *k*	Jer 38:26	4428
words that the *k* had commanded	Jer 38:27	4428
ninth year of Zedekiah *k* of Judah	Jer 39:1	4428
came Nebuchadrezzar *k* of Babylon	Jer 39:1	4428
of the *k* of Babylon came in	Jer 39:3	4428
the princes of the *k* of Babylon	Jer 39:3	4428
Zedekiah the *k* of Judah saw them	Jer 39:4	4428
him up to Nebuchadnezzar *k* of	Jer 39:5	4428
Then the *k* of Babylon slew the	Jer 39:6	4428
also the *k* of Babylon slew all	Jer 39:6	4428
Now Nebuchadrezzar *k* of Babylon	Jer 39:11	4428
all the *k* of Babylon's princes	Jer 39:13	4428
whom the *k* of Babylon hath made	Jer 40:5	4428
heard that the *k* of Babylon had	Jer 40:7	4428
serve the *k* of Babylon, and it	Jer 40:9	4428
heard that the *k* of Babylon had	Jer 40:11	4428
the *k* of the Ammonites hath sent	Jer 40:14	4428
royal, and the princes of the *k*	Jer 41:1	4428
whom the *k* of Babylon had made	Jer 41:2	4428
was it which Asa the *k* had made	Jer 41:9	4428
for fear of Baasha *k* of Israel	Jer 41:9	4428
whom the *k* of Babylon made	Jer 41:18	4428
Be not afraid of the *k* of Babylon	Jer 42:11	4428
Nebuchadrezzar the *k* of Babylon	Jer 43:10	4428
I will give Pharaoh-hophra *k* of	Jer 44:30	4428
as I gave Zedekiah *k* of Judah	Jer 44:30	4428
of Nebuchadrezzar *k* of Babylon	Jer 44:30	4428
the son of Josiah *k* of Judah	Jer 45:1	4428
army of Pharaoh-necho *k* of Egypt	Jer 46:2	4428
which Nebuchadrezzar *k* of Babylon	Jer 46:2	4428
the son of Josiah *k* of Judah	Jer 46:2	4428
how Nebuchadrezzar *k* of Babylon	Jer 46:13	4428
Pharaoh *k* of Egypt is but a noise	Jer 46:17	4428
As I live, saith the *K*, whose	Jer 46:18	4428
of Nebuchadrezzar *k* of Babylon	Jer 46:26	4428
to the slaughter, saith the *K*	Jer 48:15	4428
why then doth their *k* inherit Gad	Jer 49:1	4428
for their *k* shall go into	Jer 49:3	4428
which Nebuchadrezzar *k* of Babylon	Jer 49:28	4428
for Nebuchadrezzar *k* of Babylon	Jer 49:30	4428
the reign of Zedekiah *k* of Judah	Jer 49:34	4428
and will destroy from thence the *k*	Jer 49:38	4428
first the *k* of Assyria hath	Jer 50:17	4428
last this Nebuchadrezzar *k* of	Jer 50:17	4428
I will punish the *k* of Babylon	Jer 50:18	4428
I have punished the *k* of Assyria	Jer 50:18	4428
The *k* of Babylon hath heard the	Jer 50:43	4428
to shew the *k* of Babylon that his	Jer 51:31	4428
Nebuchadrezzar the *k* of Babylon	Jer 51:34	4428
sleep, and not wake, saith the *K*	Jer 51:57	4428
k of Judah into Babylon in the	Jer 51:59	4428
rebelled against the *k* of Babylon	Jer 52:3	4428
Nebuchadnezzar *k* of Babylon came	Jer 52:4	4428
the eleventh year of Zedekiah	Jer 52:5	4428
the Chaldeans pursued after the *k*	Jer 52:8	4428
Then they took the *k*	Jer 52:9	4428
carried him up unto the *k* of	Jer 52:9	4428
the *k* of Babylon slew the sons of	Jer 52:10	4428
the *k* of Babylon bound him in	Jer 52:11	4428
of Nebuchadrezzar *k* of Babylon	Jer 52:12	4428
which served the *k* of Babylon	Jer 52:12	4428
that fell to the *k* of Babylon	Jer 52:15	4428
which *k* Solomon had made in the	Jer 52:20	4428
brought them to the *k* of Babylon	Jer 52:26	4428
the *k* of Babylon smote them, and	Jer 52:27	4428
of Jehoiachin *k* of Judah, in the	Jer 52:31	4428
that Evil-merodach *k* of Babylon	Jer 52:31	4428
the head of Jehoiachin *k* of Judah	Jer 52:31	4428
given him of the *k* of Babylon	Jer 52:34	4428
indignation of his anger the *k*	Lam 2:6	4428
her *k* and her princes are among	Lam 2:9	4428
year of *k* Jehoiachin's captivity	Eze 1:2	4428
The *k* shall mourn, and the prince	Eze 7:27	4428
the *k* of Babylon is come to	Eze 17:12	4428
and hath taken the *k* thereof	Eze 17:12	4428
the *k* dwelleth that made him *k*	Eze 17:16	4428
the *k* dwelleth that made him *k*	Eze 17:16	4427
brought him to the *k* of Babylon	Eze 19:9	4428
of the *k* of Babylon may come	Eze 21:19	4428
For the *k* of Babylon stood at the	Eze 21:21	4428
the *k* of Babylon set himself	Eze 21:21	4428
the *k* of Babylon set himself	Eze 24:2	4428
Tyrus Nebuchadrezzar *k* of Babylon	Eze 26:7	4428
a *k* of kings, from the north,	Eze 26:7	4428

K

a lamentation upon the *k* of Tyrus	Eze 28:12	4428
face against Pharaoh *k* of Egypt	Eze 29:2	4428
Pharaoh *k* of Egypt, the great	Eze 29:3	4428
Nebuchadrezzar *k* of Babylon	Eze 29:18	4428
unto Nebuchadrezzar *k* of Babylon	Eze 29:19	4428
of Nebuchadrezzar *k* of Babylon	Eze 30:10	4428
the arm of Pharaoh *k* of Egypt	Eze 30:21	4428
I am against Pharaoh *k* of Egypt	Eze 30:22	4428
the arms of the *k* of Babylon	Eze 30:24	4428
the arms of the *k* of Babylon	Eze 30:25	4428
into the hand of the *k* of Babylon	Eze 30:25	4428
speak unto Pharaoh *k* of Egypt	Eze 31:2	4428
for Pharaoh *k* of Egypt, and say	Eze 32:2	4428
The sword of the *k* of Babylon	Eze 32:11	4428
one *k* shall be *k* to them all	Eze 37:22	4428
my servant shall be *k* over them	Eze 37:24	4428
k of Judah came Nebuchadnezzar	Dan 1:1	4428
k of Babylon unto Jerusalem	Dan 1:1	4428
k of Judah into his hand, with	Dan 1:2	4428
the *k* spake unto Ashpenaz the	Dan 1:3	4428
the *k* appointed them a daily	Dan 1:5	4428
they might stand before the *k*	Dan 1:5	4428
unto Daniel, I fear my lord the *k*	Dan 1:10	4428
make me endanger my head to the *k*	Dan 1:10	4428
k had said he should bring them	Dan 1:18	4428
And the *k* communed with them	Dan 1:19	4428
therefore stood they before the *k*	Dan 1:19	4428
that the *k* enquired of them, he	Dan 1:20	4428
unto the first year of *k* Cyrus	Dan 1:21	4428
Then he *k* commanded to call the	Dan 2:2	4428
for to shew the *k* his dreams	Dan 2:2	4428
they came and stood before the *k*	Dan 2:2	4428
the *k* said unto them, I have	Dan 2:3	4428
the Chaldeans to the *k* in Syriack	Dan 2:4	4428
O *k*, live for ever	Dan 2:4	4430
The *k* answered and said to the	Dan 2:5	4430
Let the *k* tell his servants the	Dan 2:7	4430
The *k* answered and said, I know of	Dan 2:8	4430
Chaldeans answered before the *k*	Dan 2:10	4430
therefore there is no *k*, lord	Dan 2:10	4430
a rare thing that the *k* requireth	Dan 2:11	4430
that can shew it before the *k*	Dan 2:11	4430
For this cause the *k* was angry	Dan 2:12	4430
is the decree so hasty from the *k*	Dan 2:15	4430
desired of the *k* that he would	Dan 2:16	4430
shew the *k* the interpretation	Dan 2:16	4430
whom he *k* had ordained to	Dan 2:24	4430
bring me in before the *k*, and I	Dan 2:24	4430
unto the *k* the interpretation	Dan 2:24	4430
in Daniel before the *k* in haste	Dan 2:25	4430
unto the *k* the interpretation	Dan 2:25	4430
The *k* answered and said to Daniel,	Dan 2:26	4430
answered in the presence of the *k*	Dan 2:27	4430
The secret which the *k* hath	Dan 2:27	4430
the soothsayers, shew unto the *k*	Dan 2:27	4430
secrets, and maketh known to the *k*	Dan 2:28	4430
As for thee, O *k*, thy thoughts	Dan 2:29	4430
known the interpretation to the *k*	Dan 2:30	4430
Thou, O *k*, sawest, and behold a	Dan 2:31	4430
thereof before the *k*	Dan 2:36	4430
Thou, O *k*, art a *k* of kings	Dan 2:37	4430
to the *k* what shall come to pass	Dan 2:45	4430
Then the *k* Nebuchadnezzar fell	Dan 2:46	4430
The *k* answered unto Daniel, and	Dan 2:47	4430
Then the *k* made Daniel a great	Dan 2:48	4430
Then Daniel requested of the *k*	Dan 2:49	4430
Daniel sat in the gate of the *k*	Dan 2:49	4430
Nebuchadnezzar the *k* made an	Dan 3:1	4430
Then Nebuchadnezzar the *k* sent to	Dan 3:2	4430
Nebuchadnezzar the *k* had set up	Dan 3:2	4430
Nebuchadnezzar the *k* had set up	Dan 3:3	4430
Nebuchadnezzar the *k* hath set up	Dan 3:5	4430
Nebuchadnezzar the *k* had set up	Dan 3:7	4430
to the *k* Nebuchadnezzar, O *k*	Dan 3:9	4430
Thou, O *k*, hast made a decree,	Dan 3:10	4430
these men, O *k*, have not regarded	Dan 3:12	4430
brought these men before the *k*	Dan 3:13	4430
answered and said to the *k*	Dan 3:16	4430
deliver us out of thine hand, O *k*	Dan 3:17	4430
not, be it known unto thee, O *k*	Dan 3:18	4430
Nebuchadnezzar the *k* was astonied	Dan 3:24	4430
and said unto the *k*, True, O *k*	Dan 3:24	4430
Then the *k* promoted Shadrach	Dan 3:30	4430
Nebuchadnezzar the *k*, unto all	Dan 4:1	4430
This dream I *k* Nebuchadnezzar	Dan 4:18	4430
The *k* spake, and said,	Dan 4:19	4430
It is thou, O *k*, that art grown	Dan 4:22	4430
whereas the *k* saw a watcher and an	Dan 4:23	4430
This is the interpretation, O *k*	Dan 4:24	4430
which is come upon my lord the *k*	Dan 4:24	4430
Wherefore, O *k*, let my counsel be	Dan 4:27	4430

came upon the *k* Nebuchadnezzar	Dan 4:28	4430
The *k* spake, and said, Is not this	Dan 4:30	4430
O *k* Nebuchadnezzar, to thee it is	Dan 4:31	4430
extol and honour the *K* of heaven	Dan 4:37	4430
Belshazzar the *k* made a great	Dan 5:1	4430
that the *k*, and his princes, his	Dan 5:2	4430
and the *k*, and his princes, his	Dan 5:3	4430
the *k* saw the part of the hand	Dan 5:5	4430
The *k* cried aloud to bring in the	Dan 5:7	4430
the *k* spake, and said to the wise	Dan 5:7	4430
nor make known to the *k* the	Dan 5:8	4430
Then was *k* Belshazzar greatly	Dan 5:9	4430
by reason of the words of the *k*	Dan 5:10	4430
and the queen spake and said, O *k*	Dan 5:10	4430
whom the *k* Nebuchadnezzar thy	Dan 5:11	4430
Nebuchadnezzar thy father, the *k*	Dan 5:11	4430
whom the *k* named Belteshazzar	Dan 5:12	4430
Daniel brought in before the *k*	Dan 5:13	4430
the *k* spake and said unto Daniel,	Dan 5:13	4430
whom the *k* my father brought out	Dan 5:13	4430
answered and said before the *k*	Dan 5:17	4430
will read the writing unto the *k*	Dan 5:17	4430
O thou *k*, the most high God gave	Dan 5:18	4430
the *k* of the Chaldeans slain	Dan 5:30	4430
the *k* should have no damage	Dan 6:2	4430
the *k* thought to set him over the	Dan 6:3	4430
assembled together to the *k*	Dan 6:6	4430
unto him, *K* Darius, live for ever	Dan 6:6	4430
thirty days, save of thee, O *k*	Dan 6:7	4430
Now, O *k*, establish the decree,	Dan 6:8	4430
Wherefore *k* Darius signed the	Dan 6:9	4430
spake before the *k* concerning the	Dan 6:12	4430
thirty days, save of thee, O *k*	Dan 6:12	4430
The *k* answered and said, The thing	Dan 6:12	4430
they and said before the *k*	Dan 6:13	4430
of Judah, regardeth not thee, O *k*	Dan 6:13	4430
Then the *k*, when he heard these	Dan 6:14	4430
these men assembled unto the *k*	Dan 6:15	4430
and said unto the *k*, Know, O *k*	Dan 6:15	4430
the *k* establisheth may be changed	Dan 6:15	4430
Then the *k* commanded, and they	Dan 6:16	4430
Now the *k* spake and said unto	Dan 6:16	4430
the *k* sealed it with his own	Dan 6:17	4430
Then the *k* went to his palace, and	Dan 6:18	4430
Then the *k* arose very early in	Dan 6:19	4430
the *k* spake and said to Daniel, O	Dan 6:20	4430
said Daniel unto the *k*, O *k*	Dan 6:21	4430
and also before thee, O *k*, have I	Dan 6:22	4430
Then was the *k* exceeding glad for	Dan 6:23	4430
the *k* commanded, and they brought	Dan 6:24	4430
Then *k* Darius wrote unto all	Dan 6:25	4430
k of Babylon Daniel had a dream	Dan 7:1	4430
of *k* Belshazzar a vision appeared	Dan 8:1	4428
the rough goat is the *k* of Grecia	Dan 8:21	4428
between his eyes is the first *k*	Dan 8:21	4428
a *k* of fierce countenance, and	Dan 8:23	4428
which was made *k* over the realm	Dan 9:1	4427
In the third year of Cyrus *k* of	Dan 10:1	4428
a mighty *k* shall stand up, that	Dan 11:3	4428
the *k* of the south shall be	Dan 11:5	4428
to the *k* of the north to make an	Dan 11:6	4428
fortress of the *k* of the north	Dan 11:7	4428
years than the *k* of the north	Dan 11:8	4428
So the *k* of the south shall come	Dan 11:9	4428
the *k* of the south shall be moved	Dan 11:11	4428
him, even with the *k* of the north	Dan 11:11	4428
For the *k* of the north shall	Dan 11:13	4428
up against the *k* of the south	Dan 11:14	4428
So the *k* of the north shall come,	Dan 11:15	4428
his courage against the *k* of the	Dan 11:25	4428
the *k* of the south shall be	Dan 11:25	4428
the *k* shall do according to his	Dan 11:36	4428
the *k* of the south push at him	Dan 11:40	4428
the *k* of the north shall come	Dan 11:40	4428
the son of Joash, *k* of Israel	Hos 1:1	4428
shall abide many days without a *k*	Hos 3:4	4428
LORD their God, and David their *k*	Hos 3:5	4428
and give ye ear, O house of the *k*	Hos 5:1	4428
the Assyrian, and sent to *k* Jareb	Hos 5:13	4428
They make the *k* glad with their	Hos 7:3	4428
In the day of our *k* the princes	Hos 7:5	4428
the burden of the *k* of princes	Hos 8:10	4428
now they shall say, We have no *k*	Hos 10:3	4428
what then should a *k* do to us	Hos 10:3	4428
Assyria for a present to *k* Jareb	Hos 10:6	4428
her *k* is cut off as the foam upon	Hos 10:7	4428
in a morning shall the *k* of	Hos 10:15	4428
but the Assyrian shall be his *k*	Hos 11:5	4428
I will be thy *k*	Hos 13:10	4428
of whom thou saidst, Give me a *k*	Hos 13:10	4428
I gave thee a *k* in mine anger	Hos 13:11	4428

KINGDOM

K

I stablish the throne of thy *k*	2Chr 7:18	4438
was not the like made in any *k*	2Chr 9:19	4467
bring the *k* again to Rehoboam	2Chr 11:1	4467
they strengthened the *k* of Judah	2Chr 11:17	4438
Rehoboam had established the *k*	2Chr 12:1	4438
k over Israel to David for ever	2Chr 13:5	4467
now ye think to withstand the *k*	2Chr 13:8	4467
the *k* was quiet before him	2Chr 14:5	4467
Lord stablished the *k* in his hand	2Chr 17:5	4467
but the *k* gave he to Jehoram	2Chr 21:3	4467
risen up to the *k* of his father	2Chr 21:4	4467
had no power to keep still the *k*	2Chr 22:9	4467
the king upon the throne of the *k*	2Chr 23:20	4467
when the *k* was established to him	2Chr 29:21	4467
for a sin offering for the *k*	2Chr 29:21	4467
for no god of any nation or *k* was	2Chr 32:15	4467
him again to Jerusalem into his *k*	2Chr 33:13	4438
the reign of the *k* of Persia	2Chr 36:20	4438
proclamation throughout all his *k*	2Chr 36:22	4438
proclamation throughout all his *k*	Ezr 1:1	4438
have not served thee in their *k*	Neh 9:35	4438
sat on the throne of his *k*	Est 1:2	4438
the riches of his glorious *k*	Est 1:4	4438
and which sat the first in the *k*	Est 1:14	4438
in all the provinces of his *k*	Est 2:3	4438
the whole *k* of Ahasuerus, even	Est 3:6	4438
in all the provinces of thy *k*	Est 3:8	4438
to the *k* for such a time as this	Est 4:14	4438
given thee to the half of the *k*	Est 5:3	4438
of the *k* it shall be performed	Est 5:6	4438
even to the half of the *k*	Est 7:2	4438
provinces of the *k* of Ahasuerus	Est 9:30	4438
For the *k* is the Lord's	Ps 22:28	4410
of thy *k* is a right sceptre	Ps 45:6	4438
and his *k* ruleth over all	Ps 103:19	4438
from one *k* to another people	Ps 105:13	4467
shall speak of the glory of thy *k*	Ps 145:11	4438
and the glorious majesty of his *k*	Ps 145:12	4438
Thy *k* is an everlasting *k*	Ps 145:13	4438
is born in his *k* becometh poor	Eccl 4:14	4438
throne of David, and upon his *k*	Is 9:7	4467
the *k* from Damascus, and the	Is 17:3	4467
city, and *k* against *k*	Is 19:2	4467
call the nobles thereof to the *k*	Is 34:12	4410
k that will not serve thee shall	Is 60:12	4467
a nation, and concerning a *k*	Jer 18:7	4467
a nation, and concerning a *k*	Jer 18:9	4467
k which will not serve the same	Jer 27:8	4467
he hath polluted the *k* and the	Lam 2:2	4467
and thou didst prosper into a *k*	Eze 16:13	4410
That the *k* might be base, that it	Eze 17:14	4467
and they shall be there a base *k*	Eze 29:14	4467
God of heaven hath given thee a *k*	Dan 2:37	4437
arise another *k* inferior to thee	Dan 2:39	4437
and another third *k* of brass	Dan 2:39	4437
the fourth *k* shall be strong as	Dan 2:40	4437
of iron, the *k* shall be divided	Dan 2:41	4437
so the *k* shall be partly strong	Dan 2:42	4437
the God of heaven shall set up a *k*	Dan 2:44	4437
the *k* shall not be left to other	Dan 2:44	4437
his *k* is an everlasting *k*,	Dan 4:3	4437
most High ruleth in the *k* of men	Dan 4:17	4437
as all the wise men of my *k* are	Dan 4:18	4437
most High ruleth in the *k* of men	Dan 4:25	4437
thy *k* shall be sure unto thee	Dan 4:26	4437
in the palace of the *k* of Babylon	Dan 4:29	4437
of the *k* by the might of my power	Dan 4:30	4437
The *k* is departed from thee	Dan 4:31	4437
most High ruleth in the *k* of men	Dan 4:32	4437
his *k* is from generation to	Dan 4:34	4437
and for the glory of my *k*, mine	Dan 4:36	4437
and I was established in my *k*	Dan 4:36	4437
shall be the third ruler in the *k*	Dan 5:7	4437
There is a man in thy *k*, in whom	Dan 5:11	4437
shalt be the third ruler in the *k*	Dan 5:16	4437
Nebuchadnezzar thy father a *k*	Dan 5:18	4437
high God ruled in the *k* of men	Dan 5:21	4437
God hath numbered thy *k*, and	Dan 5:26	4437
Thy *k* is divided, and given to the	Dan 5:28	4437
be the third ruler in the *k*	Dan 5:29	4437
And Darius the Median took the *k*	Dan 5:31	4437
to set over the *k* an hundred	Dan 6:1	4437
which should be over the whole *k*	Dan 6:1	4437
against Daniel concerning the *k*	Dan 6:4	4437
All the presidents of the *k*	Dan 6:7	4437
dominion of my *k* men tremble	Dan 6:26	4437
his *k* that which shall not be	Dan 6:26	4437
him dominion, and glory, and a *k*	Dan 7:14	4437
his *k* that which shall not be	Dan 7:14	4437
of the most High shall take the *k*	Dan 7:18	4437
and possess the *k* for ever	Dan 7:18	4437

that the saints possessed the *k*	Dan 7:22	4437
shall be the fourth *k* upon earth	Dan 7:23	4437
the ten horns out of this *k* are	Dan 7:24	4437
And the *k* and dominion	Dan 7:27	4437
the greatness of the *k* under the	Dan 7:27	4437
whose *k* is an everlasting *k*	Dan 7:27	4437
And in the latter time of their *k*	Dan 8:23	4438
But the prince of the *k* of Persia	Dan 10:13	4438
his *k* shall be broken, and shall	Dan 11:4	4438
for his *k* shall be plucked up,	Dan 11:4	4438
the south shall come into his *k*	Dan 11:9	4438
with the strength of his whole *k*	Dan 11:17	4438
of taxes in the glory of the *k*	Dan 11:20	4438
not give the honour of the *k*	Dan 11:21	4438
obtain the *k* by flatteries	Dan 11:21	4438
the *k* of the house of Israel	Hos 1:4	4468
Lord God are upon the sinful *k*	Amos 9:8	4467
the *k* shall be the Lord's	Obad 21	4410
the *k* shall come to the daughter	Mic 4:8	4467
for the *k* of heaven is at hand	Mt 3:2	932
for the *k* of heaven is at hand	Mt 4:17	*932*
and preaching the gospel of the *k*	Mt 4:23	*932*
for theirs is the *k* of heaven	Mt 5:3	*932*
for theirs is the *k* of heaven	Mt 5:10	*932*
the least in the *k* of heaven	Mt 5:19	*932*
called great in the *k* of heaven	Mt 5:19	*932*
case enter into the *k* of heaven	Mt 5:20	*932*
Thy *k* come	Mt 6:10	*932*
For thine is the *k*, and the power,	Mt 6:13	*932*
But seek ye first the *k* of God	Mt 6:33	*932*
shall enter into the *k* of heaven	Mt 7:21	*932*
and Jacob, in the *k* of heaven	Mt 8:11	*932*
But the children of the *k* shall	Mt 8:12	*932*
and preaching the gospel of the *k*	Mt 9:35	*932*
The *k* of heaven is at hand	Mt 10:7	*932*
he that is least in the *k* of	Mt 11:11	*932*
k of heaven suffereth violence	Mt 11:12	*932*
Every *k* divided against itself is	Mt 12:25	*932*
how shall then his *k* stand	Mt 12:26	*932*
then the *k* of God is come unto	Mt 12:28	*932*
the mysteries of the *k* of heaven	Mt 13:11	*932*
any one heareth the word of the *k*	Mt 13:19	*932*
The *k* of heaven is likened unto a	Mt 13:24	*932*
The *k* of heaven is like to a	Mt 13:31	*932*
The *k* of heaven is like unto	Mt 13:33	*932*
seed are the children of the *k*	Mt 13:38	*932*
of his *k* all things that offend	Mt 13:41	*932*
the sun in the *k* of their Father	Mt 13:43	*932*
the *k* of heaven is like unto	Mt 13:44	*932*
the *k* of heaven is like unto a	Mt 13:45	*932*
the *k* of heaven is like unto	Mt 13:47	*932*
k of heaven is like unto a man	Mt 13:52	*932*
thee the keys of the *k* of heaven	Mt 16:19	*932*
the Son of man coming in his *k*	Mt 16:28	*932*
the greatest in the *k* of heaven	Mt 18:1	*932*
not enter into the *k* of heaven	Mt 18:3	*932*
is greatest in the *k* of heaven	Mt 18:4	*932*
Therefore is the *k* of heaven	Mt 18:23	*932*
for the *k* of heaven's sake	Mt 19:12	*932*
for of such is the *k* of heaven	Mt 19:14	*932*
hardly enter into the *k* of heaven	Mt 19:23	*932*
man to enter into the *k* of God	Mt 19:24	*932*
For the *k* of heaven is like unto	Mt 20:1	*932*
the other on the left, in thy *k*	Mt 20:21	*932*
go into the *k* of God before you	Mt 21:31	*932*
The *k* of God shall be taken from	Mt 21:43	*932*
The *k* of heaven is like unto a	Mt 22:2	*932*
for ye shut up the *k* of heaven	Mt 23:13	*932*
nation, and *k* against *k*	Mt 24:7	*932*
this gospel of the *k* shall be	Mt 24:14	*932*
Then shall the *k* of heaven be	Mt 25:1	*932*
For the *k* of heaven is as a man	Mt 25:14	*932*
inherit the *k* prepared for you	Mt 25:34	*932*
it new with you in my Father's *k*	Mt 26:29	*932*
the gospel of the *k* of God	Mk 1:14	*932*
and the *k* of God is at hand	Mk 1:15	*932*
if a *k* be divided against itself,	Mk 3:24	*932*
that *k* cannot stand	Mk 3:24	*932*
know the mystery of the *k* of God	Mk 4:11	*932*
And he said, So is the *k* of God	Mk 4:26	*932*
shall we liken the *k* of God	Mk 4:30	*932*
it thee, unto the half of my *k*	Mk 6:23	*932*
seen the *k* of God come with power	Mk 9:1	*932*
into the *k* of God with one eye	Mk 9:47	*932*
for of such is the *k* of God	Mk 10:14	*932*
the *k* of God as a little child	Mk 10:15	*932*
riches enter into the *k* of God	Mk 10:23	*932*
riches to enter into the *k* of God	Mk 10:24	*932*
man to enter into the *k* of God	Mk 10:25	*932*
Blessed be the *k* of our father	Mk 11:10	*932*
art not far from the *k* of God	Mk 12:34	*932*

nation, and *k* against *k*	Mk 13:8	932
I drink it new in the *k* of God	Mk 14:25	932
also waited for the *k* of God	Mk 15:43	932
of his *k* there shall be no end	Lk 1:33	932
I must preach the *k* of God to	Lk 4:43	932
for yours is the *k* of God	Lk 6:20	932
the *k* of God is greater than he	Lk 7:28	932
the glad tidings of the *k* of God	Lk 8:1	932
the mysteries of the *k* of God	Lk 8:10	932
sent them to preach the *k* of God	Lk 9:2	932
spake unto them of the *k* of God	Lk 9:11	932
death, till they see the *k* of God	Lk 9:27	932
go thou and preach the *k* of God	Lk 9:60	932
back, is fit for the *k* of God	Lk 9:62	932
The *k* of God is come nigh unto	Lk 10:9	932
that the *k* of God is come nigh	Lk 10:11	932
Thy *k* come	Lk 11:2	932
Every *k* divided against itself is	Lk 11:17	932
himself, how shall his *k* stand	Lk 11:18	932
no doubt the *k* of God is come	Lk 11:20	932
But rather seek ye the *k* of God	Lk 12:31	932
good pleasure to give you the *k*	Lk 12:32	932
Unto what is the *k* of God like	Lk 13:18	932
shall I liken the *k* of God	Lk 13:20	932
all the prophets, in the *k* of God	Lk 13:28	932
and shall sit down in the *k* of God	Lk 13:29	932
shall eat bread in the *k* of God	Lk 14:15	932
time the *k* of God is preached	Lk 16:16	932
when the *k* of God should come, he	Lk 17:20	932
The *k* of God cometh not with	Lk 17:20	932
the *k* of God is within you	Lk 17:21	932
for of such is the *k* of God	Lk 18:16	932
k of God as a little child shall	Lk 18:17	932
riches enter into the *k* of God	Lk 18:24	932
man to enter into the *k* of God	Lk 18:25	932
for the *k* of God's sake,	Lk 18:29	932
the *k* of God should immediately	Lk 19:11	932
to receive for himself a *k*	Lk 19:12	932
returned, having received the *k*	Lk 19:15	932
nation, and *k* against *k*	Lk 21:10	932
know ye that the *k* of God is nigh	Lk 21:31	932
it be fulfilled in the *k* of God	Lk 22:16	932
until the *k* of God shall come	Lk 22:18	932
And I appoint unto you a *k*	Lk 22:29	932
eat and drink at my table in my *k*	Lk 22:30	932
me when thou comest into thy *k*	Lk 23:42	932
himself waited for the *k* of God	Lk 23:51	932
again, he cannot see the *k* of God	Jn 3:3	932
he cannot enter into the *k* of God	Jn 3:5	932
My *k* is not of this world	Jn 18:36	932
if my *k* were of this world, then	Jn 18:36	932
but now is my *k* not from hence	Jn 18:36	932
things pertaining to the *k* of God	Acts 1:3	932
restore again the *k* to Israel	Acts 1:6	932
things concerning the *k* of God	Acts 8:12	932
enter into the *k* of God	Acts 14:22	932
things concerning the *k* of God	Acts 19:8	932
have gone preaching the *k* of God	Acts 20:25	932
and testified the *k* of God	Acts 28:23	932
Preaching the *k* of God, and	Acts 28:31	932
For the *k* of God is not meat and	Rom 14:17	932
For the *k* of God is not in word,	1Cor 4:20	932
shall not inherit the *k* of God	1Cor 6:9	932
shall inherit the *k* of God	1Cor 6:10	932
have delivered up the *k* to God	1Cor 15:24	932
blood cannot inherit the *k* of God	1Cor 15:50	932
shall not inherit the *k* of God	Gal 5:21	932
inheritance in the *k* of Christ	Eph 5:5	932
us into the *k* of his dear Son	Col 1:13	932
fellow workers unto the *k* of God	Col 4:11	932
who hath called you unto his *k*	1Th 2:12	932
be counted worthy of the *k* of God	2Th 1:5	932
dead at his appearing and his *k*	2Ti 4:1	932
preserve me unto his heavenly *k*	2Ti 4:18	932
is the sceptre of thy *k*	Heb 1:8	932
a *k* which cannot be moved	Heb 12:28	932
heirs of the *k* which he hath	Jas 2:5	932
the everlasting *k* of our Lord	2Pet 1:11	932
in tribulation, and in the *k*	Rev 1:9	932
the *k* of our God, and the power of	Rev 12:10	932
his *k* was full of darkness	Rev 16:10	932
which have received no *k* as yet	Rev 17:12	932
give their *k* unto the beast,	Rev 17:17	932

KINGDOMS

all the *k* whither thou passest	Deut 3:21	4467
into all the *k* of the earth	Deut 28:25	4467
was the head of all those *k*	Josh 11:10	4467
and out of the hand of all *k*	1Sa 10:18	4467
Solomon reigned over all *k* from	1Kin 4:21	4467
of all the *k* of the earth	2Kin 19:15	4467

that all the *k* of the earth may	2Kin 19:19	4467
over all the *k* of the countries	1Chr 29:30	4467
service of the *k* of the countries	2Chr 12:8	4467
k of the lands that were round	2Chr 17:10	4467
over all the *k* of the heathen	2Chr 20:6	4467
on all the *k* of those countries	2Chr 20:29	4467
All the *k* of the earth hath the	2Chr 36:23	4467
given me all the *k* of the earth	Ezr 1:2	4467
Moreover thou gavest them *k*	Neh 9:22	4467
heathen raged, the *k* were moved	Ps 46:6	4467
Sing unto God, ye *k* of the earth	Ps 68:32	4467
upon the *k* that have not called	Ps 79:6	4467
are gathered together, and the *k*	Ps 102:22	4467
of Bashan, and all the *k* of Canaan	Ps 135:11	4467
hath found the *k* of the idols	Is 10:10	4467
a tumultuous noise of the *k* of	Is 13:4	4467
And Babylon, the glory of *k*	Is 13:19	4467
to tremble, that did shake *k*	Is 14:16	4467
hand over the sea, he shook the *k*	Is 23:11	4467
k of the world upon the face of	Is 23:17	4467
of all the *k* of the earth	Is 37:16	4467
that all the *k* of the earth may	Is 37:20	4467
no more be called, The lady of *k*	Is 47:5	4467
over the nations and over the *k*	Jer 1:10	4467
families of the *k* of the north	Jer 1:15	4467
of the nations, and in all their *k*	Jer 10:7	4467
removed into all *k* of the earth	Jer 15:4	4467
the *k* of the earth for their hurt	Jer 24:9	4467
all the *k* of the world, which are	Jer 25:26	4467
countries, and against great *k*	Jer 28:8	4467
removed to all the *k* of the earth	Jer 29:18	4467
all the *k* of the earth of his	Jer 34:1	4467
into all the *k* of the earth	Jer 34:17	4467
and concerning the *k* of Hazor	Jer 49:28	4467
and with thee will I destroy *k*	Jer 51:20	4467
against her the *k* of Ararat	Jer 51:27	4467
It shall be the basest of the *k*	Eze 29:15	4467
into two *k* any more at all	Eze 37:22	4467
in pieces and consume all these *k*	Dan 2:44	4437
which shall be diverse from all *k*	Dan 7:23	4437
four *k* shall stand up out of the	Dan 8:22	4438
be they better than these *k*	Amos 6:2	4467
thy nakedness, and the *k* thy shame	Nah 3:5	4467
that I may assemble the *k*	Zeph 3:8	4467
I will overthrow the throne of *k*	Hag 2:22	4467
strength of the *k* of the heathen	Hag 2:22	4467
him all the *k* of the world	Mt 4:8	932
shewed unto him all the *k* of the	Lk 4:5	932
Who through faith subdued *k*	Heb 11:33	932
The *k* of this world are become	Rev 11:15	932
are become the *k* of our Lord	Rev 11:15	932

KINGLY

he was deposed from his *k* throne	Dan 5:20	4437

KING'S

of Shaveh, which is the *k* dale	Gen 14:17	4428
a place where the *k* prisoners	Gen 39:20	4428
we will go by the *k* high way	Num 20:17	4428
will go along by the *k* high way	Num 21:22	4428
now therefore be the *k* son in law	1Sa 18:22	4428
light thing to be a *k* son in law	1Sa 18:23	4428
to be avenged of the *k* enemies	1Sa 18:25	4428
David well to be the *k* son in law	1Sa 18:26	4428
that he might be the *k* son in law	1Sa 18:27	4428
he cometh not unto the *k* table	1Sa 20:29	4428
because the *k* business required	1Sa 21:8	4428
David, which is the *k* son in law	1Sa 22:14	4428
be to deliver him into the *k* hand	1Sa 23:20	4428
And now see where the *k* spear is	1Sa 26:16	4428
and said, Behold the *k* spear	1Sa 26:22	4428
at my table, as one of the *k* sons	2Sa 9:11	4428
eat continually at the *k* table	2Sa 9:13	4428
upon the roof of the *k* house	2Sa 11:2	4428
Uriah departed out of the *k* house	2Sa 11:8	4428
k house with all the servants of	2Sa 11:9	4428
if so be that the *k* wrath arise	2Sa 11:20	4428
some of the *k* servants be dead,	2Sa 11:24	4428
he took their *k* crown from off	2Sa 12:30	4428
Why art thou, being the *k* son	2Sa 13:4	4428
the *k* daughters that were virgins	2Sa 13:18	4428
and Absalom invited all the *k* sons	2Sa 13:23	4428
all the *k* sons go with him	2Sa 13:27	4428
Then all the *k* sons arose	2Sa 13:29	4428
Absalom hath slain all the *k* sons	2Sa 13:30	4428
all the young men the *k* sons	2Sa 13:32	4428
that all the *k* sons are dead	2Sa 13:33	4428
the king, Behold, the *k* sons come	2Sa 13:35	4428
the *k* sons came, and lifted up	2Sa 13:36	4428
the *k* heart was toward Absalom	2Sa 14:1	4428
own house, and saw not the *k* face	2Sa 14:24	4428
shekels after the *k* weight	2Sa 14:26	4428

Jerusalem, and saw not the *k* face	2Sa 14:28	4428
therefore let me see the *k* face	2Sa 14:32	4428
the *k* servants said unto the king	2Sa 15:15	4428
shalt hear out of the *k* house	2Sa 15:35	4428
be for the *k* household to ride on	2Sa 16:2	4428
forth mine hand against the *k* son	2Sa 18:12	4428
a pillar, which is in the *k* dale	2Sa 18:18	4428
because the son is dead	2Sa 18:20	4428
When Joab sent the *k* servant	2Sa 18:29	4428
to carry over the *k* household	2Sa 19:18	4428
we eaten at all of the *k* cost	2Sa 19:42	4428
Notwithstanding the *k* word	2Sa 24:4	4428
all his brethren the *k* sons	1Kin 1:9	4428
the men of Judah the *k* servants	1Kin 1:9	4428
and hath called all the *k* sons	1Kin 1:25	4428
And she came into the *k* presence	1Kin 1:28	4428
him to ride upon the *k* mule	1Kin 1:44	4428
moreover the *k* servants came to	1Kin 1:47	4428
a seat to be set for the *k* mother	1Kin 2:19	4428
officer, and the *k* friend	1Kin 4:5	4428
the *k* house, and all Solomon's	1Kin 9:1	4428
of the LORD, and the *k* house,	1Kin 9:10	4428
of the LORD, and for the *k* house	1Kin 10:12	4428
the *k* merchants received the	1Kin 10:28	4428
he was of the *k* seed in Edom	1Kin 11:14	4428
the *k* hand was restored him again	1Kin 13:6	4428
and the treasures of the *k* house	1Kin 14:26	4428
kept the door of the *k* house	1Kin 14:27	4428
and the treasures of the *k* house	1Kin 15:18	4428
into the palace of the *k* house	1Kin 16:18	4428
burnt the *k* house over him with	1Kin 16:18	4428
shall deliver it into the *k* hand	1Kin 22:12	4428
the city, and to Joash the *k* son	1Kin 22:26	4428
we may go and tell the *k* household	2Kin 7:9	4428
told it to the *k* house within	2Kin 7:11	4428
for she is a *k* daughter	2Kin 9:34	4428
Now the *k* sons, being seventy	2Kin 10:6	4428
them, that they took the *k* sons	2Kin 10:7	4428
brought the heads of the *k* sons	2Kin 10:8	4428
among the *k* sons which were slain	2Kin 11:2	4428
LORD, and shewed them the *k* son	2Kin 11:4	4428
of the watch of the *k* house	2Kin 11:5	4428
And he brought forth the *k* son	2Kin 11:12	4428
the horses came into the *k* house	2Kin 11:16	4428
gate of the guard to the *k* house	2Kin 11:19	4428
with the sword beside the *k* house	2Kin 11:20	4428
in the chest, that the *k* scribe	2Kin 12:10	4428
of the LORD, and in the *k* house	2Kin 12:18	4428
put his hands upon the *k* hands	2Kin 13:16	4428
in the treasures of the *k* house	2Kin 14:14	4428
Jotham the *k* son was over the	2Kin 15:5	4428
in the palace of the *k* house	2Kin 15:25	4428
in the treasures of the *k* house	2Kin 16:8	4428
the *k* burnt sacrifice, and his	2Kin 16:15	4428
the *k* entry without, turned he	2Kin 16:18	4428
in the treasures of the *k* house	2Kin 18:15	4428
for the *k* commandment was, saying	2Kin 18:36	4428
and Asahiah a servant of the *k*	2Kin 22:12	4428
and the treasures of the *k* house	2Kin 24:13	4428
the *k* mother, and the *k* wives	2Kin 24:15	4428
walls, which is by the *k* garden	2Kin 25:4	4428
the *k* house, and all the houses of	2Kin 25:9	4428
them that were in the *k* presence	2Kin 25:19	4428
waited in the *k* gate eastward	1Chr 9:18	4428
Nevertheless the *k* word prevailed	1Chr 21:4	4428
for the *k* word was abominable to	1Chr 21:6	4428
the *k* seer in the words of God	1Chr 25:5	4428
according to the *k* order to Asaph	1Chr 25:6	4428
over the *k* treasures was Azmaveth	1Chr 27:25	4428
of Hachmoni was with the *k* sons	1Chr 27:32	4428
Ahithophel was the *k* counsellor	1Chr 27:33	4428
the Archite was the *k* companion	1Chr 27:33	4428
general of the *k* army was Joab	1Chr 27:34	4428
with the rulers of the *k* work	1Chr 29:6	4428
the *k* merchants received the	2Chr 1:16	4428
house of the LORD, and the *k* house	2Chr 7:11	4428
of the LORD, and to the *k* palace	2Chr 9:11	4428
For the *k* ships went to Tarshish	2Chr 9:21	4428
and the treasures of the *k* house	2Chr 12:9	4428
kept the entrance of the *k* house	2Chr 12:10	4428
of the LORD and of the *k* house	2Chr 16:2	4428
will deliver it into the *k* hand	2Chr 18:5	4428
the city, and to Joash the *k* son	2Chr 18:25	4428
of Judah, for all the *k* matters	2Chr 19:11	4428
that was found in the *k* house	2Chr 21:17	4428
among the *k* sons that were slain	2Chr 22:11	4428
the *k* son shall reign, as the	2Chr 23:3	4428
part shall be at the *k* house	2Chr 23:5	4428
Then they brought out the *k* son	2Chr 23:11	4428
of the horse gate by the *k* house	2Chr 23:15	4428
the high gate into the *k* house	2Chr 23:20	4428
at the *k* commandment they made a	2Chr 24:8	4428
the *k* office by the hand of the	2Chr 24:11	4428
the *k* scribe and the high priest's	2Chr 24:11	4428
Art thou made of the *k* counsel	2Chr 25:16	4428
and the treasures of the *k* house	2Chr 25:24	4428
Hananiah, one of the *k* captains	2Chr 26:11	4428
his son was over the *k* house	2Chr 26:21	4428
Ephraim, slew Maaseiah the *k* son	2Chr 28:7	4428
of David, and of Gad the *k* seer	2Chr 29:25	4428
He appointed also the *k* portion	2Chr 31:3	4428
and Asaiah a servant of the *k*	2Chr 34:20	4428
these were of the *k* substance	2Chr 35:7	4428
according to the *k* commandment	2Chr 35:10	4428
and Heman, and Jeduthun the *k* seer	2Chr 35:15	4428
maintenance from the *k* palace	Ezr 4:14	4430
for us to see the *k* dishonour	Ezr 4:14	4430
made in the *k* treasure house	Ezr 5:17	4430
be given out of the *k* house	Ezr 6:4	4430
that of the *k* goods, even of the	Ezr 6:8	4430
it out of the *k* treasure house	Ezr 7:20	4430
a thing as this in the *k* heart	Ezr 7:27	4428
before all the *k* mighty princes	Ezr 7:28	4428
they delivered the *k* commissions	Ezr 8:36	4428
unto the *k* lieutenants, and to the	Ezr 8:36	4428
For I was the *k* cupbearer	Neh 1:11	4428
Asaph the keeper of the *k* forest	Neh 2:8	4428
river, and gave them the *k* letters	Neh 2:9	4428
of the fountain, and to the *k* pool	Neh 2:14	4428
as also the *k* words that he had	Neh 2:18	4428
pool of Siloah by the *k* garden	Neh 3:15	4428
lieth out from the *k* high house	Neh 3:25	4428
borrowed money for the *k* tribute	Neh 5:4	4428
For it was the *k* commandment	Neh 11:23	4428
was at the *k* hand in all matters	Neh 11:24	4428
of the garden of the *k* palace	Est 1:5	4428
Vashti refused to come at the *k*	Est 1:12	4428
(for so was the *k* manner toward	Est 1:13	4428
and Media, which saw the *k* face	Est 1:14	4428
this day unto all the *k* princes	Est 1:18	4428
when the *k* decree which he shall	Est 1:20	4428
letters into all the *k* provinces	Est 1:22	4428
Then said the *k* servants that	Est 2:2	4428
custody of Hege the *k* chamberlain	Est 2:3	4428
when the *k* commandment and his	Est 2:8	4428
was brought also unto the *k* house	Est 2:8	4428
be given her, out of the *k* house	Est 2:9	4428
of the women unto the *k* house	Est 2:13	4428
the *k* chamberlain, which kept the	Est 2:14	4428
but what Hegai the *k* chamberlain	Est 2:15	4428
then Mordecai sat in the *k* gate	Est 2:19	4428
while Mordecai sat in the *k* gate	Est 2:21	4428
two of the *k* chamberlains,	Est 2:21	4428
all the *k* servants, that were in	Est 3:2	4428
servants, that were in the *k* gate	Est 3:2	4428
Then the *k* servants, which were	Est 3:3	4428
which were in the *k* gate	Est 3:3	4428
thou the *k* commandment	Est 3:3	4428
neither keep they the *k* laws	Est 3:8	4428
for the *k* profit to suffer them	Est 3:8	4428
to bring it into the *k* treasuries	Est 3:9	4428
Then were the *k* scribes called on	Est 3:12	4428
commanded unto the *k* lieutenants	Est 3:12	4428
and sealed with the *k* ring	Est 3:12	4428
by posts into all the *k* provinces	Est 3:13	4428
hastened by the *k* commandment	Est 3:15	4428
And came even before the *k* gate	Est 4:2	4428
the *k* gate clothed with sackcloth	Est 4:2	4428
whithersoever the *k* commandment	Est 4:3	4428
one of the *k* chamberlains, whom	Est 4:5	4428
city, which was before the *k* gate	Est 4:6	4428
to the *k* treasuries for the Jews	Est 4:7	4428
All the *k* servants, and the people	Est 4:11	4428
and the people of the *k* provinces	Est 4:11	4428
thou shalt escape in the *k* house	Est 4:13	4428
in the inner court of the *k* house	Est 5:1	4428
over against the *k* house	Est 5:1	4428
Haman saw Mordecai in the *k* gate	Est 5:9	4428
the Jew sitting at the *k* gate	Est 5:13	4428
two of the *k* chamberlains, the	Est 6:2	4428
Then said the *k* servants that	Est 6:3	4428
the outward court of the *k* house	Est 6:4	4428
the *k* servants said unto him,	Est 6:5	4428
one of the *k* most noble princes	Est 6:9	4428
Jew, that sitteth at the *k* gate	Est 6:10	4428
Mordecai came again to the *k* gate	Est 6:12	4428
came the *k* chamberlains, and	Est 6:14	4428
not countervail the *k* damage	Est 7:4	4428
the word went out of the *k* mouth	Est 7:8	4428
Then was the *k* wrath pacified	Est 7:10	4428
which are in all the *k* provinces	Est 8:5	4428
as it liketh you, in the *k* name	Est 8:8	4428

and seal it with the *k* ring .... Est 8:8   4428
which is written in the *k* name .... Est 8:8   4428
and sealed with the *k* ring .... Est 8:8   4428
Then were the *k* scribes called at .... Est 8:9   4428
and sealed it with the *k* ring .... Est 8:10   4428
pressed on by the *k* commandment .... Est 8:14   4428
whithersoever the *k* commandment ...... Est 8:17   4428
when the *k* commandment and his .... Est 9:1   4428
Mordecai was great in the *k* house .... Est 9:4   4428
in the rest of the *k* provinces .... Est 9:12   4428
k provinces gathered themselves .... Est 9:16   4428
in the heart of the *k* enemies .... Ps 45:5   4428
The *k* daughter is all glorious .... Ps 45:13   4428
shall enter into the *k* palace.................. Ps 45:15   4428
Thou wilt prolong the *k* life .... Ps 61:6   4428
thy righteousness unto the *k* son .... Ps 72:1   4428
The *k* strength also loveth...................... Ps 99:4   4428
of people is the *k* honour .... Prov 14:28   4428
The *k* favour is toward a wise .... Prov 14:35   4428
of the *k* countenance is life .... Prov 16:15   4428
The *k* wrath is as the roaring of........... Prov 19:12   4428
The *k* heart is in the hand of the .... Prov 21:1   4428
thee to keep the *k* commandment .... Eccl 8:2   4428
for the *k* commandment was, saying ..... Is 36:21   4428
LORD unto the *k* house of Judah............ Jer 22:6   4428
then they came up from the *k* .... Jer 26:10   4428
he went down into the *k* house .... Jer 36:12   4428
eunuchs which was in the *k* house .... Jer 38:7   4428
went forth out of the *k* house .... Jer 38:8   4428
night, by the way of the *k* garden .... Jer 39:4   4428
the Chaldeans burned the *k* house .... Jer 39:8   4428
even the *k* daughters, and all the .... Jer 41:10   4428
the *k* daughters, and every person .... Jer 43:6   4428
walls, which was by the *k* garden .... Jer 52:7   4428
house of the LORD, and the *k* house ...... Jer 52:13   4428
them that were near the *k* person .... Jer 52:25   4428
And hath taken of the *k* seed................. Eze 17:13   4410
of Israel, and of the *k* seed .... Dan 1:3   4410
in them to stand in the *k* palace............ Dan 1:4   4428
a daily provision of the *k* meat .... Dan 1:5   4428
with the portion of the *k* meat .... Dan 1:8   4428
eat of the portion of the *k* meat .... Dan 1:13   4428
did eat the portion of the *k* meat .... Dan 1:15   4428
earth that can shew him, and............... Dan 2:10   4430
Arioch the captain of the *k* guard .... Dan 2:14   4430
and said to Arioch the *k* captain .... Dan 2:15   4430
made known unto us the *k* matter .... Dan 2:23   4430
Therefore because the *k* .... Dan 3:22   4430
the *k* counsellors, being gathered........... Dan 3:27   4430
him, and have changed the *k* word........ Dan 3:28   4430
While the word was in the *k* mouth ...... Dan 4:31   4430
of the wall of the *k* palace .... Dan 5:5   4430
Then the *k* countenance was.................. Dan 5:6   4430
Then came in all the *k* wise men .... Dan 5:8   4430
the king concerning the *k* decree .... Dan 6:12   4430
I rose up, and did the *k* business .... Dan 8:27   4428
for the *k* daughter of the south .... Dan 11:6   4428
latter growth after the *k* mowings .... Amos 7:1   4428
for it is the *k* chapel.............................. Amos 7:13   4428
and it is the *k* court............................... Amos 7:13   4467
the *k* children, and all such as .... Zeph 1:8   4428
Hananeel unto the *k* winepresses........... Zec 14:10   4428
having made Blastus the *k*..................... Acts 12:20   *935*
was nourished by the *k* country.............. Acts 12:20   *937*
not afraid of the *k* commandment .... Heb 11:23   *935*

KINGS

the *k* that were with him, and .... Gen 14:5   4428
four *k* with five .... Gen 14:9   4428
the *k* of Sodom and Gomorrah fled, ... Gen 14:10   4428
of the *k* that were with him, at .... Gen 14:17   4428
thee, and *k* shall come out of thee .... Gen 17:6   4428
k of people shall be of her .... Gen 17:16   4428
k shall come out of thy loins .... Gen 35:11   4428
these are the *k* that reigned in .... Gen 36:31   4428
And they slew the *k* of Midian .... Num 31:8   4428
and Hur, and Reba, five *k* of Midian ...... Num 31:8   4428
k of the Amorites the land that............... Deut 3:8   4428
God hath done unto these two *k* .... Deut 3:21   4428
two *k* of the Amorites, which were......... Deut 4:47   4428
deliver their *k* into thine hand .... Deut 7:24   4428
k of the Amorites, and unto the .... Deut 31:4   4428
unto the two *k* of the Amorites .... Josh 2:10   4428
when all the *k* of the Amorites, ... Josh 5:1   4428
all the *k* of the Canaanites, ... Josh 5:1   4428
when all the *k* which were on this .... Josh 9:1   4428
did to the two *k* of the Amorites .... Josh 9:10   4428
the five *k* of the Amorites .... Josh 10:5   4428
for all the *k* of the Amorites .... Josh 10:6   4428
But these five *k* fled, and hid .... Josh 10:16   4428
The five *k* are found hid in a .... Josh 10:17   4428

bring out those five *k* unto me .... Josh 10:22   4428
five *k* unto him out of the cave .... Josh 10:23   4428
brought out those *k* unto Joshua .... Josh 10:24   4428
feet upon the necks of these *k* .... Josh 10:24   4428
and of the springs, and all their *k* .... Josh 10:40   4428
And all these *k* and their land did .... Josh 10:42   4428
to the *k* that were on the north .... Josh 11:2   4428
when all these *k* were met...................... Josh 11:5   4428
those *k*, and all the *k* of them .... Josh 11:12   4428
and all their *k* he took, and smote .... Josh 11:17   4428
war a long time with all those *k* .... Josh 11:18   4428
Now these are the *k* of the land .... Josh 12:1   4428
these are the *k* of the country .... Josh 12:7   4428
all the *k* thirty and one .... Josh 12:24   4428
even the two *k* of the Amorites .... Josh 24:12   4428
said, Threescore and ten *k* .... Judg 1:7   4428
Hear, O ye *k* .... Judg 5:3   4428
The *k* came and fought .... Judg 5:19   4428
then fought the *k* of Canaan in .... Judg 5:19   4428
Zebah and Zalmunna, *k* of Midian .... Judg 8:5   4428
them, and took the two *k* of Midian .... Judg 8:12   4428
that was on the *k* of Midian .... Judg 8:26   4428
Edom, and against the *k* of Zobah 1Sa 14:47   4428
unto the *k* of Judah unto this day 1Sa 27:6   4428
when all the *k* that were servants........... 2Sa 10:19   4428
at the time when *k* go forth to 2Sa 11:1   4428
shall not be any among the *k* like 1Kin 3:13   4428
over all the *k* on this side the 1Kin 4:24   4428
from all *k* of the earth, which 1Kin 4:34   4428
and of all the *k* of Arabia 1Kin 10:15   4428
all the *k* of the earth for riches 1Kin 10:23   4428
so for all the *k* of the Hittites,............... 1Kin 10:29   4428
for the *k* of Syria, did they 1Kin 10:29   4428
the chronicles of the *k* of Israel 1Kin 14:19   4428
the chronicles of the *k* of Judah 1Kin 14:29   4428
the chronicles of the *k* of Judah 1Kin 15:7   4428
the chronicles of the *k* of Judah 1Kin 15:23   4428
the chronicles of the *k* of Israel 1Kin 15:31   4428
the chronicles of the *k* of Israel 1Kin 16:5   4428
the chronicles of the *k* of Israel 1Kin 16:14   4428
the chronicles of the *k* of Israel 1Kin 16:20   4428
the chronicles of the *k* of Israel 1Kin 16:27   4428
k of Israel that were before him 1Kin 16:33   4428
two *k* with him, and horses, and 1Kin 20:1   4428
the *k* in the pavilions, that he 1Kin 20:12   4428
in the pavilions, he and the *k* 1Kin 20:16   4428
thirty and two *k* that helped him 1Kin 20:16   4428
And do this thing, Take the *k* away 1Kin 20:24   4428
we have heard that the *k* of the 1Kin 20:31   4428
house of Israel are merciful *k* 1Kin 20:31   4428
the chronicles of the *k* of Israel 1Kin 22:39   4428
the chronicles of the *k* of Judah 1Kin 22:45   4428
the chronicles of the *k* of Israel.............. 2Kin 1:18   4428
called these three *k* together 2Kin 3:10   4428
called these three *k* together 2Kin 3:13   4428
k were come up to fight against 2Kin 3:21   4428
the *k* are surely slain, and they 2Kin 3:23   4428
against us the *k* of the Hittites,.............. 2Kin 7:6   4428
the *k* of the Egyptians, to come 2Kin 7:6   4428
in the way of the *k* of Israel................... 2Kin 8:18   4428
the chronicles of the *k* of Judah 2Kin 8:23   4428
two *k* stood not before him.................... 2Kin 10:4   4428
the chronicles of the *k* of Israel 2Kin 10:34   4428
And he sat on the throne of the *k* 2Kin 11:19   4428
k of Judah, had dedicated, and his......... 2Kin 12:18   4428
the chronicles of the *k* of Judah 2Kin 12:19   4428
the chronicles of the *k* of Israel 2Kin 13:8   4428
the chronicles of the *k* of Israel.............. 2Kin 13:12   4428
in Samaria with the *k* of Israel............... 2Kin 13:13   4428
the chronicles of the *k* of Israel.............. 2Kin 14:15   4428
in Samaria with the *k* of Israel............... 2Kin 14:16   4428
the chronicles of the *k* of Judah 2Kin 14:18   4428
the chronicles of the *k* of Israel.............. 2Kin 14:28   4428
even with the *k* of Israel........................ 2Kin 14:29   4428
the chronicles of the *k* of Judah 2Kin 15:6   4428
the chronicles of the *k* of Israel 2Kin 15:11   4428
the chronicles of the *k* of Israel 2Kin 15:15   4428
the chronicles of the *k* of Israel 2Kin 15:21   4428
the chronicles of the *k* of Israel 2Kin 15:26   4428
the chronicles of the *k* of Israel 2Kin 15:31   4428
the chronicles of the *k* of Judah 2Kin 15:36   4428
in the way of the *k* of Israel................... 2Kin 16:3   4428
the chronicles of the *k* of Judah 2Kin 16:19   4428
but not as the *k* of Israel that 2Kin 17:2   4428
of the *k* of Israel, which they 2Kin 17:8   4428
like him among all the *k* of Judah 2Kin 18:5   4428
thou hast heard what the *k* of................ 2Kin 19:11   4428
the *k* of Assyria have destroyed 2Kin 19:17   4428
the chronicles of the *k* of Judah 2Kin 20:20   4428
the chronicles of the *k* of Judah 2Kin 21:17   4428
the chronicles of the *k* of Judah 2Kin 21:25   4428

K

whom the *k* of Judah had ordained	2Kin 23:5	4428
k of Judah had given to the sun	2Kin 23:11	4428
which the *k* of Judah had made, and	2Kin 23:12	4428
which the *k* of Israel had made to	2Kin 23:19	4428
all the days of the *k* of Israel	2Kin 23:22	4428
nor of the *k* of Judah	2Kin 23:22	4428
the chronicles of the *k* of Judah	2Kin 23:28	4428
the chronicles of the *k* of Judah	2Kin 24:5	4428
k that were with him in Babylon	2Kin 25:28	4428
Now these are the *k* that reigned	1Chr 1:43	4428
in the book of the *k* of Israel	1Chr 9:1	4428
he reproved *k* for their sakes,	1Chr 16:21	4428
the *k* that were come were by	1Chr 19:9	4428
the time that *k* go out to battle	1Chr 20:1	4428
such as none of the *k* have had	2Chr 1:12	4428
for all the *k* of the Hittites	2Chr 1:17	4428
for the *k* of Syria, by their	2Chr 1:17	4428
all the *k* of Arabia and governors	2Chr 9:14	4428
all the *k* of the earth in riches	2Chr 9:22	4428
all the *k* of the earth sought the	2Chr 9:23	4428
he reigned over all the *k* from	2Chr 9:26	4428
in the book of the *k* of Judah	2Chr 16:11	4428
in the book of the *k* of Israel	2Chr 20:34	4428
in the way of the *k* of Israel	2Chr 21:6	4428
in the way of the *k* of Israel	2Chr 21:13	4428
not in the sepulchres of the *k*	2Chr 21:20	4428
in the city of David among the *k*	2Chr 24:16	4428
not in the sepulchres of the *k*	2Chr 24:25	4428
in the story of the book of the *k*	2Chr 24:27	4428
in the book of the *k* of Judah	2Chr 25:26	4428
burial which belonged to the *k*	2Chr 26:23	4428
in the book of the *k* of Israel	2Chr 27:7	4428
in the ways of the *k* of Israel	2Chr 28:2	4428
unto the *k* of Assyria to help him	2Chr 28:16	4428
gods of the *k* of Syria help them	2Chr 28:23	4428
in the book of the *k* of Judah	2Chr 28:26	4428
the sepulchres of the *k* of Israel	2Chr 28:27	4428
of the hand of the *k* of Assyria	2Chr 30:6	4428
Why should the *k* of Assyria come,	2Chr 32:4	4428
and in the book of the *k* of Judah	2Chr 32:32	4428
in the book of the *k* of Israel	2Chr 33:18	4428
the *k* of Judah had destroyed	2Chr 34:11	4428
neither did all the *k* of Israel	2Chr 35:18	4428
in the book of the *k* of Israel	2Chr 35:27	4428
in the book of the *k* of Israel	2Chr 36:8	4428
endamage the revenue of the *k*	Ezr 4:13	4430
city, and hurtful unto *k* and	Ezr 4:15	4430
hath made insurrection against *k*	Ezr 4:19	4430
been mighty *k* also over Jerusalem	Ezr 4:20	4430
damage grow to the hurt of the *k*	Ezr 4:22	4430
name to dwell there destroy all *k*	Ezr 6:12	4430
Artaxerxes, king of *k*, unto Ezra	Ezr 7:12	4428
for our iniquities have we, our *k*	Ezr 9:7	4428
the hand of the *k* of the lands	Ezr 9:7	4428
in the sight of the *k* of Persia	Ezr 9:9	4428
into their hands, with their *k*	Neh 9:24	4428
that hath come upon us, on our *k*	Neh 9:32	4428
since the time of the *k* of	Neh 9:32	4428
Neither have our *k*, our princes,	Neh 9:34	4428
the *k* whom thou hast set over us	Neh 9:37	4428
the chronicles of the *k* of Media	Est 10:2	4428
With *k* and counsellors of the	Job 3:14	4428
He looseth the bond of *k*, and	Job 12:18	4428
but with *k* are they on the throne	Job 36:7	4428
The *k* of the earth set themselves	Ps 2:2	4428
Be wise now therefore, O ye *k*	Ps 2:10	4428
the *k* were assembled, they passed	Ps 48:4	4428
K of armies did flee apace	Ps 68:12	4428
the Almighty scattered *k* in it	Ps 68:14	4428
shall *k* bring presents unto thee	Ps 68:29	4428
The *k* of Tarshish and of the isles	Ps 72:10	4428
the *k* of Sheba and Seba shall	Ps 72:10	4428
all *k* shall fall down before him	Ps 72:11	4428
is terrible to the *k* of the earth	Ps 76:12	4428
higher than the *k* of the earth	Ps 89:27	4428
all the *k* of the earth thy glory	Ps 102:15	4428
he reproved *k* for their sakes	Ps 105:14	4428
in the chambers of their *k*	Ps 105:30	4428
through *k* in the day of his wrath	Ps 110:5	4428
of thy testimonies also before *k*	Ps 119:46	4428
great nations, and slew mighty *k*	Ps 135:10	4428
To him which smote great *k*	Ps 136:17	4428
And slew famous *k*	Ps 136:18	4428
All the *k* of the earth shall	Ps 138:4	4428
he that giveth salvation unto *k*	Ps 144:10	4428
K of the earth, and all people	Ps 148:11	4428
To bind their *k* with chains	Ps 149:8	4428
By me *k* reign, and princes decree	Prov 8:15	4428
to *k* to commit wickedness	Prov 16:12	4428
lips are the delight of *k*	Prov 16:13	4428
he shall stand before *k*	Prov 22:29	4428
but the honour of *k* is to search	Prov 25:2	4428
the heart of *k* is unsearchable	Prov 25:3	4428
ways to that which destroyeth *k*	Prov 31:3	4428
It is not for *k*, O Lemuel, it is	Prov 31:4	4428
it is not for *k* to drink wine	Prov 31:4	4428
and the peculiar treasure of *k*	Eccl 2:8	4428
Ahaz, and Hezekiah, *k* of Judah	Is 1:1	4428
shall be forsaken of both her *k*	Is 7:16	4428
Are not my princes altogether *k*	Is 10:8	4428
thrones all the *k* of the nations	Is 14:9	4428
All the *k* of the nations, even	Is 14:18	4428
of the wise, the son of ancient *k*	Is 19:11	4428
the *k* of the earth upon the earth	Is 24:21	4428
thou hast heard what the *k* of	Is 37:11	4428
the *k* of Assyria have laid waste	Is 37:18	4428
him, and made him rule over *k*	Is 41:2	4428
and I will loose the loins of *k*	Is 45:1	4428
K shall see and arise, princes	Is 49:7	4428
k shall be thy nursing fathers,	Is 49:23	4428
the *k* shall shut their mouths at	Is 52:15	4428
k to the brightness of thy rising	Is 60:3	4428
their *k* shall minister unto thee	Is 60:10	4428
that their *k* may be brought	Is 60:11	4428
and shalt suck the breast of *k*	Is 60:16	4428
righteousness, and all *k* thy glory	Is 62:2	4428
land, against the *k* of Judah	Jer 1:18	4428
they, their *k*, their princes, and	Jer 2:26	4428
out the bones of the *k* of Judah	Jer 8:1	4428
even the *k* that sit upon David's	Jer 13:13	4428
whereby the *k* of Judah come in,	Jer 17:19	4428
ye *k* of Judah, and all Judah, and	Jer 17:20	4428
into the gates of this city *k*	Jer 17:25	4428
O *k* of Judah, and inhabitants of	Jer 19:3	4428
nor the *k* of Judah, and have	Jer 19:4	4428
and the houses of the *k* of Judah	Jer 19:13	4428
all the treasures of the *k* of	Jer 20:5	4428
k sitting upon the throne of	Jer 22:4	4428
great *k* shall serve themselves of	Jer 25:14	4428
the *k* thereof, and the princes	Jer 25:18	4428
all the *k* of the land of Uz, and	Jer 25:20	4428
all the *k* of the land of the	Jer 25:20	4428
all the *k* of Tyrus	Jer 25:22	4428
all the *k* of Zidon	Jer 25:22	4428
the *k* of the isles which are	Jer 25:22	4428
all the *k* of Arabia	Jer 25:24	4428
all the *k* of the mingled people	Jer 25:24	4428
all the *k* of Zimri	Jer 25:25	4428
and all the *k* of Elam	Jer 25:25	4428
and all the *k* of the Medes	Jer 25:25	4428
all the *k* of the north, far and	Jer 25:26	4428
great *k* shall serve themselves of	Jer 27:7	4428
me to anger, they, their *k*	Jer 32:32	4428
the houses of the *k* of Judah	Jer 33:4	4428
the former *k* which were before	Jer 34:5	4428
the wickedness of the *k* of Judah	Jer 44:9	4428
done, we, and our fathers, our *k*	Jer 44:17	4428
ye, and your fathers, your *k*	Jer 44:21	4428
with their gods, and their *k*	Jer 46:25	4428
many *k* shall be raised up from	Jer 50:41	4428
the spirit of the *k* of the Medes	Jer 51:11	4428
nations with the *k* of the Medes	Jer 51:28	4428
k that were with him in Babylon	Jer 52:32	4428
The *k* of the earth, and all the	Lam 4:12	4428
king of Babylon, a king of *k*	Eze 26:7	4428
thou didst enrich the *k* of the	Eze 27:33	4428
their *k* shall be sore afraid,	Eze 27:35	4428
ground, I will lay them before *k*	Eze 28:17	4428
their *k* shall be horribly afraid	Eze 32:10	4428
There is Edom, her *k*, and all her	Eze 32:29	4428
defile, neither they, nor their *k*	Eze 43:7	4428
of their *k* in their high places	Eze 43:7	4428
and the carcases of their *k*	Eze 43:9	4428
removeth *k*, and setteth up *k*	Dan 2:21	4430
Thou, O king, art a king of *k*	Dan 2:37	4430
in the days of these *k* shall the	Dan 2:44	4430
is a God of gods, and a LORD of *k*	Dan 2:47	4430
which are four, are four *k*	Dan 7:17	4430
are ten *k* that shall arise	Dan 7:24	4430
first, and he shall subdue three *k*	Dan 7:24	4430
two horns are the *k* of Media	Dan 8:20	4428
which spake in thy name to our *k*	Dan 9:6	4428
confusion of face, to our *k*	Dan 9:8	4428
there with the *k* of Persia	Dan 10:13	4428
stand up yet three *k* in Persia	Dan 11:2	4428
k of Judah, and in the days of	Hos 1:1	4428
all their *k* are fallen	Hos 7:7	4428
They have set up *k*, but not by me	Hos 8:4	4428
k of Judah, which he saw	Mic 1:1	4428
shall be a lie to the *k* of Israel	Mic 1:14	4428
And they shall scoff at the *k*	Hab 1:10	4428
k for my sake, for a testimony	Mt 10:18	935

of whom do the *k* of the earth .... Mt 17:25   935
k for my sake, for a testimony .... Mk 13:9   935
k have desired to see those .... Lk 10:24   935
prisons, being brought before *k* .... Lk 21:12   935
The *k* of the Gentiles exercise .... Lk 22:25   935
The *k* of the earth stood up, and .... Acts 4:26   935
my name before the Gentiles, and *k* .... Acts 9:15   935
ye have reigned as *k* without us 1Cor 4:8   935
For *k*, and for all that are in 1Ti 2:2   935
and only Potentate, the King of *k* 1Ti 6:15   936
from the slaughter of the *k* .... Heb 7:1   935
the prince of the *k* of the earth .... Rev 1:5   935
And hath made us *k* and priests unto.... Rev 1:6   935
And hast made us unto our God *k* .... Rev 5:10   935
the *k* of the earth, and the great............. Rev 6:15   935
and nations, and tongues, and *k*.......... Rev 10:11   935
that the way of the *k* of the east .... Rev 16:12   935
go forth unto the *k* of the earth .... Rev 16:14   935
With whom the *k* of the earth have .... Rev 17:2   935
And there are seven *k* .... Rev 17:10   935
horns which thou sawest are ten *k* .... Rev 17:12   935
but receive power as *k* one hour .... Rev 17:12   935
he is Lord of lords, and King of *k*........... Rev 17:14   935
reigneth over the *k* of the earth .... Rev 17:18   935
the *k* of the earth have committed .... Rev 18:3   935
the *k* of the earth, who have .... Rev 18:9   935
thigh a name written, KING OF *k* .... Rev 19:16   935
That ye may eat the flesh of *k* .... Rev 19:18   935
the *k* of the earth, and their .... Rev 19:19   935
the *k* of the earth do bring their .... Rev 21:24   935

KINGS'
K daughters were among thy .... Ps 45:9   4428
her hands, and is in *k* palaces .... Prov 30:28   4428
both these *k* hearts shall be to .... Dan 11:27   4428
soft clothing are in *k* houses .... Mt 11:8   935
live delicately, are in *k* courts .... Lk 7:25   933

KINNERETH See CINNEROTH.

KINSFOLK
My *k* have failed, and my familiar .... Job 19:14   7138
and they sought him among their *k* .... Lk 2:44   4773

KINSFOLKS
against a wall, neither of his *k* 1Kin 16:11   1350
and all his great men, and his *k* 2Kin 10:11   3045
by parents, and brethren, and *k* .... Lk 21:16   4773

KINSMAN
But if the man have no *k* to .... Num 5:8   1350
his *k* that is next to him of his .... Num 27:11   7607
Naomi had a *k* of her husband's, a .... Ruth 2:1   3045
for thou art a near *k* .... Ruth 3:9   1350
it is true that I am thy near *k* .... Ruth 3:12   1350
there is a *k* nearer than I .... Ruth 3:12   1350
perform unto thee the part of a *k* .... Ruth 3:13   1350
not do the part of a *k* to thee .... Ruth 3:13   1350
will I do the part of a *k* to thee .... Ruth 3:13   1350
the *k* of whom Boaz spake came by .... Ruth 4:1   1350
And he said unto the *k*, Naomi, ... Ruth 4:3   1350
the *k* said, I cannot redeem it .... Ruth 4:6   1350
Therefore the *k* said unto Boaz, ... Ruth 4:8   1350
left thee this day without a *k* .... Ruth 4:14   1350
being his *k* whose ear Peter cut............. Jn 18:26   4773
Salute Herodion my *k* .... Rom 16:11   4773

KINSMAN'S
let him do the *k* part .... Ruth 3:13   1350

KINSMEN
of kin unto us, one of our next *k* .... Ruth 2:20   1350
and my *k* stand afar off .... Ps 38:11   7138
nor thy brethren, neither thy *k* .... Lk 14:12   4773
and had called together his *k* .... Acts 10:24   4773
my *k* according to the flesh .... Rom 9:3   4773
Salute Andronicus and Junia, my *k* .... Rom 16:7   4773
and Jason, and Sosipater, my *k* .... Rom 16:21   4773

KINSWOMAN
she is thy father's near *k* .... Lev 18:12   7607
for she is thy mother's near *k*................ Lev 18:13   7607
and call understanding thy *k* .... Prov 7:4   4129

KINSWOMEN
for they are her near *k* .... Lev 18:17   7608

KIOS See CHIOS.

KIR (*kur*) See KIR-HARESH.
1. An Assyrian district on the Kur River.
the people of it captive to *k* 2Kin 16:9   7024
shall go into captivity unto *k* .... Amos 1:5   7024
Caphtor, and the Syrians from *k* .... Amos 9:7   7024
2. A Moabite city.
because in the night *k* of Moab is.......... Is 15:1   7024

3. Inhabitants of Kir 1.
and *K* uncovered the shield .... Is 22:6   7024

KIR-HARASETH (*kur-har'-a-seth*) See KIR-HARESETH. A
Moabite city.
only in *K* left they the stones 2Kin 3:25   7025

KIR-HARESETH (*kur-har'-e-seth*) See KIR-HARESH.
Same as Kir-haraseth.
foundations of *K* shall ye mourn .... Is 16:7   7025

KIR-HARESH (*kur-ha'-resh*) See KIR-HARASETH, KIR-
HARESETH, KIR-HERES. *Same as Kir-haraseth.*
Moab, and mine inward parts for *K* .... Is 16:11   7025

KIR-HERES (*kur-he'-res*) See KIR-HARESH. *Same as Kir-*
haraseth.
shall mourn for the men of *K* .... Jer 48:31   7025
sound like pipes for the men of *K* .... Jer 48:36   7025

KIRIATH See KIRJATH.

KIRIATHAIM (*kir-e-a-thay'-im*) See KIRJATHAIM.
1. A town east of the Jordan.
in Ham, and the Emims in Shaveh *K* ..... Gen 14:5   7741
2. A city in Reuben.
K is confounded and taken...................... Jer 48:1   7156
And upon *K*, and upon Beth-gamul, ... Jer 48:23   7156
Beth-jeshimoth, Baal-meon, and *K* .... Eze 25:9   7156

KIRIATH-ARBA See KIRJATH-ARBA.

KIRIATH-ARIM See KIRJATH-ARIM.

KIRIATH-BAAL See KIRJATH-BAAL.

KIRIATH-JEARIM See KIRJATH.

KIRIATH-SANNAH See KIRJATH-SANNAH.

KIRIATH-SEPHER See KIRJATH-SEPHER.

KIRIOTH (*kir'-e-oth*) *A Moabite city.*
it shall devour the palaces of *K* .... Amos 2:2   7152

KIRJATH (*kur'-jath*) See KIRJATH-ARIM, KIRJATH-BAAL,
KIRJATH-JEARIM. *Short form of Kirjath-jearim.*
which is Jerusalem, Gibeath, and *K* .... Josh 18:28   7157

KIRJATHAIM (*jur'-jath-a'-im*)
1. A city in Reuben.
built Heshbon, and Elealeh, and *K* .... Num 32:37   7156
K, and Sibmah, and Zareth-shahar .... Josh 13:19   7156
2. A Levitical city in Naphtali.
suburbs, and *K* with her suburbs 1Chr 6:76   7156

KIRJATH-ARBA (*kur'-jath-ar'-bah*) See HEBRON. *A city*
in Judah.
And Sarah died in *K*................................. Gen 23:2   7153
the name of Hebron before was *K* .... Josh 14:15   7153
And Humtah, and *K*, which is Hebron, ... Josh 15:54   7153
in mount Ephraim, and *K* .... Josh 20:7   7153
the name of Hebron before was *K* .... Judg 1:10   7153
the children of Judah dwelt at *K* .... Neh 11:25   7153

KIRJATH-ARIM (*kur'-jath-a'-rim*) See KIRJATH-JEARIM.
Same as Kirjath-jearim.
The children of *K*, Chephirah, and.......... Ezr 2:25   7157

KIRJATH-BAAL (*kur'-jath-ba'-al*) See BAALAH, KIRJATH-
JEARIM. *Same as Kirjath-jearim.*
K, which is Kirjath-jearim, and .... Josh 15:60   7154
the goings out thereof were at *K*............. Josh 18:14   7154

KIRJATH-HUZOTH (*kur'-jath-hu'-zoth*) *Residence of*
Balak, king of Edom.
with Balak, and they came unto *K* .... Num 22:39   7155

KIRJATH-JEARIM (*kur'-jath-je'-a-rim*) See KIRJATH,
KIRJATH-ARIM, KIRJATH-BAAL.
1. A city in Judah.
and Chephirah, and Beeroth, and *K* .... Josh 9:17   7157
was drawn to Baalah, which is *K* .... Josh 15:9   7157
Kirjath-baal, which is *K*, and .... Josh 15:60   7157
were at Kirjath-baal, which is *K* .... Josh 18:14   7157
quarter was from the end of *K* .... Josh 18:15   7157
And they went up, and pitched in *K* .... Judg 18:12   7157
behold, it is behind *K* .... Judg 18:12   7157
to the inhabitants of *K*, saying, ... 1Sa 6:21   7157
And the men of *K* came, and brought 1Sa 7:1   7157
to pass, while the ark abode in *K*............ 1Sa 7:2   7157
to bring the ark of God from *K*................ 1Chr 13:5   7157
Israel, to Baalah, that is, to *K*................. 1Chr 13:6   7157
K to the place which David had 2Chr 1:4   7157
The men of *K*, Chephirah, and .... Neh 7:29   7157
Urijah the son of Shemaiah of *K* .... Jer 26:20   7157
2. A descendant of Caleb.
Shobal the father of *K*,........................... 1Chr 2:50   7157
Shobal the father of *K* had sons 1Chr 2:52   7157
And the families of *K* 1Chr 2:53   7157

K

KIRJATH-SANNAH *(kur'-jath-san'-nah) A city in Judah.*
And Dannah, and K, which is Debir, ... Josh 15:49   7158

KIRJATH-SEPHER *(kur'-jath-se'-fer)* See DEBIR, KIRJATH-SANNAH. *Same as Kirjath-sannah.*
and the name of Debir before was K ...... Josh 15:15   7158
And Caleb said, He that smiteth K .... Josh 15:16   7158
and the name of Debir before was K ...... Judg 1:11   7158
And Caleb said, He that smiteth K .... Judg 1:12   7158

KISH *(kish)*
   1. Father of King Saul.
man of Benjamin, whose name was K ...1Sa 9:1   7027
the asses of K Saul's father were 1Sa 9:3   7027
K said to Saul his son, Take now 1Sa 9:3   7027
that is come unto the son of K 1Sa 10:11   7027
and Saul the son of K was taken 1Sa 10:21   7027
And K was the father of Saul 1Sa 14:51   7027
in the sepulchre of K his father 2Sa 21:14   7027
And Ner begat K 1Chr 8:33   7027
K begat Saul 1Chr 8:33   7027
And Ner begat K 1Chr 9:39   7027
and K begat Saul 1Chr 9:39   7027
because of Saul the son of K 1Chr 12:1   7027
the seer, and Saul the son of K 1Chr 26:28   7027
   2. Son of Abi-Gibeon.
firstborn son Abdon, and Zur, and K 1Chr 8:30   7027
son Abdon, then Zur, and K 1Chr 9:36   7027
   3. A sanctuary servant.
of Mahli, Eleazar, and K 1Chr 23:21   7027
brethren the sons of K took them 1Chr 23:22   7027
Concerning K: the son of Kish 1Chr 24:29   7027
   4. A Levite.
K the son of Abdi, and Azariah the 2Chr 29:12   7027
   5. An ancestor of Mordecai.
the son of Shimei, the son of K .... Est 2:5   7027

KISHI *(kish'-i)* See KUSHAIAH. *Father of Ethan.*
Ethan the son of K, the son of 1Chr 6:44   7029

KISHION *(kish'-e-on)* See KEDESH, KISHON. *A Levitical city in Issachar.*
And Rabbith, and K, and Abez, ... Josh 19:20   7191

KISHON *(ki'-shon)* See KISHION, KISON.
   1. Same as Kishion.
K with her suburbs, Dabareh with .... Josh 21:28   7191
the Gentiles unto the river of K .... Judg 4:13   7028
The river of K swept them away, ... Judg 5:21   7028
that ancient river, the river K .... Judg 5:21   7028
brought them down to the brook K 1Kin 18:40   7028
   2. A brook near Mt. Tabor.
draw unto thee to the river K .... Judg 4:7   7028

KISLEV See CHISLEU.

KISLON See CHISLON.

KISLOTH TABOR See CHISLOTH-TABOR.

KISON *(ki'-son)* See KISHON. *Same as Kishon 2.*
as to Jabin, at the brook of K .... Ps 83:9   7028

KISS
Come near now, and k me, my son .... Gen 27:26   5401
hast not suffered me to k my sons .... Gen 31:28   5401
with the right hand to k him 2Sa 20:9   5401
k my father and my mother, and then 1Kin 19:20   5401
K the Son, lest he be angry, and .... Ps 2:12   5401
Every man shall k his lips that.............. Prov 24:26   5401
Let him k me with the kisses of .... Song 1:2   5401
find thee without, I would k thee .... Song 8:1   5401
men that sacrifice k the calves .... Hos 13:2   5401
saying, Whomsoever I shall k .... Mt 26:48   5368
saying, Whomsoever I shall k .... Mk 14:44   5368
Thou gavest me no k .... Lk 7:45   5370
in hath not ceased to k my feet .... Lk 7:45   2705
and drew near unto Jesus to k him .... Lk 22:47   5368
thou the Son of man with a k .... Lk 22:48   5370
Salute one another with an holy k .... Rom 16:16   5370
ye one another with an holy k 1Cor 16:20   5370
Greet one another with an holy k 2Cor 13:12   5370
all the brethren with an holy k 1Th 5:26   5370
one another with a k of charity.............. 1Pet 5:14   5370

KISSED
And he came near, and k him .... Gen 27:27   5401
Jacob k Rachel, and lifted up his........... Gen 29:11   5401
k him, and brought him to his .... Gen 29:13   5401
k his sons and his daughters, and .... Gen 31:55   5401
and fell on his neck, and k him .... Gen 33:4   5401
Moreover he k all his brethren,.............. Gen 45:15   5401
he k them, and embraced them .... Gen 48:10   5401
face, and wept upon him, and k him ...... Gen 50:1   5401

him in the mount of God, and k him ...... Ex 4:27   5401
law, and did obeisance, and k him.......... Ex 18:7   5401
Then she k them .... Ruth 1:9   5401
Orpah k her mother in law...................... Ruth 1:14   5401
k him, and said, Is it not because 1Sa 10:1   5401
they k one another, and wept one 1Sa 20:41   5401
and the king k Absalom 2Sa 14:33   5401
his hand, and took him, and k him......... 2Sa 15:5   5401
the king k Barzillai, and blessed 2Sa 19:39   5401
every mouth which hath not k him 1Kin 19:18   5401
or my mouth hath k my hand.................. Job 31:27   5401
and peace have k each other .... Ps 85:10   5401
k him, and with an impudent face .... Prov 7:13   5401
master; and k him .... Mt 26:49   2705
Master, master; and k him .... Mk 14:45   2705
k his feet, and anointed them with .... Lk 7:38   2705
and fell on his neck, and k him .... Lk 15:20   2705
and fell on Paul's neck, and k him, ... Acts 20:37   2705

KISSES
but the k of an enemy are .... Prov 27:6   5390
kiss me with the k of his mouth .... Song 1:2   5390

KITE
vulture, and the k after his kind .... Lev 11:14   344
And the glede, and the k, and the.......... Deut 14:13   344

KITHLISH *(kith'-lish) A city in Judah.*
And Cabbon, and Lahmam, and K .... Josh 15:40   3798

KITRON *(ki'-tron)* See KATTAH. *A city in Zebulun.*
drive out the inhabitants of K .... Judg 1:30   7003

KITTIM *(kit'-tim)* See CHITTIM. *A son of Javan.*
Elishah, and Tarshish, K, and .... Gen 10:4   3794
Elishah, and Tarshish, K, and................ 1Chr 1:7   3794

KIYYUN See CHIUN.

KNEAD
k it, and make cakes upon the .... Gen 18:6   3888
the women k their dough, to make .... Jer 7:18   3888

KNEADED
k it, and did bake unleavened 1Sa 28:24   3888
k it, and made cakes in his sight, ... 2Sa 13:8   3888
raising after he hath k the dough .... Hos 7:4   3888

KNEADINGTROUGHS
into thine ovens, and into thy k .... Ex 8:3   4863
their k being bound up in their .... Ex 12:34   4863

KNEE
they cried before him, Bow the k .... Gen 41:43
That to me every k shall bow.................. Is 45:23   1290
and they bowed the k before him .... Mt 27:29
bowed the k to the image of Baal .... Rom 11:4   *1119*
every k shall bow to me, and every .... Rom 14:11   *1119*
name of Jesus every k should bow .... Phil 2:10   *1119*

KNEEL
he made his camels to k down .... Gen 24:11   1288
let us k before the LORD our .... Ps 95:6   1288

KNEELED
k down upon his knees before all 2Chr 6:13   1288
he k upon his knees three times a.......... Dan 6:10   1289
k to him, and asked him, Good................ Mk 10:17   *1120*
cast, and k down, and prayed, ... Lk 22:41   5087,1119
he k down, and cried with a loud ... Acts 7:60   5087,1119
all forth, and k down, and prayed... Acts 9:40   5087,1119
he k down, and prayed with them .. Acts 20:36   5087,1119
k down on the shore, and prayed .... Acts 21:5   5087,1119

KNEELING
from k on his knees with his 1Kin 8:54   3766
k down to him, and saying, ... Mt 17:14   *1120*
k down to him, and saying unto him ...... Mk 1:40   *1120*

KNEES
and she shall bear upon my k .... Gen 30:3   1290
them out from between his k .... Gen 48:12   1290
were brought up upon Joseph's k .... Gen 50:23   1290
LORD shall smite thee in the k.............. Deut 28:35   1290
boweth down upon his k to drink .... Judg 7:5   1290
down upon their k to drink water .... Judg 7:6   1290
And she made him sleep upon her k ...... Judg 16:19   1290
from kneeling on his k with his 1Kin 8:54   1290
and put his face between his k 1Kin 18:42   1290
all the k which have not bowed 1Kin 19:18   1290
fell on his k before Elijah, and 2Kin 1:13   1290
mother, he sat on her k till noon 2Kin 4:20   1290
kneeled down upon his k before 2Chr 6:13   1290
and my mantle, I fell upon my k .... Ezr 9:5   1290
Why did the k prevent me .... Job 3:12   1290
hast strengthened the feeble k .... Job 4:4   1290
My k are weak through fasting .... Ps 109:24   1290

hands, and confirm the feeble *k*	Is 35:3	1290
sides, and be dandled upon her *k*	Is 66:12	1290
all *k* shall be weak as water	Eze 7:17	1290
all *k* shall be weak as water	Eze 21:7	1290
the waters were to the *k*	Eze 47:4	1290
his *k* smote one against another	Dan 5:6	755
upon his *k* three times a day	Dan 6:10	1291
me, which set me upon my *k*	Dan 10:10	1290
the *k* smite together, and much	Nah 2:10	1290
bowing their *k* worshipped him	Mk 15:19	1119
saw it, he fell down at Jesus' *k*	Lk 5:8	1119
For this cause I bow my *k* unto	Eph 3:14	1119
which hang down, and the feeble *k*	Heb 12:12	1119

KNEW

they *k* that they were naked	Gen 3:7	3045
And Adam *k* Eve his wife	Gen 4:1	3045
And Cain *k* his wife	Gen 4:17	3045
And Adam *k* his wife again	Gen 4:25	3045
so Noah *k* that the waters were	Gen 8:11	3045
k what his younger son had done	Gen 9:24	3045
and I *k* it not	Gen 28:16	3045
For Jacob *k* not that Rachel had	Gen 31:32	3045
And he *k* it, and said, It is my	Gen 37:33	5234
Onan *k* that the seed should not	Gen 38:9	3045
(for he *k* not that she was his	Gen 38:16	3045
And he *k* her again no more	Gen 38:26	3045
he *k* not ought he had, save the	Gen 39:6	3045
he *k* them, but made himself	Gen 42:7	5234
Joseph *k* his brethren	Gen 42:8	5234
his brethren, but they *k* not him	Gen 42:8	3045
they *k* not that Joseph understood	Gen 42:23	3045
over Egypt, which *k* not Joseph	Ex 1:8	3045
for I *k* not that thou stoodest in	Num 22:34	3045
k the knowledge of the most High	Num 24:16	3045
manna, which thy fathers *k* not	Deut 8:16	3045
LORD from the day that I *k* you	Deut 9:24	3045
them, gods whom they *k* not	Deut 29:26	3045
to gods whom they *k* not, to new	Deut 32:17	3045
brethren, nor *k* his own children	Deut 33:9	3045
whom the LORD *k* face to face	Deut 34:10	3045
which *k* not the LORD, nor yet the	Judg 2:10	3045
such as before *k* nothing thereof	Judg 3:2	3045
and she *k* no man	Judg 11:39	3045
For Manoah *k* not that he was an	Judg 13:16	3045
Then Manoah *k* that he was an	Judg 13:21	3045
his mother *k* not that it was of	Judg 14:4	3045
they *k* the voice of the young man	Judg 18:3	5234
and they *k* her, and abused her all	Judg 19:25	3045
but they *k* not that evil was near	Judg 20:34	3045
Elkanah *k* Hannah his wife	1Sa 1:19	3045
they *k* not the LORD	1Sa 2:12	3045
from Dan even to Beer-sheba *k*	1Sa 3:20	3045
when all that *k* him beforetime	1Sa 10:11	3045
the people *k* not that Jonathan	1Sa 14:3	3045
k that the LORD was with David	1Sa 18:28	3045
for if I *k* certainly that evil	1Sa 20:9	3045
whereby Jonathan *k* that it was	1Sa 20:33	3045
But the lad *k* not any thing	1Sa 20:39	3045
Jonathan and David *k* the matter	1Sa 20:39	3045
for thy servant *k* nothing of all	1Sa 22:15	3045
and because they *k* when he fled	1Sa 22:17	3045
I *k* it that day, when Doeg the	1Sa 22:22	3045
David *k* that Saul secretly	1Sa 23:9	3045
away, and no man saw it, nor *k* it	1Sa 26:12	3045
Saul *k* David's voice, and said, Is	1Sa 26:17	5234
but David *k* it not	2Sa 3:26	3045
where he *k* that valiant men were	2Sa 11:16	3045
k ye not that they would shoot	2Sa 11:20	3045
and they *k* not any thing	2Sa 15:11	3045
tumult, but I *k* not what it was	2Sa 18:29	3045
a people which I *k* not shall	2Sa 22:44	3045
but the king *k* her not	1Kin 1:4	3045
he *k* him, and fell on his face, and	1Kin 18:7	5234
for they *k* them not	2Kin 4:39	3045
Then Manasseh *k* that the LORD he	2Chr 33:13	3045
the rulers *k* not whither I went	Neh 2:16	3045
which *k* the times, (for so was	Est 1:13	5234
manner toward all that *k* law	Est 1:13	5234
k him not, they lifted up their	Job 2:12	5234
Oh that I *k* where I might find	Job 23:3	3045
the cause which I *k* not I	Job 29:16	3045
wonderful for me, which I *k* not	Job 42:3	3045
to my charge things that I *k* not	Ps 35:11	3045
against me, and I *k* it not	Ps 35:15	3045
thou sayest, Behold, we *k* it not	Prov 24:12	3045
blind by a way that they *k* not	Is 42:16	3045
on fire round about, yet he *k* not	Is 42:25	3045
Because I *k* that thou art	Is 48:4	1847
shouldest say, Behold, I *k* them	Is 48:7	3045

for I *k* that thou wouldest deal	Is 48:8	3045
nations that *k* not thee shall run	Is 55:5	3045
formed thee in the belly I *k* thee	Jer 1:5	3045
they that handle the law *k* me not	Jer 2:8	3045
I *k* not that they had devised	Jer 11:19	3045
Then I *k* that this was the word	Jer 32:8	3045
slain Gedaliah, and no man *k* it	Jer 41:4	3045
serve other gods, whom they *k* not	Jer 44:3	3045
Then all the men which *k* that	Jer 44:15	3045
I *k* that they were the cherubims	Eze 10:20	3045
he *k* their desolate palaces, and	Eze 19:7	3045
till he *k* that the most high God	Dan 5:21	3046
Now when Daniel *k* that the	Dan 6:10	3046
a god whom his fathers *k* not	Dan 11:38	3045
have made princes, and I *k* it not	Hos 8:4	3045
but they *k* not that I healed them	Hos 11:3	3045
For the men *k* that he fled from	Jonah 1:10	3045
for I *k* that thou art a gracious	Jonah 4:2	3045
all the nations whom they *k* not	Zec 7:14	3045
me *k* that it was the word of the	Zec 11:11	3045
k her not till she had brought	Mt 1:25	1097
profess unto them, I never *k* you	Mt 7:23	1097
But when Jesus *k* it, he withdrew	Mt 12:15	1097
Jesus *k* their thoughts, and said	Mt 12:25	1492
they *k* him not, but have done	Mt 17:12	1912
k not until the flood came, and	Mt 24:39	1097
I *k* thee that thou art an hard	Mt 25:24	1097
For he *k* that for envy they had	Mt 27:18	1492
to speak, because they *k* him	Mk 1:34	1492
saw them departing, and many *k* him	Mk 6:33	1921
And when they *k*, they say, Five	Mk 6:38	1097
the ship, straightway they *k* him	Mk 6:54	1921
And when Jesus *k* it, he saith unto	Mk 8:17	1097
for they *k* that he had spoken the	Mk 12:12	1097
For he *k* that the chief priests	Mk 15:10	1097
when he *k* it of the centurion, he	Mk 15:45	1097
Joseph and his mother *k* not of it	Lk 2:43	1097
for they *k* that he was Christ	Lk 4:41	
But he *k* their thoughts, and said	Lk 6:8	1492
when she *k* that Jesus sat at meat	Lk 7:37	1921
And the people, when they *k* it	Lk 9:11	1097
which *k* his lord's will, and	Lk 12:47	1097
But he that *k* not, and did commit	Lk 12:48	1097
neither *k* they the things which	Lk 18:34	1097
as soon as he *k* that he belonged	Lk 23:7	1921
eyes were opened, and they *k* him	Lk 24:31	1921
by him, and the world *k* him not	Jn 1:10	1097
And I *k* him not	Jn 1:31	1492
And I *k* him not	Jn 1:33	1492
made wine, and *k* not whence it was	Jn 2:9	1492
servants which drew the water *k*	Jn 2:9	1492
unto them, because he *k* all men	Jn 2:24	1097
for he *k* what was in man	Jn 2:25	1097
When therefore the Lord *k* how the	Jn 4:1	1097
So the father *k* that it was at	Jn 4:53	1097
k that he had been now a long	Jn 5:6	1097
for he himself *k* what he would do	Jn 6:6	1492
When Jesus *k* in himself that his	Jn 6:61	1492
For Jesus *k* from the beginning	Jn 6:64	1492
I *k* that thou hearest me always	Jn 11:42	1492
if any man *k* where he were, he	Jn 11:57	1097
therefore *k* that he was there	Jn 12:9	1097
when Jesus *k* that his hour was	Jn 13:1	1492
For he *k* who should betray him	Jn 13:11	1492
Now no man at the table *k* for	Jn 13:28	1097
Now Jesus *k* that they were	Jn 16:19	1492
which betrayed him, *k* the place	Jn 18:2	1492
For as yet they *k* not the	Jn 20:9	1492
and *k* not that it was Jesus	Jn 20:14	1492
but the disciples *k* not that it	Jn 21:4	1492
they *k* that it was he which sat	Acts 3:10	1921
king arose, which *k* not Joseph	Acts 7:18	1492
Which when the brethren *k*	Acts 9:30	1921
when she *k* Peter's voice, she	Acts 12:14	1921
rulers, because they *k* him not	Acts 13:27	50
for they *k* all that his father	Acts 16:3	1492
the more part *k* not wherefore	Acts 19:32	1492
But when they *k* that he was a Jew	Acts 19:34	1921
after he *k* that he was a Roman	Acts 22:29	1921
Which *k* me from the beginning, if	Acts 26:5	4267
it was day, they *k* not the land	Acts 27:39	1921
then they *k* that the island was	Acts 28:1	1921
Because that, when they *k* God	Rom 1:21	1097
God the world by wisdom *k* not God	1Cor 1:21	1097
of the princes of this world *k*	1Cor 2:8	1097
to be sin for us, who *k* no sin	2Cor 5:21	1097
I *k* a man in Christ above	2Cor 12:2	1492
I *k* such a man, (whether in the	2Cor 12:3	1492
Howbeit then, when ye *k* not God	Gal 4:8	1492
k the grace of God in truth	Col 1:6	1921

K

For I would that ye *k* what great	Col 2:1	1492
us not, because it *k* him not	1Jn 3:1	1097
though ye once *k* this, how that	Jude 5	1492
had a name written, that no man *k*	Rev 19:12	1492

KNEWEST

thee with manna, which thou *k* not	Deut 8:3	3045
which thou *k* not heretofore	Ruth 2:11	3045
for thou *k* that they dealt	Neh 9:10	3045
within me, then thou *k* my path	Ps 142:3	3045
yea, thou *k* not	Is 48:8	3045
heart, though thou *k* all this	Dan 5:22	3046
thou *k* that I reap where I sowed	Mt 25:26	1492
Thou *k* that I was an austere man,	Lk 19:22	1492
because thou *k* not the time of	Lk 19:44	1097
If thou *k* the gift of God, and who	Jn 4:10	1492

KNIFE

took the fire in his hand, and a *k*	Gen 22:6	3979
took the *k* to slay his son	Gen 22:10	3979
come into his house, he took a *k*	Judg 19:29	3979
put a *k* to thy throat, if thou be	Prov 23:2	7915
son of man, take thee a sharp *k*	Eze 5:1	2719
part, and smite about it with a *k*	Eze 5:2	2719

KNIT

the city, *k* together as one man	Judg 20:11	2270
was *k* with the soul of David	1Sa 18:1	7194
mine heart shall be *k* unto you	1Chr 12:17	3162
great sheet *k* at the four corners	Acts 10:11	1210
being *k* together in love, and unto	Col 2:2	4822
k together, increaseth with the	Col 2:19	4822

KNIVES

unto Joshua, Make thee sharp *k*	Josh 5:2	2719
And Joshua made him sharp *k*	Josh 5:3	2719
after their manner with *k*	1Kin 18:28	2719
of silver, nine and twenty *k*	Ezr 1:9	4252
swords, and their jaw teeth as *k*	Prov 30:14	3979

KNOCK

***k*, and it shall be opened unto you**	Mt 7:7	2925
***k*, and it shall be opened unto you**	Lk 11:9	2925
to *k* at the door, saying, Lord,	Lk 13:25	2925
Behold, I stand at the door, and *k*	Rev 3:20	2925

KNOCKED

as Peter *k* at the door of the	Acts 12:13	2925

KNOCKETH

is the voice of my beloved that *k*	Song 5:2	1849
to him that *k* it shall be opened	Mt 7:8	2925
to him that *k* it shall be opened	Lk 11:10	2925
that when he cometh and *k*, they	Lk 12:36	2925

KNOCKING

But Peter continued *k*	Acts 12:16	2925

KNOP

made like unto almonds, with a *k*	Ex 25:33	3730
in the other branch, with a *k*	Ex 25:33	3730
there shall be the a *k* under two	Ex 25:35	3730
a *k* under two branches of the	Ex 25:35	3730
a *k* under two branches of the	Ex 25:35	3730
of almonds in one branch, a *k*	Ex 37:19	3730
almonds in another branch, a *k*	Ex 37:19	3730
a *k* under two branches of the	Ex 37:21	3730
a *k* under two branches of the	Ex 37:21	3730
a *k* under two branches of the	Ex 37:21	3730

KNOPS

and his branches, his bowls, his *k*	Ex 25:31	3730
like unto almonds, with their *k*	Ex 25:34	3730
Their *k* and their branches shall	Ex 25:36	3730
and his branch, his bowls, his *k*	Ex 37:17	3730
bowls made like almonds, his *k*	Ex 37:20	3730
Their *k* and their branches were of	Ex 37:22	3730
house within was carved with *k*	1Kin 6:18	6497
about there were *k* compassing it	1Kin 7:24	6497
the *k* were cast in two rows, when	1Kin 7:24	6497

KNOW

For God doth *k* that in the day ye	Gen 3:5	3045
as one of us, to *k* good and evil	Gen 3:22	3045
And he said, I *k* not	Gen 4:9	3045
I *k* that thou art a fair woman to	Gen 12:11	3045
whereby shall I *k* that I shall	Gen 15:8	3045
K of a surety that thy seed shall	Gen 15:13	3045
For I *k* him, that he will command	Gen 18:19	3045
and if not, I will *k*	Gen 18:21	3045
out unto us, that we may *k* them	Gen 19:5	3045
I *k* that thou didst this in the	Gen 20:6	3045
k thou that thou shalt surely die	Gen 20:7	3045
for now I *k* that thou fearest God	Gen 22:12	3045
thereby shall I *k* that thou hast	Gen 24:14	3045
I *k* not the day of my death	Gen 27:2	3045

K ye Laban the son of Nahor	Gen 29:5	3045
And they said, We *k* him	Gen 29:5	3045
ye *k* that with all my power I	Gen 31:6	3045
k now whether it be thy son's	Gen 37:32	5234
Hereby shall I *k* that ye are true	Gen 42:33	3045
then shall I *k* that ye are no	Gen 42:34	3045
we certainly *k* that he would say	Gen 43:7	3045
Ye *k* that my wife bare me two	Gen 44:27	3045
I *k* it, my son, I *k* it	Gen 48:19	3045
for I *k* their sorrows	Ex 3:7	3045
I *k* that he can speak well	Ex 4:14	3045
I *k* not the LORD, neither will I	Ex 5:2	3045
ye shall *k* that I am the LORD	Ex 6:7	3045
shall *k* that I am the LORD	Ex 7:5	3045
thou shalt *k* that I am the LORD	Ex 7:17	3045
that thou mayest *k* that there is	Ex 8:10	3045
to the end thou mayest *k* that I	Ex 8:22	3045
that thou mayest *k* that there is	Ex 9:14	3045
that thou mayest *k* how that the	Ex 9:29	3045
I *k* that ye will not yet fear the	Ex 9:30	3045
that ye may *k* how that I am the	Ex 10:2	3045
we *k* not with what we must serve	Ex 10:26	3045
that ye may *k* how that the LORD	Ex 11:7	3045
may *k* that I am the LORD	Ex 14:4	3045
shall *k* that I am the LORD	Ex 14:18	3045
then ye shall *k* that the LORD	Ex 16:6	3045
ye shall *k* that I am the LORD	Ex 16:12	3045
Now I *k* that the LORD is greater	Ex 18:11	3045
I do make them *k* the statutes of	Ex 18:16	3045
for ye *k* the heart of a stranger,	Ex 23:9	3045
they shall *k* that I am the LORD,	Ex 29:46	3045
that ye may *k* that I am the LORD	Ex 31:13	3045
that I may *k* what to do unto thee	Ex 33:5	3045
thou hast not let me *k* whom thou	Ex 33:12	3045
I *k* thee by name, and thou hast	Ex 33:12	3045
me now thy way, that I may *k* thee	Ex 33:13	3045
in my sight, and I *k* thee by name	Ex 33:17	3045
understanding of how to work	Ex 36:1	3045
That your generations may *k* that	Lev 23:43	3045
they shall *k* the land which ye	Num 14:31	3045
ye shall *k* my breach of promise	Num 14:34	3045
Hereby ye shall *k* that the LORD	Num 16:28	3045
that I may *k* what the LORD will	Num 22:19	3045
(for I *k* that ye have much cattle	Deut 3:19	3045
that thou mightest *k* that the	Deut 4:35	3045
K therefore this day, and consider	Deut 4:39	3045
K therefore that the LORD thy God	Deut 7:9	3045
to *k* what was in thine heart,	Deut 8:2	3045
not, neither did thy fathers *k*	Deut 8:3	3045
that he might make thee *k* that	Deut 8:3	3045
And *k* ye this day	Deut 11:2	3045
to *k* whether ye love the LORD	Deut 13:3	3045
How shall we *k* the word which the	Deut 18:21	3045
unto thee, or if thou *k* him not	Deut 22:2	3045
that ye might *k* that I am the	Deut 29:6	3045
(For ye *k* how we have dwelt in	Deut 29:16	3045
for I *k* their imagination which	Deut 31:21	3045
For I *k* thy rebellion, and thy	Deut 31:27	3045
For I *k* that after my death ye	Deut 31:29	3045
I *k* that the LORD hath given you	Josh 2:9	3045
that ye may *k* the way by which ye	Josh 3:4	3045
all Israel, that they may *k* that	Josh 3:7	3045
Hereby ye shall *k* that the living	Josh 3:10	3045
Then ye shall let your children *k*	Josh 4:22	3045
might *k* the hand of the LORD	Josh 4:24	3045
he knoweth, and Israel he shall *k*	Josh 22:22	3045
K for a certainty that the LORD	Josh 23:13	3045
ye *k* in all your hearts and in all	Josh 23:14	3045
of the children of Israel might *k*	Judg 3:2	3045
to *k* whether they would hearken	Judg 3:4	3045
then shall I *k* that thou wilt	Judg 6:37	3045
Now *k* I that the LORD will do me	Judg 17:13	3045
that we may *k* whether our way	Judg 18:5	3045
Do ye *k* that there is in these	Judg 18:14	3045
thine house, that we may *k* him	Judg 19:22	3045
k that thou art a virtuous woman	Ruth 3:11	3045
up before one could *k* another	Ruth 3:14	5234
until thou *k* how the matter will	Ruth 3:18	3045
it, then tell me, that I may *k*	Ruth 4:4	3045
Now Samuel did not yet *k* the LORD	1Sa 3:7	3045
then we shall *k* that it is not	1Sa 6:9	3045
and *k* and see wherein this sin hath	1Sa 14:38	3045
I *k* thy pride, and the naughtiness	1Sa 17:28	3045
that all the earth may *k* that	1Sa 17:46	3045
all this assembly shall *k* that	1Sa 17:47	3045
he saith, Let not Jonathan *k* this	1Sa 20:3	3045
do not I *k* that thou hast chosen	1Sa 20:30	3045
Let no man *k* any thing of the	1Sa 21:2	3045
till I *k* what God will do for me	1Sa 22:3	3045
Go, I pray you, prepare yet, and *k*	1Sa 23:22	3045
k thou and see that there is	1Sa 24:11	3045

I *k* well that thou shalt surely	1Sa 24:20	3045
whom I *k* not whence they be	1Sa 25:11	3045
Now therefore *k* and consider what	1Sa 25:17	3045
K thou assuredly, that thou shalt	1Sa 28:1	3045
Surely thou shalt *k* what thy	1Sa 28:2	3045
I *k* that thou art good in my	1Sa 29:9	3045
to *k* thy going out and thy coming	2Sa 3:25	3045
in, and to *k* all that thou doest	2Sa 3:25	3045
K ye not that there is a prince	2Sa 3:38	3045
to make thy servant *k* them	2Sa 7:21	3045
to *k* all things that are in the	2Sa 14:20	3045
servant doth *k* that I have sinned	2Sa 19:20	3045
for do not I *k* that I am this day	2Sa 19:22	3045
that I may *k* the number of the	2Sa 24:2	3045
thou shalt *k* for certain that	1Kin 2:37	3045
K for a certain, on the day thou	1Kin 2:42	3045
I *k* not how to go out or come in	1Kin 3:7	3045
which thou *k* every man the	1Kin 8:38	3045
of the earth may *k* thy name	1Kin 8:43	3045
that they may *k* that this house,	1Kin 8:43	3045
earth may *k* that the LORD is God	1Kin 8:60	3045
Now by this I *k* that thou art a	1Kin 17:24	3045
shall carry thee whither I *k* not	1Kin 18:12	3045
that this people may *k* that thou	1Kin 18:37	3045
thou shalt *k* that I am the LORD	1Kin 20:13	3045
ye shall *k* that I am the LORD	1Kin 20:28	3045
K ye that Ramoth in Gilead is	1Kin 22:3	3045
And he said, Yea, I *k* it	2Kin 2:3	3045
And he answered, Yea, I *k* it	2Kin 2:5	3045
he shall *k* that there is a	2Kin 5:8	3045
now I *k* that there is no God in	2Kin 5:15	3045
They *k* that we be hungry	2Kin 7:12	3045
Because I *k* the evil that thou	2Kin 8:12	3045
unto them, Ye *k* the man, and his	2Kin 9:11	3045
K now that there shall fall unto	2Kin 10:10	3045
k not the manner of the God of	2Kin 17:26	3045
because they *k* not the manner of	2Kin 17:26	3045
may *k* that thou art the LORD God	2Kin 19:19	3045
But I *k* thy abode, and thy going	2Kin 19:27	3045
to *k* what Israel ought to do	1Chr 12:32	3045
of them to me, that I may *k* it	1Chr 21:2	3045
k thou the God of thy father, and	1Chr 28:9	3045
I *k* also, my God, that thou	1Chr 29:17	3045
for I *k* that thy servants can	2Chr 2:8	3045
every one shall *k* his own sore	2Chr 6:29	3045
of the earth may *k* thy name	2Chr 6:33	3045
may *k* that this house which I	2Chr 6:33	3045
that they may *k* my service	2Chr 12:8	3045
Ought ye not to *k* that the LORD	2Chr 13:5	3045
neither *k* we what to do	2Chr 20:12	3045
I *k* that God hath determined to	2Chr 25:16	3045
K ye not what I and my fathers	2Chr 32:13	3045
that he might *k* all that was in	2Chr 32:31	3045
k that this city is a rebellious	Ezr 4:15	3046
all such as *k* the laws of thy God	Ezr 7:25	3046
and teach ye them that *k* them not	Ezr 7:25	3046
said, They shall not *k*, neither	Neh 4:11	3045
to *k* how Esther did, and what	Est 2:11	3045
to *k* what it was, and why it was	Est 4:5	3045
of the king's provinces, do *k*	Est 4:11	3045
thou shalt *k* that thy tabernacle	Job 5:24	3045
Thou shalt *k* also that thy seed	Job 5:25	3045
it, and *k* thou it for thy good	Job 5:27	3045
shall his place *k* him any more	Job 7:10	5234
k nothing, because our days upon	Job 8:9	3045
I *k* it is so of a truth	Job 9:2	3045
the mountains, and they *k* not	Job 9:5	3045
yet would I not *k* my soul	Job 9:21	3045
I *k* that thou wilt not hold me	Job 9:28	3045
I *k* that this is with thee	Job 10:13	3045
K therefore that God exacteth of	Job 11:6	3045
what canst thou *k*	Job 11:8	3045
What ye *k*, the same do I *k*	Job 13:2	1847
ye *k*, the same do I *k* also	Job 13:2	3045
I *k* that I shall be justified	Job 13:18	3045
make me to *k* my transgression and	Job 13:23	3045
What knowest thou, that we *k* not	Job 15:9	3045
K now that God hath overthrown me	Job 19:6	3045
For I *k* that my redeemer liveth,	Job 19:25	3045
that ye may *k* there is a judgment	Job 19:29	3045
rewardeth him, and he shall *k* it	Job 21:19	3045
I *k* your thoughts, and the devices	Job 21:27	3045
do ye not *k* their tokens,	Job 21:29	5234
And thou sayest, How doth God *k*	Job 22:13	3045
I would *k* the words which he	Job 23:5	3045
do they that *k* him not see his	Job 24:1	5234
they *k* not the ways thereof, nor	Job 24:13	5234
they *k* not the light	Job 24:16	3045
if one *k* them, they are in the	Job 24:17	5234
For I *k* that thou wilt bring me	Job 30:23	3045
that God may *k* mine integrity	Job 31:6	3045

For I *k* not to give flattering	Job 32:22	3045
let us *k* among ourselves what is	Job 34:4	3045
we *k* him not, neither can the	Job 36:26	3045
that all men may *k* his work	Job 37:7	3045
Dost thou *k* when God disposed	Job 37:15	3045
Dost thou *k* the balancings of the	Job 37:16	3045
the dayspring to *k* his place	Job 38:12	3045
that thou shouldest *k* the paths	Job 38:20	995
I *k* that thou canst do every	Job 42:2	3045
But *k* that the LORD hath set	Ps 4:3	3045
they that *k* thy name will put	Ps 9:10	3045
that the nations may *k* themselves	Ps 9:20	3045
Now I that the LORD saveth his	Ps 20:6	3045
unto them that *k* thee	Ps 36:10	3045
LORD, make me to *k* mine end	Ps 39:4	3045
that I may *k* how frail I am	Ps 39:4	3045
By this I *k* that thou favourest	Ps 41:11	3045
Be still, and *k* that I am God	Ps 46:10	3045
I *k* all the fowls of the	Ps 50:11	3045
thou shalt make me to *k* wisdom	Ps 51:6	3045
enemies turn back: this I *k*	Ps 56:9	3045
let them *k* that God ruleth in	Ps 59:13	3045
for I *k* not the numbers thereof	Ps 71:15	3045
And they say, How doth God *k*	Ps 73:11	3045
When I thought to *k* this, it was	Ps 73:16	3045
generation to come might *k* them	Ps 78:6	3045
They *k* not, neither will they	Ps 82:5	3045
That men may *k* that thou, whose	Ps 83:18	3045
and Babylon to them that *k* me	Ps 87:4	3045
people that *k* the joyful sound	Ps 89:15	3045
man knowledge, shall not he *k*	Ps 94:10	3045
K ye that the LORD he is God	Ps 100:3	3045
I will not *k* a wicked person	Ps 101:4	3045
place thereof shall *k* it no more	Ps 103:16	5234
That they may *k* that this is thy	Ps 109:27	3045
I *k*, O LORD, that thy judgments	Ps 119:75	3045
that I may *k* thy testimonies	Ps 119:125	3045
For I *k* that the LORD is great,	Ps 135:5	3045
Search me, O God, and *k* my heart	Ps 139:23	3045
try me, and *k* my thoughts	Ps 139:23	3045
I *k* that the LORD will maintain	Ps 140:12	3045
there was no man that would *k* me	Ps 142:4	5234
cause me to *k* the way wherein I	Ps 143:8	3045
To *k* wisdom and instruction	Prov 1:2	3045
attend to *k* understanding	Prov 4:1	3045
they *k* not at what they stumble	Prov 4:19	3045
that thou canst not *k* them	Prov 5:6	3045
righteous *k* what is acceptable	Prov 10:32	3045
That I might make thee *k* the	Prov 22:21	3045
thy soul, doth not he *k* it	Prov 24:12	3045
lest thou *k* not what to do in the	Prov 25:8	
Be thou diligent to *k* the state	Prov 27:23	3045
the wicked regardeth not to *k* it	Prov 29:7	1847
for me, yea, four which I *k* not	Prov 30:18	3045
And I gave my heart to *k* wisdom	Eccl 1:17	3045
and to *k* madness and folly	Eccl 1:17	3045
I *k* that there is no good in them	Eccl 3:12	3045
I *k* that, whatsoever God doeth,	Eccl 3:14	3045
I applied mine heart to *k*	Eccl 7:25	3045
to *k* the wickedness of folly,	Eccl 7:25	3045
yet surely I *k* that it shall be	Eccl 8:12	3045
I applied mine heart to *k* wisdom	Eccl 8:16	3045
though a wise man think to *k* it	Eccl 8:17	3045
For the living *k* that they shall	Eccl 9:5	3045
but the dead *k* not any thing,	Eccl 9:5	3045
but *k* thou, that for all these	Eccl 11:9	3045
If thou *k* not, O thou fairest	Song 1:8	3045
but Israel doth not *k*, my people	Is 1:3	3045
nigh and come, that we may *k* it	Is 5:19	3045
that he may *k* to refuse the evil,	Is 7:15	3045
child shall *k* to refuse the evil	Is 7:16	3045
And all the people shall *k*	Is 9:9	3045
let them *k* what the LORD of hosts	Is 19:12	3045
the Egyptians shall *k* the LORD in	Is 19:21	3045
may *k* that thou art the LORD	Is 37:20	3045
But I *k* thy abode, and thy going	Is 37:28	3045
That they may see, and *k*, and	Is 41:20	3045
them, and *k* the latter end of them	Is 41:22	3045
that we may *k* that ye are gods	Is 41:23	3045
from the beginning, that we may *k*	Is 41:26	3045
that ye may *k* and believe me, and	Is 43:10	3045
shall ye not *k* it	Is 43:19	3045
I *k* not any	Is 44:8	3045
they see not, nor *k*	Is 44:9	3045
places, that thou mayest *k* that I	Is 45:3	3045
That they may *k* from the rising	Is 45:6	3045
neither shall I *k* the loss of	Is 47:8	3045
thou shalt not *k* from whence it	Is 47:11	3045
suddenly, which thou shalt not *k*	Is 47:11	3045
things, and thou didst not *k* them	Is 48:6	3045
thou shalt *k* that I am the LORD	Is 49:23	3045

K

But that ye may *k* that the Son of	Mt 9:6	1492
saying, See that no man *k* it	Mt 9:30	1097
k the mysteries of the kingdom of	Mt 13:11	1097
and said, Ye *k* not what ye ask	Mt 20:22	1492
Ye *k* that the princes of the	Mt 20:25	1492
we *k* that thou art true, and	Mt 22:16	1492
leaves, ye *k* that summer is nigh	Mt 24:32	1097
k that it is near, even at the	Mt 24:33	1097
for ye *k* not what hour your Lord	Mt 24:42	1492
But *k* this, that if the goodman	Mt 24:43	1097
I say unto you, I *k* you not	Mt 25:12	1492
for ye *k* neither the day nor the	Mt 25:13	1492
Ye *k* that after two days is the	Mt 26:2	1492
saying, I *k* not what thou sayest	Mt 26:70	1492
with an oath, I do not *k* the man	Mt 26:72	1492
to swear, saying, I *k* not the man	Mt 26:74	1492
for I *k* that ye seek Jesus, which	Mt 28:5	1492
I *k* thee who thou art, the Holy	Mk 1:24	1492
But that ye may *k* that the Son of	Mk 2:10	1492
Unto you it is given to *k* the	Mk 4:11	1097
unto them, *K* ye not this parable	Mk 4:13	1492
how then will ye *k* all parables	Mk 4:13	1097
straitly that no man should *k* it	Mk 5:43	1097
house, and would have no man *k* it	Mk 7:24	1097
not that any man should *k* it	Mk 9:30	1097
unto them, Ye *k* not what ye ask	Mk 10:38	1492
them, Ye *k* that they which are	Mk 10:42	1492
we *k* that thou art true, and	Mk 12:14	1492
because ye *k* not the scriptures,	Mk 12:24	1492
leaves, ye *k* that summer is near	Mk 13:28	1097
k that it is nigh, even at the	Mk 13:29	1097
for ye *k* not when the time is	Mk 13:33	1492
for ye *k* not when the master of	Mk 13:35	1492
I *k* not, neither understand I	Mk 14:68	1492
I *k* not this man of whom ye speak	Mk 14:71	1492
That thou mightest *k* the	Lk 1:4	1921
the angel, Whereby shall I *k* this	Lk 1:18	1097
this be, seeing I *k* not a man	Lk 1:34	1097
I *k* thee who thou art	Lk 4:34	1492
But that ye may *k* that the Son of	Lk 5:24	1492
Unto you it is given to *k* the	Lk 8:10	1097
Ye *k* not what manner of spirit ye	Lk 9:55	1492
k how to give good gifts unto	Lk 11:13	1492
And this *k*, that if the goodman of	Lk 12:39	1097
I *k* you not whence ye are	Lk 13:25	1492
I *k* you not whence ye are	Lk 13:27	1492
that he might *k* how much every	Lk 19:15	1097
we *k* that thou sayest and teachest	Lk 20:21	1492
then *k* that the desolation	Lk 21:20	1097
k of your own selves that summer	Lk 21:30	1097
k ye that the kingdom of God is	Lk 21:31	1097
him, saying, Woman, I *k* him not	Lk 22:57	1492
Man, I *k* not what thou sayest	Lk 22:60	1492
for they *k* not what they do	Lk 23:34	1492
holden that they should not *k* him	Lk 24:16	1921
one among you, whom ye *k* not	Jn 1:26	1492
we *k* that thou art a teacher come	Jn 3:2	1492
unto thee, We speak that we do *k*	Jn 3:11	1492
Ye worship ye *k* not what	Jn 4:22	1492
we *k* what we worship	Jn 4:22	1492
I *k* that Messias cometh, which is	Jn 4:25	1492
have meat to eat that ye *k* not of	Jn 4:32	1492
k that this is indeed the Christ,	Jn 4:42	1492
I *k* that the witness which he	Jn 5:32	1492
But I *k* you, that ye have not the	Jn 5:42	1097
whose father and mother we *k*	Jn 6:42	1492
he shall *k* of the doctrine,	Jn 7:17	1097
Do the rulers *k* indeed that this	Jn 7:26	1097
Howbeit we *k* this man whence he	Jn 7:27	1492
both *k* me, and ye *k* whence I am	Jn 7:28	1492
sent me is true, whom ye *k* not	Jn 7:28	1492
But I *k* him	Jn 7:29	1492
it hear him, and *k* what he doeth	Jn 7:51	1097
for I *k* whence I came, and whither	Jn 8:14	1492
Jesus answered, Ye neither *k* me	Jn 8:19	1492
man, then shall ye *k* that I am he	Jn 8:28	1097
ye shall *k* the truth, and the	Jn 8:32	1492
I *k* that ye are Abraham's seed	Jn 8:37	1097
Now we *k* that thou hast a devil	Jn 8:52	1492
but I *k* him	Jn 8:55	1492
I *k* him not, I shall be a liar	Jn 8:55	1492
but I *k* him, and keep his saying	Jn 8:55	1492
He said, I *k* not	Jn 9:12	1492
We *k* that this is our son, and	Jn 9:20	1492
what means he now seeth, we *k* not	Jn 9:21	1492
hath opened his eyes, we *k* not	Jn 9:21	1492
we *k* that this man is a sinner	Jn 9:24	1492
he be a sinner or no, I *k* not	Jn 9:25	1492

one thing I *k*, that, whereas I	Jn 9:25	1492
We *k* that God spake unto Moses	Jn 9:29	1492
we *k* not from whence he is	Jn 9:29	1492
that ye *k* not from whence he is,	Jn 9:30	1492
Now we *k* that God heareth not	Jn 9:31	1492
for they *k* his voice	Jn 10:4	1492
for they *k* not the voice of	Jn 10:5	1492
k my sheep, and am known of mine	Jn 10:14	1097
me, even so *k* I the Father	Jn 10:15	1097
I *k* them, and they follow me	Jn 10:27	1097
that ye may *k*, and believe, that	Jn 10:38	1097
But I *k*, that even now,	Jn 11:22	1492
I *k* that he shall rise again in	Jn 11:24	1492
unto them, Ye *k* nothing at all,	Jn 11:49	1492
I *k* that his commandment is life	Jn 12:50	1492
but thou shalt *k* hereafter	Jn 13:7	1097
K ye what I have done to you	Jn 13:12	1097
If ye *k* these things, happy are	Jn 13:17	1492
I *k* whom I have chosen	Jn 13:18	1492
By this shall all men *k* that ye	Jn 13:35	1097
I go ye *k*, and the way ye *k*	Jn 14:4	1492,
we *k* not whither thou goest	Jn 14:5	1492
and how can we *k* the way	Jn 14:5	
and from henceforth ye *k* him	Jn 14:7	1097
but ye *k* him	Jn 14:17	1492
At that day ye shall *k* that I am	Jn 14:20	1097
may *k* that I love the Father	Jn 14:31	1097
ye *k* that it hated me before it	Jn 15:18	1097
because they *k* not him that sent	Jn 15:21	1492
that they might *k* thee the only	Jn 17:3	1097
that the world may *k* that thou	Jn 17:23	1097
behold, they *k* what I said	Jn 18:21	1492
that ye may *k* that I find no	Jn 19:4	1097
we *k* not where they have laid him	Jn 20:2	1492
I *k* not where they have laid him	Jn 20:13	1492
we *k* that his testimony is true	Jn 21:24	1492
It is not for you to *k* the times	Acts 1:7	1097
of you, as ye yourselves also *k*	Acts 2:22	1492
the house of Israel *k* assuredly	Acts 2:36	1097
this man strong, whom ye see and *k*	Acts 3:16	1492
Ye *k* how that it is an unlawful	Acts 10:28	1987
That word, I say, ye *k*, which was	Acts 10:37	1492
Now I *k* of a surety, that the	Acts 12:11	1492
ye *k* how that a good while ago	Acts 15:7	1987
May we *k* what this new doctrine,	Acts 17:19	1097
we would *k* therefore what these	Acts 17:20	1097
said, Jesus I *k*, and Paul I *k*	Acts 19:15	1987
ye *k* that by this craft we have	Acts 19:25	1987
to him, he said unto them, Ye *k*	Acts 20:18	1987
I *k* that ye all, among whom I	Acts 20:25	1492
For I *k* this, that after my	Acts 20:29	1492
Yea, ye yourselves *k*, that these	Acts 20:34	1097
all may *k* that those things,	Acts 21:24	1097
when he could not *k* the certainty	Acts 21:34	1097
that thou shouldest *k* his will	Acts 22:14	1097
they *k* that I imprisoned and beat	Acts 22:19	1987
that he might *k* wherefore they	Acts 22:24	1921
Forasmuch as I *k* that thou hast	Acts 24:10	1987
I will *k* the uttermost of your	Acts 24:22	1231
Especially because I *k* thee to be	Acts 26:3	
at Jerusalem, *k* all the Jews	Acts 26:4	2467
I *k* that thou believest	Acts 26:27	1492
we *k* that every where it is	Acts 28:22	1110
Now we *k* that what things soever	Rom 3:19	1492
K ye not, that so many of us as	Rom 6:3	50
K ye not, that to whom ye yield	Rom 6:16	1492
K ye not, brethren, (for I speak	Rom 7:1	50
I speak to them that *k* the law	Rom 7:1	1097
For we *k* that the law is	Rom 7:14	1492
For I *k* that in me (that is, in	Rom 7:18	1492
For we *k* that the whole creation	Rom 8:22	1492
for we *k* not what we should pray	Rom 8:26	1492
we *k* that all things work	Rom 8:28	1492
But I say, Did not Israel *k*	Rom 10:19	1097
I *k*, and am persuaded by the Lord	Rom 14:14	1492
I *k* not whether I baptized any	1Cor 1:16	1492
not to *k* any thing among you	1Cor 2:2	1492
that we might *k* the things that	1Cor 2:12	1492
neither can he *k* them, because	1Cor 2:14	1097
K ye not that ye are the temple	1Cor 3:16	1492
For I *k* nothing by myself	1Cor 4:4	4892
if the Lord will, and will *k*	1Cor 4:19	1097
K ye not that a little leaven	1Cor 5:6	1492
Do ye not *k* that the saints shall	1Cor 6:2	1492
K ye not that we shall judge	1Cor 6:3	1492
K ye not that the unrighteous	1Cor 6:9	1492
K ye not that your bodies are the	1Cor 6:15	1492
k ye not that he which is joined	1Cor 6:16	1492
k ye not that your body is the	1Cor 6:19	1492
we *k* that we all have knowledge	1Cor 8:1	1492

K

nothing yet as he ought to *k*	1Cor 8:2	1097
we *k* that an idol is nothing in	1Cor 8:4	1492
Do ye not *k* that they which	1Cor 9:13	1492
K ye not that they which run in a	1Cor 9:24	1492
But I would have you *k*, that the	1Cor 11:3	1492
Ye *k* that ye were Gentiles,	1Cor 12:2	1492
For we *k* in part, and we prophesy	1Cor 13:9	1097
now I *k* in part	1Cor 13:12	1097
but then shall I *k* even as also I	1Cor 13:12	1921
Therefore if I *k* not the meaning	1Cor 14:11	1492
forasmuch as ye *k* that your	1Cor 15:58	1492
(ye *k* the house of Stephanas,	1Cor 16:15	1492
but that ye might *k* the love	2Cor 2:4	1097
that I might *k* the proof of you,	2Cor 2:9	1097
For we *k* that if our earthly	2Cor 5:1	1492
Wherefore henceforth *k* we no man	2Cor 5:16	1492
now henceforth *k* we him no more	2Cor 5:16	1097
For ye *k* the grace of our Lord	2Cor 8:9	1097
For I *k* the forwardness of your	2Cor 9:2	1492
K ye not your own selves, how	2Cor 13:5	1921
But I trust that ye shall *k* that	2Cor 13:6	1097
K ye therefore that they which	Gal 3:7	1097
Ye *k* how through infirmity of the	Gal 4:13	1492
that ye may *k* what is the hope of	Eph 1:18	1492
to *k* the love of Christ, which	Eph 3:19	1097
For this ye *k*, that no	Eph 5:5	1097
But that ye also may *k* my affairs	Eph 6:21	1492
that ye might *k* our affairs	Eph 6:22	1097
For I *k* that this shall turn to	Phil 1:19	1492
I *k* that I shall abide and	Phil 1:25	1492
good comfort, when I *k* your state	Phil 2:19	1097
But ye *k* the proof of him, that,	Phil 2:22	1097
That I may *k* him, and the power of	Phil 3:10	1097
I *k* both how to be abased	Phil 4:12	1492
and I *k* how to abound	Phil 4:12	1492
Now ye Philippians *k* also	Phil 4:15	1492
that ye may *k* how ye ought to	Col 4:6	1492
that he might *k* your estate	Col 4:8	1097
as ye *k* what manner of men we	1Th 1:5	1492
k our entrance in unto you, that	1Th 2:1	1492
shamefully entreated, as ye *k*	1Th 2:2	1492
used we flattering words, as ye *k*	1Th 2:5	1492
As ye *k* how we exhorted and	1Th 2:11	1492
for yourselves *k* that we are	1Th 3:3	1492
even as it came to pass, and ye *k*	1Th 3:4	1492
I sent to *k* your faith, lest by	1Th 3:5	1097
For ye *k* what commandments we	1Th 4:2	1492
k how to possess his vessel in	1Th 4:4	1492
as the Gentiles which *k* not God	1Th 4:5	1492
For yourselves *k* perfectly that	1Th 5:2	1492
to *k* them which labour among you,	1Th 5:12	1492
vengeance on them that *k* not God	2Th 1:8	1097
now ye *k* what withholdeth that he	2Th 2:6	1492
For yourselves *k* how ye ought to	2Th 3:7	1492
But we *k* that the law is good, if	1Ti 1:8	1492
(For if a man *k* not how to rule	1Ti 3:5	1492
that thou mayest *k* how thou	1Ti 3:15	1492
them which believe and *k* the truth	1Ti 4:3	1921
for I *k* whom I have believed, and	2Ti 1:12	1492
This *k* also, that in the last	2Ti 3:1	1097
They profess that they *k* God	Titus 1:16	1492
his brother, saying, *K* the Lord	Heb 8:11	1097
for all shall *k* me, from the	Heb 8:11	1492
For we *k* him that hath said,	Heb 10:30	1492
For ye *k* how that afterward, when	Heb 12:17	2467
K ye that our brother Timothy is	Heb 13:23	1097
But wilt thou *k*, O vain man, that	Jas 2:20	1097
k ye not that the friendship of	Jas 4:4	1492
Whereas ye *k* not what shall be on	Jas 4:14	1987
Let him *k*, that he which	Jas 5:20	1097
Forasmuch as ye *k* that ye were	1Pet 1:18	1492
of these things, though ye *k* them	2Pet 1:12	1492
seeing ye *k* these things before,	2Pet 3:17	4267
hereby we do *k* that we *k* him,	1Jn 2:3	1097
hereby we do *k* that we *k* him	1Jn 2:3	1097
I *k* him, and keepeth not his	1Jn 2:4	1097
hereby *k* we that we are in him	1Jn 2:5	1097
whereby we *k* that it is the last	1Jn 2:18	1097
the Holy One, and ye *k* all things	1Jn 2:20	1492
you because ye *k* not the truth	1Jn 2:21	1492
but because ye *k* it	1Jn 2:21	1492
If ye *k* that he is righteous	1Jn 2:29	1492
ye *k* that every one that doeth	1Jn 2:29	1097
but we *k* that, when he shall	1Jn 3:2	1492
ye *k* that he was manifested to	1Jn 3:5	1492
We *k* that we have passed from	1Jn 3:14	1492
ye *k* that no murderer hath	1Jn 3:15	1492
hereby we *k* that we are of the	1Jn 3:19	1097
hereby we *k* that he abideth in us	1Jn 3:24	1097

Hereby *k* ye the Spirit of God	1Jn 4:2	1097
Hereby *k* we the spirit of truth,	1Jn 4:6	1097
Hereby *k* we that we dwell in him,	1Jn 4:13	1097
By this we *k* that we love the	1Jn 5:2	1097
that ye may *k* that ye have	1Jn 5:13	1492
And if we *k* that he hear us,	1Jn 5:15	1492
we *k* that we have the petitions	1Jn 5:15	1492
We *k* that whosoever is born of	1Jn 5:18	1492
we *k* that we are of God, and the	1Jn 5:19	1492
we *k* that the Son of God is come,	1Jn 5:20	1492
that we may *k* him that is true,	1Jn 5:20	1097
ye *k* that our record is true	3Jn 12	1492
of those things which they *k* not	Jude 10	1492
but what they *k* naturally	Jude 10	1987
I *k* thy works, and thy labour, and	Rev 2:2	1492
I *k* thy works, and tribulation, and	Rev 2:9	1492
I *k* the blasphemy of them which	Rev 2:9	
I *k* thy works, and where thou	Rev 2:13	1492
I *k* thy works, and charity, and	Rev 2:19	1492
all the churches shall *k* that I	Rev 2:23	1097
I *k* thy works, that thou hast a	Rev 3:1	1492
thou shalt not *k* what hour I will	Rev 3:3	1097
I *k* thy works	Rev 3:8	1492
to *k* that I have loved thee	Rev 3:9	1097
I *k* thy works, that thou art	Rev 3:15	1492

KNOWEST

for thou *k* my service which I	Gen 30:26	3045
Thou *k* how I have served thee, and	Gen 30:29	3045
if thou *k* any men of activity	Gen 47:6	3045
k thou not yet that Egypt is	Ex 10:7	3045
thou *k* the people, that they are	Ex 32:22	3045
forasmuch as thou *k* how we are to	Num 10:31	3045
whom thou *k* to be the elders of	Num 11:16	3045
Thou *k* all the travail that hath	Num 20:14	3045
diseases of Egypt, which thou *k*	Deut 7:15	3045
of the Anakims, whom thou *k*	Deut 9:2	3045
Only the trees which thou *k* that	Deut 20:20	3045
a nation which thou *k* not eat up	Deut 28:33	3045
Thou *k* the thing that the LORD	Josh 14:6	3045
K thou not that the Philistines	Judg 15:11	3045
thou *k* what Saul hath done, how	1Sa 28:9	3045
How *k* thou that Saul and Jonathan	2Sa 1:5	3045
k thou not that it will be	2Sa 2:26	3045
Thou *k* Abner the son of Ner, that	2Sa 3:25	3045
for thou, Lord GOD, *k* thy servant	2Sa 7:20	3045
thou *k* thy father and his men,	2Sa 17:8	3045
my lord the king, thou *k* it not	1Kin 1:18	3045
Moreover thou *k* also what Joab	1Kin 2:5	3045
k what thou oughtest to do unto	1Kin 2:9	3045
Thou *k* that the kingdom was mine,	1Kin 2:15	3045
Thou *k* all the wickedness which	1Kin 2:44	3045
Thou *k* how that David my father	1Kin 5:3	3045
for thou *k* that there is not	1Kin 5:6	3045
to his ways, whose heart thou *k*	1Kin 8:39	3045
k the hearts of all the children	1Kin 8:39	3045
K thou that the LORD will take	2Kin 2:3	3045
K thou that the LORD will take	2Kin 2:5	3045
thou *k* that thy servant did fear	2Kin 4:1	3045
for thou *k* thy servant	1Chr 17:18	3045
all his ways, whose heart thou *k*	2Chr 6:30	3045
(for thou only *k* the hearts of	2Chr 6:30	3045
Thou *k* that I am not wicked	Job 10:7	1847
What *k* thou, that we know not	Job 15:9	3045
K thou not this of old, since man	Job 20:4	3045
therefore speak what thou *k*	Job 34:33	3045
the measures thereof, if thou *k*	Job 38:5	3045
declare if thou *k* it all	Job 38:18	3045
K thou it, because thou wast then	Job 38:21	3045
K thou the ordinances of heaven	Job 38:33	3045
K thou the time when the wild	Job 39:1	3045
or *k* thou the time when they	Job 39:2	3045
refrained my lips, O LORD, thou *k*	Ps 40:9	3045
O God, thou *k* my foolishness	Ps 69:5	3045
Thou *k* my downsitting and mine	Ps 139:2	3045
lo, O LORD, thou *k* it altogether	Ps 139:4	3045
for thou *k* not what a day may	Prov 27:1	3045
for thou *k* not what evil shall be	Eccl 11:2	3045
As thou *k* not what is the way of	Eccl 11:5	3045
even so thou *k* not the works of	Eccl 11:5	3045
for thou *k* not whether shall	Eccl 11:6	3045
call a nation that thou *k* not	Is 55:5	3045
nation whose language thou *k* not	Jer 5:15	3045
But thou, O LORD, *k* me	Jer 12:3	3045
into a land which thou *k* not	Jer 15:14	3045
O LORD, thou *k*	Jer 15:15	3045
in the land which thou *k* not	Jer 17:4	3045

thou *k*: that which came	Jer 17:16	3045
thou *k* all their counsel against	Jer 18:23	3045
mighty things, which thou *k* not	Jer 33:3	3045
And I answered, O Lord GOD, thou *k*	Eze 37:3	3045
K thou wherefore I come unto thee	Dan 10:20	3045
unto me, *K* thou not what these be	Zec 4:5	3045
and said, *K* thou not what these be	Zec 4:13	3045
K thou that the Pharisees were	Mt 15:12	1492
Thou *k* the commandments, Do not	Mk 10:19	1492
Thou *k* the commandments, Do not	Lk 18:20	1492
shalt thrice deny that thou *k* me	Lk 22:34	1492
saith unto him, Whence *k* thou me	Jn 1:48	1097
of Israel, and *k* not these things	Jn 3:10	1097
him, What I do thou *k* not now	Jn 13:7	1492
we sure that thou *k* all things	Jn 16:30	1492
k thou not what I have power to	Jn 19:10	1492
thou *k* that I love thee	Jn 21:15	1492
thou *k* that I love thee	Jn 21:16	1492
unto him, Lord, thou *k* all things	Jn 21:17	1492
thou *k* that I love thee	Jn 21:17	1097
which *k* the hearts of all men,	Acts 1:24	2589
no wrong, as thou very well *k*	Acts 25:10	1921
k his will, and approvest the	Rom 2:18	1097
For what *k* thou, O wife, whether	1Cor 7:16	1492
or how *k* thou, O man, whether	1Cor 7:16	1492
This thou *k*, that all they which	2Ti 1:15	1492
me at Ephesus, thou *k* very well	2Ti 1:18	1097
k not that thou art wretched, and	Rev 3:17	1492
And I said unto him, Sir, thou *k*	Rev 7:14	1492

KNOWETH

My lord *k* that the children are	Gen 33:13	3045
when he *k* of it, then he shall be	Lev 5:3	3045
when he *k* of it, then he shall be	Lev 5:4	3045
he *k* thy walking through this	Deut 2:7	3045
but no man *k* of his sepulchre	Deut 34:6	3045
gods, the LORD God of gods, he *k*	Josh 22:22	3045
ever for the iniquity which he *k*	1Sa 3:13	3045
Thy father certainly *k* that I	1Sa 20:3	3045
and that also Saul my father *k*	1Sa 23:17	3045
Today thy servant *k* that I have	2Sa 14:22	3045
for all Israel *k* that thy father	2Sa 17:10	3045
reign, and David our lord *k* it not	1Kin 1:11	3045
who *k* whether thou art come to	Est 4:14	3045
For he *k* vain men	Job 11:11	3045
who *k* not such things as these	Job 12:3	854
Who *k* not in all these that the	Job 12:9	3045
come to honour, and he *k* it not	Job 14:21	3045
he *k* that the day of darkness is	Job 15:23	3045
the place of him that *k* not God	Job 18:21	3045
But he *k* the way that I take	Job 23:10	3045
There is a path which no fowl *k*	Job 28:7	3045
Man *k* not the price thereof	Job 28:13	3045
and he *k* the place thereof	Job 28:23	3045
Therefore he *k* their works	Job 34:25	5234
yet he *k* it not in great	Job 35:15	3045
For the LORD *k* the way of the	Ps 1:6	3045
The LORD *k* the days of the	Ps 37:18	3045
k not who shall gather them	Ps 39:6	3045
for he *k* the secrets of the heart	Ps 44:21	3045
among us any that *k* how long	Ps 74:9	3045
Who *k* the power of thine anger	Ps 90:11	3045
A brutish man *k* not	Ps 92:6	3045
The LORD *k* the thoughts of man,	Ps 94:11	3045
For he *k* our frame	Ps 103:14	3045
the sun *k* his going down	Ps 104:19	3045
but the proud he *k* afar off	Ps 138:6	3045
and that my soul *k* right well	Ps 139:14	3045
k not that it is for his life	Prov 7:23	3045
she is simple, and *k* nothing	Prov 9:13	3045
But he *k* not that the dead are	Prov 9:18	3045
The heart *k* his own bitterness	Prov 14:10	3045
who *k* the ruin of them both	Prov 24:22	3045
who *k* whether he shall be a wise	Eccl 2:19	3045
Who *k* the spirit of man that	Eccl 3:21	3045
that *k* to walk before the living	Eccl 6:8	3045
For who *k* what is good for man in	Eccl 6:12	3045
k that thou thyself likewise hast	Eccl 7:22	3045
who *k* the interpretation of a	Eccl 8:1	3045
For he *k* not that which shall be	Eccl 8:7	3045
no man *k* either love or hatred by	Eccl 9:1	3045
For man also *k* not his time	Eccl 9:12	3045
because he *k* not how to go to the	Eccl 10:15	3045
The ox *k* his owner, and the ass	Is 1:3	3045
and who *k* us?	Is 29:15	3045
the heaven *k* her appointed times	Jer 8:7	3045
k me, that I am the LORD which	Jer 9:24	3045
he *k* what is in the darkness, and	Dan 2:22	3046
his strength, and he *k* it not	Hos 7:9	3045

and there upon him, yet he *k* not	Hos 7:9	3045
Who *k* if he will return and repent	Joel 2:14	3045
he *k* them that trust in him	Nah 1:7	3045
but the unjust *k* not shame	Zeph 3:5	3045
for your Father *k* what things ye	Mt 6:8	1492
for your heavenly Father *k* that	Mt 6:32	1492
no man *k* the Son, but the Father	Mt 11:27	1921
neither *k* any man the Father,	Mt 11:27	1921
hour *k* no man, no, not the angels	Mt 24:36	1492
spring and grow up, he *k* not how	Mk 4:27	1492
of that day and that hour *k* no man	Mk 13:32	1492
no man *k* who the Son is, but the	Lk 10:22	1097
your Father *k* that ye have need	Lk 12:30	1492
but God *k* your hearts	Lk 16:15	1097
How *k* this man letters, having	Jn 7:15	1492
cometh, no man *k* whence he is	Jn 7:27	1097
But this people who *k* not the law	Jn 7:49	1097
As the Father *k* me, even so know	Jn 10:15	1097
darkness *k* not whither he goeth	Jn 12:35	1492
it seeth him not, neither *k* him	Jn 14:17	1097
for the servant *k* not what his	Jn 15:15	1492
he *k* that he saith true, that ye	Jn 19:35	1492
which *k* the hearts, bare them	Acts 15:8	2589
what man is there that *k* not how	Acts 19:35	1097
For the king *k* of these things,	Acts 26:26	1987
he that searcheth the hearts *k*	Rom 8:27	1492
For what man *k* the things of a	1Cor 2:11	1492
so the things of God *k* no man	1Cor 2:11	1492
The Lord *k* the thoughts of the	1Cor 3:20	1097
any man think that he *k* any thing	1Cor 8:2	1492
he *k* nothing yet as he ought to	1Cor 8:2	1097
I love you not? God *k*	2Cor 11:11	1492
for evermore, *k* that I lie not	2Cor 11:31	1492
I cannot tell: God *k*	2Cor 12:2	1492
I cannot tell: God *k*	2Cor 12:3	1492
The Lord *k* them that are his	2Ti 2:19	1097
to him that *k* to do good, and	Jas 4:17	1492
The Lord *k* how to deliver the	2Pet 2:9	1492
k not whither he goeth, because	1Jn 2:11	1492
therefore the world *k* us not	1Jn 3:1	1097
than our heart, and *k* all things	1Jn 3:20	1097
he that *k* God heareth us	1Jn 4:6	1097
loveth is born of God, and *k* God	1Jn 4:7	1097
He that loveth not *k* not God	1Jn 4:8	1097
which no man *k* saving he that	Rev 2:17	1097
because he *k* that he hath but a	Rev 12:12	1492

KNOWING

shall be as gods, *k* good and evil	Gen 3:5	3045
my father David not *k* thereof	1Kin 9:33	3045
Jesus *k* their thoughts said,	Mt 9:4	1492
not *k* the scriptures, nor the	Mt 22:29	1492
immediately *k* in himself that	Mk 5:30	1921
k what was done in her, came and	Mk 5:33	1492
k that he was a just man and an	Mk 6:20	1492
k their hypocrisy, said unto them	Mk 12:15	1492
him to scorn, *k* that she was dead	Lk 8:53	1492
not *k* what he said	Lk 9:33	1492
k their thoughts, said unto them,	Lk 11:17	1492
Jesus *k* that the Father had given	Jn 13:3	1492
k all things that should come	Jn 18:4	1492
Jesus *k* that all things were now	Jn 19:28	1492
k that it was the Lord	Jn 21:12	1492
k that God had sworn with an oath	Acts 2:30	1492
not *k* what was done, came in	Acts 5:7	1492
k only the baptism of John	Acts 18:25	1987
not *k* the things that shall	Acts 20:22	1492
Who *k* the judgment of God, that	Rom 1:32	1921
not *k* that the goodness of God	Rom 2:4	50
k that tribulation worketh	Rom 5:3	1492
K this, that our old man is	Rom 6:6	1097
K that Christ being raised from	Rom 6:9	1492
k the time, that now it is high	Rom 13:11	1492
And our hope of you is stedfast, *k*	2Cor 1:7	1492
K that he which raised up the	2Cor 4:14	1492
k that, whilst we are at home in	2Cor 5:6	1492
K therefore the terror of the	2Cor 5:11	1492
K that a man is not justified by	Gal 2:16	1492
K that whatsoever good thing any	Eph 6:8	1492
k that your Master also is in	Eph 6:9	1492
k that I am set for the defence	Phil 1:17	1492
K that of the Lord ye shall	Col 3:24	1492
k that ye also have a Master in	Col 4:1	1492
K, brethren beloved, your	1Th 1:4	1492
K this, that the law is not made	1Ti 1:9	1492
k nothing, but doting about	1Ti 6:4	1987
k that they do gender strifes	2Ti 2:23	1492
k of whom thou hast learned them	2Ti 3:14	1492
K that he that is such is	Titus 3:11	1492
k that thou wilt also do more	Philem 21	1492
k in yourselves that ye have in	Heb 10:34	1097

K

went out, not *k* whither he went	Heb 11:8	1987
K this, that the trying of your	Jas 1:3	1097
k that we shall receive the	Jas 3:1	1492
k that ye are thereunto called,	1Pet 3:9	1492
k that the same afflictions are	1Pet 5:9	1492
K that shortly I must put off	2Pet 1:14	1492
K this first, that no prophecy of	2Pet 1:20	1097
K this first, that there shall	2Pet 3:3	1097

KNOWLEDGE

garden, and the tree of *k* of good	Gen 2:9	1847
But of the tree of the *k* of good	Gen 2:17	1847
and in understanding, and in *k*	Ex 31:3	1847
wisdom, in understanding, and in *k*	Ex 35:31	1847
he hath sinned, come to his *k*	Lev 4:23	3045
he hath sinned, come to his *k*	Lev 4:28	3045
without the *k* of the congregation	Num 15:24	5869
knew the *k* of the most High	Num 24:16	1847
in that day had no *k* between good	Deut 1:39	3045
that thou shouldest take *k* of me	Ruth 2:10	5234
be he that did take *k* of thee	Ruth 2:19	5234
for the LORD is a God of *k*	1Sa 2:3	1844
take *k* of all the lurking places	1Sa 23:23	3045
shipmen that had *k* of the sea	1Kin 9:27	3045
Give me now wisdom and *k*, that I	2Chr 1:10	4093
k for thyself, that thou mayest	2Chr 1:11	4093
Wisdom and *k* is granted unto thee	2Chr 1:12	4093
and servants that had *k* of the sea	2Chr 8:18	3045
taught the good *k* of the LORD	2Chr 30:22	7922
daughters, every one having *k*	Neh 10:28	3045
Should a wise man utter vain *k*	Job 15:2	1847
we desire not the *k* of thy ways	Job 21:14	1847
Shall any teach God *k*	Job 21:22	1847
and my lips shall utter *k* clearly	Job 33:3	1847
give ear unto me, ye that have *k*	Job 34:2	3045
Job hath spoken without *k*	Job 34:35	1847
he multiplieth words without *k*	Job 35:16	1847
I will fetch my *k* from afar	Job 36:3	1843
that is perfect in *k* is with thee	Job 36:4	1844
and they shall die without *k*	Job 36:12	1847
of him which is perfect in *k*	Job 37:16	1843
counsel by words without *k*	Job 38:2	1847
he that hideth counsel without *k*	Job 42:3	1847
all the workers of iniquity no *k*	Ps 14:4	3045
and night unto night sheweth *k*	Ps 19:2	1847
Have the workers of iniquity no *k*	Ps 53:4	3045
is there *k* in the most High	Ps 73:11	1844
he that teacheth man *k*, shall not	Ps 94:10	1847
Teach me good judgment and *k*	Ps 119:66	1847
Such is too wonderful for me	Ps 139:6	1847
is man, that thou takest *k* of him	Ps 144:3	3045
to the simple, to the young man *k*	Prov 1:4	1847
of the LORD is the beginning of *k*	Prov 1:7	1847
their scorning, and fools hate *k*	Prov 1:22	1847
For that they hated *k*, and did not	Prov 1:29	1847
Yea, if thou criest after *k*	Prov 2:3	998
of the LORD, and find the *k* of God	Prov 2:5	1847
out of his mouth cometh *k*	Prov 2:6	1847
k is pleasant unto thy soul	Prov 2:10	1847
By his *k* the depths are broken up	Prov 3:20	1847
and that thy lips may keep *k*	Prov 5:2	1847
and right to them that find *k*	Prov 8:9	1847
k rather than choice gold	Prov 8:10	1847
find out *k* of witty inventions	Prov 8:12	1847
and the *k* of the holy is	Prov 9:10	1847
Wise men lay up *k*	Prov 10:14	1847
but through *k* shall the just be	Prov 11:9	1847
Whoso loveth instruction loveth *k*	Prov 12:1	1847
A prudent man concealeth *k*	Prov 12:23	1847
Every prudent man dealeth with *k*	Prov 13:16	1847
but *k* is easy unto him that	Prov 14:6	1847
not in him the lips of *k*	Prov 14:7	1847
the prudent are crowned with *k*	Prov 14:18	1847
tongue of the wise useth *k* aright	Prov 15:2	1847
The lips of the wise disperse *k*	Prov 15:7	1847
that hath understanding seeketh *k*	Prov 15:14	1847
He that hath *k* spareth his words	Prov 17:27	1847
heart of the prudent getteth *k*	Prov 18:15	1847
and the ear of the wise seeketh *k*	Prov 18:15	1847
Also, that the soul be without *k*	Prov 19:2	1847
and he will understand *k*	Prov 19:25	1847
to err from the words of *k*	Prov 19:27	1847
but the lips of *k* are a precious	Prov 20:15	1847
is instructed, he receiveth *k*	Prov 21:11	1847
The eyes of the LORD preserve *k*	Prov 22:12	1847
and apply thine heart unto my *k*	Prov 22:17	1847
excellent things in counsels and *k*	Prov 22:20	1847
and thine ears to the words of *k*	Prov 23:12	1847
by *k* shall the chambers be filled	Prov 24:4	1847
a man of *k* increaseth strength	Prov 24:5	1847
So shall the *k* of wisdom be unto	Prov 24:14	3045
k the state thereof shall be	Prov 28:2	3045
nor have the *k* of the holy	Prov 30:3	1847
great experience of wisdom and *k*	Eccl 1:16	1847
increaseth *k* increaseth sorrow	Eccl 1:18	1847
labour is in wisdom, and in *k*	Eccl 2:21	1847
is good in his sight wisdom, and *k*	Eccl 2:26	1847
but the excellency of *k* is	Eccl 7:12	1847
is no work, nor device, nor *k*	Eccl 9:10	1847
he still taught the people *k*	Eccl 12:9	1847
captivity, because they have no *k*	Is 5:13	1847
the child shall have *k* to cry	Is 8:4	3045
counsel and might, the spirit of *k*	Is 11:2	1847
be full of the *k* of the LORD	Is 11:9	1844
Whom shall he teach *k*	Is 28:9	1844
of the rash shall understand *k*	Is 32:4	1847
k shall be the stability of thy	Is 33:6	1847
path of judgment, and taught him *k*	Is 40:14	1847
his heart, neither is there *k* nor	Is 44:19	1847
and maketh their *k* foolish	Is 44:25	1847
they have no *k* that set up the	Is 45:20	3045
Thy wisdom and thy *k*, it hath	Is 47:10	1847
by his *k* shall my righteous	Is 53:11	1847
our soul, and thou takest no *k*	Is 58:3	3045
which shall feed you with *k*	Jer 3:15	1844
but to do good they have no *k*	Jer 4:22	3045
Every man is brutish in his *k*	Jer 10:14	1847
And the LORD hath given me *k* of it	Jer 11:18	3045
Every man is brutish by his *k*	Jer 51:17	1847
in all wisdom, and cunning in *k*	Dan 1:4	1847
four children, God gave them *k*	Dan 1:17	4093
k to them that know understanding	Dan 2:21	998
as an excellent spirit, and *k*	Dan 5:12	998
and fro, and *k* shall be increased	Dan 12:4	1847
mercy, nor *k* of God in the land	Hos 4:1	1847
are destroyed for lack of *k*	Hos 4:6	1847
because thou hast rejected *k*	Hos 4:6	1847
the *k* of God more than burnt	Hos 6:6	1847
the *k* of the glory of the LORD	Hab 2:14	3045
the priest's lips should keep *k*	Mal 2:7	1847
men of that place had *k* of him	Mt 14:35	1921
To give *k* of salvation unto his	Lk 1:77	1108
ye have taken away the key of *k*	**Lk 11:52**	*1108*
and they took of them, that they	Acts 4:13	1921
had *k* that the word of God was	Acts 17:13	1097
mayest take *k* of all these things	Acts 24:8	1921
having more perfect *k* of that way	Acts 24:22	1492
not like to retain God in their *k*	Rom 1:28	1922
babes, which hast the form of *k*	Rom 2:20	1108
for by the law is the *k* of sin	Rom 3:20	1922
of God, but not according to *k*	Rom 10:2	1922
both of the wisdom and *k* of God	Rom 11:33	1108
of goodness, filled with all *k*	Rom 15:14	1108
in all utterance, and in all *k*	1Cor 1:5	1108
idols, we know that we all have *k*	1Cor 8:1	1108
K puffeth up, but charity	1Cor 8:1	1108
there is not in every man that *k*	1Cor 8:7	1108
hast *k* sit at meat in the idol's	1Cor 8:10	1108
through thy *k* shall the weak	1Cor 8:11	1108
the word of *k* by the same Spirit	1Cor 12:8	1108
all mysteries, and all *k*	1Cor 13:2	1108
whether there be *k*, it shall	1Cor 13:8	1108
you either by revelation, or by *k*	1Cor 14:6	1108
for some have not the *k* of God	1Cor 15:34	56
of his *k* by us in every place	2Cor 2:14	1108
to give the light of the *k* of the	2Cor 4:6	1108
By pureness, by *k*, by	2Cor 6:6	1108
in faith, and utterance, and *k*	2Cor 8:7	1108
itself against the *k* of God	2Cor 10:5	1108
I be rude in speech, yet not in *k*	2Cor 11:6	1108
and revelation in the *k* of him	Eph 1:17	1922
ye may understand my *k* in the	Eph 3:4	4907
love of Christ, which passeth *k*	Eph 3:19	1108
of the *k* of the Son of God, unto	Eph 4:13	1922
may abound yet more and more in *k*	Phil 1:9	1922
of the *k* of Christ Jesus my Lord	Phil 3:8	1108
the *k* of his will in all wisdom	Col 1:9	1922
and increasing in the *k* of God	Col 1:10	1922
all the treasures of wisdom and *k*	Col 2:3	1108
which is renewed in *k* after the	Col 3:10	1922
to come unto the *k* of the truth	1Ti 2:4	1922
to come unto the *k* of the truth	2Ti 3:7	1922
have received the *k* of the truth	Heb 10:26	1922
man and endued with *k* among you	Jas 3:13	1990
dwell with them according to *k*	1Pet 3:7	1108
unto you through the *k* of God	2Pet 1:2	1922
through the *k* of him that hath	2Pet 1:3	1922
and to virtue *k*	2Pet 1:5	1108
And to *k* temperance	2Pet 1:6	1108
in the *k* of our Lord Jesus Christ	2Pet 1:8	1922
world through the *k* of the Lord	2Pet 2:20	1922
in the *k* of our Lord and Saviour	2Pet 3:18	1108

KNOWN

daughters which have not *k* man	Gen 19:8	3045
virgin, neither had any man *k* her	Gen 24:16	3045
it could not be *k* that they had	Gen 41:21	3045
the plenty shall not be *k* in the	Gen 41:31	3045
made himself *k* unto his brethren	Gen 45:1	3045
and said, Surely this thing is *k*	Ex 2:14	3045
name JEHOVAH was I not *k* to them	Ex 6:3	3045
Or if it be *k* that the ox hath	Ex 21:36	3045
wherein shall it be *k* here that I	Ex 33:16	3045
they have sinned against it, is *k*	Lev 4:14	3045
whether he hath seen or *k* of it	Lev 5:1	3045
myself *k* unto him in a vision	Num 12:6	3045
that hath *k* man by lying with him	Num 31:17	3045
that have not *k* a man by lying	Num 31:18	3045
had not *k* man by lying with him	Num 31:35	3045
k among your tribes, and I will	Deut 1:13	3045
of your tribes, wise men, and *k*	Deut 1:15	3045
your children which have not *k*	Deut 11:2	3045
other gods, which ye have not *k*	Deut 11:28	3045
other gods, which thou hast not *k*	Deut 13:2	3045
other gods, which thou hast not *k*	Deut 13:6	3045
other gods, which ye have not *k*	Deut 13:13	3045
it be not *k* who hath slain him	Deut 21:1	3045
thou nor thy fathers have *k*	Deut 28:36	3045
thou nor thy fathers have *k*	Deut 28:64	3045
which have not *k* any thing	Deut 31:13	3045
which had *k* all the works of the	Josh 24:31	3045
had not *k* all the wars of Canaan	Judg 3:1	3045
So his strength was not *k*	Judg 16:9	3045
that had *k* no man by lying with	Judg 21:12	3045
make not thyself *k* unto the man	Ruth 3:3	3045
Let it not be *k* that a woman came	Ruth 3:14	3045
it shall be *k* to you why his hand	1Sa 6:3	3045
that thou mayest make *k* unto me	1Sa 28:15	3045
and the thing was not *k*	2Sa 17:19	3045
that thou be not *k* to be the wife	1Kin 14:2	3045
let it be *k* this day that thou	1Kin 18:36	3045
make *k* his deeds among the people	1Chr 16:8	3045
in making *k* all these great	1Chr 17:19	3045
Be it *k* unto the king, that the	Ezr 4:12	3046
Be it *k* now unto the king, that,	Ezr 4:13	3046
Be it *k* unto the king, that we	Ezr 5:8	3046
heard that it was *k* unto us	Neh 4:15	3045
madest *k* unto them thy holy	Neh 9:14	3045
And the thing was *k* to Mordecai	Est 2:22	3045
The LORD is *k* by the judgment	Ps 9:16	3045
whom I have not *k* shall serve me	Ps 18:43	3045
thou hast *k* my soul in	Ps 31:7	3045
God is *k* in her palaces for a	Ps 48:3	3045
That thy way may be *k* upon earth	Ps 67:2	3045
Thou hast *k* my reproach, and my	Ps 69:19	3045
In Judah is God *k*	Ps 76:1	3045
and thy footsteps are not *k*	Ps 77:19	3045
Which we have heard and *k*, and our	Ps 78:3	3045
make them *k* to their children	Ps 78:5	3045
the heathen that have not *k* thee	Ps 79:6	3045
let him be *k* among the heathen in	Ps 79:10	3045
thy wonders be *k* in the dark	Ps 88:12	3045
I make *k* thy faithfulness to all	Ps 89:1	3045
high, because he hath *k* my name	Ps 91:14	3045
heart, and they have not *k* my ways	Ps 95:10	3045
LORD hath made *k* his salvation	Ps 98:2	3045
He made *k* his ways unto Moses,	Ps 103:7	3045
make *k* his deeds among the people	Ps 105:1	3045
make his mighty power to be *k*	Ps 106:8	3045
those that have *k* thy testimonies	Ps 119:79	3045
I have *k* of old that thou hast	Ps 119:152	3045
thou hast searched me, and *k* me	Ps 139:1	3045
To make *k* to the sons of men his	Ps 145:12	3045
judgments, they have not *k* them	Ps 147:20	3045
I will make *k* my words unto you	Prov 1:23	3045
perverteth his ways shall be *k*	Prov 10:9	3045
A fool's wrath is presently *k*	Prov 12:16	3045
in the midst of fools is made *k*	Prov 14:33	3045
Even a child is *k* by his doings	Prov 20:11	5234
I have made *k* to thee this day,	Prov 22:19	3045
Her husband is *k* in the gates	Prov 31:23	3045
a fool's voice is *k* by multitude	Eccl 5:3	
not seen the sun, nor *k* any thing	Eccl 6:5	3045
and it is *k* that it is man	Eccl 6:10	3045
this is *k* in all the earth	Is 12:5	3045
And the LORD shall be *k* to Egypt	Is 19:21	3045
children shall make *k* thy truth	Is 38:19	3045
Have ye not *k*?	Is 40:21	3045
Hast thou not *k*?	Is 40:28	3045
in paths that they have not *k*	Is 42:16	3045
They have not *k* nor understood	Is 44:18	3045
thee, though thou hast not *k* me	Is 45:4	3045
thee, though thou hast not *k* me	Is 45:5	3045
shall be *k* among the Gentiles	Is 61:9	3045

to make thy name *k* to thine	Is 64:2	3045
shall be *k* toward his servants	Is 66:14	3045
is foolish, they have not *k* me	Jer 4:22	3045
for they know the way of the	Jer 5:5	3045
they nor their fathers have *k*	Jer 9:16	3045
they nor their fathers have *k*	Jer 19:4	3045
pass, then shall the prophet be *k*	Jer 28:9	3045
they are not *k* in the streets	Lam 4:8	5234
made myself *k* unto them in the	Eze 20:5	3045
sight I made myself *k* unto them	Eze 20:9	3045
countries which thou hast not *k*	Eze 32:9	3045
I will make myself *k* among them	Eze 35:11	3045
the Lord GOD, be it *k* unto you	Eze 36:32	3045
I will be *k* in the eyes of many	Eze 38:23	3045
name *k* in the midst of my people	Eze 39:7	3045
will not make *k* unto me the dream	Dan 2:5	3046
will not make *k* unto me the dream	Dan 2:9	3046
Arioch made the thing *k* to Daniel	Dan 2:15	3046
and made the thing *k* to Hananiah	Dan 2:17	3046
hast made *k* unto me now what we	Dan 2:23	3046
for thou hast now made *k* unto us	Dan 2:23	3046
that will make *k* unto the king	Dan 2:25	3046
Art thou able to make *k* unto me	Dan 2:26	3046
secrets, and maketh *k* to the king	Dan 2:28	3046
that revealeth secrets maketh *k*	Dan 2:29	3046
k the interpretation to the king	Dan 2:30	3046
the great God hath made *k* to the	Dan 2:45	3046
be it *k* unto thee, O king, that	Dan 3:18	3046
that they might make *k* unto me	Dan 4:6	3046
but they did not make *k* unto me	Dan 4:7	3046
make *k* unto me the interpretation	Dan 4:18	3046
have *k* that the heavens do rule	Dan 4:26	3046
nor make *k* to the king the	Dan 5:8	3046
make *k* unto me the interpretation	Dan 5:15	3046
make *k* to me the interpretation	Dan 5:16	3046
make *k* to him the interpretation	Dan 5:17	3046
them, and they have not *k* the LORD	Hos 5:4	3045
made *k* that which shall surely be	Hos 5:9	3045
You only have I *k* of all the	Amos 3:2	3045
place is not *k* where they are	Nah 3:17	3045
in the midst of the years make *k*	Hab 3:2	3045
day which shall be *k* to the LORD	Zec 14:7	3045
and hid, that shall not be *k*	Mt 10:26	*1097*
But if ye had *k* what this meaneth	Mt 12:7	*1097*
that they should not make him *k*	Mt 12:16	*5318*
for the tree is *k* by his fruit	Mt 12:33	*1097*
k in what watch the thief would	Mt 24:43	*1492*
that they should not make him *k*	Mk 3:12	*5318*
the Lord hath made *k* unto us	Lk 2:15	*1107*
they made *k* abroad the saying	Lk 2:17	*1232*
every tree is *k* by his own fruit	Lk 6:44	*1097*
were a prophet, would have *k* who	Lk 7:39	*1097*
thing hid, that shall not be *k*	Lk 8:17	*1097*
neither hid, that shall not be *k*	Lk 12:2	*1097*
k what hour the thief would come	Lk 12:39	*1492*
Saying, If thou hadst *k*, even	Lk 19:42	*1097*
hast not *k* the things which are	Lk 24:18	*1097*
how he was *k* of them in breaking	Lk 24:35	*1097*
he himself seeketh to be *k* openly	Jn 7:4	*1097*
if ye had *k* me, ye should have	Jn 8:19	*1492*
ye should have *k* my Father also	Jn 8:19	*1492*
Yet ye have not *k* him	Jn 8:55	*1097*
my sheep, and am *k* of mine	Jn 10:14	*1097*
If ye had *k* me, ye should have	Jn 14:7	*1097*
ye should have *k* my Father also	Jn 14:7	*1097*
you, and yet hast thou not *k* me	Jn 14:9	*1097*
my Father I have made *k* unto you	Jn 15:15	*1107*
they have not *k* the Father	Jn 16:3	*1097*
Now they have *k* that all things	Jn 17:7	*1097*
have *k* surely that I came out	Jn 17:8	*1097*
Father, the world hath not *k* thee	Jn 17:25	*1097*
but I have *k* thee, and these have	Jn 17:25	*1097*
these have *k* that thou hast sent	Jn 17:25	*1097*
that disciple was *k* unto the high	Jn 18:15	*1110*
which was *k* unto the high priest,	Jn 18:16	*1110*
it was *k* unto all the dwellers at	Acts 1:19	*1110*
be this *k* unto you, and hearken to	Acts 2:14	*1110*
Thou hast made *k* to me the ways	Acts 2:28	*1107*
Be it *k* unto you all, and to all	Acts 4:10	*1110*
Joseph was made *k* to his brethren	Acts 7:13	*319*
kindred was made *k* unto Pharaoh	Acts 7:13	*5318*
their laying await was *k* of Saul	Acts 9:24	*1097*
it was *k* throughout all Joppa	Acts 9:42	*1110*
Be it *k* unto you therefore, men	Acts 13:38	*1110*
K unto God are all his works from	Acts 15:18	*1110*
this was *k* to all the Jews and	Acts 19:17	*1110*
because he would have *k* the	Acts 22:30	*1097*
when I would have *k* the cause	Acts 23:28	*1097*
Be it *k* therefore unto you, that	Acts 28:28	*1110*
Because that which may be *k* of	Rom 1:19	*1110*
the way of peace have they not *k*	Rom 3:17	*1097*

Nay, I had not *k* sin, but by the	Rom 7:7	1097
for I had not *k* lust, except the	Rom 7:7	1492
his wrath, and to make his power *k*	Rom 9:22	1107
that he might make *k* the riches	Rom 9:23	1107
For who hath *k* the mind of the	Rom 11:34	1097
made *k* to all nations for the	Rom 16:26	1107
for had they *k* it, they would not	1Cor 2:8	1097
For who hath *k* the mind of the	1Cor 2:16	1097
love God, the same is *k* of him	1Cor 8:3	1097
shall I know even as also I am *k*	1Cor 13:12	1921
how shall it be *k* what is piped	1Cor 14:7	1097
how shall it be *k* what is spoken	1Cor 14:9	1097
epistle written in our hearts, *k*	2Cor 3:2	1097
though we have *k* Christ after the	2Cor 5:16	1097
As unknown, and yet well *k*	2Cor 6:9	1921
But now, after that ye have *k* God	Gal 4:9	1097
or rather are *k* of God	Gal 4:9	1097
Having made *k* unto us the mystery	Eph 1:9	1107
he made *k* unto me the mystery	Eph 3:3	1107
not made *k* unto the sons of men	Eph 3:5	1107
be *k* by the church the manifold	Eph 3:10	1107
to make *k* the mystery of the	Eph 6:19	1107
shall make *k* to you all things	Eph 6:21	1107
your moderation be *k* unto all men	Phil 4:5	1097
your requests be made *k* unto God	Phil 4:6	1107
To whom God would make *k* what is	Col 1:27	1107
They shall make *k* unto you all	Col 4:9	1107
But thou hast fully *k* my doctrine	2Ti 3:10	3877
thou hast *k* the holy scriptures	2Ti 3:15	1492
me the preaching might be fully *k*	2Ti 4:17	4135
and they have not *k* my ways	Heb 3:10	1097
when we made *k* unto you the power	2Pet 1:16	1107
have *k* the way of righteousness	2Pet 2:21	1921
than, after they have *k* it	2Pet 2:21	1921
because ye have *k* him that is	1Jn 2:13	1097
because ye have *k* the Father	1Jn 2:13	1097
because ye have *k* him that is	1Jn 2:14	1097
hath not seen him, neither *k* him	1Jn 3:6	1097
And we have *k* and believed the love	1Jn 4:16	1097
all they that have *k* the truth	2Jn 1	1097
which have not *k* the depths of	Rev 2:24	1097

KOA (ko'-ah) *An obscure tribe.*

Chaldeans, Pekod, and Shoa, and *K*	Eze 23:23	6970

KOHATH (ko'-hath) See KOHATHITES. *A son of Levi.*

Gershon, and *K*, and Merari	Gen 46:11	6955
Gershon, and *K*, and Merari	Ex 6:16	6955
And the sons of *K*	Ex 6:18	6955
life of *K* were an hundred thirty	Ex 6:18	6955
Gershon, and *K*, and Merari	Num 3:17	6955
the sons of *K* by their families	Num 3:19	6955
of *K* was the family of the	Num 3:27	6955
The families of the sons of *K*	Num 3:29	6955
of *K* from among the sons of Levi	Num 4:2	6955
of *K* in the tabernacle of the	Num 4:4	6955
the sons of *K* shall come to bear	Num 4:15	6955
of *K* in the tabernacle of the	Num 4:15	6955
unto the sons of *K* he gave none	Num 7:9	6955
the son of Izhar, the son of *K*	Num 16:1	6955
of *K*, the family of the	Num 26:57	6955
And *K* begat Amram	Num 26:58	6955
the rest of the children of *K* had	Josh 21:5	6955
the families of the children of *K*	Josh 21:20	6955
remained of the children of *K*	Josh 21:20	6955
the children of *K* that remained	Josh 21:26	6955
Gershon, *K*, and Merari	1Chr 6:1	6955
And the sons of *K*	1Chr 6:2	6955
Gershom, *K*, and Merari	1Chr 6:16	6955
And the sons of *K* were, Amram, and	1Chr 6:18	6955
The sons of *K*	1Chr 6:22	6955
The son of Izhar, the son of *K*	1Chr 6:38	6955
And unto the sons of *K*, which were	1Chr 6:61	6955
K had cities of their coasts out	1Chr 6:66	6955
of the remnant of the sons of *K*	1Chr 6:70	6955
Of the sons of *K*	1Chr 15:5	6955
sons of Levi, namely, Gershon, *K*	1Chr 23:6	6955
The sons of *K*	1Chr 23:12	6955

KOHATHITES (ko'-hath-ites) *Descendants of Kohath.*

these are the families of the *K*	Num 3:27	6956
K shall be Elizaphan the son of	Num 3:30	6956
of the *K* from among the Levites	Num 4:18	6956
of the *K* after their families	Num 4:34	6956
numbered of the families of the *K*	Num 4:37	6956
the *K* set forward, bearing the	Num 10:21	6956
of Kohath, the family of the *K*	Josh 21:4	6956
out for the families of the *K*	Josh 21:4	6956
being of the families of the *K*	Josh 21:10	6956
Of the sons of the *K*	1Chr 6:33	6956
Aaron, of the families of the *K*	1Chr 6:54	6956

brethren, of the sons of the *K*	1Chr 9:32	6956
Levites, of the children of the *K*	2Chr 20:19	6956
of Azariah, of the sons of the *K*	2Chr 29:12	6956
Meshullam, of the sons of the *K*	2Chr 34:12	6956

KOLAIAH (ko-la-i'-ah)
1. A family of exiles.

the son of Pedaiah, the son of *K*	Neh 11:7	6964

2. Father of Ahab.

of Israel, of Ahab the son of *K*	Jer 29:21	6964

KORAH (ko'-rah) See CORE, KORAHITE, KORE.
1. A son of Esau.

bare Jeush, and Jaalam, and *K*	Gen 36:5	7141
to Esau Jeush, and Jaalam, and *K*	Gen 36:14	7141
duke Jeush, duke Jaalam, duke *K*	Gen 36:18	7141
Reuel, and Jeush, and Jaalam, and *K*	1Chr 1:35	7141

2. A son of Eliphaz.

Duke *K*, duke Gatam, and duke	Gen 36:16	7141

3. A conspirator against Moses.

K, and Nepheg, and Zichri	Ex 6:21	7141
And the sons of *K*	Ex 6:24	7141
Now *K*, the son of Izhar, the son	Num 16:1	7141
And he spake unto *K* and unto all	Num 16:5	7141
Take you censers, *K*, and all his	Num 16:6	7141
And Moses said unto *K*, Hear, I	Num 16:8	7141
And Moses said unto *K*, Be thou and	Num 16:16	7141
K gathered all the congregation	Num 16:19	7141
up from about the tabernacle of *K*	Num 16:24	7141
gat up from the tabernacle of *K*	Num 16:27	7141
the men that appertained unto *K*	Num 16:32	7141
that he be not as *K*, and as his	Num 16:40	7141
that died about the matter of *K*	Num 16:49	7141
against Aaron in the company of *K*	Num 26:9	7141
swallowed them up together with *K*	Num 26:10	7141
the children of *K* died not	Num 26:11	7141
the LORD in the company of *K*	Num 27:3	7141
the son of Ebiasaph, the son of *K*	1Chr 6:37	7141
the son of Ebiasaph, the son of *K*	1Chr 9:19	7141

4. A son of Hebron.

K, and Tappuah, and Rekem	1Chr 2:43	7141

5. A grandson of Kohath.

K his son, Assir his son,	1Chr 6:22	7141
Maschil, for the sons of *K*	Ps 42:t	7141
chief Musician for the sons of *K*	Ps 44:t	7141
Shoshannim, for the sons of *K*	Ps 45:t	7141
chief Musician for the sons of *K*	Ps 46:t	7141
A Psalm for the sons of *K*	Ps 47:t	7141
A Song and Psalm for the sons of *K*	Ps 48:t	7141
A Psalm for the sons of *K*	Ps 49:t	7141
A Psalm for the sons of *K*	Ps 84:t	7141
A Psalm for the sons of *K*	Ps 85:t	7141
A Psalm or Song for the sons of *K*	Ps 87:t	7141
of *K* to the chief Musician	Ps 88:t	7141

KORAHITE (ko'-ra-hite) See KORAHITES, KORE. *A descendant of Korah.*

the firstborn of Shallum the *K*	1Chr 9:31	7145

KORAHITES (ko'-ra-hites) See KORATHITES, KORHITES.

of the house of his father, the *K*	1Chr 9:19	7145

KORATHITES (ko'-ra-thites) See KORAHITES. *Same as Korahites.*

the Mushites, the family of the *K*	Num 26:58	7145

KORAZIN See CHORAZIN.

KORE (ko'-re) See KORAH, KORAHITE.
1. Father of Shallum.

And Shallum the son of *K*, the son	1Chr 9:19	6981
was Meshelemiah the son of *K*	1Chr 26:1	6981
the porters among the sons of *K*	1Chr 26:19	7145

2. A Temple servant.

K the son of Imnah the Levite,	2Chr 31:14	6981

KORHITES (kor'-hites) See KORAHITES. *Same as Korahites.*

these are the families of the *K*	Ex 6:24	7145
and Joezer, and Jashobeam, the *K*	1Chr 12:6	7145
Of the *K* was Meshelemiah the son	1Chr 26:1	7145
and of the children of the *K*	2Chr 20:19	7145

KOUM See CUMI.

KOZ (coz) See HAKKOZ.
1. A family of exiles.

of Habaiah, the children of *K*	Ezr 2:61	6976
of Habaiah, the children of *K*	Neh 7:63	6976

2. Father of two rebuilders of the wall.

the son of Urijah, the son of *K*	Neh 3:4	6976
Urijah the son of *K* another piece	Neh 3:21	6976

KUSHAIAH (cu-shah'-yah) See KISHI. *Father of Ethan.*

brethren, Ethan the son of *K*	1Chr 15:17	6984

L

LAADAH (la'-a-dah) *Son of Shelah.*
L the father of Mareshah, and the 1Chr 4:21   3935

LAADAN (la'-a-dan) *See* LIBNI.
1. A descendant of Ephraim.
L his son, Ammihud his son, ... 1Chr 7:26   3936
2. A descendant of Gershon.
Of the Gershonites were, L....................... 1Chr 23:7   3936
The sons of L 1Chr 23:8   3936
the chief of the fathers of L..................... 1Chr 23:9   3936
As concerning the sons of L 1Chr 26:21   3936
the sons of the Gershonite L 1Chr 26:21   3936
even of L the Gershonite, were.............. 1Chr 26:21   3936

LABAN (la'-ban) *See* LABAN'S, LIBNAH.
1. Father of Rachel.
had a brother, and his name was L .... Gen 24:29   3837
L ran out unto the man, unto the .... Gen 24:29   3837
Then L and Bethuel answered and........ Gen 24:50   3837
the sister to L the Syrian...................... Gen 25:20   3837
flee thou to L my brother to .... Gen 27:43   3837
of L thy mother's brother .... Gen 28:2   3837
and he went to Padan-aram unto L .... Gen 28:5   3837
Know ye L the son of Nahor .... Gen 29:5   3837
of L his mother's brother .... Gen 29:10   3837
the sheep of L his mother's .... Gen 29:10   3837
flock of L his mother's brother .... Gen 29:10   3837
when L heard the tidings of Jacob.......... Gen 29:13   3837
he told L all these things .... Gen 29:13   3837
L said to him, Surely thou art my .... Gen 29:14   3837
L said unto Jacob, Because thou .... Gen 29:15   3837
And L had two daughters .... Gen 29:16   3837
L said, It is better that I give .... Gen 29:19   3837
And Jacob said unto L, Give me my .... Gen 29:21   3837
L gathered together all the men .... Gen 29:22   3837
L gave unto his daughter Leah .... Gen 29:24   3837
and he said to L, What is this.............. Gen 29:25   3837
L said, It must not be so done in............ Gen 29:26   3837
L gave to Rachel his daughter .... Gen 29:29   3837
Joseph, that Jacob said unto L.............. Gen 30:25   3837
L said unto him, I pray thee, if............. Gen 30:27   3837
L said, Behold, I would it might .... Gen 30:34   3837
all the brown in the flock of L................ Gen 30:40   3837
Jacob beheld the countenance of L........ Gen 31:2   3837
seen all that L doeth unto thee .... Gen 31:12   3837
L went to shear his sheep...................... Gen 31:19   3837
away unawares to L the Syrian .... Gen 31:20   3837
it was told L on the third day .... Gen 31:22   3837
God came to L the Syrian in a .... Gen 31:24   3837
Then L overtook Jacob.......................... Gen 31:25   3837
L with his brethren pitched in .... Gen 31:25   3837
L said to Jacob, What hast thou............ Gen 31:26   3837
And Jacob answered and said to L........ Gen 31:31   3837
L went into Jacob's tent, and into .... Gen 31:33   3837
L searched all the tent, but .... Gen 31:34   3837
Jacob was wroth, and chode with L ...... Gen 31:36   3837
and Jacob answered and said to L .... Gen 31:36   3837
L answered and said unto Jacob,.......... Gen 31:43   3837
L called it Jegar-sahadutha.................... Gen 31:47   3837
L said, This heap is a witness .... Gen 31:48   3837
L said to Jacob, Behold this heap .... Gen 31:51   3837
And early in the morning L rose up ...... Gen 31:55   3837
L departed, and returned unto his .... Gen 31:55   3837
thus, I have sojourned with L................ Gen 32:4   3837
whom L gave to Leah his daughter, ... Gen 46:18   3837
which L gave unto Rachel his .... Gen 46:25   3837
2. A Hebrew encampment in the wilderness.
between Paran, and Tophel, and L.......... Deut 1:1   3837

LABAN'S (la'-bans) *Refers to Laban 1.*
and Jacob fed the rest of L flocks.......... Gen 30:36   3837
and put them not unto L cattle .... Gen 30:40   3837
so the feebler were L, and the .... Gen 30:42   3837
And he heard the words of L sons .... Gen 31:1   3837

LABOUR
the l of my hands, and rebuked .... Gen 31:42   3018
travailed, and she had hard l.................. Gen 35:16   3205
to pass, when she was in hard l.............. Gen 35:17   3205
the men, that they may l therein .... Ex 5:9   6213
Six days shalt thou l, and do all .... Ex 20:9   5647
Six days thou shalt l, and do all .... Deut 5:13   5647
on our affliction, and our l .... Deut 26:7   5999
not all the people to l thither .... Josh 7:3   3021
you a land for which ye did not l .... Josh 24:13   3021
be a guard to us, and l on the day.......... Neh 4:22   4399
man from his house, and from his l........ Neh 5:13   3018
I be wicked, why then l I in vain .... Job 9:29   3021
or wilt thou leave thy l to him .... Job 39:11   3018

her l is in vain without fear .... Job 39:16   3018
and their l unto the locust .... Ps 78:46   3018
years, yet is their strength l.................... Ps 90:10   5999
to his l until the evening .... Ps 104:23   5656
inherited the l of the people .... Ps 105:44   5999
brought down their heart with l .... Ps 107:12   5999
and let the strangers spoil his l .... Ps 109:11   3018
they l in vain that build it...................... Ps 127:1   5998
shalt eat the l of thine hands .... Ps 128:2   3018
That our oxen may be strong to l .... Ps 144:14   5445
The l of the righteous tendeth to .... Prov 10:16   6468
gathereth by l shall increase.................. Prov 13:11   3027
In all l there is profit.............................. Prov 14:23   6089
for his hands refuse to l.......................... Prov 21:25   6213
L not to be rich...................................... Prov 23:4   3021
profit hath a man of all his l .... Eccl 1:3   5999
All things are full of l .... Eccl 1:8   3023
for my heart rejoiced in all my l .... Eccl 2:10   5999
this was my portion of all my l .... Eccl 2:10   5999
on the l that I had laboured to .... Eccl 2:11   5999
I hated all my l which I had.................... Eccl 2:18   5999
all my l wherein I have laboured............ Eccl 2:19   5999
the l which I took under the sun............ Eccl 2:20   5999
is a man whose l is in wisdom .... Eccl 2:21   5999
For what hath man of all his l .... Eccl 2:22   5999
make his soul enjoy good in his l .... Eccl 2:24   5999
and enjoy the good of all his l................ Eccl 3:13   5999
yet is there no end of all his l .... Eccl 4:8   5999
neither saith he, For whom do I l .... Eccl 4:8   6001
have a good reward for their l .... Eccl 4:9   5999
and shall take nothing of his l .... Eccl 5:15   5999
l that he taketh under the sun .... Eccl 5:18   5999
portion, and to rejoice in his l .... Eccl 5:19   5999
All the l of man is for his mouth .... Eccl 6:7   5999
him of his l the days of his life .... Eccl 8:15   5999
though a man l to seek it out.................. Eccl 8:17   5998
in thy l which thou takest under............ Eccl 9:9   5999
The l of the foolish wearieth.................. Eccl 10:15   5999
l not to comfort me, because of.............. Is 22:4   213
The l of Egypt, and merchandise of........ Is 45:14   3018
your l for that which satisfieth .... Is 55:2   3018
They shall not l in vain, nor .... Is 65:23   3021
For shame hath devoured the l of.......... Jer 3:24   3018
I forth out of the womb to see l .... Jer 20:18   5999
and the people shall l in vain .... Jer 51:58   3021
we l, and have no rest............................ Lam 5:5   3021
and shall take away all thy l.................. Eze 23:29   3018
him the land of Egypt for his l................ Eze 29:20   6468
l to bring forth, O daughter of................ Mic 4:10   1518
people shall l in the very fire .... Hab 2:13   3021
the l of the olive shall fail, and.............. Hab 3:17   4639
and upon all the l of the hands .... Hag 1:11   3018
Come unto me, all ye that l.................. Mt 11:28   2872
that whereon ye bestowed no l .... Jn 4:38   2872
L not for the meat which .... Jn 6:27   2038
Mary, who bestowed much l on us .... Rom 16:6   2872
and Tryphosa, who l in the Lord............ Rom 16:12   2872
own reward according to his own l 1Cor 3:8   2873
And l, working with our own hands 1Cor 4:12   2872
your l is not in vain in the Lord 1Cor 15:58   2873
Wherefore we l, that, whether................ 2Cor 5:9   5389
have bestowed upon you l in vain .... Gal 4:11   2872
but rather let him l, working.................. Eph 4:28   2872
flesh, this is the fruit of my l.................. Phil 1:22   2041
my brother, and companion in l .... Phil 2:25   4904
Whereunto I also l, striving .... Col 1:29   2872
l of love, and patience of hope in 1Th 1:3   2873
For ye remember, brethren, our l 1Th 2:9   2873
tempted you, and our l be in vain 1Th 3:5   2873
to know them which l among you.......... 1Th 5:12   2872
but wrought with l and travail 2Th 3:8   2873
For therefore we both l and suffer 1Ti 4:10   2872
especially they who l in the word 1Ti 5:17   2872
Let us l therefore to enter into .... Heb 4:11   4704
l of love, which ye have shewed .... Heb 6:10   2873
I know thy works, and thy l.................. Rev 2:2   2873

LABOURED
So we l in the work .... Neh 4:21   6213
That which he l for shall he .... Job 20:18   3022
on the labour that I had l to do .... Eccl 2:11   5998
all my labour wherein I have l .... Eccl 2:19   5998
yet to a man that hath not l .... Eccl 2:21   5998
wherein he hath l under the sun............ Eccl 2:22   6001
hath he that hath l for the wind .... Eccl 5:16   5998
thou hast l from thy youth .... Is 47:12   3021
unto thee with whom thou hast l............ Is 47:15   3021
I have l in vain, I have spent my .... Is 49:4   3021

wine, for the which thou hast *l*	Is 62:8	3021
he *l* till the going down of the	Dan 6:14	7712
for the which thou hast not *l*	Jonah 4:10	5998
other men *l*, and ye are entered	Jn 4:38	2872
Persis, which *l* much in the Lord	Rom 16:12	2872
but I *l* more abundantly than they	1Cor 15:10	2872
run in vain, neither *l* in vain	Phil 2:16	2872
which *l* with me in the gospel	Phil 4:3	4866
and for my name's sake hast *l*	Rev 2:3	2872

LABOURER

for the *l* is worthy of his hire	Lk 10:7	2040
The *l* is worthy of his reward	1Ti 5:18	2040

LABOURERS

is plenteous, but the *l* are few	Mt 9:37	2040
send forth *l* into his harvest	Mt 9:38	2040
to hire *l* into his vineyard	Mt 20:1	2040
with the *l* for a penny a day	Mt 20:2	2040
unto his steward, Call the *l*	Mt 20:8	2040
truly is great, but the *l* are few	Lk 10:2	2040
send forth *l* into his harvest	Lk 10:2	2040
For we are *l* together with God	1Cor 3:9	4904
the hire of the *l* who have reaped	Jas 5:4	2040

LABOURETH

He that *l l* for himself	Prov 16:26	6001
He that *l l* for himself	Prov 16:26	5998
that worketh in that wherein he *l*	Eccl 3:9	6001
one that helpeth with us, and *l*	1Cor 16:16	2872
The husbandman that *l* must be	2Ti 2:6	2872

LABOURING

The sleep of a *l* man is sweet	Eccl 5:12	5647
how that so *l* ye ought to support	Acts 20:35	2872
always *l* fervently for you in	Col 4:12	75
for *l* night and day, because we	1Th 2:9	2873

LABOURS

harvest, the firstfruits of thy *l*	Ex 23:16	4639
in thy *l* out of the field	Ex 23:16	4639
fruit of thy land, and all thy *l*	Deut 28:33	3018
thy *l* be in the house of a	Prov 5:10	6089
pleasure, and exact all your *l*	Is 58:3	6092
this city, and all the *l* thereof	Jer 20:5	3018
in all my *l* they shall find none	Hos 12:8	3018
hail in all the *l* of your hands	Hag 2:17	4639
and ye are entered into their *l*	Jn 4:38	2873
imprisonments, in tumults, in *l*	2Cor 6:5	2873
that is, of other men's *l*	2Cor 10:15	2873
in *l* more abundant, in stripes	2Cor 11:23	2873
that they may rest from their *l*	Rev 14:13	2873

LACE

of the ephod with a *l* of blue	Ex 28:28	6616
And thou shalt put it on a blue *l*	Ex 28:37	6616
of the ephod with a *l* of blue	Ex 39:21	6616
And they tied unto it a *l* of blue	Ex 39:31	6616

LACHISH (la'-kish) *An Amorite city.*

Jarmuth, and unto Japhia king of L	Josh 10:3	3923
king of Jarmuth, the king of L	Josh 10:5	3923
king of Jarmuth, the king of L	Josh 10:23	3923
and all Israel with him, unto L	Josh 10:31	3923
the Lord delivered L into the	Josh 10:32	3923
king of Gezer came up to help L	Josh 10:33	3923
from L Joshua passed unto Eglon,	Josh 10:34	3923
to all that he had done to L	Josh 10:35	3923
the king of L, one	Josh 12:11	3923
L, and Bozkath, and Eglon,	Josh 15:39	3923
and he fled to L	2Kin 14:19	3923
but they sent after him to L	2Kin 14:19	3923
sent to the king of Assyria to L	2Kin 18:14	3923
Rab-shakeh from L to king	2Kin 18:17	3923
heard that he was departed from L	2Kin 19:8	3923
And Adoraim, and L, and Azekah,	2Chr 11:9	3923
and he fled to L	2Chr 25:27	3923
but they sent to L after him	2Chr 25:27	3923
he himself laid siege against L	2Chr 32:9	3923
and in their villages, at L	Neh 11:30	3923
of Assyria sent Rabshakeh from L	Is 36:2	3923
heard that he was departed from L	Is 37:8	3923
Judah that were left, against L	Jer 34:7	3923
O thou inhabitant of L, bind the	Mic 1:13	3923

LACK

Peradventure there shall *l* five	Gen 18:28	2637
all the city for *l* of five	Gen 18:28	
he that gathered little had no *l*	Ex 16:18	2637
thou shalt not *l* any thing in it	Deut 8:9	2637
old lion perisheth for *l* of prey	Job 4:11	1097
God, they wander for *l* of meat	Job 38:41	1097
The young lions do *l*, and suffer	Ps 34:10	7326
giveth unto the poor shall not *l*	Prov 28:27	4270
and let thy head *l* no ointment	Eccl 9:8	2637

are destroyed for *l* of knowledge	Hos 4:6	1097
what *l* I yet	Mt 19:20	5302
that had gathered little had no *l*	2Cor 8:15	1641
to supply your *l* of service	Phil 2:30	5303
and that ye may have *l* of nothing	1Th 4:12	5332
If any of you *l* wisdom, let him	Jas 1:5	3007

LACKED

thou hast *l* nothing	Deut 2:7	2637
there *l* of David's servants	2Sa 2:30	6485
by the morning light there *l* not	2Sa 17:22	5737
they *l* nothing	1Kin 4:27	5737
him, But what hast thou *l* with me	1Kin 11:22	2638
so that they *l* nothing	Neh 9:21	2637
away, because it *l* moisture	Lk 8:6	3361,2192
scrip, and shoes, *l* ye any thing	Lk 22:35	5302
was there any among them that *l*	Acts 4:34	1729
honour to that part which *l*	1Cor 12:24	5302
careful, but ye *l* opportunity	Phil 4:10	170

LACKEST

said unto him, One thing thou *l*	Mk 10:21	5302
unto him, Yet *l* thou one thing	Lk 18:22	3007

LACKETH

there *l* not one man of us	Num 31:49	6485
on the sword, or that *l* bread	2Sa 3:29	2638
with a woman *l* understanding	Prov 6:32	2638
honoureth himself, and *l* bread	Prov 12:9	2638
But he that *l* these things is	2Pet 1:9	3361,3918

LACKING

to be *l* from thy meat offering	Lev 2:13	7673
superfluous or *l* in his parts	Lev 22:23	7038
be to day one tribe *l* in Israel	Judg 21:3	5737
And there was nothing *l* to them	1Sa 30:19	5737
dismayed, neither shall they be *l*	Jer 23:4	
for that which was *l* on your part	1Cor 16:17	5303
for that which was *l* to me the	2Cor 11:9	5303
that which is *l* in your faith	1Th 3:10	5303

LAD

in thy sight because of the *l*	Gen 21:12	5288
And God heard the voice of the *l*	Gen 21:17	5288
the voice of the *l* where he is	Gen 21:17	5288
Arise, lift up the *l*, and hold him	Gen 21:18	5288
with water, and gave the *l* drink	Gen 21:19	5288
And God was with the *l*	Gen 21:20	5288
the *l* will go yonder and worship,	Gen 22:5	5288
Lay not thine hand upon the *l*	Gen 22:12	5288
the *l* was with the sons of Bilhah	Gen 37:2	5288
his father, Send the *l* with me	Gen 43:8	5288
The *l* cannot leave his father	Gen 44:22	5288
father, and the *l* be not with us	Gen 44:30	5288
seeth that the *l* is not with us	Gen 44:31	5288
surety for the *l* unto my father	Gen 44:32	5288
of the *l* a bondman to my lord	Gen 44:33	5288
let the *l* go up with his brethren	Gen 44:33	5288
father, and the *l* be not with me	Gen 44:34	5288
Samson said unto the *l* that held	Judg 16:26	5288
And, behold, I will send a *l*	1Sa 20:21	5288
If I expressly say unto the *l*	1Sa 20:21	5288
David, and a little *l* with him	1Sa 20:35	5288
And he said unto his *l*, Run, find	1Sa 20:36	5288
And as the *l* ran, he shot an arrow	1Sa 20:36	5288
when the *l* was come to the place	1Sa 20:37	5288
shot, Jonathan cried after the *l*	1Sa 20:37	5288
And Jonathan cried after the *l*	1Sa 20:38	5288
Jonathan's *l* gathered up the	1Sa 20:38	5288
But the *l* knew not any thing	1Sa 20:39	5288
gave his artillery unto his *l*	1Sa 20:40	5288
And as soon as the *l* was gone,	1Sa 20:41	5288
Nevertheless a *l* saw them	2Sa 17:18	5288
And he said to a *l*, Carry him to	2Kin 4:19	5288
There is a *l* here, which hath	Jn 6:9	3808

LADAN See Laadan.

LADDER

behold a *l* set up on the earth,	Gen 28:12	5551

LADE

l your beasts, and go, get you	Gen 45:17	2943
did *l* you with a heavy yoke	1Kin 12:11	6006
for ye *l* men with burdens	Lk 11:46	5412

LADED

they *l* their asses with the corn,	Gen 42:26	5375
l every man his ass, and returned	Gen 44:13	6006
bare burdens, with those that *l*	Neh 4:17	6006
they *l* us with such things as	Acts 28:10	2007

LADEN

ten asses *l* with the good things	Gen 45:23	5375
and ten she asses *l* with corn	Gen 45:23	5375
And Jesse took an ass *l* with bread	1Sa 16:20	

a people *l* with iniquity, a seed	Is 1:4	3515
all ye that labour and are heavy *l*	Mt 11:28	*5412*
captive silly women *l* with sins	2Ti 3:6	*4987*

LADETH

to him that *l* himself with thick	Hab 2:6	3515

LADIES

Her wise *l* answered her, yea, she	Judg 5:29	8282
Likewise shall the *l* of Persia	Est 1:18	8282

LADING

bringing in sheaves, and *l* asses	Neh 13:15	6006
and much damage, not only of the *l*	Acts 27:10	*5414*

LAD'S

life is bound up in the *l* life	Gen 44:30	5288

LADS

me from all evil, bless the *l*	Gen 48:16	5288

LADY

more be called, The *l* of kingdoms	Is 47:5	1404
saidst, I shall be a *l* for ever	Is 47:7	1404
The elder unto the elect *l*	2Jn 1	2959
And now I beseech thee, *l*, not as	2Jn 5	2959

LAEL *(la'-el) A Levite.*

shall be Eliasaph the son of *L*	Num 3:24	3815

LAHAD *(la'-had) Great-grandson of Shobal.*

and Jahath begat Ahumai, and *L*	1Chr 4:2	3854

LAHAI-ROI *(la-hah'-ee-roy) See BEER-LAHAI-ROI. A well in Paran.*

came from the way of the well *L*	Gen 24:62	883
and Isaac dwelt by the well *L*	Gen 25:11	883

LAHMAM *(lah'-mam) A city in Judah.*

And Cabbon, and *L*, and Kithlish,	Josh 15:40	3903

LAHMAS See LAHMAM.

LAHMI *(lah'-mi) See BETHLEHEMITE. A brother of Goliath.*

slew *L* the brother of Goliath the	1Chr 20:5	3902

LAID

l it upon both their shoulders,	Gen 9:23	7760
l each piece one against another	Gen 15:10	5414
the men *l* hold upon his hand, and	Gen 19:16	
and *l* it upon Isaac his son	Gen 22:6	7760
l the wood in order, and bound	Gen 22:9	
l him on the altar upon the wood	Gen 22:9	7760
that Jacob *l* the rods before the	Gen 30:41	7760
l by her vail from her, and put on	Gen 38:19	5493
she *l* up his garment by her,	Gen 39:16	3241
l up the food in the cities	Gen 41:48	5414
every city, *l* he up in the same	Gen 41:48	5414
l it upon Ephraim's head, who was	Gen 48:14	7896
l his right hand upon the head of	Gen 48:17	7896
she *l* it in the flags by the	Ex 2:3	7760
there more work be *l* upon the men	Ex 5:9	3515
they *l* it up till the morning, as	Ex 16:24	3241
so Aaron *l* it up before the	Ex 16:34	3241
l before their faces all these	Ex 19:7	7760
If there be *l* on him a sum of	Ex 21:30	7896
his life whatsoever is *l* upon him	Ex 21:30	7896
of Israel he *l* not his hand	Ex 24:11	7971
his sons *l* their hands upon the	Lev 8:14	5564
his sons *l* their hands upon the	Lev 8:18	5564
his sons *l* their hands upon the	Lev 8:22	5564
l incense thereon, and stood in	Num 16:18	7760
Moses *l* up the rods before the	Num 17:7	3241
we have *l* them waste even unto	Num 21:30	
he *l* his hands upon him, and gave	Num 27:23	5564
us, and *l* upon us hard bondage	Deut 26:6	5414
which the LORD hath *l* upon it	Deut 29:22	2470
Is not this *l* up in store with me	Deut 32:34	3647
for Moses had *l* his hands upon	Deut 34:9	5564
which she had *l* in order upon the	Josh 2:6	
And before they were *l* down	Josh 2:8	7901
they lodged, and *l* them down there	Josh 4:8	3241
l them out before the LORD	Josh 7:23	3332
l great stones in the cave's	Josh 10:27	
their blood be *l* upon Abimelech	Judg 9:24	7760
they *l* wait against Shechem in	Judg 9:34	
l wait in the field, and looked,	Judg 9:43	
l it on his shoulder, and said	Judg 9:48	7760
l wait for him all night in the	Judg 16:2	
l hold on his concubine, and	Judg 19:29	
uncovered his feet, and *l* her down	Ruth 3:7	7901
of barley, and *l* it on her	Ruth 3:15	7896
l it in her bosom, and became	Ruth 4:16	7896
when Eli was *l* down in his place,	1Sa 3:2	7901
Samuel was *l* down to sleep	1Sa 3:3	7901
they *l* the ark of the LORD upon	1Sa 6:11	7760
book, and *l* it up before the LORD	1Sa 10:25	3241

how he *l* wait for him in the way,	1Sa 15:2	7760
Amalek, and *l* wait in the valley	1Sa 15:5	
he *l* hold upon the skirt of his	1Sa 15:27	
l it in the bed, and put a pillow	1Sa 19:13	7760
David *l* up these words in his	1Sa 21:12	7760
cakes of figs, and *l* them on asses	1Sa 25:18	7760
and he was *l* down	2Sa 13:8	7901
l her hand on her head, and went	2Sa 13:19	7760
l a very great heap of stones	2Sa 18:17	5324
l it in her bosom	1Kin 3:20	7901
l her dead child in my bosom	1Kin 3:20	7901
of the house of the LORD *l*	1Kin 6:37	
an oath be *l* upon him to cause	1Kin 8:31	5375
l it upon the ass, and brought it	1Kin 13:29	3241
he *l* his carcase in his own grave	1Kin 13:30	3241
all Israel *l* siege to Gibbethon	1Kin 15:27	
he *l* the foundation thereof in	1Kin 16:34	
abode, and *l* him upon his own bed	1Kin 17:19	7901
l him on the wood, and said, Fill	1Kin 18:33	7760
eat and drink, and *l* him down again	1Kin 19:6	7901
he *l* him down upon his bed, and	1Kin 21:4	7901
l him on the bed of the man of	2Kin 4:21	7901
l the staff upon the face of the	2Kin 4:31	7760
child was dead, and *l* upon his bed	2Kin 4:32	7901
l them upon two of his servants	2Kin 5:23	5414
the LORD *l* this burden upon them	2Kin 9:25	5375
And they *l* hands on her	2Kin 11:16	7760
they *l* it out to the carpenters	2Kin 12:11	3318
for all that was *l* out for the	2Kin 12:12	3318
l it on the boil, and he recovered	2Kin 20:7	7760
have *l* up in store unto this day	2Kin 20:17	
an oath be *l* upon him to make him	2Chr 6:22	5375
and *l* hold on other gods, and	2Chr 7:22	
l him in the bed which was filled	2Chr 16:14	7901
So they *l* hands on her	2Chr 23:15	7760
l upon Israel in the wilderness	2Chr 24:9	
of the burdens *l* upon him	2Chr 24:27	
they *l* their hands upon them	2Chr 29:23	5564
their God, and *l* them by heaps	2Chr 31:6	5414
(but he himself *l* siege against	2Chr 32:9	
temple of the LORD was not yet *l*	Ezr 3:6	
And when the builders *l* the	Ezr 3:10	
of the house of the LORD was *l*	Ezr 3:11	
house was *l* before their eyes	Ezr 3:12	
timber is *l* in the walls, and this	Ezr 5:8	7760
l the foundation of the house of	Ezr 5:16	3052
treasures were *l* up in Babylon	Ezr 6:1	5182
foundations thereof be strongly *l*	Ezr 6:3	5446
who also *l* the beams thereof, and	Neh 3:3	
they *l* the beams thereof, and set	Neh 3:6	
they *l* the meat offerings	Neh 13:5	5414
because he *l* his hand upon the	Est 8:7	7971
but on the spoil *l* they not their	Est 9:10	7971
on the prey they *l* not their hand	Est 9:15	7971
but they *l* not their hands on the	Est 9:16	7971
the king Ahasuerus *l* a tribute	Est 10:1	7760
my calamity *l* in the balances	Job 6:2	5375
The snare is *l* for him in the	Job 18:10	
l their hand on their mouth	Job 29:9	7760
or if I have *l* wait at my	Job 31:9	
Where wast thou when I *l* the	Job 38:4	
Who hath *l* the measures thereof,	Job 38:5	7760
or who *l* the corner stone thereof	Job 38:6	3384
I *l* me down and slept	Ps 3:5	7901
and majesty hast thou *l* upon him	Ps 21:5	7737
that they have *l* privily for me	Ps 31:4	2934
which thou hast *l* up for them	Ps 31:19	6845
they *l* to my charge things that I	Ps 35:11	
sheep they are *l* in the grave	Ps 49:14	8371
to be *l* in the balance, they are	Ps 62:9	5927
they have *l* Jerusalem on heaps	Ps 79:1	7760
l waste his dwelling place	Ps 79:7	
Thou hast *l* me in the lowest pit,	Ps 88:6	7896
I have *l* help upon one that is	Ps 89:19	7737
Of old hast thou *l* the foundation	Ps 102:25	
Who *l* the foundations of the	Ps 104:5	
he was *l* in iron	Ps 105:18	935
thy judgments have I *l* before me	Ps 119:30	7737
The wicked have *l* a snare for me	Ps 119:110	5414
before, and *l* thine hand upon me	Ps 139:5	7896
snares which they have *l* for me	Ps 141:9	3369
they privily *l* a snare for me	Ps 142:3	2934
the sinner is *l* up for the just	Prov 13:22	6845
old, which I have *l* up for thee	Song 7:13	6845
he *l* it upon my mouth, and said,	Is 6:7	5060
he hath *l* up his carriages	Is 10:28	6485
saying, Since thou art *l* down	Is 14:8	7901
the night Ar of Moab is *l* waste	Is 15:1	
the night Kir of Moab is *l* waste	Is 15:1	
and that which they have *l* up	Is 15:7	6486
for it is *l* waste, so that there	Is 23:1	

L

for your strength is *l* waste .... Is 23:14
shall not be treasured nor *l* up .... Is 23:18   2630
have *l* waste all the nations .... Is 37:18
have *l* up in store until this day .... Is 39:6
him, yet he *l* it not to heart .... Is 42:25   7760
temple, Thy foundation shall be *l* .... Is 44:28
hast thou very heavily *l* thy yoke .... Is 47:6
Mine hand also hath *l* the .... Is 48:13
l the foundations of the earth................. Is 51:13
thou hast *l* thy body as the .... Is 51:23   7760
the LORD hath *l* on him the .... Is 53:6   6293
me, nor *l* it to my heart .... Is 57:11   7760
our pleasant things are *l* waste .... Is 64:11
and thy cities shall be *l* waste................ Jer 4:7
should this city be *l* waste .... Jer 27:17
but they *l* up the roll in the .... Jer 36:20   6485
I have *l* a snare for thee, and .... Jer 50:24
they *l* wait for us in the .... Lam 4:19
For I have *l* upon thee the years .... Eze 4:5   5414
the cities shall be *l* waste .... Eze 6:6
that your altars may be *l* waste .... Eze 6:6
whom ye have *l* in the midst of it .... Eze 11:7   7760
are inhabited shall be *l* waste............... Eze 12:20
and he *l* waste their cities .... Eze 19:7
replenished, now she is *l* waste .... Eze 26:2
among the cities that are *l* waste .... Eze 29:12
be thou *l* with the uncircumcised .... Eze 32:19   7901
they have *l* their swords under .... Eze 32:27   5414
which with their might are *l* by .... Eze 32:29   5414
he shall be *l* in the midst of the .... Eze 32:32   7901
when I have *l* the land most .... Eze 33:29   5414
saying, They are *l* desolate................... Eze 35:12
my hand that I have *l* upon them .... Eze 39:21   7760
whereupon also they *l* the .... Eze 40:42   3240
l upon the mouth of the den .... Dan 6:17   7760
their jaws, and I *l* meat unto them .... Hos 11:4   5186
He hath *l* my vine waste, and .... Joel 1:7   7760
clods, the garners are *l* desolate......... Joel 1:17
l to pledge by every altar .... Amos 2:8
of Israel shall be *l* waste .... Amos 7:9
bread have *l* a wound under thee .... Obad 7   7760
nor have *l* hands on their .... Obad 13   7971
he *l* his robe from him, and .... Jonah 3:6   5674
he hath *l* siege against us .... Mic 5:1   7760
thee, and say, Nineveh is *l* waste .... Nah 3:7
it is *l* over with gold and silver, ... Hab 2:19   8610
from before a stone was *l* upon a .... Hag 2:15   7760
of the LORD's temple was *l* .... Hag 2:18
stone that I have *l* before Joshua .... Zec 3:9   5414
l the foundation of this house .... Zec 4:9
for they *l* the pleasant land .... Zec 7:14   7760
house of the LORD of hosts was *l*............. Zec 8:9
l his mountains and his heritage .... Mal 1:3   7760
now also the ax is *l* unto the .... Mt 3:10   2749
house, he saw his wife's mother *l* .... Mt 8:14   906
For Herod had *l* hold on John .... Mt 14:3
he *l* hands on him, and took him by ...... Mt 18:28
he *l* his hands on them, and .... Mt 19:15   2007
l hands on Jesus, and took him .... Mt 26:50   1911
the temple, and ye *l* no hold on me ...... Mt 26:55
they that had *l* hold on Jesus led .... Mt 26:57
l it in his own new tomb, which .... Mt 27:60   5087
save that he *l* his hands upon a............. Mk 6:5   2007
l hold upon John, and bound him in ...... Mk 6:17
up his corpse, and *l* it in a tomb......... Mk 6:29   5087
they *l* the sick in the streets, ... Mk 6:56   5087
and her daughter *l* upon the bed .... Mk 7:30   906
they *l* their hands on him, and............. Mk 14:46   1911
and the young men *l* hold on him .... Mk 14:51
l him in a sepulchre which was .... Mk 15:46   2698
of Joses beheld where he was *l* .... Mk 15:47   5087
behold the place where they *l* him .... Mk 16:6   5087
them *l* them up in their hearts................. Lk 1:66   5087
clothes, and *l* him in a manger .... Lk 2:7   347
now also the axe is *l* unto the .... Lk 3:9   2749
he *l* his hands on every one of............. Lk 4:40   2007
l the foundation on a rock .... Lk 6:48   5087
much goods *l* up for many years......... Lk 12:19   2749
And he *l* his hands on her .... Lk 13:13   2007
after he hath *l* the foundation, ... Lk 14:29   5087
which was *l* at his gate, full of............. Lk 16:20   906
I have kept *l* up in a napkin .... Lk 19:20   606
man, taking up that I *l* not down .... Lk 19:22   5087
they *l* hold upon one Simon, a............. Lk 23:26
and on him they *l* the cross................... Lk 23:26   2007
l it in a sepulchre that was hewn......... Lk 23:53   5087
wherein never man before was *l* .... Lk 23:53   2749
sepulchre, and how his body was *l*......... Lk 23:55   5087
the linen clothes *l* by themselves......... Lk 24:12   2749
but no man *l* hands on him, ... Jn 7:30   1911
but no man *l* hands on him .... Jn 7:44   1911

and no man *l* hands on him .... Jn 8:20
And said, Where have ye *l* him .... Jn 11:34   5087
the place where the dead was *l* .... Jn 11:41   2749
supper, and *l* aside his garments .... Jn 13:4   5087
wherein was never man yet *l* .... Jn 19:41   5087
There *l* they Jesus therefore .... Jn 19:42   5087
we know not where they have *l* him ...... Jn 20:2   5087
I know not where they have *l* him .... Jn 20:13   5087
tell me where thou hast *l* him .... Jn 20:15   5087
and fish *l* thereon, and bread .... Jn 21:9   1945
whom they *l* daily at the gate of .... Acts 3:2   5087
they *l* hands on them, and put them ...... Acts 4:3   1911
l them down at the apostles' feet........... Acts 4:35   5087
l it at the apostles' feet .... Acts 4:37   5087
l it at the apostles' feet .... Acts 5:2   5087
l them on beds and couches, that .... Acts 5:15   5087
l their hands on the apostles, and .... Acts 5:18   1911
they *l* their hands on them .... Acts 6:6   2007
l in the sepulchre that Abraham .... Acts 7:16   5087
the witnesses *l* down their .... Acts 7:58   659
Then *l* they their hands on them,......... Acts 8:17   2007
they *l* her in an upper chamber .... Acts 9:37   5087
l their hands on them, they sent .... Acts 13:3   2007
the tree, and *l* him in a sepulchre .... Acts 13:29   5087
was *l* unto his fathers, and saw .... Acts 13:36   4369
when they had *l* many stripes upon ...... Acts 16:23   2007
when Paul had *l* his hands upon............. Acts 19:6   2007
And when the Jews *l* wait for him .... Acts 20:3   1096
the people, and *l* hands on him, ... Acts 21:27   1911
but to have nothing *l* to his .... Acts 23:29   1462
that the Jews *l* wait for the man .... Acts 23:30   2071
l many and grievous complaints .... Acts 25:7   5342
the crime *l* against him .... Acts 25:16   1462
signify the crimes *l* against him .... Acts 25:27
l them on the fire, there came a............. Acts 28:2   2007
l his hands on him, and healed him ...... Acts 28:8   2007
my life *l* down their own necks .... Rom 16:4   5294
I have *l* the foundation, and 1Cor 3:10   5087
can no man lay than that is *l*................... 1Cor 3:11   5087
for necessity is *l* upon me..................... 1Cor 9:16   1945
which is *l* up for you in heaven .... Col 1:5   606
Henceforth there is *l* up for me a 2Ti 4:8   606
it may not be *l* to their charge 2Ti 5:16   3049
in the beginning hast *l* the .... Heb 1:10
because he *l* down his life for us............. 1Jn 3:16   5087
he *l* his right hand upon me, ... Rev 1:17   2007
he *l* hold on the dragon, that old .... Rev 20:2

LAIDST
thou *l* affliction upon our loins................. Ps 66:11   7760

LAIN
woman, If no man have *l* with thee .... Num 5:19   7901
some man have *l* with thee beside.......... Num 5:20   5414,7903
every woman that hath *l* by man.... Judg 21:11   3045,4904
For now should I have *l* still .... Job 3:13   7901
he found that he had *l* in the................... Jn 11:17
where the body of Jesus had *l* .... Jn 20:12   2749

LAISH (*la'-ish*) See DAN, LESHEM.
    1. *Same as the city of Dan.*
five men departed, and came to *L* .... Judg 18:7   3919
went to spy out the country of *L*............. Judg 18:14   3919
which he had, and came unto *L*............. Judg 18:27   3919
of the city was *L* at the first .... Judg 18:29   3919
cause it to be heard unto *L* .... Is 10:30   3919
    2. *Father of Phaltiel.*
wife, to Phalti the son of *L*................... 1Sa 25:44   3919
even from Phaltiel the son of *L* 2Sa 3:15   3919

LAKE
he stood by the *l* of Gennesaret............. Lk 5:1   3041
saw two ships standing by the *l*............. Lk 5:2   3041
over unto the other side of the *l* .... Lk 8:22   3041
down a storm of wind on the *l* .... Lk 8:23   3041
down a steep place into the *l* .... Lk 8:33   3041
both were cast alive into a *l* of............. Rev 19:20   3041
them was cast into the *l* of fire .... Rev 20:10   3041
hell were cast into the *l* of fire .... Rev 20:14   3041
life was cast into the *l* of fire .... Rev 20:15   3041
in the *l* which burneth with fire .... Rev 21:8   3041

LAKKUM See LAKUM.

LAKUM (*la'-kum*) *A city in Naphtali.*
Adami, Nekeb, and Jabneel, unto *L*........ Josh 19:33   3946

LAMA
saying, Eli, Eli, *l* sabachthani............... Mt 27:46   2982
saying, Eloi, Eloi, *l* sabachthani............ Mk 15:34   2982

LAMB
but where is the *l* for a burnt .... Gen 22:7   7716
himself a *l* for a burnt offering............... Gen 22:8   7716
shall take to them every man a *l*............. Ex 12:3   7716

their fathers, a *l* for an house	Ex 12:3	7716
household be too little for the *l*	Ex 12:4	7716
shall make your count for the *l*	Ex 12:4	7716
Your *l* shall be without blemish,	Ex 12:5	7716
take you a *l* according to your	Ex 12:21	6629
an ass thou shalt redeem with a *l*	Ex 13:13	7716
The one *l* thou shalt offer in the	Ex 29:39	3532
the other *l* thou shalt offer at	Ex 29:39	3532
with the one *l* a tenth deal of	Ex 29:40	3532
the other *l* thou shalt offer at	Ex 29:41	3532
an ass thou shalt redeem with a *l*	Ex 34:20	7716
If he offer a *l* for his offering,	Lev 3:7	3775
if he bring a *l* for a sin	Lev 4:32	3532
as the fat of the *l* is taken away	Lev 4:35	3775
a *l* or a kid of the goats, for a	Lev 5:6	3776
And if he be not able to bring a *l*	Lev 5:7	7716
and a calf and a *l*, both of the	Lev 9:3	3532
she shall bring a *l* of the first	Lev 12:6	3532
if she be not able to bring a *l*	Lev 12:8	7716
one ewe *l* of the first year	Lev 14:10	3535
And the priest shall take one he *l*	Lev 14:12	3532
he shall slay the *l* in the place	Lev 14:13	3532
then he shall take one *l* for a	Lev 14:21	3532
the *l* of the trespass offering	Lev 14:24	3532
he shall kill the *l* of the	Lev 14:25	3532
Israel, that killeth an ox, or *l*	Lev 17:3	3775
Either a bullock or a *l* that hath	Lev 22:23	7716
he *l* without blemish of the first	Lev 23:12	3532
shall bring a *l* of the first year	Num 6:12	3532
one he *l* of the first year	Num 6:14	3532
one ewe *l* of the first year	Num 6:14	3535
one *l* of the first year, for a	Num 7:15	3532
one *l* of the first year, for a	Num 7:21	3532
one *l* of the first year, for a	Num 7:27	3532
one *l* of the first year, for a	Num 7:33	3532
one *l* of the first year, for a	Num 7:39	3532
one *l* of the first year, for a	Num 7:45	3532
one *l* of the first year, for a	Num 7:51	3532
one *l* of the first year, for a	Num 7:57	3532
one *l* of the first year, for a	Num 7:63	3532
one *l* of the first year, for a	Num 7:69	3532
one *l* of the first year, for a	Num 7:75	3532
one *l* of the first year, for a	Num 7:81	3532
offering or sacrifice, for one *l*	Num 15:5	3532
or for one ram, or for a *l*	Num 15:11	7716
The one *l* shalt thou offer in the	Num 28:4	3532
the other *l* shalt thou offer at	Num 28:4	3532
part of an hin for the one *l*	Num 28:7	3532
the other *l* shalt thou offer at	Num 28:8	3532
for a meat offering unto one *l*	Num 28:13	3532
a fourth part of an hin unto a *l*	Num 28:14	3532
deal shalt thou offer for every *l*	Num 28:21	3532
A several tenth deal unto one *l*	Num 28:29	3532
And one tenth deal for one *l*	Num 29:4	3532
A several tenth deal for one *l*	Num 29:10	3532
to each *l* of the fourteen lambs	Num 29:15	3532
And Samuel took a sucking *l*	1Sa 7:9	2924
took a *l* out of the flock	1Sa 17:34	7716
nothing, save one little ewe *l*	2Sa 12:3	3535
but took the poor man's *l*	2Sa 12:4	3535
he shall restore the *l* fourfold	2Sa 12:6	3535
wolf also shall dwell with the *l*	Is 11:6	3532
Send ye the *l* to the ruler of the	Is 16:1	3733
brought as a *l* to the slaughter	Is 53:7	7716
the *l* shall feed together, and the	Is 65:25	2924
he that sacrificeth a *l*, as if he	Is 66:3	7716
But I was like a *l* or an ox that	Jer 11:19	3532
one *l* out of the flock, out of	Eze 45:15	7716
of a *l* of the first year without	Eze 46:13	3532
Thus shall they prepare the *l*	Eze 46:15	3532
feed them as a *l* in a large place	Hos 4:16	3532
and saith, Behold the *L* of God	Jn 1:29	286
he saith, Behold the *L* of God	Jn 1:36	286
like a *l* dumb before his shearer,	Acts 8:32	286
as of a *l* without blemish and	1Pet 1:19	286
stood a *L* as it had been slain,	Rev 5:6	721
elders fell down before the *L*	Rev 5:8	721
Worthy is the *L* that was slain to	Rev 5:12	721
throne, and unto the *L* for ever	Rev 5:13	721
I saw when the *L* opened one of	Rev 6:1	721
and from the wrath of the *L*	Rev 6:16	721
the throne, and before the *L*	Rev 7:9	721
upon the throne, and unto the *L*	Rev 7:10	721
them white in the blood of the *L*	Rev 7:14	721
For the *L* which is in the midst	Rev 7:17	721
him by the blood of the *L*	Rev 12:11	721
in the book of life of the *L*	Rev 13:8	721
and he had two horns like a *l*	Rev 13:11	721
a *L* stood on the mount Sion, and	Rev 14:1	721
the *L* whithersoever he goeth	Rev 14:4	721
firstfruits unto God and to the *L*	Rev 14:4	721
and in the presence of the *L*	Rev 14:10	721
of God, and the song of the *L*	Rev 15:3	721
These shall make war with the *L*	Rev 17:14	721
the *L* shall overcome them	Rev 17:14	721
for the marriage of the *L* is come	Rev 19:7	721
unto the marriage supper of the *L*	Rev 19:9	721
of the twelve apostles of the *L*	Rev 21:14	721
the *L* are the temple of it	Rev 21:22	721
the *L* is the light thereof	Rev 21:23	721
of the throne of God and of the *L*	Rev 22:1	721
of God and of the *L* shall be in it	Rev 22:3	721

LAMB'S

shew thee the bride, the *L* wife	Rev 21:9	721
are written in the *L* book of life	Rev 21:27	721

LAMBS

Abraham set seven ewe *l* of the	Gen 21:28	3535
ewe *l* which thou hast set by	Gen 21:29	3535
For these seven ewe *l* shalt thou	Gen 21:30	3535
And Jacob did separate the *l*	Gen 30:40	3775
two *l* of the first year day by	Ex 29:38	3532
take two he *l* without blemish	Lev 14:10	3532
offer with the bread seven *l*	Lev 23:18	3532
two *l* of the first year for a	Lev 23:19	3532
before the LORD, with the two *l*	Lev 23:20	3532
goats, five *l* of the first year	Num 7:17	3532
goats, five *l* of the first year	Num 7:23	3532
goats, five *l* of the first year	Num 7:29	3532
goats, five *l* of the first year	Num 7:35	3532
goats, five *l* of the first year	Num 7:41	3532
goats, five *l* of the first year	Num 7:47	3532
goats, five *l* of the first year	Num 7:53	3532
goats, five *l* of the first year	Num 7:59	3532
goats, five *l* of the first year	Num 7:65	3532
goats, five *l* of the first year	Num 7:71	3532
goats, five *l* of the first year	Num 7:77	3532
goats, five *l* of the first year	Num 7:83	3532
the *l* of the first year twelve,	Num 7:87	3532
the *l* of the first year sixty	Num 7:88	3532
two *l* of the first year without	Num 28:3	3532
on the sabbath day two *l* of the	Num 28:9	3532
seven *l* of the first year without	Num 28:11	3532
seven *l* of the first year	Num 28:19	3532
lamb, throughout the seven *l*	Num 28:21	3532
seven *l* of the first year	Num 28:27	3532
one lamb, throughout the seven *l*	Num 28:29	3532
seven *l* of the first year without	Num 29:2	3532
one lamb, throughout the seven *l*	Num 29:4	3532
seven *l* of the first year	Num 29:8	3532
one lamb, throughout the seven *l*	Num 29:10	3532
fourteen *l* of the first year	Num 29:13	3532
to each lamb of the fourteen *l*	Num 29:15	3532
fourteen *l* of the first year	Num 29:17	3532
for the rams, and for the *l*	Num 29:18	3532
fourteen *l* of the first year	Num 29:20	3532
for the rams, and for the *l*	Num 29:21	3532
fourteen *l* of the first year	Num 29:23	3532
for the rams, and for the *l*	Num 29:24	3532
fourteen *l* of the first year	Num 29:26	3532
for the rams, and for the *l*	Num 29:27	3532
fourteen *l* of the first year	Num 29:29	3532
for the rams, and for the *l*	Num 29:30	3532
fourteen *l* of the first year	Num 29:32	3532
for the rams, and for the *l*	Num 29:33	3532
seven *l* of the first year without	Num 29:36	3532
for the ram, and for the *l*	Num 29:37	3532
and milk of sheep, with fat of *l*	Deut 32:14	3733
and of the fatlings, and the *l*	1Sa 15:9	3733
of Israel an hundred thousand *l*	2Kin 3:4	3733
a thousand rams, and a thousand *l*	1Chr 29:21	3532
and seven rams, and seven *l*	2Chr 29:21	3532
they killed also the *l*, and they	2Chr 29:22	3532
an hundred rams, and two hundred *l*	2Chr 29:32	3532
to the people, of the flock, *l*	2Chr 35:7	3532
young bullocks, and rams, and *l*	Ezr 6:9	563
two hundred rams, four hundred *l*	Ezr 6:17	563
with this money bullocks, rams, *l*	Ezr 7:17	563
and six rams, seventy and seven *l*	Ezr 8:35	3532
the LORD shall be as the fat of *l*	Ps 37:20	3733
rams, and the little hills like *l*	Ps 114:4	1121,6629
and ye little hills, like *l*	Ps 114:6	1121,6629
The *l* are for my clothing, and	Prov 27:26	3532
in the blood of bullocks, or of *l*	Is 1:11	3532
Then shall the *l* feed after their	Is 5:17	3532
fatness, and with the blood of *l*	Is 34:6	3733
shall gather the *l* with his arm	Is 40:11	2922
them down like *l* to the slaughter	Jer 51:40	3733
they occupied with thee in *l*	Eze 27:21	3733
of the earth, of rams, of *l*	Eze 39:18	3733
shall be six *l* without blemish	Eze 46:4	3532
the meat offering for the *l* as he	Eze 46:5	3532

L

bullock without blemish, and six *l* .... Eze 46:6   3532
for the *l* according as his hand .... Eze 46:7   3532
to the *l* as he is able to give, ... Eze 46:11   3532
eat the *l* out of the flock, and .... Amos 6:4   3733
send you forth as *l* among wolves .... Lk 10:3   *704*
He saith unto him, Feed my *l* .... Jn 21:15   *721*

LAME
a blind man, or a *l*, or he that .... Lev 21:18   6455
blemish therein, as if it be *l* .... Deut 15:21   6455
had a son that was *l* of his feet 2Sa 4:4   5223
flee, that he fell, and became *l* 2Sa 4:4   6452
thou take away the blind and the *l* 2Sa 5:6   6455
smiteth the Jebusites, and the *l* 2Sa 5:8   6455
the *l* shall not come into the 2Sa 5:8   6455
yet a son, which is *l* on his feet 2Sa 9:3   5223
and was *l* on both his feet 2Sa 9:13   6455
because thy servant is *l* 2Sa 19:26   6455
the blind, and feet was I to the *l* .... Job 29:15   6455
The legs of the *l* are not equal .... Prov 26:7   6455
the *l* take the prey .... Is 33:23   6455
Then shall the *l* man leap as an .... Is 35:6   6455
and with them the blind and the *l* .... Jer 31:8   6455
and if ye offer the *l* and sick, is .... Mal 1:8   6455
that which was torn, and the *l* .... Mal 1:13   6455
the *l* walk, the lepers are .... Mt 11:5   *5560*
with them those that were *l* .... Mt 15:30   *5560*
the *l* to walk, and the blind to .... Mt 15:31   *5560*
the *l* came to him in the temple .... Mt 21:14   *5560*
the *l* walk, the lepers are .... Lk 7:22   *5560*
call the poor, the maimed, the *l* .... Lk 14:13   *5560*
a certain man *l* from his mother's .... Acts 3:2   *5560*
as the *l* man which was healed .... Acts 3:11   *5560*
with palsies, and that were *l* .... Acts 8:7   *5560*
lest that which is *l* be turned .... Heb 12:13   *5560*

LAMECH (la´-mek) *A son of Methuselah.*
and Methusael begat *L* .... Gen 4:18   3929
L took unto him two wives .... Gen 4:19   3929
L said unto his wives, Adah and .... Gen 4:23   3929
ye wives of *L*, hearken unto my .... Gen 4:23   3929
truly *L* seventy and sevenfold .... Gen 4:24   3929
eighty and seven years, and begat *L* ..... Gen 5:25   3929
he begat *L* seven hundred eighty .... Gen 5:26   3929
L lived an hundred eighty and two .... Gen 5:28   3929
L lived after he begat Noah five .... Gen 5:30   3929
all the days of *L* were seven .... Gen 5:31   3929
Henoch, Methuselah, *L*, ... 1Chr 1:3   3929
of Noe, which was the son of *L* .... Lk 3:36   *2984*

LAMENT
of Israel went yearly to *l* the .... Judg 11:40   8567
And her gates shall *l* and mourn .... Is 3:26   578
angle into the brooks shall *l* .... Is 19:8   56
They shall *l* for the teats, for .... Is 32:12   5594
this gird you with sackcloth, *l* .... Jer 4:8   5594
neither go to *l* nor bemoan them .... Jer 16:5   5594
neither shall men *l* for them .... Jer 16:6   5594
They shall not *l* for him, saying, ... Jer 22:18   5594
they shall not *l* for him, saying, ... Jer 22:18   5594
and they will *l* thee, saying, Ah .... Jer 34:5   5594
l, and run to and fro by the hedges ...... Jer 49:3   5594
made the rampart and the wall to *l* ..... Lam 2:8   56
l over thee, saying, What city is .... Eze 27:32   6969
wherewith they shall *l* her .... Eze 32:16   6969
of the nations shall *l* her .... Eze 32:16   6969
they shall *l* for her, even for .... Eze 32:16   6969
L like a virgin girded with .... Joel 1:8   421
Gird yourselves, and *l*, ye priests .... Joel 1:13   5594
l with a doleful lamentation, and .... Mic 2:4   5091
unto you, That ye shall weep and *l* .... Jn 16:20   *2354*
l for her, when they shall see .... Rev 18:9   *2875*

LAMENTABLE
he cried with a *l* voice unto .... Dan 6:20   6088

LAMENTATION
with a great and very sore *l* .... Gen 50:10   4553
lamented with this *l* over Saul 2Sa 1:17   7015
and their widows made no *l* .... Ps 78:64   1058
as for an only son, most bitter *l* .... Jer 6:26   4553
take up a *l* on high places .... Jer 7:29   7015
habitations of the wilderness a *l* .... Jer 9:10   7015
and every one her neighbour *l* .... Jer 9:20   7015
A voice was heard in Ramah, *l*, ... Jer 31:15   5092
There shall be *l* generally upon .... Jer 48:38   4553
daughter of Judah mourning and *l* .... Lam 2:5   592
Moreover take thou up a *l* for the .... Eze 19:1   7015
is a *l*, and shall be for a *l* .... Eze 19:14   7015
they shall take up a *l* for thee .... Eze 26:17   7015
son of man, take up a *l* for Tyrus .... Eze 27:2   7015
they shall take up a *l* for thee .... Eze 27:32   7015
take up a *l* upon the king of .... Eze 28:12   7015

take up a *l* for Pharaoh king of .... Eze 32:2   7015
This is the *l* wherewith they .... Eze 32:16   7015
I take up against you, even a *l* .... Amos 5:1   7015
as are skilful of *l* to wailing .... Amos 5:16   5092
and all your songs into .... Amos 8:10   7015
you, and lament with a doleful *l* .... Mic 2:4   5092
Rama was there a voice heard, *l* .... Mt 2:18   *2355*
burial, and made great *l* over him .... Acts 8:2   *2870*

LAMENTATIONS
of Josiah in their *l* to this day 2Chr 35:25   7015
behold, they are written in the *l* 2Chr 35:25   7015
and there was written therein *l* .... Eze 2:10   7015

LAMENTED
and the people *l*, because the Lᴏʀᴅ 1Sa 6:19   56
house of Israel *l* after the Lᴏʀᴅ 1Sa 7:2   5091
l him, and buried him in his house 1Sa 25:1   5594
was dead, and all Israel had *l* him 1Sa 28:3   5594
David *l* with this lamentation 2Sa 1:17   6969
the king *l* over Abner, and said, ... 2Sa 3:33   6969
And Jeremiah *l* for Josiah 2Chr 35:25   6969
they shall not be *l* .... Jer 16:4   5594
they shall not be *l*, neither .... Jer 25:33   5594
unto you, and ye have not *l* .... Mt 11:17   *2875*
which also bewailed and *l* him .... Lk 23:27   *2354*

LAMP
a burning *l* that passed between .... Gen 15:17   3940
to cause the *l* to burn always .... Ex 27:20   5216
ere the *l* of God went out in the 1Sa 3:3   5216
For thou art my *l*, O Lᴏʀᴅ 2Sa 22:29   5216
his God give him a *l* in Jerusalem 1Kin 15:4   5216
to slip with his feet is as a *l* .... Job 12:5   3940
Thy word is a *l* unto my feet .... Ps 119:105   5216
ordained a *l* for mine anointed .... Ps 132:17   5216
For the commandment is a *l* .... Prov 6:23   5216
but the *l* of the wicked shall be .... Prov 13:9   5216
his *l* shall be put out in obscure .... Prov 20:20   5216
thereof as a *l* that burneth .... Is 62:1   3940
heaven, burning as it were a *l* .... Rev 8:10   *2985*

LAMPS
shalt make the seven *l* thereof .... Ex 25:37   5216
and they shall light the *l* thereof .... Ex 25:37   5216
when he dresseth the *l*, he shall .... Ex 30:7   5216
when Aaron lighteth the *l* at even .... Ex 30:8   5216
light, and his furniture, and his *l* .... Ex 35:14   5216
And he made his seven *l*, and his .... Ex 37:23   5216
candlestick, with the *l* thereof, ... Ex 39:37   5216
even with the *l* to be set in .... Ex 39:37   5216
and light the *l* thereof .... Ex 40:4   5216
he lighted the *l* before the Lᴏʀᴅ .... Ex 40:25   5216
the light, to cause the *l* to burn .... Lev 24:2   5216
He shall order the *l* upon the .... Lev 24:4   5216
of the light, and his *l*, and his .... Num 4:9   5216
him, When thou lightest the *l* .... Num 8:2   5216
the seven *l* shall give light over .... Num 8:2   5216
he lighted the *l* thereof over .... Num 8:3   5216
and *l* within the pitchers...................... Judg 7:16   3940
held the *l* in their left hands, ... Judg 7:20   3940
with the flowers, and the *l* 1Kin 7:49   5216
of gold, and for their *l* of gold 1Chr 28:15   5216
candlestick, and for the *l* thereof 1Chr 28:15   5216
and also for the *l* thereof 1Chr 28:15   5216
the candlesticks with their *l* 2Chr 4:20   5216
And the flowers, and the *l*, and the 2Chr 4:21   5216
of gold with the *l* thereof 2Chr 13:11   5216
of the porch, and put out the *l* 2Chr 29:7   5216
Out of his mouth go burning *l* .... Job 41:19   3940
fire, and like the appearance of *l* .... Eze 1:13   3940
and his eyes as *l* of fire .... Dan 10:6   3940
top of it, and his seven *l* thereon .... Zec 4:2   5216
and seven pipes to the seven *l* .... Zec 4:2   5216
ten virgins, which took their *l* .... Mt 25:1   *2985*
that were foolish took their *l* .... Mt 25:3   *2985*
oil in their vessels with their *l* .... Mt 25:4   *2985*
virgins arose, and trimmed their *l* .... Mt 25:7   *2985*
for our *l* are gone out .... Mt 25:8   *2985*
there were seven *l* of fire .... Rev 4:5   *2985*

LANCE
They shall hold the bow and the *l* .... Jer 50:42   3591

LANCETS
their manner with knives and *l* 1Kin 18:28   7420

LAND
place, and let the dry *l* appear .... Gen 1:9
And God called the dry *l* Earth .... Gen 1:10
compasseth the whole *l* of Havilah ...... Gen 2:11   776
And the gold of that *l* is good .... Gen 2:12   776
the whole *l* of Ethiopia........................ Gen 2:13   776
Lᴏʀᴅ, and dwelt in the *l* of Nod .... Gen 4:16   776

of all that was in the dry *l*	Gen 7:22	
and Calneh, in the *l* of Shinar	Gen 10:10	776
Out of that *l* went forth Asshur,	Gen 10:11	776
found a plain in the *l* of Shinar	Gen 11:2	776
Terah in the *l* of his nativity	Gen 11:28	776
to go into the *l* of Canaan	Gen 11:31	776
unto a *l* that I will shew thee	Gen 12:1	776
forth to go into the *l* of Canaan	Gen 12:5	776
into the *l* of Canaan they came	Gen 12:5	776
the *l* unto the place of Sichem	Gen 12:6	776
the Canaanite was then in the *l*	Gen 12:6	776
Unto thy seed will I give this *l*	Gen 12:7	776
And there was a famine in the *l*	Gen 12:10	776
the famine was grievous in the *l*	Gen 12:10	776
the *l* was not able to bear them,	Gen 13:6	776
Perizzite dwelled then in the *l*	Gen 13:7	776
Is not the whole *l* before thee	Gen 13:9	776
of the LORD, like the *l* of Egypt	Gen 13:10	776
Abram dwelled in the *l* of Canaan	Gen 13:12	776
For all the *l* which thou seest,	Gen 13:15	776
walk through the *l* in the length	Gen 13:17	776
to give thee this *l* to inherit it	Gen 15:7	776
in a *l* that is not theirs	Gen 15:13	776
Unto thy seed have I given this *l*	Gen 15:18	776
ten years in the *l* of Canaan	Gen 16:3	776
the *l* wherein thou art a stranger	Gen 17:8	776
all the *l* of Canaan, for an	Gen 17:8	776
and toward all the *l* of the plain	Gen 19:28	776
said, Behold, my *l* is before thee	Gen 20:15	776
him a wife out of the *l* of Egypt	Gen 21:21	776
to the *l* wherein thou hast	Gen 21:23	776
into the *l* of the Philistines	Gen 21:32	776
in the Philistines' *l* many days	Gen 21:34	776
and get thee into the *l* of Moriah	Gen 22:2	776
same is Hebron in the *l* of Canaan	Gen 23:2	776
himself to the people of the *l*	Gen 23:7	776
before the people of the *l*	Gen 23:12	776
audience of the people of the *l*	Gen 23:13	776
the *l* is worth four hundred	Gen 23:15	776
same is Hebron in the *l* of Canaan	Gen 23:19	776
willing to follow me unto this *l*	Gen 24:5	776
the *l* from whence thou camest	Gen 24:5	776
from the *l* of my kindred, and	Gen 24:7	776
Unto thy seed will I give this *l*	Gen 24:7	776
Canaanites, in whose *l* I dwell	Gen 24:37	776
And there was a famine in the *l*	Gen 26:1	776
dwell in the *l* which I shall tell	Gen 26:2	776
Sojourn in this *l*, and I will be	Gen 26:3	776
Then Isaac sowed in that *l*	Gen 26:12	776
and we shall be fruitful in the *l*	Gen 26:22	776
are of the daughters of the *l*	Gen 27:46	776
the *l* wherein thou art a stranger	Gen 28:4	776
the *l* whereon thou liest, to thee	Gen 28:13	776
will bring thee again into this *l*	Gen 28:15	127
came into the *l* of the people of	Gen 29:1	776
Return unto the *l* of thy fathers	Gen 31:3	776
arise, get thee out from this *l*	Gen 31:13	776
return unto the *l* of thy kindred	Gen 31:13	776
his father in the *l* of Canaan	Gen 31:18	776
his brother unto the *l* of Seir	Gen 32:3	776
which is in the *l* of Canaan	Gen 33:18	776
out to see the daughters of the *l*	Gen 34:1	776
the *l* shall be before you	Gen 34:10	776
therefore let them dwell in the *l*	Gen 34:21	776
for the *l*, behold, it is large	Gen 34:21	776
among the inhabitants of the *l*	Gen 34:30	776
Luz, which is in the *l* of Canaan	Gen 35:6	776
the *l* which I gave Abraham and	Gen 35:12	776
seed after thee will I give the *l*	Gen 35:12	776
pass, when Israel dwelt in that *l*	Gen 35:22	776
born unto him in the *l* of Canaan	Gen 36:5	776
he had got in the *l* of Canaan	Gen 36:6	776
the *l* wherein they were strangers	Gen 36:7	776
came of Eliphaz in the *l* of Edom	Gen 36:16	776
came of Reuel in the *l* of Edom	Gen 36:17	776
the Horite, who inhabited the *l*	Gen 36:20	776
children of Seir in the *l* of Edom	Gen 36:21	776
their dukes in the *l* of Seir	Gen 36:30	776
that reigned in the *l* of Edom	Gen 36:31	776
Husham of the *l* of Temani reigned	Gen 36:34	776
in the *l* of their possession	Gen 36:43	776
Jacob dwelt in the *l* wherein his	Gen 37:1	776
a stranger, in the *l* of Canaan	Gen 37:1	776
away out of the *l* of the Hebrews	Gen 40:15	776
in all the *l* of Egypt for badness	Gen 41:19	776
throughout all the *l* of Egypt	Gen 41:29	776
be forgotten in the *l* of Egypt	Gen 41:30	776
and the famine shall consume the *l*	Gen 41:30	776
in the *l* by reason of that famine	Gen 41:31	776
and set him over the *l* of Egypt	Gen 41:33	776
him appoint officers over the *l*	Gen 41:34	776
take up the fifth part of the *l*	Gen 41:34	776
the *l* against the seven years of	Gen 41:36	776
which shall be in the *l* of Egypt	Gen 41:36	776
that the *l* perish not through the	Gen 41:36	776
set thee over all the *l* of Egypt	Gen 41:41	776
him ruler over all the *l* of Egypt	Gen 41:43	776
or foot in all the *l* of Egypt	Gen 41:44	776
went out over all the *l* of Egypt	Gen 41:45	776
throughout all the *l* of Egypt	Gen 41:46	776
which were in the *l* of Egypt	Gen 41:48	776
in the *l* of my affliction	Gen 41:52	776
that was in the *l* of Egypt	Gen 41:53	776
but in all the *l* of Egypt there	Gen 41:54	776
when all the *l* of Egypt was	Gen 41:55	776
waxed sore in the *l* of Egypt	Gen 41:56	776
the famine was in the *l* of Canaan	Gen 42:5	776
was the governor over the *l*	Gen 42:6	776
sold to all the people of the *l*	Gen 42:6	776
From the *l* of Canaan to buy food	Gen 42:7	776
nakedness of the *l* ye are come	Gen 42:9	776
nakedness of the *l* ye are come	Gen 42:12	776
of one man in the *l* of Canaan	Gen 42:13	776
their father unto the *l* of Canaan	Gen 42:29	776
The man, who is the lord of the *l*	Gen 42:30	776
our father in the *l* of Canaan	Gen 42:32	776
and ye shall traffick in the *l*	Gen 42:34	776
And the famine was sore in the *l*	Gen 43:1	776
fruits in the *l* in your vessels	Gen 43:11	776
unto thee out of the *l* of Canaan	Gen 44:8	776
hath the famine been in the *l*	Gen 45:6	776
throughout all the *l* of Egypt	Gen 45:8	776
shalt dwell in the *l* of Goshen	Gen 45:10	776
go, get you unto the *l* of Canaan	Gen 45:17	776
you the good of the *l* of Egypt	Gen 45:18	776
and ye shall eat the fat of the *l*	Gen 45:18	776
take you wagons out of the *l* of	Gen 45:19	776
of all the *l* of Egypt is yours	Gen 45:20	776
came into the *l* of Canaan unto	Gen 45:25	776
governor over all the *l* of Egypt	Gen 45:26	776
had gotten in the *l* of Canaan	Gen 46:6	776
and Onan died in the *l* of Canaan	Gen 46:12	776
unto Joseph in the *l* of Egypt	Gen 46:20	776
and they came into the *l* of Goshen	Gen 46:28	776
which were in the *l* of Canaan	Gen 46:31	776
ye may dwell in the *l* of Goshen	Gen 46:34	776
are come out of the *l* of Canaan	Gen 47:1	776
they are in the *l* of Goshen	Gen 47:1	776
to sojourn in the *l* are we come	Gen 47:4	776
famine is sore in the *l* of Canaan	Gen 47:4	776
servants dwell in the *l* of Goshen	Gen 47:4	776
The *l* of Egypt is before thee	Gen 47:6	776
the best of the *l* make thy father	Gen 47:6	776
in the *l* of Goshen let them dwell	Gen 47:6	776
a possession in the *l* of Egypt	Gen 47:11	776
in the best of the *l*	Gen 47:11	776
in the *l* of Rameses, as Pharaoh	Gen 47:11	776
there was no bread in all the *l*	Gen 47:13	776
very sore, so that the *l* of Egypt	Gen 47:13	776
all the *l* of Canaan fainted by	Gen 47:13	776
that was found in the *l* of Egypt	Gen 47:14	776
in the *l* of Canaan, for the corn	Gen 47:14	776
money failed in the *l* of Egypt	Gen 47:15	776
in the *l* of Canaan, all the	Gen 47:15	776
thine eyes, both we and our *l*	Gen 47:19	127
our *l* for bread, and we and our	Gen 47:19	127
our *l* will be servants unto	Gen 47:19	127
that the *l* be not desolate	Gen 47:19	127
all the *l* of Egypt for Pharaoh	Gen 47:20	127
so the *l* became Pharaoh's	Gen 47:20	776
Only the *l* of the priests bought	Gen 47:22	127
this day and your *l* for Pharaoh	Gen 47:23	127
for you, and ye shall sow the *l*	Gen 47:23	127
over the *l* of Egypt unto this day	Gen 47:26	127
except the *l* of the priests only,	Gen 47:26	127
And Israel dwelt in the *l* of Egypt	Gen 47:27	776
Jacob lived in the *l* of Egypt	Gen 47:28	776
unto me at Luz in the *l* of Canaan	Gen 48:3	776
will give this *l* to thy seed	Gen 48:4	776
were born unto thee in the *l* of	Gen 48:5	776
me in the *l* of Canaan in the way	Gen 48:7	776
again unto the *l* of your fathers	Gen 48:21	776
the *l* that it was pleasant	Gen 49:15	776
in the *l* of Canaan, which Abraham	Gen 49:30	776
digged for me in the *l* of Canaan	Gen 50:5	776
all the elders of the *l* of Egypt	Gen 50:7	776
they left in the *l* of Goshen	Gen 50:8	776
And when the inhabitants of the *l*	Gen 50:11	776
carried him into the *l* of Canaan	Gen 50:13	776
bring you out of this *l* unto the	Gen 50:24	776
the *l* which he sware to Abraham	Gen 50:24	776
the *l* was filled with them	Ex 1:7	776

L

L

L

all the people of the *l* went into	2Kin 11:18	776
guard, and all the people of the *l*	2Kin 11:19	776
all the people of the *l* rejoiced	2Kin 11:20	776
of the Moabites invaded the *l* at	2Kin 13:20	776
judging the people of the *l*	2Kin 15:5	776
of Assyria came against the *l*	2Kin 15:19	776
and stayed not there in the *l*	2Kin 15:20	776
all the *l* of Naphtali, and carried	2Kin 15:29	776
of all the people of the *l*	2Kin 16:15	776
came up throughout all the *l*	2Kin 17:5	776
them up out of the *l* of Egypt	2Kin 17:7	776
own *l* to Assyria unto this day	2Kin 17:23	127
the manner of the God of the *l*	2Kin 17:26	776
the manner of the God of the *l*	2Kin 17:26	776
the manner of the God of the *l*	2Kin 17:27	776
the *l* of Egypt with great power	2Kin 17:36	776
said to me, Go up against this *l*	2Kin 18:25	776
away to a *l* like your own	2Kin 18:32	776
a *l* of corn and wine	2Kin 18:32	776
a *l* of bread and vineyards	2Kin 18:32	776
a *l* of oil olive and of honey	2Kin 18:32	776
nations delivered at all his *l*	2Kin 18:33	776
and shall return to his own *l*	2Kin 19:7	776
to fall by the sword in his own *l*	2Kin 19:7	776
escaped into the *l* of Armenia	2Kin 19:37	776
the *l* which I gave their fathers	2Kin 21:8	127
the people of the *l* slew all them	2Kin 21:24	776
the people of the *l* made Josiah	2Kin 21:24	776
that were spied in the *l* of Judah	2Kin 23:24	776
the people of the *l* took Jehoahaz	2Kin 23:30	776
at Riblah in the *l* of Hamath	2Kin 23:33	776
put the *l* to a tribute of an	2Kin 23:33	776
but he taxed the *l* to give the	2Kin 23:35	776
the gold of the people of the *l*	2Kin 23:35	776
not again any more out of his *l*	2Kin 24:7	776
sort of the people of the *l*	2Kin 24:14	776
officers, and the mighty of the *l*	2Kin 24:15	776
no bread for the people of the *l*	2Kin 25:3	776
poor of the *l* to be vinedressers	2Kin 25:12	776
mustered the people of the *l*	2Kin 25:19	776
men of the people of the *l* that	2Kin 25:19	776
them at Riblah in the *l* of Hamath	2Kin 25:21	776
was carried away out of their *l*	2Kin 25:21	127
that remained in the *l* of Judah	2Kin 25:22	776
dwell in the *l*, and serve the king	2Kin 25:24	776
the kings that reigned in the *l*	1Chr 1:43	776
Husham of the *l* of the Temanites	1Chr 1:45	776
twenty cities in the *l* of Gilead	1Chr 2:22	776
the *l* was wide, and quiet, and	1Chr 4:40	776
multiplied in the *l* of Gilead	1Chr 5:9	776
all the east *l* of Gilead	1Chr 5:10	
in the *l* of Bashan unto Salchah	1Chr 5:11	
tribe of Manasseh dwelt in the *l*	1Chr 5:23	776
the gods of the people of the *l*	1Chr 5:25	776
them Hebron in the *l* of Judah	1Chr 6:55	776
that were born in that *l* slew	1Chr 7:21	776
armour, and sent into the *l* of the	1Chr 10:9	776
were, the inhabitants of the *l*	1Chr 11:4	776
are left in all the *l* of Israel	1Chr 13:2	776
thee will I give the *l* of Canaan	1Chr 16:18	776
the *l* of the children of Ammon to	1Chr 19:2	776
to overthrow, and to spy out the *l*	1Chr 19:3	776
even the pestilence, in the *l*	1Chr 21:12	776
that were in the *l* of Israel	1Chr 22:2	776
of the *l* into mine hand	1Chr 22:18	776
the *l* is subdued before the LORD,	1Chr 22:18	776
that ye may possess this good *l*	1Chr 28:8	776
that were in the *l* of Israel	2Chr 2:17	776
forth my people out of the *l* of	2Chr 6:5	776
the *l* which thou gavest to them	2Chr 6:25	127
and send rain upon thy *l*, which	2Chr 6:27	776
If there be dearth in the *l*	2Chr 6:28	776
them in the cities of their *l*	2Chr 6:28	776
the *l* which thou gavest unto our	2Chr 6:31	127
captives unto a *l* far off or near	2Chr 6:36	776
in the *l* whither they are carried	2Chr 6:37	776
thee in the *l* of their captivity	2Chr 6:37	776
soul in the *l* of their captivity	2Chr 6:38	776
captives, and pray toward their *l*	2Chr 6:38	776
the locusts to devour the *l*	2Chr 7:13	776
their sin, and will heal their *l*	2Chr 7:14	776
of my *l* which I have given them	2Chr 7:20	127
the LORD done thus unto this *l*	2Chr 7:21	776
them forth out of the *l* of Egypt	2Chr 7:22	776
all the *l* of his dominion	2Chr 8:6	776
who were left after them in the *l*	2Chr 8:8	776
at the sea side in the *l* of Edom	2Chr 8:17	776
heard in mine own *l* of thine acts	2Chr 9:5	776
seen before in the *l* of Judah	2Chr 9:11	776
turned, and went away to her own *l*	2Chr 9:12	776
unto the *l* of the Philistines	2Chr 9:26	776

In his days the *l* was quiet ten	2Chr 14:1	776
for the *l* had rest, and he had no	2Chr 14:6	776
while the *l* is yet before us	2Chr 14:7	776
idols out of all the *l* of Judah	2Chr 15:8	776
set garrisons in the *l* of Judah	2Chr 17:2	776
away the groves out of the *l*	2Chr 19:3	776
he set judges in the *l* throughout	2Chr 19:5	776
this *l* before thy people Israel	2Chr 20:7	776
they came out of the *l* of Egypt	2Chr 20:10	776
and Athaliah reigned over the *l*	2Chr 22:12	776
all the people of the *l* rejoiced	2Chr 23:13	776
and all the people of the *l*	2Chr 23:20	776
all the people of the *l* rejoiced	2Chr 23:21	776
judging the people of the *l*	2Chr 26:21	776
they shall come again into this *l*	2Chr 30:9	776
that came out of the *l* of Israel	2Chr 30:25	776
ran through the midst of the *l*	2Chr 32:4	776
with shame of face to his own *l*	2Chr 32:21	776
the wonder that was done in the *l*	2Chr 32:31	776
foot of Israel from out of the *l*	2Chr 33:8	127
But the people of the *l* slew all	2Chr 33:25	776
the people of the *l* made Josiah	2Chr 33:25	776
throughout all the *l* of Israel	2Chr 34:7	776
reign, when he had purged the *l*	2Chr 34:8	776
Then the people of the *l* took	2Chr 36:1	776
condemned the *l* in an hundred	2Chr 36:3	776
until the *l* had enjoyed her	2Chr 36:21	776
Then the people of the *l* weakened	Ezr 4:4	776
of the heathen of the *l*, to seek	Ezr 6:21	776
the prophets, saying, The *l*	Ezr 9:11	776
it, is an unclean *l* with the	Ezr 9:11	776
strong, and eat the good of the *l*	Ezr 9:12	776
wives of the people of the *l*	Ezr 10:2	776
from the people of the *l*, and from	Ezr 10:11	776
for a prey in the *l* of captivity	Neh 4:4	776
their governor in the *l* of Judah	Neh 5:14	776
wall, neither bought we any *l*	Neh 5:16	7704
to give the *l* of the Canaanites	Neh 9:8	776
and on all the people of his *l*	Neh 9:10	776
the midst of the sea on the dry *l*	Neh 9:11	
should go in to possess the *l*	Neh 9:15	776
so they possessed the *l* of Sihon	Neh 9:22	776
the *l* of the king of Heshbon, and	Neh 9:22	776
the *l* of Og king of Bashan	Neh 9:22	776
and broughtest them into the *l*	Neh 9:23	776
went in and possessed the *l*	Neh 9:24	776
them the inhabitants of the *l*	Neh 9:24	776
kings, and the people of the *l*	Neh 9:24	776
took strong cities, and a fat *l*	Neh 9:25	127
fat *l* which thou gavest before	Neh 9:35	776
for the *l* that thou gavest unto	Neh 9:36	776
unto the people of the *l*, nor	Neh 10:30	776
if the people of the *l* bring ware	Neh 10:31	776
the people of the *l* became Jews	Est 8:17	776
laid a tribute upon the *l*	Est 10:1	776
There was a man in the *l* of Uz	Job 1:1	776
substance is increased in the *l*	Job 1:10	776
return, even to the *l* of darkness	Job 10:21	776
A *l* of darkness, as darkness	Job 10:22	776
it found in the *l* of the living	Job 28:13	776
If my *l* cry against me, or that	Job 31:38	127
for correction, or for his *l*	Job 37:13	776
the barren *l* his dwellings	Job 39:6	
in all the *l* were no women found	Job 42:15	776
heathen are perished out of his *l*	Ps 10:16	776
the LORD in the *l* of the living	Ps 27:13	776
them that are quiet in the *l*	Ps 35:20	776
so shalt thou dwell in the *l*	Ps 37:3	776
The righteous shall inherit the *l*	Ps 37:29	776
shall exalt thee to inherit the *l*	Ps 37:34	776
thee from the *l* of Jordan	Ps 42:6	776
For they got not the *l* in	Ps 44:3	776
thee out of the *l* of the living	Ps 52:5	776
for thee in a dry and thirsty *l*	Ps 63:1	776
He turned the sea into dry *l*	Ps 66:6	776
the rebellious dwell in a dry *l*	Ps 68:6	
the synagogues of God in the *l*	Ps 74:8	776
in the *l* of Egypt, in the field	Ps 78:12	776
deep root, and it filled the *l*	Ps 80:9	776
went out through the *l* of Egypt	Ps 81:5	776
thee out of the *l* of Egypt	Ps 81:10	776
hast been favourable unto thy *l*	Ps 85:1	776
that glory may dwell in our *l*	Ps 85:9	776
our *l* shall yield her increase	Ps 85:12	776
in the *l* of forgetfulness	Ps 88:12	776
and his hands formed the dry *l*	Ps 95:5	
be upon the faithful of the *l*	Ps 101:6	776
destroy all the wicked of the *l*	Ps 101:8	776
thee will I give the *l* of Canaan	Ps 105:11	776
he called for a famine upon the *l*	Ps 105:16	776
Jacob sojourned in the *l* of Ham	Ps 105:23	776

L

and against the *l* of Israel	Eze 25:3	127
despite against the *l* of Israel	Eze 25:6	127
set glory in the *l* of the living	Eze 26:20	776
the *l* of Israel, they were thy	Eze 27:17	776
they shall stand upon the *l*	Eze 27:29	776
then shall they dwell in their *l*	Eze 28:25	127
the *l* of Egypt shall be desolate	Eze 29:9	776
I will make the *l* of Egypt	Eze 29:10	776
I will make the *l* of Egypt	Eze 29:12	776
to return into the *l* of Pathros	Eze 29:14	776
into the *l* of their habitation	Eze 29:14	776
I will give the *l* of Egypt unto	Eze 29:19	776
I have given him the *l* of Egypt	Eze 29:20	776
the men of the *l* that is in	Eze 30:5	776
shall be brought to destroy the *l*	Eze 30:11	776
fill the *l* with the slain	Eze 30:11	776
sell the *l* into the hand of the	Eze 30:12	776
and I will make the *l* waste	Eze 30:12	776
more a prince of the *l* of Egypt	Eze 30:13	776
will put a fear in the *l* of Egypt	Eze 30:13	776
it out upon the *l* of Egypt	Eze 30:25	776
broken by all the rivers of the *l*	Eze 31:12	776
Then will I leave thee upon the *l*	Eze 32:4	776
blood the *l* wherein thou swimmest	Eze 32:6	776
thee, and set darkness upon thy *l*	Eze 32:8	776
make the *l* of Egypt desolate	Eze 32:15	776
terror in the *l* of the living	Eze 32:23	776
terror in the *l* of the living	Eze 32:24	776
was caused in the *l* of the living	Eze 32:25	776
terror in the *l* of the living	Eze 32:26	776
the mighty in the *l* of the living	Eze 32:27	776
my terror in the *l* of the living	Eze 32:32	776
When I bring the sword upon a *l*	Eze 33:2	776
if the people of the *l* take a man	Eze 33:2	776
seeth the sword come upon the *l*	Eze 33:3	776
wastes of the *l* of Israel speak	Eze 33:24	127
was one, and he inherited the *l*	Eze 33:24	776
the *l* is given us for inheritance	Eze 33:24	776
and shall ye possess the *l*	Eze 33:25	776
and shall ye possess the *l*	Eze 33:26	776
I will lay the *l* most desolate	Eze 33:28	776
when I have laid the *l* most	Eze 33:29	776
and will bring them to their own *l*	Eze 34:13	127
evil beasts to cease out of the *l*	Eze 34:25	776
and they shall be safe in their *l*	Eze 34:27	127
the beast of the *l* devour them	Eze 34:28	776
consumed with hunger in the *l*	Eze 34:29	776
which have appointed my *l* into	Eze 36:5	776
concerning the *l* of Israel	Eze 36:6	127
Thou *l* devourest up men, and hast	Eze 36:13	776
of Israel dwelt in their own *l*	Eze 36:17	127
that they had shed upon the *l*	Eze 36:18	776
and are gone forth out of his *l*	Eze 36:20	776
and will bring you into your own *l*	Eze 36:24	127
ye shall dwell in the *l* that I	Eze 36:28	776
the desolate *l* shall be tilled,	Eze 36:34	776
This *l* that was desolate is	Eze 36:35	776
and bring you into the *l* of Israel	Eze 37:12	127
I shall place you in your own *l*	Eze 37:14	127
and bring them into their own *l*	Eze 37:21	127
make them one nation in the *t*	Eze 37:22	776
they shall dwell in the *l* that I	Eze 37:25	776
the *l* of Magog, the chief prince	Eze 38:2	776
l that is brought back from the	Eze 38:8	776
be like a cloud to cover the *l*	Eze 38:9	776
I will go up to the *l* of unwalled	Eze 38:11	776
that dwell in the midst of the *l*	Eze 38:12	776
Israel, as a cloud to cover the *l*	Eze 38:16	776
and I will bring thee against my *l*	Eze 38:16	776
come against the *l* of Israel	Eze 38:18	127
great shaking in the *l* of Israel	Eze 38:19	127
them, that they may cleanse the *l*	Eze 39:12	776
people of the *l* shall bury them	Eze 39:13	776
passing through the *l* to bury	Eze 39:14	776
that pass through the *l*, when any	Eze 39:15	776
Thus shall they cleanse the *l*	Eze 39:16	776
when they dwelt safely in their *l*	Eze 39:26	127
gathered them unto their own *l*	Eze 39:28	127
he me into the *l* of Israel	Eze 40:2	776
by lot the *l* for inheritance	Eze 45:1	776
LORD, an holy portion of the *l*	Eze 45:1	776
The holy portion of the *l* shall	Eze 45:4	776
In the *l* shall be his possession	Eze 45:8	776
the rest of the *l* shall they give	Eze 45:8	776
All the people of the *l* shall	Eze 45:16	776
for all the people of the *l* a	Eze 45:22	776
Likewise the people of the *l*	Eze 46:3	776
But when the people of the *l*	Eze 46:9	776
whereby ye shall inherit the *l*	Eze 47:13	776
this *l* shall fall unto you for	Eze 47:14	776
of the *l* toward the north side	Eze 47:15	776
from the *l* of Israel by Jordan,	Eze 47:18	776
So shall ye divide this *l* unto	Eze 47:21	776
this oblation of the *l* that is	Eze 48:12	776
alienate the firstfruits of the *l*	Eze 48:14	776
This is the *l* which ye shall	Eze 48:29	776
which he carried into the *l* of	Dan 1:2	776
east, and toward the pleasant *l*	Dan 8:9	
and to all the people of the *l*	Dan 9:6	776
the *l* of Egypt with a mighty hand	Dan 9:15	776
and shall return into his own *l*	Dan 11:9	127
he shall stand in the glorious *l*	Dan 11:16	776
face toward the fort of his own *l*	Dan 11:19	776
into his *l* with great riches	Dan 11:28	776
exploits, and return to his own *l*	Dan 11:28	776
and shall divide the *l* for gain	Dan 11:39	127
enter also into the glorious *l*	Dan 11:41	776
the *l* of Egypt shall not escape	Dan 11:42	776
for the *l* hath committed great	Hos 1:2	776
they shall come up out of the *l*	Hos 1:11	776
and set her like a dry *l*, and slay	Hos 2:3	776
she came up out of the *l* of Egypt	Hos 2:15	776
with the inhabitants of the *l*	Hos 4:1	776
nor knowledge of God in the *l*	Hos 4:1	776
Therefore shall the *l* mourn	Hos 4:3	776
their derision in the *l* of Egypt	Hos 7:16	776
shall not dwell in the LORD's *l*	Hos 9:3	776
to the goodness of his *l* they	Hos 10:1	776
not return into the *l* of Egypt	Hos 11:5	776
as a dove out of the *l* of Assyria	Hos 11:11	776
am the LORD thy God from the *l* of	Hos 12:9	776
LORD thy God from the *l* of Egypt	Hos 13:4	776
in the *l* of great drought	Hos 13:5	776
ear, all ye inhabitants of the *l*	Joel 1:2	776
For a nation is come up upon my *l*	Joel 1:6	776
field is wasted, the *l* mourneth	Joel 1:10	127
all the inhabitants of the *l* into	Joel 1:14	776
the inhabitants of the *l* tremble	Joel 2:1	776
the *l* is as the garden of Eden	Joel 2:3	776
the LORD be jealous for his *l*	Joel 2:18	776
and will drive him into a *l* barren	Joel 2:20	776
Fear not, O *l*	Joel 2:21	127
among the nations, and parted my *l*	Joel 3:2	776
shed innocent blood in their *l*	Joel 3:19	776
you up from the *l* of Egypt	Amos 2:10	776
to possess the *l* of the Amorite	Amos 2:10	776
I brought up from the *l* of Egypt	Amos 3:1	776
in the palaces in the *l* of Egypt	Amos 3:9	776
shall be even round about the *l*	Amos 3:11	776
she is forsaken upon her *l*	Amos 5:2	127
end of eating the grass of the *l*	Amos 7:2	776
the *l* is not able to bear all his	Amos 7:10	776
away captive out of their own *l*	Amos 7:11	127
thee away into the *l* of Judah	Amos 7:12	776
thy *l* shall be divided by line	Amos 7:17	127
and thou shalt die in a polluted *l*	Amos 7:17	127
go into captivity forth of his *l*	Amos 7:17	127
to make the poor of the *l* to fail	Amos 8:4	776
Shall not the *l* tremble for this,	Amos 8:8	776
I will send a famine in the *l*	Amos 8:11	776
hosts is he that toucheth the *l*	Amos 9:5	776
up Israel out of the *l* of Egypt	Amos 9:7	776
And I will plant them upon their *l*	Amos 9:15	127
their *l* which I have given them	Amos 9:15	127
hath made the sea and the dry *l*	Jonah 1:9	
rowed hard to bring it to the *l*	Jonah 1:13	3004
vomited out Jonah upon the dry *l*	Jonah 2:10	
Assyrian shall come into our *l*	Mic 5:5	776
they shall waste the *l* of Assyria	Mic 5:6	776
the *l* of Nimrod in the entrances	Mic 5:6	776
when he cometh into our *l*	Mic 5:6	776
will cut off the cities of thy *l*	Mic 5:11	776
thee up out of the *l* of Egypt	Mic 6:4	776
Notwithstanding the *l* shall be	Mic 7:13	776
l of Egypt will I shew unto him	Mic 7:15	776
the gates of thy *l* shall be set	Nah 3:13	776
through the breadth of the *l*	Hab 1:6	776
and for the violence of the *l*	Hab 2:8	776
and for the violence of the *l*	Hab 2:17	776
the curtains of the *l* of Midian	Hab 3:7	776
through the *l* in indignation	Hab 3:12	776
consume all things from off the *l*	Zeph 1:2	127
I will cut off man from off the *l*	Zeph 1:3	127
but the whole *l* shall be devoured	Zeph 1:18	776
of all them that dwell in the *l*	Zeph 1:18	776
the *l* of the Philistines, I will	Zeph 2:5	776
fame in every *l* where they have	Zeph 3:19	776
I called for a drought upon the *l*	Hag 1:11	776
be strong, all ye people of the *l*	Hag 2:4	776
earth, and the sea, and the dry *l*	Hag 2:6	
over the *l* of Judah to scatter it	Zec 1:21	776
and flee from the *l* of the north	Zec 2:6	776

Judah his portion in the holy *l*	Zec 2:12	127
the iniquity of that *l* in one day	Zec 3:9	776
it an house in the *l* of Shinar	Zec 5:11	776
unto all the people of the *l*	Zec 7:5	776
Thus the *l* was desolate after	Zec 7:14	776
they laid the pleasant *l* desolate	Zec 7:14	776
of the LORD in the *l* of Hadrach	Zec 9:1	776
lifted up as an ensign upon his *l*	Zec 9:16	127
again also out of the *l* of Egypt	Zec 10:10	776
bring them into the *l* of Gilead	Zec 10:10	776
pity the inhabitants of the *l*	Zec 11:6	776
and they shall smite the *l*	Zec 11:6	776
will raise up a shepherd in the *l*	Zec 11:16	776
the *l* shall mourn, every family	Zec 12:12	776
names of the idols out of the *l*	Zec 13:2	776
spirit to pass out of the *l*	Zec 13:2	776
come to pass, that in all the *l*	Zec 13:8	776
All the *l* shall be turned as a	Zec 14:10	776
for ye shall be a delightsome *l*	Mal 3:12	776
in the *l* of Juda, art not the	Mt 2:6	1093
and go into the *l* of Israel	Mt 2:20	1093
and came into the *l* of Israel	Mt 2:21	1093
The *l* of Zabulon	Mt 4:15	1093
the *l* of Nephthalim, by the way	Mt 4:15	1093
went abroad into all that *l*	Mt 9:26	1093
more tolerable for the *l* of Sodom	Mt 10:15	1093
***l* of Sodom in the day of judgment**	Mt 11:24	1093
came into the *l* of Gennesaret	Mt 14:34	1093
***l* to make one proselyte, and when**	Mt 23:15	3584
all the *l* unto the ninth hour	Mt 27:45	1093
out unto him all the *l* of Judaea	Mk 1:5	5561
multitude was by the sea on the *l*	Mk 4:1	1093
of the sea, and he alone on the *l*	Mk 6:47	1093
came into the *l* of Gennesaret	Mk 6:53	1093
the whole *l* until the ninth hour	Mk 15:33	1093
famine was throughout all the *l*	Lk 4:25	1093
thrust out a little from the *l*	Lk 5:3	1093
they had brought their ships to *l*	Lk 5:11	1093
And when he went forth to *l*	Lk 8:27	1093
It is neither fit for the *l*	Lk 14:35	1093
arose a mighty famine in that *l*	Lk 15:14	5561
shall be great distress in the *l*	Lk 21:23	1093
disciples into the *l* of Judaea	Jn 3:22	1093
was at the *l* whither they went	Jn 6:21	1093
(for they were not far from *l*	Jn 21:8	1093
soon then as they were come to *l*	Jn 21:9	1093
drew the net to *l* full of great	Jn 21:11	1093
Having *l*, sold it, and brought the	Acts 4:37	68
back part of the price of the *l*	Acts 5:3	5564
whether ye sold the *l* for so much	Acts 5:8	5564
come into the *l* which I shall	Acts 7:3	1093
he out of the *l* of the Chaldaeans	Acts 7:4	1093
dead, he removed him into this *l*	Acts 7:4	1093
should sojourn in a strange *l*	Acts 7:6	1093
a dearth over all the *l* of Egypt	Acts 7:11	1093
was a stranger in the *l* of Madian	Acts 7:29	1093
and signs in the *l* of Egypt	Acts 7:36	1093
brought us out of the *l* of Egypt	Acts 7:40	1093
he did both in the *l* of the Jews	Acts 10:39	5561
as strangers in the *l* of Egypt	Acts 13:17	1093
seven nations in the *l* of Chanaan	Acts 13:19	1093
he divided their *l* to them by lot	Acts 13:19	1093
it was day, they knew not the *l*	Acts 27:39	1093
first into the sea, and get to *l*	Acts 27:43	1093
that they escaped all safe to *l*	Acts 27:44	1093
lead them out of the *l* of Egypt	Heb 8:9	1093
he sojourned in the *l* of promise	Heb 11:9	1093
through the Red sea as by dry *l*	Heb 11:29	1093
the people out of the *l* of Egypt	Jude 5	1093

LANDED

And when he had *l* at Caesarea	Acts 18:22	2718
sailed into Syria, and *l* at Tyre	Acts 21:3	2609

LANDING

l at Syracuse, we tarried there	Acts 28:12	2609

LANDMARK

not remove thy neighbour's *l*	Deut 19:14	1366
that removeth his neighbour's *l*	Deut 27:17	1366
Remove not the ancient *l*, which	Prov 22:28	1366
Remove not the old *l*	Prov 23:10	1366

LANDMARKS

Some remove the *l*	Job 24:2	1367

LANDS

the Gentiles divided in their *l*	Gen 10:5	776
after their tongues, in their *l*	Gen 10:31	776
and the dearth was in all *l*	Gen 41:54	776
the famine was so sore in all *l*	Gen 41:57	776
my lord, but our bodies, and our *l*	Gen 47:18	127
wherefore they sold not their *l*	Gen 47:22	127

hearts in the *l* of their enemies	Lev 26:36	776
their iniquity in your enemies' *l*	Lev 26:39	776
restore those *l* again peaceably	Judg 11:13	
of Assyria have done to all *l*	2Kin 19:11	776
destroyed the nations and their *l*	2Kin 19:17	776
fame of David went out into all *l*	1Chr 14:17	776
out of Egypt, and out of all *l*	2Chr 9:28	776
manner of the nations of other *l*	2Chr 13:9	776
the *l* that were round about Judah	2Chr 17:10	776
unto all the people of other *l*	2Chr 32:13	776
gods of the nations of those *l*	2Chr 32:13	776
deliver their *l* out of mine hand	2Chr 32:13	776
gods of the nations of other *l*	2Chr 32:17	776
from the people of the *l*, doing	Ezr 9:1	776
with the people of those *l*	Ezr 9:2	776
the hand of the kings of the *l*	Ezr 9:7	776
filthiness of the people of the *l*	Ezr 9:11	776
said, We have mortgaged our *l*	Neh 5:3	7704
tribute, and that upon our *l*	Neh 5:4	7704
for other men have our *l* and	Neh 5:5	7704
to them, even this day, their *l*	Neh 5:11	7704
the hand of the people of the *l*	Neh 9:30	776
of the *l* unto the law of God	Neh 10:28	776
they call their *l* after their own	Ps 49:11	127
a joyful noise unto God, all ye *l*	Ps 66:1	776
noise unto the LORD, all ye *l*	Ps 100:1	776
gave them the *l* of the heathen	Ps 105:44	776
and to scatter them in the *l*	Ps 106:27	776
And gathered them out of the *l*	Ps 107:3	776
among all the gods of these *l*	Is 36:20	776
all *l* by destroying them utterly	Is 37:11	776
from all the *l* whither he had	Jer 16:15	776
now have I given all these *l* into	Jer 27:6	776
which is the glory of all *l*	Eze 20:6	776
which is the glory of all *l*	Eze 20:15	776
them out of their enemies' *l*	Eze 39:27	776
or wife, or children, or *l*	Mt 19:29	68
or wife, or children, or *l*	Mk 10:29	68
and mothers, and children, and *l*	Mk 10:30	68
of *l* or houses sold them, and	Acts 4:34	5564

LANES

l of the city, and bring in hither	Lk 14:21	4505

LANGUAGE

And the whole earth was of one *l*	Gen 11:1	8193
is one, and they have all one *l*	Gen 11:6	8193
down, and there confound their *l*	Gen 11:7	8193
confound the *l* of all the earth	Gen 11:9	8193
to thy servants in the Syrian *l*	2Kin 18:26	
talk not with us in the Jews' *l*	2Kin 18:26	
with a loud voice in the Jews' *l*	2Kin 18:28	
and could not speak in the Jews' *l*	Neh 13:24	
according to the *l* of each people	Neh 13:24	
and to every people after their *l*	Est 1:22	3956
to the *l* of every people	Est 1:22	3956
and to every people after their *l*	Est 3:12	3956
unto every people after their *l*	Est 8:9	3956
writing, and according to their *l*	Est 8:9	3956
There is no speech nor *l*, where	Ps 19:3	1697
where I heard a *l* that I	Ps 81:5	8193
Jacob from a people of strange *l*	Ps 114:1	3937
of Egypt speak the *l* of Canaan	Is 19:18	8193
unto thy servants in the Syrian *l*	Is 36:11	
and speak not to us in the Jews' *l*	Is 36:11	
with a loud voice in the Jews' *l*	Is 36:13	
a nation whose *l* thou knowest not	Jer 5:15	3956
a strange speech and of an hard *l*	Eze 3:5	3956
a strange speech and of an hard *l*	Eze 3:6	3956
That every people, nation, and *l*	Dan 3:29	3961
I turn to the people a pure *l*	Zeph 3:9	8193
man heard them speak in his own *l*	Acts 2:6	1258

LANGUAGES

O people, nations, and *l*,	Dan 3:4	3961
the people, the nations, and the *l*	Dan 3:7	3961
unto all people, nations, and *l*	Dan 4:1	3961
him, all people, nations, and *l*	Dan 5:19	3961
unto all people, nations, and *l*	Dan 6:25	3961
that all people, nations, and *l*	Dan 7:14	3961
hold out of all *l* of the nations	Zec 8:23	3956

LANGUISH

For the fields of Heshbon *l*	Is 16:8	535
nets upon the waters shall *l*	Is 19:8	535
haughty people of the earth do *l*	Is 24:4	535
mourneth, and the gates thereof *l*	Jer 14:2	535
one that dwelleth therein shall *l*	Hos 4:3	535

LANGUISHED

they *l* together	Lam 2:8	535

LANGUISHETH
and fadeth away, the world *l* .... Is 24:4 — 535
The new wine mourneth, the vine *l* .... Is 24:7 — 535
The earth mourneth and *l* .... Is 33:9 — 535
She that hath borne seven *l* .... Jer 15:9 — 535
new wine is dried up, the oil *l* .... Joel 1:10 — 535
is dried up, and the fig tree *l* .... Joel 1:12 — 535
Bashan *l*, and Carmel .... Nah 1:4 — 535
and the flower of Lebanon *l* .... Nah 1:4 — 535

LANGUISHING
strengthen him upon the bed of *l* .... Ps 41:3 — 1741

LANTERNS
Pharisees, cometh thither with *l* .... Jn 18:3 — 5322

LAODICEA (*la-od-i-se'-ah*) *Chief city of Phrygia.*
I have for you, and for them at *L* .... Col 2:1 — 2993
for you, and them that are in *L* .... Col 4:13 — 2993
the brethren which are in *L* .... Col 4:15 — 2993
likewise read the epistle from *L* .... Col 4:16 — 2993
to Timothy was written from *L* .... 1Ti *s*
and unto Philadelphia, and unto *L* .... Rev 1:11 — 2993

LAODICEANS (*la-od-i-se'-uns*) *Inhabitants of Laodicea.*
read also in the church of the *L* .... Col 4:16 — 2994
of the church of the *L* write .... Rev 3:14 — 2994

LAP
thereof wild gourds his *l* full .... 2Kin 4:39 — 899
Also I shook my *l*, and said, So .... Neh 5:13 — 2684
The lot is cast into the *l* .... Prov 16:33 — 2436

LAPIDOTH (*lap'-i-doth*) *Husband of Deborah.*
a prophetess, the wife of *L* .... Judg 4:4 — 3941

LAPPED
And the number of them that *l* .... Judg 7:6 — 3952
men that *l* will I save you .... Judg 7:7 — 3952

LAPPETH
Every one that *l* of the water .... Judg 7:5 — 3952
water with his tongue, as a dog *l* .... Judg 7:5 — 3952

LAPPIDOTH See LAPIDOTH.

LAPWING
heron after her kind, and the *l* .... Lev 11:19 — 1744
heron after her kind, and the *l* .... Deut 14:18 — 1744

LARGE See APPENDIX.

LARGENESS See APPENDIX.

LASCIVIOUSNESS
wickedness, deceit, *l*, an evil .... Mk 7:22 — 766
l which they have committed .... 2Cor 12:21 — 766
fornication, uncleanness, *l* .... Gal 5:19 — 766
have given themselves over unto *l* .... Eph 4:19 — 766
the Gentiles, when we walked in *l* .... 1Pet 4:3 — 766
the grace of our God into *l* .... Jude 4 — 766

LASEA (*la-se'-ah*) *A city on Crete.*
nigh whereunto was the city of *L* .... Acts 27:8 — 2996

LASHA (*la'-shah*) *A place in southern Canaan.*
and Admah, and Zeboim, even unto *L* ... Gen 10:19 — 3962

LASHARON (*lash'-ar-on*) *A Canaanite town.*
the king of *L*, one .... Josh 12:18 — 8289

LAST
shall befall you in the *l* days .... Gen 49:1 — 319
but he shall overcome at the *l* .... Gen 49:19 — 6119
and let my *l* end be like his .... Num 23:10 — 319
Why are ye the *l* to bring the .... 2Sa 19:11 — 314
ye the *l* to bring back the king .... 2Sa 19:12 — 314
Now these be the *l* words of David .... 2Sa 23:1 — 314
For by the *l* words of David the .... 1Chr 23:27 — 314
of David the king, first and *l* .... 1Chr 29:29 — 314
the acts of Solomon, first and *l* .... 2Chr 9:29 — 314
the acts of Rehoboam, first and *l* .... 2Chr 12:15 — 314
the acts of Asa, first and *l* .... 2Chr 16:11 — 314
acts of Jehoshaphat, first and *l* .... 2Chr 20:34 — 314
the acts of Amaziah, first and *l* .... 2Chr 25:26 — 314
of the acts of Uzziah, first and *l* .... 2Chr 26:22 — 314
and of all his ways, first and *l* .... 2Chr 28:26 — 314
And his deeds, first and *l*, behold, ... 2Chr 35:27 — 314
of the *l* sons of Adonikam, whose .... Ezr 8:13 — 314
from the first day unto the *l* day .... Neh 8:18 — 314
And thou mourn at the *l*, when thy .... Prov 5:11 — 319
At the *l* it biteth like a serpent .... Prov 23:32 — 319
shall come to pass in the *l* days .... Is 2:2 — 319
LORD, the first, and with the *l* .... Is 41:4 — 314
I am the first, and I am the *l* .... Is 44:6 — 314
I am the first, I also am the *l* .... Is 48:12 — 314
said, He shall not see our *l* end .... Jer 12:4 — 319
l this Nebuchadrezzar king of .... Jer 50:17 — 314
she remembereth not her *l* end .... Lam 1:9 — 319
But at the *l* Daniel came in .... Dan 4:8 — 318

other, and the higher came up *l* .... Dan 8:3 — 314
in the *l* end of the indignation .... Dan 8:19 — 319
I will slay the *l* of them with .... Amos 9:1 — 319
But in the *l* days it shall come .... Mic 4:1 — 319
the *l* state of that man is worse .... Mt 12:45 — 2078
many that are first shall be *l* .... Mt 19:30 — 2078
and the *l* shall be first .... Mt 19:30 — 2078
from the *l* unto the first .... Mt 20:8 — 2078
These *l* have wrought but one hour .... Mt 20:12 — 2078
I will give unto this *l*, even as .... Mt 20:14 — 2078
So the *l* shall be first .... Mt 20:16 — 2078
shall be first, and the first *l* .... Mt 20:16 — 2078
But *l* of all he sent unto them .... Mt 21:37 — 5305
l of all the woman died also .... Mt 22:27 — 5305
At the *l* came two false witnesses .... Mt 26:60 — 5305
so the *l* error shall be worse .... Mt 27:64 — 2078
first, the same shall be *l* of all .... Mk 9:35 — 2078
many that are first shall be *l* .... Mk 10:31 — 2078
and the *l* first .... Mk 10:31 — 2078
he sent him also *l* unto them .... Mk 12:6 — 2078
l of all the woman died also .... Mk 12:22 — 2078
the *l* state of that man is worse .... Lk 11:26 — 2078
thou hast paid the very *l* mite .... Lk 12:59 — 2078
there are *l* which shall be first, ... Lk 13:30 — 2078
there are first which shall be *l* .... Lk 13:30 — 2078
L of all the woman died also .... Lk 20:32 — 5305
raise it up again at the *l* day .... Jn 6:39 — 2078
I will raise him up at the *l* day .... Jn 6:40 — 2078
I will raise him up at the *l* day .... Jn 6:44 — 2078
I will raise him up at the *l* day .... Jn 6:54 — 2078
In the *l* day, that great day of .... Jn 7:37 — 2078
at the eldest, even unto the *l* .... Jn 8:9 — 2078
in the resurrection at the *l* day .... Jn 11:24 — 2078
same shall judge him in the *l* day .... Jn 12:48 — 2078
shall come to pass in the *l* days .... Acts 2:17 — 2078
hath set forth us the apostles *l* .... 1Cor 4:9 — 2078
l of all he was seen of me also, ... 1Cor 15:8 — 2078
The *l* enemy that shall be .... 1Cor 15:26 — 2078
the *l* Adam was made a quickening .... 1Cor 15:45 — 2078
of an eye, at the *l* trump .... 1Cor 15:52 — 2078
that now at the *l* your care of me .... Phil 4:10 — 4218
that in the *l* days perilous times .... 2Ti 3:1 — 2078
Hath in these *l* days spoken unto .... Heb 1:2 — 2078
treasure together for the *l* days .... Jas 5:3 — 2078
to be revealed in the *l* time .... 1Pet 1:5 — 2078
manifest in these *l* times for you .... 1Pet 1:20 — 2078
shall come in the *l* days scoffers .... 2Pet 3:3 — 2078
Little children, it is the *l* time .... 1Jn 2:18 — 2078
we know that it is the *l* time .... 1Jn 2:18 — 2078
should be mockers in the *l* time .... Jude 18 — 2078
and Omega, the first and the *l* .... Rev 1:11 — 2078
I am the first and the *l* .... Rev 1:17 — 2078
things saith the first and the *l* .... Rev 2:8 — 2078
the *l* to be more than the first .... Rev 2:19 — 2078
angels having the seven *l* plagues .... Rev 15:1 — 2078
vials full of the seven *l* plagues .... Rev 21:9 — 2078
and the end, the first and the *l* .... Rev 22:13 — 2078

LASTED
seven days, while their feast *l* .... Judg 14:17 — 1961

LASTING
precious things of the *l* hills .... Deut 33:15 — 5769

LATCHET
nor the *l* of their shoes be .... Is 5:27 — 8288
the *l* of whose shoes I am not .... Mk 1:7 — 2438
the *l* of whose shoes I am not .... Lk 3:16 — 2438
whose shoe's *l* I am not worthy to .... Jn 1:27 — 2438

LATE
you to rise up early, to sit up *l* .... Ps 127:2 — 309
Even of *l* my people is risen up .... Mic 2:8 — 865
the Jews of *l* sought to stone .... Jn 11:8 — 3568

LATELY
l come from Italy, with his wife .... Acts 18:2 — 4373

LATIN (*lat'-in*) *Language spoken by the Romans.*
him in letters of Greek, and *L* .... Lk 23:38 — 4513
written in Hebrew, and Greek, and *L* ..... Jn 19:20 — 4513

LATTER
believe the voice of the *l* sign .... Ex 4:8 — 314
do to thy people in the *l* days .... Num 24:14 — 319
but his *l* end shall be that he .... Num 24:20 — 319
upon thee, even in the *l* days .... Deut 4:30 — 319
to do thee good at thy *l* end .... Deut 8:16 — 319
the *l* rain, that thou mayest .... Deut 11:14 — 4456
if the *l* husband hate her, and .... Deut 24:3 — 314
or if the *l* husband die, which .... Deut 24:3 — 314
will befall you in the *l* days .... Deut 31:29 — 319
they would consider their *l* end .... Deut 32:29 — 319
the *l* end than at the beginning .... Ruth 3:10 — 314

L

will be bitterness in the *l* end 2Sa 2:26 314
yet thy *l* end should greatly........................Job 8:7 319
stand at the *l* day upon the earth ....Job 19:25 314
mouth wide as for the *l* rain....................Job 29:23 4456
So the LORD blessed the *l* end of............Job 42:12 319
is as a cloud of the *l* rain ....Prov 16:15 4456
thou mayest be wise in thy *l* end ....Prov 19:20 319
them, and know the *l* end of them ....Is 41:22 319
didst remember the *l* end of it ....Is 47:7 319
and there hath been no *l* rain................Jer 3:3 4456
rain, both the former and the *l* ....Jer 5:24 4456
in the *l* days ye shall consider ....Jer 23:20 319
in the *l* days ye shall consider ....Jer 30:24 319
captivity of Moab in the *l* days..............Jer 48:47 319
shall come to pass in the *l* days............Jer 49:39 319
in the *l* years thou shalt come ....Eze 38:8 319
it shall be in the *l* days ....Eze 38:16 319
what shall be in the *l* days....................Dan 2:28 320
in the *l* time of their kingdom, ...Dan 8:23 319
befall thy people in the *l* days ....Dan 10:14 319
not be as the former, or as the *l* ....Dan 11:29 314
and his goodness in the *l* days..............Hos 3:5 319
unto us as the rain, as the *l* ....Hos 6:3 4456
the *l* rain in the first month....................Joel 2:23 4456
the shooting up of the *l* growth ....Amos 7:1 3954
it was the *l* growth after the..................Amos 7:1 3954
The glory of this *l* house shall..............Hag 2:9 314
rain in the time of the *l* rain................Zec 10:1 4456
that in the *l* times some shall................1Ti 4:1 5305
he receive the early and *l* rain..............Jas 5:7 3797
the *l* end is worse with them than 2Pet 2:20 2078

LATTICE
a window, and cried through the *l*..........Judg 5:28 822
Ahaziah fell down through a *l* in............2Kin 1:2 7639
shewing himself through the *l* ....Song 2:9 2762

LAUD
and *l* him, all ye people ....Rom 15:11 *1867*

LAUGH
Abraham, Wherefore did Sarah *l* ....Gen 18:13 6711
but thou didst *l* ....Gen 18:15 6711
Sarah said, God hath made me to *l* ......Gen 21:6 6712
that all that hear will *l* with me............Gen 21:6 6711
and famine thou shalt *l*..........................Job 5:22 7832
he will *l* at the trial of the....................Job 9:23 3932
the innocent *l* them to scorn ....Job 22:19 3932
sitteth in the heavens shall *l* ....Ps 2:4 7832
they that see me *l* me to scorn..............Ps 22:7 3932
The LORD shall *l* at him ....Ps 37:13 7832
see, and fear, and shall *l* at him............Ps 52:6 7832
But thou, O LORD, shalt *l* at them ....Ps 59:8 7832
our enemies *l* among themselves ....Ps 80:6 3932
I also will *l* at your calamity ....Prov 1:26 7832
foolish man, whether he rage or *l*..........Prov 29:9 7832
A time to weep, and a time to *l*............Eccl 3:4 7832
for ye shall *l* ....Lk 6:21 *1070*
Woe unto you that *l* now ....Lk 6:25 *1070*

LAUGHED
Abraham fell upon his face, and *l* ....Gen 17:17 6711
Therefore Sarah *l* within herself............Gen 18:12 6711
Sarah denied, saying, I *l* not..................Gen 18:15 6711
despised thee, and *l* thee to scorn 2Kin 19:21 3932
but they *l* them to scorn, and 2Chr 30:10 7832
they *l* us to scorn, and despised ....Neh 2:19 3932
just upright man is *l* to scorn ....Job 12:4 7832
If I *l* on them, they believed it ....Job 29:24 7832
despised thee, and *l* thee to scorn ....Is 37:22 3932
thou shalt be *l* to scorn and had ....Eze 23:32 6712
And they *l* him to scorn ....Mt 9:24 *2606*
And they *l* him to scorn ....Mk 5:40 *2606*
they *l* him to scorn, knowing that..........Lk 8:53 *2606*

LAUGHETH
he *l* at the shaking of a spear ....Job 41:29 7832

LAUGHING
Till he fill thy mouth with *l*....................Job 8:21 7814

LAUGHTER
Then was our mouth filled with *l*............Ps 126:2 7814
Even in *l* the heart is sorrowful ....Prov 14:13 7814
I said of *l*, It is mad................................Eccl 2:2 7814
Sorrow is better than *l* ....Eccl 7:3 7814
a pot, so is the *l* of the fool ....Eccl 7:6 7814
A feast is made for *l*, and wine ....Eccl 10:19 7814
let your *l* be turned to mourning, ...Jas 4:9 *1071*

LAUNCH
L out into the deep, and let down ....Lk 5:4 *1877*

LAUNCHED
And they *l* forth ....Lk 8:22 *321*
were gotten from them, and had *l* ....Acts 21:1 *321*

into a ship of Adramyttium, we *l* ....Acts 27:2 *321*
And when we had *l* from thence ....Acts 27:4 *321*

LAVER
Thou shalt also make a *l* of brass ....Ex 30:18 3595
with all his vessels, and the *l*................Ex 30:28 3595
with all his furniture, and the *l*............Ex 31:9 3595
staves, and all his vessels, the *l* ....Ex 35:16 3595
And he made the *l* of brass ....Ex 38:8 3595
staves, and all his vessels, the *l* ....Ex 39:39 3595
thou shalt set the *l* between the............Ex 40:7 3595
And thou shalt anoint the *l* ....Ex 40:11 3595
he set the *l* between the tent of ....Ex 40:30 3595
and all his vessels, both the *l*................Lev 8:11 3595
under the *l* were undersetters 1Kin 7:30 3595
one *l* contained forty baths 1Kin 7:38 3595
and every *l* was four cubits 1Kin 7:38 3595
every one of the ten bases one *l*............1Kin 7:38 3595
removed the *l* from off them..................2Kin 16:17 3595

LAVERS
Then made he ten *l* of brass 1Kin 7:38 3595
And Hiram made the *l*, and the 1Kin 7:40 3595
ten bases, and ten *l* on the bases 1Kin 7:43 3595
He made also ten *l*, and put five............2Chr 4:6 3595
and *l* made he upon the bases 2Chr 4:14 3595

LAVISH
They *l* gold out of the bag, and ....Is 46:6 2107

LAW
son, and Sarai his daughter in *l* ....Gen 11:31 3618
son in *l*, and thy sons, and thy ....Gen 19:12 2859
out, and spake unto his sons in *l* ....Gen 19:14 2859
that mocked unto his sons in *l*..............Gen 19:14 2859
Judah to Tamar his daughter in *l* ....Gen 38:11 3618
Behold thy father in *l* goeth up ....Gen 38:13 2524
that she was his daughter in *l*................Gen 38:16 3618
Tamar thy daughter in *l* hath ....Gen 38:24 3618
she sent to her father in *l* ....Gen 38:25 2524
Joseph made it a *l* over the land............Gen 47:26 2706
flock of Jethro his father in *l* ....Ex 3:1 2859
to Jethro his father in *l*..........................Ex 4:18 2859
One *l* shall be to him that is ....Ex 12:49 8451
that the LORD's *l* may be in thy ....Ex 13:9 8451
whether they will walk in my *l*..............Ex 16:4 8451
of Midian, Moses' father in *l* ....Ex 18:1 2859
Then Jethro, Moses' father in *l* ....Ex 18:2 2859
And Jethro, Moses' father in *l* ....Ex 18:5 2859
I thy father in *l* Jethro am come ....Ex 18:6 2859
went out to meet his father in *l*............Ex 18:7 2859
Moses told his father in *l* all..................Ex 18:8 2859
And Jethro, Moses' father in *l* ....Ex 18:12 2859
Moses' father in *l* before God ....Ex 18:12 2859
when Moses' father in *l* saw all..............Ex 18:14 2859
Moses said unto his father in *l* ....Ex 18:15 2859
Moses' father in *l* said unto him ....Ex 18:17 2859
to the voice of his father in *l* ....Ex 18:24 2859
Moses let his father in *l* depart ....Ex 18:27 2859
give thee tables of stone, and a *l* ....Ex 24:12 8451
This is the *l* of the burnt ....Lev 6:9 8451
this is the *l* of the meat........................Lev 6:14 8451
This is the *l* of the sin offering ....Lev 6:25 8451
Likewise this is the *l* of the....................Lev 7:1 8451
there is one *l* for them............................Lev 7:7 8451
this is the *l* of the sacrifice of ....Lev 7:11 8451
This is the *l* of the burnt ....Lev 7:37 8451
This is the *l* of the beasts, and ....Lev 11:46 8451
This is the *l* for her that hath ....Lev 12:7 8451
This is the *l* of the plague of ....Lev 13:59 8451
This shall be the *l* of the leper ....Lev 14:2 8451
This is the *l* of him in whom is..............Lev 14:32 8451
This is the *l* for all manner of ....Lev 14:54 8451
this is the *l* of leprosy ....Lev 14:57 8451
This is the *l* of him that hath an............Lev 15:32 8451
nakedness of thy daughter in *l* ....Lev 18:15 3618
a man lie with his daughter in *l*............Lev 20:12 3618
Ye shall have one manner of *l* ....Lev 24:22 4941
This is the *l* of jealousies, when............Num 5:29 8451
shall execute upon her all this *l* ....Num 5:30 8451
this is the *l* of the Nazarite, ...Num 6:13 8451
This is the *l* of the Nazarite who ....Num 6:21 8451
do after the *l* of his separation ....Num 6:21 8451
the Midianite, Moses' father in *l* ....Num 10:29 2859
One *l* and one manner shall be for ....Num 15:16 8451
Ye shall have one *l* for him that ....Num 15:29 8451
This is the ordinance of the *l* ....Num 19:2 8451
This is the *l*, when a man dieth ....Num 19:14 8451
This is the ordinance of the *l* ....Num 31:21 8451
began Moses to declare this *l*................Deut 1:5 8451
so righteous as all this *l* ....Deut 4:8 8451
this is the *l* which Moses set ....Deut 4:44 8451
to the sentence of the *l* which ....Deut 17:11 8451

l in a book out of that which is	Deut 17:18	8451
to keep all the words of this *l*	Deut 17:19	8451
upon them all the words of this *l*	Deut 27:3	8451
the words of this *l* very plainly	Deut 27:8	8451
that lieth with his mother in *l*	Deut 27:23	2859
the words of this *l* to do them	Deut 27:26	8451
to do all the words of this *l*	Deut 28:58	8451
not written in the book of this *l*	Deut 28:61	8451
are written in this book of the *l*	Deut 29:21	8451
we may do all the words of this *l*	Deut 29:29	8451
are written in this book of the *l*	Deut 30:10	8451
And Moses wrote this *l*, and	Deut 31:9	8451
thou shalt read this *l* before all	Deut 31:11	8451
to do all the words of this *l*	Deut 31:12	8451
the words of this *l* in a book	Deut 31:24	8451
Take this book of the *l*, and put	Deut 31:26	8451
to do, all the words of this *l*	Deut 32:46	8451
hand went a fiery *l* for them	Deut 33:2	1881
Moses commanded us a *l*, even the	Deut 33:4	8451
thy judgments, and Israel thy *l*	Deut 33:10	8451
to do according to all the *l*	Josh 1:7	8451
This book of the *l* shall not	Josh 1:8	8451
in the book of the *l* of Moses	Josh 8:31	8451
stones a copy of the *l* of Moses	Josh 8:32	8451
he read all the words of the *l*	Josh 8:34	8451
is written in the book of the *l*	Josh 8:34	8451
to do the commandment and the *l*	Josh 22:5	8451
in the book of the *l* of Moses	Josh 23:6	8451
words in the book of the *l* of God	Josh 24:26	8451
of the Kenite, Moses' father in *l*	Judg 1:16	2859
of Hobab the father in *l* of Moses	Judg 4:11	2859
the son in *l* of the Timnite,	Judg 15:6	2859
And his father in *l*, the damsel's	Judg 19:4	2859
father said unto his son in *l*	Judg 19:5	2859
depart, his father in *l* urged him	Judg 19:7	2859
and his servant, his father in *l*	Judg 19:9	2859
she arose with her daughters in *l*	Ruth 1:6	3618
her two daughters in *l* with her	Ruth 1:7	3618
said unto her two daughters in *l*	Ruth 1:8	3618
and Orpah kissed her mother in *l*	Ruth 1:14	2545
thy sister in *l* is gone back unto	Ruth 1:15	2994
return thou after thy sister in *l*	Ruth 1:15	2994
the Moabitess, her daughter in *l*	Ruth 1:22	3618
in *l* since the death of thine	Ruth 2:11	2545
her mother in *l* saw what she had	Ruth 2:18	2545
And her mother in *l* said unto her	Ruth 2:19	2545
she shewed her mother in *l* with	Ruth 2:19	2545
Naomi said unto her daughter in *l*	Ruth 2:20	3618
said unto Ruth her daughter in *l*	Ruth 2:22	3618
and dwelt with her mother in *l*	Ruth 2:23	2545
her mother in *l* said unto her	Ruth 3:1	2545
all that her mother in *l* bade her	Ruth 3:6	2545
when she came to her mother in *l*	Ruth 3:16	2545
Go not empty unto thy mother in *l*	Ruth 3:17	2545
for thy daughter in *l*, which	Ruth 4:15	3618
And his daughter in *l*, Phinehas'	1Sa 4:19	3618
taken, and that her father in *l*	1Sa 4:19	2524
and because of her father in *l*	1Sa 4:21	2524
I should be son in *l* to the king	1Sa 18:18	2859
son in *l* in the one of the twain	1Sa 18:21	2860
therefore be the king's son in *l*	1Sa 18:22	2860
thing to be a king's son in *l*	1Sa 18:23	2860
well to be the king's son in *l*	1Sa 18:26	2860
he might be the king's son in *l*	1Sa 18:27	2860
which is the king's son in *l*	1Sa 22:14	2859
it is written in the *l* of Moses	1Kin 2:3	8451
the son in *l* of the house of Ahab	2Kin 8:27	2859
took no heed to walk in the *l* of	2Kin 10:31	8451
in the book of the *l* of Moses	2Kin 14:6	8451
according to all the *l* which I	2Kin 17:13	8451
their ordinances, or after the *l*	2Kin 17:34	8451
and the ordinances, and the *l*	2Kin 17:37	8451
according to all the *l* that my	2Kin 21:8	8451
of the *l* in the house of the LORD	2Kin 22:8	8451
the words of the book of the *l*	2Kin 22:11	8451
l which were written in the book	2Kin 23:24	8451
according to all the *l* of Moses	2Kin 23:25	8451
his daughter in *l* bare him Pharez	1Chr 2:4	3618
the same to Jacob for a *l*	1Chr 16:17	2706
is written in the *l* of the LORD	1Chr 16:40	8451
keep the *l* of the LORD thy God	1Chr 22:12	8451
heed to their way to walk in my *l*	2Chr 6:16	8451
he forsook the *l* of the LORD	2Chr 12:1	8451
of their fathers, and to do the *l*	2Chr 14:4	8451
a teaching priest, and without *l*	2Chr 15:3	8451
had the book of the *l* of the LORD	2Chr 17:9	8451
between blood and blood, between *l*	2Chr 19:10	8451
it is written in the *l* of Moses	2Chr 23:18	8451
in the *l* in the book of Moses	2Chr 25:4	8451
according to the *l* of Moses the	2Chr 30:16	8451
is written in the *l* of the LORD	2Chr 31:3	8451

encouraged in the *l* of the LORD	2Chr 31:4	8451
of the house of God, and in the *l*	2Chr 31:21	8451
them, according to the whole *l*	2Chr 33:8	8451
the *l* of the LORD given by Moses	2Chr 34:14	8451
of the *l* in the house of the LORD	2Chr 34:15	8451
king had heard the words of the *l*	2Chr 34:19	8451
was written in the *l* of the LORD	2Chr 35:26	8451
in the *l* of Moses the man of God	Ezr 3:2	8451
a ready scribe in the *l* of Moses	Ezr 7:6	8451
heart to seek the *l* of the LORD	Ezr 7:10	8451
a scribe of the *l* of the God of	Ezr 7:12	1882
according to the *l* of thy God	Ezr 7:14	1882
the scribe of the *l* of the God of	Ezr 7:21	1882
will not do the *l* of thy God	Ezr 7:26	1882
the *l* of the king, let judgment	Ezr 7:26	1882
let it be done according to the *l*	Ezr 10:3	8451
because he was the son in *l* of	Neh 6:18	2859
bring the book of the *l* of Moses	Neh 8:1	8451
Ezra the priest brought the *l*	Neh 8:2	8451
attentive unto the book of the *l*	Neh 8:3	8451
the people to understand the *l*	Neh 8:7	8451
book in the *l* of God distinctly	Neh 8:8	8451
they heard the words of the *l*	Neh 8:9	8451
to understand the words of the *l*	Neh 8:13	8451
they found written in the *l* which	Neh 8:14	8451
read in the book of the *l* of God	Neh 8:18	8451
read in the book of the *l* of the	Neh 9:3	8451
cast thy *l* behind their backs, and	Neh 9:26	8451
bring them again unto thy *l*	Neh 9:29	8451
nor our fathers, kept thy *l*	Neh 9:34	8451
of the lands unto the *l* of God	Neh 10:28	8451
into an oath, to walk in God's *l*	Neh 10:29	8451
God, as it is written in the *l*	Neh 10:34	8451
cattle, as it is written in the *l*	Neh 10:36	8451
portions of the *l* for the priests	Neh 12:44	8451
pass, when they had heard the *l*	Neh 13:3	8451
was son in *l* to Sanballat the	Neh 13:28	2859
drinking was according to the *l*	Est 1:8	1881
manner toward all that knew *l*	Est 1:13	1881
the queen Vashti according to *l*	Est 1:15	1881
there is one *l* of his to put him	Est 4:11	1881
which is not according to the *l*	Est 4:16	1881
the *l* from his mouth, and lay up	Job 22:22	8451
delight is in the *l* of the LORD	Ps 1:2	8451
in his *l* doth he meditate day and	Ps 1:2	8451
The *l* of the LORD is perfect,	Ps 19:7	8451
The *l* of his God is in his heart	Ps 37:31	8451
yea, thy *l* is within my heart	Ps 40:8	8451
Give ear, O my people, to my *l*	Ps 78:1	8451
Jacob, and appointed a *l* in Israel	Ps 78:5	8451
God, and refused to walk in his *l*	Ps 78:10	8451
and a *l* of the God of Jacob	Ps 81:4	4941
If his children forsake my *l*	Ps 89:30	8451
and teachest him out of thy *l*	Ps 94:12	8451
which frameth mischief by a *l*	Ps 94:20	2706
the same unto Jacob for a *l*	Ps 105:10	2706
who walk in the *l* of the LORD	Ps 119:1	8451
wondrous things out of thy *l*	Ps 119:18	8451
and grant me thy *l* graciously	Ps 119:29	8451
and I shall keep thy *l*	Ps 119:34	8451
So shall I keep thy *l* continually	Ps 119:44	8451
have I not declined from thy *l*	Ps 119:51	8451
of the wicked that forsake thy *l*	Ps 119:53	8451
in the night, and have kept thy *l*	Ps 119:55	8451
but I have not forgotten thy *l*	Ps 119:61	8451
but I delight in thy *l*	Ps 119:70	8451
The *l* of thy mouth is better unto	Ps 119:72	8451
for thy *l* is my delight	Ps 119:77	8451
for me, which are not after thy *l*	Ps 119:85	8451
Unless thy *l* had been my delights	Ps 119:92	8451
O how love I thy *l*	Ps 119:97	8451
yet do I not forget thy *l*	Ps 119:109	8451
but thy *l* do I love	Ps 119:113	8451
for they have made void thy *l*	Ps 119:126	8451
eyes, because they keep not thy *l*	Ps 119:136	8451
and thy *l* is the truth	Ps 119:142	8451
they are far from thy *l*	Ps 119:150	8451
for I do not forget thy *l*	Ps 119:153	8451
but thy *l* do I love	Ps 119:163	8451
peace have they which love thy *l*	Ps 119:165	8451
and thy *l* is my delight	Ps 119:174	8451
forsake not the *l* of thy mother	Prov 1:8	8451
My son, forget not my *l*	Prov 3:1	8451
doctrine, forsake ye not my *l*	Prov 4:2	8451
forsake not the *l* of thy mother	Prov 6:20	8451
and the *l* is light	Prov 6:23	8451
my *l* as the apple of thine eye	Prov 7:2	8451
The *l* of the wise is a fountain	Prov 13:14	8451
forsake the *l* praise the wicked	Prov 28:4	8451
as keep the *l* contend with them	Prov 28:4	8451
Whoso keepeth the *l* is a wise son	Prov 28:7	8451

away his ear from hearing the *l*	Prov 28:9	8451
but he that keepeth the *l*	Prov 29:18	8451
Lest they drink, and forget the *l*	Prov 31:5	2710
her tongue is the *l* of kindness	Prov 31:26	8451
give ear unto the *l* of our God	Is 1:10	8451
out of Zion shall go forth the *l*	Is 2:3	8451
away the *l* of the LORD of hosts	Is 5:24	8451
seal the *l* among my disciples	Is 8:16	8451
To the *l* and to the testimony	Is 8:20	8451
will not hear the *l* of the LORD	Is 30:9	8451
and the isles shall wait for his *l*	Is 42:4	8451
he will magnify the *l*, and make it	Is 42:21	8451
were they obedient unto his *l*	Is 42:24	8451
for a *l* shall proceed from me, and	Is 51:4	8451
the people in whose heart is my *l*	Is 51:7	8451
that they handle the *l* knew me not	Jer 2:8	8451
unto my words, nor to my *l*	Jer 6:19	8451
the *l* of the LORD is with us	Jer 8:8	8451
my *l* which I set before them	Jer 9:13	8451
me, and have not kept my *l*	Jer 16:11	8451
for the *l* shall not perish from	Jer 18:18	8451
hearken to me, to walk in my *l*	Jer 26:4	8451
I will put my *l* in their inward	Jer 31:33	8451
was sealed according to the *l*	Jer 32:11	4687
voice, neither walked in thy *l*	Jer 32:23	8451
they feared, nor walked in my *l*	Jer 44:10	8451
of the LORD, nor walked in his *l*	Jer 44:23	8451
the *l* is no more	Lam 2:9	8451
but the *l* shall perish from the	Eze 7:26	8451
lewdly defiled his daughter in *l*	Eze 22:11	3618
Her priests have violated my *l*	Eze 22:26	8451
This is the *l* of the house	Eze 43:12	8451
this is the *l* of the house	Eze 43:12	8451
him concerning the *l* of his God	Dan 6:5	1882
according to the *l* of the Medes	Dan 6:8	1882
according to the *l* of the Medes	Dan 6:12	1882
that the *l* of the Medes and	Dan 6:15	1882
Israel have transgressed thy *l*	Dan 9:11	8451
the *l* of Moses the servant of God	Dan 9:11	8451
it is written in the *l* of Moses	Dan 9:13	8451
hast forgotten the *l* of thy God	Hos 4:6	8451
and trespassed against my *l*	Hos 8:1	8451
to him the great things of my *l*	Hos 8:12	8451
have despised the *l* of the LORD	Amos 2:4	8451
for the *l* shall go forth of Zion,	Mic 4:2	8451
the daughter in *l* against her	Mic 7:6	3618
against her mother in *l*	Mic 7:6	2545
Therefore the *l* is slacked	Hab 1:4	8451
they have done violence to the *l*	Zeph 3:4	8451
now the priests concerning the *l*	Hag 2:11	8451
lest they should hear the *l*	Zec 7:12	8451
The *l* of truth was in his mouth,	Mal 2:6	8451
should seek the *l* at his mouth	Mal 2:7	8451
caused many to stumble at the *l*	Mal 2:8	8451
but have been partial in the *l*	Mal 2:9	8451
Remember ye the *l* of Moses my	Mal 4:4	8451
that I am come to destroy the *l*	Mt 5:17	3551
shall in no wise pass from the *l*	Mt 5:18	3551
if any man will sue thee at the *l*	Mt 5:40	3551
for this is the *l* and the prophets	Mt 7:12	3551
the daughter in *l* against her	Mt 10:35	3565
against her mother in *l*	Mt 10:35	3994
the *l* prophesied until John	Mt 11:13	3551
Or have ye not read in the *l*	Mt 12:5	3551
is the great commandment in the *l*	Mt 22:36	3551
two commandments hang all the *l*	Mt 22:40	3551
the weightier matters of the *l*	Mt 23:23	3551
the *l* of Moses were accomplished	Lk 2:22	3551
is written in the *l* of the Lord	Lk 2:23	3551
is said in the *l* of the Lord	Lk 2:24	3551
for him after the custom of the *l*	Lk 2:27	3551
according to the *l* of the Lord	Lk 2:39	3551
and doctors of the *l* sitting by	Lk 5:17	3547
him, What is written in the *l*	Lk 10:26	3551
the mother in *l* against her	Lk 12:53	3994
against her daughter in *l*	Lk 12:53	3565
the daughter in *l* against her	Lk 12:53	3565
against her mother in *l*	Lk 12:53	3994
The *l* and the prophets were until	Lk 16:16	3551
than one tittle of the *l* to fail	Lk 16:17	3551
were written in the *l* of Moses	Lk 24:44	3551
For the *l* was given by Moses, but	Jn 1:17	3551
found him, of whom Moses in the *l*	Jn 1:45	3551
Did not Moses give you the *l*	Jn 7:19	3551
and yet none of you keepeth the *l*	Jn 7:19	3551
that the *l* of Moses should not be	Jn 7:23	3551
who knoweth not the *l* are cursed	Jn 7:49	3551
Doth our *l* judge any man, before	Jn 7:51	3551
Now Moses in the *l* commanded us	Jn 8:5	3551
It is also written in your *l*	Jn 8:17	3551
them, Is it not written in your *l*	Jn 10:34	3551

We have heard out of the *l* that	Jn 12:34	3551
that is written in their *l*	Jn 15:25	3551
he was father in *l* to Caiaphas	Jn 18:13	3995
and judge him according to your *l*	Jn 18:31	3551
Jews answered him, We have a *l*	Jn 19:7	3551
by our *l* he ought to die, because	Jn 19:7	3551
named Gamaliel, a doctor of the *l*	Acts 5:34	3547
against this holy place, and the *l*	Acts 6:13	3551
Who have received the *l* by the	Acts 7:53	3551
And after the reading of the *l*	Acts 13:15	3551
be justified by the *l* of Moses	Acts 13:39	3551
them to keep the *l* of Moses	Acts 15:5	3551
be circumcised, and keep the *l*	Acts 15:24	3551
to worship God contrary to the *l*	Acts 18:13	3551
of words and names, and of your *l*	Acts 18:15	3551
the *l* is open, and there are	Acts 19:38	60
and they are all zealous of the *l*	Acts 21:20	3551
walkest orderly, and keepest the *l*	Acts 21:24	3551
against the people, and the *l*	Acts 21:28	3551
manner of the *l* of the fathers	Acts 22:3	3551
a devout man according to the *l*	Acts 22:12	3551
thou to judge me after the *l*	Acts 23:3	3551
to be smitten contrary to the *l*	Acts 23:3	3891
accused of questions of their *l*	Acts 23:29	3551
have judged according to our *l*	Acts 24:6	3551
things which are written in the *l*	Acts 24:14	3551
Neither against the *l* of the Jews	Acts 25:8	3551
Jesus, both out of the *l* of Moses	Acts 28:23	3551
l shall also perish without *l*	Rom 2:12	460
the *l* shall be judged by the *l*	Rom 2:12	3551
of the *l* are just before God	Rom 2:13	3551
doers of the *l* shall be justified	Rom 2:13	3551
Gentiles, which have not the *l*	Rom 2:14	3551
the things contained in the *l*	Rom 2:14	3551
these, having not the *l*	Rom 2:14	3551
the *l*, are a *l* unto themselves	Rom 2:14	3551
of the *l* written in their hearts	Rom 2:15	3551
called a Jew, and restest in the *l*	Rom 2:17	3551
being instructed out of the *l*	Rom 2:18	3551
and of the truth in the *l*	Rom 2:20	3551
that makest thy boast of the *l*	Rom 2:23	3551
through breaking the *l*	Rom 2:23	3551
profiteth, if thou keep the *l*	Rom 2:25	3551
but if thou be a breaker of the *l*	Rom 2:25	3551
keep the righteousness of the *l*	Rom 2:26	3551
is by nature, if it fulfil the *l*	Rom 2:27	3551
dost transgress the *l*	Rom 2:27	3551
what things soever the *l* saith	Rom 3:19	3551
saith to them who are under the *l*	Rom 3:19	3551
of the *l* there shall no flesh be	Rom 3:20	3551
for by the *l* is the knowledge of	Rom 3:20	3551
God without the *l* is manifested	Rom 3:21	3551
being witnessed by the *l*	Rom 3:21	3551
By what *l*?	Rom 3:27	3551
but by the *l* of faith	Rom 3:27	3551
faith without the deeds of the *l*	Rom 3:28	3551
make void the *l* through faith	Rom 3:31	3551
yea, we establish the *l*	Rom 3:31	3551
or to his seed, through the *l*	Rom 4:13	3551
they which are of the *l* be heirs	Rom 4:14	3551
Because the *l* worketh wrath	Rom 4:15	3551
for where no *l* is, there is no	Rom 4:15	3551
to that only which is of the *l*	Rom 4:16	3551
(For until the *l* sin was in the	Rom 5:13	3551
is not imputed when there is no *l*	Rom 5:13	3551
Moreover the *l* entered, that the	Rom 5:20	3551
for ye are not under the *l*	Rom 6:14	3551
because we are not under the *l*	Rom 6:15	3551
I speak to them that know the *l*	Rom 7:1	3551
how that the *l* hath dominion	Rom 7:1	3551
l to her husband so long as he	Rom 7:2	3551
loosed from the *l* of her husband	Rom 7:2	3551
be dead, she is free from that *l*	Rom 7:3	3551
to the *l* by the body of Christ	Rom 7:4	3551
of sins, which were by the *l*	Rom 7:5	3551
now we are delivered from the *l*	Rom 7:6	3551
Is the *l* sin	Rom 7:7	3551
I had not known sin, but by the *l*	Rom 7:7	3551
known lust, except the *l* had said	Rom 7:7	3551
For without the *l* sin was dead	Rom 7:8	3551
I was alive without the *l* once	Rom 7:9	3551
Wherefore the *l* is holy, and the	Rom 7:12	3551
we know that the *l* is spiritual	Rom 7:14	3551
unto the *l* that it is good	Rom 7:16	3551
I find then a *l*, that, when I	Rom 7:21	3551
For I delight in the *l* of God	Rom 7:22	3551
But I see another *l* in my members	Rom 7:23	3551
warring against the *l* of my mind	Rom 7:23	3551
me into captivity to the *l* of sin	Rom 7:23	3551
mind I myself serve the *l* of God	Rom 7:25	3551
but with the flesh the *l* of sin	Rom 7:25	3551

For the *l* of the Spirit of	Rom 8:2	3551
made me free from the *l* of sin	Rom 8:2	3551
For what the *l* could not do	Rom 8:3	3551
of the *l* might be fulfilled in us	Rom 8:4	3551
it is not subject to the *l* of God	Rom 8:7	3551
covenants, and the giving of the *l*	Rom 9:4	3548
after the *l* of righteousness	Rom 9:31	3551
to the *l* of righteousness	Rom 9:31	3551
as it were by the works of the *l*	Rom 9:32	3551
For Christ is the end of the *l*	Rom 10:4	3551
righteousness which is of the *l*	Rom 10:5	3551
another hath fulfilled the *l*	Rom 13:8	3551
love is the fulfilling of the *l*	Rom 13:10	3551
go to *l* before the unjust, and not	1Cor 6:1	2919
brother goeth to *l* with brother	1Cor 6:6	2919
ye go to *l* one with another	1Cor 6:7	2917
The wife is bound by the *l* as	1Cor 7:39	3551
or saith not the *l* the same also	1Cor 9:8	3551
it is written in the *l* of Moses	1Cor 9:9	3551
are under the *l*, as under the *l*	1Cor 9:20	3551
gain them that are under the *l*	1Cor 9:20	3551
are without *l*, as without *l*	1Cor 9:21	459
l, (being not without *l* to God	1Cor 9:21	459
but under the *l* to Christ	1Cor 9:21	1772
gain them that are without *l*	1Cor 9:21	459
In the *l* it is written, With men	1Cor 14:21	3551
obedience, as also saith the *l*	1Cor 14:34	3551
and the strength of sin is the *l*	1Cor 15:56	3551
justified by the works of the *l*	Gal 2:16	3551
and not by the works of the *l*	Gal 2:16	3551
for by the works of the *l* shall	Gal 2:16	3551
For I through the *l* am dead to	Gal 2:19	3551
through the *l* am dead to the *l*	Gal 2:19	3551
if righteousness come by the *l*	Gal 2:21	3551
the Spirit by the works of the *l*	Gal 3:2	3551
doeth he it by the works of the *l*	Gal 3:5	3551
of the *l* are under the curse	Gal 3:10	3551
in the book of the *l* to do them	Gal 3:10	3551
by the *l* in the sight of God	Gal 3:11	3551
And the *l* is not of faith	Gal 3:12	3551
us from the curse of the *l*	Gal 3:13	3551
before of God in Christ, the *l*	Gal 3:17	3551
if the inheritance be of the *l*	Gal 3:18	3551
Wherefore then serveth the *l*	Gal 3:19	3551
Is the *l* then against the	Gal 3:21	3551
for if there had been a *l* given	Gal 3:21	3551
should have been by the *l*	Gal 3:21	3551
came, we were kept under the *l*	Gal 3:23	3551
Wherefore the *l* was our	Gal 3:24	3551
made of a woman, made under the *l*	Gal 4:4	3551
redeem them that were under the *l*	Gal 4:5	3551
ye that desire to be under the *l*	Gal 4:21	3551
do ye not hear the *l*	Gal 4:21	3551
he is a debtor to do the whole *l*	Gal 5:3	3551
of you are justified by the *l*	Gal 5:4	3551
For all the *l* is fulfilled in one	Gal 5:14	3551
Spirit, ye are not under the *l*	Gal 5:18	3551
against such there is no *l*	Gal 5:23	3551
and so fulfil the *l* of Christ	Gal 6:2	3551
who are circumcised keep the *l*	Gal 6:13	3551
even the *l* of commandments	Eph 2:15	3551
as touching the *l*, a Pharisee	Phil 3:5	3551
righteousness which is in the *l*	Phil 3:6	3551
righteousness, which is of the *l*	Phil 3:9	3551
Desiring to be teachers of the *l*	1Ti 1:7	3547
But we know that the *l* is good	1Ti 1:8	3551
that the *l* is not made for a	1Ti 1:9	3551
and strivings about the *l*	Titus 3:9	3544
of the people according to the *l*	Heb 7:5	3551
it the people received the *l*	Heb 7:11	3549
necessity a change also of the *l*	Heb 7:12	3551
not after the *l* of a carnal	Heb 7:16	3551
For the *l* made nothing perfect,	Heb 7:19	3551
For the *l* maketh men high priests	Heb 7:28	3551
the oath, which was since the *l*	Heb 7:28	3551
offer gifts according to the *l*	Heb 8:4	3551
all the people according to the *l*	Heb 9:19	3551
are by the *l* purged with blood	Heb 9:22	3551
For the *l* having a shadow of good	Heb 10:1	3551
which are offered by the *l*	Heb 10:8	3551
He that despised Moses' *l* died	Heb 10:28	3551
into the perfect *l* of liberty	Jas 1:25	3551
If ye fulfil the royal *l*	Jas 2:8	3551
of the *l* as transgressors	Jas 2:9	3551
whosoever shall keep the whole *l*	Jas 2:10	3551
become a transgressor of the *l*	Jas 2:11	3551
be judged by the *l* of liberty	Jas 2:12	3551
evil of the *l*, and judgeth the *l*	Jas 4:11	3551
but if thou judge the *l*	Jas 4:11	3551
thou art not a doer of the *l*	Jas 4:11	3551

sin transgresseth also the *l*	1Jn 3:4	4160,458
sin is the transgression of the *l*	1Jn 3:4	458

LAWFUL

it shall not be *l* to impose toll	Ezr 7:24	7990
or the *l* captive delivered	Is 49:24	6662
be just, and do that which is *l*	Eze 18:5	4941
the son hath done that which is *l*	Eze 18:19	4941
statutes, and do that which is *l*	Eze 18:21	4941
and doeth that which is *l*	Eze 18:27	4941
his sin, and do that which is *l*	Eze 33:14	4941
he hath done that which is *l*	Eze 33:16	4941
wickedness, and do that which is *l*	Eze 33:19	4941
not *l* to do upon the sabbath day	Mt 12:2	1832
which was not *l* for him to eat,	Mt 12:4	1832
Is it *l* to heal on the sabbath	Mt 12:10	1832
Wherefore it is *l* to do well on	Mt 12:12	1832
It is not *l* for thee to have her	Mt 14:4	1832
Is it *l* for a man to put away his	Mt 19:3	1832
Is it not *l* for me to do what I	Mt 20:15	1833
Is it *l* to give tribute unto	Mt 22:17	1833
It is not *l* for to put them into	Mt 27:6	1833
sabbath day that which is not *l*	Mk 2:24	1833
which is not *l* to eat but for the	Mk 2:26	1833
Is it *l* to do good on the sabbath	Mk 3:4	1833
It is not *l* for thee to have thy	Mk 6:18	1833
Is it *l* for a man to put away his	Mk 10:2	1833
Is it *l* to give tribute to Caesar	Mk 12:14	1833
not *l* to do on the sabbath days	Lk 6:2	1833
which it is not *l* to eat but for	Lk 6:4	1833
Is it *l* on the sabbath days to do	Lk 6:9	1833
Is it *l* to heal on the sabbath	Lk 14:3	1833
Is it *l* for us to give tribute	Lk 20:22	1833
it is not *l* for thee to carry thy	Jn 5:10	1833
It is not *l* for us to put any man	Jn 18:31	1833
which are not *l* for us to receive	Acts 16:21	1833
be determined in a *l* assembly	Acts 19:39	1772
Is it *l* for you to scourge a man	Acts 22:25	1832
All things are *l* unto me, but all	1Cor 6:12	1832
all things are *l* for me, but I	1Cor 6:12	1832
All things are *l* for me, but all	1Cor 10:23	1832
all things are *l* for me, but all	1Cor 10:23	1832
which it is not *l* for a man to	2Cor 12:4	1832

LAWFULLY

law is good, if a man use it *l*	1Ti 1:8	3545
not crowned, except he strive *l*	2Ti 2:5	3545

LAWGIVER

nor a *l* from between his feet,	Gen 49:10	2710
it, by the direction of the *l*	Num 21:18	2710
there, in a portion of the *l*	Deut 33:21	2710
Judah is my *l*	Ps 60:7	2710
Judah is my *l*	Ps 108:8	2710
is our judge, the LORD is our *l*	Is 33:22	2710
There is one *l*, who is able to	Jas 4:12	3550

LAWLESS

a righteous man, but for the *l*	1Ti 1:9	459

LAWS

my statutes, and my *l*	Gen 26:5	8451
to keep my commandments and my *l*	Ex 16:28	8451
the statutes of God, and his *l*	Ex 18:16	8451
shalt teach them ordinances and *l*	Ex 18:20	8451
the statutes and judgments and *l*	Lev 26:46	8451
all such as know the *l* of thy God	Ezr 7:25	1882
them right judgments, and true *l*	Neh 9:13	8451
them precepts, statutes, and *l*	Neh 9:14	8451
among the *l* of the Persians	Est 1:19	1881
their *l* are diverse from all	Est 3:8	1881
neither keep they the king's *l*	Est 3:8	1881
his statutes, and keep his *l*	Ps 105:45	8541
they have transgressed the *l*	Is 24:5	8451
thereof, and all the *l* thereof	Eze 43:11	8451
of the LORD, and all the *l* thereof	Eze 44:5	8451
and they shall keep my *l* and my	Eze 44:24	8451
and think to change times and *l*	Dan 7:25	1882
LORD our God, to walk in his *l*	Dan 9:10	8451
I will put my *l* into their mind,	Heb 8:10	3551
I will put my *l* into their hearts	Heb 10:16	3551

LAWYER

Then one of them, which was a *l*	Mt 22:35	3544
And, behold, a certain *l* stood up	Lk 10:25	3544
Bring Zenas the *l* and Apollos on	Titus 3:13	3544

LAWYERS

l rejected the counsel of God	Lk 7:30	3544
Then answered one of the *l*	Lk 11:45	3544
he said, Woe unto you also, ye *l*	Lk 11:46	3544
Woe unto you, *l*	Lk 11:52	3544
Jesus answering spake unto the *l*	Lk 14:3	3544

L

LAY

But before they *l* down, the men	Gen 19:4	7901
went in, and *l* with her father	Gen 19:33	7901
he perceived not when she *l* down	Gen 19:33	7901
I *l* yesternight with my father	Gen 19:34	7901
the younger arose, and *l* with him	Gen 19:35	7901
he perceived not when she *l* down	Gen 19:35	7901
L not thine hand upon the lad,	Gen 22:12	7971
l down in that place to sleep	Gen 28:11	7901
And he *l* with her that night	Gen 30:16	7901
l with her, and defiled her	Gen 34:2	7901
l with Bilhah his father's	Gen 35:22	7901
wilderness, and *l* no hand upon him	Gen 37:22	7971
l up corn under the hand of	Gen 41:35	6651
heretofore, ye shall *l* upon them	Ex 5:8	7760
that I may *l* my hand upon Egypt	Ex 7:4	5414
the dew *l* round about the host	Ex 16:13	7902
when the dew that *l* was gone up	Ex 16:14	7902
there *l* a small round thing	Ex 16:14	
that which remaineth over *l* up	Ex 16:23	3241
l it up before the LORD, to be	Ex 16:33	3241
woman's husband will *l* upon him	Ex 21:22	7896
shalt thou *l* upon him usury	Ex 22:25	7760
l the wood in order upon the fire	Lev 1:7	
shall *l* the parts, the head, and	Lev 1:8	
the priest shall *l* them in order	Lev 1:12	
it, and *l* frankincense thereon	Lev 2:15	7760
he shall *l* his hand upon the head	Lev 3:2	5564
he shall *l* his hand upon the head	Lev 3:8	5564
he shall *l* his hand upon the head	Lev 3:13	5564
shall *l* his hand upon the	Lev 4:4	5564
of the congregation shall *l* their	Lev 4:15	5564
he shall *l* his hand upon the head	Lev 4:24	5564
he shall *l* his hand upon the head	Lev 4:29	5564
he shall *l* his hand upon the head	Lev 4:33	5564
l the burnt offering in order	Lev 6:12	
Aaron shall *l* both his hands upon	Lev 16:21	5564
let all that heard him *l* their	Lev 24:14	5564
the Levites shall *l* their hands	Num 8:12	5564
l not the sin upon us, wherein we	Num 12:11	7896
thou shalt *l* them up in the	Num 17:4	3241
l them up without the camp in a	Num 17:18	3241
he *l* down as a lion, and as a	Num 24:9	7901
spirit, and *l* thine hand upon him	Num 27:18	5564
but will *l* them upon all them	Deut 7:15	5414
Therefore shall ye *l* up these my	Deut 11:18	7760
your God shall *l* the fear of you	Deut 11:25	
shalt *l* it up within thy gates	Deut 14:28	3241
l not innocent blood unto thy	Deut 21:8	5414
his mother *l* hold on him, and	Deut 21:19	
the man that *l* with the woman	Deut 22:22	7901
only that man *l* with her shall die	Deut 22:25	7901
l hold on her, and lie with her	Deut 22:28	
Then the man that *l* with her	Deut 22:29	7901
he shall *l* the foundation thereof	Josh 6:26	
l thee an ambush for the city	Josh 8:2	7760
all that *l* near Ashdod, with	Josh 15:46	
her tent, behold, Sisera *l* dead	Judg 4:22	5307
feet he bowed, he fell, he *l* down	Judg 5:27	7901
l them upon this rock, and pour	Judg 6:20	3241
east *l* along in the valley like	Judg 7:12	5307
it, that the tent *l* along	Judg 7:13	5307
because she *l* sore upon him	Judg 14:17	
Samson *l* till midnight, and arose	Judg 16:3	7901
l thine hand upon thy mouth, and	Judg 18:19	7760
uncover his feet, and *l* thee down	Ruth 3:4	7901
and, behold, a woman *l* at his feet	Ruth 3:8	7901
she *l* at his feet until the	Ruth 3:14	7901
how they *l* with the women that	1Sa 2:22	7901
And he went and *l* down	1Sa 3:5	7901
went and *l* down in his place	1Sa 3:9	7901
Samuel *l* until the morning, and	1Sa 3:15	7901
the LORD, and *l* it upon the cart	1Sa 6:8	5414
l it for a reproach upon all	1Sa 11:2	7760
l down naked all that day and all	1Sa 19:24	5307
beheld the place where Saul *l*	1Sa 26:5	7901
Saul *l* in the trench, and the	1Sa 26:5	7901
Saul *l* sleeping within the trench	1Sa 26:7	7901
the people *l* round about him	1Sa 26:7	7901
l thee hold on one of the young	2Sa 2:21	
who *l* on a bed at noon	2Sa 4:5	7901
he *l* on his bed in his bedchamber	2Sa 4:7	7901
in unto him, and he *l* with her	2Sa 11:4	7901
l in his bosom, and was unto him	2Sa 12:3	7901
l all night upon the earth	2Sa 12:16	7901
went in unto her, and *l* with her	2Sa 12:24	7901
L thee down on thy bed, and make	2Sa 13:5	7901
So Amnon *l* down, and made himself	2Sa 13:6	7901
she, forced her, and *l* with her	2Sa 13:14	7901
his garments, and *l* on the earth	2Sa 13:31	7901
sustenance while he *l* at Mahanaim	2Sa 19:32	7871

to *l* the foundation of the house	1Kin 5:17	
that *l* on forty five pillars,	1Kin 7:3	
the altar, saying, *L* hold on him	1Kin 13:4	
l my bones beside his bones	1Kin 13:31	3241
l it on wood, and put no fire	1Kin 18:23	7760
l it on wood, and put no fire	1Kin 18:23	7760
And as he *l* and slept under a	1Kin 19:5	7901
l in sackcloth, and went softly	1Kin 21:27	7901
into the chamber, and *l* there	2Kin 4:11	7901
l my staff upon the face of the	2Kin 4:29	7760
l upon the child, and put his	2Kin 4:34	7901
for Joram to *l*	2Kin 9:16	7901
L ye them in two heaps at the	2Kin 10:8	7760
be to *l* waste fenced cities into	2Kin 19:25	
to *l* the foundation of the heaps	2Chr 31:7	
for as long as she *l* desolate she	2Chr 36:21	
of such as *l* in wait by the way	Ezr 8:31	
so again, I will *l* hands on you	Neh 13:21	7971
sought to *l* hand on the king	Est 2:21	7971
he thought scorn to *l* hands on	Est 3:6	7971
many *l* in sackcloth and ashes	Est 4:3	3331
who sought to *l* hand on the king	Est 6:2	7971
to *l* hand on such as sought their	Est 9:2	7971
that might *l* his hand upon us	Job 9:33	7896
L down now, put me in a surety	Job 17:3	7760
l your hand upon your mouth	Job 21:5	7760
l up his words in thine heart	Job 22:22	7760
Then shalt thou *l* up gold as dust	Job 22:24	7896
the dew *l* all night upon my	Job 29:19	3885
For he will not *l* upon man more	Job 34:23	7760
I will *l* mine hand upon my mouth	Job 40:4	7760
L thine hand upon him, remember	Job 41:8	7760
I will both *l* me down in peace,	Ps 4:8	7901
l mine honour in the dust	Ps 7:5	7931
after my life *l* snares for me	Ps 38:12	
they that *l* wait for my soul take	Ps 71:10	
where she may *l* her young	Ps 84:3	7896
l them down in their dens	Ps 104:22	7257
let us *l* wait for blood, let us	Prov 1:11	
they *l* wait for their own blood	Prov 1:18	
life to them that *l* hold upon her	Prov 3:18	
l up my commandments with thee	Prov 7:1	6845
Wise men *l* up knowledge	Prov 10:14	6845
L not wait, O wicked man, against	Prov 24:15	
l thine hand upon thy mouth	Prov 30:32	
to *l* hold on folly, till I might	Eccl 2:3	
the living will *l* it to his heart	Eccl 7:2	5414
And I will *l* it waste	Is 5:6	
that *l* field to field, till there	Is 5:8	7126
l hold of the prey, and shall	Is 5:29	
they shall *l* their hand upon Edom	Is 11:14	7971
anger, to *l* the land desolate	Is 13:9	
will *l* low the haughtiness of the	Is 13:11	
David will *l* upon his shoulder	Is 22:22	5414
l low, and bring to the ground,	Is 25:12	
I *l* in Zion for a foundation a	Is 28:16	
also will I *l* to the line	Is 28:17	7760
will *l* siege against thee with a	Is 29:3	
l a snare for him that reproveth	Is 29:21	
which the LORD shall *l* upon him	Is 30:32	5117
the great owl make her nest, and *l*	Is 34:15	4422
of dragons, where each *l*, shall	Is 35:7	7258
that thou shouldest be to *l* waste	Is 37:26	
l it for a plaister upon the boil	Is 38:21	
so that thou didst not *l* these	Is 47:7	7760
l the foundations of the earth,	Is 51:16	
I will *l* thy stones with fair	Is 54:11	7257
l thy foundations with sapphires	Is 54:11	
they *l* wait, as he that setteth	Jer 5:26	
I will *l* stumblingblocks before	Jer 6:21	5414
They shall *l* hold on bow and spear	Jer 6:23	
I *l* a stumblingblock before him,	Eze 3:20	5414
l it before thee, and pourtray	Eze 4:1	5414
l siege against it, and build a	Eze 4:2	5414
thou shalt *l* siege against it	Eze 4:3	5414
l the iniquity of the house of	Eze 4:4	7760
I will *l* bands upon thee, and thou	Eze 4:8	
I will *l* the dead carcases of the	Eze 6:5	5414
she *l* down among lions, she	Eze 19:2	7257
for in her youth they *l* with her	Eze 23:8	7901
I will *l* my vengeance upon Edom	Eze 25:14	5414
when I shall *l* my vengeance upon	Eze 25:17	5414
and they shall *l* thy stones	Eze 26:12	7760
l away their robes, and put off	Eze 26:16	5493
I will *l* thee before kings, that	Eze 28:17	5414
I will *l* thy flesh upon the	Eze 32:5	5414
For I will *l* the land most	Eze 33:28	5414
I will *l* thy cities waste, and	Eze 35:4	7760
it, and *l* no famine upon you	Eze 36:29	5414
whereas it *l* desolate in the	Eze 36:34	
I will *l* sinews upon you, and will	Eze 37:6	5414

there shall they *l* the most holy	Eze 42:13	3241
but there they shall *l* their	Eze 42:14	3241
l them in the holy chambers, and	Eze 44:19	3241
they *l* themselves down upon	Amos 2:8	5186
and he *l*, and was fast asleep	Jonah 1:5	7901
l not upon us innocent blood	Jonah 1:14	5414
idols thereof will I *l* desolate	Mic 1:7	7760
they shall *l* their hand upon	Mic 7:16	7760
they shall *l* hold every one on	Zec 14:13	
and if ye will not *l* it to heart	Mal 2:2	7760
because ye do not *l* it to heart	Mal 2:2	7760
L not up for yourselves treasures	Mt 6:19	
But *l* up for yourselves treasures	Mt 6:20	
man hath not where to *l* his head	Mt 8:20	2827
l thy hand upon her, and she shall	Mt 9:18	2007
day, will he not *l* hold on it	Mt 12:11	
they sought to *l* hold on him	Mt 21:46	
l them on men's shoulders	Mt 23:4	2007
see the place where the Lord *l*	Mt 28:6	2749
wife's mother *l* sick of a fever	Mk 1:30	2621
wherein the sick of the palsy *l*	Mk 2:4	2621
they went out to *l* hold on him	Mk 3:21	
l thy hands on her, that she may	Mk 5:23	2007
And they sought to *l* hold on him	Mk 12:12	
which *l* bound with them that had	Mk 15:7	
they shall *l* hands on the sick,	Mk 16:18	2007
him in, and to *l* him before him	Lk 5:18	5087
and took up that whereon he *l*	Lk 5:25	2621
years of age, and she *l* a dying	Lk 8:42	
man hath not where to *l* his head	Lk 9:58	2827
shall *l* thee even with the ground	Lk 19:44	1474
hour sought to *l* hands on him	Lk 20:19	1911
they shall *l* their hands on you,	Lk 21:12	1911
In these *l* a great multitude of	Jn 5:3	2621
I *l* down my life for the sheep	Jn 10:15	5087
because I *l* down my life, that I	Jn 10:17	5087
but I *l* it down of myself	Jn 10:18	5087
I have power to *l* it down	Jn 10:18	5087
was a cave, and a stone *l* upon it	Jn 11:38	1945
I will *l* down my life for thy	Jn 13:37	5087
Wilt thou *l* down thy life for my	Jn 13:38	5087
that a man *l* down his life for	Jn 15:13	5087
l not this sin to their charge	Acts 7:60	2476
that on whomsoever I *l* hands	Acts 8:19	2007
to *l* upon you no greater burden	Acts 15:28	2007
and no small tempest *l* on us	Acts 27:20	1945
of Publius *l* sick of a fever	Acts 28:8	2621
Who shall *l* any thing to the	Rom 8:33	1458
I *l* in Sion a stumblingstone and	Rom 9:33	5087
can no man *l* than that is laid	1Cor 3:11	5087
one of you *l* by him in store	1Cor 16:2	5087
ought not to *l* up for the parents	2Cor 12:14	2343
L hands suddenly on no man,	1Ti 5:22	2007
l hold on eternal life, whereunto	1Ti 6:12	1949
that they may *l* hold on eternal	1Ti 6:19	1949
who have fled for refuge to *l*	Heb 6:18	
let us *l* aside every weight, and	Heb 12:1	659
Wherefore *l* apart all filthiness	Jas 1:21	659
I *l* in Sion a chief corner stone,	1Pet 2:6	5087
we ought to *l* down our lives for	1Jn 3:16	5087

LAYEDST

takest up that thou *l* not down	Lk 19:21	5087

LAYEST

that thou *l* the burden of all	Num 11:11	7760
wherefore then *l* thou a snare for	1Sa 28:9	

LAYETH

God *l* up his iniquity for his	Job 21:19	6845
yet God *l* not folly to them	Job 24:12	7760
of him that *l* hold that cannot hold	Job 41:26	5381
he *l* up the depth in storehouses	Ps 33:7	5414
Who *l* the beams of his chambers	Ps 104:3	7760
He *l* up sound wisdom for the	Prov 2:7	6845
but a fool *l* open his folly	Prov 13:16	
lips, and *l* up deceit within him	Prov 26:24	7896
She *l* her hands to the spindle,	Prov 31:19	7971
the lofty city, he *l* it low	Is 26:5	
he *l* it low, even to the ground	Is 26:5	
the son of man that *l* hold on it	Is 56:2	
and no man *l* it to heart	Is 57:1	7760
mouth, but in heart he *l* his wait	Jer 9:8	7760
because no man *l* it to heart	Jer 12:11	7760
l the foundation of the earth, and	Zec 12:1	
So is he that *l* up treasure for	Lk 12:21	
he *l* it on his shoulders,	Lk 15:5	2007

LAYING

or hurl at him by *l* of wait	Num 35:20	
him any thing without *l* of wait	Num 35:22	
they commune of *l* snares privily	Ps 64:5	2934
For *l* aside the commandment of	Mk 7:8	863

L wait for him, and seeking to	Lk 11:54	1748
when Simon saw that through *l* on	Acts 8:18	1936
But their *l* await was known of	Acts 9:24	1917
l wait in the way to kill him	Acts 25:3	4160
with the *l* on of the hands of the	1Ti 4:14	1936
L up in store for themselves a	1Ti 6:19	597
not *l* again the foundation of	Heb 6:1	2598
and of *l* on of hands, and of	Heb 6:2	1936
Wherefore *l* aside all malice, and	1Pet 2:1	659

LAZARUS *(laz'-a-rus)*
1. Name for a beggar in a parable of Jesus.

was a certain beggar named *L*	Lk 16:20	2976
afar off, and *L* in his bosom	Lk 16:23	2976
have mercy on me, and send *L*	Lk 16:24	2976
things, and likewise *L* evil things	Lk 16:25	2976

2. Man raised from the dead by Jesus.

a certain man was sick, named *L*	Jn 11:1	2976
hair, whose brother *L* was sick	Jn 11:2	2976
loved Martha, and her sister, and *L*	Jn 11:5	2976
unto them, Our friend *L* sleepeth	Jn 11:11	2976
unto them plainly, *L* is dead	Jn 11:14	2976
he cried with a loud voice, *L*	Jn 11:43	2976
where *L* was which had been dead,	Jn 12:1	2976
but *L* was one of them that sat at	Jn 12:2	2976
but that they might see *L* also	Jn 12:9	2976
they might put *L* also to death	Jn 12:10	2976
when he called *L* out of his grave	Jn 12:17	2976

LEAD

I will *l* on softly, according as	Gen 33:14	5095
of a cloud, to *l* them the way	Ex 13:21	5148
they sank as *l* in the mighty	Ex 15:10	5777
l the people unto the place of	Ex 32:34	5148
them, and which may *l* them out	Num 27:17	3318
the iron, the tin, and the *l*	Num 31:22	5777
whither the Lord shall *l* you	Deut 4:27	5090
of the armies to *l* the people	Deut 20:9	7218
whither the Lord shall *l* thee	Deut 28:37	5090
So the Lord alone did *l* him	Deut 32:12	5148
l thy captivity captive, thou son	Judg 5:12	
that they may *l* them away	1Sa 30:22	5090
before them that *l* them captive	2Chr 30:9	
them by day, to *l* them in the way	Neh 9:19	5148
pen and *l* in the rock for ever	Job 19:24	5777
L me, O Lord, in thy	Ps 5:8	5148
L me in thy truth, and teach me	Ps 25:5	1869
l me in a plain path, because of	Ps 27:11	5148
for thy name's sake *l* me, and	Ps 31:3	5148
let them *l* me	Ps 43:3	5148
who will *l* me into Edom	Ps 60:9	5148
l me to the rock that is higher	Ps 61:2	5148
who will *l* me into Edom	Ps 108:10	5148
the Lord shall *l* them forth with	Ps 125:5	3212
Even there shall thy hand *l* me	Ps 139:10	5148
l me in the way everlasting	Ps 139:24	5148
l me into the land of uprightness	Ps 143:10	5148
When thou goest, it shall *l* thee	Prov 6:22	5148
I *l* in the way of righteousness,	Prov 8:20	1980
I would *l* thee, and bring thee	Song 8:2	5090
they which *l* thee cause thee to	Is 3:12	833
and a little child shall *l* them	Is 11:6	5090
l away the Egyptians prisoners	Is 20:4	5090
shall gently *l* those that are	Is 40:11	5095
I will *l* them in paths that they	Is 42:16	1869
hath mercy on them shall *l* them	Is 49:10	5090
I will *l* him also, and restore	Is 57:18	5148
so didst thou *l* thy people	Is 63:14	5090
the *l* is consumed of the fire	Jer 6:29	5777
with supplications will I *l* them	Jer 31:9	2986
he shall *l* Zedekiah to Babylon,	Jer 32:5	3212
are brass, and tin, and iron, and *l*	Eze 22:18	5777
silver, and brass, and iron, and *l*	Eze 22:20	5777
with silver, iron, tin, and *l*	Eze 27:12	5777
her maids shall *l* her as with the	Nah 2:7	5090
there was lifted up a talent of *l*	Zec 5:7	5777
he cast the weight of *l* upon the	Zec 5:8	5777
l us not into temptation, but	Mt 6:13	1533
And if the blind *l* the blind	Mt 15:14	3594
But when they shall *l* you	Mk 13:11	71
take him, and *l* him away safely	Mk 14:44	520
them, Can the blind *l* the blind	Lk 6:39	3594
And *l* us not into temptation	Lk 11:4	1533
stall, and *l* him away to watering	Lk 13:15	520
seeking some to *l* him by the hand	Acts 13:11	5497
we not power to *l* about a sister	1Cor 9:5	4013
that we may *l* a quiet and	1Ti 2:2	1236
l captive silly women laden with	2Ti 3:6	162
l them out of the land of Egypt	Heb 8:9	1806
them, and shall *l* them unto living	Rev 7:17	3594

L

LEADER

was the *l* of the Aaronites	1Chr 12:27	5057
and hundreds, and with every *l*	1Chr 13:1	5057
for a witness to the people, a *l*	Is 55:4	5057

LEADERS

mighty men of valour, and the *l*	2Chr 32:21	5057
For the *l* of this people cause	Is 9:16	833
they be blind *l* of the blind	Mt 15:14	3595

LEADEST

thou that *l* Joseph like a flock	Ps 80:1	5090

LEADETH

unto the way that *l* to Ophrah	1Sa 13:17	
He *l* counsellors away spoiled, and	Job 12:17	3212
He *l* princes away spoiled, and	Job 12:19	3212
he *l* me beside the still waters	Ps 23:2	5095
he *l* me in the paths of	Ps 23:3	5090
l him into the way that is not	Prov 16:29	3212
which *l* thee by the way that thou	Is 48:17	1869
that *l* to destruction, and many	Mt 7:13	520
which *l* unto life, and few there	Mt 7:14	520
l them up into an high mountain	Mk 9:2	399
own sheep by name, and *l* them out	Jn 10:3	1806
iron gate that *l* unto the city	Acts 12:10	5342
of God *l* thee to repentance	Rom 2:4	71
He that *l* into captivity shall go	Rev 13:10	4863

LEAF

mouth was an olive *l* pluckt off	Gen 8:11	5929
of a shaken *l* shall chase them	Lev 26:36	5929
Wilt thou break a *l* driven to	Job 13:25	5929
his *l* also shall not wither	Ps 1:3	5929
shall be as an oak whose *l* fadeth	Is 1:30	5929
as the *l* falleth off from the	Is 34:4	5929
and we all do fade as a *l*	Is 64:6	5929
the fig tree, and the *l* shall fade	Jer 8:13	5929
cometh, but her *l* shall be green	Jer 17:8	5929
whose *l* shall not fade, neither	Eze 47:12	5929
the *l* thereof for medicine	Eze 47:12	5929

LEAGUE

now therefore make ye a *l* with us	Josh 9:6	1285
and how shall we make a *l* with you	Josh 9:7	1285
therefore now make ye a *l* with us	Josh 9:11	1285
made a *l* with them, to let them	Josh 9:15	1285
after they had made a *l* with them	Josh 9:16	1285
ye shall make no *l* with the	Judg 2:2	1285
made a *l* with the son of Jesse	1Sa 22:8	3772
saying also, Make thy *l* with me	2Sa 3:12	1285
I will make a *l* with thee	2Sa 3:13	1285
that they may make a *l* with thee	2Sa 3:21	1285
king David make a *l* with them in	2Sa 5:3	1285
and they two made a *l* together	1Kin 5:12	1285
There is a *l* between me and thee,	1Kin 15:19	1285
break thy *l* with Baasha king of	1Kin 15:19	1285
There is a *l* between me and thee,	2Chr 16:3	1285
break thy *l* with Baasha king of	2Chr 16:3	1285
For thou shalt be in *l* with the	Job 5:23	1285
the men of the land that is in *l*	Eze 30:5	1285
after the *l* made with him he	Dan 11:23	2266

LEAH (*le'-ah*) See LEAH'S. *Wife of Jacob.*

the name of the elder was *L*	Gen 29:16	3812
L was tender eyed	Gen 29:17	3812
that he took *L* his daughter	Gen 29:23	3812
Laban gave unto his daughter *L*	Gen 29:24	3812
in the morning, behold, it was *L*	Gen 29:25	3812
he loved also Rachel more than *L*	Gen 29:30	3812
the LORD saw that *L* was hated	Gen 29:31	3812
L conceived, and bare a son, and	Gen 29:32	3812
When *L* saw that she had left	Gen 30:9	3812
And *L* said, A troop cometh	Gen 30:11	3812
L said, Happy am I, for the	Gen 30:13	3812
and brought them unto his mother *L*	Gen 30:14	3812
Then Rachel said to *L*, Give me, I	Gen 30:14	3812
L went out to meet him, and said,	Gen 30:16	3812
And God hearkened unto *L*, and she	Gen 30:17	3812
L said, God hath given me my hire	Gen 30:18	3812
L conceived again, and bare Jacob	Gen 30:19	3812
L said, God hath endued me with a	Gen 30:20	3812
L to the field unto his flock,	Gen 31:4	3812
L answered and said unto him, Is	Gen 31:14	3812
And he divided the children unto *L*	Gen 33:1	3812
and their children foremost, and *L*	Gen 33:2	3812
L also with her children came	Gen 33:7	3812
And Dinah the daughter of *L*	Gen 34:1	3812
The sons of *L*; Reuben	Gen 35:23	3812
These be the sons of *L*, which she	Gen 46:15	3812
whom Laban gave to *L* his daughter	Gen 46:18	3812
and there I buried *L*	Gen 49:31	3812
thine house like Rachel and like *L*	Ruth 4:11	3812

LEAH'S (*le'-ahs*)

Zilpah *L* maid bare Jacob a son	Gen 30:10	3812
Zilpah *L* maid bare Jacob a second	Gen 30:12	3812
into Jacob's tent, and into *L* tent	Gen 31:33	3812
Then went he out of *L* tent	Gen 31:33	3812
And the sons of Zilpah, *L* handmaid	Gen 35:26	3812

LEAN

And the *l* and the ill favoured kine	Gen 41:20	7534
land is, whether it be fat or *l*	Num 13:20	7330
standeth, that I may *l* upon them	Judg 16:26	8172
the king's son, *l* from day to day	2Sa 13:4	1800
upon Egypt, on which if a man *l*	2Kin 18:21	5564
He shall *l* upon his house, but it	Job 8:15	8172
and *l* not unto thine own	Prov 3:5	8172
fatness of his flesh shall wax *l*	Is 17:4	7329
whereon if a man *l*, it will go	Is 36:6	5564
cattle and between the *l* cattle	Eze 34:20	7330
yet will they *l* upon the LORD	Mic 3:11	8172

LEANED

behold, Saul *l* upon his spear	2Sa 1:6	8172
king answered the man of God	2Kin 7:2	8172
the lord on whose hand he *l* to	2Kin 7:17	8172
and when they *l* upon thee, thou	Eze 29:7	8172
l his hand on the wall, and a	Amos 5:19	5564
which also *l* on his breast at	Jn 21:20	377

LEANETH

or that *l* on a staff, or that	2Sa 3:29	2388
he *l* on my hand, and I bow myself	2Kin 5:18	8127

LEANFLESHED

of the river, ill favoured and *l*	Gen 41:3	1851,1320
l kine did eat up the seven well	Gen 41:4	1851,1320
poor and very ill favoured and *l*	Gen 41:19	7534

LEANING

wilderness, *l* upon her beloved	Song 8:5	7514
Now there was *l* on Jesus' bosom	Jn 13:23	345
l upon the top of his staff	Heb 11:21	

LEANNESS

my *l* rising up in me beareth	Job 16:8	3585
but sent *l* into their soul	Ps 106:15	7332
hosts, send among his fat ones *l*	Is 10:16	7332
But I said, My *l*, my *l*,	Is 24:16	7334

LEANNOTH (*le-an'-noth*) *A musical choir.*

chief Musician upon Mahalath *L*	Ps 88:*t*	6030

LEAP

all the rams which *l* upon the	Gen 31:12	5927
to *l* withal upon the earth	Lev 11:21	5425
he shall *l* from Bashan	Deut 33:22	2178
lamps, and sparks of fire *l* out	Job 41:19	4422
Why *l* ye, ye high hills	Ps 68:16	7520
shall the lame man *l* as an hart	Is 35:6	1801
tops of mountains shall they *l*	Joel 2:5	7540
all those that *l* on the threshold	Zeph 1:9	1801
ye in that day, and *l* for joy	Lk 6:23	4640

LEAPED

the rams which *l* upon the cattle	Gen 31:10	5927
by my God have I *l* over a wall	2Sa 22:30	1801
they *l* upon the altar which was	1Kin 18:26	6452
and by my God have I *l* over a wall	Ps 18:29	1801
of Mary, the babe *l* in her womb	Lk 1:41	4640
the babe *l* in my womb for joy	Lk 1:44	4640
And he *l* and walked	Acts 14:10	242
the evil spirit was *l* on them	Acts 19:16	2177

LEAPING

a window, and saw king David *l*	2Sa 6:16	6339
he cometh *l* upon the mountains,	Song 2:8	1801
he *l* up stood, and walked, and	Acts 3:8	1814
into the temple, walking, and *l*	Acts 3:8	242

LEARN

that they may *l* to fear me all	Deut 4:10	3925
ears this day, that ye may *l* them	Deut 5:1	3925
that thou mayest *l* to fear the	Deut 14:23	3925
that he may *l* to fear the LORD	Deut 17:19	3925
thou shalt not *l* to do after the	Deut 18:9	3925
they may hear, and that they may *l*	Deut 31:12	3925
l to fear the LORD your God, as	Deut 31:13	3925
that I might *l* thy statutes	Ps 119:71	3925
that I may *l* thy commandments	Ps 119:73	3925
Lest thou *l* his ways, and get a	Prov 22:25	502
L to do well	Is 1:17	3925
neither shall they *l* war any more	Is 2:4	3925
of the world will *l* righteousness	Is 26:9	3925
yet will he not *l* righteousness	Is 26:10	3925
that murmured shall *l* doctrine	Is 29:24	3925
L not the way of the heathen, and	Jer 10:2	3925
l the ways of my people, to swear	Jer 12:16	3925

neither shall they *l* war any more	Mic 4:3	3925
l what that meaneth, I will have	Mt 9:13	3129
Take my yoke upon you, and *l* of me	Mt 11:29	3129
Now *l* a parable of the fig tree	Mt 24:32	3129
Now *l* a parable of the fig tree	Mk 13:28	3129
that ye might *l* in us not to	1Cor 4:6	3129
one by one, that all may *l*	1Cor 14:31	3129
And if they will *l* any thing	1Cor 14:35	3129
This only would I *l* of you	Gal 3:2	3129
that they may *l* not to blaspheme	1Ti 1:20	3811
Let the woman *l* in silence with	1Ti 2:11	3129
let them *l* first to shew piety at	1Ti 5:4	3129
And withal they *l* to be idle	1Ti 5:13	3129
let ours also *l* to maintain good	Titus 3:14	3129
no man could *l* that song but the	Rev 14:3	3129

LEARNED

for I have *l* by experience that	Gen 30:27	5172
the heathen, and *l* their works	Ps 106:35	3925
when I shall have *l* thy righteous	Ps 119:7	3925
I neither *l* wisdom, nor have the	Prov 30:3	3925
men deliver to one that is *l*	Is 29:11	3045,5612
is delivered to him that is not *l*	Is 29:12	3045,5612
and he saith, I am not *l*	Is 29:12	3045,5612
hath given me the tongue of the *l*	Is 50:4	3928
mine ear to hear as the *l*	Is 50:4	3928
lion, and it *l* to catch the prey	Eze 19:3	3925
l to catch the prey, and devoured	Eze 19:6	3925
hath *l* of the Father, cometh unto	Jn 6:45	3129
this man letters, having never *l*	Jn 7:15	3129
Moses was *l* in all the wisdom of	Acts 7:22	3811
to the doctrine which ye have *l*	Rom 16:17	3129
But ye have not so *l* Christ	Eph 4:20	3129
things, which ye have both *l*	Phil 4:9	3129
for I have *l*, in whatsoever state	Phil 4:11	3129
As ye also *l* of Epaphras our dear	Col 1:7	3129
in the things which thou hast *l*	2Ti 3:14	3129
knowing of whom thou hast *l* them	2Ti 3:14	3129
yet *l* he obedience by the things	Heb 5:8	3129

LEARNING

man will hear, and will increase *l*	Prov 1:5	3948
man, and he will increase in *l*	Prov 9:9	3948
of the lips increaseth *l*	Prov 16:21	3948
mouth, and addeth *l* to his lips	Prov 16:23	3948
and whom they might teach the *l*	Dan 1:4	5612
them knowledge and skill in all *l*	Dan 1:17	5612
much *l* doth make thee mad	Acts 26:24	1121
aforetime were written for our *l*	Rom 15:4	1319
Ever *l*, and never able to come to	2Ti 3:7	3129

LEASING

ye love vanity, and seek after *l*	Ps 4:2	3577
shalt destroy them that speak *l*	Ps 5:6	3577

LEAST See APPENDIX.

LEATHER

a girdle of *l* about his loins	2Kin 1:8	5785

LEATHERN

a *l* girdle about his loins	Mt 3:4	1193

LEAVE See APPENDIX.

LEAVED

open before him the two *l* gates	Is 45:1	1817

LEAVEN

put away *l* out of your houses	Ex 12:15	7603
be no *l* found in your houses	Ex 12:19	7603
neither shall there be *l* seen	Ex 13:7	7603
the blood of my sacrifice with *l*	Ex 34:25	2557
the LORD, shall be made with *l*	Lev 2:11	2557
for ye shall burn no *l*, nor any	Lev 2:11	7603
It shall not be baken with *l*	Lev 6:17	2557
eat it without *l* beside the altar	Lev 10:12	4682
they shall be baken with *l*	Lev 23:17	2557
sacrifice of thanksgiving with *l*	Amos 4:5	2557
kingdom of heaven is like unto *l*	Mt 13:33	2219
beware of the *l* of the Pharisees	Mt 16:6	2219
beware of the *l* of the Pharisees	Mt 16:11	2219
them not beware of the *l* of bread	Mt 16:12	2219
beware of the *l* of the Pharisees,	Mk 8:15	2219
and of the *l* of Herod	Mk 8:15	2219
ye of the *l* of the Pharisees	Lk 12:1	2219
It is like *l*, which a woman took	Lk 13:21	2219
little *l* leaveneth the whole lump	1Cor 5:6	2219
Purge out therefore the old *l*	1Cor 5:7	2219
us keep the feast, not with old *l*	1Cor 5:8	2219
neither with the *l* of malice	1Cor 5:8	2219
A little *l* leaveneth the whole	Gal 5:9	2219

LEAVENED

for whosoever eateth *l* bread from	Ex 12:15	2557
whosoever eateth that which is *l*	Ex 12:19	2557
Ye shall eat nothing *l*	Ex 12:20	2557
took their dough before it was *l*	Ex 12:34	2557
out of Egypt, for it was not *l*	Ex 12:39	2557
there shall no *l* bread be eaten	Ex 13:3	2557
there shall no *l* bread be seen	Ex 13:7	2557
of my sacrifice with *l* bread	Ex 23:18	2557
l bread with the sacrifice of	Lev 7:13	2557
Thou shalt eat no *l* bread with it	Deut 16:3	2557
there shall be no *l* bread seen	Deut 16:4	7603
kneaded the dough, until it be *l*	Hos 7:4	2557
of meal, till the whole was *l*	Mt 13:33	2220
of meal, till the whole was *l*	Lk 13:21	2220

LEAVENETH

a little leaven *l* the whole lump	1Cor 5:6	2220
A little leaven *l* the whole lump	Gal 5:9	2220

LEAVES

and they sewed fig *l* together	Gen 3:7	2529
the two *l* of the one door were	1Kin 6:34	6763
the two *l* of the other door were	1Kin 6:34	7050
in them, when they cast their *l*	Is 6:13	
Jehudi had read three or four *l*	Jer 36:23	1817
wither in all the *l* of her spring	Eze 17:9	2964
two *l* apiece, two turning *l*	Eze 41:24	1817
two *l* for the one door	Eze 41:24	
and two *l* for the other door	Eze 41:24	1817
The *l* thereof were fair, and the	Dan 4:12	6074
off his branches, shake off his *l*	Dan 4:14	6074
Whose *l* were fair, and the fruit	Dan 4:21	6074
but *l* only, and said unto it, Let	Mt 21:19	5444
is yet tender, and putteth forth *l*	Mt 24:32	5444
a fig tree afar off having *l*	Mk 11:13	5444
to it, he found nothing but *l*	Mk 11:13	5444
is yet tender, and putteth forth *l*	Mk 13:28	5444
the *l* of the tree were for the	Rev 22:2	5444

LEAVETH

Which *l* her eggs in the earth, and	Job 39:14	5800
A good man *l* an inheritance to	Prov 13:22	
a sweeping rain which *l* no food	Prov 28:3	
idol shepherd that *l* the flock	Zec 11:17	5800
Then the devil *l* him, and, behold,	Mt 4:11	863
coming, and *l* the sheep, and fleeth	Jn 10:12	863

LEAVING See APPENDIX.

LEBANA (leb'-a-nah) See LEBANAH. *A family of exiles.*

The children of *L*, the children	Neh 7:48	3848

LEBANAH (leb'-a-nah) *Same as Lebana.*

The children of *L*, the children	Ezr 2:45	3848

LEBANON (leb'-a-non) *Chief mountain range in Syria.*

land of the Canaanites, and unto *L*	Deut 1:7	3844
that goodly mountain, and *L*	Deut 3:25	3844
from the wilderness and *L*, from	Deut 11:24	3844
this *L* even unto the great river,	Josh 1:4	3844
of the great sea over against *L*	Josh 9:1	3844
valley of *L* under mount Hermon	Josh 11:17	3844
of *L* even unto the mount Halak	Josh 12:7	3844
land of the Giblites, and all *L*	Josh 13:5	3844
from *L* unto Misrephoth-maim	Josh 13:6	3844
the Hivites that dwelt in mount *L*	Judg 3:3	3844
and devour the cedars of *L*	Judg 9:15	3844
is in *L* even unto the hyssop that	1Kin 4:33	3844
they hew me cedar trees out of *L*	1Kin 5:6	3844
them down from *L* unto the sea	1Kin 5:9	3844
And he sent them to *L*, ten	1Kin 5:14	3844
a month they were in *L*, and two	1Kin 5:14	3844
also the house of the forest of *L*	1Kin 7:2	3844
to build in Jerusalem, and in *L*	1Kin 9:19	3844
in the house of the forest of *L*	1Kin 10:17	3844
the forest of *L* were of pure gold	1Kin 10:21	3844
The thistle that was in *L* sent to	2Kin 14:9	3844
sent to the cedar that was in *L*	2Kin 14:9	3844
by a wild beast that was in *L*	2Kin 14:9	3844
the mountains, to the sides of *L*	2Kin 19:23	3844
trees, and algum trees, out of *L*	2Chr 2:8	3844
can skill to cut timber in *L*	2Chr 2:8	3844
And we will cut wood out of *L*	2Chr 2:16	3844
to build in Jerusalem, and in *L*	2Chr 8:6	3844
in the house of the forest of *L*	2Chr 9:16	3844
the forest of *L* were of pure gold	2Chr 9:20	3844
The thistle that was in *L* sent to	2Chr 25:18	3844
sent to the cedar that was in *L*	2Chr 25:18	3844
by a wild beast that was in *L*	2Chr 25:18	3844
trees unto the sea of *L* to Joppa	Ezr 3:7	3844
the LORD breaketh the cedars of *L*	Ps 29:5	3844
L and Sirion like a young unicorn	Ps 29:6	3844
fruit thereof shall shake like *L*	Ps 72:16	3844
he shall grow like a cedar in *L*	Ps 92:12	3844
the cedars of *L*, which he hath	Ps 104:16	3844
a chariot of the wood of *L*	Song 3:9	3844

L

Come with me from *L*, my spouse,	Song 4:8	3844
with me from *L*	Song 4:8	3844
garments is like the smell of *L*	Song 4:11	3844
living waters, and streams from *L*	Song 4:15	3844
his countenance is as *L*,	Song 5:15	3844
thy nose is as the tower of *L*	Song 7:4	3844
And upon all the cedars of *L*	Is 2:13	3844
L shall fall by a mighty one	Is 10:34	3844
at thee, and the cedars of *L*	Is 14:8	3844
L shall be turned into a fruitful	Is 29:17	3844
L is ashamed and hewn down	Is 33:9	3844
the glory of *L* shall be given	Is 35:2	3844
the mountains, to the sides of *L*	Is 37:24	3844
L is not sufficient to burn, nor	Is 40:16	3844
The glory of *L* shall come unto	Is 60:13	3844
Will a man leave the snow of *L*	Jer 18:14	3844
Gilead unto me, and the head of *L*	Jer 22:6	3844
Go up to *L*, and cry	Jer 22:20	3844
O inhabitant of *L*, that makest	Jer 22:23	3844
had divers colours, came unto *L*	Eze 17:3	3844
from *L* to make masts for thee	Eze 27:5	3844
a cedar in *L* with fair branches	Eze 31:3	3844
I caused *L* to mourn for him, and	Eze 31:15	3844
of Eden, the choice and best of *L*	Eze 31:16	3844
and cast forth his roots as *L*	Hos 14:5	3844
the olive tree, and his smell as *L*	Hos 14:6	3844
thereof shall be as the wine of *L*	Hos 14:7	3844
and the flower of *L* languisheth	Nah 1:4	3844
violence of *L* shall cover thee	Hab 2:17	3844
them into the land of Gilead and *L*	Zec 10:10	3844
Open thy doors, O *L*, that the	Zec 11:1	3844

LEBAOTH (leb'-a-oth) See BETH-LEBAOTH. *A city in Judah.*
And *L*, and Shilhim, and Ain, and	Josh 15:32	3822

LEBBAEUS (leb-be'-us) See JUDAS, THADDAEUS. *Same as Thaddaeus.*
James the son of Alphaeus, and *L*	Mt 10:3	3002

LEB-KAMAI See MIDST.

LEBONAH (le-bo'-nah) *A city in Ephraim.*
to Shechem, and on the south of *L*	Judg 21:19	3829

LECAH (le'-cah) *Son of Er.*
of Judah were, Er the father of *L*	1Chr 4:21	3922

LED
the LORD *l* me to the house of my	Gen 24:27	5148
which had *l* me in the right way	Gen 24:48	5148
he *l* the flock to the backside of	Ex 3:1	5090
that God *l* them not through the	Ex 13:17	5148
But God *l* the people about,	Ex 13:18	5437
Thou in thy mercy hast *l* forth	Ex 15:13	5148
l thee these forty years in the	Deut 8:2	3212
Who *l* thee through that great and	Deut 8:15	3212
I have *l* you forty years in the	Deut 29:5	3212
he *l* him about, he instructed him	Deut 32:10	5437
l him throughout all the land of	Josh 24:3	3212
which *l* them away captive, and	1Kin 8:48	
But he *l* them to Samaria	2Kin 6:19	3212
Joab *l* forth the power of the	1Chr 20:1	5090
l forth his people, and went to	2Chr 25:11	5090
thou hast *l* captivity captive	Ps 68:18	
also he *l* them with a cloud	Ps 78:14	5148
he *l* them on safely, so that they	Ps 78:53	5148
so he *l* them through the depths,	Ps 106:9	3212
he *l* them forth by the right way,	Ps 107:7	1869
To him which *l* his people through	Ps 136:16	3212
I have *l* thee in right paths	Prov 4:11	1869
they that are *l* of them are	Is 9:16	833
he *l* them through the deserts	Is 48:21	3212
joy, and be *l* forth with peace	Is 55:12	2986
That *l* them by the right hand of	Is 63:12	3212
That *l* them through the deep, as	Is 63:13	3212
that *l* us through the wilderness,	Jer 2:6	3212
when he *l* thee by the way	Jer 2:17	3212
whither they have *l* him captive	Jer 22:12	
which *l* the seed of the house of	Jer 23:8	935
He hath *l* me, and brought me into	Lam 3:2	5090
l them with him to Babylon	Eze 17:12	935
which caused them to be *l* into	Eze 39:28	
l me about the way without unto	Eze 47:2	5437
l you forty years through the	Amos 2:10	3212
Israel shall surely be *l* away	Amos 7:11	
And Huzzab shall be *l* away captive	Nah 2:7	
Then was Jesus *l* up of the spirit	Mt 4:1	321
that had laid hold on Jesus *l* him	Mt 26:57	520
they *l* him away, and delivered him	Mt 27:2	520
l him away to crucify him	Mt 27:31	520
hand, and *l* him out of the town	Mk 8:23	1806
they *l* Jesus away to the high	Mk 14:53	520
the soldiers *l* him away into the	Mk 15:16	520

him, and *l* him out to crucify him	Mk 15:20	1806
was *l* by the Spirit into the	Lk 4:1	71
l him unto the brow of the hill	Lk 4:29	71
shall be *l* away captive into all	Lk 21:24	163
l him, and brought him into the	Lk 22:54	71
l him into their council, saying,	Lk 22:66	321
them arose, and *l* him unto Pilate	Lk 23:1	71
as they *l* him away, they laid	Lk 23:26	520
l with him to be put to death	Lk 23:32	71
he *l* them out as far as to	Lk 24:50	1806
l him away to Annas first	Jn 18:13	520
Then *l* they Jesus from Caiaphas	Jn 18:28	71
And they took Jesus, and *l* him away	Jn 19:16	520
He was *l* as a sheep to the	Acts 8:32	71
but they *l* him by the hand, and	Acts 9:8	5496
Paul was to be *l* into the castle	Acts 21:37	1521
being *l* by the hand of them that	Acts 22:11	5496
For as many as are *l* by the	Rom 8:14	71
dumb idols, even as ye were *l*	1Cor 12:2	71
But if ye be *l* of the Spirit, ye	Gal 5:18	71
he *l* captivity captive, and gave	Eph 4:8	162
l away with divers lusts,	2Ti 3:6	71
being *l* away with the error of	2Pet 3:17	4879

LEDDEST
over us, thou wast he that *l* out	2Sa 5:2	3318
was king, thou wast he that *l* out	1Chr 11:2	3318
Moreover thou *l* them in the day	Neh 9:12	5148
Thou *l* thy people like a flock by	Ps 77:20	5148
l out into the wilderness four	Acts 21:38	1806

LEDGES
and the borders were between the *l*	1Kin 7:28	7948
were between the *l* were lions	1Kin 7:29	7948
upon the *l* there was a base above	1Kin 7:29	7948
the top of the base the *l* thereof	1Kin 7:35	3027
on the plates of the *l* thereof	1Kin 7:36	3027

LEEKS
and the melons, and the, *l*, and the	Num 11:5	2682

LEES
things, a feast of wines on the *l*	Is 25:6	8105
of wines on the *l* well refined	Is 25:6	8105
and he hath settled on his *l*	Jer 48:11	8105
men that are settled on their *l*	Zeph 1:12	8105

LEFT
they *l* off to build the city	Gen 11:8	2308
if thou wilt take the *l* hand	Gen 13:9	8040
hand, then I will go to the *l*	Gen 13:9	8041
which is on the *l* hand of	Gen 14:15	8040
he *l* off talking with him, and God	Gen 17:22	3615
as soon as he had *l* communing	Gen 18:33	3615
who hath not *l* destitute my	Gen 24:27	5800
to the right hand, or to the *l*	Gen 24:49	8040
and *l* bearing	Gen 29:35	5975
Leah saw that she had *l* bearing	Gen 30:9	5975
company which is *l* shall escape	Gen 32:8	7604
And Jacob was *l* alone	Gen 32:24	3498
he *l* all that he had in Joseph's	Gen 39:6	5800
he *l* his garment in her hand, and	Gen 39:12	5800
he had *l* his garment in her hand	Gen 39:13	5800
that he *l* his garment with me, and	Gen 39:15	5800
that he *l* his garment with me, and	Gen 39:18	5800
very much, until he *l* numbering	Gen 41:49	2308
brother is dead, and he is *l* alone	Gen 42:38	7604
the eldest, and *l* at the youngest	Gen 44:12	3615
he alone is *l* of his mother, and	Gen 44:20	3498
there is not ought *l* in the sight	Gen 47:18	7604
right hand toward Israel's *l* hand	Gen 48:13	8040
Manasseh in his *l* hand toward	Gen 48:13	8040
his *l* hand upon Manasseh's head,	Gen 48:14	8040
they *l* in the land of Goshen	Gen 50:8	5800
why is it that ye have *l* the man	Ex 2:20	5800
word of the LORD *l* his servants	Ex 9:21	5800
even all that the hail hath *l*	Ex 10:12	7604
of the trees which the hail had *l*	Ex 10:15	3498
shall not an hoof be *l* behind	Ex 10:26	7604
their right hand, and on their *l*	Ex 14:22	8040
their right hand, and on their *l*	Ex 14:29	8040
but some of them *l* of it until	Ex 16:20	3498
passover be *l* unto the morning	Ex 34:25	3885
that which is *l* of the meat	Lev 2:10	3498
Ithamar, his sons that were *l*	Lev 10:12	3498
sons of Aaron which were *l* alive	Lev 10:16	3498
into the palm of his own *l* hand	Lev 14:15	8042
in the oil that is in his *l* hand	Lev 14:16	8042
into the palm of his own *l* hand	Lev 14:26	8042
his *l* hand seven times before the	Lev 14:27	8042
upon them that are *l* alive of you	Lev 26:36	7604
they that are *l* of you shall pine	Lev 26:39	7604
The land also shall be *l* of them	Lev 26:43	5800

to the right hand nor to the *l*	Num 20:17	8040
until there was none *l* him alive	Num 21:35	7604
to the right hand or to the *l*	Num 22:26	8040
And there was not *l* a man of them	Num 26:65	3498
unto the right hand nor to the *l*	Deut 2:27	8040
every city, we *l* none to remain	Deut 2:34	7604
until none was *l* to him remaining	Deut 3:3	7604
ye shall be *l* few in number among	Deut 4:27	7604
to the right hand or to the *l*	Deut 5:32	8040
among them, until they that are *l*	Deut 7:20	7604
to the right hand, nor to the *l*	Deut 17:11	8040
to the right hand, or to the *l*	Deut 17:20	8040
to the right hand, or to the *l*	Deut 28:14	8040
hath nothing *l* him in the siege	Deut 28:55	7604
ye shall be *l* few in number,	Deut 28:62	7604
and there is none shut up, or *l*	Deut 32:36	5800
it to the right hand or to the *l*	Josh 1:7	8040
l them without the camp of Israel	Josh 6:23	3241
was not a man *l* in Ai or Beth-el	Josh 8:17	7604
they *l* the city open, and pursued	Josh 8:17	5800
until he had *l* him none remaining	Josh 10:33	7604
he *l* none remaining, according to	Josh 10:37	7604
he *l* none remaining	Josh 10:39	7604
he *l* none remaining, but utterly	Josh 10:40	7604
until they *l* him none remaining	Josh 11:8	7604
there was not any *l* to breathe	Josh 11:11	3498
neither *l* they any to breathe	Josh 11:14	7604
he *l* nothing undone of all that	Josh 11:15	5493
There was none of the Anakims *l*	Josh 11:22	3498
goeth unto Cabul on the *l* hand	Josh 19:27	8040
Ye have not *l* your brethren these	Josh 22:3	5800
to the right hand or to the *l*	Josh 23:6	8040
which Joshua *l* when he died	Judg 2:21	5800
the LORD *l* those nations, without	Judg 2:23	3241
are the nations which the LORD *l*	Judg 3:1	3241
And Ehud put forth his *l* hand	Judg 3:21	8040
and there was not a man *l*	Judg 4:16	7604
l no sustenance for Israel,	Judg 6:4	7604
held the lamps in their *l* hands	Judg 7:20	8040
all that were *l* of all the hosts	Judg 8:10	3498
youngest son of Jerubbaal was *l*	Judg 9:5	3498
hand, and the other with his *l*	Judg 16:29	8040
and she was *l*, and her two sons	Ruth 1:3	7604
the woman was *l* of her two sons	Ruth 1:5	7604
then she *l* speaking unto her	Ruth 1:18	2308
and how thou hast *l* thy father	Ruth 2:11	5800
did eat, and was sufficed, and *l*	Ruth 2:14	3498
who hath not *l* off his kindness	Ruth 2:20	5800
which hath not *l* thee this day	Ruth 4:14	7673
that every one that is *l* in thine	1Sa 2:36	3498
the stump of Dagon was *l* to him	1Sa 5:4	7604
to the right hand or to the *l*	1Sa 6:12	8040
said, Behold that which is *l*	1Sa 9:24	7604
thy father hath *l* the care of the	1Sa 10:2	5203
two of them were not *l* together	1Sa 11:11	7604
l the sheep with a keeper, and	1Sa 17:20	5203
David *l* his carriage in the hand	1Sa 17:22	5203
with whom hast thou *l* those few	1Sa 17:28	5203
surely there had not been *l* unto	1Sa 25:34	3498
l neither man nor woman alive, and	1Sa 27:9	
those that were *l* behind stayed	1Sa 30:9	3498
and my master *l* me, because three	1Sa 30:13	5800
nor to the *l* from following Abner	2Sa 2:19	8040
to thy right hand or to thy *l*	2Sa 2:21	8040
there they *l* their images, and	2Sa 5:21	5800
that is *l* of the house of Saul	2Sa 9:1	3498
and there is not one of them *l*	2Sa 13:30	3498
shall quench my coal which is *l*	2Sa 14:7	7604
the *l* from ought that my lord the	2Sa 14:19	8041
the king *l* ten women, which were	2Sa 15:16	5800
on his right hand and on his *l*	2Sa 16:6	8040
which he hath *l* to keep the house	2Sa 16:21	3240
shall not be *l* so much as one	2Sa 17:12	3498
whom he had *l* to keep the house,	2Sa 20:3	3240
and he set up the *l* pillar	1Kin 7:21	8042
five on the *l* side of the house	1Kin 7:39	8040
Solomon *l* all the vessels	1Kin 7:47	3240
the right side, and five on the *l*	1Kin 7:49	8040
that were *l* of the Amorites	1Kin 9:20	3498
were *l* after them in the land	1Kin 9:21	3498
l in Israel, and will take away	1Kin 14:10	5800
the gold that were *l* in the	1Kin 15:18	3498
that he *l* off building of Ramah,	1Kin 15:21	2308
he *l* not to Jeroboam any that	1Kin 15:29	7604
he *l* him not one that pisseth	1Kin 16:11	7604
that there was no breath *l* in him	1Kin 17:17	3498
to Judah, and *l* his servant there	1Kin 19:3	3240
and I, even I only, am *l*	1Kin 19:10	3498
and I, even I only, am *l*	1Kin 19:14	3498
Yet I have *l* me seven thousand in	1Kin 19:18	7604
he *l* the oxen, and ran after	1Kin 19:20	5800

thousand of the men that were *l*	1Kin 20:30	3498
that is shut up and *l* in Israel,	1Kin 21:21	5800
him on his right hand and on his *l*	1Kin 22:19	8040
only in Kir-haraseth *l* they the	2Kin 3:25	7604
l thereof, according to the word	2Kin 4:44	3498
l their tents, and their horses,	2Kin 7:7	5800
which are *l* in the city, (behold,	2Kin 7:13	7604
of Israel that are *l* in it	2Kin 7:13	7604
since the day that she *l* the land	2Kin 8:6	5800
that is shut up and *l* in Israel	2Kin 9:8	6113
until he *l* him none remaining	2Kin 10:11	7604
neither *l* he any of them	2Kin 10:14	7604
was not a man *l* that came not	2Kin 10:21	7604
to the *l* corner of the temple	2Kin 11:11	8042
was not any shut up, nor any *l*	2Kin 14:26	5800
they *l* all the commandments of	2Kin 17:16	5800
there was none *l* but the tribe of	2Kin 17:18	7604
prayer for the remnant that are *l*	2Kin 19:4	4672
nothing shall be *l*, saith the	2Kin 20:17	3498
to the right hand and on his *l*	2Kin 22:2	8040
which were on a man's *l* hand at	2Kin 23:8	8040
people that were *l* in the city	2Kin 25:11	7604
But the captain of the guard *l* of	2Kin 25:12	7604
king of Babylon had *l*, even over	2Kin 25:22	7604
of Merari stood on the *l* hand	1Chr 6:44	8040
which were *l* of the family of	1Chr 6:61	3498
the *l* in hurling stones and	1Chr 12:2	8040
that are *l* in all the land of	1Chr 13:2	7604
when they had *l* their gods there,	1Chr 14:12	5800
So he *l* there before the ark of	1Chr 16:37	5800
right hand, and the other on the *l*	2Chr 3:17	8040
and the name of that on the *l* Boaz	2Chr 3:17	8042
the right hand, and five on the *l*	2Chr 4:6	8040
the right hand, and five on the *l*	2Chr 4:7	8040
the right side, and five on the *l*	2Chr 4:8	8040
that were *l* of the Hittites	2Chr 8:7	3498
who were *l* after them in the land	2Chr 8:8	3498
For the Levites *l* their suburbs	2Chr 11:14	5800
therefore have I also *l* you in	2Chr 12:5	5800
that he *l* off building of Ramah,	2Chr 16:5	2308
on his right hand and on his *l*	2Chr 18:18	8040
that there was never a son *l* him	2Chr 21:17	7604
to the *l* side of the temple	2Chr 23:10	8042
they *l* the house of the LORD God	2Chr 24:18	5800
(for they *l* him in great diseases	2Chr 24:25	5800
other ten thousand *l* alive did	2Chr 25:12	
So the armed men *l* the captives	2Chr 28:14	5800
enough to eat, and have *l* plenty	2Chr 31:10	3498
that which is *l* is this great	2Chr 31:10	3498
was done in the land, God *l* him	2Chr 32:31	5800
to the right hand, nor to the *l*	2Chr 34:2	8040
and for them that are *l* in Israel	2Chr 34:21	7604
which were *l* of the captivity, and	Neh 1:2	7604
The remnant that are *l* of the	Neh 1:3	7604
there was no breach *l* therein	Neh 6:1	3498
and on his *l* hand, Pedaiah, and	Neh 8:4	8040
There shall none of his meat be *l*	Job 20:21	8300
him that is *l* in his tabernacle	Job 20:26	8300
On the *l* hand, where he doth work	Job 23:9	8040
they *l* off speaking	Job 32:15	6275
he hath *l* off to be wise, and to	Ps 36:3	2308
there was not one of them *l*	Ps 106:11	3498
in her *l* hand riches and honour	Prov 3:16	8040
to the right hand nor to the *l*	Prov 4:27	8040
but a child *l* to himself bringeth	Prov 29:15	7971
but a fool's heart at his *l*	Eccl 10:2	8040
His *l* hand is under my head, and	Song 2:6	8040
His *l* hand should be under my	Song 8:3	8040
the daughter of Zion is *l* as a	Is 1:8	3498
l unto us a very small remnant	Is 1:9	3498
pass, that he that is *l* in Zion	Is 4:3	7604
one eat that is *l* in the land	Is 7:22	3498
and he shall eat on the *l* hand	Is 9:20	8040
as one gathereth eggs that are *l*	Is 10:14	5800
of his people, which shall be *l*	Is 11:11	7604
of his people, which shall be *l*	Is 11:16	7604
gleaning grapes shall be *l* in it	Is 17:6	7604
which they *l* because of the	Is 17:9	5800
They shall be *l* together unto the	Is 18:6	5800
earth be burned, and few men *l*	Is 24:6	7604
In the city is *l* desolation	Is 24:12	7604
forsaken, and *l* like a wilderness	Is 27:10	5800
till ye be *l* as a beacon upon the	Is 30:17	3498
hand, and when ye turn to the *l*	Is 30:21	8041
multitude of the city shall be *l*	Is 32:14	5800
prayer for the remnant that is *l*	Is 37:4	4672
nothing shall be *l*, saith the	Is 39:6	3498
Behold, I was *l* alone	Is 49:21	7604
on the right hand and on the *l*	Is 54:3	8040
house, I have *l* mine heritage	Jer 12:7	5203
such as are *l* in this city from	Jer 21:7	7604

L

are *l* in the house of the LORD	Jer 27:18	3498
The people which were *l* of the	Jer 31:2	8300
the cities of Judah that were *l*	Jer 34:7	3498
all the women that are *l* in the	Jer 38:22	7604
So they *l* off speaking with him	Jer 38:27	2790
the captain of the guard *l* of the	Jer 39:10	7604
people that were *l* in the land	Jer 40:6	7604
Babylon had *l* a remnant of Judah	Jer 40:11	5414
(for we are *l* but a few of many,	Jer 42:2	7604
the captain of the guard had *l*	Jer 43:6	3240
But since we *l* off to burn	Jer 44:18	2308
How is the city of praise not *l*	Jer 49:25	5800
let nothing of her be *l*	Jer 50:26	7611
the captain of the guard *l*	Jer 52:16	7604
the face of an ox on the *l* side	Eze 1:10	8040
Lie thou also upon thy *l* side	Eze 4:4	8042
were slaying them, and I was *l*	Eze 9:8	7604
therein being *l* a remnant that	Eze 14:22	3498
that dwell at thy *l* hand	Eze 16:46	8040
on the right hand, or on the *l*	Eze 21:16	8041
Neither *l* she her whoredoms	Eze 23:8	5800
ye have *l* shall fall by the sword	Eze 24:21	5800
have cut him off, and have *l* him	Eze 31:12	5203
from his shadow, and have *l* him	Eze 31:12	5203
Then the heathen that are *l* round	Eze 36:36	7604
smite thy bow out of thy *l* hand	Eze 39:3	8040
have *l* none of them any more	Eze 39:28	3498
that which was *l* was the place of	Eze 41:9	3240
were toward the place that was *l*	Eze 41:11	3240
was *l* was five cubits round about	Eze 41:11	3240
that are *l* in the breadth over	Eze 48:15	3498
shall not be *l* to other people	Dan 2:44	7662
Therefore I was *l* alone, and saw	Dan 10:8	7604
neither is there breath *l* in me	Dan 10:17	7604
his *l* hand unto heaven, and sware	Dan 12:7	8040
because they have *l* off to take	Hos 4:10	5800
that there shall not be a man *l*	Hos 9:12	
hath *l* hath the locust eaten	Joel 1:4	3499
hath *l* hath the cankerworm eaten	Joel 1:4	3499
hath *l* hath the caterpiller eaten	Joel 1:4	3499
their right hand and their *l* hand	Jonah 4:11	8040
Who is *l* among you that saw this	Hag 2:3	7604
the other upon the *l* side thereof	Zec 4:3	8040
and upon the *l* side thereof	Zec 4:11	8040
on the right hand and on the *l*	Zec 12:6	8040
but the third shall be *l* therein	Zec 13:8	3498
that every one that is *l* of all	Zec 14:16	3498
And they straightway *l* their nets	Mt 4:20	863
And they immediately *l* the ship	Mt 4:22	863
let not thy *l* hand know what thy	Mt 6:3	710
her hand, and the fever *l* her	Mt 8:15	863
that was *l* seven baskets full	Mt 15:37	4052
And he *l* them, and departed	Mt 16:4	2641
right hand, and the other on the *l*	Mt 20:21	2176
sit on my right hand, and on my *l*	Mt 20:23	2176
he *l* them, and went out of the	Mt 21:17	2641
and *l* him, and went their way	Mt 22:22	863
l his wife unto his brother	Mt 22:25	863
your house is *l* unto you desolate	Mt 23:38	863
There shall not be *l* here one	Mt 24:2	863
shall be taken, and the other *l*	Mt 24:40	863
shall be taken, and the other *l*	Mt 24:41	863
hand, but the goats on the *l*	Mt 25:33	2176
say also unto them on the *l* hand	Mt 25:41	2176
he *l* them, and went away again, and	Mt 26:44	863
right hand, and another on the *l*	Mt 27:38	2176
they *l* their father Zebedee in	Mk 1:20	863
and immediately the fever *l* her	Mk 1:31	863
meat that was *l* seven baskets	Mk 8:8	4051
he *l* them, and entering into the	Mk 8:13	863
say unto him, Lo, we have *l* all	Mk 10:28	863
There is no man that hath *l* house	Mk 10:29	863
hand, and the other on thy *l* hand	Mk 10:37	2176
on my *l* hand is not mine to give	Mk 10:40	2176
and they *l* him, and went their way	Mk 12:12	863
took a wife, and dying *l* no seed	Mk 12:20	863
and died, neither *l* he any seed	Mk 12:21	863
the seven had her, and *l* no seed	Mk 12:22	863
there shall not be *l* one stone	Mk 13:2	863
journey, who *l* his house, and gave	Mk 13:34	863
he *l* the linen cloth, and fled	Mk 14:52	2641
right hand, and the other on his *l*	Mk 15:27	2176
and it *l* her	Lk 4:39	863
Now when he had *l* speaking	Lk 5:4	3973
he *l* all, rose up, and followed	Lk 5:28	2641
sister hath *l* me to serve alone	Lk 10:40	2641
your house is *l* unto you desolate	Lk 13:35	863
be taken, and the other shall be *l*	Lk 17:34	863
shall be taken, and the other *l*	Lk 17:35	863
shall be taken, and the other *l*	Lk 17:36	863
Peter said, Lo, we have *l* all	Lk 18:28	863

There is no man that hath *l* house	Lk 18:29	863
they *l* no children, and died	Lk 20:31	2641
not be *l* one stone upon another	Lk 21:6	863
right hand, and the other on the *l*	Lk 23:33	710
He *l* Judaea, and departed again	Jn 4:3	863
The woman then *l* her waterpot	Jn 4:28	863
the seventh hour the fever *l* him	Jn 4:52	863
and Jesus was *l* alone, and the	Jn 8:9	2641
the Father hath not *l* me alone	Jn 8:29	863
that his soul was not *l* in hell	Acts 2:31	2641
Nevertheless he *l* not himself	Acts 14:17	863
came to Ephesus, and *l* them there	Acts 18:19	2641
we *l* it on the *l* hand, and	Acts 21:3	2641
Cyprus, we *l* it on the *l* hand	Acts 21:3	2176
soldiers, they *l* beating of Paul	Acts 21:32	3973
On the morrow they *l* the horsemen	Acts 23:32	1439
the Jews a pleasure, *l* Paul bound	Acts 24:27	2641
a certain man *l* in bonds by Felix	Acts 25:14	2641
Lord of Sabaoth had *l* us a seed	Rom 9:29	1459
I am *l* alone, and they seek my	Rom 11:3	5275
on the right hand and on the *l*	2Cor 6:7	710
it good to be *l* at Athens alone	1Th 3:1	2641
The cloke that I *l* at Troas with	2Ti 4:13	620
have I *l* at Miletum sick	2Ti 4:20	620
For this cause I *l* thee in Crete,	Titus 1:5	2641
he *l* nothing that is not put	Heb 2:8	863
a promise being *l* us of entering	Heb 4:1	2641
but *l* their own habitation, he	Jude 6	620
thou hast *l* thy first love	Rev 2:4	863
sea, and his *l* foot on the earth,	Rev 10:2	2176

LEFTEST

therefore *l* thou them in the hand	Neh 9:28	5800

LEFTHANDED

of Gera, a Benjamite, a man *l*..	Judg 3:15	334,3027,3225
seven hundred chosen men *l*	Judg 20:16	334,3027,3225

LEG

thy locks, make bare the *l*	Is 47:2	7640

LEGION

he answered, saying, My name is *L*	Mk 5:9	3003
with the devil, and had the *l*	Mk 5:15	3003
And he said, *L*	Lk 8:30	3003

LEGIONS

me more than twelve *l* of angels	Mt 26:53	3003

LEGS

his head with his *l*, and with the	Ex 12:9	3767
wash the inwards of him, and his *l*	Ex 29:17	3767
his *l* shall he wash in water	Lev 1:9	3767
the inwards and the *l* with water	Lev 1:13	3767
with his head, and with his *l*	Lev 4:11	3767
the inwards and the *l* in water	Lev 8:21	3767
he did wash the inwards and the *l*	Lev 9:14	3767
which have *l* above their feet, to	Lev 11:21	3767
thee in the knees, and in the *l*	Deut 28:35	7785
had greaves of brass upon his *l*	1Sa 17:6	7272
not pleasure in the *l* of a man	Ps 147:10	7785
The *l* of the lame are not equal	Prov 26:7	7785
His *l* are as pillars of marble,	Song 5:15	7785
and the ornaments of the *l*	Is 3:20	6807
His *l* of iron, his feet part of	Dan 2:33	8243
of the mouth of the lion two *l*	Amos 3:12	3767
that their *l* might be broken	Jn 19:31	4628
brake the *l* of the first, and of	Jn 19:32	4628
already, they brake not his *l*	Jn 19:33	4628

LEHAB See LEHABIM.

LEHABIM (le'·ha·bim) *A son of Mizraim.*

begat Ludim, and Anamim, and *L*	Gen 10:13	3853
begat Ludim, and Anamim, and *L*	1Chr 1:11	3853

LEHABITES See LEHABIM.

LEHI (le'·hi) See RAMATH-LEHI. *A district near Jerusalem.*

Judah, and spread themselves in *L*	Judg 15:9	3896
And when he came unto *L*, the	Judg 15:14	3896
which is in *L* unto this day	Judg 15:19	3896

LEISURE

they had no *l* so much as to eat	Mk 6:31	2119

LEMUEL (lem'·u·el) *A king mentioned in Proverbs.*

The words of king *L*, the prophecy	Prov 31:1	3927
It is not for kings, O *L*, it is	Prov 31:4	3927

LEND

If thou *l* money to any of my	Ex 22:25	3867
nor *l* him thy victuals for	Lev 25:37	5414
thou shalt *l* unto many nations,	Deut 15:6	5670
shalt surely *l* him sufficient for	Deut 15:8	5670
Thou shalt not *l* upon usury to	Deut 23:19	5391
stranger thou mayest *l* upon usury	Deut 23:20	5391

thou shalt not *l* upon usury	Deut 23:20	5391
When thou dost *l* thy brother any	Deut 24:10	5383
the man to whom thou dost *l* shall	Deut 24:11	5383
thou shalt *l* unto many nations,	Deut 28:12	3867
He shall *l* to thee, and thou shalt	Deut 28:44	3867
and thou shalt not *l* to him	Deut 28:44	3867
if ye *l* to them of whom ye hope	Lk 6:34	*1155*
for sinners also *l* to sinners	Lk 6:34	*1155*
ye your enemies, and do good, and *l*	Lk 6:35	*1155*
him, Friend, *l* me three loaves	Lk 11:5	*5531*

LENDER

the borrower is servant to the *l*	Prov 22:7	3867
as with the *l*, so with the	Is 24:2	3867

LENDETH

Every creditor that *l* ought unto	Deut 15:2	5383
He is ever merciful, and *l*	Ps 37:26	3867
A good man sheweth favour, and *l*	Ps 112:5	3867
upon the poor *l* unto the LORD	Prov 19:17	3867

LENGTH

The *l* of the ark shall be three	Gen 6:15	753
through the land in the *l* of it	Gen 13:17	753
and a half shall be the *l* thereof	Ex 25:10	753
and a half shall be the *l* thereof	Ex 25:17	753
two cubits shall be the *l* thereof	Ex 25:23	753
The *l* of one curtain shall be	Ex 26:2	753
The *l* of one curtain shall be	Ex 26:8	753
the *l* of the curtains of the tent	Ex 26:13	753
cubits shall be the *l* of a board	Ex 26:16	753
l there shall be hangings of an	Ex 27:11	753
The *l* of the court shall be an	Ex 27:18	753
a span shall be the *l* thereof	Ex 28:16	753
A cubit shall be the *l* thereof	Ex 30:2	753
The *l* of one curtain was twenty	Ex 36:9	753
The *l* of one curtain was thirty	Ex 36:15	753
The *l* of a board was ten cubits	Ex 36:21	753
cubits and a half was the *l* of it	Ex 37:1	753
and a half was the *l* thereof	Ex 37:6	753
two cubits was the *l* thereof	Ex 37:10	753
the *l* of it was a cubit, and the	Ex 37:25	753
five cubits was the *l* thereof	Ex 38:1	753
and twenty cubits was the	Ex 38:18	753
a span was the *l* thereof, and a	Ex 39:9	753
nine cubits was the *l* thereof	Deut 3:11	753
is thy life, and the *l* of thy days	Deut 30:20	753
which had two edges, of a cubit *l*	Judg 3:16	753
the *l* thereof was threescore	1Kin 6:2	753
twenty cubits was the *l* thereof	1Kin 6:3	753
forepart was twenty cubits in *l*	1Kin 6:20	753
the *l* thereof was an hundred	1Kin 7:2	753
the *l* thereof was fifty cubits,	1Kin 7:6	753
four cubits was the *l* of one base	1Kin 7:27	753
The *l* by cubits after the first	2Chr 3:3	753
the *l* of it was according to the	2Chr 3:4	753
the *l* whereof was according to	2Chr 3:8	753
twenty cubits the *l* thereof	2Chr 4:1	753
in *l* of days understanding	Job 12:12	753
even *l* of days for ever and ever	Ps 21:4	753
For *l* of days, and long life, and	Prov 3:2	753
L of days is in her right hand	Prov 3:16	753
have him become his son at the *l*	Prov 29:21	319
in the *l* of his branches	Eze 31:7	753
the *l* of the gate, thirteen	Eze 40:11	753
the *l* of the gates was the lower	Eze 40:18	753
north, the *l* thereof	Eze 40:20	753
the *l* thereof was fifty cubits,	Eze 40:21	753
the *l* was fifty cubits, and the	Eze 40:25	753
the *l* was fifty cubits, and the	Eze 40:36	753
The *l* of the porch was twenty	Eze 40:49	753
and he measured the *l* thereof	Eze 41:2	753
So he measured the *l* thereof	Eze 41:4	753
the *l* thereof ninety cubits	Eze 41:12	753
he measured the *l* of the building	Eze 41:15	753
high, and the *l* thereof two cubits	Eze 41:22	753
the *l* thereof, and the walls	Eze 41:22	753
Before the *l* of an hundred cubits	Eze 42:2	753
the *l* thereof was fifty cubits	Eze 42:7	753
For the *l* of the chambers that	Eze 42:8	753
the *l* shall be the *l* of five	Eze 45:1	753
the sanctuary five hundred in *l*	Eze 45:2	
shalt thou measure the *l* of five	Eze 45:3	753
the five and twenty thousand of *l*	Eze 45:5	753
the *l* shall be over against one	Eze 45:7	753
in *l* as one of the other parts,	Eze 48:8	753
of five and twenty thousand in *l*	Eze 48:9	753
five and twenty thousand in *l*	Eze 48:10	753
five and twenty thousand in *l*	Eze 48:10	753
have five and twenty thousand in *l*	Eze 48:13	753
all the *l* shall be five and twenty	Eze 48:13	753
the residue in *l* over against the	Eze 48:18	753

thereof, and what is the *l* thereof	Zec 2:2	753
the *l* thereof is twenty cubits,	Zec 5:2	753
if by any means now at *l* I might	Rom 1:10	*4218*
saints what is the breadth, and *l*	Eph 3:18	*3372*
the *l* is as large as the breadth	Rev 21:16	*3372*
The *l* and the breadth and the	Rev 21:16	*3372*

LENGTHEN

did walk, then I will *l* thy days	1Kin 3:14	748
l thy cords, and strengthen thy	Is 54:2	748

LENGTHENED

that thy days may be *l* in the	Deut 25:15	748

LENGTHENING

if it may be a *l* of thy	Dan 4:27	754

LENT

so that they *l* unto them such	Ex 12:36	7592
of any thing that is *l* upon usury	Deut 23:19	5391
also I have *l* him to the LORD	1Sa 1:28	7592
liveth he shall be *l* to the LORD	1Sa 1:28	7592
the loan which is *l* to the LORD	1Sa 2:20	7592
I have neither *l* on usury	Jer 15:10	5383
nor men have *l* to me on usury	Jer 15:10	5383

LENTILES

gave Esau bread and pottage of *l*	Gen 25:34	5742
and parched corn, and beans, and *l*	2Sa 17:28	5742
was a piece of ground full of *l*	2Sa 23:11	5742
wheat, and barley, and beans, and *l*	Eze 4:9	5742

LEOPARD

the *l* shall lie down with the kid	Is 11:6	5246
a *l* shall watch over their cities	Jer 5:6	5246
his skin, or the *l* his spots	Jer 13:23	5246
I beheld, and lo another, like a *l*	Dan 7:6	5245
as a *l* by the way will I observe	Hos 13:7	5246
which I saw was like unto a *l*	Rev 13:2	*3917*

LEOPARDS

dens, from the mountains of the *l*	Song 4:8	5246
also are swifter than the *l*	Hab 1:8	5246

LEPER

the *l* in whom the plague is, his	Lev 13:45	6879
the *l* in the day of his cleansing	Lev 14:2	6879
of leprosy be healed in the *l*	Lev 14:3	6879
of the seed of Aaron is a *l*	Lev 22:4	6879
they put out of the camp every *l*	Num 5:2	6879
hath an issue, or that is a *l*	2Sa 3:29	6879
man in valour, but he was a *l*	2Kin 5:1	6879
over the place, and recover the *l*	2Kin 5:11	6879
his presence a *l* as white as snow	2Kin 5:27	6879
so that he was a *l* unto the day	2Kin 15:5	6879
Uzziah the king was a *l* unto the	2Chr 26:21	6879
in a several house, being a *l*	2Chr 26:21	6879
for they said, He is a *l*	2Chr 26:23	6879
And, behold, there came a *l*	Mt 8:2	*3015*
in the house of Simon the *l*	Mt 26:6	*3015*
And there came a *l* to him,	Mk 1:40	*3015*
in the house of Simon the *l*	Mk 14:3	*3015*

LEPERS

And when these *l* came to the	2Kin 7:8	6879
Heal the sick, cleanse the *l*	Mt 10:8	*3015*
the *l* are cleansed, and the deaf	Mt 11:5	*3015*
many *l* were in Israel in the time	Lk 4:27	*3015*
the *l* are cleansed, the deaf hear	Lk 7:22	*3015*
there met him ten men that were *l*	Lk 17:12	*3015*

LEPROSY

of his flesh like the plague of *l*	Lev 13:2	6883
of his flesh, it is a plague of *l*	Lev 13:3	6883
it is a *l*	Lev 13:8	6883
When the plague of *l* is in a man	Lev 13:9	6883
It is an old *l* in the skin of his	Lev 13:11	6883
if a *l* break out abroad in the	Lev 13:12	6883
the *l* cover all the skin of him	Lev 13:12	6883
if the *l* have covered all his	Lev 13:13	6883
it is a *l*	Lev 13:15	6883
it is a plague of *l* broken out of	Lev 13:20	6883
it is a *l* broken out of the	Lev 13:25	6883
it is the plague of *l*	Lev 13:25	6883
it is the plague of *l*	Lev 13:27	6883
even a *l* upon the head or beard	Lev 13:30	6883
it is a *l* sprung up in his bald	Lev 13:42	6883
as the *l* appeareth in the skin of	Lev 13:43	6883
also that the plague of *l* is in	Lev 13:47	6883
it is a plague of *l*, and shall be	Lev 13:49	6883
the plague is a fretting *l*	Lev 13:51	6883
for it is a fretting *l*	Lev 13:52	6883
of *l* in a garment of woollen or	Lev 13:59	6883
if the plague of *l* be healed in	Lev 14:3	6883
cleansed from the *l* seven times	Lev 14:7	6883
of him in whom is the plague of *l*	Lev 14:32	6883

I put the plague of *l* in a house	Lev 14:34	6883
it is a fretting *l* in the house	Lev 14:44	6883
law for all manner of plague of *l*	Lev 14:54	6883
for the *l* of a garment, and of a	Lev 14:55	6883
this is the law of *l*	Lev 14:57	6883
Take heed in the plague of *l*	Deut 24:8	6883
for he would recover him of his *l*	2Kin 5:3	6883
thou mayest recover him of his *l*	2Kin 5:6	6883
unto me to recover a man of his *l*	2Kin 5:7	6883
The *l* therefore of Naaman shall	2Kin 5:27	6883
the *l* even rose up in his	2Chr 26:19	6883
And immediately his *l* was cleansed	Mt 8:3	3014
immediately the *l* departed from	Mk 1:42	3014
city, behold a man full of *l*	Lk 5:12	3014
immediately the *l* departed from	Lk 5:13	3014

LEPROUS

behold, his hand was *l* as snow	Ex 4:6	6879
He is a *l* man, he is unclean	Lev 13:44	6879
and, behold, Miriam became *l*	Num 12:10	6879
Miriam, and, behold, she was *l*	Num 12:10	6879
there were four *l* men at the	2Kin 7:3	6879
he was *l* in his forehead, and they	2Chr 26:20	6879

LESHEM (le'-shem) See LAISH. *Same as Laish.*

of Dan went up to fight against *L*	Josh 19:47	3959
it, and dwelt therein, and called *L*	Josh 19:47	3959

LESS See APPENDIX.

LESSER See APPENDIX.

LEST See APPENDIX.

LET See APPENDIX.

LETHEK See HOMER.

LETTER

that David wrote a *l* to Joab	2Sa 11:14	5612
And he wrote in the *l*, saying, Set	2Sa 11:15	5612
I will send a *l* unto the king of	2Kin 5:5	5612
he brought the *l* to the king of	2Kin 5:6	5612
Now when this *l* is come unto thee	2Kin 5:6	5612
the king of Israel had read the *l*	2Kin 5:7	5612
as soon as this *l* cometh to you	2Kin 10:2	5612
Then he wrote a *l* the second time	2Kin 10:6	5612
when the *l* came to them, that	2Kin 10:7	5612
Hezekiah received the *l* of the	2Kin 19:14	5612
the writing of the *l* was written	Ezr 4:7	5406
Shimshai the scribe wrote a *l*	Ezr 4:8	104
of the *l* that they sent unto him	Ezr 4:11	104
The *l* which ye sent unto us hath	Ezr 4:18	5407
l was read before Rehum, and	Ezr 4:23	5407
by *l* concerning this matter	Ezr 5:5	5407
The copy of the *l* that Tatnai	Ezr 5:6	104
They sent a *l* unto him, wherein	Ezr 5:7	6600
Now this is the copy of the *l*	Ezr 7:11	5406
a *l* unto Asaph the keeper of the	Neh 2:8	107
time with an open *l* in his hand	Neh 6:5	107
for all the words of this *l*	Est 9:26	107
to confirm this second *l* of Purim	Est 9:29	107
Hezekiah received the *l* from the	Is 37:14	5612
l that Jeremiah the prophet sent	Jer 29:1	5612
l in the ears of Jeremiah the	Jer 29:29	5612
he wrote a *l* after this manner	Acts 23:25	1992
when the governor had read the *l*	Acts 23:34	
the law, judge thee, who by the *l*	Rom 2:27	1121
in the spirit, and not in the *l*	Rom 2:29	1121
and not in the oldness of the *l*	Rom 7:6	1121
not of the *l*, but of the spirit	2Cor 3:6	1121
for the *l* killeth, but the spirit	2Cor 3:6	1121
though I made you sorry with a *l*	2Cor 7:8	1992
Ye see how large a *l* I have	Gal 6:11	1121
nor by *l* as from us, as that the	2Th 2:2	1992
for I have written a *l* unto you	Heb 13:22	1989

LETTERS

So she wrote *l* in Ahab's name, and	1Kin 21:8	5612
sent the *l* unto the elders and to	1Kin 21:8	5612
And she wrote in the *l*, saying,	1Kin 21:9	5612
as it was written in the *l* which	1Kin 21:11	5612
And Jehu wrote *l*, and sent to	2Kin 10:1	5612
Baladan, king of Babylon, sent *l*	2Kin 20:12	5612
wrote *l* also to Ephraim and	2Chr 30:1	107
went with the *l* from the king	2Chr 30:6	107
He wrote also *l* to rail on the	2Chr 32:17	5612
king, let *l* be given me to the	Neh 2:7	107
river, and gave them the king's *l*	Neh 2:9	107
of Judah sent many *l* unto Tobiah	Neh 6:17	107
the *l* of Tobiah came unto them	Neh 6:17	
Tobiah sent *l* to put me in fear	Neh 6:19	107
For he sent *l* into all the king's	Est 1:22	5612
the *l* were sent by posts into all	Est 3:13	5612
the *l* devised by Haman the son of	Est 8:5	5612

sent *l* by posts on horseback, and	Est 8:10	5612
sent *l* unto all the Jews that	Est 9:20	5612
he commanded by *l* that his wicked	Est 9:25	5612
he sent the *l* unto all the Jews,	Est 9:30	5612
Baladan, king of Babylon, sent *l*	Is 39:1	5612
Because thou hast sent *l* in thy	Jer 29:25	5612
written over him in *l* of Greek	Lk 23:38	1121
saying, How knoweth this man *l*	Jn 7:15	1121
desired of him *l* to Damascus to	Acts 9:2	1992
they wrote *l* by them after this	Acts 15:23	
I received *l* unto the brethren	Acts 22:5	1992
We neither received *l* out of	Acts 28:21	1121
ye shall approve by your *l*	1Cor 16:3	1992
or *l* of commendation from you	2Cor 3:1	
as if I would terrify you by *l*	2Cor 10:9	1992
For his *l*, say they, are weighty	2Cor 10:10	1992
in word by *l* when we are absent	2Cor 10:11	1992

LETTEST

l such words go out of thy mouth	Job 15:13	
with a cord which thou *l* down	Job 41:1	8257
now *l* thou thy servant depart in	Lk 2:29	630

LETTETH

hands escape, he that *l* him go	2Kin 10:24	
strife is as when one *l* out water	Prov 17:14	6362
only he who now *l* will let	2Th 2:7	2722

LETTING See APPENDIX.

LETUSHIM (le-tu'-shim) *A son of Dedan.*

sons of Dedan were Asshurim, and *L*	Gen 25:3	3912

LETUSHITES See LETUSHIM.

LEUMMIM (le-um'-mim) *A son of Dedan.*

were Asshurim, and Letushim, and *L*	Gen 25:3	3817

LEVI (le'-vi) See LEVITE, LEVITICAL, MATTHEW.
    1. A son of Jacob.

therefore was his name called *L*	Gen 29:34	3878
of the sons of Jacob, Simeon and *L*	Gen 34:25	3878
And Jacob said to Simeon and *L*	Gen 34:30	3878
firstborn, then Simeon, and *L*	Gen 35:23	3878
Simeon and *L* are brethren	Gen 49:5	3878
Reuben, Simeon, *L*, and Judah,	Ex 1:2	3878
are the names of the sons of *L*	Ex 6:16	3878
life of *L* were an hundred thirty	Ex 6:16	3878
were the sons of *L* by their names	Num 3:17	3878
the son of Kohath, the son of *L*	Num 16:1	3878
was Jochebed, the daughter of *L*	Num 26:59	3878
her mother bare to *L* in Egypt	Num 26:59	3878
the son of Kohath, the son of *L*	1Chr 6:38	3878
the son of Gershom, the son of *L*	1Chr 6:43	3878
the son of Merari, the son of *L*	1Chr 6:47	3878
the sons of Mahli, the son of *L*	Ezr 8:18	3878

    2. The tribe.

And the sons of *L*	Gen 46:11	3878
went a man of the house of *L*	Ex 2:1	3878
and took to wife a daughter of *L*	Ex 2:1	3878
these are the families of *L*	Ex 6:19	3878
all the sons of *L* gathered	Ex 32:26	3878
the children of *L* did according	Ex 32:28	3878
shalt not number the tribe of *L*	Num 1:49	3878
Bring the tribe of *L* near	Num 3:6	3878
Number the children of *L* after	Num 3:15	3878
Kohath from among the sons of *L*	Num 4:2	3878
too much upon you, ye sons of *L*	Num 16:7	3878
Hear, I pray you, ye sons of *L*	Num 16:8	3878
brethren the sons of *L* with thee	Num 16:10	3878
Aaron's name upon the rod of *L*	Num 17:3	3878
for the house of *L* was budded	Num 17:8	3878
brethren also of the tribe of *L*	Num 18:2	3878
I have given the children of *L*	Num 18:21	3878
the LORD separated the tribe of *L*	Deut 10:8	3878
Wherefore *L* hath no part nor	Deut 10:9	3878
Levites, and all the tribe of *L*	Deut 18:1	3878
the sons of *L* shall come near	Deut 21:5	3878
Simeon, and *L*, and Judah, and	Deut 27:12	3878
it unto the priests the sons of *L*	Deut 31:9	3878
of *L* he said, Let thy Thummim and	Deut 33:8	3878
Only unto the tribe of *L* he gave	Josh 13:14	3878
But unto the tribe of *L* Moses	Josh 13:33	3878
who were of the children of *L*	Josh 21:10	3878
which were not of the sons of *L*	1Kin 12:31	3878
Reuben, Simeon, *L*, and Judah,	1Chr 2:1	3878
The sons of *L*; Gershon	1Chr 6:1	3878
The sons of *L*; Gershom	1Chr 6:16	3878
companies of the children of *L*	1Chr 9:18	3878
the children of *L* four thousand	1Chr 12:26	3878
But *L* and Benjamin counted he not	1Chr 21:6	3878
into courses among the sons of *L*	1Chr 23:6	3878
sons were named of the tribe of *L*	1Chr 23:14	3878
These were the sons of *L* after	1Chr 23:24	3878

rest of the sons of L were these	1Chr 24:20	3878
found there none of the sons of L	Ezr 8:15	3878
the children of L shall bring the	Neh 10:39	3878
The sons of L, the chief of the	Neh 12:23	3878
Bless the LORD, O house of L	Ps 135:20	3878
sons of Zadok among the sons of L	Eze 40:46	3878
one gate of Judah, one gate of L	Eze 48:31	3878
family of the house of L apart	Zec 12:13	3878
that my covenant might be with L	Mal 2:4	3878
have corrupted the covenant of L	Mal 2:8	3878
and he shall purify the sons of L	Mal 3:3	3878
they that are of the sons of L	Heb 7:5	3017
L also, who receiveth tithes,	Heb 7:9	3017
Of the tribe of L were sealed	Rev 7:7	3017

3. *Same as Matthew the apostle.*

he saw L the son of Alphaeus	Mk 2:14	3018
forth, and saw a publican, named L	Lk 5:27	3018
L made him a great feast in his	Lk 5:29	3018

4. *Father of Matthat; ancestor of Jesus.*

Matthat, which was the son of	Lk 3:24	3017

5. *Father of another Matthat; ancestor of Jesus.*

Matthat, which was the son of L	Lk 3:29	3017

LEVIATHAN

thou draw out l with an hook	Job 41:1	3882
brakest the heads of l in pieces	Ps 74:14	3882
there is that l, whom thou hast	Ps 104:26	3882
punish l the piercing serpent	Is 27:1	3882
even l that crooked serpent	Is 27:1	3882

LEVITE (le'-vite) See LEVITES, LEVITICAL. *A descendant of Levi.*

Is not Aaron the L thy brother	Ex 4:14	3881
the L that is within your gates	Deut 12:12	3881
the L that is within thy gates	Deut 12:18	3881
that thou forsake not the L as	Deut 12:19	3881
the L that is within thy gates	Deut 14:27	3881
And the L, (because he hath no	Deut 14:29	3881
the L that is within thy gates,	Deut 16:11	3881
and thy maidservant, and the L	Deut 16:14	3881
if a L come from any of thy gates	Deut 18:6	3881
unto thine house, thou, and the L	Deut 26:11	3881
and hast given it unto the L	Deut 26:12	3881
also have given them unto the L	Deut 26:13	3881
the family of Judah, who was a L	Judg 17:7	3881
I am a L of Beth-lehem-judah, and	Judg 17:9	3881
So the L went in	Judg 17:10	3881
the L was content to dwell with	Judg 17:11	3881
And Micah consecrated the L	Judg 17:12	3881
seeing I have a L to my priest	Judg 17:13	3881
the voice of the young man the L	Judg 18:3	3881
the house of the young man the L	Judg 18:15	3881
that there was a certain L	Judg 19:1	3881
And the L, the husband of the	Judg 20:4	3881
a L of the sons of Asaph, came	2Chr 20:14	3881
which Cononiah the L was ruler	2Chr 31:12	3881
And Kore the son of Imnah the L	2Chr 31:14	3881
and Shabbethai the L helped them	Ezr 10:15	3881
And likewise a L, when he was at	Lk 10:32	3019
The son of consolation,) a L	Acts 4:36	3019

LEVITES

the L according to their families	Ex 6:25	3881
Moses, for the service of the L	Ex 38:21	3881
the cities of the L, and the	Lev 25:32	3881
may the L redeem at any time	Lev 25:32	3881
And if a man purchase of the L	Lev 25:33	3881
L are their possession among the	Lev 25:33	3881
But the L after the tribe of	Num 1:47	3881
the L over the tabernacle of	Num 1:50	3881
forward, the L shall take it down	Num 1:51	3881
be pitched, the L shall set it up	Num 1:51	3881
But the L shall pitch round about	Num 1:53	3881
the L shall keep the charge of	Num 1:53	3881
of the L in the midst of the camp	Num 2:17	3881
But the L were not numbered among	Num 2:33	3881
thou shalt give the L unto Aaron	Num 3:9	3881
I have taken the L from among the	Num 3:12	3881
therefore the L shall be mine	Num 3:12	3881
These are the families of the L	Num 3:20	3881
be chief over the chief of the L	Num 3:32	3881
All that were numbered of the L	Num 3:39	3881
thou shalt take the L for me (I	Num 3:41	3881
the cattle of the L instead of	Num 3:41	3881
Take the L instead of all the	Num 3:45	3881
the cattle of the L instead of	Num 3:45	3881
and the L shall be mine	Num 3:45	3881
Israel, which are more than the L	Num 3:46	3881
them that were redeemed by the L	Num 3:49	3881
the Kohathites from among the L	Num 4:18	3881
those that were numbered of the L	Num 4:46	3881
thou shalt give them unto the L	Num 7:5	3881

the oxen, and gave them unto the L	Num 7:6	3881
Take the L from among the	Num 8:6	3881
thou shalt bring the L before the	Num 8:9	3881
shalt bring the L before the LORD	Num 8:10	3881
shall put their hands upon the L	Num 8:10	3881
Aaron shall offer the L before	Num 8:11	3881
the L shall lay their hands upon	Num 8:12	3881
to make an atonement for the L	Num 8:12	3881
thou shalt set the L before Aaron	Num 8:13	3881
the L from among the children of	Num 8:14	3881
and the L shall be mine	Num 8:14	3881
after that shall the L go in to	Num 8:15	3881
I have taken the L for all the	Num 8:18	3881
I have given the L as a gift to	Num 8:19	3881
did to the L according unto all	Num 8:20	3881
commanded Moses concerning the L	Num 8:20	3881
the L were purified, and they	Num 8:21	3881
after that went the L in to do	Num 8:22	3881
commanded Moses concerning the L	Num 8:22	3881
is it that belongeth unto the L	Num 8:24	3881
unto the L touching their charge	Num 8:26	3881
the L from among the children of	Num 18:6	3881
But the L shall do the service of	Num 18:23	3881
I have given to the L to inherit	Num 18:24	3881
Thus speak unto the L, and say	Num 18:26	3881
unto the L as the increase of the	Num 18:30	3881
of the L after their families	Num 26:57	3881
These are the families of the L	Num 26:58	3881
beasts, and give them unto the L	Num 31:30	3881
of beast, and gave them unto the L	Num 31:47	3881
that they give unto the L of the	Num 35:2	3881
ye shall give also unto the L	Num 35:2	3881
which ye shall give unto the L	Num 35:4	3881
which ye shall give unto the L	Num 35:6	3881
give to the L shall be forty	Num 35:7	3881
give of his cities unto the L	Num 35:8	3881
shalt come unto the priests the L	Deut 17:9	3881
which is before the priests the L	Deut 17:18	3881
The priests the L, and all the	Deut 18:1	3881
God, as all his brethren the L do	Deut 18:7	3881
the priests the L shall teach you	Deut 24:8	3881
the priests the L spake unto all	Deut 27:9	3881
the L shall speak, and say unto	Deut 27:14	3881
That Moses commanded the L	Deut 31:25	3881
and the priests the L bearing it	Josh 3:3	3881
side before the priests the L	Josh 8:33	3881
but unto the L he gave none	Josh 14:3	3881
no part unto the L in the land	Josh 14:4	3881
But the L have no part among you	Josh 18:7	3881
of the L unto Eleazar the priest	Josh 21:1	3881
of Israel gave unto the L out of	Josh 21:3	3881
the priest, which were of the L	Josh 21:4	3881
of Israel gave by lot unto the L	Josh 21:8	3881
the L which remained of the	Josh 21:20	3881
Gershon, of the families of the L	Josh 21:27	3881
of Merari, the rest of the L	Josh 21:34	3881
of the families of the L, were by	Josh 21:40	3881
All the cities of the L within	Josh 21:41	3881
the L took down the ark of the	1Sa 6:15	3881
all the L were with him, bearing	2Sa 15:24	3881
did the priests and the L bring up	1Kin 8:4	3881
the L according to their fathers	1Chr 6:19	3881
Their brethren also the L were	1Chr 6:48	3881
children of Israel gave to the L	1Chr 6:64	3881
the Israelites, the priests, L	1Chr 9:2	3881
And of the L	1Chr 9:14	3881
For these L, the four chief	1Chr 9:26	3881
And Mattithiah, one of the L	1Chr 9:31	3881
chief of the fathers of the L	1Chr 9:33	3881
These chief fathers of the L were	1Chr 9:34	3881
L which are in their cities and	1Chr 13:2	3881
to carry the ark of God but the L	1Chr 15:2	3881
the children of Aaron, and the L	1Chr 15:4	3881
the priests, and for the L	1Chr 15:11	3881
the chief of the fathers of the L	1Chr 15:12	3881
the L sanctified themselves to	1Chr 15:14	3881
the children of the Levite the	1Chr 15:15	3881
L to appoint their brethren to be	1Chr 15:16	3881
So the L appointed Heman the son	1Chr 15:17	3881
And Chenaniah, chief of the L	1Chr 15:22	3881
when God helped the L that bare	1Chr 15:26	3881
all the L that bare the ark, and	1Chr 15:27	3881
he appointed certain of the L to	1Chr 16:4	3881
Israel, with the priests and the L	1Chr 23:2	3881
Now the L were numbered from the	1Chr 23:3	3881
And also unto the L	1Chr 23:26	3881
by the last words of David the L	1Chr 23:27	3881
the scribe, one of the L, wrote	1Chr 24:6	3878
the fathers of the priests and L	1Chr 24:6	3881
of the L after the house of their	1Chr 24:30	3881
the fathers of the priests and L	1Chr 24:31	3881

L

Eastward were six L, northward	1Chr 26:17	3881
And of the L, Ahijah was over the	1Chr 26:20	3881
Of the L, Hashabiah the son of	1Chr 27:17	3881
courses of the priests and the L	1Chr 28:13	3881
courses of the priests and the L	1Chr 28:21	3881
and the L took up the ark	2Chr 5:4	3881
did the priests and the L bring up	2Chr 5:5	3881
Also the L which were the singers	2Chr 5:12	3881
the L also with instruments of	2Chr 7:6	3881
the L to their charges, to praise	2Chr 8:14	3881
L concerning any matter, or	2Chr 8:15	3881
the L that were in all Israel	2Chr 11:13	3881
For the L left their suburbs and	2Chr 11:14	3881
LORD, the sons of Aaron, and the L	2Chr 13:9	3881
the L wait upon their business	2Chr 13:10	3881
And with them he sent L, even	2Chr 17:8	3881
and Tobijah, and Tob-adonijah, L	2Chr 17:8	3881
did Jehoshaphat set of the L	2Chr 19:8	3881
also the L shall be officers	2Chr 19:11	3881
And the L, of the children of the	2Chr 20:19	3881
gathered the L out of all the	2Chr 23:2	3881
of the priests and of the L	2Chr 23:4	3881
and they that minister of the L	2Chr 23:6	3881
the L shall compass the king	2Chr 23:7	3881
So the L and all Judah did	2Chr 23:8	3881
by the hand of the priests the L	2Chr 23:18	3881
together the priests and the L	2Chr 24:5	3881
Howbeit the L hastened it not	2Chr 24:5	3881
of the L to bring in out of Judah	2Chr 24:6	3881
office by the hand of the L	2Chr 24:11	3881
brought in the priests and the L	2Chr 29:4	3881
And said unto them, Hear me, ye L	2Chr 29:5	3881
Then the L arose, Mahath the son	2Chr 29:12	3881
the L took it, to carry it out	2Chr 29:16	3881
he set the L in the house of the	2Chr 29:25	3881
the L stood with the instruments	2Chr 29:26	3881
the princes commanded the L to	2Chr 29:30	3881
brethren the L did help them	2Chr 29:34	3881
for the L were more upright in	2Chr 29:34	3881
the L were ashamed, and sanctified	2Chr 30:15	3881
received of the L the charge of	2Chr 30:16	3881
therefore the L had the charge of	2Chr 30:17	3881
and the L and the priests praised	2Chr 30:21	3881
L that taught the good knowledge	2Chr 30:22	3881
Judah, with the priests and the L	2Chr 30:25	3881
Then the priests the L arose	2Chr 30:27	3881
the L after their courses, every	2Chr 31:2	3881
L for burnt offerings and for	2Chr 31:2	3881
portion of the priests and the L	2Chr 31:4	3881
the L concerning the heaps	2Chr 31:9	3881
the L from twenty years old and	2Chr 31:17	3881
by genealogies among the L	2Chr 31:19	3881
which the L that kept the doors	2Chr 34:9	3881
were Jahath and Obadiah, the L	2Chr 34:12	3881
and other of the L, all that could	2Chr 34:12	3881
of the L there were scribes, and	2Chr 34:13	3881
and the priests, and the L	2Chr 34:30	3881
said unto the L that taught all	2Chr 35:3	3881
division of the families of the L	2Chr 35:5	3881
to the priests, and to the L	2Chr 35:8	3881
Jeiel and Jozabad, chief of the L	2Chr 35:9	3881
gave unto the L for passover	2Chr 35:9	3881
the L in their courses, according	2Chr 35:10	3881
their hands, and the L flayed them	2Chr 35:11	3881
therefore the L prepared for	2Chr 35:14	3881
brethren the L prepared for them	2Chr 35:15	3881
kept, and the priests, and the L	2Chr 35:18	3881
and the priests, and the L	Ezr 1:5	3881
The L: the children	Ezr 2:40	3881
So the priests, and the L, and some	Ezr 2:70	3881
brethren the priests and the L	Ezr 3:8	3881
and appointed the L, from twenty	Ezr 3:8	3881
sons and their brethren the L	Ezr 3:9	3881
the L the sons of Asaph with	Ezr 3:10	3881
But many of the priests and L	Ezr 3:12	3881
of Israel, the priests, and the L	Ezr 6:16	3879
the L in their courses, for the	Ezr 6:18	3879
the L were purified together, all	Ezr 6:20	3881
and of the priests, and the L	Ezr 7:7	3881
of Israel, and of his priests and L	Ezr 7:13	3879
touching any of the priests and L	Ezr 7:24	3879
for the service of the L, two	Ezr 8:20	3881
the chief of the priests and the L	Ezr 8:29	3881
the L the weight of the silver,	Ezr 8:30	3881
and Noadiah the son of Binnui, L	Ezr 8:33	3881
Israel, and the priests, and the L	Ezr 9:1	3881
and made the chief priests, the L	Ezr 10:5	3881
Also of the L	Ezr 10:23	3881
After him repaired the L, Rehum	Neh 3:17	3881
singers and the L were appointed,	Neh 7:1	3881
The L: the children	Neh 7:43	3881

So the priests, and the L, and the	Neh 7:73	3881
Jozabad, Hanan, Pelaiah, and the L	Neh 8:7	3881
the L that taught the people,	Neh 8:9	3881
So the L stilled all the people,	Neh 8:11	3881
the people, the priests, and the L	Neh 8:13	3881
up upon the stairs, of the L	Neh 9:4	3881
Then the L, Jeshua, and Kadmiel,	Neh 9:5	3881
and our princes, L, and priests,	Neh 9:38	3881
And the L: both Jeshua	Neh 10:9	3881
of the people, the priests, the L	Neh 10:28	3881
the lots among the priests, the L	Neh 10:34	3881
tithes of our ground unto the L	Neh 10:37	3881
that the same L might have the	Neh 10:37	3881
son of Aaron shall be with the L	Neh 10:38	3881
when the L take tithes	Neh 10:38	3881
the L shall bring up the tithe of	Neh 10:38	3881
Israel, the priests, and the L	Neh 11:3	3881
Also of the L	Neh 11:15	3881
and Jozabad, of the chief of the L	Neh 11:16	3881
All the L in the holy city were	Neh 11:18	3881
Israel, of the priests, and the L	Neh 11:20	3881
The overseer also of the L at	Neh 11:22	3881
of the L were divisions in Judah,	Neh 11:36	3881
and the L that went up with	Neh 12:1	3881
Moreover the L: Jeshua,	Neh 12:8	3881
The L in the days of Eliashib,	Neh 12:22	3881
And the chief of the L	Neh 12:24	3881
the L out of all their places	Neh 12:27	3881
the L purified themselves, and	Neh 12:30	3881
of the law for the priests and L	Neh 12:44	3881
priests and for the L that waited	Neh 12:44	3881
sanctified holy things unto the L	Neh 12:47	3881
the L sanctified them unto the	Neh 12:47	3881
commanded to be given to the L	Neh 13:5	3881
of the L had not been given them	Neh 13:10	3881
for the L and the singers, that	Neh 13:10	3881
and Zadok the scribe, and of the L	Neh 13:13	3881
I commanded the L that they	Neh 13:22	3881
of the priesthood, and of the L	Neh 13:29	3881
the wards of the priests and the L	Neh 13:30	3881
take of them for priests and for L	Is 66:21	3881
L want a man before me to offer	Jer 33:18	3881
with the L the priests, my	Jer 33:21	3881
the L that minister unto me	Jer 33:22	3881
L that be of the seed of Zadok	Eze 43:19	3881
the L that are gone away far from	Eze 44:10	3881
But the priests the L, the sons	Eze 44:15	3881
of breadth, shall also the L	Eze 45:5	3881
went astray, as the L went astray	Eze 48:11	3881
most holy by the border of the L	Eze 48:12	3881
the priests the L shall have five	Eze 48:13	3881
from the possession of the L	Eze 48:22	3881
L from Jerusalem to ask him, Who	Jn 1:19	3019

LEVITICAL (le-vit'-i-cal) *Belonging to the Levites.*

were by the L priesthood, (for	Heb 7:11	3020

LEVY

l a tribute unto the LORD of the	Num 31:28	7311
raised a l out of all Israel	1Kin 5:13	4522
the l was thirty thousand men	1Kin 5:13	4522
and Adoniram was over the l	1Kin 5:14	4522
the l which king Solomon raised	1Kin 9:15	4522
upon those did Solomon l a	1Kin 9:21	5927

LEWD

which are ashamed of thy l way	Eze 16:27	2154
and unto Aholibah, L women	Eze 23:44	2154
took unto them certain l fellows	Acts 17:5	4190

LEWDLY

another hath l defiled his	Eze 22:11	2154

LEWDNESS

for they have committed l	Judg 20:6	2154
she hath wrought l with many	Jer 11:15	4209
the l of thy whoredom, and thine	Jer 13:27	2154
thou shalt not commit this l	Eze 16:43	2154
Thou hast borne thy l and thine	Eze 16:58	2154
the midst of thee they commit l	Eze 22:9	2154
to remembrance the l of thy youth	Eze 23:21	2154
I make thy l to cease from thee	Eze 23:27	2154
shall be discovered, both thy l	Eze 23:29	2154
therefore bear thou also thy l	Eze 23:35	2154
Thus will I cause thy l to cease out	Eze 23:48	2154
be taught not to do after your l	Eze 23:48	2154
shall recompense your l upon you	Eze 23:49	2154
In thy filthiness is l	Eze 24:13	2154
now will I discover her l in the	Hos 2:10	5040
for they commit l	Hos 6:9	2154
a matter of wrong or wicked l	Acts 18:14	4467

LIAR

not so now, who will make me a *l*	Job 24:25	3576
a *l* giveth ear to a naughty	Prov 17:4	8267
a poor man is better than a *l*	Prov 19:22	376,3576
thee, and thou be found a *l*	Prov 30:6	3576
thou be altogether unto me as a *l*	Jer 15:18	391
for he is a *l*, and the father of	Jn 8:44	5583
I shall be a *l* like unto you	Jn 8:55	5583
God be true, but every man a *l*	Rom 3:4	5583
have not sinned, we make him a *l*	1Jn 1:10	5583
not his commandments, is a *l*	1Jn 2:4	5583
Who is a *l* but he that denieth	1Jn 2:22	5583
and hateth his brother, he is a *l*	1Jn 4:20	5583
not God hath made him a *l*	1Jn 5:10	5583

LIARS

shall be found *l* unto thee	Deut 33:29	3584
I said in my haste, All men are *l*	Ps 116:11	3576
frustrateth the tokens of the *l*	Is 44:25	907
A sword is upon the *l*	Jer 50:36	907
mankind, for menstealers, for *l*	1Ti 1:10	5583
said, The Cretians are alway *l*	Titus 1:12	5583
and are not, and hast found them *l*	Rev 2:2	5571
sorcerers, and idolaters, and all *l*	Rev 21:8	5571

LIBERAL

The *l* soul shall be made fat	Prov 11:25	1293
person shall be no more called *l*	Is 32:5	5081
But the *l* deviseth *l* things	Is 32:8	5081
by *l* things shall he stand	Is 32:8	5081
for your *l* distribution unto them	2Cor 9:13	572

LIBERALITY

to bring your *l* unto Jerusalem	1Cor 16:3	5485
unto the riches of their *l*	2Cor 8:2	572

LIBERALLY

furnish him *l* out of thy flock	Deut 15:14	6059
of God, that giveth to all men *l*	Jas 1:5	574

LIBERTINES (lib'-ur-tins) Former Jewish slaves.

is called the synagogue of the *L*	Acts 6:9	3032

LIBERTY

proclaim *l* throughout all the	Lev 25:10	1865
And I will walk at *l*	Ps 119:45	7342
to proclaim *l* to the captives, and	Is 61:1	1865
to proclaim *l* unto them	Jer 34:8	1865
in proclaiming *l* every man to his	Jer 34:15	1865
he had set at *l* at their pleasure	Jer 34:16	2670
unto me, in proclaiming *l*	Jer 34:17	1865
behold, I proclaim a *l* for you	Jer 34:17	1865
it shall be his to the year of *l*	Eze 46:17	1865
to set at *l* them that are bruised	Lk 4:18	859
keep Paul, and to let him have *l*	Acts 24:23	425
This man might have been set at *l*	Acts 26:32	630
gave him *l* to go unto his friends	Acts 27:3	2010
glorious *l* of the children of God	Rom 8:21	1657
she is at *l* to be married to whom	1Cor 7:39	1658
means this *l* of yours become a	1Cor 8:9	1849
for why is my *l* judged of another	1Cor 10:29	1657
Spirit of the Lord is, there is *l*	2Cor 3:17	1657
l which we have in Christ Jesus	Gal 2:4	1657
Stand fast therefore in the *l*	Gal 5:1	1657
ye have been called unto *l*	Gal 5:13	1657
only use not *l* for an occasion to	Gal 5:13	1657
our brother Timothy is set at *l*	Heb 13:23	630
looketh into the perfect law of *l*	Jas 1:25	1657
shall be judged by the law of *l*	Jas 2:12	1657
not using your *l* for a cloke of	1Pet 2:16	1657
While they promise them *l*	2Pet 2:19	1657

LIBNAH (lib'-nah) See LABAN.

1. A Hebrew encampment in the wilderness.

Rimmon-parez, and pitched in *L*	Num 33:20	3841
And they removed from *L*, and	Num 33:21	3841

2. A Levitical city in Judah.

and all Israel with him, unto *L*	Josh 10:29	3841
unto Libnah, and fought against *L*	Josh 10:29	3841
And Joshua passed from *L*, and all	Josh 10:31	3841
to all that he had done to *L*	Josh 10:39	3841
as he had done also to *L*, and to	Josh 10:39	3841
The king of *L*, one	Josh 12:15	3841
L, and Ether, and Ashan,	Josh 15:42	3841
and *L* with her suburbs,	Josh 21:13	3841
Then *L* revolted at the same time	2Kin 8:22	3841
king of Assyria warring against *L*	2Kin 19:8	3841
the daughter of Jeremiah of *L*	2Kin 23:31	3841
the daughter of Jeremiah of *L*	2Kin 24:18	3841
L with her suburbs, and Jattir, and	1Chr 6:57	3841
The same time also did *L* revolt	2Chr 21:10	3841
king of Assyria warring against *L*	Is 37:8	3841
the daughter of Jeremiah of *L*	Jer 52:1	3841

LIBNI (lib'-ni) See LAADAN, LIBNITES.

1. Son of Gershon.

L, and Shimi, according to their	Ex 6:17	3845
their families; *L*, and Shimei	Num 3:18	3845
of Gershom; *L*, and Shimei	1Chr 6:17	3845
L his son, Jahath his son, Zimmah	1Chr 6:20	3845

2. Grandson of Merari.

L his son, Shimei his son, Uzza	1Chr 6:29	3845

LIBNITES (lib'-nites) Descendants of Libni 1.

Gershon was the family of the *L*	Num 3:21	3864
the family of the *L*, the family	Num 26:58	3864

LIBYA (lib'-e-ah) See LIBYANS. A land in north Africa.

Ethiopia, and *L*, and Lydia, and all	Eze 30:5	6316
Persia, Ethiopia, and *L* with them	Eze 38:5	6316
and in the parts of *L* about Cyrene	Acts 2:10	3033

LIBYANS (lib'-e-uns) See LEHABIM. Inhabitants of Libya.

the Ethiopians and the *L*, that	Jer 46:9	6316
and the *L* and the Ethiopians shall	Dan 11:43	3864

LICE

that it may become *l* throughout	Ex 8:16	3654
the earth, and it became *l* in man	Ex 8:17	3654
l throughout all the land of	Ex 8:17	3654
enchantments to bring forth *l*	Ex 8:18	3654
so there were *l* upon man, and upon	Ex 8:18	3654
flies, and *l* in all their coasts	Ps 105:31	3654

LICENCE

And when he had given him *l*	Acts 21:40	2010
have a *l* to answer for himself	Acts 25:16	5117

LICK

Now shall this company *l* up all	Num 22:4	3897
of Naboth shall dogs *l* thy blood	1Kin 21:19	3952
and his enemies shall *l* the dust	Ps 72:9	3897
l up the dust of thy feet	Is 49:23	3897
They shall *l* the dust like a	Mic 7:17	3897

LICKED

l up the water that was in the	1Kin 18:38	3897
In the place where dogs *l* the	1Kin 21:19	3952
and the dogs *l* up his blood	1Kin 22:38	3952
the dogs came and *l* his sores	Lk 16:21	621

LICKETH

as the ox *l* up the grass of the	Num 22:4	3897

LID

and bored a hole in the *l* of it	2Kin 12:9	1817

LIE

we will *l* with him, that we may	Gen 19:32	7901
l with him, that we may preserve	Gen 19:34	7901
Therefore he shall *l* with thee to	Gen 30:15	7901
and she said, *L* with me	Gen 39:7	7901
to *l* by her, or to be with her	Gen 39:10	7901
by his garment, saying, *L* with me	Gen 39:12	7901
he came in unto me to *l* with me	Gen 39:14	7901
But I will *l* with my fathers, and	Gen 47:30	7901
if a man *l* not in wait, but God	Ex 21:13	6658
l with her, he shall surely endow	Ex 22:16	7901
thou shalt let it rest and *l* still	Ex 23:11	5203
l unto his neighbour in that	Lev 6:2	3584
shall *l* with seed of copulation	Lev 15:18	7901
if any man *l* with her at all, and	Lev 15:24	7901
Moreover thou shalt not *l*	Lev 18:20	5414,7903
Thou shalt not *l* with mankind	Lev 18:22	7903
Neither shalt thou *l* with any	Lev 18:23	5414,7903
before a beast to *l* down thereto	Lev 18:23	7250
falsely, neither *l* one to another	Lev 19:11	8266
if a man *l* with his daughter in	Lev 20:12	7901
If a man also *l* with mankind	Lev 20:13	7901
if a man *l* with a beast, he shall	Lev 20:15	5414,7903
l down thereto, thou shalt kill	Lev 20:16	7250
if a man shall *l* with a woman	Lev 20:18	7901
if a man shall *l* with his uncle's	Lev 20:20	7901
in the land, and ye shall *l* down	Lev 26:6	7901
a man *l* with her carnally, and it	Num 5:13	7901
then the camps that *l* on the east	Num 10:5	2583
then the camps that *l* on the	Num 10:6	2583
is not a man, that he should *l*	Num 23:19	3576
he shall not *l* down until he eat	Num 23:24	7901
l in wait for him, and rise up	Deut 19:11	693
her in the city, and *l* with her	Deut 22:23	7901
the man force her, and *l* with her	Deut 22:25	7901
l with her, and they be found	Deut 22:28	7901
judge shall cause him to *l* down	Deut 25:2	5307
and another man shall *l* with her	Deut 28:30	7693
in this book shall *l* upon him	Deut 29:20	7257
ye shall *l* in wait against the	Josh 8:4	693
and they went to *l* in ambush	Josh 8:9	
set them to *l* in ambush between	Josh 8:12	

thee, and *l* in wait in the field	Judg 9:32	
let all thy wants *l* upon me	Judg 19:20	
l in wait in the vineyards	Judg 21:20	
mark the place where he shall *l*	Ruth 3:4	7901
he went to *l* down at the end of	Ruth 3:7	7901
l down until the morning	Ruth 3:13	7901
l down again	1Sa 3:5	7901
l down again	1Sa 3:6	7901
Eli said unto Samuel, Go, *l* down	1Sa 3:9	7901
of Israel will not *l* nor repent	1Sa 15:29	8266
to *l* in wait, as at this day	1Sa 22:8	8266
to *l* in wait, as at this day	1Sa 22:13	8266
and to drink, and to *l* with my wife	2Sa 11:11	7901
at even he went out to *l* on his	2Sa 11:13	7901
he shall *l* with thy wives in the	2Sa 12:11	7901
Come *l* with me, my sister	2Sa 13:11	7901
let her *l* in thy bosom, that my	1Kin 1:2	7901
do not *l* unto thine handmaid	2Kin 4:16	3576
for it is evident unto you if I *l*	Job 6:28	3576
When I *l* down, I say, When shall	Job 7:4	7901
Also thou shalt *l* down, and none	Job 11:19	7257
which shall *l* down with him in	Job 20:11	7901
They shall *l* down alike in the	Job 21:26	7901
The rich man shall *l* down	Job 27:19	7901
Should I *l* against my right	Job 34:6	3576
abide in the covert to *l* in wait	Job 38:40	
He maketh me to *l* down in green	Ps 23:2	7257
I *l* even among them that are set	Ps 57:4	7901
they *l* in wait for my soul	Ps 59:3	
and men of high degree are a *l*	Ps 62:9	3576
the slain that *l* in the grave	Ps 88:5	7901
that I will not *l* unto David	Ps 89:35	3576
proud have forged a *l* against me	Ps 119:69	3576
yea, thou shalt *l* down, and thy	Prov 3:24	7901
wicked are to *l* in wait for blood	Prov 12:6	
A faithful witness will not *l*	Prov 14:5	3576
if two *l* together, then they have	Eccl 4:11	7901
he shall *l* all night betwixt my	Song 1:13	3885
leopard shall *l* down with the kid	Is 11:6	7257
young ones shall *l* down together	Is 11:7	7257
of the desert shall *l* there	Is 13:21	7257
l in glory, every one in his own	Is 14:18	7901
the needy shall *l* down in safety	Is 14:30	7257
be for flocks, which shall *l* down	Is 17:2	7257
feed, and there shall he *l* down	Is 27:10	7257
The highways *l* waste, the	Is 33:8	
to generation it shall *l* waste	Is 34:10	
they shall *l* down together, they	Is 43:17	7901
Is there not a *l* in my right hand	Is 44:20	3576
ye shall *l* down in sorrow	Is 50:11	7901
they *l* at the head of all the	Is 51:20	7901
people, children that will not *l*	Is 63:8	8266
place for the herds to *l* down in	Is 65:10	7258
We *l* down in our shame, and our	Jer 3:25	7901
For they prophesy a *l* unto you	Jer 27:10	8267
for they prophesy a *l* unto you	Jer 27:14	8267
yet they prophesy a *l* in my name	Jer 27:15	8267
for they prophesy a *l* unto you	Jer 27:16	8267
this people to trust in a *l*	Jer 28:15	8267
which prophesy a *l* unto you in my	Jer 29:21	8267
and he caused you to trust in a *l*	Jer 29:31	8267
causing their flocks to *l* down	Jer 33:12	7257
the old *l* on the ground in the	Lam 2:21	7901
L thou also upon thy left side,	Eze 4:4	7901
of the days that thou shalt *l*	Eze 4:4	7901
l again on thy right side, and	Eze 4:6	7901
that thou shalt *l* upon thy side	Eze 4:9	7901
whiles they divine a *l* unto thee	Eze 21:29	3576
thou shalt *l* in the midst of the	Eze 31:18	7901
they *l* uncircumcised, slain by	Eze 32:21	7901
they shall not *l* with the mighty	Eze 32:27	7901
shalt *l* with them that are slain	Eze 32:28	7901
they shall *l* with the	Eze 32:29	7901
they *l* uncircumcised with them	Eze 32:30	7901
there shall they *l* in a good fold	Eze 34:14	7257
and I will cause them to *l* down	Eze 34:15	7257
will make them to *l* down safely	Hos 2:18	7901
an oven, whiles they *l* in wait	Hos 7:6	
l all night in sackcloth, ye	Joel 1:13	3885
That *l* upon beds of ivory, and	Amos 6:4	7901
be a *l* to the kings of Israel	Mic 1:14	391
in the spirit and falsehood do *l*	Mic 2:11	3576
they all *l* in wait for blood	Mic 7:2	
the end it shall speak, and not *l*	Hab 2:3	3576
shall they *l* down in the evening	Zeph 2:7	7257
flocks shall *l* down in the midst	Zeph 2:14	7257
a place for beasts to *l* down in	Zeph 2:15	4769
l down, and none shall make them	Zeph 3:13	7257
houses, and this house *l* waste	Hag 1:4	
and the diviners have seen a *l*	Zec 10:2	8267
When Jesus saw him *l*, and knew	Jn 5:6	2621

When he speaketh a *l*, he speaketh	Jn 8:44	5579
and seeth the linen clothes *l*	Jn 20:6	2749
heart to *l* to the Holy Ghost	Acts 5:3	5574
for there *l* in wait for him of	Acts 23:21	
changed the truth of God into a *l*	Rom 1:25	5579
through my *l* unto his glory	Rom 3:7	3582
I *l* not, my conscience also	Rom 9:1	5574
evermore, knoweth that I *l* not	2Cor 11:31	5574
you, behold, before God, I *l* not	Gal 1:20	5574
whereby they *l* in wait to deceive	Eph 4:14	3180
L not one to another, seeing that	Col 3:9	5574
that they should believe a *l*	2Th 2:11	5579
the truth in Christ, and *l* not	1Ti 2:7	5574
life, which God, that cannot *l*	Titus 1:2	893
it was impossible for God to *l*	Heb 6:18	5574
not, and *l* not against the truth	Jas 3:14	5574
him, and walk in darkness, we *l*	1Jn 1:6	5574
that no *l* is of the truth	1Jn 2:21	5579
things, and is truth, and is no *l*	1Jn 2:27	5579
are Jews, and are not, but do *l*	Rev 3:9	5574
their dead bodies shall *l* in the	Rev 11:8	5574
abomination, or maketh a *l*	Rev 21:27	5579
and whosoever loveth and maketh a *l*	Rev 22:15	5579

LIED

But he *l* unto him	1Kin 13:18	3584
they *l* unto him with their	Ps 78:36	3576
or feared, that thou hast *l*	Is 57:11	3576
thou hast not *l* unto men, but	Acts 5:4	5574

LIEN

lightly have *l* with thy wife	Gen 26:10	7901
Though ye have *l* among the pots	Ps 68:13	7901
where thou hast not been *l* with	Jer 3:2	7693

LIERS

their *l* in wait on the west of	Josh 8:13	
l in ambush against him behind	Josh 8:14	
the men of Shechem set *l* in wait	Judg 9:25	
there were *l* in wait abiding in	Judg 16:12	
Israel set *l* in wait round about	Judg 20:29	
the *l* in wait of Israel came	Judg 20:33	
the *l* in wait which they had set	Judg 20:36	
the *l* in wait hasted, and rushed	Judg 20:37	
the *l* in wait drew themselves	Judg 20:37	
the *l* in wait, that they should	Judg 20:38	

LIES

thou hast mocked me, and told me *l*	Judg 16:10	3576
thou hast mocked me, and told me *l*	Judg 16:13	3576
Should thy *l* make men hold their	Job 11:3	907
But ye are forgers of *l*, ye are	Job 13:4	8267
nor such as turn aside to *l*	Ps 40:4	3576
soon as they be born, speaking *l*	Ps 58:3	3576
they delight in *l*	Ps 62:4	3576
that speak *l* shall be stopped	Ps 63:11	8267
he that telleth *l* shall not tarry	Ps 101:7	8267
A false witness that speaketh *l*	Prov 6:19	3576
but a false witness will utter *l*	Prov 14:5	3576
a deceitful witness speaketh *l*	Prov 14:25	3576
that speaketh *l* shall not escape	Prov 19:5	3576
he that speaketh *l* shall perish	Prov 19:9	3576
If a ruler hearken to *l*, all his	Prov 29:12	1697,8267
Remove far from me vanity and *l*	Prov 30:8	1697,3576
and the prophet that teacheth *l*	Is 9:15	8267
but his *l* shall not be so	Is 16:6	907
for we have made *l* our refuge	Is 28:15	3576
shall sweep away the refuge of *l*	Is 28:17	3576
your lips have spoken *l*, your	Is 59:3	8267
they trust in vanity, and speak *l*	Is 59:4	7723
tongues like their bow for *l*	Jer 9:3	8267
taught their tongue to speak *l*	Jer 9:5	8267
prophets prophesy *l* in my name	Jer 14:14	8267
our fathers have inherited *l*	Jer 16:19	8267
to whom thou hast prophesied *l*	Jer 20:6	8267
commit adultery, and walk in *l*	Jer 23:14	8267
said, that prophesy *l* in my name	Jer 23:25	8267
of the prophets that prophesy *l*	Jer 23:26	8267
cause my people to err by their *l*	Jer 23:32	8267
his *l* shall not so effect it	Jer 48:30	907
ye have spoken vanity, and seen *l*	Eze 13:8	3576
that see vanity, and that divine *l*	Eze 13:9	3576
to my people that hear your *l*	Eze 13:19	3576
Because with *l* ye have made the	Eze 13:22	3576
divining *l* unto them, saying,	Eze 22:28	3576
She hath wearied herself with *l*	Eze 24:12	8383
they shall speak *l* at one table	Dan 11:27	3576
and the princes with their *l*	Hos 7:3	3585
yet they have spoken *l* against me	Hos 7:13	3576
ye have eaten the fruit of *l*	Hos 10:13	3585
compasseth me about with *l*	Hos 11:12	3585
he daily increaseth *l* and	Hos 12:1	3576
their *l* caused them to err, after	Amos 2:4	3576

inhabitants thereof have spoken *l*	Mic 6:12	8267
it is all full of *l* and robbery	Nah 3:1	3585
molten image, and a teacher of *l*	Hab 2:18	8267
not do iniquity, nor speak *l*	Zeph 3:13	3576
for thou speakest *l* in the name	Zec 13:3	8267
Speaking *l* in hypocrisy	1Ti 4:2	5573

LIEST

the land whereon thou *l*, to thee	Gen 28:13	7901
by the way, and when thou *l* down	Deut 6:7	7901
by the way, when thou *l* down	Deut 11:19	7901
wherefore *l* thou thus upon thy	Josh 7:10	5307
When thou *l* down, thou shalt not	Prov 3:24	7901

LIETH

doest not well, sin *l* at the door	Gen 4:7	7257
of the deep that *l* under,	Gen 49:25	7257
Whosoever *l* with a beast shall	Ex 22:19	7901
l concerning it, and sweareth	Lev 6:3	3584
he that *l* in the house shall wash	Lev 14:47	7901
whereon he *l* that hath the issue,	Lev 15:4	7901
every thing that she *l* upon in	Lev 15:20	7901
bed whereon he *l* shall be unclean	Lev 15:24	7901
Every bed whereon she *l* all the	Lev 15:26	7901
of him that *l* with her that is	Lev 15:33	7901
whosoever *l* carnally with a woman	Lev 19:20	7901
the man that *l* with his father's	Lev 20:11	7901
as he *l* with a woman, both of	Lev 20:13	4904
as long as it *l* desolate	Lev 26:34	
As long as it *l* desolate it shall	Lev 26:35	
while she *l* desolate without them	Lev 26:43	
l upon the border of Moab	Num 21:15	8172
Cursed be he that *l* with his	Deut 27:20	7901
Cursed be he that *l* with any	Deut 27:21	7901
be he that *l* with his sister	Deut 27:22	7901
Cursed be he that *l* with his	Deut 27:23	7901
l before the valley of Hinnom	Josh 15:8	
Michmethah, that *l* before Shechem	Josh 17:7	
near the hill that *l* on the south	Josh 18:13	
from the hill that *l* before	Josh 18:14	
l before the valley of the son of	Josh 18:16	
which *l* in the south of Arad	Judg 1:16	
see wherein his great strength *l*	Judg 16:5	
wherein thy great strength *l*	Judg 16:6	
me wherein thy great strength *l*	Judg 16:15	
the valley that *l* by Beth-rehob	Judg 18:28	
And it shall be, when he *l* down	Ruth 3:4	7901
that *l* before Giah by the way of	2Sa 2:24	
l in the midst of the river of	2Sa 24:5	
l waste, and the gates thereof are	Neh 2:3	
we are in, how Jerusalem *l* waste	Neh 2:17	
the tower which *l* out from the	Neh 3:25	3318
the east, and the tower that *l* out	Neh 3:26	3318
the great tower that *l* out	Neh 3:27	3318
So man *l* down, and riseth not	Job 14:12	7901
He *l* under the shady trees, in	Job 40:21	7901
He *l* in wait secretly as a lion	Ps 10:9	
he *l* in wait to catch the poor	Ps 10:9	
now that he *l* he shall rise up no	Ps 41:8	7901
Thy wrath *l* hard upon me, and thou	Ps 88:7	5564
l in wait at every corner,	Prov 7:12	
She also *l* in wait as for a prey,	Prov 23:28	
thou shalt be as he that *l* down	Prov 23:34	7901
or as he that *l* upon the top of a	Prov 23:34	7901
which *l* toward the north, and	Eze 9:2	
the great dragon that *l* in the	Eze 29:3	6437
from her that *l* in thy bosom	Mic 7:5	7901
my servant *l* at home sick of the	Mt 8:6	906
My little daughter *l* at the point	Mk 5:23	2192
the region that *l* round about	Acts 14:6	
l toward the south west and north	Acts 27:12	991
be possible, as much as *l* in you	Rom 12:18	
the whole world *l* in wickedness	1Jn 5:19	2749
the city *l* foursquare, and the	Rev 21:16	2749

LIEUTENANTS

commissions unto the king's *l*	Ezr 8:36	323
had commanded unto the king's *l*	Est 3:12	323
unto the Jews, and to the *l*	Est 8:9	323
rulers of the provinces, and the *l*	Est 9:3	323

LIFE

the moving creature that hath *l*	Gen 1:20	2416
the earth, wherein there is *l*	Gen 1:30	2416
into his nostrils the breath of *l*	Gen 2:7	2416
the tree of *l* also in the midst	Gen 2:9	2416
thou eat all the days of thy *l*	Gen 3:14	2416
eat of it all the days of thy *l*	Gen 3:17	2416
and take also of the tree of *l*	Gen 3:22	2416
to keep the way of the tree of *l*	Gen 3:24	2416
flesh, wherein is the breath of *l*	Gen 6:17	2416
six hundredth year of Noah's *l*	Gen 7:11	2416
flesh, wherein is the breath of *l*	Gen 7:15	2416

nostrils was the breath of *l*	Gen 7:22	2416
But flesh with the *l* thereof	Gen 9:4	5315
will I require the *l* of man	Gen 9:5	5315
thee according to the time of *l*	Gen 18:10	2416
thee, according to the time of *l*	Gen 18:14	2416
that he said, Escape for thy *l*	Gen 19:17	5315
shewed unto me in saving my *l*	Gen 19:19	5315
were the years of the *l* of Sarah	Gen 23:1	2416
of Abraham's *l* which he lived	Gen 25:7	2416
are the years of the *l* of Ishmael	Gen 25:17	2416
I am weary of my *l* because of the	Gen 27:46	2416
land, what good shall my *l* do me	Gen 27:46	2416
to face, and my *l* is preserved	Gen 32:30	5315
By the *l* of Pharaoh ye shall not	Gen 42:15	2416
or else by the *l* of Pharaoh	Gen 42:16	2416
seeing that his *l* is bound up in	Gen 44:30	5315
is bound up in the lad's *l*	Gen 44:30	
send me before you to preserve *l*	Gen 45:5	
days of the years of my *l* been	Gen 47:9	2416
l of my fathers in the days of	Gen 47:9	2416
me all my *l* long unto this day	Gen 48:15	
men are dead which sought thy *l*	Ex 4:19	5315
the years of the *l* of Levi were	Ex 6:16	2416
the years of the *l* of Kohath were	Ex 6:18	2416
the years of the *l* of Amram were	Ex 6:20	2416
then thou shalt give *l* for *l*	Ex 21:23	5315
give for the ransom of his *l*	Ex 21:30	5315
For the *l* of the flesh is in the	Lev 17:11	5315
For it is the *l* of all flesh	Lev 17:14	5315
blood of it is for the *l* thereof	Lev 17:14	5315
for the *l* of all flesh is the	Lev 17:14	5315
beside the other in her *l* time	Lev 18:18	2416
for the *l* of a murderer, which is	Num 35:31	5315
thy heart all the days of thy *l*	Deut 4:9	2416
son's son, all the days of thy *l*	Deut 6:2	2416
for the blood is the *l*	Deut 12:23	5315
not eat the *l* with the flesh	Deut 12:23	5315
of Egypt all the days of thy *l*	Deut 16:3	2416
therein all the days of his *l*	Deut 17:19	2416
but I shall go for *l*, eye for	Deut 19:21	5315
l) to employ them in the siege	Deut 20:19	
for he taketh a man's *l* to pledge	Deut 24:6	5315
thy *l* shall hang in doubt before	Deut 28:66	2416
have none assurance of thy *l*	Deut 28:66	2416
I have set before thee this day *l*	Deut 30:15	2416
you, that I have set before you *l*	Deut 30:19	2416
therefore choose *l*, that both	Deut 30:19	2416
for he is thy *l*, and the length of	Deut 30:20	2416
because it is your *l*	Deut 32:47	2416
before thee all the days of thy *l*	Josh 1:5	2416
Our *l* for yours, if ye utter not	Josh 2:14	5315
Moses, all the days of his *l*	Josh 4:14	2416
for you, and adventured his *l* far	Judg 9:17	5315
I put my *l* in my hands, and passed	Judg 12:3	5315
than they which he slew in his *l*	Judg 16:30	2416
run upon thee, and thou lose thy *l*	Judg 18:25	5315
be unto thee a restorer of thy *l*	Ruth 4:15	5315
the LORD all the days of his *l*	1Sa 1:11	2416
Israel all the days of his *l*	1Sa 7:15	2416
and what is my *l*, or my father's	1Sa 18:18	2416
For he did put his *l* in his hand	1Sa 19:5	5315
thy father, that he seeketh my *l*	1Sa 20:1	5315
seeketh my *l* seeketh thy *l*	1Sa 22:23	5315
Saul was come out to seek his *l*	1Sa 23:15	5315
bundle of *l* with the LORD thy God	1Sa 25:29	2416
as thy *l* was much set by this day	1Sa 26:24	5315
so let my *l* be much set by in the	1Sa 26:24	5315
then layest thou a snare for my *l*	1Sa 28:9	5315
and I have put my *l* in my hand	1Sa 28:21	5315
because my *l* is yet whole in me	2Sa 1:9	5315
thine enemy, which sought thy *l*	2Sa 4:8	5315
for the *l* of his brother whom he	2Sa 14:7	5315
shall be, whether in death or *l*	2Sa 15:21	2416
forth of my bowels, seeketh my *l*	2Sa 16:11	5315
falsehood against mine own *l*	2Sa 18:13	5315
which this day have saved thy *l*	2Sa 19:5	5315
that thou mayest save thine own *l*	1Kin 1:12	5315
and the *l* of thy son Solomon	1Kin 1:12	5315
this word against his own *l*	1Kin 2:23	5315
hast not asked for thyself long *l*	1Kin 3:11	3117
hast asked the *l* of thine enemies	1Kin 3:11	5315
Solomon all the days of his *l*	1Kin 4:21	2416
his *l* for David my servant's sake	1Kin 11:34	2416
him all the days of his *l*	1Kin 15:5	2416
and Jeroboam all the days of his *l*	1Kin 15:6	2416
if I make not thy *l* as the *l*	1Kin 19:2	5315
that, he arose, and went for his *l*	1Kin 19:3	5315
now, O LORD, take away my *l*	1Kin 19:4	5315
and they seek my *l*, to take it	1Kin 19:10	5315
and they seek my *l*, to take it	1Kin 19:14	5315
peradventure he will save thy *l*	1Kin 20:31	5315

L

then shall thy *l* be for his *l*,	1Kin 20:39	5315
thy *l* shall go for his *l*	1Kin 20:42	5315
man of God, I pray thee, let my *l*	2Kin 1:13	5315
the *l* of these fifty thy servants	2Kin 1:13	
therefore let my *l* now be	2Kin 1:14	5315
according to the time of *l*	2Kin 4:16	2416
her, according to the time of *l*	2Kin 4:17	2416
as it was, and fled for their *l*	2Kin 7:7	5315
whose son he had restored to *l*	2Kin 8:1	2421
he had restored a dead body to *l*	2Kin 8:5	2421
whose son he had restored to *l*	2Kin 8:5	2421
son, whom Elisha restored to *l*	2Kin 8:5	2421
his *l* shall be for the *l* of	2Kin 10:24	2421
l shall be for the *l* of him	2Kin 10:24	5315
before him all the days of his *l*	2Kin 25:29	2416
every day, all the days of his *l*	2Kin 25:30	2416
nor the *l* of thine enemies,	2Chr 1:11	5315
neither yet hast asked long *l*	2Chr 1:11	3117
and pray for the *l* of the king	Ezr 6:10	2417
go into the temple to save his *l*	Neh 6:11	2425
let my *l* be given me at my	Est 7:3	5315
for his *l* to Esther the queen	Est 7:7	5315
together, and to stand for their *l*	Est 8:11	5315
a man hath will he give for his *l*	Job 2:4	5315
but save his *l*	Job 2:6	5315
l unto the bitter in soul	Job 3:20	2416
end, that I should prolong my *l*	Job 6:11	5315
O remember that my *l* is wind	Job 7:7	2416
and death rather than my *l*	Job 7:15	6106
I would despise my *l*	Job 9:21	2416
My soul is weary of my *l*	Job 10:1	2416
Thou hast granted me *l* and favour,	Job 10:12	2416
teeth, and put my *l* in mine hand	Job 13:14	5315
riseth up, and no man is sure of *l*	Job 24:22	2416
owners thereof to lose their *l*	Job 31:39	5315
of the Almighty hath given me *l*	Job 33:4	2421
his *l* from perishing by the sword	Job 33:18	2416
So that his *l* abhorreth bread, and	Job 33:20	2416
grave, and his *l* to the destroyers	Job 33:22	2416
his *l* shall see the light	Job 33:28	2416
not the *l* of the wicked	Job 36:6	2421
their *l* is among the unclean	Job 36:14	2416
tread down my *l* upon the earth	Ps 7:5	2416
Thou wilt shew me the path of *l*	Ps 16:11	2416
have their portion in this *l*	Ps 17:14	2416
He asked *l* of thee, and thou	Ps 21:4	2416
follow me all the days of my *l*	Ps 23:6	2416
sinners, nor my *l* with bloody men	Ps 26:9	2416
the LORD is the strength of my *l*	Ps 27:1	2416
of the LORD all the days of my *l*	Ps 27:4	2416
in his favour is *l*	Ps 30:5	2416
For my *l* is spent with grief, and	Ps 31:10	2416
they devised to take away my *l*	Ps 31:13	5315
What man is he that desireth *l*	Ps 34:12	2416
with thee is the fountain of *l*	Ps 36:9	2416
seek after my *l* lay snares for me	Ps 38:12	5315
and my prayer unto the God of my *l*	Ps 42:8	2416
Thou wilt prolong the king's *l*	Ps 61:6	3117,5921
lovingkindness is better than *l*	Ps 63:3	2416
preserve my *l* from fear of the	Ps 64:1	2416
Which holdeth our soul in *l*	Ps 66:9	2416
but gave their *l* over to the	Ps 78:50	2416
my *l* draweth nigh unto the grave	Ps 88:3	2416
With long *l* will I satisfy him,	Ps 91:16	3117
redeemeth thy *l* from destruction	Ps 103:4	2416
Jerusalem all the days of thy *l*	Ps 128:5	2416
the blessing, even *l* for evermore	Ps 133:3	2416
smitten my *l* down to the ground	Ps 143:3	2416
away the *l* of the owners thereof	Prov 1:19	5315
take they hold of the paths of *l*	Prov 2:19	2416
For length of days, and long *l*	Prov 3:2	2416
She is a tree of *l* to them that	Prov 3:18	2416
So shall they be *l* unto thy soul	Prov 3:22	2416
the years of thy *l* shall be many	Prov 4:10	2416
for she is thy *l*	Prov 4:13	2416
For they are *l* unto those that	Prov 4:22	2416
for out of it are the issues of *l*	Prov 4:23	2416
shouldest ponder the path of *l*	Prov 5:6	2416
of instruction are the way of *l*	Prov 6:23	2416
will hunt for the precious *l*	Prov 6:26	5315
knoweth not that it is for his *l*	Prov 7:23	5315
For whoso findeth me findeth *l*	Prov 8:35	2416
the years of thy *l* shall be	Prov 9:11	2416
of a righteous man is a well of *l*	Prov 10:11	2416
of the righteous tendeth to *l*	Prov 10:16	2416
He is in the way of *l* that	Prov 10:17	2416
As righteousness tendeth to *l*	Prov 11:19	2416
of the righteous is a tree of *l*	Prov 11:30	2416
man regardeth the *l* of his beast	Prov 12:10	5315
In the way of righteousness is *l*	Prov 12:28	2416
keepeth his mouth keepeth his *l*	Prov 13:3	5315
of a man's *l* are his riches	Prov 13:8	5315
desire cometh, it is a tree of *l*	Prov 13:12	2416
of the wise is a fountain of *l*	Prov 13:14	2416
of the LORD is a fountain of *l*	Prov 14:27	2416
sound heart is the *l* of the flesh	Prov 14:30	2416
A wholesome tongue is a tree of *l*	Prov 15:4	2416
The way of *l* is above to the wise	Prov 15:24	2416
of *l* abideth among the wise	Prov 15:31	2416
of the king's countenance is *l*	Prov 16:15	2416
is a wellspring of *l* unto him	Prov 16:22	2416
l are in the power of the tongue	Prov 18:21	2416
The fear of the LORD tendeth to *l*	Prov 19:23	2416
righteousness and mercy findeth *l*	Prov 21:21	2416
LORD are riches, and honour, and *l*	Prov 22:4	2416
and not evil all the days of her *l*	Prov 31:12	2416
heaven all the days of their *l*	Eccl 2:3	2416
Therefore I hated *l*	Eccl 2:17	2416
rejoice, and to do good in his *l*	Eccl 3:12	2416
the sun all the days of his *l*	Eccl 5:18	2416
much remember the days of his *l*	Eccl 5:20	2416
what is good for man in this *l*	Eccl 6:12	2416
all the days of his vain *l* which	Eccl 6:12	2416
that wisdom giveth *l* to them that	Eccl 7:12	2421
his *l* in his wickedness	Eccl 7:15	
of his labour the days of his *l*	Eccl 8:15	2416
the days of the *l* of thy vanity	Eccl 9:9	2416
for that is thy portion in this *l*	Eccl 9:9	2416
his *l* shall be grievous unto him	Is 15:4	5315
I have cut off like a weaver my *l*	Is 38:12	2416
things is the *l* of my spirit	Is 38:16	2416
of our *l* in the house of the LORD	Is 38:20	2416
men for thee, and people for thy *l*	Is 43:4	5315
hast found the *l* of thine hand	Is 57:10	2416
thee, they will seek thy *l*	Jer 4:30	5315
shall be chosen rather than *l* by	Jer 8:3	
men of Anathoth, that seek thy *l*	Jer 11:21	5315
hand of those that seek their *l*	Jer 21:7	5315
I set before you the way of *l*	Jer 21:8	2416
his *l* shall be unto him for a	Jer 21:9	5315
the hand of them that seek thy *l*	Jer 22:25	5315
hand of them that seek their *l*	Jer 34:20	5315
hand of them that seek their *l*	Jer 34:21	5315
he shall have his *l* for a prey	Jer 38:2	5315
hand of these men that seek thy *l*	Jer 38:16	5315
but thy *l* shall be for a prey	Jer 39:18	5315
the hand of them that seek his *l*	Jer 44:30	5315
his enemy, and that sought his *l*	Jer 44:30	5315
but thy *l* will I give unto thee	Jer 45:5	5315
and before them that seek their *l*	Jer 49:37	5315
before him all the days of his *l*	Jer 52:33	2416
his death, all the days of his *l*	Jer 52:34	2416
for the *l* of thy young children	Lam 2:19	5315
have cut off my *l* in the dungeon	Lam 3:53	2416
thou hast redeemed my *l*	Lam 3:58	
his wicked way, to save his *l*	Eze 3:18	2421
himself in the iniquity of his *l*	Eze 7:13	2416
wicked way, by promising him *l*	Eze 13:22	2421
moment, every man for his own *l*	Eze 32:10	5315
robbed, walk in the statutes of *l*	Eze 33:15	2416
awake, some to everlasting *l*	Dan 12:2	2416
us not perish for this man's *l*	Jonah 1:14	5315
brought up my *l* from corruption	Jonah 2:6	2416
I beseech thee, my *l* from me	Jonah 4:3	5315
My covenant was with him of *l*	Mal 2:5	2416
which sought the young child's *l*	Mt 2:20	5590
you, Take no thought for your *l*	Mt 6:25	5590
Is not the *l* more than meat, and	Mt 6:25	5590
is the way, which leadeth unto *l*	Mt 7:14	2222
that findeth his *l* shall lose it	Mt 10:39	5590
he that loseth his *l* for my sake	Mt 10:39	5590
will save his *l* shall lose it	Mt 16:25	5590
whosoever will lose his *l* for my	Mt 16:25	5590
to enter into *l* halt or maimed	Mt 18:8	2222
thee to enter into *l* with one eye	Mt 18:9	2222
I do, that I may have eternal *l*	Mt 19:16	2222
but if thou wilt enter into *l*	Mt 19:17	2222
and shall inherit everlasting *l*	Mt 19:29	2222
to give his *l* a ransom for many	Mt 20:28	5590
but the righteous into *l* eternal	Mt 25:46	2222
to save *l*, or to kill	Mk 3:4	5590
will save his *l* shall lose it	Mk 8:35	5590
shall lose his *l* for my sake	Mk 8:35	5590
for thee to enter into *l* maimed	Mk 9:43	2222
for thee to enter halt into *l*	Mk 9:45	2222
I do that I may inherit eternal *l*	Mk 10:17	2222
and in the world to come eternal *l*	Mk 10:30	2222
to give his *l* a ransom for many	Mk 10:45	5590
before him, all the days of our *l*	Lk 1:75	2222
to save *l*, or to destroy it	Lk 6:9	5590
and riches and pleasures of this *l*	Lk 8:14	979
will save his *l* shall lose it	Lk 9:24	5590

will lose his *l* for my sake	Lk 9:24	5590
shall I do to inherit eternal *l*	Lk 10:25	2222
for a man's *l* consisteth not in	Lk 12:15	2222
you, Take no thought for your *l*	Lk 12:22	5590
The *l* is more than meat, and the	Lk 12:23	5590
sisters, yea, and his own *l* also	Lk 14:26	5590
seek to save his *l* shall lose it	Lk 17:33	5590
lose his *l* shall preserve it	Lk 17:33	5590
shall I do to inherit eternal *l*	Lk 18:18	2222
the world to come *l* everlasting	Lk 18:30	2222
drunkenness, and cares of this *l*	Lk 21:34	982
In him was *l*	Jn 1:4	2222
the *l* was the light of men	Jn 1:4	2222
not perish, but have eternal *l*	Jn 3:15	2222
perish, but have everlasting *l*	Jn 3:16	2222
on the Son hath everlasting *l*	Jn 3:36	2222
not the Son shall not see *l*	Jn 3:36	2222
springing up into everlasting *l*	Jn 4:14	2222
and gathereth fruit unto *l* eternal	Jn 4:36	2222
that sent me, hath everlasting *l*	Jn 5:24	2222
but is passed from death unto *l*	Jn 5:24	2222
as the Father hath *l* in himself	Jn 5:26	2222
to the Son to have *l* in himself	Jn 5:26	2222
good, unto the resurrection of *l*	Jn 5:29	2222
them ye think ye have eternal *l*	Jn 5:39	2222
come to me, that ye might have *l*	Jn 5:40	2222
which endureth unto everlasting *l*	Jn 6:27	2222
and giveth *l* unto the world	Jn 6:33	2222
unto them, I am the bread of *l*	Jn 6:35	2222
on him, may have everlasting *l*	Jn 6:40	2222
on me hath everlasting *l*	Jn 6:47	2222
I am that bread of *l*	Jn 6:48	2222
will give for the *l* of the world	Jn 6:51	2222
his blood, ye have no *l* in you	Jn 6:53	2222
drinketh my blood, hath eternal *l*	Jn 6:54	2222
they are spirit, and they are *l*	Jn 6:63	2222
thou hast the words of eternal *l*	Jn 6:68	2222
but shall have the light of *l*	Jn 8:12	2222
I am come that they might have *l*	Jn 10:10	2222
giveth his *l* for the sheep	Jn 10:11	5590
and I lay down my *l* for the sheep	Jn 10:15	5590
love me, because I lay down my *l*	Jn 10:17	5590
And I give unto them eternal *l*	Jn 10:28	2222
I am the resurrection, and the *l*	Jn 11:25	2222
that loveth his *l* shall lose it	Jn 12:25	5590
he that hateth his *l* in this	Jn 12:25	5590
shall keep it unto *l* eternal	Jn 12:25	2222
his commandment is *l* everlasting	Jn 12:50	2222
I will lay down my *l* for thy sake	Jn 13:37	5590
thou lay down thy *l* for my sake	Jn 13:38	5590
I am the way, the truth, and the *l*	Jn 14:6	2222
lay down his *l* for his friends	Jn 15:13	5590
that he should give eternal *l* to	Jn 17:2	2222
And this is *l* eternal, that they	Jn 17:3	2222
ye might have *l* through his name	Jn 20:31	2222
made known to me the ways of *l*	Acts 2:28	2222
And killed the Prince of *l*	Acts 3:15	2222
people all the words of this *l*	Acts 5:20	2222
for his *l* is taken from the earth	Acts 8:33	2222
granted repentance unto *l*	Acts 11:18	2222
unworthy of everlasting *l*	Acts 13:46	2222
ordained to eternal *l* believed	Acts 13:48	2222
thing, seeing he giveth to all *l*	Acts 17:25	2222
for his *l* is in him	Acts 20:10	5590
count I my *l* dear unto myself	Acts 20:24	5590
My manner of *l* from my youth	Acts 26:4	981
no loss of any man's *l* among you	Acts 27:22	5590
honour and immortality, eternal *l*	Rom 2:7	2222
we shall be saved by his *l*	Rom 5:10	2222
shall reign in *l* by one, Jesus	Rom 5:17	2222
all men unto justification of *l*	Rom 5:18	2222
l by Jesus Christ our Lord	Rom 5:21	2222
also should walk in newness of *l*	Rom 6:4	2222
and the end everlasting *l*	Rom 6:22	2222
l through Jesus Christ our Lord	Rom 6:23	2222
which was ordained to *l*, I found	Rom 7:10	2222
of *l* in Christ Jesus hath made me	Rom 8:2	2222
but to be spiritually minded is *l*	Rom 8:6	2222
but the Spirit is *l* because of	Rom 8:10	2222
that neither death, nor *l*	Rom 8:38	2222
am left alone, and they seek my *l*	Rom 11:3	5590
of them be, but *l* from the dead	Rom 11:15	2222
Who have for my *l* laid down their	Rom 16:4	5590
or Cephas, or the world, or *l*	1Cor 3:22	2222
things that pertain to this *l*	1Cor 6:3	982
of things pertaining to this *l*	1Cor 6:4	982
things without *l* giving sound	1Cor 14:7	895
If in this *l* only we have hope in	1Cor 15:19	2222
that we despaired even of *l*	2Cor 1:8	2198
other the savour of *l* unto *l*	2Cor 2:16	2222
killeth, but the spirit giveth *l*	2Cor 3:6	2227

that the *l* also of Jesus might be	2Cor 4:10	2222
that the *l* also of Jesus might be	2Cor 4:11	2222
death worketh in us, but *l* in you	2Cor 4:12	2222
might be swallowed up of *l*	2Cor 5:4	2222
the *l* which I now live in the	Gal 2:20	
given which could have given *l*	Gal 3:21	2227
of the Spirit reap *l* everlasting	Gal 6:8	2222
being alienated from the *l* of God	Eph 4:18	2222
in my body, whether it be by *l*	Phil 1:20	2222
Holding forth the word of *l*	Phil 2:16	2222
unto death, not regarding his *l*	Phil 2:30	5590
whose names are in the book of *l*	Phil 4:3	2222
your *l* is hid with Christ in God	Col 3:3	2222
When Christ, who is our *l*	Col 3:4	2222
believe on him to *l* everlasting	1Ti 1:16	2222
peaceable *l* in all godliness and	1Ti 2:2	979
promise of the *l* that now is	1Ti 4:8	2222
of faith, lay hold on eternal *l*	1Ti 6:12	2222
they may lay hold on eternal *l*	1Ti 6:19	2222
of *l* which is in Christ Jesus	2Ti 1:1	2222
death, and hath brought *l* and	2Ti 1:10	2222
with the affairs of this *l*	2Ti 2:4	979
known my doctrine, manner of *l*	2Ti 3:10	72
In hope of eternal *l*, which God,	Titus 1:2	2222
to the hope of eternal *l*	Titus 3:7	2222
beginning of days, nor end of *l*	Heb 7:3	2222
after the power of an endless *l*	Heb 7:16	2222
their dead raised to *l* again	Heb 11:35	
he shall receive the crown of *l*	Jas 1:12	2222
For what is your *l*	Jas 4:14	2222
heirs together of the grace of *l*	1Pet 3:7	2222
For he that will love *l*, and see	1Pet 3:10	2222
For the time past of our *l* may	1Pet 4:3	979
us all things that pertain unto *l*	2Pet 1:3	2222
have handled, of the Word of *l*	1Jn 1:1	2222
(For the *l* was manifested, and we	1Jn 1:2	2222
and shew unto you that eternal *l*	1Jn 1:2	2222
of the eyes, and the pride of *l*	1Jn 2:16	979
hath promised us, even eternal *l*	1Jn 2:25	2222
we have passed from death unto *l*	1Jn 3:14	2222
hath eternal *l* abiding in him	1Jn 3:15	2222
because he laid down his *l* for us	1Jn 3:16	5590
God hath given to us eternal *l*	1Jn 5:11	2222
and this *l* is in his Son	1Jn 5:11	2222
He that hath the Son hath *l*	1Jn 5:12	2222
not the Son of God hath not *l*	1Jn 5:12	2222
may know that ye have eternal *l*	1Jn 5:13	2222
he shall give him *l* for them that	1Jn 5:16	2222
is the true God, and eternal *l*	1Jn 5:20	2222
Lord Jesus Christ unto eternal *l*	Jude 21	2222
I give to eat of the tree of *l*	Rev 2:7	2222
and I will give thee a crown of *l*	Rev 2:10	2222
out his name out of the book of *l*	Rev 3:5	2222
which were in the sea, and had *l*	Rev 8:9	5590
an half the Spirit of *l* from God	Rev 11:11	2222
of *l* of the Lamb slain from the	Rev 13:8	2222
he had power to give *l* unto the	Rev 13:15	4151
of *l* from the foundation of the	Rev 17:8	2222
opened, which is the book of *l*	Rev 20:12	2222
found written in the book of *l*	Rev 20:15	2222
fountain of the water of *l* freely	Rev 21:6	2222
written in the Lamb's book of *l*	Rev 21:27	2222
me a pure river of water of *l*	Rev 22:1	2222
river, was there the tree of *l*	Rev 22:2	2222
may have right to the tree of *l*	Rev 22:14	2222
him take the water of *l* freely	Rev 22:17	2222
his part out of the book of *l*	Rev 22:19	2222

LIFETIME

Now Absalom in his *l* had taken	2Sa 18:18	2416
remember that thou in thy *l*	Lk 16:25	2222
all their *l* subject to bondage	Heb 2:15	2198

LIFT

it was *l* up above the earth	Gen 7:17	7311
L up now thine eyes, and look from	Gen 13:14	5375
I have *l* up mine hand unto the	Gen 14:22	7311
he *l* up his eyes and looked, and,	Gen 18:2	5375
him, and *l* up her voice, and wept	Gen 21:16	5375
l up the lad, and hold him in	Gen 21:18	5375
L up now thine eyes, and see, all	Gen 31:12	5375
shall Pharaoh *l* up thine head	Gen 40:13	5375
l up thy head from off thee	Gen 40:19	5375
without thee shall no man *l* up	Gen 41:44	7311
But *l* thou up thy rod, and stretch	Ex 14:16	7311
for if thou *l* up thy tool upon it	Ex 20:25	5130
The LORD *l* up his countenance	Num 6:26	5375
wherefore then *l* ye up yourselves	Num 16:3	5375
l up himself as a young lion	Num 23:24	5375
l up thine eyes westward, and	Deut 3:27	5375
lest thou *l* up thine eyes unto	Deut 4:19	5375
help him to *l* them up again	Deut 22:4	6965

L

thou shalt not *l* up any iron tool	Deut 27:5	5130
For I *l* up my hand to heaven, and	Deut 32:40	5375
which no man hath *l* up any iron	Josh 8:31	5130
he *l* up his spear against eight	2Sa 23:8	
wherefore *l* up thy prayer for the	2Kin 19:4	5375
l up the head of Jehoiachin king	2Kin 25:27	5375
words of God, to *l* up the horn	1Chr 25:5	7311
blush to *l* up my face to thee, my	Ezr 9:6	7311
yet will I not *l* up my head	Job 10:15	5375
For then shalt thou *l* up thy face	Job 11:15	5375
shalt *l* up thy face unto God	Job 22:26	5375
Canst thou *l* up thy voice to the	Job 38:34	7311
l thou up the light of thy	Ps 4:6	5375
l up thyself because of the rage	Ps 7:6	5375
O God, *l* up thine hand	Ps 10:12	5375
L up your heads, O ye gates	Ps 24:7	5375
L up your heads, O ye gates	Ps 24:9	5375
even *l* them up, ye everlasting	Ps 24:9	5375
thee, O LORD, do I *l* up my soul	Ps 25:1	5375
when I *l* up my hands toward thy	Ps 28:2	5375
them also, and *l* them up for ever	Ps 28:9	5375
I will *l* up my hands in thy name	Ps 63:4	5375
L up thy feet unto the perpetual	Ps 74:3	7311
to the wicked, *L* not up the horn	Ps 75:4	7311
L not up your horn on high	Ps 75:5	7311
thee, O Lord, do I *l* up my soul	Ps 86:4	5375
the floods *l* up their waves	Ps 93:3	5375
L up thyself, thou judge of the	Ps 94:2	5375
therefore shall he *l* up the head	Ps 110:7	7311
My hands also will I *l* up unto	Ps 119:48	5375
I will *l* up mine eyes unto the	Ps 121:1	5375
Unto thee *l* I up mine eyes, O	Ps 123:1	5375
L up your hands in the sanctuary,	Ps 134:2	5375
for I *l* up my soul unto thee	Ps 143:8	5375
the one will *l* up his fellow	Eccl 4:10	6965
nation shall not *l* up sword	Is 2:4	5375
he will *l* up an ensign to the	Is 5:26	5375
itself against them that *l* it up	Is 10:15	7311
if the staff should *l* up itself	Is 10:15	7311
shall *l* up his staff against thee	Is 10:24	5375
so shall he *l* it up after the	Is 10:26	5375
L up thy voice, O daughter of	Is 10:30	6670
L ye up a banner upon the high	Is 13:2	5375
They shall *l* up their voice, they	Is 24:14	5375
now will I *l* up myself	Is 33:10	5375
wherefore *l* up thy prayer for the	Is 37:4	5375
l up thy voice with strength	Is 40:9	7311
l it up, be not afraid	Is 40:9	7311
L up your eyes on high, and behold	Is 40:26	5375
He shall not cry, nor *l* up	Is 42:2	5375
cities thereof *l* up their voice	Is 42:11	5375
L up thine eyes round about, and	Is 49:18	5375
I will *l* up mine hand to the	Is 49:22	5375
L up your eyes to the heavens, and	Is 51:6	5375
Thy watchmen shall *l* up the voice	Is 52:8	5375
l up thy voice like a trumpet, and	Is 58:1	7311
shall *l* up a standard against him	Is 59:19	5127
L up thine eyes round about, and	Is 60:4	5375
l up a standard for the people	Is 62:10	7311
L up thine eyes unto the high	Jer 3:2	5375
neither *l* up cry nor prayer for	Jer 7:16	5375
neither *l* up a cry or prayer for	Jer 11:14	5375
L up your eyes, and behold them	Jer 13:20	5375
l up thy voice in Bashan, and cry	Jer 22:20	5414
they shall *l* up a shout against	Jer 51:14	6030
l up thy hands toward him for the	Lam 2:19	5375
Let us *l* up our heart with our	Lam 3:41	5375
l up thine eyes now the way	Eze 8:5	5375
the cherubims *l* up their wings	Eze 11:22	5375
that it might not *l* itself up	Eze 17:14	5375
to *l* up the voice with shouting	Eze 21:22	7311
so that thou shalt not *l* up thine	Eze 23:27	5375
l up the buckler against thee	Eze 26:8	6965
l up your eyes toward your idols,	Eze 33:25	5375
nation shall not *l* up a sword	Mic 4:3	5375
so that no man did *l* up his head	Zec 1:21	5375
L up now thine eyes, and see what	Zec 5:5	5375
not lay hold on it, and *l* it out	Mt 12:11	*1458*
and could in no wise *l* up herself	Lk 13:11	*352*
in hell he *l* up his eyes, being	Lk 16:23	*1869*
would not *l* up so much as his	Lk 18:13	*1869*
then look up, and *l* up your heads	Lk 21:28	*1869*
L up your eyes, and look on the	Jn 4:35	*1869*
Wherefore *l* up the hands which	Heb 12:12	*461*
of the Lord, and he shall *l* you up	Jas 4:10	*5312*

LIFTED

Lot *l* up his eyes, and beheld all	Gen 13:10	5375
third day Abraham *l* up his eyes	Gen 22:4	5375
Abraham *l* up his eyes, and looked,	Gen 22:13	5375
he *l* up his eyes, and saw, and,	Gen 24:63	5375

Rebekah *l* up her eyes, and when	Gen 24:64	5375
Esau *l* up his voice, and wept	Gen 27:38	5375
and *l* up his voice, and wept	Gen 29:11	5375
that I *l* up mine eyes, and saw in	Gen 31:10	5375
Jacob *l* up his eyes, and looked,	Gen 33:1	5375
he *l* up his eyes, and saw the	Gen 33:5	5375
they *l* up their eyes and looked,	Gen 37:25	5375
l up Joseph out of the pit, and	Gen 37:28	5927
he heard that I *l* up my voice,	Gen 39:15	7311
as I *l* up my voice and cried, that	Gen 39:18	7311
he *l* up the head of the chief	Gen 40:20	5375
he *l* up his eyes, and saw his	Gen 43:29	5375
he *l* up the rod, and smote the	Ex 7:20	7311
of Israel *l* up their eyes	Ex 14:10	5375
Aaron *l* up his hand toward the	Lev 9:22	5375
the congregation *l* up their voice	Num 14:1	5375
Moses *l* up his hand, and with his	Num 20:11	7311
Balaam *l* up his eyes, and he saw	Num 24:2	5375
Then thine heart be *l* up, and thou	Deut 8:14	7311
be not *l* up above his brethren	Deut 17:20	7311
feet were *l* up unto the dry land	Josh 4:18	5423
that he *l* up his eyes and looked,	Josh 5:13	5375
that the people *l* up their voice	Judg 2:4	5375
so that they *l* up their heads no	Judg 8:28	5375
l up his voice, and cried, and said	Judg 9:7	5375
And when he had *l* up his eyes	Judg 19:17	5375
l up their voices, and wept sore	Judg 21:2	5375
they *l* up their voice, and wept	Ruth 1:9	5375
they *l* up their voice, and wept	Ruth 1:14	5375
they *l* up their eyes, and saw the	1Sa 6:13	5375
all the people *l* up their voices,	1Sa 11:4	5375
Saul *l* up his voice, and wept	1Sa 24:16	5375
were with him *l* up their voice	1Sa 30:4	5375
the king *l* up his voice, and wept	2Sa 3:32	5375
that kept the watch *l* up his eyes	2Sa 13:34	5375
came, and *l* up their voice and wept	2Sa 13:36	5375
l up his eyes, and looked, and	2Sa 18:24	5375
l up their hand against my lord	2Sa 18:28	5375
hath *l* up his hand against the	2Sa 20:21	5375
thou also hast *l* me up on high	2Sa 22:49	7311
he *l* up his spear against three	2Sa 23:18	5782
even he *l* up his hand against the	1Kin 11:26	7311
this was the cause that he *l* up	1Kin 11:27	7311
he *l* up his face to the window,	2Kin 9:32	5375
and thine heart hath *l* thee up	2Kin 14:10	5375
voice, and *l* up thine eyes on high	2Kin 19:22	5375
he *l* up his spear against three	1Chr 11:11	5782
for his kingdom was *l* up on high	1Chr 14:2	5375
David *l* up his eyes, and saw the	1Chr 21:16	5375
when they *l* up their voice with	2Chr 5:13	7311
his heart was *l* up in the ways of	2Chr 17:6	1361
his heart was *l* up to his	2Chr 26:16	1361
for his heart was *l* up	2Chr 32:25	1361
when they *l* up their eyes afar	Job 2:12	5375
they *l* up their voice, and wept	Job 2:12	5375
If I have *l* up my hand against	Job 31:21	5130
or *l* up myself when evil found	Job 31:29	5782
who hath not *l* up his soul unto	Ps 24:4	5375
and be ye *l* up, ye everlasting	Ps 24:7	5375
now shall mine head be *l* up above	Ps 27:6	7311
for thou hast *l* me up, and hast	Ps 30:1	1802
hath *l* up his heel against me	Ps 41:9	1431
l up axes upon the thick trees	Ps 74:5	935
that hate thee have *l* up the head	Ps 83:2	5375
The floods have *l* up, O LORD, the	Ps 93:3	5375
the floods have *l* up their voice	Ps 93:3	5375
for thou hast *l* me up, and cast me	Ps 102:10	5375
Therefore he *l* up his hand	Ps 106:26	5375
and their eyelids are *l* up	Prov 30:13	5375
and upon every one that is *l* up	Is 2:12	5375
l up, and upon all the oaks of	Is 2:13	5375
upon all the hills that are *l* up	Is 2:14	5375
l up, and his train filled the	Is 6:1	5375
LORD, when thy hand is *l* up	Is 26:11	5375
voice, and *l* up thine eyes on high	Is 37:23	5375
is *l* up even to the skies	Jer 51:9	5375
l up the head of Jehoiachin king	Jer 52:31	5375
were *l* up from the earth, the	Eze 1:19	5375
the earth, the wheels were *l* up	Eze 1:19	5375
the wheels were *l* up over against	Eze 1:20	5375
when those were *l* up from the	Eze 1:21	5375
the wheels were *l* up over against	Eze 1:21	5375
So the spirit *l* me up, and took me	Eze 3:14	5375
the spirit *l* me up between the	Eze 8:3	5375
So I *l* up mine eyes the way	Eze 8:5	5375
And the cherubims were *l* up	Eze 10:15	7426
when the cherubims *l* up their	Eze 10:16	5375
and when they were *l* up	Eze 10:17	7311
these *l* up themselves also	Eze 10:17	7426
the cherubims *l* up their wings,	Eze 10:19	5375
Moreover the spirit *l* me up	Eze 11:1	5375

neither hath *l* up his eyes to the ... Eze 18:6 5375
hath *l* up his eyes to the idols, ... Eze 18:12 5375
neither hath *l* up his eyes to the ... Eze 18:15 5375
l up mine hand unto the seed of ... Eze 20:5 5375
when I *l* up mine hand unto them, ... Eze 20:5 5375
In the day that I *l* up mine hand ... Eze 20:6 5375
Yet also I *l* up my hand unto them ... Eze 20:15 5375
I *l* up mine hand unto them also ... Eze 20:23 5375
for the which I *l* up mine hand to ... Eze 20:28 5375
the country for the which I *l* up ... Eze 20:42 5375
Because thine heart is *l* up ... Eze 28:2 1361
thine heart is *l* up because of ... Eze 28:5 1361
Thine heart was *l* up because of ... Eze 28:17 1361
Because thou hast *l* up thyself in ... Eze 31:10 1361
his heart is *l* up in his height ... Eze 31:10 7311
I have *l* up mine hand, Surely the ... Eze 36:7 5375
therefore have I *l* up mine hand ... Eze 44:12 5375
concerning the which I *l* up mine ... Eze 47:14 5375
l up mine eyes unto heaven ... Dan 4:34 5191
But when his heart was *l* up ... Dan 5:20 7313
But hast *l* up thyself against the ... Dan 5:23 7313
it was *l* up from the earth, and ... Dan 7:4 5191
Then I *l* up mine eyes, and saw, and ... Dan 8:3 5375
Then I *l* up mine eyes, and looked, ... Dan 10:5 5375
his heart shall be *l* up ... Dan 11:12 7311
Thine hand shall be *l* up upon ... Mic 5:9 7311
his soul which is *l* up is not ... Hab 2:4 6075
voice, and *l* up his hands on high ... Hab 3:10 5375
Then *l* I up mine eyes, and saw, and ... Zec 1:18 5375
which *l* up their horn over the ... Zec 1:21 5375
I *l* up mine eyes again, and looked ... Zec 2:1 5375
l up mine eyes, and looked, and ... Zec 5:1 5375
there was *l* up a talent of lead ... Zec 5:7
Then *l* I up mine eyes, and looked, ... Zec 5:9 5375
they *l* up the ephah between the ... Zec 5:9 5375
l up mine eyes, and looked, and, ... Zec 6:1 5375
l up as an ensign upon his land ... Zec 9:16 5264
and it shall be *l* up, and inhabited ... Zec 14:10 7213
And when they had *l* up their eyes ... Mt 17:8 *1869*
took her by the hand, and *l* her up ... Mk 1:31 *1453*
took him by the hand, and *l* him up ... Mk 9:27 *1453*
he *l* up his eyes on his disciples ... Lk 6:20 *1869*
of the company *l* up her voice ... Lk 11:27 *1869*
they *l* up their voices, and said, ... Lk 17:13 *142*
he *l* up his hands, and blessed ... Lk 24:50 *1869*
as Moses *l* up the serpent in the ... Jn 3:14 *5312*
so must the Son of man be *l* up ... Jn 3:14 *5312*
When Jesus then *l* up his eyes ... Jn 6:5 *1869*
he *l* up himself, and said unto ... Jn 8:7 *352*
When Jesus had *l* up himself ... Jn 8:10 *352*
When ye have *l* up the Son of man, ... Jn 8:28 *5312*
Jesus *l* up his eyes, and said, ... Jn 11:41 *142*
if I be *l* up from the earth, will ... Jn 12:32 *5312*
thou, The Son of man must be *l* up ... Jn 12:34 *5312*
me hath *l* up his heel against me ... Jn 13:18 *1869*
l up his eyes to heaven, and said, ... Jn 17:1 *1869*
l up his voice, and said unto them ... Acts 2:14 *1869*
by the right hand, and *l* him up ... Acts 3:7 *1453*
they *l* up their voice to God with ... Acts 4:24 *142*
l her up, and when he had called ... Acts 9:41 *450*
they *l* up their voices, saying in ... Acts 14:11 *1869*
then *l* up their voices, and said, ... Acts 22:22 *1869*
lest being *l* up with pride he ... 1Ti 3:6 *5188*
upon the earth *l* up his hand to ... Rev 10:5 *142*

LIFTER
glory, and the *l* up of mine head ... Ps 3:3 7311

LIFTEST
Thou *l* me up to the wind ... Job 30:22 5375
thou that *l* me up from the gates ... Ps 9:13 7311
thou *l* me up above those that ... Ps 18:48 7311
l up thy voice for understanding ... Prov 2:3 5414

LIFTETH
he bringeth low, and *l* up ... 1Sa 2:7 7311
l up the beggar from the dunghill ... 1Sa 2:8 7311
thine heart *l* thee up to boast ... 2Chr 25:19 5375
What time she *l* up herself on ... Job 39:18 4754
which *l* up the waves thereof ... Ps 107:25 7311
l the needy out of the dunghill ... Ps 113:7 7311
The LORD *l* up the meek ... Ps 147:6 5749
when he *l* up an ensign on the ... Is 18:3 5375
against him that *l* himself up in ... Jer 51:3 5927
The horseman *l* up both the bright ... Nah 3:3 5927

LIFTING
for *l* up his spear against three ... 1Chr 11:20 5782
by *l* up the voice with joy ... 1Chr 15:16 7311
Amen, Amen, with *l* up their hands ... Neh 8:6 4607
thou shalt say, There is *l* up ... Job 22:29 1466
the *l* up of my hands as the ... Ps 141:2 4864
done foolishly in *l* up thyself ... Prov 30:32 5375
mount up like the *l* up of smoke ... Is 9:18 1348
at the *l* up of thyself the ... Is 33:3 7427
l up holy hands, without wrath and ... 1Ti 2:8 *1869*

LIGHT
And God said, Let there be *l* ... Gen 1:3 216
and there was *l* ... Gen 1:3 216
And God saw the *l*, that it was ... Gen 1:4 216
God divided the *l* from the ... Gen 1:4 216
And God called the *l* Day, and the ... Gen 1:5 216
heaven to give *l* upon the earth ... Gen 1:15 216
the greater *l* to rule the day, and ... Gen 1:16 3974
the lesser *l* to rule the night ... Gen 1:16 3974
heaven to give *l* upon the earth ... Gen 1:17 216
to divide the *l* from the darkness ... Gen 1:18 216
As soon as the morning was *l* ... Gen 44:3 216
Israel had *l* in their dwellings ... Ex 10:23 216
a pillar of fire, to give them *l* ... Ex 13:21 216
but it gave *l* by night to these ... Ex 14:20 216
Oil for the *l*, spices for ... Ex 25:6 3974
they shall *l* the lamps thereof, ... Ex 25:37 5927
they may give *l* over against it ... Ex 25:37 216
pure oil olive beaten for the *l* ... Ex 27:20 3974
And oil for the *l*, and spices for ... Ex 35:8 3974
The candlestick also for the *l* ... Ex 35:14 3974
his lamps, with the oil for the *l* ... Ex 35:14 3974
And spice, and oil for the *l* ... Ex 35:28 3974
vessels thereof, and the oil for *l* ... Ex 39:37 3974
and *l* the lamps thereof ... Ex 40:4 5927
pure oil olive beaten for the *l* ... Lev 24:2 3974
and cover the candlestick of the *l* ... Num 4:9 3974
pertaineth the oil for the *l* ... Num 4:16 3974
the seven lamps shall give *l* over ... Num 8:2 216
and our soul loatheth this *l* bread ... Num 21:5 7052
Cursed be he that setteth *l* by ... Deut 27:16 7034
l persons, which followed him ... Judg 9:4 6348
where her lord was, till it was *l* ... Judg 19:26 216
her hap was to *l* on a part of the ... Ruth 2:3 7136
and spoil them until the morning *l* ... 1Sa 14:36 216
Seemeth it to you a *l* thing to be ... 1Sa 18:23 7043
l any that pisseth against the ... 1Sa 25:22 216
l any that pisseth against the ... 1Sa 25:34 216
less or more, until the morning *l* ... 1Sa 25:36 216
early in the morning, and have *l* ... 1Sa 29:10 216
Asahel was as *l* of foot as a wild ... 2Sa 2:18 7031
we will *l* upon him as the dew ... 2Sa 17:12 5117
by the morning *l* there lacked not ... 2Sa 17:22 216
thou quench not the *l* of Israel ... 2Sa 21:17 5216
shall be as the *l* of the morning ... 2Sa 23:4 216
l was against *l* in three ... 1Kin 7:4 4237
l was against *l* in three ... 1Kin 7:5 4237
was against *l* in three ranks ... 1Kin 7:5 216
David my servant may have a *l* ... 1Kin 11:36 5216
as if it had been a *l* thing for ... 1Kin 16:31 7043
this is but a *l* thing in the ... 2Kin 3:18 7043
if we tarry till the morning *l* ... 2Kin 7:9 216
him to give him alway a *l* ... 2Kin 8:19 5216
It is a *l* thing for the shadow to ... 2Kin 20:10 7043
as he promised to give a *l* to him ... 2Chr 21:7 5216
to give them *l* in the way wherein ... Neh 9:12 216
of fire by night, to shew them *l* ... Neh 9:19 216
The Jews had *l*, and gladness, and ... Est 8:16 219
neither let the *l* shine upon it ... Job 3:4 5105
let it look for *l*, but have none ... Job 3:9 216
as infants which never saw *l* ... Job 3:16 216
Wherefore is *l* given to him that ... Job 3:20 216
Why is *l* given to a man whose way ... Job 3:23
where the *l* is as darkness ... Job 10:22 3313
bringeth out to *l* the shadow of ... Job 12:22 216
They grope in the dark without *l* ... Job 12:25 216
the *l* is short because of ... Job 17:12 216
the *l* of the wicked shall be put ... Job 18:5 216
The *l* shall be dark in his ... Job 18:6 216
be driven from *l* into darkness ... Job 18:18 216
the *l* shall shine upon thy ways ... Job 22:28 216
of those that rebel against the *l* ... Job 24:13 216
with the *l* killeth the poor ... Job 24:14 216
they know not the *l* ... Job 24:16 216
and upon whom doth not his *l* arise ... Job 25:3 216
is hid bringeth he forth to *l* ... Job 28:11 216
when by his *l* I walked through ... Job 29:3 216
the *l* of my countenance they cast ... Job 29:24 216
and when I waited for *l*, there ... Job 30:26 216
pit, and his life shall see the *l* ... Job 33:28 216
with the *l* of the living ... Job 33:30 216
he spreadeth his *l* upon it ... Job 36:30 216
With clouds he covereth the *l* ... Job 36:32 216
caused the *l* of his cloud to ... Job 37:15 216
bright *l* which is in the clouds ... Job 37:21 216
the wicked their *l* is withholden ... Job 38:15 216
Where is the way where *l* dwelleth ... Job 38:19 216

By what way is the *l* parted	Job 38:24	216
By his neesings a *l* doth shine	Job 41:18	216
lift thou up the *l* of thy	Ps 4:6	216
For thou wilt *l* my candle	Ps 18:28	215
The LORD is my *l* and my salvation	Ps 27:1	216
in thy *l* shall we see *l*	Ps 36:9	216
in thy *l* shall we see *l*	Ps 36:9	216
forth thy righteousness as the *l*	Ps 37:6	216
as for the *l* of mine eyes, it	Ps 38:10	216
O send out thy *l* and thy truth	Ps 43:3	216
the *l* of thy countenance, because	Ps 44:3	216
they shall never see *l*	Ps 49:19	216
before God in the *l* of the living	Ps 56:13	216
thou hast prepared the *l* and the	Ps 74:16	3974
and all the night with a *l* of fire	Ps 78:14	216
in the *l* of thy countenance	Ps 89:15	216
sins in the *l* of thy countenance	Ps 90:8	3974
L is sown for the righteous, and	Ps 97:11	216
thyself with *l* as with a garment	Ps 104:2	216
and fire to give *l* in the night	Ps 105:39	216
there ariseth *l* in the darkness	Ps 112:4	216
the LORD, which hath shewed us *l*	Ps 118:27	216
unto my feet, and a *l* unto my path	Ps 119:105	216
entrance of thy words giveth *l*	Ps 119:130	216
the night shall be *l* about me	Ps 139:11	216
the *l* are both alike to thee	Ps 139:12	219
praise him, all ye stars of *l*	Ps 148:3	216
of the just is as the shining *l*	Prov 4:18	216
and the law is *l*	Prov 6:23	216
The *l* of the righteous rejoiceth	Prov 13:9	216
The *l* of the eyes rejoiceth the	Prov 15:30	3974
In the *l* of the king's	Prov 16:15	216
as far as *l* excelleth darkness	Eccl 2:13	216
Truly the *l* is sweet, and a	Eccl 11:7	216
While the sun, or the *l*, or the	Eccl 12:2	216
let us walk in the *l* of the LORD	Is 2:5	216
for *l*, and *l* for darkness	Is 5:20	216
the *l* is darkened in the heavens	Is 5:30	216
is because there is no *l* in them	Is 8:20	7837
in darkness have seen a great *l*	Is 9:2	216
upon them hath the *l* shined	Is 9:2	216
the *l* of Israel shall be for a	Is 10:17	216
thereof shall not give their *l*	Is 13:10	216
shall not cause her *l* to shine	Is 13:10	216
Moreover the *l* of the moon shall	Is 30:26	216
moon shall be as the *l* of the sun	Is 30:26	216
the *l* of the sun shall be	Is 30:26	216
as the *l* of seven days, in the	Is 30:26	216
people, for a *l* of the Gentiles	Is 42:6	216
will make darkness *l* before them	Is 42:16	216
I form the *l*, and create darkness	Is 45:7	216
It is a *l* thing that thou	Is 49:6	7043
give thee for a *l* to the Gentiles	Is 49:6	216
walketh in darkness, and hath no *l*	Is 50:10	5051
walk in the *l* of your fire, and in	Is 50:11	217
to rest for a *l* of the people	Is 51:4	216
Then shall thy *l* break forth as	Is 58:8	216
then shall thy *l* rise in	Is 58:10	216
we wait for *l*, but behold	Is 59:9	216
for thy *l* is come, and the glory	Is 60:1	216
the Gentiles shall come to thy *l*	Is 60:3	216
sun shall be no more thy *l* by day	Is 60:19	216
shall the moon give *l* unto thee	Is 60:19	216
be unto thee an everlasting *l*	Is 60:19	216
LORD shall be thine everlasting *l*	Is 60:20	216
and the heavens, and they had no *l*	Jer 4:23	216
and, while ye look for *l*, he turn	Jer 13:16	216
and the *l* of the candle	Jer 25:10	216
giveth the sun for a *l* by day	Jer 31:35	216
and of the stars for a *l* by night	Jer 31:35	216
me into darkness, but not into *l*	Lam 3:2	216
Is it a *l* thing to the house of	Eze 8:17	7043
In thee have they set *l* by father	Eze 22:7	7043
and the moon shall not give her *l*	Eze 32:7	216
and the *l* dwelleth with him	Dan 2:22	5094
and in the days of thy father *l*	Dan 5:11	5094
of the gods is in thee, and that *l*	Dan 5:14	5094
are as the *l* that goeth forth	Hos 6:5	216
of the LORD is darkness, and not *l*	Amos 5:18	216
of the LORD be darkness, and not *l*	Amos 5:20	216
when the morning is *l*, they	Mic 2:1	216
the LORD shall be a *l* unto me	Mic 7:8	216
he will bring me forth to the *l*	Mic 7:9	216
And his brightness was as the *l*	Hab 3:4	216
at the *l* of thine arrows they	Hab 3:11	216
Her prophets are *l* and treacherous	Zeph 3:4	6348
doth he bring his judgment to *l*	Zeph 3:5	216
that the *l* shall not be clear,	Zec 14:6	216
at evening time it shall be *l*	Zec 14:7	216
which sat in darkness saw great *l*	Mt 4:16	5457
and shadow of death *l* is sprung up	Mt 4:16	5457
Ye are the *l* of the world	Mt 5:14	5457
Neither do men *l* a candle	Mt 5:15	2545
it giveth *l* unto all that are in	Mt 5:15	2989
Let your *l* so shine before men,	Mt 5:16	5457
The *l* of the body is the eye	Mt 6:22	5460
thy whole body shall be full of *l*	Mt 6:22	3088
If therefore the *l* that is in	Mt 6:23	5457
in darkness, that speak ye in *l*	Mt 10:27	5457
yoke is easy, and my burden is *l*	Mt 11:30	1645
and his raiment was white as the *l*	Mt 17:2	5457
But they made *l* of it, and went	Mt 22:5	272
and the moon shall not give her *l*	Mt 24:29	5338
and the moon shall not give her *l*	Mk 13:24	5338
To give *l* to them that sit in	Lk 1:79	2014
A *l* to lighten the Gentiles, and	Lk 2:32	5457
they which enter in may see the *l*	Lk 8:16	5457
they which come in may see the *l*	Lk 11:33	5338
The *l* of the body is the eye	Lk 11:34	3088
thy whole body also is full of *l*	Lk 11:34	5460
the *l* which is in thee be not	Lk 11:35	5457
whole body therefore be full of *l*	Lk 11:36	5460
the whole shall be full of *l*	Lk 11:36	5460
of a candle doth give thee *l*	Lk 11:36	5461
darkness shall be heard in the *l*	Lk 12:3	5457
one piece, doth not *l* a candle	Lk 15:8	681
wiser than the children of *l*	Lk 16:8	5457
and the life was the *l* of men	Jn 1:4	5457
the *l* shineth in darkness	Jn 1:5	5457
witness, to bear witness of the *L*	Jn 1:7	5457
He was not that *L*, but was sent	Jn 1:8	5457
sent to bear witness of that *L*	Jn 1:8	5457
That was the true *L*, which	Jn 1:9	5457
that *l* is come into the world, and	Jn 3:19	5457
men loved darkness rather than *l*	Jn 3:19	5457
one that doeth evil hateth the *l*	Jn 3:20	5457
neither cometh to the *l*	Jn 3:20	5457
that doeth truth cometh to the *l*	Jn 3:21	5457
He was a burning and a shining *l*	Jn 5:35	3088
for a season to rejoice in his *l*	Jn 5:35	5457
saying, I am the *l* of the world	Jn 8:12	5457
but shall have the *l* of life	Jn 8:12	5457
world, I am the *l* of the world	Jn 9:5	5457
he seeth the *l* of this world	Jn 11:9	5457
because there is no *l* in him	Jn 11:10	5457
a little while is the *l* with you	Jn 12:35	5457
Walk while ye have the *l*, lest	Jn 12:35	5457
ye have *l*, believe in the *l*	Jn 12:36	5457
that ye may be the children of *l*	Jn 12:36	5457
I am come a *l* into the world,	Jn 12:46	5457
round about him a *l* from heaven	Acts 9:3	5457
him, and a *l* shined in the prison	Acts 12:7	5457
thee to be a *l* of the Gentiles	Acts 13:47	5457
Then he called for a *l*, and sprang	Acts 16:29	5457
heaven a great *l* round about me	Acts 22:6	5457
were with me saw indeed the *l*	Acts 22:9	5457
not see for the glory of that *l*	Acts 22:11	5457
I saw in the way a *l* from heaven	Acts 26:13	5457
to turn them from darkness to *l*	Acts 26:18	5457
should shew *l* unto the people, and	Acts 26:23	5457
a *l* of them which are in darkness	Rom 2:19	5457
and let us put on the armour of *l*	Rom 13:12	5457
who both will bring to *l* the	1Cor 4:5	5461
lest the *l* of the glorious gospel	2Cor 4:4	5462
who commanded the *l* to shine out	2Cor 4:6	5457
to give the *l* of the knowledge of	2Cor 4:6	5462
For our *l* affliction, which is	2Cor 4:17	1645
communion hath *l* with darkness	2Cor 6:14	5457
is transformed into an angel of *l*	2Cor 11:14	5457
but now are ye *l* in the Lord	Eph 5:8	5457
walk as children of *l*	Eph 5:8	5457
are made manifest by the *l*	Eph 5:13	5457
doth make manifest is *l*	Eph 5:13	5457
dead, and Christ shall give thee *l*	Eph 5:14	2017
inheritance of the saints in *l*	Col 1:12	5457
Ye are all the children of *l*	1Th 5:5	5457
dwelling in the *l* which no man	1Ti 6:16	5457
immortality to *l* through the	2Ti 1:10	5461
of darkness into his marvellous *l*	1Pet 2:9	5457
as unto a *l* that shineth in a	2Pet 1:19	3088
declare unto you, that God is *l*	1Jn 1:5	5457
in the *l*, as he is in the *l*	1Jn 1:7	5457
past, and the true *l* now shineth	1Jn 2:8	5457
He that saith he is in the *l*	1Jn 2:9	5457
his brother abideth in the *l*	1Jn 2:10	5457
neither shall the sun *l* on them	Rev 7:16	4098
the *l* of a candle shall shine no	Rev 18:23	5457
her *l* was like unto a stone most	Rev 21:11	5458
it, and the Lamb is the *l* thereof	Rev 21:23	3088
saved shall walk in the *l* of it	Rev 21:24	5457
no candle, neither *l* of the sun	Rev 22:5	5457
for the Lord God giveth them *l*	Rev 22:5	5461

LIGHTED

saw Isaac, she *l* off the camel	Gen 24:64	5307
he *l* upon a certain place, and	Gen 28:11	6293
he *l* the lamps before the LORD	Ex 40:25	5927
he *l* the lamps thereof over	Num 8:3	5927
and she *l* off her ass	Josh 15:18	6795
and she *l* from off her ass	Judg 1:14	6795
so that Sisera *l* down off his	Judg 4:15	3381
l off the ass, and fell before	1Sa 25:23	3381
he *l* down from the chariot to	2Kin 5:21	5307
he *l* on Jehonadab the son of	2Kin 10:15	4672
Jacob, and it hath *l* upon Israel	Is 9:8	5307
No man, when he hath *l* a candle	Lk 8:16	*681*
No man, when he hath *l* a candle	Lk 11:33	*681*

LIGHTEN

peradventure he will *l* his hand	1Sa 6:5	7043
and the LORD will *l* my darkness	2Sa 22:29	5050
that our God may *l* our eyes	Ezr 9:8	215
l mine eyes, lest I sleep the	Ps 13:3	215
into the sea, to *l* it of them	Jonah 1:5	7043
A light to *l* the Gentiles, and the	Lk 2:32	*602*
for the glory of God did *l* it	Rev 21:23	*5461*

LIGHTENED

They looked unto him, and were *l*	Ps 34:5	5102
the lightnings *l* the world	Ps 77:18	215
the next day they *l* the ship	Acts 27:18	*1546,4160*
they *l* the ship, and cast out the	Acts 27:38	*2893*
the earth was *l* with his glory	Rev 18:1	*5461*

LIGHTENETH

the LORD *l* both their eyes	Prov 29:13	215
that *l* out of the one part under	Lk 17:24	*797*

LIGHTER

yoke which he put upon us, *l*	1Kin 12:4	7043
thy father did put upon us *l*	1Kin 12:9	7043
heavy, but make thou it *l* unto us	1Kin 12:10	7043
make thou it somewhat *l* for us	2Chr 10:10	7043
they are altogether *l* than vanity	Ps 62:9	

LIGHTEST

unto him, When thou *l* the lamps	Num 8:2	5927

LIGHTETH

when Aaron *l* the lamps at even,	Ex 30:8	5927
l upon his neighbour, that he die	Deut 19:5	4672
which *l* every man that cometh	Jn 1:9	*5461*

LIGHTING

shall shew the *l* down of his arm,	Is 30:30	5183
like a dove, and *l* upon him	Mt 3:16	*2064*

LIGHTLY

might *l* have lien with thy wife	Gen 26:10	4592
l esteemed the Rock of his	Deut 32:15	5034
despise me shall be *l* esteemed	1Sa 2:30	7043
I am a poor man, and *l* esteemed	1Sa 18:23	7034
when at the first he *l* afflicted	Is 9:1	7043
and all the hills moved *l*	Jer 4:24	7043
that can *l* speak evil of me	Mk 9:39	*5035*

LIGHTNESS

through the *l* of her whoredom	Jer 3:9	6963
err by their lies, and by their *l*	Jer 23:32	6350
was thus minded, did I use *l*	2Cor 1:17	*1644*

LIGHTNING

l, and discomfited them	2Sa 22:15	1300
a way for the *l* of the thunder	Job 28:26	2385
his *l* unto the ends of the earth	Job 37:3	216
or a way for the *l* of thunder	Job 38:25	2385
Cast forth *l*, and scatter them	Ps 144:6	1300
and out of the fire went forth *l*	Eze 1:13	1300
as the appearance of a flash of *l*	Eze 1:14	965
his face as the appearance of *l*	Dan 10:6	1300
his arrow shall go forth as the *l*	Zec 9:14	1300
For as the *l* cometh out of the	Mt 24:27	*796*
His countenance was like *l*	Mt 28:3	*796*
Satan as *l* fall from heaven	Lk 10:18	*796*
For as the *l*, that lighteneth out	Lk 17:24	*796*

LIGHTNINGS

that there were thunders and *l*	Ex 19:16	1300
saw the thunderings, and the *l*	Ex 20:18	3940
Canst thou send *l*, that they may	Job 38:35	1300
and he shot out *l*, and discomfited	Ps 18:14	1300
the *l* lightened the world	Ps 77:18	1300
His *l* enlightened the world	Ps 97:4	1300
he maketh *l* for the rain	Ps 135:7	1300
he maketh *l* with rain, and	Jer 10:13	1300
he maketh *l* with rain, and	Jer 51:16	1300
they shall run like the *l*	Nah 2:4	1300
And out of the throne proceeded *l*	Rev 4:5	*796*
were voices, and thunderings, and *l*	Rev 8:5	*796*

and there were *l*, and voices, and	Rev 11:19	*796*
were voices, and thunders, and *l*	Rev 16:18	*796*

LIGHTS

Let there be *l* in the firmament	Gen 1:14	3974
And let them be for *l* in the	Gen 1:15	3974
And God made two great *l*	Gen 1:16	3974
house he made windows of narrow *l*	1Kin 6:4	8261
To him that made great *l*	Ps 136:7	216
All the bright *l* of heaven will I	Eze 32:8	3974
girded about, and your *l* burning	Lk 12:35	*3088*
there were many *l* in the upper	Acts 20:8	*2985*
whom ye shine as *l* in the world	Phil 2:15	*5458*
cometh down from the Father of *l*	Jas 1:17	*5457*

LIGN

as the trees of *l* aloes which the	Num 24:6	

LIGURE

And the third row a *l*, an agate,	Ex 28:19	3958
And the third row, a *l*, an agate,	Ex 39:12	3958

LIKE See APPENDIX.

LIKED

he *l* me to make me king over all	1Chr 28:4	7521

LIKEMINDED

grant you to be *l* one	Rom 15:5	*3588,846,5426*
Fulfil ye my joy, that ye be *l*	Phil 2:2	*3588,846,5426*
For I have no man *l*, who will	Phil 2:20	*2473*

LIKEN

To whom then will ye *l* God	Is 40:18	1819
To whom then will ye *l* me	Is 40:25	1819
To whom will ye *l* me, and make me	Is 46:5	1819
what thing shall I *l* to thee	Lam 2:13	1819
I will *l* him unto a wise man,	Mt 7:24	*3666*
shall I *l* this generation	Mt 11:16	*3666*
shall we *l* the kingdom of God	Mk 4:30	*3666*
Whereunto then shall I *l* the men	Lk 7:31	*3666*
Whereunto shall I *l* the kingdom	Lk 13:20	*3666*

LIKENED

the mighty can be *l* unto the LORD	Ps 89:6	1819
I have *l* the daughter of Zion to	Jer 6:2	1819
shall be *l* unto a foolish man,	Mt 7:26	*3666*
The kingdom of heaven is *l* unto a	Mt 13:24	*3666*
of heaven *l* unto a certain king	Mt 18:23	*3666*
of heaven be *l* unto ten virgins	Mt 25:1	*3666*

LIKENESS

man in our image, after our *l*	Gen 1:26	1823
in the *l* of God made he him	Gen 5:1	1823
and begat a son in his own *l*	Gen 5:3	1823
or any *l* of any thing that is in	Ex 20:4	8544
figure, the *l* of male or female,	Deut 4:16	8403
The *l* of any beast that is on the	Deut 4:17	8403
the *l* of any winged fowl that	Deut 4:17	8403
The *l* of any thing that creepeth	Deut 4:18	8403
the *l* of any fish that is in the	Deut 4:18	8403
or the *l* of any thing, which the	Deut 4:23	8544
or the *l* of any thing, and shall	Deut 4:25	8544
or any *l* of any thing that is in	Deut 5:8	8544
when I awake, with thy *l*	Ps 17:15	8544
or what *l* will ye compare unto	Is 40:18	1823
the *l* of four living creatures	Eze 1:5	1823
they had the *l* of a man	Eze 1:5	1823
As for the *l* of their faces, they	Eze 1:10	1823
As for the *l* of the living	Eze 1:13	1823
and they four had one *l*	Eze 1:16	1823
the *l* of the firmament upon the	Eze 1:22	1823
their heads was the *l* of a throne	Eze 1:26	1823
upon the *l* of the throne was the	Eze 1:26	1823
the *l* as the appearance of a man	Eze 1:26	1823
of the *l* of the glory of the LORD	Eze 1:28	1823
lo a *l* as the appearance of fire	Eze 8:2	1823
appearance of the *l* of a throne	Eze 10:1	1823
appearances, they four had one *l*	Eze 10:10	1823
the *l* of the hands of a man was	Eze 10:21	1823
the *l* of their faces was the same	Eze 10:22	1823
come down to us in the *l* of men	Acts 14:11	*3666*
together in the *l* of his death	Rom 6:5	*3667*
also in the *l* of his resurrection	Rom 6:5	
own Son in the *l* of sinful flesh	Rom 8:3	*3667*
and was made in the *l* of men	Phil 2:7	*3667*

LIKETH

of thy gates, where it *l* him best	Deut 23:16	2896
ye also for the Jews, as it *l* you	Est 8:8	2896
for this *l* you, O ye children of	Amos 4:5	157

LIKEWISE See APPENDIX.

LIKHI (lik'-hi) Son of Shemidah.

were, Ahian, and Shechem, and L	1Chr 7:19	3949

LIKING

Their young ones are in good *l* ....Job 39:4   2492
l than the children which are of ....Dan 1:10

LILIES

brim of a cup, with flowers of *l* 1Kin 7:26   7799
brim of a cup, with flowers of *l* 2Chr 4:5   7799
he feedeth among the *l* ....Song 2:16   7799
are twins, which feed among the *l*.........Song 4:5   7799
his lips like *l*, dropping sweet..................Song 5:13   7799
in the gardens, and to gather *l* ....Song 6:2   7799
he feedeth among the *l*...........................Song 6:3   7799
an heap of wheat set about with *l*...........Song 7:2   7799
Consider the *l* of the field.......................Mt 6:28   *2918*
Consider the *l* how they grow ....Lk 12:27   *2918*

LILY

were of *l* work in the porch 1Kin 7:19   7799
the top of the pillars was *l* work 1Kin 7:22   7799
Sharon, and the *l* of the valleys ....Song 2:1   7799
As the *l* among thorns, so is my ....Song 2:2   7799
he shall grow as the *l*, and cast ....Hos 14:5   7799

LIME

shall be as the burnings of *l*...................Is 33:12   7875
bones of the king of Edom into *l* ....Amos 2:1   7875

LIMIT

l thereof round about shall be.................Eze 43:12   1366

LIMITED

God, and *l* the Holy One of Israel..........Ps 78:41   8428

LIMITETH

he *l* a certain day, saying in ....Heb 4:7   *3724*

LINE

thou shalt bind this *l* of scarlet ....Josh 2:18   8615
bound the scarlet *l* in the window ....Josh 2:21   8515
Moab, and measured them with a *l* 2Sa 8:2   2256
and with one full *l* to keep alive.............2Sa 8:2   2256
a *l* of twelve cubits did compass 1Kin 7:15   2339
a *l* of thirty cubits did compass 1Kin 7:23   6957
over Jerusalem the *l* of Samaria............2Kin 21:13   6957
a *l* of thirty cubits did compass 2Chr 4:2   6957
who hath stretched the *l* upon it ....Job 38:5   6957
Their *l* is gone out through all ....Ps 19:4   6957
divided them an inheritance by *l*...........Ps 78:55   2256
l upon *l*, *l* upon *l*....................................Is 28:10   6957
l upon *l*, *l* upon *l*....................................Is 28:13   6957
Judgment also will I lay to the *l* ....Is 28:17   6957
out upon it the *l* of confusion ....Is 34:11   6957
hath divided it unto them by *l* ....Is 34:17   6957
he marketh it out with a *l* ....Is 44:13   8279
the measuring *l* shall yet go ....Jer 31:39   6957
he hath stretched out a *l*.........................Lam 2:8   6957
with a *l* of flax in his hand, and............Eze 40:3   6616
when the man that had the *l* in ....Eze 47:3   6957
and thy land shall be divided by *l* ....Amos 7:17   2256
a *l* shall be stretched forth upon ....Zec 1:16   6957
with a measuring *l* in his hand..............Zec 2:1   2256
l of things made ready to our 2Cor 10:16   *2583*

LINEAGE

he was of the house and *l* of David........Lk 2:4   *3965*

LINEN

arrayed him in vestures of fine *l* ....Gen 41:42   8336
and purple, and scarlet, and fine *l* ....Ex 25:4   8336
ten curtains of fine twined *l* ....Ex 26:1   8336
fine twined *l* of cunning work ....Ex 26:31   8336
and scarlet, and fine twined *l* ....Ex 26:36   8336
for the court of fine twined *l* of ....Ex 27:9   8336
and scarlet, and fine twined *l* ....Ex 27:16   8336
five cubits of fine twined *l* ....Ex 27:18   8336
and purple, and scarlet, and fine *l* ....Ex 28:5   8336
of scarlet, and fine twined *l*....................Ex 28:6   8336
and purple, and fine twined *l* ....Ex 28:8   8336
of scarlet, and of fine twined *l* ....Ex 28:15   8336
embroider the coat of fine *l* ....Ex 28:39   8336
shalt make the mitre of fine *l*.................Ex 28:39   8336
thou shalt make them *l* breeches ....Ex 28:42   906
and purple, and scarlet, and fine *l* ....Ex 35:6   8336
and purple, and scarlet, and fine *l* ....Ex 35:23   8336
and of scarlet, and of fine *l* ....Ex 35:25   8336
purple, in scarlet, and in fine *l*..............Ex 35:35   8336
ten curtains of fine twined *l*...................Ex 36:8   8336
and scarlet, and fine twined *l* ....Ex 36:35   8336
and scarlet, and fine twined *l* ....Ex 36:37   8336
the court were of fine twined *l* ....Ex 38:9   8336
round about were of fine twined *l* ....Ex 38:16   8336
and scarlet, and fine twined *l* ....Ex 38:18   8336
purple, and in scarlet, and fine *l*............Ex 38:23   8336
and scarlet, and fine twined *l* ....Ex 39:2   8336
in the scarlet, and in the fine *l*..............Ex 39:3   8336

and scarlet, and fine twined *l* ....Ex 39:5   8336
and scarlet, and fine twined *l* ....Ex 39:8   8336
purple, and scarlet, and twined *l* ....Ex 39:24
of fine *l* of woven work for Aaron ....Ex 39:27   8336
And a mitre of fine *l*...............................Ex 39:28   8336
and goodly bonnets of fine *l* ....Ex 39:28   8336
l breeches of fine twined *l*,...................Ex 39:28   906
l breeches of fine twined *l* ....Ex 39:28   8336
And a girdle of fine twined *l* ....Ex 39:29   8336
priest shall put on his *l* garment ....Lev 6:10   906
his *l* breeches shall he put upon ....Lev 6:10   906
a woollen garment, or a *l* garment ....Lev 13:47   6593
of *l*, or of woollen ....Lev 13:48   6593
warp or woof, in woollen or in *l* ....Lev 13:52   6593
in a garment of woollen or *l* ....Lev 13:59   6593
He shall put on the holy *l* coat ....Lev 16:4   906
he shall have the *l* breeches upon ....Lev 16:4   906
shall be girded with a *l* girdle................Lev 16:4   906
with the *l* mitre shall he be ....Lev 16:4   906
and shall put off the *l* garments ....Lev 16:23   906
and shall put on the *l* clothes.................Lev 16:32   906
shall a garment mingled of *l* ....Lev 19:19   8162
as of woollen and *l* together ....Deut 22:11   6593
a child, girded with a *l* ephod 1Sa 2:18   906
persons that did wear a *l* ephod 1Sa 22:18   906
David was girded with a *l* ephod 2Sa 6:14   906
brought out of Egypt, and *l* yarn 1Kin 10:28   4723
received the *l* yarn at a price...................1Kin 10:28   4723
house of them that wrought fine *l* 1Chr 4:21   948
was clothed with a robe of fine *l* 1Chr 15:27   948
also had upon him an ephod of *l* 1Chr 15:27   906
brought out of Egypt, and *l* yarn 2Chr 1:16   4723
received the *l* yarn at a price...................2Chr 1:16   4723
in purple, in blue, and in fine *l* 2Chr 2:14   948
and purple, and crimson, and fine *l* 2Chr 3:14   948
being arrayed in white *l* 2Chr 5:12   948
fastened with cords of fine *l* ....Est 1:6   948
gold, and with a garment of fine *l*...........Est 8:15   948
works, with fine *l* of Egypt ....Prov 7:16   948
She maketh fine *l*, and selleth it ....Prov 31:24   5466
The glasses, and the fine *l*......................Is 3:23   5466
me, Go and get thee a *l* girdle ....Jer 13:1   6593
man among them was clothed with *l* ......Eze 9:2   906
called to the man clothed with *l* ....Eze 9:3   906
behold, the man clothed with *l* ....Eze 9:11   906
spake unto the man clothed with *l* ....Eze 10:2   906
commanded the man clothed with *l* ....Eze 10:6   906
of him that was clothed with *l* ....Eze 10:7   906
I girded thee about with fine *l* ....Eze 16:10   8336
and thy raiment was of fine *l* ....Eze 16:13   8336
Fine *l* with broidered work from ....Eze 27:7   8336
and broidered work, and fine *l*................Eze 27:16   948
shall be clothed with *l* garments ....Eze 44:17   6593
They shall have *l* bonnets upon ....Eze 44:18   6593
shall have *l* breeches upon their............Eze 44:18   6593
behold a certain man clothed in *l* ....Dan 10:5   906
one said to the man clothed in *l* ....Dan 12:6   906
And I heard the man clothed in *l* ....Dan 12:7   906
he wrapped it in a clean *l* cloth ....Mt 27:59   *4616*
having a *l* cloth cast about his ....Mk 14:51   *4616*
And he left the *l* cloth, and fled ....Mk 14:52   *4616*
And he bought fine *l*, and took him ....Mk 15:46   *4616*
him down, and wrapped him in the *l*.......Mk 15:46   *4616*
was clothed in purple and fine *l* ....Lk 16:19   *1040*
took it down, and wrapped it in *l*............Lk 23:53   *4616*
he beheld the *l* clothes laid by ....Lk 24:12   *3608*
wound it in *l* clothes with the ....Jn 19:40   *3608*
in, saw the *l* clothes lying ....Jn 20:5   *3608*
and seeth the *l* clothes lie,.....................Jn 20:6   *3608*
not lying with the *l* clothes ....Jn 20:7   *3608*
clothed in pure and white *l* ....Rev 15:6   *3043*
stones, and of pearls, and fine *l* ....Rev 18:12   *1040*
city, that was clothed in fine *l* ....Rev 18:16   *1039*
she should be arrayed in fine *l*...............Rev 19:8   *1039*
for the fine *l* is the ....Rev 19:8   *1039*
white horses, clothed in fine *l* ....Rev 19:14   *1039*

LINES

even with two *l* measured he to 2Sa 8:2   2256
The *l* are fallen unto me in......................Ps 16:6   2256

LINGERED

And while he *l*, the men laid hold ....Gen 19:16   4102
For except we had *l*, surely now.............Gen 43:10   4102

LINGERETH

judgment now of a long time *l* not 2Pet 2:3   *691*

LINTEL

is in the bason, and strike the *l*.............Ex 12:22   4947
he seeth the blood upon the *l*.................Ex 12:23   4947
the *l* and side posts were a fifth............1Kin 6:31   352
Smite the *l* of the door, that the ....Amos 9:1   3730

LINTELS

shall lodge in the upper *l* of it	Zeph 2:14	3730

LINUS (li'-nus) *A Christian at Rome.*

greeteth thee, and Pudens, and L	2Ti 4:21	3044

LION

stooped down, he couched as a *l*	Gen 49:9	738
and as an old *l*	Gen 49:9	3833
people shall rise up as a great *l*	Num 23:24	3833
and lift up himself as a young *l*	Num 23:24	738
He couched, he lay down as a *l*	Num 24:9	738
and as a great *l*	Num 24:9	3833
he dwelleth as a *l*, and teareth	Deut 33:20	3833
a young *l* roared against him	Judg 14:5	738
aside to see the carcase of the *l*	Judg 14:8	738
and honey in the carcase of the *l*	Judg 14:8	738
honey out of the carcase of the *l*	Judg 14:9	738
And what is stronger than a *l*	Judg 14:18	738
father's sheep, and there came a *l*	1Sa 17:34	738
Thy servant slew both the *l*	1Sa 17:36	738
me out of the paw of the *l*	1Sa 17:37	738
heart is as the heart of a *l*	2Sa 17:10	738
slew a *l* in the midst of a pit in	2Sa 23:20	738
a *l* met him by the way, and slew	1Kin 13:24	738
the *l* also stood by the carcase	1Kin 13:24	738
the *l* standing by the carcase	1Kin 13:25	738
hath delivered him unto the *l*	1Kin 13:26	738
the *l* standing by the carcase	1Kin 13:28	738
the *l* had not eaten the carcase,	1Kin 13:28	738
from me, a *l* shall slay thee	1Kin 20:36	738
a *l* found him, and slew him	1Kin 20:36	738
slew a *l* in a pit in a snowy day	1Chr 11:22	738
The roaring of the *l*	Job 4:10	738
and the voice of the fierce *l*	Job 4:10	7826
The old *l* perisheth for lack of	Job 4:11	3918
Thou huntest me as a fierce *l*	Job 10:16	7826
it, nor the fierce *l* passed by it	Job 28:8	7826
Wilt thou hunt the prey for the *l*	Job 38:39	3833
Lest he tear my soul like a *l*	Ps 7:2	738
wait secretly as a *l* in his den	Ps 10:9	738
Like as a *l* that is greedy of his	Ps 17:12	738
as it were a young *l* lurking in	Ps 17:12	3715
as a ravening and a roaring *l*	Ps 22:13	738
Thou shalt tread upon the *l*	Ps 91:13	7826
the young *l* and the dragon shalt	Ps 91:13	3715
wrath is as the roaring of a *l*	Prov 19:12	3715
a king is as the roaring of a *l*	Prov 20:2	3715
man saith, There is a *l* without	Prov 22:13	738
saith, There is a *l* in the way	Prov 26:13	738
a *l* is in the streets	Prov 26:13	738
but the righteous are bold as a *l*	Prov 28:1	3715
As a roaring *l*, and a ranging bear	Prov 28:15	739
A *l* which is strongest among	Prov 30:30	3918
dog is better than a dead *l*	Eccl 9:4	738
Their roaring shall be like a *l*	Is 5:29	3833
and the calf and the young *l*	Is 11:6	3715
the *l* shall eat straw like the ox	Is 11:7	738
And he cried, A *l*	Is 21:8	738
whence come the young and old *l*	Is 30:6	3918
spoken unto me, Like as the *l*	Is 31:4	738
the young *l* roaring on his prey,	Is 31:4	3715
No *l* shall be there, nor any	Is 35:9	738
till morning, that, as a *l*	Is 38:13	738
the *l* shall eat straw like the	Is 65:25	738
prophets, like a destroying *l*	Jer 2:30	738
The *l* is come up from his thicket	Jer 4:7	738
Wherefore a *l* out of the forest	Jer 5:6	738
is unto me as a *l* in the forest	Jer 12:8	738
forsaken his covert, as the *l*	Jer 25:38	3715
he shall come up like a *l* from	Jer 49:19	738
he shall come up like a *l* from	Jer 50:44	738
wait, and as a *l* in secret places	Lam 3:10	738
face of a man, and the face of a *l*	Eze 1:10	738
man, and the third the face of a *l*	Eze 10:14	738
it became a young *l*, and it	Eze 19:3	3715
her whelps, and made him a young *l*	Eze 19:5	3715
the lions, he became a young *l*	Eze 19:6	3715
like a roaring *l* ravening the	Eze 22:25	738
art like a young *l* of the nations	Eze 32:2	3715
the face of a young *l* toward the	Eze 41:19	3715
The first was like a *l*, and had	Dan 7:4	738
For I will be unto Ephraim as a *l*	Hos 5:14	7826
as a young *l* to the house of	Hos 5:14	3715
he shall roar like a *l*	Hos 11:10	738
I will be unto them as a *l*	Hos 13:7	7826
there will I devour them like a *l*	Hos 13:8	3833
whose teeth are the teeth of a *l*	Joel 1:6	738
hath the cheek teeth of a great *l*	Joel 1:6	3833
Will a *l* roar in the forest, when	Amos 3:4	738
will a young *l* cry out of his den	Amos 3:4	3715
The *l* hath roared, who will not	Amos 3:8	738

of the mouth of the *l* two legs	Amos 3:12	738
As if a man did flee from a *l*	Amos 5:19	738
the midst of many people as a *l*	Mic 5:8	738
as a young *l* among the flocks of	Mic 5:8	3715
of the young lions, where the *l*	Nah 2:11	739
even the old *l*	Nah 2:11	3833
The *l* did tear in pieces enough	Nah 2:12	738
out of the mouth of the *l*	2Ti 4:17	3023
the devil, as a roaring *l*	1Pet 5:8	3023
And the first beast was like a *l*	Rev 4:7	3023
the L of the tribe of Juda, the	Rev 5:5	3023
a loud voice, as when a *l* roareth	Rev 10:3	3023
and his mouth as the mouth of a *l*	Rev 13:2	3023

LIONESS

A *l*: she lay down	Eze 19:2	3833

LIONESSES

whelps, and strangled for his *l*	Nah 2:12	3833

LIONLIKE

acts, he slew two *l* men of Moab	2Sa 23:20	739
he slew two *l* men of Moab	1Chr 11:22	739

LION'S

Judah is a *l* whelp	Gen 49:9	738
of Dan he said, Dan is a *l* whelp	Deut 33:22	738
the stout *l* whelps are scattered	Job 4:11	3833
The *l* whelps have not trodden it,	Job 28:8	7830
Save me from the *l* mouth	Ps 22:21	738
the *l* whelp, and none made them	Nah 2:11	738

LIONS

eagles, they were stronger than *l*	2Sa 1:23	738
were between the ledges were *l*	1Kin 7:29	738
and beneath the *l* and oxen were	1Kin 7:29	738
thereof, he graved cherubims, *l*	1Kin 7:36	738
two *l* stood beside the stays	1Kin 10:19	738
twelve *l* stood there on the one	1Kin 10:20	738
the LORD sent *l* among them	2Kin 17:25	738
he hath sent *l* among them	2Kin 17:26	738
faces were like the faces of *l*	1Chr 12:8	738
two *l* standing by the stays	2Chr 9:18	738
twelve *l* stood there on the one	2Chr 9:19	738
lion, and the teeth of the young *l*	Job 4:10	3715
fill the appetite of the young *l*	Job 38:39	3715
The young *l* do lack, and suffer	Ps 34:10	3715
my darling from the *l*	Ps 35:17	3715
My soul is among *l*	Ps 57:4	3833
the great teeth of the young *l*	Ps 58:6	3715
The young *l* roar after their prey	Ps 104:21	3715
they shall roar like young *l*	Is 5:29	3715
l upon him that escapeth of Moab,	Is 15:9	738
The young *l* roared upon him, and	Jer 2:15	3715
the *l* have driven him away	Jer 50:17	738
They shall roar together like *l*	Jer 51:38	3715
she lay down among *l*, she	Eze 19:2	738
her whelps among young *l*	Eze 19:2	3715
And he went up and down among the *l*.	Eze 19:6	738
with all the young *l* thereof	Eze 38:13	3715
shall be cast into the den of *l*	Dan 6:7	744
shall be cast into the den of *l*	Dan 6:12	744
and cast him into the den of *l*	Dan 6:16	744
went in haste unto the den of *l*	Dan 6:19	744
able to deliver thee from the *l*	Dan 6:20	744
they cast them into the den of *l*	Dan 6:24	744
the *l* had the mastery of them, and	Dan 6:24	744
Daniel from the power of the *l*	Dan 6:27	744
Where is the dwelling of the *l*	Nah 2:11	738
the feeding place of the young *l*	Nah 2:11	3715
sword shall devour thy young *l*	Nah 2:13	3715
princes within her are roaring *l*	Zeph 3:3	738
a voice of the roaring of young *l*	Zec 11:3	3715
promises, stopped the mouths of *l*	Heb 11:33	3023
teeth were as the teeth of *l*	Rev 9:8	3023
the horses were as the heads of *l*	Rev 9:17	3023

LIONS'

Shenir and Hermon, from the *l* dens	Song 4:8	738
they shall yell as *l* whelps	Jer 51:38	738
angel, and hath shut the *l* mouths	Dan 6:22	744

LIP

put a covering upon his upper *l*	Lev 13:45	822
they shoot out the *l*, they shake	Ps 22:7	8193
The *l* of truth shall be	Prov 12:19	8193

LIPS

me, who am of uncircumcised *l*	Ex 6:12	8193
Behold, I am of uncircumcised *l*	Ex 6:30	8193
pronouncing with his *l* to do evil	Lev 5:4	8193
or uttered ought out of her *l*	Num 30:6	8193
that which she uttered with her *l*	Num 30:8	8193
out of her *l* concerning her vows	Num 30:12	8193
gone out of thy *l* thou shalt keep	Deut 23:23	8193

L

only her *l* moved, but her voice	1Sa 1:13	8193
thy nose, and my bridle in thy *l*	2Kin 19:28	8193
this did not Job sin with his *l*	Job 2:10	8193
laughing, and thy *l* with rejoicing	Job 8:21	8193
speak, and open his *l* against thee	Job 11:5	8193
hearken to the pleadings of my *l*	Job 13:6	8193
thine own *l* testify against thee	Job 15:6	8193
the moving of my *l* should assuage	Job 16:5	8193
from the commandment of his *l*	Job 23:12	8193
My *l* shall not speak wickedness,	Job 27:4	8193
I will open my *l* and answer	Job 32:20	8193
my *l* shall utter knowledge	Job 33:3	8193
with flattering *l* and with a	Ps 12:2	8193
shall cut off all flattering *l*	Ps 12:3	8193
our *l* are our own	Ps 12:4	8193
nor take up their names into my *l*	Ps 16:4	8193
that goeth not out of feigned *l*	Ps 17:1	8193
by the word of thy *l* I have kept	Ps 17:4	8193
withholden the breath of his *l*	Ps 21:2	8193
Let the lying *l* be put to silence	Ps 31:18	8193
thy *l* from speaking guile	Ps 34:13	8193
lo, I have not refrained my *l*	Ps 40:9	8193
grace is poured into thy *l*	Ps 45:2	8193
O Lord, open thou my *l*	Ps 51:15	8193
swords are in their *l*	Ps 59:7	8193
the words of their *l* let them	Ps 59:12	8193
than life, my *l* shall praise thee	Ps 63:3	8193
shall praise thee with joyful *l*	Ps 63:5	8193
Which my *l* have uttered, and my	Ps 66:14	8193
My *l* shall greatly rejoice when I	Ps 71:23	8193
thing that is gone out of my *l*	Ps 89:34	8193
he spake unadvisedly with his *l*	Ps 106:33	8193
With my *l* have I declared all the	Ps 119:13	8193
My *l* shall utter praise, when	Ps 119:171	8193
my soul, O Lord, from lying *l*	Ps 120:2	8193
adders' poison is under their *l*	Ps 140:3	8193
of their own *l* cover them	Ps 140:9	8193
Keep the door of my *l*	Ps 141:3	8193
perverse *l* put far from thee	Prov 4:24	8193
that thy *l* may keep knowledge	Prov 5:2	8193
For the *l* of a strange woman drop	Prov 5:3	8193
of her *l* she forced him	Prov 7:21	8193
the opening of my *l* shall be	Prov 8:6	8193
is an abomination to my *l*	Prov 8:7	8193
In the *l* of him that hath	Prov 10:13	2193
that hideth hatred with lying *l*	Prov 10:18	8193
he that refraineth his *l* is wise	Prov 10:19	8193
The *l* of the righteous feed many	Prov 10:21	8193
The *l* of the righteous know what	Prov 10:32	8193
by the transgression of his *l*	Prov 12:13	8193
Lying *l* are abomination to the	Prov 12:22	8193
wide his *l* shall have destruction	Prov 13:3	8193
but the *l* of the wise shall	Prov 14:3	8193
not in him the *l* of knowledge	Prov 14:7	8193
but the talk of the *l* tendeth	Prov 14:23	8193
The *l* of the wise disperse	Prov 15:7	8193
sentence is in the *l* of the king	Prov 16:10	8193
Righteous *l* are the delight of	Prov 16:13	8193
of the *l* increaseth learning	Prov 16:21	8193
and addeth learning to his *l*	Prov 16:23	8193
in his *l* there is as a burning	Prov 16:27	8193
moving his *l* he bringeth evil to	Prov 16:30	8193
doer giveth heed to false *l*	Prov 17:4	8193
much less do lying *l* a prince	Prov 17:7	8193
his *l* is esteemed a man of	Prov 17:28	8193
A fool's *l* enter into contention,	Prov 18:6	8193
his *l* are the snare of his soul,	Prov 18:7	8193
of his *l* shall he be filled	Prov 18:20	8193
than he that is perverse in his *l*	Prov 19:1	8193
but the *l* of knowledge are a	Prov 20:15	8193
him that flattereth with his *l*	Prov 20:19	8193
for the grace of his *l* the king	Prov 22:11	8193
shall withal be fitted in thy *l*	Prov 22:18	8193
when thy *l* speak right things	Prov 23:16	8193
and their *l* talk of mischief	Prov 24:2	8193
Every man shall kiss his *l* that	Prov 24:26	8193
and deceive not with thy *l*	Prov 24:28	8193
Burning *l* and a wicked heart are	Prov 26:23	8193
hateth dissembleth with his *l*	Prov 26:24	8193
a stranger, and not thine own *l*	Prov 27:2	8193
but the *l* of a fool shall swallow	Eccl 10:12	8193
Thy *l* are like a thread of	Song 4:3	8193
Thy *l*, O my spouse, drop as the	Song 4:11	8193
his *l* like lilies, dropping sweet	Song 5:13	8193
causing the *l* of those that are	Song 7:9	8193
because I am a man of unclean *l*	Is 6:5	8193
midst of a people of unclean *l*	Is 6:5	8193
said, Lo, this hath touched thy *l*	Is 6:7	8193
with the breath of his *l* shall he	Is 11:4	8193
For with stammering *l* and another	Is 28:11	8193
with their *l* do honour me, but	Is 29:13	8193

his *l* are full of indignation, and	Is 30:27	8193
thy nose, and my bridle in thy *l*	Is 37:29	8193
I create the fruit of the *l*	Is 57:19	8193
your *l* have spoken lies, your	Is 59:3	8193
out of my *l* was right before thee	Jer 17:16	8193
The *l* of those that rose up	Lam 3:62	8193
upon thy feet, and cover not thy *l*	Eze 24:17	8222
ye shall not cover your *l*	Eze 24:22	8222
are taken up in the *l* of talkers	Eze 36:3	8193
of the sons of men touched my *l*	Dan 10:16	8193
we render the calves of our *l*	Hos 14:2	8193
yea, they shall all cover their *l*	Mic 3:7	8222
my *l* quivered at the voice	Hab 3:16	8193
iniquity was not found in his *l*	Mal 2:6	8193
For the priest's *l* should keep	Mal 2:7	8193
and honoureth me with their *l*	Mt 15:8	5491
people honoureth me with their *l*	Mk 7:6	5491
poison of asps is under their *l*	Rom 3:13	5491
other *l* will I speak unto this	1Cor 14:21	5491
the fruit of our *l* giving thanks	Heb 13:15	5491
his *l* that they speak no guile	1Pet 3:10	5491

LIQUOR

shall he drink any *l* of grapes	Num 6:3	4952
round goblet, which wanteth not *l*	Song 7:2	4197

LIQUORS

of thy ripe fruits, and of thy *l*	Ex 22:29	1831

LISTED

done unto him whatsoever they *l*	Mt 17:12	*2309*
done unto him whatsoever they *l*	Mk 9:13	*2309*

LISTEN

L, O isles, unto me	Is 49:1	8085

LISTETH

The wind bloweth where it *l*.	Jn 3:8	*2309*
whithersoever the governor *l*	Jas 3:4	*3730,1014*

LITTERS

horses, and in chariots, and in *l*	Is 66:20	6632

LITTLE

Let a *l* water, I pray you, be	Gen 18:4	4592
to flee unto, and it is a *l* one	Gen 19:20	4705
thither, (is it not a *l* one)	Gen 19:20	4705
drink a *l* water of thy pitcher	Gen 24:17	4592
a *l* water of thy pitcher to drink	Gen 24:43	4592
For it was *l* which thou hadst	Gen 30:30	4592
their wealth, and all their *l* ones	Gen 34:29	2945
there was but a *l* way to come to	Gen 35:16	3530
them, Go again, buy us a *l* food	Gen 43:2	4592
we, and thou, and also our *l* ones	Gen 43:8	2945
a *l* balm, and a *l* honey,	Gen 43:11	4592
a child of his old age, a *l* one	Gen 44:20	6966
Go again, and buy us a *l* food	Gen 44:25	4592
the land of Egypt for your *l* ones	Gen 45:19	2945
their father, and their *l* ones	Gen 46:5	2945
and for food for your *l* ones	Gen 47:24	2945
but a *l* way to come unto Ephrath	Gen 48:7	3530
only their *l* ones, and their	Gen 50:8	2945
will nourish you, and your *l* ones	Gen 50:21	2945
I will let you go, and your *l* ones	Ex 10:10	2945
let your *l* ones also go with you	Ex 10:24	2945
household be too *l* for the lamb	Ex 12:4	4591
and he that gathered *l* had no lack	Ex 16:18	4591
By *l* and *l* I will drive them	Ex 23:30	4592
And the *l* owl, and the cormorant,	Lev 11:17	3563
But your *l* ones, which ye said	Num 14:31	2945
their sons, and their *l* children	Num 16:27	2945
Midian captives, and their *l* ones	Num 31:9	2945
kill every male among the *l* ones	Num 31:17	2945
cattle, and cities for our *l* ones	Num 32:16	2945
our *l* ones shall dwell in the	Num 32:17	2945
Build you cities for your *l* ones	Num 32:24	2945
Our *l* ones, our wives, our flocks	Num 32:26	2945
Moreover your *l* ones, which ye	Deut 1:39	2945
the *l* ones, of every city, we	Deut 2:34	2945
But your wives, and your *l* ones	Deut 3:19	2945
before thee by *l* and *l*	Deut 7:22	4592
The *l* owl, and the great owl, and	Deut 14:16	3563
the *l* ones, and the cattle, and all	Deut 20:14	2945
field, and shalt gather but *l* in	Deut 28:38	4592
Your *l* ones, your wives, and thy	Deut 29:11	2945
Your wives, your *l* ones, and your	Josh 1:14	2945
the *l* ones, and the strangers that	Josh 8:35	2945
of Dan went out too *l* for them	Josh 19:47	
the iniquity of Peor too *l* for us	Josh 22:17	4592
I pray thee, a *l* water to drink	Judg 4:19	4592
and departed, and put the *l* ones	Judg 18:21	2945
that she tarried a *l* in the house	Ruth 2:7	4592
his mother made him a *l* coat	1Sa 2:19	6996
I tasted a *l* of this honey	1Sa 14:29	4592

I did but taste a *l* honey with	1Sa 14:43	4592
When thou wast *l* in thine own	1Sa 15:17	6996
with David, and a *l* lad with him	1Sa 20:35	6996
had nothing, save one *l* ewe lamb	2Sa 12:3	6996
and if that had been too *l*	2Sa 12:8	4592
all the *l* ones that were with him	2Sa 15:22	2945
when David was a *l* past the top	2Sa 16:1	4592
Thy servant will go a *l* way over	2Sa 19:36	4592
and I am but a *l* child	1Kin 3:7	6996
was before the LORD was too *l* to	1Kin 8:64	6996
Hadad being yet a *l* child	1Kin 11:17	6996
My *l* finger shall be thicker than	1Kin 12:10	6996
a *l* water in a vessel, that I may	1Kin 17:10	4592
a barrel, and a *l* oil in a cruse	1Kin 17:12	4592
make me thereof a *l* cake first	1Kin 17:13	6996
there ariseth a *l* cloud out of	1Kin 18:44	6996
them like two *l* flocks of kids	1Kin 20:27	2835
there came forth *l* children out	2Kin 2:23	6996
Let us make a *l* chamber, I pray	2Kin 4:10	6996
of the land of Israel a *l* maid	2Kin 5:2	6996
like unto the flesh of a *l* child	2Kin 5:14	6995
So he departed from him a *l* way	2Kin 5:19	3530
unto them, Ahab served Baal a *l*	2Kin 10:18	4592
My *l* finger shall be thicker than	2Chr 10:10	6996
the LORD, with their *l* ones	2Chr 20:13	2945
the genealogy of all their *l* ones	2Chr 31:18	2945
way for us, and for our *l* ones	Ezr 8:21	2945
now for a *l* space grace hath been	Ezr 9:8	4592
give us a *l* reviving in our	Ezr 9:8	4592
the trouble were *l* before thee	Neh 9:32	4591
l children and women, in one day,	Est 3:13	2945
would assault them, both *l* ones	Est 8:11	2945
and mine ear received a *l* thereof	Job 4:12	8102
that I may take comfort a *l*	Job 10:20	4592
forth their *l* ones like a flock	Job 21:11	5759
They are exalted for a *l* while	Job 24:24	4592
but how *l* a portion is heard of	Job 26:14	8102
Suffer me a *l*, and I will shew	Job 36:2	2191
when his wrath is kindled but a *l*	Ps 2:12	4592
him a *l* lower than the angels	Ps 8:5	4592
For yet a *l* while, and the wicked	Ps 37:10	4592
A *l* that a righteous man hath is	Ps 37:16	4592
the *l* hills rejoice on every side	Ps 65:12	
There is *l* Benjamin with their	Ps 68:27	6810
the *l* hills, by righteousness	Ps 72:3	
rams, and the *l* hills like lambs	Ps 114:4	
and ye *l* hills, like lambs	Ps 114:6	
dasheth thy *l* ones against the	Ps 137:9	5768
Yet a *l* sleep, a *l* slumber,	Prov 6:10	4592
a *l* folding of the hands to sleep	Prov 6:10	4592
heart of the wicked is *l* worth	Prov 10:20	4592
Better is *l* with the fear of the	Prov 15:16	4592
Better is a *l* with righteousness	Prov 16:8	4592
Yet a *l* sleep, a *l* slumber,	Prov 24:33	4592
a *l* folding of the hands to sleep	Prov 24:33	4592
things which are *l* upon the earth	Prov 30:24	6996
sweet, whether he eat *l* or much	Eccl 5:12	4592
There was a *l* city, and few men	Eccl 9:14	6996
so doth a *l* folly him that is in	Eccl 10:1	4592
the *l* foxes, that spoil the vines	Song 2:15	6996
It was but a *l* that I passed from	Song 3:4	4592
We have a *l* sister, and she hath	Song 8:8	6996
For yet a very *l* while, and the	Is 10:25	4592
a *l* child shall lead them	Is 11:6	6995
thyself as it were for a *l* moment	Is 26:20	4592
here a *l*, and there a *l*	Is 28:10	2191
here a *l*, and there a *l*	Is 28:13	2191
Is it not yet a very *l* while	Is 29:17	4592
up the isles as a very *l* thing	Is 40:15	1851
In a *l* wrath I hid my face from	Is 54:8	8241
A *l* one shall become a thousand,	Is 60:22	6996
have possessed it but a *l* while	Is 63:18	4705
sent their *l* ones to the waters	Jer 14:3	6810
her *l* ones have caused a cry to	Jer 48:4	6810
yet a *l* while, and the time of her	Jer 51:33	4592
maids, and *l* children, and women	Eze 9:6	2945
as a *l* sanctuary in the countries	Eze 11:16	4592
as if that were a very *l* thing	Eze 16:47	4592
sent out her *l* rivers unto all	Eze 31:4	8585
every *l* chamber was one reed long	Eze 40:7	
between the *l* chambers were five	Eze 40:7	
the *l* chambers of the gate	Eze 40:10	
The space also before the *l*	Eze 40:12	
the *l* chambers were six cubits on	Eze 40:12	
the gate from the roof of one *l*	Eze 40:13	
narrow windows to the *l* chambers	Eze 40:16	
the *l* chambers thereof were three	Eze 40:21	
the *l* chambers thereof, and the	Eze 40:29	
the *l* chambers thereof, and the	Eze 40:33	
The *l* chambers thereof, the posts	Eze 40:36	
came up among them another *l* horn	Dan 7:8	2192
one of them came forth a *l* horn	Dan 8:9	4704
shall be holpen with a *l* help	Dan 11:34	4592
for yet a *l* while, and I will	Hos 1:4	4592
they shall sorrow a *l* for the	Hos 8:10	4592
and the *l* house with clefts	Amos 6:11	6996
though thou be *l* among the	Mic 5:2	6810
Ye have sown much, and bring in *l*	Hag 1:6	4592
for much, and, lo, it came to *l*	Hag 1:9	4592
Yet once, it is a *l* while	Hag 2:6	4592
for I was but a *l* displeased	Zec 1:15	4592
turn mine hand upon the *l* ones	Zec 13:7	6819
more clothe you, O ye of *l* faith	Mt 6:30	3640
are ye fearful, O ye of *l* faith	Mt 8:26	3640
l ones a cup of cold water only	Mt 10:42	3398
said unto him, O thou of *l* faith	Mt 14:31	3640
said, Seven, and a few *l* fishes	Mt 15:34	2485
said unto them, O ye of *l* faith	Mt 16:8	3640
Jesus called a *l* child unto him	Mt 18:2	3813
and become as *l* children, ye	Mt 18:3	3813
humble himself as this *l* child	Mt 18:4	3813
whoso shall receive one such *l*	Mt 18:5	3398
these *l* ones which believe in me	Mt 18:6	3398
despise not one of these *l* ones	Mt 18:10	3398
that one of these *l* ones should	Mt 18:14	3398
there brought unto him *l* children	Mt 19:13	3813
Suffer *l* children, and forbid them	Mt 19:14	3813
And he went a *l* farther, and fell	Mt 26:39	3397
he had gone a *l* farther thence	Mk 1:19	3641
were also with him other *l* ships	Mk 4:36	4142
My *l* daughter lieth at the point	Mk 5:23	2365
these *l* ones that believe in me	Mk 9:42	3398
Suffer the *l* children to come	Mk 10:14	3813
the kingdom of God as a *l* child	Mk 10:15	3813
And he went forward a *l*, and fell	Mk 14:35	3397
a *l* after, they that stood by	Mk 14:70	3397
thrust out a *l* from the land	Lk 5:3	3641
but to whom *l* is forgiven	Lk 7:47	3641
is forgiven, the same loveth *l*	Lk 7:47	3641
he clothe you, O ye of *l* faith	Lk 12:28	3640
Fear not, *l* flock	Lk 12:32	3398
should offend one of these *l* ones	Lk 17:2	3398
Suffer *l* children to come unto me	Lk 18:16	3813
a *l* child shall in no wise enter	Lk 18:17	3813
because he was *l* of stature	Lk 19:3	3398
hast been faithful in a very *l*	Lk 19:17	1646
after a *l* while another saw him,	Lk 22:58	1024
every one of them may take a *l*	Jn 6:7	1024
Yet a *l* while am I with you, and	Jn 7:33	3398
Yet a *l* while is the light with	Jn 12:35	3398
L children, yet a *l* while I	Jn 13:33	5040
Yet a *l* while, and the world seeth	Jn 14:19	3397
A *l* while, and ye shall not see me	Jn 16:16	3397
a *l* while, and ye shall see me,	Jn 16:16	3397
A *l* while, and ye shall not see me	Jn 16:17	3397
a *l* while, and ye shall see me	Jn 16:17	3397
is this that he saith, A *l* while	Jn 16:18	3397
A *l* while, and ye shall not see me	Jn 16:19	3397
a *l* while, and ye shall see me	Jn 16:19	3397
other disciples came in a *l* ship	Jn 21:8	4142
put the apostles forth a *l* space	Acts 5:34	1024
alive, and were not a *l* comforted	Acts 20:12	3357
and when they had gone a *l* further	Acts 27:28	1024
people shewed us no *l* kindness	Acts 28:2	5177
Know ye not that a *l* leaven	1Cor 5:6	3398
that had gathered *l* had no lack	2Cor 8:15	3641
bear with me a *l* in my folly	2Cor 11:1	3397
me, that I may boast myself a *l*	2Cor 11:16	3397
My *l* children, of whom I travail	Gal 4:19	5040
A *l* leaven leaveneth the whole	Gal 5:9	3398
For bodily exercise profiteth *l*	1Ti 4:8	3641
water, but use a *l* wine for thy	1Ti 5:23	3641
Thou madest him a *l* lower than	Heb 2:7	1024
who was made a *l* lower than the	Heb 2:9	1024
For yet a *l* while, and he that	Heb 10:37	3397
Even so the tongue is a *l* member	Jas 3:5	3398
great a matter a *l* fire kindleth	Jas 3:5	3641
that appeareth for a *l* time	Jas 4:14	3641
My *l* children, these things write	1Jn 2:1	5040
l children, because your sins are	1Jn 2:12	5040
l children, because ye have known	1Jn 2:13	3813
L children, it is the last time	1Jn 2:18	3813
And now, *l* children, abide in him	1Jn 2:28	5040
L children, let no man deceive	1Jn 3:7	5040
My *l* children, let us not love in	1Jn 3:18	5040
l children, and have overcome them	1Jn 4:4	5040
L children, keep yourselves from	1Jn 5:21	5040
for thou hast a *l* strength	Rev 3:8	3398
should rest yet for a *l* season	Rev 6:11	3398
he had in his hand a *l* book open	Rev 10:2	974
take the *l* book which is open in	Rev 10:8	974
said unto him, Give me the *l* book	Rev 10:9	974

L

I took the *l* book out of the	Rev 10:10	974
that he must be loosed a *l* season	Rev 20:3	3398

LIVE

of life, and eat, and *l* for ever	Gen 3:22	2425
my soul shall *l* because of thee	Gen 12:13	2421
that Ishmael might *l* before thee	Gen 17:18	2421
and my soul shall *l*	Gen 19:20	2421
pray for thee, and thou shalt *l*	Gen 20:7	2421
And by thy sword shalt thou *l*	Gen 27:40	2421
findest thy gods, let him not *l*	Gen 31:32	2421
that we may *l*, and not die	Gen 42:2	2421
them the third day, This do, and *l*	Gen 42:18	2421
that we may *l*, and not die, both	Gen 43:8	2421
doth my father yet *l*	Gen 45:3	2416
and give us seed, that we may *l*	Gen 47:19	2421
be a daughter, then she shall *l*	Ex 1:16	2425
be beast or man, it shall not *l*	Ex 19:13	2421
then they shall sell the *l* ox	Ex 21:35	2416
shalt not suffer a witch to *l*	Ex 22:18	2421
there shall no man see me, and *l*	Ex 33:20	2425
altar, he shall bring the *l* goat	Lev 16:20	2416
hands upon the head of the *l* goat	Lev 16:21	2416
if a man do, he shall *l* in them	Lev 18:5	2425
that he may *l* with thee	Lev 25:35	2416
that thy brother may *l* with thee	Lev 25:36	2416
do unto them, that they may *l*	Num 4:19	2421
But as truly as I *l*, all the	Num 14:21	2416
Say unto them, As truly as I *l*	Num 14:28	2416
when he looketh upon it, shall *l*	Num 21:8	2425
who shall *l* when God doeth this	Num 24:23	2421
for to do them, that ye may *l*	Deut 4:1	2421
that they shall *l* upon the earth	Deut 4:10	2416
fire, as thou hast heard, and *l*	Deut 4:33	2421
one of these cities he might *l*	Deut 4:42	2425
hath commanded you, that ye may *l*	Deut 5:33	2421
ye observe to do, that ye may *l*	Deut 8:1	2421
that man doth not *l* by bread only	Deut 8:3	2421
the mouth of the Lord doth man *l*	Deut 8:3	2421
the days that ye *l* upon the earth	Deut 12:1	2416
thou follow, that thou mayest *l*	Deut 16:20	2421
shall flee thither, that he may *l*	Deut 19:5	2425
unto one of those cities, and *l*	Deut 19:5	2425
all thy soul, that thou mayest *l*	Deut 30:6	2416
his judgments, that thou mayest *l*	Deut 30:16	2421
that both thou and thy seed may *l*	Deut 30:19	2421
as long as ye *l* in the land	Deut 31:13	2416
to heaven, and say, I *l* for ever	Deut 32:40	2416
Let Reuben *l*, and not die	Deut 33:6	2421
only Rahab the harlot shall *l*	Josh 6:17	2421
a league with them, to let them *l*	Josh 9:15	2421
we will even let them *l*, lest	Josh 9:20	2421
said unto them, Let them *l*	Josh 9:21	2421
I *l* shew me the kindness of the	1Sa 20:14	2416
not *l* after that he was fallen	2Sa 1:10	2421
to me, that the child may *l*	2Sa 12:22	2416
the king, How long have I to *l*	2Sa 19:34	2416
Let my lord king David *l* for ever	1Kin 1:31	2421
thee all the days that they *l* in	1Kin 8:40	2416
saith, I pray thee, let me *l*	1Kin 20:32	2421
l thou and thy children of the	2Kin 4:7	2421
if they save us alive, we shall *l*	2Kin 7:4	2421
shall be wanting, he shall not *l*	2Kin 10:19	2421
olive and of honey, that ye may *l*	2Kin 18:32	2421
for thou shalt die, and not *l*	2Kin 20:1	2421
so long as they *l* in the land	2Chr 6:31	2416
the king, Let the king *l* for ever	Neh 2:3	2421
for them, that we may eat, and *l*	Neh 5:2	2421
if a man do, he shall *l* in them	Neh 9:29	2421
the golden sceptre, that he may *l*	Est 4:11	2421
I would not *l* alway	Job 7:16	2421
If a man die, shall he *l* again	Job 14:14	2421
Wherefore do the wicked *l*	Job 21:7	2421
not reproach me so long as I *l*	Job 27:6	3117
your heart shall *l* for ever	Ps 22:26	2421
That he should still *l* for ever	Ps 49:9	2421
shall not *l* out half their days	Ps 55:23	
Thus will I bless thee while I *l*	Ps 63:4	2416
your heart shall *l* that seek God	Ps 69:32	2421
And he shall *l*, and to him shall be	Ps 72:15	2421
sing unto the Lord as long as I *l*	Ps 104:33	2416
I call upon him as long as I *l*	Ps 116:2	3117
I shall not die, but *l*, and	Ps 118:17	2421
with thy servant, that I may *l*	Ps 119:17	2421
come unto me, that I may *l*	Ps 119:77	2421
unto thy word, that I may *l*	Ps 119:116	2421
me understanding, and I shall *l*	Ps 119:144	2421
Let my soul *l*, and it shall praise	Ps 119:175	2421
While I *l* will I praise the Lord	Ps 146:2	2416
keep my commandments, and *l*	Prov 4:4	2421
Keep my commandments, and *l*	Prov 7:2	2421

Forsake the foolish, and *l*	Prov 9:6	2421
but he that hateth gifts shall *l*	Prov 15:27	2421
l many years, so that the days of	Eccl 6:3	2421
though he *l* a thousand years	Eccl 6:6	2421
is in their heart while they *l*	Eccl 9:3	2416
L joyfully with the wife whom	Eccl 9:9	2416
But if a man *l* many years	Eccl 11:8	2421
having a *l* coal in his hand	Is 6:6	7531
They are dead, they shall not *l*	Is 26:14	2421
Thy dead men shall *l*, together	Is 26:19	2421
for thou shalt die, and not *l*	Is 38:1	2421
O Lord, by these things men *l*	Is 38:16	2421
thou recover me, and make me to *l*	Is 38:16	2421
As I *l*, saith the Lord, thou	Is 49:18	2416
hear, and your soul shall *l*	Is 55:3	2421
that besiege you, he shall *l*	Jer 21:9	2421
As I *l*, saith the Lord, though	Jer 22:24	2416
and serve him and his people, and *l*	Jer 27:12	2421
serve the king of Babylon, and *l*	Jer 27:17	2421
that ye may *l* many days in the	Jer 35:7	2421
forth to the Chaldeans shall *l*	Jer 38:2	2421
his life for a prey, and shall *l*	Jer 38:2	2425
princes, then thy soul shall *l*	Jer 38:17	2421
and thou shalt *l*, and thine house	Jer 38:17	2421
unto thee, and thy soul shall *l*	Jer 38:20	2421
As I *l*, saith the King, whose	Jer 46:18	2416
we shall *l* among the heathen	Lam 4:20	2421
doth not sin, he shall surely *l*	Eze 3:21	2421
Wherefore, as I *l*, saith the Lord	Eze 5:11	2416
the souls alive that should not *l*	Eze 13:19	2421
three men were in it, as I *l*	Eze 14:16	2416
three men were in it, as I *l*	Eze 14:18	2416
and Job, were in it, as I *l*	Eze 14:20	2416
when thou wast in thy blood, *L*	Eze 16:6	2421
when thou wast in thy blood, *L*	Eze 16:6	2421
As I *l*, saith the Lord God, Sodom	Eze 16:48	2416
As I *l*, saith the Lord God,	Eze 17:16	2416
As I *l*, surely mine oath that he	Eze 17:19	2416
As I *l*, saith the Lord God, ye	Eze 18:3	2416
he is just, he shall surely *l*	Eze 18:9	2421
shall he then *l*	Eze 18:13	2425
he shall not *l*	Eze 18:13	2421
of his father, he shall surely *l*	Eze 18:17	2421
hath done them, he shall surely *l*	Eze 18:19	2421
and right, he shall surely *l*	Eze 18:21	2421
that he hath done he shall *l*	Eze 18:22	2421
should return from his ways, and *l*	Eze 18:23	2421
the wicked man doeth, shall he *l*	Eze 18:24	2425
hath committed, he shall surely *l*	Eze 18:28	2421
turn yourselves, and *l* ye	Eze 18:32	2421
As I *l*, saith the Lord God, I	Eze 20:3	2416
a man do, he shall even *l* in them	Eze 20:11	2425
a man do, he shall even *l* in them	Eze 20:13	2425
a man do, he shall even *l* in them	Eze 20:21	2425
whereby they should not *l*	Eze 20:25	2421
As I *l*, saith the Lord God, I	Eze 20:31	2416
As I *l*, saith the Lord God	Eze 20:33	
in them, how should we then *l*	Eze 33:10	2421
Say unto them, As I *l*, saith the	Eze 33:11	2416
the wicked turn from his way and *l*	Eze 33:11	2421
to *l* for his righteousness in the	Eze 33:12	2421
righteous, that he shall surely *l*	Eze 33:13	2421
he shall surely *l*, he shall not	Eze 33:15	2421
he shall surely *l*	Eze 33:16	2421
and right, he shall *l* thereby	Eze 33:19	2421
As I *l*, surely they that are in	Eze 33:27	2416
As I *l* saith the Lord God, surely	Eze 34:8	2416
Therefore, as I *l*, saith the Lord	Eze 35:6	2416
Therefore, as I *l*, saith these Lord	Eze 35:11	2416
me, Son of man, can these bones *l*	Eze 37:3	2421
to enter into you, and ye shall *l*	Eze 37:5	2421
put breath in you, and ye shall *l*	Eze 37:6	2421
upon these slain, that they may *l*	Eze 37:9	2421
my spirit in you, and ye shall *l*	Eze 37:14	2421
the rivers shall come, shall *l*	Eze 47:9	2421
every thing shall *l* whither the	Eze 47:9	2425
in Syriack, O king, *l* for ever	Dan 2:4	2418
O king, *l* for ever	Dan 3:9	2418
spake and said, O king, *l* for ever	Dan 5:10	2414
unto him, King Darius, *l* for ever	Dan 6:6	2414
unto the king, O king, *l* for ever	Dan 6:21	2414
us up, and shall *l* in his sight	Hos 6:2	2421
Israel, Seek ye me, and ye shall *l*	Amos 5:4	2421
Seek the Lord, and ye shall *l*	Amos 5:6	2421
good, and not evil, that ye may *l*	Amos 5:14	2421
is better for me to die than to *l*	Jonah 4:3	2416
is better for me to die than to *l*	Jonah 4:8	2416
but the just shall *l* by his faith	Hab 2:4	2421
Therefore as I *l*, saith the Lord	Zeph 2:9	2416
the prophets, do they *l* for ever	Zec 1:5	2421
they shall *l* with their children,	Zec 10:9	2421

say unto him, Thou shalt not *l* .... Zec 13:3   2421
Man shall not *l* by bread alone, ... Mt 4:4   2198
thy hand upon her, and she shall *l* .... Mt 9:18   2198
and she shall *l* .... Mk 5:23   2198
man shall not *l* by bread alone .... Lk 4:4   2198
l delicately, are in kings' .... Lk 7:25   5225
this do, and thou shalt *l* .... Lk 10:28   2198
for all *l* unto him .... Lk 20:38   2198
and they that hear shall *l* .... Jn 5:25   2198
this bread, he shall *l* for ever .... Jn 6:51   2198
sent me, and I *l* by the Father .... Jn 6:57   2198
eateth me, even he shall *l* by me .... Jn 6:57   2198
of this bread shall *l* for ever .... Jn 6:58   2198
he were dead, yet shall he *l* .... Jn 11:25   2198
because I *l*, ye shall *l* also .... Jn 14:19   2198
to the end they might not *l* .... Acts 7:19   2225
For in him we *l*, and move, and have ..... Acts 17:28   2198
it is not fit that he should *l* .... Acts 22:22   2198
that he ought not to *l* any longer .... Acts 25:24   2198
yet vengeance suffereth not to *l* .... Acts 28:4   2198
The just shall *l* by faith.......................... Rom 1:17   2198
dead to sin, *l* any longer therein .... Rom 6:2   2198
that we shall also *l* with him .... Rom 6:8   4800
the flesh, to *l* after the flesh .... Rom 8:12   2198
For if ye *l* after the flesh, ye .... Rom 8:13   2198
the deeds of the body, ye shall *l*............ Rom 8:13   2198
those things shall *l* by them.................. Rom 10:5   2198
in you, *l* peaceably with all men .... Rom 12:18   1514
we *l*, we *l* unto the Lord .... Rom 14:8   2198
whether we *l* therefore, or die, ... Rom 14:8   2198
For it is written, As I *l* .... Rom 14:11   2198
minister about holy things *l* of 1Cor 9:13   2068
the gospel should *l* of the gospel........... 1Cor 9:14   2198
For we which *l* are alway....................... 2Cor 4:11   2198
that they which *l* should not.................. 2Cor 5:15   2198
not henceforth *l* unto themselves........... 2Cor 5:15   2198
as dying, and, behold, we *l* 2Cor 6:9   2198
our hearts to die and *l* with you 2Cor 7:3   4800
but we shall *l* with him by the 2Cor 13:4   2198
be of one mind, *l* in peace 2Cor 13:11   1514
the Gentiles to *l* as do the Jews .... Gal 2:14   2198
the law, that I might *l* unto God .... Gal 2:19   2198
nevertheless I *l* .... Gal 2:20   2198
the life which I now *l* in the.................. Gal 2:20   2198
l by the faith of the Son of God .... Gal 2:20   2198
for, The just shall *l* by faith .... Gal 3:11   2198
that doeth them shall *l* in them .... Gal 3:12   2198
If we *l* in the Spirit, let us.................... Gal 5:25   2198
thou mayest *l* long on the earth ...... Eph 6:3   2071,3118
For to me to *l* is Christ, and to .... Phil 1:21   2198
But if I *l* in the flesh, this is .... Phil 1:22   2198
For now we *l*, if ye stand fast in 1Th 3:8   2198
we should *l* together with him................ 1Th 5:10   2198
him, we shall also *l* with him 2Ti 2:11   4800
all that will *l* godly in Christ 2Ti 3:12   2198
lusts, we should *l* soberly .... Titus 2:12   2198
Now the just shall *l* by faith .... Heb 10:38   2198
unto the Father of spirits, and *l* .... Heb 12:9   2198
all things willing to *l* honestly.............. Heb 13:18   390
say, If the Lord will, we shall *l* .... Jas 4:15   2198
should *l* unto righteousness 1Pet 2:24   2198
That he no longer should *l* the 1Pet 4:2   980
but *l* according to God in the................ 1Pet 4:6   2198
those that after should *l* ungodly......... 2Pet 2:6
escaped from them who *l* in error 2Pet 2:18   390
that we might *l* through him.................. 1Jn 4:9   2198
the wound by a sword, and did *l* .... Rev 13:14   2198

LIVED

Adam *l* an hundred and thirty years ..... Gen 5:3   2421
that Adam *l* were nine hundred.............. Gen 5:5   2425
Seth *l* an hundred and five years, ... Gen 5:6   2421
Seth *l* after he begat Enos eight .... Gen 5:7   2421
Enos *l* ninety years, and begat .... Gen 5:9   2421
Enos *l* after he begat Cainan .... Gen 5:10   2421
Cainan *l* seventy years, and begat .... Gen 5:12   2421
And Cainan *l* after he begat.................. Gen 5:13   2421
And Mahalaleel *l* sixty and five............. Gen 5:15   2421
Mahalaleel *l* after he begat Jared .... Gen 5:16   2421
Jared *l* an hundred sixty and two .... Gen 5:18   2421
Jared *l* after he begat Enoch .... Gen 5:19   2421
And Enoch *l* sixty and five years,.......... Gen 5:21   2421
Methuselah *l* an hundred eighty and ..... Gen 5:25   2421
Methuselah *l* after he begat.................. Gen 5:26   2421
Lamech *l* an hundred eighty and two ..... Gen 5:28   2421
Lamech *l* after he begat Noah five .... Gen 5:30   2421
Noah *l* after the flood three .... Gen 9:28   2421
Shem *l* after he begat Arphaxad .... Gen 11:11   2421
And Arphaxad *l* five and thirty .... Gen 11:12   2425
Arphaxad *l* after he begat Salah .... Gen 11:13   2421
Salah *l* thirty years, and begat.............. Gen 11:14   2425

Salah *l* after he begat Eber four............. Gen 11:15   2421
And Eber *l* four and thirty years, ... Gen 11:16   2421
Eber *l* after he begat Peleg four............. Gen 11:17   2421
Peleg *l* thirty years, and begat .... Gen 11:18   2421
Peleg *l* after he begat Reu two .... Gen 11:19   2421
And Reu *l* two and thirty years, and ..... Gen 11:20   2421
Reu *l* after he begat Serug two .... Gen 11:21   2421
Serug *l* thirty years, and begat .... Gen 11:22   2421
Serug *l* after he begat Nahor two .... Gen 11:23   2421
And Nahor *l* nine and twenty years, ... Gen 11:24   2421
Nahor *l* after he begat Terah an .... Gen 11:25   2421
Terah *l* seventy years, and begat .... Gen 11:26   2421
Isaac his son, while he yet *l* .... Gen 25:6   2416
of Abraham's life which he *l*.................. Gen 25:7   2425
Jacob *l* in the land of Egypt .... Gen 47:28   2421
Joseph *l* an hundred and ten years .... Gen 50:22   2421
went to search the land, *l* still.............. Num 14:38   2421
beheld the serpent of brass, he *l* .... Num 21:9   2425
of the fire, as we have, and *l* .... Deut 5:26   2421
I perceive, that if Absalom had *l* 2Sa 19:6   2416
Solomon his father while he yet *l* 1Kin 12:6   2416
l after the death of Jehoash son 2Kin 14:17   2421
Solomon his father while he yet *l* 2Chr 10:6   2416
the son of Joash king of Judah *l* 2Chr 25:25   2421
After this *l* Job an hundred and.............. Job 42:16   2421
Though while he *l* he blessed his........... Ps 49:18   2416
breath came into them, and they *l* .... Eze 37:10   2421
had *l* with an husband seven years......... Lk 2:36   2198
I have *l* in all good conscience............... Acts 23:1   4176
of our religion I *l* a Pharisee .... Acts 26:5   2198
some time, when ye *l* in them .... Col 3:7   2198
Ye have *l* in pleasure on the.................. Jas 5:5   5171
l deliciously, so much torment and .... Rev 18:7   2198
l deliciously with her, shall .... Rev 18:9   2198
and they *l* and reigned with Christ .... Rev 20:4   2198
But the rest of the dead *l* not .... Rev 20:5   326

LIVELY

for they are *l*, and are delivered .... Ex 1:19   2422
But mine enemies are *l*, and they .... Ps 38:19   2416
who received the *l* oracles to .... Acts 7:38   2198
a *l* hope by the resurrection of.............. 1Pet 1:3   2198
as *l* stones, are built up a 1Pet 2:5   2198

LIVER

and the caul that is above the *l* .... Ex 29:13   3516
inwards, and the caul above the *l*........... Ex 29:22   3516
flanks, and the caul above the *l*............. Lev 3:4   3516
flanks, and the caul above the *l*............. Lev 3:10   3516
flanks, and the caul above the *l*............. Lev 3:15   3516
and the caul that is above the *l* .... Lev 4:9   3516
and the caul that is above the *l* .... Lev 7:4   3516
inwards, and the caul above the *l*........... Lev 8:16   3516
inwards, and the caul above the *l*........... Lev 8:25   3516
the caul above the *l* of the sin.............. Lev 9:10   3516
kidneys, and the caul above the *l* .... Lev 9:19   3516
Till a dart strike through his *l* .... Prov 7:23   3516
my *l* is poured upon the earth, ... Lam 2:11   3516
with images, he looked in the *l* .... Eze 21:21   3516

LIVES

blood of your *l* will I require .... Gen 9:5   5315
to save your *l* by a great........................ Gen 45:7   2421
they said, Thou hast saved our *l*............ Gen 47:25   2421
they made their *l* bitter with................ Ex 1:14   2416
have, and deliver our *l* from death .... Josh 2:13   5315
afraid of our *l* because of you .... Josh 9:24   5315
l unto the death in the high .... Judg 5:18   5315
with the *l* of thy household .... Judg 18:25   5315
lovely and pleasant in their *l*................. 2Sa 1:23   2416
the *l* of thy sons and of thy................... 2Sa 19:5   5315
the *l* of thy wives.................................. 2Sa 19:5   5315
and the *l* of thy concubines 2Sa 19:5   5315
that went in jeopardy of their *l* 2Sa 23:17   5315
that have put their *l* in jeopardy 1Chr 11:19   5315
of their *l* they brought it 1Chr 11:19   5315
together, and stood for their *l* .... Est 9:16   5315
they lurk privily for their own *l*............. Prov 1:18   5315
hands of them that seek their *l*.............. Jer 19:7   5315
and they that seek their *l* .... Jer 19:9   5315
hand of those that seek their *l* .... Jer 46:26   5315
Flee, save your *l*, and be like the .... Jer 48:6   5315
our *l* because of the sword of the .... Lam 5:9   5315
yet their *l* were prolonged for a............. Dan 7:12   2417
is not come to destroy men's *l* .... Lk 9:56   5590
Men that have hazarded their *l* .... Acts 15:26   5590
lading and ship, but also of our *l*........... Acts 27:10   5590
lay down our *l* for the brethren 1Jn 3:16   5590
loved not their *l* unto the death .... Rev 12:11   5590

LIVEST

as long as thou *l* upon the earth............ Deut 12:19   3117
as thou *l*, and as thy soul liveth, ... 2Sa 11:11   2416

l after the manner of Gentiles, ... Gal 2:14   *2198*
that thou hast a name that thou *l* .... Rev 3:1   *2198*

LIVETH

that *l* shall be meat for you .... Gen 9:3   2416
God doth talk with man, and he *l* .... Deut 5:24   2425
as the LORD *l*, if ye had saved .... Judg 8:19   2416
a kinsman to thee, as the LORD *l* .... Ruth 3:13   2416
said, Oh my lord, as thy soul *l* 1Sa 1:26   2416
as long as he *l* he shall be lent 1Sa 1:28   3117
For, as the LORD *l*, which saveth 1Sa 14:39   2416
as the LORD *l*, there shall not 1Sa 14:45   2416
And Abner said, As thy soul *l* 1Sa 17:55   2416
and Saul sware, As the LORD *l* 1Sa 19:6   2416
the LORD *l*, and as thy soul *l* 1Sa 20:3   2416
as the LORD *l* 1Sa 20:21   2416
son of Jesse *l* upon the ground 1Sa 20:31   2425
say to him that *l* in prosperity 1Sa 25:6   2416
the LORD *l*, and as thy soul *l* 1Sa 25:26   2416
deed, as the LORD God of Israel *l* 1Sa 25:34   2416
said furthermore, As the LORD *l* 1Sa 26:10   2416
As the LORD *l*, ye are worthy to 1Sa 26:16   2416
the LORD, saying, As the LORD *l* 1Sa 28:10   2416
unto him, Surely, as the LORD *l* 1Sa 29:6   2416
And Joab said, As God *l*, unless 2Sa 2:27   2416
and said unto them, As the LORD *l* 2Sa 4:9   2416
as thou livest, and as thy soul *l* 2Sa 11:11   2416
he said to Nathan, As the LORD *l* 2Sa 12:5   2416
And he said, As the LORD *l* 2Sa 14:11   2416
answered and said, As thy soul *l* 2Sa 14:19   2416
the king, and said, As the LORD *l* 2Sa 15:21   2416
and as my lord the king *l* 2Sa 15:21   2416
The LORD *l* 2Sa 22:47   2416
sware, and said, As the LORD *l* 1Kin 1:29   2416
Now therefore, as the LORD *l* 1Kin 2:24   2416
one saith, This is my son that *l* 1Kin 3:23   2416
Ahab, As the LORD God of Israel *l* 1Kin 17:1   2416
she said, As the LORD thy God *l* 1Kin 17:12   2416
and Elijah said, See, thy son *l* 1Kin 17:23   2416
As the LORD thy God *l*, there is 1Kin 18:10   2416
said, As the LORD of hosts *l* 1Kin 18:15   2416
And Micaiah said, As the LORD *l* 1Kin 22:14   2416
the LORD *l*, and as thy soul *l* 2Kin 2:2   2416
the LORD *l*, and as thy soul *l* 2Kin 2:4   2416
the LORD *l*, and as thy soul *l* 2Kin 2:6   2416
said, As the LORD of hosts *l* 2Kin 3:14   2416
the LORD *l*, and as thy soul *l* 2Kin 4:30   2416
But he said, As the LORD *l* 2Kin 5:16   2416
but, as the LORD *l*, I will run 2Kin 5:20   2416
And Micaiah said, As the LORD *l* 2Chr 18:13   2416
For I know that my redeemer *l* .... Job 19:25   2416
As God *l*, who hath taken away my ...... Job 27:2   2416
The LORD *l* .... Ps 18:46   2416
What man is he that *l*, and shall .... Ps 89:48   2421
And thou shalt swear, The LORD *l* .... Jer 4:2   2416
And though they say, The LORD *l* .... Jer 5:2   2416
to swear by my name, The LORD *l* .... Jer 12:16   2416
shall no more be said, The LORD *l* .... Jer 16:14   2416
But, The LORD *l*, that brought up .... Jer 16:15   2416
shall no more say, The LORD *l* .... Jer 23:7   2416
But, The LORD *l*, which brought up .... Jer 23:8   2416
Jeremiah, saying, As the LORD *l* .... Jer 38:16   2416
of Egypt, saying, The Lord GOD *l* .... Jer 44:26   2416
to pass, that every thing that *l* .... Eze 47:9   2416
and honoured him that *l* for ever .... Dan 4:34   2416
sware by him that *l* for ever that .... Dan 12:7   2416
Beth-aven, nor swear, The LORD *l* .... Hos 4:15   2416
and say, Thy god, O Dan, *l* .... Amos 8:14   2416
and, The manner of Beer-sheba *l* .... Amos 8:14   2416
thy son *l* .... Jn 4:50   *2198*
and told him, saying, Thy son *l* .... Jn 4:51   *2198*
Jesus said unto him, Thy son *l* .... Jn 4:53   *2198*
And whosoever *l* **and believeth in me** ... Jn 11:26   *2198*
in that he *l*, he *l* unto God .... Rom 6:10   *2198*
over a man as long as he *l* .... Rom 7:1   *2198*
to her husband so long as he *l* .... Rom 7:2   *2198*
So then if, while her husband *l* .... Rom 7:3   *2198*
For none of us *l* to himself .... Rom 14:7   *2198*
the law as long as her husband *l* 1Cor 7:39   *2198*
yet he *l* by the power of God 2Cor 13:4   *2198*
yet not I, but Christ *l* in me .... Gal 2:20   *2198*
But she that *l* in pleasure is 1Ti 5:6   *2198*
in pleasure is dead while she *l* 1Ti 5:6   *2198*
of whom it is witnessed that he *l* .... Heb 7:8   *2198*
by him, seeing he ever *l* to make .... Heb 7:25   *2198*
at all while the testator *l* .... Heb 9:17   *2198*
by the word of God, which *l* 1Pet 1:23   *2198*
I am he that *l*, **and was dead** .... Rev 1:18   *2198*
throne, who *l* for ever and ever, ... Rev 4:9   *2198*
and worship him that *l* for ever .... Rev 4:10   *2198*
and worshipped him that *l* for ever .... Rev 5:14   *2198*

And sware by him that *l* for ever .... Rev 10:6   *2198*
of God, who *l* for ever and ever .... Rev 15:7   *2198*

LIVING

every *l* creature that moveth, ... Gen 1:21   2416
the *l* creature after his kind .... Gen 1:24   2416
over every *l* thing that moveth .... Gen 1:28   2416
and man became a *l* soul .... Gen 2:7   2416
Adam called every *l* creature .... Gen 2:19   2416
she was the mother of all *l* .... Gen 3:20   2416
of every *l* thing of all flesh, ... Gen 6:19   2416
every *l* substance that I have .... Gen 7:4
every *l* substance was destroyed .... Gen 7:23
remembered Noah, and every *l* thing ..... Gen 8:1   2416
every *l* thing that is with thee .... Gen 8:17   2416
smite any more every thing *l* .... Gen 8:21   2416
with every *l* creature that is .... Gen 9:10   2416
every *l* creature that is with you .... Gen 9:12   2416
every *l* creature of all flesh .... Gen 9:15   2416
every *l* creature of all flesh .... Gen 9:16   2416
of any *l* thing which is in the .... Lev 11:10   2416
of every *l* creature that moveth .... Lev 11:46   2416
As for the *l* bird, he shall take .... Lev 14:6   2416
the *l* bird in the blood of the .... Lev 14:6   2416
shall let the *l* bird loose into .... Lev 14:7   2416
the *l* bird, and dip them in the .... Lev 14:51   2416
running water, and with the *l* bird .... Lev 14:52   2416
But he shall let go the *l* bird .... Lev 14:53   2416
or by any manner of *l* thing that .... Lev 20:25
stood between the dead and the *l* .... Num 16:48   2416
hath heard the voice of the *l* God .... Deut 5:26   2416
know that the *l* God is among you .... Josh 3:10   2416
left off his kindness to the *l* .... Ruth 2:20   2416
defy the armies of the *l* God 1Sa 17:26   2416
defied the armies of the *l* God 1Sa 17:36   2416
of their death, *l* in widowhood 2Sa 20:3   2424
but the *l* is my son, and the dead 1Kin 3:22   2416
is thy son, and the *l* is my son 1Kin 3:22   2416
is the dead, and my son is the *l* 1Kin 3:23   2416
Divide the *l* child in two, and 1Kin 3:25   2416
the *l* child was unto the king 1Kin 3:26   2416
O my lord, give her the *l* child 1Kin 3:26   2416
and said, Give her the *l* child 1Kin 3:27   2416
hath sent to reproach the *l* God 2Kin 19:4   2416
sent him to reproach the *l* God 2Kin 19:16   2416
hand is the soul of every *l* thing .... Job 12:10   2416
is it found in the land of the *l* .... Job 28:13   2416
it is hid from the eyes of all *l* .... Job 28:21   2416
to the house appointed for all *l* .... Job 30:23   2416
with the light of the *l* .... Job 33:30   2416
of the LORD in the land of the *l* .... Ps 27:13   2416
thirsteth for God, for the *l* God .... Ps 42:2   2416
thee out of the land of the *l* .... Ps 52:5   2416
before God in the light of the *l* .... Ps 56:13   2416
away as with a whirlwind, both *l* .... Ps 58:9   2416
blotted out of the book of the *l* .... Ps 69:28   2416
my flesh crieth out for the *l* God .... Ps 84:2   2416
the LORD in the land of the *l* .... Ps 116:9   2416
my portion in the land of the *l* .... Ps 142:5   2416
sight shall no man *l* be justified .... Ps 143:2   2416
the desire of every *l* thing .... Ps 145:16   2416
than the *l* which are yet alive .... Eccl 4:2   2416
I considered all the *l* which walk .... Eccl 4:15   2416
that knoweth to walk before the *l* .... Eccl 6:8   2416
the *l* will lay it to his heart .... Eccl 7:2   2416
joined to all the *l* there is hope .... Eccl 9:4   2416
for a *l* dog is better than a dead .... Eccl 9:4   2416
For the *l* know that they shall .... Eccl 9:5   2416
of gardens, a well of *l* waters .... Song 4:15   2416
written among the *l* in Jerusalem .... Is 4:3   2416
for the *l* to the dead .... Is 8:19   2416
hath sent to reproach the *l* God .... Is 37:4   2416
hath sent to reproach the *l* God .... Is 37:17   2416
the LORD, in the land of the *l* .... Is 38:11   2416
The *l*, the *l*, he shall .... Is 38:19   2416
cut off out of the land of the *l* .... Is 53:8   2416
me the fountain of *l* waters .... Jer 2:13   2416
is the true God, he is the *l* God .... Jer 10:10   2416
him off from the land of the *l* .... Jer 11:19   2416
LORD, the fountain of *l* waters .... Jer 17:13   2416
perverted the words of the *l* God .... Jer 23:36   2416
Wherefore doth a *l* man complain .... Lam 3:39   2416
the likeness of four *l* creatures .... Eze 1:5   2416
the likeness of the *l* creatures .... Eze 1:13   2416
up and down among the *l* creatures .... Eze 1:13   2416
the *l* creatures ran and returned .... Eze 1:14   2416
Now as I beheld the *l* creatures .... Eze 1:15   2416
upon the earth by the *l* creatures .... Eze 1:15   2416
when the *l* creatures went, the .... Eze 1:19   2416
when the *l* creatures were lifted .... Eze 1:19   2416
for the spirit of the *l* creature .... Eze 1:20   2416

for the spirit of the *l* creature	Eze 1:21	2416
l creature was as the colour of	Eze 1:22	2416
the *l* creatures that touched one	Eze 3:13	2416
This is the *l* creature that I saw	Eze 10:15	2416
of the *l* creature was in them	Eze 10:17	2416
This is the *l* creature that I saw	Eze 10:20	2416
set glory in the land of the *l*	Eze 26:20	2416
terror in the land of the *l*	Eze 32:23	2416
their terror in the land of the *l*	Eze 32:24	2416
was caused in the land of the *l*	Eze 32:25	2416
their terror in the land of the *l*	Eze 32:26	2416
the mighty in the land of the *l*	Eze 32:27	2416
my terror in the land of the *l*	Eze 32:32	2416
that I have more than any *l*	Dan 2:30	2417
to the intent that the *l* may know	Dan 4:17	2417
O Daniel, servant of the *l* God	Dan 6:20	2417
for he is the *l* God, and stedfast	Dan 6:26	2417
Ye are the sons of the *l* God	Hos 1:10	2416
that *l* waters shall go out from	Zec 14:8	2416
the Christ, the Son of the *l* God	Mt 16:16	2198
the God of the dead, but of the *l*	Mt 22:32	2198
him, I adjure thee by the *l* God	Mt 26:63	2198
of the dead, but the God of the *l*	Mk 12:27	2198
all that she had, even all her *l*	Mk 12:44	979
spent all her *l* upon physicians	Lk 8:43	979
And he divided unto them his *l*	Lk 15:12	979
his substance with riotous *l*	Lk 15:13	2198
hath devoured thy *l* with harlots	Lk 15:30	979
a God of the dead, but of the *l*	Lk 20:38	2198
cast in all the *l* that she had	Lk 21:4	979
Why seek ye the *l* among the dead	Lk 24:5	2198
he would have given the *l* water	Jn 4:10	2198
then hast thou that *l* water	Jn 4:11	2198
I am the *l* bread which came down	Jn 6:51	2198
As the *l* Father hath sent me, and	Jn 6:57	2198
that Christ, the Son of the *l* God	Jn 6:69	2198
shall flow rivers of *l* water	Jn 7:38	2198
these vanities unto the *l* God	Acts 14:15	2198
called the children of the *l* God	Rom 9:26	2198
present your bodies a *l* sacrifice	Rom 12:1	2198
be Lord both of the dead and *l*	Rom 14:9	2198
first man Adam was made a *l* soul	1Cor 15:45	2198
but with the Spirit of the *l* God	2Cor 3:3	2198
ye are the temple of the *l* God	2Cor 6:16	2198
as though *l* in the world, are ye	Col 2:20	2198
to God from idols to serve the *l*	1Th 1:9	2198
which is the church of the *l* God	1Ti 3:15	2198
because we trust in the *l* God	1Ti 4:10	2198
riches, but in the *l* God, who	1Ti 6:17	2198
l in malice and envy, hateful, and	Titus 3:3	1236
in departing from the *l* God	Heb 3:12	2198
dead works to serve the *l* God	Heb 9:14	2198
l way, which he hath consecrated	Heb 10:20	2198
fall into the hands of the *l* God	Heb 10:31	2198
and unto the city of the *l* God	Heb 12:22	2198
To whom coming, as unto a *l* stone	1Pet 2:4	2198
having the seal of the *l* God	Rev 7:2	2198
them unto *l* fountains of waters	Rev 7:17	2198
every *l* soul died in the sea	Rev 16:3	2198

LIZARD

and the chameleon, and the *l*	Lev 11:30	3911

LO

and, *l*, in her mouth was an olive	Gen 8:11	2009
and, *l*, one born in my house is	Gen 15:3	2009
and, *l*, an horror of great	Gen 15:12	2009
lift up his eyes and looked, and, *l*	Gen 18:2	2009
and, *l*, Sarah thy wife shall have	Gen 18:10	2009
of the plain, and beheld, and, *l*	Gen 19:28	2009
behold a well in the field, and, *l*	Gen 29:2	2009
And he said, *L*, it is yet high day	Gen 29:7	2005
sheaves in the field, and, *l*	Gen 37:7	2009
and, *l*, it is even in my sack	Gen 42:28	2009
l, here is seed for you, and ye	Gen 47:23	1883
and, *l*, God hath shewed me also	Gen 48:11	2009
father made me swear, saying, *L*	Gen 50:5	2009
l, he goeth unto the water	Ex 7:15	2009
l, he cometh forth to the water	Ex 8:20	2009
l, shall we sacrifice the	Ex 8:26	2005
And the LORD said unto Moses, *L*	Ex 19:9	2009
top of the mountain, saying, *L*	Num 14:40	2009
And Balaam said unto Balak, *L*	Num 22:38	2009
And he returned unto him and, *l*	Num 23:6	2009
l, the people shall dwell alone,	Num 23:9	2005
but, *l*, the LORD hath kept thee	Num 24:11	2009
And, *l*, he hath given occasions of	Deut 22:17	2009
and now, *l*, I am this day	Josh 14:10	2009
Behold, I dreamed a dream, and, *l*	Judg 7:13	2009
For, *l*, thou shalt conceive, and	Judg 13:5	2009
And when he came, *l*, Eli sat upon	1Sa 4:13	2009
and, *l*, thy father hath left the	1Sa 10:2	2009

rod that was in mine hand, and, *l*	1Sa 14:43	2114
said Achish unto his servants, *L*	1Sa 21:14	2009
and, *l*, the chariots and horsemen	2Sa 1:6	2009
l Zadok also, and all the Levites	2Sa 15:24	2009
that smote the people, and said, *L*	2Sa 24:17	2009
And, *l*, while she yet talked with	1Kin 1:22	2009
for, *l*, he hath caught hold on	1Kin 1:51	2009
l, I have given thee a wise and an	1Kin 3:12	2009
and they said one to another, *L*	2Kin 7:6	2009
and, *l*, all the way was full of	2Kin 7:15	2009
said to Nathan the prophet, *L*	1Chr 17:1	2009
l, I give thee the oxen also for	1Chr 21:23	7200
the acts of Asa, first and last, *l*	2Chr 16:11	2009
Thou sayest, *L*, thou hast smitten	2Chr 25:19	2009
and all his wars, and his ways, *l*	2Chr 27:7	2005
For, *l*, our fathers have fallen	2Chr 29:9	2009
and, *l*, we bring into bondage our	Neh 5:5	2009
And, *l*, I perceived that God had	Neh 6:12	2009
L, let that night be solitary	Job 3:7	2009
L this, we have searched it, so	Job 5:27	2009
L, he goeth by me, and I see him	Job 9:11	2005
If I speak of strength, *l*	Job 9:19	2009
L, mine eye hath seen all this,	Job 13:1	2005
L, their good is not in their	Job 21:16	2009
L, these are parts of his ways	Job 26:14	2005
L, all these things worketh God	Job 33:29	2005
L now, his strength is in his	Job 40:16	2009
For, *l*, the wicked bend their bow	Ps 11:2	2009
Yet he passed away, and, *l*	Ps 37:36	2009
Then said I, *L*, I come	Ps 40:7	2009
l, I have not refrained my lips,	Ps 40:9	2009
For, *l*, the kings were assembled,	Ps 48:4	2009
L, this is the man that made not	Ps 52:7	2009
L, then would I wander far off,	Ps 55:7	2009
For, *l*, they lie in wait for my	Ps 59:3	2009
l, he doth send out his voice, and	Ps 68:33	2005
For, *l*, they that are far from	Ps 73:27	2005
For, *l*, thine enemies make a	Ps 83:2	2009
l, thine enemies, O LORD, for, *l*	Ps 92:9	2009
L, children are an heritage of	Ps 127:3	2009
L, we heard of it at Ephratah	Ps 132:6	2009
not a word in my tongue, but, *l*	Ps 139:4	2005
And, *l*, it was all grown over with	Prov 24:31	2009
with mine own heart, saying, *L*	Eccl 1:16	2009
L, this only have I found, that	Eccl 7:29	7200
For, *l*, the winter is past, the	Song 2:11	2009
laid it upon my mouth, and said, *L*	Is 6:7	2009
it shall be said in that day, *L*	Is 25:9	2009
L, thou trustest in the staff of	Is 36:6	2009
and, *l*, these from the north and	Is 49:12	2009
l, they all shall wax old as a	Is 50:9	2005
For, *l*, I will call all the	Jer 1:15	2009
I beheld the earth, and, *l*	Jer 4:23	2009
I beheld the mountains, and, *l*	Jer 4:24	2009
I beheld, and, *l*, there was no man	Jer 4:25	2009
I beheld, and, *l*, the fruitful	Jer 4:26	2009
L, I will bring a nation upon you	Jer 5:15	2009
L, certainly in vain made he it	Jer 8:8	2009
l, they have rejected the word of	Jer 8:9	2009
For, *l*, I begin to bring evil on	Jer 25:29	2009
For, *l*, the days come, saith the	Jer 30:3	2009
for, *l*, I will save thee from	Jer 30:10	2009
and, *l*, all the princes sat there,	Jer 36:12	2009
For, *l*, I will make thee small	Jer 49:15	2009
For, *l*, I will raise and cause to	Jer 50:9	2009
and, *l*, a roll of a book was	Eze 2:9	2009
Then he said unto me, *L*, I have	Eze 4:15	7200
l a likeness as the appearance of	Eze 8:2	2009
and, *l*, they put the branch to	Eze 8:17	2009
and one built up a wall, and, *l*	Eze 13:10	2009
L, when the wall is fallen, shall	Eze 13:12	2009
by breaking the covenant, when, *l*	Eze 17:18	2009
Now, *l*, if he beget a son, that	Eze 18:14	2009
is not good among his people, *l*	Eze 18:18	2009
and, *l*, thus have they done in the	Eze 23:39	2009
and, *l*, they came	Eze 23:40	2009
for, *l*, it cometh	Eze 30:9	2009
and, *l*, it shall not be bound up	Eze 30:21	2009
And, *l*, thou art unto them as a	Eze 33:32	2009
And when this cometh to pass, (*l*	Eze 33:33	2009
and, *l*, they were very dry	Eze 37:2	2009
And when I beheld, *l*, the sinews	Eze 37:8	2009
me into the outward court, and, *l*	Eze 40:17	2009
and, *l*, before the temple were an	Eze 42:8	2009
He answered and said, *L*, I see	Dan 3:25	1888
l another, like a leopard, which	Dan 7:6	718
but, *l*, Michael, one of the chief	Dan 10:13	2009
and when I am gone forth, *l*	Dan 10:20	2009
For, *l*, they are gone because of	Hos 9:6	2009
sworn by his holiness, that, *l*	Amos 4:2	2009
For, *l*, he that formeth the	Amos 4:13	2009

L

and, *l*, it was the latter growth	Amos 7:1	2009
For, *l*, I will command, and I will	Amos 9:9	2009
For, *l*, I raise up the Chaldeans,	Hab 1:6	2009
Ye looked for much, and, *l*	Hag 1:9	2009
for, *l*, I come, and I will dwell	Zec 2:10	
but, *l*, I will deliver the men	Zec 11:6	
For, *l*, I will raise up a	Zec 11:16	
and, *l*, the star, which they saw	Mt 2:9	2400
and, *l*, the heavens were opened	Mt 3:16	2400
l a voice from heaven, saying,	Mt 3:17	2400
if any man shall say unto you, *L*	Mt 24:23	2400
l, there thou hast that is thine	Mt 25:25	2395
And while he yet spake, *l*, Judas,	Mt 26:47	2400
l, I have told you	Mt 28:7	2400
and, *l*, I am with you alway, even	Mt 28:20	2400
Peter began to say unto him, *L*	Mk 10:28	2400
if any man shall say to you, *L*	Mk 13:21	2400
or, *l*, he is there	Mk 13:21	2400
l, he that betrayeth me is at	Mk 14:42	2400
For, *l*, as soon as the voice of	Lk 1:44	2400
And, *l*, the angel of the Lord came	Lk 2:9	2400
And, *l*, a spirit taketh him, and he	Lk 9:39	2400
Abraham, whom Satan hath bound, *l*	Lk 13:16	2400
answering said to his father, *L*	Lk 15:29	2400
Neither shall they say, *L* here	Lk 17:21	2400
or, *l* there	Lk 17:21	2400
Then Peter said, *L*, we have left	Lk 18:28	2400
and, *l*, nothing worthy of death is	Lk 23:15	2400
But, *l*, he speaketh boldly, and	Jn 7:26	2396
His disciples said unto him, *L*	Jn 16:29	2396
unworthy of everlasting life, *l*	Acts 13:46	2400
and, *l*, God hath given thee all	Acts 27:24	2400
Then said I, *L*, I come (in the	Heb 10:7	2400
Then said he, *L*, I come to do thy	Heb 10:9	2400
And I beheld, and, *l*, in the midst	Rev 5:6	2400
And I beheld, and *l* a black horse	Rev 6:5	2400
had opened the sixth seal, and, *l*	Rev 6:12	2400
After this I beheld, and, *l*	Rev 7:9	2400
And I looked, and, *l*, a Lamb stood	Rev 14:1	2400

LOADEN
your carriages were heavy *l*	Is 46:1	6006

LOADETH
who daily *l* us with benefits,	Ps 68:19	6006

LOAF
one *l* of bread, and one cake of	Ex 29:23	3603
woman, to every one a *l* of bread	1Chr 16:3	3603
ship with them more than one *l*	Mk 8:14	740

LO-AMMI (lo-am'-mi) Symbolic name meaning "Not My People."
Then said God, Call his name *L*	Hos 1:9	3818

LOAN
the *l* which is lent to the LORD	1Sa 2:20	7596

LOATHE
I *l* it	Job 7:16	3988

LOATHETH
our soul *l* this light bread	Num 21:5	6973
The full soul *l* an honeycomb	Prov 27:7	947

LOATHSOME
nostrils, and it be *l* unto you	Num 11:20	2214
my skin is broken, and become *l*	Job 7:5	3988
loins are filled with a *l* disease	Ps 38:7	7033
but a wicked man is *l*, and cometh	Prov 13:5	887

LOAVES
two wave *l* of two tenth deals	Lev 23:17	3899
l of bread unto the people that	Judg 8:5	3603
another carrying three *l* of bread	1Sa 10:3	3603
thee, and give thee two *l* of bread	1Sa 10:4	
this parched corn, and these ten *l*	1Sa 17:17	3899
give me five *l* of bread in mine	1Sa 21:3	
made haste, and took two hundred *l*	1Sa 25:18	3899
upon them two hundred *l* of bread	2Sa 16:1	
And take with thee ten *l*, and	1Kin 14:3	3899
twenty *l* of barley, and full ears	2Kin 4:42	3899
unto him, We have here but five *l*	Mt 14:17	740
on the grass, and took the five *l*	Mt 14:19	740
gave the *l* to his disciples, and	Mt 14:19	740
unto them, How many *l* have ye	Mt 15:34	740
And he took the seven *l* and the	Mt 15:36	740
the five *l* of the five thousand	Mt 16:9	740
Neither the seven *l* of the four	Mt 16:10	740
unto them, How many *l* have ye	Mk 6:38	740
And when he had taken the five *l*	Mk 6:41	740
and blessed, and brake the *l*	Mk 6:41	740
they that did eat of the *l* were	Mk 6:44	740
not the miracle of the *l*	Mk 6:52	740
he asked them, How many *l* have ye	Mk 8:5	740

and he took the seven *l*, and gave	Mk 8:6	740
the five *l* among five thousand	Mk 8:19	740
said, We have no more but five *l*	Lk 9:13	740
Then he took the five *l* and the	Lk 9:16	740
unto him, Friend, lend me three *l*	Lk 11:5	740
here, which hath five barley *l*	Jn 6:9	740
And Jesus took the *l*	Jn 6:11	740
fragments of the five barley *l*	Jn 6:13	740
but because ye did eat of the *l*	Jn 6:26	740

LOCK
myrrh, upon the handles of the *l*	Song 5:5	4514
and took me by a *l* of mine head	Eze 8:3	6734

LOCKED
the parlour upon him, and *l* them	Judg 3:23	5274
the doors of the parlour were *l*	Judg 3:24	5274

LOCKS
shall let the *l* of the hair of	Num 6:5	6545
seven *l* of my head with the web	Judg 16:13	4253
shave off the seven *l* of his head	Judg 16:19	4253
the *l* thereof, and the bars	Neh 3:3	4514
the *l* thereof, and the bars	Neh 3:6	4514
the *l* thereof, and the bars	Neh 3:13	4514
the *l* thereof, and the bars	Neh 3:14	4514
the *l* thereof, and the bars	Neh 3:15	4514
hast doves' eyes within thy *l*	Song 4:1	6777
of a pomegranate within thy *l*	Song 4:3	6777
my *l* with the drops of the night	Song 5:2	6977
his *l* are bushy, and black as a	Song 5:11	6977
are thy temples within thy *l*	Song 6:7	6777
uncover thy *l*, make bare the leg,	Is 47:2	6777
nor suffer their *l* to grow long	Eze 44:20	6545

LOCUST
there remained not one *l* in all	Ex 10:19	697
the *l* after his kind, and the bald	Lev 11:22	697
the bald *l* after his kind, and the	Lev 11:22	5556
for the *l* shall consume it	Deut 28:38	697
of thy land shall the *l* consume	Deut 28:42	6767
pestilence, blasting, mildew, *l*	1Kin 8:37	697
and their labour unto the *l*	Ps 78:46	697
I am tossed up and down as the *l*	Ps 109:23	697
hath left hath the *l* eaten	Joel 1:4	697
that which the *l* hath left hath	Joel 1:4	697
the years that the *l* hath eaten	Joel 2:25	697

LOCUSTS
will I bring the *l* into thy coast	Ex 10:4	697
over the land of Egypt for the *l*	Ex 10:12	697
the east wind brought the *l*	Ex 10:13	697
the *l* went up over all the land	Ex 10:14	697
them there were no such *l* as they	Ex 10:14	697
west wind, which took away the *l*	Ex 10:19	697
there be blasting, or mildew, *l*	2Chr 6:28	697
command the *l* to devour the land	2Chr 7:13	2284
the *l* came, and caterpillers, and	Ps 105:34	697
The *l* have no king, yet go they	Prov 30:27	697
fro of *l* shall he run upon them	Is 33:4	1357
make thyself many as the *l*	Nah 3:15	697
Thy crowned are as the *l*, and thy	Nah 3:17	697
and his meat was *l* and wild honey	Mt 3:4	200
and he did eat *l* and wild honey	Mk 1:6	200
out of the smoke *l* upon the earth	Rev 9:3	200
the shapes of the *l* were like	Rev 9:7	200

LOD A city in Benjamin.
and Shamed, who built Ono, and *L*	1Chr 8:12	3850
The children of *L*, Hadid, and Ono,	Ezr 2:33	3850
The children of *L*, Hadid, and Ono,	Neh 7:37	3850
L, and Ono, the valley of	Neh 11:35	3850

LO-DEBAR (lo-de'-bar) A city in Manasseh.
Machir, the son of Ammiel, in *L*	2Sa 9:4	3810
Machir, the son of Ammiel, from *L*	2Sa 9:5	3810
and Machir the son of Ammiel of *L*	2Sa 17:27	3810

LODGE
thy father's house for us to *l* in	Gen 24:23	3885
provender enough, and room to *l* in	Gen 24:25	3885
L here this night, and I will	Num 22:8	3885
where ye shall *l* this night	Josh 4:3	3885
l here, that thine heart may be	Judg 19:9	3885
city of the Jebusites, and *l* in it	Judg 19:11	3885
of these places to *l* all night	Judg 19:13	3885
to go in and to *l* in Gibeah	Judg 19:15	3885
only I not in the street	Judg 19:20	3885
Benjamin, I and my concubine, to *l*	Judg 20:4	3885
and where thou lodgest, I will *l*	Ruth 1:16	3885
will not *l* with the people	2Sa 17:8	3885
L not this night in the plains of	2Sa 17:16	3885
his servant *l* within Jerusalem	Neh 4:22	3885
them, Why *l* ye about the wall	Neh 13:21	3885
the naked to *l* without clothing	Job 24:7	3885

stranger did not *l* in the street .... Job 31:32   3885
let us *l* in the villages .... Song 7:11   3885
as a *l* in a garden of cucumbers, ... Is 1:8   4412
the forest in Arabia shall ye *l* .... Is 21:13   3885
l in the monuments, which eat .... Is 65:4   3885
thy vain thoughts *l* within thee .... Jer 4:14   3885
the bittern shall *l* in the upper .... Zeph 2:14   3885
l in the branches thereof .... Mt 13:32   2681
air may l under the shadow of it .... Mk 4:32   2681
and country round about, and *l* .... Lk 9:12   2647
disciple, with whom we should *l* .... Acts 21:16   3579

LODGED
he *l* there that same night .... Gen 32:13   3885
himself *l* that night in the .... Gen 32:21   3885
house, named Rahab, and *l* there .... Josh 2:1   7901
l there before they passed over .... Josh 3:1   3885
them unto the place where they *l* .... Josh 4:8   4411
into the camp, and *l* in the camp .... Josh 6:11   3885
but Joshua *l* that night among the .... Josh 8:9   3885
the house of Micah, they *l* there .... Judg 18:2   3885
they did eat and drink, and *l* there .... Judg 19:4   3885
therefore he *l* there again .... Judg 19:7   3885
thither into a cave, and *l* there 1Kin 19:9   3885
they *l* round about the house of 1Chr 9:27   3885
sellers of all kind of ware *l* .... Neh 13:20   3885
righteousness *l* in it .... Is 1:21   3885
and he *l* there .... Mt 21:17   835
the fowls of the air l in the .... Lk 13:19   2681
was surnamed Peter, were *l* there .... Acts 10:18   3579
Then called he them in, and *l* them .... Acts 10:23   3579
he is *l* in the house of one Simon .... Acts 10:32   3579
l us three days courteously .... Acts 28:7   3579
children, if she have *l* strangers 1Ti 5:10   3580

LODGEST
and where thou *l*, I will lodge .... Ruth 1:16   3885

LODGETH
He *l* with one Simon a tanner, ... Acts 10:6   3579

LODGING
you, and leave them in the *l* place .... Josh 4:3   4411
took them into his house to *l* .... Judg 19:15   3885
have taken up their *l* at Geba .... Is 10:29   4411
a *l* place of wayfaring men .... Jer 9:2   4411
there came many to him into his *l* .... Acts 28:23   3578
But withal prepare me also a *l* .... Philem 22   3578

LODGINGS
enter into the *l* of his borders 2Kin 19:23   4411

LOFT
bosom, and carried him up into a *l* 1Kin 17:19   5944
and fell down from the third *l* .... Acts 20:9

LOFTILY
they speak *l* .... Ps 73:8   4791

LOFTINESS
the *l* of man shall be bowed down, ... Is 2:17   1365
(he is exceeding proud) his *l* .... Jer 48:29   1363

LOFTY
is not haughty, nor mine eyes *l* .... Ps 131:1   7311
O how *l* are their eyes .... Prov 30:13   7311
The *l* looks of man shall be .... Is 2:11   1365
upon every one that is proud and *l* .... Is 2:12   7311
the eyes of the *l* shall be .... Is 5:15   1364
the *l* city, he layeth it low .... Is 26:5   7682
Upon a *l* and high mountain hast .... Is 57:7   1364
l One that inhabiteth eternity, ... Is 57:15   5375

LOG
mingled with oil, and one *l* of oil .... Lev 14:10   3849
the *l* of oil, and wave them for a .... Lev 14:12   3849
shall take some of the *l* of oil .... Lev 14:15   3849
a meat offering, and a *l* of oil .... Lev 14:21   3849
the *l* of oil, and the priest shall .... Lev 14:24   3849

LOINS
and kings shall come out of thy *l* .... Gen 35:11   2504
and put sackcloth upon his *l* .... Gen 37:34   4975
Egypt, which came out of his *l* .... Gen 46:26   3409
the *l* of Jacob were seventy souls .... Ex 1:5   3409
with your *l* girded, your shoes on .... Ex 12:11   4975
from the *l* even unto the thighs .... Ex 28:42   4975
smite through the *l* of them that .... Deut 33:11   4975
upon his *l* in the sheath thereof 2Sa 20:8   4975
his girdle that was about his *l* 1Kin 2:5   4975
shall come forth out of thy *l* 1Kin 8:19   2504
be thicker than my father's *l* 1Kin 12:10   4975
and he girded up his *l*, and ran 1Kin 18:46   4975
pray thee, put sackcloth on our *l* 1Kin 20:31   4975
they girded sackcloth on their *l* 1Kin 20:32   4975
a girdle of leather about his *l* 2Kin 1:8   4975

he said to Gehazi, Gird up thy *l* 2Kin 4:29   4975
and said unto him, Gird up thy *l* 2Kin 9:1   4975
shall come forth out of thy *l* 2Chr 6:9   2504
be thicker than my father's *l* 2Chr 10:10   4975
and girdeth their *l* with a girdle .... Job 12:18   4975
If his *l* have not blessed me, and .... Job 31:20   2504
Gird up now thy *l* like a man .... Job 38:3   2504
Gird up thy *l* now like a man .... Job 40:7   2504
Lo now, his strength is in his *l* .... Job 40:16   4975
For my *l* are filled with a .... Ps 38:7   3689
thou laidst affliction upon our *l* .... Ps 66:11   4975
make their *l* continually to shake .... Ps 69:23   4975
She girdeth her *l* with strength .... Prov 31:17   4975
the girdle of their *l* be loosed .... Is 5:27   2504
shall be the girdle of his *l* .... Is 11:5   4975
the sackcloth from off thy *l* .... Is 20:2   4975
are my *l* filled with pain .... Is 21:3   4975
and gird sackcloth upon your *l* .... Is 32:11   2504
and I will loose the *l* of kings .... Is 45:1   4975
Thou therefore gird up thy *l* .... Jer 1:17   4975
girdle, and put it upon thy *l* .... Jer 13:1   4975
of the Lord, and put it on my *l* .... Jer 13:2   4975
hast got, which is upon thy *l* .... Jer 13:4   4975
girdle cleaveth to the *l* of a man .... Jer 13:11   4975
every man with his hands on his *l* .... Jer 30:6   2504
cuttings, and upon the *l* sackcloth .... Jer 48:37   4975
appearance of his *l* even upward .... Eze 1:27   4975
appearance of his *l* even downward ...... Eze 1:27   4975
appearance of his *l* even downward ...... Eze 8:2   4975
from his *l* even upward, as the .... Eze 8:2   4975
man, with the breaking of thy *l* .... Eze 21:6   4975
Girded with girdles upon their *l* .... Eze 23:15   4975
all their *l* to be at a stand .... Eze 29:7   4975
have linen breeches upon their *l* .... Eze 44:18   4975
the waters were to the *l* .... Eze 47:4   4975
the joints of his *l* were loosed .... Dan 5:6   2788
whose *l* were girded with fine .... Dan 10:5   4975
bring up sackcloth upon all *l* .... Amos 8:10   4975
watch the way, make thy *l* strong .... Nah 2:1   4975
and much pain is in all *l* .... Nah 2:10   4975
and a leathern girdle about his *l* .... Mt 3:4   3751
a girdle of a skin about his *l* .... Mk 1:6   3751
Let your l be girded about, and .... Lk 12:35   3751
him, that of the fruit of his *l* .... Acts 2:30   3751
having your *l* girt about with .... Eph 6:14   3751
they come out of the *l* of Abraham .... Heb 7:5   3751
he was yet in the *l* of his father .... Heb 7:10   3751
gird up the *l* of your mind 1Pet 1:13   3751

LOIS *(lo'-is) Grandmother of Timothy.*
dwelt first in thy grandmother *L* 2Ti 1:5   3090

LONG
when he had been there a *l* time .... Gen 26:8   748
me all my life *l* unto this day .... Gen 48:15   5750
How *l* wilt thou refuse to humble .... Ex 10:3   4970
How *l* shall this man be a snare .... Ex 10:7   5704
How *l* refuse ye to keep my .... Ex 16:28   5704
when the trumpet soundeth *l* .... Ex 19:13   4900
voice of the trumpet sounded *l* .... Ex 19:19
that thy days may be *l* upon the .... Ex 20:12   748
of shittim wood, five cubits *l* .... Ex 27:1   753
an hundred cubits *l* for one side .... Ex 27:9   753
hangings of an hundred cubits *l* .... Ex 27:11   753
as *l* as she is put apart for her .... Lev 18:19
as *l* as it lieth desolate, and ye .... Lev 26:34   3117
As *l* as it lieth desolate it .... Lev 26:35   3117
as *l* as the cloud abode upon the .... Num 9:18   3117
when the cloud tarried *l* upon the .... Num 9:19
How *l* will this people provoke me .... Num 14:11   5704
how *l* will it be ere they believe .... Num 14:11   5704
How *l* shall I bear with this evil .... Num 14:27   5704
we have dwelt in Egypt a *l* time .... Num 20:15   7227
Ye have dwelt *l* enough in this .... Deut 1:6   7227
compassed this mountain *l* enough .... Deut 2:3   7227
shall have remained *l* in the land .... Deut 4:25
l as thou livest upon the earth .... Deut 12:19   3117
And if the way be too *l* for thee .... Deut 14:24   7235
him, because the way is *l* .... Deut 19:6   7235
shalt besiege a city a *l* time .... Deut 20:19   7227
longing for them all the day *l* .... Deut 28:32
of *l* continuance, and sore .... Deut 28:59   7227
sicknesses, and of *l* continuance .... Deut 28:59   7227
as *l* as ye live in the land .... Deut 31:13   3117
shall cover him all the day *l* .... Deut 33:12
that when they make a *l* blast .... Josh 6:5   4900
by reason of the very *l* journey .... Josh 9:13   7230
Joshua made war a *l* time with all .... Josh 11:18   7227
How *l* are ye slack to go to .... Josh 18:3   5704
it came to pass a *l* time after .... Josh 23:1   7227
in the wilderness a *l* season .... Josh 24:7   7227
Why is his chariot so *l* in coming .... Judg 5:28   954

L

How *l* wilt thou be drunken	1Sa 1:14	3117
as *l* as he liveth he shall be	1Sa 1:28	3117
that the time was *l*	1Sa 7:2	7235
How *l* wilt thou mourn for Saul,	1Sa 16:1	5704
For as *l* as the son of Jesse	1Sa 20:31	3117
as *l* as we were conversant with	1Sa 25:15	3117
thou found in thy servant so *l* as	1Sa 29:8	3117
how *l* shall it be then, ere thou	2Sa 2:26	5704
Now there was *l* war between the	2Sa 3:1	752
had a *l* time mourned for the dead	2Sa 14:2	752
How *l* have I to live, that I	2Sa 19:34	3117
hast not asked for thyself *l* life	1Kin 3:11	7221
before it, was forty cubits *l*	1Kin 6:17	
How *l* halt ye between two	1Kin 18:21	5704
so *l* as the whoredoms of thy	2Kin 9:22	5704
Hast thou not heard *l* ago how I	2Kin 19:25	7350
neither yet hast asked *l* life	2Chr 1:11	7227
cherubims were twenty cubits *l*	2Chr 3:11	753
brasen scaffold, of five cubits *l*	2Chr 6:13	753
so *l* as they live in the land	2Chr 6:31	3117
Now for a *l* season Israel hath	2Chr 15:3	7227
as *l* as he sought the LORD, God	2Chr 26:5	3117
a *l* time in such sort as it was	2Chr 30:5	7230
for as *l* as she lay desolate she	2Chr 36:21	3117
For how *l* shall thy journey be	Neh 2:6	5704
so *l* as I see Mordecai the Jew	Est 5:13	6256
Which *l* for death, but it cometh	Job 3:21	2442
grant me the thing that I *l* for	Job 6:8	8615
How *l* wilt thou not depart from	Job 7:19	4101
How *l* wilt thou speak these	Job 8:2	5704
how *l* shall the words of thy	Job 8:2	
How *l* will it be ere ye make an	Job 18:2	5704
How *l* will ye vex my soul, and	Job 19:2	5704
not reproach me so *l* as I live	Job 27:6	3117
how *l* will ye turn my glory into	Ps 4:2	5704
how *l* will ye love vanity, and	Ps 4:2	
but thou, O LORD, how *l*	Ps 6:3	5704
How *l* wilt thou forget me, O LORD	Ps 13:1	5704
how *l* wilt thou hide thy face	Ps 13:1	5704
How *l* shall I take counsel in my	Ps 13:2	5704
how *l* shall mine enemy be exalted	Ps 13:2	5704
through my roaring all the day *l*	Ps 32:3	
LORD, how *l* wilt thou look on	Ps 35:17	5704
and of thy praise all the day *l*	Ps 35:28	
I go mourning all the day *l*	Ps 38:6	
and imagine deceits all the day *l*	Ps 38:12	
In God we boast all the day *l*	Ps 44:8	
sake are we killed all the day *l*	Ps 44:22	
How *l* will ye imagine mischief	Ps 62:3	5704
thy righteousness all the day *l*	Ps 71:24	
shall fear thee as *l* as the sun	Ps 72:5	5973
peace so *l* as the moon endureth	Ps 72:7	5704
be continued as *l* as the sun	Ps 72:17	6440
For all the day *l* have I been	Ps 73:14	
among us any that knoweth how *l*	Ps 74:9	5704
how *l* shall the adversary	Ps 74:10	5704
How *l*, LORD	Ps 79:5	5704
how *l* wilt thou be angry against	Ps 80:4	5704
How *l* will ye judge unjustly, and	Ps 82:2	5704
How *l*, LORD?	Ps 89:46	5704
Return, O LORD, how *l*	Ps 90:13	5704
With *l* life will I satisfy him,	Ps 91:16	753
how *l* shall the wicked	Ps 94:3	5704
how *l* shall the wicked triumph	Ps 94:3	5704
How *l* shall they utter and speak	Ps 94:4	5704
Forty years *l* was I grieved with	Ps 95:10	
sing unto the LORD as *l* as I live	Ps 104:33	
I call upon him as *l* as I live	Ps 116:2	3117
My soul hath *l* dwelt with him	Ps 120:6	7227
they made *l* their furrows	Ps 129:3	748
as those that have been *l* dead	Ps 143:3	5769
How *l*, ye simple ones, will ye	Prov 1:22	5704
l life, and peace, shall they add	Prov 3:2	753
How *l* wilt thou sleep, O sluggard	Prov 6:9	5704
at home, he is gone a *l* journey	Prov 7:19	7350
coveteth greedily all the day *l*	Prov 21:26	
fear of the LORD all the day *l*	Prov 23:17	
They that tarry *l* at the wine	Prov 23:30	
By *l* forbearing is a prince	Prov 25:15	753
because man goeth to his *l* home	Eccl 12:5	5769
Then said I, Lord, how *l*	Is 6:11	5704
unto him that fashioned it *l* ago	Is 22:11	7350
Hast thou not heard *l* ago	Is 37:26	5704
I have *l* time holden my peace	Is 42:14	5769
mine elect shall *l* enjoy the work	Is 65:22	
How *l* shall thy vain thoughts	Jer 4:14	5704
How *l* shall I see the standard,	Jer 4:21	5704
How *l* shall the land mourn, and	Jer 12:4	5704
How *l* shall this be in the heart	Jer 23:26	5704
saying, This captivity is *l*	Jer 29:28	752
How *l* wilt thou go about, O thou	Jer 31:22	5704

how *l* wilt thou cut thyself	Jer 47:5	5704
how *l* will it be ere thou be	Jer 47:6	5704
fruit, and children of a span *l*	Lam 2:20	
for ever, and forsake us so *l* time	Lam 5:20	753
his branches became *l* because of	Eze 31:5	748
reed of six cubits *l* by the cubit	Eze 40:5	
little chamber was one reed *l*	Eze 40:7	753
it was fifty cubits *l*, and five and	Eze 40:29	753
were five and twenty cubits *l*	Eze 40:30	753
it was fifty cubits *l*, and five and	Eze 40:33	753
offering, of a cubit and an half *l*	Eze 40:42	753
the court, an hundred cubits *l*	Eze 40:47	753
the house, an hundred cubits *l*	Eze 41:13	753
thereof, an hundred cubits *l*	Eze 41:13	753
as *l* as they, and as broad as they	Eze 42:11	753
round about, five hundred reeds *l*	Eze 42:20	753
altar shall be twelve cubits *l*	Eze 43:16	753
settle shall be fourteen cubits *l*	Eze 43:17	753
nor suffer their locks to grow *l*	Eze 44:20	
and five and twenty thousand *l*	Eze 45:6	753
courts joined of forty cubits *l*	Eze 46:22	753
How *l* shall be the vision	Dan 8:13	5704
but the time appointed was *l*	Dan 10:1	1419
How *l* shall it be to the end of	Dan 12:6	5704
how *l* will it be ere they attain	Hos 8:5	5704
for he should not stay *l* in the	Hos 13:13	
how *l* shall I cry, and thou wilt	Hab 1:2	5704
which is not his! how *l*?	Hab 2:6	5704
how *l* wilt thou not have mercy on	Zec 1:12	5704
as *l* as the bridegroom is with	Mt 9:15	*1909*
have repented *l* ago in sackcloth	Mt 11:21	*3819*
how *l* shall I be with you	Mt 17:17	*2193*
how *l* shall I suffer you	Mt 17:17	*2193*
and for a pretence make *l* prayer	Mt 23:14	*3117*
After a *l* time the lord of those	Mt 25:19	*4183*
as *l* as they have the bridegroom	Mk 2:19	*5550*
how *l* shall I be with you	Mk 9:19	*2193*
how *l* shall I suffer you	Mk 9:19	*2193*
How *l* is it ago since this came	Mk 9:21	*4214*
which love to go in *l* clothing	Mk 12:38	
and for a pretence make *l* prayers	Mk 12:40	*3117*
clothed in a *l* white garment	Mk 16:5	
he tarried so *l* in the temple	Lk 1:21	
man, which had devils *l* time	Lk 8:27	*2425*
how *l* shall I be with you, and	Lk 9:41	*2193*
him, though he bear *l* with them	Lk 18:7	*3114*
into a far country for a *l* time	Lk 20:9	*2425*
which desire to walk in *l* robes	Lk 20:46	
and for a shew make *l* prayers	Lk 20:47	*3117*
desirous to see him of a *l* season	Lk 23:8	*2425*
been now a *l* time in that case	Jn 5:6	*4183*
As *l* as I am in the world, I am	Jn 9:5	*3752*
How *l* dost thou make us to doubt	Jn 10:24	*2193*
Have I been so *l* time with you	Jn 14:9	*5118*
because that of *l* time he had	Acts 8:11	*2425*
L time therefore abode they	Acts 14:3	*2425*
there they abode *l* time with the	Acts 14:28	*3756,3641*
and as Paul was *l* preaching	Acts 20:9	*1909,4119*
and eaten, and talked a *l* while	Acts 20:11	*2425*
But not *l* after there arose	Acts 27:14	*4183*
But after *l* abstinence Paul stood	Acts 27:21	*4183*
For I *l* to see you, that I may	Rom 1:11	*1971*
over a man as *l* as he liveth	Rom 7:1	*5550*
to her husband so *l* as he liveth	Rom 7:2	
sake we are killed all the day *l*	Rom 8:36	
All day *l* I have stretched forth	Rom 10:21	
law as *l* as her husband liveth	1Cor 7:39	*5550*
you, that, if a man have *l* hair	1Cor 11:14	*2863*
But if a woman have *l* hair	1Cor 11:15	*2863*
Charity suffereth *l*, and is kind	1Cor 13:4	*3114*
which *l* after you for the	2Cor 9:14	*1971*
as *l* as he is a child, differeth	Gal 4:1	*5550*
thou mayest live *l* on the earth	Eph 6:3	*2118*
how greatly I *l* after you all in	Phil 1:8	*1971*
But if I tarry *l*, that thou	1Ti 3:15	
David, To day, after so *l* a time	Heb 4:7	*5118*
hath *l* patience for it, until he	Jas 5:7	*3114*
as *l* as ye do well, and are not	1Pet 3:6	
as *l* as I am in this tabernacle,	2Pet 1:13	
now of a *l* time lingereth not	2Pet 2:3	
with a loud voice, saying, How *l*	Rev 6:10	*2193*

LONGED

the soul of king David *l* to go	2Sa 13:39	3615
And David *l*, and said, Oh that one	2Sa 23:15	183
And David *l*, and said, Oh that one	1Chr 11:17	183
I have *l* after thy precepts	Ps 119:40	8373
for I *l* for thy commandments	Ps 119:131	2968
I have *l* for thy salvation, O	Ps 119:174	8373
For he *l* after you all, and was	Phil 2:26	1971
l for, my joy and crown, so stand	Phil 4:1	1973

LONGEDST

because thou sore *l* after thy	Gen 31:30	3700

LONGER

And when she could not *l* hide him	Ex 2:3	5750
let you go, and ye shall stay no *l*	Ex 9:28	3254
any *l* stand before their enemies	Judg 2:14	5750
but he tarried *l* than the set	2Sa 20:5	
should I wait for the LORD any *l*	2Kin 6:33	5750
thereof is *l* than the earth	Job 11:9	752
So that the LORD could no *l* bear	Jer 44:22	5750
for thou mayest be no *l* steward	Lk 16:2	2089
him to tarry *l* time with them	Acts 18:20	4119
that he ought not to live any *l*	Acts 25:24	3370
dead to sin, live any *l* therein	Rom 6:2	2089
we are no *l* under a schoolmaster	Gal 3:25	2089
when we could no *l* forbear	1Th 3:1	3370
cause, when I could no *l* forbear	1Th 3:5	3370
Drink no *l* water, but use a	1Ti 5:23	3370
That he no *l* should live the rest	1Pet 4:2	3370
that there should be time no *l*	Rev 10:6	2089

LONGETH

son Shechem *l* for your daughter	Gen 34:8	2836
because thy soul *l* to eat flesh	Deut 12:20	183
my flesh *l* for thee in a dry and	Ps 63:1	3642
My soul *l*, yea, even fainteth for	Ps 84:2	3700

LONGING

fail with *l* for them all the day	Deut 28:32	
For he satisfieth the *l* soul	Ps 107:9	8264
My soul breaketh for the *l* that	Ps 119:20	8375

LONGSUFFERING

God, merciful and gracious, *l*	Ex 34:6	750,639
The LORD is *l*, and of great mercy,	Num 14:18	750,639
of compassion, and gracious, *l*	Ps 86:15	750,639
take me not away in thy *l*	Jer 15:15	750,639
his goodness and forbearance and *l*	Rom 2:4	3115
endured with much *l* the vessels	Rom 9:22	3115
By pureness, by knowledge, by *l*	2Cor 6:6	3115
the Spirit is love, joy, peace, *l*	Gal 5:22	3115
all lowliness and meekness, with *l*	Eph 4:2	3115
all patience and *l* with joyfulness	Col 1:11	3115
humbleness of mind, meekness, *l*	Col 3:12	3115
Christ might shew forth all *l*	1Ti 1:16	3115
manner of life, purpose, faith, *l*	2Ti 3:10	3115
rebuke, exhort with all *l*	2Ti 4:2	3115
when once the *l* of God waited in	1Pet 3:20	3115
but is *l* to us-ward, not willing	2Pet 3:9	3114
account that the *l* of our Lord is	2Pet 3:15	3115

LONGWINGED

A great eagle with great wings, *l*	Eze 17:3	750,83

LOOK

I will *l* upon it, that I may	Gen 9:16	7200
thou art a fair woman to *l* upon	Gen 12:11	4758
l from the place where thou art	Gen 13:14	7200
L now toward heaven, and tell the	Gen 15:5	5027
l not behind thee, neither stay	Gen 19:17	5027
damsel was very fair to *l* upon	Gen 24:16	4758
because she was fair to *l* upon	Gen 26:7	4758
Wherefore *l* ye so sadly to day	Gen 40:7	6440
let Pharaoh *l* out a man discreet	Gen 41:33	7200
Why do ye *l* one upon another	Gen 42:1	7200
for he was afraid to *l* upon God	Ex 3:6	5027
unto them, The LORD *l* upon you	Ex 5:21	7200
l to it	Ex 10:10	7200
faces shall *l* one to another	Ex 25:20	
l that thou make them after their	Ex 25:40	7200
Moses did *l* upon all the work, and	Ex 39:43	7200
the priest shall *l* on the plague	Lev 13:3	7200
and the priest shall *l* on him	Lev 13:3	7200
the priest shall *l* on him the	Lev 13:5	7200
the priest shall *l* on him again	Lev 13:6	7200
But if the priest *l* on it	Lev 13:21	7200
Then the priest shall *l* upon it	Lev 13:25	7200
But if the priest *l* on it	Lev 13:26	7200
the priest shall *l* upon him the	Lev 13:27	7200
if the priest *l* on the plague of	Lev 13:31	7200
the priest shall *l* on the plague	Lev 13:32	7200
the priest shall *l* on the scall	Lev 13:34	7200
Then the priest shall *l* on him	Lev 13:36	7200
Then the priest shall *l*	Lev 13:39	7200
Then the priest shall *l* upon it	Lev 13:43	7200
priest shall *l* upon the plague	Lev 13:50	7200
he shall *l* on the plague the	Lev 13:51	7200
And if the priest shall *l*, and,	Lev 13:53	7200
the priest shall *l* on the plague	Lev 13:55	7200
And if the priest *l*, and, behold,	Lev 13:56	7200
and the priest shall *l*, and, behold	Lev 14:3	7200
he shall *l* on the plague, and,	Lev 14:37	7200
again the seventh day, and shall *l*	Lev 14:39	7200

Then the priest shall come and *l*	Lev 14:44	7200
l upon it, and, behold, the plague	Lev 14:48	7200
a fringe, that ye may *l* upon it	Num 15:39	7200
l not unto the stubbornness of	Deut 9:27	6437
L down from thy holy habitation,	Deut 26:15	8259
people, and thine eyes shall *l*	Deut 28:32	7200
them, L on me, and do likewise	Judg 7:17	7200
if thou wilt indeed *l* on the	1Sa 1:11	7200
L not on his countenance, or on	1Sa 16:7	5027
countenance, and goodly to *l* to	1Sa 16:12	7210
l how thy brethren fare, and take	1Sa 17:18	6485
that thou shouldest *l* upon such a	2Sa 9:8	6437
was very beautiful to *l* upon	2Sa 11:2	4758
LORD will *l* on mine affliction	2Sa 16:12	7200
Go up now, *l* toward the sea	1Kin 18:43	7200
Judah, I would not *l* toward thee	2Kin 3:14	5027
l, when the messenger cometh,	2Kin 6:32	7200
l out there Jehu the son of	2Kin 9:2	7200
L even out the best and meetest of	2Kin 10:3	7200
l that there be here with you	2Kin 10:23	7200
let us *l* one another in the face	2Kin 14:8	7200
the God of our fathers *l* thereon	1Chr 12:17	7200
died, he said, The LORD *l* upon it	2Chr 24:22	7200
for she was fair to *l* on	Est 1:11	4758
let it *l* for light, but have none	Job 3:9	6960
therefore be content, *l* upon me	Job 6:28	6437
shall no man *l* for his goods	Job 20:21	2342
L unto the heavens, and see	Job 35:5	5027
L on every one that is proud, and	Job 40:12	7200
my prayer unto thee, and will *l* up	Ps 5:3	6822
they *l* and stare upon me	Ps 22:17	5027
L upon mine affliction and my pain	Ps 25:18	7200
LORD, how long wilt thou *l* on	Ps 35:17	7200
me, so that I am not able to *l* up	Ps 40:12	7200
l down from heaven, and behold, and	Ps 80:14	5027
l upon the face of thine anointed	Ps 84:9	5027
shall *l* down from heaven	Ps 85:11	8259
him that hath an high *l* and a	Ps 101:5	5869
L thou upon me, and be merciful	Ps 119:132	6437
as the eyes of servants *l* unto	Ps 123:2	
Let thine eyes *l* right on	Prov 4:25	5027
let thine eyelids *l* straight	Prov 4:25	
A proud *l*, a lying tongue, and	Prov 6:17	5869
An high *l*, and a proud heart, and	Prov 21:4	5869
L not thou upon the wine when it	Prov 23:31	7200
flocks, and *l* well to thy herds	Prov 27:23	7896
those that *l* out of the windows	Eccl 12:3	7200
L not upon me, because I am black	Song 1:6	7200
l from the top of Amana, from the	Song 4:8	7789
return, that we may *l* upon thee	Song 6:13	2372
if one *l* unto the land, behold	Is 5:30	5027
of Jacob, and I will *l* for him	Is 8:17	6960
king and their God, and *l* upward	Is 8:21	6437
they shall *l* unto the earth	Is 8:22	5027
thee shall narrowly *l* upon thee	Is 14:16	7688
day shall a man *l* to his Maker	Is 17:7	8159
he shall not *l* to the altars, the	Is 17:8	8159
Therefore said I, L away from me	Is 22:4	8159
thou didst *l* in that day to the	Is 22:8	5027
but they *l* not unto the Holy One	Is 31:1	8159
L upon Zion, the city of our	Is 33:20	2372
and *l*, ye blind, that ye may see	Is 42:18	5027
L unto me, and be ye saved, all	Is 45:22	6437
l unto the rock whence ye are	Is 51:1	5027
L unto Abraham your father, and	Is 51:2	5027
and *l* upon the earth beneath	Is 51:6	5027
they all *l* to their own way,	Is 56:11	6437
we *l* for judgment, but there is	Is 59:11	6960
L down from heaven, and behold	Is 63:15	5027
but to this man will I *l*, even to	Is 66:2	5027
l upon the carcases of the men	Is 66:24	7200
while ye *l* for light, he turn it	Jer 13:16	6960
l well to him, and do him no harm	Jer 39:12	7760
and I will *l* well unto thee	Jer 40:4	7760
and are fled apace, and *l* not back	Jer 46:5	6437
the fathers shall not *l* back to	Jer 47:3	6437
Till the LORD *l* down, and behold	Lam 3:50	8259
all of them princes to *l* to	Eze 23:15	4758
when they shall *l* after them	Eze 29:16	6437
stairs shall *l* toward the east	Eze 43:17	6437
whose *l* was more stout than his	Dan 7:20	2376
who *l* to other gods, and love	Hos 3:1	6437
yet I will *l* again toward thy	Jonah 2:4	5027
and let our eye *l* upon Zion	Mic 4:11	2372
Therefore I will *l* unto the LORD	Mic 7:7	6822
but none shall *l* back	Nah 2:8	6437
that all they that *l* upon thee	Nah 3:7	7200
evil, and canst not *l* on iniquity	Hab 1:13	5027
that thou mayest *l* on their	Hab 2:15	5027
they shall *l* upon me whom they	Zec 12:10	5027
come, or do we *l* for another	Mt 11:3	4328

L

upon his eyes, and made him *l* up	Mk 8:25	308
or *l* we for another	Lk 7:19	4328
or *l* we for another	Lk 7:20	4328
I beseech thee, *l* upon my son	Lk 9:38	1914
begin to come to pass, then *l* up	Lk 21:28	352
up your eyes, and *l* on the fields	Jn 4:35	2300
Search, and *l*	Jn 7:52	1492
They shall *l* on him whom they	Jn 19:37	3700
upon him with John, said, *L* on us	Acts 3:4	991
or why *l* ye so earnestly on us,	Acts 3:12	816
l ye out among you seven men of	Acts 6:3	1980
names, and of your law, *l* ye to it	Acts 18:15	3700
for I *l* for him with the brethren	1Cor 16:11	1551
l to the end of that which is	2Cor 3:13	816
While we *l* not at the things	2Cor 4:18	4648
Do ye *l* on things after the	2Cor 10:7	991
L not every man on his own things	Phil 2:4	4648
whence also we *l* for the Saviour	Phil 3:20	553
unto them that *l* for him shall he	Heb 9:28	553
the angels desire to *l* into	1Pet 1:12	3879
l for new heavens and a new earth,	2Pet 3:13	4328
seeing that ye *l* for such things,	2Pet 3:14	4328
L to yourselves, that we lose not	2Jn 8	991
sat was to *l* upon like a jasper	Rev 4:3	3706
the book, neither to *l* thereon	Rev 5:3	991
the book, neither to *l* thereon	Rev 5:4	991

LOOKED

God *l* upon the earth, and, behold,	Gen 6:12	7200
the covering of the ark, and *l*	Gen 8:13	7200
Have I also here *l* after him that	Gen 16:13	7200
And he lift up his eyes and *l*	Gen 18:2	7200
up from thence, and *l* toward Sodom	Gen 18:16	8259
But his wife *l* back from behind	Gen 19:17	5027
he *l* toward Sodom and Gomorrah,	Gen 19:28	8259
Abraham lifted up his eyes, and *l*	Gen 22:13	7200
the Philistines *l* out at a window	Gen 26:8	8259
And he *l*, and behold a well in the	Gen 29:2	7200
LORD hath *l* upon my affliction	Gen 29:32	7200
And Jacob lifted up his eyes, and *l*	Gen 33:1	7200
and they lifted up their eyes and *l*	Gen 37:25	7200
The keeper of the prison *l* not to	Gen 39:23	7200
l upon them, and, behold, they	Gen 40:6	7200
brethren, and *l* on their burdens	Ex 2:11	7200
he *l* this way and that way, and	Ex 2:12	6437
God *l* upon the children of Israel,	Ex 2:25	7200
and he *l*, and, behold, the bush	Ex 3:2	7200
and that he had *l* upon their	Ex 4:31	7200
in the morning watch the LORD *l*	Ex 14:24	8259
that they *l* toward the wilderness	Ex 16:10	6437
l after Moses, until he was gone	Ex 33:8	5027
Aaron *l* upon Miriam, and, behold,	Num 12:10	6437
that they *l* toward the tabernacle	Num 16:42	6437
and they *l*, and took every man his	Num 17:9	7200
when he *l* on Amalek, he took up	Num 24:20	7200
he *l* on the Kenites, and took up	Num 24:21	7200
And I *l*, and, behold, ye had sinned	Deut 9:16	7200
l on our affliction, and our	Deut 26:7	7200
that he lifted up his eyes and *l*	Josh 5:13	7200
when the men of Ai *l* behind them	Josh 8:20	6437
of Sisera *l* out at a window	Judg 5:28	8259
And the LORD *l* upon him, and said,	Judg 6:14	6437
and laid wait in the field, and *l*	Judg 9:43	7200
and Manoah and his wife *l* on	Judg 13:19	7200
And Manoah and his wife *l* on it	Judg 13:20	7200
the Benjamites *l* behind them	Judg 20:40	6437
because they had *l* into the ark	1Sa 6:19	7200
for I have *l* upon my people,	1Sa 9:16	7200
of Saul in Gibeah of Benjamin *l*	1Sa 14:16	7200
that he *l* on Eliab and said,	1Sa 16:6	7200
And when the Philistine *l* about	1Sa 17:42	5027
when Saul *l* behind him, David	1Sa 24:8	5027
when he *l* behind him, he saw me,	2Sa 1:7	6437
Then Abner *l* behind him, and said,	2Sa 2:20	6437
daughter *l* through a window	2Sa 6:16	8259
watch lifted up his eyes, and *l*	2Sa 13:34	7200
wall, and lifted up his eyes, and *l*	2Sa 18:24	7200
They *l*, but there was none to	2Sa 22:42	8159
And Araunah *l*, and saw the king and	2Sa 24:20	8259
And he went up, and *l*, and said,	1Kin 18:43	5027
And he *l*, and, behold, there was a	1Kin 19:6	5027
l on them, and cursed them in the	2Kin 2:24	7200
by upon the wall, and the people *l*	2Kin 6:30	7200
her head, and *l* out at a window	2Kin 9:30	8259
there *l* out to him two or three	2Kin 9:32	8259
And when she *l*, behold, the king	2Kin 11:14	7200
Amaziah king of Judah *l* one	2Kin 14:11	7200
as David came to Ornan, Ornan *l*	1Chr 21:21	5027
And when Judah *l* back, behold, the	2Chr 13:14	6437
they *l* unto the multitude, and,	2Chr 20:24	6437
And she *l*, and, behold, the king	2Chr 23:13	7200

l upon him, and, behold, he was	2Chr 26:20	6437
And I *l*, and rose up, and said unto	Neh 4:14	6437
sight of all them that *l* upon her	Est 2:15	6437
The troops of Tema *l*, the	Job 6:19	5027
When I *l* for good, then evil came	Job 30:26	6960
The LORD *l* down from heaven upon	Ps 14:2	8559
They *l* unto him, and were	Ps 34:5	5027
God *l* down from heaven upon the	Ps 53:2	8259
I *l* for some to take pity, but	Ps 69:20	6960
For he hath *l* down from the	Ps 102:19	8259
when they *l* upon me they shaked	Ps 109:25	7200
I *l* on my right hand, and beheld,	Ps 142:4	5027
my house I *l* through my casement	Prov 7:6	8259
I *l* upon it, and received	Prov 24:32	7200
Then I *l* on all the works that my	Eccl 2:11	6437
because the sun hath *l* upon me	Song 1:6	7805
he *l* that it should bring forth	Is 5:2	6960
when I *l* that it should bring	Is 5:4	6960
he *l* for judgment, but behold	Is 5:7	6970
but ye have not *l* unto the maker	Is 22:11	5027
And I *l*, and there was none to help	Is 63:5	5027
things which we *l* not for	Is 64:3	6960
We *l* for peace, but no good came	Jer 8:15	6960
we *l* for peace, and there is no	Jer 14:19	6960
this is the day that we *l* for	Lam 2:16	6960
And I *l*, and, behold, a whirlwind	Eze 1:4	7200
And when I *l*, behold, an hand was	Eze 2:9	7200
and when I *l*, behold a hole in the	Eze 8:7	7200
Then I *l*, and, behold, in the	Eze 10:1	7200
And when I *l*, behold the four	Eze 10:9	7200
the head *l* they followed it	Eze 10:11	6437
l upon thee, behold, thy time was	Eze 16:8	7200
with images, he *l* in the liver	Eze 21:21	7200
court that *l* toward the north	Eze 40:20	6440
and I *l*, and, behold, the glory of	Eze 44:4	7200
priests, which *l* toward the north	Eze 46:19	6437
be I upon before thee, and the	Dan 1:13	7200
Then I lifted up mine eyes, and *l*	Dan 10:5	7200
Then I Daniel *l*, and, behold,	Dan 12:5	7200
But thou shouldest not have *l* on	Obad 12	7200
thou shouldest not have *l* on	Obad 13	7200
Ye *l* for much, and, lo, it came to	Hag 1:9	6437
I lifted up mine eyes again, and *l*	Zec 2:1	7200
And I said, I have *l*, and behold a	Zec 4:2	7200
and lifted up mine eyes, and *l*	Zec 5:1	7200
Then lifted I up mine eyes, and *l*	Zec 5:9	7200
and lifted up mine eyes, and *l*	Zec 6:1	7200
when he had *l* round about on them	Mk 3:5	4017
he *l* round about on them which	Mk 3:34	4017
he *l* round about to see her that	Mk 5:32	4017
he *l* up to heaven, and blessed, and	Mk 6:41	308
And he *l* up, and said, I see men as	Mk 8:24	308
l on his disciples, he rebuked	Mk 8:33	1492
when they had *l* round about	Mk 9:8	4017
Jesus *l* round about, and saith	Mk 10:23	4017
when he had *l* round about upon	Mk 11:11	4017
she *l* upon him, and said, And thou	Mk 14:67	1689
And when they *l*, they saw that the	Mk 16:4	308
me in the days wherein he *l* on me	Lk 1:25	1869
l for redemption in Jerusalem	Lk 2:38	4327
***l* on him, and passed by on the**	Lk 10:32	1492
Jesus came to the place, he *l* up	Lk 19:5	308
And he *l* up, and saw the rich men	Lk 21:1	308
the fire, and earnestly *l* upon him	Lk 22:56	816
the Lord turned, and *l* upon Peter	Lk 22:61	1689
the disciples *l* one on another	Jn 13:22	991
down, and *l* into the sepulchre,	Jn 20:11	
while they *l* stedfastly toward	Acts 1:10	816
l up stedfastly into heaven, and	Acts 7:55	816
And when he *l* on him, he was	Acts 10:4	816
And the same hour I *l* up upon him	Acts 22:13	308
Howbeit they *l* when he should	Acts 28:6	4328
after they had *l* a great while	Acts 28:6	4328
For he *l* for a city which hath	Heb 11:10	1551
our eyes, which we have *l* upon	1Jn 1:1	2300
After this I *l*, and, behold, a	Rev 4:1	1492
And I *l*, and behold a pale horse,	Rev 6:8	1492
And I *l*, and, lo, a Lamb stood on	Rev 14:1	1492
And I *l*, and behold a white cloud,	Rev 14:14	1492
And after that I *l*, and, behold,	Rev 15:5	1492

LOOKEST

l narrowly unto all my paths	Job 13:27	8104
wherefore *l* thou upon them that	Hab 1:13	5027

LOOKETH

foot, wheresoever the priest *l*	Lev 13:12	4758,5869
that is bitten, when he *l* upon it	Num 21:8	7200
Pisgah, which *l* toward Jeshimon	Num 21:20	8259
of Peor, that *l* toward Jeshimon	Num 23:28	8259
from the bay that *l* southward	Josh 15:2	6437
to the way of the border that *l*	1Sa 13:18	8259

for man *l* on the outward	1Sa 16:7	7200
but the LORD *l* on the heart	1Sa 16:7	7200
as a hireling *l* for the reward of	Job 7:2	6960
For he *l* to the ends of the earth	Job 28:24	5027
He *l* upon men, and if any say, I	Job 33:27	7789
The LORD *l* from heaven	Ps 33:13	5027
the place of his habitation he *l*	Ps 33:14	7688
He *l* on the earth, and it	Ps 104:32	5027
prudent man *l* well to his going	Prov 14:15	995
She *l* well to the ways of her	Prov 31:27	6822
he *l* forth at the windows,	Song 2:9	7688
Who is she that *l* forth as the	Song 6:10	8259
Lebanon which *l* toward Damascus	Song 7:4	6822
when he that *l* upon it seeth	Is 28:4	7200
gate, that *l* toward the north	Eze 8:3	6437
LORD's house, which *l* eastward	Eze 11:1	6437
the gate which *l* toward the east	Eze 40:6	6440
the gate that *l* toward the east	Eze 40:22	6440
the gate that *l* toward the east	Eze 43:1	6437
sanctuary which *l* toward the east	Eze 44:1	6437
gate of the inner court that *l*	Eze 46:1	6437
the gate that *l* toward the east	Eze 46:12	6437
gate by the way that *l* eastward	Eze 47:2	6437
That whosoever *l* on a woman to	Mt 5:28	*991*
in a day when he *l* not for him	Mt 24:50	*4328*
in a day when he *l* not for him	Lk 12:46	*4328*
But whoso *l* into the perfect law	Jas 1:25	*3879*

LOOKING

l toward Gilgal, that is before	Josh 15:7	6437
three *l* toward the north, and	1Kin 7:25	6437
three *l* toward the west	1Kin 7:25	6437
three *l* toward the south	1Kin 7:25	6437
and three *l* toward the east	1Kin 7:25	6437
Michal the daughter of Saul *l* out	1Chr 15:29	8259
three *l* toward the north, and	2Chr 4:4	6437
three *l* toward the west	2Chr 4:4	6437
three *l* toward the south	2Chr 4:4	6437
and three *l* toward the east	2Chr 4:4	6437
is strong, and as a molten *l* glass	Job 37:18	7209
mine eyes fail with *l* upward	Is 38:14	
l up to heaven, he blessed, and	Mt 14:19	*308*
l up to heaven, he sighed, and	Mk 7:34	*308*
Jesus *l* upon them saith, With men	Mk 10:27	*1689*
were also women *l* on afar off	Mk 15:40	*2334*
l round about upon them all, he	Lk 6:10	*4017*
l up to heaven, he blessed them,	Lk 9:16	*308*
l back, is fit for the kingdom of	Lk 9:62	*991*
for *l* after those things which	Lk 21:26	*4329*
l upon Jesus as he walked, he	Jn 1:36	*1689*
l in, saw the linen clothes lying	Jn 20:5	
l stedfastly on him, saw his face	Acts 6:15	*816*
l for a promise from thee	Acts 23:21	*4327*
L for that blessed hope, and the	Titus 2:13	*4327*
certain fearful *l* for of judgment	Heb 10:27	*1561*
L unto Jesus the author and	Heb 12:2	*872*
L diligently lest any man fail of	Heb 12:15	*1983*
L for and hasting unto the coming	2Pet 3:12	*4328*
l for the mercy of our Lord Jesus	Jude 21	*4327*

LOOKINGGLASSES

of the *l* of the women assembling,	Ex 38:8	4759

LOOKS

but wilt bring down high *l*	Ps 18:27	5869
The lofty *l* of man shall be	Is 2:11	5869
and the glory of his high *l*	Is 10:12	5869
words, nor be dismayed at their *l*	Eze 2:6	6400
neither be dismayed at their *l*	Eze 3:9	6400

LOOPS

thou shalt make *l* of blue upon	Ex 26:4	3924
Fifty *l* shalt thou make in the	Ex 26:5	3924
fifty *l* shalt thou make in the	Ex 26:5	3924
that the *l* may take hold one of	Ex 26:5	3924
thou shalt make fifty *l* on the	Ex 26:10	3924
fifty *l* in the edge of the	Ex 26:10	3924
and put the taches into the *l*	Ex 26:11	3924
he made *l* of blue on the edge of	Ex 36:11	3924
Fifty *l* made he in one curtain,	Ex 36:12	3924
fifty *l* made he in the edge of	Ex 36:12	3924
the *l* held one curtain to another	Ex 36:12	3924
And he made fifty *l* upon the	Ex 36:17	3924
fifty *l* made he upon the edge of	Ex 36:17	3924

LOOSE

Naphtali is a hind let *l*	Gen 49:21	7971
living bird *l* into the open field	Lev 14:7	7971
l his shoe from off his foot, and	Deut 25:9	2502
L thy shoe from off thy foot	Josh 5:15	5394
that he would let *l* his hand	Job 6:9	5425
they have also let *l* the bridle	Job 30:11	7971
Pleiades, or *l* the bands of Orion	Job 38:31	6605

to *l* those that are appointed to	Ps 102:20	6605
l the sackcloth from off thy	Is 20:2	6605
I will *l* the loins of kings, to	Is 45:1	6605
l thyself from the bands of thy	Is 52:2	6605
to *l* the bands of wickedness, to	Is 58:6	6605
I *l* thee this day from the chains	Jer 40:4	6605
and said, Lo, I see four men *l*	Dan 3:25	8271
whatsoever thou shalt *l* on earth	Mt 16:19	*3089*
whatsoever ye shall *l* on earth	Mt 18:18	*3089*
l them, and bring them unto me	Mt 21:2	*3089*
l him, and bring him	Mk 11:2	*3089*
and they *l* him	Mk 11:4	*3089*
l his ox or his ass from the	Lk 13:15	*3089*
l him, and bring him hither	Lk 19:30	*3089*
any man ask you, Why do ye *l* him	Lk 19:31	*3089*
said unto them, Why *l* ye the colt	Lk 19:33	*3089*
unto them, L him, and let him go	Jn 11:44	*3089*
of his feet I am not worthy to *l*	Acts 13:25	*3089*
him of Paul, that he might *l* him	Acts 24:26	*3089*
book, and to *l* the seals thereof	Rev 5:2	*3089*
to *l* the seven seals thereof	Rev 5:5	*3089*
L the four angels which are bound	Rev 9:14	*3089*

LOOSED

be not *l* from the ephod	Ex 28:28	2118
might not be *l* from the ephod	Ex 39:21	2118
house of him that hath his shoe *l*	Deut 25:10	2502
his bands *l* from off his hands	Judg 15:14	4549
Because he hath *l* my cord	Job 30:11	6605
or who hath *l* the bands of the	Job 39:5	6605
The king sent and *l* him	Ps 105:20	5425
thou hast *l* my bonds	Ps 116:16	6605
Or ever the silver cord be *l*	Eccl 12:6	7368
the girdle of their loins be *l*	Is 5:27	6605
Thy tacklings are *l*	Is 33:23	5203
exile hasteneth that he may be *l*	Is 51:14	6605
the joints of his loins were *l*	Dan 5:6	8271
on earth shall be *l* in heaven	Mt 16:19	*3089*
on earth shall be *l* in heaven	Mt 18:18	*3089*
l him, and forgave him the debt	Mt 18:27	*630*
and the string of his tongue was *l*	Mk 7:35	*3089*
immediately, and his tongue *l*	Lk 1:64	
thou art *l* from thine infirmity	Lk 13:12	*630*
be *l* from this bond on the	Lk 13:16	*3089*
having *l* the pains of death	Acts 2:24	*3089*
Paul and his company *l* from Paphos	Acts 13:13	*321*
and every one's bands were *l*	Acts 16:26	*447*
he *l* him from his bands, and	Acts 22:30	*3089*
not have *l* from Crete, and to have	Acts 27:21	*321*
l the rudder bands, and hoised up	Acts 27:40	*447*
she is *l* from the law of her	Rom 7:2	*2673*
seek not to be *l*	1Cor 7:27	*3089*
Art thou *l* from a wife	1Cor 7:27	*3080*
And the four angels were *l*	Rev 9:15	*3089*
that he must be *l* a little season	Rev 20:3	*3089*
Satan shall be *l* out of his	Rev 20:7	*3089*

LOOSETH

He *l* the bond of kings, and	Job 12:18	6605
The LORD *l* the prisoners	Ps 146:7	5425

LOOSING

unto them, What do ye, *l* the colt	Mk 11:5	*3089*
And as they were *l* the colt	Lk 19:33	*3089*
Therefore *l* from Troas, we came	Acts 16:11	*321*
l thence, they sailed close by	Acts 27:13	*142*

LOP

shall *l* the bough with terror	Is 10:33	5586

LORD

1. God.

day that the L God made the earth	Gen 2:4	3068
for the L God had not caused it	Gen 2:5	3068
the L God formed man of the dust	Gen 2:7	3068
the L God planted a garden	Gen 2:8	3068
out of the ground made the L God	Gen 2:9	3068
the L God took the man, and put	Gen 2:15	3068
the L God commanded the man,	Gen 2:16	3068
the L God said, It is not good	Gen 2:18	3068
out of the ground the L God	Gen 2:19	3068
the L God caused a deep sleep to	Gen 2:21	3068
which the L God had taken from	Gen 2:22	3068
field which the L God had made	Gen 3:1	3068
they heard the voice of the L God	Gen 3:8	3068
from the presence of the L God	Gen 3:8	3068
the L God called unto Adam, and	Gen 3:9	3068
the L God said unto the woman,	Gen 3:13	3068
the L God said unto the serpent,	Gen 3:14	3068
to his wife did the L God make	Gen 3:21	3068
the L God said, Behold, the man	Gen 3:22	3068
Therefore the L God sent him	Gen 3:23	3068
I have gotten a man from the L	Gen 4:1	3068

L

the ground an offering unto the L	Gen 4:3	3068
the L had respect unto Abel and to	Gen 4:4	3068
the L said unto Cain, Why art	Gen 4:6	3068
the L said unto Cain, Where is	Gen 4:9	3068
And Cain said unto the L, My	Gen 4:13	3068
the L said unto him, Therefore	Gen 4:15	3068
the L set a mark upon Cain, lest	Gen 4:15	3068
out from the presence of the L	Gen 4:16	3068
to call upon the name of the L	Gen 4:26	3068
ground which the L hath cursed	Gen 5:29	3068
the L said, My spirit shall not	Gen 6:3	3068
it repented the L that he had	Gen 6:6	3068
the L said, I will destroy man	Gen 6:7	3068
found grace in the eyes of the L	Gen 6:8	3068
the L said unto Noah, Come thou	Gen 7:1	3068
unto all that the L commanded him	Gen 7:5	3068
and the L shut him in	Gen 7:16	3068
Noah builded an altar unto the L	Gen 8:20	3068
the L smelled a sweet savour	Gen 8:21	3068
the L said in his heart, I will	Gen 8:21	3068
Blessed be the L God of Shem	Gen 9:26	3068
was a mighty hunter before the L	Gen 10:9	3068
the mighty hunter before the L	Gen 10:9	3068
the L came down to see the city	Gen 11:5	3068
the L said, Behold, the people is	Gen 11:6	3068
So the L scattered them abroad	Gen 11:8	3068
because the L did there confound	Gen 11:9	3068
from thence did the L scatter	Gen 11:9	3068
Now the L had said unto Abram	Gen 12:1	3068
as the L had spoken unto him	Gen 12:4	3068
the L appeared unto Abram, and	Gen 12:7	3068
builded he an altar unto the L	Gen 12:7	3068
he builded an altar unto the L	Gen 12:8	3068
and called upon the name of the L	Gen 12:8	3068
the L plagued Pharaoh and his	Gen 12:17	3068
Abram called on the name of the L	Gen 13:4	3068
before the L destroyed Sodom and	Gen 13:10	3068
even as the garden of the L	Gen 13:10	3068
sinners before the L exceedingly	Gen 13:13	3068
the L said unto Abram, after that	Gen 13:14	3068
built there an altar unto the L	Gen 13:18	3068
have lift up mine hand unto the L	Gen 14:22	3068
the L came unto Abram in a vision	Gen 15:1	3068
L GOD, what wilt thou give me,	Gen 15:2	136
the word of the L came unto him	Gen 15:4	3068
And he believed in the L	Gen 15:6	3068
I am the L that brought thee out	Gen 15:7	3068
L GOD, whereby shall I know that	Gen 15:8	136
In the same day the L made a	Gen 15:18	3068
the L hath restrained me from	Gen 16:2	3068
the L judge between me and thee	Gen 16:5	3068
the angel of the L found her by a	Gen 16:7	3068
the angel of the L said unto her	Gen 16:9	3068
the angel of the L said unto her	Gen 16:10	3068
the angel of the L said unto her	Gen 16:11	3068
because the L hath heard thy	Gen 16:11	3068
name of the L that spake unto her	Gen 16:13	3068
the L appeared to Abram, and said	Gen 17:1	3068
the L appeared unto him in the	Gen 18:1	3068
And said, My L, if now I have	Gen 18:3	136
And the L said unto Abraham,	Gen 18:13	3068
Is any thing too hard for the L	Gen 18:14	3068
the L said, Shall I hide from	Gen 18:17	3068
they shall keep the way of the L	Gen 18:19	3068
that the L may bring upon Abraham	Gen 18:19	3068
the L said, Because the cry of	Gen 18:20	3068
Abraham stood yet before the L	Gen 18:22	3068
the L said, If I find in Sodom	Gen 18:26	3068
taken upon me to speak unto the L	Gen 18:27	136
him, Oh let not the L be angry	Gen 18:30	136
taken upon me to speak unto the L	Gen 18:31	136
said, Oh let not the L be angry	Gen 18:32	136
the L went his way, as soon as he	Gen 18:33	3068
great before the face of the L	Gen 19:13	3068
the L hath sent us to destroy it	Gen 19:13	3068
for the L will destroy this city	Gen 19:14	3068
the L being merciful unto him	Gen 19:16	3068
Then the L rained upon Sodom and	Gen 19:24	3068
and fire from the L out of heaven	Gen 19:24	3068
place where he stood before the L	Gen 19:27	3068
and he said, L, wilt thou slay	Gen 20:4	136
For the L had fast closed up all	Gen 20:18	3068
the L visited Sarah as he had	Gen 21:1	3068
the L did unto Sarah as he had	Gen 21:1	3068
called there on the name of the L	Gen 21:33	3068
the angel of the L called unto	Gen 22:11	3068
mount of the L it shall be seen	Gen 22:14	3068
the angel of the L called unto	Gen 22:15	3068
myself have I sworn, saith the L	Gen 22:16	3068
the L had blessed Abraham in all	Gen 24:1	3068
I will make thee swear by the L	Gen 24:3	3068
The L God of heaven, which took	Gen 24:7	3068
O L God of my master Abraham, I	Gen 24:12	3068
to wit whether the L had made his	Gen 24:21	3068
his head, and worshipped the L	Gen 24:26	3068
Blessed be the L God of my master	Gen 24:27	3068
the L led me to the house of my	Gen 24:27	3068
Come in, thou blessed of the L	Gen 24:31	3068
the L hath blessed my master	Gen 24:35	3068
And he said unto me, The L	Gen 24:40	3068
O L God of my master Abraham, if	Gen 24:42	3068
the L hath appointed out for my	Gen 24:44	3068
down my head, and worshipped the L	Gen 24:48	3068
blessed the L God of my master	Gen 24:48	3068
The thing proceedeth from the L	Gen 24:50	3068
son's wife, as the L hath spoken	Gen 24:51	3068
their words, he worshipped the L	Gen 24:52	3068
seeing the L hath prospered my	Gen 24:56	3068
intreated the L for his wife	Gen 25:21	3068
the L was intreated of him, and	Gen 25:21	3068
And she went to enquire of the L	Gen 25:22	3068
the L said unto her, Two nations	Gen 25:23	3068
the L appeared unto him, and said,	Gen 26:2	3068
and the L blessed him	Gen 26:12	3068
For now the L hath made room for	Gen 26:22	3068
the L appeared unto him the same	Gen 26:24	3068
and called upon the name of the L	Gen 26:25	3068
that the L was with thee	Gen 26:28	3068
thou art now the blessed of the L	Gen 26:29	3068
thee before the L before my death	Gen 27:7	3068
Because the L thy God brought it	Gen 27:20	3068
a field which the L hath blessed	Gen 27:27	3068
the L stood above it, and said	Gen 28:13	3068
I am the L God of Abraham thy	Gen 28:13	3068
Surely the L is in this place	Gen 28:16	3068
then shall the L be my God	Gen 28:21	3068
when the L saw that Leah was	Gen 29:31	3068
Surely the L hath looked upon my	Gen 29:32	3068
Because the L hath heard that I	Gen 29:33	3068
she said, Now will I praise the L	Gen 29:35	3068
The L shall add to me another son	Gen 30:24	3068
L hath blessed me for thy sake	Gen 30:27	3068
the L hath blessed thee since my	Gen 30:30	3068
the L said unto Jacob, Return	Gen 31:3	3068
The L watch between me and thee,	Gen 31:49	3068
the L which saidst unto me,	Gen 32:9	3068
was wicked in the sight of the L	Gen 38:7	3068
and the L slew him	Gen 38:7	3068
which he did displeased the L	Gen 38:10	3068
the L was with Joseph, and he was	Gen 39:2	3068
saw that the L was with him	Gen 39:3	3068
that the L made all that he did	Gen 39:3	3068
that the L blessed the Egyptian's	Gen 39:5	3068
the blessing of the L was upon	Gen 39:5	3068
But the L was with Joseph, and	Gen 39:21	3068
because the L was with him, and	Gen 39:23	3068
he did, the L made it to prosper	Gen 39:23	3068
waited for thy salvation, O L	Gen 49:18	3068
the angel of the L appeared unto	Ex 3:2	3068
when the L saw that he turned	Ex 3:4	3068
the L said, I have surely seen	Ex 3:7	3068
The L God of your fathers, the	Ex 3:15	3068
The L God of your fathers, the	Ex 3:16	3068
The L God of the Hebrews hath met	Ex 3:18	3068
we may sacrifice to the L our God	Ex 3:18	3068
The L hath not appeared unto thee	Ex 4:1	3068
the L said unto him, What is that	Ex 4:2	3068
the L said unto Moses, Put forth	Ex 4:4	3068
that the L God of their fathers	Ex 4:5	3068
the L said furthermore unto him,	Ex 4:6	3068
And Moses said unto the L	Ex 4:10	136
O my L, I am not eloquent	Ex 4:10	3068
the L said unto him, Who hath	Ex 4:11	3068
have not I the L	Ex 4:11	3068
And he said, O my L, send, I pray	Ex 4:13	136
the anger of the L was kindled	Ex 4:14	3068
the L said unto Moses in Midian	Ex 4:19	3068
the L said unto Moses, When thou	Ex 4:21	3068
unto Pharaoh, Thus saith the L	Ex 4:22	3068
in the inn, that the L met him	Ex 4:24	3068
the L said to Aaron, Go into the	Ex 4:27	3068
words of the L who had sent him	Ex 4:28	3068
which the L had spoken unto Moses	Ex 4:30	3068
when they heard that the L had	Ex 4:31	3068
Thus saith the L God of Israel	Ex 5:1	3068
And Pharaoh said, Who is the L	Ex 5:2	3068
I know not the L, neither will I	Ex 5:2	3068
and sacrifice unto the L our God	Ex 5:3	3068
us go and do sacrifice unto the L	Ex 5:17	3068
The L look upon you, and judge	Ex 5:21	3068
And Moses returned unto the L	Ex 5:22	136
and said, L, wherefore hast	Ex 5:22	3068

Then the *L* said unto Moses, Now	Ex 6:1	3068
and said unto him, I am the *L*	Ex 6:2	3068
children of Israel, I am the *L*	Ex 6:6	3068
know that I am the *L* your God	Ex 6:7	3068
I am the *L*	Ex 6:8	3068
the *L* spake unto Moses, saying,	Ex 6:10	3068
And Moses spake before the *L*	Ex 6:12	3068
the *L* spake unto Moses and unto	Ex 6:13	3068
and Moses, to whom the *L* said	Ex 6:26	3068
to pass on the day when the *L*	Ex 6:28	3068
That the *L* spake unto Moses,	Ex 6:29	3068
unto Moses, saying, I am the *L*	Ex 6:29	3068
And Moses said before the *L*	Ex 6:30	3068
the *L* said unto Moses, See, I	Ex 7:1	3068
shall know that I am the *L*	Ex 7:5	3068
Aaron did as the *L* commanded them	Ex 7:6	3068
the *L* spake unto Moses and unto	Ex 7:8	3068
did so as the *L* had commanded	Ex 7:10	3068
as the *L* had said	Ex 7:13	3068
the *L* said unto Moses, Pharaoh's	Ex 7:14	3068
The *L* God of the Hebrews hath	Ex 7:16	3068
Thus saith the *L*, In this thou	Ex 7:17	3068
thou shalt know that I am the *L*	Ex 7:17	3068
the *L* spake unto Moses, Say unto	Ex 7:19	3068
Aaron did so, as the *L* commanded	Ex 7:20	3068
as the *L* had said	Ex 7:22	3068
after that the *L* had smitten the	Ex 7:25	3068
the *L* spake unto Moses, Go unto	Ex 8:1	3068
and say unto him, Thus saith the *L*	Ex 8:1	3068
the *L* spake unto Moses, Say unto	Ex 8:5	3068
and Aaron, and said, Intreat the *L*	Ex 8:8	3068
they may do sacrifice unto the *L*	Ex 8:8	3068
is none like unto the *L* our God	Ex 8:10	3068
Moses cried unto the *L* because of	Ex 8:12	3068
the *L* did according to the word	Ex 8:13	3068
as the *L* had said	Ex 8:15	3068
the *L* said unto Moses, Say unto	Ex 8:16	3068
as the *L* had said	Ex 8:19	3068
the *L* said unto Moses, Rise up	Ex 8:20	3068
and say unto him, Thus saith the *L*	Ex 8:20	3068
the *L* in the midst of the earth	Ex 8:22	3068
And the *L* did so	Ex 8:24	3068
of the Egyptians to the *L* our God	Ex 8:26	3068
and sacrifice to the *L* our God	Ex 8:27	3068
the *L* your God in the wilderness	Ex 8:28	3068
I will intreat the *L* that the	Ex 8:29	3068
people go to sacrifice to the *L*	Ex 8:29	3068
from Pharaoh, and intreated the *L*	Ex 8:30	3068
the *L* did according to the word	Ex 8:31	3068
Then the *L* said unto Moses, Go in	Ex 9:1	3068
Thus saith the *L* God of the	Ex 9:1	3068
the hand of the *L* is upon thy	Ex 9:3	3068
the *L* shall sever between the	Ex 9:4	3068
the *L* appointed a set time,	Ex 9:5	3068
To morrow the *L* shall do this	Ex 9:5	3068
the *L* did that thing on the	Ex 9:6	3068
the *L* said unto Moses and unto	Ex 9:8	3068
the *L* hardened the heart of	Ex 9:12	3068
as the *L* had spoken unto Moses	Ex 9:12	3068
the *L* said unto Moses, Rise up	Ex 9:13	3068
Thus saith the *L* God of the	Ex 9:13	3068
L among the servants of Pharaoh	Ex 9:20	3068
word of the *L* left his servants	Ex 9:21	3068
the *L* said unto Moses, Stretch	Ex 9:22	3068
the *L* sent thunder and hail, and	Ex 9:23	3068
the *L* rained hail upon the land	Ex 9:23	3068
the *L* is righteous, and I and my	Ex 9:27	3068
Intreat the *L* (for it is enough)	Ex 9:28	3068
spread abroad my hands unto the *L*	Ex 9:29	3068
ye will not yet fear the *L* God	Ex 9:30	3068
abroad his hands unto the *L*	Ex 9:33	3068
as the *L* had spoken by Moses	Ex 9:35	3068
the *L* said unto Moses, Go in unto	Ex 10:1	3068
ye may know how that I am the *L*	Ex 10:2	3068
Thus saith the *L* God of the	Ex 10:3	3068
they may serve the *L* their God	Ex 10:7	3068
them, Go, serve the *L* your God	Ex 10:8	3068
we must hold a feast unto the *L*	Ex 10:9	3068
Let the *L* be so with you, as I	Ex 10:10	3068
ye that are men, and serve the *L*	Ex 10:11	3068
the *L* said unto Moses, Stretch	Ex 10:12	3068
the *L* brought an east wind upon	Ex 10:13	3068
sinned against the *L* your God	Ex 10:16	3068
once, and intreat the *L* your God	Ex 10:17	3068
from Pharaoh, and intreated the *L*	Ex 10:18	3068
the *L* turned a mighty strong west	Ex 10:19	3068
But the *L* hardened Pharaoh's	Ex 10:20	3068
the *L* said unto Moses, Stretch	Ex 10:21	3068
and said, Go ye, serve the *L*	Ex 10:24	3068
may sacrifice unto the *L* our God	Ex 10:25	3068
we take to serve the *L* our God	Ex 10:26	3068
not with what we must serve the *L*	Ex 10:26	3068
But the *L* hardened Pharaoh's	Ex 10:27	3068
the *L* said unto Moses, Yet will I	Ex 11:1	3068
the *L* gave the people favour in	Ex 11:3	3068
And Moses said, Thus saith the *L*	Ex 11:4	3068
L doth put a difference between	Ex 11:7	3068
the *L* said unto Moses, Pharaoh	Ex 11:9	3068
the *L* hardened Pharaoh's heart,	Ex 11:10	3068
the *L* spake unto Moses and Aaron	Ex 12:1	3068
I am the *L*	Ex 12:12	3068
the *L* throughout your generations	Ex 12:14	3068
For the *L* will pass through to	Ex 12:23	3068
the *L* will pass over the door, and	Ex 12:23	3068
land which the *L* will give you	Ex 12:25	3068
did as the *L* had commanded Moses	Ex 12:28	3068
that at midnight the *L* smote all	Ex 12:29	3068
and go, serve the *L*, as ye have	Ex 12:31	3068
the *L* gave the people favour in	Ex 12:36	3068
that all the hosts of the *L* went	Ex 12:41	3068
to be much observed unto the *L*	Ex 12:42	3068
the *L* to be observed of all the	Ex 12:42	3068
the *L* said unto Moses and Aaron,	Ex 12:43	3068
will keep the passover to the *L*	Ex 12:48	3068
the *L* commanded Moses and Aaron	Ex 12:50	3068
that the *L* did bring the children	Ex 12:51	3068
the *L* spake unto Moses, saying,	Ex 13:1	3068
for by strength of hand the *L*	Ex 13:3	3068
it shall be when the *L* shall	Ex 13:5	3068
day shall be a feast to the *L*	Ex 13:6	3068
L did unto me when I came forth	Ex 13:8	3068
the *L* brought thee out of Egypt	Ex 13:9	3068
it shall be when the *L* shall	Ex 13:11	3068
the *L* all that openeth the matrix	Ex 13:12	3068
By strength of hand the *L* brought	Ex 13:14	3068
that the *L* slew all the firstborn	Ex 13:15	3068
the *L* all that openeth the matrix	Ex 13:15	3068
for by strength of hand the *L*	Ex 13:16	3068
the *L* went before them by day in	Ex 13:21	3068
the *L* spake unto Moses, saying,	Ex 14:1	3068
may know that I am the *L*	Ex 14:4	3068
the *L* hardened the heart of	Ex 14:8	3068
of Israel cried out unto the *L*	Ex 14:10	3068
and see the salvation of the *L*	Ex 14:13	3068
The *L* shall fight for you, and ye	Ex 14:14	3068
the *L* said unto Moses, Wherefore	Ex 14:15	3068
shall know that I am the *L*	Ex 14:18	3068
the *L* caused the sea to go back	Ex 14:21	3068
the *L* looked unto the host of the	Ex 14:24	3068
for the *L* fighteth for them	Ex 14:25	3068
the *L* said unto Moses, Stretch	Ex 14:26	3068
the *L* overthrew the Egyptians in	Ex 14:27	3068
Thus the *L* saved Israel that day	Ex 14:30	3068
the *L* did upon the Egyptians	Ex 14:31	3068
and the people feared the *L*	Ex 14:31	3068
and believed the *L*	Ex 14:31	3068
of Israel this song unto the *L*	Ex 15:1	3068
saying, I will sing unto the *L*	Ex 15:1	3068
The *L* is my strength and song, and	Ex 15:2	3068
The *L* is a man of war	Ex 15:3	3068
the *L* is his name	Ex 15:3	3068
Thy right hand, O *L*, is become	Ex 15:6	3068
thy right hand, O *L*, hath dashed	Ex 15:6	3068
Who is like unto thee, O *L*	Ex 15:11	3068
till thy people pass over, O *L*	Ex 15:16	3068
inheritance, in the place, O *L*	Ex 15:17	3068
dwell in, in the Sanctuary, O *L*	Ex 15:17	3068
The *L* shall reign for ever and	Ex 15:18	3068
the *L* brought again the waters of	Ex 15:19	3068
answered them, Sing ye to the *L*	Ex 15:21	3068
And he cried unto the *L*	Ex 15:25	3068
the *L* shewed him a tree, which	Ex 15:25	3068
to the voice of the *L* thy God	Ex 15:26	3068
for I am the *L* that healeth thee	Ex 15:26	3068
of the *L* in the land of Egypt	Ex 16:3	3068
Then said the *L* unto Moses	Ex 16:4	3068
then ye shall know that the *L*	Ex 16:6	3068
ye shall see the glory of the *L*	Ex 16:7	3068
your murmurings against the *L*	Ex 16:7	3068
when the *L* shall give you in the	Ex 16:8	3068
for that the *L* heareth your	Ex 16:8	3068
not against us, but against the *L*	Ex 16:8	3068
of Israel, Come near before the *L*	Ex 16:9	3068
the glory of the *L* appeared in	Ex 16:10	3068
the *L* spake unto Moses, saying,	Ex 16:11	3068
know that I am the *L* your God	Ex 16:12	3068
which the *L* hath given you to eat	Ex 16:15	3068
thing which the *L* hath commanded	Ex 16:16	3068
is that which the *L* hath said	Ex 16:23	3068
of the holy sabbath unto the *L*	Ex 16:23	3068
to day is a sabbath unto the *L*	Ex 16:25	3068
the *L* said unto Moses, How long	Ex 16:28	3068

for that the *L* hath given you the	Ex 16:29	3068
the thing which the *L* commandeth	Ex 16:32	3068
and lay it up before the *L*	Ex 16:33	3068
As the *L* commanded Moses, so	Ex 16:34	3068
to the commandment of the *L*	Ex 17:1	3068
wherefore do ye tempt the *L*	Ex 17:2	3068
And Moses cried unto the *L*	Ex 17:4	3068
the *L* said unto Moses, Go on	Ex 17:5	3068
and because they tempted the *L*	Ex 17:7	3068
Is the *L* among us, or not	Ex 17:7	3068
the *L* said unto Moses, Write this	Ex 17:14	3068
the *L* hath sworn that the *L*	Ex 17:16	3068
that the *L* had brought Israel out	Ex 18:1	3068
that the *L* had done unto Pharaoh	Ex 18:8	3068
way, and how the *L* delivered them	Ex 18:8	3068
which the *L* had done to Israel	Ex 18:9	3068
And Jethro said, Blessed be the *L*	Ex 18:10	3068
Now I know that the *L* is greater	Ex 18:11	3068
the *L* called unto him out of the	Ex 19:3	3068
words which the *L* commanded him	Ex 19:7	3068
All that the *L* hath spoken we	Ex 19:8	3068
words of the people unto the *L*	Ex 19:8	3068
the *L* said unto Moses, Lo, I come	Ex 19:9	3068
words of the people unto the *L*	Ex 19:9	3068
the *L* said unto Moses, Go unto	Ex 19:10	3068
for the third day the *L* will come	Ex 19:11	3068
because the *L* descended upon it	Ex 19:18	3068
the *L* came down upon mount Sinai,	Ex 19:20	3068
the *L* called Moses up to the top	Ex 19:20	3068
the *L* said unto Moses, Go down,	Ex 19:21	3068
break through unto the *L* to gaze	Ex 19:21	3068
also, which come near to the *L*	Ex 19:22	3068
lest the *L* break forth upon them	Ex 19:22	3068
And Moses said unto the *L*, The	Ex 19:23	3068
the *L* said unto him, Away, get	Ex 19:24	3068
through to come up unto the *L*	Ex 19:24	3068
I am the *L* thy God, which have	Ex 20:2	3068
for I the *L* thy God am a jealous	Ex 20:5	3068
the name of the *L* thy God in vain	Ex 20:7	3068
for the *L* will not hold him	Ex 20:7	3068
is the sabbath of the *L* thy God	Ex 20:10	3068
For in six days the *L* made heaven	Ex 20:11	3068
wherefore the *L* blessed the	Ex 20:11	3068
which the *L* thy God giveth thee	Ex 20:12	3068
the *L* said unto Moses, Thus thou	Ex 20:22	3068
of the *L* be between them both	Ex 22:11	3068
any god, save unto the *L* only	Ex 22:20	3068
shall appear before the *L* GOD	Ex 23:17	3068
into the house of the *L* thy God	Ex 23:19	3068
And ye shall serve the *L* your God	Ex 23:25	3068
unto Moses, Come up unto the *L*	Ex 24:1	3068
Moses alone shall come near the *L*	Ex 24:2	3068
the people all the words of the *L*	Ex 24:3	3068
which the *L* hath said will we do	Ex 24:3	3068
wrote all the words of the *L*	Ex 24:4	3068
offerings of oxen unto the *L*	Ex 24:5	3068
All that the *L* hath said will we	Ex 24:7	3068
which the *L* hath made with you	Ex 24:8	3068
the *L* said unto Moses, Come up to	Ex 24:12	3068
the glory of the *L* abode upon	Ex 24:16	3068
the sight of the glory of the *L*	Ex 24:17	3068
the *L* spake unto Moses, saying,	Ex 25:1	3068
evening to morning before the *L*	Ex 27:21	3068
bear their names before the *L*	Ex 28:12	3068
memorial before the *L* continually	Ex 28:29	3068
when he goeth in before the *L*	Ex 28:30	3068
heart before the *L* continually	Ex 28:30	3068
unto the holy place before the *L*	Ex 28:35	3068
of a signet, HOLINESS TO THE *L*	Ex 28:36	3068
they may be accepted before the *L*	Ex 28:38	3068
kill the bullock before the *L*	Ex 29:11	3068
it is a burnt offering unto the *L*	Ex 29:18	3068
offering made by fire unto the *L*	Ex 29:18	3068
bread that is before the *L*	Ex 29:23	3068
for a wave offering before the *L*	Ex 29:24	3068
for a sweet savour before the *L*	Ex 29:25	3068
offering made by fire unto the *L*	Ex 29:25	3068
for a wave offering before the *L*	Ex 29:26	3068
their heave offering unto the *L*	Ex 29:28	3068
offering made by fire unto the *L*	Ex 29:41	3068
of the congregation before the *L*	Ex 29:42	3068
know that I am the *L* their God	Ex 29:46	3068
I am the *L* their God	Ex 29:46	3068
the *L* throughout your generations	Ex 30:8	3068
it is most holy unto the *L*	Ex 30:10	3068
the *L* spake unto Moses, saying,	Ex 30:11	3068
a ransom for his soul unto the *L*	Ex 30:12	3068
shall be the offering of the *L*	Ex 30:13	3068
shall give an offering unto the *L*	Ex 30:14	3068
they give an offering unto the *L*	Ex 30:15	3068
children of Israel before the *L*	Ex 30:16	3068
the *L* spake unto Moses, saying,	Ex 30:17	3068
offering made by fire unto the *L*	Ex 30:20	3068
Moreover the *L* spake unto Moses,	Ex 30:22	3068
the *L* said unto Moses, Take unto	Ex 30:34	3068
shall be unto thee holy for the *L*	Ex 30:37	3068
the *L* spake unto Moses, saying,	Ex 31:1	3068
the *L* spake unto Moses, saying,	Ex 31:12	3068
I am the *L* that doth sanctify you	Ex 31:13	3068
sabbath of rest, holy to the *L*	Ex 31:15	3068
for in six days the *L* made heaven	Ex 31:17	3068
To morrow is a feast to the *L*	Ex 32:5	3068
the *L* said unto Moses, Go, get	Ex 32:7	3068
the *L* said unto Moses, I have	Ex 32:9	3068
the *L* his God, and said, *L*	Ex 32:11	3068
the *L* repented of the evil which	Ex 32:14	3068
Thus saith the *L* God of Israel	Ex 32:27	3068
yourselves to day to the *L*	Ex 32:29	3068
and now I will go up unto the *L*	Ex 32:30	3068
And Moses returned unto the *L*	Ex 32:31	3068
the *L* said unto Moses, Whosoever	Ex 32:33	3068
the *L* plagued the people, because	Ex 32:35	3068
the *L* said unto Moses, Depart, and	Ex 33:1	3068
For the *L* had said unto Moses,	Ex 33:5	3068
L went out unto the tabernacle of	Ex 33:7	3068
and the *L* talked with Moses.	Ex 33:9	
the *L* spake unto Moses face to	Ex 33:11	3068
And Moses said unto the *L*, See,	Ex 33:12	3068
the *L* said unto Moses, I will do	Ex 33:17	3068
the name of the *L* before thee	Ex 33:19	3068
the *L* said, Behold, there is a	Ex 33:21	3068
the *L* said unto Moses, Hew thee	Ex 34:1	3068
as the *L* had commanded him, and	Ex 34:4	3068
the *L* descended in the cloud, and	Ex 34:5	3068
and proclaimed the name of the *L*	Ex 34:5	3068
the *L* passed by before him, and	Ex 34:6	3068
proclaimed, The *L*, The *L* God	Ex 34:6	3068
in thy sight, O *L*, let my *L*	Ex 34:9	136
art shall see the work of the *L*	Ex 34:10	3068
for the *L*, whose name is Jealous,	Ex 34:14	3068
children appear before the *L* GOD	Ex 34:23	3068
the *L* thy God thrice in the year	Ex 34:24	3068
unto the house of the *L* thy God	Ex 34:26	3068
the *L* said unto Moses, Write thou	Ex 34:27	3068
was there with the *L* forty days	Ex 34:28	3068
in commandment all that the *L* had	Ex 34:32	3068
in before the *L* to speak with him	Ex 34:34	3068
words which the *L* hath commanded	Ex 35:1	3068
day, a sabbath of rest to the *L*	Ex 35:2	3068
the thing which the *L* commanded	Ex 35:4	3068
among you an offering unto the *L*	Ex 35:5	3068
bring it, an offering of the *L*	Ex 35:5	3068
all that the *L* hath commanded	Ex 35:10	3068
an offering of gold unto the *L*	Ex 35:22	3068
a willing offering unto the *L*	Ex 35:29	3068
which the *L* had commanded to be	Ex 35:29	3068
the *L* hath called by name	Ex 35:30	3068
man, in whom the *L* put wisdom	Ex 36:1	3068
to all that the *L* had commanded	Ex 36:1	3068
whose heart the *L* had put wisdom	Ex 36:2	3068
which the *L* commanded to make	Ex 36:5	3068
all that the *L* commanded Moses	Ex 38:22	3068
as the *L* commanded Moses	Ex 39:1	3068
as the *L* commanded Moses	Ex 39:5	3068
as the *L* commanded Moses	Ex 39:7	3068
as the *L* commanded Moses	Ex 39:21	3068
as the *L* commanded Moses	Ex 39:26	3068
as the *L* commanded Moses	Ex 39:29	3068
of a signet, HOLINESS TO THE *L*	Ex 39:30	3068
as the *L* commanded Moses	Ex 39:31	3068
to all that the *L* commanded Moses	Ex 39:32	3068
to all that the *L* commanded Moses	Ex 39:42	3068
done it as the *L* had commanded	Ex 39:43	3068
the *L* spake unto Moses, saying,	Ex 40:1	3068
to all that the *L* commanded him	Ex 40:16	3068
as the *L* commanded Moses	Ex 40:19	3068
as the *L* commanded Moses	Ex 40:21	3068
in order upon it before the *L*	Ex 40:23	3068
as the *L* had commanded Moses	Ex 40:23	3068
he lighted the lamps before the *L*	Ex 40:25	3068
as the *L* commanded Moses	Ex 40:25	3068
as the *L* commanded Moses	Ex 40:27	3068
as the *L* commanded Moses	Ex 40:29	3068
as the *L* commanded Moses	Ex 40:32	3068
the glory of the *L* filled the	Ex 40:34	3068
the glory of the *L* filled the	Ex 40:35	3068
For the cloud of the *L* was upon	Ex 40:38	3068
the *L* called unto Moses, and spake	Lev 1:1	3068
you bring an offering unto the *L*	Lev 1:2	3068
of the congregation before the *L*	Lev 1:3	3068
kill the bullock before the *L*	Lev 1:5	3068
of a sweet savour unto the *L*	Lev 1:9	3068

the altar northward before the *L*	Lev 1:11	3068
of a sweet savour unto the *L*	Lev 1:13	3068
his offering to the *L* be of fowls	Lev 1:14	3068
of a sweet savour unto the *L*	Lev 1:17	3068
offer a meat offering unto the *L*	Lev 2:1	3068
of a sweet savour unto the *L*	Lev 2:2	3068
offerings of the *L* made by fire	Lev 2:3	3068
made of these things unto the *L*	Lev 2:8	3068
of a sweet savour unto the *L*	Lev 2:9	3068
offerings of the *L* made by fire	Lev 2:10	3068
which ye shall bring unto the *L*	Lev 2:11	3068
offering of the *L* made by fire	Lev 2:11	3068
ye shall offer them unto the *L*	Lev 2:12	3068
of thy firstfruits unto the *L*	Lev 2:14	3068
offering made by fire unto the *L*	Lev 2:16	3068
it without blemish before the *L*	Lev 3:1	3068
offering made by fire unto the *L*	Lev 3:3	3068
of a sweet savour unto the *L*	Lev 3:5	3068
unto the *L* be of the flock	Lev 3:6	3068
shall he offer it before the *L*	Lev 3:7	3068
offering made by fire unto the *L*	Lev 3:9	3068
offering made by fire unto the *L*	Lev 3:11	3068
he shall offer it before the *L*	Lev 3:12	3068
offering made by fire unto the *L*	Lev 3:14	3068
the *L* spake unto Moses, saying,	Lev 4:1	3068
L concerning things which ought	Lev 4:2	3068
unto the *L* for a sin offering	Lev 4:3	3068
of the congregation before the *L*	Lev 4:4	3068
and kill the bullock before the *L*	Lev 4:4	3068
blood seven times before the *L*	Lev 4:6	3068
of sweet incense before the *L*	Lev 4:7	3068
L concerning things which should	Lev 4:13	3068
head of the bullock before the *L*	Lev 4:15	3068
shall be killed before the *L*	Lev 4:15	3068
it seven times before the *L*	Lev 4:17	3068
the altar which is before the *L*	Lev 4:18	3068
any of the commandments of the *L*	Lev 4:22	3068
the burnt offering before the *L*	Lev 4:24	3068
L concerning things which ought	Lev 4:27	3068
for a sweet savour unto the *L*	Lev 4:31	3068
offerings made by fire unto the *L*	Lev 4:35	3068
the *L* for his sin which he hath	Lev 5:6	3068
or two young pigeons, unto the *L*	Lev 5:7	3068
offerings made by fire unto the *L*	Lev 5:12	3068
the *L* spake unto Moses, saying,	Lev 5:14	3068
in the holy things of the *L*	Lev 5:15	3068
L a ram without blemish out of	Lev 5:15	3068
done by the commandments of the *L*	Lev 5:17	3068
trespassed against the *L*	Lev 5:19	3068
the *L* spake unto Moses, saying,	Lev 6:1	3068
commit a trespass against the *L*	Lev 6:2	3068
his trespass offering unto the *L*	Lev 6:6	3068
an atonement for him before the *L*	Lev 6:7	3068
the *L* spake unto Moses, saying,	Lev 6:8	3068
Aaron shall offer it before the *L*	Lev 6:14	3068
the memorial of it, unto the *L*	Lev 6:15	3068
offerings of the *L* made by fire	Lev 6:18	3068
the *L* spake unto Moses, saying,	Lev 6:19	3068
L in the day when he is anointed	Lev 6:20	3068
for a sweet savour unto the *L*	Lev 6:21	3068
is a statute for ever unto the *L*	Lev 6:22	3068
the *L* spake unto Moses, saying,	Lev 6:24	3068
offering be killed before the *L*	Lev 6:25	3068
offering made by fire unto the *L*	Lev 7:5	3068
which he shall offer unto the *L*	Lev 7:11	3068
for an heave offering unto the *L*	Lev 7:14	3068
that pertain unto the *L*, having	Lev 7:20	3068
which pertain unto the *L*	Lev 7:21	3068
the *L* spake unto Moses, saying,	Lev 7:22	3068
offering made by fire unto the *L*	Lev 7:25	3068
the *L* spake unto Moses, saying,	Lev 7:28	3068
L shall bring his oblation unto	Lev 7:29	3068
bring his oblation unto the *L* of	Lev 7:29	3068
offerings of the *L* made by fire	Lev 7:30	3068
for a wave offering before the *L*	Lev 7:30	3068
offerings of the *L* made by fire	Lev 7:35	3068
unto the *L* in the priest's office	Lev 7:35	3068
Which the *L* commanded to be given	Lev 7:36	3068
Which the *L* commanded Moses in	Lev 7:38	3068
offer their oblations unto the *L*	Lev 7:38	3068
the *L* spake unto Moses, saying,	Lev 8:1	3068
Moses did as the *L* commanded him	Lev 8:4	3068
which the *L* commanded to be done	Lev 8:5	3068
as the *L* commanded Moses	Lev 8:9	3068
as the *L* commanded Moses	Lev 8:13	3068
as the *L* commanded Moses	Lev 8:17	3068
offering made by fire unto the *L*	Lev 8:21	3068
as the *L* commanded Moses	Lev 8:21	3068
bread, that was before the *L*	Lev 8:26	3068
for a wave offering before the *L*	Lev 8:27	3068
offering made by fire unto the *L*	Lev 8:28	3068
for a wave offering before the *L*	Lev 8:29	3068
as the *L* commanded Moses	Lev 8:29	3068
so the *L* hath commanded to do, to	Lev 8:34	3068
days, and keep the charge of the *L*	Lev 8:35	3068
sons did all things which the *L*	Lev 8:36	3068
and offer them before the *L*	Lev 9:2	3068
to sacrifice before the *L*	Lev 9:4	3068
for to day the *L* will appear unto	Lev 9:4	3068
drew near and stood before the *L*	Lev 9:5	3068
the *L* commanded that ye should do	Lev 9:6	3068
the glory of the *L* shall appear	Lev 9:6	3068
as the *L* commanded	Lev 9:7	3068
as the *L* commanded Moses	Lev 9:10	3068
for a wave offering before the *L*	Lev 9:21	3068
the glory of the *L* appeared unto	Lev 9:23	3068
came a fire out from before the *L*	Lev 9:24	3068
offered strange fire before the *L*	Lev 10:1	3068
And there went out fire from the *L*	Lev 10:2	3068
them, and they died before the *L*	Lev 10:2	3068
This is it that the *L* spake	Lev 10:3	3068
burning which the *L* hath kindled	Lev 10:6	3068
oil of the *L* is upon you	Lev 10:7	3068
the *L* spake unto Aaron, saying,	Lev 10:8	3068
all the statutes which the *L* hath	Lev 10:11	3068
offerings of the *L* made by fire	Lev 10:12	3068
sacrifices of the *L* made by fire	Lev 10:13	3068
for a wave offering before the *L*	Lev 10:15	3068
as the *L* hath commanded	Lev 10:15	3068
atonement for them before the *L*	Lev 10:17	3068
their burnt offering before the *L*	Lev 10:19	3068
accepted in the sight of the *L*	Lev 10:19	3068
the *L* spake unto Moses and to	Lev 11:1	3068
For I am the *L* your God	Lev 11:44	3068
For I am the *L* that bringeth you	Lev 11:45	3068
the *L* spake unto Moses, saying,	Lev 12:1	3068
Who shall offer it before the *L*	Lev 12:7	3068
the *L* spake unto Moses and Aaron,	Lev 13:1	3068
the *L* spake unto Moses, saying,	Lev 14:1	3068
and those things, before the *L*	Lev 14:11	3068
for a wave offering before the *L*	Lev 14:12	3068
finger seven times before the *L*	Lev 14:16	3068
an atonement for him before the *L*	Lev 14:18	3068
of the congregation, before the *L*	Lev 14:23	3068
for a wave offering before the *L*	Lev 14:24	3068
hand seven times before the *L*	Lev 14:27	3068
an atonement for him before the *L*	Lev 14:29	3068
is to be cleansed before the *L*	Lev 14:31	3068
the *L* spake unto Moses and unto	Lev 14:33	3068
the *L* spake unto Moses and to	Lev 15:1	3068
come before the *L* unto the door	Lev 15:14	3068
him before the *L* for his issue	Lev 15:15	3068
before the *L* for the issue of her	Lev 15:30	3068
the *L* spake unto Moses after the	Lev 16:1	3068
when they offered before the *L*	Lev 16:1	3068
the *L* said unto Moses, Speak unto	Lev 16:2	3068
present them before the *L* at the	Lev 16:7	3068
one lot for the *L*, and the other	Lev 16:8	3068
be presented alive before the *L*	Lev 16:10	3068
from off the altar before the *L*	Lev 16:12	3068
upon the fire before the *L*	Lev 16:13	3068
the altar that is before the *L*	Lev 16:18	3068
from all your sins before the *L*	Lev 16:30	3068
he did as the *L* commanded Moses	Lev 16:34	3068
the *L* spake unto Moses, saying,	Lev 17:1	3068
thing which the *L* hath commanded	Lev 17:2	3068
L before the tabernacle of the	Lev 17:4	3068
before the tabernacle of the *L*	Lev 17:4	3068
they may bring them unto the *L*	Lev 17:5	3068
for peace offerings unto the *L*	Lev 17:5	3068
L at the door of the tabernacle	Lev 17:6	3068
fat for a sweet savour unto the *L*	Lev 17:6	3068
to offer it unto the *L*	Lev 17:9	3068
the *L* spake unto Moses, saying,	Lev 18:1	3068
unto them, I am the *L* your God	Lev 18:2	3068
I am the *L* your God	Lev 18:4	3068
I am the *L*	Lev 18:5	3068
I am the *L*	Lev 18:6	3068
I am the *L*	Lev 18:21	3068
I am the *L* your God	Lev 18:30	3068
the *L* spake unto Moses, saying,	Lev 19:1	3068
for I the *L* your God am holy	Lev 19:2	3068
I am the *L* your God	Lev 19:3	3068
I am the *L* your God	Lev 19:4	3068
of peace offerings unto the *L*	Lev 19:5	3068
the hallowed thing of the *L*	Lev 19:8	3068
I am the *L* your God	Lev 19:10	3068
I am the *L*	Lev 19:12	3068
I am the *L*	Lev 19:14	3068
I am the *L*	Lev 19:16	3068
I am the *L*	Lev 19:18	3068
his trespass offering unto the *L*	Lev 19:21	3068

L

trespass offering before the *L*	Lev 19:22	3068
be holy to praise the *L* withal	Lev 19:24	3068
I am the *L* your God	Lev 19:25	3068
I am the *L*	Lev 19:28	3068
I am the *L*	Lev 19:30	3068
I am the *L* your God	Lev 19:31	3068
I am the *L*	Lev 19:32	3068
I am the *L* your God	Lev 19:34	3068
I am the *L* your God, which	Lev 19:36	3068
I am the *L*	Lev 19:37	3068
the *L* spake unto Moses, saying,	Lev 20:1	3068
for I am the *L* your God	Lev 20:7	3068
I am the *L* which sanctify you	Lev 20:8	3068
I am the *L* your God, which have	Lev 20:24	3068
for I the *L* am holy, and have	Lev 20:26	3068
the *L* said unto Moses, Speak unto	Lev 21:1	3068
offerings of the *L* made by fire	Lev 21:6	3068
for I the *L*, which sanctify you,	Lev 21:8	3068
I am the *L*	Lev 21:12	3068
for I the *L* do sanctify him	Lev 21:15	3068
the *L* spake unto Moses, saying,	Lev 21:16	3068
offerings of the *L* made by fire	Lev 21:21	3068
for I the *L* do sanctify them	Lev 21:23	3068
the *L* spake unto Moses, saying,	Lev 22:1	3068
I am the *L*	Lev 22:2	3068
of Israel hallow unto the *L*	Lev 22:3	3068
I am the *L*	Lev 22:3	3068
I am the *L*	Lev 22:8	3068
I the *L* do sanctify them	Lev 22:9	3068
which they offer unto the *L*	Lev 22:15	3068
for I the *L* do sanctify them	Lev 22:16	3068
the *L* spake unto Moses, saying,	Lev 22:17	3068
unto the *L* for a burnt offering	Lev 22:18	3068
unto the *L* to accomplish his vow	Lev 22:21	3068
shall not offer these unto the *L*	Lev 22:22	3068
of them upon the altar unto the *L*	Lev 22:22	3068
unto the *L* that which is bruised	Lev 22:24	3068
the *L* spake unto Moses, saying,	Lev 22:26	3068
offering made by fire unto the *L*	Lev 22:27	3068
of thanksgiving unto the *L*	Lev 22:29	3068
I am the *L*	Lev 22:30	3068
I am the *L*	Lev 22:31	3068
I am the *L* which hallow you,	Lev 22:32	3068
I am the *L*	Lev 22:33	3068
the *L* spake unto Moses, saying,	Lev 23:1	3068
Concerning the feasts of the *L*	Lev 23:2	3068
of the *L* in all your dwellings	Lev 23:3	3068
These are the feasts of the *L*	Lev 23:4	3068
of unleavened bread unto the *L*	Lev 23:6	3068
by fire unto the *L* seven days	Lev 23:8	3068
the *L* spake unto Moses, saying,	Lev 23:9	3068
shall wave the sheaf before the *L*	Lev 23:11	3068
for a burnt offering unto the *L*	Lev 23:12	3068
unto the *L* for a sweet savour	Lev 23:13	3068
a new meat offering unto the *L*	Lev 23:16	3068
are the firstfruits unto the *L*	Lev 23:17	3068
for a burnt offering unto the *L*	Lev 23:18	3068
fire, of sweet savour unto the *L*	Lev 23:18	3068
for a wave offering before the *L*	Lev 23:20	3068
be holy to the *L* for the priest	Lev 23:20	3068
I am the *L* your God	Lev 23:22	3068
the *L* spake unto Moses, saying,	Lev 23:23	3068
offering made by fire unto the *L*	Lev 23:25	3068
the *L* spake unto Moses, saying,	Lev 23:26	3068
offering made by fire unto the *L*	Lev 23:27	3068
for you before the *L* your God	Lev 23:28	3068
the *L* spake unto Moses, saying,	Lev 23:33	3068
for seven days unto the *L*	Lev 23:34	3068
offering made by fire unto the *L*	Lev 23:36	3068
offering made by fire unto the *L*	Lev 23:36	3068
These are the feasts of the *L*	Lev 23:37	3068
offering made by fire unto the *L*	Lev 23:37	3068
Beside the sabbaths of the *L*	Lev 23:38	3068
which ye give unto the *L*	Lev 23:38	3068
a feast unto the *L* seven days	Lev 23:39	3068
before the *L* your God seven days	Lev 23:40	3068
unto the *L* seven days in the year	Lev 23:41	3068
I am the *L* your God	Lev 23:43	3068
of Israel the feasts of the *L*	Lev 23:44	3068
the *L* spake unto Moses, saying,	Lev 24:1	3068
morning before the *L* continually	Lev 24:3	3068
before the *L* continually	Lev 24:4	3068
upon the pure table before the *L*	Lev 24:6	3068
offering made by fire unto the *L*	Lev 24:7	3068
in order before the *L* continually	Lev 24:8	3068
the *L* made by fire by a perpetual	Lev 24:9	3068
son blasphemed the name of the *L*	Lev 24:11	3068
of the *L* might be shewed them	Lev 24:12	3068
the *L* spake unto Moses, saying,	Lev 24:13	3068
blasphemeth the name of the *L*	Lev 24:16	3068
he blasphemeth the name of the *L*	Lev 24:16	3068
for I am the *L* your God	Lev 24:22	3068
did as the *L* commanded Moses	Lev 24:23	3068
the *L* spake unto Moses in mount	Lev 25:1	3068
land keep a sabbath unto the *L*	Lev 25:2	3068
the land, a sabbath for the *L*	Lev 25:4	3068
for I am the *L* your God	Lev 25:17	3068
I am the *L* your God, which	Lev 25:38	3068
I am the *L* your God	Lev 25:55	3068
for I am the *L* your God	Lev 26:1	3068
I am the *L*	Lev 26:2	3068
I am the *L* your God, which	Lev 26:13	3068
for I am the *L* their God	Lev 26:44	3068
I am the *L*	Lev 26:45	3068
which the *L* made between him and	Lev 26:46	3068
the *L* spake unto Moses, saying,	Lev 27:1	3068
be for the *L* by thy estimation	Lev 27:2	3068
men bring an offering unto the *L*	Lev 27:9	3068
of such unto the *L* shall be holy	Lev 27:9	3068
not offer a sacrifice unto the *L*	Lev 27:11	3068
his house to be holy unto the *L*	Lev 27:14	3068
the *L* some part of a field of his	Lev 27:16	3068
jubile, shall be holy unto the *L*	Lev 27:21	3068
if a man sanctify unto the *L* a	Lev 27:22	3068
day, as a holy thing unto the *L*	Lev 27:23	3068
unto the *L* of all that he hath	Lev 27:28	3068
thing is most holy unto the *L*	Lev 27:28	3068
it is holy unto the *L*	Lev 27:30	3068
tenth shall be holy unto the *L*	Lev 27:32	3068
which the *L* commanded Moses for	Lev 27:34	3068
the *L* spake unto Moses in the	Num 1:1	3068
As the *L* commanded Moses, so he	Num 1:19	3068
For the *L* had spoken unto Moses,	Num 1:48	3068
to all that the *L* commanded Moses	Num 1:54	3068
the *L* spake unto Moses and unto	Num 2:1	3068
as the *L* commanded Moses	Num 2:33	3068
to all that the *L* commanded Moses	Num 2:34	3068
Moses in the day that the *L* spake	Num 3:1	3068
Nadab and Abihu died before the *L*	Num 3:4	3068
offered strange fire before the *L*	Num 3:4	3068
the *L* spake unto Moses, saying,	Num 3:5	3068
the *L* spake unto Moses, saying,	Num 3:11	3068
I am the *L*	Num 3:13	3068
the *L* spake unto Moses in the	Num 3:14	3068
according to the word of the *L*	Num 3:16	3068
at the commandment of the *L*	Num 3:39	3068
the *L* said unto Moses, Number all	Num 3:40	3068
the Levites for me (I am the *L*)	Num 3:41	3068
as the *L* commanded him, all the	Num 3:42	3068
the *L* spake unto Moses, saying,	Num 3:44	3068
I am the *L*	Num 3:45	3068
according to the word of the *L*	Num 3:51	3068
as the *L* commanded Moses	Num 3:51	3068
the *L* spake unto Moses and unto	Num 4:1	3068
the *L* spake unto Moses and unto	Num 4:17	3068
the *L* spake unto Moses, saying,	Num 4:21	3068
of the *L* by the hand of Moses	Num 4:37	3068
to the commandment of the *L*	Num 4:41	3068
of the *L* by the hand of Moses	Num 4:45	3068
to the commandment of the *L* they	Num 4:49	3068
of him, as the *L* commanded Moses	Num 4:49	3068
the *L* spake unto Moses, saying,	Num 5:1	3068
as the *L* spake unto Moses, so did	Num 5:4	3068
the *L* spake unto Moses, saying,	Num 5:5	3068
to do a trespass against the *L*	Num 5:6	3068
be recompensed unto the *L*	Num 5:8	3068
the *L* spake unto Moses, saying,	Num 5:11	3068
her near, and set her before the *L*	Num 5:16	3068
shall set the woman before the *L*	Num 5:18	3068
The *L* make thee a curse and an	Num 5:21	3068
when the *L* doth make thy thigh to	Num 5:21	3068
wave the offering before the *L*	Num 5:25	3068
shall set the woman before the *L*	Num 5:30	3068
the *L* spake unto Moses, saying,	Num 6:1	3068
to separate themselves unto the *L*	Num 6:2	3068
he separateth himself unto the *L*	Num 6:5	3068
L he shall come at no dead body	Num 6:6	3068
separation he is holy unto the *L*	Num 6:8	3068
the *L* the days of his separation	Num 6:12	3068
offer his offering unto the *L*	Num 6:14	3068
shall bring them before the *L*	Num 6:16	3068
of peace offerings unto the *L*	Num 6:17	3068
for a wave offering before the *L*	Num 6:20	3068
unto the *L* for his separation	Num 6:21	3068
the *L* spake unto Moses, saying,	Num 6:22	3068
The *L* bless thee, and keep thee	Num 6:24	3068
The *L* make his face shine upon	Num 6:25	3068
The *L* lift up his countenance	Num 6:26	3068
their offering before the *L*	Num 7:3	3068
the *L* spake unto Moses, saying,	Num 7:4	3068
the *L* said unto Moses, They shall	Num 7:11	3068
the *L* spake unto Moses, saying,	Num 8:1	3068

as the *L* commanded Moses	Num 8:3	3068
which the *L* had shewed Moses	Num 8:4	3068
the *L* spake unto Moses, saying,	Num 8:5	3068
bring the Levites before the *L*	Num 8:10	3068
offer the Levites before the *L*	Num 8:11	3068
may execute the service of the *L*	Num 8:11	3068
for a burnt offering, unto the *L*	Num 8:12	3068
them for an offering unto the *L*	Num 8:13	3068
according unto all that the *L*	Num 8:20	3068
them as an offering before the *L*	Num 8:21	3068
as the *L* had commanded Moses	Num 8:22	3068
the *L* spake unto Moses, saying,	Num 8:23	3068
the *L* spake unto Moses in the	Num 9:1	3068
to all that the *L* commanded Moses	Num 9:5	3068
not offer an offering of the *L* in	Num 9:7	3068
I will hear what the *L* will	Num 9:8	3068
the *L* spake unto Moses, saying,	Num 9:9	3068
keep the passover unto the *L*	Num 9:10	3068
of the *L* in his appointed season	Num 9:13	3068
will keep the passover unto the *L*	Num 9:14	3068
of the *L* the children of Israel	Num 9:18	3068
commandment of the *L* they pitched	Num 9:18	3068
Israel kept the charge of the *L*	Num 9:19	3068
the *L* they abode in their tents	Num 9:20	3068
of the *L* they journeyed	Num 9:20	3068
of the *L* they rested in the tents	Num 9:23	3068
of the *L* they journeyed	Num 9:23	3068
they kept the charge of the *L*	Num 9:23	3068
of the *L* by the hand of Moses	Num 9:23	3068
the *L* spake unto Moses, saying,	Num 10:1	3068
remembered before the *L* your God	Num 10:9	3068
I am the *L* your God	Num 10:10	3068
of the *L* by the hand of Moses	Num 10:13	3068
the place of which the *L* said	Num 10:29	3068
for the *L* hath spoken good	Num 10:29	3068
goodness the *L* shall do unto us	Num 10:32	3068
of the *L* three days' journey	Num 10:33	3068
L went before them in the three	Num 10:33	3068
the cloud of the *L* was upon them	Num 10:34	3068
that Moses said, Rise up, *L*	Num 10:35	3068
it rested, he said, Return, O *L*	Num 10:36	3068
complained, it displeased the *L*	Num 11:1	3068
and the *L* heard it	Num 11:1	3068
the fire of the *L* burnt among	Num 11:1	3068
and when Moses prayed unto the *L*	Num 11:2	3068
fire of the *L* burnt among them	Num 11:3	3068
the anger of the *L* was kindled	Num 11:10	3068
And Moses said unto the *L*,	Num 11:11	3068
the *L* said unto Moses, Gather	Num 11:16	3068
ye have wept in the ears of the *L*	Num 11:18	3068
therefore the *L* will give you	Num 11:18	3068
despised the *L* which is among you	Num 11:20	3068
the *L* said unto Moses, Is the	Num 11:23	3068
the people the words of the *L*	Num 11:24	3068
the *L* came down in a cloud, and	Num 11:25	3068
that the *L* would put his spirit	Num 11:29	3068
went forth a wind from the *L*	Num 11:31	3068
the wrath of the *L* was kindled	Num 11:33	3068
the *L* smote the people with a	Num 11:33	3068
Hath the *L* indeed spoken only by	Num 12:2	3068
And the *L* heard it	Num 12:2	3068
the *L* spake suddenly unto Moses,	Num 12:4	3068
the *L* came down in the pillar of	Num 12:5	3068
I the *L* will make myself known	Num 12:6	3068
of the *L* shall he behold	Num 12:8	3068
the anger of the *L* was kindled	Num 12:9	3068
And Moses cried unto the *L*	Num 12:13	3068
the *L* said unto Moses, If her	Num 12:14	3068
the *L* spake unto Moses, saying,	Num 13:1	3068
L sent them from the wilderness	Num 13:3	3068
wherefore hath the *L* brought us	Num 14:3	3068
If the *L* delight in us, then he	Num 14:8	3068
Only rebel not ye against the *L*	Num 14:9	3068
from them, and the *L* is with us	Num 14:9	3068
the glory of the *L* appeared in	Num 14:10	3068
the *L* said unto Moses, How long	Num 14:11	3068
And Moses said unto the *L*, Then	Num 14:13	3068
that thou *L* art among this people	Num 14:14	3068
that thou *L* art seen face to face	Num 14:14	3068
Because the *L* was not able to	Num 14:16	3068
let the power of my *L* be great	Num 14:17	136
The *L* is longsuffering, and of	Num 14:18	3068
the *L* said, I have pardoned	Num 14:20	3068
be filled with the glory of the *L*	Num 14:21	3068
the *L* spake unto Moses and unto	Num 14:26	3068
As truly as I live, saith the *L*	Num 14:28	3068
I the *L* have said, I will surely	Num 14:35	3068
died by the plague before the *L*	Num 14:37	3068
place which the *L* hath promised	Num 14:40	3068
the commandment of the *L*	Num 14:41	3068
for the *L* is not among you	Num 14:42	3068
ye are turned away from the *L*	Num 14:43	3068
therefore the *L* will not be with	Num 14:43	3068
the ark of the covenant of the *L*	Num 14:44	3068
the *L* spake unto Moses, saying,	Num 15:1	3068
an offering by fire unto the *L*	Num 15:3	3068
to make a sweet savour unto the *L*	Num 15:3	3068
the *L* bring a meat offering of a	Num 15:4	3068
for a sweet savour unto the *L*	Num 15:7	3068
or peace offerings unto the *L*	Num 15:8	3068
of a sweet savour unto the *L*	Num 15:10	3068
of a sweet savour unto the *L*	Num 15:13	3068
of a sweet savour unto the *L*	Num 15:14	3068
the stranger be before the *L*	Num 15:15	3068
the *L* spake unto Moses, saying,	Num 15:17	3068
up an heave offering unto the *L*	Num 15:19	3068
the *L* an heave offering in your	Num 15:21	3068
which the *L* hath spoken unto	Num 15:22	3068
Even all that the *L* hath	Num 15:23	3068
day that the *L* commanded Moses	Num 15:23	3068
for a sweet savour unto the *L*	Num 15:24	3068
sacrifice made by fire unto the *L*	Num 15:25	3068
their sin offering before the *L*	Num 15:25	3068
sinneth by ignorance before the *L*	Num 15:28	3068
the same reproacheth the *L*	Num 15:30	3068
hath despised the word of the *L*	Num 15:31	3068
the *L* said unto Moses, The man	Num 15:35	3068
as the *L* commanded Moses	Num 15:36	3068
the *L* spake unto Moses, saying,	Num 15:37	3068
all the commandments of the *L*	Num 15:39	3068
I am the *L* your God, which	Num 15:41	3068
I am the *L* your God	Num 15:41	3068
of them, and the *L* is among them	Num 16:3	3068
above the congregation of the *L*	Num 16:3	3068
Even to morrow the *L* will shew	Num 16:5	3068
in them before the *L* to morrow	Num 16:7	3068
the man whom the *L* doth choose	Num 16:7	3068
of the tabernacle of the *L*	Num 16:9	3068
gathered together against the *L*	Num 16:11	3068
very wroth, and said unto the *L*	Num 16:15	3068
and all thy company before the *L*	Num 16:16	3068
bring ye before the *L* every man	Num 16:17	3068
the glory of the *L* appeared unto	Num 16:19	3068
the *L* spake unto Moses and unto	Num 16:20	3068
the *L* spake unto Moses, saying,	Num 16:23	3068
L hath sent me to do all these	Num 16:28	3068
then the *L* hath not sent me	Num 16:29	3068
But if the *L* make a new thing, and	Num 16:30	3068
these men have provoked the *L*	Num 16:30	3068
there came out a fire from the *L*	Num 16:35	3068
the *L* spake unto Moses, saying,	Num 16:36	3068
they offered them before the *L*	Num 16:38	3068
to offer incense before the *L*	Num 16:40	3068
as the *L* said to him by the hand	Num 16:40	3068
have killed the people of the *L*	Num 16:41	3068
and the glory of the *L* appeared	Num 16:42	3068
the *L* spake unto Moses, saying,	Num 16:44	3068
is wrath gone out from the *L*	Num 16:46	3068
the *L* spake unto Moses, saying,	Num 17:1	3068
laid up the rods before the *L* in	Num 17:7	3068
all the rods from before the *L*	Num 17:9	3068
the *L* said unto Moses, Bring	Num 17:10	3068
as the *L* commanded him, so did he	Num 17:11	3068
the tabernacle of the *L* shall die	Num 17:13	3068
the *L* said unto Aaron, Thou and	Num 18:1	3068
are given as a gift for the *L*	Num 18:6	3068
the *L* spake unto Aaron, Behold, I	Num 18:8	3068
which they shall offer unto the *L*	Num 18:12	3068
which they shall bring unto the *L*	Num 18:13	3068
which they bring unto the *L*	Num 18:15	3068
for a sweet savour unto the *L*	Num 18:17	3068
of Israel offer unto the *L*	Num 18:19	3068
for ever before the *L* unto thee	Num 18:19	3068
the *L* spake unto Aaron, Thou	Num 18:20	3068
as an heave offering unto the *L*	Num 18:24	3068
the *L* spake unto Moses, saying,	Num 18:25	3068
an heave offering of it for the *L*	Num 18:26	3068
unto the *L* of all your tithes	Num 18:28	3068
every heave offering of the *L*	Num 18:29	3068
the *L* spake unto Moses and unto	Num 19:1	3068
law which the *L* hath commanded	Num 19:2	3068
defileth the tabernacle of the *L*	Num 19:13	3068
defiled the sanctuary of the *L*	Num 19:20	3068
our brethren died before the *L*	Num 20:3	3068
of the *L* into this wilderness	Num 20:4	3068
the glory of the *L* appeared	Num 20:6	3068
the *L* spake unto Moses, saying,	Num 20:7	3068
took the rod from before the *L*	Num 20:9	3068
the *L* spake unto Moses and Aaron,	Num 20:12	3068
of Israel strove with the *L*	Num 20:13	3068
And when we cried unto the *L*	Num 20:16	3068
the *L* spake unto Moses and Aaron	Num 20:23	3068

L

And Moses did as the L commanded	Num 20:27	3068
And Israel vowed a vow unto the L	Num 21:2	3068
the L hearkened to the voice of	Num 21:3	3068
the L sent fiery serpents among..............	Num 21:6	3068
for we have spoken against the L	Num 21:7	3068
pray unto the L, that he take	Num 21:7	3068
the L said unto Moses, Make thee	Num 21:8	3068
in the book of the wars of the L	Num 21:14	3068
whereof the L spake unto Moses	Num 21:16	3068
the L said unto Moses, Fear him	Num 21:34	3068
as the L shall speak unto me	Num 22:8	3068
for the L refuseth to give me	Num 22:13	3068
beyond the word of the L my God	Num 22:18	3068
what the L will say unto me more	Num 22:19	3068
the angel of the L stood in the	Num 22:22	3068
of the L standing in the way	Num 22:23	3068
But the angel of the L stood in a	Num 22:24	3068
the ass saw the angel of the L	Num 22:25	3068
the angel of the L went further	Num 22:26	3068
the ass saw the angel of the L	Num 22:27	3068
the L opened the mouth of the ass	Num 22:28	3068
Then the L opened the eyes of	Num 22:31	3068
of the L standing in the way	Num 22:31	3068
the angel of the L said unto him...........	Num 22:32	3068
said unto the angel of the L	Num 22:34	3068
angel of the L said unto Balaam	Num 22:35	3068
peradventure the L will come to	Num 23:3	3068
the L put a word in Balaam's.................	Num 23:5	3068
whom the L hath not defied	Num 23:8	3068
which the L hath put in my mouth........	Num 23:12	3068
while I meet the L yonder	Num 23:15	
the L met Balaam, and put a word........	Num 23:16	3068
unto him, What hath the L spoken	Num 23:17	3068
the L his God is with him, and the	Num 23:21	3068
saying, All that the L speaketh..............	Num 23:26	3068
it pleased the L to bless Israel..............	Num 24:1	3068
aloes which the L hath planted	Num 24:6	3068
the L hath kept thee back from	Num 24:11	3068
beyond the commandment of the L	Num 24:13	3068
but what the L saith, that will I	Num 24:13	3068
the anger of the L was kindled	Num 25:3	3068
the L said unto Moses, Take all	Num 25:4	3068
up before the L against the sun	Num 25:4	3068
that the fierce anger of the L	Num 25:4	3068
the L spake unto Moses, saying, ...	Num 25:10	3068
the L spake unto Moses, saying, ...	Num 25:16	3068
that the L spake unto Moses and	Num 26:1	3068
as the L commanded Moses and the	Num 26:4	3068
when they strove against the L.............	Num 26:9	3068
the L spake unto Moses, saying, ...	Num 26:52	3068
offered strange fire before the L	Num 26:61	3068
For the L had said of them, They	Num 26:65	3068
the L in the company of Korah	Num 27:3	3068
brought their cause before the L	Num 27:5	3068
the L spake unto Moses, saying, ...	Num 27:6	3068
as the L commanded Moses....................	Num 27:11	3068
the L said unto Moses, Get thee	Num 27:12	3068
And Moses spake unto the L..................	Num 27:15	3068
Let the L, the God of the spirits	Num 27:16	3068
that the congregation of the L be	Num 27:17	3068
the L said unto Moses, Take thee	Num 27:18	3068
the judgment of Urim before the L..........	Num 27:21	3068
Moses did as the L commanded him......	Num 27:22	3068
as the L commanded by the hand of	Num 27:23	3068
the L spake unto Moses, saying, ...	Num 28:1	3068
which ye shall offer unto the L..............	Num 28:3	3068
sacrifice made by fire unto the L	Num 28:6	3068
unto the L for a drink offering	Num 28:7	3068
of a sweet savour unto the L	Num 28:8	3068
offer a burnt offering unto the L	Num 28:11	3068
sacrifice made by fire unto the L	Num 28:13	3068
unto the L shall be offered	Num 28:15	3068
month is the passover of the L	Num 28:16	3068
for a burnt offering unto the L	Num 28:19	3068
of a sweet savour unto the L	Num 28:24	3068
a new meat offering unto the L	Num 28:26	3068
for a sweet savour unto the L................	Num 28:27	3068
for a sweet savour unto the L................	Num 29:2	3068
sacrifice made by fire unto the L...........	Num 29:6	3068
unto the L for a sweet savour................	Num 29:8	3068
a feast unto the L seven days	Num 29:12	3068
of a sweet savour unto the L	Num 29:13	3068
of a sweet savour unto the L	Num 29:36	3068
do unto the L in your set feasts	Num 29:39	3068
to all that the L commanded Moses.......	Num 29:40	3068
thing which the L hath commanded	Num 30:1	3068
If a man vow a vow unto the L	Num 30:2	3068
a woman also vow a vow unto the L	Num 30:3	3068
the L shall forgive her, because	Num 30:5	3068
and the L shall forgive her	Num 30:8	3068
and the L shall forgive her	Num 30:12	3068
which the L commanded Moses,............	Num 30:16	3068
the L spake unto Moses, saying, ...	Num 31:1	3068
and avenge the L of Midian	Num 31:3	3068
as the L commanded Moses...................	Num 31:7	3068
the L in the matter of Peor	Num 31:16	3068
among the congregation of the L	Num 31:16	3068
law which the L commanded Moses	Num 31:21	3068
the L spake unto Moses, saying, ...	Num 31:25	3068
levy a tribute unto the L of the	Num 31:28	3068
for an heave offering of the L	Num 31:29	3068
charge of the tabernacle of the L..........	Num 31:30	3068
did as the L commanded Moses	Num 31:31	3068
priest, as the L commanded Moses	Num 31:41	3068
charge of the tabernacle of the L..........	Num 31:47	3068
as the L commanded Moses...................	Num 31:47	3068
brought an oblation for the L	Num 31:50	3068
for our souls before the L	Num 31:50	3068
that they offered up to the L	Num 31:52	3068
children of Israel before the L..............	Num 31:54	3068
Even the country which the L	Num 32:4	3068
land which the L hath given them.........	Num 32:7	3068
land which the L had given them	Num 32:9	3068
they have wholly followed the L	Num 32:12	3068
done evil in the sight of the L...............	Num 32:13	3068
anger of the L toward Israel..................	Num 32:14	3068
will go armed before the L to war	Num 32:20	3068
armed over Jordan before the L.............	Num 32:21	3068
the land be subdued before the L	Num 32:22	3068
and be guiltless before the L	Num 32:22	3068
be your possession before the L	Num 32:22	3068
ye have sinned against the L	Num 32:23	3068
for war, before the L to battle	Num 32:27	3068
man armed to battle, before the L.........	Num 32:29	3068
As the L hath said unto thy	Num 32:31	3068
the L into the land of Canaan	Num 32:32	3068
by the commandment of the L	Num 33:2	3068
which the L had smitten among	Num 33:4	3068
also the L executed judgments	Num 33:4	3068
Hor at the commandment of the L.........	Num 33:38	3068
the L spake unto Moses in the	Num 33:50	3068
the L spake unto Moses, saying, ...	Num 34:1	3068
which the L commanded to give	Num 34:13	3068
the L spake unto Moses, saying, ...	Num 34:16	3068
the L commanded to divide the	Num 34:29	3068
the L spake unto Moses in the	Num 35:1	3068
the L spake unto Moses, saying, ...	Num 35:9	3068
for I the L dwell among the	Num 35:34	3068
The L commanded my l to give	Num 36:2	3068
was commanded by the L to give	Num 36:2	3068
according to the word of the L..............	Num 36:5	3068
the L doth command concerning the	Num 36:6	3068
Even as the L commanded Moses, so	Num 36:10	3068
which the L commanded by the hand	Num 36:13	3068
according unto all that the L had..........	Deut 1:3	3068
The L our God spake unto us in	Deut 1:6	3068
the L sware unto your fathers	Deut 1:8	3068
The L your God hath multiplied	Deut 1:10	3068
(The L God of your fathers make	Deut 1:11	3068
as the L our God commanded us	Deut 1:19	3068
which the L our God doth give	Deut 1:20	3068
the L thy God hath set the land	Deut 1:21	3068
as the L God of thy fathers hath............	Deut 1:21	3068
which the L our God doth give us	Deut 1:25	3068
the commandment of the L your God.....	Deut 1:26	3068
and said, Because the L hated us..........	Deut 1:27	3068
The L your God which goeth before	Deut 1:30	3068
how that the L thy God bare thee	Deut 1:31	3068
ye did not believe the L your God	Deut 1:32	3068
the L heard the voice of your	Deut 1:34	3068
he hath wholly followed the L	Deut 1:36	3068
Also the L was angry with me for	Deut 1:37	3068
me, We have sinned against the L	Deut 1:41	3068
that the L our God commanded us	Deut 1:41	3068
the L said unto me, Say unto them........	Deut 1:42	3068
against the commandment of the L........	Deut 1:43	3068
ye returned and wept before the L	Deut 1:45	3068
but the L would not hearken to..............	Deut 1:45	3068
Red sea, as the L spake unto me	Deut 2:1	3068
the L spake unto me, saying, ...	Deut 2:2	3068
For the L thy God hath blessed	Deut 2:7	3068
these forty years the L thy God	Deut 2:7	3068
the L said unto me, Distress not	Deut 2:9	3068
which the L gave unto them...................	Deut 2:12	3068
host, as the L sware unto them..............	Deut 2:14	3068
hand of the L was against them	Deut 2:15	3068
That the L spake unto me, saying, ...	Deut 2:17	3068
but the L destroyed them before............	Deut 2:21	3068
which the L our God giveth us	Deut 2:29	3068
for the L thy God hardened his..............	Deut 2:30	3068
the L said unto me, Behold, I	Deut 2:31	3068
the L our God delivered him	Deut 2:33	3068

the *L* our God delivered all unto	Deut 2:36	3068
the *L* our God forbad us	Deut 2:37	3068
the *L* said unto me, Fear him not	Deut 3:2	3068
So the *L* our God delivered into	Deut 3:3	3068
The *L* your God hath given you	Deut 3:18	3068
Until the *L* have given rest unto	Deut 3:20	3068
L your God hath given them beyond	Deut 3:20	3068
eyes have seen all that the *L*	Deut 3:21	3068
so shall the *L* do unto all the	Deut 3:21	3068
for the *L* your God he shall fight	Deut 3:22	3068
And I besought the *L* at that time	Deut 3:23	3068
O *L* God, thou hast begun to shew	Deut 3:24	136
But the *L* was wroth with me for	Deut 3:26	3068
the *L* said unto me, Let it	Deut 3:26	3068
possess the land which the *L* God	Deut 4:1	3068
L your God which I command you	Deut 4:2	3068
the *L* did because of Baal-peor	Deut 4:3	3068
the *L* thy God hath destroyed them	Deut 4:3	3068
L your God are alive every one of	Deut 4:4	3068
even as the *L* my God commanded me	Deut 4:5	3068
as the *L* our God is in all things	Deut 4:7	3068
before the *L* thy God in Horeb	Deut 4:10	3068
when the *L* said unto me, Gather	Deut 4:10	3068
the *L* spake unto you out of the	Deut 4:12	3068
the *L* commanded me at that time	Deut 4:14	3068
L spake unto you in Horeb out of	Deut 4:15	3068
which the *L* thy God hath divided	Deut 4:19	3068
But the *L* hath taken you, and	Deut 4:20	3068
Furthermore the *L* was angry with	Deut 4:21	3068
which the *L* thy God giveth thee	Deut 4:21	3068
the covenant of the *L* your God	Deut 4:23	3068
thing, which the *L* thy God hath	Deut 4:23	3068
For the *L* thy God is a consuming	Deut 4:24	3068
in the sight of the *L* thy God	Deut 4:25	3068
the *L* shall scatter you among the	Deut 4:27	3068
whither the *L* shall lead you	Deut 4:27	3068
thou shalt seek the *L* thy God	Deut 4:29	3068
if thou turn to the *L* thy God	Deut 4:30	3068
(For the *L* thy God is a merciful	Deut 4:31	3068
according to all that the *L* your	Deut 4:34	3068
know that the *L* he is God	Deut 4:35	3068
that the *L* he is God in heaven	Deut 4:39	3068
which the *L* thy God giveth thee,	Deut 4:40	3068
The *L* our God made a covenant	Deut 5:2	3068
The *L* made not this covenant with	Deut 5:3	3068
The *L* talked with you face to	Deut 5:4	3068
(I stood between the *L* and you at	Deut 5:5	3068
to shew you the word of the *L*	Deut 5:5	3068
I am the *L* thy God, which brought	Deut 5:6	3068
for I the *L* thy God am a jealous	Deut 5:9	3068
the name of the *L* thy God in vain	Deut 5:11	3068
for the *L* will not hold him	Deut 5:11	3068
as the *L* thy God hath commanded	Deut 5:14	3068
is the sabbath of the *L* thy God	Deut 5:14	3068
that the *L* thy God brought thee	Deut 5:15	3068
therefore the *L* thy God commanded	Deut 5:15	3068
as the *L* thy God hath commanded	Deut 5:16	3068
which the *L* thy God giveth thee	Deut 5:16	3068
These words the *L* spake unto all	Deut 5:22	3068
the *L* our God hath shewed us his	Deut 5:24	3068
voice of the *L* our God any more	Deut 5:25	3068
all that the *L* our God shall say	Deut 5:27	3068
L our God shall speak unto thee	Deut 5:27	3068
the *L* heard the voice of your	Deut 5:28	3068
the *L* said unto me, I have heard	Deut 5:28	3068
the *L* your God hath commanded	Deut 5:32	3068
the *L* your God hath commanded you	Deut 5:33	3068
which the *L* your God commanded to	Deut 6:1	3068
thou mightest fear the *L* thy God	Deut 6:2	3068
as the *L* God of thy fathers hath	Deut 6:3	3068
The *L* our God is one *L*	Deut 6:4	3068
thou shalt love the *L* thy God	Deut 6:5	3068
when the *L* thy God shall have	Deut 6:10	3068
beware lest thou forget the *L*	Deut 6:12	3068
Thou shalt fear the *L* thy God	Deut 6:13	3068
(For the *L* thy God is a jealous	Deut 6:15	3068
you) lest the anger of the *L* thy	Deut 6:15	3068
Ye shall not tempt the *L* your God	Deut 6:16	3068
commandments of the *L* your God	Deut 6:17	3068
and good in the sight of the *L*	Deut 6:18	3068
the *L* sware unto thy fathers	Deut 6:18	3068
before thee, as the *L* hath spoken	Deut 6:19	3068
which the *L* our God hath	Deut 6:20	3068
the *L* brought us out of Egypt	Deut 6:21	3068
the *L* shewed signs and wonders,	Deut 6:22	3068
the *L* commanded us to do all	Deut 6:24	3068
statutes, to fear the *L* our God	Deut 6:24	3068
commandments before the *L* our God	Deut 6:25	3068
When the *L* thy God shall bring	Deut 7:1	3068
when the *L* thy God shall deliver	Deut 7:2	3068
of the *L* be kindled against you	Deut 7:4	3068
an holy people unto the *L* thy God	Deut 7:6	3068
the *L* thy God hath chosen thee to	Deut 7:6	3068
The *L* did not set his love upon	Deut 7:7	3068
But because the *L* lov'ed you	Deut 7:8	3068
hath the *L* brought you out with a	Deut 7:8	3068
Know therefore that the *L* thy God	Deut 7:9	3068
that the *L* thy God shall keep	Deut 7:12	3068
the *L* will take away from thee	Deut 7:15	3068
all the people which the *L* thy	Deut 7:16	3068
the *L* thy God did unto Pharaoh	Deut 7:18	3068
whereby the *L* thy God brought	Deut 7:19	3068
so shall the *L* thy God do unto	Deut 7:19	3068
Moreover the *L* thy God will send	Deut 7:20	3068
for the *L* thy God is among you, a	Deut 7:21	3068
the *L* thy God will put out those	Deut 7:22	3068
But the *L* thy God shall deliver	Deut 7:23	3068
an abomination to the *L* thy God	Deut 7:25	3068
the *L* sware unto your fathers	Deut 8:1	3068
L thy God led thee these forty	Deut 8:2	3068
the mouth of the *L* doth man live	Deut 8:3	3068
so the *L* thy God chasteneth thee	Deut 8:5	3068
the commandments of the *L* thy God	Deut 8:6	3068
For the *L* thy God bringeth thee	Deut 8:7	3068
then thou shalt bless the *L* thy	Deut 8:10	3068
thou forget not the *L* thy God	Deut 8:11	3068
up, and thou forget the *L* thy God	Deut 8:14	3068
thou shalt remember the *L* thy God	Deut 8:18	3068
do at all forget the *L* thy God	Deut 8:19	3068
As the nations which the *L*	Deut 8:20	3068
unto the voice of the *L* your God	Deut 8:20	3068
that the *L* thy God is he which	Deut 9:3	3068
as the *L* hath said unto thee	Deut 9:3	3068
after that the *L* thy God hath	Deut 9:4	3068
For my righteousness the *L* hath	Deut 9:4	3068
L doth drive them out from before	Deut 9:4	3068
the *L* thy God doth drive them out	Deut 9:5	3068
the *L* sware unto thy fathers	Deut 9:5	3068
that the *L* thy God giveth thee	Deut 9:6	3068
the *L* thy God to wrath in the	Deut 9:7	3068
been rebellious against the *L*	Deut 9:7	3068
Horeb ye provoked the *L* to wrath	Deut 9:8	3068
so that the *L* was angry with you	Deut 9:8	3068
which the *L* made with you	Deut 9:9	3068
the *L* delivered unto me two	Deut 9:10	3068
which the *L* spake with you in the	Deut 9:10	3068
that the *L* gave me the two tables	Deut 9:11	3068
the *L* said unto me, Arise, get	Deut 9:12	3068
Furthermore the *L* spake unto me	Deut 9:13	3068
had sinned against the *L* your God	Deut 9:16	3068
way which the *L* had commanded you	Deut 9:16	3068
And I fell down before the *L*	Deut 9:18	3068
wickedly in the sight of the *L*	Deut 9:18	3068
wherewith the *L* was wroth against	Deut 9:19	3068
But the *L* hearkened unto me at	Deut 9:19	3068
the *L* was very angry with Aaron	Deut 9:20	3068
ye provoked the *L* to wrath	Deut 9:22	3068
Likewise when the *L* sent you from	Deut 9:23	3068
the commandment of the *L* your God	Deut 9:23	3068
been rebellious against the *L*	Deut 9:24	3068
fell down before the *L* forty days	Deut 9:25	3068
because the *L* had said he would	Deut 9:25	3068
I prayed therefore unto the *L*	Deut 9:26	3068
O *L* God, destroy not thy people	Deut 9:26	136
Because the *L* was not able to	Deut 9:28	3068
At that time the *L* said unto me	Deut 10:1	3068
which the *L* spake unto you in the	Deut 10:4	3068
and the *L* gave them unto me	Deut 10:4	3068
they be, as the *L* commanded me	Deut 10:5	3068
At that time the *L* separated the	Deut 10:8	3068
the ark of the covenant of the *L*	Deut 10:8	3068
to stand before the *L* to minister	Deut 10:8	3068
the *L* is his inheritance,	Deut 10:9	3068
according as the *L* thy God	Deut 10:9	3068
the *L* hearkened unto me at that	Deut 10:10	3068
the *L* would not destroy thee	Deut 10:10	3068
the *L* said unto me, Arise, take	Deut 10:11	3068
what doth the *L* thy God require	Deut 10:12	3068
thee, but to fear the *L* thy God	Deut 10:12	3068
to serve the *L* thy God with all	Deut 10:12	3068
To keep the commandments of the *L*	Deut 10:13	3068
Only the *L* had a delight in thy	Deut 10:15	3068
For the *L* your God is God of gods	Deut 10:17	3068
L of lords, a great God, a mighty	Deut 10:17	113
Thou shalt fear the *L* thy God	Deut 10:20	3068
now the *L* thy God hath made thee	Deut 10:22	3068
thou shalt love the *L* thy God	Deut 11:1	3068
chastisement of the *L* your God	Deut 11:2	3068
how the *L* hath destroyed them	Deut 11:4	3068
great acts of the *L* which he did	Deut 11:7	3068
which the *L* sware unto your	Deut 11:9	3068
A land which the *L* thy God careth	Deut 11:12	3068

L

the eyes of the *L* thy God are	Deut 11:12	3068
this day, to love the *L* your God	Deut 11:13	3068
good land which the *L* giveth you	Deut 11:17	3068
in the land which the *L* sware	Deut 11:21	3068
do them, to love the *L* your God	Deut 11:22	3068
Then will the *L* drive out all	Deut 11:23	3068
for the *L* your God shall lay the	Deut 11:25	3068
commandments of the *L* your God	Deut 11:27	3068
commandments of the *L* your God	Deut 11:28	3068
when the *L* thy God hath brought	Deut 11:29	3068
which the *L* your God giveth you	Deut 11:31	3068
which the *L* God of thy fathers	Deut 12:1	3068
not do so unto the *L* your God	Deut 12:4	3068
L your God shall choose out of	Deut 12:5	3068
shall eat before the *L* your God	Deut 12:7	3068
wherein the *L* thy God hath	Deut 12:7	3068
which the *L* your God giveth you	Deut 12:9	3068
dwell in the land which the *L*	Deut 12:10	3068
shall be a place which the *L* your	Deut 12:11	3068
vows which ye vow unto the *L*	Deut 12:11	3068
rejoice before the *L* your God	Deut 12:12	3068
the *L* shall choose in one of thy	Deut 12:14	3068
to the blessing of the *L* thy God	Deut 12:15	3068
thou must eat them before the *L*	Deut 12:18	3068
which the *L* thy God shall choose	Deut 12:18	3068
the *L* thy God in all that thou	Deut 12:18	3068
When the *L* thy God shall enlarge	Deut 12:20	3068
If the place which the *L* thy God	Deut 12:21	3068
which the *L* hath given thee, as I	Deut 12:21	3068
is right in the sight of the *L*	Deut 12:25	3068
place which the *L* shall choose	Deut 12:26	3068
upon the altar of the *L* thy God	Deut 12:27	3068
upon the altar of the *L* thy God	Deut 12:27	3068
in the sight of the *L* thy God	Deut 12:28	3068
When the *L* thy God shall cut off	Deut 12:29	3068
not do so unto the *L* thy God	Deut 12:31	3068
for every abomination to the *L*	Deut 12:31	3068
for the *L* your God proveth you,	Deut 13:3	3068
to know whether ye love the *L*	Deut 13:3	3068
shall walk after the *L* your God	Deut 13:4	3068
turn you away from the *L* your God	Deut 13:5	3068
thee out of the way which the *L*	Deut 13:5	3068
thee away from the *L* thy God	Deut 13:10	3068
which the *L* thy God hath given	Deut 13:12	3068
every whit, for the *L* thy God	Deut 13:16	3068
that the *L* may turn from the	Deut 13:17	3068
to the voice of the *L* thy God	Deut 13:18	3068
in the eyes of the *L* thy God	Deut 13:18	3068
the children of the *L* your God	Deut 14:1	3068
an holy people unto the *L* thy God	Deut 14:2	3068
the *L* hath chosen thee to be a	Deut 14:2	3068
an holy people unto the *L* thy God	Deut 14:21	3068
shalt eat before the *L* thy God	Deut 14:23	3068
to fear the *L* thy God always	Deut 14:23	3068
which the *L* thy God shall choose	Deut 14:24	3068
when the *L* thy God hath blessed	Deut 14:24	3068
which the *L* thy God shall choose	Deut 14:25	3068
eat there before the *L* thy God	Deut 14:26	3068
that the *L* thy God may bless thee	Deut 14:29	3068
for the *L* shall greatly bless	Deut 15:4	3068
the *L* thy God giveth thee for an	Deut 15:4	3068
unto the voice of the *L* thy God	Deut 15:5	3068
For the *L* thy God blesseth thee,	Deut 15:6	3068
which the *L* thy God giveth thee	Deut 15:7	3068
and he cry unto the *L* against thee	Deut 15:9	3068
L thy God shall bless thee in all	Deut 15:10	3068
of that wherewith the *L* thy God	Deut 15:14	3068
the *L* thy God redeemed thee	Deut 15:15	3068
the *L* thy God shall bless thee in	Deut 15:18	3068
shalt sanctify unto the *L* thy God	Deut 15:19	3068
the *L* thy God year by year in the	Deut 15:20	3068
place which the *L* shall choose	Deut 15:20	3068
sacrifice it unto the *L* thy God	Deut 15:21	3068
the passover unto the *L* thy God	Deut 16:1	3068
for in the month of Abib the *L*	Deut 16:1	3068
the passover unto the *L* thy God	Deut 16:2	3068
in the place which the *L* shall	Deut 16:2	3068
which the *L* thy God giveth thee	Deut 16:5	3068
But at the place which the *L* thy	Deut 16:6	3068
which the *L* thy God shall choose	Deut 16:7	3068
solemn assembly to the *L* thy God	Deut 16:8	3068
the *L* thy God with a tribute of a	Deut 16:10	3068
shalt give unto the *L* thy God	Deut 16:10	
according as the *L* thy God hath	Deut 16:10	3068
rejoice before the *L* thy God	Deut 16:11	3068
in the place which the *L* thy God	Deut 16:11	3068
keep a solemn feast unto the *L*	Deut 16:15	3068
place which the *L* shall choose	Deut 16:15	3068
because the *L* thy God shall bless	Deut 16:15	3068
L thy God in the place which he	Deut 16:16	3068
not appear before the *L* empty	Deut 16:16	3068
to the blessing of the *L* thy God	Deut 16:17	3068
which the *L* thy God giveth thee,	Deut 16:18	3068
which the *L* thy God giveth thee	Deut 16:20	3068
unto the altar of the *L* thy God	Deut 16:21	3068
which the *L* thy God hateth	Deut 16:22	3068
unto the *L* thy God any bullock	Deut 17:1	3068
an abomination unto the *L* thy God	Deut 17:1	3068
which the *L* thy God giveth thee	Deut 17:2	3068
in the sight of the *L* thy God	Deut 17:2	3068
which the *L* thy God shall choose	Deut 17:8	3068
L shall choose shall shew thee	Deut 17:10	3068
there before the *L* thy God	Deut 17:12	3068
which the *L* thy God giveth thee	Deut 17:14	3068
whom the *L* thy God shall choose	Deut 17:15	3068
forasmuch as the *L* hath said unto	Deut 17:16	3068
may learn to fear the *L* his God	Deut 17:19	3068
offerings of the *L* made by fire	Deut 18:1	3068
the *L* is their inheritance, as he	Deut 18:2	3068
For the *L* thy God hath chosen him	Deut 18:5	3068
to minister in the name of the *L*	Deut 18:5	3068
place which the *L* shall choose	Deut 18:6	3068
in the name of the *L* his God	Deut 18:7	3068
which stand there before the *L*	Deut 18:7	3068
which the *L* thy God giveth thee	Deut 18:9	3068
are an abomination unto the *L*	Deut 18:12	3068
of these abominations the *L* thy	Deut 18:12	3068
be perfect with the *L* thy God	Deut 18:13	3068
the *L* thy God hath not suffered	Deut 18:14	3068
The *L* thy God will raise up unto	Deut 18:15	3068
L thy God in Horeb in the day of	Deut 18:16	3068
again the voice of the *L* my God	Deut 18:16	3068
the *L* said unto me, They have	Deut 18:17	3068
word which the *L* hath not spoken	Deut 18:21	3068
speaketh in the name of the *L*	Deut 18:22	3068
thing which the *L* hath not spoken	Deut 18:22	3068
When the *L* thy God hath cut off	Deut 19:1	3068
whose land the *L* thy God giveth	Deut 19:1	3068
which the *L* thy God giveth thee	Deut 19:2	3068
which the *L* thy God giveth thee	Deut 19:3	3068
if the *L* thy God enlarge thy	Deut 19:8	3068
this day, to love the *L* thy God	Deut 19:9	3068
which the *L* thy God giveth thee	Deut 19:10	3068
inherit in the land that the *L*	Deut 19:14	3068
is, shall stand before the *L*	Deut 19:17	3068
for the *L* thy God is with thee.	Deut 20:1	3068
For the *L* your God is he that	Deut 20:4	3068
when the *L* thy God hath delivered	Deut 20:13	3068
which the *L* thy God hath given	Deut 20:14	3068
which the *L* thy God doth give	Deut 20:16	3068
as the *L* thy God hath commanded	Deut 20:17	3068
ye sin against the *L* your God	Deut 20:18	3068
slain in the land which the *L* thy	Deut 21:1	3068
for them the *L* thy God hath	Deut 21:5	3068
and to bless in the name of the *L*	Deut 21:5	3068
Be merciful, O *L*, unto thy people	Deut 21:8	3068
is right in the sight of the *L*	Deut 21:9	3068
the *L* thy God hath delivered them	Deut 21:10	3068
which the *L* thy God giveth thee	Deut 21:23	3068
abomination unto the *L* thy God	Deut 22:5	3068
into the congregation of the *L*	Deut 23:1	3068
into the congregation of the *L*	Deut 23:2	3068
into the congregation of the *L*	Deut 23:2	3068
into the congregation of the *L*	Deut 23:3	3068
congregation of the *L* for ever	Deut 23:3	3068
Nevertheless the *L* thy God would	Deut 23:5	3068
but the *L* thy God turned the	Deut 23:5	3068
because the *L* thy God loved thee	Deut 23:5	3068
the *L* in their third generation	Deut 23:8	3068
For the *L* thy God walketh in the	Deut 23:14	3068
of the *L* thy God for any vow	Deut 23:18	3068
abomination unto the *L* thy God	Deut 23:18	3068
that the *L* thy God may bless thee	Deut 23:20	3068
vow a vow unto the *L* thy God	Deut 23:21	3068
for the *L* thy God will surely	Deut 23:21	3068
hast vowed unto the *L* thy God	Deut 23:23	3068
that is abomination before the *L*	Deut 24:4	3068
which the *L* thy God giveth thee	Deut 24:4	3068
Remember what the *L* thy God did	Deut 24:9	3068
unto thee before the *L* thy God	Deut 24:13	3068
he cry against thee unto the *L*	Deut 24:15	3068
the *L* thy God redeemed thee	Deut 24:18	3068
that the *L* thy God may bless thee	Deut 24:19	3068
which the *L* thy God giveth thee	Deut 25:15	3068
an abomination unto the *L* thy God	Deut 25:16	3068
when the *L* thy God hath given	Deut 25:19	3068
in the land which the *L* thy God	Deut 25:19	3068
the *L* thy God giveth thee for an	Deut 26:1	3068
that the *L* thy God giveth thee	Deut 26:2	3068
go unto the place which the *L* thy	Deut 26:2	3068
this day unto the *L* thy God	Deut 26:3	3068
L sware unto our fathers for to	Deut 26:3	3068

before the altar of the L thy God	Deut 26:4	3068
speak and say before the L thy God	Deut 26:5	3068
unto the L God of our fathers	Deut 26:7	3068
the L heard our voice, and looked	Deut 26:7	3068
the L brought us forth out of	Deut 26:8	3068
of the land, which thou, O L	Deut 26:10	3068
shalt set it before the L thy God	Deut 26:10	3068
and worship before the L thy God	Deut 26:10	3068
L thy God hath given unto thee	Deut 26:11	3068
shalt say before the L thy God	Deut 26:13	3068
to the voice of the L my God	Deut 26:14	3068
This day the L thy God hath	Deut 26:16	3068
the L this day to be thy God	Deut 26:17	3068
the L hath avouched thee this day	Deut 26:18	3068
an holy people unto the L thy God	Deut 26:19	3068
which the L thy God giveth thee	Deut 27:2	3068
which the L thy God giveth thee	Deut 27:3	3068
as the L God of thy fathers hath	Deut 27:3	3068
build an altar unto the L thy God	Deut 27:5	3068
of the L thy God of whole stones	Deut 27:6	3068
thereon unto the L thy God	Deut 27:6	3068
and rejoice before the L thy God	Deut 27:7	3068
the people of the L thy God	Deut 27:9	3068
obey the voice of the L thy God	Deut 27:10	3068
image, an abomination unto the L	Deut 27:15	3068
unto the voice of the L thy God	Deut 28:1	3068
that the L thy God will set thee	Deut 28:1	3068
unto the voice of the L thy God	Deut 28:2	3068
The L shall cause thine enemies	Deut 28:7	3068
The L shall command the blessing	Deut 28:8	3068
which the L thy God giveth thee	Deut 28:8	3068
The L shall establish thee an	Deut 28:9	3068
the commandments of the L thy God	Deut 28:9	3068
art called by the name of the L	Deut 28:10	3068
the L shall make thee plenteous	Deut 28:11	3068
in the land which the L sware	Deut 28:11	3068
The L shall open unto thee his	Deut 28:12	3068
the L shall make thee the head,	Deut 28:13	3068
the commandments of the L thy God	Deut 28:13	3068
unto the voice of the L thy God	Deut 28:15	3068
The L shall send upon thee	Deut 28:20	3068
The L shall make the pestilence	Deut 28:21	3068
The L shall smite thee with a	Deut 28:22	3068
The L shall make the rain of thy	Deut 28:24	3068
The L shall cause thee to be	Deut 28:25	3068
The L will smite thee with the	Deut 28:27	3068
The L shall smite thee with	Deut 28:28	3068
The L shall smite thee in the	Deut 28:35	3068
The L shall bring thee, and thy	Deut 28:36	3068
whither the L shall lead thee	Deut 28:37	3068
unto the voice of the L thy God	Deut 28:45	3068
not the L thy God with joyfulness	Deut 28:47	3068
the L shall send against thee	Deut 28:48	3068
The L shall bring a nation	Deut 28:49	3068
which the L thy God hath given	Deut 28:52	3068
which the L thy God hath given	Deut 28:53	3068
and fearful name, THE L THY GOD	Deut 28:58	3068
Then the L will make thy plagues	Deut 28:59	3068
them will the L bring upon thee,	Deut 28:61	3068
obey the voice of the L thy God	Deut 28:62	3068
that as the L rejoiced over you	Deut 28:63	3068
so the L will rejoice over you to	Deut 28:63	3068
the L shall scatter thee among	Deut 28:64	3068
but the L shall give thee there a	Deut 28:65	3068
the L shall bring thee into Egypt	Deut 28:68	3068
which the L commanded Moses to	Deut 29:1	3068
Ye have seen all that the L did	Deut 29:2	3068
Yet the L hath not given you an	Deut 29:4	3068
know that I am the L your God	Deut 29:6	3068
all of you before the L your God	Deut 29:10	3068
into covenant with the L thy God	Deut 29:12	3068
which the L thy God maketh with	Deut 29:12	3068
us this day before the L our God	Deut 29:15	3068
away this day from the L our God	Deut 29:18	3068
The L will not spare him	Deut 29:20	3068
but then the anger of the L	Deut 29:20	3068
the L shall blot out his name	Deut 29:20	3068
the L shall separate him unto	Deut 29:21	3068
which the L hath laid upon it	Deut 29:22	3068
which the L overthrew in his	Deut 29:23	3068
Wherefore hath the L done thus	Deut 29:24	3068
of the L God of their fathers	Deut 29:25	3068
the anger of the L was kindled	Deut 29:27	3068
the L rooted them out of their	Deut 29:28	3068
things belong unto the L our God	Deut 29:29	3068
whither the L thy God hath driven	Deut 30:1	3068
shalt return unto the L thy God	Deut 30:2	3068
That then the L thy God will turn	Deut 30:3	3068
whither the L thy God hath	Deut 30:3	3068
will the L thy God gather thee	Deut 30:4	3068
the L thy God will bring thee	Deut 30:5	3068
the L thy God will circumcise	Deut 30:6	3068
to love the L thy God with all	Deut 30:6	3068
the L thy God will put all these	Deut 30:7	3068
return and obey the voice of the L	Deut 30:8	3068
the L thy God will make thee	Deut 30:9	3068
for the L will again rejoice over	Deut 30:9	3068
unto the voice of the L thy God	Deut 30:10	3068
if thou turn unto the L thy God	Deut 30:10	3068
this day to love the L thy God	Deut 30:16	3068
the L thy God shall bless thee in	Deut 30:16	3068
thou mayest love the L thy God	Deut 30:20	3068
the L sware unto thy fathers	Deut 30:20	3068
also the L hath said unto me,	Deut 31:2	3068
The L thy God, he will go over	Deut 31:3	3068
before thee, as the L hath said	Deut 31:3	3068
the L shall do unto them as he	Deut 31:4	3068
the L shall give them up before	Deut 31:5	3068
for the L thy God, he it is that	Deut 31:6	3068
L hath sworn unto their fathers	Deut 31:7	3068
And the L, he it is that doth go	Deut 31:8	3068
the ark of the covenant of the L	Deut 31:9	3068
is come to appear before the L	Deut 31:11	3068
may learn, and fear the L your God	Deut 31:12	3068
and learn to fear the L your God	Deut 31:13	3068
the L said unto Moses, Behold,	Deut 31:14	3068
the L appeared in the tabernacle	Deut 31:15	3068
the L said unto Moses, Behold,	Deut 31:16	3068
the ark of the covenant of the L	Deut 31:25	3068
of the covenant of the L your God	Deut 31:26	3068
been rebellious against the L	Deut 31:27	3068
do evil in the sight of the L	Deut 31:29	3068
I will publish the name of the L	Deut 32:3	3068
Do ye thus requite the L, O	Deut 32:6	3068
So the L alone did lead him, and	Deut 32:12	3068
And when the L saw it, he abhorred	Deut 32:19	3068
the L hath not done all this	Deut 32:27	3068
them, and the L had shut them up	Deut 32:30	3068
For the L shall judge his people,	Deut 32:36	3068
the L spake unto Moses that	Deut 32:48	3068
The L came from Sinai, and rose up	Deut 33:2	3068
and he said, Hear, L, the voice of	Deut 33:7	3068
Bless, L, his substance, and	Deut 33:11	3068
The beloved of the L shall dwell	Deut 33:12	3068
the L shall cover him all the day	Deut 33:12	3068
Blessed of the L be his land	Deut 33:13	3068
he executed the justice of the L	Deut 33:21	3068
full with the blessing of the L	Deut 33:23	3068
thee, O people saved by the L	Deut 33:29	3068
the L shewed him all the land of	Deut 34:1	3068
the L said unto him, This is the	Deut 34:4	3068
So Moses the servant of the L	Deut 34:5	3068
according to the word of the L	Deut 34:5	3068
did as the L commanded Moses	Deut 34:9	3068
whom the L knew face to face,	Deut 34:10	3068
which the L sent him to do in the	Deut 34:11	3068
servant of the L it came to pass	Josh 1:1	3068
that the L spake unto Joshua the	Josh 1:1	3068
for the L thy God is with thee	Josh 1:9	3068
which the L your God giveth you	Josh 1:11	3068
servant of the L commanded you	Josh 1:13	3068
The L your God hath given you	Josh 1:13	3068
Until the L have given your	Josh 1:15	3068
which the L your God giveth them	Josh 1:15	3068
only the L thy God be with thee,	Josh 1:17	3068
I know that the L hath given you	Josh 2:9	3068
For we have heard how the L dried	Josh 2:10	3068
for the L your God, he is God in	Josh 2:11	3068
pray you, swear unto me by the L	Josh 2:12	3068
when the L hath given us the land	Josh 2:14	3068
Truly the L hath delivered into	Josh 2:24	3068
of the covenant of the L your God	Josh 3:3	3068
for to morrow the L will do	Josh 3:5	3068
the L said unto Joshua, This day	Josh 3:7	3068
hear the words of the L your God	Josh 3:9	3068
L of all the earth passeth over	Josh 3:11	113
that bear the ark of the L	Josh 3:13	3068
the L of all the earth, shall	Josh 3:13	113
the ark of the covenant of the L	Josh 3:17	3068
that the L spake unto Joshua,	Josh 4:1	3068
the L your God into the midst of	Josh 4:5	3068
the ark of the covenant of the L	Josh 4:7	3068
as the L spake unto Joshua,	Josh 4:8	3068
thing was finished that the L	Josh 4:10	3068
that the ark of the L passed over	Josh 4:11	3068
over before the L unto battle	Josh 4:13	3068
On that day the L magnified	Josh 4:14	3068
the L spake unto Joshua, saying,	Josh 4:15	3068
L were come up out of the midst	Josh 4:18	3068
For the L your God dried up the	Josh 4:23	3068
as the L your God did to the Red	Josh 4:23	3068
might know the hand of the L	Josh 4:24	3068

L

fear the *L* your God for ever	Josh 4:24	3068
heard that the *L* had dried up the	Josh 5:1	3068
that time the *L* said unto Joshua	Josh 5:2	3068
obeyed not the voice of the *L*	Josh 5:6	3068
unto whom the *L* sware that he	Josh 5:6	3068
which the *L* sware unto their	Josh 5:6	3068
the *L* said unto Joshua, This day	Josh 5:9	3068
the host of the *L* am I now come	Josh 5:14	113
What saith my *l* unto his servant	Josh 5:14	3068
the *L* said unto Joshua, See, I	Josh 6:2	3068
horns before the ark of the *L*	Josh 6:6	3068
pass on before the ark of the *L*	Josh 6:7	3068
horns passed on before the *L*	Josh 6:8	3068
covenant of the *L* followed them	Josh 6:8	3068
So the ark of the *L* compassed the	Josh 6:11	3068
priests took up the ark of the *L*	Josh 6:12	3068
ark of the *L* went on continually	Josh 6:13	3068
came after the ark of the *L*	Josh 6:13	3068
for the *L* hath given you the city	Josh 6:16	3068
and all that are therein, to the *L*	Josh 6:17	3068
iron, are consecrated unto the *L*	Josh 6:19	3068
come into the treasury of the *L*	Josh 6:19	3068
treasury of the house of the *L*	Josh 6:24	3068
Cursed be the man before the *L*	Josh 6:26	3068
So the *L* was with Joshua	Josh 6:27	3068
the anger of the *L* was kindled	Josh 7:1	3068
ark of the *L* until the eventide	Josh 7:6	3068
O *L* GOD, wherefore hast thou at	Josh 7:7	136
O *L*, what shall I say, when	Josh 7:8	136
the *L* said unto Joshua, Get thee	Josh 7:10	3068
thus saith the *L* God of Israel	Josh 7:13	3068
that the tribe which the *L* taketh	Josh 7:14	3068
the family which the *L* shall take	Josh 7:14	3068
the household which the *L* shall	Josh 7:14	3068
the covenant of the *L*, and because	Josh 7:15	3068
glory to the *L* God of Israel, and	Josh 7:19	3068
against the *L* God of Israel	Josh 7:20	3068
and laid them out before the *L*	Josh 7:23	3068
the *L* shall trouble thee this day	Josh 7:25	3068
So the *L* turned from the	Josh 7:26	3068
the *L* said unto Joshua, Fear not,	Josh 8:1	3068
for the *L* your God will deliver	Josh 8:7	3068
commandment of the *L* shall ye do	Josh 8:8	3068
the *L* said unto Joshua, Stretch	Josh 8:18	3068
the *L* which he commanded Joshua	Josh 8:27	3068
the *L* God of Israel in mount Ebal	Josh 8:30	3068
the *L* commanded the children of	Josh 8:31	3068
burnt offerings unto the *L*	Josh 8:31	3068
the ark of the covenant of the *L*	Josh 8:33	3068
of the *L* had commanded before	Josh 8:33	3068
of the name of the *L* thy God	Josh 9:9	3068
not counsel at the mouth of the *L*	Josh 9:14	3068
unto them by the *L* God of Israel	Josh 9:18	3068
unto them by the *L* God of Israel	Josh 9:19	3068
how that the *L* thy God commanded	Josh 9:24	3068
and for the altar of the *L*	Josh 9:27	3068
the *L* said unto Joshua, Fear them	Josh 10:8	3068
the *L* discomfited them before	Josh 10:10	3068
that the *L* cast down great stones	Josh 10:11	3068
to the *L* in the day when the *L*	Josh 10:12	3068
that the *L* hearkened unto the	Josh 10:14	3068
for the *L* fought for Israel	Josh 10:14	3068
for the *L* your God hath delivered	Josh 10:19	3068
for thus shall the *L* do to all	Josh 10:25	3068
the *L* delivered it also, and the	Josh 10:30	3068
the *L* delivered Lachish into the	Josh 10:32	3068
as the *L* God of Israel commanded	Josh 10:40	3068
because the *L* God of Israel	Josh 10:42	3068
the *L* said unto Joshua, Be not	Josh 11:6	3068
the *L* delivered them into the	Josh 11:8	3068
did unto them as the *L* bade him	Josh 11:9	3068
the servant of the *L* commanded	Josh 11:12	3068
As the *L* commanded Moses his	Josh 11:15	3068
of all that the *L* commanded Moses	Josh 11:15	3068
For it was of the *L* to harden	Josh 11:20	3068
them, as the *L* commanded Moses	Josh 11:20	3068
to all that the *L* said unto Moses	Josh 11:23	3068
did Moses the servant of the *L*	Josh 12:6	3068
Moses the servant of the *L* gave	Josh 12:6	3068
the *L* said unto him, Thou art old	Josh 13:1	3068
the servant of the *L* gave them	Josh 13:8	3068
the sacrifices of the *L* God of	Josh 13:14	3068
the *L* God of Israel was their	Josh 13:33	3068
as the *L* commanded by the hand of	Josh 14:2	3068
As the *L* commanded Moses, so the	Josh 14:5	3068
L said unto Moses the man of God	Josh 14:6	3068
L sent me from Kadesh-barnea to	Josh 14:7	3068
I wholly followed the *L* my God	Josh 14:8	3068
hast wholly followed the *L* my God	Josh 14:9	3068
the *L* hath kept me alive, as he	Josh 14:10	3068
even since the *L* spake this word	Josh 14:10	3068
whereof the *L* spake in that day	Josh 14:12	3068
if so be the *L* will be with me,	Josh 14:12	3068
to drive them out, as the *L* said	Josh 14:12	3068
followed the *L* God of Israel	Josh 14:14	3068
commandment of the *L* to Joshua	Josh 15:13	3068
The *L* commanded Moses to give us	Josh 17:4	3068
to the commandment of the *L* he	Josh 17:4	3068
forasmuch as the *L* hath blessed	Josh 17:14	3068
which the *L* God of your fathers	Josh 18:3	3068
for you here before the *L* our God	Josh 18:6	3068
of the *L* is their inheritance	Josh 18:7	3068
the servant of the *L* gave them	Josh 18:7	3068
for you before the *L* in Shiloh	Josh 18:8	3068
for them in Shiloh before the *L*	Josh 18:10	3068
According to the word of the *L*	Josh 19:50	3068
by lot in Shiloh before the *L*	Josh 19:51	3068
The *L* also spake unto Joshua,	Josh 20:1	3068
The *L* commanded by the hand of	Josh 21:2	3068
at the commandment of the *L*	Josh 21:3	3068
as the *L* commanded by the hand of	Josh 21:8	3068
the *L* gave unto Israel all the	Josh 21:43	3068
the *L* gave them rest round about,	Josh 21:44	3068
the *L* delivered all their enemies	Josh 21:44	3068
of any good thing which the *L* had	Josh 21:45	3068
servant of the *L* commanded you	Josh 22:2	3068
the commandment of the *L* your God	Josh 22:3	3068
now the *L* your God hath given	Josh 22:4	3068
the *L* gave you on the other side	Josh 22:4	3068
the servant of the *L* charged you	Josh 22:5	3068
you, to love the *L* your God	Josh 22:5	3068
of the *L* by the hand of Moses	Josh 22:9	3068
the whole congregation of the *L*	Josh 22:16	3068
this day from following the *L*	Josh 22:16	3068
rebel this day against the *L*	Josh 22:16	3068
in the congregation of the *L*	Josh 22:17	3068
this day from following the *L*	Josh 22:18	3068
ye rebel to day against the *L*	Josh 22:18	3068
land of the possession of the *L*	Josh 22:19	3068
but rebel not against the *L*	Josh 22:19	3068
beside the altar of the *L* our God	Josh 22:19	3068
The *L* God of gods, the *L* God	Josh 22:22	3068
if in transgression against the *L*	Josh 22:22	3068
to turn from following the *L*	Josh 22:23	3068
let the *L* himself require it	Josh 22:23	3068
ye to do with the *L* God of Israel	Josh 22:24	3068
For the *L* hath made Jordan a	Josh 22:25	3068
ye have no part in the *L*	Josh 22:25	3068
children cease from fearing the *L*	Josh 22:25	3068
the *L* before him with our burnt	Josh 22:27	3068
to come, Ye have no part in the *L*	Josh 22:27	3068
the pattern of the altar of the *L*	Josh 22:28	3068
we should rebel against the *L*	Josh 22:29	3068
this day from following the *L*	Josh 22:29	3068
beside the altar of the *L* our God	Josh 22:29	3068
perceive that the *L* is among us	Josh 22:31	3068
this trespass against the *L*	Josh 22:31	3068
Israel out of the hand of the *L*	Josh 22:31	3068
between us that the *L* is God	Josh 22:34	3068
L had given rest unto Israel from	Josh 23:1	3068
ye have seen all that the *L* your	Josh 23:3	3068
for the *L* your God is he that	Josh 23:3	3068
the *L* your God, he shall expel	Josh 23:5	3068
as the *L* your God hath promised	Josh 23:5	3068
But cleave unto the *L* your God	Josh 23:8	3068
For the *L* hath driven out from	Josh 23:9	3068
for the *L* your God, for it is that	Josh 23:10	3068
that ye love the *L* your God	Josh 23:11	3068
Know for a certainty that the *L*	Josh 23:13	3068
the *L* your God hath given you	Josh 23:13	3068
L your God spake concerning you	Josh 23:14	3068
which the *L* your God promised you	Josh 23:15	3068
so shall the *L* bring upon you all	Josh 23:15	3068
the *L* your God hath given you	Josh 23:15	3068
the covenant of the *L* your God	Josh 23:16	3068
of the *L* be kindled against you	Josh 23:16	3068
Thus saith the *L* God of Israel	Josh 24:2	3068
And when they cried unto the *L*	Josh 24:7	3068
Now therefore fear the *L*, and	Josh 24:14	3068
and serve ye the *L*	Josh 24:14	3068
seem evil unto you to serve the *L*	Josh 24:15	3068
and my house, we will serve the *L*	Josh 24:15	3068
that we should forsake the *L*	Josh 24:16	3068
For the *L* our God, he it is that	Josh 24:17	3068
the *L* drave out from before us	Josh 24:18	3068
will we also serve the *L*	Josh 24:18	3068
the people, Ye cannot serve the *L*	Josh 24:19	3068
If ye forsake the *L*, and serve	Josh 24:20	3068
but we will serve the *L*	Josh 24:21	3068
that ye have chosen you the *L*	Josh 24:22	3068
heart unto the *L* God of Israel	Josh 24:23	3068
The *L* our God will we serve, and	Josh 24:24	3068

was by the sanctuary of the *L*	Josh 24:26	3068
of the *L* which he spake unto us	Josh 24:27	3068
son of Nun, the servant of the *L*	Josh 24:29	3068
Israel served the *L* all the days	Josh 24:31	3068
had known all the works of the *L*	Josh 24:31	3068
children of Israel asked the *L*	Judg 1:1	3068
the *L* said, Judah shall go up	Judg 1:2	3068
the *L* delivered the Canaanites and	Judg 1:4	3068
And the *L* was with Judah	Judg 1:19	3068
and the *L* was with them	Judg 1:22	3068
an angel of the *L* came up from	Judg 2:1	3068
when the angel of the *L* spake	Judg 2:4	3068
they sacrificed there unto the *L*	Judg 2:5	3068
the people served the *L* all the	Judg 2:7	3068
seen all the great works of the *L*	Judg 2:7	3068
son of Nun, the servant of the *L*	Judg 2:8	3068
after them, which knew not the *L*	Judg 2:10	3068
did evil in the sight of the *L*	Judg 2:11	3068
they forsook the *L* God of their	Judg 2:12	3068
them, and provoked the *L* to anger	Judg 2:12	3068
And they forsook the *L*, and served	Judg 2:13	3068
the anger of the *L* was hot	Judg 2:14	3068
the hand of the *L* was against	Judg 2:15	3068
as the *L* had said, and as the *L*	Judg 2:15	3068
the *L* raised up judges, which	Judg 2:16	3068
obeying the commandments of the *L*	Judg 2:17	3068
when the *L* raised them up judges,	Judg 2:18	3068
then the *L* was with the judge, and	Judg 2:18	3068
for it repented the *L* because of	Judg 2:18	3068
the anger of the *L* was hot	Judg 2:20	3068
the way of the *L* to walk therein	Judg 2:22	3068
Therefore the *L* left those	Judg 2:23	3068
are the nations which the *L* left	Judg 3:1	3068
unto the commandments of the *L*	Judg 3:4	3068
did evil in the sight of the *L*	Judg 3:7	3068
and forgat the *L* their God	Judg 3:7	3068
of the *L* was hot against Israel	Judg 3:8	3068
of Israel cried unto the *L*	Judg 3:9	3068
the *L* raised up a deliverer to	Judg 3:9	3068
the spirit of the *L* came upon him	Judg 3:10	3068
and the *L* delivered	Judg 3:10	3068
evil again in the sight of the *L*	Judg 3:12	3068
the *L* strengthened Eglon the king	Judg 3:12	3068
done evil in the sight of the *L*	Judg 3:12	3068
of Israel cried unto the *L*	Judg 3:15	3068
the *L* raised them up a deliverer,	Judg 3:15	3068
for the *L* hath delivered your	Judg 3:28	3068
did evil in the sight of the *L*	Judg 4:1	3068
the *L* sold them into the hand of	Judg 4:2	3068
of Israel cried unto the *L*	Judg 4:3	3068
Hath not the *L* God of Israel	Judg 4:6	3068
for the *L* shall sell Sisera into	Judg 4:9	3068
the *L* hath delivered Sisera into	Judg 4:14	3068
is not the *L* gone out before thee	Judg 4:14	3068
the *L* discomfited Sisera, and all	Judg 4:15	3068
Praise ye the *L* for the avenging	Judg 5:2	3068
I, even I, will sing unto the *L*	Judg 5:3	3068
praise to the *L* God of Israel	Judg 5:3	3068
L, when thou wentest out of Seir,	Judg 5:4	3068
melted from before the *L*, even	Judg 5:5	3068
from before the *L* God of Israel	Judg 5:5	3068
Bless ye the *L*	Judg 5:9	3068
the righteous acts of the *L*	Judg 5:11	3068
of the *L* go down to the gates	Judg 5:11	3068
the *L* made me have dominion over	Judg 5:13	3068
ye Meroz, said the angel of the *L*	Judg 5:23	3068
came not to the help of the *L*	Judg 5:23	3068
help of the *L* against the mighty	Judg 5:23	3068
let all thine enemies perish, O *L*	Judg 5:31	3068
did evil in the sight of the *L*	Judg 6:1	3068
the *L* delivered them into the	Judg 6:1	3068
of Israel cried unto the *L*	Judg 6:6	3068
of Israel cried unto the *L*	Judg 6:7	3068
That the *L* sent a prophet unto	Judg 6:8	3068
Thus saith the *L* God of Israel	Judg 6:8	3068
unto you, I am the *L* your God	Judg 6:10	3068
And there came an angel of the *L*	Judg 6:11	3068
the angel of the *L* appeared unto	Judg 6:12	3068
The *L* is with thee, thou mighty	Judg 6:12	3068
if the *L* be with us, why then is	Judg 6:13	3068
Did not the *L* bring us up from	Judg 6:13	3068
but now the *L* hath forsaken us,	Judg 6:13	3068
the *L* looked upon him, and said,	Judg 6:14	3068
And he said unto him, Oh my *L*	Judg 6:15	136
the *L* said unto him, Surely I	Judg 6:16	3068
Then the angel of the *L* put forth	Judg 6:21	3068
Then the angel of the *L* departed	Judg 6:21	3068
that he was an angel of the *L*	Judg 6:22	3068
Gideon said, Alas, O *L* GOD	Judg 6:22	136
an angel of the *L* face to face	Judg 6:22	3068
the *L* said unto him, Peace be	Judg 6:23	3068
built an altar there unto the *L*	Judg 6:24	3068
that the *L* said unto him, Take	Judg 6:25	3068
build an altar unto the *L* thy God	Judg 6:26	3068
did as the *L* had said unto him	Judg 6:27	3068
Spirit of the *L* came upon Gideon	Judg 6:34	3068
the *L* said unto Gideon, The	Judg 7:2	3068
the *L* said unto Gideon, The	Judg 7:4	3068
the *L* said unto Gideon, Every one	Judg 7:5	3068
the *L* said unto Gideon, By the	Judg 7:7	3068
that the *L* said unto him, Arise,	Judg 7:9	3068
for the *L* hath delivered into	Judg 7:15	3068
camp, and say, The sword of the *L*	Judg 7:18	3068
and they cried, The sword of the *L*	Judg 7:20	3068
the *L* set every man's sword	Judg 7:22	3068
Therefore when the *L* hath	Judg 8:7	3068
as the *L* liveth, if ye had saved	Judg 8:19	3068
the *L* shall rule over you	Judg 8:23	3068
remembered not the *L* their God	Judg 8:34	3068
evil again in the sight of the *L*	Judg 10:6	3068
the Philistines, and forsook the *L*	Judg 10:6	3068
the anger of the *L* was hot	Judg 10:7	3068
of Israel cried unto the *L*	Judg 10:10	3068
the *L* said unto the children of	Judg 10:11	3068
of Israel said unto the *L*	Judg 10:15	3068
from among them, and served the *L*	Judg 10:16	3068
the *L* deliver them before me,	Judg 11:9	3068
The *L* be witness between us, if	Judg 11:10	3068
his words before the *L* in Mizpeh	Judg 11:11	3068
the *L* God of Israel delivered	Judg 11:21	3068
So now the *L* God of Israel hath	Judg 11:23	3068
So whomsoever the *L* our God shall	Judg 11:24	3068
the *L* the Judge be judge this day	Judg 11:27	3068
of the *L* came upon Jephthah	Judg 11:29	3068
Jephthah vowed a vow unto the *L*	Judg 11:30	3068
the *L* delivered them into his	Judg 11:32	3068
I have opened my mouth unto the *L*	Judg 11:35	3068
hast opened thy mouth unto the *L*	Judg 11:36	3068
forasmuch as the *L* hath taken	Judg 11:36	3068
the *L* delivered them into my hand	Judg 12:3	3068
evil again in the sight of the *L*	Judg 13:1	3068
the *L* delivered them into the	Judg 13:1	3068
the angel of the *L* appeared unto	Judg 13:3	3068
the *L*, and said, O my *L*	Judg 13:8	3068
angel of the *L* said unto Manoah	Judg 13:13	3068
said unto the angel of the *L*	Judg 13:15	3068
angel of the *L* said unto Manoah	Judg 13:16	3068
thou must offer it unto the *L*	Judg 13:16	3068
not that he was an angel of the *L*	Judg 13:16	3068
said unto the angel of the *L*	Judg 13:17	3068
the angel of the *L* said unto him	Judg 13:18	3068
offered it upon a rock unto the *L*	Judg 13:19	3068
that the angel of the *L* ascended	Judg 13:20	3068
But the angel of the *L* did no	Judg 13:21	3068
that he was an angel of the *L*	Judg 13:21	3068
If the *L* were pleased to kill us,	Judg 13:23	3068
child grew, and the *L* blessed him	Judg 13:24	3068
the Spirit of the *L* began to move	Judg 13:25	3068
knew not that it was of the *L*	Judg 14:4	3068
the Spirit of the *L* came mightily	Judg 14:6	3068
the Spirit of the *L* came upon him	Judg 14:19	3068
the Spirit of the *L* came mightily	Judg 15:14	3068
sore athirst, and called on the *L*	Judg 15:18	3068
he wist not that the *L* was	Judg 16:20	3068
And Samson called unto the *L*	Judg 16:28	3068
O *L* GOD, remember me, I pray thee	Judg 16:28	136
said, Blessed be thou of the *L*	Judg 17:2	3068
the *L* from my hand for my son	Judg 17:3	3068
know I that the *L* will do me good	Judg 17:13	3068
before the *L* is your way wherein	Judg 18:6	3068
now going to the house of the *L*	Judg 19:18	3068
the man's house where her *l* was	Judg 19:26	113
her *l* rose up in the morning, and	Judg 19:27	113
of Gilead, unto the *L* in Mizpeh	Judg 20:1	3068
the *L* said, Judah shall go up	Judg 20:18	3068
and wept before the *L* until even	Judg 20:23	3068
and asked counsel of the *L*	Judg 20:23	3068
the *L* said, Go up against him	Judg 20:23	3068
wept, and sat there before the *L*	Judg 20:26	3068
and peace offerings before the *L*	Judg 20:26	3068
of Israel enquired of the *L*	Judg 20:27	3068
And the *L* said, Go up	Judg 20:28	3068
the *L* smote Benjamin before	Judg 20:35	3068
O *L* God of Israel, why is this	Judg 21:3	3068
with the congregation unto the *L*	Judg 21:5	3068
came not up to the *L* to Mizpeh	Judg 21:5	3068
seeing we have sworn by the *L*	Judg 21:7	3068
came not up to Mizpeh to the *L*	Judg 21:8	3068
because that the *L* had made a	Judg 21:15	3068
there is a feast of the *L* in	Judg 21:19	3068
the *L* had visited his people in	Ruth 1:6	3068
the *L* deal kindly with you, as ye	Ruth 1:8	3068

L

The *L* grant you that ye may find	Ruth 1:9	3068
of the *L* is gone out against me	Ruth 1:13	113
the *L* do so to me, and more also,	Ruth 1:17	3068
the *L* hath brought me home again	Ruth 1:21	3068
seeing the *L* hath testified	Ruth 1:21	3068
the reapers, The *L* be with you	Ruth 2:4	3068
answered him, The *L* bless thee	Ruth 2:4	3068
The *L* recompense thy work, and a	Ruth 2:12	3068
given thee of the *L* God of Israel	Ruth 2:12	3068
in law, Blessed be he of the *L*	Ruth 2:20	3068
he said, Blessed be thou of the *L*	Ruth 3:10	3068
kinsman to thee, as the *L* liveth	Ruth 3:13	3068
The *L* make the woman that is come	Ruth 4:11	3068
of the seed which the *L* shall	Ruth 4:12	3068
the *L* gave her conception, and she	Ruth 4:13	3068
said unto Naomi, Blessed be the *L*	Ruth 4:14	3068
unto the *L* of hosts in Shiloh	1Sa 1:3	3068
and Phinehas, the priests of the *L*	1Sa 1:3	3068
but the *L* had shut up her womb	1Sa 1:5	3068
because the *L* had shut up her	1Sa 1:6	3068
she went up to the house of the *L*	1Sa 1:7	3068
by a post of the temple of the *L*	1Sa 1:9	3068
of soul, and prayed unto the *L*	1Sa 1:10	3068
O *L* of hosts, if thou wilt indeed	1Sa 1:11	3068
the *L* all the days of his life	1Sa 1:11	3068
continued praying before the *L*	1Sa 1:12	3068
Hannah answered and said, No, my *l*	1Sa 1:15	113
poured out my soul before the *L*	1Sa 1:15	3068
early, and worshipped before the *L*	1Sa 1:19	3068
and the *L* remembered her	1Sa 1:19	3068
Because I have asked him of the *L*	1Sa 1:20	3068
unto the *L* the yearly sacrifice	1Sa 1:21	3068
that he may appear before the *L*	1Sa 1:22	3068
only the *L* establish his word	1Sa 1:23	3068
unto the house of the *L* in Shiloh	1Sa 1:24	3068
And she said, Oh my *l*, as thy soul	1Sa 1:26	113
by thee here, praying unto the *L*	1Sa 1:26	113
the *L* hath given me my petition	1Sa 1:27	3068
also I have lent him to the *L*	1Sa 1:28	3068
liveth he shall be lent to the *L*	1Sa 1:28	3068
And he worshipped the *L* there	1Sa 1:28	3068
said, My heart rejoiceth in the *L*	1Sa 2:1	3068
mine horn is exalted in the *L*	1Sa 2:1	3068
There is none holy as the *L*	1Sa 2:2	3068
for the *L* is a God of knowledge,	1Sa 2:3	3068
The *L* killeth, and maketh alive	1Sa 2:6	3068
The *L* maketh poor, and maketh rich	1Sa 2:7	3068
The adversaries of the *L* shall be	1Sa 2:10	3068
the *L* shall judge the ends of the	1Sa 2:10	3068
unto the *L* before Eli the priest	1Sa 2:11	3068
they knew not the *L*	1Sa 2:12	3068
men was very great before the *L*	1Sa 2:17	3068
abhorred the offering of the *L*	1Sa 2:17	3068
Samuel ministered before the *L*	1Sa 2:18	3068
The *L* give thee seed of this	1Sa 2:20	3068
the loan which is lent to the *L*	1Sa 2:20	3068
the *L* visited Hannah, so that she	1Sa 2:21	3068
child Samuel grew before the *L*	1Sa 2:21	3068
but if a man sin against the *L*	1Sa 2:25	3068
because the *L* would slay them	1Sa 2:25	3068
and was in favour both with the *L*	1Sa 2:26	3068
said unto him, Thus saith the *L*	1Sa 2:27	3068
Wherefore the *L* God of Israel	1Sa 2:30	3068
but now the *L* saith, Be it far	1Sa 2:30	3068
ministered unto the *L* before Eli	1Sa 3:1	3068
the word of the *L* was precious in	1Sa 3:1	3068
went out in the temple of the *L*	1Sa 3:3	3068
That the *L* called Samuel	1Sa 3:4	3068
the *L* called yet again, Samuel	1Sa 3:6	3068
Now Samuel did not yet know the *L*	1Sa 3:7	3068
of the *L* yet revealed unto him	1Sa 3:7	3068
the *L* called Samuel again the	1Sa 3:8	3068
that the *L* had called the child	1Sa 3:8	3068
that thou shalt say, Speak, *L*	1Sa 3:9	3068
the *L* came, and stood, and called	1Sa 3:10	3068
the *L* said to Samuel, Behold, I	1Sa 3:11	3068
the doors of the house of the *L*	1Sa 3:15	3068
that the *L* hath said unto thee	1Sa 3:17	
And he said, It is the *L*	1Sa 3:18	3068
the *L* was with him, and did let	1Sa 3:19	3068
to be a prophet of the *L*	1Sa 3:20	3068
the *L* appeared again in Shiloh	1Sa 3:21	3068
for the *L* revealed himself to	1Sa 3:21	3068
in Shiloh by the word of the *L*	1Sa 3:21	3068
Wherefore hath the *L* smitten us	1Sa 4:3	3068
of the *L* out of Shiloh unto us	1Sa 4:3	3068
of the covenant of the *L* of hosts	1Sa 4:4	3068
of the *L* came into the camp	1Sa 4:5	3068
of the *L* was come into the camp	1Sa 4:6	3068
the earth before the ark of the *L*	1Sa 5:3	3068
ground before the ark of the *L*	1Sa 5:4	3068

But the hand of the *L* was heavy	1Sa 5:6	3068
the hand of the *L* was against the	1Sa 5:9	3068
the ark of the *L* was in the	1Sa 6:1	3068
shall we do to the ark of the *L*	1Sa 6:2	3068
And take the ark of the *L*, and lay	1Sa 6:8	3068
the ark of the *L* upon the cart	1Sa 6:11	3068
kine a burnt offering unto the *L*	1Sa 6:14	3068
took down the ark of the *L*	1Sa 6:15	3068
the same day unto the *L*	1Sa 6:15	3068
a trespass offering unto the *L*	1Sa 6:17	3068
they set down the ark of the *L*	1Sa 6:18	3068
had looked into the ark of the *L*	1Sa 6:19	3068
because the *L* had smitten many of	1Sa 6:19	3068
to stand before this holy *L* God	1Sa 6:20	3068
brought again the ark of the *L*	1Sa 6:21	3068
and brought up the ark of the *L*	1Sa 7:1	3068
his son to keep the ark of the *L*	1Sa 7:1	3068
of Israel lamented after the *L*	1Sa 7:2	3068
unto the *L* with all your hearts	1Sa 7:3	3068
and prepare your hearts unto the *L*	1Sa 7:3	3068
Ashtaroth, and served the *L* only	1Sa 7:4	3068
and I will pray for you unto the *L*	1Sa 7:5	3068
and poured it out before the *L*	1Sa 7:6	3068
We have sinned against the *L*	1Sa 7:6	3068
to cry unto the *L* our God for us	1Sa 7:8	3068
burnt offering wholly unto the *L*	1Sa 7:9	3068
cried unto the *L* for Israel	1Sa 7:9	3068
and the *L* heard him	1Sa 7:9	3068
but the *L* thundered with a great	1Sa 7:10	3068
Hitherto hath the *L* helped us	1Sa 7:12	3068
the hand of the *L* was against the	1Sa 7:13	3068
he built an altar unto the *L*	1Sa 7:17	3068
And Samuel prayed unto the *L*	1Sa 8:6	3068
the *L* said unto Samuel, Hearken	1Sa 8:7	3068
told all the words of the *L* unto	1Sa 8:10	3068
the *L* will not hear you in that	1Sa 8:18	3068
them in the ears of the *L*	1Sa 8:21	3068
the *L* said to Samuel, Hearken	1Sa 8:22	3068
Now the *L* had told Samuel in his	1Sa 9:15	3068
the *L* said unto him, Behold the	1Sa 9:17	3068
Is it not because the *L* hath	1Sa 10:1	3068
the Spirit of the *L* will come	1Sa 10:6	3068
together unto the *L* to Mizpeh	1Sa 10:17	3068
Thus saith the *L* God of Israel	1Sa 10:18	3068
before the *L* by your tribes	1Sa 10:19	3068
they enquired of the *L* further	1Sa 10:22	3068
the *L* answered, Behold, he hath	1Sa 10:22	3068
See ye him whom the *L* hath chosen	1Sa 10:24	3068
book, and laid it up before the *L*	1Sa 10:25	3068
the fear of the *L* fell on the	1Sa 11:7	3068
for to day the *L* hath wrought	1Sa 11:13	3068
Saul king before the *L* in Gilgal	1Sa 11:15	3068
of peace offerings before the *L*	1Sa 11:15	3068
witness against me before the *L*	1Sa 12:3	3068
The *L* is witness against you, and	1Sa 12:5	3068
It is the *L* that advanced Moses	1Sa 12:6	3068
L of all the righteous acts of	1Sa 12:7	3068
all the righteous acts of the *L*	1Sa 12:7	3068
and your fathers cried unto the *L*	1Sa 12:8	3068
then the *L* sent Moses and Aaron,	1Sa 12:8	3068
when they forgat the *L* their God	1Sa 12:9	3068
And they cried unto the *L*, and said	1Sa 12:10	3068
because we have forsaken the *L*	1Sa 12:10	3068
the *L* sent Jerubbaal, and Bedan,	1Sa 12:11	3068
when the *L* your God was your king	1Sa 12:12	3068
the *L* hath set a king over you	1Sa 12:13	3068
If ye will fear the *L*, and serve	1Sa 12:14	3068
of the *L* then shall both ye	1Sa 12:14	3068
continue following the *L* your God	1Sa 12:14	3068
will not obey the voice of the *L*	1Sa 12:15	3068
against the commandment of the *L*	1Sa 12:15	3068
the hand of the *L* be against you	1Sa 12:15	3068
which the *L* will do before your	1Sa 12:16	3068
I will call unto the *L*, and he	1Sa 12:17	3068
have done in the sight of the *L*	1Sa 12:17	3068
So Samuel called unto the *L*	1Sa 12:18	3068
the *L* sent thunder and rain that	1Sa 12:18	3068
the people greatly feared the *L*	1Sa 12:18	3068
thy servants unto the *L* thy God	1Sa 12:19	3068
not aside from following the *L*	1Sa 12:20	3068
but serve the *L* with all your	1Sa 12:20	3068
For the *L* will not forsake his	1Sa 12:22	3068
the *L* to make you his people	1Sa 12:22	3068
the *L* in ceasing to pray for you	1Sa 12:23	3068
Only fear the *L*, and serve him in	1Sa 12:24	3068
not made supplication unto the *L*	1Sa 13:12	3068
the commandment of the *L* thy God	1Sa 13:13	3068
for now would the *L* have	1Sa 13:13	3068
the *L* hath sought him a man after	1Sa 13:14	3068
the *L* hath commanded him to be	1Sa 13:14	3068
that which the *L* commanded thee	1Sa 13:14	3068

be that the *L* will work for us	1Sa 14:6	3068
the *L* to save by many or by few	1Sa 14:6	3068
for the *L* hath delivered them	1Sa 14:10	3068
for the *L* hath delivered them	1Sa 14:12	3068
So the *L* saved Israel that day	1Sa 14:23	3068
the people sin against the *L*	1Sa 14:33	3068
sin not against the *L* in eating	1Sa 14:34	3068
And Saul built an altar unto the *L*	1Sa 14:35	3068
altar that he built unto the *L*	1Sa 14:35	3068
For, as the *L* liveth, which	1Sa 14:39	3068
said unto the *L* God of Israel	1Sa 14:41	3068
as the *L* liveth, there shall not	1Sa 14:45	3068
The *L* sent me to anoint thee to	1Sa 15:1	3068
the voice of the words of the *L*	1Sa 15:1	3068
Thus saith the *L* of hosts	1Sa 15:2	3068
the word of the *L* unto Samuel	1Sa 15:10	3068
and he cried unto the *L* all night	1Sa 15:11	3068
him, Blessed be thou of the *L*	1Sa 15:13	3068
the commandment of the *L*	1Sa 15:13	3068
to sacrifice unto the *L* thy God	1Sa 15:15	3068
I will tell thee what the *L* hath	1Sa 15:16	3068
the *L* anointed thee king over	1Sa 15:17	3068
the *L* sent thee on a journey, and	1Sa 15:18	3068
thou not obey the voice of the *L*	1Sa 15:19	3068
didst evil in the sight of the *L*	1Sa 15:19	3068
I have obeyed the voice of the *L*	1Sa 15:20	3068
gone the way which the *L* sent me	1Sa 15:20	3068
unto the *L* thy God in Gilgal	1Sa 15:21	3068
Hath the *L* as great delight in	1Sa 15:22	3068
as in obeying the voice of the *L*	1Sa 15:22	3068
hast rejected the word of the *L*	1Sa 15:23	3068
the commandment of the *L*, and thy	1Sa 15:24	3068
with me, that I may worship the *L*	1Sa 15:25	3068
hast rejected the word of the *L*	1Sa 15:26	3068
the *L* hath rejected thee from	1Sa 15:26	3068
The *L* hath rent the kingdom of	1Sa 15:28	3068
that I may worship the *L* thy God	1Sa 15:30	3068
and Saul worshipped the *L*	1Sa 15:31	3068
in pieces before the *L* in Gilgal	1Sa 15:33	3068
the *L* repented that he had made	1Sa 15:35	3068
the *L* said unto Samuel, How long	1Sa 16:1	3068
the *L* said, Take an heifer with	1Sa 16:2	3068
I am come to sacrifice to the *L*	1Sa 16:2	3068
Samuel did that which the *L* spake	1Sa 16:4	3068
I am come to sacrifice unto the *L*	1Sa 16:5	3068
But the *L* said unto Samuel, Look	1Sa 16:7	3068
for the *L* seeth not as man seeth	1Sa 16:7	3068
but the *L* looketh on the heart	1Sa 16:7	3068
Neither hath the *L* chosen this	1Sa 16:8	3068
Neither hath the *L* chosen this	1Sa 16:9	3068
The *L* hath not chosen these	1Sa 16:10	3068
the *L* said, Arise, anoint him	1Sa 16:12	3068
the Spirit of the *L* came upon	1Sa 16:13	3068
of the *L* departed from Saul	1Sa 16:14	3068
spirit from the *L* troubled him	1Sa 16:14	3068
person, and the *L* is with him	1Sa 16:18	3068
The *L* that delivered me out of	1Sa 17:37	3068
David, Go, and the *L* be with thee	1Sa 17:37	3068
in the name of the *L* of hosts	1Sa 17:45	3068
This day will the *L* deliver thee	1Sa 17:46	3068
that the *L* saveth not with sword	1Sa 17:47	3068
because the *L* was with him, and	1Sa 18:12	3068
and the *L* was with him	1Sa 18:14	3068
knew that the *L* was with David,	1Sa 18:28	3068
the *L* wrought a great salvation	1Sa 19:5	3068
and Saul sware, As the *L* liveth	1Sa 19:6	3068
spirit from the *L* was upon Saul	1Sa 19:9	3068
but truly as the *L* liveth	1Sa 20:3	3068
a covenant of the *L* with thee	1Sa 20:8	3068
O *L* God of Israel, when I have	1Sa 20:12	3068
The *L* do so and much more to	1Sa 20:13	3068
the *L* be with thee, as he hath	1Sa 20:13	3068
shew me the kindness of the *L*	1Sa 20:14	3068
not when the *L* hath cut off the	1Sa 20:15	3068
Let the *L* even require it at the	1Sa 20:16	3068
as the *L* liveth	1Sa 20:21	3068
for the *L* hath sent thee away	1Sa 20:22	3068
the *L* be between thee and me for	1Sa 20:23	3068
both of us in the name of the *L*	1Sa 20:42	3068
The *L* be between me and thee, and	1Sa 20:42	3068
that was taken from before the *L*	1Sa 21:6	3068
that day, detained before the *L*	1Sa 21:7	3068
And he enquired of the *L* for him	1Sa 22:10	3068
and slay the priests of the *L*	1Sa 22:17	3068
to fall upon the priests of the *L*	1Sa 22:17	3068
Therefore David enquired of the *L*	1Sa 23:2	3068
the *L* said unto David, Go, and	1Sa 23:2	3068
David enquired of the *L* yet again	1Sa 23:4	3068
the *L* answered him and said, Arise	1Sa 23:4	3068
O *L* God of Israel, thy servant	1Sa 23:10	3068
O *L* God of Israel, I beseech thee	1Sa 23:11	3068
the *L* said, He will come down	1Sa 23:11	3068
the *L* said, They will deliver	1Sa 23:12	3068
two made a covenant before the *L*	1Sa 23:18	3068
Saul said, Blessed be ye of the *L*	1Sa 23:21	3068
day of which the *L* said unto thee	1Sa 24:4	3068
The *L* forbid that I should do	1Sa 24:6	3068
he is the anointed of the *L*	1Sa 24:6	3068
eyes have seen how that the *L* had	1Sa 24:10	3068
The *L* judge between me and thee,	1Sa 24:12	3068
and the *L* avenge me of thee	1Sa 24:12	3068
The *L* therefore be judge, and	1Sa 24:15	3068
forasmuch as when the *L* had	1Sa 24:18	3068
wherefore the *L* reward thee good	1Sa 24:19	3068
now therefore unto me by the *L*	1Sa 24:21	3068
as the *L* liveth	1Sa 25:26	3068
seeing the *L* hath withholden thee	1Sa 25:26	3068
for the *L* will certainly make my	1Sa 25:28	3068
fighteth the battles of the *L*	1Sa 25:28	3068
bundle of life with the *L* thy God	1Sa 25:29	3068
when the *L* shall have done to my	1Sa 25:30	3068
but when the *L* shall have dealt	1Sa 25:31	3068
Blessed be the *L* God of Israel	1Sa 25:32	3068
as the *L* God of Israel liveth,	1Sa 25:34	3068
that the *L* smote Nabal, that he	1Sa 25:38	3068
dead, he said, Blessed be the *L*	1Sa 25:39	3068
for the *L* hath returned the	1Sa 25:39	3068
said furthermore, As the *L* liveth	1Sa 26:10	3068
the *L* shall smite him	1Sa 26:10	3068
The *L* forbid that I should	1Sa 26:11	3068
from the *L* was fallen upon them	1Sa 26:12	113
As the *L* liveth, ye are worthy to	1Sa 26:16	3068
If the *L* have stirred thee up	1Sa 26:19	3068
men, cursed be they before the *L*	1Sa 26:19	3068
in the inheritance of the *L*	1Sa 26:19	3068
earth before the face of the *L*	1Sa 26:20	3068
The *L* render to every man his	1Sa 26:23	3068
for the *L* delivered thee into my	1Sa 26:23	3068
much set by in the eyes of the *L*	1Sa 26:24	3068
And when Saul enquired of the *L*	1Sa 28:6	3068
the *L* answered him not, neither	1Sa 28:6	3068
the *L*, saying, As the *L* liveth	1Sa 28:10	3068
seeing the *L* is departed from	1Sa 28:16	3068
the *L* hath done to him, as he	1Sa 28:17	3068
for the *L* hath rent the kingdom	1Sa 28:17	3068
obeyedst not the voice of the *L*	1Sa 28:18	3068
therefore hath the *L* done this	1Sa 28:18	3068
Moreover the *L* will also deliver	1Sa 28:19	3068
the *L* also shall deliver the host	1Sa 28:19	3068
unto him, Surely, as the *L* liveth	1Sa 29:6	3068
himself in the *L* his God	1Sa 30:6	3068
And David enquired at the *L*	1Sa 30:8	3068
that which the *L* hath given us	1Sa 30:23	3068
the spoil of the enemies of the *L*	1Sa 30:26	3068
son, and for the people of the *L*	2Sa 1:12	3068
that David enquired of the *L*	2Sa 2:1	3068
the *L* said unto him, Go up	2Sa 2:1	3068
unto them, Blessed be ye of the *L*	2Sa 2:5	3068
now the *L* shew kindness and truth	2Sa 2:6	3068
as the *L* hath sworn to David,	2Sa 3:9	3068
for the *L* hath spoken of David,	2Sa 3:18	3068
are guiltless before the *L* for	2Sa 3:28	3068
the *L* shall reward the doer of	2Sa 3:39	3068
the *L* hath avenged my	2Sa 4:8	3068
said unto them, As the *L* liveth	2Sa 4:9	3068
the *L* said to thee, Thou shalt	2Sa 5:2	3068
with them in Hebron before the *L*	2Sa 5:3	3068
the *L* God of hosts was with him	2Sa 5:10	3068
David perceived that the *L* had	2Sa 5:12	3068
And David enquired of the *L*	2Sa 5:19	3068
the *L* said unto David, Go up	2Sa 5:19	3068
The *L* hath broken forth upon mine	2Sa 5:20	3068
And when David enquired of the *L*	2Sa 5:23	3068
shall the *L* go out before thee	2Sa 5:24	3068
as the *L* had commanded him	2Sa 5:25	3068
is called by the name of the *L* of	2Sa 6:2	3068
of Israel played before the *L* on	2Sa 6:5	3068
the anger of the *L* was kindled	2Sa 6:7	3068
because the *L* had made a breach	2Sa 6:8	3068
was afraid of the *L* that day	2Sa 6:9	3068
shall the ark of the *L* come to me	2Sa 6:9	3068
L unto him into the city of David	2Sa 6:10	3068
the ark of the *L* continued in the	2Sa 6:11	3068
the *L* blessed Obed-edom, and all	2Sa 6:11	3068
The *L* hath blessed the house of	2Sa 6:12	3068
ark of the *L* had gone six paces	2Sa 6:13	3068
before the *L* with all his might	2Sa 6:14	3068
up the ark of the *L* with shouting	2Sa 6:15	3068
as the ark of the *L* came into the	2Sa 6:16	3068
leaping and dancing before the *L*	2Sa 6:16	3068
they brought in the ark of the *L*	2Sa 6:17	3068
and peace offerings before the *L*	2Sa 6:17	3068

in the name of the *L* of hosts	2Sa 6:18	3068
unto Michal, It was before the *L*	2Sa 6:21	3068
me ruler over the people of the *L*	2Sa 6:21	3068
will I play before the *L*	2Sa 6:21	3068
the *L* had given him rest round	2Sa 7:1	3068
for the *L* is with thee	2Sa 7:3	3068
word of the *L* came unto Nathan	2Sa 7:4	3068
servant David, Thus saith the *L*	2Sa 7:5	3068
David, Thus saith the *L* of hosts	2Sa 7:8	3068
Also the *L* telleth thee that he	2Sa 7:11	3068
David in, and sat before the *L*	2Sa 7:18	3068
and he said, Who am I, O *L* God	2Sa 7:18	136
small thing in thy sight, O *L* God	2Sa 7:19	136
this the manner of man, O *L* God	2Sa 7:19	136
L God, knowest thy servant	2Sa 7:20	136
Wherefore thou art great, O *L* God	2Sa 7:22	3068
and thou, *L*, art become their God	2Sa 7:24	3068
O *L* God, the word that thou hast	2Sa 7:25	3068
The *L* of hosts is the God over	2Sa 7:26	3068
O *L* of hosts, God of Israel, hast	2Sa 7:27	3068
O *L* God, thou art that God, and	2Sa 7:28	136
for thou, O *L* God, hast spoken it	2Sa 7:29	136
And the *L* preserved David	2Sa 8:6	3068
David did dedicate unto the *L*	2Sa 8:11	3068
And the *L* preserved David	2Sa 8:14	3068
the *L* do that which seemeth him	2Sa 10:12	3068
David had done displeased the *L*	2Sa 11:27	3068
the *L* sent Nathan unto David	2Sa 12:1	3068
said to Nathan, As the *L* liveth	2Sa 12:5	3068
Thus saith the *L* God of Israel	2Sa 12:7	3068
despised the commandment of the *L*	2Sa 12:9	3068
Thus saith the *L*, Behold, I will	2Sa 12:11	3068
I have sinned against the *L*	2Sa 12:13	3068
The *L* also hath put away thy sin	2Sa 12:13	3068
the enemies of the *L* to blaspheme	2Sa 12:14	3068
the *L* struck the child that	2Sa 12:15	3068
and came into the house of the *L*	2Sa 12:20	3068
and the *L* loved him	2Sa 12:24	3068
name Jedidiah, because of the *L*	2Sa 12:25	3068
the king remember the *L* thy God	2Sa 14:11	3068
And he said, As the *L* liveth	2Sa 14:11	3068
therefore the *L* thy God will be	2Sa 14:17	3068
which I have vowed unto the *L*	2Sa 15:7	3068
If the *L* shall bring me again	2Sa 15:8	3068
then I will serve the *L*	2Sa 15:8	3068
king, and said, As the *L* liveth	2Sa 15:21	3068
find favour in the eyes of the *L*	2Sa 15:25	3068
And David said, O *L*, I pray thee,	2Sa 15:31	3068
The *L* hath returned upon thee all	2Sa 16:8	3068
the *L* hath delivered the kingdom	2Sa 16:8	3068
because the *L* hath said unto him,	2Sa 16:10	3068
for the *L* hath bidden him	2Sa 16:11	3068
It may be that the *L* will look on	2Sa 16:12	3068
that the *L* will requite me good	2Sa 16:12	3068
but whom the *L*, and this people,	2Sa 16:18	3068
For the *L* had appointed to defeat	2Sa 17:14	3068
to the intent that the *L* might	2Sa 17:14	3068
how that the *L* hath avenged him	2Sa 18:19	3068
and said, Blessed be the *L* thy God	2Sa 18:28	3068
for the *L* hath avenged thee this	2Sa 18:31	3068
for I swear by the *L*, if thou go	2Sa 19:7	3068
up the inheritance of the *L*	2Sa 20:19	3068
and David enquired of the *L*	2Sa 21:1	3068
the *L* answered, It is for Saul,	2Sa 21:1	3068
bless the inheritance of the *L*	2Sa 21:3	3068
up unto the *L* in Gibeah of Saul	2Sa 21:6	3068
of Saul, whom the *L* did choose	2Sa 21:6	3068
them in the hill before the *L*	2Sa 21:9	3068
David spake unto the *L* the words	2Sa 22:1	3068
in the day that the *L* had	2Sa 22:1	3068
The *L* is my rock, and my fortress,	2Sa 22:2	3068
I will call on the *L*, who is	2Sa 22:4	3068
my distress I called upon the *L*	2Sa 22:7	3068
The *L* thundered from heaven, and	2Sa 22:14	3068
at the rebuking of the *L*	2Sa 22:16	3068
but the *L* was my stay	2Sa 22:19	3068
The *L* rewarded me according to my	2Sa 22:21	3068
For I have kept the ways of the *L*	2Sa 22:22	3068
Therefore the *L* hath recompensed	2Sa 22:25	3068
For thou art my lamp, O *L*	2Sa 22:29	3068
the *L* will lighten my darkness	2Sa 22:29	3068
the word of the *L* is tried	2Sa 22:31	3068
For who is God, save the *L*	2Sa 22:32	3068
even unto the *L*, but he answered	2Sa 22:42	3068
The *L* liveth	2Sa 22:47	3068
I will give thanks unto thee, O *L*	2Sa 22:50	3068
The Spirit of the *L* spake by me	2Sa 23:2	3068
the *L* wrought a great victory	2Sa 23:10	3068
the *L* wrought a great victory	2Sa 23:12	3068
but poured it out unto the *L*	2Sa 23:16	3068
he said, Be it far from me, O *L*	2Sa 23:17	3068

again the anger of the *L* was	2Sa 24:1	3068
Now the *L* thy God add unto the	2Sa 24:3	3068
And David said unto the *L*, I have	2Sa 24:10	3068
and now, I beseech thee, O *L*	2Sa 24:10	3068
the word of the *L* came unto the	2Sa 24:11	3068
say unto David, Thus saith the *L*	2Sa 24:12	3068
fall now into the hand of the *L*	2Sa 24:14	3068
So the *L* sent a pestilence upon	2Sa 24:15	3068
the *L* repented him of the evil,	2Sa 24:16	3068
the angel of the *L* was by the	2Sa 24:16	3068
David spake unto the *L* when he	2Sa 24:17	3068
rear an altar unto the *L* in the	2Sa 24:18	3068
Gad, went up as the *L* commanded	2Sa 24:19	3068
to build an altar unto the *L*	2Sa 24:21	3068
The *L* thy God accept thee	2Sa 24:23	3068
L my God of that which doth cost	2Sa 24:24	3068
built there an altar unto the *L*	2Sa 24:25	3068
So the *L* was intreated for the	2Sa 24:25	3068
thou swarest by the *L* thy God	1Kin 1:17	3068
sware, and said, As the *L* liveth	1Kin 1:29	3068
unto thee by the *L* God of Israel	1Kin 1:30	3068
the *L* God of my	1Kin 1:36	3068
As the *L* hath been with my	1Kin 1:37	3068
Blessed be the *L* God of Israel	1Kin 1:48	3068
keep the charge of the *L* thy God	1Kin 2:3	3068
That the *L* may continue his word	1Kin 2:4	3068
and I sware to him by the *L*	1Kin 2:8	3068
for it was his from the *L*	1Kin 2:15	3068
Then king Solomon sware by the *L*	1Kin 2:23	3068
Now therefore, as the *L* liveth	1Kin 2:24	3068
the *L* God before David my father	1Kin 2:26	136
from being priest unto the *L*	1Kin 2:27	3068
he might fulfil the word of the *L*	1Kin 2:27	3068
fled unto the tabernacle of the *L*	1Kin 2:28	3068
fled unto the tabernacle of the *L*	1Kin 2:29	3068
came to the tabernacle of the *L*	1Kin 2:30	3068
the *L* shall return his blood upon	1Kin 2:32	3068
be peace for ever from the *L*	1Kin 2:33	3068
I not make thee to swear by the *L*	1Kin 2:42	3068
thou not kept the oath of the *L*	1Kin 2:43	3068
therefore the *L* shall return thy	1Kin 2:44	3068
established before the *L* for ever	1Kin 2:45	3068
own house, and the house of the *L*	1Kin 3:1	3068
built unto the name of the *L*	1Kin 3:2	3068
And Solomon loved the *L*, walking	1Kin 3:3	3068
In Gibeon the *L* appeared to	1Kin 3:5	3068
O *L* my God, thou hast made thy	1Kin 3:7	3068
And the speech pleased the *L*	1Kin 3:10	136
the ark of the covenant of the *L*	1Kin 3:15	3068
an house unto the name of the *L*	1Kin 5:3	3068
until the *L* put them under the	1Kin 5:3	3068
But now the *L* my God hath given	1Kin 5:4	3068
unto the name of the *L* my God	1Kin 5:5	3068
as the *L* spake unto David my	1Kin 5:5	3068
said, Blessed be the *L* this day	1Kin 5:7	3068
the *L* gave Solomon wisdom, as he	1Kin 5:12	3068
began to build the house of the *L*	1Kin 6:1	3068
king Solomon built for the *L*	1Kin 6:2	3068
the word of the *L* came to Solomon	1Kin 6:11	3068
the ark of the covenant of the *L*	1Kin 6:19	3068
of the house of the *L* laid	1Kin 6:37	3068
inner court of the house of the *L*	1Kin 7:12	3068
Solomon for the house of the *L*	1Kin 7:40	3068
Solomon for the house of the *L*	1Kin 7:45	3068
pertained unto the house of the *L*	1Kin 7:48	3068
made for the house of the *L*	1Kin 7:51	3068
treasures of the house of the *L*	1Kin 7:51	3068
of the *L* out of the city of David	1Kin 8:1	3068
they brought up the ark of the *L*	1Kin 8:4	3068
covenant of the *L* unto his place	1Kin 8:6	3068
when the *L* made a covenant with	1Kin 8:9	3068
cloud filled the house of the *L*	1Kin 8:10	3068
for the glory of the *L* had filled	1Kin 8:11	3068
had filled the house of the *L*	1Kin 8:11	3068
The *L* said that he would dwell in	1Kin 8:12	3068
Blessed be the *L* God of Israel	1Kin 8:15	3068
the name of the *L* God of Israel	1Kin 8:17	3068
the *L* said unto David my father,	1Kin 8:18	3068
the *L* hath performed his word	1Kin 8:20	3068
as the *L* promised, and have built	1Kin 8:20	3068
the name of the *L* God of Israel	1Kin 8:20	3068
wherein is the covenant of the *L*	1Kin 8:21	3068
the *L* in the presence of all the	1Kin 8:22	3068
L God of Israel, there is no God	1Kin 8:23	3068
L God of Israel, keep with thy	1Kin 8:25	3068
O *L* my God, to hearken unto the	1Kin 8:28	3068
shall pray unto the *L* toward the	1Kin 8:44	3068
our fathers out of Egypt, O *L* God	1Kin 8:53	136
prayer and supplication unto the *L*	1Kin 8:54	3068
from before the altar of the *L*	1Kin 8:54	3068
Blessed be the *L*, that hath given	1Kin 8:56	3068

The *L* our God be with us, as he	1Kin 8:57	3068
made supplication before the *L*	1Kin 8:59	3068
be nigh unto the *L* our God day	1Kin 8:59	3068
earth may know that the *L* is God	1Kin 8:60	3068
be perfect with the *L* our God	1Kin 8:61	3068
offered sacrifice before the *L*	1Kin 8:62	3068
which he offered unto the *L*	1Kin 8:63	3068
dedicated the house of the *L*	1Kin 8:63	3068
was before the house of the *L*	1Kin 8:64	3068
altar that was before the *L* was	1Kin 8:64	3068
of Egypt, before the *L* our God	1Kin 8:65	3068
for all the goodness that the *L*	1Kin 8:66	3068
building of the house of the *L*	1Kin 9:1	3068
That the *L* appeared to Solomon	1Kin 9:2	3068
the *L* said unto him, I have heard	1Kin 9:3	3068
Why hath the *L* done thus unto	1Kin 9:8	3068
they forsook the *L* their God	1Kin 9:9	3068
therefore hath the *L* brought upon	1Kin 9:9	3068
two houses, the house of the *L*	1Kin 9:10	3068
for to build the house of the *L*	1Kin 9:15	3068
altar which he built unto the *L*	1Kin 9:25	3068
the altar that was before the *L*	1Kin 9:25	3068
concerning the name of the *L*	1Kin 10:1	3068
went up unto the house of the *L*	1Kin 10:5	3068
Blessed be the *L* thy God, which	1Kin 10:9	3068
because the *L* loved Israel for	1Kin 10:9	3068
pillars for the house of the *L*	1Kin 10:12	3068
the *L* said unto the children of	1Kin 11:2	3068
not perfect with the *L* his God	1Kin 11:4	3068
did evil in the sight of the *L*	1Kin 11:6	3068
and went not fully after the *L*	1Kin 11:6	3068
the *L* was angry with Solomon,	1Kin 11:9	3068
turned from the *L* God of Israel	1Kin 11:9	3068
not that which the *L* commanded	1Kin 11:10	3068
Wherefore the *L* said unto Solomon	1Kin 11:11	3068
the *L* stirred up an adversary	1Kin 11:14	3068
for thus saith the *L*, the God of	1Kin 11:31	3068
for the cause was from the *L*	1Kin 12:15	3068
which the *L* spake by Ahijah the	1Kin 12:15	3068
Thus saith the *L*, Ye shall not go	1Kin 12:24	3068
therefore to the word of the *L*	1Kin 12:24	3068
according to the word of the *L*	1Kin 12:24	3068
the house of the *L* at Jerusalem	1Kin 12:27	3068
by the word of the *L* unto Beth-el	1Kin 13:1	3068
the altar in the word of the *L*	1Kin 13:2	3068
O altar, altar, thus saith the *L*	1Kin 13:2	3068
the sign which the *L* hath spoken	1Kin 13:3	3068
had given by the word of the *L*	1Kin 13:5	3068
now the face of the *L* thy God	1Kin 13:6	3068
And the man of God besought the *L*	1Kin 13:6	3068
charged me by the word of the *L*	1Kin 13:9	3068
said to me by the word of the *L*	1Kin 13:17	3068
unto me by the word of the *L*	1Kin 13:18	3068
that the word of the *L* came unto	1Kin 13:20	3068
Judah, saying, Thus saith the *L*	1Kin 13:21	3068
hast disobeyed the mouth of the *L*	1Kin 13:21	3068
the *L* thy God commanded thee	1Kin 13:21	3068
the which the *L* did say to thee	1Kin 13:22	
unto the word of the *L*	1Kin 13:26	3068
therefore the *L* hath delivered	1Kin 13:26	3068
according to the word of the *L*	1Kin 13:26	3068
he cried by the word of the *L*	1Kin 13:32	3068
the *L* said unto Ahijah, Behold,	1Kin 14:5	3068
Thus saith the *L* God of Israel	1Kin 14:7	3068
for the *L* hath spoken it	1Kin 14:11	3068
some good thing toward the *L* God	1Kin 14:13	3068
Moreover the *L* shall raise him up	1Kin 14:14	3068
For the *L* shall smite Israel, as	1Kin 14:15	3068
groves, provoking the *L* to anger	1Kin 14:15	3068
according to the word of the *L*	1Kin 14:18	3068
the city which the *L* did choose	1Kin 14:21	3068
did evil in the sight of the *L*	1Kin 14:22	3068
of the nations which the *L* cast	1Kin 14:24	3068
treasures of the house of the *L*	1Kin 14:26	3068
king went into the house of the *L*	1Kin 14:28	3068
not perfect with the *L* his God	1Kin 15:3	3068
for David's sake did the *L* his	1Kin 15:4	3068
was right in the eyes of the *L*	1Kin 15:5	3068
was right in the eyes of the *L*	1Kin 15:11	3068
perfect with the *L* all his days	1Kin 15:14	3068
into the house of the *L*, silver,	1Kin 15:15	3068
treasures of the house of the *L*	1Kin 15:18	3068
he did evil in the sight of the *L*	1Kin 15:26	3068
unto the saying of the *L*, which	1Kin 15:29	3068
the *L* God of Israel to anger	1Kin 15:30	3068
he did evil in the sight of the *L*	1Kin 15:34	3068
Then the word of the *L* came to	1Kin 16:1	3068
the word of the *L* against Baasha	1Kin 16:7	3068
that he did in the sight of the *L*	1Kin 16:7	3068
according to the word of the *L*	1Kin 16:12	3068
in provoking the *L* God of Israel	1Kin 16:13	3068
doing evil in the sight of the *L*	1Kin 16:19	3068
wrought evil in the eyes of the *L*	1Kin 16:25	3068
to provoke the *L* God of Israel to	1Kin 16:26	3068
did evil in the sight of the *L*	1Kin 16:30	3068
Ahab did more to provoke the *L*	1Kin 16:33	3068
according to the word of the *L*	1Kin 16:34	3068
As the *L* God of Israel liveth,	1Kin 17:1	3068
the word of the *L* came unto him	1Kin 17:2	3068
according unto the word of the *L*	1Kin 17:5	3068
the word of the *L* came unto him	1Kin 17:8	3068
As the *L* thy God liveth, I have	1Kin 17:12	3068
thus saith the *L* God of Israel	1Kin 17:14	3068
until the day that the *L* sendeth	1Kin 17:14	3068
according to the word of the *L*	1Kin 17:16	3068
And he cried unto the *L*, and said,	1Kin 17:20	3068
O *L* my God, hast thou also	1Kin 17:20	3068
three times, and cried unto the *L*	1Kin 17:21	3068
O *L* my God, I pray thee, let this	1Kin 17:21	3068
the *L* heard the voice of Elijah	1Kin 17:22	3068
that the word of the *L* in thy	1Kin 17:24	3068
that the word of the *L* came to	1Kin 18:1	3068
(Now Obadiah feared the *L* greatly	1Kin 18:3	3068
cut off the prophets of the *L*	1Kin 18:4	3068
As the *L* thy God liveth, there is	1Kin 18:10	3068
that the Spirit of the *L* shall	1Kin 18:12	3068
servant fear the *L* from my youth	1Kin 18:12	3068
slew the prophets of the *L*	1Kin 18:13	3068
As the *L* of hosts liveth, before	1Kin 18:15	3068
the commandments of the *L*	1Kin 18:18	3068
if the *L* be God, follow him	1Kin 18:21	3068
I only, remain a prophet of the *L*	1Kin 18:22	3068
I will call on the name of the *L*	1Kin 18:24	3068
of the *L* that was broken down	1Kin 18:30	3068
unto whom the word of the *L* came	1Kin 18:31	3068
an altar in the name of the *L*	1Kin 18:32	3068
L God of Abraham, Isaac, and of	1Kin 18:36	3068
Hear me, O *L*, hear me, that this	1Kin 18:37	3068
may know that thou art the *L* God	1Kin 18:37	3068
Then the fire of the *L* fell	1Kin 18:38	3068
and they said, The *L*, he is the	1Kin 18:39	3068
the *L*, he is the God	1Kin 18:39	3068
the hand of the *L* was on Elijah	1Kin 18:46	3068
now, O *L*, take away my life	1Kin 19:4	3068
the angel of the *L* came again the	1Kin 19:7	3068
the word of the *L* came to him	1Kin 19:9	3068
jealous for the *L* God of hosts	1Kin 19:10	3068
stand upon the mount before the *L*	1Kin 19:11	3068
the *L* passed by, and a great and	1Kin 19:11	3068
in pieces the rocks before the *L*	1Kin 19:11	3068
but the *L* was not in the wind	1Kin 19:11	3068
but the *L* was not in the	1Kin 19:11	3068
but the *L* was not in the fire	1Kin 19:12	3068
jealous for the *L* God of hosts	1Kin 19:14	3068
the *L* said unto him, Go, return	1Kin 19:15	3068
Israel, saying, Thus saith the *L*	1Kin 20:13	3068
thou shalt know that I am the *L*	1Kin 20:13	3068
And he said, Thus saith the *L*	1Kin 20:14	3068
Israel, and said, Thus saith the *L*	1Kin 20:28	3068
The *L* is God of the hills, but he	1Kin 20:28	3068
and ye shall know that I am the *L*	1Kin 20:28	3068
neighbour in the word of the *L*	1Kin 20:35	3068
not obeyed the voice of the *L*	1Kin 20:36	3068
said unto him, Thus saith the *L*	1Kin 20:42	3068
The *L* forbid it me, that I should	1Kin 21:3	3068
the word of the *L* came to Elijah	1Kin 21:17	3068
him, saying, Thus saith the *L*	1Kin 21:19	3068
him, saying, Thus saith the *L*	1Kin 21:19	3068
work evil in the sight of the *L*	1Kin 21:20	3068
And of Jezebel also spake the *L*	1Kin 21:23	3068
wickedness in the sight of the *L*	1Kin 21:25	3068
whom the *L* cast out before the	1Kin 21:26	3068
the word of the *L* came to Elijah	1Kin 21:28	3068
thee, at the word of the *L* to day	1Kin 22:5	3068
for the *L* shall deliver it into	1Kin 22:6	136
here a prophet of the *L* besides	1Kin 22:7	3068
by whom we may enquire of the *L*	1Kin 22:8	3068
and he said, Thus saith the *L*	1Kin 22:11	3068
for the *L* shall deliver it into	1Kin 22:12	3068
And Micaiah said, As the *L* liveth	1Kin 22:14	3068
what the *L* saith unto me, that	1Kin 22:14	3068
for the *L* shall deliver it into	1Kin 22:15	3068
is true in the name of the *L*	1Kin 22:16	3068
the *L* said, These have no master	1Kin 22:17	3068
thou therefore the word of the *L*	1Kin 22:19	3068
I saw the *L* sitting on his throne	1Kin 22:19	3068
the *L* said, Who shall persuade	1Kin 22:20	3068
a spirit, and stood before the *L*	1Kin 22:21	3068
the *L* said unto him, Wherewith	1Kin 22:22	3068
the *L* hath put a lying spirit in	1Kin 22:23	3068
the *L* hath spoken evil concerning	1Kin 22:23	3068
the *L* from me to speak unto thee	1Kin 22:24	3068

L

the *L* hath not spoken by me	1Kin 22:28	3068
the word of the *L* which he spake	1Kin 22:38	3068
was right in the eyes of the *L*	1Kin 22:43	3068
he did evil in the sight of the *L*	1Kin 22:52	3068
to anger the *L* God of Israel	1Kin 22:53	3068
But the angel of the *L* said to	2Kin 1:3	3068
Now therefore thus saith the *L*	2Kin 1:4	3068
and say unto him, Thus saith the *L*	2Kin 1:6	3068
angel of the *L* said unto Elijah	2Kin 1:15	3068
said unto him, Thus saith the *L*	2Kin 1:16	3068
of the *L* which Elijah had spoken	2Kin 1:17	3068
when the *L* would take up Elijah	2Kin 2:1	3068
for the *L* hath sent me to Beth-el	2Kin 2:2	3068
said unto him, As the *L* liveth	2Kin 2:2	3068
Knowest thou that the *L* will take	2Kin 2:3	3068
for the *L* hath sent me to Jericho	2Kin 2:4	3068
And he said, As the *L* liveth	2Kin 2:4	3068
Knowest thou that the *L* will take	2Kin 2:5	3068
for the *L* hath sent me to Jordan	2Kin 2:6	3068
And he said, As the *L* liveth	2Kin 2:6	3068
Where is the *L* God of Elijah	2Kin 2:14	3068
Spirit of the *L* hath taken him up	2Kin 2:16	3068
there, and said, Thus saith the *L*	2Kin 2:21	3068
cursed them in the name of the *L*	2Kin 2:24	3068
evil in the sight of the *L*	2Kin 3:2	3068
that the *L* hath called these	2Kin 3:10	3068
there not here a prophet of the *L*	2Kin 3:11	3068
we may enquire of the *L* by him	2Kin 3:11	3068
The word of the *L* is with him	2Kin 3:12	3068
for the *L* hath called these three	2Kin 3:13	3068
As the *L* of hosts liveth, before	2Kin 3:14	3068
the hand of the *L* came upon him	2Kin 3:15	3068
And he said, Thus saith the *L*	2Kin 3:16	3068
For thus saith the *L*, Ye shall	2Kin 3:17	3068
light thing in the sight of the *L*	2Kin 3:18	3068
that thy servant did fear the *L*	2Kin 4:1	3068
the *L* hath hid it from me, and	2Kin 4:27	3068
the child said, As the *L* liveth	2Kin 4:30	3068
them twain, and prayed unto the *L*	2Kin 4:33	3068
for thus saith the *L*, They shall	2Kin 4:43	3068
according to the word of the *L*	2Kin 4:44	3068
because by him the *L* had given	2Kin 5:1	3068
call on the name of the *L* his God	2Kin 5:11	3068
But he said, As the *L* liveth	2Kin 5:16	3068
unto other gods, but unto the *L*	2Kin 5:17	3068
In this thing the *L* pardon thy	2Kin 5:18	3068
the *L* pardon thy servant in this	2Kin 5:18	3068
but, as the *L* liveth, I will run	2Kin 5:20	3068
And Elisha prayed, and said	2Kin 6:17	3068
the *L* opened the eyes of the	2Kin 6:17	3068
to him, Elisha prayed unto the *L*	2Kin 6:18	3068
into Samaria, that Elisha said, *L*	2Kin 6:20	3068
the *L* opened their eyes, and they	2Kin 6:20	3068
If the *L* do not help thee, whence	2Kin 6:27	3068
Behold, this evil is of the *L*	2Kin 6:33	3068
I wait for the *L* any longer	2Kin 6:33	3068
said, Hear ye the word of the *L*	2Kin 7:1	3068
Thus saith the *L*, To morrow about	2Kin 7:1	3068
if the *L* would make windows in	2Kin 7:2	3068
For the *L* had made the host of	2Kin 7:6	136
according to the word of the *L*	2Kin 7:16	3068
if the *L* should make windows in	2Kin 7:19	3068
for the *L* hath called for a	2Kin 8:1	3068
God, and enquire of the *L* by him	2Kin 8:8	3068
howbeit the *L* hath shewed me that	2Kin 8:10	3068
The *L* hath shewed me that thou	2Kin 8:13	3068
he did evil in the sight of the *L*	2Kin 8:18	3068
Yet the *L* would not destroy Judah	2Kin 8:19	3068
and did evil in the sight of the *L*	2Kin 8:27	3068
head, and say, Thus saith the *L*	2Kin 9:3	3068
Thus saith the *L* God of Israel	2Kin 9:6	3068
king over the people of the *L*	2Kin 9:6	3068
of all the servants of the *L*	2Kin 9:7	3068
to me, saying, Thus saith the *L*	2Kin 9:12	3068
the *L* laid this burden upon him	2Kin 9:25	3068
blood of his sons, saith the *L*	2Kin 9:26	3068
thee in this plat, saith the *L*	2Kin 9:26	3068
according to the word of the *L*	2Kin 9:26	3068
said, This is the word of the *L*	2Kin 9:36	3068
nothing of the word of the *L*	2Kin 10:10	3068
which the *L* spake concerning the	2Kin 10:10	3068
for the *L* hath done that which he	2Kin 10:10	3068
with me, and see my zeal for the *L*	2Kin 10:16	3068
according to the saying of the *L*	2Kin 10:17	3068
you none of the servants of the *L*	2Kin 10:23	3068
the *L* said unto Jehu, Because	2Kin 10:30	3068
the *L* God of Israel with all his	2Kin 10:31	3068
In those days the *L* began to cut	2Kin 10:32	3068
in the house of the *L* six years	2Kin 11:3	3068
to him into the house of the *L*	2Kin 11:4	3068
of them in the house of the *L*	2Kin 11:4	3068
the house of the *L* about the king	2Kin 11:7	3068
that were in the temple of the *L*	2Kin 11:10	3068
people into the temple of the *L*	2Kin 11:13	3068
be slain in the house of the *L*	2Kin 11:15	3068
made a covenant between the *L*	2Kin 11:17	3068
officers over the house of the *L*	2Kin 11:18	3068
the king from the house of the *L*	2Kin 11:19	3068
L all his days wherein Jehoiada	2Kin 12:2	3068
brought into the house of the *L*	2Kin 12:4	3068
to bring into the house of the *L*	2Kin 12:4	3068
cometh into the house of the *L*	2Kin 12:9	3068
brought into the house of the *L*	2Kin 12:9	3068
was found in the house of the *L*	2Kin 12:10	3068
oversight of the house of the *L*	2Kin 12:11	3068
wrought upon the house of the *L*	2Kin 12:11	3068
breaches of the house of the *L*	2Kin 12:12	3068
house of the *L* bowls of silver	2Kin 12:13	3068
brought into the house of the *L*	2Kin 12:13	3068
therewith the house of the *L*	2Kin 12:14	3068
brought into the house of the *L*	2Kin 12:16	3068
treasures of the house of the *L*	2Kin 12:18	3068
was evil in the sight of the *L*	2Kin 13:2	3068
the anger of the *L* was kindled	2Kin 13:3	3068
And Jehoahaz besought the *L*	2Kin 13:4	3068
and the *L* hearkened unto him	2Kin 13:4	3068
the *L* gave Israel a saviour, so	2Kin 13:5	3068
was evil in the sight of the *L*	2Kin 13:11	3068
the *L* was gracious unto them, and	2Kin 13:23	3068
was right in the sight of the *L*	2Kin 14:3	3068
of Moses, wherein the *L* commanded	2Kin 14:6	3068
were found in the house of the *L*	2Kin 14:14	3068
was evil in the sight of the *L*	2Kin 14:24	3068
the word of the *L* God of Israel	2Kin 14:25	3068
For the *L* saw the affliction of	2Kin 14:26	3068
the *L* said not that he would blot	2Kin 14:27	3068
was right in the sight of the *L*	2Kin 15:3	3068
the *L* smote the king, so that he	2Kin 15:5	3068
was evil in the sight of the *L*	2Kin 15:9	3068
of the *L* which he spake unto Jehu	2Kin 15:12	3068
was evil in the sight of the *L*	2Kin 15:18	3068
was evil in the sight of the *L*	2Kin 15:24	3068
was evil in the sight of the *L*	2Kin 15:28	3068
was right in the sight of the *L*	2Kin 15:34	3068
higher gate of the house of the *L*	2Kin 15:35	3068
In those days the *L* began to send	2Kin 15:37	3068
in the sight of the *L* his God	2Kin 16:2	3068
whom the *L* cast out from before	2Kin 16:3	3068
was found in the house of the *L*	2Kin 16:8	3068
altar, which was before the *L*	2Kin 16:14	3068
the altar and the house of the *L*	2Kin 16:14	3068
of the *L* for the king of Assyria	2Kin 16:18	3068
was evil in the sight of the *L*	2Kin 17:2	3068
sinned against the *L* their God	2Kin 17:7	3068
whom the *L* cast out from before	2Kin 17:8	3068
not right against the *L* their God	2Kin 17:9	3068
the *L* carried away before them	2Kin 17:11	3068
things to provoke the *L* to anger	2Kin 17:11	3068
whereof the *L* had said unto them,	2Kin 17:12	3068
Yet the *L* testified against	2Kin 17:13	3068
not believe in the *L* their God	2Kin 17:14	3068
whom the *L* had charged them	2Kin 17:15	3068
commandments of the *L* their God	2Kin 17:16	3068
to do evil in the sight of the *L*	2Kin 17:17	3068
Therefore the *L* was very angry	2Kin 17:18	3068
commandments of the *L* their God	2Kin 17:19	3068
the *L* rejected all the seed of	2Kin 17:20	3068
drave Israel from following the *L*	2Kin 17:21	3068
Until the *L* removed Israel out of	2Kin 17:23	3068
there, that they feared not the *L*	2Kin 17:25	3068
therefore the *L* sent lions among	2Kin 17:25	3068
them how they should fear the *L*	2Kin 17:28	3068
So they feared the *L*, and made	2Kin 17:32	3068
They feared the *L*, and served	2Kin 17:33	3068
they fear not the *L*, neither do	2Kin 17:34	3068
which the *L* commanded	2Kin 17:34	3068
With whom the *L* had made a	2Kin 17:35	3068
But the *L*, who brought you up out	2Kin 17:36	3068
But the *L* your God ye shall fear	2Kin 17:39	3068
So these nations feared the *L*	2Kin 17:41	3068
was right in the sight of the *L*	2Kin 18:3	3068
He trusted in the *L* God of Israel	2Kin 18:5	3068
For he clave to the *L*, and	2Kin 18:6	3068
which the *L* commanded Moses	2Kin 18:6	3068
And the *L* was with him	2Kin 18:7	3068
not the voice of the *L* their God	2Kin 18:12	3068
the servant of the *L* commanded	2Kin 18:12	3068
was found in the house of the *L*	2Kin 18:15	3068
the doors of the temple of the *L*	2Kin 18:16	3068
me, We trust in the *L* our God	2Kin 18:22	3068
Am I now come up without the *L*	2Kin 18:25	3068
The *L* said to me, Go up against	2Kin 18:25	3068

Hezekiah make you trust in the *L*	2Kin 18:30	3068
The *L* will surely deliver us, and	2Kin 18:30	3068
saying, The *L* will deliver us	2Kin 18:32	3068
that the *L* should deliver	2Kin 18:35	3068
and went into the house of the *L*	2Kin 19:1	3068
It may be the *L* thy God will hear	2Kin 19:4	3068
which the *L* thy God hath heard	2Kin 19:4	3068
to your master, Thus saith the *L*	2Kin 19:6	3068
went up into the house of the *L*	2Kin 19:14	3068
and spread it before the *L*	2Kin 19:14	3068
And Hezekiah prayed before the *L*	2Kin 19:15	3068
O *L* God of Israel, which dwellest	2Kin 19:15	3068
L, bow down thine ear, and hear	2Kin 19:16	3068
open, *L*, thine eyes, and see	2Kin 19:16	3068
Of a truth, *L*, the kings of	2Kin 19:17	3068
O *L* our God, I beseech thee, save	2Kin 19:19	3068
may know that thou art the *L* God	2Kin 19:19	3068
Thus saith the *L* God of Israel	2Kin 19:20	3068
This is the word that the *L* hath	2Kin 19:21	3068
thou hast reproached the *L*	2Kin 19:23	3068
the zeal of the *L* of hosts shall	2Kin 19:31	3068
Therefore thus saith the *L*	2Kin 19:32	3068
come into this city, saith the *L*	2Kin 19:33	3068
that the angel of the *L* went out	2Kin 19:35	3068
said unto him, Thus saith the *L*	2Kin 20:1	3068
to the wall, and prayed unto the *L*	2Kin 20:2	3068
I beseech thee, O *L*, remember now	2Kin 20:3	3068
the word of the *L* came to him	2Kin 20:4	3068
of my people, Thus saith the *L*	2Kin 20:5	3068
go up unto the house of the *L*	2Kin 20:5	3068
the sign that the *L* will heal me	2Kin 20:8	3068
the house of the *L* the third day	2Kin 20:8	3068
sign shalt thou have of the *L*	2Kin 20:9	3068
that the *L* will do the thing that	2Kin 20:9	3068
the prophet cried unto the *L*	2Kin 20:11	3068
Hezekiah, Hear the word of the *L*	2Kin 20:16	3068
shall be left, saith the *L*	2Kin 20:17	3068
of the *L* which thou hast spoken	2Kin 20:19	3068
was evil in the sight of the *L*	2Kin 21:2	3068
whom the *L* cast out before the	2Kin 21:2	3068
of the *L*, of which the *L* said	2Kin 21:4	3068
two courts of the house of the *L*	2Kin 21:5	3068
wickedness in the sight of the *L*	2Kin 21:6	3068
of which the *L* said to David, and	2Kin 21:7	3068
L destroyed before the children	2Kin 21:9	3068
the *L* spake by his servants the	2Kin 21:10	3068
thus saith the *L* God of Israel	2Kin 21:12	3068
was evil in the sight of the *L*	2Kin 21:16	3068
was evil in the sight of the *L*	2Kin 21:20	3068
he forsook the *L* God of his	2Kin 21:22	3068
and walked not in the way of the *L*	2Kin 21:22	3068
was right in the sight of the *L*	2Kin 22:2	3068
the scribe, to the house of the *L*	2Kin 22:3	3068
brought into the house of the *L*	2Kin 22:4	3068
oversight of the house of the *L*	2Kin 22:5	3068
which is in the house of the *L*	2Kin 22:5	3068
of the law in the house of the *L*	2Kin 22:8	3068
oversight of the house of the *L*	2Kin 22:9	3068
Go ye, enquire of the *L* for me	2Kin 22:13	3068
the *L* that is kindled against us	2Kin 22:13	3068
Thus saith the *L* God of Israel	2Kin 22:15	3068
Thus saith the *L*, Behold, I will	2Kin 22:16	3068
sent you to enquire of the *L*	2Kin 22:18	3068
Thus saith the *L* God of Israel	2Kin 22:18	3068
hast humbled thyself before the *L*	2Kin 22:19	3068
also have heard thee, saith the *L*	2Kin 22:19	3068
went up into the house of the *L*	2Kin 23:2	3068
was found in the house of the *L*	2Kin 23:2	3068
and made a covenant before the *L*	2Kin 23:3	3068
to walk after the *L*	2Kin 23:3	3068
L all the vessels that were made	2Kin 23:4	3068
the grove from the house of the *L*	2Kin 23:6	3068
that were by the house of the *L*	2Kin 23:7	3068
the altar of the *L* in Jerusalem	2Kin 23:9	3068
entering in of the house of the *L*	2Kin 23:11	3068
two courts of the house of the *L*	2Kin 23:12	3068
according to the word of the *L*	2Kin 23:16	3068
made to provoke the *L* to anger	2Kin 23:19	
the passover unto the *L* your God	2Kin 23:21	3068
was holden to the *L* in Jerusalem	2Kin 23:23	3068
found in the house of the *L*	2Kin 23:24	3068
to the *L* with all his heart	2Kin 23:25	3068
Notwithstanding the *L* turned not	2Kin 23:26	3068
the *L* said, I will remove Judah	2Kin 23:27	3068
was evil in the sight of the *L*	2Kin 23:32	3068
was evil in the sight of the *L*	2Kin 23:37	3068
the *L* sent against him bands of	2Kin 24:2	3068
according to the word of the *L*	2Kin 24:2	3068
of the *L* came this upon Judah	2Kin 24:3	3068
which the *L* would not pardon	2Kin 24:4	3068
was evil in the sight of the *L*	2Kin 24:9	3068
treasures of the house of the *L*	2Kin 24:13	3068
had made in the temple of the *L*	2Kin 24:13	3068
as the *L* had said	2Kin 24:13	3068
was evil in the sight of the *L*	2Kin 24:19	3068
L it came to pass in Jerusalem	2Kin 24:20	3068
And he burnt the house of the *L*	2Kin 25:9	3068
that were in the house of the *L*	2Kin 25:13	3068
that was in the house of the *L*	2Kin 25:13	3068
had made for the house of the *L*	2Kin 25:16	3068
was evil in the sight of the *L*	1Chr 2:3	3068
when the *L* carried away Judah and	1Chr 6:15	3068
of song in the house of the *L*	1Chr 6:31	3068
the house of the *L* in Jerusalem	1Chr 6:32	3068
being over the host of the *L*	1Chr 9:19	3068
time past, and the *L* was with him	1Chr 9:20	3068
the gates of the house of the *L*	1Chr 9:23	3068
which he committed against the *L*	1Chr 10:13	3068
even against the word of the *L*	1Chr 10:13	3068
And enquired not of the *L*	1Chr 10:14	3068
the *L* thy God said unto thee,	1Chr 11:2	3068
with them in Hebron before the *L*	1Chr 11:3	3068
to the word of the *L* by Samuel	1Chr 11:3	3068
for the *L* of hosts was with him	1Chr 11:9	3068
word of the *L* concerning Israel	1Chr 11:10	3068
the *L* saved them by a great	1Chr 11:14	3068
of it, but poured it out to the *L*	1Chr 11:18	3068
according to the word of the *L*	1Chr 12:23	3068
and that it be of the *L* our God	1Chr 13:2	3068
up thence the ark of God the *L*	1Chr 13:6	3068
the anger of the *L* was kindled	1Chr 13:10	3068
because the *L* had made a breach	1Chr 13:11	3068
the *L* blessed the house of	1Chr 13:14	3068
David perceived that the *L* had	1Chr 14:2	3068
the *L* said unto him, Go up	1Chr 14:10	3068
the *L* brought the fear of him	1Chr 14:17	3068
for them hath the *L* chosen to	1Chr 15:2	3068
the ark of the *L* unto his place	1Chr 15:3	3068
L God of Israel unto the place	1Chr 15:12	3068
the *L* our God made a breach upon	1Chr 15:13	3068
up the ark of the *L* God of Israel	1Chr 15:14	3068
according to the word of the *L*	1Chr 15:15	3068
L out of the house of Obed-edom	1Chr 15:25	3068
the ark of the covenant of the *L*	1Chr 15:26	3068
covenant of the *L* with shouting	1Chr 15:28	3068
the *L* came to the city of David	1Chr 15:29	3068
the people in the name of the *L*	1Chr 16:2	3068
minister before the ark of the *L*	1Chr 16:4	3068
praise the *L* God of Israel	1Chr 16:4	3068
the *L* into the hand of Asaph	1Chr 16:7	3068
Give thanks unto the *L*, call upon	1Chr 16:8	3068
of them rejoice that seek the *L*	1Chr 16:10	3068
Seek the *L* and his strength, seek	1Chr 16:11	3068
He is the *L* our God	1Chr 16:14	3068
Sing unto the *L*, all the earth	1Chr 16:23	3068
For great is the *L*, and greatly to	1Chr 16:25	3068
but the *L* made the heavens	1Chr 16:26	3068
Give unto the *L*, ye kindreds of	1Chr 16:28	3068
the people, give unto the *L* glory	1Chr 16:28	3068
Give unto the *L* the glory due	1Chr 16:29	3068
worship the *L* in the beauty of	1Chr 16:29	3068
among the nations, The *L* reigneth	1Chr 16:31	3068
sing out at the presence of the *L*	1Chr 16:33	3068
O give thanks unto the *L*	1Chr 16:34	3068
Blessed be the *L* God of Israel	1Chr 16:36	3068
said, Amen, and praised the *L*	1Chr 16:36	3068
of the covenant of the *L* Asaph	1Chr 16:37	3068
before the tabernacle of the *L* in	1Chr 16:39	3068
the *L* upon the altar of the burnt	1Chr 16:40	3068
is written in the law of the *L*	1Chr 16:40	3068
by name, to give thanks to the *L*	1Chr 16:41	3068
of the *L* remaineth under curtains	1Chr 17:1	3068
my servant, Thus saith the *L*	1Chr 17:4	3068
David, Thus saith the *L* of hosts	1Chr 17:7	3068
I tell thee that the *L* will build	1Chr 17:10	3068
the king came and sat before the *L*	1Chr 17:16	3068
O *L* God, and what is mine house,	1Chr 17:16	3068
of a man of high degree, O *L* God	1Chr 17:17	3068
O *L*, for thy servant's sake, and	1Chr 17:19	3068
O *L*, there is none like thee,	1Chr 17:20	3068
and thou, *L*, becamest their God	1Chr 17:22	3068
Therefore now, *L*, let the thing	1Chr 17:23	3068
The *L* of hosts is the God of	1Chr 17:24	3068
And now, *L*, thou art God, and hast	1Chr 17:26	3068
for thou blessest, O *L*, and it	1Chr 17:27	3068
Thus the *L* preserved David	1Chr 18:6	3068
king David dedicated unto the *L*	1Chr 18:11	3068
Thus the *L* preserved David	1Chr 18:13	3068
let the *L* do that which is good	1Chr 19:13	3068
The *L* make his people an hundred	1Chr 21:3	3068
the *L* spake unto Gad, David's	1Chr 21:9	3068
David, saying, Thus saith the *L*	1Chr 21:10	3068

L

said unto him, Thus saith the L	1Chr 21:11	3068
three days the sword of the L	1Chr 21:12	3068
the angel of the L destroying	1Chr 21:12	3068
fall now into the hand of the L	1Chr 21:13	3068
So the L sent pestilence upon	1Chr 21:14	3068
the L beheld, and he repented him	1Chr 21:15	3068
the angel of the L stood by the	1Chr 21:15	3068
saw the angel of the L stand	1Chr 21:16	3068
O L my God, be on me, and on my	1Chr 21:17	3068
Then the angel of the L commanded	1Chr 21:18	3068
set up an altar unto the L in the	1Chr 21:18	3068
he spake in the name of the L	1Chr 21:19	3068
build an altar therein unto the L	1Chr 21:22	3068
that which is thine for the L	1Chr 21:24	3068
built there an altar unto the L	1Chr 21:26	3068
offerings, and called upon the L	1Chr 21:26	3068
the L commanded the angel	1Chr 21:27	3068
the L had answered him in the	1Chr 21:28	3068
For the tabernacle of the L	1Chr 21:29	3068
the sword of the angel of the L	1Chr 21:30	3068
This is the house of the L God	1Chr 22:1	3068
L must be exceeding magnifical	1Chr 22:5	3068
an house for the L God of Israel	1Chr 22:6	3068
unto the name of the L my God	1Chr 22:7	3068
But the word of the L came to me	1Chr 22:8	3068
Now, my son, the L be with thee	1Chr 22:11	3068
build the house of the L thy God	1Chr 22:11	3068
Only the L give thee wisdom and	1Chr 22:12	3068
keep the law of the L thy God	1Chr 22:12	3068
judgments which the L charged	1Chr 22:13	3068
prepared for the house of the L	1Chr 22:14	3068
be doing, and the L be with thee	1Chr 22:16	3068
Is not the L your God with you	1Chr 22:18	3068
the land is subdued before the L	1Chr 22:18	3068
your soul to seek the L your God	1Chr 22:19	3068
ye the sanctuary of the L God	1Chr 22:19	3068
the ark of the covenant of the L	1Chr 22:19	3068
to be built to the name of the L	1Chr 22:19	3068
the work of the house of the L	1Chr 23:4	3068
four thousand praised the L with	1Chr 23:5	3068
to burn incense before the L	1Chr 23:13	3068
the service of the house of the L	1Chr 23:24	3068
The L God of Israel hath given	1Chr 23:25	3068
the service of the house of the L	1Chr 23:28	3068
morning to thank and praise the L	1Chr 23:30	3068
unto the L in the sabbaths	1Chr 23:31	3068
them, continually before the L	1Chr 23:31	3068
the service of the house of the L	1Chr 23:32	3068
to come into the house of the L	1Chr 24:19	3068
as the L God of Israel had	1Chr 24:19	3068
to give thanks and to praise the L	1Chr 25:3	3068
for song in the house of the L	1Chr 25:6	3068
instructed in the songs of the L	1Chr 25:7	3068
to minister in the house of the L	1Chr 26:12	3068
treasures of the house of the L	1Chr 26:22	3068
to maintain the house of the L	1Chr 26:27	3068
in all the business of the L	1Chr 26:30	3068
because the L had said he would	1Chr 27:23	3068
the ark of the covenant of the L	1Chr 28:2	3068
Howbeit the L God of Israel chose	1Chr 28:4	3068
(for the L hath given me many	1Chr 28:5	3068
the kingdom of the L over Israel	1Chr 28:5	3068
Israel the congregation of the L	1Chr 28:8	3068
commandments of the L your God	1Chr 28:8	3068
for the L searcheth all hearts	1Chr 28:9	3068
for the L hath chosen thee to	1Chr 28:10	3068
the courts of the house of the L	1Chr 28:12	3068
the service of the house of the L	1Chr 28:13	3068
of service in the house of the L	1Chr 28:13	3068
the ark of the covenant of the L	1Chr 28:18	3068
the L made me understand in	1Chr 28:19	3068
for the L God, even my God, will	1Chr 28:20	3068
the service of the house of the L	1Chr 28:20	3068
is not for man, but for the L God	1Chr 29:1	3068
his service this day unto the L	1Chr 29:5	3068
treasure of the house of the L	1Chr 29:8	3068
they offered willingly to the L	1Chr 29:9	3068
the L before all the congregation	1Chr 29:10	3068
L God of Israel our father, for	1Chr 29:10	3068
Thine, O L, is the greatness, and	1Chr 29:11	3068
thine is the kingdom, O L	1Chr 29:11	3068
O L our God, all this store that	1Chr 29:16	3068
O L God of Abraham, Isaac, and of	1Chr 29:18	3068
Now bless the L your God	1Chr 29:20	3068
the L God of their fathers	1Chr 29:20	3068
their heads, and worshipped the L	1Chr 29:20	3068
sacrificed sacrifices unto the L	1Chr 29:21	3068
burnt offerings unto the L	1Chr 29:21	3068
drink before the L on that day	1Chr 29:22	3068
anointed him unto the L to be the	1Chr 29:22	3068
sat on the throne of the L as	1Chr 29:23	3068
And the L magnified Solomon	1Chr 29:25	3068
the L his God was with him, and	2Chr 1:1	3068
the L had made in the wilderness	2Chr 1:3	3068
before the tabernacle of the L	2Chr 1:5	3068
to the brasen altar before the L	2Chr 1:6	3068
O L God, let thy promise unto	2Chr 1:9	3068
an house for the name of the L	2Chr 2:1	3068
house to the name of the L my God	2Chr 2:4	3068
solemn feasts of the L our God	2Chr 2:4	3068
Because the L hath loved his	2Chr 2:11	3068
Blessed be the L God of Israel	2Chr 2:12	3068
might build an house for the L	2Chr 2:12	3068
L at Jerusalem in mount Moriah	2Chr 3:1	3068
where the L appeared unto David	2Chr 3:1	3068
house of the L of bright brass	2Chr 4:16	3068
the house of the L was finished	2Chr 5:1	3068
of the L out of the city of David	2Chr 5:2	3068
covenant of the L unto his place	2Chr 5:7	3068
when the L made a covenant with	2Chr 5:10	3068
in praising and thanking the L	2Chr 5:13	3068
of musick, and praised the L	2Chr 5:13	3068
a cloud, even the house of the L	2Chr 5:13	3068
for the glory of the L had filled	2Chr 5:14	3068
The L hath said that he would	2Chr 6:1	3068
Blessed be the L God of Israel	2Chr 6:4	3068
the name of the L God of Israel	2Chr 6:7	3068
But the L said to David my father	2Chr 6:8	3068
The L therefore hath performed	2Chr 6:10	3068
as the L promised, and have built	2Chr 6:10	3068
the name of the L God of Israel	2Chr 6:10	3068
wherein is the covenant of the L	2Chr 6:11	3068
the L in the presence of all the	2Chr 6:12	3068
O L God of Israel, there is no	2Chr 6:14	3068
O L God of Israel, keep with thy	2Chr 6:16	3068
O L God of Israel, let thy word	2Chr 6:17	3068
O L my God, to hearken unto the	2Chr 6:19	3068
O L God, into thy resting place,	2Chr 6:41	3068
priests, O L God, be clothed with	2Chr 6:41	3068
O L God, turn not away the face	2Chr 6:42	3068
glory of the L filled the house	2Chr 7:1	3068
not enter into the house of the L	2Chr 7:2	3068
because the glory of the L had	2Chr 7:2	3068
the glory of the L upon the house	2Chr 7:3	3068
and worshipped, and praised the L	2Chr 7:3	3068
offered sacrifices before the L	2Chr 7:4	3068
instruments of musick of the L	2Chr 7:6	3068
the king had made to praise the L	2Chr 7:6	3068
was before the house of the L	2Chr 7:7	3068
that the L had shewed unto David	2Chr 7:10	3068
finished the house of the L	2Chr 7:11	3068
to make in the house of the L	2Chr 7:11	3068
the L appeared to Solomon by	2Chr 7:12	3068
Why hath the L done thus unto	2Chr 7:21	3068
the L God of their fathers	2Chr 7:22	3068
had built the house of the L	2Chr 8:1	3068
the ark of the L hath come	2Chr 8:11	3068
the L on the altar of the L	2Chr 8:12	3068
foundation of the house of the L	2Chr 8:16	3068
the house of the L was perfected	2Chr 8:16	3068
went up into the house of the L	2Chr 9:4	3068
Blessed be the L thy God, which	2Chr 9:8	3068
to be king for the L thy God	2Chr 9:8	3068
terraces to the house of the L	2Chr 9:11	3068
that the L might perform his word	2Chr 10:15	3068
But the word of the L came to	2Chr 11:2	3068
Thus saith the L, Ye shall not go	2Chr 11:4	3068
And they obeyed the words of the L	2Chr 11:4	3068
the priest's office unto the L	2Chr 11:14	3068
L God of Israel came to Jerusalem	2Chr 11:16	3068
unto the L God of their fathers	2Chr 11:16	3068
he forsook the law of the L	2Chr 12:1	3068
had transgressed against the L	2Chr 12:2	3068
said unto them, Thus saith the L	2Chr 12:5	3068
and they said, The L is righteous	2Chr 12:6	3068
when the L saw that they humbled	2Chr 12:7	3068
the word of the L came to	2Chr 12:7	3068
treasures of the house of the L	2Chr 12:9	3068
entered into the house of the L	2Chr 12:11	3068
wrath of the L turned from him	2Chr 12:12	3068
the city which the L had chosen	2Chr 12:13	3068
not his heart to seek the L	2Chr 12:14	3068
Ought ye not to know that the L	2Chr 13:5	3068
the L in the hand of the sons of	2Chr 13:8	3068
not cast out the priests of the L	2Chr 13:9	3068
the L is our God, and we have not	2Chr 13:10	3068
which minister unto the L	2Chr 13:10	3068
burn unto the L every morning	2Chr 13:11	3068
keep the charge of the L our God	2Chr 13:11	3068
against the L God of your fathers	2Chr 13:12	3068
and they cried unto the L, and the	2Chr 13:14	3068
upon the L God of their fathers	2Chr 13:18	3068

the *L* struck him, and he died	2Chr 13:20	3068
in the eyes of the *L* his God	2Chr 14:2	3068
seek the *L* God of their fathers	2Chr 14:4	3068
because the *L* had given him rest	2Chr 14:6	3068
we have sought the *L* our God	2Chr 14:7	3068
unto the *L* his God, and said, *L*	2Chr 14:11	3068
help us, O *L* our God	2Chr 14:11	3068
O *L*, thou art our God	2Chr 14:11	3068
So the *L* smote the Ethiopians	2Chr 14:12	3068
they were destroyed before the *L*	2Chr 14:13	3068
the fear of the *L* came upon them	2Chr 14:14	3068
The *L* is with you, while ye be	2Chr 15:2	3068
did turn unto the *L* God of Israel	2Chr 15:4	3068
and renewed the altar of the *L*	2Chr 15:8	3068
was before the porch of the *L*	2Chr 15:8	3068
that the *L* his God was with him	2Chr 15:9	3068
offered unto the *L* the same time	2Chr 15:11	3068
into a covenant to seek the *L* God	2Chr 15:12	3068
whosoever would not seek the *L*	2Chr 15:13	3068
unto the *L* with a loud voice	2Chr 15:14	3068
the *L* gave them rest round about	2Chr 15:15	3068
treasures of the house of the *L*	2Chr 16:2	3068
and not relied on the *L* thy God	2Chr 16:7	3068
because thou didst rely on the *L*	2Chr 16:8	3068
For the eyes of the *L* run to	2Chr 16:9	3068
disease he sought not to the *L*	2Chr 16:12	3068
the *L* was with Jehoshaphat,	2Chr 17:3	3068
sought to the *L* God of his father	2Chr 17:4	3068
Therefore the *L* stablished the	2Chr 17:5	3068
lifted up in the ways of the *L*	2Chr 17:6	3068
of the law of the *L* with them	2Chr 17:9	3068
the fear of the *L* fell upon all	2Chr 17:10	3068
offered himself unto the *L*	2Chr 17:16	3068
thee, at the word of the *L* to day	2Chr 18:4	3068
here a prophet of the *L* besides	2Chr 18:6	3068
by whom we may enquire of the *L*	2Chr 18:7	3068
iron, and said, Thus saith the *L*	2Chr 18:10	3068
for the *L* shall deliver it into	2Chr 18:11	3068
And Micaiah said, As the *L* liveth	2Chr 18:13	3068
truth to me in the name of the *L*	2Chr 18:15	3068
the *L* said, These have no master	2Chr 18:16	3068
Therefore hear the word of the *L*	2Chr 18:18	3068
I saw the *L* sitting upon his	2Chr 18:18	3068
the *L* said, Who shall entice Ahab	2Chr 18:19	3068
a spirit, and stood before the *L*	2Chr 18:20	3068
the *L* said unto him, Wherewith	2Chr 18:20	3068
the *L* said, Thou shalt entice him	2Chr 18:21	
the *L* hath put a lying spirit in	2Chr 18:22	3068
the *L* hath spoken evil against	2Chr 18:22	3068
the *L* from me to speak unto thee	2Chr 18:23	3068
then hath not the *L* spoken by me	2Chr 18:27	3068
cried out, and the *L* helped him	2Chr 18:31	3068
and love them that hate the *L*	2Chr 19:2	3068
wrath upon thee from before the *L*	2Chr 19:2	3068
unto the *L* God of their fathers	2Chr 19:4	3068
judge not for man, but for the *L*	2Chr 19:6	3068
let the fear of the *L* be upon you	2Chr 19:7	3068
is no iniquity with the *L* our God	2Chr 19:7	3068
Israel, for the judgment of the *L*	2Chr 19:8	3068
shall ye do in the fear of the *L*	2Chr 19:9	3068
they trespass not against the *L*	2Chr 19:10	3068
over you in all matters of the *L*	2Chr 19:11	3068
the *L* shall be with the good	2Chr 19:11	3068
and set himself to seek the *L*	2Chr 20:3	3068
together, to ask help of the *L*	2Chr 20:4	3068
of Judah they came to seek the *L*	2Chr 20:4	3068
Jerusalem, in the house of the *L*	2Chr 20:5	3068
O *L* God of our fathers, art not	2Chr 20:6	3068
And all Judah stood before the *L*	2Chr 20:13	3068
of the *L* in the midst of the	2Chr 20:14	3068
Thus saith the *L* unto you	2Chr 20:15	3068
the salvation of the *L* with you	2Chr 20:17	3068
for the *L* will be with you	2Chr 20:17	3068
the *L*, worshipping the *L*	2Chr 20:18	3068
stood up to praise the *L* God of	2Chr 20:19	3068
Believe in the *L* your God	2Chr 20:20	3068
he appointed singers unto the *L*	2Chr 20:21	3068
the army, and to say, Praise the *L*	2Chr 20:21	3068
the *L* set ambushments against the	2Chr 20:22	3068
for there they blessed the *L*	2Chr 20:26	3068
for the *L* had made them to	2Chr 20:27	3068
trumpets unto the house of the *L*	2Chr 20:28	3068
when they had heard that the *L*	2Chr 20:29	3068
was right in the sight of the *L*	2Chr 20:32	3068
the *L* hath broken thy works	2Chr 20:37	3068
was evil in the eyes of the *L*	2Chr 21:6	3068
Howbeit the *L* would not destroy	2Chr 21:7	3068
forsaken the *L* God of his fathers	2Chr 21:10	3068
Thus saith the *L* God of David thy	2Chr 21:12	3068
will the *L* smite thy people	2Chr 21:14	3068
Moreover the *L* stirred up against	2Chr 21:16	3068
after all this the *L* smote him in	2Chr 21:18	3068
of the *L* like the house of Ahab	2Chr 22:4	3068
whom the *L* had anointed to cut	2Chr 22:7	3068
who sought the *L* with all his	2Chr 22:9	3068
as the *L* hath said of the sons of	2Chr 23:3	3068
the courts of the house of the *L*	2Chr 23:5	3068
none come into the house of the *L*	2Chr 23:6	3068
shall keep the watch of the *L*	2Chr 23:6	3068
people into the house of the *L*	2Chr 23:12	3068
her not in the house of the *L*	2Chr 23:14	3068
L by the hand of the priests the	2Chr 23:18	3068
distributed in the house of the *L*	2Chr 23:18	3068
the burnt offerings of the *L*	2Chr 23:18	3068
the gates of the house of the *L*	2Chr 23:19	3068
the king from the house of the *L*	2Chr 23:20	3068
L all the days of Jehoiada the	2Chr 24:2	3068
to repair the house of the *L*	2Chr 24:4	3068
of Moses the servant of the *L*	2Chr 24:6	3068
things of the house of the *L* did	2Chr 24:7	3068
at the gate of the house of the *L*	2Chr 24:8	3068
to bring in to the *L* the	2Chr 24:9	3068
the service of the house of the *L*	2Chr 24:12	3068
to repair the house of the *L*	2Chr 24:12	3068
brass to mend the house of the *L*	2Chr 24:12	3068
vessels for the house of the *L*	2Chr 24:14	3068
the *L* continually all the days of	2Chr 24:14	3068
of the *L* God of their fathers	2Chr 24:18	3068
to bring them again unto the *L*	2Chr 24:19	3068
ye the commandments of the *L*	2Chr 24:20	3068
because ye have forsaken the *L*	2Chr 24:20	3068
the court of the house of the *L*	2Chr 24:21	3068
The *L* look upon it, and require it	2Chr 24:22	3068
the *L* delivered a very great host	2Chr 24:24	3068
the *L* God of their fathers	2Chr 24:24	3068
was right in the sight of the *L*	2Chr 25:2	3068
of Moses, where the *L* commanded	2Chr 25:4	3068
for the *L* is not with Israel, to	2Chr 25:7	3068
The *L* is able to give thee much	2Chr 25:9	3068
Wherefore the anger of the *L* was	2Chr 25:15	3068
turn away from following the *L*	2Chr 25:27	3068
was right in the sight of the *L*	2Chr 26:4	3068
and as long as he sought the *L*	2Chr 26:5	3068
against the *L* his God	2Chr 26:16	3068
went into the temple of the *L* to	2Chr 26:16	3068
him fourscore priests of the *L*	2Chr 26:17	3068
to burn incense unto the *L*	2Chr 26:18	3068
for thine honour from the *L* God	2Chr 26:18	3068
the priests in the house of the *L*	2Chr 26:19	3068
because the *L* had smitten him	2Chr 26:20	3068
cut off from the house of the *L*	2Chr 26:21	3068
was right in the sight of the *L*	2Chr 27:2	3068
not into the temple of the *L*	2Chr 27:2	3068
high gate of the house of the *L*	2Chr 27:3	3068
his ways before the *L* his God	2Chr 27:6	3068
was right in the sight of the *L*	2Chr 28:1	3068
the *L* had cast out before the	2Chr 28:3	3068
Wherefore the *L* his God delivered	2Chr 28:5	3068
the *L* God of their fathers	2Chr 28:6	3068
But a prophet of the *L* was there	2Chr 28:9	3068
because the *L* God of your fathers	2Chr 28:9	3068
you, sins against the *L* your God	2Chr 28:10	3068
fierce wrath of the *L* is upon you	2Chr 28:11	3068
offended against the *L* already	2Chr 28:13	3068
For the *L* brought Judah low	2Chr 28:19	3068
transgressed sore against the *L*	2Chr 28:19	3068
portion out of the house of the *L*	2Chr 28:21	3068
trespass yet more against the *L*	2Chr 28:22	3068
the doors of the house of the *L*	2Chr 28:24	3068
to anger the *L* God of his fathers	2Chr 28:25	3068
was right in the sight of the *L*	2Chr 29:2	3068
the doors of the house of the *L*	2Chr 29:3	3068
of the *L* God of your fathers	2Chr 29:5	3068
evil in the eyes of the *L* our God	2Chr 29:6	3068
from the habitation of the *L*	2Chr 29:6	3068
the wrath of the *L* was upon Judah	2Chr 29:8	3068
covenant with the *L* God of Israel	2Chr 29:10	3068
for the *L* hath chosen you to	2Chr 29:11	3068
the king, by the words of the *L*	2Chr 29:15	3068
to cleanse the house of the *L*	2Chr 29:15	3068
inner part of the house of the *L*	2Chr 29:16	3068
L into the court of the house of	2Chr 29:16	3068
the court of the house of the *L*	2Chr 29:16	3068
came they to the porch of the *L*	2Chr 29:17	3068
the house of the *L* in eight days	2Chr 29:17	3068
cleansed all the house of the *L*	2Chr 29:18	3068
are before the altar of the *L*	2Chr 29:19	3068
and went up to the house of the *L*	2Chr 29:20	3068
offer them on the altar of the *L*	2Chr 29:21	3068
the house of the *L* with cymbals	2Chr 29:25	3068
of the *L* by his prophets	2Chr 29:25	3068
the song of the *L* began also with	2Chr 29:27	3068

L

the *L* with the words of David	2Chr 29:30	3068
consecrated yourselves unto the *L*	2Chr 29:31	3068
offerings into the house of the *L*	2Chr 29:31	3068
for a burnt offering to the *L*	2Chr 29:32	3068
house of the *L* was set in order	2Chr 29:35	3068
the house of the *L* at Jerusalem	2Chr 30:1	3068
passover unto the *L* God of Israel	2Chr 30:1	3068
the *L* God of Israel at Jerusalem	2Chr 30:5	3068
again unto the *L* God of Abraham	2Chr 30:6	3068
the *L* God of their fathers	2Chr 30:7	3068
but yield yourselves unto the *L*	2Chr 30:8	3068
and serve the *L* your God, that the	2Chr 30:8	3068
For if ye turn again unto the *L*	2Chr 30:9	3068
for the *L* your God is gracious and	2Chr 30:9	3068
the princes, by the word of the *L*	2Chr 30:12	3068
offerings into the house of the *L*	2Chr 30:15	3068
to sanctify them unto the *L*	2Chr 30:17	3068
The good *L* pardon every one	2Chr 30:18	3068
the *L* God of his fathers, though	2Chr 30:19	3068
the *L* hearkened to Hezekiah, and	2Chr 30:20	3068
priests praised the *L* day by day	2Chr 30:21	3068
with loud instruments unto the *L*	2Chr 30:21	3068
the good knowledge of the *L*	2Chr 30:22	3068
to the *L* God of their fathers	2Chr 30:22	3068
the gates of the tents of the *L*	2Chr 31:2	3068
it is written in the law of the *L*	2Chr 31:3	3068
be encouraged in the law of the *L*	2Chr 31:4	3068
consecrated unto the *L* their God	2Chr 31:6	3068
saw the heaps, they blessed the *L*	2Chr 31:8	3068
offerings into the house of the *L*	2Chr 31:10	3068
for the *L* hath blessed his people	2Chr 31:10	3068
chambers in the house of the *L*	2Chr 31:11	3068
distribute the oblations of the *L*	2Chr 31:14	3068
entereth into the house of the *L*	2Chr 31:16	3068
and truth before the *L* his God	2Chr 31:20	3068
us is the *L* our God to help us	2Chr 32:8	3068
The *L* our God shall deliver us	2Chr 32:11	3068
spake yet more against the *L* God	2Chr 32:16	3068
to rail on the *L* God of Israel	2Chr 32:17	3068
the *L* sent an angel, which cut	2Chr 32:21	3068
Thus the *L* saved Hezekiah and the	2Chr 32:22	3068
gifts unto the *L* to Jerusalem	2Chr 32:23	3068
the death, and prayed unto the *L*	2Chr 32:24	3068
so that the wrath of the *L* came	2Chr 32:26	3068
was evil in the sight of the *L*	2Chr 33:2	3068
whom the *L* had cast out before	2Chr 33:2	3068
altars in the house of the *L*	2Chr 33:4	3068
whereof the *L* had said	2Chr 33:4	3068
two courts of the house of the *L*	2Chr 33:5	3068
much evil in the sight of the *L*	2Chr 33:6	3068
whom the *L* had destroyed before	2Chr 33:9	3068
the *L* spake to Manasseh, and to	2Chr 33:10	3068
Wherefore the *L* brought upon them	2Chr 33:11	3068
he besought the *L* his God	2Chr 33:12	3068
knew that the *L* he was God	2Chr 33:13	3068
idol out of the house of the *L*	2Chr 33:15	3068
the mount of the house of the *L*	2Chr 33:15	3068
And he repaired the altar of the *L*	2Chr 33:16	3068
to serve the *L* God of Israel	2Chr 33:16	3068
yet unto the *L* their God only	2Chr 33:17	3068
the name of the *L* God of Israel	2Chr 33:18	3068
was evil in the sight of the *L*	2Chr 33:22	3068
humbled not himself before the *L*	2Chr 33:23	3068
was right in the sight of the *L*	2Chr 34:2	3068
repair the house of the *L* his God	2Chr 34:8	3068
oversight of the house of the *L*	2Chr 34:10	3068
wrought in the house of the *L*	2Chr 34:10	3068
brought into the house of the *L*	2Chr 34:14	3068
the law of the *L* given by Moses	2Chr 34:14	3068
of the law in the house of the *L*	2Chr 34:15	3068
was found in the house of the *L*	2Chr 34:17	3068
Go, enquire of the *L* for me	2Chr 34:21	3068
the *L* that is poured out upon us	2Chr 34:21	3068
have not kept the word of the *L*	2Chr 34:21	3068
Thus saith the *L* God of Israel	2Chr 34:23	3068
Thus saith the *L*, Behold, I will	2Chr 34:24	3068
who sent you to enquire of the *L*	2Chr 34:26	3068
Thus saith the *L* God of Israel	2Chr 34:26	3068
even heard thee also, saith the *L*	2Chr 34:27	3068
went up into the house of the *L*	2Chr 34:30	3068
was found in the house of the *L*	2Chr 34:30	3068
and made a covenant before the *L*	2Chr 34:31	3068
to walk after the *L*	2Chr 34:31	3068
even to serve the *L* their God	2Chr 34:33	3068
departed not from following the *L*	2Chr 34:33	3068
passover unto the *L* in Jerusalem	2Chr 35:1	3068
the service of the house of the *L*	2Chr 35:2	3068
which were holy unto the *L*	2Chr 35:3	3068
serve now the *L* your God, and his	2Chr 35:3	3068
of the *L* by the hand of Moses	2Chr 35:6	3068
the people, to offer unto the *L*	2Chr 35:12	3068
the *L* was prepared the same day	2Chr 35:16	3068
offerings upon the altar of the *L*	2Chr 35:16	3068
was written in the law of the *L*	2Chr 35:26	3068
in the sight of the *L* his God	2Chr 36:5	3068
of the house of the *L* to Babylon	2Chr 36:7	3068
was evil in the sight of the *L*	2Chr 36:9	3068
vessels of the house of the *L*	2Chr 36:10	3068
in the sight of the *L* his God	2Chr 36:12	3068
speaking from the mouth of the *L*	2Chr 36:12	3068
turning unto the *L* God of Israel	2Chr 36:13	3068
of the *L* which he had hallowed in	2Chr 36:14	3068
the *L* God of their fathers sent	2Chr 36:15	3068
until the wrath of the *L* arose	2Chr 36:16	3068
treasures of the house of the *L*	2Chr 36:18	3068
of the *L* by the mouth of Jeremiah	2Chr 36:21	3068
that the word of the *L* spoken by	2Chr 36:22	3068
the *L* stirred up the spirit of	2Chr 36:22	3068
hath the *L* God of heaven given me	2Chr 36:23	3068
The *L* his God be with him, and let	2Chr 36:23	3068
that the word of the *L* by the	Ezr 1:1	3068
the *L* stirred up the spirit of	Ezr 1:1	3068
The *L* God of heaven hath given me	Ezr 1:2	3068
the house of the *L* God of Israel	Ezr 1:3	3068
of the *L* which is in Jerusalem	Ezr 1:5	3068
the vessels of the house of the *L*	Ezr 1:7	3068
of the *L* which is at Jerusalem	Ezr 2:68	3068
offerings thereon unto the *L*	Ezr 3:3	3068
of the *L* that were consecrated	Ezr 3:5	3068
a freewill offering unto the *L*	Ezr 3:5	3068
offer burnt offerings unto the *L*	Ezr 3:6	3068
temple of the *L* was not yet laid	Ezr 3:6	3068
the work of the house of the *L*	Ezr 3:8	3068
foundation of the temple of the *L*	Ezr 3:10	3068
with cymbals, to praise the *L*	Ezr 3:10	3068
and giving thanks unto the *L*	Ezr 3:11	3068
shout, when they praised the *L*	Ezr 3:11	3068
of the house of the *L* was laid	Ezr 3:11	3068
temple unto the *L* God of Israel	Ezr 4:1	3068
build unto the *L* God of Israel	Ezr 4:3	3068
to seek the *L* God of Israel, did	Ezr 6:21	3068
for the *L* had made them joyful,	Ezr 6:22	3068
which the *L* God of Israel had	Ezr 7:6	3068
hand of the *L* his God upon him	Ezr 7:6	3068
heart to seek the law of the *L*	Ezr 7:10	3068
of the commandments of the *L*	Ezr 7:11	3068
Blessed be the *L* God of our	Ezr 7:27	3068
of the *L* which is in Jerusalem	Ezr 7:27	3068
hand of the *L* my God was upon me	Ezr 7:28	3068
unto them, Ye are holy unto the *L*	Ezr 8:28	3068
unto the *L* God of your fathers	Ezr 8:28	3068
chambers of the house of the *L*	Ezr 8:29	3068
was a burnt offering unto the *L*	Ezr 8:35	3068
out my hands unto the *L* my God	Ezr 9:5	3068
been shewed from the *L* our God	Ezr 9:8	3068
O *L* God of Israel, thou art	Ezr 9:15	3068
unto the *L* God of your fathers	Ezr 10:11	3068
O *L* God of heaven, the great and	Neh 1:5	3068
O *L*, I beseech thee, let now	Neh 1:11	136
necks to the work of their *L*	Neh 3:5	113
remember the *L*, which is great and	Neh 4:14	136
said, Amen, and praised the *L*	Neh 5:13	3068
which the *L* had commanded to	Neh 8:1	3068
And Ezra blessed the *L*, the great	Neh 8:6	3068
worshipped the *L* with their faces	Neh 8:6	3068
day is holy unto the *L* your God	Neh 8:9	3068
for this day is holy unto our *L*	Neh 8:10	113
the joy of the *L* is your strength	Neh 8:10	3068
the *L* had commanded by Moses	Neh 8:14	3068
L their God one fourth part of	Neh 9:3	3068
and worshipped the *L* their God	Neh 9:3	3068
a loud voice unto the *L* their God	Neh 9:4	3068
bless the *L* your God for ever and	Neh 9:5	3068
Thou, even thou, art *L* alone	Neh 9:6	3068
Thou art the *L* the God, who didst	Neh 9:7	3068
commandments of the *L* our *L*	Neh 10:29	3068
commandments of the *L* our *L*	Neh 10:29	113
upon the altar of the *L* our God	Neh 10:34	3068
by year, unto the house of the *L*	Neh 10:35	3068
present themselves before the *L*	Job 1:6	3068
the *L* said unto Satan, Whence	Job 1:7	3068
Then Satan answered the *L*	Job 1:7	3068
the *L* said unto Satan, Hast thou	Job 1:8	3068
Then Satan answered the *L*	Job 1:9	3068
the *L* said unto Satan, Behold,	Job 1:12	3068
forth from the presence of the *L*	Job 1:12	3068
the *L* gave, and the *L* hath	Job 1:21	3068
blessed be the name of the *L*	Job 1:21	3068
present themselves before the *L*	Job 2:1	3068
to present himself before the *L*	Job 2:1	3068
the *L* said unto Satan, From	Job 2:2	3068
And Satan answered the *L*, and said,	Job 2:2	3068

the *L* said unto Satan, Hast thou	Job 2:3	3068
And Satan answered the *L*, and said,	Job 2:4	3068
the *L* said unto Satan, Behold, he	Job 2:6	3068
forth from the presence of the *L*	Job 2:7	3068
hand of the *L* hath wrought this	Job 12:9	3068
said, Behold, the fear of the *L*	Job 28:28	136
Then the *L* answered Job out of	Job 38:1	3068
Moreover the *L* answered Job	Job 40:1	3068
Then Job answered the *L*, and said,	Job 40:3	3068
Then answered the *L* unto Job out	Job 40:6	3068
Then Job answered the *L*, and said,	Job 42:1	3068
that after the *L* had spoken these	Job 42:7	3068
the *L* said to Eliphaz the	Job 42:7	3068
according as the *L* commanded them	Job 42:9	3068
the *L* also accepted Job	Job 42:9	3068
the *L* turned the captivity of Job	Job 42:10	3068
also the *L* gave Job twice as much	Job 42:10	3068
that the *L* had brought upon him	Job 42:11	3068
So the *L* blessed the latter end	Job 42:12	3068
delight is in the law of the *L*	Ps 1:2	3068
For the *L* knoweth the way of the	Ps 1:6	3068
counsel together, against the *L*	Ps 2:2	3068
the *L* shall have them in derision	Ps 2:4	136
The *L* hath said unto me, Thou art	Ps 2:7	3068
Serve the *L* with fear, and rejoice	Ps 2:11	3068
L, how are they increased that	Ps 3:1	3068
But thou, O *L*, art a shield for	Ps 3:3	3068
I cried unto the *L* with my voice	Ps 3:4	3068
for the *L* sustained me	Ps 3:5	3068
Arise, O *L*	Ps 3:7	3068
Salvation belongeth unto the *L*	Ps 3:8	3068
But know that the *L* hath set	Ps 4:3	3068
the *L* will hear when I call unto	Ps 4:3	3068
and put your trust in the *L*	Ps 4:5	3068
L, lift thou up the light of thy	Ps 4:6	3068
for thou, *L*, only makest me dwell	Ps 4:8	3068
Give ear to my words, O *L*	Ps 5:1	3068
thou hear in the morning, O *L*	Ps 5:3	3068
the *L* will abhor the bloody and	Ps 5:6	3068
Lead me, O *L*, in thy	Ps 5:8	3068
For thou, *L*, wilt bless the	Ps 5:12	3068
O *L*, rebuke me not in thine anger	Ps 6:1	3068
Have mercy upon me, O *L*	Ps 6:2	3068
O *L*, heal me	Ps 6:2	3068
but thou, O *L*, how long	Ps 6:3	3068
Return, O *L*, deliver my soul	Ps 6:4	3068
for the *L* hath heard the voice of	Ps 6:8	3068
The *L* hath heard my supplication	Ps 6:9	3068
the *L* will receive my prayer	Ps 6:9	3068
David, which he sang unto the *L*	Ps 7:*t*	3068
O *L* my God, in thee do I put my	Ps 7:1	3068
O *L* my God, if I have done this	Ps 7:3	3068
Arise, O *L*, in thine anger, lift	Ps 7:6	3068
The *L* shall judge the people	Ps 7:8	3068
judge me, O *L*, according to my	Ps 7:8	3068
I will praise the *L* according to	Ps 7:17	3068
to the name of the *L* most high	Ps 7:17	3068
O *L*	Ps 8:1	3068
our *L*, how excellent is	Ps 8:1	113
O *L*	Ps 8:9	3068
our *L*, how excellent is	Ps 8:9	113
I will praise thee, O *L*, with my	Ps 9:1	3068
But the *L* shall endure for ever	Ps 9:7	3068
The *L* also will be a refuge for	Ps 9:9	3068
for thou, *L*, hast not forsaken	Ps 9:10	3068
Sing praises to the *L*, which	Ps 9:11	3068
Have mercy upon me, O *L*	Ps 9:13	3068
The *L* is known by the judgment	Ps 9:16	3068
Arise, O *L*	Ps 9:19	3068
Put them in fear, O *L*	Ps 9:20	3068
Why standest thou afar off, O *L*	Ps 10:1	3068
covetous, whom the *L* abhorreth	Ps 10:3	3068
Arise, O *L*	Ps 10:12	3068
The *L* is King for ever and ever	Ps 10:16	3068
L, thou hast heard the desire of	Ps 10:17	3068
In the *L* put I my trust	Ps 11:1	3068
The *L* is in his holy temple, the	Ps 11:4	3068
The *L* trieth the righteous	Ps 11:5	3068
For the righteous *L* loveth	Ps 11:7	3068
Help, *L*; for the	Ps 12:1	3068
The *L* shall cut off all	Ps 12:3	3068
now will I arise, saith the *L*	Ps 12:5	3068
The words of the *L* are pure words	Ps 12:6	3068
Thou shalt keep them, O *L*	Ps 12:7	3068
How long wilt thou forget me, O *L*	Ps 13:1	3068
Consider and hear me, O *L* my God	Ps 13:3	3068
I will sing unto the *L*, because	Ps 13:6	3068
The *L* looked down from heaven	Ps 14:2	3068
eat bread, and call not upon the *L*	Ps 14:4	3068
because the *L* is his refuge	Ps 14:6	3068
when the *L* bringeth back the	Ps 14:7	3068
L, who shall abide in thy	Ps 15:1	3068
he honoureth them that fear the *L*	Ps 15:4	3068
soul, thou hast said unto the *L*	Ps 16:2	3068
Thou art my *L*	Ps 16:2	136
The *L* is the portion of mine	Ps 16:5	3068
I will bless the *L*, who hath	Ps 16:7	3068
I have set the *L* always before me	Ps 16:8	3068
Hear the right, O *L*, attend unto	Ps 17:1	3068
Arise, O *L*, disappoint him, cast	Ps 17:13	3068
From men which are thy hand, O *L*	Ps 17:14	3068
of David, the servant of the *L*	Ps 18:*t*	3068
who spake unto the *L* the words of	Ps 18:*t*	3068
this song in the day that the *L*	Ps 18:*t*	3068
I will love thee, O *L*, my	Ps 18:1	3068
The *L* is my rock, and my fortress,	Ps 18:2	3068
I will call upon the *L*, who is	Ps 18:3	3068
my distress I called upon the *L*	Ps 18:6	3068
The *L* also thundered in the	Ps 18:13	3068
discovered at thy rebuke, O *L*	Ps 18:15	3068
but the *L* was my stay	Ps 18:18	3068
The *L* rewarded me according to my	Ps 18:20	3068
For I have kept the ways of the *L*	Ps 18:21	3068
Therefore hath the *L* recompensed	Ps 18:24	3068
the *L* my God will enlighten my	Ps 18:28	3068
the word of the *L* is tried	Ps 18:30	3068
For who is God save the *L*	Ps 18:31	3068
even unto the *L*, but he answered	Ps 18:41	3068
The *L* liveth	Ps 18:46	3068
will I give thanks unto thee, O *L*	Ps 18:49	3068
The law of the *L* is perfect	Ps 19:7	3068
the testimony of the *L* is sure	Ps 19:7	3068
The statutes of the *L* are right	Ps 19:8	3068
the commandment of the *L* is pure	Ps 19:8	3068
The fear of the *L* is clean	Ps 19:9	3068
the judgments of the *L* are true	Ps 19:9	3068
be acceptable in thy sight, O *L*	Ps 19:14	3068
The *L* hear thee in the day of	Ps 20:1	3068
the *L* fulfil all thy petitions	Ps 20:5	3068
I that the *L* saveth his anointed	Ps 20:6	3068
the name of the *L* our God	Ps 20:7	3068
Save, *L*	Ps 20:9	3068
shall joy in thy strength, O *L*	Ps 21:1	3068
For the king trusteth in the *L*	Ps 21:7	3068
the *L* shall swallow them up in	Ps 21:9	3068
Be thou exalted, *L*, in thine own	Ps 21:13	3068
He trusted on the *L* that he would	Ps 22:8	3068
But be not thou far from me, O *L*	Ps 22:19	3068
Ye that fear the *L*, praise him	Ps 22:23	3068
shall praise the *L* that seek him	Ps 22:26	3068
shall remember and turn unto the *L*	Ps 22:27	3068
to the *L* for a generation	Ps 22:30	136
The *L* is my shepherd	Ps 23:1	3068
in the house of the *L* for ever	Ps 23:6	3068
ascend into the hill of the *L*	Ps 24:3	3068
receive the blessing from the *L*	Ps 24:5	3068
The *L* strong and mighty, the *L*	Ps 24:8	3068
The *L* of hosts, he is the King of	Ps 24:10	3068
Unto thee, O *L*, do I lift up my	Ps 25:1	3068
Shew me thy ways, O *L*	Ps 25:4	3068
Remember, O *L*, thy tender mercies	Ps 25:6	3068
me for thy goodness' sake, O *L*	Ps 25:7	3068
Good and upright is the *L*	Ps 25:8	3068
All the paths of the *L* are mercy	Ps 25:10	3068
For thy name's sake, O *L*, pardon	Ps 25:11	3068
What man is he that feareth the *L*	Ps 25:12	3068
The secret of the *L* is with them	Ps 25:14	3068
Mine eyes are ever toward the *L*	Ps 25:15	3068
Judge me, O *L*	Ps 26:1	3068
I have trusted also in the *L*	Ps 26:1	3068
Examine me, O *L*, and prove me	Ps 26:2	3068
will I compass thine altar, O *L*	Ps 26:6	3068
L, I have loved the habitation of	Ps 26:8	3068
congregations will I bless the *L*	Ps 26:12	3068
The *L* is my light and my salvation	Ps 27:1	3068
the *L* is the strength of my life	Ps 27:1	3068
One thing have I desired of the *L*	Ps 27:4	3068
of the *L* all the days of my life	Ps 27:4	3068
to behold the beauty of the *L*	Ps 27:4	3068
I will sing praises unto the *L*	Ps 27:6	3068
Hear, O *L*, when I cry with my	Ps 27:7	3068
heart said unto thee, Thy face, *L*	Ps 27:8	3068
then the *L* will take me up	Ps 27:10	3068
Teach me thy way, O *L*, and lead me	Ps 27:11	3068
the *L* in the land of the living	Ps 27:13	3068
Wait on the *L*	Ps 27:14	3068
wait, I say, on the *L*	Ps 27:14	3068
Unto thee will I cry, O *L* my rock	Ps 28:1	3068
regard not the works of the *L*	Ps 28:5	3068
Blessed be the *L*, because he hath	Ps 28:6	3068
The *L* is my strength and my shield	Ps 28:7	3068
The *L* is their strength, and he is	Ps 28:8	3068

L

Give unto the *L*, O ye mighty,	Ps 29:1	3068
give unto the *L* glory	Ps 29:1	3068
Give unto the *L* the glory due	Ps 29:2	3068
worship the *L* in the beauty of	Ps 29:2	3068
The voice of the *L* is upon the	Ps 29:3	3068
the *L* is upon many waters	Ps 29:3	3068
The voice of the *L* is powerful	Ps 29:4	3068
the voice of the *L* is full of	Ps 29:4	3068
The voice of the *L* breaketh the	Ps 29:5	3068
the *L* breaketh the cedars of	Ps 29:5	3068
The voice of the *L* divideth the	Ps 29:7	3068
The voice of the *L* shaketh the	Ps 29:8	3068
the *L* shaketh the wilderness of	Ps 29:8	3068
The voice of the *L* maketh the	Ps 29:9	3068
The *L* sitteth upon the flood	Ps 29:10	3068
the *L* sitteth King for ever	Ps 29:10	3068
The *L* will give strength unto his	Ps 29:11	3068
the *L* will bless his people with	Ps 29:11	3068
I will extol thee, O *L*	Ps 30:1	3068
O *L* my God, I cried unto thee, and	Ps 30:2	3068
O *L*, thou hast brought up my soul	Ps 30:3	3068
Sing unto the *L*, O ye saints of	Ps 30:4	3068
L, by thy favour thou hast made	Ps 30:7	3068
I cried to thee, O *L*	Ps 30:8	3068
unto the *L* I made supplication	Ps 30:8	3068
Hear, O *L*, and have mercy upon me	Ps 30:10	3068
L, be thou my helper	Ps 30:10	3068
O *L* my God, I will give thanks	Ps 30:12	3068
IN thee, O *L*, do I put my trust	Ps 31:1	3068
redeemed me, O *L* God of truth	Ps 31:5	3068
but I trust in the *L*	Ps 31:6	3068
Have mercy upon me, O *L*, for I am	Ps 31:9	3068
But I trusted in thee, O *L*	Ps 31:14	3068
Let me not be ashamed, O *L*	Ps 31:17	3068
Blessed be the *L*	Ps 31:21	3068
O love the *L*, all ye his saints	Ps 31:23	3068
for the *L* preserveth the faithful	Ps 31:23	3068
heart, all ye that hope in the *L*	Ps 31:24	3068
whom the *L* imputeth not iniquity	Ps 32:2	3068
my transgressions unto the *L*	Ps 32:5	3068
but he that trusteth in the *L*	Ps 32:10	3068
Be glad in the *L*, and rejoice, ye	Ps 32:11	3068
Rejoice in the *L*, O ye righteous	Ps 33:1	3068
Praise the *L* with harp	Ps 33:2	3068
For the word of the *L* is right	Ps 33:4	3068
is full of the goodness of the *L*	Ps 33:5	3068
By the word of the *L* were the	Ps 33:6	3068
Let all the earth fear the *L*	Ps 33:8	3068
The *L* bringeth the counsel of the	Ps 33:10	3068
of the *L* standeth for ever	Ps 33:11	3068
is the nation whose God is the *L*	Ps 33:12	3068
The *L* looketh from heaven	Ps 33:13	3068
the eye of the *L* is upon them	Ps 33:18	3068
Our soul waiteth for the *L*	Ps 33:20	3068
Let thy mercy, O *L*, be upon us,	Ps 33:22	3068
I will bless the *L* at all times	Ps 34:1	3068
shall make her boast in the *L*	Ps 34:2	3068
O magnify the *L* with me, and let	Ps 34:3	3068
I sought the *L*, and he heard me,	Ps 34:4	3068
the *L* heard him, and saved him out	Ps 34:6	3068
The angel of the *L* encampeth	Ps 34:7	3068
O taste and see that the *L* is good	Ps 34:8	3068
O fear the *L*, ye his saints	Ps 34:9	3068
but they that seek the *L* shall	Ps 34:10	3068
will teach you the fear of the *L*	Ps 34:11	3068
The eyes of the *L* are upon the	Ps 34:15	3068
The face of the *L* is against them	Ps 34:16	3068
the *L* heareth, and delivereth them	Ps 34:17	3068
The *L* is nigh unto them that are	Ps 34:18	3068
but the *L* delivereth him out of	Ps 34:19	3068
The *L* redeemeth the soul of his	Ps 34:22	3068
Plead my cause, O *L*, with them	Ps 35:1	3068
let the angel of the *L* chase them	Ps 35:5	3068
the angel of the *L* persecute them	Ps 35:6	3068
my soul shall be joyful in the *L*	Ps 35:9	3068
All my bones shall say, *L*	Ps 35:10	3068
L, how long wilt thou look on	Ps 35:17	136
This thou hast seen, O *L*	Ps 35:22	3068
O *L*, be not far from me	Ps 35:22	3068
unto my cause, my God and my *L*	Ps 35:23	136
O *L* my God, according to thy	Ps 35:24	3068
Let the *L* be magnified, which	Ps 35:27	3068
of David, the servant of the *L*	Ps 36:t	3068
Thy mercy, O *L*, is in the heavens	Ps 36:5	3068
O *L*, thou preservest man and beast	Ps 36:6	3068
Trust in the *L*, and do good	Ps 37:3	3068
Delight thyself also in the *L*	Ps 37:4	3068
Commit thy way unto the *L*	Ps 37:5	3068
Rest in the *L*, and wait patiently	Ps 37:7	3068
but those that wait upon the *L*	Ps 37:9	3068
The *L* shall laugh at him	Ps 37:13	136
but the *L* upholdeth the righteous	Ps 37:17	3068
The *L* knoweth the days of the	Ps 37:18	3068
the enemies of the *L* shall be as	Ps 37:20	3068
a good man are ordered by the *L*	Ps 37:23	3068
for the *L* upholdeth him with his	Ps 37:24	3068
For the *L* loveth judgment, and	Ps 37:28	3068
The *L* will not leave him in his	Ps 37:33	3068
Wait on the *L*, and keep his way,	Ps 37:34	3068
of the righteous is of the *L*	Ps 37:39	3068
the *L* shall help them, and deliver	Ps 37:40	3068
O *L*, rebuke me not in thy wrath	Ps 38:1	3068
L, all my desire is before thee	Ps 38:9	136
For in thee, O *L*, do I hope	Ps 38:15	3068
thou wilt hear, O *L* my God	Ps 38:15	136
Forsake me not, O *L*	Ps 38:21	3068
to help me, O *L* my salvation	Ps 38:22	136
L, make me to know mine end, and	Ps 39:4	3068
And now, *L*, what wait I for	Ps 39:7	136
Hear my prayer, O *L*, and give ear	Ps 39:12	3068
I waited patiently for the *L*	Ps 40:1	3068
and fear, and shall trust in the *L*	Ps 40:3	3068
man that maketh the *L* his trust	Ps 40:4	3068
O *L* my God, are thy wonderful	Ps 40:5	3068
I have not refrained my lips, O *L*	Ps 40:9	3068
thy tender mercies from me, O *L*	Ps 40:11	3068
Be pleased, O *L*, to deliver me	Ps 40:13	3068
O *L*, make haste to help me	Ps 40:13	3068
continually, The *L* be magnified	Ps 40:16	3068
yet the *L* thinketh upon me	Ps 40:17	136
the *L* will deliver him in time of	Ps 41:1	3068
The *L* will preserve him, and keep	Ps 41:2	3068
The *L* will strengthen him upon	Ps 41:3	3068
I said, *L*, be merciful unto me	Ps 41:4	3068
But thou, O *L*, be merciful unto	Ps 41:10	3068
Blessed be the *L* God of Israel	Ps 41:13	3068
Yet the *L* will command his	Ps 42:8	3068
Awake, why sleepest thou, O *L*	Ps 44:23	136
for he is thy *L*	Ps 45:11	113
The *L* of hosts is with us	Ps 46:7	3068
Come, behold the works of the *L*	Ps 46:8	3068
The *L* of hosts is with us	Ps 46:11	3068
For the *L* most high is terrible	Ps 47:2	3068
the *L* with the sound of a trumpet	Ps 47:5	3068
Great is the *L*, and greatly to be	Ps 48:1	3068
in the city of the *L* of hosts	Ps 48:8	3068
The mighty God, even the *L*	Ps 50:1	3068
O *L*, open thou my lips	Ps 51:15	136
the *L* is with them that uphold my	Ps 54:4	136
I will praise thy name, O *L*	Ps 54:6	3068
Destroy, O *L*, and divide their	Ps 55:9	136
and the *L* shall save me	Ps 55:16	3068
Cast thy burden upon the *L*	Ps 55:22	3068
in the *L* will I praise his word	Ps 56:10	3068
I will praise thee, O *L*, among	Ps 57:9	136
teeth of the young lions, O *L*	Ps 58:6	3068
nor for my sin, O *L*	Ps 59:3	3068
O *L* God of hosts, the God of	Ps 59:5	3068
But thou, O *L*, shalt laugh at	Ps 59:8	3068
bring them down, O *L* our shield	Ps 59:11	136
Also unto thee, O *L*, belongeth	Ps 62:12	136
righteous shall be glad in the *L*	Ps 64:10	3068
my heart, the *L* will not hear me	Ps 66:18	136
The *L* gave the word	Ps 68:11	136
the *L* will dwell in it for ever	Ps 68:16	3068
the *L* is among them, as in Sinai,	Ps 68:17	136
that the *L* God might dwell among	Ps 68:18	136
Blessed be the *L*, who daily	Ps 68:19	136
unto God the *L* belong the issues	Ps 68:20	136
The *L* said, I will bring again	Ps 68:22	136
in the congregations, even the *L*	Ps 68:26	136
O sing praises unto the *L*	Ps 68:32	136
O *L* God of hosts, be ashamed for	Ps 69:6	136
me, my prayer is unto thee, O *L*	Ps 69:13	3068
Hear me, O *L*	Ps 69:16	3068
This also shall please the *L*	Ps 69:31	3068
For the *L* heareth the poor, and	Ps 69:33	3068
make haste to help me, O *L*	Ps 70:1	3068
O *L*, make no tarrying	Ps 70:5	3068
In thee, O *L*, do I put my trust	Ps 71:1	3068
For thou art my hope, O *L* God	Ps 71:5	136
go in the strength of the *L* God	Ps 71:16	136
Blessed be the *L* God, the God of	Ps 72:18	3068
so, O *L*, when thou awakest, thou	Ps 73:20	136
I have put my trust in the *L* God	Ps 73:28	136
the enemy hath reproached, O *L*	Ps 74:18	3068
the hand of the *L* there is a cup	Ps 75:8	3068
Vow, and pay unto the *L* your God	Ps 76:11	3068
day of my trouble I sought the *L*	Ps 77:2	136
Will the *L* cast off for ever	Ps 77:7	136
will remember the works of the *L*	Ps 77:11	3050
to come the praises of the *L*	Ps 78:4	3068

Therefore the *L* heard this	Ps 78:21	3068
Then the *L* awaked as one out of	Ps 78:65	136
How long, *L*?	Ps 79:5	3068
they have reproached thee, O *L*	Ps 79:12	136
O *L* God of hosts, how long wilt	Ps 80:4	3068
O *L* God of hosts, cause thy face	Ps 80:19	3068
I am the *L* thy God, which brought	Ps 81:10	3068
The haters of the *L* should have	Ps 81:15	3068
that they may seek thy name, O *L*	Ps 83:16	3068
are thy tabernacles, O *L* of hosts	Ps 84:1	3068
fainteth for the courts of the *L*	Ps 84:2	3068
O *L* of hosts, my King, and my God	Ps 84:3	3068
O *L* God of hosts, hear my prayer	Ps 84:8	3068
For the *L* God is a sun and shield	Ps 84:11	3068
the *L* will give grace and glory	Ps 84:11	3068
O *L* of hosts, blessed is the man	Ps 84:12	3068
L, thou hast been favourable unto	Ps 85:1	3068
Shew us thy mercy, O *L*, and grant	Ps 85:7	3068
hear what God the *L* will speak	Ps 85:8	3068
the *L* shall give that which is	Ps 85:12	3068
Bow down thine ear, O *L*, hear me	Ps 86:1	3068
Be merciful unto me, O *L*	Ps 86:3	136
for unto thee, O *L*, do I lift up	Ps 86:4	136
For thou, *L*, art good, and ready	Ps 86:5	136
Give ear, O *L*, unto my prayer	Ps 86:6	3068
there is none like unto thee, O *L*	Ps 86:8	136
come and worship before thee, O *L*	Ps 86:9	136
Teach me thy way, O *L*	Ps 86:11	3068
O *L* my God, with all my heart	Ps 86:12	136
But thou, O *L*, art a God full of	Ps 86:15	136
because thou, *L*, hast holpen me	Ps 86:17	3068
The *L* loveth the gates of Zion	Ps 87:2	3068
The *L* shall count, when he	Ps 87:6	3068
O *L* God of my salvation, I have	Ps 88:1	3068
L, I have called daily upon thee	Ps 88:9	3068
But unto thee have I cried, O *L*	Ps 88:13	3068
L, why castest thou off my soul	Ps 88:14	3068
of the mercies of the *L* for ever	Ps 89:1	3068
shall praise thy wonders, O *L*	Ps 89:5	3068
heaven can be compared unto the *L*	Ps 89:6	3068
mighty can be likened unto the *L*	Ps 89:6	3068
O *L* God of hosts, who is a strong	Ps 89:8	3050
who is a strong *L* like unto thee	Ps 89:8	3068
they shall walk, O *L*, in the	Ps 89:15	3068
For the *L* is our defence	Ps 89:18	3068
How long, *L*?	Ps 89:46	3068
L, where are thy former	Ps 89:49	136
Remember, *L*, the reproach of thy	Ps 89:50	136
enemies have reproached, O *L*	Ps 89:51	3068
Blessed be the *L* for evermore	Ps 89:52	3068
L, thou hast been our dwelling	Ps 90:1	136
Return, O *L*, how long	Ps 90:13	3068
of the *L* our God be upon us	Ps 90:17	3068
I will say of the *L*, He is my	Ps 91:2	3068
Because thou hast made the *L*	Ps 91:9	3068
thing to give thanks unto the *L*	Ps 92:1	3068
For thou, *L*, hast made me glad	Ps 92:4	3068
O *L*, how great are thy works	Ps 92:5	3068
But thou, *L*, art most high for	Ps 92:8	3068
For, lo, thine enemies, O *L*	Ps 92:9	3068
be planted in the house of the *L*	Ps 92:13	3068
To shew that the *L* is upright	Ps 92:15	3068
The *L* reigneth, he is clothed	Ps 93:1	3068
the *L* is clothed with strength	Ps 93:1	3068
The floods have lifted up, O *L*	Ps 93:3	3068
The *L* on high is mightier than	Ps 93:4	3068
becometh thine house, O *L*	Ps 93:5	3068
O *L* God, to whom vengeance	Ps 94:1	3068
L, how long shall the wicked, how	Ps 94:3	3068
break in pieces thy people, O *L*	Ps 94:5	3068
The *L* shall not see, neither	Ps 94:7	3050
The *L* knoweth the thoughts of man	Ps 94:11	3068
the man whom thou chastenest, O *L*	Ps 94:12	3050
For the *L* will not cast off his	Ps 94:14	3068
Unless the *L* had been my help, my	Ps 94:17	3068
thy mercy, O *L*, held me up	Ps 94:18	3068
But the *L* is my defence	Ps 94:22	3068
the *L* our God shall cut them off	Ps 94:23	3068
O come, let us sing unto the *L*	Ps 95:1	3068
For the *L* is a great God, and a	Ps 95:3	3068
us kneel before the *L* our maker	Ps 95:6	3068
O sing unto the *L* a new song	Ps 96:1	3068
sing unto the *L*, all the earth	Ps 96:1	3068
Sing unto the *L*, bless his name	Ps 96:2	3068
For the *L* is great, and greatly to	Ps 96:4	3068
but the *L* made the heavens	Ps 96:5	3068
Give unto the *L*, O ye kindreds of	Ps 96:7	3068
the people, give unto the *L* glory	Ps 96:7	3068
Give unto the *L* the glory due	Ps 96:8	3068
O worship the *L* in the beauty of	Ps 96:9	3068
the heathen that the *L* reigneth	Ps 96:10	3068
Before the *L*: for he cometh	Ps 96:13	3068
The *L* reigneth	Ps 97:1	3068
like wax at the presence of the *L*	Ps 97:5	113
of the *L* of the whole earth	Ps 97:5	3068
because of thy judgments, O *L*	Ps 97:8	3068
For thou, *L*, art high above all	Ps 97:9	3068
Ye that love the *L*, hate evil	Ps 97:10	3068
Rejoice in the *L*, ye righteous	Ps 97:12	3068
O sing unto the *L* a new song	Ps 98:1	3068
The *L* hath made known his	Ps 98:2	3068
Make a joyful noise unto the *L*	Ps 98:4	3068
Sing unto the *L* with the harp	Ps 98:5	3068
make a joyful noise before the *L*	Ps 98:6	3068
Before the *L*; for he cometh	Ps 98:9	3068
The *L* reigneth	Ps 99:1	3068
The *L* is great in Zion	Ps 99:2	3068
Exalt ye the *L* our God, and	Ps 99:5	3068
they called upon the *L*, and he	Ps 99:6	3068
Thou answeredst them, O *L* our God	Ps 99:8	3068
Exalt the *L* our God, and worship	Ps 99:9	3068
for the *L* our God is holy	Ps 99:9	3068
Make a joyful noise unto the *L*	Ps 100:1	3068
Serve the *L* with gladness	Ps 100:2	3068
Know ye that the *L* he is God	Ps 100:3	3068
For the *L* is good	Ps 100:5	3068
unto thee, O *L*, will I sing	Ps 101:1	3068
doers from the city of the *L*	Ps 101:8	3068
out his complaint before the *L*	Ps 102:*t*	3068
Hear my prayer, O *L*, and let my	Ps 102:1	3068
But thou, O *L*, shalt endure for	Ps 102:12	3068
shall fear the name of the *L*	Ps 102:15	3068
When the *L* shall build up Zion	Ps 102:16	3068
be created shall praise the *L*	Ps 102:18	3050
heaven did the *L* behold the earth	Ps 102:19	3068
declare the name of the *L* in Zion	Ps 102:21	3068
and the kingdoms, to serve the *L*	Ps 102:22	3068
Bless the *L*, O my soul	Ps 103:1	3068
Bless the *L*, O my soul, and forget	Ps 103:2	3068
The *L* executeth righteousness and	Ps 103:6	3068
The *L* is merciful and gracious,	Ps 103:8	3068
so the *L* pitieth them that fear	Ps 103:13	3068
But the mercy of the *L* is from	Ps 103:17	3068
The *L* hath prepared his throne in	Ps 103:19	3068
Bless the *L*, ye his angels, that	Ps 103:20	3068
Bless ye the *L*, all ye his hosts	Ps 103:21	3068
Bless the *L*, all his works in all	Ps 103:22	3068
bless the *L*, O my soul	Ps 103:22	3068
Bless the *L*, O my soul	Ps 104:1	3068
O *L* my God, thou art very great	Ps 104:1	3068
trees of the *L* are full of sap	Ps 104:16	3068
O *L*, how manifold are thy works	Ps 104:24	3068
The glory of the *L* shall endure	Ps 104:31	3068
the *L* shall rejoice in his works	Ps 104:31	3068
sing unto the *L* as long as I live	Ps 104:33	3068
I will be glad in the *L*	Ps 104:34	3068
Bless thou the *L*, O my soul	Ps 104:35	3050
Praise ye the *L*	Ps 104:35	3050
O give thanks unto the *L*	Ps 105:1	3050
of them rejoice that seek the *L*	Ps 105:3	3050
Seek the *L*, and his strength	Ps 105:4	3050
He is the *L* our God	Ps 105:7	3050
the word of the *L* tried him	Ps 105:19	3050
Praise ye the *L*	Ps 105:45	3050
Praise ye the *L*	Ps 106:1	3050
O give thanks unto the *L*	Ps 106:1	3068
utter the mighty acts of the *L*	Ps 106:2	3068
Remember me, O *L*, with the favour	Ps 106:4	3068
camp, and Aaron the saint of the *L*	Ps 106:16	3068
not unto the voice of the *L*	Ps 106:25	3068
whom the *L* commanded them	Ps 106:34	3068
the *L* kindled against his people	Ps 106:40	3068
O *L* our God, and gather us from	Ps 106:47	3068
Blessed be the *L* God of Israel	Ps 106:48	3068
Praise ye the *L*	Ps 106:48	3050
O give thanks unto the *L*, for he	Ps 107:1	3068
Let the redeemed of the *L* say so	Ps 107:2	3068
cried unto the *L* in their trouble	Ps 107:6	3068
praise the *L* for his goodness	Ps 107:8	3068
cried unto the *L* in their trouble	Ps 107:13	3068
praise the *L* for his goodness	Ps 107:15	3068
cry unto the *L* in their trouble	Ps 107:19	3068
praise the *L* for his goodness	Ps 107:21	3068
These see the works of the *L*	Ps 107:24	3068
cry unto the *L* in their trouble	Ps 107:28	3068
praise the *L* for his goodness	Ps 107:31	3068
the lovingkindness of the *L*	Ps 107:43	3068
I will praise thee, O *L*, among	Ps 108:3	3068
fathers be remembered with the *L*	Ps 109:14	3068
them be before the *L* continually	Ps 109:15	3068
of mine adversaries from the *L*	Ps 109:20	3068
But do thou for me, O GOD the *L*	Ps 109:21	136

L

Help me, O *L* my God	Ps 109:26	3068
that thou, *L*, hast done it	Ps 109:27	3068
praise the *L* with my mouth	Ps 109:30	3068
The *L* said unto my	Ps 110:1	3068
said unto my *L*, Sit thou	Ps 110:1	113
The *L* shall send the rod of thy	Ps 110:2	3068
The *L* hath sworn, and will not	Ps 110:4	3068
The *L* at thy right hand shall	Ps 110:5	136
Praise ye the *L*	Ps 111:1	3050
I will praise the *L* with my whole	Ps 111:1	3068
The works of the *L* are great	Ps 111:2	3068
the *L* is gracious and full of	Ps 111:4	3068
The fear of the *L* is the	Ps 111:10	3068
Praise ye the *L*	Ps 112:1	3050
is the man that feareth the *L*	Ps 112:1	3068
heart is fixed, trusting in the *L*	Ps 112:7	3068
Praise ye the *L*	Ps 113:1	3050
Praise, O ye servants of the *L*	Ps 113:1	3068
praise the name of the *L*	Ps 113:1	3068
of the *L* from this time forth	Ps 113:2	3068
The *L* is high above all nations,	Ps 113:4	3068
Who is like unto the *L* our God	Ps 113:5	3068
Praise ye the *L*	Ps 113:9	3050
earth, at the presence of the *L*	Ps 114:7	113
Not unto us, O *L*, not unto us,	Ps 115:1	3068
O Israel, trust thou in the *L*	Ps 115:9	3068
O house of Aaron, trust in the *L*	Ps 115:10	3068
fear the *L*, trust in the *L*	Ps 115:11	3068
The *L* hath been mindful of us	Ps 115:12	3068
will bless them that fear the *L*	Ps 115:13	3068
The *L* shall increase you more and	Ps 115:14	3068
of the *L* which made heaven	Ps 115:15	3068
The dead praise not the *L*	Ps 115:17	3050
bless the *L* from this time forth	Ps 115:18	3050
Praise the *L*	Ps 115:18	3050
I love the *L*, because he hath	Ps 116:1	3068
called I upon the name of the *L*	Ps 116:4	3068
O *L*, I beseech thee, deliver my	Ps 116:4	3068
Gracious is the *L*, and righteous	Ps 116:5	3068
The *L* preserveth the simple	Ps 116:6	3068
for the *L* hath dealt bountifully	Ps 116:7	3068
I will walk before the *L* in the	Ps 116:9	3068
What shall I render unto the *L*	Ps 116:12	3068
and call upon the name of the *L*	Ps 116:13	3068
I will pay my vows unto the *L* now	Ps 116:14	3068
the *L* is the death of his saints	Ps 116:15	3068
O *L*, truly I am thy servant	Ps 116:16	3068
will call upon the name of the *L*	Ps 116:17	3068
I will pay my vows unto the *L* now	Ps 116:18	3068
Praise ye the *L*	Ps 116:19	3050
O praise the *L*, all ye nations	Ps 117:1	3068
the truth of the *L* endureth for	Ps 117:2	3068
Praise ye the *L*	Ps 117:2	3050
O give thanks unto the *L*	Ps 118:1	3068
Let them now that fear the *L* say	Ps 118:4	3068
I called upon the *L* in distress	Ps 118:5	3050
the *L* answered me, and set me in a	Ps 118:5	3050
The *L* is on my side	Ps 118:6	3068
The *L* taketh my part with them	Ps 118:7	3068
It is better to trust in the *L*	Ps 118:8	3068
the *L* than to put confidence in	Ps 118:9	3068
name of the *L* I will destroy them	Ps 118:10	3068
name of the *L* I will destroy them	Ps 118:11	3068
name of the *L* I will destroy them	Ps 118:12	3068
but the *L* helped me	Ps 118:13	3068
The *L* is my strength and song, and	Ps 118:14	3050
hand of the *L* doeth valiantly	Ps 118:15	3068
right hand of the *L* is exalted	Ps 118:16	3068
hand of the *L* doeth valiantly	Ps 118:16	3068
and declare the works of the *L*	Ps 118:17	3050
The *L* hath chastened me sore	Ps 118:18	3050
into them, and I will praise the *L*	Ps 118:19	3050
This gate of the *L*, into which	Ps 118:20	3068
is the day which the *L* hath made	Ps 118:24	3068
Save now, I beseech thee, O *L*	Ps 118:25	3068
O *L*, I beseech thee, send now	Ps 118:25	3068
that cometh in the name of the *L*	Ps 118:26	3068
you out of the house of the *L*	Ps 118:26	3068
God is the *L*, which hath shewed	Ps 118:27	3068
O give thanks unto the *L*	Ps 118:29	3068
way, who walk in the law of the *L*	Ps 119:1	3068
Blessed art thou, O *L*	Ps 119:12	3068
O *L*, put me not to shame	Ps 119:31	3068
Teach me, O *L*, the way of thy	Ps 119:33	3068
mercies come also unto me, O *L*	Ps 119:41	3068
thy judgments of old, O *L*	Ps 119:52	3068
I have remembered thy name, O *L*	Ps 119:55	3068
Thou art my portion, O *L*	Ps 119:57	3068
The earth, O *L*, is full of thy	Ps 119:64	3068
dealt well with thy servant, O *L*	Ps 119:65	3068
I know, O *L*, that thy judgments	Ps 119:75	3068
For ever, O *L*, thy word is	Ps 119:89	3068
quicken me, O *L*, according unto	Ps 119:107	3068
offerings of my mouth, O *L*	Ps 119:108	3068
It is time for thee, *L*, to work	Ps 119:126	3068
Righteous art thou, O *L*, and	Ps 119:137	3068
hear me, O *L*	Ps 119:145	3068
O *L*, quicken me according to thy	Ps 119:149	3068
Thou art near, O *L*	Ps 119:151	3068
Great are thy tender mercies, O *L*	Ps 119:156	3068
quicken me, O *L*, according to thy	Ps 119:159	3068
L, I have hoped for thy salvation	Ps 119:166	3068
my cry come near before thee, O *L*	Ps 119:169	3068
longed for thy salvation, O *L*	Ps 119:174	3068
In my distress I cried unto the *L*	Ps 120:1	3068
Deliver my soul, O *L*, from lying	Ps 120:2	3068
My help cometh from the *L*	Ps 121:2	3068
The *L* is thy keeper	Ps 121:5	3068
the *L* is thy shade upon thy right	Ps 121:5	3068
The *L* shall preserve thee from	Ps 121:7	3068
The *L* shall preserve thy going	Ps 121:8	3068
Let us go into the house of the *L*	Ps 122:1	3068
tribes go up, the tribes of the *L*	Ps 122:4	3050
thanks unto the name of the *L*	Ps 122:4	3068
Because of the house of the *L* our	Ps 122:9	3068
our eyes wait upon the *L* our God	Ps 123:2	3068
Have mercy upon us, O *L*, have	Ps 123:3	3068
been the *L* who was on our side	Ps 124:1	3068
been the *L* who was on our side	Ps 124:2	3068
Blessed be the *L*, who hath not	Ps 124:6	3068
Our help is in the name of the *L*	Ps 124:8	3068
in the *L* shall be as mount Zion	Ps 125:1	3068
so the *L* is round about his	Ps 125:2	3068
Do good, O *L*, unto those that be	Ps 125:4	3068
the *L* shall lead them forth with	Ps 125:5	3068
When the *L* turned again the	Ps 126:1	3068
The *L* hath done great things for	Ps 126:2	3068
The *L* hath done great things for	Ps 126:3	3068
Turn again our captivity, O *L*	Ps 126:4	3068
Except the *L* build the house,	Ps 127:1	3068
except the *L* keep the city, the	Ps 127:1	3068
children are an heritage of the *L*	Ps 127:3	3068
is every one that feareth the *L*	Ps 128:1	3068
man be blessed that feareth the *L*	Ps 128:4	3068
The *L* shall bless thee out of	Ps 128:5	3068
The *L* is righteous	Ps 129:4	3068
The blessing of the *L* be upon you	Ps 129:8	3068
we bless you in the name of the *L*	Ps 129:8	3068
have I cried unto thee, O *L*	Ps 130:1	3068
L, hear my voice	Ps 130:2	136
If thou, *L*, shouldest mark	Ps 130:3	3050
shouldest mark iniquities, O *L*	Ps 130:3	136
I wait for the *L*, my soul doth	Ps 130:5	3068
My soul waiteth for the *L* more	Ps 130:6	136
Let Israel hope in the *L*	Ps 130:7	3068
for with the *L* there is mercy, and	Ps 130:7	3068
L, my heart is not haughty, nor	Ps 131:1	3068
hope in the *L* from henceforth	Ps 131:3	3068
L, remember David, and all his	Ps 132:1	3068
How he sware unto the *L*, and vowed	Ps 132:2	3068
I find out a place for the *L*	Ps 132:5	3068
Arise, O *L*, into thy rest	Ps 132:8	3068
The *L* hath sworn in truth unto	Ps 132:11	3068
For the *L* hath chosen Zion	Ps 132:13	3068
for there the *L* commanded the	Ps 133:3	3068
Behold, bless ye the *L*	Ps 134:1	3068
all ye servants of the *L*	Ps 134:1	3068
night stand in the house of the *L*	Ps 134:1	3068
in the sanctuary, and bless the *L*	Ps 134:2	3068
The *L* that made heaven and earth	Ps 134:3	3068
Praise ye the *L*	Ps 135:1	3050
Praise ye the name of the *L*	Ps 135:1	3068
him, O ye servants of the *L*	Ps 135:1	3068
that stand in the house of the *L*	Ps 135:2	3068
Praise the *L*	Ps 135:3	3050
for the *L* is good	Ps 135:3	3068
For the *L* hath chosen Jacob unto	Ps 135:4	3050
For I know that the *L* is great	Ps 135:5	3068
that our *L* is above all gods	Ps 135:5	113
Whatsoever the *L* pleased, that	Ps 135:6	3068
Thy name, O *L*, endureth for ever	Ps 135:13	3068
and thy memorial, O *L*, throughout	Ps 135:13	3068
For the *L* will judge his people	Ps 135:14	3068
Bless the *L*, O house of Israel	Ps 135:19	3068
bless the *L*, O house of Aaron	Ps 135:19	3068
Bless the *L*, O house of Levi	Ps 135:20	3068
that fear the *L*, bless the *L*	Ps 135:20	3068
Blessed be the *L* out of Zion	Ps 135:21	3068
Praise ye the *L*	Ps 135:21	3050
O Give thanks unto the *L*	Ps 136:1	3068
O give thanks to the *L* of lords	Ps 136:3	113
Remember, O *L*, the children of	Ps 137:7	3068

the earth shall praise thee, O *L*	Ps 138:4	3068	The blessing of the *L*, it maketh	Prov 10:22	3068
shall sing in the ways of the *L*	Ps 138:5	3068	The fear of the *L* prolongeth days	Prov 10:27	3068
for great is the glory of the *L*	Ps 138:5	3068	The way of the *L* is strength to	Prov 10:29	3068
Though the *L* be high, yet hath he	Ps 138:6	3068	balance is abomination to the *L*	Prov 11:1	3068
The *L* will perfect that which	Ps 138:8	3068	heart are abomination to the *L*	Prov 11:20	3068
thy mercy, O *L*, endureth for ever	Ps 138:8	3068	man obtaineth favour of the *L*	Prov 12:2	3068
O *l*, thou hast searched me, and	Ps 139:1	3068	lips are abomination to the *L*	Prov 12:22	3068
a word in my tongue, but, lo, O *L*	Ps 139:4	3068	in his uprightness feareth the *L*	Prov 14:2	3068
Do not I hate them, O *L*, that	Ps 139:21	3068	In the fear of the *L* is strong	Prov 14:26	3068
Deliver me, O *L*, from the evil	Ps 140:1	3068	The fear of the *L* is a fountain	Prov 14:27	3068
Keep me, O *L*, from the hands of	Ps 140:4	3068	The eyes of the *L* are in every	Prov 15:3	3068
I said unto the *L*, Thou art my	Ps 140:6	3068	wicked is an abomination to the *L*	Prov 15:8	3068
voice of my supplications, O *L*	Ps 140:6	3068	is an abomination unto the *L*	Prov 15:9	3068
O God the *L*, the strength of my	Ps 140:7	136	and destruction are before the *L*	Prov 15:11	3068
Grant me, O *L*, the desires of	Ps 140:8	3068	fear of the *L* than great treasure	Prov 15:16	3068
I know that the *L* will maintain	Ps 140:12	3068	The *L* will destroy the house of	Prov 15:25	3068
L, I cry unto thee	Ps 141:1	3068	are an abomination to the *L*	Prov 15:26	3068
Set a watch, O *L*, before my mouth	Ps 141:3	3068	The *L* is far from the wicked	Prov 15:29	3068
eyes are unto thee, O GOD the *L*	Ps 141:8	136	The fear of the *L* is the	Prov 15:33	3068
I cried unto the *L* with my voice	Ps 142:1	3068	of the tongue, is from the *L*	Prov 16:1	3068
with my voice unto the *L* did I	Ps 142:1	3068	but the *L* weigheth the spirits	Prov 16:2	3068
I cried unto thee, O *L*	Ps 142:5	3068	Commit thy works unto the *L*	Prov 16:3	3068
Hear my prayer, O *L*, give ear to	Ps 143:1	3068	The *L* hath made all things for	Prov 16:4	3068
Hear me speedily, O *L*	Ps 143:7	3068	heart is an abomination to the *L*	Prov 16:5	3068
Deliver me, O *L*, from mine	Ps 143:9	3068	by the fear of the *L* men depart	Prov 16:6	3068
Quicken me, O *L*, for thy name's	Ps 143:11	3068	When a man's ways please the *L*	Prov 16:7	3068
Blessed be the *L* my strength	Ps 144:1	3068	but the *L* directeth his steps	Prov 16:9	3068
L, what is man, that thou takest	Ps 144:3	3068	and whoso trusteth in the *L*	Prov 16:20	3068
Bow thy heavens, O *L*, and come	Ps 144:5	3068	disposing thereof is of the *L*	Prov 16:33	3068
that people, whose God is the *L*	Ps 144:15	3068	but the *L* trieth the hearts	Prov 17:3	3068
Great is the *L*, and greatly to be	Ps 145:3	3068	both are abomination to the *L*	Prov 17:15	3068
The *L* is gracious, and full of	Ps 145:8	3068	The name of the *L* is a strong	Prov 18:10	3068
The *L* is good to all	Ps 145:9	3068	and obtaineth favour of the *L*	Prov 18:22	3068
thy works shall praise thee, O *L*	Ps 145:10	3068	his heart fretteth against the *L*	Prov 19:3	3068
The *L* upholdeth all that fall, and	Ps 145:14	3068	and a prudent wife is from the *L*	Prov 19:14	3068
The *L* is righteous in all his	Ps 145:17	3068	upon the poor lendeth unto the *L*	Prov 19:17	3068
The *L* is nigh unto all them that	Ps 145:18	3068	nevertheless the counsel of the *L*	Prov 19:21	3068
The *L* preserveth all them that	Ps 145:20	3068	The fear of the *L* tendeth to life	Prov 19:23	3068
shall speak the praise of the *L*	Ps 145:21	3068	are alike abomination to the *L*	Prov 20:10	3068
Praise ye the *L*	Ps 146:1	3050	the *L* hath made even both of them	Prov 20:12	3068
Praise the *L*, O my soul	Ps 146:1	3068	but wait on the *L*, and he shall	Prov 20:22	3068
While I live will I praise the *L*	Ps 146:2	3068	are an abomination unto the *L*	Prov 20:23	3068
whose hope is in the *L* his God	Ps 146:5	3068	Man's goings are of the *L*	Prov 20:24	3068
The *L* looseth the prisoners	Ps 146:7	3068	of man is the candle of the *L*	Prov 20:27	3068
The *L* openeth the eyes of the	Ps 146:8	3068	heart is in the hand of the *L*	Prov 21:1	3068
the *L* raiseth them that are bowed	Ps 146:8	3068	but the *L* pondereth the hearts	Prov 21:2	3068
the *L* loveth the righteous	Ps 146:8	3068	to the *L* than sacrifice	Prov 21:3	3068
The *L* preserveth the strangers	Ps 146:9	3068	nor counsel against the *L*	Prov 21:30	3068
The *L* shall reign for ever, even	Ps 146:10	3068	but safety is of the *L*	Prov 21:31	3068
Praise ye the *L*	Ps 146:10	3050	the *L* is the maker of them all	Prov 22:2	3068
Praise ye the *L*	Ps 147:1	3050	and the fear of the *L* are riches	Prov 22:4	3068
The *L* doth build up Jerusalem	Ps 147:2	3068	The eyes of the *L* preserve	Prov 22:12	3068
Great is our *L*, and of great power	Ps 147:5	113	of the *L* shall fall therein	Prov 22:14	3068
The *L* lifteth up the meek	Ps 147:6	3068	That thy trust may be in the *L*	Prov 22:19	3068
Sing unto the *L* with thanksgiving	Ps 147:7	3068	For the *L* will plead their cause,	Prov 22:23	3068
The *L* taketh pleasure in them	Ps 147:11	3068	fear of the *L* all the day long	Prov 23:17	3068
Praise the *L*, O Jerusalem	Ps 147:12	3068	Lest the *L* see it, and it	Prov 24:18	3068
Praise ye the *L*	Ps 147:20	3050	My son, fear thou the *L* and the	Prov 24:21	3068
Praise ye the *L*	Ps 148:1	3050	head, and the *L* shall reward thee	Prov 25:22	3068
Praise ye the *L* from the heavens	Ps 148:1	3068	seek the *L* understand all things	Prov 28:5	3068
Let them praise the name of the *L*	Ps 148:5	3068	trust in the *L* shall be made fat	Prov 28:25	3068
Praise the *L* from the earth, ye	Ps 148:7	3068	the *L* lighteneth both their eyes	Prov 29:13	3068
Let them praise the name of the *L*	Ps 148:13	3068	his trust in the *L* shall be safe	Prov 29:25	3068
Praise ye the *L*	Ps 148:14	3050	man's judgment cometh from the *L*	Prov 29:26	3068
Praise ye the *L*	Ps 149:1	3050	deny thee, and say, Who is the *L*	Prov 30:9	3068
Sing unto the *L* a new song	Ps 149:1	3068	but a woman that feareth the *L*	Prov 31:30	3068
For the *L* taketh pleasure in his	Ps 149:4	3068	for the *L* hath spoken, I have	Is 1:2	3068
Praise ye the *L*	Ps 149:9	3050	they have forsaken the *L*, they	Is 1:4	3068
Praise ye the *L*	Ps 150:1	3050	Except the *L* of hosts had left	Is 1:9	3068
that hath breath praise the *L*	Ps 150:6	3050	Hear the word of the *L*, ye rulers	Is 1:10	3068
Praise ye the *L*	Ps 150:6	3050	saith the *L*	Is 1:11	3068
The fear of the *L* is the	Prov 1:7	3068	us reason together, saith the *L*	Is 1:18	3068
did not choose the fear of the *L*	Prov 1:29	3068	the mouth of the *L* hath spoken it	Is 1:20	3068
thou understand the fear of the *L*	Prov 2:5	3068	Therefore saith the *L*, the *L*	Is 1:24	113
For the *L* giveth wisdom	Prov 2:6	3068	the *L* of hosts, the mighty One of	Is 1:24	3068
Trust in the *L* with all thine	Prov 3:5	3068	forsake the *L* shall be consumed	Is 1:28	3068
fear the *L*, and depart from evil	Prov 3:7	3068	us go up to the mountain of the *L*	Is 2:3	3068
Honour the *L* with thy substance,	Prov 3:9	3068	the word of the *L* from Jerusalem	Is 2:3	3068
not the chastening of the *L*	Prov 3:11	3068	let us walk in the light of the *L*	Is 2:5	3068
For whom the *L* loveth he	Prov 3:12	3068	in the dust, for fear of the *L*	Is 2:10	3068
The *L* by wisdom hath founded the	Prov 3:19	3068	the *L* alone shall be exalted in	Is 2:11	3068
For the *L* shall be thy confidence	Prov 3:26	3068	For the day of the *L* of hosts	Is 2:12	3068
froward is abomination to the *L*	Prov 3:32	3068	the *L* alone shall be exalted in	Is 2:17	3068
The curse of the *L* is in the	Prov 3:33	3068	of the earth, for fear of the *L*	Is 2:19	3068
man are before the eyes of the *L*	Prov 5:21	3068	ragged rocks, for fear of the *L*	Is 2:21	3068
These six things doth the *L* hate	Prov 6:16	3068	For, behold, the *L*, the *L* of	Is 3:1	113
The fear of the *L* is to hate evil	Prov 8:13	3068	the *L* of hosts, doth take away	Is 3:1	3068
The *L* possessed me in the	Prov 8:22	3068	and their doings are against the *L*	Is 3:8	3068
and shall obtain favour of the *L*	Prov 8:35	3068	The *L* standeth up to plead, and	Is 3:13	3068
The fear of the *L* is the	Prov 9:10	3068	The *L* will enter into judgment	Is 3:14	3068
The *L* will not suffer the soul of	Prov 10:3	3068	saith the *L* GOD of hosts	Is 3:15	136

L

Moreover the *L* saith, Because the	Is 3:16	3068
Therefore the *L* will smite with a	Is 3:17	136
the *L* will discover their secret	Is 3:17	3068
In that day the *L* will take away	Is 3:18	136
the branch of the *L* be beautiful	Is 4:2	3068
When the *L* shall have washed away	Is 4:4	136
the *L* will create upon every	Is 4:5	3068
For the vineyard of the *L* of	Is 5:7	3068
In mine ears said the *L* of hosts	Is 5:9	3068
they regard not the work of the *L*	Is 5:12	3068
But the *L* of hosts shall be	Is 5:16	3068
away the law of the *L* of hosts	Is 5:24	3068
the *L* kindled against his people	Is 5:25	3068
also the *L* sitting upon a throne	Is 6:1	136
holy, holy, is the *L* of hosts	Is 6:3	3068
seen the King, the *L* of hosts	Is 6:5	3068
Also I heard the voice of the *L*	Is 6:8	136
Then said I, *L*, how long	Is 6:11	136
the *L* have removed men far away,	Is 6:12	3068
Then said the *L* unto Isaiah	Is 7:3	3068
Thus saith the *L* GOD, It shall	Is 7:7	136
Moreover the *L* spake again unto	Is 7:10	3068
Ask thee a sign of the *L* thy God	Is 7:11	3068
ask, neither will I tempt the *L*	Is 7:12	3068
Therefore the *L* himself shall	Is 7:14	136
The *L* shall bring upon thee, and	Is 7:17	3068
that the *L* shall hiss for the fly	Is 7:18	3068
In the same day shall the *L* shave	Is 7:20	136
Moreover the *L* said unto me	Is 8:1	3068
Then said the *L* to me, Call his	Is 8:3	3068
The *L* spake also unto me again,	Is 8:5	3068
the *L* bringeth up upon them the	Is 8:7	136
For the *L* spake thus to me with a	Is 8:11	3068
Sanctify the *L* of hosts himself	Is 8:13	3068
And I will wait upon the *L*	Is 8:17	3068
the children whom the *L* hath	Is 8:18	3068
in Israel from the *L* of hosts	Is 8:18	3068
The zeal of the *L* of hosts will	Is 9:7	3068
The *L* sent a word into Jacob, and	Is 9:8	3068
Therefore the *L* shall set up the	Is 9:11	3068
do they seek the *L* of hosts	Is 9:13	3068
Therefore the *L* will cut off from	Is 9:14	3068
Therefore the *L* shall have no joy	Is 9:17	136
Through the wrath of the *L* of	Is 9:19	3068
that when the *L* hath performed	Is 10:12	136
Therefore shall the *L*	Is 10:16	113
the *L* of hosts, send among his	Is 10:16	136
but shall stay upon the *L*	Is 10:20	3068
For the *L* GOD of hosts shall make	Is 10:23	136
thus saith the *L* GOD of hosts	Is 10:24	136
the *L* of hosts shall stir up a	Is 10:26	3068
Behold, the *L*	Is 10:33	113
the *L* of hosts, shall lop the	Is 10:33	3068
the spirit of the *L* shall rest	Is 11:2	3068
knowledge and of the fear of the *L*	Is 11:2	3068
in the fear of the *L*	Is 11:3	3068
be full of the knowledge of the *L*	Is 11:9	3068
that the *L* shall set his hand	Is 11:11	136
the *L* shall utterly destroy the	Is 11:15	3068
in that day thou shalt say, O *L*	Is 12:1	3068
for the *L* JEHOVAH is my strength	Is 12:2	3050
day shall ye say, Praise the *L*	Is 12:4	3068
Sing unto the *L*	Is 12:5	3068
the *L* of hosts mustereth the host	Is 13:4	3068
the end of heaven, even the *L*	Is 13:5	3068
for the day of the *L* is at hand	Is 13:6	3068
Behold, the day of the *L* cometh	Is 13:9	3068
in the wrath of the *L* of hosts	Is 13:13	3068
For the *L* will have mercy on	Is 14:1	3068
in the land of the *L* for servants	Is 14:2	3068
to pass in the day that the *L*	Is 14:3	3068
The *L* hath broken the staff of	Is 14:5	3068
them, saith the *L* of hosts	Is 14:22	3068
and son, and nephew, saith the *L*	Is 14:22	3068
destruction, saith the *L* of hosts	Is 14:23	3068
The *L* of hosts hath sworn, saying	Is 14:24	3068
For the *L* of hosts hath purposed,	Is 14:27	3068
That the *L* hath founded Zion, and	Is 14:32	3068
This is the word that the *L* hath	Is 16:13	3068
But now the *L* hath spoken	Is 16:14	3068
of Israel, saith the *L* of hosts	Is 17:3	3068
saith the *L* God of Israel	Is 17:6	3068
For so the *L* said unto me, I will	Is 18:4	3068
L of hosts of a people scattered	Is 18:7	3068
of the name of the *L* of hosts	Is 18:7	3068
the *L* rideth upon a swift cloud,	Is 19:1	3068
shall rule over them, saith the *L*	Is 19:4	113
the *L* of hosts	Is 19:4	3068
let them know what the *L* of hosts	Is 19:12	3068
The *L* hath mingled a perverse	Is 19:14	3068
of the hand of the *L* of hosts	Is 19:16	3068
of the counsel of the *L* of hosts	Is 19:17	3068
and swear to the *L* of hosts	Is 19:18	3068
the *L* in the midst of the land of	Is 19:19	3068
at the border thereof to the *L*	Is 19:19	3068
for a witness unto the *L* of hosts	Is 19:20	3068
the *L* because of the oppressors	Is 19:20	3068
the *L* shall be known to Egypt, and	Is 19:21	3068
shall know the *L* in that day	Is 19:21	3068
they shall vow a vow unto the *L*	Is 19:21	3068
And the *L* shall smite Egypt	Is 19:22	3068
they shall return even to the *L*	Is 19:22	3068
Whom the *L* of hosts shall bless,	Is 19:25	3068
the *L* by Isaiah the son of Amoz	Is 20:2	3068
the *L* said, Like as my servant	Is 20:3	3068
For thus hath the *L* said unto me	Is 21:6	136
I have heard of the *L* of hosts	Is 21:10	3068
For thus hath the *L* said unto me	Is 21:16	136
for the *L* God of Israel hath	Is 21:17	3068
of perplexity by the *L* GOD of	Is 22:5	136
in that day did the *L* GOD of	Is 22:12	136
in mine ears by the *L* of hosts	Is 22:14	3068
ye die, saith the *L* GOD of hosts	Is 22:14	136
Thus saith the *L* GOD of hosts	Is 22:15	136
the *L* will carry thee away with a	Is 22:17	3068
In that day, saith the *L* of hosts	Is 22:25	3068
for the *L* hath spoken it	Is 22:25	3068
The *L* of hosts hath purposed it,	Is 23:9	3068
the *L* hath given a commandment	Is 23:11	3068
that the *L* will visit Tyre, and	Is 23:17	3068
hire shall be holiness to the *L*	Is 23:18	3068
for them that dwell before the *L*	Is 23:18	3068
the *L* maketh the earth empty, and	Is 24:1	3068
for the *L* hath spoken this word	Is 24:3	3068
sing for the majesty of the *L*	Is 24:14	3068
glorify ye the *L* in the fires	Is 24:15	3068
even the name of the *L* God of	Is 24:15	3068
that the *L* shall punish the host	Is 24:21	3068
when the *L* of hosts shall reign	Is 24:23	3068
O *L*, thou art my God	Is 25:1	3068
in this mountain shall the *L* of	Is 25:6	3068
the *L* GOD will wipe away tears	Is 25:8	136
for the *L* hath spoken it	Is 25:8	3068
this is the *L*	Is 25:9	3068
shall the hand of the *L* rest	Is 25:10	3068
Trust ye in the *L* for ever	Is 26:4	3068
for in the *L* JEHOVAH is	Is 26:4	3050
in the way of thy judgments, O *L*	Is 26:8	3068
not behold the majesty of the *L*	Is 26:10	3068
L, when thy hand is lifted up,	Is 26:11	3068
L, thou wilt ordain peace for us	Is 26:12	3068
O *L* our God, other lords besides	Is 26:13	3068
hast increased the nation, O *L*	Is 26:15	3068
L, in trouble have they visited	Is 26:16	3068
so have we been in thy sight, O *L*	Is 26:17	3068
the *L* cometh out of his place to	Is 26:21	3068
In that day the *L* with his sore	Is 27:1	3068
I the *L* do keep it	Is 27:3	3068
that the *L* shall beat off from	Is 27:12	3068
shall worship the *L* in the holy	Is 27:13	3068
the *L* hath a mighty and strong one	Is 28:2	136
In that day shall the *L* of hosts	Is 28:5	3068
But the word of the *L* was unto	Is 28:13	3068
Wherefore hear the word of the *L*	Is 28:14	3068
Therefore thus saith the *L* GOD	Is 28:16	136
For the *L* shall rise up as in	Is 28:21	3068
for I have heard from the *L* GOD	Is 28:22	136
cometh forth from the *L* of hosts	Is 28:29	3068
of the *L* of hosts with thunder	Is 29:6	3068
For the *L* hath poured out upon	Is 29:10	3068
Wherefore the *L* said, Forasmuch	Is 29:13	136
to hide their counsel from the *L*	Is 29:15	3068
shall increase their joy in the *L*	Is 29:19	3068
Therefore thus saith the *L*	Is 29:22	3068
rebellious children, saith the *L*	Is 30:1	3068
will not hear the law of the *L*	Is 30:9	3068
For thus saith the *L* GOD, the	Is 30:15	136
And therefore will the *L* wait	Is 30:18	3068
for the *L* is a God of judgment	Is 30:18	3068
though the *L* give you the bread	Is 30:20	136
in the day that the *L* bindeth up	Is 30:26	3068
the name of the *L* cometh from far	Is 30:27	3068
come into the mountain of the *L*	Is 30:29	3068
the *L* shall cause his glorious	Is 30:30	3068
L shall the Assyrian be beaten	Is 30:31	3068
which the *L* shall lay upon him,	Is 30:32	3068
the breath of the *L*, like a	Is 30:33	3068
One of Israel, neither seek the *L*	Is 31:1	3068
When the *L* shall stretch out his	Is 31:3	3068
thus hath the *L* spoken unto me	Is 31:4	3068
so shall the *L* of hosts come down	Is 31:4	3068
so will the *L* of hosts defend	Is 31:5	3068

afraid of the ensign, saith the *L*	Is 31:9	3068
and to utter error against the *L*	Is 32:6	3068
O *L*, be gracious unto us	Is 33:2	3068
The *L* is exalted	Is 33:5	3068
the fear of the *L* is his treasure	Is 33:6	3068
Now will I rise, saith the *L*	Is 33:10	3068
But there the glorious *L* will be	Is 33:21	3068
For the *L* is our judge	Is 33:22	3068
the *L* is our lawgiver	Is 33:22	3068
the *L* is our king	Is 33:22	3068
of the *L* is upon all nations	Is 34:2	3068
The sword of the *L* is filled with	Is 34:6	3068
for the *L* hath a sacrifice in	Is 34:6	3068
Seek ye out of the book of the *L*	Is 34:16	3068
they shall see the glory of the *L*	Is 35:2	3068
ransomed of the *L* shall return	Is 35:10	3068
to me, We trust in the *L* our God	Is 36:7	3068
am I now come up without the *L*	Is 36:10	3068
the *L* said unto me, Go up against	Is 36:10	3068
Hezekiah make you trust in the *L*	Is 36:15	3068
The *L* will surely deliver us	Is 36:15	3068
saying, The *L* will deliver us	Is 36:18	3068
that the *L* should deliver	Is 36:20	3068
and went into the house of the *L*	Is 37:1	3068
It may be the *L* thy God will hear	Is 37:4	3068
which the *L* thy God hath heard	Is 37:4	3068
your master, Thus saith the *L*	Is 37:6	3068
went up unto the house of the *L*	Is 37:14	3068
and spread it before the *L*	Is 37:14	3068
And Hezekiah prayed unto the *L*	Is 37:15	3068
O *L* of hosts, God of Israel, that	Is 37:16	3068
Incline thine ear, O *L*, and hear	Is 37:17	3068
open thine eyes, O *L*, and see	Is 37:17	3068
Of a truth, *L*, the kings of	Is 37:18	3068
O *L* our God, save us from his	Is 37:20	3068
may know that thou art the *L*	Is 37:20	3068
Thus saith the *L* God of Israel	Is 37:21	3068
the *L* hath spoken concerning him	Is 37:22	3068
hast thou reproached the *L*	Is 37:24	136
the zeal of the *L* of hosts shall	Is 37:32	3068
Therefore thus saith the *L*	Is 37:33	3068
come into this city, saith the *L*	Is 37:34	3068
the angel of the *L* went forth	Is 37:36	3068
said unto him, Thus saith the *L*	Is 38:1	3068
the wall, and prayed unto the *L*	Is 38:2	3068
And said, Remember now, O *L*	Is 38:3	3068
came the word of the *L* to Isaiah	Is 38:4	3068
say to Hezekiah, Thus saith the *L*	Is 38:5	3068
be a sign unto thee from the *L*	Is 38:7	3068
that the *L* will do this thing	Is 38:7	3068
not see the *L*, even the *L*	Is 38:11	3050
O *L*, I am oppressed	Is 38:14	3068
O *L*, by these things men live, and	Is 38:16	136
The *L* was ready to save me	Is 38:20	3068
of our life in the house of the *L*	Is 38:20	3068
shall go up to the house of the *L*	Is 38:22	3068
Hear the word of the *L* of hosts	Is 39:5	3068
shall be left, saith the *L*	Is 39:6	3068
of the *L* which thou hast spoken	Is 39:8	3068
Prepare ye the way of the *L*	Is 40:3	3068
the glory of the *L* shall be	Is 40:5	3068
the mouth of the *L* hath spoken it	Is 40:5	3068
spirit of the *L* bloweth upon it	Is 40:7	3068
the *L* God will come with strong	Is 40:10	136
hath directed the Spirit of the *L*	Is 40:13	3068
Israel, My way is hid from the *L*	Is 40:27	3068
that the everlasting God, the *L*	Is 40:28	3068
the *L* shall renew their strength	Is 40:31	3068
I the *L*, the first, and with the	Is 41:4	3068
For I the *L* thy God will hold thy	Is 41:13	3068
I will help thee, saith the *L*	Is 41:14	3068
and thou shalt rejoice in the *L*	Is 41:16	3068
I the *L* will hear them, I the God	Is 41:17	3068
the hand of the *L* hath done this	Is 41:20	3068
Produce your cause, saith the *L*	Is 41:21	3068
Thus saith God the *L*, he that	Is 42:5	3068
I the *L* have called thee in	Is 42:6	3068
I am the *L*	Is 42:8	3068
Sing unto the *L* a new song	Is 42:10	3068
Let them give glory unto the *L*	Is 42:12	3068
The *L* shall go forth as a mighty	Is 42:13	3068
The *L* is well pleased for his	Is 42:21	3068
did not the *L*, he against whom we	Is 42:24	3068
saith the *L* that created thee	Is 43:1	3068
For I am the *L* thy God, the Holy	Is 43:3	3068
Ye are my witnesses, saith the *L*	Is 43:10	3068
I, even I, am the *L*	Is 43:11	3068
ye are my witnesses, saith the *L*	Is 43:12	3068
Thus saith the *L*, your redeemer	Is 43:14	3068
I am the *L*, your Holy One, the	Is 43:15	3068
Thus saith the *L*, which maketh a	Is 43:16	3068
Thus saith the *L* that made thee	Is 44:2	3068
with his hand unto the *L*, and	Is 44:5	3068
Thus saith the *L* the King of	Is 44:6	3068
and his redeemer the *L* of hosts	Is 44:6	3068
for the *L* hath done it	Is 44:23	3068
for the *L* hath redeemed Jacob, and	Is 44:23	3068
Thus saith the *L*, thy redeemer	Is 44:24	3068
I am the *L* that maketh all things	Is 44:24	3068
Thus saith the *L* to his anointed	Is 45:1	3068
thou mayest know that I, the *L*	Is 45:3	3068
I am the *L*, and there is none else	Is 45:5	3068
I am the *L*, and there is none else	Is 45:6	3068
I the *L* do all these things	Is 45:7	3068
I the *L* have created it	Is 45:8	3068
Thus saith the *L*, the Holy One of	Is 45:11	3068
nor reward, saith the *L* of hosts	Is 45:13	3068
Thus saith the *L*, The labour of	Is 45:14	3068
Israel shall be saved in the *L*	Is 45:17	3068
For thus saith the *L* that created	Is 45:18	3068
I am the *L*	Is 45:18	3068
I the *L* speak righteousness, I	Is 45:19	3068
have not I the *L*	Is 45:21	3068
in the *L* have I righteousness and	Is 45:24	3068
In the *L* shall all the seed of	Is 45:25	3068
the *L* of hosts is his name, the	Is 47:4	3068
which swear by the name of the *L*	Is 48:1	3068
The *L* of hosts is his name	Is 48:2	3068
The *L* hath loved him	Is 48:14	3068
and now the *L* GOD, and his Spirit	Is 48:16	136
Thus saith the *L*, thy Redeemer	Is 48:17	3068
I am the *L* thy God which teacheth	Is 48:17	3068
The *L* hath redeemed his servant	Is 48:20	3068
There is no peace, saith the *L*	Is 48:22	3068
The *L* hath called me from the	Is 49:1	3068
surely my judgment is with the *L*	Is 49:4	3068
saith the *L* that formed me from	Is 49:5	3068
be glorious in the eyes of the *L*	Is 49:5	3068
Thus saith the *L*, the Redeemer of	Is 49:7	3068
because of the *L* that is faithful	Is 49:7	3068
Thus saith the *L*, In an	Is 49:8	3068
for the *L* hath comforted his	Is 49:13	3068
The *L* hath forsaken me	Is 49:14	3068
and my *L* hath forgotten me	Is 49:14	136
As I live, saith the *L*, thou	Is 49:18	3068
Thus saith the *L* GOD, Behold, I	Is 49:22	136
thou shalt know that I am the *L*	Is 49:23	3068
But thus saith the *L*, Even the	Is 49:25	3068
know that I the *L* am thy Saviour	Is 49:26	3068
Thus saith the *L*, Where is the	Is 50:1	3068
The *L* GOD hath given me the	Is 50:4	136
The *L* GOD hath opened mine ear,	Is 50:5	136
For the *L* GOD will help me	Is 50:7	136
Behold, the *L* GOD will help me	Is 50:9	136
is among you that feareth the *L*	Is 50:10	3068
him trust in the name of the *L*	Is 50:10	3068
righteousness, ye that seek the *L*	Is 51:1	3068
For the *L* shall comfort Zion	Is 51:3	3068
desert like the garden of the *L*	Is 51:3	3068
put on strength, O arm of the *L*	Is 51:9	3068
redeemed of the *L* shall return	Is 51:11	3068
And forgettest the *L* thy maker	Is 51:13	3068
But I am the *L* thy God, that	Is 51:15	3068
The *L* of hosts is his name	Is 51:15	3068
hand of the *L* the cup of his fury	Is 51:17	3068
are full of the fury of the *L*	Is 51:20	3068
Thus saith thy *L*	Is 51:22	113
the *L*, and thy God	Is 51:22	3068
For thus saith the *L*, Ye have	Is 52:3	3068
For thus saith the *L* GOD, My	Is 52:4	136
what have I here, saith the *L*	Is 52:5	3068
make them to howl, saith the *L*	Is 52:5	3068
when the *L* shall bring again Zion	Is 52:8	3068
for the *L* hath comforted his	Is 52:9	3068
The *L* hath made bare his holy arm	Is 52:10	3068
that bear the vessels of the *L*	Is 52:11	3068
for the *L* will go before you	Is 52:12	3068
whom is the arm of the *L* revealed	Is 53:1	3068
the *L* hath laid on him the	Is 53:6	3068
it pleased the *L* to bruise him	Is 53:10	3068
the pleasure of the *L* shall	Is 53:10	3068
of the married wife, saith the *L*	Is 54:1	3068
the *L* of hosts is his name	Is 54:5	3068
For the *L* hath called thee as a	Is 54:6	3068
on thee, saith the *L* thy Redeemer	Is 54:8	3068
saith the *L* that hath mercy on	Is 54:10	3068
children shall be taught of the *L*	Is 54:13	3068
heritage of the servants of the *L*	Is 54:17	3068
is of me, saith the *L*	Is 54:17	3068
thee because of the *L* thy God	Is 55:5	3068
Seek ye the *L* while he may be	Is 55:6	3068
and let him return unto the *L*	Is 55:7	3068

L

your ways my ways, saith the L	Is 55:8	3068
it shall be to the L for a name	Is 55:13	3068
Thus saith the L, Keep ye	Is 56:1	3068
that hath joined himself to the L	Is 56:3	3068
The L hath utterly separated me	Is 56:3	3068
For thus saith the L unto the	Is 56:4	3068
that join themselves to the L	Is 56:6	3068
him, and to love the name of the L	Is 56:6	3068
The L GOD which gathereth the	Is 56:8	136
to him that is near, saith the L	Is 57:19	3068
and an acceptable day to the L	Is 58:5	3068
the glory of the L shall be thy	Is 58:8	3068
thou call, and the L shall answer	Is 58:9	3068
And the L shall guide thee	Is 58:11	3068
a delight, the holy of the L	Is 58:13	3068
thou delight thyself in the L	Is 58:14	3068
the mouth of the L hath spoken it	Is 58:14	3068
and lying against the L, and	Is 59:13	3068
the L saw it, and it displeased	Is 59:15	3068
the name of the L from the west	Is 59:19	3068
the Spirit of the L shall lift up	Is 59:19	3068
in Jacob, saith the L	Is 59:20	3068
covenant with them, saith the L	Is 59:21	3068
of thy seed's seed, saith the L	Is 59:21	3068
the glory of the L is risen upon	Is 60:1	3068
but the L shall arise upon thee,	Is 60:2	3068
shew forth the praises of the L	Is 60:6	3068
unto the name of the L thy God	Is 60:9	3068
call thee, The city of the L	Is 60:14	3068
know that I the L am thy Saviour	Is 60:16	3068
but the L shall be unto thee an	Is 60:19	3068
for the L shall be thine	Is 60:20	3068
I the L will hasten it in his	Is 60:22	3068
Spirit of the L GOD is upon me	Is 61:1	136
because the L hath anointed me to	Is 61:1	3068
the acceptable year of the L	Is 61:2	3068
the planting of the L, that he	Is 61:3	3068
be named the Priests of the L	Is 61:6	3068
For I the L love judgment, I hate	Is 61:8	3068
the seed which the L hath blessed	Is 61:9	3068
I will greatly rejoice in the L	Is 61:10	3068
so the L GOD will cause	Is 61:11	136
the mouth of the L shall name	Is 62:2	3068
of glory in the hand of the L	Is 62:3	3068
for the L delighteth in thee, and	Is 62:4	3068
ye that make mention of the L	Is 62:6	3068
The L hath sworn by his right	Is 62:8	3068
it shall eat it, and praise the L	Is 62:9	3068
the L hath proclaimed unto the	Is 62:11	3068
people, The redeemed of the L	Is 62:12	3068
the lovingkindnesses of the L	Is 63:7	3068
and the praises of the L	Is 63:7	3068
that the L hath bestowed on us	Is 63:7	3068
the Spirit of the L caused him to	Is 63:14	3068
thou, O L, art our father, our	Is 63:16	3068
O L, why hast thou made us to err	Is 63:17	3068
But now, O L, thou art our father	Is 64:8	3068
Be not wroth very sore, O L	Is 64:9	3068
thyself for these things, O L	Is 64:12	3068
fathers together, saith the L	Is 65:7	3068
Thus saith the L, As the new wine	Is 65:8	3068
ye are they that forsake the L	Is 65:11	3068
Therefore thus saith the L GOD	Is 65:13	136
for the L GOD shall slay thee, and	Is 65:15	136
the seed of the blessed of the L	Is 65:23	3068
all my holy mountain, saith the L	Is 65:25	3068
Thus saith the L, The heaven is	Is 66:1	3068
things have been, saith the L	Is 66:2	3068
Hear the word of the L, ye that	Is 66:5	3068
said, Let the L be glorified	Is 66:5	3068
a voice of the L that rendereth	Is 66:6	3068
saith the L	Is 66:9	3068
For thus saith the L, Behold, I	Is 66:12	3068
the hand of the L shall be known	Is 66:14	3068
the L will come with fire, and	Is 66:15	3068
will the L plead with all flesh	Is 66:16	3068
the slain of the L shall be many	Is 66:16	3068
be consumed together, saith the L	Is 66:17	3068
for an offering unto the L out of	Is 66:20	3068
mountain Jerusalem, saith the L	Is 66:20	3068
vessel into the house of the L	Is 66:20	3068
and for Levites, saith the L	Is 66:21	3068
remain before me, saith the L	Is 66:22	3068
to worship before me, saith the L	Is 66:23	3068
To whom the word of the L came in	Jer 1:2	3068
the word of the L came unto me	Jer 1:4	3068
Then said I, Ah, L GOD	Jer 1:6	136
But the L said unto me, Say not,	Jer 1:7	3068
thee to deliver thee, saith the L	Jer 1:8	3068
Then the L put forth his hand, and	Jer 1:9	3068
the L said unto me, Behold, I	Jer 1:9	3068
the word of the L came unto me	Jer 1:11	3068
Then said the L unto me, Thou	Jer 1:12	3068
the word of the L came unto me	Jer 1:13	3068
Then the L said unto me, Out of	Jer 1:14	3068
of the north, saith the L	Jer 1:15	3068
for I am with thee, saith the L	Jer 1:19	3068
the word of the L came to me	Jer 2:1	3068
saying, Thus saith the L	Jer 2:2	3068
Israel was holiness unto the L	Jer 2:3	3068
shall come upon them, saith the L	Jer 2:3	3068
Hear ye the word of the L	Jer 2:4	3068
Thus saith the L, What iniquity	Jer 2:5	3068
Where is the L that brought us up	Jer 2:6	3068
priests said not, Where is the L	Jer 2:8	3068
yet plead with you, saith the L	Jer 2:9	3068
be ye very desolate, saith the L	Jer 2:12	3068
thou hast forsaken the L thy God	Jer 2:17	3068
thou hast forsaken the L thy God	Jer 2:19	3068
in thee, saith the L GOD of hosts	Jer 2:19	136
marked before me, saith the L GOD	Jer 2:22	136
against me, saith the L	Jer 2:29	3068
see ye the word of the L	Jer 2:31	3068
for the L hath rejected thy	Jer 2:37	3068
return again to me, saith the L	Jer 3:1	3068
The L said also unto me in the	Jer 3:6	3068
heart, but feignedly, saith the L	Jer 3:10	3068
And the L said unto me, The	Jer 3:11	3068
backsliding Israel, saith the L	Jer 3:12	3068
for I am merciful, saith the L	Jer 3:12	3068
against the L thy God, and hast	Jer 3:13	3068
not obeyed my voice, saith the L	Jer 3:13	3068
backsliding children, saith the L	Jer 3:14	3068
land, in those days, saith the L	Jer 3:16	3068
The ark of the covenant of the L	Jer 3:16	3068
Jerusalem the throne of the L	Jer 3:17	3068
unto it, to the name of the L	Jer 3:17	3068
O house of Israel, saith the L	Jer 3:20	3068
have forgotten the L their God	Jer 3:21	3068
for thou art the L our God	Jer 3:22	3068
truly in the L our God is the	Jer 3:23	3068
have sinned against the L our God	Jer 3:25	3068
obeyed the voice of the L our God	Jer 3:25	3068
return, O Israel, saith the L	Jer 4:1	3068
The L liveth, in truth, in	Jer 4:2	3068
For thus saith the L to the men	Jer 4:3	3068
Circumcise yourselves to the L	Jer 4:4	3068
the L is not turned back from us	Jer 4:8	3068
to pass at that day, saith the L	Jer 4:9	3068
Then said I, Ah, L GOD	Jer 4:10	136
against me, saith the L	Jer 4:17	3068
down at the presence of the L	Jer 4:26	3068
For thus hath the L said, The	Jer 4:27	3068
And though they say, The L liveth	Jer 5:2	3068
O L, are not thine eyes upon the	Jer 5:3	3068
they know not the way of the L	Jer 5:4	3068
they have known the way of the L	Jer 5:5	3068
for these things? saith the L	Jer 5:9	3068
against me, saith the L	Jer 5:11	3068
They have belied the L, and said,	Jer 5:12	3068
thus saith the L God of hosts	Jer 5:14	3068
O house of Israel, saith the L	Jer 5:15	3068
in those days, saith the L	Jer 5:18	3068
Wherefore doeth the L our God all	Jer 5:19	3068
Fear ye not me? saith the L	Jer 5:22	3068
Let us now fear the L our God	Jer 5:24	3068
these things? saith the L	Jer 5:29	3068
For thus hath the L of hosts said	Jer 6:6	3068
Thus saith the L of hosts	Jer 6:9	3068
the word of the L is unto them a	Jer 6:10	3068
I am full of the fury of the L	Jer 6:11	3068
of the land, saith the L	Jer 6:12	3068
shall be cast down, saith the L	Jer 6:15	3068
Thus saith the L, Stand ye in the	Jer 6:16	3068
Therefore thus saith the L	Jer 6:21	3068
Thus saith the L, Behold, a	Jer 6:22	3068
because the L hath rejected them	Jer 6:30	3068
that came to Jeremiah from the L	Jer 7:1	3068
and say, Hear the word of the L	Jer 7:2	3068
at these gates to worship the L	Jer 7:2	3068
Thus saith the L of hosts	Jer 7:3	3068
saying, The temple of the L	Jer 7:4	3068
of the L, The temple of the L	Jer 7:4	3068
even I have seen it, saith the L	Jer 7:11	3068
done all these works, saith the L	Jer 7:13	3068
to anger? saith the L	Jer 7:19	3068
Therefore thus saith the L GOD	Jer 7:20	136
Thus saith the L of hosts	Jer 7:21	3068
not the voice of the L their God	Jer 7:28	3068
for the L hath rejected and	Jer 7:29	3068
evil in my sight, saith the L	Jer 7:30	3068
the days come, saith the L	Jer 7:32	3068

At that time, saith the *L*	Jer 8:1	3068
driven them, saith the *L* of hosts	Jer 8:3	3068
say unto them, Thus saith the *L*	Jer 8:4	3068
know not the judgment of the *L*	Jer 8:7	3068
and the law of the *L* is with us	Jer 8:8	3068
have rejected the word of the *L*	Jer 8:9	3068
shall be cast down, saith the *L*	Jer 8:12	3068
surely consume them, saith the *L*	Jer 8:13	3068
for the *L* our God hath put us to	Jer 8:14	3068
we have sinned against the *L*	Jer 8:14	3068
they shall bite you, saith the *L*	Jer 8:17	3068
Is not the *L* in Zion	Jer 8:19	3068
and they know not me, saith the *L*	Jer 9:3	3068
refuse to know me, saith the *L*	Jer 9:6	3068
thus saith the *L* of hosts	Jer 9:7	3068
these things? saith the *L*	Jer 9:9	3068
the mouth of the *L* hath spoken	Jer 9:12	3068
the *L* saith, Because they have	Jer 9:13	3068
thus saith the *L* of hosts	Jer 9:15	3068
Thus saith the *L* of hosts	Jer 9:17	3068
Yet hear the word of the *L*	Jer 9:20	3068
Speak, Thus saith the *L*, Even the	Jer 9:22	3068
Thus saith the *L*, Let not the	Jer 9:23	3068
that I am the *L* which exercise	Jer 9:24	3068
things I delight, saith the *L*	Jer 9:24	3068
the days come, saith the *L*	Jer 9:25	3068
which the *L* speaketh unto you	Jer 10:1	3068
Thus saith the *L*, Learn not the	Jer 10:2	3068
there is none like unto thee, O *L*	Jer 10:6	3068
But the *L* is the true God, he is	Jer 10:10	3068
The *L* of hosts is his name	Jer 10:16	3068
For thus saith the *L*, Behold, I	Jer 10:18	3068
brutish, and have not sought the *L*	Jer 10:21	3068
O *L*, I know that the way of man	Jer 10:23	3068
O *L*, correct me, but with	Jer 10:24	3068
that came to Jeremiah from the *L*	Jer 11:1	3068
Thus saith the *L* God of Israel	Jer 11:3	3068
I, and said, So be it, O *L*	Jer 11:5	3068
Then the *L* said unto me, Proclaim	Jer 11:6	3068
the *L* said unto me, A conspiracy	Jer 11:9	3068
Therefore thus saith the *L*	Jer 11:11	3068
The *L* called thy name, A green	Jer 11:16	3068
For the *L* of hosts, that planted	Jer 11:17	3068
the *L* hath given me knowledge of	Jer 11:18	3068
O *L* of hosts, that judgest	Jer 11:20	3068
the *L* of the men of Anathoth	Jer 11:21	3068
Prophesy not in the name of the *L*	Jer 11:21	3068
thus saith the *L* of hosts	Jer 11:22	3068
Righteous art thou, O *L*, when I	Jer 12:1	3068
But thou, O *L*, knowest me	Jer 12:3	3068
for the sword of the *L* shall	Jer 12:12	3068
of the fierce anger of the *L*	Jer 12:13	3068
Thus saith the *L* against all mine	Jer 12:14	3068
to swear by my name, The *L* liveth	Jer 12:16	3068
destroy that nation, saith the *L*	Jer 12:17	3068
Thus saith the *L* unto me, Go and	Jer 13:1	3068
according to the word of the *L*	Jer 13:2	3068
the word of the *L* came unto me	Jer 13:3	3068
Euphrates, as the *L* commanded me	Jer 13:5	3068
that the *L* said unto me, Arise,	Jer 13:6	3068
the word of the *L* came unto me	Jer 13:8	3068
Thus saith the *L*, After this	Jer 13:9	3068
whole house of Judah, saith the *L*	Jer 13:11	3068
Thus saith the *L* God of Israel	Jer 13:12	3068
say unto them, Thus saith the *L*	Jer 13:13	3068
and the sons together, saith the *L*	Jer 13:14	3068
for the *L* hath spoken	Jer 13:15	3068
Give glory to the *L* your God	Jer 13:16	3068
thy measures from me, saith the *L*	Jer 13:25	3068
The word of the *L* that came to	Jer 14:1	3068
O *L*, though our iniquities	Jer 14:7	3068
yet thou, O *L*, art in the midst	Jer 14:9	3068
Thus saith the *L* unto this people	Jer 14:10	3068
therefore the *L* doth not accept	Jer 14:10	3068
Then said the *L* unto me, Pray not	Jer 14:11	3068
Then said I, Ah, *L* God	Jer 14:13	136
Then the *L* said unto me, The	Jer 14:14	3068
Therefore thus saith the *L*	Jer 14:15	3068
We acknowledge, O *L*, our	Jer 14:20	3068
art not thou he, O *L* our God	Jer 14:22	3068
Then said the *L* unto me, Though	Jer 15:1	3068
shalt tell them, Thus saith the *L*	Jer 15:2	3068
over them four kinds, saith the *L*	Jer 15:3	3068
hast forsaken me, saith the *L*	Jer 15:6	3068
before their enemies, saith the *L*	Jer 15:9	3068
The *L* said, Verily it shall be	Jer 15:11	3068
O *L*, thou knowest	Jer 15:15	3068
by thy name, O *L* God of hosts	Jer 15:16	3068
Therefore thus saith the *L*	Jer 15:19	3068
and to deliver thee, saith the *L*	Jer 15:20	3068
The word of the *L* came also unto	Jer 16:1	3068
For thus saith the *L* concerning	Jer 16:3	3068
For thus saith the *L*, Enter not	Jer 16:5	3068
from this people, saith the *L*	Jer 16:5	3068
For thus saith the *L* of hosts	Jer 16:9	3068
Wherefore hath the *L* pronounced	Jer 16:10	3068
committed against the *L* our God	Jer 16:10	3068
have forsaken me, saith the *L*	Jer 16:11	3068
the days come, saith the *L*	Jer 16:14	3068
The *L* liveth, that brought up the	Jer 16:14	3068
The *L* liveth, that brought up the	Jer 16:15	3068
for many fishers, saith the *L*	Jer 16:16	3068
O *L*, my strength, and my fortress,	Jer 16:19	3068
shall know that my name is The *L*	Jer 16:21	3068
Thus saith the *L*	Jer 17:5	3068
whose heart departeth from the *L*	Jer 17:5	3068
is the man that trusteth in the *L*	Jer 17:7	3068
and whose hope the *L* is	Jer 17:7	3068
I the *L* search the heart, I try	Jer 17:10	3068
O *L*, the hope of Israel, all that	Jer 17:13	3068
because they have forsaken the *L*	Jer 17:13	3068
Heal me, O *L*, and I shall be	Jer 17:14	3068
me, Where is the word of the *L*	Jer 17:15	3068
Thus said the *L* unto me	Jer 17:19	3068
them, Hear ye the word of the *L*	Jer 17:20	3068
Thus saith the *L*	Jer 17:21	3068
hearken unto me, saith the *L*	Jer 17:24	3068
praise, unto the house of the *L*	Jer 17:26	3068
which came to Jeremiah from the *L*	Jer 18:1	3068
Then the word of the *L* came to me	Jer 18:5	3068
this potter? saith the *L*	Jer 18:6	3068
saying, Thus saith the *L*	Jer 18:11	3068
Therefore thus saith the *L*	Jer 18:13	3068
Give heed to me, O *L*, and hearken	Jer 18:19	3068
Yet, *L*, thou knowest all their	Jer 18:23	3068
Thus saith the *L*, Go and get a	Jer 19:1	3068
And say, Hear ye the word of the *L*	Jer 19:3	3068
Thus saith the *L* of hosts	Jer 19:3	3068
the days come, saith the *L*	Jer 19:6	3068
them, Thus saith the *L* of hosts	Jer 19:11	3068
I do unto this place, saith the *L*	Jer 19:12	3068
whither the *L* had sent him to	Jer 19:14	3068
Thus saith the *L* of hosts	Jer 19:15	3068
governor in the house of the *L*	Jer 20:1	3068
which was by the house of the *L*	Jer 20:2	3068
The *L* hath not called thy name	Jer 20:3	3068
For thus saith the *L*, Behold, I	Jer 20:4	3068
O *L*, thou hast deceived me, and I	Jer 20:7	3068
because the word of the *L* was	Jer 20:8	3068
But the *L* is with me as a mighty	Jer 20:11	3068
O *L* of hosts, that triest the	Jer 20:12	3068
unto the *L*, praise ye the *L*	Jer 20:13	3068
the cities which the *L* overthrew	Jer 20:16	3068
came unto Jeremiah from the *L*	Jer 21:1	3068
I pray thee, of the *L* for us	Jer 21:2	3068
if so be that the *L* will deal	Jer 21:2	3068
Thus saith the *L* God of Israel	Jer 21:4	3068
And afterward, saith the *L*	Jer 21:7	3068
thou shalt say, Thus saith the *L*	Jer 21:8	3068
and not for good, saith the *L*	Jer 21:10	3068
say, Hear ye the word of the *L*	Jer 21:11	3068
house of David, thus saith the *L*	Jer 21:12	3068
and rock of the plain, saith the *L*	Jer 21:13	3068
fruit of your doings, saith the *L*	Jer 21:14	3068
Thus saith the *L*	Jer 22:1	3068
And say, Hear the word of the *L*	Jer 22:2	3068
Thus saith the *L*	Jer 22:3	3068
I swear by myself, saith the *L*	Jer 22:5	3068
For thus saith the *L* unto the	Jer 22:6	3068
Wherefore hath the *L* done thus	Jer 22:8	3068
the covenant of the *L* their God	Jer 22:9	3068
For thus saith the *L* touching	Jer 22:11	3068
know me? saith the *L*	Jer 22:16	3068
Therefore thus saith the *L*	Jer 22:18	3068
As I live, saith the *L*, though	Jer 22:24	3068
earth, hear the word of the *L*	Jer 22:29	3068
Thus saith the *L*, Write ye this	Jer 22:30	3068
my pasture! saith the *L*	Jer 23:1	3068
Therefore thus saith the *L* God of	Jer 23:2	3068
evil of your doings, saith the *L*	Jer 23:2	3068
they be lacking, saith the *L*	Jer 23:4	3068
the days come, saith the *L*	Jer 23:5	3068
called, The *L* our Righteousness	Jer 23:6	3068
the days come, saith the *L*	Jer 23:7	3068
The *L* liveth, which brought up	Jer 23:7	3068
The *L* liveth, which brought up and	Jer 23:8	3068
hath overcome, because of the *L*	Jer 23:9	3068
their wickedness, saith the *L*	Jer 23:11	3068
of their visitation, saith the *L*	Jer 23:12	3068
the *L* of hosts concerning the	Jer 23:15	3068
Thus saith the *L* of hosts	Jer 23:16	3068
and not out of the mouth of the *L*	Jer 23:16	3068

L

The *L* hath said, Ye shall have	Jer 23:17	3068
stood in the counsel of the *L*	Jer 23:18	3068
a whirlwind of the *L* is gone	Jer 23:19	3068
anger of the *L* shall not return	Jer 23:20	3068
Am I a God at hand, saith the *L*	Jer 23:23	3068
see him? saith the *L*	Jer 23:24	3068
and earth? saith the *L*	Jer 23:24	3068
the wheat? saith the *L*	Jer 23:28	3068
a fire? saith the *L*	Jer 23:29	3068
against the prophets, saith the *L*	Jer 23:30	3068
against the prophets, saith the *L*	Jer 23:31	3068
false dreams, saith the *L*	Jer 23:32	3068
this people at all, saith the *L*	Jer 23:32	3068
What is the burden of the *L*	Jer 23:33	3068
even forsake you, saith the *L*	Jer 23:33	3068
shall say, The burden of the *L*	Jer 23:34	3068
brother, What hath the *L* answered	Jer 23:35	3068
and, What hath the *L* spoken	Jer 23:35	3068
the burden of the *L* shall ye	Jer 23:36	3068
of the *L* of hosts our God	Jer 23:36	3068
What hath the *L* answered thee	Jer 23:37	3068
and, What hath the *L* spoken	Jer 23:37	3068
since ye say, The burden of the *L*	Jer 23:38	3068
therefore thus saith the *L*	Jer 23:38	3068
this word, The burden of the *L*	Jer 23:38	3068
not say, The burden of the *L*	Jer 23:38	3068
The *L* shewed me, and, behold, two	Jer 24:1	3068
set before the temple of the *L*	Jer 24:1	3068
Then said the *L* unto me, What	Jer 24:3	3068
the word of the *L* came unto me	Jer 24:4	3068
Thus saith the *L*, the God of	Jer 24:5	3068
heart to know me, that I am the *L*	Jer 24:7	3068
surely thus saith the *L*, So will	Jer 24:8	3068
the word of the *L* hath come unto	Jer 25:3	3068
the *L* hath sent unto you all his	Jer 25:4	3068
that the *L* hath given unto you	Jer 25:5	3068
hearkened unto me, saith the *L*	Jer 25:7	3068
thus saith the *L* of hosts	Jer 25:8	3068
of the north, saith the *L*	Jer 25:9	3068
and that nation, saith the *L*	Jer 25:12	3068
For thus saith the *L* God of	Jer 25:15	3068
unto whom the *L* had sent me	Jer 25:17	3068
them, Thus saith the *L* of hosts	Jer 25:27	3068
them, Thus saith the *L* of hosts	Jer 25:28	3068
the earth, saith the *L* of hosts	Jer 25:29	3068
The *L* shall roar from on high, and	Jer 25:30	3068
for the *L* hath a controversy with	Jer 25:31	3068
wicked to the sword, saith the *L*	Jer 25:31	3068
Thus saith the *L* of hosts	Jer 25:32	3068
the slain of the *L* shall be at	Jer 25:33	3068
for the *L* hath spoiled their	Jer 25:36	3068
of the fierce anger of the *L*	Jer 25:37	3068
Judah came this word from the *L*	Jer 26:1	3068
Thus saith the *L*	Jer 26:2	3068
say unto them, Thus saith the *L*	Jer 26:4	3068
these words in the house of the *L*	Jer 26:7	3068
L had commanded him to speak unto	Jer 26:8	3068
prophesied in the name of the *L*	Jer 26:9	3068
Jeremiah in the house of the *L*	Jer 26:9	3068
house unto the house of the *L*	Jer 26:10	3068
The *L* sent me to prophesy against	Jer 26:12	3068
obey the voice of the *L* your God	Jer 26:13	3068
the *L* will repent him of the evil	Jer 26:13	3068
for of a truth the *L* hath sent me	Jer 26:15	3068
us in the name of the *L* our God	Jer 26:16	3068
saying, Thus saith the *L* of hosts	Jer 26:18	3068
did he not fear the *L*, and	Jer 26:19	3068
fear the *L*, and besought the *L*	Jer 26:19	3068
prophesied in the name of the *L*	Jer 26:20	3068
word unto Jeremiah from the *L*	Jer 27:1	3068
Thus saith the *L* to me	Jer 27:2	3068
Thus saith the *L* of hosts	Jer 27:4	3068
nation will I punish, saith the *L*	Jer 27:8	3068
in their own land, saith the *L*	Jer 27:11	3068
as the *L* hath spoken against the	Jer 27:15	3068
I have not sent them, saith the *L*	Jer 27:15	3068
people, saying, Thus saith the *L*	Jer 27:16	3068
if the word of the *L* be with them	Jer 27:18	3068
intercession to the *L* of hosts	Jer 27:18	3068
are left in the house of the *L*	Jer 27:18	3068
For thus saith the *L* of hosts	Jer 27:19	3068
Yea, thus saith the *L* of hosts	Jer 27:21	3068
that remain in the house of the *L*	Jer 27:21	3068
that I visit them, saith the *L*	Jer 27:22	3068
unto me in the house of the *L*	Jer 28:1	3068
Thus speaketh the *L* of hosts	Jer 28:2	3068
went into Babylon, saith the *L*	Jer 28:4	3068
that stood in the house of the *L*	Jer 28:5	3068
the *L* do so	Jer 28:6	3068
the *L* perform thy words which	Jer 28:6	3068
that the *L* hath truly sent him	Jer 28:9	3068
people, saying, Thus saith the *L*	Jer 28:11	3068
Then the word of the *L* came unto	Jer 28:12	3068
saying, Thus saith the *L*	Jer 28:13	3068
For thus saith the *L* of hosts	Jer 28:14	3068
The *L* hath not sent thee	Jer 28:15	3068
Therefore thus saith the *L*	Jer 28:16	3068
taught rebellion against the *L*	Jer 28:16	3068
Thus saith the *L* of hosts	Jer 29:4	3068
and pray unto the *L* for it	Jer 29:7	3068
For thus saith the *L* of hosts	Jer 29:8	3068
I have not sent them, saith the *L*	Jer 29:9	3068
For thus saith the *L*, That after	Jer 29:10	3068
I think toward you, saith the *L*	Jer 29:11	3068
will be found of you, saith the *L*	Jer 29:14	3068
I have driven you, saith the *L*	Jer 29:14	3068
The *L* hath raised us up prophets	Jer 29:15	3068
Know that thus saith the *L* of the	Jer 29:16	3068
Thus saith the *L* of hosts	Jer 29:17	3068
to my words, saith the *L*, which I	Jer 29:19	3068
ye would not hear, saith the *L*	Jer 29:19	3068
ye therefore the word of the *L*	Jer 29:20	3068
Thus saith the *L* of hosts	Jer 29:21	3068
The *L* make thee like Zedekiah and	Jer 29:22	3068
and am a witness, saith the *L*	Jer 29:23	3068
Thus speaketh the *L* of hosts	Jer 29:25	3068
The *L* hath made thee priest in	Jer 29:26	3068
be officers in the house of the *L*	Jer 29:26	3068
the word of the *L* unto Jeremiah	Jer 29:30	3068
Thus saith the *L* concerning	Jer 29:31	3068
Therefore thus saith the *L*	Jer 29:32	3068
do for my people, saith the *L*	Jer 29:32	3068
taught rebellion against the *L*	Jer 29:32	3068
that came to Jeremiah from the *L*	Jer 30:1	3068
Thus speaketh the *L* God of Israel	Jer 30:2	3068
lo, the days come, saith the *L*	Jer 30:3	3068
Israel and Judah, saith the *L*	Jer 30:3	3068
the *L* spake concerning Israel	Jer 30:4	3068
For thus saith the *L*	Jer 30:5	3068
in that day, saith the *L* of hosts	Jer 30:8	3068
they shall serve the *L* their God	Jer 30:9	3068
O my servant Jacob, saith the *L*	Jer 30:10	3068
For I am with thee, saith the *L*	Jer 30:11	3068
For thus saith the *L*, Thy bruise	Jer 30:12	3068
thee of thy wounds, saith the *L*	Jer 30:17	3068
Thus saith the *L*	Jer 30:18	3068
unto me? saith the *L*	Jer 30:21	3068
the whirlwind of the *L* goeth	Jer 30:23	3068
anger of the *L* shall not return	Jer 30:24	3068
At the same time, saith the *L*	Jer 31:1	3068
Thus saith the *L*, The people	Jer 31:2	3068
The *L* hath appeared of old unto	Jer 31:3	3068
go up to Zion unto the *L* our God	Jer 31:6	3068
For thus saith the *L*	Jer 31:7	3068
ye, praise ye, and say, O *L*	Jer 31:7	3068
Hear the word of the *L*, O ye	Jer 31:10	3068
For the *L* hath redeemed Jacob, and	Jer 31:11	3068
together to the goodness of the *L*	Jer 31:12	3068
with my goodness, saith the *L*	Jer 31:14	3068
Thus saith the *L*	Jer 31:15	3068
Thus saith the *L*	Jer 31:16	3068
shall be rewarded, saith the *L*	Jer 31:16	3068
is hope in thine end, saith the *L*	Jer 31:17	3068
for thou art the *L* my God	Jer 31:18	3068
have mercy upon him, saith the *L*	Jer 31:20	3068
for the *L* hath created a new	Jer 31:22	3068
Thus saith the *L* of hosts	Jer 31:23	3068
The *L* bless thee, O habitation of	Jer 31:23	3068
the days come, saith the *L*	Jer 31:27	3068
build, and to plant, saith the *L*	Jer 31:28	3068
the days come, saith the *L*	Jer 31:31	3068
an husband unto them, saith the *L*	Jer 31:32	3068
After those days, saith the *L*	Jer 31:33	3068
his brother, saying, Know the *L*	Jer 31:34	3068
the greatest of them, saith the *L*	Jer 31:34	3068
Thus saith the *L*, which giveth	Jer 31:35	3068
The *L* of hosts is his name	Jer 31:35	3068
from before me, saith the *L*	Jer 31:36	3068
Thus saith the *L*	Jer 31:37	3068
that they have done, saith the *L*	Jer 31:37	3068
the days come, saith the *L*	Jer 31:38	3068
the city shall be built to the *L*	Jer 31:38	3068
east, shall be holy unto the *L*	Jer 31:40	3068
L in the tenth year of Zedekiah	Jer 32:1	3068
and say, Thus saith the *L*	Jer 32:3	3068
be until I visit him, saith the *L*	Jer 32:5	3068
The word of the *L* came unto me	Jer 32:6	3068
according to the word of the *L*	Jer 32:8	3068
that this was the word of the *L*	Jer 32:8	3068
Thus saith the *L* of hosts	Jer 32:14	3068
For thus saith the *L* of hosts	Jer 32:15	3068
of Neriah, I prayed unto the *L*	Jer 32:16	3068

L

The word of the *L* that came to	Jer 49:34	3068
Thus saith the *L* of hosts	Jer 49:35	3068
even my fierce anger, saith the *L*	Jer 49:37	3068
king and the princes, saith the *L*	Jer 49:38	3068
captivity of Elam, saith the *L*	Jer 49:39	3068
The word that the *L* spake against	Jer 50:1	3068
and in that time, saith the *L*	Jer 50:4	3068
shall go, and seek the *L* their God	Jer 50:4	3068
L in a perpetual covenant that	Jer 50:5	3068
they have sinned against the *L*	Jer 50:7	3068
habitation of justice, even the *L*	Jer 50:7	3068
shall be satisfied, saith the *L*	Jer 50:10	3068
the *L* it shall not be inhabited	Jer 50:13	3068
for she hath sinned against the *L*	Jer 50:14	3068
for it is the vengeance of the *L*	Jer 50:15	3068
thus saith the *L* of hosts	Jer 50:18	3068
and in that time, saith the *L*	Jer 50:20	3068
destroy after them, saith the *L*	Jer 50:21	3068
thou hast striven against the *L*	Jer 50:24	3068
The *L* hath opened his armoury, and	Jer 50:25	3068
for this is the work of the *L* God	Jer 50:25	136
the vengeance of the *L* our God	Jer 50:28	3068
she hath been proud against the *L*	Jer 50:29	3068
cut off in that day, saith the *L*	Jer 50:30	3068
proud, saith the *L* God of hosts	Jer 50:31	136
Thus saith the *L* of hosts	Jer 50:33	3068
the *L* of hosts is his name	Jer 50:34	3068
upon the Chaldeans, saith the *L*	Jer 50:35	3068
cities thereof, saith the *L*	Jer 50:40	3068
hear ye the counsel of the *L*	Jer 50:45	3068
Thus saith the *L*	Jer 51:1	3068
of his God, of the *L* of hosts	Jer 51:5	3068
The *L* hath brought forth our	Jer 51:10	3068
in Zion the work of the *L* our God	Jer 51:10	3068
the *L* hath raised up the spirit	Jer 51:11	3068
it is the vengeance of the *L*	Jer 51:11	3068
for the *L* hath both devised and	Jer 51:12	3068
The *L* of hosts hath sworn by	Jer 51:14	3068
the *L* of hosts is his name	Jer 51:19	3068
Zion in your sight, saith the *L*	Jer 51:24	3068
destroying mountain, saith the *L*	Jer 51:25	3068
be desolate for ever, saith the *L*	Jer 51:26	3068
for every purpose of the *L* shall	Jer 51:29	3068
For thus saith the *L* of hosts	Jer 51:33	3068
Therefore thus saith the *L*	Jer 51:36	3068
sleep, and not wake, saith the *L*	Jer 51:39	3068
from the fierce anger of the *L*	Jer 51:45	3068
her from the north, saith the *L*	Jer 51:48	3068
remember the *L* afar off, and let	Jer 51:50	3068
the days come, saith the *L*	Jer 51:52	3068
come unto her, saith the *L*	Jer 51:53	3068
Because the *L* hath spoiled	Jer 51:55	3068
for the *L* God of recompences	Jer 51:56	3068
whose name is the *L* of hosts	Jer 51:57	3068
Thus saith the *L* of hosts	Jer 51:58	3068
Then shalt thou say, O *L*, thou	Jer 51:62	3068
was evil in the eye of the *L*	Jer 52:2	3068
L it came to pass in Jerusalem	Jer 52:3	3068
And burned the house of the *L*	Jer 52:13	3068
that were in the house of the *L*	Jer 52:17	3068
that was in the house of the *L*	Jer 52:17	3068
had made in the house of the *L*	Jer 52:20	3068
for the *L* hath afflicted her for	Lam 1:5	3068
O *L*, behold my affliction	Lam 1:9	3068
see, O *L*, and consider	Lam 1:11	3068
wherewith the *L* hath afflicted me	Lam 1:12	3068
the *L* hath delivered me into	Lam 1:14	136
The *L* hath trodden under foot all	Lam 1:15	136
the *L* hath trodden the virgin,	Lam 1:15	136
the *L* hath commanded concerning	Lam 1:17	3068
The *L* is righteous	Lam 1:18	3068
Behold, O *L*	Lam 1:20	3068
How hath the *L* covered the	Lam 2:1	136
The *L* hath swallowed up all the	Lam 2:2	136
The *L* was as an enemy	Lam 2:5	136
the *L* hath caused the solemn	Lam 2:6	3068
The *L* hath cast off his altar, he	Lam 2:7	136
a noise in the house of the *L*	Lam 2:7	3068
The *L* hath purposed to destroy	Lam 2:8	3068
also find no vision from the *L*	Lam 2:9	3068
The *L* hath done that which he had	Lam 2:17	3068
Their heart cried unto the *L*	Lam 2:18	136
water before the face of the *L*	Lam 2:19	136
Behold, O *L*, and consider to whom	Lam 2:20	3068
slain in the sanctuary of the *L*	Lam 2:20	136
and my hope is perished from the *L*	Lam 3:18	3068
The *L* is my portion, saith my	Lam 3:24	3068
The *L* is good unto them that wait	Lam 3:25	3068
wait for the salvation of the *L*	Lam 3:26	3068
For the *L* will not cast off for	Lam 3:31	136
in his cause, the *L* approveth not	Lam 3:36	136

when the *L* commandeth it not	Lam 3:37	
our ways, and turn again to the *L*	Lam 3:40	136
Till the *L* look down, and behold	Lam 3:50	3068
I called upon thy name, O *L*		136
O *L*, thou hast pleaded the causes	Lam 3:50	3068
O *L*, thou hast seen my wrong	Lam 3:55	3068
hast heard their reproach, O *L*	Lam 3:58	136
unto them a recompence, O *L*		3068
from under the heavens of the *L*		3068
The *L* hath accomplished his fury	Lam	3068
The anger of the *L* hath divided	Lam	3068
nostrils, the anointed of the *L*	Lam	3068
Remember, O *L*, what is come upon	Lam	
Thou, O *L*, remainest for ever	Lam 5:	
Turn thou us unto thee, O *L*	Lam 5:2	
The word of the *L* came expressly	Eze 1:3	
the hand of the *L* was there upon	Eze 1:3	
likeness of the glory of the *L*	Eze 1:28	
unto them, Thus saith the *L* God	Eze 2:4	
tell them, Thus saith the *L* God	Eze 3:11	
the glory of the *L* from his place	Eze 3:12	
hand of the *L* was strong upon me	Eze 3:14	3068
the word of the *L* came unto me	Eze 3:16	3068
the hand of the *L* was there upon	Eze 3:22	3068
the glory of the *L* stood there	Eze 3:23	3068
unto them, Thus saith the *L* God	Eze 3:27	136
the *L* said, Even thus shall the	Eze 4:13	3068
Then said I, Ah *L* God	Eze 4:14	136
Thus saith the *L* God	Eze 5:5	136
Therefore thus saith the *L* God	Eze 5:7	136
Therefore thus saith the *L* God	Eze 5:8	136
as I live, saith the *L* God	Eze 5:11	136
I the *L* have spoken it in my zeal	Eze 5:13	3068
I the *L* have spoken it	Eze 5:15	3068
I the *L* have spoken it	Eze 5:17	3068
And the word of the *L* came unto me	Eze 6:1	3068
hear the word of the *L*	Eze 6:3	136
Thus saith the *L* God to the	Eze 6:3	136
and ye shall know that I am the *L*	Eze 6:7	3068
they shall know that I am the *L*	Eze 6:10	3068
Thus saith the *L* God	Eze 6:11	136
shall ye know that I am the *L*	Eze 6:13	3068
they shall know that I am the *L*	Eze 6:14	3068
the word of the *L* came unto me	Eze 7:1	3068
thus saith the *L* God unto the	Eze 7:2	136
and ye shall know that I am the *L*	Eze 7:4	3068
Thus saith the *L* God	Eze 7:5	136
know that I am the *L* that smiteth	Eze 7:9	3068
in the day of the wrath of the *L*	Eze 7:19	3068
they shall know that I am the *L*	Eze 7:27	3068
that the hand of the *L* God fell	Eze 8:1	136
for they say, The *L* seeth us not	Eze 8:12	3068
the *L* hath forsaken the earth	Eze 8:12	3068
the door of the temple of the *L*	Eze 8:16	3068
backs toward the temple of the *L*	Eze 8:16	3068
the *L* said unto him, Go through	Eze 9:4	3068
face, and cried, and said, Ah *L* God	Eze 9:8	136
The *L* hath forsaken the earth	Eze 9:9	3068
and the *L* seeth not	Eze 9:9	3068
Then the glory of the *L* went up	Eze 10:4	3068
Then the glory of the *L* departed	Eze 10:18	3068
the Spirit of the *L* fell upon me	Eze 11:5	3068
Thus saith the *L*	Eze 11:5	3068
Therefore thus saith the *L* God	Eze 11:7	136
a sword upon you, saith the *L* God	Eze 11:8	136
and ye shall know that I am the *L*	Eze 11:10	3068
And ye shall know that I am the *L*	Eze 11:12	3068
a loud voice, and said, Ah *L* God	Eze 11:13	136
the word of the *L* came unto me	Eze 11:14	3068
have said, Get you far from the *L*	Eze 11:15	3068
say, Thus saith the *L* God	Eze 11:16	136
say, Thus saith the *L* God	Eze 11:17	136
their own heads, saith the *L* God	Eze 11:21	136
the glory of the *L* went up from	Eze 11:23	3068
things that the *L* had shewed me	Eze 11:25	3068
The word of the *L* also came unto	Eze 12:1	3068
came the word of the *L* unto me	Eze 12:8	3068
unto them, Thus saith the *L* God	Eze 12:10	136
they shall know that I am the *L*	Eze 12:15	3068
they shall know that I am the *L*	Eze 12:16	3068
the word of the *L* came to me	Eze 12:17	3068
Thus saith the *L* God of the	Eze 12:19	136
and ye shall know that I am the *L*	Eze 12:20	3068
And the word of the *L* came unto me	Eze 12:21	3068
therefore, Thus saith the *L* God	Eze 12:23	136
For I am the *L*	Eze 12:25	3068
will perform it, saith the *L* God	Eze 12:25	136
the word of the *L* came to me	Eze 12:26	3068
unto them, Thus saith the *L* God	Eze 12:28	136
shall be done, saith the *L* God	Eze 12:28	136
And the word of the *L* came unto me	Eze 13:1	3068

hearts, Hear ye the word of the *L*	Eze 13:2	3068
Thus saith the *L* God	Eze 13:3	136
in the battle in the day of the *L*	Eze 13:5	3068
divination, saying, The *L* saith	Eze 13:6	3068
and the *L* hath not sent them	Eze 13:6	3068
whereas ye say, The *L* saith it	Eze 13:7	3068
Therefore thus saith the *L* God	Eze 13:8	136
I am against you, saith the *L* God	Eze 13:8	136
ye shall know that I am the *L* God	Eze 13:9	136
Therefore thus saith the *L* God	Eze 13:13	136
and ye shall know that I am the *L*	Eze 13:14	3068
is no peace, saith the *L* God	Eze 13:16	136
And say, Thus saith the *L* God	Eze 13:18	136
Wherefore thus saith the *L* God	Eze 13:20	136
and ye shall know that I am the *L*	Eze 13:21	3068
and ye shall know that I am the *L*	Eze 13:23	3068
And the word of the *L* came unto me	Eze 14:2	3068
unto them, Thus saith the *L* God	Eze 14:4	136
I the *L* will answer him that	Eze 14:4	3068
of Israel, Thus saith the *L* God	Eze 14:6	136
I the *L* will answer him by myself	Eze 14:7	3068
and ye shall know that I am the *L*	Eze 14:8	3068
I the *L* have deceived that	Eze 14:9	3068
may be their God, saith the *L* God	Eze 14:11	136
The word of the *L* came again to	Eze 14:12	3068
righteousness, saith the *L* God	Eze 14:14	136
in it, as I live, saith the *L* God	Eze 14:16	136
in it, as I live, saith the *L* God	Eze 14:18	136
in it, as I live, saith the *L* God	Eze 14:20	136
For thus saith the *L* God	Eze 14:21	136
have done in it, saith the *L* God	Eze 14:23	136
And the word of the *L* came unto me	Eze 15:1	3068
Therefore thus saith the *L* God	Eze 15:6	136
and ye shall know that I am the *L*	Eze 15:7	3068
a trespass, saith the *L* God	Eze 15:8	136
the word of the *L* came unto me	Eze 16:1	3068
Thus saith the *L* God unto	Eze 16:3	136
with thee, saith the *L* God	Eze 16:8	136
put upon thee, saith the *L* God	Eze 16:14	136
and thus it was, saith the *L* God	Eze 16:19	136
saith the *L* God	Eze 16:23	136
is thine heart, saith the *L* God	Eze 16:30	136
O harlot, hear the word of the *L*	Eze 16:35	3068
Thus saith the *L* God	Eze 16:36	136
upon thine head, saith the *L* God	Eze 16:43	136
As I live, saith the *L* God	Eze 16:48	136
thine abominations, saith the *L*	Eze 16:58	3068
For thus saith the *L* God	Eze 16:59	136
thou shalt know that I am the *L*	Eze 16:62	3068
thou hast done, saith the *L* God	Eze 16:63	136
And the word of the *L* came unto me	Eze 17:1	3068
And say, Thus saith the *L* God	Eze 17:3	136
Say thou, Thus saith the *L* God	Eze 17:9	136
the word of the *L* came unto me	Eze 17:11	3068
As I live, saith the *L* God	Eze 17:16	136
Therefore thus saith the *L* God	Eze 17:19	136
know that I the *L* have spoken it	Eze 17:21	3068
Thus saith the *L* God	Eze 17:22	136
L have brought down the high tree	Eze 17:24	3068
I the *L* have spoken and have done	Eze 17:24	3068
The word of the *L* came unto me	Eze 18:1	3068
As I live, saith the *L* God	Eze 18:3	136
surely live, saith the *L* God	Eze 18:9	136
saith the *L* God	Eze 18:23	136
The way of the *L* is not equal	Eze 18:25	136
The way of the *L* is not equal	Eze 18:29	136
to his ways, saith the *L* God	Eze 18:30	136
him that dieth, saith the *L* God	Eze 18:32	136
Israel came to enquire of the *L*	Eze 20:1	3068
came the word of the *L* unto me	Eze 20:2	3068
unto them, Thus saith the *L* God	Eze 20:3	136
As I live, saith the *L* God	Eze 20:3	136
unto them, Thus saith the *L* God	Eze 20:5	136
them, saying, I am the *L* your God	Eze 20:5	3068
I am the *L* your God	Eze 20:7	3068
I am the *L* that sanctify them	Eze 20:12	3068
I am the *L* your God	Eze 20:19	3068
may know that I am the *L* your God	Eze 20:20	3068
they might know that I am the *L*	Eze 20:26	3068
unto them, Thus saith the *L* God	Eze 20:27	136
of Israel, Thus saith the *L* God	Eze 20:30	136
As I live, saith the *L* God	Eze 20:31	136
As I live, saith the *L* God	Eze 20:33	136
I plead with you, saith the *L* God	Eze 20:36	136
and ye shall know that I am the *L*	Eze 20:38	3068
of Israel, thus saith the *L* God	Eze 20:39	136
height of Israel, saith the *L* God	Eze 20:40	136
And ye shall know that I am the *L*	Eze 20:42	3068
And ye shall know that I am the *L*	Eze 20:44	3068
house of Israel, saith the *L* God	Eze 20:44	136
the word of the *L* came unto me	Eze 20:45	3068
the south, Hear the word of the *L*	Eze 20:47	3068
Thus saith the *L* God	Eze 20:47	136
see that I the *L* have kindled it	Eze 20:48	3068
Then said I, Ah *L* God	Eze 20:49	136
And the word of the *L* came unto me	Eze 21:1	3068
land of Israel, Thus saith the *L*	Eze 21:3	3068
L have drawn forth my sword out	Eze 21:5	3068
brought to pass, saith the *L* God	Eze 21:7	136
the word of the *L* came unto me	Eze 21:8	3068
and say, Thus saith the *L*	Eze 21:9	3068
shall be no more, saith the *L* God	Eze 21:13	136
I the *L* have said it	Eze 21:17	3068
The word of the *L* came unto me	Eze 21:18	3068
Therefore thus saith the *L* God	Eze 21:24	136
Thus saith the *L* God	Eze 21:26	136
Thus saith the *L* God concerning	Eze 21:28	136
for I the *L* have spoken it	Eze 21:32	3068
the word of the *L* came unto me	Eze 22:1	3068
say thou, Thus saith the *L* God	Eze 22:3	136
forgotten me, saith the *L* God	Eze 22:12	136
I the *L* have spoken it, and will	Eze 22:14	3068
thou shalt know that I am the *L*	Eze 22:16	3068
And the word of the *L* came unto me	Eze 22:17	3068
Therefore thus saith the *L* God	Eze 22:19	136
ye shall know that I the *L* have	Eze 22:22	3068
And the word of the *L* came unto me	Eze 22:23	3068
saying, Thus saith the *L* God	Eze 22:28	136
when the *L* hath not spoken	Eze 22:28	3068
upon their heads, saith the *L* God	Eze 22:31	136
The word of the *L* came again unto	Eze 23:1	3068
O Aholibah, thus saith the *L* God	Eze 23:22	136
For thus saith the *L* God	Eze 23:28	136
Thus saith the *L* God	Eze 23:32	136
I have spoken it, saith the *L* God	Eze 23:34	136
Therefore thus saith the *L* God	Eze 23:35	136
The *L* said moreover unto me	Eze 23:36	3068
For thus saith the *L* God	Eze 23:46	136
ye shall know that I am the *L* God	Eze 23:49	136
the word of the *L* came unto me	Eze 24:1	3068
unto them, Thus saith the *L* God	Eze 24:3	136
Wherefore thus saith the *L* God	Eze 24:6	136
Therefore thus saith the *L* God	Eze 24:9	136
I the *L* have spoken it	Eze 24:14	3068
they judge thee, saith the *L* God	Eze 24:14	136
the word of the *L* came unto me	Eze 24:15	3068
The word of the *L* came unto me	Eze 24:20	3068
of Israel, Thus saith the *L* God	Eze 24:21	136
ye shall know that I am the *L* God	Eze 24:24	136
they shall know that I am the *L*	Eze 24:27	3068
The word of the *L* came again unto	Eze 25:1	3068
Hear the word of the *L* God	Eze 25:3	136
Thus saith the *L* God	Eze 25:3	136
and ye shall know that I am the *L*	Eze 25:5	3068
For thus saith the *L* God	Eze 25:6	136
thou shalt know that I am the *L*	Eze 25:7	3068
Thus saith the *L* God	Eze 25:8	136
they shall know that I am the *L*	Eze 25:11	3068
Thus saith the *L* God	Eze 25:12	136
Therefore thus saith the *L* God	Eze 25:13	136
my vengeance, saith the *L* God	Eze 25:14	136
Thus saith the *L* God	Eze 25:15	136
Therefore thus saith the *L* God	Eze 25:16	136
they shall know that I am the *L*	Eze 25:17	3068
the word of the *L* came unto me	Eze 26:1	3068
Therefore thus saith the *L* God	Eze 26:3	136
I have spoken it, saith the *L* God	Eze 26:5	136
they shall know that I am the *L*	Eze 26:6	3068
For thus saith the *L* God	Eze 26:7	136
for I the *L* have spoken it	Eze 26:14	3068
have spoken it, saith the *L* God	Eze 26:14	136
Thus saith the *L* God to Tyrus	Eze 26:15	136
For thus saith the *L* God	Eze 26:19	136
be found again, saith the *L* God	Eze 26:21	136
The word of the *L* came again unto	Eze 27:1	3068
many isles, Thus saith the *L* God	Eze 27:3	136
The word of the *L* came again unto	Eze 28:1	3068
of Tyrus, Thus saith the *L* God	Eze 28:2	136
Therefore thus saith the *L* God	Eze 28:6	136
I have spoken it, saith the *L* God	Eze 28:10	136
the word of the *L* came unto me	Eze 28:11	3068
unto him, Thus saith the *L* God	Eze 28:12	136
the word of the *L* came unto me	Eze 28:20	3068
And say, Thus saith the *L* God	Eze 28:22	136
they shall know that I am the *L*	Eze 28:22	3068
they shall know that I am the *L*	Eze 28:23	3068
shall know that I am the *L* God	Eze 28:24	136
Thus saith the *L* God	Eze 28:25	136
know that I am the *L* their God	Eze 28:26	3068
the word of the *L* came unto me	Eze 29:1	3068
and say, Thus saith the *L* God	Eze 29:3	136
Egypt shall know that I am the *L*	Eze 29:6	3068

L

Therefore thus saith the *L* God	Eze 29:8	136
they shall know that I am the *L*	Eze 29:9	3068
Yet thus saith the *L* God	Eze 29:13	136
shall know that I am the *L* God	Eze 29:16	136
the word of the *L* came unto me	Eze 29:17	3068
Therefore thus saith the *L* God	Eze 29:19	136
wrought for me, saith the *L* God	Eze 29:20	136
they shall know that I am the *L*	Eze 29:21	3068
The word of the *L* came again unto	Eze 30:1	3068
and say, Thus saith the *L* God	Eze 30:2	136
even the day of the *L* is near	Eze 30:3	3068
Thus saith the *L*	Eze 30:6	3068
it by the sword, saith the *L* God	Eze 30:6	136
they shall know that I am the *L*	Eze 30:8	3068
Thus saith the *L* God	Eze 30:10	136
I the *L* have spoken it	Eze 30:12	3068
Thus saith the *L* God	Eze 30:13	136
they shall know that I am the *L*	Eze 30:19	3068
the word of the *L* came unto me	Eze 30:20	3068
Therefore thus saith the *L* God	Eze 30:22	136
they shall know that I am the *L*	Eze 30:25	3068
they shall know that I am the *L*	Eze 30:26	3068
the word of the *L* came unto me	Eze 31:1	3068
Therefore thus saith the *L* God	Eze 31:10	136
Thus saith the *L* God	Eze 31:15	136
his multitude, saith the *L* God	Eze 31:18	136
the word of the *L* came unto me	Eze 32:1	3068
Thus saith the *L* God	Eze 32:3	136
upon thy land, saith the *L* God	Eze 32:8	136
For thus saith the *L* God	Eze 32:11	136
to run like oil, saith the *L* God	Eze 32:14	136
shall they know that I am the *L*	Eze 32:15	3068
her multitude, saith the *L* God	Eze 32:16	136
the word of the *L* came unto me	Eze 32:17	3068
by the sword, saith the *L* God	Eze 32:31	136
his multitude, saith the *L* God	Eze 32:32	136
the word of the *L* came unto me	Eze 33:1	3068
them, As I live, saith the *L* God	Eze 33:11	136
The way of the *L* is not equal	Eze 33:17	136
The way of the *L* is not equal	Eze 33:20	136
Now the hand of the *L* was upon me	Eze 33:22	3068
the word of the *L* came unto me	Eze 33:23	3068
unto them, Thus saith the *L* God	Eze 33:25	136
unto them, Thus saith the *L* God	Eze 33:27	136
shall they know that I am the *L*	Eze 33:29	3068
word that cometh forth from the *L*	Eze 33:30	3068
And the word of the *L* came unto me	Eze 34:1	3068
Thus saith the *L* God unto the	Eze 34:2	136
shepherds, hear the word of the *L*	Eze 34:7	3068
As I live saith the *L* God	Eze 34:8	136
shepherds, hear the word of the *L*	Eze 34:9	3068
Thus saith the *L* God	Eze 34:10	136
For thus saith the *L* God	Eze 34:11	136
them to lie down, saith the *L* God	Eze 34:15	136
O my flock, thus saith the *L* God	Eze 34:17	136
thus saith the *L* God unto them	Eze 34:20	136
I the *L* will be their God, and my	Eze 34:24	3068
I the *L* have spoken it	Eze 34:24	3068
and shall know that I am the *L*	Eze 34:27	3068
I the *L* their God am with them	Eze 34:30	3068
are my people, saith the *L* God	Eze 34:30	136
and I am your God, saith the *L* God	Eze 34:31	136
the word of the *L* came unto me	Eze 35:1	3068
say unto it, Thus saith the *L* God	Eze 35:3	136
thou shalt know that I am the *L*	Eze 35:4	3068
as I live, saith the *L* God	Eze 35:6	136
and ye shall know that I am the *L*	Eze 35:9	3068
whereas the *L* was there	Eze 35:10	3068
as I live, saith the *L* God	Eze 35:11	136
thou shalt know that I am the *L*	Eze 35:12	3068
Thus saith the *L* God	Eze 35:14	136
they shall know that I am the *L*	Eze 35:15	3068
of Israel, hear the word of the *L*	Eze 36:1	3068
Thus saith the *L* God	Eze 36:2	136
and say, Thus saith the *L* God	Eze 36:3	136
hear the word of the *L* God	Eze 36:4	136
Thus saith the *L* God to the	Eze 36:4	136
Therefore thus saith the *L* God	Eze 36:5	136
the valleys, Thus saith the *L* God	Eze 36:6	136
Therefore thus saith the *L* God	Eze 36:7	136
and ye shall know that I am the *L*	Eze 36:11	3068
Thus saith the *L* God	Eze 36:13	136
nations any more, saith the *L* God	Eze 36:14	136
to fall any more, saith the *L* God	Eze 36:15	136
the word of the *L* came unto me	Eze 36:16	3068
These are the people of the *L*	Eze 36:20	3068
of Israel, that profaned the *L* God	Eze 36:22	136
shall know that I am the *L*	Eze 36:23	3068
saith the *L* God	Eze 36:23	136
sakes do I this, saith the *L* God	Eze 36:32	136
Thus saith the *L* God	Eze 36:33	136

I the *L* build the ruined places	Eze 36:36	3068
I the *L* have spoken it, and I will	Eze 36:36	3068
Thus saith the *L* God	Eze 36:37	136
they shall know that I am the *L*	Eze 36:38	3068
The hand of the *L* was upon me	Eze 37:1	3068
me out in the spirit of the *L*	Eze 37:1	3068
I answered, O *L* God, thou knowest	Eze 37:3	136
dry bones, hear the word of the *L*	Eze 37:4	3068
Thus saith the *L* God unto these	Eze 37:5	136
and ye shall know that I am the *L*	Eze 37:6	3068
to the wind, Thus saith the *L* God	Eze 37:9	136
unto them, Thus saith the *L* God	Eze 37:12	136
And ye shall know that I am the *L*	Eze 37:13	3068
know that I the *L* have spoken it	Eze 37:14	3068
and performed it, saith the *L*	Eze 37:14	136
The word of the *L* came again unto	Eze 37:15	3068
unto them, Thus saith the *L* God	Eze 37:19	136
unto them, Thus saith the *L* God	Eze 37:21	136
that I the *L* do sanctify Israel	Eze 37:28	3068
And the word of the *L* came unto me	Eze 38:1	3068
And say, Thus saith the *L* God	Eze 38:3	136
Thus saith the *L* God	Eze 38:10	136
unto Gog, Thus saith the *L* God	Eze 38:14	136
Thus saith the *L* God	Eze 38:17	136
land of Israel, saith the *L* God	Eze 38:18	136
all my mountains, saith the *L* God	Eze 38:21	136
they shall know that I am the *L*	Eze 38:23	3068
Gog, and say, Thus saith the *L* God	Eze 39:1	136
I have spoken it, saith the *L* God	Eze 39:5	136
they shall know that I am the *L*	Eze 39:6	3068
shall know that I am the *L*	Eze 39:7	3068
and it is done, saith the *L* God	Eze 39:8	136
that robbed them, saith the *L* God	Eze 39:10	136
be glorified, saith the *L* God	Eze 39:13	136
son of man, thus saith the *L* God	Eze 39:17	136
all men of war, saith the *L* God	Eze 39:20	136
am the *L* their God from that day	Eze 39:22	3068
Therefore thus saith the *L* God	Eze 39:25	136
know that I am the *L* their God	Eze 39:28	3068
house of Israel, saith the *L* God	Eze 39:29	136
day the hand of the *L* was upon me	Eze 40:1	3068
to the *L* to minister unto him	Eze 40:46	3068
is the table that is before the *L*	Eze 41:22	3068
L shall eat the most holy things	Eze 42:13	3068
the glory of the *L* came into the	Eze 43:4	3068
glory of the *L* filled the house	Eze 43:5	3068
Son of man, thus saith the *L* God	Eze 43:18	136
minister unto me, saith the *L* God	Eze 43:19	136
shalt offer them before the *L*	Eze 43:24	3068
for a burnt offering unto the *L*	Eze 43:24	3068
will accept you, saith the *L* God	Eze 43:27	136
Then said the *L* unto me	Eze 44:2	3068
because the *L*, the God of Israel,	Eze 44:2	3068
in it to eat bread before the *L*	Eze 44:3	3068
L filled the house of the *L*	Eze 44:4	3068
the *L* said unto me, Son of man,	Eze 44:5	3068
ordinances of the house of the *L*	Eze 44:5	3068
of Israel, Thus saith the *L* God	Eze 44:6	136
Thus saith the *L* God	Eze 44:9	136
against them, saith the *L* God	Eze 44:12	136
fat and the blood, saith the *L* God	Eze 44:15	136
his sin offering, saith the *L* God	Eze 44:27	136
offer an oblation unto the *L*	Eze 45:1	3068
come near to minister unto the *L*	Eze 45:4	3068
Thus saith the *L* God	Eze 45:9	136
from my people, saith the *L* God	Eze 45:9	136
for them, saith the *L* God	Eze 45:15	136
Thus saith the *L* God	Eze 45:18	136
prepare a burnt offering to the *L*	Eze 45:23	3068
Thus saith the *L* God	Eze 46:1	136
gate before the *L* in the sabbaths	Eze 46:3	3068
L in the sabbath day shall be six	Eze 46:4	3068
before the *L* in the solemn feasts	Eze 46:9	3068
offerings voluntarily unto the *L*	Eze 46:12	3068
a burnt offering unto the *L* of a	Eze 46:13	3068
a perpetual ordinance unto the *L*	Eze 46:14	3068
Thus saith the *L* God	Eze 46:16	136
Thus saith the *L* God	Eze 47:13	136
his inheritance, saith the *L* God	Eze 47:23	136
offer unto the *L* shall be of five	Eze 48:9	3068
the sanctuary of the *L* shall be	Eze 48:10	3068
for it is holy unto the *L*	Eze 48:14	3068
their portions, saith the *L* God	Eze 48:29	136
that day shall be, The *L* is there	Eze 48:35	3068
the *L* gave Jehoiakim king	Dan 1:2	136
a *L* of kings, and a revealer of	Dan 2:47	4756
thyself against the *L* of heaven	Dan 5:23	4756
whereof the word of the *L* came to	Dan 9:2	3068
And I set my face unto the *L* God	Dan 9:3	136
And I prayed unto the *L* my God	Dan 9:4	3068
made my confession, and said, O *L*	Dan 9:4	136

O L, righteousness belongeth unto	Dan 9:7	136
O L, to us belongeth confusion of	Dan 9:8	136
To the L our God belong mercies	Dan 9:9	136
obeyed the voice of the L our God	Dan 9:10	3068
our prayer before the L our God	Dan 9:13	3068
Therefore hath the L watched upon	Dan 9:14	3068
for the L our God is righteous in	Dan 9:14	3068
O L our God, that hast brought	Dan 9:15	136
O L, according to all thy	Dan 9:16	136
O L, hear	Dan 9:19	136
O L, forgive	Dan 9:19	136
O L, hearken and do	Dan 9:19	136
my supplication before the L my	Dan 9:20	3068
then said I, O my L, what shall	Dan 12:8	113
The word of the L that came unto	Hos 1:1	3068
of the word of the L by Hosea	Hos 1:2	3068
the L said to Hosea, Go, take	Hos 1:2	3068
whoredom, departing from the L	Hos 1:2	3068
the L said unto him, Call his	Hos 1:4	3068
will save them by the L their God	Hos 1:7	3068
lovers, and forgat me, saith the L	Hos 2:13	3068
shall be at that day, saith the L	Hos 2:16	3068
and thou shalt know the L	Hos 2:20	3068
day, I will hear, saith the L	Hos 2:21	3068
Then said the L unto me, Go yet,	Hos 3:1	3068
according to the love of the L	Hos 3:1	3068
seek the L their God, and David	Hos 3:5	3068
and shall fear the L and his	Hos 3:5	3068
Hear the word of the L, ye	Hos 4:1	3068
for the L hath a controversy with	Hos 4:1	3068
left off to take heed to the L	Hos 4:10	3068
nor swear, The L liveth	Hos 4:15	3068
now the L will feed them as a	Hos 4:16	3068
and they have not known the L	Hos 5:4	3068
and with their herds to seek the L	Hos 5:6	3068
dealt treacherously against the L	Hos 5:7	3068
Come, and let us return unto the L	Hos 6:1	3068
if we follow on to know the L	Hos 6:3	3068
do not return to the L their God	Hos 7:10	3068
eagle against the house of the L	Hos 8:1	3068
but the L accepteth them not	Hos 8:13	3068
not offer wine offerings to the L	Hos 9:4	3068
not come into the house of the L	Hos 9:4	3068
in the day of the feast of the L	Hos 9:5	3068
Give them, O L	Hos 9:14	3068
king, because we feared not the L	Hos 10:3	3068
for it is time to seek the L	Hos 10:12	3068
They shall walk after the L	Hos 11:10	3068
them in their houses, saith the L	Hos 11:11	3068
The L hath also a controversy	Hos 12:2	3068
Even the L God of hosts	Hos 12:5	3068
the L is his memorial	Hos 12:5	3068
I that am the L thy God from the	Hos 12:9	3068
by a prophet the L brought Israel	Hos 12:13	3068
shall his L return unto him	Hos 12:14	113
Yet I am the L thy God from the	Hos 13:4	3068
the wind of the L shall come up	Hos 13:15	3068
Israel, return unto the L thy God	Hos 14:1	3068
with you words, and turn to the L	Hos 14:2	3068
for the ways of the L are right	Hos 14:9	3068
The word of the L that came to	Joel 1:1	3068
cut off from the house of the L	Joel 1:9	3068
into the house of the L your God	Joel 1:14	3068
and cry unto the L	Joel 1:14	3068
for the day of the L is at hand	Joel 1:15	3068
O L, to thee will I cry	Joel 1:19	3068
for the day of the L cometh	Joel 2:1	3068
the L shall utter his voice	Joel 2:11	3068
for the day of the L is great	Joel 2:11	3068
Therefore also now, saith the L	Joel 2:12	3068
and turn unto the L your God	Joel 2:13	3068
offering unto the L your God	Joel 2:14	3068
priests, the ministers of the L	Joel 2:17	3068
them say, Spare thy people, O L	Joel 2:17	3068
Then will the L be jealous for	Joel 2:18	3068
the L will answer and say unto his	Joel 2:19	3068
for the L will do great things	Joel 2:21	3068
and rejoice in the L your God	Joel 2:23	3068
praise the name of the L your God	Joel 2:26	3068
and that I am the L your God	Joel 2:27	3068
and the terrible day of the L come	Joel 2:31	3068
name of the L shall be delivered	Joel 2:32	3068
as the L hath said, and in the	Joel 2:32	3068
the remnant whom the L shall call	Joel 2:32	3068
for the L hath spoken it	Joel 3:8	3068
thy mighty ones to come down, O L	Joel 3:11	3068
for the day of the L is near in	Joel 3:14	3068
The L also shall roar out of Zion	Joel 3:16	3068
but the L will be the hope of his	Joel 3:16	3068
the L your God dwelling in Zion	Joel 3:17	3068
come forth of the house of the L	Joel 3:18	3068
for the L dwelleth in Zion	Joel 3:21	3068
The L will roar from Zion, and	Amos 1:2	3068
Thus saith the L	Amos 1:3	3068
captivity unto Kir, saith the L	Amos 1:5	3068
Thus saith the L	Amos 1:6	3068
shall perish, saith the L GOD	Amos 1:8	136
Thus saith the L	Amos 1:9	3068
Thus saith the L	Amos 1:11	3068
Thus saith the L	Amos 1:13	3068
his princes together, saith the L	Amos 1:15	3068
Thus saith the L	Amos 2:1	3068
thereof with him, saith the L	Amos 2:3	3068
Thus saith the L	Amos 2:4	3068
have despised the law of the L	Amos 2:4	3068
Thus saith the L	Amos 2:6	3068
saith the L	Amos 2:11	3068
naked in that day, saith the L	Amos 2:16	3068
the L hath spoken against you	Amos 3:1	3068
a city, and the L hath not done it	Amos 3:6	3068
Surely the L GOD will do nothing,	Amos 3:7	136
the L GOD hath spoken, who can	Amos 3:8	136
know not to do right, saith the L	Amos 3:10	3068
Therefore thus saith the L GOD	Amos 3:11	136
Thus saith the L	Amos 3:12	3068
house of Jacob, saith the L GOD	Amos 3:13	136
shall have an end, saith the L	Amos 3:15	3068
The L GOD hath sworn by his	Amos 4:2	136
them into the palace, saith the L	Amos 4:3	3068
of Israel, saith the L GOD	Amos 4:5	136
not returned unto me, saith the L	Amos 4:6	3068
not returned unto me, saith the L	Amos 4:8	3068
not returned unto me, saith the L	Amos 4:9	3068
not returned unto me, saith the L	Amos 4:10	3068
not returned unto me, saith the L	Amos 4:11	3068
high places of the earth, The L	Amos 4:13	3068
For thus saith the L GOD	Amos 5:3	136
For thus saith the L unto the	Amos 5:4	3068
Seek the L, and ye shall live	Amos 5:6	3068
The L is his name	Amos 5:8	3068
and so the L, the God of hosts,	Amos 5:14	3068
it may be that the L God of hosts	Amos 5:15	3068
Therefore the L, the God of hosts	Amos 5:16	3068
the God of hosts, the L	Amos 5:16	136
pass through thee, saith the L	Amos 5:17	3068
you that desire the day of the L	Amos 5:18	3068
the day of the L is darkness	Amos 5:18	3068
not the day of the L be darkness	Amos 5:20	3068
beyond Damascus, saith the L	Amos 5:27	3068
The L GOD hath sworn by himself,	Amos 6:8	136
saith the L the God of hosts, I	Amos 6:8	3068
make mention of the name of the L	Amos 6:10	3068
the L commandeth, and he will	Amos 6:11	3068
saith the L the God of hosts	Amos 6:14	3068
Thus hath the L GOD shewed unto	Amos 7:1	136
O L GOD, forgive, I beseech thee	Amos 7:2	136
The L repented for this	Amos 7:3	3068
It shall not be, saith the L	Amos 7:3	3068
Thus hath the L GOD shewed unto	Amos 7:4	136
the L GOD called to contend by	Amos 7:4	136
O L GOD, cease, I beseech thee	Amos 7:5	136
The L repented for this	Amos 7:6	3068
shall not be, saith the L GOD	Amos 7:6	136
the L stood upon a wall made by a	Amos 7:7	136
the L said unto me, Amos, what	Amos 7:8	3068
Then said the L, Behold, I will	Amos 7:8	136
the L took me as I followed the	Amos 7:15	3068
the L said unto me, Go, prophesy	Amos 7:15	3068
hear thou the word of the L	Amos 7:16	3068
Therefore thus saith the L	Amos 7:17	3068
Thus hath the L GOD shewed unto	Amos 8:1	136
Then said the L unto me, The end	Amos 8:2	3068
in that day, saith the L GOD	Amos 8:3	136
The L hath sworn by the	Amos 8:7	3068
pass in that day, saith the L GOD	Amos 8:9	136
the days come, saith the L GOD	Amos 8:11	136
but of hearing the words of the L	Amos 8:11	3068
and fro to seek the word of the L	Amos 8:12	3068
I saw the L standing upon the	Amos 9:1	136
the L GOD of hosts is he that	Amos 9:5	136
The L is his name	Amos 9:6	3068
of Israel? saith the L	Amos 9:7	3068
the eyes of the L GOD are upon	Amos 9:8	136
the house of Jacob, saith the L	Amos 9:8	3068
saith the L that doeth this	Amos 9:12	3068
the days come, saith the L	Amos 9:13	3068
given them, saith the L thy God	Amos 9:15	3068
Thus saith the L GOD concerning	Obad 1	136
We have heard a rumour from the L	Obad 1	3068
I bring thee down, saith the L	Obad 4	3068
I not in that day, saith the L	Obad 8	3068
For the day of the L is near upon	Obad 15	3068

L

for the *L* hath spoken it	Obad 18	3068
Now the word of the *L* came unto	Jonah 1:1	3068
from the presence of the *L*	Jonah 1:3	3068
from the presence of the *L*	Jonah 1:3	3068
But the *L* sent out a great wind	Jonah 1:4	3068
and I fear the *L*, the God of	Jonah 1:9	3068
fled from the presence of the *L*	Jonah 1:10	3068
Wherefore they cried unto the *L*	Jonah 1:14	3068
and said, We beseech thee, O *L*	Jonah 1:14	3068
for thou, O *L*, hast done as it	Jonah 1:14	3068
the men feared the *L* exceedingly	Jonah 1:16	3068
and offered a sacrifice unto the *L*	Jonah 1:16	3068
Now the *L* had prepared a great	Jonah 1:17	3068
Then Jonah prayed unto the *L* his	Jonah 2:1	3068
of mine affliction unto the *L*	Jonah 2:2	3068
life from corruption, O *L* my God	Jonah 2:6	3068
within me I remembered the *L*	Jonah 2:7	3068
Salvation is of the *L*	Jonah 2:9	3068
the *L* spake unto the fish, and it	Jonah 2:10	3068
the word of the *L* came unto Jonah	Jonah 3:1	3068
according to the word of the *L*	Jonah 3:3	3068
And he prayed unto the *L*	Jonah 4:2	3068
and said, I pray thee, O *L*	Jonah 4:2	3068
Therefore now, O *L*, take, I	Jonah 4:3	3068
Then said the *L*, Doest thou well	Jonah 4:4	3068
the *L* God prepared a gourd, and	Jonah 4:6	3068
Then said the *L*, Thou hast had	Jonah 4:10	3068
The word of the *L* that came to	Mic 1:1	3068
let the *L* GOD be witness against	Mic 1:2	136
the *L* from his holy temple	Mic 1:2	136
the *L* cometh forth out of his	Mic 1:3	3068
the *L* unto the gate of Jerusalem	Mic 1:12	3068
Therefore thus saith the *L*	Mic 2:3	3068
lot in the congregation of the *L*	Mic 2:5	3068
is the spirit of the *L* straitened	Mic 2:7	3068
the *L* on the head of them	Mic 2:13	3068
Then shall they cry unto the *L*	Mic 3:4	3068
Thus saith the *L* concerning the	Mic 3:5	3068
of power by the spirit of the *L*	Mic 3:8	3068
yet will they lean upon the *L*	Mic 3:11	3068
and say, Is not the *L* among us	Mic 3:11	3068
mountain of the house of the *L*	Mic 4:1	3068
us go up to the mountain of the *L*	Mic 4:2	3068
the word of the *L* from Jerusalem	Mic 4:2	3068
for the mouth of the *L* of hosts	Mic 4:4	3068
name of the *L* our God for ever	Mic 4:5	3068
In that day, saith the *L*, will I	Mic 4:6	3068
the *L* shall reign over them in	Mic 4:7	3068
there the *L* shall redeem thee	Mic 4:10	3068
know not the thoughts of the *L*	Mic 4:12	3068
consecrate their gain unto the *L*	Mic 4:13	3068
unto the *L* of the whole earth	Mic 4:13	113
and feed in the strength of the *L*	Mic 5:4	3068
of the name of the *L* his God	Mic 5:4	3068
many people as a dew from the *L*	Mic 5:7	3068
to pass in that day, saith the *L*	Mic 5:10	3068
Hear ye now what the *L* saith	Mic 6:1	3068
for the *L* hath a controversy with	Mic 6:2	3068
know the righteousness of the *L*	Mic 6:5	3068
shall I come before the *L*	Mic 6:6	3068
Will the *L* be pleased with	Mic 6:7	3068
what doth the *L* require of thee,	Mic 6:8	3068
Therefore I will look unto the *L*	Mic 7:7	3068
the *L* shall be a light unto me	Mic 7:8	3068
bear the indignation of the *L*	Mic 7:9	3068
unto me, Where is the *L* thy God	Mic 7:10	3068
shall be afraid of the *L* our God	Mic 7:17	3068
is jealous, and the *L* revengeth	Nah 1:2	3068
the *L* revengeth, and is furious	Nah 1:2	3068
the *L* will take vengeance on his	Nah 1:2	3068
The *L* is slow to anger, and great	Nah 1:3	3068
the *L* hath his way in the	Nah 1:3	3068
The *L* is good, a strong hold in	Nah 1:7	3068
What do ye imagine against the *L*	Nah 1:9	3068
that imagineth evil against the *L*	Nah 1:11	3068
Thus saith the *L*	Nah 1:12	3068
the *L* hath given a commandment	Nah 1:14	3068
For the *L* hath turned away the	Nah 2:2	3068
thee, saith the *L* of hosts	Nah 2:13	3068
thee, saith the *L* of hosts	Nah 3:5	3068
O *L*, how long shall I cry, and	Hab 1:2	3068
O *L* my God, mine Holy One	Hab 1:12	3068
O *L*, thou hast ordained them for	Hab 1:12	3068
the *L* answered me, and said, Write	Hab 2:2	3068
is it not of the *L* of hosts that	Hab 2:13	3068
knowledge of the glory of the *L*	Hab 2:14	3068
But the *L* is in his holy temple	Hab 2:20	3068
O *L*, I have heard thy speech, and	Hab 3:2	3068
O *L*, revive thy work in the midst	Hab 3:2	3068
Was the *L* displeased against the	Hab 3:8	3068
Yet I will rejoice in the *L*	Hab 3:18	3068
The *L* God is my strength, and he	Hab 3:19	3068
The word of the *L* which came unto	Zeph 1:1	3068
from off the land, saith the *L*	Zeph 1:2	3068
from off the land, saith the *L*	Zeph 1:3	3068
worship and that swear by the *L*	Zeph 1:5	3068
that are turned back from the *L*	Zeph 1:6	3068
those that have not sought the *L*	Zeph 1:6	3068
at the presence of the *L* GOD	Zeph 1:7	136
for the day of the *L* is at hand	Zeph 1:7	3068
for the *L* hath prepared a	Zeph 1:7	3068
to pass in that day, saith the *L*	Zeph 1:10	3068
The *L* will not do good, neither	Zeph 1:12	3068
The great day of the *L* is near	Zeph 1:14	3068
the voice of the day of the *L*	Zeph 1:14	3068
they have sinned against the *L*	Zeph 1:17	3068
anger of the *L* come upon you	Zeph 2:2	3068
Seek ye the *L*, all ye meek of the	Zeph 2:3	3068
the word of the *L* is against you	Zeph 2:5	3068
for the *L* their God shall visit	Zeph 2:7	3068
as I live, saith the *L* of hosts	Zeph 2:9	3068
the people of the *L* of hosts	Zeph 2:10	3068
The *L* will be terrible unto them	Zeph 2:11	3068
she trusted not in the *L*	Zeph 3:2	3068
The just *L* is in the midst	Zeph 3:5	3068
wait ye upon me, saith the *L*	Zeph 3:8	3068
all call upon the name of the *L*	Zeph 3:9	3068
shall trust in the name of the *L*	Zeph 3:12	3068
The *L* hath taken away thy	Zeph 3:15	3068
the king of Israel, even the *L*	Zeph 3:15	3068
The *L* thy God in the midst of	Zeph 3:17	3068
before your eyes, saith the *L*	Zeph 3:20	3068
came the word of the *L* by Haggai	Hag 1:1	3068
Thus speaketh the *L* of hosts	Hag 1:2	3068
of the *L* by Haggai the prophet	Hag 1:3	3068
thus saith the *L* of hosts	Hag 1:5	3068
Thus saith the *L* of hosts	Hag 1:7	3068
I will be glorified, saith the *L*	Hag 1:8	3068
saith the *L* of hosts	Hag 1:9	3068
the voice of the *L* their God	Hag 1:12	3068
as the *L* their God had sent him,	Hag 1:12	3068
the people did fear before the *L*	Hag 1:12	3068
I am with you, saith the *L*	Hag 1:13	3068
the *L* stirred up the spirit of	Hag 1:14	3068
in the house of the *L* of hosts	Hag 1:14	3068
came the word of the *L* by the	Hag 2:1	3068
strong, O Zerubbabel, saith the *L*	Hag 2:4	3068
people of the land, saith the *L*	Hag 2:4	3068
am with you, saith the *L* of hosts	Hag 2:4	3068
For thus saith the *L* of hosts	Hag 2:6	3068
with glory, saith the *L* of hosts	Hag 2:7	3068
is mine, saith the *L* of hosts	Hag 2:8	3068
the former, saith the *L* of hosts	Hag 2:9	3068
give peace, saith the *L* of hosts	Hag 2:9	3068
came the word of the *L* by Haggai	Hag 2:10	3068
Thus saith the *L* of hosts	Hag 2:11	3068
nation before me, saith the *L*	Hag 2:14	3068
a stone in the temple of the *L*	Hag 2:15	3068
ye turned not to me, saith the *L*	Hag 2:17	3068
again the word of the *L* came unto	Hag 2:20	3068
In that day, saith the *L* of hosts	Hag 2:23	3068
the son of Shealtiel, saith the *L*	Hag 2:23	3068
chosen thee, saith the *L* of hosts	Hag 2:23	3068
the word of the *L* unto Zechariah	Zec 1:1	3068
The *L* hath been sore displeased	Zec 1:2	3068
them, Thus saith the *L* of hosts	Zec 1:3	3068
ye unto me, saith the *L* of hosts	Zec 1:3	3068
unto you, saith the *L* of hosts	Zec 1:3	3068
saying, Thus saith the *L* of hosts	Zec 1:4	3068
nor hearken unto me, saith the *L*	Zec 1:4	3068
Like as the *L* of hosts thought to	Zec 1:6	3068
the word of the *L* unto Zechariah	Zec 1:7	3068
whom the *L* hath sent to walk to	Zec 1:10	3068
the *L* that stood among the myrtle	Zec 1:11	3068
Then the angel of the *L* answered	Zec 1:12	3068
O *L* of hosts, how long wilt thou	Zec 1:12	3068
the *L* answered the angel that	Zec 1:13	3068
saying, Thus saith the *L* of hosts	Zec 1:14	3068
Therefore thus saith the *L*	Zec 1:16	3068
built in it, saith the *L* of hosts	Zec 1:16	3068
saying, Thus saith the *L* of hosts	Zec 1:17	3068
the *L* shall yet comfort Zion, and	Zec 1:17	3068
the *L* shewed me four carpenters	Zec 1:20	3068
For I, saith the *L*, will be unto	Zec 2:5	3068
land of the north, saith the *L*	Zec 2:6	3068
winds of the heaven, saith the *L*	Zec 2:6	3068
For thus saith the *L* of hosts	Zec 2:8	3068
that the *L* of hosts hath sent me	Zec 2:9	3068
in the midst of thee, saith the *L*	Zec 2:10	3068
be joined to the *L* in that day	Zec 2:11	3068
thou shalt know that the *L* of	Zec 2:11	3068
the *L* shall inherit Judah his	Zec 2:12	3068

silent, O all flesh, before the *L*	Zec 2:13	3068
before the angel of the *L*	Zec 3:1	3068
the *L* said unto Satan	Zec 3:2	3068
The *L* rebuke thee, O Satan	Zec 3:2	3068
even the *L* that hath chosen	Zec 3:2	3068
And the angel of the *L* stood by	Zec 3:5	3068
the angel of the *L* protested unto	Zec 3:6	3068
Thus saith the *L* of hosts	Zec 3:7	3068
thereof, saith the *L* of hosts	Zec 3:9	3068
In that day, saith the *L* of hosts	Zec 3:10	3068
the word of the *L* unto Zerubbabel	Zec 4:6	3068
my spirit, saith the *L* of hosts	Zec 4:6	3068
the word of the *L* came unto me	Zec 4:8	3068
thou shalt know that the *L* of	Zec 4:9	3068
they are the eyes of the *L*	Zec 4:10	3068
that stand by the *L* of the whole	Zec 4:14	113
it forth, saith the *L* of hosts	Zec 5:4	3068
before the *L* of all the earth	Zec 6:5	113
And the word of the *L* came unto me	Zec 6:9	3068
Thus speaketh the *L* of hosts	Zec 6:12	3068
shall build the temple of the *L*	Zec 6:12	3068
shall build the temple of the *L*	Zec 6:13	3068
a memorial in the temple of the *L*	Zec 6:14	3068
and build in the temple of the *L*	Zec 6:15	3068
ye shall know that the *L* of hosts	Zec 6:15	3068
obey the voice of the *L* your God	Zec 6:15	3068
that the word of the *L* came unto	Zec 7:1	3068
their men, to pray before the *L*	Zec 7:2	3068
in the house of the *L* of hosts	Zec 7:3	3068
word of the *L* of hosts unto me	Zec 7:4	3068
the *L* hath cried by the former	Zec 7:7	3068
the word of the *L* came unto	Zec 7:8	3068
Thus speaketh the *L* of hosts	Zec 7:9	3068
the words which the *L* of hosts	Zec 7:12	3068
a great wrath from the *L* of hosts	Zec 7:12	3068
not hear, saith the *L* of hosts	Zec 7:13	3068
word of the *L* of hosts came to me	Zec 8:1	3068
Thus saith the *L* of hosts	Zec 8:2	3068
Thus saith the *L*	Zec 8:3	3068
the mountain of the *L* of hosts	Zec 8:3	3068
Thus saith the *L* of hosts	Zec 8:4	3068
Thus saith the *L* of hosts	Zec 8:6	3068
saith the *L* of hosts	Zec 8:6	3068
Thus saith the *L* of hosts	Zec 8:7	3068
Thus saith the *L* of hosts	Zec 8:9	3068
house of the *L* of hosts was laid	Zec 8:9	3068
former days, saith the *L* of hosts	Zec 8:11	3068
For thus saith the *L* of hosts	Zec 8:14	3068
me to wrath, saith the *L* of hosts	Zec 8:14	3068
things that I hate, saith the *L*	Zec 8:17	3068
the word of the *L* of hosts came	Zec 8:18	3068
Thus saith the *L* of hosts	Zec 8:19	3068
Thus saith the *L* of hosts	Zec 8:20	3068
go speedily to pray before the *L*	Zec 8:21	3068
and to seek the *L* of hosts	Zec 8:21	3068
seek the *L* of hosts in Jerusalem	Zec 8:22	3068
and to pray before the *L*	Zec 8:22	3068
Thus saith the *L* of hosts	Zec 8:23	3068
of the *L* in the land of Hadrach	Zec 9:1	3068
of Israel, shall be toward the *L*	Zec 9:1	3068
the *L* will cast her out, and he	Zec 9:4	136
the *L* shall be seen over them, and	Zec 9:14	3068
the *L* GOD shall blow the trumpet,	Zec 9:14	136
The *L* of hosts shall defend them	Zec 9:15	3068
the *L* their God shall save them	Zec 9:16	3068
Ask ye of the *L* rain in the time	Zec 10:1	3068
so the *L* shall make bright clouds	Zec 10:1	3068
for the *L* of hosts hath visited	Zec 10:3	3068
because the *L* is with them, and	Zec 10:5	3068
for I am the *L* their God, and will	Zec 10:6	3068
heart shall rejoice in the *L*	Zec 10:7	3068
I will strengthen them in the *L*	Zec 10:12	3068
and down in his name, saith the *L*	Zec 10:12	3068
Thus saith the *L* my God	Zec 11:4	3068
sell them say, Blessed be the *L*	Zec 11:5	3068
of the land, saith the *L*	Zec 11:6	3068
that it was the word of the *L*	Zec 11:11	3068
the *L* said unto me, Cast it unto	Zec 11:13	3068
the potter in the house of the *L*	Zec 11:13	3068
the *L* said unto me, Take unto	Zec 11:15	3068
of the word of the *L* for Israel	Zec 12:1	3068
for Israel, saith the *L*	Zec 12:1	3068
In that day, saith the *L*, I will	Zec 12:4	3068
in the *L* of hosts their God	Zec 12:5	3068
The *L* also shall save the tents	Zec 12:7	3068
In that day shall the *L* defend	Zec 12:8	3068
as the angel of the *L* before them	Zec 12:8	3068
in that day, saith the *L* of hosts	Zec 13:2	3068
lies in the name of the *L*	Zec 13:3	3068
my fellow, saith the *L* of hosts	Zec 13:7	3068
that in all the land, saith the *L*	Zec 13:8	3068

they shall say, The *L* is my God	Zec 13:9	3068
Behold, the day of the *L* cometh	Zec 14:1	3068
Then shall the *L* go forth	Zec 14:3	3068
the *L* my God shall come, and all	Zec 14:5	3068
day which shall be known to the *L*	Zec 14:7	3068
the *L* shall be king over all the	Zec 14:9	3068
in that day shall there be one *L*	Zec 14:9	3068
be the plague wherewith the *L*	Zec 14:12	3068
from the *L* shall be among them	Zec 14:13	3068
the *L* of hosts, and to keep the	Zec 14:16	3068
the *L* of hosts, even upon them	Zec 14:17	3068
wherewith the *L* will smite the	Zec 14:18	3068
the horses, HOLINESS UNTO THE *L*.	Zec 14:20	3068
be holiness unto the *L* of hosts	Zec 14:21	3068
in the house of the *L* of hosts	Zec 14:21	3068
of the *L* to Israel by Malachi	Mal 1:1	3068
I have loved you, saith the *L*	Mal 1:2	3068
Jacob's brother? saith the *L*	Mal 1:2	3068
thus saith the *L* of hosts	Mal 1:4	3068
the *L* hath indignation for ever	Mal 1:4	3068
The *L* will be magnified from the	Mal 1:5	3068
saith the *L* of hosts unto you, O	Mal 1:6	3068
table of the *L* is contemptible	Mal 1:7	3068
saith the *L* of hosts	Mal 1:8	3068
saith the *L* of hosts	Mal 1:9	3068
in you, saith the *L* of hosts	Mal 1:10	3068
the heathen, saith the *L* of hosts	Mal 1:11	3068
The table of the *L* is polluted	Mal 1:12	3068
at it, saith the *L* of hosts	Mal 1:13	3068
your hand? saith the *L*	Mal 1:13	3068
unto the *L* a corrupt thing	Mal 1:14	136
great King, saith the *L* of hosts	Mal 1:14	3068
my name, saith the *L* of hosts	Mal 2:2	3068
with Levi, saith the *L* of hosts	Mal 2:4	3068
the messenger of the *L* of hosts	Mal 2:7	3068
of Levi, saith the *L* of hosts	Mal 2:8	3068
holiness of the *L* which he loved	Mal 2:11	3068
The *L* will cut off the man that	Mal 2:12	3068
an offering unto the *L* of hosts	Mal 2:12	3068
the altar of the *L* with tears	Mal 2:13	3068
Because the *L* hath been witness	Mal 2:14	3068
For the *L*, the God of Israel,	Mal 2:16	3068
his garment, saith the *L* of hosts	Mal 2:16	3068
wearied the *L* with your words	Mal 2:17	3068
is good in the sight of the *L*	Mal 2:17	3068
and the *L*, whom ye seek, shall	Mal 3:1	113
shall come, saith the *L* of hosts	Mal 3:1	3068
L an offering in righteousness	Mal 3:3	3068
Jerusalem be pleasant unto the *L*	Mal 3:4	3068
fear not me, saith the *L* of hosts	Mal 3:5	3068
For I am the *L*, I change not	Mal 3:6	3068
unto you, saith the *L* of hosts	Mal 3:7	3068
herewith, saith the *L* of hosts	Mal 3:10	3068
the field, saith the *L* of hosts	Mal 3:11	3068
land, saith the *L* of hosts	Mal 3:12	3068
stout against me, saith the *L*	Mal 3:13	3068
mournfully before the *L* of hosts	Mal 3:14	3068
Then they that feared the *L* spake	Mal 3:16	3068
the *L* hearkened, and heard it, and	Mal 3:16	3068
him for them that feared the *L*	Mal 3:16	3068
be mine, saith the *L* of hosts	Mal 3:17	3068
them up, saith the *L* of hosts	Mal 4:1	3068
do this, saith the *L* of hosts	Mal 4:3	3068
great and dreadful day of the *L*	Mal 4:5	3068
the angel of the *L* appeared unto	Mt 1:20	2962
spoken of the *L* by the prophet	Mt 1:22	2962
the angel of the *L* had bidden him	Mt 1:24	2962
the angel of the *L* appeareth to	Mt 2:13	2962
spoken of the *L* by the prophet	Mt 2:15	2962
an angel of the *L* appeareth in a	Mt 2:19	2962
Prepare ye the way of the *L*	Mt 3:3	2962
shalt not tempt the *L* thy God	Mt 4:7	2962
Thou shalt worship the *L* thy God	Mt 4:10	2962
perform unto the *L* thine oaths	Mt 5:33	2962
one that saith unto me, *L*, *L*	Mt 7:21	2962
say to me in that day, *L*	Mt 7:22	2962
and worshipped him, saying, *L*	Mt 8:2	2962
And saying, *L*, my servant lieth at	Mt 8:6	2962
The centurion answered and said, *L*	Mt 8:8	2962
of his disciples said unto him, *L*	Mt 8:21	2962
to him, and awoke him, saying, *L*	Mt 8:25	2962
They said unto him, Yea, *L*	Mt 9:28	2962
ye therefore the *L* of the harvest	Mt 9:38	2962
***L* of heaven and earth, because**	Mt 11:25	2962
For the Son of man is *L* even of	Mt 12:8	2962
They say unto him, Yea, *L*	Mt 13:51	2962
And Peter answered him and said, *L*	Mt 14:28	2962
to sink, he cried, saying, *L*	Mt 14:30	2962
saying, Have mercy on me, O *L*	Mt 15:22	2962
she and worshipped him, saying, *L*	Mt 15:25	2962
And she said, Truth, *L*	Mt 15:27	2962

L

saying, Be it far from thee, *L*	Mt 16:22	2962
Peter, and said unto Jesus, *L*	Mt 17:4	2962
L, have mercy on my son	Mt 17:15	2962
came Peter to him, and said, *L*	Mt 18:21	2962
and worshipped him, saying, *L*	Mt 18:26	2962
saying, Have mercy on us, O *L*	Mt 20:30	2962
saying, Have mercy on us, O *L*	Mt 20:31	2962
They say unto him, *L*, that our	Mt 20:33	2962
say, The *L* hath need of them	Mt 21:3	2962
that cometh in the name of the *L*	Mt 21:9	2962
When the *l* therefore the	Mt 21:40	2962
Thou shalt love the *L* thy God	Mt 22:37	2962
doth David in spirit call him *L*	Mt 22:43	2962
The *L* said unto my *L*, Sit thou	Mt 22:44	2962
If David then call him *L*	Mt 22:45	2962
that cometh in the name of the *L*	Mt 23:39	2962
not what hour your *L* doth come	Mt 24:42	2962
other virgins, saying, *L*, *L*	Mt 25:11	2962
righteous answer him, saying, *L*	Mt 25:37	2962
they also answer him, saying, *L*	Mt 25:44	2962
one of them to say unto him, *L*	Mt 26:22	2962
field, as the *L* appointed me	Mt 27:10	2962
for the angel of the *L* descended	Mt 28:2	2962
see the place where the *L* lay	Mt 28:6	2962
Prepare ye the way of the *L*	Mk 1:3	2962
of man is *L* also of the sabbath	Mk 2:28	2962
things the *L* hath done for thee	Mk 5:19	2962
answered and said unto him, Yes, *L*	Mk 7:28	2962
cried out, and said with tears, *L*	Mk 9:24	2962
The blind man said unto him, *L*	Mk 10:51	4462
say ye that the *L* hath need of	Mk 11:3	2962
that cometh in the name of the *L*	Mk 11:9	2962
that cometh in the name of the *L*	Mk 11:10	2962
The *L* our God is one *L*	Mk 12:29	2962
thou shalt love the *L* thy God	Mk 12:30	2962
The *L* said to my *L*, Sit thou	Mk 12:36	2962
therefore himself calleth him *L*	Mk 12:37	2962
except that the *L* had shortened	Mk 13:20	2962
So then after the *L* had spoken	Mk 16:19	2962
the *L* working with them, and	Mk 16:20	2962
and ordinances of the *L* blameless	Lk 1:6	2962
he went into the temple of the *L*	Lk 1:9	2962
unto him an angel of the *L*	Lk 1:11	2962
be great in the sight of the *L*	Lk 1:15	2962
shall he turn to the *L* their God	Lk 1:16	2962
ready a people prepared for the *L*	Lk 1:17	2962
Thus hath the *L* dealt with me in	Lk 1:25	2962
favoured, the *L* is with thee	Lk 1:28	2962
the *L* God shall give unto him the	Lk 1:32	2962
Behold the handmaid of the *L*	Lk 1:38	2962
mother of my *L* should come to me	Lk 1:43	2962
which were told her from the *L*	Lk 1:45	2962
said, My soul doth magnify the *L*	Lk 1:46	2962
her cousins heard how the *L* had	Lk 1:58	2962
And the hand of the *L* was with him	Lk 1:66	2962
Blessed be the *L* God of Israel	Lk 1:68	2962
face of the *L* to prepare his ways	Lk 1:76	2962
the angel of the *L* came upon them	Lk 2:9	2962
the glory of the *L* shone round	Lk 2:9	2962
a Saviour, which is Christ the *L*	Lk 2:11	2962
which the *L* hath made known unto	Lk 2:15	2962
to present him to the *L*	Lk 2:22	2962
it is written in the law of the *L*	Lk 2:23	2962
shall be called holy to the *L*	Lk 2:23	2962
which is said in the law of the *L*	Lk 2:24	2962
L, now lettest thou thy servant	Lk 2:29	1203
gave thanks likewise unto the *L*	Lk 2:38	2962
according to the law of the *L*	Lk 2:39	2962
Prepare ye the way of the *L*	Lk 3:4	2962
Thou shalt worship the *L* thy God	Lk 4:8	2962
shalt not tempt the *L* thy God	Lk 4:12	2962
The Spirit of the *L* is upon me	Lk 4:18	2962
the acceptable year of the *L*	Lk 4:19	2962
for I am a sinful man, O *L*	Lk 5:8	2962
face, and besought him, saying, *L*	Lk 5:12	2962
the power of the *L* was present to	Lk 5:17	2962
of man is *L* also of the sabbath	Lk 6:5	2962
And why call ye me, *L*, *L*	Lk 6:46	2962
to him, saying unto him, *L*	Lk 7:6	2962
And when the *L* saw her, he had	Lk 7:13	2962
the *L* said, Whereunto then shall	Lk 7:31	2962
and John saw this, they said, *L*	Lk 9:54	2962
a certain man said unto him, *L*	Lk 9:57	2962
But he said, *L*, suffer me first	Lk 9:59	2962
And another also said, *L*, I will	Lk 9:61	2962
After these things the *L*	Lk 10:1	2962
ye therefore the *L* of the harvest	Lk 10:2	2962
again with joy, saying, *L*	Lk 10:17	2962
L of heaven and earth, that thou	Lk 10:21	2962
Thou shalt love the *L* thy God	Lk 10:27	2962
and came to him, and said, *L*	Lk 10:40	2962
of his disciples said unto him, *L*	Lk 11:1	2962
the *L* said unto him, Now do ye	Lk 11:39	2962
Then Peter said unto him, *L*	Lk 12:41	2962
the *L* said, Who then is that	Lk 12:42	2962
And he answering said unto him, *L*	Lk 13:8	2962
The *L* then answered him, and said,	Lk 13:15	2962
Then said one unto him, *L*	Lk 13:23	2962
at the door, saying, *L*, *L*	Lk 13:25	2962
that cometh in the name of the *L*	Lk 13:35	2962
And the apostles said unto the *L*	Lk 17:5	2962
the *L* said, If ye had faith as a	Lk 17:6	2962
and said unto him, Where, *L*	Lk 17:37	2962
the *L* said, Hear what the unjust	Lk 18:6	2962
And he said, *L*, that I may receive	Lk 18:41	2962
stood, and said unto the *L*	Lk 19:8	2962
Behold, *L*, the half of my goods I	Lk 19:8	2962
Then came the first, saying, *L*	Lk 19:16	2962
And the second came, saying, *L*	Lk 19:18	2962
And another came, saying, *L*	Lk 19:20	2962
(And they said unto him, *L*	Lk 19:25	2962
Because the *L* hath need of him	Lk 19:31	2962
they said, The *L* hath need of him	Lk 19:34	2962
that cometh in the name of the *L*	Lk 19:38	2962
calleth the *L* the God of Abraham	Lk 20:37	2962
The *L* said unto my *L*, Sit thou	Lk 20:42	2962
David therefore calleth him *L*	Lk 20:44	2962
the *L* said, Simon, Simon, behold,	Lk 22:31	2962
And he said unto him, *L*, I am	Lk 22:33	2962
And they said, *L*, behold, here are	Lk 22:38	2962
follow, they said unto him, *L*	Lk 22:49	2962
the *L* turned, and looked upon	Lk 22:61	2962
remembered the word of the *L*	Lk 22:61	2962
And he said unto Jesus, *L*,	Lk 23:42	2962
found not the body of the *L* Jesus	Lk 24:3	2962
The *L* is risen indeed, and hath	Lk 24:34	2962
Make straight the way of the *L*	Jn 1:23	2962
When therefore the *L* knew how the	Jn 4:1	2962
after that the *L* had given thanks,	Jn 6:23	2962
Then said they unto him, *L*	Jn 6:34	2962
Then Simon Peter answered him, *L*	Jn 6:68	2962
She said, No man, *L*,	Jn 8:11	2962
He answered and said, Who is he, *L*	Jn 9:36	2962
And he said, *L*, I believe	Jn 9:38	2962
anointed the *L* with ointment	Jn 11:2	2962
sisters sent unto him, saying, *L*	Jn 11:3	2962
Then said his disciples, *L*	Jn 11:12	2962
Then said Martha unto Jesus, *L*	Jn 11:21	2962
She saith unto him, Yea, *L*	Jn 11:27	2962
at his feet, saying unto him, *L*	Jn 11:32	2962
They said unto him, *L*, come and	Jn 11:34	2962
that was dead, saith unto him, *L*	Jn 11:39	2962
that cometh in the name of the *L*	Jn 12:13	2962
be fulfilled, which he spake, *L*	Jn 12:38	2962
the arm of the *L* been revealed	Jn 12:38	2962
and Peter saith unto him, *L*	Jn 13:6	2962
Simon Peter saith unto him, *L*	Jn 13:9	2962
Ye call me Master and *L*	Jn 13:13	2962
If I then, your *L* and Master, have	Jn 13:14	2962
Jesus' breast saith unto him, *L*	Jn 13:25	2962
Simon Peter said unto him, *L*	Jn 13:36	2962
Peter said unto him, *L*, why	Jn 13:37	2962
Thomas saith unto him, *L*, we know	Jn 14:5	2962
Philip saith unto him, *L*, shew us	Jn 14:8	2962
saith unto him, not Iscariot, *L*	Jn 14:22	2962
away the *L* out of the sepulchre	Jn 20:2	2962
Because they have taken away my *L*	Jn 20:13	2962
disciples that she had seen the *L*	Jn 20:18	2962
glad, when they saw the *L*	Jn 20:20	2962
said unto him, We have seen the *L*	Jn 20:25	2962
answered and said unto him, My *L*	Jn 20:28	2962
saith unto Peter, It is the *L*	Jn 21:7	2962
Peter heard that it was the *L*	Jn 21:7	2962
knowing that it was the *L*	Jn 21:12	2962
He saith unto him, Yea, *L*	Jn 21:15	2962
He saith unto him, Yea, *L*	Jn 21:16	2962
And he said unto him, *L*, thou	Jn 21:17	2962
his breast at supper, and said, *L*	Jn 21:20	2962
seeing him saith to Jesus, *L*	Jn 21:21	2962
they asked of him, saying, *L*	Acts 1:6	2962
the time that the *L* Jesus went in	Acts 1:21	2962
And they prayed, and said, Thou, *L*	Acts 1:24	2962
and notable day of the *L* come	Acts 2:20	2962
the name of the *L* shall be saved	Acts 2:21	2962
I foresaw the *L* always before my	Acts 2:25	2962
The *L* said unto my *L*, Sit thou	Acts 2:34	2962
whom ye have crucified, both *L*	Acts 2:36	2962
many as the *L* our God shall call	Acts 2:39	2962
the *L* added to the church daily	Acts 2:47	2962
come from the presence of the *L*	Acts 3:19	2962
A prophet shall the *L* your God	Acts 3:22	2962
God with one accord, and said, *L*	Acts 4:24	1203

gathered together against the L	Acts 4:26	2962
And now, L, behold their	Acts 4:29	2962
the resurrection of the L Jesus	Acts 4:33	2962
to tempt the Spirit of the L	Acts 5:9	2962
were the more added to the L	Acts 5:14	2962
But the angel of the L by night	Acts 5:19	2962
L in a flame of fire in a bush	Acts 7:30	2962
the voice of the L came unto him	Acts 7:31	2962
Then said the L to him, Put off	Acts 7:33	2962
A prophet shall the L your God	Acts 7:37	2962
build me? saith the L	Acts 7:49	2962
L Jesus, receive my spirit	Acts 7:59	2962
and cried with a loud voice, L	Acts 7:60	2962
in the name of the L Jesus	Acts 8:16	2962
and said, Pray ye to the L for me	Acts 8:24	2962
and preached the word of the L	Acts 8:25	2962
the angel of the L spake unto	Acts 8:26	2962
the Spirit of the L caught away	Acts 8:39	2962
against the disciples of the L	Acts 9:1	2962
And he said, Who art thou, L	Acts 9:5	2962
the L said, I am Jesus whom	Acts 9:5	2962
trembling and astonished said, L	Acts 9:6	2962
the L said unto him, Arise, and go	Acts 9:6	2962
and to him said the L in a vision	Acts 9:10	2962
And he said, Behold, I am here, L	Acts 9:10	2962
the L said unto him, Arise, and go	Acts 9:11	2962
Then Ananias answered, L, I have	Acts 9:13	2962
But the L said unto him, Go thy	Acts 9:15	2962
on him said, Brother Saul, the L	Acts 9:17	2962
how he had seen the L in the way	Acts 9:27	2962
boldly in the name of the L Jesus	Acts 9:29	2962
and walking in the fear of the L	Acts 9:31	2962
Saron saw him, and turned to the L	Acts 9:35	2962
and many believed in the L	Acts 9:42	2962
afraid, and said, What is it, L	Acts 10:4	2962
But Peter said, Not so, L	Acts 10:14	2962
(he is L of all	Acts 10:36	2962
be baptized in the name of the L	Acts 10:48	2962
But I said, Not so, L	Acts 11:8	2962
remembered I the word of the L	Acts 11:16	2962
believed on the L Jesus Christ	Acts 11:17	2962
Grecians, preaching the L Jesus	Acts 11:20	2962
the hand of the L was with them	Acts 11:21	2962
believed, and turned unto the L	Acts 11:21	2962
they would cleave unto the L	Acts 11:23	2962
much people was added unto the L	Acts 11:24	2962
the angel of the L came upon him	Acts 12:7	2962
that the L hath sent his angel,	Acts 12:11	2962
the L had brought him out of the	Acts 12:17	2962
the angel of the L smote him	Acts 12:23	2962
As they ministered to the L	Acts 13:2	2962
pervert the right ways of the L	Acts 13:10	2962
the hand of the L is upon thee	Acts 13:11	2962
at the doctrine of the L	Acts 13:12	2962
For so hath the L commanded us	Acts 13:47	2962
and glorified the word of the L	Acts 13:48	2962
the word of the L was published	Acts 13:49	2962
they speaking boldly in the L	Acts 14:3	2962
they commended them to the L	Acts 14:23	2962
that through the grace of the L	Acts 15:11	2962
of men might seek after the L	Acts 15:17	2962
my name is called, saith the L	Acts 15:17	2962
the name of our L Jesus Christ	Acts 15:26	2962
and preaching the word of the L	Acts 15:35	2962
have preached the word of the L	Acts 15:36	2962
assuredly gathering that the L	Acts 16:10	2962
whose heart the L opened, that	Acts 16:14	2962
judged me to be faithful to the L	Acts 16:15	2962
Believe on the L Jesus Christ	Acts 16:31	2962
spake unto him the word of the L	Acts 16:32	2962
seeing that he is L of heaven	Acts 17:24	2962
That they should seek the L	Acts 17:27	2962
believed on the L with all his	Acts 18:8	2962
Then spake the L to Paul in the	Acts 18:9	2962
instructed in the way of the L	Acts 18:25	2962
diligently the things of the L	Acts 18:25	2962
in the name of the L Jesus	Acts 19:5	2962
heard the word of the L Jesus	Acts 19:10	2962
spirits the name of the L Jesus	Acts 19:13	2962
the name of the L Jesus was	Acts 19:17	2962
Serving the L with all humility	Acts 20:19	2962
faith toward our L Jesus Christ	Acts 20:21	2962
I have received of the L Jesus	Acts 20:24	2962
remember the words of the L Jesus	Acts 20:35	2962
for the name of the L Jesus	Acts 21:13	2962
saying, The will of the L be done	Acts 21:14	2962
heard it, they glorified the L	Acts 21:20	2962
And I said, Who art thou, L	Acts 22:8	2962
the L said unto me, Arise, and go	Acts 22:10	2962
calling on the name of the L	Acts 22:16	2962
And I said, L, they know that I	Acts 22:19	2962
following the L stood by him	Acts 23:11	2962
And I said, Who art thou, L	Acts 26:15	2962
which concern the L Jesus Christ	Acts 28:31	2962
his Son Jesus Christ our L	Rom 1:3	2962
our Father, and the L Jesus Christ	Rom 1:7	2962
to whom the L will not impute sin	Rom 4:8	2962
up Jesus our L from the dead	Rom 4:24	2962
God through our L Jesus Christ	Rom 5:1	2962
in God through our L Jesus Christ	Rom 5:11	2962
life by Jesus Christ our L	Rom 5:21	2962
God through Jesus Christ our L	Rom 6:11	2962
life through Jesus Christ our L	Rom 6:23	2962
God through Jesus Christ our L	Rom 7:25	2962
which is in Christ Jesus our L	Rom 8:39	2962
will the L make upon the earth	Rom 9:28	2962
Except the L of Sabaoth had left	Rom 9:29	2962
with thy mouth the L Jesus	Rom 10:9	2962
for the same L over all is rich	Rom 10:12	2962
the name of the L shall be saved	Rom 10:13	2962
For Esaias saith, L, who hath	Rom 10:16	2962
L, they have killed thy prophets,	Rom 11:3	2962
who hath known the mind of the L	Rom 11:34	2962
fervent in spirit; serving the L	Rom 12:11	2962
I will repay, saith the L	Rom 12:19	2962
But put ye on the L Jesus Christ	Rom 13:14	2962
the day, regardeth it unto the L	Rom 14:6	2962
to the L he doth not regard it	Rom 14:6	2962
He that eateth, eateth to the L	Rom 14:6	2962
to the L he eateth not, and giveth	Rom 14:6	2962
we live, we live unto the L	Rom 14:8	2962
whether we die, we die unto the L	Rom 14:8	2962
he might be L both of the dead	Rom 14:9	2961
written, As I live, saith the L	Rom 14:11	2962
and am persuaded by the L Jesus	Rom 14:14	2962
the Father of our L Jesus Christ	Rom 15:6	2962
And again, Praise the L, all ye	Rom 15:11	2962
for the L Jesus Christ's sake, and	Rom 15:30	2962
That ye receive her in the L	Rom 16:2	2962
Greet Amplias my beloved in the L	Rom 16:8	2962
of Narcissus, which are in the L	Rom 16:11	2962
and Tryphosa, who labour in the L	Rom 16:12	2962
which laboured much in the L	Rom 16:12	2962
Salute Rufus chosen in the L	Rom 16:13	2962
such serve not our L Jesus Christ	Rom 16:18	2962
The grace of our L Jesus Christ	Rom 16:20	2962
this epistle, salute you in the L	Rom 16:22	2962
The grace of our L Jesus Christ	Rom 16:24	2962
the name of Jesus Christ our L	1Cor 1:2	2962
and from the L Jesus Christ	1Cor 1:3	2962
the coming of our L Jesus Christ	1Cor 1:7	2962
in the day of our L Jesus Christ	1Cor 1:8	2962
of his Son Jesus Christ our L	1Cor 1:9	2962
by the name of our L Jesus Christ	1Cor 1:10	2962
glorieth, let him glory in the L	1Cor 1:31	2962
not have crucified the L of glory	1Cor 2:8	2962
who hath known the mind of the L	1Cor 2:16	2962
even as the L gave to every man	1Cor 3:5	2962
The L knoweth the thoughts of the	1Cor 3:20	2962
but he that judgeth me is the L	1Cor 4:4	2962
before the time, until the L come	1Cor 4:5	2962
beloved son, and faithful in the L	1Cor 4:17	2962
to you shortly, if the L will	1Cor 4:19	2962
In the name of our L Jesus Christ	1Cor 5:4	2962
the power of our L Jesus Christ	1Cor 5:4	2962
saved in the day of the L Jesus	1Cor 5:5	2962
in the name of the L Jesus	1Cor 6:11	2962
for fornication, but for the L	1Cor 6:13	2962
and the L for the body	1Cor 6:13	2962
And God hath both raised up the L	1Cor 6:14	2962
joined unto the L is one spirit	1Cor 6:17	2962
I command, yet not I, but the L	1Cor 7:10	2962
to the rest speak I, not the L	1Cor 7:12	2962
as the L hath called every one,	1Cor 7:17	2962
For he that is called in the L	1Cor 7:22	2962
I have no commandment of the L	1Cor 7:25	2962
mercy of the L to be faithful	1Cor 7:25	2962
the things that belong to the L	1Cor 7:32	2962
how he may please the L	1Cor 7:32	2962
careth for the things of the L	1Cor 7:34	2962
upon the L without distraction	1Cor 7:35	2962
whom she will; only in the L	1Cor 7:39	2962
one L Jesus Christ, by whom are	1Cor 8:6	2962
I not seen Jesus Christ our L	1Cor 9:1	2962
are not ye my work in the L	1Cor 9:1	2962
mine apostleship are ye in the L	1Cor 9:2	2962
and as the brethren of the L	1Cor 9:5	2962
Even so hath the L ordained that	1Cor 9:14	2962
Ye cannot drink the cup of the L	1Cor 10:21	2962
Do we provoke the L to jealousy	1Cor 10:22	2962
woman without the man, in the L	1Cor 11:11	2962

L

For I have received of the *L* that............1Cor 11:23   2962
That the *L* Jesus the same night............1Cor 11:23   2962
bread, and drink this cup of the *L*..........1Cor 11:27   2962
of the body and blood of the *L*..........1Cor 11:27   2962
judged, we are chastened of the *L*..........1Cor 11:32   2962
man can say that Jesus is the *L*............1Cor 12:3   2962
administrations, but the same *L*..........1Cor 12:5   2962
they not hear me, saith the *L*............1Cor 14:21   2962
you are the commandments of the *L*......1Cor 14:37   2962
I have in Christ Jesus our *L*..................1Cor 15:31   2962
second man is the *L* from heaven..........1Cor 15:47   2962
through our *L* Jesus Christ..................1Cor 15:57   2962
abounding in the work of the *L*............1Cor 15:58   2962
labour is not in vain in the *L*............1Cor 15:58   2962
a while with you, if the *L* permit............1Cor 16:7   2962
for he worketh the work of the *L*............1Cor 16:10   2962
salute you much in the *L*, with............1Cor 16:19   2962
man love not the *L* Jesus Christ............1Cor 16:22   2962
The grace of our *L* Jesus Christ............1Cor 16:23   2962
and from the *L* Jesus Christ..................2Cor 1:2   2962
the Father of our *L* Jesus Christ............2Cor 1:3   2962
ours in the day of the *L* Jesus................2Cor 1:14   2962
door was opened unto me of the *L*..........2Cor 2:12   2962
when it shall turn to the *L*..................2Cor 3:16   2962
Now the *L* is that Spirit..........................2Cor 3:17   2962
and where the Spirit of the *L* is............2Cor 3:17   2962
as in a glass the glory of the *L*............2Cor 3:18   2962
even as by the Spirit of the *L*............2Cor 3:18   2962
ourselves, but Christ Jesus the *L*..........2Cor 4:5   2962
the body the dying of the *L* Jesus..........2Cor 4:10   2962
that he which raised up the *L*............2Cor 4:14   2962
body, we are absent from the *L*............2Cor 5:6   2962
body, and to be present with the *L*..........2Cor 5:8   2962
therefore the terror of the *L*..................2Cor 5:11   2962
and be ye separate, saith the *L*..........2Cor 6:17   2962
daughters, saith the *L* Almighty............2Cor 6:18   2962
gave their own selves to the *L*................2Cor 8:5   2962
the grace of our *L* Jesus Christ............2Cor 8:9   2962
by us to the glory of the same *L*..........2Cor 8:19   2962
not only in the sight of the *L*..............2Cor 8:21   2962
which the *L* hath given us for............2Cor 10:8   2962
glorieth, let him glory in the *L*................2Cor 10:17   2962
but whom the *L* commendeth..................2Cor 10:18   2962
speak, I speak it not after the *L*............2Cor 11:17   2962
and Father of our *L* Jesus Christ............2Cor 11:31   2962
visions and revelations of the *L*............2Cor 12:1   2962
thing I besought the *L* thrice................2Cor 12:8   2962
to the power which the *L* hath............2Cor 13:10   2962
The grace of the *L* Jesus Christ............2Cor 13:14   2962
and from our *L* Jesus Christ, ...Gal 1:3   2962
confidence in you through the *L*............Gal 5:10   2962
the cross of our *L* Jesus Christ............Gal 6:14   2962
my body the marks of the *L* Jesus........Gal 6:17   2962
the grace of our *L* Jesus Christ............Gal 6:18   2962
and from the *L* Jesus Christ..................Eph 1:2   2962
and Father of our *L* Jesus Christ............Eph 1:3   2962
of your faith in the *L* Jesus..................Eph 1:15   2962
the God of our *L* Jesus Christ................Eph 1:17   2962
unto an holy temple in the *L*..................Eph 2:21   2962
he purposed in Christ Jesus our *L*........Eph 3:11   2962
the Father of our *L* Jesus Christ............Eph 3:14   2962
therefore, the prisoner of the *L*................Eph 4:1   2962
One *L*, one faith, one baptism, ...Eph 4:5   2962
therefore, and testify in the *L*..................Eph 4:17   2962
but now are ye light in the *L*................Eph 5:8   2962
what is acceptable unto the *L*............Eph 5:10   2962
what the will of the *L* is..........................Eph 5:17   2962
melody in your heart to the *L*..............Eph 5:19   2962
in the name of our *L* Jesus Christ..........Eph 5:20   2962
your own husbands, as unto the *L*..........Eph 5:22   2962
it, even as the *L* the church..................Eph 5:29   2962
obey your parents in the *L*....................Eph 6:1   2962
nurture and admonition of the *L*............Eph 6:4   2962
will doing service, as to the *L*................Eph 6:7   2962
same shall he receive of the *L*..............Eph 6:8   2962
my brethren, be strong in the *L*............Eph 6:10   2962
and faithful minister in the *L*............Eph 6:21   2962
the Father and the *L* Jesus Christ........Eph 6:23   2962
our *L* Jesus Christ in sincerity..............Eph 6:24   2962
and from the *L* Jesus Christ..................Phil 1:2   2962
And many of the brethren in the *L*........Phil 1:14   2962
confess that Jesus Christ is *L*................Phil 2:11   2962
But I trust in the *L* Jesus to..................Phil 2:19   2962
But I trust in the *L* that I also ....Phil 2:24   2962
in the *L* with all gladness....................Phil 2:29   2962
my brethren, rejoice in the *L*................Phil 3:1   2962
knowledge of Christ Jesus my *L*............Phil 3:8   2962
the Saviour, the *L* Jesus Christ............Phil 3:20   2962
and crown, so stand fast in the *L*..........Phil 4:1   2962
they be of the same mind in the *L*, ...Phil 4:2   2962
Rejoice in the *L* alway ....Phil 4:4   2962

The *L* is at hand ....Phil 4:5   2962
But I rejoiced in the *L* greatly................Phil 4:10   2962
The grace of our *L* Jesus Christ..............Phil 4:23   2962
our Father and the *L* Jesus Christ........Col 1:2   2962
the Father of our *L* Jesus Christ............Col 1:3   2962
worthy of the *L* unto all pleasing............Col 1:10   2962
received Christ Jesus the *L*......................Col 2:6   2962
grace in your hearts to the *L*..................Col 3:16   2962
do all in the name of the *L* Jesus..........Col 3:17   2962
husbands, as it is fit in the *L*................Col 3:18   2962
this is well pleasing unto the *L*..............Col 3:20   2962
do, do it heartily, as to the *L*................Col 3:23   2962
Knowing that of the *L* ye shall................Col 3:24   2962
for ye serve the *L* Christ........................Col 3:24   2962
and fellowservant in the *L*......................Col 4:7   2962
which thou hast received in the *L*............Col 4:17   2962
Father and in the *L* Jesus Christ 1Th 1:1   2962
our Father, and the *L* Jesus Christ..........1Th 1:1   2962
of hope in our *L* Jesus Christ 1Th 1:3   2962
followers of us, and of the *L*..................1Th 1:6   2962
of the *L* not only in Macedonia..............1Th 1:8   2962
Who both killed the *L* Jesus 1Th 2:15   2962
our *L* Jesus Christ at his coming............1Th 2:19   2962
live, if ye stand fast in the *L*..................1Th 3:8   2962
our *L* Jesus Christ, direct our................1Th 3:11   2962
the *L* make you to increase and 1Th 3:12   2962
at the coming of our *L* Jesus 1Th 3:13   2962
and exhort you by the *L* Jesus 1Th 4:1   2962
we gave you by the *L* Jesus....................1Th 4:2   2962
because that the *L* is the avenger..........1Th 4:6   2962
say unto you by the word of the *L* 1Th 4:15   2962
L shall not prevent them which 1Th 4:15   2962
For the *L* himself shall descend 1Th 4:16   2962
clouds, to meet the *L* in the air 1Th 4:17   2962
and so shall we ever be with the *L* 1Th 4:17   2962
the *L* so cometh as a thief in the 1Th 5:2   2962
salvation by our *L* Jesus Christ 1Th 5:9   2962
you, and are over you in the *L* 1Th 5:12   2962
the coming of our *L* Jesus Christ............1Th 5:23   2962
I charge you by the *L* that this 1Th 5:27   2962
The grace of our *L* Jesus Christ..............1Th 5:28   2962
our Father and the *L* Jesus Christ 2Th 1:1   2962
our Father and the *L* Jesus Christ 2Th 1:2   2962
when the *L* Jesus shall be 2Th 1:7   2962
the gospel of our *L* Jesus Christ 2Th 1:8   2962
from the presence of the *L* 2Th 1:9   2962
That the name of our *L* Jesus 2Th 1:12   2962
of our God and the *L* Jesus Christ..........2Th 1:12   2962
the coming of our *L* Jesus Christ 2Th 2:1   2962
whom the *L* shall consume with the 2Th 2:8   2962
you, brethren beloved of the *L* 2Th 2:13   2962
the glory of our *L* Jesus Christ 2Th 2:14   2962
Now our *L* Jesus Christ himself,............2Th 2:16   2962
of the *L* may have free course 2Th 3:1   2962
But the *L* is faithful, who shall................2Th 3:3   2962
confidence in the *L* touching you 2Th 3:4   2962
the *L* direct your hearts into the 2Th 3:5   2962
in the name of our *L* Jesus Christ 2Th 3:6   2962
and exhort by our *L* Jesus Christ 2Th 3:12   2962
Now the *L* of peace himself give............2Th 3:16   2962
The *L* be with you all................................2Th 3:16   2962
The grace of our *L* Jesus Christ..............2Th 3:18   2962
L Jesus Christ, which is our hope 1Ti 1:1   2962
our Father and Jesus Christ our *L*..........1Ti 1:2   2962
And I thank Christ Jesus our *L* 1Ti 1:12   2962
the grace of our *L* was exceeding 1Ti 1:14   2962
the *L* Jesus Christ, and the elect 1Ti 5:21   2962
the words of our *L* Jesus Christ 1Ti 6:3   2962
appearing of our *L* Jesus Christ 1Ti 6:14   2962
the King of kings, and *L* of lords............1Ti 6:15   2962
the Father and Christ Jesus our *L* 2Ti 1:2   2962
ashamed of the testimony of our *L* 2Ti 1:8   2962
The *L* give mercy unto the house............2Ti 1:16   2962
The *L* grant unto him that he may 2Ti 1:18   2962
find mercy of the *L* in that day 2Ti 1:18   2962
the *L* give thee understanding in 2Ti 2:7   2962
charging them before the *L* that 2Ti 2:14   2962
The *L* knoweth them that are his 2Ti 2:19   2962
call on the *L* out of a pure heart............2Ti 2:22   2962
servant of the *L* must not strive 2Ti 2:24   2962
of them all the *L* delivered me 2Ti 3:11   2962
the *L* Jesus Christ, who shall 2Ti 4:1   2962
of righteousness, which the *L*..................2Ti 4:8   2962
the *L* reward him according to his 2Ti 4:14   2962
the *L* stood with me, and 2Ti 4:17   2962
the *L* shall deliver me from every 2Ti 4:18   2962
The *L* Jesus Christ be with thy 2Ti 4:22   2962
the *L* Jesus Christ our Saviour ....Titus 1:4   2962
our Father and the *L* Jesus Christ ....Philem 3   2962
thou hast toward the *L* Jesus ....Philem 5   2962
both in the flesh, and in the *L*................Philem 16   2962

let me have joy of thee in the *L*	Philem 20	2962
refresh my bowels in the *L*	Philem 20	2962
The grace of our *L* Jesus Christ	Philem 25	2962
And, Thou, *L*, in the beginning	Heb 1:10	2962
first began to be spoken by the *L*	Heb 2:3	2962
that our *L* sprang out of Juda	Heb 7:14	2962
The *L* sware and will not repent,	Heb 7:21	2962
tabernacle, which the *L* pitched	Heb 8:2	2962
the days come, saith the *L*	Heb 8:8	2962
I regarded them not, saith the *L*	Heb 8:9	2962
after those days, saith the *L*	Heb 8:10	2962
his brother, saying, Know the *L*	Heb 8:11	2962
after those days, saith the *L*	Heb 10:16	2962
I will recompense, saith the *L*	Heb 10:30	2962
The *L* shall judge his people	Heb 10:30	2962
not thou the chastening of the *L*	Heb 12:5	2962
For whom the *L* loveth he	Heb 12:6	2962
which no man shall see the *L*	Heb 12:14	2962
The *L* is my helper, and I will not	Heb 13:6	2962
again from the dead our *L* Jesus	Heb 13:20	2962
of the *L* Jesus Christ, to the	Jas 1:1	2962
shall receive any thing of the *L*	Jas 1:7	2962
which the *L* hath promised to them	Jas 1:12	2962
the faith of our *L* Jesus Christ	Jas 2:1	2962
the *L* of glory, with respect of	Jas 2:1	
yourselves in the sight of the *L*	Jas 4:10	2962
ye ought to say, If the *L* will	Jas 4:15	2962
into the ears of the *L* of Sabaoth	Jas 5:4	2962
unto the coming of the *L*	Jas 5:7	2962
the coming of the *L* draweth nigh	Jas 5:8	2962
have spoken in the name of the *L*	Jas 5:10	2962
and have seen the end of the *L*	Jas 5:11	2962
that the *L* is very pitiful, and of	Jas 5:11	2962
him with oil in the name of the *L*	Jas 5:14	2962
sick, and the *L* shall raise him up	Jas 5:15	2962
and Father of our *L* Jesus Christ	1Pet 1:3	2962
word of the *L* endureth for ever	1Pet 1:25	2962
tasted that the *L* is gracious	1Pet 2:3	2962
For the eyes of the *L* are over	1Pet 3:12	2962
but the face of the *L* is against	1Pet 3:12	2962
But sanctify the *L* God in your	1Pet 3:15	2962
of God, and of Jesus our *L*	2Pet 1:2	2962
knowledge of our *L* Jesus Christ	2Pet 1:8	2962
the everlasting kingdom of our *L*	2Pet 1:11	2962
even as our *L* Jesus Christ hath	2Pet 1:16	2962
and coming of our *L* Jesus Christ	2Pet 1:16	2962
denying the *L* that bought them	2Pet 2:1	1203
The *L* knoweth how to deliver the	2Pet 2:9	2962
against them before the *L*	2Pet 2:11	2962
through the knowledge of the *L*	2Pet 2:20	2962
of us the apostles of the *L*	2Pet 3:2	2962
is with the *L* as a thousand years	2Pet 3:8	2962
The *L* is not slack concerning his	2Pet 3:9	2962
But the day of the *L* will come as	2Pet 3:10	2962
of our *L* is salvation	2Pet 3:15	2962
and in the knowledge of our *L*	2Pet 3:18	2962
from the *L* Jesus Christ, the Son	2Jn 3	2962
and denying the only *L* God	Jude 4	2962
and our *L* Jesus Christ	Jude 4	2962
ye once knew this, how that the *L*	Jude 5	2962
but said, The *L* rebuke thee	Jude 9	2962
the *L* cometh with ten thousands	Jude 14	2962
apostles of our *L* Jesus Christ	Jude 17	2962
looking for the mercy of our *L*	Jude 21	2962
and the ending, saith the *L*	Rev 1:8	2962
L God Almighty, which was, and is,	Rev 4:8	2962
Thou art worthy, O *L*, to receive	Rev 4:11	2962
loud voice, saying, How long, O *L*	Rev 6:10	1203
where also our *L* was crucified	Rev 11:8	2962
are become the kingdoms of our *L*	Rev 11:15	2962
O *L* God Almighty, which art, and	Rev 11:17	2962
die in the *L* from henceforth	Rev 14:13	2962
are thy works, *L* God Almighty	Rev 15:3	2962
Who shall not fear thee, O *L*	Rev 15:4	2962
say, Thou art righteous, O *L*	Rev 16:5	2962
L God Almighty, true and righteous	Rev 16:7	2962
for he is *L* of lords, and King of	Rev 17:14	2962
for strong is the *L* God who	Rev 18:8	2962
and power, unto the *L* our God	Rev 19:1	2962
for the *L* God omnipotent reigneth	Rev 19:6	2962
KING OF KINGS, AND *L* OF LORDS	Rev 19:16	2962
for the *L* God Almighty and the	Rev 21:22	2962
for the *L* God giveth them light	Rev 22:5	2962
the *L* God of the holy prophets	Rev 22:6	2962
Even so, come, *L* Jesus	Rev 22:20	2962
The grace of our *L* Jesus Christ	Rev 22:21	2962

2. A human title of honor.

pleasure, my *l* being old also	Gen 18:12	113
said unto them, Oh, not so, my *l*	Gen 19:18	113
Hear us, my *l*	Gen 23:6	113
Nay, my *l*, hear me	Gen 23:11	113

My *l*, hearken unto me	Gen 23:15	113
And she said, Drink, my *l*	Gen 24:18	113
be *l* over thy brethren, and let	Gen 27:29	1376
Behold, I have made him thy *l*	Gen 27:37	1376
Let it not displease my *l* that I	Gen 31:35	113
shall ye speak unto my *l* Esau	Gen 32:4	113
and I have sent to tell my *l*	Gen 32:5	113
is a present sent unto my *l* Esau	Gen 32:18	113
find grace in the sight of my *l*	Gen 33:8	113
My *l* knoweth that the children	Gen 33:13	113
Let my *l*, I pray thee, pass over	Gen 33:14	113
until I come unto my *l* unto Seir	Gen 33:14	113
find grace in the sight of my *l*	Gen 33:15	113
by her, until his *l* came home	Gen 39:16	113
their *l* the king of Egypt	Gen 40:1	113
And they said unto him, Nay, my *l*	Gen 42:10	113
who is the *l* of the land, spake	Gen 42:30	113
the *l* of the country, said unto	Gen 42:33	113
this it in which my *l* drinketh	Gen 44:5	113
Wherefore saith my *l* these words	Gen 44:7	113
said, What shall we say unto my *l*	Gen 44:16	113
near unto him, and said, Oh my *l*	Gen 44:18	113
My *l* asked his servants, saying,	Gen 44:19	113
And we said unto my *l*, We have a	Gen 44:20	113
And we said unto my *l*, The lad	Gen 44:22	113
we told him the words of my *l*	Gen 44:24	113
of the lad a bondman to my *l*	Gen 44:33	113
l of all his house, and a ruler	Gen 45:8	113
God hath made me *l* of all Egypt	Gen 45:9	113
We will not hide it from my *l*	Gen 47:18	113
my *l* also hath our herds of	Gen 47:18	113
ought left in the sight of my *l*	Gen 47:18	113
find grace in the sight of my *l*	Gen 47:25	113
Let not the anger of my *l* wax hot	Ex 32:22	113
and said, My *l* Moses, forbid them	Num 11:28	113
Aaron said unto Moses, Alas, my *l*	Num 12:11	113
will do as my *l* commandeth	Num 32:25	113
to battle, as my *l* saith	Num 32:27	113
their *l* was fallen down dead on	Judg 3:25	113
and said unto him, Turn in, my *l*	Judg 4:18	3068
And Gideon said unto him, Oh my *l*	Judg 6:13	113
me find favour in thy sight, my *l*	Ruth 2:13	3068
my lord, as thy soul liveth, my *l*	1Sa 1:26	113
Let our *l* now command thy	1Sa 16:16	113
And he answered, Here I am, my *l*	1Sa 22:12	113
after Saul, saying, My *l* the king	1Sa 24:8	113
put forth mine hand against my *l*	1Sa 24:10	113
his feet, and said, Upon me, my *l*	1Sa 25:24	113
Let not my *l*, I pray thee, regard	1Sa 25:25	113
saw not the young men of my *l*	1Sa 25:25	113
and they that seek evil to my *l*	1Sa 25:26	113
handmaid hath brought unto my *l*	1Sa 25:27	113
the young men that follow my *l*	1Sa 25:27	113
certainly make my *l* a sure house	1Sa 25:28	113
because my *l* fighteth the battles	1Sa 25:28	113
but the soul of my *l* shall be	1Sa 25:29	113
l according to all the good that	1Sa 25:30	113
nor offence of heart unto my *l*	1Sa 25:31	136
or that my *l* hath avenged himself	1Sa 25:31	136
shall have dealt well with my *l*	1Sa 25:31	113
the feet of the servants of my *l*	1Sa 25:41	113
hast thou not kept thy *l* the king	1Sa 26:15	113
in to destroy the king my *l*	1Sa 26:15	3068
David said, It is my voice, my *l*	1Sa 26:17	113
Wherefore doth my *l* thus pursue	1Sa 26:18	113
let my *l* the king hear the words	1Sa 26:19	113
the enemies of my *l* the king	1Sa 29:8	113
brought them hither unto my *l*	2Sa 1:10	113
shewed this kindness unto your *l*	2Sa 2:5	113
all Israel unto my *l* the king	2Sa 3:21	113
According to all that my *l* the	2Sa 9:11	113
of Ammon said unto Hanun their *l*	2Sa 10:3	113
with all the servants of his *l*	2Sa 11:9	113
my *l* Joab, and the servants of my	2Sa 11:11	113
Joab, and the servants of my *l*	2Sa 11:11	113
bed with the servants of his *l*	2Sa 11:13	113
Let not my *l* suppose that they	2Sa 13:32	113
Now therefore let not my *l* the	2Sa 13:33	113
Tekoah said unto the king, My *l*	2Sa 14:9	113
speak one word unto my *l* the king	2Sa 14:12	113
of this thing unto my *l* the king	2Sa 14:15	113
The word of my *l* the king shall	2Sa 14:17	113
so is my *l* the king to discern	2Sa 14:17	113
Let my *l* the king now speak	2Sa 14:18	113
my *l* the king, none can turn to	2Sa 14:19	113
that my *l* the king hath spoken	2Sa 14:19	113
my *l* is wise, according to the	2Sa 14:20	113
found grace in thy sight, my *l*	2Sa 14:22	113
my *l* the king shall appoint	2Sa 15:15	113
as my *l* the king liveth, surely	2Sa 15:21	113
what place my *l* the king shall be	2Sa 15:21	113

L

may find grace in thy sight, my *l*	2Sa 16:4	113
this dead dog curse my *l* the king	2Sa 16:9	113
their hand against my *l* the king	2Sa 18:28	113
said, Tidings, my *l* the king	2Sa 18:31	113
The enemies of my *l* the king	2Sa 18:32	113
Let not my *l* impute iniquity unto	2Sa 19:19	113
l the king went out of Jerusalem	2Sa 19:19	113
to go down to meet my *l* the king	2Sa 19:20	113
And he answered, My *l*, O king, my	2Sa 19:26	113
thy servant unto my *l* the king	2Sa 19:27	113
but my *l* the king is as an angel	2Sa 19:27	113
but dead men before my *l* the king	2Sa 19:28	113
forasmuch as my *l* the king is	2Sa 19:30	113
yet a burden unto my *l* the king	2Sa 19:35	113
him go over with my *l* the king	2Sa 19:37	3068
eyes of my *l* the king may see it	2Sa 24:3	113
but why doth my *l* the king	2Sa 24:3	113
Wherefore is my *l* the king come	2Sa 24:21	113
Let my *l* the king take and offer	2Sa 24:22	113
for my *l* the king a young virgin	1Kin 1:2	113
that my *l* the king may get heat	1Kin 1:2	113
David our *l* knoweth it not	1Kin 1:11	113
unto him, Didst not thou, my *l*	1Kin 1:13	113
And she said unto him, My *l*	1Kin 1:17	113
my *l* the king, thou knowest it	1Kin 1:18	113
And thou, my *l*, O king, the eyes	1Kin 1:20	113
throne of my *l* the king after him	1Kin 1:20	113
when my *l* the king shall sleep	1Kin 1:21	113
And Nathan said, My *l*, O king,	1Kin 1:24	113
this thing done by my *l* the king	1Kin 1:27	113
throne of my *l* the king after him	1Kin 1:27	113
Let my *l* king David live for ever	1Kin 1:31	113
with you the servants of your *l*	1Kin 1:33	113
the throne of my *l* king David	1Kin 1:37	113
Verily our *l* king David hath made	1Kin 1:43	113
came to bless our *l* king David	1Kin 1:47	113
as my *l* the king hath said, so	1Kin 2:38	113
And the one woman said, O my *l*	1Kin 3:17	113
upon her son, and she said, O my *l*	1Kin 3:26	113
which fled from his *l* Hadadezer	1Kin 11:23	113
people turn again unto their *l*	1Kin 12:27	3068
said, Art thou that my *l* Elijah	1Kin 18:7	113
go, tell thy *l*, Behold, Elijah is	1Kin 18:8	113
whither my *l* hath not sent to	1Kin 18:10	113
now thou sayest, Go, tell thy *l*	1Kin 18:11	3068
Was it not told my *l* what I did	1Kin 18:13	113
now thou sayest, Go, tell thy *l*	1Kin 18:14	113
of Israel answered and said, My *l*	1Kin 20:4	113
Tell my *l* the king, All that thou	1Kin 20:9	113
city is pleasant, as my *l* seeth	2Kin 2:19	113
And she said, Nay, my *l*, thou man	2Kin 4:16	113
said, Did I desire a son of my *l*	2Kin 4:28	113
Would God my *l* were with the	2Kin 5:3	113
And one went in, and told his *l*	2Kin 5:4	113
of his servants said, None, my *l*	2Kin 6:12	113
unto him, saying, Help, my *l*	2Kin 6:26	113
Then a *l* on whose hand the king	2Kin 7:2	7991
the king appointed the *l* on whose	2Kin 7:17	7991
that *l* answered the man of God,	2Kin 7:19	7991
And Gehazi said, My *l*, O king,	2Kin 8:5	113
And Hazael said, Why weepeth my *l*	2Kin 8:12	113
forth to the servants of his *l*	2Kin 9:11	113
give pledges to my *l* the king of	2Kin 18:23	113
my *l* the king, are they not all	1Chr 21:3	113
why then doth my *l* require this	1Chr 21:3	113
let my *l* the king do that which	1Chr 21:23	113
men of my *l* David thy father	2Chr 2:14	113
which my *l* hath spoken of, let	2Chr 2:15	113
and hath rebelled against his *l*	2Chr 13:6	113
according to the counsel of my *l*	Ezr 10:3	136
who is *l* over us	Ps 12:4	113
He made him *l* of his house, and	Ps 105:21	3050
over into the hand of a cruel *l*	Is 19:4	113
My *l*, I stand continually upon	Is 21:8	136
not lament for him, saying, Ah *l*	Jer 22:18	113
will lament thee, saying, Ah *l*	Jer 34:5	113
now, I pray thee, O my *l* the king	Jer 37:20	113
My *l* the king, these men have	Jer 38:9	113
unto Daniel, I fear my *l* the king	Dan 1:10	113
therefore there is no king, *l*	Dan 2:10	7229
answered and said, My *l*, the dream	Dan 4:19	4756
which is come upon my *l* the king	Dan 4:24	4756
him that stood before me, O my *l*	Dan 10:16	113
this my *l* talk with this my lord	Dan 10:17	113
and said, Let my *l* speak	Dan 10:19	113
Then said I, O my *l*, what are	Zec 1:9	113
me, saying, What are these, my *l*	Zec 4:4	113
And I said, No, my *l*	Zec 4:5	113
And I said, No, my *l*	Zec 4:13	113
with me, What are these, my *l*	Zec 6:4	113
nor the servant above his *l*	Mt 10:24	2962

master, and the servant as his *l*	Mt 10:25	2962
his *l* commanded him to be sold,	Mt 18:25	2962
Then the *l* of that servant was	Mt 18:27	2962
told unto their *l* all that was	Mt 18:31	2962
Then his *l*, after that he had	Mt 18:32	2962
his *l* was wroth, and delivered him	Mt 18:34	2962
the *l* of the vineyard saith unto	Mt 20:8	2962
whom his *l* hath made ruler over	Mt 24:45	2962
whom his *l* when he cometh shall	Mt 24:46	2962
heart, My *l* delayeth his coming	Mt 24:48	2962
The *l* of that servant shall come	Mt 24:50	2962
After a long time the *l* of those	Mt 25:19	2962
other five talents, saying, L	Mt 25:20	2962
His *l* said unto him, Well done,	Mt 25:21	2962
enter thou into the joy of thy *l*	Mt 25:21	2962
two talents came and said, L	Mt 25:22	2962
His *l* said unto him, Well done,	Mt 25:23	2962
enter thou into the joy of thy *l*	Mt 25:23	2962
the one talent came and said, L	Mt 25:24	2962
His *l* answered and said unto him,	Mt 25:26	2962
the *l* of the vineyard do	Mk 12:9	2962
unto men that wait for their *l*	Lk 12:36	2962
whom the *l* when he cometh shall	Lk 12:37	2962
whom his *l* shall make ruler over	Lk 12:42	2962
whom his *l* when he cometh shall	Lk 12:43	2962
heart, My *l* delayeth his coming	Lk 12:45	2962
The *l* of that servant will come	Lk 12:46	2962
shewed his *l* these things	Lk 14:21	2962
And the servant said, L, it is	Lk 14:22	2962
the *l* said unto the servant, Go	Lk 14:23	2962
for my *l* taketh away from me the	Lk 16:3	2962
How much owest thou unto my *l*	Lk 16:5	2962
the *l* commended the unjust	Lk 16:8	2962
Then said the *l* of the vineyard,	Lk 20:13	2962
What therefore shall the *l* of the	Lk 20:15	2962
servant is not greater than his *l*	Jn 13:16	2962
knoweth not what his *l* doeth	Jn 15:15	2962
servant is not greater than his *l*	Jn 15:20	2962
certain thing to write unto my *l*	Acts 25:26	2962
a servant, though he be *l* of all	Gal 4:1	2962
obeyed Abraham, calling him *l*	1Pet 3:6	2962

LORDLY

brought forth butter in a *l* dish	Judg 5:25	117

LORD'S

1. Refers to Lord 1.

know how that the earth is the L	Ex 9:29	3068
it is the L passover	Ex 12:11	3068
the sacrifice of the L passover	Ex 12:27	3068
that the L law may be in thy	Ex 13:9	3068
the males shall be the L	Ex 13:12	3068
and said, Who is on the L side	Ex 32:26	3068
they brought the L offering to	Ex 35:21	3068
and brass brought the L offering	Ex 35:24	3068
all the fat is the L	Lev 3:16	3068
goat upon which the L lot fell	Lev 16:9	3068
month at even is the L passover	Lev 23:5	3068
which should be the L firstling	Lev 27:26	3068
it is the L	Lev 27:26	3068
the fruit of the tree, is the L	Lev 27:30	3068
Is the L hand waxed short	Num 11:23	3068
all the L people were prophets	Num 11:29	3068
ye shall give thereof the L heave	Num 18:28	3068
the L tribute of the sheep was	Num 31:37	3068
of which the L tribute was	Num 31:38	3068
of which the L tribute was	Num 31:39	3068
of which the L tribute was thirty	Num 31:40	3068
which was the L heave offering,	Num 31:41	3068
the L anger was kindled the same	Num 32:10	3068
the L anger was kindled against	Num 32:13	3068
of heavens is the L thy God	Deut 10:14	3068
then the L wrath be kindled	Deut 11:17	3068
it is called the L release	Deut 15:2	3068
For the L portion is his people	Deut 32:9	3068
which Moses the L servant gave	Josh 1:15	3068
the captain of the L host said	Josh 5:15	3068
wherein the L tabernacle dwelleth	Josh 22:19	3068
of Ammon, shall surely be the L	Judg 11:31	3068
pillars of the earth are the L	1Sa 2:8	3068
ye make the L people to	1Sa 2:24	3068
the L priest in Shiloh, wearing	1Sa 14:3	3068
Surely the L anointed is before	1Sa 16:6	3068
for the battle is the L, and he	1Sa 17:47	3068
for me, and fight the L battles	1Sa 18:17	3068
that Saul had slain the L priests	1Sa 22:21	3068
the L anointed, to stretch forth	1Sa 24:6	3068
for he is the L anointed	1Sa 24:10	3068
his hand against the L anointed	1Sa 26:9	3068
mine hand against the L anointed	1Sa 26:11	3068
kept your master, the L anointed	1Sa 26:16	3068
mine hand against the L anointed	1Sa 26:23	3068

hand to destroy the *L* anointed 2Sa 1:14   3068
I have slain the *L* anointed 2Sa 1:16   3068
because he cursed the *L* anointed 2Sa 19:21   3068
because of the *L* oath that was 2Sa 21:7   3068
the *L* prophets by fifty in a cave 1Kin 18:13   3068
that they should be the *L* people 2Kin 11:17   3068
The arrow of the *L* deliverance 2Kin 13:17   3068
the Lᴏʀᴅ had filled the *L* house 2Chr 7:2   3068
that they should be the *L* people 2Chr 23:16   3068
the *L* throne is in heaven .... Ps 11:4   3068
For the kingdom is the *L* .... Ps 22:28   3068
The earth is the *L*, and the .... Ps 24:1   3068
same the *L* name is to be praised .... Ps 113:3   3068
even the heavens, are the *L* .... Ps 115:16   3068
In the courts of the *L* house .... Ps 116:19   3068
This is the *L* doing .... Ps 118:23   3068
How shall we sing the *L* song in a .... Ps 137:4   3068
just weight and balance are the *L* .... Prov 16:11   3068
that the mountain of the *L* house .... Is 2:2   3068
it is the day of the *L* vengeance .... Is 34:8   3068
L hand double for all her sins .... Is 40:2   3068
and blind as the *L* servant .... Is 42:19   3068
One shall say, I am the *L* .... Is 44:5   3068
the *L* hand is not shortened, that .... Is 59:1   3068
for they are not the *L* .... Jer 5:10   3068
Stand in the gate of the *L* house .... Jer 7:2   3068
because the *L* flock is carried .... Jer 13:17   3068
stood in the court of the *L* house .... Jer 19:14   3068
Then took I the cup at the *L* hand .... Jer 25:17   3068
Stand in the court of the *L* house .... Jer 26:2   3068
come to worship in the *L* house .... Jer 26:2   3068
of the new gate of the *L* house .... Jer 26:10   3068
the vessels of the *L* house shall .... Jer 27:16   3068
all the vessels of the *L* house .... Jer 28:3   3068
again the vessels of the *L* house .... Jer 28:6   3068
the *L* house upon the fasting day .... Jer 36:6   3068
words of the Lᴏʀᴅ in the *L* house .... Jer 36:8   3068
of the new gate of the *L* house .... Jer 36:10   3068
is the time of the *L* vengeance .... Jer 51:6   3068
been a golden cup in the *L* hand .... Jer 51:7   3068
the sanctuaries of the *L* house .... Jer 51:51   3068
so that in the day of the *L* anger .... Lam 2:22   3068
It is of the *L* mercies that we .... Lam 3:22   3068
the *L* house which was toward the .... Eze 8:14   3068
the inner court of the *L* house .... Eze 8:16   3068
of the brightness of the *L* glory .... Eze 10:4   3068
of the east gate of the *L* house .... Eze 10:19   3068
unto the east gate of the *L* house .... Eze 11:1   3068
that is desolate, for the *L* sake .... Dan 9:17   136
shall not dwell in the *L* land .... Hos 9:3   3068
priests, the *L* ministers, mourn .... Joel 1:9   3068
and the kingdom shall be the *L* .... Obad 21   3068
the *L* controversy, and ye strong .... Mic 6:2   3068
The *L* voice crieth unto the city, ... Mic 6:9   3068
the cup of the *L* right hand shall .... Hab 2:16   3068
in the day of the *L* sacrifice .... Zeph 1:8   3068
them in the day of the *L* wrath .... Zeph 1:18   3068
day of the *L* anger come upon you .... Zeph 2:2   3068
be hid in the day of the *L* anger............. Zeph 2:3   3068
the time that the *L* house should .... Hag 1:2   3068
Then spake Haggai the *L* messenger ..... Hag 1:13   3068
in the *L* message unto the people .... Hag 1:13   3068
of the *L* temple was laid,...................... Hag 2:18   3068
the pots in the *L* house shall be .... Zec 14:20   3068
this is the *L* doing, and it is .... Mt 21:42   2962
This was the *L* doing, and it is .... Mk 12:11   2962
before he had seen the *L* Christ .... Lk 2:26   2962
therefore, or die, we are the *L* .... Rom 14:8   2962
being a servant, is the *L* freeman 1Cor 7:22   2962
be partakers of the *L* table 1Cor 10:21   2962
For the earth is the *L*, and the 1Cor 10:26   2962
for the earth is the *L*, and the 1Cor 10:28   2962
this is not to eat the *L* supper 1Cor 11:20   2960
ye do shew the *L* death till he 1Cor 11:26   2962
not discerning the *L* body 1Cor 11:29   2962
I none, save James the *L* brother .... Gal 1:19   2962
ordinance of man for the *L* sake 1Pet 2:13   2962
I was in the Spirit on the *L* day .... Rev 1:10   2960
  2. *Refers to Lord 2.*
him in the ward of his *l* house .... Gen 40:7   113
out of thy *l* house silver or gold .... Gen 44:8   113
and we also will be my *l* bondmen .... Gen 44:9   113
behold, we are my *l* servants .... Gen 44:16   113
thee, speak a word in my *l* ears .... Gen 44:18   113
take thou thy *l* servants, and 2Sa 20:6   113
are they not all my *l* servants 1Chr 21:3   113
shall be the shame of thy *l* house .... Is 22:18   113
in the earth, and hid his *l* money .... Mt 25:18   2962
servant, which knew his *l* will .... Lk 12:47   2962

one of his *l* debtors unto him .... Lk 16:5   2962

LORDS

And he said, Behold now, my *l* .... Gen 19:2   113
the *l* of the high places of Arnon .... Num 21:28   1167
God is God of gods, and Lord of *l* .... Deut 10:17   113
five *l* of the Philistines .... Josh 13:3   5633
five *l* of the Philistines, and all .... Judg 3:3   5633
the *l* of the Philistines came up .... Judg 16:5   5633
Then the *l* of the Philistines .... Judg 16:8   5633
sent and called for the *l* of the .... Judg 16:18   5633
Then the *l* of the Philistines .... Judg 16:18   5633
Then the *l* of the Philistines .... Judg 16:23   5633
all the *l* of the Philistines were .... Judg 16:27   5633
and the house fell upon the *l* .... Judg 16:30   5633
gathered all the *l* of the 1Sa 5:8   5633
all the *l* of the Philistines 1Sa 5:11   5633
of the *l* of the Philistines 1Sa 6:4   5633
was on you all, and on your *l* 1Sa 6:4   5633
the *l* of the Philistines went 1Sa 6:12   5633
And when the five *l* of the 1Sa 6:16   5633
belonging to the five *l*, both of 1Sa 6:18   5633
the *l* of the Philistines went up 1Sa 7:7   5633
the *l* of the Philistines passed 1Sa 29:2   5633
the *l* favour thee not............................ 1Sa 29:6   5633
not the *l* of the Philistines 1Sa 29:7   5633
for the *l* of the Philistines upon 1Chr 12:19   5633
and his counsellors, and his *l* .... Ezr 8:25   8269
O give thanks to the Lord of *l* .... Ps 136:3   113
the *l* of the heathen have broken .... Is 16:8   1167
other *l* besides thee have had .... Is 26:13   113
wherefore say my people, We are *l* .... Jer 2:31   7300
men, captains and rulers, great *l* .... Eze 23:23   7991
and my *l* sought unto me .... Dan 4:36   7261
feast to a thousand of his *l* .... Dan 5:1   7261
in him, and his *l* were astonied .... Dan 5:9   7261
of the words of the king and his *l* .... Dan 5:10   7261
before thee, and thou, and thy *l* .... Dan 5:23   7261
and with the signet of his *l* .... Dan 6:17   7261
birthday made a supper to his *l* .... Mk 6:21   3175
there be gods many, and *l* many,) 1Cor 8:5   2962
the King of kings, and Lord of *l* 1Ti 6:15   2961
Neither as being *l* over God's 1Pet 5:3   2634
for he is Lord of *l*, and King of .... Rev 17:14   2962
KING OF KINGS, AND LORD OF *L* ...... Rev 19:16   2962

LORDSHIP

the Gentiles exercise *l* over them .... Mk 10:42   2634
the Gentiles exercise *l* over them .... Lk 22:25   2961

LO-RUHAMAH *(lo-ru-ha'-mah) Symbolic name meaning "Not pitied."*

said unto him, Call her name *L* .... Hos 1:6   3819
Now when she had weaned *L* .... Hos 1:8   3819

LOSE

thou *l* thy life, with the lives .... Judg 18:25   622
that we *l* not all the beasts................... 1Kin 18:5   3772
owners thereof to *l* their life .... Job 31:39   5307
vomit up, and *l* thy sweet words .... Prov 23:8   7843
A time to get, and a time to *l* .... Eccl 3:6   6
that findeth his life shall *l* it .... Mt 10:39   622
he shall in no wise *l* his reward .... Mt 10:42   622
will save his life shall *l* it .... Mt 16:25   622
whosoever will *l* his life for my .... Mt 16:25   622
whole world, and *l* his own soul .... Mt 16:26   2210
will save his life shall *l* it .... Mk 8:35   622
but whosoever shall *l* his life .... Mk 8:35   622
whole world, and *l* his own soul .... Mk 8:36   2210
you, he shall not *l* his reward .... Mk 9:41   622
will save his life shall *l* it .... Lk 9:24   622
but whosoever will *l* his life for .... Lk 9:24   622
***l* himself, or be cast away** .... Lk 9:25   622
if he *l* one of them, doth not .... Lk 15:4   622
if she *l* one piece, doth not .... Lk 15:8   622
seek to save his life shall *l* it .... Lk 17:33   622
whosoever shall *l* his life shall .... Lk 17:33   622
hath given me I should *l* nothing .... Jn 6:39   622
that loveth his life shall *l* it .... Jn 12:25   622
that we *l* not those things which 2Jn 8   622

LOSETH

he that *l* his life for my sake .... Mt 10:39   622

LOSS

I bare the *l* of it .... Gen 31:39   2398
shall pay for the *l* of his time .... Ex 21:19   7674
shall I know the *l* of children .... Is 47:8   7921
the *l* of children, and widowhood .... Is 47:9   7921
and to have gained this harm and *l* .... Acts 27:21   2209
for there shall be no *l* of any .... Acts 27:22   580
be burned, he shall suffer *l* 1Cor 3:15   2210
me, those I counted *l* for Christ .... Phil 3:7   2209

L

I count all things but *l* for the	Phil 3:8	2209
have suffered the *l* of all things	Phil 3:8	2210

LOST

or for any manner of *l* thing	Ex 22:9	9
Or have found that which was *l*	Lev 6:3	9
or the *l* thing which he found,	Lev 6:4	9
days that were before shall be *l*	Num 6:12	5307
and with all *l* things of thy	Deut 22:3	9
of thy brother's, which he hath *l*	Deut 22:3	6
of Kish Saul's father were *l*	1Sa 9:3	6
asses that were *l* three days ago	1Sa 9:20	6
like the army that thou hast *l*	1Kin 20:25	5307
I have gone astray like a *l* sheep	Ps 119:176	6
have, after thou hast *l* the other	Is 49:20	7923
seeing I have *l* my children	Is 49:21	7908
My people hath been *l* sheep	Jer 50:6	6
she had waited, and her hope was *l*	Eze 19:5	6
have ye sought that which was *l*	Eze 34:4	6
I will seek that which was *l*	Eze 34:16	6
bones are dried, and our hope is *l*	Eze 37:11	6
but if the salt have *l* his savour	Mt 5:13	3471
But go rather to the *l* sheep of	Mt 10:6	622
I am not sent but unto the *l*	Mt 15:24	622
is come to save that which was *l*	Mt 18:11	622
if the salt have *l* his saltness	Mk 9:50	358,1096
but if the salt have *l* his savour	Lk 14:34	3471
and go after that which is *l*	Lk 15:4	622
I have found my sheep which was *l*	Lk 15:6	622
found the piece which I had *l*	Lk 15:9	622
he was *l*, and is found	Lk 15:24	622
and was *l*, and is found	Lk 15:32	622
seek and to save that which was *l*	Lk 19:10	622
that remain, that nothing be *l*	Jn 6:12	622
I have kept, and none of them is *l*	Jn 17:12	622
thou gavest me have I *l* none	Jn 18:9	622
hid, it is hid to them that are *l*	2Cor 4:3	622

LOT (lot) See LOT'S.

1. Abraham's nephew.

and Haran begat *L*	Gen 11:27	3876
L the son of Haran his son's son,	Gen 11:31	3876
and *L* went with him	Gen 12:4	3876
L his brother's son, and all their	Gen 12:5	3876
L with him, into the south	Gen 13:1	3876
L also, which went with Abram,	Gen 13:5	3876
And Abram said unto *L*, Let there	Gen 13:8	3876
L lifted up his eyes, and beheld	Gen 13:10	3876
Then *L* chose him all the plain of	Gen 13:11	3876
and *L* journeyed east	Gen 13:11	3876
L dwelled in the cities of the	Gen 13:12	3876
after that *L* was separated from	Gen 13:14	3876
And they took *L*, Abram's brother's	Gen 14:12	3876
also brought again his brother *L*	Gen 14:16	3876
L sat in the gate of Sodom	Gen 19:1	3876
L seeing them rose up to meet	Gen 19:1	3876
And they called unto *L*, and said	Gen 19:5	3876
L went out at the door unto them,	Gen 19:6	3876
pressed sore upon the man, even *L*	Gen 19:9	3876
pulled *L* into the house to them,	Gen 19:10	3876
And the men said unto *L*, Hast thou	Gen 19:12	3876
L went out, and spake unto his	Gen 19:14	3876
arose, then the angels hastened *L*	Gen 19:15	3876
L said unto them, Oh, not so, my	Gen 19:18	3876
earth when *L* entered into Zoar	Gen 19:23	3876
sent *L* out of the midst of the	Gen 19:29	3876
the cities in the which *L* dwelt	Gen 19:29	3876
L went up out of Zoar, and dwelt	Gen 19:30	3876
of *L* with child by their father	Gen 19:36	3876
children of *L* for a possession	Deut 2:9	3876
children of *L* for a possession	Deut 2:19	3876
have holpen the children of *L*	Ps 83:8	3876
also as it was in the days of *L*	Lk 17:28	3091
But the same day that *L* went out	Lk 17:29	3091
And delivered just *L*, vexed with	2Pet 2:7	3091

2. A die.

one *l* for the LORD, and the other *l*	Lev 16:8	1486
goat upon which the LORD's *l* fell	Lev 16:9	1486
on which the *l* fell to be the	Lev 16:10	1486
the land shall be divided by *l*	Num 26:55	1486
According to the *l* shall the	Num 26:56	1486
ye shall divide the land by *l* for	Num 33:54	1486
in the place where his *l* falleth	Num 33:54	1486
land which ye shall inherit by *l*	Num 34:13	1486
by *l* to the children of Israel	Num 36:2	1486
from the *l* of our inheritance	Num 36:3	1486
Jacob is the *l* of his inheritance	Deut 32:9	2256
only divide thou it by *l* unto the	Josh 13:6	1486
By *l* was their inheritance, as	Josh 14:2	1486
This then was the *l* of the tribe	Josh 15:1	1486

the *l* of the children of Joseph	Josh 16:1	1486
There was also a *l* for the tribe	Josh 17:1	1486
There was also a *l* for the rest	Josh 17:2	
Why hast thou given me but one *l*	Josh 17:14	1486
thou shalt not have one *l* only	Josh 17:17	1486
the *l* of the tribe of the	Josh 18:11	1486
the coast of their *l* came forth	Josh 18:11	1486
the second *l* came forth to Simeon	Josh 19:1	1486
the third *l* came up for the	Josh 19:10	1486
the fourth *l* came out to Issachar	Josh 19:17	1486
the fifth *l* came out for the	Josh 19:24	1486
The sixth *l* came out to the	Josh 19:32	1486
the seventh *l* came out for the	Josh 19:40	1486
by *l* in Shiloh before the LORD	Josh 19:51	1486
the *l* came out for the families	Josh 21:4	1486
had by *l* out of the tribe of	Josh 21:4	1486
by *l* out of the families of the	Josh 21:5	1486
by *l* out of the families of the	Josh 21:6	1486
l unto the Levites these cities	Josh 21:8	1486
for theirs was the first *l*	Josh 21:10	1486
l out of the tribe of Ephraim	Josh 21:20	1486
were by their *l* twelve cities	Josh 21:40	1486
by *l* these nations that remain	Josh 23:4	
Come up with me into my *l*	Judg 1:3	1486
will go with thee into thy *l*	Judg 1:3	1486
we will go up by *l* against it	Judg 20:9	1486
God of Israel, Give a perfect *l*	1Sa 14:41	
for theirs was the *l*	1Chr 6:54	1486
the half tribe of Manasseh, by *l*	1Chr 6:61	1486
sons of Merari were given by *l*	1Chr 6:63	1486
they gave by *l* out of the tribe	1Chr 6:65	1486
the *l* of your inheritance	1Chr 16:18	2256
Thus were they divided by *l*	1Chr 24:5	1486
Now the first *l* came forth to	1Chr 24:7	1486
Now the first *l* came forth for	1Chr 25:9	1486
the *l* eastward fell to Shelemiah	1Chr 26:14	1486
and his *l* came out northward	1Chr 26:14	1486
Hosah the *l* came forth westward,	1Chr 26:16	
they cast Pur, that is, the *l*	Est 3:7	1486
and had cast Pur, that is, the *l*	Est 9:24	1486
thou maintainest my *l*	Ps 16:5	1486
the *l* of your inheritance	Ps 105:11	2256
rest upon the *l* of the righteous	Ps 125:3	1486
Cast in thy *l* among us	Prov 1:14	1486
The *l* is cast into the lap	Prov 16:33	1486
The *l* causeth contentions to	Prov 18:18	1486
the *l* of them that rob us	Is 17:14	1486
And he hath cast the *l* for them	Is 34:17	1486
they, they are thy *l*	Is 57:6	
This is thy *l*, the portion of thy	Jer 13:25	1486
let no *l* fall upon it	Eze 24:6	1486
when ye shall divide by *l* the	Eze 45:1	
that ye shall divide it by *l* for	Eze 48:29	
l unto the tribes of Israel for	Eze 48:29	
stand in thy *l* at the end of the	Dan 12:13	1486
lots, and the *l* fell upon Jonah	Jonah 1:7	1486
none that shall cast a cord by *l*	Mic 2:5	1486
his *l* was to burn incense when he	Lk 1:9	2975
and the *l* fell upon Matthias	Acts 1:26	2819
neither part nor *l* in this matter	Acts 8:21	2819
divided their land to them by *l*	Acts 13:19	2624

LOTAN (lo'-tan) See LOTAN'S. *Son of Seir.*

L, and Shobal, and Zibeon, and Anah,	Gen 36:20	3877
And the children of *L* were Hori	Gen 36:22	3877
duke *L*, duke Shobal, duke Zibeon,	Gen 36:29	3877
L, and Shobal, and Zibeon, and Anah,	1Chr 1:38	3877
And the sons of *L*	1Chr 1:39	3877

LOTAN'S (lo'-tans)

and *L* sister was Timna	Gen 36:22	3877
and Timna was *L* sister	1Chr 1:39	3877

LOTHE

the Egyptians shall *l* to drink of	Ex 7:18	3811
they shall *l* themselves for the	Eze 6:9	6962
ye shall *l* yourselves in your own	Eze 20:43	6962
shall *l* yourselves in your own	Eze 36:31	6962

LOTHED

hath thy soul *l* Zion	Jer 14:19	1602
which *l* their husbands and their	Eze 16:45	1602
and my soul *l* them, and their soul	Zec 11:8	7114

LOTHETH

that *l* her husband and her	Eze 16:45	1602

LOTHING

to the *l* of thy person, in the	Eze 16:5	1604

LOT'S (lots)

cattle and the herdmen of *L* cattle	Gen 13:7	3876
Remember *L* wife	Lk 17:32	

LOTS

Aaron shall cast *l* upon the two	Lev 16:8	1486
that I may cast *l* for you here	Josh 18:6	1486
that I may here cast *l* for you	Josh 18:8	1486
Joshua cast *l* for them in Shiloh	Josh 18:10	1486
Cast *l* between me and Jonathan my	1Sa 14:42	
These likewise cast *l* over	1Chr 24:31	1486
And they cast *l*, ward against ward	1Chr 25:8	1486
And they cast *l*, as well the small	1Chr 26:13	1486
a wise counsellor, they cast *l*	1Chr 26:14	1486
we cast the *l* among the priests,	Neh 10:34	1486
rest of the people also cast *l*	Neh 11:1	1486
them, and cast *l* upon my vesture	Ps 22:18	1486
And they have cast *l* for my people	Joel 3:3	1486
cast *l* upon Jerusalem, even thou	Obad 11	1486
fellow, Come, and let us cast *l*	Jonah 1:7	1486
So they cast *l*, and the lot fell	Jonah 1:7	1486
they cast *l* for her honourable	Nah 3:10	1486
and parted his garments, casting *l*	Mt 27:35	2819
upon my vesture did they cast *l*	Mt 27:35	2819
casting upon them, what every	Mk 15:24	2819
parted his raiment, and cast *l*	Lk 23:34	2819
us not rend it, but cast *l* for it	Jn 19:24	2819
and for my vesture they did cast *l*	Jn 19:24	2975
And they gave forth their *l*	Acts 1:26	2819

LOUD

me, and I cried with a *l* voice	Gen 39:14	1419
voice of the trumpet exceeding *l*	Ex 19:16	2389
the men of Israel with a *l* voice	Deut 27:14	7311
Samuel, she cried with a *l* voice	1Sa 28:12	1419
the country wept with a *l* voice	2Sa 15:23	1419
and the king cried with a *l* voice	2Sa 19:4	1419
of Israel with a *l* voice, saying,	1Kin 8:55	1419
cried with a *l* voice in the Jews'	2Kin 18:28	1419
unto the LORD with a *l* voice	2Chr 15:14	1419
of Israel with a *l* voice on high	2Chr 20:19	1419
singing with *l* instruments unto	2Chr 30:21	5797
Then they cried with a *l* voice in	2Chr 32:18	1419
their eyes, wept with a *l* voice	Ezr 3:12	1419
the people shouted with a *l* shout	Ezr 3:13	1419
answered and said with a *l* voice	Ezr 10:12	1419
cried with a *l* voice unto the	Neh 9:4	1419
And the singers sang *l*, with	Neh 12:42	8085
of the city, and cried with a *l*	Est 4:1	1419
play skilfully with a *l* noise	Ps 33:3	
make a *l* noise, and rejoice, and	Ps 98:4	
Praise him upon the *l* cymbals	Ps 150:5	8085
(She is *l* and stubborn	Prov 7:11	1993
his friend with a *l* voice	Prov 27:14	1419
cried with a *l* voice in the Jews'	Is 36:13	1419
cry in mine ears with a *l* voice	Eze 8:18	1419
also in mine ears with a *l* voice	Eze 9:1	1419
my face, and cried with a *l* voice	Eze 11:13	1419
hour Jesus cried with a *l* voice	Mt 27:46	3173
he had cried again with a *l* voice	Mt 27:50	3173
torn him, and cried with a *l* voice	Mk 1:26	3173
And cried with a *l* voice, and said,	Mk 5:7	3173
hour Jesus cried with a *l* voice	Mk 15:34	3173
And Jesus cried with a *l* voice	Mk 15:37	3173
And she spake out with a *l* voice	Lk 1:42	3173
and cried out with a *l* voice	Lk 4:33	3173
with a *l* voice said, What have I	Lk 8:28	3173
with a *l* voice glorified God,	Lk 17:15	3173
praise God with a *l* voice for all	Lk 19:37	3173
they were instant with *l* voices	Lk 23:23	3173
Jesus had cried with a *l* voice	Lk 23:46	3173
spoken, he cried with a *l* voice	Jn 11:43	3173
they cried out with a *l* voice	Acts 7:57	3173
down, and cried with a *l* voice	Acts 7:60	3173
spirits, crying with *l* voice	Acts 8:7	3173
Said with a *l* voice, Stand	Acts 14:10	3173
But Paul cried with a *l* voice	Acts 16:28	3173
Festus said with a *l* voice	Acts 26:24	3173
angel proclaiming with a *l* voice	Rev 5:2	3173
Saying with a *l* voice, Worthy is	Rev 5:12	3173
And they cried with a *l* voice	Rev 6:10	3173
he cried with a *l* voice to the	Rev 7:2	3173
And cried with a *l* voice, saying,	Rev 7:10	3173
of heaven, saying with a *l* voice	Rev 8:13	3173
And cried with a *l* voice, as when	Rev 10:3	3173
I heard a *l* voice saying in	Rev 12:10	3173
Saying with a *l* voice, Fear God,	Rev 14:7	3173
them, saying with a *l* voice	Rev 14:9	3173
crying with a *l* voice to him that	Rev 14:15	3173
cried with a *l* cry to him that	Rev 14:18	3173
and he cried with a *l* voice	Rev 19:17	3173

LOUDER

long, and waxed *l* and *l*	Ex 19:19	3966

LOVE

make me savoury meat, such as I *l*	Gen 27:4	157
few days, for the *l* he had to her	Gen 29:20	160
therefore my husband will *l* me	Gen 29:32	157
unto thousands of them that *l* me	Ex 20:6	157
I *l* my master, my wife, and my	Ex 21:5	157
but thou shalt *l* thy neighbour as	Lev 19:18	157
thou shalt *l* him as thyself	Lev 19:34	157
unto thousands of them that *l* me	Deut 5:10	157
thou shalt *l* the LORD thy God	Deut 6:5	157
LORD did not set his *l* upon you	Deut 7:7	2836
and mercy with them that *l* him	Deut 7:9	157
And he will *l* thee, and bless thee,	Deut 7:13	157
to *l* him, and to serve the LORD	Deut 10:12	157
delight in thy fathers to *l* them	Deut 10:15	157
L ye therefore the stranger	Deut 10:19	157
thou shalt *l* the LORD thy God	Deut 11:1	157
to *l* the LORD your God, and to	Deut 11:13	157
to *l* the LORD your God, to walk	Deut 11:22	157
to know whether ye *l* the LORD	Deut 13:3	157
to *l* the LORD thy God, and to walk	Deut 19:9	157
to *l* the LORD thy God with all	Deut 30:6	157
this day to *l* the LORD thy God	Deut 30:16	157
thou mayest *l* the LORD thy God	Deut 30:20	157
to *l* the LORD your God, and to	Josh 22:5	157
that ye *l* the LORD your God	Josh 23:11	157
but let them that *l* him be as the	Judg 5:31	157
I *l* thee, when thine heart is not	Judg 16:15	157
thee, and all his servants *l* thee	1Sa 18:22	157
thy *l* to me was wonderful,	2Sa 1:26	160
passing the *l* of women	2Sa 1:26	160
I *l* Tamar, my brother Absalom's	2Sa 13:4	157
the *l* wherewith he had loved her	2Sa 13:15	160
Solomon clave unto these in *l*	1Kin 11:2	160
l them that hate the LORD	2Chr 19:2	157
and mercy for them that *l* him	Neh 1:5	157
how long will ye *l* vanity	Ps 4:2	157
let them also that *l* thy name be	Ps 5:11	157
I will *l* thee, O LORD, my	Ps 18:1	7355
O *l* the LORD, all ye his saints	Ps 31:23	157
let such as *l* thy salvation say	Ps 40:16	157
they that *l* his name shall dwell	Ps 69:36	157
let such as *l* thy salvation say	Ps 70:4	157
Because he hath set his *l* upon me	Ps 91:14	2836
Ye that *l* the LORD, hate evil	Ps 97:10	157
For my *l* they are my adversaries	Ps 109:4	160
evil for good, and hatred for my *l*	Ps 109:5	160
I *l* the LORD, because he hath	Ps 116:1	157
O how *l* I thy law	Ps 119:97	157
but thy law do I *l*	Ps 119:113	157
therefore I *l* thy testimonies	Ps 119:119	157
Therefore I *l* thy commandments	Ps 119:127	157
to do unto those that *l* thy name	Ps 119:132	157
Consider how I *l* thy precepts	Ps 119:159	157
but thy law do I *l*	Ps 119:163	157
peace have they which *l* thy law	Ps 119:165	157
and I *l* them exceedingly	Ps 119:167	157
they shall prosper that *l* thee	Ps 122:6	157
preserveth all them that *l* him	Ps 145:20	157
simple ones, will ye *l* simplicity	Prov 1:22	157
l her, and she shall keep thee	Prov 4:6	157
thou ravished always with her *l*	Prov 5:19	160
our fill of *l* until the morning	Prov 7:18	1730
I *l* them that *l* me	Prov 8:17	157
that *l* me to inherit substance	Prov 8:21	157
all they that hate me *l* death	Prov 8:36	157
a wise man, and he will *l* thee	Prov 9:8	157
but *l* covereth all sins	Prov 10:12	160
is a dinner of herbs where *l* is	Prov 15:17	160
they *l* him that speaketh right	Prov 16:13	157
a transgression seeketh *l*	Prov 17:9	160
they that *l* it shall eat the	Prov 18:21	157
L not sleep, lest thou come to	Prov 20:13	157
rebuke is better than secret *l*	Prov 27:5	160
A time to *l*, and a time to hate	Eccl 3:8	157
no man knoweth either *l* or hatred	Eccl 9:1	160
Also their *l*, and their hatred, and	Eccl 9:6	160
for thy *l* is better than wine	Song 1:2	1730
therefore do the virgins *l* thee	Song 1:3	157
remember thy *l* more than wine	Song 1:4	1730
the upright *l* thee	Song 1:4	157
I have compared thee, O my *l*	Song 1:9	7474
Behold, thou art fair, my *l*	Song 1:15	7474
so is my *l* among the daughters	Song 2:2	7474
and his banner over me was *l*	Song 2:4	160
for I am sick of *l*	Song 2:5	160
ye stir not up, nor awake my *l*	Song 2:7	160
and said unto me, Rise up, my *l*	Song 2:10	7474

L

Arise, my *l*, my fair one, and come	Song 2:13	7474
ye stir not up, nor awake my *l*	Song 3:5	160
midst thereof being paved with *l*	Song 3:10	160
Behold, thou art fair, my *l*	Song 4:1	7474
Thou art all fair, my *l*	Song 4:7	7474
How fair is thy *l*, my sister, my	Song 4:10	1730
much better is thy *l* than wine	Song 4:10	1730
Open to me, my sister, my *l*	Song 5:2	7474
ye tell him, that I am sick of *l*	Song 5:8	160
Thou art beautiful, O my *l*	Song 6:4	7474
and how pleasant art thou, O *l*	Song 7:6	160
ye stir not up, nor awake my *l*	Song 8:4	160
for *l* is strong as death	Song 8:6	160
Many waters cannot quench *l*	Song 8:7	160
the substance of his house for *l*	Song 8:7	160
but thou hast in *l* to my soul	Is 38:17	2836
to *l* the name of the LORD, to be	Is 56:6	157
For I the LORD *l* judgment	Is 61:8	157
in his *l* and in his pity he	Is 63:9	160
glad with her, all ye that *l* her	Is 66:10	157
the *l* of thine espousals, when	Jer 2:2	160
trimmest thou thy way to seek *l*	Jer 2:33	160
my people *l* to have it so	Jer 5:31	157
loved thee with an everlasting *l*	Jer 31:3	160
thy time was the time of *l*	Eze 16:8	1730
in her inordinate *l* than she	Eze 23:11	5691
came to her into the bed of *l*	Eze 23:17	1730
with their mouth they shew much *l*	Eze 33:31	5690
tender *l* with the prince of the	Dan 1:9	
and mercy to them that *l* him	Dan 9:4	157
l a woman beloved of her friend,	Hos 3:1	157
according to the *l* of the LORD	Hos 3:1	160
other gods, and *l* flagons of wine	Hos 3:1	157
her rulers with shame do *l*	Hos 4:18	157
mine house, I will *l* them no more	Hos 9:15	160
cords of a man, with bands of *l*	Hos 11:4	160
backsliding, I will *l* them freely	Hos 14:4	157
l the good, and establish judgment	Amos 5:15	157
Who hate the good, and *l* the evil	Mic 3:2	157
to *l* mercy, and to walk humbly	Mic 6:8	160
he will rest in his *l*, he will	Zeph 3:17	160
and *l* no false oath	Zec 8:17	157
therefore *l* the truth and peace	Zec 8:19	157
Thou shalt *l* thy neighbour, and	Mt 5:43	25
L your enemies, bless them that	Mt 5:44	25
For if ye *l* them which *l* you,	Mt 5:46	25
for they *l* to pray standing in	Mt 6:5	5368
will hate the one, and *l* the other	Mt 6:24	25
Thou shalt *l* thy neighbour as	Mt 19:19	25
Thou shalt *l* the Lord thy God	Mt 22:37	25
Thou shalt *l* thy neighbour as	Mt 22:39	25
***l* the uppermost rooms at feasts,**	Mt 23:6	5368
the *l* of many shall wax cold	Mt 24:12	26
thou shalt *l* the Lord thy God	Mk 12:30	25
Thou shalt *l* thy neighbour as	Mk 12:31	25
to *l* him with all the heart, and	Mk 12:33	25
to *l* his neighbour as himself, is	Mk 12:33	25
which *l* to go in long clothing,	Mk 12:38	2309
***l* salutations in the marketplaces**	Mk 12:38	
L your enemies, do good to them	Lk 6:27	25
For if ye *l* them which *l* you	Lk 6:32	25
also *l* those that *l* them	Lk 6:32	25
But *l* ye your enemies, and do good	Lk 6:35	25
which of them will *l* him most	Lk 7:42	25
Thou shalt *l* the Lord thy God	Lk 10:27	25
over judgment and the *l* of God	Lk 11:42	26
for ye *l* the uppermost seats in	Lk 11:43	25
will hate the one, and *l* the other	Lk 16:13	25
***l* greetings in the markets, and**	Lk 20:46	5368
ye have not the *l* of God in you	Jn 5:42	26
were your Father, ye would *l* me	Jn 8:42	25
Therefore doth my Father *l* me	Jn 10:17	25
unto you, That ye *l* one another	Jn 13:34	25
you, that ye also *l* one another	Jn 13:34	25
if ye have *l* one to another	Jn 13:35	26
If ye *l* me, keep my commandments	Jn 14:15	25
of my Father, and I will *l* him	Jn 14:21	25
and said unto him, If a man *l* me	Jn 14:23	25
and my Father will *l* him, and we	Jn 14:23	25
may know that I *l* the Father	Jn 14:31	25
continue ye in my *l*.	Jn 15:9	26
ye shall abide in my *l*	Jn 15:10	26
commandments, and abide in his *l*	Jn 15:10	26
That ye *l* one another, as I have	Jn 15:12	25
Greater *l* hath no man than this,	Jn 15:13	26
you, that ye *l* one another	Jn 15:17	25
world, the world would *l* his own	Jn 15:19	5368
that the *l* wherewith thou hast	Jn 17:26	26
thou knowest that I *l* thee	Jn 21:15	5368

thou knowest that I *l* thee	Jn 21:16	5368
thou knowest that I *l* thee	Jn 21:17	5368
because the *l* of God is shed	Rom 5:5	26
God commendeth his *l* toward us	Rom 5:8	26
for good to them that *l* God	Rom 8:28	25
separate us from the *l* of Christ	Rom 8:35	26
to separate us from the *l* of God	Rom 8:39	26
Let *l* be without dissimulation	Rom 12:9	26
one to another with brotherly *l*	Rom 12:10	5360
any thing, but to *l* one another	Rom 13:8	25
Thou shalt *l* thy neighbour as	Rom 13:9	25
L worketh no ill to his neighbour	Rom 13:10	26
therefore *l* is the fulfilling of	Rom 13:10	26
for the *l* of the Spirit, that ye	Rom 15:30	26
hath prepared for them that *l* him	1Cor 2:9	25
come unto you with a rod, or in *l*	1Cor 4:21	26
But if any man *l* God, the same is	1Cor 8:3	25
If any man *l* not the Lord Jesus	1Cor 16:22	5368
My *l* be with you all in Christ	1Cor 16:24	26
but that ye might know the *l*	2Cor 2:4	26
would confirm your *l* toward him	2Cor 2:8	26
For the *l* of Christ constraineth	2Cor 5:14	26
the Holy Ghost, by *l* unfeigned,	2Cor 6:6	26
all diligence, and in your *l* to us	2Cor 8:7	26
to prove the sincerity of your *l*	2Cor 8:8	26
the churches, the proof of your *l*	2Cor 8:24	26
because I *l* you not	2Cor 11:11	25
the more abundantly I *l* you	2Cor 12:15	25
and the God of *l* and peace shall be	2Cor 13:11	26
the *l* of God, and the communion of	2Cor 13:14	26
but faith which worketh by *l*	Gal 5:6	26
but by *l* serve one another	Gal 5:13	26
Thou shalt *l* thy neighbour as	Gal 5:14	25
But the fruit of the Spirit is *l*	Gal 5:22	26
and without blame before him in *l*	Eph 1:4	26
Jesus, and *l* unto all the saints,	Eph 1:15	26
for his great *l* wherewith he	Eph 2:4	26
ye, being rooted and grounded in *l*	Eph 3:17	26
And to know the *l* of Christ	Eph 3:19	26
forbearing one another in *l*	Eph 4:2	26
But speaking the truth in *l*	Eph 4:15	26
unto the edifying of itself in *l*	Eph 4:16	26
And walk in *l*, as Christ also hath	Eph 5:2	26
l your wives, even as Christ also	Eph 5:25	25
So ought men to *l* their wives as	Eph 5:28	25
so *l* his wife even as himself	Eph 5:33	25
l with faith, from God the Father	Eph 6:23	26
that *l* our Lord Jesus Christ in	Eph 6:24	25
that your *l* may abound yet more	Phil 1:9	26
But the other of *l*, knowing that	Phil 1:17	26
in Christ, if any comfort of *l*	Phil 2:1	26
be likeminded, having the same *l*	Phil 2:2	26
of the *l* which ye have to all the	Col 1:4	26
unto us your *l* in the Spirit	Col 1:8	26
being knit together in *l*	Col 2:2	26
l your wives, and be not bitter	Col 3:19	25
work of faith, and labour of *l*	1Th 1:3	26
abound in *l* one toward another,	1Th 3:12	26
But as touching brotherly *l* ye	1Th 4:9	5360
taught of God to *l* one another	1Th 4:9	25
on the breastplate of faith and *l*	1Th 5:8	26
highly in *l* for their work's sake	1Th 5:13	26
received not the *l* of the truth	2Th 2:10	26
your hearts into the *l* of God	2Th 3:5	26
l which is in Christ Jesus	1Ti 1:14	26
For the *l* of money is the root of	1Ti 6:10	5365
godliness, faith, *l*, patience,	1Ti 6:11	26
but of power, and of *l*, and of a	2Ti 1:7	26
l which is in Christ Jesus	2Ti 1:13	26
them also that *l* his appearing	2Ti 4:8	25
be sober, to *l* their husbands	Titus 2:4	5362
to *l* their children	Titus 2:4	5388
l of God our Saviour toward man	Titus 3:4	5363
Greet them that *l* us in the faith	Titus 3:15	5368
Hearing of thy *l* and faith, which	Philem 5	26
great joy and consolation in thy *l*	Philem 7	26
forget your work and labour of *l*	Heb 6:10	26
one another to provoke unto *l*	Heb 10:24	26
Let brotherly *l* continue	Heb 13:1	5360
hath promised to them that *l* him	Jas 1:12	25
hath promised to them that *l* him	Jas 2:5	25
Thou shalt *l* thy neighbour as	Jas 2:8	25
Whom having not seen, ye *l*	1Pet 1:8	25
unto unfeigned *l* of the brethren	1Pet 1:22	5360
see that ye *l* one another with a	1Pet 1:22	25
L the brotherhood	1Pet 2:17	25
l as brethren, be pitiful, be	1Pet 3:8	5361
For he that will *l* life, and see	1Pet 3:10	25
verily is the *l* of God perfected	1Jn 2:5	26

L not the world, neither the	1Jn 2:15	25
If any man *l* the world	1Jn 2:15	25
the *l* of the Father is not in him	1Jn 2:15	26
what manner of *l* the Father hath	1Jn 3:1	26
that we should *l* one another	1Jn 3:11	25
because we *l* the brethren	1Jn 3:14	25
Hereby perceive we the *l* of God	1Jn 3:16	26
how dwelleth the *l* of God in him	1Jn 3:17	26
children, let us not *l* in word	1Jn 3:18	25
l one another, as he gave us	1Jn 3:23	25
Beloved, let us *l* one another	1Jn 4:7	25
for *l* is of God	1Jn 4:7	26
for God is *l*	1Jn 4:8	26
manifested the *l* of God toward us	1Jn 4:9	26
Herein is *l*, not that we loved	1Jn 4:10	26
we ought also to *l* one another	1Jn 4:11	25
If we *l* one another, God dwelleth	1Jn 4:12	25
us, and his *l* is perfected in us	1Jn 4:12	26
believed the *l* that God hath to	1Jn 4:16	26
God is *l*	1Jn 4:16	26
dwelleth in *l* dwelleth in God	1Jn 4:16	26
Herein is our *l* made perfect	1Jn 4:17	26
There is no fear in *l*	1Jn 4:18	26
but perfect *l* casteth out fear	1Jn 4:18	26
feareth is not made perfect in *l*	1Jn 4:18	26
We *l* him, because he first loved	1Jn 4:19	25
I *l* God, and hateth his brother	1Jn 4:20	25
how can he *l* God whom he hath not	1Jn 4:20	25
who loveth God *l* his brother also	1Jn 4:21	25
that we *l* the children of God	1Jn 5:2	25
children of God, when we *l* God	1Jn 5:2	25
For this is the *l* of God, that we	1Jn 5:3	26
children, whom I *l* in the truth	2Jn 1	25
Son of the Father, in truth and *l*	2Jn 3	26
beginning, that we *l* one another	2Jn 5	25
And this is *l*, that we walk after	2Jn 6	26
Gaius, whom I *l* in the truth	3Jn 1	25
Mercy unto you, and peace, and *l*	Jude 2	26
Keep yourselves in the *l* of God	Jude 21	26
thou hast left thy first *l*	Rev 2:4	26
As many as I *l*, I rebuke and	Rev 3:19	5368

LOVED

his wife; and he *l* her	Gen 24:67	157
And Isaac *l* Esau, because he did	Gen 25:28	157
but Rebekah *l* Jacob	Gen 25:28	157
meat, such as his father *l*	Gen 27:14	157
And Jacob *l* Rachel	Gen 29:18	157
he *l* also Rachel more than Leah,	Gen 29:30	157
he *l* the damsel, and spake kindly	Gen 34:3	157
Now Israel *l* Joseph more than all	Gen 37:3	157
l him more than all his brethren	Gen 37:4	157
because he *l* thy fathers	Deut 4:37	157
But because the LORD *l* you	Deut 7:8	160
because the LORD thy God *l* thee	Deut 23:5	157
Yea, he *l* the people	Deut 33:3	2245
that he *l* a woman in the valley	Judg 16:4	157
for he *l* Hannah	1Sa 1:5	157
and he *l* him greatly	1Sa 16:21	157
Jonathan *l* him as his own soul	1Sa 18:1	157
because he *l* him as his own soul	1Sa 18:3	160
But all Israel and Judah *l* David	1Sa 18:16	157
And Michal Saul's daughter *l* David	1Sa 18:20	157
that Michal Saul's daughter *l* him	1Sa 18:28	157
to swear again, because he *l* him	1Sa 20:17	160
for he *l* him as he	1Sa 20:17	157
him as he *l* his own soul	1Sa 20:17	160
and the LORD *l* him	2Sa 12:24	157
and Amnon the son of David *l* her	2Sa 13:1	157
the love wherewith he had *l* her	2Sa 13:15	157
Solomon *l* the LORD, walking in	1Kin 3:3	157
the LORD *l* Israel for ever	1Kin 10:9	160
But king Solomon *l* many strange	1Kin 11:1	157
the LORD hath *l* his people	2Chr 2:11	160
because thy God *l* Israel, to	2Chr 9:8	160
Rehoboam *l* Maachah the daughter	2Chr 11:21	157
for he *l* husbandry	2Chr 26:10	157
the king *l* Esther above all the	Est 2:17	157
they whom I *l* are turned against	Job 19:19	157
I have *l* the habitation of thy	Ps 26:8	157
the excellency of Jacob whom he *l*	Ps 47:4	157
Judah, the mount Zion which he *l*	Ps 78:68	157
As he *l* cursing, so let it come	Ps 109:17	157
thy commandments, which I have *l*	Ps 119:47	157
thy commandments, which I have *l*	Ps 119:48	157
been honourable, and I have *l* thee	Is 43:4	157
The LORD hath *l* him	Is 48:14	157
for I have *l* strangers, and after	Jer 2:25	157
host of heaven, whom they have *l*	Jer 8:2	157

Thus have they *l* to wander	Jer 14:10	157
I have *l* thee with an everlasting	Jer 31:3	157
and all them that thou hast *l*	Eze 16:37	157
thou hast *l* a reward upon every	Hos 9:1	157
were according as they *l*	Hos 9:10	157
Israel was a child, then I *l* him	Hos 11:1	157
I have *l* you, saith the LORD	Mal 1:2	157
ye say, Wherein hast thou *l* us	Mal 1:2	157
yet I *l* Jacob,	Mal 1:2	157
holiness of the LORD which he *l*	Mal 2:11	157
Then Jesus beholding him *l* him	Mk 10:21	25
for she *l* much	Lk 7:47	25
For God so *l* the world, that he	Jn 3:16	25
men *l* darkness rather than light,	Jn 3:19	25
Now Jesus *l* Martha, and her sister	Jn 11:5	25
the Jews, Behold how he *l* him	Jn 11:36	5368
For they *l* the praise of men more	Jn 12:43	25
having *l* his own which were in	Jn 13:1	25
the world, he *l* them unto the end	Jn 13:1	25
of his disciples, whom Jesus *l*	Jn 13:23	25
as I have *l* you, that ye also	Jn 13:34	25
loveth me shall be *l* of my Father	Jn 14:21	25
If ye *l* me, ye would rejoice,	Jn 14:28	25
hath *l* me, so have I *l* you	Jn 15:9	25
love one another, as I have *l* you	Jn 15:12	25
loveth you, because ye have *l* me	Jn 16:27	5368
thou hast sent me, and hast *l* them	Jn 17:23	25
as thou hast *l* me	Jn 17:23	25
thou hast *l* me may be in them	Jn 17:26	25
disciple standing by, whom he *l*	Jn 19:26	25
the other disciple, whom Jesus *l*	Jn 20:2	5368
whom Jesus *l* saith unto Peter	Jn 21:7	25
disciple whom Jesus *l* following	Jn 21:20	25
conquerors through him that *l* us	Rom 8:37	25
As it is written, Jacob have I *l*	Rom 9:13	25
I love you, the less I be *l*	2Cor 12:15	25
faith of the Son of God, who *l* me	Gal 2:20	25
his great love wherewith he *l* us	Eph 2:4	25
in love, as Christ also hath *l* us	Eph 5:2	26
even as Christ also *l* the church	Eph 5:25	25
even our Father, which hath *l* us	2Th 2:16	25
having *l* this present world, and	2Ti 4:10	25
Thou hast *l* righteousness, and	Heb 1:9	25
son of Bosor, who *l* the wages of	2Pet 2:15	25
Herein is love, not that we *l* God	1Jn 4:10	25
but that he *l* us	1Jn 4:10	25
Beloved, if God so *l* us, we ought	1Jn 4:11	25
love him, because he first *l* us	1Jn 4:19	25
Unto him that *l* us, and washed us	Rev 1:5	25
and to know that I have *l* thee	Rev 3:9	25
they *l* not their lives unto the	Rev 12:11	25

LOVEDST

thou *l* their bed where thou	Is 57:8	157
for thou *l* me before the	Jn 17:24	25

LOVELY

Saul and Jonathan were *l* and	2Sa 1:23	157
yea, he is altogether *l*	Song 5:16	4261
a very *l* song of one that hath a	Eze 33:32	5690
are pure, whatsoever things are *l*	Phil 4:8	4375

LOVER

for Hiram was ever a *l* of David	1Kin 5:1	157
L and friend hast thou put far	Ps 88:18	157
But a *l* of hospitality	Titus 1:8	5382
a *l* of good men, sober, just,	Titus 1:8	5358

LOVERS

My *l* and my friends stand aloof	Ps 38:11	157
played the harlot with many *l*	Jer 3:1	7453
thy *l* will despise thee, they	Jer 4:30	5689
for all thy *l* are destroyed	Jer 22:20	157
thy *l* shall go into captivity	Jer 22:22	157
All thy *l* have forgotten thee	Jer 30:14	157
among all her *l* she hath none to	Lam 1:2	157
I called for my *l*, but they	Lam 1:19	157
givest thy gifts to all thy *l*	Eze 16:33	157
through thy whoredoms with thy *l*	Eze 16:36	157
therefore I will gather all thy *l*	Eze 16:37	157
and she doted on her *l*, on the	Eze 23:5	157
her into the hand of her *l*	Eze 23:9	157
will raise up thy *l* against thee	Eze 23:22	157
she said, I will go after my *l*	Hos 2:5	157
And she shall follow after her *l*	Hos 2:7	157
lewdness in the sight of her *l*	Hos 2:10	157
rewards that my *l* have given me	Hos 2:12	157
jewels, and she went after her *l*	Hos 2:13	157
Ephraim hath hired *l*	Hos 8:9	158
For men shall be *l* of their own	2Ti 3:2	5367
l of pleasures more than	2Ti 3:4	5369

of pleasures more than *l* of God 2Ti 3:4   5377

LOVE'S
Yet for *l* sake I rather beseech ....Philem 9   26

LOVES
of Korah, A Maschil, A Song of *l* ....Ps 45:*t*   3039
let us solace ourselves with *l* ....Prov 7:18   159
there will I give thee my *l* ....Song 7:12   1730

LOVEST
thine only son Isaac, whom thou *l* ....Gen 22:2   157
dost but hate me, and *l* me not ....Judg 14:16   157
In that thou *l* thine enemies, and 2Sa 19:6   157
Thou *l* righteousness, and hatest...........Ps 45:7   157
Thou *l* evil more than good ....Ps 52:3   157
Thou *l* all devouring words, O.................Ps 52:4   157
with the wife whom thou *l* all the ....Eccl 9:9   157
behold, he whom thou *l* is sick ....Jn 11:3   5368
l thou me more than these ....Jn 21:15   25
Simon, son of Jonas, l thou me ....Jn 21:16   25
Simon, son of Jonas, l thou me ....Jn 21:17   5368
him the third time, L thou me ....Jn 21:17   5368

LOVETH
meat for thy father, such as he *l* ....Gen 27:9   157
his mother, and his father I him ....Gen 44:20   157
l the stranger, in giving him ....Deut 10:18   157
because he *l* thee and thine house, ...Deut 15:16   157
thy daughter in law, which *l* thee...........Ruth 4:15   157
him that *l* violence his soul ....Ps 11:5   157
righteous LORD *l* righteousness ....Ps 11:7   157
He *l* righteousness and judgment ....Ps 33:5   157
l many days, that he may see good ....Ps 34:12   157
For the LORD *l* judgment, and.................Ps 37:28   157
The LORD *l* the gates of Zion more.........Ps 87:2   157
king's strength also *l* judgment ....Ps 99:4   157
therefore thy servant *l* it ....Ps 119:140   157
the LORD *l* the righteous ....Ps 146:8   157
For whom the LORD *l* he correcteth ....Prov 3:12   157
l instruction *l* knowledge ....Prov 12:1   157
but he that *l* him chasteneth him ....Prov 13:24   157
but he *l* him that followeth after ....Prov 15:9   157
A scorner *l* not one that..........................Prov 15:12   157
A friend *l* at all times, and a ....Prov 17:17   157
He *l* transgression that..........................Prov 17:19   157
transgression that *l* strife......................Prov 17:19   157
getteth wisdom *l* his own soul ....Prov 19:8   157
He that *l* pleasure shall be a..................Prov 21:17   157
he that *l* wine and oil shall not ....Prov 21:17   157
He that *l* pureness of heart, for..............Prov 22:11   157
Whoso *l* wisdom rejoiceth his ....Prov 29:3   157
He that *l* silver shall not be....................Eccl 5:10   157
nor he that *l* abundance with..................Eccl 5:10   157
Tell me, O thou whom my soul *l* ....Song 1:7   157
bed I sought him whom my soul *l* ....Song 3:1   157
I will seek him whom my soul *l* ....Song 3:2   157
I said, Saw ye him whom my soul *l* ....Song 3:3   157
but I found him whom my soul *l*..............Song 3:4   157
every one *l* gifts, and followeth...............Is 1:23   157
and *l* to tread out the corn ....Hos 10:11   157
he *l* to oppress......................................Hos 12:7   157
He that l father or mother more............Mt 10:37   5368
he that l son or daughter more ....Mt 10:37   5368
For he *l* our nation, and he hath ....Lk 7:5   25
is forgiven, the same l little ....Lk 7:47   25
The Father *l* the Son, and hath ....Jn 3:35   25
For the Father l the Son, and ....Jn 5:20   5368
He that l his life shall lose it ....Jn 12:25   5368
keepeth them, he it is that l me ....Jn 14:21   25
he that l shall be loved of my ....Jn 14:21   25
He that l me not keepeth not my...........Jn 14:24   25
For the Father himself l you ....Jn 16:27   5368
for he *l* another hath............................Rom 13:8   25
for God *l* a cheerful giver 2Cor 9:7   25
He that *l* his wife *l* himself....................Eph 5:28   25
For whom the Lord *l* he chasteneth........Heb 12:6   25
He that *l* his brother abideth in 1Jn 2:10   25
neither he that *l* not his brother 1Jn 3:10   25
He that *l* not his brother abideth 1Jn 3:14   25
every one that *l* is born of God 1Jn 4:7   25
He that *l* not knoweth not God................1Jn 4:8   25
for he that *l* not his brother....................1Jn 4:20   25
That he who *l* God love his 1Jn 4:21   25
every one that *l* him that begat 1Jn 5:1   25
l him also that is begotten of 1Jn 5:1   25
who *l* to have the preeminence 3Jn 9   5383
and idolaters, and whosoever *l* ....Rev 22:15   5368

LOVING
Let her be as the *l* hind and ....Prov 5:19   158
l favour rather than silver and...............Prov 22:1   2896
lying down, *l* to slumber ....Is 56:10   157

LOVINGKINDNESS
Shew thy marvellous *l*, O thou...............Ps 17:7   2617
For thy *l* is before mine eyes ....Ps 26:3   2617
How excellent is thy *l*, O God..................Ps 36:7   2617
O continue thy *l* unto them that ....Ps 36:10   2617
I have not concealed thy *l* ....Ps 40:10   2617
let thy *l* and thy truth............................Ps 40:11   2617
will command his *l* in the daytime ....Ps 42:8   2617
We have thought of thy *l*, O God,............Ps 48:9   2617
me, O God, according to thy *l* ....Ps 51:1   2617
Because thy *l* is better than life..............Ps 63:3   2617
for thy *l* is good ....Ps 69:16   2617
Shall thy *l* be declared in the.................Ps 88:11   2617
Nevertheless my *l* will I not ....Ps 89:33   2617
shew forth thy *l* in the morning ....Ps 92:2   2617
who crowneth thee with *l* and ....Ps 103:4   2617
understand the *l* of the LORD...................Ps 107:43   2617
Quicken me after thy *l*............................Ps 119:88   2617
my voice according unto thy *l* ....Ps 119:149   2617
me, O LORD, according to thy *l* ....Ps 119:159   2617
and praise thy name for thy *l* ....Ps 138:2   2617
me to hear thy *l* in the morning ....Ps 143:8   2617
I am the LORD which exercise *l*................Jer 9:24   2617
people, saith the LORD, even *l* ....Jer 16:5   2617
therefore with *l* have I drawn..................Jer 31:3   2617
Thou shewest *l* unto thousands, and .....Jer 32:18   2617
and in judgment, and in *l*, and in ....Hos 2:19   2617

LOVINGKINDNESSES
LORD, thy tender mercies and thy *l*........Ps 25:6   2617
Lord, where are thy former *l* ....Ps 89:49   2617
I will mention the *l* of the LORD..............Is 63:7   2617
to the multitude of his *l* ....Is 63:7   2617

LOW See APPENDIX.

LOWER See APPENDIX.

LOWEST See APPENDIX.

LOWETH
or *l* the ox over his fodder ....Job 6:5   1600

LOWING
l as they went, and turned not 1Sa 6:12   1600
the *l* of the oxen which I hear 1Sa 15:14   6963

LOWLINESS
With all *l* and meekness, with ....Eph 4:2   5012
but in *l* of mind let each esteem ....Phil 2:3   5012

LOWLY
yet hath he respect unto the *l* ....Ps 138:6   8217
but he giveth grace unto the *l*................Prov 3:34   6041
but with the *l* is wisdom ....Prov 11:2   6800
be of an humble spirit with the *l* ....Prov 16:19   6041
l, and riding upon an ass, and upon.......Zec 9:9   6041
for I am meek and l in heart ....Mt 11:29   5011

LOWRING
for the sky is red and l...........................Mt 16:3   4768

LUBIM (lu'-bim) See LUBIMS. *An African race.*
the *L*, the Sukkiims, and the 2Chr 12:3   3864
Put and *L* were thy helpers ....Nah 3:9   3864

LUBIMS (lu'-bims) See LEHABIM, LUBIM. *Same as Lubim.*
the *L* a huge host, with very many 2Chr 16:8   3864

LUCAS (lu'-cas) See LUKE. *Same as Luke.*
city of Macedonia, by Titus and *L* ....2Cor *s*   3065
Marcus, Aristarchus, Demas, *L* ....Philem 24   3065

LUCIFER (lu'-sif-ur) *Title applied to king of Babylon.*
art thou fallen from heaven, O *L* ....Is 14:12   1966

LUCIUS (lu'-she-us)
    1. *A Christian from Cyrene.*
L of Cyrene, and Manaen, which had ....Acts 13:1   3066
    2. *A relative of Paul.*
Timotheus my workfellow, and *L* ....Rom 16:21   3066

LUCRE
ways, but turned aside after *l* 1Sa 8:3   1215
striker, not greedy of filthy *l*..................1Ti 3:3   866
much wine, not greedy of filthy *l* 1Ti 3:8   146
no striker, not given to filthy *l* ....Titus 1:7   146
not for filthy *l*, but of a ready 1Pet 5:2   147

LUCRE'S
they ought not, for filthy *l* sake ....Titus 1:11   2771

LUD (lud) See LUDIM, LYDIA.
    1. *Son of Shem.*
and Asshur, and Arphaxad, and *L*..........Gen 10:22   3865
and Asshur, and Arphaxad, and *L*..........1Chr 1:17   3865
    2. *Descendants of Lud 1.*
nations, to Tarshish, Pul, and *L* ....Is 66:19   3865

They of Persia and of *L* and of Phut .... Eze 27:10   3865

LUDIM *(lu'-dim)* See LUD. *Son of Mizraim.*
Mizraim begat *L*, and Anamim, and ...... Gen 10:13   3866
And Mizraim begat *L*, and Anamim 1Chr 1:11   3866

LUHITH *(lu'-hith)* A Moabite city.
for by the mounting up of *L* with .... Is 15:5   3872
For in the going up of *L* .... Jer 48:5   3872

LUKE *(luke)* See LUCAS. *A companion of Paul.*
L, the beloved physician, and .... Col 4:14   3065
Only *L* is with me 2Ti 4:11   3065

LUKEWARM
So then because thou art *l* .... Rev 3:16   5513

LUMP
And Isaiah said, Take a *l* of figs 2Kin 20:7   1690
said, Let them take a *l* of figs .... Is 38:21   1690
of the same *l* to make one vessel .... Rom 9:21   5445
be holy, the *l* is also holy .... Rom 11:16   5445
leaven leaveneth the whole *l* 1Cor 5:6   5445
leaven, that ye may be a new *l* 1Cor 5:7   5445
leaven leaveneth the whole *l* .... Gal 5:9   5445

LUNATICK
devils, and those which were *l* .... Mt 4:24   4583
for he is *l*, and sore vexed..................... Mt 17:15   4583

LURK
let us *l* privily for the innocent............... Prov 1:11   6845
they *l* privily for their own .... Prov 1:18   6845

LURKING
take knowledge of all the *l* 1Sa 23:23   4224
He sitteth in the *l* places of the............. Ps 10:8   3993
a young lion *l* in secret places .... Ps 17:12   3427

LUST
my *l* shall be satisfied upon them .... Ex 15:9   5315
heart by asking meat for their *l*............. Ps 78:18   5315
were not estranged from their *l* .... Ps 78:30   8378
them up unto their own hearts' *l* .... Ps 81:12   8307
L not after her beauty in thine............... Prov 6:25   2530
to *l* after her hath committed .... Mt 5:28   1937
burned in their *l* one toward .... Rom 1:27   3715
for I had not known *l*, except the.......... Rom 7:7   1939
we should not *l* after evil things...... 1Cor 10:6   1511,1938
not fulfil the *l* of the flesh .... Gal 5:16   1939
Not in the *l* of concupiscence, ... 1Th 4:5   3806
he is drawn away of his own *l* .... Jas 1:14   1939
Then when *l* hath conceived, it .... Jas 1:15   1939
Ye *l*, and have not............................... Jas 4:2   1937
that is in the world through *l* 2Pet 1:4   1939
the flesh in the *l* of uncleanness 2Pet 2:10   1939
the *l* of the flesh 1Jn 2:16   1939
the *l* of the eyes, and the pride............... 1Jn 2:16   1939
passeth away, and the *l* thereof 1Jn 2:17   1939

LUSTED
they buried the people that *l*............... Num 11:34   183
But *l* exceedingly in the.......................... Ps 106:14   183
after evil things, as they also *l*............... 1Cor 10:6   1937
the fruits that thy soul *l* after .... Rev 18:14   1937

LUSTETH
whatsoever thy soul *l* after..................... Deut 12:15   183
whatsoever thy soul *l* after..................... Deut 12:20   183
gates whatsoever thy soul *l* after .... Deut 12:21   183
for whatsoever thy soul *l* after .... Deut 14:26   183
For the flesh *l* against the .... Gal 5:17   1937
that dwelleth in us *l* to envy.................. Jas 4:5   1971

LUSTING
that was among them fell a *l* .... Num 11:4   8378

LUSTS
the *l* of other things entering in .... Mk 4:19   1939
the *l* of your father ye will do .... Jn 8:44   1939
through the *l* of their own hearts .... Rom 1:24   1939
should obey it in the *l* thereof................ Rom 6:12   1939
flesh, to fulfil the *l* thereof .... Rom 13:14   1939
flesh with the affections and *l*................ Gal 5:24   1939
times past in the *l* of our flesh .... Eph 2:3   1939
according to the deceitful *l* .... Eph 4:22   1939
and into many foolish and hurtful *l*........ 1Ti 6:9   1939
Flee also youthful *l* 2Ti 2:22   1939
with sins, led away with divers *l* 2Ti 3:6   1939
but after their own *l* shall they 2Ti 4:3   1939
denying ungodliness and worldly *l* .... Titus 2:12   1939
deceived, serving divers *l* .... Titus 3:3   1939
even of your *l* that war in your .... Jas 4:1   2237
ye may consume it upon your *l*............... Jas 4:3   2237
to the former *l* in your ignorance 1Pet 1:14   1939
pilgrims, abstain from fleshly *l*............... 1Pet 2:11   1939
time in the flesh to the *l* of men 1Pet 4:2   1939

we walked in lasciviousness, *l* 1Pet 4:3   1939
allure through the *l* of the flesh 2Pet 2:18   1939
walking after their own *l* 2Pet 3:3   1939
walking after their own *l* .... Jude 16   1939
walk after their own ungodly *l* .... Jude 18   1939

LUSTY
about ten thousand men, all *l* .... Judg 3:29   8082

LUZ *(luz)* See BETH-EL.
   1. A Cananite city.
city was called *L* at the first .... Gen 28:19   3870
So Jacob came to *L*, which is in .... Gen 35:6   3870
me at *L* in the land of Canaan .... Gen 48:3   3870
And goeth out from Beth-el to *L* .... Josh 16:2   3870
toward *L*, to the side of *L* .... Josh 18:13   3870
the name of the city before was *L*.......... Judg 1:23   3870
   2. A Hittite city.
and called the name thereof *L* .... Judg 1:26   3870

LYCAONIA *(li-ca-o'-ne-ah)* A Roman province in Asia
   Minor.
unto Lystra and Derbe, cities of *L* .... Acts 14:6   3071
voices, saying in the speech of *L* .... Acts 14:11   3071

LYCAONIAN See LYCAONIA.

LYCIA *(lish'-e-ah)* A Roman province in Asia Minor.
we came to Myra, a city of *L* .... Acts 27:5   3073

LYDDA *(lid'-dah)* See LOD. *A city in Judea.*
to the saints which dwelt at *L* .... Acts 9:32   3069
And all that dwelt at *L* and Saron .... Acts 9:35   3069
forasmuch as *L* was nigh to Joppa, ... Acts 9:38   3069

LYDIA *(lid'-e-ah)* See LUDIM, LYDIANS.
   1. A people in North Africa.
Ethiopia, and Libya, and *L*, and all .... Eze 30:5   3865
   2. A Christian woman.
And a certain woman named *L* .... Acts 16:14   3070
and entered into the house of *L* .... Acts 16:40   3070

LYDIANS *(lid'-e-uns)* Same as Lydia 1.
and the *L*, that handle and bend the ...... Jer 46:9   3866

LYING
three flocks of sheep *l* by it .... Gen 29:2   7257
Israel in *l* with Jacob's daughter............ Gen 34:7   7901
hateth thee *l* under his burden .... Ex 23:5   7257
that hath known man by *l* with him....... Num 31:17   4904
not known a man by *l* with him .... Num 31:18   4904
had not known man by *l* with him .... Num 31:35   4904
l in the field, and it be not .... Deut 21:1   5307
If a man be found *l* with a woman .... Deut 22:22   7901
were with him, from *l* in wait .... Judg 9:35
Now there were men *l* in wait .... Judg 16:9
known no man by *l* with any male .... Judg 21:12   4904
I will be a *l* spirit in the mouth 1Kin 22:22   8267
the LORD hath put a *l* spirit in 1Kin 22:23   8267
be a *l* spirit in the mouth of all 2Chr 18:21   8267
the LORD hath put a *l* spirit in 2Chr 18:22   8267
hated them that regard *l* vanities .... Ps 31:6   7723
Let the *l* lips be put to silence................ Ps 31:18   8267
and *l* rather than to speak .... Ps 52:3   8267
for cursing and *l* which they speak .... Ps 59:12   3585
spoken against me with a *l* tongue .... Ps 109:2   8267
Remove from me the way of *l*................. Ps 119:29   8267
I hate and abhor *l*................................. Ps 119:163   8267
my soul, O LORD, from *l* lips.................. Ps 120:2   8267
my *l* down, and art acquainted with .... Ps 139:3   7252
a *l* tongue, and hands that shed .... Prov 6:17   8267
He hideth hatred with *l* lips .... Prov 10:18   8267
but a *l* tongue is but for a...................... Prov 12:19   8267
L lips are abomination to the .... Prov 12:22   8267
A righteous man hateth *l* .... Prov 13:5
much less do *l* lips a prince .... Prov 17:7   8267
a *l* tongue is a vanity tossed to............... Prov 21:6   8267
A *l* tongue hateth those that are .... Prov 26:28   8267
l children, children that will .... Is 30:9   3586
to destroy the poor with *l* words............ Is 32:7   8267
l down, loving to slumber .... Is 56:10   7901
l against the LORD, and departing .... Is 59:13   3584
Trust ye not in *l* words, saying............... Jer 7:4   8267
Behold, ye trust in *l* words .... Jer 7:8   8267
have spoken *l* words in my name, ... Jer 29:23   8267
was unto me as a bear *l* in wait .... Lam 3:10
l divination, saying, The LORD............... Eze 13:7   3577
have ye not spoken a *l* divination........... Eze 13:7   3577
by your *l* to my people that hear .... Eze 13:19   3576
for ye have prepared *l* and corrupt .... Dan 2:9   3538
By swearing, and *l*, and killing, and....... Hos 4:2   3584
They that observe *l* vanities .... Jonah 2:8   7723
man sick of the palsy, *l* on a bed........... Mt 9:2   906
in where the damsel was *l*...................... Mk 5:40   345

swaddling clothes, *l* in a manger ....Lk 2:12   2749
Joseph, and the babe *l* in a manger ....Lk 2:16   2749
He then *l* on Jesus' breast saith..............Jn 13:25   1968
in, saw the linen clothes *l* ....Jn 20:5   2749
not *l* with the linen clothes, but ....Jn 20:7   2749
me by the *l* in wait of the Jews................Acts 20:19
son heard of their *l* in wait ....Acts 23:16
Wherefore putting away *l*, speak ....Eph 4:25   5579
all power and signs and *l* wonders, ...2Th 2:9   5579

LYSANIAS (*li-sa'-ne-as*) *Governor of Abilene.*
L the tetrarch of Abilene,.........................Lk 3:1   3078

LYSIAS (*lis'-e-as*) *A Roman commander.*
Claudius *L* unto the most ....Acts 23:26   3079
the chief captain *L* came upon us...........Acts 24:7   3079
When *L* the chief captain shall...............Acts 24:22   3079

LYSTRA (*lis'-trah*) *A city in Lycaonia.*
were ware of it, and fled unto *L* ....Acts 14:6   3082
And there sat a certain man at *L* ....Acts 14:8   3082
many, they returned again to *L* ....Acts 14:21   3082
Then came he to Derbe and *L*.................Acts 16:1   3082
of by the brethren that were at *L*............Acts 16:2   3082
me at Antioch, at Iconium, at *L* 2Ti 3:11   3082

M

MAACAH (*ma'-a-kah*) See Maachah.
   1. A wife of David.
Absalom the son of *M* the daughter........2Sa 3:3   4601
   2. A king of Maacah 3.
of king *M* a thousand men, and of 2Sa 10:6   4601
   3. A district of Syria.
and of Rehob, and Ish-tob, and *M* 2Sa 10:8   4601

MAACATH See Maachathite.

MAACATHITE See Maachathite.

MAACHAH (*ma'-a-kah*) See Beth-maachah, Maachah,
   Maachathite, Syria-maachah.
   1. A son of Nahor.
and Gaham, and Thahash, and *M* ....Gen 22:24   4601
   2. Father of Achish.
unto Achish son of *M* king of Gath 1Kin 2:39   4601
   3. Wife of King Rehoboam.
And his mother's name was *M* 1Kin 15:2   4601
And his mother's name was *M* 1Kin 15:10   4601
after her he took *M* the daughter 2Chr 11:20   4601
Rehoboam loved *M* the daughter of........2Chr 11:21   4601
Abijah the son of *M* the chief 2Chr 11:22   4601
   4. Mother of King Asa.
also *M* his mother, even her he...............1Kin 15:13   4601
also concerning *M* the mother of 2Chr 15:16   4601
   5. Concubine of Caleb.
M, Caleb's concubine, bare Sheber 1Chr 2:48   4601
   6. A wife of David.
Absalom the son of *M* the daughter........1Chr 3:2   4601
   7. A wife of Machir.
whose sister's name was *M* 1Chr 7:15   4601
M the wife of Machir bare a son,.............1Chr 7:16   4601
   8. Wife of Jehiel.
whose wife's name was *M* 1Chr 8:29   4601
Jehiel, whose wife's name was *M* 1Chr 9:35   4601
   9. Father of Hanan.
Hanan the son of *M*, and Joshaphat.......1Chr 11:43   4601
   10. A district of Syria.
chariots, and the king of *M* 1Chr 19:7   4601
   11. Father of Shephatiah.
Shephatiah the son of *M*...........................1Chr 27:16   4601

MAACHATHI (*ma-ak'-a-thi*) See Maachathite. *Inhab-*
   itants of Maachah 10.
unto the coasts of Geshuri and *M* ....Deut 3:14   4602

MAACHATHITE (*ma-ak'-a-thite*) See Maachathi, Maachathites. *Same as Maachathi.*
son of Ahasbai, the son of the *M* 2Sa 23:34   4602
and Jaazaniah the son of a *M* 2Kin 25:23   4602
the Garmite, and Eshtemoa the *M* 1Chr 4:19   4602
and Jezaniah the son of a *M* ....Jer 40:8   4602

MAACHATHITES
border of the Geshurites and the *M* ....Josh 12:5   4602
the border of the Geshurites and *M* ....Josh 13:11   4602
not the Geshurites, nor the *M* ....Josh 13:13   4602
the *M* dwell among the Israelites............Josh 13:13   4602

MAADAI (*ma'-a-dahee*) *Married a foreigner in exile.*
M, Amram, and Uel,................................Ezr 10:34   4572

MAADIAH (*ma-a-di'-ah*) See Moadiah. *A priest with*
   Zerubbabel.
Miamin, *M*, Bilgah, ...Neh 12:5   4573

MAAI (*ma'-ahee*) *A priest.*
and Azarael, Milalai, Gilalai, *M* ....Neh 12:36   4597

MAALEH-ACRABBIM (*ma'-a-leh-ac-rab'-bim*) See Akrabbim. *A pass on Judah's southern border.*
went out to the south side to *M*..............Josh 15:3   4610

MAARATH (*ma'-a-rath*) *A city in Judah.*
And *M*, and Beth-anoth, and Eltekon .....Josh 15:59   4638

MAAREH-GEBA See Gibeah.

MAASAI See Maasiai.

MAASEIAH (*ma-a-si'-ah*).
   1. A priest who relocated the Ark.
and Unni, Eliab, and Benaiah, and *M* 1Chr 15:18   4641
Jehiel, and Unni, and Eliab, and *M* 1Chr 15:20   4641
   2. Son of Adaiah.
Obed, and *M* the son of Adaiah, and......2Chr 23:1   4641
   3. An officer of King Uzziah.
M the ruler, under the hand of 2Chr 26:11   4641
   4. A son of King Ahaz.
slew *M* the king's son, and Azrikam.......2Chr 28:7   4641
   5. A governor of Jerusalem.
M the governor of the city, and 2Chr 34:8   4641
   6. A priest who married a foreigner.
M, and Eliezer, and Jarib, and ....Ezr 10:18   4641
   7. A priest of the Harim family.
M, and Elijah, and Shemaiah, and ....Ezr 10:21   4641
   8. A priest of the Pashur family.
Elioenai, *M*, Ishmael, Nethaneel,............Ezr 10:22   4641
   9. A priest of the Pahath-moab family.
Adna, and Chelal, Benaiah, *M* ....Ezr 10:30   4641
   10. Father of Azariah.
M the son of Ananiah by his house ....Neh 3:23   4641
   11. A priest with Ezra.
and Urijah, and Hilkiah, and *M* ....Neh 8:4   4641
   12. Another priest with Ezra.
Akkub, Shabbethai, Hodijah, *M*...............Neh 8:7   4641
   13. An Israelite who renewed the covenant.
Rehum, Hashabnah, *M*,...........................Neh 10:25   4641
   14. A family of exiles.
M the son of Baruch, the son of ....Neh 11:5   4641
   15. A descendant of Benjamin.
the son of Kolaiah, the son of *M* ....Neh 11:7   4641
   16. A priest who dedicated the wall.
Eliakim, *M*, Miniamin, Michaiah,...........Neh 12:41   4641
   17. Another priest who dedicated the wall.
And *M*, and Shemaiah, and Eleazar ....Neh 12:42   4641
   18. Father of Zephaniah.
Zephaniah the son of *M* the priest..........Jer 21:1   4641
Zephaniah the son of *M* the priest..........Jer 29:25   4641
Zephaniah the son of *M* the priest..........Jer 37:3   4641
   19. Father of Zedekiah.
and of Zedekiah the son of *M* ....Jer 29:21   4641
   20. A Temple officer.
chamber of *M* the son of Shallum ....Jer 35:4   4641
   21. Grandfather of Baruch.
the son of Neriah, the son of *M* ....Jer 32:12   4271
the son of Neriah, the son of *M* ....Jer 51:59   4271

MAASIAI (*ma-a'-see-ahee*) *A family of exiles.*
M the son of Adiel, the son of 1Chr 9:12   4640

MAATH (*ma'-ath*) *Father of Nagge; ancestor of Jesus.*
Which was the son of *M*, which was ......Lk 3:26   3092

MAAZ (*ma'-az*) *A son of Ram.*
firstborn of Jerahmeel were, *M* 1Chr 2:27   4619

MAAZIAH (*ma-a-zi'-ah*)
   1. A sanctuary servant.
the four and twentieth to *M*......................1Chr 24:18   4590
   2. A priest who renewed the covenant.
M, Bilgai, Shemaiah ....Neh 10:8   4590

MACBENNAH See Machbennah.

MACEDONIA (*mas-e-do'-nee-ah*) See Macedonian. *A*
   Roman province north of Greece.
There stood a man of *M*, and prayed .....Acts 16:9   3110
him, saying, Come over into *M*................Acts 16:9   3109
we endeavoured to go into *M* ....Acts 16:10   3109
the chief city that part of *M* ....Acts 16:12   3109
and Timotheus were come from *M* ....Acts 18:5   3109
when he had passed through *M* ....Acts 19:21   3109
So he sent into *M* two of them ....Acts 19:22   3109
Gaius and Aristarchus, men of *M*...........Acts 19:29   3110

and departed for to go into *M*	Acts 20:1	3109
he purposed to return through *M*	Acts 20:3	3109
For it hath pleased them of *M*	Rom 15:26	3109
you, when I shall pass through *M*	1Cor 16:5	3109
for I do pass through *M*	1Cor 16:5	3109
And to pass by you into *M*	2Cor 1:16	3109
to come again out of *M* unto you	2Cor 1:16	3109
them, I went from thence into *M*	2Cor 2:13	3109
For, when we were come into *M*	2Cor 7:5	3109
God bestowed on the churches of *M*	2Cor 8:1	3109
which I boast of you to them of *M*	2Cor 9:2	3110
haply if they of *M* come with me	2Cor 9:4	3110
which came from *M* supplied	2Cor 11:9	3109
from Philippi, a city of *M*	2Cor s	3109
gospel, when I departed from *M*	Phil 4:15	3109
to all that believe in *M*	1Th 1:7	3109
word of the Lord not only in *M*	1Th 1:8	3109
the brethren which are in all *M*	1Th 4:10	3109
at Ephesus, when I went into *M*	1Ti 1:3	3109
the Cretians, from Nicopolis of *M*	Titus s	3109

MACEDONIAN *(mas-e-do'-nee-an) An inhabitant of Macedonia.*

a *M* of Thessalonica, being with	Acts 27:2	3110

MACHBANAI *(mak'-ba-nahee) A warrior in David's army.*

the tenth, *M* the eleventh	1Chr 12:13	4344

MACHBANNAI See MACEBANAI.

MACHBENA See MACHBENAH.

MACHBENAH *(mak'-be-nah) A descendant of Caleb.*

Madmannah, Sheva the father of *M*	1Chr 2:49	4343

MACHI *(ma'-ki) Father of Geuel.*

tribe of Gad, Geuel the son of *M*	Num 13:15	4352

MACHIR *(ma'-kur) See MACHIRITE.*
  1. Son of Manasseh.

the children also of *M* the son of	Gen 50:23	4353
of *M*, the family of the	Num 26:29	4353
and *M* begat Gilead	Num 26:29	4353
the son of Gilead, the son of *M*	Num 27:1	4353
the children of *M* the son of	Num 32:39	4353
Gilead unto *M* the son of Manasseh	Num 32:40	4353
children of Gilead, the son of *M*	Num 36:1	4353
And I gave Gilead unto *M*	Deut 3:15	4353
children of *M* the son of Manasseh	Josh 13:31	4353
children of *M* by their families	Josh 13:31	4353
for *M* the firstborn of Manasseh	Josh 17:1	4353
the son of Gilead, the son of *M*	Josh 17:3	4353
out of *M* came down governors, and	Judg 5:14	4353
of *M* the father of Gilead	1Chr 2:21	4353
sons of *M* the father of Gilead	1Chr 2:23	4353
bare *M* the father of Gilead	1Chr 7:14	4353
M took to wife the sister of	1Chr 7:15	4353
Maachah the wife of *M* bare a son	1Chr 7:16	4353
the sons of Gilead, the son of *M*	1Chr 7:17	4353

  2. Son of Ammiel.

Behold, he is in the house of *M*	2Sa 9:4	4353
fetched him out of the house of *M*	2Sa 9:5	4353
M the son of Ammiel of Lo-debar,	2Sa 17:27	4353

MACHIRITES *(ma'-kur-ites) Descendants of Machir 1.*

of Machir, the family of the *M*	Num 26:29	4354

MACHNADEBAI *(mak-nad'-e-bahee) Married a foreigner in exile.*

M, Shashai, Sharai,	Ezr 10:40	4367

MACHPELAH *(mak-pe'-lah) Burial place of Abraham.*

That he may give me the cave of *M*	Gen 23:9	4375
field of Ephron, which was in *M*	Gen 23:17	4375
of the field of *M* before Mamre	Gen 23:19	4375
buried him in the cave of *M*	Gen 25:9	4375
cave that is in the field of *M*	Gen 49:30	4375
him in the cave of the field of *M*	Gen 50:13	4375

MAD

So that thou shalt be *m* for the	Deut 28:34	7696
feigned himself *m* in their hands	1Sa 21:13	1984
servants, Lo, ye see the man is *m*	1Sa 21:14	7696
Have I need of *m* men, that ye	1Sa 21:15	7696
to play the *m* man in my presence	1Sa 21:15	7696
came this *m* fellow to thee	2Kin 9:11	7696
they that are *m* against me are	Ps 102:8	1984
As a *m* man who casteth firebrands	Prov 26:18	3856
I said of laughter, It is *m*	Eccl 2:2	1984
oppression maketh a wise man *m*	Eccl 7:7	1984
the liars, and maketh diviners *m*	Is 44:25	1984
shall drink, and be moved, and be *m*	Jer 25:16	7696
the Lord, for every man that is *m*	Jer 29:26	7696
they are *m* upon their idols	Jer 50:38	1984
therefore the nations are *m*	Jer 51:7	1984

is a fool, the spiritual man is *m*	Hos 9:7	7696
said, He hath a devil, and is *m*	Jn 10:20	3105
And they said unto her, Thou art *m*	Acts 12:15	3105
being exceedingly *m* against them	Acts 26:11	1693
much learning doth make thee *m*	Acts 26:24	1519,3130
But he said, I am not *m*, most	Acts 26:25	3105
will they not say that ye are *m*	1Cor 14:23	3105

MADAI *(ma'-dahee) See MEDE, MEDIA. Son of Japheth.*

Gomer, and Magog, and *M*, and Javan,	Gen 10:2	4074
Gomer, and Magog, and *M*, and Javan,	1Chr 1:5	4074

MADE See APPENDIX.

MADEST See APPENDIX.

MADIAN *(ma'-de-an) See MIDIAN. Same as Midian 2.*

was a stranger in the land of *M*	Acts 7:29	3099

MADMANNAH *(mad-man'-nah)*
  1. A city in Judah.

And Ziklag, and *M*, and Sansannah,	Josh 15:31	4089

  2. Grandson of Caleb.

bare also Shaaph the father of *M*	1Chr 2:49	4089

MADMEN *(mad'-men) See MADMENAH. A Moabite city.*

Also thou shalt be cut down, O *M*	Jer 48:2	4086

MADMENAH *(mad-me'-nah) See MADMEN. A city in Benjamin.*

M is removed	Is 10:31	4088

MADNESS

The LORD shall smite thee with *m*	Deut 28:28	7697
to know wisdom, and to know *m*	Eccl 1:17	1947
myself to behold wisdom, and *m*	Eccl 2:12	1947
folly, even of foolishness and *m*	Eccl 7:25	1947
m is in their heart while they	Eccl 9:3	1947
end of his talk is mischievous *m*	Eccl 10:13	1948
astonishment, and his rider with *m*	Zec 12:4	7697
And they were filled with *m*	Lk 6:11	454
voice forbad the *m* of the prophet	2Pet 2:16	3913

MADON *(ma'-don) A Canaanite city.*

that he sent to Jobab king of *M*	Josh 11:1	4068
The king of *M*, one	Josh 12:19	4068

MAGADAN See MAGDALA.

MAGBISH *(mag'-bish) A family of exiles.*

The children of *M*, an hundred	Ezr 2:30	4019

MAGDALA *(mag'-da-lah) See MAGDALENE. A city in Galilee.*

and came into the coasts of *M*	Mt 15:39	3093

MAGDALENE *(mag'-da-leen) A woman acquaintance of Jesus.*

Among which was Mary *M*, and Mary	Mt 27:56	3094
And there was Mary *M*, and the other	Mt 27:61	3094
day of the week, came Mary *M*	Mt 28:1	3094
among whom was Mary *M*, and Mary	Mk 15:40	3094
And Mary *M* and Mary the mother of	Mk 15:47	3094
when the sabbath was past, Mary *M*	Mk 16:1	3094
week, he appeared first to Mary *M*	Mk 16:9	3094
and infirmities, Mary called *M*	Lk 8:2	3094
It was Mary *M*, and Joanna, and Mary	Lk 24:10	3094
the wife of Cleophas, and Mary *M*	Jn 19:25	3094
of the week cometh Mary *M* early	Jn 20:1	3094
Mary *M* came and told the disciples	Jn 20:18	3094

MAGDIEL *(mag'-de-el) A duke of Edom.*

Duke *M*, duke Iram	Gen 36:43	4025
Duke *M*, duke Iram	1Chr 1:54	4025

MAGICIAN

that asked such things at any *m*	Dan 2:10	2749

MAGICIANS

and called for all the *m* of Egypt	Gen 41:8	2748
and I told this unto the *m*	Gen 41:24	2748
now the *m* of Egypt, they also did	Ex 7:11	2748
the *m* of Egypt did so with their	Ex 7:22	2748
And the *m* did so with their	Ex 8:7	2748
And the *m* did so with their	Ex 8:18	2748
Then the *m* said unto Pharaoh,	Ex 8:19	2748
the *m* could not stand before	Ex 9:11	2748
for the boil was upon the *m*	Ex 9:11	2748
ten times better than all the *m*	Dan 1:20	2748
the king commanded to call the *m*	Dan 2:2	2748
wise men, the astrologers, the *m*	Dan 2:27	2749
Then came in the *m*, the	Dan 4:7	2749
O Belteshazzar, master of the *m*	Dan 4:9	2749
thy father, made master of the *m*	Dan 5:11	2749

MAGISTRATE

and there was no *m* in the land	Judg 18:7	3423,6114
with thine adversary to the *m*	Lk 12:58	758

M

MAGISTRATES

God, that is in thine hand, set *m*	Ezr 7:25	8200
unto the synagogues, and unto *m*	Lk 12:11	*746*
And brought them to the, *m*, saying,	Acts 16:20	4755
the *m* rent off their clothes, and	Acts 16:22	4755
the *m* sent the serjeants, saying,	Acts 16:35	4755
The *m* have sent to let you go	Acts 16:36	4755
told these words unto the *m*	Acts 16:38	4755
and powers, to obey *m*, to be ready	Titus 3:1	*3980*

MAGNIFICAL

for the LORD must be exceeding *m*	1Chr 22:5	1431

MAGNIFICENCE

her *m* should be destroyed, whom	Acts 19:27	*3168*

MAGNIFIED

sight, and thou hast *m* thy mercy	Gen 19:19	1431
On that day the LORD *m* Joshua in	Josh 4:14	1431
And let thy name be *m* for ever	2Sa 7:26	1431
that thy name may be *m* for ever	1Chr 17:24	1431
the LORD *m* Solomon exceedingly in	1Chr 29:25	1431
with him, and *m* him exceedingly	2Chr 1:1	1431
so that he was *m* in the sight of	2Chr 32:23	5375
continually, Let the LORD be *m*	Ps 35:27	1431
say continually, The LORD be *m*	Ps 40:16	1431
say continually, Let God be *m*	Ps 70:4	1431
for thou hast *m* thy word above	Ps 138:2	1431
for he *m* himself against the LORD	Jer 48:26	1431
because he hath *m* himself against	Jer 48:42	1431
for the enemy hath *m* himself	Lam 1:9	1431
he *m* himself even to the prince	Dan 8:11	1431
m themselves against their border	Zeph 2:8	1431
m themselves against the people	Zeph 2:10	1431
The LORD will be *m* from the	Mal 1:5	1431
but the people *m* them	Acts 5:13	3170
the name of the Lord Jesus was *m*	Acts 19:17	3170
also Christ shall be *m* in my body	Phil 1:20	3170

MAGNIFY

This day will I begin to *m* thee	Josh 3:7	1431
is man, that thou shouldest *m* him	Job 7:17	1431
If indeed ye will *m* yourselves	Job 19:5	1431
Remember that thou *m* his work	Job 36:24	7679
O *m* the LORD with me, and let us	Ps 34:3	1431
dishonour that *m* themselves	Ps 35:26	1431
they *m* themselves against me	Ps 38:16	1431
me that did *m* himself against me	Ps 55:12	1431
will *m* him with thanksgiving	Ps 69:30	1431
or shall the saw *m* itself against	Is 10:15	1431
he will *m* the law, and make it	Is 42:21	1431
Thus will I *m* myself, and sanctify	Eze 38:23	1431
he shall *m* himself in his heart,	Dan 8:25	1431
m himself above every god, and	Dan 11:36	1431
for he shall *m* himself above all	Dan 11:37	1431
do not themselves against Judah	Zec 12:7	1431
said, My soul doth *m* the Lord	Lk 1:46	3170
them speak with tongues, and *m* God	Acts 10:46	3170
of the Gentiles, I *m* mine office	Rom 11:13	*1392*

MAGOG (ma'-gog)

1. A son of Japheth.

Gomer, and *M*, and Madai, and Javan,	Gen 10:2	4031
Gomer, and *M*, and Madai, and Javan,	1Chr 1:5	4031

2. Descendants of Magog.

face against Gog, the land of *M*	Eze 38:2	4031
And I will send a fire on *M*	Eze 39:6	4031
quarters of the earth, Gog and *M*	Rev 20:8	*3098*

MAGOR-MISSABIB (ma'-gor-mis'-sa-bib) *A symbolic name of Pashur.*

not called thy name Pashur, but *M*	Jer 20:3	4036

MAGPIASH (mag'-pe-ash) *A chief Israelite who renewed the covenant.*

M, Meshullam, Hezir,	Neh 10:20	4047

MAHALAH (ma'-ha-lah) See MAHLAH. *Great-grandson of Manasseh.*

bare Ishod, and Abiezer, and *M*	1Chr 7:18	4244

MAHALALEEL (ma-hal'-a-le-el) See MALELEEL.

1. Son of Cainan.

lived seventy years, and begat *M*	Gen 5:12	4111
after he begat *M* eight hundred	Gen 5:13	4111
M lived sixty and five years, and	Gen 5:15	4111
M lived after he begat Jared	Gen 5:16	4111
all the days of *M* were eight	Gen 5:17	4111
Kenan, *M*, Jered,	1Chr 1:2	4111

2. A family of exiles.

son of Shephatiah, the son of *M*	Neh 11:4	4111

MAHALALEL See MAHALEEL.

MAHALATH (ma'-ha-lath) See BASHEMATH.

1. A daughter of Ishmael.

he had *M* the daughter of Ishmael	Gen 28:9	4258

2. A granddaughter of David.

Rehoboam took him *M* the daughter	2Chr 11:18	4258

3. A musical choir.

To the chief Musician upon *M*	Ps 53:t	4257
chief Musician upon *M* Leannoth	Ps 88:t	4257

MAHALI (ma'-ha-li) See MAHLI. *Same as Lahli 1.*

sons of Merari; *M* and Mushi	Ex 6:19	4249

MAHANAIM (ma-ha-na'-im) *A town east of the Jordan.*

called the name of that place *M*	Gen 32:2	4266
from *M* unto the border of Debir	Josh 13:26	4266
And their coast was from *M*	Josh 13:30	4266
and *M* with her suburbs,	Josh 21:38	4266
of Saul, and brought him over to *M*	2Sa 2:8	4266
Saul, went out from *M* to Gibeon	2Sa 2:12	4266
all Bithron, and they came to *M*	2Sa 2:29	4266
Then David came to *M*	2Sa 17:24	4266
to pass, when David was come to *M*	2Sa 17:27	4266
of sustenance while he lay at *M*	2Sa 19:32	4266
curse in the day when I went to *M*	1Kin 2:8	4266
Ahinadab the son of Iddo had *M*	1Kin 4:14	4266
suburbs, and *M* with her suburbs,	1Chr 6:80	4266

MAHANEH-DAN (ma'-ha-neh-dan) *A place in Judah.*

called that place *M* unto this day	Judg 18:12	4265

MAHARAI (ma'-ha-rahee) *A warrior of David.*

the Ahohite, *M* the Netophathite,	2Sa 23:28	4121
M the Netophathite, Heled the son	1Chr 11:30	4121
month was *M* the Netophathite	1Chr 27:13	4121

MAHATH (ma'-hath)

1. A descendant of Kohath.

the son of Elkanah, the son of *M*	1Chr 6:35	4287
M the son of Amasai, and Joel the	2Chr 29:12	4287

2. A Temple servant.

and Eliel, and Ismachiah, and *M*	2Chr 31:13	4287

MAHAVITE (ma'-ha-vite) *Family name of Eliel.*

Eliel the *M*, and Jeribai, and	1Chr 11:46	4233

MAHAZIOTH (ma-ha'-ze-oth) *A sanctuary servant.*

Mallothi, Hothir, and *M*	1Chr 25:4	4238
The three and twentieth to *M*	1Chr 25:30	4238

MAHER-SHALAL-HASH-BAZ (ma'-her-sha'-lal-hash'-baz) *A son of Isaiah.*

it with a man's pen concerning *M*	Is 8:1	4122
the LORD to me, Call his name *M*	Is 8:3	4122

MAHLAH (mah'-lah) *A daughter of Zelophehad.*

daughters of Zelophehad were *M*	Num 26:33	4244
M, Noah, and Hoglah, and Milcah	Num 27:1	4244
For *M*, Tirzah, and Hoglah, and	Num 36:11	4244
are the names of his daughters, *M*	Josh 17:3	4244

MAHLI (mah'-li) See MAHALI, MAHLITES.

1. Son of Merari.

their families; *M*, and Mushi	Num 3:20	4249
of Merari; *M*, and Mushi	1Chr 6:19	4249
M, Libni his son, Shimei his son,	1Chr 6:29	4249
M, and Mushi. The sons of *M*	1Chr 23:21	4249
The sons of Merari were *M*	1Chr 24:26	4249
Of *M* came Eleazar, who had no	1Chr 24:28	4249
understanding, of the sons of *M*	Ezr 8:18	4249

2. Son of Mushi.

The son of *M*, the son of Mushi,	1Chr 6:47	4249
M, and Eder, and Jeremoth, three	1Chr 23:23	4249
M, and Eder, and Jerimoth	1Chr 24:30	4249

MAHLITES (mah'-lites) *Descendants of Mahli 1.*

Of Merari was the family of the *M*	Num 3:33	4250
Hebronites, the family of the *M*	Num 26:58	4250

MAHLON (mah'-lon) See MAHLON'S. *A son of Naomi.*

and the name of his two sons *M*	Ruth 1:2	4248
And *M* and Chilion died also both of	Ruth 1:5	4248
Ruth the Moabitess, the wife of *M*	Ruth 4:10	4248

MAHLON'S (mah'-lons)

and all that was Chilion's and *M*	Ruth 4:9	4248

MAHOL (ma'-hol) *Father of some wise men.*

Chalcol, and Darda, the sons of *M*	1Kin 4:31	4235

MAHSEIAH See MASEIAH.

MAID

I pray thee, go in unto my *m*	Gen 16:2	8198
took Hagar her *m* the Egyptian	Gen 16:3	8198
I have given my *m* into thy bosom	Gen 16:5	8198
Behold, thy *m* is in thy hand	Gen 16:6	8198
And he said, Hagar, Sarai's *m*	Gen 16:8	8198
Leah Zilpah his *m* for an handmaid	Gen 29:24	8198
Bilhah his handmaid to be her *m*	Gen 29:29	8198
And she said, Behold my *m* Bilhah	Gen 30:3	519
Bilhah Rachel's *m* conceived again	Gen 30:7	8198
bearing, she took Zilpah her *m*	Gen 30:9	8198

Zilpah Leah's *m* bare Jacob a son .... Gen 30:10   8198
Zilpah Leah's *m* bare Jacob a .... Gen 30:12   8198
flags, she sent her *m* to fetch it .... Ex 2:5   519
the *m* went and called the child's .... Ex 2:8   5959
a man smite his servant, or his *m* .... Ex 21:20   519
his servant, or the eye of his *m* .... Ex 21:26   519
if a man entice a *m* that is not .... Ex 22:16   1330
But if she bear a *m* child .... Lev 12:5   5347
and for thy servant, and for thy *m* .... Lev 25:6   519
came to her, I found her not a *m* .... Deut 22:14   1331
I found not thy daughter a *m* .... Deut 22:17   1331
of the land of Israel a little *m* 2Kin 5:2   5291
thus said the *m* that is of the 2Kin 5:4   5291
the *m* was fair and beautiful .... Est 2:7   5291
why then should I think upon a *m* .... Job 31:1   1330
and the way of a man with a *m* .... Prov 30:19   5959
as with the *m*, so with her .... Is 24:2   8198
Can a *m* forget her ornaments, or .... Jer 2:32   1330
in pieces the young man and the *m* ...... Jer 51:22   1330
father will go in unto the same *m* .... Amos 2:7   5291
for the *m* is not dead, but .... Mt 9:24   2877
her by the hand, and the *m* arose .... Mt 9:25   2877
into the porch, another *m* saw him .... Mt 26:71
a *m* saw him again, and began to .... Mk 14:69   *3814*
by the hand, and called, saying, *M* .... Lk 8:54   *3816*
But a certain *m* beheld him as he .... Lk 22:56   *3814*

MAIDEN

I have given my *m* to my husband .... Gen 30:18   8198
Behold, here is my daughter a *m* .... Judg 19:24   1330
no compassion upon young man or *m* ... 2Chr 36:17   1330
let the *m* which pleaseth the king .... Est 2:4   5291
the *m* pleased him, and she .... Est 2:9   5291
thus came every *m* unto the king .... Est 2:13   5291
as the eyes of a *m* unto the hand .... Ps 123:2   8198
the father and the mother of the *m* .... Lk 8:51   *3816*

MAIDENS

her *m* walked along by the river's .... Ex 2:5   5291
but abide here fast by my *m* .... Ruth 2:8   5291
that thou go out with his *m* .... Ruth 2:22   5291
So she kept fast by the *m* of Boaz .... Ruth 2:23   5291
kindred, with whose *m* thou wast .... Ruth 3:2   5291
they found young *m* going out to 1Sa 9:11   5291
when many *m* were gathered .... Est 2:8   5291
as belonged to her, and seven *m* .... Est 2:9   5291
I also and my *m* will fast likewise .... Est 4:16   5291
or wilt thou bind him for thy *m* .... Job 41:5   5291
their *m* were not given to .... Ps 78:63   1330
Both young men, and *m* .... Ps 148:12   1330
She hath sent forth her *m* .... Prov 9:3   5291
and for the maintenance for thy *m* .... Prov 27:27   5291
household, and a portion to her *m* .... Prov 31:15   5291
I got me servants and *m*, and had .... Eccl 2:7   8198
but they shall take *m* of the seed .... Eze 44:22   1330
to beat the menservants and *m* .... Lk 12:45   *3814*

MAID'S

Now when every *m* turn was come to .... Est 2:12   5291

MAIDS

Beside their servants and their *m* .... Ezr 2:65   519
her *m* unto the best place of the .... Est 2:9   5291
So Esther's and her chamberlains ...... Est 4:4   5291
that dwell in mine house, and my *m* .... Job 19:15   519
the *m* in the cities of Judah .... Lam 5:11   1330
Slay utterly old and young, both *m* .... Eze 9:6   1330
her *m* shall lead her as with the .... Nah 2:7   519
men cheerful, and new wine the *m* .... Zec 9:17   1330
one of the *m* of the high priest .... Mk 14:66   *3814*

MAIDSERVANT

of the *m* that is behind the mill .... Ex 11:5   8198
thy manservant, nor thy *m* .... Ex 20:10   519
nor his manservant, nor his *m* .... Ex 20:17   519
a man sell his daughter to be a *m* .... Ex 21:7   519
ox shall push a manservant or a *m* .... Ex 21:32   519
nor thy manservant, nor thy *m* .... Deut 5:14   519
thy *m* may rest as well as thou .... Deut 5:14   519
or his manservant, or his *m* .... Deut 5:21   519
and thy manservant, and thy *m* .... Deut 12:18   519
also unto thy *m* thou shalt do .... Deut 15:17   519
and thy manservant, and thy *m* .... Deut 16:11   519
and thy manservant, and thy *m* .... Deut 16:14   519
made Abimelech, the son of his *m* .... Judg 9:18   519
cause of my manservant or of my *m* ...... Job 31:13   519
manservant, and every man his *m* .... Jer 34:9   8198
manservant, and every one his *m* .... Jer 34:10   8198

MAIDSERVANT'S

tooth, or his *m* tooth .... Ex 21:27   519

MAIDSERVANTS

and he asses, and menservants, and *m* . Gen 12:16   8198
Abimelech, and his wife, and his *m* .... Gen 20:17   519
and gold, and menservants, and *m* .... Gen 24:35   8198
and had much cattle, and *m* .... Gen 30:43   8198
and your menservants, and your *m* .... Deut 12:12   519
take your menservants, and your *m* 1Sa 8:16   8198
of the *m* which thou hast spoken 2Sa 6:22   519
and oxen, and menservants, and *m* 2Kin 5:26   8198
their manservants and their *m* .... Neh 7:67   519

MAIDSERVANTS'

tent, and into the two *m* tents .... Gen 31:33   519

MAIL

and he was armed with a coat of *m* 1Sa 17:5   7193
he armed him with a coat of *m* 1Sa 17:38   7193

MAIMED

Blind, or broken, or *m*, or having .... Lev 22:22   2782
that were lame, blind, dumb, *m* .... Mt 15:30   2948
the *m* to be whole, the lame to .... Mt 15:31   2948
thee to enter into life halt or *m* .... Mt 18:8   2948
for thee to enter into life *m* .... Mk 9:43   2948
a feast, call the poor, the *m* .... Lk 14:13   *376*
in hither the poor, and the *m* .... Lk 14:21   *376*

MAINSAIL

and hoised up the *m* to the wind .... Acts 27:40   *736*

MAINTAIN

supplication, and *m* their cause 1Kin 8:45   6213
dwelling place, and *m* their cause, ... 1Kin 8:49   6213
that he *m* the cause of his 1Kin 8:59   6213
to *m* the house of the LORD 1Chr 26:27   2388
supplication, and *m* their cause 2Chr 6:35   6213
m their cause, and forgive thy 2Chr 6:39   6213
but I will *m* mine own ways before .... Job 13:15   3198
I know that the LORD will *m* the .... Ps 140:12   6213
might be careful to *m* good works .... Titus 3:8   4291
let ours also learn to *m* good .... Titus 3:14   4291

MAINTAINED

For thou hast *m* my right and my .... Ps 9:4   6213

MAINTAINEST

thou *m* my lot .... Ps 16:5   8551

MAINTENANCE

Now because we have *m* from the .... Ezr 4:14   4415
for the *m* for thy maidens .... Prov 27:27   2416

MAJESTY

glory, and the victory, and the *m* 1Chr 29:11   1935
m as had not been on any king 1Chr 29:25   1935
of his excellent *m* many days .... Est 1:4   1420
with God is terrible in .... Job 37:22   1935
Deck thyself now with *m* and .... Job 40:10   1347
m hast thou laid upon him .... Ps 21:5   1926
voice of the LORD is full of *m* .... Ps 29:4   1926
mighty, with thy glory and thy *m* .... Ps 45:3   1926
in thy *m* ride prosperously .... Ps 45:4   1926
reigneth, he is clothed with *m* .... Ps 93:1   1348
Honour and *m* are before him .... Ps 96:6   1926
thou art clothed with honour and *m* .... Ps 104:1   1926
of the glorious honour of thy *m* .... Ps 145:5   1935
the glorious *m* of his kingdom .... Ps 145:12   1926
LORD, and for the glory of his *m* .... Is 2:10   1347
LORD, and for the glory of his *m* .... Is 2:19   1347
LORD, and for the glory of his *m* .... Is 2:21   1347
shall sing for the *m* of the LORD .... Is 24:14   1347
will not behold the *m* of the LORD .... Is 26:10   1348
of his ornament, he set it in *m* .... Eze 7:20   1347
power, and for the honour of my *m* .... Dan 4:30   1923
excellent *m* was added unto me .... Dan 4:36   7238
thy father a kingdom and *m* .... Dan 5:18   7238
for the *m* that he gave him, all .... Dan 5:19   7238
in the *m* of the name of the LORD .... Mic 5:4   1347
the right hand of the *M* on high .... Heb 1:3   *3172*
throne of the *M* in the heavens .... Heb 8:1   *3172*
but were eyewitnesses of his *m* 2Pet 1:16   *3168*
God our Saviour, be glory and *m* .... Jude 25   *3172*

MAKAZ (ma'-kaz) A town in Judah.

The son of Dekar, in *M*, and in 1Kin 4:9   4739

MAKE See APPENDIX.

MAKER See APPENDIX.

MAKERS

together that are *m* of idols .... Is 45:16   2796

MAKEST See APPENDIX.

MAKETH See APPENDIX.

M

MAKHELOTH (mak'-he-loth) *An Israelite encampment in the wilderness.*

from Haradah, and pitched in M .... Num 33:25   4721
And they removed from M, and .... Num 33:26   4721

MAKI See MACHI.

MAKING

task in m brick both yesterday .... Ex 5:14
in m war against it to take it, ... Deut 20:19
Now as they were m their hearts............ Judg 19:22
eating and drinking, and m merry 1Kin 4:20
m a noise with psalteries and 1Chr 15:28
in m known all these great things 1Chr 17:19
m confession to the LORD God of 2Chr 30:22
LORD is sure, m wise the simple............ Ps 19:7
of m many books there is no end.......... Eccl 12:12   6213
m a tinkling with their feet .... Is 3:16
m him very glad .... Jer 20:15
multitude of the wares of thy m .... Eze 27:16   4639
multitude of the wares of thy m .... Eze 27:18   4639
m supplication before his God .... Dan 6:11
swearing falsely in m a covenant .... Hos 10:4   3772
m the ephah small, and the shekel .... Amos 8:5
in m thee desolate because of thy .... Mic 6:13
minstrels and the people m a noise....... Mt 9:23   2350
M the word of God of none effect .... Mk 7:13   208
Father, m himself equal with God........ Jn 5:18   4160
M request, if by any means now at .... Rom 1:10   1189
as poor, yet m many rich........................ 2Cor 6:10   4148
m mention of you in my prayers .... Eph 1:16   4160
of twain one new man, so m peace .... Eph 2:15   4160
m melody in your heart to the .... Eph 5:19   5567
for you all m request with joy .... Phil 1:4   4160
m mention of you in our prayers............ 1Th 1:2   4160
m mention of thee always in my .... Philem 4   4160
m them an ensample unto those 2Pet 2:6   4160
have compassion, m a difference .... Jude 22   1252

MAKIR See MACHIR.

MAKIRITE See MACHIRITES.

MAKKEDAH (mak'-ke-dah) *A city in Judah.*

smote them to Azekah, and unto M .... Josh 10:10   4719
and hid themselves in a cave at M .... Josh 10:16   4719
are found hid in a cave at M .... Josh 10:17   4719
the camp to Joshua at M in peace.......... Josh 10:21   4719
And that day Joshua took M .... Josh 10:28   4719
he did to the king of M as he did .... Josh 10:28   4719
Then Joshua passed from M .... Josh 10:29   4719
The king of M, one .... Josh 12:16   4719
Beth-dagon, and Naamah, and M.......... Josh 15:41   4719

MAKTESH (mak'-tesh) *A district near Jerusalem.*

Howl, ye inhabitants of M....................... Zeph 1:11   4389

MALACHI (mal'-a-ki) *A prophet.*

word of the LORD to Israel by M .... Mal 1:1   4401

MALCAM See MALCHAM.

MALCHAM (mal'-kam) See MILCOM.
  1. Son of Shaharaim.

Jobab, and Zibia, and Mesha, and M 1Chr 8:9   4445
  2. An Ammonite idol.

by the LORD, and that swear by M .... Zeph 1:5   4445

MALCHIAH (mal-ki'-ah) See MALCHIJAH, MELCHIAH.
  1. Father of Baaseiah.

the son of Baaseiah, the son of M 1Chr 6:40   4441
  2. A descendant of Parosh.

Ramiah, and Jeziah, and M, and .... Ezr 10:25   4441
the son of Pashur, the son of M .... Neh 11:12   4441
  3. Another descendant of Parosh.

Eliezer, Ishijah, M, Shemaiah,................. Ezr 10:31   4441
  4. A repairer of Jerusalem's wall.

gate repaired M the son of Rechab .... Neh 3:14   4441
  5. Another repairer of Jerusalem's wall.

After him repaired M the .... Neh 3:31   4441
  6. A priest who aided Ezra.

hand, Pedaiah, and Mishael, and M .... Neh 8:4   4441
  7. A priest who dedicated the wall.

Shelemiah, and Pashur the son of M...... Jer 38:1   4441
dungeon of M the son of Hammelech ...... Jer 38:6   4441

MALCHIEL (mal'-ke-el) See MALCHIELITES. *A son of Beriah.*

Heber, and M .... Gen 46:17   4439
of M, the family of the.............................. Num 26:45   4439
Heber, and M, who is the father of 1Chr 7:31   4439

MALCHIELITES (mal'-ke-el-ites) *Descendants of Malchiel.*

of Malchiel, the family of the M .... Num 26:45   4440

MALCHIJAH (mal-ki'-jah) See MALCHIAH.
  1. A family of exiles.

the son of Pashur, the son of M 1Chr 9:12   4441
  2. A sanctuary servant.

The fifth to M, the sixth to 1Chr 24:9   4441
  3. Married a foreigner in exile.

and Miamin, and Eleazar, and M .... Ezr 10:25   4441
  4. A rebuilder of Jerusalem's wall.

M the son of Harim, and Hashub the ..... Neh 3:11   4441
  5. A priest who dedicated the wall.

Pashur, Amariah, M,................................. Neh 10:3   4441
and Uzzi, and Jehohanan, and M .... Neh 12:42   4441

MALCHIRAM (mal'-ki-ram) *A descendant of King Jehoiakim.*

M also, and Pedaiah, and Shenazar, ... 1Chr 3:18   4443

MALCHI-SHUA (mal'-ki-shu'-ah) See MELCHISHUA. *A son of King Saul.*

and Saul begat Jonathan, and M........... 1Chr 8:33   4444
and Saul begat Jonathan, and M........... 1Chr 9:39   4444
slew Jonathan, and Abinadab, and M 1Chr 10:2   4444

MALCHUS (mal'-kus) *A servant wounded by Simon Peter.*

The servant's name was M .... Jn 18:10   3124

MALE

m and female created he them .... Gen 1:27   2145
M and female created he them .... Gen 5:2   2145
they shall be m and female .... Gen 6:19   2145
take to thee by sevens, the m.................. Gen 7:2   376
that are not clean by two, the m............ Gen 7:2   376
also of the air by sevens, the m .... Gen 7:3   2145
two unto Noah into the ark, the m .... Gen 7:9   2145
And they that went in, went in m............ Gen 7:16   2145
money, every m among the men of .... Gen 17:23   2145
as we be, that every m of you be .... Gen 34:15   2145
people, if every m among us be .... Gen 34:22   2145
every m was circumcised, all that .... Gen 34:24   2145
blemish, a m of the first year................ Ex 12:5   2145
whether ox or sheep, that is m................ Ex 34:19   2142
let him offer a m without blemish .... Lev 1:3   2145
bring it a m without blemish .... Lev 1:10   2145
whether it be a m or female .... Lev 3:1   2145
m or female, he shall offer it .... Lev 3:6   2145
of the goats, a m without blemish .... Lev 4:23   2145
Every m among the priests shall .... Lev 7:6   2145
that hath born a m or a female .... Lev 12:7   2145
your own will a m without blemish ...... Lev 22:19   2145
thy estimation shall be of the m .... Lev 27:3   2145
shall be of the m twenty shekels............ Lev 27:5   2145
of the m five shekels of silver .... Lev 27:6   2145
if it be a m, then thy estimation .... Lev 27:7   2145
names, every m by their polls .... Num 1:2   2145
every m from twenty years old and ...... Num 1:20   2145
every m from twenty years old and ...... Num 1:22   2145
every m from a month old and .... Num 3:15   2145
Both m and female shall ye put out .... Num 5:3   2145
every m shall eat it .... Num 18:10   2145
every m among the little ones .... Num 31:17   2145
the likeness of m or female .... Deut 4:16   2145
there shall not be m or female .... Deut 7:14
thou shalt smite every m thereof .... Deut 20:13   2138
these were the m children of.................. Josh 17:2   2145
Ye shall utterly destroy every m .... Judg 21:11   2145
known no man by lying with any m ...... Judg 21:12   2145
he had smitten every m in Edom 1Kin 11:15   2145
he had cut off every m in Edom............ 1Kin 11:16   2145
which hath in his flock a m .... Mal 1:14   2145
them at the beginning made them m .... Mt 19:4   730
of the creation God made them m ...... Mk 10:6   730
Every m that openeth the womb............ Lk 2:23   730
there is neither m nor female .... Gal 3:28   730

MALEFACTOR

said unto him, If he were not a m......... Jn 18:30   2555

MALEFACTORS

And there were also two others, m .... Lk 23:32   2557
they crucified him, and the m .... Lk 23:33   2557
one of the m which were hanged .... Lk 23:39   2557

MALELEEL (mal'-e-le-el) See MAHALALEEL. *Son of Cainan; ancestor of Jesus.*

of Jared, which was the son of M............ Lk 3:37   3121

MALES

city boldly, and slew all the m .... Gen 34:25   2145
let all his m be circumcised, and.......... Ex 12:48   2145
the m shall be the LORD's .... Ex 13:12   2145
that openeth the matrix, being m.......... Ex 13:15   2145
m shall appear before the Lord .... Ex 23:17   2138
All the m among the children of .... Lev 6:18   2145
All the m among the priests shall .... Lev 6:29   2145

to the number of all the *m* .... Num 3:22   2145
In the number of all the *m* .... Num 3:28   2145
to the number of all the *m* .... Num 3:34   2145
all the *m* from a month old and .... Num 3:39   2145
m of the children of Israel from .... Num 3:40   2145
all the firstborn *m* by the number .... Num 3:43   2145
all *m* from a month old and upward ...... Num 26:62   2145
and they slew all the *m* .... Num 31:7   2145
All the firstling *m* that come of .... Deut 15:19   2145
times in a year shall all thy *m* .... Deut 16:16   2138
came out of Egypt, that were *m* .... Josh 5:4   2145
Beside their genealogy of *m* 2Chr 31:16   2145
to all the *m* among the priests 2Chr 31:19   2145
by genealogy of the *m* an hundred .... Ezr 8:3   2145
and with him two hundred *m* .... Ezr 8:4   2145
and with him three hundred *m* .... Ezr 8:5   2145
of Jonathan, and with him fifty *m* .... Ezr 8:6   2145
Athaliah, and with him seventy *m* .... Ezr 8:7   2145
Michael, and with him fourscore *m* ...... Ezr 8:8   2145
him two hundred and eighteen *m* .... Ezr 8:9   2145
him an hundred and threescore *m* .... Ezr 8:10   2145
and with them twenty and eight *m* ...... Ezr 8:11   2145
and with him an hundred and ten *m* ..... Ezr 8:12   2145
and with them threescore *m* .... Ezr 8:13   2145
Zabbud, and with them seventy *m* .... Ezr 8:14   2145

MALICE
neither with the leaven of *m* 1Cor 5:8   2549
howbeit in *m* be ye children, but 1Cor 14:20   2549
be put away from you, with all *m* .... Eph 4:31   2549
anger, wrath, *m*, blasphemy, ... Col 3:8   2549
lusts and pleasures, living in *m* .... Titus 3:3   2549
Wherefore laying aside all *m* 1Pet 2:1   2549

MALICIOUS
prating against us with *m* words 3Jn 10   4190

MALICIOUSNESS
wickedness, covetousness, *m* .... Rom 1:29   2549
your liberty for a cloke of *m* 1Pet 2:16   2549

MALIGNITY
envy, murder, debate, deceit, *m* .... Rom 1:29   2550

MALLOTHI (mal'-lo-thi) A son of Heman.
and Romamti-ezer, Joshbekashah, *M* 1Chr 25:4   4413
The nineteenth to *M*, he, his sons 1Chr 25:26   4413

MALLOWS
Who cut up *m* by the bushes, and .... Job 30:4   4408

MALLUCH (mal'-luk) See MELICU.
1. Ancestor of Ethan.
the son of Abdi, the son of *M* 1Chr 6:44   4409
2. A son of Bani.
Meshullam, *M*, and Adaiah, Jashub, ... Ezr 10:29   4409
3. A descendant of Harim.
Benjamin, *M*, and Shemariah .... Ezr 10:32   4409
4. A priest who renewed the covenant.
Hattush, Shebaniah, *M*, ... Neh 10:4   4409
Amariah, *M*, Hattush, ... Neh 12:2   4409
5. A clan leader who renewed the covenant.
M, Harim, Baanah .... Neh 10:27   4409

MALLUCHI See MELICU.

MALTA See MELITA.

MAMMON
Ye cannot serve God and *m* .... Mt 6:24   3126
of the *m* of unrighteousness .... Lk 16:9   3126
faithful in the unrighteous *m* .... Lk 16:11   3126
Ye cannot serve God and *m* .... Lk 16:13   3126

MAMRE (mam'-re)
1. A place near Hebron.
came and dwelt in the plain of *M* .... Gen 13:18   4471
unto him in the plains of *M* .... Gen 18:1   4471
in Machpelah, which was before *M* .... Gen 23:17   4471
the field of Machpelah before *M* .... Gen 23:19   4471
the Hittite, which is before *M* .... Gen 25:9   4471
came unto Isaac his father unto *M* .... Gen 35:27   4471
of Machpelah, which before *M* .... Gen 49:30   4471
of Ephron the Hittite, before *M* .... Gen 50:13   4471
2. An Amorite ally of Abraham.
in the plain of *M* the Amorite .... Gen 14:13   4471
went with me, Aner, Eshcol, and *M* .... Gen 14:24   4471

MAN
Let us make *m* in our image, after .... Gen 1:26   120
So God created *m* in his own image ...... Gen 1:27   120
there was not a *m* to till the .... Gen 2:5   120
the LORD God formed *m* of the dust .... Gen 2:7   120
and *m* became a living soul .... Gen 2:7   120
there he put the *m* whom he had .... Gen 2:8   120
And the LORD God took the *m* .... Gen 2:15   120
And the LORD God commanded the *m* ... Gen 2:16   120

good that the *m* should be alone .... Gen 2:18   120
the LORD God had taken from *m* .... Gen 2:22   120
woman, and brought her unto the *m* ...... Gen 2:22   120
because she was taken out of *M* .... Gen 2:23   376
shall a *m* leave his father .... Gen 2:24   376
And they were both naked, the *m* .... Gen 2:25   120
the *m* said, The woman whom thou .... Gen 3:12   120
the *m* is become as one of us, to .... Gen 3:22   120
So he drove out the *m* .... Gen 3:24   120
I have gotten a *m* from the LORD .... Gen 4:1   376
I have slain a *m* to my wounding .... Gen 4:23   376
and a young *m* to my hurt .... Gen 4:23
In the day that God created *m* .... Gen 5:1   120
shall not always strive with *m* .... Gen 6:3   120
of *m* was great in the earth .... Gen 6:5   120
that he had made *m* on the earth .... Gen 6:6   120
I will destroy *m* whom I have .... Gen 6:7   120
both *m*, and beast, and the creeping ...... Gen 6:7   120
Noah was a just *m* and perfect in .... Gen 6:9   376
upon the earth, and every *m* .... Gen 7:21   120
the face of the ground, both *m* .... Gen 7:23   120
I require it, and at the hand of *m* .... Gen 9:5   120
will I require the life of *m* .... Gen 9:5   120
by *m* shall his blood be shed .... Gen 9:6   120
for in the image of God made he *m* .... Gen 9:6   120
so that if a *m* can number the .... Gen 13:16   376
And he will be a wild *m* .... Gen 16:12   120
his hand will be against every *m* .... Gen 16:12
Every *m* child among you shall be .... Gen 17:10   2145
every *m* child in your generations .... Gen 17:12   2145
the uncircumcised *m* child whose .... Gen 17:14   2145
good, and gave it unto a young *m* .... Gen 18:7
daughters which have not known *m* .... Gen 19:8   376
And they pressed sore upon the *m* .... Gen 19:9   376
there is not a *m* in the earth to .... Gen 19:31   376
Behold, thou art but a dead *m* .... Gen 20:3   376
therefore restore the *m* his wife .... Gen 20:7   376
neither had any *m* known her .... Gen 24:16   376
the *m* wondering at her held his .... Gen 24:21   376
that the *m* took a golden earring .... Gen 24:22   376
the *m* bowed down his head, and .... Gen 24:26   376
and Laban ran out unto the *m* .... Gen 24:29   376
saying, Thus spake the *m* unto me .... Gen 24:30   376
that he came unto the *m* .... Gen 24:30   376
the *m* came into the house .... Gen 24:32   376
her, Wilt thou go with this *m* .... Gen 24:58   376
the camels, and followed the *m* .... Gen 24:61   376
What *m* is this that walketh in .... Gen 24:65   376
died in a good old age, an old *m* .... Gen 25:8
cunning hunter, a *m* of the field .... Gen 25:27   376
and Jacob was a plain *m*, dwelling .... Gen 25:27   376
He that toucheth this *m* or his .... Gen 26:11   376
the *m* waxed great, and went .... Gen 26:13   376
Esau my brother is a hairy *m* .... Gen 27:11   376
and I am a smooth *m* .... Gen 27:11   376
I should give her to another *m* .... Gen 29:19   376
the *m* increased exceedingly, and .... Gen 30:43   376
my daughters, no *m* is with us .... Gen 31:50   376
there wrestled a *m* with him until .... Gen 32:24   376
the young *m* deferred not to do .... Gen 34:19   376
brethren, took each *m* his sword .... Gen 34:25   376
And a certain *m* found him, and, ... Gen 37:15   376
the *m* asked him, saying, What .... Gen 37:15   376
the *m* said, They are departed .... Gen 37:17   376
father in law, saying, By the *m* .... Gen 38:25   376
Joseph, and he was a prosperous *m* .... Gen 39:2   376
each *m* his dream in one night, ... Gen 40:5   376
each *m* according to the .... Gen 40:5   376
we dreamed each *m* according to .... Gen 41:11   376
there was there with us a young *m* .... Gen 41:12   376
to each *m* according to his dream .... Gen 41:12   376
let Pharaoh look out a *m* discreet .... Gen 41:33   376
a *m* in whom the Spirit of God is .... Gen 41:38   376
without thee shall no *m* lift up .... Gen 41:44   376
the sons of one *m* in the land of .... Gen 42:13   376
The *m*, who is the lord of the .... Gen 42:30   376
And the *m*, the lord of the country .... Gen 42:33   376
The *m* did solemnly protest unto .... Gen 43:3   376
for the *m* said unto us, Ye shall .... Gen 43:5   376
as to tell the *m* whether ye had .... Gen 43:6   376
The *m* asked us straitly of our .... Gen 43:7   376
and carry down the *m* a present .... Gen 43:11   376
and arise, go again unto the *m* .... Gen 43:13   376
give you mercy before the *m* .... Gen 43:14   376
And the *m* did as Joseph bade .... Gen 43:17   376
the *m* brought the men into .... Gen 43:17   376
the *m* brought the men into .... Gen 43:24   376
the old *m* of whom ye spake .... Gen 43:27
every *m* his sack to the ground .... Gen 44:11   376
and opened every *m* his sack .... Gen 44:11   376
clothes, and laded every *m* his ass .... Gen 44:13   376

M

wot ye not that such a *m* as I can	Gen 44:15	376
but the *m* in whose hand the cup	Gen 44:17	376
lord, We have a father, an old *m*	Gen 44:20	376
Cause every *m* to go out from me	Gen 45:1	376
And there stood no *m* with him	Gen 45:1	376
he gave each *m* changes of raiment	Gen 45:22	376
Egyptians sold every *m* his field	Gen 47:20	376
for in their anger they slew a *m*	Gen 49:6	376
every *m* and his household came	Ex 1:1	376
there went a *m* of the house of	Ex 2:1	376
when he saw that there was no *m*	Ex 2:12	376
why is it that ye have left the *m*	Ex 2:20	376
was content to dwell with the *m*	Ex 2:21	376
they cast down every *m* his rod	Ex 7:12	376
the earth, and it became lice in *m*	Ex 8:17	120
so there were lice upon *m*	Ex 8:18	120
breaking forth with blains upon *m*	Ex 9:9	120
breaking forth with blains upon *m*	Ex 9:10	120
for upon every *m* and beast which	Ex 9:19	120
in all the land of Egypt, upon *m*	Ex 9:22	120
all that was in the field, both *m*	Ex 9:25	120
shall this *m* be a snare unto us	Ex 10:7	
let every *m* borrow of his	Ex 11:2	376
Moreover the *m* Moses was very	Ex 11:3	376
his tongue, against *m* or beast	Ex 11:7	376
shall take to them every *m* a lamb	Ex 12:3	376
every *m* according to his eating	Ex 12:4	376
in the land of Egypt, both *m*	Ex 12:12	120
save that which every *m* must eat	Ex 12:16	5315
the children of Israel, both of *m*	Ex 13:2	120
all the firstborn of *m* among thy	Ex 13:13	120
of Egypt, both the firstborn of *m*	Ex 13:15	120
The LORD is a *m* of war	Ex 15:3	376
Gather of it every *m* according to	Ex 16:16	376
his eating, an omer for every *m*	Ex 16:16	1538
take ye every *m* for them which	Ex 16:16	376
they gathered every *m* according	Ex 16:18	376
Let no *m* leave of it till the	Ex 16:19	376
every *m* according to his eating	Ex 16:21	376
much bread, two omers for one *m*	Ex 16:22	
abide ye every *m* in his place	Ex 16:29	376
let no *m* go out of his place on	Ex 16:29	376
whether it be beast or *m*, it	Ex 19:13	376
if a *m* sell his daughter to be a	Ex 21:7	376
He that smiteth a *m*, so that he	Ex 21:12	376
if a *m* lie not in wait, but God	Ex 21:13	
But if a *m* come presumptuously	Ex 21:14	376
And he that stealeth a *m*, and	Ex 21:16	376
if a *m* smite his servant, or his	Ex 21:20	376
if a *m* smite the eye of his	Ex 21:26	376
If an ox gore a *m* or a woman	Ex 21:28	376
he hath killed a *m* or a woman	Ex 21:29	376
if a *m* shall open a pit	Ex 21:33	376
or if a *m* shall dig a pit, and not	Ex 21:33	376
If a *m* shall steal an ox, or a	Ex 22:1	376
If a *m* shall cause a field or	Ex 22:5	376
If a *m* shall deliver unto his	Ex 22:7	376
If a *m* deliver unto his neighbour	Ex 22:10	376
or driven away, no *m* seeing it	Ex 22:10	
if a *m* borrow ought of his	Ex 22:14	376
if a *m* entice a maid that is not	Ex 22:16	376
countenance a poor *m* in his cause	Ex 23:3	
if any *m* have any matters to do	Ex 24:14	1167
of every *m* that giveth it	Ex 25:2	376
then shall they give every *m* a	Ex 30:12	376
the *m* that brought us up out of	Ex 32:1	376
the *m* that brought us up out of	Ex 32:23	376
Put every *m* his sword by his side	Ex 32:27	376
slay every *m* his brother, and	Ex 32:27	376
every *m* his companion	Ex 32:27	376
and every *m* his neighbour	Ex 32:27	376
even every *m* upon his son, and	Ex 32:29	376
no *m* did put on him his ornaments	Ex 33:4	376
stood every *m* at his tent door	Ex 33:8	376
every *m* in his tent door	Ex 33:10	376
as a *m* speaketh unto his friend	Ex 33:11	376
Joshua, the son of Nun, a young *m*	Ex 33:11	
for there shall no *m* see me	Ex 33:20	120
no *m* shall come up with thee	Ex 34:3	376
neither let any *m* be seen	Ex 34:3	376
shall any *m* desire thy land	Ex 34:24	376
every *m* that offered offered an	Ex 35:22	376
And every *m*, with whom was found	Ex 35:23	376
and every *m*, with whom was found	Ex 35:24	376
offering unto the LORD, every *m*	Ex 35:29	376
Aholiab, and every wise hearted *m*	Ex 36:1	376
Aholiab, and every wise hearted *m*	Ex 36:2	376
came every *m* from his work which	Ex 36:4	376
Let neither *m* nor woman make any	Ex 36:6	376
every wise hearted *m* among them	Ex 36:8	
A bekah for every *m*, that is,	Ex 38:26	1538

If any *m* of you bring an offering	Lev 1:2	120
if he touch the uncleanness of *m*	Lev 5:3	120
that a *m* shall be defiled withal	Lev 5:3	
whatsoever it be that a *m* shall	Lev 5:4	120
any of all these that a *m* doeth	Lev 6:3	120
thing, as the uncleanness of *m*	Lev 7:21	120
conceived seed, and born a *m* child	Lev 12:2	2145
When a *m* shall have in the skin	Lev 13:2	120
the plague of leprosy is in a *m*	Lev 13:9	120
If a *m* or woman have a plague	Lev 13:29	376
If a *m* also or a woman have in	Lev 13:38	376
the *m* whose hair is fallen off	Lev 13:40	376
He is a leprous *m*, he is unclean	Lev 13:44	376
the *m* that is to be made clean	Lev 14:11	376
When any *m* hath a running issue	Lev 15:2	376
whom *m* shall lie with seed of	Lev 15:18	376
if any *m* lie with her at all, and	Lev 15:24	376
him that hath an issue, of the *m*	Lev 15:33	2145
there shall be no *m* in the	Lev 16:17	120
of a fit *m* into the wilderness	Lev 16:21	376
What *m* soever there be of the	Lev 17:3	376
shall be imputed unto that *m*	Lev 17:4	376
that *m* shall be cut off from	Lev 17:4	376
Whatsoever *m* there be of the	Lev 17:8	376
even that *m* shall be cut off from	Lev 17:9	376
whatsoever *m* there be of the	Lev 17:10	376
whatsoever *m* there be of the	Lev 17:13	376
which if a *m* do, he shall live in	Lev 18:5	120
Ye shall fear every *m* his mother	Lev 19:3	376
and honour the face of the old *m*	Lev 19:32	
I will set my face against that *m*	Lev 20:3	376
ways hide their eyes from the *m*	Lev 20:4	376
I will set my face against that *m*	Lev 20:5	376
the *m* that committeth adultery	Lev 20:10	376
the *m* that lieth with his	Lev 20:11	376
if a *m* lie with his daughter in	Lev 20:12	376
If a *m* also lie with mankind, as	Lev 20:13	376
if a *m* take a wife and her mother,	Lev 20:14	376
if a *m* lie with a beast, he shall	Lev 20:15	376
if a *m* shall take his sister, his	Lev 20:17	376
if a *m* shall lie with a woman	Lev 20:18	376
if a *m* shall lie with his uncle's	Lev 20:20	376
if a *m* shall take his brother's	Lev 20:21	376
A *m* also or woman that hath a	Lev 20:27	376
being a chief *m* among his people,	Lev 21:4	1167
For whatsoever *m* he be that hath	Lev 21:18	376
a blind *m*, or a lame, or he that	Lev 21:18	376
Or a *m* that is brokenfooted, or	Lev 21:19	376
No *m* that hath a blemish of the	Lev 21:21	376
What *m* soever of the seed of	Lev 22:4	376
or a *m* whose seed goeth from him	Lev 22:4	376
or a *m* of whom he may take	Lev 22:5	120
if a *m* eat of the holy thing	Lev 22:14	376
a *m* of Israel strove together in	Lev 24:10	376
he that killeth any *m* shall	Lev 24:17	
if a *m* cause a blemish in his	Lev 24:19	376
he hath caused a blemish in a *m*	Lev 24:20	120
and he that killeth a *m*, he shall	Lev 24:21	120
every *m* unto his possession	Lev 25:10	376
return every *m* unto his family	Lev 25:10	376
every *m* unto his possession	Lev 25:13	376
if the *m* have none to redeem it,	Lev 25:26	376
unto the *m* to whom he sold it	Lev 25:27	376
if a *m* sell a dwelling house in a	Lev 25:29	376
if a *m* purchase of the Levites,	Lev 25:33	
When a *m* shall make a singular	Lev 27:2	376
all that any *m* giveth of such	Lev 27:9	
when a *m* shall sanctify his house	Lev 27:14	376
if a *m* shall sanctify unto the	Lev 27:16	376
have sold the field to another *m*	Lev 27:20	376
if a *m* sanctify unto the LORD a	Lev 27:22	
firstling, no *m* shall sanctify it	Lev 27:26	376
that a *m* shall devote unto the	Lev 27:28	376
of all that he hath, both of *m*	Lev 27:28	120
if a *m* will at all redeem ought	Lev 27:31	376
there shall be a *m* of every tribe	Num 1:4	376
every *m* by his own camp, and every	Num 1:52	376
every *m* by his own standard,	Num 1:52	376
Every *m* of the children of Israel	Num 2:2	376
every *m* in his place by their	Num 2:17	376
the firstborn in Israel, both *m*	Num 3:13	120
When a *m* or woman shall commit	Num 5:6	376
But if the *m* have no kinsman to	Num 5:8	376
whatsoever any *m* giveth	Num 5:10	376
a *m* lie with her carnally, and it	Num 5:13	376
Then shall the *m* bring his wife	Num 5:15	376
If no *m* have lain with thee, and	Num 5:19	376
some *m* have lain with thee beside	Num 5:20	376
Then shall the *m* be guiltless	Num 5:31	376
When either *m* or woman shall	Num 6:2	376
if any *m* die very suddenly by him	Num 6:9	

to every *m* according to his	Num 7:5	376
of Israel are mine, both *m*	Num 8:17	120
defiled by the dead body of a *m*	Num 9:6	120
defiled by the dead body of a *m*	Num 9:7	120
If any *m* of you or of your	Num 9:10	376
But the *m* that is clean, and is	Num 9:13	376
that *m* shall bear his sin	Num 9:13	376
every *m* in the door of his tent	Num 11:10	376
And there ran a young *m*, and told	Num 11:27	
(Now the *m* Moses was very meek,	Num 12:3	376
their fathers shall ye send a *m*	Num 13:2	376
kill all this people as one *m*	Num 14:15	376
they found a *m* that gathered	Num 15:32	376
The *m* shall be surely put to	Num 15:35	376
it shall be that the *m* whom the	Num 16:7	376
And take every *m* his censer	Num 16:17	376
the LORD every *m* his censer	Num 16:17	376
And they took every *m* his censer	Num 16:18	376
of all flesh, shall one *m* sin	Num 16:22	376
looked, and took every *m* his rod	Num 17:9	376
of *m* shalt thou surely redeem	Num 18:15	120
a *m* that is clean shall gather up	Num 19:9	376
any *m* shall be unclean seven days	Num 19:11	120
dead body of any *m* that is dead	Num 19:13	120
the law, when a *m* dieth in a tent	Num 19:14	120
or a dead body, or a bone of a *m*	Num 19:16	120
But the *m* that shall be unclean,	Num 19:20	376
if a serpent had bitten any *m*	Num 21:9	376
God is not a *m*, that he should	Num 23:19	376
neither the son of *m*, that he	Num 23:19	120
the *m* whose eyes are open hath	Num 24:3	1397
the *m* whose eyes are open hath	Num 24:15	1397
he went after the *m* of Israel	Num 25:8	376
the *m* of Israel, and the woman	Num 25:8	376
was not a *m* of them whom Moses	Num 26:64	376
And there was not left a *m* of them	Num 26:65	376
of Israel, saying, If a *m* die	Num 27:8	376
set a *m* over the congregation,	Num 27:16	376
a *m* in whom is the spirit, and lay	Num 27:18	376
If a *m* vow a vow unto the LORD,	Num 30:2	376
commanded Moses, between a *m*	Num 30:16	376
hath known *m* by lying with him	Num 31:17	376,2145
not known a *m* by lying with him	Num 31:18	2145
prey that was taken, both of *m*	Num 31:26	120
had not known *m* by lying with him	Num 31:35	2145
one portion of fifty, both of *m*	Num 31:47	120
and there lacketh not one *m* of us	Num 31:49	376
what every *m* hath gotten, of	Num 31:50	376
taken spoil, every *m* for himself	Num 31:53	376
inherited every *m* his inheritance	Num 32:18	376
every *m* armed for war, before the	Num 32:27	
every *m* armed to battle, before	Num 32:29	
any stone, wherewith a *m* may die	Num 35:23	
of Israel may enjoy every *m* the	Num 36:8	376
judge righteously between every *m*	Deut 1:16	376
not be afraid of the face of *m*	Deut 1:17	376
as a *m* doth bear his son, in all	Deut 1:31	376
on every *m* his weapons of war	Deut 1:41	376
of it, after the cubit of a *m*	Deut 3:11	376
every *m* unto his possession	Deut 3:20	376
that God created *m* upon the earth	Deut 4:32	120
day that God doth talk with *m*	Deut 5:24	120
there shall no *m* be able to stand	Deut 7:24	375
m doth not live by bread only	Deut 8:3	120
the mouth of the LORD doth *m* live	Deut 8:3	120
as a *m* chasteneth his son, so the	Deut 8:5	376
There shall no *m* be able to stand	Deut 11:25	376
every *m* whatsoever is right in	Deut 12:8	376
If there be among you a poor *m* of	Deut 15:7	
And if thy brother, an Hebrew *m*	Deut 15:12	
Every *m* shall give as he is able,	Deut 16:17	376
m or woman, that hath wrought	Deut 17:2	376
bring forth that *m* or that woman	Deut 17:5	376
even that *m* or that woman, and	Deut 17:5	376
the *m* that will do presumptuously	Deut 17:12	376
the judge, even that *m* shall die	Deut 17:12	376
As when a *m* goeth into the wood	Deut 19:5	
But if any *m* hate his neighbour,	Deut 19:11	376
up against a *m* for any iniquity	Deut 19:15	376
any *m* to testify against him that	Deut 19:16	376
What *m* is there that hath built a	Deut 20:5	376
battle, and another *m* dedicate it	Deut 20:5	376
what *m* is he that hath planted a	Deut 20:6	376
battle, and another *m* eat of it	Deut 20:6	376
what *m* is there that hath	Deut 20:7	376
the battle, and another *m* take her	Deut 20:7	376
What *m* is there that is fearful	Deut 20:8	376
which is next unto the slain *m*	Deut 21:3	376
that are next unto the slain *m*	Deut 21:6	
If a *m* have two wives, one	Deut 21:15	376
If a *m* have a stubborn and	Deut 21:18	376

if a *m* have committed a sin	Deut 21:22	376
that which pertaineth unto a *m*	Deut 22:5	1397
neither shall a *m* put on a	Deut 22:5	1397
if any *m* fall from thence	Deut 22:8	
If any *m* take a wife, and go in	Deut 22:13	376
my daughter unto this *m* to wife	Deut 22:16	376
of that city shall take that *m*	Deut 22:18	376
If a *m* be found lying with a	Deut 22:22	376
both the *m* that lay with the	Deut 22:22	376
a *m* find her in the city, and lie	Deut 22:23	376
and the *m*, because he hath humbled	Deut 22:24	376
But if a *m* find a betrothed	Deut 22:25	376
the *m* force her, and lie with her	Deut 22:25	376
then the *m* only that lay with her	Deut 22:25	376
for as when a *m* riseth against	Deut 22:26	376
If a *m* find a damsel that is a	Deut 22:28	376
Then the *m* that lay with her	Deut 22:29	376
A *m* shall not take his father's	Deut 22:30	376
If there be among you any *m*	Deut 23:10	376
When a *m* hath taken a wife, and	Deut 24:1	376
When a *m* hath taken a new wife,	Deut 24:5	376
No *m* shall take the nether or the	Deut 24:6	
If a *m* be found stealing any of	Deut 24:7	376
the *m* to whom thou dost lend	Deut 24:11	376
if the *m* be poor, thou shalt not	Deut 24:12	376
every *m* shall be put to death for	Deut 24:16	376
if the wicked *m* be worthy to be	Deut 25:2	
if the *m* like not to take his	Deut 25:7	376
that *m* that will not build up his	Deut 25:9	376
Cursed be the *m* that maketh any	Deut 27:15	376
no *m* shall fray them away	Deut 28:26	
evermore, and no *m* shall save thee	Deut 28:29	
another *m* shall lie with her	Deut 28:30	376
So that the *m* that is tender	Deut 28:54	376
bondwomen, and no *m* shall buy you	Deut 28:68	
Lest there should be among you *m*	Deut 29:18	376
shall smoke against that *m*	Deut 29:20	376
shall destroy both the young *m*	Deut 32:25	
also with the *m* of gray hairs	Deut 32:25	376
wherewith Moses the *m* of God	Deut 33:1	376
but no *m* knoweth of his sepulchre	Deut 34:6	376
There shall not any *m* be able to	Josh 1:5	376
remain any more courage in any *m*	Josh 2:11	376
of Israel, out of every tribe a *m*	Josh 3:12	376
people, out of every tribe a *m*	Josh 4:2	376
of Israel, out of every tribe a *m*	Josh 4:4	376
take you up every *m* of you a	Josh 4:5	376
there stood a *m* over against him	Josh 5:13	376
up every *m* straight before him	Josh 6:5	376
every *m* straight before him, and	Josh 6:20	376
all that was in the city, both *m*	Josh 6:21	376
Cursed be the *m* before the LORD,	Josh 6:26	376
shall take shall come in by *m*	Josh 7:14	1397
family of the Zarhites *m* by *m*	Josh 7:17	1397
he brought his household *m* by *m*	Josh 7:18	1397
there was not a *m* left in Ai or	Josh 8:17	376
over which no *m* hath lift up any	Josh 8:31	
there shall not a *m* of them stand	Josh 10:8	376
hearkened unto the voice of a *m*	Josh 10:14	376
but every *m* they smote with the	Josh 11:14	120
Moses the *m* of God concerning me	Josh 14:6	376
was a great *m* among the Anakims	Josh 14:15	120
because he was a *m* of war	Josh 17:1	376
there stood not a *m* of all their	Josh 21:44	376
that *m* perished not alone in his	Josh 22:20	376
no *m* hath been able to stand	Josh 23:9	376
One of you shall chase a	Josh 23:10	376
every *m* unto his inheritance	Josh 24:28	376
the spies saw a *m* come forth out	Judg 1:24	376
but they let go the *m* and all his	Judg 1:25	376
the *m* went into the land of the	Judg 1:26	376
children of Israel went every *m*	Judg 2:6	376
Gera, a Benjamite, a *m* lefthanded	Judg 3:15	376
and Eglon was a very fat *m*	Judg 3:17	376
and suffered not a *m* to pass over	Judg 3:28	376
and there escaped not a *m*	Judg 3:29	376
and there was not a *m* left	Judg 4:16	
when any *m* doth come and enquire	Judg 4:20	376
thee, and say, Is there any *m* here	Judg 4:20	376
shew thee the *m* whom thou seekest	Judg 4:22	376
to every *m* a damsel or two	Judg 5:30	1397
thee, thou mighty *m* of valour	Judg 6:12	
smite the Midianites as one *m*	Judg 6:16	376
people go every *m* unto his place	Judg 7:7	376
of Israel every *m* unto his tent	Judg 7:8	376
there was a *m* that told a dream	Judg 7:13	376
the son of Joash, a *m* of Israel	Judg 7:14	376
they stood every *m* in his place	Judg 7:21	376
caught a young *m* of the men of	Judg 8:14	
for as the *m* is, so is his	Judg 8:21	376
every *m* the earrings of his prey	Judg 8:24	376

M

did cast therein every *m* the	Judg 8:25	376
by me they honour God and *m*	Judg 9:9	376
my wine, which cheereth God and *m*	Judg 9:13	376
cut down every *m* his bough	Judg 9:49	376
unto the young *m* his armourbearer	Judg 9:54	
his young *m* thrust him through,	Judg 9:54	
departed every *m* unto his place	Judg 9:55	376
the son of Dodo, a *m* of Issachar	Judg 10:1	376
What *m* is he that will begin to	Judg 10:18	376
was a mighty *m* of valour, and he	Judg 11:1	
and she knew no *m*	Judg 11:39	376
And there was a certain *m* of Zorah	Judg 13:2	376
A *m* of God came unto me, and his	Judg 13:6	376
let the *m* of God which thou didst	Judg 13:8	376
the *m* hath appeared unto me, that	Judg 13:10	376
after his wife, and came to the *m*	Judg 13:11	376
Art thou the *m* that spakest unto	Judg 13:11	376
I be weak, and be as another *m*	Judg 16:7	120
I be weak, and be as another *m*	Judg 16:11	120
weak, and be like any other *m*	Judg 16:17	120
and she called for a *m*, and she	Judg 16:19	376
there was a *m* of mount Ephraim,	Judg 17:1	376
the *m* Micah had an house of gods,	Judg 17:5	376
but every *m* did that which was	Judg 17:6	376
there was a young *m* out of	Judg 17:7	
the *m* departed out of the city	Judg 17:8	376
was content to dwell with the *m*	Judg 17:11	376
the young *m* was unto him as one	Judg 17:11	
the young *m* became his priest, and	Judg 17:12	
voice of the young *m* the Levite	Judg 18:3	
and had no business with any *m*	Judg 18:7	120
house of the young *m* the Levite	Judg 18:15	
a priest unto the house of one *m*	Judg 18:19	376
they had no business with any *m*	Judg 18:28	120
father had said unto the *m*	Judg 19:6	376
when the *m* rose up to depart, his	Judg 19:7	376
when the *m* rose up to depart, he,	Judg 19:9	376
But the *m* would not tarry that	Judg 19:10	376
for there was no *m* that took them	Judg 19:15	376
there came an old *m* from his work	Judg 19:16	376
he saw a wayfaring *m* in the	Judg 19:17	376
and the old *m* said, Whither goest	Judg 19:17	376
there is no *m* that receiveth me	Judg 19:18	376
for the young *m* which is with thy	Judg 19:19	
And the old *m* said, Peace be with	Judg 19:20	376
master of the house, the old *m*	Judg 19:22	376
Bring forth the *m* that came into	Judg 19:22	376
And the *m*, the master of the house	Judg 19:23	376
seeing that this *m* is come into	Judg 19:23	376
but unto this *m* do not so vile a	Judg 19:24	376
so the *m* took his concubine, and	Judg 19:25	376
Then the *m* took her up upon an	Judg 19:28	376
the *m* rose up, and gat him unto	Judg 19:28	376
was gathered together as one *m*	Judg 20:1	376
And all the people arose as one *m*	Judg 20:8	376
the city, knit together as one *m*	Judg 20:11	376
every man that hath lain by *m*	Judg 21:11	2145
that had known no *m* by lying with	Judg 21:12	376
catch you every *m* his wife of the	Judg 21:21	376
not to each *m* his wife in the war	Judg 21:22	376
every *m* to his tribe and to his	Judg 21:24	376
thence every *m* to his inheritance	Judg 21:24	376
every *m* did that which was right	Judg 21:25	376
a certain *m* of Beth-lehem-judah	Ruth 1:1	376
the name of the *m* was Elimelech	Ruth 1:2	376
a mighty *m* of wealth, of the	Ruth 2:1	376
The *m* is near of kin unto us, one	Ruth 2:20	376
make not thyself known unto the *m*	Ruth 3:3	376
that the *m* was afraid, and turned	Ruth 3:8	376
all that the *m* had done to her	Ruth 3:16	376
for the *m* will not be in rest,	Ruth 3:18	376
a *m* plucked off his shoe, and gave	Ruth 4:7	376
a certain *m* of Ramathaim-zophim	1Sa 1:1	376
this *m* went up out of his city	1Sa 1:3	376
unto thine handmaid a *m* child	1Sa 1:11	582
the *m* Elkanah, and all his house,	1Sa 1:21	376
by strength shall no *m* prevail	1Sa 2:9	376
when any *m* offered sacrifice, the	1Sa 2:13	376
said to the *m* that sacrificed,	1Sa 2:15	376
if any *m* said unto him, Let them	1Sa 2:16	376
If one *m* sin against another, the	1Sa 2:25	376
but if a *m* sin against the LORD,	1Sa 2:25	376
there came a *m* of God unto Eli,	1Sa 2:27	376
not be an old *m* in thine house	1Sa 2:31	
an old *m* in thine house for ever	1Sa 2:32	
the *m* of thine, whom I shall not	1Sa 2:33	376
they fled every *m* into his tent	1Sa 4:10	376
there ran a *m* of Benjamin out of	1Sa 4:12	376
when the *m* came into the city, and	1Sa 4:13	376
the *m* came in hastily, and told	1Sa 4:14	376
the *m* said unto Eli, I am he that	1Sa 4:16	376

for he was an old *m*, and heavy	1Sa 4:18	376
Go ye every *m* unto his city	1Sa 8:22	376
Now there was a *m* of Benjamin	1Sa 9:1	376
a Benjamite, a mighty *m* of power	1Sa 9:1	376
name was Saul, a choice young *m*	1Sa 9:2	
there is in this city a *m* of God	1Sa 9:6	376
and he is an honourable *m*	1Sa 9:6	376
we go, what shall we bring the *m*	1Sa 9:7	376
present to bring to the *m* of God	1Sa 9:7	376
that will I give to the *m* of God	1Sa 9:8	376
when a *m* went to enquire of God,	1Sa 9:9	376
the city where the *m* of God was	1Sa 9:10	376
a *m* out of the land of Benjamin	1Sa 9:16	376
Behold the *m* whom I spake to thee	1Sa 9:17	376
and shalt be turned into another *m*	1Sa 10:6	376
if the *m* should yet come thither	1Sa 10:22	376
people away, every *m* to his house	1Sa 10:25	376
said, How shall this *m* save us	1Sa 10:27	
then, if there be no *m* to save us	1Sa 11:3	
There shall not a *m* be put to	1Sa 11:13	376
he sent every *m* to his tent	1Sa 13:2	376
him a *m* after his own heart	1Sa 13:14	376
to sharpen every *m* his share	1Sa 13:20	376
the young *m* that bare his armour	1Sa 14:1	
the young *m* that bare his armour	1Sa 14:6	
Cursed be the *m* that eateth any	1Sa 14:24	376
but no *m* put his hand to his	1Sa 14:26	
Cursed be the *m* that eateth any	1Sa 14:28	376
Bring me hither every *m* his ox	1Sa 14:34	376
every *m* his sheep, and slay them	1Sa 14:34	376
m his ox with him that night	1Sa 14:34	376
and let us not leave a *m* of them	1Sa 14:36	376
But there was not a *m* among all	1Sa 14:39	
and when Saul saw any strong *m*	1Sa 14:52	376
or any valiant *m*	1Sa 14:52	1121
but slay both *m* and woman, infant	1Sa 15:3	376
for he is not a *m*, that he should	1Sa 15:29	120
for the LORD seeth not as *m* seeth	1Sa 16:7	120
for *m* looketh on the outward	1Sa 16:7	120
are before thee, to seek out a *m*	1Sa 16:16	376
Provide me now a *m* that can play	1Sa 16:17	376
in playing, and a mighty valiant *m*	1Sa 16:18	
a *m* of war, and prudent in matters	1Sa 16:18	376
choose you a *m* for you, and let	1Sa 17:8	376
give me a *m*, that we may fight	1Sa 17:10	376
the *m* went among men for an old	1Sa 17:12	376
for an old *m* in the days of Saul	1Sa 17:12	
of Israel, when they saw the *m*	1Sa 17:24	376
ye seen this *m* that is come up	1Sa 17:25	376
that the *m* who killeth him, the	1Sa 17:25	376
What shall be done to the *m* that	1Sa 17:26	376
be done to the *m* that killeth him	1Sa 17:27	376
he a *m* of war from his youth	1Sa 17:33	376
the *m* that bare the shield went	1Sa 17:41	376
Whose son art thou, thou young *m*	1Sa 17:58	
in law, seeing that I am a poor *m*	1Sa 18:23	376
if I say thus unto the young *m*	1Sa 20:22	5958
art thou alone, and no *m* with thee	1Sa 21:1	376
Let no *m* know any thing of the	1Sa 21:2	376
Now a certain *m* of the servants	1Sa 21:7	376
servants, Lo, ye see the *m* is mad	1Sa 21:14	376
to play the mad *m* in my presence	1Sa 21:15	
For if a *m* find his enemy, will	1Sa 24:19	376
And there was a *m* in Maon, whose	1Sa 25:2	376
the *m* was very great, and he had	1Sa 25:2	376
Now the name of the *m* was Nabal	1Sa 25:3	376
but the *m* was churlish and evil in	1Sa 25:3	376
away every *m* from his master	1Sa 25:10	376
men, Gird ye on every *m* his sword	1Sa 25:13	376
they girded on every *m* his sword	1Sa 25:13	376
that a *m* cannot speak to him	1Sa 25:17	
thee, regard this *m* of Belial	1Sa 25:25	376
Yet a *m* is risen to pursue thee,	1Sa 25:29	120
no *m* saw it, nor knew it, neither	1Sa 26:12	
Abner, Art not thou a valiant *m*	1Sa 26:15	376
to every *m* his righteousness	1Sa 26:23	376
every *m* with his household, even	1Sa 27:3	376
left neither *m* nor woman alive,	1Sa 27:9	376
saved neither *m* nor woman alive	1Sa 27:11	376
And she said, An old *m* cometh up	1Sa 28:14	376
every *m* for his sons and for his	1Sa 30:6	376
he said, I am a young *m* of Egypt	1Sa 30:13	
and there escaped not a *m* of them	1Sa 30:17	376
save to every *m* his wife	1Sa 30:22	376
a *m* came out of the camp from	2Sa 1:2	376
unto the young *m* that told him	2Sa 1:5	
the young *m* that told him said,	2Sa 1:13	
unto the young *m* that told him	2Sa 1:13	
every *m* with his household	2Sa 2:3	376
as a *m* falleth before wicked men,	2Sa 3:34	1121
a great *m* fallen this day in	2Sa 3:38	

And is this the manner of *m*	2Sa 7:19	120
The rich *m* had exceeding many	2Sa 12:2	
But the poor *m* had nothing	2Sa 12:3	
came a traveller unto the rich *m*	2Sa 12:4	376
m that was come unto him	2Sa 12:4	
dressed it for the *m* that was	2Sa 12:4	376
was greatly kindled against the *m*	2Sa 12:5	376
the *m* that hath done this thing	2Sa 12:5	376
said to David, Thou art the *m*	2Sa 12:7	376
and Jonadab was a very subtil *m*	2Sa 13:3	376
And they went out every *m* from him	2Sa 13:9	376
every *m* gat him up upon his mule	2Sa 13:29	376
the young *m* that kept the watch	2Sa 13:34	
of the *m* that would destroy me	2Sa 14:16	376
bring the young *m* Absalom again	2Sa 14:21	
that when any *m* that had a	2Sa 15:2	376
but there is no *m* deputed of the	2Sa 15:3	
that every *m* which hath any suit	2Sa 15:4	376
that when any *m* came nigh to him	2Sa 15:5	376
with him covered every *m* his head	2Sa 15:30	376
thence came out a *m* of the family	2Sa 16:5	376
bloody *m*, and thou *m* of Belial	2Sa 16:7	376
because thou art a bloody *m*	2Sa 16:8	376
was as if a *m* had enquired at the	2Sa 16:23	376
the *m* whom thou seekest is as if	2Sa 17:3	376
and thy father is a *m* of war	2Sa 17:8	376
that thy father is a mighty *m*	2Sa 17:10	
for my sake with the young *m*	2Sa 18:5	
And a certain *m* saw it, and told	2Sa 18:10	376
said unto the *m* that told him	2Sa 18:11	376
the *m* said unto Joab, Though I	2Sa 18:12	376
none touch the young *m* Absalom	2Sa 18:12	
and behold a *m* running alone	2Sa 18:24	376
watchman saw another *m* running	2Sa 18:26	376
Behold another *m* running alone	2Sa 18:26	376
And the king said, He is a good *m*	2Sa 18:27	376
said, Is the young *m* Absalom safe	2Sa 18:29	
Is the young *m* Absalom safe	2Sa 18:32	
thee hurt, be as that young *m* is	2Sa 18:32	
had fled every *m* to his tent	2Sa 19:8	376
Judah, even as the heart of one *m*	2Sa 19:14	376
shall there any *m* be put to death	2Sa 19:22	376
Now Barzillai was a very aged *m*	2Sa 19:32	
for he was a very great *m*	2Sa 19:32	376
to be there a *m* of Belial	2Sa 20:1	376
every *m* to his tents, O Israel	2Sa 20:1	376
So every *m* of Israel went up from	2Sa 20:2	376
when the *m* saw that all the	2Sa 20:12	376
but a *m* of mount Ephraim, Sheba	2Sa 20:21	376
the city, every *m* to his tent	2Sa 20:22	376
shalt thou kill any *m* in Israel	2Sa 21:4	376
The *m* that consumed us, and that	2Sa 21:5	376
where was a *m* of great stature	2Sa 21:20	376
with the upright *m* thou wilt shew	2Sa 22:26	
delivered me from the violent *m*	2Sa 22:49	376
the *m* who was raised up on high	2Sa 23:1	1397
But the *m* that shall touch them	2Sa 23:7	376
Jehoiada, the son of a valiant *m*	2Sa 23:20	376
he slew an Egyptian, a goodly *m*	2Sa 23:21	376
me not fall into the hand of *m*	2Sa 24:14	120
and he also was a very goodly *m*	1Kin 1:6	
for thou art a valiant *m*, and	1Kin 1:42	376
rose up, and went every *m* his way	1Kin 1:49	376
he will shew himself a worthy *m*	1Kin 1:52	1121
therefore, and shew thyself a *m*	1Kin 2:2	376
he) a *m* on the throne of Israel	1Kin 2:4	376
for thou art a wise *m*, and knowest	1Kin 2:9	376
each *m* his month in a year made	1Kin 4:7	
every *m* under his vine and under	1Kin 4:25	376
table, every *m* in his month	1Kin 4:27	376
every *m* according to his charge	1Kin 4:28	376
and his father was a *m* of Tyre	1Kin 7:14	376
a *m* in my sight to sit on the	1Kin 8:25	376
If any *m* trespass against his	1Kin 8:31	376
soever be made by any *m*, or by	1Kin 8:38	120
which know every *m* the	1Kin 8:38	376
give to every *m* according to his	1Kin 8:39	376
there is no *m* that sinneth not	1Kin 8:46	120
a *m* upon the throne of Israel	1Kin 9:5	376
they brought every *m* his present	1Kin 10:25	376
the *m* Jeroboam was a mighty	1Kin 11:28	376
Jeroboam was a mighty *m* of valour	1Kin 11:28	
young *m* that he was industrious	1Kin 11:28	
came unto Shemaiah the *m* of God	1Kin 12:22	376
return every *m* to his house	1Kin 12:24	376
there came a *m* of God out of	1Kin 13:1	376
heard the saying of the *m* of God	1Kin 13:4	376
m of God had given by the word of	1Kin 13:5	376
and said unto the *m* of God	1Kin 13:6	376
the *m* of God besought the LORD	1Kin 13:6	376
the king said unto the *m* of God	1Kin 13:7	376

the *m* of God said unto the king	1Kin 13:8	376
the *m* of God had done that day in	1Kin 13:11	376
seen what way the *m* of God went	1Kin 13:12	376
And went after the *m* of God	1Kin 13:14	376
Art thou the *m* of God that camest	1Kin 13:14	376
he cried unto the *m* of God that	1Kin 13:21	376
he said, It is the *m* of God	1Kin 13:26	376
up the carcase of the *m* of God	1Kin 13:29	376
wherein the *m* of God is buried	1Kin 13:31	376
as a *m* taketh away dung, till it	1Kin 14:10	
to do with thee, O thou *m* of God	1Kin 17:18	376
I know that thou art a *m* of God	1Kin 17:24	376
see how this *m* seeketh mischief	1Kin 20:7	
And they slew every one his *m*	1Kin 20:20	376
every *m* out of his place, and put	1Kin 20:24	376
And there came a *m* of God, and	1Kin 20:28	376
a certain *m* of the sons of the	1Kin 20:35	376
the *m* refused to smite him	1Kin 20:35	376
Then he found another *m*, and said	1Kin 20:37	376
the *m* smote him, so that in	1Kin 20:37	376
a *m* turned aside, and brought a	1Kin 20:39	376
m unto me, and said, Keep this *m*	1Kin 20:39	376
a *m* whom I appointed to utter	1Kin 20:42	376
Jehoshaphat, There is yet one *m*	1Kin 22:8	376
every *m* to his house in peace	1Kin 22:17	376
a certain *m* drew a bow at a	1Kin 22:34	376
Every *m* to his city	1Kin 22:36	376
every *m* to his own country	1Kin 22:36	376
There came a *m* up to meet us, and	2Kin 1:6	376
What manner of *m* was he which	2Kin 1:7	376
answered him, He was an hairy *m*	2Kin 1:8	376
Thou *m* of God, the king hath said	2Kin 1:9	376
of fifty, If I be a *m* of God	2Kin 1:10	376
O *m* of God, thus hath the king	2Kin 1:11	376
unto them, If I be a *m* of God	2Kin 1:12	376
O *m* of God, I pray thee, let my	2Kin 1:13	376
of land cast every *m* his stone	2Kin 3:25	376
she came and told the *m* of God	2Kin 4:7	376
that this is an holy *m* of God	2Kin 4:9	376
thou *m* of God, do not lie unto	2Kin 4:16	376
him on the bed of the *m* of God	2Kin 4:21	376
that I may run to the *m* of God	2Kin 4:22	376
came unto the *m* of God to mount	2Kin 4:25	376
when the *m* of God saw her afar	2Kin 4:25	376
came to the *m* of God to the hill	2Kin 4:27	376
the *m* of God said, Let her alone	2Kin 4:27	376
if thou meet any *m*, salute him	2Kin 4:29	376
out, and said, O thou *m* of God	2Kin 4:40	376
there came a *m* from Baal-shalisha	2Kin 4:42	376
brought the *m* of God bread of the	2Kin 4:42	376
was a great *m* with his master, and	2Kin 5:1	376
he was also a mighty *m* in valour	2Kin 5:1	376
that this *m* doth send unto me to	2Kin 5:7	
me to recover of his leprosy	2Kin 5:7	376
when Elisha the *m* of God had	2Kin 5:8	376
to the saying of the *m* of God	2Kin 5:14	376
And he returned to the *m* of God	2Kin 5:15	376
servant of Elisha the *m* of God	2Kin 5:20	376
when the *m* turned again from his	2Kin 5:26	376
and take thence every *m* a beam	2Kin 6:2	376
the *m* of God said, Where fell it	2Kin 6:6	376
the *m* of God sent unto the king	2Kin 6:9	376
place which the *m* of God told him	2Kin 6:10	376
of the *m* of God was risen early	2Kin 6:15	376
opened the eyes of the young *m*	2Kin 6:17	
bring you to the *m* whom ye seek	2Kin 6:19	376
the king sent a *m* from before him	2Kin 6:32	376
king leaned answered the *m* of God	2Kin 7:2	376
behold, there was no *m* there	2Kin 7:5	376
and, behold, there was no *m* there	2Kin 7:10	376
neither voice of *m*	2Kin 7:10	120
as the *m* of God had said, who	2Kin 7:17	376
it came to pass as the *m* of God	2Kin 7:18	376
that lord answered the *m* of God	2Kin 7:19	376
after the saying of the *m* of God	2Kin 8:2	376
the servant of the *m* of God	2Kin 8:4	376
The *m* of God is come hither	2Kin 8:7	376
hand, and go, meet the *m* of God	2Kin 8:8	376
and the *m* of God wept	2Kin 8:11	376
So the young *m*, even the young	2Kin 9:4	
even the young *m* the prophet	2Kin 9:4	376
he said unto them, Ye know the *m*	2Kin 9:11	376
took every *m* his garment, and put	2Kin 9:13	376
was not a *m* left that came not	2Kin 10:21	376
every *m* with his weapons in his	2Kin 11:8	376
they took every *m* his men that	2Kin 11:9	376
every *m* with his weapons in his	2Kin 11:11	376
the money that every *m* is set at	2Kin 12:4	5315
every *m* of his acquaintance	2Kin 12:5	376
the *m* of God was wroth with him	2Kin 13:19	376
to pass, as they were burying a *m*	2Kin 13:21	376

M

wilderness, wherein there is no *m* ....Job 38:26 ... 120
Gird up thy loins now like a *m* ....Job 40:7 ... 1397
every *m* also gave him a piece of ....Job 42:11 ... 376
Blessed is the *m* that walketh not ....Ps 1:1 ... 376
abhor the bloody and deceitful *m*...........Ps 5:6 ... 376
What is *m*, that thou art mindful ....Ps 8:4 ... 582
and the son of *m*, that thou ....Ps 8:4 ... 120
let not *m* prevail......................................Ps 9:19 ... 582
arm of the wicked and the evil *m* ....Ps 10:15
that the *m* of the earth may no ....Ps 10:18 ... 582
for the godly *m* ceaseth ....Ps 12:1 ... 376
with an upright *m* thou wilt shew ....Ps 18:25 ... 1397
delivered me from the violent *m* ....Ps 18:48 ... 376
as a strong *m* to run a race ....Ps 19:5
But I am a worm, and no *m* ....Ps 22:6 ... 376
What *m* is he that feareth the ....Ps 25:12 ... 376
forgotten as a dead *m* out of mind ....Ps 31:12
thy presence from the pride of *m*...........Ps 31:20 ... 376
Blessed is the *m* unto whom the.............Ps 32:2 ... 120
a mighty *m* is not delivered by ....Ps 33:16
This poor *m* cried, and the LORD ....Ps 34:6
blessed is the *m* that trusteth in ....Ps 34:8 ... 1397
What *m* is he that desireth life, ...Ps 34:12 ... 376
O LORD, thou preservest *m* ....Ps 36:6 ... 120
because of the *m* who bringeth ....Ps 37:7 ... 376
A little that a righteous *m* hath ....Ps 37:16
The steps of a good *m* are ordered ....Ps 37:23 ... 1397
Mark the perfect *m*, and behold the ......Ps 37:37
for the end of that *m* is peace ....Ps 37:37 ... 376
But I, as a deaf *m*, heard not ....Ps 38:13
I was as a dumb *m* that openeth ....Ps 38:13
Thus I was as a *m* that heareth ....Ps 38:14 ... 376
verily every *m* at his best state..............Ps 39:5 ... 120
Surely every *m* walketh in a vain ....Ps 39:6 ... 376
dost correct *m* for iniquity ....Ps 39:11 ... 376
surely every *m* is vanity ....Ps 39:11 ... 120
Blessed is that *m* that maketh the ....Ps 40:4 ... 1397
me from the deceitful and unjust *m* ....Ps 43:1 ... 376
Nevertheless *m* being in honour ....Ps 49:12 ... 120
M that is in honour, and..........................Ps 49:20 ... 120
thyself in mischief, O mighty *m*..............Ps 52:1
this is the *m* that made not God.............Ps 52:7 ... 1397
a *m* mine equal, my guide, and mine .....Ps 55:13 ... 582
for *m* would swallow me up ....Ps 56:1 ... 582
be afraid what *m* can do unto me ....Ps 56:11 ... 120
So that a *m* shall say, Verily ....Ps 58:11 ... 120
for vain is the help of *m*..........................Ps 60:11 ... 120
ye imagine mischief against a *m*.............Ps 62:3 ... 376
to every *m* according to his work ....Ps 62:12 ... 376
Blessed is the *m* whom thou ....Ps 65:4
of the unrighteous and cruel *m* ....Ps 71:4
A *m* was famous according as he ....Ps 74:5
foolish *m* reproacheth thee daily ....Ps 74:22
the wrath of *m* shall praise thee.............Ps 76:10 ... 120
M did eat angels' food ....Ps 78:25 ... 376
like a mighty *m* that shouteth by ....Ps 78:65
be upon the *m* of thy right hand............Ps 80:17 ... 376
upon the son of *m* whom thou ....Ps 80:17 ... 120
Blessed is the *m* whose strength ....Ps 84:5 ... 120
blessed is the *m* that trusteth in ....Ps 84:12 ... 120
this *m* was born there..............................Ps 87:4
This and that *m* was born in her ....Ps 87:5 ... 376
that this *m* was born there......................Ps 87:6
I am as a *m* that hath no strength ....Ps 88:4 ... 1397
What *m* is he that liveth, and................Ps 89:48 ... 1397
A Prayer of Moses, the *m* of God ....Ps 90:t ... 376
Thou turnest *m* to destruction ....Ps 90:3 ... 582
A brutish *m* knoweth not ....Ps 92:6 ... 376
he that teacheth *m* knowledge...............Ps 94:10 ... 120
LORD knoweth the thoughts of *m* ....Ps 94:11 ... 120
Blessed is the *m* whom thou ....Ps 94:12 ... 1397
As for *m*, his days are as grass ....Ps 103:15 ... 582
and herb for the service of *m* ....Ps 104:14 ... 120
that maketh glad the heart of *m* ....Ps 104:15 ... 582
M goeth forth unto his work and to........Ps 104:23 ... 120
He suffered no *m* to do them wrong ....Ps 105:14 ... 120
He sent a *m* before them, even ....Ps 105:17 ... 376
fro, and stagger like a drunken *m*..........Ps 107:27
for vain is the help of *m*.........................Ps 108:12 ... 120
Set thou a wicked *m* over him ....Ps 109:6
persecuted the poor and needy *m* ....Ps 109:16 ... 376
Blessed is the *m* that feareth the ....Ps 112:1 ... 376
A good *m* sheweth favour, and...............Ps 112:5 ... 376
what can *m* do unto me...........................Ps 118:6 ... 120
LORD than to put confidence in *m* ....Ps 118:8 ... 120
shall a young *m* cleanse his way ....Ps 119:9
me from the oppression of *m*..................Ps 119:134 ... 120
are in the hand of a mighty *m* ....Ps 127:4
Happy is the *m* that hath his.................Ps 127:5 ... 1397
that thus shall the *m* be blessed............Ps 128:4 ... 1397
the firstborn of Egypt, both of *m* ....Ps 135:8 ... 120

me, O LORD, from the evil *m* ....Ps 140:1 ... 120
preserve me from the violent *m* ....Ps 140:1 ... 376
preserve me from the violent *m* ....Ps 140:4 ... 376
the violent *m* to overthrow him ....Ps 140:11 ... 376
but there was no *m* that would ....Ps 142:4
no *m* cared for my soul ....Ps 142:4
shall no *m* living be justified.................Ps 143:2
LORD, what is *m*, that thou takest.........Ps 144:3 ... 120
or the son of *m*, that thou makest ....Ps 144:3 ... 582
M is like to vanity ....Ps 144:4 ... 120
in princes, nor in the son of *m* ....Ps 146:3 ... 120
not pleasure in the legs of a *m* ....Ps 147:10 ... 376
simple, to the young *m* knowledge ....Prov 1:4
A wise *m* will hear, and will ....Prov 1:5
a *m* of understanding shall attain ....Prov 1:5
out my hand, and no *m* regarded ....Prov 1:24
thee from the way of the evil *m* ....Prov 2:12
from the *m* that speaketh froward ....Prov 2:12 ... 376
in the sight of God and *m* ....Prov 3:4 ... 120
Happy is the *m* that findeth ....Prov 3:13 ... 120
the *m* that getteth understanding ....Prov 3:13 ... 120
Strive not with a *m* without cause ....Prov 3:30 ... 120
For the ways of *m* are before the ....Prov 5:21 ... 376
and thy want as an armed *m* ....Prov 6:11 ... 376
A naughty person, a wicked *m* ....Prov 6:12 ... 376
by means of a whorish woman a *m* ....Prov 6:26
Can a *m* take fire in his bosom, ...Prov 6:27 ... 376
For jealousy is the rage of a *m*.............Prov 6:34 ... 1397
a young *m* void of understanding, ...Prov 7:7
and my voice is to the sons of *m* ....Prov 8:4 ... 120
Blessed is the *m* that heareth me,.........Prov 8:34 ... 120
a wicked *m* getteth himself a blot ....Prov 9:7
rebuke a wise *m*, and he will love ....Prov 9:8
Give instruction to a wise *m* ....Prov 9:9
teach a just *m*, and he will ....Prov 9:9
a righteous *m* is a well of life ....Prov 10:11
but a *m* of understanding hath ....Prov 10:23 ... 376
When a wicked *m* dieth, his ....Prov 11:7 ... 120
but a *m* of understanding holdeth ....Prov 11:12 ... 376
The merciful *m* doeth good to his..........Prov 11:17 ... 376
A good *m* obtaineth favour of the ....Prov 12:2
but a *m* of wicked devices will he ....Prov 12:2 ... 376
A *m* shall not be established by ....Prov 12:3 ... 120
A *m* shall be commended according ......Prov 12:8 ... 376
A righteous *m* regardeth the life ....Prov 12:10
A *m* shall be satisfied with good ....Prov 12:14 ... 376
but a prudent *m* covereth shame...........Prov 12:16
A prudent *m* concealeth knowledge ......Prov 12:23 ... 120
in the heart of *m* maketh it stoop ....Prov 12:25 ... 376
The slothful *m* roasteth not that ....Prov 12:27
of a diligent *m* is precious ....Prov 12:27 ... 120
A *m* shall eat good by the fruit..............Prov 13:2 ... 376
A righteous *m* hateth lying ....Prov 13:5
but a wicked *m* is loathsome ....Prov 13:5
Every prudent *m* dealeth with ....Prov 13:16
A good *m* leaveth an inheritance...........Prov 13:22
from the presence of a foolish *m* ....Prov 14:7 ... 376
way which seemeth right unto a *m* ....Prov 14:12 ... 376
a good *m* shall be satisfied from ....Prov 14:14 ... 376
but the prudent *m* looketh well to..........Prov 14:15
A wise *m* feareth, and departeth ....Prov 14:16
a *m* of wicked devices is hated ....Prov 14:17 ... 376
A wrathful *m* stirreth up strife ....Prov 15:18 ... 376
The way of the slothful *m* is as ....Prov 15:19
but a foolish *m* despiseth his ....Prov 15:20 ... 120
but a *m* of understanding walketh ....Prov 15:21 ... 376
A *m* hath joy by the answer of his ....Prov 15:23 ... 376
preparations of the heart in *m*..............Prov 16:1 ... 120
All the ways of a *m* are clean in ....Prov 16:2 ... 376
but a wise *m* will pacify it.....................Prov 16:14 ... 376
a way that seemeth right unto a *m* ....Prov 16:25 ... 376
An ungodly *m* diggeth up evil ....Prov 16:27 ... 376
A froward *m* soweth strife.....................Prov 16:28 ... 376
A violent *m* enticeth his........................Prov 16:29 ... 376
entereth more into a wise *m* than ....Prov 17:10
An evil *m* seeketh only rebellion ....Prov 17:11
robbed of her whelps meet a *m* ....Prov 17:12 ... 376
A *m* void of understanding....................Prov 17:18 ... 120
A wicked *m* taketh a gift out of ....Prov 17:23
a *m* of understanding is of an ....Prov 17:27 ... 376
is esteemed a *m* of understanding ....Prov 17:28
Through desire a *m*, having....................Prov 18:1
the heart of *m* is haughty ....Prov 18:12 ... 376
The spirit of a *m* will sustain ....Prov 18:14 ... 376
A *m* that hath friends must shew ....Prov 18:24 ... 376
of *m* perverteth his way........................Prov 19:3 ... 120
every *m* is a friend to him that ....Prov 19:6
of a *m* deferreth his anger.....................Prov 19:11 ... 120
A *m* of great wrath shall suffer ....Prov 19:19
The desire of a *m* is his kindness ....Prov 19:22 ... 120
a poor *m* is better than a liar ....Prov 19:22

M

A slothful *m* hideth his hand in	Prov 19:24	
for a *m* to cease from strife	Prov 20:3	376
the heart of *m* is like deep water	Prov 20:5	376
but a *m* of understanding will	Prov 20:5	376
but a faithful *m* who can find	Prov 20:6	376
The just *m* walketh in his	Prov 20:7	
Bread of deceit is sweet to a *m*	Prov 20:17	376
how can a *m* then understand his	Prov 20:24	120
It is a snare to the *m* who	Prov 20:25	120
The spirit of *m* is the candle of	Prov 20:27	
Every way of a *m* is right in his	Prov 21:2	376
The way of *m* is froward and	Prov 21:8	376
The righteous *m* wisely	Prov 21:12	
The *m* that wandereth out of the	Prov 21:16	120
loveth pleasure shall be a poor *m*	Prov 21:17	376
but a foolish *m* spendeth it up	Prov 21:20	120
A wise *m* scaleth the city of the	Prov 21:22	
but the *m* that heareth speaketh	Prov 21:28	376
A wicked *m* hardeneth his face	Prov 21:29	376
A prudent *m* foreseeth the evil,	Prov 22:3	
The slothful *m* saith, There is a	Prov 22:13	
no friendship with an angry *m*	Prov 22:24	1167
with a furious *m* thou shalt not	Prov 22:24	376
Seest thou a *m* diligent in his	Prov 22:29	376
if thou be a *m* given to appetite	Prov 23:2	1167
shall clothe a *m* with rags	Prov 23:21	
A wise *m* is strong	Prov 24:5	1397
a *m* of knowledge increaseth	Prov 24:5	376
to every *m* according to his works	Prov 24:12	120
Lay not wait, O wicked *m*, against	Prov 24:15	376
For a just *m* falleth seven times,	Prov 24:16	
shall be no reward to the evil *m*	Prov 24:20	
Every *m* shall kiss his lips that	Prov 24:26	
I will render to the *m* according	Prov 24:29	376
of the *m* void of understanding	Prov 24:30	120
and thy want as an armed *m*	Prov 24:34	376
A *m* that beareth false witness	Prov 25:18	376
Confidence in an unfaithful *m* in	Prov 25:19	
A righteous *m* falling down before	Prov 25:26	
Seest thou a *m* wise in his own	Prov 26:12	376
The slothful *m* saith, There is a	Prov 26:13	
As a mad *m* who casteth firebrands	Prov 26:18	
So is the *m* that deceiveth his	Prov 26:19	376
a contentious *m* to kindle strife	Prov 26:21	376
Let another *m* praise thee	Prov 27:2	
so is a *m* that wandereth from his	Prov 27:8	376
A prudent *m* foreseeth the evil,	Prov 27:12	
so a *m* sharpeneth the countenance	Prov 27:17	376
to face, so the heart of *m* to *m*	Prov 27:19	120
so the eyes of *m* are never	Prov 27:20	120
so is a *m* to his praise	Prov 27:21	376
wicked flee when no *m* pursueth	Prov 28:1	
but by a *m* of understanding and	Prov 28:2	120
A poor *m* that oppresseth the poor	Prov 28:3	1397
The rich *m* is wise in his own	Prov 28:11	376
the wicked rise, a *m* is hidden	Prov 28:12	120
Happy is the *m* that feareth alway	Prov 28:14	120
A *m* that doeth violence to the	Prov 28:17	120
let no *m* stay him	Prov 28:17	376
A faithful *m* shall abound with	Prov 28:20	376
of bread that *m* will transgress	Prov 28:21	1397
He that rebuketh a *m* afterwards	Prov 28:23	120
A *m* that flattereth his neighbour	Prov 29:5	1397
of an evil *m* there is a snare	Prov 29:6	376
m contendeth with a foolish *m*	Prov 29:9	376
but a wise *m* keepeth it in till	Prov 29:11	
and the deceitful *m* meet together	Prov 29:13	376
Seest thou a *m* that is hasty in	Prov 29:20	376
An angry *m* stirreth up strife	Prov 29:22	376
and a furious *m* aboundeth in	Prov 29:22	1167
The fear of *m* bringeth a snare	Prov 29:25	120
An unjust *m* is an abomination to	Prov 29:27	376
the *m* spake unto Ithiel, even	Prov 30:1	1397
I am more brutish than any *m*	Prov 30:2	376
have not the understanding of a *m*	Prov 30:2	120
and the way of a *m* with a maid	Prov 30:19	1397
What profit hath a *m* of all his	Eccl 1:3	120
m cannot utter it	Eccl 1:8	376
of *m* to be exercised therewith	Eccl 1:13	120
for what can the *m* do that cometh	Eccl 2:12	120
And how dieth the wise *m*	Eccl 2:16	
unto the *m* that shall be after me	Eccl 2:18	120
he shall be a wise *m* or a fool	Eccl 2:19	
For there is a *m* whose labour is	Eccl 2:21	120
yet to a *m* that hath not laboured	Eccl 2:21	120
For what hath *m* of all his labour	Eccl 2:22	120
There is nothing better for a *m*	Eccl 2:24	120
For God giveth to a *m* that is	Eccl 2:26	120
so that no *m* can find out the	Eccl 3:11	120
but for a *m* to rejoice, and to do	Eccl 3:12	
And also that every *m* should eat	Eccl 3:13	120
so that a *m* hath no preeminence	Eccl 3:19	120
the spirit of *m* that goeth upward	Eccl 3:21	1121,120
than that a *m* should rejoice in	Eccl 3:22	120
that for this a *m* is envied of	Eccl 4:4	376
sleep of a labouring *m* is sweet	Eccl 5:12	
Every *m* also to whom God hath	Eccl 5:19	120
A *m* to whom God hath given riches	Eccl 6:2	376
If a *m* beget an hundred children,	Eccl 6:3	376
the labour of *m* is for his mouth	Eccl 6:7	120
and it is known that it is *m*	Eccl 6:10	120
vanity, what is *m* the better	Eccl 6:11	120
what is good for *m* in this life	Eccl 6:12	120
for who can tell a *m* what shall	Eccl 6:12	120
than for a *m* to hear the song of	Eccl 7:5	376
oppression maketh a wise *m* mad	Eccl 7:7	
to the end that *m* should find	Eccl 7:14	120
there is a just *m* that perisheth	Eccl 7:15	
and there is a wicked *m* that	Eccl 7:15	
there is not a just *m* upon earth	Eccl 7:20	120
one *m* among a thousand have I	Eccl 7:28	120
that God hath made *m* upright	Eccl 7:29	120
Who is as the wise *m*	Eccl 8:1	376
the misery of *m* is great upon him	Eccl 8:6	120
There is no *m* that hath power	Eccl 8:8	120
there is a time wherein one *m*	Eccl 8:9	120
because a *m* hath no better thing	Eccl 8:15	120
that a *m* cannot find out the work	Eccl 8:17	120
because though a *m* labour to seek	Eccl 8:17	120
though a wise *m* think to know it,	Eccl 8:17	
no *m* knoweth either love or	Eccl 9:1	120
For *m* also knoweth not his time	Eccl 9:12	120
was found in it a poor wise *m*	Eccl 9:15	376
m remembered that same poor *m*	Eccl 9:15	376
a *m* cannot tell what shall be	Eccl 10:14	120
But if a *m* live many years, and	Eccl 11:8	120
Rejoice, O young *m*, in thy youth	Eccl 11:9	
because *m* goeth to his long home,	Eccl 12:5	120
for this is the whole duty of *m*	Eccl 12:13	120
every *m* hath his sword upon his	Song 3:8	376
if a *m* would give all the	Song 8:7	376
the mean *m* boweth down, and the	Is 2:9	1201
the great *m* humbleth himself	Is 2:9	376
lofty looks of *m* shall be humbled	Is 2:11	120
the loftiness of *m* shall be bowed	Is 2:17	120
In that day a *m* shall cast his	Is 2:20	120
Cease ye from *m*, whose breath is	Is 2:22	120
The mighty *m*, and the	Is 3:2	
the *m* of war, the judge, and the	Is 3:2	376
of fifty, and the honourable *m*	Is 3:3	
When a *m* shall take hold of his	Is 3:6	376
women shall take hold of one *m*	Is 4:1	376
the mean *m* shall be brought down,	Is 5:15	120
the mighty *m* shall be humbled, and	Is 5:15	376
because I am a *m* of unclean lips,	Is 6:5	376
and the houses without *m*, and the	Is 6:11	120
that a *m* shall nourish a young	Is 7:21	376
no *m* shall spare his brother	Is 9:19	376
they shall eat every *m* the flesh	Is 9:20	376
the inhabitants like a valiant *m*	Is 10:13	
I will make a *m* more precious	Is 13:12	582
even a *m* than the golden wedge of	Is 13:12	120
and as a sheep that no *m* taketh up	Is 13:14	
they shall every *m* turn to his	Is 13:14	376
Is this the *m* that made the earth	Is 14:16	376
day shall a *m* look to his Maker	Is 17:7	120
as a drunken *m* staggereth in his	Is 19:14	
is shut up, that no *m* may come in	Is 24:10	935
a *m* can stretch himself on it	Is 28:20	376
be as when an hungry *m* dreameth	Is 29:8	
or as when a thirsty *m* dreameth	Is 29:8	
That make a *m* an offender for a	Is 29:21	120
For in that day every *m* shall	Is 31:7	376
with the sword, not of a mighty *m*	Is 31:8	376
and the sword, not of a mean *m*	Is 31:8	120
a *m* shall be as an hiding place	Is 32:2	376
waste, the wayfaring *m* ceaseth	Is 33:8	
the cities, he regardeth no *m*	Is 33:8	582
shall the lame *m* leap as an hart	Is 35:6	
whereon if a *m* lean, it will go	Is 36:6	376
I shall behold *m* no more with the	Is 38:11	120
up the righteous *m* from the east	Is 41:2	
For I beheld, and there was no *m*	Is 41:28	376
Lord shall go forth as a mighty *m*	Is 42:13	376
stir up jealousy like a *m* of war	Is 42:13	376
maketh it after the figure of a *m*	Is 44:13	376
according to the beauty of a *m*	Is 44:13	376
Then shall it be for a *m* to burn	Is 44:15	120
the earth, and created *m* upon it	Is 45:12	120
the *m* that executeth my counsel	Is 46:11	376
and I will not meet thee as a *m*	Is 47:3	120
Holy One, to him whom *m* despiseth	Is 49:7	5315

when I came, was there no *m*	Is 50:2	376
be afraid of a *m* that shall die	Is 51:12	582
of the son of *m* which shall be	Is 51:12	120
was so marred more than any *m*	Is 52:14	376
a *m* of sorrows, and acquainted	Is 53:3	376
and the unrighteous *m* his thoughts	Is 55:7	376
Blessed is the *m* that doeth this,	Is 56:2	582
the son of *m* that layeth hold on	Is 56:2	120
and no *m* layeth it to heart	Is 57:1	376
a day for a *m* to afflict his soul	Is 58:5	120
And he saw that there was no *m*	Is 59:16	376
so that no *m* went through thee, I	Is 60:15	
For as a young *m* marrieth a	Is 62:5	
nor an old *m* that hath not filled	Is 65:20	
but to this *m* will I look	Is 66:2	
an ox is as if he slew a *m*	Is 66:3	376
she was delivered of a *m* child	Is 66:7	2145
a land that no *m* passed through	Jer 2:6	376
and where no *m* dwelt	Jer 2:6	120
If a *m* put away his wife, and she	Jer 3:1	376
I beheld, and, lo, there was no *m*	Jer 4:25	120
and not a *m* dwell therein	Jer 4:29	376
thereof, if ye can find a *m*	Jer 5:1	376
execute judgment between a *m*	Jer 7:5	376
out upon this place, upon *m*	Jer 7:20	120
no *m* repented him of his	Jer 8:6	376
Who is the wise *m*, that may	Jer 9:12	376
Let not the wise *m* glory in his	Jer 9:23	
the mighty *m* glory in his might	Jer 9:23	
let not the rich *m* glory in his	Jer 9:23	
Every *m* is brutish in his	Jer 10:14	120
the way of *m* is not in himself	Jer 10:23	120
it is not in *m* that walketh to	Jer 10:23	
Cursed be the *m* that obeyeth not	Jer 11:3	376
because no *m* layeth it to heart	Jer 12:11	376
every *m* to his heritage	Jer 12:15	376
and every *m* to his land	Jer 12:15	376
cleaveth to the loins of a *m*	Jer 13:11	376
as a wayfaring *m* that turneth	Jer 14:8	
shouldest thou be as a *m* astonied	Jer 14:9	376
as a mighty *m* that cannot save	Jer 14:9	376
thou hast borne me a *m* of strife	Jer 15:10	376
a *m* of contention to the whole	Jer 15:10	376
Shall a *m* make gods unto himself,	Jer 16:20	120
Cursed be the *m* that trusteth in	Jer 17:5	1397
that trusteth in *m*	Jer 17:5	120
Blessed is the *m* that trusteth in	Jer 17:7	1397
even to give every *m* according to	Jer 17:10	376
Will a *m* leave the snow of	Jer 18:14	
Cursed be the *m* who brought	Jer 20:15	376
A *m* child is born unto thee	Jer 20:15	2145
let that *m* be as the cities which	Jer 20:16	376
inhabitants of this city, both *m*	Jer 21:6	120
say every *m* to his neighbour	Jer 22:8	376
Is this *m* Coniah a despised	Jer 22:28	376
LORD, Write ye this *m* childless	Jer 22:30	376
a *m* that shall not prosper in his	Jer 22:30	1397
for no *m* of his seed shall	Jer 22:30	376
I am like a drunken *m*, and like a	Jer 23:9	376
like a *m* whom wine hath overcome,	Jer 23:9	1397
tell every *m* to his neighbour	Jer 23:27	376
LORD, I will even punish that *m*	Jer 23:34	376
turn every *m* from his evil way,	Jer 26:3	376
saying, This *m* is worthy to die	Jer 26:11	376
This *m* is not worthy to die	Jer 26:16	376
And there was also a *m* that	Jer 26:20	376
I have made the earth, the *m*	Jer 27:5	120
for every *m* that is mad, and	Jer 29:26	376
he shall not have a *m* to dwell	Jer 29:32	376
see whether a *m* doth travail with	Jer 30:6	2145
wherefore do I see every *m* with	Jer 30:6	1397
is Zion, whom no *m* seeketh after	Jer 30:17	
earth, A woman shall compass a *m*	Jer 31:22	1397
house of Judah with the seed of *m*	Jer 31:27	120
every *m* that eateth the sour	Jer 31:30	120
no more every *m* his neighbour	Jer 31:34	376
every *m* his brother, saying, Know	Jer 31:34	376
It is desolate without *m* or beast	Jer 32:43	120
say shall be desolate without *m*	Jer 33:10	120
that are desolate, without *m*	Jer 33:10	120
which is desolate without *m*	Jer 33:12	120
David shall never want a *m* to sit	Jer 33:17	376
want a *m* before me to offer burnt	Jer 33:18	376
That every *m* should let his	Jer 34:9	376
every *m* his maidservant, being an	Jer 34:9	376
go every *m* his brother an Hebrew	Jer 34:14	376
liberty every *m* to his neighbour	Jer 34:15	376
and caused every *m* his servant	Jer 34:16	376
every *m* his handmaid, whom he had	Jer 34:16	376
and every *m* to his neighbour	Jer 34:17	376
a *m* of God, which was by the	Jer 35:4	376

ye now every *m* from his evil way	Jer 35:15	376
a *m* to stand before me for ever	Jer 35:19	376
return every *m* from his evil way	Jer 36:3	376
let no *m* know where ye be	Jer 36:19	376
cause to cease from thence *m*	Jer 36:29	120
they rise up every *m* in his tent	Jer 37:10	376
let this *m* be put to death	Jer 38:4	376
for this *m* seeketh not the	Jer 38:4	376
Let no *m* know of these words, and	Jer 38:24	376
Nethaniah, and no *m* shall know it	Jer 40:15	376
slain Gedaliah, and no *m* knew it,	Jer 41:4	376
and no *m* dwelleth therein,	Jer 44:2	
your souls, to cut off from you *m*	Jer 44:7	376
any *m* of Judah in all the land of	Jer 44:26	376
away, nor the mighty *m* escape	Jer 46:6	
for the mighty *m* hath stumbled	Jer 46:12	
be driven out every *m* right forth	Jer 49:5	376
no *m* shall abide there, neither	Jer 49:18	376
shall a son of *m* dwell in it	Jer 49:18	120
and who is a chosen *m*, that I may	Jer 49:19	
there shall no *m* abide there	Jer 49:33	376
nor any son of *m* dwell in it	Jer 49:33	120
remove, they shall depart, both *m*	Jer 50:3	120
shall be as of a mighty expert *m*	Jer 50:9	
so shall no *m* abide there	Jer 50:40	376
shall any son of *m* dwell therein	Jer 50:40	120
like a *m* to the battle, against	Jer 50:42	376
and who is a chosen *m*, that I may	Jer 50:44	
and deliver every *m* his soul	Jer 51:6	376
Every *m* is brutish by his	Jer 51:17	120
also will I break in pieces *m*	Jer 51:22	376
I break in pieces the young *m*	Jer 51:22	
a land wherein no *m* dwelleth	Jer 51:43	376
doth any son of *m* pass thereby	Jer 51:43	120
deliver ye every *m* his soul from	Jer 51:45	376
neither *m* nor beast, but that it	Jer 51:62	120
I am the *m* that hath seen	Lam 3:1	1397
is good that a *m* should both hope	Lam 3:26	
It is good for a *m* that he bear	Lam 3:27	1397
a *m* before the face of the most	Lam 3:35	1397
To subvert a *m* in his cause	Lam 3:36	120
doth a living *m* complain	Lam 3:39	120
a *m* for the punishment of his	Lam 3:39	1397
no *m* breaketh it unto them	Lam 4:4	
they had the likeness of a *m*	Eze 1:5	120
they had the hands of a *m* under	Eze 1:8	120
they four had the face of a *m*	Eze 1:10	120
appearance of a *m* above upon it	Eze 1:26	120
And he said unto me, Son of *m*	Eze 2:1	120
And he said unto me, Son of *m*	Eze 2:3	120
And thou, son of *m*, be not afraid	Eze 2:6	120
But thou, son of *m*, hear what I	Eze 2:8	120
he said unto me, Son of *m*	Eze 3:1	120
And he said unto me, Son of *m*	Eze 3:3	120
And he said unto me, Son of *m*	Eze 3:4	120
he said unto me, Son of *m*	Eze 3:10	120
Son of *m*, I have made thee a	Eze 3:17	120
the same wicked *m* shall die in	Eze 3:18	
When a righteous *m* doth turn from	Eze 3:20	
if thou warn the righteous *m*	Eze 3:21	
But thou, O son of *m*, behold,	Eze 3:25	120
Thou also, son of *m*, take thee a	Eze 4:1	120
it with dung that cometh out of *m*	Eze 4:12	120
he said unto me, Son of *m*	Eze 4:16	120
And thou, son of *m*, take thee a	Eze 5:1	120
Son of *m*, set thy face toward the	Eze 6:2	120
Also, thou son of *m*, thus saith	Eze 7:2	120
Then said he unto me, Son of *m*	Eze 8:5	120
furthermore unto me, Son of *m*	Eze 8:6	120
Then said he unto me, Son of *m*	Eze 8:8	120
with every *m* his censer in his	Eze 8:11	376
Then said he unto me, Son of *m*	Eze 8:12	120
every *m* in the chambers of his	Eze 8:12	376
Hast thou seen this, O son of *m*	Eze 8:15	120
Hast thou seen this, O son of *m*	Eze 8:17	120
even every *m* with his destroying	Eze 9:1	376
every *m* a slaughter weapon in his	Eze 9:2	376
one *m* among them was clothed with	Eze 9:2	376
he called to the *m* clothed with	Eze 9:3	376
near any *m* upon whom is the mark	Eze 9:6	376
the *m* clothed with linen, which	Eze 9:11	376
he spake unto the *m* clothed with	Eze 10:2	376
of the house, when the *m* went in	Eze 10:3	376
the *m* clothed with linen, saying,	Eze 10:6	376
second face was the face of a *m*	Eze 10:14	120
of a *m* was under their wings	Eze 10:21	120
Then said he unto me, Son of *m*	Eze 11:2	120
them, prophesy, O son of *m*	Eze 11:4	120
Son of *m*, thy brethren, even thy	Eze 11:15	120
Son of *m*, thou dwellest in the	Eze 12:2	120
Therefore, thou son of *m*, prepare	Eze 12:3	120

M

Son of *m*, hath not the house of	Eze 12:9	120	
Son of *m*, eat thy bread with	Eze 12:18	120	
Son of *m*, what is that proverb	Eze 12:22	120	
Son of *m*, behold, they of the	Eze 12:27	120	
Son of *m*, prophesy against the	Eze 13:2	120	
Likewise, thou son of *m*, set thy	Eze 13:17	120	
Son of *m*, these men have set up	Eze 14:3	120	
Every *m* of the house of Israel	Eze 14:4	376	
I will set my face against that *m*	Eze 14:8	376	
Son of *m*, when the land sinneth	Eze 14:13	120	
famine upon it, and will cut off *m*	Eze 14:13	120	
that no *m* may pass through	Eze 14:15		
so that I cut off *m* and beast from	Eze 14:17	120	
it in blood, to cut off from it *m*	Eze 14:19	120	
pestilence, to cut off from it *m*	Eze 14:21	120	
Son of *m*, What is the vine tree	Eze 15:2	120	
Son of *m*, cause Jerusalem to know	Eze 16:2	120	
Son of *m*, put forth a riddle, and	Eze 17:2	120	
But if a *m* be just, and do that	Eze 18:5	376	
true judgment between *m* and *m*	Eze 18:8	376	
that the wicked *m* doeth, shall he	Eze 18:24		
When a righteous *m* turneth away	Eze 18:26		
when the wicked *m* turneth away	Eze 18:27		
Son of *m*, speak unto the elders	Eze 20:3	120	
Wilt thou judge them, son of *m*	Eze 20:4	120	
them, Cast ye away every *m* the	Eze 20:7	376	
they did not every *m* cast away	Eze 20:8	376	
my judgments, which if a *m* do	Eze 20:11	120	
my judgments, which if a *m* do	Eze 20:13	120	
to do them, which if a *m* do	Eze 20:21	120	
Therefore, son of *m*, speak unto	Eze 20:27	120	
Son of *m*, set thy face toward the	Eze 20:46	120	
Son of *m*, set thy face toward	Eze 21:2	120	
Sigh therefore, thou son of *m*	Eze 21:6	120	
Son of *m*, prophesy, and say, Thus	Eze 21:9	120	
Cry and howl, son of *m*,	Eze 21:12	120	
Thou therefore, son of *m*,	Eze 21:14	120	
Also, thou son of *m*, appoint thee	Eze 21:19	120	
And thou, son of *m*, prophesy and	Eze 21:28	120	
Now, thou son of *m*, wilt thou	Eze 22:2	120	
Son of *m*, the house of Israel is	Eze 22:18	120	
Son of *m*, say unto her, Thou art	Eze 22:24	120	
And I sought for a *m* among them	Eze 22:30	376	
Son of *m*, there were two women,	Eze 23:2	120	
Son of *m*, wilt thou judge Aholah	Eze 23:36	120	
Son of *m*, write thee the name of	Eze 24:2	120	
Son of *m*, behold, I take away	Eze 24:16	120	
Also, thou son of *m*, shall it not	Eze 24:25	120	
Son of *m*, set thy face against	Eze 25:2	120	
hand upon Edom, and will cut off *m*	Eze 25:13	120	
Son of *m*, because Tyrus hath	Eze 26:2	120	
Now, thou son of *m*, take up a	Eze 27:2	120	
Son of *m*, say unto the prince of	Eze 28:2	120	
yet thou art a *m*, and not God,	Eze 28:2	120	
but thou shalt be a *m*, and no God,	Eze 28:9	120	
Son of *m*, take up a lamentation	Eze 28:12	120	
Son of *m*, set thy face against	Eze 28:21	120	
Son of *m*, set thy face against	Eze 29:2	120	
a sword upon thee, and cut off *m*	Eze 29:8	120	
No foot of *m* shall pass through	Eze 29:11	120	
Son of *m*, Nebuchadrezzar king of	Eze 29:18	120	
Son of *m*, prophesy and say, Thus	Eze 30:2	120	
Son of *m*, I have broken the arm	Eze 30:21	120	
groanings of a deadly wounded *m*	Eze 30:24		
Son of *m*, speak unto Pharaoh king	Eze 31:2	120	
Son of *m*, take up a lamentation	Eze 32:2	120	
every *m* for his own life, in the	Eze 32:10	376	
foot of *m* trouble them any more	Eze 32:13	120	
Son of *m*, wail for the multitude	Eze 32:18	120	
Son of *m*, speak to the children	Eze 33:2	120	
the land take a *m* of their coasts	Eze 33:2	376	
So thou, O son of *m*, I have set	Eze 33:7	120	
I say unto the wicked, O wicked *m*	Eze 33:8		
that wicked *m* shall die in his	Eze 33:8		
Therefore, O thou son of *m*	Eze 33:10	120	
Therefore, thou son of *m*, say	Eze 33:12	120	
Son of *m*, they that inhabit those	Eze 33:24	120	
Also, thou son of *m*, the children	Eze 33:30	120	
Son of *m*, prophesy against the	Eze 34:2	120	
Son of *m*, set thy face against	Eze 35:2	120	
Also, thou son of *m*, prophesy	Eze 36:1	120	
And I will multiply upon you *m*	Eze 36:11	120	
Son of *m*, when the house of	Eze 36:17	120	
And he said unto me, Son of *m*	Eze 37:3	120	
unto the wind, prophesy, son of *m*	Eze 37:9	120	
Then he said unto me, Son of *m*	Eze 37:11	120	
Moreover, thou son of *m*, take	Eze 37:16	120	
Son of *m*, set thy face against	Eze 38:2	120	
Therefore, son of *m*, prophesy and	Eze 38:14	120	
Therefore, thou son of *m*,	Eze 39:1	120	
And, thou son of *m*, thus saith the	Eze 39:17	120	
and, behold, there was a *m*	Eze 40:3	376	
And the *m* said unto me	Eze 40:4	376	
said unto me, Son of *m*	Eze 40:4	120	
So that the face of a *m* was	Eze 41:19	120	
and the *m* stood by me	Eze 43:6	376	
And he said unto me, Son of *m*	Eze 43:7	120	
Thou son of *m*, shew the house to	Eze 43:10	120	
And he said unto me, Son of *m*	Eze 43:18	120	
no *m* shall enter in by it	Eze 44:2	376	
the LORD said unto me, Son of *m*	Eze 44:5	120	
every *m* from his possession	Eze 46:18	376	
when the *m* that had the line in	Eze 47:3	376	
And he said unto me, Son of *m*	Eze 47:6	120	
till a *m* come over against Hamath	Eze 47:20		
There is not a *m* upon the earth	Dan 2:10	606	
I have found a *m* of the captives	Dan 2:25	1400	
the king made Daniel a great *m*	Dan 2:48		
that every *m* that shall hear the	Dan 3:10	606	
There is a *m* in thy kingdom, in	Dan 5:11	1400	
of any God or *m* for thirty days	Dan 6:7	606	
that every *m* that shall ask a	Dan 6:12	606	
any God or *m* within thirty days	Dan 6:12	606	
made stand upon the feet as a *m*	Dan 7:4	606	
horn were eyes like the eyes of *m*	Dan 7:8	606	
one like the Son of *m* came with	Dan 7:13	606	
me as the appearance of a *m*	Dan 8:15	1397	
make this *m* to understand the	Dan 8:16		
unto me, Understand, O son of *m*	Dan 8:17	120	
in prayer, even the *m* Gabriel	Dan 9:21	376	
a certain *m* clothed in linen	Dan 10:5	376	
a *m* greatly beloved, understand	Dan 10:11	376	
me one like the appearance of a *m*	Dan 10:18	120	
O *m* greatly beloved, fear not	Dan 10:19	376	
one said to the *m* clothed in	Dan 12:6	376	
I heard the *m* clothed in linen,	Dan 12:7	376	
thou shalt not be for another *m*	Hos 3:3	376	
Yet let no *m* strive, nor reprove	Hos 4:4	376	
as troops of robbers wait for a *m*	Hos 6:9	376	
is a fool, the spiritual *m* is mad	Hos 9:7	376	
that there shall not be a *m* left	Hos 9:12	120	
I drew them with cords of a *m*	Hos 11:4	120	
for I am God, and not *m*	Hos 11:9	376	
and a *m* and his father will go in	Amos 2:7	376	
declareth unto *m* what is his	Amos 4:13	120	
As if a *m* did flee from a lion,	Amos 5:19	376	
cried every *m* unto his god, and	Jonah 1:5		
saying, Let neither *m* nor beast	Jonah 3:7	120	
But let *m* and beast be covered	Jonah 3:8	120	
so they oppress a *m* and his house,	Mic 2:2	1397	
and his house, even a *m*	Mic 2:2	376	
If a *m* walking in the spirit and	Mic 2:11	376	
shall sit every *m* under his vine	Mic 4:4	376	
this *m* shall be the peace, when	Mic 5:5		
grass, that tarrieth not for *m*	Mic 5:7	376	
He hath shewed thee, O *m*, what is	Mic 6:8	120	
the *m* of wisdom shall see thy	Mic 6:9		
The good *m* is perished out of the	Mic 7:2		
they hunt every *m* his brother	Mic 7:2	376	
and the great *m*, he uttereth his	Mic 7:3		
mountains, and no *m* gathereth them	Nah 3:18		
when the wicked devoureth the *m*	Hab 1:13		
by wine, he is a proud *m*, neither	Hab 2:5	1397	
I will consume *m* and beast	Zeph 1:3	120	
I will cut off *m* from off the	Zeph 1:3	120	
the mighty *m* shall cry there	Zeph 1:14		
destroyed, so that there is no *m*	Zeph 3:6	376	
ye run every *m* unto his own house	Hag 1:9	376	
behold a *m* riding upon a red	Zec 1:8	376	
the *m* that stood among the myrtle	Zec 1:10	376	
so that no *m* did lift up his head	Zec 1:21	376	
behold a *m* with a measuring line	Zec 2:1	376	
him, Run, speak to this young *m*	Zec 2:4		
shall ye call every *m* his	Zec 3:10		
as a *m* that is wakened out of his	Zec 4:1	376	
Behold the *m* whose name is The	Zec 6:12	376	
every *m* to his brother	Zec 7:9	376	
that no *m* passed through nor	Zec 7:14		
every *m* with his staff in his	Zec 8:4	376	
days there was no hire for *m*	Zec 8:10	120	
Speak ye every *m* the truth to his	Zec 8:16	376	
when the eyes of *m*, as of all the	Zec 9:1	120	
thee as the sword of a mighty *m*	Zec 9:13		
Ephraim shall be like a mighty *m*	Zec 10:7		
the spirit of *m* within him	Zec 12:1	120	
for *m* taught me to keep cattle	Zec 13:5	120	
against the *m* that is my fellow,	Zec 13:7	1397	
every *m* against his brother	Mal 2:10	376	
cut off the *m* that doeth this	Mal 2:12	376	
Will a *m* rob God	Mal 3:8	120	
as a *m* spareth his own son that	Mal 3:17	376	
her husband, being a just *m*	Mt 1:19		

M shall not live by bread alone,............ Mt 4:4	444
if any *m* will sue thee at the law .... Mt 5:40	
No *m* can serve two masters.................. Mt 6:24	3762
Or what *m* is there of you, whom .... Mt 7:9	444
I will liken him unto a wise *m*.............. Mt 7:24	435
shall be likened unto a foolish *m* .... Mt 7:26	435
unto him, See thou tell no *m* .... Mt 8:4	3367
For I am a *m* under authority,.............. Mt 8:9	444
and I say to this *m*, Go, and he .... Mt 8:9	
but the Son of *m* hath not where........... Mt 8:20	444
saying, What manner of *m* is this .... Mt 8:27	
so that no *m* might pass by that .... Mt 8:28	5100
to him a *m* sick of the palsy.................. Mt 9:2	
themselves, This *m* blasphemeth .... Mt 9:3	
ye may know that the Son of *m* .... Mt 9:6	444
forth from thence, he saw a *m* .... Mt 9:9	444
No *m* putteth a piece of new cloth .... Mt 9:16	3762
saying, See that no *m* know it .... Mt 9:30	3367
a dumb *m* possessed with a devil........... Mt 9:32	444
Israel, till the Son of *m* be come .... Mt 10:23	444
For I am come to set a *m* at .... Mt 10:35	444
he that receiveth a righteous *m* .... Mt 10:41	
in the name of a righteous *m* .... Mt 10:41	
A *m* clothed in soft raiment.................. Mt 11:8	444
The Son of *m* came eating and.............. Mt 11:19	444
Behold, a *m* gluttonous, and a.............. Mt 11:19	444
no *m* knoweth the Son, but the .... Mt 11:27	3762
neither knoweth any *m* the Father .... Mt 11:27	
For the Son of *m* is Lord even of .... Mt 12:8	444
there was a *m* which had his hand......... Mt 12:10	444
What *m* shall there be among you, ... Mt 12:11	444
How much then is a *m* better than .... Mt 12:12	444
Then saith he to the *m*, Stretch .... Mt 12:13	444
neither shall any *m* hear his .... Mt 12:19	
except he first bind the strong *m* .... Mt 12:29	
a word against the Son of *m* .... Mt 12:32	444
A good *m* out of the good treasure .... Mt 12:35	444
an evil *m* out of the evil...................... Mt 12:35	444
shall the Son of *m* be three days........... Mt 12:40	444
unclean spirit is gone out of a *m* .... Mt 12:43	444
the last state of that *m* is worse........... Mt 12:45	444
of heaven is likened unto a *m* .... Mt 13:24	444
of mustard seed, which a *m* took........... Mt 13:31	444
the good seed is the Son of *m*............... Mt 13:37	444
The Son of *m* shall send forth his .... Mt 13:41	444
the which when a *m* hath found .... Mt 13:44	444
heaven is like unto a merchant *m*.......... Mt 13:45	444
unto a *m* that is an householder............ Mt 13:52	444
Whence hath this *m* this wisdom .... Mt 13:54	
then hath this *m* all these things............ Mt 13:56	
goeth into the mouth defileth a *m* .... Mt 15:11	444
of the mouth, this defileth a *m* .... Mt 15:11	444
and they defile the *m* .... Mt 15:18	444
are the things which defile a *m* .... Mt 15:20	444
unwashen hands defileth not a *m* .... Mt 15:20	444
do men say that I the Son of *m* am........ Mt 16:13	444
that they should tell no *m* that .... Mt 16:20	3367
If any *m* will come after me, let .... Mt 16:24	
For what is a *m* profited, if he .... Mt 16:26	444
or what shall a *m* give in...................... Mt 16:26	444
For the Son of *m* shall come in .... Mt 16:27	444
every *m* according to his works .... Mt 16:27	
Son of *m* coming in his kingdom .... Mt 16:28	444
up their eyes, they saw no *m*................. Mt 17:8	3762
saying, Tell the vision to no *m* .... Mt 17:9	3367
until the Son of *m* be risen again .... Mt 17:9	444
also the Son of *m* suffer of them .... Mt 17:12	444
there came to him a certain *m* .... Mt 17:14	444
The Son of *m* shall be betrayed............. Mt 17:22	444
but woe to that *m* by whom the .... Mt 18:7	444
For the Son of *m* is come to save .... Mt 18:11	444
if a *m* have an hundred sheep, and .... Mt 18:12	444
him be unto thee as an heathen *m* .... Mt 18:17	
Is it lawful for a *m* to put away............. Mt 19:3	444
this cause shall a *m* leave father .... Mt 19:5	444
together, let not *m* put asunder............. Mt 19:6	444
If the case of the *m* be so with............. Mt 19:10	444
The young *m* saith unto him, All .... Mt 19:20	3495
the young *m* heard that saying............. Mt 19:22	3495
That a rich *m* shall hardly enter .... Mt 19:23	
than for a rich *m* to enter into............. Mt 19:24	
regeneration when the Son of *m* .... Mt 19:28	444
unto a *m* that is an householder............ Mt 20:1	444
Because no *m* hath hired us.................. Mt 20:7	3762
they received every *m* a penny .... Mt 20:9	
likewise received every *m* a penny .... Mt 20:10	
the Son of *m* shall be betrayed .... Mt 20:18	444
Even as the Son of *m* came not to .... Mt 20:28	444
if any *m* say ought unto you, ye .... Mt 21:3	
A certain *m* had two sons .... Mt 21:28	444
he saw there a *m* which had not on....... Mt 22:11	444

neither carest thou for any *m* .... Mt 22:16	3762
Master, Moses said, If a *m* die .... Mt 22:24	5100
no *m* was able to answer him a .... Mt 22:46	3762
neither durst any *m* from that day .... Mt 22:46	
call no *m* your father upon the............. Mt 23:9	
Take heed that no *m* deceive you .... Mt 24:4	5100
Then if any *m* shall say unto you,......... Mt 24:23	
the coming of the Son of *m* be.............. Mt 24:27	444
sign of the Son of *m* in heaven............. Mt 24:30	444
they shall see the Son of *m*................... Mt 24:30	444
of that day and hour knoweth no *m* ...... Mt 24:36	3762
the coming of the Son of *m* be.............. Mt 24:37	444
the coming of the Son of *m* be.............. Mt 24:39	444
ye think not the Son of *m* cometh .... Mt 24:44	444
hour wherein the Son of *m* cometh .... Mt 25:13	444
a *m* travelling into a far country .... Mt 25:14	444
to every *m* according to his .... Mt 25:15	
knew thee that thou art an hard *m*........ Mt 25:24	444
When the Son of *m* shall come in .... Mt 25:31	444
the Son of *m* is betrayed to be.............. Mt 26:2	444
Go into the city to such a *m*.................. Mt 26:18	
The Son of *m* goeth as it is .... Mt 26:24	444
but woe unto that *m* by whom the .... Mt 26:24	444
by whom the Son of *m* is betrayed........ Mt 26:24	444
that *m* if he had not been born .... Mt 26:24	444
the Son of *m* is betrayed into the .... Mt 26:45	444
shall ye see the Son of *m* sitting .... Mt 26:64	444
with an oath, I do not know the *m* .... Mt 26:72	444
swear, saying, I know not the *m* .... Mt 26:74	444
nothing to do with that just *m* .... Mt 27:19	
out, they found a *m* of Cyrene .... Mt 27:32	444
said, This *m* calleth for Elias .... Mt 27:47	
there came a rich *m* of Arimathaea .... Mt 27:57	444
a *m* with an unclean spirit.................... Mk 1:23	444
See thou say nothing to any *m*.............. Mk 1:44	3367
Why doth this *m* thus speak................. Mk 2:7	
ye may know that the Son of *m* .... Mk 2:10	444
No *m* also seweth a piece of new .... Mk 2:21	3762
no *m* putteth new wine into old .... Mk 2:22	3762
them, The sabbath was made for *m* .... Mk 2:27	444
and not *m* for the sabbath .... Mk 2:27	444
Therefore the Son of *m* is Lord .... Mk 2:28	444
there was a *m* there which had a .... Mk 3:1	444
he saith unto the *m* which had the........ Mk 3:3	444
their hearts, he saith to the *m* .... Mk 3:5	444
No *m* can enter into a strong................ Mk 3:27	3762
he will first bind the strong *m* .... Mk 3:27	2478
If any *m* have ears to hear, let .... Mk 4:23	
as if a *m* should cast seed into .... Mk 4:26	444
another, What manner of *m* is this........ Mk 4:41	
tombs a *m* with an unclean spirit.......... Mk 5:2	444
no *m* could bind him, no, not with .... Mk 5:3	3762
neither could any *m* tame him .... Mk 5:4	
said unto him, Come out of the *m* .... Mk 5:8	444
And he suffered no *m* to follow him....... Mk 5:37	3762
straitly that no *m* should know it .... Mk 5:43	3367
whence hath this *m* these things............ Mk 6:2	
knowing that he was a just *m*................ Mk 6:20	435
If a *m* shall say to his father or............. Mk 7:11	444
There is nothing from without a *m* .... Mk 7:15	444
those are they that defile the *m* .... Mk 7:15	444
If any *m* have ears to hear, let .... Mk 7:16	
from without entereth into the *m* .... Mk 7:18	444
of the *m*, that defileth the *m* .... Mk 7:20	444
come from within, and defile the *m* ...... Mk 7:23	444
house, and would have no *m* know it...... Mk 7:24	3762
them that they should tell no *m* .... Mk 7:36	3367
From whence can a *m* satisfy these .... Mk 8:4	5100
and they bring a blind *m* unto him .... Mk 8:22	
he took the blind *m* by the hand........... Mk 8:23	
restored, and saw every *m* clearly......... Mk 8:25	
that they should tell no *m* of him.......... Mk 8:30	3367
that the Son of *m* must suffer .... Mk 8:31	444
For what shall it profit a *m*................... Mk 8:36	444
Or what shall a *m* give in .... Mk 8:37	444
shall the Son of *m* be ashamed .... Mk 8:38	444
about, they saw no *m* any more............ Mk 9:8	3762
no *m* what things they had seen .... Mk 9:9	3367
till the Son of *m* were risen from .... Mk 9:9	444
how it is written of the Son of *m* .... Mk 9:12	444
not that any *m* should know it .... Mk 9:30	
The Son of *m* is delivered into.............. Mk 9:31	444
If any *m* desire to be first, the.............. Mk 9:35	
for there is no *m* which shall do .... Mk 9:39	3762
Is it lawful for a *m* to put away............. Mk 10:2	435
cause shall a *m* leave his father .... Mk 10:7	444
together, let not *m* put asunder............. Mk 10:9	444
than for a rich *m* to enter into.............. Mk 10:25	
There is no *m* that hath left .... Mk 10:29	3762
the Son of *m* shall be delivered............. Mk 10:33	444
For even the Son of *m* came not to .... Mk 10:45	444

M

And they call the blind *m*, saying .... Mk 10:49	Son of *m* be to this generation................ Lk 11:30	444
The blind *m* said unto him, Lord, ... Mk 10:51	No *m*, when he hath lighted a................ Lk 11:33	3762
a colt tied, whereon never *m* sat .... Mk 11:2	444	him shall the Son of *m* also.................... Lk 12:8	444
if any *m* say unto you, Why do ye .... Mk 11:3	speak a word against the Son of *m* ...... Lk 12:10	444
No *m* eat fruit of thee hereafter .... Mk 11:14	3367	And he said unto him, *M*, who made...... Lk 12:14	444
would not suffer that any *m* .... Mk 11:16	rich *m* brought forth plentifully .... Lk 12:16	444
A certain *m* planted a vineyard, ... Mk 12:1	444	for the Son of *m* cometh at an .... Lk 12:40	444
thou art true, and carest for no *m* .... Mk 12:14	444	A certain *m* had a fig tree .... Lk 13:6
no *m* after that durst ask him any .... Mk 12:34	3762	of mustard seed, which a *m* took .... Lk 13:19	444
Take heed lest any *m* deceive you. ...... Mk 13:5	there was a certain *m* before him .... Lk 14:2	444
then if any *m* shall say to you, ... Mk 13:21	art bidden of any *m* to a wedding .... Lk 14:8
then shall they see the Son of *m* .... Mk 13:26	444	lest a more honourable *m* than .... Lk 14:8
day and that hour knoweth no *m* .... Mk 13:32	3762	and say to thee, Give this *m* place .... Lk 14:9
For the Son of *m* is as a........................ Mk 13:34	A certain *m* made a great supper,........ Lk 14:16	444
is as a *m* taking a far journey.............. Mk 13:34	444	If any *m* come to me, and hate not ...... Lk 14:26
servants, and to every *m* his work .... Mk 13:34	This *m* began to build, and was not .... Lk 14:30	444
there shall meet you a *m* bearing .... Mk 14:13	444	This *m* receiveth sinners, and............... Lk 15:2
The Son of *m* indeed goeth, as it .... Mk 14:21	444	**What *m* of you, having an hundred** ..... Lk 15:4	444
but woe to that *m* by whom the Son ...... Mk 14:21	444	he said, A certain *m* had two sons........ Lk 15:11	444
by whom the Son of *m* is betrayed ...... Mk 14:21	444	and no *m* gave unto him .... Lk 15:16	3762
good were it for that *m* if he had .... Mk 14:21	444	There was a certain rich *m* .... Lk 16:1	444
the Son of *m* is betrayed into the .... Mk 14:41	444	and every *m* presseth into it .... Lk 16:16
followed him a certain young *m*.............. Mk 14:51	3495	There was a certain rich *m* .... Lk 16:19	444
ye shall see the Son of *m* sitting .... Mk 14:62	444	the rich *m* also died, and was .... Lk 16:22
I know not this *m* of whom ye .... Mk 14:71	444	one of the days of the Son of *m* .... Lk 17:22	444
them, what every *m* should take .... Mk 15:24	also the Son of *m* be in his day .... Lk 17:24	444
Truly this *m* was the Son of God .... Mk 15:39	444	also in the days of the Son of *m* .... Lk 17:26	444
they saw a young *m* sitting on the......... Mk 16:5	3495	day when the Son of *m* is revealed .... Lk 17:30	444
to any *m* for they were afraid.................. Mk 16:8	3762	not God, neither regarded *m* .... Lk 18:2	444
for I am an old *m*, and my wife............... Lk 1:18	I fear not God, nor regard *m* .... Lk 18:4	444
to a *m* whose name was Joseph.............. Lk 1:27	435	when the Son of *m* cometh, shall .... Lk 18:8	444
this be, seeing I know not a *m*................ Lk 1:34	435	this *m* went down to his house .... Lk 18:14
there was a *m* in Jerusalem, whose........ Lk 2:25	444	than for a rich *m* to enter into .... Lk 18:25
and the same *m* was just and devout, ... Lk 2:25	444	There is no *m* that hath left .... Lk 18:29	3762
and in favour with God and *m*................ Lk 2:52	444	Son of *m* shall be accomplished .... Lk 18:31	444
unto them, Do violence to no *m* .... Lk 3:14	3367	a certain blind *m* sat by the way .... Lk 18:35
That *m* shall not live by bread .... Lk 4:4	444	there was a *m* named Zacchaeus,.......... Lk 19:2	435
And in the synagogue there was a *m*..... Lk 4:33	444	guest with a *m* that is a sinner.............. Lk 19:7	435
for I am a sinful *m*, O Lord .... Lk 5:8	435	from any *m* by false accusation............. Lk 19:8
behold a *m* full of leprosy........................ Lk 5:12	435	For the Son of *m* is come to seek .... Lk 19:10	444
And he charged him to tell no *m* .... Lk 5:14	3367	not have this *m* to reign over us .... Lk 19:14
men brought in a bed a *m* which .... Lk 5:18	444	every *m* had gained by trading .... Lk 19:15
their faith, he said unto him, *M* .... Lk 5:20	because thou art an austere *m* .... Lk 19:21	444
Son of *m* hath power upon earth to ...... Lk 5:24	444	knewest that I was an austere *m*........... Lk 19:22	444
No *m* putteth a piece of a new .... Lk 5:36	3762	tied, whereon yet never *m* sat .... Lk 19:30	444
no *m* putteth new wine into old .... Lk 5:37	3762	if any *m* ask you, Why do ye loose ...... Lk 19:31
No *m* also having drunk old wine .... Lk 5:39	3762	A certain *m* planted a vineyard, ... Lk 20:9	444
That the Son of *m* is Lord also of ...... Lk 6:5	444	of *m* coming in a cloud with power ...... Lk 21:27	444
there was a *m* whose right hand .... Lk 6:6	444	and to stand before the Son of *m* .... Lk 21:36	444
said to the *m* which had the.................... Lk 6:8	444	city, there shall a *m* meet you .... Lk 22:10	444
upon them all, he said unto the *m*......... Lk 6:10	444	And truly the Son of *m* goeth............... Lk 22:22	444
Give to every *m* that asketh of .... Lk 6:30	but woe unto that *m* by whom he is...... Lk 22:22	444
A good *m* out of the good treasure ...... Lk 6:45	444	thou the Son of *m* with a kiss............... Lk 22:48	444
an evil *m* out of the evil........................... Lk 6:45	444	and said, This *m* was also with him ...... Lk 22:56
He is like a *m* which built an .... Lk 6:48	444	And Peter said, *M*, I am not .... Lk 22:58	444
is like a *m* that without a..................... Lk 6:49	444	And Peter said, *M*, I know not what ...... Lk 22:60	444
For I also am a *m* set under .... Lk 7:8	444	**Hereafter shall the Son of *m* sit** .... Lk 22:69	444
there was a dead *m* carried out.............. Lk 7:12	people, I find no fault in this *m* .... Lk 23:4	444
And he said, Young *m*, I say unto .... Lk 7:14	3495	whether the *m* were a Galilaean .... Lk 23:6	444
A *m* clothed in soft raiment.................. Lk 7:25	444	Ye have brought this *m* unto me .... Lk 23:14	444
The Son of *m* is come eating and .... Lk 7:34	444	have found no fault in this *m* .... Lk 23:14	444
and ye say, Behold a gluttonous *m* .... Lk 7:34	444	at once, saying, Away with this *m* .... Lk 23:18
within himself, saying, This *m*................. Lk 7:39	but this *m* hath done nothing .... Lk 23:41
No *m*, when he hath lighted a............. Lk 8:16	3762	Certainly this was a righteous *m* .... Lk 23:47	444
another, What manner of *m* is this........ Lk 8:25	there was a *m* named Joseph, a............. Lk 23:50	435
him out of the city a certain *m* .... Lk 8:27	435	and he was a good *m*, and a just........... Lk 23:50	435
spirit to come out of the *m* .... Lk 8:29	444	This *m* went unto Pilate, and .... Lk 23:52
Then went the devils out of the *m* .... Lk 8:33	444	wherein never *m* before was laid .... Lk 23:53	3762
and came to Jesus, and found the *m* ...... Lk 8:35	444	The Son of *m* must be delivered .... Lk 24:7	444
Now the *m* out of whom the devils .... Lk 8:38	435	There was a *m* sent from God,............... Jn 1:6	444
there came a *m* named Jairus .... Lk 8:41	435	which lighteth every *m* that .... Jn 1:9	444
house, he suffered no *m* to go in .... Lk 8:51	3762	the flesh, nor of the will of *m* .... Jn 1:13	435
should tell no *m* what was done............. Lk 8:56	3367	No *m* hath seen God at any time .... Jn 1:18	3762
them to tell no *m* that thing .... Lk 9:21	3367	After me cometh a *m* which is .... Jn 1:30	435
The Son of *m* must suffer many .... Lk 9:22	444	**and descending upon the Son of *m*** ..... Jn 1:51	444
If any *m* will come after me, let .... Lk 9:23	Every *m* at the beginning doth set .... Jn 2:10	444
For what is a *m* advantaged .... Lk 9:25	444	not that any should testify of *m* .... Jn 2:25	444
him shall the Son of *m* be ashamed ...... Lk 9:26	444	for he knew what was in *m* .... Jn 2:25	444
told no *m* in those days any of .... Lk 9:36	3762	There was a *m* of the Pharisees,........... Jn 3:1	444
a *m* of the company cried out, ... Lk 9:38	435	for no *m* can do these miracles.............. Jn 3:2	3762
for the Son of *m* shall be .... Lk 9:44	444	Except a *m* be born again, he .... Jn 3:3	5100
For the Son of *m* is not come to .... Lk 9:56	444	How can a *m* be born when he is .... Jn 3:4	444
a certain *m* said unto him, Lord, ... Lk 9:57	**Except a *m* be born of water and of** ...... Jn 3:5	5100
but the Son of *m* hath not where .... Lk 9:58	444	no *m* hath ascended up to heaven, ... Jn 3:13	3762
And Jesus said unto him, No *m* .... Lk 9:62	3762	even the Son of *m* which is in .... Jn 3:13	444
and salute no *m* by the way................... Lk 10:4	3367	so must the Son of *m* be lifted up .... Jn 3:14	444
no *m* knoweth who the Son is, but .... Lk 10:22	3762	A *m* can receive nothing, except .... Jn 3:27	444
A certain *m* went down from .... Lk 10:30	444	no *m* receiveth his testimony .... Jn 3:32	3762
When a strong *m* armed keepeth his .... Lk 11:21	yet no *m* said, What seekest thou .... Jn 4:27	3762
unclean spirit is gone out of a *m* .... Lk 11:24	444	Come, see a *m*, which told me all .... Jn 4:29	444
the last state of that *m* is worse............ Lk 11:26	444	Hath any *m* brought him ought to .... Jn 4:33

the *m* believed the word that ....Jn 4:50	444	**your joy no *m* taketh from you** ....Jn 16:22	3762
And a certain *m* was there, which ....Jn 5:5	444	not that any *m* should ask thee ....Jn 16:30	
The impotent *m* answered him ....Jn 5:7		**every *m* to his own, and shall** ....Jn 16:32	
answered him, Sir, I have no *m* ....Jn 5:7	444	one *m* should die for the people ....Jn 18:14	444
immediately the *m* was made whole ......Jn 5:9	444	bring ye against this *m* ....Jn 18:29	444
What *m* is that which said unto ....Jn 5:12	444	for us to put any *m* to death ....Jn 18:31	3762
The *m* departed, and told the Jews ......Jn 5:15	444	all again, saying, Not this *m* ....Jn 18:40	444
For the Father judgeth no *m* ....Jn 5:22	3762	saith unto them, Behold the *m* ....Jn 19:5	444
also, because he is the Son of *m* ....Jn 5:27	444	saying, If thou let this *m* go ....Jn 19:12	444
I receive not testimony from *m* ....Jn 5:34	444	wherein was never *m* yet laid ....Jn 19:41	3762
which the Son of *m* shall give ....Jn 6:27	444	Lord, and what shall this *m* do ....Jn 21:21	
No *m* can come to me, except the ....Jn 6:44	3762	Now this *m* purchased a field with ....Acts 1:18	
Every *m* therefore that hath heard ....Jn 6:45		and let no *m* dwell therein ....Acts 1:20	
Not that any *m* hath seen the ....Jn 6:46		because that every *m* heard them ....Acts 2:6	1520
that a *m* may eat thereof, and not ....Jn 6:50	5100	hear we every *m* in our own tongue ......Acts 2:8	1520
if any *m* eat of this bread, he ....Jn 6:51		a *m* approved of God among you by ......Acts 2:22	435
How can this *m* give us his flesh ....Jn 6:52		to all men, as every *m* had need............Acts 2:45	
ye eat the flesh of the Son of *m* ....Jn 6:53	444	a certain *m* lame from his ....Acts 3:2	435
if ye shall see the Son of *m* ....Jn 6:62	444	as the lame *m* which was healed ....Acts 3:11	
that no *m* can come unto me, ...Jn 6:65	3762	we had made this *m* to walk ....Acts 3:12	
For there is no *m* that doeth any ....Jn 7:4	3762	his name hath made this *m* strong ....Acts 3:16	
for some said, He is a good *m* ....Jn 7:12		good deed done to the impotent *m* ....Acts 4:9	444
Howbeit no *m* spake openly of him ......Jn 7:13	3762	even by him doth this *m* stand ....Acts 4:10	
How knoweth this *m* letters ....Jn 7:15		beholding the *m* which was healed ....Acts 4:14	444
If any *m* will do his will, he ....Jn 7:17		henceforth to no *m* in this name ....Acts 4:17	444
on the sabbath day circumcise a *m* ......Jn 7:22	444	For the *m* was above forty years ....Acts 4:22	444
If a *m* on the sabbath day receive ......Jn 7:23	444	was made unto every *m* according ....Acts 4:35	
because I have made a *m* every ....Jn 7:23	444	But a certain *m* named Ananias ....Acts 5:1	435
we know this *m* whence he is ....Jn 7:27		durst no *m* join himself to them ....Acts 5:13	3762
no *m* knoweth whence he is ....Jn 7:27	3762	had opened, we found no *m* within........Acts 5:23	3762
but no *m* laid hands on him, ...Jn 7:30	3762	After this *m* rose up Judas of................Acts 5:37	
than these which this *m* hath done ....Jn 7:31		a *m* full of faith and of the Holy ....Acts 6:5	435
and cried, saying, If any *m* thirst ....Jn 7:37		This *m* ceaseth not to speak..................Acts 6:13	444
but no *m* laid hands on him ....Jn 7:44	3762	the Son of *m* standing on the ....Acts 7:56	444
Never *m* spake like this *m* ....Jn 7:46	444	But there was a certain *m* ....Acts 8:9	435
Doth our law judge any *m*, before ....Jn 7:51	444	This *m* is the great power of God ....Acts 8:10	
every *m* went unto his own house..........Jn 7:53		a *m* of Ethiopia, an eunuch of ....Acts 8:27	435
hath no *m* condemned thee ....Jn 8:10	3762	except some *m* should guide me ....Acts 8:31	
She said, No *m*, Lord ....Jn 8:11	3762	of himself, or of some other *m* ....Acts 8:34	
I judge no *m* ....Jn 8:15	3762	hearing a voice, but seeing no *m*............Acts 9:7	3367
and no *m* laid hands on him ....Jn 8:20	3762	his eyes were opened, he saw no *m* ....Acts 9:8	3762
ye have lifted up the Son of *m* ....Jn 8:28	444	**a *m* named Ananias coming in** ....Acts 9:12	435
and were never in bondage to any *m* .....Jn 8:33		I have heard by many of this *m* ....Acts 9:13	435
a *m* that hath told you the truth, ...Jn 8:40	444	he found a certain *m* named Aeneas ......Acts 9:33	444
If a *m* keep my saying, he shall ....Jn 8:51	5100	There was a certain *m* in Caesarea ....Acts 10:1	435
If a *m* keep my saying, he shall ....Jn 8:52	5100	A devout *m*, and one that feared ....Acts 10:2	
he saw a *m* which was blind from ....Jn 9:1	444	Cornelius the centurion, a just *m* ....Acts 10:22	435
Master, who did sin, this *m* ....Jn 9:2		I myself also am a *m*...............................Acts 10:26	444
Neither hath this *m* sinned ....Jn 9:3		a *m* that is a Jew to keep company ....Acts 10:28	435
night cometh, when no *m* can work .....Jn 9:4	3762	not call any *m* common or unclean ....Acts 10:28	444
eyes of the blind *m* with the clay ....Jn 9:6		a *m* stood before me in bright.................Acts 10:30	435
A *m* that is called Jesus made ....Jn 9:11	444	Can any *m* forbid water, that ....Acts 10:47	5100
This *m* is not of God, because he............Jn 9:16	444	For he was a good *m*, and full of ....Acts 11:24	435
How can a *m* that is a sinner do............Jn 9:16	444	every *m* according to his ability,............Acts 11:29	1538
They say unto the blind *m* again ....Jn 9:17		the voice of a god, and not of a *m* ....Acts 12:22	444
that if any *m* did confess that he ....Jn 9:22		Sergius Paulus, a prudent *m* ....Acts 13:7	435
called they the *m* that was blind ....Jn 9:24	444	a *m* of the tribe of Benjamin, by...........Acts 13:21	435
we know that this *m* is a sinner.............Jn 9:24	444	a *m* after mine own heart, which...........Acts 13:22	435
The *m* answered and said unto them, ...Jn 9:30	444	that through this *m* is preached.............Acts 13:38	
but if any *m* be a worshipper of.............Jn 9:31		though a *m* declare it unto you..............Acts 13:41	5100
m opened the eyes of one that was ....Jn 9:32		there sat a certain *m* at Lystra ....Acts 14:8	435
If this *m* were not of God, he ....Jn 9:33		There stood a *m* of Macedonia ....Acts 16:9	435
by me if any *m* enter in, he shall ....Jn 10:9		by that *m* whom he hath ordained ....Acts 17:31	435
No *m* taketh it from me, but I lay ....Jn 10:18	3762	**no *m* shall set on thee to hurt** ....Acts 18:10	3762
neither shall any *m* pluck them ....Jn 10:28		born at Alexandria, an eloquent *m*.........Acts 18:24	435
no *m* is able to pluck them out of........Jn 10:29	3762	This *m* was instructed in the way..........Acts 18:25	
and because that thou, being a *m* ....Jn 10:33	444	the *m* in whom the evil spirit was ....Acts 19:16	444
John spake of this *m* were true..............Jn 10:41		For a certain *m* named Demetrius, ...Acts 19:24	
Now a certain *m* was sick, named ....Jn 11:1		what *m* is there that knoweth not ....Acts 19:35	444
If any *m* walk in the day, he ....Jn 11:9		him, have a matter against any *m* ....Acts 19:38	
But if a *m* walk in the night, he ....Jn 11:10	5100	a certain young *m* named Eutychus ....Acts 20:9	3494
of them said, Could not this *m* ....Jn 11:37		And they brought the young *m* alive ......Acts 20:12	
even this *m* should not have died ....Jn 11:37		the same *m* had four daughters, ...Acts 21:9	
for this *m* doeth many miracles.............Jn 11:47	444	the *m* that owneth this girdle ....Acts 21:11	435
that one *m* should die for the ....Jn 11:50	444	This is the *m*, that teacheth all ....Acts 21:28	444
if any *m* knew where he were, he..........Jn 11:57		I am a *m* which am a Jew of Tarsus ....Acts 21:39	444
that the Son of *m* should be ....Jn 12:23	444	I am verily a *m* which am a Jew, ...Acts 22:3	435
If any *m* serve me, let him follow ....Jn 12:26		a devout *m* according to the law, ...Acts 22:12	435
if any *m* serve me, him will my ....Jn 12:26		to scourge a *m* that is a Roman ....Acts 22:25	444
The Son of *m* must be lifted up ....Jn 12:34	444	for this *m* is a Roman ....Acts 22:26	444
who is this Son of *m* ....Jn 12:34	444	saying, We find no evil in this *m* ....Acts 23:9	444
if any *m* hear my words, and ....Jn 12:47		Bring this young *m* unto the chief ....Acts 23:17	3494
Now no *m* at the table knew for ....Jn 13:28	3762	to bring this young *m* unto thee ....Acts 23:18	3494
Now is the Son of *m* glorified ....Jn 13:31	444	then let the young *m* depart..................Acts 23:22	3494
no *m* cometh unto the Father, but........Jn 14:6	3762	See thou tell no *m* that thou hast ....Acts 23:22	3367
If a *m* love me, he will keep my ....Jn 14:23	5100	This *m* was taken of the Jews, and........Acts 23:27	435
If a *m* abide not in me, he is ....Jn 15:6	5100	that the Jews laid wait for the *m* ....Acts 23:30	435
Greater love hath no *m* than this ....Jn 15:13	3762	found this *m* a pestilent fellow ....Acts 24:5	435
that a *m* lay down his life for ....Jn 15:13	5100	the temple disputing with any *m* ....Acts 24:12	
the works which none other *m* did ....Jn 15:24		go down with me, and accuse this *m* ......Acts 25:5	435
for joy that a *m* is born into the ....Jn 16:21	444	no *m* may deliver me unto them ....Acts 25:11	3762

M

There is a certain *m* left in	Acts 25:14	435
Romans to deliver any *m* to die	Acts 25:16	444
commanded the *m* to be brought	Acts 25:17	435
I would also hear the *m* myself	Acts 25:22	444
present with us, ye see this *m*	Acts 25:24	
This *m* doeth nothing worthy of	Acts 26:31	444
This *m* might have been set at	Acts 26:32	444
No doubt this *m* is a murderer	Acts 28:4	444
of the chief of the island	Acts 28:7	
confidence, no *m* forbidding him	Acts 28:31	
image made like to corruptible *m*	Rom 1:23	444
thou art inexcusable, O *m*	Rom 2:1	444
And thinkest thou this, O *m*	Rom 2:3	444
to every *m* according to his deeds	Rom 2:6	
every soul of *m* that doeth evil	Rom 2:9	444
to every *m* that worketh good, to	Rom 2:10	3956
preachest a *m* should not steal	Rom 2:21	
Thou that sayest a *m* should not	Rom 2:22	
God be true, but every *m* a liar	Rom 3:4	444
(I speak as a *m*)	Rom 3:5	444
Therefore we conclude that a *m* is	Rom 3:28	444
the blessedness of the *m*, unto	Rom 4:6	444
Blessed is the *m* to whom the Lord	Rom 4:8	435
for a righteous *m* will one die	Rom 5:7	
m some would even dare to die	Rom 5:7	
as by one *m* sin entered into the	Rom 5:12	444
gift by grace, which is by one *m*	Rom 5:15	
that our old *m* is crucified with	Rom 6:6	444
over a *m* as long as he liveth	Rom 7:1	444
she be married to another *m*	Rom 7:3	435
she be married to another *m*	Rom 7:3	435
the law of God after the inward *m*	Rom 7:22	444
O wretched *m* that I am	Rom 7:24	444
Now if any *m* have not the Spirit	Rom 8:9	
for what a *m* seeth, why doth he	Rom 8:24	5100
Nay but, O *m*, who art thou that	Rom 9:20	444
That the *m* which doeth those	Rom 10:5	444
For with the heart *m* believeth	Rom 10:10	
to every *m* that is among you, not	Rom 12:3	
to every *m* the measure of faith	Rom 12:3	
Recompense to no *m* evil for evil	Rom 12:17	3367
Owe no *m* any thing, but to love	Rom 13:8	3367
One *m* esteemeth one day above	Rom 14:5	
Let every *m* be fully persuaded in	Rom 14:5	
himself, and no *m* dieth to himself	Rom 14:7	3762
that no *m* put a stumblingblock or	Rom 14:13	
that *m* who eateth with offence	Rom 14:20	444
have entered into the heart of *m*	1Cor 2:9	444
For what *m* knoweth the things of	1Cor 2:11	444
knoweth the things of a *m*	1Cor 2:11	444
the spirit of *m* which is in him	1Cor 2:11	444
so the things of God knoweth no *m*	1Cor 2:11	3762
But the natural *m* receiveth not	1Cor 2:14	444
yet he himself is judged of no *m*	1Cor 2:15	3762
even as the Lord gave to every *m*	1Cor 3:5	
every *m* shall receive his own	1Cor 3:8	
But let every *m* take heed how he	1Cor 3:10	
can no *m* lay than that is laid	1Cor 3:11	3762
Now if any *m* build upon this	1Cor 3:12	
If any *m* defile the temple of God	1Cor 3:17	
Let no *m* deceive himself	1Cor 3:18	3367
If any *m* among you seemeth to be	1Cor 3:18	
Therefore let no *m* glory in men	1Cor 3:21	3367
Let a *m* so account of us, as of	1Cor 4:1	444
that a *m* be found faithful	1Cor 4:2	5100
then shall every *m* have praise of	1Cor 4:5	
if any *m* that is called a brother	1Cor 5:11	
there is not a wise *m* among you	1Cor 6:5	
Every sin that a *m* doeth is	1Cor 6:18	444
It is good for a *m* not to touch a	1Cor 7:1	444
let every *m* have his own wife, and	1Cor 7:2	
But every *m* hath his proper gift	1Cor 7:7	
or how knowest thou, O *m*, whether	1Cor 7:16	435
God hath distributed to every *m*	1Cor 7:17	
Is any *m* called being circumcised	1Cor 7:18	
Let every *m* abide in the same	1Cor 7:20	
Brethren, let every *m*, wherein he	1Cor 7:24	
that it is good for a *m* so to be	1Cor 7:26	444
But if any *m* think that he	1Cor 7:36	
if any *m* think that he knoweth	1Cor 8:2	
But if any *m* love God, the same	1Cor 8:3	
is not in every *m* that knowledge	1Cor 8:7	3956
For if any *m* see thee which hast	1Cor 8:10	
Say I these things as a *m*	1Cor 9:8	444
than that any *m* should make my	1Cor 9:15	
every *m* that striveth for the	1Cor 9:25	
you but such as is common to *m*	1Cor 10:13	442
Let no *m* seek his own	1Cor 10:24	3367
but every *m* another's wealth	1Cor 10:24	
But if any *m* say unto you, This	1Cor 10:28	
the head of every *m* is Christ	1Cor 11:3	435
and the head of the woman is the *m*	1Cor 11:3	435
Every *m* praying or prophesying,	1Cor 11:4	435
For a *m* indeed ought not to cover	1Cor 11:7	435
the woman is the glory of the *m*	1Cor 11:7	435
For the *m* is not of the woman	1Cor 11:8	435
but the woman of the *m*	1Cor 11:8	435
Neither was the *m* created for the	1Cor 11:9	435
but the woman for the *m*	1Cor 11:9	435
is the *m* without the woman	1Cor 11:11	435
neither the woman without the *m*	1Cor 11:11	435
For as the woman is of the *m*	1Cor 11:12	435
even so is the *m* also by the	1Cor 11:12	435
if a *m* have long hair, it is a	1Cor 11:14	435
But if any *m* seem to be	1Cor 11:16	
But let a *m* examine himself, and	1Cor 11:28	444
And if any *m* hunger, let him eat	1Cor 11:34	
that no *m* speaking by the Spirit	1Cor 12:3	3762
that no *m* can say that Jesus is	1Cor 12:3	3762
given to every *m* to profit withal	1Cor 12:7	1538
dividing to every *m* severally as	1Cor 12:11	1538
but when I became a *m*, I put away	1Cor 13:11	435
for no *m* understandeth him	1Cor 14:2	3762
If any *m* speak in an unknown	1Cor 14:27	
If any *m* think himself to be a	1Cor 14:37	
But if any *m* be ignorant, let him	1Cor 14:38	
For since by *m* came death	1Cor 15:21	444
by *m* came also the resurrection	1Cor 15:21	444
But every *m* in his own order	1Cor 15:23	
But some *m* will say, How are the	1Cor 15:35	
The first *m* Adam was made a	1Cor 15:45	444
The first *m* is of the earth,	1Cor 15:47	444
the second *m* is the Lord from	1Cor 15:47	444
Let no *m* therefore despise him	1Cor 16:11	5100
If any *m* love not the Lord Jesus	1Cor 16:22	
to such a *m* is this punishment	2Cor 2:6	
but though our outward *m* perish	2Cor 4:16	444
yet the inward *m* is renewed day	2Cor 4:16	
know we no *m* after the flesh	2Cor 5:16	3762
Therefore if any *m* be in Christ	2Cor 5:17	
we have wronged no *m*	2Cor 7:2	3762
we have corrupted no *m*	2Cor 7:2	3762
we have defrauded no *m*	2Cor 7:2	3762
according to that a *m* hath	2Cor 8:12	5100
that no *m* should blame us in this	2Cor 8:20	5100
Every *m* according as he purposeth	2Cor 9:7	
If any *m* trust to himself that he	2Cor 10:7	
wanted, I was chargeable to no *m*	2Cor 11:9	3762
no *m* shall stop me of this	2Cor 11:10	
again, Let no *m* think me a fool	2Cor 11:16	5100
if a *m* bring you into bondage	2Cor 11:20	5100
if a *m* devour you	2Cor 11:20	5100
if a *m* take of you	2Cor 11:20	5100
if a *m* exalt himself	2Cor 11:20	5100
if a *m* smite you on the face	2Cor 11:20	5100
I knew a *m* in Christ above	2Cor 12:2	444
And I knew such a *m*, (whether in	2Cor 12:3	444
it is not lawful for a *m* to utter	2Cor 12:4	444
lest any *m* should think of me	2Cor 12:6	
(not of men, neither by *m*	Gal 1:1	444
If any *m* preach any other gospel	Gal 1:9	
was preached the *m* is not after *m*	Gal 1:11	444
For I neither received it of *m*	Gal 1:12	444
Knowing that a *m* is not justified	Gal 2:16	444
But that no *m* is justified by the	Gal 3:11	3762
The *m* that doeth them shall live	Gal 3:12	444
no *m* disannulleth, or addeth	Gal 3:15	3762
to every *m* that is circumcised	Gal 5:3	444
if a *m* be overtaken in a fault,	Gal 6:1	444
For if a *m* think himself to be	Gal 6:3	5100
But let every *m* prove his own	Gal 6:4	
For every *m* shall bear his own	Gal 6:5	
for whatsoever a *m* soweth	Gal 6:7	444
henceforth let no *m* trouble me	Gal 6:17	3367
of works, lest any *m* should boast	Eph 2:9	
in himself of twain one new *m*	Eph 2:15	444
by his Spirit in the inner *m*	Eph 3:16	444
the Son of God, unto a perfect *m*	Eph 4:13	435
the former conversation the old *m*	Eph 4:22	444
And that ye put on the new *m*	Eph 4:24	444
speak every *m* truth with his	Eph 4:25	
unclean person, nor covetous *m*	Eph 5:5	444
Let no *m* deceive you with vain	Eph 5:6	3367
For no *m* ever yet hated his own	Eph 5:29	3762
cause shall a *m* leave his father	Eph 5:31	444
whatsoever good thing any *m* doeth	Eph 6:8	
Look not every *m* on his own	Phil 2:4	
but every *m* also on the things of	Phil 2:4	
And being found in fashion as a *m*	Phil 2:8	444
For I have no *m* likeminded	Phil 2:20	3762
If any other *m* thinketh that he	Phil 3:4	
Whom we preach, warning every *m*	Col 1:28	444

and teaching every *m* in all wisdom	Col 1:28	444
every *m* perfect in Christ Jesus	Col 1:28	444
lest any *m* should beguile you	Col 2:4	
Beware lest any *m* spoil you	Col 2:8	
Let no *m* therefore judge you in	Col 2:16	5100
Let no *m* beguile you of your	Col 2:18	3367
put off the old *m* with his deeds	Col 3:9	444
And have put on the new *m*, which	Col 3:10	
if any *m* have a quarrel against	Col 3:13	
how ye ought to answer every *m*	Col 4:6	1520
That no *m* should be moved by	1Th 3:3	3367
That no *m* go beyond and defraud	1Th 4:6	
that despiseth, despiseth not *m*	1Th 4:8	444
render evil for evil unto any *m*	1Th 5:15	
Let no *m* deceive you by any means	2Th 2:3	5100
that *m* of sin be revealed, the	2Th 2:3	444
if any *m* obey not our word by	2Th 3:14	
word by this epistle, note that *m*	2Th 3:14	
is good, if a *m* use it lawfully	1Ti 1:8	5100
law is not made for a righteous *m*	1Ti 1:9	
God and men, the *m* Christ Jesus	1Ti 2:5	444
nor to usurp authority over the *m*	1Ti 2:12	435
If a *m* desire the office of a	1Ti 3:1	5100
(For if a *m* know not how to rule	1Ti 3:5	5100
Let no *m* despise thy youth	1Ti 4:12	3367
having been the wife of one *m*	1Ti 5:9	435
If any *m* or woman that believeth	1Ti 5:16	
Lay hands suddenly on no *m*	1Ti 5:22	3367
If any *m* teach otherwise, and	1Ti 6:3	
O *m* of God, flee these things	1Ti 6:11	444
which no *m* can approach unto	1Ti 6:16	
whom no *m* hath seen, nor can see	1Ti 6:16	444
No *m* that warreth entangleth	2Ti 2:4	3762
if a *m* also strive for masteries,	2Ti 2:5	5100
If a *m* therefore purge himself	2Ti 2:21	5100
That the *m* of God may be perfect,	2Ti 3:17	444
first answer no *m* stood with me	2Ti 4:16	3762
Let no *m* despise thee	Titus 2:15	3367
To speak evil of no *m*, to be no	Titus 3:2	3367
God our Saviour toward *m* appeared	Titus 3:4	
A *m* that is an heretick after the	Titus 3:10	444
testified, saying, What is *m*	Heb 2:6	444
or the son of *m*, that thou	Heb 2:6	444
should taste death for every *m*	Heb 2:9	
For this *m* was counted worthy of	Heb 3:3	
every house is builded by some *m*	Heb 3:4	
lest any *m* fall after the same	Heb 4:11	
no *m* taketh this honour unto	Heb 5:4	5100
Now consider how great this *m* was	Heb 7:4	
of which no *m* gave attendance at	Heb 7:13	3762
But this *m*, because he continueth	Heb 7:24	
which the Lord pitched, and not *m*	Heb 8:2	444
m have somewhat also to offer	Heb 8:3	
not teach every *m* his neighbour	Heb 8:11	
every *m* his brother, saying, Know	Heb 8:11	
But this *m*, after he had offered	Heb 10:12	
but if any *m* draw back, my soul	Heb 10:38	
without which no *m* shall see the	Heb 12:14	3762
any *m* fail of the grace of God	Heb 12:15	
not fear what *m* shall do unto me	Heb 13:6	444
For let not that *m* think that he	Jas 1:7	444
A double minded *m* is unstable in	Jas 1:8	435
the rich *m* fade away in his ways	Jas 1:11	
Blessed is the *m* that endureth	Jas 1:12	435
Let no *m* say when he is tempted,	Jas 1:13	3367
evil, neither tempteth he any *m*	Jas 1:13	3762
But every *m* is tempted, when he	Jas 1:14	
let every *m* be swift to hear,	Jas 1:19	444
For the wrath of *m* worketh not	Jas 1:20	435
he is like unto a *m* beholding his	Jas 1:23	435
what manner of *m* he was	Jas 1:24	
this *m* shall be blessed in his	Jas 1:25	
If any *m* among you seem to be	Jas 1:26	
assembly a *m* with a gold ring	Jas 2:2	435
in also a poor *m* in vile raiment	Jas 2:2	
though a *m* say he hath faith, and	Jas 2:14	5100
a *m* may say, Thou hast faith, and	Jas 2:18	5100
But wilt thou know, O vain *m*	Jas 2:20	444
that by works a *m* is justified	Jas 2:24	444
If any *m* offend not in word	Jas 3:2	
the same is a perfect *m*	Jas 3:2	435
But the tongue can no *m* tame	Jas 3:8	444
Who is a wise *m* and endued with	Jas 3:13	
of a righteous *m* availeth much	Jas 5:16	
Elias was a *m* subject to like	Jas 5:17	444
all the glory of *m* as the flower	1Pet 1:24	444
of *m* for the Lord's sake	1Pet 2:13	442
if a *m* for conscience toward God	1Pet 2:19	5100
it be the hidden *m* of the heart	1Pet 3:4	444
to give an answer to every *m* that	1Pet 3:15	
As every *m* hath received the gift	1Pet 4:10	

If any *m* speak, let him speak as	1Pet 4:11	
if any *m* minister, let him do it	1Pet 4:11	
Yet if any *m* suffer as a	1Pet 4:16	
not in old time by the will of *m*	2Pet 1:21	444
righteous *m* dwelling among them	2Pet 2:8	
for of whom a *m* is overcome	2Pet 2:19	5100
And if any *m* sin, we have an	1Jn 2:1	
If any *m* love the world, the love	1Jn 2:15	
ye need not that any *m* teach you	1Jn 2:27	
every *m* that hath this hope in	1Jn 3:3	
children, let no *m* deceive you	1Jn 3:7	3367
No *m* hath seen God at any time	1Jn 4:12	3762
If a *m* say, I love God, and hateth	1Jn 4:20	
If any *m* see his brother sin a	1Jn 5:16	
one like unto the Son of *m*	Rev 1:13	444
which no *m* knoweth saving he that	Rev 2:17	3762
he that openeth, and no *m* shutteth	Rev 3:7	3762
and shutteth, and no *m* openeth	Rev 3:7	3762
an open door, and no *m* can shut it	Rev 3:8	3762
hast, that no *m* take thy crown	Rev 3:11	3367
if any *m* hear my voice, and open	Rev 3:20	
the third beast had a face as a *m*	Rev 4:7	444
no *m* in heaven, nor in earth,	Rev 5:3	3762
because no *m* was found worthy to	Rev 5:4	3762
and every bondman, and every free *m*	Rev 6:15	
which no *m* could number, of all	Rev 7:9	3762
a scorpion, when he striketh a *m*	Rev 9:5	444
if any *m* will hurt them, fire	Rev 11:5	
if any *m* will hurt them, he must	Rev 11:5	
And she brought forth a *m* child	Rev 12:5	730
which brought forth the *m* child	Rev 12:13	730
If any *m* have an ear, let him	Rev 13:9	
that no *m* might buy or sell, save	Rev 13:17	5100
for it is the number of a *m*	Rev 13:18	444
no *m* could learn that song but	Rev 14:3	3762
If any *m* worship the beast and his	Rev 14:9	
one sat like unto the Son of *m*	Rev 14:14	444
no *m* was able to enter into the	Rev 15:8	3762
became as the blood of a dead *m*	Rev 16:3	
for no *m* buyeth their merchandise	Rev 18:11	3762
a name written, that no *m* knew	Rev 19:12	3762
and they were judged every *m*	Rev 20:13	
according to the measure of *m*	Rev 21:17	444
to give every *m* according as his	Rev 22:12	
For I testify unto every *m* that	Rev 22:18	3956
If any *m* shall add unto these	Rev 22:18	
if any *m* shall take away from the	Rev 22:19	

MANAEN *(man´-a-en) A Christian teacher at Antioch.*

Niger, and Lucius of Cyrene, and M	Acts 13:1	3127

MANAHATH *(man´-a-hath)*
> 1. *A son of Shobal.*

Alvan, and M, and Ebal, Shepho, and	Gen 36:23	4506
Alian, and M, and Ebal, Shephi, and	1Chr 1:40	4506

> 2. *A city in Benjamin.*

Geba, and they removed them to M	1Chr 8:6	4506

MANAHETHITES *(man´-a-heth-ites) Descendants of Shobal.*

Haroeh, and half of the M	1Chr 2:52	2679
house of Joab, and half of the M	1Chr 2:54	2680

MANASSEH *(ma-nas´-seh)* See MANASSEH'S, MAN-
ASSES, MANASSITES.
> 1. *A son of Joseph.*

the name of the firstborn M	Gen 41:51	4519
in the land of Egypt were born M	Gen 46:20	4519
he took with him his two sons, M	Gen 48:1	4519
And now thy two sons, Ephraim and M	Gen 48:5	4519
M in his left hand toward	Gen 48:13	4519
for M was the firstborn	Gen 48:14	4519
God make thee as Ephraim and as M	Gen 48:20	4519
and he set Ephraim before M	Gen 48:20	4519
also of Machir the son of M were	Gen 50:23	4519
after their families were M	Num 26:28	4519
Of the sons of M	Num 26:29	4519
the son of Machir, the son of M	Num 27:1	4519
families of M the son of Joseph	Num 27:1	4519
the son of M went to Gilead	Num 32:39	4519
Gilead unto Machir the son of M	Num 32:40	4519
And Jair the son of M went	Num 32:41	4519
the son of Machir, the son of M	Num 36:1	4519
Jair the son of M took all the	Deut 3:14	4519
children of Machir the son of M	Josh 13:31	4519
for M the firstborn of M	Josh 17:1	4519
of M the son of Joseph by their	Josh 17:2	4519
the son of Machir, the son of M	Josh 17:3	4519
the towns of Jair the son of M	1Kin 4:13	4519
The sons of M	1Chr 7:14	4519
the son of Machir, the son of M	1Chr 7:17	4519

2. Descendants and land of Manasseh 1.

of M; Gamaliel the son	Num 1:10	4519
Of the children of M, by their	Num 1:34	4519
of them, even of the tribe of M	Num 1:35	4519
And by him shall be the tribe of M	Num 2:20	4519
of M shall be Gamaliel the son of	Num 2:20	4519
prince of the children of M	Num 7:54	4519
of M was Gamaliel the son of	Num 10:23	4519
Joseph, namely, of the tribe of M	Num 13:11	4519
These are the families of M	Num 26:34	4519
the tribe of M the son of Joseph	Num 32:33	4519
half the tribe of M have received	Num 34:14	4519
the tribe of the children of M	Num 34:23	4519
the sons of M the son of Joseph	Num 36:12	4519
gave I unto the half tribe of M	Deut 3:13	4519
and to the half tribe of M	Deut 29:8	4520
and they are the thousands of M	Deut 33:17	4519
and the land of Ephraim, and M	Deut 34:2	4519
and to half the tribe of M	Josh 1:12	4519
of Gad, and half the tribe of M	Josh 4:12	4519
Gadites, and the half tribe of M	Josh 12:6	4519
tribes, and the half tribe of M	Josh 13:7	4519
unto the half tribe of M	Josh 13:29	4519
children of M by their families	Josh 13:29	4519
of Joseph were two tribes, M	Josh 14:4	4519
So the children of Joseph, M	Josh 16:4	4519
inheritance of the children of M	Josh 16:9	4519
was also a lot for the tribe of M	Josh 17:1	4519
children of M by their families	Josh 17:2	4519
And there fell ten portions to M	Josh 17:5	4519
Because the daughters of M had an	Josh 17:6	4519
the coast of M was from Asher to	Josh 17:7	4519
Now M had the land of Tappuah	Josh 17:8	4519
of M belonged to the children of	Josh 17:8	4519
Ephraim are among the cities of M	Josh 17:9	4519
the coast of M also was on the	Josh 17:9	4519
M had in Issachar and in Asher	Josh 17:11	4519
Yet the children of M could not	Josh 17:12	4519
Joseph, even to Ephraim and to M	Josh 17:17	4519
and Reuben, and half the tribe of M	Josh 18:7	4519
in Bashan out of the tribe of M	Josh 20:8	4519
and out of the half tribe of M	Josh 21:5	4519
of the half tribe of M in Bashan	Josh 21:6	4519
And out of the half tribe of M	Josh 21:25	4519
M they gave Golan in Bashan with	Josh 21:27	4519
Gadites, and the half tribe of M	Josh 22:1	4519
M Moses had given possession in	Josh 22:7	4519
and the half tribe of M returned	Josh 22:9	4519
the half tribe of M built there	Josh 22:10	4519
the half tribe of M have built an	Josh 22:11	4519
of Gad, and to the half tribe of M	Josh 22:13	4519
of Gad, and to the half tribe of M	Josh 22:15	4519
and the half tribe of M answered	Josh 22:21	4519
of Gad and the children of M spake	Josh 22:30	4519
of Gad, and to the children of M	Josh 22:31	4519
Neither did M drive out the	Judg 1:27	4519
behold, my family is poor in M	Judg 6:15	4519
sent messengers throughout all M	Judg 6:35	4519
and out of Asher, and out of all M	Judg 7:23	4519
and he passed over Gilead, and M	Judg 11:29	4519
Gadites, and half the tribe of M	1Chr 5:18	4519
half tribe of M dwelt in the land	1Chr 5:23	4519
Gadites, and the half tribe of M	1Chr 5:26	4519
out of the half tribe of M	1Chr 6:61	4519
out of the tribe of M in Bashan	1Chr 6:62	4519
And out of the half tribe of M	1Chr 6:70	4519
the family of the half tribe of M	1Chr 6:71	4519
the borders of the children of M	1Chr 7:29	4519
of the children of Ephraim, and M	1Chr 9:3	4519
And there fell some of M to David	1Chr 12:19	4519
to Ziklag, there fell to him of M	1Chr 12:20	4519
of the thousands that were of M	1Chr 12:20	4519
half tribe of M eighteen thousand	1Chr 12:31	4519
and of the half tribe of M	1Chr 12:37	4519
Gadites, and the half tribe of M	1Chr 26:32	4520
of the half tribe of M, Joel the	1Chr 27:20	4519
Of the half tribe of M in Gilead	1Chr 27:21	4519
with them out of Ephraim and M	2Chr 15:9	4519
letters also to Ephraim and M	2Chr 30:1	4519
of Ephraim and M even unto Zebulun	2Chr 30:10	4519
Nevertheless divers of Asher and M	2Chr 30:11	4519
even many of Ephraim, and M	2Chr 30:18	4519
and Benjamin, in Ephraim also and M	2Chr 31:1	4519
And so did he in the cities of M	2Chr 34:6	4519
had gathered of the hand of M	2Chr 34:9	4519
Gilead is mine, and M is mine	Ps 60:7	4519
M stir up thy strength, and come	Ps 80:2	4519
M is mine	Ps 108:8	4519
M, Ephraim; and Ephraim	Is 9:21	4519
and Ephraim, M	Is 9:21	4519

the west side, a portion for M	Eze 48:4	4519
And by the border of M, from the	Eze 48:5	4519

3. Grandfather of Jonathan.

the son of Gershom, the son of M	Judg 18:30	4519

4. Son of King Hezekiah.

M his son reigned in his stead	2Kin 20:21	4519
M was twelve years old when he	2Kin 21:1	4519
M seduced them to do more evil	2Kin 21:9	4519
Because M king of Judah hath done	2Kin 21:11	4519
Moreover M shed innocent blood	2Kin 21:16	4519
Now the rest of the acts of M	2Kin 21:17	4519
M slept with his fathers, and was	2Kin 21:18	4519
of the LORD, as his father M did	2Kin 21:20	4519
the altars which M had made in	2Kin 23:12	4519
that M had provoked him withal	2Kin 23:26	4519
of his sight, for the sins of M	2Kin 24:3	4519
son, Hezekiah his son, M his son,	1Chr 3:13	4519
M his son reigned in his stead	2Chr 32:33	4519
M was twelve years old when he	2Chr 33:1	4519
So M made Judah and the	2Chr 33:9	4519
And the LORD spake to M, and to his	2Chr 33:10	4519
which took M among the thorns, and	2Chr 33:11	4519
Then M knew that the LORD he was	2Chr 33:13	4519
Now the rest of the acts of M	2Chr 33:18	4519
So M slept with his fathers, and	2Chr 33:20	4519
of the LORD, as did M his father	2Chr 33:22	4519
which M his father had made	2Chr 33:22	4519
as M his father had humbled	2Chr 33:23	4519
because of M the son of Hezekiah	Jer 15:4	4519

5. Married a foreigner in exile.

Bezaleel, and Binnui, and M	Ezr 10:30	4519

6. A descendant of Hashum.

Zabad, Eliphelet, Jeremai, M	Ezr 10:33	4519

MANASSEH'S (ma-nas'-sez)

1. Refers to Manasseh 1.

and his left hand upon M head	Gen 48:14	4519
from Ephraim's head unto M head	Gen 48:17	4519
the rest of M sons had the land	Josh 17:6	4519

2. Refers to Manasseh 2.

Ephraim's, and northward it was M	Josh 17:10	4519

MANASSES (ma-nas'-seez) See MANASSEH.

1. Greek form of Manasseh; ancestor of Jesus.

And Ezekias begat M	Mt 1:10	3128
and M begat Amon	Mt 1:10	3128

2. Greek form of Manasseh 2.

Of the tribe of M were sealed	Rev 7:6	3128

MANASSITES (ma-nas'-sites) Same as Manasseh 2.

and Golan in Bashan, of the M	Deut 4:43	4520
the Ephraimites, and among the M	Judg 12:4	4520
and the Reubenites, and the M	2Kin 10:33	4520

MANDRAKES

found m in the field, and brought	Gen 30:14	1736
me, I pray thee, of thy son's m	Gen 30:14	1736
thou take away my son's m also	Gen 30:15	1736
thee to night for thy son's m	Gen 30:15	1736
I have hired thee with my son's m	Gen 30:16	1736
The m give a smell, and at our	Song 7:13	1736

MANEH

fifteen shekels, shall be your m	Eze 45:12	4488

MANGER

clothes, and laid him in a m	Lk 2:7	5336
swaddling clothes, lying in a m	Lk 2:12	5336
Joseph, and the babe lying in a m	Lk 2:16	5336

MANIFEST

of men, that God might m them	Eccl 3:18	1305
secret, that shall not be made m	Lk 8:17	5318
he should be made m to Israel	Jn 1:31	5319
that his deeds may be made m	Jn 3:21	5319
of God should be made m in him	Jn 9:3	5319
love him, and will m myself to him	Jn 14:21	1718
that thou wilt m thyself unto us	Jn 14:22	1718
is m to all them that dwell in	Acts 4:16	5318
may be known of God is m in them	Rom 1:19	5319
I was made m unto them that asked	Rom 10:20	1717
But now is made m, and by the	Rom 16:26	5319
Every man's work shall be made m	1Cor 3:13	5318
will make m the counsels of the	1Cor 4:5	5319
approved may be made m among you	1Cor 11:19	5318
the secrets of his heart made m	1Cor 14:25	5318
it is m that he is excepted	1Cor 15:27	1212
maketh m the savour of his	2Cor 2:14	5319
Jesus might be made m in our body	2Cor 4:10	5319
be made m in our mortal flesh	2Cor 4:11	5319
but we are made m unto God	2Cor 5:11	5319
are made m in your consciences	2Cor 5:11	5319
made m among you in all things	2Cor 11:6	5319
Now the works of the flesh are m	Gal 5:19	5318

reproved are made *m* by the light	Eph 5:13	5319
whatsoever doth make *m* is light	Eph 5:13	5319
in Christ are *m* in all the palace	Phil 1:13	5318
but now is made *m* to his saints	Col 1:26	5319
That I may make it *m*, as I ought	Col 4:4	5319
Which is a *m* token of the	2Th 1:5	
God was *m* in the flesh, justified	1Ti 3:16	5319
works of some are *m* beforehand	1Ti 5:25	4271
But is now made *m* by the	2Ti 1:10	5319
folly shall be *m* unto all men	2Ti 3:9	1552
that is not *m* in his sight	Heb 4:13	852
holiest of all was not yet made *m*	Heb 9:8	5319
but was *m* in these last times for	1Pet 1:20	5319
that they might be made *m* that	1Jn 2:19	5319
In this the children of God are *m*	1Jn 3:10	5318
for thy judgments are made *m*	Rev 15:4	5319

MANIFESTATION

for the *m* of the sons of God	Rom 8:19	602
But the *m* of the Spirit is given	1Cor 12:7	5321
but by *m* of the truth commending	2Cor 4:2	5321

MANIFESTED

nothing hid, which shall not be *m*	Mk 4:22	5319
of Galilee, and *m* forth his glory	Jn 2:11	5319
I have *m* thy name unto the men	Jn 17:6	5319
of God without the law is *m*	Rom 3:21	5319
But hath in due times *m* his word	Titus 1:3	5319
(For the life was *m*, and we have	1Jn 1:2	5319
with the Father, and was *m* unto us	1Jn 1:2	5319
ye know that he was *m* to take	1Jn 3:5	5319
this purpose the Son of God was *m*	1Jn 3:8	5319
In this was *m* the love of God	1Jn 4:9	5319

MANIFESTLY

Forasmuch as ye are *m* declared to	2Cor 3:3	5319

MANIFOLD

Yet thou in thy *m* mercies	Neh 9:19	7227
according to thy *m* mercies thou	Neh 9:27	7227
O LORD, how *m* are thy works	Ps 104:24	7231
For I know your *m* transgressions	Amos 5:12	7227
Who shall not receive *m* more in	Lk 18:30	4179
by the church the *m* wisdom of God	Eph 3:10	4182
heaviness through *m* temptations	1Pet 1:6	4164
stewards of the *m* grace of God	1Pet 4:10	4164

MANKIND

Thou shalt not lie with *m*	Lev 18:22	2145
If a man also lie with *m*, as he	Lev 20:13	2145
thing, and the breath of all *m*	Job 12:10	1320,376
nor abusers of themselves with *m*	1Cor 6:9	733
that defile themselves with *m*	1Ti 1:10	733
and hath been tamed of *m*	Jas 3:7	5449,442

MANNA

they said one to another, It is *m*	Ex 16:15	4478
Israel called the name thereof *M*	Ex 16:31	4478
and put an omer full of *m* therein	Ex 16:33	4478
of Israel did eat *m* forty years	Ex 16:35	4478
they did eat *m*, until they came	Ex 16:35	4478
is nothing at all, beside this *m*	Num 11:6	4478
the *m* was as coriander seed, and	Num 11:7	4478
in the night, the *m* fell upon it	Num 11:9	4478
to hunger, and fed thee with *m*	Deut 8:3	4478
fed thee in the wilderness with *m*	Deut 8:16	4478
the *m* ceased on the morrow after	Josh 5:12	4478
the children of Israel *m* any more	Josh 5:12	4478
not thy *m* from their mouth	Neh 9:20	4478
had rained down *m* upon them to	Ps 78:24	4478
fathers did eat *m* in the desert	Jn 6:31	3131
did eat *m* in the wilderness	Jn 6:49	3131
not as your fathers did eat *m*	Jn 6:58	3131
was the golden pot that had *m*	Heb 9:4	3131
I give to eat of the hidden *m*	Rev 2:17	3131

MANNER

with Sarah after the *m* of women	Gen 18:11	734
far from thee to do after this *m*	Gen 18:25	1697
us after the *m* of all the earth	Gen 19:31	1870
womb, and two *m* of people shall be	Gen 25:23	
On this *m* shall ye speak unto	Gen 32:19	1697
After this *m* did thy servant to	Gen 39:19	1697
after the former *m* when thou wast	Gen 40:13	4941
basket there was of all *m* of	Gen 40:17	
his father he sent after this *m*	Gen 45:23	
in all *m* of service in the field	Ex 1:14	
they also did in like *m* with	Ex 7:11	3651
no *m* of work shall be done in	Ex 12:16	
with her after the *m* of daughters	Ex 21:9	4941
For all *m* of trespass, whether it	Ex 22:9	1697
or for any *m* of lost thing, which	Ex 22:9	
In like *m* thou shalt deal with	Ex 23:11	3651
and in all *m* of workmanship,	Ex 31:3	

to work in all *m* of workmanship	Ex 31:5	
to bring for all *m* of work	Ex 35:29	
and in all *m* of workmanship	Ex 35:31	
to make any *m* of cunning work	Ex 35:33	
of heart, to work all *m* of work	Ex 35:35	3605
to know how to work all *m* of work	Ex 36:1	
offering, according to the *m*	Lev 5:10	4941
saying, Ye shall eat no *m* of fat	Lev 7:23	
ye shall eat no *m* of blood	Lev 7:26	
it be that eateth any *m* of blood	Lev 7:27	
and offered it according to the *m*	Lev 9:16	4941
among all *m* of beasts that go on	Lev 11:27	
ye defile yourselves with any *m*	Lev 11:44	
for all *m* of plague of leprosy	Lev 14:54	
you, that eateth any *m* of blood	Lev 17:10	
eat the blood of no *m* of flesh	Lev 17:14	
planted all *m* of trees for food	Lev 19:23	
or by any *m* of living thing that	Lev 20:25	
Ye shall do no *m* of work	Lev 23:31	
Ye shall have one *m* of law	Lev 24:22	4941
neither she be taken with *m*	Num 5:13	
and according to the *m* thereof	Num 9:14	4941
do these things after this *m*	Num 15:13	3541
one *m* shall be for you, and for	Num 15:16	4941
offering, according to the *m*	Num 15:24	4941
ye shall do no *m* of servile work	Num 28:18	
After this *m* ye shall offer daily	Num 28:24	
offerings, according unto their *m*	Num 29:6	4941
to their number, after the *m*	Num 29:18	4941
to their number, after the *m*	Num 29:21	4941
to their number, after the *m*	Num 29:24	4941
to their number, after the *m*	Num 29:27	4941
to their number, after the *m*	Num 29:30	4941
to their number, after the same *m*	Num 29:33	4941
to their number, after the *m*	Num 29:37	4941
of all *m* of beasts, and give them	Num 31:30	
for ye saw no *m* of similitude on	Deut 4:15	
this is the *m* of the release	Deut 15:2	1697
In like *m* shalt thou do with his	Deut 22:3	3651
he that lieth with any *m* of beast	Deut 27:21	
city after the same *m* seven times	Josh 6:15	4941
What *m* of men were they whom ye	Judg 8:18	
in like *m* they sent unto the king	Judg 11:17	
after the *m* of the Zidonians,	Judg 18:7	4941
Now this was the *m* in former time	Ruth 4:7	
shew them the *m* of the king that	1Sa 8:9	4941
This will be the *m* of the king	1Sa 8:11	4941
the people the *m* of the kingdom	1Sa 10:25	4941
people answered him after this *m*	1Sa 17:27	1697
and spake after the same *m*	1Sa 17:30	1697
him again after the former *m*	1Sa 17:30	1697
saying, On this *m* spake David	1Sa 18:24	1697
before Samuel in like *m*, and lay	1Sa 19:24	1571
and the bread is in a *m* common	1Sa 21:5	1870
so will be his *m* all the while he	1Sa 27:11	3541
played before the LORD on all *m*	2Sa 6:5	
And is this the *m* of man, O Lord	2Sa 7:19	8452
king, and speak on this *m* unto him	2Sa 14:3	1697
on this *m* did Absalom to all	2Sa 15:6	1697
hath spoken after this *m*	2Sa 17:6	1697
work of the bases was on this *m*	1Kin 7:28	
After this *m* he made the ten	1Kin 7:37	
after their *m* with knives	1Kin 18:28	4941
And one said on this *m*	1Kin 22:20	3541
and another said on that *m*	1Kin 22:20	3541
What *m* of man was he which came	2Kin 1:7	4941
stood by a pillar, as the *m* was	2Kin 11:14	4941
know not the *m* of the God of the	2Kin 17:26	4941
not the *m* of the God of the land	2Kin 17:26	4941
them the *m* of the God of the land	2Kin 17:27	4941
after the *m* of the nations whom	2Kin 17:33	4941
but they did after their former *m*	2Kin 17:40	4941
m of service of the tabernacle of	1Chr 6:48	
with all *m* of instruments of war	1Chr 12:37	
with him all *m* of vessels of gold	1Chr 18:10	
all *m* of cunning men for every	1Chr 22:15	
cunning men for every *m* of work	1Chr 22:15	
for all *m* of measure and size	1Chr 23:29	
of the LORD, according to their *m*	1Chr 24:19	4941
instruments of all *m* of service	1Chr 28:14	
shall be with thee for all *m* of	1Chr 28:21	
skilful man, for any *m* of service	1Chr 28:21	
all *m* of precious stones, and	1Chr 29:2	
for all *m* of work to be made by	1Chr 29:5	
also to grave any *m* of graving	2Chr 2:14	
after the *m* before the oracle	2Chr 4:20	4941
m of the nations of other lands	2Chr 13:9	
And one spake saying after this *m*	2Chr 18:19	3541
and another saying after that *m*	2Chr 18:19	
in their place after their *m*	2Chr 30:16	4941
you, nor persuade you on this *m*	2Chr 32:15	

for all *m* of pleasant jewels	2Chr 32:27	
and stalls for all *m* of beasts	2Chr 32:28	
the work in any *m* of service	2Chr 34:13	
said we unto them after this *m*	Ezr 5:4	
I answered them after the same *m*	Neh 6:4	1697
m the fifth time with an open	Neh 6:5	1697
assembly, according unto the *m*	Neh 8:18	4941
and the fruit of all *m* of trees	Neh 10:37	
all *m* of burdens, which they	Neh 13:15	
all *m* of ware, and sold on the	Neh 13:16	
(for so was the king's *m* toward	Est 1:13	1697
according to the *m* of the women	Est 2:12	1881
soul abhorreth all *m* of meat	Ps 107:18	
be full, affording all *m* of store	Ps 144:13	2177
are full of pleasant fruits	Song 7:13	
the lambs feed after their *m*	Is 5:17	1699
thee, after the *m* of Egypt	Is 10:24	1870
lift it up after the *m* of Egypt	Is 10:26	1870
dwell therein shall die in like *m*	Is 51:6	3654
After this *m* will I mar the pride	Jer 13:9	3541
hath been thy *m* from thy youth	Jer 22:21	1870
shall remain after the *m* thereof	Jer 30:18	4941
after the *m* of your fathers	Eze 20:30	1870
after the *m* of the Babylonians	Eze 23:15	1823
them after the *m* of adulteresses	Eze 23:45	4941
after the *m* of women that shed	Eze 23:45	4941
no *m* of hurt was found upon him	Dan 6:23	
pestilence after the *m* of Egypt	Amos 4:10	1870
The *m* of Beer-sheba liveth	Amos 8:14	1870
and healing all *m* of sickness	Mt 4:23	
all *m* of disease among the people	Mt 4:23	
shall say all *m* of evil against	Mt 5:11	
After this *m* therefore pray ye	Mt 6:9	3779
What *m* of man is this, that even	Mt 8:27	4217
out, and to heal all *m* of sickness	Mt 10:1	
of sickness and all *m* of disease	Mt 10:1	
All *m* of sin and blasphemy shall	Mt 12:31	
What *m* of man is this, that even	Mk 4:41	686
see what *m* of stones and what	Mk 13:1	4217
So ye in like *m*, when ye shall	Mk 13:29	3779
cast in her mind what *m* of	Lk 1:29	4217
What *m* of child shall this be	Lk 1:66	686
for in the like *m* did their	Lk 6:23	
what *m* of woman this is that	Lk 7:39	4217
to another, What *m* of man is this	Lk 8:25	686
Ye know not what *m* of spirit ye	Lk 9:55	3634
all *m* of herbs, and pass over	Lk 11:42	
and in like *m* the seven also	Lk 20:31	5615
What *m* of communications are	Lk 24:17	
after the *m* of the purifying of	Jn 2:6	
What *m* of saying is this that he	Jn 7:36	
as the *m* of the Jews is to bury	Jn 19:40	1485
shall so come in like *m* as ye	Acts 1:11	5158
Wherein were all *m* of fourfooted	Acts 10:12	1485
circumcised after the *m* of Moses	Acts 15:1	1485
letters by them after this *m*	Acts 15:23	3592
And Paul, as his *m* was, went in	Acts 17:2	1486
after what *m* I have been with you	Acts 20:18	4458
m of the law of the fathers	Acts 22:3	195
And he wrote a letter after this *m*	Acts 23:25	5179
It is not the *m* of the Romans to	Acts 25:16	1485
I doubted of such *m* of questions	Acts 25:20	4012
My *m* of life from my youth, which	Acts 26:4	981
I speak after the *m* of men	Rom 6:19	442
in me all *m* of concupiscence	Rom 7:8	
gift of God, one after this *m*	1Cor 7:9	
After the same *m* also he took the	1Cor 11:25	3779
If after the *m* of men I have	1Cor 15:32	5615
were made sorry after a godly *m*	2Cor 7:9	
livest after the *m* of Gentiles	Gal 2:14	1483
I speak after the *m* of men	Gal 3:15	
as ye know what *m* of men we were	1Th 1:5	3634
m of entering in we had unto you	1Th 1:9	3697
In like *m* also, that women adorn	1Ti 2:9	
m of life, purpose, faith,	2Ti 3:10	72
together, as the *m* of some is	Heb 10:25	1485
forgetteth what *m* of man he was	Jas 1:24	3697
or what *m* of time the Spirit of	1Pet 1:11	4169
ye holy in all *m* of conversation	1Pet 1:15	
For after this *m* in the old time	1Pet 3:5	3779
what *m* of persons ought ye to be	2Pet 3:11	4217
what *m* of love the Father hath	1Jn 3:1	4217
the cities about them in like *m*	Jude 7	5158
them, he must in this *m* be killed	Rev 11:5	3779
all *m* vessels of ivory	Rev 18:12	
all *m* vessels of most precious	Rev 18:12	
with all *m* of precious stones	Rev 21:19	
which bare twelve *m* of fruits	Rev 22:2	

MANNERS

not walk in the *m* of the nation	Lev 20:23	2708
day they do after the former *m*	2Kin 17:34	4941
but have done after the *m* of the	Eze 11:12	4941
he their *m* in the wilderness	Acts 13:18	5159
communications corrupt good *m*	1Cor 15:33	2239
in divers *m* spake in time past	Heb 1:1	4187

MANOAH (ma-no'-ah) *Father of Samson.*

of the Danites, whose name was *M*	Judg 13:2	4495
Then *M* intreated the LORD, and	Judg 13:8	4495
God hearkened to the voice of *M*	Judg 13:9	4495
but *M* her husband was not with	Judg 13:9	4495
M arose, and went after his wife	Judg 13:11	4495
M said, Now let thy words come to	Judg 13:12	4495
the angel of the LORD said unto *M*	Judg 13:13	4495
M said unto the angel of the LORD	Judg 13:15	4495
the angel of the LORD said unto *M*	Judg 13:16	4495
For *M* knew not that he was an	Judg 13:16	4495
M said unto the angel of the LORD	Judg 13:17	4495
So *M* took a kid with a meat	Judg 13:19	4495
and *M* and his wife looked on	Judg 13:19	4495
And *M* and his wife looked on it, and	Judg 13:20	4495
the LORD did no more appear to *M*	Judg 13:21	4495
Then *M* knew that he was an angel	Judg 13:21	4495
M said unto his wife, We shall	Judg 13:22	4495
the buryingplace of *M* his father	Judg 16:31	4495

MAN'S See APPENDIX.

MANSERVANT

thy son, nor thy daughter, thy *m*	Ex 20:10	5650
thy neighbour's wife, nor his *m*	Ex 20:17	5650
shall push a *m* or a maidservant	Ex 21:32	5650
son, nor thy daughter, nor thy *m*	Deut 5:14	5650
that thy *m* and thy maidservant may	Deut 5:14	5650
house, his field, or his *m*	Deut 5:21	5650
son, and thy daughter, and thy *m*	Deut 12:18	5650
son, and thy daughter, and thy *m*	Deut 16:11	5650
son, and thy daughter, and thy *m*	Deut 16:14	5650
of my *m* or of my maidservant	Job 31:13	5650
That every man should let his *m*	Jer 34:9	5650
that every one should let his *m*	Jer 34:10	5650

MANSERVANT'S

And if he smite out his *m* tooth	Ex 21:27	5650

MANSERVANTS

Beside their *m* and their	Neh 7:67	5650

MANSIONS

In my Father's house are many *m*	Jn 14:2	3438

MANSLAYER

which ye shall appoint for the *m*	Num 35:6	7523
that the *m* die not, until he	Num 35:12	7523

MANSLAYERS

and murderers of mothers, for *m*	1Ti 1:9	409

MANTLE

tent, she covered him with a *m*	Judg 4:18	8063
laid hold upon the skirt of his *m*	1Sa 15:27	4598
and he is covered with a *m*	1Sa 28:14	4598
that he wrapped his face in his *m*	1Kin 19:13	155
by him, and cast his *m* upon him	1Kin 19:19	155
And Elijah took his *m*, and wrapped	2Kin 2:8	155
He took up also the *m* of Elijah	2Kin 2:13	155
he took the *m* of Elijah that fell	2Kin 2:14	155
thing, I rent my garment and my *m*	Ezr 9:3	4598
having rent my garment and my *m*	Ezr 9:5	4598
Then Job arose, and rent his *m*	Job 1:20	4598
and they rent every one his *m*	Job 2:12	4598
their own confusion, as with a *m*	Ps 109:29	4598

MANTLES

suits of apparel, and the *m*	Is 3:22	4595

MANY See APPENDIX.

MAOCH (ma'-ok) *Father of Achish.*

him unto Achish, the son of *M*	1Sa 27:2	4582

MAON (ma'-on) See MAONITES.
  1. A city in Judah.

M, Carmel, and Ziph, and Juttah,	Josh 15:55	4584
And there was a man in *M*, whose	1Sa 25:2	4584

  2. A descendant of Caleb.

And the son of Shammai was *M*	1Chr 2:45	4584
M was the father of Beth-zur	1Chr 2:45	4584

  3. A wilderness in Judah.

men were in the wilderness of *M*	1Sa 23:24	4584
and abode in the wilderness of *M*	1Sa 23:25	4584
David in the wilderness of *M*	1Sa 23:25	4584

MAONITES (ma'-on-ites) See MEHUNIM. *An enemy tribe of Israel.*

also, and the Amalekites, and the *M*	Judg 10:12	4584

MAR
neither shalt thou *m* the corners	Lev 19:27	7843
lest I *m* mine own inheritance	Ruth 4:6	7843
of your mice that *m* the land	1Sa 6:5	7843
m every good piece of land with	2Kin 3:19	3510
They *m* my path, they set forward	Job 30:13	5420
will I *m* the pride of Judah	Jer 13:9	7843

MARA (ma'-rah) *Another name for Naomi.*
Call me not Naomi, call me *M*	Ruth 1:20	4755

MARAH (ma'-rah) *An Israelite encampment in the wilderness.*
And when they came to *M*, they	Ex 15:23	4785
not drink of the waters of *M*	Ex 15:23	4785
the name of it was called *M*	Ex 15:23	4785
of Etham, and pitched in *M*	Num 33:8	4785
And they removed from *M*, and came	Num 33:9	4785

MARALAH (mar'-a-lah) *A city in Zebulun.*
went up toward the sea, and *M*	Josh 19:11	4831

MARANATHA
Christ, let him be Anathema *M*	1Cor 16:22	*3134*

MARBLE
stones, and *m* stones in abundance	1Chr 29:2	7898
to silver rings and pillars of *m*	Est 1:6	8338
and blue, and white, and black, *m*	Est 1:6	8336
His legs are as pillars of *m*	Song 5:15	8336
wood, and of brass, and iron, and *m*	Rev 18:12	*3139*

MARCH
when thou didst *m* through the	Ps 68:7	6805
for they shall *m* with an army	Jer 46:22	3212
they shall *m* every one on his	Joel 2:7	3212
which shall *m* through the breadth	Hab 1:6	1980
Thou didst *m* through the land in	Hab 3:12	6805

MARCHED
the Egyptians *m* after them	Ex 14:10	5265

MARCHEDST
when thou *m* out of the field of	Judg 5:4	6805

MARCUS (mar'-cus) *See* MARK. *Latin form of Mark.*
fellowprisoner saluteth you, and *M*	Col 4:10	*3138*
M, Aristarchus, Demas, Lucas, my	Philem 24	*3138*
and so doth *M* my son	1Pet 5:13	*3138*

MARDUK *See* MERODACH.

MAREAL *See* MARALAH.

MARESHAH
1. *A city in Judah.*
And Keilah, and Achzib, and *M*	Josh 15:44	4762
And Gath, and *M*, and Ziph,	2Chr 11:8	4762
and came unto *M*	2Chr 14:9	4762
in the valley of Zephathah at *M*	2Chr 14:10	4762
Eliezer the son of Dodavah of *M*	2Chr 20:37	4762
heir unto thee, O inhabitant of *M*	Mic 1:15	4762

2. *Father of Hebron.*
the sons of *M* the father of	1Chr 2:42	4762

3. *A descendant of Shelah.*
Lecah, and Laadah the father of *M*	1Chr 4:21	4762

MARINERS
of Zidon and Arvad were thy *m*	Eze 27:8	7751
m were in thee to occupy thy	Eze 27:9	4419
thy fairs, thy merchandise, thy *m*	Eze 27:27	4419
And all that handle the oar, the *m*	Eze 27:29	4419
Then the *m* were afraid, and cried	Jonah 1:5	4419

MARISHES
the *m* thereof shall not be healed	Eze 47:11	1360

MARK *See* MARCUS.
And the LORD set a *m* upon Cain	Gen 4:15	226
that thou shalt *m* the place where	Ruth 3:4	3045
thereof, as though I shot at a *m*	1Sa 20:20	4307
M ye now when Amnon's heart is	2Sa 13:28	7200
elders of the land, and said, *M*	1Kin 20:7	3045
him, Go, strengthen thyself, and *m*	1Kin 20:22	3045
thou set me as a *m* against thee	Job 7:20	4645
to pieces, and set me up for his *m*	Job 16:12	4307
m, and afterwards we will speak	Job 18:2	995
M me, and be astonished, and lay	Job 21:5	6437
M well, O Job, hearken unto me	Job 33:31	7181
or canst thou *m* when the hinds do	Job 39:1	8104
M the perfect man, and behold the	Ps 37:37	8104
M ye well her bulwarks, consider	Ps 48:13	7896
they *m* my steps, when they wait	Ps 56:6	8104
shouldest *m* iniquities, O Lord,	Ps 130:3	8104
set me as a *m* for the arrow	Lam 3:12	4307
set a *m* upon the foreheads of the	Eze 9:4	8420
near any man upon whom is the *m*	Eze 9:6	8420
m well, and behold with thine eyes	Eze 44:5	7760
m well the entering in of the	Eze 44:5	7760

m them which cause divisions and	Rom 16:17	*4648*
I press toward the *m* for the	Phil 3:14	*4649*
m them which walk so as ye have	Phil 3:17	*4648*
to receive a *m* in their right	Rev 13:16	*5480*
or sell, save he that had the *m*	Rev 13:17	*5480*
receive his *m* in his forehead, or	Rev 14:9	*5480*
receiveth the *m* of his name	Rev 14:11	*5480*
and over his image, and over his *m*	Rev 15:2	*5480*
men which had the *m* of the beast	Rev 16:2	*5480*
had received the *m* of the beast	Rev 19:20	*5480*
his *m* upon their foreheads	Rev 20:4	*5480*

Companion of Paul..
of John, whose surname was *M*	Acts 12:12	*3138*
them John, whose surname was *M*	Acts 12:25	*3138*
them John, whose surname was *M*	Acts 15:37	*3138*
and so Barnabas took *M*, and sailed	Acts 15:39	*3138*
Take *M*, and bring him with thee	2Ti 4:11	*3138*

MARKED
the LORD, that Eli *m* her mouth	1Sa 1:12	8104
Hast thou *m* the old way which	Job 22:15	8104
which they had *m* for themselves	Job 24:16	2856
yet thine iniquity is *m* before me	Jer 2:22	3799
who hath *m* his word, and heard it	Jer 23:18	7181
when he *m* how they chose out the	Lk 14:7	*1907*

MARKEST
If I sin, then thou *m* me, and thou	Job 10:14	8104

MARKET
men and vessels of brass in thy *m*	Eze 27:13	4627
traded in thy *m* wheat of Minnith	Eze 27:17	4627
cassia, and calamus, were in thy *m*	Eze 27:19	4627
did sing of thee in thy *m*	Eze 27:25	4627
And when they come from the *m*	Mk 7:4	*58*
Jerusalem by the sheep *m* a pool	Jn 5:2	
in the *m* daily with them that met	Acts 17:17	*58*

MARKETH
in the stocks, he *m* all my paths	Job 33:11	8104
he *m* it out with a line	Is 44:13	8388
he *m* it out with the compass, and	Is 44:13	8388

MARKETPLACE
saw others standing idle in the *m*	Mt 20:3	*58*
unto children sitting in the *m*	Lk 7:32	*58*
them into the *m* unto the rulers	Acts 16:19	*58*

MARKETPLACES
and love salutations in the *m*	Mk 12:38	*58*

MARKETS
unto children sitting in the *m*	Mt 11:16	*58*
And greetings in the *m*, and to be	Mt 23:7	*58*
synagogues, and greetings in the *m*	Lk 11:43	*58*
robes, and love greetings in the *m*	Lk 20:46	*58*

MARKS
dead, nor print any *m* upon you	Lev 19:28	7085
my body the *m* of the Lord Jesus	Gal 6:17	4742

MAROTH (ma'-roth) *A city in Judah.*
For the inhabitant of *M* waited	Mic 1:12	4796

MARRED
visage was so *m* more than any man	Is 52:14	4893
and, behold, the girdle was *m*	Jer 13:7	7843
was *m* in the hand of the potter	Jer 18:4	7843
out, and *m* their vine branches	Nah 2:2	7843
spilled, and the bottles will be *m*	Mk 2:22	*622*

MARRIAGE
her raiment, and her duty of *m*	Ex 21:10	5772
their maidens were not given to *m*	Ps 78:63	1984
king, which made a *m* for his son	Mt 22:2	*1062*
are ready: come unto the *m*	Mt 22:4	*1062*
as ye shall find, bid to the *m*	Mt 22:9	*1062*
neither marry, nor are given in *m*	Mt 22:30	*1548*
drinking, marrying and giving in *m*	Mt 24:38	*1547*
ready went in with him to the *m*	Mt 25:10	*1062*
neither marry, nor are given in *m*	Mk 12:25	*1061*
wives, they were given in *m*	Lk 17:27	*1548*
world marry, and are given in *m*	Lk 20:34	*1548*
neither marry, nor are given in *m*	Lk 20:35	*1548*
there was a *m* in Cana of Galilee	Jn 2:1	*1062*
and his disciples, to the *m*	Jn 2:2	*1062*
that giveth her in *m* doeth well	1Cor 7:38	*1547*
giveth her not in *m* doeth better	1Cor 7:38	*1547*
M is honourable in all, and the	Heb 13:4	*1062*
for the *m* of the Lamb is come, and	Rev 19:7	*1062*
unto the *m* supper of the Lamb	Rev 19:9	*1062*

MARRIAGES
And make ye *m* with us, and give	Gen 34:9	2859
shalt thou make *m* with them	Deut 7:3	2859
you, and shall make *m* with them	Josh 23:12	2859

M

MARRIED

which *m* his daughters, and said,	Gen 19:14	3947
if he were *m*, then his wife shall	Ex 21:3	1166,802
also be *m* unto a stranger	Lev 22:12	
the Ethiopian woman whom he had *m*	Num 12:1	3947
for he had *m* an Ethiopian woman	Num 12:1	3947
if they be *m* to any of the sons	Num 36:3	802
were *m* unto their father's	Num 36:11	802
they were *m* into the families of	Num 36:12	802
with a woman *m* to an husband	Deut 22:22	1166
m her, and it come to pass that	Deut 24:1	1166
whom he *m* when he was threescore	1Chr 2:21	3947
m fourteen wives, and begat twenty	2Chr 13:21	5375
I Jews that had *m* wives of Ashdod	Neh 13:23	3427
For an odious woman when she is *m*	Prov 30:23	1166
than the children of the *m* wife	Is 54:1	1166
in thee, and thy land shall be *m*	Is 62:4	1166
for I am *m* unto you	Jer 3:14	1166
hath *m* the daughter of a strange	Mal 2:11	1166
the first, when he had *m* a wife	Mt 22:25	1060
for he had *m* her.	Mk 6:17	1060
be *m* to another, she committeth	Mk 10:12	1060
And another said, I have *m* a wife	Lk 14:20	1060
they *m* wives, they were given in	Lk 17:27	1060
she be *m* to another man, she	Rom 7:3	1096
though she be *m* to another man	Rom 7:3	1096
that ye should be *m* to another	Rom 7:4	1096
unto the *m* I command, yet not I,	1Cor 7:10	1060
But he that is *m* careth for the	1Cor 7:33	1060
but she that is *m* careth for the	1Cor 7:34	1060
liberty to be *m* to whom she will	1Cor 7:39	1060

MARRIETH

For as a young man *m* a virgin	Is 62:5	1166
whoso *m* her which is put away	Mt 19:9	1060
m another, committeth adultery	Lk 16:18	1060
whosoever *m* her that is put away	Lk 16:18	1060

MARROW

and his bones are moistened with *m*	Job 21:24	4221
soul shall be satisfied as with *m*	Ps 63:5	2459
to thy navel, and *m* to thy bones	Prov 3:8	8250
the lees, of fat things full of *m*	Is 25:6	4229
and spirit, and of the joints and *m*	Heb 4:12	3452

MARRY

m her, and raise up seed to thy	Gen 38:8	2992
Let them *m* to whom they think	Num 36:6	802
of their father shall they *m*	Num 36:6	802
not *m* without unto a stranger	Deut 25:5	1961,3176
virgin, so shall thy sons *m* thee	Is 62:5	1166
whosoever shall *m* her that is	Mt 5:32	1060
shall *m* another, committeth	Mt 19:9	1060
his wife, it is not good to *m*	Mt 19:10	1060
his brother shall *m* his wife	Mt 22:24	1918
the resurrection they neither *m*	Mt 22:30	1060
m another, committeth adultery	Mk 10:11	1060
from the dead, they neither *m*	Mk 12:25	1060
The children of this world *m*	Lk 20:34	1060
from the dead, neither *m*, nor are	Lk 20:35	1060
they cannot contain, let them *m*	1Cor 7:9	1060
it is better to *m* than to burn	1Cor 7:9	1060
But and if thou *m*, thou hast not	1Cor 7:28	1060
and if a virgin *m*, she hath not	1Cor 7:28	1060
he sinneth not: let them *m*	1Cor 7:36	1060
Forbidding to *m*, and commanding to	1Ti 4:3	1060
against Christ, they will *m*	1Ti 5:11	1060
that the younger women *m*, bear	1Ti 5:14	1060

MARRYING

our God in *m* strange wives	Neh 13:27	3427
they were eating and drinking, *m*	Mt 24:38	1060

MARS' *(marz) Refers to a landmark in Athens.*

Paul stood in the midst of *M* hill	Acts 17:22	697

MARSENA *(mar'-se-nah) A prince of Media and Persia.*

Admatha, Tarshish, Meres, *M*	Est 1:14	4826

MART

and she is a *m* of nations	Is 23:3	5505

MARTHA *(mar'-thah) Sister of Lazarus.*

a certain woman named *M* received	Lk 10:38	3136
But *M* was cumbered about much	Lk 10:40	3136
and said unto her, *M*, *M*	Lk 10:41	3136
the town of Mary and her sister *M*	Jn 11:1	3136
Now Jesus loved *M*, and her sister,	Jn 11:5	3136
And many of the Jews came to *M*	Jn 11:19	3136
Then *M*, as soon as she heard that	Jn 11:20	3136
Then said *M* unto Jesus, Lord, if	Jn 11:21	3136
M saith unto him, I know that he	Jn 11:24	3136
was in that place where *M* met him	Jn 11:30	3136
M, the sister of him that was	Jn 11:39	3136
a supper; and *M* served	Jn 12:2	3136

MARTYR

blood of thy *m* Stephen was shed	Acts 22:20	3144
wherein Antipas was my faithful *m*	Rev 2:13	3144

MARTYRS

with the blood of the *m* of Jesus	Rev 17:6	3144

MARVEL

a province, *m* not at the matter	Eccl 5:8	8539
and all men did *m*	Mk 5:20	2296
M not that I said unto thee, Ye	Jn 3:7	2296
works than these, that ye may *m*	Jn 5:20	2296
M not at this	Jn 5:28	2296
I have done one work, and ye all *m*	Jn 7:21	2296
men of Israel, why *m* ye at this	Acts 3:12	2296
And no *m*; for Satan himself	2Cor 11:14	2296
I *m* that ye are so soon removed	Gal 1:6	2296
M not, my brethren, if the world	1Jn 3:13	2296
unto me, Wherefore didst thou *m*	Rev 17:7	2296

MARVELLED

and the men *m* one at another	Gen 43:33	8539
They saw it, and so they *m*	Ps 48:5	8539
When Jesus heard it, he *m*	Mt 8:10	2296
But the men *m*, saying, What	Mt 8:27	2296
the multitudes saw it, they *m*	Mt 9:8	2296
and the multitudes *m*, saying, It	Mt 9:33	2296
when the disciples saw it, they *m*	Mt 21:20	2296
had heard these words, they *m*	Mt 22:22	2296
that the governor *m* greatly	Mt 27:14	2296
he *m* because of their unbelief	Mk 6:6	2296
And they *m* at him	Mk 12:17	2296
so that Pilate *m*	Mk 15:5	2296
Pilate *m* if he were already dead	Mk 15:44	2296
m that he tarried so long in the	Lk 1:21	2296
And they *m* all	Lk 1:63	2296
his mother *m* at those things	Lk 2:33	2296
he *m* at him, and turned him about,	Lk 7:9	2296
he *m* that he had not first washed	Lk 11:38	2296
they *m* at his answer, and held	Lk 20:26	2296
m that he talked with the woman	Jn 4:27	2296
And the Jews *m*, saying, How	Jn 7:15	2296
And they were all amazed and *m*	Acts 2:7	2296
unlearned and ignorant men, they *m*	Acts 4:13	2296

MARVELLOUS

Remember his *m* works that he hath	1Chr 16:12	6381
his *m* works among all nations	1Chr 16:24	6381
m things without number	Job 5:9	6381
thou shewest thyself *m* upon me	Job 10:16	6381
I will shew forth all thy *m* works	Ps 9:1	6381
Shew thy *m* lovingkindness, O thou	Ps 17:7	6395
his *m* kindness in a strong city	Ps 31:21	6381
M things did he in the sight of	Ps 78:12	6382
for he hath done *m* things	Ps 98:1	6381
Remember his *m* works that he hath	Ps 105:5	6381
it is *m* in our eyes	Ps 118:23	6381
m are thy works	Ps 139:14	6381
to do a *m* work among this people	Is 29:14	6381
among this people, even a *m* work	Is 29:14	6381
shall speak *m* things against the	Dan 11:36	6381
will I shew unto him *m* things	Mic 7:15	6381
If it be *m* in the eyes of the	Zec 8:6	6381
should it also be *m* in mine eyes	Zec 8:6	6381
doing, and it is *m* in our eyes	Mt 21:42	2298
doing, and it is *m* in our eyes	Mk 12:11	2298
them, Why herein is a *m* thing	Jn 9:30	2298
out of darkness into his *m* light	1Pet 2:9	2298
sign in heaven, great and *m*	Rev 15:1	2298
m are thy works, Lord God	Rev 15:3	2298

MARVELLOUSLY

for he was *m* helped, till he was	2Chr 26:15	6381
God thundereth *m* with his voice	Job 37:5	6381
heathen, and regard, and wonder *m*	Hab 1:5	8539

MARVELS

before all thy people I will do *m*	Ex 34:10	6381

MARY *(ma'-ry)*
    1. Mother of Jesus.

begat Joseph the husband of *M*	Mt 1:16	3137
When as his mother *M* was espoused	Mt 1:18	3137
not to take unto thee *M* thy wife	Mt 1:20	3137
the young child with *M* his mother	Mt 2:11	3137
is not his mother called *M*	Mt 13:55	3137
this the carpenter, the son of *M*	Mk 6:3	3137
and the virgin's name was *M*	Lk 1:27	3137
angel said unto her, Fear not, *M*	Lk 1:30	3137
Then said *M* unto the angel, How	Lk 1:34	3137
M said, Behold, the handmaid of	Lk 1:38	3137
M arose in those days, and went	Lk 1:39	3137
heard the salutation of *M*	Lk 1:41	3137
M said, My soul doth magnify the	Lk 1:46	3137

M abode with her about three .... Lk 1:56	3137
To be taxed with *M* his espoused .... Lk 2:5	3137
they came with haste, and found *M* ...... Lk 2:16	3137
But *M* kept all these things, and .... Lk 2:19	3137
said unto *M* his mother, Behold, ... Lk 2:34	3137
M the mother of Jesus, and with .... Acts 1:14	3137
2. A woman of Magdala.	
Among which was *M* Magdalene .... Mt 27:56	3137
And there was *M* Magdalene, and the..... Mt 27:61	3137
came *M* Magdalene and the other .... Mt 28:1	3137
among whom was *M* Magdalene .... Mk 15:40	3137
M Magdalene and Mary the mother of .. Mk 15:47	3137
he appeared first to *M* Magdalene .... Mk 16:9	3137
M called Magdalene, out of whom .... Lk 8:2	3137
It was *M* Magdalene, and Joanna, and .. Lk 24:10	3137
wife of Cleophas, and *M* Magdalene...... Jn 19:25	3137
the week cometh *M* Magdalene early ..... Jn 20:1	3137
But *M* stood without at the .... Jn 20:11	3137
Jesus saith unto her, *M* .... Jn 20:16	3137
M Magdalene came and told the .... Jn 20:18	3137
3. Mother of James and Joses.	
M the mother of James and Joses,........ Mt 27:56	3137
Mary Magdalene, and the other *M*........ Mt 27:61	3137
the other *M* to see the sepulchre .... Mt 28:1	3137
M the mother of James the less and ..... Mk 15:40	3137
M the mother of Joses beheld.................. Mk 15:47	3137
M Magdalene, and Mary the mother ..... Mk 16:1	3137
M the mother of James, and Salome, ... Mk 16:1	3137
M the mother of James, and other .... Lk 24:10	3137
4. Wife of Cleophas.	
M the wife of Cleophas, and Mary .... Jn 19:25	3137
5. Sister of Lazarus.	
And she had a sister called *M* .... Lk 10:39	3137
M hath chosen that good part, ... Lk 10:42	3137
of Bethany, the town of *M*........................ Jn 11:1	3137
(It was that *M* which anointed the .... Jn 11:2	3137
of the Jews came to Martha and *M* .... Jn 11:19	3137
but *M* sat still in the house...................... Jn 11:20	3137
called *M* her sister secretly,.................... Jn 11:28	3137
and comforted her, when they saw *M* .... Jn 11:31	3137
Then when *M* was come where Jesus .... Jn 11:32	3137
many of the Jews which came to *M*........ Jn 11:45	3137
Then took *M* a pound of ointment........... Jn 12:3	3137
6. Mother of John Mark.	
the house of *M* the mother of John .... Acts 12:12	3137
7. A Christian in Rome.	
Greet *M*, who bestowed much labour..... Rom 16:6	3137

MASCHIL *(mas'-kil) A didactic poem.*
A Psalm of David, A *M* .... Ps 32:*t*	4905
To the chief Musician, *M*, for the .... Ps 42:*t*	4905
Musician for the sons of Korah, *M* .... Ps 44:*t*	4905
for the sons of Korah, A *M* .... Ps 45:*t*	4905
To the chief Musician, *M*, A Psalm .... Ps 52:*t*	4905
chief Musician upon Mahalath, *M*........... Ps 53:*t*	4905
the chief Musician on Neginoth, *M*......... Ps 54:*t*	4905
the chief Musician on Neginoth, *M*......... Ps 55:*t*	4905
M of Asaph .... Ps 74:*t*	4905
M of Asaph .... Ps 78:*t*	4905
Leannoth, *M* of Heman the Ezrahite ...... Ps 88:*t*	4905
M of Ethan the Ezrahite............................ Ps 89:*t*	4905
M of David .... Ps 142:*t*	4905

MASH *(mash) A son of Aram.*
Uz, and Hul, and Gether, and *M* .... Gen 10:23	4851

MASHAL *(ma'-shal) A Levitical city in Asher.*
M with her suburbs, and Abdon with 1Chr 6:74	4913

MASONS
cedar trees, and carpenters, and *m* 2Sa 5:11	
And to *m*, and hewers of stone, and 2Kin 12:12	1443
carpenters, and builders, and *m* 2Kin 22:6	1443
and timber of cedars, with *m* 1Chr 14:1	
he set *m* to hew wrought stones to 1Chr 22:2	2672
the house of the LORD, and hired *m*........ 2Chr 24:12	2672
They gave money also unto the *m* .... Ezr 3:7	2672

MASREKAH *(mas'-re-kah) A place in Edom.*
Samlah of *M* reigned in his stead .... Gen 36:36	4957
Samlah of *M* reigned in his stead 1Chr 1:47	4957

MASSA *(mas'-sah) A son of Ishmael.*
And Mishma, and Dumah, and *M*........... Gen 25:14	4854
Mishma, and Dumah, *M*, Hadad, and 1Chr 1:30	4854

MASSAH *(mas'-sah) See MERIBAH. A place in the wilderness where the Israelites murmured.*
he called the name of the place *M* .... Ex 17:7	4532
your God, as ye tempted him in *M* .... Deut 6:16	4532
And at Taberah, and at *M*, and at .... Deut 9:22	4532
one, whom thou didst prove at *M* .... Deut 33:8	4532

MAST
he that lieth upon the top of a *m* .... Prov 23:34	2260
could not well strengthen their *m* .... Is 33:23	8650

MASTER
under the thigh of Abraham his *m* .... Gen 24:9	113
ten camels of the camels of his *m* .... Gen 24:10	113
goods of his *m* were in his hand .... Gen 24:10	113
said, O LORD God of my *m* Abraham ..... Gen 24:12	113
shew kindness unto my *m* Abraham ...... Gen 24:12	113
hast shewed kindness unto my *m* .... Gen 24:14	113
be the LORD God of my *m* Abraham ...... Gen 24:27	113
left destitute my *m* of his mercy .... Gen 24:27	113
LORD hath blessed my *m* greatly............ Gen 24:35	113
a son to my *m* when she was old............ Gen 24:36	113
my *m* made me swear, saying, Thou ...... Gen 24:37	113
And I said unto my *m*, Peradventure ...... Gen 24:39	113
said, O LORD God of my *m* Abraham ..... Gen 24:42	113
the LORD God of my *m* Abraham............ Gen 24:48	113
deal kindly and truly with my *m* .... Gen 24:49	113
he said, Send me away unto my *m* .... Gen 24:54	113
me away that I may go to my *m* .... Gen 24:56	113
the servant had said, It is my *m* .... Gen 24:65	113
the house of his *m* the Egyptian .... Gen 39:2	113
his *m* saw that the LORD was with......... Gen 39:3	113
my *m* wotteth not what is with me .... Gen 39:8	113
when his *m* heard the words of his......... Gen 39:19	113
And Joseph's *m* took him, and put .... Gen 39:20	113
If his *m* have given him a wife,.............. Ex 21:4	113
shall plainly say, I love my *m* .... Ex 21:5	113
Then his *m* shall bring him unto .... Ex 21:6	113
his *m* shall bore his ear through .... Ex 21:6	113
If she please not her *m*, who hath .... Ex 21:8	113
their *m* thirty shekels of silver .... Ex 21:32	113
then the *m* of the house shall be........... Ex 22:8	1167
m the servant which is escaped .... Deut 23:15	113
is escaped from his *m* unto thee........... Deut 23:15	113
and the servant said unto his *m* .... Judg 19:11	113
his *m* said unto him, We will not .... Judg 19:12	113
and spake to the *m* of the house .... Judg 19:22	1167
the *m* of the house, went out unto .... Judg 19:23	1167
up the arrows, and came to his *m*......... 1Sa 20:38	113
I should do this thing unto my *m* 1Sa 24:6	113
break away every man from his *m* 1Sa 25:10	113
of the wilderness to salute our *m*.......... 1Sa 25:14	113
evil is determined against our *m* 1Sa 25:17	113
because ye have not kept your *m* 1Sa 26:16	113
he reconcile himself unto his *m* 1Sa 29:4	113
my *m* left me, because three days 1Sa 30:13	113
deliver me into the hands of my *m* 1Sa 30:15	113
for your *m* Saul is dead, and also......... 2Sa 2:7	113
and the LORD said, These have no *m* 1Kin 22:17	113
away thy *m* from thy head to day 2Kin 2:3	113
away thy *m* from thy head to day 2Kin 2:5	113
go, we pray thee, and seek thy *m* 2Kin 2:16	113
Syria, was a great man with his *m* 2Kin 5:1	113
that when my *m* goeth into the 2Kin 5:18	113
my *m* hath spared Naaman this 2Kin 5:20	113
My *m* hath sent me, saying, Behold 2Kin 5:22	113
he went in, and stood before his *m* 2Kin 5:25	113
and he cried, and said, Alas, *m* 2Kin 6:5	113
servant said unto him, Alas, my *m*........ 2Kin 6:15	113
eat and drink, and go to their *m* 2Kin 6:22	113
away, and they went to their *m* 2Kin 6:23	113
from Elisha, and came to his *m*............. 2Kin 8:14	113
smite the house of Ahab thy *m* 2Kin 9:7	113
Had Zimri peace, who slew his *m* 2Kin 9:31	113
behold, I conspired against my *m* 2Kin 10:9	113
Hath my *m* sent me to thy *m*, ... 2Kin 18:27	113
his *m* hath sent to reproach the 2Kin 19:4	113
them, Thus shall ye say to your *m* 2Kin 19:6	113
He will fall to his *m* Saul to the 1Chr 12:19	113
Chenaniah the *m* of the song with 1Chr 15:27	8269
and the LORD said, These have no *m* 2Chr 18:16	113
and the servant is free from his *m* .... Job 3:19	113
on his *m* shall be honoured .... Prov 27:18	113
Accuse not a servant unto his *m* .... Prov 30:10	113
with the servant, so with his *m* .... Is 24:2	113
to my *m* the king of Assyria, and I........ Is 36:8	113
Hath my *m* sent me to thy *m*, ... Is 36:12	113
his *m* hath sent to reproach the .... Is 37:4	113
Thus shall ye say unto your *m* .... Is 37:6	113
Ashpenaz the *m* of his eunuchs............ Dan 1:3	7227
m of the magicians, because I .... Dan 4:9	729
father, made *m* of the magicians,.......... Dan 5:11	729
his father, and a servant his *m* .... Mal 1:6	113
and if I be a *m*, where is my fear........... Mal 1:6	113
the man that doeth this, the *m* .... Mal 2:12	5782
scribe came, and said unto him, *M*........ Mt 8:19	1320
Why eateth your *M* with publicans .... Mt 9:11	1320
The disciple is not above his *m* .... Mt 10:24	1320

M

the disciple that he be as his *m* .... Mt 10:25   1320
the *m* of the house Beelzebub................ Mt 10:25   1320
the Pharisees answered, saying, *M* ...... Mt 12:38   1320
said, Doth not your *m* pay tribute .... Mt 17:24   1320
one came and said unto him, Good *M*.... Mt 19:16   1320
with the Herodians, saying, ... Mt 22:16   1320
Saying, *M*, Moses said, If a man .... Mt 22:24   1320
M, which is the great commandment ..... Mt 22:36   1320
for one is your *M*, even Christ .... Mt 23:8   2519
for one is your *M*, even Christ .... Mt 23:10   2519
The *M* saith, My time is at hand .... Mt 26:18   1320
betrayed him, answered and said, *M*..... Mt 26:25   4461
came to Jesus, and said, Hail, *m* .... Mt 26:49   4461
awake him, and say unto him, *M* .... Mk 4:38   1320
troublest thou the *M* any further .... Mk 5:35   1320
answered and said to Jesus, *M* .... Mk 9:5   4461
the multitude answered and said, *M* ...... Mk 9:17   1320
And John answered him, saying, *M*........ Mk 9:38   1320
to him, and asked him, Good *M* .... Mk 10:17   1320
he answered and said unto him, *M*........ Mk 10:20   1320
Zebedee, came unto him, saying, *M* ...... Mk 10:35   1320
to remembrance saith unto him, *M*........ Mk 11:21   4461
were come, they say unto him, *M*.......... Mk 12:14   1320
M, Moses wrote unto us, If a.............. Mk 12:19   1320
the scribe said unto him, Well, *M* .... Mk 12:32   1320
his disciples saith unto him, *M* .... Mk 13:1   1320
when the *m* of the house cometh............ Mk 13:35   2962
The *M* saith, Where is the .... Mk 14:14   1320
to him, and saith, *M*, *m* .... Mk 14:45   4461
be baptized, and said unto him, *M*.......... Lk 3:12   1320
Simon answering said unto him, *M* ...... Lk 5:5   1988
The disciple is not above his *m* .... Lk 6:40   1320
that is perfect shall be as his *m* .... Lk 6:40   1320
And he saith, *M*, say on .... Lk 7:40   1320
and awoke him, saying, *M*, *m*.............. Lk 8:24   1988
they that were with him said, *M* .... Lk 8:45   1988
trouble not the *M*.................................... Lk 8:49   1320
him, Peter said unto Jesus, *M* .... Lk 9:33   1988
the company cried out, saying, *M*.......... Lk 9:38   1320
And John answered and said, *M* .... Lk 9:49   1988
up, and tempted him, saying, *M* .... Lk 10:25   1320
the lawyers, and said unto him, *M*........ Lk 11:45   1320
of the company said unto him, *M* .... Lk 12:13   1320
When once the *m* of the house is .... Lk 13:25   3617
Then the *m* of the house being .... Lk 14:21   3617
their voices, and said, Jesus, *M*............ Lk 17:13   1988
ruler asked him, saying, Good *M* .... Lk 18:18   1320
the multitude said unto him, *M* .... Lk 19:39   1320
And they asked him, saying, *M* .... Lk 20:21   1320
Saying, *M*, Moses wrote unto us,............ Lk 20:28   1320
of the scribes answering said, *M*............ Lk 20:39   1320
And they asked him, saying, *M* .... Lk 21:7   1320
The *M* saith unto thee, Where is .... Lk 22:11   1320
is to say, being interpreted, *M*.............. Jn 1:38   1320
unto him, Art thou a *m* of Israel .... Jn 3:10   1320
disciples prayed him, saying, *M*............ Jn 4:31   4461
They say unto him, *M*, this woman........ Jn 8:4   1320
disciples asked him, saying, *M* .... Jn 9:2   4461
His disciples say unto him, *M* .... Jn 11:8   4461
The *M* is come, and calleth for.............. Jn 11:28   1320
Ye call me *M* and Lord .... Jn 13:13   1320
If I then, your Lord and *M* .... Jn 13:14   1320
which is to say, *M*,................................ Jn 20:16   1320
the centurion believed the *m*................ Acts 27:11   2942
to his own *m* he standeth or .... Rom 14:4   2962
that your *M* also is in heaven.............. Eph 6:9   2962
that ye also have a *M* in heaven.......... Col 4:1   2962

MASTERBUILDER
is given unto me, as a wise *m* 1Cor 3:10   753

MASTERIES
And if a man also strive for *m*................ 2Ti 2:5

MASTER'S
me to the house of my *m* brethren .... Gen 24:27   113
Sarah my *m* wife bare a son to my .... Gen 24:36   113
hath appointed out for my *m* son .... Gen 24:44   113
me in the right way to take my *m* .... Gen 24:48   113
and let her be thy *m* son's wife .... Gen 24:51   113
that his *m* wife cast her eyes .... Gen 39:7   113
refused, and said unto his *m* wife.......... Gen 39:8   113
and her children shall be her *m*.............. Ex 21:4   113
thy *m* servants that are come with........ 1Sa 29:10   113
I have given unto thy *m* son all 2Sa 9:9   113
that thy *m* son may have food to 2Sa 9:10   113
but Mephibosheth thy *m* son shall 2Sa 9:10   113
And I gave thee thy *m* house 2Sa 12:8   113
thy *m* wives into thy bosom, and.......... 2Sa 12:8   113
king said, And where is thy *m* son 2Sa 16:3   113
sound of his *m* feet behind him 2Kin 6:32   113
seeing your *m* sons are with you,........ 2Kin 10:2   113

best and meetest of your *m* sons 2Kin 10:3   113
throne, and fight for your *m* house 2Kin 10:3   113
the heads of the men your *m* sons........ 2Kin 10:6   113
of the least of my *m* servants 2Kin 18:24   113
his owner, and the ass his *m* crib .... Is 1:3   1167
of the least of my *m* servants .... Is 36:9   113
sanctified, and meet for the *m* use 2Ti 2:21   1203

MASTERS
look unto the hand of their *m* .... Ps 123:2   113
he refresheth the soul of his *m* .... Prov 25:13   113
fastened by the *m* of assemblies............ Eccl 12:11   1167
command them to say unto their *m* .... Jer 27:4   113
Thus shall ye say unto your *m*................ Jer 27:4   113
the needy, which say to their *m*............ Amos 4:1   113
No man can serve two *m* .... Mt 6:24   2962
Neither be ye called *m* .... Mt 23:10   2519
No servant can serve two *m* .... Lk 16:13   2962
which brought her *m* much gain by .... Acts 16:16   2962
when her *m* saw that the hope of .... Acts 16:19   2962
are your *m* according to the flesh .... Eph 6:5   2962
And, ye *m*, do the same things unto ...... Eph 6:9   2962
your *m* according to the flesh.................. Col 3:22   2962
M, give unto your servants that .... Col 4:1   2962
their own *m* worthy of all honour 1Ti 6:1   1203
And they that have believing *m* 1Ti 6:2   1203
to be obedient unto their own *m*............ Titus 2:9   1203
My brethren, be not many *m* .... Jas 3:1   1320
subject to your *m* with all fear................ 1Pet 2:18   1203

MASTERS'
which fill their *m* houses with .... Zeph 1:9   113
which fall from their *m* table .... Mt 15:27   2962

MASTERY
voice of them that shout for *m* .... Ex 32:18   1369
and the lions had the *m* of them............ Dan 6:24   6981
the *m* is temperate in all things............ 1Cor 9:25

MASTS
from Lebanon to make *m* for thee .... Eze 27:5   8650

MATE
be gathered, every one with her *m* .... Is 34:15   7468
shall fail, none shall want her *m* .... Is 34:16   7468

MATHUSALA (*ma-thu'-sa-lah*) See METHUSELAH. *Son of Enoch; ancestor of Jesus.*
Which was the son of *M*, which was ...... Lk 3:37   3103

MATRED (*ma'-tred*) *Mother of Mehetabel.*
was Mehetabel, the daughter of *M* .... Gen 36:39   4308
was Mehetabel, the daughter of *M* 1Chr 1:50   4308

MATRI (*ma'-tri*) *An ancestoral family of King Saul.*
the family of *M* was taken 1Sa 10:21   4309

MATRITE See MATRI.

MATRIX
the LORD all that openeth the *m* .... Ex 13:12   7358
the LORD all that openeth the *m* .... Ex 13:15   7358
All that openeth the *m* is mine .... Ex 34:19   7358
m among the children of Israel.............. Num 3:12   7358
that openeth the *m* in all flesh.............. Num 18:15   7358

MATTAN (*mat'-tan*)
1. A priest of Baal.
slew *M* the priest of Baal before 2Kin 11:18   4977
slew *M* the priest of Baal before 2Chr 23:17   4977
2. Father of Shephatiah.
Then Shephatiah the son of *M* .... Jer 38:1   4977

MATTANAH (*mat'-ta-nah*) *An encampment of Israel in the wilderness.*
the wilderness they went to *M* .... Num 21:18   4980
And from *M* to Nahaliel.......................... Num 21:19   4980

MATTANIAH (*mat-ta-ni'-ah*) See ZEDEKIAH.
1. Same as Zedekiah, king of Judah.
the king of Babylon made *M* his 2Kin 24:17   4983
2. A family of exiles.
M the son of Micah, the son of................ 1Chr 9:15   4983
the son of Jeiel, the son of *M* 2Chr 20:14   4983
M the son of Micha, the son of .... Neh 11:17   4983
son of Hashabiah, the son of *M* .... Neh 11:22   4983
Kadmiel, Sherebiah, Judah, and *M*........ Neh 12:8   4983
M, and Bakbukiah, Obadiah,.................. Neh 12:25   4983
the son of Shemaiah, the son of *M* .... Neh 12:35   4983
3. A sanctuary servant.
Bukkiah, *M*, Uzziel, Shebuel, and........ 1Chr 25:4   4983
The ninth to *M*, he, his sons, and............ 1Chr 25:16   4983
4. A descendant of Asaph.
Zechariah, and *M*.................................. 2Chr 29:13   4983
5. A descendant of Elam.
M, Zechariah, and Jehiel, and Abdi,...... Ezr 10:26   4983
6. A descendant of Zattu.
Elioenai, Eliashib, *M*, and .... Ezr 10:27   4983

7. *A descendant of Pahath-Moab.*
and Chelal, Benaiah, Maaseiah, M .... Ezr 10:30   4983
8. *A descendant of Bani.*
M, Mattenai, and Jaasau, ... Ezr 10:37   4983
9. *Father of Zaccur.*
the son of Zaccur, the son of M .... Neh 13:13   4983

MATTATHA (mat'-ta-thah) See MATTATHAH. *A son of Nathan; ancestor of Jesus.*
of Menan, which was the son of M .... Lk 3:31   3160

MATTATHAH (mat'-ta-thah) See MATTATHA. *Married a foreigner in exile.*
Mattenai, M, Zabad, Eliphelet, ... Ezr 10:33   4992

MATTATHIAH See MATTATHIAS.

MATTATHIAS (mat-ta-thi'-as) See MATTITHIAH.
1. *A son of Amos; ancestor of Jesus.*
Which was the son of M, which was ...... Lk 3:25   3161
2. *A son of Semei; ancestor of Jesus.*
of Maath, which was the son of M .... Lk 3:26   3161

MATTATTAH See MATTATHAH.

MATTENAI (mat'-te-nahee)
1. *A descendant of Hashum.*
M, Mattathah, Zabad, Eliphelet, ... Ezr 10:33   4982
2. *A descendant of Bani.*
Mattaniah, M, and Jaasau, ... Ezr 10:37   4982
3. *A priest.*
And of Joiarib, M................................... Neh 12:19   4982

MATTER See APPENDIX.

MATTERS See APPENDIX.

MATTHAN (mat'-than) *Son of Eleazar; ancestor of Jesus.*
and Eleazar begat M .... Mt 1:15   3157
and M begat Jacob.................................. Mt 1:15   3157

MATTHAT (mat'-that)
1. *Son of Levi; an ancestor of Jesus.*
Which was the son of M, which was ...... Lk 3:24   3158
2. *Father of Jorim; an ancestor of Jesus.*
of Jorim, which was the son of M .... Lk 3:29   3158

MATTHEW (math'-ew) See LEVI. *A disciple of Jesus.*
thence, he saw a man, named M .... Mt 9:9   3156
Thomas, and M the publican .... Mt 10:3   3156
and Philip, and Bartholomew, and M..... Mk 3:18   3156
M and Thomas, James the son of .... Lk 6:15   3156
and Thomas, Bartholomew, and M .... Acts 1:13   3156

MATTHIAS (mat'-thias) *Successor to Judas Iscariot as apostle.*
who was surnamed Justus, and M .... Acts 1:23   3159
and the lot fell upon M .... Acts 1:26   3159

MATTITHIAH (mat-tith-i'-ah) See MATTATHIAS.
1. *A son of Shallum.*
And M, one of the Levites, who was 1Chr 9:31   4993
2. *A Levite gatekeeper.*
and Benaiah, and Maaseiah, and M 1Chr 15:18   4993
And M, and Eliphelah, and Mikneiah, ... 1Chr 15:21   4993
and Shemiramoth, and Jehiel, and M 1Chr 16:5   4993
3. *Son of Jeduthun.*
and Jeshaiah, Hashabiah, and M 1Chr 25:3   4993
The fourteenth to M, he, his sons 1Chr 25:21   4993
4. *Married a foreigner in exile.*
Jeiel, M, Zabad, Zebina, Jadau, ... Ezr 10:43   4993
5. *A priest who aided Ezra.*
and beside him stood M, and Shema, ... Neh 8:4   4993

MATTOCK
his coulter, and his ax, and his m 1Sa 13:20   4281
that shall be digged with the m.............. Is 7:25   4576

MATTOCKS
Yet they had a file for the m................... 1Sa 13:21   4281
with their m round about 2Chr 34:6   2719

MAUL
against his neighbour is a m .... Prov 25:18   4650

MAW
and the two cheeks, and the m .... Deut 18:3   6896

MAY See APPENDIX.

MAYEST See APPENDIX.

MAZZAROTH (maz'-za-roth) *The twelve signs of the Zodiac.*
thou bring forth M in his season .... Job 38:32   4216

ME See APPENDIX.

MEADOW
and they fed in a m................................ Gen 41:2   260
and they fed in a m................................ Gen 41:18   260

MEADOWS
even out of the m of Gibeah.................... Judg 20:33   4629

MEAH (me'-ah) *A tower on Jerusalem's wall.*
the tower of M they sanctified it .... Neh 3:1   3968
of Hananeel, and the tower of M............. Neh 12:39   3968

MEAL
three measures of fine m................. Gen 18:6   7058,5560
part of an ephah of barley m .... Num 5:15   7058
and threescore measures of m............... 1Kin 4:22   7058
but an handful of m in a barrel 1Kin 17:12   7058
The barrel of m shall not waste, ... 1Kin 17:14   7058
And the barrel of m wasted not 1Kin 17:16   7058
But he said, Then bring m................... 2Kin 4:41   7058
on mules, and on oxen, and meat, m 1Chr 12:40   7058
Take the millstones, and grind m .... Is 47:2   7058
the bud shall yield no m .... Hos 8:7   7058
and hid in three measures of m .... Mt 13:33   224
and hid in three measures of m .... Lk 13:21   224

MEALTIME
m come thou hither, and eat of........ Ruth 2:14   6256,400

MEAN
What m these seven ewe lambs .... Gen 21:29
What m ye by this service .... Ex 12:26
What m the testimonies, and the .... Deut 6:20
What m ye by these stones .... Josh 4:6
come, saying, What m these stones .... Josh 4:21
came to pass in the m while 1Kin 18:45   5704,3541
he shall not stand before m men .... Prov 22:29   2823
the m man boweth down, and the .... Is 2:9   120
What m ye that ye beat my people .... Is 3:15
the m man shall be brought down, ... Is 5:15   120
and the sword, not of a m man .... Is 31:8   120
Know ye not what these things m .... Eze 17:12
What m ye, that ye use this.................... Eze 18:2
the rising from the dead should m .... Mk 9:10   2076
In the m time, when there were .... Lk 12:1
In the m while his disciples.................... Jn 4:31   3342
vision which he had seen should m .... Acts 10:17   1498
what these things m .... Acts 17:20   2309,1511
What m ye to weep and to break .... Acts 21:13   4160
Cilicia, a citizen of no m city .... Acts 21:39   767
their thoughts the m while .... Rom 2:15   3342
For I m not that other men be................ 2Cor 8:13

MEANEST
What m thou by all this drove............... Gen 33:8
unto Ziba, What m thou by these 2Sa 16:2
not shew us what thou m by these .... Eze 37:18
and said unto him, What m thou............ Jonah 1:6

MEANETH
what m the heat of this great .... Deut 29:24
What m the noise of this great.............. 1Sa 4:6
What m the noise of this tumult............. 1Sa 4:14
What m then this bleating of the 1Sa 15:14
Howbeit he m not so, neither doth.......... Is 10:7   1819
But go ye and learn what that m .... Mt 9:13   2076
But if ye had known what this m .... Mt 12:7   2076
one to another, What m this............ Acts 2:12   2309,1511

MEANING
the vision, and sought for the m .... Dan 8:15   998
m to sail by the coasts of Asia.............. Acts 27:2   3195
if I know not the m of the voice 1Cor 14:11   1411

MEANS
that will by no m clear the .... Ex 34:7
by no m clearing the guilty,................... Num 14:18
broken by the m of the pransings.......... Judg 5:22
by what m we may prevail against .... Judg 16:5
yet doth he devise m, that his 2Sa 14:14   4284
they bring them out by their m.............. 1Kin 10:29   3027
if by any m he be missing, then............ 1Kin 20:39
the kings of Syria, by their m 2Chr 1:17   3027
by this m thou shalt have no .... Ezr 4:16   6903
can by any m redeem his brother .... Ps 49:7
For by m of a whorish woman a man...... Prov 6:26   1157
the priests bear rule by their m.............. Jer 5:31   3027
this hath been by your m .... Mal 1:9   3027
shalt by no m come out thence .... Mt 5:26   3361
they sought m to bring him in, and .... Lk 5:18
m he that was possessed of the .... Lk 8:36   4459
nothing shall by any m hurt you .... Lk 10:19   3364
But by what m he now seeth, we .... Jn 9:21   4459
by what m he is made whole.................. Acts 4:9
I must by all m keep this feast .... Acts 18:21   3843
if by any m they might attain to .... Acts 27:12   4458
if by any m now at length I might .... Rom 1:10   4458
If by any m I may provoke to .... Rom 11:14   4458
But take heed lest by any m this 1Cor 8:9   4458
that I might by all m save some 1Cor 9:22   3843

M

lest that by any *m*, when I have	1Cor 9:27	4458
gift bestowed upon us by the *m* of	2Cor 1:11	
But I fear, lest by any *m*	2Cor 11:3	4458
lest by any *m* I should run, or	Gal 2:2	4458
If by any *m* I might attain unto	Phil 3:11	4458
lest by some *m* the tempter have	1Th 3:5	4458
Let no man deceive you by any *m*	2Th 2:3	5158
give you peace always by all *m*	2Th 3:16	5158
that by *m* of death, for the	Heb 9:15	1096
m of those miracles which he had	Rev 13:14	

MEANT

but God *m* it unto good, to bring	Gen 50:20	2803
and asked what these things *m*	Lk 15:26	*1498*
pass by, he asked what it *m*	Lk 18:36	*1498*

MEARAH (*me'-a-rah*) *A place near Sidon.*

M that is beside the Sidonians,	Josh 13:4	4632

MEASURE

of the curtains shall have one *m*	Ex 26:2	4060
curtains shall be all of one *m*	Ex 26:8	4060
in meteyard, in weight, or in *m*	Lev 19:35	4884
ye shall *m* from without the city	Num 35:5	4058
they shall *m* unto the cities	Deut 21:2	4058
perfect and just *m* shalt thou have	Deut 25:15	374
about two thousand cubits by *m*	Josh 3:4	4060
both the cherubims were of one *m*	1Kin 6:25	4060
of them had one casting, one *m*	1Kin 7:37	4060
a *m* of fine flour be sold for a	2Kin 7:1	5429
So a *m* of fine flour was sold for	2Kin 7:16	5429
a *m* of fine flour for a shekel,	2Kin 7:18	5429
is fried, and for all manner of *m*	1Chr 23:29	4884
the first *m* was threescore cubits	2Chr 3:3	4060
The *m* thereof is longer than the	Job 11:9	4055
and he weigheth the waters by *m*	Job 28:25	4060
the *m* of my days, what it is	Ps 39:4	4060
them tears to drink in great *m*	Ps 80:5	7991
and opened her mouth without *m*	Is 5:14	2706
In *m*, when it shooteth forth,	Is 27:8	5432
the dust of the earth in a *m*	Is 40:12	7991
therefore will I *m* their former	Is 65:7	4058
but I will correct thee in *m*	Jer 30:11	4941
of thee, but correct thee in *m*	Jer 46:28	4941
the *m* of thy covetousness	Jer 51:13	520
Thou shalt drink also water by *m*	Eze 4:11	4884
and they shall drink water by *m*	Eze 4:16	4884
they three were of one *m*	Eze 40:10	4060
the posts had one *m* on this side	Eze 40:10	4060
after the *m* of the first gate	Eze 40:21	4060
were after the *m* of the gate that	Eze 40:22	4060
about within and without, by *m*	Eze 41:17	4060
and let them *m* the pattern	Eze 43:10	4058
of this *m* shalt thou	Eze 45:3	4060
shalt thou *m* the length of five	Eze 45:3	4058
and the bath shall be of one *m*	Eze 45:11	8506
the *m* thereof shall be after the	Eze 45:11	4971
these four corners were of one *m*	Eze 46:22	4060
east side ye shall *m* from Hauran	Eze 47:18	4058
the scant *m* that is abominable	Mic 6:10	374
To *m* Jerusalem, to see what is	Zec 2:2	4058
and with what *m* ye mete, it shall	Mt 7:2	*3358*
ye up then the *m* of your fathers	Mt 23:32	*3358*
with what *m* ye mete, it shall be	Mk 4:24	*3358*
amazed in themselves beyond *m*	Mk 6:51	4053
And were beyond *m* astonished	Mk 7:37	5249
And they were astonished out of *m*	Mk 10:26	4057
good *m*, pressed down, and shaken	Lk 6:38	*3358*
For with the same *m* that ye mete	Lk 6:38	*3358*
not the Spirit by *m* unto him	Jn 3:34	*3358*
dealt to every man the *m* of faith	Rom 12:3	*3358*
that we were pressed out of *m*	2Cor 1:8	5236
not boast of things without our *m*	2Cor 10:13	280
but according to the *m* of the	2Cor 10:13	*3358*
a *m* to reach even unto you	2Cor 10:13	*3358*
not ourselves beyond our *m*	2Cor 10:14	
boasting of things without our *m*	2Cor 10:15	280
more abundant, in stripes above *m*	2Cor 11:23	5234
m through the abundance of the	2Cor 12:7	
lest I should be exalted above *m*	2Cor 12:7	
how that beyond *m* I persecuted	Gal 1:13	5236
to the *m* of the gift of Christ	Eph 4:7	*3358*
unto the *m* of the stature of the	Eph 4:13	*3358*
working in the *m* of every part	Eph 4:16	*3358*
A *m* of wheat for a penny, and	Rev 6:6	5518
m the temple of God, and the altar	Rev 11:1	*3354*
the temple leave out, and *m* it not	Rev 11:2	*3354*
had a golden reed to *m* the city	Rev 21:15	*3354*
according to the *m* of a man	Rev 21:17	*3358*

MEASURED

he *m* six measures of barley, and	Ruth 3:15	4058
m them with a line, casting them	2Sa 8:2	4058

two lines *m* he to put to death	2Sa 8:2	4058
Who hath *m* the waters in the	Is 40:12	4058
If heaven above can be *m*, and the	Jer 31:37	4058
neither the sand of the sea *m*	Jer 33:22	4058
so he *m* the breadth of the	Eze 40:5	4058
m the threshold of the gate,	Eze 40:6	4058
He *m* also the porch of the gate	Eze 40:8	4058
Then *m* he the porch of the gate,	Eze 40:9	4058
he *m* the breadth of the entry of	Eze 40:11	4058
He *m* then the gate from the roof	Eze 40:13	4058
Then he *m* the breadth from the	Eze 40:19	4058
he *m* the length thereof, and the	Eze 40:20	4058
he *m* from gate to gate an hundred	Eze 40:23	4058
he *m* the posts thereof and the	Eze 40:24	4058
he *m* from gate to gate toward the	Eze 40:27	4058
he *m* the south gate according to	Eze 40:28	4058
he *m* the gate according to these	Eze 40:32	4058
m it according to these measures	Eze 40:35	4058
So he *m* the court, an hundred	Eze 40:47	4058
m each post of the porch, five	Eze 40:48	4058
m the posts, six cubits broad on	Eze 41:1	4058
he *m* the length thereof, forty	Eze 41:2	4058
m the post of the door, two	Eze 41:3	4058
So he *m* the length thereof,	Eze 41:4	4058
After he *m* the wall of the house,	Eze 41:5	4058
So he *m* the house, an hundred	Eze 41:13	4058
he *m* the length of the building	Eze 41:15	4058
the east, and *m* it round about	Eze 42:15	4058
He *m* the east side with the	Eze 42:16	4058
He *m* the north side, five hundred	Eze 42:17	4058
He *m* the south side, five hundred	Eze 42:18	4058
m five hundred reeds with the	Eze 42:19	4058
He *m* it by the four sides	Eze 42:20	4058
he *m* a thousand cubits, and he	Eze 47:3	4058
Again he *m* a thousand, and brought	Eze 47:4	4058
Again he *m* a thousand, and brought	Eze 47:4	4058
Afterward he *m* a thousand	Eze 47:5	4058
which cannot be *m* nor numbered	Hos 1:10	4058
He stood, and *m* the earth	Hab 3:6	4128
it shall be *m* to you again	Mt 7:2	*488*
ye mete, it shall be *m* to you	Mk 4:24	*3354*
withal it shall be *m* to you again	Lk 6:38	*488*
he *m* the city with the reed,	Rev 21:16	*3354*
he *m* the wall thereof, an hundred	Rev 21:17	*3354*

MEASURES

quickly three *m* of fine meal	Gen 18:6	5429
not have in thine house divers *m*	Deut 25:14	374
it, he measured six *m* of barley	Ruth 3:15	
These six *m* of barley gave he me	Ruth 3:17	
five *m* of parched corn, and an	1Sa 25:18	5429
day was thirty *m* of fine flour	1Kin 4:22	3734
and threescore *m* of meal	1Kin 4:22	3734
m of wheat for food to his	1Kin 5:11	3734
and twenty *m* of pure oil	1Kin 5:11	3734
to the *m* of hewed stones, sawed	1Kin 7:9	4060
after the *m* of hewed stones, and	1Kin 7:11	4060
as would contain two *m* of seed	1Kin 18:32	5429
two *m* of barley for a shekel, in	2Kin 7:1	5429
two *m* of barley for a shekel,	2Kin 7:16	5429
Two *m* of barley for a shekel, and	2Kin 7:18	5429
twenty thousand *m* of beaten wheat	2Chr 2:10	3734
and twenty thousand *m* of barley	2Chr 2:10	3734
and ten thousand *m* of wheat	2Chr 27:5	3734
and to an hundred *m* of wheat	Ezr 7:22	3734
Who hath laid the *m* thereof	Job 38:5	4461
Divers weights, and divers *m*	Prov 20:10	374
lot, the portion of thy *m* from me	Jer 13:25	4055
thereof according to these *m*	Eze 40:24	4060
south gate according to these *m*	Eze 40:28	4060
thereof, according to these *m*	Eze 40:29	4060
the gate according to these *m*	Eze 40:32	4060
were according to these *m*	Eze 40:33	4060
measured it according to these *m*	Eze 40:35	4060
these are the *m* of the altar	Eze 43:13	4060
And these shall be the *m* thereof	Eze 48:16	4060
four thousand and five hundred *m*	Eze 48:30	4060
four thousand and five hundred *m*	Eze 48:33	4060
round about eighteen thousand *m*	Eze 48:35	
one came to an heap of twenty *m*	Hag 2:16	
took, and hid in three *m* of meal	Mt 13:33	*4568*
took and hid in three *m* of meal	Lk 13:21	*4568*
And he said, An hundred *m* of oil	Lk 16:6	*943*
And he said, An hundred *m* of wheat	Lk 16:7	*2884*
three *m* of barley for a penny	Rev 6:6	5518

MEASURING

the *m* line shall yet go forth	Jer 31:39	4060
of flax in his hand, and a *m* reed	Eze 40:3	4060
in the man's hand a *m* reed of six	Eze 40:5	4060
made an end of *m* the inner house	Eze 42:15	4060
the east side with the *m* reed	Eze 42:16	4060

with the *m* reed round about	Eze 42:16	4060
with the *m* reed round about	Eze 42:17	4060
hundred reeds, with the *m* reed	Eze 42:18	4060
hundred reeds with the *m* reed	Eze 42:19	4060
a man with a *m* line in his hand	Zec 2:1	4060
but they *m* themselves by	2Cor 10:12	*3354*

MEAT

to you it shall be for *m*	Gen 1:29	402
have given every green herb for *m*	Gen 1:30	402
that liveth shall be *m* for you	Gen 9:3	402
there was set *m* before him to eat	Gen 24:33	
And make me savoury *m*, such as I	Gen 27:4	
me venison, and make me savoury *m*	Gen 27:7	
them savoury *m* for thy father	Gen 27:9	
and his mother made savoury *m*	Gen 27:14	
And she gave the savoury *m*	Gen 27:17	
And he also had made savoury *m*	Gen 27:31	
m for his father by the way	Gen 45:23	4202
to the *m* offering of the morning	Ex 29:41	
burnt sacrifice, nor *m* offering	Ex 30:9	
burnt offering and the *m* offering	Ex 40:29	
when any will offer a *m* offering	Lev 2:1	
the remnant of the *m* offerings	Lev 2:3	
of a *m* offering baken in the oven	Lev 2:4	
if thy oblation be a *m* offering	Lev 2:5	
it is a *m* offering	Lev 2:6	
if thy oblation be a *m* offering	Lev 2:7	
thou shalt bring the *m* offering	Lev 2:8	
the *m* offering a memorial thereof	Lev 2:9	
the *m* offering shall be Aaron's	Lev 2:10	
No *m* offering, which ye shall	Lev 2:11	
every oblation of thy *m* offering	Lev 2:13	
to be lacking from thy *m* offering	Lev 2:13	
if thou offer a *m* offering of thy	Lev 2:14	
thou shalt offer for the *m*	Lev 2:14	
it is a *m* offering	Lev 2:15	
be the priest's, as a *m* offering	Lev 5:13	
this is the law of the *m* offering	Lev 6:14	
of the flour of the *m* offering	Lev 6:15	
which is upon the *m* offering	Lev 6:15	
flour for a *m* offering perpetual	Lev 6:20	
the baken pieces of the *m*	Lev 6:21	
For every *m* offering for the	Lev 6:23	
all the *m* offering that is baken	Lev 7:9	
every *m* offering, mingled with	Lev 7:10	
of the *m* offering, and of the sin	Lev 7:37	
a *m* offering mingled with oil	Lev 9:4	
And he brought the *m* offering	Lev 9:17	
left, Take the *m* offering that	Lev 10:12	
Of all *m* which may be eaten, that	Lev 11:34	400
of fine flour for a *m* offering	Lev 14:10	
the *m* offering upon the altar	Lev 14:20	
mingled with oil for a *m* offering	Lev 14:21	
offering, with the *m* offering	Lev 14:31	
they shall eat of his *m*	Lev 22:11	3899
she shall eat of her father's *m*	Lev 22:13	3899
the *m* offering thereof shall be	Lev 23:13	
ye shall offer a new *m* offering	Lev 23:16	
the Lord, with their *m* offering	Lev 23:18	
a *m* offering, a sacrifice, and	Lev 23:37	
of the land shall be *m* for you	Lev 25:6	402
all the increase thereof be *m*	Lev 25:7	398
incense, and the daily *m* offering	Num 4:16	
their *m* offering, and their drink	Num 6:15	
shall offer also his *m* offering	Num 6:17	
mingled with oil for a *m* offering	Num 7:13	
mingled with oil for a *m* offering	Num 7:19	
mingled with oil for a *m* offering	Num 7:25	
mingled with oil for a *m* offering	Num 7:31	
mingled with oil for a *m* offering	Num 7:37	
mingled with oil for a *m* offering	Num 7:43	
mingled with oil for a *m* offering	Num 7:49	
mingled with oil for a *m* offering	Num 7:55	
mingled with oil for a *m* offering	Num 7:61	
mingled with oil for a *m* offering	Num 7:67	
mingled with oil for a *m* offering	Num 7:73	
mingled with oil for a *m* offering	Num 7:79	
twelve, with their *m* offering	Num 7:87	
young bullock with his *m* offering	Num 8:8	
a *m* offering of a tenth deal of	Num 15:4	
thou shalt prepare for a *m*	Num 15:6	
a *m* offering of three tenth deals	Num 15:9	
the Lord, with his *m* offering	Num 15:24	
every *m* offering of theirs, and	Num 18:9	
ephah for a *m* offering, and	Num 28:5	
as the *m* offering of the morning,	Num 28:8	
deals of flour for a *m* offering	Num 28:9	
deals of flour for a *m* offering	Num 28:12	
deals of flour for a *m* offering	Num 28:12	
for a *m* offering unto one lamb	Num 28:13	

their *m* offering shall be of	Num 28:20	
the *m* of the sacrifice made by	Num 28:24	3899
when ye bring a new *m* offering	Num 28:26	
their *m* offering of flour mingled	Num 28:28	
his *m* offering, (they shall be	Num 28:31	
their *m* offering shall be of	Num 29:3	
his *m* offering, and the daily	Num 29:6	
his *m* offering, and their drink	Num 29:6	
their *m* offering shall be of	Num 29:9	
the *m* offering of it, and their	Num 29:11	
their *m* offering shall be of	Num 29:14	
his *m* offering, and his drink	Num 29:16	
their *m* offering and their drink	Num 29:18	
the *m* offering thereof, and their	Num 29:19	
their *m* offering and their drink	Num 29:21	
his *m* offering, and his drink	Num 29:22	
Their *m* offering and their drink	Num 29:24	
his *m* offering, and his drink	Num 29:25	
their *m* offering and their drink	Num 29:27	
his *m* offering, and his drink	Num 29:28	
their *m* offering and his drink	Num 29:30	
his *m* offering, and his drink	Num 29:31	
their *m* offering and his drink	Num 29:33	
his *m* offering, and his drink	Num 29:34	
Their *m* offering and their drink	Num 29:37	
his *m* offering, and his drink	Num 29:38	
for your *m* offerings, and for your	Num 29:39	
Ye shall buy *m* of them for money,	Deut 2:6	400
Thou shalt sell me *m* for money	Deut 2:28	400
that they be not trees for *m*	Deut 20:20	3978
thy carcase shall be *m* unto all	Deut 28:26	3978
burnt offering or *m* offering	Josh 22:23	
for *m* offerings, or for	Josh 22:29	
gathered their *m* under my table	Judg 1:7	
took a kid with a *m* offering	Judg 13:19	
a *m* offering at our hands,	Judg 13:23	
Out of the eater came forth *m*	Judg 14:14	3978
fail to sit with the king at *m*	1Sa 20:5	398
the king sat him down to eat *m*	1Sa 20:24	3899
cometh not the son of Jesse to *m*	1Sa 20:27	3899
did eat no *m* the second day of	1Sa 20:34	3899
to eat *m* while it was yet day	2Sa 3:35	3899
him a mess of *m* from the king	2Sa 11:8	
it did eat of his own *m*, and drank	2Sa 12:3	6595
sister Tamar come, and give me *m*	2Sa 13:5	3899
dress the *m* in my sight, that I	2Sa 13:5	1279
Amnon's house, and dress him *m*	2Sa 13:7	1279
Bring the *m* into the chamber,	2Sa 13:10	1279
m offerings, and the fat of the	1Kin 8:64	
m offerings, and the fat of the	1Kin 8:64	
the *m* of his table, and the	1Kin 10:5	3978
the strength of that *m* forty days	1Kin 19:8	396
when the *m* offering was offered,	1Kin 3:20	
his *m* offering, and poured his	2Kin 16:13	
and the evening *m* offering	2Kin 16:15	
his *m* offering, with the burnt	2Kin 16:15	
their *m* offering, and their drink	2Kin 16:15	
and on mules, and on oxen, and *m*	1Chr 12:40	3978
and the wheat for the *m* offering	1Chr 21:23	
for the fine flour for *m* offering	1Chr 23:29	
the *m* offerings, and the fat	2Chr 7:7	
the *m* of his table, and the	2Chr 9:4	3978
and *m*, and drink, and oil, unto them	Ezr 3:7	3978
lambs, with their *m* offerings	Ezr 7:17	
and for the continual *m* offering	Neh 10:33	
they laid the *m* offerings	Neh 13:5	
house of God, with the *m* offering	Neh 13:9	
to touch are as my sorrowful *m*	Job 6:7	3899
and the mouth taste his *m*	Job 12:11	400
Yet his *m* in his bowels is turned	Job 20:14	3899
There shall none of his *m* be left	Job 20:21	400
and juniper roots for their *m*	Job 30:4	3899
bread, and his soul dainty *m*	Job 33:20	3978
words, as the mouth tasteth *m*	Job 34:3	398
he giveth *m* in abundance	Job 36:31	400
God, they wander for lack of *m*	Job 38:41	400
My tears have been my *m* day	Ps 42:3	3899
us like sheep appointed for *m*	Ps 44:11	3978
Let them wander up and down for *m*	Ps 59:15	398
They gave me also gall for my *m*	Ps 69:21	1267
gavest him to be *m* to the people	Ps 74:14	3978
heart by asking *m* for their lust	Ps 78:18	400
he sent them *m* to the full	Ps 78:25	6720
but while their *m* was yet in	Ps 78:30	400
be *m* unto the fowls of the heaven	Ps 79:2	3978
prey, and seek their *m* from God	Ps 104:21	400
give them their *m* in due season	Ps 104:27	400
soul abhorreth all manner of *m*	Ps 107:18	400
He hath given *m* unto them that	Ps 111:5	2964
givest them their *m* in due season	Ps 145:15	400
Provideth her *m* in the summer	Prov 6:8	3899

M

for they are deceitful *m*	Prov 23:3	3899
a fool when he is filled with *m*	Prov 30:22	3899
prepare their *m* in the summer	Prov 30:25	3899
giveth *m* to her household, and a	Prov 31:15	2964
thou hast offered a *m* offering	Is 57:6	
corn to be *m* for thine enemies	Is 62:8	3978
and dust shall be the serpent's *m*	Is 65:25	3899
of this people shall be *m* for the	Jer 7:33	3978
be *m* for the fowls of heaven	Jer 16:4	3978
m offerings, and incense, and	Jer 17:26	
carcases will I give to be *m* for	Jer 19:7	3978
and to kindle *m* offerings	Jer 33:18	
m unto the fowls of the heaven	Jer 34:20	3978
things for *m* to relieve the soul	Lam 1:11	400
their *m* to relieve their souls	Lam 1:19	400
they were their *m* in the	Lam 4:10	1262
thy *m* which thou shalt eat shall	Eze 4:10	3978
My *m* also which I gave thee, fine	Eze 16:19	3899
I have given thee for *m* to the	Eze 29:5	402
they became *m* to all the beasts	Eze 34:5	402
my flock became *m* to every beast	Eze 34:8	402
that they may not be *m* for them	Eze 34:10	402
the *m* offering, and the sin	Eze 42:13	
They shall eat the *m* offering	Eze 44:29	
for a *m* offering, and for a burnt	Eze 45:15	
m offerings, and drink offerings,	Eze 45:17	
the *m* offering, and the burnt	Eze 45:17	
he shall prepare a *m* offering of	Eze 45:24	
and according to the *m* offering	Eze 45:25	
the *m* offering shall be an ephah	Eze 46:5	
the *m* offering for the lambs as	Eze 46:5	
And he shall prepare a *m* offering	Eze 46:7	
in the solemnities the *m* offering	Eze 46:11	
thou shalt prepare a *m* offering	Eze 46:14	
a *m* offering continually by a	Eze 46:14	
the *m* offering, and the oil, every	Eze 46:15	
they shall bake the *m* offering	Eze 46:20	
side, shall grow all trees for *m*	Eze 47:12	3978
the fruit thereof shall be for *m*	Eze 47:12	3978
a daily provision of the king's *m*	Dan 1:5	6598
with the portion of the king's *m*	Dan 1:8	6598
king, who hath appointed your *m*	Dan 1:10	3978
of the portion of the king's *m*	Dan 1:13	6598
eat the portion of the king's *m*	Dan 1:15	6598
took away the portion of their *m*	Dan 1:16	6598
much, and in it was *m* for all	Dan 4:12	4203
much, and in it was *m* for all	Dan 4:21	4203
of his *m* shall destroy him	Dan 11:26	6598
their jaws, and I laid *m* unto them	Hos 11:4	398
The *m* offering and the drink	Joel 1:9	
for the *m* offering and the drink	Joel 1:13	
Is not the *m* cut off before our	Joel 1:16	400
even a *m* offering and a drink	Joel 2:14	
your *m* offerings, I will not	Amos 5:22	
is fat, and their *m* plenteous	Hab 1:16	3978
and the fields shall yield no *m*	Hab 3:17	400
or wine, or oil, or any *m*	Hag 2:12	3978
and the fruit thereof, even his *m*	Mal 1:12	400
that there may be *m* in mine house	Mal 3:10	2964
his *m* was locusts and wild honey	Mt 3:4	5160
Is not the life more than *m*	Mt 6:25	5160
as Jesus sat at *m* in the house	Mt 9:10	
the workman is worthy of his *m*	Mt 10:10	5160
and them which sat with him at *m*	Mt 14:9	
they took up of the broken *m* that	Mt 15:37	
to give them *m* in due season	Mt 24:45	5160
I was an hungred, and ye gave me *m*	Mt 25:35	5315
an hungred, and ye gave me no *m*	Mt 25:42	5315
it on his head, as he sat at *m*	Mt 26:7	
as Jesus sat at *m* in his house	Mk 2:15	
they took up of the broken *m* that	Mk 8:8	
Simon the leper, as he sat at *m*	Mk 14:3	
unto the eleven as they sat at *m*	Mk 16:14	
and he that hath *m*, let him do	Lk 3:11	1033
house, and sat down to *m*	Lk 7:36	
sat at *m* in the Pharisee's house	Lk 7:37	
they that sat at *m* with him began	Lk 7:49	
and he commanded to give her *m*	Lk 8:55	5315
buy *m* for all this people	Lk 9:13	1033
and he went in, and sat down to *m*	Lk 11:37	
The life is more than *m*, and the	Lk 12:23	5160
and make them to sit down to *m*	Lk 12:37	
their portion of *m* in due season	Lk 12:42	4620
of them that sit at *m* with thee	Lk 14:10	
at *m* with him heard these things	Lk 14:15	
the field, Go and sit down to *m*	Lk 17:7	
is greater, he that sitteth at *m*	Lk 22:27	
is not he that sitteth at *m*	Lk 22:27	
to pass, as he sat at *m* with them	Lk 24:30	
unto them, Have ye here any *m*	Lk 24:41	1034
gone away unto the city to buy *m*	Jn 4:8	5160

I have *m* to eat that ye know not	Jn 4:32	1035
My *m* is to do the will of him	Jn 4:34	1033
not for the *m* which perisheth	Jn 6:27	1035
but for that *m* which endureth	Jn 6:27	1035
For my flesh is *m* indeed, and my	Jn 6:55	1035
them, Children, have ye any *m*	Jn 21:5	4371
did eat their *m* with gladness	Acts 2:46	5160
And when he had received *m*	Acts 9:19	5160
he set *m* before them, and rejoiced	Acts 16:34	5132
Paul besought them all to take *m*	Acts 27:33	5160
I pray you to take some *m*	Acts 27:34	5160
cheer, and they also took some *m*	Acts 27:36	5160
thy brother be grieved with thy *m*	Rom 14:15	1033
Destroy not him with thy *m*	Rom 14:15	1033
For the kingdom of God is not *m*	Rom 14:17	1035
For *m* destroy not the work of God	Rom 14:20	1033
fed you with milk, and not with *m*	1Cor 3:2	1033
But *m* commendeth us not to God	1Cor 8:8	1033
sit at *m* in the idol's temple	1Cor 8:10	
if *m* make my brother to offend, I	1Cor 8:13	1033
did all eat the same spiritual *m*	1Cor 10:3	1033
no man therefore judge you in *m*	Col 2:16	1035
need of milk, and not of strong *m*	Heb 5:12	5160
But strong *m* belongeth to them	Heb 5:14	5160
morsel of *m* sold his birthright	Heb 12:16	1035

MEATS

neither desire thou his dainty *m*	Prov 23:6	
into the draught, purging all *m*	Mk 7:19	1033
abstain from *m* offered to idols	Acts 15:29	
M for the belly, and the belly for	1Cor 6:13	1033
for the belly, and the belly for *m*	1Cor 6:13	1033
and commanding to abstain from *m*	1Ti 4:3	1033
Which stood only in *m* and drinks,	Heb 9:10	1033
not with *m*, which have not	Heb 13:9	1033

MEBUNNAI (me-bun'-nahee) See SIBBECHAI. A "mighty man" of David.

Anethothite, *M* the Hushathite,	2Sa 23:27	4012

MECHERATHITE (me-ker'-ath-ite) A family name of a "mighty man" of David.

Hepher the *M*, Ahijah the Pelonite	1Chr 11:36	4382

MECONAH See MEKONAH.

MEDAD (me'-dad) An elder of Israel.

Eldad, and the name of the other *M*	Num 11:26	4312
M do prophesy in the camp	Num 11:27	4312

MEDAN (me'-dan) A son of Abraham.

bare him Zimran, and Jokshan, and *M*	Gen 25:2	4091
she bare Zimran, and Jokshan, and *M*	1Chr 1:32	4091

MEDDLE

M not with them	Deut 2:5	1624
them not, nor *m* with them	Deut 2:19	1624
why shouldest thou *m* to thy hurt	2Kin 14:10	1624
shouldest thou *m* to thine hurt	2Chr 25:19	1624
therefore *m* not with him that	Prov 20:19	6148
m not with them that are given to	Prov 24:21	6148

MEDDLED

contention, before it be *m* with	Prov 17:14	1566

MEDDLETH

m with strife belonging not to	Prov 26:17	5674

MEDDLING

forbear thee from *m* with God	2Chr 35:21	
but every fool will be *m*	Prov 20:3	1566

MEDE (meed) See MEDES, MEDIAN. An inhabitant of Media.

in the first year of Darius the *M*	Dan 11:1	4075

MEDEBA (med'-e-bah) A city in Reuben.

Nophah, which reacheth unto *M*	Num 21:30	4311
and all the plain of *M* unto Dibon	Josh 13:9	4311
the river, and all the plain by *M*	Josh 13:16	4311
who came and pitched before *M*	1Chr 19:7	4311
shall howl over Nebo, and over *M*	Is 15:2	4311

MEDES (meeds)

Gozan, and in the cities of the *M*	2Kin 17:6	4074
Gozan, and in the cities of the *M*	2Kin 18:11	4074
that is in the province of the *M*	Ezr 6:2	4074
the laws of the Persians and the *M*	Est 1:19	4074
I will stir up the *M* against them	Is 13:17	4074
Elam, and all the kings of the *M*	Jer 25:25	4074
the spirit of the kings of the *M*	Jer 51:11	4074
nations with the kings of the *M*	Jer 51:28	4074
is divided, and given to the *M*	Dan 5:28	4076
according to the law of the *M*	Dan 6:8	4076
according to the law of the *M*	Dan 6:12	4076
O king, that the law of the *M*	Dan 6:15	4076
Ahasuerus, of the seed of the *M*	Dan 9:1	4074
Parthians, and *M*, and Elamites, and	Acts 2:9	3370

MEDIA *(me'-de-ah)* See Madai, Mede, Median. *A country north of Persia.*

the power of Persia and M, the	Est 1:3	4074
the seven princes of Persia and M	Est 1:14	4074
M say this day unto all the	Est 1:18	4074
the chronicles of the kings of M	Est 10:2	4074
besiege, O M	Is 21:2	4074
two horns are the kings of M	Dan 8:20	4074

MEDIAN *(me'-de-an)* See Mede. *A native of Media.*

Darius the M took the kingdom,	Dan 5:31	4077

MEDIATOR

by angels in the hand of a m	Gal 3:19	3316
Now a m is not a	Gal 3:20	3316
is not a m of one	Gal 3:20	
one m between God and men, the man	1Ti 2:5	3316
he is the m of a better covenant	Heb 8:6	3316
he is the m of the new testament	Heb 9:15	3316
to Jesus the m of the new	Heb 12:24	3316

MEDICINE

A merry heart doeth good like a m	Prov 17:22	1456
meat, and the leaf thereof for m	Eze 47:12	8644

MEDICINES

thou hast no healing m	Jer 30:13	7499
in vain shalt thou use many m	Jer 46:11	7499

MEDITATE

Isaac went out to m in the field	Gen 24:63	7742
but thou shalt therein day	Josh 1:8	1897
and in his law doth he m day	Ps 1:2	1897
m on thee in the night watches	Ps 63:6	1897
I will m also of all thy work, and	Ps 77:12	1897
I will m in thy precepts, and have	Ps 119:15	7878
thy servant did m in thy statutes	Ps 119:23	7878
and I will m in thy statutes	Ps 119:48	7878
but I will m in thy precepts	Ps 119:78	7878
that I might m in thy word	Ps 119:148	7878
I m on all thy works	Ps 143:5	1897
Thine heart shall m terror	Is 33:18	1897
not to m before what ye shall	Lk 21:14	4304
M upon these things	1Ti 4:15	3191

MEDITATION

consider my m	Ps 5:1	1901
the m of my heart, be acceptable	Ps 19:14	1902
the m of my heart shall be of	Ps 49:3	1900
My m of him shall be sweet	Ps 104:34	7879
it is my m all the day	Ps 119:97	7881
for thy testimonies are my m	Ps 119:99	7881

MEEK

(Now the man Moses was very m	Num 12:3	6035
The m shall eat and be satisfied	Ps 22:26	6035
The m will he guide in judgment	Ps 25:9	6035
the m will he teach his way	Ps 25:9	6035
But the m shall inherit the earth	Ps 37:11	6035
to save all the m of the earth	Ps 76:9	6035
The Lord lifteth up the m	Ps 147:6	6035
beautify the m with salvation	Ps 149:4	6035
equity for the m of the earth	Is 11:4	6035
The m also shall increase their	Is 29:19	6035
to preach good tidings unto the m	Is 61:1	6035
and turn aside the way of the m	Amos 2:7	6035
all ye m of the earth, which have	Zeph 2:3	6035
Blessed are the m	Mt 5:5	4239
for I am m and lowly in heart	Mt 11:29	4235
thy King cometh unto thee, m	Mt 21:5	4239
even the ornament of a m	1Pet 3:4	4239

MEEKNESS

because of truth and m and	Ps 45:4	6037
seek righteousness, seek m	Zeph 2:3	6038
or in love, and in the spirit of m	1Cor 4:21	4236
Paul myself beseech you by the m	2Cor 10:1	4236
M, temperance	Gal 5:23	4236
such an one in the spirit of m	Gal 6:1	4236
With all lowliness and m, with	Eph 4:2	4236
kindness, humbleness of mind, m	Col 3:12	4236
faith, love, patience, m	1Ti 6:11	4236
In m instructing those that	2Ti 2:25	4236
shewing all m unto all men	Titus 3:2	4236
receive with m the engrafted word	Jas 1:21	4240
his works with m of wisdom	Jas 3:13	4240
of the hope that is in you with m	1Pet 3:15	4240

MEET

I will make him an help m for him	Gen 2:18	5828
was not found an help m for him	Gen 2:20	5828
m him after his return from the	Gen 14:17	7125
he ran to m them from the tent	Gen 18:2	7125
Lot seeing them rose up to m them	Gen 19:1	7125
And the servant ran to m her	Gen 24:17	7125

that walketh in the field to m us	Gen 24:65	7125
son, that he ran to m him	Gen 29:13	7125
and Leah went out to m him	Gen 30:16	7125
Esau, and also he cometh to m thee	Gen 32:6	7125
Esau ran to m him, and embraced	Gen 33:4	7125
went up to m Israel his father,	Gen 46:29	7125
behold, he cometh forth to m thee	Ex 4:14	7125
Go into the wilderness to m Moses	Ex 4:27	7125
Moses said, It is not m so to do	Ex 8:26	3559
went out to m his father in law	Ex 18:7	7125
out of the camp to m with God	Ex 19:17	7125
If thou m thine enemy's ox or his	Ex 23:4	6293
And there I will m with thee	Ex 25:22	3259
where I will m you, to speak	Ex 29:42	3259
there I will m with the children	Ex 29:43	3259
where I will m with thee	Ex 30:6	3259
where I will m with thee	Ex 30:36	3259
where I will m with you	Num 17:4	3259
he went out to m him unto a city	Num 22:36	7125
the Lord will come to m me	Num 23:3	7125
while I m the Lord yonder	Num 23:15	7136
went forth to m them without the	Num 31:13	7125
all that are m for the war	Deut 3:18	1121
mountain, lest the pursuers m you	Josh 2:16	6293
for the journey, and go to m them	Josh 9:11	7125
And Jael went out to m Sisera	Judg 4:18	7125
Sisera, Jael came out to m him	Judg 4:22	7125
m for the necks of them that take	Judg 5:30	
and they came up to m them	Judg 6:35	7125
of the doors of my house to m me	Judg 11:31	7125
came out to m him with timbrels	Judg 11:34	7125
saw him, he rejoiced to m him	Judg 19:3	7125
that they m thee not in any other	Ruth 2:22	6293
there shall m thee three men	1Sa 10:3	4672
that thou shalt m a company of	1Sa 10:5	6293
and Saul went out to m him	1Sa 13:10	7125
early to m Saul in the morning	1Sa 15:12	7125
and came and drew nigh to m David	1Sa 17:48	7125
the army to m the Philistine	1Sa 17:48	7125
to m king Saul, with tabrets,	1Sa 18:6	7125
which sent thee this day to m me	1Sa 25:32	7125
thou hadst hasted and come to m me	1Sa 25:34	7125
and they went forth to m David	1Sa 30:21	7125
to m the people that were with	1Sa 30:21	7125
of Saul came out to m David	2Sa 6:20	7125
it unto David, he sent to m them	2Sa 10:5	7125
came to m him with his coat rent	2Sa 15:32	7125
to Gilgal, to go to m the king	2Sa 19:15	7125
the men of Judah to m king David	2Sa 19:16	7125
to go down to m my lord the king	2Sa 19:20	7125
of Saul came down to m the king	2Sa 19:24	7125
come to Jerusalem to m the king	2Sa 19:25	7125
he came down to m me at Jordan	1Kin 2:8	7125
And the king rose up to m her	1Kin 2:19	7125
So Obadiah went to m Ahab	1Kin 18:16	7125
and Ahab went to m Elijah	1Kin 18:16	7125
go down to m Ahab king of Israel,	1Kin 21:18	7125
go up to m the messengers of the	2Kin 1:3	7125
him, There came a man up to m us	2Kin 1:6	7125
man was he which came up to m you	2Kin 1:7	7125
And they came to m him, and bowed	2Kin 2:15	7125
to m her, and say unto her, Is it	2Kin 4:26	7125
if thou m any man, salute him not	2Kin 4:29	4672
Wherefore he went again to m him	2Kin 4:31	7125
down from the chariot to m him	2Kin 5:21	7125
again from his chariot to m thee	2Kin 5:26	7125
m the man of God, and enquire of	2Kin 8:8	7125
So Hazael went to m him, and took	2Kin 8:9	7125
an horseman, and send to m them	2Kin 9:17	7125
went one on horseback to m him	2Kin 9:18	7125
the son of Rechab coming to m him	2Kin 10:15	7125
king Ahaz went to Damascus to m	2Kin 16:10	7125
And David went out to m them	1Chr 14:8	6440
And he sent to m them	1Chr 19:5	7125
And he went out to m Asa, and said	2Chr 15:2	6440
Hanani the seer went out to m him	2Chr 19:2	6440
it was not m for us to see the	Ezr 4:14	749
let us m together in some one of	Neh 6:2	3259
Let us m together in the house of	Neh 6:10	3259
which were m to be given her, out	Est 2:9	7200
They m with darkness in the	Job 5:14	6298
Surely it is m to be said unto	Job 34:31	
he goeth on to m the armed men	Job 39:21	7125
Therefore came I forth to m thee	Prov 7:15	7125
that withholdeth more than is m	Prov 11:24	3476
bear robbed of her whelps in a man	Prov 17:12	6298
The rich and poor m together	Prov 22:2	6298
and the deceitful man m together	Prov 29:13	6298
Isaiah, Go forth now to m Ahaz	Is 7:3	7125
for thee to m thee at thy coming	Is 14:9	7125
m with the wild beasts of the	Is 34:14	6298

M

I will not *m* thee as a man .... Is 47:3   6293
me as seemeth good and *m* unto you ..... Jer 26:14   3477
it unto whom it seemed *m* unto me .... Jer 27:5   3474
went forth from Mizpah to *m* them .... Jer 41:6   7125
One post shall run to *m* another .... Jer 51:31   7125
and one messenger to *m* another .... Jer 51:31   7125
Is it *m* for any work .... Eze 15:4   6743
was whole, it was *m* for no work .... Eze 15:5   6213
shall it be *m* yet for any work .... Eze 15:5   6213
I will *m* them as a bear that is .... Hos 13:8   6298
unto them, prepare to *m* thy God .... Amos 4:12   7125
another angel went out to *m* him .... Zec 2:3   7125
therefore fruits *m* for repentance .... Mt 3:8   *514*
whole city came out to *m* Jesus .... Mt 8:34   4877
and said, It is not *m* to take the .... Mt 15:26   2570
went forth to *m* the bridegroom .... Mt 25:1   *529*
go ye out to *m* him .... Mt 25:6   *529*
for it is not *m* to take the .... Mk 7:27   2570
there shall *m* you a man bearing a .... Mk 14:13   *528*
to *m* him that cometh against him .... Lk 14:31   *528*
It was *m* that we should make .... Lk 15:32   *1163*
the city, there shall a man *m* you .... Lk 22:10   4876
trees, and went forth to *m* him .... Jn 12:13   5222
do works *m* for repentance .... Acts 26:20   *514*
they came to *m* us as far as Appii .... Acts 28:15   *529*
of their error which was *m* .... Rom 1:27   *1163*
that am not to be called an 1Cor 15:9   2425
if it be *m* that I go also, they 1Cor 16:4   *514*
Even as it is *m* for me to think .... Phil 1:7   *1342*
which hath made us *m* to be .... Col 1:12   2427
clouds, to *m* the Lord in the air 1Th 4:17   *529*
for you, brethren, as it is *m* 2Th 1:3   *514*
m for the master's use, and 2Ti 2:21   *2173*
bringeth forth herbs *m* for them .... Heb 6:7   *2111*
Yea, I think it *m*, as long as I 2Pet 1:13   *1342*

MEETEST
m of your master's sons, and set 2Kin 10:3   3477
Thou *m* him that rejoiceth and .... Is 64:5   6293

MEETETH
When Esau my brother *m* thee .... Gen 32:17   6298
when he *m* him, he shall slay him .... Num 35:19   6293
slay the murderer, when he *m* him .... Num 35:21   6293

MEETING
was afraid at the *m* of David 1Sa 21:1   7125
it is iniquity, even the solemn *m* .... Is 1:13   6116

MEGIDDO (me-ghid'-do) See MEGIDDON. *A city on the plain of Jezreel.*
the king of *M*, one .... Josh 12:21   4023
towns, and the inhabitants of *M* .... Josh 17:11   4023
towns, nor the inhabitants of *M* .... Judg 1:27   4023
in Taanach by the waters of *M* .... Judg 5:19   4023
to him pertained Taanach and *M* 1Kin 4:12   4023
wall of Jerusalem, and Hazor, and *M* 1Kin 9:15   4023
And he fled to *M*, and died there 2Kin 9:27   4023
and he slew him at *M*, when he had 2Kin 23:29   4023
him in a chariot dead from *M* 2Kin 23:30   4023
towns, Taanach and her towns, *M* 1Chr 7:29   4023
came to fight in the valley of *M* 2Chr 35:22   4023

MEGIDDON (me-ghid'-don) See ARMAGEDDON, ME-GIDDO. *Same as Megiddo.*
of Hadadrimmon in the valley of *M* .... Zec 12:11   4023

MEHETABEEL (me-het'-a-be-el) See MEHETABEL. *Father of Delaiah.*
the son of Delaiah the son of *M* .... Neh 6:10   4105

MEHETABEL (me-het'-a-bel) See MEHETABEEL. *Wife of Hadar.*
and his wife's name was *M*, the .... Gen 36:39   4105
and his wife's name was *M*, the 1Chr 1:50   4105

MEHIDA (me-hi'-dah) *A family of exiles.*
of Bazluth, the children of *M* .... Ezr 2:52   4240
of Bazlith, the children of *M* .... Neh 7:54   4240

MEHIR (me'-hur) *A son of Chelub.*
the brother of Shuah begat *M* 1Chr 4:11   4243

MEHOLATHITE (me-ho'-lath-ite) *An inhabitant of a city in Issachar.*
given unto Adriel the *M* to wife 1Sa 18:19   4259
Adriel the son of Barzillai the *M* 2Sa 21:8   4259

MEHUJAEL (me-hu'-ja-el) *Son of Irad.*
and Irad begat *M* .... Gen 4:18   4232
and *M* begat Methusael .... Gen 4:18   4232

MEHUMAN (me-hu'-man) *A servant of King Ahasuerus.*
merry with wine, he commanded *M* .... Est 1:10   4104

MEHUNIM (me-hu'-nim) See MAONITE, MEHUNIMS, MEUNIM. *A family of exiles.*
of Asnah, the children of *M* .... Ezr 2:50   4586

MEHUNIMS (me-hu'-nims) See MEHUNIM. *A people who lived in Arabia.*
that dwelt in Gur-baal, and the *M* 2Chr 26:7   4586

ME-JARKON (me-jar'-kon) *A city in Dan.*
And *M*, and Rakkon, with the border ..... Josh 19:46   4313

MEKERATHITE See MECHERATHITE.

MEKONAH (me-ko'-nah) *A city in Judah.*
And at Ziklag, and at *M*, and in the .... Neh 11:28   4368

MELATIAH (mel-a-ti'-ah) *A repairer of Jerusalem's wall.*
them repaired *M* the Gibeonite .... Neh 3:7   4424

MELCHI (mel'-ki) See MELCHI-SHUA, MELCHIZEDEK.
  1. Son of Janna; ancestor of Jesus.
of Levi, which was the son of *M* .... Lk 3:24   *3197*
  2. Son of Addi; ancestor of Jesus.
Which was the son of *M*, which was ...... Lk 3:28   *3197*

MELCHIAH (mel-ki'-ah) See MALCHIAH. *Father of Pashur.*
sent unto him Pashur the son of *M* .... Jer 21:1   4441

MELCHISEDEC (mel-kis'-e-dek) See MELCHIZEDEK. *Greek form of Melchizedek.*
for ever after the order of *M* .... Heb 5:6   *3198*
high priest after the order of *M* .... Heb 5:10   *3198*
for ever after the order of *M* .... Heb 6:20   *3198*
For this *M*, king of Salem, priest .... Heb 7:1   *3198*
of his father, when *M* met him .... Heb 7:10   *3198*
should rise after the order of *M* .... Heb 7:11   *3198*
of *M* there ariseth another priest .... Heb 7:15   *3198*
for ever after the order of *M* .... Heb 7:17   *3198*
for ever after the order of *M* .... Heb 7:21   *3198*

MELCHI-SHUA (mel'-ki-shu'-ah) See MALCHISHUA. *A son of King Saul.*
were Jonathan, and Ishui, and *M* 1Sa 14:49   4444
slew Jonathan, and Abinadab, and *M* 1Sa 31:2   4444

MELCHIZEDEK (mel-kiz'-e-dek) See MELCHISEDEC. *King and priest of Salem.*
M king of Salem brought forth .... Gen 14:18   4442
for ever after the order of *M* .... Ps 110:4   4442

MELEA (mel'-e-ah) *Son of Menan; an ancestor of Jesus.*
Which was the son of *M*, which was ...... Lk 3:31   *3190*

MELECH (me'-lek) See EBED-MELECH, HAM-MELECH, NATHAN-MELECH, REGEM-MELECH. *A son of Micah.*
sons of Micah were, Pithon, and *M* 1Chr 8:35   4429
sons of Micah were, Pithon, and *M* 1Chr 9:41   4429

MELICHU See MELICU.

MELICU (mel'-i-cu) See MALLUCH. *A priest.*
Of *M*, Jonathan .... Neh 12:14   4409

MELITA (mel'-i-tah) *A Mediterranean island.*
knew that the island was called *M* .... Acts 28:1   *3194*

MELODY
make sweet *m*, sing many songs, ... Is 23:16   5059
thanksgiving, and the voice of *m* .... Is 51:3   2172
will not hear the *m* of thy viols .... Amos 5:23   2172
making *m* in your heart to the .... Eph 5:19   *5567*

MELONS
the cucumbers, and the *m*, and the .... Num 11:5   20

MELT
of Canaan shall *m* away .... Ex 15:15   4127
these things, our hearts did *m* .... Josh 2:11   4549
me made the heart of the people *m* .... Josh 14:8   4529
heart of a lion, shall utterly *m* 2Sa 17:10   4549
Let them *m* away as waters which .... Ps 58:7   3988
gnash with his teeth, and *m* away .... Ps 112:10   4549
and every man's heart shall *m* .... Is 13:7   4549
Egypt shall *m* in the midst of it .... Is 19:1   4549
of hosts, Behold, I will *m* them .... Jer 9:7   6884
and every heart shall *m*, and all .... Eze 21:7   4549
to blow the fire upon it, to *m* it .... Eze 22:20   5413
I will leave you there, and *m* you .... Eze 22:20   5413
toucheth the land, and it shall *m* .... Amos 9:5   4127
wine, and all the hills shall *m* .... Amos 9:13   4127
quake at him, and the hills *m* .... Nah 1:5   4127
shall *m* with fervent heat 2Pet 3:10   *3089*
shall *m* with fervent heat 2Pet 3:12   *5080*

MELTED
and when the sun waxed hot, it *m* .... Ex 16:21   4549
passed over, that their heart *m* .... Josh 5:1   4549
the hearts of the people *m* .... Josh 7:5   4549
The mountains *m* from before the .... Judg 5:5   5140
and, behold, the multitude *m* away 1Sa 14:16   4127

it is *m* in the midst of my bowels .... Ps 22:14   4549
he uttered his voice, the earth *m* .... Ps 46:6   4127
The hills *m* like wax at the .... Ps 97:5   4549
their soul is *m* because of .... Ps 107:26   4127
shall be *m* with their blood .... Is 34:3   4549
ye shall be *m* in the midst .... Eze 22:21   5413
As silver is *m* in the midst of .... Eze 22:22   2046
so shall ye be *m* in the midst .... Eze 22:22   5413

MELTETH
As a snail which *m*, let every one .... Ps 58:8   8557
as wax *m* before the fire, so let .... Ps 68:2   4549
My soul *m* for heaviness....................... Ps 119:28   1811
sendeth out his word, and *m* them .... Ps 147:18   4549
The workman *m* a graven image, and ... Is 40:19   5258
the founder *m* in vain .... Jer 6:29   6884
and the heart *m*, and the knees .... Nah 2:10   4549

MELTING
As when the *m* fire burneth, the .... Is 64:2   2003

MELZAR *(mel'-zar) Babylonian officer charged with Daniel and his companions.*
Then said Daniel to *M*, whom the .... Dan 1:11   4453
Thus *M* took away the portion of .... Dan 1:16   4453

MEMBER
or hath his privy *m* cut off .... Deut 23:1
For the body is not one *m* 1Cor 12:14   *3196*
And if they were all one *m* 1Cor 12:19   *3196*
And whether one *m* suffer, all the 1Cor 12:26   *3196*
or one *m* be honoured, all the 1Cor 12:26   *3196*
Even so the tongue is a little *m* .... Jas 3:5   *3196*

MEMBERS
and all my *m* are as a shadow .... Job 17:7   3338
in thy book all my *m* were written .... Ps 139:16
that one of thy *m* should perish .... Mt 5:29   *3196*
that one of thy *m* should perish .... Mt 5:30   *3196*
yield ye your *m* as instruments of .... Rom 6:13   *3196*
dead, and your *m* as instruments of....... Rom 6:13   *3196*
your *m* servants to uncleanness .... Rom 6:19   *3196*
even so now yield your *m* servants........ Rom 6:19   *3196*
did work in our *m* to bring forth .... Rom 7:5   *3196*
But I see another law in my *m* .... Rom 7:23   *3196*
the law of sin which is in my *m* .... Rom 7:23   *3196*
For as we have many *m* in one body ..... Rom 12:4   *3196*
all *m* have not the same office .... Rom 12:4   *3196*
every one *m* one of another .... Rom 12:5   *3196*
your bodies are the *m* of Christ............. 1Cor 6:15   *3196*
shall I then take the *m* of Christ 1Cor 6:15   *3196*
and make them the *m* of an harlot......... 1Cor 6:15   *3196*
the body is one, and hath many *m* 1Cor 12:12   *3196*
all the *m* of that one body, being 1Cor 12:12   *3196*
But now hath God set the *m* every 1Cor 12:18   *3196*
But now are they many *m*, yet but 1Cor 12:20   *3196*
much more those *m* of the body 1Cor 12:22   *3196*
those *m* of the body, which we 1Cor 12:23
but that the *m* should have the 1Cor 12:25   *3196*
suffer, all the *m* suffer with it 1Cor 12:26   *3196*
all the *m* rejoice with it........................... 1Cor 12:26   *3196*
of Christ, and *m* in particular................. 1Cor 12:27   *3196*
for we are *m* one of another .... Eph 4:25   *3196*
For we are *m* of his body, of his .... Eph 5:30   *3196*
Mortify therefore your *m* which .... Col 3:5   *3196*
so is the tongue among our *m* .... Jas 3:6   *3196*
of your lusts that war in your *m* .... Jas 4:1   *3196*

MEMORIAL
this is my *m* unto all generations .... Ex 3:15   2143
day shall be unto you for a *m* .... Ex 12:14   2146
for a *m* between thine eyes, that .... Ex 13:9   2146
Write this for a *m* in a book .... Ex 17:14   2146
of the ephod for stones of *m* unto .... Ex 28:12   2146
upon his two shoulders for a *m* .... Ex 28:12   2146
place, for a *m* before the LORD .... Ex 28:29   2146
that it may be a *m* unto the .... Ex 30:16   2146
for a *m* to the children of Israel .... Ex 39:7   2146
burn the *m* of it upon the altar .... Lev 2:2   234
the meat offering a *m* thereof .... Lev 2:9   234
the priest shall burn the *m* of it .... Lev 2:16   234
even a *m* thereof, and burn it on............ Lev 5:12   234
a sweet savour, even the *m* of it .... Lev 6:15   234
a *m* of blowing of trumpets, an.............. Lev 23:24   2146
it may be on the bread for a *m* .... Lev 24:7   234
of jealousy, an offering of *m* .... Num 5:15   2146
the offering of *m* in her hands............... Num 5:18   2146
the offering, even the *m* thereof .... Num 5:26   234
be to you for a *m* before your God......... Num 10:10   2146
To be a *m* unto the children of .... Num 16:40   2146
for a *m* for the children of .... Num 31:54   2146
these stones shall be for a *m* .... Josh 4:7   2146
have no portion, nor right, nor *m*........... Neh 2:20   2146
nor the *m* of them perish from .... Est 9:28   2143

their *m* is perished with them .... Ps 9:6   2143
and thy *m*, O LORD, throughout all......... Ps 135:13   2143
the LORD is his *m* .... Hos 12:5   2143
for a *m* in the temple of the LORD .... Zec 6:14   2146
hath done, be told for a *m* of her .... Mt 26:13   *3422*
shall be spoken of for a *m* of her .... Mk 14:9   *3422*
are come up for a *m* before God............ Acts 10:4   *3422*

MEMORY
off the *m* of them from the earth .... Ps 109:15   2143
utter the *m* of thy great goodness .... Ps 145:7   2143
The *m* of the just is blessed .... Prov 10:7   2143
for the *m* of them is forgotten .... Eccl 9:5   2143
and made all their *m* to perish............... Is 26:14   2143
if ye keep in *m* what I preached 1Cor 15:2

MEMPHIS *(mem'-fis)* See NOPH. *A city in Egypt.*
gather them up, *M* shall bury them......... Hos 9:6   4644

MEMUCAN *(mem-u'-can) A prince of Media and Persia.*
Tarshish, Meres, Marsena, and *M* .... Est 1:14   4462
M answered before the king and the ...... Est 1:16   4462
did according to the word of *M* .... Est 1:21   4462

MEN See APPENDIX.

MENAHEM *(men'-a-hem) Son of Gadi.*
For *M* the son of Gadi went up................ 2Kin 15:14   4505
Then *M* smote Tiphsah, and all that 2Kin 15:16   4505
M the son of Gadi to reign over 2Kin 15:17   4505
M gave Pul a thousand talents of 2Kin 15:19   4505
M exacted the money of Israel,............... 2Kin 15:20   4505
And the rest of the acts of *M* 2Kin 15:21   4505
And *M* slept with his fathers 2Kin 15:22   4505
of Judah Pekahiah the son of *M* 2Kin 15:23   4505

MENAN *(me'-nan) Father of Melea; ancestor of Jesus.*
of Melea, which was the son of *M*........... Lk 3:31   *3104*

MEND
brass to *m* the house of the LORD 2Chr 24:12   2388

MENDING
their father, *m* their nets......................... Mt 4:21   2675
were in the ship *m* their nets .... Mk 1:19   2675

MENE *(me'-ne) Part of "the handwriting on the wall".*
writing that was written, *M*, *M* .... Dan 5:25   4484
M; God hath numbered .... Dan 5:26   4484

MENI See MENAN.

MENNA See MENAN.

MENPLEASERS
Not with eyeservice, as *m* .... Eph 6:6   *441*
not with eyeservice, as *m* .... Col 3:22   *441*

MEN'S See APPENDIX.

MENSERVANTS
sheep, and oxen, and he asses, and *m* ... Gen 12:16   5650
took sheep, and oxen, and *m*.................. Gen 20:14   5650
herds, and silver, and gold, and *m* .... Gen 24:35   5650
cattle, and maidservants, and *m* .... Gen 30:43   5650
have oxen, and asses, flocks, and *m* ...... Gen 32:5   5650
she shall not go out as the *m* do .... Ex 21:7   5650
and your daughters, and your *m* .... Deut 12:12   5650
And he will take your *m*, and your 1Sa 8:16   5650
and sheep, and oxen, and *m*, and 2Kin 5:26   5650
and shall begin to beat the *m* .... Lk 12:45   *3816*

MENSTEALERS
themselves with mankind, for *m* 1Ti 1:10   *405*

MENSTRUOUS
shalt cast them away as a *m* cloth .... Is 30:22   1739
is as a *m* woman among them................ Lam 1:17   5079
hath come near to a *m* woman............... Eze 18:6   5079

MENTION
make *m* unto me unto Pharaoh, and .... Gen 40:14   2142
make no *m* of the name of other .... Ex 23:13   2142
neither make *m* of the names of .... Josh 23:7   2142
when he made *m* of the ark of God,....... 1Sa 4:18   2142
No *m* shall be made of coral, or............. Job 28:18   2142
I will make *m* of thy............................... Ps 71:16   2142
I will make *m* of Rahab and Babylon..... Ps 87:4   2142
make *m* that his name is exalted .... Is 12:4   2142
every one that maketh *m* thereof........... Is 19:17   2142
only will we make *m* of thy name........... Is 26:13   2142
make *m* of the God of Israel, but........... Is 48:1   2142
mother hath he made *m* of my name..... Is 49:1   2142
ye that make *m* of the LORD .... Is 62:6   2142
I will make *m* of the lovingkindnesses of .... Is 63:7   2142
Make ye *m* to the nations...................... Jer 4:16   2142
I said, I will not make *m* of him.............. Jer 20:9   2142
of the LORD shall ye *m* no more .... Jer 23:36   2142
for we may not make *m* of the name...... Amos 6:10   2142

m of you always in my prayers .... Rom 1:9   3417
making *m* of you in my prayers .... Eph 1:16   3417
making *m* of you in our prayers 1Th 1:2   3417
making *m* of thee always in my .... Philem 4   3417
made *m* of the departing of the .... Heb 11:22   3421

MENTIONED
cities which are here *m* by name .... Josh 21:9   7121
These *m* by their names were 1Chr 4:38   935
who is *m* in the book of the kings 2Chr 20:34   5927
For thy sister Sodom was not *m* by .... Eze 16:56   8052
they shall not be *m* unto him .... Eze 18:22   2142
that he hath done shall not be *m* .... Eze 18:24   2142
committed shall be *m* unto him .... Eze 33:16   2142

MENUHOTH See MANAHETHITES.

MEONENIM (*me-on'-e-nim*) A place near Shechem.
come along by the plain of *M* .... Judg 9:37   6049

MEONOTHAI (*me-on'-o-thahee*) Descendant of Judah.
And *M* begat Ophrah 1Chr 4:14   4587

MEPHAATH (*mef-a-ath*) A Levitical city in Reuben.
And Jahaza, and Kedemoth, and *M* .... Josh 13:18   4158
suburbs, and *M* with her suburbs .... Josh 21:37   4158
suburbs, and *M* with her suburbs 1Chr 6:79   4158
Holon, and upon Jahazah, and upon *M* . Jer 48:21   4158

MEPHIBOSHETH (*me-fib'-o-sheth*) See MERIBBAAL.
1. Son of Jonathan.
And his name was *M* 2Sa 4:4   4648
Now when *M*, the son of Jonathan, ... 2Sa 9:6   4648
And David said, *M* 2Sa 9:6   4648
but *M* thy master's son shall eat 2Sa 9:10   4648
As for *M*, said the king, he shall 2Sa 9:11   4648
M had a young son, whose name was 2Sa 9:12   4648
of Ziba were servants unto *M* 2Sa 9:12   4648
So *M* dwelt in Jerusalem 2Sa 9:13   4648
Ziba the servant of *M* met him 2Sa 16:1   4648
are all that pertained unto *M* 2Sa 16:4   4648
M the son of Saul came down to 2Sa 19:24   4648
wentest not thou with me, *M* 2Sa 19:25   4648
M said unto the king, Yea, let 2Sa 19:30   4648
But the king spared *M*, the son of 2Sa 21:7   4648
2. Son of Rizpah.
she bare unto Saul, Armoni and *M* 2Sa 21:8   4648

MERAB (*me'-rab*) Daughter of King Saul.
the name of the firstborn *M* 1Sa 14:49   4764
David, Behold my elder daughter *M* 1Sa 18:17   4764
M Saul's daughter should have 1Sa 18:19   4764

MERAIAH (*mer-a-i'-ah*) A priest.
fathers: of Seraiah, *M* .... Neh 12:12   4811

MERAIOTH (*me-rah'-yoth*) See MEREMOTH.
1. An ancestor of Azariah.
Zerahiah, and Zerahiah begat *M* 1Chr 6:6   4812
M begat Amariah, and Amariah begat .. 1Chr 6:7   4812
M his son, Amariah his son, ... 1Chr 6:52   4812
the son of Azariah, the son of *M* .... Ezr 7:3   4812
2. Another ancestor of Azariah.
the son of Zadok, the son of *M* 1Chr 9:11   4812
the son of Zadok, the son of *M* .... Neh 11:11   4812
3. A priest in exile.
of *M*, Helkai .... Neh 12:15   4812

MERARI (*me-ra'-ri*) See MERARITES. A son of Levi.
Gershon, Kohath, and *M* .... Gen 46:11   4847
Gershon, and Kohath, and *M* .... Ex 6:16   4847
And the sons of *M* .... Ex 6:19   4847
Gershon, and Kohath, and *M* .... Num 3:17   4847
the sons of *M* by their families .... Num 3:20   4847
Of *M* was the family of the .... Num 3:33   4847
these are the families of *M* .... Num 3:33   4847
M was Zuriel the son of Abihail .... Num 3:35   4847
charge of the sons of *M* shall be .... Num 3:36   4847
As for the sons of *M*, thou shalt .... Num 4:29   4847
of the families of the sons of *M* .... Num 4:33   4847
of the families of the sons of *M* .... Num 4:42   4847
of the families of the sons of *M* .... Num 4:45   4847
oxen he gave unto the sons of *M* .... Num 7:8   4847
and the sons of *M* set forward .... Num 10:17   4847
of *M*, the family of the Merarites .... Num 26:57   4847
The children of *M* by their .... Josh 21:7   4847
the families of the children of *M* .... Josh 21:34   4847
children of *M* by their families .... Josh 21:40   4847
Gershon, Kohath, and *M* 1Chr 6:1   4847
Gershom, Kohath, and *M* 1Chr 6:16   4847
The sons of *M*; Mahli, and 1Chr 6:19   4847
The sons of *M*; Mahli, Libni, ... 1Chr 6:29   4847
sons of *M* stood on the left hand 1Chr 6:44   4847
the son of Mushi, the son of *M* 1Chr 6:47   4847
Unto the sons of *M* were given by 1Chr 6:63   4847
the rest of the children of *M* 1Chr 6:77   4847

of Hashabiah, of the sons of *M* 1Chr 9:14   4847
Of the sons of *M* 1Chr 15:6   4847
of the sons of *M* their brethren 1Chr 15:17   4847
namely, Gershon, Kohath, and *M* 1Chr 23:6   4847
The sons of *M*; Mahli, and 1Chr 23:21   4847
The sons of *M* were Mahli and Mushi 1Chr 24:26   4847
The sons of *M* by Jaaziah 1Chr 24:27   4847
Also Hosah, of the children of *M* 1Chr 26:10   4847
of Kore, and among the sons of *M* 1Chr 26:19   4847
and of the sons of *M*, Kish the son 2Chr 29:12   4847
the Levites, of the sons of *M* 2Chr 34:12   4847
him Jeshaiah of the sons of *M* .... Ezr 8:19   4847

MERARITES (*me-ra'-rites*) Descendants of Merari.
of Merari, the family of the *M* .... Num 26:57   4848

MERATHAIM (*mer-a-tha'-im*) A symbolic name for Babylon.
Go up against the land of *M* .... Jer 50:21   4850

MERCHANDISE
thou shalt not make *m* of her .... Deut 21:14   6014
of Israel, and maketh *m* of him .... Deut 24:7   6014
For the *m* of it is better than .... Prov 3:14   5504
it is better than the *m* of silver .... Prov 3:14   5505
She perceiveth that her *m* is good .... Prov 31:18   5504
And her *m* and her hire shall be .... Is 23:18   5504
for her *m* shall be for them that .... Is 23:18   5504
m of Ethiopia and of the Sabeans, ... Is 45:14   5505
riches, and make a prey of thy *m* .... Eze 26:12   7404
were in thee to occupy thy *m* .... Eze 27:9   4627
isles were the *m* of thine hand .... Eze 27:15   5506
and made of cedar, among thy *m* .... Eze 27:24   4819
Thy riches, and thy fairs, thy *m* .... Eze 27:27   4627
and the occupiers of thy *m* .... Eze 27:27   4627
of thy riches and of thy *m* .... Eze 27:33   4627
in the depths of the waters thy *m* .... Eze 27:34   4627
By the multitude of thy *m* they .... Eze 28:16   7404
one to his farm, another to his *m* .... Mt 22:5   *1711*
my Father's house an house of *m* .... Jn 2:16   *1712*
with feigned words make *m* of you 2Pet 2:3
no man buyeth their *m* any more .... Rev 18:11   *1117*
The *m* of gold, and silver, and .... Rev 18:12   *1117*

MERCHANT
silver, current money with the *m* .... Gen 23:16
and delivereth girdles unto the *m* .... Prov 31:24   5503
with all powders of the *m* .... Song 3:6   7402
a commandment against the *m* city .... Is 23:11   3667
which art a *m* of the people for .... Eze 27:3   7402
Tarshish was thy *m* by reason of .... Eze 27:12   5503
Syria was thy *m* by reason of the .... Eze 27:16   5503
Damascus was thy *m* in the .... Eze 27:18   5503
Dedan was thy *m* in precious .... Eze 27:20   7402
He is a *m*, the balances of deceit .... Hos 12:7   3667
for all the *m* people are cut down .... Zeph 1:11   3667
of heaven is unto a *m* man .... Mt 13:45   *1713*

MERCHANTMEN
Then there passed by Midianites *m* .... Gen 37:28   5503
Beside that he had of the *m* 1Kin 10:15   8446

MERCHANTS
and of the traffick of the spice *m* 1Kin 10:15   7402
the king's *m* received the linen 1Kin 10:28   5503
the king's *m* received the linen 2Chr 1:16   5503
that which chapmen and *m* brought 2Chr 9:14   5503
of the Nethinims, and of the *m* .... Neh 3:31   7402
repaired the goldsmiths and the *m* .... Neh 3:32   7402
So the *m* and sellers of all kind .... Neh 13:20   7402
shall they part him among the *m* .... Job 41:6   3669
thou whom the *m* of Zidon, that .... Is 23:2   5503
whose *m* are princes, whose .... Is 23:8   5503
thou hast laboured, even thy *m* .... Is 47:15   5503
he set it in a city of *m* .... Eze 17:4   7402
and Meshech, they were thy *m* .... Eze 27:13   7402
The men of Dedan were thy *m* .... Eze 27:15   7402
land of Israel, they were thy *m* .... Eze 27:17   7402
in these were they thy *m* .... Eze 27:21   5503
The *m* of Sheba and Raamah .... Eze 27:22   7402
Sheba and Raamah, they were thy *m* .... Eze 27:22   7402
the *m* of Sheba, Asshur, and .... Eze 27:23   7402
and Chilmad, were thy *m* .... Eze 27:23   7402
These were thy *m* in all sorts of .... Eze 27:24   7402
The *m* among the people shall hiss .... Eze 27:36   5503
the *m* of Tarshish, with all the .... Eze 38:13   5503
Thou hast multiplied thy *m* above .... Nah 3:16   7402
the *m* of the earth are waxed rich .... Rev 18:3   *1713*
the *m* of the earth shall weep and .... Rev 18:11   *1713*
The *m* of these things, which were .... Rev 18:15   *1713*
for thy *m* were the great men of .... Rev 18:23   *1713*

MERCHANTS'
She is like the *m* ships .... Prov 31:14   5503

MERCIES

worthy of the least of all the *m*	Gen 32:10	2617
for his *m* are great	2Sa 24:14	7356
for very great are his	1Chr 21:13	7356
remember the *m* of David thy	2Chr 6:42	2617
Yet thou in thy manifold *m*	Neh 9:19	7356
m thou gavest them saviours	Neh 9:27	7356
deliver them according to thy *m*	Neh 9:28	7356
Remember, O LORD, thy tender *m*	Ps 25:6	7356
not thou thy tender *m* from me	Ps 40:11	7356
m blot out my transgressions	Ps 51:1	7356
to the multitude of thy tender *m*	Ps 69:16	7356
he in anger shut up his tender *m*	Ps 77:9	7356
let thy tender *m* speedily prevent	Ps 79:8	7356
I will sing of the *m* of the LORD	Ps 89:1	2617
with lovingkindness and tender *m*	Ps 103:4	7356
not the multitude of thy *m*	Ps 106:7	2617
to the multitude of his *m*	Ps 106:45	2617
Let thy *m* come also unto me, O	Ps 119:41	2617
Let thy tender *m* come unto me	Ps 119:77	7356
Great are thy tender *m*, O LORD	Ps 119:156	7356
his tender *m* are over all his	Ps 145:9	7356
but the tender *m* of the wicked	Prov 12:10	7356
but with great *m* will I gather	Is 54:7	7356
you, even the sure *m* of David	Is 55:3	2617
on them according to his *m*	Is 63:7	7356
thy bowels and of thy *m* toward me	Is 63:15	7356
LORD, even lovingkindness and *m*	Jer 16:5	7356
And I will shew *m* unto you	Jer 42:12	7356
It is of the LORD's *m* that we are	Lam 3:22	2617
to the multitude of his *m*	Lam 3:32	2617
That they would desire of the	Dan 2:18	7359
To the Lord our God belong *m*	Dan 9:9	7356
but for thy great *m*	Dan 9:18	7356
and in lovingkindness, and in *m*	Hos 2:19	7356
I am returned to Jerusalem with *m*	Zec 1:16	7356
will give you the sure *m* of David	Acts 13:34	3741
brethren, by the *m* of God	Rom 12:1	3628
Jesus Christ, the Father of *m*	2Cor 1:3	3628
of the Spirit, if any bowels and *m*	Phil 2:1	3628
God, holy and beloved, bowels of *m*	Col 3:12	3628

MERCIES'

Nevertheless for thy great *m* sake	Neh 9:31	7356
oh save me for thy *m* sake	Ps 6:4	2617
save me for thy *m* sake	Ps 31:16	2617
help, and redeem us for thy *m* sake	Ps 44:26	2617

MERCIFUL

the LORD being *m* unto him	Gen 19:16	2551
The LORD, The LORD God, *m*	Ex 34:6	7349
(For the LORD thy God is a *m* God	Deut 4:31	7349
Be *m*, O LORD, unto thy people	Deut 21:8	3722
will be *m* unto his land, and to	Deut 32:43	3722
With the *m* thou wilt shew thyself	2Sa 22:26	2623
thou wilt shew thyself *m*	2Sa 22:26	2616
the house of Israel are *m* kings	1Kin 20:31	2617
LORD your God is gracious and *m*	2Chr 30:9	7349
ready to pardon, gracious and *m*	Neh 9:17	7349
for thou art a gracious and *m* God	Neh 9:31	7349
With the *m* thou wilt shew thyself	Ps 18:25	2623
thou wilt shew thyself *m*	Ps 18:25	2616
redeem me, and be *m* unto me	Ps 26:11	2603
He is ever *m*, and lendeth	Ps 37:26	2603
I said, LORD, be *m* unto me	Ps 41:4	2603
be *m* unto me, and raise me up,	Ps 41:10	2603
Be *m* unto me, O God	Ps 56:1	2603
Be *m* unto me, O God, be	Ps 57:1	2603
be not *m* to any wicked	Ps 59:5	2603
God be *m* unto us, and bless us	Ps 67:1	2603
Be *m* unto me, O Lord	Ps 86:3	2603
The LORD is *m* and gracious, slow	Ps 103:8	7349
yea, our God is *m*	Ps 116:5	7355
For his *m* kindness is great	Ps 117:2	2617
be *m* unto me according to thy	Ps 119:58	2603
thy *m* kindness be for my comfort,	Ps 119:76	2617
be *m* unto me, as thou usest to do	Ps 119:132	2603
The *m* man doeth good to his own	Prov 11:17	2617
m men are taken away, none	Is 57:1	2617
for I am *m*, saith the LORD, and I	Jer 3:12	2623
for he is gracious and *m*, slow to	Joel 2:13	7349
thou art a gracious God, and *m*	Jonah 4:2	7349
Blessed are the *m*	Mt 5:7	*1655*
Be ye therefore *m*, as your Father	Lk 6:36	*3629*
as your Father also is *m*	Lk 6:36	*3629*
saying, God be *m* to me a sinner	Lk 18:13	*2433*
brethren, that he might be a *m*	Heb 2:17	*1655*
For I will be *m* to their	Heb 8:12	*2436*

MERCURIUS (*mer-cu'-re-us*) A Roman god.

and Paul, *M*, because he was the	Acts 14:12	*2060*

MERCY

and thou hast magnified thy *m*	Gen 19:19	2617
left destitute my master of his *m*	Gen 24:27	2617
was with Joseph, and shewed him *m*	Gen 39:21	2617
give you *m* before the man	Gen 43:14	7356
Thou in thy *m* hast led forth the	Ex 15:13	2617
shewing *m* unto thousands of them	Ex 20:6	2617
shalt make a *m* seat of pure gold	Ex 25:17	3727
in the two ends of the *m* seat	Ex 25:18	3727
even of the *m* seat shall ye make	Ex 25:19	3727
covering the *m* seat with their	Ex 25:20	3727
toward the *m* seat shall the faces	Ex 25:20	3727
thou shalt put the *m* seat above	Ex 25:21	3727
with thee from above the *m* seat	Ex 25:22	3727
thou shalt put the *m* seat upon	Ex 26:34	3727
before the *m* seat that is over	Ex 30:6	3727
the *m* seat that is thereupon, and	Ex 31:7	3727
shew *m* on whom I will shew *m*	Ex 33:19	7355
Keeping *m* for thousands,	Ex 34:7	2617
staves thereof, with the *m* seat	Ex 35:12	3727
he made the *m* seat of pure gold	Ex 37:6	3727
on the two ends of the *m* seat	Ex 37:7	3727
out of the *m* seat made he the	Ex 37:8	3727
with their wings over the *m* seat	Ex 37:9	3727
even to the *m* seatward were the	Ex 37:9	3727
staves thereof, and the *m* seat,	Ex 39:35	3727
put the *m* seat above upon the ark	Ex 40:20	3727
within the vail before the *m* seat	Lev 16:2	3727
in the cloud upon the *m* seat	Lev 16:2	3727
of the incense may cover the *m*	Lev 16:13	3727
finger upon the *m* seat eastward	Lev 16:14	3727
before the *m* seat shall he	Lev 16:14	3727
and sprinkle it upon the *m* seat	Lev 16:15	3727
and before the *m* seat	Lev 16:15	3727
m seat that was upon the ark of	Num 7:89	3727
is longsuffering, and of great *m*	Num 14:18	2617
unto the greatness of thy *m*	Num 14:19	2617
shewing *m* unto thousands of them	Deut 5:10	2617
with them, nor shew *m* unto them	Deut 7:2	2603
m with them that love him and keep	Deut 7:9	2617
the *m* which he sware unto thy	Deut 7:12	2617
of his anger, and shew thee *m*	Deut 13:17	7356
the city, and we will shew thee *m*	Judg 1:24	2617
But my *m* shall not depart away	2Sa 7:15	2617
m and truth be with the	2Sa 15:20	2617
sheweth *m* to his anointed, unto	2Sa 22:51	2617
servant David my father great *m*	1Kin 3:6	2617
m with thy servants that walk	1Kin 8:23	2617
for his *m* endureth for ever	1Chr 16:34	2617
because his *m* endureth for ever	1Chr 16:41	2617
will not take my *m* away from him	1Chr 17:13	2617
and of the place of the *m* seat	1Chr 28:11	3727
great *m* unto David my father	2Chr 1:8	2617
for his *m* endureth for ever	2Chr 5:13	2617
shewest *m* unto thy servants, that	2Chr 6:14	2617
for his *m* endureth for ever	2Chr 7:3	2617
because his *m* endureth for ever,	2Chr 7:6	2617
for his *m* endureth for ever	2Chr 20:21	2617
for his *m* endureth for ever	Ezr 3:11	2617
hath extended *m* unto me before	Ezr 7:28	2617
but hath extended *m* unto us in	Ezr 9:9	2617
m for them that love him and	Neh 1:5	2617
grant him *m* in the sight of this	Neh 1:11	7356
God, who keepest covenant and *m*	Neh 9:32	2617
to the greatness of thy *m*	Neh 13:22	2617
or for his land, or for *m*	Job 37:13	2617
have *m* upon me, and hear my prayer	Ps 4:1	2603
house in the multitude of thy *m*	Ps 5:7	2617
Have *m* upon me, O LORD	Ps 6:2	2603
Have *m* upon me, O LORD	Ps 9:13	2603
But I have trusted in thy *m*	Ps 13:5	2617
sheweth *m* to his anointed, to	Ps 18:50	2617
through the *m* of the most High he	Ps 21:7	2617
m shall follow me all the days of	Ps 23:6	2617
according to thy *m* remember thou	Ps 25:7	2617
All the paths of the LORD are *m*	Ps 25:10	2617
thee unto me, and have *m* upon me	Ps 25:16	2603
have *m* also upon me, and answer me	Ps 27:7	2603
Hear, O LORD, and have *m* upon me	Ps 30:10	2603
will be glad and rejoice in thy *m*	Ps 31:7	2617
Have *m* upon me, O LORD, for I am	Ps 31:9	2603
m shall compass him about	Ps 32:10	2617
him, upon them that hope in his *m*	Ps 33:18	2617
Let thy *m*, O LORD, be upon us,	Ps 33:22	2617
Thy *m*, O LORD, is in the heavens	Ps 36:5	2617
but the righteous sheweth *m*	Ps 37:21	2603
Have *m* upon me, O God, according	Ps 51:1	2603
I trust in the *m* of God for ever	Ps 52:8	2617
God shall send forth his *m*	Ps 57:3	2617
For thy *m* is great unto the	Ps 57:10	2617
The God of my *m* shall prevent me	Ps 59:10	2617

M

aloud of thy *m* in the morning	Ps 59:16	2617
is my defence, and the God of my *m*	Ps 59:17	2617
O prepare *m* and truth, which may	Ps 61:7	2617
unto thee, O Lord, belongeth *m*	Ps 62:12	2617
away my prayer, nor his *m* from me	Ps 66:20	2617
in the multitude of thy *m* hear me	Ps 69:13	2617
Is his *m* clean gone for ever	Ps 77:8	2617
Shew us thy *m*, O Lord, and grant	Ps 85:7	2617
M and truth are met together	Ps 85:10	2617
plenteous in *m* unto all them that	Ps 86:5	2617
For great is thy *m* toward me	Ps 86:13	2617
longsuffering, and plenteous in *m*	Ps 86:15	2617
O turn unto me, and have *m* upon me	Ps 86:16	2603
M shall be built up for ever	Ps 89:2	2617
m and truth shall go before thy	Ps 89:14	2617
and my *m* shall be with him	Ps 89:24	2617
My *m* will I keep for him for	Ps 89:28	2617
O satisfy us early with thy *m*	Ps 90:14	2617
thy *m*, O Lord, held me up	Ps 94:18	2617
He hath remembered his *m* and his	Ps 98:3	2617
his *m* is everlasting	Ps 100:5	2617
I will sing of *m* and judgment	Ps 101:1	2617
shalt arise, and have *m* upon Zion	Ps 102:13	7355
slow to anger, and plenteous in *m*	Ps 103:8	2617
so great is his *m* toward them	Ps 103:11	2617
But the *m* of the Lord is from	Ps 103:17	2617
for his *m* endureth for ever	Ps 106:1	2617
for his *m* endureth for ever	Ps 107:1	2617
For thy *m* is great above the	Ps 108:4	2617
be none to extend *m* unto him	Ps 109:12	2617
that he remembered not to shew *m*	Ps 109:16	2617
because thy *m* is good, deliver	Ps 109:21	2617
O save me according to thy *m*	Ps 109:26	2617
thy name give glory, for thy *m*	Ps 115:1	2617
because his *m* endureth for ever	Ps 118:1	2617
that his *m* endureth for ever	Ps 118:2	2617
that his *m* endureth for ever	Ps 118:3	2617
that his *m* endureth for ever	Ps 118:4	2617
for his *m* endureth for ever	Ps 118:29	2617
earth, O Lord, is full of thy *m*	Ps 119:64	2617
thy servant according unto thy *m*	Ps 119:124	2617
God, until that he have *m* upon us	Ps 123:2	2603
Have *m* upon us, O Lord, have	Ps 123:3	2603
upon us, O Lord, have *m* upon us	Ps 123:3	2603
for with the Lord there is *m*	Ps 130:7	2617
for his *m* endureth for ever	Ps 136:1	2617
for his *m* endureth for ever	Ps 136:2	2617
for his *m* endureth for ever	Ps 136:3	2617
for his *m* endureth for ever	Ps 136:4	2617
for his *m* endureth for ever	Ps 136:5	2617
for his *m* endureth for ever	Ps 136:6	2617
for his *m* endureth for ever	Ps 136:7	2617
for his *m* endureth for ever	Ps 136:8	2617
for his *m* endureth for ever	Ps 136:9	2617
for his *m* endureth for ever	Ps 136:10	2617
for his *m* endureth for ever	Ps 136:11	2617
for his *m* endureth for ever	Ps 136:12	2617
for his *m* endureth for ever	Ps 136:13	2617
for his *m* endureth for ever	Ps 136:14	2617
for his *m* endureth for ever	Ps 136:15	2617
for his *m* endureth for ever	Ps 136:16	2617
for his *m* endureth for ever	Ps 136:17	2617
for his *m* endureth for ever	Ps 136:18	2617
for his *m* endureth for ever	Ps 136:19	2617
for his *m* endureth for ever	Ps 136:20	2617
for his *m* endureth for ever	Ps 136:21	2617
for his *m* endureth for ever	Ps 136:22	2617
for his *m* endureth for ever	Ps 136:23	2617
for his *m* endureth for ever	Ps 136:24	2617
for his *m* endureth for ever	Ps 136:25	2617
for his *m* endureth for ever	Ps 136:26	2617
thy, O Lord, endureth for ever	Ps 138:8	2617
of thy *m* cut off mine enemies, and	Ps 143:12	2617
slow to anger, and of great *m*	Ps 145:8	2617
him, in those that hope in his *m*	Ps 147:11	2617
Let not *m* and truth forsake thee	Prov 3:3	2617
but he that hath *m* on the poor	Prov 14:21	2603
but *m* and truth shall be to them	Prov 14:22	2617
honoureth him hath *m* on the poor	Prov 14:31	2603
By *m* and truth iniquity is purged	Prov 16:6	2617
M and truth preserve the king	Prov 20:28	2617
and his throne is upholden by *m*	Prov 20:28	2617
m findeth life, righteousness, and	Prov 21:21	2617
and forsaketh them shall have *m*	Prov 28:13	7355
neither shall have *m* on their	Is 9:17	7355
For the Lord will have *m* on Jacob	Is 14:1	7355
And in *m* shall the throne be	Is 16:5	2617
made them will not have *m* on them	Is 27:11	7355
that he may have *m* upon you	Is 30:18	7355
thou didst shew them no *m*	Is 47:6	7356
for he that hath *m* on them shall	Is 49:10	7355

will have *m* upon his afflicted	Is 49:13	7355
kindness will I have *m* on thee	Is 54:8	7355
the Lord that hath *m* on thee	Is 54:10	7355
Lord, and he will have *m* upon him	Is 55:7	7355
in my favour have I had *m* on thee	Is 60:10	7355
they are cruel, and have no *m*	Jer 6:23	7355
not pity, nor spare, nor have *m*	Jer 13:14	7355
neither have pity, nor have *m*	Jer 21:7	7355
have *m* on his dwellingplaces	Jer 30:18	7355
I will surely have *m* upon him	Jer 31:20	7355
for his *m* endureth for ever	Jer 33:11	2617
to return, and have *m* on them	Jer 33:26	7355
you, that he may have *m* upon you	Jer 42:12	7355
are cruel, and will not shew *m*	Jer 50:42	7355
have *m* upon the whole house of	Eze 39:25	7355
by shewing *m* to the poor	Dan 4:27	2604
m to them that love him, and to	Dan 9:4	2617
for I will no more have *m* upon	Hos 1:6	7355
But I will have *m* upon the house	Hos 1:7	7355
I will not have *m* upon her	Hos 2:4	7355
I will have *m* upon her that had	Hos 2:23	7355
upon her that had not obtained *m*	Hos 2:23	7355
because there is no truth, nor *m*	Hos 4:1	2617
For I desired *m*, and not sacrifice	Hos 6:6	2617
in righteousness, reap in *m*	Hos 10:12	2617
keep *m* and judgment, and wait on	Hos 12:6	2617
in thee the fatherless findeth *m*	Hos 14:3	7355
vanities forsake their own *m*	Jonah 2:8	2617
but to do justly, and to love *m*	Mic 6:8	2617
ever, because he delighteth in *m*	Mic 7:18	2617
the *m* to Abraham, which thou hast	Mic 7:20	2617
in wrath remember *m*	Hab 3:2	2617
wilt thou not have *m* on Jerusalem	Zec 1:12	7355
Execute true judgment, and shew *m*	Zec 7:9	2617
for I have *m* upon them	Zec 10:6	7355
for they shall obtain *m*	Mt 5:7	*1653*
what this meaneth, I will have *m*	Mt 9:13	*1656*
Thou son of David, have *m* on us	Mt 9:27	*1653*
what this meaneth, I will have *m*	Mt 12:7	*1656*
Have *m* on me, O Lord, thou son of	Mt 15:22	*1653*
Lord, have *m* on my son	Mt 17:15	*1653*
Have *m* on us, O Lord, thou son of	Mt 20:30	*1653*
Have *m* on us, O Lord, thou son of	Mt 20:31	*1653*
matters of the law, judgment, *m*	Mt 23:23	*1656*
thou son of David, have *m* on me	Mk 10:47	*1653*
Thou son of David, have *m* on me	Mk 10:48	*1653*
his *m* is on them that fear him	Lk 1:50	*1656*
Israel, in remembrance of his *m*	Lk 1:54	*1656*
Lord had shewed great *m* upon her	Lk 1:58	*1656*
To perform the *m* promised to our	Lk 1:72	*1656*
Through the tender *m* of our God	Lk 1:78	*1656*
he said, He that shewed *m* on him	Lk 10:37	*1656*
have *m* on me, and send Lazarus,	Lk 16:24	*1653*
said, Jesus, Master, have *m* on us	Lk 17:13	*1653*
thou son of David, have *m* on me	Lk 18:38	*1653*
Thou son of David, have *m* on me	Lk 18:39	*1653*
I will have *m* on whom I will have	Rom 9:15	*1653*
have *m* on whom I will have *m*	Rom 9:15	*1653*
but of God that sheweth *m*	Rom 9:16	*1653*
Therefore hath he *m* on whom he	Rom 9:18	*1653*
on whom he will have *m*	Rom 9:18	
of his glory on the vessels of *m*	Rom 9:23	*1656*
yet have now obtained *m* through	Rom 11:30	*1653*
that through your *m* they also may	Rom 11:31	*1656*
they also may obtain *m*	Rom 11:31	*1653*
that he might have *m* upon all	Rom 11:32	*1653*
he that sheweth *m*, with	Rom 12:8	*1653*
might glorify God for his *m*	Rom 15:9	*1656*
as one that hath obtained *m*	1Cor 7:25	*1653*
ministry, as we have received *m*	2Cor 4:1	*1653*
this rule, peace be on them, and *m*	Gal 6:16	*1656*
But God, who is rich in *m*	Eph 2:4	*1656*
but God had *m* on him	Phil 2:27	*1653*
Grace, and peace, from God our	1Ti 1:2	*1656*
but I obtained *m*, because I did	1Ti 1:13	*1653*
for this cause I obtained *m*	1Ti 1:16	*1653*
Grace, *m*, and peace, from God the	2Ti 1:2	*1656*
The Lord give *m* unto the house of	2Ti 1:16	*1656*
find *m* of the Lord in that day	2Ti 1:18	*1656*
Grace, *m*, and peace, from God the	Titus 1:4	*1656*
according to his *m* he saved us	Titus 3:5	*1656*
of grace, that we may obtain *m*	Heb 4:16	*1656*
Moses' law died without *m* under	Heb 10:28	*3628*
he shall have judgment without *m*	Jas 2:13	*448*
that hath shewed no *m*	Jas 2:13	*1656*
m rejoiceth against judgment	Jas 2:13	*1656*
easy to be intreated, full of *m*	Jas 3:17	*1656*
is very pitiful, and of tender *m*	Jas 5:11	*3629*
m hath begotten us again unto a	1Pet 1:3	*1656*
which had not obtained *m*	1Pet 2:10	*1653*
but now have obtained *m*	1Pet 2:10	*1653*

Grace be with you, *m*, and peace, ... 2Jn 3　*1656*
M unto you, and peace, and love, be ...... Jude 2　*1656*
looking for the *m* of our Lord .... Jude 21　*1656*

MERCYSEAT
of glory shadowing the *m* .... Heb 9:5　*2435*

MERED *(me'-red) A descendant of Judah.*
sons of Ezra were, Jether, and *M* .... 1Chr 4:17　*4778*
daughter of Pharaoh, which *M* took .... 1Chr 4:18　*4778*

MEREMOTH *(mer'-e-moth)* See MERAIOTH.
　1. Son of Uriah the priest.
of *M* the son of Uriah the priest .... Ezr 8:33　*4822*
them repaired *M* the son of Urijah .... Neh 3:4　*4822*
After him repaired *M* the son of .... Neh 3:21　*4822*
　2. Married a foreigner in exile.
Vaniah, *M*, Eliashib, ... Ezr 10:36　*4822*
　3. A priest who renewed the covenant.
Harim, *M*, Obadiah, ... Neh 10:5　*4822*
Shechaniah, Rehum, *M*, ... Neh 12:3　*4822*

MERES *(me'-res) A prince of Media and Persia.*
Shethar, Admatha, Tarshish, *M* .... Est 1:14　*4825*

MERIBAH *(mer'-i-bah)* See MASSAH, MERIBAH-KADESH.
　Same as Meribah-Kadesh.
name of the place Massah, and *M* .... Ex 17:7　*4809*
This is the water of *M* .... Num 20:13　*4809*
against my word at the water of *M* .... Num 20:24　*4809*
that is the water of *M* in Kadesh .... Num 27:14　*4809*
didst strive at the waters of *M* .... Deut 33:8　*4809*
I proved thee at the waters of *M* .... Ps 81:7　*4809*

MERIBAH-KADESH *(mer'-i-bah-ka'-desh) A place be-*
　tween Zin and Sinai.
of Israel at the waters of *M* .... Deut 32:51

MERIBATH-KADESH See MERIBAH-KADESH.

MERIB-BAAL *(me-rib'-ba-al)* See MEPHIBOSHETH. *Son*
　of Jonathan.
And the son of Jonathan was *M* .... 1Chr 8:34　*4807*
and *M* begat Micah .... 1Chr 8:34　*4807*
And the son of Jonathan was *M* .... 1Chr 9:40　*4807*
and *M* begat Micah .... 1Chr 9:40　*4810*

MERODACH *(mer'-o-dak)* See BERODACH, EVIL-
　MERODACH, MERODACH-BALADAN. *A Babylonian god*
　of war.
confounded, *M* is broken in pieces .... Jer 50:2　*4781*

MERODACH-BALADAN *(mer'-o-dak-bal'-a-dan)* See
　BERODACH-BALADAN. *A king of Babylon.*
At that time *M*, the son of .... Is 39:1　*4757*

MEROM *(me'-rom) A small lake north of the Sea of*
　Chinneroth.
together at the waters of *M* .... Josh 11:5　*4792*
them by the waters of *M* suddenly .... Josh 11:7　*4792*

MERONOTHITE *(me-ron'-o-thite) An inhabitant of a*
　district of Zebulun.
over the asses was Jehdeiah the *M* .... 1Chr 27:30　*4824*
the Gibeonite, and Jadon the *M* .... Neh 3:7　*4824*

MEROZ *(me'-roz) A place near Lake Merom.*
Curse ye *M*, said the angel of the .... Judg 5:23　*4789*

MERRILY
then go thou in *m* with the king .... Est 5:14　*8056*

MERRY
And they drank, and were *m* with him .. Gen 43:34　*7937*
and trode the grapes, and made *m* .... Judg 9:27　*1974*
to pass, when their hearts were *m* .... Judg 16:25　*2896*
night, and let thine heart be *m* .... Judg 19:6　*3190*
here, that thine heart may be *m* .... Judg 19:9　*3190*
they were making their hearts *m* .... Judg 19:22　*3190*
and drunk, and his heart was *m* .... Ruth 3:7　*3190*
Nabal's heart was *m* within him .... 1Sa 25:36　*2896*
when Amnon's heart is *m* with wine ...... 2Sa 13:28　*2896*
eating and drinking, and making *m* ...... 1Kin 4:20　*8056*
bread, and let thine heart be *m* .... 1Kin 21:7　*3190*
m in heart for the goodness that .... 2Chr 7:10　*2896*
heart of the king was *m* with wine .... Est 1:10　*2896*
A *m* heart maketh a cheerful .... Prov 15:13　*8056*
but he that is of a *m* heart hath .... Prov 15:15　*2896*
A *m* heart doeth good like a .... Prov 17:22　*8056*
to eat, and to drink, and to be *m* .... Eccl 8:15　*8055*
and drink thy wine with a *m* heart .... Eccl 9:7　*2896*
for laughter, and wine maketh *m* .... Eccl 10:19　*8055*
and the voice of them that make *m* .... Jer 30:19　*7832*
in the dances of them that make *m* .... Jer 31:4　*7832*
thine ease, eat, drink, and be *m* .... Lk 12:19　*2165*
and let us eat, and be *m* .... Lk 15:23　*2165*
And they began to be *m* .... Lk 15:24　*2165*
I might make *m* **with my friends** ...... Lk 15:29　*2165*
It was meet that we should make *m* ... Lk 15:32　*2165*

Is any *m*? .... Jas 5:13　*2114*
rejoice over them, and make *m* .... Rev 11:10　*2165*

MERRYHEARTED
languisheth, all the *m* do sigh .... Is 24:7

MESECH *(me'-sek)* See MESHECH. *A tribe joined to*
　Kedar.
Woe is me, that I sojourn in *M* .... Ps 120:5　*4902*

MESHA *(me'-shah)*
　1. A place in southeastern Arabia.
And their dwelling was from *M* .... Gen 10:30　*4852*
　2. A king of Moab.
M king of Moab was a sheepmaster, ... 2Kin 3:4　*4337*
　3. A son of Caleb.
M his firstborn, which was the .... 1Chr 2:42　*4338*
　4. A son of Shaharaim.
his wife, Jobab, and Zibia, and *M* .... 1Chr 8:9　*4331*

MESHACH *(me'-shak) A companion of Daniel.*
and to Mishael, of *M* .... Dan 1:7　*4335*
the king, and he set Shadrach, *M* .... Dan 2:49　*4336*
province of Babylon, Shadrach, *M* .... Dan 3:12　*4336*
commanded to bring Shadrach, *M* .... Dan 3:13　*4336*
them, Is it true, O Shadrach, *M* .... Dan 3:14　*4336*
Shadrach, *M*, and Abed-nego, ... Dan 3:16　*4336*
was changed against Shadrach, *M* .... Dan 3:19　*4336*
in his army to bind Shadrach, *M* .... Dan 3:20　*4336*
men that took up Shadrach, *M* .... Dan 3:22　*4336*
And these three men, Shadrach, *M* .... Dan 3:23　*4336*
and spake, and said, Shadrach, *M* .... Dan 3:26　*4336*
Then Shadrach, *M*, and Abed-nego, ... Dan 3:26　*4336*
Blessed be the God of Shadrach, *M* .... Dan 3:28　*4336*
against the God of Shadrach, *M* .... Dan 3:29　*4336*
the king promoted Shadrach, *M* .... Dan 3:30　*4336*

MESHECH *(me'-shek)* See MESECH.
　1. A son of Japheth.
Madai, and Javan, and Tubal, and *M* ..... Gen 10:2　*4902*
Madai, and Javan, and Tubal, and *M* ..... 1Chr 1:5　*4902*
　2. A son of Shem.
and Uz, and Hul, and Gether, and *M* ...... 1Chr 1:17　*4902*
　3. Descendants of Meshech 1.
Javan, Tubal, and *M*, they were thy .... Eze 27:13　*4902*
There is *M*, Tubal, and all her .... Eze 32:26　*4902*
of Magog, the chief prince of *M* .... Eze 38:2　*4902*
O Gog, the chief prince of *M* .... Eze 38:3　*4902*
O Gog, the chief prince of *M* .... Eze 39:1　*4902*

MESHELEMIAH *(me-shel-e-mi'ah)* See MESHULLAM,
　SHELEMIAH, SHALLUM. *Father of Zechariah.*
Zechariah the son of *M* was porter .... 1Chr 9:21　*4920*
Korhites was *M* the son of Kore .... 1Chr 26:1　*4920*
And the sons of *M* were, Zechariah .... 1Chr 26:2　*4920*
M had sons and brethren, strong .... 1Chr 26:9　*4920*

MESHEZABEEL *(me-shez'-a-be-el)*
　1. Father of Berechiah.
son of Berechiah, the son of *M* .... Neh 3:4　*4898*
　2. An Israelite who renewed the covenant.
M, Zadok, Jaddua, ... Neh 10:21　*4898*
And Pethahiah the son of *M* .... Neh 11:24　*4898*

MESHEZABEL See MESHEZABEEL.

MESHILLEMITH *(me-shil'-le-mith)* See MESHILLEMOTH.
　A family of exiles.
son of Meshullam, the son of *M* .... 1Chr 9:12　*4921*

MESHILLEMOTH *(me-shil'-le-moth)* See MESHILLE-
　MITH.
　1. Father of Berechiah.
Johanan, Berechiah the son of *M* .... 2Chr 28:12　*4919*
　2. A family of exiles.
the son of Ahasai, the son of *M* .... Neh 11:13　*4919*

MESHOBAB *(me-sho'-bab) A chief of Simeon.*
And *M*, and Jamlech, and Joshah the .... 1Chr 4:34　*4877*

MESHULLAM *(me-shul'-lam)* See MESHELLEMIAH.
　1. A scribe in Josiah's time.
the son of Azaliah, the son of *M* .... 2Kin 22:3　*4918*
　2. A descendant of Jeconiah.
M, and Hananiah, and Shelomith .... 1Chr 3:19　*4918*
　3. Head of a Gadite family.
their fathers were, Michael, and *M* .... 1Chr 5:13　*4918*
　4. A Benjamite of the Elpaal family.
Zebadiah, and *M*, and Hezeki, and .... 1Chr 8:17　*4918*
　5. Father of Sallu.
Sallu the son of *M*, the son of .... 1Chr 9:7　*4918*
　6. Son of Shephatiah.
M the son of Shephatiah, the son .... 1Chr 9:8　*4918*
　7. Father of Hilkiah.
the son of Hilkiah, the son of *M* .... 1Chr 9:11　*4918*
the son of Hilkiah, the son of *M* .... Neh 11:11　*4918*

M

8. *Son of Meshillemith.*
the son of Jahzerah, the son of M 1Chr 9:12   4918
   9. *A Kohathite repairer of the wall.*
and Zechariah and M, of the sons of 2Chr 34:12   4918
   10. *A clan leader with Ezra.*
and for Zechariah, and for M .... Ezr 8:16   4918
   11. *A priest who accounted for the foreign wives.*
and M and Shabbethai the Levite .... Ezr 10:15   4918
   12. *A son of Bani.*
M, Malluch, and Adaiah, Jashub, and ... Ezr 10:29   4918
   13. *A son of Berechiah.*
repaired M the son of Berechiah .... Neh 3:4   4918
After him repaired M the son of .... Neh 3:30   4918
of M the son of Berechiah....................... Neh 6:18   4918
   14. *A son of Besodeiah.*
Paseah, and M the son of Besodeiah...... Neh 3:6   4918
   15. *A Levite who aided Ezra.*
and Hashbadana, Zechariah, and M...... Neh 8:4   4918
   16. *A priest who renewed the covenant.*
M, Abijah, Mijamin, ... Neh 10:7   4918
   17. *A clan leader who renewed the covenant.*
Magpiash, M, Hezir, ... Neh 10:20   4918
   18. *A family of exiles.*
Sallu the son of M, the son of .... Neh 11:7   4918
   19. *A priest who dedicated the wall.*
Of Ezra, M .... Neh 12:13   4918
And Azariah, Ezra, and M, ... Neh 12:33   4918
   20. *A descendant of Ginnethon.*
of Ginnethon, M.................................... Neh 12:16   4918
   21. *A Levite gatekeeper.*
and Bakbukiah, Obadiah, M................. Neh 12:25   4918

MESHULLEMETH (me-shul'-le-meth) *Mother of King Amon.*
And his mother's name was M 2Kin 21:19   4922

MESOBAITE (me-so'-ba-ite) *Family name of Jasiel.*
Eliel, and Obed, and Jasiel the M 1Chr 11:47   4677

MESOPOTAMIA (mes-o-po-ta'-me-ah) *See* ARAM, NAHA-RAIM. *Land between the Tigris and Euphrates Rivers.*
and he arose, and went to M .... Gen 24:10   763
the son of Beor of Pethor of M .... Deut 23:4   763
of Chushan-rishathaim king of M .... Judg 3:8   763
king of M into his hand.......................... Judg 3:10   763
chariots and horsemen out of M 1Chr 19:6   763
and Elamites, and the dwellers in M ...... Acts 2:9   3318
father Abraham, when he was in M .... Acts 7:2   3318

MESS
but Benjamin's m was five times .... Gen 43:34   4864
there followed him a m of meat 2Sa 11:8   4864

MESSAGE
I have a m from God unto thee............... Judg 3:20   1697
pass, when Ben-hadad heard this m 1Kin 20:12   1697
He that sendeth a m by the hand .... Prov 26:6   1697
in the LORD's m unto the people............. Hag 1:13   4400
sent a m after him, saying, We .... Lk 19:14   4242
This then is the m which we have 1Jn 1:5   1860
For this is the m that ye heard 1Jn 3:11   31

MESSENGER
And they sent a m unto Joseph.............. Gen 50:16   6680
the m answered and said, Israel is......... 1Sa 4:17   1319
But there came a m unto Saul 1Sa 23:27   4397
And charged the m, saying, When 2Sa 11:19   4397
So the m went, and came and shewed ... 2Sa 11:22   4397
the m said unto David, Surely the 2Sa 11:23   4397
Then David said unto the m.................... 2Sa 11:25   4397
And there came a m to David 2Sa 15:13   5046
Then Jezebel sent a m unto Elijah 1Kin 19:2   4397
the m that was gone to call 1Kin 22:13   4397
And Elisha sent a m unto him 2Kin 5:10   4397
but ere the m came to him 2Kin 6:32   4397
look, when the m cometh, shut the 2Kin 6:32   4397
behold, the m came down unto him 2Kin 6:33   4397
The m came to them, but he cometh 2Kin 9:18   4397
And there came a m, and told him, ... 2Kin 10:8   4397
the m that went to call Micaiah 2Chr 18:12   4397
And there came a m unto Job .... Job 1:14   4397
If there be a m with an .... Job 33:23   4397
A wicked m falleth into mischief .... Prov 13:17   4397
therefore a cruel m shall be sent .... Prov 17:11   4397
so is a faithful m to them that .... Prov 25:13   6735
or deaf, as my m that I sent................... Is 42:19   4397
one m to meet another, to shew .... Jer 51:31   5046
from far, unto whom a m was sent .... Eze 23:40   4397
Then spake Haggai the LORD's m in........ Hag 1:13   4397
for he is the m of the LORD of .... Mal 2:7   4397
Behold, I will send my m, and he........... Mal 3:1   4397
even the m of the covenant, whom .... Mal 3:1   4397
I send my m before thy face, ... Mt 11:10   32

I send my m before thy face, ... Mk 1:2   32
I send my m before thy face, ... Lk 7:27   32
the m of Satan to buffet me, lest 2Cor 12:7   32
and fellow soldier, but your m .... Phil 2:25   652

MESSENGERS
Jacob sent m before him to Esau .... Gen 32:3   4397
the m returned to Jacob, saying, ... Gen 32:6   4397
Moses sent m from Kadesh unto the ...... Num 20:14   4397
Israel sent m unto Sihon king of .... Num 21:21   4397
He sent m therefore unto Balaam .... Num 22:5   4397
Spake I not also to thy m which .... Num 24:12   4397
I sent m out of the wilderness of............ Deut 2:26   4397
she hid the m that we sent .... Josh 6:17   4397
because she hid the m, which .... Josh 6:25   4397
So Joshua sent m, and they ran .... Josh 7:22   4397
he sent m throughout all Manasseh ...... Judg 6:35   4397
he sent m unto Asher, and unto .... Judg 6:35   4397
Gideon sent m throughout all .... Judg 7:24   4397
he sent m unto Abimelech privily .... Judg 9:31   4397
Jephthah sent m unto the king of .... Judg 11:12   4397
answered unto the m of Jephthah.......... Judg 11:13   4397
Jephthah sent m again unto the .... Judg 11:14   4397
Then Israel sent m unto the king .... Judg 11:17   4397
Israel sent m unto Sihon king of .... Judg 11:19   4397
they sent m to the inhabitants of 1Sa 6:21   4397
that we may send m unto all the 1Sa 11:3   4397
Then came the m to Gibeah of Saul....... 1Sa 11:4   4397
of Israel by the hands of m 1Sa 11:7   4397
And they said unto the m that came 1Sa 11:9   4397
the m came and shewed it to the 1Sa 11:9   4397
Wherefore Saul sent m unto Jesse 1Sa 16:19   4397
Saul also sent m unto David's................ 1Sa 19:11   4397
And when Saul sent m to take David 1Sa 19:14   4397
Saul sent the m again to see.................. 1Sa 19:15   4397
when the m were come in, behold, ... 1Sa 19:16   4397
Saul sent m to take David 1Sa 19:20   4397
of God was upon the m of Saul.............. 1Sa 19:20   4397
it was told Saul, he sent other m 1Sa 19:21   4397
Saul sent m again the third time,.......... 1Sa 19:21   4397
Behold, David sent m out of the 1Sa 25:14   4397
and she went after the m of David 1Sa 25:42   4397
David sent m unto the men of................ 2Sa 2:5   4397
Abner sent m to David on his 2Sa 3:12   4397
David sent m to Ish-bosheth 2Sa 3:14   4397
he sent m after Abner, which 2Sa 3:26   4397
king of Tyre sent m to David 2Sa 5:11   4397
And David sent m, and took her 2Sa 11:4   4397
And Joab sent m to David, and said,..... 2Sa 12:27   4397
he sent m to Ahab king of Israel 1Kin 20:2   4397
the m came again, and said, Thus 1Kin 20:5   4397
he said unto the m of Ben-hadad 1Kin 20:9   4397
the m departed, and brought him 1Kin 20:9   4397
and he sent m, and said unto them, ... 2Kin 1:2   4397
go up to meet the m of the king 2Kin 1:3   4397
when the m turned back unto him, ... 2Kin 1:5   4397
Forasmuch as thou hast sent m to 2Kin 1:16   4397
the m returned, and told the king 2Kin 7:15   4397
Then Amaziah sent m to Jehoash 2Kin 14:8   4397
So Ahaz sent m to Tiglath-pileser 2Kin 16:7   4397
for he had sent m to So king of 2Kin 17:4   4397
he sent m again unto Hezekiah,............ 2Kin 19:9   4397
the letter of the hand of the m 2Kin 19:14   4397
By thy m thou hast reproached the........ 2Kin 19:23   4397
king of Tyre sent m to David 1Chr 14:1   4397
David sent m to comfort him 1Chr 19:2   4397
worse before Israel, they sent m 1Chr 19:16   4397
fathers sent to them by his m 2Chr 36:15   4397
But they mocked the m of God 2Chr 36:16   4397
I sent m unto them, saying, I am .... Neh 6:3   4397
wrath of a king is as m of death............ Prov 16:14   4397
then answer the m of the nation .... Is 14:32   4397
waters, saying, Go, ye swift m .... Is 18:2   4397
he sent m to Hezekiah, saying,............. Is 37:9   4397
the letter from the hand of the m .... Is 37:14   4397
performeth the counsel of his m .... Is 44:26   4397
and didst send thy m far off................... Is 57:9   6735
by the hand of the m which come .... Jer 27:3   4397
sent m unto them into Chaldea .... Eze 23:16   4397
In that day shall m go forth from .... Eze 30:9   4397
the voice of thy m shall no more............ Nah 2:13   4397
when the m of John were departed,....... Lk 7:24   32
And sent m before his face .... Lk 9:52   32
they are the m of the churches, ... 2Cor 8:23   652
when she had received the m .... Jas 2:25   32

MESSES
sent m unto them from before him .... Gen 43:34   4864

MESSIAH (mes-si'-ah) See Messias. *The great Deliverer of Israel.*
to build Jerusalem unto the *M* the .... Dan 9:25 — 4899
and two weeks shall *M* be cut off .... Dan 9:26 — 4899

MESSIAS (mes-si'-as) See Messiah. *Greek form of Messiah.*
unto him, We have found the *M* .... Jn 1:41 — 3323
unto him, I know that *M* cometh .... Jn 4:25 — 3323

MET
way, and the angels of God *m* him .... Gen 32:1 — 6293
thou by all this drove which I *m* .... Gen 33:8 — 6298
God of the Hebrews hath *m* with us .... Ex 3:18 — 7136
in the inn, that the Lord *m* him.............. Ex 4:24 — 6298
m him in the mount of God, and.............. Ex 4:27 — 6298
God of the Hebrews hath *m* with us...... Ex 5:3 — 7122
they *m* Moses and Aaron, who stood .... Ex 5:20 — 6293
And God *m* Balaam .... Num 23:4 — 7136
And the Lord *m* Balaam, and put a....... Num 23:16 — 7136
Because they *m* you not with bread ...... Deut 23:4 — 6923
How he *m* thee by the way, and .... Deut 25:18 — 7136
all these kings were *m* together.............. Josh 11:5 — 3259
they *m* together in Asher on the .... Josh 17:10 — 6293
a company of prophets *m* him .... 1Sa 10:10 — 7125
and she *m* him .... 1Sa 25:20 — 6298
m together by the pool of Gibeon .... 2Sa 2:13 — 6298
the servant of Mephibosheth *m* him...... 2Sa 16:1 — 7135
Absalom *m* the servants of David .... 2Sa 18:9 — 7122
a lion *m* him by the way, and slew.......... 1Kin 13:24 — 4672
in the way, behold, Elijah *m* him .... 1Kin 18:7 — 7125
m him in the portion of Naboth.............. 2Kin 9:21 — 4672
Jehu *m* with the brethren of.................... 2Kin 10:13 — 4672
Because they *m* not the children .... Neh 13:2 — 6923
Mercy and truth are *m* together............ Ps 85:10 — 6298
there *m* him a woman with the.............. Prov 7:10 — 7125
and it came to pass, as he *m* them.......... Jer 41:6 — 6298
flee from a lion, and a bear *m* him.......... Amos 5:19 — 6293
there *m* him two possessed with .... Mt 8:28 — 5221
disciples, behold, Jesus *m* them .... Mt 28:9 — 528
immediately there *m* him out of .... Mk 5:2 — 528
in a place where two ways *m* .... Mk 11:4 — 296
there *m* him out of the city a .... Lk 8:27 — 5221
from the hill, much people *m* him .... Lk 9:37 — 4876
there *m* him ten men that were .... Lk 17:12 — 528
going down, his servants *m* him .... Jn 4:51 — 528
Jesus was coming, went and *m* him ...... Jn 11:20 — 5221
in that place where Martha *m* him .... Jn 11:30 — 5221
this cause the people also *m* him .... Jn 12:18 — 5221
was coming in, Cornelius *m* him .... Acts 10:25 — 4876
with a spirit of divination *m* us .... Acts 16:16 — 528
daily with them that *m* with him .... Acts 17:17 — 3909
when he *m* with us at Assos, we............ Acts 20:14 — 4820
into a place where two seas *m*................ Acts 27:41 — 4876
who *m* Abraham returning from the...... Heb 7:1 — 4876
father, when Melchisedec *m* him .... Heb 7:10 — 4876

METE
when they did *m* it with an omer, ... Ex 16:18 — 4058
m out the valley of Succoth.................... Ps 60:6 — 4058
m out the valley of Succoth.................... Ps 108:7 — 4058
and with what measure ye *m* .... Mt 7:2 — 3354
with what measure ye *m*, it shall ...... Mk 4:24 — 3354
with the same measure that ye *m* .... Lk 6:38 — 3354

METED
a nation *m* out and trodden down, ... Is 18:2 — 6978
a nation *m* out and trodden under .... Is 18:7 — 6978
m out heaven with the span, and .... Is 40:12 — 8505

METEYARD
unrighteousness in judgment, in *m* .... Lev 19:35 — 4060

METHEG-AMMAH (me'-theg-am'-mah) *A place in Philistia.*
David took *M* out of the hand of .... 2Sa 8:1 — 4965

METHUSAEL (me-thu'-sa-el) *A descendant of Cain.*
and Mehujael begat *M*............................ Gen 4:18 — 4967
and *M* begat Lamech .... Gen 4:18 — 4967

METHUSELAH (me-thu'-se-lah) See Mathusala. *Son of Enoch.*
sixty and five years, and begat *M* .... Gen 5:21 — 4968
he begat *M* three hundred years .... Gen 5:22 — 4968
M lived an hundred eighty and .... Gen 5:25 — 4968
M lived after he begat Lamech .... Gen 5:26 — 4968
all the days of *M* were nine .... Gen 5:27 — 4968
Henoch, *M*, Lamech, ... 1Chr 1:3 — 4968

METHUSHAEL See Methusael.

MEUNIM (me-u'-nim) See Mehunim. *A family of exiles.*
of Besai, the children of *M*...................... Neh 7:52 — 4586

MEUNITES See Mehunims.

MEZAHAB (mez'-a-hab) *Grandmother of Mehetabel.*
of Matred, the daughter of *M* .... Gen 36:39 — 4314
of Matred, the daughter of *M* .... 1Chr 1:50 — 4314

MEZOBAITE See Mesobaite.

MIAMIN (mi'-a-min) See Mijamin, Miniamin.
  1. Married a foreigner in exile.
and Jeziah, and Malchiah, and *M* .... Ezr 10:25 — 4326
  2. A priest with Zerubbabel.
M, Maadiah, Bilgah, ... Neh 12:5 — 4326

MIBHAR (mib'-har) *A "mighty man" of David.*
of Nathan, *M* the son of Haggeri, ... 1Chr 11:38 — 4006

MIBSAM (mib'-sam)
  1. A son of Ishmael.
and Kedar, and Adbeel, and *M*................ Gen 25:13 — 4017
then Kedar, and Adbeel, and *M* .... 1Chr 1:29 — 4017
  2. A son of Simeon.
M his son, Mishma his son...................... 1Chr 4:25 — 4017

MIBZAR (mib'-zar) *A descendant of Esau.*
Duke Kenaz, duke Teman, duke *M*.......... Gen 36:42 — 4014
Duke Kenaz, duke Teman, duke *M* .... 1Chr 1:53 — 4014

MICA See Micha.

MICAH (mi'-cah) See Micaiah, Micah's, Michah.
  1. An Ephraimite who set up idols.
mount Ephraim, whose name was *M* ...... Judg 17:1 — 4319
and they were in the house of *M* .... Judg 17:4 — 4319
the man *M* had an house of gods, ... Judg 17:5 — 4318
mount Ephraim to the house of *M* .... Judg 17:8 — 4318
M said unto him, Whence comest .... Judg 17:9 — 4319
M said unto him, Dwell with me, ... Judg 17:10 — 4319
And *M* consecrated the Levite .... Judg 17:12 — 4318
priest, and was in the house of *M* .... Judg 17:12 — 4318
Then said *M*, Now know I that the .... Judg 17:13 — 4318
mount Ephraim, to the house of *M* .... Judg 18:2 — 4318
When they were by the house of *M* .... Judg 18:3 — 4318
Thus and thus dealeth *M* with me .... Judg 18:4 — 4318
and came unto the house of *M* .... Judg 18:13 — 4318
Levite, even unto the house of *M* .... Judg 18:15 — 4318
a good way from the house of *M* .... Judg 18:22 — 4318
their faces, and said unto *M*.................... Judg 18:23 — 4318
when *M* saw that they were too .... Judg 18:26 — 4318
took the things which *M* had made........ Judg 18:27 — 4318
  2. Head of a Reubenite family.
M his son, Reaia his son, Baal................ 1Chr 5:5 — 4318
  3. Son of Merib-baal.
and Merib-baal begat *M* .... 1Chr 8:34 — 4318
And the sons of *M* were, Pithon, and ...... 1Chr 8:35 — 4318
and Merib-baal begat *M* .... 1Chr 9:40 — 4318
And the sons of *M* were, Pithon, and ...... 1Chr 9:41 — 4318
  4. A family of exiles.
Galal, and Mattania the son of *M* .... 1Chr 9:15 — 4316
  5. A sanctuary servant.
M the first, and Jesiah the second .... 1Chr 23:20 — 4318
  6. Father of Abdon.
of Shaphan, and Abdon the son of *M* ...... 2Chr 34:20 — 4318
  7. A prophet.
M the Morasthite prophesied in.............. Jer 26:18 — 4320
M the Morasthite in the days of.............. Mic 1:1 — 4318

MICAH'S (mi'-cahs) *Refers to Micah 1.*
And these went into *M* house .... Judg 18:18 — 4318
to *M* house were gathered together .... Judg 18:22 — 4318
they set them up *M* graven image .... Judg 18:31 — 4318

MICAIAH (mi-ka-i'-ah) See Micha, Michaiiah. *A prophet who foretold Ahab's fall.*
M the son of Imlah, by whom we .... 1Kin 22:8 — 4321
Hasten hither *M* the son of Imlah .... 1Kin 22:9 — 4321
was gone to call *M* spake unto him .... 1Kin 22:13 — 4321
M said, As the Lord liveth, what .... 1Kin 22:14 — 4321
And the king said unto him, *M* .... 1Kin 22:15 — 4321
smote *M* on the cheek, and said,.............. 1Kin 22:24 — 4321
M said, Behold, thou shalt see in .... 1Kin 22:25 — 4321
the king of Israel said, Take *M*................ 1Kin 22:26 — 4321
M said, If thou return at all in .... 1Kin 22:28 — 4321
the same is *M* the son of Imla................ 2Chr 18:7 — 4321
Fetch quickly *M* the son of Imla.............. 2Chr 18:8 — 4319
that went to call *M* spake to him .... 2Chr 18:12 — 4321
M said, As the Lord liveth, even .... 2Chr 18:13 — 4321
king, the king said unto him, *M*.............. 2Chr 18:14 — 4318
smote *M* upon the cheek, and said, ... 2Chr 18:23 — 4321
M said, Behold, thou shalt see on .... 2Chr 18:24 — 4321
king of Israel said, Take ye *M* .... 2Chr 18:25 — 4321
M said, If thou certainly return .... 2Chr 18:27 — 4321

MICE
golden emerods, and five golden *m* .... 1Sa 6:4 — 5909
images of your *m* that mar the................ 1Sa 6:5 — 5909

M

and the coffer with the *m* of gold	1Sa 6:11	5909
And the golden *m*, according to the	1Sa 6:18	5909

MICHA (mi'-cah) See MICAH, MICAIAH.
1. Son of Mephibosheth.

had a young son, whose name was M	2Sa 9:12	4316

2. A Levite who renewed the covenant.

M, Rehob, Hashabiah,	Neh 10:11	4316

3. A family of exiles.

And Mattaniah the son of M	Neh 11:17	4316
son of Mattaniah, the son of M	Neh 11:22	4316

MICHAEL (mi'-ka-el)
1. Father of Sethur.

of Asher, Sethur the son of M	Num 13:13	4317

2. A Gadite who settled in Bashan.

house of their fathers were, M	1Chr 5:13	4317

3. Son of Jeshishai.

the son of Gilead, the son of M	1Chr 5:14	4317

4. Son of Baaseiah.

The son of M, the son of Baaseiah	1Chr 6:40	4317

5. A chief man of Issachar.

M, and Obadiah, and Joel, Ishiah,	1Chr 7:3	4317

6. A Benjamite in Jerusalem.

And M, and Ispah, and Joha, the sons	1Chr 8:16	4317

7. A warrior in David's army.

and Jozabad, and Jediael, and M	1Chr 12:20	4317

8. Father of Omri.

of Issachar, Omri the son of M	1Chr 27:18	4317

9. A son of Jehoshaphat.

and Zechariah, and Azariah, and M	2Chr 21:2	4317

10. A family of exiles.

Zebadiah the son of M, and with	Ezr 8:8	4317

11. Angelic messenger who came to Daniel.

but, lo, M, one of the chief	Dan 10:13	4317
these things, but M your prince	Dan 10:21	4317
And at that time shall M stand up	Dan 12:1	4317
Yet M the archangel, when	Jude 9	3413
M and his angels fought against	Rev 12:7	3413

MICHAH (mi'-cah) See MICAH, MICHAIAH. *A sanctuary servant.*

sons of Uzziel; M	1Chr 24:24	4318
of the sons of M	1Chr 24:24	4318
The brother of M was Isshiah	1Chr 24:25	4318

MICHAIAH (mi-ka-i'-ah) See MICAH, MICAIAH.
1. Father of Achbor.

Shaphan, and Achbor the son of M	2Kin 22:12	4320

2. Wife of King Rehoboam.

His mother's name also was M the	2Chr 13:2	4322

3. A prince of Judah.

and to Nethaneel, and to M	2Chr 17:7	4322

4. A priest with Zerubbabel.

son of Mattaniah, the son of M	Neh 12:35	4320
Eliakim, Maaseiah, Miniamin, M	Neh 12:41	4320

5. Son of Gemariah.

When M the son of Gemariah, the	Jer 36:11	4321
Then M declared unto them all the	Jer 36:13	4321

MICHAL (mi'-kal) See EGLAH. *A wife of David.*

and the name of the younger M	1Sa 14:49	4324
M Saul's daughter loved David	1Sa 18:20	4324
Saul gave him M his daughter to	1Sa 18:27	4324
that M Saul's daughter loved him	1Sa 18:28	4324
M David's wife told him, saying,	1Sa 19:11	4324
So M let David down through a	1Sa 19:12	4324
M took an image, and laid it in	1Sa 19:13	4324
And Saul said unto M, Why hast	1Sa 19:17	4324
M answered Saul, He said unto me,	1Sa 19:17	4324
But Saul had given M his daughter	1Sa 25:44	4324
first bring M Saul's daughter	2Sa 3:13	4324
son, saying, Deliver me my wife M	2Sa 3:14	4324
M Saul's daughter looked through	2Sa 6:16	4324
M the daughter of Saul came out	2Sa 6:20	4324
And David said unto M, It was	2Sa 6:21	4324
Therefore M the daughter of Saul	2Sa 6:23	4324
the five sons of M the daughter	2Sa 21:8	4324
that M the daughter of Saul	1Chr 15:29	4324

MICHMAS (mik'-mas) See MICHMASH. *Home of some exiles.*

The men of M, an hundred twenty	Ezr 2:27	4363
The men of M, an hundred and	Neh 7:31	4363

MICHMASH (mik'-mash) See MICHMAS. *A city near Jerusalem.*

two thousand were with Saul in M	1Sa 13:2	4363
and they came up, and pitched in M	1Sa 13:5	4363
gathered themselves together at M	1Sa 13:11	4363
but the Philistines encamped in M	1Sa 13:16	4363
went out to the passage of M	1Sa 13:23	4363
situate northward over against M	1Sa 14:5	4363
that day from M to Aijalon	1Sa 14:31	4363

of Benjamin from Geba dwelt at M	Neh 11:31	4363
at M he hath laid up his	Is 10:28	4363

MICHMETHAH (mik'-me-thah) *A city between Ephraim and Manasseh.*

the sea to M on the north side	Josh 16:6	4366
of Manasseh was from Asher to M	Josh 17:7	4366

MICHMETHATH See MICHMETHAH.

MICHRI (mik'-ri) *Father of Uzzi.*

the son of Uzzi, the son of M	1Chr 9:8	4381

MICHTAM (mik'-tam) *A type of psalm.*

M of David	Ps 16:t	4387
a M of David, when the	Ps 56:t	4387
M of David, when he fled from	Ps 57:t	4387
Musician, Altaschith, M of David	Ps 58:t	4387
Musician, Altaschith, M of David	Ps 59:t	4387
M of David, to teach	Ps 60:t	4387

MICMASH See MICHMASH.

MICMETHAH See MICHMETHAH.

MICRI See MICHRI.

MIDDAY

to pass, when *m* was past, and they	1Kin 18:29	6672
gate from the morning until *m*	Neh 8:3	4276,3117
At *m*, O king, I saw in the way a	Acts 26:13	2250,3319

MIDDIN (mid'-din) *A city in the wilderness south of Judah.*

In the wilderness, Beth-arabah, M	Josh 15:61	4081

MIDDLE

the *m* bar in the midst of the	Ex 26:28	8432
he made the *m* bar to shoot	Ex 36:33	8484
from the *m* of the river, and from	Josh 12:2	8484
in the beginning of the *m* watch	Judg 7:19	8484
people down by the *m* of the land	Judg 9:37	2872
Samson took hold of the two *m*	Judg 16:29	8432
out, as out of the *m* of a sling	1Sa 25:29	8432
cut off their garments in the *m*	2Sa 10:4	2677
the *m* was six cubits broad, and	1Kin 6:6	8484
The door for the *m* chamber was in	1Kin 6:8	8484
winding stairs into the *m* chamber	1Kin 6:8	8484
out of the *m* into the third	1Kin 6:8	8484
day did the king hallow the *m* of	1Kin 8:64	8432
was gone out into the *m* court	2Kin 20:4	8484
m of the court that was before	2Chr 7:7	8484
came in, and sat in the *m* gate	Jer 39:3	8484
were a wheel in the *m* of a wheel	Eze 1:16	8432
hath broken down the *m* wall of	Eph 2:14	3320

MIDDLEMOST

than the *m* of the building	Eze 42:5	8484
lowest and the *m* from the ground	Eze 42:6	8484

MIDIAN (mid'-e-an) See MADIAN, MIDIANITE.
1. A son of Abraham.

and Jokshan, and Medan, and M	Gen 25:2	4080
And the sons of M	Gen 25:4	4080
and Jokshan, and Medan, and M	1Chr 1:32	4080
And the sons of M	1Chr 1:33	4080

2. A nation on the southern border of Israel.

who smote M in the field of Moab,	Gen 36:35	4080
and dwelt in the land of M	Ex 2:15	4080
Now the priest of M had seven	Ex 2:16	4080
father in law, the priest of M	Ex 3:1	4080
And the LORD said unto Moses in M	Ex 4:19	4080
When Jethro, the priest of M	Ex 18:1	4080
And Moab said unto the elders of M	Num 22:4	4080
the elders of M departed with the	Num 22:7	4080
people, and of a chief house in M	Num 25:15	4080
the daughter of a prince of M	Num 25:18	4080
and avenge the LORD of M	Num 31:3	4080
And they slew the kings of M	Num 31:8	4080
and Hur, and Reba, five kings of M	Num 31:8	4080
took all the women of M captives	Num 31:9	4080
Moses smote with the princes of M	Josh 13:21	4080
into the hand of M seven years	Judg 6:1	4080
the hand of M prevailed against	Judg 6:2	4080
the host of M was beneath him in	Judg 7:8	4080
bread tumbled into the host of M	Judg 7:13	4080
his hand hath God delivered M	Judg 7:14	4080
into your hand the host of M	Judg 7:15	4080
winepress of Zeeb, and pursued M	Judg 7:25	4080
into your hands the princes of M	Judg 8:3	4080
Zebah and Zalmunna, kings of M	Judg 8:5	4080
them, and took the two kings of M	Judg 8:12	4080
delivered us from the hand of M	Judg 8:22	4080
that was on the kings of M	Judg 8:26	4080
Thus was M subdued before the	Judg 8:28	4080
you out of the hand of M	Judg 9:17	4080
And they arose out of M, and came	1Kin 11:18	4080

which smote *M* in the field of 1Chr 1:46   4080
his oppressor, as in the day of *M* .... Is 9:4   4080
of *M* at the rock of Oreb .... Is 10:26   4080
cover thee, the dromedaries of *M* .... Is 60:6   4080
of the land of *M* did tremble .... Hab 3:7   4080

MIDIANITE (mid'-e-an-ite) See MIDIANITES, MIDIANI-
TISH. *A descendant of Midian.*
Hobab, the son of Raguel the *M* .... Num 10:29   4084

MIDIANITES (mid'-e-an-ites) See KENITES.
there passed by *M* merchantmen .... Gen 37:28   4084
the *M* sold him into Egypt unto .... Gen 37:36   4092
Vex the *M*, and smite them .... Num 25:17   4084
the children of Israel of the *M* .... Num 31:2   4084
war, and let them go against the *M* .... Num 31:3   4080
And they warred against the *M* .... Num 31:7   4080
because of the *M* the children of .... Judg 6:2   4080
had sown, that the *M* came up .... Judg 6:3   4080
impoverished because of the *M* .... Judg 6:6   4080
unto the LORD because of the *M* .... Judg 6:7   4080
winepress, to hide it from the *M* .... Judg 6:11   4080
us into the hands of the *M* .... Judg 6:13   4080
Israel from the hand of the *M* .... Judg 6:14   4080
thou shalt smite the *M* as one man .... Judg 6:16   4080
Then all the *M* and the Amalekites .... Judg 6:33   4080
so that the host of the *M* were on .... Judg 7:1   4080
me to give the *M* into their hands .... Judg 7:2   4080
deliver the *M* into thine hand .... Judg 7:7   4080
And the *M* and the Amalekites and all .. Judg 7:12   4080
Manasseh, and pursued after the *M* ...... Judg 7:23   4080
saying, Come down against the *M* .... Judg 7:24   4080
And they took two princes of the *M* ...... Judg 7:25   4080
thou wentest to fight with the *M* .... Judg 8:1   4080
Do unto them as unto the *M* .... Ps 83:9   4080

MIDIANITISH (mid'-e-an-i'-tish) *Belonging to the land*
of Midian.
a *M* woman in the sight of Moses .... Num 25:6   4084
that was slain with the *M* woman .... Num 25:14   4084
the name of the *M* woman that was .... Num 25:15   4084

MIDNIGHT
About *m* will I go out into the .... Ex 11:4   2676,3915
at *m* the LORD smote all the .... Ex 12:29   2677,3915
lay till *m*, and arose at *m* .... Judg 16:3   2677,3915
it came to pass at *m*, that the .... Ruth 3:8   2677,3915
arose at *m*, and took my son 1Kin 3:20   8432,3915
the people shall be troubled at *m* ... Job 34:20   2676,3915
At *m* I will rise to give thanks .... Ps 119:62   2676,3915
m there was a cry made, Behold .... Mt 25:6   3319,3571
house cometh, at even, or at *m* .... Mk 13:35   3317
and shall go unto him at *m* .... Lk 11:5   3317
at *m* Paul and Silas prayed, and .... Acts 16:25   3317
and continued his speech until *m* .... Acts 20:7   3317
about *m* the shipmen deemed .... Acts 27:27   3319,3571

MIDST See APPENDIX.

MIDWIFE
that the *m* said unto her, Fear .... Gen 35:17   3205
the *m* took and bound upon his hand .... Gen 38:28   3205
office of a *m* to the Hebrew women .... Ex 1:16   3205

MIDWIVES
of Egypt spake to the Hebrew *m* .... Ex 1:15   3205
But the *m* feared God, and did .... Ex 1:17   3205
king of Egypt called for the *m* .... Ex 1:18   3205
the *m* said unto Pharaoh, Because .... Ex 1:19   3205
ere the *m* come in unto them .... Ex 1:19   3205
God dealt well with the *m* .... Ex 1:20   3205
to pass, because the *m* feared God .... Ex 1:21   3205

MIGDAL EDER See EDAR.

MIGDAL-EL (mig'-dal-el) *A city in Naphtali.*
And Iron, and *M*, Horem, and .... Josh 19:38   4027

MIGDAL-GAD (mig'-dal-gad) *A city in Judah.*
Zenan, and Hadashah, and *M*, ... Josh 15:37   4028

MIGDOL (mig'-dol)
   1. *A place west of the Red Sea.*
before Pi-hahiroth, between *M* .... Ex 14:2   4024
and they pitched before *M* .... Num 33:7   4024
   2. *A place in northern Egypt.*
land of Egypt, which dwell at *M* .... Jer 44:1   4024
ye in Egypt, and publish in *M* .... Jer 46:14   4024

MIGHT See APPENDIX.

MIGHTEST
that thou *m* know that the LORD he .... Deut 4:35
That thou *m* fear the LORD thy God .... Deut 6:2
wherewith thou *m* be bound to .... Judg 16:6
thee, wherewith thou *m* be bound .... Judg 16:10
tell me wherewith thou *m* be bound ...... Judg 16:13
down that thou *m* see the battle 1Sa 17:28

that thou *m* bring them again unto .... Neh 9:29
that thou *m* still the enemy and .... Ps 8:2
that thou *m* be justified when .... Ps 51:4
that thou *m* answer the words of .... Prov 22:21
that thou *m* know the thoughts of .... Dan 2:30
thou *m* **be profited by me** .... Mt 15:5
thou *m* **be profited by me** .... Mk 7:11
That thou *m* know the certainty of .... Lk 1:4
that thou *m* receive thy sight, and .... Acts 9:17
That thou *m* be justified in thy .... Rom 3:4
m overcome when thou art judged .... Rom 3:4
that thou *m* charge some that they 1Ti 1:3
that thou by them *m* war a good 1Ti 1:18

MIGHTIER
for thou art much *m* than we .... Gen 26:16   6105
of Israel are more and *m* than we .... Ex 1:9   6099
a greater nation and *m* than they .... Num 14:12   6099
m than thou art, to bring thee in .... Deut 4:38   6099
nations greater and *m* than thou .... Deut 7:1   6099
m than thyself, cities great and .... Deut 9:1   6099
and I will make of thee a nation *m* .... Deut 9:14   6099
nations and *m* than yourselves .... Deut 11:23   6099
The LORD on high is *m* than the .... Ps 93:4   117
with him that is *m* than he .... Eccl 6:10   8623
that cometh after me is *m* than I .... Mt 3:11   2478
cometh one *m* than I after me .... Mk 1:7   2478
but one *m* than I cometh, the .... Lk 3:16   2478

MIGHTIES
who was one of the three *m* 1Chr 11:12   1368
and had the name among the three *m* ... 1Chr 11:24   1368

MIGHTIEST
These things did these three *m* 1Chr 11:19   1368

MIGHTILY
thee, and that ye may increase *m* .... Deut 6:3   3966
twenty years he *m* oppressed the .... Judg 4:3   2393
of the LORD came *m* upon him .... Judg 14:6
of the LORD came *m* upon him .... Judg 15:14
he shall *m* roar upon his .... Jer 25:30
with sackcloth, and cry *m* unto God ...... Jonah 3:8   2393
loins strong, fortify thy power *m* .... Nah 2:1   3966
For he *m* convinced the Jews, and .... Acts 18:28   2159
So *m* grew the word of God and ..... Acts 19:20   2596,2904
which worketh in me *m* .... Col 1:29   1722,1411
he cried *m* with a strong voice, ... Rev 18:2   1722,2479

MIGHTY
the same became *m* men which were..... Gen 6:4   1368
began to be a *m* one in the earth........... Gen 10:8   1368
He was a *m* hunter before the LORD ...... Gen 10:9   1368
Even as Nimrod the *m* hunter .... Gen 10:9   1368
m nation, and all the nations of .... Gen 18:18   6099
thou art a *m* prince among us .... Gen 23:6   430
the hands of the *m* God of Jacob .... Gen 49:24   46
multiplied, and waxed exceeding *m* ...... Ex 1:7   6105
multiplied, and waxed very *m* .... Ex 1:20   6105
let you go, no, not by a *m* hand .... Ex 3:19   2389
there be no more *m* thunderings............ Ex 9:28   430
LORD turned a *m* strong west wind ...... Ex 10:19   3966
they sank as lead in the *m* waters.......... Ex 15:10   117
the *m* men of Moab, trembling .... Ex 15:15   352
great power, and with a *m* hand .... Ex 32:11   2389
nor honour the person of the *m* .... Lev 19:15   1419
for they are too *m* for me .... Num 22:6   6099
thy greatness, and thy *m* hand .... Deut 3:24   2389
and by war, and by a *m* hand................. Deut 4:34   2389
with his *m* power out of Egypt .... Deut 4:37   1419
thee out thence through a *m* hand .... Deut 5:15   2389
us out of Egypt with a *m* hand .... Deut 6:21   2389
brought you out with a *m* hand .... Deut 7:8   2389
the *m* hand, and the stretched out .... Deut 7:19   2389
is among you, a *m* God and terrible ...... Deut 7:21   1419
destroy them with a *m* destruction .... Deut 7:23   1419
forth out of Egypt with a *m* hand .... Deut 9:26   2389
broughtest out by thy *m* power .... Deut 9:29   1419
Lord of lords, a great God, a *m* .... Deut 10:17   1368
his *m* hand, and his stretched out .... Deut 11:2   2389
became there a nation, great, *m*............ Deut 26:5   6099
forth out of Egypt with a *m* hand .... Deut 26:8   2389
And in all that *m* hand, and in all .... Deut 34:12   2389
all the *m* men of valour, and help .... Josh 1:14   1368
hand of the LORD, that it is *m* .... Josh 4:24   2389
thereof, and the *m* men of valour .... Josh 6:2   1368
thirty thousand *m* men of valour .... Josh 8:3   1368
Ai, and all the men thereof were *m* .... Josh 10:2   1368
him, and all the *m* men of valour .... Josh 10:7   1368
made have dominion over the *m*............ Judg 5:13   1368
the pransings of their *m* ones .... Judg 5:22   47
help of the LORD against the *m* .... Judg 5:23   1368
with thee, thou *m* man of valour .... Judg 6:12   1368

M

Gileadite was a *m* man of valour	Judg 11:1	1368
a *m* man of wealth, of the family	Ruth 2:1	1368
The bows of the *m* men are broken	1Sa 2:4	1368
out of the hand of these *m* Gods	1Sa 4:8	117
a Benjamite, a *m* man of power	1Sa 9:1	1368
a *m* valiant man, and a man of war,	1Sa 16:18	1368
how are the *m* fallen	2Sa 1:19	1368
of the *m* is vilely cast away	2Sa 1:21	1368
the slain, from the fat of the *m*	2Sa 1:22	1368
How are the *m* fallen in the midst	2Sa 1:25	1368
How are the *m* fallen, and the	2Sa 1:27	1368
and all the host of the *m* men	2Sa 10:7	1368
all the *m* men were on his right	2Sa 16:6	1368
and his men, that they be *m* men	2Sa 17:8	1368
that thy father is a *m* man	2Sa 17:10	1368
the Pelethites, and all the *m* men	2Sa 20:7	1368
names of the *m* men whom David had	2Sa 23:8	1368
one of the three *m* men with David	2Sa 23:9	1368
the three *m* men brake through the	2Sa 23:16	1368
things did these three *m* men	2Sa 23:17	1368
had the name among three *m* men	2Sa 23:22	1368
the *m* men which belonged to David	1Kin 1:8	1368
prophet, and Benaiah, and the *m* men	1Kin 1:10	1368
Jeroboam was a *m* man of valour	1Kin 11:28	1368
he was also a *m* man in valour	2Kin 5:1	1368
even of all the *m* men of wealth	2Kin 15:20	1368
all the *m* men of valour, even ten	2Kin 24:14	1368
the *m* of the land, those carried	2Kin 24:15	193
he began to be *m* upon the earth	1Chr 1:10	1368
m men of valour, famous men, and	1Chr 5:24	1368
of their fathers, *m* men of valour	1Chr 7:7	1368
m men of valour, was twenty	1Chr 7:9	1368
m men of valour, were seventeen	1Chr 7:11	1368
m men of valour, chief of the	1Chr 7:40	1368
sons of Ulam were *m* men of valour	1Chr 8:40	1368
chief of the *m* men whom David had	1Chr 11:10	1368
of the *m* men whom David had	1Chr 11:11	1368
and they were among the *m* men	1Chr 12:1	1368
a *m* man among the thirty, and over	1Chr 12:4	1368
for they were all *m* men of valour	1Chr 12:21	1368
m men of valour for the war,	1Chr 12:25	1368
And Zadok, a young man *m* of valour	1Chr 12:28	1368
hundred, *m* men of valour, famous	1Chr 12:30	1368
and all the host of the *m* men	1Chr 19:8	1368
for they were *m* men of valour	1Chr 26:6	1368
them *m* men of valour at Jazer of	1Chr 26:31	1368
who was *m* among the thirty, and	1Chr 27:6	1368
the officers, and with the *m* men	1Chr 28:1	1368
And all the princes, and the *m* men	1Chr 29:24	1368
thy *m* hand, and thy stretched out	2Chr 6:32	2389
chosen men, being *m* men of valour	2Chr 13:3	1368
But Abijah waxed *m*, and married	2Chr 13:21	2388
all these were *m* men of valour	2Chr 14:8	1368
of war, *m* men of valour, were in	2Chr 17:13	1368
with him *m* men of valour three	2Chr 17:14	1368
hundred thousand *m* men of valour	2Chr 17:16	1368
Eliada a *m* man of valour, and with	2Chr 17:17	1368
hired also an hundred thousand *m*	2Chr 25:6	1368
m men of valour were two thousand	2Chr 26:12	1368
that made war with *m* power	2Chr 26:13	2428
So Jotham became *m*, because he	2Chr 27:6	2388
a *m* man of Ephraim, slew Maaseiah	2Chr 28:7	1368
his *m* men to stop the waters of	2Chr 32:3	1368
cut off all the *m* men of valour	2Chr 32:21	1368
There have been *m* kings also over	Ezr 4:20	8624
before all the king's *m* princes	Ezr 7:28	1368
made, and unto the house of the *m*	Neh 3:16	1368
as a stone into the *m* waters	Neh 9:11	5794
our God, the great, the *m*	Neh 9:32	1368
m men of valour, an hundred	Neh 11:14	1368
mouth, and from the hand of the *m*	Job 5:15	2389
Redeem me from the hand of the *m*	Job 6:23	6184
wise in heart, and *m* in strength	Job 9:4	533
spoiled, and overthroweth the *m*	Job 12:19	386
weakeneth the strength of the *m*	Job 12:21	650
become old, yea, are *m* in power	Job 21:7	1396
But as for the *m* man, he had the	Job 22:8	2220
draweth also the *m* with his power	Job 24:22	47
the *m* shall be taken away without	Job 34:20	47
in pieces *m* men without number	Job 34:24	3524
out by reason of the arm of the *m*	Job 35:9	7227
Behold, God is *m*, and despiseth	Job 36:5	3524
he is *m* in strength and wisdom	Job 36:5	3524
up himself, the *m* are afraid	Job 41:25	410
and *m*, the LORD *m* in battle	Ps 24:8	1368
Give unto the LORD, O ye *m*	Ps 29:1	1121,410
a *m* man is not delivered by much	Ps 33:16	1368
sword upon thy thigh, O most *m*	Ps 45:3	1368
The *m* God, even the LORD, hath	Ps 50:1	410
thou thyself in mischief, O *m* man	Ps 52:1	1368
the *m* are gathered against me	Ps 59:3	5794
out his voice, and that a *m* voice	Ps 68:33	5797
mine enemies wrongfully, are *m*	Ps 69:4	6105
thou driedst up *m* rivers	Ps 74:15	386
like a *m* man that shouteth by	Ps 78:65	1368
in the congregation of the *m*	Ps 82:1	410
who among the sons of the *m* can	Ps 89:6	410
Thou hast a *m* arm	Ps 89:13	1369
have laid help upon one that is *m*	Ps 89:19	1368
the reproach of all the *m* people	Ps 89:50	7227
than the *m* waves of the sea	Ps 93:4	117
can utter the *m* acts of the LORD	Ps 106:2	1369
make his *m* power to be known	Ps 106:8	1369
His seed shall be *m* upon earth	Ps 112:2	1368
Sharp arrows of the *m*, with coals	Ps 120:4	1368
arrows are in the hand of a *m* man	Ps 127:4	1368
and vowed unto the *m* God of Jacob	Ps 132:2	46
habitation for the *m* God of Jacob	Ps 132:5	46
great nations, and slew *m* kings	Ps 135:10	6099
and shall declare thy *m* acts	Ps 145:4	1369
to the sons of men his *m* acts	Ps 145:12	1369
Praise him for his *m* acts	Ps 150:2	1369
to anger is better than the *m*	Prov 16:32	1368
cease, and parteth between the *m*	Prov 18:18	6099
man scaleth the city of the *m*	Prov 21:22	1368
For their redeemer is *m*	Prov 23:11	2389
the wise more than ten *m* men	Eccl 7:19	7989
bucklers, all shields of *m* men	Song 4:4	1368
the *m* One of Israel, Ah, I will	Is 1:24	46
The *m* man, and the man of war, the	Is 3:2	1368
by the sword, and thy *m* in the war	Is 3:25	1369
the *m* man shall be humbled, and	Is 5:15	376
them that are *m* to drink wine	Is 5:22	1368
Wonderful, Counsellor, The *m* God	Is 9:6	1368
remnant of Jacob, unto the *m* God	Is 10:21	1368
and Lebanon shall fall by a *m* one	Is 10:34	117
with his *m* wind shall he shake	Is 11:15	5868
called my *m* ones for mine anger	Is 13:3	1368
like the rushing of *m* waters	Is 17:12	3524
the *m* men of the children of	Is 21:17	1368
thee away with a *m* captivity	Is 22:17	1397
Behold, the Lord hath a *m*	Is 28:2	2389
storm, as a flood of *m* waters	Is 28:2	3524
the LORD, to the *m* One of Israel	Is 30:29	6697
with the sword, not of a *m* man	Is 31:8	376
LORD shall go forth as a *m* man	Is 42:13	1368
sea, and a path in the *m* waters	Is 43:16	5794
the prey be taken from the *m*	Is 49:24	1368
of the *m* shall be taken away	Is 49:25	1368
thy Redeemer, the *m* One of Jacob	Is 49:26	46
thy Redeemer, the *m* One of Jacob	Is 60:16	46
speak in righteousness, *m* to save	Is 63:1	7227
it is a *m* nation, it is an	Jer 5:15	386
sepulchre, they are all *m* men	Jer 5:16	1368
neither let the *m* man glory in	Jer 9:23	1368
as a *m* man that cannot save	Jer 14:9	1368
is with me as a *m* terrible one	Jer 20:11	1368
the king, with all his *m* men	Jer 26:21	1368
the Great, the *M* God, the LORD of	Jer 32:18	1368
Great in counsel, and *m* in work	Jer 32:19	7227
m things, which thou knowest not	Jer 33:3	1219
even *m* men of war, and the women,	Jer 41:16	1397
their *m* ones are beaten down, and	Jer 46:5	1368
flee away, nor the *m* man escape	Jer 46:6	1368
and let the *m* men come forth	Jer 46:9	1368
for the *m* man hath stumbled	Jer 46:12	1368
man hath stumbled against the *m*	Jer 46:12	1368
How say ye, We are *m* and strong	Jer 48:14	1368
the *m* men's hearts in Moab at	Jer 48:41	1368
m men of Edom be as the heart of	Jer 49:22	1368
shall be as of a *m* expert man	Jer 50:9	1368
a sword is upon her *m* men	Jer 50:36	1368
The *m* men of Babylon have forborn	Jer 51:30	1368
her *m* men are taken, every one of	Jer 51:56	1368
and her rulers, and her *m* men	Jer 51:57	1368
all my *m* men in the midst of me	Lam 1:15	47
hath also taken the *m* of the land	Eze 17:13	352
shall Pharaoh with his *m* army	Eze 17:17	1419
Lord GOD, surely with a *m* hand	Eze 20:33	2389
ye are scattered, with a *m* hand	Eze 20:34	2389
hand of the *m* one of the heathen	Eze 31:11	410
By the swords of the *m* will I	Eze 32:12	1368
The strong among the *m* shall	Eze 32:21	1368
with the *m* that are fallen of the	Eze 32:27	1368
the *m* in the land of the living	Eze 32:27	1368
a great company, and a *m* army	Eze 38:15	7227
Ye shall eat the flesh of the *m*	Eze 39:18	1368
horses and chariots, with *m* men	Eze 39:20	1368
he commanded the most *m* men that	Dan 3:20	1401
and how *m* are his wonders	Dan 4:3	8624
And his power shall be *m*, but not	Dan 8:24	6105
practise, and shall destroy the *m*	Dan 8:24	6099

the land of Egypt with a *m* hand	Dan 9:15	2389
a *m* king shall stand up, that	Dan 11:3	1368
with a very great and *m* army	Dan 11:25	6099
in the multitude of thy *m* men	Hos 10:13	1368
They shall run like *m* men	Joel 2:7	1368
Prepare war, wake up the *m* men	Joel 3:9	1368
cause thy *m* ones to come down	Joel 3:11	1368
shall the *m* deliver himself	Amos 2:14	1368
m shall flee away naked in that	Amos 2:16	1368
transgressions and your *m* sins	Amos 5:12	6099
and righteousness as a *m* stream	Amos 5:24	386
And thy *m* men, O Teman, shall be	Obad 9	1368
there was a *m* tempest in the sea,	Jonah 1:4	1419
shield of his *m* men is made red	Nah 2:3	1368
O *m* God, thou hast established	Hab 1:12	6697
the *m* man shall cry there	Zeph 1:14	1368
thy God in the midst of thee is *m*	Zeph 3:17	1368
made thee as the sword of a *m* man	Zec 9:13	1368
And they shall be as *m* men	Zec 10:5	1368
of Ephraim shall be like a *m* man	Zec 10:7	1368
because the *m* are spoiled	Zec 11:2	117
most of his *m* works were done	Mt 11:20	1411
for if the *m* works, which were	Mt 11:21	*1411*
for if the *m* works, which have	Mt 11:23	*1411*
man this wisdom, and these *m* works	Mt 13:54	*1411*
he did not many *m* works there	Mt 13:58	*1411*
therefore *m* works do shew forth	Mt 14:2	*1411*
that even such *m* works are	Mk 6:2	*1411*
And he could there do no *m* work	Mk 6:5	*1411*
therefore *m* works do shew forth	Mk 6:14	*1411*
For he that is *m* hath done to me	Lk 1:49	1415
put down the *m* from their seats	Lk 1:52	*1413*
all amazed at the *m* power of God	Lk 9:43	*3168*
for if the *m* works had been done	Lk 10:13	*1411*
there arose a *m* famine in that	Lk 15:14	*2478*
the *m* works that they had seen	Lk 19:37	*1411*
which was a prophet *m* in deed	Lk 24:19	1415
heaven as of a rushing *m* wind	Acts 2:2	972
was *m* in words and in deeds	Acts 7:22	1415
m in the scriptures, came to	Acts 18:24	1415
Through *m* signs and wonders, by	Rom 15:19	*1411*
men after the flesh, not many *m*	1Cor 1:26	1415
confound the things which are *m*	1Cor 1:27	*2478*
but *m* through God to the pulling	2Cor 10:4	1415
in signs, and wonders, and *m* deeds	2Cor 12:12	*1411*
is not weak, but is *m* in you	2Cor 13:3	*1414*
the same was *m* in me toward the	Gal 2:8	*1754*
to the working of his *m* power	Eph 1:19	*2479*
from heaven with his *m* angels	2Th 1:7	*1411*
therefore under the *m* hand of God	1Pet 5:6	*2900*
when she is shaken of a *m* wind	Rev 6:13	*3173*
the chief captains, and the *m* men	Rev 6:15	1415
I saw another *m* angel come down	Rev 10:1	*2478*
so *m* an earthquake, and so great	Rev 16:18	*5082*
great city Babylon, that *m* city	Rev 18:10	*2478*
a *m* angel took up a stone like a	Rev 18:21	*2478*
and as the voice of *m* thunderings	Rev 19:6	*2478*
captains, and the flesh of *m* men	Rev 19:18	*2478*

MIGRON *(mi'-gron) A city in Benjamin.*

a pomegranate tree which is in *M*	1Sa 14:2	4051
come to Aiath, he is passed to *M*	Is 10:28	4051

MIJAMIN *(mij'-a-min)* See MIAMIN.
1. A priest in David's time.

to Malchijah, the sixth to *M*	1Chr 24:9	4326

2. A priest who renewed the covenant.

Meshullam, Abijah, *M*,	Neh 10:7	4326

MIKLOTH *(mik'-loth)*
1. A Benjamite in Jerusalem.

And *M* begat Shimeah	1Chr 8:32	4732
and Ahio, and Zechariah, and *M*	1Chr 9:37	4732
And *M* begat Shimeam	1Chr 9:38	4732

2. A ruler of David's guard.

his course was *M* also the ruler	1Chr 27:4	4732

MIKNEIAH *(mik-ne-i'-ah) A Levite musician.*

and Mattithiah, and Elipheleh, and *M*	1Chr 15:18	4737
And Mattithiah, and Elipheleh, and *M*	1Chr 15:21	4737

MILALAI *(mil'-a-lahee) A priest who purified the wall.*

brethren, Shemaiah, and Azarael, *M*	Neh 12:36	4450

MILCAH *(mil'-cah)*
1. Daughter of Haran.

and the name of Nahor's wife, *M*	Gen 11:29	4435
of Haran, the father of *M*	Gen 11:29	4435
told Abraham, saying, Behold, *M*	Gen 22:20	4435
these eight *M* did bear to Nahor,	Gen 22:23	4435
who was born to Bethuel, son of *M*	Gen 24:15	4435
daughter of Bethuel the son of *M*	Gen 24:24	4435
Nahor's son, whom *M* bare unto him	Gen 24:47	4435

2. A daughter of Zelophehad.

were Mahlah, and Noah, Hoglah, *M*	Num 26:33	4435
Mahlah, Noah, and Hoglah, and *M*	Num 27:1	4435
Mahlah, Tirzah, and Hoglah, and *M*	Num 36:11	4435
Mahlah, and Noah, Hoglah, *M*	Josh 17:3	4435

MILCH

Thirty *m* camels with their colts,	Gen 32:15	3243
a new cart, and take two *m* kine	1Sa 6:7	5763
and took two *m* kine, and tied them	1Sa 6:10	5763

MILCHAM See MILCOM.

MILCOM *(mil'-com)* See MALCHAM, MOLECH. *Chief god of the Ammonites.*

after *M* the abomination of the	1Kin 11:5	4445
M the god of the children of	1Kin 11:33	4445
for *M* the abomination of the	2Kin 23:13	4445

MILDEW

and with blasting, and with *m*	Deut 28:22	3420
there be pestilence, blasting, *m*	1Kin 8:37	3420
if there be blasting, or *m*	2Chr 6:28	3420
smitten you with blasting and *m*	Amos 4:9	3420
smote you with blasting and with *m*	Hag 2:17	3420

MILE

shall compel thee to go a *m*	Mt 5:41	*3400*

MILETUM *(mi-le'-tum)* See MILETUS. *A city in the Roman province of Caria.*

Trophimus have I left at *M* sick	2Ti 4:20	*3399*

MILETUS *(mi-le-tus)* See MILETUM. *Same as Miletum.*

and the next day we came to *M*	Acts 20:15	*3399*
from *M* he sent to Ephesus, and	Acts 20:17	*3399*

MILK

And he took butter, and *m*, and the	Gen 18:8	2461
wine, and his teeth white with *m*	Gen 49:12	2461
large, unto a land flowing with *m*	Ex 3:8	2461
unto a land flowing with *m*	Ex 3:17	2461
give thee, a land flowing with *m*	Ex 13:5	2461
seethe a kid in his mother's *m*	Ex 23:19	2461
Unto a land flowing with *m*	Ex 33:3	2461
seethe a kid in his mother's *m*	Ex 34:26	2461
it, a land that floweth with *m*	Lev 20:24	2461
us, and surely it floweth with *m*	Num 13:27	2461
a land which floweth with *m*	Num 14:8	2461
out of a land that floweth with *m*	Num 16:13	2461
into a land that floweth with *m*	Num 16:14	2461
in the land that floweth with *m*	Deut 6:3	2461
seed, a land that floweth with *m*	Deut 11:9	2461
seethe a kid in his mother's *m*	Deut 14:21	2461
even a land that floweth with *m*	Deut 26:9	2461
a land that floweth with *m*	Deut 26:15	2461
thee, a land that floweth with *m*	Deut 27:3	2461
fathers, that floweth with *m*	Deut 31:20	2461
m of sheep, with fat of lambs, and	Deut 32:14	2461
us, a land that floweth with *m*	Josh 5:6	2461
And she opened a bottle of *m*	Judg 4:19	2461
He asked water, and she gave him *m*	Judg 5:25	2461
Hast thou not poured me out as *m*	Job 10:10	2461
His breasts are full of *m*	Job 21:24	2461
have goats' *m* enough for thy food	Prov 27:27	2461
of *m* bringeth forth butter	Prov 30:33	2461
honey and *m* are under thy tongue	Song 4:11	2461
I have drunk my wine with my *m*	Song 5:1	2461
rivers of waters, washed with *m*	Song 5:12	2461
of *m* that they shall give	Is 7:22	2461
them that are weaned from the *m*	Is 28:9	2461
m without money and without price	Is 55:1	2461
also suck the *m* of the Gentiles	Is 60:16	2461
that ye may *m* out, and be	Is 66:11	4711
give them a land flowing with *m*	Jer 11:5	2461
give them, a land flowing with *m*	Jer 32:22	2461
snow, they were whiter than *m*	Lam 4:7	2461
espied for them, flowing with *m*	Eze 20:6	2461
I had given them, flowing with *m*	Eze 20:15	2461
fruit, and they shall drink thy *m*	Eze 25:4	2461
and the hills shall flow with *m*	Joel 3:18	2461
I have fed you with *m*, and not	1Cor 3:2	*1051*
eateth not of the *m* of the flock	1Cor 9:7	*1051*
are become such as have need of *m*	Heb 5:12	*1051*
For every one that useth *m* is	Heb 5:13	*1051*
desire the sincere *m* of the word	1Pet 2:2	*1051*

MILL

maidservant that is behind the *m*	Ex 11:5	7347
women shall be grinding at the *m*	Mt 24:41	*3459*

MILLET

and beans, and lentiles, and *m*	Eze 4:9	1764

MILLIONS

thou the mother of thousands of *m*	Gen 24:60	7233

MILLO (mil'-lo)
1. A fort near Shechem.
together, and all the house of M .... Judg 9:6   4407
men of Shechem, and the house of M ..... Judg 9:20   4407
Shechem, and from the house of M .... Judg 9:20   4407
2. A fort near Jerusalem.
And David built round about from M 2Sa 5:9   4407
the LORD, and his own house, and M 1Kin 9:15   4407
then did he build M 1Kin 9:24   4407
Solomon built M, and repaired the 1Kin 11:27   4407
and slew Joash in the house of M 2Kin 12:20 4407
about, even from M round about 1Chr 11:8   4407
repaired M in the city of David, ... 2Chr 32:5   4407

MILLS
and gathered it, and ground it in m .... Num 11:8   7347

MILLSTONE
nether or the upper m to pledge .... Deut 24:6   7347
of a m upon Abimelech's head .... Judg 9:53   7393
of a m upon him from the wall 2Sa 11:21   7393
hard as a piece of the nether m .... Job 41:24
m were hanged about his neck ...... Mt 18:6   3458,3684
m were hanged about his neck ...... Mk 9:42   3037,3457
m were hanged about his neck ...... Lk 17:2   3458,3684
took up a stone like a great m .... Rev 18:21   3458
the sound of a m shall be heard .... Rev 18:22   3458

MILLSTONES
Take the m, and grind meal .... Is 47:2   7347
of the bride, the sound of the m .... Jer 25:10   7347

MINCING
m as they go, and making a .... Is 3:16   2952

MIND
If it be your m that I should .... Gen 23:8   5315
were a grief of m unto Isaac .... Gen 26:35   7307
that the m of the LORD might be .... Lev 24:12   6310
have not done them of mine own m .... Num 16:28   3820
either good or bad of mine own m .... Num 24:13   3820
m unto the place which the LORD .... Deut 18:6   5315
failing of eyes, and sorrow of m .... Deut 28:65   5315
them to m among all the nations .... Deut 30:1   3824
which is in mine heart and in my m 1Sa 2:35   5315
days ago, set not thy m on them 1Sa 9:20   3820
it was in my m to build an house 1Chr 22:7   3824
perfect heart and with a willing m 1Chr 28:9   5315
for the people had a m to work.............. Neh 4:6   3820
But he is in one m, and who can .... Job 23:13
Should it be according to thy m .... Job 34:33   5973
forgotten as a dead man out of m .... Ps 31:12   3820
he bringeth it with a wicked m .... Prov 21:27
A fool uttereth all his m .... Prov 29:11   7307
whose m is stayed on thee .... Is 26:3   3336
bring it again to m, O ye .... Is 46:8   3820
be remembered, nor come into m .... Is 65:17   3820
neither shall it come to m .... Jer 3:16   3820
yet my m could not be toward this .... Jer 15:1   5315
it, neither came it into my m .... Jer 19:5   3820
not, neither came it into my m .... Jer 32:35   3820
them, and came it not into his m .... Jer 44:21   3820
and let Jerusalem come into your m ...... Jer 51:50   3824
This I recall to my m, therefore .... Lam 3:21   3820
the things that come into your m .... Eze 11:5   7307
into your m shall not be at all .... Eze 20:32   7307
her m was alienated from them .... Eze 23:17   5315
then my m was alienated from her, ... Eze 23:18   5315
like as my m was alienated from........... Eze 23:22   5315
from whom thy m is alienated .... Eze 23:22   5315
them from whom thy m is alienated ...... Eze 23:28   5315
time shall things come into thy m .... Eze 38:10   3824
came into thy m upon thy bed .... Dan 2:29
his m hardened in pride, he was............ Dan 5:20   7307
Then shall his m change, and he .... Hab 1:11   7307
all thy soul, and with all thy m .... Mt 22:37   1271
and clothed, and in his right m .... Mk 5:15   4993
all thy soul, and with all thy m .... Mk 12:30   1271
Peter called to the m the word that .... Mk 14:72   363
cast in her m what manner of................ Lk 1:29
Jesus, clothed, and in his right m .... Lk 8:35   4993
thy strength, and with all thy m .... Lk 10:27   1271
neither be ye of doubtful m .... Lk 12:29
the word with all readiness of m .... Acts 17:11   4288
the Lord with all humility of m .... Acts 20:19
gave them over to a reprobate m .... Rom 1:28   3563
warring against the law of my m .... Rom 7:23   3563
So then with the m I myself serve .... Rom 7:25   3563
do the things of the flesh .... Rom 8:5   5426
Because the carnal m is enmity .... Rom 8:7   5427
what is the m of the Spirit...................... Rom 8:27   5427
who hath known the m of the Lord .... Rom 11:34   3563
by the renewing of your m..................... Rom 12:2   3563

Be of the same m one toward.................. Rom 12:16   5426
M not high things, but condescend........ Rom 12:16   5426
be fully persuaded in his own m .... Rom 14:5   3563
That ye may with one m and one .... Rom 15:6   3661
in some sort, as putting you in m .... Rom 15:15   1878
joined together in the same m 1Cor 1:10   3563
who hath known the m of the Lord 1Cor 2:16   3563
But we have the m of Christ 1Cor 2:16   3563
your fervent m toward me 2Cor 7:7
For if there be first a willing m 2Cor 8:12   4288
and declaration of your ready m 2Cor 8:19   4288
I know the forwardness of your m 2Cor 9:2   4288
be of good comfort, be of one m............ 2Cor 13:11   5426
desires of the flesh and of the m............ Eph 2:3   1271
walk, in the vanity of their m .... Eph 4:17   3563
renewed in the spirit of your m............. Eph 4:23   3563
with one m striving together for .... Phil 1:27   5590
being of one accord, of one m .... Phil 2:2   5426
but in lowliness of m let each................ Phil 2:3   5012
Let this m be in you, which was .... Phil 2:5   5426
rule, let us m the same thing .... Phil 3:16   5426
their shame, who m earthly things .... Phil 3:19   5426
they be of the same m in the Lord......... Phil 4:2   5426
enemies in your m by wicked works ...... Col 1:21   1271
vainly puffed up by his fleshly m .... Col 2:18   3563
kindness, humbleness of m .... Col 3:12
That ye be not soon shaken in m 2Th 2:2   3563
and of love, and of a sound m 2Ti 1:7   4995
but even their m and conscience is .... Titus 1:15   3563
Put them in m to be subject to .... Titus 3:1   5279
But without thy m would I do .... Philem 14   1106
I will put my laws into their m .... Heb 8:10   1271
gird up the loins of your m 1Pet 1:13   1271
Finally, be ye all of one m..................... 1Pet 3:8   3675
likewise with the same m 1Pet 4:1   1771
filthy lucre, but of a ready m................. 1Pet 5:2   4290
here is the m which hath wisdom .... Rev 17:9   3563
These have one m, and shall give .... Rev 17:13   1106

MINDED
was stedfastly m to go with her .... Ruth 1:18
Joash was m to repair the 2Chr 24:4   5973,3820
which are m of their own freewill .... Ezr 7:13
was m to put her away privily .... Mt 1:19   1014
shore, into the which they were m .... Acts 27:39   1014
For to be carnally m is death .... Rom 8:6   5427
but to be spiritually m is life .... Rom 8:6   5427
I was m to come unto you before 2Cor 1:15   1014
When I therefore was thus m 2Cor 1:17   1011
that ye will be none otherwise m .... Gal 5:10   5426
as many as be perfect, be thus m .... Phil 3:15   5426
if in any thing ye be otherwise m .... Phil 3:15   5426
men likewise exhort to be sober m .... Titus 2:6   4993
A double m man is unstable in all.......... Jas 1:8   1374
purify your hearts, ye double m .... Jas 4:8   1374

MINDFUL
Be ye m always of his covenant............ 1Chr 16:15   2142
neither were m of thy wonders .... Neh 9:17   2142
is man, that thou art m of him .... Ps 8:4   2142
he will ever be m of his covenant .... Ps 111:5   2142
The LORD hath been m of us .... Ps 115:12   2142
hast not been m of the rock of .... Is 17:10   2142
being m of thy tears, that I may 2Ti 1:4   3403
is man, that thou art m of him .... Heb 2:6   3403
if they had been m of that...................... Heb 11:15   3421
That ye may be m of the words 2Pet 3:2   3403

MINDING
appointed, m himself to go afoot............ Acts 20:13   3195

MINDS
it, take advice, and speak your m .... Judg 19:30
men, may be chafed in their m.............. 2Sa 17:8   5315
And Jehu said, If it be your m 2Kin 9:15   5315
that whereupon they set their m .... Eze 24:25   5315
their heart, with despiteful m .... Eze 36:5   5315
made their m evil affected .... Acts 14:2   5590
come to him, they changed their m .... Acts 28:6   5315
But their m were blinded....................... 2Cor 3:14   3540
the m of them which believe not........... 2Cor 4:4   3540
so your m should be corrupted 2Cor 11:3   3540
hearts and m through Christ Jesus........ Phil 4:7   3540
disputings of men of corrupt m 1Ti 6:5   3563
men of corrupt m, reprobate 2Ti 3:8   3563
in their m will I write them .... Heb 10:16   1271
ye be wearied and faint in your m .... Heb 12:3   5590
your pure m by way of remembrance..... 2Pet 3:1   1271

MINE See APPENDIX.

MINGLE
men of strength to m strong drink .... Is 5:22   4537
they shall m themselves with the .... Dan 2:43   6151

MINGLED

fire *m* with the hail, very	Ex 9:24	3947
m with the fourth part of an hin	Ex 29:40	1101
cakes of fine flour *m* with oil	Lev 2:4	1101
fine flour unleavened, *m* with oil	Lev 2:5	1101
m with oil, and dry, shall all the	Lev 7:10	1101
unleavened cakes *m* with oil	Lev 7:12	1101
cakes *m* with oil, of fine flour,	Lev 7:12	1101
and a meat offering *m* with oil	Lev 9:4	1101
m with oil, and one log of oil	Lev 14:10	1101
m with oil for a meat offering	Lev 14:21	1101
not sow thy field with *m* seed	Lev 19:19	3610
shall a garment *m* of linen	Lev 19:19	3610
deals of fine flour *m* with oil	Lev 23:13	1101
cakes of fine flour *m* with oil	Num 6:15	1101
m with oil for a meat offering	Num 7:13	1101
m with oil for a meat offering	Num 7:19	1101
m with oil for a meat offering	Num 7:25	1101
m with oil for a meat offering	Num 7:31	1101
m with oil for a meat offering	Num 7:37	1101
m with oil for a meat offering	Num 7:43	1101
m with oil for a meat offering	Num 7:49	1101
m with oil for a meat offering	Num 7:55	1101
m with oil for a meat offering	Num 7:61	1101
m with oil for a meat offering	Num 7:67	1101
m with oil for a meat offering	Num 7:73	1101
m with oil for a meat offering	Num 7:79	1101
even fine flour *m* with oil	Num 8:8	1101
of a tenth deal of flour *m* with	Num 15:4	1101
two tenth deals of flour *m* with	Num 15:6	1101
flour *m* with half an hin of oil	Num 15:9	1101
m with the fourth part of an hin	Num 28:5	1101
m with oil, and the drink offering	Num 28:9	1101
m with oil, for one bullock	Num 28:12	1101
offering, *m* with oil, for one ram	Num 28:12	1101
m with oil for a meat offering	Num 28:13	1101
shall be of flour *m* with oil	Num 28:20	1101
meat offering of flour *m* with oil	Num 28:28	1101
shall be of flour *m* with oil	Num 29:3	1101
shall be of flour *m* with oil	Num 29:9	1101
shall be of flour *m* with oil	Num 29:14	1101
so that the holy seed have *m*	Ezr 9:2	6148
and *m* my drink with weeping,	Ps 102:9	4537
But were *m* among the heathen, and	Ps 106:35	6148
she hath *m* her wine	Prov 9:2	4537
drink of the wine which I have *m*	Prov 9:5	4537
The LORD hath *m* a perverse spirit	Is 19:14	4537
And all the *m* people, and all the	Jer 25:20	6154
all the kings of the *m* people	Jer 25:24	6154
upon all the *m* people that are in	Jer 50:37	6154
and Lydia, and all the *m* people	Eze 30:5	6154
him vinegar to drink *m* with gall	Mt 27:34	3396
him to drink wine *m* with myrrh	Mk 15:23	3396
had *m* with their sacrifices	Lk 13:1	3396
fire *m* with blood, and they were	Rev 8:7	3396
were a sea of glass *m* with fire	Rev 15:2	3396

MINIAMIN (*min'-e-a-min*) See MIAMIN.
1. A Levite.

And next him were Eden, and *M*	2Chr 31:15	4509

2. A priest with Zerubbabel.

of *M*, of Moadiah, Piltai	Neh 12:17	4509
Eliakim, Maaseiah, *M*, Michaiah,	Neh 12:41	4509

MINISH

Ye shall not *m* ought from your	Ex 5:19	1639

MINISHED

Again, they are *m* and brought low	Ps 107:39	4591

MINISTER

And Moses rose up, and his *m* Joshua	Ex 24:13	8334
that he may *m* unto me in the	Ex 28:1	
that he may *m* unto me in the	Ex 28:3	
that he may *m* unto me in the	Ex 28:4	
And it shall be upon Aaron to *m*	Ex 28:35	8334
that they may *m* unto me in the	Ex 28:41	
the altar to *m* in the holy place	Ex 28:43	8334
to *m* unto me in the priest's	Ex 29:1	
to *m* in the holy place	Ex 29:30	8334
to *m* to me in the priest's office	Ex 29:44	
they come near to the altar to *m*	Ex 30:20	8334
that they may *m* unto me in the	Ex 30:30	
to *m* in the priest's office,	Ex 31:10	
to *m* in the priest's office	Ex 35:19	8334
about the hem of the robe to *m* in	Ex 39:26	8334
to *m* in the priest's office	Ex 39:41	8334
that he may *m* unto me in the	Ex 40:13	
that they may *m* unto me in the	Ex 40:15	
m unto the LORD in the priest's	Lev 7:35	
whom he shall consecrate to *m* in	Lev 16:32	
and they shall *m* unto it, and shall	Num 1:50	8334
to *m* in the priest's office	Num 3:3	

priest, that they may *m* unto him	Num 3:6	8334
of the sanctuary wherewith they *m*	Num 3:31	8334
thereof, wherewith they *m* unto it	Num 4:9	8334
wherewith they *m* in the sanctuary	Num 4:12	8334
wherewith they *m* about it	Num 4:14	8334
But shall *m* with their brethren	Num 8:26	8334
the congregation to *m* unto them	Num 16:9	8334
joined unto thee, and *m* unto thee	Num 18:2	8334
shall *m* before the tabernacle of	Num 18:2	
before the LORD to *m* unto him	Deut 10:8	8334
the priest that standeth to *m*	Deut 17:12	8334
to stand to *m* in the name of the	Deut 18:5	8334
Then he shall *m* in the name of	Deut 18:7	8334
thy God hath chosen to *m* unto him	Deut 21:5	8334
Joshua the son of Nun, Moses' *m*	Josh 1:1	8334
the child did *m* unto the LORD	1Sa 2:11	8334
stand to *m* because of the cloud	1Kin 8:11	8334
of God, and to *m* unto him for ever	1Chr 15:2	8334
certain of the Levites to *m*	1Chr 16:4	8334
to *m* before the ark continually,	1Chr 16:37	8334
to *m* unto him, and to bless in his	1Chr 23:13	8334
to *m* in the house of the LORD	1Chr 26:12	8334
stand to *m* by reason of the cloud	2Chr 5:14	8334
m before the priests, as the duty	2Chr 8:14	8334
which *m* unto the LORD, are the	2Chr 13:10	8334
they that *m* of the Levites	2Chr 23:6	8334
of the LORD, even vessels to *m*	2Chr 24:14	8335
him, and that ye should *m* unto him	2Chr 29:11	8334
and for peace offerings, to *m*	2Chr 31:2	8334
unto the priests that *m* in the	Neh 10:36	8334
sanctuary, and the priests that *m*	Neh 10:39	8334
he shall *m* judgment to the people	Ps 9:8	1777
of Nebaioth shall *m* unto thee	Is 60:7	8334
and their kings shall *m* unto thee	Is 60:10	8334
and the Levites that *m* unto me	Jer 33:22	8334
near to the LORD to *m* unto him	Eze 40:46	8334
lay their garments wherein they *m*	Eze 42:14	8334
to *m* unto me, saith the Lord GOD,	Eze 43:19	8334
stand before them to *m* unto them	Eze 44:11	8334
come near to me to *m* unto me	Eze 44:15	8334
to *m* unto me, and they shall keep	Eze 44:16	8334
whiles they *m* in the gates of the	Eze 44:17	8334
to *m* in the sanctuary, he shall	Eze 44:27	8334
come near to *m* unto the LORD	Eze 45:4	8334
among you, let him be your *m*	Mt 20:26	1249
to be ministered unto, but to *m*	Mt 20:28	1247
in prison, and did not *m* unto thee	Mt 25:44	1247
great among you, shall be your *m*	Mk 10:43	1249
to be ministered unto, but to *m*	Mk 10:45	1247
and he gave it again to the *m*	Lk 4:20	5257
and they had also John to their *m*	Acts 13:5	5257
to *m* or come unto him	Acts 24:23	5256
this purpose, to make thee a *m*	Acts 26:16	5257
For he is the *m* of God to thee	Rom 13:4	1249
for he is the *m* of God, a	Rom 13:4	1249
a *m* of the circumcision for the	Rom 15:8	1249
That I should be the *m* of Jesus	Rom 15:16	3011
Jerusalem to *m* unto the saints	Rom 15:25	1247
their duty is also to *m* unto them	Rom 15:27	3008
m about holy things live of the	1Cor 9:13	2038
sower both *m* bread for your food	2Cor 9:10	5524
is therefore Christ the *m* of sin	Gal 2:17	1249
Whereof I was made a *m*, according	Eph 3:7	1249
that it may *m* grace unto the	Eph 4:29	1325
faithful *m* in the Lord, shall	Eph 6:21	1249
is for you a faithful *m* of Christ	Col 1:7	1249
whereof I Paul am made a *m*	Col 1:23	1249
Whereof I am made a *m*, according	Col 1:25	1249
beloved brother, and a faithful *m*	Col 4:7	1249
m of God, and our fellowlabourer	1Th 3:2	1249
which *m* questions, rather than	1Ti 1:4	3930
shalt be a good *m* of Jesus Christ	1Ti 4:6	1249
sent forth to *m* for them who	Heb 1:14	1248
ministered to the saints, and do *m*	Heb 6:10	1247
A *m* of the sanctuary, and of the	Heb 8:2	3011
but unto us they did *m* the things	1Pet 1:12	1247
even so *m* the same one to another	1Pet 4:10	1247
if any man *m*, let him do it as of	1Pet 4:11	1247

MINISTERED

Ithamar *m* in the priest's office	Num 3:4	
Eleazar his son *m* in the priest's	Deut 10:6	
But Samuel *m* before the LORD,	1Sa 2:18	8334
the child Samuel *m* unto the LORD	1Sa 3:1	8334
his servant than to *m* unto him	2Sa 13:17	8334
cherished the king, and *m* to him	1Kin 1:4	8334
the Shunammite *m* unto the king	1Kin 1:15	8334
went after Elijah, and *m* unto him	1Kin 19:21	8334
vessels of brass wherewith they *m*	2Kin 25:14	8334
they *m* before the dwelling place	1Chr 6:32	8334
that *m* to the king by course	1Chr 28:1	8334

M

that *m* to Ahaziah, he slew them	2Chr 22:8	8334
king's servants that *m* unto him	Est 2:2	8334
king's servants that *m* unto him	Est 6:3	8334
vessels of brass wherewith they *m*	Jer 52:18	8334
Because they *m* unto them before	Eze 44:12	8334
off their garments wherein they *m*	Eze 44:19	8334
thousand thousands *m* unto him	Dan 7:10	8120
behold, angels came and *m* unto him	Mt 4:11	1247
and she arose, and *m* unto them	Mt 8:15	1247
Son of man came not to be *m* unto	Mt 20:28	1247
and the angels *m* unto him	Mk 1:13	1247
left her, and she *m* unto them	Mk 1:31	1247
Son of man came not to be *m* unto	Mk 10:45	1247
followed him, and *m* unto him	Mk 15:41	1247
she arose and *m* unto them	Lk 4:39	1247
which *m* unto him of their	Lk 8:3	1247
As they *m* to the Lord, and fasted,	Acts 13:2	3008
two of them that *m* unto him	Acts 19:22	1247
hands have *m* unto my necessities	Acts 20:34	5256
be the epistle of Christ *m* by us	2Cor 3:3	1247
and he that *m* to my wants	Phil 2:25	3011
and bands having nourishment *m*	Col 2:19	2023
things he *m* unto me at Ephesus	2Ti 1:18	1247
m unto me in the bonds of the	Philem 13	1247
in that ye have *m* to the saints	Heb 6:10	1247
For so an entrance shall be *m*	2Pet 1:11	2023

MINISTERETH

Now he that *m* seed to the sower	2Cor 9:10	2023
that *m* to you the Spirit, and	Gal 3:5	2023

MINISTERING

had the charge of the *m* vessels	1Chr 9:28	5656
of the house, and *m* to the house	Eze 44:14	8334
Jesus from Galilee, *m* unto him	Mt 27:55	1247
Or ministry, let us wait on our *m*	Rom 12:7	1248
m the gospel of God, that the	Rom 15:16	2418
fellowship of the *m* to the saints	2Cor 8:4	1248
as touching the *m* to the saints	2Cor 9:1	1248
Are they not all *m* spirits	Heb 1:14	3010
And every priest standeth daily *m*	Heb 10:11	3008

MINISTERS

and the attendance of his *m*	1Kin 10:5	8334
and the attendance of his *m*	2Chr 9:4	8334
or *m* of this house of God, it	Ezr 7:24	6399
us *m* for the house of our God	Ezr 8:17	8334
ye *m* of his, that do his pleasure	Ps 103:21	8334
his *m* a flaming fire	Ps 104:4	8334
shall call you the *M* of our God	Is 61:6	8334
the Levites the priests, my *m*	Jer 33:21	8334
they shall be *m* in my sanctuary	Eze 44:11	8334
priests the *m* of the sanctuary	Eze 45:4	8334
the *m* of the house, have for	Eze 45:5	8334
where the *m* of the house shall	Eze 46:24	8334
the priests, the LORD'S *m*	Joel 1:9	8334
howl, ye *m* of the altar	Joel 1:13	8334
in sackcloth, ye *m* of my God	Joel 1:13	8334
the *m* of the LORD, weep between	Joel 2:17	8334
eyewitnesses, and *m* of the word	Lk 1:2	5257
for they are God's *m*, attending	Rom 13:6	3011
but *m* by whom ye believed, even	1Cor 3:5	1249
of us, as of the *m* of Christ	1Cor 4:1	5257
us able *m* of the new testament	2Cor 3:6	1249
ourselves as the *m* of God	2Cor 6:4	1249
his *m* also be transformed as the	2Cor 11:15	1249
as the *m* of righteousness	2Cor 11:15	1249
Are they *m* of Christ?	2Cor 11:23	1249
spirits, and his *m* a flame of fire	Heb 1:7	3011

MINISTRATION

days of his *m* were accomplished	Lk 1:23	3009
were neglected in the daily *m*	Acts 6:1	1248
But if the *m* of death, written and	2Cor 3:7	1248
How shall not the *m* of the spirit	2Cor 3:8	1248
For if the *m* of condemnation be	2Cor 3:9	1248
be glory, much more doth the *m* of	2Cor 3:9	1248
this *m* they glorify God for your	2Cor 9:13	1248

MINISTRY

take all the instruments of *m*	Num 4:12	8335
came to do the service of the *m*	Num 4:47	5656
when David praised by their *m*	2Chr 7:6	3027
by the *m* of the prophets	Hos 12:10	3027
and had obtained part of this *m*	Acts 1:17	1248
That he may take part of this *m*	Acts 1:25	1248
prayer, and to the *m* of the word	Acts 6:4	1248
when they had fulfilled their *m*	Acts 12:25	1248
my course with joy, and the *m*	Acts 20:24	1248
among the Gentiles by his *m*	Acts 21:19	1248
Or *m*, let us wait on our	Rom 12:7	1248
themselves to the *m* of the saints	1Cor 16:15	1248
Therefore, seeing we have this *m*	2Cor 4:1	1248

to us the *m* of reconciliation	2Cor 5:18	1248
thing, that the *m* be not blamed	2Cor 6:3	1248
the saints, for the work of the *m*	Eph 4:12	1248
Take heed to the *m* which thou	Col 4:17	1248
faithful, putting me into the *m*	1Ti 1:12	1248
make full proof of thy *m*	2Ti 4:5	1248
he is profitable to me for the *m*	2Ti 4:11	1248
he obtained a more excellent *m*	Heb 8:6	3009
and all the vessels of the *m*	Heb 9:21	3009

MINJAMIN See MINIAMIN.

MINNI (min'-ni) A district in Armenia.

her the kingdoms of Ararat, *M*	Jer 51:27	4508

MINNITH (min'-nith) An Ammonite city.

Aroer, even till thou come to *M*	Judg 11:33	4511
traded in thy market wheat of *M*	Eze 27:17	4511

MINSTREL

But now bring me a *m*	2Kin 3:15	5059
came to pass, when the *m* played	2Kin 3:15	5059

MINSTRELS

the ruler's house, and saw the *m*	Mt 9:23	834

MINT

for ye pay tithe of *m* and anise and	Mt 23:23	2238
for ye tithe *m* and rue and all	Lk 11:42	2238

MIPHKAD (mif'-kad) A gate of Jerusalem.

over against the gate *M*, and to	Neh 3:31	4663

MIRACLE

you, saying, Shew a *m* for you	Ex 7:9	4159
not the *m* of the loaves	Mk 6:52	
man which shall do a *m* in my name	Mk 9:39	1411
to have seen some *m* done by him	Lk 23:8	4592
again the second *m* that Jesus did	Jn 4:54	4592
had seen the *m* that Jesus did	Jn 6:14	4592
unto him, and said, John did no *m*	Jn 10:41	4592
heard that he had done this *m*	Jn 12:18	4592
m hath been done by them is	Acts 4:16	4592
on whom this *m* of healing was	Acts 4:22	4592

MIRACLES

which have seen my glory, and my *m*	Num 14:22	226
And his *m*, and his acts, which he	Deut 11:3	226
seen, the signs, and those great *m*	Deut 29:3	4159
where be all his *m* which our	Judg 6:13	6381
This beginning of *m* did Jesus in	Jn 2:11	4592
when they saw the *m* which he did	Jn 2:23	4592
can do these *m* that thou doest	Jn 3:2	4592
because they saw his *m* which he	Jn 6:2	4592
seek me, not because ye saw the *m*	Jn 6:26	4592
will he do more *m* than these	Jn 7:31	4592
a man that is a sinner do such *m*	Jn 9:16	4592
for this man doeth many *m*	Jn 11:47	4592
he had done so many *m* before them	Jn 12:37	4592
approved of God among you by *m*	Acts 2:22	1411
wonders and *m* among the people	Acts 6:8	4592
seeing the *m* which he did	Acts 8:6	4592
and wondered, beholding the *m*	Acts 8:13	1411
and Paul, declaring what *m*	Acts 15:12	4592
God wrought special *m* by the	Acts 19:11	1411
To another the working of *m*	1Cor 12:10	1411
thirdly teachers, after that *m*	1Cor 12:28	1411
are all workers of *m*?	1Cor 12:29	1411
worketh *m* among you, doeth he it	Gal 3:5	1411
and wonders, and with divers *m*	Heb 2:4	1411
m which he had power to do in the	Rev 13:14	4592
the spirits of devils, working *m*	Rev 16:14	4592
prophet that wrought *m* before him	Rev 19:20	4592

MIRE

stamp them as the *m* of the street	2Sa 22:43	2916
Can the rush grow up without *m*	Job 8:11	1207
He hath cast me into the *m*	Job 30:19	2563
sharp pointed things upon the *m*	Job 41:30	2916
I sink in deep *m*, where there is	Ps 69:2	3121
Deliver me out of the *m*, and let	Ps 69:14	2916
down like the *m* of the streets	Is 10:6	2563
rest, whose waters cast up *m*	Is 57:20	7516
dungeon there was no water, but *m*	Jer 38:6	2916
so Jeremiah sunk in the *m*	Jer 38:6	2916
thy feet are sunk in the *m*	Jer 38:22	1206
down as the *m* of the streets	Mic 7:10	2916
fine gold as the *m* of the streets	Zec 9:3	2916
m of the streets in the battle	Zec 10:5	2916
washed to her wallowing in the *m*	2Pet 2:22	1004

MIRIAM (mir'-e-am) See MARY.
1. Sister of Aaron.

M the prophetess, the sister of	Ex 15:20	4813
M answered them, Sing ye to the	Ex 15:21	4813
M and Aaron spake against Moses	Num 12:1	4813

Moses, and unto Aaron, and unto *M*	Num 12:4	4813
tabernacle, and called Aaron and *M*	Num 12:5	4813
M became leprous, white as snow	Num 12:10	4813
and Aaron looked upon *M*, and,	Num 12:10	4813
M was shut out from the camp	Num 12:15	4813
not till *M* was brought in again	Num 12:15	4813
M died there, and was buried there	Num 20:1	4813
Aaron and Moses, and *M* their sister	Num 26:59	4813
thy God did unto *M* by the way	Deut 24:9	4813
Aaron, and Moses, and *M*	1Chr 6:3	4813
before thee Moses, Aaron, and *M*	Mic 6:4	4813
2. *A daughter of Ezra.*		
and she bare *M*, and Shammai, and	1Chr 4:17	4813

MIRMA (*mur'-mah*) *Son of Shaharaim.*

And Jeuz, and Shachia, and *M*	1Chr 8:10	4821

MIRMAH See MIRMA.

MIRTH

might have sent thee away with *m*	Gen 31:27	8057
send portions, and to make great *m*	Neh 8:12	8057
that wasted us required of us *m*	Ps 137:3	8057
and the end of that *m* is heaviness	Prov 14:13	8057
to now, I will prove thee with *m*	Eccl 2:1	8057
and of *m*, What doeth it	Eccl 2:2	8057
of fools is in the house of *m*	Eccl 7:4	8057
Then I commended *m*, because a man	Eccl 8:15	8057
The *m* of tabrets ceaseth, the	Is 24:8	4885
the *m* of the land is gone	Is 24:11	4885
of Jerusalem, the voice of *m*	Jer 7:34	8342
and in your days, the voice of *m*	Jer 16:9	8342
take from them the voice of *m*	Jer 25:10	8342
should we then make *m*?	Eze 21:10	7797
also cause all her *m* to cease	Hos 2:11	4885

MIRY

horrible pit, out of the *m* clay	Ps 40:2	3121
But the *m* places thereof and the	Eze 47:11	1207
sawest the iron mixed with *m* clay	Dan 2:41	2917
sawest iron mixed with *m* clay	Dan 2:43	2917

MISCARRYING

give them a *m* womb and dry breasts	Hos 9:14	7921

MISCHIEF

Lest peradventure *m* befall him	Gen 42:4	611
if *m* befall him by the way in the	Gen 42:38	611
m befall him, then shall bring down	Gen 44:29	611
from her, and yet no *m* follow	Ex 21:22	611
And if any *m* follow, then thou	Ex 21:23	611
For *m* did he bring them out, to	Ex 32:12	7451
people, that they are set on *m*	Ex 32:22	7451
secretly practised *m* against him	1Sa 23:9	7451
behold, thou art taken in thy *m*	2Sa 16:8	7451
beside the *m* that Hadad did	1Kin 11:25	7451
and see how this man seeketh *m*	1Kin 20:7	7451
light, some *m* will come upon us	2Kin 7:9	5771
But they thought to do me *m*	Neh 6:2	7451
away the *m* of Haman the Agagite	Est 8:3	7451
They conceive *m*, and bring forth	Job 15:35	5999
iniquity, and hath conceived *m*	Ps 7:14	5999
His *m* shall return upon his own	Ps 7:16	5999
under his tongue is *m* and vanity	Ps 10:7	5999
for thou beholdest *m* and spite, to	Ps 10:14	5999
In whose hands is *m*, and their	Ps 26:10	2154
but *m* is in their hearts	Ps 28:3	7451
He deviseth *m* upon his bed	Ps 36:4	205
Why boastest thou thyself in *m*	Ps 52:1	7451
m also and sorrow are in the midst	Ps 55:10	205
will ye imagine *m* against a man	Ps 62:3	205
thee, which frameth *m* by a law	Ps 94:20	5999
draw nigh that follow after *m*	Ps 119:150	2154
let the *m* of their own lips cover	Ps 140:9	5999
not, except they have done *m*	Prov 4:16	7489
heart, he deviseth *m* continually	Prov 6:14	7451
that be swift in running to *m*	Prov 6:18	7451
It is as sport to a fool to do *m*	Prov 10:23	2154
but he that seeketh *m*, it shall	Prov 11:27	7451
the wicked shall be filled with *m*	Prov 12:21	7451
A wicked messenger falleth into *m*	Prov 13:17	7451
a perverse tongue falleth into *m*	Prov 17:20	7451
and their lips talk of *m*	Prov 24:2	5999
but the wicked shall fall into *m*	Prov 24:16	7451
his heart shall fall into *m*	Prov 28:14	7451
and *m* shall fall upon thee	Is 47:11	1943
they conceive *m*, and bring forth	Is 59:4	5999
M shall come upon *m*	Eze 7:26	1943
these are the men that devise *m*	Eze 11:2	205
kings' hearts shall be to do *m*	Dan 11:27	4827
yet do they imagine *m* against me	Hos 7:15	7451
O full of all subtilty and all *m*	Acts 13:10	4468

MISCHIEFS

I will heap *m* upon them	Deut 32:23	7451
Thy tongue deviseth *m*	Ps 52:2	1942
Which imagine *m* in their heart	Ps 140:2	7451

MISCHIEVOUS

they imagined a *m* device, which	Ps 21:11	4209
that seek my hurt speak *m* things	Ps 38:12	1942
evil shall be called a *m* person	Prov 24:8	4209
the end of his talk is *m* madness	Eccl 10:13	7451
man, he uttereth his *m* desire	Mic 7:3	1942

MISERABLE

m comforters are ye all	Job 16:2	5999
Christ, we are of all men most *m*	1Cor 15:19	*1652*
not that thou art wretched, and *m*	Rev 3:17	*1652*

MISERABLY

He will *m* destroy those wicked	Mt 21:41	*2560*

MISERIES

of her *m* all her pleasant things	Lam 1:7	4788
howl for your *m* that shall come	Jas 5:1	*5004*

MISERY

was grieved for the *m* of Israel	Judg 10:16	5999
light given to him that is in *m*	Job 3:20	6001
Because thou shalt forget thy *m*	Job 11:16	5999
and remember his *m* no more	Prov 31:7	5999
therefore the *m* of man is great	Eccl 8:6	7451
mine affliction and my *m*, the	Lam 3:19	4788
and *m* are in their ways	Rom 3:16	*5004*

MISGAB (*mis'-gab*) *The mountainous area in Moab.*

M is confounded and dismayed	Jer 48:1	4869

MISHAEL (*mish'-a-el*) See MISHAL.
    1. A son of Uzziel.

M, and Elzaphan, and Zithri	Ex 6:22	4332
Moses called *M* and Elzaphan, and	Lev 10:4	4332
of Judah, Daniel, Hananiah, *M*	Dan 1:6	4332
and to *M*, of Meshach	Dan 1:7	4332
had set over Daniel, Hananiah, *M*	Dan 1:11	4332
none like Daniel, Hananiah, *M*	Dan 1:19	4332
the thing known to Hananiah, *M*	Dan 2:17	4332
2. A priest who aided Ezra.		
on his left hand, Pedaiah, and *M*	Neh 8:4	4332

MISHAL (*mi'-shal*) See MISHEAL. *A Levitical city in Asher.*

M with her suburbs, Abdon with	Josh 21:30	4861

MISHAM (*mi'-sham*) *Son of Elpaal.*

Eber, and *M*, and Shamed, who built	1Chr 8:12	4936

MISHEAL (*mish'-e-al*) *Same as Mishal.*

And Alammelech, and Amad, and *M*	Josh 19:26	4861

MISHMA (*mish'-mah*) *A son of Ishmeal.*

And *M*, and Dumah, and Massa,	Gen 25:14	4927
M, and Dumah, Massa, Hadad, and	1Chr 1:30	4927
son, Mibsam his son, *M* his son	1Chr 4:25	4927
And the sons of *M*	1Chr 4:26	4927

MISHMANNAH (*mish-man'-nah*) *A warrior in David's army.*

M the fourth, Jeremiah the fifth,	1Chr 12:10	4925

MISHRAITES (*mish'-ra-ites*) *A family of Kirjath-jearim.*

and the Shumathites, and the *M*	1Chr 2:53	4954

MISPAR See MIZPAR.

MISPERETH (*mis-pe'-reth*) See MIZPAR. *An exile with Ezra.*

Nahamani, Mordecai, Bilshan, *M*	Neh 7:7	4559

MISREPHOTH-MAIM *Same as Zarephath.*

them unto great Zidon, and unto *M*	Josh 11:8	4956
hill country from Lebanon unto *M*	Josh 13:6	4956

MISS

at an hair breadth, and not *m*	Judg 20:16	2398
If thy father at all *m* me	1Sa 20:6	6485

MISSED

and thou shalt be *m*, because thy	1Sa 20:18	6485
neither we any thing, as long	1Sa 25:15	6485
so that nothing was *m* of all that	1Sa 25:21	6485

MISSING

was there ought *m* unto them	1Sa 25:7	6485
if by any means he be *m*, then	1Kin 20:39	6485

MIST

there went up a *m* from the earth	Gen 2:6	108
immediately there fell on him a *m*	Acts 13:11	887
to whom the *m* of darkness is	2Pet 2:17	2217

MISTRESS

her *m* was despised in her eyes	Gen 16:4	1404
flee from the face of my *m* Sarai	Gen 16:8	1404

M

said unto her, Return to thy *m*	Gen 16:9	1404
the *m* of the house, fell sick	1Kin 17:17	1172
And she said unto her *m*, Would God	2Kin 5:3	1404
a maiden unto the hand of her *m*	Ps 123:2	1404
an handmaid that is heir to her *m*	Prov 30:23	1404
as with the maid, so with her *m*	Is 24:2	1404
the *m* of witchcrafts, that	Nah 3:4	1172

MISUSED

m his prophets, until the wrath	2Chr 36:16	8591

MITE

thou hast paid the very last *m*	Lk 12:59	*3016*

MITES

poor widow, and she threw in two *m*	Mk 12:42	*3016*
widow casting in thither two *m*	Lk 21:2	*3016*

MITHCAH (mith'-cah) *An Israelite encampment in the wilderness.*

from Tarah, and pitched in *M*	Num 33:28	4989
And they went from *M*, and pitched	Num 33:29	4989

MITHCAK See MITHCAH.

MITHKAH See MITHCAH.

MITHNITE (mith'-nite) *Family name of Joshaphat.*

of Maachah, and Joshaphat the *M*	1Chr 11:43	4981

MITHREDATH (mith'-re-dath) *Treasurer for King Cyrus of Persia.*

by the hand of *M* the treasurer	Ezr 1:8	4990
of Artaxerxes wrote Bishlam, *M*	Ezr 4:7	4990

MITRE

a robe, and a broidered coat, a *m*	Ex 28:4	4701
lace, that it may be upon the *m*	Ex 28:37	4701
forefront of the *m* it shall be	Ex 28:37	4701
shalt make the *m* of fine linen	Ex 28:39	4701
shalt put the *m* upon his head	Ex 29:6	4701
and put the holy crown upon the *m*	Ex 29:6	4701
a *m* of fine linen, and goodly	Ex 39:28	4701
to fasten it on high upon the *m*	Ex 39:31	4701
he put the *m* upon his head	Lev 8:9	4701
also upon the *m*, even upon his	Lev 8:9	4701
with the linen *m* shall he be	Lev 16:4	4701
them set a fair *m* upon his head	Zec 3:5	6797
they set a fair *m* upon his head	Zec 3:5	6797

MITYLENE (mit-i-le'-ne) *Major city of the island of Lesbos.*

we took him in, and came to *M*	Acts 20:14	*3412*

MIXED

a *m* multitude went up also with	Ex 12:38	6154
from Israel all the *m* multitude	Neh 13:3	6154
they that go to seek *m* wine	Prov 23:30	4469
dross, thy wine *m* with water	Is 1:22	4107
sawest the iron *m* with miry clay	Dan 2:41	6151
thou sawest iron *m* with miry clay	Dan 2:43	6151
even as iron is not *m* with clay	Dan 2:43	6151
he hath *m* himself among the	Hos 7:8	1101
not being *m* with faith in them	Heb 4:2	*4786*

MIXT

the *m* multitude that was among	Num 11:4	

MIXTURE

it is full of *m*	Ps 75:8	4538
by night, and brought a *m* of myrrh	Jn 19:39	*3395*
which is poured out without *m*	Rev 14:10	194

MIZAR (mi'-zar) *A hill near Hermon.*

the Hermonites, from the hill *M*	Ps 42:6	4706

MIZPAH (miz'-pah) See MIZPEH.

1. A city in Gad.

And *M*; for he said	Gen 31:49	4709

2. A city in Benjamin.

with them Geba of Benjamin, and *M*	1Kin 15:22	4709
the men of Gibeon, and of *M*	Neh 3:7	4709

3. A city in Judah.

there came to Gedaliah to *M*	2Kin 25:23	4709
Chaldees that were with him at *M*	2Kin 25:25	4709
and he built therewith Geba and *M*	2Chr 16:6	4709
Gedaliah the son of Ahikam to *M*	Jer 40:6	4708
Then they came to Gedaliah to *M*	Jer 40:8	4708
I will dwell at *M* to serve the	Jer 40:10	4708
of Judah, to Gedaliah, unto *M*	Jer 40:12	4708
the fields, came to Gedaliah to *M*	Jer 40:13	4708
spake to Gedaliah in *M* secretly	Jer 40:15	4709
Gedaliah the son of Ahikam to *M*	Jer 41:1	4709
they did eat bread together in *M*	Jer 41:1	4709
him, even with Gedaliah, at *M*	Jer 41:3	4709
went forth from *M* to meet them	Jer 41:6	4709
of the people that were in *M*	Jer 41:10	4709
all the people that remained in *M*	Jer 41:10	4709
away captive from *M* cast about	Jer 41:14	4709

the son of Nethaniah, from *M*	Jer 41:16	4709
because ye have been a snare on *M*	Hos 5:1	4709

4. A district ruled by Shallum.

Colhozeh, the ruler of part of *M*	Neh 3:15	4709

5. A place ruled by Ezer.

the son of Jeshua, the ruler of *M*	Neh 3:19	4709

MIZPAR (miz'-par) See MISPERETH. *A clan leader with Zerubbabel.*

Reelaiah, Mordecai, Bilshan, *M*	Ezr 2:2	4558

MIZPEH (miz'-peh) See MIZPAH, RAMATH-MIZPEH.

1. A valley near Mt. Hermon.

under Hermon in the land of *M*	Josh 11:3	4709
and unto the valley of *M* eastward	Josh 11:8	4708

2. A city in Judah.

And Dilean, and *M*, and Joktheel,	Josh 15:38	4708
of Gilead, unto the LORD in *M*	Judg 20:1	4709
of Israel were gone up to *M*	Judg 20:3	4709
the men of Israel had sworn in *M*	Judg 21:1	4709
that came not up to the LORD to *M*	Judg 21:5	4709
that came not up to *M* to the LORD	Judg 21:8	4709
said, Gather all Israel to *M*	1Sa 7:5	4708
And they gathered together to *M*	1Sa 7:6	4709
the children of Israel in *M*	1Sa 7:6	4708
were gathered together to *M*	1Sa 7:7	4708
the men of Israel went out of *M*	1Sa 7:11	4709
took a stone, and set it between *M*	1Sa 7:12	4709
to Beth-el, and Gilgal, and *M*	1Sa 7:16	4709
together unto the LORD to *M*	1Sa 10:17	4709

3. A city in Benjamin.

And *M*, and Chephirah, and Mozah,	Josh 18:26	4708

4. A city in Gad.

together, and encamped in *M*	Judg 10:17	4709
his words before the LORD in *M*	Judg 11:11	4709
and passed over *M* of Gilead	Judg 11:29	4709
from *M* of Gilead he passed over	Judg 11:29	4708
Jephthah came to *M* unto his house	Judg 11:34	4709

5. A city in Moab.

And David went thence to *M* of Moab	1Sa 22:3	4708

MIZRAIM (miz'-ra-im) See ABEL-MIZRAIM. *Son of Ham.*

Cush, and *M*, and Phut, and Canaan	Gen 10:6	4714
M begat Ludim, and Anamim, and	Gen 10:13	4714
Cush, and *M*, Put, and Canaan	1Chr 1:8	4714
M begat Ludim, and Anamim, and	1Chr 1:11	4714

MIZZAH (miz'-zah) *Son of Reuel.*

Nahath, and Zerah, Shammah, and *M*	Gen 36:13	4199
duke Zerah, duke Shammah, duke *M*	Gen 36:17	4199
Nahath, Zerah, Shammah, and *M*	1Chr 1:37	4199

MNASON (na'-son) *A Christian in Jerusalem.*

brought with them one *M* of Cyprus	Acts 21:16	*3416*

MOAB (mo'-ab)

1. A nation east of Israel.

smote Midian in the field of *M*	Gen 36:35	4124
the mighty men of *M*, trembling	Ex 15:15	4124
the wilderness which is before *M*	Num 21:11	4124
is the border of *M*, between *M*	Num 21:13	4124
Ar, and lieth upon the border of *M*	Num 21:15	4124
that is in the country of *M*	Num 21:20	4124
against the former king of *M*	Num 21:26	4124
it hath consumed Ar of *M*, and the	Num 21:28	4124
Woe to thee, *M*	Num 21:29	4124
pitched in the plains of *M* on	Num 22:1	4124
M was sore afraid of the people,	Num 22:3	4124
M was distressed because of the	Num 22:3	4124
M said unto the elders of Midian,	Num 22:4	4124
And the elders of *M* and the elders	Num 22:7	4124
the princes of *M* abode with	Num 22:8	4124
the son of Zippor, king of *M*	Num 22:10	4124
And the princes of *M* rose up,	Num 22:14	4124
and went with the princes of *M*	Num 22:21	4124
out to meet him unto a city of *M*	Num 22:36	4124
he, and all the princes of *M*	Num 23:6	4124
Balak the king of *M* hath brought	Num 23:7	4124
and the princes of *M* with him	Num 23:17	4124
and shall smite the corners of *M*	Num 24:17	4124
whoredom with the daughters of *M*	Num 25:1	4124
of *M* by Jordan near Jericho	Num 26:3	4124
of *M* by Jordan near Jericho	Num 26:63	4124
unto the camp at the plains of *M*	Num 31:12	4124
in Ije-abarim, in the border of *M*	Num 33:44	4124
of *M* by Jordan near Jericho	Num 33:48	4124
Abel-shittim in the plains of *M*	Num 33:49	4124
in the plains of *M* by Jordan	Num 33:50	4124
of *M* by Jordan near Jericho	Num 35:1	4124
of *M* by Jordan near Jericho	Num 36:13	4124
side Jordan, in the land of *M*	Deut 1:5	4124
by the way of the wilderness of *M*	Deut 2:8	4124
over through Ar, the coast of *M*	Deut 2:18	4124
of Israel in the land of *M*	Deut 29:1	4124

Nebo, which is in the land of *M* .... Deut 32:49 4124
of *M* unto the mountain of Nebo .... Deut 34:1 4124
LORD died there in the land of *M* .... Deut 34:5 4124
him in a valley in the land of *M* .... Deut 34:6 4124
in the plains of *M* thirty days................. Deut 34:8 4124
inheritance in the plains of *M* .... Josh 13:32 4124
the son of Zippor, king of *M*.................... Josh 24:9 4124
the king of *M* against Israel.................... Judg 3:12 4124
the king of *M* eighteen years .... Judg 3:14 4124
present unto Eglon the king of *M* .... Judg 3:15 4124
the present unto Eglon king of *M* .... Judg 3:17 4124
took the fords of Jordan toward *M*......... Judg 3:28 4124
they slew of *M* at that time about .... Judg 3:29 4124
So *M* was subdued that day under .... Judg 3:30 4124
gods of Zidon, and the gods of *M*......... Judg 10:6 4124
took not away the land of *M* .... Judg 11:15 4124
they sent unto the king of *M* .... Judg 11:17 4124
land of Edom, and the land of *M*......... Judg 11:18 4124
by the east side of the land of *M* .... Judg 11:18 4124
came not within the border of *M* .... Judg 11:18 4124
for Arnon was the border of *M* .... Judg 11:18 4124
the son of Zippor, king of *M*.................. Judg 11:25 4124
to sojourn in the country of *M* .... Ruth 1:1 4124
they came into the country of *M* .... Ruth 1:2 4124
took them wives of the women of *M* ...... Ruth 1:4 4125
return from the country of *M* .... Ruth 1:6 4124
M how that the LORD had visited............ Ruth 1:6 4124
returned out of the country of *M* .... Ruth 1:22 4124
Naomi out of the country of *M* .... Ruth 2:6 4124
again out of the country of *M* .... Ruth 4:3 4124
and into the hand of the king of *M* 1Sa 12:9 4124
enemies on every side, against *M* 1Sa 14:47 4124
David went thence to Mizpeh of *M*....... 1Sa 22:3 4124
and he said unto the king of *M* 1Sa 22:3 4124
brought them before the king of *M* 1Sa 22:4 4124
And he smote *M*, and measured them ...2Sa 8:2 4124
Of Syria, and of *M*, and of the 2Sa 8:12 4124
he slew two lionlike men of *M* 2Sa 23:20 4124
for Chemosh, the abomination of *M* 1Kin 11:7 4124
Then *M* rebelled against Israel................ 2Kin 1:1 4124
Mesha king of *M* was a sheepmaster ... 2Kin 3:4 4124
that the king of *M* rebelled.................... 2Kin 3:5 4124
The king of *M* hath rebelled 2Kin 3:7 4124
go with me against *M* to battle.............. 2Kin 3:7 4124
deliver them into the hand of *M*.......... 2Kin 3:10 4124
deliver them into the hand of *M* 2Kin 3:13 4124
now therefore, *M*, to the spoil 2Kin 3:23 4124
when the king of *M* saw that the 2Kin 3:26 4124
smote Midian in the field of *M* 1Chr 1:46 4124
Saraph, who had the dominion in *M* 1Chr 4:22 4124
children in the country of *M*................... 1Chr 8:8 4124
he slew two lionlike men of *M* 1Chr 11:22 4124
And he smote *M* 1Chr 18:2 4124
from Edom, and from *M*, and from the ... 1Chr 18:11 4124
this also, that the children of *M*.............. 2Chr 20:1 4124
the children of Ammon and *M* 2Chr 20:10 4124
against the children of Ammon, *M* 2Chr 20:22 4124
Ammon and *M* stood up against the 2Chr 20:23 4124
of Ashdod, of Ammon, and of *M* .... Neh 13:23 4125
M is my washpot .... Ps 60:8 4124
of *M*, and the Hagarenes .... Ps 83:6 4124
M is my washpot .... Ps 108:9 4124
lay their hand upon Edom and *M* .... Is 11:14 4124
The burden of *M*.. Is 15:1 4124
the night Ar of *M* is laid waste................ Is 15:1 4124
the night Kir of *M* is laid waste .... Is 15:1 4124
M shall howl over Nebo, and .... Is 15:2 4124
armed soldiers of *M* shall cry out .... Is 15:4 4124
My heart shall cry out for *M*..................... Is 15:5 4124
gone round about the borders of *M* .... Is 15:8 4124
lions upon him that escapeth of *M* .... Is 15:9 4124
so the daughters of *M* shall be at .... Is 16:2 4124
mine outcasts dwell with thee, *M* .... Is 16:4 4124
We have heard of the pride of *M* .... Is 16:6 4124
Therefore shall *M* howl for *M* .... Is 16:7 4124
Therefore shall *M* howl for *M* .... Is 16:7 4124
shall sound like an harp for *M*................ Is 16:11 4124
when it is seen that *M* is weary .... Is 16:12 4124
concerning *M* since that time.................. Is 16:13 4124
the glory of *M* shall be contemned .... Is 16:14 4124
M shall be trodden down under him ...... Is 25:10 4124
and the children of Ammon, and *M*......... Jer 9:26 4124
Edom, and *M*, and the children of .... Jer 25:21 4124
king of Edom, and to the king of *M* .... Jer 27:3 4124
when all the Jews that were in *M* .... Jer 40:11 4124
Against *M* thus saith the LORD of .... Jer 48:1 4124
shall be no more praise of *M*.................. Jer 48:2 4124
M is destroyed .... Jer 48:4 4124
Give wings unto *M*, that it may .... Jer 48:9 4124
M hath been at ease from his .... Jer 48:11 4124
M shall be ashamed of Chemosh, as ...... Jer 48:13 4124

M is spoiled, and gone up out of .... Jer 48:15 4124
The calamity of *M* is near to come .... Jer 48:16 4124
for the spoiler of *M* shall come .... Jer 48:18 4124
M is confounded .... Jer 48:20 4124
it in Arnon, that *M* is spoiled, ... Jer 48:20 4124
all the cities of the land of *M*.................. Jer 48:24 4124
The horn of *M* is cut off, and his .... Jer 48:25 4124
M also shall wallow in his vomit,........... Jer 48:26 4124
O ye that dwell in *M*, leave the .... Jer 48:28 4124
We have heard the pride of *M*................. Jer 48:29 4124
Therefore will I howl for *M* .... Jer 48:31 4124
and I will cry out for all *M* .... Jer 48:31 4124
field, and from the land of *M*................... Jer 48:33 4124
I will cause to cease in *M*........................ Jer 48:35 4124
shall sound for *M* like pipes .... Jer 48:36 4124
upon all the housetops of *M* .... Jer 48:38 4124
for I have broken *M* like a vessel............ Jer 48:38 4124
how hath *M* turned the back with .... Jer 48:39 4124
so shall *M* be a derision and a .... Jer 48:39 4124
and shall spread his wings over *M* .... Jer 48:40 4124
the mighty men's hearts in *M* at .... Jer 48:41 4124
M shall be destroyed from being a .... Jer 48:42 4124
be upon thee, O inhabitant of *M*............. Jer 48:43 4124
I will bring upon it, even upon *M*............ Jer 48:44 4124
and shall devour the corner of *M* .... Jer 48:45 4124
Woe be unto thee, O *M*............................ Jer 48:46 4124
captivity of *M* in the latter days .... Jer 48:47 4124
Thus far is the judgment of *M* .... Jer 48:47 4124
Because that *M* and Seir do say, ... Eze 25:8 4124
the side of *M* from the cities .... Eze 25:9 4124
I will execute judgments upon *M* .... Eze 25:11 4124
out of his hand, even Edom, and *M* .... Dan 11:41 4124
For three transgressions of *M* .... Amos 2:1 4124
But I will send a fire upon *M* .... Amos 2:2 4124
M shall die with tumult, with .... Amos 2:2 4124
what Balak king of *M* consulted .... Mic 6:5 4124
I have heard the reproach of *M* .... Zeph 2:8 4124
Surely *M* shall be as Sodom, and .... Zeph 2:9 4124
   2. *Son of Lot.*
bare a son, and called his name *M* .... Gen 19:37 4124

MOABITE *(mo'-ab-ite)* See MOABITES, MOABITISS,
  MOABITISH. *An inhabitant of Moab.*
An Ammonite or *M* shall not enter .... Deut 23:3 4125
sons of Elnaam, and Ithmah the *M* 1Chr 11:46 4125
the *M* should not come into the.............. Neh 13:1 4125

MOABITES *(mo'-ab-ites)*
the father of the *M* unto this day .... Gen 19:37 4124
was king of the *M* at that time............... Num 22:4 4124
said unto me, Distress not the *M* .... Deut 2:9 4124
but the *M* call them Emims.................... Deut 2:11 4125
the *M* which dwell in Ar, did unto .... Deut 2:29 4125
your enemies the *M* into your hand .... Judg 3:28 4124
so the *M* became David's servants, ... 2Sa 8:2 4124
of Pharaoh, women of the *M*.................. 1Kin 11:1 4125
Chemosh the god of the *M* 1Kin 11:33 4124
deliver the *M* also into your hand.......... 2Kin 3:18 4124
when all the *M* heard that the 2Kin 3:21 4124
the *M* saw the water on the other 2Kin 3:22 4124
Israelites rose up and smote the *M* 2Kin 3:24 4124
they went forward smiting the *M* 2Kin 3:24 4124
the bands of the *M* invaded the 2Kin 13:20 4124
Chemosh the abomination of *M* 2Kin 23:13 4124
of the Syrians, and bands of the *M* 2Kin 24:2 4124
the *M* became David's servants, and 1Chr 18:2 4124
Jebusites, the Ammonites, the *M* .... Ezr 9:1 4124

MOABITESS *(mo'-ab-i-tess) A female Moabite.*
So Naomi returned, and Ruth the *M*...... Ruth 1:22 4125
Ruth the *M* said unto Naomi, Let .... Ruth 2:2 4125
And Ruth the *M* said, He said unto .... Ruth 2:21 4125
must buy it also of Ruth the *M* .... Ruth 4:5 4125
Moreover Ruth the *M*, the wife of .... Ruth 4:10 4125
Jehozabad the son of Shimrith a *M* 2Chr 24:26 4125

MOABITISH *(mo'-ab-i-tish) Belonging to the Moabites.*
It is the *M* damsel that came back........ Ruth 2:6 4125

MOADIAH *(mo-ad-i'-ah)* See MAADIAH. *A priest.*
of Miniamin, of *M*, Piltai....................... Neh 12:17 4153

MOCK
in an Hebrew unto us to *m*..us............... Gen 39:14 6711
unto us, came in unto me to *m* me .... Gen 39:17 6711
mocketh another, do ye so *m* him .... Job 13:9 2048
and after that I have spoken, *m* on .... Job 21:3 3932
I will *m* when your fear cometh............. Prov 1:26 3932
Fools make a *m* at sin........................... Prov 14:9 3887
me into their hand, and they *m* me .... Jer 38:19 5953
saw her, and did *m* at her sabbaths .... Lam 1:7 7832
be far from thee, shall *m* thee................ Eze 22:5 7046
deliver him to the Gentiles to *m*............ Mt 20:19 *1702*

M

And they shall *m* him, and shall	Mk 10:34	1702
all that behold it begin to *m* him	Lk 14:29	1702

MOCKED

one that *m* unto his sons in law	Gen 19:14	6711
the ass, Because thou hast *m* me	Num 22:29	5953
Samson, Behold, thou hast *m* me	Judg 16:10	2048
Samson, Hitherto thou hast *m* me	Judg 16:13	2048
thou hast *m* me these three times,	Judg 16:15	2048
pass at noon, that Elijah *m* them	1Kin 18:27	2048
m him, and said unto him, Go up,	2Kin 2:23	7046
laughed them to scorn, and *m* them	2Chr 30:10	3932
But they *m* the messengers of God,	2Chr 36:16	3931
great indignation, and *m* the Jews	Neh 4:1	3932
I am as one *m* of his neighbour,	Job 12:4	7832
saw that he was *m* of the wise men	Mt 2:16	1702
m him, saying, Hail, King of the	Mt 27:29	1702
And after that they had *m* him	Mt 27:31	1702
And when they had *m* him, they took	Mk 15:20	1702
unto the Gentiles, and shall be *m*	Lk 18:32	1702
And the men that held Jesus *m* him	Lk 22:63	1702
m him, and arrayed him in a	Lk 23:11	1702
And the soldiers also *m* him	Lk 23:36	1702
resurrection of the dead, some *m*	Acts 17:32	5512
God is not *m*	Gal 6:7	3456

MOCKER

Wine is a *m*, strong drink is	Prov 20:1	3887

MOCKERS

Are there not *m* with me	Job 17:2	2049
With hypocritical *m* in feasts	Ps 35:16	3934
Now therefore be ye not *m*	Is 28:22	3887
sat not in the assembly of the *m*	Jer 15:17	7832
should be *m* in the last time	Jude 18	1703

MOCKEST

and when thou *m*, shall no man make	Job 11:3	3932

MOCKETH

or as one man *m* another, do ye so	Job 13:9	2048
He *m* at fear, and is not	Job 39:22	7832
Whoso *m* the poor reproacheth his	Prov 17:5	3932
The eye that *m* at his father, and	Prov 30:17	3932
in derision daily, every one *m* me	Jer 20:7	3932

MOCKING

she had born unto Abraham, *m*	Gen 21:9	6711
heathen, and a *m* to all countries	Eze 22:4	7048
also the chief priests *m* him	Mt 27:41	1702
m said among themselves with the	Mk 15:31	1702
Others *m* said, These men are full	Acts 2:13	5512

MOCKINGS

And others had trial of cruel *m*	Heb 11:36	1701

MODERATELY

hath given you the former rain *m*	Joel 2:23	6666

MODERATION

Let your *m* be known unto all men	Phil 4:5	1933

MODEST

adorn themselves in *m* apparel	1Ti 2:9	2887

MOIST

of grapes, nor eat *m* grapes	Num 6:3	3892

MOISTENED

and his bones are *m* with marrow	Job 21:24	8248

MOISTURE

my *m* is turned into the drought	Ps 32:4	3955
away, because it lacked *m*	Lk 8:6	2429

MOLADAH (mo-la´-dah) *A city in Judah.*

Amam, and Shema, and M,	Josh 15:26	4137
Beer-sheba, or Sheba, and M	Josh 19:2	4137
And they dwelt at Beer-sheba, and M	1Chr 4:28	4137
And at Jeshua, and at M, and at	Neh 11:26	4137

MOLE

lizard, and the snail, and the *m*	Lev 11:30	8580

MOLECH (mo´-lek) *See* MALCHAM, MOLOCH. *An Ammonite god.*

seed pass through the fire to M	Lev 18:21	4432
giveth of his seed unto M	Lev 20:2	4432
he hath given of his seed unto M	Lev 20:3	4432
when he giveth of his seed unto M	Lev 20:4	4432
him, to commit whoredom with M	Lev 20:5	4432
is before Jerusalem, and for M	1Kin 11:7	4432
to pass through the fire to M	2Kin 23:10	4432
to pass through the fire unto M	Jer 32:35	4432

MOLES

for himself to worship, to the *m*	Is 2:20	2661

MOLID (mo´-lid) *A descendant of Jerahmeel.*

and she bare him Ahban, and M	1Chr 2:29	4140

MOLLIFIED

bound up, neither *m* with ointment	Is 1:6	7401

MOLOCH (mo´-loch) *See* MILCHOM, MOLECH. *Same as Molech.*

borne the tabernacle of your M	Amos 5:26	4432
ye took up the tabernacle of M	Acts 7:43	3434

MOLTEN

after he had made it a *m* calf	Ex 32:4	4541
they have made them a *m* calf	Ex 32:8	4541
Thou shalt make thee no *m* gods	Ex 34:17	4541
nor make to yourselves *m* gods	Lev 19:4	4541
and destroy all their *m* images	Num 33:52	4541
they have made them a *m* image	Deut 9:12	4541
God, and had made you a *m* calf	Deut 9:16	4541
that maketh any graven or *m* image	Deut 27:15	4541
make a graven image and a *m* image	Judg 17:3	4541
a graven image and a *m* image	Judg 17:4	4541
and a graven image, and a *m* image,	Judg 18:14	4541
and the teraphim, and the *m* image	Judg 18:17	4541
and the teraphim, and the *m* image	Judg 18:18	4541
he made two chapiters of *m* brass	1Kin 7:16	3332
And he made a *m* sea, ten cubits	1Kin 7:23	3332
the laver were undersetters *m*	1Kin 7:30	3332
and their spokes, were all *m*	1Kin 7:33	3332
m images, to provoke me to anger,	1Kin 14:9	4541
their God, and made them *m* images	2Kin 17:16	4541
Also he made a *m* sea of ten	2Chr 4:2	3332
made also *m* images for Baalim	2Chr 28:2	4541
carved images, and the *m* images	2Chr 34:3	4541
the *m* images, he brake in pieces,	2Chr 34:4	4541
when they had made them a *m* calf	Neh 9:18	4541
brass is *m* out of the stone	Job 28:2	6694
strong, and as a *m* looking glass	Job 37:18	3332
Horeb, and worshipped the *m* image	Ps 106:19	4541
ornament of thy *m* images of gold	Is 30:22	4541
their *m* images are wind and	Is 41:29	5262
images, that say to the *m* images	Is 42:17	4541
or *m* a graven image that is	Is 44:10	5258
my *m* image, hath commanded them	Is 48:5	5262
for his *m* image is falsehood, and	Jer 10:14	5262
for his *m* image is falsehood, and	Jer 51:17	5262
filthiness of it may be *m* in it	Eze 24:11	5413
have made them *m* images of their	Hos 13:2	4541
mountains shall be *m* under him	Mic 1:4	4549
the graven image and the *m* image	Nah 1:14	4541
the *m* image, and a teacher of lies	Hab 2:18	4541

MOMENT

up into the midst of thee in a *m*	Ex 33:5	7281
that I may consume them in a *m*	Num 16:21	7281
that I may consume them as in a *m*	Num 16:45	7281
every morning, and try him every *m*	Job 7:18	7281
joy of the hypocrite but for a *m*	Job 20:5	7281
in a *m* go down to the grave	Job 21:13	7281
In a *m* shall they die, and the	Job 34:20	7281
For his anger endureth but a *m*	Ps 30:5	7281
into desolation, as in a *m*	Ps 73:19	7281
but a lying tongue is but for a *m*	Prov 12:19	7281
thyself as it were for a little *m*	Is 26:20	7281
I will water it every *m*	Is 27:3	7281
come to thee in a *m* in one day	Is 47:9	7281
For a small *m* have I forsaken	Is 54:7	7281
I hid my face from thee for a *m*	Is 54:8	7281
spoiled, and my curtains in a *m*	Jer 4:20	7281
that was overthrown as in a *m*	Lam 4:6	7281
and shall tremble at every *m*	Eze 26:16	7281
and they shall tremble at every *m*	Eze 32:10	7281
of the world in a *m* of time	Lk 4:5	4743
In a *m*, in the twinkling of an	1Cor 15:52	823
affliction, which is but for a *m*	2Cor 4:17	3901

MONEY

or bought with *m* of any stranger	Gen 17:12	3701
and he that is bought with thy *m*	Gen 17:13	3701
all that were bought with his *m*	Gen 17:23	3701
bought with *m* of the stranger,	Gen 17:27	3701
for as much *m* as it is worth he	Gen 23:9	3701
I will give thee *m* for the field	Gen 23:13	3701
current *m* with the merchant	Gen 23:16	3701
and hath quite devoured also our *m*	Gen 31:15	3701
for an hundred pieces of *m*	Gen 33:19	7192
every man's *m* into his sack	Gen 42:25	3701
in the inn, he espied his *m*	Gen 42:27	3701
his brethren, My *m* is restored	Gen 42:28	3701
man's bundle of *m* was in his sack	Gen 42:35	3701
their father saw the bundles of *m*	Gen 42:35	3701
take double *m* in your hand	Gen 43:12	3701
the *m* that was brought again in	Gen 43:12	3701
they took double *m* in their hand	Gen 43:15	3701
Because of the *m* that was	Gen 43:18	3701
every man's *m* was in the mouth of	Gen 43:21	3701

of his sack, our *m* in full weight	Gen 43:21	3701
other *m* have we brought down in	Gen 43:22	3701
tell who put our *m* in our sacks	Gen 43:22	3701
I had your *m*	Gen 43:23	3701
put every man's *m* in his sack's	Gen 44:1	3701
of the youngest, and his corn *m*	Gen 44:2	3701
Behold, the *m*, which we found in	Gen 44:8	3701
Joseph gathered up all the *m* that	Gen 47:14	3701
Joseph brought the *m* into	Gen 47:14	3701
when *m* failed in the land of	Gen 47:15	3701
for the *m* faileth	Gen 47:15	3701
you for your cattle, if *m* fail	Gen 47:16	3701
my lord, how that our *m* is spent	Gen 47:18	3701
servant that is bought for *m*	Ex 12:44	3701
shall she go out free without *m*	Ex 21:11	3701
for he is his *m*	Ex 21:21	3701
there be laid on him a sum of *m*	Ex 21:30	
give *m* unto the owner of them	Ex 21:34	3701
live ox, and divide the *m* of it	Ex 21:35	3701
his neighbour *m* or stuff to keep	Ex 22:7	3701
he shall pay *m* according to the	Ex 22:17	3701
If thou lend *m* to any of my	Ex 22:25	3701
m of the children of Israel	Ex 30:16	3701
priest buy any soul with his *m*	Lev 22:11	3701
not give him thy *m* upon usury	Lev 25:37	3701
of the *m* that he was bought for	Lev 25:51	3701
the *m* of thy estimation unto it	Lev 27:15	3701
shall reckon unto him the *m*	Lev 27:18	3701
the *m* of thy estimation unto it	Lev 27:19	3701
And thou shalt give the *m*,	Num 3:48	3701
m of them that were over and above	Num 3:49	3701
children of Israel took he the *m*	Num 3:50	3701
Moses gave the *m* of them that	Num 3:51	3701
for the *m* of five shekels, after	Num 18:16	3701
Ye shall buy meat of them for *m*	Deut 2:6	3701
also buy water of them for *m*	Deut 2:6	3701
Thou shalt sell me meat for *m*	Deut 2:28	3701
and give me water for *m*, that I	Deut 2:28	3701
Then shalt thou turn it into *m*	Deut 14:25	3701
bind up the *m* in thine hand, and	Deut 14:25	3701
thou shalt bestow that *m* for	Deut 14:26	3701
shalt not sell her at all for *m*	Deut 21:14	3701
usury of *m*, usury of victuals,	Deut 23:19	3701
they took no gain of *m*	Judg 5:19	3701
her, and brought in their hand	Judg 16:18	3701
he restored the *m* unto his mother	Judg 17:4	3701
give thee the worth of it in *m*	1Kin 21:2	3701
him, Give me thy vineyard for *m*	1Kin 21:6	3701
he refused to give thee for *m*	1Kin 21:15	3701
Is it a time to receive *m*	2Kin 5:26	3701
All the *m* of the dedicated things	2Kin 12:4	3701
even the *m* of every one that	2Kin 12:4	3701
the *m* that every man is set at,	2Kin 12:4	3701
all the *m* that cometh into any	2Kin 12:4	3701
no more *m* of your acquaintance	2Kin 12:7	3701
receive no more *m* of the people	2Kin 12:8	3701
the door put therein all the *m*	2Kin 12:9	3701
there was much *m* in the chest	2Kin 12:10	3701
told the *m* that was found in the	2Kin 12:10	3701
And they gave the *m*, being told,	2Kin 12:11	3701
of the *m* that was brought into	2Kin 12:13	3701
the *m* to be bestowed on workmen	2Kin 12:15	3701
The trespass *m* and sin *m* was	2Kin 12:16	3701
Menahem exacted the *m* of Israel	2Kin 15:20	3701
m that was delivered into their	2Kin 22:7	3701
the *m* that was found in the house	2Kin 22:9	3701
he taxed the land to give the *m*	2Kin 23:35	3701
gather of all Israel *m* to repair	2Chr 24:5	3701
they saw that there was much *m*	2Chr 24:11	3701
day, and gathered *m* in abundance	2Chr 24:11	3701
the rest of the *m* before the king	2Chr 24:14	3701
they delivered the *m* that was	2Chr 34:9	3701
when they brought out the *m* that	2Chr 34:14	3701
m that was found in the house of	2Chr 34:17	3701
They gave *m* also unto the masons,	Ezr 3:7	3701
buy speedily with this *m* bullocks	Ezr 7:17	3702
We have borrowed *m* for the king's	Neh 5:4	3701
servants, might exact of them *m*	Neh 5:10	3701
also the hundredth part of the *m*	Neh 5:11	3701
of the sum of the *m* that Haman	Est 4:7	3701
the fruits thereof without *m*	Job 31:39	3701
man also gave him a piece of *m*	Job 42:11	7192
putteth not out his *m* to usury	Ps 15:5	3701
He hath taken a bag of *m* with him	Prov 7:20	3701
is a defence, and *m* is a defence.	Eccl 7:12	3701
but *m* answereth all things	Eccl 10:19	3701
bought me no sweet cane with *m*	Is 43:24	3701
and ye shall be redeemed without *m*	Is 52:3	3701
the waters, and he that hath no *m*	Is 55:1	3701
come, buy wine and milk without *m*	Is 55:1	3701
Wherefore do ye spend *m* for that	Is 55:2	3701

in Anathoth, and weighed him the *m*	Jer 32:9	3701
weighed him the *m* in the balances	Jer 32:10	3701
GOD, Buy thee the field for *m*	Jer 32:25	3701
Men shall buy fields for *m*	Jer 32:44	3701
We have drunken our water for *m*	Lam 5:4	3701
the prophets thereof divine for *m*	Mic 3:11	3701
received tribute *m* came to Peter	Mt 17:24	
thou shalt find a piece of *m*	Mt 17:27	4715
Shew me the tribute *m*	Mt 22:19	3546
in the earth, and hid his lord's *m*	Mt 25:18	694
have put my *m* to the exchangers	Mt 25:27	694
they gave large *m* unto the	Mt 28:12	694
So they took the *m*, and did as	Mt 28:15	694
no bread, no *m* in their purse	Mk 6:8	5475
people cast *m* into the treasury	Mk 12:41	5475
glad, and promised to give him *m*	Mk 14:11	694
scrip, neither bread, neither *m*	Lk 9:3	694
him, to whom he had given the *m*	Lk 19:15	694
not thou my *m* into the bank	Lk 19:23	694
glad, and covenanted to give him *m*	Lk 22:5	694
and the changers of *m* sitting	Jn 2:14	2773
and poured out the changers' *m*	Jn 2:15	2772
land, sold it, and brought the *m*	Acts 4:37	5536
Abraham bought for a sum of *m* of	Acts 7:16	694
was given, he offered them *m*	Acts 8:18	5536
Thy *m* perish with thee, because	Acts 8:20	694
of God may be purchased with *m*	Acts 8:20	5536
He hoped also that *m* should have	Acts 24:26	5536
For the love of *m* is the root of	1Ti 6:10	5365

MONEYCHANGERS

and overthrew the tables of the *m*	Mt 21:12	2855
and overthrew the tables of the *m*	Mk 11:15	2855

MONSTERS

Even the sea *m* draw out the	Lam 4:3	8577

MONTH

of Noah's life, in the second *m*	Gen 7:11	2320
the seventeenth day of the *m*	Gen 7:11	2320
the ark rested in the seventh *m*	Gen 8:4	2320
on the seventeenth day of the *m*	Gen 8:4	2320
continually until the tenth *m*	Gen 8:5	2320
in the tenth *m*, on the first day	Gen 8:5	
on the first day of the *m*	Gen 8:5	2320
and first year, in the first *m*	Gen 8:13	
the first day of the *m*	Gen 8:13	2320
And in the second *m*, on the seven	Gen 8:14	2320
seven and twentieth day of the *m*	Gen 8:14	2320
abode with him the space of a *m*	Gen 29:14	2320
This *m* shall be unto you the	Ex 12:2	2320
be the first *m* of the year to you	Ex 12:2	2320
In the tenth day of this *m* they	Ex 12:3	2320
the fourteenth day of the same *m*	Ex 12:6	2320
In the first *m*, on the fourteenth	Ex 12:18	
fourteenth day of the *m* at even	Ex 12:18	2320
and twentieth day of the *m* at even	Ex 12:18	2320
day came ye out in the *m* Abib	Ex 13:4	2320
shalt keep this service in this *m*	Ex 13:5	2320
m after their departing out of	Ex 16:1	2320
In the third *m*, when the children	Ex 19:1	2320
the time appointed of the *m* Abib	Ex 23:15	2320
thee, in the time of the *m* Abib	Ex 34:18	2320
for in the *m* Abib thou camest out	Ex 34:18	2320
the first *m* shalt thou set up the	Ex 40:2	2320
in the first *m* in the second year	Ex 40:17	2320
on the first day of the *m*	Ex 40:17	2320
that in the seventh *m*, on the	Lev 16:29	2320
m, on the tenth day of the *m*	Lev 16:29	2320
m at even is the LORD's passover	Lev 23:5	2320
same *m* is the feast of unleavened	Lev 23:6	2320
Israel, saying, In the seventh *m*	Lev 23:24	2320
in the first day of the *m*	Lev 23:24	2320
seventh *m* there shall be a day of	Lev 23:27	2320
in the ninth day of the *m* at even	Lev 23:32	2320
seventh *m* shall be the feast of	Lev 23:34	2320
fifteenth day of the seventh *m*	Lev 23:39	2320
celebrate it in the seventh *m*	Lev 23:41	2320
on the tenth day of the seventh *m*	Lev 25:9	2320
if it be from a *m* old even unto	Lev 27:6	2320
on the first day of the second *m*	Num 1:1	2320
on the first day of the second *m*	Num 1:18	2320
every male from a *m* old and upward	Num 3:15	2320
of all the males, from a *m* old	Num 3:22	2320
of all the males, from a *m* old	Num 3:28	2320
of all the males, from a *m* old	Num 3:34	2320
all the males from a *m* old	Num 3:39	2320
children of Israel from a *m* old	Num 3:40	2320
the number of names, from a *m* old	Num 3:43	2320
in the first *m* of the second year	Num 9:1	2320
In the fourteenth day of this *m*	Num 9:3	2320
m at even in the wilderness of	Num 9:5	2320

M

M

so long as I see *M* the Jew .... Est 5:13   4782
king that *M* may be hanged thereon ...... Est 5:14   4782
that *M* had told of Bigthana and .... Est 6:2   4782
hath been done to *M* for this .... Est 6:3   4782
hang *M* on the gallows that he had .... Est 6:4   4782
said, and do even so to *M* the Jew .... Est 6:10   4782
and the horse, and arrayed *M* .... Est 6:11   4782
M came again to the king's gate .... Est 6:12   4782
If *M* be of the seed of the Jews, ... Est 6:13   4782
high, which Haman had made for *M* ..... Est 7:9   4782
that he had prepared for *M* .... Est 7:10   4782
And *M* came before the king .... Est 8:1   4782
from Haman, and gave it unto *M* .... Est 8:2   4782
Esther set *M* over the house of .... Est 8:2   4782
to *M* the Jew, Behold, I have .... Est 8:7   4782
that *M* commanded unto the Jews .... Est 8:9   4782
M went out from the presence of .... Est 8:15   4782
the fear of *M* fell upon them .... Est 9:3   4782
For *M* was great in the king's .... Est 9:4   4782
for this man *M* waxed greater and .... Est 9:4   4782
M wrote these things, and sent .... Est 9:20   4782
as *M* had written unto them .... Est 9:23   4782
M the Jew, wrote with all .... Est 9:29   4782
appointed, according as *M* .... Est 9:31   4782
declaration of the greatness of *M* .... Est 10:2   4782
For *M* the Jew was next unto king .... Est 10:3   4782

MORDECAI'S (*mor'-de-cahees*) *Refers to Mordecai 2.*
the king thereof in *M* name .... Est 2:22   4782
to see whether *M* matters would .... Est 3:4   4782

MORE See APPENDIX.

MOREH (*mo'-reh*)
   1. A place in Ephraim.
of Sichem, unto the plain of *M* .... Gen 12:6   4176
Gilgal, beside the plains of *M* .... Deut 11:30   4176
   2. A place in Issachar.
side of them, by the hill of *M* .... Judg 7:1   4176

MOREOVER See APPENDIX.

MORESHETH See MORASTHITE.

MORESHETH-GATH (*mor'-e-sheth-gath*) See
   MORASTHITE. *A city in Judah.*
shalt thou give presents to *M* .... Mic 1:14   4182

MORIAH (*mo-ri'-ah*) *The Temple Mount.*
and get thee into the land of *M* .... Gen 22:2   4179
the LORD at Jerusalem in mount *M* 2Chr 3:1   4179

MORNING
and the *m* were the first day .... Gen 1:5   1242
the *m* were the second day .... Gen 1:8   1242
and the *m* were the third day .... Gen 1:13   1242
the *m* were the fourth day .... Gen 1:19   1242
and the *m* were the fifth day .... Gen 1:23   1242
and the *m* were the sixth day .... Gen 1:31   1242
And when the *m* arose, then the .... Gen 19:15   7837
the *m* to the place where he stood .... Gen 19:27   1242
Abimelech rose early in the *m* .... Gen 20:8   1242
And Abraham rose up early in the *m* .... Gen 21:14   1242
And Abraham rose up early in the *m* .... Gen 22:3   1242
and they rose up in the *m*, and he .... Gen 24:54   1242
And they rose up betimes in the *m* .... Gen 26:31   1242
And Jacob rose up early in the *m* .... Gen 28:18   1242
And it came to pass, that in the *m* .... Gen 29:25   1242
early in the *m* Laban rose up, and .... Gen 31:55   1242
Joseph came in unto them in the *m* ...... Gen 40:6   1242
it came to pass in the *m* that his .... Gen 41:8   1242
As soon as the *m* was light .... Gen 44:3   1242
in the *m* he shall devour the prey .... Gen 49:27   1242
Get thee unto Pharaoh in the *m* .... Ex 7:15   1242
Moses, Rise up early in the *m* .... Ex 8:20   1242
Moses, Rise up early in the *m* .... Ex 9:13   1242
and when it was *m*, the east wind .... Ex 10:13   1242
nothing of it remain until the *m* .... Ex 12:10   1242
the *m* ye shall burn with fire .... Ex 12:10   1242
the door of his house until the *m* .... Ex 12:22   1242
that in the *m* watch the LORD .... Ex 14:24   1242
his strength when the *m* appeared .... Ex 14:27   1242
And in the *m*, then ye shall see .... Ex 16:7   1242
in the *m* bread to the full .... Ex 16:8   1242
in the *m* ye shall be filled with .... Ex 16:12   1242
in the *m* the dew lay round about .... Ex 16:13   1242
Let no man leave of it till the *m* .... Ex 16:19   1242
of them left of it until the *m* .... Ex 16:20   1242
And they gathered it every *m* .... Ex 16:21   1242
up for you to be kept until the *m* .... Ex 16:23   1242
And they laid it up till the *m* .... Ex 16:24   1242
Moses from the *m* unto the evening ...... Ex 18:13   1242
stand by thee from *m* unto even .... Ex 18:14   1242
to pass on the third day in the *m* .... Ex 19:16   1242
my sacrifice remain until the *m* .... Ex 23:18   1242

LORD, and rose up early in the *m* .... Ex 24:4   1242
from evening to *m* before the LORD .... Ex 27:21   1242
of the bread, remain unto the *m* .... Ex 29:34   1242
lamb thou shalt offer in the *m* .... Ex 29:39   1242
to the meat offering of the *m* .... Ex 29:41   1242
thereon sweet incense every *m* .... Ex 30:7   1242
And be ready in the *m*, and come up ..... Ex 34:2   1242
come up in the *m* unto mount Sinai ...... Ex 34:2   1242
and Moses rose up early in the *m* .... Ex 34:4   1242
the passover be left unto the *m* .... Ex 34:25   1242
unto him free offerings every *m* .... Ex 36:3   1242
the altar all night unto the *m* .... Lev 6:9   1242
shall burn wood on it every *m* .... Lev 6:12   1242
perpetual, half of it in the *m* .... Lev 6:20   1242
not leave any of it until the *m* .... Lev 7:15   1242
the burnt sacrifice of the *m* .... Lev 9:17   1242
with thee all night until the *m* .... Lev 19:13   1242
the *m* before the LORD continually .... Lev 24:3   1242
shall leave none of it unto the *m* .... Num 9:12   1242
appearance of fire, until the *m* .... Num 9:15   1242
cloud abode from even unto the *m* .... Num 9:21   1242
the cloud was taken up in the *m* .... Num 9:21   1242
And they rose up early in the *m* .... Num 14:40   1242
And Balaam rose up in the *m* .... Num 22:13   1242
And Balaam rose up in the *m* .... Num 22:21   1242
lamb shalt thou offer in the *m* .... Num 28:4   1242
as the meat offering of the *m* .... Num 28:8   1242
the burnt offering in the *m* .... Num 28:23   1242
remain all night until the *m* .... Deut 16:4   1242
and thou shalt turn in the *m* .... Deut 16:7   1242
In the *m* thou shalt say, Would .... Deut 28:67   1242
shalt say, Would God it were *m* .... Deut 28:67   1242
And Joshua rose early in the *m* .... Josh 3:1   1242
And Joshua rose early in the *m* .... Josh 6:12   1242
In the *m* therefore ye shall be .... Josh 7:14   1242
So Joshua rose up early in the *m* .... Josh 7:16   1242
And Joshua rose up early in the *m* .... Josh 8:10   1242
of the city arose early in the *m* .... Judg 6:28   1242
put to death whilst it is yet *m* .... Judg 6:31   1242
And it shall be, that in the *m* .... Judg 9:33   1242
all the night, saying, In the *m* .... Judg 16:2   1242
when they arose early in the *m* .... Judg 19:5   1242
he arose early in the *m* on the .... Judg 19:8   1242
her all the night until the *m* .... Judg 19:25   1242
And her lord rose up in the *m* .... Judg 19:27   1242
of Israel rose up in the *m* .... Judg 20:19   1242
even from the *m* until now .... Ruth 2:7   1242
night, and it shall be in the *m* .... Ruth 3:13   1242
lie down until the *m* .... Ruth 3:13   1242
she lay at his feet until the *m* .... Ruth 3:14   1242
And they rose up in the *m* early 1Sa 1:19   1242
And Samuel lay until the *m* 1Sa 3:15   1242
they arose early on the morrow *m* 1Sa 5:4   1242
midst of the host in the *m* watch 1Sa 11:11   1242
and spoil them until the *m* light 1Sa 14:36   1242
rose early to meet Saul in the *m* 1Sa 15:12   1242
And the Philistine drew near *m* 1Sa 17:16   7925
And David rose up early in the *m* 1Sa 17:20   1242
take heed to thyself until the *m* 1Sa 19:2   1242
him, and to slay him in the *m* 1Sa 19:11   1242
And it came to pass in the *m* 1Sa 20:35   1242
m light any that pisseth against 1Sa 25:22   1242
m light any that pisseth against 1Sa 25:34   1242
less or more, until the *m* light 1Sa 25:36   1242
But it came to pass in the *m* 1Sa 25:37   1242
now rise up early in the *m* with 1Sa 29:10   1242
soon as ye be up early in the *m* 1Sa 29:10   1242
rose up early to depart in the *m* 1Sa 29:11   1242
surely then in the *m* the people 2Sa 2:27   1242
And it came to pass in the *m* 2Sa 11:14   1242
by the *m* light there lacked not 2Sa 17:22   1242
he shall be as the light of the *m* 2Sa 23:4   1242
riseth, even a *m* without clouds 2Sa 23:4   1242
For when David was up in the *m* 2Sa 24:11   1242
the *m* even to the time appointed 2Sa 24:15   1242
when I rose in the *m* to give my 1Kin 3:21   1242
when I had considered in the *m* 1Kin 3:21   1242
him bread and flesh in the *m* 1Kin 17:6   1242
of Baal from *m* even until noon 1Kin 18:26   1242
And it came to pass in the *m* 2Kin 3:20   1242
And they rose up early in the *m* 2Kin 3:22   1242
if we tarry till the *m* light 2Kin 7:9   1242
in of the gate until the *m* 2Kin 10:8   1242
And it came to pass in the *m* 2Kin 10:9   1242
altar burn the *m* burnt offering 2Kin 16:15   1242
and when they arose early in the *m* 2Kin 19:35   1242
thereof every *m* pertained to them 1Chr 9:27   1242
the burnt offering continually *m* 1Chr 16:40   1242
And to stand every *m* to thank 1Chr 23:30   1242
and for the burnt offerings *m* 2Chr 2:4   1242
they burn unto the LORD every *m* 2Chr 13:11   1242

And they rose early in the *m*	2Chr 20:20	1242
offerings, to wit, for the *m*	2Chr 31:3	1242
the LORD, even burnt offerings *m*	Ezr 3:3	1242
of the *m* till the stars appeared	Neh 4:21	7837
gate from the *m* until midday	Neh 8:3	216
them, and rose up early in the *m*	Job 1:5	1242
are destroyed from *m* to evening	Job 4:20	1242
thou shouldest visit him every *m*	Job 7:18	1242
and thou shalt seek me in the *m*	Job 7:21	7836
forth, thou shalt be as the *m*	Job 11:17	1242
For the *m* is to them even as the	Job 24:17	1242
When the *m* stars sang together,	Job 38:7	1242
commanded the *m* since my days	Job 38:12	1242
are like the eyelids of the *m*	Job 41:18	7837
My voice shalt thou hear in the *m*	Ps 5:3	1242
in the *m* will I direct my prayer	Ps 5:3	1242
a night, but joy cometh in the *m*	Ps 30:5	1242
have dominion over them in the *m*	Ps 49:14	1242
Evening, and *m*, and at noon, will I	Ps 55:17	1242
sing aloud of thy mercy in the *m*	Ps 59:16	1242
makest the outgoings of the *m*	Ps 65:8	1242
plagued, and chastened every *m*	Ps 73:14	1242
in the *m* shall my prayer prevent	Ps 88:13	1242
in the *m* they are like grass	Ps 90:5	1242
In the *m* it flourisheth, and	Ps 90:6	1242
forth thy lovingkindness in the *m*	Ps 92:2	1242
holiness from the womb of the *m*	Ps 110:3	4891
I prevented the dawning of the *m*	Ps 119:147	
than they that watch for the *m*	Ps 130:6	1242
than they that watch for the *m*	Ps 130:6	1242
If I take the wings of the *m*	Ps 139:9	7837
hear thy lovingkindness in the *m*	Ps 143:8	1242
take our fill of love until the *m*	Prov 7:18	1242
loud voice, rising early in the *m*	Prov 27:14	1242
and thy princes eat in the *m*	Eccl 10:16	1242
In the *m* sow thy seed, and in the	Eccl 11:6	1242
she that looketh forth as the *m*	Song 6:10	7837
them that rise up early in the *m*	Is 5:11	1242
heaven, O Lucifer, son of the *m*	Is 14:12	7837
in the *m* shalt thou make thy seed	Is 17:11	1242
and before the *m* he is not	Is 17:14	1242
The *m* cometh, and also the night	Is 21:12	1242
for *m* by *m* shall it pass	Is 28:19	1242
be thou their arm every *m*	Is 33:2	1242
and when they arose early in the *m*	Is 37:36	1242
I reckoned till *m*, that, as a	Is 38:13	1242
he wakeneth *m* by *m*, he	Is 50:4	1242
thy light break forth as the *m*	Is 58:8	7837
They were as fed horses in the *m*	Jer 5:8	7904
and let him hear the cry in the *m*	Jer 20:16	1242
Execute judgment in the *m*	Jer 21:12	1242
They are new every *m*	Lam 3:23	1242
The *m* is come unto thee, O thou	Eze 7:7	6843
the *m* is gone forth	Eze 7:10	6843
in the *m* came the word of the	Eze 12:8	1242
I spake unto the people in the *m*	Eze 24:18	1242
I did in the *m* as I was commanded	Eze 24:18	1242
until he came to me in the *m*	Eze 33:22	1242
thou shalt prepare it every *m*	Eze 46:13	1242
a meat offering for it every *m*	Eze 46:14	1242
every *m* for a continual burnt	Eze 46:15	1242
king arose very early in the *m*	Dan 6:19	5053
the *m* which was told is true	Dan 8:26	1242
going forth is prepared as the *m*	Hos 6:3	7837
for your goodness is as a *m* cloud	Hos 6:4	1242
in the *m* it burneth as a flaming	Hos 7:6	1242
in a *m* shall the king of Israel	Hos 10:15	7837
they shall be as the *m* cloud	Hos 13:3	1242
as the *m* spread upon the	Joel 2:2	7837
and bring your sacrifices every *m*	Amos 4:4	1242
that maketh the *m* darkness	Amos 4:13	7837
the shadow of death into the *m*	Amos 5:8	1242
worm when the *m* rose the next day	Jonah 4:7	7837
when the *m* is light, they	Mic 2:1	1242
every *m* doth he bring his	Zeph 3:5	1242
And in the *m*, It will be foul	Mt 16:3	4404
the *m* to hire labourers into his	Mt 20:1	
Now in the *m* as he returned into	Mt 21:18	4405
When the *m* was come, all the	Mt 27:1	4405
And in the *m*, rising up a great	Mk 1:35	4404
And in the *m*, as they passed by,	Mk 11:20	4404
at the cockcrowing, or in the *m*	Mk 13:35	4404
straightway in the *m* the chief	Mk 15:1	4404
very early in the *m* the first day	Mk 16:2	
in the *m* to him in the temple	Lk 21:38	
of the week, very early in the *m*	Lk 24:1	
And early in the *m* he came	Jn 8:1	
early in the *m* he came again into	Jn 8:2	
But when the *m* was now come	Jn 21:4	4405
into the temple early in the *m*	Acts 5:21	
the prophets, from *m* till evening	Acts 28:23	4404

And I will give him the *m* star	Rev 2:28	4407
of David, and the bright and *m* star	Rev 22:16	3720

MORROW

And it came to pass on the *m*	Gen 19:34	4283
And he said, To *m*	Ex 8:10	4279
to *m* shall this sign be	Ex 8:23	4279
and from his people, to *m*	Ex 8:29	4279
To *m* the LORD shall do this thing	Ex 9:5	4279
the LORD did that thing on the *m*	Ex 9:6	4283
to *m* about this time I will cause	Ex 9:18	4279
to *m* will I bring the locusts	Ex 10:4	4279
To *m* is the rest of the holy	Ex 16:23	4279
to *m* I will stand on the top of	Ex 17:9	4279
And it came to pass on the *m*	Ex 18:13	4283
and sanctify them to day and to *m*	Ex 19:10	4279
To *m* is a feast to the LORD	Ex 32:5	4279
And they rose up early on the *m*	Ex 32:6	4283
And it came to pass on the *m*	Ex 32:30	4283
on the *m* also the remainder of it	Lev 7:16	4283
same day ye offer it, and on the *m*	Lev 19:6	4283
leave none of it until the *m*	Lev 22:30	1242
on the *m* after the sabbath the	Lev 23:11	4283
you from the *m* after the sabbath	Lev 23:15	4283
Even unto the *m* after the seventh	Lev 23:16	4283
Sanctify yourselves against to *m*	Num 11:18	4279
) To *m* turn you, and get you into	Num 14:25	4279
Even to *m* the LORD will shew who	Num 16:5	1242
in them before the LORD to *m*	Num 16:7	4279
thou, and they, and Aaron, to *m*	Num 16:16	4279
But on the *m* all the congregation	Num 16:41	4283
that on the *m* Moses went into the	Num 17:8	4283
And it came to pass on the *m*	Num 22:41	1242
on the *m* after the passover the	Num 33:3	4283
for to *m* the LORD will do wonders	Josh 3:5	4279
land on the *m* after the passover	Josh 5:11	4283
the manna ceased on the *m* after	Josh 5:12	4283
Sanctify yourselves against to *m*	Josh 7:13	4279
for to *m* about this time will I	Josh 11:6	4279
that to *m* he will be wroth with	Josh 22:18	4279
for he rose up early on the *m*	Judg 6:38	4283
And it came to pass on the *m*	Judg 9:42	4283
to *m* get you early on your way,	Judg 19:9	4279
for to *m* I will deliver them into	Judg 20:28	4279
And it came to pass on the *m*	Judg 21:4	4283
of Ashdod arose early on the *m*	1Sa 5:3	4283
they arose early on the *m* morning	1Sa 5:4	4283
To *m* about this time I will send	1Sa 9:16	4279
to *m* I will let thee go, and will	1Sa 9:19	1242
the men of Jabesh-gilead, To *m*	1Sa 11:9	4279
To *m* we will come out unto you,	1Sa 11:10	4279
And it was so on the *m*, that Saul	1Sa 11:11	4283
And it came to pass on the *m*	1Sa 18:10	4283
night, to *m* thou shalt be slain	1Sa 19:11	4279
to *m* is the new moon, and I should	1Sa 20:5	4279
my father about to *m* any time	1Sa 20:12	4279
to David, To *m* is the new moon	1Sa 20:18	4279
And it came to pass on the *m*	1Sa 20:27	4283
to *m* shalt thou and thy sons be	1Sa 28:19	4279
And it came to pass on the *m*	1Sa 31:8	4283
to *m* I will let thee depart	2Sa 11:12	4279
in Jerusalem that day, and the *m*	2Sa 11:12	4283
of them by to *m* about this time	1Kin 19:2	4279
unto thee to *m* about this time	1Kin 20:6	4279
day, and we will eat my son to *m*	2Kin 6:28	4279
To *m* about this time shall a	2Kin 7:1	4279
shall be to *m* about this time in	2Kin 7:18	4279
And it came to pass on the *m*	2Kin 8:15	4283
me to Jezreel by to *m* this time	2Kin 10:6	4279
And it came to pass on the *m*	1Chr 10:8	4283
on the *m* after that day, even a	1Chr 29:21	4283
To *m* go ye down against them	2Chr 20:16	4279
to *m* go out against them	2Chr 20:17	4279
on the *m* she returned into the	Est 2:14	1242
I will do to *m* as the king hath	Est 5:8	4279
to *m* am I invited unto her also	Est 5:12	4279
to *m* speak thou unto the king	Est 5:14	1242
which are in Shushan to do to *m*	Est 9:13	4279
come again, and to *m* I will give	Prov 3:28	4279
Boast not thyself of to *m*	Prov 27:1	4279
for to *m* we shall die	Is 22:13	4279
to *m* shall be as this day, and	Is 56:12	4279
And it came to pass on the *m*	Jer 20:3	4283
gnaw not the bones till the *m*	Zeph 3:3	1242
to *m* is cast into the oven, shall	Mt 6:30	839
therefore no thought for the *m*	Mt 6:34	839
for the *m* shall take thought for	Mt 6:34	839
And on the *m*, when they were come	Mk 11:12	1887
on the *m* when he departed, he	Lk 10:35	839
to *m* is cast into the oven	Lk 12:28	839
and I do cures to day and to *m*	Lk 13:32	839

M

I must walk to day, and to *m*	Lk 13:33	*839*
And it came to pass on the *m*	Acts 4:5	*839*
On the *m*, as they went on their	Acts 10:9	*1887*
on the *m* Peter went away with	Acts 10:23	*1887*
the *m* after they entered into	Acts 10:24	*1887*
them, ready to depart on the *m*	Acts 20:7	*1887*
On the *m*, because he would have	Acts 22:30	*1887*
he bring him down unto you to *m*	Acts 23:15	*839*
down Paul to *m* into the council	Acts 23:20	*839*
On the *m* they left the horsemen	Acts 23:32	*1887*
without any delay on the *m* I sat	Acts 25:17	*1836*
To *m*, said he, thou shalt hear	Acts 25:22	*839*
And on the *m*, when Agrippa was	Acts 25:23	*1887*
for to *m* we die	1Cor 15:32	*839*
To day or to *m* we will go into	Jas 4:13	*839*
know not what shall be on the *m*	Jas 4:14	*839*

MORSEL

And I will fetch a *m* of bread	Gen 18:5	*6595*
thine heart with a *m* of bread	Judg 19:5	*6595*
and dip thy *m* in the vinegar	Ruth 2:14	*6595*
a *m* of bread, and shall say, Put	1Sa 2:36	*3603*
let me set a *m* of bread before	1Sa 28:22	*6595*
a *m* of bread in thine hand	1Kin 17:11	*6595*
Or have eaten my *m* myself alone	Job 31:17	*6595*
Better is a dry *m*, and quietness	Prov 17:1	*6595*
The *m* which thou hast eaten shalt	Prov 23:8	*6595*
who for one *m* of meat sold his	Heb 12:16	*1035*

MORSELS

He casteth forth his ice like *m*	Ps 147:17	*6595*

MORTAL

Shall *m* man be more just than God	Job 4:17	*582*
therefore reign in your *m* body	Rom 6:12	*2349*
your *m* bodies by his Spirit that	Rom 8:11	*2349*
this *m* must put on immortality	1Cor 15:53	*2349*
and this *m* shall have put on	1Cor 15:54	*2349*
be made manifest in our *m* flesh	2Cor 4:11	*2349*

MORTALITY

that *m* might be swallowed up of	2Cor 5:4	*2349*

MORTALLY

smite him *m* that he die, and	Deut 19:11	*5315*

MORTAR

it in mills, or beat it in a *m*	Num 11:8	*4085*
in a *m* among wheat with a pestle	Prov 27:22	*4388*

MORTER

stone, and slime had they for *m*	Gen 11:3	*2563*
bitter with hard bondage, in *m*	Ex 1:14	*2563*
and he shall take other *m*, and	Lev 14:42	*6083*
and all the *m* of the house	Lev 14:45	*6083*
shall come upon princes as upon *m*	Is 41:25	*2563*
daubed it with untempered *m*	Eze 13:10	
which daub it with untempered *m*	Eze 13:11	
ye have daubed it with untempered *m*	Eze 13:14	
have daubed it with untempered *m*	Eze 13:15	
daubed them with untempered *m*	Eze 22:28	
go into clay, and tread the *m*	Nah 3:14	*2563*

MORTGAGED

We have *m* our lands, vineyards,	Neh 5:3	*6148*

MORTIFY

Spirit do *m* the deeds of the body	Rom 8:13	*2289*
M therefore your members which	Col 3:5	*3499*

MOSERA (mo-se'-rah) See MOSEROTH. *Where Aaron was buried.*

of the children of Jaakan to *M*	Deut 10:6	*4149*

MOSERAH See MOSERA.

MOSEROTH (mo-se'-roth) See MOSERA. *An Israelite encampment in the wilderness.*

from Hashmonah, and encamped at *M*.	Num 33:30	*4149*
And they departed from *M*, and	Num 33:31	*4149*

MOSES (mo'-zez) See MOSES'. *Led Israel out of Egypt.*

And she called his name *M*	Ex 2:10	*4872*
when *M* was grown, that he went	Ex 2:11	*4872*
M feared, and said, Surely this	Ex 2:14	*4872*
this thing, he sought to slay *M*	Ex 2:15	*4872*
But *M* fled from the face of	Ex 2:15	*4872*
but *M* stood up and helped them, and	Ex 2:17	*4872*
M was content to dwell with the	Ex 2:21	*4872*
he gave *M* Zipporah his daughter	Ex 2:21	*4872*
Now *M* kept the flock of Jethro	Ex 3:1	*4872*
M said, I will now turn aside, and	Ex 3:3	*4872*
of the bush, and said, *M*, *M*	Ex 3:4	*4872*
And *M* hid his face	Ex 3:6	*4872*
M said unto God, Who am I, that I	Ex 3:11	*4872*
M said unto God, Behold, when I	Ex 3:13	*4872*
And God said unto *M*, I AM THAT I	Ex 3:14	*4872*

And God said moreover unto *M*	Ex 3:15	*4872*
M answered and said, But, behold,	Ex 4:1	*4872*
and *M* fled from before it	Ex 4:3	*4872*
And the LORD said unto *M*, Put	Ex 4:4	*4872*
M said unto the LORD, O my Lord,	Ex 4:10	*4872*
of the LORD was kindled against *M*	Ex 4:14	*4872*
M went and returned to Jethro his	Ex 4:18	*4872*
And Jethro said to *M*, Go in peace	Ex 4:18	*4872*
And the LORD said unto *M* in Midian	Ex 4:19	*4872*
M took his wife and his sons, and	Ex 4:20	*4872*
M took the rod of God in his hand	Ex 4:20	*4872*
And the LORD said unto *M*, When	Ex 4:21	*4872*
Go into the wilderness to meet *M*	Ex 4:27	*4872*
M told Aaron all the words of the	Ex 4:28	*4872*
And *M* and Aaron went and gathered	Ex 4:29	*4872*
which the LORD had spoken unto *M*	Ex 4:30	*4872*
And afterward *M* and Aaron went in,	Ex 5:1	*4872*
unto them, Wherefore do ye, *M*	Ex 5:4	*4872*
And they met *M* and Aaron, who stood	Ex 5:20	*4872*
M returned unto the LORD, and said	Ex 5:22	*4872*
Then the LORD said unto *M*	Ex 6:1	*4872*
And God spake unto *M*, and said unto	Ex 6:2	*4872*
M spake so unto the children of	Ex 6:9	*4872*
not unto *M* for anguish of spirit	Ex 6:9	*4872*
And the LORD spake unto *M*, saying,	Ex 6:10	*4872*
M spake before the LORD, saying,	Ex 6:12	*4872*
And the LORD spake unto *M* and unto	Ex 6:13	*4872*
and she bare him Aaron and *M*	Ex 6:20	*4872*
These are that Aaron and *M*	Ex 6:26	*4872*
these are that *M* and Aaron	Ex 6:27	*4872*
spake unto *M* in the land of Egypt	Ex 6:28	*4872*
That the LORD spake unto *M*	Ex 6:29	*4872*
M said before the LORD, Behold, I	Ex 6:30	*4872*
And the LORD said unto *M*, See, I	Ex 7:1	*4872*
And *M* and Aaron did as the LORD	Ex 7:6	*4872*
M was fourscore years old, and	Ex 7:7	*4872*
And the LORD spake unto *M* and unto	Ex 7:8	*4872*
And *M* and Aaron went in unto	Ex 7:10	*4872*
And the LORD said unto *M*,	Ex 7:14	*4872*
And the LORD spake unto *M*, Say	Ex 7:19	*4872*
And *M* and Aaron did so, as the LORD	Ex 7:20	*4872*
And the LORD said unto *M*, Go unto	Ex 8:1	*4872*
And the LORD said unto *M*, Say	Ex 8:5	*4872*
Then Pharaoh called for *M*	Ex 8:8	*4872*
M said unto Pharaoh, Glory over	Ex 8:9	*4872*
And *M* and Aaron went out from	Ex 8:12	*4872*
M cried unto the LORD because of	Ex 8:12	*4872*
did according to the word of *M*	Ex 8:13	*4872*
And the LORD said unto *M*, Say unto	Ex 8:16	*4872*
And the LORD said unto *M*, Rise up	Ex 8:20	*4872*
And Pharaoh called for *M* and for	Ex 8:25	*4872*
M said, It is not meet so to do	Ex 8:26	*4872*
M said, Behold, I go out from	Ex 8:29	*4872*
M went out from Pharaoh, and	Ex 8:30	*4872*
did according to the word of *M*	Ex 8:31	*4872*
Then the LORD said unto *M*	Ex 9:1	*4872*
And the LORD said unto *M* and unto	Ex 9:8	*4872*
let *M* sprinkle it toward the	Ex 9:8	*4872*
M sprinkled it up toward heaven	Ex 9:10	*4872*
before *M* because of the boils	Ex 9:11	*4872*
as the LORD had spoken unto *M*	Ex 9:12	*4872*
And the LORD said unto *M*, Rise up	Ex 9:13	*4872*
And the LORD said unto *M*, Stretch	Ex 9:22	*4872*
M stretched forth his rod toward	Ex 9:23	*4872*
And Pharaoh sent, and called for *M*	Ex 9:27	*4872*
M said unto him, As soon as I am	Ex 9:29	*4872*
M went out of the city from	Ex 9:33	*4872*
as the LORD had spoken by *M*	Ex 9:35	*4872*
And the LORD said unto *M*, Go in	Ex 10:1	*4872*
And *M* and Aaron came in unto	Ex 10:3	*4872*
And *M* and Aaron were brought again	Ex 10:8	*4872*
M said, We will go with our young	Ex 10:9	*4872*
And the LORD said unto *M*, Stretch	Ex 10:12	*4872*
M stretched forth his rod over	Ex 10:13	*4872*
Then Pharaoh called for *M*	Ex 10:16	*4872*
And the LORD said unto *M*, Stretch	Ex 10:21	*4872*
M stretched forth his hand toward	Ex 10:22	*4872*
And Pharaoh called unto *M*, and said	Ex 10:24	*4872*
M said, Thou must give us also	Ex 10:25	*4872*
M said, Thou hast spoken well, I	Ex 10:29	*4872*
And the LORD said unto *M*, Yet will	Ex 11:1	*4872*
Moreover the man *M* was very great	Ex 11:3	*4872*
M said, Thus saith the LORD,	Ex 11:4	*4872*
And the LORD said unto *M*, Pharaoh	Ex 11:9	*4872*
And *M* and Aaron did all these	Ex 11:10	*4872*
the LORD spake unto *M* and Aaron	Ex 12:1	*4872*
Then *M* called for all the elders	Ex 12:21	*4872*
did as the LORD had commanded *M*	Ex 12:28	*4872*
And he called for *M* and Aaron by	Ex 12:31	*4872*
did according to the word of *M*	Ex 12:35	*4872*

And the LORD said unto *M* and Aaron,...	Ex 12:43	4872
the LORD commanded *M* and Aaron,......	Ex 12:50	4872
And the LORD spake unto *M*, saying,......	Ex 13:1	4872
M said unto the people, Remember	Ex 13:3	4872
M took the bones of Joseph with	Ex 13:19	4872
And the LORD spake unto *M*, saying,......	Ex 14:1	4872
And they said unto *M*, Because	Ex 14:11	4872
M said unto the people, Fear ye	Ex 14:13	4872
And the LORD said unto *M*,................	Ex 14:15	4872
M stretched out his hand over the	Ex 14:21	4872
And the LORD said unto *M*, Stretch	Ex 14:26	4872
M stretched forth his hand over	Ex 14:27	4872
the LORD, and his servant *M*	Ex 14:31	4872
Then sang *M* and the children of	Ex 15:1	4872
So *M* brought Israel from the Red........	Ex 15:22	4872
And the people murmured against *M*	Ex 15:24	4872
of Israel murmured against *M*.............	Ex 16:2	4872
Then said the LORD unto *M*	Ex 16:4	4872
And *M* and Aaron said unto all the	Ex 16:6	4872
M said, This shall be, when the	Ex 16:8	4872
M spake unto Aaron, Say unto all	Ex 16:9	4872
And the LORD spake unto *M*, saying,......	Ex 16:11	4872
M said unto them, This is the	Ex 16:15	4872
M said, Let no man leave of it	Ex 16:19	4872
they hearkened not unto *M*	Ex 16:20	4872
and *M* was wroth with them	Ex 16:20	4872
the congregation came and told *M*	Ex 16:22	4872
it up till the morning, as *M* bade	Ex 16:24	4872
And *M* said, Eat that to day	Ex 16:25	4872
And the LORD said unto *M*, How long	Ex 16:28	4872
M said, This is the thing which	Ex 16:32	4872
M said unto Aaron, Take a pot, and	Ex 16:33	4872
As the LORD commanded *M*, so Aaron	Ex 16:34	4872
the people did chide with *M*	Ex 17:2	4872
M said unto them, Why chide ye	Ex 17:2	4872
and the people murmured against *M*	Ex 17:3	4872
M cried unto the LORD, saying, ...	Ex 17:4	4872
And the LORD said unto *M*, Go on..........	Ex 17:5	4872
M did so in the sight of the	Ex 17:6	4872
M said unto Joshua, Choose us out	Ex 17:9	4872
Joshua did as *M* had said to him	Ex 17:10	4872
and *M*, Aaron, and Hur went up to	Ex 17:10	4872
when *M* held up his hand, that	Ex 17:11	4872
And the LORD said unto *M*, Write	Ex 17:14	4872
M built an altar, and called the...........	Ex 17:15	4872
of all that God had done for *M*...........	Ex 18:1	4872
sons and his wife unto *M* into the........	Ex 18:5	4872
And he said unto *M*, I thy father.........	Ex 18:6	4872
M went out to meet his father in	Ex 18:7	4872
M told his father in law all that	Ex 18:8	4872
that *M* sat to judge the people	Ex 18:13	4872
the people stood by *M* from the	Ex 18:13	4872
M said unto his father in law,.............	Ex 18:15	4872
So *M* hearkened to the voice of	Ex 18:24	4872
M chose able men out of all	Ex 18:25	4872
hard causes they brought unto *M*...........	Ex 18:26	4872
M let his father in law depart.............	Ex 18:27	4872
M went up unto God, and the LORD	Ex 19:3	4872
M came and called for the elders	Ex 19:7	4872
M returned the words of the	Ex 19:8	4872
And the LORD said unto *M*, Lo, I	Ex 19:9	4872
M told the words of the people	Ex 19:9	4872
And the LORD said unto *M*, Go unto	Ex 19:10	4872
M went down from the mount unto	Ex 19:14	4872
M brought forth the people out of..........	Ex 19:17	4872
M spake, and God answered him by a ...	Ex 19:19	4872
the LORD called *M* up to the top............	Ex 19:20	4872
and *M* went up..................................	Ex 19:20	4872
And the LORD said unto *M*, Go down,......	Ex 19:21	4872
M said unto the LORD, The people	Ex 19:23	4872
So *M* went down unto the people, ...	Ex 19:25	4872
And they said unto *M*, Speak thou	Ex 20:19	4872
M said unto the people, Fear not	Ex 20:20	4872
M drew near unto the thick.................	Ex 20:21	4872
And the LORD said unto *M*, Thus	Ex 20:22	4872
And he said unto *M*, Come up unto	Ex 24:1	4872
M alone shall come near the LORD.........	Ex 24:2	4872
M came and told the people all the	Ex 24:3	4872
M wrote all the words of the LORD........	Ex 24:4	4872
M took half of the blood, and put	Ex 24:6	4872
M took the blood, and sprinkled it	Ex 24:8	4872
Then went up *M*, and Aaron, Nadab, ...	Ex 24:9	4872
And the LORD said unto *M*, Come up.......	Ex 24:12	4872
M rose up, and his minister Joshua	Ex 24:13	4872
M went up into the mount of God	Ex 24:13	4872
M went up into the mount, and a	Ex 24:15	4872
M out of the midst of the cloud	Ex 24:16	4872
M went into the midst of the	Ex 24:18	4872
M was in the mount forty days and	Ex 24:18	4872
And the LORD spake unto *M*, saying, ...	Ex 25:1	4872
And the LORD spake unto *M*, saying, ...	Ex 30:11	4872
And the LORD spake unto *M*, saying, ...	Ex 30:17	4872
Moreover the LORD spake unto *M*	Ex 30:22	4872
And the LORD said unto *M*, Take	Ex 30:34	4872
And the LORD spake unto *M*, saying, ...	Ex 31:1	4872
And the LORD spake unto *M*, saying, ...	Ex 31:12	4872
And he gave unto *M*, when he had	Ex 31:18	4872
when the people saw that *M*	Ex 32:1	4872
for as for this *M*, the man that............	Ex 32:1	4872
And the LORD said unto *M*, Go, get........	Ex 32:7	4872
And the LORD said unto *M*, I have	Ex 32:9	4872
M besought the LORD his God, and	Ex 32:11	4872
M turned, and went down from the	Ex 32:15	4872
as they shouted, he said unto *M*	Ex 32:17	4872
M said unto Aaron, What did this	Ex 32:21	4872
for as for this *M*, the man that..............	Ex 32:23	4872
when *M* saw that the people were	Ex 32:25	4872
Then *M* stood in the gate of the............	Ex 32:26	4872
did according to the word of *M*	Ex 32:28	4872
For *M* had said, Consecrate	Ex 32:29	4872
that *M* said unto the people, Ye	Ex 32:30	4872
M returned unto the LORD, and said......	Ex 32:31	4872
And the LORD said unto *M*,...................	Ex 32:33	4872
And the LORD said unto *M*, Depart, ...	Ex 33:1	4872
For the LORD had said unto *M*...............	Ex 33:5	4872
M took the tabernacle, and pitched........	Ex 33:7	4872
to pass, when *M* went out unto the	Ex 33:8	4872
his tent door, and looked after *M*	Ex 33:8	4872
as *M* entered into the tabernacle, ...	Ex 33:9	4872
and the LORD talked with *M*.................	Ex 33:9	4872
LORD spake unto *M* face to face............	Ex 33:11	4872
M said unto the LORD, See, thou	Ex 33:12	4872
And the LORD said unto *M*, I will	Ex 33:17	4872
And the LORD said unto *M*, Hew thee	Ex 34:1	4872
M rose up early in the morning, ...	Ex 34:4	4872
M made haste, and bowed his head	Ex 34:8	4872
And the LORD said unto *M*, Write	Ex 34:27	4872
when *M* came down from mount Sinai	Ex 34:29	4872
that *M* wist not that the skin of	Ex 34:29	4872
all the children of Israel saw *M*	Ex 34:30	4872
And *M* called unto them	Ex 34:31	4872
and *M* talked with them	Ex 34:31	4872
till *M* had done speaking with	Ex 34:33	4872
But when *M* went in before the	Ex 34:34	4872
of Israel saw the face of *M*	Ex 34:35	4872
M put the vail upon his face	Ex 34:35	4872
M gathered all the congregation	Ex 35:1	4872
M spake unto all the congregation	Ex 35:4	4872
departed from the presence of *M*...........	Ex 35:20	4872
to be made by the hand of *M*	Ex 35:29	4872
M said unto the children of	Ex 35:30	4872
M called Bezaleel and Aholiab, and	Ex 36:2	4872
received of *M* all the offering	Ex 36:3	4872
And they spake unto *M*, saying, The	Ex 36:5	4872
M gave commandment, and they	Ex 36:6	4872
according to the commandment of *M*.......	Ex 38:21	4872
all that the LORD commanded *M*	Ex 38:22	4872
as the LORD commanded *M*...................	Ex 39:1	4872
as the LORD commanded *M*...................	Ex 39:5	4872
as the LORD commanded *M*...................	Ex 39:7	4872
as the LORD commanded *M*...................	Ex 39:21	4872
as the LORD commanded *M*...................	Ex 39:26	4872
as the LORD commanded *M*...................	Ex 39:29	4872
as the LORD commanded *M*...................	Ex 39:31	4872
to all that the LORD commanded *M*	Ex 39:32	4872
brought the tabernacle unto *M*.............	Ex 39:33	4872
to all that the LORD commanded *M*	Ex 39:42	4872
M did look upon all the work	Ex 39:43	4872
and *M* blessed them...........................	Ex 39:43	4872
And the LORD spake unto *M*, saying, ...	Ex 40:1	4872
Thus did *M*.....................................	Ex 40:16	4872
M reared up the tabernacle, and............	Ex 40:18	4872
as the LORD commanded *M*...................	Ex 40:19	4872
as the LORD commanded *M*...................	Ex 40:21	4872
as the LORD had commanded *M*	Ex 40:23	4872
as the LORD commanded *M*...................	Ex 40:25	4872
as the LORD commanded *M*...................	Ex 40:27	4872
as the LORD commanded *M*...................	Ex 40:29	4872
M and Aaron and his sons washed	Ex 40:31	4872
as the LORD commanded *M*...................	Ex 40:32	4872
So *M* finished the work.......................	Ex 40:33	4872
M was not able to enter into the	Ex 40:35	4872
And the LORD called unto *M*	Lev 1:1	4872
And the LORD spake unto *M*, saying, ...	Lev 4:1	4872
And the LORD spake unto *M*, saying, ...	Lev 5:14	4872
And the LORD spake unto *M*, saying, ...	Lev 6:1	4872
And the LORD spake unto *M*, saying, ...	Lev 6:8	4872
And the LORD spake unto *M*, saying, ...	Lev 6:19	4872
And the LORD spake unto *M*, saying, ...	Lev 6:24	4872

M

And the LORD spake unto *M*, saying,	Lev 7:22	4872
And the LORD spake unto *M*, saying,	Lev 7:28	4872
LORD commanded *M* in mount Sinai	Lev 7:38	4872
And the LORD spake unto *M*, saying,	Lev 8:1	4872
M did as the LORD commanded him	Lev 8:4	4872
M said unto the congregation,	Lev 8:5	4872
M brought Aaron and his sons, and	Lev 8:6	4872
as the LORD commanded *M*	Lev 8:9	4872
M took the anointing oil, and	Lev 8:10	4872
M brought Aaron's sons, and put	Lev 8:13	4872
as the LORD commanded *M*	Lev 8:13	4872
M took the blood, and put it upon	Lev 8:15	4872
M burned it upon the altar	Lev 8:16	4872
as the LORD commanded *M*	Lev 8:17	4872
M sprinkled the blood upon the	Lev 8:19	4872
M burnt the head, and the pieces,	Lev 8:20	4872
M burnt the whole ram upon the	Lev 8:21	4872
as the LORD commanded *M*	Lev 8:21	4872
M took of the blood of it, and put	Lev 8:23	4872
M put of the blood upon the tip	Lev 8:24	4872
M sprinkled the blood upon the	Lev 8:24	4872
M took them from off their hands,	Lev 8:28	4872
M took the breast, and waved it	Lev 8:29	4872
as the LORD commanded *M*	Lev 8:29	4872
M took of the anointing oil, and	Lev 8:30	4872
M said unto Aaron and to his sons,	Lev 8:31	4872
LORD commanded by the hand of *M*	Lev 8:36	4872
that *M* called Aaron and his sons,	Lev 9:1	4872
they brought that which *M*	Lev 9:5	4872
M said, This is the thing which	Lev 9:6	4872
M said unto Aaron, Go unto the	Lev 9:7	4872
as the LORD commanded *M*	Lev 9:10	4872
as *M* commanded	Lev 9:21	4872
And *M* and Aaron went into the	Lev 9:23	4872
Then *M* said unto Aaron, This is	Lev 10:3	4872
M called Mishael and Elzaphan, and	Lev 10:4	4872
as *M* had said	Lev 10:5	4872
M said unto Aaron, and unto	Lev 10:6	4872
did according to the word of *M*	Lev 10:7	4872
spoken unto them by the hand of *M*	Lev 10:11	4872
M spake unto Aaron, and unto	Lev 10:12	4872
M diligently sought the goat of	Lev 10:16	4872
And Aaron said unto *M*, Behold,	Lev 10:19	4872
when *M* heard that, he was content	Lev 10:20	4872
And the LORD spake unto *M* and to	Lev 11:1	4872
And the LORD spake unto *M*, saying,	Lev 12:1	4872
the LORD spake unto *M* and Aaron	Lev 13:1	4872
And the LORD spake unto *M*, saying,	Lev 14:1	4872
And the LORD spake unto *M* and unto	Lev 14:33	4872
And the LORD spake unto *M* and to	Lev 15:1	4872
the LORD spake unto *M* after the	Lev 16:1	4872
And the LORD said unto *M*, Speak	Lev 16:2	4872
he did as the LORD commanded *M*	Lev 16:34	4872
And the LORD spake unto *M*, saying,	Lev 17:1	4872
And the LORD spake unto *M*, saying,	Lev 18:1	4872
And the LORD spake unto *M*, saying,	Lev 19:1	4872
And the LORD spake unto *M*, saying,	Lev 20:1	4872
And the LORD said unto *M*, Speak	Lev 21:1	4872
And the LORD spake unto *M*, saying,	Lev 21:16	4872
M told it unto Aaron, and to his	Lev 21:24	4872
And the LORD spake unto *M*, saying,	Lev 22:1	4872
And the LORD spake unto *M*, saying,	Lev 22:17	4872
And the LORD spake unto *M*, saying,	Lev 22:26	4872
And the LORD spake unto *M*, saying,	Lev 23:1	4872
And the LORD spake unto *M*, saying,	Lev 23:9	4872
And the LORD spake unto *M*, saying,	Lev 23:23	4872
And the LORD spake unto *M*, saying,	Lev 23:26	4872
And the LORD spake unto *M*, saying,	Lev 23:33	4872
M declared unto the children of	Lev 23:44	4872
And the LORD spake unto *M*, saying,	Lev 24:1	4872
And they brought him unto *M*	Lev 24:11	4872
And the LORD spake unto *M*, saying,	Lev 24:13	4872
M spake to the children of Israel	Lev 24:23	4872
did as the LORD commanded *M*	Lev 24:23	4872
LORD spake unto *M* in mount Sinai	Lev 25:1	4872
in mount Sinai by the hand of *M*	Lev 26:46	4872
And the LORD spake unto *M*, saying,	Lev 27:1	4872
which the LORD commanded *M* for	Lev 27:34	4872
the LORD spake unto *M* in the	Num 1:1	4872
And *M* and Aaron took these men	Num 1:17	4872
As the LORD commanded *M*, so he	Num 1:19	4872
those that were numbered, which *M*	Num 1:44	4872
For the LORD had spoken unto *M*	Num 1:48	4872
to all that the LORD commanded *M*	Num 1:54	4872
And the LORD spake unto *M* and unto	Num 2:1	4872
as the LORD commanded *M*	Num 2:33	4872
to all that the LORD commanded *M*	Num 2:34	4872
M in the day that the LORD spake	Num 3:1	4872
LORD spake with *M* in mount Sinai	Num 3:1	4872
And the LORD spake unto *M*, saying,	Num 3:5	4872
And the LORD spake unto *M*, saying,	Num 3:11	4872
the LORD spake unto *M* in the	Num 3:14	4872
M numbered them according to the	Num 3:16	4872
congregation eastward, shall be *M*	Num 3:38	4872
numbered of the Levites, which *M*	Num 3:39	4872
And the LORD said unto *M*, Number	Num 3:40	4872
M numbered, as the LORD commanded	Num 3:42	4872
And the LORD spake unto *M*, saying,	Num 3:44	4872
M took the redemption money of	Num 3:49	4872
M gave the money of them that	Num 3:51	4872
the LORD, as the LORD commanded *M*	Num 3:51	4872
And the LORD spake unto *M* and unto	Num 4:1	4872
And the LORD spake unto *M* and unto	Num 4:17	4872
And the LORD spake unto *M*, saying,	Num 4:21	4872
And *M* and Aaron and the chief of the	Num 4:34	4872
of the congregation, which *M*	Num 4:37	4872
of the LORD by the hand of *M*	Num 4:37	4872
of the congregation, whom *M*	Num 4:41	4872
of the sons of Merari, whom *M*	Num 4:45	4872
word of the LORD by the hand of *M*	Num 4:45	4872
numbered of the Levites, whom *M*	Num 4:46	4872
were numbered by the hand of *M*	Num 4:49	4872
of him, as the LORD commanded *M*	Num 4:49	4872
And the LORD spake unto *M*, saying,	Num 5:1	4872
as the LORD spake unto *M*, so did	Num 5:4	4872
And the LORD spake unto *M*, saying,	Num 5:5	4872
And the LORD spake unto *M*, saying,	Num 5:11	4872
And the LORD spake unto *M*, saying,	Num 6:1	4872
And the LORD spake unto *M*, saying,	Num 6:22	4872
M had fully set up the tabernacle	Num 7:1	4872
And the LORD spake unto *M*, saying,	Num 7:4	4872
M took the wagons and the oxen, and	Num 7:6	4872
And the LORD said unto *M*, They	Num 7:11	4872
And when *M* was gone into the	Num 7:89	4872
And the LORD spake unto *M*, saying,	Num 8:1	4872
as the LORD commanded *M*	Num 8:3	4872
which the LORD had shewed *M*	Num 8:4	4872
And the LORD spake unto *M*, saying,	Num 8:5	4872
And *M*, and Aaron, and all the	Num 8:20	4872
M concerning the Levites, so did	Num 8:20	4872
M concerning the Levites, so did	Num 8:22	4872
And the LORD spake unto *M*, saying,	Num 8:23	4872
the LORD spake unto *M* in the	Num 9:1	4872
M spake unto the children of	Num 9:4	4872
to all that the LORD commanded *M*	Num 9:5	4872
and they came before *M* and before	Num 9:6	4872
M said unto them, Stand still, and	Num 9:8	4872
And the LORD spake unto *M*, saying,	Num 9:9	4872
of the LORD by the hand of *M*	Num 9:23	4872
And the LORD spake unto *M*, saying,	Num 10:1	4872
of the LORD by the hand of *M*	Num 10:13	4872
M said unto Hobab, the son of	Num 10:29	4872
the ark set forward, that *M* said	Num 10:35	4872
And the people cried unto *M*	Num 11:2	4872
when *M* prayed unto the LORD, the	Num 11:2	4872
Then *M* heard the people weep	Num 11:10	4872
M also was displeased	Num 11:10	4872
M said unto the LORD, Wherefore	Num 11:11	4872
And the LORD said unto *M*, Gather	Num 11:16	4872
M said, The people, among whom I	Num 11:21	4872
And the LORD said unto *M*, Is the	Num 11:23	4872
M went out, and told the people	Num 11:24	4872
there ran a young man, and told *M*	Num 11:27	4872
the son of Nun, the servant of *M*	Num 11:28	4872
men, answered and said, My lord *M*	Num 11:28	4872
M said unto him, Enviest thou for	Num 11:29	4872
M gat him into the camp, he and	Num 11:30	4872
Aaron spake against *M* because of	Num 12:1	4872
the LORD indeed spoken only by *M*	Num 12:2	4872
(Now the man *M* was very meek,	Num 12:3	4872
And the LORD spake suddenly unto *M*	Num 12:4	4872
My servant *M* is not so, who is	Num 12:7	4872
to speak against my servant *M*	Num 12:8	4872
And Aaron said unto *M*, Alas, my	Num 12:11	4872
M cried unto the LORD, saying,	Num 12:13	4872
And the LORD said unto *M*, If her	Num 12:14	4872
And the LORD spake unto *M*, saying,	Num 13:1	4872
M by the commandment of the LORD	Num 13:3	4872
which *M* sent to spy out the land	Num 13:16	4872
M called Oshea the son of Nun	Num 13:16	4872
M sent them to spy out the land	Num 13:17	4872
And they went and came to *M*	Num 13:26	4872
Caleb stilled the people before *M*	Num 13:30	4872
of Israel murmured against *M*	Num 14:2	4872
Then *M* and Aaron fell on their	Num 14:5	4872
And the LORD said unto *M*, How long	Num 14:11	4872
M said unto the LORD, Then the	Num 14:13	4872
And the LORD spake unto *M* and unto	Num 14:26	4872
which *M* sent to search the land,	Num 14:36	4872
M told these sayings unto all the	Num 14:39	4872
M said, Wherefore now do ye	Num 14:41	4872

of Israel, as *M* spake unto them .... Josh 4:12   4872
they feared him, as they feared *M* .... Josh 4:14   4872
As *M* the servant of the LORD .... Josh 8:31   4872
in the book of the law of *M* .... Josh 8:31   4872
the stones a copy of the law of *M* .... Josh 8:32   4872
as *M* the servant of the LORD had .... Josh 8:33   4872
a word of all that *M* commanded .... Josh 8:35   4872
M to give you all the land .... Josh 9:24   4872
as *M* the servant of the LORD .... Josh 11:12   4872
the LORD commanded *M* his servant ...... Josh 11:15   4872
so did *M* command Joshua, and so .... Josh 11:15   4872
of all that the LORD commanded *M* .... Josh 11:15   4872
them, as the LORD commanded *M* .... Josh 11:20   4872
to all that the LORD said unto *M* .... Josh 11:23   4872
Them did *M* the servant of the .... Josh 12:6   4872
M the servant of the LORD gave it .... Josh 12:6   4872
which *M* gave them, beyond Jordan .... Josh 13:8   4872
even as *M* the servant of the LORD .... Josh 13:8   4872
for these did *M* smite, and cast .... Josh 13:12   4872
M gave unto the tribe of .... Josh 13:15   4872
whom *M* smote with the princes of .... Josh 13:21   4872
M gave inheritance unto the tribe .... Josh 13:24   4872
M gave inheritance unto the half .... Josh 13:29   4872
These are the countries which *M* .... Josh 13:32   4872
Levi *M* gave not any inheritance .... Josh 13:33   4872
LORD commanded by the hand of *M* .... Josh 14:2   4872
For *M* had given the inheritance .... Josh 14:3   4872
As the LORD commanded *M*, so the .... Josh 14:5   4872
M the man of God concerning me .... Josh 14:6   4872
Forty years old was I when *M* the .... Josh 14:7   4872
M sware on that day, saying, ... Josh 14:9   4872
the LORD spake this word unto *M* .... Josh 14:10   4872
I was in the day that *M* sent me .... Josh 14:11   4872
The LORD commanded *M* to give us .... Josh 17:4   4872
which *M* the servant of the LORD .... Josh 18:7   4872
I spake unto you by the hand of *M* .... Josh 20:2   4872
M to give us cities to dwell in .... Josh 21:2   4872
LORD commanded by the hand of *M* .... Josh 21:8   4872
Ye have kept all that the *M* the .... Josh 22:2   4872
which *M* the servant of the LORD .... Josh 22:4   4872
which *M* the servant of the LORD .... Josh 22:5   4872
half of the tribe of Manasseh *M* .... Josh 22:7   4872
word of the LORD by the hand of *M* .... Josh 22:9   4872
in the book of the law of *M* .... Josh 23:6   4872
I sent *M* also and Aaron, and I .... Josh 24:5   4872
gave Hebron unto Caleb, as *M* said ...... Judg 1:20   4872
their fathers by the hand of *M* .... Judg 3:4   4872
of Hobab the father in law of *M* .... Judg 4:11   4872
It is the LORD that advanced *M* 1Sa 12:6   4872
the LORD, then the LORD sent *M* 1Sa 12:8   4872
as it is written in the law of *M* 1Kin 2:3   4872
which *M* put there at Horeb, when 1Kin 8:9   4872
by the hand of *M* thy servant 1Kin 8:53   4872
by the hand of *M* his servant 1Kin 8:56   4872
in the book of the law of *M* 2Kin 14:6   4872
brasen serpent that *M* had made 2Kin 18:4   4872
which the LORD commanded *M* 2Kin 18:6   4872
all that *M* the servant of the 2Kin 18:12   4872
that my servant *M* commanded them 2Kin 21:8   4872
according to all the law of *M* 2Kin 23:25   4872
Aaron, and *M*, and Miriam 1Chr 6:3   4872
according to all that *M* the 1Chr 6:49   4872
as *M* commanded according to the 1Chr 15:15   4872
which *M* made in the wilderness, ... 1Chr 21:29   4872
charged *M* with concerning Israel 1Chr 22:13   4872
of Amram; Aaron and *M* 1Chr 23:13   4872
Now concerning *M* the man of God 1Chr 23:14   4872
The sons of *M* were, Gershom, and 1Chr 23:15   4872
the son of Gershom, the son of *M* 1Chr 26:24   4872
which *M* the servant of the LORD 2Chr 1:3   4872
which *M* put therein at Horeb 2Chr 5:10   4872
according to the commandment of *M* 2Chr 8:13   4872
as it is written in the law of *M* 2Chr 23:18   4872
of *M* the servant of the LORD 2Chr 24:6   4872
M the servant of God laid upon 2Chr 24:9   4872
in the law in the book of *M* 2Chr 25:4   4872
to the law of *M* the man of God 2Chr 30:16   4872
the ordinances by the hand of *M* 2Chr 33:8   4872
of the law of the LORD given by *M* 2Chr 34:14   4872
word of the LORD by the hand of *M* 2Chr 35:6   4872
as it is written in the book of *M* 2Chr 35:12   4872
in the law of *M* the man of God .... Ezr 3:2   4872
as it is written in the book of *M* .... Ezr 6:18   4873
a ready scribe in the law of *M* .... Ezr 7:6   4872
thou commandedst thy servant *M* .... Neh 1:7   4872
thou commandedst thy servant *M* .... Neh 1:8   4872
to bring the book of the law of *M* .... Neh 8:1   4872
which the LORD had commanded by *M* .. Neh 8:14   4872
by the hand of *M* thy servant .... Neh 9:14   4872
was given by *M* the servant of God .... Neh 10:29   4872

day they read in the book of *M* in .... Neh 13:1   4872
like a flock by the hand of *M* .... Ps 77:20   4872
A Prayer of *M*, the man of God .... Ps 90:t   4872
M and Aaron among his priests, and .... Ps 99:6   4872
He made known his ways unto *M* .... Ps 103:7   4872
He sent *M* his servant .... Ps 105:26   4872
They envied *M* also in the camp, ... Ps 106:16   4872
had not *M* his chosen stood before .... Ps 106:23   4872
went ill with *M* for their sakes .... Ps 106:32   4872
he remembered the days of old, *M* .... Is 63:11   4872
hand of *M* with his glorious arm .... Is 63:12   4872
said the LORD unto me, Though *M* .... Jer 15:1   4872
the law of *M* the servant of God .... Dan 9:11   4872
As it is written in the law of *M* .... Dan 9:13   4872
and I sent before thee *M*, Aaron, ... Mic 6:4   4872
ye the law of *M* my servant .... Mal 4:4   4872
offer the gift that *M* commanded .... Mt 8:4   3475
there appeared unto them *M* .... Mt 17:3   3475
one for thee, and one for *M* .... Mt 17:4   3475
Why did *M* then command to give a ...... Mt 19:7   3475
M because of the hardness of your ...... Mt 19:8   3475
M said, If a man die, having no .... Mt 22:24   3475
those things which *M* commanded ...... Mk 1:44   3475
For *M* said, Honour thy father and ...... Mk 7:10   3475
appeared unto them Elias with *M* .... Mk 9:4   3475
one for thee, and one for *M* .... Mk 9:5   3475
unto them, What did *M* command you .. Mk 10:3   3475
M suffered to write a bill of .... Mk 10:4   3475
M wrote unto us, If a man's .... Mk 12:19   3475
have ye not read in the book of *M* .... Mk 12:26   3475
to the law of *M* were accomplished .... Lk 2:22   3475
according as *M* commanded .... Lk 5:14   3475
with him two men, which were *M* .... Lk 9:30   3475
one for thee, and one for *M* .... Lk 9:33   3475
saith unto him, They have *M* .... Lk 16:29   3475
said unto him, If they hear not *M* .... Lk 16:31   3475
M wrote unto us, If any man's .... Lk 20:28   3475
even *M* shewed at the bush, when .... Lk 20:37   3475
And beginning at *M* and all the .... Lk 24:27   3475
were written in the law of *M* .... Lk 24:44   3475
For the law was given by *M* .... Jn 1:17   3475
of whom *M* in the law, and the .... Jn 1:45   3475
as *M* lifted up the serpent in the .... Jn 3:14   3475
is one that accuseth you, even *M* .... Jn 5:45   3475
For had ye believed *M*, ye would .... Jn 5:46   3475
M gave you not that bread from .... Jn 6:32   3475
Did not *M* give you the law, and .... Jn 7:19   3475
M therefore gave unto you .... Jn 7:22   3475
(not because it is of *M*, but of .... Jn 7:22   3475
that the law of *M* should not be .... Jn 7:23   3475
Now *M* in the law commanded us, ... Jn 8:5   3475
We know that God spake unto *M* .... Jn 9:29   3475
For *M* truly said unto the fathers .... Acts 3:22   3475
speak blasphemous words against *M* ..... Acts 6:11   3475
the customs which *M* delivered us .... Acts 6:14   3475
In which time *M* was born, and was ...... Acts 7:20   3475
M was learned in all the wisdom .... Acts 7:22   3475
Then fled *M* at this saying, and .... Acts 7:29   3475
When *M* saw it, he wondered at the ...... Acts 7:31   3475
Then *M* trembled, and durst not .... Acts 7:32   3475
This *M* whom they refused, saying, ... Acts 7:35   3475
This is that *M*, which said unto .... Acts 7:37   3475
for as for this *M*, which brought .... Acts 7:40   3475
he had appointed, speaking unto *M* ...... Acts 7:44   3475
not be justified by the law of *M* .... Acts 13:39   3475
circumcised after the manner of *M* .... Acts 15:1   3475
command them to keep the law of *M* ..... Acts 15:5   3475
For *M* of old time hath in every .... Acts 15:21   3475
among the Gentiles to forsake *M* .... Acts 21:21   3475
prophets and *M* did say should come .... Acts 26:22   3475
Jesus, both out of the law of *M* .... Acts 28:23   3475
death reigned from Adam to *M* .... Rom 5:14   3475
For he saith to *M*, I will have .... Rom 9:15   3475
For *M* describeth the .... Rom 10:5   3475
First *M* saith, I will provoke you .... Rom 10:19   3475
For it is written in the law of *M* 1Cor 9:9   3475
all baptized unto *M* in the cloud 1Cor 10:2   3475
face of *M* for the glory of his 2Cor 3:7   3475
And not as *M*, which put a vail 2Cor 3:13   3475
when *M* is read, the vail is upon 2Cor 3:15   3475
as Jannes and Jambres withstood *M* 2Ti 3:8   3475
as also *M* was faithful in all his .... Heb 3:2   3475
worthy of more glory than *M* .... Heb 3:3   3475
M verily was faithful in all his .... Heb 3:5   3475
all that came out of Egypt by *M* .... Heb 3:16   3475
of which tribe *M* spake nothing .... Heb 7:14   3475
as *M* was admonished of God when .... Heb 8:5   3475
For when *M* had spoken every .... Heb 9:19   3475
By faith *M*, when he was born, was .... Heb 11:23   3475
By faith *M*, when he was come to .... Heb 11:24   3475

was the sight, that *M* said .... Heb 12:21   3475
he disputed about the body of *M* .... Jude 9   3475
the song of *M* the servant of God .... Rev 15:3   3475

MOSES'
But *M* hands were heavy .... Ex 17:12   4872
M father in law, heard of all .... Ex 18:1   4872
M father in law, took Zipporah,............. Ex 18:2   4872
M wife, after he had sent her .... Ex 18:2   4872
M father in law, came with his .... Ex 18:5   4872
M father in law, took a burnt................. Ex 18:12   4872
to eat bread with *M* father in law .... Ex 18:12   4872
when *M* father in law saw all that .... Ex 18:14   4872
M father in law said unto him, ... Ex 18:17   4872
M anger waxed hot, and he cast the ...... Ex 32:19   4872
two tables of testimony in *M* hand .... Ex 34:29   4872
that the skin of *M* face shone .... Ex 34:35   4872
ram of consecration it was *M* part .... Lev 8:29   4872
M father in law, We are .... Num 10:29   4872
son of Nun, *M* minister, saying,............. Josh 1:1   4872
M father in law, went up out of .... Judg 1:16   4872
and the Pharisees sit in *M* seat .... Mt 23:2   3475
but we are *M* disciples .... Jn 9:28   3475
He that despised *M* law died.................. Heb 10:28   3475

MOST See APPENDIX.

MOTE
why beholdest thou the *m* that is .... Mt 7:3   2595
pull out the *m* out of thine eye .... Mt 7:4   2595
the *m* out of thy brother's eye .... Mt 7:5   2595
why beholdest thou the *m* that is .... Lk 6:41   2595
let me pull out the *m* that is in .... Lk 6:42   2595
see clearly to pull out the *m* .... Lk 6:42   2595

MOTH
which are crushed before the *m* .... Job 4:19   6211
as a garment that is *m* eaten................. Job 13:28   6211
He buildeth his house as a *m*................. Job 27:18   6211
beauty to consume away like a *m* .... Ps 39:11   6211
the *m* shall eat them up .... Is 50:9   6211
For the *m* shall eat them up like .... Is 51:8   6211
will I be unto Ephraim as a *m* .... Hos 5:12   6211
treasures upon earth, where *m* .... Mt 6:19   4597
where neither *m* nor rust doth............... Mt 6:20   4597
approacheth, neither *m* corrupteth ...... Lk 12:33   4597

MOTHEATEN
corrupted, and your garments are *m* ..... Jas 5:2   4598

MOTHER
a man leave his father and his *m* .... Gen 2:24   517
she was the *m* of all living .... Gen 3:20   517
and she shall be a *m* of nations............. Gen 17:16
but not the daughter of my *m* .... Gen 20:12   517
his *m* took him a wife out of the .... Gen 21:21   517
and to her *m* precious things .... Gen 24:53   517
her *m* said, Let the damsel abide........... Gen 24:55   517
be thou the *m* of thousands of .... Gen 24:60
her into his *m* Sarah's tent..................... Gen 24:67   517
And Jacob said to Rebekah his *m* .... Gen 27:11   517
his *m* said unto him, Upon me be .... Gen 27:13   517
fetched, and brought them to his *m* ...... Gen 27:14   517
his *m* made savoury meat, such as .... Gen 27:14   517
of Rebekah, Jacob's and Esau's *m* .... Gen 28:5   517
Jacob obeyed his father and his *m* .... Gen 28:7   517
and brought them unto his *m* Leah .... Gen 30:14   517
me, and the *m* with the children............ Gen 32:11   517
Shall I and thy *m* and thy brethren .... Gen 37:10   517
and he alone is left of his *m* .... Gen 44:20   517
maid went and called the child's *m* .... Ex 2:8   517
Honour thy father and thy *m* .... Ex 20:12   517
that smiteth his father, or his *m* .... Ex 21:15   517
that curseth his father, or his *m* .... Ex 21:17   517
father, or the nakedness of thy *m* .... Lev 18:7   517
she is thy *m* .... Lev 18:7   517
thy father, or daughter of thy *m* .... Lev 18:9   517
Ye shall fear every man his *m* .... Lev 19:3   517
m shall be surely put to death............... Lev 20:9   517
hath cursed his father or his *m* .... Lev 20:9   517
And if a man take a wife and her *m* ...... Lev 20:14   517
near unto him, that is, for his *m* .... Lev 21:2   517
for his father, or for his *m*...................... Lev 21:11   517
for his father, or for his *m* .... Num 6:7   517
whom her *m* bare to Levi in Egypt........ Num 26:59   517
Honour thy father and thy *m* .... Deut 5:16   517
If thy brother, the son of thy *m* .... Deut 13:6   517
her father and her *m* a full month .... Deut 21:13   517
his father, or the voice of his *m* .... Deut 21:18   517
his *m* lay hold on him, and bring........... Deut 21:19   517
father of the damsel, and her *m* .... Deut 22:15   517
light by his father or his *m* .... Deut 27:16   517
father, or the daughter of his *m* .... Deut 27:22   517

he that lieth with his *m* in law .... Deut 27:23   2859
said unto his father and to his *m* .... Deut 33:9   517
save alive my father, and my *m* .... Josh 2:13   517
shalt bring thy father, and thy *m* .... Josh 2:18   517
Rahab, and her father, and her *m* .... Josh 6:23   517
arose, that I arose a *m* in Israel............. Judg 5:7   517
The *m* of Sisera looked out at a .... Judg 5:28   517
brethren, even the sons of my *m* .... Judg 8:19   517
up, and told his father and his *m* .... Judg 14:2   517
his *m* said unto him, Is there .... Judg 14:3   517
his *m* knew not that it was of the .... Judg 14:4   517
down, and his father and his *m* .... Judg 14:5   517
father or his *m* what he had done.......... Judg 14:6   517
and came to his father and *m* .... Judg 14:9   517
not told it my father nor my *m* .... Judg 14:16   517
And he said unto his *m*, The eleven ...... Judg 17:2   517
his *m* said, Blessed be thou of .... Judg 17:2   517
shekels of silver to his *m* .... Judg 17:3   517
his *m* said, I had wholly .... Judg 17:3   517
he restored the money unto his *m* .... Judg 17:4   517
his *m* took two hundred shekels of .... Judg 17:4   517
and Orpah kissed her *m* in law .... Ruth 1:14   2545
that thou hast done unto thy *m* in .... Ruth 2:11   2545
hast left thy father and thy *m* .... Ruth 2:11   517
her *m* in law saw what she had .... Ruth 2:18   2545
her *m* in law said unto her, Where .... Ruth 2:19   2545
she shewed her *m* in law with whom ..... Ruth 2:19   2545
and dwelt with her *m* in law .... Ruth 2:23   2545
Then Naomi her *m* in law said unto ...... Ruth 3:1   2545
to all that her *m* in law bade her .... Ruth 3:6   2545
And when she came to her *m* in law ...... Ruth 3:16   2545
Go not empty unto thy *m* in law .... Ruth 3:17   2545
Moreover his *m* made him a little 1Sa 2:19   517
so shall thy *m* be childless among......... 1Sa 15:33   517
of Moab, Let my father and my *m* 1Sa 22:3   517
sister to Zeruiah Joab's *m* 2Sa 17:25   517
the grave of my father and of my *m* 2Sa 19:37   517
destroy a city and a *m* in Israel 2Sa 20:19   517
his *m* bare him after Absalom 1Kin 1:6
unto Bath-sheba the *m* of Solomon 1Kin 1:11   517
to Bath-sheba the *m* of Solomon 1Kin 2:13   517
a seat to be set for the king's *m* 1Kin 2:19   517
king said unto her, Ask on, my *m* 1Kin 2:20   517
answered and said unto his *m* 1Kin 2:22   517
she is the *m* thereof............................... 1Kin 3:27   517
And also Maachah his *m*, even her 1Kin 15:13   517
and delivered him unto his *m* 1Kin 17:23   517
pray thee, kiss my father and my *m* 1Kin 19:20   517
father, and in the way of his *m* 1Kin 22:52   517
like his father, and like his *m* 2Kin 3:2   517
and to the prophets of thy *m* 2Kin 3:13   517
said to a lad, Carry him to his *m* 2Kin 4:19   517
him, and brought him to his *m* 2Kin 4:20   517
the *m* of the child said, As the 2Kin 4:30   517
as the whoredoms of thy *m* Jezebel...... 2Kin 9:22   517
when Athaliah the *m* of Ahaziah 2Kin 11:1   517
the king of Babylon, he, and his *m* 2Kin 24:12   517
to Babylon, and the king's *m*................. 2Kin 24:15   517
she was the *m* of Onam 1Chr 2:26   517
his *m* called his name Jabez, ... 1Chr 4:9   517
Maachah the *m* of Asa the king 2Chr 15:16   517
for his *m* was his counsellor to 2Chr 22:3   517
But when Athaliah the *m* of................... 2Chr 22:10   517
for she had neither father nor *m* .... Est 2:7   517
m were dead, took for his own .... Est 2:7   517
to the worm, Thou art my *m* .... Job 17:14   517
my *m* forsake me, then the LORD .... Ps 27:10   517
as one that mourneth for his *m* .... Ps 35:14   517
and in sin did my *m* conceive me .... Ps 51:5   517
the sin of his *m* be blotted out............... Ps 109:14   517
and to be a joyful *m* of children............. Ps 113:9   517
a child that is weaned of his *m* .... Ps 131:2   517
and forsake not the law of thy *m* .... Prov 1:8   517
only beloved in the sight of my *m* .... Prov 4:3   517
and forsake not the law of thy *m* .... Prov 6:20   517
son is the heaviness of his *m* .... Prov 10:1   517
but a foolish man despiseth his *m* .... Prov 15:20   517
his father, and chaseth away his *m* .... Prov 19:26   517
Whoso curseth his father or his *m*......... Prov 20:20   517
despise not thy *m* when she is old .... Prov 23:22   517
thy *m* shall be glad, and she that .... Prov 23:25   517
Whoso robbeth his father or his *m*........ Prov 28:24   517
himself bringeth his *m* to shame .... Prov 29:15   517
father, and doth not bless their *m* .... Prov 30:11   517
and despiseth to obey his *m* .... Prov 30:17   517
prophecy that his *m* taught him .... Prov 31:1   517
with the crown wherewith his *m*............ Song 3:11   517
she is the only one of her *m* .... Song 6:9   517
that sucked the breasts of my *m* .... Song 8:1   517

there thy *m* brought thee forth	Song 8:5	517
to cry, My father, and my *m*	Is 8:4	517
from the bowels of my *m* hath he	Is 49:1	517
transgressions is your *m* put away	Is 50:1	517
As one whom his *m* comforteth	Is 66:13	517
m of the young men a spoiler at	Jer 15:8	517
Woe is me, my *m*, that thou hast	Jer 15:10	517
for their father or for their *m*	Jer 16:7	517
wherein my *m* bare me be blessed	Jer 20:14	517
or that my *m* might have been my	Jer 20:17	517
thy *m* that bare thee, into	Jer 22:26	517
Your *m* shall be sore confounded	Jer 50:12	517
an Amorite, and thy *m* an Hittite	Eze 16:3	517
against thee, saying, As is the *m*	Eze 16:44	517
your *m* was an Hittite, and your	Eze 16:45	517
And say, What is thy *m*	Eze 19:2	517
Thy *m* is like a vine in thy blood	Eze 19:10	517
they set light by father and *m*	Eze 22:7	517
two women, the daughters of one *m*	Eze 23:2	517
but for father, or for *m*, or for	Eze 44:25	517
Plead with your *m*, plead	Hos 2:2	517
For their *m* hath played the	Hos 2:5	517
night, and I will destroy thy *m*	Hos 4:5	517
the *m* was dashed in pieces upon	Hos 10:14	517
daughter riseth up against her *m*	Mic 7:6	517
in law against her *m* in law	Mic 7:6	2545
his *m* that begat him shall say	Zec 13:3	517
his *m* that begat him shall thrust	Zec 13:3	517
When as his *m* Mary was espoused	Mt 1:18	3384
the young child with Mary his *m*	Mt 2:11	3384
and take the young child and his *m*	Mt 2:13	3384
his *m* by night, and departed into	Mt 2:14	3384
and take the young child and his *m*	Mt 2:20	3384
and took the young child and his *m*	Mt 2:21	3384
house, he saw his wife's *m* laid	Mt 8:14	3994
and the daughter against her *m*	Mt 10:35	3384
in law against her *m* in law	Mt 10:35	3994
He that loveth father or *m* more	Mt 10:37	3384
to the people, behold, his *m*	Mt 12:46	3384
one said unto him, Behold, thy *m*	Mt 12:47	3384
him that told him, Who is my *m*	Mt 12:48	3384
disciples, and said, Behold my *m*	Mt 12:49	3384
is my brother, and sister, and *m*	Mt 12:50	3384
is not his *m* called Mary	Mt 13:55	3384
being before instructed of her *m*	Mt 14:8	3384
and she brought it to her *m*	Mt 14:11	3384
saying, Honour thy father and *m*	Mt 15:4	3384
and, He that curseth father or *m*	Mt 15:4	3384
shall say to his father or his *m*	Mt 15:5	3384
And honour not his father or his *m*	Mt 15:6	3384
shall a man leave father and *m*	Mt 19:5	3384
Honour thy father and thy *m*	Mt 19:19	3384
or sisters, or father, or *m*	Mt 19:29	3384
Then came to him the *m* of	Mt 20:20	3384
Magdalene, and Mary the *m* of James	Mt 27:56	3384
the *m* of Zebedee's children	Mt 27:56	3384
But Simon's wife's *m* lay sick of	Mk 1:30	3994
came then his brethren and his *m*	Mk 3:31	3384
they said unto him, Behold, thy *m*	Mk 3:32	3384
them, saying, Who is my *m*	Mk 3:33	3384
about him, and said, Behold my *m*	Mk 3:34	3384
is my brother, and my sister, and *m*	Mk 3:35	3384
the *m* of the damsel, and them that	Mk 5:40	3384
went forth, and said unto her *m*	Mk 6:24	3384
and the damsel gave it to her *m*	Mk 6:28	3384
said, Honour thy father and thy *m*	Mk 7:10	3384
and, Whoso curseth father or *m*	Mk 7:10	3384
man shall say to his father or *m*	Mk 7:11	3384
do ought for his father or his *m*	Mk 7:12	3384
shall a man leave his father and *m*	Mk 10:7	3384
not, Honour thy father and *m*	Mk 10:19	3384
or sisters, or father, or *m*	Mk 10:29	3384
Mary the *m* of James the less and	Mk 15:40	3384
Mary the *m* of Joses beheld where	Mk 15:47	3384
Magdalene, and Mary the *m* of James	Mk 16:1	3384
that the *m* of my Lord should come	Lk 1:43	3384
his *m* answered and said, Not so	Lk 1:60	3384
his *m* marvelled at those things	Lk 2:33	3384
them, and said unto Mary his *m*	Lk 2:34	3384
and Joseph and his *m* knew not of it	Lk 2:43	3384
his *m* said unto him, Son, why	Lk 2:48	3384
but his *m* kept all these sayings	Lk 2:51	3384
Simon's wife's *m* was taken with a	Lk 4:38	3994
out, the only son of his *m*	Lk 7:12	3384
And he delivered him to his *m*	Lk 7:15	3384
Then came to him his *m* and his	Lk 8:19	3384
him by certain which said, Thy *m*	Lk 8:20	3384
answered and said unto them, My *m*	Lk 8:21	3384
the father and the *m* of the maiden	Lk 8:51	3384
the *m* against the daughter	Lk 12:53	3384
and the daughter against the *m*	Lk 12:53	3384

the *m* in law against her daughter	Lk 12:53	3994
in law against her *m* in law	Lk 12:53	3994
me, and hate not his father, and *m*	Lk 14:26	3384
Honour thy father and thy *m*	Lk 18:20	3384
and Joanna, and Mary the *m* of James	Lk 24:10	
and the *m* of Jesus was there	Jn 2:1	3384
the *m* of Jesus saith unto him,	Jn 2:3	3384
His *m* saith unto the servants,	Jn 2:5	3384
down to Capernaum, he, and his *m*	Jn 2:12	3384
Joseph, whose father and *m* we know	Jn 6:42	3384
stood by the cross of Jesus his *m*	Jn 19:25	3384
When Jesus therefore saw his *m*	Jn 19:26	3384
he loved, he saith unto his *m*	Jn 19:26	3384
he to the disciple, Behold thy *m*	Jn 19:27	3384
the women, and Mary the *m* of Jesus	Acts 1:14	3384
the house of Mary the *m* of John	Acts 12:12	3384
chosen in the Lord, and his *m*	Rom 16:13	3384
is free, which is the *m* of us all	Gal 4:26	3384
shall a man leave his father and *m*	Eph 5:31	3384
Honour thy father and *m*	Eph 6:2	3384
grandmother Lois, and thy *m* Eunice	2Ti 1:5	3384
Without father, without *m*	Heb 7:3	282
THE *M* OF HARLOTS AND	Rev 17:5	3384

MOTHER'S

told them of her *m* house these	Gen 24:28	517
was comforted after his *m* death	Gen 24:67	517
let thy *m* sons bow down to thee	Gen 27:29	517
the house of Bethuel thy *m* father	Gen 28:2	517
daughters of Laban thy *m* brother	Gen 28:2	517
daughter of Laban his *m* brother	Gen 29:10	517
the sheep of Laban his *m* brother	Gen 29:10	517
the flock of Laban his *m* brother	Gen 29:10	517
his brother Benjamin, his *m* son	Gen 43:29	517
not seethe a kid in his *m* milk	Ex 23:19	517
not seethe a kid in his *m* milk	Ex 34:26	517
the nakedness of thy *m* sister	Lev 18:13	517
for she is thy *m* near kinswoman	Lev 18:13	517
or his *m* daughter, and see her	Lev 20:17	517
the nakedness of thy *m* sister	Lev 20:19	517
his *m* name was Shelomith, the	Lev 24:11	517
when he cometh out of his *m* womb	Num 12:12	517
not seethe a kid in his *m* milk	Deut 14:21	517
to Shechem unto his *m* brethren	Judg 9:1	517
of the house of his *m* father	Judg 9:1	517
his *m* brethren spake of him in	Judg 9:3	517
Nazarite unto God from my *m* womb	Judg 16:17	517
Go, return each to her *m* house	Ruth 1:8	517
the confusion of thy *m* nakedness	1Sa 20:30	517
whose *m* name was Zeruah, a widow	1Kin 11:26	517
And his *m* name was Naamah an	1Kin 14:21	517
And his *m* name was Naamah an	1Kin 14:31	517
his *m* name was Maachah, the	1Kin 15:2	517
his *m* name was Maachah, the	1Kin 15:10	517
his *m* name was Azubah the	1Kin 22:42	517
his *m* name was Athaliah, the	2Kin 8:26	517
And his *m* name was Zibiah of	2Kin 12:1	517
his *m* name was Jehoaddan of	2Kin 14:2	517
his *m* name was Jecoliah of	2Kin 15:2	517
his *m* name was Jerusha, the	2Kin 15:33	517
His *m* name also was Abi, the	2Kin 18:2	517
his *m* name was Hephzi-bah	2Kin 21:1	517
his *m* name was Meshullemeth, the	2Kin 21:19	517
his *m* name was Jedidah, the	2Kin 22:1	517
his *m* name was Hamutal, the	2Kin 23:31	517
his *m* name was Zebudah, the	2Kin 23:36	517
his *m* name was Nehushta, the	2Kin 24:8	517
his *m* name was Hamutal, the	2Kin 24:18	517
And his *m* name was Naamah an	2Chr 12:13	517
His *m* name also was Michaiah the	2Chr 13:2	517
his *m* name was Azubah the	2Chr 20:31	517
His *m* name also was Athaliah the	2Chr 22:2	517
His *m* name also was Zibiah of	2Chr 24:1	517
his *m* name was Jehoaddan of	2Chr 25:1	517
His *m* name also was Jecoliah of	2Chr 26:3	517
His *m* name also was Jerushah, the	2Chr 27:1	517
his *m* name was Abijah, the	2Chr 29:1	517
Naked came I out of my *m* womb	Job 1:21	517
not up the doors of my *m* womb	Job 3:10	
I have guided her from my *m* womb	Job 31:18	517
hope when I was upon my *m* breasts	Ps 22:9	517
thou art my God from my *m* belly	Ps 22:10	517
thou slanderest thine own *m* son	Ps 50:20	517
and an alien unto my *m* children	Ps 69:8	517
that took me out of my *m* bowels	Ps 71:6	517
thou hast covered me in my *m* womb	Ps 139:13	517
As he came forth of his *m* womb	Eccl 5:15	517
my *m* children were angry with me	Song 1:6	517
I had brought him into my *m* house	Song 3:4	517
and bring thee into my *m* house	Song 8:2	517
is the bill of your *m* divorcement	Is 50:1	517

his *m* name was Hamutal the ....Jer 52:1   517
Thou art thy *m* daughter, that................Eze 16:45   517
were so born from their *m* womb ....Mt 19:12   3384
Holy Ghost, even from his *m* womb ....Lk 1:15   3384
the second time into his *m* womb ....Jn 3:4   3384
his *m* sister, Mary the wife of................Jn 19:25   3384
lame from his *m* womb was carried ....Acts 3:2   3384
being a cripple from his *m* womb ....Acts 14:8   3384
who separated me from my *m* womb .....Gal 1:15   3384

MOTHERS
and their queens thy nursing *m* ....Is 49:23
concerning their *m* that bare them ....Jer 16:3   517
They say to their *m*, Where is.................Lam 2:12   517
fatherless, our *m* are as widows ....Lam 5:3   517
and brethren, and sisters, and *m* ....Mk 10:30   3384
of fathers and murderers of *m* 1Ti 1:9   3389
The elder women as *m* 1Ti 5:2   3384

MOTHERS'
was poured out into their *m* bosom........Lam 2:12   517

MOTIONS
the *m* of sins, which were by the ....Rom 7:5   3804

MOULDY
of their provision was dry and *m*...........Josh 9:5   5350
behold, it is dry, and it is *m*.....................Josh 9:12   5350

MOUNT
goest unto Sephar a *m* of the east ....Gen 10:30   2022
And the Horites in their *m* Seir ....Gen 14:6   2042
In the *m* of the Lord it shall be ....Gen 22:14   2022
set his face toward the *m* Gilead...........Gen 31:21   2022
they overtook him in the *m* Gilead.........Gen 31:23   2022
had pitched his tent in the *m*.................Gen 31:25   2022
pitched in the *m* of Gilead.....................Gen 31:25   2022
offered sacrifice upon the *m* ....Gen 31:54   2022
and tarried all night in the *m* ....Gen 31:54   2022
Thus dwelt Esau in *m* Seir ....Gen 36:8   2022
father of the Edomites in *m* Seir ....Gen 36:9   2022
went, and met him in the *m* of God ....Ex 4:27   2022
where he encamped at the *m* of God .....Ex 18:5   2022
there Israel camped before the *m*...........Ex 19:2   2022
of all the people upon *m* Sinai...............Ex 19:11   2022
that ye go not up into the *m* ....Ex 19:12   2022
whosoever toucheth the *m* shall be ....Ex 19:12   2022
long, they shall come up to the *m*..........Ex 19:13   2022
down from the *m* unto the people ....Ex 19:14   2022
and a thick cloud upon the *m* ....Ex 19:16   2022
stood at the nether part of the *m* ....Ex 19:17   2022
m Sinai was altogether on a smoke........Ex 19:18   2022
the whole *m* quaked greatly.....................Ex 19:18   2022
m Sinai, on the top of the *m* ....Ex 19:20   2022
Moses up to the top of the *m* ....Ex 19:20   2022
people cannot come up to *m* Sinai ....Ex 19:23   2022
saying, Set bounds about the *m* ....Ex 19:23   2022
Moses, Come up to me into the *m* ....Ex 24:12   2022
Moses went up into the *m* of God ....Ex 24:13   2022
And Moses went up into the *m* ....Ex 24:15   2022
and a cloud covered the *m* ....Ex 24:15   2022
of the Lord abode upon *m* Sinai ....Ex 24:16   2022
fire on the top of the *m* in the ....Ex 24:17   2022
cloud, and gat him up into the *m*..........Ex 24:18   2022
and Moses was in the *m* forty days ....Ex 24:18   2022
which was shewed thee in the *m* ....Ex 25:40   2022
which was shewed thee in the *m* ....Ex 26:30   2022
as it was shewed thee in the *m* ....Ex 27:8   2022
communing with him upon *m* Sinai ....Ex 31:18   2022
delayed to come down out of the *m* ....Ex 32:1   2022
turned, and went down from the *m* ....Ex 32:15   2022
and brake them beneath the *m* ....Ex 32:19   2022
of their ornaments by the *m* Horeb ....Ex 33:6   2022
up in the morning unto *m* Sinai ....Ex 34:2   2022
there to me in the top of the *m* ....Ex 34:2   2022
man be seen throughout all the *m* ....Ex 34:3   2022
nor herds feed before that *m* ....Ex 34:3   2022
morning, and went up unto *m* Sinai......Ex 34:4   2022
when Moses came down from the *m* .....Ex 34:29   2022
when he came down from the *m* ....Ex 34:29   2022
had spoken with him in *m* Sinai.............Ex 34:32   2022
Lord commanded Moses in *m* Sinai .....Lev 7:38   2022
Lord spake unto Moses in *m* Sinai ....Lev 25:1   2022
the children of Israel in *m* Sinai ....Lev 26:46   2022
the children of Israel in *m* Sinai ....Lev 27:34   2022
Lord spake with Moses in *m* Sinai ....Num 3:1   2022
they departed from the *m* of the ....Num 10:33   2022
from Kadesh, and came unto *m* Hor.......Num 20:22   2022
unto Moses and Aaron in *m* Hor.............Num 20:23   2022
son, and bring them up unto *m* Hor.......Num 20:25   2022
they went up into *m* Hor in the ....Num 20:27   2022
died there in the top of the *m*................Num 20:28   2022
and Eleazar came down from the *m* ......Num 20:28   2022

they journeyed from *m* Hor by the.........Num 21:4   2022
Get thee up into this *m* Abarim...............Num 27:12   2022
which was ordained in *m* Sinai for........Num 28:6   2022
and pitched in *m* Shapher ....Num 33:23   2022
And they removed from *m* Shapher ....Num 33:24   2022
from Kadesh, and pitched in *m* Hor ....Num 33:37   2022
m Hor at the commandment of the ....Num 33:38   2022
years old when he died in *m* Hor...........Num 33:39   2022
And they departed from *m* Hor ....Num 33:41   2022
ye shall point out for you *m* Hor.............Num 34:7   2022
From *m* Hor ye shall point out ....Num 34:8   2022
way of *m* Seir unto Kadesh-barnea ....Deut 1:2   2022
have dwelt long enough in this *m* ....Deut 1:6   2022
go to the *m* of the Amorites, and ....Deut 1:7   2022
we compassed *m* Seir many days..........Deut 2:1   2022
because I have given *m* Seir unto ....Deut 2:5   2022
the river of Arnon unto *m* Hermon ....Deut 3:8   2022
half *m* Gilead, and the cities ....Deut 3:12   2022
even unto *m* Sion which is Hermon, ...Deut 4:48   2022
m out of the midst of the fire ....Deut 5:4   2022
fire, and went not up into the *m* ....Deut 5:5   2022
m out of the midst of the fire ....Deut 5:22   2022
When I was gone up into the *m* to ....Deut 9:9   2022
then I abode in the *m* forty days ....Deut 9:9   2022
the Lord spake with you in the *m* ....Deut 9:10   2022
I turned and came down from the *m*......Deut 9:15   2022
and the *m* burned with fire ....Deut 9:15   2022
brook that descended out of the *m*........Deut 9:21   2022
and come up unto me into the *m* ....Deut 10:1   2022
the first, and went up into the *m* ....Deut 10:3   2022
the Lord spake unto you in the *m* ....Deut 10:4   2022
myself and came down from the *m* ....Deut 10:5   2022
And I stayed in the *m*, according ....Deut 10:10   2022
put the blessing upon *m* Gerizim ....Deut 11:29   2022
and the curse upon *m* Ebal....................Deut 11:29   2022
in *m* Ebal, and thou shalt plaister ....Deut 27:4   2022
These shall stand upon *m* Gerizim........Deut 27:12   2022
shall stand upon *m* Ebal to curse..........Deut 27:13   2022
this mountain Abarim, unto *m* Nebo .....Deut 32:49   2022
die in the *m* whither thou goest.............Deut 32:50   2022
Aaron thy brother died in *m* Hor.............Deut 32:50   2022
he shined forth from *m* Paran.................Deut 33:2   2022
the Lord God of Israel in *m* Ebal...........Josh 8:30   2022
of them over against *m* Gerizim ....Josh 8:33   2022
half of them over against *m* Ebal ....Josh 8:33   2022
Even from the *m* Halak, that goeth ....Josh 11:17   2022
valley of Lebanon under *m* Hermon ....Josh 11:17   2022
the river Arnon unto *m* Hermon ....Josh 12:1   2022
And reigned in *m* Hermon, and in ....Josh 12:5   2022
of Lebanon even unto the *m* Halak ....Josh 12:7   2022
from Baal-gad under *m* Hermon unto .....Josh 13:5   2022
all *m* Hermon, and all Bashan unto ....Josh 13:11   2022
in the *m* of the valley, ...Josh 13:19   2022
out to the cities of *m* Ephron..................Josh 15:9   2022
from Baalah westward unto *m* Seir ....Josh 15:10   2022
along unto the side of *m* Jearim ....Josh 15:10   2022
and passed along to *m* Baalah ....Josh 15:11   2022
from Jericho throughout *m* Beth-el........Josh 16:1   2022
if *m* Ephraim be too narrow for..............Josh 17:15   2022
even Timnath-serah in *m* Ephraim.........Josh 19:50   2022
Kedesh in Galilee in *m* Naphtali ....Josh 20:7   2022
and Shechem in *m* Ephraim ....Josh 20:7   2022
with her suburbs in *m* Ephraim ....Josh 21:21   2022
and I gave unto Esau *m* Seir ....Josh 24:4   2022
which is in *m* Ephraim, on the................Josh 24:30   2022
which was given him in *m* Ephraim ....Josh 24:33   2022
would dwell in *m* Heres in Aijalon ....Judg 1:35   2022
in the *m* of Ephraim, on the north ....Judg 2:9   2022
Hivites that dwelt in *m* Lebanon.............Judg 3:3   2022
from *m* Baal-hermon unto the ....Judg 3:3   2022
went down with him from the *m* ....Judg 3:27   2022
Ramah and Beth-el in *m* Ephraim ....Judg 4:5   2022
saying, Go and draw toward *m* Tabor ....Judg 4:6   2022
of Abinoam was gone up to *m* Tabor......Judg 4:12   2022
So Barak went down from *m* Tabor........Judg 4:14   2022
and depart early from *m* Gilead ....Judg 7:3   2022
throughout all *m* Ephraim, saying..........Judg 7:24   2022
and stood in the top of *m* Gerizim..........Judg 9:7   2022
Abimelech gat him up to *m* Zalmon ....Judg 9:48   2022
he dwelt in Shamir in *m* Ephraim ....Judg 10:1   2022
in the *m* of the Amalekites.....................Judg 12:15   2022
And there was a man of *m* Ephraim ....Judg 17:1   2022
he came to *m* Ephraim to the house ......Judg 17:8   2022
who when they came to *m* Ephraim ....Judg 18:2   2022
they passed thence unto *m* Ephraim ......Judg 18:13   2022
on the side of *m* Ephraim, who ....Judg 19:1   2022
even, which was also of *m* Ephraim ....Judg 19:16   2022
toward the side of *m* Ephraim.................Judg 19:18   2022
of *m* Ephraim, and his name was 1Sa 1:1   2022
And he passed through *m* Ephraim 1Sa 9:4   2022

in *m* Beth-el, and a thousand were	1Sa 13:2	2022
had hid themselves in *m* Ephraim	1Sa 14:22	2022
and fell down slain in *m* Gilboa	1Sa 31:1	2022
his three sons fallen in *m* Gilboa	1Sa 31:8	2022
happened by chance upon *m* Gilboa	2Sa 1:6	2022
went up by the ascent of *m* Olivet	2Sa 15:30	
was come to the top of the *m*	2Sa 15:32	
but a man of *m* Ephraim, Sheba the	2Sa 20:21	
The son of Hur, in *m* Ephraim	1Kin 4:8	2022
built Shechem in *m* Ephraim	1Kin 12:25	2022
to me all Israel unto *m* Carmel	1Kin 18:19	2022
prophets together unto *m* Carmel	1Kin 18:20	2022
nights unto Horeb the *m* of God	1Kin 19:8	2022
stand upon the *m* before the LORD	1Kin 19:11	2022
he went from thence to *m* Carmel	2Kin 2:25	2022
unto the man of God to *m* Carmel	2Kin 4:25	2022
m Ephraim two young men of the	2Kin 5:22	2022
and they that escape out of *m* Zion	2Kin 19:31	2022
right hand of the *m* of corruption	2Kin 23:13	2022
that were there in the *m*, and sent	2Kin 23:16	2022
five hundred men, went to *m* Seir	1Chr 4:42	2022
and Senir, and unto *m* Hermon	1Chr 5:23	2022
Shechem in *m* Ephraim with her	1Chr 6:67	2022
and fell down slain in *m* Gilboa	1Chr 10:1	2022
and his sons fallen in *m* Gilboa	1Chr 10:8	2022
the LORD at Jerusalem in *m* Moriah	2Chr 3:1	2022
Abijah stood up upon *m* Zemaraim	2Chr 13:4	2022
Zemaraim, which is in *m* Ephraim	2Chr 13:4	2022
which he had taken from *m* Ephraim	2Chr 15:8	2022
from Beer-sheba to *m* Ephraim	2Chr 19:4	2022
m Seir, whom thou wouldest not	2Chr 20:10	2022
m Seir, which were come against	2Chr 20:22	2022
against the inhabitants of *m* Seir	2Chr 20:23	2022
in the *m* of the house of the LORD	2Chr 33:15	2022
saying, Go forth unto the *m*	Neh 8:15	2022
camest down also upon *m* Sinai	Neh 9:13	2022
excellency *m* up to the heavens	Job 20:6	5927
Doth the eagle *m* up at thy	Job 39:27	1361
is *m* Zion, on the sides of the	Ps 48:2	2022
Let *m* Zion rejoice, let the	Ps 48:11	2022
this *m* Zion, wherein thou hast	Ps 74:2	2022
the *m* Zion which he loved	Ps 78:68	2022
They *m* up to the heaven, they go	Ps 107:26	5927
in the LORD shall be as *m* Zion	Ps 125:1	2022
goats, that appear from *m* Gilead	Song 4:1	2022
every dwelling place of *m* Zion	Is 4:5	2022
hosts, which dwelleth in *m* Zion	Is 8:18	2022
they shall *m* up like the lifting	Is 9:18	55
his whole work upon *m* Zion	Is 10:12	2022
the *m* of the daughter of Zion	Is 10:32	2022
upon the *m* of the congregation	Is 14:13	2022
unto the *m* of the daughter of	Is 16:1	2022
of the LORD of hosts, the *m* Zion	Is 18:7	2022
of hosts shall reign in *m* Zion	Is 24:23	2022
LORD in the holy *m* at Jerusalem	Is 27:13	2022
shall rise up as in *m* Perazim	Is 28:21	2022
lay siege against thee with a *m*	Is 29:3	4674
be, that fight against *m* Zion	Is 29:8	2022
come down to fight for *m* Zion	Is 31:4	2022
and they that escape out of *m* Zion	Is 37:32	2022
they shall *m* up with wings as	Is 40:31	5927
affliction from *m* Ephraim	Jer 4:15	2022
cast a *m* against Jerusalem	Jer 6:6	5550
upon the *m* Ephraim shall cry	Jer 31:6	2022
shall be satisfied upon *m* Ephraim	Jer 50:19	2022
Babylon should *m* up to heaven	Jer 51:53	5927
it, and cast a *m* against it	Eze 4:2	5550
wings to *m* up from the earth	Eze 10:16	7311
against the gates, to cast a *m*	Eze 21:22	5550
cast a *m* against thee, and lift up	Eze 26:8	5550
man, set thy face against *m* Seir	Eze 35:2	2022
O *m* Seir, I am against thee, and I	Eze 35:3	2022
Thus will I make *m* Seir most	Eze 35:7	2022
O *m* Seir, and all Idumea, even all	Eze 35:15	2022
north shall come, and cast up a *m*	Dan 11:15	5550
for in *m* Zion and in Jerusalem	Joel 2:32	2022
out of the *m* of Esau	Obad 8	2022
the *m* of Esau may be cut off by	Obad 9	2022
But upon *m* Zion shall be	Obad 17	2022
south shall possess the *m* of Esau	Obad 19	2022
m Zion to judge the *m* of Esau	Obad 21	2022
them in *m* Zion from henceforth	Mic 4:7	2022
and the Holy One from *m* Paran	Hab 3:3	2022
in that day upon the *m* of Olives	Zec 14:4	2022
the *m* of Olives shall cleave in	Zec 14:4	2022
unto the *m* of Olives, then sent	Mt 21:1	3735
And as he sat upon the *m* of Olives	Mt 24:3	3735
went out into the *m* of Olives	Mt 26:30	3735
at the *m* of Olives, he sendeth	Mk 11:1	3735
as he sat upon the *m* of Olives	Mk 13:3	3735
went out into the *m* of Olives	Mk 14:26	3735
at the *m* called the *m* of	Lk 19:29	3735
called the *m* of Olives	Lk 19:29	
at the descent of the *m* of Olives	Lk 19:37	3735
abode in the *m* that is called the	Lk 21:37	3735
that is called the *m* of Olives	Lk 21:37	
he was wont, to the *m* of Olives	Lk 22:39	3735
Jesus went unto the *m* of Olives	Jn 8:1	3735
from the *m* called Olivet, which	Acts 1:12	3735
to him in the wilderness of *m*	Acts 7:30	3735
which spake to him in the *m* Sina	Acts 7:38	3735
the one from the *m* Sinai, which	Gal 4:24	3735
this Agar is *m* Sinai in Arabia	Gal 4:25	3735
pattern shewed to thee in the *m*	Heb 8:5	3735
unto the *m* that might be touched	Heb 12:18	3735
But ye are come unto *m* Sion	Heb 12:22	3735
we were with him in the holy *m*	2Pet 1:18	3735
lo, a Lamb stood on the *m* Sion	Rev 14:1	3735

MOUNTAIN

unto a *m* on the east of Beth-el	Gen 12:8	2022
they that remained fled to the *m*	Gen 14:10	2022
escape to the *m*, lest thou be	Gen 19:17	2022
and I cannot escape to the *m*	Gen 19:19	2022
up out of Zoar, and dwelt in the *m*	Gen 19:30	2022
desert, and came to the *m* of God	Ex 3:1	2022
ye shall serve God upon this *m*	Ex 3:12	2022
plant them in the *m* of thine	Ex 15:17	2022
LORD called unto him out of the *m*	Ex 19:3	2022
of the trumpet, and the *m* smoking	Ex 20:18	2022
southward, and go up into the *m*	Num 13:17	2022
gat them up into the top of the *m*	Num 14:40	2022
the way of the *m* of the Amorites	Deut 1:19	2022
come unto the *m* of the Amorites	Deut 1:20	2022
they turned and went up into the *m*	Deut 1:24	2022
Amorites, which dwelt in that *m*	Deut 1:44	2022
have compassed this *m* long enough	Deut 2:3	2022
is beyond Jordan, that goodly *m*	Deut 3:25	2022
ye came near and stood under the *m*	Deut 4:11	2022
the *m* burned with fire unto the	Deut 4:11	2022
(for the *m* did burn with fire,)	Deut 5:23	2022
Get thee up into this *m* Abarim	Deut 32:49	2022
shall call the people unto the *m*	Deut 33:19	2022
plains of Moab unto the *m* of Nebo	Deut 34:1	2022
said unto them, Get you to the *m*	Josh 2:16	2022
And they went, and came unto the *m*	Josh 2:22	2022
returned, and descended from the *m*	Josh 2:23	2022
the *m* of Israel, and the valley of	Josh 11:16	2022
Now therefore give me this *m*	Josh 14:12	2022
went up to the top of the *m* that	Josh 15:8	2022
But the *m* shall be thine	Josh 17:18	2022
came down to the end of the *m*	Josh 18:16	2022
is Hebron, in the *m* of Judah	Josh 20:7	2022
Canaanites, that dwelt in the *m*	Judg 1:9	2022
out the inhabitants of the *m*	Judg 1:19	2022
the children of Dan into the *m*	Judg 1:34	2022
a trumpet in the *m* of Ephraim	Judg 3:27	2022
stood on a *m* on the one side	1Sa 17:3	2022
stood on a *m* on the other side	1Sa 17:3	2022
remained in a *m* in the wilderness	1Sa 23:14	2022
Saul went on this side of the *m*	1Sa 23:26	2022
and his men on that side of the *m*	1Sa 23:26	2022
him up, and cast him upon some *m*	2Kin 2:16	2022
the *m* was full of horses and	2Kin 6:17	2022
thousand to hew in the *m*, and	2Chr 2:2	2022
thousand to be hewers in the *m*	2Chr 2:18	2022
surely the *m* falling cometh to	Job 14:18	2022
my soul, Flee as a bird to your *m*	Ps 11:1	2022
hast made my *m* to stand strong	Ps 30:7	2042
our God, in the *m* of his holiness	Ps 48:1	2022
of his sanctuary, even to this *m*	Ps 78:54	2022
I will get me to the *m* of myrrh	Song 4:6	2022
that the of the LORD's house	Is 2:2	2022
let us go up to the *m* of the LORD	Is 2:3	2022
hurt nor destroy in all my holy *m*	Is 11:9	2022
ye up a banner upon the high *m*	Is 13:2	2022
in this *m* shall the LORD of hosts	Is 25:6	2022
he will destroy in this *m* the	Is 25:7	2022
For in this *m* shall the hand of	Is 25:10	2022
as a beacon upon the top of a *m*	Is 30:17	2022
there shall be upon every high *m*	Is 30:25	2022
to come into the *m* of the LORD	Is 30:29	2022
shall be exalted, and every *m*	Is 40:4	2022
get thee up into the high *m*	Is 40:9	2022
them will I bring to my holy *m*	Is 56:7	2022
high *m* hast thou set thy bed	Is 57:7	2022
land, and shall inherit my holy *m*	Is 57:13	2022
the LORD, that forget my holy *m*	Is 65:11	2022
hurt nor destroy in all my holy *m*	Is 65:25	2022
beasts, to my holy *m* Jerusalem	Is 66:20	2022
she is gone up upon every high *m*	Jer 3:6	2022
they shall hunt them from every *m*	Jer 16:16	2022

O my *m* in the field, I will give	Jer 17:3	2042
the *m* of the house as the high	Jer 26:18	2022
of justice, and *m* of holiness	Jer 31:23	2022
they have gone from *m* to hill	Jer 50:6	2022
I am against thee, O destroying *m*	Jer 51:25	2022
and will make thee a burnt *m*	Jer 51:25	2022
Because of the *m* of Zion, which	Lam 5:18	2022
stood upon the *m* which is on the	Eze 11:23	2022
and will plant it upon an high *m*	Eze 17:22	2022
In the *m* of the height of Israel	Eze 17:23	2022
For in mine holy *m*	Eze 20:40	2022
in the *m* of the height of Israel,	Eze 20:40	2022
thou wast upon the holy *m* of God	Eze 28:14	2022
as profane out of the *m* of God	Eze 28:16	2022
and set me upon a very high *m*	Eze 40:2	2022
Upon the top of the *m* the whole	Eze 43:12	2022
smote the image became a great *m*	Dan 2:35	2906
cut out of the *m* without hands	Dan 2:45	2906
thy city Jerusalem, thy holy *m*	Dan 9:16	2022
my God for the holy *m* of my God	Dan 9:20	2022
the seas in the glorious holy *m*	Dan 11:45	2022
and sound an alarm in my holy *m*	Joel 2:1	2022
God dwelling in Zion, my holy *m*	Joel 3:17	2022
that are in the *m* of Samaria	Amos 4:1	2022
and trust in the *m* of Samaria	Amos 6:1	2022
as ye have drunk upon my holy *m*	Obad 16	2022
the *m* of the house as the high	Mic 3:12	2022
that the *m* of the house of the	Mic 4:1	2022
let us go up to the *m* of the LORD	Mic 4:2	2022
sea to sea, and from *m* to *m*	Mic 7:12	2022
be haughty because of my holy *m*	Zeph 3:11	2022
Go up to the *m*, and bring wood, and	Hag 1:8	2022
Who art thou, O great *m*	Zec 4:7	2022
the *m* of the LORD of hosts the	Zec 8:3	2022
of the LORD of hosts the holy *m*	Zec 8:3	2022
half of the *m* shall remove toward	Zec 14:4	2022
him up into an exceeding high *m*	Mt 4:8	3735
multitudes, he went up into a *m*	Mt 5:1	3735
When he was come down from the *m*	Mt 8:1	3735
he went up into a *m* apart to pray	Mt 14:23	3735
and went up into a *m*, and sat down	Mt 15:29	3735
them up into an high *m* apart	Mt 17:1	3735
And as they came down from the *m*	Mt 17:9	3735
seed, ye shall say unto this *m*	Mt 17:20	3735
also if ye shall say unto this *m*	Mt 21:21	3735
Galilee, into a *m* where Jesus had	Mt 28:16	3735
And he goeth up into a *m*, and	Mk 3:13	3735
he departed into a *m* to pray	Mk 6:46	3735
an high *m* apart by themselves	Mk 9:2	3735
And as they came down from the *m*	Mk 9:9	3735
whosoever shall say unto this *m*	Mk 11:23	3735
shall be filled, and every *m*	Lk 3:5	3735
taking him up into an high *m*	Lk 4:5	3735
that he went out into a *m* to pray	Lk 6:12	3735
of many swine feeding on the *m*	Lk 8:32	3735
and went up into a *m* to pray	Lk 9:28	3735
Our fathers worshipped in this *m*	Jn 4:20	3735
when ye shall neither in this *m*	Jn 4:21	3735
And Jesus went up into a *m*	Jn 6:3	3735
again into a *m* himself alone	Jn 6:15	3735
if so much as a beast touch the *m*	Heb 12:20	3735
and every *m* and island were moved	Rev 6:14	3735
as it were a great *m* burning with	Rev 8:8	3735
the spirit to a great and high *m*	Rev 21:10	3735

MOUNTAINS

and the *m* were covered	Gen 7:20	2022
the month, upon the *m* of Ararat	Gen 8:4	2022
were the tops of the *m* seen	Gen 8:5	2022
the *m* which I will tell thee of	Gen 22:2	2022
them out, to slay them in the *m*	Ex 32:12	2022
and the Amorites, dwell in the *m*	Num 13:29	2022
out of the *m* of the east, saying,	Num 23:7	2042
and pitched in the *m* of Abarim	Num 33:47	2022
departed from the *m* of Abarim	Num 33:48	2022
nor unto the cities in the *m*	Deut 2:37	2022
their gods, upon the high *m*	Deut 12:2	2022
on fire the foundations of the *m*	Deut 32:22	2022
the chief things of the ancient *m*	Deut 33:15	2042
m are gathered together against	Josh 10:6	2022
that were on the north of the *m*	Josh 11:2	2022
and the Jebusite in the *m*	Josh 11:3	2022
and cut off the Anakims from the *m*	Josh 11:21	2022
Anab, and from all the *m* of Judah	Josh 11:21	2022
and from all the *m* of Israel	Josh 11:21	2022
In the *m*, and in the valleys, and	Josh 12:8	2022
And in the *m*, Shamir, and Jattir,	Josh 15:48	2022
and went up through the *m* westward	Josh 18:12	2022
The *m* melted from before the LORD	Judg 5:5	2022
them the dens which are in the *m*	Judg 6:2	2022
wait for him in the top of the *m*	Judg 9:25	2022

people down from the top of the *m*	Judg 9:36	2022
of the *m* as if they were men	Judg 9:36	2022
I may go up and down upon the *m*	Judg 11:37	2022
bewailed her virginity upon the *m*	Judg 11:38	2022
doth hunt a partridge in the *m*	1Sa 26:20	2022
Ye *m* of Gilboa, let there be no	2Sa 1:21	2022
thousand hewers in the *m*	1Kin 5:15	2022
a great and strong wind rent the *m*	1Kin 19:11	2022
am come up to the height of the *m*	2Kin 19:23	2022
as swift as the roes upon the *m*	1Chr 12:8	2022
all Israel scattered upon the *m*	2Chr 18:16	2022
high places in the *m* of Judah	2Chr 21:11	2022
also, and vine dressers in the *m*	2Chr 26:10	2022
he built cities in the *m* of Judah	2Chr 27:4	2022
Which removeth the *m*, and they	Job 9:5	2022
are wet with the showers of the *m*	Job 24:8	2022
he overturneth the *m* by the roots	Job 28:9	2022
The range of the *m* is his pasture	Job 39:8	2022
Surely the *m* bring him forth food	Job 40:20	2022
righteousness is like the great *m*	Ps 36:6	2042
though the *m* be carried into the	Ps 46:2	2022
though the *m* shake with the	Ps 46:3	2022
I know all the fowls of the *m*	Ps 50:11	2022
his strength setteth fast the *m*	Ps 65:6	2022
The *m* shall bring peace to the	Ps 72:3	2022
the earth upon the top of the *m*	Ps 72:16	2022
and excellent than the *m* of prey	Ps 76:4	2042
the flame setteth the *m* on fire	Ps 83:14	2022
His foundation is in the holy *m*	Ps 87:1	2042
Before the *m* were brought forth,	Ps 90:2	2022
the waters stood above the *m*	Ps 104:6	2022
They go up by the *m*	Ps 104:8	2022
The *m* skipped like rams, and the	Ps 114:4	2022
Ye *m*, that ye skipped like rams	Ps 114:6	2022
As the *m* are round about	Ps 125:2	2022
that descended upon the *m* of Zion	Ps 133:3	2042
touch the *m*, and they shall smoke	Ps 144:5	2022
maketh grass to grow upon the *m*	Ps 147:8	2022
M, and all hills	Ps 148:9	2022
Before the *m* were settled, before	Prov 8:25	2022
and herbs of the *m* are gathered	Prov 27:25	2022
he cometh leaping upon the *m*	Song 2:8	2022
a young hart upon the *m* of Bether	Song 2:17	2022
from the *m* of the leopards	Song 4:8	2042
a young hart upon the *m* of spices	Song 8:14	2022
established in the top of the *m*	Is 2:2	2022
And upon all the high *m*, and upon	Is 2:14	2022
The noise of a multitude in the *m*	Is 13:4	2022
upon my *m* tread him under foot	Is 14:25	2022
chaff of the *m* before the wind	Is 17:13	2022
he lifteth up an ensign on the *m*	Is 18:3	2022
together unto the fowls of the *m*	Is 18:6	2022
the walls, and of crying to the *m*	Is 22:5	2022
the *m* shall be melted with their	Is 34:3	2022
I come up to the height of the *m*	Is 37:24	2022
and weighed the *m* in scales	Is 40:12	2022
thou shalt thresh the *m*, and beat	Is 41:15	2022
them shout from the top of the *m*	Is 42:11	2022
I will make waste *m* and hills, and	Is 42:15	2022
break forth into singing, ye *m*	Is 44:23	2022
And I will make all my *m* a way	Is 49:11	2022
and break forth into singing, O *m*	Is 49:13	2022
How beautiful upon the *m* are the	Is 52:7	2022
For the *m* shall depart, and the	Is 54:10	2022
the *m* and the hills shall break	Is 55:12	2022
that the *m* might flow down at thy	Is 64:1	2022
the *m* flowed down at thy presence	Is 64:3	2022
have burned incense upon the *m*	Is 65:7	2022
out of Judah an inheritor of my *m*	Is 65:9	2022
hills, and from the multitude of *m*	Jer 3:23	2022
I beheld the *m*, and, lo, they	Jer 4:24	2022
For the *m* will I take up a	Jer 9:10	2022
your feet stumble upon the dark *m*	Jer 13:16	2022
and from the plain, and from the *m*	Jer 17:26	2022
plant vines upon the *m* of Samaria	Jer 31:5	2022
Judah, and in the cities of the *m*	Jer 32:44	2022
In the cities of the *m*, in the	Jer 33:13	2022
Surely as Tabor is among the *m*	Jer 46:18	2022
have turned them away on the *m*	Jer 50:6	2022
they pursued us upon the *m*	Lam 4:19	2022
thy face toward the *m* of Israel	Eze 6:2	2022
Ye *m* of Israel, hear the word of	Eze 6:3	2022
Thus saith the Lord GOD to the *m*	Eze 6:3	2022
hill, in all the tops of the *m*	Eze 6:13	2022
not the sounding again of the *m*	Eze 7:7	2022
shall be on the *m* like doves of	Eze 7:16	2022
And hath not eaten upon the *m*	Eze 18:6	2022
but even hath eaten upon the *m*	Eze 18:11	2022
That hath not eaten upon the *m*	Eze 18:15	2022
be heard upon the *m* of Israel	Eze 19:9	2022
and in thee they eat upon the *m*	Eze 22:9	2022

M

upon the *m* and in all the valleys	Eze 31:12	2022
I will lay thy flesh upon the *m*	Eze 32:5	2022
thou swimmest, even to the *m*	Eze 32:6	2022
the *m* of Israel shall be desolate	Eze 33:28	2022
sheep wandered through all the *m*	Eze 34:6	2022
feed them upon the *m* of Israel by	Eze 34:13	2022
upon the high *m* of Israel shall	Eze 34:14	2022
they feed upon the *m* of Israel	Eze 34:14	2022
I will fill his *m* with his slain	Eze 35:8	2022
spoken against the *m* of Israel	Eze 35:12	2022
prophesy unto the *m* of Israel	Eze 36:1	2022
Ye *m* of Israel, hear the word of	Eze 36:1	2022
ye *m* of Israel, hear the word of	Eze 36:4	2022
Thus saith the Lord GOD to the *m*	Eze 36:4	2022
land of Israel, and say unto the *m*	Eze 36:6	2022
O *m* of Israel, ye shall shoot	Eze 36:8	2022
in the land upon the *m* of Israel	Eze 37:22	2022
people, against the *m* of Israel	Eze 38:8	2022
the *m* shall be thrown down, and	Eze 38:20	2022
against him throughout all my *m*	Eze 38:21	2022
bring thee upon the *m* of Israel	Eze 39:2	2022
shalt fall upon the *m* of Israel	Eze 39:4	2022
sacrifice upon the *m* of Israel	Eze 39:17	2022
sacrifice upon the tops of the *m*	Hos 4:13	2022
and they shall say to the *m*	Hos 10:8	2022
as the morning spread upon the *m*	Joel 2:2	2022
on the tops of *m* shall they leap	Joel 2:5	2022
that the *m* shall drop down new	Joel 3:18	2022
yourselves upon the *m* of Samaria	Amos 3:9	2022
For, lo, he that formeth the *m*	Amos 4:13	2022
the *m* shall drop sweet wine, and	Amos 9:13	2022
went down to the bottoms of the *m*	Jonah 2:6	2022
the *m* shall be molten under him,	Mic 1:4	2022
established in the top of the *m*	Mic 4:1	2022
Arise, contend thou before the *m*	Mic 6:1	2022
Hear ye, O *m*, the LORD's	Mic 6:2	2022
The *m* quake at him, and the hills	Nah 1:5	2022
Behold upon the *m* the feet of him	Nah 1:15	2022
people is scattered upon the *m*	Nah 3:18	2022
the everlasting *m* were scattered	Hab 3:6	2042
The *m* saw thee, and they trembled	Hab 3:10	2022
upon the land, and upon the *m*	Hag 1:11	2022
chariots out from between two *m*	Zec 6:1	2022
and the *m* were *m* of brass	Zec 6:1	2022
shall flee to the valley of the *m*	Zec 14:5	2022
of the *m* shall reach unto Azal	Zec 14:5	2022
And I hated Esau, and laid his *m*	Mal 1:3	2022
and nine, and goeth into the *m*	Mt 18:12	3735
be in Judaea flee into the *m*	Mt 24:16	3735
night and day, he was in the *m*	Mk 5:5	3735
m a great herd of swine feeding	Mk 5:11	3735
that be in Judaea flee to the *m*	Mk 13:14	3735
which are in Judaea flee to the *m*	Lk 21:21	3735
shall they begin to say to the *m*	Lk 23:30	3735
faith, so that I could remove *m*	1Cor 13:2	3735
they wandered in deserts, and in *m*	Heb 11:38	3735
the dens and in the rocks of the *m*	Rev 6:15	3735
And said to the *m* and rocks, Fall	Rev 6:16	3735
away, and the *m* were not found	Rev 16:20	3735
The seven heads are seven *m*	Rev 17:9	3735

MOUNTED
m up from the earth in my sight	Eze 10:19	7426

MOUNTING
for by the *m* up of Luhith with	Is 15:5	4608

MOUNTS
Behold the *m*, they are come unto	Jer 32:24	5550
which are thrown down by the *m*	Jer 33:4	5550
him in the war, by casting up *m*	Eze 17:17	5550

MOURN
and Abraham came to *m* for Sarah	Gen 23:2	5594
How long wilt thou *m* for Saul	1Sa 16:1	56
with sackcloth, and *m* before Abner	2Sa 3:31	5594
prophet came to the city, to *m*	1Kin 13:29	5594
And all Israel shall *m* for him	1Kin 14:13	5594
m not, nor weep	Neh 8:9	56
together to come to *m* with him	Job 2:11	5110
that those which *m* may be exalted	Job 5:11	6937
and his soul within him shall *m*	Job 14:22	56
I *m* in my complaint, and make a	Ps 55:2	7300
thou *m* at the last, when thy	Prov 5:11	5098
wicked beareth rule, the people *m*	Prov 29:2	584
a time to *m*, and a time to dance	Eccl 3:4	5594
And her gates shall lament and *m*	Is 3:26	56
of Kir-haresheth shall ye *m*	Is 16:7	1897
The fishers also shall *m*, and all	Is 19:8	578
I did *m* as a dove	Is 38:14	1897
like bears, and *m* sore like doves	Is 59:11	1897
to comfort all that *m*	Is 61:2	57
appoint unto them that *m* in Zion	Is 61:3	57

with her, all ye that *m* for her	Is 66:10	56
For this should the earth *m*	Jer 4:28	56
How long shall the land *m*	Jer 12:4	56
mine heart shall *m* for the men of	Jer 48:31	1897
The ways of Zion do *m*, because	Lam 1:4	57
buyer rejoice, nor the seller *m*	Eze 7:12	56
The king shall *m*, and the prince	Eze 7:27	56
yet neither shalt thou *m* nor weep	Eze 24:16	5594
ye shall not *m* nor weep	Eze 24:23	5594
and *m* one toward another	Eze 24:23	5098
and I caused Lebanon to *m* for him	Eze 31:15	6937
Therefore shall the land *m*	Hos 4:3	56
people thereof shall *m* over it	Hos 10:5	56
priests, the LORD's ministers, *m*	Joel 1:9	56
of the shepherds shall *m*, and the	Amos 1:2	56
every one *m* that dwelleth therein	Amos 8:8	56
and all that dwell therein shall *m*	Amos 9:5	56
pierced, and they shall *m* for him	Zec 12:10	5594
And the land shall *m*, every family	Zec 12:12	5594
Blessed are they that *m*	Mt 5:4	3996
children of the bridechamber *m*	Mt 9:15	3996
all the tribes of the earth *m*	Mt 24:30	2875
for ye shall *m* and weep	Lk 6:25	3996
Be afflicted, and *m*, and weep	Jas 4:9	3996
earth shall weep and *m* over her	Rev 18:11	3996

MOURNED
loins, and *m* for his son many days	Gen 37:34	56
and the Egyptians *m* for him	Gen 50:3	1058
there they *m* with a great and very	Gen 50:10	5594
heard these evil tidings, they *m*	Ex 33:4	56
and the people *m* greatly	Num 14:39	56
they *m* for Aaron thirty days,	Num 20:29	1058
nevertheless Samuel *m* for Saul	1Sa 15:35	56
And they *m*, and wept, and fasted	2Sa 1:12	5594
was dead, she *m* for her husband	2Sa 11:26	5594
David *m* for his son every day	2Sa 13:37	56
had a long time for the dead	2Sa 14:2	56
they *m* over him, saying, Alas, my	1Kin 13:30	5594
and all Israel *m* for him,	1Kin 14:18	5594
Ephraim their father *m* many days	1Chr 7:22	56
Judah and Jerusalem *m* for Josiah	2Chr 35:24	56
for he *m* because of the	Ezr 10:6	56
m certain days, and fasted, and	Neh 1:4	56
m in the fifth and seventh month,	Zec 7:5	5594
we have *m* unto you, and ye have	Mt 11:17	2354
that had been with him, as they *m*	Mk 16:10	3996
we have *m* to you, and ye have not	Lk 7:32	2354
puffed up, and have not rather *m*	1Cor 5:2	3996

MOURNER
thee, feign thyself to be a *m*	2Sa 14:2	56

MOURNERS
as one that comforteth the *m*	Job 29:25	57
the *m* go about the streets	Eccl 12:5	5594
comforts unto him and to his *m*	Is 57:18	57
be unto them as the bread of *m*	Hos 9:4	205

MOURNETH
the king weepeth and *m* for Absalom	2Sa 19:1	56
as one that *m* for his mother	Ps 35:14	57
Mine eye *m* by reason of	Ps 88:9	1669
The earth and fadeth away, the	Is 24:4	56
The new wine *m*, the vine	Is 24:7	56
The earth *m* and languisheth	Is 33:9	56
and being desolate it *m* unto me	Jer 12:11	56
Judah *m*, and the gates thereof	Jer 14:2	56
because of swearing the land *m*	Jer 23:10	56
The field is wasted, the land *m*	Joel 1:10	56
as one *m* for his only son, and	Zec 12:10	5594

MOURNFULLY
that we have walked *m* before the	Mal 3:14	6941

MOURNING
The days of *m* for my father are	Gen 27:41	60
down into the grave unto my son *m*	Gen 37:35	57
when the days of his *m* were past	Gen 50:4	1086
he made a *m* for his father seven	Gen 50:10	60
saw the *m* in the floor of Atad,	Gen 50:11	60
is a grievous *m* to the Egyptians	Gen 50:11	60
I have not eaten thereof in my *m*	Deut 26:14	205
weeping and *m* for Moses were ended	Deut 34:8	60
And when the *m* was past, David	2Sa 11:27	60
mourner, and put on now *m* apparel	2Sa 14:2	60
turned into *m* unto all the people	2Sa 19:2	60
there was great *m* among the Jews	Est 4:3	60
But Haman hasted to his house *m*	Est 6:12	57
to joy, and from *m* into a good day	Est 9:22	60
who are ready to raise up their *m*	Job 3:8	3382
I went *m* without the sun	Job 30:28	6937
My harp also is turned to *m*	Job 30:31	60
turned for me my *m* into dancing	Ps 30:11	4553

I go *m* all the day long	Ps 38:6	6937
why go I *m* because of the	Ps 42:9	6937
Why go I *m* because of the	Ps 43:2	6937
is better to go to the house of *m*	Eccl 7:2	60
of the wise is in the house of *m*	Eccl 7:4	60
of hosts call to weeping, and to *m*	Is 22:12	4553
and sorrow and *m* shall flee away	Is 51:11	585
the days of thy *m* shall be ended	Is 60:20	60
for ashes, the oil of joy for *m*	Is 61:3	60
make thee *m*, as for an only son,	Jer 6:26	60
ye, and call for the *m* women	Jer 9:17	6969
Enter not into the house of *m*	Jer 16:5	4798
men tear themselves for them in *m*	Jer 16:7	60
for I will turn their *m* into joy	Jer 31:13	60
in the daughter of Judah *m*	Lam 2:5	8386
our dance is turned into *m*	Lam 5:15	60
therein lamentations, and *m*	Eze 2:10	1899
of the valleys, all of them in *m*	Eze 7:16	1993
make no *m* for the dead, bind the	Eze 24:17	60
down to the grave I caused a *m*	Eze 31:15	56
I Daniel was *m* three full weeks	Dan 10:2	56
and with weeping, and with *m*	Joel 2:12	4553
shall call the husbandman to *m*	Amos 5:16	60
And I will turn your feasts into *m*	Amos 8:10	60
make it as the *m* of an only son	Amos 8:10	60
the dragons, and *m* as the owls	Mic 1:8	60
not forth in the house of Beth-ezel	Mic 1:11	4553
there be a great *m* in Jerusalem	Zec 12:11	4553
as the *m* of Hadadrimmon in the	Zec 12:11	4553
and weeping, and great *m*, Rachel	Mt 2:18	3602
us your earnest desire, your *m*	2Cor 7:7	3602
let your laughter be turned to *m*	Jas 4:9	3997
come in one day, death, and *m*	Rev 18:8	3997

MOUSE

the weasel, and the *m*, and the	Lev 11:29	5909
and the abomination, and the *m*	Is 66:17	5909

MOUTH

which hath opened her *m* to	Gen 4:11	6310
in her *m* was an olive leaf pluckt	Gen 8:11	6310
the damsel, and enquire at her *m*	Gen 24:57	6310
great stone was upon the well's *m*	Gen 29:2	6310
the stone from the well's *m*	Gen 29:3	6310
upon the well's *m* in his place	Gen 29:3	6310
roll the stone from the well's *m*	Gen 29:8	6310
the stone from the well's *m*	Gen 29:10	6310
behold, it was in his sack's *m*	Gen 42:27	6310
again in the *m* of your sacks	Gen 43:12	6310
money was in the *m* of his sack	Gen 43:21	6310
every man's money in his sack's *m*	Gen 44:1	6310
in the sack's *m* of the youngest,	Gen 44:2	6310
that it is my *m* that speaketh	Gen 45:12	6310
unto him, Who hath made man's *m*	Ex 4:11	6310
go, and I will be with thy *m*	Ex 4:12	6310
unto him, and put words in his *m*	Ex 4:15	6310
be with thy *m*, and with his *m*	Ex 4:15	6310
shall be to thee instead of a *m*	Ex 4:16	6310
the LORD's law may be in thy *m*	Ex 13:9	6310
let it be heard out of thy *m*	Ex 23:13	6310
With him will I speak *m* to *m*	Num 12:8	6310
With him will I speak *m* to *m*	Num 12:8	6310
thing, and the earth open her *m*	Num 16:30	6310
And the earth opened her *m*	Num 16:32	6310
the LORD opened the *m* of the ass	Num 22:28	6310
the word that God putteth in my *m*	Num 22:38	6310
the LORD put a word in Balaam's *m*	Num 23:5	6310
which the LORD hath put in my *m*	Num 23:12	6310
Balaam, and put a word in his *m*	Num 23:16	6310
And the earth opened her *m*	Num 26:10	6310
all that proceedeth out of his *m*	Num 30:2	6310
hath proceeded out of your *m*	Num 32:24	6310
to death by the *m* of witnesses	Num 35:30	6310
the *m* of the LORD doth man live	Deut 8:3	6310
how the earth opened her *m*	Deut 11:6	6310
At the *m* of two witnesses, or	Deut 17:6	6310
but at the *m* of one witness he	Deut 17:6	6310
and will put my words in his *m*	Deut 18:18	6310
at the *m* of two witnesses	Deut 19:15	6310
or at the *m* of three witnesses,	Deut 19:15	6310
thou hast promised with thy *m*	Deut 23:23	6310
is very nigh unto thee, in thy *m*	Deut 30:14	6310
hear, O earth, the words of my *m*	Deut 32:1	6310
law shall not depart out of thy *m*	Josh 1:8	6310
any word proceed out of your *m*	Josh 6:10	6310
not counsel at the *m* of the LORD	Josh 9:14	6310
stones upon the *m* of the cave	Josh 10:18	6310
Open the *m* of the cave, and bring	Josh 10:22	6310
laid great stones in the cave's *m*	Josh 10:27	6310
putting their hand to their *m*	Judg 7:6	6310
unto him, Where is now thy *m*	Judg 9:38	6310
I have opened my *m* unto the LORD	Judg 11:35	6310

hast opened thy *m* unto the LORD	Judg 11:36	6310
which hath proceeded out of thy *m*	Judg 11:36	6310
peace, lay thine hand upon thy *m*	Judg 18:19	6310
the LORD, that Eli marked her *m*	1Sa 1:12	6310
my *m* is enlarged over mine	1Sa 2:1	6310
not arrogancy come out of your *m*	1Sa 2:3	6310
but no man put his hand to his *m*	1Sa 14:26	6310
and put his hand to his *m*	1Sa 14:27	6310
him, and delivered it out of his *m*	1Sa 17:35	6310
for thy *m* hath testified against	2Sa 1:16	6310
So Joab put the words in her *m*	2Sa 14:3	6310
words in the *m* of thine handmaid	2Sa 14:19	6310
a covering over the well's *m*	2Sa 17:19	6310
alone, there is tidings in his *m*	2Sa 18:25	6310
and fire out of his *m* devoured	2Sa 22:9	6310
the *m* of it within the chapter	1Kin 7:31	6310
but the *m* thereof was round after	1Kin 7:31	6310
also upon the *m* of it were	1Kin 7:31	6310
with his *m* unto David my father	1Kin 8:15	6310
thou spakest also with thy *m*	1Kin 8:24	6310
hast disobeyed the *m* of the LORD	1Kin 13:21	6310
of the LORD in thy *m* is truth	1Kin 17:24	6310
every *m* which hath not kissed him	1Kin 19:18	6310
good unto the king with one *m*	1Kin 22:13	6310
in the *m* of all his prophets	1Kin 22:22	6310
the *m* of all these thy prophets	1Kin 22:23	6310
and put his *m* upon his *m*	2Kin 4:34	6310
and the judgments of his *m*	1Chr 16:12	6310
with his *m* to my father David	2Chr 6:4	6310
and spakest with thy *m*, and hast	2Chr 6:15	6310
in the *m* of all his prophets	2Chr 18:21	6310
in the *m* of these thy prophets	2Chr 18:22	6310
words of Necho from the *m* of God	2Chr 35:22	6310
speaking from the *m* of the LORD	2Chr 36:12	6310
of the LORD by the *m* of Jeremiah	2Chr 36:21	6310
by the *m* of Jeremiah might be	2Chr 36:22	6310
the word of the LORD by the *m* of	Ezr 1:1	6310
not thy manna from their *m*	Neh 9:20	6310
the word went out of the king's *m*	Est 7:8	6310
After this opened Job his *m*	Job 3:1	6310
poor from the sword, from their *m*	Job 5:15	6310
hope, and iniquity stoppeth her *m*	Job 5:16	6310
Therefore I will not refrain my *m*	Job 7:11	6310
of thy *m* be like a strong wind	Job 8:2	6310
Till he fill thy *m* with laughing	Job 8:21	6310
mine own *m* shall condemn me	Job 9:20	6310
and the *m* taste his meat	Job 12:11	2441
For thy *m* uttereth thine iniquity	Job 15:5	6310
Thine own *m* condemneth thee, and	Job 15:6	6310
such words go out of thy *m*	Job 15:13	6310
breath of his *m* shall he go away	Job 15:30	6310
I would strengthen you with my *m*	Job 16:5	6310
have gaped upon me with their *m*	Job 16:10	6310
I intreated him with my *m*	Job 19:16	6310
wickedness be sweet in his *m*	Job 20:12	6310
but keep it still within his *m*	Job 20:13	2441
and lay your hand upon your *m*	Job 21:5	6310
I pray thee, the law from his *m*	Job 22:22	6310
him, and fill my *m* with arguments	Job 23:4	6310
his *m* more than my necessary food	Job 23:12	6310
and laid their hand on their *m*	Job 29:9	6310
cleaved to the roof of their *m*	Job 29:10	2441
they opened their *m* wide as for	Job 29:23	6310
or my *m* hath kissed my hand	Job 31:27	6310
(Neither have I suffered my *m* to	Job 31:30	2441
in the *m* of these three men	Job 32:5	6310
Behold, now I have opened my *m*	Job 33:2	6310
my tongue hath spoken in my *m*	Job 33:2	2441
words, as the *m* tasteth meat	Job 34:3	2441
doth Job open his *m* in vain	Job 35:16	6310
the sound that goeth out of his *m*	Job 37:2	6310
I will lay mine hand upon my *m*	Job 40:4	6310
he can draw up Jordan into his *m*	Job 40:23	6310
Out of his *m* go burning lamps, and	Job 41:19	6310
and a flame goeth out of his *m*	Job 41:21	6310
is no faithfulness in their *m*	Ps 5:9	6310
Out of the *m* of babes and	Ps 8:2	6310
His *m* is full of cursing and	Ps 10:7	6310
that my *m* shall not transgress	Ps 17:3	6310
with their *m* they speak proudly	Ps 17:10	6310
and fire out of his *m* devoured	Ps 18:8	6310
Let the words of my *m*, and the	Ps 19:14	6310
Save me from the lion's *m*	Ps 22:21	6310
whose *m* must be held in with bit	Ps 32:9	5716
of them by the breath of his *m*	Ps 33:6	6310
shall continually be in my *m*	Ps 34:1	6310
opened their *m* wide against me	Ps 35:21	6310
The words of his *m* are iniquity	Ps 36:3	6310
The *m* of the righteous speaketh	Ps 37:30	6310
a dumb man that openeth not his *m*	Ps 38:13	6310
in whose *m* are no reproofs	Ps 38:14	6310

M

I will keep my *m* with a bridle	Ps 39:1	6310
I was dumb, I opened not my *m*	Ps 39:9	6310
And he hath put a new song in my *m*	Ps 40:3	6310
My *m* shall speak of wisdom	Ps 49:3	6310
take my covenant in thy *m*	Ps 50:16	6310
Thou givest thy *m* to evil	Ps 50:19	6310
my *m* shall shew forth thy praise	Ps 51:15	6310
give ear to the words of my *m*	Ps 54:2	6310
The words of his *m* were smoother	Ps 55:21	6310
their teeth, O God, in their *m*	Ps 58:6	6310
they belch out with their *m*	Ps 59:7	6310
For the sin of their *m* and the	Ps 59:12	6310
they bless with their *m*, but they	Ps 62:4	6310
my *m* shall praise thee with	Ps 63:5	6310
but the *m* of them that speak lies	Ps 63:11	6310
my *m* hath spoken, when I was in	Ps 66:14	6310
I cried unto him with my *m*	Ps 66:17	6310
not the pit shut her *m* upon me	Ps 69:15	6310
Let my *m* be filled with thy	Ps 71:8	6310
My *m* shall shew forth thy	Ps 71:15	6310
They set their *m* against the	Ps 73:9	6310
your ears to the words of my *m*	Ps 78:1	6310
I will open my *m* in a parable	Ps 78:2	6310
they did flatter him with their *m*	Ps 78:36	6310
open thy *m* wide, and I will fill	Ps 81:10	6310
with my *m* will I make known thy	Ps 89:1	6310
satisfieth thy *m* with good things	Ps 103:5	5716
and the judgments of his *m*	Ps 105:5	6310
and all iniquity shall stop her *m*	Ps 107:42	6310
For the *m* of the wicked and the	Ps 109:2	6310
the *m* of the deceitful are opened	Ps 109:2	6310
greatly praise the LORD with my *m*	Ps 109:30	6310
all the judgments of thy *m*	Ps 119:13	6310
word of truth utterly out of my *m*	Ps 119:43	6310
The law of thy *m* is better unto	Ps 119:72	6310
I keep the testimony of thy *m*	Ps 119:88	6310
yea, sweeter than honey to my *m*	Ps 119:103	6310
the freewill offerings of my *m*	Ps 119:108	6310
I opened my *m*, and panted	Ps 119:131	6310
Then was our *m* filled with	Ps 126:2	6310
tongue cleave to the roof of my *m*	Ps 137:6	2441
when they hear the words of thy *m*	Ps 138:4	6310
Set a watch, O LORD, before my *m*	Ps 141:3	6310
are scattered at the grave's *m*	Ps 141:7	6310
Whose *m* speaketh vanity, and their	Ps 144:8	6310
whose *m* speaketh vanity, and their	Ps 144:11	6310
My *m* shall speak the praise of	Ps 145:21	6310
high praises of God be in their *m*	Ps 149:6	1627
out of his *m* cometh knowledge and	Prov 2:6	6310
decline from the words of my *m*	Prov 4:5	6310
Put away from thee a froward *m*	Prov 4:24	6310
her *m* is smoother than oil	Prov 5:3	2441
depart not from the words of my *m*	Prov 5:7	6310
snared with the words of thy *m*	Prov 6:2	6310
art taken with the words of thy *m*	Prov 6:2	6310
man, walketh with a froward *m*	Prov 6:12	6310
and attend to the words of my *m*	Prov 7:24	6310
For my *m* shall speak truth	Prov 8:7	2441
All the words of my *m* are in	Prov 8:8	6310
and the evil way, and the froward *m*	Prov 8:13	6310
covereth the *m* of the wicked	Prov 10:6	6310
The *m* of a righteous man is a	Prov 10:11	6310
covereth the *m* of the wicked	Prov 10:11	6310
but the *m* of the foolish is near	Prov 10:14	6310
The *m* of the just bringeth forth	Prov 10:31	6310
but the *m* of the wicked speaketh	Prov 10:32	6310
An hypocrite with his *m*	Prov 11:9	6310
overthrown by the *m* of the wicked	Prov 11:11	6310
but the *m* of the upright shall	Prov 12:6	6310
with good by the fruit of his *m*	Prov 12:14	6310
eat good by the fruit of his *m*	Prov 13:2	6310
keepeth his *m* keepeth his life	Prov 13:3	6310
In the *m* of the foolish is a rod	Prov 14:3	6310
but the *m* of fools poureth out	Prov 15:2	6310
but the *m* of fools feedeth on	Prov 15:14	6310
hath joy by the answer of his *m*	Prov 15:23	6310
but the *m* of the wicked poureth	Prov 15:28	6310
his *m* transgresseth not in	Prov 16:10	6310
heart of the wise teacheth his *m*	Prov 16:23	6310
for his *m* craveth it of him	Prov 16:26	6310
of a man's *m* are as deep waters	Prov 18:4	6310
his *m* calleth for strokes	Prov 18:6	6310
A fool's *m* is his destruction, and	Prov 18:7	6310
satisfied with the fruit of his *m*	Prov 18:20	6310
much as bring it to his *m* again	Prov 19:24	6310
the *m* of the wicked devoureth	Prov 19:28	6310
but afterwards his *m* shall be	Prov 20:17	6310
Whoso keepeth his *m* and his tongue	Prov 21:23	6310
The *m* of strange women is a deep	Prov 22:14	6310
he openeth not his *m* in the gate	Prov 24:7	6310
so is a parable in the *m* of fools	Prov 26:7	6310
so is a parable in the *m* of fools	Prov 26:9	6310
him to bring it again to his *m*	Prov 26:15	6310
and a flattering *m* worketh ruin	Prov 26:28	6310
praise thee, and not thine own *m*	Prov 27:2	6310
she eateth, and wipeth her *m*	Prov 30:20	6310
evil, lay thine hand upon thy *m*	Prov 30:32	6310
Open thy *m* for the dumb in the	Prov 31:8	6310
Open thy *m*, judge righteously, and	Prov 31:9	6310
She openeth her *m* with wisdom	Prov 31:26	6310
Be not rash with thy *m*, and let	Eccl 5:2	6310
Suffer not thy *m* to cause thy	Eccl 5:6	6310
the labour of man is for his *m*	Eccl 6:7	6310
of a wise man's *m* are gracious	Eccl 10:12	6310
the words of his *m* is foolishness	Eccl 10:13	6310
kiss me with the kisses of his *m*	Song 1:2	6310
His *m* is most sweet	Song 5:16	2441
the roof of thy *m* like the best	Song 7:9	2441
for the *m* of the LORD hath spoken	Is 1:20	6310
opened her *m* without measure	Is 5:14	6310
And he laid it upon my *m*, and said,	Is 6:7	6310
shall devour Israel with open *m*	Is 9:12	6310
and every *m* speaketh folly	Is 9:17	6310
moved the wing, or opened the *m*	Is 10:14	6310
the earth with the rod of his *m*	Is 11:4	6310
by the *m* of the brooks, and every	Is 19:7	6310
people draw near me with their *m*	Is 29:13	6310
Egypt, and have not asked at my *m*	Is 30:2	6310
for my *m* it hath commanded, and	Is 34:16	6310
for the *m* of the LORD hath spoken	Is 40:5	6310
gone out of my *m* in righteousness	Is 45:23	6310
and they went forth out of my *m*	Is 48:3	6310
he hath made my *m* like a sharp	Is 49:2	6310
And I have put my words in thy *m*	Is 51:16	6310
yet he opened not his *m*	Is 53:7	6310
is dumb, so he openeth not his *m*	Is 53:7	6310
neither was any deceit in his *m*	Is 53:9	6310
be that goeth forth out of my *m*	Is 55:11	6310
against whom make ye a wide *m*	Is 57:4	6310
for the *m* of the LORD hath spoken	Is 58:14	6310
words which I have put in thy *m*	Is 59:21	6310
shall not depart out of thy *m*	Is 59:21	6310
nor out of the *m* of thy seed	Is 59:21	6310
nor out of the *m* of thy seed's	Is 59:21	6310
which the *m* of the LORD shall	Is 62:2	6310
forth his hand, and touched my *m*	Jer 1:9	6310
I have put my words in thy *m*	Jer 1:9	6310
will make my words in thy *m* fire	Jer 5:14	6310
and is cut off from their *m*	Jer 7:28	6310
to his neighbour with his *m*	Jer 9:8	6310
who is he to whom the *m* of the	Jer 9:12	6310
ear receive the word of his *m*	Jer 9:20	6310
thou art near in their *m*, and far	Jer 12:2	6310
the vile, thou shalt be as my *m*	Jer 15:19	6310
and not out of the *m* of the LORD	Jer 23:16	6310
shall speak with him *m* to *m*	Jer 32:4	6310
shall speak with thee *m* to *m*	Jer 34:3	6310
Baruch wrote from the *m* of	Jer 36:4	6310
which thou hast written from my *m*	Jer 36:6	6310
write all these words at his *m*	Jer 36:17	6310
these words unto me with his *m*	Jer 36:18	6310
Baruch wrote at the *m* of Jeremiah	Jer 36:27	6310
who wrote therein from the *m* of	Jer 36:32	6310
goeth forth out of our own *m*	Jer 44:17	6310
shall no more be named in the *m*	Jer 44:26	6310
in a book at the *m* of Jeremiah	Jer 45:1	6310
nest in the sides of the hole's *m*	Jer 48:28	6310
I will bring forth out of his *m*	Jer 51:44	6310
have opened their *m* against thee	Lam 2:16	6310
He putteth his *m* in the dust	Lam 3:29	6310
Out of the *m* of the most High	Lam 3:38	6310
to the roof of his *m* for thirst	Lam 4:4	2441
open thy *m*, and eat that I give	Eze 2:8	6310
So I opened my *m*, and he caused me	Eze 3:2	6310
it was in my *m* as honey for	Eze 3:3	6310
therefore hear the word at my *m*	Eze 3:17	6310
cleave to the roof of thy *m*	Eze 3:26	2441
with thee, I will open thy *m*	Eze 3:27	6310
there abominable flesh into my *m*	Eze 4:14	6310
by thy *m* in the day of thy pride	Eze 16:56	6310
never open thy *m* any more because	Eze 16:63	6310
to open the *m* in the slaughter,	Eze 21:22	6310
In that day shall thy *m* be opened	Eze 24:27	6310
In that day shall thy *m* be opened	Eze 29:21	6310
of the *m* in the midst of them	Eze 29:21	6310
thou shalt hear the word at my *m*	Eze 33:7	6310
and had opened my *m*, until he came	Eze 33:22	6310
my *m* was opened, and I was no more	Eze 33:22	6310
for with their *m* they shew much	Eze 33:31	6310
deliver my flock from their *m*	Eze 34:10	6310
Thus with your *m* ye have boasted	Eze 35:13	6310
m of the burning fiery furnace	Dan 3:26	8651
the word was in the king's *m*	Dan 4:31	6433

and laid upon the *m* of the den .... Dan 6:17   6433
it had three ribs in the *m* of it .... Dan 7:5   6433
a *m* speaking great things .... Dan 7:8   6433
a *m* that spake very great things, ... Dan 7:20   6433
came flesh nor wine in my *m* .... Dan 10:3   6310
then I opened my *m*, and spake, and .... Dan 10:16   6310
the names of Baalim out of her *m* .... Hos 2:17   6310
slain them by the words of my *m* .... Hos 6:5   6310
Set the trumpet to thy *m* .... Hos 8:1   2441
for it is cut off from your *m* .... Joel 1:5   6310
out of the *m* of the lion two legs .... Amos 3:12   6310
for the *m* of the Lord of hosts .... Mic 4:4   6310
tongue is deceitful in their *m* .... Mic 6:12   6310
keep the doors of thy *m* from her .... Mic 7:5   6310
shall lay their hand upon their *m* .... Mic 7:16   6310
even fall into the *m* of the eater .... Nah 3:12   6310
tongue be found in their *m* .... Zeph 3:13   6310
weight of lead upon the *m* thereof .... Zec 5:8   6310
words by the *m* of the prophets .... Zec 8:9   6310
take away his blood out of his *m* .... Zec 9:7   6310
shall consume away in their *m* .... Zec 14:12   6310
The law of truth was in his *m* .... Mal 2:6   6310
they should seek the law at his *m* .... Mal 2:7   6310
proceedeth out of the *m* of God .... Mt 4:4   4750
And he opened his *m*, and taught .... Mt 5:2   4750
of the heart the *m* speaketh .... Mt 12:34   4750
I will open my *m* in parables .... Mt 13:35   4750
draweth nigh unto me with their *m* ..... Mt 15:8   4750
goeth into the *m* defileth a man .... Mt 15:11   4750
that which cometh out of the *m* .... Mt 15:11   4750
in at the *m* goeth into the belly .... Mt 15:17   4750
the *m* come forth from the heart .... Mt 15:18   4750
and when thou hast opened his *m* .... Mt 17:27   4750
that in the *m* of two or three .... Mt 18:16   4750
never read, Out of the *m* of babes .... Mt 21:16   4750
his *m* was opened immediately, and ..... Lk 1:64   4750
As he spake by the *m* of his holy .... Lk 1:70   4750
which proceeded out of his *m* .... Lk 4:22   4750
of the heart his *m* speaketh .... Lk 6:45   4750
to catch something out of his *m* .... Lk 11:54   4750
Out of thine own *m* will I judge .... Lk 19:22   4750
For I will give you a *m* and wisdom ..... Lk 21:15   4750
ourselves have heard of his own *m* .... Lk 22:71   4750
upon hyssop, and put it to his *m* .... Jn 19:29   4750
by the *m* of David spake before .... Acts 1:16   4750
by the *m* of all his prophets .... Acts 3:18   4750
which God hath spoken by the *m* .... Acts 3:21   4750
Who by the *m* of thy servant David ...... Acts 4:25   4750
shearer, so opened he not his *m* .... Acts 8:32   4750
Then Philip opened his *m*, and .... Acts 8:35   4750
Then Peter opened his *m*, and said, ... Acts 10:34   4750
at any time entered into my *m* .... Acts 11:8   4750
that the Gentiles by my *m* should .... Acts 15:7   4750
tell you the same things by *m* .... Acts 15:27   3056
Paul was now about to open his *m* .... Acts 18:14   4750
shouldest hear the voice of his *m* .... Acts 22:14   4750
by him to smite him on the *m* .... Acts 23:2   4750
Whose *m* is full of cursing and .... Rom 3:14   4750
that every *m* may be stopped, and .... Rom 3:19   4750
word is nigh thee, even in thy *m* .... Rom 10:8   4750
confess with thy *m* the Lord Jesus .... Rom 10:9   4750
with the *m* confession is made .... Rom 10:10   4750
one *m* glorify God, even the .... Rom 15:6   4750
Thou shalt not muzzle the *m* of 1Cor 9:9
our *m* is open unto you, our heart 2Cor 6:11   4750
In the *m* of two or three 2Cor 13:1   4750
proceed out of your *m*, but that .... Eph 4:29   4750
me, that I may open my *m* boldly .... Eph 6:19   4750
communication out of your *m* .... Col 3:8   4750
consume with the spirit of his *m* 2Th 2:8   4750
out of the *m* of the lion 2Ti 4:17   4750
Out of the same *m* proceedeth .... Jas 3:10   4750
neither was guile found in his *m* 1Pet 2:22   4750
their *m* speaketh great swelling .... Jude 16   4750
out of his *m* went a sharp .... Rev 1:16   4750
them with the sword of my *m* .... Rev 2:16   4750
hot, I will spue thee out of my *m* .... Rev 3:16   4750
For their power is in their *m* .... Rev 9:19   4750
shall be in thy *m* sweet as honey .... Rev 10:9   4750
it was in my *m* sweet as honey .... Rev 10:10   4750
fire proceedeth out of their *m* .... Rev 11:5   4750
his *m* water as a flood after the .... Rev 12:15   4750
woman, and the earth opened her *m* ..... Rev 12:16   4750
the dragon cast out of his *m* .... Rev 12:16   4750
his *m* as the *m* of a lion .... Rev 13:2   4750
and his *m* as the *m* of a lion .... Rev 13:2   4750
him a *m* speaking great things .... Rev 13:5   4750
he opened his *m* in blasphemy .... Rev 13:6   4750
in their *m* was found no guile .... Rev 14:5   4750
come out of the *m* of the dragon .... Rev 16:13   4750
out of the *m* of the beast .... Rev 16:13   4750

out of the *m* of the false prophet .... Rev 16:13   *4750*
out of his *m* goeth a sharp sword, ... Rev 19:15   *4750*
sword proceeded out of his *m* .... Rev 19:21   *4750*

MOUTHS
which we found in our sacks' *m* .... Gen 44:8   6310
put it in their *m*, that this song .... Deut 31:19   6310
out of the *m* of their seed .... Deut 31:21   6310
They gaped upon me with their *m* .... Ps 22:13   6310
their meat was yet in their *m* .... Ps 78:30   6310
They have *m*, but they speak not .... Ps 115:5   6310
They have *m*, but they speak not .... Ps 135:16   6310
is there any breath in their *m* .... Ps 135:17   6310
kings shall shut their *m* at him .... Is 52:15   6310
have both spoken with your *m* .... Jer 44:25   6310
have opened their *m* against us .... Lam 3:46   6310
angel, and hath shut the lions' *m* .... Dan 6:22   6433
he that putteth not into their *m* .... Mic 3:5   6310
Whose *m* must be stopped, who .... Titus 1:11   *1993*
promises, stopped the *m* of lions .... Heb 11:33   *4750*
we put bits in the horses' *m* .... Jas 3:3   *4750*
and out of their *m* issued fire .... Rev 9:17   *4750*
which issued out of their *m* .... Rev 9:18   *4750*

MOVE
shall not a dog *m* his tongue .... Ex 11:7   2782
of all that *m* in the waters, and .... Lev 11:10   8318
but thou shalt not *m* a sickle .... Deut 23:25   5130
I will *m* them to jealousy with .... Deut 32:21
m him at times in the camp of Dan .... Judg 13:25   6470
place of their own, and *m* no more 2Sa 7:10   7264
m any more out of the land which 2Kin 21:8   5110
let no man *m* his bones 2Kin 23:18   5128
and with hammers, that it *m* not .... Jer 10:4   6328
they shall *m* out of their holes .... Mic 7:17   7264
but they themselves will not *m* .... Mt 23:4   2795
For in him we live, and *m*, and have ...... Acts 17:28   2795
But none of these things *m* me .... Acts 20:24   3056,4160

MOVEABLE
the path of life, her ways are *m* .... Prov 5:6   5128

MOVED
the Spirit of God *m* upon the face .... Gen 1:2   7363
flesh died that *m* upon the earth .... Gen 7:21   7430
They have *m* me to jealousy with .... Deut 32:21
none *m* his tongue against any of .... Josh 10:21   2782
that she *m* him to ask of her .... Josh 15:18   5496
that she *m* him to ask of her .... Judg 1:14   5496
all the city was *m* about them .... Ruth 1:19   1949
only her lips *m*, but her voice 1Sa 1:13   5128
And the king was much *m*, and went 2Sa 18:33   7264
the foundations of heaven *m* 2Sa 22:8   7264
he *m* David against them to say, ... 2Sa 24:1   5496
shall be stable, that it be not *m* 1Chr 16:30   4131
place, and shall be *m* no more 1Chr 17:9   7264
God *m* them to depart from him 2Chr 18:31   5496
that they have *m* sedition within .... Ezr 4:15   5648
nor *m* for him, he was full of .... Est 5:9   2111
and is *m* out of his place .... Job 37:1   5425
they cannot be *m* .... Job 41:23   4131
in his heart, I shall not be *m* .... Ps 10:6   4131
trouble me rejoice when I am *m* .... Ps 13:4   4131
these things shall never be *m* .... Ps 15:5   4131
my right hand, I shall not be *m* .... Ps 16:8   4131
foundations also of the hills *m* .... Ps 18:7   7264
the most High he shall not be *m* .... Ps 21:7   4131
I said, I shall never be *m* .... Ps 30:6   4131
she shall not be *m* .... Ps 46:5   4131
raged, the kingdoms were *m* .... Ps 46:6   4131
suffer the righteous to be *m* .... Ps 55:22   4131
I shall not be greatly *m* .... Ps 62:2   4131
I shall not be *m* .... Ps 62:6   4131
and suffereth not our feet to be *m* .... Ps 66:9   4132
even Sinai itself was *m* at the .... Ps 68:8   4131
m him to jealousy with their .... Ps 78:58
stablished, that it cannot be *m* .... Ps 93:1   4131
that it shall not be *m* .... Ps 96:10   4131
let the earth be *m* .... Ps 99:1   5120
Surely he shall not be *m* for ever .... Ps 112:6   4131
will not suffer thy foot to be *m* .... Ps 121:3   4132
of the righteous shall not be *m* .... Prov 12:3   4131
door, and my bowels were *m* for him ..... Song 5:4   1993
the posts of the door *m* at the .... Is 6:4   5128
And his heart was *m*, and the heart ...... Is 7:2   5128
of the wood are *m* with the wind .... Is 7:2   5128
and there was none that *m* the wing ..... Is 10:14   5074
Hell from beneath is *m* for thee .... Is 14:9   7264
Egypt shall be *m* at his presence .... Is 19:1   5128
the earth is *m* exceedingly .... Is 24:19   4132
graven image, that shall not be *m* .... Is 40:20   4131
nails, that it should not be *m* .... Is 41:7   4131
and all the hills *m* lightly .... Jer 4:24   7043

M

And they shall drink, and be *m*	Jer 25:16	1607
whose waters are *m* as the rivers	Jer 46:7	1607
his waters are *m* like the rivers	Jer 46:8	1607
The earth is *m* at the noise of	Jer 49:21	7493
taking of Babylon the earth is *m*	Jer 50:46	7493
he was *m* with choler against him,	Dan 8:7	
the south shall be *m* with choler	Dan 11:11	
he was *m* with compassion on them,	Mt 9:36	4697
was *m* with compassion toward them	Mt 14:14	4697
servant was *m* with compassion	Mt 18:27	4697
they were *m* with indignation	Mt 20:24	23
Jerusalem, all the city was *m*	Mt 21:10	4579
m with compassion, put forth his	Mk 1:41	4697
was *m* with compassion toward them	Mk 6:34	4697
the chief priests *m* the people	Mk 15:11	383
hand, that I should not be *m*	Acts 2:25	4531
m with envy, sold Joseph into	Acts 7:9	2206
m with envy, took unto them	Acts 17:5	2206
And all the city was *m*, and the	Acts 21:30	2795
be not *m* away from the hope of	Col 1:23	3334
should be *m* by these afflictions	1Th 3:3	4525
m with fear, prepared an ark to	Heb 11:7	2125
a kingdom which cannot be *m*	Heb 12:28	761
as they were *m* by the Holy Ghost	2Pet 1:21	5342
island were *m* out of their places	Rev 6:14	2795

MOVEDST

although thou *m* me against him,	Job 2:3	5496

MOVER

a *m* of sedition among all the	Acts 24:5	2795

MOVETH

and every living creature that *m*	Gen 1:21	7430
thing that *m* upon the earth	Gen 1:28	7430
upon all that *m* upon the earth,	Gen 9:2	7430
creature that *m* in the waters	Lev 11:46	7430
He *m* his tail like a cedar	Job 40:17	2654
and every thing that *m* therein	Ps 69:34	7430
the cup, when it *m* itself aright	Prov 23:31	1980
every thing that liveth, which *m*	Eze 47:9	8317

MOVING

the *m* creature that hath life	Gen 1:20	8318
Every *m* thing that liveth shall	Gen 9:3	7430
the *m* of my lips should assuage	Job 16:5	5205
m his lips he bringeth evil to	Prov 16:30	7169
waiting for the *m* of the water	Jn 5:3	2796

MOWER

Wherewith the *m* filleth not his	Ps 129:7	7114

MOWINGS

latter growth after the king's *m*	Amos 7:1	1488

MOWN

down like rain upon the *m* grass	Ps 72:6	1488

MOZA (mo'-zah)
1. *A son of Caleb.*

concubine, bare Haran, and *M*	1Chr 2:46	4162

2. *Descendant of King Saul.*

and Zimri begat *M*,	1Chr 8:36	4162
And *M* begat Binea	1Chr 8:37	4162
and Zimri begat *M*,	1Chr 9:42	4162
And *M* begat Binea	1Chr 9:43	4162

MOZAH (mo'-zah) *A city in Benjamin.*

And Mizpeh, and Chephirah, and *M*	Josh 18:26	4681

MUCH See APPENDIX.

MUFFLERS

and the bracelets, and the *m*	Is 3:19	7479

MULBERRY

them over against the *m* trees	2Sa 5:23	1057
going in the tops of the *m* trees	2Sa 5:24	1057
them over against the *m* trees	1Chr 14:14	1057
going in the tops of the *m* trees	1Chr 14:15	1057

MULE

every man gat him up upon his *m*	2Sa 13:29	6505
And Absalom rode upon a *m*, and the	2Sa 18:9	6505
the *m* went under the thick boughs	2Sa 18:9	6505
the *m* that was under him went	2Sa 18:9	6505
my son to ride upon mine own *m*	1Kin 1:33	6506
to ride upon king David's *m*	1Kin 1:38	6506
him to ride upon the king's *m*	1Kin 1:44	6506
ye not as the horse, or as the *m*	Ps 32:9	
the plague of the horse, of the *m*	Zec 14:15	6505

MULES

found the *m* in the wilderness	Gen 36:24	3222
armour, and spices, horses, and *m*	1Kin 10:25	6505
m alive, that we lose not all the	1Kin 18:5	6505
on asses, and on camels, and on *m*	1Chr 12:40	6505
harness, and spices, horses, and *m*	2Chr 9:24	6505

their *m*, two hundred forty and	Ezr 2:66	6505
their *m*, two hundred forty and	Neh 7:68	6505
on horseback, and riders on *m*	Est 8:10	7409
So the posts that rode upon *m*	Est 8:14	7409
and in litters, and upon *m*	Is 66:20	6505
with horses and horsemen and *m*	Eze 27:14	6505

MULES'

thy servant two *m* burden of earth	2Kin 5:17	6505

MULTIPLIED

and grew, and *m* exceedingly	Gen 47:27	7235
and increased abundantly, and *m*	Ex 1:7	7235
afflicted them, the more they *m*	Ex 1:12	7235
and the people *m*, and waxed very	Ex 1:20	7235
may be *m* in the land of Egypt	Ex 1:20	7235
The LORD your God hath *m* you	Deut 1:10	7235
and thy silver and thy gold is *m*	Deut 8:13	7235
and all that thou hast is *m*	Deut 8:13	7235
That your days may be *m*, and the	Deut 11:21	7235
m his seed, and gave him Isaac	Josh 24:3	7235
were *m* in the land of Gilead	1Chr 5:9	7235
If his children be *m*, it is for	Job 27:14	7235
or if thy transgressions be *m*	Job 35:6	7231
Their sorrows shall be *m* that	Ps 16:4	7235
that hate me wrongfully are *m*	Ps 38:19	7231
also, so that they are *m* greatly	Ps 107:38	7235
For by me thy days shall be *m*	Prov 9:11	7235
When the wicked are *m*,	Prov 29:16	7235
Thou hast *m* the nation, and not	Is 9:3	7235
transgressions are *m* before thee	Is 59:12	7231
shall come to pass, when ye be *m*	Jer 3:16	7235
Because ye *m* more than the	Eze 5:7	1995
Ye have *m* your slain in this city	Eze 11:6	7235
passed by, and *m* thy whoredoms	Eze 16:25	7235
Thou hast moreover *m* thy	Eze 16:29	7235
but thou hast *m* thine	Eze 16:51	7235
may be *m*, and their ruins be *m*	Eze 21:15	7235
Yet she *m* her whoredoms, in	Eze 23:19	7235
the field, and his boughs were *m*	Eze 31:5	7235
have *m* your words against me	Eze 35:13	6280
Peace be *m* unto you.	Dan 4:1	7680
Peace be *m* unto you.	Dan 6:25	7680
m her silver and gold, which they	Hos 2:8	7235
Judah hath *m* fenced cities	Hos 8:14	7235
I have *m* visions, and used	Hos 12:10	7235
Thou hast *m* thy merchants above	Nah 3:16	7235
the number of the disciples was *m*	Acts 6:1	4129
disciples *m* in Jerusalem greatly	Acts 6:7	4129
the people grew and *m* in Egypt,	Acts 7:17	4129
comfort of the Holy Ghost, were *m*	Acts 9:31	4129
But the word of God grew and *m*	Acts 12:24	4129
Grace unto you, and peace, be *m*	1Pet 1:2	4129
peace be *m* unto you through the	2Pet 1:2	4129
unto you, and peace, and love, be *m*	Jude 2	4129

MULTIPLIEDST

Their children also *m* thou as the	Neh 9:23	7235

MULTIPLIETH

m my wounds without cause	Job 9:17	7235
us, and *m* his words against God	Job 34:37	7235
he *m* words without knowledge	Job 35:16	3527

MULTIPLY

them, saying, Be fruitful, and *m*	Gen 1:22	7235
seas, and let fowl *m* in the earth	Gen 1:22	7235
said unto them, Be fruitful, and *m*	Gen 1:28	7235
said, I will greatly *m* thy sorrow	Gen 3:16	7235
when men began to *m* on the face	Gen 6:1	7231
be fruitful, and *m* upon the earth	Gen 8:17	7235
said unto them, Be fruitful, and *m*	Gen 9:1	7235
And you, be ye fruitful, and *m*	Gen 9:7	7235
in the earth, and *m* therein	Gen 9:7	7235
I will *m* thy seed exceedingly,	Gen 16:10	7235
thee, and will *m* thee exceedingly	Gen 17:2	7235
and will *m* him exceedingly	Gen 17:20	7235
in multiplying I will *m* thy seed	Gen 22:17	7235
seed to *m* as the stars of heaven	Gen 26:4	7235
m thy seed for my servant	Gen 26:24	7235
m thee, that thou mayest be *m*	Gen 28:3	7235
be fruitful and *m*	Gen 35:11	7235
m thee, and I will make of thee a	Gen 48:4	7235
lest they *m*, and it come to pass,	Ex 1:10	7235
m my signs and my wonders in the	Ex 7:3	7235
beast of the field *m* against thee	Ex 23:29	7227
I will *m* your seed as the stars	Ex 32:13	7235
m you, and establish my covenant	Lev 26:9	7235
thee, and bless thee, and *m* thee	Deut 7:13	7235
to do, that ye may live, and *m*	Deut 8:1	7235
And when thy herds and thy flocks *m*	Deut 8:13	7235
m thee, as he hath sworn unto thy	Deut 13:17	7235
But he shall not *m* horses to	Deut 17:16	7235

the end that he should *m* horses	Deut 17:16	7235
shall he *m* wives to himself	Deut 17:17	7235
he greatly *m* to himself silver	Deut 17:17	7235
you to do you good, and to *m* you	Deut 28:63	7235
good, and *m* thee above thy fathers	Deut 30:5	7235
that thou mayest live and *m*	Deut 30:16	7235
neither did all their family *m*	1Chr 4:27	7235
I shall *m* my days as the sand	Job 29:18	7235
and I will *m* them, and they shall	Jer 30:19	7235
so will I *m* the seed of David my	Jer 33:22	7235
I have caused thee to *m* as the	Eze 16:7	7233
I will *m* men upon you, all the	Eze 36:10	7235
I will *m* upon you man and beast	Eze 36:11	7235
I will *m* the fruit of the tree,	Eze 36:30	7235
m them, and will set my sanctuary	Eze 37:26	7235
at Gilgal *m* transgression	Amos 4:4	7235
m your seed sown, and increase the	2Cor 9:10	4129
and multiplying I will *m* thee	Heb 6:14	4129

MULTIPLYING

in *m* I will multiply thy seed as	Gen 22:17	7235
thee, and *m* I will multiply thee	Heb 6:14	4129

MULTITUDE

it shall not be numbered for *m*	Gen 16:10	7230
that thou mayest be a *m* of people	Gen 28:3	6951
and it is now increased unto a *m*	Gen 30:30	7230
which cannot be numbered for *m*	Gen 32:12	7230
I will make of thee a *m* of people	Gen 48:4	6951
let them grow into a *m* in the	Gen 48:16	7230
seed shall become a *m* of nations	Gen 48:19	4393
a mixed *m* went up also with them	Ex 12:38	7227
shalt not follow a *m* to do evil	Ex 23:2	7227
According to the *m* of years thou	Lev 25:16	7230
the mixt *m* that was among them	Num 11:4	628
Gad had a very great *m* of cattle	Num 32:1	7227
day as the stars of heaven for *m*	Deut 1:10	7230
thee as the stars of heaven for *m*	Deut 10:22	7230
were as the stars of heaven for *m*	Deut 28:62	7230
that is upon the sea shore in *m*	Josh 11:4	7230
army, with his chariots and his *m*	Judg 4:7	1995
they came as grasshoppers for *m*	Judg 6:5	7230
valley like grasshoppers for *m*	Judg 7:12	7230
as the sand by the sea side for *m*	Judg 7:12	7230
which is on the sea shore in *m*	1Sa 13:5	7230
the *m* melted away, and they went	1Sa 14:16	1995
even among the whole *m* of Israel	2Sa 6:19	1995
the sand that is by the sea for *m*	2Sa 17:11	7230
be numbered nor counted for *m*	1Kin 3:8	7230
the sand which is by the sea in *m*	1Kin 4:20	7230
not be told nor numbered for *m*	1Kin 8:5	7230
Hast thou seen all this great *m*	1Kin 20:13	1995
all this great *m* into thine hand	1Kin 20:28	
they are as all the *m* of Israel	2Kin 7:13	1995
they are even as all the *m* of the	2Kin 7:13	1995
With the *m* of my chariots I am	2Kin 19:23	7393
with the remnant of the *m*	2Kin 25:11	1995
like the dust of the earth in *m*	2Chr 1:9	7227
not be told nor numbered for *m*	2Chr 5:6	7230
and ye be a great *m*, and there are	2Chr 13:8	1995
in thy name we go against this *m*	2Chr 14:11	1995
There cometh a great *m* against	2Chr 20:2	1995
by reason of this great *m*	2Chr 20:15	1995
they looked unto the *m*, and	2Chr 20:24	1995
away a great *m* of them captives	2Chr 28:5	
For a *m* of the people, even many	2Chr 30:18	4768
nor for all the *m* that is with	2Chr 32:7	1995
from Israel all the mixed *m*	Neh 13:3	6154
the *m* of his children, and all the	Est 5:11	7230
accepted of the *m* of his brethren	Est 10:3	7230
Should not the *m* of words be	Job 11:2	7230
Did I fear a great *m*, or did the	Job 31:34	1995
m of years should teach wisdom	Job 32:7	7230
the *m* of his bones with strong	Job 33:19	7379
By reason of the *m* of oppressions	Job 35:9	7230
He scorneth the *m* of the city	Job 39:7	1995
thy house in the *m* of thy mercy	Ps 5:7	7230
cast them out in the *m* of their	Ps 5:10	7230
no king saved by the *m* of an host	Ps 33:16	7230
for I had gone with the *m*	Ps 42:4	5519
with a *m* that kept holyday	Ps 42:4	1995
in the *m* of their riches	Ps 49:6	7230
according unto the *m* of thy	Ps 51:1	7230
the *m* of the bulls, with the	Ps 68:30	5712
in the *m* of thy mercy hear me, in	Ps 69:13	7230
to the *m* of thy tender mercies	Ps 69:16	7230
unto the *m* of the wicked	Ps 74:19	2416
In the *m* of my thoughts within me	Ps 94:19	7230
let the *m* of isles be glad	Ps 97:1	7227
not the *m* of thy mercies	Ps 106:7	7230
according to the *m* of his mercies	Ps 106:45	7230
I will praise him among the *m*	Ps 109:30	7227

In the *m* of words there wanteth	Prov 10:19	7230
but in the *m* of counsellors there	Prov 11:14	7230
In the *m* of people is the king's	Prov 14:28	7230
but in the *m* of counsellors they	Prov 15:22	7230
There is gold, and a *m* of rubies	Prov 20:15	7230
in *m* of counsellors there is	Prov 24:6	7230
cometh through the *m* of business	Eccl 5:3	7230
voice is known by *m* of words	Eccl 5:3	7230
For in the *m* of dreams and many	Eccl 5:7	7230
To what purpose is the *m* of your	Is 1:11	7230
their *m* dried up with thirst	Is 5:13	1995
and their glory, and their *m*	Is 5:14	1995
The noise of a *m* in the mountains	Is 13:4	1995
contemned, with all that great *m*	Is 16:14	1995
Woe to the *m* of many people,	Is 17:12	1995
Moreover the *m* of thy strangers	Is 29:5	1995
the *m* of the terrible ones shall	Is 29:5	1995
the *m* of all the nations that	Is 29:7	1995
so shall the *m* of all the nations	Is 29:8	1995
when a *m* of shepherds is called	Is 31:4	4393
the *m* of the city shall be left	Is 32:14	1995
By the *m* of my chariots am I come	Is 37:24	7230
for the *m* of thy sorceries	Is 47:9	7230
with the *m* of thy sorceries,	Is 47:12	7230
wearied in the *m* of thy counsels	Is 47:13	7230
The *m* of camels shall cover thee,	Is 60:6	8229
according to the *m* of his	Is 63:7	7230
hills, and from the *m* of mountains	Jer 3:23	1995
there is a *m* of waters in the	Jer 10:13	1995
they have called a *m* after thee	Jer 12:6	4392
for the *m* of thine iniquity	Jer 30:14	7230
for the *m* of thine iniquity	Jer 30:15	7230
women that stood by, a great *m*	Jer 44:15	6951
Behold, I will punish the *m* of No	Jer 46:25	582
the *m* of their cattle a spoil	Jer 49:32	527
there is a *m* of waters in the	Jer 51:16	527
with the *m* of the waves thereof	Jer 51:42	527
of Babylon, and the rest of the *m*	Jer 52:15	527
for the *m* of her transgressions	Lam 1:5	7230
according to the *m* of his mercies	Lam 3:32	7230
them shall remain, nor of their *m*	Eze 7:11	1995
wrath is upon all the *m* thereof	Eze 7:12	1995
is touching the whole *m* thereof	Eze 7:13	1995
wrath is upon all the *m* thereof	Eze 7:14	1995
according to the *m* of his idols	Eze 14:4	7230
height with the *m* of her branches	Eze 19:11	7230
a voice of a *m* being at ease was	Eze 23:42	1995
of the *m* of all kind of riches	Eze 27:12	7230
the *m* of the wares of thy making	Eze 27:16	7230
was thy merchant in the *m* of the	Eze 27:18	7230
making, for the *m* of all riches	Eze 27:18	7230
earth with the *m* of thy riches	Eze 27:33	7230
By the *m* of thy merchandise they	Eze 28:16	7230
by the *m* of thine iniquities	Eze 28:18	7230
and he shall take her *m*, and take	Eze 29:19	1995
and they shall take away her *m*	Eze 30:4	1995
I will also make the *m* of Egypt	Eze 30:10	1995
and I will cut off the *m* of No	Eze 30:15	1995
king of Egypt, and to his *m*	Eze 31:2	1995
long because of the *m* of waters	Eze 31:5	7227
him fair by the *m* of his branches	Eze 31:9	7230
This is Pharaoh and all his *m*	Eze 31:18	1995
mighty will I cause thy *m* to fall	Eze 32:12	1995
all the *m* thereof shall be	Eze 32:12	1995
even for Egypt, and for all her *m*	Eze 32:16	1995
of man, wail for the *m* of Egypt	Eze 32:18	1995
all her *m* round about her grave,	Eze 32:24	1995
midst of the slain with all her *m*	Eze 32:25	1995
is Meshech, Tubal, and all her *m*	Eze 32:26	1995
shall be comforted over all his *m*	Eze 32:31	1995
sword, even Pharaoh and all his *m*	Eze 32:32	1995
shall they bury Gog and all his *m*	Eze 39:11	1995
shall be a very great *m* of fish	Eze 47:9	
his words like the voice of a *m*	Dan 10:6	1995
assemble a *m* of great forces	Dan 11:10	1995
and he shall set forth a great *m*	Dan 11:11	1995
but the *m* shall be given into his	Dan 11:11	1995
And when he hath taken away the *m*	Dan 11:12	1995
shall set forth a *m* greater than	Dan 11:13	1995
for the *m* of thine iniquity, and	Hos 9:7	7230
according to the *m* of his fruit	Hos 10:1	7230
in the *m* of thy mighty men	Hos 10:13	7230
noise by reason of the *m* of men	Mic 2:12	
and there is a *m* of slain, and a	Nah 3:3	7230
Because of the *m* of the whoredoms	Nah 3:4	7230
without walls for the *m* of men	Zec 2:4	7230
the whole *m* stood on the shore	Mt 13:2	3793
Jesus unto the *m* in parables	Mt 13:34	3793
Then Jesus sent the *m* away	Mt 13:36	3793
put him to death, he feared the *m*	Mt 14:5	3793
went forth, and saw a great *m*	Mt 14:14	3793

M

send the *m* away, that they may go	Mt 14:15	3793
he commanded the *m* to sit down on	Mt 14:19	3793
and the disciples to the *m*	Mt 14:19	3793
And he called the *m*, and said unto	Mt 15:10	3793
Insomuch that the *m* wondered	Mt 15:31	3793
said, I have compassion on the *m*	Mt 15:32	3793
as to fill so great a *m*	Mt 15:33	3793
he commanded the *m* to sit down on	Mt 15:35	3793
and the disciples to the *m*	Mt 15:36	3793
And he sent away the *m*, and took	Mt 15:39	3793
And when they were come to the *m*	Mt 17:14	3793
Jericho, a great *m* followed him	Mt 20:29	3793
the *m* rebuked them, because they	Mt 20:31	3793
a very great *m* spread their	Mt 21:8	3793
the *m* said, This is Jesus the	Mt 21:11	3793
hands on him, they feared the *m*	Mt 21:46	3793
when the *m* heard this, they were	Mt 22:33	3793
Then spake Jesus to the *m*	Mt 23:1	3793
and with him a great *m* with swords	Mt 26:47	3793
elders persuaded the *m* that they	Mt 27:20	3793
and washed his hands before the *m*	Mt 27:24	3793
all the *m* resorted unto him, and	Mk 2:13	3793
a great *m* from Galilee followed	Mk 3:7	4128
about Tyre and Sidon, a great *m*	Mk 3:8	4128
wait on him because of the *m*	Mk 3:9	3793
the *m* cometh together again, so	Mk 3:20	3793
the *m* sat about him, and they said	Mk 3:32	3793
was gathered unto him a great *m*	Mk 4:1	3793
the whole *m* was by the sea on the	Mk 4:1	3793
And when they had sent away the *m*	Mk 4:36	3793
Thou seest the *m* thronging thee	Mk 5:31	3793
And he took him aside from the *m*	Mk 7:33	3793
those days the *m* being very great	Mk 8:1	3793
I have compassion on the *m*	Mk 8:2	3793
he saw a great *m* about them	Mk 9:14	3793
And one of the *m* answered and said,	Mk 9:17	3793
and with him a great *m* with swords	Mk 14:43	3793
the *m* crying aloud began to	Mk 15:8	3793
the whole *m* of the people were	Lk 1:10	4128
there was with the angel a *m* of	Lk 2:13	4128
Then said he to the *m* that came	Lk 3:7	3793
they inclosed a great *m* of fishes	Lk 5:6	4128
bring him in because of the *m*	Lk 5:19	3793
a great *m* of people out of all	Lk 6:17	4128
the whole *m* sought to touch him	Lk 6:19	3793
Then the whole *m* of the country	Lk 8:37	4128
the *m* throng thee and press thee,	Lk 8:45	3793
and said unto him, Send the *m* away	Lk 9:12	3793
the disciples to set before the *m*	Lk 9:16	3793
an innumerable *m* of people	Lk 12:1	3461
And hearing the *m* pass by, he	Lk 18:36	3793
the whole *m* of the disciples	Lk 19:37	4128
from among the *m* said unto him	Lk 19:39	3793
unto them in the absence of the *m*	Lk 22:6	3793
And while he yet spake, behold a *m*	Lk 22:47	3793
the whole *m* of them arose, and led	Lk 23:1	4128
lay a great *m* of impotent folk	Jn 5:3	4128
away, a *m* being in that place	Jn 5:13	3793
a great *m* followed him, because	Jn 6:2	3793
to draw it for the *m* of fishes	Jn 21:6	4128
the *m* came together, and were	Acts 2:6	4128
the *m* of them that believed were	Acts 4:32	4128
There came also a *m* out of the	Acts 5:16	4128
the *m* of the disciples unto them	Acts 6:2	4128
And the saying pleased the whole *m*	Acts 6:5	4128
that a great *m* both of the Jews	Acts 14:1	4128
But the *m* of the city was divided	Acts 14:4	4128
Then all the *m* kept silence	Acts 15:12	4128
they had gathered the *m* together	Acts 15:30	4128
the *m* rose up together against	Acts 16:22	3793
and of the devout Greeks a great *m*	Acts 17:4	4128
evil of that way before the *m*	Acts 19:9	4128
they drew Alexander out of the *m*	Acts 19:33	3793
the *m* must needs come together	Acts 21:22	4128
thing, some another, among the *m*	Acts 21:34	3793
For the *m* of the people followed	Acts 21:36	4128
and the *m* was divided	Acts 23:7	4128
in the temple, neither with *m*	Acts 24:18	3793
about whom all the *m* of the Jews	Acts 25:24	4128
many as the stars of the sky in *m*	Heb 11:12	4128
death, and shall hide a *m* of sins	Jas 5:20	4128
charity shall cover the *m* of sins	1Pet 4:8	4128
this I beheld, and, lo, a great *m*	Rev 7:9	3793
as it were the voice of a great *m*	Rev 19:6	3793

MULTITUDES

draw her and all her *m*	Eze 32:20	1995
M, *m* in the valley of	Joel 3:14	1995
great *m* of people from Galilee	Mt 4:25	3793
And seeing the *m*, he went up into	Mt 5:1	3793
mountain, great *m* followed him	Mt 8:1	3793

when Jesus saw great *m* about him	Mt 8:18	3793
But when the *m* saw it, they	Mt 9:8	3793
the *m* marvelled, saying, It was	Mt 9:33	3793
But when he saw the *m*, he was	Mt 9:36	3793
to say unto the *m* concerning John	Mt 11:7	3793
great *m* followed him, and he	Mt 12:15	3793
great *m* were gathered together	Mt 13:2	3793
side, while he sent the *m* away	Mt 14:22	3793
And when he had sent the *m* away	Mt 14:23	3793
great *m* came unto him, having	Mt 15:30	3793
And great *m* followed him	Mt 19:2	3793
the *m* that went before, and that	Mt 21:9	3793
same hour said Jesus to the *m*	Mt 26:55	3793
great *m* came together to hear, and	Lk 5:15	3793
And there went great *m* with him	Lk 14:25	3793
the Lord, *m* both of men and women	Acts 5:14	4128
But when the Jews saw the *m*	Acts 13:45	3793
whore sitteth, are peoples, and *m*	Rev 17:15	3793

MUNITION

that fight against her and her *m*	Is 29:7	4685
keep the *m*, watch the way, make	Nah 2:1	4694

MUNITIONS

defence shall be the *m* of rocks	Is 33:16	4679

MUPPIM *(mup'-pim)* See Shuppim. *A son of Benjamin.*

Gera, and Naaman, Ehi, and Rosh, *M*	Gen 46:21	4649

MURDER

places doth he *m* the innocent	Ps 10:8	2026
the stranger, and *m* the fatherless	Ps 94:6	7523
Will ye steal, *m*, and commit	Jer 7:9	7523
priests *m* in the way by consent	Hos 6:9	7523
Jesus said, Thou shalt do no *m*	Mt 19:18	5407
who had committed *m* in the	Mk 15:7	5408
made in the city, and for *m*	Lk 23:19	5408
m was cast into prison, whom thou	Lk 23:25	5408
full of envy, *m*, debate, deceit,	Rom 1:29	5408

MURDERER

iron, so that he die, he is a *m*	Num 35:16	7523
the *m* shall surely be put to	Num 35:16	7523
he may die, and he die, he is a *m*	Num 35:17	7523
the *m* shall surely be put to	Num 35:17	7523
he may die, and he die, he is a *m*	Num 35:18	7523
the *m* shall surely be put to	Num 35:18	7523
of blood himself shall slay the *m*	Num 35:19	7523
for he is a *m*	Num 35:21	7523
of blood shall slay the *m*	Num 35:21	7523
the *m* shall be put to death by	Num 35:30	7523
satisfaction for the life of a *m*	Num 35:31	7523
See ye how this son of a *m* hath	2Kin 6:32	7523
The *m* rising with the light	Job 24:14	7523
bring forth his children to the *m*	Hos 9:13	2026
He was a *m* from the beginning, and	Jn 8:44	443
desired a *m* to be granted unto	Acts 3:14	5406
No doubt this man is a *m*	Acts 28:4	5406
But let none of you suffer as a *m*	1Pet 4:15	5406
hateth his brother is a *m*	1Jn 3:15	443
ye know that no *m* hath eternal	1Jn 3:15	443

MURDERERS

the children of the *m* he slew not	2Kin 14:6	5221
lodged in it; but now *m*	Is 1:21	7523
my soul is wearied because of *m*	Jer 4:31	2026
his armies, and destroyed those *m*	Mt 22:7	5406
have been now the betrayers and *m*	Acts 7:52	5406
four thousand men that were *m*	Acts 21:38	4607
for *m* of fathers and *m* of	1Ti 1:9	3964
m of mothers, for manslayers,	1Ti 1:9	3389
and the abominable, and, *m*, and	Rev 21:8	5406
sorcerers, and whoremongers, and *m*	Rev 22:15	5406

MURDERS

heart proceed evil thoughts, *m*	Mt 15:19	5408
adulteries, fornications, *m*	Mk 7:21	5408
Envyings, *m*, drunkenness,	Gal 5:21	5408
Neither repented they of their *m*	Rev 9:21	5408

MURMUR

what are we, that ye *m* against us	Ex 16:7	3885
murmurings which ye *m* against him	Ex 16:8	3885
congregation, which *m* against me	Num 14:27	3885
Israel, which they *m* against me	Num 14:27	3885
the congregation to *m* against him	Num 14:36	3885
is Aaron, that ye *m* against him	Num 16:11	3885
whereby they *m* against you	Num 17:5	3885
unto them, *M* not among yourselves	Jn 6:43	1111
Neither *m* ye, as some of them	1Cor 10:10	1111

MURMURED

the people *m* against Moses,	Ex 15:24	3885
of Israel *m* against Moses	Ex 16:2	3885
the people *m* against Moses, and	Ex 17:3	3885

of Israel *m* against Moses	Num 14:2	3885
upward, which have *m* against me	Num 14:29	3885
of Israel *m* against Moses	Num 16:41	3885
ye *m* in your tents, and said,	Deut 1:27	7279
m against the princes	Josh 9:18	3885
But *m* in their tents, and	Ps 106:25	7279
they that *m* shall learn doctrine	Is 29:24	7279
they *m* against the goodman of the	Mt 20:11	*1111*
And they *m* against her	Mk 14:5	*1690*
Pharisees *m* against his disciples	Lk 5:30	*1111*
And the Pharisees and scribes *m*	Lk 15:2	*1234*
And when they saw it, they all *m*	Lk 19:7	*1234*
The Jews then *m* at him, because	Jn 6:41	*1111*
that his disciples *m* at it	Jn 6:61	*1111*
m such things concerning him	Jn 7:32	*1111*
murmur ye, as some of them also *m*	1Cor 10:10	*1111*

MURMURERS
These are *m*, complainers, walking	Jude 16	*1113*

MURMURING
there was much *m* among the people	Jn 7:12	*1112*
there arose a *m* of the Grecians	Acts 6:1	*1112*

MURMURINGS
heareth your *m* against the LORD	Ex 16:7	8519
m which ye murmur against him	Ex 16:8	8519
your *m* are not against us, but	Ex 16:8	8519
for he hath heard your *m*	Ex 16:9	8519
I have heard the *m* of the	Ex 16:12	8519
I have heard the *m* of the	Num 14:27	8519
the *m* of the children of Israel	Num 17:5	8519
quite take away their *m* from me	Num 17:10	8519
Do all things without *m* and	Phil 2:14	*1112*

MURRAIN
there shall be a very grievous *m*	Ex 9:3	1698

MUSE
I *m* on the work of thy hands	Ps 143:5	7878

MUSED
all men *m* in their hearts of John	Lk 3:15	*1260*

MUSHI (mu'-shi) See MUSHITES. A son of Merari.
of Merari; Mahali and *M*	Ex 6:19	4187
families; Mahli, and *M*	Num 3:20	4187
Merari; Mahli, and *M*	1Chr 6:19	4187
The son of Mahli, the son of *M*	1Chr 6:47	4187
Merari; Mahli, and *M*	1Chr 23:21	4187
The sons of *M*; Mahli	1Chr 23:23	4187
sons of Merari were Mahli and *M*	1Chr 24:26	4187
The sons also of *M*	1Chr 24:30	4187

MUSHITES (mu'-shites) The family of Mushi.
Mahlites, and the family of the *M*	Num 3:33	4188
the Mahlites, the family of the *M*	Num 26:58	4188

MUSICAL
with *m* instruments of God	1Chr 16:42	7892
with the *m* instruments of David	Neh 12:36	7892
as *m* instruments, and that of all	Eccl 2:8	7705

MUSICIAN
To the chief *M* on Neginoth	Ps 4:t	5329
To the chief *M* upon Nehiloth, A	Ps 5:t	5329
To the chief *M* on Neginoth upon	Ps 6:t	5329
To the chief *M* upon Gittith	Ps 8:t	5329
To the chief *M* upon Muth-labben,	Ps 9:t	5329
To the chief *M*, A Psalm of David	Ps 11:t	5329
To the chief *M* upon Sheminith, A	Ps 12:t	5329
To the chief *M*, A Psalm of David	Ps 13:t	5329
To the chief *M*, A Psalm of David	Ps 14:t	5329
To the chief *M*, A Psalm of David	Ps 18:t	5329
To the chief *M*, A Psalm of David	Ps 19:t	5329
To the chief *M*, A Psalm of David	Ps 20:t	5329
To the chief *M*, A Psalm of David	Ps 21:t	5329
To the chief *M* upon Aijeleth	Ps 22:t	5329
To the chief *M*, A Psalm of David	Ps 31:t	5329
To the chief *M*, A Psalm of David	Ps 36:t	5329
To the chief *M*, even to Jeduthun,	Ps 39:t	5329
To the chief *M*, A Psalm of David	Ps 40:t	5329
To the chief *M*, A Psalm of David	Ps 41:t	5329
To the chief *M*, Maschil, for the	Ps 42:t	5329
To the chief *M* for the sons of	Ps 44:t	5329
To the chief *M* upon Shoshannim,	Ps 45:t	5329
To the chief *M* for the sons of	Ps 46:t	5329
To the chief *M*, A Psalm for the	Ps 47:t	5329
To the chief *M*, A Psalm for the	Ps 49:t	5329
To the chief *M*, A Psalm of David	Ps 51:t	5329
To the chief *M*, Maschil, A Psalm	Ps 52:t	5329
To the chief *M* upon Mahalath,	Ps 53:t	5329
To the chief *M* on Neginoth	Ps 54:t	5329
To the chief *M* on Neginoth	Ps 55:t	5329
To the chief *M* upon	Ps 56:t	5329
To the chief *M*, Altaschith,	Ps 57:t	5329

To the chief *M*, Altaschith,	Ps 58:t	5329
To the chief *M*, Altaschith,	Ps 59:t	5329
To the chief *M* upon Shushan-eduth	Ps 60:t	5329
To the chief *M* upon Neginah	Ps 61:t	5329
To the chief *M*, to Jeduthun, A	Ps 62:t	5329
To the chief *M*, A Psalm of David	Ps 64:t	5329
To the chief *M*, A Psalm and Song	Ps 65:t	5329
To the chief *M*, A Song or Psalm	Ps 66:t	5329
To the chief *M* on Neginoth	Ps 67:t	5329
To the chief *M*, A Psalm or Song	Ps 68:t	5329
To the chief *M* upon Shoshannim, A	Ps 69:t	5329
To the chief *M*, A Psalm of David,	Ps 70:t	5329
To the chief *M*, Altaschith, A	Ps 75:t	5329
To the chief *M* on Neginoth	Ps 76:t	5329
To the chief *M*, to Jeduthun, A	Ps 77:t	5329
To the chief *M* upon	Ps 80:t	5329
To the chief *M* upon Gittith	Ps 81:t	5329
To the chief *M* upon Gittith	Ps 84:t	5329
To the chief *M*, A Psalm for the	Ps 85:t	5329
chief *M* upon Mahalath Leannoth	Ps 88:t	5329
To the chief *M*, A Psalm of David	Ps 109:t	5329
To the chief *M*, A Psalm of David	Ps 139:t	5329
To the chief *M*, A Psalm of David	Ps 140:t	5329

MUSICIANS
And the voice of harpers, and *m*	Rev 18:22	3451

MUSICK
joy, and with instruments of *m*	1Sa 18:6	7892
the singers with instruments of *m*	1Chr 15:16	7892
and cymbals and instruments of *m*	2Chr 5:13	7892
with instruments of *m* of the LORD	2Chr 7:6	7892
the singers with instruments of *m*	2Chr 23:13	7892
could skill of instruments of *m*	2Chr 34:12	7892
of *m* shall be brought low	Eccl 12:4	7892
I am their *m*	Lam 3:63	4485
gate, the young men from their *m*	Lam 5:14	5058
dulcimer, and all kinds of *m*	Dan 3:5	2170
psaltery, and all kinds of *m*	Dan 3:7	2170
and dulcimer, and all kinds of *m*	Dan 3:10	2170
and dulcimer, and all kinds of *m*	Dan 3:15	2170
of *m* brought before him	Dan 6:18	
to themselves instruments of *m*	Amos 6:5	7892
nigh to the house, he heard *m*	Lk 15:25	*4858*

MUSING
while I was *m* the fire burned	Ps 39:3	1901

MUST
thy money, *m* needs be circumcised	Gen 17:13	
m I needs bring thy son again	Gen 24:5	
It *m* not be so done in our	Gen 29:26	
and said, Thou *m* come in unto me	Gen 30:16	
If it *m* be so now, do this	Gen 43:11	
time drew nigh that Israel *m* die	Gen 47:29	
for we *m* hold a feast unto the	Ex 10:9	
Thou *m* give us also sacrifices and	Ex 10:25	
for thereof *m* we take to serve	Ex 10:26	
not with what we *m* serve the LORD	Ex 10:26	
save that which every man *m* eat	Ex 12:16	
them the way wherein they *m* walk	Ex 18:20	
walk, and the work that they *m* do	Ex 18:20	
it *m* be put into water, and it	Lev 11:32	
seven days ye *m* eat unleavened	Lev 23:6	
so he *m* do after the law of his	Num 6:21	
Neither *m* the children of Israel	Num 18:22	
m we fetch you water out of this	Num 20:10	
M I not take heed to speak that	Num 23:12	
the LORD speaketh, that I *m* do	Num 23:26	
word again by what way we *m* go up	Deut 1:22	
But I *m* die in this land, I *m*	Deut 4:22	
But thou *m* eat them before the	Deut 12:18	
for thou *m* go with this people	Deut 31:7	
thy days approach that thou *m* die	Deut 31:14	
may know the way by which ye *m* go	Josh 3:4	
But that ye *m* turn away this day	Josh 22:18	
thou *m* offer it unto the LORD	Judg 13:16	
There *m* be an inheritance for	Judg 21:17	
thou *m* buy it also of Ruth the	Ruth 4:5	
was in mine hand, and, lo, I *m* die	1Sa 14:43	
For we *m* needs die, and are as	2Sa 14:14	
He that ruleth over men *m* be just	2Sa 23:3	
touch them *m* be fenced with iron	2Sa 23:7	
he sleepeth, and *m* be awaked	1Kin 18:27	
thou *m* go to be with thy fathers	1Chr 17:11	
LORD *m* be exceeding magnifical	1Chr 22:5	
As thou hast said, so *m* we do	Ezr 10:12	
whose mouth *m* be held in with bit	Ps 32:9	
friends *m* shew himself friendly	Prov 18:24	
him, yet thou *m* do it again	Prov 19:19	
then *m* he put to more strength	Eccl 10:10	
m have a thousand, and those that	Song 8:12	

For precept *m* be upon precept,	Is 28:10	
they *m* needs be borne, because	Jer 10:5	
this is a grief, and I *m* bear it	Jer 10:19	
but ye *m* tread down with your	Eze 34:18	
but ye *m* foul the residue with	Eze 34:18	
how that he *m* go unto Jerusalem,	Mt 16:21	1163
scribes that Elias *m* first come	Mt 17:10	1163
for it *m* needs be that offences	Mt 18:7	318
all these things *m* come to pass	Mt 24:6	1163
be fulfilled, that thus it *m* be	Mt 26:54	1163
but new wine *m* be put into new	Mk 2:22	
Son of man *m* suffer many things	Mk 8:31	1163
scribes that Elias *m* first come	Mk 9:11	1163
that he *m* suffer many things, and	Mk 9:12	
for such things *m* needs be	Mk 13:7	1163
the gospel *m* first be published	Mk 13:10	1163
but the scriptures *m* be fulfilled	Mk 14:49	2443
wist ye not that I *m* be about my	Lk 2:49	1163
I *m* preach the kingdom of God to	Lk 4:43	1163
But new wine *m* be put into new	Lk 5:38	
The Son of man *m* suffer many	Lk 9:22	1163
Nevertheless I *m* walk to day	Lk 13:33	1163
ground, and I *m* needs go and see it	Lk 14:18	2192
But first *m* he suffer many things	Lk 17:25	1163
for to day I *m* abide at thy house	Lk 19:5	1163
for these things *m* first come to	Lk 21:9	1163
when the passover *m* be killed	Lk 22:7	1163
m yet be accomplished in me	Lk 22:37	1163
(For of necessity he *m* release	Lk 23:17	
The Son of man *m* be delivered	Lk 24:7	1163
that all things *m* be fulfilled	Lk 24:44	1163
unto thee, Ye *m* be born again	Jn 3:7	1163
even so *m* the Son of man be	Jn 3:14	1163
He *m* increase, but I	Jn 3:30	1163
increase, but I *m* decrease	Jn 3:30	
he *m* needs go through Samaria	Jn 4:4	
him *m* worship him in spirit	Jn 4:24	1163
I *m* work the works of him that	Jn 9:4	1163
them also I *m* bring, and they	Jn 10:16	1163
The Son of man *m* be lifted up	Jn 12:34	1163
that he *m* rise again from the	Jn 20:9	1163
this scripture *m* needs have been	Acts 1:16	1163
m one be ordained to be a witness	Acts 1:22	1163
Whom the heaven *m* receive until	Acts 3:21	1163
among men, whereby we *m* be saved	Acts 4:12	1163
shall be told thee what thou *m* do	Acts 9:6	1163
he *m* suffer for my name's sake	Acts 9:16	1163
faith, and that we *m* through much	Acts 14:22	1163
Ye *m* be circumcised, and keep the	Acts 15:24	
Sirs, what *m* I do to be saved	Acts 16:30	1163
that Christ *m* needs have suffered	Acts 17:3	1163
I *m* by all means keep this feast	Acts 18:21	1163
been there, I *m* also see Rome	Acts 19:21	1163
the multitude *m* needs come	Acts 21:22	1163
so *m* thou bear witness also at	Acts 23:11	1163
thou *m* be brought before Caesar	Acts 27:24	1163
Howbeit we *m* be cast upon a	Acts 27:26	1163
Wherefore ye *m* needs be subject,	Rom 13:5	
for then *m* ye needs go out of the	1Cor 5:10	3784
For there *m* be also heresies	1Cor 11:19	1163
For he *m* reign, till he hath put	1Cor 15:25	1163
corruptible *m* put on incorruption	1Cor 15:53	1163
this mortal *m* put on immortality	1Cor 15:53	
For we *m* all appear before the	2Cor 5:10	1163
If I *m* needs glory, I will glory	2Cor 11:30	1163
A bishop then *m* be blameless	1Ti 3:2	1163
Moreover he *m* have a good report	1Ti 3:7	1163
Likewise *m* the deacons be grave,	1Ti 3:8	
Even so *m* their wives be grave,	1Ti 3:11	
The husbandman that laboureth *m*	2Ti 2:6	1163
servant of the Lord *m* not strive	2Ti 2:24	1163
For a bishop *m* be blameless	Titus 1:7	1163
Whose mouths *m* be stopped	Titus 1:11	1163
that some *m* enter therein	Heb 4:6	
there *m* also of necessity be the	Heb 9:16	
For then *m* he often have suffered	Heb 9:26	1163
to God *m* believe that he is	Heb 11:6	1163
as they that *m* give account	Heb 13:17	
m begin at the house of God	1Pet 4:17	
Knowing that shortly I *m* put off	2Pet 1:14	
which *m* shortly come to pass	Rev 1:1	1163
thee things which *m* be hereafter	Rev 4:1	1163
Thou *m* prophesy again before many	Rev 10:11	1163
he *m* in this manner be killed	Rev 13:10	1163
sword *m* be killed with the sword	Rev 13:10	1163
he *m* continue a short space	Rev 17:10	1163
after that he *m* be loosed a	Rev 20:3	1163
things which *m* shortly be done	Rev 22:6	1163

MUSTARD

is like to a grain of *m* seed	Mt 13:31	4615
have faith as a grain of *m* seed	Mt 17:20	4615
It is like a grain of *m* seed	Mk 4:31	4615
It is like a grain of *m* seed	Lk 13:19	4615
ye had faith as a grain of *m* seed	Lk 17:6	4615

MUSTERED

which *m* the people of the land,	2Kin 25:19	6633
who *m* the people of the land	Jer 52:25	6633

MUSTERETH

the Lord of hosts *m* the host of	Is 13:4	6485

MUTH-LABBEN (muth-lab'-ben) A muscial notation.

To the chief Musician upon *M*	Ps 9:t	4192

MUTTER

unto wizards that peep, and that *m*	Is 8:19	1897

MUTTERED

your tongue hath *m* perverseness	Is 59:3	1897

MUTUAL

you by the *m* faith both of you	Rom 1:12	1722,240

MUZZLE

Thou shalt not *m* the ox when he	Deut 25:4	2629
Thou shalt not *m* the mouth of the	1Cor 9:9	5392
Thou shalt not *m* the ox that	1Ti 5:18	5392

MY See APPENDIX.

MYRA (mi'-rah) A city in Lycia.

and Pamphylia, we came to *M*	Acts 27:5	3460

MYRRH

bearing spicery and balm and *m*	Gen 37:25	3910
and a little honey, spices, and *m*	Gen 43:11	3910
of pure *m* five hundred shekels	Ex 30:23	4753
to wit, six months with oil of *m*	Est 2:12	4753
All thy garments smell of *m*	Ps 45:8	4753
I have perfumed my bed with *m*	Prov 7:17	4753
A bundle of *m* is my wellbeloved	Song 1:13	4753
pillars of smoke, perfumed with *m*	Song 3:6	4753
will get me to the mountain of *m*	Song 4:6	4753
m and aloes, with all the chief	Song 4:14	4753
have gathered my *m* with my spice	Song 5:1	4753
and my hands dropped with *m*	Song 5:5	4753
my fingers with sweet smelling *m*	Song 5:5	4753
lilies, dropping sweet smelling *m*	Song 5:13	4753
gold, and frankincense, and *m*	Mt 2:11	4666
him to drink wine mingled with *m*	Mk 15:23	4669
night, and brought a mixture of *m*	Jn 19:39	4666

MYRTLE

m branches, and palm branches, and	Neh 8:15	1918
cedar, the shittah tree, and the *m*	Is 41:19	1918
brier shall come up the *m* tree	Is 55:13	1918
he stood among the *m* trees that	Zec 1:8	1918
stood among the *m* trees answered	Zec 1:10	1918
Lord that stood among the *m* trees	Zec 1:11	1918

MYSELF See APPENDIX.

MYSIA (miz'-ye-ah) A Roman province in Asia Minor.

After they were come to *M*	Acts 16:7	3463
they passing by *M* came down to	Acts 16:8	3463

MYSTERIES

the *m* of the kingdom of heaven	Mt 13:11	3466
know the *m* of the kingdom of God	Lk 8:10	3466
and stewards of the *m* of God	1Cor 4:1	3466
of prophecy, and understand all *m*	1Cor 13:2	3466
in the spirit he speaketh *m*	1Cor 14:2	3466

MYSTERY

know the *m* of the kingdom of God	Mk 4:11	3466
ye should be ignorant of this *m*	Rom 11:25	3466
to the revelation of the *m*	Rom 16:25	3466
we speak the wisdom of God in a *m*	1Cor 2:7	3466
Behold, I shew you a *m*	1Cor 15:51	3466
known unto us the *m* of his will	Eph 1:9	3466
he made known unto me the *m*	Eph 3:3	3466
my knowledge in the *m* of Christ)	Eph 3:4	3466
what is the fellowship of the *m*	Eph 3:9	3466
This is a great *m*	Eph 5:32	3466
to make known the *m* of the gospel	Eph 6:19	3466
Even the *m* which hath been hid	Col 1:26	3466
of this *m* among the Gentiles	Col 1:27	3466
acknowledgement of the *m* of God	Col 2:2	3466
to speak the *m* of Christ	Col 4:3	3466
For the *m* of iniquity doth	2Th 2:7	3466
Holding the *m* of the faith in a	1Ti 3:9	3466
great is the *m* of godliness	1Ti 3:16	3466
The *m* of the seven stars which	Rev 1:20	3466
the *m* of God should be finished,	Rev 10:7	3466
forehead was a name written, *M*	Rev 17:5	3466
will tell thee the *m* of the woman	Rev 17:7	3466

N

NAAM (na'-am) *A son of Caleb.*
Iru, Elah, and *N* 1Chr 4:15   5277

NAAMAH (na'-a-mah) See NAAMATHITE.
   1. Sister of Tubal-cain.
and the sister of Tubal-cain was *N* .... Gen 4:22   5279
   2. Mother of King Rehoboam.
mother's name was *N* an Ammonitess ... 1Kin 14:21   5279
mother's name was *N* an Ammonitess ... 1Kin 14:31   5279
mother's name was *N* an Ammonitess ... 2Chr 12:13   5279
   3. A city in Judah.
And Gederoth, Beth-dagon, and *N* .... Josh 15:41   5279

NAAMAN (na'-a-man) See NAAMAN'S, NAAMITES.
   1. A son of Benjamin.
and Becher, and Ashbel, Gera, and *N* .... Gen 46:21   5283
   2. A son of Bela.
And the sons of Bela were Ard and *N* .... Num 26:40   5283
and of *N*, the family of the .... Num 26:40   5283
And Abishua, and *N*, and Ahoah, ... 1Chr 8:4   5283
   3. A son of Ehud.
And *N*, and Ahiah, and Gera, he 1Chr 8:7   5283
   4. A Syrian captain.
Now *N*, captain of the host of the 2Kin 5:1   5283
sent *N* my servant to thee 2Kin 5:6   5283
So *N* came with his horses and with 2Kin 5:9   5283
But *N* was wroth, and went away, and .. 2Kin 5:11   5283
N said, Shall there not then, I 2Kin 5:17   5283
master hath spared *N* this Syrian......... 2Kin 5:20   5283
So Gehazi followed after *N*...................... 2Kin 5:21   5283
when *N* saw him running after him, ... 2Kin 5:21   5283
N said, Be content, take two 2Kin 5:23   5283
of *N* shall cleave unto thee 2Kin 5:27   5283
was cleansed, saving *N* the Syrian .... Lk 4:27   *3497*

NAAMAN'S (na'-a-mans) *Refers to Naaman 4.*
and she waited on *N* wife 2Kin 5:2   5283

NAAMATHITE (na'-a-math-ite) *Family name of Zophar.*
the Shuhite, and Zophar the *N* .... Job 2:11   5284
Then answered Zophar the *N*................... Job 11:1   5284
Then answered Zophar the *N*................... Job 20:1   5284
the Shuhite and Zophar the *N* went .... Job 42:9   5284

NAAMITES (na'-a-mites) *Descendants of Naaman 3.*
and of Naaman, the family of the *N* .... Num 26:40   5280

NAARAH (na'-a-rah) See NAARAN, NAARATH. *A wife of Ashur.*
Tekoa had two wives, Helah and *N* 1Chr 4:5   5292
N bare him Ahuzam, and Hepher, and ... 1Chr 4:6   5292
These were the sons of *N* 1Chr 4:6   5292

NAARAI (na'-a-rahee) See PAARAI. *A "mighty man" of David.*
Carmelite, *N* the son of Ezbai, ... 1Chr 11:37   5293

NAARAN (na'-a-ran) *A city in Ephraim.*
the towns thereof, and eastward *N*......... 1Chr 7:28   5295

NAARATH (na'-a-rath) See NAARAH, NAARAN. *Same as Naaran.*
from Janohah to Ataroth, and to *N* .... Josh 16:7   5292

NAASHON (na'-a-shon) See NAHSHON. *Brother of Elisheba.*
of Amminadab, sister of *N* .... Ex 6:23   5177

NAASSON (na'-as-son) See NAASHON. *Father of Salmon.*
and Aminadab begat *N* .... Mt 1:4   *3476*
and *N* begat Salmon .... Mt 1:4   *3476*
of Salmon, which was the son of *N* .... Lk 3:32   *3476*

NABAJOTH See NABOTH.

NABAL (na'-bal) See NABAL'S. *A wife of David.*
Now the name of the man was *N* 1Sa 25:3   5037
that *N* did shear his sheep 1Sa 25:4   5037
Get you up to Carmel, and go to *N* 1Sa 25:5   5037
they spake to *N* according to all............. 1Sa 25:9   5037
N answered David's servants, and 1Sa 25:10   5037
But she told not her husband *N* 1Sa 25:19   5037
regard this man of Belial, even *N*........... 1Sa 25:25   5037
N is his name, and folly is with 1Sa 25:25   5037
seek evil to my lord, be as *N* 1Sa 25:26   5037
there had not been left unto *N* by 1Sa 25:34   5037
And Abigail came to *N* 1Sa 25:36   5037
when the wine was gone out of *N* 1Sa 25:37   5037
days after, that the LORD smote *N* 1Sa 25:38   5037
when David heard that *N* was dead 1Sa 25:39   5037
of my reproach from the hand of *N* 1Sa 25:39   5037
wickedness of *N* upon his own head 1Sa 25:39   5037

the wife of *N* the Carmelite 1Sa 30:5   5037
the wife of *N* the Carmelite 2Sa 3:3   5037

NABAL'S (na'-balz)
N wife, saying, Behold, David.............. 1Sa 25:14   5037
N heart was merry within him for 1Sa 25:36   5037
Abigail the Carmelitess, *N* wife 1Sa 27:3   5037
Abigail *N* wife the Carmelite.................. 2Sa 2:2   5037

NABOTH (na'-both) *A Jezreelite of Issachar.*
that *N* the Jezreelite had a...................... 1Kin 21:1   5022
And Ahab spake unto *N*, saying, ... 1Kin 21:2   5022
N said to Ahab, The LORD forbid 1Kin 21:3   5022
because of the word which *N* the........... 1Kin 21:4   5022
I spake unto *N* the Jezreelite 1Kin 21:6   5022
the vineyard of *N* the Jezreelite 1Kin 21:7   5022
were in his city, dwelling with *N* 1Kin 21:8   5022
set *N* on high among the people 1Kin 21:9   5022
set *N* on high among the people 1Kin 21:12   5022
against him, even against *N* 1Kin 21:13   5022
N did blaspheme God and the king 1Kin 21:13   5022
saying, *N* is stoned, and is dead 1Kin 21:14   5022
Jezebel heard that *N* was stoned 1Kin 21:15   5022
the vineyard of *N* the Jezreelite 1Kin 21:15   5022
for *N* is not alive, but dead..................... 1Kin 21:15   5022
when Ahab heard that *N* was dead 1Kin 21:16   5022
the vineyard of *N* the Jezreelite 1Kin 21:16   5022
he is in the vineyard of *N* 1Kin 21:18   5022
of *N* shall dogs lick thy blood................. 1Kin 21:19   5022
the portion of *N* the Jezreelite................ 2Kin 9:21   5022
of the field of *N* the Jezreelite 2Kin 9:25   5022
seen yesterday the blood of *N* 2Kin 9:26   5022

NACHON See NACHON'S.

NACHON'S (na'-kons)
they came to *N* threshingfloor 2Sa 6:6   5225

NACHOR (na'-kor) See NAHOR.
   1. Brother of Abraham.
of Abraham, and the father of *N* .... Josh 24:2   5152
   2. Father of Thara; ancestor of Jesus.
of Thara, which was the son of *N* .... Lk 3:34   *3493*

NACON See NACHON'S.

NADAB (na'-dab)
   1. Son of Aaron.
and she bare him *N*, and Abihu, ... Ex 6:23   5070
unto the LORD, thou, and Aaron, *N* .... Ex 24:1   5070
Then went up Moses, and Aaron, *N* .... Ex 24:9   5070
priest's office, even Aaron, *N* .... Ex 28:1   5070
And *N* and Abihu, the sons of Aaron, ... Lev 10:1   5070
N the firstborn, and Abihu, ... Num 3:2   5070
And *N* and Abihu died before the .... Num 3:4   5070
And unto Aaron was born *N*, and.......... Num 26:60   5070
And *N* and Abihu died, when they.......... Num 26:61   5070
N, and Abihu, Eleazar, and Ithamar....... 1Chr 6:3   5070
N, and Abihu, Eleazar, and Ithamar....... 1Chr 24:1   5070
But *N* and Abihu died before their 1Chr 24:2   5070
   2. Son of King Jeroboam 1.
N his son reigned in his stead 1Kin 14:20   5070
N the son of Jeroboam began to 1Kin 15:25   5070
for *N* and all Israel laid siege to 1Kin 15:27   5070
Now the rest of the acts of *N* 1Kin 15:31   5070
   3. Great-grandson of Jerahmeel.
Shammai; *N*, and 1Chr 2:28   5070
And the sons of *N*.................................... 1Chr 2:30   5070
   4. A descendant of King Saul.
and Zur, and Kish, and Baal, and *N* 1Chr 8:30   5070
and Kish, and Baal, and Ner, and *N* 1Chr 9:36   5070

NAGGAI See NAGGE.

NAGGE (nag'-e) See NEARIAH. *Father of Esli; ancestor of Jesus.*
of Esli, which was the son of *N* .... Lk 3:25   *3477*

NAHALAL (na'-ha-lal) *A Levitical city in Zebulun.*
her suburbs, *N* with her suburbs .... Josh 21:35   5096

NAHALIEL (na-ha'-le-el) *An Israelite encampment in the wilderness.*
And from Mattanah to *N*......................... Num 21:19   5160
and from *N* to Bamoth............................. Num 21:19   5160

NAHALLAL (na'-hal-el) See NAHALAL. *Same as Nahalal.*
And Kattath, and *N*, and Shimron, and . Josh 19:15   5096

NAHALOL (na'-ha-lol) *Same as Nahalal.*
Kitron, nor the inhabitants of *N*............. Judg 1:30   5096

NAHAM (na'-ham) See ISHBAH. *A descendant of Caleb.*
his wife Hodiah the sister of *N*................ 1Chr 4:19   5163

NAHAMANI (na-ham'-a-ni) A clan chief with Zerubbabel.
Nehemiah, Azariah, Raamiah, N .... Neh 7:7   5167

NAHARAI (na'-ha-rahee) See NAHARI. A "mighty man" of David.
N the Berothite, the armourbearer 1Chr 11:39   5171

NAHARI (na'-ha-ri) See NAHARAI. Same as Naharai.
N the Beerothite, armourbearer to 2Sa 23:37   5171

NAHASH (na'-hash) See IR-NAHASH.
1. An Ammonite king.
Then N the Ammonite came up, and 1Sa 11:1   5176
all the men of Jabesh said unto N 1Sa 11:1   5176
N the Ammonite answered them, On 1Sa 11:2   5176
when ye saw that N the king of 1Sa 12:12   5176
2. Father of Shobi and Hanun.
kindness unto Hanun the son of N 2Sa 10:2   5176
that Shobi the son of N of Rabbah 2Sa 17:27   5176
that N the king of the children 1Chr 19:1   5176
kindness unto Hanun the son of N 1Chr 19:2   5176
3. Mother of Abigail.
in to Abigail the daughter of N 2Sa 17:25   5176

NAHATH (na'-hath) See TOHU.
1. A son of Reuel.
N, and Zerah, Shammah, and Mizzah ... Gen 36:13   5184
duke N, duke Zerah, duke Shammah, ... Gen 36:17   5184
N, Zerah, Shammah, and Mizzah 1Chr 1:37   5184
2. Son of Zophi.
Zophai his son, and N his son, ... 1Chr 6:26   5184
3. A Temple servant.
And Jehiel, and Azaziah, and N 2Chr 31:13   5184

NAHBI (nah'-bi) A spy sent to the Promised Land.
of Naphtali, N the son of Vophsi .... Num 13:14   5147

NAHOR (na'-hor) See NACHOR, NAHOR'S.
1. Grandfather of Abraham.
lived thirty years, and begat N .... Gen 11:22   5152
he begat N two hundred years................ Gen 11:23   5152
N lived nine and twenty years, and .... Gen 11:24   5152
N lived after he begat Terah an .... Gen 11:25   5152
Serug, N, Terah,................................... 1Chr 1:26   5152
2. Son of Terah.
seventy years, and begat Abram, N .... Gen 11:26   5152
Terah begat Abram, N, and Haran .... Gen 11:27   5152
And Abram and N took them wives ...... Gen 11:29   5152
born children unto thy brother N .... Gen 22:20   5152
these eight Milcah did bear to N .... Gen 22:23   5152
Mesopotamia, unto the city of N .... Gen 24:10   5152
son of Milcah, the wife of N .... Gen 24:15   5152
of Milcah, which she bare unto N .... Gen 24:24   5152
them, Know ye Laban the son of N .... Gen 29:5   5152
God of Abraham, and the God of N .... Gen 31:53   5152

NAHOR'S (na'-hors) Refers to Nahor 2.
and the name of N wife, Milcah, ... Gen 11:29   5152
N son, whom Milcah bare unto him .... Gen 24:47   5152

NAHSHON (nah-shon) See NAASHON, NAASSON. Son of Amminadab.
N the son of Amminadab .... Num 1:7   5177
N the son of Amminadab shall be .... Num 2:3   5177
day was N the son of Amminadab .... Num 7:12   5177
of N the son of Amminadab .... Num 7:17   5177
over his host was N the son of .... Num 10:14   5177
And Amminadab begat N, and N .... Ruth 4:20   5177
begat N, and N begat Salmon,.............. Ruth 4:20   5177
and Amminadab begat N, prince of 1Chr 2:10   5177
N begat Salma, and Salma begat 1Chr 2:11   5177

NAHUM (na'-hum) See NAUM. A prophet who spoke against Nineveh.
of the vision of N the Elkoshite .... Nah 1:1   5151

NAIL
Heber's wife took a n of the tent .... Judg 4:21   3489
smote the n into his temples, and .... Judg 4:22   3489
dead, and the n was in his temples .... Judg 4:22   3489
She put her hand to the n .... Judg 5:26   3489
to give us a n in his holy place, ... Ezr 9:8   3489
fasten him as a n in a sure place .... Is 22:23   3489
shall the n that is fastened in .... Is 22:25   3489
the corner, out of him the n .... Zec 10:4   3489

NAILING
out of the way, n it to his cross .... Col 2:14   4338

NAILS
shave her head, and pare her n .... Deut 21:12   6856
iron in abundance for the n for.............. 1Chr 22:3   4548
the weight of the n was fifty 2Chr 3:9   4548
as n fastened by the masters of .... Eccl 12:11   4930
and he fastened it with n, that it .... Is 41:7   4548
they fasten it with n and with .... Jer 10:4   4548

and his n like birds' claws .... Dan 4:33   2953
were of iron, and his n of brass.............. Dan 7:19   2953
in his hands the print of the n .... Jn 20:25   2247
my finger into the print of the n .... Jn 20:25   2247

NAIN (nane) A city in Galilee.
that he went into a city called N .... Lk 7:11   *3484*

NAIOTH (nay'-yoth) A place in Ramah.
he and Samuel went and dwelt in N 1Sa 19:18   5121
Behold, David is at N in Ramah 1Sa 19:19   5121
Behold, they be at N in Ramah.............. 1Sa 19:22   5121
And he went thither to N in Ramah 1Sa 19:23   5121
until he came to N in Ramah 1Sa 19:23   5121
And David fled from N in Ramah.......... 1Sa 20:1   5121

NAKED
And they were both n, the man and ...... Gen 2:25   6174
and they knew that they were n .... Gen 3:7   5903
and I was afraid, because I was n .... Gen 3:10   5903
Who told thee that thou wast n .... Gen 3:11   5903
Moses saw that the people were n.......... Ex 32:25   6544
(for Aaron had made them n unto .... Ex 32:25   6544
lay down n all that day and all.............. 1Sa 19:24   6174
all that were n among them 2Chr 28:15   4636
for he made Judah n, and 2Chr 28:19   6544
N came I out of my mother's womb, ... Job 1:21   6174
and n shall I return thither .... Job 1:21   6174
stripped the n of their clothing.............. Job 22:6   6174
They cause the n to lodge without......... Job 24:7   6174
him to go n without clothing.................. Job 24:10   6174
Hell is n before him, and .... Job 26:6   6174
n shall he return to go as he.................. Eccl 5:15   6174
And he did so, walking n and .... Is 20:2   6174
my servant Isaiah hath walked n .... Is 20:3   6174
captives, young and old, n .... Is 20:4   6174
when thou seest the n, that thou .... Is 58:7   6174
drunken, and shalt make thyself n........ Lam 4:21   6168
is grown, whereas thou wast n .... Eze 16:7   5903
of thy youth, when thou wast n .... Eze 16:22   5903
thy fair jewels, and leave thee n .... Eze 16:39   5903
hath covered the n with a garment .... Eze 18:7   5903
hath covered the n with a garment .... Eze 18:16   5903
thy labour, and shall leave thee n......... Eze 23:29   5903
Lest I strip her n, and set her as .... Hos 2:3   6174
shall flee away n in that day .... Amos 2:16   6174
and howl, I will go stripped and n........ Mic 1:8   6174
of Saphir, having thy shame n .... Mic 1:11   6181
Thy bow was made quite n, ... Hab 3:9   5783
N, and ye clothed me .... Mt 25:36   *1131*
or n, and clothed thee .... Mt 25:38   *1131*
n, and ye clothed me not .... Mt 25:43   *1131*
or athirst, or a stranger, or n .... Mt 25:44   *1131*
linen cloth cast about his n body .... Mk 14:51   *1131*
linen cloth, and fled from them n .... Mk 14:52   *1131*
coat unto him, (for he was n................. Jn 21:7   *1131*
they fled out of that house n .... Acts 19:16   *1131*
both hunger, and thirst, and are n......... 1Cor 4:11   *1130*
clothed we shall not be found n 2Cor 5:3   *1131*
but all things are n and opened .... Heb 4:13   *1131*
If a brother or sister be n .... Jas 2:15   *1131*
and poor, and blind, and n.................... Rev 3:17   *1131*
his garments, lest he walk n .... Rev 16:15   *1131*
and shall make her desolate and n .... Rev 17:16   *1131*

NAKEDNESS
saw the n of his father, and told .... Gen 9:22   6172
covered the n of their father.................. Gen 9:23   6172
and they saw not their father's n .... Gen 9:23   6172
to see the n of the land ye are .... Gen 42:9   6172
but to see the n of the land ye .... Gen 42:12   6172
that thy n be not discovered .... Ex 20:26   6172
linen breeches to cover their n.............. Ex 28:42   6172
of kin to him, to uncover their n .... Lev 18:6   6172
The n of thy father .... Lev 18:7   6172
or the n of thy mother, shalt .... Lev 18:7   6172
thou shalt not uncover her n .... Lev 18:7   6172
The n of thy father's wife shalt .... Lev 18:8   6172
it is thy father's n .... Lev 18:8   6172
The n of thy sister, the daughter .... Lev 18:9   6172
even their n thou shalt not .... Lev 18:9   6172
The n of thy son's daughter, or .... Lev 18:10   6172
even their n thou shalt not .... Lev 18:10   6172
for theirs is thine own n .... Lev 18:10   6172
The n of thy father's wife's .... Lev 18:11   6172
thou shalt not uncover her n .... Lev 18:11   6172
the n of thy father's sister .... Lev 18:12   6172
the n of thy mother's sister .... Lev 18:13   6172
the n of thy father's brother .... Lev 18:14   6172
the n of thy daughter in law .... Lev 18:15   6172
thou shalt not uncover her n .... Lev 18:15   6172
the n of thy brother's wife .... Lev 18:16   6172
it is thy brother's n .... Lev 18:16   6172

not uncover the n of a woman	Lev 18:17	6172
daughter, to uncover her n	Lev 18:17	6172
to vex her, to uncover her n	Lev 18:18	6172
unto a woman to uncover her n	Lev 18:19	6172
hath uncovered his father's n	Lev 20:11	6172
her n, and she see his n	Lev 20:17	6172
he hath uncovered his sister's n	Lev 20:17	6172
sickness, and shall uncover her n	Lev 20:18	6172
the n of thy mother's sister	Lev 20:19	6172
he hath uncovered his uncle's n	Lev 20:20	6172
he hath uncovered his brother's n	Lev 20:21	6172
in hunger, and in thirst, and in n	Deut 28:48	5903
the confusion of thy mother's n	1Sa 20:30	6172
Thy n shall be uncovered, yea,	Is 47:3	6172
her, because they have seen her n	Lam 1:8	6172
skirt over thee, and covered thy n	Eze 16:8	6172
thy n discovered through thy	Eze 16:36	6172
and will discover thy n unto them	Eze 16:37	6172
that they may see all thy n	Eze 16:37	6172
they discovered their fathers' n	Eze 22:10	6172
These discovered her n	Eze 23:10	6172
whoredoms, and discovered her n	Eze 23:18	6172
the n of thy whoredoms shall be	Eze 23:29	6172
and my flax given to cover her n	Hos 2:9	6172
and I will shew the nations thy n	Nah 3:5	4626
that thou mayest look on their n	Hab 2:15	4589
or persecution, or famine, or n	Rom 8:35	1132
in fastings often, in cold and n	2Cor 11:27	1132
the shame of thy n do not appear	Rev 3:18	1132

NAME

The n of the first is Pison	Gen 2:11	8034
the n of the second river is	Gen 2:13	8034
the n of the third river is	Gen 2:14	8034
creature, that was the n thereof	Gen 2:19	8034
And Adam called his wife's n Eve	Gen 3:20	8034
called the n of the city	Gen 4:17	8034
after the n of his son, Enoch	Gen 4:17	8034
the n of the one was Adah, and the	Gen 4:19	8034
the n of the other Zillah	Gen 4:19	8034
And his brother's n was Jubal	Gen 4:21	8034
bare a son, and called his n Seth	Gen 4:25	8034
and he called his n Enos	Gen 4:26	8034
to call upon the n of the LORD	Gen 4:26	8034
them, and called their n Adam	Gen 5:2	8034
and called his n Seth	Gen 5:3	8034
And he called his n Noah, saying,	Gen 5:29	8034
the n of one was Peleg	Gen 10:25	8034
and his brother's n was Joktan	Gen 10:25	8034
and let us make us a n, lest we be	Gen 11:4	8034
Therefore is the n of it called	Gen 11:9	8034
the n of Abram's wife was Sarai	Gen 11:29	8034
the n of Nahor's wife, Milcah,	Gen 11:29	8034
bless thee, and make thy n great	Gen 12:2	8034
and called upon the n of the LORD	Gen 12:8	8034
Abram called on the n of the LORD	Gen 13:4	8034
an Egyptian, whose n was Hagar	Gen 16:1	8034
son, and shalt call his n Ishmael	Gen 16:11	8034
she called the n of the LORD that	Gen 16:13	8034
and Abram called his son's n	Gen 16:15	8034
Neither shall thy n any more be	Gen 17:5	8034
but thy n shall be Abraham	Gen 17:5	8034
thou shalt not call her n Sarai	Gen 17:15	8034
Sarai, but Sarah shall her n be	Gen 17:15	8034
and thou shalt call his n Isaac	Gen 17:19	8034
Therefore the n of the city was	Gen 19:22	8034
bare a son, and called his n Moab	Gen 19:37	8034
a son, and called his n Ben-ammi	Gen 19:38	8034
Abraham called the n of his son	Gen 21:3	8034
called there on the n of the LORD	Gen 21:33	8034
Abraham called the n of that	Gen 22:14	8034
whose n was Reumah, she bare also	Gen 22:24	8034
had a brother, and his n was Laban	Gen 24:29	8034
took a wife, and her n was Keturah	Gen 25:1	8034
and they called his n Esau	Gen 25:25	8034
and his n was called Jacob	Gen 25:26	8034
therefore was his n called Edom	Gen 25:30	8034
he called the n of the well Esek	Gen 26:20	8034
and he called the n of it Sitnah	Gen 26:21	8034
he called the n of it Rehoboth	Gen 26:22	8034
and called upon the n of the LORD	Gen 26:25	8034
therefore the n of the city is	Gen 26:33	8034
he called the n of that place	Gen 28:19	8034
but the n of that city was called	Gen 28:19	8034
the n of the elder was Leah, and	Gen 29:16	8034
the n of the younger was Rachel	Gen 29:16	8034
a son, and she called his n Reuben	Gen 29:32	8034
and she called his n Simeon	Gen 29:33	8034
therefore was his n called Levi	Gen 29:34	8034
therefore she called his n Judah	Gen 29:35	8034
therefore called she his n Dan	Gen 30:6	8034

and she called his n Naphtali	Gen 30:8	8034
and she called his n Gad	Gen 30:11	8034
and she called his n Asher	Gen 30:13	8034
and she called his n Issachar	Gen 30:18	8034
and she called his n Zebulun	Gen 30:20	8034
a daughter, and called her n Dinah	Gen 30:21	8034
And she called his n Joseph	Gen 30:24	8034
Therefore was the n of it called	Gen 31:48	8034
he called the n of that place	Gen 32:2	8034
he said unto him, What is thy n	Gen 32:27	8034
Thy n shall be called no more	Gen 32:28	8034
said, Tell me, I pray thee, thy n	Gen 32:29	8034
it that thou dost ask after my n	Gen 32:29	8034
Jacob called the n of the place	Gen 32:30	8034
therefore the n of the place is	Gen 33:17	8034
and the n of it was called	Gen 35:8	8034
God said unto him, Thy n is Jacob	Gen 35:10	8034
thy n shall not be called any	Gen 35:10	8034
Jacob, but Israel shall be thy n	Gen 35:10	8034
and he called his n Israel	Gen 35:10	8034
Jacob called the n of the place	Gen 35:15	8034
that she called his n Ben-oni	Gen 35:18	8034
the n of his city was Dinhabah	Gen 36:32	8034
the n of his city was Avith	Gen 36:35	8034
the n of his city was Pau	Gen 36:39	8034
his wife's n was Mehetabel, the	Gen 36:39	8034
Adullamite, whose n was Hirah	Gen 38:1	8034
Canaanite, whose n was Shuah	Gen 38:2	8034
and he called his n Er	Gen 38:3	8034
and she called his n Onan	Gen 38:4	8034
and called his n Shelah	Gen 38:5	8034
his firstborn, whose n was Tamar	Gen 38:6	8034
therefore his n was called Pharez	Gen 38:29	8034
and his n was called Zarah	Gen 38:30	8034
Joseph's n Zaphnath-paaneah	Gen 41:45	8034
Joseph called the n of the	Gen 41:51	8034
the n of the second called he	Gen 41:52	8034
shall be called after the n of	Gen 48:6	8034
let my n be named on them, and the	Gen 48:16	8034
the n of my fathers Abraham and	Gen 48:16	8034
wherefore the n of it was called	Gen 50:11	8034
of which the n of the one was	Ex 1:15	8034
and the n of the other Puah	Ex 1:15	8034
And she called his n Moses	Ex 2:10	8034
a son, and he called his n Gershom	Ex 2:22	8034
shall say to me, What is his n	Ex 3:13	8034
this is my n for ever, and this is	Ex 3:15	8034
came to Pharaoh to speak in thy n	Ex 5:23	8034
by the n of God Almighty, but	Ex 6:3	
but by my n JEHOVAH was I not	Ex 6:3	8034
that my n may be declared	Ex 9:16	8034
the LORD is his n	Ex 15:3	8034
therefore the n of it was called	Ex 15:23	8034
Israel called the n thereof Manna	Ex 16:31	8034
he called the n of the place	Ex 17:7	8034
called the n of it Jehovah-nissi	Ex 17:15	8034
of which the n of the one was	Ex 18:3	8034
the n of the other was Eliezer	Ex 18:4	8034
Thou shalt not take the n of the	Ex 20:7	8034
that taketh his n in vain	Ex 20:7	8034
record my n I will come unto thee	Ex 20:24	8034
no mention of the n of other gods	Ex 23:13	8034
for my n is in him	Ex 23:21	8034
every one with his n shall they	Ex 28:21	8034
I have called by n Bezaleel the	Ex 31:2	8034
thou hast said, I know thee by n	Ex 33:12	8034
in my sight, and I know thee by n	Ex 33:17	8034
I will proclaim the n of the LORD	Ex 33:19	8034
and proclaimed the n of the LORD	Ex 34:5	8034
whose n is Jealous, is a jealous	Ex 34:14	8034
by n Bezaleel the son of Uri	Ex 35:30	8034
of a signet, every one with his n	Ex 39:14	8034
thou profane the n of thy God	Lev 18:21	8034
shall not swear by my n falsely	Lev 19:12	8034
thou profane the n of thy God	Lev 19:12	8034
and to profane my holy n	Lev 20:3	8034
and not profane the n of their God	Lev 21:6	8034
holy n in those things which they	Lev 22:2	8034
shall ye profane my holy n	Lev 22:32	8034
son blasphemed the n of the LORD	Lev 24:11	8034
his mother's n was Shelomith, the	Lev 24:11	8034
blasphemeth the n of the LORD	Lev 24:16	8034
he blasphemeth the n of the LORD	Lev 24:16	8034
and by n ye shall reckon the	Num 4:32	8034
they shall put my n upon the	Num 6:27	8034
he called the n of the place	Num 11:3	8034
the n of the one was Eldad	Num 11:26	8034
and the n of the other Medad	Num 11:26	8034
he called the n of that place	Num 11:34	8034
thou every man's n upon his rod	Num 17:2	8034
Aaron's n upon the rod of Levi	Num 17:3	8034

N

he called the *n* of the place	Num 21:3	8034
Now the *n* of the Israelite that	Num 25:14	8034
the *n* of the Midianitish woman	Num 25:15	8034
the *n* of the daughter of Asher	Num 26:46	8034
the *n* of Amram's wife was	Num 26:59	8034
Why should the *n* of our father be	Num 27:4	8034
called it Nobah, after his own *n*	Num 32:42	8034
and called them after his own *n*	Deut 3:14	8034
Thou shalt not take the *n* of the	Deut 5:11	8034
that taketh his *n* in vain	Deut 5:11	8034
him, and shalt swear by his *n*	Deut 6:13	8034
destroy their *n* from under heaven	Deut 7:24	8034
blot out their *n* from under	Deut 9:14	8034
unto him, and to bless in his *n*	Deut 10:8	8034
thou cleave, and swear by his *n*	Deut 10:20	8034
your tribes to put his *n* there	Deut 12:5	8034
to cause his *n* to dwell there	Deut 12:11	8034
his *n* there be too far from thee	Deut 12:21	8034
shall choose to place his *n* there	Deut 14:23	8034
shall choose to set his *n* there	Deut 14:24	8034
shall choose to place his *n* there	Deut 16:2	8034
shall choose to place his *n* in	Deut 16:6	8034
hath chosen to place his *n* there	Deut 16:11	8034
to minister in the *n* of the Lord	Deut 18:5	8034
in the *n* of the Lord his God	Deut 18:7	8034
which he shall speak in my *n*	Deut 18:19	8034
presume to speak a word in my *n*	Deut 18:20	8034
speak in the *n* of other gods	Deut 18:20	8034
speaketh in the *n* of the Lord	Deut 18:22	8034
and to bless in the *n* of the Lord	Deut 21:5	8034
and bring up an evil *n* upon her	Deut 22:14	8034
an evil *n* upon a virgin of Israel	Deut 22:19	8034
n of his brother which is dead	Deut 25:6	8034
that his *n* be not put out of	Deut 25:6	8034
up unto his brother a *n* in Israel	Deut 25:7	8034
his *n* shall be called in Israel,	Deut 25:10	8034
shall choose to place his *n* there	Deut 26:2	8034
he hath made, in praise, and in *n*	Deut 26:19	8034
art called by the *n* of the Lord	Deut 28:10	8034
fear this glorious and fearful *n*	Deut 28:58	8034
blot out his *n* from under heaven	Deut 29:20	8034
I will publish the *n* of the Lord	Deut 32:3	8034
Wherefore the *n* of the place is	Josh 5:9	8034
cut off our *n* from the earth	Josh 7:9	8034
wilt thou do unto thy great *n*	Josh 7:9	8034
Wherefore the *n* of that place was	Josh 7:26	8034
of the *n* of the Lord thy God	Josh 9:9	8034
the *n* of Hebron before was	Josh 14:15	8034
the *n* of Debir before was	Josh 15:15	8034
after the *n* of Dan their father	Josh 19:47	8034
which are here mentioned by *n*	Josh 21:9	8034
(now the *n* of Hebron before was	Judg 1:10	8034
the *n* of Debir before was	Judg 1:11	8034
the *n* of the city was called	Judg 1:17	8034
(Now the *n* of the city before was	Judg 1:23	8034
city, and called the *n* thereof Luz	Judg 1:26	8034
which is the *n* thereof unto this	Judg 1:26	8034
they called the *n* of that place	Judg 2:5	8034
whose *n* he called Abimelech	Judg 8:31	8034
the Danites, whose *n* was Manoah	Judg 13:2	8034
he was, neither told he me his *n*	Judg 13:6	8034
angel of the Lord, What is thy *n*	Judg 13:17	8034
Why askest thou thus after my *n*	Judg 13:18	8034
a son, and called his *n* Samson	Judg 13:24	8034
called the *n* thereof En-hakkore	Judg 15:19	8034
of Sorek, whose *n* was Delilah	Judg 16:4	8034
mount Ephraim, whose *n* was Micah	Judg 17:1	8034
they called the *n* of the city Dan	Judg 18:29	8034
after the *n* of Dan their father,	Judg 18:29	8034
howbeit the *n* of the city was	Judg 18:29	8034
the *n* of the man was Elimelech,	Ruth 1:2	8034
the *n* of his wife Naomi, and the	Ruth 1:2	8034
the *n* of his two sons Mahlon and	Ruth 1:2	8034
the *n* of the one was Orpah	Ruth 1:4	8034
and the *n* of the other Ruth	Ruth 1:4	8034
and his *n* was Boaz	Ruth 2:1	8034
The man's *n* with whom I wrought	Ruth 2:19	8034
to raise up the *n* of the dead	Ruth 4:5	8034
to raise up the *n* of the dead	Ruth 4:10	8034
that the *n* of the dead be not cut	Ruth 4:10	8034
that his *n* may be famous in	Ruth 4:14	8034
women her neighbours gave it a *n*	Ruth 4:17	8034
and they called his *n* Obed	Ruth 4:17	8034
his *n* was Elkanah, the son of	1Sa 1:1	8034
the *n* of the one was Hannah, and	1Sa 1:2	8034
the *n* of the other Peninnah	1Sa 1:2	8034
a son, and called his *n* Samuel	1Sa 1:20	8034
called the *n* of it Eben-ezer	1Sa 7:12	8034
Now the *n* of his firstborn was	1Sa 8:2	8034
the *n* of his second, Abiah	1Sa 8:2	8034
whose *n* was Kish, the son of	1Sa 9:1	8034

whose *n* was Saul, a choice young	1Sa 9:2	8034
the *n* of the one was Bozez	1Sa 14:4	8034
and the *n* of the other Seneh	1Sa 14:4	8034
the *n* of the firstborn Merab, and	1Sa 14:49	8034
the *n* of the younger Michal	1Sa 14:49	8034
the *n* of Saul's wife was Ahinoam,	1Sa 14:50	8034
the *n* of the captain of his host	1Sa 14:50	8034
unto me him whom I *n* unto thee	1Sa 16:3	559
whose *n* was Jesse	1Sa 17:12	8034
Philistine of Gath, Goliath by *n*	1Sa 17:23	8034
in the *n* of the Lord of hosts	1Sa 17:45	8034
so that his *n* was much set by	1Sa 18:30	8034
both of us in the *n* of the Lord	1Sa 20:42	8034
his *n* was Doeg, an Edomite, the	1Sa 21:7	8034
my *n* out of my father's house	1Sa 24:21	8034
Now the *n* of the man was Nabal	1Sa 25:3	8034
the *n* of his wife Abigail	1Sa 25:3	8034
go to Nabal, and greet him in my *n*	1Sa 25:5	8034
all those words in the *n* of David	1Sa 25:9	8034
for as his *n* is, so is he	1Sa 25:25	8034
Nabal is his *n*, and folly is with	1Sa 25:25	8034
him up, whom I shall *n* unto thee	1Sa 28:8	559
whose *n* was Rizpah, the daughter	2Sa 3:7	8034
the *n* of the one was Baanah, and	2Sa 4:2	8034
the *n* of the other Rechab, the	2Sa 4:2	8034
And his *n* was Mephibosheth	2Sa 4:4	8034
Therefore he called the *n* of that	2Sa 5:20	8034
whose *n* is called by the *n* of	2Sa 6:2	8034
he called the *n* of the place	2Sa 6:8	
in the *n* of the Lord of hosts	2Sa 6:18	8034
and have made thee a great *n*	2Sa 7:9	8034
like unto the *n* of the great men	2Sa 7:9	8034
He shall build an house for my *n*	2Sa 7:13	8034
to himself, and to make him a *n*	2Sa 7:23	8034
let thy *n* be magnified for ever,	2Sa 7:26	8034
David gat him a *n* when he	2Sa 8:13	8034
Saul a servant whose *n* was Ziba	2Sa 9:2	8034
a young son, whose *n* was Micha	2Sa 9:12	8034
a son, and he called his *n* Solomon	2Sa 12:24	8034
and he called his *n* Jedidiah	2Sa 12:25	8034
city, and it be called after my *n*	2Sa 12:28	8034
a fair sister, whose *n* was Tamar	2Sa 13:1	8034
whose *n* was Jonadab, the son of	2Sa 13:3	8034
n nor remainder upon the earth	2Sa 14:7	8034
one daughter, whose *n* was Tamar	2Sa 14:27	8034
whose *n* was Shimei, the son of	2Sa 16:5	8034
whose *n* was Ithra an Israelite,	2Sa 17:25	8034
son to keep my *n* in remembrance	2Sa 18:18	8034
called the pillar after his own *n*	2Sa 18:18	8034
whose *n* was Sheba, the son of	2Sa 20:1	8034
Sheba the son of Bichri by *n*	2Sa 20:21	8034
them, and had the *n* among three	2Sa 23:18	8034
had the *n* among three mighty men	2Sa 23:22	8034
n of Solomon better than thy *n*	1Kin 1:47	8034
built unto the *n* of the Lord	1Kin 3:2	8034
the *n* of the Lord his God for the	1Kin 5:3	8034
unto the *n* of the Lord my God	1Kin 5:5	8034
he shall build an house unto my *n*	1Kin 5:5	8034
called the *n* thereof Jachin	1Kin 7:21	8034
called the *n* thereof Boaz	1Kin 7:21	8034
that my *n* might be therein	1Kin 8:16	8034
the *n* of the Lord God of Israel	1Kin 8:17	8034
heart to build an house unto my *n*	1Kin 8:18	8034
shall build the house unto my *n*	1Kin 8:19	8034
the *n* of the Lord God of Israel	1Kin 8:20	8034
hast said, My *n* shall be there	1Kin 8:29	8034
again to thee, and confess thy *n*	1Kin 8:33	8034
this place, and confess thy *n*	1Kin 8:35	8034
they shall hear of thy great *n*	1Kin 8:42	8034
of the earth may know thy *n*	1Kin 8:43	8034
have builded, is called by thy *n*	1Kin 8:43	8034
house that I have built for thy *n*	1Kin 8:44	8034
which I have built for thy *n*	1Kin 8:48	8034
to put my *n* there for ever	1Kin 9:3	8034
which I have hallowed for my *n*	1Kin 9:7	8034
concerning the *n* of the Lord	1Kin 10:1	8034
whose mother's *n* was Zeruah	1Kin 11:26	8034
have chosen me to put my *n* there	1Kin 11:36	8034
the house of David, Josiah by *n*	1Kin 13:2	8034
of Israel, to put his *n* there	1Kin 14:21	8034
his mother's *n* was Naamah an	1Kin 14:21	8034
his mother's *n* was Naamah an	1Kin 14:31	8034
And his mother's *n* was Maachah	1Kin 15:2	8034
And his mother's *n* was Maachah	1Kin 15:10	8034
called the *n* of the city which he	1Kin 16:24	8034
he built, after the *n* of Shemer	1Kin 16:24	8034
And call ye on the *n* of your gods	1Kin 18:24	8034
I will call on the *n* of the Lord	1Kin 18:24	8034
call on the *n* of your gods, but	1Kin 18:25	8034
called on the *n* of Baal from	1Kin 18:26	8034
saying, Israel shall be thy *n*	1Kin 18:31	8034

an altar in the *n* of the LORD	1Kin 18:32	8034
So she wrote letters in Ahab's *n*	1Kin 21:8	8034
is true in the *n* of the LORD	1Kin 22:16	8034
his mother's *n* was Azubah the	1Kin 22:42	8034
cursed them in the *n* of the LORD	2Kin 2:24	8034
call on the *n* of the LORD his God	2Kin 5:11	8034
And his mother's *n* was Athaliah	2Kin 8:26	8034
his mother's *n* was Zibiah of	2Kin 12:1	8034
his mother's *n* was Jehoaddan of	2Kin 14:2	8034
called the *n* of it Joktheel unto	2Kin 14:7	8034
the *n* of Israel from under heaven	2Kin 14:27	8034
his mother's *n* was Jecholiah of	2Kin 15:2	8034
And his mother's *n* was Jerusha	2Kin 15:33	8034
His mother's *n* also was Abi	2Kin 18:2	8034
his mother's *n* was Hephzi-bah	2Kin 21:1	8034
In Jerusalem will I put my *n*	2Kin 21:4	8034
Israel, will I put my *n* for ever	2Kin 21:7	8034
his mother's *n* was Meshullemeth,	2Kin 21:19	8034
And his mother's *n* was Jedidah	2Kin 22:1	8034
which I said, My *n* shall be there	2Kin 23:27	8034
And his mother's *n* was Hamutal	2Kin 23:31	8034
turned his *n* to Jehoiakim, and	2Kin 23:34	8034
And his mother's *n* was Zebudah	2Kin 23:36	8034
And his mother's *n* was Nehushta	2Kin 24:8	8034
and changed his *n* to Zedekiah	2Kin 24:17	8034
And his mother's *n* was Hamutal	2Kin 24:18	8034
the *n* of the one was Peleg	1Chr 1:19	8034
and his brother's *n* was Joktan	1Chr 1:19	8034
the *n* of his city was Dinhabah	1Chr 1:43	8034
the *n* of his city was Avith	1Chr 1:46	8034
the *n* of his city was Pai	1Chr 1:50	8034
his wife's *n* was Mehetabel, the	1Chr 1:50	8034
another wife, whose *n* was Atarah	1Chr 2:26	8034
the *n* of the wife of Abishur was	1Chr 2:29	8034
an Egyptian, whose *n* was Jarha	1Chr 2:34	8034
the *n* of their sister was	1Chr 4:3	8034
and his mother called his *n* Jabez	1Chr 4:9	8034
these written by *n* came in the	1Chr 4:41	8034
whose sister's *n* was Maachah	1Chr 7:15	8034
and the *n* of the second was	1Chr 7:15	8034
a son, and she called his *n* Peresh	1Chr 7:16	8034
the *n* of his brother was Sheresh	1Chr 7:16	8034
a son, and he called his *n* Beriah	1Chr 7:23	8034
whose wife's *n* was Maachah	1Chr 8:29	8034
whose wife's *n* was Maachah	1Chr 9:35	8034
them, and had a *n* among the three	1Chr 11:20	8034
had the *n* among the three	1Chr 11:24	8034
which were expressed by *n*	1Chr 12:31	8034
whose *n* is called on it	1Chr 13:6	8034
therefore they called the *n* of	1Chr 14:11	8034
the people in the *n* of the LORD	1Chr 16:2	8034
unto the LORD, call upon his *n*	1Chr 16:8	8034
Glory ye in his holy *n*	1Chr 16:10	8034
the LORD the glory due unto his *n*	1Chr 16:29	8034
we may give thanks to thy holy *n*	1Chr 16:35	8034
chosen, who were expressed by *n*	1Chr 16:41	8034
have made thee a *n* like the *n*	1Chr 17:8	8034
n of the great men that are in	1Chr 17:8	8034
to make thee a *n* of greatness	1Chr 17:21	8034
that thy *n* may be magnified for	1Chr 17:24	8034
he spake in the *n* of the LORD	1Chr 21:19	8034
unto the *n* of the LORD my God	1Chr 22:7	8034
not build an house unto my *n*	1Chr 22:8	8034
for his *n* shall be Solomon, and I	1Chr 22:9	8034
He shall build an house for my *n*	1Chr 22:10	8034
to be built to the *n* of the LORD	1Chr 22:19	8034
and to bless his *n* for ever	1Chr 23:13	8034
shalt not build an house for my *n*	1Chr 28:3	8034
thee, and praise thy glorious *n*	1Chr 29:13	8034
thine holy *n* cometh of thine hand	1Chr 29:16	8034
an house for the *n* of the LORD	2Chr 2:1	8034
house to the *n* of the LORD my God	2Chr 2:4	8034
called the *n* of that on the right	2Chr 3:17	8034
the *n* of that on the left Boaz	2Chr 3:17	8034
in, that my *n* might be there	2Chr 6:5	8034
that my *n* might be there	2Chr 6:6	8034
the *n* of the LORD God of Israel	2Chr 6:7	8034
heart to build an house for my *n*	2Chr 6:8	8034
he shall build the house for my *n*	2Chr 6:9	8034
the *n* of the LORD God of Israel	2Chr 6:10	8034
thou wouldest put thy *n* there	2Chr 6:20	8034
and shall return and confess thy *n*	2Chr 6:24	8034
this place, and confess thy *n*	2Chr 6:26	8034
of the earth may know thy *n*	2Chr 6:33	8034
I have built is called by thy *n*	2Chr 6:33	8034
which I have built for thy *n*	2Chr 6:34	8034
which I have built for thy *n*	2Chr 6:38	8034
people, which are called by my *n*	2Chr 7:14	8034
that my *n* may be there for ever	2Chr 7:16	8034
which I have sanctified for my *n*	2Chr 7:20	8034
of Israel, to put his *n* there	2Chr 12:13	8034

his mother's *n* was Naamah an	2Chr 12:13	8034
His mother's *n* also was Michaiah	2Chr 13:2	8034
in thy *n* we go against this	2Chr 14:11	8034
truth to me in the *n* of the LORD	2Chr 18:15	8034
a sanctuary therein for thy *n*	2Chr 20:8	8034
(for thy *n* is in this house,) and	2Chr 20:9	8034
therefore the *n* of the same place	2Chr 20:26	8034
his mother's *n* was Azubah the	2Chr 20:31	8034
His mother's *n* also was Athaliah	2Chr 22:2	8034
His mother's *n* was Zibiah of	2Chr 24:1	8034
his mother's *n* was Jehoaddan of	2Chr 25:1	8034
His mother's *n* also was Jecoliah	2Chr 26:3	8034
his *n* spread abroad even to the	2Chr 26:8	8034
And his *n* spread far abroad	2Chr 26:15	8034
His mother's *n* also was Jerushah,	2Chr 27:1	8034
LORD was there, whose *n* was Oded	2Chr 28:9	8034
which were expressed by *n* rose up	2Chr 28:15	8034
And his mother's *n* was Abijah	2Chr 29:1	8034
the men that were expressed by *n*	2Chr 31:19	8034
Jerusalem shall my *n* be for ever	2Chr 33:4	8034
Israel, will I put my *n* for ever	2Chr 33:7	8034
the *n* of the LORD God of Israel	2Chr 33:18	8034
turned his *n* to Jehoiakim	2Chr 36:4	8034
and was called after their *n*	Ezr 2:61	8034
Jerusalem in the *n* of the God of	Ezr 5:1	8036
whose *n* was Sheshbazzar, whom he	Ezr 5:14	8036
his *n* to dwell there destroy all	Ezr 6:12	8036
all of them were expressed by *n*	Ezr 8:20	8034
I have chosen to set my *n* there	Neh 1:9	8034
who desire to fear thy *n*	Neh 1:11	8034
wife, and was called after their *n*	Neh 7:63	8034
and blessed be thy glorious *n*	Neh 9:5	8034
and gavest him the *n* of Abraham	Neh 9:7	8034
So didst thou get thee a *n*	Neh 9:10	8034
whose *n* was Mordecai, the son of	Est 2:5	8034
her, and that she were called by *n*	Est 2:14	8034
the king thereof in Mordecai's *n*	Est 2:22	8034
in the *n* of king Ahasuerus was it	Est 3:12	8034
as it liketh you, in the king's *n*	Est 8:8	8034
which is written in the king's *n*	Est 8:8	8034
he wrote in the king Ahasuerus' *n*	Est 8:10	8034
days Purim after the *n* of Pur	Est 9:26	8034
the land of Uz, whose *n* was Job	Job 1:1	8034
blessed be the *n* of the LORD	Job 1:21	8034
he shall have no *n* in the street	Job 18:17	8034
And he called the *n* of the first	Job 42:14	8034
the *n* of the second, Kezia	Job 42:14	8034
the *n* of the third, Keren-happuch	Job 42:14	8034
that love thy *n* be joyful in thee	Ps 5:11	8034
to the *n* of the LORD most high	Ps 7:17	8034
is thy *n* in all the earth	Ps 8:1	8034
is thy *n* in all the earth	Ps 8:9	8034
I will sing praise to thy *n*	Ps 9:2	8034
hast put out their *n* for ever	Ps 9:5	8034
they that know thy *n* will put	Ps 9:10	8034
and sing praises unto thy *n*	Ps 18:49	8034
the *n* of the God of Jacob defend	Ps 20:1	8034
in the *n* of our God we will set	Ps 20:5	8034
the *n* of the LORD our God	Ps 20:7	8034
declare thy *n* unto my brethren	Ps 22:22	8034
the LORD the glory due unto his *n*	Ps 29:2	8034
we have trusted in his holy *n*	Ps 33:21	8034
and let us exalt his *n* together	Ps 34:3	8034
shall he die, and his *n* perish	Ps 41:5	8034
through thy *n* will we tread them	Ps 44:5	8034
long, and praise thy *n* for ever	Ps 44:8	8034
have forgotten the *n* of our God	Ps 44:20	8034
I will make thy *n* to be	Ps 45:17	8034
According to thy *n*, O God, so is	Ps 48:10	8034
and I will wait on thy *n*	Ps 52:9	8034
Save me, O God, by thy *n*, and	Ps 54:1	8034
I will praise thy *n*, O LORD	Ps 54:6	8034
heritage of those that fear thy *n*	Ps 61:5	8034
I sing praise unto thy *n* for ever	Ps 61:8	8034
I will lift up my hands in thy *n*	Ps 63:4	8034
Sing forth the honour of his *n*	Ps 66:2	8034
they shall sing to thy *n*	Ps 66:4	8034
unto God, sing praises to his *n*	Ps 68:4	8034
upon the heavens by his *n* JAH	Ps 68:4	8034
I will praise the *n* of God with a	Ps 69:30	8034
they that love his *n* shall dwell	Ps 69:36	8034
His *n* shall endure for ever	Ps 72:17	8034
his *n* shall be continued as long	Ps 72:17	8034
be his glorious *n* for ever	Ps 72:19	8034
place of thy *n* to the ground	Ps 74:7	8034
enemy blaspheme thy *n* for ever	Ps 74:10	8034
people have blasphemed thy *n*	Ps 74:18	8034
the poor and needy praise thy *n*	Ps 74:21	8034
for that thy *n* is near thy	Ps 75:1	8034
his *n* is great in Israel	Ps 76:1	8034
that have not called upon thy *n*	Ps 79:6	8034

N

salvation, for the glory of thy *n*	Ps 79:9	8034
us, and we will call upon thy *n*	Ps 80:18	8034
that the *n* of Israel may be no	Ps 83:4	8034
that they may seek thy *n*, O LORD	Ps 83:16	8034
whose *n* alone is JEHOVAH, art the	Ps 83:18	8034
and shall glorify thy *n*	Ps 86:9	8034
unite my heart to fear thy *n*	Ps 86:11	8034
I will glorify thy *n* for evermore	Ps 86:12	8034
and Hermon shall rejoice in thy *n*	Ps 89:12	8034
In thy *n* shall they rejoice all	Ps 89:16	8034
in my *n* shall his horn be exalted	Ps 89:24	8034
high, because he hath known my *n*	Ps 91:14	8034
and to sing praises unto thy *n*	Ps 92:1	8034
Sing unto the LORD, bless his *n*	Ps 96:2	8034
the LORD the glory due unto his *n*	Ps 96:8	8034
praise thy great and terrible *n*	Ps 99:3	8034
among them that call upon his *n*	Ps 99:6	8034
thankful unto him, and bless his *n*	Ps 100:4	8034
shall fear the *n* of the LORD	Ps 102:15	8034
To declare the *n* of the LORD in	Ps 102:21	8034
is within me, bless his holy *n*	Ps 103:1	8034
call upon his *n*	Ps 105:1	8034
Glory ye in his holy *n*	Ps 105:3	8034
to give thanks unto thy holy *n*	Ps 106:47	8034
let their *n* be blotted out	Ps 109:13	8034
holy and reverend is his *n*	Ps 111:9	8034
LORD, praise the *n* of the LORD	Ps 113:1	8034
Blessed be the *n* of the LORD from	Ps 113:2	8034
the LORD's *n* is to be praised	Ps 113:3	8034
us, but unto thy *n* give glory	Ps 115:1	8034
called I upon the *n* of the LORD	Ps 116:4	8034
and call upon the *n* of the LORD	Ps 116:13	8034
will call upon the *n* of the LORD	Ps 116:17	8034
but in the *n* of the LORD will I	Ps 118:10	8034
but in the *n* of the LORD I will	Ps 118:11	8034
for in the *n* of the LORD I will	Ps 118:12	8034
that cometh in the *n* of the LORD	Ps 118:26	8034
I have remembered thy *n*, O LORD,	Ps 119:55	8034
to do unto those that love thy *n*	Ps 119:132	8034
thanks unto the *n* of the LORD	Ps 122:4	8034
Our help is in the *n* of the LORD	Ps 124:8	8034
we bless you in the *n* of the LORD	Ps 129:8	8034
Praise ye the *n* of the LORD	Ps 135:1	8034
sing praises unto his *n*	Ps 135:3	8034
Thy *n*, O LORD, endureth for ever	Ps 135:13	8034
temple, and praise thy *n* for thy	Ps 138:2	8034
thy word above all thy *n*	Ps 138:2	8034
thine enemies take thy *n* in vain	Ps 139:20	8034
shall give thanks unto thy *n*	Ps 140:13	8034
prison, that I may praise thy *n*	Ps 142:7	8034
and I will bless thy *n* for ever	Ps 145:1	8034
and I will praise thy *n* for ever	Ps 145:2	8034
flesh bless his holy *n* for ever	Ps 145:21	8034
Let them praise the *n* of the LORD	Ps 148:5	8034
Let them praise the *n* of the LORD	Ps 148:13	8034
for his *n* alone is excellent	Ps 148:13	8034
them praise his *n* in the dance	Ps 149:3	8034
but the *n* of the wicked shall rot	Prov 10:7	8034
The *n* of the LORD is a strong	Prov 18:10	8034
Proud and haughty scorner is his *n*	Prov 21:24	8034
A good *n* is rather to be chosen	Prov 22:1	8034
his *n*, and what is his son's *n*	Prov 30:4	8034
take the *n* of my God in vain	Prov 30:9	8034
his *n* shall be covered with	Eccl 6:4	8034
A good *n* is better than precious	Eccl 7:1	8034
of thy good ointments thy *n* is as	Song 1:3	8034
only let us be called by thy *n*	Is 4:1	8034
son, and shall call his *n* Immanuel	Is 7:14	8034
Call his *n* Maher-shalal-hash-baz	Is 8:3	8034
his *n* shall be called Wonderful,	Is 9:6	8034
Praise the LORD, call upon his *n*	Is 12:4	8034
mention that his *n* is exalted	Is 12:4	8034
and cut off from Babylon the *n*	Is 14:22	8034
to the place of the *n* of the LORD	Is 18:7	8034
even the *n* of the LORD God of	Is 24:15	8034
exalt thee, I will praise thy *n*	Is 25:1	8034
desire of our soul is to thy *n*	Is 26:8	8034
will we make mention of thy *n*	Is 26:13	8034
of him, they shall sanctify my *n*	Is 29:23	8034
the *n* of the LORD cometh from far	Is 30:27	8034
the sun shall he call upon my *n*	Is 41:25	8034
that is my *n*	Is 42:8	8034
thee, I have called thee by thy *n*	Is 43:1	8034
every one that is called by my *n*	Is 43:7	8034
call himself by the *n* of Jacob	Is 44:5	8034
himself by the *n* of Israel	Is 44:5	8034
LORD, which call thee by thy *n*	Is 45:3	8034
I have even called thee by thy *n*	Is 45:4	8034
the LORD of hosts is his *n*	Is 47:4	8034
are called by the *n* of Israel	Is 48:1	8034
which swear by the *n* of the LORD	Is 48:1	8034
The LORD of hosts is his *n*	Is 48:2	8034
for how should my *n* be polluted	Is 48:11	8034
his *n* should not have been cut	Is 48:19	8034
hath he made mention of my *n*	Is 49:1	8034
him trust in the *n* of the LORD	Is 50:10	8034
The LORD of hosts is his *n*	Is 51:15	8034
my *n* continually every day is	Is 52:5	8034
my people shall know my *n*	Is 52:6	8034
the LORD of hosts is his *n*	Is 54:5	8034
it shall be to the LORD for a *n*	Is 55:13	8034
a *n* better than of sons and of	Is 56:5	8034
I will give them an everlasting *n*	Is 56:5	8034
him, and to love the *n* of the LORD	Is 56:6	8034
eternity, whose *n* is Holy	Is 57:15	8034
So shall they fear the *n* of the	Is 59:19	8034
unto the *n* of the LORD thy God,	Is 60:9	8034
thou shalt be called by a new *n*	Is 62:2	8034
the mouth of the LORD shall *n*	Is 62:2	8034
to make himself an everlasting *n*	Is 63:12	8034
to make thyself a glorious *n*	Is 63:14	8034
thy *n* is from everlasting	Is 63:16	8034
they were not called by thy *n*	Is 63:19	8034
to make thy *n* known to thine	Is 64:2	8034
is none that calleth upon thy *n*	Is 64:7	8034
that was not called by my *n*	Is 65:1	8034
ye shall leave your *n* for a curse	Is 65:15	8034
and call his servants by another *n*	Is 65:15	8034
shall your seed and your *n* remain	Is 66:22	8034
unto it, to the *n* of the LORD, to	Jer 3:17	8034
house, which is called by my *n*	Jer 7:10	8034
house, which is called by my *n*	Jer 7:11	8034
where I set my *n* at the first	Jer 7:12	8034
house, which is called by my *n*	Jer 7:14	8034
the house which is called by my *n*	Jer 7:30	8034
great, and thy *n* is great in might	Jer 10:6	8034
The LORD of hosts is his *n*	Jer 10:16	8034
families that call not on thy *n*	Jer 10:25	8034
The LORD called thy *n*, A green	Jer 11:16	8034
that his *n* may be no more	Jer 11:19	8034
Prophesy not in the *n* of the	Jer 11:21	8034
of my people, to swear by my *n*	Jer 12:16	8034
unto me for a people, and for a *n*	Jer 13:11	8034
of us, and we are called by thy *n*	Jer 14:9	8034
prophets prophesy lies in my *n*	Jer 14:14	8034
prophets that prophesy in my *n*	Jer 14:15	8034
for I am called by thy *n*, O LORD	Jer 15:16	8034
shall know that my *n* is The LORD	Jer 16:21	8034
LORD hath not called thy *n* Pashur	Jer 20:3	8034
him, nor speak any more in his *n*	Jer 20:9	8034
this is his *n* whereby he shall be	Jer 23:6	8034
said, that prophesy lies in my *n*	Jer 23:25	8034
n by their dreams which they tell	Jer 23:27	8034
have forgotten my *n* for Baal	Jer 23:27	8034
the city which is called by my *n*	Jer 25:29	8034
prophesied in the *n* of the LORD	Jer 26:9	8034
us in the *n* of the LORD our God	Jer 26:16	8034
prophesied in the *n* of the LORD	Jer 26:20	8034
yet they prophesy a lie in my *n*	Jer 27:15	8034
prophesy falsely unto you in my *n*	Jer 29:9	8034
prophesy a lie unto you in my *n*	Jer 29:21	8034
have spoken lying words in my *n*	Jer 29:23	8034
thou hast sent letters in thy *n*	Jer 29:25	8034
The LORD of hosts is his *n*	Jer 31:35	8034
God, the LORD of hosts, is his *n*	Jer 32:18	8034
and hast made thee a *n*, as at this	Jer 32:20	8034
house, which is called by my *n*	Jer 32:34	8034
the LORD is his *n*	Jer 33:2	8034
And it shall be to me a *n* of joy	Jer 33:9	8034
this is the *n* wherewith she shall	Jer 33:16	
the house which is called by my *n*	Jer 34:15	8034
But ye turned and polluted my *n*	Jer 34:16	8034
whose *n* was Irijah, the son of	Jer 37:13	8034
unto us in the *n* of the LORD	Jer 44:16	8034
I have sworn by my great *n*	Jer 44:26	8034
that my *n* shall no more be named	Jer 44:26	8034
whose *n* is the LORD of hosts,	Jer 46:18	8034
whose *n* is the LORD of hosts	Jer 48:15	8034
and all ye that know his *n*	Jer 48:17	8034
the LORD of hosts is his *n*	Jer 50:34	8034
the LORD of hosts is his *n*	Jer 51:19	8034
whose *n* is the LORD of hosts	Jer 51:57	8034
his mother's *n* was Hamutal the	Jer 52:1	8034
I called upon thy *n*, O LORD, out	Lam 3:55	8034
the *n* thereof is called Bamah	Eze 20:29	8034
but pollute ye my holy *n* no more	Eze 20:39	8034
man, write thee the *n* of the day	Eze 24:2	8034
went, they profaned my holy *n*	Eze 36:20	8034
But I had pity for mine holy *n*	Eze 36:21	8034
And I will sanctify my great *n*	Eze 36:23	8034
So will I make my holy *n* known in	Eze 39:7	8034
them pollute my holy *n* any more	Eze 39:7	8034

also the *n* of the city shall be	Eze 39:16	8034
and will be jealous for my holy *n*	Eze 39:25	8034
of Israel for ever, and my holy *n*	Eze 43:7	8034
they have even defiled my holy *n*	Eze 43:8	8034
the *n* of the city from that day	Eze 48:35	8034
unto Daniel the *n* of Belteshazzar	Dan 1:7	8034
Blessed be the *n* of God for ever	Dan 2:20	8036
whose *n* was Belteshazzar, Art	Dan 2:26	8036
whose *n* was Belteshazzar,	Dan 4:8	8036
according to the *n* of my god	Dan 4:8	8036
whose *n* was Belteshazzar, was	Dan 4:19	8036
which spake in thy *n* to our kings	Dan 9:6	8034
the city which is called by thy *n*	Dan 9:18	8034
and thy people are called by thy *n*	Dan 9:19	8034
whose *n* was called Belteshazzar	Dan 10:1	8034
said unto him, Call his *n* Jezreel	Hos 1:4	8034
unto him, Call her *n* Lo-ruhamah	Hos 1:6	8034
Then said God, Call his *n* Lo-ammi	Hos 1:9	8034
no more be remembered by their *n*	Hos 2:17	8034
praise the *n* of the LORD your God	Joel 2:26	8034
whosoever shall call on the *n* of	Joel 2:32	8034
same maid, to profane my holy *n*	Amos 2:7	8034
LORD, The God of hosts, is his *n*	Amos 4:13	8034
The LORD is his *n*	Amos 5:8	8034
whose *n* is The God of hosts	Amos 5:27	8034
make mention of the *n* of the LORD	Amos 6:10	8034
The LORD is his *n*	Amos 9:6	8034
heathen, which are called by my *n*	Amos 9:12	8034
every one in the *n* of his god	Mic 4:5	8034
we will walk in the *n* of the LORD	Mic 4:5	8034
of the *n* of the LORD his God	Mic 5:4	8034
the man of wisdom shall see thy *n*	Mic 6:9	8034
that no more of thy *n* be sown	Nah 1:14	8034
the *n* of the Chemarims with the	Zeph 1:4	8034
all call upon the *n* of the LORD	Zeph 3:9	8034
shall trust in the *n* of the LORD	Zeph 3:12	8034
for I will make you a *n* and a	Zeph 3:20	8034
him that sweareth falsely by my *n*	Zec 5:4	8034
the man whose *n* is The BRANCH	Zec 6:12	8034
shall walk up and down in his *n*	Zec 10:12	8034
lies in the *n* of the LORD	Zec 13:3	8034
they shall call on my *n*, and I	Zec 13:9	8034
there be one LORD, and his *n* one	Zec 14:9	8034
you, O priests, that despise my *n*	Mal 1:6	8034
Wherein have we despised thy *n*	Mal 1:6	8034
my *n* shall be great among the	Mal 1:11	8034
shall be offered unto my *n*	Mal 1:11	8034
for my *n* shall be great among the	Mal 1:11	8034
my *n* is dreadful among the	Mal 1:14	8034
to heart, to give glory unto my *n*	Mal 2:2	8034
me, and was afraid before my *n*	Mal 2:5	8034
LORD, and that thought upon his *n*	Mal 3:16	8034
But unto you that fear my *n* shall	Mal 4:2	8034
and thou shalt call his *n* JESUS	Mt 1:21	3686
and they shall call his *n* Emmanuel	Mt 1:23	3686
and he called his *n* JESUS	Mt 1:25	3686
art in heaven, Hallowed be thy *n*	Mt 6:9	3686
have we not prophesied in thy *n*	Mt 7:22	3686
in thy *n* have cast out devils	Mt 7:22	3686
in thy *n* done many wonderful	Mt 7:22	3686
n of a prophet shall receive a	Mt 10:41	3686
a righteous man in the *n* of a	Mt 10:41	3686
water only in the *n* of a disciple	Mt 10:42	3686
in his *n* shall the Gentiles trust	Mt 12:21	3686
little child in my *n* receiveth me	Mt 18:5	3686
are gathered together in my *n*	Mt 18:20	3686
that cometh in the *n* of the Lord	Mt 21:9	3686
that cometh in the *n* of the Lord	Mt 23:39	3686
For many shall come in my *n*	Mt 24:5	3686
found a man of Cyrene, Simon by *n*	Mt 27:32	3686
them in the *n* of the Father	Mt 28:19	3686
And he asked him, What is thy *n*	Mk 5:9	3686
answered, saying, My *n* is Legion	Mk 5:9	3686
of the synagogue, Jairus by *n*	Mk 5:22	3686
(for his *n* was spread abroad	Mk 6:14	3686
one of such children in my *n*	Mk 9:37	3686
one casting out devils in thy *n*	Mk 9:38	3686
which shall do a miracle in my *n*	Mk 9:39	3686
a cup of water to drink in my *n*	Mk 9:41	3686
that cometh in the *n* of the Lord	Mk 11:9	3686
that cometh in the *n* of the Lord	Mk 11:10	3686
For many shall come in my *n*	Mk 13:6	3686
In my *n* shall they cast out	Mk 16:17	3686
of Aaron, and her *n* was Elisabeth	Lk 1:5	3686
and thou shalt call his *n* John	Lk 1:13	3686
to a man whose *n* was Joseph	Lk 1:27	3686
and the virgin's *n* was Mary	Lk 1:27	3686
a son, and shalt call his *n* JESUS	Lk 1:31	3686
and holy is his *n*	Lk 1:49	3686
after the *n* of his father	Lk 1:59	3686
kindred that is called by this *n*	Lk 1:61	3686

and wrote, saying, His *n* is John	Lk 1:63	3686
his *n* was called JESUS, which was	Lk 2:21	3686
in Jerusalem, whose *n* was Simeon	Lk 2:25	3686
you, and cast out your *n* as evil	Lk 6:22	3686
asked him, saying, What is thy *n*	Lk 8:30	3686
this child in my *n* receiveth me	Lk 9:48	3686
one casting out devils in thy *n*	Lk 9:49	3686
are subject unto us through thy *n*	Lk 10:17	3686
art in heaven, Hallowed be thy *n*	Lk 11:2	3686
that cometh in the *n* of the Lord	Lk 13:35	3686
that cometh in the *n* of the Lord	Lk 19:38	3686
for many shall come in my *n*	Lk 21:8	3686
whose *n* was Cleopas, answering	Lk 24:18	3686
in his *n* among all nations	Lk 24:47	3686
sent from God, whose *n* was John	Jn 1:6	3686
to them that believe on his *n*	Jn 1:12	3686
feast day, many believed in his *n*	Jn 2:23	3686
he hath not believed in the *n* of	Jn 3:18	3686
I am come in my Father's *n*	Jn 5:43	3686
another shall come in his own *n*	Jn 5:43	3686
and he calleth his own sheep by *n*	Jn 10:3	3686
works that I do in my Father's *n*	Jn 10:25	3686
that cometh in the *n* of the Lord	Jn 12:13	3686
Father, glorify thy *n*	Jn 12:28	3686
whatsoever ye shall ask in my *n*	Jn 14:13	3686
If ye shall ask any thing in my *n*	Jn 14:14	3686
whom the Father will send in my *n*	Jn 14:26	3686
shall ask of the Father in my *n*	Jn 15:16	3686
ye shall ask the Father in my *n*	Jn 16:23	3686
have ye asked nothing in my *n*	Jn 16:24	3686
At that day ye shall ask in my *n*	Jn 16:26	3686
I have manifested thy *n* unto the	Jn 17:6	3686
keep through thine own *n* those	Jn 17:11	3686
the world, I kept them in thy *n*	Jn 17:12	3686
I have declared unto them thy *n*	Jn 17:26	3686
The servant's *n* was Malchus	Jn 18:10	3686
ye might have life through his *n*	Jn 20:31	3686
the *n* of the Lord shall be saved	Acts 2:21	3686
in the *n* of Jesus Christ for the	Acts 2:38	3686
In the *n* of Jesus Christ of	Acts 3:6	3686
his *n* through faith in his *n*	Acts 3:16	3686
By what power, or by what *n*	Acts 4:7	3686
that by the *n* of Jesus Christ of	Acts 4:10	3686
for there is none other *n* under	Acts 4:12	3686
henceforth to no man in this *n*	Acts 4:17	3686
all nor teach in the *n* of Jesus	Acts 4:18	3686
by the *n* of thy holy child Jesus	Acts 4:30	3686
ye should not teach in this *n*	Acts 5:28	3686
not speak in the *n* of Jesus	Acts 5:40	3686
worthy to suffer shame for his *n*	Acts 5:41	3686
man's feet, whose *n* was Saul	Acts 7:58	2564
the *n* of Jesus Christ, they were	Acts 8:12	3686
in the *n* of the Lord Jesus	Acts 8:16	3686
to bind all that call on thy *n*	Acts 9:14	3686
to bear my *n* before the Gentiles,	Acts 9:15	3686
called on this *n* in Jerusalem	Acts 9:21	3686
at Damascus in the *n* of Jesus	Acts 9:27	3686
boldly in the *n* of the Lord Jesus	Acts 9:29	3686
that through his *n* whosoever	Acts 10:43	3686
be baptized in the *n* of the Lord	Acts 10:48	3686
a Jew, whose *n* was Bar-jesus	Acts 13:6	3686
the sorcerer (for so is his *n* by	Acts 13:8	3686
out of them a people for his *n*	Acts 15:14	3686
upon whom my *n* is called	Acts 15:17	3686
the *n* of our Lord Jesus Christ	Acts 15:26	3686
I command thee in the *n* of Jesus	Acts 16:18	3686
in the *n* of the Lord Jesus	Acts 19:5	3686
spirits the *n* of the Lord Jesus	Acts 19:13	3686
the *n* of the Lord Jesus was	Acts 19:17	3686
for the *n* of the Lord Jesus	Acts 21:13	3686
calling on the *n* of the Lord	Acts 22:16	3686
to the *n* of Jesus of Nazareth	Acts 26:9	3686
the island, whose *n* was Publius	Acts 28:7	3686
among all nations, for his *n*	Rom 1:5	3686
For the *n* of God is blasphemed	Rom 2:24	3686
that my *n* might be declared	Rom 9:17	3686
the *n* of the Lord shall be saved	Rom 10:13	3686
the Gentiles, and sing unto thy *n*	Rom 15:9	3686
the *n* of Jesus Christ our Lord	1Cor 1:2	3686
by the *n* of our Lord Jesus Christ	1Cor 1:10	3686
were ye baptized in the *n* of Paul	1Cor 1:13	3686
that I had baptized in mine own *n*	1Cor 1:15	3686
In the *n* of our Lord Jesus Christ	1Cor 5:4	3686
in the *n* of the Lord Jesus	1Cor 6:11	3686
every *n* that is named, not only	Eph 1:21	3686
the Father in the *n* of our Lord	Eph 5:20	3686
him a *n* which is above every *n*	Phil 2:9	3686
That at the *n* of Jesus every knee	Phil 2:10	3686
do all in the *n* of the Lord Jesus	Col 3:17	3686
That the *n* of our Lord Jesus	2Th 1:12	3686
in the *n* of our Lord Jesus Christ	2Th 3:6	3686

N

of all honour, that the *n* of God 1Ti 6:1   3686
Let every one that nameth the *n* 2Ti 2:19   3686
a more excellent *n* than they................. Heb 1:4   3686
declare thy *n* unto my brethren........... Heb 2:12   3686
which ye have shewed toward his *n* .... Heb 6:10   3686
our lips giving thanks to his *n* .... Heb 13:15   3686
n by the which ye are called.................. Jas 2:7   3686
have spoken in the *n* of the Lord .... Jas 5:10   3686
him with oil in the *n* of the Lord .... Jas 5:14   3686
be reproached for the *n* of Christ 1Pet 4:14   3686
on the *n* of his Son Jesus Christ 1Jn 3:23   3686
on the *n* of the Son of God 1Jn 5:13   3686
on the *n* of the Son of God 1Jn 5:13   3686
Greet the friends by *n*........................ 3Jn 14   3686
and thou holdest fast my *n* .... Rev 2:13   3686
and in the stone a new *n* written .... Rev 2:17   3686
thou hast a *n* that thou livest .... Rev 3:1   3686
out his *n* out of the book of life .... Rev 3:5   3686
confess his *n* before my Father............. Rev 3:5   3686
my word, and hast not denied my *n* ..... Rev 3:8   3686
write upon him the *n* of my God .... Rev 3:12   3686
the *n* of the city of my God, ... Rev 3:12   3686
and I will write upon him my new *n* ...... Rev 3:12   3686
his *n* that sat on him was Death, ... Rev 6:8   3686
the *n* of the star is called .... Rev 8:11   3686
whose *n* in the Hebrew tongue is .... Rev 9:11   3686
Greek tongue hath his *n* Apollyon.......... Rev 9:11   3686
saints, and them that fear thy *n* .... Rev 11:18   3686
upon his heads the *n* of blasphemy .... Rev 13:1   3686
against God, to blaspheme his *n* .... Rev 13:6   3686
or the *n* of the beast, or the .... Rev 13:17   3686
the beast, or the number of his *n* .... Rev 13:17   3686
having his Father's *n* written in .... Rev 14:1   3686
receiveth the mark of his *n* .... Rev 14:11   3686
mark, and over the number of his *n* .... Rev 15:2   3686
thee, O Lord, and glorify thy *n* .... Rev 15:4   3686
heat, and blasphemed the *n* of God .... Rev 16:9   3686
upon her forehead was a *n* written .... Rev 17:5   3686
and he had a *n* written, that no .... Rev 19:12   3686
his *n* is called The Word of God .... Rev 19:13   3686
and on his thigh a *n* written .... Rev 19:16   3686
his *n* shall be in their foreheads .... Rev 22:4   3686

NAMED

which he had *n* in the audience of.......... Gen 23:16   1696
said, Is not he rightly *n* Jacob......... Gen 27:36   7121,8034
and let my name be *n* on them.............. Gen 48:16   7121
house, *n* Rahab, and lodged there .... Josh 2:1   8034
she *n* the child I-chabod, saying, ... 1Sa 4:21   7121
n Goliath, of Gath, whose height 1Sa 17:4   8034
n Abiathar, escaped, and fled 1Sa 22:20   8034
of Jacob, whom he *n* Israel 2Kin 17:34   8034
his sons were *n* of the tribe of 1Chr 23:14   7121
That which hath been is *n* already Eccl 6:10   8034,7121
But ye shall be *n* the Priests of.............. Is 61:6   7121
be *n* in the mouth of any man of .... Jer 44:26   7121
whom the king *n* Belteshazzar .... Dan 5:12   8036
which are *n* chief of the nations,........... Amos 6:1   5344
O thou that art *n* the house of .... Mic 2:7   559
n Matthew, sitting at the receipt .... Mt 9:9   3004
n Joseph, who also himself was............. Mt 27:57   3686
to a place which was *n* Gethsemane .... Mk 14:32   3686
And there was one *n* Barabbas.............. Mk 15:7   3004
a certain priest *n* Zacharias .... Lk 1:5   3686
a city of Galilee, *n* Nazareth,................ Lk 1:26   3686
which was so *n* of the angel.................. Lk 2:21   2564
n Levi, sitting at the receipt of .... Lk 5:27   3686
twelve, whom also he *n* apostles .... Lk 6:13   3687
Simon, (whom he also *n* Peter .... Lk 6:14   3687
behold, there came a man *n* Jairus .... Lk 8:41   3686
a certain woman *n* Martha received .... Lk 10:38   3686
was a certain beggar *n* Lazarus .... Lk 16:20   3686
there was a man *n* Zacchaeus .... Lk 19:2   2564
behold, there was a man *n* Joseph.......... Lk 23:50   3686
n Nicodemus, a ruler of the Jews .... Jn 3:1   3686
n Lazarus, of Bethany, the town .... Jn 11:1
n Caiaphas, being the high priest .... Jn 11:49
But a certain man *n* Ananias .... Acts 5:1   3686
n Gamaliel, a doctor of the law,........... Acts 5:34   3686
disciple at Damascus, *n* Ananias........... Acts 9:10   3686
vision a man *n* Ananias coming in ... Acts 9:12   3686
he found a certain man *n* Aeneas .... Acts 9:33   3686
a certain disciple *n* Tabitha.................. Acts 9:36   3686
stood up one of them *n* Agabus............. Acts 11:28   3686
a damsel came to hearken, *n* Rhoda...... Acts 12:13   3686
n Timotheus, the son of a certain .... Acts 16:1   3686
And a certain woman *n* Lydia .... Acts 16:14   3686
Areopagite, and a woman *n* Damaris .... Acts 17:34   3686
And found a certain Jew *n* Aquila .... Acts 18:2   3686
n Justus, one that worshipped God....... Acts 18:7   3686
And a certain Jew *n* Apollos .... Acts 18:24   3686

For a certain man *n* Demetrius .... Acts 19:24   3686
a certain young man *n* Eutychus .... Acts 20:9   3686
a certain prophet, *n* Agabus .... Acts 21:10   3686
with a certain orator *n* Tertullus .... Acts 24:1   3686
other prisoners unto one *n* Julius .... Acts 27:1   3686
gospel, not where Christ was *n* .... Rom 15:20   3687
so much as *n* among the Gentiles.......... 1Cor 5:1   3687
dominion, and every name that is *n* ...... Eph 1:21   3687
family in heaven and earth is *n* .... Eph 3:15   3687
let it not be once *n* among you.............. Eph 5:3   3687

NAMELY See APPENDIX.

NAME'S

his people for his great *n* sake 1Sa 12:22   8034
of a far country for thy *n* sake 1Kin 8:41   8034
far country for thy great *n* sake 2Chr 6:32   8034
of righteousness for his *n* sake .... Ps 23:3   8034
For thy *n* sake, O LORD, pardon .,.......... Ps 25:11   8034
therefore for thy *n* sake lead me .... Ps 31:3   8034
away our sins, for thy *n* sake .... Ps 79:9   8034
he saved them for his *n* sake .... Ps 106:8   8034
O GOD the Lord, for thy *n* sake............. Ps 109:21   8034
me, O LORD, for thy *n* sake .... Ps 143:11   8034
For my *n* sake will I defer mine .... Is 48:9   8034
that cast you out for my *n* sake .... Is 66:5   8034
us, do thou it for thy *n* sake .... Jer 14:7   8034
Do not abhor us, for thy *n* sake .... Jer 14:21   8034
But I wrought for my *n* sake .... Eze 20:9   8034
But I wrought for my *n* sake .... Eze 20:14   8034
hand, and wrought for my *n* sake .... Eze 20:22   8034
wrought with you for my *n* sake .... Eze 20:44   8034
Israel, but for mine holy *n* sake .... Eze 36:22   8034
be hated of all men for my *n* sake ...... Mt 10:22   3686
children, or lands, for my *n* sake .... Mt 19:29   3686
of all nations for my *n* sake .... Mt 24:9   3686
be hated of all men for my *n* sake ...... Mk 13:13   3686
kings and rulers for my *n* sake .... Lk 21:12   3686
be hated of all men for my *n* sake ...... Lk 21:17   3686
they do unto you for my *n* sake.......... Jn 15:21   3686
he must suffer for my *n* sake................. Acts 9:16   3686
are forgiven you for his *n* sake 1Jn 2:12   3686
for his *n* sake they went forth 3Jn 7   3686
for my *n* sake hast laboured, and ...... Rev 2:3   3686

NAMES

Adam gave *n* to all cattle, and to .... Gen 2:20   8034
these are the *n* of the sons of .... Gen 25:13   8034
the sons of Ishmael, by their *n* .... Gen 25:13   8034
of Ishmael, and these are their *n* .... Gen 25:16   8034
he called their *n* after the *n* .... Gen 26:18   8034
These are the *n* of Esau's sons............... Gen 36:10   8034
these are the *n* of the dukes that .... Gen 36:40   8034
after their places, by their *n* .... Gen 36:40   8034
these are the *n* of the children .... Gen 46:8   8034
Now these are the *n* of the .... Ex 1:1   8034
these are the *n* of the sons of .... Ex 6:16   8034
grave on them the *n* of the .... Ex 28:9   8034
Six of their *n* on one stone .... Ex 28:10   8034
the other six *n* of the rest on .... Ex 28:10   8034
the *n* of the children of Israel................ Ex 28:11   8034
Aaron shall bear their *n* before .... Ex 28:12   8034
the *n* of the children of Israel................ Ex 28:21   8034
twelve, according to their *n* .... Ex 28:21   8034
Aaron shall bear the *n* of the................. Ex 28:29   8034
with the *n* of the children of .... Ex 39:6   8034
the *n* of the children of Israel................ Ex 39:14   8034
twelve, according to their *n* .... Ex 39:14   8034
with the number of their *n* .... Num 1:2   8034
these are the *n* of the men that .... Num 1:5   8034
which are expressed by their *n* .... Num 1:17   8034
according to the number of the *n* .... Num 1:18   8034
according to the number of the *n* .... Num 1:20   8034
according to the number of the *n* .... Num 1:22   8034
according to the number of the *n* .... Num 1:24   8034
according to the number of the *n* .... Num 1:26   8034
according to the number of the *n* .... Num 1:28   8034
according to the number of the *n* .... Num 1:30   8034
according to the number of the *n* .... Num 1:32   8034
according to the number of the *n* .... Num 1:34   8034
according to the number of the *n* .... Num 1:36   8034
according to the number of the *n* .... Num 1:38   8034
according to the number of the *n* .... Num 1:40   8034
according to the number of the *n* .... Num 1:42   8034
these are the *n* of the sons of .... Num 3:2   8034
These are the *n* of the sons of .... Num 3:3   8034
were the sons of Levi by their *n* .... Num 3:17   8034
these are the *n* of the sons of .... Num 3:18   8034
and take the number of their *n* .... Num 3:40   8034
males by the number of *n*, from a .... Num 3:43   8034
And these were their *n* .... Num 13:4   8034
These are the *n* of the men which .... Num 13:16   8034

the *n* of the daughters of	Num 26:33	8034
according to the number of *n*	Num 26:53	8034
according to the *n* of the tribes	Num 26:55	8034
these are the *n* of his daughters	Num 27:1	8034
(their *n* being changed,) and	Num 32:38	8034
gave other *n* unto the cities	Num 32:38	8034
These are the *n* of the men which	Num 34:17	8034
the *n* of the men are these	Num 34:19	8034
destroy the *n* of them out of that	Deut 12:3	8034
these are the *n* of his daughters,	Josh 17:3	8034
mention of the *n* of their gods	Josh 23:7	8034
the *n* of his two daughters were	1Sa 14:49	8034
the *n* of his three sons that went	1Sa 17:13	8034
these be the *n* of those that were	2Sa 5:14	8034
These be the *n* of the mighty men	2Sa 23:8	8034
And these are their *n*	1Kin 4:8	8034
These mentioned by their *n* were	1Chr 4:38	8034
these be the *n* of the sons of	1Chr 6:17	8034
which are called by their *n*	1Chr 6:65	8034
whose *n* are these, Azrikam,	1Chr 8:38	8034
whose *n* are these, Azrikam,	1Chr 9:44	8034
Now these are the *n* of his	1Chr 14:4	8034
by number of *n* by their polls	1Chr 23:24	8034
What are the *n* of the men that	Ezr 5:4	8036
We asked their *n* also, to certify	Ezr 5:10	8036
that we might write the *n* of the	Ezr 5:10	8036
whose *n* are these, Eliphelet,	Ezr 8:13	8034
and all of them by their *n*	Ezr 10:16	8034
nor take up their *n* into my lips	Ps 16:4	8034
their lands after their own *n*	Ps 49:11	8034
he calleth them all by their *n*	Ps 147:4	8034
he calleth them all by *n* by the	Is 40:26	8034
the *n* of them were Aholah the	Eze 23:4	8034
Thus were their *n*	Eze 23:4	8034
Now these are the *n* of the tribes	Eze 48:1	8034
the *n* of the tribes of Israel	Eze 48:31	8034
the prince of the eunuchs gave *n*	Dan 1:7	8034
For I will take away the *n* of	Hos 2:17	8034
that I will cut off the *n* of the	Zec 13:2	8034
Now the *n* of the twelve apostles	Mt 10:2	3686
because your *n* are written in	Lk 10:20	3686
(the number of *n* together were	Acts 1:15	3686
if it be a question of words and *n*	Acts 18:15	3686
whose *n* are in the book of life	Phil 4:3	3686
Thou hast a few *n* even in Sardis	Rev 3:4	3686
whose *n* are not written in the	Rev 13:8	3686
full of *n* of blasphemy, having	Rev 17:3	3686
whose *n* were not written in the	Rev 17:8	3686
n written thereon, which are the	Rev 21:12	3686
which are the *n* of the twelve	Rev 21:12	3686
in them the *n* of the twelve	Rev 21:14	3686

NAMETH
Let every one that *n* the name of	2Ti 2:19	3687

NAOMI (na'-o-mee) See NAOMI'S. *Mother-in-law of Ruth.*
and the name of his wife *N*	Ruth 1:2	5281
N said unto her two daughters in	Ruth 1:8	5281
N said, Turn again, my daughters	Ruth 1:11	5281
them, and they said, Is this *N*	Ruth 1:19	5281
she said unto them, Call me not *N*	Ruth 1:20	5281
why then call ye me *N*, seeing the	Ruth 1:21	5281
So *N* returned, and Ruth the	Ruth 1:22	5281
N had a kinsman of her husband's,	Ruth 2:1	5281
And Ruth the Moabitess said unto *N*	Ruth 2:2	5281
with *N* out of the country of Moab	Ruth 2:6	5281
N said unto her daughter in law,	Ruth 2:20	5281
N said unto her, The man is near	Ruth 2:20	5281
N said to Ruth her daughter in	Ruth 2:22	5281
Then *N* her mother in law said	Ruth 3:1	5281
And he said unto the kinsman, *N*	Ruth 4:3	5281
buyest the field of the hand of *N*	Ruth 4:5	5281
and Mahlon's, of the hand of *N*	Ruth 4:9	5281
And the women said unto *N*, Blessed	Ruth 4:14	5281
N took the child, and laid it in	Ruth 4:16	5281
saying, There is a son born to *N*	Ruth 4:17	5281

NAOMI'S (na'-o-meze)
And Elimelech *N* husband died	Ruth 1:3	5281

NAPHATH See DOR.

NAPHATH DOR See DOR.

NAPHETH See DOR.

NAPHISH (na'-fish) See NEPHISH. *A son of Ishmael.*
Hadar, and Tema, Jetur, *N*, and	Gen 25:15	5305
Jetur, *N*, and Kedemah	1Chr 1:31	5305

NAPHTALI (naf-ta-li) See NEPHTHALIM.
1. A son of Jacob.
and she called his name *N*	Gen 30:8	5321
handmaid; Dan, and *N*	Gen 35:25	5321

And the sons of *N*	Gen 46:24	5321
N is a hind let loose	Gen 49:21	5321
Dan, and *N*, Gad, and Asher	Ex 1:4	5321
Dan, Joseph, and Benjamin, *N*	1Chr 2:2	5321
The sons of *N*	1Chr 7:13	5321
one gate of Asher, one gate of *N*	Eze 48:34	5321
2. The tribe and land.		
Of *N*; Ahira the son	Num 1:15	5321
Of the children of *N*, throughout	Num 1:42	5321
of them, even of the tribe of *N*	Num 1:43	5321
Then the tribe of *N*	Num 2:29	5321
N shall be Ahira the son of Enan	Num 2:29	5321
Enan, prince of the children of *N*	Num 7:78	5321
of *N* was Ahira the son of Enan	Num 10:27	5321
Of the tribe of *N*, Nahbi the son	Num 13:14	5321
Of the sons of *N* after their	Num 26:48	5321
These are the families of *N*	Num 26:50	5321
of the tribe of the children of *N*	Num 34:28	5321
and Asher, and Zebulun, Dan, and *N*	Deut 27:13	5321
And of Naphtali he said, O *N*	Deut 33:23	5321
And all *N*, and the land of Ephraim,	Deut 34:2	5321
lot came out to the children of *N*	Josh 19:32	5321
even for the children of *N*	Josh 19:32	5321
of *N* according to their families	Josh 19:39	5321
Kedesh in Galilee in mount *N*	Josh 20:7	5321
Asher, and out of the tribe of *N*	Josh 21:6	5321
And out of the tribe of *N*, Kedesh	Josh 21:32	5321
Neither did *N* drive out the	Judg 1:33	5321
thousand men of the children of *N*	Judg 4:6	5321
called Zebulun and *N* to Kedesh	Judg 4:10	5321
N were a people that jeoparded	Judg 5:18	5321
Asher, and unto Zebulun, and unto *N*	Judg 6:35	5321
themselves together out of *N*	Judg 7:23	5321
Ahimaaz was in *N*	1Kin 4:15	5321
a widow's son of the tribe of *N*	1Kin 7:14	5321
Cinneroth, with all the land of *N*	1Kin 15:20	5321
and Galilee, all the land of *N*	2Kin 15:29	5321
Asher, and out of the tribe of *N*	1Chr 6:62	5321
And out of the tribe of *N*	1Chr 6:76	5321
of *N* a thousand captains, and with	1Chr 12:34	5321
unto Issachar and Zebulun and *N*	1Chr 12:40	5321
of *N*, Jerimoth the son of Azriel	1Chr 27:19	5321
and all the store cities of *N*	2Chr 16:4	5321
Ephraim, and Simeon, even unto *N*	2Chr 34:6	5321
of Zebulun, and the princes of *N*	Ps 68:27	5321
land of Zebulun and the land of *N*	Is 9:1	5321
the west side, a portion for *N*	Eze 48:3	5321
And by the border of *N*, from the	Eze 48:4	5321

NAPHTUHIM (naf-too-him) *Inhabitants of central Egypt.*
and Anamim, and Lehabim, and *N*	Gen 10:13	5320

NAPKIN
which I have kept laid up in a *n*	Lk 19:20	4676
his face was bound about with a *n*	Jn 11:44	4676
And the *n*, that was about his head	Jn 20:7	4676

NAPHTHUHIM
and Anamim, and Lehabim, and *N*	1Chr 1:11	5320

NARCISSUS (nar-sis'-sus) *A Christian in Rome.*
that be of the household of *N*	Rom 16:11	3488

NARROW
further, and stood in a *n* place	Num 22:26	6862
mount Ephraim be too *n* for thee	Josh 17:15	213
house he made windows of *n* lights	1Kin 6:4	331
and a strange woman is a *n* pit	Prov 23:27	6862
shall even now be too *n* by reason	Is 49:19	3334
there were *n* windows to the	Eze 40:16	331
the *n* windows, and the galleries	Eze 41:16	331
And there were *n* windows and palm	Eze 41:26	331
n is the way, which leadeth unto	Mt 7:14	2346

NARROWED
house he made *n* rests round about	1Kin 6:6	4052

NARROWER
the covering *n* than that he can	Is 28:20	6887

NARROWLY
lookest *n* unto all my paths	Job 13:27	8104
see thee shall *n* look upon thee	Is 14:16	

NATHAN (na'-than) See NATHAN-MELECH.
1. A son of David.
Shammuah, and Shobab, and *N*	2Sa 5:14	5416
Shimea, and Shobab, and *N*, and	1Chr 3:5	5416
and Shobab, *N*, and Solomon	1Chr 14:4	5416
Mattatha, which was the son of *N*	Lk 3:31	3481
2. A prophet in David's court.		
the king said unto *N* the prophet	2Sa 7:2	5416
N said to the king, Go, do all	2Sa 7:3	5416
the word of the LORD came unto *N*	2Sa 7:4	5416

N

so did N speak unto David	2Sa 7:17	5416
And the LORD sent N unto David	2Sa 12:1	5416
and he said to N, As the LORD	2Sa 12:5	5416
N said to David, Thou art the man	2Sa 12:7	5416
And David said unto N, I have	2Sa 12:13	5416
N said unto David, The LORD also	2Sa 12:13	5416
N departed unto his house	2Sa 12:15	5416
sent by the hand of N the prophet	2Sa 12:25	5416
N the prophet, and Shimei, and Rei,....	1Kin 1:8	5416
But N the prophet, and Benaiah, and....	1Kin 1:10	5416
Wherefore N spake unto Bath-sheba	1Kin 1:11	5416
N the prophet also came in	1Kin 1:22	5416
saying, Behold N the prophet	1Kin 1:23	5416
N said, My lord, O king, hast	1Kin 1:24	5416
N the prophet, and Benaiah the son	1Kin 1:32	5416
N the prophet anoint him there	1Kin 1:34	5416
N the prophet, and Benaiah the son	1Kin 1:38	5416
N the prophet, and Benaiah the son	1Kin 1:44	5416
N the prophet have anointed him	1Kin 1:45	5416
that David said to N the prophet	1Chr 17:1	5416
Then N said unto David, Do all	1Chr 17:2	5416
that the word of God came to N	1Chr 17:3	5416
so did N speak unto David	1Chr 17:15	5416
and in the book of N the prophet	1Chr 29:29	5416
in the book of N the prophet	2Chr 9:29	5416
the king's seer, and N the prophet	2Chr 29:25	5416
when N the prophet came unto him,	Ps 51:t	5416

3. Father of Igal.

Igal the son of N of Zobah	2Sa 23:36	5416

4. Father of Azariah.

Azariah the son of N was over the	1Kin 4:5	5416

5. Father of Zebud.

Zabud the son of N was principal	1Kin 4:5	5416

6. Son of Attai.

And Attai begat N	1Chr 2:36	5416
and N begat Zabad	1Chr 2:36	5416

7. Brother of Joel.

Joel the brother of N, Mibhar the	1Chr 11:38	5416

8. A clan leader with Ezra.

Jarib, and for Elnathan, and for N	Ezr 8:16	5416

9. Married a foreigner in exile.

And Shelemiah, and N, and Adaiah,	Ezr 10:39	5416

10. A family leader.

family of the house of N apart	Zec 12:12	5416

NATHANAEL (na-than'-a-el) See BARTHOLOMEW. *A disciple of Jesus.*

Philip findeth N, and saith unto	Jn 1:45	3482
N said unto him, Can there any	Jn 1:46	3482
Jesus saw N coming to him, and	Jn 1:47	3482
N saith unto him, Whence knowest	Jn 1:48	3482
N answered and saith unto him,	Jn 1:49	3482
N of Cana in Galilee, and the sons	Jn 21:2	3482

NATHAN-MELECH (na'-than-me'-lek) *A servant of King Josiah.*

the chamber of N the chamberlain	2Kin 23:11	5419

NATION

And I will make of thee a great n	Gen 12:2	1471
And also that n, whom they shall	Gen 15:14	1471
and I will make him a great n	Gen 17:20	1471
surely become a great and mighty n	Gen 18:18	1471
wilt thou slay also a righteous n	Gen 20:4	1471
of the bondwoman will I make a n	Gen 21:13	1471
for I will make him a great n	Gen 21:18	1471
a n and a company of nations shall	Gen 35:11	1471
will there make of thee a great n	Gen 46:3	1471
land of Egypt since it became a n	Ex 9:24	1471
kingdom of priests, and an holy n	Ex 19:6	1471
strange n he shall have no power	Ex 21:8	5971
and I will make of thee a great n	Ex 32:10	1471
that this n is thy people	Ex 33:13	1471
in all the earth, nor in any n	Ex 34:10	1471
neither any of your own n	Lev 18:26	249
not walk in the manners of the n	Lev 20:23	1471
and will make of thee a greater n	Num 14:12	1471
Surely this great n is a wise	Deut 4:6	1471
For what n is there so great, who	Deut 4:7	1471
what n is there so great, that	Deut 4:8	1471
take him a n from the midst of	Deut 4:34	1471
from the midst of another n	Deut 4:34	1471
I will make of thee a n mightier	Deut 9:14	1471
with a few, and became there a n	Deut 26:5	1471
shall a n which thou knowest not	Deut 28:33	5971
unto a n which neither thou nor	Deut 28:36	1471
bring a n against thee from far	Deut 28:49	1471
a n whose tongue thou shalt not	Deut 28:49	1471
A n of fierce countenance, which	Deut 28:50	1471
them to anger with a foolish n	Deut 32:21	1471
For they are a n void of counsel,	Deut 32:28	1471
what one n in the earth is like	2Sa 7:23	1471

liveth, there is no n or kingdom	1Kin 18:10	1471
took an oath of the kingdom and n	1Kin 18:10	1471
Howbeit every n made gods of	2Kin 17:29	1471
every n in their cities wherein	2Kin 17:29	1471
when they went from n to n	1Chr 16:20	1471
what one n in the earth is like	1Chr 17:21	1471
And n was destroyed of n	2Chr 15:6	1471
for no god of any n or kingdom	2Chr 32:15	1471
whether it be done against a n	Job 34:29	1471
Blessed is the n whose God is the	Ps 33:12	1471
my cause against an ungodly n	Ps 43:1	1471
us cut them off from being a n	Ps 83:4	1471
they went from one n to another	Ps 105:13	1471
rejoice in the gladness of thy n	Ps 106:5	1471
He hath not dealt so with any n	Ps 147:20	1471
Righteousness exalteth a n	Prov 14:34	1471
Ah sinful n, a people laden with	Is 1:4	1471
n shall not lift up sword against	Is 2:4	1471
shall not lift up sword against n	Is 2:4	1471
Thou hast multiplied the n	Is 9:3	1471
him against an hypocritical n	Is 10:6	1471
answer the messengers of the n	Is 14:32	1471
to a n scattered and peeled, to a	Is 18:2	1471
a n meted out and trodden down,	Is 18:2	1471
a n meted out and trodden under	Is 18:7	1471
that the righteous n which	Is 26:2	1471
Thou hast increased the n	Is 26:15	1471
O LORD, thou hast increased the n	Is 26:15	1471
to him whom the n abhorreth	Is 49:7	1471
and give ear unto me, O my n	Is 51:4	3816
thou shalt call a n that thou	Is 55:5	1471
as a n that did righteousness, and	Is 58:2	1471
For the n and kingdom that will	Is 60:12	1471
and a small one a strong n	Is 60:22	1471
unto a n that was not called by	Is 65:1	1471
or shall a n be born at once	Is 66:8	1471
Hath a n changed their gods,	Jer 2:11	1471
be avenged on such a n as this	Jer 5:9	1471
I will bring a n upon you from	Jer 5:15	1471
mighty n, it is an ancient n	Jer 5:15	1471
a n whose language thou knowest	Jer 5:15	1471
be avenged on such a n as this	Jer 5:29	1471
a great n shall be raised from	Jer 6:22	1471
This is a n that obeyeth not the	Jer 7:28	1471
be avenged on such a n as this	Jer 9:9	1471
pluck up and destroy that n	Jer 12:17	1471
I shall speak concerning a n	Jer 18:7	1471
If that n, against whom I have	Jer 18:8	1471
I shall speak concerning a n	Jer 18:9	1471
the king of Babylon, and that n	Jer 25:12	1471
shall go forth from n to n	Jer 25:32	1471
it shall come to pass, that the n	Jer 27:8	1471
that n will I punish, saith the	Jer 27:8	1471
LORD hath spoken against the n	Jer 27:13	1471
from being a n before me for ever	Jer 31:36	1471
should be no more a n before them	Jer 33:24	1471
let us cut it off from being a n	Jer 48:2	1471
get you up unto the wealthy n	Jer 49:31	1471
there shall be no n whither the	Jer 49:36	1471
there cometh up a n against her	Jer 50:3	1471
come from the north, and a great n	Jer 50:41	1471
for a n that could not save us	Lam 4:17	1471
to a rebellious n that hath	Eze 2:3	1471
I will make them one n in the	Eze 37:22	1471
a decree, That every people, n	Dan 3:29	524
shall stand up out of the n	Dan 8:22	1471
was a n even to that same time	Dan 12:1	1471
For a n is come up upon my land,	Joel 1:6	1471
I will raise up against you a n	Amos 6:14	1471
n shall not lift up a sword	Mic 4:3	1471
not lift up a sword against n	Mic 4:3	1471
that was cast far off a strong n	Mic 4:7	1471
Chaldeans, that bitter and hasty n	Hab 1:6	1471
gather together, O n not desired	Zeph 2:1	1471
coast, the n of the Cherethites	Zeph 2:5	1471
people, and so is this n before me	Hag 2:14	1471
have robbed me, even this whole n	Mal 3:9	1471
given to a n bringing forth the	Mt 21:43	1484
For n shall rise against n,	Mt 24:7	1484
was a Greek, a Syrophenician by n	Mk 7:26	1085
For n shall rise against n,	Mk 13:8	1484
For he loveth our n, and he hath	Lk 7:5	1484
N shall rise against n, and	Lk 21:10	1484
this fellow perverting the n	Lk 23:2	1484
and take away both our place and n	Jn 11:48	1484
and that the whole n perish not	Jn 11:50	1484
that Jesus should die for that n	Jn 11:51	1484
And not for that n only, but that	Jn 11:52	1484
Thine own n and the chief priests	Jn 18:35	1484
men, out of every n under heaven	Acts 2:5	1484
the n to whom they shall be in	Acts 7:7	1484

among all the *n* of the Jews .... Acts 10:22   *1484*
or come unto one of another *n* .... Acts 10:28   *246*
But in every *n* he that feareth................ Acts 10:35   *1484*
unto this *n* by thy providence .... Acts 24:2   *1484*
of many years a judge unto this *n* .... Acts 24:10   *1484*
I came to bring alms to my *n* .... Acts 24:17   *1484*
among mine own *n* at Jerusalem .... Acts 26:4   *1484*
I had ought to accuse my *n* of .... Acts 28:19   *1484*
by a foolish *n* I will anger you .... Rom 10:19   *1484*
many my equals in mine own *n* .... Gal 1:14   *1085*
midst of a crooked and perverse *n* .... Phil 2:15   *1074*
a royal priesthood, an holy *n* 1Pet 2:9   *1484*
and tongue, and people, and *n* .... Rev 5:9   *1484*
dwell on the earth, and to every *n* .... Rev 14:6   *1484*

NATIONS

after their families, in their *n*.............. Gen 10:5   *1471*
in their countries, and in their *n*.......... Gen 10:20   *1471*
in their lands, after their *n*.................. Gen 10:31   *1471*
their generations, in their *n* .... Gen 10:32   *1471*
by these were the *n* divided in .... Gen 10:32   *1471*
king of Elam, and Tidal king of *n* .... Gen 14:1   *1471*
of Elam, and with Tidal king of *n* .... Gen 14:9   *1471*
thou shalt be a father of many *n* .... Gen 17:4   *1471*
father of many *n* have I made thee .... Gen 17:5   *1471*
and I will make *n* of thee .... Gen 17:6   *1471*
and she shall be a mother of *n* .... Gen 17:16   *1471*
all the *n* of the earth shall be .... Gen 18:18   *1471*
all the *n* of the earth be blessed............ Gen 22:18   *1471*
princes according to their *n* .... Gen 25:16   *523*
Two *n* are in thy womb, and two .... Gen 25:23   *1471*
all the *n* of the earth be blessed............ Gen 26:4   *1471*
serve thee, and *n* bow down to thee ...... Gen 27:29   *3816*
a company of *n* shall be of thee, ... Gen 35:11   *1471*
shall become a multitude of *n* .... Gen 48:19   *1471*
I will cast out the *n* before thee .... Ex 34:24   *1471*
for in all these the *n* are .... Lev 18:24   *1471*
as it spued out the *n* that were .... Lev 18:28   *1471*
then the *n* which have heard the .... Num 14:15   *1471*
shall not be reckoned among the *n* .... Num 23:9   *1471*
he shall eat up the *n* his enemies .... Num 24:8   *1471*
Amalek was the first of the *n* .... Num 24:20   *1471*
the fear of thee upon the *n* that............ Deut 2:25   *5971*
in the sight of the *n*, which.................. Deut 4:6   *5971*
unto all *n* under the whole heaven .... Deut 4:19   *5971*
shall scatter you among the *n*................ Deut 4:27   *5971*
To drive out *n* from before thee .... Deut 4:38   *1471*
hath cast out many *n* before thee.......... Deut 7:1   *1471*
seven *n* greater and mightier than .... Deut 7:1   *1471*
heart, These *n* are more than I.............. Deut 7:17   *1471*
out those *n* before thee by little .... Deut 7:22   *1471*
As the *n* which the LORD .... Deut 8:20   *1471*
to go in to possess *n* greater.................. Deut 9:1   *1471*
n the LORD doth drive them out .... Deut 9:4   *1471*
n the LORD thy God doth drive .... Deut 9:5   *1471*
out all these *n* from before you .... Deut 11:23   *1471*
and ye shall possess greater *n* .... Deut 11:23   *1471*
wherein the *n* which ye shall .... Deut 12:2   *1471*
cut off the *n* from before thee .... Deut 12:29   *1471*
How did these *n* serve their gods .... Deut 12:30   *1471*
above all the *n* that are upon the .... Deut 14:2   *5971*
and thou shalt lend unto many *n* .... Deut 15:6   *1471*
and thou shalt reign over many *n* .... Deut 15:6   *1471*
like as all the *n* that are about .... Deut 17:14   *1471*
after the abominations of those *n* .... Deut 18:9   *1471*
For these *n*, which thou shalt................ Deut 18:14   *1471*
LORD thy God hath cut off the *n* .... Deut 19:1   *1471*
are not of the cities of these *n*.............. Deut 20:15   *1471*
above all *n* which he hath made .... Deut 26:19   *1471*
on high above all *n* of the earth .... Deut 28:1   *1471*
and thou shalt lend unto many *n*.......... Deut 28:12   *1471*
among all *n* whither the LORD .... Deut 28:37   *5971*
among these *n* shalt thou find no .... Deut 28:65   *1471*
through the *n* which ye passed by .... Deut 29:16   *1471*
go and serve the gods of these *n* .... Deut 29:18   *1471*
Even all *n* shall say, Wherefore .... Deut 29:24   *1471*
call them to mind among all the *n* .... Deut 30:1   *1471*
and gather thee from all the *n* .... Deut 30:3   *5971*
destroy these *n* from before thee .... Deut 31:3   *1471*
to the *n* their inheritance...................... Deut 32:8   *1471*
Rejoice, O ye *n*, with his people .... Deut 32:43   *1471*
the king of the *n* of Gilgal .... Josh 12:23   *1471*
unto all these *n* because of you .... Josh 23:3   *1471*
you by lot these *n* that remain................ Josh 23:4   *1471*
with all the *n* that I have cut .... Josh 23:4   *1471*
That ye come not among these *n* .... Josh 23:7   *1471*
out from before you great *n* .... Josh 23:9   *1471*
unto the remnant of these *n*.................. Josh 23:12   *1471*
any of these *n* from before you .... Josh 23:13   *1471*
n which Joshua left when he died........ Judg 2:21   *1471*
Therefore the LORD left those *n* .... Judg 2:23   *1471*

Now these are the *n* which the .... Judg 3:1   *1471*
a king to judge us like all the *n* 1Sa 8:5   *1471*
we also may be like all the *n* 1Sa 8:20   *1471*
for those *n* were of old the 1Sa 27:8
to thee from Egypt, from the *n* 2Sa 7:23   *1471*
of all *n* which he subdued 2Sa 8:11   *1471*
his fame was in all *n* round about 1Kin 4:31   *1471*
Of the *n* concerning which the.............. 1Kin 11:2   *1471*
n which the LORD cast out before 1Kin 14:24   *1471*
The *n* which thou hast removed, and 2Kin 17:26   *1471*
after the manner of the *n* whom 2Kin 17:33   *1471*
So these *n* feared the LORD, and............2Kin 17:41   *1471*
Hath any of the gods of the *n* 2Kin 18:33   *1471*
Have the gods of the *n* delivered 2Kin 19:12   *1471*
of Assyria have destroyed the *n* 2Kin 19:17   *1471*
to do more evil than did the *n* 2Kin 21:9   *1471*
the fear of him upon all *n* 1Chr 14:17   *1471*
his marvellous works among all *n*........1Chr 16:24   *5971*
and let men say among the *n*................1Chr 16:31   *1471*
by driving out *n* from before thy 1Chr 17:21   *1471*
that he brought from all these *n* 1Chr 18:11   *1471*
a proverb and a byword among all *n* 2Chr 7:20   *5971*
manner of the *n* of other lands 2Chr 13:9   *5971*
were the gods of the *n* of those 2Chr 32:13   *1471*
those *n* that my fathers utterly 2Chr 32:14   *1471*
As the gods of the *n* of other 2Chr 32:17   *1471*
sight of all *n* from thenceforth 2Chr 32:23   *1471*
the rest of the *n* whom the great ....Ezr 4:10   *524*
scatter you abroad among the *n*.............. Neh 1:8   *5971*
thou gavest them kingdoms and *n* .... Neh 9:22   *1471*
yet among many *n* was there no .... Neh 13:26   *1471*
He increaseth the *n*, and .... Job 12:23   *1471*
he enlargeth the *n*, and .... Job 12:23   *1471*
all the *n* that forget God .... Ps 9:17   *1471*
that the *n* may know themselves to ...... Ps 9:20   *1471*
all the kindreds of the *n* shall .... Ps 22:27   *1471*
and he is the governor among the *n* ...... Ps 22:28   *1471*
under us, and the *n* under our feet ...... Ps 47:3   *3816*
I will sing unto thee among the *n* .... Ps 57:9   *3816*
his eyes behold the *n* .... Ps 66:7   *1471*
thy saving health among all *n* .... Ps 67:2   *1471*
O let the *n* be glad and sing for............ Ps 67:4   *3816*
and govern the *n* upon earth .... Ps 67:4   *3816*
all *n* shall serve him .... Ps 72:11   *1471*
all *n* shall call him blessed .... Ps 72:17   *1471*
for thou shalt inherit all *n* .... Ps 82:8   *1471*
All *n* whom thou hast made shall........ Ps 86:9   *1471*
all the gods of the *n* are idols................ Ps 96:5   *5971*
their seed also among the *n* .... Ps 106:27   *1471*
They did not destroy the *n* .... Ps 106:34   *5971*
praises unto thee among the *n* .... Ps 108:3   *3816*
The LORD is high above all *n* .... Ps 113:4   *1471*
O praise the LORD, all ye *n* .... Ps 117:1   *1471*
All *n* compassed me about.................... Ps 118:10   *1471*
Who smote great *n*, and slew mighty ....Ps 135:10   *1471*
people curse, *n* shall abhor him .... Prov 24:24   *3816*
and all *n* shall flow unto it .... Is 2:2   *1471*
And he shall judge among the *n* .... Is 2:4   *1471*
up an ensign to the *n* from far.............. Is 5:26   *1471*
Jordan, in Galilee of the *n*.................... Is 9:1   *1471*
to destroy and cut off *n* not a few.......... Is 10:7   *1471*
shall set up an ensign for the *n* .... Is 11:12   *1471*
kingdoms of *n* gathered together............ Is 13:4   *1471*
he that ruled the *n* in anger .... Is 14:6   *1471*
thrones all the kings of the *n* .... Is 14:9   *1471*
ground, which didst weaken the *n*........ Is 14:12   *1471*
All the kings of the *n*, even all .... Is 14:18   *1471*
is stretched out upon all the *n* .... Is 14:26   *1471*
and to the rushing of *n*, that make........ Is 17:12   *3816*
The *n* shall rush like the rushing .... Is 17:13   *3816*
and she is a mart of *n* .... Is 23:3   *1471*
of the terrible *n* shall fear thee .... Is 25:3   *1471*
vail that is spread over all *n* .... Is 25:7   *1471*
the *n* that fight against Ariel .... Is 29:7   *1471*
the multitude of all the *n* be .... Is 29:8   *1471*
to sift the *n* with the sieve of................ Is 30:28   *1471*
of thyself the *n* were scattered.............. Is 33:3   *1471*
Come near, ye *n*, to hear...................... Is 34:1   *1471*
of the LORD is upon all *n* .... Is 34:2   *1471*
Hath any of the gods of the *n* .... Is 36:18   *1471*
Have the gods of the *n* delivered .... Is 37:12   *1471*
Assyria have laid waste all the *n* ....Is 37:18   *776*
the *n* are as a drop of a bucket,.............. Is 40:15   *1471*
All *n* before him are as nothing............ Is 40:17   *1471*
gave the *n* before him, and made .... Is 41:2   *1471*
Let all the *n* be gathered .... Is 43:9   *1471*
holden, to subdue *n* before him............ Is 45:1   *1471*
ye that are escaped of the *n* .... Is 45:20   *1471*
holy arm in the eyes of all the *n* .... Is 52:10   *1471*
So shall he sprinkle many *n* .... Is 52:15   *1471*
n that knew not thee shall run .... Is 55:5   *1471*

N

those *n* shall be utterly wasted	Is 60:12	1471
to spring forth before all the *n*	Is 61:11	1471
that the *n* may tremble at thy	Is 64:2	1471
come, that I will gather all *n*	Is 66:18	1471
that escape of them unto the *n*	Is 66:19	1471
the LORD out of all *n* upon horses	Is 66:20	1471
thee a prophet unto the *n*	Jer 1:5	1471
have this day set thee over the *n*	Jer 1:10	1471
all the *n* shall be gathered unto	Jer 3:17	1471
goodly heritage of the hosts of *n*	Jer 3:19	1471
the *n* shall bless themselves in	Jer 4:2	1471
Make ye mention to the *n*	Jer 4:16	1471
Therefore hear, ye *n*, and know, O	Jer 6:18	1471
for all these *n* are uncircumcised	Jer 9:26	1471
would not fear thee, O King of *n*	Jer 10:7	1471
among all the wise men of the *n*	Jer 10:7	1471
the *n* shall not be able to abide	Jer 10:10	1471
many *n* shall pass by this city,	Jer 22:8	1471
against all these *n* round about	Jer 25:9	1471
these *n* shall serve the king of	Jer 25:11	1471
hath prophesied against all the *n*	Jer 25:13	1471
For many *n* and great kings shall	Jer 25:14	1471
at my hand, and cause all the *n*	Jer 25:15	1471
hand, and made all the *n* to drink	Jer 25:17	1471
hath a controversy with the *n*	Jer 25:31	1471
a curse to all the *n* of the earth	Jer 26:6	1471
all *n* shall serve him, and his son	Jer 27:7	1471
and then many *n* and great kings	Jer 27:7	1471
But the *n* that bring their neck	Jer 27:11	1471
n within the space of two full	Jer 28:11	1471
iron upon the neck of all these *n*	Jer 28:14	1471
I will gather you from all the *n*	Jer 29:14	1471
among all the *n* whither I have	Jer 29:18	1471
n whither I have scattered thee	Jer 30:11	1471
and shout among the chief of the *n*	Jer 31:7	1471
Hear the word of the LORD, O ye *n*	Jer 31:10	1471
before all the *n* of the earth	Jer 33:9	1471
Judah, and against all the *n*	Jer 36:2	1471
that were returned from all *n*	Jer 43:5	1471
among all the *n* of the earth	Jer 44:8	1471
The *n* have heard of thy shame, and	Jer 46:12	1471
the *n* whither I have driven thee	Jer 46:28	1471
Declare ye among the *n*, and	Jer 50:2	1471
of great *n* from the north country	Jer 50:9	1471
of the *n* shall be a wilderness	Jer 50:12	1471
become a desolation among the *n*	Jer 50:23	1471
and the cry is heard among the *n*	Jer 50:46	1471
the *n* have drunken of her wine	Jer 51:7	1471
therefore the *n* are mad	Jer 51:7	1471
thee will I break in pieces the *n*	Jer 51:20	1471
blow the trumpet among the *n*	Jer 51:27	1471
prepare the *n* against her	Jer 51:27	1471
Prepare against her the *n* with	Jer 51:28	1471
an astonishment among the *n*	Jer 51:41	1471
the *n* shall not flow together any	Jer 51:44	1471
she that was great among the *n*	Lam 1:1	1471
have set it in the midst of the *n*	Eze 5:5	1471
into wickedness more than the *n*	Eze 5:6	1471
the *n* that are round about you	Eze 5:7	1471
to the judgments of the *n* that	Eze 5:7	1471
of thee in the sight of the *n*	Eze 5:8	1471
a reproach among the *n* that are	Eze 5:14	1471
an astonishment unto the *n* that	Eze 5:15	1471
escape the sword among the *n*	Eze 6:8	1471
n whither they shall be carried	Eze 6:9	1471
I shall scatter them among the *n*	Eze 12:15	1471
The *n* also heard of him	Eze 19:4	1471
Then the *n* set against him on	Eze 19:8	1471
may not be remembered among the *n*	Eze 25:10	1471
will cause many *n* to come up	Eze 26:3	1471
it shall become a spoil to the *n*	Eze 26:5	1471
upon thee, the terrible of the *n*	Eze 28:7	1471
scatter the Egyptians among the *n*	Eze 29:12	1471
exalt itself any more above the *n*	Eze 29:15	1471
shall no more rule over the *n*	Eze 29:15	1471
with him, the terrible of the *n*	Eze 30:11	1471
scatter the Egyptians among the *n*	Eze 30:23	1471
scatter the Egyptians among the *n*	Eze 30:26	1471
his shadow dwelt all great *n*	Eze 31:6	1471
strangers, the terrible of the *n*	Eze 31:12	1471
I made the *n* to shake at the	Eze 31:16	1471
art like a young lion of the *n*	Eze 32:2	1471
bring thy destruction among the *n*	Eze 32:9	1471
to fall, the terrible of the *n*	Eze 32:12	1471
of the *n* shall lament her	Eze 32:16	1471
and the daughters of the famous *n*	Eze 32:18	1471
thou hast said, These two *n*	Eze 35:10	1471
up men, and hast bereaved thy *n*	Eze 36:13	1471
neither bereave thy *n* any more	Eze 36:14	1471
thou cause thy *n* to fall any more	Eze 36:15	1471
and they shall be no more two *n*	Eze 37:22	1471

it is brought forth out of the *n*	Eze 38:8	1471
that are gathered out of the *n*	Eze 38:12	1471
be known in the eyes of many *n*	Eze 38:23	1471
in them in the sight of many *n*	Eze 39:27	1471
you it is commanded, O people, *n*	Dan 3:4	524
of musick, all the people, the *n*	Dan 3:7	524
the king, unto all people, *n*	Dan 4:1	524
that he gave him, all people,	Dan 5:19	524
Darius wrote unto all people, *n*	Dan 6:25	524
and a kingdom, that all people, *n*	Dan 7:14	524
they have hired among the *n*	Hos 8:10	1471
shall be wanderers among the *n*	Hos 9:17	1471
I will also gather all *n*, and will	Joel 3:2	1471
they have scattered among the *n*	Joel 3:2	1471
which are named chief of the *n*	Amos 6:1	1471
the house of Israel among all *n*	Amos 9:9	1471
many *n* shall come, and say, Come,	Mic 4:2	1471
and rebuke strong *n* afar off	Mic 4:3	1471
Now also many *n* are gathered	Mic 4:11	1471
The *n* shall see and be confounded	Mic 7:16	1471
that selleth *n* through her	Nah 3:4	1471
I will shew the *n* thy nakedness	Nah 3:5	1471
spare continually to slay the *n*	Hab 1:17	1471
but gathereth unto him all *n*	Hab 2:5	1471
Because thou hast spoiled many *n*	Hab 2:8	1471
he beheld, and drove asunder the *n*	Hab 3:6	1471
of her, all the beasts of the *n*	Zeph 2:14	1471
I have cut off the *n*	Zeph 3:6	1471
determination is to gather the *n*	Zeph 3:8	1471
I will shake all *n*	Hag 2:7	1471
and the desire of all *n* shall come	Hag 2:7	1471
me unto the *n* which spoiled you	Zec 2:8	1471
many *n* shall be joined to the	Zec 2:11	1471
all the *n* whom they knew not	Zec 7:14	1471
strong *n* shall come to seek the	Zec 8:22	1471
out of all languages of the *n*	Zec 8:23	1471
the *n* that come against Jerusalem	Zec 12:9	1471
For I will gather all *n* against	Zec 14:2	1471
forth, and fight against those *n*	Zec 14:3	1471
one that is left of all the *n*	Zec 14:16	1471
the punishment of all *n* that come	Zec 14:19	1471
all *n* shall call you blessed	Mal 3:12	1471
hated of all *n* for my name's sake	Mt 24:9	1484
world for a witness unto all *n*	Mt 24:14	1484
him shall be gathered all *n*	Mt 25:32	1484
Go ye therefore, and teach all *n*	Mt 28:19	1484
of all *n* the house of prayer	Mk 11:17	1484
first be published among all *n*	Mk 13:10	1484
do the *n* of the world seek after	Lk 12:30	1484
be led away captive into all *n*	Lk 21:24	1484
and upon the earth distress of *n*	Lk 21:25	1484
preached in his name among all *n*	Lk 24:47	1484
seven *n* in the land of Chanaan	Acts 13:19	1484
all *n* to walk in their own ways	Acts 14:16	1484
hath made of one blood all *n* of	Acts 17:26	1484
to the faith among all *n*, for his	Rom 1:5	1484
have made thee a father of many *n*	Rom 4:17	1484
might become the father of many *n*	Rom 4:18	1484
made known to all *n* for the	Rom 16:26	1484
In thee shall all *n* be blessed	Gal 3:8	1484
him will I give power over the *n*	Rev 2:26	1484
no man could number, of all *n*	Rev 7:9	1484
again before many peoples, and *n*	Rev 10:11	1484
n shall see their dead bodies	Rev 11:9	1484
the *n* were angry, and thy wrath is	Rev 11:18	1484
to rule all *n* with a rod of iron	Rev 12:5	1484
all kindreds, and tongues, and *n*	Rev 13:7	1484
because she made all *n* drink of	Rev 14:8	1484
for all *n* shall come and worship	Rev 15:4	1484
and the cities of the *n* fell	Rev 16:19	1484
are peoples, and multitudes, and *n*	Rev 17:15	1484
For all *n* have drunk of the wine	Rev 18:3	1484
thy sorceries were all *n* deceived	Rev 18:23	1484
with it he should smite the *n*	Rev 19:15	1484
he should deceive the *n* no more	Rev 20:3	1484
shall go out to deceive the *n*	Rev 20:8	1484
the *n* of them which are saved	Rev 21:24	1484
glory and honour of the *n* into it	Rev 21:26	1484
were for the healing of the *n*	Rev 22:2	1484

NATIVE

no more, nor see his *n* country	Jer 22:10	4138

NATIVITY

father Terah in the land of his *n*	Gen 11:28	4138
thy mother, and the land of thy *n*	Ruth 2:11	4138
people, and to the land of our *n*	Jer 46:16	4138
thy *n* is of the land of Canaan	Eze 16:3	4138
And as for thy *n*, in the day thou	Eze 16:4	4138
created, in the land of thy *n*	Eze 21:30	4351
of Chaldea, the land of their *n*	Eze 23:15	4138

NATURAL

not dim, nor his *n* force abated	Deut 34:7	3893
n use into that which is against	Rom 1:26	5446
leaving the *n* use of the woman,	Rom 1:27	5446
without *n* affection, implacable,	Rom 1:31	
if God spared not the *n* branches	Rom 11:21	2596,6449
these, which be the *n* branches	Rom 11:24	2596,6449
But the *n* man receiveth not the	1Cor 2:14	5591
It is sown a *n* body	1Cor 15:44	5591
There is a *n* body, and there is a	1Cor 15:44	5591
is spiritual, but that which is *n*	1Cor 15:46	5591
Without *n* affection,	2Ti 3:3	
beholding his *n* face in a glass	Jas 1:23	1083
as *n* brute beasts, made to be	2Pet 2:12	5446

NATURALLY

who will *n* care for your state	Phil 2:20	1103
but what they know *n*, as brute	Jude 10	5447

NATURE

use into that which is against *n*	Rom 1:26	5449
do by *n* the things contained in	Rom 2:14	5449
not uncircumcision which is by *n*	Rom 2:27	5449
the olive tree which is wild by *n*	Rom 11:24	5449
to *n* into a good olive tree	Rom 11:24	5449
Doth not even *n* itself teach you,	1Cor 11:14	5449
We who are Jews by *n*, and not	Gal 2:15	5449
unto them which by *n* are no gods	Gal 4:8	5449
were by *n* the children of wrath,	Eph 2:3	5449
took not on him the *n* of angels	Heb 2:16	5449
setteth on fire the course of *n*	Jas 3:6	1078
be partakers of the divine *n*	2Pet 1:4	5449

NAUGHT

but the water is *n*, and the ground	2Kin 2:19	7451
It is *n*, it is *n*, saith the	Prov 20:14	7451

NAUGHTINESS

pride, and the *n* of thine heart	1Sa 17:28	7455
shall be taken in their own *n*	Prov 11:6	1942
filthiness and superfluity of *n*	Jas 1:21	2549

NAUGHTY

A *n* person, a wicked man, walketh	Prov 6:12	1100
a liar giveth ear to a *n* tongue	Prov 17:4	1942
the other basket had very *n* figs	Jer 24:2	7451

NAUM (na'-um) See NAHUM. *Father of Amos; ancestor of Jesus.*

of Amos, which was the son of *N*	Lk 3:25	3486

NAVEL

force is in the *n* of his belly	Job 40:16	8306
It shall be health to thy *n*	Prov 3:8	8270
Thy *n* is like a round goblet,	Song 7:2	8326
thou wast born thy *n* was not cut	Eze 16:4	8270

NAVES

their axletrees, and their *n*	1Kin 7:33	1354

NAVY

king Solomon made a *n* of ships in	1Kin 9:26	590
Hiram sent in the *n* his servants	1Kin 9:27	590
the *n* also of Hiram, that brought	1Kin 10:11	590
For the king had at sea a *n* of	1Kin 10:22	590
of Tharshish with the *n* of Hiram	1Kin 10:22	590
years came the *n* of Tharshish	1Kin 10:22	590

NAY

And he said, *N*; but thou didst	Gen 18:15	3808
And they said, *N*; but we will	Gen 19:2	
N, my lord, hear me	Gen 23:11	3808
And Jacob said, *N*, I pray thee, if	Gen 33:10	408
And they said unto him, *N*, my lord	Gen 42:10	3808
And he said unto them, *N*, but to	Gen 42:12	3808
And he said, *N*	Num 22:30	3808
And he said, *N*; but as captain	Josh 5:14	3808
And the people said unto Joshua, *N*	Josh 24:21	3808
If he said, *N*	Judg 12:5	3808
unto them, and said unto them, *N*	Judg 19:23	408
my brethren, *n*, I pray you	Judg 19:23	
n, my daughters; for it	Ruth 1:13	408
then he would answer him, *N*	1Sa 2:16	
N, my sons; for it is	1Sa 2:24	408
and they said, *N*; but we will	1Sa 8:19	3808
and ye have said unto him, *N*	1Sa 10:19	
against you, ye said unto me, *N*	1Sa 12:12	3808
And she answered him, *N*, my	2Sa 13:12	408
And the king said to Absalom, *N*	2Sa 13:25	408
And Hushai said unto Absalom, *N*	2Sa 16:18	3808
And the king said unto Araunah, *N*	2Sa 24:24	3808
king, (for he will not say thee *n*	1Kin 2:17	
I pray thee, say me not *n*	1Kin 2:20	6440
for I will not say thee *n*	1Kin 2:20	
And he said, *N*; but I	1Kin 2:30	3808
And the other woman said, *N*	1Kin 3:22	3808

and the other saith, *N*	1Kin 3:23	3808
king of Israel said unto him, *N*	2Kin 3:13	408
And she said, *N*, my lord, thou man	2Kin 4:16	408
n, but let the shadow return	2Kin 20:10	3808
And king David said to Ornan, *N*	1Chr 21:24	3808
n, they were not at all ashamed,	Jer 6:15	1571
n, they were not at all ashamed,	Jer 8:12	1571
be, Yea, yea; *N*, *n*	Mt 5:37	3756
But he said, *N*; lest while	Mt 13:29	3756
I tell you, *N*; but rather	Lk 12:51	3780
I tell you, *N*: but, except	Lk 13:3	3780
I tell you, *N*: but, except	Lk 13:5	3780
And he said, *N*, father Abraham	Lk 16:30	3780
others said, *N*; but he	Jn 7:12	3756
n verily; but let them	Acts 16:37	3756
N: but by the law	Rom 3:27	3780
N, I had not known sin, but by	Rom 7:7	235
N, in all these things we are	Rom 8:37	235
N but, O man, who art thou that	Rom 9:20	3304
N, ye do wrong, and defraud, and	1Cor 6:8	235
N, much more those members of the	1Cor 12:22	235
there should be yea yea, and *n n*	2Cor 1:17	3756
word toward you was not yea and *n*	2Cor 1:18	3756
and Timotheus, was not yea and *n*	2Cor 1:19	3756
be yea; and your *n*, *n*	Jas 5:12	3756

NAZARENE (naz-a-reen') See NAZARENES. *Native to Nazareth.*

prophets, He shall be called a *N*	Mt 2:23	3480

NAZARENES (naz-a-reens')

a ringleader of the sect of the *N*	Acts 24:5	3480

NAZARETH (naz'-a-reth) See NAZARENE. *A city in Galilee.*

came and dwelt in a city called *N*	Mt 2:23	3478
And leaving *N*, he came and dwelt in	Mt 4:13	3478
Jesus the prophet of *N* of Galilee	Mt 21:11	3478
fellow was also with Jesus of *N*	Mt 26:71	3478
that Jesus came from *N* of Galilee	Mk 1:9	3478
to do with thee, thou Jesus of *N*	Mk 1:24	3478
he heard that it was Jesus of *N*	Mk 10:47	3478
And thou also wast with Jesus of *N*	Mk 14:67	3478
Ye seek Jesus of *N*, which was	Mk 16:6	3478
unto a city of Galilee, named *N*	Lk 1:26	3478
Galilee, out of the city of *N*	Lk 2:4	3478
into Galilee, to their own city *N*	Lk 2:39	3478
went down with them, and came to *N*	Lk 2:51	3478
And he came to *N*, where he had	Lk 4:16	3478
to do with thee, thou Jesus of *N*	Lk 4:34	3478
him, that Jesus of *N* passeth by	Lk 18:37	3478
unto him, Concerning Jesus of *N*	Lk 24:19	3478
prophets, did write, Jesus of *N*	Jn 1:45	3478
any good thing come out of *N*	Jn 1:46	3478
They answered him, Jesus of *N*	Jn 18:5	3478
And they said, Jesus of *N*	Jn 18:7	3478
JESUS OF *N* THE KING OF THE	Jn 19:19	3478
Jesus of *N*, a man approved of God	Acts 2:22	3478
name of Jesus Christ of *N* rise up	Acts 3:6	3478
by the name of Jesus Christ of *N*	Acts 4:10	3478
that this Jesus of *N* shall	Acts 6:14	3478
Jesus of *N* with the Holy Ghost	Acts 10:38	3478
he said unto me, I am Jesus of *N*	Acts 22:8	3478
to the name of Jesus of *N*	Acts 26:9	3478

NAZARITE (naz'-a-rite) See NAZARITES. *Title applied to one making a special vow of abstention.*

themselves to vow a vow of a *N*	Num 6:2	5139
And this is the law of the *N*	Num 6:13	5139
the *N* shall shave the head of his	Num 6:18	5139
put them upon the hands of the *N*	Num 6:19	5139
after that the *N* may drink wine	Num 6:20	5139
the law of the *N* who hath vowed	Num 6:21	5139
be a *N* unto God from the womb	Judg 13:5	5139
for the child shall be a *N* to God	Judg 13:7	5139
for I have been a *N* unto God from	Judg 16:17	5139

NAZARITES (naz'-a-rites)

Her *N* were purer than snow, they	Lam 4:7	5139
and of your young men for *N*	Amos 2:11	5139
But ye gave the *N* wine to drink	Amos 2:12	5139

NEAH (ne'-ah) *A city in Zebulun.*

goeth out to Remmon-methoar to *N*	Josh 19:13	5269

NEAPOLIS (ne-ap'-o-lis) *A Macedonian seaport.*

Samothracia, and the next day to *N*	Acts 16:11	3496

NEAR See APPENDIX.

NEARER See APPENDIX.

NEARIAH (ne-a-ri'-ah) See NAGGE.
1. *A son of Shemiah.*

and Igeal, and Bariah, and *N*	1Chr 3:22	5294
And the sons of *N*	1Chr 3:23	5294

N

2. A son of Ishi.
for their captains Pelatiah, and *N* 1Chr 4:42   5294

NEBAI *(ne'-bahee) A renewer of the covenant.*
Hariph, Anathoth, *N,* .... Neh 10:19   5109

NEBAIOTH *(ne-bah'-yoth)* See NEBAJOTH.
  1. A son of Ishmael.
The firstborn of Ishmael, *N* 1Chr 1:29   5032
  2. Descendants of Ishmael.
the rams of *N* shall minister unto .... Is 60:7   5032

NEBAJOTH *(ne-ba'-joth)* See NEBAIOTH. *Same as Nebaioth 1.*
the firstborn of Ishmael, *N* .... Gen 25:13   5032
Abraham's son, the sister of *N* .... Gen 28:9   5032
Ishmael's daughter, sister of *N* .... Gen 36:3   5032

NEBALLAT *(ne-bal'-lat) A Benjamite city.*
Hadid, Zeboim, *N,* .... Neh 11:34   5041

NEBAT *(ne'-bat) Father of King Jeroboam.*
And Jeroboam the son of *N,* an 1Kin 11:26   5028
pass, when Jeroboam the son of *N* 1Kin 12:2   5028
unto Jeroboam the son of *N* 1Kin 12:15   5028
of *N* reigned Abijam over Judah 1Kin 15:1   5028
house of Jeroboam the son of *N* 1Kin 16:3   5028
the way of Jeroboam the son of *N* 1Kin 16:26   5028
the sins of Jeroboam the son of *N* 1Kin 16:31   5028
house of Jeroboam the son of *N* 1Kin 21:22   5028
the way of Jeroboam the son of *N* 1Kin 22:52   5028
the sins of Jeroboam the son of *N* 2Kin 3:3   5028
house of Jeroboam the son of *N* 2Kin 9:9   5028
the sins of Jeroboam the son of *N* 2Kin 10:29   5028
the sins of Jeroboam the son of *N* 2Kin 13:2   5028
the sins of Jeroboam the son of *N* 2Kin 13:11   5028
the sins of Jeroboam the son of *N* 2Kin 14:24   5028
the sins of Jeroboam the son of *N* 2Kin 15:9   5028
the sins of Jeroboam the son of *N* 2Kin 15:18   5028
the sins of Jeroboam the son of *N* 2Kin 15:24   5028
the sins of Jeroboam the son of *N* 2Kin 15:28   5028
made Jeroboam the son of *N* king 2Kin 17:21   5028
place which Jeroboam the son of *N* 2Kin 23:15   5028
against Jeroboam the son of *N* 2Chr 9:29   5028
pass, when Jeroboam the son of *N* 2Chr 10:2   5028
to Jeroboam the son of *N* 2Chr 10:15   5028
Yet Jeroboam the son of *N* 2Chr 13:6   5028

NEBO *(ne'-bo)* See PISGAH, SAMGAR-NEBO.
  1. A city in Reuben.
and Elealeh, and Shebam, and *N* .... Num 32:3   5015
And *N,* and Baal-meon, (their names...... Num 32:38   5015
the mountains of Abarim, before *N* .... Num 33:47   5015
who dwelt in Aroer, even unto *N* 1Chr 5:8   5015
Moab shall howl over *N,* and over .... Is 15:2   5015
Woe unto *N* .... Jer 48:1   5015
And upon Dibon, and upon *N,* .... Jer 48:22   5015
  2. A mountain east of the Jordan.
mountain Abarim, unto mount *N* .... Deut 32:49   5015
of Moab unto the mountain of *N* .... Deut 34:1   5015
  3. A city in Judah.
The children of *N,* fifty and two .... Ezr 2:29   5015
The men of the other *N,* fifty and.......... Neh 7:33   5015
  4. A Chaldean idol.
N stoopeth, their idols were upon .... Is 46:1   5015
  5. Father of several who married foreigners.
Of the sons of *N* .... Ezr 10:43   5015

NEBO-SARSEKIM See SARSECHIM.

NEBUCHADNEZZAR *(neb-u-kad-nez'-zar)* See NEBU-CHADREZZAR. *King of Babylon.*
In his days *N* king of Babylon 2Kin 24:1   5019
At that time the servants of *N* 2Kin 24:10   5019
N king of Babylon came against............. 2Kin 24:11   5019
that *N* king of Babylon came, he,........... 2Kin 25:1   5019
year of king *N* king of Babylon 2Kin 25:8   5019
whom *N* king of Babylon had left,.......... 2Kin 25:22   5019
and Jerusalem by the hand of *N* 1Chr 6:15   5019
him came up *N* king of Babylon 2Chr 36:6   5019
N also carried of the vessels of.............. 2Chr 36:7   5019
the year was expired, king *N* sent 2Chr 36:10   5019
he also rebelled against king *N* 2Chr 36:13   5019
which *N* had brought forth out of .... Ezr 1:7   5019
whom *N* the king of Babylon had .... Ezr 2:1   5019
the hand of *N* the king of Babylon .... Ezr 5:12   5020
which *N* took out of the temple .... Ezr 5:14   5020
which *N* took forth out of the .... Ezr 6:5   5020
whom *N* the king of Babylon had .... Neh 7:6   5019
whom *N* the king of Babylon had .... Est 2:6   5019
the hand of *N* the king of Babylon .... Jer 27:6   5019
the same *N* king of Babylon .... Jer 27:8   5019
Which *N* king of Babylon took not, ... Jer 27:20   5019
that *N* king of Babylon took away .... Jer 28:3   5019
so will I break the yoke of *N* .... Jer 28:11   5019

they may serve *N* king of Babylon .... Jer 28:14   5019
to all the people whom *N* had .... Jer 29:1   5019
to *N* king of Babylon) saying .... Jer 29:3   5019
when *N* king of Babylon, and all............. Jer 34:1   5019
they brought him up to *N* king of .... Jer 39:5   5019
N king of Babylon unto Jerusalem .... Dan 1:1   5019
eunuchs brought them in before *N* .... Dan 1:18   5019
the second year of the reign of *N*........... Dan 2:1   5019
N dreamed dreams, wherewith his........ Dan 2:1   5019
maketh known to the king *N* what .... Dan 2:28   5020
Then the king *N* fell upon his................. Dan 2:46   5020
N the king made an image of gold, ... Dan 3:1   5020
Then *N* the king sent to gather .... Dan 3:2   5020
image which *N* the king had set up .... Dan 3:2   5020
image that *N* the king had set up .... Dan 3:3   5020
the image that *N* had set up .... Dan 3:3   5020
image that *N* the king hath set up .... Dan 3:5   5020
image that *N* the king had set up .... Dan 3:7   5020
They spake and said to the king *N*......... Dan 3:9   5020
Then *N* in his rage and fury................... Dan 3:13   5020
N spake and said unto them, Is it .... Dan 3:14   5020
answered and said to the king, O *N* .... Dan 3:16   5020
Then was *N* full of fury, and the .... Dan 3:19   5020
Then *N* the king was astonied, and .... Dan 3:24   5020
Then *N* came near to the mouth of .... Dan 3:26   5020
Then *N* spake, and said, Blessed be ...... Dan 3:28   5020
N the king, unto all people, ... Dan 4:1   5020
I *N* was at rest in mine house, and........ Dan 4:4   5020
This dream I king *N* have seen .... Dan 4:18   5020
All this came upon the king *N* .... Dan 4:28   5020
from heaven, saying, O king *N* .... Dan 4:31   5020
was the thing fulfilled upon *N* .... Dan 4:33   5020
at the end of the days I *N* lifted .... Dan 4:34   5020
Now I *N* praise and extol and honour .... Dan 4:37   5020
N had taken out of the temple .... Dan 5:2   5020
whom the king *N* thy father .... Dan 5:11   5020
God gave *N* thy father a kingdom .... Dan 5:18   5020

NEBUCHADREZZAR *(neb-u-kad-rez'-zar)* See NEBU-CHADNEZZAR. *Same as Nebuchadnezzar.*
for *N* king of Babylon maketh war .... Jer 21:2   5019
the hand of *N* king of Babylon .... Jer 21:7   5019
the hand of *N* king of Babylon .... Jer 22:25   5019
after that *N* king of Babylon had............ Jer 24:1   5019
first year of *N* king of Babylon................ Jer 25:1   5019
N the king of Babylon, my servant .... Jer 25:9   5019
the hand of *N* king of Babylon .... Jer 29:21   5019
was the eighteenth year of *N* .... Jer 32:1   5019
the hand of *N* king of Babylon .... Jer 32:28   5019
when *N* king of Babylon came up .... Jer 35:11   5019
whom *N* king of Babylon made king ...... Jer 37:1   5019
came *N* king of Babylon and all his .... Jer 39:1   5019
Now *N* king of Babylon gave charge ...... Jer 39:11   5019
take *N* the king of Babylon, my .... Jer 43:10   5019
the hand of *N* king of Babylon .... Jer 44:30   5019
which *N* king of Babylon smote in.......... Jer 46:2   5019
how *N* king of Babylon should come...... Jer 46:13   5019
the hand of *N* king of Babylon .... Jer 46:26   5019
which *N* king of Babylon shall .... Jer 49:28   5019
for *N* king of Babylon hath taken .... Jer 49:30   5019
last this *N* king of Babylon hath .... Jer 50:17   5019
N the king of Babylon hath .... Jer 51:34   5019
that *N* king of Babylon came, he .... Jer 52:4   5019
year of *N* king of Babylon...................... Jer 52:12   5019
whom *N* carried away captive .... Jer 52:28   5019
In the eighteenth year of *N* he .... Jer 52:29   5019
twentieth year of *N* Nebuzar-adan .... Jer 52:30   5019
upon Tyrus *N* king of Babylon .... Eze 26:7   5019
N king of Babylon caused his army .... Eze 29:18   5019
of Egypt unto *N* king of Babylon .... Eze 29:19   5019
by the hand of *N* king of Babylon .... Eze 30:10   5019

NEBUSHASBAN *(neb-u-shas'-ban) A Babylonian prince.*
captain of the guard sent, and *N* .... Jer 39:13   5021

NEBUSHAZBAN See NEBUSHASBAN.

NEBUZAR-ADAN *(neb-u-zar'-a-dan) Commander of Nebuchadnezzar's army.*
king of Babylon, came *N,* captain.......... 2Kin 25:8   5018
did *N* the captain of the guard............... 2Kin 25:11   5018
N captain of the guard took these 2Kin 25:20   5018
Then *N* the captain of the guard .... Jer 39:9   5018
But *N* the captain of the guard .... Jer 39:10   5018
to *N* the captain of the guard................. Jer 39:11   5018
So *N* the captain of the guard .... Jer 39:13   5018
after that *N* the captain of the .... Jer 40:1   5018
whom *N* the captain of the guard........... Jer 41:10   5018
every person that *N* the captain............. Jer 43:6   5018
king of Babylon, came *N,* captain.......... Jer 52:12   5018
Then *N* the captain of the guard .... Jer 52:15   5018
But *N* the captain of the guard .... Jer 52:16   5018

So *N* the captain of the guard .... Jer 52:26   5018
year of Nebuchadrezzar *N* the .... Jer 52:30   5018

NEBUZARADAN See NEBUZAR-ADAN.

NECESSARY
of his mouth more than my *n* food .... Job 23:12   2706
It was *n* that the word of God .... Acts 13:46   *316*
burden than these *n* things .... Acts 15:28   *1876*
us with such things as were *n* . Acts 28:10   *4314,3588,5532*
seem to be more feeble, are *n* 1Cor 12:22   *316*
it *n* to exhort the brethren 2Cor 9:5   *316*
Yet I supposed it *n* to send to .... Phil 2:25   *316*
to maintain good works for *n* uses .... Titus 3:14   *316*
It was therefore *n* that the .... Heb 9:23   *318*

NECESSITIES
hands have ministered unto my *n* .... Acts 20:34   *5532*
patience, in afflictions, in *n* 2Cor 6:4   *318*
infirmities, in reproaches, in *n* 2Cor 12:10   *318*

NECESSITY
(For of *n* he must release one .... Lk 23:17   *2192,318*
Distributing to the *n* of saints .... Rom 12:13   *5532*
in his heart, having no *n* 1Cor 7:37   *318*
for *n* is laid upon me 1Cor 9:16   *318*
not grudgingly, or of *n* 2Cor 9:7   *318*
ye sent once and again unto my *n* .... Phil 4:16   *5532*
should not be as it were of *n* .... Philem 14   *318*
there is made of *n* a change also .... Heb 7:12   *318*
wherefore it is of *n* that this .... Heb 8:3   *316*
there must also of *n* be the death .... Heb 9:16   *318*

NECHO (ne'-ko) See PHARAOH-NECHOH. *A king of Egypt.*
N king of Egypt came up to fight 2Chr 35:20   5224
words of *N* from the mouth of God 2Chr 35:22   5224
N took Jehoahaz his brother, and 2Chr 36:4   5224

NECK
and upon the smooth of his *n* .... Gen 27:16   6677
break his yoke from off thy *n* .... Gen 27:40   6677
and embraced him, and fell on his *n* ...... Gen 33:4   6677
and put a gold chain about his *n* .... Gen 41:42   6677
upon his brother Benjamin's *n* .... Gen 45:14   6677
and Benjamin wept upon his *n* .... Gen 45:14   6677
and he fell on his *n*, and wept on .... Gen 46:29   6677
wept on his *n* a good while .... Gen 46:29   6677
be in the *n* of thine enemies .... Gen 49:8   6203
it, then thou shalt break his *n* .... Ex 13:13   6203
not, then shalt thou break his *n* .... Ex 34:20   6203
and wring off his head from his *n* .... Lev 5:8   6203
heifer's *n* there in the valley .... Deut 21:4   6203
put a yoke of iron upon thy *n* .... Deut 28:48   6677
thy rebellion, and thy stiff *n* .... Deut 31:27   6203
gate, and his *n* brake, and he died 1Sa 4:18   4665
like to the *n* of their fathers, ... 2Kin 17:14   6203
but he stiffened his *n*, and 2Chr 36:13   6203
the shoulder, and hardened their *n* .... Neh 9:29   6203
runneth upon him, even on his *n* .... Job 15:26   6677
he hath also taken me by my *n* .... Job 16:12   6203
thou clothed his *n* with thunder............ Job 39:19   6677
In his *n* remaineth strength, and........... Job 41:22   6677
speak not with a stiff *n* .... Ps 75:5   6677
thy head, and chains about thy *n* .... Prov 1:9   1621
bind them about thy *n* .... Prov 3:3   1621
unto thy soul, and grace to thy *n* .... Prov 3:22   1621
heart, and tie them about thy *n* .... Prov 6:21   1621
often reproved hardeneth his *n*............. Prov 29:1   6203
thy *n* with chains of gold .... Song 1:10   6677
Thy *n* is like the tower of David .... Song 4:4   6677
eyes, with one chain of thy *n* .... Song 4:9   6677
Thy *n* is as a tower of ivory .... Song 7:4   6677
he shall reach even to the *n* .... Is 8:8   6677
and his yoke from off thy *n* .... Is 10:27   6677
shall reach to the midst of the *n* .... Is 30:28   6677
thy *n* is an iron sinew, and thy .... Is 48:4   6203
thyself from the bands of thy *n* .... Is 52:2   6677
lamb, as if he cut off a dog's *n* .... Is 66:3   6202
their ear, but hardened their *n* .... Jer 7:26   6202
their ear, but made their *n* stiff .... Jer 17:23   6202
and yokes, and put them upon thy *n*..... Jer 27:2   6677
that will not put their *n* under .... Jer 27:8   6677
the nations that bring their *n* .... Jer 27:11   6677
from off the prophet Jeremiah's *n*........ Jer 28:10   6677
king of Babylon from the *n* of all .... Jer 28:11   6677
off the *n* of the prophet Jeremiah .... Jer 28:12   6677
upon the *n* of all these nations .... Jer 28:14   6677
break his yoke from off thy *n* .... Jer 30:8   6677
wreathed, and come up upon my *n* .... Lam 1:14   6677
thy hands, and a chain on thy *n* .... Eze 16:11   1627
have a chain of gold about his *n* .... Dan 5:7   6676
have a chain of gold about thy *n* .... Dan 5:16   6676
put a chain of gold about his *n* .... Dan 5:29   6676

but I passed over upon her fair *n* .... Hos 10:11   6676
the foundation unto the *n* .... Hab 3:13   6676
millstone were hanged about his *n* ...... Mt 18:6   *5137*
millstone were hanged about his *n* ...... Mk 9:42   *5137*
and ran, and fell on his *n* .... Lk 15:20   *5137*
millstone were hanged about his *n* ...... Lk 17:2   *5137*
yoke upon the *n* of the disciples .... Acts 15:10   *5137*
wept sore, and fell on Paul's *n* .... Acts 20:37   *5137*

NECKS
feet upon the *n* of these kings .... Josh 10:24   6677
put their feet upon the *n* of them .... Josh 10:24   6677
meet for the *n* of them that take .... Judg 5:30   6677
that were on their camels' *n* .... Judg 8:21   6677
that were about their camels' *n* .... Judg 8:26   6677
given me the *n* of mine enemies 2Sa 22:41   6203
not hear, but hardened their *n* 2Kin 17:14   6203
their *n* to the work of their Lord .... Neh 3:5   6677
proudly, and hardened their *n* .... Neh 9:16   6203
but hardened their *n*, and in their .... Neh 9:17   6203
given me the *n* of mine enemies .... Ps 18:40   6203
and walk with stretched forth *n* .... Is 3:16   1627
they have hardened their *n* .... Jer 19:15   6203
Bring your *n* under the yoke of .... Jer 27:12   6677
Our *n* are under persecution .... Lam 5:5   6677
upon the *n* of them that are slain .... Eze 21:29   6677
which ye shall not remove your *n* .... Mic 2:3   6677
for my life laid down their own *n* .... Rom 16:4   *5137*

NECO See NECHOH.

NECROMANCER
spirits, or a wizard, or a *n* .... Deut 18:11   1875,4191

NEDABIAH (ned-a-bi'-ah) Son of Jeconiah.
Shenazar, Jecamiah, Hoshama, and *N* .. 1Chr 3:18   5072

NEED
lend him sufficient for his *n* .... Deut 15:8   4270
Have I *n* of mad men, that ye have 1Sa 21:15   2638
Lebanon, as much as thou shalt *n* 2Chr 2:16   6878
Ye shall not *n* to fight in this 2Chr 20:17
And that which they have *n* of .... Ezr 6:9   2818
that he shall have no *n* of spoil .... Prov 31:11   2637
I have *n* to be baptized of thee, ... Mt 3:14   *5532*
knoweth what things ye have *n* of .... Mt 6:8   *5532*
ye have *n* of all these things .... Mt 6:32   *5535*
that be whole *n* not a physician ..... Mt 9:12   *2192,5532*
said unto them, They *n* not depart . Mt 14:16   *2192,5532*
say, The Lord hath *n* of them .... Mt 21:3   *5532*
what further *n* have we of .... Mt 26:65   *5532*
whole have no *n* of the physician ...... Mk 2:17   *5532*
what David did, when he had *n* .... Mk 2:25   *5532*
ye that the Lord hath *n* of him .... Mk 11:3   *5532*
What *n* we any further witnesses ... Mk 14:63   *2192,5532*
that are whole *n* not a physician ... Lk 5:31   *2192,5532*
healed that had *n* of healing .... Lk 9:11   *5532*
that ye have *n* of these things .... Lk 12:30   *5535*
persons, which *n* no repentance ..... Lk 15:7   *2192,5532*
Because the Lord hath *n* of him .... Lk 19:31   *5532*
they said, The Lord hath *n* of him .... Lk 19:34   *5532*
What *n* we any further witness .... Lk 22:71   *2192,5532*
we have *n* of against the feast .... Jn 13:29   *5532*
to all men, as every man had *n* .... Acts 2:45   *5532*
every man according as he had *n* .... Acts 4:35   *5532*
business she hath *n* of you .... Rom 16:2   *5535*
n so require, let him do what he 1Cor 7:36   *3784*
the hand, I have no *n* of thee 1Cor 12:21   *5532*
to the feet, I have no *n* of you 1Cor 12:21   *5532*
For our comely parts have no *n* 1Cor 12:24   *5532*
or *n* we, as some others, epistles 2Cor 3:1   *5535*
both to abound and to suffer *n* .... Phil 4:12   *5532*
your *n* according to his riches in .... Phil 4:19   *5532*
so that we *n* not to speak any 1Th 1:8   *2192,5532*
ye *n* not that I write unto you 1Th 4:9   *5532*
ye have no *n* that I write unto 1Th 5:1   *5532*
find grace to help in time of *n* .... Heb 4:16   *2121*
ye have *n* that one teach you .... Heb 5:12   *5532*
are become such as have *n* of milk .... Heb 5:12   *5532*
what further *n* was there that .... Heb 7:11   *5532*
For ye have *n* of patience .... Heb 10:36   *5532*
though now for a season, if *n* be 1Pet 1:6   *1163*
ye *n* not that any man teach you.... 1Jn 2:27   *2192,5532*
good, and seeth his brother have *n* 1Jn 3:17   *5532*
with goods, and have *n* of nothing ..... Rev 3:17   *5532*
And the city had no *n* of the sun .... Rev 21:23   *5532*
they *n* no candle, neither light .... Rev 22:5   *5532*

NEEDED
n not that any should testify of....... Jn 2:25   *2192,5532*
hands, as though he *n* any thing .... Acts 17:25   *4326*

NEEDEST
n not that any man should ask....... Jn 16:30   *2192,5532*

N

NEEDETH

And he said, What n it	Gen 33:15	
rise and give him as many as he n	Lk 11:8	5535
He that is washed n **not save to**	Jn 13:10	2192,5532
he may have to give to him that n	Eph 4:28	5532
a workman that n not to be	2Ti 2:15	422
Who n not daily, as those high	Heb 7:27	2192,318

NEEDFUL

be n for the house of thy God	Ezr 7:20	2819
But one thing is n	Lk 10:42	5532
That it was n to circumcise them,	Acts 15:5	1163
in the flesh is more n for you	Phil 1:24	316
things which are n to the body	Jas 2:16	2006
it was n for me to write unto you	Jude 3	318

NEEDLE

to go through the eye of a n	Mt 19:24	4476
to go through the eye of a n	Mk 10:25	4476

NEEDLE'S

for a camel to go through a n **eye**	Lk 18:25	4476

NEEDLEWORK

fine twined linen, wrought with n	Ex 26:36	4639,7551
fine twined linen, wrought with n	Ex 27:16	7551
thou shalt make the girdle of n	Ex 28:39	7551
and fine twined linen, of n	Ex 36:37	7551
for the gate of the court was n	Ex 38:18	7551
blue, and purple, and scarlet, of n	Ex 39:29	7551
a prey of divers colours of n	Judg 5:30	7553
divers colours of n on both sides	Judg 5:30	7553
unto the king in raiment of n	Ps 45:14	7553

NEEDS

thy money, must n be circumcised	Gen 17:13	
sojourn, and he will n be a judge	Gen 19:9	
must I n bring thy son again unto	Gen 24:5	
though thou wouldest n be gone	Gen 31:30	
For we must n die, and are as	2Sa 14:14	
they must n be borne, because	Jer 10:5	
for it must n be that offences	Mt 18:7	318
for such things must n be	Mk 13:7	
a piece of ground, and I must n go	Lk 14:18	318
he must n go through Samaria	Jn 4:4	
must n have been fulfilled	Acts 1:16	
that Christ must n have suffered	Acts 17:3	
multitude must n come together	Acts 21:22	3843
Wherefore ye must n be subject	Rom 13:5	318
for then must ye n go out of the	1Cor 5:10	
If I must n glory, I will glory	2Cor 11:30	

NEEDY

brother, to thy poor, and to thy n	Deut 15:11	34
hired servant that is poor and n	Deut 24:14	34
They turn the n out of the way	Job 24:4	34
the light killeth the poor and n	Job 24:14	34
For the n shall not alway be	Ps 9:18	34
poor, for the sighing of the n	Ps 12:5	34
the n from him that spoileth him	Ps 35:10	34
bow, to cast down the poor and n	Ps 37:14	34
But I am poor and n	Ps 40:17	34
But I am poor and n	Ps 70:5	34
shall save the children of the n	Ps 72:4	34
deliver the n when he crieth	Ps 72:12	34
He shall spare the poor and n	Ps 72:13	34
and shall save the souls of the n	Ps 72:13	34
let the poor and n praise thy name	Ps 74:21	34
do justice to the afflicted and n	Ps 82:3	7326
Deliver the poor and n	Ps 82:4	34
for I am poor and n	Ps 86:1	34
n man, that he might even slay	Ps 109:16	34
For I am poor and n, and my heart	Ps 109:22	34
lifteth the n out of the dunghill	Ps 113:7	34
earth, and the n from among men	Prov 30:14	34
plead the cause of the poor and n	Prov 31:9	34
reacheth forth her hands to the n	Prov 31:20	34
To turn aside the n from judgment	Is 10:2	1800
the n shall lie down in safety	Is 14:30	34
strength to the n in his distress	Is 25:4	34
the poor, and the steps of the n	Is 26:6	1800
even when the n speaketh right	Is 32:7	34
n seek water, and there is none,	Is 41:17	34
the right of the n do they not	Jer 5:28	34
judged the cause of the poor and n	Jer 22:16	34
the hand of the poor and n	Eze 16:49	34
Hath oppressed the poor and n	Eze 18:12	34
and have vexed the poor and n	Eze 22:29	34
the poor, which crush the n	Amos 4:1	34
this, O ye that swallow up the n	Amos 8:4	34
the n for a pair of shoes	Amos 8:6	34

NEESINGS

By his n a light doth shine, and	Job 41:18	5846

NEGEV See SOUTH.

NEGINAH (neg'-i-nah) See NEGINOTH. A stringed instrument.

To the chief Musician upon N	Ps 61:t	5058

NEGINOTH (neg'-i-noth) See NEGINAH. Same as Neginah.

To the chief Musician on N	Ps 4:t	5058
Musician on N upon Sheminith	Ps 6:t	5058
To the chief Musician on N	Ps 54:t	5058
To the chief Musician on N	Ps 55:t	5058
To the chief Musician on N	Ps 67:t	5058
To the chief Musician on N	Ps 76:t	5058

NEGLECT

if he shall n **to hear them, tell**	Mt 18:17	3878
but if he n **to hear the church,**	Mt 18:17	3878
N not the gift that is in thee,	1Ti 4:14	272
if we n so great salvation	Heb 2:3	272

NEGLECTED

were n in the daily ministration	Acts 6:1	3865

NEGLECTING

and humility, and n of the body	Col 2:23	857

NEGLIGENT

My sons, be not now n	2Chr 29:11	7952
not be n to put you always in	2Pet 1:12	272

NEHELAM See NEHELAMITE.

NEHELAMITE (ne-hel'-am-ite) Family name of Shemaiah.

thou also speak to Shemaiah the N	Jer 29:24	5161
LORD concerning Shemaiah the N	Jer 29:31	5161
I will punish Shemaiah the N	Jer 29:32	5161

NEHEMIAH (ne-he-mi'-ah)

1. *A clan leader with Zerubbabel.*

Jeshua, N, Seraiah, Reelaiah,	Ezr 2:2	5166
came with Zerubbabel, Jeshua, N	Neh 7:7	5166

2. *Governor of Jerusalem.*

The words of N the son of	Neh 1:1	5166
And N, which is the Tirshatha, and	Neh 8:9	5166
Now those that sealed were, N	Neh 10:1	5166
and in the days of N the governor	Neh 12:26	5166
Zerubbabel, and in the days of N	Neh 12:47	5166

3. *A rebuilder of Jerusalem's wall.*

him repaired N the son of Azbuk	Neh 3:16	5166

NEHILOTH (ne'-hi-loth) A musical choir or instrument.

To the chief Musician upon N	Ps 5:t	5155

NEHUM (ne'-hum) See REHUM. A clan leader with Zerubbabel.

Bilshan, Mispereth, Bigvai, N	Neh 7:7	5149

NEHUSHTA (ne-hush'-tah) Mother of King Jehoiachin.

And his mother's name was N	2Kin 24:8	5179

NEHUSHTAN (ne-hush'-tan) Name given to the brazen serpents.

and he called it N	2Kin 18:4	5180

NEIEL (ne-i'-el) A city in Asher.

the north side of Beth-emek, and N	Josh 19:27	5272

NEIGHBOUR

every woman shall borrow of her n	Ex 3:22	7934
and let every man borrow of his n	Ex 11:2	7453
and every woman of her n, jewels	Ex 11:2	7468
his n next unto his house take it	Ex 12:4	7934
bear false witness against thy n	Ex 20:16	7453
come presumptuously upon his n	Ex 21:14	7453
unto his n money or stuff to keep	Ex 22:7	7453
he shall pay double unto his n	Ex 22:9	7453
a man deliver unto his n an ass	Ex 22:10	7453
And if a man borrow ought of his n	Ex 22:14	7453
his companion, and every man his n	Ex 32:27	7138
lie unto his n in that which was	Lev 6:2	5997
violence, or hath deceived his n	Lev 6:2	5997
Thou shalt not defraud thy n	Lev 19:13	7453
shalt thou judge thy n	Lev 19:15	5997
stand against the blood of thy n	Lev 19:16	7453
shalt in any wise rebuke thy n	Lev 19:17	5997
thou shalt love thy n as thyself	Lev 19:18	7453
if a man cause a blemish in his n	Lev 24:19	5997
And if thou sell ought unto thy n	Lev 25:14	5997
jubile thou shalt buy of thy n	Lev 25:15	5997
which should kill his n unawares	Deut 4:42	7453
bear false witness against thy n	Deut 5:20	7453
ought unto his n shall release it	Deut 15:2	7453
he shall not exact it of his n	Deut 15:2	7453
Whoso killeth his n ignorantly	Deut 19:4	7453
the wood with his n to hew wood	Deut 19:5	7453
the helve, and lighteth upon his n	Deut 19:5	7453

But if any man hate his *n* .... Deut 19:11   7453
when a man riseth against his *n* .... Deut 22:26   7453
into the standing corn of thy *n* .... Deut 23:25   7453
be he that smiteth his *n* secretly .... Deut 27:24   7453
he smote his *n* unwittingly .... Josh 20:5   7453
off his shoe, and gave it to his *n* .... Ruth 4:7   7453
and hath given it to a *n* of thine 1Sa 15:28   7453
thine hand, and given it to thy *n* 1Sa 28:17   7453
eyes, and give them unto thy *n* 2Sa 12:11   7453
If any man trespass against his *n* 1Kin 8:31   7453
his *n* in the word of the LORD 1Kin 20:35   7453
If a man sin against his *n* 2Chr 6:22   7453
I am as one mocked of his *n* .... Job 12:4   7453
God, as a man pleadeth for his *n* .... Job 16:21   7453
speak vanity every one with his *n* .... Ps 12:2   7453
tongue, nor doeth evil to his *n* .... Ps 15:3   7453
up a reproach against his *n* .... Ps 15:3   7138
Whoso privily slandereth his *n* .... Ps 101:5   7453
Say not unto thy *n*, Go, and come .... Prov 3:28   7453
Devise not evil against thy *n* .... Prov 3:29   7453
with his mouth destroyeth his *n* .... Prov 11:9   7453
is void of wisdom despiseth his *n* .... Prov 11:12   7453
is more excellent than his *n* .... Prov 12:26   7453
poor is hated even of his own *n* .... Prov 14:20   7453
He that despiseth his *n* sinneth .... Prov 14:21   7453
A violent man enticeth his *n* .... Prov 16:29   7453
but his *n* cometh and searcheth him ..... Prov 18:17   7453
the poor is separated from his *n* .... Prov 19:4   7453
his *n* findeth no favour in his .... Prov 21:10   7453
against thy *n* without cause .... Prov 24:28   7453
when thy *n* hath put thee to shame ...... Prov 25:8   7453
thy cause with thy *n* himself .... Prov 25:9   7453
witness against his *n* is a maul .... Prov 25:18   7453
is the man that deceiveth his *n* .... Prov 26:19   7453
for better is a *n* that is near .... Prov 27:10   7934
A man that flattereth his *n* .... Prov 29:5   7453
for this a man is envied of his *n* .... Eccl 4:4   7453
by another, and every one by his *n* .... Is 3:5   7453
and every one against his *n* .... Is 19:2   7453
They helped every one his *n* .... Is 41:6   7453
the *n* and his friend shall perish .... Jer 6:21   7934
judgment between a man and his *n* .... Jer 7:5   7453
Take ye heed every one of his *n* .... Jer 9:4   7453
every *n* will walk with slanders .... Jer 9:4   7453
they will deceive every one his *n* .... Jer 9:5   7453
peaceably to his *n* with his mouth .... Jer 9:8   7453
and every one her *n* lamentation .... Jer 9:20   7468
they shall say every man to his *n* .... Jer 22:8   7453
they tell every man to his *n* .... Jer 23:27   7453
my words every one from his *n* .... Jer 23:30   7453
shall ye say every one to his *n* .... Jer 23:35   7453
teach no more every man his *n* .... Jer 31:34   7453
liberty every man to his *n* .... Jer 34:15   7453
brother, and every man to his *n* .... Jer 34:17   7453
the *n* cities thereof, saith the .... Jer 49:18   7934
the *n* cities thereof, saith the .... Jer 50:40   7934
unto him that giveth his *n* drink .... Hab 2:15   7453
every man his *n* under the vine .... Zec 3:10   7453
all men every one against his *n* .... Zec 8:10   7453
ye every man the truth to his *n* .... Zec 8:16   7453
evil in your hearts against his *n* .... Zec 8:17   7453
every one on the hand of his *n* .... Zec 14:13   7453
rise up against the hand of his *n* .... Zec 14:13   7453
been said, Thou shalt love thy *n* .... Mt 5:43   *4139*
Thou shalt love thy *n* as thyself .... Mt 19:19   *4139*
Thou shalt love thy *n* as thyself .... Mt 22:39   *4139*
Thou shalt love thy *n* as thyself .... Mk 12:31   *4139*
and to love his *n* as himself .... Mk 12:33   *4139*
and thy *n* as thyself .... Lk 10:27   *4139*
said unto Jesus, And who is my *n* .... Lk 10:29   *4139*
was *n* unto him that fell among .... Lk 10:36   *4139*
But he that did his *n* wrong .... Acts 7:27   *4139*
Thou shalt love thy *n* as thyself .... Rom 13:9   *4139*
Love worketh no ill to his *n* .... Rom 13:10   *4139*
his *n* for his good to edification .... Rom 15:2   *4139*
Thou shalt love thy *n* as thyself .... Gal 5:14   *4139*
speak every man truth with his *n* .... Eph 4:25   *4139*
shall not teach every man his *n* .... Heb 8:11   *4139*
Thou shalt love thy *n* as thyself .... Jas 2:8   *4139*

NEIGHBOUR'S
Thou shalt not covet thy *n* house .... Ex 20:17   7453
thou shalt not covet thy *n* wife .... Ex 20:17   7453
ass, nor any thing that is thy *n* .... Ex 20:17   7453
put his hand unto his *n* goods .... Ex 22:8   7453
not put his hand unto his *n* goods .... Ex 22:11   7453
all take thy *n* raiment to pledge .... Ex 22:26   7453
not lie carnally with thy *n* wife .... Lev 18:20   5997
adultery with his *n* wife, the .... Lev 20:10   7453
or buyest ought of thy *n* hand .... Lev 25:14   5997

shalt thou desire thy *n* wife .... Deut 5:21   7453
shalt thou covet thy *n* house .... Deut 5:21   7453
ass, or any thing that is thy *n* .... Deut 5:21   7453
shalt not remove thy *n* landmark .... Deut 19:14   7453
he hath humbled his *n* wife .... Deut 22:24   7453
thou comest into thy *n* vineyard .... Deut 23:24   7453
a sickle unto thy *n* standing corn .... Deut 23:25   7453
he that removeth his *n* landmark .... Deut 27:17   7453
if I have laid wait at my *n* door .... Job 31:9   7453
So he that goeth in to his *n* wife .... Prov 6:29   7453
thy foot from thy *n* house .... Prov 25:17   7453
one neighed after his *n* wife .... Jer 5:8   7453
that useth his *n* service without .... Jer 22:13   7453
neither hath defiled his *n* wife .... Eze 18:6   7453
mountains, and defiled his *n* wife .... Eze 18:11   7453
hath not defiled his *n* wife .... Eze 18:15   7453
abomination with his *n* wife .... Eze 22:11   7453
and ye defile every one his *n* wife .... Eze 33:26   7453
the men every one into his *n* hand .... Zec 11:6   7453

NEIGHBOURS
they heard that they were their *n* .... Josh 9:16   7138
the women her *n* gave it a name, ... Ruth 4:17   7934
thee vessels abroad of all thy *n* 2Kin 4:3   7934
which speak peace to their *n* .... Ps 28:3   7453
but especially among my *n* .... Ps 31:11   7934
makest us a reproach to our *n* .... Ps 44:13   7934
We are become a reproach to our *n* ...... Ps 79:4   7934
render unto our *n* sevenfold into .... Ps 79:12   7934
makest us a strife unto our *n* .... Ps 80:6   7934
he is a reproach to his *n* .... Ps 89:41   7934
the LORD against all mine evil *n* .... Jer 12:14   7934
and his brethren, and his *n* .... Jer 49:10   7934
with the Egyptians thy *n*, great .... Eze 16:26   7934
gained of thy *n* by extortion .... Eze 22:12   7453
lovers, on the Assyrians her *n* .... Eze 23:5   7138
doted upon the Assyrians her *n* .... Eze 23:12   7138
And her *n* and her cousins heard how .. Lk 1:58   *4040*
thy kinsmen, nor thy rich *n* .... Lk 14:12   *1069*
calleth together his friends and .... Lk 15:6   *1069*
her *n* together, saying, Rejoice .... Lk 15:9   *1069*
The *n* therefore, and they which .... Jn 9:8   *1069*

NEIGHBOURS'
adultery with their *n* wives .... Jer 29:23   7453
NEIGHED
every one *n* after his neighbour's .... Jer 5:8   6670
NEIGHING
sound of the *n* of his strong ones .... Jer 8:16   4684
NEIGHINGS
seen thine adulteries, and thy *n* .... Jer 13:27   4684
NEITHER See APPENDIX.

NEKEB *(ne'-keb) A city in Naphtali.*
Allon to Zaanannim, and Adami, N ...... Josh 19:33   5346
NEKODA *(ne-ko'-dah)*
    1. A family of exiles.
of Rezin, the children of N .... Ezr 2:48   5353
of Rezin, the children of N .... Neh 7:50   5353
    2. A family of uncertain origin.
of Tobiah, the children of N .... Ezr 2:60   5353
of Tobiah, the children of N .... Neh 7:62   5353

NEMUEL *(ne-mu'-el) See* JEMUEL, NEMUELITES.
    1. Son of Eliab.
N, and Dathan, and Abiram .... Num 26:9   5241
    2. A son of Simeon.
of N, the family of the .... Num 26:12   5241
The sons of Simeon were, N 1Chr 4:24   5241

NEMUELITES *(ne-mu'-el-ites) Descendants of Nemuel 2.*
of Nemuel, the family of the N .... Num 26:12   5242
NEPHEG *(ne'-feg)*
    1. A son of Izhar.
Korah, and N, and Zichri .... Ex 6:21   5298
    2. A son of David.
Ibhar also, and Elishua, and N 2Sa 5:15   5298
And Nogah, and N, and Japhia, ... 1Chr 3:7   5298
And Nogah, and N, and Japhia, ... 1Chr 14:6   5298

NEPHEW
have son nor *n* among his people .... Job 18:19   5220
name, and remnant, and son, and *n* ...... Is 14:22   5220
NEPHEWS
And he had forty sons and thirty *n* .... Judg 12:14   1121
if any widow have children or *n* 1Ti 5:4   *1549*

NEPHILIM See GIANTS.
NEPHISH *(ne'-fish) See* NAPHISH. *Descendants of*
    Naphish.
the Hagarites, with Jetur, and N 1Chr 5:19   5305

N

NEPHISHESIM (ne-fish'-e-sim) See Nephusim. A family of exiles.
of Meunim, the children of N................Neh 7:52   5300

NEPHISIM See Nephusim.

NEPHTHALIM (nef-tha-lim) See Naphtali. Country and tribe of Naphtali.
in the borders of Zabulon and N.............Mt 4:13   3508
land of Zabulon, and the land of N........Mt 4:15   3508

NEPHTOAH (nef-to'-ah) A stream near Jerusalem.
the fountain of the water of N.................Josh 15:9   5318
out to the well of waters of N.................Josh 18:15   5318

NEPHUSHESIM See Nephishesim.

NEPHUSIM (ne-fu'-sim) See Nephishesim. A family of exiles.
of Mehunim, the children of N...............Ezr 2:50   5304

NEPTHALIM
Of the tribe of N were sealed.................Rev 7:6   3508

NER (nur) Grandfather of King Saul.
his host was Abner, the son of N.............1Sa 14:50   5369
N the father of Abner was the son..........1Sa 14:51   5369
Saul lay, and Abner the son of N.............1Sa 26:5   5369
people, and to Abner the son of N............1Sa 26:14   5369
But Abner the son of N, captain.............2Sa 2:8   5369
And Abner the son of N, and the............2Sa 2:12   5369
the son of N came to the king.................2Sa 3:23   5369
Thou knowest Abner the son of N..........2Sa 3:25   5369
the blood of Abner the son of N............2Sa 3:28   5369
king to slay Abner the son of N..............2Sa 3:37   5369
Israel, unto Abner the son of N...............1Kin 2:5   5369
to wit, Abner the son of N.......................1Kin 2:32   5369
N begat Kish, and Kish begat Saul,.......1Chr 8:33   5369
then Zur, and Kish, and Baal, and N......1Chr 9:36   5369
And N begat Kish.................................1Chr 9:39   5369
of Kish, and Abner the son of N.............1Chr 26:28   5369

NERAIAH See Neriah.

NEREUS (ne'-re-us) A Christian acquaintance of Paul.
Salute Philologus, and Julia, N...............Rom 16:15   3517

NERGAL (nur'-gal) See Nergal-sharezer. War god of Cuth.
and the men of Cuth made N.................2Kin 17:30   5370

NERGAL-SHAREZER (nur'-gal-sha-re'-zur)
1. A Babylonian prince.
and sat in the middle gate, even N.........Jer 39:3   5371
2. Another Babylonian prince.
Sarsechim, Rab-saris, N, Rab-mag.........Jer 39:3   5371
and Nebushasban, Rab-saris, and N......Jer 39:13   5371

NERI (ne'-ri) Father of Salathiel; ancestor of Jesus.
Salathiel, which was the son of N...........Lk 3:27   3518

NERIAH (ne-ri'-ah) Father of Baruch.
purchase unto Baruch the son of N........Jer 32:12   5374
purchase unto Baruch the son of N........Jer 32:16   5374
called Baruch the son of N....................Jer 36:4   5374
Baruch the son of N did according........Jer 36:8   5374
So Baruch the son of N took the.............Jer 36:14   5374
Baruch the scribe, the son of N.............Jer 36:32   5374
But Baruch the son of N setteth.............Jer 43:3   5374
prophet, and Baruch the son of N..........Jer 43:6   5374
spake unto Baruch the son of N.............Jer 45:1   5374
commanded Seraiah the son of N..........Jer 51:59   5374

NERO (ne'-ro) Emperor of Rome.
brought before N the second time..........2Ti s   3505

NEST
and thou puttest thy n in a rock............Num 24:21   7064
If a bird's n chance to be before............Deut 22:6   7064
As an eagle stirreth up her n.................Deut 32:11   7064
Then I said, I shall die in my n...............Job 29:18   7064
command, and make her n on high........Job 39:27   7064
and the swallow a n for herself..............Ps 84:3   7064
a bird that wandereth from her n............Prov 27:8   7064
my hand hath found as a n the.............Is 10:14   7064
wandering bird cast out of the n............Is 16:2   7064
shall the great owl make her n.............Is 34:15   7077
that makest thy n in the cedars.............Jer 22:23   7077
her n in the sides of the hole's..............Jer 48:28   7077
make thy n as high as the eagle............Jer 49:16   7064
thou set thy n among the stars...............Obad 4   7064
that he may set his n on high................Hab 2:9   7064

NESTS
Where the birds make their n.................Ps 104:17   7077
heaven made their n in his boughs........Eze 31:6   7077
and the birds of the air have n.............Mt 8:20   2682
holes, and birds of the air have n..........Lk 9:58   2682

NET
upon the n shalt thou make four...........Ex 27:4   7568
that the n may be even to the.................Ex 27:5   7568
is cast into a n by his own feet...............Job 18:8   7568
and hath compassed me with his n........Job 19:6   4685
in the n which they hid is their..............Ps 9:15   7568
when he draweth him into his n.............Ps 10:9   7568
shall pluck my feet out of the n.............Ps 25:15   7568
Pull me out of the n that they................Ps 31:4   7568
they hid for me their n in a pit...............Ps 35:7   7568
let his n that he hath hid catch..............Ps 35:8   7568
have prepared a n for my steps..............Ps 57:6   7568
Thou broughtest us into the n...............Ps 66:11   4685
have spread a n by the wayside..............Ps 140:5   7568
Surely in vain the n is spread in...........Prov 1:17   7568
wicked desireth the n of evil men..........Prov 12:12   4686
spreadeth a n for his feet......................Prov 29:5   7568
that are taken in an evil n....................Eccl 9:12   4686
streets, as a wild bull in a n..................Is 51:20   4364
he hath spread a n for my feet...............Lam 1:13   7568
My n also will I spread upon him,.........Eze 12:13   7568
And I will spread my n upon him,..........Eze 17:20   7568
and spread their n over him..................Eze 19:8   7568
my n over thee with a company of.........Eze 32:3   7568
they shall bring thee up in my n...........Eze 32:3   2764
Mizpah, and a n spread upon Tabor.......Hos 5:1   7568
go, I will spread my n upon them,..........Hos 7:12   7568
every man his brother with a n.............Mic 7:2   2764
angle, they catch them in their n...........Hab 1:15   2764
they sacrifice unto their n....................Hab 1:16   2764
they therefore empty their n.................Hab 1:17   2764
brother, casting a n into the sea...........Mt 4:18   293
of heaven is like unto a n..................Mt 13:47   4522
brother casting a n into the sea............Mk 1:16   293
at thy word I will let down the n............Lk 5:5   1350
and their n brake...............................Lk 5:6   1350
Cast the n on the right side of..........Jn 21:6   1350
dragging the n with fishes....................Jn 21:8   1350
drew the n to land full of great.............Jn 21:11   1350
so many, yet was not the n broken.........Jn 21:11   1350

NETAIM See Plants.

NETHANEAL See Nethaneel.

NETHANEEL (ne-than'-e-el)
1. A son of Zuar.
N the son of Zuar...............................Num 1:8   5417
N the son of Zuar shall be....................Num 2:5   5417
the second day N the son of Zuar..........Num 7:18   5417
the offering of N the son of Zuar............Num 7:23   5417
of Issachar was N the son of Zuar..........Num 10:15   5417
2. A brother of David.
N the fourth, Raddai the fifth,..............1Chr 2:14   5417
3. A priest who relocated the Ark.
Shebaniah, and Jehoshaphat, and N......1Chr 15:24   5417
4. A sanctuary servant.
Shemaiah the son of N the scribe..........1Chr 24:6   5417
5. A son of Obed-edom.
Sacar the fourth, and N the fifth,..........1Chr 26:4   5417
6. A prince of Judah.
Obadiah, and to Zechariah, and to N....2Chr 17:7   5417
7. A chief Levite.
Conaniah also, and Shemaiah and N....2Chr 35:9   5417
8. Married a foreigner in exile.
Elioenai, Maaseiah, Ishmael, N.............Ezr 10:22   5417
9. A priest with Zerubbabel.
of Jedaiah, N......................................Neh 12:21   5417
10. A priest who dedicated the wall.
Milalai, Gilalai, Maai, N.......................Neh 12:36   5417

NETHANEL See Nethaneel.

NETHANIAH (neth-a-ni'-ah)
1. Father of Ishmael.
Mizpah, even Ishmael the son of N........2Kin 25:23   5418
month, that Ishmael the son of N...........2Kin 25:25   5418
Mizpah, even Ishmael the son of N........Jer 40:8   5418
Ishmael the son of N to slay thee..........Jer 40:14   5418
I will slay Ishmael the son of N.............Jer 40:15   5418
the son of N the son of Elishama............Jer 41:1   5418
Then arose Ishmael the son of N...........Jer 41:2   5418
Ishmael the son of N went forth............Jer 41:6   5418
Ishmael the son of N slew them............Jer 41:7   5418
Ishmael the son of N filled it.................Jer 41:9   5418
Ishmael the son of N carried them.........Jer 41:10   5418
Ishmael the son of N had done..............Jer 41:11   5418
fight with Ishmael the son of N.............Jer 41:12   5418
But Ishmael the son of N escaped..........Jer 41:15   5418
from Ishmael the son of N.....................Jer 41:16   5418
because Ishmael the son of N had..........Jer 41:18   5418

NETHER (continued)

2. *A sanctuary servant.*

Zaccur, and Joseph, and N, and	1Chr 25:2	5418
The fifth to N, he, his sons, and	1Chr 25:12	5418

3. *A Levite.*

sent Levites, even Shemaiah, and N	2Chr 17:8	5418

4. *Father of Jehudi.*

princes sent Jehudi the son of N	Jer 36:14	5418

NETHER

stood at the n part of the mount	Ex 19:17	8482
No man shall take the n or the	Deut 24:6	7347
upper springs, and the n springs	Josh 15:19	8482
the coast of Beth-horon the n	Josh 16:3	8481
south side of the n Beth-horon	Josh 18:13	8481
upper springs and the n springs	Judg 1:15	8482
built Gezer, and Beth-horon the n	1Kin 9:17	8481
who built Beth-horon the n	1Chr 7:24	8481
the upper, and Beth-horon the n	2Chr 8:5	8481
as a piece of the n millstone	Job 41:24	8482
to the n parts of the earth, in	Eze 31:14	8482
in the n parts of the earth	Eze 31:16	8482
unto the n parts of the earth	Eze 31:18	8482
unto the n parts of the earth	Eze 32:18	8482
into the n parts of the earth	Eze 32:24	8482

NETHERMOST

The n chamber was five cubits	1Kin 6:6	8481

NETHINIM See NETHINIMS.

NETHINIMS *(neth'-in-ims) Assistants to the Levites.*

the priests, Levites, and the N	1Chr 9:2	5411
The N: the children of Ziha	Ezr 2:43	5411
All the N, and the children of	Ezr 2:58	5411
singers, and the porters, and the N	Ezr 2:70	5411
singers, and the porters, and the N	Ezr 7:7	5411
and Levites, singers, porters, N	Ezr 7:24	5412
Iddo, and to his brethren the N	Ezr 8:17	5411
Also of the N, whom David and the	Ezr 8:20	5411
Levites, two hundred and twenty N	Ezr 8:20	5411
Moreover the N dwelt in Ophel,	Neh 3:26	5411
son unto the place of the N	Neh 3:31	5411
The N: the children of Ziha	Neh 7:46	5411
All the N, and the children of	Neh 7:60	5411
and some of the people, and the N	Neh 7:73	5411
the porters, the singers, the N	Neh 10:28	5411
priests, and the Levites, and the N	Neh 11:3	5411
But the N dwelt in Ophel	Neh 11:21	5411
and Ziha and Gispa were over the N	Neh 11:21	5411

NETOPHAH *(ne-to'-fah)* See NETOPHATHITE. *A city in Judah.*

The men of N, fifty and six	Ezr 2:22	5199
The men of Beth-lehem and N	Neh 7:26	5199

NETOPHATHI *(ne-to'-fa-thi)* See NETOPHATHITE. *An inhabitant of Netophah.*

and from the villages of N	Neh 12:28	5200

NETOPHATHITE *(ne-to'-fa-thite)* See NETOPHATHI, NETHOPHATHITES. *Same as Netophathi.*

Zalmon the Ahohite, Maharai the N	2Sa 23:28	5200
Heleb the son of Baanah, a N	2Sa 23:29	5200
the son of Tanhumeth the N	2Kin 25:23	5200
Maharai the N, Heled the son of	1Chr 11:30	5200
Heled the son of Baanah the N	1Chr 11:30	5200
the tenth month was Maharai the N	1Chr 27:13	5200
twelfth month was Heldai the N	1Chr 27:15	5200
and the sons of Ephai the N	Jer 40:8	5200

NETOPHATHITES *(ne-to'-fa-thites)*

Beth-lehem, and the N, Ataroth	1Chr 2:54	5200
dwelt in the villages of the N	1Chr 9:16	5200

NETS

n of checker work, and wreaths of	1Kin 7:17	7638
the wicked fall into their own n	Ps 141:10	4365
woman, whose heart is snares and n	Eccl 7:26	2764
they that spread n upon the	Is 19:8	4364
of n in the midst of the sea	Eze 26:5	2764
shalt be a place to spread n upon	Eze 26:14	2764
be a place to spread forth n	Eze 47:10	2764
And they straightway left their n	Mt 4:20	1350
their father, mending their n	Mt 4:21	1350
straightway they forsook their n	Mk 1:18	1350
were in the ship mending their n	Mk 1:19	1350
of them, and were washing their n	Lk 5:2	1350
and let down your n for a draught	Lk 5:4	1350

NETTLES

under the n they were gathered	Job 30:7	2738
n had covered the face thereof,	Prov 24:31	2738
shall come up in her palaces, n	Is 34:13	7057
silver, n shall possess them	Hos 9:6	7057
Gomorrah, even the breeding of n	Zeph 2:9	2738

NETWORK

make for it a grate of n of brass	Ex 27:4	4640,7568
of n under the compass thereof	Ex 38:4	4640,7568
rows round about upon the one n	1Kin 7:18	7639
the belly which was by the n	1Kin 7:20	7639
rows of pomegranates for one n	1Kin 7:42	7639
chapiter was five cubits, with n	Jer 52:22	7639
the n were an hundred round about	Jer 52:23	7639

NETWORKS

and the two n, to cover the two	1Kin 7:41	7639
pomegranates for the two n	1Kin 7:42	7639
fine flax, and they that weave n	Is 19:9	2355

NEVER See APPENDIX.

NEVERTHELESS See APPENDIX.

NEW

arose up a n king over Egypt	Ex 1:8	2319
ye shall offer a n meat offering	Lev 23:16	2319
forth the old because of the n	Lev 26:10	2319
But if the LORD make a n thing	Num 16:30	1278
when ye bring a n meat offering	Num 28:26	2319
there that hath built a n house	Deut 20:5	2319
When thou buildest a n house	Deut 22:8	2319
When a man hath taken a n wife	Deut 24:5	2319
to n gods that came newly up,	Deut 32:17	2319
of wine, which we filled, were n	Josh 9:13	2319
They chose n gods	Judg 5:8	2319
they bound him with two n cords	Judg 15:13	2319
he found a n jawbone of an ass,	Judg 15:15	2961
If they bind me fast with n ropes	Judg 16:11	2319
Delilah therefore took n ropes	Judg 16:12	2319
Now therefore make a n cart	1Sa 6:7	2319
Behold, to morrow is the n moon	1Sa 20:5	2320
to David, To morrow is the n moon	1Sa 20:18	2320
when the n moon was come, the	1Sa 20:24	2320
set the ark of God upon a n cart	2Sa 6:3	2319
of Abinadab, drave the n cart	2Sa 6:3	2319
he being girded with a n sword	2Sa 21:16	2319
had clad himself with a n garment	1Kin 11:29	2319
Ahijah caught the n garment that	1Kin 11:30	2319
And he said, Bring me a n cruse	2Kin 2:20	2319
it is neither n moon, nor sabbath	2Kin 4:23	2320
in a n cart out of the house of	1Chr 13:7	2319
in the sabbaths, in the n moons	1Chr 23:31	2320
the sabbaths, and on the n moons	2Chr 2:4	2320
the sabbaths, and on the n moons	2Chr 8:13	2320
of the LORD, before the n court	2Chr 20:5	2319
the sabbaths, and for the n moons	2Chr 31:3	2320
offering, both of the n moons	Ezr 3:5	2320
stones, and a row of n timber	Ezr 6:4	2323
of the sabbaths, of the n moons	Neh 10:33	2319
of the corn, of the n wine	Neh 10:39	8492
the n wine and the oil, which was	Neh 13:5	8492
the n wine and the oil unto the	Neh 13:12	8492
is ready to burst like n bottles	Job 32:19	2319
Sing unto the LORD a n song	Ps 33:3	2319
he hath put a n song in my mouth,	Ps 40:3	2319
Blow up the trumpet in the n moon	Ps 81:3	2320
O sing unto the LORD a n song	Ps 96:1	2319
O sing unto the LORD a n song	Ps 98:1	2319
I will sing a n song unto thee, O	Ps 144:9	2319
Sing unto the LORD a n song	Ps 149:1	2319
shall burst out with n wine	Prov 3:10	8492
there is no n thing under the sun	Eccl 1:9	2319
it may be said, See, this is n	Eccl 1:10	2319
all manner of pleasant fruits, n	Song 7:13	2319
the n moons and sabbaths, the	Is 1:13	2320
Your n moons and your appointed	Is 1:14	2320
The n wine mourneth, the vine	Is 24:7	8492
I will make thee a n sharp	Is 41:15	2319
to pass, and n things do I declare	Is 42:9	2319
Sing unto the LORD a n song	Is 42:10	2319
Behold, I will do a n thing	Is 43:19	2319
I have shewed thee n things from	Is 48:6	2319
thou shalt be called by a n name	Is 62:2	2319
As the n wine is found in the	Is 65:8	8492
I create n heavens and a n earth	Is 65:17	2319
For as the n heavens	Is 66:22	2319
the n earth, which I will make,	Is 66:22	2319
that from one n moon to another,	Is 66:23	2320
of the n gate of the LORD's house	Jer 26:10	2319
created a n thing in the earth	Jer 31:22	2319
that I will make a n covenant	Jer 31:31	2319
at the entry of the n gate of the	Jer 36:10	2319
They are n every morning	Lam 3:23	2319
I will put a n spirit within you	Eze 11:19	2319
you a n heart and a n spirit	Eze 18:31	2319
A n heart also will I give you,	Eze 36:26	2319
a n spirit will I put within you,	Eze 36:26	2319
in the feasts, and in the n moons	Eze 45:17	2320

N

in the day of the *n* moon it shall	Eze 46:1	2320
in the sabbaths and in the *n* moons	Eze 46:3	2320
in the day of the *n* moon it shall	Eze 46:6	2320
it shall bring forth *n* fruit	Eze 47:12	1069
her *n* moons, and her sabbaths, and	Hos 2:11	2320
n wine take away the heart	Hos 4:11	8492
the *n* wine shall fail in her	Hos 9:2	8492
of wine, because of the *n* wine	Joel 1:5	
the *n* wine is dried up, the oil	Joel 1:10	8492
mountains shall drop down wine	Joel 3:18	
When will the *n* moon be gone	Amos 8:5	2320
upon the corn, and upon the *n* wine	Hag 1:11	8492
men cheerful, and *n* wine the maids	Zec 9:17	8492
of *n* cloth unto an old garment	Mt 9:16	46
Neither do men put *n* wine into	Mt 9:17	3501
but they put *n* wine into	Mt 9:17	3501
wine into *n* bottles	Mt 9:17	2537
out of his treasure things *n*	Mt 13:52	2537
is my blood of the *n* testament	Mt 26:28	2537
until that day when I drink it *n*	Mt 26:29	2537
And laid it in his own *n* tomb	Mt 27:60	2537
what *n* doctrine is this	Mk 1:27	2537
of *n* cloth on an old garment	Mk 2:21	46
else the *n* piece that filled it	Mk 2:21	2537
no man putteth *n* wine into old	Mk 2:22	3501
else the *n* wine doth burst the	Mk 2:22	3501
but *n* wine must be put into	Mk 2:22	3501
wine must be put into *n* bottles	Mk 2:22	2537
is my blood of the *n* testament	Mk 14:24	2537
drink it *n* in the kingdom of God	Mk 14:25	2537
they shall speak with *n* tongues	Mk 16:17	2537
piece of a *n* garment upon an old	Lk 5:36	2537
then both the *n* maketh a rent	Lk 5:36	2537
of the *n* agreeth not with the old	Lk 5:36	2537
no man putteth *n* wine into old	Lk 5:37	3501
else the *n* wine will burst the	Lk 5:37	3501
But *n* wine must be put into	Lk 5:38	3501
wine must be put into *n* bottles	Lk 5:38	2537
old wine straightway desireth *n*	Lk 5:39	2537
This cup is the *n* testament in my	Lk 22:20	2537
A *n* commandment I give unto you,	Jn 13:34	2537
and in the garden a *n* sepulchre	Jn 19:41	2537
These men are full of *n* wine	Acts 2:13	1098
May we know what this *n* doctrine	Acts 17:19	2537
to tell, or to hear some *n* thing	Acts 17:21	2537
leaven, that ye may be a *n* lump	1Cor 5:7	3501
This cup is the *n* testament in my	1Cor 11:25	2537
able ministers of the *n* testament	2Cor 3:6	2537
be in Christ, he is a *n* creature	2Cor 5:17	2537
behold, all things are become *n*	2Cor 5:17	2537
uncircumcision, but a *n* creature	Gal 6:15	2537
in himself of twain one *n* man	Eph 2:15	2537
And that ye put on the *n* man	Eph 4:24	2537
of an holyday, or of the *n* moon	Col 2:16	3561
And have put on the *n* man, which	Col 3:10	3501
when I will make a *n* covenant	Heb 8:8	2537
A *n* covenant, he hath made the	Heb 8:13	2537
the mediator of the *n* testament	Heb 9:15	2537
By a *n* and living way, which he	Heb 10:20	4372
the mediator of the *n* covenant	Heb 12:24	3501
his promise, look for *n* heavens	2Pet 3:13	2537
a *n* earth, wherein dwelleth	2Pet 3:13	2537
I write *n* commandment unto you	1Jn 2:7	2537
a *n* commandment I write unto you,	1Jn 2:8	2537
I wrote a *n* commandment unto thee	2Jn 5	2537
and in the stone a *n* name written	Rev 2:17	2537
which is *n* Jerusalem, which	Rev 3:12	2537
I will write upon him my *n* name	Rev 3:12	2537
And they sung a *n* song, saying,	Rev 5:9	2537
were a *n* song before the throne	Rev 14:3	2537
I saw a *n* heaven and a *n* earth	Rev 21:1	2537
n Jerusalem, coming down from God	Rev 21:2	2537
said, Behold, I make all things *n*	Rev 21:5	2537

NEWBORN

As *n* babes, desire the sincere	1Pet 2:2	738

NEWLY

not, to new gods that came *n* up	Deut 32:17	7138
they had but *n* set the watch	Judg 7:19	6965

NEWNESS

we also should walk in *n* of life	Rom 6:4	2538
we should serve in *n* of spirit	Rom 7:6	2538

NEWS

so is good *n* from a far country	Prov 25:25	8052

NEXT See APPENDIX.

NEZIAH *(ne-zi'-ah) A family of exiles.*

The children of *N*, the children	Ezr 2:54	5335
The children of *N*, the children	Neh 7:56	5335

NEZIB *(ne'-zib) A city in Judah.*

And Jiphtah, and Ashnah, and *N*	Josh 15:43	5334

NIBHAZ *(nib'-haz) A god of the Avites.*

And the Avites made *N* and Tartak,	2Kin 17:31	5026

NIBSHAN *(nib'-shan) A city in Judah.*

And *N*, and the city of Salt, and	Josh 15:62	5044

NICANOR *(ni-ca'-nor) A leader in the Jerusalem church.*

and Philip, and Prochorus, and *N*	Acts 6:5	3527

NICODEMUS *(nic-o-de'-mus) A Pharisee sympathetic to Jesus.*

a man of the Pharisees, named *N*	Jn 3:1	3530
N saith unto him, How can a man	Jn 3:4	3530
N answered and said unto him, How	Jn 3:9	3530
N saith unto them, (he that came	Jn 7:50	3530
And there came also *N*, which at	Jn 19:39	3530

NICOLAITANES *(nic-o-la'-i-tans) A group condemned in Revelation.*

thou hatest the deeds of the *N*	Rev 2:6	3531
that hold the doctrine of the *N*	Rev 2:15	3531

NICOLAITANS See NICOLAITANES.

NICOLAS *(nic'-o-las) A leader in the Jerusalem church.*

and *N* a proselyte of Antioch	Acts 6:5	3532

NICOLAUS See NICOLAS.

NICOPOLIS *(ni-cop'-o-lis) A city in Thrace.*

be diligent to come unto me to *N*	Titus 3:12	3533
the Cretians, from *N* of Macedonia	Titus *s*	3533

NIGER *(ni'-jur) See* SIMEON. *A Christian teacher and prophet at Antioch.*

and Simeon that was called *N*	Acts 13:1	3526

NIGH

the time drew *n* that Israel must	Gen 47:29	7126
And he said, Draw not *n* hither	Ex 3:5	7126
And when Pharaoh drew *n*, the	Ex 14:10	7126
but they shall not come *n*	Ex 24:2	5066
soon as he came *n* unto the camp	Ex 32:19	7126
and they were afraid to come *n* him	Ex 34:30	5066
all the children of Israel came *n*	Ex 34:32	5066
sanctified in them that come *n* me	Lev 10:3	7138
that is *n* unto him, which hath	Lev 21:3	7138
n to offer the offerings of the	Lev 21:21	5066
he shall not come *n* to offer the	Lev 21:21	5066
nor come *n* unto the altar,	Lev 21:23	5066
or any that is *n* of kin unto him	Lev 25:49	7607
cometh *n* shall be put to death	Num 1:51	7126
cometh *n* shall be put to death	Num 3:10	7126
cometh *n* shall be put to death	Num 3:38	7126
Israel come *n* unto the sanctuary	Num 8:19	5066
only they shall not come *n* the	Num 18:3	7126
shall not come *n* unto you	Num 18:4	7126
cometh *n* shall be put to death	Num 18:7	7126
come *n* the tabernacle of the	Num 18:22	7126
I shall behold him, but not *n*	Num 24:17	7126
unto all the places *n* thereunto	Deut 1:7	7934
when thou comest *n* over against	Deut 2:19	7126
who hath God so *n* unto them	Deut 4:7	7126
n unto thee, or far off from thee	Deut 13:7	7126
ye are come *n* unto the battle	Deut 20:2	7126
When thou comest *n* unto a city to	Deut 20:10	7126
if thy brother be not *n* unto thee	Deut 22:2	7126
But the word is very *n* unto thee	Deut 30:14	7126
were with him, went up, and drew *n*	Josh 8:11	5066
drew *n* to meet David, that David	1Sa 17:48	7126
And Joab drew *n*, and the people	2Sa 10:13	5066
Wherefore approached ye so *n* unto	2Sa 11:20	
why went ye *n* the wall	2Sa 11:21	5066
that when any man came *n* to him	2Sa 15:5	7126
David drew *n* that he should die	1Kin 2:1	7126
be *n* unto the LORD our God day and	1Kin 8:59	7126
Moreover they that were *n* them	1Chr 12:40	7126
n before the Syrians unto the	1Chr 19:14	5066
of the king Ahasuerus, both *n*	Est 9:20	7126
they shall not come *n* unto him	Ps 32:6	5060
The LORD is *n* unto them that are	Ps 34:18	7126
Draw *n* unto my soul, and redeem it	Ps 69:18	7126
my steps had well *n* slipped	Ps 73:2	4952
salvation is *n* them that fear him	Ps 85:9	7138
my life draweth *n* unto the grave	Ps 88:3	5060
but it shall not come *n* thee	Ps 91:7	5066
any plague come *n* thy dwelling	Ps 91:10	7126
They draw *n* that follow after	Ps 119:150	7126
The LORD is *n* unto all them that	Ps 145:18	7138
come not *n* the door of her house	Prov 5:8	7126
come not, nor the years draw *n*	Eccl 12:1	5060
of the Holy One of Israel draw *n*	Is 5:19	7126
LORD cometh, for it is *n* at hand	Joel 2:1	7126

This people draweth *n* unto me	Mt 15:8	*1448*
came *n* unto the sea of Galilee	Mt 15:29	*3844*
when they drew *n* unto Jerusalem	Mt 21:1	*1448*
leaves, ye know that summer is *n*	Mt 24:32	*1451*
not come *n* unto him for the press	Mk 2:4	
Now there was there *n* unto the	Mk 5:11	*4314*
and he was *n* unto the sea	Mk 5:21	*3844*
And when they came *n* to Jerusalem	Mk 11:1	
come to pass, know that it is *n*	Mk 13:29	*1451*
Now when he came *n* to the gate of	Lk 7:12	*1448*
kingdom of God is come *n* unto you	Lk 10:9	*1448*
kingdom of God is come *n* unto you	Lk 10:11	*1448*
drew *n* to the house, he heard	Lk 15:25	*1448*
as he was come *n* unto Jericho	Lk 18:35	*1448*
because he was *n* to Jerusalem	Lk 19:11	*1451*
when he was come *n* to Bethphage	Lk 19:29	*1448*
And when he was come *n*, even now	Lk 19:37	*1448*
that the desolation thereof is *n*	Lk 21:20	*1448*
for your redemption draweth *n*	Lk 21:28	*1448*
that summer is now *n* at hand	Lk 21:30	*1451*
the kingdom of God is *n* at hand	Lk 21:31	*1451*
feast of unleavened bread drew *n*	Lk 22:1	*1448*
they drew *n* unto the village,	Lk 24:28	*1448*
a feast of the Jews, was *n*	Jn 6:4	*1451*
sea, and drawing *n* unto the ship	Jn 6:19	*1451*
n unto the place where they did	Jn 6:23	*1451*
Now Bethany was *n* unto Jerusalem	Jn 11:18	*1451*
the Jews' passover was *n* at hand	Jn 11:55	*1451*
was crucified was *n* to the city	Jn 19:20	*1451*
for the sepulchre was *n* at hand	Jn 19:42	*1451*
the time of the promise drew *n*	Acts 7:17	*1448*
forasmuch as Lydda was *n* to Joppa	Acts 9:38	*1451*
drew *n* unto the city, Peter went	Acts 10:9	*1448*
was come *n* unto Damascus about	Acts 22:6	*1448*
n whereunto was the city of Lasea	Acts 27:8	*1451*
The word is *n* thee, even in thy	Rom 10:8	*1451*
are made *n* by the blood of Christ	Eph 2:13	*1451*
afar off, and to them that were *n*	Eph 2:17	*1451*
indeed he was sick *n* unto death	Phil 2:27	*3897*
of Christ he was *n* unto death	Phil 2:30	*1448*
is rejected, and is *n* unto cursing	Heb 6:8	*1451*
by the which we draw *n* unto God	Heb 7:19	*1448*
Draw *n* to God, and he will draw	Jas 4:8	*1448*
to God, and he will draw *n* to you	Jas 4:8	*1448*
the coming of the Lord draweth *n*	Jas 5:8	*1448*

NIGHT

Day, and the darkness he called *N*	Gen 1:5	3915
to divide the day from the *n*	Gen 1:14	3915
and the lesser light to rule the *n*	Gen 1:16	3915
rule over the day and over the *n*	Gen 1:18	3915
and day and *n* shall not cease	Gen 8:22	3915
them, he and his servants, by *n*	Gen 14:15	3915
servant's house, and tarry all *n*	Gen 19:2	
we will abide in the street all *n*	Gen 19:2	
men which came in to thee this *n*	Gen 19:5	3915
their father drink wine that *n*	Gen 19:33	3915
make him drink wine this *n* also	Gen 19:34	3915
father drink wine that *n* also	Gen 19:35	3915
came to Abimelech in a dream by *n*	Gen 20:3	3915
were with him, and tarried all *n*	Gen 24:54	
LORD appeared unto him the same *n*	Gen 26:24	3915
place, and tarried there all *n*	Gen 28:11	
thee to *n* for thy son's mandrakes	Gen 30:15	3915
And he lay with her that *n*	Gen 30:16	3915
Laban the Syrian in a dream by *n*	Gen 31:24	3915
stolen by day, or stolen by *n*	Gen 31:39	3915
consumed me, and the frost by *n*	Gen 31:40	3915
tarried all *n* in the mount	Gen 31:54	
And he lodged there that same *n*	Gen 32:13	3915
lodged that *n* in the company	Gen 32:21	3915
And he rose up that *n*, and took his	Gen 32:22	3915
them, each man his dream in one *n*	Gen 40:5	3915
And we dreamed a dream in one *n*	Gen 41:11	3915
Israel in the visions of the *n*	Gen 46:2	3915
at *n* he shall divide the spoil	Gen 49:27	6153
land all that day, and all that *n*	Ex 10:13	3915
shall eat the flesh in that *n*	Ex 12:8	3915
through the land of Egypt this *n*	Ex 12:12	3915
And Pharaoh rose up in the *n*	Ex 12:30	3915
he called for Moses and Aaron by *n*	Ex 12:31	3915
It is a *n* to be much observed	Ex 12:42	3915
this is that *n* of the LORD to be	Ex 12:42	3915
by *n* in a pillar of fire, to give	Ex 13:21	3915
to go by day and *n*	Ex 13:21	3915
day, nor the pillar of fire by *n*	Ex 13:22	3915
but it gave light by *n* to these	Ex 14:20	3915
came not near the other all the *n*	Ex 14:20	3915
by a strong east wind all that *n*	Ex 14:21	3915
by day, and fire was on it by *n*	Ex 40:38	3915
the altar all *n* unto the morning	Lev 6:9	3915
the morning, and half thereof at *n*	Lev 6:20	6153
n seven days, and keep the charge	Lev 8:35	3915
the *n* hawk, and the cuckow, and the	Lev 11:16	8464
with thee all *n* until the morning	Lev 19:13	
and the appearance of fire by *n*	Num 9:16	3915
by *n* that the cloud was taken up	Num 9:21	3915
dew fell upon the camp in the *n*	Num 11:9	3915
up all that day, and all that *n*	Num 11:32	3915
and the people wept that *n*	Num 14:1	3915
and in a pillar of fire by *n*	Num 14:14	3915
said unto them, Lodge here this *n*	Num 22:8	3915
you, tarry ye also here this *n*	Num 22:19	3915
And God came unto Balaam at *n*	Num 22:20	3915
pitch your tents in, in fire by *n*	Deut 1:33	3915
the *n* hawk, and the cuckow, and the	Deut 14:15	8464
thee forth out of Egypt by *n*	Deut 16:1	3915
remain all *n* until the morning	Deut 16:4	
not remain all *n* upon the tree	Deut 21:23	
that chanceth him by *n*, then	Deut 23:10	3915
and thou shalt fear day and *n*	Deut 28:66	3915
shalt meditate therein day and *n*	Josh 1:8	3915
there came men in hither to *n* of	Josh 2:2	3915
where ye shall lodge this *n*	Josh 4:3	3915
of valour, and sent them away by *n*	Josh 8:3	3915
lodged that *n* among the people	Josh 8:9	3915
Joshua went that *n* into the midst	Josh 8:13	3915
and went up from Gilgal all *n*	Josh 10:9	3915
And it came to pass the same *n*	Judg 6:25	3915
do it by day, that he did it by *n*	Judg 6:27	3915
And God did so that *n*	Judg 6:40	3915
And it came to pass the same *n*	Judg 7:9	3915
Now therefore up by *n*, thou and	Judg 9:32	3915
people that were with him, by *n*	Judg 9:34	3915
laid wait for him all *n* in the	Judg 16:2	3915
the city, and were quiet all the *n*	Judg 16:2	3915
I pray thee, and tarry all *n*	Judg 19:6	
evening, I pray you tarry all *n*	Judg 19:9	
the man would not tarry that *n*	Judg 19:10	
of these places to lodge all *n*	Judg 19:13	
her all the *n* until the morning	Judg 19:25	3915
house round about upon me by *n*	Judg 20:5	3915
should have an husband also to *n*	Ruth 1:12	3915
barley to *n* in the threshingfloor	Ruth 3:2	3915
Tarry this *n*, and it shall be in	Ruth 3:13	3915
every man his ox with him that *n*	1Sa 14:34	3915
down after the Philistines by *n*	1Sa 14:36	3915
and he cried unto the LORD all *n*	1Sa 15:11	3915
the LORD hath said to me this *n*	1Sa 15:16	3915
and David fled, and escaped that *n*	1Sa 19:10	3915
saying, If thou save not thy to *n*	1Sa 19:11	3915
naked all that day and all that *n*	1Sa 19:24	3915
were a wall unto us both by *n*	1Sa 25:16	3915
Abishai came to the people by *n*	1Sa 26:7	3915
and they came to the woman by *n*	1Sa 28:8	3915
bread all the day, nor all the *n*	1Sa 28:20	3915
they rose up, and went away that *n*	1Sa 28:25	3915
valiant men arose, and went all *n*	1Sa 31:12	3915
all that *n* through the plain	2Sa 2:29	3915
And Joab and his men went all *n*	2Sa 2:32	3915
them away through the plain all *n*	2Sa 4:7	3915
And it came to pass that *n*	2Sa 7:4	3915
in, and lay all *n* upon the earth	2Sa 12:16	
and pursue after David this *n*	2Sa 17:1	3915
Lodge not this *n* in the plains of	2Sa 17:16	3915
not tarry one with thee this *n*	2Sa 19:7	3915
nor the beasts of the field by *n*	2Sa 21:10	3915
to Solomon in a dream by *n*	1Kin 3:5	3915
this woman's child died in the *n*	1Kin 3:19	3915
may be open toward this house *n*	1Kin 8:29	3915
unto the LORD our God day and *n*	1Kin 8:59	3915
and they came by *n*, and compassed	2Kin 6:14	3915
And the king arose in the *n*	2Kin 7:12	3915
and he rose by *n*, and smote the	2Kin 8:21	3915
And it came to pass that *n*	2Kin 19:35	3915
all the men of war fled by *n* by	2Kin 25:4	3915
employed in that work day and *n*	1Chr 9:33	3915
And it came to pass the same *n*	1Chr 17:3	3915
In that *n* did God appear unto	2Chr 1:7	3915
be open upon this house day and *n*	2Chr 6:20	3915
the LORD appeared to Solomon by *n*	2Chr 7:12	3915
and he rose up by *n*, and smote the	2Chr 21:9	3915
offerings and the fat until *n*	2Chr 35:14	3915
I pray before thee now, day and *n*	Neh 1:6	3915
And I arose in the *n*, I and some	Neh 2:12	3915
I went out by *n* by the gate of	Neh 2:13	3915
went I up in the *n* by the brook	Neh 2:15	3915
set a watch against them day and *n*	Neh 4:9	3915
that in the *n* they may be a guard	Neh 4:22	3915
in the *n* will they come to slay	Neh 6:10	3915
in the *n* by a pillar of fire, to	Neh 9:12	3915
neither the pillar of fire by *n*	Neh 9:19	3915

N

NIGHTS

forty *n* unto Horeb the mount of	1Kin 19:8	3915
the ground seven days and seven *n*	Job 2:13	3915
wearisome *n* are appointed to me	Job 7:3	3915
and I am set in my ward whole *n*	Is 21:8	3915
of the fish three days and three *n*	Jonah 1:17	3915
had fasted forty days and forty *n*	Mt 4:2	3571
three *n* in the whale's belly	Mt 12:40	3571
three *n* in the heart of the earth	Mt 12:40	3571

NILE See BROOKS, FLOOD, RIVER.

NIMRAH (nim'-rah) See BETH-NIMRAH. *A city in Gad.*

Ataroth, and Dibon, and Jazer, and *N*	Num 32:3	5247

NIMRIM (nim'-rim) *A body of water on the border of Gad.*

the waters of *N* shall be desolate	Is 15:6	5249
also of *N* shall be desolate	Jer 48:34	5249

NIMROD (nim'-rod) *Son of Cush.*

And Cush begat *N*	Gen 10:8	5248
Even as *N* the mighty hunter	Gen 10:9	5248
And Cush begat *N*	1Chr 1:10	5248
the land of *N* in the entrances	Mic 5:6	5248

NIMSHI (nim'-shi) *Grandfather of Jehu.*

Jehu the son of *N* shalt thou	1Kin 19:16	5250
son of Jehoshaphat the son of *N*	2Kin 9:2	5250
son of *N* conspired against Joram	2Kin 9:14	5250
the driving of Jehu the son of *N*	2Kin 9:20	5250
Jehoram against Jehu the son of *N*	2Chr 22:7	5250

NINE

that Adam lived were *n* hundred	Gen 5:5	8672
the days of Seth were *n* hundred	Gen 5:8	8672
the days of Enos were *n* hundred	Gen 5:11	8672
the days of Cainan were *n* hundred	Gen 5:14	8672
of Jared were *n* hundred sixty	Gen 5:20	8672
n hundred sixty and *n* years	Gen 5:27	8672
the days of Noah were *n* hundred	Gen 9:29	8672
n years, and begat sons and	Gen 11:19	8672
And Nahor lived *n* and twenty years,	Gen 11:24	8672
Abram was ninety years old and *n*	Gen 17:1	8672
Abraham was ninety years old and *n*	Gen 17:24	8672
n talents, and seven hundred and	Ex 38:24	8672
be unto the forty and *n* years	Lev 25:8	8672
n thousand and three hundred	Num 1:23	8672
n thousand and three hundred	Num 2:13	8672
And on the fifth day *n* bullocks	Num 29:26	8672
to give unto the *n* tribes	Num 34:13	8672
n cubits was the length thereof,	Deut 3:11	8672
an inheritance unto the *n* tribes	Josh 13:7	8672
hand of Moses, for the *n* tribes	Josh 14:2	8672
all the cities are twenty and *n*	Josh 15:32	8672
n cities with their villages	Josh 15:44	8672
n cities with their villages	Josh 15:54	8672
n cities out of those two tribes	Josh 21:16	8672
for he had *n* hundred chariots of	Judg 4:3	8672
even as *n* hundred chariots of iron,	Judg 4:13	8672
Jerusalem at the end of *n* months	2Sa 24:8	8672
twenty and *n* years in Jerusalem	2Kin 14:2	8672
of Jabesh began to reign in the *n*	2Kin 15:13	8672
In the *n* and thirtieth year of	2Kin 15:17	8672
in Samaria over Israel *n* years	2Kin 17:1	8672
twenty and *n* years in Jerusalem	2Kin 18:2	8672
and Eliada, and Eliphelet, *n*	1Chr 3:8	8672
n hundred and fifty and six	1Chr 9:9	8672
twenty and *n* years in Jerusalem	2Chr 25:1	8672
twenty years old, and he reigned *n*	2Chr 29:1	8672
a thousand chargers of silver, *n*	Ezr 1:9	8672
of Zattu, *n* hundred forty and five	Ezr 2:8	8672
n hundred seventy and three	Ezr 2:36	8672
in all an hundred thirty and *n*	Ezr 2:42	8672
Senaah, three thousand *n* hundred	Neh 7:38	8672
n hundred seventy and three	Neh 7:39	8672
n parts to dwell in other cities	Neh 11:1	8672
n hundred twenty and eight	Neh 11:8	8672
doth he not leave the ninety and *n*	Mt 18:12	1768
ninety and *n* which went not astray	Mt 18:13	1768
n in the wilderness, and go after	Lk 15:4	1768
n just persons, which need no	Lk 15:7	1768
but where are the *n*	Lk 17:17	1767

NINETEEN

n years, and begat sons and	Gen 11:25	8672,6240
n cities with their villages	Josh 19:38	8672,6240
lacked of David's servants *n* men	2Sa 2:30	8672,6240

NINETEENTH

which is the *n* year of king	2Kin 25:8	8672,6240
The *n* to Pethahiah, the twentieth	1Chr 24:16	8672,6240
The *n* to Mallothi, he, his sons,	1Chr 25:26	8672,6240
month, which was the *n* year of	Jer 52:12	8672,6240

NINETY

And Enos lived *n* years, and begat	Gen 5:9	8673
Mahalaleel were eight hundred *n*	Gen 5:17	8673
he begat Noah five hundred *n*	Gen 5:30	8673
And when Abram was *n* years old	Gen 17:1	8673
that is *n* years old, bear	Gen 17:17	8673
And Abraham was *n* years old	Gen 17:24	8673
Now Eli was *n* and eight years old	1Sa 4:15	8673
their brethren, six hundred and *n*	1Chr 9:6	8673
children of Ater of Hezekiah, *n*	Ezr 2:16	8673
The children of Gibbar, *n*	Ezr 2:20	8673
servants, were three hundred *n*	Ezr 2:58	8673
twelve bullocks for all Israel, *n*	Ezr 8:35	8673
children of Ater of Hezekiah, *n*	Neh 7:21	8673
The children of Gibeon, *n*	Neh 7:25	8673
servants, were three hundred *n*	Neh 7:60	8673
And there were *n* and six	Jer 52:23	8673
the days, three hundred and *n* days	Eze 4:5	8673
n days shalt thou eat thereof	Eze 4:9	8673
and the length thereof *n* cubits	Eze 41:12	8673
a thousand two hundred and *n* days	Dan 12:11	8673
astray, doth he not leave the *n*	Mt 18:12	1768
more of that sheep, than of the *n*	Mt 18:13	1768
one of them, doth not leave the *n*	Lk 15:4	1768
that repenteth, more than over *n*	Lk 15:7	1768

NINEVE (nen'-e-ve) See NINEVEH, NINEVITES. *Same as Nineveh.*

The men of *N* shall rise up in the	Lk 11:32	3535

NINEVEH (nin'-e-veh) See NINEVE. *Capital of Assyria.*

went forth Asshur, and builded *N*	Gen 10:11	5210
And Resen between *N* and Calah	Gen 10:12	5210
went and returned, and dwelt at *N*	2Kin 19:36	5210
went and returned, and dwelt at *N*	Is 37:37	5210
Arise, go to *N*, that great city,	Jonah 1:2	5210
Arise, go unto *N*, that great city	Jonah 3:2	5210
So Jonah arose, and went unto *N*	Jonah 3:3	5210
Now *N* was an exceeding great city	Jonah 3:3	5210
days, and *N* shall be overthrown	Jonah 3:4	5210
So the people of *N* believed God	Jonah 3:5	5210
For word came unto the king of *N*	Jonah 3:6	5210
published through *N* by the decree	Jonah 3:7	5210
And should not I spare *N*, that	Jonah 4:11	5210
The burden of *N*	Nah 1:1	5210
But *N* is of old like a pool of	Nah 2:8	5210
thee, and say, *N* is laid waste	Nah 3:7	5210
will make *N* a desolation, and dry	Zeph 2:13	5210
The men of *N* shall rise in	Mt 12:41	3536

NINEVITES (nin'-e-vites) *Inhabitants of Nineveh.*

as Jonas was a sign unto the *N*	Lk 11:30	3536

NINTH

in the *n* day of the month at even	Lev 23:32	8672
yet of old fruit until the *n* year	Lev 25:22	8671
On the *n* day Abidan the son of	Num 7:60	8671
In the *n* year of Hoshea the king	2Kin 17:6	8671
that is the *n* year of Hoshea king	2Kin 18:10	8672
pass in the *n* year of his reign	2Kin 25:1	8671
on the *n* day of the fourth month	2Kin 25:3	8672
Johanan the eighth, Elzabad the *n*	1Chr 12:12	8671
The *n* to Jeshua, the tenth to	1Chr 24:11	8671
The *n* to Mattaniah, he, his sons,	1Chr 25:16	8671
The *n* captain for the *n* month	1Chr 27:12	8671
for the *n* month was Abiezer the	1Chr 27:12	8671
n year of his reign was diseased	2Chr 16:12	8672
It was the *n* month, on the	Ezr 10:9	8671
king of Judah, in the *n* month	Jer 36:9	8671
in the winterhouse in the *n* month	Jer 36:22	8671
In the *n* year of Zedekiah king of	Jer 39:1	8671
the *n* day of the month, the city	Jer 39:2	8672
pass in the *n* year of his reign	Jer 52:4	8671
in the *n* day of the month, the	Jer 52:6	8672
Again in the *n* year, in the tenth	Eze 24:1	8671
and twentieth day of the *n* month	Hag 2:10	8671
and twentieth day of the *n* month	Hag 2:18	8671
in the fourth day of the *n* month	Zec 7:1	8671
sixth and *n* hour, and did likewise	Mt 20:5	1766
over all the land unto the *n* hour	Mt 27:45	1766
about the *n* hour Jesus cried with	Mt 27:46	1766
the whole land until the *n* hour	Mk 15:33	1766
at the *n* hour Jesus cried with a	Mk 15:34	1766
all the earth until the *n* hour	Lk 23:44	1766
hour of prayer, being the *n* hour	Acts 3:1	1766
n hour of the day an angel of God	Acts 10:3	1766
at the *n* hour I prayed in my	Acts 10:30	1766
the *n*, a topaz	Rev 21:20	1766

NISAN (ni'-san) See ABIB. *First month of the Hebrew year.*

And it came to pass in the month *N*	Neh 2:1	5212
first month, that is, the month *N*	Est 3:7	5212

N

NISROCH (nis'-rok) *An Assyrian god.*
in the house of *N* his god..........................2Kin 19:37   5268
in the house of *N* his god..........................Is 37:38   5268

NITRE
weather, and as vinegar upon *n*..............Prov 25:20   5427
For though thou wash thee with *n*..............Jer 2:22   5427

NO (*Also see* APPENDIX.) *A city on the Nile.*
I will punish the multitude of *N*..............Jer 46:25   4996
and will execute judgments in *N*..............Eze 30:14   4996
I will cut off the multitude of *N*..............Eze 30:15   4996
N shall be rent asunder, and Noph........Eze 30:16   4996
Art thou better than populous *N*............Nah 3:8   4996

NOADIAH (no-a-di'-ah)
  1. Son of Binnui.
N the son of Binnui, Levites ....Ezr 8:33   5129
  2. An opponent of Nehemiah.
works, and on the prophetess *N*..............Neh 6:14   5129

NOAH (no'-ah) See NOAH'S, NOE.
  1. Son of Lamech; built the ark.
And he called his name *N*, saying, ...Gen 5:29   5146
he begat *N* five hundred ninety ....Gen 5:30   5146
N was five hundred years old ....Gen 5:32   5146
N begat Shem, Ham, and Japheth.........Gen 5:32   5146
But *N* found grace in the eyes of ....Gen 6:8   5146
These are the generations of *N* ....Gen 6:9   5146
N was a just man and perfect in ....Gen 6:9   5146
generations, and *N* walked with God .....Gen 6:9   5146
N begat three sons, Shem, Ham, and.....Gen 6:10   5146
And God said unto *N*, The end of ....Gen 6:13   5146
Thus did *N* ....Gen 6:22   5146
And the LORD said unto *N*, Come ....Gen 7:1   5146
N did according unto all that the ....Gen 7:5   5146
N was six hundred years old when ....Gen 7:6   5146
N went in, and his sons, and his ....Gen 7:7   5146
two unto *N* into the ark, the male...........Gen 7:9   5146
female, as God had commanded *N* ....Gen 7:9   5146
In the selfsame day entered *N* ....Gen 7:13   5146
and Ham, and Japheth, the sons of *N* ....Gen 7:13   5146
they went in unto *N* into the ark.............Gen 7:15   5146
N only remained alive, and they.............Gen 7:23   5146
And God remembered *N*, and every ......Gen 8:1   5146
that *N* opened the window of the ....Gen 8:6   5146
so *N* knew that the waters were..............Gen 8:11   5146
N removed the covering of the ark ....Gen 8:13   5146
And God spake unto *N*, saying, ...Gen 8:15   5146
N went forth, and his sons, and his ....Gen 8:18   5146
N builded an altar unto the LORD ....Gen 8:20   5146
And God blessed *N* and his sons, and.....Gen 9:1   5146
And God spake unto *N*, and to his ....Gen 9:8   5146
And God said unto *N*, This is the ....Gen 9:17   5146
And the sons of *N*, that went forth........Gen 9:18   5146
These are the three sons of *N* ....Gen 9:19   5146
N began to be an husbandman, and.......Gen 9:20   5146
N awoke from his wine, and knew ....Gen 9:24   5146
N lived after the flood three ....Gen 9:28   5146
all the days of *N* were nine ....Gen 9:29   5146
the generations of the sons of *N*..............Gen 10:1   5146
are the families of the sons of *N* ....Gen 10:32   5146
N, Shem, Ham, and Japheth 1Chr 1:4   5146
is as the waters of *N* unto me..................Is 54:9   5146
of *N* should no more go over the ....Is 54:9   5146
Though these three men, *N* ....Eze 14:14   5146
Though *N*, Daniel, and Job, were in.......Eze 14:20   5146
By faith *N*, being warned of God ....Heb 11:7   3575
of God waited in the days of *N* 1Pet 3:20   3575
but saved *N* the eighth person, a............2Pet 2:5   3575
  2. A daughter of Zelophehad.
of Zelophehad were Mahlah, and *N*........Num 26:33   5270
Mahlah, *N*, and Hoglah, and Milcah,.....Num 27:1   5270
and Hoglah, and Milcah, and *N* ....Num 36:11   5270
of his daughters, Mahlah, and *N* ....Josh 17:3   5270

NOAH'S (no'-ahz) *Refers to Noah 1.*
the six hundredth year of *N* life ....Gen 7:11   5146
N wife, and the three wives of his ....Gen 7:13   5146

NO-AMON See NO.

NOB (nob) *A Levitical city in Benjamin.*
Then came David to *N* to Ahimelech......1Sa 21:1   5011
saw the son of Jesse coming to *N* 1Sa 22:9   5011
house, the priests that were in *N* 1Sa 22:11   5011
And *N*, the city of the priests, ...1Sa 22:19   5011
And at Anathoth, *N*, Ananiah,.................Neh 11:32   5011
yet shall he remain at *N* that day...........Is 10:32   5011

NOBAH (no'-bah) See KENAH, NOPHAH.
  1. A Manassite who captured an Amorite city.
N went and took Kenah, and the ....Num 32:42   5025
villages thereof, and called it *N* ....Num 32:42   5025

  2. A city in the Trachonitis.
dwelt in tents on the east of *N* ....Judg 8:11   5025

NOBLE
n Asnapper brought over, and set ....Ezr 4:10   3358
one of the king's most *n* princes ....Est 6:9   6579
Yet I had planted thee a *n* vine ....Jer 2:21   2104
These were more *n* than those in ....Acts 17:11   2104
places, most *n* Felix, with all.................Acts 24:3   2908
said, I am not mad, most *n* Festus ....Acts 26:25   2908
not many mighty, not many *n* 1Cor 1:26   2104

NOBLEMAN
A certain *n* went into a far..............Lk 19:12   2104,444
And there was a certain *n*, whose ....Jn 4:46   937
The *n* saith unto him, Sir, come ....Jn 4:49   937

NOBLES
upon the *n* of the children of..................Ex 24:11   678
the *n* of the people digged it, by ....Num 21:18   5081
over the *n* among the people ....Judg 5:13   117
to the *n* that were in his city,.................1Kin 21:8   2715
the *n* who were the inhabitants in 1Kin 21:11   2715
captains of hundreds, and the *n* 2Chr 23:20   117
nor to the priests, nor to the *n* ....Neh 2:16   2715
but their *n* put not their necks................Neh 3:5   117
and rose up, and said unto the *n* ....Neh 4:14   2715
And I said unto the *n*, and to the ....Neh 4:19   2715
with myself, and I rebuked the *n* ....Neh 5:7   2715
Moreover in those days the *n* of ....Neh 6:17   2715
heart to gather together the *n* ....Neh 7:5   2715
clave to their brethren, their *n*...............Neh 10:29   117
I contended with the *n* of Judah ....Neh 13:17   2715
power of Persia and Media, the *n* ....Est 1:3   6579
The *n* held their peace, and their ....Job 29:10   5057
Make their *n* like Oreb, and like............Ps 83:11   5081
their *n* with fetters of iron ....Ps 149:8   3513
By me princes rule, and *n*, even ....Prov 8:16   5081
when thy king is the son of *n*.................Eccl 10:17   2715
may go into the gates of the *n* ....Is 13:2   5081
They shall call the *n* thereof to ....Is 34:12   2715
and have brought down all their *n* ....Is 43:14   1281
their *n* have sent their little...................Jer 14:3   117
all the *n* of Judah and Jerusalem ....Jer 27:20   2715
their *n* shall be of themselves, ...Jer 30:21   117
Babylon slew all the *n* of Judah.............Jer 39:6   2715
the decree of the king and his *n* ....Jonah 3:7   1419
thy *n* shall dwell in the dust...................Nah 3:18   117

NOD (nod) *A land east of Eden.*
LORD, and dwelt in the land of *N*............Gen 4:16   5113

NODAB (no'-dab) *Name of tribe east of the Jordan.*
with Jetur, and Nephish, and *N*..............1Chr 5:19   5114

NOE (no'-e) See NOAH. *Greek form of Noah.*
But as the days of *N* were ....Mt 24:37   3575
until the day that *N* entered into ....Mt 24:38   3575
of Sem, which was the son of *N* ....Lk 3:36   3575
And as it was in the days of *N*...............Lk 17:26   3575
until the day that *N* entered into ....Lk 17:27   3575

NOGAH (no'-gah) *A son of David.*
And *N*, and Nepheg, and Japhia, ...1Chr 3:7   5052
And *N*, and Nepheg, and Japhia, ...1Chr 14:6   5052

NOHAH (no'-hah) *A son of Benjamin.*
N the fourth, and Rapha the fifth 1Chr 8:2   5119

NOISE
the *n* of the trumpet, and the..................Ex 20:18   6963
when Joshua heard the *n* of the..............Ex 32:17   6963
There is a *n* of war in the camp..............Ex 32:17   6963
but the *n* of them that sing do I..............Ex 32:18   6963
nor make any *n* with your voice, ...Josh 6:10   8085
the *n* of archers in the places of ....Judg 5:11   6963
heard the *n* of the shout, they 1Sa 4:6   6963
What meaneth the *n* of this great 1Sa 4:6   6963
Eli heard the *n* of the crying 1Sa 4:14   6963
What meaneth the *n* of this tumult 1Sa 4:14   6963
that the *n* that was in the host 1Sa 14:19   1995
Wherefore is this *n* of the city................1Kin 1:41   6963
This is the *n* that ye have heard.............1Kin 1:45   6963
Syrians to hear a *n* of chariots 2Kin 7:6   6963
a *n* of horses, even the *n* of 2Kin 7:6   6963
Athaliah heard the *n* of the guard 2Kin 11:13   6963
making a *n* with psalteries and..............1Chr 15:28   8085
heard the *n* of the people running 2Chr 23:12   6963
n of the shout of joy from the ....Ezr 3:13   6963
n of the weeping of the people ....Ezr 3:13   6963
and the *n* was heard afar off..................Ezr 3:13   6963
or the *n* of his tabernacle.......................Job 36:29   8663
The *n* thereof sheweth concerning.........Job 36:33   7452
attentively the *n* of his voice ....Job 37:2   7267
play skilfully with a loud *n* ....Ps 33:3   8643

deep at the *n* of thy waterspouts	Ps 42:7	6963
in my complaint, and make a *n*	Ps 55:2	1949
they make a *n* like a dog, and go	Ps 59:6	1993
and let them make a *n* like a dog	Ps 59:14	1993
Which stilleth the *n* of the seas	Ps 65:7	7588
the *n* of their waves, and the	Ps 65:7	7588
Make a joyful *n* unto God, all ye	Ps 66:1	
make a joyful *n* unto the God of	Ps 81:1	
than the *n* of many waters	Ps 93:4	6963
let us make a joyful *n* to the	Ps 95:1	
make a joyful *n* unto him with	Ps 95:2	
Make a joyful *n* unto the LORD	Ps 98:4	
make a loud *n*, and rejoice, and	Ps 98:4	6476
make a joyful *n* before the LORD	Ps 98:6	
Make a joyful *n* unto the LORD	Ps 100:1	
of the warrior is with confused *n*	Is 9:5	
The *n* of a multitude in the	Is 13:4	6963
a tumultuous *n* of the kingdoms of	Is 13:4	6963
the grave, and the *n* of thy viols	Is 14:11	1998
a *n* like the *n* of the seas	Is 17:12	1993
the *n* of them that rejoice endeth	Is 24:8	7588
that he who fleeth from the *n* of	Is 24:18	6963
bring down the *n* of strangers	Is 25:5	7588
and with earthquake, and great *n*	Is 29:6	6963
abase himself for the *n* of them	Is 31:4	1995
At the *n* of the tumult the people	Is 33:3	6963
A voice of *n* from the city, a	Is 66:6	7588
my heart maketh a *n* in me	Jer 4:19	1993
flee for the *n* of the horsemen	Jer 4:29	6963
the *n* of the bruit is come, and a	Jer 10:22	6963
with the *n* of a great tumult he	Jer 11:16	6963
A *n* shall come even to the ends	Jer 25:31	7588
Pharaoh king of Egypt is but a *n*	Jer 46:17	7588
At the *n* of the stamping of the	Jer 47:3	6963
is moved at the *n* of their fall	Jer 49:21	6963
at the cry the *n* thereof was	Jer 49:21	6963
At the *n* of the taking of Babylon	Jer 50:46	6963
a *n* of their voice is uttered	Jer 51:55	7588
they have made a *n* in the house	Lam 2:7	6963
I heard the *n* of their wings,	Eze 1:24	6963
like the *n* of great waters, as	Eze 1:24	6963
of speech, as the *n* of an host	Eze 1:24	6963
I heard also the *n* of the wings	Eze 3:13	6963
the *n* of the wheels over against	Eze 3:13	6963
them, and a *n* of a great rushing	Eze 3:13	6963
thereof, by the *n* of his roaring	Eze 19:7	6963
shake at the *n* of the horsemen	Eze 26:10	6963
I will cause the *n* of thy songs	Eze 26:13	1995
and as I prophesied, there was a *n*	Eze 37:7	6963
voice was like a *n* of many waters	Eze 43:2	6963
Like the *n* of chariots on the	Joel 2:5	6963
like the *n* of a flame of fire	Joel 2:5	6963
away from me the *n* of thy songs	Amos 5:23	1995
they shall make great *n* by reason	Mic 2:12	1949
The *n* of a whip, and the *n* of	Nah 3:2	6963
that there shall be the *n* of a	Zeph 1:10	6963
and make a *n* as through wine	Zec 9:15	6963
and the people making a *n*,	Mt 9:23	2350
shall pass away with a great *n*	2Pet 3:10	4500
as it were the *n* of thunder	Rev 6:1	5456

NOISED

his fame was *n* throughout all the	Josh 6:27	
it was *n* that he was in the house	Mk 2:1	*191*
all these sayings were *n* abroad	Lk 1:65	*1255*
Now when this was *n* abroad	Acts 2:6	*1096,5408*

NOISOME

fowler, and from the *n* pestilence	Ps 91:3	1942
If I cause *n* beasts to pass	Eze 14:15	7451
the *n* beast, and the pestilence,	Eze 14:21	7451
and there fell a *n* and grievous	Rev 16:2	2556

NON *(non)* See NUN. *Son of Elishama.*

N his son, Jehoshuah his son	1Chr 7:27	5126

NONE See APPENDIX.

NOON

these men shall dine with me at *n*	Gen 43:16	6672
present against Joseph came at *n*	Gen 43:25	6672
who lay on a bed at *n*	2Sa 4:5	6672
of Baal from morning even until *n*	1Kin 18:26	6672
And it came to pass at *n*, that	1Kin 18:27	6672
And they went out at *n*	1Kin 20:16	6672
he sat on her knees till *n*	2Kin 4:20	6672
Evening, and morning, and at *n*	Ps 55:17	6672
makest thy flock to rest at *n*	Song 1:7	6672
arise, and let us go up at *n*	Jer 6:4	6672
cause the sun to go down at *n*	Amos 8:9	6672
come nigh unto Damascus about *n*	Acts 22:6	3314

NOONDAY

And thou shalt grope at *n*, as the	Deut 28:29	6672
grope in the *n* as in the night	Job 5:14	6672
age shall be clearer than the *n*	Job 11:17	6672
light, and thy judgment as the *n*	Ps 37:6	6672
the destruction that wasteth at *n*	Ps 91:6	6672
the night in the midst of the *n*	Is 16:3	6672
and thy darkness be as the *n*	Is 58:10	6672
we stumble at *n* as in the night	Is 59:10	6672
of the young men a spoiler at *n*	Jer 15:8	6672
shall drive out Ashdod at the *n*	Zeph 2:4	6672

NOONTIDE

morning, and the shouting at *n*	Jer 20:16	6256,6672

NOPH *(nof)* See MEMPHIS. *Same as Memphis.*

the princes of *N* are deceived	Is 19:13	5297
Also the children of *N* and	Jer 2:16	5297
Migdol, and at Tahpanhes, and at *N*	Jer 44:1	5297
in Migdol, and publish in *N*	Jer 46:14	5297
for *N* shall be waste and desolate	Jer 46:19	5297
their images to cease out of *N*	Eze 30:13	5297
N shall have distresses daily	Eze 30:16	5297

NOPHAH *(no'-fah)* See NOBAH. *A city in Sihon.*

have laid them waste even unto *N*	Num 21:30	5302

NOR See APPENDIX.

NORTH

west, and to the east, and to the *n*	Gen 28:14	6828
the *n* side there shall be twenty	Ex 26:20	6828
shalt put the table on the *n* side	Ex 26:35	6828
likewise for the *n* side in length	Ex 27:11	6828
which is toward the *n* corner	Ex 36:25	6828
for the *n* side the hangings were	Ex 38:11	6828
be on the *n* side by their armies	Num 2:25	6828
And this shall be your *n* border	Num 34:7	6828
this shall be your *n* border	Num 34:9	6828
on the *n* side two thousand cubits	Num 35:5	6828
and pitched on the *n* side of Ai	Josh 8:11	6828
that was on the *n* of the city	Josh 8:13	6828
were on the *n* of the mountains	Josh 11:2	6828
their border in the *n* quarter was	Josh 15:5	6828
along by the *n* of Beth-arabah	Josh 15:6	6828
which is Chesalon, on the *n* side	Josh 15:10	6828
sea to Michmethah on the *n* side	Josh 16:6	6828
was on the *n* of the river	Josh 17:9	6828
met together in Asher on the *n*	Josh 17:10	6828
abide in their coasts on the *n*	Josh 18:5	6828
their border on the *n* side was	Josh 18:12	6828
the side of Jericho on the *n* side	Josh 18:12	6828
the valley of the giants on the *n*	Josh 18:16	6828
And was drawn from the *n*, and went	Josh 18:17	6828
of the border were at the *n* bay	Josh 18:19	6828
it on the *n* side to Hannathon	Josh 19:14	6828
toward the *n* side of Beth-emek	Josh 19:27	6828
on the *n* side of the hill	Josh 24:30	6828
on the *n* side of the hill Gaash	Judg 2:9	6828
were on the *n* side of them	Judg 7:1	6828
which is on the *n* side of Beth-el	Judg 21:19	6828
oxen, three looking toward the *n*	1Kin 7:25	6828
put it on the *n* side of the altar	2Kin 16:14	6828
porters, toward the east, west, *n*	1Chr 9:24	6828
oxen, three looking toward the *n*	2Chr 4:4	6828
out the *n* over the empty place	Job 26:7	6828
and cold out of the *n*	Job 37:9	4215
Fair weather cometh out of the *n*	Job 37:22	6828
mount Zion, on the sides of the *n*	Ps 48:2	6828
The *n* and the south thou hast	Ps 89:12	6828
and from the west, from the *n*	Ps 107:3	6828
The *n* wind driveth away rain	Prov 25:23	6828
and turneth about unto the *n*	Eccl 1:6	6828
toward the south, or toward the *n*	Eccl 11:3	6828
Awake, O *n* wind	Song 4:16	6828
in the sides of the *n*	Is 14:13	6828
shall come from the *n* a smoke	Is 14:31	6828
I have raised up one from the *n*	Is 41:25	6828
I will say to the *n*, Give up	Is 43:6	6828
and, lo, these from the *n* and from	Is 49:12	6828
the face thereof is toward the *n*	Jer 1:13	6828
Out of the *n* an evil shall break	Jer 1:14	6828
families of the kingdoms of the *n*	Jer 1:15	6828
proclaim these words toward the *n*	Jer 3:12	6828
n to the land that I have given	Jer 3:18	6828
for I will bring evil from the *n*	Jer 4:6	6828
for evil appeareth out of the *n*	Jer 6:1	6828
people cometh from the *n* country	Jer 6:22	6828
commotion out of the *n* country	Jer 10:22	6828
behold them that come from the *n*	Jer 13:20	6828
of Israel from the land of the *n*	Jer 16:15	6828
of Israel out of the *n* country	Jer 23:8	6828
and take all the families of the *n*	Jer 25:9	6828

N

NORTHERN (cont.)

And all the kings of the *n*	Jer 25:26	6828
bring them from the *n* country	Jer 31:8	6828
fall toward the *n* by the river	Jer 46:6	6828
hosts hath a sacrifice in the *n*	Jer 46:10	6828
it cometh out of the *n*	Jer 46:20	6828
the hand of the people of the *n*	Jer 46:24	6828
waters rise up out of the *n*	Jer 47:2	6828
For out of the *n* there cometh up	Jer 50:3	6828
great nations from the *n* country	Jer 50:9	6828
a people shall come from the *n*	Jer 50:41	6828
shall come unto her from the *n*	Jer 51:48	6828
a whirlwind came out of the *n*	Eze 1:4	6828
gate, that looketh toward the *n*	Eze 8:3	6828
eyes now the way toward the *n*	Eze 8:5	6828
up mine eyes the way toward the *n*	Eze 8:5	6828
house which was toward the *n*	Eze 8:14	6828
gate, which lieth toward the *n*	Eze 9:2	6828
to the *n* shall be burned therein	Eze 20:47	6828
all flesh from the south to the *n*	Eze 21:4	6828
a king of kings, from the *n*	Eze 26:7	6828
There be the princes of the *n*	Eze 32:30	6828
of Togarmah of the *n* quarters	Eze 38:6	6828
from thy place out of the *n* parts	Eze 38:15	6828
thee to come up from the *n* parts	Eze 39:2	6828
court that looked toward the *n*	Eze 40:20	6828
against the gate toward the *n*	Eze 40:23	6828
And he brought me to the *n* gate	Eze 40:35	6828
up to the entry of the *n* gate	Eze 40:40	6828
was at the side of the *n* gate	Eze 40:44	6828
having the prospect toward the *n*	Eze 40:44	6828
toward the *n* is for the priests	Eze 40:46	6828
was left, one door toward the *n*	Eze 41:11	6828
utter court, the way toward the *n*	Eze 42:1	6828
before the building toward the *n*	Eze 42:1	6828
an hundred cubits was the *n* door	Eze 42:2	6828
and their doors toward the *n*	Eze 42:4	6828
chambers which were toward the *n*	Eze 42:11	6828
The *n* chambers and the south	Eze 42:13	6828
He measured the *n* side, five	Eze 42:17	6828
of the *n* gate before the house	Eze 44:4	6828
entereth in by the way of the *n*	Eze 46:9	6828
go forth by the way of the *n* gate	Eze 46:9	6828
which looked toward the *n*	Eze 46:19	6828
of the land toward the *n* side	Eze 47:15	6828
the *n* northward, and the border of	Eze 47:17	6828
And this is the *n* side	Eze 47:17	6828
From the *n* end to the coast of	Eze 48:1	6828
toward the *n* five and twenty	Eze 48:10	6828
the *n* side four thousand and five	Eze 48:16	6828
shall be toward the *n* two hundred	Eze 48:17	6828
out of the city on the *n* side	Eze 48:30	6828
of the *n* to make an agreement	Dan 11:6	6828
the fortress of the king of the *n*	Dan 11:7	6828
more years than the king of the *n*	Dan 11:8	6828
him, even with the king of the *n*	Dan 11:11	6828
the king of the *n* shall return	Dan 11:13	6828
So the king of the *n* shall come	Dan 11:15	6828
the king of the *n* shall come	Dan 11:40	6828
out of the *n* shall trouble him	Dan 11:44	6828
from the *n* even to the east, they	Amos 8:12	6828
out his hand against the *n*	Zeph 2:13	6828
and flee from the land of the *n*	Zec 2:6	6828
go forth into the *n* country	Zec 6:6	6828
these that go toward the *n*	Zec 6:8	6828
my spirit in the *n* country	Zec 6:8	6828
shall remove toward the *n*	Zec 14:4	6828
and from the west, and from the *n*	Lk 13:29	1005
toward the south west and *n* west	Acts 27:12	5566
on the *n* three gates	Rev 21:13	1005

NORTHERN

Shall iron break the *n* iron	Jer 15:12	6828
far off from you the *n* army	Joel 2:20	6830

NORTHWARD

from the place where thou art *n*	Gen 13:14	6828
upon the side of the tabernacle *n*	Ex 40:22	6828
of the altar *n* before the LORD	Lev 1:11	6828
on the side of the tabernacle *n*	Num 3:35	6828
turn you *n*	Deut 2:3	6828
lift up thine eyes westward, and *n*	Deut 3:27	6828
even unto the borders of Ekron *n*	Josh 13:3	6828
from the valley of Achor, and so *n*	Josh 15:7	6828
end of the valley of the giants *n*	Josh 15:8	6828
went out unto the side of Ekron *n*	Josh 15:11	6828
n it was Manasseh's, and the sea	Josh 17:10	6828
the side over against Arabah *n*	Josh 18:18	6828
to the side of Beth-hoglah *n*	Josh 18:19	6828
themselves together, and went *n*	Judg 12:1	6828
situate *n* over against Michmash	1Sa 14:5	6828
and his lot came out *n*	1Chr 26:14	6828
n four a day, southward four a	1Chr 26:17	6828

behold *n* at the gate of the altar	Eze 8:5	6828
an hundred cubits eastward and *n*	Eze 40:19	6828
me out of the way of the gate *n*	Eze 47:2	6828
of Damascus, and the north *n*	Eze 47:17	6828
the border of Damascus *n*	Eze 48:1	6828
three gates *n*; one gate	Eze 48:31	6828
the ram pushing westward, and *n*	Dan 8:4	6828

NOSE

a lame, or he that hath a flat *n*	Lev 21:18	2763
I will put my hook in thy *n*	2Kin 19:28	639
his *n* pierceth through snares	Job 40:24	639
Canst thou put an hook into his *n*	Job 41:2	639
the wringing of the *n* bringeth	Prov 30:33	639
thy *n* is as the tower of Lebanon	Song 7:4	639
and the smell of thy *n* like apples	Song 7:8	639
The rings, and *n* jewels	Is 3:21	639
will I put my hook in thy *n*	Is 37:29	639
These are a smoke in my *n*	Is 65:5	639
they put the branch to their *n*	Eze 8:17	639
they shall take away thy *n*	Eze 23:25	639

NOSES

n have they, but they smell not	Ps 115:6	639
stop the *n* of the passengers	Eze 39:11	

NOSTRILS

breathed into his *n* the breath of	Gen 2:7	639
All in whose *n* was the breath of	Gen 7:22	639
with the blast of thy *n* the	Ex 15:8	639
until it come out at your *n*	Num 11:20	639
went up a smoke out of his *n*	2Sa 22:9	639
the blast of the breath of his *n*	2Sa 22:16	639
breath of his *n* are they consumed	Job 4:9	639
and the spirit of God is in my *n*	Job 27:3	639
the glory of his *n* is terrible	Job 39:20	5170
Out of his *n* goeth smoke, as out	Job 41:20	5156
went up a smoke out of his *n*	Ps 18:8	639
the blast of the breath of thy *n*	Ps 18:15	639
man, whose breath is in his *n*	Is 2:22	639
The breath of our *n*, the anointed	Lam 4:20	639
your camps to come up unto your *n*	Amos 4:10	639

NOT See APPENDIX.

NOTABLE

the goat had a *n* horn between his	Dan 8:5	2380
for it came up four *n* ones toward	Dan 8:8	2380
And they had then a *n* prisoner	Mt 27:16	1978
great and *n* day of the Lord come	Acts 2:20	2016
for that indeed a *n* miracle hath	Acts 4:16	1110

NOTE

n it in a book, that it may be	Is 30:8	2710
who are of *n* among the apostles	Rom 16:7	1978
n that man, and have no company	2Th 3:14	4593

NOTED

is *n* in the scripture of truth	Dan 10:21	7559

NOTHING See APPENDIX.

NOTICE

And all the people took *n* of it	2Sa 3:36	5234
bounty, whereof ye had *n* before	2Cor 9:5	4293

NOTWITHSTANDING

N they hearkened not unto Moses	Ex 16:20	
N, if he continue a day or two,	Ex 21:21	389
N the cities of the Levites, and	Lev 25:32	
N no devoted thing, that a man	Lev 27:28	389
N the children of Korah died not	Num 26:11	
N the land shall be divided by	Num 26:55	
N ye would not go up, but	Deut 1:26	
N thou mayest kill and eat flesh	Deut 12:15	7535
N, if the land of your possession	Josh 22:19	389
n the journey that thou takest	Judg 4:9	657
n yet Jotham the youngest son of	Judg 9:5	
N they hearkened not unto the	1Sa 2:25	
n, if there be in me iniquity,	1Sa 20:8	
n the princes of the Philistines	1Sa 29:9	389
N the king's word prevailed	2Sa 24:4	
N in thy days I will not do it	1Kin 11:12	389
N they would not hear, but	2Kin 17:14	
N the LORD turned not from the	2Kin 23:26	389
N thou shalt not build the house	2Chr 6:9	7535
N Hezekiah humbled himself for	2Chr 32:26	
n I have spoken unto you, rising	Jer 35:14	
N the children rebelled against	Eze 20:21	
N the land shall be desolate	Mic 7:13	
n, being warned of God in a dream	Mt 2:22	
n he that is least in the kingdom	Mt 11:11	
N, lest we should offend them, go	Mt 17:27	
n be ye sure of this, that the	Lk 10:11	4133
N in this rejoice not, that the	Lk 10:20	4133
N it pleased Silas to abide there	Acts 15:34	

N, that I be not further tedious .... Acts 24:4
n, every way, whether in pretence .... Phil 1:18   4133
N ye have well done, that ye did .... Phil 4:14   4133
N she shall be saved in 1Ti 2:15
N the Lord stood with me, and 2Ti 4:17
n ye give them not those things .... Jas 2:16
N **I have a few things against** .... Rev 2:20   235

NOUGHT
thou therefore serve me for n .... Gen 29:15   2600
there shall cleave n of the .... Deut 13:17   408,3972
brother, and thou givest him n .... Deut 15:9   3808
destroy you, and to bring you to n .... Deut 28:63   8045
had brought their counsel to n .... Neh 4:15   6565
and said, Doth Job fear God for n .... Job 1:9   2600
of the wicked shall come to n .... Job 8:22   369
the mountain falling cometh to n .... Job 14:18   5034
a pledge from thy brother for n .... Job 22:6   2600
the counsel of the heathen to n .... Ps 33:10   6331
Thou sellest thy people for n .... Ps 44:12   3808,1952
ye have set at n all my counsel .... Prov 1:25   6544
together, and it shall come to n .... Is 8:10   6565
the terrible one is brought to n .... Is 29:20   656
aside the just for a thing of n .... Is 29:21   8414
be as nothing, and as a thing of n .... Is 41:12   657
are of nothing, and your work of n .... Is 41:24   659
I have spent my strength for n .... Is 49:4   8414
Ye have sold yourselves for n .... Is 52:3   2600
my people is taken away for n .... Is 52:5   2600
and divination, and a thing of n .... Jer 14:14   434
and Beth-el shall come to n .... Amos 5:5   205
Ye which rejoice in a thing of n ...... Amos 6:13   3808,1697
that would shut the doors for n .... Mal 1:10
kindle fire on mine altar for n .... Mal 1:10   2600
many things, and be set at n .... Mk 9:12   1847
with his men of war set him at n .... Lk 23:11   1848
was set at n of you builders .... Acts 4:11   1848
were scattered, and brought to n .... Acts 5:36   3762
work of men, it will come to n .... Acts 5:38   2647
craft is in danger to be set at n .... Acts 19:27   557
dost thou set at n thy brother .... Rom 14:10   1848
to bring to n things that are 1Cor 1:28   2673
of this world, that come to n 1Cor 2:6   2673
did we eat any man's bread for n 2Th 3:8   1432
hour so great riches is come to n .... Rev 18:17   2049

NOURISH
And there will I n thee .... Gen 45:11   3557
I will n you, and your little ones .... Gen 50:21   3557
that a man shall n a young cow .... Is 7:21   2421
neither do I n up young men .... Is 23:4   1431
an ash, and the rain doth n it .... Is 44:14   1431

NOURISHED
Joseph n his father, and his .... Gen 47:12   3557
lamb, which he had bought and n up 2Sa 12:3   2421
the LORD hath spoken, I have n .... Is 1:2   1431
she n her whelps among young .... Eze 19:2   7235
n up in his father's house three .... Acts 7:20   397
him up, and n him for her own son .... Acts 7:21   397
was n by the king's country .... Acts 12:20   5142
n up in the words of faith and of 1Ti 4:6   1789
ye have n your hearts, as in a .... Jas 5:5   5142
place, where she is n for a time .... Rev 12:14   5142

NOURISHER
thy life, and a n of thine old age .... Ruth 4:15   3557

NOURISHETH
but n and cherisheth it, even as .... Eph 5:29   1625

NOURISHING
so n them three years, that at .... Dan 1:5   1431

NOURISHMENT
and bands having n ministered .... Col 2:19   2023

NOVICE
Not a n, lest being lifted up 1Ti 3:6   3504

NOW See APPENDIX.

NUMBER
so that if a man can n the dust .... Gen 13:16   4487
stars, if thou be able to n them .... Gen 15:5   5608
and I being few in n, they shall .... Gen 34:30   4557
for it was without n .... Gen 41:49   4557
according to the n of the souls .... Ex 12:4   4373
to the n of your persons .... Ex 16:16   4557
the n of thy days I will fulfil .... Ex 23:26   4557
children of Israel after their n .... Ex 30:12   6485
then he shall n to himself seven .... Lev 15:13   5608
then she shall n to herself seven .... Lev 15:28   5608
sabbath shall ye n fifty days .... Lev 23:16   5608
thou shalt n seven sabbaths of .... Lev 25:8   5608
According to the n of years after .... Lev 25:15   4557

according unto the n of years of .... Lev 25:15   4557
for according to the n of the .... Lev 25:16   4557
be according unto the n of years .... Lev 25:50   4557
your cattle, and make you few in n ...... Lev 26:22
with the n of their names, every .... Num 1:2   4557
Aaron shall n them by their .... Num 1:3   6485
according to the n of the names .... Num 1:18   4557
according to the n of the names .... Num 1:20   4557
according to the n of the names .... Num 1:22   4557
according to the n of the names .... Num 1:24   4557
according to the n of the names .... Num 1:26   4557
according to the n of the names .... Num 1:28   4557
according to the n of the names .... Num 1:30   4557
according to the n of the names .... Num 1:32   4557
according to the n of the names .... Num 1:34   4557
according to the n of the names .... Num 1:36   4557
according to the n of the names .... Num 1:38   4557
according to the n of the names .... Num 1:40   4557
according to the n of the names .... Num 1:42   4557
shalt not n the tribe of Levi .... Num 1:49   6485
N the children of Levi after the .... Num 3:15   6485
old and upward shalt thou n them .... Num 3:15   6485
to the n of all the males .... Num 3:22   4557
In the n of all the males, from a .... Num 3:28   4557
to the n of all the males .... Num 3:34   4557
N all the firstborn of the males .... Num 3:40   6485
take the n of their names .... Num 3:40   4557
firstborn males by the n of names .... Num 3:43   4557
wherewith the odd n of them is to .... Num 3:48   5736
fifty years old shalt thou n them .... Num 4:23   6485
thou shalt n them after their .... Num 4:29   6485
fifty years old shalt thou n them .... Num 4:30   6485
Aaron did n according to the .... Num 4:37   6485
Aaron did n according to the .... Num 4:41   6485
of you, according to your whole n .... Num 14:29   4557
After the n of the days in which .... Num 14:34   4557
According to the n that ye shall .... Num 15:12   4557
to every one according to their n .... Num 15:12   4557
the n of the fourth part of .... Num 23:10   4557
according to the n of names .... Num 26:53   4557
shall be according to their n .... Num 29:18   4557
shall be according to their n .... Num 29:21   4557
shall be according to their n .... Num 29:24   4557
shall be according to their n .... Num 29:27   4557
shall be according to their n .... Num 29:30   4557
shall be according to their n .... Num 29:33   4557
shall be according to their n .... Num 29:37   4557
was in n three hundred thousand .... Num 31:36   4557
left few in n among the heathen .... Deut 4:27   4557
ye were more in n than any people .... Deut 7:7
weeks shalt thou n unto thee .... Deut 16:9   5608
begin to n the seven weeks from .... Deut 16:9   5608
to his fault, by a certain n .... Deut 25:2   4557
And ye shall be left few in n .... Deut 28:62
the n of the children of Israel .... Deut 32:8   4557
according unto the n of the .... Josh 4:5   4557
according to the n of the tribes .... Josh 4:8   4557
and their camels were without n .... Judg 6:5   4557
the n of them that lapped, ... Judg 7:6   4557
and their camels were without n .... Judg 7:12   4557
them wives, according to their n .... Judg 21:23   4557
according to the n of the lords 1Sa 6:4   4557
according to the n of all the 1Sa 6:18   4557
N now, and see who is gone from us 1Sa 14:17   6485
went over by n twelve of Benjamin 2Sa 2:15   4557
six toes, four and twenty in n 2Sa 21:20   4557
to say, Go, n Israel and Judah 2Sa 24:1   4487
n ye the people, that I may know 2Sa 24:2   6485
I may know the n of the people 2Sa 24:2   4557
to n the people of Israel 2Sa 24:4   6485
the n of the people unto the king 2Sa 24:9   4662
according to the n of the tribes 1Kin 18:31   4557
n thee an army, like the army 1Kin 20:25   4487
whose n was in the days of David 1Chr 7:2   4557
the n of them, after their 1Chr 7:9   3187
the n throughout the genealogy of . 1Chr 7:40   4557,3187
this is the n of the mighty men 1Chr 11:11   4557
and provoked David to n Israel 1Chr 21:1   4487
n Israel from Beer-sheba even to 1Chr 21:2   5608
bring the n of them to me, that I 1Chr 21:2   4557
of the n of the people unto David 1Chr 21:5   4662
brass, and the iron, there is no n 1Chr 22:16   4557
their n by their polls, man by 1Chr 23:3   4557
by n of names by their polls 1Chr 23:24   4557
moons, and on the set feasts, by n 1Chr 23:31   4557
the n of the workmen according to 1Chr 25:1   4557
So the n of them, with their 1Chr 25:7   4557
children of Israel after their n 1Chr 27:1   4557
But David took not the n of them 1Chr 27:23   4557
the son of Zeruiah began to n 1Chr 27:24   4487
neither was the n put in the 1Chr 27:24   4557

N

the people were without *n* that	2Chr 12:3	4557
according to the *n* of their	2Chr 26:11	4557
The whole *n* of the chief of the	2Chr 26:12	4557
the *n* of the burnt offerings,	2Chr 29:32	4557
a great *n* of priests sanctified	2Chr 30:24	4557
to the *n* of thirty thousand, and	2Chr 35:7	4557
And this is the *n* of them	Ezr 1:9	4557
The *n* of the men of the people of	Ezr 2:2	4557
the daily burnt offerings by *n*	Ezr 3:4	4557
according to the *n* of the tribes	Ezr 6:17	4510
By *n* and by weight of every one	Ezr 8:34	4557
The *n*, I say, of the men of the	Neh 7:7	4557
On that day the *n* of those that	Est 9:11	4557
according to the *n* of them all	Job 1:5	4557
not come into the *n* of the months	Job 3:6	4557
marvellous things without *n*	Job 5:9	4557
yea, and wonders without *n*	Job 9:10	4557
the *n* of his months are with thee	Job 14:5	4557
the *n* of years is hidden to the	Job 15:20	4557
when the *n* of his months is cut	Job 21:21	4557
Is there any *n* of his armies	Job 25:3	4557
unto him the *n* of my steps	Job 31:37	4557
in pieces mighty men without *n*	Job 34:24	2714
neither can the *n* of his years be	Job 36:26	4557
or because the *n* of thy days is	Job 38:21	4557
Who can *n* the clouds in wisdom	Job 38:37	5608
Canst thou *n* the months that they	Job 39:2	5608
So teach us to *n* our days	Ps 90:12	4487
When they were but a few men in *n*	Ps 105:12	4557
caterpillers, and that without *n*	Ps 105:34	4557
they are more in *n* than the sand	Ps 139:18	
He telleth the *n* of the stars	Ps 147:4	4557
concubines, and virgins without *n*	Song 6:8	4557
the residue of the *n* of archers	Is 21:17	4557
that bringeth out their host by *n*	Is 40:26	4557
the drink offering unto that *n*	Is 65:11	4507
will I *n* you to the sword	Is 65:12	4487
for according to the *n* of thy	Jer 2:28	4557
have forgotten me days without *n*	Jer 2:32	4557
For according to the *n* of thy	Jer 11:13	4557
according to the *n* of the streets	Jer 11:13	4557
Yet a small *n* that escape the	Jer 44:28	4557
according to the *n* of the days	Eze 4:4	4557
according to the *n* of the days	Eze 4:5	4557
according to the *n* of the days	Eze 4:9	4557
also take thereof a few in *n*	Eze 5:3	4557
by books the *n* of the years	Dan 9:2	4557
Yet the *n* of the children of	Hos 1:10	4557
my land, strong, and without *n*	Joel 1:6	4557
slain, and a great *n* of carcases	Nah 3:3	
a great *n* of people, blind	Mk 10:46	3793
being of the *n* of the twelve	Lk 22:3	706
down, in *n* about five thousand	Jn 6:10	706
(the *n* of names together were	Acts 1:15	3793
the *n* of the men was about five	Acts 4:4	706
to whom a *n* of men, about four	Acts 5:36	706
when the *n* of the disciples was	Acts 6:1	
the *n* of the disciples multiplied	Acts 6:7	706
a great *n* believed, and turned	Acts 11:21	706
faith, and increased in *n* daily	Acts 16:5	706
Though the *n* of the children of	Rom 9:27	706
dare not make ourselves of the *n*	2Cor 10:12	1469
the *n* under threescore years old	1Ti 5:9	2639
the *n* of them was ten thousand	Rev 5:11	706
I heard the *n* of them which were	Rev 7:4	706
multitude, which no man could *n*	Rev 7:9	705
the *n* of the army of the horsemen	Rev 9:16	706
and I heard the *n* of them	Rev 9:16	706
the beast, or the *n* of his name	Rev 13:17	706
count the *n* of the beast	Rev 13:18	706
for it is the *n* of a man	Rev 13:18	706
his *n* is six hundred threescore	Rev 13:18	706
over the *n* of his name, stand on	Rev 15:2	706
the *n* of whom is as the sand of	Rev 20:8	706

NUMBERED

then shall thy seed also be *n*	Gen 13:16	4487
it shall not be *n* for multitude	Gen 16:10	5608
which cannot be *n* for multitude	Gen 32:12	5608
passeth among them that are *n*	Ex 30:13	6485
passeth among them that are *n*	Ex 30:14	6485
were *n* of the congregation was an	Ex 38:25	6485
for every one that went to be *n*	Ex 38:26	6485
so he *n* them in the wilderness of	Num 1:19	6485
Those that were *n* of them	Num 1:21	6485
those that were *n* of them	Num 1:22	6485
Those that were *n* of them	Num 1:23	6485
Those that were *n* of them	Num 1:25	6485
Those that were *n* of them	Num 1:27	6485
Those that were *n* of them	Num 1:29	6485
Those that were *n* of them	Num 1:31	6485

Those that were *n* of them	Num 1:33	6485
Those that were *n* of them	Num 1:35	6485
Those that were *n* of them	Num 1:37	6485
Those that were *n* of them	Num 1:39	6485
Those that were *n* of them	Num 1:41	6485
Those that were *n* of them	Num 1:43	6485
n, which Moses and Aaron *n*	Num 1:44	6485
were *n* of the children of Israel	Num 1:45	6485
Even all they that were *n* were	Num 1:46	6485
fathers were not *n* among them	Num 1:47	6485
and those that were *n* of them	Num 2:4	6485
and those that were *n* thereof	Num 2:6	6485
and those that were *n* thereof	Num 2:8	6485
All that were *n* in the camp of	Num 2:9	6485
and those that were *n* thereof	Num 2:11	6485
and those that were *n* of them	Num 2:13	6485
and those that were *n* of them	Num 2:15	6485
All that were *n* in the camp of	Num 2:16	6485
and those that were *n* of them	Num 2:19	6485
and those that were *n* of them	Num 2:21	6485
and those that were *n* of them	Num 2:23	6485
All that were *n* of the camp of	Num 2:24	6485
and those that were *n* of them	Num 2:26	6485
and those that were *n* of them	Num 2:28	6485
and those that were *n* of them	Num 2:30	6485
All they that were *n* in the camp	Num 2:31	6485
These are those which were *n* of	Num 2:32	6485
all those that were *n* of the	Num 2:32	6485
But the Levites were not *n* among	Num 2:33	6485
Moses *n* them according to the	Num 3:16	6485
Those that were *n* of them	Num 3:22	6485
even those that were *n* of them	Num 3:22	6485
And those that were *n* of them	Num 3:34	6485
All that were *n* of the Levites,	Num 3:39	6485
Aaron *n* at the commandment of the	Num 3:39	6485
Moses *n*, as the LORD commanded	Num 3:42	6485
of those that were *n* of them	Num 3:43	6485
n the sons of the Kohathites	Num 4:34	6485
those that were *n* of them by	Num 4:36	6485
were *n* of the families of the	Num 4:37	6485
those that were *n* of the sons of	Num 4:38	6485
Even those that were *n* of them	Num 4:40	6485
These are they that were *n* of the	Num 4:41	6485
those that were *n* of the families	Num 4:42	6485
Even those that were *n* of them	Num 4:44	6485
These be those that were *n* of the	Num 4:45	6485
Aaron *n* according to the word of	Num 4:45	6485
those that were *n* of the Levites	Num 4:46	6485
and Aaron and the chief of Israel *n*	Num 4:46	6485
Even those that were *n* of them	Num 4:48	6485
they were *n* by the hand of Moses	Num 4:49	6485
thus were they *n* of him, as the	Num 4:49	6485
and were over them that were *n*	Num 7:2	6485
and all that were *n* of you	Num 1:29	6485
they that were *n* of them were	Num 26:7	6485
to those that were *n* of them	Num 26:18	6485
to those that were *n* of them	Num 26:22	6485
to those that were *n* of them	Num 26:25	6485
to those that were *n* of them	Num 26:27	6485
and those that were *n* of them	Num 26:34	6485
to those that were *n* of them	Num 26:37	6485
they that were *n* of them were	Num 26:41	6485
to those that were *n* of them	Num 26:43	6485
to those that were *n* of them	Num 26:47	6485
they that were *n* of them were	Num 26:50	6485
These were the *n* of the children	Num 26:51	6485
to those that were *n* of him	Num 26:54	6485
these are they that were *n* of the	Num 26:57	6485
those that were *n* of them were	Num 26:62	6485
for they were not *n* among the	Num 26:62	6485
are they that were *n* by Moses	Num 26:63	6485
who *n* the children of Israel in	Num 26:63	6485
whom Moses and Aaron the priest *n*	Num 26:64	6485
when they *n* the children of	Num 26:64	6485
n the people, and went up, he and	Josh 8:10	6485
the children of Benjamin were *n*	Judg 20:15	6485
which were *n* seven hundred chosen	Judg 20:15	6485
were *n* four hundred thousand men	Judg 20:17	6485
For the people were *n*, and, behold	Judg 21:9	6485
when he *n* them in Bezek, the	1Sa 11:8	6485
Saul the people that were	1Sa 13:15	6485
And when they had *n*, behold,	1Sa 14:17	6485
n them in Telaim, two hundred	1Sa 15:4	6485
David *n* the people that were with	2Sa 18:1	6485
after that he had *n* the people	2Sa 24:10	5608
that cannot be *n* nor counted for	1Kin 3:8	4487
not be told nor *n* for multitude	1Kin 8:5	4487
Then he *n* the young men of the	1Kin 20:15	6485
after them he *n* all the people,	1Kin 20:15	6485
that Ben-hadad *n* the Syrians	1Kin 20:26	6485
And the children of Israel were *n*	1Kin 20:27	6485

the same time, and *n* all Israel 2Kin 3:6   6485
that commanded the people to be *n* 1Chr 21:17   4487
Now the Levites were *n* from the 1Chr 23:3   5608
were *n* from twenty years old 1Chr 23:27   4557
Solomon *n* all the strangers that 2Chr 2:17   5608
David his father had *n* them 2Chr 2:17   5608
not be told nor *n* for multitude 2Chr 5:6   4487
he *n* them from twenty years old 2Chr 25:5   6485
n them unto Sheshbazzar, the .... Ezr 1:8   5608
them, they are more than can be *n* .... Ps 40:5   5608
that which is wanting cannot be *n* .... Eccl 1:15   4487
ye have in the houses of Jerusalem .... Is 22:10   5608
he was *n* with the transgressors .... Is 53:12   4487
As the host of heaven cannot be *n* .... Jer 33:22   5608
God hath *n* thy kingdom, and .... Dan 5:26   4483
which cannot be measured nor *n* .... Hos 1:10   5608
very hairs of your head are all *n* .... Mt 10:30   705
he was *n* with the transgressors .... Mk 15:28   3049
very hairs of your head are all *n* .... Lk 12:7   705
For he was *n* with us, and had .... Acts 1:17   2674
he was *n* with the eleven apostles .... Acts 1:26   4785

NUMBEREST
unto the Lord, when thou *n* them .... Ex 30:12   6485
among them, when thou *n* them .... Ex 30:12   6485
For now thou *n* my steps .... Job 14:16   5608

NUMBERING
sea, very much, until he left *n* .... Gen 41:49   5608
after the *n* wherewith David his 2Chr 2:17   5610

NUMBERS
these are the *n* of the bands that 1Chr 12:23   4557
these are the *n* of them according 2Chr 17:14   6486
for I know not the *n* thereof .... Ps 71:15   5615

NUN (nun) See Non. *Father of Joshua.*
his servant Joshua, the son of *N* .... Ex 33:11   5126
And Joshua the son of *N*, the .... Num 11:28   5126
of Ephraim, Oshea the son of *N* .... Num 13:8   5126
Oshea the son of *N* Jehoshua .... Num 13:16   5126
And Joshua the son of *N*, and Caleb ...... Num 14:6   5126
Jephunneh, and Joshua the son of *N* ..... Num 14:30   5126
But Joshua the son of *N*, and Caleb .... Num 14:38   5126
Jephunneh, and Joshua the son of *N* ..... Num 26:65   5126
Take thee Joshua the son of *N* .... Num 27:18   5126
Kenezite, and Joshua the son of *N* .... Num 32:12   5126
priest, and Joshua the son of *N* .... Num 32:28   5126

priest, and Joshua the son of *N* .... Num 34:17   5126
But Joshua the son of *N*, which .... Deut 1:38   5126
gave Joshua the son of *N* a charge .... Deut 31:23   5126
he, and Hoshea the son of *N* .... Deut 32:44   5126
Joshua the son of *N* was full of .... Deut 34:9   5126
spake unto Joshua the son of *N* .... Josh 1:1   5126
Joshua the son of *N* sent out of .... Josh 2:1   5126
and came to Joshua the son of *N* .... Josh 2:23   5126
Joshua the son of *N* called the .... Josh 6:6   5126
priest, and Joshua the son of *N* .... Josh 14:1   5126
and before Joshua the son of *N* .... Josh 17:4   5126
to Joshua the son of *N* among them ...... Josh 19:49   5126
priest, and Joshua the son of *N* .... Josh 19:51   5126
and unto Joshua the son of *N* .... Josh 21:1   5126
things, that Joshua the son of *N* .... Josh 24:29   5126
And Joshua the son of *N*, the .... Judg 2:8   5126
he spake by Joshua the son of *N* 1Kin 16:34   5126
of *N* unto that day had not the .... Neh 8:17   5126

NURSE
Rebekah their sister, and her *n* .... Gen 24:59   3243
But Deborah Rebekah's *n* died .... Gen 35:8   3243
call to thee a *n* of the Hebrew .... Ex 2:7   3243
that she may *n* the child for thee .... Ex 2:7   3243
n it for me, and I will give thee .... Ex 2:9   3243
in her bosom, and became *n* unto it .... Ruth 4:16   539
his *n* took him up, and 2Sa 4:4   539
they hid him, even him and his *n* 2Kin 11:2   3243
put him and his *n* in a bedchamber 2Chr 22:11   3243
even as a *n* cherisheth her 1Th 2:7   5162

NURSED
the woman took the child, and *n* it .... Ex 2:9   5134
daughters shall be *n* at thy side .... Is 60:4   539

NURSING
as a *n* father beareth the sucking .... Num 11:12   539
And kings shall be thy *n* fathers .... Is 49:23   539
and their queens thy *n* mothers .... Is 49:23   3243

NURTURE
but bring them up in the *n* .... Eph 6:4   3809

NUTS
little honey, spices, and myrrh, *n* .... Gen 43:11   992
I went down into the garden of *n* .... Song 6:11   93

NYMPHA See Nymphas.

NYMPHAS (nim'-fas) A Christian at Colosse.
which are in Laodicea, and *N* .... Col 4:15   3564

O

O See APPENDIX.

OAK
under the *o* which was by Shechem .... Gen 35:4   424
buried beneath Beth-el under an *o* .... Gen 35:8   437
and set it up there under an *o* .... Josh 24:26   427
sat under an *o* which was in .... Judg 6:11   424
it out unto him under the *o* .... Judg 6:19   424
the thick boughs of a great *o* 2Sa 18:9   424
and his head caught hold of the *o* 2Sa 18:9   424
I saw Absalom hanged in an *o* 2Sa 18:10   424
yet alive in the midst of the *o* 2Sa 18:14   424
and found him sitting under an *o* 1Kin 13:14   424
their bones under the *o* in Jabesh 1Chr 10:12   424
be as an *o* whose leaf fadeth .... Is 1:30   424
as a teil tree, and as an *o* .... Is 6:13   437
and taketh the cypress and the *o* .... Is 44:14   437
tree, and under every thick *o* .... Eze 6:13   424

OAKS
of the *o* which ye have desired .... Is 1:29   352
up, and upon all the *o* of Bashan .... Is 2:13   437
Of the *o* of Bashan have they made ...... Eze 27:6   437
incense upon the hills, under *o* .... Hos 4:13   437
cedars, and he was strong as the *o* .... Amos 2:9   437
howl, O ye *o* of Bashan .... Zec 11:2   437

OAR
And all that handle the *o*, the .... Eze 27:29   4880

OARS
wherein shall go no galley with *o* .... Is 33:21   7885
of Bashan have they made thine *o* .... Eze 27:6   4880

OATH
shalt be clear from this my *o* .... Gen 24:8   7621
thou be clear from this my *o* .... Gen 24:41   423
thou shalt be clear from my *o* .... Gen 24:41   423
I will perform the *o* which I .... Gen 26:3   7621
Let there be now an *o* betwixt us .... Gen 26:28   423
Joseph took an *o* of the children .... Gen 50:25   7650

Then shall an *o* of the Lord be .... Ex 22:11   7621
a man shall pronounce with an *o* .... Lev 5:4   7621
priest shall charge her by an *o* .... Num 5:19   7650
the woman with an *o* of cursing .... Num 5:21   7621
an *o* among thy people, when the .... Num 5:21   7621
or swear an *o* to bind his soul .... Num 30:2   7621
her soul by a bond with an *o* .... Num 30:10   7621
every binding *o* to afflict the .... Num 30:13   7621
because he would keep the *o* which ...... Deut 7:8   7621
the Lord thy God, and into his *o* .... Deut 29:12   423
do I make this covenant and this *o* .... Deut 29:14   423
o which thou hast made us swear .... Josh 2:17   7621
o which thou hast made us to .... Josh 2:20   7621
because of the *o* which we sware .... Josh 9:20   7621
For they had made a great *o* .... Judg 21:5   7621
for the people feared the *o* 1Sa 14:26   7621
charged the people with the *o* 1Sa 14:27   7650
charged the people with an *o* 1Sa 14:28   7650
Lord's *o* that was between them 2Sa 21:7   7621
thou not kept the *o* of the Lord 1Kin 2:43   7621
an *o* be laid upon him to cause 1Kin 8:31   423
the *o* come before thine altar in 1Kin 8:31   423
he took an *o* of the kingdom and 1Kin 18:10   7650
took an *o* of them in the house of 2Kin 11:4   7650
Abraham, and of his *o* unto Isaac 1Chr 16:16   7621
an *o* be laid upon him to make him 2Chr 6:22   423
the *o* come before thine altar in 2Chr 6:22   423
And all Judah rejoiced at the *o* 2Chr 15:15   7621
the priests, and took an *o* of them .... Neh 5:12   7650
into a curse, and into an *o* .... Neh 10:29   7621
with Abraham, and his *o* unto Isaac ..... Ps 105:9   7621
and that in regard of the *o* of God .... Eccl 8:2   7621
sweareth, as he that feareth an *o* .... Eccl 9:2   7621
That I may perform the *o* which I .... Jer 11:5   7621
which hast despised the *o* in .... Eze 16:59   423
him, and hath taken an *o* of him .... Eze 17:13   423
whose *o* he despised, and whose .... Eze 17:16   423
Seeing he despised the *o* by .... Eze 17:18   423

surely mine *o* that he hath	Eze 17:19	423
the *o* that is written in the law	Dan 9:11	7621
and love no false *o*	Zec 8:17	7621
an *o* to give her whatsoever she	Mt 14:7	3727
And again he denied with an *o*	Mt 26:72	3727
The *o* which he sware to our	Lk 1:73	3727
God had sworn with an *o* to him	Acts 2:30	3727
have bound themselves with an *o*	Acts 23:21	332
an *o* for confirmation is to them	Heb 6:16	3727
his counsel, confirmed it by an *o*	Heb 6:17	3727
without an *o* he was made priest	Heb 7:20	3728
priests were made without an *o*	Heb 7:21	3728
but this with an *o* by him that	Heb 7:21	3728
but the word of the *o*, which was	Heb 7:28	3728
the earth, neither by any other *o*	Jas 5:12	3727

OATH'S

nevertheless for the *o* sake	Mt 14:9	3727
yet for his *o* sake, and for their	Mk 6:26	3727

OATHS

sight, to them that have sworn *o*	Eze 21:23	7621
according to the *o* of the tribes	Hab 3:9	7621
perform unto the Lord thine *o*	Mt 5:33	3727

OBADIAH (o-ba-di'-ah)
1. An officer in Ahab's court.

And Ahab called *O*, which was the	1Kin 18:3	5662
(Now *O* feared the Lord greatly	1Kin 18:3	5662
that *O* took an hundred prophets,	1Kin 18:4	5662
And Ahab said unto *O*, Go into the	1Kin 18:5	5662
O went another way by himself	1Kin 18:6	5662
as *O* was in the way, behold,	1Kin 18:7	5662
So *O* went to meet Ahab, and told	1Kin 18:16	5662

2. A descendant of David.

the sons of Arnan, the sons of *O*	1Chr 3:21	5662

3. A descendant of Tola.

Michael, and *O*, and Joel, Ishiah,	1Chr 7:3	5662

4. Son of Azel.

and Ishmael, and Sheariah, and *O*	1Chr 8:38	5662
and Ishmael, and Sheariah, and *O*	1Chr 9:44	5662

5. Son of Shemaiah.

O the son of Shemaiah, the son of	1Chr 9:16	5662

6. A warrior in David's army.

O the second, Eliab the third,	1Chr 12:9	5662

7. A prince of Zebulun.

Of Zebulun, Ishmaiah the son of *O*	1Chr 27:19	5662

8. A prince of Judah.

even to Ben-hail, and to *O*	2Chr 17:7	5662

9. A Levite in Josiah's time.

of them were Jahath and *O*, the	2Chr 34:12	5662

10. A clan leader with Ezra.

O the son of Jehiel, and with him	Ezr 8:9	5662

11. A priest who renewed the covenant.

Harim, Meremoth, *O*,	Neh 10:5	5662

12. A Temple gatekeeper.

Mattaniah, and Bakbukiah, *O*	Neh 12:25	5662

13. A prophet.

The vision of *O*	Obad 1	5662

OBAL (o'-bal) *A son of Joktan.*

And *O*, and Abimael, and Sheba,	Gen 10:28	5745

OBED (o'-bed) See OBED-EDOM.
1. Father of Jesse.

and they called his name *O*	Ruth 4:17	5744
begat Boaz, and Boaz begat *O*	Ruth 4:21	5744
O begat Jesse, and Jesse begat	Ruth 4:22	5744
And Boaz begat *O*, and *O* begat	1Chr 2:12	5744
and Booz begat *O* of Ruth	Mt 1:5	5601
and *O* begat Jesse	Mt 1:5	5601
of Jesse, which was the son of *O*	Lk 3:32	5601

2. A descendant of Judah.

begat Ephlal, and Ephlal begat *O*	1Chr 2:37	5744
O begat Jehu, and Jehu begat	1Chr 2:38	5744

3. A "mighty man" of David.

Eliel, and *O*, and Jasiel the	1Chr 11:47	5744

4. A sanctuary servant.

Othni, and Rephael, and *O*, Elzabad,	1Chr 26:7	5744

5. Father of Azariah.

and Azariah the son of *O*, and	2Chr 23:1	5744

OBED-EDOM (o'-bed-e'-dom)
1. A Levite.

into the house of *O* the Gittite	2Sa 6:10	5654
of *O* the Gittite three months	2Sa 6:11	5654
and the Lord blessed *O*, and all his	2Sa 6:11	5654
Lord hath blessed the house of *O*	2Sa 6:12	5654
of *O* into the city of David with	2Sa 6:12	5654
into the house of *O* the Gittite	1Chr 13:13	5654
of *O* in his house three months	1Chr 13:14	5654
the Lord blessed the house of *O*	1Chr 13:14	5654
and *O* and Jehiah were doorkeepers	1Chr 15:24	5654
out of the house of *O* with joy	1Chr 15:25	5654

2. A priest who relocated the Ark.

and Elipheleh, and Mikneiah, and *O*	1Chr 15:18	5654
and Elipheleh, and Mikneiah, and *O*	1Chr 15:21	5654
Moreover the sons of *O* were	1Chr 26:4	5654
All these of the sons of *O*	1Chr 26:8	5654
were threescore and two of *O*	1Chr 26:8	5654
To *O* southward	1Chr 26:15	5654

3. Another priest who relocated the Ark.

and Eliab, and Benaiah, and *O*	1Chr 16:5	5654
O with their brethren, threescore	1Chr 16:38	5654

4. Son of Jeduthun.

O also the son of Jeduthun and	1Chr 16:38	5654

5. A Temple servant.

found in the house of God with *O*	2Chr 25:24	5654

OBEDIENCE

for *o* to the faith among all	Rom 1:5	5218
so by the *o* of one shall many be	Rom 5:19	5218
or of *o* unto righteousness	Rom 6:16	5218
For your *o* is come abroad unto	Rom 16:19	5218
to all nations for the *o* of faith	Rom 16:26	5218
they are commanded to be under *o*	1Cor 14:34	5293
he remembereth the *o* of you all	2Cor 7:15	5218
every thought to the *o* of Christ	2Cor 10:5	5218
when your *o* is fulfilled	2Cor 10:6	5218
in thy *o* I wrote unto thee	Philem 21	5218
yet learned he *o* by the things	Heb 5:8	5218
of the Spirit, unto *o* and	1Pet 1:2	5218

OBEDIENT

hath said will we do, and be *o*	Ex 24:7	8085
the children of Israel may be *o*	Num 27:20	8085
shalt be *o* unto his voice	Deut 4:30	8085
because ye would not be *o* unto	Deut 8:20	8085
hear, they shall be *o* unto me	2Sa 22:45	8085
is a wise reprover upon an *o* ear	Prov 25:12	8085
If ye be willing and *o*, ye shall	Is 1:19	8085
neither were they *o* unto his law	Is 42:24	8085
the priests were *o* to the faith	Acts 6:7	5219
by me, to make the Gentiles *o*	Rom 15:18	5218
whether ye be *o* in all things	2Cor 2:9	5255
be *o* to them that are your	Eph 6:5	5219
became *o* unto death, even the	Phil 2:8	5255
o to their own husbands, that the	Titus 2:5	5293
Exhort servants to be *o* unto	Titus 2:9	5293
As *o* children, not fashioning	1Pet 1:14	5218

OBEISANCE

about, and made *o* to my sheaf	Gen 37:7	7812
and the eleven stars made *o* to me	Gen 37:9	7812
bowed down their heads, and made *o*	Gen 43:28	7812
meet his father in law, and did *o*	Ex 18:7	7812
he fell to the earth, and did *o*	2Sa 1:2	7812
her face to the ground, and did *o*	2Sa 14:4	7812
man came nigh to him to do him *o*	2Sa 15:5	7812
bowed, and did *o* unto the king	1Kin 1:16	7812
of Judah, and made *o* to the king	2Chr 24:17	7812

OBEY

o my voice according to that	Gen 27:8	8085
only *o* my voice, and go fetch me	Gen 27:13	8085
Now therefore, my son, *o* my voice	Gen 27:43	8085
that I should *o* his voice to let	Ex 5:2	8085
if ye will *o* my voice indeed, and	Ex 19:5	8085
o his voice, provoke him not	Ex 23:21	8085
if thou shalt indeed *o* his voice	Ex 23:22	8085
if ye *o* the commandments of the	Deut 11:27	8085
if ye will not *o* the commandments	Deut 11:28	8085
o his voice, and ye shall serve	Deut 13:4	8085
which will not *o* the voice of his	Deut 21:18	8085
he will not *o* our voice	Deut 21:20	8085
Thou shalt therefore *o* the voice	Deut 27:10	8085
because thou wouldest not *o* the	Deut 28:62	8085
shalt *o* his voice according to	Deut 30:2	8085
o the voice of the Lord, and do	Deut 30:8	8085
and that thou mayest *o* his voice	Deut 30:20	8085
we serve, and his voice will we *o*	Josh 24:24	8085
refused to *o* the voice of Samuel	1Sa 8:19	8085
o his voice, and not rebel against	1Sa 12:14	8085
But if ye will not *o* the voice of	1Sa 12:15	8085
thou not *o* the voice of the Lord	1Sa 15:19	8085
to *o* is better than sacrifice, and	1Sa 15:22	8085
And refused to *o*, neither were	Neh 9:17	8085
If they *o* and serve him, they	Job 36:11	8085
But if they *o* not, they shall	Job 36:12	8085
they hear of me, they shall *o* me	Ps 18:44	8085
and despiseth to *o* his mother	Prov 30:17	3349
children of Ammon shall *o* them	Is 11:14	4928
O my voice, and I will be your God	Jer 7:23	8085
O my voice, and do them, according	Jer 11:4	8085
and protesting, saying, *O* my voice	Jer 11:7	8085
But if they will not *o*, I will	Jer 12:17	8085
that it *o* not my voice, then I	Jer 18:10	8085

o the voice of the LORD your God	Jer 26:13	8085
but *o* their father's commandment	Jer 35:14	8085
O, I beseech thee, the voice of	Jer 38:20	8085
we will *o* the voice of the LORD	Jer 42:6	8085
when we *o* the voice of the LORD	Jer 42:6	8085
neither *o* the voice of the LORD	Jer 42:13	8085
dominions shall serve and *o* him	Dan 7:27	8086
that they might not *o* thy voice	Dan 9:11	8085
if ye will diligently *o* the voice	Zec 6:15	8085
even the winds and the sea *o* him	Mt 8:27	5219
unclean spirits, and they do *o* him	Mk 1:27	5219
even the wind and the sea *o* him	Mk 4:41	5219
the winds and water, and they *o* him	Lk 8:25	5219
and it should *o* you	Lk 17:6	5219
We ought to *o* God rather than men	Acts 5:29	3980
God hath given to them that *o* him	Acts 5:32	3980
To whom our fathers would not *o*	Acts 7:39	5255,1036
do not *o* the truth	Rom 2:8	544
but *o* unrighteousness	Rom 2:8	3982
that ye should *o* it in the lusts	Rom 6:12	5219
ye yield yourselves servants to *o*	Rom 6:16	5218
his servants ye are to whom ye *o*	Rom 6:16	5219
that ye should not *o* the truth	Gal 3:1	3982
that ye should not *o* the truth	Gal 5:7	3982
o your parents in the Lord	Eph 6:1	5219
o your parents in all things	Col 3:20	5219
o in all things your masters	Col 3:22	5219
that *o* not the gospel of our Lord	2Th 1:8	5219
if any man *o* not our word by this	2Th 3:14	5219
to *o* magistrates, to be ready to	Titus 3:1	3980
unto all them that *o* him	Heb 5:9	5219
O them that have the rule over	Heb 13:17	3982
mouths, that they may *o* us	Jas 3:3	3982
if any *o* not the word, they also	1Pet 3:1	544
them that *o* not the gospel of God	1Pet 4:17	544

OBEYED

because thou hast *o* my voice	Gen 22:18	8085
Because that Abraham *o* my voice	Gen 26:5	8085
And that Jacob *o* his father	Gen 28:7	8085
because they *o* not the voice of	Josh 5:6	8085
have *o* my voice in all that I	Josh 22:2	8085
but ye have not *o* my voice	Judg 2:2	8085
but ye have not *o* my voice	Judg 6:10	8085
I have *o* the voice of the LORD,	1Sa 15:20	8085
the people, and *o* their voice	1Sa 15:24	8085
thine handmaid hath *o* thy voice	1Sa 28:21	8085
hast not *o* the voice of the LORD	1Kin 20:36	8085
Because they *o* not the voice of	2Kin 18:12	8085
and all Israel *o* him	1Chr 29:23	8085
they *o* the words of the LORD, and	2Chr 11:4	8085
have not *o* the voice of my	Prov 5:13	8085
tree, and ye have not *o* my voice	Jer 3:13	8085
have not *o* the voice of the LORD	Jer 3:25	8085
them, and have not *o* my voice	Jer 9:13	8085
Yet they *o* not, nor inclined	Jer 11:8	8085
But they *o* not, neither inclined	Jer 17:23	8085
but they *o* not thy voice, neither	Jer 32:23	8085
of them any more, then they *o*	Jer 34:10	8085
Thus have we *o* the voice of	Jer 35:8	8085
we have dwelt in tents, and have *o*	Jer 35:10	8085
Because ye have *o* the commandment	Jer 35:18	8085
have not *o* his voice, therefore	Jer 40:3	8085
but ye have not *o* the voice of,	Jer 42:21	8085
o not the voice of the LORD, to	Jer 43:4	8085
for they *o* not the voice of the	Jer 43:7	8085
have not *o* the voice of the LORD,	Jer 44:23	8085
Neither have we *o* the voice of	Dan 9:10	8085
for we *o* not his voice	Dan 9:14	8085
She *o* not the voice	Zeph 3:2	8085
o the voice of the LORD their God	Hag 1:12	8085
and all, as many as *o* him, were	Acts 5:36	3982
and all, even as many as *o* him	Acts 5:37	3982
but ye have *o* from the heart that	Rom 6:17	5219
they have not all *o* the gospel	Rom 10:16	5219
my beloved, as ye have always *o*	Phil 2:12	5219
receive for an inheritance, *o*	Heb 11:8	5219
Even as Sarah *o* Abraham, calling	1Pet 3:6	5219

OBEYEDST

Because thou *o* not the voice of	1Sa 28:18	8085
youth, that thou *o* not my voice	Jer 22:21	8085

OBEYETH

that *o* the voice of his servant,	Is 50:10	8085
This is a nation that *o* not the	Jer 7:28	8085
Cursed be the man that *o* not the	Jer 11:3	8085

OBEYING

o the commandments of the LORD	Judg 2:17	8085
as in *o* the voice of the LORD	1Sa 15:22	8085
in *o* the truth through the Spirit	1Pet 1:22	5218

OBIL (o'-bil) An Ishmaelite camel driver.

camels also was *O* the Ishmaelite	1Chr 27:30	179

OBJECT

have been here before thee, and *o*	Acts 24:19	2723

OBLATION

if thou bring an *o* of a meat	Lev 2:4	7133
if thy *o* be a meat offering baken	Lev 2:5	7133
if thy *o* be a meat offering baken	Lev 2:7	7133
As for the *o* of the firstfruits,	Lev 2:12	7133
every *o* of thy meat offering	Lev 2:13	7133
if his *o* be a sacrifice of peace	Lev 3:1	7133
offer one out of the whole *o* for	Lev 7:14	7133
unto the LORD shall bring his *o*	Lev 7:29	7133
will offer his *o* for all his vows	Lev 22:18	7133
every *o* of theirs, every meat	Num 18:9	7133
brought an *o* for the LORD	Num 31:50	7133
day, and shall do sacrifice and *o*	Is 19:21	4503
o chooseth a tree that will not	Is 40:20	8641
he that offereth an *o*, as if he	Is 66:3	4503
they offer burnt offering and an *o*	Jer 14:12	4503
every *o* of all, of every sort of	Eze 44:30	8641
ye shall offer an *o* unto the LORD	Eze 45:1	8641
over against the *o* of the holy	Eze 45:6	8641
side of the *o* of the holy portion	Eze 45:7	8641
before the *o* of the holy portion,	Eze 45:7	8641
This is the *o* that ye shall offer	Eze 45:13	8641
this *o* for the prince in Israel	Eze 45:16	8641
The *o* that ye shall offer unto	Eze 48:9	8641
the priests, shall be this holy *o*	Eze 48:10	8641
this *o* of the land that is	Eze 48:12	8642
in length over against the *o* of	Eze 48:18	8641
against the *o* of the holy portion	Eze 48:18	8641
All the *o* shall be five and twenty	Eze 48:20	8641
shall offer the holy *o* foursquare	Eze 48:20	8641
and on the other of the holy *o*	Eze 48:21	8641
of the *o* toward the east border	Eze 48:21	8641
and it shall be the holy *o*	Eze 48:21	8641
that they should offer an *o*	Dan 2:46	4541
about the time of the evening *o*	Dan 9:21	4503
the *o* to cease, and for the	Dan 9:27	4503

OBLATIONS

to offer their *o* unto the LORD	Lev 7:38	7133
to distribute the *o* of the LORD	2Chr 31:14	8641
Bring no more vain *o*	Is 1:13	4503
and the firstfruits of your *o*	Eze 20:40	4864
of all, of every sort of your *o*	Eze 44:30	8641

OBOTH (o'-both) An Israelite encampment in the wilderness.

set forward, and pitched in *O*	Num 21:10	88
And they journeyed from *O*, and	Num 21:11	88
from Punon, and pitched in *O*	Num 33:43	88
And they departed from *O*, and	Num 33:44	88

OBSCURE

shall be put out in *o* darkness	Prov 20:20	380

OBSCURITY

of the blind shall see out of *o*	Is 29:18	652
then shall thy light rise in *o*	Is 58:10	2822
we wait for light, but behold *o*	Is 59:9	2822

OBSERVATION

kingdom of God cometh not with *o*	Lk 17:20	3907

OBSERVE

And ye shall *o* the feast of	Ex 12:17	8104
therefore shall ye *o* this day in	Ex 12:17	8104
ye shall *o* this thing for an	Ex 12:24	8104
to *o* the sabbath throughout their	Ex 31:16	6213
O thou that which I command thee	Ex 34:11	8104
thou shalt *o* the feast of weeks,	Ex 34:22	6213
ye use enchantment, nor *o* times	Lev 19:26	6049
shall ye *o* all my statutes	Lev 19:37	8104
shall ye *o* to offer unto me in	Num 28:2	8104
Ye shall *o* to do therefore as the	Deut 5:32	8104
O Israel, and *o* to do it	Deut 6:3	8104
if we *o* to do all these	Deut 6:25	8104
thee this day shall ye *o* to do	Deut 8:1	8104
ye shall *o* to do all the statutes	Deut 11:32	8104
which ye shall *o* to do in the	Deut 12:1	8104
O and hear all these words which I	Deut 12:28	8104
soever I command you, *o* to do it	Deut 12:32	8104
to *o* to do all these commandments	Deut 15:5	8104
O the month of Abib, and keep the	Deut 16:1	8104
and thou shalt *o* and do these	Deut 16:12	8104
Thou shalt *o* the feast of	Deut 16:13	6213
thou shalt *o* to do according to	Deut 17:10	8104
that thou *o* diligently, and do	Deut 24:8	8104
them, so ye shall *o* to do	Deut 24:8	8104
voice of the LORD thy God, to *o*	Deut 28:1	8104
I command thee this day, to *o*	Deut 28:13	8104

to o to do all his commandments	Deut 28:15	8104
If thou wilt not o to do all the	Deut 28:58	8104
o to do all the words of this law	Deut 31:12	8104
command your children to o to do	Deut 32:46	8104
that thou mayest o to do	Josh 1:7	8104
night, that thou mayest o to do	Josh 1:8	8104
that I commanded her let her o	Judg 13:14	8104
Now the men did diligently o	1Kin 20:33	5172
ye shall o to do for evermore	2Kin 17:37	8104
only if they will o to do	2Kin 21:8	8104
shalt o my statutes and my	2Chr 7:17	8104
love him and o his commandments	Neh 1:5	8104
Moses the servant of God, and to o	Neh 10:29	8104
That they might o his statutes	Ps 105:45	8104
will o these things, even they	Ps 107:43	8104
I shall o it with my whole heart	Ps 119:34	8104
and let thine eyes o my ways	Prov 23:26	5341
the swallow o the time of their	Jer 8:7	8104
neither o their judgments, nor	Eze 20:18	8104
o my statutes, and do them	Eze 37:24	8104
leopard by the way will I o them	Hos 13:7	7789
They that o lying vanities	Jonah 2:8	8104
they bid you o, that o	Mt 23:3	5083
Teaching them to o all things	Mt 28:20	5083
for us to receive, neither to o	Acts 16:21	4160
that they o no such thing	Acts 21:25	5083
Ye o days, and months, and times,	Gal 4:10	3906
that thou o these things without	1Ti 5:21	5442

OBSERVED

but his father o the saying	Gen 37:11	8104
It is a night to be much o unto	Ex 12:42	8107
o of all the children of Israel	Ex 12:42	8107
not o all these commandments,	Num 15:22	6213
for they have o thy word, and kept	Deut 33:9	8104
to pass, when Joab o the city	2Sa 11:16	8104
o times, and used enchantments, and	2Kin 21:6	6049
also he o times, and used	2Chr 33:6	6049
I have heard him, and o him	Hos 14:8	7789
a just man and an holy, and o him	Mk 6:20	4933
all these have I o from my youth	Mk 10:20	5442

OBSERVER

or an o of times, or an enchanter	Deut 18:10	6049

OBSERVERS

hearkened unto o of times	Deut 18:14	6049

OBSERVEST

many things, but thou o not	Is 42:20	8104

OBSERVETH

He that o the wind shall not sow	Eccl 11:4	8104

OBSTINATE

his spirit, and made his heart o	Deut 2:30	553
Because I knew that thou art o	Is 48:4	7186

OBTAIN

be that I may o children by her	Gen 16:2	1129
shall o favour of the LORD	Prov 8:35	6329
they shall o joy and gladness, and	Is 35:10	5381
they shall o gladness and joy	Is 51:11	5381
o the kingdom by flatteries	Dan 11:21	2388
for they shall o mercy	Mt 5:7	1653
accounted worthy to o that world	Lk 20:35	5177
your mercy they also may o mercy	Rom 11:31	1653
So run, that ye may o	1Cor 9:24	2638
Now they do it to o a corruptible	1Cor 9:25	2983
but to o salvation by our Lord	1Th 5:9	4047
sakes, that they may also o the	2Ti 2:10	5177
of grace, that we may o mercy	Heb 4:16	2983
that they might o a better	Heb 11:35	5177
and desire to have, and cannot o	Jas 4:2	2013

OBTAINED

after certain days o I leave of	Neh 13:6	7592
him, and she o kindness of him	Est 2:9	5375
Esther o favour in the sight of	Est 2:15	5375
she o grace and favour in his	Est 2:17	5375
that she o favour in his sight	Est 5:2	5375
upon her that had not o mercy	Hos 2:23	5375
had o part of this ministry	Acts 1:17	2975
With a great sum o I this freedom	Acts 22:28	2932
Having therefore o help of God	Acts 26:22	5177
that they had o their purpose	Acts 27:13	2902
Israel hath not o that which he	Rom 11:7	2013
but the election hath o it	Rom 11:7	2013
yet have now o mercy through	Rom 11:30	1653
as one that hath o mercy of the	1Cor 7:25	1653
also we have o an inheritance	Eph 1:11	2820
but I o mercy, because I did it	1Ti 1:13	1653
Howbeit for this cause I o mercy	1Ti 1:16	1653
as he hath by inheritance o a	Heb 1:4	2816
endured, he o the promise	Heb 6:15	2013

But now hath he o a more	Heb 8:6	5177
having o eternal redemption for	Heb 9:12	2147
by it the elders o a good report	Heb 11:2	3140
by which he o witness that he was	Heb 11:4	3140
o promises, stopped the mouths of	Heb 11:33	2013
having o a good report through	Heb 11:39	3140
which had not o mercy	1Pet 2:10	1653
but now have o mercy	1Pet 2:10	1653
to them that have o like precious	2Pet 1:1	2975

OBTAINETH

A good man o favour of the LORD	Prov 12:2	6329
thing, and o favour of the LORD	Prov 18:22	6329

OBTAINING

to the o of the glory of our Lord	2Th 2:14	4047

OCCASION

that he may seek o against us	Gen 43:18	1556
do to them as thou shalt find o	Judg 9:33	4672
that he sought an o against the	Judg 14:4	8385
that thou do as o serve thee	1Sa 10:7	4672
o to the enemies of the LORD to	2Sa 12:14	5006
which thou shalt have o to bestow	Ezr 7:20	5308
in her o who can turn her away	Jer 2:24	8385
ye shall not have o any more to	Eze 18:3	4911
princes sought to find o against	Dan 6:4	5931
they could find none o nor fault	Dan 6:4	5931
find any o against this Daniel	Dan 6:5	5931
taking o by the commandment,	Rom 7:8	874
taking o by the commandment,	Rom 7:11	874
an o to fall in his brother's way	Rom 14:13	4625
but give you o to glory on our	2Cor 5:12	874
but by o of the forwardness of	2Cor 8:8	1223
o from them which desire o	2Cor 11:12	874
not liberty for an o to the flesh	Gal 5:13	874
give none o to the adversary to	1Ti 5:14	874
there is none o of stumbling in	1Jn 2:10	4625

OCCASIONED

I have o the death of all the	1Sa 22:22	5437

OCCASIONS

give o of speech against her, and	Deut 22:14	5949
he hath given o of speech against	Deut 22:17	5949
Behold, he findeth o against me	Job 33:10	8569

OCCUPATION

you, and shall say, What is your o	Gen 46:33	4639
unto his brethren, What is your o	Gen 47:3	4639
What is thine o	Jonah 1:8	4399
for by their o they were	Acts 18:3	5078
with the workmen of like o	Acts 19:25	

OCCUPIED

All the gold that was o for the	Ex 38:24	6213
with new ropes that never were o	Judg 16:11	6213,4399
they o in thy fairs with emeralds	Eze 27:16	5414
going to and fro o in thy fairs	Eze 27:19	5414
they o with thee in lambs, and	Eze 27:21	5503
they o in thy fairs with chief of	Eze 27:22	5414
them that have been o therein	Heb 13:9	4043

OCCUPIERS

the o of thy merchandise, and all	Eze 27:27	6148

OCCUPIETH

how shall he that o the room of	1Cor 14:16	378

OCCUPY

were in thee to o thy merchandise	Eze 27:9	6148
and said unto them, O till I come	Lk 19:13	4231

OCCURRENT

is neither adversary nor evil o	1Kin 5:4	6294

OCHRAN See OCRAN.

OCRAN (o'-cran) *An Asherite who counted the people.*

Pagiel the son of O	Num 1:13	5918
shall be Pagiel the son of O	Num 2:27	5918
eleventh day Pagiel the son of O	Num 7:72	5918
offering of Pagiel the son of O	Num 7:77	5918
of Asher was Pagiel the son of O	Num 10:26	5918

ODD

wherewith the o number of them is	Num 3:48	5736

ODED (o'-ded)
　1. *Father of Azariah.*

came upon Azariah the son of O	2Chr 15:1	5752
and the prophecy of O the prophet	2Chr 15:8	5752

　2. *A prophet of Samaria.*

LORD was there, whose name was O	2Chr 28:9	5752

ODIOUS

had made themselves o to David	1Chr 19:6	887
For an o woman when she is	Prov 30:23	8130

ODOUR

filled with the o of the ointment	Jn 12:3	3744
you, an o of a sweet smell, a	Phil 4:18	3744

ODOURS

smell the savour of your sweet o	Lev 26:31	5207
bed which was filled with sweet o	2Chr 16:14	1314
myrrh, and six months with sweet o	Est 2:12	1314
so shall they burn o for thee	Jer 34:5	
an oblation and sweet o unto him	Dan 2:46	5208
harps, and golden vials full of o	Rev 5:8	2368
And cinnamon, and o, and ointments,	Rev 18:13	2368

OF See APPENDIX.

OFF See APPENDIX.

OFFENCE

nor o of heart unto my lord,	1Sa 25:31	4383
for a rock of o to both the	Is 8:14	4383
till they acknowledge their o	Hos 5:15	816
thou art an o unto me	Mt 16:23	4625
to that man by whom the o cometh	Mt 18:7	4625
a conscience void of o toward God	Acts 24:16	677
But not as the o, so also is the	Rom 5:15	3900
For if through the o of one many	Rom 5:15	3900
For if by one man's o death	Rom 5:17	3900
Therefore as by the o of one	Rom 5:18	3900
entered, that the o might abound	Rom 5:20	3900
a stumblingstone and rock of o	Rom 9:33	4625
for that man who eateth with o	Rom 14:20	4348
Give none o, neither to the Jews,	1Cor 10:32	677
Giving no o in any thing, that	2Cor 6:3	4349
Have I committed an o in abasing	2Cor 11:7	266
then is the o of the cross ceased	Gal 5:11	4625
without o till the day of Christ	Phil 1:10	677
of stumbling, and a rock of o	1Pet 2:8	4625

OFFENCES

for yielding pacifieth great o	Eccl 10:4	2399
Woe unto the world because of o	Mt 18:7	4625
for it must needs be that o come	Mt 18:7	4625
impossible but that o will come	Lk 17:1	4625
Who was delivered for our o	Rom 4:25	3900
is of many o unto justification	Rom 5:16	3900
o contrary to the doctrine which	Rom 16:17	4625

OFFEND

I will not o any more	Job 34:31	2254
I should o against the generation	Ps 73:15	898
and nothing shall o them	Ps 119:165	4383
all that devour him shall o	Jer 2:3	816
We o not, because they have	Jer 50:7	816
the harlot, yet let not Judah o	Hos 4:15	816
and he shall pass over, and o	Hab 1:11	816
And if thy right eye o thee	Mt 5:29	4624
And if thy right hand o thee	Mt 5:30	4624
of his kingdom all things that o	Mt 13:41	4625
lest we should o them, go thou	Mt 17:27	4624
But whoso shall o one of these	Mt 18:6	4624
if thy hand or thy foot o thee	Mt 18:8	4624
And if thine eye o thee, pluck it	Mt 18:9	4624
whosoever shall o one of these	Mk 9:42	4624
And if thy hand o thee, cut it off	Mk 9:43	4624
And if thy foot o thee, cut it off	Mk 9:45	4624
And if thine eye o thee, pluck it	Mk 9:47	4624
than that he should o one of	Lk 17:2	4624
said unto them, Doth this o you	Jn 6:61	4624
if meat make my brother to o	1Cor 8:13	4624
lest I make my brother to o	1Cor 8:13	4624
yet o in one point, he is guilty	Jas 2:10	4417
For in many things we o all	Jas 3:2	4417
If any man o not in word, the	Jas 3:2	4417

OFFENDED

and what have I o thee, that thou	Gen 20:9	2398
his baker had o their lord the	Gen 40:1	2398
to Lachish, saying, I have o	2Kin 18:14	2398
for whereas I have o against the	2Chr 28:13	819
A brother o is harder to be won	Prov 18:19	6586
What have I o against thee, or	Jer 37:18	2398
vengeance, and hath greatly o	Eze 25:12	816
but when he o in Baal, he died	Hos 13:1	816
whosoever shall not be o in me	Mt 11:6	4624
of the word, by and by he is o	Mt 13:21	4624
And they were o in him	Mt 13:57	4624
thou that the Pharisees were o	Mt 15:12	4624
And then shall many be o, and shall	Mt 24:10	4624
All ye shall be o because of me	Mt 26:31	4624
men shall be o because of thee	Mt 26:33	4624
yet will I never be o	Mt 26:33	4624
sake, immediately they are o	Mk 4:17	4624
And they were o at him	Mk 6:3	4624
All ye shall be o because of me	Mk 14:27	4624

unto him, Although all shall be o	Mk 14:29	4624
whosoever shall not be o in me	Lk 7:23	4624
unto you, that ye should not be o	Jn 16:1	4624
have I o any thing at all	Acts 25:8	264
thy brother stumbleth, or is o	Rom 14:21	4624
who is o, and I burn not	2Cor 11:29	4624

OFFENDER

That make a man an o for a word	Is 29:21	2398
For if I be an o, or have	Acts 25:11	91

OFFENDERS

my son Solomon shall be counted o	1Kin 1:21	2400

OFFER

o him there for a burnt offering	Gen 22:2	5927
Thou shalt not delay to o the	Ex 22:29	
Thou shalt not o the blood of my	Ex 23:18	2076
thou shalt o every day a bullock	Ex 29:36	6213
which thou shalt o upon the altar	Ex 29:38	6213
lamb thou shalt o in the morning	Ex 29:39	6213
other lamb thou shalt o at even	Ex 29:39	6213
other lamb thou shalt o at even	Ex 29:41	6213
Ye shall o no strange incense	Ex 30:9	5927
Thou shalt not o the blood of my	Ex 34:25	7819
Every one that did o an offering	Ex 35:24	7311
let him o a male without blemish	Lev 1:3	7126
he shall o it of his own	Lev 1:3	7126
when any will o a meat offering	Lev 2:1	7126
ye shall o them unto the LORD	Lev 2:12	7126
thine offerings thou shalt o salt	Lev 2:13	7126
if thou o a meat offering of thy	Lev 2:14	7126
thou shalt o for the meat	Lev 2:14	7126
offering, if he o it of the herd	Lev 3:1	7126
he shall o it without blemish	Lev 3:1	7126
he shall o of the sacrifice of	Lev 3:3	7126
he shall o it without blemish	Lev 3:6	7126
If he o a lamb for his offering,	Lev 3:7	7126
then shall he o it before the	Lev 3:7	7126
he shall o of the sacrifice of	Lev 3:9	7126
then he shall o it before the	Lev 3:12	7126
he shall o thereof his offering,	Lev 3:14	7126
o a young bullock for the sin	Lev 4:14	7126
who shall o that which is for the	Lev 5:8	7126
he shall o the second for a burnt	Lev 5:10	6213
Aaron shall o it before the LORD	Lev 6:14	7126
which they shall o unto the LORD	Lev 6:20	7126
o for a sweet savour unto the	Lev 6:21	7126
anointed in his stead shall o it	Lev 6:22	6213
he shall o of it all the fat	Lev 7:3	7126
which he shall o unto the LORD	Lev 7:11	7126
If he o it for a thanksgiving,	Lev 7:12	7126
then he shall o with the	Lev 7:12	7126
he shall o for his offering	Lev 7:13	7126
of it he shall o one out of the	Lev 7:14	7126
of which men o an offering made	Lev 7:25	7126
the children of Israel to o their	Lev 7:38	7126
and o them before the LORD	Lev 9:2	7126
o thy sin offering, and thy burnt	Lev 9:7	6213
o the offering of the people, and	Lev 9:7	6213
Who shall o it before the LORD,	Lev 12:7	7126
o him for a trespass offering, and	Lev 14:12	7126
priest shall o the sin offering	Lev 14:19	6213
the priest shall o the burnt	Lev 14:20	5927
he shall o the one of the	Lev 14:30	6213
And the priest shall o them	Lev 15:15	6213
the priest shall o the one for a	Lev 15:30	6213
Aaron shall o his bullock of the	Lev 16:6	7126
fell, and o it for a sin offering,	Lev 16:9	6213
o his burnt offering, and the	Lev 16:24	6213
to o an offering unto the LORD	Lev 17:4	7126
which they o in the open field,	Lev 17:5	2076
o them for peace offerings unto	Lev 17:5	2076
they shall no more o their	Lev 17:7	2076
to o it unto the LORD	Lev 17:9	6213
if ye o a sacrifice of peace	Lev 19:5	2076
ye shall o it at your own will	Lev 19:5	2076
be eaten the same day ye o it	Lev 19:6	2077
the bread of their God, they do o	Lev 21:6	7126
to o the bread of his God	Lev 21:17	7126
the priest shall come nigh to o	Lev 21:21	7126
nigh to o the bread of his God	Lev 21:21	7126
which they o unto the LORD	Lev 22:15	7311
that will o his oblation for all	Lev 22:18	7126
which they o unto the LORD	Lev 22:18	7126
Ye shall o at your own will a	Lev 22:19	
a blemish, that shall ye not o	Lev 22:20	7126
ye shall not o these unto the LORD	Lev 22:22	7126
that mayest thou o for a freewill	Lev 22:23	6213
Ye shall not o unto the LORD that	Lev 22:24	7126
o the bread of your God of any of	Lev 22:25	7126
when ye will o a sacrifice of	Lev 22:29	2076

O

the LORD, o it at your own will	Lev 22:29	2076
But ye shall o an offering made	Lev 23:8	7126
ye shall o that day when ye wave	Lev 23:12	6213
ye shall o a new meat offering	Lev 23:16	7126
ye shall o with the bread seven	Lev 23:18	7126
but ye shall o an offering made	Lev 23:25	7126
o an offering made by fire unto	Lev 23:27	7126
Seven days ye shall o an offering	Lev 23:36	7126
ye shall o an offering made by	Lev 23:36	7126
to o an offering made by fire	Lev 23:37	7126
beast, of which they do not o a	Lev 27:11	7126
the LORD, and o it upon the altar	Num 5:25	7126
the priest shall o the one for a	Num 6:11	6213
he shall o his offering unto the	Num 6:14	7126
shall o his sin offering, and his	Num 6:16	6213
And he shall o the ram for a	Num 6:17	6213
the priest shall o also his meat	Num 6:17	6213
They shall o their offering, each	Num 7:11	7126
Zuar, prince of Issachar, did o	Num 7:18	7126
of the children of Zebulun, did o	Num 7:24	
of the children of Reuben, did o	Num 7:30	
of the children of Simeon, did o	Num 7:36	
Aaron shall o the Levites before	Num 8:11	5130
thou shalt o the one for a sin	Num 8:12	6213
o them for an offering unto the	Num 8:13	5130
them, and o them for an offering	Num 8:15	5130
that we may not o an offering of	Num 9:7	6213
o the third part of an hin of	Num 15:7	7126
will o an offering made by fire,	Num 15:14	6213
ye shall o up an heave offering	Num 15:19	7311
Ye shall o up a cake of the first	Num 15:20	7311
o one young bullock for a burnt	Num 15:24	6213
come near to o incense before the	Num 16:40	
which they shall o unto the LORD	Num 18:12	5414
of Israel o unto the LORD	Num 18:19	7311
which they o as an heave offering	Num 18:24	7311
then ye shall o up an heave	Num 18:26	7311
Thus ye also shall o an heave	Num 18:28	7311
o every heave offering of the	Num 18:29	7311
shall ye observe to o unto me in	Num 28:2	7126
which ye shall o unto the LORD	Num 28:3	7126
lamb shalt thou o in the morning	Num 28:4	6213
other lamb shalt thou o at even	Num 28:4	6213
other lamb shalt thou o at even	Num 28:8	6213
offering thereof, thou shalt o it	Num 28:8	6213
of your months ye shall o a burnt	Num 28:11	7126
But ye shall o a sacrifice made	Num 28:19	7126
deals shall ye o for a bullock	Num 28:20	6213
deal shalt thou o for every lamb	Num 28:21	6213
Ye shall o these beside the burnt	Num 28:23	6213
this manner ye shall o daily	Num 28:24	6213
But ye shall o the burnt offering	Num 28:27	6213
Ye shall o them beside the	Num 28:31	6213
ye shall o a burnt offering for a	Num 29:2	6213
But ye shall o a burnt offering	Num 29:8	7126
ye shall o a burnt offering, a	Num 29:13	7126
ye shall o twelve young bullocks	Num 29:17	
But ye shall o a burnt offering,	Num 29:36	7126
thou o not thy burnt offerings in	Deut 12:13	5927
there thou shalt o thy burnt	Deut 12:14	5927
thou shalt o thy burnt offerings,	Deut 12:27	6213
from them that o a sacrifice	Deut 18:3	5927
thou shalt o burnt offerings	Deut 27:6	5927
thou shalt o peace offerings, and	Deut 27:7	2076
there they shall o sacrifices of	Deut 33:19	2076
or if to o thereon burnt offering	Josh 22:23	5927
or if to o peace offerings	Josh 22:23	6213
had made an end to o the present	Judg 3:18	7126
o a burnt sacrifice with the wood	Judg 6:26	
I will o it up for a burnt	Judg 11:31	5927
if thou wilt o a burnt offering,	Judg 13:16	6213
thou must o it unto the LORD	Judg 13:16	5927
to o a great sacrifice unto Dagon	Judg 16:23	2076
went up to o unto the LORD the	1Sa 1:21	2076
husband to o the yearly sacrifice	1Sa 2:19	2076
to o upon mine altar, to burn	1Sa 2:28	5927
to o burnt offerings, and to	1Sa 10:8	5927
the LORD, I o thee three things	2Sa 24:12	5190
o up what seemeth good unto him	2Sa 24:22	5927
neither will I o of burnt offerings	2Sa 24:24	5927
did Solomon o upon that altar	1Kin 3:4	5927
did Solomon o burnt offerings	1Kin 9:25	5927
upon thee shall he o the priests	1Kin 13:2	2076
o neither burnt offering nor	2Kin 5:17	6213
when they went in to o sacrifices	2Kin 10:24	6213
To o burnt offerings unto the	1Chr 16:40	5927
the LORD, I o thee three things	1Chr 21:10	5186
nor o burnt offerings without	1Chr 21:24	5927
to o all burnt sacrifices unto	1Chr 23:31	5927
that we should be able to o so	1Chr 29:14	
here, to o willingly unto thee	1Chr 29:17	

to o the burnt offerings of the	2Chr 23:18	5927
to o withal, and spoons, and	2Chr 24:14	5927
priests the sons of Aaron to o	2Chr 29:21	5927
Hezekiah commanded to o the burnt	2Chr 29:27	5927
to o unto the LORD, as it is	2Chr 35:12	7126
to o burnt offerings upon the	2Chr 35:16	5927
to o burnt offerings thereon, as	Ezr 3:2	5927
o burnt offerings unto the LORD	Ezr 3:6	5927
That they may o sacrifices of	Ezr 6:10	7127
o them upon the altar of the	Ezr 7:17	7127
o up for yourselves a burnt	Job 42:8	5927
O the sacrifices of righteousness	Ps 4:5	2076
offerings of blood will I not o	Ps 16:4	5258
therefore will I o in his	Ps 27:6	2076
O unto God thanksgiving	Ps 50:14	2076
then shall they o bullocks upon	Ps 51:19	5927
I will o unto thee burnt	Ps 66:15	5927
I will o bullocks with goats	Ps 66:15	6213
of Sheba and Seba shall o gifts	Ps 72:10	7126
I will o to thee the sacrifice of	Ps 116:17	2076
wentest thou up to o sacrifice	Is 57:7	2076
the gods unto whom they o incense	Jer 11:12	
when they o burnt offering and an	Jer 14:12	5927
before me to o burnt offerings	Jer 33:18	5927
the place where they did o sweet	Eze 6:13	5414
For when ye o your gifts, when ye	Eze 20:31	5375
to o burnt offerings thereon, and	Eze 43:18	5927
o a kid of the goats without	Eze 43:22	7126
thou shalt o a young bullock	Eze 43:23	7126
thou shalt o them before the LORD	Eze 43:24	7126
they shall o them up for a burnt	Eze 43:24	5927
when ye o my bread, the fat and	Eze 44:7	7126
before me to o unto me the fat	Eze 44:15	7126
he shall o his sin offering,	Eze 44:27	7126
ye shall o an oblation unto the	Eze 45:1	7311
is the oblation that ye shall o	Eze 45:13	7311
ye shall o the tenth part of a	Eze 45:14	
o unto the LORD in the sabbath	Eze 46:4	7126
offering which ye shall o of five	Eze 48:8	7311
The oblation that ye shall o unto	Eze 48:9	7311
ye shall o the holy oblation	Eze 48:20	7311
that they should o an oblation	Dan 2:46	5260
They shall not o wine offerings	Hos 9:4	5258
o a sacrifice of thanksgiving	Amos 4:5	6999
Though ye o me burnt offerings and	Amos 5:22	5927
that which they o there is	Hag 2:14	7126
Ye o polluted bread upon mine	Mal 1:7	5066
if ye o the blind for sacrifice,	Mal 1:8	5066
if ye o the lame and sick, is it	Mal 1:8	5066
o it now unto thy governor	Mal 1:8	7126
that they may o unto the LORD an	Mal 3:3	5066
and then come and o thy gift	Mt 5:24	*4374*
o the gift that Moses commanded,	Mt 8:4	*4374*
o for thy cleansing those things	Mk 1:44	*4374*
to o a sacrifice according to	Lk 2:24	*1325*
o for thy cleansing, according as	Lk 5:14	*4374*
on the one cheek o also the other	Lk 6:29	*3930*
an egg, will he o him a scorpion	Lk 11:12	*1929*
to God, that he may o both gifts	Heb 5:1	*4374*
also for himself, to o for sins	Heb 5:3	*4374*
to o up sacrifice, first for his	Heb 7:27	*399*
priest is ordained to o gifts	Heb 8:3	*4374*
this man have somewhat also to o	Heb 8:3	*4374*
that o gifts according to the law	Heb 8:4	*4374*
that he should o himself often	Heb 9:25	*4374*
By him therefore let us o the	Heb 13:15	*399*
to o up spiritual sacrifices,	1Pet 2:5	*399*
that he should o it with the	Rev 8:3	*1325*

OFFERED

o burnt offerings on the altar	Gen 8:20	5927
o him up for a burnt offering in	Gen 22:13	5927
Then Jacob o sacrifice upon the	Gen 31:54	2076
o sacrifices unto the God of his	Gen 46:1	2076
which o burnt offerings, and	Ex 24:5	5927
o burnt offerings, and brought	Ex 32:6	5927
every man that o	Ex 35:22	5130
o an offering of gold	Ex 35:22	
o upon it the burnt offering and	Ex 40:29	5927
burnt offering which he hath o	Lev 7:8	7126
eaten the same day that it is o	Lev 7:15	7133
o it for sin, as the first	Lev 9:15	2398
o it according to the manner	Lev 9:16	6213
o strange fire before the LORD,	Lev 10:1	7126
have they o their sin offering	Lev 10:19	7126
when they o before the LORD, and	Lev 16:1	7126
when they o strange fire before	Num 3:4	7126
over them that were numbered, o	Num 7:2	7126
the princes o for dedicating of	Num 7:10	7126
even the princes o their offering	Num 7:10	7126
he that o his offering the first	Num 7:12	7126

He o for his offering one silver	Num 7:19	7126
prince of the children of Gad, o	Num 7:42	
of the children of Ephraim, o	Num 7:48	
On the eighth day o Gamaliel the	Num 7:54	
of the children of Benjamin, o	Num 7:60	
prince of the children of Dan, o	Num 7:66	
of the children of Asher, o	Num 7:72	
of the children of Naphtali, o	Num 7:78	
Aaron o them as an offering	Num 8:21	5130
and fifty men that o incense	Num 16:35	7126
for they o them before the LORD,	Num 16:38	7126
they that were burnt had o	Num 16:39	7126
And Balak o oxen and sheep, and sent	Num 22:40	2076
Balaam o on every altar a bullock	Num 23:2	5927
I have o upon every altar a	Num 23:4	5927
o a bullock and a ram on every	Num 23:14	5927
o a bullock and a ram on every	Num 23:30	5927
when they o strange fire before	Num 26:61	7126
offering unto the LORD shall be o	Num 28:15	6213
it shall be o beside the	Num 28:24	6213
that they o up to the LORD	Num 31:52	7311
they o burnt offerings	Josh 8:31	5927
the people willingly o themselves	Judg 5:2	
that o themselves willingly among	Judg 5:9	
the second bullock was o upon the	Judg 6:28	5927
o it upon a rock unto the LORD	Judg 13:19	5927
o burnt offerings and peace	Judg 20:26	5927
o burnt offerings and peace	Judg 21:4	5927
when the time was that Elkanah o	1Sa 1:4	2076
that, when any man o sacrifice	1Sa 2:13	2076
o the kine a burnt offering unto	1Sa 6:14	5927
of Beth-shemesh o burnt offerings	1Sa 6:15	5927
o it for a burnt offering wholly	1Sa 7:9	5927
And he o the burnt offering	1Sa 13:9	5927
therefore, and o a burnt offering	1Sa 13:12	5927
David o burnt offerings and peace	2Sa 6:17	5927
from Giloh, while he o sacrifices	2Sa 15:12	2076
o burnt offerings and peace	2Sa 24:25	5927
o up burnt offerings	1Kin 3:15	5927
o peace offerings, and made a	1Kin 3:15	6213
o sacrifice before the LORD	1Kin 8:62	2076
Solomon o a sacrifice of peace	1Kin 8:63	2076
which he o unto the LORD, two and	1Kin 8:63	2076
for there he o burnt offerings,	1Kin 8:64	6213
in Judah, and he o upon the altar	1Kin 12:32	5927
So he o upon the altar which he	1Kin 12:33	5927
he o upon the altar, and burnt	1Kin 12:33	5927
for the people o and burnt incense	1Kin 22:43	2076
when the meat offering was o	2Kin 3:20	5927
o him for a burnt offering upon	2Kin 3:27	5927
to the altar, and o thereon	2Kin 16:12	5927
his sons o upon the altar of the	1Chr 6:49	6999
that they o seven bullocks and	1Chr 15:26	2076
they o burnt sacrifices and peace	1Chr 16:1	7126
o burnt offerings and peace	1Chr 21:26	5927
of the king's work, o willingly,	1Chr 29:6	
for that they o willingly	1Chr 29:9	
they o willingly to the LORD	1Chr 29:9	
have willingly o all these things	1Chr 29:17	
o burnt offerings unto the LORD,	1Chr 29:21	5927
o a thousand burnt offerings upon	2Chr 1:6	5927
such things as they o for the	2Chr 4:6	4639
all the people o sacrifices	2Chr 7:4	2076
king Solomon o a sacrifice of	2Chr 7:5	2076
for there he o burnt offerings,	2Chr 7:7	6213
Then Solomon o burnt offerings	2Chr 8:12	5927
they o unto the LORD the same	2Chr 15:11	2076
who willingly o himself unto the	2Chr 17:16	
they o burnt offerings in the	2Chr 24:14	5927
nor o burnt offerings in the holy	2Chr 29:7	5927
beside all that was willingly o	Ezr 1:6	
o freely for the house of God to	Ezr 2:68	
they o burnt offerings thereon	Ezr 3:3	5927
o the daily burnt offerings by	Ezr 3:4	
afterward o the continual burnt	Ezr 3:5	
of every one that willingly o a	Ezr 3:5	5068
the place where they o sacrifices	Ezr 6:3	1684
o at the dedication of this house	Ezr 6:17	7127
freely unto the God of Israel	Ezr 7:15	5069
all Israel there present, had o	Ezr 8:25	7311
o burnt offerings unto the God of	Ezr 8:35	7126
they o a ram of the flock for	Ezr 10:19	
that willingly o themselves to	Neh 11:2	
that day they o great sacrifices	Neh 12:43	2076
o burnt offerings according to	Job 1:5	5927
thou hast o a meat offering	Is 57:6	5927
as if he o swine's blood	Is 66:3	5927
they have o incense unto Baal	Jer 32:29	6999
they o there their sacrifices, and	Eze 20:28	2076
oblation of the land that is o	Eze 48:12	8641
the reproach o by him to cease	Dan 11:18	

Have ye o unto me sacrifices and	Amos 5:25	5066
o a sacrifice unto the LORD, and	Jonah 1:16	2076
incense shall be o unto my name	Mal 1:11	5066
o sacrifice unto the idol, and	Acts 7:41	321
have ye o to me slain beasts and	Acts 7:42	4374
Ghost was given, he o them money,	Acts 8:18	4374
ye abstain from meats o to idols	Acts 15:29	1494
themselves from things o to idols	Acts 21:25	1494
should be o for every one of them	Acts 21:26	4374
as touching things o unto idols	1Cor 8:1	1494
are o in sacrifice unto idols	1Cor 8:4	1494
eat it as a thing o unto an idol	1Cor 8:7	1494
those things which are o to idols	1Cor 8:10	1494
or that which is o in sacrifice	1Cor 10:19	1494
This is o in sacrifice unto idols	1Cor 10:28	1494
if I be o upon the sacrifice and	Phil 2:17	4689
For I am now ready to be o	2Ti 4:6	4689
flesh, when he had o up prayers	Heb 5:7	4374
he did once, when he o up himself	Heb 7:27	
which he o for himself, and for	Heb 9:7	4374
in which were o both gifts	Heb 9:9	
o himself without spot to God	Heb 9:14	4374
So Christ was once o to bear the	Heb 9:28	4374
those sacrifices which they o	Heb 10:1	4374
they not have ceased to be o	Heb 10:2	4374
which are o by the law	Heb 10:8	4374
after he had o one sacrifice for	Heb 10:12	4374
By faith Abel o unto God a more	Heb 11:4	4374
when he was tried, o up Isaac	Heb 11:17	4374
o up his only begotten son	Heb 11:17	4374
when he had o Isaac his son upon	Jas 2:21	399

OFFERETH

The priest that o it for sin	Lev 6:26	2398
the priest that o any man's burnt	Lev 7:8	7126
shall be the priest's that o it	Lev 7:9	7126
same day that he o his sacrifice	Lev 7:16	7126
it be imputed unto him that o it	Lev 7:18	7126
He that o the sacrifice of his	Lev 7:29	7126
that o the blood of the peace	Lev 7:33	7126
that o a burnt offering or	Lev 17:8	5926
for he o the bread of thy God	Lev 21:8	7126
whosoever o a sacrifice of peace	Lev 22:21	7126
Then shall he that o his offering	Num 15:4	7126
Whoso o praise glorifieth me	Ps 50:23	2076
he that o an oblation, as if he	Is 66:3	5927
him that o in the high places, and	Jer 48:35	5927
him that o an offering unto the	Mal 2:12	5066

OFFERING

of the ground an o unto the LORD	Gen 4:3	4503
had respect unto Abel and to his o	Gen 4:4	4503
to his o he had not respect	Gen 4:5	4503
offer him there for a burnt o	Gen 22:2	
and clave the wood for the burnt o	Gen 22:3	
took the wood of the burnt o	Gen 22:6	
where is the lamb for a burnt o	Gen 22:7	
himself a lamb for a burnt o	Gen 22:8	
a burnt o in the stead of his son	Gen 22:13	
and he poured a drink o thereon	Gen 35:14	
father in law, took a burnt o	Ex 18:12	
Israel, that they bring me an o	Ex 25:2	8641
with his heart ye shall take my o	Ex 25:2	8641
this is the o which ye shall take	Ex 25:3	8641
it is a sin o	Ex 29:14	
it is a burnt o unto the LORD	Ex 29:18	
an o made by fire unto the LORD	Ex 29:18	
them for a wave o before the LORD	Ex 29:24	
them upon the altar for a burnt o	Ex 29:25	
it is an o made by fire unto the	Ex 29:25	
it for a wave o before the LORD	Ex 29:26	
sanctify the breast of the wave o	Ex 29:27	
and the shoulder of the heave o	Ex 29:27	8641
for it is an heave o	Ex 29:28	8641
it shall be an heave o from the	Ex 29:28	8641
even their heave o unto the LORD	Ex 29:28	8641
bullock for a sin o for atonement	Ex 29:36	
of an hin of wine for a drink o	Ex 29:40	
to the meat o of the morning	Ex 29:41	4503
according to the drink o thereof	Ex 29:41	
an o made by fire unto the LORD	Ex 29:41	
o throughout your generations at	Ex 29:42	
nor burnt sacrifice, nor meat o	Ex 30:9	4503
shall ye pour drink o thereon	Ex 30:9	
blood of the sin o of atonements	Ex 30:10	
shekel shall be the o of the LORD	Ex 30:13	8641
shall give an o unto the LORD	Ex 30:14	8641
when they give an o unto the LORD	Ex 30:15	8641
to burn o made by fire unto the	Ex 30:20	
the altar of burnt o with all his	Ex 30:28	
the altar of burnt o with all his	Ex 31:9	
from among you an o unto the LORD	Ex 35:5	8641

O

him bring it, an *o* of the LORD	Ex 35:5	8641
The altar of burnt *o*, with his	Ex 35:16	
they brought the LORD's *o* to the	Ex 35:21	8641
an *o* of gold unto the LORD	Ex 35:22	
one that did offer an *o* of silver	Ex 35:24	8641
and brass brought the LORD's *o*	Ex 35:24	8641
brought a willing *o* unto the LORD	Ex 35:29	
they received of Moses all the *o*	Ex 36:3	8641
work for the *o* of the sanctuary	Ex 36:6	8641
altar of burnt *o* of shittim wood	Ex 38:1	
place, even the gold of the *o*	Ex 38:24	8573
the brass of the *o* was seventy	Ex 38:29	8573
burnt *o* before the door of the	Ex 40:6	
anoint the altar of the burnt *o*	Ex 40:10	
he put the altar of burnt *o* by	Ex 40:29	
and offered upon it the burnt *o*	Ex 40:29	
and the meat *o*	Ex 40:29	4503
of you bring an *o* unto the LORD	Lev 1:2	7133
shall bring your *o* of the cattle	Lev 1:2	7133
If his *o* be a burnt sacrifice of	Lev 1:3	7133
hand upon the head of the burnt *o*	Lev 1:4	
And he shall flay the burnt *o*	Lev 1:6	
an *o* made by fire, of a sweet	Lev 1:9	
if his *o* be of the flocks, namely	Lev 1:10	7133
an *o* made by fire, of a sweet	Lev 1:13	
for his *o* to the LORD be of fowls	Lev 1:14	7133
shall bring his *o* of turtledoves	Lev 1:14	7133
an *o* made by fire, of a sweet	Lev 1:17	
will offer a meat *o* unto the LORD	Lev 2:1	7133
his *o* shall be of fine flour	Lev 2:1	7133
to be an *o* made by fire, of a	Lev 2:2	
of a meat *o* baken in the oven	Lev 2:4	4503
be a meat *o* baken in a pan	Lev 2:5	4503
it is a meat *o*.	Lev 2:6	4503
a meat *o* baken in the frying pan	Lev 2:7	4503
thou shalt bring the meat *o* that	Lev 2:8	4503
the meat *o* a memorial thereof	Lev 2:9	4503
it is an *o* made by fire, of a	Lev 2:9	
of the meat *o* shall be Aaron's	Lev 2:10	4503
No meat *o*, which ye shall bring	Lev 2:11	4503
in any *o* of the LORD made by fire	Lev 2:11	
every oblation of thy meat *o*	Lev 2:13	4503
God to be lacking from thy meat *o*	Lev 2:13	4503
if thou offer a meat *o* of thy	Lev 2:14	4503
o of thy firstfruits green ears	Lev 2:14	4503
it is a meat *o*.	Lev 2:15	4503
it is an *o* made by fire unto the	Lev 2:16	
be a sacrifice of peace *o*	Lev 3:1	
his hand upon the head of his *o*	Lev 3:2	7133
of the peace *o* an *o* made	Lev 3:3	
it is an *o* made by fire, of a	Lev 3:5	
if his *o* for a sacrifice of peace	Lev 3:6	7133
for a sacrifice of peace *o* unto	Lev 3:6	
If he offer a lamb for his *o*	Lev 3:7	7133
his hand upon the head of his *o*	Lev 3:8	7133
of the peace *o* an *o* made	Lev 3:9	
it is the food of the *o* made by	Lev 3:11	
if his *o* be a goat, then he shall	Lev 3:12	7133
And he shall offer thereof his *o*	Lev 3:14	7133
even an *o* made by fire unto the	Lev 3:14	
it is the food of the *o* made by	Lev 3:16	
blemish unto the LORD for a sin *o*	Lev 4:3	
of the altar of the burnt *o*	Lev 4:7	
fat of the bullock for the sin *o*	Lev 4:8	
upon the altar of the burnt *o*	Lev 4:10	
of the altar of the burnt *o*	Lev 4:18	
did with the bullock for a sin *o*	Lev 4:20	
it is a sin *o* for the	Lev 4:21	
he shall bring his *o*, a kid of	Lev 4:23	7133
kill the burnt *o* before the LORD	Lev 4:24	
it is a sin *o*	Lev 4:24	
of the sin *o* with his finger	Lev 4:25	
the horns of the altar of burnt *o*	Lev 4:25	
bottom of the altar of burnt *o*	Lev 4:25	
then he shall bring his *o*	Lev 4:28	7133
hand upon the head of the sin *o*	Lev 4:29	
slay the sin *o* in the place of	Lev 4:29	
in the place of the burnt *o*	Lev 4:29	
the horns of the altar of burnt *o*	Lev 4:30	
And if he bring a lamb for a sin *o*	Lev 4:32	7133
hand upon the head of the sin *o*	Lev 4:33	
slay it for a sin *o* in the place	Lev 4:33	
place where they kill the burnt *o*	Lev 4:33	
of the sin *o* with his finger	Lev 4:34	
the horns of the altar of burnt *o*	Lev 4:34	
he shall bring his trespass *o*	Lev 5:6	
a kid of the goats, for a sin *o*	Lev 5:6	817
one for a sin *o*, and the other for	Lev 5:7	
and the other for a burnt *o*	Lev 5:7	
that which is for the sin *o* first	Lev 5:8	
of the blood of the sin *o* upon	Lev 5:9	

it is a sin *o*	Lev 5:9	
offer the second for a burnt *o*	Lev 5:10	
o the tenth part of an ephah of	Lev 5:11	7133
ephah of fine flour for a sin *o*	Lev 5:11	
for it is a sin *o*	Lev 5:11	
it is a sin *o*	Lev 5:12	
be the priest's, as a meat *o*	Lev 5:13	4503
the sanctuary, for a trespass *o*	Lev 5:15	
with the ram of the trespass *o*	Lev 5:16	
thy estimation, for a trespass *o*	Lev 5:18	
It is a trespass *o*	Lev 5:19	
in the day of his trespass *o*	Lev 6:5	
his trespass *o* unto the LORD	Lev 6:6	
thy estimation, for a trespass *o*	Lev 6:6	
This is the law of the burnt *o*	Lev 6:9	
It is the burnt *o*, because of the	Lev 6:9	
with the burnt *o* on the altar	Lev 6:10	
lay the burnt *o* in order upon it	Lev 6:12	
And this is the law of the meat *o*	Lev 6:14	4503
of the flour of the meat *o*	Lev 6:15	4503
which is upon the meat *o*, and	Lev 6:15	4503
it is most holy, as is the sin *o*	Lev 6:17	
and as the trespass *o*.	Lev 6:17	
This is the *o* of Aaron and of his	Lev 6:20	7133
fine flour for a meat *o* perpetual	Lev 6:20	4503
o shalt thou offer for a sweet	Lev 6:21	4503
For every meat *o* for the priest	Lev 6:23	4503
This is the law of the sin *o*	Lev 6:25	
burnt *o* is killed shall the sin	Lev 6:25	
is killed shall the sin *o* be	Lev 6:25	
And no sin *o*, whereof any of the	Lev 6:30	
this is the law of the trespass *o*	Lev 7:1	
o shall they kill the trespass *o*	Lev 7:2	
shall they kill the trespass *o*	Lev 7:2	
an *o* made by fire unto the LORD	Lev 7:5	
it is a trespass *o*.	Lev 7:5	
o is, so is the trespass *o*	Lev 7:7	
that offereth any man's burnt *o*	Lev 7:8	
the burnt *o* which he hath offered	Lev 7:8	
all the meat *o* that is baken in	Lev 7:9	4503
And every meat *o*, mingled with oil	Lev 7:10	4503
he shall offer for his *o* leavened	Lev 7:13	7133
for an heave *o* unto the LORD	Lev 7:14	8641
the sacrifice of his *o* be a vow	Lev 7:16	7133
be a vow, or a voluntary *o*	Lev 7:16	
of which men offer an *o* made by	Lev 7:25	
for a wave *o* before the LORD	Lev 7:30	
unto the priest for an heave *o* of	Lev 7:32	8641
This is the law of the burnt *o*	Lev 7:37	
of the meat *o*	Lev 7:37	4503
o, and of the trespass *o*	Lev 7:37	
oil, and a bullock for the sin *o*	Lev 8:2	
brought the bullock for the sin *o*	Lev 8:14	
head of the bullock for the sin *o*	Lev 8:14	
brought the ram for the burnt *o*	Lev 8:18	5930
an *o* made by fire unto the LORD	Lev 8:21	
them for a wave *o* before the LORD	Lev 8:27	
on the altar upon the burnt *o*	Lev 8:28	
it is an *o* made by fire unto the	Lev 8:28	
it for a wave *o* before the LORD	Lev 8:29	
o, and a ram for a burnt *o*	Lev 9:2	
ye a kid of the goats for a sin *o*	Lev 9:3	
without blemish, for a burnt *o*	Lev 9:3	
a meat *o* mingled with oil	Lev 9:4	4503
the altar, and offer thy sin *o*	Lev 9:7	
and thy burnt *o*	Lev 9:7	
offer the *o* of the people, and	Lev 9:7	7133
and slew the calf of the sin *o*	Lev 9:8	
caul above the liver of the sin *o*	Lev 9:10	
And he slew the burnt *o*	Lev 9:12	
presented the burnt *o* unto him	Lev 9:13	
upon the burnt *o* on the altar	Lev 9:14	
And he brought the people's *o*	Lev 9:15	7133
was the sin *o* for the people	Lev 9:15	
And he brought the burnt *o*	Lev 9:16	
And he brought the meat *o*, and took	Lev 9:17	4503
for a wave *o* before the LORD	Lev 9:21	
came down from *o* of the sin	Lev 9:22	6213
the sin *o*, and the burnt *o*	Lev 9:22	
upon the altar the burnt *o*	Lev 9:24	
Take the meat *o* that remaineth of	Lev 10:12	4503
it for a wave *o* before the LORD	Lev 10:15	
sought the goat of the sin *o*	Lev 10:16	
eaten the sin *o* in the holy place	Lev 10:17	
day have they offered their sin *o*	Lev 10:19	
their burnt *o* before the LORD	Lev 10:19	
if I had eaten the sin *o* to day	Lev 10:19	
of the first year for a burnt *o*	Lev 12:6	
or a turtledove, for a sin *o*	Lev 12:6	
the one for the burnt *o*	Lev 12:8	
and the other for a sin *o*	Lev 12:8	

deals of fine flour for a meat o .... Lev 14:10	
and offer him for a trespass o .... Lev 14:12	
them for a wave o before the LORD .... Lev 14:12	
the sin o and the burnt o .... Lev 14:13	
for as the sin o is the priest's, ... Lev 14:13	
so is the trespass o .... Lev 14:13	
of the blood of the trespass o .... Lev 14:14	
upon the blood of the trespass o .... Lev 14:17	
the priest shall offer the sin o .... Lev 14:19	
he shall kill the burnt o .... Lev 14:19	
priest shall offer the burnt o .... Lev 14:20	
the meat o upon the altar .... Lev 14:20	4503
lamb for a trespass o to be waved .... Lev 14:21	
mingled with oil for a meat o .... Lev 14:21	4503
o, and the other a burnt o .... Lev 14:22	
take the lamb of the trespass o .... Lev 14:24	
them for a wave o before the LORD .... Lev 14:24	
kill the lamb of the trespass o .... Lev 14:25	
of the blood of the trespass o .... Lev 14:25	
of the blood of the trespass o .... Lev 14:28	
able to get, the one for a sin o .... Lev 14:31	
and the other for a burnt o .... Lev 14:31	
with the meat o .... Lev 14:31	4503
offer them, the one for a sin o .... Lev 15:15	
and the other for a burnt o .... Lev 15:15	
shall offer the one for a sin o .... Lev 15:30	
and the other for a burnt o .... Lev 15:30	
o, and a ram for a burnt o .... Lev 16:3	
two kids of the goats for a sin o .... Lev 16:5	
and one ram for a burnt o .... Lev 16:5	
offer his bullock of the sin o .... Lev 16:6	
fell, and offer him for a sin o .... Lev 16:9	
bring the bullock of the sin o .... Lev 16:11	
of the sin o which is for himself .... Lev 16:11	
he kill the goat of the sin o .... Lev 16:15	
come forth, and offer his burnt o .... Lev 16:24	
the burnt o of the people, and .... Lev 16:24	
the fat of the sin o shall he .... Lev 16:25	
And the bullock for the sin o .... Lev 16:27	
and the goat for the sin o .... Lev 16:27	
to offer an o unto the LORD .... Lev 17:4	7133
offereth a burnt o or sacrifice .... Lev 17:8	
his trespass o unto the LORD .... Lev 19:21	
even a ram for a trespass o .... Lev 19:21	
o before the LORD for his sin .... Lev 19:22	
eat of an o of the holy things .... Lev 22:12	8641
offer unto the LORD for a burnt o .... Lev 22:18	
or a freewill o in beeves or .... Lev 22:21	
nor make an o by fire of them .... Lev 22:22	
thou offer for a freewill o .... Lev 22:23	
make any o thereof in your land .... Lev 22:24	
an o made by fire unto the LORD .... Lev 22:27	
But ye shall offer an o made by .... Lev 23:8	
year for a burnt o unto the LORD .... Lev 23:12	
the meat o thereof shall be two .... Lev 23:13	4503
an o made by fire unto the LORD .... Lev 23:13	
the drink o thereof shall be of .... Lev 23:13	
have brought an o unto your God .... Lev 23:14	7133
brought the sheaf of the wave o .... Lev 23:15	
offer a new meat o unto the LORD .... Lev 23:16	4503
be for a burnt o unto the LORD .... Lev 23:18	
unto the LORD, with their meat o .... Lev 23:18	4503
even an o made by fire, of sweet .... Lev 23:18	
one kid of the goats for a sin o .... Lev 23:19	
for a wave o before the LORD .... Lev 23:20	
but ye shall offer an o made by .... Lev 23:25	
offer an o made by fire unto the .... Lev 23:27	
an o made by fire unto the LORD .... Lev 23:36	
ye shall offer an o made by fire .... Lev 23:36	
to offer an o made by fire unto .... Lev 23:37	
by fire unto the LORD, a burnt o .... Lev 23:37	
and a meat o .... Lev 23:37	4503
even an o made by fire unto the .... Lev 24:7	
men bring an o unto the LORD .... Lev 27:9	7133
incense, and the daily meat o .... Num 4:16	4503
every o of all the holy things of .... Num 5:9	8641
and he shall bring her o for her .... Num 5:15	7133
for it is an o of jealousy .... Num 5:15	4503
an o of memorial, bringing .... Num 5:15	4503
put the o of memorial in her .... Num 5:18	4503
hands, which is the jealousy o .... Num 5:18	4503
o out of the woman's hand .... Num 5:25	4503
shall wave the o before the LORD, ... Num 5:25	4503
shall take an handful of the o .... Num 5:26	4503
shall offer the one for a sin o .... Num 6:11	
and the other for a burnt o .... Num 6:11	
the first year for a trespass o .... Num 6:12	
shall offer his o unto the LORD .... Num 6:14	7133
without blemish for a burnt o .... Num 6:14	
year without blemish for a sin o .... Num 6:14	
with oil, and their meat o .... Num 6:15	4503

his sin o, and his burnt o .... Num 6:16	
shall offer also his meat o .... Num 6:17	4503
and his drink o .... Num 6:17	
them for a wave o before the LORD .... Num 6:20	
of his o unto the LORD for his .... Num 6:21	7133
brought their o before the LORD .... Num 7:3	7133
offered their o before the altar .... Num 7:10	7133
Moses, They shall offer their o .... Num 7:11	7133
he that offered his o the first .... Num 7:12	7133
his o was one silver charger, the .... Num 7:13	7133
mingled with oil for a meat o .... Num 7:13	4503
of the first year, for a burnt o .... Num 7:15	
One kid of the goats for a sin o .... Num 7:16	
this was the o of Nahshon the son .... Num 7:17	7133
for his o one silver charger .... Num 7:19	7133
mingled with oil for a meat o .... Num 7:19	4503
of the first year, for a burnt o .... Num 7:21	
One kid of the goats for a sin o .... Num 7:22	
this was the o of Nethaneel the .... Num 7:23	7133
His o was one silver charger, the .... Num 7:25	7133
mingled with oil for a meat o .... Num 7:25	4503
of the first year, for a burnt o .... Num 7:27	
One kid of the goats for a sin o .... Num 7:28	
this was the o of Eliab the son .... Num 7:29	7133
His o was one silver charger of .... Num 7:31	7133
mingled with oil for a meat o .... Num 7:31	4503
of the first year, for a burnt o .... Num 7:33	
One kid of the goats for a sin o .... Num 7:34	
this was the o of Elizur the son .... Num 7:35	7133
His o was one silver charger, the .... Num 7:37	7133
mingled with oil for a meat o .... Num 7:37	4503
of the first year, for a burnt o .... Num 7:39	
One kid of the goats for a sin o .... Num 7:40	
this was the o of Shelumiel the .... Num 7:41	7133
His o was one silver charger of .... Num 7:43	7133
mingled with oil for a meat o .... Num 7:43	4503
of the first year, for a burnt o .... Num 7:45	
One kid of the goats for a sin o .... Num 7:46	
this was the o of Eliasaph the .... Num 7:47	7133
His o was one silver charger, the .... Num 7:49	7133
mingled with oil for a meat o .... Num 7:49	4503
of the first year, for a burnt o .... Num 7:51	
One kid of the goats for a sin o .... Num 7:52	
this was the o of Elishama the .... Num 7:53	7133
His o was one silver charger of .... Num 7:55	7133
mingled with oil for a meat o .... Num 7:55	4503
of the first year, for a burnt o .... Num 7:57	
One kid of the goats for a sin o .... Num 7:58	
this was the o of Gamaliel the .... Num 7:59	7133
His o was one silver charger, the .... Num 7:61	7133
mingled with oil for a meat o .... Num 7:61	4503
of the first year, for a burnt o .... Num 7:63	
One kid of the goats for a sin o .... Num 7:64	
this was the o of Abidan the son .... Num 7:65	7133
His o was one silver charger, the .... Num 7:67	7133
mingled with oil for a meat o .... Num 7:67	4503
of the first year, for a burnt o .... Num 7:69	
One kid of the goats for a sin o .... Num 7:70	
this was the o of Ahiezer the son .... Num 7:71	7133
His o was one silver charger, the .... Num 7:73	7133
mingled with oil for a meat o .... Num 7:73	4503
of the first year, for a burnt o .... Num 7:75	
One kid of the goats for a sin o .... Num 7:76	
this was the o of Pagiel the son .... Num 7:77	7133
His o was one silver charger, the .... Num 7:79	7133
mingled with oil for a meat o .... Num 7:79	4503
of the first year, for a burnt o .... Num 7:81	
One kid of the goats for a sin o .... Num 7:82	
this was the o of Ahira the son .... Num 7:83	7133
the burnt o were twelve bullocks .... Num 7:87	
year twelve, with their meat o .... Num 7:87	4503
of the goats for sin o twelve .... Num 7:87	
a young bullock with his meat o .... Num 8:8	4503
shalt thou take for a sin o .... Num 8:8	
an o of the children of Israel .... Num 8:11	8573
shalt offer the one for a sin o .... Num 8:12	
and the other for a burnt o .... Num 8:12	
offer them for an o unto the LORD .... Num 8:13	8573
them, and offer them for an o .... Num 8:15	8573
them as an o before the LORD .... Num 8:21	8573
that we may not offer an o of the .... Num 9:7	7133
because he brought not the o of .... Num 9:13	7133
will make an o by fire unto the .... Num 15:3	
by fire unto the LORD, a burnt o .... Num 15:3	
a vow, or in a freewill o .... Num 15:3	
his o unto the LORD bring a meat .... Num 15:4	7133
a meat o of a tenth deal of flour .... Num 15:4	4503
o shalt thou prepare with the .... Num 15:5	
with the burnt o or sacrifice .... Num 15:5	
a meat o two tenth deals of flour .... Num 15:6	4503
for a drink o thou shalt offer .... Num 15:7	

O

preparest a bullock for a burnt *o* Num 15:8
o of three tenth deals of flour Num 15:9 4503
for a drink *o* half an hin of wine Num 15:10
for an *o* made by fire, of a sweet Num 15:10
after this manner, in *o* Num 15:13 7126
an *o* made by fire Num 15:13
and will offer an *o* made by fire Num 15:14
offer up an heave *o* unto the LORD Num 15:19 8641
of your dough for an heave *o* Num 15:20 8641
as ye do the heave *o* of the Num 15:20 8641
an heave *o* in your generations Num 15:21 8641
one young bullock for a burnt *o* Num 15:24
unto the LORD, with his meat *o* Num 15:24 4503
and his drink *o* Num 15:24
one kid of the goats for a sin *o* Num 15:24
and they shall bring their *o* Num 15:25 7133
their sin *o* before the LORD, for Num 15:25
of the first year for a sin *o* Num 15:27
LORD, Respect not thou their *o* Num 16:15 4503
of theirs, every meat *o* of theirs Num 18:9 4503
and every sin *o* of theirs Num 18:9
and every trespass *o* of theirs Num 18:9
the heave *o* of their gift, with Num 18:11 8641
their fat for an *o* made by fire Num 18:17
offer as an heave *o* unto the LORD Num 18:24 8641
up an heave *o* of it for the LORD Num 18:26 8641
this your heave *o* shall be Num 18:27 8641
heave *o* unto the LORD of all your Num 18:28 8641
heave *o* to Aaron the priest Num 18:28 8641
offer every heave *o* of the LORD Num 18:29 8641
unto Balak, Stand by thy burnt *o* Num 23:3
Balak, Stand here by thy burnt *o* Num 23:15
behold, he stood by his burnt *o* Num 23:17
of Israel, and say unto them, My *o* Num 28:2 7133
This is the *o* made by fire which Num 28:3
by day, for a continual burnt *o* Num 28:3
of an ephah of flour for a meat *o* Num 28:5 4503
It is a continual burnt *o* Num 28:6
the drink *o* thereof shall be the Num 28:7
unto the LORD for a drink *o* Num 28:7
as the meat *o* of the morning, and Num 28:8 4503
and as the drink *o* thereof Num 28:8
tenth deals of flour for a meat *o* Num 28:9 4503
with oil, and the drink *o* thereof Num 28:9
is the burnt *o* of every sabbath Num 28:10
burnt *o*, and his drink *o* Num 28:10
offer a burnt *o* unto the LORD Num 28:11
tenth deals of flour for a meat *o* Num 28:12 4503
tenth deals of flour for a meat *o* Num 28:12 4503
oil for a meat *o* unto one lamb Num 28:13 4503
for a burnt *o* of a sweet savour, Num 28:13
this is the burnt *o* of every Num 28:14
o unto the LORD shall be offered Num 28:15
burnt *o*, and his drink *o* Num 28:15
fire for a burnt *o* unto the LORD Num 28:19
their meat *o* shall be of flour Num 28:20 4503
And one goat for a sin *o*, to make Num 28:22
beside the burnt *o* in the morning Num 28:23
which is for a continual burnt *o* Num 28:23
burnt *o*, and his drink *o* Num 28:24
bring a new meat *o* unto the LORD Num 28:26 4503
o for a sweet savour unto the Num 28:27
their meat *o* of flour mingled Num 28:28 4503
them beside the continual burnt *o* Num 28:31
and his meat *o* Num 28:31 4503
ye shall offer a burnt *o* for a Num 29:2
their meat *o* shall be of flour Num 29:3 4503
one kid of the goats for a sin *o* Num 29:5
Beside the burnt *o* of the month Num 29:6
of the month, and his meat *o* Num 29:6 4503
and the daily burnt *o* Num 29:6
and his meat *o* Num 29:6 4503
burnt *o* unto the LORD for a sweet Num 29:8
their meat *o* shall be of flour Num 29:9 4503
One kid of the goats for a sin *o* Num 29:11
beside the sin *o* of atonement Num 29:11
and the continual burnt *o* Num 29:11
and the meat *o* of it Num 29:11 4503
And ye shall offer a burnt *o* Num 29:13
their meat *o* shall be of flour Num 29:14 4503
one kid of the goats for a sin *o* Num 29:16
beside the continual burnt *o* Num 29:16
his meat *o* Num 29:16 4503
his meat *o*, and his drink *o* Num 29:16
And their meat *o* and their drink Num 29:18 4503
one kid of the goats for a sin *o* Num 29:19
beside the continual burnt *o* Num 29:19
and the meat *o* thereof Num 29:19 4503
And their meat *o* and their drink Num 29:21 4503
And one goat for a sin *o* Num 29:22
beside the continual burnt *o* Num 29:22
and his meat *o* Num 29:22 4503
and his drink *o* Num 29:22
Their meat *o* and their drink Num 29:24 4503
one kid of the goats for a sin *o* Num 29:25
beside the continual burnt *o* Num 29:25
his meat *o*, and his drink Num 29:25 4503
and his drink *o*. Num 29:25
And their meat *o* and their drink Num 29:27 4503
And one goat for a sin *o* Num 29:28
beside the continual burnt *o* Num 29:28
and his meat *o* Num 29:28 4503
and his drink *o* Num 29:28
And their meat *o* and their drink Num 29:30 4503
And one goat for a sin *o* Num 29:31
beside the continual burnt *o* Num 29:31
his meat *o*, and his drink Num 29:31 4503
and his drink *o* Num 29:31
And their meat *o* and their drink Num 29:33 4503
And one goat for a sin *o* Num 29:34
beside the continual burnt *o* Num 29:34
his meat *o*, and his drink Num 29:34 4503
and his drink *o* Num 29:34
But ye shall offer a burnt *o* Num 29:36
Their meat *o* and their drink Num 29:37 4503
And one goat for a sin *o* Num 29:38
beside the continual burnt *o* Num 29:38
and his meat *o* Num 29:38 4503
and his drink *o* Num 29:38
for an heave *o* of the LORD Num 31:29 8641
which was the LORD's heave *o* Num 31:41 8641
all the gold of the *o* that they Num 31:52 8641
the heave *o* of your hand, and all Deut 12:11 8641
or heave *o* of thine hand Deut 12:17 8641
of a freewill *o* of thine hand Deut 16:10
even a freewill *o*, according as Deut 23:23
thereon burnt *o* or meat Josh 22:23
or meat *o*, or if Josh 22:23 4503
us an altar, not for burnt *o* Josh 22:26
I will offer it up for a burnt *o* Judg 11:31
and if thou wilt offer a burnt *o* Judg 13:16
Manoah took a kid with a meat *o* Judg 13:19 4503
would not have received a burnt *o* Judg 13:23
a meat *o* at our hands, neither Judg 13:23 4503
men abhorred the *o* of the LORD 1Sa 2:17 4503
ye at my sacrifice and at mine *o* 1Sa 2:29 4503
with sacrifice nor *o* for ever 1Sa 3:14 4503
any wise return him a trespass *o* 1Sa 6:3
What shall be the trespass *o* 1Sa 6:4
ye return him for a trespass *o* 1Sa 6:8
the kine a burnt *o* unto the LORD 1Sa 6:14
for a trespass *o* unto the LORD 1Sa 6:17
a burnt *o* wholly unto the LORD 1Sa 7:9
as Samuel was *o* up the burnt 1Sa 7:10 5927
up the burnt *o* 1Sa 7:10
Bring hither a burnt *o* to me 1Sa 13:9
And he offered the burnt *o* 1Sa 13:9
an end of *o* the burnt 1Sa 13:10 5927
the burnt *o*, behold 1Sa 13:10
therefore, and offered a burnt *o* 1Sa 13:12
against me, let him accept an *o* 1Sa 26:19 4503
made an end of *o* burnt offerings 2Sa 6:18 5927
until the time of the *o* of the 1Kin 18:29 5927
of the *o* of the evening sacrifice 1Kin 18:36 5927
when the meat *o* was offered 2Kin 3:20 4503
him for a burnt *o* upon the wall 2Kin 3:27
o nor sacrifice unto other gods 2Kin 5:17
an end of *o* the burnt 2Kin 10:25 6213
the burnt *o*, that Jehu 2Kin 10:25
And he burnt his burnt *o* and his 2Kin 16:13
and his meat *o* 2Kin 16:13 4503
and poured his drink *o* 2Kin 16:13
altar burn the morning burnt *o* 2Kin 16:15
and the evening meat *o* 2Kin 16:15 4503
burnt sacrifice, and his meat *o* 2Kin 16:15
with the burnt *o* of all the 2Kin 16:15
of the land, and their meat *o* 2Kin 16:15 4503
it all the blood of the burnt *o* 2Kin 16:15
upon the altar of the burnt *o* 1Chr 6:49
an end of *o* the burnt offerings 1Chr 16:2 5927
bring an *o*, and come before him 1Chr 16:29 4503
the burnt *o* continually morning 1Chr 16:40
wood, and the wheat for the meat *o* 1Chr 21:23 4503
by fire upon the altar of burnt *o* 1Chr 21:26
and the altar of the burnt *o* 1Chr 21:29
altar of the burnt *o* for Israel 1Chr 22:1
and for the fine flour for meat *o* 1Chr 23:29 4503
the burnt *o* they washed in them 2Chr 4:6
heaven, and consumed the burnt *o* 2Chr 7:1
o according to the commandment of 2Chr 8:13 5927
the LORD, and the altar of burnt *o* 2Chr 29:18
for a sin *o* for the kingdom, and 2Chr 29:21

for the sin *o* before the king 2Chr 29:23
king commanded that the burnt *o* 2Chr 29:24
the sin *o* should be made for all 2Chr 29:24
offer the burnt *o* upon the altar 2Chr 29:27
And when the burnt *o* began 2Chr 29:27
until the burnt *o* was finished 2Chr 29:28
And when they had made an end of *o* ...2Chr 29:29   5927
were for a burnt *o* to the LORD 2Chr 29:32
drink offerings for every burnt *o* 2Chr 29:35
o peace offerings, and making 2Chr 30:22   2076
busied in *o* of burnt offerings 2Chr 35:14   5927
beside the freewill *o* for the ....Ezr 1:4
offered the continual burnt *o* ....Ezr 3:5
a freewill *o* unto the LORD ....Ezr 3:5
for a sin *o* for all Israel, ...Ezr 6:17
with the freewill *o* of the people ....Ezr 7:16
o willingly for the house of ....Ezr 7:16
even the *o* of the house of our ....Ezr 8:25   8641
the gold are a freewill *o* unto ....Ezr 8:28
twelve he goats for a sin *o* ....Ezr 8:35
this was a burnt *o* unto the LORD ....Ezr 8:35
and for the continual meat *o* ....Neh 10:33   4503
and for the continual burnt *o* ....Neh 10:33
and the people, for the wood *o* ....Neh 10:34   7133
shall bring the *o* of the corn ....Neh 10:39   8641
the house of God, with the meat *o* ....Neh 13:9   4503
And for the wood *o*, at times ....Neh 13:31   7133
offer up for yourselves a burnt *o* ....Job 42:8
and *o* thou didst not desire ....Ps 40:6   4503
burnt *o* and sin *o* hast thou ....Ps 40:6
thou delightest not in burnt *o* ....Ps 51:16
burnt *o* and whole burnt *o* ....Ps 51:19
bring an *o*, and come into his ....Ps 96:8   4503
thereof sufficient for a burnt *o* ....Is 40:16
caused thee to serve with an *o* ....Is 43:23   4503
shalt make his soul an *o* for sin ....Is 53:10
them hast thou poured a drink *o* ....Is 57:6
thou hast offered a meat *o* ....Is 57:6   4503
I hate robbery for burnt *o* ....Is 61:8
the drink *o* unto that number ....Is 65:11
for an *o* unto the LORD out of all ....Is 66:20   4503
an *o* in a clean vessel into the ....Is 66:20   4503
to anger in *o* incense unto Baal ....Jer 11:17
and when they offer burnt *o* ....Jer 14:12
the provocation of their *o* ....Eze 20:28   7133
where they washed the burnt *o* ....Eze 40:38
side, to slay thereon the burnt *o* ....Eze 40:39
sin *o* and the trespass *o* ....Eze 40:39
of hewn stone for the burnt *o* ....Eze 40:42
wherewith they slew the burnt *o* ....Eze 40:42
the tables was the flesh of the *o* ....Eze 40:43   7133
most holy things, and the meat *o* ....Eze 42:13   4503
sin *o*, and the trespass *o* ....Eze 42:13
GOD, a young bullock for a sin *o* ....Eze 43:19
the bullock also of the sin *o* ....Eze 43:21
goats without blemish for a sin *o* ....Eze 43:22
up for a burnt *o* unto the LORD ....Eze 43:24
every day a goat for a sin *o* ....Eze 43:25
they shall slay the burnt *o* ....Eze 44:11
he shall offer his sin *o* ....Eze 44:27
They shall eat the meat *o* ....Eze 44:29   4503
sin *o*, and the trespass *o* ....Eze 44:29
for a meat *o*, and for a burnt ....Eze 45:15   4503
and for a burnt *o* ....Eze 45:15
he shall prepare the sin *o* ....Eze 45:17
and the meat *o* ....Eze 45:17   4503
and the burnt *o* ....Eze 45:17
take of the blood of the sin *o* ....Eze 45:19
of the land a bullock for a sin *o* ....Eze 45:22
prepare a burnt *o* to the LORD ....Eze 45:23
of the goats daily for a sin *o* ....Eze 45:23
he shall prepare a meat *o* of an ....Eze 45:24   4503
days, according to the sin *o* ....Eze 45:25
according to the burnt *o* ....Eze 45:25
and according to the meat *o* ....Eze 45:25   4503
priests shall prepare his burnt *o* ....Eze 46:2
the burnt *o* that the prince shall ....Eze 46:4
the meat *o* shall be an ephah for ....Eze 46:5   4503
the meat *o* for the lambs as he ....Eze 46:5   4503
And he shall prepare a meat *o* ....Eze 46:7   4503
in the solemnities the meat *o* ....Eze 46:11   4503
o or peace offerings voluntarily ....Eze 46:12
and he shall prepare his burnt *o* ....Eze 46:12
shalt daily prepare a burnt *o* ....Eze 46:13
a meat *o* for it every morning ....Eze 46:14   4503
a meat *o* continually by a ....Eze 46:14   4503
prepare the lamb, and the meat *o* ....Eze 46:15   4503
morning for a continual burnt *o* ....Eze 46:15
trespass *o* and the sin *o* ....Eze 46:20
where they shall bake the meat *o* ....Eze 46:20   4503
shall be the *o* which ye shall ....Eze 48:8   8641

The meat *o* and the drink ....Joel 1:9   4503
the drink *o* is cut off from the ....Joel 1:9
for the meat *o* and the drink ....Joel 1:13   4503
the drink *o* is withholden from ....Joel 1:13
even a meat *o* and a drink ....Joel 2:14   4503
a drink *o* unto the LORD your God ....Joel 2:14
my dispersed, shall bring mine *o* ....Zeph 3:10   4503
will I accept an *o* at your hand ....Mal 1:10   4503
offered unto my name, and a pure *o* ......Mal 1:11   4503
thus ye brought an *o* ....Mal 1:13   4503
him that offereth an *o* unto the ....Mal 2:12   4503
he regardeth not the *o* any more ....Mal 2:13   4503
the LORD an *o* in righteousness ....Mal 3:3   4503
Then shall the *o* of Judah ....Mal 3:4   4503
coming to him, and *o* him vinegar, ...Lk 23:36   4374
until that an *o* should be offered ....Acts 21:26   4376
that the *o* up of the Gentiles ....Rom 15:16   4376
and hath given himself for us an *o* ....Eph 5:2   4376
o thou wouldest not, but a body ....Heb 10:5   4376
when he said, Sacrifice and *o* ....Heb 10:8   4376
o for sin thou wouldest not, ...Heb 10:8
the *o* of the body of Jesus Christ ....Heb 10:10   4376
o oftentimes the same sacrifices, ...Heb 10:11   4374
For by one *o* he hath perfected ....Heb 10:14   4376
is, there is no more *o* for sin ....Heb 10:18   4376

OFFERINGS
and offered burnt *o* on the altar ....Gen 8:20
us also sacrifices and burnt *o* ....Ex 10:25
sacrifice thereon thy burnt *o* ....Ex 20:24
burnt *o*, and thy peace *o* ....Ex 20:24
of Israel, which offered burnt *o* ....Ex 24:5
sacrificed peace *o* of oxen unto ....Ex 24:5   2077
of the sacrifice of their peace *o* ....Ex 29:28
on the morrow, and offered burnt *o* ....Ex 32:6
o, and brought peace *o* ....Ex 32:6
yet unto him free *o* every morning ....Ex 36:3
of the meat *o* shall be Aaron's ....Lev 2:3
of the *o* of the LORD made by fire ....Lev 2:3
of the *o* of the LORD made by fire ....Lev 2:10
with all thine *o* thou shalt offer ....Lev 2:13   7133
of the sacrifice of peace *o* ....Lev 4:10
fat of the sacrifice of peace *o* ....Lev 4:26
from off the sacrifice of peace *o* ....Lev 4:31
from the sacrifice of the peace *o* ....Lev 4:35
according to the *o* made by fire ....Lev 4:35
according to the *o* made by fire ....Lev 5:12
thereon the fat of the peace *o* ....Lev 6:12
portion of my *o* made by fire ....Lev 6:17
the *o* of the LORD made by fire ....Lev 6:18
law of the sacrifice of peace *o* ....Lev 7:11
of thanksgiving of his peace *o* ....Lev 7:13
the blood of the peace *o* ....Lev 7:14
of the sacrifice of his peace *o* ....Lev 7:15
o be eaten at all on the third ....Lev 7:18
flesh of the sacrifice of peace *o* ....Lev 7:20
flesh of the sacrifice of peace *o* ....Lev 7:21
the sacrifice of his peace *o* unto ....Lev 7:29
of the sacrifice of peace *o* ....Lev 7:29
the *o* of the LORD made by fire ....Lev 7:30
of the sacrifices of your peace *o* ....Lev 7:32
offereth the blood of the peace *o* ....Lev 7:33
the sacrifices of their peace *o* ....Lev 7:34
out of the *o* of the LORD made by ....Lev 7:35
of the sacrifice of the peace *o* ....Lev 7:37
a bullock and a ram for peace *o* ....Lev 9:4
ram for a sacrifice of peace *o* ....Lev 9:18
and the burnt offering, and peace *o* ......Lev 9:22
of the *o* of the LORD made by fire ....Lev 10:12
peace *o* of the children of Israel ....Lev 10:14
the *o* made by fire of the fat ....Lev 10:15
them for peace *o* unto the LORD ....Lev 17:5   2077
of peace *o* unto the LORD, ye ....Lev 19:5
for the *o* of the LORD made by ....Lev 21:6
the *o* of the LORD made by fire ....Lev 21:21
vows, and for all his freewill *o* ....Lev 22:18
offereth a sacrifice of peace *o* ....Lev 22:21
meat offering, and their drink *o* ....Lev 23:18
year for a sacrifice of peace *o* ....Lev 23:19
offering, a sacrifice, and drink *o* ....Lev 23:37
and beside all your freewill *o* ....Lev 23:38
o of the LORD made by fire by a ....Lev 24:9
ram without blemish for peace *o* ....Num 6:14
meat offering, and their drink *o* ....Num 6:15
of peace *o* unto the LORD, with ....Num 6:17
the sacrifice of the peace *o* ....Num 6:18
And for a sacrifice of peace *o* ....Num 7:17
And for a sacrifice of peace *o* ....Num 7:23
And for a sacrifice of peace *o* ....Num 7:29
And for a sacrifice of peace *o* ....Num 7:35
And for a sacrifice of peace *o* ....Num 7:41

O

And for a sacrifice of peace o	Num 7:47	
And for a sacrifice of peace o	Num 7:53	
And for a sacrifice of peace o	Num 7:59	
And for a sacrifice of peace o	Num 7:65	
And for a sacrifice of peace o	Num 7:71	
And for a sacrifice of peace o	Num 7:77	
And for a sacrifice of peace o	Num 7:83	
of the peace o were twenty	Num 7:88	
the trumpets over your burnt o	Num 10:10	
the sacrifices of your peace o	Num 10:10	
a vow, or peace o unto the LORD	Num 15:8	
o of all the hallowed things of	Num 18:8	8641
with all the wave o of the	Num 18:11	
All the heave o of the holy	Num 18:19	8641
their drink o shall be half an	Num 28:14	
without blemish) and their drink o	Num 28:31	
meat offering, and their drink o	Num 29:6	
offering of it, and their drink o	Num 29:11	
their drink o for the bullocks,	Num 29:18	
thereof, and their drink o	Num 29:19	
their drink o for the bullocks,	Num 29:21	
their drink o for the bullocks,	Num 29:24	
their drink o for the bullocks,	Num 29:27	
their drink o for the bullocks,	Num 29:30	
their drink o for the bullocks,	Num 29:33	
their drink o for the bullock,	Num 29:37	
your vows, and your freewill o	Num 29:39	
for your burnt o	Num 29:39	
and for your meat o	Num 29:39	4503
and for your drink o	Num 29:39	
and for your peace o	Num 29:39	
ye shall bring your burnt o	Deut 12:6	
heave o of your hand, and your	Deut 12:6	
and your vows, and your freewill o	Deut 12:6	
your burnt o, and your sacrifices,	Deut 12:11	
that thou offer not thy burnt o	Deut 12:13	
thou shalt offer thy burnt o	Deut 12:14	
thou vowest, nor thy freewill o	Deut 12:17	
And thou shalt offer thy burnt o	Deut 12:27	
they shall eat the o of the LORD	Deut 18:1	
thou shalt offer burnt o thereon	Deut 27:6	
And thou shalt offer peace o	Deut 27:7	
drank the wine of their drink o	Deut 32:38	
thereon burnt o unto the LORD	Josh 8:31	
the LORD, and sacrificed peace o	Josh 8:31	
or if to offer peace o thereon	Josh 22:23	2077
LORD before him with our burnt o	Josh 22:27	
sacrifices, and with our peace o	Josh 22:27	
our fathers made, not for burnt o	Josh 22:28	
to build an altar for burnt o	Josh 22:29	
for burnt o, for meat o	Josh 22:29	4503
until even, and offered burnt o	Judg 20:26	
and peace o before the LORD	Judg 20:26	
burnt o and peace o	Judg 21:4	
o made by fire of the children of	1Sa 2:28	
of all the o of Israel my people	1Sa 2:29	4503
of Beth-shemesh offered burnt o	1Sa 6:15	
down unto thee, to offer burnt o	1Sa 10:8	
sacrifice sacrifices of peace o	1Sa 10:8	
of peace o before the LORD	1Sa 11:15	
burnt offering to me, and peace o	1Sa 13:9	
LORD as great delight in burnt o	1Sa 15:22	
rain, upon you, nor fields of o	2Sa 1:21	8641
and David offered burnt o and peace	2Sa 6:17	
and peace o before the LORD	2Sa 6:17	
burnt o and peace o	2Sa 6:18	
neither will I offer burnt o unto	2Sa 24:24	
burnt o and peace o	2Sa 24:25	
a thousand burnt o did Solomon	1Kin 3:4	
the LORD, and offered up burnt o	1Kin 3:15	
o, and offered peace o	1Kin 3:15	
offered a sacrifice of peace o	1Kin 8:63	
for there he offered burnt o	1Kin 8:64	
and meat o	1Kin 8:64	4503
and the fat of the peace o	1Kin 8:64	
too little to receive the burnt o	1Kin 8:64	
and meat o	1Kin 8:64	4503
and the fat of the peace o	1Kin 8:64	
a year did Solomon offer burnt o	1Kin 9:25	
peace o upon the altar which he	1Kin 9:25	
in to offer sacrifices and burnt o	2Kin 10:24	
the blood of his peace o, upon	2Kin 16:13	
meat offering, and their drink o	2Kin 16:15	
sacrifices and peace o before God	1Chr 16:1	
burnt o and the peace o	1Chr 16:2	
To offer burnt o unto the LORD	1Chr 16:40	
thee the oxen also for burnt o	1Chr 21:23	
nor offer burnt o without cost	1Chr 21:24	
burnt o and peace o	1Chr 21:26	
and offered burnt o unto the LORD	1Chr 29:21	
lambs, with their drink o	1Chr 29:21	

a thousand burnt o upon it	2Chr 1:6	
and for the burnt o morning	2Chr 2:4	
for there he offered burnt o	2Chr 7:7	
and the fat of the peace o	2Chr 7:7	
not able to receive the burnt o	2Chr 7:7	
and the meat o	2Chr 7:7	4503
Then Solomon offered burnt o unto	2Chr 8:12	
to offer the burnt o of the LORD	2Chr 23:18	
they offered burnt o in the house	2Chr 24:14	
incense nor offered burnt o in	2Chr 29:7	
thank o into the house of the	2Chr 29:31	
brought in sacrifices and thank o	2Chr 29:31	
as were of a free heart burnt o	2Chr 29:31	
And the number of the burnt o	2Chr 29:32	
could not flay all the burnt o	2Chr 29:34	
And also the burnt o were in	2Chr 29:35	
with the fat of the peace o	2Chr 29:35	
the drink o for every burnt	2Chr 29:35	
brought in the burnt o into the	2Chr 30:15	
seven days, offering peace o	2Chr 30:22	2077
priests and Levites for burnt o	2Chr 31:2	
and for peace o	2Chr 31:2	
of his substance for the burnt o	2Chr 31:3	
the morning and evening burnt o	2Chr 31:3	
the burnt o for the sabbaths, and	2Chr 31:3	
the o into the house of the LORD	2Chr 31:10	8641
And brought in the o and the tithes	2Chr 31:12	8641
was over the freewill o of God	2Chr 31:14	8641
and sacrificed thereon peace o	2Chr 33:16	2077
and thank o, and commanded	2Chr 33:16	
and kids, all for the passover o	2Chr 35:7	
for the passover o two thousand	2Chr 35:8	
o five thousand small cattle	2Chr 35:9	
And they removed the burnt o	2Chr 35:12	
the other holy o sod they in pots	2Chr 35:13	
busied in offering of burnt o	2Chr 35:14	
to offer burnt o upon the altar	2Chr 35:16	
Israel, to offer burnt o thereon	Ezr 3:2	
they offered burnt o thereon unto	Ezr 3:3	
the LORD, even burnt o morning	Ezr 3:3	
the daily burnt o by number	Ezr 3:4	
to offer burnt o unto the LORD	Ezr 3:6	
for the burnt o of the God of	Ezr 6:9	
rams, lambs, with their meat o	Ezr 7:17	4503
and their drink o	Ezr 7:17	
offered burnt o unto the God of	Ezr 8:35	
and for the sin o to make an	Neh 10:33	
of our dough, and our o, and the	Neh 10:37	8641
for the treasures, for the o	Neh 12:44	8641
aforetime they laid the meat o	Neh 13:5	4503
and the o of the priests	Neh 13:5	4503
offered burnt o according to the	Job 1:5	
their drink o of blood will I not	Ps 16:4	
Remember all thy o, and accept thy	Ps 20:3	4503
for thy sacrifices or thy burnt o	Ps 50:8	
go into thy house with burnt o	Ps 66:13	
thee, the freewill o of my mouth	Ps 119:108	
I have peace o with me	Prov 7:14	
I am full of the burnt o of rams	Is 1:11	
the small cattle of thy burnt o	Is 43:23	
their burnt o and their sacrifices	Is 56:7	
your burnt o are not acceptable,	Jer 6:20	
pour out drink o unto other gods	Jer 7:18	5262
Put your burnt o unto your	Jer 7:21	
concerning burnt o or sacrifices	Jer 7:22	
from the south, bringing burnt o	Jer 17:26	
and sacrifices, and meat o	Jer 17:26	4503
with fire for burnt o unto Baal	Jer 19:5	
out drink o unto other gods	Jer 19:13	
out drink o unto other gods	Jer 32:29	
a man before me to offer burnt o	Jer 33:18	
and to kindle meat o	Jer 33:18	4503
and having cut themselves, with o	Jer 41:5	4503
and to pour out drink o unto her	Jer 44:17	
and to pour out drink o unto her	Jer 44:18	
and poured out drink o unto her	Jer 44:19	
and pour out drink o unto her	Jer 44:19	
and to pour out drink o unto her	Jer 44:25	
and poured out there their drink o	Eze 20:28	
and there will I require your o	Eze 20:40	8641
make it, to offer burnt o thereon	Eze 43:18	
make your burnt o upon the altar	Eze 43:27	
upon the altar, and your peace o	Eze 43:27	
a burnt offering, and for peace o	Eze 45:15	
the prince's part to give burnt o	Eze 45:17	
and meat o, and drink	Eze 45:17	4503
and drink o, in the	Eze 45:17	
burnt offering, and the peace o	Eze 45:17	
his burnt offering and his peace o	Eze 46:2	
burnt offering or peace o	Eze 46:12	
his burnt offering and his peace o	Eze 46:12	

of God more than burnt o .... Hos 6:6
for the sacrifices of mine o .... Hos 8:13   1890
not offer wine o to the LORD .... Hos 9:4
and proclaim and publish the free o ...... Amos 4:5
Though ye offer me burnt o .... Amos 5:22
and your meat o .... Amos 5:22   4503
the peace o of your fat beasts................. Amos 5:22
o in the wilderness forty years, ... Amos 5:25   4503
I come before him with burnt o .... Mic 6:6
In tithes and o .... Mal 3:8   8641
is more than all whole burnt o .... Mk 12:33   *3646*
cast in unto the o of God .... Lk 21:4   *1435*
to bring alms to my nation, and o .... Acts 24:17   4376
In burnt o and sacrifices for sin .... Heb 10:6   *3646*
Sacrifice and offering and burnt o......... Heb 10:8   *3646*

OFFICE

me he restored unto mine o .... Gen 41:13   3653
When ye do the o of a midwife to .... Ex 1:16
unto me in the priest's o .... Ex 28:1
unto me in the priest's o .... Ex 28:3
unto me in the priest's o .... Ex 28:4
unto me in the priest's o .... Ex 28:41
unto me in the priest's o .... Ex 29:1
the priest's o shall be theirs .... Ex 29:9
minister to me in the priest's o .... Ex 29:44
unto me in the priest's o .... Ex 30:30
to minister in the priest's o .... Ex 31:10
to minister in the priest's o .... Ex 35:19
to minister in the priest's o .... Ex 39:41
unto me in the priest's o .... Ex 40:13
unto me in the priest's o .... Ex 40:15
unto the LORD in the priest's o .... Lev 7:35
priest's o in his father's stead .... Lev 16:32
to minister in the priest's o .... Num 3:3
ministered in the priest's o in .... Num 3:4
shall wait on their priest's o .... Num 3:10
to the o of Eleazar the son of................. Num 4:16   6486
o for every thing of the altar .... Num 18:7
I have given your priest's o unto .... Num 18:7
in the priest's o in his stead .... Deut 10:6
o in the temple that Solomon 1Chr 6:10
their o according to their order 1Chr 6:32   5656
seer did ordain in their set o 1Chr 9:22
porters, were in their set o 1Chr 9:26
had the set o over the things 1Chr 9:31
Because their o was to wait on 1Chr 23:28   4612
Ithamar executed their priest's o 1Chr 24:2
the priest's o unto the LORD 2Chr 11:14
o by the hand of the Levites 2Chr 24:11   6486
of the priests, in their set o 2Chr 31:15
for in their set o they 2Chr 31:18
their o was to distribute unto................. Neh 13:13
and let another take his o .... Ps 109:8   6486
to do the o of a priest unto me, ... Eze 44:13
o before God in the order of his .... Lk 1:8   2407
to the custom of the priest's o .... Lk 1:9   2405
of the Gentiles, I magnify mine o .... Rom 11:13   1248
all members have not the same o .... Rom 12:4   4234
If a man desire the o of a bishop 1Ti 3:1   1984
let them use the o of a deacon 1Ti 3:10   1247
For they that have used the o 1Ti 3:13   1247
of Levi, who receive the o of the .... Heb 7:5   2405

OFFICER

an o of Pharaoh's, and captain of........... Gen 37:36   5631
an o of Pharaoh, captain of the .... Gen 39:1   5631
and Zebul his o .... Judg 9:28   6496
the son of Nathan was principal o 1Kin 4:5   5324
he was the o of which was in 1Kin 4:19   5333
the king of Israel called an o 1Kin 22:9   5631
appointed unto her a certain o 2Kin 8:6   5631
out of the city he took an o that 2Kin 25:19   5631
and the high priest's o came 2Chr 24:11   6496
the judge deliver thee to the o .... Mt 5:25   5257
the judge deliver thee to the o .... Lk 12:58   4233
the o cast thee into prison .... Lk 12:58   4233

OFFICERS

was wroth against two of his o .... Gen 40:2   5631
he asked Pharaoh's o that were............. Gen 40:7   5631
let him appoint o over the land.............. Gen 41:34   6496
of the people, and their o........................ Ex 5:6   7860
the people went out, and their o .... Ex 5:10   7860
the o of the children of Israel, ... Ex 5:14   7860
Then the o of the children of .... Ex 5:15   7860
the o of the children of Israel................. Ex 5:19   7860
of the people, and o over them .... Num 11:16   7860
was wroth with the o of the host .... Num 31:14   6485
the o which were over thousands .... Num 31:48   6485
over tens, and o among your tribes .... Deut 1:15   7860
o shalt thou make thee in all thy .... Deut 16:18   7860

the o shall speak unto the people .... Deut 20:5   7860
the o shall speak further unto .... Deut 20:8   7860
when the o have made an end of .... Deut 20:9   7860
tribes, your elders, and your o .... Deut 29:10   7860
elders of your tribes, and your o .... Deut 31:28   7860
commanded the o of the people .... Josh 1:10   7860
that the o went through the host .... Josh 3:2   7860
all Israel, and their elders, and o .... Josh 8:33   7860
for their judges, and for their o .... Josh 23:2   7860
for their judges, and for their o .... Josh 24:1   7860
your vineyards, and give to his o 1Sa 8:15   5631
the son of Nathan was over the o 1Kin 4:5   5324
had twelve o over all Israel.................... 1Kin 4:7   5324
those o provided victual for king 1Kin 4:27   5324
unto the place where the o were 1Kin 4:28
o which were over the work 1Kin 5:16   5324
These were the chief of the o................. 1Kin 9:23   5324
the o of the host, and said unto 2Kin 11:15   6485
the priest appointed o over the.............. 2Kin 11:18   6486
and his princes, and his o 2Kin 24:12   5631
and the king's wives, and his o 2Kin 24:15   5631
and six thousand were o and judges 1Chr 23:4   7860
business over Israel, for o 1Chr 26:29   7860
were o among them of Israel on 1Chr 26:30   6486
their o that served the king in 1Chr 27:1   7860
king, and of his sons, with the o 1Chr 28:1   5631
the chief of king Solomon's o 2Chr 8:10   5324
of Israel called for one of his o 2Chr 18:8   5631
the Levites shall be o before you 2Chr 19:11   7860
Levites there were scribes, and o........... 2Chr 34:13   7860
to all the o of his house .... Est 1:8   7227
let the king appoint o in all the .... Est 2:3   6496
o of the king, helped the Jews................ Est 9:3   6213
I will also make thy o peace .... Is 60:17   6496
that ye should be o in the house .... Jer 29:26   6496
chief priests sent o to take him.............. Jn 7:32   5257
Then came the o to the chief................... Jn 7:45   5257
The o answered, Never man spake........ Jn 7:46   5257
o from the chief priests and .... Jn 18:3   5257
o of the Jews took Jesus, and .... Jn 18:12   5257
o stood there, who had made a .... Jn 18:18   5257
one of the o which stood by.................... Jn 18:22   5257
o saw him, they cried out, saying .... Jn 19:6   5257
But when the o came, and found .... Acts 5:22   5257
Then went the captain with the o .... Acts 5:26   5257

OFFICES

thee, into one of the priests' o 1Sa 2:36
to their o in their service........................ 1Chr 24:3   6486
And the priests waited on their o 2Chr 7:6   4931
Also Jehoiada appointed the o of 2Chr 23:18   6486
of my God, and for the o thereof............ Neh 13:14   4929

OFFSCOURING

Thou hast made us as the o..................... Lam 3:45   5501
are the o of all things unto this 1Cor 4:13   4067

OFFSPRING

thine o as the grass of the earth .... Job 5:25   6631
their o before their eyes......................... Job 21:8   6631
his o shall not be satisfied with.............. Job 27:14   6631
yea, let my o be rooted out .... Job 31:8   6631
of his father's house, the o...................... Is 22:24   6631
seed, and my blessing upon thine o .... Is 44:3   6631
the o of thy bowels like the..................... Is 48:19   6631
and their o among the people .... Is 61:9   6631
of the LORD, and their o with them .... Is 65:23   6631
have said, For we are also his o .... Acts 17:28   1085
then as we are the o of God .... Acts 17:29   1085
the o of David, and the bright and........ Rev 22:16   1085

OFT

that as o as he passed by, he 2Kin 4:8   1767
How o is the candle of the wicked .... Job 21:17
how o cometh their destruction .... Job 21:17
How o did they provoke him in the........ Ps 78:40
Why do we and the Pharisees fast o ...... Mt 9:14   *4183*
the fire, and o into the water.................. Mt 17:15   *4178*
how o shall my brother sin...................... Mt 18:21   *4212*
except they wash their hands o .... Mk 7:3   *4435*
I punished them o in every .... Acts 26:11   *4178*
do ye, as o as ye drink it, in 1Cor 11:25   *3740*
more frequent, in deaths o 2Cor 11:23   *4178*
for he o refreshed me, and was not 2Ti 1:16   *4178*
in the rain that cometh o upon it............ Heb 6:7   *4178*

OFTEN See APPENDIX.

OFTENER

wherefore he sent for him the o .... Acts 24:26   *4437*

OFTENTIMES

things worketh God o with man ..... Job 33:29   6471,7969
For o also thine own heart .... Eccl 7:22   6471,7227

O

For *o* it had caught him	Lk 8:29	4183,5550
that *o* I purposed to come unto	Rom 1:13	4178
whom we have *o* proved diligent in	2Cor 8:22	4178
offering *o* the same sacrifices,	Heb 10:11	4178

OFTTIMES
for *o* he falleth into the fire,	Mt 17:15	4178
o it hath cast him into the fire,	Mk 9:22	4178
for Jesus *o* resorted thither with	Jn 18:2	4178

OG (og) An Amorite king.
O the king of Bashan went out	Num 21:33	5747
the kingdom of *O* king of Bashan	Num 32:33	5747
O the king of Bashan, which dwelt	Deut 1:4	5747
O the king of Bashan came out	Deut 3:1	5747
delivered into our hands *O* also	Deut 3:3	5747
Argob, the kingdom of *O* in Bashan	Deut 3:4	5747
of the kingdom of *O* in Bashan	Deut 3:10	5747
For only *O* king of Bashan	Deut 3:11	5747
Bashan, being the kingdom of *O*	Deut 3:13	5747
the land of *O* king of Bashan, two	Deut 4:47	5747
O the king of Bashan, came out	Deut 29:7	5747
them as he did to Sihon and to *O*	Deut 31:4	5747
the other side Jordan, Sihon and *O*	Josh 2:10	5747
to *O* king of Bashan, which was at	Josh 9:10	5747
the coast of *O* king of Bashan,	Josh 12:4	5747
All the kingdom of *O* in Bashan	Josh 13:12	5747
the kingdom of *O* king of Bashan	Josh 13:30	5747
of the kingdom of *O* in Bashan	Josh 13:31	5747
Amorites, and of *O* king of Bashan	1Kin 4:19	5747
the land of *O* king of Bashan	Neh 9:22	5747
O king of Bashan, and all the	Ps 135:11	5747
And *O* the king of Bashan	Ps 136:20	5747

OH See APPENDIX.

OHAD (o'-had) A son of Simeon.
Jemuel, and Jamin, and *O*, and Jachin	Gen 46:10	161
Jemuel, and Jamin, and *O*, and Jachin	Ex 6:15	161

OHEL (o'-hel) A son of Zerubbabel.
And Hashubah, and *O*, and Berechiah,	1Chr 3:20	169

OHOLAH See AHOLAH.

OHOLIAB See AHOLIAB.

OHOLIBAH See AHOLIBAH.

OHOLIBAMAH See AHOLIBAMAH.

OIL
poured *o* upon the top of it	Gen 28:18	8081
thereon, and he poured *o* thereon	Gen 35:14	8081
O for the light, spices for	Ex 25:6	8081
the light, spices for anointing *o*	Ex 25:6	8081
that they bring thee pure *o* olive	Ex 27:20	8081
cakes unleavened tempered with *o*	Ex 29:2	8081
wafers unleavened anointed with *o*	Ex 29:2	8081
shalt thou take the anointing *o*	Ex 29:7	8081
the altar, and of the anointing *o*	Ex 29:21	8081
fourth part of an hin of beaten *o*	Ex 29:40	8081
sanctuary, and of *o* olive an hin	Ex 30:24	8081
make it an *o* of holy ointment	Ex 30:25	8081
it shall be an holy anointing *o*	Ex 30:25	8081
o unto me throughout your	Ex 30:31	8081
And the anointing *o*, and sweet	Ex 31:11	8081
o for the light, and spices for	Ex 35:8	8081
light, and spices for anointing *o*	Ex 35:8	8081
with the *o* for the light,	Ex 35:14	8081
and his staves, and the anointing *o*	Ex 35:15	8081
o for the light, and for the	Ex 35:28	8081
the light, and for the anointing *o*	Ex 35:28	8081
And he made the holy anointing *o*	Ex 37:29	8081
thereof, and the *o* for light,	Ex 39:37	8081
golden altar, and the anointing *o*	Ex 39:38	8081
thou shalt take the anointing *o*	Ex 40:9	8081
and he shall pour *o* upon it	Lev 2:1	8081
of the *o* thereof, with all the	Lev 2:2	8081
of fine flour mingled with *o*	Lev 2:4	8081
unleavened wafers anointed with *o*	Lev 2:4	8081
flour unleavened, mingled with *o*	Lev 2:6	8081
it in pieces, and pour *o* thereon	Lev 2:6	8081
be made of fine flour with *o*	Lev 2:7	8081
And thou shalt put *o* upon it	Lev 2:15	8081
thereof, and part of the *o* thereof	Lev 2:16	8081
he shall put no *o* upon it	Lev 5:11	8081
of the *o* thereof, and all the	Lev 6:15	8081
In a pan it shall be made with *o*	Lev 6:21	8081
meat offering, mingled with *o*	Lev 7:10	8081
unleavened cakes mingled with *o*	Lev 7:12	8081
with *o*, and cakes mingled with *o*	Lev 7:12	8081
the garments, and the anointing *o*	Lev 8:2	8081
And Moses took the anointing *o*	Lev 8:10	8081
the anointing *o* upon Aaron's head	Lev 8:12	8081
And Moses took of the anointing *o*	Lev 8:30	8081
and a meat offering mingled with *o*	Lev 9:4	8081
for the anointing of the LORD	Lev 10:7	8081
mingled with *o*, and one log of *o*	Lev 14:10	8081
offering, and the log of *o*	Lev 14:12	8081
shall take some of the log of *o*	Lev 14:15	8081
in the *o* that is in his left hand	Lev 14:16	8081
shall sprinkle of the *o* with his	Lev 14:16	8081
of the rest of the *o* that is in	Lev 14:17	8081
the remnant of the *o* that is in	Lev 14:18	8081
with *o* for a meat offering	Lev 14:21	8081
a meat offering, and a log of *o*	Lev 14:21	8081
offering, and the log of *o*	Lev 14:24	8081
the priest shall pour of the *o*	Lev 14:26	8081
his right finger some of the *o*	Lev 14:27	8081
the priest shall put of the *o*	Lev 14:28	8081
the rest of the *o* that is in the	Lev 14:29	8081
head the anointing *o* was poured	Lev 21:10	8081
o of his God is upon him	Lev 21:12	8081
of fine flour mingled with *o*	Lev 23:13	8081
pure *o* olive beaten for the light	Lev 24:2	8081
all the *o* vessels thereof,	Num 4:9	8081
pertaineth the *o* for the light	Num 4:16	8081
meat offering, and the anointing *o*	Num 4:16	8081
he shall pour *o* upon it	Num 5:15	8081
of fine flour mingled with *o*	Num 6:15	8081
unleavened bread anointed with *o*	Num 6:15	8081
with *o* for a meat offering	Num 7:13	8081
with *o* for a meat offering	Num 7:19	8081
with *o* for a meat offering	Num 7:25	8081
with *o* for a meat offering	Num 7:31	8081
with *o* for a meat offering	Num 7:37	8081
with *o* for a meat offering	Num 7:43	8081
with *o* for a meat offering	Num 7:49	8081
with *o* for a meat offering	Num 7:55	8081
with *o* for a meat offering	Num 7:61	8081
with *o* for a meat offering	Num 7:67	8081
with *o* for a meat offering	Num 7:73	8081
with *o* for a meat offering	Num 7:79	8081
even fine flour mingled with *o*	Num 8:8	8081
of it was as the taste of fresh *o*	Num 11:8	8081
the fourth part of an hin of *o*	Num 15:4	8081
the third part of an hin of *o*	Num 15:6	8081
mingled with half an hin of *o*	Num 15:9	8081
All the best of the *o*, and all the	Num 18:12	8081
fourth part of an hin of beaten *o*	Num 28:5	8081
a meat offering, mingled with *o*	Num 28:9	8081
a meat offering, mingled with *o*	Num 28:12	8081
a meat offering, mingled with *o*	Num 28:12	8081
deal of flour mingled with *o* for	Num 28:13	8081
shall be of flour mingled with *o*	Num 28:20	8081
offering of flour mingled with *o*	Num 28:28	8081
shall be of flour mingled with *o*	Num 29:3	8081
shall be of flour mingled with *o*	Num 29:9	8081
shall be of flour mingled with *o*	Num 29:14	8081
was anointed with the holy *o*	Num 35:25	8081
thy corn, and thy wine, and thine *o*	Deut 7:13	3323
a land of olive, and honey,	Deut 8:8	8081
thy corn, and thy wine, and thine *o*	Deut 11:14	3323
corn, or of thy wine, or of thy *o*	Deut 12:17	3323
corn, of thy wine, and of thine *o*	Deut 14:23	3323
corn, of thy wine, and of thine *o*	Deut 18:4	3323
not anoint thyself with the *o*	Deut 28:40	8081
thee either corn, wine, or *o*	Deut 28:51	3323
rock, and *o* out of the flinty rock	Deut 32:13	8081
and let him dip his foot in *o*	Deut 33:24	8081
Then Samuel took a vial of *o*	1Sa 10:1	8081
fill thine horn with *o*, and go, I	1Sa 16:1	8081
Then Samuel took the horn of *o*	1Sa 16:13	8081
he had not been anointed with *o*	2Sa 1:21	8081
and anoint not thyself with *o*	2Sa 14:2	8081
horn of *o* out of the tabernacle	1Kin 1:39	8081
and twenty measures of pure *o*	1Kin 5:11	8081
barrel, and a little *o* in a cruse	1Kin 17:12	8081
neither shall the cruse of *o* fail	1Kin 17:14	8081
neither did the cruse of *o* fail	1Kin 17:16	8081
in the house, save a pot of *o*	2Kin 4:2	8081
And he stayed	2Kin 4:6	8081
And he said, Go, sell the *o*	2Kin 4:7	8081
take this box of *o* in thine hand	2Kin 9:1	8081
Then take the box of *o*, and pour	2Kin 9:3	8081
and he poured the *o* on his head	2Kin 9:6	8081
and vineyards, and a land of olive	2Kin 18:32	3323
fine flour, and the wine, and the *o*	1Chr 9:29	8081
bunches of raisins, and wine, and *o*	1Chr 12:40	8081
over the cellars of *o* was Joash	1Chr 27:28	8081
and twenty thousand baths of *o*	2Chr 2:10	8081
the wheat, and the barley, the *o*	2Chr 2:15	8081
and store of victual, and of *o*	2Chr 11:11	8081
firstfruits of corn, and wine, and *o*	2Chr 31:5	3323
increase of corn, and wine, and *o*	2Chr 32:28	3323
and meat, and drink, and *o*, unto	Ezr 3:7	8081

heaven, wheat, salt, wine, and o	Ezr 6:9	4887
wine, and to an hundred baths of o	Ezr 7:22	4887
of the corn, the wine, and the o	Neh 5:11	3323
manner of trees, of wine and of o	Neh 10:37	3323
corn, of the new wine, and the o	Neh 10:39	3323
the corn, the new wine, and the o	Neh 13:5	3323
the o unto the treasuries	Neh 13:12	3323
wit, six months with o of myrrh	Est 2:12	8081
Which make o within their walls,	Job 24:11	6671
rock poured me out rivers of o	Job 29:6	8081
thou anointest my head with o	Ps 23:5	8081
hath anointed thee with the o of	Ps 45:7	8081
his words were softer than o	Ps 55:21	8081
with my holy o have I anointed	Ps 89:20	8081
I shall be anointed with fresh o	Ps 92:10	8081
o to make his face to shine, and	Ps 104:15	8081
water, and like o into his bones	Ps 109:18	8081
it shall be an excellent o	Ps 141:5	8081
and her mouth is smoother than o	Prov 5:3	8081
wine and o shall not be rich	Prov 21:17	8081
o in the dwelling of the wise	Prov 21:20	8081
and the myrtle, and the o tree	Is 41:19	8081
the o of joy for mourning, the	Is 61:3	8081
for wheat, and for wine, and for o	Jer 31:12	3323
ye wine, and summer fruits, and o	Jer 40:10	8081
of wheat, and of barley, and of o	Jer 41:8	8081
thee, and I anointed thee with o	Eze 16:9	8081
eat fine flour, and honey, and o	Eze 16:13	8081
and thou hast set mine o and mine	Eze 16:18	8081
I gave thee, fine flour, and o	Eze 16:19	8081
hast set mine incense and mine o	Eze 23:41	8081
and Pannag, and honey, and o	Eze 27:17	8081
cause their rivers to run like o	Eze 32:14	8081
ordinance of o, the bath of o	Eze 45:14	8081
ram, and an hin of o for an ephah	Eze 45:24	8081
offering, and according to the o	Eze 45:25	8081
give, and an hin of o to an ephah	Eze 46:5	8081
unto, and an hin of o to an ephah	Eze 46:7	8081
give, and an hin of o to an ephah	Eze 46:11	8081
and the third part of an hin of o	Eze 46:14	8081
and the meat offering, and the o	Eze 46:15	8081
water, my wool and my flax, mine o	Hos 2:5	8081
I gave her corn, and wine, and o	Hos 2:8	3323
the corn, and the wine, and the o	Hos 2:22	3323
and o is carried into Egypt	Hos 12:1	8081
is dried up, the o languisheth	Joel 1:10	3323
will send you corn, and wine, and o	Joel 2:19	3323
shall overflow with wine and o	Joel 2:24	3323
with ten thousands of rivers of o	Mic 6:7	8081
thou shalt not anoint thee with o	Mic 6:15	8081
upon the new wine, and upon the o	Hag 1:11	3323
bread, or pottage, or wine, or o	Hag 2:12	8081
the golden o out of themselves	Zec 4:12	
lamps, and took no o with them	Mt 25:3	1637
But the wise took o in their	Mt 25:4	1637
unto the wise, Give us of your o	Mt 25:8	1637
anointed with o many that were	Mk 6:13	1637
My head with o thou didst not	Lk 7:46	1637
bound up his wounds, pouring in o	Lk 10:34	1637
he said, An hundred measures of o	Lk 16:6	1637
hath anointed thee with the o of	Heb 1:9	1637
anointing him with o in the name	Jas 5:14	1637
and see thou hurt not the o	Rev 6:6	1637
and frankincense, and wine, and o	Rev 18:13	1637

OILED

of bread, and one cake of o bread	Ex 29:23	8081
cake, and a cake of o bread	Lev 8:26	8081

OINTMENT

shalt make it an oil of holy o	Ex 30:25	4888
an o compound after the art of	Ex 30:25	7545
and the spices, and the precious o	2Kin 20:13	8081
priests made the o of the spices	1Chr 9:30	4842
he maketh the sea like a pot of o	Job 41:31	4841
like the precious o upon the head	Ps 133:2	8081
O and perfume rejoice the heart	Prov 27:9	8081
the o of his right hand, which	Prov 27:16	8081
name is better than precious o	Eccl 7:1	8081
and let thy head lack no o	Eccl 9:8	8081
Dead flies cause the o of the	Eccl 10:1	8081
thy name is as o poured forth	Song 1:3	8081
up, neither mollified with o	Is 1:6	8081
and the spices, and the precious o	Is 39:2	8081
thou wentest to the king with o	Is 57:9	8081
alabaster box of very precious o	Mt 26:7	3464
For this o might have been sold	Mt 26:9	3464
she hath poured this o on my body	Mt 26:12	3464
of o of spikenard very precious	Mk 14:3	3464
Why was this waste of the o made	Mk 14:4	3464
brought an alabaster box of o	Lk 7:37	3464
feet, and anointed them with the o	Lk 7:38	3464

hath anointed my feet with o	Lk 7:46	3464
which anointed the Lord with o	Jn 11:2	3464
Mary a pound of o of spikenard	Jn 12:3	3464
filled with the odour of the o	Jn 12:3	3464
Why was not this o sold for three	Jn 12:5	3464

OINTMENTS

of the savour of thy good o thy	Song 1:3	8081
smell of thine o than all spices	Song 4:10	8081
themselves with the chief o		8081
returned, and prepared spices and o	Lk 23:56	3464
And cinnamon, and odours, and o	Rev 18:13	3464

OLD

And Noah was five hundred years o	Gen 5:32	1121
became mighty men which were of o	Gen 6:4	5769
Noah was six hundred years o when	Gen 7:6	1121
Shem was an hundred years o	Gen 11:10	1121
five years o when he departed out	Gen 12:4	1121
me an heifer of three years o	Gen 15:9	8027
and a she goat of three years o	Gen 15:9	8027
and a ram of three years o	Gen 15:9	8027
shalt be buried in a good o age	Gen 15:15	7872
was fourscore and six years o	Gen 16:16	1121
And when Abram was ninety years o	Gen 17:1	1121
he that is eight days o shall be	Gen 17:12	1121
him that is an hundred years o	Gen 17:17	1121
Sarah, that is ninety years o	Gen 17:17	1323
And Abraham was ninety years o	Gen 17:24	1121
his son was thirteen years o	Gen 17:25	1121
Now Abraham and Sarah were o	Gen 18:11	2205
After I am waxed o shall I have	Gen 18:12	1086
pleasure, my lord being o also	Gen 18:12	2204
a surety bear a child, which am o	Gen 18:13	2204
compassed the house round, both o	Gen 19:4	2205
unto the younger, Our father is o	Gen 19:31	2204
bare Abraham a son in his o age	Gen 21:2	2208
his son Isaac being eight days o	Gen 21:4	1121
And Abraham was an hundred years o	Gen 21:5	1121
have born him a son in his o age	Gen 21:7	2208
and seven and twenty years o	Gen 23:1	2416
And Abraham was o, and well	Gen 24:1	2204
a son to my master when she was o	Gen 24:36	2209
ghost, and died in a good o age	Gen 25:8	7872
an o man, and full of years	Gen 25:8	2205
Isaac was forty years o when he	Gen 25:20	1121
years o when she bare them	Gen 25:26	1121
Esau was forty years o when he	Gen 26:34	1121
to pass, that when Isaac was o	Gen 27:1	2204
And he said, Behold now, I am o	Gen 27:2	2204
gathered unto his people, being o	Gen 35:29	2205
Joseph, being seventeen years o	Gen 37:2	1121
he was the son of his o age	Gen 37:3	2208
Joseph was thirty years o when he	Gen 41:46	1121
the o man of whom ye spake	Gen 43:27	2205
o man, and a child of his o age	Gen 44:20	2208
unto Jacob, How o art thou	Gen 47:8	3117,8140,3117
as a lion, and as an o lion	Gen 49:9	3833
being an hundred and ten years o	Gen 50:26	1121
And Moses was fourscore years o	Ex 7:7	1121
Aaron fourscore and three years o	Ex 7:7	1121
go with our young and with our o	Ex 10:9	2205
are numbered, from twenty years o	Ex 30:14	1121
be numbered, from twenty years o	Ex 38:26	1121
It is an o leprosy in the skin of	Lev 13:11	3462
and honour the face of the o man	Lev 19:32	2205
eat yet of o fruit until the	Lev 25:22	3465
in ye shall eat of the o store	Lev 25:22	3465
And ye shall eat o store	Lev 26:10	3462
bring forth the o because of the	Lev 26:10	3465
years o even unto sixty years	Lev 27:3	1121
o even unto twenty years	Lev 27:5	1121
month o even unto five years o	Lev 27:6	1121
And if it be from sixty years o	Lev 27:7	1121
From twenty years o and upward,	Num 1:3	1121
of the names, from twenty years o	Num 1:18	1121
every male from twenty years o	Num 1:20	1121
every male from twenty years o	Num 1:22	1121
of the names, from twenty years o	Num 1:24	1121
of the names, from twenty years o	Num 1:26	1121
of the names, from twenty years o	Num 1:28	1121
of the names, from twenty years o	Num 1:30	1121
of the names, from twenty years o	Num 1:32	1121
of the names, from twenty years o	Num 1:34	1121
of the names, from twenty years o	Num 1:36	1121
of the names, from twenty years o	Num 1:38	1121
of the names, from twenty years o	Num 1:40	1121
of the names, from twenty years o	Num 1:42	1121
fathers, from twenty years o	Num 1:45	1121
every male from a month o	Num 3:15	1121
of all the males, from a month o	Num 3:22	1121
of all the males, from a month o	Num 3:28	1121

O

of all the males, from a month o	Num 3:34	1121
all the males from a month o	Num 3:39	1121
children of Israel from a month o	Num 3:40	1121
number of names, from a month o	Num 3:43	1121
From thirty years o and upward	Num 4:3	1121
upward even until fifty years o	Num 4:3	1121
From thirty years o and upward	Num 4:23	1121
years o shalt thou number them	Num 4:23	1121
From thirty years o and upward	Num 4:30	1121
years o shalt thou number them	Num 4:30	1121
From thirty years o and upward	Num 4:35	1121
and upward even unto fifty years o	Num 4:35	1121
From thirty years o and upward	Num 4:39	1121
and upward even unto fifty years o	Num 4:39	1121
From thirty years o and upward	Num 4:43	1121
and upward even unto fifty years o	Num 4:43	1121
From thirty years o and upward	Num 4:47	1121
and upward even unto fifty years o	Num 4:47	1121
from twenty and five years o	Num 8:24	1121
whole number, from twenty years o	Num 14:29	1121
from a month o shalt thou redeem	Num 18:16	1121
of Israel, from twenty years o	Num 26:2	1121
the people, from twenty years o	Num 26:4	1121
all males from a month o	Num 26:62	1121
out of Egypt, from twenty years o	Num 32:11	1121
three years o when he died in	Num 33:39	1121
giants dwelt therein in o time	Deut 2:20	6440
Thy raiment waxed not o upon thee	Deut 8:4	1086
which they of o time have set in	Deut 19:14	7223
not regard the person of the o	Deut 28:50	2205
clothes are not waxen o upon you	Deut 29:5	1086
shoe is not waxen o upon thy foot	Deut 29:5	1086
and twenty years o this day	Deut 31:2	1121
Remember the days of o, consider	Deut 32:7	5769
and twenty years o when he died	Deut 34:7	1121
they did eat of the o corn of the	Josh 5:11	5669
eaten of the o corn of the land	Josh 5:12	5669
both man and woman, young and o	Josh 6:21	5288
took o sacks upon their asses, and	Josh 9:4	1087
their asses, and wine bottles, o	Josh 9:4	1087
o shoes and clouted upon their	Josh 9:5	1087
feet, and o garments upon them	Josh 9:5	1087
our shoes are become o by reason	Josh 9:13	1086
Now Joshua was o and stricken in	Josh 13:1	2204
LORD said unto him, Thou art o	Josh 13:1	2204
Forty years o was I when Moses	Josh 14:7	1121
day fourscore and five years o	Josh 14:10	1121
round about, that Joshua waxed o	Josh 23:1	2204
and said unto them, I am o	Josh 23:2	2204
other side of the flood in o time	Josh 24:2	5769
being an hundred and ten years o	Josh 24:29	1121
being an hundred and ten years o	Judg 2:8	1121
second bullock of seven years o	Judg 6:25	
son of Joash died in a good o age	Judg 8:32	7872
there came an o man from his work	Judg 19:16	2205
the o man said, Whither goest	Judg 19:17	2205
the o man said, Peace be with	Judg 19:20	2205
master of the house, the o man	Judg 19:22	2205
for I am too o to have an husband	Ruth 1:12	2204
and a nourisher of thine o age	Ruth 4:15	7872
Now Eli was very o, and heard all	1Sa 2:22	2204
not be an o man in thine house	1Sa 2:31	2205
there shall not be an o man in	1Sa 2:32	2205
Eli was ninety and eight years o	1Sa 4:15	1121
for he was an o man, and heavy	1Sa 4:18	2204
came to pass, when Samuel was o	1Sa 8:1	2204
said unto him, Behold, thou art o	1Sa 8:5	2204
and I am o and grayheaded	1Sa 12:2	2204
for an o man in the days of Saul	1Sa 17:12	2204
for those nations were of o	1Sa 27:8	5769
And she said, An o man cometh up	1Sa 28:14	2205
Saul's son was forty years o when	2Sa 2:10	1121
He was five years o when the	2Sa 4:4	1121
years o when he began to reign	2Sa 5:4	1121
aged man, even fourscore years o	2Sa 19:32	1121
I am this day fourscore years o	2Sa 19:35	1121
They were wont to speak in o time	2Sa 20:18	7223
Now king David was o and stricken	1Kin 1:1	2204
and the king was very o	1Kin 1:15	2204
came to pass, when Solomon was o	1Kin 11:4	2209
Rehoboam consulted with the o men	1Kin 12:6	2205
forsook the counsel of the o men	1Kin 12:8	2205
forsook the o men's counsel that	1Kin 12:13	2205
dwelt an o prophet in Beth-el	1Kin 13:11	2205
city where the o prophet dwelt	1Kin 13:25	2205
the o prophet came to the city,	1Kin 13:29	2205
one years o when he began to	1Kin 14:21	1121
o age he was diseased in his feet	1Kin 15:23	2209
five years o when he began to	1Kin 22:42	1121
no child, and her husband is o	2Kin 4:14	2204
two years o was he when he began	2Kin 8:17	1121
twenty years o was Ahaziah when	2Kin 8:26	1121
Seven years o was Jehoash when he	2Kin 11:21	1121
five years o when he began to	2Kin 14:2	1121
which was sixteen years o	2Kin 14:21	1121
Sixteen years o was he when he	2Kin 15:2	1121
twenty years o was he when he	2Kin 15:33	1121
Twenty years o was Ahaz when he	2Kin 16:2	1121
five years o when he began	2Kin 18:2	1121
years o when he began to reign	2Kin 21:1	1121
two years o when he began to	2Kin 21:19	1121
years o when he began to reign	2Kin 22:1	1121
three years o when he began to	2Kin 23:31	1121
five years o when he began to	2Kin 23:36	1121
years o when he began to reign	2Kin 24:8	1121
one years o when he began to	2Kin 24:18	1121
when he was threescore years o	1Chr 2:21	1121
they of Ham had dwelt there of o	1Chr 4:40	6440
So when David was o and full of	1Chr 23:1	2204
were numbered from twenty years o	1Chr 23:27	1121
of them from twenty years o	1Chr 27:23	1121
And he died in a good o age	1Chr 29:28	7872
the o men that had stood before	2Chr 10:6	2205
counsel which the o men gave him	2Chr 10:8	2205
forsook the counsel of the o men	2Chr 10:13	2205
forty years o when he began to	2Chr 12:13	1121
five years o when he began to	2Chr 20:31	1121
two years o when he began to	2Chr 21:5	1121
two years o was he when he began	2Chr 21:20	1121
two years o was Ahaziah when he	2Chr 22:2	1121
Joash was seven years o when he	2Chr 24:1	1121
But Jehoiada waxed o, and was full	2Chr 24:15	2204
thirty years o was he when he	2Chr 24:15	1121
five years o when he began to	2Chr 25:1	1121
numbered them from twenty years o	2Chr 25:5	1121
Uzziah, who was sixteen years o	2Chr 26:1	1121
Sixteen years o was Uzziah when	2Chr 26:3	1121
five years o when he began to	2Chr 27:1	1121
twenty years o when he began to	2Chr 27:8	1121
Ahaz was twenty years o when he	2Chr 28:1	1121
he was five and twenty years o	2Chr 29:1	1121
of males, from three years o	2Chr 31:16	1121
the Levites from twenty years o	2Chr 31:17	1121
years o when he began to reign	2Chr 33:1	1121
twenty years o when he began to	2Chr 33:21	1121
years o when he began to reign	2Chr 34:1	1121
three years o when he began to	2Chr 36:2	1121
five years o when he began to	2Chr 36:5	1121
years o when he began to reign	2Chr 36:9	1121
twenty years o when he began to	2Chr 36:11	1121
o man, or him that stooped for	2Chr 36:17	2205
the Levites, from twenty years o	Ezr 3:8	1121
within the same of o time	Ezr 4:15	5957
of o time hath made insurrection	Ezr 4:19	5957
Moreover the o gate repaired	Neh 3:6	3465
their clothes waxed not o	Neh 9:21	1086
of Ephraim, and above the o gate	Neh 12:39	3465
Asaph of o there were chief of	Neh 12:46	6924
perish, all Jews, both young and o	Est 3:13	2205
The o lion perisheth for lack of	Job 4:11	
root thereof wax o in the earth	Job 14:8	2204
Knowest thou not this of o	Job 20:4	5703
do the wicked live, become o	Job 21:7	6275
Hast thou marked the o way which	Job 22:15	5769
in whom o age was perished	Job 30:2	
I am young, and ye are very o	Job 32:6	3453
So Job died, being o and full of	Job 42:17	2205
it waxeth o because of all mine	Ps 6:7	6275
for they have been ever of o	Ps 25:6	5769
my bones waxed o through my	Ps 32:3	1086
I have been young, and now am o	Ps 37:25	2204
in their days, in the times of o	Ps 44:1	6924
them, even that abideth of o	Ps 55:19	6924
of heavens, which were of o	Ps 68:33	6924
me not off in the time of o age	Ps 71:9	2209
Now also when I am o and	Ps 71:18	2209
which thou hast purchased of o	Ps 74:2	6924
For God is my King of o, working	Ps 74:12	6924
I have considered the days of o	Ps 77:5	6924
I will remember thy wonders of o	Ps 77:11	6924
I will utter dark sayings of o	Ps 78:2	6924
still bring forth fruit in o age	Ps 92:14	7872
Thy throne is established of o	Ps 93:2	227
Of o hast thou laid the	Ps 102:25	6440
them shall wax o like a garment	Ps 102:26	1086
I remembered thy judgments of o	Ps 119:52	5769
I have known of o that thou hast	Ps 119:152	6924
I remember the days of o	Ps 143:5	6924
o men, and children	Ps 148:12	2205
of his way, before his works of o	Prov 8:22	227
children are the crown of o men	Prov 17:6	2205
the beauty of o men is the grey	Prov 20:29	2205

and when he is *o*, he will not	Prov 22:6	2204
Remove not the *o* landmark	Prov 23:10	5769
not thy mother when she is *o*	Prov 23:22	2204
it hath been already of *o* time	Eccl 1:10	5769
a poor and a wise child than an *o*	Eccl 4:13	2205
of pleasant fruits, new and *o*	Song 7:13	3465
Zoar, an heifer of three years *o*	Is 15:5	7992
Ethiopians captives, young and *o*	Is 20:4	2205
walls for the water of the *o* pool	Is 22:11	3465
thy counsels of *o* are	Is 25:1	7350
o lion, the viper and fiery flying	Is 30:6	3918
For Tophet is ordained of *o*	Is 30:33	865
neither consider the things of *o*	Is 43:18	6931
And even to your *o* age I am he	Is 46:4	2209
Remember the former things of *o*	Is 46:9	5769
they all shall wax *o* as a garment	Is 50:9	1086
earth shall wax *o* like a garment	Is 51:6	1086
days, in the generations of *o*	Is 51:9	5769
not I held my peace even of *o*	Is 57:11	5769
shall build the *o* waste places	Is 58:12	5769
And they shall build the *o* wastes	Is 61:4	5769
and carried them all the days of *o*	Is 63:9	5769
Then he remembered the days of *o*	Is 63:11	5769
nor an *o* man that hath not filled	Is 65:20	2205
shall die an hundred years *o*	Is 65:20	1121
hundred years *o* shall be accursed	Is 65:20	1121
For of *o* time I have broken thy	Jer 2:20	5769
and see, and ask for the *o* paths	Jer 6:16	5769
before thee of *o* prophesied both	Jer 28:8	5769
Lord hath appeared of *o* unto me	Jer 31:3	7350
both young men and *o* together	Jer 31:13	2205
and took thence *o* cast clouts	Jer 38:11	1094
o rotten rags, and let them down	Jer 38:11	1094
Put now these *o* cast clouts	Jer 38:12	1094
be inhabited, as in the days of *o*	Jer 46:26	6924
as an heifer of three years *o*	Jer 48:34	7992
thee will I break in pieces *o*	Jer 51:22	2205
twenty years *o* when he began to	Jer 52:1	1121
that she had in the days of *o*	Lam 1:7	6924
he had commanded in the days of *o*	Lam 2:17	6924
the *o* lie on the ground in the	Lam 2:21	2205
flesh and my skin hath he made *o*	Lam 3:4	1086
places, as they that be dead of *o*	Lam 3:6	5769
renew our days as of *o*	Lam 5:21	6924
Slay utterly *o* and young, both	Eze 9:6	2205
unto her that was *o* in adulteries	Eze 23:43	1087
to destroy it for the *o* hatred	Eze 25:15	5769
pit, with the people of *o* time	Eze 26:20	5769
earth, in places desolate of *o*	Eze 26:20	5769
settle you after your *o* estates	Eze 36:11	6927
in *o* time by my servants the	Eze 38:17	6931
about threescore and two years *o*	Dan 5:31	1247
ye *o* men, and give ear, all ye	Joel 1:2	2205
your *o* men shall dream dreams,	Joel 2:28	2205
will build it as in the days of *o*	Amos 9:11	5769
goings forth have been from of *o*	Mic 5:2	6924
with calves of a year *o*	Mic 6:6	1121
and Gilead, as in the days of *o*	Mic 7:14	5769
our fathers from the days of *o*	Mic 7:20	6924
But Nineveh is of *o* like a pool	Nah 2:8	3117
where the lion, even the *o* lion	Nah 2:11	
There shall yet *o* men	Zec 8:4	2205
o women dwell in the streets of	Zec 8:4	2205
the Lord, as in the days of *o*	Mal 3:4	5769
coasts thereof, from two years *o*	Mt 2:16	1332
it was said by them of *o* time	Mt 5:21	744
it was said by them of *o* time	Mt 5:27	744
hath been said by them of *o* time	Mt 5:33	744
of new cloth unto an *o* garment	Mt 9:16	3820
men put new wine into *o* bottles	Mt 9:17	3820
of his treasure things new and *o*	Mt 13:52	3820
of new cloth on an *o* garment	Mk 2:21	3820
it up taketh away from the *o*	Mk 2:21	3820
putteth new wine into *o* bottles	Mk 2:22	3820
for I am an *o* man, and my wife	Lk 1:18	4246
also conceived a son in her *o* age	Lk 1:36	1094
And when he was twelve years *o*	Lk 2:42	
piece of a new garment upon an *o*	Lk 5:36	3820
of the new agreeth not with the *o*	Lk 5:36	3820
putteth new wine into *o* bottles	Lk 5:37	3820
No man also having drunk *o* wine	Lk 5:39	3820
for he saith, The *o* is better	Lk 5:39	3820
that one of the *o* prophets was	Lk 9:8	744
that one of the *o* prophets is	Lk 9:19	744
yourselves bags which wax not *o*	Lk 12:33	3822
can a man be born when he is *o*	Jn 3:4	1088
Thou art not yet fifty years *o*	Jn 8:57	
but when thou shalt be *o*, thou	Jn 21:18	1095
your *o* men shall dream dreams	Acts 2:17	4245
the man was above forty years *o*	Acts 4:22	
And when he was full forty years *o*	Acts 7:23	5550

For Moses of *o* time hath in every	Acts 15:21	744
an *o* disciple, with whom we	Acts 21:16	744
he was about an hundred years *o*	Rom 4:19	1541
that our *o* man is crucified with	Rom 6:6	3820
Purge out therefore the *o* leaven	1Cor 5:7	3820
keep the feast, not with *o* leaven	1Cor 5:8	3820
in the reading of the *o* testament	2Cor 3:14	3820
o things are passed away	2Cor 5:17	744
the former conversation the *o* man	Eph 4:22	3820
put off the *o* man with his deeds	Col 3:9	3820
o wives' fables, and exercise	1Ti 4:7	1126
number under threescore years *o*	1Ti 5:9	
all shall wax *o* as doth a garment	Heb 1:11	3822
he hath made the first *o*	Heb 8:13	3822
waxeth *o* is ready to vanish away	Heb 8:13	1095
in the *o* time the holy women also	1Pet 3:5	4218
he was purged from his *o* sins	2Pet 1:9	3819
not in time by the will of man	2Pet 1:21	4218
And spared not the *o* world	2Pet 2:5	744
word of God the heavens were of *o*	2Pet 3:5	1597
but an *o* commandment which ye had	1Jn 2:7	3820
The *o* commandment is the word	1Jn 2:7	3820
who were before of *o* ordained to	Jude 4	3819
that *o* serpent, called the Devil,	Rev 12:9	744
that *o* serpent, which is the	Rev 20:2	744

OLDNESS

not in the *o* of the letter	Rom 7:6	3821

OLIVE

mouth was an *o* leaf pluckt off	Gen 8:11	2132
pure oil *o* beaten for the light	Ex 27:20	2132
the sanctuary, and of oil *o* an hin	Ex 30:24	2132
pure oil *o* beaten for the light	Lev 24:2	2132
o trees, which thou plantedst not	Deut 6:11	2132
a land of oil *o*, and honey	Deut 8:8	2132
When thou beatest thine *o* tree	Deut 24:20	2132
Thou shalt have *o* trees	Deut 28:40	2132
for thine *o* shall cast his fruit	Deut 28:40	2132
and they said unto the *o* tree	Judg 9:8	2132
But the *o* tree said unto them,	Judg 9:9	2132
he made two cherubims of *o* tree	1Kin 6:23	8081
oracle he made doors of *o* tree	1Kin 6:31	8081
The two doors also were of *o* tree	1Kin 6:32	8081
of the temple posts of *o* tree	1Kin 6:33	8081
and vineyards, a land of oil *o*	2Kin 18:32	2132
And over the *o* trees and the	1Chr 27:28	2132
fetch *o* branches, and pine	Neh 8:15	2132
cast off his flower as the *o*	Job 15:33	2132
But I am like a green *o* tree in	Ps 52:8	2132
thy children like *o* plants round	Ps 128:3	2132
it, as the shaking of an *o* tree	Is 17:6	2132
be as the shaking of an *o* tree	Is 24:13	2132
called thy name, A green *o* tree	Jer 11:16	2132
his beauty shall be as the *o* tree	Hos 14:6	2132
your *o* trees increased, the	Amos 4:9	2132
the labour of the *o* shall fail	Hab 3:17	2132
the *o* tree, hath not brought	Hag 2:19	2132
two *o* trees by it, one upon the	Zec 4:3	2132
What are these two *o* trees upon	Zec 4:11	2132
What be these two *o* branches	Zec 4:12	2132
off, and thou, being a wild *o* tree	Rom 11:17	65
the root and fatness of the *o* tree	Rom 11:17	1636
o tree which is wild by nature	Rom 11:24	65
to nature into a good *o* tree	Rom 11:24	2565
be graffed into their own *o* tree	Rom 11:24	1636
tree, my brethren, bear *o* berries	Jas 3:12	1636
These are the two *o* trees	Rev 11:4	1636

OLIVES

corn, with the vineyards and *o*	Judg 15:5	2132
thou shalt tread the *o*, but thou	Mic 6:15	2132
in that day upon the mount of *O*	Zec 14:4	2132
the mount of *O* shall cleave in	Zec 14:4	2132
to Bethphage, unto the mount of *O*	Mt 21:1	1636
And as he sat upon the mount of *O*	Mt 24:3	1636
they went out into the mount of *O*	Mt 26:30	1636
and Bethany, at the mount of *O*	Mk 11:1	1636
of *O* over against the temple	Mk 13:3	1636
they went out into the mount of *O*	Mk 14:26	1636
the mount called the mount of *O*	Lk 19:29	1636
at the descent of the mount of *O*	Lk 19:37	1636
that is called the mount of *O*	Lk 21:37	1636
as he was wont, to the mount of *O*	Lk 22:39	1636
Jesus went unto the mount of *O*	Jn 8:1	1636

OLIVET See Mount, Olives. *Hills east of Jerusalem.*

went up by the ascent of mount *O*	2Sa 15:30	2132
Jerusalem from the mount called *O*	Acts 1:12	1638

OLIVEYARD

with thy vineyard, and with thy *o*	Ex 23:11	2132

OLIVEYARDS
o which ye planted not do ye eat .... Josh 24:13   2132
and your vineyards, and your o 1Sa 8:14   2132
and to receive garments, and o 2Kin 5:26   2132
lands, their vineyards, their o .... Neh 5:11   2132
wells digged, vineyards, and o .... Neh 9:25   2132

OLYMPAS (o-lim'-pas) *A Christian acquaintance of Paul.*
Nereus, and his sister, and O .... Rom 16:15   3632

OMAR (o'-mar) *A son of Eliphaz.*
the sons of Eliphaz were Teman, O .... Gen 36:11   201
duke Teman, duke Zepho, ... Gen 36:15   201
Teman, and O, Zephi, and Gatam, ... 1Chr 1:36   201

OMEGA (o'-me-gah) *Last letter of Greek alphabet; a title applied to Jesus.*
I am Alpha and O, the beginning and .. Rev 1:8   5598
Saying, I am Alpha and O, the .... Rev 1:11   5598
I am Alpha and O, the beginning and .. Rev 21:6   5598
I am Alpha and O, the beginning and .. Rev 22:13   5598

OMER
an o for every man, according to .... Ex 16:16   6016
when they did mete it with an o .... Ex 16:18   6016
Fill an o of it to be kept for .... Ex 16:32   6016
put an o full of manna therein, ... Ex 16:33   6016
Now an o is the tenth part of an .... Ex 16:36   6016

OMERS
as much bread, two o for one man .... Ex 16:22   6016

OMITTED
have o the weightier matters of .... Mt 23:23   863

OMNIPOTENT
for the Lord God o reigneth .... Rev 19:6   3841

OMRI (om'-ri)
1. A king of Israel.
wherefore all Israel made O 1Kin 16:16   6018
O went up from Gibbethon, and all 1Kin 16:17   6018
and half followed O 1Kin 16:21   6018
O prevailed against the people 1Kin 16:22   6018
so Tibni died, and O reigned.................. 1Kin 16:22   6018
began O to reign over Israel 1Kin 16:23   6018
But O wrought evil in the eyes of 1Kin 16:25   6018
of the acts of O which he did 1Kin 16:27   6018
So O slept with his fathers, and 1Kin 16:28   6018
the son of O to reign over Israel 1Kin 16:29   6018
Ahab the son of O reigned over 1Kin 16:29   6018
Ahab the son of O did evil in the 1Kin 16:30   6018
the daughter of O king of Israel............. 2Kin 8:26   6018
was Athaliah the daughter of O............. 2Chr 22:2   6018
For the statutes of O are kept .... Mic 6:16   6018
2. Son of Becher.
and Eliezer, and Elioenai, and O............. 1Chr 7:8   6018
3. A descendant of Pharez.
the son of Ammihud, the son of O 1Chr 9:4   6018
4. A ruler of Issachar.
of Issachar, O the son of Michael............ 1Chr 27:18   6018

ON (*Also see* APPENDIX.)
1. Capital of Lower Egypt.
of Poti-pherah priest of O........................ Gen 41:45   204
priest of O bare unto him .... Gen 41:50   204
priest of O bare unto him .... Gen 46:20   204
2. Son of Peleth.
Abiram, the sons of Eliab, and O .... Num 16:1   203

ONAM (o'-nam)
1. A son of Shobal.
Manahath, and Ebal, Shepho, and O ..... Gen 36:23   208
Manahath, and Ebal, Shephi, and O 1Chr 1:40   208
2. A son of Jerahmeel.
she was the mother of O 1Chr 2:26   208
And the sons of O were, Shammai,........ 1Chr 2:28   208

ONAN (o'-nan) *A son of Judah.*
and she called his name O .... Gen 38:4   209
And Judah said unto O, Go in unto .... Gen 38:8   209
O knew that the seed should not .... Gen 38:9   209
Er, and O, and Shelah, and Pharez, ... Gen 46:12   209
O died in the land of Canaan.................. Gen 46:12   209
The sons of Judah were Er and O........... Num 26:19   209
O died in the land of Canaan.................. Num 26:19   209
Er, and O, and Shelah 1Chr 2:3   209

ONCE
and I will speak yet but this o .... Gen 18:32   6471
I pray thee, my sin only this o .... Ex 10:17   6471
atonement upon the horns of it o .... Ex 30:10   259
o in the year shall he make.................... Ex 30:10   259
for all their sins o a year .... Lev 16:34   259
Moses, and said, Let us go up at o .... Num 13:30
thou mayest not consume them at o ...... Deut 7:22   4118

war, and go round about the city o .... Josh 6:3   259
the city, going about it o .... Josh 6:11   259
day they compassed the city o .... Josh 6:14   259
me, and I will speak but this o .... Judg 6:39   6471
but this o with the fleece .... Judg 6:39   6471
saying, Come up this o, for he .... Judg 16:18   6471
me, I pray thee, only this o .... Judg 16:28   6471
that I may be at o avenged of the.......... Judg 16:28
the spear even to the earth at o 1Sa 26:8   6471,259
o in three years came the navy of 1Kin 10:22   259
himself there, not o nor twice 2Kin 6:10   259
every three years o came the................. 2Chr 9:21   259
o in ten days store of all sorts................ Neh 5:18   996
without Jerusalem o or twice .... Neh 13:20   6471
For God speaketh o, yea twice,............... Job 33:14   259
O have I spoken...................................... Job 40:5   259
God hath spoken o.................................. Ps 62:11   259
work thereof at o with axes.................... Ps 74:6
thy sight when o thou art angry .... Ps 76:7   227
O have I sworn by my holiness .... Ps 89:35   259
in his ways shall fall at o .... Prov 28:18   259
I will destroy and devour at o .... Is 42:14   3162
or shall a nation be born at o .... Is 66:8   6471
inhabitants of the land at this o .... Jer 10:18   6471
when shall it o be .... Jer 13:27   5750
I will this o cause them to know, ... Jer 16:21   6471
Yet o, it is a little while, and I .... Hag 2:6   259
When o the master of the house is........ Lk 13:25
And they cried out all at o .... Lk 23:18   3826
that he died, he died unto sin o .... Rom 6:10   2178
For I was alive without the law o........... Rom 7:9   4218
above five hundred brethren at o........... 1Cor 15:6   2178
o was I stoned, thrice I suffered 2Cor 11:25   530
the faith which o he destroyed............... Gal 1:23   4218
let it not be o named among you, ... Eph 5:3   3366
even in Thessalonica ye sent o............... Phil 4:16   530
come unto you, even I Paul, o................. 1Th 2:18   530
for those who were o enlightened .... Heb 6:4   530
for this he did o, when he .... Heb 7:27   2178
high priest alone o every year .... Heb 9:7   530
entered in o into the holy place.............. Heb 9:12   2178
but now in the end of the world .... Heb 9:26   530
it is appointed unto men o to die........... Heb 9:27   530
So Christ was o offered to bear .... Heb 9:28   530
because that the worshippers o .... Heb 10:2   530
body of Jesus Christ o for all .... Heb 10:10   2178
Yet o more I shake not the earth .... Heb 12:26   530
Yet o more, signifieth the .... Heb 12:27   530
also hath o suffered for sins................... 1Pet 3:18   530
when o the longsuffering of God 1Pet 3:20   530
was o delivered unto the saints .... Jude 3   530
though ye o knew this, how that............ Jude 5   530

ONE See APPENDIX.

ONE'S See APPENDIX.

ONES See APPENDIX.

ONESIMUS (o-nes'-i-mus) *A Christian of Colosse.*
With O, a faithful and beloved................ Col 4:9   3682
the Colossians by Tychicus and O .... Col s   3682
I beseech thee for my son O.................... Philem 10   3682
from Rome to Philemon, by O .... Philem s   3682

ONESIPHORUS (o-ne-sif'-o-rus) *A Christian of Ephesus.*
give mercy unto the house of O 2Ti 1:16   3683
and Aquila, and the household of O........ 2Ti 4:19   3683

ONIONS
melons, and the leeks, and the o............ Num 11:5   1211

ONLY See APPENDIX.

ONO (o'-no)
1. A city in Benjamin.
Misham, and Shamed, who built O 1Chr 8:12   207
The children of Lod, Hadid, and O.......... Ezr 2:33   207
The children of Lod, Hadid, and O .... Neh 7:37   207
Lod, and O, the valley of........................ Neh 11:35   207
2. A valley near Jerusalem.
of the villages in the plain of O.............. Neh 6:2   207

ONWARD
went o in all their journeys..................... Ex 40:36

ONYCHA
thee sweet spices, stacte, and o .... Ex 30:34   7827

ONYX
there is bdellium and the o stone........... Gen 2:12   7718
O stones, and stones to be set in .... Ex 25:7   7718
And thou shalt take two o stones........... Ex 28:9   7718
the fourth row a beryl, and an o .... Ex 28:20   7718
o stones, and stones to be set for........... Ex 35:9   7718
And the rulers brought o stones............. Ex 35:27   7718

they wrought *o* stones inclosed in	Ex 39:6	7718
And the fourth row, a beryl, an *o*	Ex 39:13	7718
o stones, and stones to be set,	1Chr 29:2	7718
of Ophir, with the precious *o*	Job 28:16	7718
and the diamond, the beryl, the *o*	Eze 28:13	7718

OPEN

in the *o* firmament of heaven	Gen 1:20	6440
herself, and sat in an *o* place	Gen 38:14	5869
And if a man shall *o* a pit	Ex 21:33	6605
bird loose into the *o* field	Lev 14:7	6440
out of the city into the *o* fields	Lev 14:53	6440
which they offer in the *o* field	Lev 17:5	6440
instead of such as *o* every womb	Num 8:16	6363
thing, and the earth *o* her mouth	Num 16:30	6475
every *o* vessel, which hath no	Num 19:15	6605
with a sword in the *o* fields	Num 19:16	6440
man whose eyes are *o* hath said	Num 24:3	8365
a trance, but having his eyes *o*	Num 24:4	1540
man whose eyes are *o* hath said	Num 24:15	8365
a trance, but having his eyes *o*	Num 24:16	1540
But thou shalt *o* thine hand wide	Deut 15:8	6605
Thou shalt *o* thine hand wide unto	Deut 15:11	6605
o unto thee, then it shall be,	Deut 20:11	6605
The LORD shall *o* unto thee his	Deut 28:12	6605
and they left the city *o*, and	Josh 8:17	6605
O the mouth of the cave, and bring	Josh 10:22	6605
there was no *o* vision	1Sa 3:1	6555
are encamped in the *o* fields	2Sa 11:11	6440
carved with knops and *o* flowers	1Kin 6:18	6358
o flowers, within and without	1Kin 6:29	6358
o flowers, and overlaid them with	1Kin 6:32	6358
and palm trees and *o* flowers	1Kin 6:35	6358
That thine eyes may be *o* toward	1Kin 8:29	6605
That thine eyes may be *o* unto the	1Kin 8:52	6605
o his eyes, that he may see	2Kin 6:17	6491
o the eyes of these men, that	2Kin 6:20	6491
Then *o* the door, and flee, and	2Kin 9:3	6605
And he said, *O* the window eastward	2Kin 13:17	6605
o, LORD, thine eyes, and see	2Kin 19:16	6491
eyes may be *o* upon this house day	2Chr 6:20	6605
I beseech thee, thine eyes be *o*	2Chr 6:40	6605
Now mine eyes shall be *o*, and mine	2Chr 7:15	6605
now be attentive, and thine eyes *o*	Neh 1:6	6605
time with an *o* letter in his hand	Neh 6:5	6605
speak, and *o* his lips against thee	Job 11:5	6605
dost thou *o* thine eyes upon such	Job 14:3	6491
I will *o* my lips and answer	Job 32:20	6605
men in the *o* sight of others	Job 34:26	4725
doth Job *o* his mouth in vain	Job 35:16	6475
Who can *o* the doors of his face	Job 41:14	6605
their throat is an *o* sepulchre	Ps 5:9	6605
his ears are *o* unto their cry	Ps 34:15	
I will *o* my dark saying upon the	Ps 49:4	6605
O Lord, *o* thou my lips	Ps 51:15	6605
I will *o* my mouth in a parable	Ps 78:2	6605
o thy mouth wide, and I will fill	Ps 81:10	
O to me the gates of	Ps 118:19	6605
O thou mine eyes, that I may	Ps 119:18	1540
but a fool layeth *o* his folly	Prov 13:16	6566
o thine eyes, and thou shalt be	Prov 20:13	6491
O rebuke is better than secret	Prov 27:5	1540
O thy mouth for the dumb in the	Prov 31:8	6605
O thy mouth, judge righteously,	Prov 31:9	6605
O to me, my sister, my love, my	Song 5:2	6605
I rose up to *o* to my beloved	Song 5:5	6605
shall devour Israel with *o* mouth	Is 9:12	3605
so he shall *o*, and none shall shut	Is 22:22	6605
and he shall shut, and none shall *o*	Is 22:22	6605
the windows from on high are *o*	Is 24:18	6605
O ye the gates, that the	Is 26:2	6605
doth he *o* and break the clods of	Is 28:24	6605
o thine eyes, O LORD, and see	Is 37:17	6491
I will *o* rivers in high places,	Is 41:18	6605
To *o* the blind eyes, to bring out	Is 42:7	6491
to *o* before him the two leaved	Is 45:1	6605
let the earth *o*, and let them	Is 45:8	6605
thy gates shall be *o* continually	Is 60:11	6605
Their quiver is as an *o* sepulchre	Jer 5:16	6605
fall as dung upon the *o* field	Jer 9:22	6440
be shut up, and none shall *o* them	Jer 13:19	6605
and custom, and that which was *o*	Jer 32:11	1540
and this evidence which is *o*	Jer 32:14	1540
for thine eyes are *o* upon all the	Jer 32:19	6491
utmost border, and *her* storehouses	Jer 50:26	6605
o thy mouth, and eat that I give	Eze 2:8	6475
I will *o* thy mouth, and thou shalt	Eze 3:27	6605
thou wast cast out in the *o* field	Eze 16:5	6440
never *o* thy mouth any more	Eze 16:63	6610
to *o* the mouth in the slaughter,	Eze 21:22	6605
I will *o* the side of Moab from	Eze 25:9	6605

thou shalt fall upon the *o* fields	Eze 29:5	6440
cast thee forth upon the *o* field	Eze 32:4	6440
him that is in the *o* field will	Eze 33:27	6440
were very many in the *o* valley	Eze 37:2	6440
I will *o* your graves, and cause	Eze 37:12	6605
Thou shalt fall upon the *o* field	Eze 39:5	6440
one shall then *o* him the gate	Eze 46:12	6605
his windows being *o* in his	Dan 6:10	6606
o thine eyes, and behold our	Dan 9:18	6491
be set wide *o* unto thine enemies	Nah 3:13	6605
O thy doors, O Lebanon, that the	Zec 11:1	6605
I will *o* mine eyes upon the house	Zec 12:4	6491
if I will not *o* you the windows	Mal 3:10	6605
I will *o* my mouth in parables	Mt 13:35	455
saying, Lord, Lord, *o* to us	Mt 25:11	455
they may *o* unto him immediately	Lk 12:36	455
saying, Lord, Lord, *o* unto us	Lk 13:25	455
Hereafter ye shall see heaven *o*	Jn 1:51	455
Can a devil *o* the eyes of the	Jn 10:21	455
and seeing the prison doors *o*	Acts 16:27	455
Paul was now about to *o* his mouth	Acts 18:14	455
against any man, the law is *o*	Acts 19:38	71
To *o* their eyes, and to turn them	Acts 26:18	455
Their throat is an *o* sepulchre	Rom 3:13	455
with *o* face beholding as in a	2Cor 3:18	343
our mouth is *o* unto you, our	2Cor 6:11	455
that I may *o* my mouth boldly, to	Eph 6:19	1722,457
that God would *o* unto us a door	Col 4:3	455
Some men's sins are *o* beforehand	1Ti 5:24	4271
afresh, and put him to an *o* shame	Heb 6:6	3856
his ears are *o* unto their prayers	1Pet 3:12	
I have set before thee an *o* door	Rev 3:8	455
o the door, I will come in to him	Rev 3:20	455
Who is worthy to *o* the book	Rev 5:2	455
the earth, was able to *o* the book	Rev 5:3	455
no man was found worthy to *o*	Rev 5:4	455
hath prevailed to *o* the book	Rev 5:5	455
book, and to *o* the seals thereof	Rev 5:9	455
had in his hand a little book *o*	Rev 10:2	455
take the little book which is *o*	Rev 10:8	455

OPENED

then your eyes shall be *o*	Gen 3:5	6491
And the eyes of them both were *o*	Gen 3:7	6491
which hath *o* her mouth to receive	Gen 4:11	6475
and the windows of heaven were *o*	Gen 7:11	6605
that Noah *o* the window of the ark	Gen 8:6	6605
God *o* her eyes, and she saw a well	Gen 21:19	6491
Leah was hated, he *o* her womb	Gen 29:31	6605
hearkened to her, and *o* her womb	Gen 30:22	6605
Joseph *o* all the storehouses, and	Gen 41:56	6605
as one of them *o* his sack to give	Gen 42:27	6605
that we *o* our sacks, and, behold,	Gen 43:21	6605
ground, and *o* every man his sack	Gen 44:11	6605
And when she had *o* it, she saw the	Ex 2:6	6605
And the earth *o* her mouth, and	Num 16:32	6605
the LORD *o* the mouth of the ass,	Num 22:28	6605
Then the LORD *o* the eyes of	Num 22:31	1540
And the earth *o* her mouth, and	Num 26:10	6605
how the earth *o* her mouth	Deut 11:6	6475
he *o* not the doors of the parlour	Judg 3:25	6605
they took a key, and *o* them	Judg 3:25	6605
she *o* a bottle of milk, and gave	Judg 4:19	6605
for I have *o* my mouth unto the	Judg 11:35	6475
if thou hast *o* thy mouth unto the	Judg 11:36	6475
o the doors of the house, and went	Judg 19:27	6605
o the doors of the house of the	1Sa 3:15	6605
times, and the child *o* his eyes	2Kin 4:35	6491
the LORD *o* the eyes of the young	2Kin 6:17	6491
the LORD *o* their eyes, and they	2Kin 6:20	6491
And he *o* the door, and fled	2Kin 9:10	6605
And he *o* it	2Kin 13:17	6605
because they *o* not to him	2Kin 15:16	6605
o the doors of the house of the	2Chr 29:3	6605
be *o* until the sun be hot	Neh 7:3	6605
Ezra *o* the book in the sight of	Neh 8:5	6605
and when he *o* it, all the people	Neh 8:5	6605
not be *o* till after the sabbath	Neh 13:19	6605
After this *o* Job his mouth, and	Job 3:1	6605
they *o* their mouth wide as for	Job 29:23	6473
but I *o* my doors to the traveller	Job 31:32	6605
Behold, now I have *o* my mouth	Job 33:2	6605
gates of death been *o* unto thee	Job 38:17	1540
they *o* their mouth wide against	Ps 35:21	6473
I was dumb, I *o* not my mouth	Ps 39:9	6605
mine ears hast thou *o*	Ps 40:6	3738
above, and *o* the doors of heaven,	Ps 78:23	6605
He *o* the rock, and the waters	Ps 105:41	6605
The earth *o* and swallowed up	Ps 106:17	6605
of the deceitful are *o* against me	Ps 109:2	6605
I *o* my mouth, and panted	Ps 119:131	6473

I o to my beloved .... Song 5:6   6605
o her mouth without measure .... Is 5:14   6473
or o the mouth, or peeped .... Is 10:14   6475
that o not the house of his .... Is 14:17   6605
the eyes of the blind shall be o .... Is 35:5   6491
time that thine ear was not o .... Is 48:8   6605
The Lord GOD hath o mine ear .... Is 50:5   6605
afflicted, yet he o not his mouth .... Is 53:7   6605
for unto thee have I o my cause .... Jer 20:12   1540
The LORD hath o his armoury .... Jer 50:25   6605
All thine enemies have o their .... Lam 2:16   6475
All our enemies have o their .... Lam 3:46   6475
Chebar, that the heavens were o .... Eze 1:1   6605
So I o my mouth, and he caused me ..... Eze 3:2   6605
hast o thy feet to every one that .... Eze 16:25   6589
be o to him which is escaped .... Eze 24:27   6605
had o my mouth, until he came to .... Eze 33:22   6605
and my mouth was o, and I was no ...... Eze 33:22   6605
LORD, when I have o your graves .... Eze 37:13   6605
shall be shut, it shall not be o .... Eze 44:2   6605
but on the sabbath it shall be o .... Eze 46:1   6605
day of the new moon it shall be o .... Eze 46:1   6605
was set, and the books were o .... Dan 7:10   6606
then I o my mouth, and spake, and .... Dan 10:16   6605
gates of the rivers shall be o .... Nah 2:6   6605
fountain to the house of David, ... Zec 13:1   6605
when they had o their treasures, ... Mt 2:11   455
lo, the heavens were o unto him .... Mt 3:16   455
he o his mouth, and taught them, ... Mt 5:2   455
knock, and it shall be o unto you .... Mt 7:7   455
him that knocketh it shall be o .... Mt 7:8   455
And their eyes were o .... Mt 9:30   455
and when thou hast o his mouth .... Mt 17:27   455
him, Lord, that our eyes may be o .... Mt 20:33   455
And the graves were o .... Mt 27:52   455
the water, he saw the heavens o .... Mk 1:10   4977
him, Ephphatha, that is, Be o .... Mk 7:34   1272
And straightway his ears were o .... Mk 7:35   1272
And his mouth was o immediately .... Lk 1:64   455
and praying, the heaven was o .... Lk 3:21   455
And when he had o the book .... Lk 4:17   380
knock, and it shall be o unto you .... Lk 11:9   455
him that knocketh it shall be o .... Lk 11:10   455
And their eyes were o, and they .... Lk 24:31   1272
while he o to us the scriptures .... Lk 24:32   1272
Then o he their understanding, ... Lk 24:45   1272
unto him, How were thine eyes o .... Jn 9:10   455
made the clay, and o his eyes .... Jn 9:14   455
of him, that he hath o thine eyes .... Jn 9:17   455
or who hath o his eyes, we know .... Jn 9:21   455
how o he thine eyes .... Jn 9:26   455
he is, and yet he hath o mine eyes .... Jn 9:30   455
o the eyes of one that was born .... Jn 9:32   455
which o the eyes of the blind, ... Jn 11:37   455
Lord by night o the prison doors .... Acts 5:19   455
but when we had o, we found no .... Acts 5:23   455
said, Behold, I see the heavens o .... Acts 7:56   455
shearer, so o he not his mouth .... Acts 8:32   455
Then Philip o his mouth, and began ..... Acts 8:35   455
and when his eyes were o, he saw .... Acts 9:8   455
And she o her eyes .... Acts 9:40   455
And saw heaven o, and a certain .... Acts 10:11   455
Then Peter o his mouth, and said, ... Acts 10:34   455
which o to them of his own accord .... Acts 12:10   455
she o not the gate for gladness, ... Acts 12:14   455
and when they had o the door .... Acts 12:16   455
how he had o the door of faith .... Acts 14:27   455
whose heart the Lord o, that she .... Acts 16:14   1272
immediately all the doors were o .... Acts 16:26   455
door and effectual is o unto me 1Cor 16:9   455
a door was o unto me of the Lord, ... 2Cor 2:12   455
o unto the eyes of him with whom .... Heb 4:13   5136
behold, a door was o in heaven .... Rev 4:1   455
when the Lamb o one of the seals .... Rev 6:1   455
when he had o the second seal, I .... Rev 6:3   455
when he had o the third seal, I .... Rev 6:5   455
when he had o the fourth seal, I .... Rev 6:7   455
when he had o the fifth seal, I .... Rev 6:9   455
when he had o the sixth seal .... Rev 6:12   455
when he had o the seventh seal, ... Rev 8:1   455
And he o the bottomless pit .... Rev 9:2   455
the temple of God was o in heaven .... Rev 11:19   455
woman, and the earth o her mouth ...... Rev 12:16   455
he o his mouth in blasphemy .... Rev 13:6   455
of the testimony in heaven was o .... Rev 15:5   455
And I saw heaven o, and behold a .... Rev 19:11   455
and the books were o .... Rev 20:12   455
And another book was o, which is .... Rev 20:12   455

OPENEST
thou o thine hand, they are .... Ps 104:28   6605
Thou o thine hand, and satisfiest .... Ps 145:16   6605

OPENETH
whatsoever o the womb among the .... Ex 13:2   6363
the LORD all that o the matrix .... Ex 13:12   6363
to the LORD all that o the matrix .... Ex 13:15   6363
All that o the matrix is mine .... Ex 34:19   6363
of all the firstborn that o the .... Num 3:12   6363
Every thing that o the matrix in .... Num 18:15   6363
he o his eyes, and he is not .... Job 27:19   6491
Then he o the ears of men, and .... Job 33:16   1540
He o also their ear to discipline .... Job 36:10   1540
o their ears in oppression........................ Job 36:15   1540
a dumb man that o not his mouth .... Ps 38:13   6605
The LORD o the eyes of the blind .... Ps 146:8   6491
but he that o wide his lips shall .... Prov 13:3   6589
he o not his mouth in the gate .... Prov 24:7   6605
She o her mouth with wisdom .... Prov 31:26   6605
is dumb, so he o not his mouth .... Is 53:7   6605
the fire all that o the womb .... Eze 20:26   6363
Every male that o the womb shall .... Lk 2:23   1272
To him the porter o .... Jn 10:3   455
hath the key of David, he that o .... Rev 3:7   455
and shutteth, and no man o .... Rev 3:7   455

OPENING
the o thereof every morning 1Chr 9:27   4668
up a man, and there can be no o .... Job 12:14   6605
the o of my lips shall be right .... Prov 8:6   4669
o the ears, but he heareth not .... Is 42:20   6491
the o of the prison to them that .... Is 61:1   6495
I will give thee the o of the .... Eze 29:21   6610
O and alleging, that Christ must .... Acts 17:3   1272

OPENINGS
concourse, in the o of the gates .... Prov 1:21   6607

OPENLY
that was o by the way side .... Gen 38:21   5879
his righteousness hath he o .... Ps 98:2
himself shall reward thee o ..... Mt 6:4   1722,3588,5318
in secret shall reward thee o .. Mt 6:6   1722,3588,5318
in secret, shall reward thee o . Mt 6:18   1722,3588,5318
no more o enter into the city .... Mk 1:45   5320
And he spake that saying o .... Mk 8:32   3954
he himself seeketh to be known o .. Jn 7:4   1722,3954
he also up unto the feast, not o .... Jn 7:10   5320
Howbeit no man spake o of him for .... Jn 7:13   3954
walked no more o among the Jews .... Jn 11:54   3954
him, I spake o to the world .... Jn 18:20   3954
up the third day, and shewed him o ..... Acts 10:40   1717
They have beaten us o uncondemned .... Acts 16:37   1219
powers, he made a shew of them o . Col 2:15   1722,3954

OPERATION
nor the o of his hands, he shall .... Ps 28:5   4639
consider the o of his hands .... Is 5:12   4639
through the faith of the o of God .... Col 2:12   1753

OPERATIONS
And there are diversities of o 1Cor 12:6   1755

OPHEL (o'-fel) A fortified place near Jerusalem.
and on the wall of O he built much 2Chr 27:3   6077
fish gate, and compassed about O 2Chr 33:14   6077
Moreover the Nethinims dwelt in O .... Neh 3:26   6077
out, even unto the wall of O .... Neh 3:27   6077
But the Nethinims dwelt in O .... Neh 11:21   6077

OPHIR (o'-fur)
   1. A son of Joktan.
And O, and Havilah, and Jobab .... Gen 10:29   211
And O, and Havilah, and Jobab 1Chr 1:23   211
   2. A place in southern Arabia.
And they came to O, and fetched 1Kin 9:28   211
Hiram, that brought gold from O 1Kin 10:11   211
brought in from O great plenty of.......... 1Kin 10:11   211
of Tharshish to go to O for gold 1Kin 22:48   211
talents of gold, of the gold of O 1Chr 29:4   211
with the servants of Solomon to O 2Chr 8:18   211
which brought gold from O 2Chr 9:10   211
the gold of O as the stones of .... Job 22:24   211
be valued with the gold of O .... Job 28:16   211
did stand the queen in gold of O .... Ps 45:9   211
a man than the golden wedge of O......... Is 13:12   211

OPHNI (of'-ni) A place in Benjamin.
And Chephar-haammonai, and O .... Josh 18:24   6078

OPHRAH (of'-rah) See APHRAH.
   1. A city in Benjamin.
And Avim, and Parah, and O, ... Josh 18:23   6084
unto the way that leadeth to O 1Sa 13:17   6084

2. A city in Manasseh.

sat under an oak which was in O	Judg 6:11	6084
it is yet in O of the Abi-ezrites	Judg 6:24	6084
and put it in his city, even in O	Judg 8:27	6084
father, in O of the Abi-ezrites	Judg 8:32	6084
went unto his father's house at O	Judg 9:5	6084

3. Head of a family in Judah.

And Meonothai begat O	1Chr 4:14	6084

OPINION

and durst not shew you mine o	Job 32:6	1843
I also will shew mine o	Job 32:10	1843
my part, I also will shew mine o	Job 32:17	1843

OPINIONS

How long halt ye between two o	1Kin 18:21	5587

OPPORTUNITY

time he sought o to betray him	Mt 26:16	2120
sought o to betray him unto them	Lk 22:6	2120
As we have therefore o, let us do	Gal 6:10	2540
also careful, but ye lacked o	Phil 4:10	170
might have had o to have returned	Heb 11:15	2540

OPPOSE

those that o themselves	2Ti 2:25	475

OPPOSED

when they o themselves, and	Acts 18:6	498

OPPOSEST

hand thou o thyself against me	Job 30:21	7852

OPPOSETH

Who o and exalteth himself above	2Th 2:4	480

OPPOSITIONS

o of science falsely so called	1Ti 6:20	477

OPPRESS

wherewith the Egyptians o them	Ex 3:9	3905
neither vex a stranger, nor o him	Ex 22:21	3905
Also thou shalt not o a stranger	Ex 23:9	3905
hand, ye shall not o one another	Lev 25:14	3238
shall not therefore o one another	Lev 25:17	3238
thou shalt not o him	Deut 23:16	3238
Thou shalt not o an hired servant	Deut 24:14	6231
and the Maonites, did o you	Judg 10:12	3905
unto thee that thou shouldest o	Job 10:3	6231
man of the earth may no more o	Ps 10:18	6206
From the wicked that o me	Ps 17:9	7703
let not the proud o me	Ps 119:122	6231
neither o the afflicted in the	Prov 22:22	1792
I will feed them that o thee with	Is 49:26	3238
If ye o not the stranger, the	Jer 7:6	6231
and I will punish all that o them	Jer 30:20	3905
princes shall no more o my people	Eze 45:8	3238
he loveth to o	Hos 12:7	6231
which o the poor, which crush the	Amos 4:1	6231
so they o a man and his house,	Mic 2:2	6231
And o not the widow, nor the	Zec 7:10	6231
against those that o the hireling	Mal 3:5	6231
Do not rich men o you, and draw	Jas 2:6	2616

OPPRESSED

and thou shalt be only o and	Deut 28:29	6231
and thou shalt be only o and	Deut 28:33	6231
by reason of them that o them	Judg 2:18	3905
mightily o the children of Israel	Judg 4:3	3905
out of the hand of all that o you	Judg 6:9	3905
vexed and o the children of Israel	Judg 10:8	7533
kingdoms, and of them that o you	1Sa 10:18	3905
whom have I o	1Sa 12:3	7533
hast not defrauded us, nor o us	1Sa 12:4	7533
because the king of Syria o them	2Kin 13:4	3905
But Hazael king of Syria o Israel	2Kin 13:22	3905
Asa o some of the people the same	2Chr 16:10	7533
Because he hath o and hath	Job 20:19	7533
they make the o to cry	Job 35:9	
also will be a refuge for the o	Ps 9:9	1790
To judge the fatherless and the o	Ps 10:18	1790
O let not the o return ashamed	Ps 74:21	1790
and judgment for all that are o	Ps 103:6	6231
Their enemies also o them	Ps 106:42	3905
executeth judgment for the o	Ps 146:7	6231
the tears of such as were o	Eccl 4:1	6231
seek judgment, relieve the o	Is 1:17	2541
And the people shall be o, every	Is 3:5	5065
no more rejoice, O thou o virgin	Is 23:12	6231
O LORD, I am o	Is 38:14	6234
the Assyrian o them without cause	Is 52:4	6231
He was o, and he was afflicted,	Is 53:7	5065
burdens, and to let the o go free	Is 58:6	7533
children of Judah were o together	Jer 50:33	6231
And hath not o any, but hath	Eze 18:7	3238
Hath o the poor and needy, hath	Eze 18:12	3238

Neither hath o any, hath not	Eze 18:16	3238
his father, because he cruelly o	Eze 18:18	6231
yea, they have o the stranger	Eze 22:29	6231
Ephraim is o and broken in	Hos 5:11	6231
the o in the midst thereof	Amos 3:9	6217
him, and avenged him that was o	Acts 7:24	2669
all that were o of the devil	Acts 10:38	2616

OPPRESSETH

land against the enemy that o you	Num 10:9	6887
he fighting daily o me	Ps 56:1	3905
He that o the poor reproacheth	Prov 14:31	6231
He that o the poor to increase	Prov 22:16	6231
A poor man that o the poor is	Prov 28:3	6231

OPPRESSING

of our nativity, from the o sword	Jer 46:16	3238
for fear of the o sword they	Jer 50:16	3238
filthy and polluted, to the o city	Zeph 3:1	3238

OPPRESSION

I have also seen the o wherewith	Ex 3:9	3906
and our labour, and our o	Deut 26:7	3906
for he saw the o of Israel	2Kin 13:4	3906
and openeth their ears in o	Job 36:15	3906
For the o of the poor, for the	Ps 12:5	7701
because of the o of the enemy	Ps 42:9	3906
because of the o of the enemy	Ps 43:2	3906
our affliction and our o	Ps 44:24	3906
because of the o of the wicked	Ps 55:3	6125
Trust not in o, and become not	Ps 62:10	6233
and speak wickedly concerning o	Ps 73:8	6233
minished and brought low through o	Ps 107:39	6115
Deliver me from the o of man	Ps 119:134	6233
If thou seest the o of the poor	Eccl 5:8	6233
Surely o maketh a wise man mad	Eccl 7:7	6233
looked for judgment, but behold o	Is 5:7	4939
despise this word, and trust in o	Is 30:12	6233
thou shalt be far from o	Is 54:14	6233
away from our God, speaking o	Is 59:13	6233
she is wholly o in the midst of	Jer 6:6	6233
to shed innocent blood, and for o	Jer 22:17	6233
they dealt by o with the stranger	Eze 22:7	6233
people of the land have used o	Eze 22:29	6233
of the people's inheritance by o	Eze 46:18	3238

OPPRESSIONS

By reason of the multitude of o	Job 35:9	6217
considered all the o that are	Eccl 4:1	6217
he that despiseth the gain of o	Is 33:15	4642

OPPRESSOR

they hear not the voice of the o	Job 3:18	5065
of years is hidden to the o	Job 15:20	6184
and shall break in pieces the o	Ps 72:4	6231
Envy thou not the o, and choose	Prov 3:31	376,2555
understanding is also a great o	Prov 28:16	4642
of his shoulder, the rod of his o	Is 9:4	5065
and say, How hath the o ceased	Is 14:4	5065
day because of the fury of the o	Is 51:13	6693
and where is the fury of the o	Is 51:13	6693
spoiled out of the hand of the o	Jer 21:12	6231
spoiled out of the hand of the o	Jer 22:3	6216
of the fierceness of the o	Jer 25:38	3238
no o shall pass through them any	Zec 9:8	5065
bow, out of him every o together	Zec 10:4	5065

OPPRESSORS

with God, and the heritage of o	Job 27:13	6184
me, and o seek after my soul	Ps 54:3	6184
leave me not to mine o	Ps 119:121	6231
side of their o there was power	Eccl 4:1	6231
my people, children are their o	Is 3:12	5065
and they shall rule over their o	Is 14:2	5065
the o are consumed out of the	Is 16:4	7429
unto the LORD because of the o	Is 19:20	3905

OR See APPENDIX.

ORACLE

man had enquired at the o of God	2Sa 16:23	1697
both of the temple and of the o	1Kin 6:5	1687
for it within, even for the o	1Kin 6:16	1687
the o he prepared in the house	1Kin 6:19	1687
the o in the forepart was twenty	1Kin 6:20	1687
the chains of gold before the o	1Kin 6:21	1687
by the o he overlaid with gold	1Kin 6:22	1687
And within the o he made two	1Kin 6:23	1687
for the entering of the o he made	1Kin 6:31	1687
and five on the left, before the o	1Kin 7:49	1687
into the o of the house, to the	1Kin 8:6	1687
in the holy place before the o	1Kin 8:8	1687
And he made chains, as in the o	2Chr 3:16	1687
after the manner before the o	2Chr 4:20	1687
to the o of the house, into the	2Chr 5:7	1687

O

seen from the ark before the o	2Chr 5:9	1687
up my hands toward thy holy o	Ps 28:2	1687

ORACLES

the lively o to give unto us	Acts 7:38	3051
them were committed the o of God	Rom 3:2	3051
first principles of the o of God	Heb 5:12	3051
let him speak as the o of God	1Pet 4:11	3051

ORATION

throne, and made an o unto them	Acts 12:21	1215

ORATOR

artificer, and the eloquent o	Is 3:3	3908
with a certain o named Tertullus,	Acts 24:1	4489

ORCHARD

plants are an o of pomegranates	Song 4:13	6508

ORCHARDS

I made me gardens and o, and I	Eccl 2:5	6508

ORDAIN

seer did o in their set office	1Chr 9:22	3245
Also I will o a place for my	1Chr 17:9	7760
Lord, thou wilt o peace for us	Is 26:12	8239
And so I in all churches	1Cor 7:17	1299
o elders in every city, as I had	Titus 1:5	2525

ORDAINED

which was o in mount Sinai for a	Num 28:6	6213
Jeroboam o a feast in the eighth	1Kin 12:32	6213
o a feast unto the children of	1Kin 12:33	6213
had o to burn incense in the high	2Kin 23:5	5414
he o him priests for the high	2Chr 11:15	5975
singing, as it was o by David	2Chr 23:18	
with the instruments o by David	2Chr 29:27	
The Jews o, and took upon them, and	Est 9:27	6965
sucklings hast thou o strength	Ps 8:2	3245
and the stars, which thou hast o	Ps 8:3	3559
This he o in Joseph for a	Ps 81:5	7760
I have o a lamp for mine anointed	Ps 132:17	6186
For Tophet is o of old	Is 30:33	6186
I o thee a prophet unto the	Jer 1:5	5414
whom the king had o to destroy	Dan 2:24	4483
thou hast o them for judgment	Hab 1:12	7760
he o twelve, that they should be	Mk 3:14	4160
o you, that ye should go and bring	Jn 15:16	5087
must one be o to be a witness	Acts 1:22	1096
o of God to be the Judge of quick	Acts 10:42	3724
as many as were o to eternal life	Acts 13:48	5021
when they had o them elders in	Acts 14:23	5500
that were o of the apostles and	Acts 16:4	2919
by that man whom he hath o	Acts 17:31	3724
commandment, which was o to life	Rom 7:10	
the powers that be are o of God	Rom 13:1	5021
which God o before the world unto	1Cor 2:7	4304
Even so hath the Lord o that they	1Cor 9:14	1299
it was o by angels in the hand of	Gal 3:19	1299
which God hath before o that we	Eph 2:10	4282
Whereunto I am o a preacher	1Ti 2:7	5087
o the first bishop of the church	2Ti s	5500
o the first bishop of the church	Titus s	5500
priest taken from among men is o	Heb 5:1	2525
high priest is o to offer gifts	Heb 8:3	2525
Now when these things were thus o	Heb 9:6	2680
of old o to this condemnation	Jude 4	4270

ORDAINETH

he o his arrows against the	Ps 7:13	6466

ORDER

there, and laid the wood in o	Gen 22:9	
set in o one against another	Ex 26:17	7947
his sons shall o it from evening	Ex 27:21	6186
with the lamps to be set in o	Ex 39:37	4634
set in o the things that are to	Ex 40:4	6186
that are to be set in o upon it	Ex 40:4	6187
he set the bread in o upon it	Ex 40:23	6186
lay the wood in o upon the fire	Lev 1:7	6186
in o upon the wood that is on the	Lev 1:8	6186
the priest shall lay them in o on	Lev 6:12	6186
the burnt offering in o upon it	Lev 6:12	6186
shall Aaron o it from the evening	Lev 24:3	6186
He shall o the lamps upon the	Lev 24:4	6186
sabbath he shall set it in o	Lev 24:8	6186
she had laid in o upon the roof	Josh 2:6	
How shall we o the child, and how	Judg 13:12	4941
city, and put his household in o	2Sa 17:23	6680
And he put the wood in o, and cut	1Kin 18:33	6186
he said, Who shall o the battle	1Kin 20:14	631
the Lord, Set thine house in o	2Kin 20:1	6680
and the priests of the second	2Kin 23:4	
their office according to their o	1Chr 6:32	4941
we sought him not after the due o	1Chr 15:13	4941

according to the o commanded unto	1Chr 23:31	4941
according to the o of the king	1Chr 25:2	3027
to the king's o to Asaph,	1Chr 25:6	3027
according to the o of David his	2Chr 8:14	4941
set they in o upon the pure table	2Chr 13:11	
house of the Lord was set in o	2Chr 29:35	3559
shadow of death, without any o	Job 10:22	5468
I would o my cause before him, and	Job 23:4	6186
me, set thy words in o before me	Job 33:5	6186
for we cannot o our speech by	Job 37:19	6186
be reckoned up in o unto thee	Ps 40:5	6186
set them in o before thine eyes	Ps 50:21	6186
ever after the o of Melchizedek	Ps 110:4	1700
O my steps in thy word	Ps 119:133	3559
out, and set in o many proverbs	Eccl 12:9	8626
and upon his kingdom, to o it	Is 9:7	3559
the Lord, Set thine house in o	Is 38:1	6680
declare it, and set it in o for me	Is 44:7	6186
O ye the buckler and shield, and	Jer 46:3	6186
one over another, and thirty in o	Eze 41:6	6471
o a declaration of those things	Lk 1:1	1299
first, to write unto thee in o	Lk 1:3	2517
before God in the o of his course	Lk 1:8	5010
and expounded it by o unto them	Acts 11:4	2517
of Galatia and Phrygia in o	Acts 18:23	2517
rest will I set in o when I come	1Cor 11:34	1299
things be done decently and in o	1Cor 14:40	5010
But every man in his own o	1Cor 15:23	5001
as I have given o to the churches	1Cor 16:1	1299
joying and beholding your o	Col 2:5	5010
that thou shouldest set in o the	Titus 1:5	1930
ever after the o of Melchisedec	Heb 5:6	5010
priest after the o of Melchisedec	Heb 5:10	5010
ever after the o of Melchisedec	Heb 6:20	5010
rise after the o of Melchisedec	Heb 7:11	5010
be called after the o of Aaron	Heb 7:11	5010
ever after the o of Melchisedec	Heb 7:17	5010
ever after the o of Melchisedec	Heb 7:21	5010

ORDERED

top of this rock, in the o place	Judg 6:26	4634
o in all things, and sure	2Sa 23:5	6186
Behold now, I have o my cause	Job 13:18	6186
of a good man are o by the Lord	Ps 37:23	3559

ORDERETH

to him that o his conversation	Ps 50:23	7760

ORDERINGS

These were the o of them in their	1Chr 24:19	6486

ORDERLY

that thou thyself also walkest o	Acts 21:24	4748

ORDINANCE

keep it a feast by an o for ever	Ex 12:14	2708
your generations by an o for ever	Ex 12:17	2708
this thing for an o to thee	Ex 12:24	2706
This is the o of the passover	Ex 12:43	2708
Thou shalt therefore keep this o	Ex 13:10	2708
made for them a statute and an o	Ex 15:25	4941
Therefore shall ye keep mine o	Lev 18:30	4931
They shall therefore keep mine o	Lev 22:9	4931
to the o of the passover, and	Num 9:14	2708
ye shall have one o, both for the	Num 9:14	2708
for an o for ever throughout your	Num 10:8	2708
One o shall be both for you of	Num 15:15	2708
an o for ever in your generations	Num 15:15	2708
and to thy sons, by an o for ever	Num 18:8	2706
This is the o of the law which	Num 19:2	2708
This is the o of the law which	Num 31:21	2708
them a statute and an o in Shechem	Josh 24:25	4941
an o for Israel unto this day	1Sa 30:25	4941
This is an o for ever to Israel	2Chr 2:4	
with fire according to the o,	2Chr 35:13	4941
day, and made them an o in Israel	2Chr 35:25	2706
after the o of David king of	Ezr 3:10	3027
and the o that he gave them	Ps 99:7	2706
the laws, changed the o, broken	Is 24:5	2706
and forsook not the o of their God	Is 58:2	4941
Concerning the o of oil, the bath	Eze 45:14	2706
by a perpetual o unto the Lord	Eze 46:14	2708
is it that we have kept his o	Mal 3:14	4931
the power, resisteth the o of God	Rom 13:2	1296
o of man for the Lord's sake	1Pet 2:13	2937

ORDINANCES

And thou shalt teach them o	Ex 18:20	2706
neither shall ye walk in their o	Lev 18:3	2708
do my judgments, and keep mine o	Lev 18:4	2708
according to all the o of the	Num 9:3	
their statutes, or after their o	2Kin 17:34	4941
And the statutes, and the o	2Kin 17:37	4941
the o by the hand of Moses	2Chr 33:8	4941

Also we made o for us, to charge ....Neh 10:32	4687
Knowest thou the o of heaven ....Job 38:33	2708
this day according to thine o ....Ps 119:91	4941
they ask of me the o of justice ....Is 58:2	4941
the o of the moon and of the stars ....Jer 31:35	2708
If those o depart from before me, ...Jer 31:36	2706
not appointed the o of heaven..................Jer 33:25	2708
in my statutes, and keep mine o ....Eze 11:20	4941
thereof, and all the o thereof ....Eze 43:11	2708
thereof, and all the o thereof ....Eze 43:11	2708
These are the o of the altar in ....Eze 43:18	2708
the o of the house of the LORD.................Eze 44:5	2708
ye are gone away from mine o ....Mal 3:7	2706
and o of the Lord blameless...................Lk 1:6	1345
me in all things, and keep the o 1Cor 11:2	3862
of commandments contained in o ....Eph 2:15	1378
of o that was against us, which ....Col 2:14	1378
in the world, are ye subject to o ....Col 2:20	1379
had also o of divine service.....................Heb 9:1	1345
and divers washings, and carnal o ....Heb 9:10	1345

ORDINARY

and have diminished thine o food ....Eze 16:27	2706

OREB (o'-reb)
   1. A prince of Midian.

two princes of the Midianites, O ....Judg 7:25	6157
they slew O upon the rock O, ...Judg 7:25	6157
Midian, and brought the heads of O ......Judg 7:25	6157
hands the princes of Midian, O................Judg 8:3	6157
Make their nobles like O, and like ....Ps 83:11	6157

   2. A rock east of the Jordan.

of Midian at the rock of O ....Is 10:26	6157

OREN (o'-ren) *A son of Jerahmeel.*

Ram the firstborn, and Bunah, and O....1Chr 2:25	767

ORGAN

all such as handle the harp and o ....Gen 4:21	5748
and rejoice at the sound of the o ....Job 21:12	5748
my o into the voice of them that.............Job 30:31	5748

ORGANS

with stringed instruments and o ....Ps 150:4	5748

ORION (o'-ri'-on) *A constellation of stars.*

Which maketh Arcturus, O, and ....Job 9:9	3685
Pleiades, or loose the bands of O ....Job 38:31	3685
that maketh the seven stars and O ....Amos 5:8	3685

ORNAMENT

For they shall be an o of grace ....Prov 1:9	3880
give to thine head an o of grace............Prov 4:9	3880
an o of fine gold, so is a wise ....Prov 25:12	2481
the o of thy molten images of ....Is 30:22	642
thee with them all, as with an o ....Is 49:18	5716
As for the beauty of his o ....Eze 7:20	5716
even the o of a meek and quiet 1Pet 3:4	

ORNAMENTS

and no man did put on him his o ....Ex 33:4	5716
now put off thy o from thee ....Ex 33:5	5716
of their o by the mount Horeb ....Ex 33:6	5716
took away the o that were on ....Judg 8:21	7720
beside o, and collars, and purple ....Judg 8:26	7720
who put on o of gold upon your 2Sa 1:24	5716
their tinkling o about their feet ....Is 3:18	5914
the o of the legs, and the ....Is 3:20	6807
bridegroom decketh himself with o ....Is 61:10	6287
Can a maid forget her o, or a ....Jer 2:32	5716
thou deckest thee with o of gold ....Jer 4:30	5716
and thou art come to excellent o ....Eze 16:7	5716
I decked thee also with o ....Eze 16:11	5716
eyes, and deckedst thyself with o ....Eze 23:40	5716

ORNAN (or'-nan) See ARAUNAH. *A Jebusite prince.*

threshingfloor of O the Jebusite.............1Chr 21:15	771
threshingfloor of O the Jebusite.............1Chr 21:18	771
O turned back, and saw the angel...........1Chr 21:20	771
Now O was threshing wheat 1Chr 21:20	771
And as David came to O, O 1Chr 21:21	771
Then David said to O, Grant me 1Chr 21:22	771
O said unto David, Take it to..................1Chr 21:23	771
And king David said to O, Nay 1Chr 21:24	771
So David gave to O for the place 1Chr 21:25	771
threshingfloor of O the Jebusite.............1Chr 21:28	771
threshingfloor of O the Jebusite.............2Chr 3:1	771

ORPAH (or'-pah) *Daughter-in-law of Naomi.*

the name of the one was O ....Ruth 1:4	6204
O kissed her mother in law ....Ruth 1:14	6204

ORPHANS

We are o and fatherless, our ....Lam 5:3	3490

OSEE (o'-see) See HOSEA, JOSHUA, OSHEA. *Greek form of Hoshea.*

As he saith also in O, I will ....Rom 9:25	5617

OSHEA (o-she'-ah) See HOSHEA, OSEE. *Same as Joshua, son of Nun.*

of Ephraim, O the son of Nun ....Num 13:8	1954
Moses called O the son of Nun ....Num 13:16	1954

OSNAPPAR See ASNAPPER.

OSPRAY

eagle, and the ossifrage, and the o.........Lev 11:13	5822
eagle, and the ossifrage, and the o.........Deut 14:12	5822

OSSIFRAGE

the eagle, and the o, and the..................Lev 11:13	6538
the eagle, and the o, and the..................Deut 14:12	6538

OSTRICH

or wings and feathers unto the o ....Job 39:13	5133

OSTRICHES

like the o in the wilderness.....................Lam 4:3	3283

OTHER See APPENDIX.

OTHERS See APPENDIX.

OTHERWISE See APPENDIX.

OTHNI (oth'-ni) *A son of Shemiah.*

O, and Rephael, and Obed, Elzabad, ...1Chr 26:7	6273

OTHNIEL (oth'-ne-el)
   1. A brother of Caleb.

O the son of Kenaz, the brother ....Josh 15:17	6274
O the son of Kenaz, Caleb's....................Judg 1:13	6274
even O the son of Kenaz, Caleb's...........Judg 3:9	6274
And O the son of Kenaz died ....Judg 3:11	6274
O, and Seraiah 1Chr 4:13	6274
and the sons of O 1Chr 4:13	6274

   2. Tribe or family of Othniel 1.

was Heldai the Netophathite, of O 1Chr 27:15	6274

OUCHES

make them to be set in o of gold ....Ex 28:11	4865
And thou shalt make o of gold ....Ex 28:13	4865
the wreathen chains to the o ....Ex 28:14	4865
thou shalt fasten in the two o ....Ex 28:25	4865
onyx stones inclosed in o of gold ....Ex 39:6	4865
they were inclosed in o of gold ....Ex 39:13	4865
And they made two o of gold ....Ex 39:16	4865
chains they fastened in the two o ....Ex 39:18	4865

OUGHT See APPENDIX.

OUGHTEST

what thou o to do unto him 1Kin 2:9	
Thou o therefore to have put my..........Mt 25:27	1163
shall tell thee what thou o to do ....Acts 10:6	1163
o to behave thyself in the house 1Ti 3:15	1163

OUR See APPENDIX.

OURS See APPENDIX.

OURSELVES See APPENDIX.

OUT See APPENDIX.

OUTCAST

because they called thee an O ....Jer 30:17	5080

OUTCASTS

together the o of Israel ....Ps 147:2	1760
and shall assemble the o of Israel..........Is 11:12	1760
hide the o..Is 16:3	5080
Let mine o dwell with thee, Moab ....Is 16:4	5080
the o in the land of Egypt, and ....Is 27:13	5080
gathereth the o of Israel saith ....Is 56:8	1760
the o of Elam shall not come ....Jer 49:36	5080

OUTER

was heard even to the o court.................Eze 10:5	2435
shall be cast out into o darkness...........Mt 8:12	1857
away, and cast him into o darkness......Mt 22:13	1857
servant into o darkness ....Mt 25:30	1857

OUTGOINGS

the o of it were at the sea.......................Josh 17:9	8444
the o of it shall be thine.........................Josh 17:18	8444
the o of the border were at the ....Josh 18:19	8444
the o thereof are in the valley ....Josh 19:14	8444
the o of their border were at ....Josh 19:22	8444
the o thereof are at the sea from ....Josh 19:29	8444
the o thereof were at Jordan ....Josh 19:33	8444
thou makest the o of the morning ....Ps 65:8	4161

OUTLANDISH

even him did o women cause to sin ....Neh 13:26	5237

O

OUTLIVED
of the elders that o Joshua .... Judg 2:7   748,3117,310

OUTMOST
curtain that is o in the coupling	Ex 26:10	7020
o coast of the salt sea eastward	Num 34:3	7097
out unto the o parts of heaven	Deut 30:4	7097
four or five in the o fruitful	Is 17:6	

OUTRAGEOUS
Wrath is cruel, and anger is o .... Prov 27:4   7858

OUTRUN
and the other disciple did o Peter ... Jn 20:4   4370,5032

OUTSIDE See APPENDIX.

OUTSTRETCHED
a mighty hand, and with an o arm	Deut 26:8	5186
fight against you with an o hand	Jer 21:5	5186
by my great power and by my o arm	Jer 27:5	5186

OUTWARD
o a thousand cubits round about	Num 35:4	2435
man looketh on the o appearance	1Sa 16:7	5869
for the o business over Israel	1Chr 26:29	2435
had the oversight of the o	Neh 11:16	2435
the o court of the king's house	Est 6:4	2435
brought he me into the o court	Eze 40:17	2435
the gate of the o court that	Eze 40:20	2435
thereof were toward the o court	Eze 40:34	2435
o sanctuary which looketh toward	Eze 44:1	2435
which indeed appear beautiful o	Mt 23:27	1855
which is o in the flesh	Rom 2:28	1722,3588,5318
but though our o man perish	2Cor 4:16	1854
on things after the o appearance	2Cor 10:7	4383
adorning let it not be that o	1Pet 3:3	1855

OUTWARDLY
Even so ye also o appear	Mt 23:28	1855
he is not a Jew, which is one o	Rom 2:28	1722,5318

OUTWENT
o them, and came together unto him ..... Mk 6:33   4281

OVEN
of a meat offering baken in the o	Lev 2:4	8574
offering that is baken in the o	Lev 7:9	8574
whether it be o, or ranges for	Lev 11:35	8574
shall bake your bread in one o	Lev 26:26	8574
o in the time of thine anger	Ps 21:9	8574
Our skin was black like an o	Lam 5:10	8574
as an o heated by the baker, who	Hos 7:4	8574
made ready their heart like an o	Hos 7:6	8574
They are all hot as an o, and have	Hos 7:7	8574
cometh, that shall burn as an o	Mal 4:1	8574
and to morrow is cast into the o	Mt 6:30	2823
and to morrow is cast into the o	Lk 12:28	2823

OVENS
upon thy people, and into thine o .... Ex 8:3   8574

OVER See APPENDIX.

OVERCAME
o them, and prevailed against them	Acts 19:16	2634
me in my throne, even as I also o	Rev 3:21	3528
they o him by the blood of the	Rev 12:11	3528

OVERCHARGE
that I may not o you all 2Cor 2:5   1912

OVERCHARGED
your hearts be o with surfeiting .... Lk 21:34   925

OVERCOME
Gad, a troop shall o him	Gen 49:19	1464
but he shall o at the last	Gen 49:19	1464
of them that cry for being o	Ex 32:18	2476
for we are well able to o it	Num 13:30	3201
I shall be able to o them	Num 22:11	3898
Ahaz, but could not o him	2Kin 16:5	3898
eyes from me, for they have o me	Song 6:5	7292
of them that are o with wine	Is 28:1	1986
and like a man whom wine hath o	Jer 23:9	5674
o him, he taketh from him all his	Lk 11:22	3528
I have o the world	Jn 16:33	3528
mightest o when thou art judged	Rom 3:4	3528
Be not o of evil, but o	Rom 12:21	3528
for of whom a man is o, of the	2Pet 2:19	2274
are again entangled therein, and o	2Pet 2:20	2274
because ye have o the wicked one	1Jn 2:13	3528
you, and ye have o the wicked one	1Jn 2:14	3528
little children, and have o them	1Jn 4:4	3528
war against them, and shall o them	Rev 11:7	3528
war with the saints, and to o them	Rev 13:7	3528
Lamb, and the Lamb shall o them	Rev 17:14	3528

OVERCOMETH
is born of God o the world	1Jn 5:4	3528
is the victory that o the world	1Jn 5:4	3528
Who is he that o the world	1Jn 5:5	3528
To him that o will I give to eat	Rev 2:7	3528
He that o shall not be hurt of	Rev 2:11	3528
To him that o will I give to eat	Rev 2:17	3528
And he that o, and keepeth my works	Rev 2:26	3528
He that o, the same shall be	Rev 3:5	3528
Him that o will I make a pillar	Rev 3:12	3528
To him that o will I grant to sit	Rev 3:21	3528
He that o shall inherit all	Rev 21:7	3528

OVERDRIVE
and if men should o them one day .... Gen 33:13   1849

OVERFLOW
the water of the Red sea to o	Deut 11:4	6687
waters, where the floods o me	Ps 69:2	7857
Let not the waterflood o me	Ps 69:15	7857
he shall o and go over, he shall	Is 8:8	7857
shall o with righteousness	Is 10:22	7857
waters shall o the hiding place	Is 28:17	7857
the rivers, they shall not o thee	Is 43:2	7857
shall o the land, and all that is	Jer 47:2	7857
and one shall certainly come, and o	Dan 11:10	7857
destroy him, and his army shall o	Dan 11:26	7857
into the countries, and shall o	Dan 11:40	7857
and the fats shall o with wine	Joel 2:24	7783
for the press is full, the fats o	Joel 3:13	7783

OVERFLOWED
gushed out, and the streams o	Ps 78:20	7857
being o with water, perished	2Pet 3:6	2626

OVERFLOWETH
(for Jordan o all his banks all .... Josh 3:15   4390

OVERFLOWING
He bindeth the floods from o	Job 28:11	1065
a watercourse for the o of waters	Job 38:25	7858
as a flood of mighty waters o	Is 28:2	7857
when the o scourge shall pass	Is 28:15	7857
when the o scourge shall pass	Is 28:18	7857
as an o stream, shall reach to	Is 30:28	7857
the north, and shall be an o flood	Jer 47:2	7857
there shall be an o shower	Eze 13:11	7857
there shall be an o shower in	Eze 13:13	7857
o rain, and great hailstones, fire	Eze 38:22	7857
the o of the water passed by	Hab 3:10	2230

OVERFLOWN
when it had o all his banks	1Chr 12:15	4390
foundation was o with a flood	Job 22:16	3332
shall they be o from before him	Dan 11:22	7857

OVERLAID
of shittim wood o with gold	Ex 26:32	6823
he o the boards with gold, and	Ex 36:34	6823
the bars, and o the bars with gold	Ex 36:34	6823
shittim wood, and o them with gold	Ex 36:36	6823
he o their chapiters and their	Ex 36:38	6823
he o it with pure gold within and	Ex 37:2	6823
shittim wood, and o them with gold	Ex 37:4	6823
he o it with pure gold, and made	Ex 37:11	6823
o them with gold, to bear the	Ex 37:15	6823
he o it with pure gold, both the	Ex 37:26	6823
shittim wood, and o them with gold	Ex 37:28	6823
and he o it with brass	Ex 38:2	6823
wood, and o them with brass	Ex 38:6	6823
o their chapiters, and filleted	Ex 38:28	6823
because she o it	1Kin 3:19	7901
and he o it with pure gold	1Kin 6:20	6823
So Solomon o the house within	1Kin 6:21	6823
and he o it with gold	1Kin 6:21	6823
And the whole house he o with gold	1Kin 6:22	6823
was by the oracle he o with gold	1Kin 6:22	6823
he o the cherubims with gold	1Kin 6:28	6823
floor of the house he o with gold	1Kin 6:30	6823
o them with gold, and spread gold	1Kin 6:32	6823
ivory, and o it with the best gold	1Kin 10:18	6823
Hezekiah king of Judah had o	2Kin 18:16	6823
he o it within with pure gold	2Chr 3:4	6823
which he o with fine gold, and set	2Chr 3:5	2645
He o also the house, the beams,	2Chr 3:7	2645
he o it with fine gold, amounting	2Chr 3:8	2645
he o the upper chambers with gold	2Chr 3:9	2645
image work, and o them with gold	2Chr 3:10	6823
o the doors of them with brass	2Chr 4:9	6823
of ivory, and o it with pure gold	2Chr 9:17	6823
as bright ivory o with sapphires	Song 5:14	5968
covenant o round about with gold	Heb 9:4	4028

OVERLAY

thou shalt o it with pure gold,	Ex 25:11	6823
within and without shalt thou o it	Ex 25:11	6823
shittim wood, and o them with gold	Ex 25:13	6823
thou shalt o it with pure gold,	Ex 25:24	6823
o them with gold, that the table	Ex 25:28	6823
thou shalt o the boards with gold	Ex 26:29	6823
thou shalt o the bars with gold	Ex 26:29	6823
o them with gold, and their hooks	Ex 26:37	6823
thou shalt o it with brass	Ex 27:2	6823
wood, and o them with brass	Ex 27:6	6823
thou shalt o it with pure gold,	Ex 30:3	6823
shittim wood, and o them with gold	Ex 30:5	6823
to o the walls of the houses	1Chr 29:4	2902

OVERLAYING

the o of their chapiters of	Ex 38:17	6826
the o of their chapiters and their	Ex 38:19	6826

OVERLIVED

days of the elders that o Joshua	Josh 24:31	

OVERMUCH

be swallowed up with o sorrow	2Cor 2:7	4055

OVERPASS

they o the deeds of the wicked	Jer 5:28	5674

OVERPAST

until these calamities be o	Ps 57:1	5674
until the indignation be o	Is 26:20	5674

OVERPLUS

restore the o unto the man to	Lev 25:27	5736

OVERRAN

the way of the plain, and o Cushi	2Sa 18:23	5674

OVERRUNNING

But with an o flood he will make	Nah 1:8	5674

OVERSEE

were appointed to o the vessels	1Chr 9:29	
thousand and six hundred to o them	2Chr 2:2	5329

OVERSEER

he made him o over his house, and	Gen 39:4	6485
he had made him o in his house	Gen 39:5	6485
the son of Zichri was their o	Neh 11:9	6496
their o was Zabdiel, the son of	Neh 11:14	6496
The o also of the Levites at	Neh 11:22	6496
sang loud, with Jezrahiah their o	Neh 12:42	6496
Which having no guide, o, or	Prov 6:7	7860

OVERSEERS

six hundred o to set the people a	2Chr 2:18	5329
were o under the hand of Cononiah	2Chr 31:13	6496
the o of them were Jahath and	2Chr 34:12	6485
were o of all that wrought the	2Chr 34:13	5329
it into the hand of the o	2Chr 34:17	6485
the Holy Ghost hath made you o	Acts 20:28	1985

OVERSHADOW

power of the Highest shall o thee	Lk 1:35	1982
passing by might o some of them	Acts 5:15	1982

OVERSHADOWED

behold, a bright cloud o them	Mt 17:5	1982
And there was a cloud that o them	Mk 9:7	1982
there came a cloud, and o them	Lk 9:34	1982

OVERSIGHT

peradventure it was an o	Gen 43:12	4870
have the o of them that keep the	Num 3:32	6486
the o of all the tabernacle, and	Num 4:16	6486
that had the o of the house of	2Kin 12:11	6485
that have the o of the house of	2Kin 22:5	6485
that have the o of the house of	2Kin 22:9	6485
their children had the o of the	1Chr 9:23	5921
the o of the house of the LORD	2Chr 34:10	6485
had the o of the outward business	Neh 11:16	5921
having the o of the chamber of	Neh 13:4	5414
among you, taking the o thereof	1Pet 5:2	1983

OVERSPREAD

and of them was the whole earth o	Gen 9:19	5310

OVERSPREADING

for the o of abominations he	Dan 9:27	3671

OVERTAKE

and when thou dost o them, say	Gen 44:4	5381
said, I will pursue, I will o	Ex 15:9	5381
o him, because the way is long,	Deut 19:6	5381
o thee, if thou shalt hearken	Deut 28:2	5381
shall come upon thee, and o thee	Deut 28:15	5381
o thee, till thou be destroyed	Deut 28:45	5381
for ye shall o them	Josh 2:5	5381
shall I o them	1Sa 30:8	5381
for thou shalt surely o them	1Sa 30:8	5381

lest he o us suddenly, and bring	2Sa 15:14	5381
us, neither doth justice o us	Is 59:9	5381
shall o you there in the land of	Jer 42:16	5381
lovers, but she shall not o them	Hos 2:7	5381
of iniquity did not o them	Hos 10:9	5381
evil shall not o nor prevent us	Amos 9:10	5066
the plowman shall o the reaper	Amos 9:13	5066
that day should o you as a thief	1Th 5:4	2638

OVERTAKEN

pursued mine enemies, and o them	Ps 18:37	5381
if a man be o in a fault	Gal 6:1	4301

OVERTAKETH

the sword of thine enemies o thee	1Chr 21:12	5381

OVERTHREW

he o those cities, and all the	Gen 19:25	2015
when he o the cities in the which	Gen 19:29	2015
the LORD o the Egyptians in the	Ex 14:27	5287
which the LORD o in his anger	Deut 29:23	2015
But o Pharaoh and his host in the	Ps 136:15	5286
shall be as when God o Sodom	Is 13:19	4114
be as the cities which the LORD o	Jer 20:16	2015
As God o Sodom and Gomorrah	Jer 50:40	4114
some of you, as God o Sodom	Amos 4:11	4114
o the tables of the moneychangers	Mt 21:12	2690
o the tables of the moneychangers	Mk 11:15	2690
changers' money, and o the tables	Jn 2:15	390

OVERTHROW

also, that I will not o this city	Gen 19:21	2015
Lot out of the midst of the o	Gen 19:29	2018
but thou shalt utterly o them	Ex 23:24	2040
ye shall o their altars, and break	Deut 12:3	5422
therein, like the o of Sodom	Deut 29:23	4114
and to spy it out, and to o it	2Sa 10:3	2015
strong against the city, and o it	2Sa 11:25	2040
unto thee for to search, and to o	1Chr 19:3	2015
to o them in the wilderness	Ps 106:26	5307
To o their seed also among the	Ps 106:27	5307
who have purposed to o my goings	Ps 140:4	1760
hunt the violent man to o him	Ps 140:11	4073
to o the righteous in judgment	Prov 18:5	5186
As in the o of Sodom and Gomorrah	Jer 49:18	4114
I will o the throne of kingdoms,	Hag 2:22	2015
I will o the chariots, and those	Hag 2:22	2015
if it be of God, ye cannot o it	Acts 5:39	2647
and o the faith of some	2Ti 2:18	396
ashes condemned them with an o	2Pet 2:6	2692

OVERTHROWETH

away spoiled, and o the mighty	Job 12:19	5557
but wickedness o the sinner	Prov 13:6	5557
but God o the wicked for their	Prov 21:12	5557
and he o the words of the	Prov 22:12	5557
but he that receiveth gifts o it	Prov 29:4	2040

OVERTHROWN

of thine excellency thou hast o	Ex 15:7	2040
fled before him, and many were o	Judg 9:40	5307
some of them be o at the first	2Sa 17:9	5307
and the Ethiopians were o, that	2Chr 14:13	5307
Know now that God hath o me	Job 19:6	5791
judges are o in stony places	Ps 141:6	8058
but it is o by the mouth of the	Prov 11:11	2040
The wicked are o, and are not	Prov 12:7	2015
house of the wicked shall be o	Prov 14:11	8045
it is desolate, as o by strangers	Is 1:7	4114
but let them be o before thee	Jer 18:23	3782
that was o as in a moment, and no	Lam 4:6	2015
and many countries shall be o	Dan 11:41	3782
I have o some of you, as God	Amos 4:11	2015
forty days, and Nineveh shall be o	Jonah 3:4	2015
for they were o in the wilderness	1Cor 10:5	2693

OVERTOOK

they o him in the mount Gilead	Gen 31:23	1692
Then Laban o Jacob	Gen 31:25	5381
he o them, and he spake unto them	Gen 44:6	5381
o them encamping by the sea,	Ex 14:9	5381
and o the children of Dan	Judg 18:22	1692
but the battle o them	Judg 20:42	1692
o him in the plains of Jericho	2Kin 25:5	5381
o Zedekiah in the plains of	Jer 39:5	5381
o Zedekiah in the plains of	Jer 52:8	5381
all her persecutors o her between	Lam 1:3	5381

OVERTURN

them out, and they o the earth	Job 12:15	2015
I will o, o, o	Eze 21:27	5754

OVERTURNED

o it, that the tent lay along	Judg 7:13	2015

OVERTURNETH

which o them in his anger	Job 9:5	2015
he o the mountains by the roots	Job 28:9	2015
he o them in the night, so that	Job 34:25	2015

OVERWHELM

ye o the fatherless, and ye dig a	Job 6:27	5307

OVERWHELMED

come upon me, and horror hath o me	Ps 55:5	3680
cry unto thee, when my heart is o	Ps 61:2	5848
I complained, and my spirit was o	Ps 77:3	5848
but the sea o their enemies	Ps 78:53	3680
of the afflicted, when he is o	Ps 102:t	5848
Then the waters had o us, the	Ps 124:4	7857
When my spirit was o within me	Ps 142:3	5848
is my spirit o within me	Ps 143:4	5848

OWE

O no man any thing, but to love	Rom 13:8	3784

OWED

which o him ten thousand talents	Mt 18:24	3781
which o him an hundred pence	Mt 18:28	3784
the one o five hundred pence, and	Lk 7:41	3784

OWEST

saying, Pay me that thou o	Mt 18:28	3784
How much o thou unto my lord	Lk 16:5	3784
he to another, And how much o thou	Lk 16:7	3784
o unto me even thine own self	Philem 19	4359

OWETH

or o thee ought, put that on mine	Philem 18	3784

OWL

And the o, and the night hawk, and	Lev 11:16	1323,3284
And the little o, and the cormorant	Lev 11:17	3563
and the cormorant, and the great o	Lev 11:17	3244
And the o, and the night hawk	Deut 14:15	1323,3284
The little o, and the great	Deut 14:16	3563
and the great o	Deut 14:16	3244
I am like an o of the desert	Ps 102:6	3563
the o also and the raven shall	Is 34:11	3244
the screech o also shall rest	Is 34:14	3917
shall the great o make her nest	Is 34:15	7091

OWLS

to dragons, and a companion to o	Job 30:29	1323,3284
o shall dwell there, and satyrs	Is 13:21	1323,3284
of dragons, and a court for o	Is 34:13	1323,3284
honour me, the dragons and the o	Is 43:20	1323,3284
the o shall dwell therein	Jer 50:39	1323,3284
dragons, and mourning as the o	Mic 1:8	1323,3284

OWN

So God created man in his o image	Gen 1:27	
and begat a son in his o likeness	Gen 5:3	249
servants, born in his o house	Gen 14:14	249
o bowels shall be thine heir	Gen 15:4	249
that I may go unto mine o place	Gen 30:25	
I provide for mine o house also	Gen 30:30	
he put his o flocks by themselves	Gen 30:40	
and four parts shall be your o	Gen 47:24	
the fault is in thine o people	Ex 5:16	
he went his way into his o land	Ex 18:27	
and the dead shall be his o	Ex 21:36	
of the best of his o field	Ex 22:5	
and of the best of his o vineyard	Ex 22:5	
whom thou swarest by thine o self	Ex 32:13	
he shall offer it of his o	Lev 1:3	
His o hands shall bring the	Lev 7:30	
into the palm of his o left hand	Lev 14:15	3548
into the palm of his o left hand	Lev 14:26	3548
it be one of your o country	Lev 16:29	249
it be one of your o country	Lev 17:15	249
for theirs is thine o nakedness	Lev 18:10	
neither any of your o nation	Lev 18:26	249
ye shall offer it at your o will	Lev 19:5	
a virgin of his o people to wife	Lev 21:14	
Ye shall offer at your o will a	Lev 22:19	
the LORD, offer it at your o will	Lev 22:29	
as for one of your o country	Lev 24:22	249
That which groweth of its o	Lev 25:5	
and shall return unto his o family	Lev 25:41	
tents, every man by his o camp	Num 1:52	
and every man by his o standard	Num 1:52	
shall pitch by his o standard	Num 2:2	
but I will depart to mine o land	Num 10:30	
we were in our o sight as	Num 13:33	
ye seek not after your o heart	Num 15:39	
your o heart and your o eyes	Num 15:39	
have not done them of mine o mind	Num 16:28	
sinners against their o souls	Num 16:38	
either good or bad of mine o mind	Num 24:13	

but died in his o sin, and had no	Num 27:3	
called it Nobah, after his o name	Num 32:42	
keep himself to his o inheritance	Num 36:9	
and called them after his o name	Deut 3:14	
whatsoever is right in his o eyes	Deut 12:8	
friend, which is as thine o soul	Deut 13:6	
shalt bring it unto thine o house	Deut 22:2	
thy fill at thine o pleasure	Deut 23:24	
he may sleep in his o raiment	Deut 24:13	
be put to death for his o sin	Deut 24:16	
eat the fruit of their o body	Deut 28:53	
brethren, nor knew his o children	Deut 33:9	
put it even among their o stuff	Josh 7:11	
his o city, and unto his o house	Josh 20:6	
ceased not from their o doings	Judg 2:19	
Mine o hand hath saved me	Judg 7:2	
went and dwelt in his o house	Judg 8:29	
which was right in his o eyes	Judg 17:6	
which was right in his o eyes	Judg 21:25	
lest I mar mine o inheritance	Ruth 4:6	
And they went unto their o home	1Sa 2:20	
and let it go again to his o place	1Sa 5:11	
of his o coast to Beth-shemesh	1Sa 6:9	
him a man after his o heart	1Sa 13:14	
Philistines went to their o place	1Sa 14:46	
thou valse little in thine o sight	1Sa 15:17	
Jonathan loved him as his o soul	1Sa 18:1	
he loved him as his o soul	1Sa 18:3	
loved him as he loved his o soul	1Sa 20:17	
son of Jesse to thine o confusion	1Sa 20:30	
thyself with thine o hand	1Sa 25:26	
avenging myself with mine o hand	1Sa 25:33	
of Nabal upon his o head	1Sa 25:39	
him in Ramah, even in his o city	1Sa 28:3	
in his o house upon his bed	2Sa 4:11	
and will be base in mine o sight	2Sa 6:22	
may dwell in a place of their o	2Sa 7:10	
and according to thine o heart	2Sa 7:21	
o meat, and drank of his o cup	2Sa 12:3	
of his o flock and of his o herd	2Sa 12:4	
against thee out of thine o house	2Sa 12:11	
then he came to his o house	2Sa 12:20	
said, Let him turn to his o house	2Sa 14:24	
Absalom returned to his o house	2Sa 14:24	
go to battle in thine o person	2Sa 17:11	
falsehood against mine o life	2Sa 18:13	
the pillar after his o name	2Sa 18:18	
that did eat at thine o table	2Sa 19:28	
again in peace unto his o house	2Sa 19:30	
that I may die in mine o city	2Sa 19:37	
and he returned unto his o place	2Sa 19:39	
and slew him with his o spear	2Sa 23:21	
thou mayest save thine o life	1Kin 1:12	
my son to ride upon mine o mule	1Kin 1:33	
this word against his o life	1Kin 2:23	
to Anathoth, unto thine o fields	1Kin 2:26	
return his blood upon his o head	1Kin 2:32	
he was buried in his o house in	1Kin 2:34	
blood shall be upon thine o head	1Kin 2:37	
thy wickedness upon thine o head	1Kin 2:44	
an end of building his o house	1Kin 3:1	
his o house thirteen years	1Kin 7:1	
man the plague of his o heart	1Kin 8:38	
his o house, and Millo, and the	1Kin 9:15	
heard in mine o land of thy acts	1Kin 10:6	
turned and went to her o country	1Kin 10:13	249
to wife the sister of his o wife	1Kin 11:19	
that I may go to mine o country	1Kin 11:21	
seekest to go to thine o country	1Kin 11:22	
now see to thine o house, David	1Kin 12:16	
he had devised of his o heart	1Kin 12:33	
laid his carcase in his o grave	1Kin 13:30	
get thee to thine o house	1Kin 14:12	
abode, and laid him upon his o bed	1Kin 17:19	
and every man to his o country	1Kin 22:36	
and he took hold of his o clothes	2Kin 2:12	249
him, and returned to their o land	2Kin 3:27	
I dwell among mine o people	2Kin 4:13	
his o hallowed things, and all the	2Kin 12:18	
be put to death for his o sin	2Kin 14:6	
carried away out of their o land	2Kin 17:23	
every nation made gods of their o	2Kin 17:29	
the LORD, and served their o gods	2Kin 17:33	
that they may eat their o dung	2Kin 18:27	
drink their o piss with you	2Kin 18:27	
eat ye every man of his o vine	2Kin 18:31	
away to a land like your o land	2Kin 18:32	
and shall return to his o land	2Kin 19:7	
fall by the sword in his o land	2Kin 19:7	
city, to save it, for mine o sake	2Kin 19:34	
defend this city for mine o sake	2Kin 20:6	

in the garden of his o house	2Kin 21:18	
and slew the king in his o house	2Kin 21:23	
and buried him in his o sepulchre	2Kin 23:30	
and slew him with his o spear	1Chr 11:23	
and according to thine o heart	1Chr 17:19	
went to redeem to be his o people	1Chr 17:21	
thou make thine o people for ever	1Chr 17:22	
God, I have of mine o proper good	1Chr 29:3	
of thine o have we given thee	1Chr 29:14	
of thine hand, and is all thine o	1Chr 29:16	
his way upon his o head	2Chr 6:23	
every one shall know his o sore	2Chr 6:29	
his o grief, and shall spread	2Chr 6:29	
of the LORD, and in his o house	2Chr 7:11	
of the LORD, and his o house,	2Chr 8:1	
in mine o land of thine acts	2Chr 9:5	
and went away to her o land	2Chr 9:12	
now, David, see to thine o house	2Chr 10:16	
buried him in his o sepulchres	2Chr 16:14	
his o servants conspired against	2Chr 24:25	249
every man shall die for his o sin	2Chr 25:4	
their o people out of thine hand	2Chr 25:15	
possession, into their o cities	2Chr 31:1	
with shame of face to his o land	2Chr 32:21	
they that came forth of his o	2Chr 32:21	
and they buried him in his o house	2Chr 33:20	
him, and slew him in his o house	2Chr 33:24	
which are minded of their o	Ezr 7:13	
their reproach upon their o head	Neh 4:4	
them out of thine o heart	Neh 6:8	
much cast down in their o eyes	Neh 6:16	
should bear rule in his o house	Est 1:22	
dead, took for his o daughter	Est 2:7	
should return upon his o head	Est 9:25	
came every one from his o place	Job 2:11	
the wise in their o craftiness	Job 5:13	
mine o mouth shall condemn me	Job 9:20	
mine o clothes shall abhor me	Job 9:31	
maintain mine o ways before him	Job 13:15	
Thine o mouth condemneth thee, and	Job 15:6	
thine o lips testify against thee	Job 15:6	
his o counsel shall cast him down	Job 18:7	
is cast into a net by his o feet	Job 18:8	
children's sake of mine o body	Job 19:17	
perish for ever like his o dung	Job 20:7	
he was righteous in his o eyes	Job 32:1	
thine o right hand can save thee	Job 40:14	
commune with your o heart upon	Ps 4:4	
let them fall by their o counsels	Ps 5:10	
shall return upon his o head	Ps 7:16	
shall come down upon his o pate	Ps 7:16	
they hid is their o foot taken	Ps 9:15	
snared in the work of his o hands	Ps 9:16	
our lips are our o	Ps 12:4	
He that sweareth to his o hurt	Ps 15:4	
They are inclosed in their o fat	Ps 17:10	249
thee according to thine o heart	Ps 20:4	
LORD, in thine o strength	Ps 21:13	
and none can keep alive his o soul	Ps 22:29	
hath chosen for his o inheritance	Ps 33:12	
prayer returned into mine o bosom	Ps 35:13	
flattereth himself in his o eyes	Ps 36:2	
shall enter into their o heart	Ps 37:15	
mine o familiar friend, in whom I	Ps 41:9	
in possession by their o sword	Ps 44:3	
neither did their o arm save them	Ps 44:3	
forget also thine o people	Ps 45:10	
their lands after their o names	Ps 49:11	
slanderest thine o mother's son	Ps 50:20	
So they shall make their o tongue	Ps 64:8	
and God, even our o God, shall	Ps 67:6	
Arise, O God, plead thine o cause	Ps 74:22	
I commune with mine o heart	Ps 77:6	
for he gave them their o desire	Ps 78:29	
But made his o people to go forth	Ps 78:52	
them up unto their o hearts' lust	Ps 81:12	
they walked in their o counsels	Ps 81:12	
bring upon them their o iniquity	Ps 94:23	
them off in their o wickedness	Ps 94:23	
they defiled with their o works	Ps 106:39	
a whoring with their o inventions	Ps 106:39	
he abhorred his o inheritance	Ps 106:40	
themselves with their o confusion	Ps 109:29	
not the works of thine o hands	Ps 138:8	
of their o lips cover them	Ps 140:9	
the wicked fall into their o nets	Ps 141:10	249
they lay wait for their o blood	Prov 1:18	
lurk privily for their o lives	Prov 1:18	
eat of the fruit of their o way	Prov 1:31	
and be filled with their o devices	Prov 1:31	
not unto thine o understanding	Prov 3:5	

Be not wise in thine o eyes	Prov 3:7	
waters out of thine o cistern	Prov 5:15	
waters out of thine o well	Prov 5:15	
Let them be only thine o, and not	Prov 5:17	249
His o iniquities shall take the	Prov 5:22	249
doeth it destroyeth his o soul	Prov 6:32	
against me wrongeth his o soul	Prov 8:36	
shall fall by his o wickedness	Prov 11:5	
be taken in their o naughtiness	Prov 11:6	
man doeth good to his o soul	Prov 11:17	
is cruel troubleth his o flesh	Prov 11:17	
evil pursueth it to his o death	Prov 11:19	
He that troubleth his o house	Prov 11:29	
of a fool is right in his o eyes	Prov 12:15	
heart knoweth his o bitterness	Prov 14:10	5315
shall be filled with his o ways	Prov 14:14	
is hated even of his o neighbour	Prov 14:20	
of gain troubleth his o house	Prov 15:27	
instruction despiseth his o soul	Prov 15:32	
of a man are clean in his o eyes	Prov 16:2	
as an high wall in his o conceit	Prov 18:11	
first in his o cause seemeth just	Prov 18:17	
getteth wisdom loveth his o soul	Prov 19:8	
commandment keepeth his o soul	Prov 19:16	
anger sinneth against his o soul	Prov 20:2	
proclaim every one his o goodness	Prov 20:6	
a man then understand his o way	Prov 20:24	
of a man is right in his o eyes	Prov 21:2	
cease from thine o wisdom	Prov 23:4	
search their o glory is not glory	Prov 25:27	
o spirit is like a city that is	Prov 25:28	
lest he be wise in his o conceit	Prov 26:5	
thou a man wise in his o conceit	Prov 26:12	
The sluggard is wiser in his o	Prov 26:16	
praise thee, and not thine o mouth	Prov 27:2	
a stranger, and not thine o lips	Prov 27:2	
Thine o friend, and thy father's	Prov 27:10	
shall fall himself into his o pit	Prov 28:10	
rich man is wise in his o conceit	Prov 28:11	
trusteth in his o heart is a fool	Prov 28:26	
with a thief hateth his o soul	Prov 29:24	
that are pure in their o eyes	Prov 30:12	
let her o works praise her in the	Prov 31:31	
I communed with mine o heart	Eccl 1:16	
man should rejoice in his o works	Eccl 3:22	
together, and eateth his o flesh	Eccl 4:5	
For oftentimes also thine o heart	Eccl 7:22	
ruleth over another to his o hurt	Eccl 8:9	
but mine o vineyard have I not	Song 1:6	
worship the work of their o hands	Is 2:8	
that which their o fingers have	Is 2:8	
saying, We will eat our o bread	Is 4:1	
o bread, and wear our o apparel	Is 4:1	
that are wise in their o eyes	Is 5:21	
and prudent in their o sight	Is 5:21	
every man the flesh of his o arm	Is 9:20	
every man turn to his o people	Is 13:14	
and flee every one into his o land	Is 13:14	
and set them in their o land	Is 14:1	
glory, every one in his o house	Is 14:18	
her o feet shall carry her afar	Is 23:7	
which your o hands have made unto	Is 31:7	
that they may eat their o dung	Is 36:12	
drink their o piss with you	Is 36:12	
one the waters of his o cistern	Is 36:16	
away to a land like your o land	Is 36:17	
a rumour, and return to his o land	Is 37:7	
fall by the sword in his o land	Is 37:7	
city to save it for mine o sake	Is 37:35	
transgressions for mine o sake	Is 43:25	
and they are their o witnesses	Is 44:9	
o sake, even for mine o sake	Is 48:11	
oppress thee with their o flesh	Is 49:26	
be drunken with their o blood	Is 49:26	
turned every one to his o way	Is 53:6	
they all look to their o way	Is 56:11	
not thyself from thine o flesh	Is 58:7	
him, not doing thine o ways	Is 58:13	
nor finding thine o pleasure	Is 58:13	
nor speaking thine o words	Is 58:13	
therefore mine o arm brought	Is 63:5	
not good, after their o thoughts	Is 65:2	
they have chosen their o ways	Is 66:3	
the works of their o hands	Jer 1:16	249
Thine o wickedness shall correct	Jer 2:19	
your o sword hath devoured your	Jer 2:30	
to the confusion of their o faces	Jer 7:19	
the imagination of their o heart	Jer 9:14	
we will walk after our o devices	Jer 18:12	
they shall dwell in their o land	Jer 23:8	
speak a vision of their o heart	Jer 23:16	

O

the imagination of his o heart	Jer 23:17	
of the deceit of their o heart	Jer 23:26	
of your hands to your o hurt	Jer 25:7	
to the works of their o hands	Jer 25:14	
let remain still in their o land	Jer 27:11	
shall be builded upon her o heap	Jer 30:18	
come again to their o border	Jer 31:17	
one shall die for his o iniquity	Jer 31:30	
return to Egypt into their o land	Jer 37:7	
you to return to your o land	Jer 42:12	
your o wickedness, and the	Jer 44:9	
goeth forth out of our o mouth	Jer 44:17	
let us go again to our o people	Jer 46:16	
flee every one to his o land	Jer 50:16	
go every one into his o country	Jer 51:9	
away captive out of his o land	Jer 52:27	
have sodden their o children	Lam 4:10	
their way upon their o heads	Eze 11:21	
prophesy out of their o hearts	Eze 13:2	
that follow their o spirit	Eze 13:3	
prophesy out of their o heart	Eze 13:17	
house of Israel in their o heart	Eze 14:5	
o souls by their righteousness	Eze 14:14	
o souls by their righteousness	Eze 14:20	
thee polluted in thine o blood	Eze 16:6	
didst trust in thine o beauty	Eze 16:15	
bear thine o shame for thy sins	Eze 16:52	
thou mayest bear thine o shame	Eze 16:54	
will I recompense upon his o head	Eze 17:19	
I polluted them in their o gifts	Eze 20:26	
o sight for all your evils that	Eze 20:43	
their o way have I recompensed	Eze 22:31	
and pluck off thine o breasts	Eze 23:34	
hath said, My river is mine o	Eze 29:3	
moment, every man for his o life	Eze 32:10	
blood shall be upon his o head	Eze 33:4	
he trust to his o righteousness	Eze 33:13	
will bring them to their o land	Eze 34:13	
of Israel dwelt in their o land	Eze 36:17	
they defiled it by their o way	Eze 36:17	
will bring you into your o land	Eze 36:24	
ye remember your o evil ways	Eze 36:31	
your o sight for your iniquities	Eze 36:31	
and confounded for your o ways	Eze 36:32	
I shall place you in your o land	Eze 37:14	
and bring them into their o land	Eze 37:21	
gathered them unto their o land	Eze 39:28	
out of his o possession	Eze 46:18	
any god, except their o God	Dan 3:28	
king sealed it with his o signet	Dan 6:17	
be mighty, but not by his o power	Dan 8:24	
defer not, for thine o sake	Dan 9:19	
and shall return into his o land	Dan 11:9	
shall do according to his o will	Dan 11:16	7522
but a prince for his o behalf	Dan 11:18	
without his o reproach he shall	Dan 11:18	
toward the fort of his o land	Dan 11:19	
exploits, and return to his o land	Dan 11:28	
now their o doings have beset	Hos 7:2	
shall be ashamed of his o counsel	Hos 10:6	
them, because of their o counsels	Hos 11:6	
to their o understanding, all of	Hos 13:2	
your recompence upon your o head	Joel 3:4	
your recompence upon your o head	Joel 3:7	
to us horns by our o strength	Amos 6:13	
away captive out of their o land	Amos 7:11	
shall return upon thine o head	Obad 15	
vanities forsake their o mercy	Jonah 2:8	
are the men of his o house	Mic 7:6	
ye run every man unto his o house	Hag 1:9	
and set there upon her o base	Zec 5:11	
their o shepherds pity them not	Zec 11:5	
be inhabited again in her o place	Zec 12:6	
his o son that serveth him	Mal 3:18	
into their o country another way	Mt 2:12	
the beam that is in thine o eye	Mt 7:3	
behold, a beam is in thine o eye	Mt 7:4	
out the beam out of thine o eye	Mt 7:5	
over, and came into his o city	Mt 9:1	2398
shall be they of his o household	Mt 10:36	
he was come into his o country	Mt 13:54	
o country, and in his o house	Mt 13:57	
whole world, and lose his o soul	Mt 16:26	
of their o children, or of	Mt 17:25	
me to do what I will with mine o	Mt 20:15	
who called his o servants	Mt 25:14	2398
have received mine o with usury	Mt 25:27	
put his o raiment on him, and led	Mt 27:31	
And laid it in his o new tomb	Mt 27:60	
and came into his o country	Mk 6:1	

honour, but in his o country	Mk 6:4	
his o kin, and in his o house	Mk 6:4	
that ye may keep your o tradition	Mk 7:9	
away fasting to their o houses	Mk 8:3	
whole world, and lose his o soul	Mk 8:36	
put his o clothes on him, and led	Mk 15:20	2398
he departed to his o house	Lk 1:23	
and returned to her o house	Lk 1:56	
taxed, every one into his o city	Lk 2:3	2398
pierce through thy o soul also	Lk 2:35	
Galilee, to their o city Nazareth	Lk 2:39	
is accepted in his o country	Lk 4:24	
lay, and departed to his o house	Lk 5:25	
him a great feast in his o house	Lk 5:29	
the beam that is in thine o eye	Lk 6:41	2398
the beam that is in thine o eye	Lk 6:42	
first the beam out of thine o eye	Lk 6:42	
tree is known by his o fruit	Lk 6:44	2398
Return to thine o house, and shew	Lk 8:39	
when he shall come in his o glory	Lk 9:26	
wine, and set him on his o beast	Lk 10:34	2398
his o life also, he cannot be my	Lk 14:26	1438
give you that which is your o	Lk 16:12	
shall not God avenge his o elect	Lk 18:7	
Out of thine o mouth will I judge	Lk 19:22	
have required mine o with usury	Lk 19:23	
know of your o selves that summer	Lk 21:30	
have heard of his o mouth	Lk 22:71	1438
He came unto his o	Jn 1:11	
and his o received him not	Jn 1:11	
first findeth his o brother Simon	Jn 1:41	
believed because of his o word	Jn 4:41	
hath no honour in his o country	Jn 4:44	2398
I can of mine o self do nothing	Jn 5:30	
because I seek not mine o will	Jn 5:30	
another shall come in his o name	Jn 5:43	2398
heaven, not to do mine o will	Jn 6:38	
of himself seeketh his o glory	Jn 7:18	2398
every man went unto his o house	Jn 7:53	
convicted by their o conscience	Jn 8:9	
a lie, he speaketh of his o	Jn 8:44	2398
And I seek not mine o glory	Jn 8:50	
and he calleth his o sheep by name	Jn 10:3	2398
when he putteth forth his o sheep	Jn 10:4	2398
whose o the sheep are not, seeth	Jn 10:12	2398
having loved his o which were in	Jn 13:1	2398
world, the world would love his o	Jn 15:19	2398
be scattered, every man to his o	Jn 16:32	2398
glorify thou me with thine o self	Jn 17:5	4572
keep through thine o name those	Jn 17:11	
Thine o nation and the chief	Jn 18:35	
disciple took her unto his o home	Jn 19:27	2398
went away again unto their o home	Jn 20:10	1438
Father hath put in his o power	Acts 1:7	2398
that he might go to his o place	Acts 1:25	2398
them speak in his o language	Acts 2:6	2398
hear we every man in our o tongue	Acts 2:8	2398
as though by our o power or	Acts 3:12	2398
go, they went to their o company	Acts 4:23	2398
which he possessed was his o	Acts 4:32	2398
it remained, was it not thine o	Acts 5:4	
sold, was it not in thine o power	Acts 5:4	
and nourished him for her o son	Acts 7:21	1438
in the works of their o hands	Acts 7:41	
opened to them of his o accord	Acts 12:10	848
Jesse, a man after mine o heart	Acts 13:22	
after he had served his o	Acts 13:36	2398
nations to walk in their o ways	Acts 14:16	848
to send chosen men of their o	Acts 15:22	
also of your o poets have said	Acts 17:28	2596
Your blood be upon your o heads	Acts 18:6	
hath purchased with his o blood	Acts 20:28	2398
Also of your o selves shall men	Acts 20:30	
girdle, and bound his o hands	Acts 21:11	848
him of their o superstition	Acts 25:19	2398
among mine o nation at Jerusalem	Acts 26:4	
o hands the tackling of the ship	Acts 27:19	849
whole years in his o hired house	Acts 28:30	2398
the lusts of their o hearts	Rom 1:24	
to dishonour their o bodies	Rom 1:24	
not his o body now dead, when he	Rom 4:19	1438
God sending his o Son in the	Rom 8:3	1438
He that spared not his o Son	Rom 8:32	2398
establish their o righteousness	Rom 10:3	2398
graffed into their o olive tree	Rom 11:24	2398
should be wise in your o conceits	Rom 11:25	1438
Be not wise in your o conceits	Rom 12:16	1438
to his o master he standeth or	Rom 14:4	2398
be fully persuaded in his o mind	Rom 14:5	2398
my life laid down their o necks	Rom 16:4	1438

Jesus Christ, but their o belly	Rom 16:18	1438
I had baptized in mine o name	1Cor 1:15	
his o reward according to his o	1Cor 3:8	2398
reward according to his o labour	1Cor 3:8	2398
the wise in their o craftiness	1Cor 3:19	
yea, I judge not mine o self	1Cor 4:3	1683
labour, working with our o hands	1Cor 4:12	2398
also raise us up by his o power	1Cor 6:14	848
sinneth against his o body	1Cor 6:18	2398
have of God, and ye are not your o	1Cor 6:19	1438
let every man have his o wife	1Cor 7:2	1438
every woman have her o husband	1Cor 7:2	2398
wife hath not power of her o body	1Cor 7:4	2398
hath not power of his o body	1Cor 7:4	2398
And this I speak for your o profit	1Cor 7:35	846
but hath power over his o will	1Cor 7:37	2398
warfare any time at his o charges	1Cor 9:7	2398
Let no man seek his o, but every	1Cor 10:24	1438
Conscience, I say, not thine o	1Cor 10:29	1438
things, not seeking mine o profit	1Cor 10:33	1683
taketh before other his o supper	1Cor 11:21	2398
unseemly, seeketh not her o	1Cor 13:5	1438
But every man in his o order	1Cor 15:23	2398
him, and to every seed his o body	1Cor 15:38	2398
of me Paul with mine o hand	1Cor 16:21	1699
are straitened in your o bowels	2Cor 6:12	
gave their o selves to the Lord	2Cor 8:5	
of his o accord he went unto you	2Cor 8:17	830
in perils by mine o countrymen	2Cor 11:26	
prove your o selves	2Cor 13:5	
Know ye not your o selves	2Cor 13:5	
many my equals in mine o nation	Gal 1:14	
have plucked out your o eyes	Gal 4:15	
let every man prove his o work	Gal 6:4	1438
every man shall bear his o burden	Gal 6:5	2398
written unto you with mine o hand	Gal 6:11	
after the counsel of his o will	Eph 1:11	848
set him at his o right hand in	Eph 1:20	848
yourselves unto your o husbands	Eph 5:22	2398
their o husbands in every thing	Eph 5:24	2398
their wives as their o bodies	Eph 5:28	1438
no man ever yet hated his o flesh	Eph 5:29	1438
not every man on his o things	Phil 2:4	1438
work out your o salvation with	Phil 2:12	1438
For all seek their o, not the	Phil 2:21	
not having mine o righteousness	Phil 3:9	1699
yourselves unto your o husbands	Col 3:18	2398
of God only, but also our o souls	1Th 2:8	1438
like things of your o countrymen	1Th 2:14	2398
their o prophets, and have	1Th 2:15	2398
quiet, and to do your o business	1Th 4:11	2398
and to work with your o hands	1Th 4:11	2398
they work, and eat their o bread	2Th 3:12	1438
of Paul with mine o hand, which	2Th 3:17	
Timothy, my o son in the faith	1Ti 1:2	1103
One that ruleth well his o house	1Ti 3:4	2398
know not how to rule his o house	1Ti 3:5	2398
children and their o houses well	1Ti 3:12	2398
But if any provide not for his o	1Ti 5:8	2398
for those of his o house, he hath	1Ti 5:8	2398
o masters worthy of all honour	1Ti 6:1	2398
but according to his o purpose	2Ti 1:9	2398
shall be lovers of their o selves	2Ti 3:2	
but after their o lusts shall	2Ti 4:3	2398
mine o son after the common faith	Titus 1:4	1103
even a prophet of their o	Titus 1:12	2398
obedient to their o husbands	Titus 2:5	2398
be obedient unto their o masters	Titus 2:9	2398
him, that is, mine o bowels	Philem 12	
have written it with mine o hand	Philem 19	
unto me even thine o self besides	Philem 19	4572
Ghost, according to his o will	Heb 2:4	
Christ as a son over his o house	Heb 3:6	848
also hath ceased from his o works	Heb 4:10	848
sacrifice, first for his o sins	Heb 7:27	2398
but by his o blood he entered in	Heb 9:12	2398
us after their o pleasure	Heb 12:10	848
the people with his o blood	Heb 13:12	2398
he is drawn away of his o lust	Jas 1:14	
Of his o will begat he us with	Jas 1:18	
only, deceiving your o selves	Jas 1:22	
tongue, but deceiveth his o heart	Jas 1:26	848
Who his o self bare our sins in	1Pet 2:24	848
sins in his o body on the tree	1Pet 2:24	848
in subjection to your o husbands	1Pet 3:1	2398
subjection unto their o husbands	1Pet 3:5	2398
perish in their o corruption	2Pet 2:12	848
o deceivings while they feast	2Pet 2:13	848
is turned to his o vomit again	2Pet 2:22	2398
walking after their o lusts	2Pet 3:3	2398

unto their o destruction	2Pet 3:16	2398
fall from your o stedfastness	2Pet 3:17	2398
Because his o works were evil, and	1Jn 3:12	
but left their o habitation	Jude 6	2398
sea, foaming out their o shame	Jude 13	1438
walking after their o lusts	Jude 16	848
walk after their o ungodly lusts	Jude 18	1438
us from our sins in his o blood	Rev 1:5	848

OWNER

but the o of the ox shall be quit	Ex 21:28	1167
it hath been testified to his o	Ex 21:29	1167
his o also shall be put to death	Ex 21:29	1167
The o of the pit shall make it	Ex 21:34	1167
and give money unto the o of them	Ex 21:34	1167
his o hath not kept him in	Ex 21:36	1167
the o of it shall accept thereof,	Ex 22:11	1167
restitution unto the o thereof	Ex 22:12	1167
the o thereof being not with it,	Ex 22:14	1167
But if the o thereof be with it,	Ex 22:15	1167
of Shemer, o of the hill, Samaria	1Kin 16:24	113
The ox knoweth his o, and the ass	Is 1:3	7069
the o of the ship, more than	Acts 27:11	3490

OWNERS

or have caused the o thereof to	Job 31:39	1167
away the life of the o thereof	Prov 1:19	1167
good is there to the o thereof	Eccl 5:11	1167
riches kept for the o thereof to	Eccl 5:13	1167
the o thereof said unto them, Why	Lk 19:33	2962

OWNETH

he that o the house shall come and	Lev 14:35	
bind the man that o this girdle	Acts 21:11	2076

OX

nor his maidservant, nor his o	Ex 20:17	7794
If an o gore a man or a woman,	Ex 21:28	7794
then the o shall be surely stoned	Ex 21:28	7794
the owner of the o shall be quit	Ex 21:28	7794
But if the o were wont to push	Ex 21:29	7794
the o shall be stoned, and his	Ex 21:29	7794
If the o shall push a manservant	Ex 21:32	7794
silver, and the o shall be stoned	Ex 21:32	7794
an o or an ass fall therein	Ex 21:33	7794
if one man's o hurt another's,	Ex 21:35	7794
then they shall sell the live o	Ex 21:35	7794
the dead o also they shall divide	Ex 21:35	7794
Or if it be known that the o hath	Ex 21:36	7794
he shall surely pay o for o	Ex 21:36	7794
If a man shall steal an o	Ex 22:1	7794
shall restore five oxen for an o	Ex 22:1	7794
his hand alive, whether it be o	Ex 22:4	7794
of trespass, whether it be for o	Ex 22:9	7794
his neighbour an ass, or an o	Ex 22:10	7794
enemy's o or his ass going astray	Ex 23:4	7794
that thine o and thine ass may	Ex 23:12	7794
whether o or sheep, that is male	Ex 34:19	7794
shall eat no manner of fat, of o	Lev 7:23	7794
of Israel, that killeth an o	Lev 17:3	7794
whether it be o, or sheep	Lev 27:26	7794
the princes, and for each one an o	Num 7:3	7794
as the o licketh up the grass of	Num 22:4	7794
nor thy maidservant, nor thine o	Deut 5:14	7794
or his maidservant, his o	Deut 5:21	7794
the o, the sheep, and the goat,	Deut 14:4	7794
and the pygarg, and the wild o	Deut 14:5	8377
whether it be o or sheep	Deut 18:3	7794
o or his sheep go astray, and hide	Deut 22:1	7794
ass or his o fall down by the way	Deut 22:4	7794
Thou shalt not plow with an o	Deut 22:10	7794
Thou shalt not muzzle the o when	Deut 25:4	7794
Thine o shall be slain before	Deut 28:31	7794
man and woman, young and old, and o	Josh 6:21	7794
six hundred men with an o goad	Judg 3:31	1241
for Israel, neither sheep, nor o	Judg 6:4	7794
whose o have I taken	1Sa 12:3	7794
Bring me hither every man his o	1Sa 14:34	7794
man his o with him that night	1Sa 14:34	7794
and woman, infant and suckling, o	1Sa 15:3	7794
prepared for me daily was one o	Neh 5:18	7794
or loweth the o over his fodder	Job 6:5	7794
take the widow's o for a pledge	Job 24:3	7794
he eateth grass as an o	Job 40:15	1241
an o or bullock that hath horns	Ps 69:31	7794
of an o that eateth grass	Ps 106:20	7794
as an o goeth to the slaughter,	Prov 7:22	7794
is by the strength of the o	Prov 14:4	7794
where love is, than a stalled o	Prov 15:17	7794
The o knoweth his owner, and the	Is 1:3	7794
lion shall eat straw like the o	Is 11:7	1241
forth thither the feet of the o	Is 32:20	7794

O

He that killeth an *o* is as if he	Is 66:3	7794
or an *o* that is brought to the	Jer 11:19	441
the face of an *o* on the left side	Eze 1:10	7794
his *o* or his ass from the stall	Lk 13:15	*1016*
an ass or an *o* fallen into a pit	Lk 14:5	*1016*
the *o* that treadeth out the corn	1Cor 9:9	*1016*
Thou shalt not muzzle the *o* that	1Ti 5:18	*1016*

OXEN

and he had sheep, and *o*, and he	Gen 12:16	1241
And Abimelech took sheep, and *o*	Gen 20:14	1241
And Abraham took sheep and *o*	Gen 21:27	1241
And I have *o*, and asses, flocks, and	Gen 32:5	7794
They took their sheep, and their *o*	Gen 34:28	1241
upon the camels, upon the *o*	Ex 9:3	1241
offerings, thy sheep, and thine *o*	Ex 20:24	1241
he shall restore *o* for an ox	Ex 22:1	1241
shalt thou do with thine *o*	Ex 22:30	7794
offerings of *o* unto the LORD	Ex 24:5	6499
six covered wagons, and twelve *o*	Num 7:3	1241
And Moses took the wagons and the *o*	Num 7:6	1241
four *o* he gave unto the sons of	Num 7:7	1241
eight *o* he gave unto the sons of	Num 7:8	1241
of peace offerings, two *o*	Num 7:17	1241
of peace offerings, two *o*	Num 7:23	1241
of peace offerings, two *o*	Num 7:29	1241
of peace offerings, two *o*	Num 7:35	1241
of peace offerings, two *o*	Num 7:41	1241
of peace offerings, two *o*	Num 7:47	1241
of peace offerings, two *o*	Num 7:53	1241
of peace offerings, two *o*	Num 7:59	1241
of peace offerings, two *o*	Num 7:65	1241
of peace offerings, two *o*	Num 7:71	1241
of peace offerings, two *o*	Num 7:77	1241
of peace offerings, two *o*	Num 7:83	1241
All the *o* for the burnt offering	Num 7:87	1241
all the *o* for the sacrifice of	Num 7:88	1241
And Balak offered *o* and sheep, and	Num 22:40	1241
and prepare me here seven *o*	Num 23:1	6499
thy soul lusteth after, for *o*	Deut 14:26	1241
sons, and his daughters, and his *o*	Josh 7:24	7794
And he took a yoke of *o*, and hewed	1Sa 11:7	1241
so shall it be done unto his *o*	1Sa 11:7	1241
which a yoke of *o* might plow	1Sa 14:14	1241
the spoil, and took sheep, and *o*	1Sa 14:32	1241
best of the sheep, and of the *o*	1Sa 15:9	1241
the lowing of the *o* which I hear	1Sa 15:14	1241
the best of the sheep and of the *o*	1Sa 15:15	1241
took of the spoil, sheep and *o*	1Sa 15:21	1241
children and sucklings, and *o*	1Sa 22:19	7794
and took away the sheep, and the *o*	1Sa 27:9	7794
for the *o* shook it	2Sa 6:6	1241
gone six paces, he sacrificed *o*	2Sa 6:13	7794
here be *o* for burnt sacrifice, and	2Sa 24:22	1241
instruments of the *o* for wood	2Sa 24:22	1241
the *o* for fifty shekels of silver	2Sa 24:24	1241
And Adonijah slew sheep and *o*	1Kin 1:9	1241
And he hath slain *o* and fat cattle	1Kin 1:19	7794
down this day, and hath slain *o*	1Kin 1:25	7794
Ten fat *o*, and twenty *o* out of	1Kin 4:23	1241
It stood upon twelve *o*, three	1Kin 7:25	1241
between the ledges were lions, *o*	1Kin 7:29	1241

o were certain additions made of	1Kin 7:29	1241
sea, and twelve *o* under the sea	1Kin 7:44	1241
the ark, sacrificing sheep and *o*	1Kin 8:5	1241
LORD, two and twenty thousand *o*	1Kin 8:63	1241
with twelve yoke of *o* before him	1Kin 19:19	
And he left the *o*, and ran after	1Kin 19:20	1241
from him, and took a yoke of *o*	1Kin 19:21	1241
with the instruments of the *o*	1Kin 19:21	1241
and vineyards, and sheep, and *o*	2Kin 5:26	1241
the brasen *o* that were under it	2Kin 16:17	1241
on camels, and on mules, and on *o*	1Chr 12:40	1241
of raisins, and wine, and oil, and *o*	1Chr 12:40	1241
for the *o* stumbled	1Chr 13:9	1241
I give thee the *o* also for burnt	1Chr 21:23	1241
under it was the similitude of *o*	2Chr 4:3	1241
Two rows of *o* were cast, when it	2Chr 4:3	1241
It stood upon twelve *o*, three	2Chr 4:4	1241
One sea, and twelve *o* under it	2Chr 4:15	1241
the ark, sacrificed sheep and *o*	2Chr 5:6	1241
of twenty and two thousand *o*	2Chr 7:5	1241
they had brought, seven hundred *o*	2Chr 15:11	1241
o for him in abundance, and for	2Chr 18:2	1241
things were six hundred *o*	2Chr 29:33	1241
also brought in the tithe of *o*	2Chr 31:6	1241
small cattle, and three hundred *o*	2Chr 35:8	1241
small cattle, and five hundred *o*	2Chr 35:9	1241
And so did they with the *o*	2Chr 35:12	1241
camels, and five hundred yoke of *o*	Job 1:3	1241
The *o* were plowing, and the asses	Job 1:14	1241
camels, and a thousand yoke of *o*	Job 42:12	1241
All sheep and *o*, yea, and the	Ps 8:7	504
That our *o* may be strong to	Ps 144:14	441
Where no *o* are, the crib is clean	Prov 14:4	5091
be for the sending forth of *o*	Is 7:25	7794
behold joy and gladness, slaying *o*	Is 22:13	1241
The *o* likewise and the young asses	Is 30:24	504
the husbandman and his yoke of *o*	Jer 51:23	
shall make thee to eat grass as *o*	Dan 4:25	8450
shall make thee to eat grass as *o*	Dan 4:32	8450
from men, and did eat grass as *o*	Dan 4:33	8450
they fed him with grass like *o*	Dan 5:21	8450
will one plow there with *o*	Amos 6:12	1241
my *o* and my fatlings are killed,	Mt 22:4	5022
I have bought five yoke of *o*	Lk 14:19	*1016*
in the temple those that sold *o*	Jn 2:14	*1016*
temple, and the sheep, and the *o*	Jn 2:15	*1016*
was before their city, brought *o*	Acts 14:13	5022
Doth God take care for *o*	1Cor 9:9	*1016*

OZEM (*o'-zem*)
1. Son of Jesse.

O the sixth, David the seventh	1Chr 2:15	684

2. Son of Jerahmeel.

and Bunah, and Oren, and *O*, and	1Chr 2:25	684

OZIAS (*o-zi'-as*) See UZZIAH. *Son of Joram; ancestor of Jesus.*

and Joram begat *O*	Mt 1:8	3604
And *O* begat Joatham	Mt 1:9	3604

OZNI (*oz'-ni*) See OZNITES. *A son of Gad.*

Of *O*, the family of the Oznites	Num 26:16	244

OZNITES (*oz'-nites*) *Descendants of Ozni.*

Of Ozni, the family of the *O*	Num 26:16	244

P

PAARAI (*pa'-ar-ahee*) See NAARAI. *A "mighty man" of David.*

the Carmelite, *P* the Arbite,	2Sa 23:35	6474

PACATIANA (*pa-ca-she-a'-nah*) *A region of Phrygia in Asia Minor.*

is the chiefest city of Phrygia *P*	1Ti *s*	3818

PACES

ark of the LORD had gone six *p*	2Sa 6:13	6806

PACIFIED

Then was the king's wrath *p*	Est 7:10	7918
when I am *p* toward thee for all	Eze 16:63	3722

PACIFIETH

A gift in secret *p* anger	Prov 21:14	3711
for yielding *p* great offences	Eccl 10:4	3240

PACIFY

but a wise man will *p* it	Prov 16:14	3722

PADAN (*pa'-dan*) See PADAN-ARAM. *Same as Padan-aram.*

And as for me, when I came from *P*	Gen 48:7	6307

PADAN-ARAM (*pa'-dan-a'-ram*) *The plains of Mesopotamia.*

of Bethuel the Syrian of *P*	Gen 25:20	6307
Arise, go to *P*, to the house of	Gen 28:2	6307
and he went to *P* unto Laban	Gen 28:5	6307
Jacob, and sent him away to *P*	Gen 28:6	6307
and his mother, and was gone to *P*	Gen 28:7	6307
getting, which he had gotten in *P*	Gen 31:18	6307
of Canaan, when he came from *P*	Gen 33:18	6307
again, when he came out of *P*	Gen 35:9	6307
which were born to him in *P*	Gen 35:26	6307
which she bare unto Jacob in *P*	Gen 46:15	6307

PADDLE

shalt have a *p* upon thy weapon	Deut 23:13	3489

PADON (*pa'-don*) *A family of exiles.*

of Siaha, the children of *P*	Ezr 2:44	6303
of Sia, the children of *P*	Neh 7:47	6303

PAGIEL (*pa'-ghe-el*) *An Asherite who counted the people.*

P the son of Ocran	Num 1:13	6295
Asher shall be *P* the son of Ocran	Num 2:27	6295

eleventh day *P* the son of Ocran .... Num 7:72   6295
offering of *P* the son of Ocran .... Num 7:77   6295
of Asher was *P* the son of Ocran .... Num 10:26   6295

PAHATH-MOAB *(pa'-hath-mo'-ab)*
   1. A family of exiles.
The children of *P*, of the .... Ezr 2:6   6355
And of the sons of *P* .... Ezr 10:30   6355
of Harim, and Hashub the son of *P* ...... Neh 3:11   6355
The children of *P*, of the .... Neh 7:11   6355
   2. Another family of exiles.
Of the sons of *P* .... Ezr 8:4   6355
   3. A family who renewed the covenant.
Parosh, *P*, Elam, Zatthu, Bani, ... Neh 10:14   6355

PAI *(pa'-i)* See Pau. *A city in Edom.*
and the name of his city was *P* 1Chr 1:50   6464

PAID
and custom, was *p* unto them .... Ezr 4:20   3052
so he *p* the fare thereof, and went .... Jonah 1:3   5414
till thou hast *p* the uttermost .... Mt 5:26   *591*
till thou hast *p* the very last .... Lk 12:59   *591*

PAIN
his flesh upon him shall have *p* .... Job 14:22   3510
travaileth with *p* all his days .... Job 15:20
also with *p* upon his bed, and the .... Job 33:19   4341
of his bones with strong *p* .... Job 33:19
Look upon mine affliction and my *p* ...... Ps 25:18   5999
took hold upon them there, and *p* .... Ps 48:6   2427
they shall be in *p* as a woman .... Is 13:8   2342
are my loins filled with *p* .... Is 21:3   2479
the time of her delivery, is in *p* .... Is 26:17   2342
with child, we have been in *p* .... Is 26:18   2342
before her *p* came, she was .... Is 66:7   2256
hath taken hold of us, and *p* .... Jer 6:24   2427
they have put themselves to *p* .... Jer 12:13   2470
Why is my *p* perpetual, and my .... Jer 15:18   3511
the *p* as of a woman in travail .... Jer 22:23   2427
it shall fall with *p* upon the .... Jer 30:23   2342
take balm for her *p*, if so be she .... Jer 51:8   4341
great *p* shall be in Ethiopia, ... Eze 30:4   2479
great *p* shall come upon them, as .... Eze 30:9   2479
Sin shall have great *p*, and No .... Eze 30:16   2342
Be in *p*, and labour to bring forth .... Mic 4:10   2342
much *p* is in all loins, and the .... Nah 2:10   2479
travaileth in *p* together until .... Rom 8:22
they gnawed their tongues for *p* .... Rev 16:10   *4192*
neither shall there be any more *p* .... Rev 21:4   *4192*

PAINED
My heart is sore *p* within me .... Ps 55:4   2342
be sorely *p* at the report of Tyre .... Is 23:5   2342
I am *p* at my very heart .... Jer 4:19   3176
face the people shall be much *p* .... Joel 2:6   2342
in birth, and *p* to be delivered .... Rev 12:2   *928*

PAINFUL
to know this, it was too *p* for me .... Ps 73:16   5999

PAINFULNESS
In weariness and *p*, in watchings 2Cor 11:27   *3449*

PAINS
for her *p* came upon her 1Sa 4:19   6735
the *p* of hell gat hold upon me .... Ps 116:3   4712
up, having loosed the *p* of death.......... Acts 2:24   *5604*
God of heaven because of their *p* .... Rev 16:11   *4192*

PAINTED
she *p* her face, and tired her head .. 2Kin 9:30   7760,6320
with cedar, and *p* with vermilion .... Jer 22:14   4886

PAINTEDST
p thy eyes, and deckedst thyself .... Eze 23:40   3583

PAINTING
thou rentest thy face with *p* .... Jer 4:30   6320

PAIR
and the poor for a *p* of shoes .... Amos 2:6
and the needy for a *p* of shoes .... Amos 8:6
A *p* of turtledoves, or two young............ Lk 2:24   *2201*
had a *p* of balances in his hand............ Rev 6:5   *2218*

PALACE
into the *p* of the king's house 1Kin 16:18   759
hard by the *p* of Ahab king of 1Kin 21:1   1964
in the *p* of the king's house, ... 2Kin 15:25   759
in the *p* of the king of Babylon.............. 2Kin 20:18   1964
for the *p* is not for man, but for 1Chr 29:1   1002
these things, and to build the *p* 1Chr 29:19   1002
of the Lord, and to the king's *p* 2Chr 9:11   1004
maintenance from the king's *p* .... Ezr 4:14   1964
in the *p* that is in the province.............. Ezr 6:2   1002
year, as I was in Shushan the *p* .... Neh 1:1   1002
p which appertained to the house .... Neh 2:8   1002

and Hananiah the ruler of the *p*............ Neh 7:2   1002
which was in Shushan the *p* .... Est 1:2   1002
were present in Shushan the *p* .... Est 1:5   1002
of the garden of the king's *p* .... Est 1:5   1055
young virgins unto Shushan the *p* .... Est 2:3   1002
Now in Shushan the *p* there was a........ Est 2:5   1002
together unto Shushan the *p* .... Est 2:8   1002
decree was given in Shushan the *p*........ Est 3:15   1002
his wrath went into the *p* garden .... Est 7:7   1055
p garden into the place of the .... Est 7:8   1055
decree was given at Shushan the *p* .... Est 8:14   1002
And in Shushan the *p* the Jews slew ...... Est 9:6   1002
the *p* was brought before the king.......... Est 9:11   1002
five hundred men in Shushan the *p*........ Est 9:12   1002
shall enter into the king's *p* .... Ps 45:15   1964
after the similitude of a *p* .... Ps 144:12   1964
will build upon her a *p* of silver .... Song 8:9   2918
a *p* of strangers to be no city .... Is 25:2   759
in the *p* of the king of Babylon .... Is 39:7   1964
the *p* shall remain after the .... Jer 30:18   759
in them to stand in the king's *p* .... Dan 1:4   1964
house, and flourishing in my *p* .... Dan 4:4   1965
the *p* of the kingdom of Babylon .... Dan 4:29   1965
of the wall of the king's *p* .... Dan 5:5   1965
Then the king went to his *p* .... Dan 6:18   1965
that I was at Shushan in the *p* .... Dan 8:2   1002
of his *p* between the seas in the .... Dan 11:45   643
and ye shall cast them into the *p* .... Amos 4:3   2038
and the *p* shall be dissolved.................. Nah 2:6   1964
unto the *p* of the high priest, ... Mt 26:3   *833*
afar off unto the high priest's *p* .... Mt 26:58   *833*
Now Peter sat without in the *p* .... Mt 26:69   *833*
even into the *p* of the high .... Mk 14:54   *833*
And as Peter was beneath in the *p*........ Mk 14:66   *833*
a strong man armed keepeth his *p* .... Lk 11:21   *833*
into the *p* of the high priest .... Jn 18:15   *833*
Christ are manifest in all the *p* .... Phil 1:13   *4232*

PALACES
burnt all the *p* thereof with fire 2Chr 36:19   759
and cassia, out of the ivory *p* .... Ps 45:8   1964
is known in her *p* for a refuge .... Ps 48:3   759
well her bulwarks, consider her *p* .... Ps 48:13   759
built his sanctuary like high *p* .... Ps 78:69   759
walls, and prosperity within thy *p*.......... Ps 122:7   759
with her hands, and is in kings' *p* .... Prov 30:28   1964
and dragons in their pleasant *p* .... Is 13:22   1964
they raised up the *p* thereof .... Is 23:13   759
Because the *p* shall be forsaken .... Is 32:14   759
And thorns shall come up in her *p* .... Is 34:13   759
by night, and let us destroy her *p* .... Jer 6:5   759
windows, and is entered into our *p*........ Jer 9:21   759
shall devour the *p* of Jerusalem .... Jer 17:27   759
shall consume the *p* of Ben-hadad .... Jer 49:27   759
he hath swallowed up all her *p* .... Lam 2:5   759
of the enemy the walls of her *p* .... Lam 2:7   759
And he knew their desolate *p* .... Eze 19:7
and they shall set their *p* in thee .... Eze 25:4   2918
and it shall devour the *p* thereof .... Hos 8:14   759
shall devour the *p* of Ben-hadad .... Amos 1:4   759
which shall devour the *p* thereof............ Amos 1:7   759
which shall devour the *p* thereof............ Amos 1:10   759
shall devour the *p* of Bozrah.................. Amos 1:12   759
and it shall devour the *p* thereof............ Amos 1:14   759
it shall devour the *p* of Kirioth.............. Amos 2:2   759
shall devour the *p* of Jerusalem .... Amos 2:5   759
Publish in the *p* at Ashdod .... Amos 3:9   759
in the *p* in the land of Egypt, and.......... Amos 3:9   759
up violence and robbery in their *p*.......... Amos 3:10   759
thee, and thy *p* shall be spoiled.............. Amos 3:11   759
of Jacob, and hate his *p*........................ Amos 6:8   759
and when he shall tread in our *p* .... Mic 5:5   759

PALAL *(pa'-lal) A rebuilder of Jerusalem's wall.*
P the son of Uzai, over against .... Neh 3:25   6420

PALE
neither shall his face now wax *p* .... Is 29:22   2357
And I looked, and behold a *p* horse .... Rev 6:8   *5515*

PALENESS
and all faces are turned into *p* .... Jer 30:6   3420

PALESTINA *(pal-es-ti'-nah)* See Palestine, Philistia.
   The west coast of Canaan.
take hold on the inhabitants of *P* .... Ex 15:14   6429
Rejoice not thou, whole *P* .... Is 14:29   6429
thou, whole *P*, art dissolved .... Is 14:31   6429

PALESTINE *(pal-es-tine)* See Palestina. *Same as Palestina.*
and Zidon, and all the coasts of *P* .... Joel 3:4   6429

P

PALLU

PALLU (pal'-lu) See PALLUITES, PHALLU. *A son of Reuben.*

Hanoch, and P, Hezron, and Carmi	Ex 6:14	6396
of P, the family of the Palluites	Num 26:5	6396
And the sons of P	Num 26:8	6396
of Israel were, Hanoch, and P	1Chr 5:3	6396

PALLUITES (pal'-lu-ites) *Descendants of Pallu.*

of Pallu, the family of the P	Num 26:5	6384

PALM

and threescore and ten p trees	Ex 15:27	8558
pour it into the p of his own	Lev 14:15	3709
into the p of his own left hand	Lev 14:26	3709
goodly trees, branches of p trees	Lev 23:40	8558
and threescore and ten p trees	Num 33:9	8558
of Jericho, the city of p trees	Deut 34:3	8558
of p trees with the children of	Judg 1:16	8558
and possessed the city of p trees	Judg 3:13	8558
she dwelt under the p tree of..................	Judg 4:5	8560
p trees and open flowers, within	1Kin 6:29	8561
p trees and open flowers, and	1Kin 6:32	8561
cherubims, and upon the p trees	1Kin 6:32	8561
and p trees and open flowers	1Kin 6:35	8561
p trees, according to the	1Kin 7:36	8561
fine gold, and set thereon p trees	2Chr 3:5	8561
to Jericho, the city of p trees	2Chr 28:15	8558
p branches, and branches of thick..........	Neh 8:15	8558
shall flourish like the p tree	Ps 92:12	8558
thy stature is like to a p tree	Song 7:7	8558
said, I will go up to the p tree	Song 7:8	8558
They are upright as the p tree	Jer 10:5	8560
and upon each post were p trees............	Eze 40:16	8561
and their arches, and their p trees	Eze 40:22	8561
and it had p trees, one on this	Eze 40:26	8561
p trees were upon the posts	Eze 40:31	8561
p trees were upon the posts	Eze 40:34	8561
p trees were upon the posts	Eze 40:37	8561
toward the p tree on the one side	Eze 41:19	8561
the p tree on the other side	Eze 41:19	8561
p trees made, and on the wall of	Eze 41:20	8561
p trees, like as were made upon	Eze 41:25	8561
p trees on the one side and on the	Eze 41:26	8561
the p tree also, and the apple	Joel 1:12	8558
Took branches of p trees, and went	Jn 12:13	5404
Jesus with the p of his hand..................	Jn 18:22	4475

PALMERWORM

That which the p hath left hath	Joel 1:4	1501
and the caterpiller, and the p	Joel 2:25	1501
increased, the p devoured them..............	Amos 4:9	1501

PALMS

both the p of his hands were cut	1Sa 5:4	3709
the feet, and the p of her hands	2Kin 9:35	3709
thee upon the p of my hands	Is 49:16	3709
knees and upon the p of my hands	Dan 10:10	3709
him with the p of their hands..................	Mt 26:67	4474
him with the p of their hands..................	Mk 14:65	4475
white robes, and p in their hands	Rev 7:9	5404

PALSIES

and many taken with p, and that	Acts 8:7	3886

PALSY

lunatick, and those that had the p	Mt 4:24	3885
lieth at home sick of the p	Mt 8:6	3885
to him a man sick of the p	Mt 9:2	3885
faith said unto the sick of the p	Mt 9:2	3885
saith he to the sick of the p	Mt 9:6	3885
him, bringing one sick of the p	Mk 2:3	3885
bed wherein the sick of the p lay	Mk 2:4	3885
he said unto the sick of the p	Mk 2:5	3885
to say to the sick of the p	Mk 2:9	3885
(he saith to the sick of the p...................	Mk 2:10	3885
a man which was taken with a p.............	Lk 5:18	3886
(he said unto the sick of the p	Lk 5:24	3886
eight years, and was sick of the p	Acts 9:33	3886

PALTI

PALTI (pal'-ti) *A spy sent to the Promised Land.*

of Benjamin, P the son of Raphu.............	Num 13:9	6406

PALTIEL

PALTIEL (pal'-te-el) See PHALTIEL. *A chief of Issachar.*

of Issachar, P the son of Azzan...............	Num 34:26	6409

PALTITE

PALTITE (pal'-tite) See PELONITE. *A resident of Beth-palet.*

Helez the P, Ira the son of......................	2Sa 23:26	6407

PAMPHYLIA

PAMPHYLIA (pam-fil'-e-ah) *A province of Asia Minor.*

Phrygia, and P, in Egypt, and in	Acts 2:10	3828
Paphos, they came to Perga in P............	Acts 13:13	3828
Pisidia, they came to P	Acts 14:24	3828
who departed from them from P............	Acts 15:38	3828
over the sea of Cilicia and P	Acts 27:5	3828

PAN

be a meat offering baken in a p.............	Lev 2:5	4227
offering baken in the frying p	Lev 2:7	4227
In a p it shall be made with oil...............	Lev 6:21	4227
in the fryingpan, and in the p	Lev 7:9	4227
And he struck it into the p	1Sa 2:14	3595
And she took a p, and poured them	2Sa 13:9	4958
for that which is baked in the p..............	1Chr 23:29	4227
take thou unto thee an iron p	Eze 4:3	4227

PANGS

p and sorrows shall take hold of.............	Is 13:8	6735
p have taken hold upon me, as the	Is 21:3	6735
upon me, as the p of a woman that	Is 21:3	6735
in pain, and crieth out in her p	Is 26:17	2256
thou shalt be when p come upon thee	Jer 22:23	2256
as the heart of a woman in her p............	Jer 48:41	6887
as the heart of a woman in her p............	Jer 49:22	6887
p as of a woman in travail.......................	Jer 50:43	2427
for p have taken thee as a woman.........	Mic 4:9	2427

PANNAG

PANNAG (pan'-nag) *A place on the Damascus-Baalbeck road.*

thy market wheat of Minnith, and P	Eze 27:17	6436

PANS

thou shalt make his p to receive............	Ex 27:3	5518
it in a mortar, and baked it in p..............	Num 11:8	6517
things that were made in the p...............	1Chr 9:31	2281
in pots, and in caldrons, and in p	2Chr 35:13	6745

PANT

That p after the dust of the	Amos 2:7	7602

PANTED

I opened my mouth, and p	Ps 119:131	7602
My heart p, fearfulness	Is 21:4	8582

PANTETH

My heart p, my strength faileth	Ps 38:10	5503
As the hart p after the water	Ps 42:1	6165
so p my soul after thee, O God	Ps 42:1	6165

PAPER

The p reeds by the brooks, by the	Is 19:7	6169
you, I would not write with p	2Jn 12	5489

PAPHOS

PAPHOS (pa'-fos) *Capital of Cyprus.*

had gone through the isle unto P...........	Acts 13:6	3974
Paul and his company loosed from P	Acts 13:13	3974

PAPS

Egyptians for the p of thy youth.............	Eze 23:21	7699
the p which thou hast sucked	Lk 11:27	3149
the p which never gave suck	Lk 23:29	3149
girt about the p with a golden	Rev 1:13	3149

PARABLE

And he took up his p, and said, ...	Num 23:7	4912
And he took up his p, and said, ...	Num 23:18	4912
And he took up his p, and said, ...	Num 24:3	4912
And he took up his p, and said, ...	Num 24:15	4912
on Amalek, he took up his p	Num 24:20	4912
on the Kenites, and took up his p	Num 24:21	4912
And he took up his p, and said, ...	Num 24:23	4912
Moreover Job continued his p	Job 27:1	4912
Moreover Job continued his p	Job 29:1	4912
I will incline mine ear to a p	Ps 49:4	4912
I will open my mouth in a p	Ps 78:2	4912
so is a p in the mouth of fools	Prov 26:7	4912
so is a p in the mouth of fools	Prov 26:9	4912
speak a p unto the house of	Eze 17:2	4912
utter a p unto the rebellious...................	Eze 24:3	4912
shall one take up a p against you	Mic 2:4	4912
all these take up a p against him	Hab 2:6	4912
ye therefore the p of the sower.........	Mt 13:18	3850
Another p put he forth unto them,........	Mt 13:24	3850
Another p put he forth unto them,........	Mt 13:31	3850
Another p spake he unto them	Mt 13:33	3850
without a p spake he not unto	Mt 13:34	3850
Declare unto us the p of the	Mt 13:36	3850
unto him, Declare unto us this p	Mt 15:15	3850
Hear another p......................................	Mt 21:33	3850
Now learn a p of the fig tree	Mt 24:32	3850
the twelve asked of him the p	Mk 4:10	3850
unto them, Know ye not this p	Mk 4:13	3850
But without a p spake he not unto	Mk 4:34	3850
asked him concerning the p	Mk 7:17	3850
he had spoken the p against them	Mk 12:12	3850
Now learn a p of the fig tree	Mk 13:28	3850
And he spake also a p unto the	Lk 5:36	3850
And he spake a p unto them	Lk 6:39	3850
of every city, he spake by a p	Lk 8:4	3850
him, saying, What might this p be	Lk 8:9	3850
Now the p is this	Lk 8:11	3850
And he spake a p unto them	Lk 12:16	3850

speakest thou this *p* unto us	Lk 12:41	3850
He spake also this *p*	Lk 13:6	3850
he put forth a *p* to those which	Lk 14:7	3850
And he spake this *p* unto them	Lk 15:3	3850
he spake a *p* unto them to this	Lk 18:1	3850
he spake this *p* unto certain	Lk 18:9	3850
things, he added and spake a *p*	Lk 19:11	3850
he to speak to the people this *p*	Lk 20:9	3850
he had spoken this *p* against them	Lk 20:19	3850
And he spake to them a *p*	Lk 21:29	3850
This *p* spake Jesus unto them	Jn 10:6	3942

PARABLES

say of me, Doth he not speak *p*	Eze 20:49	4912
spake many things unto them in *p*	Mt 13:3	3850
Why speakest thou unto them in *p*	Mt 13:10	3850
Therefore speak I to them in *p*	Mt 13:13	3850
Jesus unto the multitude in *p*	Mt 13:34	3850
saying, I will open my mouth in *p*	Mt 13:35	3850
when Jesus had finished these *p*	Mt 13:53	3850
and Pharisees had heard his *p*	Mt 21:45	3850
and spake unto them again by *p*	Mt 22:1	3850
unto him, and said unto them in *p*	Mk 3:23	3850
he taught them many things by *p*	Mk 4:2	3850
all these things are done in *p*	Mk 4:11	3850
and how then will ye know all *p*	Mk 4:13	3850
with many such *p* spake he the	Mk 4:33	3850
he began to speak unto them by *p*	Mk 12:1	3850
but to others in *p*	Lk 8:10	3850

PARADISE

To day shalt thou be with me in *p*	Lk 23:43	3857
How that he was caught up into *p*	2Cor 12:4	3857
is in the midst of the *p* of God	Rev 2:7	3857

PARAH *(pa'-rah) A city in Benjamin.*

And Avim, and P, and Ophrah,	Josh 18:23	6511

PARAMOURS

For she doted upon their *p*	Eze 23:20	6370

PARAN *(pa'-ran) A wilderness south of Canaan.*

he dwelt in the wilderness of P	Gen 21:21	6290
rested in the wilderness of P	Num 10:12	6290
and pitched in the wilderness of P	Num 12:16	6290
them from the wilderness of P	Num 13:3	6290
Israel, unto the wilderness of P	Num 13:26	6290
against the Red sea, between P	Deut 1:1	6290
he shined forth from mount P	Deut 33:2	6290
went down to the wilderness of P	1Sa 25:1	6290
arose out of Midian, and came to P	1Kin 11:18	6290
they took men with them out of P	1Kin 11:18	6290
and the Holy One from mount P	Hab 3:3	6290

PARBAR *(par'-bar) A place near the Temple in Jerusalem.*

At P westward, four at the	1Chr 26:18	6503
four at the causeway, and two at P	1Chr 26:18	6503

PARCEL

And he bought a *p* of a field	Gen 33:19	2513
in a *p* of ground which Jacob	Josh 24:32	2513
of Moab, selleth a *p* of land	Ruth 4:3	2513
where was a *p* of ground full of	1Chr 11:13	2513
themselves in the midst of that *p*	1Chr 11:14	2513
near to the *p* of ground that	Jn 4:5	5564

PARCHED

nor *p* corn, nor green ears, until	Lev 23:14	7039
p corn in the selfsame day	Josh 5:11	
and he reached her *p* corn, and she	Ruth 2:14	7039
brethren an ephah of this *p* corn	1Sa 17:17	7039
and five measures of *p* corn	1Sa 25:18	7039
p corn, and beans, and lentiles, and	2Sa 17:28	7039
beans, and lentiles, and *p* pulse,	2Sa 17:28	7039
the *p* ground shall become a pool,	Is 35:7	8273
but shall inhabit the *p* places in	Jer 17:6	2788

PARCHMENTS

the books, but especially the *p*	2Ti 4:13	3200

PARDON

for he will not *p* your	Ex 23:21	5375
p our iniquity and our sin, and	Ex 34:9	5545
P, I beseech thee, the iniquity	Num 14:19	5545
p my sin, and turn again with me,	1Sa 15:25	5375
this thing the LORD *p* thy servant	2Kin 5:18	5545
the LORD *p* thy servant in this	2Kin 5:18	5545
which the LORD would not *p*	2Kin 24:4	5545
saying, The good LORD *p* every one	2Chr 30:18	3722
but thou art a God ready to *p*	Neh 9:17	5547
dost thou not *p* my transgression	Job 7:21	5375
sake, O LORD, *p* mine iniquity	Ps 25:11	5545
our God, for he will abundantly *p*	Is 55:7	5545
and I will *p* it	Jer 5:1	5545
How shall I *p* thee for this	Jer 5:7	5545

I will *p* all their iniquities,	Jer 33:8	5545
for I will *p* them whom I reserve	Jer 50:20	5545

PARDONED

I have *p* according to thy word	Num 14:20	5545
that her iniquity is *p*	Is 40:2	7521
thou hast not *p*	Lam 3:42	5545

PARDONETH

that *p* iniquity, and passeth by	Mic 7:18	5375

PARE

shave her head, and *p* her nails	Deut 21:12	6213

PARENTS

shall rise up against their *p*	Mt 10:21	1118
shall rise up against their *p*	Mk 13:12	1118
when the *p* brought in the child	Lk 2:27	1118
Now his *p* went to Jerusalem every	Lk 2:41	1118
And her *p* were astonished	Lk 8:56	1118
no man that hath left house, or *p*	Lk 18:29	1118
And ye shall be betrayed both by *p*	Lk 21:16	1118
who did sin, this man, or his *p*	Jn 9:2	1118
hath this man sinned, nor his *p*	Jn 9:3	1118
until they called the *p* of him	Jn 9:18	1118
His *p* answered them and said, We	Jn 9:20	1118
These words spake his *p*, because	Jn 9:22	1118
Therefore said his *p*, He is of	Jn 9:23	1118
of evil things, disobedient to *p*	Rom 1:30	1118
ought not to lay up for the *p*	2Cor 12:14	1118
but the *p* for the children	2Cor 12:14	1118
Children, obey your *p* in the Lord	Eph 6:1	1118
obey your *p* in all things	Col 3:20	1118
at home, and to requite their *p*	1Ti 5:4	4269
blasphemers, disobedient to *p*	2Ti 3:2	1118
was hid three months of his *p*	Heb 11:23	3962

PARLOUR

and he was sitting in a summer *p*	Judg 3:20	5944
shut the doors of the *p* upon him	Judg 3:23	5944
the doors of the *p* were locked	Judg 3:24	5944
he opened not the doors of the *p*	Judg 3:25	5944
and brought them into the *p*	1Sa 9:22	3957

PARLOURS

and of the inner *p* thereof	1Chr 28:11	2315

PARMASHTA *(par-mash'-tah) A son of Haman.*

And P, and Arisai, and Aridai, and	Est 9:9	6534

PARMENAS *(par'-me-nas) A leader in the Jerusalem church.*

and Nicanor, and Timon, and P	Acts 6:5	3937

PARNACH *(par'-nak) A Zebulunite who apportioned the Promised Land.*

Zebulun, Elizaphan the son of P	Num 34:25	6535

PAROSH *(pa'-rosh) See PHAROSH.*
1. A family of exiles.

The children of P, two thousand	Ezr 2:3	6551
The children of P, two thousand	Neh 7:8	6551

2. Married a foreigner in exile.

of the sons of P	Ezr 10:25	6551

3. Father of Pedaiah.

After him Pedaiah the son of P	Neh 3:25	6551

4. A family who renewed the covenant.

P, Pahath-moab, Elam, Zatthu,	Neh 10:14	6551

PARSHANDATHA *(par-shan'-da-thah) A son of Haman.*

And P, and Dalphon, and Aspatha,	Est 9:7	6577

PART See APPENDIX.

PARTAKER

hast been *p* with adulterers	Ps 50:18	2506
in hope should be *p* of his hope	1Cor 9:10	3348
that I might be *p* thereof with	1Cor 9:23	4791
For if I by grace be a *p*, why am	1Cor 10:30	3348
neither be *p* of other men's sins	1Ti 5:22	2841
but be thou *p* of the afflictions	2Ti 1:8	4777
must be first *p* of the fruits	2Ti 2:6	3335
also a *p* of the glory that shall	1Pet 5:1	2844
God speed is *p* of his evil deeds	2Jn 11	2841

PARTAKERS

we would not have been *p* with	Mt 23:30	2844
made of their spiritual things	Rom 15:27	2841
If others be *p* of this power over	1Cor 9:12	3348
at the altar are *p* with the altar	1Cor 9:13	4829
for we are all *p* of that one	1Cor 10:17	3348
of the sacrifices *p* of the altar	1Cor 10:18	2844
ye cannot be *p* of the Lord's	1Cor 10:21	3348
knowing, that as ye are *p* of the	2Cor 1:7	2844
p of his promise in Christ by the	Eph 3:6	4830
Be not ye therefore *p* with them	Eph 5:7	4830
gospel, ye all are *p* of my grace	Phil 1:7	4791

P

to be *p* of the inheritance of the .... Col 1:12   3310
and beloved, *p* of the benefit 1Ti 6:2   482
as the children are *p* of flesh .... Heb 2:14   2841
p of the heavenly calling,....................... Heb 3:1   3353
For we are made *p* of Christ .... Heb 3:14   3353
were made *p* of the Holy Ghost, ... Heb 6:4   3353
chastisement, whereof all are *p* .... Heb 12:8   3353
we might be *p* of his holiness .... Heb 12:10   3335
inasmuch as ye are *p* of Christ's 1Pet 4:13   2841
might be *p* of the divine nature 2Pet 1:4   2844
that ye be not *p* of her sins.................... Rev 18:4   4790

PARTAKEST
   with them *p* of the root and .... Rom 11:17   1096,4791

PARTED
   and from thence it was *p*, and................ Gen 2:10   6504
   of fire, and *p* them both asunder 2Kin 2:11   6504
   waters, they *p* hither and thither 2Kin 2:14   2673
   By what way is the light *p*..................... Job 38:24   2505
   among the nations, and *p* my land .... Joel 3:2   2505
   p his garments, casting lots .... Mt 27:35   1266
   They *p* my garments among them, and . Mt 27:35   1266
   they *p* his garments, casting lots .... Mk 15:24   1266
   they *p* his raiment, and cast lots .... Lk 23:34   1266
   he was *p* from them, and carried up ...... Lk 24:51   1339
   They *p* my raiment among them, and ... Jn 19:24   1266
   p them to all men, as every man .... Acts 2:45   1266

PARTETH
   Whatsoever *p* the hoof, and is .... Lev 11:3   6536
   And every beast that *p* the hoof .... Deut 14:6   6536
   to cease, and *p* between the mighty .... Prov 18:18   6504

PARTHIANS (*par-the'-uns*) *Inhabitants of Parthia, now Iran.*
   P, and Medes, and Elamites, and the...... Acts 2:9   3934

PARTIAL
   ways, but have been *p* in the law .... Mal 2:9   5375,6440
   Are ye not then *p* in yourselves .... Jas 2:4   1252

PARTIALITY
   another, doing nothing by *p* 1Ti 5:21   4346
   mercy and good fruits, without *p* .... Jas 3:17   87

PARTICULAR
   body of Christ, and members in *p* 1Cor 12:27   3313
   let every one of you in *p* so love ...... Eph 5:33   3588,1520

PARTICULARLY
   declared *p* what things God .... Acts 21:19   1520,1538,2596
   of which we cannot now speak *p*.... Heb 9:5   2596,3313

PARTIES
   the cause of both *p* shall come ...... Ex 22:9

PARTING
   Babylon stood at the *p* of the way .... Eze 21:21   517

PARTITION
   he made a *p* by the chains of gold 1Kin 6:21   5674
   the middle wall of *p* between us .... Eph 2:14   5418

PARTLY
   be *p* strong, and *p* broken .... Dan 2:42   7118
   and I *p* believe it................................. 1Cor 11:18   3313,5100
   P, whilst ye were made a .... Heb 10:33   5124,3303
   and *p*, whilst ye became companions ... Heb 10:33   1161

PARTNER
   Whoso is *p* with a thief hateth .... Prov 29:24   2505
   do enquire of Titus, he is my *p*.............. 2Cor 8:23   2844
   If thou count me therefore a *p* .... Philem 17   2844

PARTNERS
   And they beckoned unto their *p* .... Lk 5:7   3353
   Zebedee, which were *p* with Simon .... Lk 5:10   2844

PARTRIDGE
   doth hunt a *p* in the mountains 1Sa 26:20   7124
   As the *p* sitteth on eggs, and .... Jer 17:11   7124

PARTS See APPENDIX.

PARUAH (*par'-u-ah*) *Father of Jehoshaphat.*
   Jehoshaphat the son of *P*, in 1Kin 4:17   6515

PARVAIM (*par-va'-im*) *A place rich in gold.*
   and the gold was gold of *P*...................... 2Chr 3:6   6516

PARZITES See PHARZITES.

PASACH (*pa'-sak*) *A son of Japhet.*
   P, and Bimhal, and Ashvath 1Chr 7:33   6457

PAS-DAMMIM (*pas-dam'-mim*) *A place in Judah.*
   He was with David at *P*, and there.......... 1Chr 11:13   6450

PASEAH (*pa-se'-ah*) See PHASEAH.
   1. A son of Eshton.
   And Eshton begat Beth-rapha, and *P* 1Chr 4:12   6454

   2. A family of exiles.
   of Uzza, the children of *P* .... Ezr 2:49   6454
   3. Father of Jehoiada.
   repaired Jehoiada the son of *P* .... Neh 3:6   6454

PASHUR (*pash'-ur*)
   1. Head of a priestly family.
   the son of Jeroham, the son of *P* 1Chr 9:12   6583
   The children of *P*, a thousand two .... Ezr 2:38   6583
   And of the sons of *P* .... Ezr 10:22   6583
   The children of *P*, a thousand two .... Neh 7:41   6583
   son of Zechariah, the son of *P* .... Neh 11:12   6583
   2. A priest who renewed the covenant.
   P, Amariah, Malchijah, ... Neh 10:3   6583
   3. A son of Immer.
   Now *P* the son of Immer the priest .... Jer 20:1   6583
   Then *P* smote Jeremiah the prophet .... Jer 20:2   6583
   that *P* brought forth Jeremiah out.......... Jer 20:3   6583
   LORD hath not called thy name *P* .... Jer 20:3   6583
   And thou, *P*, and all that dwell in .... Jer 20:6   6583
   Mattan, and Gedaliah the son of *P* .... Jer 38:1   6583
   4. A son of Melchiah/Malchiah.
   unto him *P* the son of Melchiah .... Jer 21:1   6583
   P the son of Malchiah, heard the .... Jer 38:1   6583

PASS See APPENDIX.

PASSAGE
   give Israel *p* through his border .... Num 20:21   5674
   at the *p* of the children of .... Josh 22:11   1552
   went out to the *p* of Michmash 1Sa 13:23   4569
   They are gone over the *p* .... Is 10:29   4569

PASSAGES
   took the *p* of Jordan before the .... Judg 12:5   4569
   and slew him at the *p* of Jordan .... Judg 12:6   4569
   And between the *p*, by which 1Sa 14:4   4569
   in Bashan, and cry from the *p* .... Jer 22:20   5676
   that the *p* are stopped, and the .... Jer 51:32   4569

PASSED See APPENDIX.

PASSEDST
   Wherefore *p* thou over to fight .... Judg 12:1   5674

PASSENGERS
   To call *p* who go right on their .... Prov 9:15   5674,1870
   the valley of the *p* on the east................ Eze 39:11   5674
   it shall stop the noses of the *p* .... Eze 39:11   5674
   the land to bury with the *p* those .... Eze 39:14   5674
   the *p* that pass through the land, ... Eze 39:15   5674

PASSEST See APPENDIX.

PASSETH See APPENDIX.

PASSING See APPENDIX.

PASSION
   his *p* by many infallible proofs .... Acts 1:3   3958

PASSIONS
   also are men of like *p* with you.............. Acts 14:15   3663
   a man subject to like *p* as we are........... Jas 5:17   3663

PASSOVER
   it is the LORD's *p* .... Ex 12:11   6453
   to your families, and kill the *p* .... Ex 12:21   6453
   is the sacrifice of the LORD's *p* .... Ex 12:27   6453
   This is the ordinance of the *p* .... Ex 12:43   6453
   and will keep the *p* to the LORD .... Ex 12:48   6453
   of the *p* be left until the morning .... Ex 34:25   6453
   month at even is the LORD's *p* .... Lev 23:5   6453
   the *p* at his appointed season................ Num 9:2   6453
   that they should keep the *p*.................... Num 9:4   6453
   they kept the *p* on the fourteenth .... Num 9:5   6453
   could not keep the *p* on that day .... Num 9:6   6453
   he shall keep the *p* unto the LORD .... Num 9:10   6453
   of the *p* they shall keep it .... Num 9:12   6453
   and forbeareth to keep the *p*................. Num 9:13   6453
   and will keep the *p* unto the LORD .... Num 9:14   6453
   to the ordinance of the *p* .... Num 9:14   6453
   first month is the *p* of the LORD .... Num 28:16   6453
   on the morrow after the *p* .... Num 33:3   6453
   keep the *p* unto the LORD thy God .... Deut 16:1   6453
   the *p* unto the LORD thy God .... Deut 16:2   6453
   the *p* within any of thy gates .... Deut 16:5   6453
   shalt sacrifice the *p* at even .... Deut 16:6   6453
   kept the *p* on the fourteenth day .... Josh 5:10   6453
   land on the morrow after the *p* .... Josh 5:11   6453
   Keep the *p* unto the LORD your God 2Kin 23:21   6453
   a *p* from the days of the judges............. 2Kin 23:22   6453
   wherein this *p* was holden to the 2Kin 23:23   6453
   to keep the *p* unto the LORD God 2Chr 30:1   6453
   to keep the *p* in the second month 2Chr 30:2   6453
   they should come to keep the *p*............. 2Chr 30:5   6453
   Then they killed the *p* on the 2Chr 30:15   6453
   yet did they eat the *p* otherwise 2Chr 30:18   6453

Moreover Josiah kept a *p* unto the	2Chr 35:1	6453
and they killed the *p* on the	2Chr 35:1	6453
So kill the *p*, and sanctify	2Chr 35:6	6453
and kids, all for the *p* offerings	2Chr 35:7	6453
for the *p* offerings two thousand	2Chr 35:8	6453
gave unto the Levites for *p*	2Chr 35:9	6453
And they killed the *p*, and the	2Chr 35:11	6453
they roasted the *p* with fire	2Chr 35:13	6453
the same day, to keep the *p*	2Chr 35:16	6453
present kept the *p* at that time	2Chr 35:17	6453
there was no *p* like to that kept	2Chr 35:18	6453
keep such a *p* as Josiah kept	2Chr 35:18	6453
reign of Josiah was this *p* kept	2Chr 35:19	6453
of the captivity kept the *p* upon	Ezr 6:19	6453
killed the *p* for all the children	Ezr 6:20	6453
of the month, ye shall have the *p*	Eze 45:21	6453
two days is the feast of the *p*	Mt 26:2	3957
we prepare for thee to eat the *p*	Mt 26:17	3957
I will keep the *p* at thy house	Mt 26:18	3957
and they made ready the *p*	Mt 26:19	3957
two days was the feast of the *p*	Mk 14:1	3957
bread, when they killed the *p*	Mk 14:12	3957
that thou mayest eat the *p*	Mk 14:12	3957
shall eat the *p* with my disciples	Mk 14:14	3957
and they made ready the *p*	Mk 14:16	3957
every year at the feast of the *p*	Lk 2:41	3957
drew nigh, which is called the *P*	Lk 22:1	3957
when the *p* must be killed	Lk 22:7	3957
saying, Go and prepare us the *p*	Lk 22:8	3957
shall eat the *p* with my disciples	Lk 22:11	3957
and they made ready the *p*	Lk 22:13	3957
this *p* with you before I suffer	Lk 22:15	3957
the Jews' *p* was at hand, and Jesus	Jn 2:13	3957
when he was in Jerusalem at the *p*	Jn 2:23	3957
And the *p*, a feast of the Jews,	Jn 6:4	3957
the Jews' *p* was nigh at hand	Jn 11:55	3957
up to Jerusalem before the *p*	Jn 11:55	3957
days before the *p* came to Bethany	Jn 12:1	3957
Now before the feast of the *p*	Jn 13:1	3957
but that they might eat the *p*	Jn 18:28	3957
release unto you one at the *p*	Jn 18:39	3957
it was the preparation of the *p*	Jn 19:14	3957
For even Christ our *p* is	1Cor 5:7	3957
Through faith he kept the *p*	Heb 11:28	3957

PASSOVERS

the *p* for every one that was not	2Chr 30:17	6453

PAST

the days of his mourning were *p*	Gen 50:4	5674
to push with his horn in time *p*	Ex 21:29	8032
ox hath used to push in time *p*	Ex 21:36	8032
way, until we be by thy borders	Num 21:22	5674
Emims dwelt therein in times *p*	Deut 2:10	
ask now of the days that are *p*	Deut 4:32	7223
and hated him not in times *p*	Deut 4:42	8032
whom he hated not in time *p*	Deut 19:4	8032
as he hated him not in time *p*	Deut 19:6	8032
the bitterness of death is *p*	1Sa 15:32	5493
in his presence, as in times *p*	1Sa 19:7	8032
in times *p* to be king over you	2Sa 3:17	8032
Also in time *p*, when Saul was	2Sa 5:2	8032
And when the mourning was *p*	2Sa 11:27	5493
a little *p* the top of the hill	2Sa 16:1	5674
came to pass, when midday was *p*	1Kin 18:29	5674
was the ruler over them in time *p*	1Chr 9:20	
And moreover in time *p*, even when	1Chr 11:2	8032
doeth great things *p* finding out	Job 9:10	369
me secret, until thy wrath be *p*	Job 14:13	7725
My days are *p*, my purposes are	Job 17:11	5674
Oh that I were as in months *p*	Job 29:2	6924
are but as yesterday when it is *p*	Ps 90:4	5674
and God requireth that which is *p*	Eccl 3:15	7291
For, lo, the winter is *p*, the	Song 2:11	5674
The harvest is *p*, the summer is	Jer 8:20	5674
place, and the time is now *p*	Mt 14:15	3928
And when the sabbath was *p*	Mk 16:1	1230
And when the voice was *p*, Jesus	Lk 9:36	1096
When they were *p* the first	Acts 12:10	1330
Who in times *p* suffered all	Acts 14:16	3944
the fast was now already *p*	Acts 27:9	3928
the remission of sins that are *p*	Rom 3:25	4266
For as ye in times *p* have not	Rom 11:30	
and his ways *p* finding out	Rom 11:33	421
in time *p* in the Jews' religion	Gal 1:13	
p now preacheth the faith which	Gal 1:23	
as I have also told you in time *p*	Gal 5:21	4302
Wherein in time *p* ye walked	Eph 2:2	
times *p* in the lusts of our flesh	Eph 2:3	
in time *p* Gentiles in the flesh	Eph 2:11	
Who being *p* feeling have given	Eph 4:19	524
the resurrection is *p* already	2Ti 2:18	1096

Which in time *p* was to thee	Philem 11	
in time *p* unto the fathers by the	Heb 1:1	3819
of a child when she was *p* age	Heb 11:11	3844
Which in time *p* were not a people	1Pet 2:10	
For the time *p* of our life may	1Pet 4:3	3928
because the darkness is *p*	1Jn 2:8	3855
One woe is *p*	Rev 9:12	565
The second woe is *p*	Rev 11:14	565

PASTOR

from being a *p* to follow thee	Jer 17:16	7462

PASTORS

the *p* also transgressed against	Jer 2:8	7462
I will give you *p* according to	Jer 3:15	7462
For the *p* are become brutish, and	Jer 10:21	7462
Many *p* have destroyed my vineyard	Jer 12:10	7462
The wind shall eat up all thy *p*	Jer 22:22	7462
Woe be unto the *p* that destroy	Jer 23:1	7462
against the *p* that feed my people	Jer 23:2	7462
and some, *p* and teachers	Eph 4:11	4166

PASTURE

have no *p* for their flocks	Gen 47:4	4829
to seek *p* for their flocks	1Chr 4:39	4829
And they found fat *p* and good, and	1Chr 4:40	4829
because there was *p* there for	1Chr 4:41	4829
range of the mountains is his *p*	Job 39:8	4829
smoke against the sheep of thy *p*	Ps 74:1	4830
sheep of thy *p* will give thee	Ps 79:13	4830
and we are the people of his *p*	Ps 95:7	4830
his people, and the sheep of his *p*	Ps 100:3	4830
joy of wild asses, a *p* of flocks	Is 32:14	4829
and scatter the sheep of my *p*	Jer 23:1	4830
for the LORD hath spoiled their *p*	Jer 25:36	4830
become like harts that find no *p*	Lam 1:6	4829
I will feed them in a good *p*	Eze 34:14	4829
in a fat *p* shall they feed upon	Eze 34:14	4829
you to have eaten up the good *p*	Eze 34:18	4829
And ye my flock, the flock of my *p*	Eze 34:31	4830
According to their *p*, so were	Hos 13:6	4830
perplexed, because they have no *p*	Joel 1:18	4829
and shall go in and out, and find *p*	Jn 10:9	3542

PASTURES

oxen, and twenty oxen out of the *p*	1Kin 4:23	7471
maketh me to lie down in green *p*	Ps 23:2	4999
drop upon the *p* of the wilderness	Ps 65:12	4999
The *p* are clothed with flocks	Ps 65:13	3733
shall thy cattle feed in large *p*	Is 30:23	3733
their *p* shall be in all high	Is 49:9	4830
your feet the residue of your *p*	Eze 34:18	4829
out of the fat *p* of Israel	Eze 45:15	4945
devoured the *p* of the wilderness	Joel 1:19	4999
devoured the *p* of the wilderness	Joel 1:20	4999
for the *p* of the wilderness do	Joel 2:22	4999

PATARA (pat'-a-rah) *A city in Lycia in Asia Minor.*

Rhodes, and from thence unto *P*	Acts 21:1	3959

PATE

shall come down upon his own *p*	Ps 7:16	6936

PATH

by the way, an adder in the *p*	Gen 49:17	734
stood in a *p* of the vineyards	Num 22:24	4934
There is a *p* which no fowl	Job 28:7	5410
They mar my *p*, they set forward	Job 30:13	5410
He maketh a *p* to shine after him	Job 41:32	5410
Thou wilt shew me the *p* of life	Ps 16:11	734
O LORD, and lead me in a plain *p*	Ps 27:11	734
thy *p* in the great waters, and thy	Ps 77:19	7635
go in the *p* of thy commandments	Ps 119:35	5410
my feet, and a light unto my *p*	Ps 119:105	5410
Thou compassest my *p* and my lying	Ps 139:3	734
within me, then thou knewest my *p*	Ps 142:3	5410
refrain thy foot from their *p*	Prov 1:15	5410
yea, every good *p*	Prov 2:9	4570
not into the *p* of the wicked	Prov 4:14	734
But the *p* of the just is as the	Prov 4:18	734
Ponder the *p* of thy feet, and let	Prov 4:26	4570
shouldest ponder the *p* of life	Prov 5:6	734
dost weigh the *p* of the just	Is 26:7	4570
the way, turn aside out of the *p*	Is 30:11	734
taught him in the *p* of judgment	Is 40:14	734
sea, and a *p* in the mighty waters	Is 43:16	5410
shall walk every one in his *p*	Joel 2:8	4546

PATHROS (path'-ros) *See PATHRUSIM. A name for Upper Egypt.*

Assyria, and from Egypt, and from *P*	Is 11:11	6624
at Noph, and in the country of *P*	Jer 44:1	6624
dwelt in the land of Egypt, in *P*	Jer 44:15	6624
them to return into the land of *P*	Eze 29:14	6624
And I will make *P* desolate	Eze 30:14	6624

P

PATHRUS See Pathros.

PATHRUSIM (path-ru'-sim) *A descendant of Mizraim.*
And P, and Casluhim, (out of whom .... Gen 10:14　　6625
And P, and Casluhim, (of whom came .... 1Chr 1:12　　6625

PATHS
The p of their way are turned .... Job 6:18　　734
So are the p of all that forget .... Job 8:13　　734
and lookest narrowly unto all my p .... Job 13:27　　734
and he hath set darkness in my p .... Job 19:8　　5410
nor abide in the p thereof .... Job 24:13　　5410
the stocks, he marketh all my p .... Job 33:11　　734
know the p to the house thereof .... Job 38:20　　5410
passeth through the p of the seas .... Ps 8:8　　734
me from the p of the destroyer .... Ps 17:4　　734
Hold up my goings in thy p .... Ps 17:5　　4570
he leadeth me in the p of .... Ps 23:3　　4570
teach me thy p .... Ps 25:4　　734
All the p of the Lord are mercy .... Ps 25:10　　734
and thy p drop fatness .... Ps 65:11　　4570
He keepeth the p of judgment .... Prov 2:8　　734
Who leave the p of uprightness, ... Prov 2:13　　734
and they froward in their p .... Prov 2:15　　4570
death, and her p unto the dead .... Prov 2:18　　4570
take they hold of the p of life .... Prov 2:19　　734
keep the p of the righteous .... Prov 2:20　　734
him, and he shall direct thy p .... Prov 3:6　　734
and all her p are peace .... Prov 3:17　　5410
I have led thee in right p .... Prov 4:11　　4570
her ways, go not astray in her p .... Prov 7:25　　5410
by the way in the places of the p .... Prov 8:2　　5410
in the midst of the p of judgment .... Prov 8:20　　5410
ways, and we will walk in his p .... Is 2:3　　734
err, and destroy the way of thy p .... Is 3:12　　734
I will lead them in p that they .... Is 42:16　　5410
The restorer of p to dwell in .... Is 58:12　　5410
and destruction are in their p .... Is 59:7　　4546
they have made them crooked p .... Is 59:8　　5410
and see, and ask for the old p .... Jer 6:16　　5410
in their ways from the ancient p .... Jer 18:15　　7635
the ancient p, to walk in p .... Jer 18:15　　5410
stone, he hath made my p crooked .... Lam 3:9　　5410
that she shall not find her p .... Hos 2:6　　5410
ways, and we will walk in his p .... Mic 4:2　　734
of the Lord, make his p straight .... Mt 3:3　　5147
of the Lord, make his p straight .... Mk 1:3　　5147
of the Lord, make his p straight .... Lk 3:4　　5147
And make straight p for your feet .... Heb 12:13　　5163

PATHWAY
in the p thereof there is no .... Prov 12:28　　1870,5410

PATIENCE
have p with me, and I will pay .... Mt 18:26　　3114
Have p with me, and I will pay .... Mt 18:29　　3114
it, and bring forth fruit with p .... Lk 8:15　　5281
In your p possess ye your souls .... Lk 21:19　　5281
that tribulation worketh p .... Rom 5:3　　5281
And p, experience .... Rom 5:4　　5281
then do we with p wait for it .... Rom 8:25　　5281
our learning, that we through p .... Rom 15:4　　5281
Now the God of p and consolation .... Rom 15:5　　5281
the ministers of God, in much p .... 2Cor 6:4　　5281
were wrought among you in all p .... 2Cor 12:12　　5281
to his glorious power, unto all p .... Col 1:11　　5281
p of hope in our Lord Jesus .... 1Th 1:3　　5281
in the churches of God for your p .... 2Th 1:4　　5281
godliness, faith, love, p .... 1Ti 6:11　　5281
faith, longsuffering, charity, p .... 2Ti 3:10　　5281
sound in faith, in charity, in p .... Titus 2:2　　5281
faith and p inherit the promises .... Heb 6:12　　3115
For ye have need of p, that, ... Heb 10:36　　5281
let us run with p the race that .... Heb 12:1　　5281
trying of your faith worketh p .... Jas 1:3　　5281
But let p have her perfect work, ... Jas 1:4　　5281
the earth, and hath long p for it .... Jas 5:7　　3114
of suffering affliction, and of p .... Jas 5:10　　3115
Ye have heard of the p of Job .... Jas 5:11　　5281
and to temperance p .... 2Pet 1:6　　5281
and to p godliness .... 2Pet 1:6　　5281
p of Jesus Christ, was in the .... Rev 1:9　　5281
works, and thy labour, and thy p .... Rev 2:2　　5281
And hast borne, and hast p, and for ..... Rev 2:3　　5281
and service, and faith, and thy p .... Rev 2:19　　5281
thou hast kept the word of my p .... Rev 3:10　　5281
Here is the p and the faith of the .... Rev 13:10　　5281
Here is the p of the saints .... Rev 14:12　　5281

PATIENT
the p in spirit is better than .... Eccl 7:8　　750
To them who by p continuance in .... Rom 2:7　　5281
p in tribulation .... Rom 12:12　　5278

the weak, be p toward all men .... 1Th 5:14　　3114
into the p waiting for Christ .... 2Th 3:5　　5281
but p, not a brawler, not .... 1Ti 3:3　　1933
unto all men, apt to teach, p .... 2Ti 2:24　　420
Be p therefore, brethren, unto .... Jas 5:7　　3114
Be ye also p .... Jas 5:8　　3114

PATIENTLY
in the Lord, and wait p for him .... Ps 37:7　　2342
I waited p for the Lord .... Ps 40:1　　6960
I beseech thee to hear me p .... Acts 26:3　　3116
And so, after he had p endured .... Heb 6:15　　3114
your faults, ye shall take it p .... 1Pet 2:20　　5278
and suffer for it, ye take it p .... 1Pet 2:20　　5278

PATMOS (pat'-mos) *An island off the west coast of Asia Minor.*
was in the isle that is called P .... Rev 1:9　　3963

PATRIARCH
speak unto you of the p David .... Acts 2:29　　3966
unto whom even the p Abraham gave, ... Heb 7:4　　3966

PATRIARCHS
and Jacob begat the twelve p .... Acts 7:8　　3966
And the p, moved with envy, sold .... Acts 7:9　　3966

PATRIMONY
which cometh of the sale of his p .... Deut 18:8

PATROBAS (pat'-ro-bas) *A Christian in Rome.*
Asyncritus, Phlegon, Hermas, P .... Rom 16:14　　3969

PATTERN
after the p of the tabernacle, and .... Ex 25:9　　8403
the p of all the instruments .... Ex 25:9　　8403
that thou make them after their p .... Ex 25:40　　8403
according unto the p which the .... Num 8:4　　4758
Behold the p of the altar of the .... Josh 22:28　　8403
the p of it, according to all the .... 2Kin 16:10　　8403
his son the p of the porch .... 1Chr 28:11　　8403
the p of all that he had by the .... 1Chr 28:12　　8403
gold for the p of the chariot of .... 1Chr 28:18　　8403
me, even all the works of this p .... 1Chr 28:19　　8403
and let them measure the p .... Eze 43:10　　8508
for a p to them which should .... 1Ti 1:16　　5296
shewing thyself a p of good works .... Titus 2:7　　5179
the p shewed to thee in the mount .... Heb 8:5　　5179

PATTERNS
therefore necessary that the p of .... Heb 9:23　　5262

PAU (pa'-u) See Pai. *City of King Hagar of Edom.*
and the name of his city was P .... Gen 36:39　　6464

PAUL (pawl) See Paul's, Paulus, Saul. *The apostle to the Gentiles.*
Then Saul, (who also is called P .... Acts 13:9　　3972
Now when P and his company loosed .... Acts 13:13　　3972
Then P stood up, and beckoning .... Acts 13:16　　3972
religious proselytes followed P .... Acts 13:43　　3972
things which were spoken by P .... Acts 13:45　　3972
Then P and Barnabas waxed bold, and .. Acts 13:46　　3972
and raised persecution against P .... Acts 13:50　　3972
The same heard P speak .... Acts 14:9　　3972
the people saw what P had done .... Acts 14:11　　3972
and P, Mercurius, because he was .... Acts 14:12　　3972
when the apostles, Barnabas and P .... Acts 14:14　　3972
the people, and, having stoned P .... Acts 14:19　　3972
When therefore P and Barnabas had ..... Acts 15:2　　3972
with them, they determined that P .... Acts 15:2　　3972
and gave audience to Barnabas and P ... Acts 15:12　　3972
own company to Antioch with P .... Acts 15:22　　3972
with our beloved Barnabas and P .... Acts 15:25　　3972
P also and Barnabas continued in .... Acts 15:35　　3972
some days after P said unto .... Acts 15:36　　3972
But P thought not good to take .... Acts 15:38　　3972
P chose Silas, and departed, being .... Acts 15:40　　3972
Him would P have to go forth with .... Acts 16:3　　3972
vision appeared to P in the night .... Acts 16:9　　3972
the things which were spoken of P .... Acts 16:14　　3972
The same followed P and us, and .... Acts 16:17　　3972
But P, being grieved, turned and .... Acts 16:18　　3972
gains was gone, they caught P .... Acts 16:19　　3972
And at midnight P and Silas prayed, ... Acts 16:25　　3972
But P cried with a loud voice, ... Acts 16:28　　3972
trembling, and fell down before P .... Acts 16:29　　3972
the prison told this saying to P .... Acts 16:36　　3972
But P said unto them, They have .... Acts 16:37　　3972
And P, as his manner was, went in .... Acts 17:2　　3972
believed, and consorted with P .... Acts 17:4　　3972
brethren immediately sent away P .... Acts 17:10　　3972
of God was preached of P at Berea .... Acts 17:13　　3972
the brethren sent away P to go as .... Acts 17:14　　3972
they that conducted P brought him .... Acts 17:15　　3972
Now while P waited for them at .... Acts 17:16　　3972

Then *P* stood in the midst of .... Acts 17:22	3972
So *P* departed from among them .... Acts 17:33	3972
After these things *P* departed .... Acts 18:1	3972
P was pressed in the spirit, and .... Acts 18:5	3972
Then spake the Lord to *P* in the .... Acts 18:9	3972
with one accord against *P* .... Acts 18:12	3972
when *P* was now about to open his .... Acts 18:14	3972
P after this tarried there yet a .... Acts 18:18	3972
P having passed through the upper .... Acts 19:1	3972
Then said *P*, John verily baptized .... Acts 19:4	3972
when *P* had laid his hands upon .... Acts 19:6	3972
miracles by the hands of *P* .... Acts 19:11	3972
you by Jesus whom *P* preacheth .... Acts 19:13	3972
said, Jesus I know, and *P* I know .... Acts 19:15	3972
P purposed in the spirit, when he .... Acts 19:21	3972
this *P* hath persuaded and turned .... Acts 19:26	3972
when *P* would have entered in unto .... Acts 19:30	3972
P called unto him the disciples, ... Acts 20:1	3972
P preached unto them, ready to .... Acts 20:7	3972
as *P* was long preaching, he sunk .... Acts 20:9	3972
P went down, and fell on him, and .... Acts 20:10	3972
there intending to take in *P* .... Acts 20:13	3972
For *P* had determined to sail by .... Acts 20:16	3972
who said to *P* through the Spirit, ... Acts 21:4	3972
Then *P* answered, What mean ye to .... Acts 21:13	3972
the day following *P* went in with .... Acts 21:18	3972
Then *P* took the men, and the next .... Acts 21:26	3972
whom they supposed that *P* had .... Acts 21:29	3972
and they took *P*, and drew him out .... Acts 21:30	3972
soldiers, they left beating of *P* .... Acts 21:32	3972
as *P* was to be led into the .... Acts 21:37	3972
But *P* said, I am a man which am a .... Acts 21:39	3972
P stood on the stairs, and .... Acts 21:40	3972
P said unto the centurion that .... Acts 22:25	3972
P said, But I was free born .... Acts 22:28	3972
to appear, and brought *P* down .... Acts 22:30	3972
And *P*, earnestly beholding the .... Acts 23:1	3972
Then said *P* unto him, God shall .... Acts 23:3	3972
Then said *P*, I wist not, brethren .... Acts 23:5	3972
But when *P* perceived that the one .... Acts 23:6	3972
fearing lest *P* should have been .... Acts 23:10	3972
him, and said, Be of good cheer, *P* ...... Acts 23:11	3972
nor drink till they had killed *P* .... Acts 23:12	3972
eat nothing until we have slain *P* .... Acts 23:14	3972
into the castle, and told *P* .... Acts 23:16	3972
Then *P* called one of the .... Acts 23:17	3972
P the prisoner called me unto him .... Acts 23:18	3972
down *P* to morrow into the council .... Acts 23:20	3972
beasts, that they may set *P* on .... Acts 23:24	3972
as it was commanded them, took *P* .... Acts 23:31	3972
presented *P* also before him .... Acts 23:33	3972
informed the governor against *P* .... Acts 24:1	3972
Then *P*, after that the governor .... Acts 24:10	3972
commanded a centurion to keep *P* .... Acts 24:23	3972
which was a Jewess, he sent for *P* .... Acts 24:24	3972
should have been given him of *P* .... Acts 24:26	3972
the Jews a pleasure, left *P* bound .... Acts 24:27	3972
the Jews informed him against *P* .... Acts 25:2	3972
that *P* should be kept at Caesarea .... Acts 25:4	3972
seat commanded *P* to be brought .... Acts 25:6	3972
and grievous complaints against *P* .... Acts 25:7	3972
the Jews a pleasure, answered *P* .... Acts 25:9	3972
Then said *P*, I stand at Caesar's .... Acts 25:10	3972
whom *P* affirmed to be alive .... Acts 25:19	3972
But when *P* had appealed to be .... Acts 25:21	3972
commandment *P* was brought forth .... Acts 25:23	3972
Then Agrippa said unto *P*, Thou .... Acts 26:1	3972
Then *P* stretched forth the hand, ... Acts 26:1	3972
Festus said with a loud voice, *P* .... Acts 26:24	3972
Then Agrippa said unto *P*, Almost .... Acts 26:28	3972
P said, I would to God, that not .... Acts 26:29	3972
sail into Italy, they delivered *P* .... Acts 27:1	3972
And Julius courteously entreated *P* .... Acts 27:3	3972
already past, *P* admonished them, ... Acts 27:9	3972
things which were spoken by *P* .... Acts 27:11	3972
But after long abstinence *P* stood .... Acts 27:21	3972
Saying, Fear not, *P* .... Acts 27:24	3972
P said to the centurion and to the .... Acts 27:31	3972
P besought them all to take meat, ... Acts 27:33	3972
the centurion, willing to save *P* .... Acts 27:43	3972
when *P* had gathered a bundle of .... Acts 28:3	3972
to whom *P* entered in, and prayed, ... Acts 28:8	3972
whom when *P* saw, he thanked God, ... Acts 28:15	3972
but *P* was suffered to dwell by .... Acts 28:16	3972
that after three days *P* called .... Acts 28:17	3972
after that *P* had spoken one word, ... Acts 28:25	3972
P dwelt two whole years in his .... Acts 28:30	3972
P, a servant of Jesus Christ, ... Rom 1:1	3972
P, called to be an apostle of 1Cor 1:1	3972
every one of you saith, I am of *P* 1Cor 1:12	3972
was *P* crucified for you 1Cor 1:13	3972

were ye baptized in the name of *P* 1Cor 1:13	3972
For while one saith, I am of *P* 1Cor 3:4	3972
Who then is *P*, and who is Apollos, ... 1Cor 3:5	3972
Whether *P*, or Apollos, or Cephas, ... 1Cor 3:22	3972
of me *P* with mine own hand 1Cor 16:21	3972
P, an apostle of Jesus Christ by 2Cor 1:1	3972
Now I *P* myself beseech you by the 2Cor 10:1	3972
P, an apostle, (not of men, ... Gal 1:1	3972
I *P* say unto you, that if ye be .... Gal 5:2	3972
P, an apostle of Jesus Christ by .... Eph 1:1	3972
For this cause I *P*, the prisoner .... Eph 3:1	3972
P and Timotheus, the servants of .... Phil 1:1	3972
P, an apostle of Jesus Christ by .... Col 1:1	3972
whereof I *P* am made a minister .... Col 1:23	3972
salutation by the hand of me *P* .... Col 4:18	3972
P, and Silvanus, and Timotheus, ... 1Th 1:1	3972
have come unto you, even I *P* 1Th 2:18	3972
P, and Silvanus, and Timotheus, ... 2Th 1:1	3972
The salutation of *P* with mine own 2Th 3:17	3972
P, an apostle of Jesus Christ by 1Ti 1:1	3972
P, an apostle of Jesus Christ by 2Ti 1:1	3972
when *P* was brought before Nero .... 2Ti *s*	3972
P, a servant of God, and an .... Titus 1:1	3972
P, a prisoner of Jesus Christ, and .... Philem 1	3972
being such an one as *P* the aged .... Philem 9	3972
I *P* have written it with mine own .... Philem 19	3972
even as our beloved brother *P* 2Pet 3:15	3972

PAUL'S *(pawls)*

P companions in travel, they .... Acts 19:29	3972
all wept sore, and fell on *P* neck .... Acts 20:37	3972
that were of *P* company departed .... Acts 21:8	3972
come unto us, he took *P* girdle .... Acts 21:11	3972
when *P* sister's son heard of .... Acts 23:16	3972
Festus declared *P* cause unto the .... Acts 25:14	3972

PAULUS See PAUL. *A Roman proconsul.*

deputy of the country, Sergius *P* .... Acts 13:7	3972

PAVED

were a *p* work of a sapphire stone .... Ex 24:10	3840
midst thereof being *p* with love .... Song 3:10	7528

PAVEMENT

it, and put it upon a *p* of stones 2Kin 16:17	4837
faces to the ground upon the *p* 2Chr 7:3	7531
gold and silver, upon a *p* of red .... Est 1:6	7531
a *p* made for the court round .... Eze 40:17	7531
thirty chambers were upon the *p* .... Eze 40:17	7531
the *p* by the side of the gates .... Eze 40:18	7531
of the gates was the lower *p* .... Eze 40:18	7531
over against the *p* which was for .... Eze 42:3	7531
in a place that is called the *P* .... Jn 19:13	3037

PAVILION

his *p* round about him were dark .... Ps 18:11	5521
trouble he shall hide me in his *p* .... Ps 27:5	5520
in a *p* from the strife of tongues .... Ps 31:20	5521
spread his royal *p* over them .... Jer 43:10	8237

PAVILIONS

made darkness *p* round about him 2Sa 22:12	5521
he and the kings in the *p* 1Kin 20:12	5521
drinking himself drunk in the *p* 1Kin 20:16	5521

PAW

me out of the *p* of the lion 1Sa 17:37	3027
out of the *p* of the bear, he will 1Sa 17:37	3027

PAWETH

He *p* in the valley, and rejoiceth .... Job 39:21	2658

PAWS

And whatsoever goeth upon his *p* .... Lev 11:27	3709

PAY

only he shall *p* for the loss of .... Ex 21:19	5414
and he shall *p* as the judges .... Ex 21:22	5414
he shall surely *p* ox for ox .... Ex 21:36	7999
thief be found, let him *p* double .... Ex 22:7	7999
he shall *p* double unto his .... Ex 22:9	7999
he shall *p* money according to the .... Ex 22:17	8254
thy water, then I will *p* for it .... Num 20:19	5414,4377
God, thou shalt not slack to *p* it .... Deut 23:21	7999
p my vow, which I have vowed unto 2Sa 15:7	7999
thou shalt *p* a talent of silver 1Kin 20:39	8254
p thy debt, and live thou and thy 2Kin 4:7	7999
make to *p* tribute until this day 2Chr 8:8	5927
the children of Ammon *p* unto him 2Chr 27:5	7725
again, then will they not *p* toll .... Ezr 4:13	5415
I will *p* ten thousand talents of .... Est 3:9	8254
that Haman had promised to *p* to .... Est 4:7	8254
thee, and thou shalt *p* thy vows .... Job 22:27	7999
I will *p* my vows before them that .... Ps 22:25	7999
p thy vows unto the most High .... Ps 50:14	7999
I will *p* thee my vows, ... Ps 66:13	7999

P

Vow, and *p* unto the LORD your God	Ps 76:11	7999
I will *p* my vows unto the LORD	Ps 116:14	7999
I will *p* my vows unto the LORD	Ps 116:18	7999
he hath given will he *p* him again	Prov 19:17	7999
If thou hast nothing to *p*	Prov 22:27	7999
a vow unto God, defer not to *p* it	Eccl 5:4	7999
p that which thou hast vowed	Eccl 5:4	7999
that thou shouldest vow and not *p*	Eccl 5:5	7999
I will *p* that that I have vowed	Jonah 2:9	7999
Doth not your master *p* tribute	Mt 17:24	5055
But forasmuch as he had not to *p*	Mt 18:25	591
with me, and I will *p* thee all	Mt 18:26	591
saying, *P* me that thou owest	Mt 18:28	591
with me, and I will *p* thee all	Mt 18:29	591
prison, till he should *p* the debt	Mt 18:30	591
till he should *p* all that was due	Mt 18:34	591
for ye *p* tithe of mint and anise	Mt 23:23	586
And when they had nothing to *p*	Lk 7:42	591
for this cause *p* ye tribute also	Rom 13:6	5055

PAYED

this day have I *p* my vows	Prov 7:14	7999
tithes, *p* tithes in Abraham	Heb 7:9	1183

PAYETH

wicked borroweth, and *p* not again	Ps 37:21	7999

PAYMENT

all that he had, and *p* to be made	Mt 18:25	591

PEACE

thou shalt go to thy fathers in *p*	Gen 15:15	7965
man wondering at her held his *p*	Gen 24:21	2790
good, and have sent thee away in *p*	Gen 26:29	7965
and they departed from him in *p*	Gen 26:31	7965
again to my father's house in *p*	Gen 28:21	7965
Jacob held his *p* until they were	Gen 34:5	2790
shall give Pharaoh an answer of *p*	Gen 41:16	7965
And he said, *P* be to you, fear not	Gen 43:23	7965
get you up in *p* unto your father	Gen 44:17	7965
And Jethro said to Moses, Go in *p*	Ex 4:18	7965
for you, and ye shall hold your *p*	Ex 14:14	2790
shall also go to their place in *p*	Ex 18:23	7965
thy *p* offerings, thy sheep, and	Ex 20:24	8002
sacrificed *p* offerings of oxen	Ex 24:5	8002
sacrifice of their *p* offerings	Ex 29:28	8002
offerings, and brought *p* offerings	Ex 32:6	8002
be a sacrifice of *p* offering	Lev 3:1	8002
p offering an offering made by	Lev 3:3	8002
of *p* offering unto the LORD be of	Lev 3:6	8002
p offering an offering made by	Lev 3:9	8002
of the sacrifice of *p* offerings	Lev 4:10	8002
of the sacrifice of *p* offerings	Lev 4:26	8002
off the sacrifice of *p* offerings	Lev 4:31	8002
the sacrifice of the *p* offerings	Lev 4:35	8002
the fat of the *p* offerings	Lev 6:12	8002
of the sacrifice of *p* offerings	Lev 7:11	8002
thanksgiving of his *p* offerings	Lev 7:13	8002
the blood of the *p* offerings	Lev 7:14	8002
his *p* offerings for thanksgiving	Lev 7:15	8002
p offerings be eaten at all on	Lev 7:18	8002
of the sacrifice of *p* offerings	Lev 7:20	8002
of the sacrifice of *p* offerings	Lev 7:21	8002
p offerings unto the LORD shall	Lev 7:29	8002
the sacrifice of his *p* offerings	Lev 7:29	8002
sacrifices of your *p* offerings	Lev 7:32	8002
the blood of the *p* offerings	Lev 7:33	8002
sacrifices of their *p* offerings	Lev 7:34	8002
the sacrifice of the *p* offerings	Lev 7:37	8002
bullock and a ram for *p* offerings	Lev 9:4	8002
for a sacrifice of *p* offerings	Lev 9:18	8002
burnt offering, and *p* offerings	Lev 9:22	8002
And Aaron held his *p*	Lev 10:3	1826
of *p* offerings of the children of	Lev 10:14	8002
offer them for *p* offerings unto	Lev 17:5	8002
of *p* offerings unto the LORD	Lev 19:5	8002
offereth a sacrifice of *p*	Lev 22:21	8002
for a sacrifice of *p* offerings	Lev 23:19	8002
And I will give *p* in the land	Lev 26:6	7965
without blemish for *p* offerings	Num 6:14	8002
of *p* offerings unto the LORD	Num 6:17	8002
the sacrifice of the *p* offerings	Num 6:18	8002
upon thee, and give thee *p*	Num 6:26	7965
And for a sacrifice of *p* offerings	Num 7:17	8002
And for a sacrifice of *p* offerings	Num 7:23	8002
And for a sacrifice of *p* offerings	Num 7:29	8002
And for a sacrifice of *p* offerings	Num 7:35	8002
And for a sacrifice of *p* offerings	Num 7:41	8002
And for a sacrifice of *p* offerings	Num 7:47	8002
And for a sacrifice of *p* offerings	Num 7:53	8002
And for a sacrifice of *p* offerings	Num 7:59	8002
And for a sacrifice of *p* offerings	Num 7:65	8002
And for a sacrifice of *p* offerings	Num 7:71	8002
And for a sacrifice of *p* offerings	Num 7:77	8002
And for a sacrifice of *p* offerings	Num 7:83	8002
of the *p* offerings were twenty	Num 7:88	8002
sacrifices of your *p* offerings	Num 10:10	8002
or *p* offerings unto the LORD	Num 15:8	8002
I give unto him my covenant of *p*	Num 25:12	7965
and for your *p* offerings	Num 29:39	8002
father shall hold his *p* at her	Num 30:4	2790
held his *p* at her in the day that	Num 30:7	2790
heard it, and held his *p* at her	Num 30:11	2790
hold his *p* at her from day to day	Num 30:14	2790
because he held his *p* at her in	Num 30:14	2790
king of Heshbon with words of *p*	Deut 2:26	7965
it, then proclaim *p* unto it	Deut 20:10	7965
be, if it make thee answer of *p*	Deut 20:11	7965
And if it will make no *p* with thee	Deut 20:12	7999
Thou shalt not seek their *p* nor	Deut 23:6	7965
And thou shalt offer *p* offerings	Deut 27:7	8002
his heart, saying, I shall have *p*	Deut 29:19	7965
LORD, and sacrificed *p* offerings	Josh 8:31	8002
And Joshua made *p* with them	Josh 9:15	7965
of Gibeon had made *p* with Israel	Josh 10:1	7999
for it hath made *p* with Joshua	Josh 10:4	7999
camp to Joshua at Makkedah in *p*	Josh 10:21	7965
p with the children of Israel	Josh 11:19	7999
or if to offer *p* offerings	Josh 22:23	8002
and with our *p* offerings	Josh 22:27	8002
for there was *p* between Jabin the	Judg 4:17	7965
said unto him, *P* be unto thee	Judg 6:23	7965
saying, When I come again in *p*	Judg 8:9	7965
when I return in *p* from the	Judg 11:31	7965
priest said unto them, Go in *p*	Judg 18:6	7965
And they said unto him, Hold thy *p*	Judg 18:19	2790
the old man said, *P* be with thee	Judg 19:20	7965
p offerings before the LORD	Judg 20:26	8002
burnt offerings and *p* offerings	Judg 21:4	8002
Eli answered and said, Go in *p*	1Sa 1:17	7965
there was *p* between Israel and the	1Sa 7:14	7965
sacrifices of *p* offerings	1Sa 10:8	8002
But he held his *p*	1Sa 10:27	2790
of *p* offerings before the LORD	1Sa 11:15	8002
offering to me, and *p* offerings	1Sa 13:9	8002
thy servant shall have *p*	1Sa 20:7	7965
away, that thou mayest go in *p*	1Sa 20:13	7965
for there is *p* to thee, and no	1Sa 20:21	7965
Jonathan said to David, Go in *p*	1Sa 20:42	7965
P be both to thee	1Sa 25:6	7965
p be to thine house	1Sa 25:6	7965
p be unto all that thou hast	1Sa 25:6	7965
Go up in *p* to thine house	1Sa 25:35	7965
Wherefore now return, and go in *p*	1Sa 29:7	7965
and he went in *p*	2Sa 3:21	7965
him away, and he was gone in *p*	2Sa 3:22	7965
sent him away, and he is gone in *p*	2Sa 3:23	7965
p offerings before the LORD	2Sa 6:17	8002
p offerings, he blessed the	2Sa 6:18	8002
they made *p* with Israel, and	2Sa 10:19	7999
but hold now thy *p*, my sister	2Sa 13:20	2790
the king said unto him, Go in *p*	2Sa 15:9	7965
return into the city in *p*	2Sa 15:27	7965
so all the people shall be in *p*	2Sa 17:3	7965
until the day he came again in *p*	2Sa 19:24	7965
again in *p* unto his own house	2Sa 19:30	7965
burnt offerings and *p* offerings	2Sa 24:25	8002
and shed the blood of war in *p*	1Kin 2:5	7965
head go down to the grave in *p*	1Kin 2:6	7965
shall there be *p* for ever from	1Kin 2:33	7965
offered *p* offerings, and made a	1Kin 3:15	8002
he had *p* on all sides round about	1Kin 4:24	7965
there was *p* between Hiram and	1Kin 5:12	7965
a sacrifice of *p* offerings	1Kin 8:63	8002
and the fat of the *p* offerings	1Kin 8:64	8002
and the fat of the *p* offerings	1Kin 8:64	8002
p offerings upon the altar which	1Kin 9:25	8002
Whether they be come out for *p*	1Kin 20:18	7965
every man to his house in *p*	1Kin 22:17	7965
of affliction, until I come in *p*	1Kin 22:27	7965
said, If thou return at all in *p*	1Kin 22:28	7965
Jehoshaphat made *p* with the king	1Kin 22:44	7999
hold ye your *p*	2Kin 2:3	2814
hold ye your *p*	2Kin 2:5	2814
And he said unto him, Go in *p*	2Kin 5:19	7965
of good tidings, and we hold our *p*	2Kin 7:9	2814
them, and let him say, Is it *p*	2Kin 9:17	7965
Thus saith the king, Is it *p*	2Kin 9:18	7965
said, What hast thou to do with *p*	2Kin 9:18	7965
Thus saith the king, Is it *p*	2Kin 9:19	7965
What hast thou to do with *p*	2Kin 9:19	7965
saw Jehu, that he said, Is it *p*	2Kin 9:22	7965
And he answered, What *p*, so long	2Kin 9:22	7965
the gate, she said, Had Zimri *p*	2Kin 9:31	7965

the blood of his *p* offerings	2Kin 16:13	8002
But the people held their *p*	2Kin 18:36	2790
And he said, Is it not good, if *p*	2Kin 20:19	7965
be gathered into thy grave in *p*	2Kin 22:20	7965
p, p be unto thee, and *p*	1Chr 12:18	7965
thee, and *p* be to thine helpers	1Chr 12:18	7965
and *p* offerings before God	1Chr 16:1	8002
the *p* offerings, he blessed the	1Chr 16:2	8002
they made *p* with David, and became	1Chr 19:19	7999
p offerings, and called upon the	1Chr 21:26	8002
be Solomon, and I will give *p*	1Chr 22:9	7965
and the fat of the *p* offerings	2Chr 7:7	8002
was no *p* to him that went out	2Chr 15:5	7965
every man to his house in *p*	2Chr 18:16	7965
affliction, until I return in *p*	2Chr 18:26	7965
If thou certainly return in *p*	2Chr 18:27	7965
to his house in *p* to Jerusalem	2Chr 19:1	7965
with the fat of the *p* offerings	2Chr 29:35	8002
offering *p* offerings, and making	2Chr 30:22	8002
for *p* offerings, to minister, and	2Chr 31:2	8002
and sacrificed thereon *p* offerings	2Chr 33:16	8002
be gathered to thy grave in *p*	2Chr 34:28	7965
unto the rest beyond the river, *P*	Ezr 4:17	8001
Unto Darius the king, all *p*	Ezr 5:7	8001
of the God of heaven, perfect *p*	Ezr 7:12	
nor seek their *p* or their wealth	Ezr 9:12	7965
Then held their *p*, and found	Neh 5:8	2790
the people, saying, Hold your *p*	Neh 8:11	2013
holdest thy *p* at this time	Est 4:14	2790
of Ahasuerus, with words of *p*	Est 9:30	7965
speaking *p* to all his seed	Est 10:3	7965
the field shall be at *p* with thee	Job 5:23	7999
that thy tabernacle shall be in *p*	Job 5:24	7965
thy lies make men hold their *p*	Job 11:3	2790
ye would altogether hold your *p*	Job 13:5	2790
Hold your *p*, let me alone, that I	Job 13:13	2790
now thyself with him, and be at *p*	Job 22:21	7999
he maketh *p* in his high places	Job 25:2	7965
The nobles held their *p*, and their	Job 29:10	6963
hold thy *p*, and I will speak	Job 33:31	2790
hold thy *p*, and I shall teach thee	Job 33:33	2790
I will both lay me down in *p*	Ps 4:8	7965
unto him that was at *p* with me	Ps 7:4	7999
which speak *p* to their neighbours	Ps 28:3	7965
LORD will bless his people with *p*	Ps 29:11	7965
seek *p*, and pursue it	Ps 34:14	7965
For they speak not *p*	Ps 35:20	7965
themselves in the abundance of *p*	Ps 37:11	7965
for the end of that man is *p*	Ps 37:37	7965
dumb with silence, I held my *p*	Ps 39:2	2814
hold not thy *p* at my tears	Ps 39:12	2790
in *p* from the battle that was	Ps 55:18	7965
against such as be at *p* with him	Ps 55:20	7965
shall bring *p* to the people	Ps 72:3	7965
abundance of *p* so long as the	Ps 72:7	7965
hold not thy *p*, and be not still,	Ps 83:1	2790
he will speak *p* unto his people	Ps 85:8	7965
and *p* have kissed each other	Ps 85:10	7965
Hold not thy *p*, O God of my	Ps 109:1	2790
Great *p* have they which love thy	Ps 119:165	7965
long dwelt with him that hateth *p*	Ps 120:6	7965
I am for *p*	Ps 120:7	7965
Pray for the *p* of Jerusalem	Ps 122:6	7965
P be within thy walls, and	Ps 122:7	7965
I will now say, *P* be within thee	Ps 122:8	7965
but *p* shall be upon Israel	Ps 125:5	7965
children, and *p* upon Israel	Ps 128:6	7965
He maketh *p* in thy borders, and	Ps 147:14	7965
of days, and long life, and *p*	Prov 3:2	7965
and all her paths are *p*	Prov 3:17	7965
I have *p* offerings with me	Prov 7:14	8002
of understanding holdeth his *p*	Prov 11:12	2790
to the counsellors of *p* is joy	Prov 12:20	7965
his enemies to be at *p* with him	Prov 16:7	7999
a fool, when he holdeth his *p*	Prov 17:28	2790
a time of war, and a time of *p*	Eccl 3:8	7965
Father, The Prince of *P*	Is 9:6	7965
p there shall be no end, upon the	Is 9:7	7965
Thou wilt keep him in perfect *p*	Is 26:3	7965
LORD, thou wilt ordain *p* for us	Is 26:12	7965
that he may make *p* with me	Is 27:5	7965
and he shall make *p* with me	Is 27:5	7965
work of righteousness shall be *p*	Is 32:17	7965
the ambassadors of *p* shall weep	Is 33:7	7965
But they held their *p*, and	Is 36:21	2790
for *p* I had great bitterness	Is 38:17	7965
moreover, For there shall be *p*	Is 39:8	7965
I have long time holden my *p*	Is 42:14	2814
I make *p*, and create evil	Is 45:7	7965
then had thy *p* been as a river,	Is 48:18	7965
There is no *p*, saith the LORD,	Is 48:22	7965

good tidings, that publisheth *p*	Is 52:7	7965
of our *p* was upon him	Is 53:5	7965
the covenant of my *p* be removed	Is 54:10	7965
shall be the *p* of thy children	Is 54:13	7965
with joy, and be led forth with *p*	Is 55:12	7965
He shall enter into *p*	Is 57:2	7965
have not I held my *p* even of old	Is 57:11	2814
P, p to him that is far off,	Is 57:19	7965
There is no *p*, saith my God, to	Is 57:21	7965
The way of *p* they know not	Is 59:8	7965
goeth therein shall not know *p*	Is 59:8	7965
I will also make thy officers *p*	Is 60:17	7965
Zion's sake will I not hold my *p*	Is 62:1	2814
never hold their *p* day nor night	Is 62:6	2814
wilt thou hold thy *p*, and afflict	Is 64:12	2814
I will extend *p* to her like a	Is 66:12	7965
saying, Ye shall have *p*	Jer 4:10	7965
I cannot hold my *p*, because thou	Jer 4:19	2790
people slightly, saying, *P, p*	Jer 6:14	7965
when there is no *p*	Jer 6:14	7965
people slightly, saying, *P, p*	Jer 8:11	7965
when there is no *p*	Jer 8:11	7965
We looked for *p*, but no good came	Jer 8:15	7965
and if in the land of *p*, wherein	Jer 12:5	7965
no flesh shall have *p*	Jer 12:12	7965
give you assured *p* in this place	Jer 14:13	7965
we looked for *p*, and there is no	Jer 14:19	7965
taken away my *p* from this people	Jer 16:5	7965
LORD hath said, Ye shall have *p*	Jer 23:17	7965
prophet which prophesieth of *p*	Jer 28:9	7965
seek the *p* of the city whither I	Jer 29:7	7965
the *p* thereof shall ye have *p*	Jer 29:7	7965
saith the LORD, thoughts of *p*	Jer 29:11	7965
trembling, of fear, and not of *p*	Jer 30:5	7965
unto them the abundance of *p*	Jer 33:6	7965
But thou shalt die in *p*	Jer 34:5	7965
shall go forth from thence in *p*	Jer 43:12	7965
removed my soul far off from *p*	Lam 3:17	7965
and they shall seek *p*, and there	Eze 7:25	7965
have seduced my people, saying, *P*	Eze 13:10	7965
and there was no *p*	Eze 13:10	7965
p for her, and there is no *p*	Eze 13:16	7965
make with them a covenant of *p*	Eze 34:25	7965
make a covenant of *p* with them	Eze 37:26	7965
the altar, and your *p* offerings	Eze 43:27	8002
and for *p* offerings, to make	Eze 45:15	8002
and the *p* offerings, to make	Eze 45:17	8002
his *p* offerings, and he shall	Eze 46:2	8002
a voluntary burnt offering or *p*	Eze 46:12	8002
his *p* offerings, as he did on the	Eze 46:12	8002
P be multiplied unto you	Dan 4:1	8001
P be multiplied unto you	Dan 6:25	8001
heart, and by *p* shall destroy many	Dan 8:25	7962
p be unto thee, be strong, yea,	Dan 10:19	7965
neither will I regard the *p*	Amos 5:22	8002
the men that were at *p* with thee	Obad 7	7965
bite with their teeth, and cry, *P*	Mic 3:5	7965
And this man shall be the *p*	Mic 5:5	7965
good tidings, that publisheth *p*	Nah 1:15	7965
Hold thy *p* at the presence of the	Zeph 1:7	2013
and in this place will I give *p*	Hag 2:9	7965
the counsel of *p* shall be between	Zec 6:13	7965
neither was there any *p* to him	Zec 8:10	7965
of truth and *p* in your gates	Zec 8:16	7965
therefore love the truth and *p*	Zec 8:19	7965
he shall speak *p* unto the heathen	Zec 9:10	7965
was with him of life and *p*	Mal 2:5	7965
he walked with me in *p* and equity,	Mal 2:6	7965
worthy, let your *p* come upon it	Mt 10:13	*1515*
worthy, let your *p* return to you	Mt 10:13	*1515*
that I am come to send *p* on earth	Mt 10:34	*1515*
I came not to send *p*, but a sword	Mt 10:34	*1515*
because they should hold their *p*	Mt 20:31	*4623*
But Jesus held his *p*	Mt 26:63	*4623*
rebuked him, saying, Hold thy *p*	Mk 1:25	*5392*
But they held their *p*	Mk 3:4	*4623*
the wind, and said unto the sea, *P*	Mk 4:39	*4623*
go in *p*, and be whole of thy	Mk 5:34	*1515*
But they held their *p*	Mk 9:34	*4623*
and have *p* one with another	Mk 9:50	*1518*
him that he should hold his *p*	Mk 10:48	*4623*
But he held his *p*, and answered	Mk 14:61	*4623*
guide our feet into the way of *p*	Lk 1:79	*1515*
God in the highest, and on earth *p*	Lk 2:14	*1515*
thou thy servant depart in *p*	Lk 2:29	*1515*
rebuked him, saying, Hold thy *p*	Lk 4:35	*5392*
go in *p*	Lk 7:50	*1515*
go in *p*	Lk 8:48	*1515*
first say, *P* be to this house	Lk 10:5	*1515*
And if the son of *p* be there	Lk 10:6	*1515*
your *p* shall rest upon it	Lk 10:6	*1515*

P

his palace, his goods are in p	Lk 11:21	1515
that I am come to give p on earth	Lk 12:51	1515
And they held their p	Lk 14:4	2270
and desireth conditions of p	Lk 14:32	1515
him, that he should hold his p	Lk 18:39	4263
p in heaven, and glory in the	Lk 19:38	1515
if these should hold their p	Lk 19:40	4623
things which belong unto thy p	Lk 19:42	1515
at his answer, and held their p	Lk 20:26	4601
and saith unto them, P be unto you	Lk 24:36	1515
P I leave with you, my p I	Jn 14:27	1515
you, that in me ye might have p	Jn 16:33	1515
and saith unto them, P be unto you	Jn 20:19	1515
to them again, P be unto you	Jn 20:21	1515
the midst, and said, P be unto you	Jn 20:26	1515
preaching p by Jesus Christ	Acts 10:36	1515
these things, they held their p	Acts 11:18	2270
with the hand to hold their p	Acts 12:17	4601
their friend, desired p	Acts 12:20	1515
And after they had held their p	Acts 15:13	4601
they were let go in p from the	Acts 15:33	1515
now therefore depart, and go in p	Acts 16:36	1515
but speak, and hold not thy p	Acts 18:9	4623
p from God our Father, and the	Rom 1:7	1515
But glory, honour, and p, to every	Rom 2:10	1515
the way of p have they not known	Rom 3:17	1515
we have p with God through our	Rom 5:1	1515
spiritually minded is life and p	Rom 8:6	1515
them that preach the gospel of p	Rom 10:15	1515
but righteousness, and p, and joy	Rom 14:17	1515
after the things which make for p	Rom 14:19	1515
p in believing, that ye may	Rom 15:13	1515
Now the God of p be with you all	Rom 15:33	1515
the God of p shall bruise Satan	Rom 16:20	1515
Grace to you, and p, from God	1Cor 1:3	1515
but God hath called us to p	1Cor 7:15	1515
by, let the first hold his p	1Cor 14:30	4601
the author of confusion, but of p	1Cor 14:33	1515
but conduct him forth in p	1Cor 16:11	1515
p from God our Father, and from	2Cor 1:2	1515
be of one mind, live in p	2Cor 13:11	1518
of love and p shall be with you	2Cor 13:11	1515
p from God the Father, and from	Gal 1:3	1515
of the Spirit is love, joy, p	Gal 5:22	1515
p be on them, and mercy, and upon	Gal 6:16	1515
Grace be to you, and p, from God	Eph 1:2	1515
For he is our p, who hath made	Eph 2:14	1515
of twain one new man, so making p	Eph 2:15	1515
preached p to you which were afar	Eph 2:17	1515
of the Spirit in the bond of p	Eph 4:3	1515
preparation of the gospel of p	Eph 6:15	1515
P be to the brethren, and love	Eph 6:23	1515
Grace be unto you, and p, from God	Phil 1:2	1515
the p of God, which passeth all	Phil 4:7	1515
the God of p shall be with you	Phil 4:9	1515
Grace be unto you, and p, from God	Col 1:2	1515
having made p through the blood	Col 1:20	1517
let the p of God rule in your	Col 3:15	1515
Grace be unto you, and p, from God	1Th 1:1	1515
For when they shall say, P	1Th 5:3	1515
And be at p among yourselves	1Th 5:13	1518
the very God of p sanctify you	1Th 5:23	1515
Grace unto you, and p, from God	2Th 1:2	1515
Now the Lord of p himself give	2Th 3:16	1515
give you p always by all means	2Th 3:16	1515
Grace, mercy, and p, from God our	1Ti 1:2	1515
Grace, mercy, and p, from God the	2Ti 1:2	1515
righteousness, faith, charity, p	2Ti 2:22	1515
Grace, mercy, and p, from God the	Titus 1:4	1515
Grace to you, and p, from God our	Philem 3	1515
of Salem, which is, King of p	Heb 7:2	1515
she had received the spies with p	Heb 11:31	1515
Follow p with all men, and	Heb 12:14	1515
Now the God of p, that brought	Heb 13:20	1515
of you say unto them, Depart in p	Jas 2:16	1515
sown in p of them that make p	Jas 3:18	1515
Grace unto you, and p, be	1Pet 1:2	1515
let him seek p, and ensue it	1Pet 3:11	1515
P be with you all that are in	1Pet 5:14	1515
p be multiplied unto you through	2Pet 1:2	1515
that ye may be found of him in p	2Pet 3:14	1515
Grace be with you, mercy, and p	2Jn 3	1515
P be to thee	3Jn 14	1515
Mercy unto you, and p, and love, be	Jude 2	1515
Grace be unto you, and p, from him	Rev 1:4	1515
thereon to take p from the earth	Rev 6:4	1515

PEACEABLE

These men are p with us	Gen 34:21	8003
I am one of them that are p	2Sa 20:19	7999
the land was wide, and quiet, and p	1Chr 4:40	7961

shall dwell in a p habitation	Is 32:18	7965
the p habitations are cut down	Jer 25:37	7965
p life in all godliness and	1Ti 2:2	2272
afterward it yieldeth the p fruit	Heb 12:11	1516
from above is first pure, then p	Jas 3:17	1516

PEACEABLY

and could not speak p unto him	Gen 37:4	7965
restore those lands again p	Judg 11:13	7965
Rimmon, and to call p unto them	Judg 21:13	7965
coming, and said, Comest thou p	1Sa 16:4	7965
And he said, P	1Sa 16:5	7965
And she said, Comest thou p	1Kin 2:13	7965
And he said, P	1Kin 2:13	7965
If ye be come p unto me to help	1Chr 12:17	7965
one speaketh p to his neighbour	Jer 9:8	7965
but he shall come in p, and obtain	Dan 11:21	7962
He shall enter p even upon the	Dan 11:24	7962
lieth in you, live p with all men	Rom 12:18	1518

PEACEMAKERS

Blessed are the p	Mt 5:9	1518

PEACOCKS

and silver, ivory, and apes, and p	1Kin 10:22	8500
and silver, ivory, and apes, and p	2Chr 9:21	8500
thou the goodly wings unto the p	Job 39:13	7443

PEARL

he had found one p of great price	Mt 13:46	3135
every several gate was of one p	Rev 21:21	3135

PEARLS

shall be made of coral, or of p	Job 28:18	1378
cast ye your p before swine	Mt 7:6	3135
a merchant man, seeking goodly p	Mt 13:45	3135
with broided hair, or gold, or p	1Ti 2:9	3135
with gold and precious stones and p	Rev 17:4	3135
and precious stones, and of p	Rev 18:12	3135
gold, and precious stones, and p	Rev 18:16	3135
And the twelve gates were twelve p	Rev 21:21	3135

PECULIAR

then ye shall be a p treasure	Ex 19:5	5459
to be a p people unto himself	Deut 14:2	5459
thee this day to be his p people	Deut 26:18	5459
and Israel for his p treasure	Ps 135:4	5459
the p treasure of kings and of the	Eccl 2:8	5459
and purify unto himself a p people	Titus 2:14	4041
an holy nation, a p people	1Pet 2:9	1519,4047

PEDAHEL (ped'-a-hel) *A Naphtalite who apportioned the Promised Land.*

of Naphtali, P the son of Ammihud	Num 34:28	6300

PEDAHZUR (pe-dah'-zur) *Father of Gamaliel.*

Gamaliel the son of P	Num 1:10	6301
shall be Gamaliel the son of P	Num 2:20	6301
day offered Gamaliel the son of P	Num 7:54	6301
offering of Gamaliel the son of P	Num 7:59	6301
was Gamaliel the son of P	Num 10:23	6301

PEDAIAH (pe-dah'-yah)
  1. Grandfather of King Josiah.

the daughter of P of Rumah	2Kin 23:36	6305

  2. Descendant of Jeconiah.

Malchiram also, and P, and Shenazar	1Chr 3:18	6305
And the sons of P were, Zerubbabel	1Chr 3:19	6305

  3. Father of Joel.

of Manasseh, Joel the son of P	1Chr 27:20	6305

  4. Son of Parosh.

After him P the son of Parosh	Neh 3:25	6305

  5. A priest who aided Ezra.

and on his left hand, P, and	Neh 8:4	6305
the scribe, and of the Levites, P	Neh 13:13	6305

  6. A family of exiles.

the son of Joed, the son of P	Neh 11:7	6305

PEDIGREES

they declared their p after their	Num 1:18	3205

PEELED

to a nation scattered and p	Is 18:2	4178
hosts of a people scattered and p	Is 18:7	4178
bald, and every shoulder was p	Eze 29:18	4803

PEEP

spirits, and unto wizards that p	Is 8:19	6850

PEEPED

wing, or opened the mouth, or p	Is 10:14	6850

PEKAH (pe'-kah) *A king of Israel.*

But P the son of Remaliah, a	2Kin 15:25	6492
P the son of Remaliah began to	2Kin 15:27	6492
In the days of P king of Israel	2Kin 15:29	6492
against P the son of Remaliah	2Kin 15:30	6492
And the rest of the acts of P	2Kin 15:31	6492

In the second year of *P* the son	2Kin 15:32	6492
Syria, and *P* the son of Remaliah	2Kin 15:37	6492
In the seventeenth year of *P* the	2Kin 16:1	6492
P son of Remaliah king of Israel	2Kin 16:5	6492
For *P* the son of Remaliah slew in	2Chr 28:6	6492
P the son of Remaliah, king of	Is 7:1	6492

PEKAHIAH *(pe-ka-hi'-ah)* Son of King Menahem.

P his son reigned in his stead	2Kin 15:22	6494
P the son of Menahem began to	2Kin 15:23	6494
And the rest of the acts of *P*	2Kin 15:26	6494

PEKOD *(pe'-kod)* Symbolic name for Chaldea.

and against the inhabitants of *P*	Jer 50:21	6489
and all the Chaldeans, *P*, and Shoa	Eze 23:23	6489

PELAIAH *(pel-a-i'-ah)*
  1. A son of Elioenai.

were, Hodaiah, and Eliashib, and *P*	1Chr 3:24	6411

  2. A priest who aided Ezra.

Azariah, Jozabad, Hanan, *P*	Neh 8:7	6411

  3. A Levite who renewed the covenant.

Shebaniah, Hodijah, Kelita, *P*	Neh 10:10	6411

PELALIAH *(pel-a-li'-ah)* A family of exiles.

the son of Jeroham, the son of *P*	Neh 11:12	6421

PELATIAH *(pel-a-ti'-ah)*
  1. Son of Hananiah.

of Hananiah; *P*, and Jesaiah	1Chr 3:21	6410

  2. A Simeonite captain.

Seir, having for their captains *P*	1Chr 4:42	6410

  3. A family who renewed the covenant.

P, Hanan, Anaiah,	Neh 10:22	6410

  4. Son of Benaiah.

P the son of Benaiah, princes of	Eze 11:1	6410
that *P* the son of Benaiah died	Eze 11:13	6410

PELEG *(pe'-leg)* See PHALEC. A son of Eber.

the name of one was *P*	Gen 10:25	6389
four and thirty years, and begat *P*	Gen 11:16	6389
after he begat *P* four hundred	Gen 11:17	6389
P lived thirty years, and begat	Gen 11:18	6389
P lived after he begat Reu two	Gen 11:19	6389
the name of the one was *P*	1Chr 1:19	6389
Eber, *P*, Reu,	1Chr 1:25	6389

PELET *(pe'-let)* See BETH-PALET.
  1. A son of Jahdai.

Jotham, and Gesham, and *P*	1Chr 2:47	6404

  2. A captain in David's army.

and Jeziel, and *P*, the sons of	1Chr 12:3	6404

PELETH *(pe'-leth)*
  1. Father of On.

of Eliab, and On, the son of *P*	Num 16:1	6431
of Jonathan; *P*, and Zaza	1Chr 2:33	6431

PELETHITES *(pel'-e-thites)* A company of David's
  bodyguards.

both the Cherethites and the *P*	2Sa 8:18	6432
all the Cherethites, and all the *P*	2Sa 15:18	6432
men, and the Cherethites, and the *P*	2Sa 20:7	6432
the Cherethites and over the *P*	2Sa 20:23	6432
and the Cherethites, and the *P*	1Kin 1:38	6432
and the Cherethites, and the *P*	1Kin 1:44	6432
was over the Cherethites and the *P*	1Chr 18:17	6432

PELICAN

And the swan, and the *p*, and the	Lev 11:18	6893
And the *p*, and the gier eagle, and	Deut 14:17	6893
I am like a *p* of the wilderness	Ps 102:6	6893

PELONITE *(pel'-o-nite)* See PALTITE.
  1. Family name of Helez.

the Harorite, Helez the *P*	1Chr 11:27	6397
the seventh month was Helez the *P*	1Chr 27:10	6397

  2. Family name of Ahijah.

the Mecherathite, Ahijah the *P*	1Chr 11:36	6397

PELUSIUM See SIN.

PEN

that handle the *p* of the writer	Judg 5:14	7626
they were graven with an iron *p*	Job 19:24	5842
my tongue is the *p* of a ready	Ps 45:1	5842
in it with a man's *p* concerning	Is 8:1	2747
the *p* of the scribes is in vain	Jer 8:8	5842
Judah is written with a *p* of iron	Jer 17:1	5842
not with ink and *p* write unto thee	3Jn 13	2563

PENCE

which owed him an hundred *p*	Mt 18:28	1220
for more than three hundred *p*	Mk 14:5	1220
the one owed five hundred *p*	Lk 7:41	1220
he departed, he took out two *p*	Lk 10:35	1220
ointment sold for three hundred *p*	Jn 12:5	1220

PENIEL *(pe-ni'-el)* See PENUEL. Same as Penuel.

called the name of the place *P*	Gen 32:30	6439

PENINNAH *(pe-nin'-nah)* A wife of Elkanah.

and the name of the other *P*	1Sa 1:2	6444
P had children, but Hannah had no	1Sa 1:2	6444
offered, he gave to *P* his wife	1Sa 1:4	6444

PENKNIFE

four leaves, he cut it with the *p*	Jer 36:23	8593

PENNY

with the labourers for a *p* a day	Mt 20:2	*1220*
hour, they received every man a *p*	Mt 20:9	*1220*
likewise received every man a *p*	Mt 20:10	*1220*
not thou agree with me for a *p*	Mt 20:13	*1220*
And they brought unto him a *p*	Mt 22:19	*1220*
bring me a *p*, that I may see it	Mk 12:15	*1220*
Shew me a *p*	Lk 20:24	*1220*
say, A measure of wheat for a *p*	Rev 6:6	*1220*
three measures of barley for a *p*	Rev 6:6	*1220*

PENNYWORTH

go and buy two hundred *p* of bread	Mk 6:37	*1220*
Two hundred *p* of bread is not	Jn 6:7	*1220*

PENTECOST *(pen'-te-cost)* Greek name for Passover.

when the day of *P* was fully come	Acts 2:1	*4005*
to be at Jerusalem the day of *P*	Acts 20:16	*4005*
I will tarry at Ephesus until *P*	1Cor 16:8	*4005*

PENUEL *(pe-nu'-el)* See PENIEL.
  1. Where Jacob wrestled God.

as he passed over *P* the sun rose	Gen 32:31	6439
And he went up thence to *P*	Judg 8:8	6439
the men of *P* answered him as the	Judg 8:8	6439
he spake also unto the men of *P*	Judg 8:9	6439
And he beat down the tower of *P*	Judg 8:17	6439

  2. Father of Gedor.

P the father of Gedor, and Ezer	1Chr 4:4	6439

  3. A son of Shashak.

And Iphedeiah, and *P*, the sons of	1Chr 8:25	6439

PENURY

of the lips tendeth only to *p*	Prov 14:23	4270
but she of her *p* hath cast in all	Lk 21:4	5303

PEOPLE

the *p* is one, and they have all	Gen 11:6	5971
and the women also, and the *p*	Gen 14:16	5971
soul shall be cut off from his *p*	Gen 17:14	5971
kings of *p* shall be of her	Gen 17:16	5971
all the *p* from every quarter	Gen 19:4	5971
himself to the *p* of the land	Gen 23:7	5971
the sons of my *p* give I it thee	Gen 23:11	5971
himself before the *p* of the land	Gen 23:12	5971
the audience of the *p* of the land	Gen 23:13	5971
and was gathered to his *p*	Gen 25:8	5971
and was gathered unto his *p*	Gen 25:17	5971
womb, and two manner of *p* shall be	Gen 25:23	3816
the one *p* shall be stronger than	Gen 25:23	3816
be stronger than the other *p*	Gen 25:23	3816
one of the *p* might lightly have	Gen 26:10	5971
And Abimelech charged all his *p*	Gen 26:11	5971
Let *p* serve thee, and nations bow	Gen 27:29	5971
thou mayest be a multitude of *p*	Gen 28:3	5971
the land of the *p* of the east	Gen 29:1	1121
he divided the *p* that was with	Gen 32:7	5971
with you, and we will become one *p*	Gen 34:16	5971
for to dwell with us, to be one *p*	Gen 34:22	5971
all the *p* that were with him	Gen 35:6	5971
died, and was gathered unto his *p*	Gen 35:29	5971
thy word shall all my *p* be ruled	Gen 41:40	5971
the *p* cried to Pharaoh for bread	Gen 41:55	5971
sold to all the *p* of the land	Gen 42:6	5971
And as for the *p*, he removed them	Gen 47:21	5971
Then Joseph said unto the *p*	Gen 47:23	5971
make of thee a multitude of *p*	Gen 48:4	5971
he also shall become a *p*, and he	Gen 48:19	5971
shall the gathering of the *p* be	Gen 49:10	5971
Dan shall judge his *p*, as one of	Gen 49:16	5971
I am to be gathered unto my *p*	Gen 49:29	5971
ghost, and was gathered unto his *p*	Gen 49:33	5971
this day, to save much *p* alive	Gen 50:20	5971
And he said unto his *p*, Behold,	Ex 1:9	5971
the *p* of the children of Israel	Ex 1:9	5971
the *p* multiplied, and waxed very	Ex 1:20	5971
And Pharaoh charged all his *p*	Ex 1:22	5971
of my *p* which are in Egypt	Ex 3:7	5971
p the children of Israel out of	Ex 3:10	5971
brought forth the *p* out of Egypt	Ex 3:12	5971
I will give this *p* favour in the	Ex 3:21	5971
shall be thy spokesman unto the *p*	Ex 4:16	5971
that he shall not let the *p* go	Ex 4:21	5971
the signs in the sight of the *p*	Ex 4:30	5971

And the *p* believed	Ex 4:31	5971
LORD God of Israel, Let my *p* go	Ex 5:1	5971
let the *p* from their works	Ex 5:4	5971
the *p* of the land now are many,	Ex 5:5	5971
same day the taskmasters of the *p*	Ex 5:6	5971
give the *p* straw to make brick	Ex 5:7	5971
the taskmasters of the *p* went out	Ex 5:10	5971
officers, and they spake to the *p*	Ex 5:10	5971
So the *p* were scattered abroad	Ex 5:12	5971
but the fault is in thine own *p*	Ex 5:16	5971
thou so evil entreated this *p*	Ex 5:22	5971
name, he hath done evil to this *p*	Ex 5:23	5971
hast thou delivered thy *p* at all	Ex 5:23	5971
And I will take you to me for a *p*	Ex 6:7	5971
my *p* the children of Israel, out	Ex 7:4	5971
he refuseth to let the *p* go	Ex 7:14	5971
me unto thee, saying, Let my *p* go	Ex 7:16	5971
Thus saith the LORD, Let my *p* go	Ex 8:1	5971
of thy servants, and upon thy *p*	Ex 8:3	5971
up both on thee, and upon thy *p*	Ex 8:4	5971
the frogs from me, and from my *p*	Ex 8:8	5971
and I will let the *p* go, that they	Ex 8:8	5971
and for thy servants, and for thy *p*	Ex 8:9	5971
from thy servants, and from thy *p*	Ex 8:11	5971
Thus saith the LORD, Let my *p* go	Ex 8:20	5971
if thou wilt not let my *p* go	Ex 8:21	5971
upon thy servants, and upon thy *p*	Ex 8:21	5971
of Goshen, in which my *p* dwell	Ex 8:22	5971
between my *p* and thy *p*	Ex 8:23	5971
from his servants, and from his *p*	Ex 8:29	5971
the *p* go to sacrifice to the LORD	Ex 8:29	5971
from his servants, and from his *p*	Ex 8:31	5971
neither would he let the *p* go	Ex 8:32	5971
God of the Hebrews, Let my *p* go	Ex 9:1	5971
and he did not let the *p* go	Ex 9:7	5971
God of the Hebrews, Let my *p* go	Ex 9:13	5971
upon thy servants, and upon thy *p*	Ex 9:14	5971
thee and thy *p* with pestilence	Ex 9:15	5971
thou thyself against my *p*	Ex 9:17	5971
and I and my *p* are wicked	Ex 9:27	5971
let my *p* go, that they may serve	Ex 10:3	5971
if thou refuse to let my *p* go	Ex 10:4	5971
Speak now in the ears of the *p*	Ex 11:2	5971
the LORD gave the *p* favour in the	Ex 11:3	5971
and in the sight of the *p*	Ex 11:3	5971
all the *p* that follow thee	Ex 11:8	5971
And he bowed the head and	Ex 12:27	5971
and get you forth from among my *p*	Ex 12:31	5971
Egyptians were urgent upon the *p*	Ex 12:33	5971
the *p* took their dough before it	Ex 12:34	5971
the LORD gave the *p* favour in the	Ex 12:36	5971
And Moses said unto the *p*,	Ex 13:3	5971
when Pharaoh had let the *p* go	Ex 13:17	5971
Lest peradventure the *p* repent	Ex 13:17	5971
But God led the *p* about, through	Ex 13:18	5971
fire by night, from before the *p*	Ex 13:22	5971
the king of Egypt that the *p* fled	Ex 14:5	5971
servants was turned against the *p*	Ex 14:5	5971
chariot, and took his *p* with him	Ex 14:6	5971
And Moses said unto the *p*, Fear ye	Ex 14:13	5971
the *p* feared the LORD, and	Ex 14:31	5971
the *p* which thou hast redeemed	Ex 15:13	5971
The *p* shall hear, and be afraid	Ex 15:14	5971
till thy *p* pass over, O LORD,	Ex 15:16	5971
till the *p* pass over, which thou	Ex 15:16	5971
the *p* murmured against Moses,	Ex 15:24	5971
the *p* shall go out and gather a	Ex 16:4	5971
the *p* on the seventh day for to	Ex 16:27	5971
So the *p* rested on the seventh	Ex 16:30	5971
was no water for the *p* to drink	Ex 17:1	5971
Wherefore the *p* did chide with	Ex 17:2	5971
the *p* thirsted there for water	Ex 17:3	5971
the *p* murmured against Moses, and	Ex 17:3	5971
What shall I do unto this *p*	Ex 17:4	5971
unto Moses, Go on before the *p*	Ex 17:5	5971
out of it, that the *p* may drink	Ex 17:6	5971
his *p* with the edge of the sword	Ex 17:13	5971
for Moses, and for Israel his *p*	Ex 18:1	5971
who hath delivered the *p* from	Ex 18:10	5971
that Moses sat to judge the *p*	Ex 18:13	5971
the *p* stood by Moses from the	Ex 18:13	5971
law saw all that he did to the *p*	Ex 18:14	5971
thing that thou doest to the *p*	Ex 18:14	5971
all the *p* stand by thee from	Ex 18:14	5971
Because the *p* come unto me to	Ex 18:15	5971
thou, and this *p* that is with thee	Ex 18:18	5971
Be thou for the *p* to God-ward	Ex 18:19	5971
provide out of all the *p* able men	Ex 18:21	5971
them judge the *p* at all seasons	Ex 18:22	5971
all this *p* shall also go to their	Ex 18:23	5971
and made them heads over the *p*	Ex 18:25	5971
they judged the *p* at all seasons	Ex 18:26	5971
treasure unto me above all *p*	Ex 19:5	5971
and called for the elders of the *p*	Ex 19:7	5971
all the *p* answered together, and	Ex 19:8	5971
the words of the *p* unto the LORD	Ex 19:8	5971
that the *p* may hear when I speak	Ex 19:9	5971
the words of the *p* unto the LORD	Ex 19:9	5971
said unto Moses, Go unto the *p*	Ex 19:10	5971
of all the *p* upon mount Sinai	Ex 19:11	5971
set bounds unto the *p* round about	Ex 19:12	5971
down from the mount unto the *p*	Ex 19:14	5971
and sanctified the *p*	Ex 19:14	5971
And he said unto the *p*, Be ready	Ex 19:15	5971
so that all the *p* that was in the	Ex 19:16	5971
Moses brought forth the *p* out of	Ex 19:17	5971
unto Moses, Go down, charge the *p*	Ex 19:21	5971
The *p* cannot come up to mount	Ex 19:23	5971
the *p* break through to come up	Ex 19:24	5971
So Moses went down unto the *p*	Ex 19:25	5971
all the *p* saw the thunderings, and	Ex 20:18	5971
and when the *p* saw it, they	Ex 20:18	5971
And Moses said unto the *p*, Fear	Ex 20:20	5971
the *p* stood afar off, and Moses	Ex 20:21	5971
any of my *p* that is poor by thee	Ex 22:25	5971
nor curse the ruler of thy *p*	Ex 22:28	5971
that the poor of thy *p* may eat	Ex 23:11	5971
will destroy all the *p* to whom	Ex 23:27	5971
shall the *p* go up with him	Ex 24:2	5971
told the *p* all the words of the	Ex 24:3	5971
all the *p* answered with one voice	Ex 24:3	5971
and read in the audience of the *p*	Ex 24:7	5971
blood, and sprinkled it on the *p*	Ex 24:8	5971
shall even be cut off from his *p*	Ex 30:33	5971
shall even be cut off from his *p*	Ex 30:38	5971
shall be cut off from among his *p*	Ex 31:14	5971
when the *p* saw that Moses delayed	Ex 32:1	5971
the *p* gathered themselves	Ex 32:1	5971
all the *p* brake off the golden	Ex 32:3	5971
the *p* sat down to eat and to drink	Ex 32:6	5971
for thy *p*, which thou broughtest	Ex 32:7	5971
unto Moses, I have seen this *p*	Ex 32:9	5971
and, behold, it is a stiffnecked *p*	Ex 32:9	5971
thy wrath wax hot against thy *p*	Ex 32:11	5971
repent of this evil against thy *p*	Ex 32:12	5971
which he thought to do unto his *p*	Ex 32:14	5971
noise of the *p* as they shouted	Ex 32:17	5971
Aaron, What did this *p* unto thee	Ex 32:21	5971
thou knowest the *p*, that they are	Ex 32:22	5971
Moses saw that the *p* were naked	Ex 32:25	5971
there fell of the *p* that day	Ex 32:28	5971
that Moses said unto the *p*	Ex 32:30	5971
this *p* have sinned a great sin,	Ex 32:31	5971
lead the *p* unto the place of	Ex 32:34	5971
And the LORD plagued the *p*	Ex 32:35	5971
the *p* which thou hast brought up	Ex 33:1	5971
for thou art a stiffnecked *p*	Ex 33:3	5971
when the *p* heard these evil	Ex 33:4	5971
of Israel, Ye are a stiffnecked *p*	Ex 33:5	5971
that all the *p* rose up, and stood	Ex 33:8	5971
all the *p* saw the cloudy pillar	Ex 33:10	5971
and all the *p* rose up and	Ex 33:10	5971
sayest unto me, Bring up this *p*	Ex 33:12	5971
that this nation is thy *p*	Ex 33:13	5971
thy *p* have found grace in thy	Ex 33:16	5971
shall we be separated, I and thy *p*	Ex 33:16	5971
from all the *p* that are upon the	Ex 33:16	5971
for it is a stiffnecked *p*	Ex 34:9	5971
before all thy *p* I will do	Ex 34:10	5971
all the *p* among which thou art	Ex 34:10	5971
The *p* bring much more than enough	Ex 36:5	5971
So the *p* were restrained from	Ex 36:6	5971
sin according to the sin of the *p*	Lev 4:3	5971
common *p* sin through ignorance	Lev 4:27	5971
soul shall be cut off from his *p*	Lev 7:20	5971
soul shall be cut off from his *p*	Lev 7:21	5971
it shall be cut off from his *p*	Lev 7:25	5971
soul shall be cut off from his *p*	Lev 7:27	5971
for thyself, and for the *p*	Lev 9:7	5971
and offer the offering of the *p*	Lev 9:7	5971
was the sin offering for the *p*	Lev 9:15	5971
offerings, which was for the *p*	Lev 9:18	5971
lifted up his hand toward the *p*	Lev 9:22	5971
and came out, and blessed the *p*	Lev 9:23	5971
the LORD appeared unto all the *p*	Lev 9:23	5971
which when all the *p* saw, they	Lev 9:24	5971
before all the *p* I will be	Lev 10:3	5971
and lest wrath come upon all the *p*	Lev 10:6	5712
sin offering, that is for the *p*	Lev 16:15	5971
and the burnt offering of the *p*	Lev 16:24	5971
for himself, and for the *p*	Lev 16:24	5971
for all the *p* of the congregation	Lev 16:33	5971

shall be cut off from among his *p*	Lev 17:4	5971
shall be cut off from among his *p*	Lev 17:9	5971
will cut him off from among his *p*	Lev 17:10	5971
be cut off from among their *p*	Lev 18:29	5971
shall be cut off from among his *p*	Lev 19:8	5971
down as a talebearer among thy *p*	Lev 19:16	5971
against the children of thy *p*	Lev 19:18	5971
the *p* of the land shall stone him	Lev 20:2	5971
will cut him off from among his *p*	Lev 20:3	5971
if the *p* of the land do any ways	Lev 20:4	5971
with Molech, from among their *p*	Lev 20:5	5971
will cut him off from among his *p*	Lev 20:6	5971
cut off in the sight of their *p*	Lev 20:17	5971
be cut off from among their *p*	Lev 20:18	5971
have separated you from other *p*	Lev 20:24	5971
and have severed you from other *p*	Lev 20:26	5971
defiled for the dead among his *p*	Lev 21:1	5971
being a chief man among his *p*	Lev 21:4	5971
a virgin of his own *p* to wife	Lev 21:14	5971
he profane his seed among his *p*	Lev 21:15	5971
shall be cut off from among his *p*	Lev 23:29	5971
will I destroy from among his *p*	Lev 23:30	5971
be your God, and ye shall be my *p*	Lev 26:12	5971
a curse and an oath among thy *p*	Num 5:21	5971
shall be a curse among her *p*	Num 5:27	5971
shall be cut off from among his *p*	Num 9:13	5971
when the *p* complained, it	Num 11:1	5971
And the *p* cried unto Moses	Num 11:2	5971
the *p* went about, and gathered it,	Num 11:8	5971
Then Moses heard the *p* weep	Num 11:10	5971
the burden of all this *p* upon me	Num 11:11	5971
Have I conceived all this *p*	Num 11:12	5971
flesh to give unto all this *p*	Num 11:13	5971
not able to bear all this *p* alone	Num 11:14	5971
knowest to be the elders of the *p*	Num 11:16	5971
the burden of the *p* with thee	Num 11:17	5971
And say thou unto the *p*, Sanctify	Num 11:18	5971
And Moses said, The *p*, among whom	Num 11:21	5971
told the *p* the words of the LORD,	Num 11:24	5971
men of the elders of the *p*	Num 11:24	5971
all the LORD's *p* were prophets	Num 11:29	5971
the *p* stood up all that day, and	Num 11:32	5971
LORD was kindled against the *p*	Num 11:33	5971
the LORD smote the *p* with a very	Num 11:33	5971
they buried the *p* that lusted	Num 11:34	5971
And the *p* journeyed from	Num 11:35	5971
the *p* journeyed not till Miriam	Num 12:15	5971
afterward the *p* removed from	Num 12:16	5971
the *p* that dwelleth therein,	Num 13:18	5971
Nevertheless the *p* be strong that	Num 13:28	5971
Caleb stilled the *p* before Moses	Num 13:30	5971
not able to go up against the *p*	Num 13:31	5971
all the *p* that we saw in it are	Num 13:32	5971
and the *p* wept that night	Num 14:1	5971
neither fear ye the *p* of the land	Num 14:9	5971
How long will this *p* provoke me	Num 14:11	5971
p in thy might from among them	Num 14:13	5971
that thou LORD art among this *p*	Num 14:14	5971
shalt kill all this *p* as one man	Num 14:15	5971
p into the land which he sware	Num 14:16	5971
the iniquity of this *p* according	Num 14:19	5971
and as thou hast forgiven this *p*	Num 14:19	5971
and the *p* mourned greatly	Num 14:39	5971
seeing all the *p* were in	Num 15:26	5971
shall be cut off from among his *p*	Num 15:30	5971
Ye have killed the *p* of the LORD	Num 16:41	5971
the plague was begun among the *p*	Num 16:47	5971
and made an atonement for the *p*	Num 16:47	5971
and the *p* abode in Kadesh	Num 20:1	5971
the *p* chode with Moses, and spake,	Num 20:3	5971
came out against him with much *p*	Num 20:20	5971
shall be gathered unto his *p*	Num 20:24	5971
shall be gathered unto his *p*	Num 20:26	5971
deliver this *p* into my hand	Num 21:2	5971
the soul of the *p* was much	Num 21:4	5971
the *p* spake against God, and	Num 21:5	5971
sent fiery serpents among the *p*	Num 21:6	5971
and they bit the *p*	Num 21:6	5971
and much *p* of Israel died	Num 21:6	5971
Therefore the *p* came to Moses	Num 21:7	5971
And Moses prayed for the *p*	Num 21:7	5971
unto Moses, Gather the *p* together	Num 21:16	5971
the nobles of the *p* digged it	Num 21:18	5971
Sihon gathered all his *p* together	Num 21:23	5971
thou art undone, O *p* of Chemosh	Num 21:29	5971
against them, he, and all his *p*	Num 21:33	5971
him into thy hand, and all his *p*	Num 21:34	5971
him, and his sons, and all his *p*	Num 21:35	5971
And Moab was sore afraid of the *p*	Num 22:3	5971
the land of the children of his *p*	Num 22:5	5971
there is a *p* come out from Egypt	Num 22:5	5971
I pray thee, curse me this *p*	Num 22:6	5971
there is a *p* come out of Egypt,	Num 22:11	5971
thou shalt not curse the *p*	Num 22:12	5971
I pray thee, curse me this *p*	Num 22:17	5971
see the utmost part of the *p*	Num 22:41	5971
the *p* shall dwell alone, and shall	Num 23:9	5971
the *p* shall rise up as a great	Num 23:24	5971
And now, behold, I go unto my *p*	Num 24:14	5971
p shall do to thy *p* in the	Num 24:14	5971
the *p* began to commit whoredom	Num 25:1	5971
they called the *p* unto the	Num 25:2	5971
the *p* did eat, and bowed down to	Num 25:2	5971
Take all the heads of the *p*	Num 25:4	5971
he was head over a *p*, and of a	Num 25:15	523
Take the sum of the *p*, from	Num 26:4	5971
also shalt be gathered unto thy *p*	Num 27:13	5971
shalt thou be gathered unto thy *p*	Num 31:2	5971
And Moses spake unto the *p*	Num 31:3	5971
and ye shall destroy all this *p*	Num 32:15	5971
was no water for the *p* to drink	Num 33:14	5971
The *p* is greater and taller than	Deut 1:28	5971
And command thou the *p*, saying, Ye	Deut 2:4	5971
a *p* great, and many, and tall, as	Deut 2:10	5971
consumed and dead from among the *p*	Deut 2:16	5971
A *p* great, and many, and tall, as	Deut 2:21	5971
out against us, he and all his *p*	Deut 2:32	5971
him, and his sons, and all his *p*	Deut 2:33	5971
out against us, he and all his *p*	Deut 3:1	5971
I will deliver him, and all his *p*	Deut 3:2	5971
the king of Bashan, and all his *p*	Deut 3:3	5971
he shall go over before this *p*	Deut 3:28	5971
is a wise and understanding *p*	Deut 4:6	5971
unto me, Gather me the *p* together	Deut 4:10	5971
to be unto him a *p* of inheritance	Deut 4:20	5971
Did ever *p* hear the voice of God	Deut 4:33	5971
the voice of the words of this *p*	Deut 5:28	5971
of the gods of the *p* which are	Deut 6:14	5971
For thou art an holy *p* unto the	Deut 7:6	5971
to be a special *p* unto himself	Deut 7:6	5971
above all *p* that are upon the	Deut 7:6	5971
ye were more in number than any *p*	Deut 7:7	5971
for ye were the fewest of all *p*	Deut 7:7	5971
Thou shalt be blessed above all *p*	Deut 7:14	5971
thou shalt consume all the *p*	Deut 7:16	5971
all the *p* of whom thou art afraid	Deut 7:19	5971
A *p* great and tall, the children	Deut 9:2	5971
for thou art a stiffnecked *p*	Deut 9:6	5971
for thy *p* which thou hast brought	Deut 9:12	5971
me, saying, I have seen this *p*	Deut 9:13	5971
and, behold, it is a stiffnecked *p*	Deut 9:13	5971
O Lord GOD, destroy not thy *p*	Deut 9:26	5971
unto the stubbornness of this *p*	Deut 9:27	5971
Yet they are thy *p* and thine	Deut 9:29	5971
take thy journey before the *p*	Deut 10:11	5971
after them, even you above all *p*	Deut 10:15	5971
of the gods of the *p* which are	Deut 13:7	5971
afterwards the hand of all the *p*	Deut 13:9	5971
For thou art an holy *p* unto the	Deut 14:2	5971
to be a peculiar *p* unto himself	Deut 14:2	5971
for thou art an holy *p* unto the	Deut 14:21	5971
judge the *p* with just judgment	Deut 16:18	5971
afterward the hands of all the *p*	Deut 17:7	5971
all the *p* shall hear, and fear, and	Deut 17:13	5971
nor cause the *p* to return to	Deut 17:16	5971
be the priest's due from the *p*	Deut 18:3	5971
a *p* more than thou, be not afraid	Deut 20:1	5971
approach and speak unto the *p*	Deut 20:2	5971
officers shall speak unto the *p*	Deut 20:5	5971
shall speak further unto the *p*	Deut 20:8	5971
an end of speaking unto the *p*	Deut 20:9	5971
of the armies to lead the *p*	Deut 20:9	5971
that all the *p* that is found	Deut 20:11	5971
But of the cities of these *p*	Deut 20:16	5971
O LORD, unto thy *p* Israel	Deut 21:8	5971
unto thy *p* of Israel's charge	Deut 21:8	5971
heaven, and bless thy *p* Israel	Deut 26:15	5971
this day to be his peculiar *p*	Deut 26:18	5971
an holy *p* unto the LORD thy God	Deut 26:19	5971
elders of Israel commanded the *p*	Deut 27:1	5971
become the *p* of the LORD thy God	Deut 27:9	5971
Moses charged the *p* the same day	Deut 27:11	5971
upon mount Gerizim to bless the *p*	Deut 27:12	5971
all the *p* shall answer and say,	Deut 27:15	5971
all the *p* shall say, Amen	Deut 27:16	5971
all the *p* shall say, Amen	Deut 27:17	5971
all the *p* shall say, Amen	Deut 27:18	5971
all the *p* shall say, Amen	Deut 27:19	5971
all the *p* shall say, Amen	Deut 27:20	5971
all the *p* shall say, Amen	Deut 27:21	5971
all the *p* shall say, Amen	Deut 27:22	5971
all the *p* shall say, Amen	Deut 27:23	5971

P

all the *p* shall say, Amen	Deut 27:24	5971
all the *p* shall say, Amen	Deut 27:25	5971
all the *p* shall say, Amen	Deut 27:26	5971
thee an holy *p* unto himself	Deut 28:9	5971
all *p* of the earth shall see that	Deut 28:10	5971
shall be given unto another *p*	Deut 28:32	5971
shall scatter thee among all *p*	Deut 28:64	5971
thee to day for a *p* unto himself	Deut 29:13	5971
for thou must go with this *p* unto	Deut 31:7	5971
Gather the *p* together, men, and	Deut 31:12	5971
this *p* will rise up, and go a	Deut 31:16	5971
requite the Lord, O foolish *p*	Deut 32:6	5971
he set the bounds of the *p*	Deut 32:8	5971
For the Lord's portion is his *p*	Deut 32:9	5971
with those which are not a *p*	Deut 32:21	5971
For the Lord shall judge his *p*	Deut 32:36	5971
Rejoice, O ye nations, with his *p*	Deut 32:43	5971
unto his land, and to his *p*	Deut 32:43	5971
of this song in the ears of the *p*	Deut 32:44	5971
up, and be gathered unto thy *p*	Deut 32:50	5971
Hor, and was gathered unto his *p*	Deut 32:50	5971
Yea, he loved the *p*	Deut 33:3	5971
Jeshurun, when the heads of the *p*	Deut 33:5	5971
of Judah, and bring him unto his *p*	Deut 33:7	5971
the *p* together to the ends of the	Deut 33:19	5971
call the *p* unto the mountain	Deut 33:19	5971
he came with the heads of the *p*	Deut 33:21	5971
O *p* saved by the Lord, the shield	Deut 33:29	5971
this Jordan, thou, and all this *p*	Josh 1:2	5971
for unto this *p* shalt thou divide	Josh 1:6	5971
commanded the officers of the *p*	Josh 1:10	5971
the host, and command the *p*	Josh 1:11	5971
And they commanded the *p*, saying,	Josh 3:3	5971
And Joshua said unto the *p*	Josh 3:5	5971
and pass over before the *p*	Josh 3:6	5971
covenant, and went before the *p*	Josh 3:6	5971
when the *p* removed from their	Josh 3:14	5971
ark of the covenant before the *p*	Josh 3:14	5971
the *p* passed over right against	Josh 3:16	5971
until all the *p* were passed clean	Josh 3:17	1471
when all the *p* were clean passed	Josh 4:1	1471
Take you twelve men out of the *p*	Josh 4:2	5971
Joshua to speak unto the *p*	Josh 4:10	5971
the *p* hasted and passed over	Josh 4:10	5971
when all the *p* were clean passed	Josh 4:11	5971
priests, in the presence of the *p*	Josh 4:11	5971
the *p* came up out of Jordan on	Josh 4:19	5971
That all the *p* of the earth might	Josh 4:24	5971
All the *p* that came out of Egypt,	Josh 5:4	5971
Now all the *p* that came out were	Josh 5:5	5971
but all the *p* that were born in	Josh 5:5	5971
till all the *p* that were men of	Josh 5:6	1471
had done circumcising all the *p*	Josh 5:8	1471
all the *p* shall shout with a	Josh 6:5	5971
the *p* shall ascend up every man	Josh 6:5	5971
And he said unto the *p*, Pass on,	Josh 6:7	5971
when Joshua had spoken unto the *p*	Josh 6:8	5971
And Joshua had commanded the *p*	Josh 6:10	5971
trumpets, Joshua said unto the *p*	Josh 6:16	5971
So the *p* shouted when the priests	Josh 6:20	5971
when the *p* heard the sound of the	Josh 6:20	5971
the *p* shouted with a great shout,	Josh 6:20	5971
so that the *p* went up into the	Josh 6:20	5971
unto him, Let not all the *p* go up	Josh 7:3	5971
make not all the *p* to labour	Josh 7:3	5971
of the *p* about three thousand men	Josh 7:4	5971
the hearts of the *p* melted	Josh 7:5	5971
at all brought this *p* over Jordan	Josh 7:7	5971
Up, sanctify the *p*, and say,	Josh 7:13	5971
take all the *p* of war with thee,	Josh 8:1	5971
thy hand the king of Ai, and his *p*	Josh 8:1	5971
Joshua arose, and all the *p* of war	Josh 8:3	5971
all the *p* that are with me, will	Josh 8:5	5971
lodged that night among the *p*	Josh 8:9	5971
in the morning, and numbered the *p*	Josh 8:10	5971
of Israel, before the *p* to Ai	Josh 8:10	5971
And all the *p*, even the	Josh 8:11	5971
even the *p* of war that were with	Josh 8:11	5971
And when they had set the *p*	Josh 8:13	5971
Israel to battle, he and all his *p*	Josh 8:14	5971
all the *p* that were in Ai were	Josh 8:16	5971
the *p* that fled to the wilderness	Josh 8:20	5971
they should bless the *p* of Israel	Josh 8:33	5971
all the *p* of war with him, and all	Josh 10:7	5971
stayed, until the *p* had avenged	Josh 10:13	1471
all the *p* returned to the camp to	Josh 10:21	5971
and Joshua smote him and his *p*	Josh 10:33	5971
all their hosts with them, much *p*	Josh 11:4	5971
all the *p* of war with him,	Josh 11:7	5971
me made the heart of the *p* melt	Josh 14:8	5971
to inherit, seeing I am a great *p*	Josh 17:14	5971

them, If thou be a great *p*	Josh 17:15	5971
saying, Thou art a great *p*	Josh 17:17	5971
And Joshua said unto all the *p*	Josh 24:2	5971
the *p* answered and said, God	Josh 24:16	5971
among all the *p* through whom we	Josh 24:17	5971
out from before us all the *p*	Josh 24:18	5971
And Joshua said unto the *p*	Josh 24:19	5971
the *p* said unto Joshua, Nay	Josh 24:21	5971
And Joshua said unto the *p*	Josh 24:22	5971
the *p* said unto Joshua, The Lord	Josh 24:24	5971
a covenant with the *p* that day	Josh 24:25	5971
And Joshua said unto all the *p*	Josh 24:27	5971
So Joshua let the *p* depart	Josh 24:28	5971
and they went and dwelt among the *p*	Judg 1:16	5971
that the *p* lifted up their voice,	Judg 2:4	5971
And when Joshua had let the *p* go	Judg 2:6	5971
the *p* served the Lord all the	Judg 2:7	5971
of the gods of the *p* that were	Judg 2:12	5971
he said, Because that this *p* hath	Judg 2:20	1471
he sent away the *p* that bare the	Judg 3:18	5971
all the *p* that were with him,	Judg 4:13	5971
when the *p* willingly offered	Judg 5:2	5971
themselves willingly among the *p*	Judg 5:9	5971
then shall the *p* of the Lord go	Judg 5:11	5971
over the nobles among the *p*	Judg 5:13	5971
after thee, Benjamin, among thy *p*	Judg 5:14	5971
Naphtali were a *p* that jeoparded	Judg 5:18	5971
all the *p* that were with him,	Judg 7:1	5971
The *p* that are with thee are too	Judg 7:2	5971
to, proclaim in the ears of the *p*	Judg 7:3	5971
And there returned of the *p* twenty	Judg 7:3	5971
Gideon, The *p* are yet too many	Judg 7:4	5971
brought down the *p* unto the water	Judg 7:5	5971
but all the rest of the *p* bowed	Judg 7:6	5971
let all the other *p* go every man	Judg 7:7	5971
So the *p* took victuals in their	Judg 7:8	5971
bread unto the *p* that follow me	Judg 8:5	5971
would to God this *p* were under my	Judg 9:29	5971
the *p* that is with thee, and lie	Judg 9:32	5971
the *p* that is with him come out	Judg 9:33	5971
all the *p* that were with him, by	Judg 9:34	5971
the *p* that were with him, from	Judg 9:35	5971
And when Gaal saw the *p*, he said	Judg 9:36	5971
there come *p* down from the top of	Judg 9:36	5971
See there come *p* down by the	Judg 9:37	5971
is not this the *p* that thou hast	Judg 9:38	5971
that the *p* went out into the	Judg 9:42	5971
And he took the *p*, and divided them	Judg 9:43	5971
the *p* were come forth out of the	Judg 9:43	5971
all the *p* that were in the fields	Judg 9:44	5971
slew the *p* that was therein, and	Judg 9:45	5971
all the *p* that were with him	Judg 9:48	5971
said unto the *p* that were with	Judg 9:48	5971
all the *p* likewise cut down every	Judg 9:49	5971
And the *p* and princes of Gilead	Judg 10:18	5971
the *p* made him head and captain	Judg 11:11	5971
Sihon gathered all his *p* together	Judg 11:20	5971
all his *p* into the hand of Israel	Judg 11:21	5971
Amorites from before his *p* Israel	Judg 11:23	5971
my *p* were at great strife with	Judg 12:2	5971
thy brethren, or among all my *p*	Judg 14:3	5971
riddle unto the children of my *p*	Judg 14:16	5971
riddle to the children of her *p*	Judg 14:17	5971
And when the *p* saw him, they	Judg 16:24	5971
upon all the *p* that were therein	Judg 16:30	5971
saw the *p* that were therein, how	Judg 18:7	5971
go, ye shall come unto a *p* secure	Judg 18:10	5971
and went in the midst of the *p*	Judg 18:20	5971
unto a *p* that were at quiet and	Judg 18:27	5971
And the chief of all the *p*	Judg 20:2	5971
in the assembly of the *p* of God	Judg 20:2	5971
all the *p* arose as one man,	Judg 20:8	5971
to fetch victual for the *p*,	Judg 20:10	5971
Among all this *p* there were seven	Judg 20:16	5971
And the *p* the men of Israel	Judg 20:22	5971
children of Israel, and all the *p*	Judg 20:26	5971
Benjamin went out against the *p*	Judg 20:31	5971
and they began to smite of the *p*	Judg 20:31	5971
the *p* came to the house of God,	Judg 21:2	5971
that the *p* rose early, and built	Judg 21:4	5971
For the *p* were numbered, and,	Judg 21:9	5971
the *p* repented them for Benjamin,	Judg 21:15	5971
his *p* in giving them bread	Ruth 1:6	5971
will return with thee unto thy *p*	Ruth 1:10	5971
in law is gone back unto her *p*	Ruth 1:15	5971
thy *p* shall be my *p*, and thy	Ruth 1:16	5971
art come unto a *p* which thou	Ruth 2:11	5971
for all the city of my *p* doth	Ruth 3:11	5971
and before the elders of my *p*	Ruth 4:4	5971
the elders, and unto all the *p*	Ruth 4:9	5971
all the *p* that were in the gate,	Ruth 4:11	5971

priest's custom with the *p* was	1Sa 2:13	5971
your evil dealings by all this *p*	1Sa 2:23	5971
make the LORD's *p* to transgress	1Sa 2:24	5971
all the offerings of Israel my *p*	1Sa 2:29	5971
when the *p* were come into the	1Sa 4:3	5971
So the *p* sent to Shiloh, that	1Sa 4:4	5971
a great slaughter among the *p*	1Sa 4:17	5971
Israel to us, to slay us and our *p*	1Sa 5:10	5971
that it slay us not, and our *p*	1Sa 5:11	5971
them, did they not let the *p* go	1Sa 6:6	
he smote of the *p* fifty thousand	1Sa 6:19	5971
the *p* lamented, because the LORD	1Sa 6:19	5971
of the *p* with a great slaughter	1Sa 6:19	5971
Hearken unto the voice of the *p*	1Sa 8:7	5971
the *p* that asked of him a king	1Sa 8:10	5971
Nevertheless the *p* refused to	1Sa 8:19	5971
heard all the words of the *p*	1Sa 8:21	5971
he was higher than any of the *p*	1Sa 9:2	5971
of the *p* to day in the high place	1Sa 9:12	5971
for the *p* will not eat until he	1Sa 9:13	5971
to be captain over my *p* Israel	1Sa 9:16	5971
that he may save my *p* out of the	1Sa 9:16	5971
for I have looked upon my *p*	1Sa 9:16	5971
this same shall reign over my *p*	1Sa 9:17	5971
I said, I have invited the *p*	1Sa 9:24	5971
then the *p* said one to another,	1Sa 10:11	5971
Samuel called the *p* together unto	1Sa 10:17	5971
and when he stood among the *p*	1Sa 10:23	5971
any of the *p* from his shoulders	1Sa 10:23	5971
And Samuel said to all the *p*	1Sa 10:24	5971
is none like him among all the *p*	1Sa 10:24	5971
And all the *p* shouted, and said,	1Sa 10:24	5971
Then Samuel told the *p* the manner	1Sa 10:25	5971
And Samuel sent all the *p* away	1Sa 10:25	5971
the tidings in the ears of the *p*	1Sa 11:4	5971
all the *p* lifted up their voices,	1Sa 11:4	5971
What aileth the *p* that they weep	1Sa 11:5	5971
fear of the LORD fell on the *p*	1Sa 11:7	5971
that Saul put the *p* in three	1Sa 11:11	5971
the *p* said unto Samuel, Who is he	1Sa 11:12	5971
Then said Samuel to the *p*	1Sa 11:14	5971
And all the *p* went to Gilgal	1Sa 11:15	5971
And Samuel said unto the *p*	1Sa 12:6	5971
all the *p* greatly feared the LORD	1Sa 12:18	5971
all the *p* said unto Samuel, Pray	1Sa 12:19	5971
And Samuel said unto the *p*	1Sa 12:20	5971
his *p* for his great name's sake	1Sa 12:22	5971
the LORD to make you his *p*	1Sa 12:22	5971
the rest of the *p* he sent every	1Sa 13:2	5971
the *p* were called together after	1Sa 13:4	5971
p as the sand which is on the sea	1Sa 13:5	5971
(for the *p* were distressed,)	1Sa 13:6	5971
then the *p* did hide themselves	1Sa 13:6	5971
all the *p* followed him trembling	1Sa 13:7	5971
the *p* were scattered from him	1Sa 13:8	5971
that the *p* were scattered from me	1Sa 13:11	5971
him to be captain over his *p*	1Sa 13:14	5971
Saul numbered the *p* that were	1Sa 13:15	5971
the *p* that were present with them	1Sa 13:16	5971
any of the *p* that were with Saul	1Sa 13:22	5971
the *p* that were with him were	1Sa 14:2	5971
the *p* knew not that Jonathan was	1Sa 14:3	5971
in the field, and among all the *p*	1Sa 14:15	5971
unto the *p* that were with him	1Sa 14:17	5971
all the *p* that were with him	1Sa 14:20	5971
for Saul had adjured the *p*	1Sa 14:24	5971
So none of the *p* tasted any food	1Sa 14:24	5971
when the *p* were come into the	1Sa 14:26	5971
for the *p* feared the oath	1Sa 14:26	5971
charged the *p* with the oath	1Sa 14:27	5971
Then answered one of the *p*	1Sa 14:28	5971
charged the *p* with an oath	1Sa 14:28	5971
And the *p* were faint	1Sa 14:28	5971
if haply the *p* had eaten freely	1Sa 14:30	5971
and the *p* were very faint	1Sa 14:31	5971
the *p* flew upon the spoil, and	1Sa 14:32	5971
the *p* did eat them with the blood	1Sa 14:32	5971
the *p* sin against the LORD, in	1Sa 14:33	5971
Disperse yourselves among the *p*	1Sa 14:34	5971
all the *p* brought every man his	1Sa 14:34	5971
hither, all the chief of the *p*	1Sa 14:38	5971
among all the *p* that answered him	1Sa 14:39	5971
the *p* said unto Saul, Do what	1Sa 14:40	5971
but the *p* escaped	1Sa 14:41	5971
the *p* said unto Saul, Shall	1Sa 14:45	5971
So the *p* rescued Jonathan, that	1Sa 14:45	5971
anoint thee to be king over his *p*	1Sa 15:1	5971
And Saul gathered the *p* together	1Sa 15:4	5971
utterly destroyed all the *p* with	1Sa 15:8	5971
the *p* spared Agag, and the best of	1Sa 15:9	5971
for the *p* spared the best of the	1Sa 15:15	5971

But the *p* took of the spoil,	1Sa 15:21	5971
because I feared the *p*, and obeyed	1Sa 15:24	5971
thee, before the elders of my *p*	1Sa 15:30	5971
the *p* answered him after this	1Sa 17:27	5971
the *p* answered him again after	1Sa 17:30	5971
in the sight of all the *p*	1Sa 18:5	5971
went out and came in before the *p*	1Sa 18:13	5971
called all the *p* together to war	1Sa 23:8	5971
the *p* pitched round about him	1Sa 26:5	5971
and Abishai came to the *p* by night	1Sa 26:7	5971
the *p* lay round about him	1Sa 26:7	5971
And David cried to the *p*, and to	1Sa 26:14	5971
for there came one of the *p* in to	1Sa 26:15	5971
He hath made his *p* Israel utterly	1Sa 27:12	5971
the *p* that were with him lifted	1Sa 30:4	5971
for the *p* spake of stoning him,	1Sa 30:6	5971
the soul of all the *p* was grieved	1Sa 30:6	5971
to meet the *p* that were with him	1Sa 30:21	5971
and when David came near to the *p*	1Sa 30:21	5971
of their idols, and among the *p*	1Sa 31:9	5971
That the *p* are fled from the	2Sa 1:4	5971
many of the *p* also are fallen and	2Sa 1:4	5971
for the *p* of the LORD, and for the	2Sa 1:12	5971
ere thou bid the *p* return from	2Sa 2:26	5971
the *p* had gone up every one from	2Sa 2:27	5971
all the *p* stood still, and pursued	2Sa 2:28	5971
had gathered all the *p* together	2Sa 2:30	5971
p Israel out of the hand of the	2Sa 3:18	5971
to all the *p* that were with him,	2Sa 3:31	5971
and all the *p* wept	2Sa 3:32	5971
all the *p* wept again over him	2Sa 3:34	5971
when all the *p* came to cause	2Sa 3:35	5971
all the *p* took notice of it, and	2Sa 3:36	5971
the king did pleased all the *p*	2Sa 3:36	5971
For all the *p* and all Israel	2Sa 3:37	5971
thee, Thou shalt feed my *p* Israel	2Sa 5:2	5971
kingdom for his *p* Israel's sake	2Sa 5:12	5971
went with all the *p* that were	2Sa 6:2	5971
he blessed the *p* in the name of	2Sa 6:18	5971
And he dealt among all the *p*	2Sa 6:19	5971
So all the *p* departed every one	2Sa 6:19	5971
me ruler over the *p* of the LORD	2Sa 6:21	5971
I commanded to feed my *p* Israel	2Sa 7:7	5971
the sheep, to be ruler over my *p*	2Sa 7:8	5971
appoint a place for my *p* Israel	2Sa 7:10	5971
judges to be over my *p* Israel	2Sa 7:11	5971
nation in the earth is like thy *p*	2Sa 7:23	5971
went to redeem for a *p* to himself	2Sa 7:23	5971
for thy land, before thy *p*	2Sa 7:23	5971
hast confirmed to thyself thy *p*	2Sa 7:24	5971
to be a *p* unto thee for ever	2Sa 7:24	5971
and justice unto all his *p*	2Sa 8:15	5971
the rest of the *p* he delivered	2Sa 10:10	5971
and let us play the men for our *p*	2Sa 10:12	5971
the *p* that were with him, unto	2Sa 10:13	5971
how Joab did, and how the *p* did	2Sa 11:7	5971
there fell some of the *p* of the	2Sa 11:17	5971
gather the rest of the *p* together	2Sa 12:28	5971
David gathered all the *p* together	2Sa 12:29	5971
forth the *p* that were therein	2Sa 12:31	5971
all the *p* returned unto Jerusalem	2Sa 12:31	5971
there came much *p* by the way of	2Sa 13:34	5971
such a thing against the *p* of God	2Sa 14:13	5971
it is because the *p* have made me	2Sa 14:15	5971
for the *p* increased continually	2Sa 15:12	5971
all the *p* after him, and tarried	2Sa 15:17	5971
voice, and all the *p* passed over	2Sa 15:23	5971
all the *p* passed over, toward the	2Sa 15:23	5971
until all the *p* had done passing	2Sa 15:24	5971
all the *p* that was with him	2Sa 15:30	5971
and all the *p* and all the mighty	2Sa 16:6	5971
all the *p* that were with him,	2Sa 16:14	5971
all the *p* the men of Israel, came	2Sa 16:15	5971
but whom the LORD, and this *p*	2Sa 16:18	5971
all the *p* that are with him shall	2Sa 17:2	5971
bring back all the *p* unto thee	2Sa 17:3	5971
so all the *p* shall be in peace	2Sa 17:3	5971
war, and will not lodge with the *p*	2Sa 17:8	5971
among the *p* that follow Absalom	2Sa 17:9	5971
all the *p* that are with him	2Sa 17:16	5971
all the *p* that were with him, and	2Sa 17:22	5971
for the *p* that were with him, to	2Sa 17:29	5971
The *p* is hungry, and weary, and	2Sa 17:29	5971
numbered the *p* that were with him	2Sa 18:1	5971
of the *p* under the hand of Joab	2Sa 18:2	5971
And the king said unto the *p*	2Sa 18:2	5971
But the *p* answered, Thou shalt	2Sa 18:3	5971
all the *p* came out by hundreds and	2Sa 18:4	5971
all the *p* heard when the king	2Sa 18:5	5971
So the *p* went out into the field	2Sa 18:6	5971
Where the *p* of Israel were slain	2Sa 18:7	5971

P

the wood devoured more *p* that day	2Sa 18:8	5971
the *p* returned from pursuing	2Sa 18:16	5971
for Joab held back the *p*	2Sa 18:16	5971
into mourning unto all the *p*	2Sa 19:2	5971
for the *p* heard say that day how	2Sa 19:2	5971
the *p* gat them by stealth that	2Sa 19:3	5971
as *p* being ashamed steal away	2Sa 19:3	5971
And they told unto all the *p*	2Sa 19:8	5971
all the *p* came before the king	2Sa 19:8	5971
And all the *p* were at strife	2Sa 19:9	5971
all the *p* went over Jordan	2Sa 19:39	5971
all the *p* of Judah conducted the	2Sa 19:40	5971
and also half the *p* of Israel	2Sa 19:40	5971
saw that all the *p* stood still	2Sa 20:12	5971
all the *p* went on after Joab, to	2Sa 20:13	376
all the *p* that were with Joab	2Sa 20:15	5971
went unto all the *p* in her wisdom	2Sa 20:22	5971
the afflicted *p* thou wilt save	2Sa 22:28	5971
me from the strivings of my *p*	2Sa 22:44	5971
a *p* which I knew not shall serve	2Sa 22:44	5971
that bringeth down the *p* under me	2Sa 22:48	5971
the *p* returned after him only to	2Sa 23:10	5971
the *p* fled from the Philistines	2Sa 23:11	5971
to Beer-sheba, and number ye the *p*	2Sa 24:2	5971
I may know the number of the *p*	2Sa 24:2	5971
the LORD thy God add unto the *p*	2Sa 24:3	5971
king, to number the *p* of Israel	2Sa 24:4	5971
the number of the *p* unto the king	2Sa 24:9	5971
after that he had numbered the *p*	2Sa 24:10	5971
there died of the *p* from Dan even	2Sa 24:15	5971
to the angel that destroyed the *p*	2Sa 24:16	5971
he saw the angel that smote the *p*	2Sa 24:17	5971
plague may be stayed from the *p*	2Sa 24:21	5971
and all the *p* said, God save king	1Kin 1:39	5971
all the *p* came up after him, and	1Kin 1:40	5971
the *p* piped with pipes, and	1Kin 1:40	5971
Only the *p* sacrificed in high	1Kin 3:2	5971
of thy *p* which thou hast chosen	1Kin 3:8	5971
which thou hast chosen, a great *p*	1Kin 3:8	5971
heart to judge thy *p*, that I may	1Kin 3:9	5971
to judge this thy so great a *p*	1Kin 3:9	5971
there came of all *p* to hear the	1Kin 4:34	5971
a wise son over this great *p*	1Kin 5:7	5971
which ruled over the *p* that	1Kin 5:16	5971
and will not forsake my *p* Israel	1Kin 6:13	5971
forth my *p* Israel out of Egypt	1Kin 8:16	5971
David to be over my *p* Israel	1Kin 8:16	5971
thy servant, and of thy *p* Israel	1Kin 8:30	5971
When thy *p* Israel be smitten down	1Kin 8:33	5971
forgive the sin of thy *p* Israel	1Kin 8:34	5971
thy servants, and of thy *p* Israel	1Kin 8:36	5971
given to thy *p* for an inheritance	1Kin 8:36	5971
any man, or by all thy *p* Israel	1Kin 8:38	5971
that is not of thy *p* Israel	1Kin 8:41	5971
that all *p* of the earth may know	1Kin 8:43	5971
to fear thee, as do thy *p* Israel	1Kin 8:43	5971
If thy *p* go out to battle against	1Kin 8:44	5971
forgive thy *p* that have sinned	1Kin 8:50	5971
For they be thy *p*, and thine	1Kin 8:51	5971
the supplication of thy *p* Israel	1Kin 8:52	5971
from among all the *p* of the earth	1Kin 8:53	5971
hath given rest unto his *p* Israel	1Kin 8:56	5971
the cause of his *p* Israel at all	1Kin 8:59	5971
That all the *p* of the earth may	1Kin 8:60	5971
the eighth day he sent the *p* away	1Kin 8:66	5971
his servant, and for Israel his *p*	1Kin 8:66	5971
a proverb and a byword among all *p*	1Kin 9:7	5971
all the *p* that were left of the	1Kin 9:20	5971
the *p* that wrought in the work	1Kin 9:23	5971
And the *p* departed	1Kin 12:5	5971
advise that I may answer this *p*	1Kin 12:6	5971
be a servant unto this *p* this day	1Kin 12:7	5971
give ye that we may answer this *p*	1Kin 12:9	5971
unto this *p* that spake unto thee	1Kin 12:10	5971
all the *p* came to Rehoboam the	1Kin 12:12	5971
the king answered the *p* roughly	1Kin 12:13	5971
the king hearkened not unto the *p*	1Kin 12:15	5971
the *p* answered the king, saying,	1Kin 12:16	5971
and to the remnant of the *p*	1Kin 12:23	5971
If this *p* go up to do sacrifice	1Kin 12:27	5971
this *p* turn again unto their lord	1Kin 12:27	5971
for the *p* went to worship before	1Kin 12:30	5971
priests of the lowest of the *p*	1Kin 12:31	5971
the *p* priests of the high places	1Kin 13:33	5971
that I should be king over this *p*	1Kin 14:2	5971
I exalted thee from among the *p*	1Kin 14:7	5971
made thee prince over my *p* Israel	1Kin 14:7	5971
made thee prince over my *p* Israel	1Kin 16:2	5971
hast made my *p* Israel to sin, to	1Kin 16:2	5971
the *p* were encamped against	1Kin 16:15	5971
the *p* that were encamped heard	1Kin 16:16	5971
Then were the *p* of Israel divided	1Kin 16:21	5971
half of the *p* followed Tibni the	1Kin 16:21	5971
But the *p* that followed Omri	1Kin 16:22	5971
Omri prevailed against the *p* that	1Kin 16:22	5971
And Elijah came unto all the *p*	1Kin 18:21	5971
the *p* answered him not a word	1Kin 18:21	5971
Then said Elijah unto the *p*	1Kin 18:22	5971
all the *p* answered and said, It is	1Kin 18:24	5971
And Elijah said unto all the *p*	1Kin 18:30	5971
all the *p* came near unto him	1Kin 18:30	5971
that this *p* may know that thou	1Kin 18:37	5971
And when all the *p* saw it, they	1Kin 18:39	5971
of the oxen, and gave unto the *p*	1Kin 19:21	5971
all the *p* said unto him, Hearken	1Kin 20:8	5971
for all the *p* that follow me	1Kin 20:10	5971
after them he numbered all the *p*	1Kin 20:15	5971
his life, and thy *p* for his *p*	1Kin 20:42	5971
and set Naboth on high among the *p*	1Kin 21:9	5971
and set Naboth on high among the *p*	1Kin 21:12	5971
Naboth, in the presence of the *p*	1Kin 21:13	5971
as thou art, my *p* as thy *p*	1Kin 22:4	5971
And he said, Hearken, O *p*, every	1Kin 22:28	5971
for the *p* offered and burnt	1Kin 22:43	5971
as thou art, my *p* as thy *p*	2Kin 3:7	5971
I dwell among mine own *p*	2Kin 4:13	5971
and he said, Pour out for the *p*	2Kin 4:41	5971
And he said, Give unto the *p*	2Kin 4:42	5971
He said again, Give the *p*	2Kin 4:43	5971
the LORD, and said, Smite this *p*	2Kin 6:18	1471
the *p* looked, and, behold, he had	2Kin 6:30	5971
the *p* went out, and spoiled the	2Kin 7:16	5971
the *p* trode upon him in the gate,	2Kin 7:17	5971
for the *p* trode upon him in the	2Kin 7:20	5971
the *p* fled into their tents	2Kin 8:21	5971
thee king over the *p* of the LORD	2Kin 9:6	5971
and stood, and said to all the *p*	2Kin 10:9	5971
Jehu gathered all the *p* together	2Kin 10:18	5971
noise of the guard and of the *p*	2Kin 11:13	5971
she came to the *p* into the temple	2Kin 11:13	5971
all the *p* of the land rejoiced,	2Kin 11:14	5971
the LORD and the king and the *p*	2Kin 11:17	5971
that they should be the LORD's *p*	2Kin 11:17	5971
between the king also and the *p*	2Kin 11:17	5971
all the *p* of the land went into	2Kin 11:18	5971
guard, and all the *p* of the land	2Kin 11:19	5971
all the *p* of the land rejoiced,	2Kin 11:20	5971
the *p* still sacrificed and burnt	2Kin 12:3	5971
to receive no more money of the *p*	2Kin 12:8	5971
Neither did he leave of the *p* to	2Kin 13:7	5971
as yet the *p* did sacrifice and	2Kin 14:4	5971
all the *p* of Judah took Azariah,	2Kin 14:21	5971
the *p* sacrificed and burnt incense	2Kin 15:4	5971
house, judging the *p* of the land	2Kin 15:5	5971
him, and smote him before the *p*	2Kin 15:10	5971
the *p* sacrificed and burned	2Kin 15:35	5971
carried the *p* of it captive to	2Kin 16:9	5971
offering of all the *p* of the land	2Kin 16:15	5971
of the *p* that are on the wall	2Kin 18:26	5971
But the *p* held their peace, and	2Kin 18:36	5971
tell Hezekiah the captain of my *p*	2Kin 20:5	5971
the *p* of the land slew all them	2Kin 21:24	5971
the *p* of the land made Josiah his	2Kin 21:24	5971
the door have gathered of the *p*	2Kin 22:4	5971
of the LORD for me, and for the *p*	2Kin 22:13	5971
and the prophets, and all the *p*	2Kin 23:2	5971
all the *p* stood to the covenant	2Kin 23:3	5971
graves of the children of the *p*	2Kin 23:6	5971
And the king commanded all the *p*	2Kin 23:21	5971
the *p* of the land took Jehoahaz	2Kin 23:30	5971
and the gold of the *p* of the land	2Kin 23:35	5971
poorest sort of the *p* of the land	2Kin 24:14	5971
no bread for the *p* of the land	2Kin 25:3	5971
Now the rest of the *p* that were	2Kin 25:11	5971
which mustered the *p* of the land	2Kin 25:19	5971
threescore men of the *p* of the	2Kin 25:19	5971
as for the *p* that remained in the	2Kin 25:22	5971
And all the *p*, both small and great	2Kin 25:26	5971
the gods of the *p* of the land	1Chr 5:25	5971
unto their idols, and to the *p*	1Chr 10:9	5971
thee, Thou shalt feed my *p* Israel	1Chr 11:2	5971
shalt be ruler over my *p* Israel	1Chr 11:2	5971
the *p* fled from before the	1Chr 11:13	5971
right in the eyes of all the *p*	1Chr 13:4	5971
on high, because of his *p* Israel	1Chr 14:2	5971
he blessed the *p* in the name of	1Chr 16:2	5971
make known his deeds among the *p*	1Chr 16:8	5971
and from one kingdom to another *p*	1Chr 16:20	5971
all the gods of the *p* are idols	1Chr 16:26	5971
the LORD, ye kindreds of the *p*	1Chr 16:28	5971
And all the *p* said, Amen, and	1Chr 16:36	5971
all the *p* departed every man to	1Chr 16:43	5971

whom I commanded to feed my *p*	1Chr 17:6	5971
be ruler over my *p* Israel	1Chr 17:7	5971
ordain a place for my *p* Israel	1Chr 17:9	5971
judges to be over my *p* Israel	1Chr 17:10	5971
in the earth is like thy *p* Israel	1Chr 17:21	5971
went to redeem to be his own *p*	1Chr 17:21	5971
out nations from before thy *p*	1Chr 17:21	5971
For thy *p* Israel didst thou make	1Chr 17:22	5971
thou make thine own *p* for ever	1Chr 17:22	5971
and justice among all his *p*	1Chr 18:14	5971
and the king of Maachah and his *p*	1Chr 19:7	5971
the rest of the *p* he delivered	1Chr 19:11	5971
ourselves valiantly for our *p*	1Chr 19:13	5971
the *p* that were with him drew	1Chr 19:14	5971
brought out the *p* that were in it	1Chr 20:3	5971
all the *p* returned to Jerusalem	1Chr 20:3	5971
to Joab and to the rulers of the *p*	1Chr 21:2	5971
The LORD make his *p* an hundred	1Chr 21:3	5971
of the number of the *p* unto David	1Chr 21:5	5971
commanded the *p* to be numbered	1Chr 21:17	5971
but not on thy *p*, that they	1Chr 21:17	5971
plague may be stayed from the *p*	1Chr 21:22	5971
before the LORD, and before his *p*	1Chr 22:18	5971
Israel hath given rest unto his *p*	1Chr 23:25	5971
Hear me, my brethren, and my *p*	1Chr 28:2	5971
all the *p* will be wholly at thy	1Chr 28:21	5971
Then the *p* rejoiced, for that	1Chr 29:9	5971
But who am I, and what is my *p*	1Chr 29:14	5971
and now have I seen with joy thy *p*	1Chr 29:17	5971
thoughts of the heart of thy *p*	1Chr 29:18	5971
a *p* like the dust of the earth in	2Chr 1:9	5971
go out and come in before this *p*	2Chr 1:10	5971
for who can judge this thy *p*	2Chr 1:10	5971
that thou mayest judge my *p*	2Chr 1:11	5971
Because the LORD hath loved his *p*	2Chr 2:11	5971
overseers to set the *p* a work	2Chr 2:18	5971
my *p* out of the land of Egypt I	2Chr 6:5	5971
to be a ruler over my *p* Israel	2Chr 6:5	5971
David to be over my *p* Israel	2Chr 6:6	5971
thy servant, and of thy *p* Israel	2Chr 6:21	5971
if thy *p* Israel be put to the	2Chr 6:24	5971
forgive the sin of thy *p* Israel	2Chr 6:25	5971
thy servants, and of thy *p* Israel	2Chr 6:27	5971
unto thy *p* for an inheritance	2Chr 6:27	5971
any man, or of all thy *p* Israel	2Chr 6:29	5971
which is not of thy *p* Israel	2Chr 6:32	5971
that all *p* of the earth may know	2Chr 6:33	5971
fear thee, as doth thy *p* Israel	2Chr 6:33	5971
If thy *p* go out to war against	2Chr 6:34	5971
forgive thy *p* which have sinned	2Chr 6:39	5971
all the *p* offered sacrifices	2Chr 7:4	5971
all the *p* dedicated the house of	2Chr 7:5	5971
sent the *p* away into their tents	2Chr 7:10	5971
and to Solomon, and to Israel his *p*	2Chr 7:10	5971
if I send pestilence among my *p*	2Chr 7:13	5971
If my *p*, which are called by my	2Chr 7:14	5971
As for all the *p* that were left	2Chr 8:7	5971
fifty, that bare rule over the *p*	2Chr 8:10	5971
And the *p* departed	2Chr 10:5	5971
ye me to return answer to this *p*	2Chr 10:6	5971
saying, If thou be kind to this *p*	2Chr 10:7	5971
we may return answer to this *p*	2Chr 10:9	5971
answer the *p* that spake unto thee	2Chr 10:10	5971
all the *p* came to Rehoboam on the	2Chr 10:12	5971
the king hearkened not unto the *p*	2Chr 10:15	5971
the *p* answered the king, saying,	2Chr 10:16	5971
the *p* were without number that	2Chr 12:3	5971
his *p* slew them with a great	2Chr 13:17	5971
the *p* that were with him pursued	2Chr 14:13	5971
some of the *p* the same time	2Chr 16:10	5971
cities of Judah, and taught the *p*	2Chr 17:9	5971
for the *p* that he had with him,	2Chr 18:2	5971
thou art, and my *p* as thy *p*	2Chr 18:3	5971
And he said, Hearken, all ye *p*	2Chr 18:27	5971
the *p* from Beer-sheba to mount	2Chr 19:4	5971
of this land before thy *p* Israel	2Chr 20:7	5971
when he had consulted with the *p*	2Chr 20:21	5971
his *p* came to take away the spoil	2Chr 20:25	5971
for as yet the *p* had not prepared	2Chr 20:33	5971
plague will the LORD smite thy *p*	2Chr 21:14	5971
his *p* made no burning for him,	2Chr 21:19	5971
all the *p* shall be in the courts	2Chr 23:5	5971
but all the *p* shall keep the	2Chr 23:6	5971
And he set all the *p*, every man	2Chr 23:10	5971
heard the noise of the *p* running	2Chr 23:12	5971
she came to the *p* into the house	2Chr 23:12	5971
all the *p* of the land rejoiced,	2Chr 23:13	5971
between him, and between all the *p*	2Chr 23:16	5971
that they should be the LORD's *p*	2Chr 23:16	5971
Then all the *p* went to the house	2Chr 23:17	5971
nobles, and the governors of the *p*	2Chr 23:20	5971

all the *p* of the land, and brought	2Chr 23:20	5971
all the *p* of the land rejoiced	2Chr 23:21	5971
all the *p* rejoiced, and brought in	2Chr 24:10	5971
priest, which stood above the *p*	2Chr 24:20	5971
of the *p* from among the *p*	2Chr 24:23	5971
himself, and led forth his *p*	2Chr 25:11	5971
sought after the gods of the *p*	2Chr 25:15	5971
their own *p* out of thine hand	2Chr 25:15	5971
Then all the *p* of Judah took	2Chr 26:1	5971
house, judging the *p* of the land	2Chr 26:21	5971
And the *p* did yet corruptly	2Chr 27:2	5971
Hezekiah rejoiced, and all the *p*	2Chr 29:36	5971
that God had prepared the *p*	2Chr 29:36	5971
neither had the *p* gathered	2Chr 30:3	5971
assembled at Jerusalem much *p* to	2Chr 30:13	5971
For a multitude of the *p*, even	2Chr 30:18	5971
to Hezekiah, and healed the *p*	2Chr 30:20	5971
Levites arose and blessed the *p*	2Chr 30:27	5971
Moreover he commanded the *p* that	2Chr 31:4	5971
blessed the LORD, and his *p* Israel	2Chr 31:8	5971
Since the *p* began to bring the	2Chr 31:10	
for the LORD hath blessed his *p*	2Chr 31:10	5971
was gathered much *p* together	2Chr 32:4	5971
he set captains of war over the *p*	2Chr 32:6	5971
the *p* rested themselves upon the	2Chr 32:8	5971
unto all the *p* of other lands	2Chr 32:13	5971
deliver his *p* out of mine hand	2Chr 32:14	5971
to deliver his *p* out of mine hand	2Chr 32:15	5971
their *p* out of mine hand, so	2Chr 32:17	5971
deliver his *p* out of mine hand	2Chr 32:17	5971
in the Jews' speech unto the *p* of	2Chr 32:18	5971
the gods of the *p* of the earth	2Chr 32:19	5971
spake to Manasseh, and to his *p*	2Chr 33:10	5971
Nevertheless the *p* did sacrifice	2Chr 33:17	5971
But the *p* of the land slew all	2Chr 33:25	5971
the *p* of the land made Josiah his	2Chr 33:25	5971
and the Levites, and all the *p*	2Chr 34:30	5971
LORD your God, and his *p* Israel,	2Chr 35:3	5971
fathers of your brethren the *p*	2Chr 35:5	
And Josiah gave to the *p*, of the	2Chr 35:7	
princes gave willingly unto the *p*	2Chr 35:8	5971
of the families of the *p*, to	2Chr 35:12	
them speedily among all the *p*	2Chr 35:13	
Then the *p* of the land took	2Chr 36:1	5971
chief of the priests, and the *p*	2Chr 36:14	5971
he had compassion on his *p*	2Chr 36:15	5971
of the LORD arose against his *p*	2Chr 36:16	5971
is there among you of all his *p*	2Chr 36:23	5971
of the men of the *p* of Israel	Ezr 1:3	5971
and the Levites, and some of the *p*	Ezr 2:2	5971
the *p* gathered themselves	Ezr 2:70	5971
of the *p* of those countries	Ezr 3:1	5971
all the *p* shouted with a great	Ezr 3:3	5971
So that the *p* could not discern	Ezr 3:11	5971
the noise of the weeping of the *p*	Ezr 3:13	5971
for the *p* shouted with a loud	Ezr 3:13	5971
Then the *p* of the land weakened	Ezr 3:13	5971
the hands of the *p* of Judah	Ezr 4:4	5971
carried the *p* away into Babylon	Ezr 4:4	5971
there destroy all kings and *p*	Ezr 5:12	5972
that all they of the *p* of Israel	Ezr 6:12	5972
the freewill offering of the *p*	Ezr 7:13	5972
which may judge all the *p* that	Ezr 7:16	5972
and I viewed the *p*, and the priests	Ezr 7:25	5972
and they furthered the *p*, and the	Ezr 8:15	5971
The *p* of Israel, and the priests,	Ezr 8:36	5971
from the *p* of those lands, doing	Ezr 9:1	5971
with the *p* of those lands	Ezr 9:1	5971
filthiness of the *p* of the lands,	Ezr 9:2	5971
with the *p* of these abominations	Ezr 9:11	5971
for the *p* wept very sore	Ezr 9:14	5971
wives of the *p* of the land	Ezr 10:1	5971
all the *p* sat in the street of	Ezr 10:2	5971
yourselves from the *p* of the land	Ezr 10:9	5971
But the *p* are many, and it is a	Ezr 10:11	5971
these are thy servants and thy *p*	Ezr 10:13	5971
for the *p* had a mind to work	Neh 1:10	5971
I even set the *p* after their	Neh 4:6	5971
rulers, and to the rest of the *p*	Neh 4:13	5971
rulers, and to the rest of the *p*	Neh 4:14	5971
the same time said I unto the *p*	Neh 4:19	5971
And there was a great cry of the *p*	Neh 4:22	5971
the *p* did according to this	Neh 5:1	5971
me were chargeable unto the *p*	Neh 5:13	5971
servants bare rule over the *p*	Neh 5:15	5971
the bondage was heavy upon this *p*	Neh 5:15	5971
all that I have done for this *p*	Neh 5:18	5971
but the *p* were few therein, and	Neh 5:19	5971
nobles, and the rulers, and the *p*	Neh 7:4	5971
of the men of the *p* of Israel was	Neh 7:5	5971
	Neh 7:7	5971

P

that which the rest of the p gave	Neh 7:72	5971
and the singers, and some of the p	Neh 7:73	5971
all the p gathered themselves	Neh 8:1	5971
the ears of all the p were	Neh 8:3	5971
the book in the sight of all p	Neh 8:5	5971
(for he was above all the p	Neh 8:5	5971
he opened it, all the p stood up	Neh 8:5	5971
all the p answered, Amen, Amen,	Neh 8:6	5971
caused the p to understand the	Neh 8:7	5971
the p stood in their place	Neh 8:7	5971
and the Levites that taught the p	Neh 8:9	5971
said unto all the p	Neh 8:9	5971
For all the p wept, when they	Neh 8:9	5971
So the Levites stilled all the p	Neh 8:11	5971
all the p went their way to eat,	Neh 8:12	5971
chief of the fathers of all the p	Neh 8:13	5971
So the p went forth, and brought	Neh 8:16	5971
and on all the p of his land	Neh 9:10	5971
the p of the land, that they	Neh 9:24	5971
the hand of the p of the lands	Neh 9:30	5971
on our fathers, and on all thy p	Neh 9:32	5971
The chief of the p	Neh 10:14	5971
And the rest of the p, the priests	Neh 10:28	5971
p of the lands unto the law of	Neh 10:28	5971
daughters unto the p of the land	Neh 10:30	5971
if the p of the land bring ware	Neh 10:31	5971
priests, the Levites, and the p	Neh 10:34	5971
the rulers of the p dwelt at	Neh 11:1	5971
the rest of the p also cast lots	Neh 11:1	5971
the p blessed all the men, that	Neh 11:2	5971
in all matters concerning the p	Neh 11:24	5971
themselves, and purified the p	Neh 12:30	5971
the half of the p upon the wall	Neh 12:38	5971
of Moses in the audience of the p	Neh 13:1	5971
to the language of each p	Neh 13:24	5971
p that were present in Shushan	Est 1:5	5971
the crown royal, to shew the p	Est 1:11	5971
to all the p that are in all the	Est 1:16	5971
to every p after their language,	Est 1:22	5971
to the language of every p	Est 1:22	5971
not shewed her p nor her kindred	Est 2:10	5971
yet shewed her kindred nor her p	Est 2:20	5971
had shewed him the p of Mordecai	Est 3:6	5971
Ahasuerus, even the p of Mordecai	Est 3:6	5971
is a certain p scattered abroad	Est 3:8	5971
dispersed among the p in all the	Est 3:8	5971
their laws are diverse from all p	Est 3:8	5971
the p also, to do with them as it	Est 3:11	5971
to the rulers of every p of every	Est 3:12	5971
to every p after their language	Est 3:12	5971
province was published unto all p	Est 3:14	5971
make request before him for her p	Est 4:8	5971
the p of the king's provinces, do	Est 4:11	5971
petition, and my p at my request	Est 7:3	5971
For we are sold, I and my p	Est 7:4	5971
evil that shall come unto my p	Est 8:6	5971
unto every p after their language	Est 8:9	5971
to perish, all the power of the p	Est 8:11	5971
province was published unto all p	Est 8:13	5971
many of the p of the land became	Est 8:17	5971
the fear of them fell upon all p	Est 9:2	5971
seeking the wealth of his p	Est 10:3	5971
No doubt but ye are the p	Job 12:2	5971
the chief of the p of the earth	Job 12:24	5971
made me also a byword of the p	Job 17:6	5971
have son nor nephew among his p	Job 18:19	5971
the p shall be troubled at	Job 34:20	5971
reign not, lest the p be ensnared	Job 34:30	5971
when p are cut off in their place	Job 36:20	5971
For by them judgeth he the p	Job 36:31	5971
the p imagine a vain thing	Ps 2:1	3816
be afraid of ten thousands of p	Ps 3:6	5971
thy blessing is upon thy p	Ps 3:8	5971
of the p compass thee about	Ps 7:7	3816
The LORD shall judge the p	Ps 7:8	5971
judgment to the p in uprightness	Ps 9:8	3816
declare among the p his doings	Ps 9:11	5971
who eat up my p as they eat bread	Ps 14:4	5971
back the captivity of his p	Ps 14:7	5971
thou wilt save the afflicted p	Ps 18:27	5971
me from the strivings of the p	Ps 18:43	5971
a p whom I have not known shall	Ps 18:43	5971
me, and subdueth the p under me	Ps 18:47	5971
of men, and despised of the p	Ps 22:6	5971
unto a p that shall be born	Ps 22:31	5971
Save thy p, and bless thine	Ps 28:9	5971
will give strength unto his p	Ps 29:11	5971
LORD will bless his p with peace	Ps 29:11	5971
devices of the p of none effect	Ps 33:10	5971
the p whom he hath chosen for his	Ps 33:12	5971
I will praise thee among much p	Ps 35:18	5971

how thou didst afflict the p	Ps 44:2	3816
Thou sellest thy p for nought	Ps 44:12	5971
a shaking of the head among the p	Ps 44:14	3816
whereby the p fall under thee	Ps 45:5	5971
forget also thine own p, and thy	Ps 45:10	5971
even the rich among the p shall	Ps 45:12	5971
therefore shall the p praise thee	Ps 45:17	5971
O clap your hands, all ye p	Ps 47:1	5971
He shall subdue the p under us	Ps 47:3	5971
The princes of the p are gathered	Ps 47:9	5971
even the p of the God of Abraham	Ps 47:9	5971
Hear this, all ye p	Ps 49:1	5971
earth, that he may judge his p	Ps 50:4	5971
Hear, O my p, and I will speak	Ps 50:7	5971
who eat up my p as they eat bread	Ps 53:4	5971
back the captivity of his p	Ps 53:6	5971
in thine anger cast down the p	Ps 56:7	5971
praise thee, O Lord, among the p	Ps 57:9	5971
Slay them not, lest my p forget	Ps 59:11	5971
hast shewed thy p hard things	Ps 60:3	5971
ye p, pour out your heart before	Ps 62:8	5971
waves, and the tumult of the p	Ps 65:7	3816
O bless our God, ye p, and make	Ps 66:8	5971
Let the p praise thee, O God	Ps 67:3	5971
let all the p praise thee	Ps 67:3	5971
shalt judge the p righteously	Ps 67:4	5971
Let the p praise thee, O God	Ps 67:5	5971
let all the p praise thee	Ps 67:5	5971
thou wentest forth before thy p	Ps 68:7	5971
I will bring my p again from the	Ps 68:22	
bulls, with the calves of the p	Ps 68:30	5971
scatter thou the p that delight	Ps 68:30	5971
strength and power unto his p	Ps 68:35	5971
judge thy p with righteousness	Ps 72:2	5971
shall bring peace to the p	Ps 72:3	5971
He shall judge the poor of the p	Ps 72:4	5971
Therefore his p return hither	Ps 73:10	5971
the p inhabiting the wilderness	Ps 74:14	5971
LORD, and that the foolish p have	Ps 74:18	5971
declared thy strength among the p	Ps 77:14	5971
with thine arm redeemed thy p	Ps 77:15	5971
Thou leddest thy p like a flock	Ps 77:20	5971
Give ear, O my p, to my law	Ps 78:1	5971
can he provide flesh for his p	Ps 78:20	5971
But made his own p to go forth	Ps 78:52	5971
He gave his p over also unto the	Ps 78:62	5971
brought him to feed Jacob his p	Ps 78:71	5971
So we thy p and sheep of thy	Ps 79:13	5971
angry against the prayer of thy p	Ps 80:4	5971
Hear, O my p, and I will testify	Ps 81:8	5971
But my p would not hearken to my	Ps 81:11	5971
Oh that my p had hearkened unto	Ps 81:13	5971
crafty counsel against thy p	Ps 83:3	5971
forgiven the iniquity of thy p	Ps 85:2	5971
that thy p may rejoice in thee	Ps 85:6	5971
he will speak peace unto his p	Ps 85:8	5971
count, when he writeth up the p	Ps 87:6	5971
Blessed is the p that know the	Ps 89:15	5971
exalted one chosen out of the p	Ps 89:19	5971
the reproach of all the mighty p	Ps 89:50	5971
They break in pieces thy p	Ps 94:5	5971
ye brutish among the p	Ps 94:8	5971
the LORD will not cast off his p	Ps 94:14	5971
we are the p of his pasture, and	Ps 95:7	5971
It is a p that do err in their	Ps 95:10	5971
heathen, his wonders among all p	Ps 96:3	5971
the LORD, O ye kindreds of the p	Ps 96:7	5971
he shall judge the p righteously	Ps 96:10	5971
and the p with his truth	Ps 96:13	5971
and all the p see his glory	Ps 97:6	5971
the world, and the p with equity	Ps 98:9	5971
let the p tremble	Ps 99:1	5971
and he is high above all the p	Ps 99:2	5971
we are his p, and the sheep of his	Ps 100:3	5971
the p which shall be created	Ps 102:18	5971
When the p are gathered together,	Ps 102:22	5971
make known his deeds among the p	Ps 105:1	5971
from one kingdom to another p	Ps 105:13	5971
even the ruler of the p, and let	Ps 105:20	5971
And he increased his p greatly	Ps 105:24	5971
turned their heart to hate his p	Ps 105:25	5971
The p asked, and he brought quails	Ps 105:40	
he brought forth his p with joy	Ps 105:43	5971
inherited the labour of the p	Ps 105:44	3816
that thou bearest unto thy p	Ps 106:4	5971
of the LORD kindled against his p	Ps 106:40	5971
and let all the p say, Amen	Ps 106:48	5971
also in the congregation of the p	Ps 107:32	5971
praise thee, O LORD, among the p	Ps 108:3	5971
Thy p shall be willing in the day	Ps 110:3	5971
He hath shewed his p the power of	Ps 111:6	5971

He sent redemption unto his *p*	Ps 111:9	5971
even with the princes of his *p*	Ps 113:8	5971
from a *p* of strange language	Ps 114:1	5971
now in the presence of all his *p*	Ps 116:14	5971
now in the presence of all his *p*	Ps 116:18	5971
praise him, all ye *p*	Ps 117:1	528
p from henceforth even for ever	Ps 125:2	5971
an heritage unto Israel his *p*	Ps 135:12	5971
For the LORD will judge his *p*	Ps 135:14	5971
To him which led his *p* through	Ps 136:16	5971
who subdueth my *p* under me	Ps 144:2	5971
Happy is that *p*, that is in such	Ps 144:15	5971
yea, happy is that *p*, whose God	Ps 144:15	5971
Kings of the earth, and all *p*	Ps 148:11	3816
also exalteth the horn of his *p*	Ps 148:14	5971
of Israel, a *p* near unto him	Ps 148:14	5971
the LORD taketh pleasure in his *p*	Ps 149:4	5971
and punishments upon the *p*	Ps 149:7	3816
Where no counsel is, the *p* fall	Prov 11:14	5971
corn, the *p* shall curse him	Prov 11:26	3816
In the multitude of *p* is the	Prov 14:28	5971
but in the want of *p* is the	Prov 14:28	3816
but sin is a reproach to any *p*	Prov 14:34	3816
him shall the *p* curse, nations	Prov 24:24	5971
is a wicked ruler over the poor *p*	Prov 28:15	5971
are in authority, the *p* rejoice	Prov 29:2	5971
wicked beareth rule, the *p* mourn	Prov 29:2	5971
there is no vision, the *p* perish	Prov 29:18	5971
The ants are a *p* not strong	Prov 30:25	5971
There is no end of all the *p*	Eccl 4:16	5971
he still taught the *p* knowledge	Eccl 12:9	5971
not know, my *p* doth not consider	Is 1:3	5971
a *p* laden with iniquity, a seed	Is 1:4	5971
law of our God, ye *p* of Gomorrah	Is 1:10	5971
many *p* shall go and say, Come ye,	Is 2:3	5971
nations, and shall rebuke many *p*	Is 2:4	5971
forsaken thy *p* the house of Jacob	Is 2:6	5971
the *p* shall be oppressed, every	Is 3:5	5971
make me not a ruler of the *p*	Is 3:7	5971
As for my *p*, children are their	Is 3:12	5971
O my *p*, they which lead thee	Is 3:12	5971
plead, and standeth to judge the *p*	Is 3:13	5971
with the ancients of his *p*	Is 3:14	5971
ye that ye beat my *p* to pieces	Is 3:15	5971
Therefore my *p* are gone into	Is 5:13	5971
of the LORD kindled against his *p*	Is 5:25	5971
the midst of a *p* of unclean lips	Is 6:5	5971
And he said, Go, and tell this *p*	Is 6:9	5971
Make the heart of this *p* fat	Is 6:10	5971
was moved, and the heart of his *p*	Is 7:2	5971
be broken, that it be not a *p*	Is 7:8	5971
bring upon thee, and upon thy *p*	Is 7:17	5971
Forasmuch as this *p* refuseth the	Is 8:6	5971
Associate yourselves, O ye *p*	Is 8:9	5971
not walk in the way of this *p*	Is 8:11	5971
all them to whom this *p* shall say	Is 8:12	5971
should not a *p* seek unto their	Is 8:19	5971
The *p* that walked in darkness	Is 9:2	5971
all the *p* shall know, even	Is 9:9	5971
For the *p* turneth not unto him	Is 9:13	5971
of this *p* cause them to err	Is 9:16	5971
the *p* shall be as the fuel of the	Is 9:19	5971
the right from the poor of my *p*	Is 10:2	5971
against the *p* of my wrath will I	Is 10:6	5971
have removed the bounds of the *p*	Is 10:13	5971
as a nest the riches of the *p*	Is 10:14	5971
For though thy *p* Israel be as the	Is 10:22	5971
O my *p* that dwellest in Zion, be	Is 10:24	5971
stand for an ensign of the *p*	Is 11:10	5971
to recover the remnant of his *p*	Is 11:11	5971
highway for the remnant of his *p*	Is 11:16	5971
declare his doings among the *p*	Is 12:4	5971
mountains, like as of a great *p*	Is 13:4	5971
shall every man turn to his own *p*	Is 13:14	5971
the *p* shall take them, and bring	Is 14:2	5971
He who smote the *p* in wrath with	Is 14:6	5971
thy land, and slain thy *p*	Is 14:20	5971
the poor of his *p* shall trust in	Is 14:32	5971
Woe to the multitude of many *p*	Is 17:12	5971
to a *p* terrible from their	Is 18:2	5971
LORD of hosts of a *p* scattered	Is 18:7	5971
from a *p* terrible from their	Is 18:7	5971
saying, Blessed be Egypt my *p*	Is 19:25	5971
spoiling of the daughter of my *p*	Is 22:4	5971
this *p* was not, til the Assyrian	Is 23:13	5971
And it shall be, as with the *p*	Is 24:2	5971
the haughty *p* of the earth do	Is 24:4	5971
the midst of the land among the *p*	Is 24:13	5971
shall the strong *p* glorify thee	Is 25:3	5971
unto all *p* a feast of fat things	Is 25:6	5971
of the covering cast over all *p*	Is 25:7	5971
the rebuke of his *p* shall he take	Is 25:8	5971
ashamed for their envy at the *p*	Is 26:11	5971
Come, my *p*, enter thou into thy	Is 26:20	5971
for it is a *p* of no understanding	Is 27:11	5971
beauty, unto the residue of his *p*	Is 28:5	5971
tongue will he speak to this *p*	Is 28:11	5971
that rule this *p* which is in	Is 28:14	5971
Forasmuch as this *p* draw near me	Is 29:13	5971
do a marvellous work among this *p*	Is 29:14	5971
of a *p* that could not profit them	Is 30:5	5971
to a *p* that shall not profit them	Is 30:6	5971
That this is a rebellious *p*	Is 30:9	5971
For the *p* shall dwell in Zion at	Is 30:19	5971
bindeth up the breach of his *p*	Is 30:26	5971
be a bridle in the jaws of the *p*	Is 30:28	5971
Upon the land of my *p* shall come	Is 32:13	5971
my *p* shall dwell in a peaceable	Is 32:18	5971
noise of the tumult the *p* fled	Is 33:3	5971
the *p* shall be as the burnings of	Is 33:12	5971
Thou shalt not see a fierce *p*	Is 33:19	5971
a *p* of a deeper speech than thou	Is 33:19	5971
the *p* that dwell therein shall be	Is 33:24	5971
and hearken, ye *p*	Is 34:1	3816
upon the *p* of my curse, to	Is 34:5	5971
in the ears of the *p* that are on	Is 36:11	5971
Comfort ye, comfort ye my *p*	Is 40:1	5971
surely the *p* is grass	Is 40:7	5971
let the *p* renew their strength	Is 41:1	3816
giveth breath unto the *p* upon it	Is 42:5	5971
give thee for a covenant of the *p*	Is 42:6	5971
But this is a *p* robbed and spoiled	Is 42:22	5971
men for thee, and *p* for thy life	Is 43:4	3816
forth the blind that have eyes	Is 43:8	5971
and let the *p* be assembed	Is 43:9	3816
the desert, to give drink to my *p*	Is 43:20	5971
This *p* have I formed for myself	Is 43:21	5971
since I appointed the ancient *p*	Is 44:7	5971
I was wroth with my *p*, I have	Is 47:6	5971
and hearken, ye *p*, from far	Is 49:1	3816
give thee for a covenant of the *p*	Is 49:8	5971
for the LORD hath comforted his *p*	Is 49:13	5971
and set up my standard to the *p*	Is 49:22	5971
Hearken unto me, my *p*	Is 51:4	5971
to rest for a light of the *p*	Is 51:4	5971
and mine arms shall judge the *p*	Is 51:5	5971
the *p* in whose heart is my law	Is 51:7	5971
and say unto Zion, Thou art my *p*	Is 51:16	5971
that pleadeth the cause of his *p*	Is 51:22	5971
My *p* went down aforetime into	Is 52:4	5971
that my *p* is taken away for	Is 52:5	5971
Therefore my *p* shall know my name	Is 52:6	5971
for the LORD hath comforted his *p*	Is 52:9	5971
of my *p* was he stricken	Is 53:8	5971
given him for a witness to the *p*	Is 55:4	3816
a leader and commander to the *p*	Is 55:4	3816
utterly separated me from his *p*	Is 56:3	5971
an house of prayer for all *p*	Is 56:7	5971
out of the way of my *p*	Is 57:14	5971
shew my *p* their transgression, and	Is 58:1	5971
earth, and gross darkness the *p*	Is 60:2	3816
Thy *p* also shall be all righteous	Is 60:21	5971
and their offspring among the *p*	Is 61:9	5971
prepare ye the way of the *p*	Is 62:10	5971
lift up a standard for the *p*	Is 62:10	5971
they shall call them, The holy *p*	Is 62:12	5971
of the *p* there was none with me	Is 63:3	5971
tread down the *p* in mine anger	Is 63:6	5971
For he said, Surely they are my *p*	Is 63:8	5971
the days of old, Moses, and his *p*	Is 63:11	5971
so didst thou lead thy *p*, to make	Is 63:14	5971
The *p* of thy holiness have	Is 63:18	5971
we beseech thee, we are all thy *p*	Is 64:9	5971
all the day unto a rebellious *p*	Is 65:2	5971
A *p* that provoketh me to anger	Is 65:3	5971
for my *p* that have sought me	Is 65:10	5971
a rejoicing, and her *p* a joy	Is 65:18	5971
in Jerusalem, and joy in my *p*	Is 65:19	5971
of a tree are the days of my *p*	Is 65:22	5971
and against the *p* of the land	Jer 1:18	5971
but my *p* have changed their glory	Jer 2:11	5971
For my *p* have committed two evils	Jer 2:13	5971
wherefore say my *p*, We are lords	Jer 2:31	5971
yet my *p* have forgotten me days	Jer 2:32	5971
thou hast greatly deceived this *p*	Jer 4:10	5971
time shall it be said to this *p*	Jer 4:11	5971
toward the daughter of my *p*	Jer 4:11	5971
For my *p* is foolish, they have	Jer 4:22	5971
in thy mouth fire, and this *p* wood	Jer 5:14	5971
Hear now this, O foolish *p*	Jer 5:21	5971
But this *p* hath a revolting and a	Jer 5:23	5971
For among my *p* are found wicked	Jer 5:26	5971

P

and my *p* love to have it so	Jer 5:31	5971
of the daughter of my *p* slightly	Jer 6:14	5971
I will bring evil upon this *p*	Jer 6:19	5971
lay stumblingblocks before this *p*	Jer 6:21	5971
a *p* cometh from the north country	Jer 6:22	5971
O daughter of my *p*, gird thee	Jer 6:26	5971
a tower and a fortress among my *p*	Jer 6:27	5971
for the wickedness of my *p* Israel	Jer 7:12	5971
pray not thou for this *p*, neither	Jer 7:16	5971
be your God, and ye shall be my *p*	Jer 7:23	5971
the carcases of this *p* shall be	Jer 7:33	5971
Why then is this *p* of Jerusalem	Jer 8:5	5971
but my *p* know not the judgment of	Jer 8:7	5971
of the daughter of my *p* slightly	Jer 8:11	5971
the cry of the daughter of my *p*	Jer 8:19	5971
of the daughter of my *p* am I hurt	Jer 8:21	5971
of the daughter of my *p* recovered	Jer 8:22	5971
the slain of the daughter of my *p*	Jer 9:1	5971
that I might leave my *p*, and go	Jer 9:2	5971
I do for the daughter of my *p*	Jer 9:7	5971
I will feed them, even this *p*	Jer 9:15	5971
For the customs of the *p* are vain	Jer 10:3	5971
so shall ye be my *p*, and I will	Jer 11:4	5971
pray not thou for this *p*, neither	Jer 11:14	5971
caused my *p* Israel to inherit	Jer 12:14	5971
diligently learn the ways of my *p*	Jer 12:16	5971
they taught my *p* to swear by Baal	Jer 12:16	5971
be built in the midst of my *p*	Jer 12:16	5971
This evil *p*, which refuse to hear	Jer 13:10	5971
they might be unto me for a *p*	Jer 13:11	5971
Thus saith the LORD unto this *p*	Jer 14:10	5971
not for this *p* for their good	Jer 14:11	5971
the *p* to whom they prophesy shall	Jer 14:16	5971
p is broken with a great breach	Jer 14:17	5971
mind could not be toward this *p*	Jer 15:1	5971
of children, I will destroy my *p*	Jer 15:7	5971
unto this *p* a fenced brasen wall	Jer 15:20	5971
taken away my peace from this *p*	Jer 16:5	5971
shalt shew this *p* all these words	Jer 16:10	5971
the gate of the children of the *p*	Jer 17:19	5971
Because my *p* hath forgotten me,	Jer 18:15	5971
and take of the ancients of the *p*	Jer 19:1	5971
Even so will I break this *p*	Jer 19:11	5971
and said to all the *p*,	Jer 19:14	5971
Judah, and his servants, and the *p*	Jer 21:7	5971
unto this *p* thou shalt say, Thus	Jer 21:8	5971
thy *p* that enter in by these	Jer 22:2	5971
he, and his servants, and his *p*	Jer 22:4	5971
the pastors that feed my *p*	Jer 23:2	5971
caused my *p* Israel to err	Jer 23:13	5971
had caused my *p* to hear my words,	Jer 23:22	5971
Which think to cause my *p* to	Jer 23:27	5971
cause my *p* to err by their lies,	Jer 23:32	5971
shall not profit this *p* at all	Jer 23:32	5971
And when this *p*, or the prophet,	Jer 23:33	5971
prophet, and the priest, and the *p*	Jer 23:34	5971
and they shall be my *p*, and I will	Jer 24:7	5971
p of Judah in the fourth year of	Jer 25:1	5971
spake unto all the *p* of Judah	Jer 25:2	5971
and his princes, and all his *p*	Jer 25:19	5971
And all the mingled *p*, and all the	Jer 25:20	5971
p that dwell in the desert	Jer 25:24	5971
all the *p* heard Jeremiah speaking	Jer 26:7	5971
him to speak unto all the *p*	Jer 26:8	5971
all the *p* took him, saying, Thou	Jer 26:8	5971
all the *p* were gathered against	Jer 26:9	5971
unto the princes and to all the *p*	Jer 26:11	5971
all the princes and to all the *p*	Jer 26:12	5971
all the *p* unto the priests and to	Jer 26:16	5971
to all the assembly of the *p*	Jer 26:17	5971
and spake to all the *p* of Judah	Jer 26:18	5971
into the graves of the common *p*	Jer 26:23	5971
hand of the *p* to put him to death	Jer 26:24	5971
of Babylon, and serve him and his *p*	Jer 27:12	5971
Why will ye die, thou and thy *p*	Jer 27:13	5971
to the priests and to all this *p*	Jer 27:16	5971
of the priests and of all the *p*	Jer 28:1	5971
in the presence of all the *p* that	Jer 28:5	5971
ears, and in the ears of all the *p*	Jer 28:7	5971
in the presence of all the *p*	Jer 28:11	5971
makest this *p* to trust in a lie	Jer 28:15	5971
to all the *p* whom Nebuchadnezzar	Jer 29:1	5971
of all the *p* that dwelleth in	Jer 29:16	5971
all the *p* that are at Jerusalem	Jer 29:25	5971
have a man to dwell among this *p*	Jer 29:32	5971
the good that I will do for my *p*	Jer 29:32	5971
the captivity of my *p* Israel	Jer 30:3	5971
And ye shall be my *p*, and I will be	Jer 30:22	5971
of Israel, and they shall be my *p*	Jer 31:1	5971
The *p* which were left of the	Jer 31:2	5971
ye, and say, O LORD, save thy *p*	Jer 31:7	5971

my *p* shall be satisfied with my	Jer 31:14	5971
their God, and they shall be my *p*	Jer 31:33	5971
hast brought forth thy *p* Israel	Jer 32:21	5971
And they shall be my *p*, and I will	Jer 32:38	5971
all this great evil upon this *p*	Jer 32:42	5971
thou not what this *p* have spoken	Jer 33:24	5971
thus they have despised my *p*	Jer 33:24	5971
of his dominion, and all the *p*	Jer 34:1	5971
all the *p* which were at Jerusalem	Jer 34:8	5971
all the princes, and all the *p*	Jer 34:10	5971
all the *p* of the land, which	Jer 34:19	5971
but this *p* hath not hearkened	Jer 35:16	5971
p in the LORD's house upon the	Jer 36:6	5971
hath pronounced against this *p*	Jer 36:7	5971
LORD to all the *p* in Jerusalem	Jer 36:9	5971
to all the *p* that came from the	Jer 36:9	5971
house, in the ears of all the *p*	Jer 36:10	5971
the book in the ears of the *p*	Jer 36:13	5971
hast read in the ears of the *p*	Jer 36:14	5971
nor the *p* of the land, did	Jer 37:2	5971
came in and went out among the *p*	Jer 37:4	5971
thence in the midst of the *p*	Jer 37:12	5971
thy servants, or against this *p*	Jer 37:18	5971
had spoken unto all the *p*	Jer 38:1	5971
city, and the hands of all the *p*	Jer 38:4	5971
seeketh not the welfare of this *p*	Jer 38:4	5971
house, and the houses of the *p*	Jer 39:8	5971
the *p* that remained in the city	Jer 39:9	5971
the rest of the *p* that remained	Jer 39:9	5971
guard left of the poor of the *p*	Jer 39:10	5971
so he dwelt among the *p*	Jer 39:14	5971
and dwell with him among the *p*	Jer 40:5	5971
dwelt with him among the *p* that	Jer 40:6	5971
of the *p* that were in Mizpah	Jer 41:10	5971
all the *p* that remained in Mizpah	Jer 41:10	5971
that when all the *p* which were	Jer 41:13	5971
So all the *p* that Ishmael had	Jer 41:14	5971
all the remnant of the *p* whom he	Jer 41:16	5971
all the *p* from the least even	Jer 42:1	5971
all the *p* from the least even to	Jer 42:8	5971
p all the words of the LORD their	Jer 43:1	5971
of the forces, and all the *p*	Jer 43:4	5971
even all the *p* that dwelt in the	Jer 44:15	5971
Then Jeremiah said unto all the *p*	Jer 44:20	5971
to all the *p* which had given him	Jer 44:20	5971
the *p* of the land, did not the	Jer 44:21	5971
Jeremiah said unto all the *p*	Jer 44:24	5971
and let us go again to our own *p*	Jer 46:16	5971
the hand of the *p* of the north	Jer 46:24	5971
shall be destroyed from being a *p*	Jer 48:42	5971
the *p* of Chemosh perisheth	Jer 48:46	5971
his *p* dwell in his cities	Jer 49:1	5971
My *p* hath been lost sheep	Jer 50:6	5971
shall turn every one to his *p*	Jer 50:16	5971
upon all the mingled *p* that are	Jer 50:37	5971
a *p* shall come from the north, and	Jer 50:41	5971
My *p*, go ye out of the midst of	Jer 51:45	5971
the *p* shall labour in vain, and	Jer 51:58	5971
no bread for the *p* of the land	Jer 52:6	5971
certain of the poor of the *p*	Jer 52:15	5971
the residue of the *p* that	Jer 52:15	5971
who mustered the *p* of the land	Jer 52:25	5971
men of the *p* of the land, that	Jer 52:25	5971
This is the *p* whom Nebuchadrezzar	Jer 52:28	5971
sit solitary, that was full of *p*	Lam 1:1	5971
when her *p* fell into the hand of	Lam 1:7	5971
All her *p* sigh, they seek bread	Lam 1:11	5971
hear, I pray you, all *p*, and	Lam 1:18	5971
of the daughter of my *p*	Lam 2:11	5971
I was a derision to all my *p*	Lam 3:14	5971
and refuse in the midst of the *p*	Lam 3:45	5971
of the daughter of my *p*	Lam 3:48	5971
daughter of my *p* is become cruel	Lam 4:3	5971
p is greater than the punishment	Lam 4:6	5971
of the daughter of my *p*	Lam 4:10	5971
sent to a *p* of a strange speech	Eze 3:5	5971
Not to many *p* of a strange speech	Eze 3:6	5971
unto the children of thy *p*	Eze 3:11	5971
the hands of the *p* of the land	Eze 7:27	5971
son of Benaiah, princes of the *p*	Eze 11:1	5971
I will even gather you from the *p*	Eze 11:17	5971
and they shall be my *p*, and I will	Eze 11:20	5971
And say unto the *p* of the land	Eze 12:19	5971
not be in the assembly of my *p*	Eze 13:9	5971
because they have seduced my *p*	Eze 13:10	5971
against the daughters of thy *p*	Eze 13:17	5971
Will ye hunt the souls of my *p*	Eze 13:18	5971
among my *p* for handfuls of barley	Eze 13:19	5971
lying to my *p* that hear your lies	Eze 13:19	5971
deliver my *p* out of your hand, and	Eze 13:21	5971
deliver my *p* out of your hand	Eze 13:23	5971

him off from the midst of my *p*	Eze 14:8	5971
him from the midst of my *p* Israel	Eze 14:9	5971
but that they may be my *p*	Eze 14:11	5971
p to pluck it up by the roots	Eze 17:9	5971
might give him horses and much *p*	Eze 17:15	5971
which is not good among his *p*	Eze 18:18	5971
I will bring you out from the *p*	Eze 20:34	5971
you into the wilderness of the *p*	Eze 20:35	5971
when I bring you out from the *p*	Eze 20:41	5971
for it shall be upon my *p*	Eze 21:12	5971
of the sword shall be upon my *p*	Eze 21:12	5971
The *p* of the land have used	Eze 22:29	5971
wheels, and with an assembly of *p*	Eze 23:24	5971
I spake unto the *p* in the morning	Eze 24:18	5971
the *p* said unto me, Wilt thou not	Eze 24:19	5971
and I will cut thee off from the *p*	Eze 25:7	5971
Edom by the hand of my *p* Israel	Eze 25:14	5971
that was the gates of the *p*	Eze 26:2	5971
horsemen, and companies, and much *p*	Eze 26:7	5971
he shall slay thy *p* by the sword	Eze 26:11	5971
with the *p* of old time, and shall	Eze 26:20	5971
merchant of the *p* for many isles	Eze 27:3	5971
of the seas, thou filledst many *p*	Eze 27:33	5971
among the *p* shall hiss at thee	Eze 27:36	5971
the *p* shall be astonished at thee	Eze 28:19	5971
the house of Israel from the *p*	Eze 28:25	5971
the *p* whither they were scattered	Eze 29:13	5971
and Lydia, and all the mingled *p*	Eze 30:5	
his *p* with him, the terrible of	Eze 30:11	5971
all the *p* of the earth are gone	Eze 31:12	5971
thee with a company of many *p*	Eze 32:3	5971
also vex the hearts of many *p*	Eze 32:9	5971
I will make many *p* amazed at thee	Eze 32:10	5971
speak to the children of thy *p*	Eze 33:2	5971
if the *p* of the land take a man	Eze 33:2	5971
blow the trumpet, and warn the *p*	Eze 33:3	5971
trumpet, and the *p* be not warned	Eze 33:6	5971
say unto the children of thy *p*	Eze 33:12	5971
Yet the children of thy *p* say	Eze 33:17	5971
the children of thy *p* still are	Eze 33:30	5971
come unto thee as the *p* cometh	Eze 33:31	5971
and they sit before thee as my *p*	Eze 33:31	5971
I will bring them out from the *p*	Eze 34:13	5971
the house of Israel, are my *p*	Eze 34:30	5971
and are an infamy of the *p*	Eze 36:3	5971
your fruit to my *p* of Israel	Eze 36:8	5971
walk upon you, even my *p* Israel	Eze 36:12	5971
the reproach of the *p* any more	Eze 36:15	5971
them, These are the *p* of the LORD	Eze 36:20	5971
and ye shall be my *p*, and I will be	Eze 36:28	5971
Behold, O my *p*, I will open your	Eze 37:12	5971
I have opened your graves, O my *p*	Eze 37:13	5971
of thy *p* shall speak unto thee	Eze 37:18	5971
so shall they be my *p*, and I will	Eze 37:23	5971
their God, and they shall be my *p*	Eze 37:27	5971
and many *p* with thee	Eze 38:6	5971
and is gathered out of many *p*	Eze 38:8	5971
thy bands, and many *p* with thee	Eze 38:9	5971
upon the *p* that are gathered out	Eze 38:12	5971
In that day when my *p* of Israel	Eze 38:14	5971
many *p* with thee, all of them	Eze 38:15	5971
come up against my *p* of Israel	Eze 38:16	5971
upon the many *p* that are with him	Eze 38:22	5971
bands, and the *p* that is with thee	Eze 39:4	5971
known in the midst of my *p* Israel	Eze 39:7	5971
all the *p* of the land shall bury	Eze 39:13	5971
brought them again from the *p*	Eze 39:27	5971
those things which are for the *p*	Eze 42:14	5971
and the sacrifice for the *p*	Eze 44:11	5971
into the utter court to the *p*	Eze 44:19	5971
the *p* with their garments	Eze 44:19	5971
they shall teach my *p* the	Eze 44:23	5971
shall no more oppress my *p*	Eze 45:8	5971
away your exactions from my *p*	Eze 45:9	5971
All the *p* of the land shall give	Eze 45:16	5971
for all the *p* of the land a	Eze 45:22	5971
Likewise the *p* of the land shall	Eze 46:3	5971
But when the *p* of the land shall	Eze 46:9	5971
that my *p* be not scattered every	Eze 46:18	5971
utter court, to sanctify the *p*	Eze 46:20	5971
shall boil the sacrifice of the *p*	Eze 46:24	5971
shall not be left to other *p*	Dan 2:44	5972
To you it is commanded, O *p*	Dan 3:4	5972
when all the *p* heard the sound of	Dan 3:7	5972
and all kinds of musick, all the *p*	Dan 3:7	5972
I make a decree, That every *p*	Dan 3:29	5972
the king, unto all *p*, nations, and	Dan 4:1	5972
majesty that he gave him, all *p*	Dan 5:19	5972
Then king Darius wrote unto all *p*	Dan 6:25	5972
glory, and a kingdom, that all *p*	Dan 7:14	5972
shall be given to the *p* of the	Dan 7:27	5972

destroy the mighty and the holy *p*	Dan 8:24	5971
and to all the *p* of the land	Dan 9:6	5971
that hast brought thy *p* forth out	Dan 9:15	5971
thy *p* are become a reproach to	Dan 9:16	5971
thy *p* are called by thy name	Dan 9:19	5971
my sin and the sin of my *p* Israel	Dan 9:20	5971
weeks are determined upon thy *p*	Dan 9:24	5971
the *p* of the prince that shall	Dan 9:26	5971
befall thy *p* in the latter days	Dan 10:14	5971
also the robbers of thy *p* shall	Dan 11:14	5971
withstand, neither his chosen *p*	Dan 11:15	5971
become strong with a small *p*	Dan 11:23	1471
but the *p* that do know their God	Dan 11:32	5971
among the *p* shall instruct many	Dan 11:33	5971
for the children of thy *p*	Dan 12:1	5971
at that time thy *p* shall be	Dan 12:1	5971
scatter the power of the holy *p*	Dan 12:7	5971
for ye are not my *p*, and I will	Hos 1:9	5971
said unto them, Ye are not my *p*	Hos 1:10	5971
were not my *p*, Thou art my *p*	Hos 2:23	5971
for thy *p* are as they that strive	Hos 4:4	5971
My *p* are destroyed for lack of	Hos 4:6	5971
They eat up the sin of my *p*	Hos 4:8	5971
And there shall be, like *p*	Hos 4:9	5971
My *p* ask counsel at their stocks	Hos 4:12	5971
therefore the *p* that doth not	Hos 4:14	5971
I returned the captivity of my *p*	Hos 6:11	5971
he hath mixed himself among the *p*	Hos 7:8	5971
O Israel, for joy, as other *p*	Hos 9:1	5971
for the *p* thereof shall mourn	Hos 10:5	5971
the *p* shall be gathered against	Hos 10:10	5971
shall a tumult arise among thy *p*	Hos 10:14	5971
my *p* are bent to backsliding from	Hos 11:7	5971
a great *p* and a strong	Joel 2:2	5971
as a strong *p* set in battle array	Joel 2:5	5971
face the *p* shall be much pained	Joel 2:6	5971
Gather the *p*, sanctify the	Joel 2:16	5971
and let them say, Spare thy *p*	Joel 2:17	5971
should they say among the *p*	Joel 2:17	5971
for his land, and pity his *p*	Joel 2:18	5971
will answer and say unto his *p*	Joel 2:19	5971
my *p* shall never be ashamed	Joel 2:26	5971
my *p* shall never be ashamed	Joel 2:27	5971
plead with them there for my *p*	Joel 3:2	5971
And they have cast lots for my *p*	Joel 3:3	5971
to the Sabeans, to a *p* far off	Joel 3:8	1471
LORD will be the hope of his *p*	Joel 3:16	5971
the *p* of Syria shall go into	Amos 1:5	5971
the city, and the *p* not be afraid	Amos 3:6	5971
in the midst of my *p* Israel	Amos 7:8	5971
me, Go, prophesy unto my *p* Israel	Amos 7:15	5971
end is come upon my *p* of Israel	Amos 8:2	5971
All the sinners of my *p* shall die	Amos 9:10	5971
the captivity of my *p* of Israel	Amos 9:14	5971
entered into the gate of my *p* in	Obad 13	5971
and of what *p* art thou	Jonah 1:8	5971
So the *p* of Nineveh believed God,	Jonah 3:5	582
Hear, all ye *p*	Mic 1:2	5971
he is come unto the gate of my *p*	Mic 1:9	5971
hath changed the portion of my *p*	Mic 2:4	5971
Even of late my *p* is risen up as	Mic 2:8	5971
The women of my *p* have ye cast	Mic 2:9	5971
even be the prophet of this *p*	Mic 2:11	5971
Who also eat the flesh of my *p*	Mic 3:3	5971
the prophets that make my *p* err	Mic 3:5	5971
and *p* shall flow unto it	Mic 4:1	5971
And he shall judge among many *p*	Mic 4:3	5971
For all *p* will walk every one in	Mic 4:5	5971
thou shalt beat in pieces many *p*	Mic 4:13	5971
of many *p* as a dew from the LORD	Mic 5:7	5971
p as a lion among the beasts of	Mic 5:8	5971
hath a controversy with his *p*	Mic 6:2	5971
O my *p*, what have I done unto	Mic 6:3	5971
O my *p*, remember now what Balak	Mic 6:5	5971
shall bear the reproach of my *p*	Mic 6:16	5971
Feed thy *p* with thy rod, the	Mic 7:14	5971
thy *p* in the midst of thee are	Nah 3:13	5971
thy *p* is scattered upon the	Nah 3:18	5971
and heapeth unto him all *p*	Hab 2:5	5971
remnant of the *p* shall spoil thee	Hab 2:8	5971
thy house by cutting off many *p*	Hab 2:10	5971
p shall labour in the very fire	Hab 2:13	5971
the *p* shall weary themselves for	Hab 2:13	3816
forth for the salvation of thy *p*	Hab 3:13	5971
when he cometh up unto the *p*	Hab 3:16	5971
all the merchant *p* are cut down	Zeph 1:11	5971
whereby they have reproached my *p*	Zeph 2:8	5971
residue of my *p* shall spoil them	Zeph 2:9	5971
the remnant of my *p* shall possess	Zeph 2:9	1471
the *p* of the LORD of hosts	Zeph 2:10	5971
I turn to the *p* a pure language	Zeph 3:9	5971

P

of thee an afflicted and poor *p*	Zeph 3:12	5971
a praise among all *p* of the earth	Zeph 3:20	5971
LORD of hosts, saying, This I say	Hag 1:2	5971
with all the remnant of the *p*	Hag 1:12	5971
the *p* did fear before the LORD	Hag 1:12	5971
in the LORD's message unto the *p*	Hag 1:13	5971
of all the remnant of the *p*	Hag 1:14	5971
and to the residue of the *p*	Hag 2:2	5971
all ye *p* of the land, saith the	Hag 2:4	5971
Haggai, and said, So is this *p*	Hag 2:14	5971
in that day, and shall be my *p*	Zec 2:11	5971
Speak unto all the *p* of the land	Zec 7:5	5971
remnant of this *p* in these days	Zec 8:6	5971
I will save my *p* from the east	Zec 8:7	5971
and they shall be my *p*, and I will	Zec 8:8	5971
of this *p* as in the former days	Zec 8:11	5971
p to possess all these things	Zec 8:12	5971
to pass, that there shall come *p*	Zec 8:20	5971
Yea, many *p* and strong nations	Zec 8:22	5971
in that day as the flock of his *p*	Zec 9:16	5971
And I will sow them among the *p*	Zec 10:9	5971
which I had made with all the *p*	Zec 11:10	5971
unto all the *p* round about	Zec 12:2	5971
a burdensome stone for all *p*	Zec 12:3	5971
though all the *p* of the earth be	Zec 12:3	1471
horse of the *p* with blindness	Zec 12:4	5971
devour all the *p* round about	Zec 12:6	5971
I will say, It is my *p*	Zec 13:9	5971
the residue of the *p* shall not be	Zec 14:2	5971
the *p* that have fought against	Zec 14:12	5971
The *p* against whom the LORD hath	Mal 1:4	5971
and base before all the *p*,	Mal 2:9	5971
shall save his *p* from their sins	Mt 1:21	2992
and scribes of the *p* together	Mt 2:4	2992
that shall rule my *p* Israel	Mt 2:6	2992
The *p* which sat in darkness saw	Mt 4:16	2992
all manner of disease among the *p*	Mt 4:23	2992
p that were taken with divers	Mt 4:24	
multitudes of *p* from Galilee	Mt 4:25	
the *p* were astonished at his	Mt 7:28	3793
and the *p* making a noise,	Mt 9:23	3793
But when the *p* were put forth, he	Mt 9:25	3793
and every disease among the *p*	Mt 9:35	2992
all the *p* were amazed, and said,	Mt 12:23	2992
While he yet talked to the *p*	Mt 12:46	3793
when the *p* had heard thereof,	Mt 14:13	3793
This *p* draweth nigh unto me with	Mt 15:8	2992
the elders of the *p* came unto him	Mt 21:23	2992
we fear the *p*	Mt 21:26	3793
scribes, and the elders of the *p*	Mt 26:3	2992
there be an uproar among the *p*	Mt 26:5	2992
chief priests and elders of the *p*	Mt 26:47	2992
elders of the *p* took counsel	Mt 27:1	2992
to release unto the *p* a prisoner	Mt 27:15	3793
Then answered all the *p*, and said,	Mt 27:25	2992
steal him away, and say unto the *p*	Mt 27:64	2992
side, much *p* gathered unto him	Mk 5:21	3793
much *p* followed him, and thronged	Mk 5:24	3793
the *p* saw them departing, and many	Mk 6:33	3793
when he came out, saw much *p*	Mk 6:34	3793
while he sent away the *p*	Mk 6:45	3793
This *p* honoureth me with their	Mk 7:6	2992
he had called all the *p* unto him	Mk 7:14	3793
entered into the house from the *p*	Mk 7:17	3793
he commanded the *p* to sit down on	Mk 8:6	3793
and they did set them before the *p*	Mk 8:6	3793
when he had called the *p* unto him	Mk 8:34	3793
And straightway all the *p*, when	Mk 9:15	3793
that the *p* came running together	Mk 9:25	3793
the *p* resort unto him again	Mk 10:1	3793
disciples and a great number of *p*	Mk 10:46	3793
because all the *p* was astonished	Mk 11:18	3793
they feared the *p*	Mk 11:32	2992
lay hold on him, but feared the *p*	Mk 12:12	3793
the common *p* heard him gladly	Mk 12:37	3793
beheld how the *p* cast money into	Mk 12:41	3793
lest there be an uproar of the *p*	Mk 14:2	2992
But the chief priests moved the *p*	Mk 15:11	3793
Pilate, willing to content the *p*	Mk 15:15	3793
the whole multitude of the *p* were	Lk 1:10	2992
to make ready a *p* prepared for	Lk 1:17	2992
the *p* waited for Zacharias, and	Lk 1:21	2992
he hath visited and redeemed his *p*	Lk 1:68	2992
p by the remission of their sins	Lk 1:77	2992
joy, which shall be to all *p*	Lk 2:10	2992
prepared before the face of all *p*	Lk 2:31	2992
and the glory of thy *p* Israel	Lk 2:32	2992
the *p* asked him, saying, What	Lk 3:10	3793
as the *p* were in expectation, and	Lk 3:15	2992
preached he unto the *p*	Lk 3:18	2992
Now when all the *p* were baptized	Lk 3:21	2992
the *p* sought him, and came unto	Lk 4:42	3793
as the *p* pressed upon him to hear	Lk 5:1	3793
taught the *p* out of the ship	Lk 5:3	3793
multitude of *p* out of all Judaea	Lk 6:17	2992
sayings in the audience of the *p*	Lk 7:1	2992
said unto the *p* that followed him	Lk 7:9	3793
went with him, and much *p*	Lk 7:11	3793
much *p* of the city was with her	Lk 7:12	3793
and, That God hath visited his *p*	Lk 7:16	2992
speak unto the *p* concerning John	Lk 7:24	3793
all the *p* that heard him, and the	Lk 7:29	2992
when much *p* were gathered	Lk 8:4	3793
the *p* gladly received him	Lk 8:40	3793
But as he went the *p* thronged him	Lk 8:42	3793
unto him before all the *p* for	Lk 8:47	2992
And the *p*, when they knew it,	Lk 9:11	3793
go and buy meat for all this *p*	Lk 9:13	2992
saying, Whom say the *p* that I am	Lk 9:18	3793
from the hill, much *p* met him	Lk 9:37	3793
and the *p* wondered	Lk 11:14	3793
when the *p* were gathered thick	Lk 11:29	3793
an innumerable multitude of *p*	Lk 12:1	3793
And he said also to the *p*, When ye	Lk 12:54	3793
sabbath day, and said unto the *p*	Lk 13:14	3793
all the *p* rejoiced for all the	Lk 13:17	3793
and all the *p*, when they saw it,	Lk 18:43	2992
the chief of the *p* sought to	Lk 19:47	2992
for all the *p* were very attentive	Lk 19:48	2992
as he taught the *p* in the temple	Lk 20:1	2992
all the *p* will stone us	Lk 20:6	2992
he to speak to the *p* this parable	Lk 20:9	2992
and they feared the *p*	Lk 20:19	2992
hold of his words before the *p*	Lk 20:26	2992
the *p* he said unto his disciples	Lk 20:45	2992
in the land, and wrath upon this *p*	Lk 21:23	2992
all the *p* came early in the	Lk 21:38	2992
for they feared the *p*	Lk 22:2	2992
it was day, the elders of the *p*	Lk 22:66	2992
to the chief priests and to the *p*	Lk 23:4	3793
saying, He stirreth up the *p*	Lk 23:5	2992
priests and the rulers and the *p*	Lk 23:13	2992
me, as one that perverteth the *p*	Lk 23:14	2992
followed him a great company of *p*	Lk 23:27	2992
And the *p* stood beholding	Lk 23:35	2992
all the *p* that came together to	Lk 23:48	3793
and word before God and all the *p*	Lk 24:19	2992
when the *p* which stood on the	Jn 6:22	3793
When the *p* therefore saw that	Jn 6:24	3793
among the *p* concerning him	Jn 7:12	3793
but he deceiveth the *p*	Jn 7:12	3793
The *p* answered and said, Thou hast	Jn 7:20	3793
many of the *p* believed on him, and	Jn 7:31	3793
The Pharisees heard that the *p*	Jn 7:32	3793
Many of the *p* therefore, when	Jn 7:40	3793
among the *p* because of him	Jn 7:43	3793
But this *p* who knoweth not the	Jn 7:49	3793
and all the *p* came unto him	Jn 8:2	2992
but because of the *p* which stand	Jn 11:42	3793
that one man should die for the *p*	Jn 11:50	2992
Much *p* of the Jews therefore knew	Jn 12:9	3793
On the next day much *p* that were	Jn 12:12	3793
The *p* therefore that was with him	Jn 12:17	3793
For this cause the *p* also met him	Jn 12:18	3793
The *p* therefore, that stood by,	Jn 12:29	3793
The *p* answered him, We have heard	Jn 12:34	3793
that one man should die for the *p*	Jn 18:14	2992
and having favour with all the *p*	Acts 2:47	2992
all the *p* saw him walking and	Acts 3:9	2992
all the *p* ran together unto them	Acts 3:11	2992
saw it, he answered unto the *p*	Acts 3:12	2992
be destroyed from among the *p*	Acts 3:23	2992
And as they spake unto the *p*	Acts 4:1	2992
grieved that they taught the *p*	Acts 4:2	2992
unto them, Ye rulers of the *p*	Acts 4:8	2992
all, and to all the *p* of Israel	Acts 4:10	2992
it spread no further among the *p*	Acts 4:17	2992
punish them, because of the *p*	Acts 4:21	2992
the *p* imagine vain things	Acts 4:25	2992
the *p* of Israel, were gathered	Acts 4:27	2992
and wonders wrought among the *p*	Acts 5:12	2992
but the *p* magnified them	Acts 5:13	2992
the *p* all the words of this life	Acts 5:20	2992
in the temple, and teaching the *p*	Acts 5:25	2992
for they feared the *p*, lest they	Acts 5:26	2992
had in reputation among all the *p*	Acts 5:34	2992
and drew away much *p* after him	Acts 5:37	2992
wonders and miracles among the *p*	Acts 6:8	2992
And they stirred up the *p*, and the	Acts 6:12	2992
the *p* grew and multiplied in Egypt	Acts 7:17	2992
of my *p* which is in Egypt	Acts 7:34	2992
the *p* with one accord gave heed	Acts 8:6	3793

and bewitched the *p* of Samaria .... Acts 8:9 — 1484
which gave much alms to the *p* .... Acts 10:2 — 2992
Not to all the *p*, but unto .... Acts 10:41 — 2992
commanded us to preach unto the *p*...... Acts 10:42 — 2992
much *p* was added unto the Lord ...... Acts 11:24 — 3793
with the church, and taught much *p* ...... Acts 11:26 — 3793
to bring him forth to the *p* .... Acts 12:4 — 2992
expectation of the *p* of the Jews .... Acts 12:11 — 2992
the *p* gave a shout, saying, It is .... Acts 12:22 — 1218
any word of exhortation for the *p* .... Acts 13:15 — 2992
The God of this *p* of Israel chose .... Acts 13:17 — 2992
exalted the *p* when they dwelt as .... Acts 13:17 — 2992
repentance to all the *p* of Israel .... Acts 13:24 — 2992
who are his witnesses unto the *p* .... Acts 13:31 — 2992
when the *p* saw what Paul had done ...... Acts 14:11 — 3793
have done sacrifice with the *p* .... Acts 14:13 — 3793
clothes, and ran in among the *p* .... Acts 14:14 — 3793
scarce restrained they the *p* .... Acts 14:18 — 3793
and Iconium, who persuaded the *p* .... Acts 14:19 — 1484
take out of them a *p* for his name .... Acts 15:14 — 2992
sought to bring them out to the *p* .... Acts 17:5 — 1218
And they troubled the *p* and the .... Acts 17:8 — 3793
thither also, and stirred up the *p* .... Acts 17:13 — 3793
for I have much *p* in this city .... Acts 18:10 — 2992
of repentance, saying unto the *p* .... Acts 19:4 — 2992
persuaded and turned away much *p*...... Acts 19:26 — 3793
would have entered in unto the *p*.......... Acts 19:30 — 1218
have made his defence unto the *p* .... Acts 19:33 — 1218
the townclerk had appeased the *p* .... Acts 19:35 — 3793
the temple, stirred up all the *p* .... Acts 21:27 — 3793
all men every where against the *p* .... Acts 21:28 — 2992
was moved, and the *p* ran together .... Acts 21:30 — 2992
for the violence of the *p* .... Acts 21:35 — 3793
multitude of the *p* followed after .... Acts 21:36 — 2992
suffer me to speak unto the *p* .... Acts 21:39 — 2992
beckoned with the hand unto the *p* .... Acts 21:40 — 2992
speak evil of the ruler of thy *p* .... Acts 23:5 — 2992
any man, neither raising up the *p* .... Acts 24:12 — 3793
Delivering thee from the *p*... .... Acts 26:17 — 2992
and should shew light unto the *p* .... Acts 26:23 — 2992
the barbarous *p* shewed us no .... Acts 28:2 —
committed nothing against the *p* .... Acts 28:17 — 2992
Saying, Go unto this *p*, and say, ... Acts 28:26 — 2992
heart of this *p* is waxed gross .... Acts 28:27 — 2992
my *p*, which were not my *p* .... Rom 9:25 — 2992
said unto them, Ye are not my *p* .... Rom 9:26 — 2992
to jealousy by them that are no *p*.......... Rom 10:19 — 1484
a disobedient and gainsaying *p* .... Rom 10:21 — 2992
then, Hath God cast away his *p*.............. Rom 11:1 — 2992
cast away his *p* which he foreknew .... Rom 11:2 — 2992
Rejoice, ye Gentiles, with his *p* .... Rom 15:10 — 2992
and laud him, all ye *p* .... Rom 15:11 — 2992
The *p* sat down to eat and drink, ... 1Cor 10:7 — 2992
lips will I speak unto this *p* .... 1Cor 14:21 — 2992
their God, and they shall be my *p* .... 2Cor 6:16 — 2992
purify unto himself a peculiar *p* .... Titus 2:14 — 2992
for the sins of the *p* .... Heb 2:17 — 2992
therefore a rest to the *p* of God............ Heb 4:9 — 2992
hereof he ought, as for the *p* .... Heb 5:3 — 2992
of the *p* according to the law .... Heb 7:5 — 2992
under it the *p* received the law .... Heb 7:11 — 2992
a God, and they shall be to me a *p*.......... Heb 8:10 — 2992
and for the errors of the *p* .... Heb 9:7 — 2992
to all the *p* according to the law .... Heb 9:19 — 2992
both the book, and all the *p* .... Heb 9:19 — 2992
again, The Lord shall judge his *p* .... Heb 10:30 — 2992
affliction with the *p* of God .... Heb 11:25 — 2992
sanctify the *p* with his own blood .... Heb 13:12 — 2992
an holy nation, a peculiar *p* .... 1Pet 2:9 — 2992
Which in time past were not a *p* .... 1Pet 2:10 — 2992
but are now the *p* of God...................... 1Pet 2:10 — 2992
false prophets also among the *p* .... 2Pet 2:1 — 2992
having saved the *p* out of the .... Jude 5 — 2992
of every kindred, and tongue, and *p*...... Rev 5:9 — 2992
of all nations, and kindreds, and *p*........ Rev 7:9 — 2992
And they of the *p* and kindreds and .... Rev 11:9 — 2992
and kindred, and tongue, and *p* .... Rev 14:6 — 2992
saying, Come out of her, my *p* .... Rev 18:4 — 2992
a great voice of much *p* in heaven .... Rev 19:1 — 3793
with them, and they shall be his *p* .... Rev 21:3 — 2992

PEOPLE'S See APPENDIX.

PEOPLES See APPENDIX.

PEOR (pe'-or) See BAAL-PEOR, BETH-PEOR, PEOR'S.
   1. A Moabite god.
beguiled in the matter of *P* .... Num 25:18 — 6465
the LORD in the matter of *P* .... Num 31:16 — 6465
iniquity of *P* too little for us.................. Josh 22:17 — 6465
   2. A mountain.
brought Balaam unto the top of *P* .... Num 23:28 — 6465

PEOR'S
   the day of the plague for *P* sake .... Num 25:18 — 6465

PERADVENTURE
P there be fifty righteous within .... Gen 18:24 — 194
P there shall lack five of the.................. Gen 18:28 — 194
P there shall be forty found .... Gen 18:29 — 194
P there shall thirty be found .... Gen 18:30 — 194
P there shall be twenty found................ Gen 18:31 — 194
P ten shall be found there...................... Gen 18:32 — 194
P the woman will not be willing.............. Gen 24:5 — 194
P the woman will not follow me .... Gen 24:39 — 194
My father *p* will feel me, and I .... Gen 27:12 — 194
P thou wouldest take by force thy.......... Gen 31:31 — 6435
p he will accept of me............................ Gen 32:20 — 194
Lest *p* he die also, as his .... Gen 38:11 — 194
Lest *p* mischief befall him .... Gen 42:4 —
p it was an oversight.............................. Gen 43:12 — 194
lest *p* I see the evil that shall................ Gen 44:34 —
they said, Joseph will *p* hate us .... Gen 50:15 — 3863
Lest *p* the people repent when .... Ex 13:17 —
p I shall make an atonement for............ Ex 32:30 — 194
p I shall prevail, that we may .... Num 22:6 — 194
p I shall be able to overcome .... Num 22:11 — 194
p the LORD will come to meet me............ Num 23:3 — 194
p it will please God that thou .... Num 23:27 — 194
the Hivites, *P* ye dwell among us .... Josh 9:7 — 194
p he will lighten his hand from .... 1Sa 6:5 — 194
p he can shew us our way that we.......... 1Sa 9:6 — 194
p we may find grass to save the .... 1Kin 18:5 — 194
or *p* he sleepeth, and must be .... 1Kin 18:27 — 194
p he will save thy life .... 1Kin 20:31 — 194
lest *p* the Spirit of the LORD .... 2Kin 2:16 —
P he will be enticed, and we shall.......... Jer 20:10 — 194
yet *p* for a good man some would .... Rom 5:7 — 5029
if God *p* will give them .... 2Ti 2:25 — 3379

PERAZIM (per'-a-zim) *Where David defeated the Philistines.*
   LORD shall rise up as in mount *P*............ Is 28:21

PERCEIVE
hath not given you an heart to *p* .... Deut 29:4 — 3045
This day we *p* that the LORD is .... Josh 22:31 — 3045
that ye may *p* and see that your.............. 1Sa 12:17 — 3045
for this day I *p*, that if Absalom .... 2Sa 19:6 — 3045
I *p* that this is an holy man of................ 2Kin 4:9 — 3045
passeth on also, but I *p* him not .... Job 9:11 — 995
and backward, but I cannot *p* him .... Job 23:8 — 3045
to *p* the words of understanding .... Prov 1:2 —
Wherefore I *p* that there is .... Eccl 3:22 — 7200
and see ye indeed, but *p* not .... Is 6:9 — 3045
a deeper speech than thou canst *p* .... Is 33:19 — 8085
ye shall see, and shall not *p* .... Mt 13:14 — 1492
seeing they may see, and not *p* .... Mk 4:12 — 1492
Do ye not *p*, that whatsoever .... Mk 7:18 — 3539
***p* ye not yet, neither understand**............ Mk 8:17 — 3539
for I *p* that virtue is gone out .... Lk 8:46 — 1097
I *p* that thou art a prophet .... Jn 4:19 — 2334
P ye how ye prevail nothing.................... Jn 12:19 — 2334
For I *p* that thou art in the gall.............. Acts 8:23 — 3708
Of a truth I *p* that God is no.................. Acts 10:34 — 2638
I *p* that in all things ye are too.............. Acts 17:22 — 2334
I *p* that this voyage will be with .... Acts 27:10 — 2334
and seeing ye shall see, and not *p*........ Acts 28:26 — 1492
for I *p* that the same epistle .... 2Cor 7:8 — 991
Hereby *p* we the love of God,.................. 1Jn 3:16 — 1097

PERCEIVED
he *p* not when she lay down, nor .... Gen 19:33 — 3045
he *p* not when she lay down, nor .... Gen 19:35 — 3045
when Gideon *p* that he was an .... Judg 6:22 — 7200
Eli *p* that the LORD had called .... 1Sa 3:8 — 995
Saul *p* that it was Samuel, and he........ 1Sa 28:14 — 3045
David *p* that the LORD had .... 2Sa 5:12 — 3045
David *p* that the child was dead .... 2Sa 12:19 — 995
p that the king's heart was .... 2Sa 14:1 — 3045
p that it was not the king of .... 1Kin 22:33 — 7200
David *p* that the LORD had .... 1Chr 14:2 — 3045
p that it was not the king of .... 2Chr 18:32 — 7200
I *p* that God had not sent him .... Neh 6:12 — 5234
for they *p* that this work was .... Neh 6:16 — 3045
I *p* that the portions of the .... Neh 13:10 — 3045
When Mordecai *p* all that was done ...... Est 4:1 — 3045
Hast thou *p* the breadth of the .... Job 38:18 — 995
I *p* that this also is vexation of .... Eccl 1:17 — 3045
I myself also *p* that one event .... Eccl 2:14 — 3045
nor *p* by the ear, neither hath .... Is 64:4 — 238
counsel of the LORD, and hath *p* .... Jer 23:18 — 7200
for the matter was not *p* .... Jer 38:27 — 8085
Which when Jesus *p*, he said unto .... Mt 16:8 — 1097
they *p* that he spake of them .... Mt 21:45 — 1097
But Jesus *p* their wickedness, and .... Mt 22:18 — 1097

P

immediately when Jesus *p* in his .... Mk 2:8 — *1921*
they *p* that he had seen a vision .... Lk 1:22 — *1921*
But when Jesus *p* their thoughts .... Lk 5:22 — *1921*
hid from them, that they *p* it not .... Lk 9:45 — *143*
for they *p* that he had spoken .... Lk 20:19 — *1097*
But he *p* their craftiness, and .... Lk 20:23 — *2657*
therefore *p* that they would come .... Jn 6:15 — *1097*
p that they were unlearned and.............. Acts 4:13 — *2638*
But when Paul *p* that the one part .... Acts 23:6 — *1097*
Whom I *p* to be accused of .... Acts 23:29 — *2147*
p the grace that was given unto .... Gal 2:9 — *1097*

PERCEIVEST
when thou *p* not in him the lips .... Prov 14:7 — *3045*
but *p* not the beam that is in .... Lk 6:41 — *2657*

PERCEIVETH
low, but he *p* it not of them .... Job 14:21 — *995*
once, yea twice, yet man *p* it not .... Job 33:14 — *7789*
She *p* that her merchandise is .... Prov 31:18 — *2938*

PERCEIVING
p that he had answered them well,.......... Mk 12:28 — *1492*
p the thought of their heart, ... Lk 9:47 — *1492*
p that he had faith to be healed, ... Acts 14:9 — *1492*

PERDITION
of them is lost, but the son of *p* .... Jn 17:12 — *684*
is to them an evident token of *p*............. Phil 1:28 — *684*
of sin be revealed, the son of *p* .... 2Th 2:3 — *684*
drown men in destruction and *p*............. 1Ti 6:9 — *684*
not of them who draw back unto *p*........ Heb 10:39 — *684*
of judgment and *p* of ungodly men .... 2Pet 3:7 — *684*
the bottomless pit, and go into *p* .... Rev 17:8 — *684*
is of the seven, and goeth into *p* .... Rev 17:11 — *684*

PERES (pe'-res) Portion of "the handwriting on the wall."
P; Thy kingdom is.................................... Dan 5:28 — *6537*

PERESH (pe'-resh) A son of Machir.
a son, and she called his name *P* .... 1Chr 7:16 — *6570*

PEREZ (pe'-rez) See PEREZ-UZZAH, PHARES.
1. An ancestor of Jashobeam.
Of the children of *P* was the .... 1Chr 27:3 — *6557*
2. A son of Judah; same as Pharez.
Mahalaleel, of the children of *P* .... Neh 11:4 — *6557*
All the sons of *P* that dwelt at .... Neh 11:6 — *6557*

PEREZITES See PHARZITES.

PEREZ-UZZA (pe'-rez-uz'-zah) See PEREZ-UZZAH. *Where Uzza died.*
place is called *P* to this day .... 1Chr 13:11 — *6560*

PEREZ-UZZAH (pe'-rez-uz'-zah) See PEREZ-UZZA. *Same as Perez-uzza.*
name of the place *P* to this day .... 2Sa 6:8 — *6560*

PERFECT
p in his generations, and Noah .... Gen 6:9 — *8549*
walk before me, and be thou *p*............... Gen 17:1 — *8549*
it shall be *p* to be accepted .... Lev 22:21 — *8549*
Thou shalt be *p* with the LORD thy .... Deut 18:13 — *8549*
a *p* and just weight, a *p* .... Deut 25:15 — *8003*
He is the Rock, his work is *p* .... Deut 32:4 — *8549*
LORD God of Israel, Give a *p* lot .... 1Sa 14:41 — *8549*
As for God, his way is *p*.......................... 2Sa 22:31 — *8549*
and he maketh my way *p* .... 2Sa 22:33 — *8549*
be *p* with the LORD our God .... 1Kin 8:61 — *8003*
his heart was not *p* with the LORD .... 1Kin 11:4 — *8003*
his heart was not *p* with the LORD .... 1Kin 15:3 — *8003*
was *p* with the LORD all his days .... 1Kin 15:14 — *8003*
thee in truth and with a *p* heart .... 2Kin 20:3 — *8003*
came with a *p* heart to Hebron, to......... 1Chr 12:38 — *8003*
and serve him with a *p* heart................. 1Chr 28:9 — *8003*
because with *p* heart they offered .... 1Chr 29:9 — *8003*
unto Solomon my son a *p* heart .... 1Chr 29:19 — *8003*
made he of gold, and that *p* gold .... 2Chr 4:21 — *4357*
heart of Asa was *p* all his days.............. 2Chr 15:17 — *8003*
them whose heart is *p* toward him .... 2Chr 16:9 — *8003*
faithfully, and with a *p* heart .... 2Chr 19:9 — *8003*
the LORD, but not with a *p* heart .... 2Chr 25:2 — *8003*
p peace, and at such a time .... Ezr 7:12 — *1585*
and that man was *p* and upright, and ... Job 1:1 — *8535*
none like him in the earth, a *p*............... Job 1:8 — *8535*
none like him in the earth, a *p*............... Job 2:3 — *8535*
God will not cast away a *p* man .... Job 8:20 — *8535*
if I say, I am *p*, it shall also .... Job 9:20 — *8535*
Though I were *p*, yet would I not .... Job 9:21 — *8535*
I said it, He destroyeth the *p*................. Job 9:22 — *8535*
him, that thou makest thy ways *p* .... Job 22:3 — *8552*
he that is *p* in knowledge is with .... Job 36:4 — *8549*
of him which is *p* in knowledge .... Job 37:16 — *8549*
As for God, his way is *p*.......................... Ps 18:30 — *8549*

with strength, and maketh my way *p* .... Ps 18:32 — *8549*
The law of the LORD is *p*,........................ Ps 19:7 — *8549*
Mark the *p* man, and behold the .... Ps 37:37 — *8535*
they may shoot in secret at the *p* .... Ps 64:4 — *8535*
behave myself wisely in a *p* way .... Ps 101:2 — *8549*
within my house with a *p* heart .... Ps 101:2 — *8537*
he that walketh in a *p* way .... Ps 101:6 — *8549*
The LORD will *p* that which .... Ps 138:8 — *1584*
I hate them with *p* hatred .... Ps 139:22 — *8503*
land, and the *p* shall remain in it .... Prov 2:21 — *8549*
more and more unto the *p* day .... Prov 4:18 — *3559*
of the *p* shall direct his way .... Prov 11:5 — *8549*
the harvest, when the bud is *p* .... Is 18:5 — *8552*
Thou wilt keep him in *p* peace .... Is 26:3
thee in truth and with a *p* heart .... Is 38:3 — *8003*
who is blind as he that is *p*.................... Is 42:19 — *7999*
for it was *p* through my .... Eze 16:14 — *3632*
thou hast said, I am of *p* beauty .... Eze 27:3 — *3632*
they have made thy beauty *p*................. Eze 27:11 — *3634*
full of wisdom, and *p* in beauty............. Eze 28:12 — *3632*
Thou wast *p* in thy ways from the .... Eze 28:15 — *8549*
Be ye therefore *p*, even as your .... Mt 5:48 — *5046*
Father which is in heaven is *p* .... Mt 5:48 — *5046*
said unto him, If thou wilt be *p* .... Mt 19:21 — *5046*
having had *p* understanding of all......... Lk 1:3 — *199*
but every one that is *p* shall be .... Lk 6:40 — *2675*
that they may be made *p* in one............ Jn 17:23 — *5048*
p soundness in the presence of .... Acts 3:16 — *3647*
taught according to the *p* manner .... Acts 22:3 — *195*
having more *p* knowledge of that .... Acts 24:22 — *197*
is that good, and acceptable, and *p* ...... Rom 12:2 — *5046*
wisdom among them that are *p* .... 1Cor 2:6 — *5046*
But when that which is *p* is come .... 1Cor 13:10 — *5046*
my strength is made *p* in weakness .... 2Cor 12:9 — *5048*
Be *p*, be of good comfort, be of .... 2Cor 13:11 — *2675*
are ye now made *p* by the flesh .... Gal 3:3 — *2005*
of the Son of God, unto a *p* man .... Eph 4:13 — *5046*
attained, either were already *p*.............. Phil 3:12 — *5048*
Let us therefore, as many as be *p* .... Phil 3:15 — *5046*
every man *p* in Christ Jesus .... Col 1:28 — *5046*
in prayers, that ye may stand *p* .... Col 4:12 — *5046*
might *p* that which is lacking in .... 1Th 3:10 — *2675*
That the man of God may be *p*............... 2Ti 3:17 — *739*
salvation *p* through sufferings .... Heb 2:10 — *5048*
And being made *p*, he became the .... Heb 5:9 — *5048*
For the law made nothing *p* .... Heb 7:19 — *5048*
make him that did the service *p* .... Heb 9:9 — *5048*
more *p* tabernacle, not made with......... Heb 9:11 — *5048*
make the comers thereunto *p* .... Heb 10:1 — *5048*
without us should not be made *p*........... Heb 11:40 — *5048*
to the spirits of just men made *p* .... Heb 12:23 — *5048*
Make you *p* in every good work to .... Heb 13:21 — *2675*
But let patience have her *p* work .... Jas 1:4 — *5046*
that ye may be *p* .... Jas 1:4 — *5046*
every *p* gift is from above, and .... Jas 1:17 — *5046*
looketh into the *p* law of liberty .... Jas 1:25 — *5046*
and by works was faith made *p* .... Jas 2:22 — *5048*
not in word, the same is a *p* man .... Jas 3:2 — *5046*
have suffered a while, make you *p* .... 1Pet 5:10 — *2675*
Herein is our love made *p* .... 1Jn 4:17 — *5048*
but *p* love casteth out fear .... 1Jn 4:18 — *5046*
feareth is not made *p* in love .... 1Jn 4:18 — *5048*
not found thy works *p* before God .... Rev 3:2 — *4137*

PERFECTED
So the house of the LORD was *p*............. 2Chr 8:16 — *8003*
and the work was *p* by them .... 2Chr 24:13 — *5927,724*
thy builders have *p* thy beauty .... Eze 27:4 — *3634*
and sucklings thou hast *p* praise .... Mt 21:16 — *2675*
and the third day I shall be *p*................. Lk 13:32 — *5048*
he hath *p* for ever them that are........... Heb 10:14 — *5048*
him verily is the love of God *p* .... 1Jn 2:5 — *5048*
in us, and his love is *p* in us .... 1Jn 4:12 — *5048*

PERFECTING
p holiness in the fear of God .... 2Cor 7:1 — *2005*
For the *p* of the saints, for the .... Eph 4:12 — *2677*

PERFECTION
thou find out the Almighty unto *p* .... Job 11:7 — *8503*
the *p* thereof upon the earth .... Job 15:29 — *4512*
darkness, and searcheth out all *p* .... Job 28:3 — *8503*
the *p* of beauty, God hath shined .... Ps 50:2 — *4359*
I have seen an end of all *p* .... Ps 119:96 — *8502*
their *p* for the multitude of thy.............. Is 47:9 — *8537*
that men call The *p* of beauty .... Lam 2:15 — *3632*
this life, and bring no fruit to *p* .... Lk 8:14 — *5052*
and this also we wish, even your *p*......... 2Cor 13:9 — *2676*
of Christ, let us go on unto *p* .... Heb 6:1 — *5051*
If therefore *p* were by the .... Heb 7:11 — *5050*

PERFECTLY
days ye shall consider it *p* .... Jer 23:20   998
many as touched were made *p* whole .... Mt 14:36   1295
unto him the way of God more *p* .... Acts 18:26   197
something more *p* concerning him .... Acts 23:15   197
enquire somewhat of him more *p* .... Acts 23:20   197
but that ye be *p* joined together............. 1Cor 1:10   2675
For yourselves know *p* that the 1Th 5:2   199

PERFECTNESS
charity, which is the bond of *p* .... Col 3:14   5047

PERFORM
I will *p* the oath which I sware .... Gen 26:3   6965
not able to *p* it thyself alone................... Ex 18:18   6213
that enter in to *p* the service .... Num 4:23   6633
which he commanded you to *p* .... Deut 4:13   6213
that he may *p* the word which the .... Deut 9:5   6965
of thy lips thou shalt keep and *p* .... Deut 23:23   6213
p the duty of an husband's .... Deut 25:5
he will not *p* the duty of my .... Deut 25:7
that if he will *p* unto thee the .... Ruth 3:13
In that day I will *p* against Eli............... 1Sa 3:12   6965
p the request of his handmaid 2Sa 14:15   6213
then will I *p* my word with thee, ... 1Kin 6:12   6965
LORD, that he might *p* his saying 1Kin 12:15   6965
to *p* the words of this covenant 2Kin 23:3   6965
that he might *p* the words of the............ 2Kin 23:24   6965
that the LORD might *p* his word 2Chr 10:15   6965
to *p* the words of the covenant 2Chr 34:31   6213
to *p* my request, let the king and.......... Est 5:8   6213
hands cannot *p* their enterprise .... Job 5:12
which they are not able to *p* .... Ps 21:11
ever, that I may daily *p* my vows .... Ps 61:8   7999
I have sworn, and I will *p* it .... Ps 119:106   6965
heart to *p* thy statutes alway .... Ps 119:112   6213
of the LORD of hosts will *p* this.............. Is 9:7   6213
vow a vow unto the LORD, and *p* it .... Is 19:21   7999
and shall *p* all my pleasure .... Is 44:28   7999
for I will hasten my word to *p* it .... Jer 1:12   6213
That I may *p* the oath which I .... Jer 11:5   6965
the LORD *p* thy words which thou .... Jer 28:6   6965
p my good word toward you, in .... Jer 29:10   6965
that I will *p* that good thing.................. Jer 33:14   6965
We will surely *p* our vows that we.......... Jer 44:25   6213
your vows, and surely *p* your vows........ Jer 44:25   6213
will I say the word, and will *p* it............ Eze 12:25   6213
Thou wilt *p* the truth to Jacob, ... Mic 7:20   5414
thy solemn feasts, *p* thy vows .... Nah 1:15   7999
but shalt *p* unto the Lord thine. .... Mt 5:33   591
To *p* the mercy promised to our .... Lk 1:72   4160
promised, he was able also to *p* .... Rom 4:21   4160
but how to *p* that which is good I .... Rom 7:18   2716
Now therefore *p* the doing of it 2Cor 8:11   2005
will *p* it until the day of Jesus .... Phil 1:6   2005

PERFORMANCE
for there shall be a *p* of those .... Lk 1:45   5050
so there may be a *p* also out of.............. 2Cor 8:11   2005

PERFORMED
hath not *p* my commandments 1Sa 15:11   6965
I have *p* the commandment of the 1Sa 15:13   6965
and they *p* all that the king.................. 2Sa 21:14   6213
the LORD hath *p* his word that he 1Kin 8:20   6965
The LORD therefore hath *p* his............... 2Chr 6:10   6965
to his seed, and hast *p* thy words .... Neh 9:8   6965
because she hath not *p* the .... Est 1:15   6213
half of the kingdom it shall be *p* .... Est 5:6   6213
and it shall be *p*, even to the .... Est 7:2   6213
and unto thee shall the vow be *p* .... Ps 65:1   7999
that when the Lord hath *p* his .... Is 10:12   1214
till he have *p* the thoughts of .... Jer 23:20   6965
until he have *p* the intents of................ Jer 30:24   6965
which have not *p* the words of the .... Jer 34:18   6965
his sons not to drink wine, are *p* .... Jer 35:14   6965
Jonadab the son of Rechab have *p* .... Jer 35:16   6965
LORD shall be *p* against Babylon .... Jer 51:29   6965
it, and *p* it, saith the LORD .... Eze 37:14   6213
day that these things shall be *p* .... Lk 1:20   1096
when they had *p* all things.................... Lk 2:39   5055
When therefore I have *p* this .... Rom 15:28   2005

PERFORMETH
that *p* not this promise, even .... Neh 5:13   6965
For he *p* the thing that is .... Job 23:14   7999
unto God that *p* all things for me .... Ps 57:2   1584
p the counsel of his messengers .... Is 44:26   7999

PERFORMING
or a sacrifice in *p* a vow .... Num 15:3   6381
or for a sacrifice in *p* a vow .... Num 15:8   6381

PERFUME
And thou shalt make it a *p* .... Ex 30:35   7004
as for the *p* which thou shalt .... Ex 30:37   7004
Ointment and *p* rejoice the heart .... Prov 27:9   7004

PERFUMED
I have *p* my bed with myrrh, aloes .... Prov 7:17   5130
p with myrrh and frankincense, ... Song 3:6   6999

PERFUMES
ointment, and didst increase thy *p* .... Is 57:9   7547

PERGA (pur'-gah) Capital of Pamphylia.
they came to *P* in Pamphylia................... Acts 13:13   4011
But when they departed from *P* .... Acts 13:14   4011
they had preached the word in *P*............ Acts 14:25   4011

PERGAMOS (pur'-ga-mos) A city in Mysia in Asia Minor.
and unto Smyrna, and unto *P* .... Rev 1:11   4010
angel of the church in *P* write............... Rev 2:12   4010

PERGAMUM See PERGAMOS.

PERHAPS See APPENDIX.

PERIDA (per-i'-dah) A family of exiles.
of Sophereth, the children of *P*............... Neh 7:57   6514

PERIL
We gat our bread with the *p* of.............. Lam 5:9
or famine, or nakedness, or *p* .... Rom 8:35   2794

PERILOUS
the last days *p* times shall come 2Ti 3:1   5467

PERILS
in *p* of waters 2Cor 11:26   2794
in *p* of robbers 2Cor 11:26   2794
in *p* by mine own countrymen 2Cor 11:26   2794
in *p* by the heathen................................. 2Cor 11:26   2794
in *p* in the city 2Cor 11:26   2794
in *p* in the wilderness.............................. 2Cor 11:26   2794
in *p* in the sea... 2Cor 11:26   2794
in *p* among false brethren 2Cor 11:26   2794

PERISH
that the land *p* not through the .... Gen 41:36   3772
LORD to gaze, and many of them *p*.......... Ex 19:21   5307
or the eye of his maid, that it *p*.............. Ex 21:26   7843
ye shall *p* among the heathen, and........ Lev 26:38   6
we die, we *p*, we all *p* .... Num 17:12   6
end shall be that he *p* for ever .... Num 24:20   8
Eber, and he also shall *p* for ever .... Num 24:24   8
that ye shall soon utterly *p* from .... Deut 4:26   6
this day that ye shall surely *p* .... Deut 8:19   6
before your face, so shall ye *p* .... Deut 8:20   6
lest ye *p* quickly from off the................. Deut 11:17   6
A Syrian ready to *p* was my father .... Deut 26:5   6
and until thou *p* quickly .... Deut 28:20   6
shall pursue thee until thou *p*................ Deut 28:22   6
this day, that ye shall surely *p* .... Deut 30:18   6
until ye *p* from off this good................... Josh 23:13   6
ye shall *p* quickly from off the .... Josh 23:16   6
So let all thine enemies *p*...................... Judg 5:31   6
shall descend into battle, and *p* 1Sa 26:10   5595
I shall now *p* one day by the hand 1Sa 27:1   5595
the whole house of Ahab shall *p* 2Kin 9:8   6
to kill, and to cause to *p* .... Est 3:13   6
and if I *p*, I *p* .... Est 4:16   6
destroyed, to be slain, and to *p*.............. Est 7:4   6
to slay, and to cause to *p* .... Est 8:11   6
of them *p* from their seed...................... Est 9:28   5486
Let the day *p* wherein I was born, ... Job 3:3   6
By the blast of God they *p* .... Job 4:9   6
they *p* for ever without any .... Job 4:20   6
they go to nothing, and *p* .... Job 6:18   6
and the hypocrite's hope shall *p* .... Job 8:13   6
shall *p* from the earth, and he .... Job 18:17   6
Yet he shall *p* for ever like his............... Job 20:7   6
that was ready to *p* came upon me .... Job 29:13   6
If I have seen any *p* for want of .... Job 31:19   6
All flesh shall *p* together....................... Job 34:15   1478
they shall *p* by the sword, and .... Job 36:12   5674
the way of the ungodly shall *p* .... Ps 1:6   6
ye *p* from the way, when his wrath .... Ps 2:12   6
shall fall and *p* at thy presence .... Ps 9:3   6
of the poor shall not *p* for ever .... Ps 9:18   6
But the wicked shall *p*, and the .... Ps 37:20   6
When shall he die, and his name *p* .... Ps 41:5   6
the fool and the brutish person *p* .... Ps 49:10   6
he is like the beasts that *p* .... Ps 49:12   1820
not, is like the beasts that *p*.................. Ps 49:20   1820
so let the wicked *p* at the .... Ps 68:2   6
that are far from thee shall *p*................. Ps 73:27   6
they *p* at the rebuke of thy .... Ps 80:16   6

P

let them be put to shame, and p	Ps 83:17	6
for, lo, thine enemies shall p	Ps 92:9	6
They shall p, but thou shalt	Ps 102:26	6
the desire of the wicked shall p	Ps 112:10	6
in that very day his thoughts p	Ps 146:4	6
expectation of the wicked shall p	Prov 10:28	6
dieth, his expectation shall p	Prov 11:7	6
and when the wicked p, there is	Prov 11:10	6
and he that speaketh lies shall p	Prov 19:9	6
A false witness shall p	Prov 21:28	6
but when they p, the righteous	Prov 28:28	6
there is no vision, the people p	Prov 29:18	6544
drink unto him that is ready to p	Prov 31:6	6
those riches p by evil travail	Eccl 5:14	6
and made all their memory to p	Is 26:14	6
ready to p in the land of Assyria	Is 27:13	6
wisdom of their wise men shall p	Is 29:14	6
that strive with thee shall p	Is 41:11	6
that will not serve thee shall p	Is 60:12	6
the heart of the king shall p	Jer 4:9	6
neighbour and his friend shall p	Jer 6:21	6
even they shall p from the earth	Jer 10:11	7
of their visitation they shall p	Jer 10:15	6
law shall not p from the priest	Jer 18:18	6
drive you out, and ye should p	Jer 27:10	6
drive you out, and that ye might p	Jer 27:15	6
and the remnant in Judah p	Jer 40:15	6
the valley also shall p, and the	Jer 48:8	6
of their visitation they shall p	Jer 51:18	6
the law shall p from the priest	Eze 7:26	6
thee to p out of the countries	Eze 25:7	6
his fellows should not p with the	Dan 2:18	7
of the Philistines shall p	Amos 1:8	6
the flight shall p from the swift	Amos 2:14	6
and the houses of ivory shall p	Amos 3:15	6
will think upon us, that we p not	Jonah 1:6	6
let us not p for this man's life,	Jonah 1:14	6
his fierce anger, that we p not	Jonah 3:9	6
and the king shall p from Gaza	Zec 9:5	6
that one of thy members should p	Mt 5:29	622
that one of thy members should p	Mt 5:30	622
Lord, save us: we p	Mt 8:25	622
runneth out, and the bottles p	Mt 9:17	622
one of these little ones should p	Mt 18:14	622
the sword shall p with the sword	Mt 26:52	622
Master, carest thou not that we p	Mk 4:38	622
spilled, and the bottles shall p	Lk 5:37	622
him, saying, Master, master, we p	Lk 8:24	622
repent, ye shall all likewise p	Lk 13:3	622
repent, ye shall all likewise p	Lk 13:5	622
that a prophet p out of Jerusalem	Lk 13:33	622
and to spare, and I p with hunger	Lk 15:17	622
shall not an hair of your head p	Lk 21:18	622
believeth in him should not p	Jn 3:15	622
believeth in him should not p	Jn 3:16	622
and they shall never p, neither	Jn 10:28	622
and that the whole nation p not	Jn 11:50	622
him, Thy money with thee	Acts 8:20	1510,1519,604
ye despisers, and wonder, and p	Acts 13:41	853
law shall also p without law	Rom 2:12	622
is to them that p foolishness	1Cor 1:18	622
shall the weak brother p, for	1Cor 8:11	622
that are saved, and in them that p	2Cor 2:15	622
but though our outward man p	2Cor 4:16	1311
Which all are to p with the using	Col 2:22	5356
of unrighteousness in them that p	2Th 2:10	622
They shall p; but thou	Heb 1:11	622
shall utterly p in their own	2Pet 2:12	2704
not willing that any should p	2Pet 3:9	622

PERISHED

and they p from among the	Num 16:33	6
Heshbon is p even unto Dibon, and	Num 21:30	6
that man p not alone in his	Josh 22:20	1478
fallen, and the weapons of war p	2Sa 1:27	6
Remember, I pray thee, who ever p	Job 4:7	6
profit me, in whom old age was p	Job 30:2	6
their memorial is p with them	Ps 9:6	6
the heathen are p out of his land	Ps 10:16	6
Which p at En-dor	Ps 83:10	8045
then have p in mine affliction	Ps 119:92	6
hatred, and their envy, is now p	Eccl 9:6	6
truth is p, and is cut off from	Jer 7:28	6
riches that he hath gotten are p	Jer 48:36	6
is counsel p from the prudent	Jer 49:7	6
my hope is p from the Lord	Lam 3:18	6
the harvest of the field is p	Joel 1:11	6
up in a night, and p in a night	Jonah 4:10	6
is thy counsellor p	Mic 4:9	6
The good man is p out of the	Mic 7:2	6
into the sea, and p in the waters	Mt 8:32	599

which p between the altar and the	Lk 11:51	622
after him: he also p	Acts 5:37	622
are fallen asleep in Christ are p	1Cor 15:18	622
By faith the harlot Rahab p not	Heb 11:31	4881
being overflowed with water, p	2Pet 3:6	622
p in the gainsaying of Core	Jude 11	622

PERISHETH

The old lion p for lack of prey,	Job 4:11	6
and the hope of unjust men p	Prov 11:7	6
man that p in his righteousness	Eccl 7:15	6
The righteous p, and no man layeth	Is 57:1	6
declare it, for what the land p	Jer 9:12	6
the people of Chemosh p	Jer 48:46	6
Labour not for the meat which p	Jn 6:27	622
the grace of the fashion of it p	Jas 1:11	622
more precious than of gold that p	1Pet 1:7	622

PERISHING

and his life from p by the sword	Job 33:18	5674

PERIZZITE (per'-iz-zite) See PERIZZITES. *A tribe in Judah.*

the P dwelled then in the land	Gen 13:7	6522
Amorite, and the Hittite, and the P	Ex 33:2	6522
and the Hittite, and the P	Ex 34:11	6522
the Amorite, the Canaanite, the P	Josh 9:1	6522
Amorite, and the Hittite, and the P	Josh 11:3	6522

PERIZZITES (per'-iz-zites)

And the Hittites, and the P	Gen 15:20	6522
among the Canaanites and the P	Gen 34:30	6522
and the Amorites, and the P	Ex 3:8	6522
and the Hittites, and the P	Ex 3:17	6522
and the Hittites, and the P	Ex 23:23	6522
and the Canaanites, and the P	Deut 7:1	6522
the Canaanites, and the P	Deut 20:17	6522
and the Hivites, and the P	Josh 3:10	6522
and the Canaanites, and the P	Josh 12:8	6522
there in the land of the P	Josh 17:15	6522
you, the Amorites, and the P	Josh 24:11	6522
and the P into their hand	Judg 1:4	6522
they slew the Canaanites and the P	Judg 1:5	6522
Hittites, and Amorites, and P	Judg 3:5	6522
left of the Amorites, Hittites, P	1Kin 9:20	6522
and the Amorites, and the P	2Chr 8:7	6522
Canaanites, the Hittites, the P	Ezr 9:1	6522
Hittites, the Amorites, and the P	Neh 9:8	6522

PERJURED

for p persons, and if there be any	1Ti 1:10	1965

PERMISSION

But I speak this by p, and not of	1Cor 7:6	4774

PERMIT

a while with you, if the Lord p	1Cor 16:7	2010
And this will we do, if God p	Heb 6:3	2010

PERMITTED

Thou art p to speak for thyself	Acts 26:1	2010
for it is not p unto them to	1Cor 14:34	2010

PERNICIOUS

And many shall follow their p ways	2Pet 2:2	684

PERPETUAL

is with you, for p generations	Gen 9:12	5769
shall be theirs for a p statute	Ex 29:9	5769
a p incense before the Lord	Ex 30:8	8548
generations, for a p covenant	Ex 31:16	5769
It shall be a p statute for your	Lev 3:17	5769
fine flour for a meat offering p	Lev 6:20	8548
Lord made by fire by a p statute	Lev 24:9	5769
for it is their p possession	Lev 25:34	5769
it shall be a p statute unto them	Num 19:21	5769
destructions are come to a p end	Ps 9:6	5331
thy feet unto the p desolations	Ps 74:3	5331
he put them to a p reproach	Ps 78:66	5769
bound of the sea by a p decree	Jer 5:22	5769
slidden back by a p backsliding	Jer 8:5	5331
Why is my pain p, and my wound	Jer 15:18	5331
land desolate, and a p hissing	Jer 18:16	5769
a p shame, which shall not be	Jer 23:40	5769
and an hissing, and p desolations	Jer 25:9	5769
and will make it p desolations	Jer 25:12	5769
cities thereof shall be p wastes	Jer 49:13	5769
in a p covenant that shall not be	Jer 50:5	5769
may rejoice, and sleep a p sleep	Jer 51:39	5769
and they shall sleep a p sleep	Jer 51:57	5769
Because thou hast had a p hatred	Eze 35:5	5769
I will make thee p desolations	Eze 35:9	5769
by a p ordinance unto the Lord	Eze 46:14	5769
scattered, the p hills did bow	Hab 3:6	5769
and saltpits, and a p desolation	Zeph 2:9	5769

PERPETUALLY
and mine heart shall be there *p* ...... 1Kin 9:3 — 3605,3711
and mine heart shall be there *p* ...... 2Chr 7:16 — 3605,3711
all pity, and his anger did tear *p* .... Amos 1:11 — 5703

PERPLEXED
but the city Shushan was *p* .... Est 3:15 — 943
the herds of cattle are *p* .... Joel 1:18 — 943
and he was *p*, because that it was .... Lk 9:7 — 1280
as they were much *p* thereabout .... Lk 24:4 — 1280
we are *p*, but not in despair .... 2Cor 4:8 — 639

PERPLEXITY
of *p* by the Lord GOD of hosts in .... Is 22:5 — 3998
now shall be their *p* .... Mic 7:4 — 3998
earth distress of nations, with *p* .... Lk 21:25 — 640

PERSECUTE
Why do ye *p* me as God, and are not ..... Job 19:22 — 7291
Why *p* we him, seeing the root of .... Job 19:28 — 7291
save me from all them that *p* me .... Ps 7:1 — 7291
Let the enemy *p* my soul, and take .... Ps 7:5 — 7291
in his pride doth *p* the poor .... Ps 10:2 — 1814
enemies, and from them that *p* me .... Ps 31:15 — 7291
the way against them that *p* me .... Ps 35:3 — 7291
let the angel of the LORD *p* them .... Ps 35:6 — 7291
For they *p* him whom thou hast .... Ps 69:26 — 7291
p and take him .... Ps 71:11 — 7291
So *p* them with thy tempest, and .... Ps 83:15 — 7291
judgment on them that *p* me .... Ps 119:84 — 7291
they *p* me wrongfully .... Ps 119:86 — 7291
Let them be confounded that *p* me .... Jer 17:18 — 7291
I will *p* them with the sword, ... Jer 29:18 — 7921,310
P and destroy them in anger from .... Lam 3:66 — 7291
***p* you, and shall say all manner of** ...... Mt 5:11 — 1377
despitefully use you, and *p* you .... Mt 5:44 — 1377
But when they *p* you in this city, ... Mt 10:23 — 1377
and *p* them from city to city .... Mt 23:34 — 1377
some of them they shall slay and *p* ...... Lk 11:49 — 1559
***p* you, delivering you up to the** .... Lk 21:12 — 1377
And therefore did the Jews *p* Jesus ...... Jn 5:16 — 1377
me, they will also *p* you .... Jn 15:20 — 1377
Bless them which *p* you .... Rom 12:14 — 1377

PERSECUTED
them that hate thee, which *p* thee .... Deut 30:7 — 7291
but *p* the poor and needy man, that ...... Ps 109:16 — 7291
Princes have *p* me without a cause .... Ps 119:161 — 7291
For the enemy hath *p* my soul .... Ps 143:3 — 7291
ruled the nations in anger, is *p* .... Is 14:6 — 4783
hast covered with anger, and *p* us .... Lam 3:43 — 7291
are *p* for righteousness' sake .... Mt 5:10 — 1377
for so *p* they the prophets which .... Mt 5:12 — 1377
If they have *p* me, they will also .... Jn 15:20 — 1377
prophets have not your fathers *p* .... Acts 7:52 — 1377
I *p* this way unto the death, ... Acts 22:4 — 1377
I *p* them even unto strange cities .... Acts 26:11 — 1377
being *p*, we suffer it .... 1Cor 4:12 — 1377
because I *p* the church of God .... 1Cor 15:9 — 1377
P, but not forsaken .... 2Cor 4:9 — 1377
measure I *p* the church of God .... Gal 1:13 — 1377
That he which *p* us in times past .... Gal 1:23 — 1377
p him that was born after the .... Gal 4:29 — 1377
their own prophets, and have *p* us .... 1Th 2:15 — 1559
he *p* the woman which brought .... Rev 12:13 — 1377

PERSECUTEST
him, Saul, Saul, why *p* thou me .... Acts 9:4 — 1377
Lord said, I am Jesus whom thou *p* ...... Acts 9:5 — 1377
me, Saul, Saul, why *p* thou me .... Acts 22:7 — 1377
am Jesus of Nazareth, whom thou *p* ..... Acts 22:8 — 1377
tongue, Saul, Saul, why *p* thou me .... Acts 26:14 — 1377
he said, I am Jesus whom thou *p* .... Acts 26:15 — 1377

PERSECUTING
Concerning zeal, *p* the church .... Phil 3:6 — 1377

PERSECUTION
Our necks are under *p* .... Lam 5:5 — 7291
for when tribulation or *p* ariseth .... Mt 13:21 — 1375
when affliction or *p* ariseth for .... Mk 4:17 — 1375
at that time there was a great *p* .... Acts 8:1 — 1375
the *p* that arose about Stephen .... Acts 11:19 — 2347
raised *p* against Paul and Barnabas ...... Acts 13:50 — 1375
tribulation, or distress, or *p* .... Rom 8:35 — 1375
why do I yet suffer *p* .... Gal 5:11 — 1377
suffer *p* for the cross of Christ .... Gal 6:12 — 1377
in Christ Jesus shall suffer *p* .... 2Ti 3:12 — 1377

PERSECUTIONS
and children, and lands, with *p* .... Mk 10:30 — 1375
reproaches, in necessities, in *p* .... 2Cor 12:10 — 1375
patience and faith in all your *p* .... 2Th 1:4 — 1375
P, afflictions, which came unto .... 2Ti 3:11 — 1375
what *p* I endured .... 2Ti 3:11 — 1375

PERSECUTOR
was before a blasphemer, and a *p* .... 1Ti 1:13 — 1376

PERSECUTORS
their *p* thou threwest into the .... Neh 9:11 — 7291
his arrows against the *p* .... Ps 7:13 — 1814
Many are my *p* and mine enemies .... Ps 119:157 — 7291
deliver me from my *p* .... Ps 142:6 — 7291
visit me, and revenge me of my *p* .... Jer 15:15 — 7291
therefore my *p* shall stumble, and .... Jer 20:11 — 7291
all her *p* overtook her between .... Lam 1:3 — 7291
Our *p* are swifter than the eagles .... Lam 4:19 — 7291

PERSEVERANCE
and watching thereunto with all *p* .... Eph 6:18 — 4343

PERSIA (*per'-she-ah*) See ELAM, PERSIAN. *An ancient world power located in present-day Iran.*
the reign of the kingdom of *P* .... 2Chr 36:20 — 6539
the first year of Cyrus king of *P* .... 2Chr 36:22 — 6539
up the spirit of Cyrus king of *P* .... 2Chr 36:22 — 6539
Thus saith Cyrus king of *P* .... 2Chr 36:23 — 6539
the first year of Cyrus king of *P* .... Ezr 1:1 — 6539
up the spirit of Cyrus king of *P* .... Ezr 1:1 — 6539
Thus saith Cyrus king of *P* .... Ezr 1:2 — 6539
of *P* bring forth by the hand of .... Ezr 1:8 — 6539
that they had of Cyrus king of *P* .... Ezr 3:7 — 6539
the king of *P* hath commanded us .... Ezr 4:3 — 6539
all the days of Cyrus king of *P* .... Ezr 4:5 — 6539
the reign of Darius king of *P* .... Ezr 4:5 — 6539
unto Artaxerxes king of *P* .... Ezr 4:7 — 6539
of the reign of Darius king of *P* .... Ezr 4:24 — 6540
Darius, and Artaxerxes king of *P* .... Ezr 6:14 — 6540
the reign of Artaxerxes king of *P* .... Ezr 7:1 — 6539
us in the sight of the kings of *P* .... Ezr 9:9 — 6539
the power of *P* and Media, the .... Est 1:3 — 6539
Memucan, the seven princes of *P* .... Est 1:14 — 6539
Likewise shall the ladies of *P* .... Est 1:18 — 6539
of the kings of Media and *P* .... Est 10:2 — 6539
They of *P* and of Lud and of Phut .... Eze 27:10 — 6539
P, Ethiopia, and Libya with them .... Eze 38:5 — 6539
horns are the kings of Media and *P* .... Dan 8:20 — 6539
of *P* a thing was revealed unto .... Dan 10:1 — 6539
the kingdom of *P* withstood me one ...... Dan 10:13 — 6539
there with the kings of *P* .... Dan 10:13 — 6539
to fight with the prince of *P* .... Dan 10:20 — 6539
stand up yet three kings in *P* .... Dan 11:2 — 6539

PERSIAN (*per'-she-un*) *A native of Persia.*
to the reign of Darius the *P* .... Neh 12:22 — 6542
and in the reign of Cyrus the *P* .... Dan 6:28 — 6523

PERSIANS (*per'-she-uns*) See ELAMITES.
written among the laws of the *P* .... Est 1:19 — 6539
and given to the Medes and *P* .... Dan 5:28 — 6540
to the law of the Medes and *P* .... Dan 6:8 — 6540
to the law of the Medes and *P* .... Dan 6:12 — 6540
P is, That no decree nor statute .... Dan 6:15 — 6540

PERSIS (*pur'-sis*) *A Christian in Rome.*
Salute the beloved *P*, which .... Rom 16:12 — 4069

PERSON
And Joseph was a goodly *p*, and well ..... Gen 39:6
uncircumcised *p* shall eat thereof .... Ex 12:48
not respect the *p* of the poor .... Lev 19:15 — 6440
nor honour the *p* of the mighty .... Lev 19:15 — 6440
the LORD, and that *p* be guilty .... Num 5:6 — 5315
for an unclean *p* they shall take .... Num 19:17
a clean *p* shall take hyssop, and ..... Num 19:18 — 376,120
the clean *p* shall sprinkle upon .... Num 19:19
whatsoever the unclean *p* toucheth .... Num 19:22
whosoever hath killed any *p* .... Num 31:19 — 5315
which killeth any *p* at unawares .... Num 35:11 — 5315
any *p* unawares may flee thither .... Num 35:15 — 5315
Whoso killeth any *p*, the murderer .... Num 35:30 — 5315
against any *p* to cause him to die .... Num 35:30 — 5315
the clean *p* shall eat it alike, ... Deut 15:22
reward to slay an innocent *p* .... Deut 27:25 — 5315
shall not regard the *p* of the old .... Deut 28:50 — 6440
that killeth any *p* unawares .... Josh 20:3 — 5315
that whosoever killeth any *p* at .... Josh 20:9 — 5315
of Israel a goodlier *p* than he .... 1Sa 9:2 — 376
prudent in matters, and a comely *p* .... 1Sa 16:18 — 376
thy voice, and have accepted thy *p* .... 1Sa 25:35 — 6440
men have slain a righteous *p* in .... 2Sa 4:11 — 376
neither doth God respect any *p* .... 2Sa 14:14 — 5315
thou go to battle in thine own *p* .... 2Sa 17:11 — 6440
Will ye accept his *p* .... Job 13:8 — 6440
and he shall save the humble *p* .... Job 22:29
I pray you, accept any man's *p* .... Job 32:21 — 6440
whose eyes a vile *p* is contemned .... Ps 15:4
the fool and the brutish *p* perish .... Ps 49:10
I will not know a wicked *p* .... Ps 101:4

one feeble *p* among their tribes .... Ps 105:37
A naughty *p*, a wicked man, ... Prov 6:12 | 120
to accept the *p* of the wicked .... Prov 18:5 | 6440
shall be called a mischievous *p* .... Prov 24:8 | 1167
of any *p* shall flee to the pit .... Prov 28:17 | 5315
The vile *p* shall be no more .... Is 32:5
For the vile *p* will speak villany .... Is 32:6
every *p* that Nebuzar-adan the .... Jer 43:6 | 5315
them that were near the king's *p* .... Jer 52:25 | 6440
field, to the lothing of thy *p* .... Eze 16:5 | 5315
take any *p* from among them, he is .... Eze 33:6 | 5315
at no dead *p* to defile themselves .... Eze 44:25 | 120
estate shall stand up a vile *p* .... Dan 11:21
with thee, or accept thy *p* .... Mal 1:8 | 6440
thou regardest not the *p* of men .... Mt 22:16 | 4383
of the blood of this just *p* .... Mt 27:24
thou regardest not the *p* of men .... Mk 12:14 | 4383
acceptest thou the *p* of any .... Lk 20:21 | 4383
among yourselves that wicked *p* 1Cor 5:13
forgave I it in the *p* of Christ .... 2Cor 2:10 | 4383
God accepteth no man's *p* .... Gal 2:6 | 4383
no whoremonger, nor unclean *p* .... Eph 5:5
and the express image of his *p* .... Heb 1:3 | 5287
be any fornicator, or profane *p* .... Heb 12:16
but saved Noah the eighth *p* 2Pet 2:5

PERSONS
said unto Abram, Give me the *p* .... Gen 14:21 | 5315
all the *p* of his house, and his .... Gen 36:6 | 5315
according to the number of your *p* .... Ex 16:16 | 5315
the *p* shall be for the LORD by .... Lev 27:2 | 5315
upon the *p* that were there, and .... Num 19:18 | 5315
of five hundred, both of the *p* .... Num 31:28 | 120
one portion of fifty, of the *p* .... Num 31:30 | 120
thirty and two thousand *p* in all ..... Num 31:35 | 5315,120
the *p* were sixteen thousand .... Num 31:40 | 5315,120
tribute was thirty and two *p* .... Num 31:40 | 5315,120
And sixteen thousand *p* .... Num 31:46 | 5315,120
shall not respect in judgment .... Deut 1:17 | 6440
a terrible, which regardeth not *p* .... Deut 10:17 | 6440
Egypt with threescore and ten *p* .... Deut 10:22 | 5315
thou shalt not respect *p*, neither .... Deut 16:19 | 6440
which are threescore and ten *p* .... Judg 9:2 | 376
Abimelech hired vain and light *p* .... Judg 9:4 | 582
being threescore and ten *p* .... Judg 9:5 | 376
his sons, threescore and ten *p* .... Judg 9:18 | 376
the men of Israel about thirty *p* .... Judg 20:39 | 376
bidden, which were about thirty *p* ...... 1Sa 9:22 | 376
five *p* that did wear a linen .... 1Sa 22:18 | 376
all the *p* of thy father's house .... 1Sa 22:22 | 5315
the king's sons, being seventy *p* .... 2Kin 10:6 | 376
king's sons, and slew seventy *p* .... 2Kin 10:7 | 376
LORD our God, nor respect of *p* .... 2Chr 19:7 | 6440
you, if ye do secretly accept *p* .... Job 13:10 | 6440
accepteth not the *p* of princes .... Job 34:19 | 6440
I have not sat with vain *p* .... Ps 26:4 | 4962
accept the *p* of the wicked .... Ps 82:2 | 6440
vain *p* is void of understanding .... Prov 12:11
to have respect of *p* in judgment .... Prov 24:23 | 6440
vain *p* shall have poverty enough .... Prov 28:19
To have respect of *p* is not good .... Prov 28:21 | 6440
eight hundred thirty and two *p* .... Jer 52:29 | 5315
seven hundred forty and five *p* .... Jer 52:30 | 5315
all the *p* were four thousand and .... Jer 52:30 | 5315
not the *p* of the priests, they .... Lam 4:16 | 6440
building forts, to cut off many *p* .... Eze 17:17 | 5315
they traded the *p* of men and .... Eze 27:13 | 5315
p that cannot discern between .... Jonah 4:11 | 120
are light and treacherous *p* .... Zeph 3:4 | 582
will he regard your *p* .... Mal 1:9 | 6440
than ever ninety and nine just *p* .... Lk 15:7
that God is no respecter of *p* .... Acts 10:34 | 4381
the Jews, and with the devout *p* .... Acts 17:17
there is no respect of *p* with God .... Rom 2:11 | 4382
upon us by the means of many *p* .... 2Cor 1:11 | 4383
is there respect of *p* with him .... Eph 6:9 | 4382
and there is no respect of *p* .... Col 3:25 | 4382
for liars, for perjured *p* .... 1Ti 1:10 | 678
Lord of glory, with respect of *p* .... Jas 2:1 | 4382
But if ye have respect to *p* .... Jas 2:9 | 4380
who without respect of *p* judgeth ...... 1Pet 1:17 | 678
what manner of *p* ought ye to be 2Pet 3:11
having men's *p* in admiration .... Jude 16 | 4383

PERSUADE
the LORD said, Who shall *p* Ahab ...... 1Kin 22:20 | 6601
the LORD, and said, I will *p* him .... 1Kin 22:21 | 6601
And he said, Thou shalt *p* him .... 1Kin 22:22 | 6601
Doth not Hezekiah *p* you to give .... 2Chr 32:11 | 5496
nor *p* you on this manner, neither ...... 2Chr 32:15 | 5496
Beware lest Hezekiah *p* you .... Is 36:18 | 5496
governor's ears, we will *p* him .... Mt 28:14 | 3982

the terror of the Lord, we *p* men .... 2Cor 5:11 | 3982
For do I now *p* men, or God .... Gal 1:10 | 3982

PERSUADED
p him to go up with him to .... 2Chr 18:2 | 5496
By long forbearing is a prince *p* .... Prov 25:15 | 6601
elders *p* the multitude that they .... Mt 27:20 | 3982
prophets, neither will they be *p* ...... Lk 16:31 | 3982
for they be *p* that John was a .... Lk 20:6 | 3982
p them to continue in the grace .... Acts 13:43 | 3982
who *p* the people, and, having .... Acts 14:19 | 3982
and *p* the Jews and the Greeks .... Acts 18:4 | 3982
all Asia, this Paul hath *p* .... Acts 19:26 | 3982
And when he would not be *p* .... Acts 21:14 | 3982
for I am *p* that none of these .... Acts 26:26 | 3982
And being fully *p* that, what he .... Rom 4:21 | 4135
For I am *p*, that neither death, ... Rom 8:38 | 3982
man be fully *p* in his own mind .... Rom 14:5 | 4135
am *p* by the Lord Jesus, that .... Rom 14:14 | 3982
And I myself also am *p* of you .... Rom 15:14 | 3982
and I am *p* that in thee also .... 2Ti 1:5 | 3982
am *p* that he is able to keep that ..... 2Ti 1:12 | 3982
we are *p* better things of you, and .... Heb 6:9 | 3982
were *p* of them, and embraced them, ... Heb 11:13 | 3982

PERSUADEST
Paul, Almost thou *p* me to be a .... Acts 26:28 | 3982

PERSUADETH
not unto Hezekiah, when he *p* you ..... 2Kin 18:32 | 5496
This fellow *p* men to worship God ...... Acts 18:13 | 374

PERSUADING
p the things concerning the .... Acts 19:8 | 3982
p them concerning Jesus, both out ..... Acts 28:23 | 3982

PERSUASION
This *p* cometh not of him that .... Gal 5:8 | 3988

PERTAIN
that *p* unto the LORD, having his .... Lev 7:20
which *p* unto the LORD, even that ...... Lev 7:21
if I leave of all that *p* to him 1Sa 25:22
in those things which *p* to God .... Rom 15:17
more things that *p* to this life 1Cor 6:3
us all things that *p* unto life 2Pet 1:3

PERTAINED
(Now the half that *p* unto the .... Num 31:43
a hill that *p* to Phinehas his son ...... Josh 24:33
that *p* unto Joash the Abi-ezrite .... Judg 6:11
was missed of all that *p* unto him 1Sa 25:21
which *p* to Ish-bosheth the son of 2Sa 2:15
master's son all that *p* unto Saul ...... 2Sa 9:9 | 1961
are all that *p* unto Mephibosheth 2Sa 16:4
to him *p* Sochoh, and all the land 1Kin 4:10
to him *p* Taanach and Megiddo, and ... 1Kin 4:12
to him *p* the towns of Jair the 1Kin 4:13
to him also *p* the region of Argob 1Kin 4:13
made all the vessels that *p* unto 1Kin 7:48
all that *p* to the king of Egypt 2Kin 24:7
thereof every morning *p* to them 1Chr 9:27
that *p* to the children of 1Chr 11:31
fenced cities which *p* to Judah 2Chr 12:4
that *p* to the children of Israel 2Chr 34:33

PERTAINETH
get that which *p* to his cleansing ...... Lev 14:32
priest *p* the oil for the light .... Num 4:16
not wear that which *p* unto a man ..... Deut 22:5 | 3627
wherefore Ziklag *p* unto the kings ..... 1Sa 27:6 | 1961
Obed-edom, and all that *p* unto him ... 2Sa 6:12
to whom *p* the adoption, and the ...... Rom 9:4
are spoken *p* to another tribe .... Heb 7:13 | 3348

PERTAINING
were *p* unto the children of .... Josh 13:31
for every matter *p* to God 1Chr 26:32
things *p* to the kingdom of God .... Acts 1:3 | 4012
as *p* to the flesh, hath found .... Rom 4:1
of things *p* to this life, set 1Cor 6:4
high priest in things *p* to God .... Heb 2:17
for men in things *p* to God .... Heb 5:1
perfect, as *p* to the conscience ...... Heb 9:9

PERUDA (per'-u-dah) See PERIDA. *A family of exiles.*
of Sophereth, the children of P .... Ezr 2:55 | 6514

PERVERSE
because thy way is *p* before me .... Num 22:32 | 3399
they are a *p* and crooked .... Deut 32:5 | 6141
Thou son of the *p* rebellious .... 1Sa 20:30 | 5753
cannot my taste discern *p* things .... Job 6:30 | 1942
perfect, it shall also prove me *p* .... Job 9:20 | 6140
and *p* lips put far from thee .... Prov 4:24 | 3891
is nothing froward or *p* in them ..... Prov 8:8 | 6141

but he that is of a *p* heart shall	Prov 12:8	5753
but he that is *p* in his ways	Prov 14:2	3868
he that hath a *p* tongue falleth	Prov 17:20	2015
than he that is *p* in his lips	Prov 19:1	6141
thine heart shall utter *p* things	Prov 23:33	8419
than he that is *p* in his ways	Prov 28:6	6141
but he that is *p* in his ways	Prov 28:18	6140
The LORD hath mingled a *p* spirit	Is 19:14	5773
p generation, how long shall I be	Mt 17:17	*1294*
p generation, how long shall I be	Lk 9:41	*1294*
men arise, speaking *p* things	Acts 20:30	*1294*
p nation, among whom ye shine as	Phil 2:15	*1294*
P disputings of men of corrupt	1Ti 6:5	*3859*

PERVERSELY

that which thy servant did *p* the	2Sa 19:19	5753
We have sinned, and have done *p*	1Kin 8:47	5753
for they dealt *p* with me without	Ps 119:78	5791

PERVERSENESS

neither hath he seen *p* in Israel	Num 23:21	5999
but the *p* of transgressors shall	Prov 11:3	5558
but *p* therein is a breach in the	Prov 15:4	5558
word, and trust in oppression and *p*	Is 30:12	3868
lies, your tongue hath muttered *p*	Is 59:3	5766
of blood, and the city full of *p*	Eze 9:9	4297

PERVERT

p the words of the righteous	Deut 16:19	5557
Thou shalt not *p* the judgment of	Deut 24:17	5186
Doth God *p* judgment	Job 8:3	5791
or doth the Almighty *p* justice	Job 8:3	5791
will the Almighty *p* judgment	Job 34:12	5791
bosom to *p* the ways of judgment	Prov 17:23	5186
p the judgment of any of the	Prov 31:5	8138
abhor judgment, and *p* all equity	Mic 3:9	6140
wilt thou not cease to *p* the	Acts 13:10	*1294*
would *p* the gospel of Christ	Gal 1:7	*3344*

PERVERTED

and took bribes, and *p* judgment	1Sa 8:3	5186
p that which was right, and it	Job 33:27	5753
and thy knowledge, it hath *p* thee	Is 47:10	7725
for they have *p* their way	Jer 3:21	5753
for ye have *p* the words of the	Jer 23:36	2015

PERVERTETH

p the words of the righteous	Ex 23:8	5557
Cursed be he that *p* the judgment	Deut 27:19	5186
but he that *p* his ways shall be	Prov 10:9	6140
The foolishness of man *p* his way	Prov 19:3	5557
unto me, as one that *p* the people	Lk 23:14	*654*

PERVERTING

violent *p* of judgment and justice	Eccl 5:8	
We found this fellow *p* the nation	Lk 23:2	*1294*

PESTILENCE

lest he fall upon us with *p*	Ex 5:3	1698
smite thee and thy people with *p*	Ex 9:15	1698
I will send the *p* among you	Lev 26:25	1698
I will smite them with the *p*	Num 14:12	1698
shall make the *p* cleave unto thee	Deut 28:21	1698
be three days' *p* in thy land	2Sa 24:13	1698
So the LORD sent a *p* upon Israel	2Sa 24:15	1698
in the land famine, if there be *p*	1Kin 8:37	1698
the sword of the LORD, even the *p*	1Chr 21:12	1698
So the LORD sent *p* upon Israel	1Chr 21:14	1698
dearth in the land, if there be *p*	2Chr 6:28	1698
or if I send *p* among my people	2Chr 7:13	1698
us, as the sword, judgment, or *p*	2Chr 20:9	1698
but gave their life over to the *p*	Ps 78:50	1698
the fowler, and from the noisome *p*	Ps 91:3	1698
Nor for the *p* that walketh in	Ps 91:6	1698
and by the famine, and by the *p*	Jer 14:12	1698
they shall die of a great *p*	Jer 21:6	1698
are left in this city from the *p*	Jer 21:7	1698
and by the famine, and by the *p*	Jer 21:9	1698
the sword, the famine, and the *p*	Jer 24:10	1698
and with the famine, and with the *p*	Jer 27:8	1698
sword, by the famine, and by the *p*	Jer 27:13	1698
of war, and of evil, and of *p*	Jer 28:8	1698
the sword, the famine, and the *p*	Jer 29:17	1698
with the famine, and with the *p*	Jer 29:18	1698
and of the famine, and of the *p*	Jer 32:24	1698
and by the famine, and by the *p*	Jer 32:36	1698
the LORD, to the sword, to the *p*	Jer 34:17	1698
sword, by the famine, and by the *p*	Jer 38:2	1698
sword, by the famine, and by the *p*	Jer 42:17	1698
sword, by the famine, and by the *p*	Jer 42:22	1698
sword, by the famine, and by the *p*	Jer 44:13	1698
part of thee shall die with the *p*	Eze 5:12	1698
and *p* and blood shall pass through	Eze 5:17	1698
sword, the famine, and by the *p*	Eze 6:11	1698

is far off shall die of the *p*	Eze 6:12	1698
The sword is without, and the *p*	Eze 7:15	1698
famine and *p* shall devour him	Eze 7:15	1698
from the famine, and from the *p*	Eze 12:16	1698
Or if I send a *p* into that land	Eze 14:19	1698
and the noisome beast, and the *p*	Eze 14:21	1698
For I will send into her *p*	Eze 28:23	1698
in the caves shall die of the *p*	Eze 33:27	1698
I will plead against him with *p*	Eze 38:22	1698
the *p* after the manner of Egypt	Amos 4:10	1698
Before him went the *p*, and burning	Hab 3:5	1698

PESTILENCES

and there shall be famines, and *p*	Mt 24:7	*3061*
divers places, and famines, and *p*	Lk 21:11	*3061*

PESTILENT

we have found this man a *p* fellow	Acts 24:5	*3061*

PESTLE

in a mortar among wheat with a *p*	Prov 27:22	5940

PETER *(pe'-tur)* See CEPHAS, PETER'S, SIMON. *A disciple of Jesus.*

saw two brethren, Simon called *P*	Mt 4:18	*4074*
The first, Simon, who is called *P*	Mt 10:2	*4074*
P answered him and said, Lord, if	Mt 14:28	*4074*
when *P* was come down out of the	Mt 14:29	*4074*
Then answered *P* and said unto him,	Mt 15:15	*4074*
Simon *P* answered and said, Thou	Mt 16:16	*4074*
also unto thee, That thou art *P*	Mt 16:18	*4074*
Then *P* took him, and began to	Mt 16:22	*4074*
But he turned, and said unto *P*	Mt 16:23	*4074*
And after six days Jesus taketh *P*	Mt 17:1	*4074*
Then answered *P*, and said unto	Mt 17:4	*4074*
received tribute money came to *P*	Mt 17:24	*4074*
P saith unto him, Of strangers	Mt 17:26	*4074*
Then came *P* to him, and said, Lord	Mt 18:21	*4074*
Then answered *P* and said unto,	Mt 19:27	*4074*
P answered and said unto him,	Mt 26:33	*4074*
P said unto him, Though I should	Mt 26:35	*4074*
And he took with him *P* and the two	Mt 26:37	*4074*
them asleep, and saith unto *P*	Mt 26:40	*4074*
But *P* followed him afar off unto	Mt 26:58	*4074*
Now *P* sat without in the palace	Mt 26:69	*4074*
they stood by, and said to *P*	Mt 26:73	*4074*
P remembered the word of Jesus,	Mt 26:75	*4074*
And Simon he surnamed *P*	Mk 3:16	*4074*
no man to follow him, save *P*	Mk 5:37	*4074*
P answereth and saith unto him,	Mk 8:29	*4074*
P took him, and began to rebuke	Mk 8:32	*4074*
on his disciples, he rebuked *P*	Mk 8:33	*4074*
six days Jesus taketh with him *P*	Mk 9:2	*4074*
P answered and said to Jesus,	Mk 9:5	*4074*
Then *P* began to say unto him, Lo,	Mk 10:28	*4074*
P calling to remembrance saith	Mk 11:21	*4074*
Olives over against the temple, *P*	Mk 13:3	*4074*
But *P* said unto him, Although all	Mk 14:29	*4074*
And he taketh with him *P* and James	Mk 14:33	*4074*
them sleeping, and saith unto *P*	Mk 14:37	*4074*
P followed him afar off, even	Mk 14:54	*4074*
as *P* was beneath in the palace,	Mk 14:66	*4074*
when she saw *P* warming himself,	Mk 14:67	*4074*
that stood by said again to *P*	Mk 14:70	*4074*
P called to mind the word that	Mk 14:72	*4074*
P that he goeth before you into	Mk 16:7	*4074*
When Simon *P* saw it, he fell down	Lk 5:8	*4074*
Simon, (whom he also named *P*	Lk 6:14	*4074*
When all denied, *P* and they that	Lk 8:45	*4074*
suffered no man to go in, save *P*	Lk 8:51	*4074*
P answering said, The Christ of	Lk 9:20	*4074*
after these sayings, he took *P*	Lk 9:28	*4074*
But *P* and they that were with him	Lk 9:32	*4074*
P said unto Jesus, Master, it is	Lk 9:33	*4074*
Then *P* said unto him, Lord,	Lk 12:41	*4074*
Then *P* said, Lo, we have left all	Lk 18:28	*4074*
And he sent *P* and John, saying, Go	Lk 22:8	*4074*
And he said, I tell thee, *P*	Lk 22:34	*4074*
And *P* followed afar off	Lk 22:54	*4074*
together, *P* sat down among them	Lk 22:55	*4074*
And *P* said, Man, I am not	Lk 22:58	*4074*
P said, Man, I know not what thou	Lk 22:60	*4074*
the Lord turned, and looked upon *P*	Lk 22:61	*4074*
P remembered the word of the Lord	Lk 22:61	*4074*
P went out, and wept bitterly	Lk 22:62	*4074*
Then arose *P*, and ran unto the	Lk 24:12	*4074*
the city of Andrew and *P*	Jn 1:44	*4074*
Then Simon *P* answered him, Lord,	Jn 6:68	*4074*
Then cometh he to Simon *P*	Jn 13:6	*4074*
P saith unto him, Lord, dost thou	Jn 13:6	
P saith unto him, Thou shalt	Jn 13:8	
Simon *P* saith unto him, Lord, not	Jn 13:9	*4074*
Simon *P* therefore beckoned to him	Jn 13:24	*4074*

P

Simon P said unto him, Lord,	Jn 13:36	4074
P said unto him, Lord, why cannot	Jn 13:37	4074
Then Simon P having a sword drew	Jn 18:10	4074
Then said Jesus unto P, Put up	Jn 18:11	4074
Simon P followed Jesus, and so did	Jn 18:15	4074
But P stood at the door without	Jn 18:16	4074
kept the door, and brought in P	Jn 18:16	4074
damsel that kept the door unto P	Jn 18:17	4074
P stood with them, and warmed	Jn 18:18	4074
And Simon P stood and warmed	Jn 18:25	4074
his kinsman whose ear P cut off	Jn 18:26	4074
P then denied again	Jn 18:27	4074
she runneth, and cometh to Simon P	Jn 20:2	4074
P therefore went forth, and that	Jn 20:3	4074
the other disciple did outrun P	Jn 20:4	4074
Then cometh Simon P following him	Jn 20:6	4074
There were together Simon P	Jn 21:2	4074
Simon P saith unto them, I go a	Jn 21:3	4074
whom Jesus loved saith unto P	Jn 21:7	4074
Now when Simon P heard that it	Jn 21:7	4074
Simon P went up, and drew the net	Jn 21:11	4074
had dined, Jesus saith to Simon P	Jn 21:15	4074
P was grieved because he said	Jn 21:17	4074
Then P, turning about, seeth the	Jn 21:20	4074
P seeing him saith to Jesus, Lord	Jn 21:21	4074
an upper room, where abode both P	Acts 1:13	4074
in those days P stood up in the	Acts 1:15	4074
But P, standing up with the	Acts 2:14	4074
in their heart, and said unto P	Acts 2:37	4074
Then P said unto them, Repent, and	Acts 2:38	4074
Now P and John went up together	Acts 3:1	4074
Who seeing P and John about to go	Acts 3:3	4074
And P, fastening his eyes upon him	Acts 3:6	4074
Then P said, Silver and gold have	Acts 3:6	4074
lame man which was healed held P	Acts 3:11	4074
when P saw it, he answered unto	Acts 3:12	4074
Then P, filled with the Holy	Acts 4:8	4074
when they saw the boldness of P	Acts 4:13	4074
But P and John answered and asked	Acts 4:19	4074
But P said, Ananias, why hath	Acts 5:3	4074
P answered unto her, Tell me	Acts 5:8	4074
Then P said unto her, How is it	Acts 5:9	4074
of P passing by might overshadow	Acts 5:15	4074
Then P and the other apostles	Acts 5:29	4074
of God, they sent unto them P	Acts 8:14	4074
But P said unto him, Thy money	Acts 8:20	4074
as P passed throughout all	Acts 9:32	4074
P said unto him, Aeneas, Jesus	Acts 9:34	4074
had heard that P was there	Acts 9:38	4074
Then P arose and went with them	Acts 9:39	4074
But P put them all forth, and	Acts 9:40	4074
and when she saw P, she sat up	Acts 9:40	4074
for one Simon, whose surname is P	Acts 10:5	4074
P went up upon the housetop to	Acts 10:9	4074
came a voice to him, Rise, P	Acts 10:13	4074
But P said, Not so, Lord	Acts 10:14	4074
Now while P doubted in himself	Acts 10:17	4074
Simon, which was surnamed P	Acts 10:18	4074
While P thought on the vision,	Acts 10:19	4074
Then P went down to the men which	Acts 10:21	4074
on the morrow P went away with	Acts 10:23	4074
as P was coming in, Cornelius met	Acts 10:25	4074
But P took him up, saying, Stand	Acts 10:26	4074
hither Simon, whose surname is P	Acts 10:32	4074
Then P opened his mouth, and said,	Acts 10:34	4074
While P yet spake these words,	Acts 10:44	4074
as many as came with P, because	Acts 10:45	4074
Then answered P,	Acts 10:46	4074
when P was come up to Jerusalem,	Acts 11:2	4074
But P rehearsed the matter from	Acts 11:4	4074
a voice saying unto me, Arise, P	Acts 11:7	4074
for Simon, whose surname is P	Acts 11:13	4074
proceeded further to take P also	Acts 12:3	4074
P therefore was kept in prison	Acts 12:5	4074
the same night P was sleeping	Acts 12:6	4074
he smote P on the side, and raised	Acts 12:7	4074
when P was come to himself, he	Acts 12:11	4074
as P knocked at the door of the	Acts 12:13	4074
told how P stood before the gate	Acts 12:14	4074
But P continued knocking	Acts 12:16	4074
soldiers, what was become of P	Acts 12:18	4074
P rose up, and said unto them, Men	Acts 15:7	4074
I went up to Jerusalem to see P	Gal 1:18	4074
of the circumcision was unto P	Gal 2:7	4074
in P to the apostleship of the	Gal 2:8	4074
But when P was come to Antioch, I	Gal 2:11	4074
I said unto P before them all, If	Gal 2:14	4074
P, an apostle of Jesus Christ, to	1Pet 1:1	4074
Simon P, a servant and an apostle	2Pet 1:1	4074

PETER'S (pe'-turz)

when Jesus was come into P house	Mt 8:14	4074
him, was Andrew, Simon P brother	Jn 1:40	4074
Simon P brother, saith unto him,	Jn 6:8	4074
And when she knew P voice, she	Acts 12:14	4074

PETHAHIAH (peth-a-hi'-ah)
   1. A sanctuary servant.

The nineteenth to P, the	1Chr 24:16	6611

   2. Married a foreigner.

Kelaiah, (the same is Kelita,) P	Ezr 10:23	6611

   3. A Levite who helped Ezra.

Hodijah, Shebaniah, and P	Neh 9:5	6611

   4. An aide to Nehemiah.

P the son of Meshezabeel, of the	Neh 11:24	6611

PETHOR (pe'-thor) *A city in Mesopotamia.*

unto Balaam the son of Beor to P	Num 22:5	6604
son of Beor of P of Mesopotamia	Deut 23:4	6604

PETHUEL *Father of Joel the prophet.*

that came to Joel the son of P	Joel 1:1	6602

PETITION

thy p that thou hast asked of him	1Sa 1:17	7596
me my p which I asked of him	1Sa 1:27	7596
And now I ask one p of thee	1Kin 2:16	7596
I desire one small p of thee	1Kin 2:20	7596
banquet of wine, What is thy p	Est 5:6	7596
answered Esther, and said, My p	Est 5:7	7596
it please the king to grant my p	Est 5:8	7596
banquet of wine, What is thy p	Est 7:2	7596
let my life be given me at my p	Est 7:3	7596
now what is thy p	Est 9:12	7596
that whosoever shall ask a p of	Dan 6:7	1159
p of any God or man within thirty	Dan 6:12	1159
but maketh his p three times a	Dan 6:13	1159

PETITIONS

the LORD fulfil all thy p	Ps 20:5	4862
have the p that we desired of him	1Jn 5:15	155

PEULLETHAI See PEULTHAI.

PEULTHAI (pe-ul'-thahee) *A sanctuary servant.*

the seventh, P the eighth	1Chr 26:5	6469

PHALEC (fa'-lek) See PELEG. *Father of Ragau; ancestor*
   of Jesus.

of Ragau, which was the son of P	Lk 3:35	5317

PHALLU (fal'-lu) *Son of Reuben.*

and P, and Hezron, and Carmi	Gen 46:9	6396

PHALTI (fal'-ti) See PHALTIEL. *Son of Laish.*

to P the son of Laish, which was	1Sa 25:44	6406

PHALTIEL (fal'-te-el) See PHALTI. *Same as Phalti.*

even from P the son of Laish	2Sa 3:15	6409

PHANUEL (fan-u'-el) *Mother of Anna.*

a prophetess, the daughter of P	Lk 2:36	5323

PHARAOH (fa'-ra-o) See PHARAOH'S, PHARAOH-HOPHRA,
   PHARAOH-NECHO.
   1. Ruler of Egypt in Abraham's time.

The princes also of P saw her	Gen 12:15	6547
and commended her before P	Gen 12:15	6547
And the LORD plagued P and his	Gen 12:17	6547
P called Abram, and said, What is	Gen 12:18	6547
P commanded his men concerning	Gen 12:20	6547

   2. Ruler of Egypt in Joseph's time.

and Potiphar, an officer of P	Gen 39:1	6547
P was wroth against two of his	Gen 40:2	6547
days shall P lift up thine head	Gen 40:13	6547
me, and make mention of me unto P	Gen 40:14	6547
of all manner of bakemeats for P	Gen 40:17	6547
Yet within three days shall P	Gen 40:19	6547
of two full years, that P dreamed	Gen 41:1	6547
So P awoke	Gen 41:4	6547
P awoke, and, behold, it was a	Gen 41:7	6547
and P told them his dream	Gen 41:8	6547
that could interpret them unto P	Gen 41:8	6547
spake the chief butler unto P	Gen 41:9	6547
P was wroth with his servants, and	Gen 41:10	6547
Then P sent and called Joseph, and	Gen 41:14	6547
his raiment, and came in unto P	Gen 41:14	6547
P said unto Joseph, I have	Gen 41:15	6547
And Joseph answered P, saying, It	Gen 41:16	6547
God shall give P an answer of	Gen 41:16	6547
P said unto Joseph, In my dream,	Gen 41:17	6547
And Joseph said unto P	Gen 41:25	6547
The dream of P is one	Gen 41:25	6547
God hath shewed P what he is	Gen 41:25	6547
thing which I have spoken unto P	Gen 41:28	6547
is about to do he sheweth unto P	Gen 41:28	6547
dream was doubled unto P twice	Gen 41:32	6547
Now therefore let P look out a	Gen 41:33	6547

Let *P* do this, and let him appoint .... Gen 41:34 6547
lay up corn under the hand of *P* .... Gen 41:35 6547
thing was good in the eyes of *P* .... Gen 41:37 6547
P said unto his servants, Can we .... Gen 41:38 6547
P said unto Joseph, Forasmuch as .... Gen 41:39 6547
P said unto Joseph, See, I have .... Gen 41:41 6547
P took off his ring from his hand .... Gen 41:42 6547
P said unto Joseph, I am Pharaoh, ... Gen 41:44 6547
And *P* called Joseph's name .... Gen 41:45 6547
he stood before *P* king of Egypt .... Gen 41:46 6547
went out from the presence of *P* .... Gen 41:46 6547
the people cried to *P* for bread .... Gen 41:55 6547
P said unto all the Egyptians, Go .... Gen 41:55 6547
By the life of *P* ye shall not go .... Gen 42:15 6547
the life of *P* surely ye are spies .... Gen 42:16 6547
for thou art even as *P* .... Gen 44:18 6547
Egyptians, and the house of *P* heard ...... Gen 45:2 6547
and he hath made me a father to *P* .... Gen 45:8 6547
and it pleased *P* well, and his .... Gen 45:16 6547
P said unto Joseph, Say unto thy .... Gen 45:17 6547
according to the commandment of *P* ...... Gen 45:21 6547
in the wagons which *P* had sent to .... Gen 46:5 6547
house, I will go up, and shew *P* .... Gen 46:31 6547
when *P* shall call you, and shall .... Gen 46:33 6547
Then Joseph came and told *P* .... Gen 47:1 6547
men, and presented them unto *P* .... Gen 47:2 6547
P said unto his brethren, What is .... Gen 47:3 6547
And they said unto *P*, Thy servants .... Gen 47:3 6547
They said moreover unto *P* .... Gen 47:4 6547
P spake unto Joseph, saying, Thy .... Gen 47:5 6547
his father, and set him before *P* .... Gen 47:7 6547
and Jacob blessed *P* .... Gen 47:7 6547
P said unto Jacob, How old art .... Gen 47:8 6547
And Jacob said unto *P*, The days of .... Gen 47:9 6547
And Jacob blessed *P* .... Gen 47:10 6547
and went out from before *P* .... Gen 47:10 6547
of Rameses, as *P* had commanded .... Gen 47:11 6547
our land will be servants unto *P* .... Gen 47:19 6547
all the land of Egypt for *P* .... Gen 47:20 6547
had a portion assigned them of *P* .... Gen 47:22 6547
their portion which *P* gave them............ Gen 47:22 6547
you this day and your land for *P* .... Gen 47:23 6547
shall give the fifth part unto *P* .... Gen 47:24 6547
that *P* should have the fifth part .... Gen 47:26 6547
Joseph spake unto the house of *P* .... Gen 50:4 6547
I pray you, in the ears of *P* .... Gen 50:4 6547
P said, Go up, and bury thy father .... Gen 50:6 6547
him went up all the servants of *P* .... Gen 50:7 6547
in the sight of *P* king of Egypt .... Acts 7:10 5328
kindred was made known unto *P* .... Acts 7:13 5328

3. *Ruler of Egypt during Moses' infancy.*
they built for *P* treasure cities,................ Ex 1:11 6547
And the midwives said unto *P*................. Ex 1:19 6547
P charged all his people, saying, ... Ex 1:22 6547
the daughter of *P* came down to .... Ex 2:5 6547

4. *Ruler of Egypt during Moses' adulthood.*
Now when *P* heard this thing, he............ Ex 2:15 6547
But Moses fled from the face of *P*........... Ex 2:15 6547

5. *Ruler of Egypt when Moses returned to Egypt.*
and I will send thee unto *P* .... Ex 3:10 6547
Who am I, that I should go unto *P* .... Ex 3:11 6547
do all those wonders before *P* .... Ex 4:21 6547
And thou shalt say unto *P*, Thus .... Ex 4:22 6547
Moses and Aaron went in, and told *P*.... Ex 5:1 6547
P said, Who is the LORD, that I .... Ex 5:2 6547
P said, Behold, the people of the .... Ex 5:5 6547
P commanded the same day the .... Ex 5:6 6547
the people, saying, Thus saith *P* .... Ex 5:10 6547
of Israel came and cried unto *P* .... Ex 5:15 6547
way, as they came forth from *P* .... Ex 5:20 6547
to be abhorred in the eyes of *P* .... Ex 5:21 6547
For since I came to *P* to speak in .... Ex 5:23 6547
thou see what I will do to *P* .... Ex 6:1 6547
speak unto *P* king of Egypt, that .... Ex 6:11 6547
how then shall *P* hear me, who am........ Ex 6:12 6547
unto *P* king of Egypt, to bring .... Ex 6:13 6547
which spake to *P* king of Egypt .... Ex 6:27 6547
speak thou unto *P* king of Egypt .... Ex 6:29 6547
how shall *P* hearken unto me .... Ex 6:30 6547
See, I have made thee a god to *P* .... Ex 7:1 6547
thy brother shall speak unto *P* .... Ex 7:2 6547
But *P* shall not hearken unto you,........ Ex 7:4 6547
years old, when they spake unto *P* .... Ex 7:7 6547
When *P* shall speak unto you, ... Ex 7:9 6547
Take thy rod, and cast it before *P* .... Ex 7:9 6547
And Moses and Aaron went in unto *P*.... Ex 7:10 6547
Aaron cast down his rod before *P* .... Ex 7:10 6547
Then *P* also called the wise men .... Ex 7:11 6547
Get thee unto *P* in the morning .... Ex 7:15 6547
in the river, in the sight of *P* .... Ex 7:20 6547
P turned and went into his house, ... Ex 7:23 6547

LORD spake unto Moses, Go unto *P*........ Ex 8:1 6547
Then *P* called for Moses and Aaron, ... Ex 8:8 6547
And Moses said unto *P*, Glory over .... Ex 8:9 6547
And Moses and Aaron went out from *P* . Ex 8:12 6547
which he had brought against *P*............. Ex 8:12 6547
But when *P* saw that there was .... Ex 8:15 6547
Then the magicians said unto *P* .... Ex 8:19 6547
in the morning, and stand before *P* .... Ex 8:20 6547
of flies into the house of *P* .... Ex 8:24 6547
P called for Moses and for Aaron, ... Ex 8:25 6547
P said, I will let you go, that.................. Ex 8:28 6547
swarms of flies may depart from *P* .... Ex 8:29 6547
but let not *P* deal deceitfully .... Ex 8:29 6547
And Moses went out from *P*, and .... Ex 8:30 6547
the swarms of flies from *P* .... Ex 8:31 6547
P hardened his heart at this time .... Ex 8:32 6547
said unto Moses, Go in unto *P* .... Ex 9:1 6547
P sent, and, behold, there was not .... Ex 9:7 6547
And the heart of *P* was hardened .... Ex 9:7 6547
the heaven in the sight of *P* .... Ex 9:8 6547
of the furnace, and stood before *P*.......... Ex 9:10 6547
the LORD hardened the heart of *P*........... Ex 9:12 6547
in the morning, and stand before *P* .... Ex 9:13 6547
servants of *P* made his servants .... Ex 9:20 6547
P sent, and called for Moses and .... Ex 9:27 6547
Moses went out of the city from *P* .... Ex 9:33 6547
when *P* saw that the rain and the.......... Ex 9:34 6547
And the heart of *P* was hardened .... Ex 9:35 6547
said unto Moses, Go in unto *P* .... Ex 10:1 6547
And Moses and Aaron came in unto *P*... Ex 10:3 6547
himself, and went out from *P* .... Ex 10:6 6547
Aaron were brought again unto *P* .... Ex 10:8 6547
Then *P* called for Moses and Aaron ...... Ex 10:16 6547
And he went out from *P*, and .... Ex 10:18 6547
P called unto Moses, and said, Go....... Ex 10:24 6547
P said unto him, Get thee from me........ Ex 10:28 6547
I bring one plague more upon *P* .... Ex 11:1 6547
from the firstborn of *P* that .... Ex 11:5 6547
went out from *P* in a great anger........... Ex 11:8 6547
P shall not hearken unto you .... Ex 11:9 6547
did all these wonders before *P* .... Ex 11:10 6547
from the firstborn of *P* that sat .... Ex 12:29 6547
P rose up in the night, he, and............. Ex 12:30 6547
when *P* would hardly let us go, ... Ex 13:15 6547
when *P* had let the people go, ... Ex 13:17 6547
For *P* will say of the children of............. Ex 14:3 6547
and I will be honoured upon *P* .... Ex 14:4 6547
and the heart of *P* and of his .... Ex 14:5 6547
the heart of *P* king of Egypt .... Ex 14:8 6547
all the horses and chariots of *P* .... Ex 14:9 6547
when *P* drew nigh, the children of .... Ex 14:10 6547
and I will get me honour upon *P*........... Ex 14:17 6547
I have gotten me honour upon *P* .... Ex 14:18 6547
all the host of *P* that came into .... Ex 14:28 6547
For the horse of *P* went in with .... Ex 15:19 6547
delivered me from the sword of *P* .... Ex 18:4 6547
all that the LORD had done unto *P* .... Ex 18:8 6547
and out of the hand of *P*, who .... Ex 18:10 6547
great and sore, upon Egypt, upon *P* ...... Deut 6:22 6547
from the hand of *P* king of Egypt .... Deut 7:8 6547
what the LORD thy God did unto *P* .... Deut 7:18 6547
of Egypt unto *P* the king of Egypt .... Deut 11:3 6547
eyes in the land of Egypt unto *P* .... Deut 29:2 6547
to do in the land of Egypt to *P* .... Deut 34:11 6547
and *P* hardened their hearts 1Sa 6:6 6547
under the hand of *P* king of Egypt......... 2Kin 17:7 6547
shewedst signs and wonders upon *P* ...... Neh 9:10 6547
midst of thee, O Egypt, upon *P* .... Ps 135:9 6547
But overthrew *P* and his host in .... Ps 136:15 6547
For the scripture saith unto *P* .... Rom 9:17 5328

6. *Ruler of Egypt in Solomon's time.*
affinity with *P* king of Egypt 1Kin 3:1 6547
For *P* king of Egypt had gone up, ... 1Kin 9:16 6547
together with the daughter of *P* 1Kin 11:1 6547
to Egypt, unto *P* king of Egypt............. 1Kin 11:18 6547
great favour in the sight of *P* 1Kin 11:19 6547
household among the sons of *P* 1Kin 11:20 6547
host was dead, Hadad said to *P*............. 1Kin 11:21 6547
Then *P* said unto him, But what 1Kin 11:22 6547
brought up the daughter of *P* out 2Chr 8:11 6547

7. *Ruler of Egypt in Isaiah's time.*
of *P* is become brutish .... Is 19:11 6547
how say ye unto *P*, I am the son .... Is 19:11 6547
themselves in the strength of *P* .... Is 30:2 6547
the strength of *P* be your shame............. Is 30:3 6547
so is *P* king of Egypt to all that .... Is 36:6 6547

8. *Ruler of Egypt in Jeremiah's time.*
so is *P* king of Egypt unto all.................. 2Kin 18:21 6547
gave the silver and the gold to *P*............. 2Kin 23:35 6547
according to the commandment of *P*...... 2Kin 23:35 6547
sons of Bithiah the daughter of *P* 1Chr 4:18 6547

P

P king of Egypt, and his servants,	Jer 25:19	6547
P king of Egypt is but a noise	Jer 46:17	6547
punish the multitude of No, and *P*	Jer 46:25	6547
even *P*, and all them that trust in	Jer 46:25	6547
before that *P* smote Gaza	Jer 47:1	6547
Neither shall *P* with his mighty	Eze 17:17	6547
thy face against *P* king of Egypt	Eze 29:2	6547
P king of Egypt, the great dragon	Eze 29:3	6547
broken the arm of *P* king of Egypt	Eze 30:21	6547
I am against *P* king of Egypt, and	Eze 30:22	6547
the arms of *P* shall fall down	Eze 30:25	6547
speak unto *P* king of Egypt, and to	Eze 31:2	6547
This is *P* and all his multitude,	Eze 31:18	6547
a lamentation for *P* king of Egypt	Eze 32:2	6547
P shall see them, and shall be	Eze 32:31	6547
over all his multitude, even *P*	Eze 32:31	6547
are slain with the sword, even *P*	Eze 32:32	6547

PHARAOH-HOPHRA *(fa'-ra-o-hof'-rah) Same as Pharaoh 8.*

I will give *P* king of Egypt into	Jer 44:30	6548

PHARAOH-NECHO *(fa'-ra-o-ne'-ko) See* PHARAOH-NECHOH. *Egyptian ruler during Josiah's time.*

the army of *P* king of Egypt	Jer 46:2	6549

PHARAOH-NECHOH *(fa'-ra-o-ne'-ko) See* PHARAOH-NECHO. *Same as Pharaoh-necho.*

In his days *P* king of Egypt went	2Kin 23:29	6549
P put him in bands at Riblah in	2Kin 23:33	6549
P made Eliakim the son of Josiah	2Kin 23:34	6549
his taxation, to give it unto *P*	2Kin 23:35	6549

PHARAOH'S *(fa'-ra-oze)*

the woman was taken into *P* house	Gen 12:15	6547
unto Potiphar, an officer of *P*	Gen 37:36	6547
he asked *P* officers that were	Gen 40:7	6547
And *P* cup was in my hand	Gen 40:11	6547
and pressed them into *P* cup	Gen 40:11	6547
and I gave the cup into *P* hand	Gen 40:11	6547
shalt deliver *P* cup into his hand	Gen 40:13	6547
third day, which was *P* birthday	Gen 40:20	6547
and he gave the cup into *P* hand	Gen 40:21	6547
fame thereof was heard in *P* house	Gen 45:16	6547
brought the money into *P* house	Gen 47:14	6547
so the land became *P*	Gen 47:20	6547
my lord, and we will be *P* servants	Gen 47:25	6547
priests only, which became not *P*	Gen 47:26	6547
said his sister to *P* daughter	Ex 2:7	6547
P daughter said to her, Go	Ex 2:8	6547
P daughter said unto her, Take	Ex 2:9	6547
she brought him unto *P* daughter	Ex 2:10	6547
which *P* taskmasters had set over	Ex 5:14	6547
And I will harden *P* heart, and	Ex 7:3	6547
And he hardened *P* heart, that he	Ex 7:13	6547
P heart is hardened, he refuseth	Ex 7:14	6547
P heart was hardened, neither did	Ex 7:22	6547
P heart was hardened, and he	Ex 8:19	6547
P servants said unto him, How	Ex 10:7	6547
were driven out from *P* presence	Ex 10:11	6547
But the LORD hardened *P* heart	Ex 10:20	6547
But the LORD hardened *P* heart	Ex 10:27	6547
Egypt, in the sight of *P* servants	Ex 11:3	6547
and the LORD hardened *P* heart	Ex 11:10	6547
And I will harden *P* heart, that he	Ex 14:4	6547
of the sea, even all *P* horses	Ex 14:23	6547
P chariots and his host hath he	Ex 15:4	6547
We were *P* bondmen in Egypt	Deut 6:21	6547
they were in Egypt in *P* house	1Sa 2:27	6547
took *P* daughter, and brought her	1Kin 3:1	6547
made also an house for *P* daughter	1Kin 7:8	6547
But *P* daughter came up out of the	1Kin 9:24	6547
whom Tahpenes weaned in *P* house	1Kin 11:20	6547
Genubath was in *P* household among	1Kin 11:20	6547
a company of horses in *P* chariots	Song 1:9	6547
Then *P* army was come forth out of	Jer 37:5	6547
P army, which is come forth to	Jer 37:7	6547
from Jerusalem for fear of *P* army	Jer 37:11	6547
the entry of *P* house in Tahpanhes	Jer 43:9	6547
but I will break *P* arms, and he	Eze 30:24	6547
P daughter took him up, and	Acts 7:21	5328
be called the son of *P* daughter	Heb 11:24	5328

PHARES *(fa'-rez) See* PHAREZ. *Same as Pharez.*

And Judas begat *P* and Zara of	Mt 1:3	5329
and *P* begat Esrom	Mt 1:3	5329
of Esrom, which was the son of *P*	Lk 3:33	5329

PHAREZ *(fa'-rez) See* PEREZ, PHARES, PHARZITES. *A son of Judah.*

therefore his name was called *P*	Gen 38:29	6557
Er, and Onan, and Shelah, and *P*	Gen 46:12	6557
And the sons of *P* were Hezron	Gen 46:12	6557
of *P*, the family of the Pharzites	Num 26:20	6557

And the sons of *P* were	Num 26:21	6557
thy house be like the house of *P*	Ruth 4:12	6557
these are the generations of *P*	Ruth 4:18	6557
P begat Hezron,	Ruth 4:18	6557
his daughter in law bare him *P*	1Chr 2:4	6557
The sons of *P*	1Chr 2:5	6557
P, Hezron, and Carmi, and Hur, and	1Chr 4:1	6557
children of *P* the son of Judah	1Chr 9:4	6557

PHARISAIC See PHARISEES.

PHARISEE *(far'-i-see) See* PHARISEE'S, PHARISEES. *A member of a Jewish sect.*

Thou blind *P*, cleanse first that	Mt 23:26	*5330*
Now when the *P* which had bidden	Lk 7:39	*5330*
a certain *P* besought him to dine	Lk 11:37	*5330*
And when the *P* saw it, he	Lk 11:38	*5330*
the one a *P*, and the other a	Lk 18:10	*5330*
The *P* stood and prayed thus with	Lk 18:11	*5330*
there up one in the council, a *P*	Acts 5:34	*5330*
I am a *P*, the son of a *P*	Acts 23:6	*5330*
sect of our religion I lived a *P*	Acts 26:5	*5330*
as touching the law, a *P*	Phil 3:5	*5330*

PHARISEE'S *(far'-i-seze)*

And he went into the *P* house	Lk 7:36	*5330*
Jesus sat at meat in the *P* house	Lk 7:37	*5330*

PHARISEES *(far'-i-seze) See* PHARISEES'. *A Jewish sect.*

But when he saw many of the *P*	Mt 3:7	*5330*
righteousness of the scribes and *P*	Mt 5:20	*5330*
And when the *P* saw it, they said	Mt 9:11	*5330*
the *P* fast oft, but thy disciples	Mt 9:14	*5330*
But the *P* said, He casteth out	Mt 9:34	*5330*
But when the *P* saw it, they said	Mt 12:2	*5330*
Then the *P* went out, and held a	Mt 12:14	*5330*
But when the *P* heard it, they	Mt 12:24	*5330*
of the *P* answered, saying, Master	Mt 12:38	*5330*
Then came to Jesus scribes and *P*	Mt 15:1	*5330*
thou that the *P* were offended	Mt 15:12	*5330*
The *P* also with the Sadducees	Mt 16:1	*5330*
and beware of the leaven of the *P*	Mt 16:6	*5330*
beware of the leaven of the *P*	Mt 16:11	*5330*
but of the doctrine of the *P*	Mt 16:12	*5330*
The *P* also came unto him,	Mt 19:3	*5330*
P had heard his parables, they	Mt 21:45	*5330*
Then went the *P*, and took counsel	Mt 22:15	*5330*
But when the *P* had heard that he	Mt 22:34	*5330*
While the *P* were gathered	Mt 22:41	*5330*
and the *P* sit in Moses' seat	Mt 23:2	*5330*
But woe unto you, scribes and *P*	Mt 23:13	*5330*
Woe unto you, scribes and *P*	Mt 23:14	*5330*
Woe unto you, scribes and *P*	Mt 23:15	*5330*
Woe unto you, scribes and *P*	Mt 23:23	*5330*
Woe unto you, scribes and *P*	Mt 23:25	*5330*
Woe unto you, scribes and *P*	Mt 23:27	*5330*
Woe unto you, scribes and *P*	Mt 23:29	*5330*
P came together unto Pilate,	Mt 27:62	*5330*
P saw him eat with publicans and	Mk 2:16	*5330*
of John and of the *P* used to fast	Mk 2:18	*5330*
of John and of the *P* fast, but thy	Mk 2:18	*5330*
the *P* said unto him, Behold, why	Mk 2:24	*5330*
the *P* went forth, and straightway	Mk 3:6	*5330*
Then came together unto him the *P*	Mk 7:1	*5330*
For the *P*, and all the Jews,	Mk 7:3	*5330*
Then the *P* and scribes asked him,	Mk 7:5	*5330*
the *P* came forth, and began to	Mk 8:11	*5330*
beware of the leaven of the *P*	Mk 8:15	*5330*
the *P* came to him, and asked him,	Mk 10:2	*5330*
send unto him certain of the *P*	Mk 12:13	*5330*
was teaching, that there were *P*	Lk 5:17	*5330*
the *P* began to reason, saying,	Lk 5:21	*5330*
P murmured against his disciples,	Lk 5:30	*5330*
likewise the disciples of the *P*	Lk 5:33	*5330*
certain of the *P* said unto them	Lk 6:2	*5330*
P watched him, whether he would	Lk 6:7	*5330*
But the *P* and lawyers rejected the	Lk 7:30	*5330*
one of the *P* desired him that he	Lk 7:36	*5330*
Now do ye *P* make clean the	Lk 11:39	*5330*
But woe unto you, *P*	Lk 11:42	*5330*
Woe unto you, *P*	Lk 11:43	*5330*
Woe unto you, scribes and *P*	Lk 11:44	*5330*
and the *P* began to urge him	Lk 11:53	*5330*
Beware of the leaven of the *P*	Lk 12:1	*5330*
day there came certain of the *P*	Lk 13:31	*5330*
the house of one of the chief *P*	Lk 14:1	*5330*
spake unto the lawyers and *P*	Lk 14:3	*5330*
And the *P* and scribes murmured,	Lk 15:2	*5330*
the *P* also, who were covetous,	Lk 16:14	*5330*
And when he was demanded of the *P*	Lk 17:20	*5330*
some of the *P* from among the	Lk 19:39	*5330*
which were sent were of the *P*	Jn 1:24	*5330*
There was a man of the *P*, named	Jn 3:1	*5330*

the *P* had heard that Jesus made	Jn 4:1	5330
The *P* heard that the people	Jn 7:32	5330
and the *P* and the chief priests	Jn 7:32	5330
to the chief priests and *P*	Jn 7:45	5330
Then answered them the *P,* Are ye	Jn 7:47	5330
or of the *P* believed on him	Jn 7:48	5330
P brought unto him a woman taken	Jn 8:3	5330
The *P* therefore said unto him,	Jn 8:13	5330
They brought to the *P* him that	Jn 9:13	5330
Then again the *P* also asked him	Jn 9:15	5330
Therefore said some of the *P*	Jn 9:16	5330
some of the *P* which were with him	Jn 9:40	5330
of them went their ways to the *P*	Jn 11:46	5330
the *P* a council, and said, What do	Jn 11:47	5330
the *P* had given a commandment,	Jn 11:57	5330
The *P* therefore said among	Jn 12:19	5330
but because of the *P* they did not	Jn 12:42	5330
from the chief priests and *P*	Jn 18:3	5330
the sect of the *P* which believed	Acts 15:5	5330
were Sadducees, and the other *P*	Acts 23:6	5330
arose a dissension between the *P*	Acts 23:7	5330
but the *P* confess both	Acts 23:8	5330

PHARISEES' *(far'-i-seez)*
that were of the *P* part arose	Acts 23:9	5330

PHAROSH *(fa'-rosh) A family of exiles.*
of Shechaniah, of the sons of *P*	Ezr 8:3	6551

PHARPAR *(far'-par) A river near Damascus.*
Are not Abana and *P,* rivers of	2Kin 5:12	6554

PHARZITES *(far'-zites) Descendants of Pharez.*
of Pharez, the family of the *P*	Num 26:20	6558

PHASEAH *(fa-se'-ah) See* PASEAH. *A family of exiles.*
of Uzza, the children of *P*	Neh 7:51	6454

PHEBE *(fe'-be) A Christian acquaintance of Paul.*
I commend unto you *P* our sister	Rom 16:1	5402
sent by *P* servant of the church	Rom *s*	5402

PHENICE *(fe-ni'-se) See* PHENICIA.
1. Same as Phenicia.
Stephen travelled as far as *P*	Acts 11:19	5403
the church, they passed through *P*	Acts 15:3	5403

2. A harbor on Crete.
any means they might attain to *P*	Acts 27:12	5405

PHENICIA *(fe-nish'-e-ah) See* PHENICE. *Coastal region of northern Palestine.*
a ship sailing over unto *P*	Acts 21:2	5403

PHICHOL *The commander of Abimelech's army.*
P the chief captain of his host	Gen 21:22	6369
P the chief captain of his host,	Gen 21:32	6369
P the chief captain of his army	Gen 26:26	6369

PHICOL *(fi'-col) See* PHICHOL. *A Philistine commander.*

PHILADELPHIA *(fil-a-del'-fe-ah) A city in Lydia in Asia Minor.*
and unto Sardis, and unto *P*	Rev 1:11	5359
angel of the church in *P* write	Rev 3:7	5359

PHILEMON *(fi-le'-mon) A recipient of a New Testament epistle.*
unto *P* our dearly beloved, and	Philem 1	5371
Written from Rome to *P,* by	Philem *s*	5371

PHILETUS *(fi-le'tus) A false Christian teacher.*
of whom is Hymenaeus and *P*	2Ti 2:17	5372

PHILIP *(fil'-ip) See* PHILIP'S.
1. An apostle.
P, and Bartholomew	Mt 10:3	5376
And Andrew, and *P,* and Bartholomew,	Mk 3:18	5376
his brother, James and John, *P*	Lk 6:14	5376
forth into Galilee, and findeth *P*	Jn 1:43	5376
Now *P* was of Bethsaida, the city	Jn 1:44	5376
P findeth Nathanael, and saith	Jn 1:45	5376
P saith unto him, Come and see	Jn 1:46	5376
him, Before that *P* called thee	Jn 1:48	5376
come unto him, he saith unto *P*	Jn 6:5	5376
P answered him, Two hundred	Jn 6:7	5376
The same came therefore to *P*	Jn 12:21	5376
P cometh and telleth Andrew	Jn 12:22	5376
and again Andrew and *P* tell Jesus	Jn 12:22	5376
P saith unto him, Lord, shew us	Jn 14:8	5376
and yet hast thou not known me, *P*	Jn 14:9	5376
and James, and John, and Andrew, *P*	Acts 1:13	5376

2. A son of Herod the Great.
his brother *P* tetrarch of Ituraea	Lk 3:1	5376

3. The evangelist.
faith and of the Holy Ghost, and *P*	Acts 6:5	5376
Then *P* went down to the city of	Acts 8:5	5376
unto those things which *P* spake	Acts 8:6	5376
But when they believed *P*	Acts 8:12	5376

was baptized, he continued with *P*	Acts 8:13	5376
angel of the Lord spake unto *P*	Acts 8:26	5376
Then the Spirit said unto *P*	Acts 8:29	5376
P ran thither to him, and heard	Acts 8:30	5376
he desired *P* that he would come	Acts 8:31	5376
And the eunuch answered *P,* and said	Acts 8:34	5376
Then *P* opened his mouth, and began	Acts 8:35	5376
P said, If thou believest with	Acts 8:37	5376
down both into the water, both *P*	Acts 8:38	5376
Spirit of the Lord caught away *P*	Acts 8:39	5376
But *P* was found at Azotus	Acts 8:40	5376
the house of *P* the evangelist	Acts 21:8	5376

PHILIPPI *(fil-ip'-pi) See* PHILIPPIANS.
1. A town in northern Palestine.
into the coasts of Caesarea *P*	Mt 16:13	5375
into the towns of Caesarea *P*	Mk 8:27	5375

2. A Macedonian city.
And from thence to *P,* which is the	Acts 16:12	5375
we sailed away from *P* after the	Acts 20:6	5375
was written from *P* by Stephanus	1Cor *s*	5375
Corinthians was written from *P*	1Cor *s*	5375
in Christ Jesus which are at *P*	Phil 1:1	5375
entreated, as ye know, at *P*	1Th 2:2	5375

PHILIPPIANS *(fil-ip'-pe-uns) Residents of Philippi 2.*
Now ye *P* know also, that in the	Phil 4:15	5374
It was written to the *P* from Rome	Phil *s*	

PHILIP'S *(fil'-ips) Refers to Philip 2.*
sake, his brother *P* wife	Mt 14:3	5376
sake, his brother *P* wife	Mk 6:17	5376
for Herodias his brother *P* wife	Lk 3:19	5376

PHILISTIA *(fil-is'-te-ah) See* PALESTINE, PHILISTINE. *Land of the Philistines.*
P, triumph thou because of me	Ps 60:8	6429
behold *P,* and Tyre, with Ethiopia	Ps 87:4	6429
over *P* will I triumph	Ps 108:9	6429

PHILISTIM *(fil-is'-tim) See* PHILISTINES. *Descendents of Casluhim.*
and Casluhim, (out of whom came *P*	Gen 10:14	6430

PHILISTINE *(fil-is'-tin) See* PHILISTINES. *An inhabitant of Philistia.*
am not I a *P,* and ye servants to	1Sa 17:8	6430
the *P* said, I defy the armies of	1Sa 17:10	6430
Israel heard those words of the *P*	1Sa 17:11	6430
the *P* drew near morning and	1Sa 17:16	6430
the *P* of Gath, Goliath by name,	1Sa 17:23	6430
to the man that killeth this *P*	1Sa 17:26	6430
for who is this uncircumcised *P*	1Sa 17:26	6430
will go and fight with this *P*	1Sa 17:32	6430
against this *P* to fight with him	1Sa 17:33	6430
this uncircumcised *P* shall be as	1Sa 17:36	6430
me out of the hand of this *P*	1Sa 17:37	6430
and he drew near to the *P*	1Sa 17:40	6430
the *P* came on and drew near unto	1Sa 17:41	6430
when the *P* looked about, and saw	1Sa 17:42	6430
the *P* said unto David, Am I a dog	1Sa 17:43	6430
the *P* cursed David by his gods	1Sa 17:43	6430
the *P* said to David, Come to me,	1Sa 17:44	6430
Then said David to the *P,* Thou	1Sa 17:45	6430
it came to pass, when the *P* arose	1Sa 17:48	6430
ran toward the army to meet the *P*	1Sa 17:48	6430
smote the *P* in his forehead, that	1Sa 17:49	6430
prevailed over the *P* with a sling	1Sa 17:50	6430
and with a stone, and smote the *P*	1Sa 17:50	6430
David ran, and stood upon the *P*	1Sa 17:51	6430
And David took the head of the *P*	1Sa 17:54	6430
saw David go forth against the *P*	1Sa 17:55	6430
from the slaughter of the *P*	1Sa 17:57	6430
the head of the *P* in his hand	1Sa 17:57	6430
from the slaughter of the *P*	1Sa 18:6	6430
life in his hand, and slew the *P*	1Sa 19:5	6430
said, The sword of Goliath the *P*	1Sa 21:9	6430
him the sword of Goliath the *P*	1Sa 22:10	6430
succoured him, and smote the *P*	2Sa 21:17	6430

PHILISTINES *(fil-is'-tinz) See* PHILISTIM, PHILISTINES'.
returned into the land of the *P*	Gen 21:32	6430
king of the *P* unto Gerar	Gen 26:1	6430
of the *P* looked out at a window	Gen 26:8	6430
and the *P* envied him	Gen 26:14	6430
the *P* had stopped them, and filled	Gen 26:15	6430
for the *P* had stopped them after	Gen 26:18	6430
the way of the land of the *P*	Ex 13:17	6430
sea even unto the sea of the *P*	Ex 23:31	6430
all the borders of the *P,* and all	Josh 13:2	6430
five lords of the *P*	Josh 13:3	6430
Namely, five lords of the *P*	Judg 3:3	6430
which slew of the *P* six hundred	Judg 3:31	6430
of Ammon, and the gods of the *P*	Judg 10:6	6430

sold them into the hands of the *P*	Judg 10:7	6430
children of Ammon, and from the *P*	Judg 10:11	6430
the hand of the *P* forty years	Judg 13:1	6430
Israel out of the hand of the *P*	Judg 13:5	6430
Timnath of the daughters of the *P*	Judg 14:1	6430
Timnath of the daughters of the *P*	Judg 14:2	6430
a wife of the uncircumcised *P*	Judg 14:3	6430
sought an occasion against the *P*	Judg 14:4	6430
for at that time the *P* had	Judg 14:4	6430
I be more blameless than the *P*	Judg 15:3	6430
into the standing corn of the *P*	Judg 15:5	6430
Then the *P* said, Who hath done	Judg 15:6	6430
the *P* came up, and burnt her and	Judg 15:6	6430
Then the *P* went up, and pitched in	Judg 15:9	6430
not that the *P* are rulers over us	Judg 15:11	6430
thee into the hand of the *P*	Judg 15:12	6430
the *P* shouted against him	Judg 15:14	6430
in the days of the *P* twenty years	Judg 15:20	6430
lords of the *P* came up unto her	Judg 16:5	6430
Then the lords of the *P* brought	Judg 16:8	6430
The *P* be upon thee, Samson	Judg 16:9	6430
The *P* be upon thee, Samson	Judg 16:12	6430
The *P* be upon thee, Samson	Judg 16:14	6430
and called for the lords of the *P*	Judg 16:18	6430
lords of the *P* came up unto her	Judg 16:18	6430
The *P* be upon thee, Samson	Judg 16:20	6430
But the *P* took him, and put out	Judg 16:21	6430
Then the lords of the *P* gathered	Judg 16:23	6430
all the lords of the *P* were there	Judg 16:27	6430
avenged of the *P* for my two eyes	Judg 16:28	6430
said, Let me die with the *P*	Judg 16:30	6430
went out against the *P* to battle	1Sa 4:1	6430
and the *P* pitched in Aphek	1Sa 4:1	6430
the *P* put themselves in array	1Sa 4:2	6430
Israel was smitten before the *P*	1Sa 4:2	6430
smitten us to day before the *P*	1Sa 4:3	6430
when the *P* heard the noise of the	1Sa 4:6	6430
the *P* were afraid, for they said,	1Sa 4:7	6430
quit yourselves like men, O ye *P*	1Sa 4:9	6430
the *P* fought, and Israel was	1Sa 4:10	6430
said, Israel is fled before the *P*	1Sa 4:17	6430
the *P* took the ark of God, and	1Sa 5:1	6430
When the *P* took the ark of God,	1Sa 5:2	6430
all the lords of the *P* unto them	1Sa 5:8	6430
together all the lords of the *P*	1Sa 5:11	6430
the country of the *P* seven months	1Sa 6:1	6430
the *P* called for the priests and	1Sa 6:2	6430
the number of the lords of the *P*	1Sa 6:4	6430
the lords of the *P* went after	1Sa 6:12	6430
five lords of the *P* had seen it	1Sa 6:16	6430
the *P* returned for a trespass	1Sa 6:17	6430
the *P* belonging to the five lords	1Sa 6:18	6430
The *P* have brought again the ark	1Sa 6:21	6430
you out of the hand of the *P*	1Sa 7:3	6430
when the *P* heard that the	1Sa 7:7	6430
the lords of the *P* went up	1Sa 7:7	6430
it, they were afraid of the *P*	1Sa 7:7	6430
save us out of the hand of the *P*	1Sa 7:8	6430
the *P* drew near to battle against	1Sa 7:10	6430
thunder on that day upon the *P*	1Sa 7:10	6430
out of Mizpeh, and pursued the *P*	1Sa 7:11	6430
So the *P* were subdued, and they	1Sa 7:13	6430
the *P* all the days of Samuel	1Sa 7:13	6430
the cities which the *P* had taken	1Sa 7:14	6430
deliver out of the hands of the *P*	1Sa 7:14	6430
people out of the hand of the *P*	1Sa 9:16	6430
where is the garrison of the *P*	1Sa 10:5	6430
Hazor, and into the hand of the *P*	1Sa 12:9	6430
of the *P* that was in Geba	1Sa 13:3	6430
and the *P* heard of it	1Sa 13:3	6430
had smitten a garrison of the *P*	1Sa 13:4	6430
was had in abomination with the *P*	1Sa 13:4	6430
the *P* gathered themselves	1Sa 13:5	6430
that the *P* gathered themselves	1Sa 13:11	6430
The *P* will come down now upon me	1Sa 13:12	6430
but the *P* encamped in Michmash	1Sa 13:16	6430
camp of the *P* in three companies	1Sa 13:17	6430
for the *P* said, Lest the Hebrews	1Sa 13:19	6430
the Israelites went down to the *P*	1Sa 13:20	6430
the garrison of the *P* went out to	1Sa 13:23	6430
unto the garrison of the *P*	1Sa 14:11	6430
the *P* said, Behold, the Hebrews	1Sa 14:11	6430
was in the host of the *P* went on	1Sa 14:19	6430
were with the *P* before that time	1Sa 14:21	6430
when they heard that the *P* fled	1Sa 14:22	6430
greater slaughter among the *P*	1Sa 14:30	6430
they smote the *P* that day from	1Sa 14:31	6430
us go down after the *P* by night	1Sa 14:36	6430
God, Shall I go down after the *P*	1Sa 14:37	6430
Saul went up from following the *P*	1Sa 14:46	6430
the *P* went to their own place	1Sa 14:46	6430
kings of Zobah, and against the *P*	1Sa 14:47	6430
the *P* all the days of Saul	1Sa 14:52	6430
Now the *P* gathered together their	1Sa 17:1	6430
the battle in array against the *P*	1Sa 17:2	6430
the *P* stood on a mountain on the	1Sa 17:3	6430
champion out of the camp of the *P*	1Sa 17:4	6430
of Elah, fighting with the *P*	1Sa 17:19	6430
the *P* had put the battle in array	1Sa 17:21	6430
name, out of the armies of the *P*	1Sa 17:23	6430
P this day unto the fowls of the	1Sa 17:46	6430
when the *P* saw their champion was	1Sa 17:51	6430
and shouted, and pursued the *P*	1Sa 17:52	6430
the wounded of the *P* fell down by	1Sa 17:52	6430
returned from chasing after the *P*	1Sa 17:53	6430
let the hand of the *P* be upon him	1Sa 18:17	6430
hand of the *P* may be against him	1Sa 18:21	6430
but an hundred foreskins of the *P*	1Sa 18:25	6430
David fall by the hand of the *P*	1Sa 18:25	6430
slew of the *P* two hundred men	1Sa 18:27	6430
the princes of the *P* went forth	1Sa 18:30	6430
went out, and fought with the *P*	1Sa 19:8	6430
the *P* fight against Keilah, and	1Sa 23:1	6430
Shall I go and smite these *P*	1Sa 23:2	6430
unto David, Go, and smite the *P*	1Sa 23:2	6430
against the armies of the *P*	1Sa 23:3	6430
deliver the *P* into thine hand	1Sa 23:4	6430
to Keilah, and fought with the *P*	1Sa 23:5	6430
for the *P* have invaded the land	1Sa 23:27	6430
David, and went against the *P*	1Sa 23:28	6430
was returned from following the *P*	1Sa 24:1	6430
escape into the land of the *P*	1Sa 27:1	6430
country of the *P* was a full year	1Sa 27:7	6430
dwelleth in the country of the *P*	1Sa 27:11	6430
that the *P* gathered their armies	1Sa 28:1	6430
the *P* gathered themselves	1Sa 28:4	6430
when Saul saw the host of the *P*	1Sa 28:5	6430
for the *P* make war against me, and	1Sa 28:15	6430
with thee into the hand of the *P*	1Sa 28:19	6430
of Israel into the hand of the *P*	1Sa 28:19	6430
Now the *P* gathered together all	1Sa 29:1	6430
the lords of the *P* passed on by	1Sa 29:2	6430
Then said the princes of the *P*	1Sa 29:3	6430
said unto the princes of the *P*	1Sa 29:3	6430
the princes of the *P* were wroth	1Sa 29:4	6430
princes of the *P* said unto him	1Sa 29:4	6430
displease not the lords of the *P*	1Sa 29:7	6430
the princes of the *P* have said	1Sa 29:9	6430
to return into the land of the *P*	1Sa 29:11	6430
And the *P* went up to Jezreel	1Sa 29:11	6430
taken out of the land of the *P*	1Sa 30:16	6430
Now the *P* fought against Israel	1Sa 31:1	6430
of Israel fled from before the *P*	1Sa 31:1	6430
the *P* followed hard upon Saul and	1Sa 31:2	6430
the *P* slew Jonathan, and Abinadab,	1Sa 31:2	6430
the *P* came and dwelt in them	1Sa 31:7	6430
when the *P* came to strip the	1Sa 31:8	6430
the land of the *P* round about	1Sa 31:9	6430
that which the *P* had done to Saul	1Sa 31:11	6430
the daughters of the *P* rejoice	2Sa 1:20	6430
for an hundred foreskins of the *P*	2Sa 3:14	6430
Israel out of the hand of the *P*	2Sa 3:18	6430
But when the *P* heard that they	2Sa 5:17	6430
all the *P* came up to seek David	2Sa 5:17	6430
The *P* also came and spread	2Sa 5:18	6430
saying, Shall I go up to the *P*	2Sa 5:19	6430
deliver the *P* into thine hand	2Sa 5:19	6430
the *P* came up yet again, and	2Sa 5:22	6430
thee, to smite the host of the *P*	2Sa 5:24	6430
smote the *P* from Geba until thou	2Sa 5:25	6430
to pass, that David smote the *P*	2Sa 8:1	6430
out of the hand of the *P*	2Sa 8:1	6430
children of Ammon, and of the *P*	2Sa 8:12	6430
us out of the hand of the *P*	2Sa 19:9	6430
where the *P* had hanged them	2Sa 21:12	6430
when the *P* had slain Saul in	2Sa 21:12	6430
Moreover the *P* had yet war again	2Sa 21:15	6430
with him, and fought against the *P*	2Sa 21:15	6430
again a battle with the *P* at Gob	2Sa 21:18	6430
again a battle in Gob with the *P*	2Sa 21:19	6430
when they defied the *P* that were	2Sa 23:9	6430
smote the *P* until his hand was	2Sa 23:10	6430
the *P* were gathered together into	2Sa 23:11	6430
and the people fled from the *P*	2Sa 23:11	6430
and defended it, and slew the *P*	2Sa 23:12	6430
the troop of the *P* pitched in the	2Sa 23:13	6430
the garrison of the *P* was then in	2Sa 23:14	6430
brake through the host of the *P*	2Sa 23:16	6430
the river unto the land of the *P*	1Kin 4:21	6430
which belonged to the *P*	1Kin 15:27	6430
which belonged to the *P*	1Kin 16:15	6430
in the land of the *P* seven years	2Kin 8:2	6430

returned out of the land of the P	2Kin 8:3	6430
He smote the P, even unto Gaza,	2Kin 18:8	6430
and Casluhim, (of whom came the P	1Chr 1:12	6430
Now the P fought against Israel	1Chr 10:1	6430
of Israel fled from before the P	1Chr 10:1	6430
the P followed hard after Saul,	1Chr 10:2	6430
the P slew Jonathan, and Abinadab,	1Chr 10:2	6430
the P came and dwelt in them	1Chr 10:7	6430
when the P came to strip the	1Chr 10:8	6430
the land of the P round about	1Chr 10:9	6430
all that the P had done to Saul	1Chr 10:11	6430
there the P were gathered	1Chr 11:13	6430
the people fled from before the P	1Chr 11:13	6430
and delivered it, and slew the P	1Chr 11:14	6430
the host of the P encamped in the	1Chr 11:15	6430
brake through the host of the P	1Chr 11:18	6430
when he came with the P against	1Chr 12:19	6430
for the lords of the P upon	1Chr 12:19	6430
when the P heard that David was	1Chr 14:8	6430
all the P went up to seek David	1Chr 14:8	6430
the P came and spread themselves	1Chr 14:9	6430
Shall I go up against the P	1Chr 14:10	6430
the P yet again spread themselves	1Chr 14:13	6430
thee to smite the host of the P	1Chr 14:15	6430
the P from Gibeon even to Gazer	1Chr 14:16	6430
to pass, that David smote the P	1Chr 18:1	6430
towns out of the hand of the P	1Chr 18:1	6430
children of Ammon, and from the P	1Chr 18:11	6430
arose war at Gezer with the P	1Chr 20:4	6430
And there was war again with the P	1Chr 20:5	6430
river even unto the land of the P	2Chr 9:26	6430
Also some of the P brought	2Chr 17:11	6430
Jehoram the spirit of the P	2Chr 21:16	6430
forth and warred against the P	2Chr 26:6	6430
about Ashdod, and among the P	2Chr 26:6	6430
And God helped him against the P	2Chr 26:7	6430
The P also had invaded the cities	2Chr 28:18	6430
when the P took him in Gath	Ps 56:t	6430
the P with the inhabitants of	Ps 83:7	6430
and are soothsayers like the P	Is 2:6	6430
Syrians before, and the P behind	Is 9:12	6430
of the P toward the west	Is 11:14	6430
the kings of the land of the P	Jer 25:20	6430
the prophet against the P	Jer 47:1	6430
that cometh to spoil all the P	Jer 47:4	6430
for the LORD will spoil the P	Jer 47:4	6430
hate thee, the daughters of the P	Eze 16:27	6430
about her, the daughters of the P	Eze 16:57	6430
Because the P have dealt by	Eze 25:15	6430
stretch out mine hand upon the P	Eze 25:16	6430
the remnant of the P shall perish	Amos 1:8	6430
then go down to Gath of the P	Amos 6:2	6430
the P from Caphtor, and the	Amos 9:7	6430
and they of the plain the P	Obad 19	6430
O Canaan, the land of the P	Zeph 2:5	6430
I will cut off the pride of the P	Zec 9:6	6430

PHILISTINES' *(fil-is'-tinz)*

sojourned in the P land many days	Gen 21:34	6430
let us go over to the P garrison	1Sa 14:1	6430
to go over unto the P garrison	1Sa 14:4	6430
the P garrison was then at	1Chr 11:16	6430

PHILOLOGUS *(fil-ol'-o-gus) A Christian in Rome.*

Salute P, and Julia, Nereus, and	Rom 16:15	5378

PHILOSOPHERS

Then certain p of the Epicureans,	Acts 17:18	5386

PHILOSOPHY

lest any man spoil you through p	Col 2:8	5385

PHINEHAS *(fin'-e-has)* See PHINEHAS'.
1. *A son of Eleazar.*

and she bare him P	Ex 6:25	6372
And when P, the son of Eleazar,	Num 25:7	6372
P, the son of Eleazar, the son of	Num 25:11	6372
P the son of Eleazar the priest,	Num 31:6	6372
P the son of Eleazar the priest,	Josh 22:13	6372
when P the priest, and the princes	Josh 22:30	6372
P the son of Eleazar the priest	Josh 22:31	6372
P the son of Eleazar the priest,	Josh 22:32	6372
hill that pertained to P his son	Josh 24:33	6372
And P the son of Eleazar, the son	Judg 20:28	6372
Eleazar begat P	1Chr 6:4	6372
P begat Abishua	1Chr 6:4	6372
P his son, Abishua his son,	1Chr 6:50	6372
P the son of Eleazar was the	1Chr 9:20	6372
The son of Abishua, the son of P	Ezr 7:5	6372
Of the sons of P	Ezr 8:2	6372
Then stood up P, and executed	Ps 106:30	6372

2. *A son of Eli.*

the two sons of Eli, Hophni and P	1Sa 1:3	6372
upon thy two sons, on Hophni and P	1Sa 2:34	6372
the two sons of Eli, Hophni and P	1Sa 4:4	6372
the two sons of Eli, Hophni and P	1Sa 4:11	6372
and thy two sons also, Hophni and P	1Sa 4:17	6372
I-chabod's brother, the son of P	1Sa 14:3	6372

3. *Father of Eleazar.*

with him was Eleazar the son of P	Ezr 8:33	6372

PHINEHAS' *(fin'-e-has) Refers to Phinehas 2.*

P wife, was with child, near to	1Sa 4:19	6372

PHLEGON *(fle'-gon) A Christian in Rome.*

Salute Asyncritus, P, Hermas,	Rom 16:14	5393

PHOENIX See PHENICE.

PHRYGIA *(frij'-e-ah) A Roman province in Asia Minor.*

P, and Pamphylia, in Egypt, and in	Acts 2:10	5435
when they had gone throughout P	Acts 16:6	5435
P in order, strengthening all the	Acts 18:23	5435
the chiefest city of P Pacatiana	1Ti s	5435

PHURAH *(fu'-rah) A servant of Gideon.*

go thou with P thy servant down	Judg 7:10	6513
Then went he down with P his	Judg 7:11	6513

PHUT *(fut)* See PUT.
1. *A son of Ham.*

and Mizraim, and P, and Canaan	Gen 10:6	6316

2. *Land of Phut's descendants.*

of P were in thine army, they men	Eze 27:10	6316

PHUVAH *(fu'-vah)* See PUAH. *A son of Issachar.*

Tola, and P, and Job, and Shimron	Gen 46:13	6312

PHYGELLUS *(fi-jel'-lus) An unfaithful Christian.*

of whom are P and Hermogenes	2Ti 1:15	5436

PHYGELUS See PHYGELLUS.

PHYLACTERIES

they make broad their p, and	Mt 23:5	5440

PHYSICIAN

is there no p there	Jer 8:22	7495
They that be whole need not a p	Mt 9:12	2395
are whole have no need of the p	Mk 2:17	2395
say unto me this proverb, P	Lk 4:23	2395
They that are whole need not a p	Lk 5:31	2395
Luke, the beloved p, and Demas,	Col 4:14	2395

PHYSICIANS

the p to embalm his father	Gen 50:2	7495
and the p embalmed Israel	Gen 50:2	7495
not to the LORD, but to the p	2Chr 16:12	7495
of lies, ye are all p of no value	Job 13:4	7495
suffered many things of many p	Mk 5:26	2395
had spent all her living upon p	Lk 8:43	2395

PI-BESETH *A city in Egypt.*

of P shall fall by the sword	Eze 30:17	6364

PICK

of the valley shall p it out	Prov 30:17	5365

PICTURES

you, and destroy all their p	Num 33:52	4906
apples of gold in p of silver	Prov 25:11	4906
Tarshish, and upon all pleasant p	Is 2:16	7914

PIECE

laid each p one against another	Gen 15:10	1335
beaten out of one p made he them	Ex 37:7	4749
of a whole p shalt thou make them	Num 10:2	
a certain woman cast a p of a	Judg 9:53	6400
crouch to him for a p of silver	1Sa 2:36	95
that I may eat a p of bread	1Sa 2:36	6595
they gave him a p of a cake of	1Sa 30:12	6400
a good p of flesh, and a flagon of	2Sa 6:19	829
did not a woman cast a p of a	2Sa 11:21	6400
where was a p of ground full of	2Sa 23:11	2513
mar every good p of land with	2Kin 3:19	2513
on every good p of land cast	2Kin 3:25	2513
a good p of flesh, and a flagon of	1Chr 16:3	829
Pahath-moab, repaired the other p	Neh 3:11	4060
another p over against the going	Neh 3:19	4060
earnestly repaired the other p	Neh 3:20	4060
Urijah the son of Koz another p	Neh 3:21	4060
the son of Henadad another p	Neh 3:24	4060
the Tekoites repaired another p	Neh 3:27	4060
sixth upon of Zalaph, another p	Neh 3:30	4060
as hard as a p of the nether	Job 41:24	6400
man also gave him a p of money	Job 42:11	
a man is brought to a p of bread	Prov 6:26	3603
for for a p of bread that man	Prov 28:21	6595
thy temples are like a p of a	Song 4:3	6400
As a p of a pomegranate are thy	Song 6:7	6400

P

a *p* of bread out of the bakers' ....Jer 37:21   3603
into it, even every good *p* ....Eze 24:4   5409
bring it out by *p* by *p* ....Eze 24:6   5409
lion two legs, or a *p* of an ear ....Amos 3:12   915
one *p* was rained upon ....Amos 4:7
the *p* whereupon it rained not................Amos 4:7
No man putteth a *p* of new cloth ....Mt 9:16   *1915*
thou shalt find a *p* of money ....Mt 17:27
No man also seweth a *p* of new ....Mk 2:21   *1915*
else the new *p* that filled it up ....Mk 2:21   *4138*
No man putteth a *p* of a new ....Lk 5:36   *1915*
the *p* that was taken out of the ....Lk 5:36   *1915*
him, I have bought a *p* of ground ....Lk 14:18
of silver, if she lose one *p* ....Lk 15:8   *1406*
have found the *p* which I had lost ....Lk 15:9   *1406*
they gave him a *p* of a broiled ....Lk 24:42   *3313*

PIECES
lamp that passed between those *p* ....Gen 15:17   *1506*
brother a thousand *p* of silver ....Gen 20:16
father, for an hundred *p* of money ....Gen 33:19
for twenty *p* of silver ....Gen 37:28
Joseph is without doubt rent in *p* ....Gen 37:33
and I said, Surely he is torn in *p* ....Gen 44:28
he gave three hundred *p* of silver ....Gen 45:22
LORD, hath dashed in *p* the enemy ....Ex 15:6
If it be torn in *p*, then let him ....Ex 22:13
And thou shalt cut the ram in *p* ....Ex 29:17   5409
his legs, and put them unto his *p* ....Ex 29:17   5409
offering, and cut it into his *p* ....Lev 1:6   5409
And he shall cut it into his *p* ....Lev 1:12   5409
Thou shalt part it in *p*, and pour ....Lev 2:6   6595
the baken *p* of the meat offering ....Lev 6:21   6595
And he cut the ram into *p* ....Lev 8:20   5409
and Moses burnt the head, and the *p* ....Lev 8:20   5409
unto him, with the *p* thereof ....Lev 9:13   5409
for an hundred *p* of silver ....Josh 24:32
ten *p* of silver out of the house ....Judg 9:4
of us eleven hundred *p* of silver ....Judg 16:5
with her bones, into twelve *p* ....Judg 19:29   5409
my concubine, and cut her in *p* ....Judg 20:6
of the LORD shall be broken to *p* 1Sa 2:10
yoke of oxen, and hewed them in *p* 1Sa 11:7
Samuel hewed Agag in *p* before the 1Sa 15:33
on him, and rent it in twelve *p* 1Kin 11:30   7168
said to Jeroboam, Take thee ten *p* 1Kin 11:31   7168
for themselves, and cut it in *p* 1Kin 18:23
in order, and cut the bullock in *p* 1Kin 18:33
brake in *p* the rocks before the 1Kin 19:11
clothes, and rent them in two *p* 2Kin 2:12   7168
silver, and six thousand *p* of gold 2Kin 5:5
sold for fourscore *p* of silver 2Kin 6:25
dove's dung for five *p* of silver 2Kin 6:25
images brake they in *p* thoroughly........2Kin 11:18
brake in *p* the brasen serpent 2Kin 18:4
And he brake in *p* the images................2Kin 23:14
cut in *p* all the vessels of gold 2Kin 24:13
LORD, did the Chaldees break in *p* 2Kin 25:13
his altars and his images in *p*................2Chr 23:17
that they all were broken in *p* 2Chr 25:12
cut in *p* the vessels of the house............2Chr 28:24
Judah, and brake the images in *p* 2Chr 31:1
the molten images, he brake in *p* 2Chr 34:4
me by my neck, and shaken me to *p* ......Job 16:12
soul, and break me in *p* with words ......Job 19:2
He shall break in *p* mighty men ....Job 34:24
bones are as strong of brass ....Job 40:18
them in *p* like a potter's vessel ....Ps 2:9
soul like a lion, rending it in *p* ....Ps 7:2
forget God, lest I tear you in *p*................Ps 50:22
arrows, let them be as cut in *p* ....Ps 58:7
submit himself with *p* of silver ....Ps 68:30   7518
and shall break in *p* the oppressor........Ps 72:4
the heads of leviathan in *p* ....Ps 74:14
Thou hast broken Rahab in *p* ....Ps 89:10
They break in *p* thy people ....Ps 94:5
to bring a thousand *p* of silver ....Song 8:11
ye that ye beat my people to *p* ....Is 3:15
and ye shall be broken in *p* ....Is 8:9
and ye shall be broken in *p* ....Is 8:9
and ye shall be broken in *p* ....Is 8:9
be dashed to *p* before their eyes ....Is 13:16
shall dash the young men to *p* ....Is 13:18
vessel that is broken in *p* ....Is 30:14
I will break in *p* the gates of ....Is 45:2
out thence shall be torn in *p* ....Jer 5:6
that breaketh the rock in *p* ....Jer 23:29
Merodach is broken in *p*..........................Jer 50:2
her images are broken in *p*......................Jer 50:2
will I break in *p* the nations....................Jer 51:20
thee will I break in *p* the horse................Jer 51:21

will I break in *p* the chariot ....Jer 51:21
thee also will I break in *p* man................Jer 51:22
with thee will I break in *p* old ....Jer 51:22
will I break in *p* the young man ....Jer 51:22
I will also break in *p* with thee ....Jer 51:23
will I break in *p* the husbandman ....Jer 51:23
thee will I break in *p* captains................Jer 51:23
aside my ways, and pulled me in *p* ....Lam 3:11
dieth of itself, or is torn in *p*..................Eze 4:14
for *p* of bread, to slay the souls..............Eze 13:19   6595
Gather the *p* thereof into it......................Eze 24:4   5409
thereof, ye shall be cut in *p* ....Dan 2:5   1917
iron and clay, and brake them to *p*..........Dan 2:34
and the gold, broken to *p* together..........Dan 2:35
forasmuch as iron breaketh in *p* ....Dan 2:40
all these, shall it break in *p* ....Dan 2:40
people, but it shall break in *p* ....Dan 2:44
and that it brake in *p* the iron ....Dan 2:45
and Abed-nego, shall be cut in *p* ....Dan 3:29   *1917*
brake all their bones in *p* or....................Dan 6:24
it devoured and brake in *p* ....Dan 7:7
which devoured, brake in *p*......................Dan 7:19
tread it down, and break it in *p* ....Dan 7:23
her to me for fifteen *p* of silver ....Hos 3:2
of Samaria shall be broken in *p*..............Hos 8:6
was dashed in *p* upon her children ....Hos 10:14
infants shall be dashed in *p* ....Hos 13:16
thereof shall be beaten to *p* ....Mic 1:7
their bones, and chop them in *p* ....Mic 3:3
thou shalt beat in *p* many people ....Mic 4:13
treadeth down, and teareth in *p* ....Mic 5:8
He that dasheth in *p* is come up ....Nah 2:1
The lion did tear in *p* enough for ....Nah 2:12
children also were dashed in *p* at ....Nah 3:10
for my price thirty *p* of silver ....Zec 11:12
And I took the thirty *p* of silver ....Zec 11:13
the fat, and tear their claws in *p* ....Zec 11:16
with it shall be cut in *p*............................Zec 12:3
with him for thirty-*p* of silver ....Mt 26:15
brought again the thirty *p* of ....Mt 27:3
he cast down the *p* of silver in ....Mt 27:5
chief priests took the silver *p* ....Mt 27:6
they took the thirty *p* of silver ....Mt 27:9
him, and the fetters broken in *p* ....Mk 5:4
what woman having ten *p* of silver ......Lk 15:8   *1406*
it fifty thousand *p* of silver ....Acts 19:19
have been pulled in *p* of them................Acts 23:10   *1288*
and some on broken *p* of the ship..........Acts 27:44

PIERCE
p them through with his arrows ....Num 24:8   4272
it will go into his hand, and *p* it 2Kin 18:21   5344
it will go into his hand, and *p* it ....Is 36:6   5344
a sword shall *p* through thy own ....Lk 2:35   *1330*

PIERCED
off his head, when she had *p* ....Judg 5:26   4272
My bones are *p* in me in the night ....Job 30:17   5365
they *p* my hands and my feet ....Ps 22:16   738
look upon me whom they have *p* ....Zec 12:10   1856
soldiers with a spear *p* his side..............Jn 19:34   *3572*
shall look on him whom they *p* ....Jn 19:37   *1574*
p themselves through with many 1Ti 6:10   *4044*
see him, and they also which *p* him ......Rev 1:7   *1574*

PIERCETH
his nose *p* through snares......................Job 40:24   5344

PIERCING
punish leviathan the *p* serpent ....Is 27:1   1281
p even to the dividing asunder of ....Heb 4:12   *1338*

PIERCINGS
speaketh like the *p* of a sword ....Prov 12:18   4094

PIETY
learn first to shew *p* at home 1Ti 5:4   *2151*

PIGEON
and a turtledove, and a young *p* ....Gen 15:9   1469
a burnt offering, and a young *p* ....Lev 12:6   3123

PIGEONS
of turtledoves, or of young *p* ....Lev 1:14   3123
two turtledoves, or two young *p*..............Lev 5:7   3123
two turtledoves, or two young *p*..............Lev 5:11   3123
bring two turtles, or two young *p* ....Lev 12:8   3123
two turtledoves, or two young *p*............Lev 14:22   3123
turtledoves, or of the young *p* ....Lev 14:30   3123
two turtledoves, or two young *p* ....Lev 15:14   3123
her two turtles, or two young *p* ....Lev 15:29   3123
bring two turtles, or two young *p* ....Num 6:10   3123
of turtledoves, or two young *p* ....Lk 2:24   *4058*

PI-HAHIROTH *A wilderness encampment.*

that they turn and encamp before *P*	Ex 14:2	6367
encamping by the sea, beside *P*	Ex 14:9	6367
Etham, and turned again unto *P*	Num 33:7	6367
And they departed from before *P*	Num 33:8	6367

PILATE *(pi'-lut) A Roman procurator of Judea.*

him to Pontius *P* the governor	Mt 27:2	4091
Then said *P* unto him, Hearest	Mt 27:13	4091
P said unto them, Whom will ye	Mt 27:17	4091
P saith unto them, What shall I	Mt 27:22	4091
When *P* saw that he could prevail	Mt 27:24	4091
He went to *P*, and begged the body	Mt 27:58	4091
Then *P* commanded the body to be	Mt 27:58	4091
and Pharisees came together unto *P*	Mt 27:62	4091
P said unto them, Ye have a watch	Mt 27:65	4091
him away, and delivered him to *P*	Mk 15:1	4091
P asked him, Art thou the King of	Mk 15:2	4091
P asked him again, saying,	Mk 15:4	4091
so that *P* marvelled	Mk 15:5	4091
But *P* answered them, saying, Will	Mk 15:9	4091
P answered and said again unto	Mk 15:12	4091
Then *P* said unto them, Why, what	Mk 15:14	4091
And so *P*, willing to content the	Mk 15:15	4091
came, and went in boldly unto *P*	Mk 15:43	4091
P marvelled if he were already	Mk 15:44	4091
Pontius *P* being governor of	Lk 3:1	4091
whose blood *P* had mingled with	Lk 13:1	4091
of them arose, and led him unto *P*	Lk 23:1	4091
P asked him, saying, Art thou the	Lk 23:3	4091
Then said *P* to the chief priests	Lk 23:4	4091
When *P* heard of Galilee, he asked	Lk 23:6	4091
robe, and sent him again to *P*	Lk 23:11	4091
And the same day *P* and Herod were	Lk 23:12	4091
And *P*, when he had called together	Lk 23:13	4091
P therefore, willing to release	Lk 23:20	4091
P gave sentence that it should be	Lk 23:24	4091
This man went unto *P*, and begged	Lk 23:52	4091
P then went out unto them, and	Jn 18:29	4091
Then said *P* unto them, Take ye	Jn 18:31	4091
Then *P* entered into the judgment	Jn 18:33	4091
P answered, Am I a Jew	Jn 18:35	4091
P therefore said unto him, Art	Jn 18:37	4091
P saith unto him, What is truth	Jn 18:38	4091
Then *P* therefore took Jesus, and	Jn 19:1	4091
P therefore went forth again, and	Jn 19:4	4091
P saith unto them, Behold the man	Jn 19:5	4091
P saith unto them, Take ye him,	Jn 19:6	4091
When *P* therefore heard that	Jn 19:8	4091
Then saith *P* unto him, Speakest	Jn 19:10	4091
from thenceforth *P* sought to	Jn 19:12	4091
When *P* therefore heard that	Jn 19:13	4091
P saith unto them, Shall I	Jn 19:15	4091
P wrote a title, and put it on the	Jn 19:19	4091
chief priests of the Jews to *P*	Jn 19:21	4091
P answered, What I have written I	Jn 19:22	4091
besought *P* that their legs might	Jn 19:31	4091
besought *P* that he might take	Jn 19:38	4091
and *P* gave him leave	Jn 19:38	4091
denied him in the presence of *P*	Acts 3:13	4091
both Herod, and Pontius *P*	Acts 4:27	4091
yet desired they *P* that he should	Acts 13:28	4091
who before Pontius *P* witnessed a	1Ti 6:13	4091

PILDASH *(pil'-dash) A son of Nahor.*

And Chesed, and Hazo, and *P*, and	Gen 22:22	6394

PILE

the *p* thereof is fire and much	Is 30:33	4071
even make the *p* for fire great	Eze 24:9	4071

PILEHA *(pil'-e-hah) A renewer of the covenant.*

Hallohesh, *P*, Shobek,	Neh 10:24	6401

PILGRIMAGE

the years of my *p* are an hundred	Gen 47:9	4033
my fathers in the days of their *p*	Gen 47:9	4033
of Canaan, the land of their *p*	Ex 6:4	4033
my songs in the house of my *p*	Ps 119:54	4033

PILGRIMS

were strangers and *p* on the earth	Heb 11:13	3927
I beseech you as strangers and *p*	1Pet 2:11	3927

PILHA See PILEHA.

PILLAR

him, and she became a *p* of salt	Gen 19:26	5333
his pillows, and set it up for a *p*	Gen 28:18	4676
stone, which I have set for a *p*	Gen 28:22	4676
where thou anointedst the *p*	Gen 31:13	4676
a stone, and set it up for a *p*	Gen 31:45	4676
this heap, and behold this *p*	Gen 31:51	4676
this *p* be witness, that I will	Gen 31:52	4676
heap, and this *p* unto me, for harm	Gen 31:52	4676

Jacob set up a *p* in the place	Gen 35:14	4676
with him, even a *p* of stone	Gen 35:14	4678
Jacob set a *p* upon her grave	Gen 35:20	4676
that is the *p* of Rachel's grave	Gen 35:20	4678
them by day in a *p* of a cloud	Ex 13:21	5982
and by night in a *p* of fire	Ex 13:21	5982
away the *p* of the cloud by day	Ex 13:22	5982
nor the *p* of fire by night, from	Ex 13:22	5982
the *p* of the cloud went from	Ex 14:19	5982
Egyptians through the *p* of fire	Ex 14:24	5982
the cloudy *p* descended, and stood	Ex 33:9	5982
p stand at the tabernacle door	Ex 33:10	5982
came down in the *p* of the cloud	Num 12:5	5982
by daytime in a *p* of a cloud	Num 14:14	5982
and in a *p* of fire by night	Num 14:14	5982
the tabernacle in a *p* of a cloud	Deut 31:15	5982
the *p* of the cloud stood over the	Deut 31:15	5982
of the *p* that was in Shechem	Judg 9:6	5324
out of the city with a *p* of smoke	Judg 20:40	5982
and reared up for himself a *p*	2Sa 18:18	4678
he called the *p* after his own	2Sa 18:18	4678
and he set up the right *p*, and	1Kin 7:21	5982
and he set up the left *p*, and	1Kin 7:21	5982
behold, the king stood by a *p*	2Kin 11:14	5982
And the king stood by a *p*, and made	2Kin 23:3	5982
of the one *p* was eighteen cubits	2Kin 25:17	5982
the second *p* with wreathen work	2Kin 25:17	5982
stood at his *p* at the entering in	2Chr 23:13	5982
them in the day by a cloudy *p*	Neh 9:12	5982
and in the night by a *p* of fire	Neh 9:12	5982
the *p* of the cloud departed not	Neh 9:19	5982
neither the *p* of fire by night,	Neh 9:19	5982
spake unto them in the cloudy *p*	Ps 99:7	5982
a *p* at the border thereof to the	Is 19:19	4676
day a defenced city, and an iron *p*	Jer 1:18	5982
the height of one *p* was eighteen	Jer 52:21	5982
The second *p* also and the	Jer 52:22	5982
church of the living God, the *p*	1Ti 3:15	4769
make a *p* in the temple of my God	Rev 3:12	4769

PILLARS

altar under the hill, and twelve *p*	Ex 24:4	4676
thou shalt hang it upon four *p* of	Ex 26:32	5982
hanging five *p* of shittim wood	Ex 26:37	5982
And the twenty *p* thereof and their	Ex 27:10	5982
the hooks of the *p* and their	Ex 27:10	5982
cubits long, and his twenty *p*	Ex 27:11	5982
the hooks of the *p* and their	Ex 27:11	5982
their *p* ten, and their sockets ten	Ex 27:12	5982
their *p* three, and their sockets	Ex 27:14	5982
their *p* three, and their sockets	Ex 27:15	5982
their *p* shall be four, and their	Ex 27:16	5982
All the *p* round about the court	Ex 27:17	5982
and his boards, his bars, his *p*	Ex 35:11	5982
The hangings of the court, his *p*	Ex 35:17	5982
thereunto four *p* of shittim wood	Ex 36:36	5982
the five *p* of it with their hooks	Ex 36:38	5982
Their *p* were twenty, and their	Ex 38:10	5982
the hooks of the *p* and their	Ex 38:10	5982
their *p* were twenty, and their	Ex 38:11	5982
the hooks of the *p* and their	Ex 38:11	5982
of fifty cubits, their *p* ten	Ex 38:12	5982
the hooks of the *p* and their	Ex 38:12	5982
their *p* three, and their sockets	Ex 38:14	5982
their *p* three, and their sockets	Ex 38:15	5982
sockets for the *p* were of brass	Ex 38:17	5982
the hooks of the *p* and their	Ex 38:17	5982
all the *p* of the court were	Ex 38:17	5982
their *p* were four, and their	Ex 38:19	5982
shekels he made hooks for the *p*	Ex 38:28	5982
his boards, his bars, and his *p*	Ex 39:33	5982
The hangings of the court, his *p*	Ex 39:40	5982
bars thereof, and reared up his *p*	Ex 40:18	5982
the *p* thereof, and the sockets	Num 3:36	5982
the *p* of the court round about,	Num 3:37	5982
the *p* thereof, and sockets thereof	Num 4:31	5982
the *p* of the court round about,	Num 4:32	5982
their altars, and break their *p*	Deut 12:3	4676
and they set him between the *p*	Judg 16:25	5982
p whereupon the house standeth	Judg 16:26	5982
p upon which the house stood	Judg 16:29	5982
for the *p* of the earth are the	1Sa 2:8	4690
cubits, upon four rows of cedar *p*	1Kin 7:2	5982
with cedar beams upon the *p*	1Kin 7:2	5982
beams, that lay on forty five *p*	1Kin 7:3	5982
And he made a porch of *p*	1Kin 7:6	5982
and the other *p* and the thick beam	1Kin 7:6	5982
For he cast two *p* of brass	1Kin 7:15	5982
to set upon the tops of the *p*	1Kin 7:16	5982
which were upon the top of the *p*	1Kin 7:17	5982
And he made the *p*, and two rows	1Kin 7:18	5982

P

that were upon the top of the *p* 1Kin 7:19   5982
the chapiters upon the two *p* had 1Kin 7:20   5982
he set up the *p* in the porch of 1Kin 7:21   5982
the top of the *p* was lily work 1Kin 7:22   5982
so was the work of the *p* finished 1Kin 7:22   5982
The two *p*, and the two bowls of 1Kin 7:41   5982
that were on the top of the two *p* 1Kin 7:41   5982
which were upon the top of the *p* 1Kin 7:41   5982
chapiters that were upon the *p* 1Kin 7:42   5982
trees *p* for the house of the LORD 1Kin 10:12   4552
from the *p* which Hezekiah king of 2Kin 18:16   547
the *p* of brass that were in the 2Kin 25:13   5982
The two *p*, one sea, and the bases 2Kin 25:16   5982
made the brasen sea, and the *p* 1Chr 18:8   5982
before the house two *p* of thirty 2Chr 3:15   5982
and put them on the heads of the *p* 2Chr 3:16   5982
he reared up the *p* before the 2Chr 3:17   5982
To wit, the two *p*, and the pommels 2Chr 4:12   5982
were on the top of the two *p* 2Chr 4:12   5982
which were on the top of the *p* 2Chr 4:12   5982
chapiters which were upon the *p* 2Chr 4:13   5982
to silver rings and *p* of marble...............Est 1:6   5982
place, and the *p* thereof tremble ....Job 9:6   5982
The *p* of heaven tremble, and are ....Job 26:11   5982
I bear up the *p* of it ....Ps 75:3   5982
she hath hewn out her seven *p* ....Prov 9:1   5982
of the wilderness like *p* of smoke ....Song 3:6   8490
He made the *p* thereof of silver, ...Song 3:10   5982
His legs are as *p* of marble ....Song 5:15   5982
LORD of hosts concerning the *p* ....Jer 27:19   5982
Also the *p* of brass that were in ....Jer 52:17   5982
The two *p*, one sea, and twelve ....Jer 52:20   5982
And concerning the *p*, the height ....Jer 52:21   5982
there were *p* by the posts, one on ....Eze 40:49   5982
p as the *p* of the courts....................Eze 46:2   5982
blood, and fire, and *p* of smoke ....Joel 2:30   8490
and John, who seemed to be *p* ....Gal 2:9   4769
the sun, and his feet as *p* of fire ....Rev 10:1   4769

PILLED
p white strakes in them, and made ....Gen 30:37   6478
he had *p* before the flocks in the ....Gen 30:38   6478

PILLOW
put a *p* of goats' hair for his...................1Sa 19:13   3523
with a *p* of goats' hair for his 1Sa 19:16   3523
part of the ship, asleep on a *p* ....Mk 4:38   4344

PILLOWS
that place, and put them for his *p* ....Gen 28:11   4763
stone that he had put for his *p* ....Gen 28:18   4763
women that sew *p* to all armholes ....Eze 13:18   3704
Behold, I am against your *p* ....Eze 13:20   3704

PILOTS
that were in thee, were thy *p*.................Eze 27:8   2259
thy mariners, and thy *p*, thy ....Eze 27:27   2259
at the sound of the cry of thy *p* ....Eze 27:28   2259
all the *p* of the sea, shall come ....Eze 27:29   2259

PILTAI (pil'-tahee) *A priest.*
of Miniamin, of Moadiah, *P*....................Neh 12:17   6408

PIN
And she fastened it with the *p* ....Judg 16:14   3489
went away with the *p* of the beam ......Judg 16:14   3489
or will men take a *p* of it to ....Eze 15:3   3489

PINE
p away in their iniquity in your ....Lev 26:39   4743
shall they *p* away with them ....Lev 26:39   4743
p branches, and myrtle branches, .. Neh 8:15   6086,8081
the desert the fir tree, and the *p* ....Is 41:19   8410
the *p* tree, and the box together, ...Is 60:13   8410
for these *p* away, stricken ....Lam 4:9   2100
but ye shall *p* away for your ....Eze 24:23   4743
we *p* away in them, how should we ....Eze 33:10   4743

PINETH
with his teeth, and *p* away ....Mk 9:18   3583

PINING
will cut me off with *p* sickness ....Is 38:12   1803

PINNACLE
setteth him on a *p* of the temple............Mt 4:5   4419
set him on a *p* of the temple, and ....Lk 4:9   4419

PINON
Aholibamah, duke Elah, duke *P*...........Gen 36:41   6373
Aholibamah, duke Elah, duke *P*.............1Chr 1:52   6373

PINS
thereof, and all the *p* thereof ....Ex 27:19   3489
all the *p* of the court, shall be ....Ex 27:19   3489
The *p* of the tabernacle, and the............Ex 35:18   3489
p of the court, and their ....Ex 35:18   3489

all the *p* of the tabernacle, and ....Ex 38:20   3489
all the *p* of the tabernacle, and..............Ex 38:31   3489
all the *p* of the court round ....Ex 38:31   3489
court gate, his cords, and his *p*...............Ex 39:40   3489
and their sockets, and their *p* ....Num 3:37   3489
and their sockets, and their *p* ....Num 4:32   3489
and the wimples, and the crisping *p* ......Is 3:22

PIPE
a psaltery, and a tabret, and a *p* 1Sa 10:5   2485
and the viol, the tabret, and *p*...............Is 5:12   2485
as when one goeth with a *p* to ....Is 30:29   2485
giving sound, whether *p* or harp.............1Cor 14:7   836

PIPED
him, and the people *p* with pipes...........1Kin 1:40   2490
We have *p* unto you, and ye have .... Mt 11:17   832
We have *p* unto you, and ye have .... Lk 7:32   832
it be known what is *p* or harped 1Cor 14:7   832

PIPERS
of harpers, and musicians, and of *p* .... Rev 18:22   834

PIPES
him, and the people piped with *p* 1Kin 1:40   2485
heart shall sound for Moab like *p* ....Jer 48:36   2485
like *p* for the men of Kir-heres...............Jer 48:36   2485
of thy *p* was prepared in thee in ....Eze 28:13   5345
seven *p* to the seven lamps, which ....Zec 4:2   4166
p empty the golden oil out of...................Zec 4:12   6804

PIRAM (pi'-ram) *An Amorite king.*
unto *P* king of Jarmuth, and unto............Josh 10:3   6502

PIRATHON (pir'-a-thon) *See* PIRATHONITE. *A place in Ephraim.*
was buried in *P* in the land of ....Judg 12:15   6552

PIRATHONITE (pir'-a-thon-ite) *An inhabitant of Pirathon.*
him Abdon the son of Hillel, a *P* ....Judg 12:13   6553
the son of Hillel the *P* died ....Judg 12:15   6553
Benaiah the *P*, Hiddai of the....................2Sa 23:30   6553
of Benjamin, Benaiah the *P* 1Chr 11:31   6553
eleventh month was Benaiah the *P* 1Chr 27:14   6553

PISGAH (piz'-gah) *A mountain peak in Moab.*
country of Moab, to the top of *P* ....Num 21:20   6449
field of Zophim, to the top of *P* ....Num 23:14   6449
Get thee up into the top of *P* ....Deut 3:27   6449
the plain, under the springs of *P* ....Deut 4:49   6449
mountain of Nebo, to the top of *P* ....Deut 34:1   6449

PISHON See PISON.

PISIDIA (pi-sid'-e-ah) *A Roman province in Asia Minor.*
Perga, they came to Antioch in *P*............Acts 13:14   4099
they had passed throughout *P* ....Acts 14:24   4099

PISIDIAN ANTIOCH See PISIDIA.

PISON (pi'-son) *A river of Eden.*
The name of the first is *P* ....Gen 2:11   6376

PISPA See PISPAH.

PISPAH (piz'-pah) *A son of Jether.*
Jephunneh, and *P*, and Ara.....................1Chr 7:38   6462

PISS
and drink their own *p* with you 2Kin 18:27   7890
and drink their own *p* with you ....Is 36:12   7890

PISSETH
light any that *p* against the wall 1Sa 25:22   8366
light any that *p* against the wall 1Sa 25:34   8366
him that *p* against the wall....................1Kin 14:10   8366
him not one that *p* against a wall 1Kin 16:11   8366
Ahab him that *p* against the wall.........1Kin 21:21   8366
Ahab him that *p* against the wall............2Kin 9:8   8366

PIT
slay him, and cast him into some *p* ....Gen 37:20   953
but cast him into this *p* that is ....Gen 37:22   953
took him, and cast him into a *p* ....Gen 37:24   953
the *p* was empty, there was no ....Gen 37:24   953
and lifted up Joseph out of the *p* ....Gen 37:28   953
And Reuben returned unto the *p* ....Gen 37:29   953
behold, Joseph was not in the *p* ....Gen 37:29   953
And if a man shall open a *p*...................Ex 21:33   953
or if a man shall dig a *p* ....Ex 21:33   953
The owner of the *p* shall make it ....Ex 21:34   953
Nevertheless a fountain or *p* ....Lev 11:36   953
and they go down quick into the *p* ....Num 16:30   7585
them, went down alive into the *p* ....Num 16:33   7585
Behold, he is hid now in some *p* 2Sa 17:9   6354
him into a great *p* in the wood 2Sa 18:17   6354
the midst of a *p* in time of snow............2Sa 23:20   953
slew them at the *p* of the 2Kin 10:14   953
slew a lion in a *p* in a snowy day............1Chr 11:22   953

ye dig a *p* for your friend	Job 6:27	
go down to the bars of the *p*	Job 17:16	7585
keepeth back his soul from the *p*	Job 33:18	7845
him from going down to the *p*	Job 33:24	7845
his soul from going into the *p*	Job 33:28	7845
To bring back his soul from the *p*	Job 33:30	7845
He made a *p*, and digged it, and is	Ps 7:15	953
sunk down in the *p* that they made	Ps 9:15	7845
like them that go down into the *p*	Ps 28:1	953
I should not go down to the *p*	Ps 30:3	953
my blood, when I go down to the *p*	Ps 30:9	7845
they hid for me their net in a *p*	Ps 35:7	7845
me up also out of an horrible *p*	Ps 40:2	953
down into the *p* of destruction	Ps 55:23	875
they have digged a *p* before me	Ps 57:6	7882
let not the *p* shut her mouth upon	Ps 69:15	875
with them that go down into the *p*	Ps 88:4	953
Thou hast laid me in the lowest *p*	Ps 88:6	953
until the *p* be digged for the	Ps 94:13	7845
unto them that go down into the *p*	Ps 143:7	953
as those that go down into the *p*	Prov 1:12	953
of strange women is a deep *p*	Prov 22:14	7745
and a strange woman is a narrow *p*	Prov 23:27	875
Whoso diggeth a *p* shall fall	Prov 26:27	7845
shall fall himself into his own *p*	Prov 28:10	7816
of any person shall flee to the *p*	Prov 28:17	953
He that diggeth a *p* shall fall	Eccl 10:8	1475
to hell, to the sides of the *p*	Is 14:15	953
go down to the stones of the *p*	Is 14:19	953
Fear, and the *p*, and the snare, are	Is 24:17	6354
of the fear shall fall into the *p*	Is 24:18	6354
up out of the midst of the *p*	Is 24:18	6354
prisoners are gathered in the *p*	Is 24:22	953
to take water withal out of the *p*	Is 30:14	1360
it from the *p* of corruption	Is 38:17	7845
the *p* cannot hope for thy truth	Is 38:18	953
to the hole of the *p* whence ye	Is 51:1	953
that he should not die in the *p*	Is 51:14	7845
they have digged a *p* for my soul	Jer 18:20	7745
they have digged a *p* to take me	Jer 18:22	7743,7882
cast them into the midst of the *p*	Jer 41:7	953
Now the *p* wherein Ishmael had	Jer 41:9	953
Fear, and the *p*, and the snare,	Jer 48:43	6354
the fear shall fall into the *p*	Jer 48:44	6354
the *p* shall be taken in the snare	Jer 48:44	6354
he was taken in their *p*, and they	Eze 19:4	7845
he was taken in their *p*	Eze 19:8	7845
with them that descend into the *p*	Eze 26:20	953
with them that go down to the *p*	Eze 26:20	953
shall bring thee down to the *p*	Eze 28:8	7845
with them that go down to the *p*	Eze 31:14	953
with them that descend into the *p*	Eze 31:16	953
with them that go down into the *p*	Eze 32:18	953
are set in the sides of the *p*	Eze 32:23	953
with them that go down to the *p*	Eze 32:24	953
with them that go down to the *p*	Eze 32:25	953
with them that go down to the *p*	Eze 32:29	953
with them that go down to the *p*	Eze 32:30	953
out of the *p* wherein is no water	Zec 9:11	953
if it fall into a *p* on the	Mt 12:11	999
an ass or an ox fallen into a *p*	Lk 14:5	5421
given the key of the bottomless *p*	Rev 9:1	5421
And he opened the bottomless *p*	Rev 9:2	5421
there arose a smoke out of the *p*	Rev 9:2	5421
by reason of the smoke of the *p*	Rev 9:2	5421
is the angel of the bottomless *p*	Rev 9:11	
p shall make war against them	Rev 11:7	
ascend out of the bottomless *p*	Rev 17:8	
the key of the bottomless *p*	Rev 20:1	
And cast him into the bottomless *p*	Rev 20:3	

PITCH

p it within and without with *p*	Gen 6:14	3724
and daubed it with slime and with *p*	Ex 2:3	2203
of Israel shall *p* their tents	Num 1:52	2583
But the Levites shall *p* round	Num 1:53	2583
shall *p* by his own standard	Num 2:2	2583
of the congregation shall they *p*	Num 2:2	2583
Judah *p* throughout their armies	Num 2:3	2583
those that do *p* next unto him	Num 2:5	2583
those which by him shall be the	Num 2:12	2583
of the Gershonites shall *p* behind	Num 3:23	2583
of the sons of Kohath shall *p* on	Num 3:29	2583
these shall *p* on the side of the	Num 3:35	2583
out a place to *p* your tents in	Deut 1:33	2583
of Jordan, did Joshua *p* in Gilgal	Josh 4:20	6965
shall the Arabian *p* tent there	Is 13:20	167
thereof shall be turned into *p*	Is 34:9	2203
thereof shall become burning *p*	Is 34:9	2203
they shall *p* their tents against	Jer 6:3	8628

PITCHED

p his tent, having Beth-el on the	Gen 12:8	5186
plain, and *p* his tent toward Sodom	Gen 13:12	167
p his tent in the valley of Gerar	Gen 26:17	2583
of the LORD, and *p* his tent there	Gen 26:25	5186
Now Jacob had *p* his tent in the	Gen 31:25	8628
brethren *p* in the mount of Gilead	Gen 31:25	8628
p his tent before the city	Gen 33:18	2583
of the LORD, and *p* in Rephidim	Ex 17:1	2583
Sinai, and had *p* in the wilderness	Ex 19:2	2583
p it without the camp, afar off	Ex 33:7	5186
and when the tabernacle is to be *p*	Num 1:51	2583
so they *p* by their standards, and	Num 2:34	2583
children of Israel *p* their tents	Num 9:17	2583
commandment of the LORD they *p*	Num 9:18	2583
p in the wilderness of Paran	Num 12:16	2583
Israel set forward, and *p* in Oboth	Num 21:10	2583
Oboth, and *p* at Ije-abarim, in the	Num 21:11	2583
and *p* in the valley of Zared	Num 21:12	2583
p on the other side of Arnon,	Num 21:13	2583
p in the plains of Moab on this	Num 22:1	2583
from Rameses, and *p* in Succoth	Num 33:5	2583
p in Etham, which is in the edge	Num 33:6	2583
and they *p* before Migdol	Num 33:7	2583
of Etham, and *p* in Marah	Num 33:8	2583
and they *p* there	Num 33:9	2583
p in the wilderness of Sinai	Num 33:15	2583
Sinai, and *p* at Kibroth-hattaavah	Num 33:16	2583
from Hazeroth, and *p* in Rithmah	Num 33:18	2583
Rithmah, and *p* at Rimmon-parez	Num 33:19	2583
from Rimmon-parez, and *p* in Libnah	Num 33:20	2583
from Libnah, and *p* at Rissah	Num 33:21	2583
from Rissah, and *p* in Kehelathah	Num 33:22	2583
Kehelathah, and *p* in mount Shapher	Num 33:23	2583
from Haradah, and *p* in Makheloth	Num 33:25	2583
from Tahath, and *p* at Tarah	Num 33:27	2583
from Tarah, and *p* in Mithcah	Num 33:28	2583
from Mithcah, and *p* in Hashmonah	Num 33:29	2583
Moseroth, and *p* in Bene-jaakan	Num 33:31	2583
Hor-hagidgad, and *p* in Jotbathah	Num 33:33	2583
p in the wilderness of Zin, which	Num 33:36	2583
p in mount Hor, in the edge of	Num 33:37	2583
from mount Hor, and *p* in Zalmonah	Num 33:41	2583
from Zalmonah, and *p* in Punon	Num 33:42	2583
from Punon, and *p* in Oboth	Num 33:43	2583
p in Ije-abarim, in the border of	Num 33:44	2583
from Iim, and *p* in Dibon-gad	Num 33:45	2583
p in the mountains of Abarim,	Num 33:47	2583
p in the plains of Moab by Jordan	Num 33:48	2583
And they *p* by Jordan, from	Num 33:49	2583
p on the north side of Ai	Josh 8:11	2583
p together at the waters of Merom	Josh 11:5	2583
p his tent unto the plain of	Judg 4:11	5186
p in the valley of Jezreel	Judg 6:33	2583
p beside the well of Harod	Judg 7:1	2583
p on the other side of Arnon, but	Judg 11:18	2583
p in Jahaz, and fought against	Judg 11:20	2583
p in Judah, and spread themselves	Judg 15:9	2583
p in Kirjath-jearim, in Judah	Judg 18:12	2583
to battle, and *p* beside Eben-ezer	1Sa 4:1	2583
and the Philistines *p* in Aphek	1Sa 4:1	2583
p in Michmash, eastward from	1Sa 13:5	2583
p between Shochoh and Azekah, in	1Sa 17:1	2583
p by the valley of Elah, and set	1Sa 17:2	2583
Saul *p* in the hill of Hachilah,	1Sa 26:3	2583
to the place where Saul had *p*	1Sa 26:5	2583
the people *p* round about him	1Sa 26:5	2583
together, and came and *p* in Shunem	1Sa 28:4	2583
together, and they *p* in Gilboa	1Sa 28:4	2583
the Israelites *p* by a fountain	1Sa 29:1	2583
that David had *p* for it	2Sa 6:17	5186
Absalom *p* in the land of Gilead	2Sa 17:26	2583
p in the valley of Rephaim	2Sa 23:13	2583
p in Aroer, on the right side of	2Sa 24:5	2583
the children of Israel *p* before	1Kin 20:27	2583
they *p* one over against the other	1Kin 20:29	2583
Jerusalem, and *p* against it	2Kin 25:1	2583
ark of God, and *p* for it a tent	1Chr 15:1	5186
the tent that David had *p* for it	1Chr 16:1	5186
who came and *p* before Medeba	1Chr 19:7	2583
for he had *p* a tent for it at	2Chr 1:4	5186
p against it, and built forts	Jer 52:4	2583
true tabernacle, which the Lord *p*	Heb 8:2	4078

PITCHER

whom I shall say, Let down thy *p*	Gen 24:14	3537
with her *p* upon her shoulder	Gen 24:15	3537
down to the well, and filled her *p*	Gen 24:16	3537
drink a little water of thy *p*	Gen 24:17	3537
let down her *p* upon her hand, and	Gen 24:18	3537
emptied her *p* into the trough, and	Gen 24:20	3537

P

a little water of thy *p* to drink	Gen 24:43	3537
forth with her *p* on her shoulder	Gen 24:45	3537
let down her *p* from her shoulder,	Gen 24:46	3537
or the *p* be broken at the	Eccl 12:6	3537
you a man bearing a *p* of water	Mk 14:13	2765
meet you, bearing a *p* of water	Lk 22:10	2765

PITCHERS
in every man's hand, with empty *p*	Judg 7:16	3537
and lamps within the *p*	Judg 7:16	3537
brake the *p* that were in their	Judg 7:19	3537
blew the trumpets, and brake the *p*	Judg 7:20	3537
are they esteemed as earthen *p*	Lam 4:2	5035

PITHOM (pi'-thom) A city in Lower Egypt.
for Pharaoh treasure cities, P	Ex 1:11	6619

PITHON (pi'-thon) A son of Micah.
And the sons of Micah were, P	1Chr 8:35	6377
And the sons of Micah were, P	1Chr 9:41	6377

PITIED
He made them also to be *p* of all	Ps 106:46	7356
of Jacob, and hath not *p*	Lam 2:2	2550
hath thrown down, and hath not *p*	Lam 2:17	2550
thou hast killed, and not *p*	Lam 2:21	2550
thou hast slain, thou hast not *p*	Lam 3:43	2550
None eye *p* thee, to do any of	Eze 16:5	2347

PITIETH
Like as a father *p* his children	Ps 103:13	7355
so the Lord *p* them that fear him	Ps 103:13	7355
eyes, and that which your soul *p*	Eze 24:21	4263

PITIFUL
The hands of the *p* women have	Lam 4:10	7362
that the Lord is very *p*, and of	Jas 5:11	*4184*
another, love as brethren, be *p*	1Pet 3:8	*2155*

PITS
rocks, and in high places, and in *p*	1Sa 13:6	953
The proud have digged *p* for me	Ps 119:85	7882
into deep *p*, that they rise not	Ps 140:10	
through a land of deserts and of *p*	Jer 2:6	7745
they came to the *p*, and found no	Jer 14:3	1356
of the Lord, was taken in their *p*	Lam 4:20	7825

PITY
eye shall have no *p* upon them	Deut 7:16	2347
neither shall thine eye *p* him	Deut 13:8	2347
Thine eye shall not *p* him	Deut 19:13	2347
And thine eye shall not *p*	Deut 19:21	2347
hand, thine eye shall not *p* her	Deut 25:12	2347
thing, and because he had no *p*	2Sa 12:6	2550
To him that is afflicted *p* should	Job 6:14	2617
Have *p* upon me, have *p* upon me	Job 19:21	2603
and I looked for some to take *p*	Ps 69:20	5110
He that hath *p* upon the poor	Prov 19:17	2603
it for him that will *p* the poor	Prov 28:8	2603
they shall have no *p* on the fruit	Is 13:18	7355
in his *p* he redeemed them	Is 63:9	2551
I will not *p*, nor spare, nor have	Jer 13:14	2550
For who shall have *p* upon thee	Jer 15:5	2550
not spare them, neither have *p*	Jer 21:7	2550
spare, neither will I have any *p*	Eze 5:11	2550
spare thee, neither will I have *p*	Eze 7:4	2550
not spare, neither will I have *p*	Eze 7:9	2550
not spare, neither will I have *p*	Eze 8:18	2550
your eye spare, neither have ye *p*	Eze 9:5	2550
not spare, neither will I have *p*	Eze 9:10	2550
But I had *p* for mine holy name,	Eze 36:21	2550
for his land, and *p* his people	Joel 2:18	2550
the sword, and did cast off all *p*	Amos 1:11	7356
Thou hast had *p* on the gourd	Jonah 4:10	2347
and their own shepherds *p* them not	Zec 11:5	2550
For I will no more *p* the	Zec 11:6	2550
even as I had *p* on thee	Mt 18:33	*1653*

PLACE See APPENDIX.

PLACED See APPENDIX.

PLACES
thee in all *p* whither thou goest	Gen 28:15	
to their families, after their *p*	Gen 36:40	4725
in all *p* where I record my name I	Ex 20:24	4725
border shall the rings be for *p*	Ex 25:27	1004
rings of gold for the bars	Ex 26:29	1004
they shall be for *p* for the	Ex 30:4	1004
of gold to be *p* for the bars	Ex 36:34	1004
the *p* for the staves to bear the	Ex 37:14	1004
to be *p* for the staves to bear it	Ex 37:27	1004
of brass, to be *p* for the staves	Ex 38:5	1004
And I will destroy your high *p*	Lev 26:30	
the lords of the high *p* of Arnon	Num 21:28	
him up into the high *p* of Baal	Num 22:41	

quite pluck down all their high *p*	Num 33:52	
unto all the *p* nigh thereunto, in	Deut 1:7	
shall utterly destroy all the *p*	Deut 12:2	4725
ride on the high *p* of the earth	Deut 32:13	
shalt tread upon their high *p*	Deut 33:29	
they abode in their *p* in the camp	Josh 5:8	8478
archers in the *p* of drawing water	Judg 5:11	
death in the high *p* of the field	Judg 5:18	
one of these *p* to lodge all night	Judg 19:13	4725
Israel came forth out of their *p*	Judg 20:33	4725
and judged Israel in all those *p*	1Sa 7:16	4725
and in rocks, and in high *p*	1Sa 13:6	
lurking *p* where he hideth himself	1Sa 23:23	
to all the *p* where David himself	1Sa 30:31	4725
Israel is slain upon thy high *p*	2Sa 1:19	
thou wast slain in thine high *p*	2Sa 1:25	
In all the *p* wherein I have	2Sa 7:7	
and setteth me upon my high *p*	2Sa 22:34	
be afraid out of their close *p*	2Sa 22:46	
the people sacrificed in high *p*	1Kin 3:2	
and burnt incense in high *p*	1Kin 3:3	
And he made an house of high *p*	1Kin 12:31	
of the high *p* which he had made	1Kin 12:32	
p that burn incense upon thee	1Kin 13:2	
high *p* which are in the cities of	1Kin 13:32	
the people priests of the high *p*	1Kin 13:33	
one of the priests of the high *p*	1Kin 13:33	
For they also built their high *p*	1Kin 14:23	
But the high *p* were not removed	1Kin 15:14	
the high *p* were not taken away	1Kin 22:43	
burnt incense yet in the high *p*	1Kin 22:43	
But the high *p* were not taken	2Kin 12:3	
and burnt incense in the high *p*	2Kin 12:3	
Howbeit the high *p* were not taken	2Kin 14:4	
and burnt incense on the high *p*	2Kin 14:4	
that the high *p* were not removed	2Kin 15:4	
burnt incense still on the high *p*	2Kin 15:4	
the high *p* were not removed	2Kin 15:35	
incense still in the high *p*	2Kin 15:35	
and burnt incense in the high *p*	2Kin 16:4	
them high *p* in all their cities	2Kin 17:9	
burnt incense in all the high *p*	2Kin 17:11	
p which the Samaritans had made	2Kin 17:29	
of them priests of the high *p*	2Kin 17:32	
them in the houses of the high *p*	2Kin 17:32	
He removed the high *p*, and brake	2Kin 18:4	
is not that he, whose high *p*	2Kin 18:22	
up all the rivers of besieged *p*	2Kin 19:24	
p which Hezekiah his father had	2Kin 21:3	
the high *p* in the cities of Judah	2Kin 23:5	
in the *p* round about Jerusalem	2Kin 23:5	
defiled the high *p* where the	2Kin 23:8	
brake down the high *p* of the	2Kin 23:8	
the priests of the high *p* came	2Kin 23:9	
the high *p* that were before	2Kin 23:13	
filled their *p* with the bones of	2Kin 23:14	4725
high *p* that were in the cities of	2Kin 23:19	
all the priests of the high *p*	2Kin 23:20	
p throughout their castles in	1Chr 6:54	
of Israel, because the *p* are holy	2Chr 8:11	
him priests for the high *p*	2Chr 11:15	
the strange gods, and the high *p*	2Chr 14:3	
the cities of Judah the high *p*	2Chr 14:5	
But the high *p* were not taken	2Chr 15:17	
moreover he took away the high *p*	2Chr 17:6	
Howbeit the high *p* were not taken	2Chr 20:33	
Moreover he made high *p* in the	2Chr 21:11	
and burnt incense in the high *p*	2Chr 28:4	
city of Judah he made high *p* to	2Chr 28:25	
groves, and threw down the high *p*	2Chr 31:1	
Hezekiah taken away his high *p*	2Chr 32:12	
For he built again the high *p*	2Chr 33:3	
did sacrifice still in the high *p*	2Chr 33:17	
the *p* wherein he built high	2Chr 33:19	4725
wherein he built high *p*	2Chr 33:19	
and Jerusalem from the high *p*	2Chr 34:3	
From all *p* whence ye shall return	Neh 4:12	4725
I in the lower *p* behind the wall	Neh 4:13	4725
the wall, and on the higher *p*	Neh 4:13	
the Levites out of all their *p*	Neh 12:27	4725
built desolate *p* for themselves	Job 3:14	2723
shall be hid in his secret *p*	Job 20:26	
are the dwelling *p* of the wicked	Job 21:28	168
he maketh peace in his high *p*	Job 25:2	
into dens, and remain in their *p*	Job 37:8	4585
in the lurking *p* of the villages	Ps 10:8	
in the secret *p* doth he murder	Ps 10:8	
are fallen unto me in pleasant *p*	Ps 16:6	
a young lion lurking in secret *p*	Ps 17:12	
and setteth me upon my high *p*	Ps 18:33	
and be afraid out of their close *p*	Ps 18:45	

ever, and their dwelling p to all	Ps 49:11	
art terrible out of thy holy p	Ps 68:35	
thou didst set them in slippery p	Ps 73:18	
for the dark p of the earth are	Ps 74:20	
him to anger with their high p	Ps 78:58	
hand are the deep p of the earth	Ps 95:4	
works in all p of his dominion	Ps 103:22	4725
ran in the dry p like a river	Ps 105:41	
also out of their desolate p	Ps 109:10	
he shall fill the p with the dead	Ps 110:6	
earth, in the seas, and all deep p	Ps 135:6	
judges are overthrown in stony p	Ps 141:6	3027
She standeth in the top of high p	Prov 8:2	
by the way in the p of the paths	Prov 8:2	1004
upon the highest p of the city	Prov 9:3	
a seat in the high p of the city	Prov 9:14	
in the secret p of the stairs	Song 2:14	
the waste p of the fat ones shall	Is 5:17	
Bajith, and to Dibon, the high p	Is 15:2	
dwellings, and in quiet resting p	Is 32:18	
is it not he, whose high p	Is 36:7	
all the rivers of the besieged p	Is 37:25	
straight, and the rough p plain	Is 40:4	
I will open rivers in high p	Is 41:18	
raise up the decayed p thereof	Is 44:26	
and make the crooked p straight	Is 45:2	
and hidden riches of secret p	Is 45:3	
pastures be in all high p	Is 49:9	
For thy waste and thy desolate p	Is 49:19	
he will comfort all her waste p	Is 51:3	
together, ye waste p of Jerusalem	Is 52:9	
thee shall build the old waste p	Is 58:12	
ride upon the high p of the earth	Is 58:14	
we are in desolate p as dead men	Is 59:10	
up thine eyes unto the high p	Jer 3:2	
A voice was heard upon the high p	Jer 3:21	
A dry wind of the high p in the	Jer 4:11	
from those p shall come unto me	Jer 4:12	
and seek in the broad p thereof	Jer 5:1	
take up a lamentation on high p	Jer 7:29	
have built the high p of Tophet	Jer 7:31	
which remain in all the p whither	Jer 8:3	4725
all high p through the wilderness	Jer 12:12	
weep in secret p for your pride	Jer 13:17	
asses did stand in the high p	Jer 14:6	
the spoil, and thy high p for sin	Jer 17:3	
the parched p in the wilderness	Jer 17:6	
from the p about Jerusalem, and	Jer 17:26	5439
built also the high p of Baal	Jer 19:5	
the pleasant p of the wilderness	Jer 23:10	
secret p that I shall not see him	Jer 23:24	
in all p whither I shall drive	Jer 24:9	4725
house as the high p of a forest	Jer 26:18	
from all the p whither I have	Jer 29:14	4725
And they built the high p of Baal	Jer 32:35	
in the p about Jerusalem, and in	Jer 32:44	
in the p about Jerusalem, and in	Jer 33:13	
of all p whither they were driven	Jer 40:12	4725
prey in all p whither thou goest	Jer 45:5	4725
him that offereth in the high p	Jer 48:35	
I have uncovered his secret p	Jer 49:10	
destroyed his p of the assembly	Lam 2:6	
He hath set me in dark p, as they	Lam 3:6	
in wait, and as a lion in secret p	Lam 3:10	
and I will destroy your high p	Eze 6:3	
the high p shall be desolate	Eze 6:6	
their holy p shall be defiled	Eze 7:24	
deckedst thy high p with divers	Eze 16:16	
and shall break down thy high p	Eze 16:39	
drop thy word toward the holy p	Eze 21:2	
in p desolate of old, with them	Eze 26:20	
will deliver them out of all p	Eze 34:12	4725
the inhabited of the country	Eze 34:13	
the p round about my hill a	Eze 34:26	
even the ancient high p are ours	Eze 36:2	
I the Lord build the ruined p	Eze 36:36	
desolate p that are now inhabited	Eze 38:12	
the steep p shall fall, and every	Eze 38:20	
of their kings in their high p	Eze 43:7	
it was made with boiling p under	Eze 46:23	
These are the p of them that boil	Eze 46:24	1004
But the miry p thereof and the	Eze 47:11	
the fattest p of the province	Dan 11:24	
the pleasant p for their silver,	Hos 9:6	
The high p also of Aven, the sin	Hos 10:8	
and want of bread in all your p	Amos 4:6	4725
upon the high p of the earth	Amos 4:13	
the high p of Isaac shall be	Amos 7:9	
upon the high p of the earth	Mic 1:3	
and what are the high p of Judah	Mic 1:5	
house as the high p of the forest	Mic 3:12	

make me to walk upon mine high p	Hab 3:19	
I will give thee p to walk among	Zec 3:7	
return and build the desolate p	Mal 1:4	
a man, he walketh through dry p	Mt 12:43	*5117*
Some fell upon stony p, where	Mt 13:5	
received the seed into stony p	Mt 13:20	
and earthquakes, in divers p	Mt 24:7	*5117*
city, but was without in desert p	Mk 1:45	*5117*
shall be earthquakes in divers p	Mk 13:8	*5117*
a man, he walketh through dry p	Lk 11:24	*5117*
earthquakes shall be in divers p	Lk 21:11	*5117*
We accept it always, and in all p	Acts 24:3	*3837*
blessings in heavenly p in Christ	Eph 1:3	
own right hand in the heavenly p	Eph 1:20	
in heavenly p in Christ Jesus	Eph 2:6	
powers in heavenly p might be	Eph 3:10	
spiritual wickedness in high p	Eph 6:12	
all the palace, and in all other p	Phil 1:13	
into the holy p made with hands	Heb 9:24	
island were moved out of their p	Rev 6:14	*5117*

PLAGUE

I bring one p more upon Pharaoh	Ex 11:1	5061
the p shall not be upon you to	Ex 12:13	5063
that there be no p among them	Ex 30:12	5063
his flesh like the p of leprosy	Lev 13:2	5061
on the p in the skin of the flesh	Lev 13:3	5061
the hair in the p is turned white	Lev 13:3	5061
the p in sight be deeper than the	Lev 13:3	5061
his flesh, it is a p of leprosy	Lev 13:3	5061
up him that hath the p seven days	Lev 13:4	5061
if the p in his sight be at a	Lev 13:5	5061
the p spread not in the skin	Lev 13:5	5061
if the p be somewhat dark	Lev 13:6	5061
the p spread not in the skin	Lev 13:6	5061
When the p of leprosy is in a man	Lev 13:9	5061
the skin of him that hath the p	Lev 13:12	5061
him clean that hath the p	Lev 13:13	5061
if the p be turned into white	Lev 13:17	5061
him clean that hath the p	Lev 13:17	5061
it is a p of leprosy broken out	Lev 13:20	5061
it is a p	Lev 13:22	5061
it is the p of leprosy	Lev 13:25	5061
it is the p of leprosy	Lev 13:27	5061
If a man or woman have a p upon	Lev 13:29	5061
Then the priest shall see the p	Lev 13:30	5061
priest look on the p of the scall	Lev 13:31	5061
the p of the scall seven days	Lev 13:31	5061
the priest shall look on the p	Lev 13:32	5061
his p is in his head	Lev 13:44	5061
And the leper in whom the p is	Lev 13:45	5061
All the days wherein the p shall	Lev 13:46	5061
also that the p of leprosy is in	Lev 13:47	5061
if the p be greenish or reddish	Lev 13:49	5061
it is a p of leprosy, and shall be	Lev 13:49	5061
the priest shall look upon the p	Lev 13:50	5061
up it that hath the p seven days	Lev 13:50	5061
look on the p on the seventh day	Lev 13:51	5061
if the p be spread in the garment	Lev 13:51	5061
the p is a fretting leprosy	Lev 13:51	5061
thing of skin, wherein the p is	Lev 13:52	5061
the p be not spread in the	Lev 13:53	5061
wash the thing wherein the p is	Lev 13:54	5061
And the priest shall look on the p	Lev 13:55	5061
if the p have not changed his	Lev 13:55	5061
colour, and the p be not spread	Lev 13:55	5061
the p be somewhat dark after the	Lev 13:56	5061
it is a spreading p	Lev 13:57	
that wherein the p is with fire	Lev 13:57	5061
if the p be departed from them,	Lev 13:58	5061
This is the law of the p of	Lev 13:59	
if the p of leprosy be healed in	Lev 14:3	5061
him in whom is the p of leprosy	Lev 14:32	5061
I put the p of leprosy in a house	Lev 14:34	5061
is as it were a p in the house	Lev 14:35	5061
priest go into it to see the p	Lev 14:36	5061
And he shall look on the p	Lev 14:37	5061
if the p be in the walls of the	Lev 14:37	5061
if the p be spread in the walls	Lev 14:39	5061
away the stones in which the p is	Lev 14:40	5061
if the p come again, and break out	Lev 14:43	5061
if the p be spread in the house,	Lev 14:44	5061
the p hath not spread in the	Lev 14:48	5061
clean, because the p is healed	Lev 14:48	5061
for all manner of p of leprosy	Lev 14:54	5061
that there be no p among the	Num 8:19	5063
the people with a very great p	Num 11:33	4347
died by the p before the Lord	Num 14:37	4046
the p is begun	Num 16:46	5063
the p was begun among the people	Num 16:47	5063
and the p was stayed	Num 16:48	4046

in the *p* were fourteen thousand	Num 16:49	4046
and the *p* was stayed	Num 16:50	4046
So the *p* was stayed from the	Num 25:8	4046
that died in the *p* were twenty	Num 25:9	4046
the day of the *p* for Peor's sake	Num 25:18	4046
And it came to pass after the *p*	Num 26:1	4046
Peor, and there was a *p* among the	Num 31:16	4046
Take heed in the *p* of leprosy	Deut 24:8	5061
Also every sickness, and every *p*	Deut 28:61	4347
although there was a *p* in the	Josh 22:17	5063
for one *p* was on you all, and on	1Sa 6:4	4046
that the *p* may be stayed from the	2Sa 24:21	4046
the *p* was stayed from Israel	2Sa 24:25	4046
whatsoever *p*, whatsoever sickness	1Kin 8:37	5061
every man the *p* of his own heart	1Kin 8:38	5061
that the *p* may be stayed from the	1Chr 21:22	4046
with a great *p* will the LORD	2Chr 21:14	4046
his face, and *p* them that hate him	Ps 89:23	5063
neither shall any *p* come nigh thy	Ps 91:10	5061
and the *p* brake in upon them	Ps 106:29	4046
and so the *p* was stayed	Ps 106:30	4046
this shall be the *p* wherewith the	Zec 14:12	4046
And so shall be the *p* of the horse	Zec 14:15	4046
be in these tents, as this *p*	Zec 14:15	4046
there shall be the *p*, wherewith	Zec 14:18	4046
that she was healed of that *p*	Mk 5:29	*3148*
go in peace, and be whole of thy *p*	Mk 5:34	*3148*
God because of the *p* of the hail	Rev 16:21	4127
for the *p* thereof was exceeding	Rev 16:21	*4127*

PLAGUED

And the LORD *p* Pharaoh and his	Gen 12:17	5060
the LORD *p* the people, because	Ex 32:35	5062
I *p* Egypt, according to that	Josh 24:5	5062
thy people, that they should be *p*	1Chr 21:17	4046
neither are they *p* like other men	Ps 73:5	5060
all the day long have I been *p*	Ps 73:14	5060

PLAGUES

his house with great *p* because of	Gen 12:17	5061
send all my *p* upon thine heart	Ex 9:14	4046
I will bring seven times more *p*	Lev 26:21	4347
LORD will make thy *p* wonderful	Deut 28:59	4347
p of thy seed, even great *p*	Deut 28:59	4347
when they see the *p* of that land	Deut 29:22	4347
with all the *p* in the wilderness	1Sa 4:8	4347
hiss because of all the *p* thereof	Jer 19:8	4347
shall hiss at all the *p* thereof	Jer 49:17	4347
astonished, and hiss at all her *p*	Jer 50:13	4347
O death, I will be thy *p*	Hos 13:14	1698
to touch him, as many as had *p*	Mk 3:10	*3148*
many of their infirmities and *p*	Lk 7:21	*3148*
p yet repented not of the works	Rev 9:20	4127
and to smite the earth with all *p*	Rev 11:6	*4127*
angels having the seven last *p*	Rev 15:1	*4127*
of the temple, having the seven *p*	Rev 15:6	*4127*
till the seven *p* of the seven	Rev 15:8	*4127*
which hath power over these *p*	Rev 16:9	*4127*
and that ye receive not of her *p*	Rev 18:4	*4127*
shall her *p* come in one day	Rev 18:8	*4127*
vials full of the seven last *p*	Rev 21:9	*4127*
God shall add unto him the *p* that	Rev 22:18	*4127*

PLAIN

that they found a *p* in the land	Gen 11:2	1237
of Sichem, unto the *p* of Moreh	Gen 12:6	436
and beheld all the *p* of Jordan	Gen 13:10	3603
Lot chose him all the *p* of Jordan	Gen 13:11	3603
dwelled in the cities of the *p*	Gen 13:12	3603
came and dwelt in the *p* of Mamre	Gen 13:18	436
for he dwelt in the *p* of Mamre	Gen 14:13	436
neither stay thou in all the *p*	Gen 19:17	3603
those cities, and all the *p*	Gen 19:25	3603
and toward all the land of the *p*	Gen 19:28	3603
God destroyed the cities of the *p*	Gen 19:29	3603
and Jacob was a *p* man, dwelling in	Gen 25:27	8535
in the *p* over against the Red sea	Deut 1:1	6160
places nigh thereunto, in the *p*	Deut 1:7	6160
the way of the *p* from Elath	Deut 2:8	6160
All the cities of the *p*, and all	Deut 3:10	4334
The *p* also, and Jordan, and the	Deut 3:17	6160
even unto the sea of the *p*	Deut 3:17	6160
in the *p* country, of the	Deut 4:43	4334
all the *p* on this side Jordan	Deut 4:49	6160
even unto the sea of the *p*	Deut 4:49	6160
the *p* of the valley of Jericho	Deut 34:3	3603
came down toward the sea of the *p*	Josh 3:16	6160
at a time appointed, before the *p*	Josh 8:14	6160
Goshen, and the valley, and the *p*	Josh 11:16	6160
Hermon, and all the *p* on the east	Josh 12:1	6160
And from the *p* to the sea of	Josh 12:3	6160
east, and unto the sea of the *p*	Josh 12:3	6160

all the *p* of Medeba unto Dibon	Josh 13:9	4334
the river, and all the *p* by Medeba	Josh 13:16	4334
all her cities that are in the *p*	Josh 13:17	4334
And all the cities of the *p*	Josh 13:21	4334
the *p* out of the tribe of Reuben	Josh 20:8	4334
his tent unto the *p* of Zaanaim	Judg 4:11	436
by the *p* of the pillar that was	Judg 9:6	436
come along by the *p* of Meonenim	Judg 9:37	436
unto the *p* of the vineyards, with	Judg 11:33	58
thou shalt come to the *p* of Tabor	1Sa 10:3	436
in the *p* on the south of Jeshimon	1Sa 23:24	6160
all that night through the *p*	2Sa 2:29	6160
them away through the *p* all night	2Sa 4:7	6160
tarry in the *p* of the wilderness	2Sa 15:28	6160
Ahimaaz ran by the way of the *p*	2Sa 18:23	3603
In the *p* of Jordan did the king	1Kin 7:46	3603
us fight against them in the *p*	1Kin 20:23	4334
will fight against them in the *p*	1Kin 20:25	4334
of Hamath unto the sea of the *p*	2Kin 14:25	6160
king went the way toward the *p*	2Kin 25:4	6160
In the *p* of Jordan did the king	2Chr 4:17	3603
the priests, the men of the *p*	Neh 3:22	3603
of the villages in the *p* of Ono	Neh 6:2	436
both out of the *p* country round	Neh 12:28	3603
O LORD, and lead me in a *p* path	Ps 27:11	4334
They are all *p* to him that	Prov 8:9	5228
way of the righteous is made *p*	Prov 15:19	5549
he hath made *p* the face thereof	Is 28:25	7737
straight, and the rough places *p*	Is 40:4	1237
land of Benjamin, and from the *p*	Jer 17:26	8219
of the valley, and rock of the *p*	Jer 21:13	4334
and he went out the way of the *p*	Jer 39:4	6160
the *p* shall be destroyed, as the	Jer 48:8	4334
is come upon the *p* country	Jer 48:21	4334
) and they went by the way of the *p*	Jer 52:7	6160
me, Arise, go forth into the *p*	Eze 3:22	1237
I arose, and went forth into the *p*	Eze 3:23	1237
to the vision that I saw in the *p*	Eze 8:4	1237
he set it up in the *p* of Dura	Dan 3:1	1236
the inhabitant from the *p* of Aven	Amos 1:5	1237
they of the *p* the Philistines	Obad 19	8219
make it *p* upon tables, that he	Hab 2:2	874
Zerubbabel thou shalt become a *p*	Zec 4:7	4334
men inhabited the south and the *p*	Zec 7:7	8219
a *p* from Geba to Rimmon south of	Zec 14:10	6160
tongue was loosed, and he spake *p*	Mk 7:35	*3723*
with them, and stood in the *p*	Lk 6:17	*5117,3977*

PLAINLY

And if the servant shall *p* say	Ex 21:5	559
all the words of this law very *p*	Deut 27:8	874
Did I *p* appear unto the house of	1Sa 2:27	1540
He told us *p* that the asses were	1Sa 10:16	5046
us hath been *p* read before me	Ezr 4:18	6568
shall be ready to speak *p*	Is 32:4	6703
If thou be the Christ, tell us *p*	Jn 10:24	*3954*
Then said Jesus unto them *p*	Jn 11:14	*3954*
I shall shew you *p* of the Father	Jn 16:25	*3954*
unto him, Lo, now speakest thou *p*	Jn 16:29	*3954*
p that they seek a country	Heb 11:14	*1718*

PLAINNESS

hope, we use great *p* of speech	2Cor 3:12	*3954*

PLAINS

unto him in the *p* of Mamre	Gen 18:1	436
pitched in the *p* of Moab on this	Num 22:1	6160
priest spake with them in the *p*	Num 26:3	6160
the children of Israel in the *p*	Num 26:63	6160
unto the camp at the *p* of Moab	Num 31:12	6160
pitched in the *p* of Moab by	Num 33:48	6160
Abel-shittim in the *p* of Moab	Num 33:49	6160
Moses in the *p* of Moab by Jordan	Num 33:50	6160
LORD spake unto Moses in the *p* of	Num 35:1	6160
the children of Israel in the *p*	Num 36:13	6160
Gilgal, beside the *p* of Moreh	Deut 11:30	436
Moses went up from the *p* of Moab	Deut 34:1	6160
in the *p* of Moab thirty days	Deut 34:8	6160
unto battle, to the *p* of Jericho	Josh 4:13	6160
month at even in the *p* of Jericho	Josh 5:10	6160
of the *p* south of Chinneroth, and	Josh 11:2	6160
and in the valleys, and in the *p*	Josh 12:8	6160
for inheritance in the *p* of Moab	Josh 13:32	6160
night in the *p* of the wilderness	2Sa 17:16	6160
overtook him in the *p* of Jericho	2Kin 25:5	6160
trees that were in the low *p* was	1Chr 27:28	8219
are in the low *p* in abundance	2Chr 9:27	8219
in the low country, and in the *p*	2Chr 26:10	4334
Zedekiah in the *p* of Jericho	Jer 39:5	6160
Zedekiah in the *p* of Jericho	Jer 52:8	6160

PLAISTER

morter, and shall *p* the house	Lev 14:42	2902
stones, and *p* them with *p*	Deut 27:2	7874
thou shalt *p* them with *p*	Deut 27:4	7874
lay it for a *p* upon the boil, and	Is 38:21	4799
the candlestick upon the *p* of the	Dan 5:5	1528

PLAISTERED

the house, and after it is *p*	Lev 14:43	2902
the house, after the house was *p*	Lev 14:48	2902

PLAITING

outward adorning of *p* the hair	1Pet 3:3	*1708*

PLANES

he fitteth it with *p*, and he	Is 44:13	4741

PLANETS

sun, and to the moon, and to the *p*	2Kin 23:5	4208

PLANKS

floor of the house with *p* of fir	1Kin 6:15	6763
there were thick *p* upon the face	Eze 41:25	6086
chambers of the house, and thick *p*	Eze 41:26	5646

PLANT

every *p* of the field before it	Gen 2:5	7880
p them in the mountain of thine	Ex 15:17	5193
Thou shalt not *p* thee a grove of	Deut 16:21	5193
thou shalt *p* a vineyard, and shalt	Deut 28:30	5193
Thou shalt *p* vineyards, and dress	Deut 28:39	5193
my people Israel, and will *p* them	2Sa 7:10	5193
p vineyards, and eat the fruits	2Kin 19:29	5193
my people Israel, and will *p* them	1Chr 17:9	5193
and bring forth boughs like a *p*	Job 14:9	5194
p vineyards, which may yield	Ps 107:37	5193
a time to *p*, and a time to pluck	Eccl 3:2	5193
the men of Judah his pleasant *p*	Is 5:7	5194
shalt thou *p* pleasant plants	Is 17:10	5193
day shalt thou make thy *p* to grow	Is 17:11	5194
p vineyards, and eat the fruit	Is 37:30	5193
I will *p* in the wilderness the	Is 41:19	5414
that I may *p* the heavens, and lay	Is 51:16	5193
grow up before him as a tender *p*	Is 53:2	
and they shall *p* vineyards	Is 65:21	5193
they shall not *p*, and another eat	Is 65:22	5193
to throw down, to build, and to *p*	Jer 1:10	5193
p of a strange vine unto me	Jer 2:21	
a kingdom, to build and to *p* it	Jer 18:9	5193
and I will *p* them, and not pluck	Jer 24:6	5193
p gardens, and eat the fruit of	Jer 29:5	5193
p gardens, and eat the fruit of	Jer 29:28	5193
Thou shalt yet *p* vines upon the	Jer 31:5	5193
the planters shall *p*, and shall	Jer 31:5	5193
over them, to build, and to *p*	Jer 31:28	5193
I will *p* them in this land	Jer 32:41	5193
nor *p* vineyard, nor have any	Jer 35:7	5193
pull you down, and I will *p* you	Jer 42:10	5193
will *p* it upon an high mountain	Eze 17:22	8362
the height of Israel will I *p* it	Eze 17:23	8362
build houses, and *p* vineyards	Eze 28:26	5193
raise up for them a *p* of renown	Eze 34:29	4302
and *p* that was desolate	Eze 36:36	5193
he shall *p* the tabernacles of his	Dan 11:45	5193
and they shall *p* vineyards	Amos 9:14	5193
I will *p* them upon their land, and	Amos 9:15	5193
and they shall *p* vineyards	Zeph 1:13	5193
But he answered and said, Every *p*	Mt 15:13	*5451*

PLANTATION

water it by the furrows of her *p*	Eze 17:7	4302

PLANTED

the LORD God *p* a garden eastward	Gen 2:8	5193
an husbandman, and he *p* a vineyard	Gen 9:20	5193
Abraham *p* a grove in Beer-sheba,	Gen 21:33	5193
shall have *p* all manner of trees	Lev 19:23	5193
lign aloes which the LORD hath *p*	Num 24:6	5193
man is he that hath *p* a vineyard	Deut 20:6	5193
which ye *p* not do ye eat	Josh 24:13	5193
a tree *p* by the rivers of water	Ps 1:3	8362
cast out the heathen, and *p* it	Ps 80:8	5193
which thy right hand hath *p*	Ps 80:15	5193
Those that be *p* in the house of	Ps 92:13	8362
He that *p* the ear, shall he not	Ps 94:9	5193
of Lebanon, which he hath *p*	Ps 104:16	5193
I *p* me vineyards	Eccl 2:4	5193
I *p* trees in them of all kind of	Eccl 2:5	5193
time to pluck up that which is *p*	Eccl 3:2	5193
p it with the choicest vine, and	Is 5:2	5193
Yea, they shall not be *p*	Is 40:24	5193
Yet I had *p* thee a noble vine	Jer 2:21	5193
the LORD of hosts, that *p* thee	Jer 11:17	5193
Thou hast *p* them, yea, they have	Jer 12:2	5193
be as a tree *p* by the waters	Jer 17:8	8362

which I have *p* I will pluck up	Jer 45:4	5193
land, and *p* it in a fruitful field	Eze 17:5	
It was *p* in a good soil by great	Eze 17:8	8362
Yea, behold, being *p*, shall it	Eze 17:10	8362
in thy blood, *p* by the waters	Eze 19:10	8362
now she is *p* in the wilderness	Eze 19:13	8362
Tyrus, is *p* in a pleasant place	Hos 9:13	8362
ye have *p* pleasant vineyards, but	Amos 5:11	5193
my heavenly Father hath not *p*	Mt 15:13	5452
which *p* a vineyard, and hedged it	Mt 21:33	5452
A certain man *p* a vineyard	Mk 12:1	5452
had a fig tree *p* in his vineyard	Lk 13:6	5452
the root, and be thou *p* in the sea	Lk 17:6	5452
they bought, they sold, they *p*	Lk 17:28	5452
A certain man *p* a vineyard	Lk 20:9	5452
For if we have been *p* together in	Rom 6:5	*4854*
I have *p*, Apollos watered	1Cor 3:6	5452

PLANTEDST

and olive trees, which thou *p* not	Deut 6:11	5193
heathen with thy hand, and *p* them	Ps 44:2	5193

PLANTERS

the *p* shall plant, and shall eat	Jer 31:5	5193

PLANTETH

of her hands she *p* a vineyard	Prov 31:16	5192
he *p* an ash, and the rain doth	Is 44:14	5192
neither is he that *p* any thing	1Cor 3:7	5452
Now he that *p* and he that watereth	1Cor 3:8	5452
who a vineyard, and eateth not	1Cor 9:7	5452

PLANTING

land for ever, the branch of my *p*	Is 60:21	4302
the *p* of the LORD, that he might	Is 61:3	4302

PLANTINGS

the field, and as *p* of a vineyard	Mic 1:6	4302

PLANTS

and those that dwelt among *p*	1Chr 4:23	5194
olive *p* round about thy table	Ps 128:3	8363
be as *p* grown up in their youth	Ps 144:12	5195
Thy *p* are an orchard of	Song 4:13	7973
down the principal *p* thereof	Is 16:8	8291
shalt thou plant pleasant *p*	Is 17:10	5194
thy *p* are gone over the sea, they	Jer 48:32	5189
rivers running round about his *p*	Eze 31:4	4302

PLAT

and I will requite thee in this *p*	2Kin 9:26	2513
and cast him into the *p* of ground	2Kin 9:26	2513

PLATE

thou shalt make a *p* of pure gold	Ex 28:36	6731
they made the *p* of the holy crown	Ex 39:30	6731
did he put the golden *p*, the	Lev 8:9	6731

PLATES

did beat the gold into thin *p*	Ex 39:3	6341
let them make them broad *p* for a	Num 16:38	6341
they were made broad *p* for a	Num 16:39	
four brasen wheels, and *p* of brass	1Kin 7:30	5633
For on the *p* of the ledges	1Kin 7:36	3871
Silver spread into *p* is brought	Jer 10:9	

PLATTED

when they had *p* a crown of thorns	Mt 27:29	*4120*
p a crown of thorns, and put it	Mk 15:17	*4120*
the soldiers *p* a crown of thorns,	Jn 19:2	*4120*

PLATTER

outside of the cup and of the *p*	Mt 23:25	*3953*
that which is within the cup and *p*	Mt 23:26	*3953*
the outside of the cup and the *p*	Lk 11:39	*4094*

PLAY

eat and to drink, and rose up to *p*	Ex 32:6	6711
to *p* the whore in her father's	Deut 22:21	
that he shall *p* with his hand	1Sa 16:16	5059
me now a man that can *p* well	1Sa 16:17	5059
to *p* the mad man in my presence	1Sa 21:15	
men now arise, and *p* before us	2Sa 2:14	7832
will I *p* before the LORD	2Sa 6:21	7832
let us *p* the men for our people,	2Sa 10:12	
all the beasts of the field *p*	Job 40:20	7832
Wilt thou *p* with him as with a	Job 41:5	7832
p skilfully with a loud noise	Ps 33:3	5059
whom thou hast made to *p* therein	Ps 104:26	7832
shall *p* on the hole of the asp	Is 11:8	8173
can *p* well on an instrument	Eze 33:32	5059
thou shalt not *p* the harlot	Hos 3:3	
p the harlot, yet let not Judah	Hos 4:15	
to eat and drink, and rose up to *p*	1Cor 10:7	*3815*

PLAYED

daughter in law hath *p* the harlot	Gen 38:24	
his concubine *p* the whore against	Judg 19:2	

took an harp, and *p* with his hand	1Sa 16:23	5059
answered one another as they *p*	1Sa 18:7	7832
David *p* with his hand, as at	1Sa 18:10	5059
and David *p* with his hand	1Sa 19:9	5059
I have *p* the fool, and have erred	1Sa 26:21	
all the house of Israel *p* before	2Sa 6:5	7832
came to pass, when the minstrel *p*	2Kin 3:15	5059
all Israel *p* before God with all	1Chr 13:8	7832
but thou hast *p* the harlot with	Jer 3:1	
tree, and there hath *p* the harlot	Jer 3:6	
but went and *p* the harlot also	Jer 3:8	
Thou hast *p* the whore also with	Eze 16:28	
thou hast *p* the harlot with them,	Eze 16:28	
Aholah *p* the harlot when she was	Eze 23:5	
wherein she had *p* the harlot in	Eze 23:19	
their mother hath *p* the harlot	Hos 2:5	

PLAYEDST

p the harlot because of thy	Eze 16:15	
and *p* the harlot thereupon	Eze 16:16	

PLAYER

who is a cunning *p* on an harp	1Sa 16:16	5059

PLAYERS

the *p* on instruments followed	Ps 68:25	5059
As well the singers as the *p* on	Ps 87:7	2490

PLAYETH

in unto a woman that *p* the harlot	Eze 23:44	

PLAYING

profane herself by *p* the whore	Lev 21:9	
that is cunning in *p*, and a	1Sa 16:18	5059
saw king David dancing and *p*	1Chr 15:29	7832
were the damsels *p* with timbrels	Ps 68:25	
tree thou wanderest, *p* the harlot	Jer 2:20	
thee to cease from *p* the harlot	Eze 16:41	
girls *p* in the streets thereof	Zec 8:5	7832

PLEA

blood and blood, between *p* and *p*	Deut 17:8	1779

PLEAD

against him, Will ye *p* for Baal	Judg 6:31	7378
he that will *p* for him, let him	Judg 6:31	7378
let him *p* for himself, because	Judg 6:31	7378
Let Baal *p* against him, because	Judg 6:32	7378
p my cause, and deliver me out of	1Sa 24:15	7378
who shall set me a time to *p*	Job 9:19	
Who is he that will *p* with me	Job 13:19	7378
Oh that one might *p* for a man	Job 16:21	3198
me, and *p* against me my reproach	Job 19:5	3198
Will he *p* against me with his	Job 23:6	7378
P my cause, O LORD, with them	Ps 35:1	7378
p my cause against an ungodly	Ps 43:1	7378
Arise, O God, *p* thine own cause	Ps 74:22	7378
P my cause, and deliver me	Ps 119:154	7378
For the LORD will *p* their cause	Prov 22:23	7378
he shall *p* their cause with thee	Prov 23:11	7378
p the cause of the poor and needy	Prov 31:9	1777
the fatherless, *p* for the widow	Is 1:17	7378
The LORD standeth up to *p*	Is 3:13	7378
let us *p* together	Is 43:26	8199
will the LORD *p* with all flesh	Is 66:16	8199
Wherefore I will yet *p* with you	Jer 2:9	7378
your children's children will I *p*	Jer 2:9	7378
Wherefore will ye *p* with me	Jer 2:29	7378
I will *p* with thee, because thou	Jer 2:35	8199
thou, O LORD, when I *p* with thee	Jer 12:1	7378
nations, he will *p* with all flesh	Jer 25:31	8199
There is none to *p* thy cause	Jer 30:13	1777
he shall throughly *p* their cause	Jer 50:34	7378
I will *p* thy cause, and take	Jer 51:36	7378
will *p* with him there for his	Eze 17:20	8199
there will I *p* with you face to	Eze 20:35	8199
of Egypt, so will I *p* with you	Eze 20:36	8199
I will *p* against him with	Eze 38:22	8199
P with your mother, *p*	Hos 2:2	7378
will *p* with them there for my	Joel 3:2	8199
people, and he will *p* with Israel	Mic 6:2	3198
against him, until he *p* my cause	Mic 7:9	7378

PLEADED

that hath *p* the cause of my	1Sa 25:39	7378
thou hast *p* the causes of my soul	Lam 3:58	7378
Like as I *p* with your fathers in	Eze 20:36	8199

PLEADETH

as a man *p* for his neighbour	Job 16:21	
thy God that *p* the cause of his	Is 51:22	7378
for justice, nor any *p* for truth	Is 59:4	8199

PLEADINGS

and hearken to the *p* of my lips	Job 13:6	7379

PLEASANT

every tree that is *p* to the sight	Gen 2:9	2530
and that it was *p* to the eyes	Gen 3:6	8378
good, and the land that it was *p*	Gen 49:15	5276
p in their lives, and in their	2Sa 1:23	5273
very *p* hast thou been unto me	2Sa 1:26	5276
whatsoever is *p* in thine eyes	1Kin 20:6	4261
the situation of this city is *p*	2Kin 2:19	2896
and for all manner of *p* jewels	2Chr 32:27	2532
are fallen unto me in *p* places	Ps 16:6	5273
the *p* harp with the psaltery	Ps 81:2	5273
Yea, they despised the *p* land	Ps 106:24	2532
how *p* it is for brethren to dwell	Ps 133:1	5273
for it is *p*	Ps 135:3	5273
knowledge is *p* unto thy soul	Prov 2:10	5276
be as the loving hind and *p* roe	Prov 5:19	2580
and bread eaten in secret is *p*	Prov 9:17	5276
the words of the pure are *p* words	Prov 15:26	5278
P words are as an honeycomb,	Prov 16:24	5278
For it is a *p* thing if thou keep	Prov 22:18	5273
with all precious and *p* riches	Prov 24:4	5273
a *p* thing it is for the eyes to	Eccl 11:7	2896
thou art fair, my beloved, yea, *p*	Song 1:16	5273
of pomegranates, with *p* fruits	Song 4:13	4022
his garden, and eat his *p* fruits	Song 4:16	4022
how *p* art thou, O love, for	Song 7:6	5276
gates are all manner of *p* fruits	Song 7:13	4022
Tarshish, and upon all *p* pictures	Is 2:16	2532
and the men of Judah his *p* plant	Is 5:7	8191
and dragons in their *p* palaces	Is 13:22	6027
shalt thou plant *p* plants	Is 17:10	2532
for the teats, for the *p* fields	Is 32:12	2531
and all thy borders of *p* stones	Is 54:12	2656
all our *p* things are laid waste	Is 64:11	4261
children, and give thee a *p* land	Jer 3:19	2532
they have made my *p* portion a	Jer 12:10	2532
the *p* places of the wilderness	Jer 23:10	4999
and ye shall fall like a *p* vessel	Jer 25:34	2532
is he a *p* child	Jer 31:20	8191
of her miseries all her *p* things	Lam 1:7	4262
his hand upon all her *p* things	Lam 1:10	4261
they have given their *p* things	Lam 1:11	4262
slew all that were *p* to the eye	Lam 2:4	4262
walls, and destroy thy *p* houses	Eze 26:12	2532
song of one that hath a *p* voice	Eze 33:32	3303
the east, and toward the *p* land	Dan 8:9	6643
I ate no *p* bread, neither came	Dan 10:3	2530
with precious stones, and *p* things	Dan 11:38	2530
the *p* places for their silver,	Hos 9:6	4261
Tyrus, is planted in a *p* place	Hos 9:13	5116
the treasure of all *p* vessels	Hos 13:15	2532
your temples my goodly *p* things	Joel 3:5	4261
ye have planted *p* vineyards	Amos 5:11	2531
ye cast out from their *p* houses	Mic 2:9	8588
glory out of all the *p* furniture	Nah 2:9	2532
for they laid the *p* land desolate	Zec 7:14	2532
Jerusalem be *p* unto the LORD, as	Mal 3:4	6148

PLEASANTNESS

Her ways are ways of *p*, and all	Prov 3:17	5278

PLEASE

If she *p* not her master, who hath	Ex 21:8	7451,5869
peradventure it will *p* God that	Num 23:27	3477,5869
but if it *p* my father to do thee	1Sa 20:13	3190
Therefore now let it *p* thee to	2Sa 7:29	2894
or else, if it *p* thee, I will	1Kin 21:6	2655
Now therefore let it *p* thee to	1Chr 17:27	2894
p them, and speak good words to	2Chr 10:7	7521
If it *p* the king, and if thy	Neh 2:5	2895
If it *p* the king, let letters be	Neh 2:7	2895
If it *p* the king, let there go a	Est 1:19	2895
If it *p* the king, let it be	Est 3:9	2895
if it *p* the king to grant my	Est 5:8	2895
if it *p* the king, let my life be	Est 7:3	2895
If it *p* the king, and if I have	Est 8:5	2896
If it *p* the king, let it be	Est 9:13	2896
that it would *p* God to destroy me	Job 6:9	2894
children shall seek to *p* the poor	Job 20:10	7521
This also shall *p* the LORD better	Ps 69:31	3190
When a man's ways *p* the LORD,	Prov 16:7	7521
up, nor awake my love, till he *p*	Song 2:7	2654
up, nor awake my love, till he *p*	Song 3:5	2654
up, nor awake my love, until he *p*	Song 8:4	2654
they *p* themselves in the children	Is 2:6	5606
shall accomplish that which I *p*	Is 55:11	2654
and choose the things that *p* me	Is 56:4	2654
do always those things that *p* him	Jn 8:29	701
are in the flesh cannot *p* God	Rom 8:8	700
the weak, and not to *p* ourselves	Rom 15:1	700
Let every one of us *p* his	Rom 15:2	700
the Lord, how he may *p* the Lord	1Cor 7:32	700

the world, how he may *p* his wife 1Cor 7:33   *700*
world, how she may *p* her husband 1Cor 7:34   *700*
Even as I *p* all men in all things 1Cor 10:33   *700*
or do I seek to *p* men .... Gal 1:10   *700*
they *p* not God, and are contrary 1Th 2:15   *700*
to *p* God, so ye would abound more 1Th 4:1   *700*
that he may *p* him who hath chosen 2Ti 2:4   *700*
to *p* them well in all things .... Titus 2:9   *2001,1511*
faith it is impossible to *p* him .... Heb 11:6   *2100*

PLEASED
of Canaan *p* not Isaac his father .... Gen 28:8   *7451,5869*
of God, and thou wast *p* with me .... Gen 33:10   *7521*
And their words *p* Hamor, and .... Gen 34:18   *3190,5869*
it *p* Pharaoh well, and his .... Gen 45:16   *3190,5869*
when Balaam saw that it *p* the .... Num 24:1   *2895*
And the saying *p* me well .... Deut 1:23   *3190,5869*
of Manasseh spake, it *p* them .... Josh 22:30   *3190,5869*
the thing *p* the children of .... Josh 22:33   *3190,5869*
If the LORD were *p* to kill us .... Judg 13:23   *2654*
and she *p* Samson well .... Judg 14:7   *3477,5869*
because it hath *p* the LORD to 1Sa 12:22   *2974*
told Saul, and the thing *p* him 1Sa 18:20   *3477,5869*
it *p* David well to be the king's........ 1Sa 18:26   *3477,5869*
took notice of it, and it *p* them 2Sa 3:36   *3190,5869*
the king did *p* all the people............ 2Sa 3:36   *2896,5869*
the saying *p* Absalom well, and all . 2Sa 17:4   *3477,5869*
this day, then it had *p* thee well 2Sa 19:6   *3477,5869*
And the speech *p* the Lord, that 1Kin 3:10   *3190,5869*
desire which he was *p* to do 1Kin 9:1   *2654*
and they *p* him not 1Kin 9:12   *3477,5869*
And the thing *p* the king and all.... 2Chr 30:4   *3477,5869*
So it *p* the king to send me .... Neh 2:6   *3190*
And the saying *p* the king and the . Est 1:21   *3190,5869*
And the thing *p* the king .... Est 2:4   *3190,5869*
And the maiden *p* him, and she ...... Est 2:9   *3190,5869*
And the thing *p* Haman........................... Est 5:14   *3190*
Be *p*, O LORD, to deliver me.................... Ps 40:13   *7521*
Then shalt thou be *p* with the .... Ps 51:19   *2654*
he hath done whatsoever he hath *p* ..... Ps 115:3   *2654*
Whatsoever the LORD *p*, that did .... Ps 135:6   *2654*
The LORD is well *p* for his .... Is 42:21   *2654*
Yet it *p* the LORD to bruise him .... Is 53:10   *2654*
It *p* Darius to set over the .... Dan 6:1   *8232*
O LORD, hast done as it *p* thee .... Jonah 1:14   *2654*
Will the LORD be *p* with thousands .... Mic 6:7   *7521*
will he be *p* with thee, or accept .... Mal 1:8   *7521*
beloved Son, in whom I am well *p* .... Mt 3:17   *2106*
in whom my soul is well *p* .... Mt 12:18   *2106*
danced before them, and *p* Herod .... Mt 14:6   *700*
beloved Son, in whom I am well *p* .... Mt 17:5   *2106*
beloved Son, in whom I am well *p* .... Mk 1:11   *2106*
p Herod and them that sat with him ...... Mk 6:22   *700*
in thee I am well *p* .... Lk 3:22   *2106*
the saying *p* the whole multitude .... Acts 6:5   *700*
And because he saw it *p* the Jews .... Acts 12:3   *701*
Then it *p* the apostles and elders,.......... Acts 15:22   *1380*
Notwithstanding it *p* Silas to .... Acts 15:34   *1380*
For even Christ *p* not himself.................. Rom 15:3   *700*
For it hath *p* them of Macedonia .... Rom 15:26   *2106*
It hath *p* them verily .... Rom 15:27   *2106*
it *p* God by the foolishness of................ 1Cor 1:21   *2106*
she be *p* to dwell with him, let 1Cor 7:12   *4909*
if he be *p* to dwell with her, let 1Cor 7:13   *4909*
many of them God was not well *p* 1Cor 10:5   *2106*
in the body, as it hath *p* him 1Cor 12:18   *2309*
giveth it a body as it hath *p* him 1Cor 15:38   *2309*
for if I yet *p* men, I should not .... Gal 1:10   *700*
But when it *p* God, who separated .... Gal 1:15   *2106*
For it *p* the Father that in him .... Col 1:19   *2106*
had this testimony, that he *p* God .... Heb 11:5   *2100*
such sacrifices God is well *p* .... Heb 13:16   *2100*
beloved Son, in whom I am well *p* 2Pet 1:17   *2106*

PLEASETH
do to her as it *p* thee .... Gen 16:6   *2896,5869*
dwell where it *p* thee .... Gen 20:15   *2896,5869*
for she *p* me well .... Judg 14:3   *3477,5869*
let the maiden which *p* the king .... Est 2:4   *3190,5869*
p God shall escape from her .... Eccl 7:26   *2896,6440*
for he doeth whatsoever *p* him .... Eccl 8:3   *2654*

PLEASING
I be *p* in his eyes, let it be .... Est 8:5   *2896*
neither shall they be *p* unto him............ Hos 9:4   *6148*
worthy of the Lord unto all *p* .... Col 1:10   *699*
for this is well *p* unto the Lord .... Col 3:20   *700*
not as *p* men, but God, which 1Th 2:4   *700*
things that are *p* in his sight 1Jn 3:22   *701*

PLEASURE
I am waxed old shall I have *p* .... Gen 18:12   *5730*
grapes thy fill at thine own *p*................. Deut 23:24   *5315*

heart, and hast *p* in uprightness 1Chr 29:17   *7521*
let the king send his *p* to us .... Ezr 5:17   *7470*
God of your fathers, and do his *p* .... Ezr 10:11   *7522*
and over our cattle, at their *p* .... Neh 9:37   *7522*
do according to every man's *p* .... Est 1:8   *7522*
For what *p* hath he in his house .... Job 21:21   *2656*
his soul, and never eateth with *p*........... Job 21:25   *2896*
Is it any *p* to the Almighty, that.............. Job 22:3   *2656*
a God that hath *p* in wickedness .... Ps 5:4   *2655*
which hath *p* in the prosperity of .... Ps 35:27   *2655*
Do good in thy good *p* unto Zion .... Ps 51:18   *7522*
thy servants take *p* in her stones........... Ps 102:14   *7521*
ministers of his, that do his *p*................. Ps 103:21   *7522*
To bind his princes at his *p* .... Ps 105:22   *5315*
of all them that have *p* therein .... Ps 111:2   *2656*
he taketh not *p* in the legs of a .... Ps 147:10   *7521*
The LORD taketh *p* in them that............. Ps 147:11   *7521*
the LORD taketh *p* in his people .... Ps 149:4   *7521*
He that loveth *p* shall be a poor .... Prov 21:17   *8057*
with mirth, therefore enjoy *p* .... Eccl 2:1   *2896*
for he hath no *p* in fools........................... Eccl 5:4   *2656*
shalt say, I have no *p* in them .... Eccl 12:1   *2656*
the night of my *p* hath he turned .... Is 21:4   *2837*
and shall perform all my *p*...................... Is 44:28   *2656*
stand, and I will do all my *p* .... Is 46:10   *2656*
he will do his *p* on Babylon .... Is 48:14   *2656*
the *p* of the LORD shall prosper .... Is 53:10   *2656*
in the day of your fast ye find *p* .... Is 58:3   *2656*
from doing thy *p* on my holy day .... Is 58:13   *2656*
own ways, nor finding thine own *p* .... Is 58:13   *2656*
snuffeth up the wind at her *p* .... Jer 2:24   *185,5315*
is he a vessel wherein is no *p*................. Jer 22:28   *2656*
he had set at liberty at their *p* .... Jer 34:16   *5315*
like a vessel wherein is no *p* .... Jer 48:38   *2656*
with whom thou hast taken *p* .... Eze 16:37   *6148*
Have I any *p* at all that the..................... Eze 18:23   *2654*
For I have no *p* in the death of................ Eze 18:32   *2654*
I have no *p* in the death of the .... Eze 33:11   *2654*
as a vessel wherein is no *p*..................... Hos 8:8   *2656*
and I will take *p* in it, and I will .... Hag 1:8   *7521*
I have no *p* in you, saith .... Mal 1:10   *2656*
good *p* to give you the kingdom .... Lk 12:32   *2106*
willing to shew the Jews a *p* .... Acts 24:27   *5485*
willing to do the Jews a *p* .... Acts 25:9   *5485*
but have *p* in them that do them .... Rom 1:32   *4909*
Therefore I take *p* in infirmities 2Cor 12:10   *2106*
to the good *p* of his will .... Eph 1:5   *2107*
according to his good *p* which he........... Eph 1:9   *2107*
to will and to do of his good *p* .... Phil 2:13   *2107*
all the good *p* of his goodness 2Th 1:11   *2107*
but had *p* in unrighteousness 2Th 2:12   *2106*
But she that liveth in *p* is dead.............. 1Ti 5:6   *4684*
for sin thou hast had no *p* .... Heb 10:6   *2106*
not, neither hadst *p* therein .... Heb 10:8   *2106*
my soul shall have no *p* in him .... Heb 10:38   *2106*
chastened us after their own *p* ...... Heb 12:10   *3588,1380*
Ye have lived in *p* on the earth .... Jas 5:5   *5171*
as they that count it *p* to riot 2Pet 2:13   *2237*
for thy *p* they are and were .... Rev 4:11   *2307*

PLEASURES
prosperity, and their years in *p* .... Job 36:11   *5273*
hand there are *p* for evermore .... Ps 16:11   *5273*
them drink of the river of thy *p* .... Ps 36:8   *5730*
this, thou that art given to *p* .... Is 47:8   *5719*
p of this life, and bring no fruit .... Lk 8:14   *2237*
lovers of *p* more than lovers of 2Ti 3:4   *5569*
serving divers lusts and *p* .... Titus 3:3   *2237*
than to enjoy the *p* of sin for a............... Heb 11:25

PLEDGE
she said, Wilt thou give me a *p* .... Gen 38:17   *6162*
he said, What *p* shall I give thee .... Gen 38:18   *6162*
to receive his *p* from the woman's .... Gen 38:20   *6162*
take thy neighbour's raiment to *p* .... Ex 22:26   *2254*
or the upper millstone to *p* .... Deut 24:6   *2254*
for he taketh a man's life to *p* .... Deut 24:6   *2254*
go into his house to fetch his *p* .... Deut 24:10   *5667*
bring out the *p* abroad unto thee .... Deut 24:11   *5667*
thou shalt not sleep with his *p* .... Deut 24:12   *5667*
p again when the sun goeth down .... Deut 24:13   *5667*
nor take a widow's raiment to *p*............. Deut 24:17   *2254*
brethren fare, and take their *p* 1Sa 17:18   *6161*
For thou hast taken a *p* from thy .... Job 22:6   *2254*
they take the widow's ox for a *p* .... Job 24:3   *2254*
breast, and take a *p* of the poor .... Job 24:9   *2254*
take a *p* of him for a strange .... Prov 20:16   *2254*
take a *p* of him for a strange .... Prov 27:13   *2254*
hath restored to the debtor his *p* .... Eze 18:7   *2258*
violence, hath not restored the *p* .... Eze 18:12   *2258*
any, hath not withholden the *p* .... Eze 18:16   *2258*

P

If the wicked restore the *p*	Eze 33:15	2258
clothes laid to *p* by every altar	Amos 2:8	2254

PLEDGES
give *p* to my lord the king of	2Kin 18:23	6148
Now therefore give *p*, I pray thee	Is 36:8	6148

PLEIADES (ple'-ya-dez) A constellation of stars.
maketh Arcturus, Orion, and *P*	Job 9:9	3598
bind the sweet influences of *P*	Job 38:31	3598

PLENTEOUS
of Egypt in the seven *p* years	Gen 41:34	7647
in the seven *p* years the earth	Gen 41:47	7647
LORD shall make thee *p* in goods	Deut 28:11	3498
p in every work of thine hand	Deut 30:9	3498
gold at Jerusalem as *p* as stones	2Chr 1:15	8082
p in mercy unto all them that	Ps 86:5	7227
and *p* in mercy and truth	Ps 86:15	7227
slow to anger, and *p* in mercy	Ps 103:8	7227
and with him is *p* redemption	Ps 130:7	7235
earth, and it shall be fat and *p*	Is 30:23	8082
portion is fat, and their meat *p*	Hab 1:16	1277
disciples, The harvest truly is *p*	Mt 9:37	*4180*

PLENTEOUSNESS
And the seven years of *p*, that was	Gen 41:53	7647
of the diligent tend only to *p*	Prov 21:5	4195

PLENTIFUL
Thou, O God, didst send a *p* rain	Ps 68:9	5071
away, and joy out of the *p* field	Is 16:10	3759
And I brought you into a *p* country	Jer 2:7	3759
is taken from the *p* field	Jer 48:33	3759

PLENTIFULLY
how hast thou *p* declared the	Job 26:3	7230
p rewardeth the proud doer	Ps 31:23	3499
certain rich man brought forth *p*	Lk 12:16	*2164*

PLENTY
the earth, and *p* of corn and wine	Gen 27:28	7230
p throughout all the land of	Gen 41:29	7647
all the *p* shall be forgotten in	Gen 41:30	7647
the *p* shall not be known in the	Gen 41:31	7647
pit, wherein there is *p* of water	Lev 11:36	4723
from Ophir great *p* of almug trees	1Kin 10:11	7235
had enough to eat, and have left *p*	2Chr 31:10	7230
and thou shalt have *p* of silver	Job 22:25	8443
in judgment, and in *p* of justice	Job 37:23	7230
shall thy barns be filled with *p*	Prov 3:10	7647
his land shall have *p* of bread	Prov 28:19	7646
for then had we *p* of victuals	Jer 44:17	7646
And ye shall eat in *p*, and be	Joel 2:26	398

PLOTTETH
The wicked *p* against the just, and	Ps 37:12	2161

PLOUGH
man, having put his hand to the *p*	Lk 9:62	*723*

PLOW
Thou shalt not *p* with an ox	Deut 22:10	2790
which a yoke of oxen might *p*	1Sa 14:14	2790
I have seen, they that *p* iniquity	Job 4:8	2790
will not *p* by reason of the cold	Prov 20:4	2790
Doth the plowman *p* all day to sow	Is 28:24	2790
Judah shall *p*, and Jacob shall	Hos 10:11	2790
will one *p* there with oxen	Amos 6:12	2790
he that ploweth should *p* in hope	1Cor 9:10	722

PLOWED
If ye had not *p* with my heifer,	Judg 14:18	2790
The plowers *p* upon my back	Ps 129:3	2790
Zion shall be *p* like a field	Jer 26:18	2790
Ye have *p* wickedness, ye have	Hos 10:13	2790
for your sake be *p* as a field	Mic 3:12	2790

PLOWERS
The *p* plowed upon my back	Ps 129:3	2790

PLOWETH
that he that *p* should plow in	1Cor 9:10	

PLOWING
who was *p* with twelve yoke of	1Kin 19:19	2790
Job, and said, The oxen were *p*	Job 1:14	2790
the *p* of the wicked, is sin	Prov 21:4	5215
having a servant *p* or feeding	Lk 17:7	*722*

PLOWMAN
Doth the *p* plow all day to sow	Is 28:24	2790
that the *p* shall overtake the	Amos 9:13	2790

PLOWMEN
sons of the alien shall be your *p*	Is 61:5	406
the *p* were ashamed, they covered	Jer 14:4	406

PLOWSHARES
shall beat their swords into *p*	Is 2:4	855
Beat your *p* into swords, and your	Joel 3:10	855
shall beat their swords into *p*	Mic 4:3	855

PLUCK
he shall *p* away his crop with his	Lev 1:16	5493
quite *p* down all their high	Num 33:52	8045
then thou mayest *p* the ears with	Deut 23:25	6998
Then will I *p* them up by the	2Chr 7:20	5428
They *p* the fatherless from the	Job 24:9	1497
for he shall *p* my feet out of the	Ps 25:15	3318
p thee out of thy dwelling place,	Ps 52:5	5255
p it out of thy bosom	Ps 74:11	3615
which pass by the way do *p* her	Ps 80:12	717
a time to *p* up that which is	Eccl 3:2	6131
I will *p* them out of their land,	Jer 12:14	5428
p out the house of Judah from	Jer 12:14	5428
not obey, I will utterly *p* up	Jer 12:17	5428
and concerning a kingdom, to *p* up	Jer 18:7	5428
hand, yet would I *p* thee thence	Jer 22:24	5423
will plant them, and not *p* them up	Jer 24:6	5428
I have watched over them, to *p* up	Jer 31:28	5428
I will plant you, and not *p* you up	Jer 42:10	5428
which I have planted I will *p* up	Jer 45:4	5428
to *p* it up by the roots thereof	Eze 17:9	5375
and *p* off thine own breasts	Eze 23:34	5423
who *p* off their skin from off	Mic 3:2	1497
I will *p* up thy groves out of the	Mic 5:14	5428
p* it out, and cast it from thee	Mt 5:29	*1808*
began to *p* the ears of corn, and	Mt 12:1	5089
p* it out, and cast it from thee	Mt 18:9	*1807*
they went, to *p* the ears of corn	Mk 2:23	5089
thine eye offend thee, *p* it out	Mk 9:47	*1544*
any man *p* them out of my hand	Jn 10:28	*726*
no man is able to *p* them out of	Jn 10:29	*726*

PLUCKED
p it out of his bosom, and, behold	Ex 4:7	3318
ye shall be *p* from off the land	Deut 28:63	5255
a man *p* off his shoe, and gave it	Ruth 4:7	8025
p the spear out of the Egyptian's	2Sa 23:21	1497
p the spear out of the Egyptian's	1Chr 11:23	1497
p off the hair of my head and of	Ezr 9:3	4803
p off their hair, and made them	Neh 13:25	4803
p the spoil out of his teeth	Job 29:17	7993
to them that *p* off the hair	Is 50:6	4803
for the wicked are not *p* away	Jer 6:29	5423
after that I have *p* them out I	Jer 12:15	5428
it shall not be *p* up, nor thrown	Jer 31:40	5428
But she was *p* up in fury, she was	Eze 19:12	5428
till the wings thereof were *p*	Dan 7:4	4804
the first horns *p* up by the roots	Dan 7:8	6132
for his kingdom shall be *p* up	Dan 11:4	5428
a firebrand *p* out of the burning	Amos 4:11	5337
this a brand *p* out of the fire	Zec 3:2	5337
chains had been *p* asunder by him	Mk 5:4	*1288*
his disciples *p* the ears of corn,	Lk 6:1	*5089*
Be thou *p* up by the root, and be	Lk 17:6	*1610*
ye would have *p* out your own eyes	Gal 4:15	*1846*
twice dead, *p* up by the roots	Jude 12	*1610*

PLUCKETH
but the foolish *p* it down with	Prov 14:1	2040

PLUCKT
her mouth was an olive leaf *p* off	Gen 8:11	2965

PLUMBLINE
stood upon a wall made by a *p*	Amos 7:7	594
with a *p* in his hand	Amos 7:7	594
And I said, A *p*	Amos 7:8	594
I will set a *p* in the midst of my	Amos 7:8	594

PLUMMET
the *p* of the house of Ahab	2Kin 21:13	4949
line, and righteousness to the *p*	Is 28:17	4949
shall see the *p* in the hand of	Zec 4:10	68,913

PLUNGE
Yet shalt thou *p* me in the ditch,	Job 9:31	2881

POCHERETH (po-ke'-reth) A family of exiles.
the children of *P* of Zebaim	Ezr 2:57	6380
the children of *P* of Zebaim	Neh 7:59	6380

POETS
also of your own *p* have said	Acts 17:28	*4163*

POINT
Behold, I am at the *p* to die	Gen 25:32	1980
ye shall *p* out for you mount Hor	Num 34:7	8376
From mount Hor ye shall *p* out	Num 34:8	8376
ye shall *p* out your east border	Num 34:10	184
iron, and with the *p* of a diamond	Jer 17:1	6856
I have set the *p* of the sword	Eze 21:15	19

daughter lieth at the *p* of death	Mk 5:23	2079
for he was at the *p* of death	Jn 4:47	3195
whole law, and yet offend in one *p*	Jas 2:10	

POINTED

he spreadeth sharp *p* things upon	Job 41:30	2742

POINTS

evil, that in all *p* as he came	Eccl 5:16	5980
but was in all *p* tempted like as	Heb 4:15	

POISON

with the *p* of serpents of the	Deut 32:24	2534
Their wine is the *p* of dragons	Deut 32:33	2534
the *p* whereof drinketh up my	Job 6:4	2534
He shall suck the *p* of asps	Job 20:16	7219
p is like the *p* of a serpent	Ps 58:4	2534
adders' *p* is under their lips	Ps 140:3	2534
the *p* of asps is under their lips	Rom 3:13	2447
an unruly evil, full of deadly *p*	Jas 3:8	2447

POLE

fiery serpent, and set it upon a *p*	Num 21:8	5251
of brass, and put it upon a *p*	Num 21:9	5251

POLICY

through his *p* also he shall cause	Dan 8:25	7922

POLISHED

p after the similitude of a	Ps 144:12	2404
he hid me, and made me a *p* shaft	Is 49:2	1305
feet like in colour to *p* brass	Dan 10:6	7044

POLISHING

rubies, their *p* was of sapphire	Lam 4:7	1508

POLL

take five shekels apiece by the *p*	Num 3:47	1538
they shall only *p* their heads	Eze 44:20	3697
p thee for thy delicate children	Mic 1:16	1494

POLLED

when he *p* his head, (for it was	2Sa 14:26	1548
at every year's end that he *p* it	2Sa 14:26	1548
heavy on him, therefore he *p* it	2Sa 14:26	1548

POLLS

names, every male by their *p*	Num 1:2	1538
years old and upward, by their *p*	Num 1:18	1538
number of the names, by their *p*	Num 1:20	1538
number of the names, by their *p*	Num 1:22	1538
and their number by their *p*	1Chr 23:3	1538
by number of names by their *p*	1Chr 23:24	1538

POLLUTE

neither shall ye *p* the holy	Num 18:32	2490
So ye shall not *p* the land	Num 35:33	2610
is called by my name, to *p* it	Jer 7:30	2930
and they shall *p* it	Eze 7:21	2490
they shall *p* my secret place	Eze 7:22	2490
will ye *p* me among my people for	Eze 13:19	2490
ye *p* yourselves with all your	Eze 20:31	2930
but *p* ye my holy name no more	Eze 20:39	2490
I will not let them *p* my holy	Eze 39:7	2490
to be in my sanctuary, to *p* it	Eze 44:7	2490
they shall *p* the sanctuary of	Dan 11:31	2490

POLLUTED

thy tool upon it, thou hast *p* it	Ex 20:25	2490
p it, according to the word of	2Kin 23:16	2930
p the house of the LORD which he	2Chr 36:14	2930
therefore were they, as *p*	Ezr 2:62	1351
therefore were they, as *p*	Neh 7:64	1351
and the land was *p* with blood	Ps 106:38	2610
I have *p* mine inheritance, and	Is 47:6	2490
for how should my name be *p*	Is 48:11	2490
How canst thou say, I am not *p*	Jer 2:23	2930
shall not that land be greatly *p*	Jer 3:1	2610
thou hast *p* the land with thy	Jer 3:2	2610
p my name, and caused every man	Jer 34:16	2490
he hath *p* the kingdom and the	Lam 2:2	2490
they have *p* themselves with blood	Lam 4:14	1351
behold, my soul hath not been *p*	Eze 4:14	2930
neither be *p* any more with all	Eze 14:11	2930
saw thee *p* in thine own blood, I	Eze 16:6	947
and bare, and wast *p* in thy blood	Eze 16:22	947
not be *p* before the heathen	Eze 20:9	2490
and my sabbaths they greatly *p*	Eze 20:13	2490
not be *p* before the heathen	Eze 20:14	2490
in my statutes, but *p* my sabbaths	Eze 20:16	2490
they *p* my sabbaths	Eze 20:21	2490
that it should not be *p* in the	Eze 20:22	2490
had *p* my sabbaths, and their eyes	Eze 20:24	2490
I *p* them in their own gifts, in	Eze 20:26	2930
Are ye *p* after the manner of your	Eze 20:30	2930
she was *p* with them, and her mind	Eze 23:17	2930
thou art *p* with their idols	Eze 23:30	2930

idols wherewith they had *p* it	Eze 36:18	2930
work iniquity, and is *p* with blood	Hos 6:8	6121
all that eat thereof shall be *p*	Hos 9:4	2930
and thou shalt die in a *p* land	Amos 7:17	2931
because it is *p*, it shall destroy	Mic 2:10	2930
Woe to her that is filthy and *p*	Zeph 3:1	1351
her priests have *p* the sanctuary	Zeph 3:4	2490
Ye offer *p* bread upon mine altar	Mal 1:7	1351
and ye say, Wherein have we *p* thee	Mal 1:7	1351
say, The table of the LORD is *p*	Mal 1:12	1351
temple, and hath *p* this holy place	Acts 21:28	2840

POLLUTING

keepeth the sabbath from *p* it	Is 56:2	2490
keepeth the sabbath from *p* it	Is 56:6	2490

POLLUTION

her that was set apart for *p*	Eze 22:10	2931

POLLUTIONS

that they abstain from *p* of idols	Acts 15:20	234
the *p* of the world through the	2Pet 2:20	3393

POLLUX *A Roman god.*

isle, whose sign was Castor and *P*	Acts 28:11	1359

POMEGRANATE

A golden bell and a *p*, a golden	Ex 28:34	7416
p, a golden bell and a *p*	Ex 28:34	7416
A bell and a *p*, a bell and a	Ex 39:26	7416
and a *p*, a bell and a *p*	Ex 39:26	7416
part of Gibeah under a *p* tree	1Sa 14:2	7416
a piece of a *p* within thy locks	Song 4:3	7416
As a piece of a *p* are thy temples	Song 6:7	7416
spiced wine of the juice of my *p*	Song 8:2	7416
the *p* tree, the palm tree also,	Joel 1:12	7416
vine, and the fig tree, and the *p*	Hag 2:19	7416

POMEGRANATES

of it thou shalt make *p* of blue	Ex 28:33	7416
the hems of the robe of blue	Ex 39:24	7416
the *p* upon the hem of the robe	Ex 39:25	7416
robe, round about between the *p*	Ex 39:25	7416
and they brought of the *p*, and of	Num 13:23	7416
or of figs, or of vines, or of *p*	Num 20:5	7416
and vines, and fig trees, and *p*	Deut 8:8	7416
that were upon the top, with *p*	1Kin 7:18	7416
the two pillars had *p* also above	1Kin 7:20	7416
the *p* were two hundred in rows	1Kin 7:20	7416
four hundred *p* for the two	1Kin 7:42	7416
two rows of *p* for one network	1Kin 7:42	7416
p upon the chapiter round about	2Kin 25:17	7416
and made an hundred *p*, and put them	2Chr 3:16	7416
four hundred *p* on the two wreaths	2Chr 4:13	7416
two rows of *p* on each wreath, to	2Chr 4:13	7416
Thy plants are an orchard of *p*	Song 4:13	7416
vine flourished, and the *p* budded	Song 6:11	7416
grape appear, and the *p* bud forth	Song 7:12	7416
p upon the chapiters round about,	Jer 52:22	7416
the *p* were like unto these	Jer 52:22	7416
were ninety and six *p* on a side	Jer 52:23	7416
all the *p* upon the network were	Jer 52:23	7416

POMMELS

To wit, the two pillars, and the *p*	2Chr 4:12	1543
two wreaths to cover the two *p* of	2Chr 4:12	1543
to cover the two *p* of the	2Chr 4:13	1543

POMP

and their multitude, and their *p*	Is 5:14	7588
Thy *p* is brought down to the	Is 14:11	1347
I will also make the *p* of the	Eze 7:24	1347
the *p* of her strength shall cease	Eze 30:18	1347
they shall spoil the *p* of Egypt	Eze 32:12	1347
the *p* of her strength shall cease	Eze 33:28	1347
come, and Bernice, with great *p*	Acts 25:23	5325

PONDER

P the path of thy feet, and let	Prov 4:26	6424
thou shouldest *p* the path of life	Prov 5:6	6424

PONDERED

things, and *p* them in her heart	Lk 2:19	4820

PONDERETH

the LORD, and he *p* all his goings	Prov 5:21	6424
but the LORD *p* the hearts	Prov 21:2	8505
doth not he that *p* the heart	Prov 24:12	8505

PONDS

their rivers, and upon their *p*	Ex 7:19	98
over the rivers, and over the *p*	Ex 8:5	98
that make sluices and *p* for fish	Is 19:10	99

PONTIUS *(pon'-she-us) The family name of Pilate.*

delivered him to *P* Pilate the	Mt 27:2	4194
P Pilate being governor of Judaea	Lk 3:1	4194

P

P Pilate, with the Gentiles, and	Acts 4:27	4194
who before P Pilate witnessed a	1Ti 6:13	4194

PONTUS (pon'-tus) *A Roman province in Asia Minor.*

and in Judaea, and Cappadocia, in P	Acts 2:9	4195
Jew named Aquila, born in P	Acts 18:2	4195
strangers scattered throughout P	1Pet 1:1	4195

POOL

met together by the p of Gibeon	2Sa 2:13	1295
the one on the one side of the p	2Sa 2:13	1295
other on the other side of the p	2Sa 2:13	1295
them up over the p in Hebron	2Sa 4:12	1295
the chariot in the p of Samaria	1Kin 22:38	1295
by the conduit of the upper p	2Kin 18:17	1295
all his might, and how he made a p	2Kin 20:20	1295
the fountain, and to the king's p	Neh 2:14	1295
the wall of the p of Siloah by	Neh 3:15	1295
to the p that was made, and unto	Neh 3:16	1295
p in the highway of the fuller's	Is 7:3	1295
the waters of the lower p	Is 22:9	1295
walls for the water of the old p	Is 22:11	1295
parched ground shall become a p	Is 35:7	98
by the conduit of the upper p in	Is 36:2	1295
make the wilderness a p of water	Is 41:18	98
is of old like a p of water	Nah 2:8	1295
Jerusalem by the sheep market a p	Jn 5:2	2861
at a certain season into the p	Jn 5:4	2861
is troubled, to put me into the p	Jn 5:7	2861
him, Go, wash in the p of Siloam	Jn 9:7	2861
unto me, Go to the p of Siloam	Jn 9:11	2861

POOLS

and upon all their p of water	Ex 7:19	4723
the rain also filleth the p	Ps 84:6	1293
I made me p of water, to water	Eccl 2:6	1295
for the bittern, and p of water	Is 14:23	98
islands, and I will dry up the p	Is 42:15	98

POOR

other kine came up after them, p	Gen 41:19	1800
of my people that is p by thee	Ex 22:25	6041
countenance a p man in his cause	Ex 23:3	1800
judgment of thy p in his cause	Ex 23:6	34
that the p of thy people may eat	Ex 23:11	34
the p shall not give less than	Ex 30:15	1800
And if he be p, and cannot get so	Lev 14:21	1800
thou shalt leave them for the p	Lev 19:10	6041
not respect the person of the p	Lev 19:15	1800
thou shalt leave them unto the p	Lev 23:22	6041
If thy brother be waxen p	Lev 25:25	4134
And if thy brother be waxen p	Lev 25:35	4134
that dwelleth by thee be waxen p	Lev 25:39	4134
that dwelleth by him wax p	Lev 25:47	4134
there shall be no p among you	Deut 15:4	34
If there be among you a p man of	Deut 15:7	34
thine hand from thy p brother	Deut 15:7	34
eye be evil against thy p brother	Deut 15:9	34
For the p shall never cease out	Deut 15:11	34
wide unto thy brother, to thy p	Deut 15:11	6041
And if the man be p, thou shalt	Deut 24:12	6041
an hired servant that is p	Deut 24:14	6041
for he is p, and setteth his heart	Deut 24:15	6041
my family is p in Manasseh	Judg 6:15	1800
not young men, whether p or rich	Ruth 3:10	1800
The LORD maketh p, and maketh rich	1Sa 2:7	3423
raiseth up the p out of the dust	1Sa 2:8	1800
in law, seeing that I am a p man	1Sa 18:23	7326
the one rich, and the other p	2Sa 12:1	7326
But the p man had nothing, save	2Sa 12:3	7326
but took the p man's lamb	2Sa 12:4	7326
of the guard left of the p of the	2Kin 25:12	1803
one to another, and gifts to the p	Est 9:22	34
he saveth the p from the sword	Job 5:15	34
So the p hath hope, and iniquity	Job 5:16	1800
shall seek to please the p	Job 20:10	1800
oppressed and hath forsaken the p	Job 20:19	1800
the p of the earth hide	Job 24:4	6035
breast, and take a pledge of the p	Job 24:9	6041
with the light killeth the p	Job 24:14	6041
I delivered the p that cried	Job 29:12	6041
I was a father to the p	Job 29:16	34
was not my soul grieved for the p	Job 30:25	34
withheld the p from their desire	Job 31:16	1800
or any p without covering	Job 31:19	34
the rich more than the p	Job 34:19	1800
the cry of the p to come unto him	Job 34:28	1800
but giveth right to the p	Job 36:6	6041
the p in his affliction, and	Job 36:15	6041
the expectation of the p shall	Ps 9:18	6041
in his pride doth persecute the p	Ps 10:2	6041
are privily set against the p	Ps 10:8	2489
he lieth in wait to catch the p	Ps 10:9	6041

he doth catch the p, when he	Ps 10:9	6041
that the p may fall by his strong	Ps 10:10	2489
the p committeth himself unto	Ps 10:14	2489
For the oppression of the p	Ps 12:5	6041
have shamed the counsel of the p	Ps 14:6	6041
This p man cried, and the LORD	Ps 34:6	6041
which deliverest the p from him	Ps 35:10	6041
is too strong for him, yea, the p	Ps 35:10	6041
their bow, to cast down the p	Ps 37:14	6041
But I am p and needy	Ps 40:17	6041
is he that considereth the p	Ps 41:1	1800
Both low and high, rich and p	Ps 49:2	34
of thy goodness for the p	Ps 68:10	6041
But I am p and sorrowful	Ps 69:29	6041
For the LORD heareth the p	Ps 69:33	34
But I am p and needy	Ps 70:5	6041
and thy p with judgment	Ps 72:2	6041
shall judge the p of the people	Ps 72:4	6041
the p also, and him that hath no	Ps 72:12	6041
He shall spare the p and needy, and	Ps 72:13	1800
congregation of thy p for ever	Ps 74:19	6041
let the p and needy praise thy	Ps 74:21	6041
Defend the p and fatherless	Ps 82:3	1800
Deliver the p and needy	Ps 82:4	1800
for I am p and needy	Ps 86:1	6041
Yet setteth he the p on high from	Ps 107:41	34
shew mercy, but persecuted the p	Ps 109:16	6041
For I am p and needy, and my heart	Ps 109:22	6041
stand at the right hand of the p	Ps 109:31	34
dispersed, he hath given to the p	Ps 112:9	34
raiseth up the p out of the dust	Ps 113:7	1800
I will satisfy her p with bread	Ps 132:15	34
afflicted, and the right of the p	Ps 140:12	34
He becometh p that dealeth with a	Prov 10:4	7326
of the p is their poverty	Prov 10:15	1800
there is that maketh himself p	Prov 13:7	7326
but the p heareth not rebuke	Prov 13:8	7326
food is in the tillage of the p	Prov 13:23	7326
The p is hated even of his own	Prov 14:20	7326
but he that hath mercy on the p	Prov 14:21	6035,6041
the p reproacheth his Maker	Prov 14:31	1800
honoureth him hath mercy on the p	Prov 14:31	34
Whoso mocketh the p reproacheth	Prov 17:5	7326
The p useth intreaties	Prov 18:23	7326
Better is the p that walketh in	Prov 19:1	7326
but the p is separated from his	Prov 19:4	7326
the brethren of the p do hate him	Prov 19:7	7326
upon the p lendeth unto the LORD	Prov 19:17	1800
a p man is better than a liar	Prov 19:22	7326
his ears at the cry of the p	Prov 21:13	1800
loveth pleasure shall be a p man	Prov 21:17	4270
The rich and p meet together	Prov 22:2	7326
The rich ruleth over the p	Prov 22:7	7326
he giveth of his bread to the p	Prov 22:9	1800
the p to increase his riches	Prov 22:16	1800
Rob not the p, because he is p	Prov 22:22	1800
A p man that oppresseth the	Prov 28:3	7326
p is like a sweeping rain which	Prov 28:3	1800
Better is the p that walketh in	Prov 28:6	1800
it for him that will pity the p	Prov 28:8	1800
but the p that hath understanding	Prov 28:11	1800
a wicked ruler over the p people	Prov 28:15	1800
giveth unto the p shall not lack	Prov 28:27	7326
considereth the cause of the p	Prov 29:7	1800
The p and the deceitful man meet	Prov 29:13	7326
that faithfully judgeth the p	Prov 29:14	1800
or lest I be p, and steal, and take	Prov 30:9	3423
to devour the p from off the	Prov 30:14	6041
and plead the cause of the p	Prov 31:9	6041
stretcheth out her hand to the p	Prov 31:20	6041
Better is a p and a wise child	Eccl 4:13	4542
is born in his kingdom becometh p	Eccl 4:14	7326
seest the oppression of the p	Eccl 5:8	7326
what hath the p, that knoweth to	Eccl 6:8	6041
was found in it a p wise man	Eccl 9:15	4542
no man remembered that same p man	Eccl 9:15	4542
nevertheless the p man's wisdom	Eccl 9:16	4542
the spoil of the p is in your	Is 3:14	6041
and grind the faces of the p	Is 3:15	6041
the right from the p of my people	Is 10:2	6041
be heard unto Laish, O p Anathoth	Is 10:30	6041
shall he judge the p, and reprove	Is 11:4	1800
the firstborn of the p shall feed	Is 14:30	1800
the p of his people shall trust	Is 14:32	6041
hast been a strength to the p	Is 25:4	1800
it down, even the feet of the p	Is 26:6	6041
the p among men shall rejoice in	Is 29:19	34
to destroy the p with lying words	Is 32:7	6035,6041
When the p and needy seek water,	Is 41:17	6041
that thou bring the p that are	Is 58:7	6041
I look, even to him that is p	Is 66:2	6041

of the souls of the *p* innocents	Jer 2:34	34
I said, Surely these are *p*	Jer 5:4	1800
the *p* from the hand of evildoers	Jer 20:13	34
He judged the cause of the *p*	Jer 22:16	6041
guard left of the *p* of the people	Jer 39:10	1800
of the *p* of the land, of them	Jer 40:7	1803
certain of the *p* of the people	Jer 52:15	1803
p of the land for vinedressers	Jer 52:16	1803
she strengthen the hand of the *p*	Eze 16:49	6041
Hath oppressed the *p* and needy,	Eze 18:12	6041
taken off his hand from the *p*	Eze 18:17	6041
robbery, and have vexed the *p*	Eze 22:29	6041
by shewing mercy to the *p*	Dan 4:27	6033
the *p* for a pair of shoes	Amos 2:6	34
of the earth on the head of the *p*	Amos 2:7	1800
of Samaria, which oppress the *p*	Amos 4:1	1800
as your treading is upon the *p*	Amos 5:11	1800
they turn aside the *p* in the gate	Amos 5:12	1800
even to make the *p* of the land to	Amos 8:4	6035,6041
That we may buy the *p* for silver	Amos 8:6	1800
was as to devour the *p* secretly	Hab 3:14	6041
p people, and they shall trust in	Zeph 3:12	1800
the stranger, nor the *p*	Zec 7:10	6041
even you, O *p* of the flock	Zec 11:7	6041
so the *p* of the flock that waited	Zec 11:11	6041
Blessed are the *p* in spirit	Mt 5:3	4434
the *p* have the gospel preached to ,	Mt 11:5	4434
that thou hast, and give to the *p*	Mt 19:21	4434
sold for much, and given to the *p*	Mt 26:9	4434
For ye have the *p* always with you	Mt 26:11	4434
thou hast, and give to the *p*	Mk 10:21	4434
And there came a certain *p* widow	Mk 12:42	4434
That this *p* widow hath cast more	Mk 12:43	4434
and have been given to the *p*	Mk 14:5	4434
For ye have the *p* with you always	Mk 14:7	4434
me to preach the gospel to the *p*	Lk 4:18	4434
and said, Blessed be ye *p*	Lk 6:20	4434
to the *p* the gospel is preached	Lk 7:22	4434
thou makest a feast, call the *p*	Lk 14:13	4434
city, and bring in hither the *p*	Lk 14:21	4434
hast, and distribute unto the *p*	Lk 18:22	4434
half of my goods I give to the *p*	Lk 19:8	4434
he saw also a certain *p* widow	Lk 21:2	3998
that this *p* widow hath cast in	Lk 21:3	4434
hundred pence, and given to the *p*	Jn 12:5	4434
said, not that he cared for the *p*	Jn 12:6	4434
For the *p* always ye have with you	Jn 12:8	4434
he should give something to the *p*	Jn 13:29	4434
p saints which are at Jerusalem	Rom 15:26	4434
bestow all my goods to feed the *p*	1Cor 13:3	
as *p*, yet making many rich	2Cor 6:10	4434
yet for your sakes he became *p*	2Cor 8:9	4433
he hath given to the *p*	2Cor 9:9	3993
that we should remember the *p*	Gal 2:10	4434
in also a *p* man in vile raiment	Jas 2:2	4434
and say to the *p*, Stand thou there	Jas 2:3	4434
Hath not God chosen the *p* of this	Jas 2:5	4434
But ye have despised the *p*	Jas 2:6	4434
art wretched, and miserable, and *p*	Rev 3:17	4434
both small and great, rich and *p*	Rev 13:16	4434

POORER

But if he be *p* than thy	Lev 27:8	4134

POOREST

save the *p* sort of the people of	2Kin 24:14	1803

POPLAR

And Jacob took him rods of green *p*	Gen 30:37	3839

POPLARS

upon the hills, under oaks and *p*	Hos 4:13	3839

POPULOUS

a nation, great, mighty, and *p*	Deut 26:5	7227
Art thou better than *p* No	Nah 3:8	527

PORATHA (por'-a-thah) *A son of Haman.*

And *P*, and Adalia, and Aridatha,	Est 9:8	6334

PORCH

Ehud went forth through the *p*	Judg 3:23	4528
the *p* before the temple of the	1Kin 6:3	197
And he made a *p* of pillars	1Kin 7:6	197
and the *p* was before them	1Kin 7:6	197
Then he made a *p* for the throne	1Kin 7:7	197
judge, even the *p* of judgment	1Kin 7:7	197
had another court within the *p*	1Kin 7:8	197
taken to wife, like unto this *p*	1Kin 7:8	197
Lord, and for the *p* of the house	1Kin 7:12	197
were of lily work in the *p*	1Kin 7:19	197
pillars in the *p* of the temple	1Kin 7:21	197
his son the pattern of the *p*	1Chr 28:11	197
the *p* that was in the front of	2Chr 3:4	197

which he had built before the *p*	2Chr 8:12	197
that was before the *p* of the Lord	2Chr 15:8	197
have shut up the doors of the *p*	2Chr 29:7	197
came they to to the *p* of the Lord	2Chr 29:17	197
temple of the Lord, between the *p*	Eze 8:16	197
threshold of the gate by the *p* of	Eze 40:7	197
also the *p* of the gate within	Eze 40:8	197
measured he the *p* of the gate	Eze 40:9	197
the *p* of the gate was inward	Eze 40:9	197
p of the inner gate were fifty	Eze 40:15	197
in the *p* of the gate were two	Eze 40:39	197
which was at the *p* of the gate	Eze 40:40	197
brought me to the *p* of the house	Eze 40:48	197
and measured each post of the *p*	Eze 40:48	197
length of the *p* was twenty cubits	Eze 40:49	197
upon the face of the *p* without	Eze 41:25	197
other side, on the sides of the *p*	Eze 41:26	197
by the way of the *p* of that gate	Eze 44:3	197
way of the *p* of that gate without	Eze 46:2	197
by the way of the *p* of that gate	Eze 46:8	197
of the Lord, weep between the *p*	Joel 2:17	197
when he was gone out into the *p*	Mt 26:71	4440
And he went out into the *p*	Mk 14:68	4259
in the temple in Solomon's *p*	Jn 10:23	4745
in the *p* that is called Solomon's	Acts 3:11	4745
with one accord in Solomon's *p*	Acts 5:12	4745

PORCHES

temple, and the *p* of the court	Eze 41:15	197
tongue Bethesda, having five *p*	Jn 5:2	4745

PORCIUS (por'-she-us) *Family name of Festus.*

But after two years *P* Festus came	Acts 24:27	4201

PORT

the dragon well, and to the dung *p*	Neh 2:13	8179

PORTER

and the watchman called unto the *p*	2Sa 18:26	7778
and called unto the *p* of the city	2Kin 7:10	7778
the son of Meshelemiah was *p* of	1Chr 9:21	7778
the *p* toward the east, was over	2Chr 31:14	7778
work, and commanded the *p* to watch	Mk 13:34	2377
To him the *p* openeth	Jn 10:3	2377

PORTERS

And he called the *p*	2Kin 7:11	7778
the *p* were, Shallum, and Akkub, and	1Chr 9:17	7778
they were *p* in the companies of	1Chr 9:18	7778
p in the gates were two hundred	1Chr 9:22	7778
In four quarters were the *p*	1Chr 9:24	7778
these Levites, the four chief *p*	1Chr 9:26	7778
and Obed-edom, and Jeiel, the *p*	1Chr 15:18	7778
son of Jeduthun and Hosah to be *p*	1Chr 16:38	7778
And the sons of Jeduthun were *p*	1Chr 16:42	8179
Moreover four thousand were *p*	1Chr 23:5	7778
Concerning the divisions of the *p*	1Chr 26:1	7778
these were the divisions of the *p*	1Chr 26:12	7778
of the *p* among the sons of Kore	1Chr 26:19	7778
the *p* also by their courses at	2Chr 8:14	7778
Levites, shall be *p* of the doors	2Chr 23:4	7778
he set the *p* at the gates of the	2Chr 23:19	7778
were scribes, and officers, and *p*	2Chr 34:13	7778
the *p* waited at every gate	2Chr 35:15	7778
The children of the *p*	Ezr 2:42	7778
people, and the singers, and the *p*	Ezr 2:70	7778
Levites, and the singers, and the *p*	Ezr 7:7	7778
priests and Levites, singers, *p*	Ezr 7:24	8652
the *p*; Shallum, and Telem	Ezr 10:24	7778
I had set up the doors, and the *p*	Neh 7:1	7778
The *p*: the children of Shallum	Neh 7:45	7778
priests, and the Levites, and the *p*	Neh 7:73	7778
the priests, the Levites, the *p*	Neh 10:28	7778
priests that minister, and the *p*	Neh 10:39	7778
Moreover the *p*, Akkub, Talmon, and	Neh 11:19	7778
were *p* keeping the ward at the	Neh 12:25	7778
the *p* kept the ward of their God,	Neh 12:45	7778
portions of the singers and the *p*	Neh 12:47	7778
Levites, and the singers, and the *p*	Neh 13:5	7778

PORTION

the *p* of the men which went with	Gen 14:24	2506
let them take their *p*	Gen 14:24	2506
Is there yet any *p* or inheritance	Gen 31:14	2506
for the priests had a *p* assigned	Gen 47:22	2706
did eat their *p* which Pharaoh	Gen 47:22	2706
to thee one *p* above thy brethren	Gen 48:22	7926
p of my offerings made by fire	Lev 6:17	2506
This is the *p* of the anointing of	Lev 7:35	
thou shalt take one *p* of fifty	Num 31:30	270
which was the *p* of them that went	Num 31:36	2506
half, Moses took one *p* of fifty	Num 31:47	270
a double *p* of all that he hath	Deut 21:17	6310
For the Lord's *p* is his people	Deut 32:9	2506

in a *p* of the lawgiver, was he .... Deut 33:21 — 2513
one *p* to inherit, seeing I am a .... Josh 17:14 — 2256
Out of the *p* of the children of .... Josh 19:9 — 2256
unto Hannah he gave a worthy *p* .... 1Sa 1:5 — 4490
Bring the *p* which I gave thee, of .... 1Sa 9:23 — 4490
saying, What *p* have we in David .... 1Kin 12:16 — 2506
let a double *p* of thy spirit be .... 2Kin 2:9 — 6310
eat Jezebel in the *p* of Jezreel .... 2Kin 9:10 — 2506
met him in the *p* of Naboth the .... 2Kin 9:21 — 2513
cast him in the *p* of the field of .... 2Kin 9:25 — 2513
In the *p* of Jezreel shall dogs .... 2Kin 9:36 — 2506
of the field in the *p* of Jezreel .... 2Kin 9:37 — 2506
saying, What *p* have we in David .... 2Chr 10:16 — 2506
For Ahaz took away a *p* out of the .... 2Chr 28:21 — 2505
He appointed also the king's *p* of .... 2Chr 31:3 — 4521
to give the *p* of the priests .... 2Chr 31:4 — 4521
his daily *p* for their service in .... 2Chr 31:16 — 1697
have no *p* on this side the river .... Ezr 4:16 — 2508
but ye have no *p*, nor right, nor .... Neh 2:20 — 2506
that a certain *p* should be for .... Neh 11:23
and the porters, every day his *p* .... Neh 12:47 — 1697
This is the *p* of a wicked man .... Job 20:29 — 2506
their *p* is cursed in the earth .... Job 24:18 — 2513
how little a *p* is heard of him .... Job 26:14 — 1697
This is the *p* of a wicked man .... Job 27:13 — 2506
For what *p* of God is there from .... Job 31:2 — 2506
this shall be the *p* of their cup .... Ps 11:6 — 4521
The LORD is my *p* of mine .... Ps 16:5 — 4490
which have their *p* in this life .... Ps 17:14 — 2506
they shall be a *p* for foxes .... Ps 63:10 — 4521
of my heart, and my *p* for ever .... Ps 73:26 — 2506
Thou art my *p*, O LORD .... Ps 119:57 — 2506
my *p* in the land of the living .... Ps 142:5 — 2506
household, and a *p* to her maidens .... Prov 31:15 — 2706
this was my *p* of all my labour .... Eccl 2:10 — 2506
shall he leave it for his *p* .... Eccl 2:21 — 2506
for that is his *p* .... Eccl 3:22 — 2506
for it is his *p* .... Eccl 5:18 — 2506
to eat thereof, and to take his *p* .... Eccl 5:19 — 2506
neither have they any more a *p* .... Eccl 9:6 — 2506
for that is thy *p* in this life .... Eccl 9:9 — 2506
Give a *p* to seven, and also to .... Eccl 11:2 — 2506
This is the *p* of them that spoil .... Is 17:14 — 2506
I divide him a *p* with the great .... Is 53:12
stones of the stream thy *p* .... Is 57:6 — 2506
they shall rejoice in their *p* .... Is 61:7 — 2506
The *p* of Jacob is not like them .... Jer 10:16 — 2506
they have trodden my *p* under foot .... Jer 12:10 — 2513
pleasant *p* a desolate wilderness .... Jer 12:10 — 2513
the *p* of thy measures from me, ... Jer 13:25 — 4490
The *p* of Jacob is not like them .... Jer 51:19 — 2506
every day a *p* until the day of .... Jer 52:34 — 1697
The LORD is my *p*, saith my soul .... Lam 3:24 — 2506
the LORD, an holy *p* of the land .... Eze 45:1
The holy *p* of the land shall be .... Eze 45:4
the oblation of the holy *p* .... Eze 45:6
a *p* shall be for the prince on .... Eze 45:7
of the oblation of the holy *p* .... Eze 45:7
before the oblation of the holy *p* .... Eze 45:7
a *p* for Dan .... Eze 48:1
unto the west side, a *p* for Asher .... Eze 48:2
the west side, a *p* for Naphtali .... Eze 48:3
the west side, a *p* for Manasseh .... Eze 48:4
the west side, a *p* for Ephraim .... Eze 48:5
the west side, a *p* for Reuben .... Eze 48:6
unto the west side, a *p* for Judah .... Eze 48:7
the oblation of the holy *p* shall .... Eze 48:18
the oblation of the holy *p* .... Eze 48:18
side, Benjamin shall have a *p* .... Eze 48:23
west side, Simeon shall have a *p* .... Eze 48:24
unto the west side, Issachar a *p* .... Eze 48:25
unto the west side, Zebulun a *p* .... Eze 48:26
side unto the west side, Gad a *p* .... Eze 48:27
with the *p* of the king's meat .... Dan 1:8 — 6598
eat of the *p* of the king's meat .... Dan 1:13 — 6598
did eat the *p* of the king's meat .... Dan 1:16 — 6598
took away the *p* of their meat .... Dan 1:16 — 6598
let his *p* be with the beasts in .... Dan 4:15 — 2508
let his *p* be with the beasts of .... Dan 4:23 — 2508
they that feed of the *p* of his .... Dan 11:26 — 6598
hath changed the *p* of my people .... Mic 2:4 — 2506
because by them their *p* is fat .... Hab 1:16 — 2506
Judah his *p* in the holy land .... Zec 2:12 — 2506
appoint him his *p* with the .... Mt 24:51 — **3313**
to give them their *p* of meat in .... Lk 12:42 — **4620**
him his *p* with the unbelievers .... Lk 12:46 — **3313**
give me the *p* of goods that .... Lk 15:12 — **3313**

PORTIONS

They shall have like *p* to eat .... Deut 18:8 — 2506
And there fell ten *p* to Manasseh .... Josh 17:5 — 2256

all her sons and her daughters, *p* .... 1Sa 1:4 — 4490
to give *p* to all the males among .... 2Chr 31:19 — 4490
send *p* unto them for whom nothing ...... Neh 8:10 — 4490
to eat, and to drink, and to send *p* .... Neh 8:12 — 4490
the *p* of the law for the priests .... Neh 12:44 — 4521
gave the *p* of the singers and the .... Neh 12:47 — 4521
I perceived that the *p* of the .... Neh 13:10 — 4521
of sending *p* one to another .... Est 9:19 — 4490
of sending *p* one to another, and .... Est 9:22 — 4490
be over against one of the *p* .... Eze 45:7 — 2506
Joseph shall have two *p* .... Eze 47:13 — 2256
over against the *p* for the prince .... Eze 48:21 — 2506
inheritance, and these are their *p* .... Eze 48:29 — 4256
a month devour them with their *p* .... Hos 5:7 — 2506

POSSESS

thy seed shall *p* the gate of his .... Gen 22:17 — 3423
let thy seed *p* the gate of those .... Gen 24:60 — 3423
I will give it unto you to *p* it .... Lev 20:24 — 3423
Let us go up at once, and *p* it .... Num 13:30 — 3423
and his seed shall *p* it .... Num 14:24 — 3423
of his family, and he shall *p* it .... Num 27:11 — 3423
I have given you the land to *p* it .... Num 33:53 — 3423
p the land which the LORD sware .... Deut 1:8 — 3423
p it, as the LORD God of thy .... Deut 1:21 — 3423
I give it, and they shall *p* it .... Deut 1:39 — 3423
begin to *p* it, and contend with .... Deut 2:24 — 3423
begin to *p*, that thou mayest .... Deut 2:31 — 3423
hath given you this land to *p* it .... Deut 3:18 — 3423
until they also *p* the land which .... Deut 3:20 — 3423
p the land which the LORD God of .... Deut 4:1 — 3423
in the land whither ye go to *p* it .... Deut 4:5 — 3423
land whither ye go over to *p* it .... Deut 4:14 — 3423
go over, and *p* that good land .... Deut 4:22 — 3423
ye go over Jordan to *p* it .... Deut 4:26 — 3423
land which I give them to *p* it .... Deut 5:31 — 3423
days in the land which ye shall *p* .... Deut 5:33 — 3423
in the land whither ye go to *p* it .... Deut 6:1 — 3423
p the good land which the LORD .... Deut 6:18 — 3423
land whither thou goest to *p* it .... Deut 7:1 — 3423
p the land which the LORD sware .... Deut 8:1 — 3423
to go in to *p* nations greater and .... Deut 9:1 — 3423
hath brought me in to *p* this land .... Deut 9:4 — 3423
dost thou go to *p* their land .... Deut 9:5 — 3423
to *p* it for thy righteousness .... Deut 9:6 — 3423
p the land which I have given you .... Deut 9:23 — 3423
p the land, which I sware unto .... Deut 10:11 — 3423
p the land, whither ye go .... Deut 11:8 — 3423
the land, whither ye go to *p* it .... Deut 11:8 — 3423
whither thou goest in to *p* it .... Deut 11:10 — 3423
the land, whither ye go to *p* it .... Deut 11:11 — 3423
ye shall *p* greater nations and .... Deut 11:23 — 3423
land whither thou goest to *p* it .... Deut 11:29 — 3423
to *p* the land which the LORD your .... Deut 11:31 — 3423
God giveth you, and ye shall *p* it .... Deut 11:31 — 3423
thy fathers giveth thee to *p* it .... Deut 12:1 — 3423
ye shall *p* served their gods .... Deut 12:2 — 3423
whither thou goest to *p* them .... Deut 12:29 — 3423
thee for an inheritance to *p* it .... Deut 15:4 — 3423
God giveth thee, and shalt *p* it .... Deut 17:14 — 3423
these nations, which thou shalt *p* .... Deut 18:14 — 3423
LORD thy God giveth thee to *p* it .... Deut 19:2 — 3423
LORD thy God giveth thee to *p* it .... Deut 19:14 — 3423
LORD thy God giveth thee to *p* it .... Deut 21:1 — 3423
land whither thou goest to *p* it .... Deut 23:20 — 3423
thee for an inheritance to *p* it .... Deut 25:19 — 3423
land, whither thou goest to *p* it .... Deut 28:21 — 3423
land whither thou goest to *p* it .... Deut 28:63 — 3423
possessed, and thou shalt *p* it .... Deut 30:5 — 3423
land whither thou goest to *p* it .... Deut 30:16 — 3423
passest over Jordan to go to *p* it .... Deut 30:18 — 3423
before thee, and thou shalt *p* them .... Deut 31:3 — 3423
whither ye go over Jordan to *p* it .... Deut 31:13 — 3423
whither ye go over Jordan to *p* it .... Deut 32:47 — 3423
p thou the west and the south .... Deut 33:23 — 3423
Jordan, to go in to *p* the land .... Josh 1:11 — 3423
LORD your God giveth you to *p* it .... Josh 1:11 — 3423
are ye slack to go to *p* the land .... Josh 18:3 — 3423
ye shall *p* their land, as the .... Josh 23:5 — 3423
unto Esau mount Seir, to *p* it .... Josh 24:4 — 3423
hand, that ye might *p* their land .... Josh 24:8 — 3423
his inheritance to *p* the land .... Judg 2:6 — 3423
Israel, and shouldest thou *p* it .... Judg 11:23 — 3423
Wilt not thou *p* that which .... Judg 11:24 — 3423
Chemosh thy god giveth thee to *p* .... Judg 11:24 — 3423
from before us, them will we *p* .... Judg 11:24 — 3423
to go, and to enter to *p* the land .... Judg 18:9 — 3423
whither he is gone down to *p* it .... 1Kin 21:18 — 3423
that ye may *p* this good land, and .... 1Chr 28:8 — 3423
land, unto which ye go to *p* it .... Ezr 9:11 — 3423
them that they should go in to *p* .... Neh 9:15 — 3423

that they should go in to *p* it	Neh 9:23	3423
So am I made to *p* months of	Job 7:3	5157
makest me to *p* the iniquities of	Job 13:26	3423
the house of Israel shall *p* them	Is 14:2	5157
nor *p* the land, nor fill the face	Is 14:21	3423
and the bittern shall *p* it	Is 34:11	3423
they shall *p* it for ever, from	Is 34:17	3423
his trust in me shall *p* the land	Is 57:13	5157
land they shall *p* the double	Is 61:7	3423
their fathers, and they shall *p* it	Jer 30:3	3423
they shall *p* their houses	Eze 7:24	3423
and shall ye *p* the land	Eze 33:25	3423
and shall ye *p* the land	Eze 33:26	3423
shall be mine, and we will *p* it	Eze 35:10	3423
and they shall *p* thee, and thou	Eze 36:12	3423
p the kingdom for ever, even for	Dan 7:18	2631
silver, nettles shall *p* them	Hos 9:6	3423
to *p* the land of the Amorite	Amos 2:10	3423
That they may *p* the remnant of	Amos 9:12	3423
Jacob shall *p* their possessions	Obad 17	3423
south shall *p* the mount of Esau	Obad 19	3423
they shall *p* the fields of	Obad 19	3423
and Benjamin shall *p* Gilead	Obad 19	3423
shall *p* that of the Canaanites	Obad 20	
shall *p* the cities of the south	Obad 20	423
to *p* the dwellingplaces that are	Hab 1:6	423
remnant of my people shall *p* them	Zeph 2:9	5157
this people to *p* all these things	Zec 8:12	5157
I give tithes of all that I *p*	Lk 18:12	2932
In your patience *p* ye your souls	Lk 21:19	2932
to *p* his vessel in sanctification	1Th 4:4	2932

POSSESSED

p his land from Arnon unto Jabbok	Num 21:24	3423
and they *p* his land	Num 21:35	3423
which we *p* at that time, from	Deut 3:12	3423
they *p* his land, and the land of	Deut 4:47	3423
into the land which thy fathers *p*	Deut 30:5	3423
they also have *p* the land which	Josh 1:15	3423
p their land on the other side	Josh 12:1	3423
yet very much land to be *p*	Josh 13:1	3423
p it, and dwelt therein, and called	Josh 19:47	3423
and they *p* it, and dwelt therein	Josh 21:43	3423
possession, whereof they were *p*	Josh 22:9	270
and *p* the city of palm trees	Judg 3:13	3423
so Israel *p* all the land of the	Judg 11:21	3423
they *p* all the coasts of the	Judg 11:22	3423
they *p* Samaria, and dwelt in the	2Kin 17:24	3423
so they *p* the land of Sihon, and	Neh 9:22	3423
p the land, and thou subduedst	Neh 9:24	3423
p houses full of all goods, wells	Neh 9:25	3423
For thou hast *p* my reins	Ps 139:13	7069
The LORD *p* me in the beginning of	Prov 8:22	7069
have *p* it but a little while	Is 63:18	
shall be *p* again in this land	Jer 32:15	7069
And they came in, and *p* it	Jer 32:23	3423
that the saints *p* the kingdom	Dan 7:22	2631
and those which were *p* with devils	Mt 4:24	1139
him many that were *p* with devils	Mt 8:16	1139
there met him two *p* with devils	Mt 8:28	1139
befallen to the *p* of the devils	Mt 8:33	1139
to him a dumb man *p* with a devil	Mt 9:32	1139
unto him one *p* with a devil	Mt 12:22	1139
and them that were *p* with devils	Mk 1:32	1139
see him that was *p* with the devil	Mk 5:15	1139
to him that was *p* with the devil	Mk 5:16	1139
he that had been *p* with the devil	Mk 5:18	1139
was *p* of the devils was healed	Lk 8:36	1139
the things which he *p* was his own	Acts 4:32	5224
out of many that were *p* with them	Acts 8:7	2192
a certain damsel *p* with a spirit	Acts 16:16	2192
that buy, as though they *p* not	1Cor 7:30	2722

POSSESSEST

p it, and dwellest therein	Deut 26:1	3423

POSSESSETH

that *p* an inheritance in any	Num 36:8	3423
of the things which he *p*	Lk 12:15	5224

POSSESSING

nothing, and yet *p* all things	2Cor 6:10	2722

POSSESSION

of Canaan, for an everlasting *p*	Gen 17:8	272
give me a *p* of a buryingplace	Gen 23:4	272
a *p* of a buryingplace amongst you	Gen 23:9	272
Unto Abraham for a *p* in the	Gen 23:18	4736
made sure unto Abraham for a *p* of	Gen 23:20	272
For he had *p* of flocks, and	Gen 26:14	4735
p of herds, and great store of	Gen 26:14	4735
in the land of their *p*	Gen 36:43	272
gave them a *p* in the land of	Gen 47:11	272

after thee for an everlasting *p*	Gen 48:4	272
Hittite for a *p* of a buryingplace	Gen 49:30	272
bought with the field for a *p* of	Gen 50:13	272
which I give to you for a *p*	Lev 14:34	272
in a house of the land of your *p*	Lev 14:34	272
shall return every man unto his *p*	Lev 25:10	272
shall return every man unto his *p*	Lev 25:13	272
in all the land of your *p* ye	Lev 25:24	272
and hath sold away some of his *p*	Lev 25:25	272
that he may return unto his *p*	Lev 25:27	272
and he shall return unto his *p*	Lev 25:28	272
houses of the cities of their *p*	Lev 25:32	272
was sold, and the city of his *p*	Lev 25:33	272
p among the children of Israel	Lev 25:33	272
for it is their perpetual *p*	Lev 25:34	272
unto the *p* of his fathers shall	Lev 25:41	272
and they shall be your *p*	Lev 25:45	272
you, to inherit them for a *p*	Lev 25:46	272
some part of a field of his *p*	Lev 27:16	272
the *p* thereof shall be the	Lev 27:21	272
is not of the fields of his *p*	Lev 27:22	272
whom the *p* of the land did belong	Lev 27:24	272
beast, and of the field of his *p*	Lev 27:28	272
And Edom shall be a *p*	Num 24:18	3424
also shall be a *p* for his enemies	Num 24:18	3424
According to the lot shall the *p*	Num 26:56	5159
Give unto us therefore a *p* among	Num 27:4	272
a *p* of an inheritance among their	Num 27:7	272
given unto thy servants for a *p*	Num 32:5	272
shall be your *p* before the LORD	Num 32:22	272
them the land of Gilead for a *p*	Num 32:29	272
that the *p* of our inheritance on	Num 32:32	272
of their *p* cities to dwell in	Num 35:2	272
the *p* of the children of Israel	Num 35:8	272
return into the land of his *p*	Num 35:28	272
mount Seir unto Esau for a *p*	Deut 2:5	3425
give thee of their land for a *p*	Deut 2:9	3425
unto the children of Lot for a *p*	Deut 2:9	3425
Israel did unto the land of his *p*	Deut 2:12	3425
of the children of Ammon any *p*	Deut 2:19	3425
unto the children of Lot for a *p*	Deut 2:19	3425
ye return every man unto his *p*	Deut 3:20	3425
the substance that was in their *p*	Deut 11:6	7272
the children of Israel for a *p*	Deut 32:49	272
return unto the land of your *p*	Josh 1:15	272
it for a *p* unto the Reubenites	Josh 12:6	3425
a *p* according to their divisions	Josh 12:7	3425
this was the *p* of the half tribe	Josh 13:29	
the son of Jephunneh for his *p*	Josh 21:12	272
of the Levites within the *p* of	Josh 24:11	272
tents, and unto the land of your *p*	Josh 22:4	272
Moses had given *p* in Bashan	Josh 22:7	
of Gilead, to the land of their *p*	Josh 22:9	272
if the land of your *p* be unclean	Josh 22:19	272
the land of the *p* of the LORD	Josh 22:19	272
dwelleth, and take *p* among us	Josh 22:19	270
take *p* of the vineyard of Naboth	1Kin 21:15	3423
the Jezreelite, to take *p* of it	1Kin 21:16	3423
Hast thou killed, and also taken *p*	1Kin 21:19	3423
p of the king, and of his sons,	1Chr 28:1	4735
left their suburbs and their *p*	2Chr 11:14	272
to come to cast us out of thy *p*	2Chr 20:11	3425
returned, every man to his *p*	2Chr 31:1	272
one in his *p* in their cities	Neh 11:3	272
parts of the earth for thy *p*	Ps 2:8	272
the land in *p* by their own sword	Ps 44:3	3423
may dwell there, and have it in *p*	Ps 69:35	3423
ourselves the houses of God in *p*	Ps 83:12	3423
shall have good things in *p*	Prov 28:10	5157
also make it a *p* for the bittern	Is 14:23	4180
unto us is this land given in *p*	Eze 11:15	4181
to the men of the east for a *p*	Eze 25:4	4181
Ammonites, and will give them in *p*	Eze 25:10	4181
ancient high places are ours in *p*	Eze 36:2	4181
that ye might be a *p* unto the	Eze 36:3	4181
appointed my land into their *p*	Eze 36:5	4181
ye shall give them no *p* in Israel	Eze 44:28	272
I am their *p*	Eze 44:28	272
for a *p* for twenty chambers	Eze 45:5	272
ye shall appoint the *p* of the	Eze 45:6	272
of the *p* of the city, before the	Eze 45:7	272
before the *p* of the city, from	Eze 45:7	272
the land shall be his *p* in Israel	Eze 45:8	272
shall be their *p* by inheritance	Eze 46:16	272
to thrust them out of their *p*	Eze 46:18	272
sons inheritance out of his own *p*	Eze 46:18	272
scattered every man from his *p*	Eze 46:18	272
with the *p* of the city	Eze 48:20	272
of the *p* of the city, over	Eze 48:21	272
from the *p* of the Levites	Eze 48:22	272
from the *p* of the city, being in	Eze 48:22	272

P

with Sapphira his wife, sold a *p*.............Acts 5:1   2933
he would give it to him for a *p* ....Acts 7:5   2697
Jesus into the *p* of the Gentiles..............Acts 7:45   2697
the redemption of the purchased *p* ....Eph 1:14   4047

POSSESSIONS
ye therein, and get you *p* therein ....Gen 34:10   270
and they had *p* therein, and grew, ...Gen 47:27   270
they shall have *p* among you in ....Num 32:30   270
in Maon, whose *p* were in Carmel 1Sa 25:2   4639
And their *p* and habitations were, ...1Chr 7:28   272
in their *p* in their cities were 1Chr 9:2   272
p of flocks and herds in abundance.......2Chr 32:29   4735
also I had great *p* of great ....Eccl 2:7   4735
of Jacob shall possess their *p* ....Obad 17   4180
for he had great *p* ....Mt 19:22   2933
for he had great *p* ....Mk 10:22   2933
And sold their *p* and goods, and ....Acts 2:45   2933
In the same quarters were *p* of ....Acts 28:7   5564

POSSESSOR
high God, *p* of heaven and earth ....Gen 14:19   7069
the *p* of heaven and earth, ...Gen 14:22   7069

POSSESSORS
Whose *p* slay them, and hold ....Zec 11:5   7069
for as many as were *p* of lands or ....Acts 4:34   2935

POSSIBLE
but with God all things are *p* ....Mt 19:26   *1415*
insomuch that, if it were *p* ....Mt 24:24   *1415*
saying, O my Father, if it be *p* ....Mt 26:39   *1415*
all things are *p* to him that ....Mk 9:23   *1415*
for with God all things are *p* ....Mk 10:27   *1415*
wonders, to seduce, if it were *p* ....Mk 13:22   *1415*
and prayed that, if it were *p*...................Mk 14:35   *1415*
all things are *p* unto thee ....Mk 14:36   *1415*
with men are *p* with God ....Lk 18:27   *1415*
because it was not *p* that he ....Acts 2:24   *1415*
he hasted, if it were *p* for him ....Acts 20:16   *1415*
they were minded, if it were *p* ....Acts 27:39   *1410*
If it be *p*, as much as lieth in ....Rom 12:18   *1415*
record, that, if it had been *p* ....Gal 4:15   *1415*
For it is not *p* that the blood of ....Heb 10:4   *102*

POST
on the upper door *p* of the houses ....Ex 12:7   4947
to the door, or unto the door *p* ....Ex 21:6   4201
by a *p* of the temple of the LORD 1Sa 1:9   4201
Now my days are swifter than a *p* ....Job 9:25   7323
One *p* shall run to meet another, ...Jer 51:31   7323
even unto the *p* of the court ....Eze 40:14   352
upon each *p* were palm trees ....Eze 40:16   352
and measured each *p* of the porch ....Eze 40:48   352
and measured the *p* of the door ....Eze 41:3   352
their *p* by my posts, and the wall ....Eze 43:8   4201
shall stand by the *p* of the gate ....Eze 46:2   4201

POSTERITY
to preserve you a *p* in the earth ....Gen 45:7   7611
If any man of you or of your *p* ....Num 9:10   1755
I will take away the *p* of Baasha 1Kin 16:3   310
of Baasha, and the *p* of his house.........1Kin 16:3   310
thee, and will take away thy *p* 1Kin 21:21   310
yet their *p* approve their sayings ....Ps 49:13   310
Let his *p* be cut off................................Ps 109:13   319
and not to his *p*, nor according to ....Dan 11:4   319
hooks, and your *p* with fishhooks ....Amos 4:2   319

POSTS
and strike it on the two side *p*................Ex 12:7   4201
the two side *p* with the blood ....Ex 12:22   4201
the lintel, and on the two side *p* ....Ex 12:23   4201
them upon the *p* of thy house ....Deut 6:9   4201
upon the door *p* of thine house ....Deut 11:20   4201
gate of the city, and the two *p* ....Judg 16:3   4201
side *p* were a fifth part of the 1Kin 6:31   4201
of the temple of olive tree......................1Kin 6:33   4201
p were square, with the windows...........1Kin 7:5   4201
also the house, the beams, the *p* 2Chr 3:7   5592
So the *p* went with the letters 2Chr 30:6   7323
So the *p* passed from city to city 2Chr 30:10   7323
the letters were sent by *p* into ....Est 3:13   7323
The *p* went out, being hastened by........Est 3:15   7323
and sent letters by *p* on horseback........Est 8:10   7323
So the *p* that rode upon mules and ....Est 8:14   7323
waiting at the *p* of my doors ....Prov 8:34   4201
the *p* of the door moved at the ....Is 6:4   520
the *p* hast thou set up thy ....Is 57:8   4201
the *p* thereof, two cubits ....Eze 40:9   352
the *p* had one measure on this ....Eze 40:10   352
He made also *p* of threescore ....Eze 40:14   352
to their *p* within the gate round.............Eze 40:16   352
the *p* thereof and the arches ....Eze 40:21   352

and he measured the *p* thereof ....Eze 40:24   352
on that side, upon the *p* thereof............Eze 40:26   352
the *p* thereof, and the arches ....Eze 40:29   352
trees were upon the *p* thereof ....Eze 40:31   352
the *p* thereof, and the arches ....Eze 40:34   352
trees were upon the *p* thereof ....Eze 40:34   352
the *p* thereof, and the arches ....Eze 40:36   352
the *p* thereof were toward the ....Eze 40:37   352
trees were upon the *p* thereof ....Eze 40:37   352
were by the *p* of the gates ....Eze 40:38   352
and there were pillars by the *p* ....Eze 40:49   352
to the temple, and measured the *p* ....Eze 41:1   352
The door *p*, and the narrow windows......Eze 41:16   5592
The *p* of the temple were squared,.........Eze 41:21   4201
thresholds, and their post by my *p* ....Eze 43:8   4201
and put it upon the *p* of the house ....Eze 45:19   4201
upon the *p* of the gate of the ....Eze 45:19   4201
of the door, that the *p* may shake ....Amos 9:1   5592

POT
Moses said unto Aaron, Take a *p* ....Ex 16:33   6803
and if it be sodden in a brasen *p*..........Lev 6:28   3627
and he put the broth in a *p* ....Judg 6:19   6517
pan, or kettle, or caldron, or *p*..............1Sa 2:14   6517
in the house, save a *p* of oil 2Kin 4:2   610
his servant, Set on the great *p*..............2Kin 4:38   5518
shred them into the *p* of pottage 2Kin 4:39   5518
of God, there is death in the *p* 2Kin 4:40   5518
And he cast it into the *p*.......................2Kin 4:41   5518
And there was no harm in the *p* 2Kin 4:41   5518
as out of a seething *p* or caldron...........Job 41:20   1731
maketh the deep to boil like a *p* ....Job 41:31   5518
the sea like a *p* of ointment ....Job 41:31   5518
The fining *p* is for silver, and................Prov 17:3   4715
As the fining *p* for silver ....Prov 27:21   4715
the crackling of thorns under a *p* ....Eccl 7:6   5518
and I said, I see a seething *p* ....Jer 1:13   5518
Set on a *p*, set it on, and also...............Eze 24:3   5518
to the *p* whose scum is therein, ...Eze 24:6   5518
chop them in pieces, as for the *p* ....Mic 3:3   5518
every *p* in Jerusalem and in Judah........Zec 14:21   5518
was the golden *p* that had manna ....Heb 9:4   *4713*

POTENTATE
who is the blessed and only *P* 1Ti 6:15   *1413*

POTIPHAR (pot'i-far) A captain of Pharaoh's guard.
sold him into Egypt unto *P* ....Gen 37:36   6318
and *P*, an officer of Pharaoh, ...Gen 39:1   6318

POTI-PHERAH Priest of On.
the daughter of *P* priest of On................Gen 41:45   6319
of *P* priest of On bare unto him ....Gen 41:50   6319
of *P* priest of On bare unto him ....Gen 46:20   6319

POTS
Egypt, when we sat by the flesh *p* ....Ex 16:3   5518
the vessels of the altar, the *p*................Ex 38:3   5518
it be oven, or ranges for *p* ....Lev 11:35
And the *p*, and the shovels, and the 1Kin 7:45   5518
And the *p*, and the shovels, and the 2Kin 25:14   5518
And Huram made the *p*, and the 2Chr 4:11   5518
The *p* also, and the shovels, and............2Chr 4:16   5518
holy offerings seethe they in *p* 2Chr 35:13   5518
Before your *p* can feel the thorns ....Ps 58:9   5518
Though ye have lien among the *p*...........Ps 68:13   8240
hands were delivered from the *p* ....Ps 81:6   1731
of the Rechabites *p* full of wine.............Jer 35:5   1375
the *p* in the LORD's house shall ....Zec 14:20   5518
as the washing of cups, and *p*...............Mk 7:4   *3582*
of men, as the washing of *p* ....Mk 7:8   *3582*

POTSHERD
he took him a *p* to scrape himself ....Job 2:8   2789
My strength is dried up like a *p* ....Ps 22:15   2789
a *p* covered with silver dross ....Prov 26:23   2789
Let the *p* strive with the ....Is 45:9   2789

POTSHERDS
strive with the *p* of the earth ....Is 45:9   2789

POTTAGE
And Jacob sod *p*...................................Gen 25:29   5138
I pray thee, with that same red *p* ....Gen 25:30   5138
gave Esau bread and *p* of lentiles..........Gen 25:34   5138
seethe *p* for the sons of the 2Kin 4:38   5138
and shred them into the pot of *p* 2Kin 4:39   5138
as they were eating of the *p*..................2Kin 4:40   5138
his skirt do touch bread, or *p*.................Hag 2:12   5138

POTTER
morter, and as the *p* treadeth clay ....Is 41:25   3335
we are the clay, and thou our *p*..............Is 64:8   3335
was marred in the hand of the *p* ....Jer 18:4   3335
seemed good to the *p* to make it ....Jer 18:4   3335

cannot I do with you as this *p*	Jer 18:6	3335
the work of the hands of the *p*	Lam 4:2	3335
said unto me, Cast it unto the *p*	Zec 11:13	3335
cast them to the *p* in the house	Zec 11:13	3335
Hath not the *p* power over the	Rom 9:21	2763
as the vessels of a *p* shall they	Rev 2:27	2764

POTTER'S

them in pieces like a *p* vessel	Ps 2:9	3335
shall be esteemed as the *p* clay	Is 29:16	3335
Arise, and go down to the *p* house	Jer 18:2	3335
Then I went down to the *p* house	Jer 18:3	3335
as the clay is in the *p* hand	Jer 18:6	3335
get a *p* earthen bottle, and take	Jer 19:1	3335
city, as one breaketh a *p* vessel	Jer 19:11	3335
and bought with them the *p* field	Mt 27:7	2763
And gave them for the *p* field	Mt 27:10	2763

POTTERS

These were the *p*, and those that	1Chr 4:23	3335

POTTERS'

p vessel that is broken in pieces	Is 30:14	3335
the feet and toes, part of *p* clay	Dan 2:41	6353

POUND

three *p* of gold went to one	1Kin 10:17	4488
and five thousand *p* of silver	Ezr 2:69	4488
thy *p* hath gained ten pounds	Lk 19:16	3414
thy *p* hath gained five pounds	Lk 19:18	3414
Lord, behold, here is thy *p*	Lk 19:20	3414
stood by, Take from him the *p*	Lk 19:24	3414
Then took Mary a *p* of ointment of	Jn 12:3	3046
aloes, about an hundred *p* weight	Jn 19:39	3046

POUNDS

and two hundred *p* of silver	Neh 7:71	4488
gold, and two thousand *p* of silver	Neh 7:72	4488
servants, and delivered them ten *p*	Lk 19:13	3414
Lord, thy pound hath gained ten *p*	Lk 19:16	3414
thy pound hath gained five *p*	Lk 19:18	3414
and give it to him that hath ten *p*	Lk 19:24	3414
unto him, Lord, he hath ten *p*	Lk 19:25	3414

POUR

river, and *p* it upon the dry land	Ex 4:9	8210
p it upon his head, and anoint him	Ex 29:7	3332
p all the blood beside the bottom	Ex 29:12	8210
neither shall ye *p* drink offering	Ex 30:9	5258
he shall *p* oil upon it, and put	Lev 2:1	3332
it in pieces, and *p* oil thereon	Lev 2:6	3332
shall *p* all the blood of the	Lev 4:7	8210
shall *p* out all the blood at the	Lev 4:18	8210
shall *p* out his blood at the	Lev 4:25	8210
shall *p* out all the blood thereof	Lev 4:30	8210
shall *p* out all the blood thereof	Lev 4:34	8210
p it into the palm of his own	Lev 14:15	3332
in the priest's hand he shall *p*	Lev 14:18	5414
the priest shall *p* of the oil	Lev 14:26	3332
they shall *p* out the dust that	Lev 14:41	8210
he shall even *p* out the blood	Lev 17:13	8210
he shall *p* no oil upon it, nor	Num 5:15	3332
He shall *p* the water out of his	Num 24:7	5140
ye shall *p* it upon the earth as	Deut 12:16	8210
thou shalt *p* it upon the earth as	Deut 12:24	8210
thou shalt *p* it upon the ground	Deut 15:23	8210
this rock, and *p* out the broth	Judg 6:20	8210
p it on the burnt sacrifice, and	1Kin 18:33	3332
P out for the people, that they	2Kin 4:41	3332
p it on his head, and say, Thus	2Kin 9:3	3332
they *p* down rain according to the	Job 36:27	2212
things, I *p* out my soul in me	Ps 42:4	8210
p out your heart before him	Ps 62:8	8210
P out thine indignation upon them	Ps 69:24	8210
P out thy wrath upon the heathen	Ps 79:6	8210
I will *p* out my spirit unto you,	Prov 1:23	5042
For I will *p* water upon him that	Is 44:3	3332
I will *p* my spirit upon thy seed,	Is 44:3	3332
above, and let the skies *p* down	Is 45:8	5140
I will *p* it out upon the children	Jer 6:11	8210
to *p* out drink offerings unto	Jer 7:18	5258
P out thy fury upon the heathen	Jer 10:25	8210
for I will *p* their wickedness	Jer 14:16	8210
p out their blood by the force of	Jer 18:21	5064
to *p* out drink offerings unto her	Jer 44:17	5258
to *p* out drink offerings unto her	Jer 44:18	5258
p out drink offerings unto her,	Jer 44:19	5258
to *p* out drink offerings unto her	Jer 44:25	5258
p out thine heart like water	Lam 2:19	8210
Now will I shortly *p* out my fury	Eze 7:8	8210
p out my fury upon it in blood,	Eze 14:19	8210
I will *p* out my fury upon them,	Eze 20:8	8210
I would *p* out my fury upon them	Eze 20:13	8210

I would *p* out my fury upon them,	Eze 20:21	8210
I will *p* out mine indignation	Eze 21:31	8210
it on, and also *p* water into it	Eze 24:3	3332
I will *p* my fury upon Sin, the	Eze 30:15	8210
therefore I will *p* out my wrath	Hos 5:10	8210
that I will *p* out my spirit upon	Joel 2:28	8210
those days will I *p* out my spirit	Joel 2:29	8210
I will *p* down the stones thereof	Mic 1:6	5064
to *p* upon them mine indignation,	Zeph 3:8	8210
I will *p* upon the house of David,	Zec 12:10	8210
p you out a blessing, that there	Mal 3:10	7324
I will *p* out of my Spirit upon	Acts 2:17	1632
on my handmaidens I will *p* out in	Acts 2:18	1632
p out the vials of the wrath of	Rev 16:1	1632

POURED

and *p* oil upon the top of it	Gen 28:18	3332
he *p* a drink offering thereon	Gen 35:14	5258
and he *p* oil thereon	Gen 35:14	3332
the rain was not *p* upon the earth	Ex 9:33	5413
man's flesh shall it not be *p*	Ex 30:32	3251
place, where the ashes are *p* out	Lev 4:12	8211
where the ashes are *p* out shall	Lev 4:12	8211
he *p* of the anointing oil upon	Lev 8:12	3332
p the blood at the bottom of the	Lev 8:15	3332
p out the blood at the bottom of	Lev 9:9	3332
head the anointing oil was *p*	Lev 21:10	3332
to be *p* unto the LORD for a drink	Num 28:7	5258
of thy sacrifices shall be *p* out	Deut 12:27	8210
but have *p* out my soul before the	1Sa 1:15	8210
p it out before the LORD, and	1Sa 7:6	8210
p it upon his head, and kissed him	1Sa 10:1	3332
a pan, and *p* them out before him	2Sa 13:9	3332
but *p* it out unto the LORD	2Sa 23:16	5258
that are upon it shall be *p* out	1Kin 13:3	8210
the ashes *p* out from the altar,	1Kin 13:5	8210
which *p* water on the hands of	2Kin 3:11	3332
and she *p* out	2Kin 4:5	3332
So they *p* out for the men to eat	2Kin 4:40	3332
he *p* the oil on his head, and said	2Kin 9:6	3332
and *p* his drink offering, and	2Kin 16:13	5258
but *p* it out to the LORD,	1Chr 11:18	5258
my wrath shall not be *p* out upon	2Chr 12:7	5413
of the LORD that is *p* out upon us	2Chr 34:21	5413
shall be *p* out upon this place	2Chr 34:25	5413
my roarings are *p* out like the	Job 3:24	5413
Hast thou not *p* me out as milk,	Job 10:10	5413
the rock *p* me out rivers of oil	Job 29:6	6694
And now my soul is *p* out upon me	Job 30:16	8210
I am *p* out like water, and all my	Ps 22:14	8210
grace is *p* into thy lips	Ps 45:2	3332
The clouds *p* out water	Ps 77:17	2229
I *p* out my complaint before him	Ps 142:2	8210
thy name is as ointment *p* forth	Song 1:3	7324
they *p* out a prayer when thy	Is 26:16	6694
For the LORD hath *p* out upon you	Is 29:10	5258
Until the spirit be *p* upon us	Is 32:15	6168
Therefore he hath *p* upon him the	Is 42:25	8210
because he hath *p* out his soul	Is 53:12	6168
them hast thou *p* a drink offering	Is 57:6	8210
my fury shall be *p* out upon this	Jer 7:20	5413
have *p* out drink offerings unto	Jer 19:13	5258
p out drink offerings unto other	Jer 32:29	5258
my fury hath been *p* forth upon	Jer 42:18	5413
shall my fury be *p* forth upon you	Jer 42:18	5413
my fury and mine anger was *p* forth	Jer 44:6	5413
p out drink offerings unto her,	Jer 44:19	5258
he *p* out his fury like fire	Lam 2:4	8210
my liver is *p* upon the earth, for	Lam 2:11	8210
when their soul was *p* out into	Lam 2:12	8210
p out in the top of every street	Lam 4:1	8210
he hath *p* out his fierce anger,	Lam 4:11	8210
Because thy filthiness was *p* out	Eze 16:36	8210
p out there their drink offerings	Eze 20:28	5258
out arm, and with fury *p* out	Eze 20:33	8210
out arm, and with fury *p* out.	Eze 20:34	8210
LORD have *p* out my fury upon you	Eze 22:22	8210
Therefore have I *p* out mine	Eze 22:31	8210
p their whoredom upon her	Eze 23:8	8210
she *p* it not upon the ground, to	Eze 24:7	8210
Wherefore I *p* my fury upon them	Eze 36:18	8210
for I have *p* out my spirit upon	Eze 39:29	8210
therefore the curse is *p* upon us	Dan 9:11	5413
shall be *p* upon the desolate	Dan 9:27	5413
that are *p* down a steep place	Mic 1:4	5064
his fury is *p* out like fire, and	Nah 1:6	5413
blood shall be *p* out as dust	Zeph 1:17	8210
p it on his head, as he sat at	Mt 26:7	2708
For in that she hath *p* this	Mt 26:12	906
the box, and *p* it on his head	Mk 14:3	2708
p out the changers' money, and	Jn 2:15	1632

P

that on the Gentiles also was *p*	Acts 10:45	*1632*
which is *p* out without mixture	Rev 14:10	*2767*
p out his vial upon the earth	Rev 16:2	*1632*
the second angel *p* out his vial	Rev 16:3	*1632*
the third angel *p* out his vial	Rev 16:4	*1632*
the fourth angel *p* out his vial	Rev 16:8	*1632*
the fifth angel *p* out his vial	Rev 16:10	*1632*
the sixth angel *p* out his vial	Rev 16:12	*1632*
the seventh angel *p* out his vial	Rev 16:17	*1632*

POUREDST
p out thy fornications on every	Eze 16:15	8210

POURETH
He *p* contempt upon princes, and	Job 12:21	8210
he *p* out my gall upon the ground	Job 16:13	8210
but mine eye *p* out tears unto God	Job 16:20	1811
and he *p* out of the same	Ps 75:8	5064
p out his complaint before the	Ps 102:*t*	8210
He *p* contempt upon princes, and	Ps 107:40	8210
mouth of fools *p* out foolishness	Prov 15:2	5042
of the wicked *p* out evil things	Prov 15:28	5042
p them out upon the face of the	Amos 5:8	8210
p them out upon the face of the	Amos 9:6	8210
After that he *p* water into a	Jn 13:5	*906*

POURING
the residue of Israel in thy *p*	Eze 9:8	8210
p in oil and wine, and set him on	Lk 10:34	

POURTRAY
thee, and *p* upon it the city, even	Eze 4:1	2710

POURTRAYED
p upon the wall round about	Eze 8:10	2707
when she saw men *p* upon the wall	Eze 23:14	2707
of the Chaldeans *p* with vermilion	Eze 23:14	2710

POVERTY
and all that thou hast, come to *p*	Gen 45:11	3423
So shall thy *p* come as one that	Prov 6:11	7389
of the poor is their *p*	Prov 10:15	7389
than is meet, but it tendeth to *p*	Prov 11:24	4270
P and shame shall be to him that	Prov 13:18	7389
not sleep, lest thou come to *p*	Prov 20:13	3423
and the glutton shall come to *p*	Prov 23:21	3423
So shall thy *p* come as one that	Prov 24:34	7389
vain persons shall have *p* enough	Prov 28:19	7389
not that *p* shall come upon him	Prov 28:22	2639
give me neither *p* nor riches	Prov 30:8	7389
Let him drink, and forget his *p*	Prov 31:7	7389
their deep *p* abounded unto the	2Cor 8:2	*4432*
ye through his *p* might be rich	2Cor 8:9	*4432*
thy works, and tribulation, and *p*	Rev 2:9	*4432*

POWDER
it in the fire, and ground it to *p*	Ex 32:20	1854
shall make the rain of thy land *p*	Deut 28:24	80
Kidron, and stamped it small to *p*	2Kin 23:6	6083
cast the *p* thereof upon the	2Kin 23:6	6083
place, and stamped it small to *p*	2Kin 23:15	6083
beaten the graven images into *p*	2Chr 34:7	1854
fall, it will grind him to *p*	Mt 21:44	*3039*
fall, it will grind him to *p*	Lk 20:18	*3039*

POWDERS
with all *p* of the merchant	Song 3:6	81

POWER
ye know that with all my *p* I have	Gen 31:6	3581
It is in the *p* of my hand to do	Gen 31:29	410
as a prince hast thou *p* with God	Gen 32:28	8280
dignity, and the excellency of *p*	Gen 49:3	5794
thee up, for to shew in thee my *p*	Ex 9:16	3581
O Lord, is become glorious in *p*	Ex 15:6	3581
strange nation he shall have no *p*	Ex 21:8	4910
of the land of Egypt with great *p*	Ex 32:11	3581
I will break the pride of your *p*	Lev 26:19	5797
ye shall have no *p* to stand	Lev 26:37	8617
let the *p* of my Lord be great,	Num 14:17	3581
have I now any *p* at all to say	Num 22:38	3201
with his mighty *p* out of Egypt	Deut 4:37	3581
And thou say in thine heart, My *p*	Deut 8:17	3581
that giveth thee *p* to get wealth	Deut 8:18	3581
broughtest out by thy mighty *p*	Deut 9:29	3581
he seeth that their *p* is gone	Deut 32:36	3027
they had no *p* to flee this way or	Josh 8:20	3027
a great people, and hast great *p*	Josh 17:17	3581
a Benjamite, a mighty man of *p*	1Sa 9:1	2428
until they had no more *p* to weep	1Sa 30:4	3581
God is my strength and *p*	2Sa 22:33	2428
of the land of Egypt with great *p*	2Kin 17:36	3581
their inhabitants were of small *p*	2Kin 19:26	3027
Joab led forth the *p* of the army	1Chr 20:1	2428
Lord, is the greatness, and the *p*	1Chr 29:11	1369

and in thine hand is *p* and might	1Chr 29:12	3581
many, or with them that have no *p*	2Chr 14:11	3581
and in thine hand is there not *p*	2Chr 20:6	3581
no *p* to keep still the kingdom	2Chr 22:9	3581
for God hath *p* to help, and to	2Chr 25:8	3581
that made war with mighty *p*	2Chr 26:13	3581
all his *p* with him,) unto	2Chr 32:9	4475
made them to cease by force and *p*	Ezr 4:23	2429
but his *p* and his wrath is against	Ezr 8:22	5797
thou hast redeemed by thy great *p*	Neh 1:10	3581
is it in our *p* to redeem them	Neh 5:5	3027
the *p* of Persia and Media, the	Est 1:3	2428
all the *p* of the people and	Est 8:11	2428
Jews hoped to have *p* over them	Est 9:1	7980
And all the acts of his *p* and of	Est 10:2	8633
all that he hath is in thy *p*	Job 1:12	3027
and in war from the *p* of the sword	Job 5:20	3027
become old, yea, are mighty in *p*	Job 21:7	2428
plead against me with his great *p*	Job 23:6	3581
also the mighty with his *p*	Job 24:22	3581
thou helped him that is without *p*	Job 26:2	3581
He divideth the sea with his *p*	Job 26:12	3581
of his *p* who can understand	Job 26:14	1369
Behold, God exalteth by his *p*	Job 36:22	3581
he is excellent in *p*, and in	Job 37:23	3581
not conceal his parts, nor his *p*	Job 41:12	1369
so will we sing and praise thy *p*	Ps 21:13	1369
my darling from the *p* of the dog	Ps 22:20	3027
I have seen the wicked in great *p*	Ps 37:35	6184
my soul from the *p* of the grave	Ps 49:15	3027
scatter them by thy *p*	Ps 59:11	2428
But I will sing of thy *p*	Ps 59:16	5797
that *p* belongeth unto God	Ps 62:11	5797
To see thy *p* and thy glory, so as	Ps 63:2	5797
being girded with *p*	Ps 65:6	1369
thy *p* shall thine enemies submit	Ps 66:3	5797
He ruleth by his *p* for ever	Ps 66:7	1369
strength and *p* unto his people	Ps 68:35	8592
thy *p* to every one that is to	Ps 71:18	1369
by his *p* he brought in the south	Ps 78:26	5797
to the greatness of thy *p*	Ps 79:11	2220
Who knoweth the *p* of thine anger	Ps 90:11	5797
make his mighty *p* to be known	Ps 106:8	1369
be willing in the day of thy *p*	Ps 110:3	2428
his people the *p* of his works	Ps 111:6	3581
of thy kingdom, and talk of thy *p*	Ps 145:11	1369
Great is our Lord, and of great *p*	Ps 147:5	3581
him in the firmament of his *p*	Ps 150:1	5797
when it is in the *p* of thine hand	Prov 3:27	410
life are in the *p* of the tongue	Prov 18:21	3027
of their oppressors there was *p*	Eccl 4:1	3581
hath given him *p* to eat thereof	Eccl 5:19	7980
giveth him not *p* to eat thereof	Eccl 6:2	7980
the word of a king is, there is *p*	Eccl 8:4	7983
There is no man that hath *p* over	Eccl 8:8	7989
neither hath he *p* in the day of	Eccl 8:8	7983
their inhabitants were of small *p*	Is 37:27	3027
might, for that he is strong in *p*	Is 40:26	3581
He giveth *p* to the faint	Is 40:29	3581
and horse, the army and the *p*	Is 43:17	5808
from the *p* of the flame	Is 47:14	3027
or have I no *p* to deliver	Is 50:2	3581
He hath made the earth by his *p*	Jer 10:12	3581
upon the ground, by my great *p*	Jer 27:5	3581
and the earth by thy great *p*	Jer 32:17	3581
He hath made the earth by his *p*	Jer 51:15	3581
even without great *p* or many	Eze 17:9	2220
in thee to their *p* to shed blood	Eze 22:6	2220
pride of her *p* shall come down	Eze 30:6	5797
hath given thee a kingdom, *p*	Dan 2:37	2632
whose bodies the fire had no *p*	Dan 3:27	7981
the kingdom by the might of my *p*	Dan 4:30	2632
Daniel from the *p* of the lions	Dan 6:27	3028
ran unto him in the fury of his *p*	Dan 8:6	3581
there was no *p* in the ram to	Dan 8:7	3581
of the nation, but not in his *p*	Dan 8:22	3581
his *p* shall be mighty	Dan 8:24	3581
but not by his own *p*	Dan 8:24	3581
shall not retain the *p* of the arm	Dan 11:6	3581
And he shall stir up his *p*	Dan 11:25	3581
But he shall have *p* over the	Dan 11:43	4910
scatter the *p* of the holy people	Dan 12:7	3027
by his strength he had *p* with God	Hos 12:3	8280
he had *p* over the angel, and	Hos 12:4	7786
them from the *p* of the grave	Hos 13:14	3027
it is in the *p* of their hand	Mic 2:1	410
But truly I am full of *p* by the	Mic 3:8	3581
is slow to anger, and great in *p*	Nah 1:3	3581
strong, fortify thy *p* mightily	Nah 2:1	3581
imputing this his *p* unto his god	Hab 1:11	3581
be delivered from the *p* of evil	Hab 2:9	3709

and there was the hiding of his *p* .... Hab 3:4 — 5797
saying, Not by might, nor by *p* .... Zec 4:6 — 3581
and he will smite her *p* in the sea.......... Zec 9:4 — 2428
thine is the kingdom, and the *p* .... Mt 6:13 — 1411
hath *p* on earth to forgive sins............ Mt 9:6 — 1849
which had given such *p* unto men............ Mt 9:8 — 1849
he gave them *p* against unclean............ Mt 10:1 — 1849
the scriptures, nor the *p* of God...... Mt 22:29 — 1411
in the clouds of heaven with *p*.............. Mt 24:30 — 1411
sitting on the right hand of *p* .... Mt 26:64 — 1411
All *p* is given unto me in heaven .... Mt 28:18 — 1849
hath *p* on earth to forgive sins.............. Mk 2:10 — 1849
to have *p* to heal sicknesses, and .... Mk 3:15 — 1849
gave them *p* over unclean spirits........... Mk 6:7 — 1849
the kingdom of God come with *p* ...... Mk 9:1 — 1411
scriptures, neither the *p* of God........... Mk 12:24 — 1411
coming in the clouds with great *p* ...... Mk 13:26 — 1411
sitting on the right hand of *p* .... Mk 14:62 — 1411
p of Elias, to turn the hearts of.............. Lk 1:17 — 1411
the *p* of the Highest shall .... Lk 1:35 — 1411
All this *p* will I give thee, and .... Lk 4:6 — 1849
Jesus returned in the *p* of the .... Lk 4:14 — 1411
for his word was with *p* .... Lk 4:32 — 1849
p he commandeth the unclean.............. Lk 4:36 — 1411
the *p* of the Lord was present to .... Lk 5:17 — 1411
hath *p* upon earth to forgive sins .... Lk 5:24 — 1849
together, and gave them *p* and............ Lk 9:1 — 1411
all amazed at the mighty *p* of God .... Lk 9:43 — 3168
I give unto you *p* to tread on .... Lk 10:19 — 1849
and over all the *p* of the enemy.............. Lk 10:19 — 1411
killed hath *p* to cast into hell.................. Lk 12:5 — 1849
they might deliver him unto the *p* .... Lk 20:20 — 746
of man coming in a cloud with *p* .... Lk 21:27 — 1411
your hour, and the *p* of darkness........... Lk 22:53 — 1849
on the right hand of the *p* of God .... Lk 22:69 — 1411
ye be endued with *p* from on high .... Lk 24:49 — 1411
to them gave he *p* to become the .... Jn 1:12 — 1849
I have *p* to lay it down, and I .... Jn 10:18 — 1849
I have *p* to take it again........................ Jn 10:18 — 1849
hast given him *p* over all flesh.............. Jn 17:2 — 1849
not that I have *p* to crucify thee .... Jn 19:10 — 1849
and have *p* to release thee .... Jn 19:10 — 1849
have no *p* at all against me .... Jn 19:11 — 1849
the Father hath put in his own *p*........... Acts 1:7 — 1849
But ye shall receive *p*, after .... Acts 1:8 — 1411
as though by our own *p* or .... Acts 3:12 — 1411
the midst, they asked, By what *p* .... Acts 4:7 — 1411
with great *p* gave the apostles............ Acts 4:33 — 1849
sold, was it not in thine own *p* .... Acts 5:4 — 1849
And Stephen, full of faith and *p* .... Acts 6:8 — 1411
This man is the great *p* of God .... Acts 8:10 — 1411
Saying, Give me also this *p*.................. Acts 8:19 — 1849
with the Holy Ghost and with *p*............ Acts 10:38 — 1411
from the *p* of Satan unto God,............ Acts 26:18 — 1849
to be the Son of God with *p* .... Rom 1:4 — 1411
for it is the *p* of God unto .... Rom 1:16 — 1411
that are made, even his eternal *p*.......... Rom 1:20 — 1411
that I might shew my *p* in thee .... Rom 9:17 — 1411
not the potter *p* over the clay .... Rom 9:21 — 1849
his wrath, and to make his *p* known...... Rom 9:22 — 1415
For there is no *p* but of God .... Rom 13:1 — 1849
therefore resisteth the *p* .... Rom 13:2 — 1849
thou then not be afraid of the *p* .... Rom 13:3 — 1849
through the *p* of the Holy Ghost .... Rom 15:13 — 1411
by the *p* of the Spirit of God.................. Rom 15:19 — 1411
Now to him that is of *p* to .... Rom 16:25 — 1410
are saved it is the *p* of God .... 1Cor 1:18 — 1411
and Greeks, Christ the *p* of God............ 1Cor 1:24 — 1411
of the Spirit and of *p*.............................. 1Cor 2:4 — 1411
of men, but in the *p* of God .... 1Cor 2:5 — 1411
which are puffed up, but the *p*............... 1Cor 4:19 — 1411
of God is not in word, but in *p*............... 1Cor 4:20 — 1411
with the *p* of our Lord Jesus .... 1Cor 5:4 — 1411
not be brought under the *p* of any .... 1Cor 6:12 — 1850
also raise us up by his own *p* .... 1Cor 6:14 — 1411
wife hath not *p* of her own body .... 1Cor 7:4 — 1850
hath not *p* of his own body .... 1Cor 7:4 — 1850
but hath *p* over his own will, and .... 1Cor 7:37 — 1849
Have we not *p* to eat and to drink .... 1Cor 9:4 — 1849
Have we not *p* to lead about a .... 1Cor 9:5 — 1849
have not we *p* to forbear working........... 1Cor 9:6 — 1849
be partakers of this *p* over you .... 1Cor 9:12 — 1849
we have not used this *p*........................ 1Cor 9:12 — 1849
I abuse not my *p* in the gospel .... 1Cor 9:18 — 1849
have *p* on her head because of the .... 1Cor 11:10 — 1849
all rule and all authority and *p*.............. 1Cor 15:24 — 1411
it is raised in *p* .... 1Cor 15:43 — 1411
excellency of the *p* may be of God .... 2Cor 4:7 — 1411
word of truth, by the *p* of God .... 2Cor 6:7 — 1411
For to their *p*, I bear record,.................. 2Cor 8:3 — 1411
beyond their *p* they were willing.......... 2Cor 8:3 — 1411

that the *p* of Christ may rest .... 2Cor 12:9 — 1411
yet he liveth by the *p* of God.................. 2Cor 13:4 — 1411
him by the *p* of God toward you .... 2Cor 13:4 — 1411
according to the *p* which the Lord........ 2Cor 13:10 — 1849
of his *p* to us-ward who believe.............. Eph 1:19 — 1411
to the working of his mighty *p* .... Eph 1:19 — 2904
Far above all principality, and *p*............ Eph 1:21 — 1849
to the prince of the *p* of the air .... Eph 2:2 — 1849
by the effectual working of his *p* .... Eph 3:7 — 1411
according to the *p* that worketh .... Eph 3:20 — 1411
Lord, and in the *p* of his might .... Eph 6:10 — 2904
the *p* of his resurrection, and the .... Phil 3:10 — 1411
according to his glorious *p* .... Col 1:11 — 2904
us from the *p* of darkness...................... Col 1:13 — 1849
the head of all principality and *p* .... Col 2:10 — 1849
you in word only, but also in *p* .... 1Th 1:5 — 1411
Lord, and from the glory of his *p* .... 2Th 1:9 — 2479
and the work of faith with *p*.................. 2Th 1:11 — 1411
the working of Satan with all *p* .... 2Th 2:9 — 1411
Not because we have not *p* .... 2Th 3:9 — 1849
whom be honour and *p* everlasting .... 1Ti 6:16 — 2904
but of *p*, and of love, and of a.............. 2Ti 1:7 — 1411
gospel according to the *p* of God............ 2Ti 1:8 — 1411
but denying the *p* thereof .... 2Ti 3:5 — 1411
all things by the word of his *p* .... Heb 1:3 — 1411
him that had the *p* of death .... Heb 2:14 — 2904
but after the *p* of an endless .... Heb 7:16 — 1411
Who are kept by the *p* of God .... 1Pet 1:5 — 1411
According as his divine *p* hath .... 2Pet 1:3 — 1411
when we made known unto you the *p* .... 2Pet 1:16 — 1411
angels, which are greater in *p* .... 2Pet 2:11 — 2479
glory and majesty, dominion and *p* .... Jude 25 — 1849
will I give *p* over the nations .... Rev 2:26 — 1849
to receive glory and honour and *p*.......... Rev 4:11 — 1411
Lamb that was slain to receive *p*............ Rev 5:12 — 1411
and honour, and glory, and *p* .... Rev 5:13 — 2904
p was given to him that sat.................... Rev 6:4 — 1849
p was given unto them over the .... Rev 6:8 — 1849
and thanksgiving, and honour, and *p* .... Rev 7:12 — 1411
and unto them was given *p*, as the .... Rev 9:3 — 1849
the scorpions of the earth have *p* .... Rev 9:3 — 1849
their *p* was to hurt men five .... Rev 9:10 — 1849
For their *p* is in their mouth, and.......... Rev 9:19 — 1849
I will give *p* unto my two .... Rev 11:3
These have *p* to shut heaven, that.......... Rev 11:6 — 1849
have *p* over waters to turn them .... Rev 11:6 — 1849
hast taken to thee thy great *p* .... Rev 11:17 — 1411
our God, and the *p* of his Christ .... Rev 12:10 — 1849
and the dragon gave him his *p* .... Rev 13:2 — 1411
which gave *p* unto the beast .... Rev 13:4 — 1849
p was given unto him to continue.......... Rev 13:5 — 1849
p was given him over all kindreds .... Rev 13:7 — 1849
he exerciseth all the *p* of the .... Rev 13:12 — 1849
of those miracles which he had *p* .... Rev 13:14 — 1325
he had *p* to give life unto the .... Rev 13:15 — 1325
the altar, which had *p* over fire.............. Rev 14:18 — 1849
the glory of God, and from his *p* .... Rev 15:8 — 1411
p was given unto him to scorch .... Rev 16:8
which hath *p* over these plagues .... Rev 16:9 — 1849
but receive *p* as kings one hour .... Rev 17:12 — 1849
one mind, and shall give their *p* .... Rev 17:13 — 1411
down from heaven, having great *p* .... Rev 18:1 — 1849
and glory, and honour, and *p* .... Rev 19:1 — 1411
such the second death hath no *p* .... Rev 20:6 — 1849

POWERFUL
The voice of the LORD is *p* .... Ps 29:4 — 3581
say they, are weighty and *p*.................. 2Cor 10:10 — 2478
the word of God is quick, and *p* .... Heb 4:12 — 1756

POWERS
the *p* of the heavens shall be .... Mt 24:29 — 1411
the *p* that are in heaven shall be .... Mk 13:25 — 1411
and unto magistrates, and *p*.............. Lk 12:11 — 1849
for the *p* of heaven shall be .... Lk 21:26 — 1411
angels, nor principalities, nor .... Rom 8:38 — 1411
soul be subject unto the higher *p* .... Rom 13:1 — 1849
the *p* that be are ordained of God .... Rom 13:1 — 1849
p in heavenly places might be .... Eph 3:10 — 1849
against principalities, against *p* .... Eph 6:12 — 1849
or principalities, or *p* .... Col 1:16 — 1849
spoiled principalities and *p*.................. Col 2:15 — 1849
be subject to principalities and *p* .... Titus 3:1 — 1849
the *p* of the world to come, ... Heb 6:5 — 1411
p being made subject unto him .... 1Pet 3:22 — 1411

PRACTICES
have exercised with covetous *p*.............. 2Pet 2:14

PRACTISE
to *p* wicked works with men that .... Ps 141:4 — 5953
to *p* hypocrisy, and to utter error .... Is 32:6 — 6213

P

and shall prosper, and *p*, and shall .... Dan 8:24 6213
the morning is light, they *p* it .... Mic 2:1 6213

PRACTISED
secretly *p* mischief against him 1Sa 23:9 2790
and it *p*, and prospered .... Dan 8:12 6213

PRAETORIUM *(pre-to'-re-um) Palace of the Roman procurator in Jerusalem.*
him away into the hall, called *P* .... Mk 15:16 *4232*

PRAISE
she said, Now will I *p* the LORD .... Gen 29:35 3034
art he whom thy brethren shall *p* .... Gen 49:8 3034
be holy to *p* the LORD withal .... Lev 19:24 1974
He is thy *p*, and he is thy God, ... Deut 10:21 8416
nations which he hath made, in *p* .... Deut 26:19 8416
P ye the LORD for the avenging of .... Judg 5:2 1288
I will sing *p* to the LORD God of .... Judg 5:3
thank and *p* the LORD God of Israel 1Chr 16:4 1984
thy holy name, and glory in thy *p* 1Chr 16:35 8416
made, said David, to *p* therewith 1Chr 23:5 1984
p the LORD, and likewise at even 1Chr 23:30 1984
to give thanks and to *p* the LORD 1Chr 25:3 1984
thee, and *p* thy glorious name 1Chr 29:13 1984
the king had made to *p* the LORD 2Chr 7:6 3034
Levites to their charges, to *p* 2Chr 8:14 1984
stood up to *p* the LORD God of 2Chr 20:19 1984
that should *p* the beauty of 2Chr 20:21 1984
the army, and to say, *P* the LORD 2Chr 20:21 3034
when they began to sing and to *p* 2Chr 20:22 8416
and such as taught to sing *p* 2Chr 23:13 1984
commanded the Levites to sing *p* 2Chr 29:30 1984
to *p* in the gates of the tents of 2Chr 31:2 1984
cymbals, to *p* the LORD, after the .... Ezr 3:10 1984
exalted above all blessing and *p* .... Neh 9:5 8416
brethren over against them, to *p* .... Neh 12:24 1984
of the singers, and songs of *p* .... Neh 12:46 8416
I will *p* the LORD according to .... Ps 7:17 3034
will sing *p* to the name of the .... Ps 7:17
I will *p* thee, O LORD, with my .... Ps 9:1 3034
I will sing *p* to thy name .... Ps 9:2
That I may shew forth all thy *p* .... Ps 9:14 8416
so will we sing and *p* thy power .... Ps 21:13 2167
of the congregation will I *p* thee .... Ps 22:22 1984
Ye that fear the LORD, *p* him .... Ps 22:23 1984
My *p* shall be of thee in the .... Ps 22:25 8416
they shall *p* the LORD that seek .... Ps 22:26 1984
and with my song will I *p* him .... Ps 28:7 3034
shall the dust *p* thee .... Ps 30:9 3034
that my glory may sing *p* to thee .... Ps 30:12
for *p* is comely for the upright .... Ps 33:1 8416
P the LORD with harp .... Ps 33:2 3034
his *p* shall continually be in my .... Ps 34:1 8416
I will *p* thee among much people .... Ps 35:18 1984
of thy *p* all the day long .... Ps 35:28 8416
in my mouth, even *p* unto our God .... Ps 40:3 8416
God, with the voice of joy and *p* .... Ps 42:4 8426
for I shall yet *p* him for the .... Ps 42:5 3034
for I shall yet *p* him, who is the .... Ps 42:11 3034
yea, upon the harp will I *p* thee .... Ps 43:4 3034
for I shall yet *p* him, who is the .... Ps 43:5 3034
day long, and *p* thy name for ever .... Ps 44:8 3034
shall the people *p* thee for ever .... Ps 45:17 3034
so is thy *p* unto the ends of the .... Ps 48:10 8416
his soul, and men will *p* thee .... Ps 49:18 3034
Whoso offereth *p* glorifieth me .... Ps 50:23 8426
my mouth shall shew forth thy *p* .... Ps 51:15 8416
I will *p* thee for ever, because .... Ps 52:9 3034
I will *p* thy name, O LORD .... Ps 54:6 3034
In God I will *p* his word, in God .... Ps 56:4 1984
In God will I *p* his word .... Ps 56:10 1984
in the LORD will I *p* his word .... Ps 56:10 1984
I will sing and give *p* .... Ps 57:7 2167
I will *p* thee, O Lord, among the .... Ps 57:9 3034
So will I sing *p* unto thy name .... Ps 61:8
than life, my lips shall *p* thee .... Ps 63:3 7623
my mouth shall *p* thee with joyful .... Ps 63:5 1984
P waiteth for thee, O God in Sion .... Ps 65:1 8416
make his *p* glorious .... Ps 66:2 8416
the voice of his *p* to be heard .... Ps 66:8 8416
Let the people *p* thee, O God .... Ps 67:3 3034
let all the people *p* thee .... Ps 67:3 3034
Let the people *p* thee, O God .... Ps 67:5 3034
let all the people *p* thee .... Ps 67:5 3034
I will *p* the name of God with a .... Ps 69:30 1984
Let the heaven and earth *p* him .... Ps 69:34 1984
my *p* shall be continually of thee .... Ps 71:6 8416
Let my mouth be filled with thy *p* .... Ps 71:8 8416
will yet *p* thee more and more .... Ps 71:14 8416
I will also *p* thee with the .... Ps 71:22 3034
let the poor and needy *p* thy name .... Ps 74:21 1984
the wrath of man shall *p* thee .... Ps 76:10 3034
forth thy *p* to all generations .... Ps 79:13 8416
I will *p* thee, O Lord my God, ... Ps 86:12 3034
shall the dead arise and *p* thee .... Ps 88:10 3034
the heavens shall *p* thy wonders .... Ps 89:5 3034
loud noise, and rejoice, and sing *p* .... Ps 98:4
Let them *p* thy great and terrible .... Ps 99:3 3034
A Psalm of *p* .... Ps 100:*t* 8426
and into his courts with *p* .... Ps 100:4 8416
shall be created shall *p* the LORD .... Ps 102:18 1984
in Zion, and his *p* in Jerusalem .... Ps 102:21 8416
I will sing *p* to my God while I .... Ps 104:33
P ye the LORD .... Ps 104:35 1984
P ye the LORD .... Ps 105:45 1984
P ye the LORD .... Ps 106:1 1984
who can shew forth all his *p* .... Ps 106:2 8416
they sang his *p* .... Ps 106:12 8416
holy name, and to triumph in thy *p* .... Ps 106:47 8416
P ye the LORD .... Ps 106:48 1984
Oh that men would *p* the LORD for .... Ps 107:8 3034
Oh that men would *p* the LORD for .... Ps 107:15 3034
Oh that men would *p* the LORD for .... Ps 107:21 3034
Oh that men would *p* the LORD for .... Ps 107:31 3034
p him in the assembly of the .... Ps 107:32 1984
I will sing and give *p*, even with .... Ps 108:1 2167
I will *p* thee, O LORD, among the .... Ps 108:3 3034
Hold not thy peace, O God of my *p* .... Ps 109:1 8416
I will greatly *p* the LORD with my .... Ps 109:30 3034
I will *p* him among the multitude .... Ps 109:30 1984
P ye the LORD .... Ps 111:1 1984
I will *p* the LORD with my whole .... Ps 111:1 3034
his *p* endureth for ever .... Ps 111:10 8416
P ye the LORD .... Ps 112:1 1984
P ye the LORD .... Ps 113:1 1984
P, O ye servants of the LORD, ... Ps 113:1 1984
p the name of the LORD .... Ps 113:1 1984
P ye the LORD .... Ps 113:9 1984
The dead *p* not the LORD, neither .... Ps 115:17 1984
P the LORD .... Ps 115:18 1984
P ye the LORD .... Ps 116:19 1984
O *p* the LORD, all ye nations .... Ps 117:1 1984
p him, all ye people .... Ps 117:1 7623
P ye the LORD .... Ps 117:2 1984
into them, and I will *p* the LORD .... Ps 118:19 3034
I will *p* thee .... Ps 118:21 3034
Thou art my God, and I will *p* thee .... Ps 118:28 3034
I will *p* thee with uprightness of .... Ps 119:7 3034
Seven times a day do I *p* thee .... Ps 119:164 1984
My lips shall utter *p*, when thou .... Ps 119:171 8416
my soul live, and it shall *p* thee .... Ps 119:175 1984
P ye the LORD .... Ps 135:1 1984
P ye the name of the LORD .... Ps 135:1 1984
p him, O ye servants of the LORD .... Ps 135:1 1984
P the LORD .... Ps 135:3 1984
P ye the LORD .... Ps 135:21 1984
I will *p* thee with my whole heart .... Ps 138:1 3034
the gods will I sing *p* unto thee .... Ps 138:1 2167
p thy name for thy lovingkindness .... Ps 138:2 3034
kings of the earth shall *p* thee .... Ps 138:4 3034
I will *p* thee .... Ps 139:14 3034
of prison, that I may *p* thy name .... Ps 142:7 3034
David's Psalm of *p* .... Ps 145:*t* 8416
I will *p* thy name for ever and .... Ps 145:2 1984
shall *p* thy works to another .... Ps 145:4 7623
All thy works shall *p* thee .... Ps 145:10 3034
shall speak the *p* of the LORD .... Ps 145:21 8416
P ye the LORD .... Ps 146:1 1984
P the LORD, O my soul .... Ps 146:1 1984
While I live will I *p* the LORD .... Ps 146:2 1984
P ye the LORD .... Ps 146:10 1984
P ye the LORD .... Ps 147:1 1984
and *p* is comely .... Ps 147:1 8416
sing *p* upon the harp unto our God .... Ps 147:7
P the LORD, O Jerusalem .... Ps 147:12 7623
p thy God, O Zion .... Ps 147:12 1984
P ye the LORD .... Ps 147:20 1984
P ye the LORD .... Ps 148:1 1984
P ye the LORD from the heavens .... Ps 148:1 1984
p him in the heights .... Ps 148:1 1984
P ye him, all his angels .... Ps 148:2 1984
p ye him, all his hosts .... Ps 148:2 1984
P ye him, sun and moon .... Ps 148:3 1984
p him, all ye stars of light .... Ps 148:3 1984
P him, ye heavens of heavens, and .... Ps 148:4 1984
Let them *p* the name of the LORD .... Ps 148:5 1984
P the LORD from the earth, ye .... Ps 148:7 1984
Let them *p* the name of the LORD .... Ps 148:13 1984
people, the *p* of all his saints .... Ps 148:14 8416
P ye the LORD .... Ps 148:14 1984
P ye the LORD .... Ps 149:1 1984
his *p* in the congregation of .... Ps 149:1 8416

Let them *p* his name in the dance	Ps 149:3	1984
P ye the LORD	Ps 149:9	1984
P ye the LORD	Ps 150:1	1984
P God in his sanctuary	Ps 150:1	1984
p him in the firmament of his	Ps 150:1	1984
P him for his mighty acts	Ps 150:2	1984
p him according to his excellent	Ps 150:2	1984
P him with the sound of the	Ps 150:3	1984
p him with the psaltery and harp	Ps 150:3	1984
P him with the timbrel and dance	Ps 150:4	1984
p him with stringed instruments	Ps 150:4	1984
P him upon the loud cymbals	Ps 150:5	1984
p him upon the high sounding	Ps 150:5	1984
thing that hath breath *p* the LORD	Ps 150:6	1984
P ye the LORD	Ps 150:6	1984
Let another man *p* thee, and not	Prov 27:2	1984
so is a man to his *p*	Prov 27:21	4110
that forsake the law *p* the wicked	Prov 28:4	1984
her own works *p* her in the gates	Prov 31:31	1984
shalt say, O LORD, I will *p* thee	Is 12:1	3034
P the LORD, call upon his name,	Is 12:4	3034
exalt thee, I will *p* thy name	Is 25:1	3034
For the grave cannot *p* thee	Is 38:18	3034
the living, he shall *p* thee	Is 38:19	3034
neither my *p* to graven images	Is 42:8	8416
his *p* from the end of the earth,	Is 42:10	8416
declare his *p* in the islands	Is 42:12	8416
they shall shew forth my *p*	Is 43:21	8416
for my *p* will I refrain for thee,	Is 48:9	8416
walls Salvation, and thy gates *P*	Is 60:18	8416
the garment of *p* for the spirit	Is 61:3	8416
p to spring forth before all the	Is 61:11	8416
make Jerusalem a *p* in the earth	Is 62:7	8416
it shall eat it, and *p* the LORD	Is 62:9	1984
people, and for a name, and for a *p*	Jer 13:11	8416
for thou art my *p*	Jer 17:14	8416
and bringing sacrifices of *p*	Jer 17:26	8426
Sing unto the LORD, *p* ye the LORD	Jer 20:13	1984
p ye, and say, O LORD, save thy	Jer 31:7	1984
shall be to me a name of joy, a *p*	Jer 33:9	8416
shall say, *P* the LORD of hosts	Jer 33:11	3034
of *p* into the house of the LORD	Jer 33:11	8426
There shall be no more *p* of Moab	Jer 48:2	8416
How is the city of *p* not left	Jer 49:25	8416
how is the *p* of the whole earth	Jer 51:41	8416
p thee, O thou God of my fathers,	Dan 2:23	7624
Now I Nebuchadnezzar *p* and extol	Dan 4:37	7624
p the name of the LORD your God,	Joel 2:26	1984
and the earth was full of his *p*	Hab 3:3	8416
and I will get them *p* and fame in	Zeph 3:19	8416
a *p* among all people of the earth	Zeph 3:20	8416
sucklings thou hast perfected *p*	Mt 21:16	136
when they saw it, gave *p* unto God	Lk 18:43	136
p God with a loud voice for all	Lk 19:37	134
and said unto him, Give God the *p*	Jn 9:24	1391
For they loved the *p* of men more	Jn 12:43	1391
of men more than the *p* of God	Jn 12:43	1391
whose *p* is not of men, but of God	Rom 2:29	1868
and thou shalt have *p* of the same	Rom 13:3	1868
P the Lord, all ye Gentiles	Rom 15:11	134
shall every man have *p* of God	1Cor 4:5	1868
Now I *p* you, brethren, that ye	1Cor 11:2	1867
I declare unto you I *p* you not	1Cor 11:17	1867
shall I *p* you in this	1Cor 11:22	1867
I *p* you not	1Cor 11:22	1868
brother, whose *p* is in the gospel	2Cor 8:18	1868
To the *p* of the glory of his	Eph 1:6	1868
should be to the *p* of his glory	Eph 1:12	1868
unto the *p* of his glory	Eph 1:14	1868
unto the glory and *p* of God	Phil 1:11	1868
any virtue, and if there be any *p*	Phil 4:8	1868
church will I sing *p* unto thee	Heb 2:12	5214
sacrifice of *p* to God continually	Heb 13:15	133
with fire, might be found unto *p*	1Pet 1:7	1868
for the *p* of them that do well	1Pet 2:14	1868
Jesus Christ, to whom be *p*	1Pet 4:11	1391
P our God, all ye his servants,	Rev 19:5	134

PRAISED

people saw him, they *p* their god	Judg 16:24	1984
much *p* as Absalom for his beauty	2Sa 14:25	1984
the LORD, who is worthy to be *p*	2Sa 22:4	1984
is the LORD, and greatly to be *p*	1Chr 16:25	1984
people said, Amen, and *p* the LORD	1Chr 16:36	1984
four thousand *p* the LORD with the	1Chr 23:5	1984
p the LORD, saying, For he is	2Chr 5:13	1984
p the LORD, saying, For he is	2Chr 7:3	3034
when David *p* by their ministry	2Chr 7:6	1984
the priests *p* the LORD day by day	2Chr 30:21	1984
great shout, when they *p* the LORD	Ezr 3:11	1984
said, Amen, and *p* the LORD	Neh 5:13	1984

the LORD, who is worthy to be *p*	Ps 18:3	1984
greatly to be *p* in the city of	Ps 48:1	1984
and daily shall he be *p*	Ps 72:15	1288
LORD is great, and greatly to be *p*	Ps 96:4	1984
same the LORD's name is to be *p*	Ps 113:3	1984
is the LORD, and greatly to be *p*	Ps 145:3	1984
feareth the LORD, she shall be *p*	Prov 31:30	1984
Wherefore I *p* the dead which are	Eccl 4:2	7623
and the concubines, and they *p* her	Song 6:9	1984
house, where our fathers *p* thee	Is 64:11	1984
I blessed the most High, and I *p*	Dan 4:34	7624
p the gods of gold, and of silver,	Dan 5:4	7624
thou hast *p* the gods of silver,	Dan 5:23	7624
loosed, and he spake, and *p* God	Lk 1:64	2127

PRAISES

in holiness, fearful in *p*	Ex 15:11	8416
they sang *p* with gladness, and	2Chr 29:30	1984
Sing *p* to the LORD, which	Ps 9:11	
heathen, and sing *p* unto thy name	Ps 18:49	
that inhabitest the *p* of Israel	Ps 22:3	8416
I will sing *p* unto the LORD	Ps 27:6	
Sing *p* to God, sing *p*	Ps 47:6	
p unto our King, sing *p*	Ps 47:6	
sing ye *p* with understanding	Ps 47:7	
I will render *p* unto thee	Ps 56:12	8426
Sing unto God, sing *p* to his name	Ps 68:4	
O sing *p* unto the Lord	Ps 68:32	
I will sing *p* to the God of Jacob	Ps 75:9	
to come the *p* of the LORD	Ps 78:4	8416
to sing *p* unto thy name, O most	Ps 92:1	
I will sing *p* unto thee among the	Ps 108:3	
sing *p* unto his name	Ps 135:3	
strings will I sing *p* unto thee	Ps 144:9	
I will sing *p* unto my God while I	Ps 146:2	
it is good to sing *p* unto our God	Ps 147:1	
let them sing *p* unto him with the	Ps 149:3	
Let the high *p* of God be in their	Ps 149:6	
shew forth the *p* of the LORD	Is 60:6	8416
the *p* of the LORD, according to	Is 63:7	8416
Silas prayed, and sang *p* unto God	Acts 16:25	
that ye should shew forth the *p*	1Pet 2:9	703

PRAISETH

her husband also, and he *p* her	Prov 31:28	1984

PRAISING

make one sound to be heard in *p*	2Chr 5:13	1984
p the king, she came to the	2Chr 23:12	1984
they sang together by course in *p*	Ezr 3:11	1984
they will be still *p* thee	Ps 84:4	1984
of the heavenly host *p* God	Lk 2:13	134
p God for all the things that	Lk 2:20	134
were continually in the temple, *p*	Lk 24:53	134
P God, and having favour with all	Acts 2:47	134
walking, and leaping, and *p* God	Acts 3:8	134
people saw him walking and *p* God	Acts 3:9	134

PRANSING

of the wheels, and of the *p* horses	Nah 3:2	1725

PRANSINGS

broken by the means of the *p*	Judg 5:22	1726
the *p* of their mighty ones	Judg 5:22	1726

PRATING

but a *p* fool shall fall	Prov 10:8	8193
but a *p* fool shall fall	Prov 10:10	8193
p against us with malicious words	3Jn 10	5396

PRAY

I *p* thee, thou art my sister	Gen 12:13	4994
I *p* thee, between me and thee, and	Gen 13:8	4994
thyself, I *p* thee, from me	Gen 13:9	4994
I *p* thee, go in unto my maid	Gen 16:2	4994
I *p* thee, from thy servant	Gen 18:3	4994
I *p* you, be fetched, and wash your	Gen 18:4	4994
I *p* you, into your servant's	Gen 19:2	4994
I *p* you, brethren, do not so	Gen 19:7	4994
I *p* you, bring them out unto you,	Gen 19:8	4994
a prophet, and he shall *p* for thee	Gen 20:7	6419
wilt give it, I *p* thee, hear me	Gen 23:13	3863
I *p* thee, thy hand under my thigh	Gen 24:2	4994
I *p* thee, send me good speed this	Gen 24:12	4994
I *p* thee, that I may drink	Gen 24:14	4994
I *p* thee, drink a little water of	Gen 24:17	4994
tell me, I *p* thee	Gen 24:23	4994
I *p* thee, a little water of thy	Gen 24:43	4994
unto her, Let me drink, I *p* thee	Gen 24:45	4994
I *p* thee, with that same red	Gen 25:30	4994
I *p* thee, thy weapons, thy quiver	Gen 27:3	4994
I *p* thee, sit and eat of my	Gen 27:19	4994
I *p* thee, that I may feel thee,	Gen 27:21	4994
I *p* thee, of thy son's mandrakes	Gen 30:14	4994

I *p* thee, if I have found favour	Gen 30:27	4994
I *p* thee, from the hand of my	Gen 32:11	4994
said, Tell me, I *p* thee, thy name	Gen 32:29	4994
I *p* thee, if now I have found	Gen 33:10	4994
I *p* thee, my blessing that is	Gen 33:11	4994
I *p* thee, pass over before his	Gen 33:14	4994
I *p* you give her him to wife	Gen 34:8	4994
I *p* you, this dream which I have	Gen 37:6	4994
I *p* thee, see whether it be well	Gen 37:14	4994
I *p* thee, where they feed their	Gen 37:16	4994
I *p* thee, let me come in unto	Gen 38:16	4994
I *p* thee, whose are these, the	Gen 38:25	4994
tell me them, I *p* you	Gen 40:8	4994
I *p* thee, unto me, and make	Gen 40:14	4994
I *p* thee, speak a word in my	Gen 44:18	4994
I *p* thee, let thy servant abide	Gen 44:33	4994
Come near to me, I *p* you	Gen 45:4	4994
we *p* thee, let thy servants dwell	Gen 47:4	4994
I *p* thee, thy hand under my thigh	Gen 47:29	4994
bury me not, I *p* thee, in Egypt	Gen 47:29	4994
I *p* thee, unto me, and I will	Gen 48:9	4994
I *p* you, in the ears of Pharaoh,	Gen 50:4	4994
I *p* thee, and bury my father, and I	Gen 50:5	4994
I *p* thee now, the trespass of thy	Gen 50:17	577
we *p* thee, forgive the trespass	Gen 50:17	4994
I *p* thee, by the hand of him whom	Ex 4:13	4994
I *p* thee, and return unto my	Ex 4:18	4994
we *p* thee, three days' journey	Ex 5:3	4994
I *p* thee, my sin only this once,	Ex 10:17	4994
I *p* thee, out of thy book which	Ex 32:32	4994
I *p* thee, if I have found grace	Ex 33:13	4994
my Lord, I *p* thee, go among us	Ex 34:9	4994
he said, Leave us not, I *p* thee	Num 10:31	4994
I *p* thee, out of hand, if I have	Num 11:15	4994
Hear, I *p* you, ye sons of Levi	Num 16:8	4994
I *p* you, from the tents of these	Num 16:26	4994
I *p* thee, through thy country	Num 20:17	4994
p unto the LORD, that he take	Num 21:7	6419
I *p* thee, curse me this people	Num 22:6	4994
I *p* thee, hinder thee from coming	Num 22:16	4994
I *p* thee, curse me this people	Num 22:17	4994
I *p* you, tarry ye also here this	Num 22:19	4994
I *p* thee, with me unto another	Num 23:13	4994
I *p* thee, I will bring thee unto	Num 23:27	4994
I *p* thee, let me go over, and see	Deut 3:25	4994
I *p* you, swear unto me by the	Josh 2:12	4994
I *p* thee, glory to the LORD God	Josh 7:19	4994
we *p* thee, the entrance into the	Judg 1:24	4994
I *p* thee, a little water to drink	Judg 4:19	4994
I *p* thee, until I come unto thee,	Judg 6:18	4994
I *p* thee, but this once with the	Judg 6:39	4994
I *p* you, loaves of bread unto the	Judg 8:5	4994
I *p* you, in the ears of all the	Judg 9:2	4994
I *p* now, and fight with them	Judg 9:38	4994
us only, we *p* thee, this day	Judg 10:15	4994
I *p* thee, pass through thy land	Judg 11:17	4994
we *p* thee, through thy land into	Judg 11:19	4994
I *p* thee, and drink not wine nor	Judg 13:4	4994
I *p* thee, let us detain thee,	Judg 13:15	4994
her, I *p* thee, instead of her	Judg 15:2	4994
I *p* thee, wherein thy great	Judg 16:6	4994
I *p* thee, wherewith thou mightest	Judg 16:10	4994
I *p* thee, and strengthen me	Judg 16:28	4994
I *p* thee, only this once, O God,	Judg 16:28	4994
we *p* thee, of God, that we may	Judg 18:5	4994
I *p* thee, and tarry all night, and	Judg 19:6	4994
Comfort thine heart, I *p* thee	Judg 19:8	4994
evening, I *p* you tarry all night	Judg 19:9	4994
I *p* thee, and let us turn in into	Judg 19:11	4994
I *p* you, do not so wickedly	Judg 19:23	4994
I *p* you, let me glean and gather	Ruth 2:7	4994
I *p* thee, into one of the	1Sa 2:36	4994
I *p* thee hide it not from me	1Sa 3:17	4994
I will *p* for you unto the LORD	1Sa 7:5	6419
I *p* thee, where the seer's house	1Sa 9:18	4994
I *p* thee, what Samuel said unto	1Sa 10:15	4994
P for thy servants unto the LORD	1Sa 12:19	6419
the LORD in ceasing to *p* for you	1Sa 12:23	6419
I *p* you, how mine eyes have been	1Sa 14:29	4994
I *p* thee, pardon my sin, and turn	1Sa 15:25	4994
I *p* thee, before the elders of my	1Sa 15:30	4994
I *p* thee, stand before me	1Sa 16:22	4994
I *p* thee, take heed to thyself	1Sa 19:2	4994
And he said, Let me go, I *p* thee	1Sa 20:29	4994
I *p* thee, see my brethren	1Sa 20:29	4994
I *p* thee, come forth, and be with	1Sa 22:3	4994
I *p* you, prepare yet, and know and	1Sa 23:22	4994
I *p* thee, whatsoever cometh to	1Sa 25:8	4994
I *p* thee, speak in thine audience	1Sa 25:24	4994
I *p* thee, regard this man of	1Sa 25:25	4994
I *p* thee, forgive the trespass of	1Sa 25:28	4994

I *p* thee, with the spear even to	1Sa 26:8	4994
I *p* thee, take thou now the spear	1Sa 26:11	4994
I *p* thee, let my lord the king	1Sa 26:19	4994
I *p* thee, divine unto me by the	1Sa 28:8	4994
I *p* thee, hearken thou also unto	1Sa 28:22	4994
I *p* thee, bring me hither the	1Sa 30:7	4994
I *p* thee, tell me	2Sa 1:4	4994
I *p* thee, upon me, and slay me	2Sa 1:9	4994
heart to *p* this prayer unto thee	2Sa 7:27	6419
I *p* thee, let my sister Tamar	2Sa 13:5	4994
I *p* thee, let Tamar my sister	2Sa 13:6	4994
I *p* thee, speak unto the king	2Sa 13:13	4994
I *p* thee, let my brother Amnon go	2Sa 13:26	4994
I *p* thee, feign thyself to be a	2Sa 14:2	4994
I *p* thee, let the king remember	2Sa 14:11	4994
I *p* thee, speak one word unto my	2Sa 14:12	4994
I *p* thee, the thing that I shall	2Sa 14:18	4994
I *p* thee, let me go and pay my vow	2Sa 15:7	4994
I *p* thee, turn the counsel of	2Sa 15:31	4994
I *p* thee, and take off his head	2Sa 16:9	4994
I *p* thee, also run after Cushi	2Sa 18:22	4994
I *p* thee, turn back again, that I	2Sa 19:37	4994
I *p* you, unto Joab, Come near	2Sa 20:16	4994
I *p* thee, be against me, and	2Sa 24:17	4994
I *p* thee, give thee counsel, that	1Kin 1:12	4994
I *p* thee, unto Solomon the king,	1Kin 2:17	4994
I *p* thee, say me not nay	1Kin 2:20	
I *p* thee, be verified, which thou	1Kin 8:26	4994
when they shall *p* toward this	1Kin 8:30	6419
thee, and confess their name, and *p*	1Kin 8:33	6419
if they *p* toward this place, and	1Kin 8:35	6419
shall come and *p* toward this house	1Kin 8:42	6419
shall *p* unto the LORD toward the	1Kin 8:44	6419
p unto thee toward their land,	1Kin 8:48	6419
p for me, that my hand may be	1Kin 13:6	6419
I *p* thee, and disguise thyself,	1Kin 14:2	4994
I *p* thee, a little water in a	1Kin 17:10	4994
I *p* thee, a morsel of bread in	1Kin 17:11	4994
I *p* thee, let this child's soul	1Kin 17:21	4994
I *p* thee, kiss my father and my	1Kin 19:20	4994
I *p* you, and see how this man	1Kin 20:7	4994
I *p* thee, put sackcloth on our	1Kin 20:31	4994
saith, I *p* thee, let me live	1Kin 20:32	4994
of the LORD, Smite me, I *p* thee	1Kin 20:35	4994
man, and said, Smite me, I *p* thee	1Kin 20:37	4994
I *p* thee, at the word of the LORD	1Kin 22:5	4994
I *p* thee, be like the word of one	1Kin 22:13	4994
I *p* thee, let my life, and the	2Kin 1:13	4994
unto Elisha, Tarry here, I *p* thee	2Kin 2:2	4994
him, Elisha, tarry here, I *p* thee	2Kin 2:4	4994
unto him, Tarry, I *p* thee, here	2Kin 2:6	4994
I *p* thee, let a double portion of	2Kin 2:9	4994
we *p* thee, and seek thy master	2Kin 2:16	4994
I *p* thee, the situation of this	2Kin 2:19	4994
chamber, I *p* thee, on the wall	2Kin 4:10	4994
I *p* thee, one of the young men,	2Kin 4:22	4994
I *p* thee, to meet her, and say	2Kin 4:26	4994
I *p* you, and see how he seeketh a	2Kin 5:7	4994
I *p* thee, take a blessing of thy	2Kin 5:15	4994
I *p* thee, be given to thy servant	2Kin 5:17	4994
I *p* thee, a talent of silver, and	2Kin 5:22	4994
we *p* thee, unto Jordan, and take	2Kin 6:2	4994
I *p* thee, and go with thy servants	2Kin 6:3	4994
I *p* thee, open his eyes, that he	2Kin 6:17	4994
people, I *p* thee, with blindness	2Kin 6:18	4994
I *p* thee, five of the horses that	2Kin 7:13	4994
I *p* thee, all the great things	2Kin 8:4	4994
I *p* thee, give pledges to my lord	2Kin 18:23	4994
I *p* thee, to thy servants in the	2Kin 18:26	4994
in his heart to *p* before thee	1Chr 17:25	6419
I *p* thee, O LORD my God, be on me	1Chr 21:17	4994
return and confess thy name, and *p*	2Chr 6:24	6419
yet if they *p* toward this place,	2Chr 6:26	6419
if they come and *p* in this house	2Chr 6:32	6419
they *p* unto thee toward this city	2Chr 6:34	
p unto thee in the land of their	2Chr 6:37	2603
p toward their land, which thou	2Chr 6:38	6419
shall humble themselves, and *p*	2Chr 7:14	6419
I *p* thee, at the word of the LORD	2Chr 18:4	4994
I *p* thee, be like one of theirs,	2Chr 18:12	4994
p for the life of the king, and of	Ezr 6:10	6739
which I *p* before thee now, day and	Neh 1:6	6419
I *p* thee, thy servant this day,	Neh 1:11	4994
I *p* you, let us leave off this	Neh 5:10	4994
I *p* you, to them, even this day,	Neh 5:11	4994
I *p* you, who ever perished,	Job 4:7	4994
I *p* you, let it not be iniquity	Job 6:29	4994
I *p* thee, of the former age, and	Job 8:8	4994
should we have, if we *p* unto him	Job 21:15	6293
I *p* thee, the law from his mouth,	Job 22:22	4994
I *p* you, accept any man's person,	Job 32:21	4994

I *p* thee, hear my speeches, and .... Job 33:1   4994
He shall *p* unto God, and he will .... Job 33:26   6279
and my servant Job shall *p* for you .... Job 42:8   6419
for unto thee will I *p* .... Ps 5:2   6419
p unto thee in a time when thou .... Ps 32:6   6419
and morning, and at noon, will I *p* ...... Ps 55:17   7878
I *p* thee, thy merciful kindness.............. Ps 119:76   7592
P for the peace of Jerusalem .... Ps 122:6   7592
I *p* you, betwixt me and my .... Is 5:3   4994
shall come to his sanctuary to *p*............ Is 16:12   6419
saying, Read this, I *p* thee .... Is 29:11   4994
saying, Read this, I *p* thee .... Is 29:12   4994
I *p* thee, to my master the king .... Is 36:8   4994
I *p* thee, unto thy servants in .... Is 36:11   4994
p unto a god that cannot save .... Is 45:20   6419
Therefore *p* not thou for this .... Jer 7:16   6419
Therefore *p* not thou for this .... Jer 11:14   6419
P not for this people for their .... Jer 14:11   6419
I *p* thee, of the LORD for us .... Jer 21:2   4994
and *p* unto the LORD for it .... Jer 29:7   6419
p unto me, and I will hearken unto .... Jer 29:12   6419
I *p* thee, that is in Anathoth,.............. Jer 32:8   4994
P now unto the LORD our God for .... Jer 37:3   6419
I *p* thee, O my lord the king .... Jer 37:20   4994
I *p* thee, be accepted before thee .... Jer 37:20   4994
I *p* thee, and I will slay Ishmael .... Jer 40:15   4994
p for us unto the LORD thy God,.............. Jer 42:2   6419
I will *p* unto the LORD your God .... Jer 42:4   6419
P for us unto the LORD our God .... Jer 42:20   6419
I *p* you, all people, and behold my .... Lam 1:18   4994
I *p* you, and hear what is the word ...... Eze 33:30   4994
we *p* thee, for whose cause this .... Jonah 1:8   4994
I *p* thee, O LORD, was not this my .... Jonah 4:2   577
I *p* you, O heads of Jacob, and ye .... Mic 3:1   4994
I *p* you, ye heads of the house of .... Mic 3:9   4994
I *p* you, consider from this day.............. Hag 2:15   4994
their men, to *p* before the LORD,............ Zec 7:2   2470
go speedily to *p* before the LORD........... Zec 8:21   2470
and to *p* before the LORD .... Zec 8:22   2470
I *p* you, beseech God that he will .... Mal 1:9   4994
p for them which despitefully use.......... Mt 5:44   4336
for they love to p standing in .... Mt 6:5   4336
p to thy Father which is in .... Mt 6:6   4336
But when ye p, use not vain .... Mt 6:7   4336
After this manner therefore p ye .... Mt 6:9   4336
P ye therefore the Lord of the .... Mt 9:38   1189
up into a mountain apart to *p* .... Mt 14:23   4336
put his hands on them, and *p* .... Mt 19:13   4336
But *p* ye that your flight be not .... Mt 24:20   4336
ye here, while I go and *p* yonder .... Mt 26:36   4336
Watch and p, that ye enter not .... Mt 26:41   4336
that I cannot now p to my Father........ Mt 26:53   3870
they began to *p* him to depart out........ Mk 5:17   3870
I *p* thee, come and lay thy hands........... Mk 5:23
he departed into a mountain to *p* .... Mk 6:46   4336
soever ye desire, when ye p .... Mk 11:24   4336
p ye that your flight be not in .... Mk 13:18   4336
Take ye heed, watch and p................... Mk 13:33   4336
Sit ye here, while I shall p.................... Mk 14:32   4336
Watch ye and p, lest ye enter into ...... Mk 14:38   4336
he went out into a mountain to *p* .... Lk 6:12   4336
p for them which despitefully use .... Lk 6:28   4336
and went up into a mountain to *p* .... Lk 9:28   4336
p ye therefore the Lord of the .... Lk 10:2   1189
unto him, Lord, teach us to *p*.................. Lk 11:1   4336
And he said unto them, When ye p ...... Lk 11:2   4336
I *p* thee have me excused..................... Lk 14:18   2065
I *p* thee have me excused..................... Lk 14:19   2065
I *p* thee therefore, father, that .... Lk 16:27   2065
end, that men ought always to *p* .... Lk 18:1   4336
men went up into the temple to *p* .... Lk 18:10   4336
and p always, that ye may be................ Lk 21:36   1189
them, P that ye enter not into .... Lk 22:40   4336
rise and p, lest ye enter into .... Lk 22:46   4336
I will *p* the Father, and he shall .... Jn 14:16   2065
that I will *p* the Father for you .... Jn 16:26   2065
I *p* for them .... Jn 17:9   2065
I *p* not for the world, but for .... Jn 17:9   2065
I *p* not that thou shouldest take........... Jn 17:15   2065
Neither p I for these alone, but .... Jn 17:20   2065
p God, if perhaps the thought of .... Acts 8:22   1189
P ye to the Lord for me, that .... Acts 8:24   1189
I *p* thee, of whom speaketh the .... Acts 8:34   1189
to *p* about the sixth hour........................ Acts 10:9   4336
I *p* thee that thou wouldest hear .... Acts 24:4   3870
Wherefore I *p* you to take some .... Acts 27:34   3870
what we should *p* for as we ought .... Rom 8:26   4336
that a woman *p* unto God uncovered..... 1Cor 11:13   4336
tongue *p* that he may interpret.............. 1Cor 14:13   4336
For if I *p* in an unknown tongue, ... 1Cor 14:14   4336
I will *p* with the spirit, and I 1Cor 14:15   4336

I will *p* with the understanding.............. 1Cor 14:15   4336
we *p* you in Christ's stead, be ye 2Cor 5:20   1189
Now I *p* to God that ye do no evil.......... 2Cor 13:7   2172
And this I *p*, that your love may .... Phil 1:9   4336
it, do not cease to *p* for you .... Col 1:9   4336
P without ceasing 1Th 5:17   4336
I *p* God your whole spirit and soul 1Th 5:23
Brethren, *p* for us 1Th 5:25   4336
also we *p* always for you, that................ 2Th 1:11   4336
p for us, that the word of the................ 2Th 3:1   4336
therefore that men *p* every where 1Ti 2:8   4336
I *p* God that it may not be laid 2Ti 4:16
P for us .... Heb 13:18   4336
let him *p*.. Jas 5:13   4336
and let them *p* over him, anointing .... Jas 5:14   4336
p one for another, that ye may be .... Jas 5:16   2172
do not say that he shall *p* for it 1Jn 5:16   2065

PRAYED
So Abraham *p* unto God .... Gen 20:17   6419
when Moses *p* unto the LORD, the........... Num 11:2   6419
And Moses *p* for the people..................... Num 21:7   6419
I *p* for Aaron also the same time .... Deut 9:20   6419
I *p* therefore unto the LORD, and .... Deut 9:26   6419
p unto the LORD, and wept sore 1Sa 1:10   6419
For this child I *p* 1Sa 1:27   6419
And Hannah *p*, and said, My heart........... 1Sa 2:1   6419
And Samuel *p* unto the LORD 1Sa 8:6   6419
them twain, and *p* unto the LORD 2Kin 4:33   6419
And Elisha *p*, and said, LORD, I.............. 2Kin 6:17   6419
Elisha *p* unto the LORD, and said,.......... 2Kin 6:18   6419
Hezekiah *p* before the LORD, and............ 2Kin 19:15   6419
That which thou hast *p* to me 2Kin 19:20   6419
wall, and *p* unto the LORD, saying,........... 2Kin 20:2   6419
But Hezekiah *p* for them, saying, ... 2Chr 30:18   6419
prophet Isaiah the son of Amoz, *p*......... 2Chr 32:20   6419
to the death, and *p* unto the LORD 2Chr 32:24   6419
And *p* unto him 2Chr 33:13   6419
Now when Ezra had *p*, and when he....... Ezr 10:1   6419
p before the God of heaven, ... Neh 1:4   6419
So I *p* to the God of heaven.................... Neh 2:4   6419
when he *p* for his friends .... Job 42:10   6419
Hezekiah *p* unto the LORD, saying, ... Is 37:15   6419
Whereas thou hast *p* to me against ...... Is 37:21   6419
the wall, and *p* unto the LORD, ... Is 38:2   6419
I *p* unto the LORD, saying,...................... Jer 32:16   6419
his knees three times a day, and *p* .... Dan 6:10   6739
I *p* unto the LORD my God, and made ... Dan 9:4   6419
Then Jonah *p* unto the LORD his .... Jonah 2:1   6419
he *p* unto the LORD, and said, I .... Jonah 4:2   6419
and fell on his face, and *p* .... Mt 26:39   4336
away again the second time, and *p* .... Mt 26:42   4336
p the third time, saying the same .... Mt 26:44   4336
into a solitary place, and there *p* .... Mk 1:35   4336
p him that he might be with him............ Mk 5:18   3870
p that, if it were possible, the................ Mk 14:35   4336
And again he went away, and *p* .... Mk 14:39   4336
p him that he would thrust out a .... Lk 5:3   2065
himself into the wilderness, and *p* .... Lk 5:16   4336
And as he *p*, the fashion of his.............. Lk 9:29   4336
p thus with himself, God, I thank......... Lk 18:11   4336
But I have p for thee, that thy .... Lk 22:32   1189
cast, and kneeled down, and *p* .... Lk 22:41   4336
in an agony he *p* more earnestly........... Lk 22:44   4336
mean while his disciples *p* him............... Jn 4:31   2065
And they *p*, and said, Thou, Lord,........... Acts 1:24   4336
And when they had *p*, the place was...... Acts 4:31   1189
and when they had *p*, they laid .... Acts 6:6   4336
p for them, that they might .... Acts 8:15   4336
all forth, and kneeled down, and *p* .... Acts 9:40   4336
to the people, and *p* to God alway .... Acts 10:2   1189
at the ninth hour I *p* in my house .... Acts 10:30   4336
Then *p* they him to tarry certain .... Acts 10:48   2065
And when they had fasted and *p*............ Acts 13:3   4336
and had *p* with fasting, they .... Acts 14:23   4336
p him, saying, Come over into................ Acts 16:9   3870
And at midnight Paul and Silas *p*........... Acts 16:25   4336
kneeled down, and *p* with them all .... Acts 20:36   4336
kneeled down on the shore, and *p* .... Acts 21:5   4336
even while I *p* in the temple, I................ Acts 22:17   4336
p me to bring this young man unto .... Acts 23:18   2065
to whom Paul entered in, and *p* .... Acts 28:8   4336
he *p* earnestly that it might not .... Jas 5:17   4336
he *p* again, and the heaven gave .... Jas 5:18   4336

PRAYER
heart to pray this *p* unto thee 2Sa 7:27   8605
respect unto the *p* of thy servant 1Kin 8:28   8605
hearken unto the cry and to the *p*.......... 1Kin 8:28   8605
p which thy servant shall make.............. 1Kin 8:29   8605
What *p* and supplication soever be 1Kin 8:38   8605
Then hear thou in heaven their *p* 1Kin 8:45   8605

P

Then hear thou their *p* and their	1Kin 8:49	8605
made an end of praying all this *p*	1Kin 8:54	8605
said unto him, I have heard thy *p*	1Kin 9:3	8605
wherefore lift up thy *p* for the	2Kin 19:4	8605
thy father, I have heard thy *p*	2Kin 20:5	8605
therefore to the *p* of thy servant	2Chr 6:19	8605
the *p* which thy servant prayeth	2Chr 6:19	8605
to hearken unto the *p* which thy	2Chr 6:20	8605
Then what *p* or what supplication	2Chr 6:29	8605
thou from the heavens their *p*	2Chr 6:35	8605
from thy dwelling place, their *p*	2Chr 6:39	8605
the *p* that is made in this place	2Chr 6:40	8605
said unto him, I have heard thy *p*	2Chr 7:12	8605
mine ears attent unto the *p* that	2Chr 7:15	8605
their *p* came up to his holy	2Chr 30:27	8605
his *p* unto his God, and the words	2Chr 33:18	8605
His *p* also, and how God was	2Chr 33:19	8605
mayest hear the *p* of thy servant	Neh 1:6	8605
attentive to the *p* of thy servant	Neh 1:11	8605
to the *p* of thy servants, who	Neh 1:11	8605
we made our *p* unto our God	Neh 4:9	6419
to begin the thanksgiving in *p*	Neh 11:17	8605
fear, and restrainest *p* before God	Job 15:4	7878
also my *p* is pure	Job 16:17	8605
Thou shalt make thy *p* unto him	Job 22:27	6279
have mercy upon me, and hear my *p*	Ps 4:1	8605
will I direct my *p* unto thee	Ps 5:3	
the LORD will receive my *p*	Ps 6:9	8605
A *P* of David	Ps 17:*t*	8605
unto my cry, give ear unto my *p*	Ps 17:1	8605
my *p* returned into mine own bosom	Ps 35:13	8605
Hear my *p*, O LORD, and give ear	Ps 39:12	8605
my *p* unto the God of my life	Ps 42:8	8605
Hear my *p*, O God	Ps 54:2	8605
Give ear to my *p*, O God	Ps 55:1	8605
attend unto my *p*	Ps 61:1	8605
Hear my voice, O God, in my *p*	Ps 64:1	7879
O thou that hearest *p*, unto thee	Ps 65:2	8605
attended to the voice of my *p*	Ps 66:19	8605
which hath not turned away my *p*	Ps 66:20	8605
my *p* is unto thee, O LORD, in an	Ps 69:13	8605
p also shall be made for him	Ps 72:15	6419
angry against the *p* of thy people	Ps 80:4	8605
O LORD God of hosts, hear my *p*	Ps 84:8	8605
A *P* of David	Ps 86:*t*	8605
Give ear, O LORD, unto my *p*	Ps 86:6	8605
Let my *p* come before thee	Ps 88:2	8605
morning shall my *p* prevent thee	Ps 88:13	8605
A *P* of Moses, the man of God	Ps 90:*t*	8605
A *P* of the afflicted, when he is	Ps 102:*t*	8605
Hear my *p*, O LORD, and let my cry	Ps 102:1	8605
regard the *p* of the destitute	Ps 102:17	8605
and not despise their *p*	Ps 102:17	8605
but I give myself unto *p*	Ps 109:4	8605
and let his *p* become sin	Ps 109:7	8605
Let my *p* be set forth before thee	Ps 141:2	8605
for yet my *p* also shall be in	Ps 141:5	8605
A *P* when he was in the cave	Ps 142:*t*	8605
Hear my *p*, O LORD, give ear to my	Ps 143:1	8605
but the *p* of the upright is his	Prov 15:8	8605
he heareth the *p* of the righteous	Prov 15:29	8605
even his *p* shall be abomination	Prov 28:9	8605
they poured out a *p* when thy	Is 26:16	3908
wherefore lift up thy *p* for the	Is 37:4	8605
thy father, I have heard thy *p*	Is 38:5	8605
make them joyful in my house of *p*	Is 56:7	8605
an house of *p* for all people	Is 56:7	8605
lift up cry nor *p* for them	Jer 7:16	8605
lift up a cry or *p* for them	Jer 11:14	8605
and shout, he shutteth out my *p*	Lam 3:8	8605
that our *p* should not pass	Lam 3:44	8605
unto the Lord God, to seek by *p*	Dan 9:3	8605
yet made we not our *p* before the	Dan 9:13	2470
hear the *p* of thy servant, and his	Dan 9:17	8605
Yea, whiles I was speaking in *p*	Dan 9:21	8605
my *p* came in unto thee, into	Jonah 2:7	8605
A *p* of Habakkuk the prophet upon	Hab 3:1	
this kind goeth not out but by *p*	Mt 17:21	4335
shall be called the house of *p*	Mt 21:13	4335
whatsoever ye shall ask in *p*	Mt 21:22	4335
and for a pretence make long *p*	Mt 23:14	4336
come forth by nothing, but by *p*	Mk 9:29	4335
of all nations the house of *p*	Mk 11:17	4335
for thy *p* is heard	Lk 1:13	1162
continued all night in *p* to God	Lk 6:12	4335
My house is the house of *p*	Lk 19:46	4335
And when he rose up from *p*	Lk 22:45	4335
continued with one accord in *p*	Acts 1:14	4335
into the temple at the hour of *p*	Acts 3:1	4335
give ourselves continually to *p*	Acts 6:4	4335
thy *p* is heard, and thine alms are	Acts 10:31	4335

but *p* was made without ceasing of	Acts 12:5	4335
where *p* was wont to be made	Acts 16:13	4335
it came to pass, as we went to *p*	Acts 16:16	4335
p to God for Israel is, that they	Rom 10:1	1162
continuing instant in *p*	Rom 12:12	4335
give yourselves to fasting and *p*	1Cor 7:5	4335
also helping together by *p* for us	2Cor 1:11	1162
And by their *p* for you, which long	2Cor 9:14	1162
Praying always with all *p*	Eph 6:18	4335
Always in every *p* of mine for you	Phil 1:4	1162
to my salvation through your *p*	Phil 1:19	1162
but in every thing by *p* and	Phil 4:6	4335
Continue in *p*, and watch in the	Col 4:2	4335
by the word of God and *p*	1Ti 4:5	1783
the *p* of faith shall save the	Jas 5:15	2171
The effectual fervent *p* of a	Jas 5:16	1162
therefore sober, and watch unto *p*	1Pet 4:7	4335

PRAYERS

The *p* of David the son of Jesse	Ps 72:20	8605
yea, when ye make many *p*, I will	Is 1:15	8605
and for a pretence make long *p*	Mk 12:40	4336
with fastings and *p* night and day	Lk 2:37	1162
of John fast often, and make *p*	Lk 5:33	1162
houses, and for a shew make long *p*	Lk 20:47	4336
and in breaking of bread, and in *p*	Acts 2:42	4335
And he said unto him, Thy *p*	Acts 10:4	4335
mention of you always in my *p*	Rom 1:9	4335
with me in your *p* to God for me	Rom 15:30	4335
making mention of you in my *p*	Eph 1:16	4335
labouring fervently for you in *p*	Col 4:12	4335
making mention of you in our *p*	1Th 1:2	4335
first of all, supplications, *p*	1Ti 2:1	4335
supplications *p* night and day	1Ti 5:5	4335
remembrance of thee in my *p* night	2Ti 1:3	1162
mention of thee always in my *p*	Philem 4	4335
your *p* I shall be given unto you	Philem 22	4335
flesh, when he had offered up *p*	Heb 5:7	1162
that your *p* be not hindered	1Pet 3:7	4335
and his ears are open unto their *p*	1Pet 3:12	1162
odours, which are the *p* of saints	Rev 5:8	4335
he should offer it with the *p* of	Rev 8:3	4335
came with the *p* of the saints	Rev 8:4	4335

PRAYEST

And when thou *p*, thou shalt not be	Mt 6:5	4336
But thou, when thou *p*, enter into	Mt 6:6	4336

PRAYETH

which thy servant *p* before thee	1Kin 8:28	6419
which thy servant *p* before thee	2Chr 6:19	6419
thy servant *p* toward this place	2Chr 6:20	6419
p unto it, and saith, Deliver me	Is 44:17	6419
for, behold, he *p*,	Acts 9:11	4336
But every woman that *p* or	1Cor 11:5	4336
in an unknown tongue, my spirit *p*	1Cor 14:14	4336

PRAYING

she continued *p* before the LORD	1Sa 1:12	6419
by thee here, *p* unto the LORD	1Sa 1:26	6419
made an end of *p* all this prayer	1Kin 8:54	6419
when Solomon had made an end of *p*	2Chr 7:1	6419
men assembled, and found Daniel *p*	Dan 6:11	1156
And whiles I was speaking, and *p*	Dan 9:20	6419
And when ye stand *p*, forgive, if	Mk 11:25	4336
multitude of the people were *p*	Lk 1:10	4336
Jesus also being baptized, and *p*	Lk 3:21	4336
came to pass, as he was alone *p*	Lk 9:18	4336
as he was *p* in a certain place,	Lk 11:1	4336
I was in the city of Joppa *p*	Acts 11:5	4336
many were gathered together *p*	Acts 12:12	4336
Every man *p* or prophesying,	1Cor 11:4	4336
P us with much intreaty that we	2Cor 8:4	1189
P always with all prayer and	Eph 6:18	4336
Jesus Christ, *p* always for you,	Col 1:3	4336
Withal *p* also for us, that God	Col 4:3	4336
day *p* exceedingly that we might	1Th 3:10	1189
holy faith, *p* in the Holy Ghost,	Jude 20	4336

PREACH

to *p* of thee at Jerusalem	Neh 6:7	7121
to *p* good tidings unto the meek	Is 61:1	1319
p unto it the preaching that I	Jonah 3:2	7121
From that time Jesus began to *p*	Mt 4:17	2784
And as ye go, *p*, saying, The	Mt 10:7	2784
that *p* ye upon the housetops	Mt 10:27	2784
to teach and to *p* in their cities	Mt 11:1	2784
p the baptism of repentance for	Mk 1:4	2784
towns, that I may *p* there also	Mk 1:38	2784
he might send them forth to *p*	Mk 3:14	2784
p the gospel to every creature	Mk 16:15	2784
me to *p* the gospel to the poor	Lk 4:18	2097
to *p* deliverance to the captives,	Lk 4:18	2784

To *p* the acceptable year of the	Lk 4:19	2784
I must *p* the kingdom of God to	Lk 4:43	2097
he sent them to *p* the kingdom of	Lk 9:2	2784
go thou and *p* the kingdom of God	Lk 9:60	1229
not to teach and *p* Jesus Christ	Acts 5:42	2097
commanded us to *p* unto the people	Acts 10:42	2784
p unto you that ye should turn	Acts 14:15	2097
in every city them that *p* him	Acts 15:21	2784
Holy Ghost to *p* the word in Asia	Acts 16:6	2980
us for to *p* the gospel unto them	Acts 16:10	2097
whom I *p* unto you, is Christ	Acts 17:3	2605
I am ready to *p* the gospel to you	Rom 1:15	2097
is, the word of faith, which we *p*	Rom 10:8	2784
And how shall they *p*, except they	Rom 10:15	2784
them that *p* the gospel of peace	Rom 10:15	2097
so have I strived to *p* the gospel	Rom 15:20	2097
to baptize, but to *p* the gospel	1Cor 1:17	2097
But we *p* Christ crucified, unto	1Cor 1:23	2784
p the gospel should live of the	1Cor 9:14	2605
For though I *p* the gospel	1Cor 9:16	2097
is unto me, if I *p* not the gospel	1Cor 9:16	2097
when I *p* the gospel, I may make	1Cor 9:18	2097
it were I or they, so we *p*	1Cor 15:11	2784
to Troas to *p* Christ's gospel	2Cor 2:12	
For we *p* not ourselves, but	2Cor 4:5	2784
To *p* the gospel in the regions	2Cor 10:16	2097
p any other gospel unto you than	Gal 1:8	2097
If any man *p* any other gospel	Gal 1:9	2097
that I might *p* him among the	Gal 1:16	2097
which I *p* among the Gentiles	Gal 2:2	2784
if I yet *p* circumcision, why do I	Gal 5:11	2784
that I should *p* among the	Eph 3:8	2097
Some indeed *p* Christ even of envy	Phil 1:15	2784
The one *p* Christ of contention,	Phil 1:16	2605
Whom we *p*, warning every man, and	Col 1:28	2605
P the word	2Ti 4:2	2784
the everlasting gospel to *p* unto	Rev 14:6	2097

PREACHED

I have *p* righteousness in the	Ps 40:9	1319
poor have the gospel *p* to them	Mt 11:5	2097
p in all the world for a witness	Mt 24:14	2784
shall be *p* in the whole world	Mt 26:13	2784
And *p*, saying, There cometh one	Mk 1:7	2784
And he *p* in their synagogues	Mk 1:39	2784
and he *p* the word unto them	Mk 2:2	2980
out, and *p* that men should repent	Mk 6:12	2784
this gospel shall be *p* throughout	Mk 14:9	2784
p every where, the Lord working	Mk 16:20	2784
exhortation *p* he unto the people	Lk 3:18	2097
he *p* in the synagogues of Galilee	Lk 4:44	2784
to the poor the gospel is *p*	Lk 7:22	2097
that time the kingdom of God is *p*	Lk 16:16	2097
p the gospel, the chief priests	Lk 20:1	2097
remission of sins should be *p* in	Lk 24:47	2784
which before was *p* unto you	Acts 3:20	4296
p through Jesus the resurrection	Acts 4:2	2605
of Samaria, and *p* Christ unto them	Acts 8:5	2784
p the word of the Lord, returned	Acts 8:25	2980
p the gospel in many villages of	Acts 8:25	2097
scripture, and *p* unto him Jesus	Acts 8:35	2097
through he *p* in all the cities	Acts 8:40	2097
straightway he *p* Christ in the	Acts 9:20	2784
how he had *p* boldly at Damascus	Acts 9:27	3954
after the baptism which John *p*	Acts 10:37	2784
they *p* the word of God in the	Acts 13:5	2605
When John had first *p* before his	Acts 13:24	4296
that through this man is *p* unto	Acts 13:38	2605
be *p* to them the next sabbath	Acts 13:42	2980
And there they *p* the gospel	Acts 14:7	2097
when they had *p* the gospel to	Acts 14:21	2097
when they had *p* the word in Perga	Acts 14:25	2980
we have *p* the word of the Lord	Acts 15:36	2605
of God was *p* of Paul at Berea	Acts 17:13	2605
because he *p* unto them Jesus, and	Acts 17:18	2907
Paul *p* unto them, ready to depart	Acts 20:7	1256
I have fully *p* the gospel of	Rom 15:19	4137
means, when I have *p* to others	1Cor 9:27	2784
you the gospel which I *p* unto you	1Cor 15:1	2097
keep in memory what I *p* unto you	1Cor 15:2	2097
Now if Christ be *p* that he rose	1Cor 15:12	2784
who was *p* among you by us, even	2Cor 1:19	2784
another Jesus, whom we have not *p*	2Cor 11:4	2784
because I have *p* to you the	2Cor 11:7	2097
that which we have *p* unto you	Gal 1:8	2097
was *p* of me is not after man	Gal 1:11	2097
p before the gospel unto Abraham,	Gal 3:8	4283
infirmity of the flesh I *p* the	Gal 4:13	2097
p peace to you which were afar	Eph 2:17	2097
or in truth, Christ is *p*	Phil 1:18	2605
which was *p* to every creature	Col 1:23	2784

we *p* unto you the gospel of God	1Th 2:9	2784
p unto the Gentiles, believed on	1Ti 3:16	2784
For unto us was the gospel *p*	Heb 4:2	2097
but the word *p* did not profit	Heb 4:2	189
first *p* entered not in because of	Heb 4:6	2097
unto you by them that have *p* the	1Pet 1:12	2097
which by the gospel is *p* unto you	1Pet 1:25	2097
p unto the spirits in prison	1Pet 3:19	2784
p also to them that are dead	1Pet 4:6	2097

PREACHER

The words of the *P*, the son of	Eccl 1:1	6953
Vanity of vanities, saith the *P*	Eccl 1:2	6953
I the *P* was king over Israel in	Eccl 1:12	6953
this have I found, saith the *p*	Eccl 7:27	6953
Vanity of vanities, saith the *p*	Eccl 12:8	6953
moreover, because the *p* was wise	Eccl 12:9	6953
The *p* sought to find out	Eccl 12:10	6953
how shall they hear without a *p*	Rom 10:14	2784
Whereunto I am ordained a *p*	1Ti 2:7	2783
Whereunto I am appointed a *p*	2Ti 1:11	2783
a *p* of righteousness, bringing in	2Pet 2:5	2783

PREACHEST

thou that *p* a man should not	Rom 2:21	2784

PREACHETH

adjure you by Jesus whom Paul *p*	Acts 19:13	2784
if he that cometh *p* another Jesus	2Cor 11:4	2784
now *p* the faith which once he	Gal 1:23	2097

PREACHING

unto it the *p* that I bid thee	Jonah 3:2	7150
p in the wilderness of Judaea,	Mt 3:1	2784
p the gospel of the kingdom, and	Mt 4:23	2784
p the gospel of the kingdom, and	Mt 9:35	2784
they repented at the *p* of Jonas	Mt 12:41	2782
p the gospel of the kingdom of	Mk 1:14	2784
p the baptism of repentance for	Lk 3:3	2784
every city and village, *p* and	Lk 8:1	2784
p the gospel, and healing every	Lk 9:6	2097
they repented at the *p* of Jonas	Lk 11:32	2782
went every where *p* the word	Acts 8:4	2097
p the things concerning the	Acts 8:12	2097
Israel, *p* peace by Jesus Christ	Acts 10:36	2097
p the word to none but unto the	Acts 11:19	2980
the Grecians, *p* the Lord Jesus	Acts 11:20	2097
p the word of the Lord, with many	Acts 15:35	2097
and as Paul was long *p*, he sunk	Acts 20:9	1256
I have gone *p* the kingdom of God	Acts 20:25	2784
P the kingdom of God, and teaching	Acts 28:31	2784
the *p* of Jesus Christ, according	Rom 16:25	2784
For the *p* of the cross is to them	1Cor 1:18	3056
of *p* to save them that believe	1Cor 1:21	2782
my *p* was not with enticing words	1Cor 2:4	2782
be not risen, then is our *p* vain	1Cor 15:14	2782
also in *p* the gospel of Christ	2Cor 10:14	
that by me the *p* might be fully	2Ti 4:17	2782
manifested his word through *p*	Titus 1:3	2782

PRECEPT

For *p* must be upon *p*,	Is 28:10	6673
p upon *p*; line upon line	Is 28:10	6673
LORD was unto them *p* upon *p*	Is 28:13	6673
p upon *p*; line upon line	Is 28:13	6673
me is taught by the *p* of men	Is 29:13	4687
of your heart he wrote you this *p*	Mk 10:5	1785
p to all the people according to	Heb 9:19	1785

PRECEPTS

sabbath, and commandedst them *p*	Neh 9:14	4687
us to keep thy *p* diligently	Ps 119:4	6490
I will meditate in thy *p*, and have	Ps 119:15	6490
me to understand the way of thy *p*	Ps 119:27	6490
Behold, I have longed after thy *p*	Ps 119:40	6490
for I seek thy *p*	Ps 119:45	6490
This I had, because I kept thy *p*	Ps 119:56	6490
thee, and of them that keep thy *p*	Ps 119:63	6490
keep thy *p* with my whole heart	Ps 119:69	6490
but I will meditate in thy *p*	Ps 119:78	6490
but I forsook not thy *p*	Ps 119:87	6490
I will never forget thy *p*	Ps 119:93	6490
for I have sought thy *p*	Ps 119:94	6490
ancients, because I keep thy *p*	Ps 119:100	6490
Through thy *p* I get understanding	Ps 119:104	6490
yet I erred not from thy *p*	Ps 119:110	6490
Therefore I esteem all thy *p*	Ps 119:128	6490
so will I keep thy *p*	Ps 119:134	6490
yet do not I forget thy *p*	Ps 119:141	6490
Consider how I love thy *p*	Ps 119:159	6490
I have kept thy *p* and thy	Ps 119:168	6490
for I have chosen thy *p*	Ps 119:173	6490
your father, and kept all his *p*	Jer 35:18	4687
even by departing from thy *p*	Dan 9:5	4687

P

PRECIOUS

brother and to her mother p things	Gen 24:53	4030
for the p things of heaven, for	Deut 33:13	4022
for the p fruits brought forth by	Deut 33:14	4022
for the p things put forth by the	Deut 33:14	4022
for the p things of the lasting	Deut 33:15	4022
for the p things of the earth and	Deut 33:16	4022
of the LORD was p in those days	1Sa 3:1	3368
because my soul was p in thine	1Sa 26:21	3365
talent of gold with the p stones	2Sa 12:30	3368
and very much gold, and p stones	1Kin 10:2	3368
very great store, and p stones	1Kin 10:10	3368
of almug trees, and p stones	1Kin 10:11	3368
thy servants, be p in thy sight	2Kin 1:13	3365
let my life now be p in thy sight	2Kin 1:14	3365
all the house of his p things	2Kin 20:13	5238
the p ointment, and all the house	2Kin 20:13	2896
there were p stones in it	1Chr 20:2	3368
and all manner of p stones	1Chr 29:2	3368
they with whom p stones were	1Chr 29:8	
house with p stones for beauty	2Chr 3:6	3368
and gold in abundance, and p stones	2Chr 9:1	3368
great abundance, and p stones	2Chr 9:9	3368
brought algum trees and p stones	2Chr 9:10	3368
p jewels, which they stripped off	2Chr 20:25	2530
of p things, with fenced cities	2Chr 21:3	4030
for p stones, and for spices, and	2Chr 32:27	3368
with p things, beside all that	Ezr 1:6	4030
vessels of fine copper, p as gold	Ezr 8:27	2530
and his eye seeth every p thing	Job 28:10	3366
gold of Ophir, with the p onyx	Job 28:16	3368
the redemption of their soul is p	Ps 49:8	3365
p shall their blood be in his	Ps 72:14	3365
P in the sight of the LORD is the	Ps 116:15	3368
forth and weepeth, bearing p seed	Ps 126:6	4901
It is like the p ointment upon	Ps 133:2	2896
How p also are thy thoughts unto	Ps 139:17	3365
We shall find all p substance	Prov 1:13	3368
She is more p than rubies	Prov 3:15	3368
will hunt for the p life	Prov 6:26	3368
substance of a diligent man is p	Prov 12:27	3368
A gift is as a p stone in the	Prov 17:8	2580
lips of knowledge are a p jewel	Prov 20:15	3366
the chambers be filled with all p	Prov 24:4	3368
name is better than p ointment	Eccl 7:1	2896
make a man more p than fine gold	Is 13:12	3365
stone, a p corner stone, a sure	Is 28:16	3368
them the house of his p things	Is 39:2	5238
the p ointment, and all the house	Is 39:2	2896
Since thou wast p in my sight	Is 43:4	3365
take forth the p from the vile	Jer 15:19	3368
all the p things thereof, and	Jer 20:5	3366
The p sons of Zion, comparable to	Lam 4:2	3368
taken the treasure and p things	Eze 22:25	3366
in p clothes for chariots	Eze 27:20	2667
all spices, and with all p stones	Eze 27:22	3368
every p stone was thy covering	Eze 28:13	3368
with their p vessels of silver and	Dan 11:8	2532
with p stones, and pleasant things	Dan 11:38	3368
over all the p things of Egypt	Dan 11:43	2530
alabaster box of very p ointment	Mt 26:7	927
of ointment of spikenard very p	Mk 14:3	4185
p stones, wood, hay, stubble	1Cor 3:12	5093
for the p fruit of the earth	Jas 5:7	5093
being much more p than of gold	1Pet 1:7	5093
But with the p blood of Christ,	1Pet 1:19	5093
of men, but chosen of God, and p	1Pet 2:4	1784
a chief corner stone, elect, p	1Pet 2:6	1784
therefore which believe he is p	1Pet 2:7	5092
like p faith with us through the	2Pet 1:1	2472
us exceeding great and p promises	2Pet 1:4	5093
p stones and pearls, having a	Rev 17:4	5093
p stones, and of pearls, and fine	Rev 18:12	5093
all manner vessels of most p wood	Rev 18:12	5093
with gold, and p stones, and pearls	Rev 18:16	5093
was like unto a stone most p	Rev 21:11	5093
with all manner of p stones	Rev 21:19	5093

PREDESTINATE

he also did p to be conformed to	Rom 8:29	4309
Moreover whom he did p, them he	Rom 8:30	4309

PREDESTINATED

Having p us unto the adoption of	Eph 1:5	4309
being p according to the purpose	Eph 1:11	4309

PREEMINENCE

a man hath no p above a beast	Eccl 3:19	4195
in all things he might have the p	Col 1:18	4409
loveth to have the p among them	3Jn 9	5383

PREFER

if I p not Jerusalem above my	Ps 137:6	5927

PREFERRED

he p her and her maids unto the	Est 2:9	8138
Daniel was p above the presidents	Dan 6:3	5330
cometh after me is p before me	Jn 1:15	1096
coming after me is p before me	Jn 1:27	1096
cometh a man which is p before me	Jn 1:30	1096

PREFERRING

in honour p one another	Rom 12:10	4285
without p one before another	1Ti 5:21	4299

PREMEDITATE

ye shall speak, neither do ye p	Mk 13:11	3191

PREPARATION

will therefore now make p for it	1Chr 22:5	3559
torches in the day of his p	Nah 2:3	3559
that followed the day of the p	Mt 27:62	3904
was come, because it was the p	Mk 15:42	3904
And that day was the p, and the	Lk 23:54	3904
it was the p of the passover, and	Jn 19:14	3904
therefore, because it was the p	Jn 19:31	3904
because of the Jews' p day	Jn 19:42	3904
with the p of the gospel of peace	Eph 6:15	2091

PREPARATIONS

The p of the heart in man, and the	Prov 16:1	4633

PREPARE

I will p him an habitation	Ex 15:2	
shall p that which they bring in	Ex 16:5	3559
thou p with the burnt offering or	Num 15:5	6213
thou shalt p for a meat offering	Num 15:6	6213
to the number that ye shall p	Num 15:12	6213
p me here seven oxen and seven	Num 23:1	3559
p me here seven bullocks and seven	Num 23:29	3559
Thou shalt p thee a way, and	Deut 19:3	3559
people, saying, P you victuals	Josh 1:11	3559
Let us now p to build us an altar	Josh 22:26	6213
p your hearts unto the LORD, and	1Sa 7:3	3559
p yet, and know and see his place	1Sa 23:22	3559
P thy chariot, and get thee down,	1Kin 18:44	631
shewbread, to p it every sabbath	1Chr 9:32	3559
and p their heart unto thee	1Chr 29:18	3559
Even to p me timber in abundance	2Chr 2:9	3559
Then Hezekiah commanded to p	2Chr 31:11	3559
p yourselves by the houses of	2Chr 35:4	3559
p your brethren, that they may do	2Chr 35:6	3559
banquet that I shall p for them	Est 5:8	6213
p thyself to the search of their	Job 8:8	3559
If thou p thine heart, and stretch	Job 11:13	3559
dust, and p raiment as the clay	Job 27:16	3559
He may p it, but the just shall	Job 27:17	3559
thou wilt p their heart, thou	Ps 10:17	3559
p themselves without my fault	Ps 59:4	3559
O p mercy and truth, which may	Ps 61:7	4487
that they may p a city for	Ps 107:36	3559
P thy work without, and make it	Prov 24:27	3559
yet they p their meat in the	Prov 30:25	3559
P slaughter for his children for	Is 14:21	3559
P the table, watch in the	Is 21:5	6186
P ye the way of the LORD, make	Is 40:3	6437
workman to p a graven image	Is 40:20	3559
ye up, p the way, take up the	Is 57:14	6437
p ye the way of the people	Is 62:10	6437
that p a table for that troop, and	Is 65:11	6186
P ye war against her	Jer 6:4	6942
p them for the day of slaughter	Jer 12:3	6942
I will p destroyers against thee,	Jer 22:7	6942
say ye, Stand fast, and p thee	Jer 46:14	3559
up the watchmen, p the ambushes	Jer 51:12	3559
p the nations against her, call	Jer 51:27	6942
P against her the nations with	Jer 51:28	6942
thou shalt p thy bread therewith	Eze 4:15	6213
p thee stuff for removing, and	Eze 12:3	6213
I will p thee unto blood, and	Eze 35:6	6213
p for thyself, thou, and all thy	Eze 38:7	3559
Seven days shalt thou p every day	Eze 43:25	6213
they shall also p a young bullock	Eze 43:25	3559
he shall p the sin offering, and	Eze 45:17	3559
shall the prince p for himself	Eze 45:22	3559
days of the feast he shall p a	Eze 45:23	3559
he shall p a meat offering of an	Eze 45:24	3559
the priests shall p his burnt	Eze 46:2	3559
he shall p a meat offering, an	Eze 46:7	3559
Now when the prince shall p a	Eze 46:12	3559
he shall p his burnt offering and	Eze 46:12	3559
Thou shalt daily p a burnt	Eze 46:13	3559
thou shalt p it every morning	Eze 46:13	3559
thou shalt p a meat offering for	Eze 46:14	3559
Thus shall they p the lamb	Eze 46:15	3559
P war, wake up the mighty men,	Joel 3:9	6942
p to meet thy God, O Israel	Amos 4:12	3559

they even *p* war against him	Mic 3:5	6942
he shall *p* the way before me	Mal 3:1	6437
P ye the way of the Lord, make	Mt 3:3	2090
which shall *p* thy way before thee	Mt 11:10	2680
Where wilt thou that we *p* for	Mt 26:17	2090
which shall *p* thy way before thee	Mk 1:2	2680
P ye the way of the Lord, make	Mk 1:3	2090
p that thou mayest eat the	Mk 14:12	2090
face of the Lord to *p* his ways	Lk 1:76	2090
P ye the way of the Lord, make	Lk 3:4	2090
which shall *p* thy way before thee	Lk 7:27	2680
p us the passover, that we may	Lk 22:8	2090
him, Where wilt thou that we *p*	Lk 22:9	2090
I go to *p* a place for you	Jn 14:2	2090
p a place for you, I will come	Jn 14:3	2090
who shall *p* himself to the battle	1Cor 14:8	3903
But withal *p* me also a lodging	Philem 22	2090

PREPARED

for I have *p* the house, and room	Gen 24:31	6437
and the bread, which she had *p*	Gen 27:17	6213
neither had they *p* for themselves	Ex 12:39	6213
into the place which I have *p*	Ex 23:20	3559
the city of Sihon be built and *p*	Num 21:27	3559
I have *p* seven altars, and I have	Num 23:4	6186
whom he had *p* of the children of	Josh 4:4	3559
About forty thousand *p* for war	Josh 4:13	2502
this, that Absalom *p* him chariots	2Sa 15:1	6213
he *p* him chariots and horsemen, and	1Kin 1:5	6213
so they *p* timber and stones to	1Kin 5:18	3559
the oracle he *p* in the house	1Kin 6:19	3559
he *p* great provision for them	2Kin 6:23	3739
for their brethren had *p* for them	1Chr 12:39	3559
p a place for the ark of God, and	1Chr 15:1	3559
his place, which he had *p* for it	1Chr 15:3	3559
the place that I have *p* for it	1Chr 15:12	3559
David *p* iron in abundance for the	1Chr 22:3	3559
So David *p* abundantly before his	1Chr 22:5	3559
in my trouble I have *p* for the	1Chr 22:14	3559
timber also and stone have I *p*	1Chr 22:14	3559
Now I have *p* with all my might	1Chr 29:2	3559
that I have *p* for the holy house	1Chr 29:3	3559
have *p* to build thee an house for	1Chr 29:16	3559
place which David had *p* for it	2Chr 1:4	3559
in the place that David had *p* in	2Chr 3:1	3559
p unto the day of the foundation	2Chr 8:16	3559
because he *p* not his heart to	2Chr 12:14	3559
divers kinds of spices *p* by the	2Chr 16:14	7543
thousand ready *p* for the war	2Chr 17:18	2502
hast *p* thine heart to seek God	2Chr 19:3	3559
p their hearts unto the God of	2Chr 20:33	3559
Uzziah *p* for them throughout all	2Chr 26:14	3559
because he *p* his ways before the	2Chr 27:6	3559
in his transgression, have we *p*	2Chr 29:19	3559
people, that God had *p* the people	2Chr 29:36	3559
and they *p* them,	2Chr 31:11	3559
So the service was *p*, and the	2Chr 35:10	3559
the Levites *p* for themselves	2Chr 35:14	3559
brethren the Levites *p* for them	2Chr 35:15	3559
of the Lord was *p* the same day	2Chr 35:16	3559
when Josiah had *p* the temple	2Chr 35:20	3559
For Ezra had *p* his heart to seek	Ezr 7:10	3559
Now that which was *p* for me daily	Neh 5:18	6213
also fowls were *p* for me, and once	Neh 5:18	6213
unto them for whom nothing is *p*	Neh 8:10	3559
he had *p* for him a great chamber,	Neh 13:5	6213
the banquet that I have *p* for him	Est 5:4	6213
to the banquet that Esther had *p*	Est 5:5	6213
banquet that she had *p* but myself	Est 5:12	6213
the gallows that he had *p* for him	Est 6:4	3559
the banquet that Esther had *p*	Est 6:14	6213
that he had *p* for Mordecai	Est 7:10	3559
he *p* it, yea, and searched it out	Job 28:27	3559
when I *p* my seat in the street	Job 29:7	3559
He hath also *p* for him the	Ps 7:13	3559
he hath *p* his throne for judgment	Ps 9:7	3559
They have *p* a net for my steps	Ps 57:6	3559
hast *p* of thy goodness for the	Ps 68:10	3559
thou hast *p* the light and the sun	Ps 74:16	3559
The Lord hath *p* his throne in the	Ps 103:19	3559
When he *p* the heavens, I was	Prov 8:27	3559
Judgments are *p* for scorners	Prov 19:29	3559
The horse is *p* against the day of	Prov 21:31	3559
yea, for the king it is *p*	Is 30:33	3559
what he hath *p* for him that	Is 64:4	6213
a table *p* before it, whereupon	Eze 23:41	6186
of thy pipes was *p* in thee the	Eze 28:13	3559
Be thou *p*, and prepare for thyself	Eze 38:7	3559
for ye have *p* lying and corrupt	Dan 2:9	2164
and gold, which they *p* for Baal	Hos 2:8	6213
going forth is *p* as the morning	Hos 6:3	3559

Now the Lord had *p* a great fish	Jonah 1:17	4487
And the Lord God *p* a gourd	Jonah 4:6	4487
But God *p* a worm when the morning	Jonah 4:7	4487
that God *p* a vehement east wind	Jonah 4:8	4487
and the defence shall be *p*	Nah 2:5	3559
for the Lord hath *p* a sacrifice	Zeph 1:7	3559
for whom it is *p* of my Father	Mt 20:23	2090
Behold, I have *p* my dinner	Mt 22:4	2090
inherit the kingdom *p* for you	Mt 25:34	2090
p for the devil and his angels	Mt 25:41	2090
be given to them for whom it is *p*	Mk 10:40	2090
a large upper room furnished and *p*	Mk 14:15	2092
ready a people *p* for the Lord	Lk 1:17	2680
Which thou hast *p* before the face	Lk 2:31	2090
p not himself, neither did	Lk 12:47	2090
and *p* spices and ointments	Lk 23:56	2090
the spices which they had *p*	Lk 24:1	2090
which he had afore *p* unto glory	Rom 9:23	4282
God hath *p* for them that love him	1Cor 2:9	2090
use, and *p* unto every good work	2Ti 2:21	2090
not, but a body hast thou *p* me	Heb 10:5	2675
p an ark to the saving of his	Heb 11:7	2680
for he hath *p* for them a city	Heb 11:16	2090
trumpets *p* themselves to sound	Rev 8:6	2090
like unto horses *p* unto battle	Rev 9:7	2090
which were *p* for an hour, and a	Rev 9:15	2090
where she hath a place *p* of God	Rev 12:6	2090
the kings of the east might be *p*	Rev 16:12	2090
p as a bride adorned for her	Rev 21:2	2090

PREPAREDST

Thou *p* room before it, and didst	Ps 80:9	6437

PREPAREST

when thou *p* a bullock for a burnt	Num 15:8	6213
Thou *p* a table before me in the	Ps 23:5	6186
thou *p* them corn, when thou hast	Ps 65:9	3559

PREPARETH

That *p* his heart to seek God, the	2Chr 30:19	3559
vanity, and their belly *p* deceit	Job 15:35	3559
who *p* rain for the earth, who	Ps 147:8	3559

PREPARING

in *p* him a chamber in the courts	Neh 13:7	6213
of Noah, while the ark was a *p*	1Pet 3:20	2680

PRESBYTERY

laying on of the hands of the *p*	1Ti 4:14	4244

PRESCRIBED

grievousness which they have *p*	Is 10:1	3789

PRESCRIBING

oil, and salt without *p* how much	Ezr 7:22	3792

PRESENCE

the *p* of the Lord God amongst the	Gen 3:8	6440
went out from the *p* of the Lord	Gen 4:16	6440
in the *p* of all his brethren	Gen 16:12	6440
in the *p* of the sons of my people	Gen 23:11	5869
in the *p* of the children of Heth	Gen 23:18	5869
he died in the *p* of all his	Gen 25:18	6440
from the *p* of Isaac his father	Gen 27:30	6440
went out from the *p* of Pharaoh	Gen 41:46	6440
for they were troubled at his *p*	Gen 45:3	6440
for why should we die in thy *p*	Gen 47:15	5048
were driven out from Pharaoh's *p*	Ex 10:11	5869
My *p* shall go with thee, and I	Ex 33:14	6440
If thy *p* go not with me, carry us	Ex 33:15	6440
departed from the *p* of Moses	Ex 35:20	6440
soul shall be cut off from my *p*	Lev 22:3	6440
Aaron went from the *p* of the	Num 20:6	6440
unto him in the *p* of the elders	Deut 25:9	5869
priests, in the *p* of the people	Josh 4:11	6440
which he wrote in the *p* of the	Josh 8:32	6440
David avoided out of his *p* twice	1Sa 18:11	6440
David to Saul, and he was in his *p*	1Sa 19:7	6440
he slipped away out of Saul's *p*	1Sa 19:10	6440
to play the mad man in my *p*	1Sa 21:15	5921
I not serve in the *p* of his son	2Sa 16:19	6440
I have served in thy father's *p*	2Sa 16:19	6440
so will I be in thy *p*	2Sa 16:19	6440
went out from the *p* of the king	2Sa 24:4	6440
And she came into the king's *p*	1Kin 1:28	6440
the *p* of all the congregation of	1Kin 8:22	5048
fled from the *p* of king Solomon	1Kin 12:2	6440
in the *p* of the people, saying,	1Kin 21:13	5048
the *p* of Jehoshaphat the king of	2Kin 3:14	6440
he went out from his *p* a leper as	2Kin 5:27	6440
cast he them from his *p* as yet	2Kin 13:23	6440
he had cast them out from his *p*	2Kin 24:20	6440
of them that were in the king's *p*	2Kin 25:19	6440
Glory and honour are in his *p*	1Chr 16:27	6440
sing out at the *p* of the Lord	1Chr 16:33	6440

P

Aaron in the p of David the king	1Chr 24:31	6440
the p of all the congregation of	2Chr 6:12	5048
the earth sought the p of Solomon	2Chr 9:23	6440
from the p of Solomon the king	2Chr 10:2	6440
before this house, and in thy p	2Chr 20:9	6440
the altars of Baalim in his p	2Chr 34:4	6440
not been beforetime sad in his p	Neh 2:1	6440
in the p of Ahasuerus the king	Est 1:10	6440
Mordecai went out from the p of	Est 8:15	6440
went forth from the p of the LORD	Job 1:12	6440
forth from the p of the LORD	Job 2:7	6440
Therefore am I troubled at his p	Job 23:15	6440
shall fall and perish at thy p	Ps 9:3	6440
in thy p is fulness of joy	Ps 16:11	6440
my sentence come forth from thy p	Ps 17:2	6440
me in the p of mine enemies	Ps 23:5	5048
of thy p from the pride of man	Ps 31:20	6440
Cast me not away from thy p	Ps 51:11	6440
the wicked perish at the p of God	Ps 68:2	6440
also dropped at the p of God	Ps 68:8	6440
itself was moved at the p of God	Ps 68:8	6440
before his p with thanksgiving	Ps 95:2	6440
like wax at the p of the LORD	Ps 97:5	6440
at the p of the LORD of the whole	Ps 97:5	6440
come before his p with singing	Ps 100:2	6440
at the p of the Lord	Ps 114:7	6440
at the p of the God of Jacob	Ps 114:7	6440
now in the p of all his people	Ps 116:14	5048
now in the p of all his people	Ps 116:18	6440
whither shall I flee from thy p	Ps 139:7	6440
the upright shall dwell in thy p	Ps 140:13	6440
Go from the p of a foolish man,	Prov 14:7	5048
surety in the p of his friend	Prov 17:18	6440
thyself in the p of the king	Prov 25:6	6440
p of the prince whom thine eyes	Prov 25:7	6440
strangers devour it in your p	Is 1:7	5048
of Egypt shall be moved at his p	Is 19:1	6440
and the angel of his p saved them	Is 63:9	6440
might flow down at thy p,	Is 64:1	6440
the nations may tremble at thy p	Is 64:2	6440
mountains flowed down at thy p	Is 64:3	6440
broken down at the p of the LORD	Jer 4:26	6440
will ye not tremble at my p	Jer 5:22	6440
fathers, and cast you out of my p	Jer 23:39	6440
in the p of the priests and of all	Jer 28:1	5869
Hananiah in the p of the priests	Jer 28:5	5869
in the p of all the people that	Jer 28:5	5869
spake in the p of all the people	Jer 28:11	5869
in the p of the witnesses that	Jer 32:12	5869
he had cast them out from his p	Jer 52:3	6440
of the earth, shall shake at my p	Eze 38:20	6440
answered in the p of the king	Dan 2:27	6925
Tarshish from the p of the LORD	Jonah 1:3	6440
Tarshish from the p of the LORD	Jonah 1:3	6440
he fled from the p of the LORD	Jonah 1:10	6440
and the earth is burned at his p	Nah 1:5	6440
peace at the p of the Lord GOD	Zeph 1:7	6440
that stand in the p of God	Lk 1:19	1799
We have eaten and drunk in thy p	Lk 13:26	1799
p of them that sit at meat with	Lk 14:10	1799
there is joy in the p of the	Lk 15:10	1799
Jesus in the p of his disciples	Jn 20:30	1799
and denied him in the p of Pilate	Acts 3:13	4383
soundness in the p of you all	Acts 3:16	561
shall come from the p of the Lord	Acts 3:19	4383
from the p of the council	Acts 5:41	4383
thanks to God in p of them all	Acts 27:35	1799
no flesh should glory in his p	1Cor 1:29	1799
who in p am base among you, but	2Cor 10:1	4383
but his bodily p is weak, and his	2Cor 10:10	3952
obeyed, not as in my p only	Phil 2:12	3952
from you for a short time in p	1Th 2:17	4383
Are not even ye in the p of our	1Th 2:19	1715
from the p of the Lord, and from	2Th 1:9	4383
to appear in the p of God for us	Heb 9:24	4383
you faultless before the p of his	Jude 24	2714
brimstone in the p of the holy	Rev 14:10	1799
angels, and in the p of the Lamb	Rev 14:10	1799

PRESENT

his hand a p for Esau his brother	Gen 32:13	4503
it is a p sent unto my lord Esau	Gen 32:18	4503
with the p that goeth before me	Gen 32:20	4503
So went the p over before him	Gen 32:21	4503
then receive my p at my hand	Gen 33:10	4503
and carry down the man a p	Gen 43:11	4503
And the men took that p, and they	Gen 43:15	4503
they made ready the p against	Gen 43:25	4503
they brought him the p which was	Gen 43:26	4503
p thyself there to me in the top	Ex 34:2	5324
p the man that is to be made	Lev 14:11	5975

p them before the LORD at the	Lev 16:7	5975
then he shall p himself before	Lev 27:8	5975
then he shall p the beast before	Lev 27:11	5975
p them before Aaron the priest,	Num 3:6	5975
p yourselves in the tabernacle of	Deut 31:14	3320
a p unto Eglon the king of Moab	Judg 3:15	4503
he brought the p unto Eglon king	Judg 3:17	4503
he had made an end to offer the p	Judg 3:18	4503
away the people that bare the p	Judg 3:18	4503
unto thee, and bring forth my p	Judg 6:18	4503
there is not a p to bring to the	1Sa 9:7	8670
Now therefore p yourselves before	1Sa 10:19	3320
the people that were p with him	1Sa 13:15	4672
the people that were p with them	1Sa 13:16	4672
in mine hand, or what there is p	1Sa 21:3	4672
Behold a p for you of the spoil	1Sa 30:26	1293
three days, and be thou here p	2Sa 11:12	5975
given it for a p unto his	1Kin 9:16	7964
And they brought every man his p	1Kin 10:25	4503
have sent unto thee a p of silver	1Kin 15:19	7810
were numbered, and were all p	1Kin 20:27	3557
Take a p in thine hand, and go,	2Kin 8:8	4503
took a p with him, even of every	2Kin 8:9	4503
sent it for a p to the king of	2Kin 16:8	7810
brought no p to the king of	2Kin 17:4	4503
Make an agreement with me by a p	2Kin 18:31	1293
sent letters and a p unto Hezekiah	2Kin 20:12	4503
joy thy people, which are p here	1Chr 29:17	4672
that were p were sanctified	2Chr 5:11	4672
And they brought every man his p	2Chr 9:24	4503
all that were p with him bowed	2Chr 29:29	4672
children of Israel that were p at	2Chr 30:21	4672
all Israel that were p went out	2Chr 31:1	4672
all that were p in Jerusalem	2Chr 34:32	4672
that were p in Israel to serve	2Chr 34:33	4672
offerings, for all that were p	2Chr 35:7	4672
children of Israel that were p	2Chr 35:17	4672
all Judah and Israel that were p	2Chr 35:18	4672
his lords, and all Israel there p	Ezr 8:25	4672
that were p in Shushan the palace	Est 1:5	4672
the Jews that are p in Shushan	Est 4:16	4672
to p themselves before the LORD	Job 1:6	3320
to p themselves before the LORD	Job 2:1	3320
them to p himself before the LORD	Job 2:1	3320
a very p help in trouble	Ps 46:1	4672
In that time shall the p be	Is 18:7	7862
Make an agreement with me by a p	Is 36:16	1293
sent letters and a p to Hezekiah	Is 39:1	4503
It may be they will p their	Jer 36:7	5307
unto whom ye sent me to p your	Jer 42:9	5307
thee for a p horns of ivory	Eze 27:15	814
for we do not p our supplications	Dan 9:18	5307
Assyria for a p to king Jareb	Hos 10:6	4503
Jerusalem, to p him to the Lord	Lk 2:22	3936
of the Lord was p to heal them	Lk 5:17	
There were p at that season some	Lk 13:1	3918
manifold more in this p time	Lk 18:30	3918
unto you, being yet p with you	Jn 14:25	3306
are we all here p before God	Acts 10:33	3918
and all the elders were p	Acts 21:18	3854
all men which are here p with us	Acts 25:24	4840
every one, because of the p rain	Acts 28:2	2186
for to will is p with me	Rom 7:18	3873
would do good, evil is p with me	Rom 7:21	3873
this p time are not worthy to be	Rom 8:18	3568
nor powers, nor things p	Rom 8:38	1764
Even so then at this p time also	Rom 11:5	3568
that ye p your bodies a living	Rom 12:1	3936
or life, or death, or things p	1Cor 3:22	1764
Even unto this p hour we both	1Cor 4:11	737
but p in spirit, have judged	1Cor 5:3	3918
already, as though I were p	1Cor 5:3	3918
this is good for the p distress	1Cor 7:26	1764
greater part remain unto this p	1Cor 15:6	737
by Jesus, and shall us with you	2Cor 4:14	3936
body, and to be p with the Lord	2Cor 5:8	1736
whether p or absent, we may be	2Cor 5:9	1736
when I am p with that confidence	2Cor 10:2	3918
we be also in deed when we are p	2Cor 10:11	3918
that I may p you as a chaste	2Cor 11:2	3936
And when I was p with you, and	2Cor 11:9	3918
and foretell you, as if I were p	2Cor 13:2	3918
lest being p I should use	2Cor 13:10	3918
deliver us from this p evil world	Gal 1:4	1764
and not only when I am p with you	Gal 4:18	3918
I desire to be p with you now	Gal 4:20	3918
That he might p it to himself a	Eph 5:27	3936
to p you holy and unblameable and	Col 1:22	3936
that we may p every man perfect	Col 1:28	3936
me, having loved this p world	2Ti 4:10	3568
and godly, in this p world	Titus 2:12	3568

was a figure for the time then *p* .... Heb 9:9   *1764*
for the *p* seemeth to be joyous .... Heb 12:11   *3918*
and be established in the *p* truth 2Pet 1:12   *3918*
to *p* you faultless before the .... Jude 24   *2476*

PRESENTED
to Goshen, and *p* himself unto him .... Gen 46:29   *7200*
five men, and *p* them unto Pharaoh ...... Gen 47:2   *3322*
when it is *p* unto the priest, he .... Lev 2:8   *7126*
in the day when he *p* them to .... Lev 7:35   *7126*
Aaron's sons *p* unto him the blood .... Lev 9:12   *4672*
they *p* the burnt offering unto .... Lev 9:13   *4672*
Aaron's sons *p* unto him the blood .... Lev 9:18   *4672*
shall be *p* alive before the LORD, ... Lev 16:10   *5975*
p themselves in the tabernacle of.......... Deut 31:14   *3320*
they *p* themselves before God .... Josh 24:1   *3320*
unto him under the oak, and *p* it .... Judg 6:19   *5066*
p themselves in the assembly of .... Judg 20:2   *3320*
evening, and *p* himself forty days.......... 1Sa 17:16   *3320*
I *p* my supplication before the .... Jer 38:26   *5307*
there they *p* the provocation of .... Eze 20:28   *5414*
treasures, they *p* unto him gifts............. Mt 2:11   *4374*
the saints and widows, *p* her alive .... Acts 9:41   *3936*
governor, *p* Paul also before him .... Acts 23:33   *3936*

PRESENTING
p my supplication before the LORD .... Dan 9:20   *5307*

PRESENTLY
them not fail to burn the fat *p* 1Sa 2:16   *3117*
A fool's wrath is *p* known .... Prov 12:16   *3117*
p the fig tree withered away .... Mt 21:19   *3916*
he shall *p* give me more than .... Mt 26:53   *3936*
Him therefore I hope to send *p* .... Phil 2:23   *1824*

PRESENTS
despised him, and brought him no *p*...... 1Sa 10:27   *4503*
they brought *p*, and served Solomon 1Kin 4:21   *4503*
became his servant, and gave him *p*...... 2Kin 17:3   *4503*
Judah brought to Jehoshaphat *p* 2Chr 17:5   *4503*
Philistines brought Jehoshaphat *p* 2Chr 17:11   *4503*
p to Hezekiah king of Judah 2Chr 32:23   *4030*
shall kings bring *p* unto thee .... Ps 68:29   *7862*
and of the isles shall bring *p*................... Ps 72:10   *4503*
bring *p* unto him that ought to be .... Ps 76:11   *7862*
thou give *p* to Moresheth-gath .... Mic 1:14   *7964*

PRESERVE
that we may *p* seed of our father .... Gen 19:32   *2421*
that we may *p* seed of our father .... Gen 19:34   *2421*
did send me before you to *p* life .... Gen 45:5   *4241*
God sent me before you to *p* you a .... Gen 45:7   *7760*
always, that he might *p* us alive .... Deut 6:24   *2421*
thou shalt *p* them from this .... Ps 12:7   *5341*
P me, O God .... Ps 16:1   *8104*
Let integrity and uprightness *p* me .... Ps 25:21   *5341*
thou shalt *p* me from trouble................... Ps 32:7   *5341*
and thy truth continually *p* me .... Ps 40:11   *5341*
The LORD will *p* him, and keep him .... Ps 41:2   *8104*
mercy and truth, which may *p* him .... Ps 61:7   *5341*
p my life from fear of the enemy .... Ps 64:1   *5341*
p thou those that are appointed .... Ps 79:11   *3498*
P my soul .... Ps 86:2   *8104*
The LORD shall *p* thee from all................ Ps 121:7   *8104*
he shall *p* thy soul .... Ps 121:7   *8104*
The LORD shall *p* thy going out .... Ps 121:8   *8104*
p me from the violent man .... Ps 140:1   *5341*
p me from the violent man .... Ps 140:4   *5341*
Discretion shall *p* thee, ... Prov 2:11   *8104*
her not, and she shall *p* thee .... Prov 4:6   *8104*
the lips of the wise shall *p* them .... Prov 14:3   *8104*
Mercy and truth *p* the king .... Prov 20:28   *5341*
The eyes of the LORD *p* knowledge .... Prov 22:12   *5341*
and passing over he will *p* it .... Is 31:5   *4422*
and I will *p* thee, and give thee .... Is 49:8   *5341*
children, I will *p* them alive.................... Jer 49:11   *2421*
shall lose his life shall *p* it .... Lk 17:33   *2225*
will *p* me unto his heavenly 2Ti 4:18   *4982*

PRESERVED
God face to face, and my life is *p* .... Gen 32:30   *5337*
p us in all the way wherein we .... Josh 24:17   *8104*
LORD hath given us, who hath *p* us 1Sa 30:23   *8104*
the LORD *p* David whithersoever he 2Sa 8:6   *3467*
the LORD *p* David whithersoever he 2Sa 8:14   *3467*
Thus the LORD *p* David 1Chr 18:6   *3467*
Thus the LORD *p* David 1Chr 18:13   *3467*
thy visitation hath *p* my spirit .... Job 10:12   *8104*
as in the days when God *p* me .... Job 29:2   *8104*
they are *p* for ever .... Ps 37:28   *8104*
and to restore the *p* of Israel .... Is 49:6   *5336*
Egypt, and by a prophet was he *p*........... Hos 12:13   *8104*
into new bottles, and both are *p*......... Mt 9:17   *4933*
and both are *p*.................................... Lk 5:38   *4933*

body be *p* blameless unto the 1Th 5:23   *5083*
p in Jesus Christ, and called................... Jude 1   *5083*

PRESERVER
I do unto thee, O thou *p* of men .... Job 7:20   *5314*

PRESERVEST
is therein, and thou *p* them all .... Neh 9:6   *2421*
O LORD, thou *p* man and beast .... Ps 36:6   *3467*

PRESERVETH
He *p* not the life of the wicked .... Job 36:6   *2421*
for the LORD *p* the faithful .... Ps 31:23   *5341*
he *p* the souls of his saints .... Ps 97:10   *8104*
The LORD *p* the simple .... Ps 116:6   *8104*
The LORD *p* all them that love him .... Ps 145:20   *8104*
The LORD *p* the strangers....................... Ps 146:9   *8104*
and *p* the way of his saints .... Prov 2:8   *8104*
that keepeth his way *p* his soul .... Prov 16:17   *8104*

PRESIDENTS
And over these three *p* .... Dan 6:2   *5632*
Daniel was preferred above the *p*........... Dan 6:3   *5632*
Then the *p* and princes sought to .... Dan 6:4   *5632*
Then these *p* and princes assembled ..... Dan 6:6   *5632*
All the *p* of the kingdom, the.................. Dan 6:7   *5632*

PRESS
for the *p* is full, the fats .... Joel 3:13   *1660*
out fifty vessels out of the *p* .... Hag 2:16   *6333*
not come nigh unto him for the *p* .... Mk 2:4   *3793*
of Jesus, came in the *p* behind............... Mk 5:27   *3793*
of him, turned him about in the *p* .... Mk 5:30   *3793*
could not come at him for the *p* .... Lk 8:19   *3793*
p thee, and sayest thou, Who................. Lk 8:45   *598*
and could not for the *p*, because............ Lk 19:3   *3793*
I *p* toward the mark for the prize .... Phil 3:14   *1377*

PRESSED
And he *p* upon them greatly .... Gen 19:3   *6484*
they *p* sore upon the man, even............. Gen 19:9   *6484*
p them into Pharaoh's cup, and I .... Gen 40:11   *7818*
when she *p* him daily with her .... Judg 16:16   *6693*
And he *p* him 2Sa 13:25   *6555*
But Absalom *p* him, that he let 2Sa 13:27   *6555*
p on by the king's commandment .... Est 8:14   *1765*
there were their breasts *p* .... Eze 23:3   *4600*
I am *p* under you, as a cart is................. Amos 2:13   *5781*
as a cart is *p* that is full of .... Amos 2:13   *5781*
insomuch that they *p* upon him for.......... Mk 3:10   *1968*
as the people *p* upon him to hear.......... Lk 5:1   *1945*
p down, and shaken together, and .... Lk 6:38   *4085*
Paul was *p* in the spirit, and.................. Acts 18:5   *4912*
that we were *p* out of measure,.............. 2Cor 1:8   *916*

PRESSES
thy *p* shall burst out with new .... Prov 3:10   *3342*
tread out no wine in their *p* .... Is 16:10   *3342*

PRESSETH
fast in me, and thy hand *p* me sore .... Ps 38:2   *5181*
preached, and every man *p* into it .... Lk 16:16   *971*

PRESSFAT
when one came to the *p* for to .... Hag 2:16   *3342*

PRESUME
which shall *p* to speak a word in........... Deut 18:20   *2102*
that durst *p* in his heart to do................ Est 7:5   *4390*

PRESUMED
But they *p* to go up unto the hill........... Num 14:44   *6075*

PRESUMPTUOUS
back thy servant also from *p* sins .... Ps 19:13   *2086*
P are they, selfwilled, they are 2Pet 2:10   *5113*

PRESUMPTUOUSLY
But if a man come *p* upon his................ Ex 21:14   *2102*
But the soul that doeth ought *p* .... Num 15:30   *3027*
LORD, and went *p* up into the hill........... Deut 1:43   *2102*
And the man that will do *p* .... Deut 17:12   *2087*
hear, and fear, and do no more *p* .... Deut 17:13   *2102*
but the prophet hath spoken it *p* .... Deut 18:22   *2087*

PRETENCE
and for a *p* make long prayer .... Mt 23:14   *4392*
for a *p* make long prayers .... Mk 12:40   *4392*
every way, whether in *p*, or in .... Phil 1:18   *4392*

PREVAIL
cubits upward did the waters *p*............... Gen 7:20   *1396*
peradventure I shall *p*, that we............... Num 22:6   *3201*
what means we may *p* against him .... Judg 16:5   *3201*
for by strength shall no man *p* 1Sa 2:9   *1396*
but if I *p* against him, and kill............... 1Sa 17:9   *3201*
things, and also shalt still *p* 1Sa 26:25   *3201*
shalt persuade him, and *p* also.............. 1Kin 22:22   *3201*
let not man *p* against thee 2Chr 14:11   *6113*

P

entice him, and thou shalt also p	2Chr 18:21	3201
thou shalt not p against him	Est 6:13	3201
they shall p against him, as a	Job 15:24	8630
and the robber shall p against him	Job 18:9	2388
let not man p	Ps 9:19	5810
said, With our tongue will we p	Ps 12:4	1396
Iniquities p against me	Ps 65:3	1396
if one p against him, two shall	Eccl 4:12	8630
it, but could not p against it	Is 7:1	3898
but he shall not p	Is 16:12	3201
he shall p against his enemies	Is 42:13	1396
to profit, if so be thou mayest p	Is 47:12	6206
but they shall not p against thee	Jer 1:19	3201
themselves, yet can they not p	Jer 5:22	3201
but they shall not p against thee	Jer 15:20	3201
we shall p against him, and we	Jer 20:10	3201
stumble, and they shall not p	Jer 20:11	3201
deal against them, and shall p	Dan 11:7	2388
of hell shall not p against it	Mt 16:18	2729
saw that he could p nothing	Mt 27:24	5623
Perceive ye how ye p nothing	Jn 12:19	5623

PREVAILED

And the waters p, and were	Gen 7:18	1396
the waters p exceedingly upon the	Gen 7:19	1396
the waters p upon the earth an	Gen 7:24	1396
with my sister, and I have p	Gen 30:8	3201
he saw that he p not against him	Gen 32:25	3201
with God and with men, and hast p	Gen 32:28	3201
because the famine p over them	Gen 47:20	2388
have p above the blessings of my	Gen 49:26	1396
held up his hand, that Israel p	Ex 17:11	1396
he let down his hand, Amalek p	Ex 17:11	1396
the hand of the house of Joseph p	Judg 1:35	3513
and his hand p against	Judg 3:10	5810
p against Jabin the king of	Judg 4:24	7186
hand of Midian p against Israel	Judg 6:2	5810
So David p over the Philistine	1Sa 17:50	2388
Surely the men p against us	2Sa 11:23	1396
the king's word p against Joab	2Sa 24:4	2388
Omri p against the people that	1Kin 16:22	2388
month the famine p in the city	2Kin 25:3	2388
For Judah p above his brethren,	1Chr 5:2	1396
the king's word p against Joab	1Chr 21:4	2388
to Hamath-zobah, and p against it	2Chr 8:3	2388
time, and the children of Judah p	2Chr 13:18	553
the Ammonites, and p against them	2Chr 27:5	2388
enemy say, I have p against him	Ps 13:4	3201
yet they have not p against me	Ps 129:2	3201
art stronger than I, and hast p	Jer 20:7	3201
thee on, and have p against thee	Jer 38:22	3201
are desolate, because the enemy p	Lam 1:16	1396
the saints, and p against them	Dan 7:21	3202
he had power over the angel, and p	Hos 12:4	3201
deceived thee, and p against thee	Obad 7	3201
of them and of the chief priests p	Lk 23:23	2729
p against them, so that they fled	Acts 19:16	2480
grew the word of God and p	Acts 19:20	2480
hath p to open the book, and to	Rev 5:5	3528
And p not	Rev 12:8	2480

PREVAILEST

Thou p for ever against him, and	Job 14:20	8630

PREVAILETH

my bones, and it p against them	Lam 1:13	7287

PREVENT

Why did the knees p me	Job 3:12	6923
The God of my mercy shall p me	Ps 59:10	6923
thy tender mercies speedily p us	Ps 79:8	6923
morning shall my prayer p thee	Ps 88:13	6923
Mine eyes p the night watches,	Ps 119:148	6923
evil shall not overtake nor p us	Amos 9:10	6923
shall not p them which are asleep	1Th 4:15	5348

PREVENTED

the snares of death p me	2Sa 22:6	6923
They p me in the day of my	2Sa 22:19	6923
the days of affliction p me	Job 30:27	6923
Who hath p me, that I should	Job 41:11	6923
the snares of death p me	Ps 18:5	6923
They p me in the day of my	Ps 18:18	6923
I p the dawning of the morning,	Ps 119:147	6923
they p with their bread him that	Is 21:14	6923
come into the house, Jesus p him	Mt 17:25	4399

PREVENTEST

For thou p him with the blessings	Ps 21:3	6923

PREY

from the p, my son, thou art gone	Gen 49:9	2964
the morning he shall devour the p	Gen 49:27	5706
and our children should be a p	Num 14:3	957

ones, which ye said should be a p	Num 14:31	957
lie down until he eat of the p	Num 23:24	2964
took all the spoil, and all the p	Num 31:11	4455
brought the captives, and the p	Num 31:12	4455
the sum of the p that was taken	Num 31:26	4455
divide the p into two parts	Num 31:27	4455
being the rest of the p which the	Num 31:32	957
ones, which ye said should be a p	Deut 1:39	957
we took for a p unto ourselves	Deut 2:35	962
we took for a p to ourselves	Deut 3:7	962
ye take for a p unto yourselves	Josh 8:2	962
took for a p unto themselves	Josh 8:27	962
took for a p unto themselves	Josh 11:14	962
have they not divided the p	Judg 5:30	7998
to Sisera of divers colours,	Judg 5:30	7998
a p of divers colours of	Judg 5:30	7998
every man the earrings of his p	Judg 8:24	7998
every man the earrings of his p	Judg 8:25	7998
and they shall become a p and a	2Kin 21:14	957
give them for a p in the land of	Neh 4:4	961
to take the spoil of them for a p	Est 3:13	962
to take the spoil of them for a p	Est 8:11	962
but on the p they laid not their	Est 9:15	961
laid not their hands on the p	Est 9:16	961
old lion perisheth for lack of p	Job 4:11	2964
the eagle that hasteth to the p	Job 9:26	400
rising betimes for a p	Job 24:5	2964
Wilt thou hunt the p for the lion	Job 38:39	2964
From thence she seeketh the p	Job 39:29	400
as a lion that is greedy of his p	Ps 17:12	2963
excellent than the mountains of p	Ps 76:4	2964
young lions roar after their p	Ps 104:21	2964
given us as a p to their teeth	Ps 124:6	2964
She also lieth in wait as for a p	Prov 23:28	2863
shall roar, and lay hold of the p	Is 5:29	2964
that widows may be their p	Is 10:2	7998
take the spoil, and to take the p	Is 10:6	957
the young lion roaring on his p	Is 31:4	2964
then is the p of a great spoil	Is 33:23	5706
the lame take the p	Is 33:23	957
they are for a p, and none	Is 42:22	957
Shall the p be taken from the	Is 49:24	4455
the p of the terrible shall be	Is 49:25	4455
from evil maketh himself a p	Is 59:15	7997
life shall be unto him for a p	Jer 21:9	7998
all that p upon thee will I give	Jer 30:16	962
upon thee will I give for a p	Jer 30:16	7998
he shall have his life for a p	Jer 38:2	7998
life shall be for a p unto thee	Jer 39:18	7998
a p in all places whither thou	Jer 45:5	7998
hands of the strangers for a p	Eze 7:21	957
and it learned to catch the p	Eze 19:3	2964
lion, and learned to catch the p	Eze 19:6	2964
a roaring lion ravening the p	Eze 22:25	2964
are like wolves ravening the p	Eze 22:27	2964
make a p of thy merchandise	Eze 26:12	962
and take her spoil, and take her p	Eze 29:19	957
because my flock became a p	Eze 34:8	957
and they shall no more be a p	Eze 34:22	957
no more be a p to the heathen	Eze 34:28	957
are forsaken, which became a p	Eze 36:4	957
minds, to cast it out for a p	Eze 36:5	957
To take a spoil, and to take a p	Eze 38:12	957
gathered thy company to take a p	Eze 38:13	957
he shall scatter among them the p	Dan 11:24	961
in the forest, when he hath no p	Amos 3:4	2964
and filled his holes with p	Nah 2:12	2964
will cut off thy p from the earth	Nah 2:13	2964
the p departeth not	Nah 3:1	2964
the day that I rise up to the p	Zeph 3:8	5706

PRICE

thou shalt increase the p thereof	Lev 25:16	4736
thou shalt diminish the p of it	Lev 25:16	4736
the p of his sale shall be	Lev 25:50	3701
p of his redemption out of the	Lev 25:51	
him again the p of his redemption	Lev 25:52	
or the p of a dog, into the house	Deut 23:18	4242
will surely buy it of thee at a p	2Sa 24:24	4242
received the linen yarn at a p	1Kin 10:28	4242
shalt grant it me for the full p	1Chr 21:22	3701
will verily buy it for the full p	1Chr 21:24	3701
received the linen yarn at a p	2Chr 1:16	4242
Man knoweth not the p thereof	Job 28:13	6187
be weighed for the p thereof	Job 28:15	4242
for the p of wisdom is above	Job 28:18	4901
increase thy wealth by their p	Ps 44:12	4242
Wherefore is there a p in the	Prov 17:16	4242
the goats are the p of the field	Prov 27:26	4242
for her p is far above rubies	Prov 31:10	4377
not for p nor reward, saith the	Is 45:13	4242

milk without money and without *p*	Is 55:1	4242
I give to the spoil without *p*	Jer 15:13	4242
If ye think good, give me my *p*	Zec 11:12	7939
So they weighed for my *p* thirty	Zec 11:12	7939
a goodly *p* that I was prised at	Zec 11:13	3365
he had found one pearl of great *p*	Mt 13:46	*4186*
because it is the *p* of blood	Mt 27:6	5092
the *p* of him that was valued	Mt 27:9	5092
And kept back part of the *p*	Acts 5:2	5092
back part of the *p* of the land	Acts 5:3	5092
and they counted the *p* of them	Acts 19:19	5092
For ye are bought with a *p*	1Cor 6:20	5092
Ye are bought with a *p*	1Cor 7:23	5092
is in the sight of God of great *p*	1Pet 3:4	*4185*

PRICES
brought the *p* of the things that	Acts 4:34	5092

PRICKED
grieved, and I was *p* in my reins	Ps 73:21	8150
they were *p* in their heart, and	Acts 2:37	2669

PRICKING
there shall be no more a *p* brier	Eze 28:24	3992

PRICKS
of them shall be *p* in your eyes	Num 33:55	7899
for thee to kick against the *p*	Acts 9:5	2759
for thee to kick against the *p*	Acts 26:14	2759

PRIDE
I will break the *p* of your power	Lev 26:19	1347
I know thy *p*, and the naughtiness	1Sa 17:28	2087
himself for the *p* of his heart	2Chr 32:26	1363
his purpose, and hide *p* from man	Job 33:17	1466
because of the *p* of evil men	Job 35:12	1347
His scales are his *p*, shut up	Job 41:15	1346
a king over all the children of *p*	Job 41:34	7830
The wicked in his *p* doth	Ps 10:2	1346
through the *p* of his countenance,	Ps 10:4	1363
of thy presence from the *p* of man	Ps 31:20	7407
not the foot of *p* come against me	Ps 36:11	1346
let them even be taken in their *p*	Ps 59:12	1347
Therefore *p* compasseth them about	Ps 73:6	1346
p, and arrogancy, and the evil way,	Prov 8:13	1344
When *p* cometh, then cometh shame	Prov 11:2	2087
Only by *p* cometh contention	Prov 13:10	2087
of the foolish is a rod of *p*	Prov 14:3	1346
P goeth before destruction, and an	Prov 16:18	1347
A man's *p* shall bring him low	Prov 29:23	1346
of Samaria, that say in the *p*	Is 9:9	1346
We have heard of the *p* of Moab	Is 16:6	1347
even of his haughtiness, and his *p*	Is 16:6	1347
it, to stain the *p* of all glory	Is 23:9	1347
he shall bring down their *p*	Is 25:11	1346
Woe to the crown of *p*, to the	Is 28:1	1348
The crown of *p*, the drunkards of	Is 28:3	1348
manner will I mar the *p* of Judah	Jer 13:9	1347
and the great *p* of Jerusalem	Jer 13:9	1347
weep in secret places for your *p*	Jer 13:17	1466
We have heard the *p* of Moab	Jer 48:29	1347
and his arrogancy, and his *p*	Jer 48:29	1347
the *p* of thine heart, O thou that	Jer 49:16	2087
rod hath blossomed, *p* hath budded	Eze 7:10	2087
iniquity of thy sister Sodom, *p*	Eze 16:49	1347
by thy mouth in the day of thy *p*	Eze 16:56	1347
the *p* of her power shall come	Eze 30:6	1347
those that walk in *p* he is able	Dan 4:37	1466
up, and his mind hardened in *p*	Dan 5:20	2103
the *p* of Israel doth testify to	Hos 5:5	1347
the *p* of Israel testifieth to his	Hos 7:10	1347
The *p* of thine heart hath	Obad 3	2087
This shall they have for their *p*	Zeph 2:10	1347
thee them that rejoice in thy *p*	Zeph 3:11	1346
cut off the *p* of the Philistines	Zec 9:6	1347
the *p* of Assyria shall be brought	Zec 10:11	1347
for the *p* of Jordan is spoiled	Zec 11:3	1347
an evil eye, blasphemy, *p*	Mk 7:22	5243
lest being lifted up with *p* he	1Ti 3:6	5187
the *p* of life, is not of the	1Jn 2:16	212

PRIEST
he was the *p* of the most high God	Gen 14:18	3548
daughter of Poti-pherah *p* of On	Gen 41:45	3548
Poti-pherah *p* of On bare unto him	Gen 41:50	3548
Poti-pherah *p* of On bare unto him	Gen 46:20	3548
Now the *p* of Midian had seven	Ex 2:16	3548
father in law, the *p* of Midian	Ex 3:1	3548
the *p* of Midian, Moses' father in	Ex 18:1	3548
that son that is *p* in his stead	Ex 29:30	3548
the holy garments for Aaron the *p*	Ex 31:10	3548
the holy garments for Aaron the *p*	Ex 35:19	3548
of Ithamar, son to Aaron the *p*	Ex 38:21	3548
the holy garments for Aaron the *p*	Ex 39:41	3548

the sons of Aaron the *p* shall put	Lev 1:7	3548
the *p* shall burn all on the altar	Lev 1:9	3548
the *p* shall lay them in order on	Lev 1:12	3548
the *p* shall bring it all, and burn	Lev 1:13	3548
the *p* shall bring it unto the	Lev 1:15	3548
the *p* shall burn it upon the	Lev 1:17	3548
the *p* shall burn the memorial of	Lev 2:2	3548
when it is presented unto the *p*	Lev 2:8	3548
the *p* shall take from the meat	Lev 2:9	3548
the *p* shall burn the memorial of	Lev 2:16	3548
the *p* shall burn it upon the	Lev 3:11	3548
the *p* shall burn them upon the	Lev 3:16	3548
If the *p* that is anointed do sin	Lev 4:3	3548
the *p* that is anointed shall take	Lev 4:5	3548
the *p* shall dip his finger in the	Lev 4:6	3548
the *p* shall put some of the blood	Lev 4:7	3548
the *p* shall burn them upon the	Lev 4:10	3548
the *p* that is anointed shall	Lev 4:16	3548
the *p* shall dip his finger in	Lev 4:17	3548
the *p* shall make an atonement for	Lev 4:20	3548
the *p* shall take of the blood of	Lev 4:25	3548
the *p* shall make an atonement for	Lev 4:26	3548
the *p* shall take of the blood	Lev 4:30	3548
the *p* shall burn it upon the	Lev 4:31	3548
the *p* shall make an atonement for	Lev 4:31	3548
the *p* shall take of the blood of	Lev 4:34	3548
the *p* shall burn them upon the	Lev 4:35	3548
the *p* shall make an atonement for	Lev 4:35	3548
the *p* shall make an atonement for	Lev 5:6	3548
And he shall bring them unto the *p*	Lev 5:8	3548
the *p* shall make an atonement for	Lev 5:10	3548
Then shall he bring it to the *p*	Lev 5:12	3548
the *p* shall take his handful of	Lev 5:12	3548
the *p* shall make an atonement for	Lev 5:13	3548
thereto, and give it unto the *p*	Lev 5:16	3548
the *p* shall make an atonement for	Lev 5:16	3548
a trespass offering, unto the *p*	Lev 5:18	3548
the *p* shall make an atonement for	Lev 5:18	3548
a trespass offering, unto the *p*	Lev 6:6	3548
the *p* shall make an atonement for	Lev 6:7	3548
the *p* shall put on his linen	Lev 6:10	3548
the *p* shall burn wood on it every	Lev 6:12	3548
the *p* of his sons that is	Lev 6:22	3548
for the *p* shall be wholly burnt	Lev 6:23	3548
The *p* that offereth it for sin	Lev 6:26	3548
the *p* shall burn them upon the	Lev 7:5	3548
the *p* that maketh atonement	Lev 7:7	3548
the *p* that offereth any man's	Lev 7:8	3548
even the *p* shall have to himself	Lev 7:8	3548
the *p* shall burn the fat upon the	Lev 7:31	3548
p for an heave offering of the	Lev 7:32	3548
have given them unto Aaron the *p*	Lev 7:34	3548
of the congregation, unto the *p*	Lev 12:6	3548
the *p* shall make an atonement for	Lev 12:8	3548
shall be brought unto Aaron the *p*	Lev 13:2	3548
the *p* shall look on the plague in	Lev 13:3	3548
the *p* shall look on him, and	Lev 13:3	3548
then the *p* shall shut up him that	Lev 13:4	3548
the *p* shall look on him the	Lev 13:5	3548
then the *p* shall shut him up	Lev 13:5	3548
the *p* shall look on him again the	Lev 13:6	3548
the *p* pronounce him clean	Lev 13:6	3548
seen of the *p* for his cleansing	Lev 13:7	3548
he shall be seen of the *p* again	Lev 13:7	3548
if the *p* see that, behold, the	Lev 13:8	3548
then the *p* shall pronounce him	Lev 13:8	3548
he shall be brought unto the *p*	Lev 13:9	3548
And the *p* shall see him	Lev 13:10	3548
the *p* shall pronounce him unclean	Lev 13:11	3548
foot, wheresoever the *p* looketh	Lev 13:12	3548
Then the *p* shall consider	Lev 13:13	3548
the *p* shall see the raw flesh, and	Lev 13:15	3548
white, he shall come unto the *p*	Lev 13:16	3548
And the *p* shall see him	Lev 13:17	3548
then the *p* shall pronounce him	Lev 13:17	3548
reddish, and it be shewed to the *p*	Lev 13:19	3548
And if, when the *p* seeth it	Lev 13:20	3548
the *p* shall pronounce him unclean	Lev 13:20	3548
But if the *p* look on it, and,	Lev 13:21	3548
then the *p* shall shut him up	Lev 13:21	3548
then the *p* shall pronounce him	Lev 13:22	3548
the *p* shall pronounce him clean	Lev 13:23	3548
Then the *p* shall look upon it	Lev 13:25	3548
wherefore the *p* shall pronounce	Lev 13:25	3548
But if the *p* look on it, and,	Lev 13:26	3548
then the *p* shall shut him up	Lev 13:26	3548
the *p* shall look upon him the	Lev 13:27	3548
then the *p* shall pronounce him	Lev 13:27	3548
the *p* shall pronounce him clean	Lev 13:28	3548
Then the *p* shall see the plague	Lev 13:30	3548
then the *p* shall pronounce him	Lev 13:30	3548

P

if the *p* look on the plague of	Lev 13:31	3548
then the *p* shall shut up him that	Lev 13:31	3548
in the seventh day the *p* shall	Lev 13:32	3548
the *p* shall shut up him that hath	Lev 13:33	3548
in the seventh day the *p* shall	Lev 13:34	3548
then the *p* shall pronounce him	Lev 13:34	3548
Then the *p* shall look on him	Lev 13:36	3548
the *p* shall not seek for yellow	Lev 13:36	3548
the *p* shall pronounce him clean	Lev 13:37	3548
Then the *p* shall look	Lev 13:39	3548
Then the *p* shall look upon it	Lev 13:43	3548
the *p* shall pronounce him utterly	Lev 13:44	3548
and shall be shewed unto the *p*	Lev 13:49	3548
the *p* shall look upon the plague,	Lev 13:50	3548
if the *p* shall look, and, behold,	Lev 13:53	3548
Then the *p* shall command that	Lev 13:54	3548
the *p* shall look on the plague,	Lev 13:55	3548
And if the *p* look, and, behold, the	Lev 13:56	3548
He shall be brought unto the *p*	Lev 14:2	3548
the *p* shall go forth out of the	Lev 14:3	3548
the *p* shall look, and, behold, if	Lev 14:3	3548
Then shall the *p* command to take	Lev 14:4	3548
the *p* shall command that one of	Lev 14:5	3548
the *p* that maketh him clean shall	Lev 14:11	3548
the *p* shall take one he lamb, and	Lev 14:12	3548
the *p* shall take some of the	Lev 14:14	3548
the *p* shall put it upon the tip	Lev 14:14	3548
the *p* shall take some of the log	Lev 14:15	3548
the *p* shall dip his right finger	Lev 14:16	3548
p put upon the tip of the right	Lev 14:17	3548
the *p* shall make an atonement for	Lev 14:18	3548
the *p* shall offer the sin	Lev 14:19	3548
the *p* shall offer the burnt	Lev 14:20	3548
the *p* shall make an atonement for	Lev 14:20	3548
day for his cleansing unto the *p*	Lev 14:23	3548
the *p* shall take the lamb of the	Lev 14:24	3548
the *p* shall wave them for a wave	Lev 14:24	3548
the *p* shall take some of the	Lev 14:25	3548
the *p* shall pour of the oil into	Lev 14:26	3548
the *p* shall sprinkle with his	Lev 14:27	3548
the *p* shall put of the oil that	Lev 14:28	3548
the *p* shall make an atonement for	Lev 14:31	3548
house shall come and tell the *p*	Lev 14:35	3548
Then the *p* shall command that	Lev 14:36	3548
before the *p* go into it to see	Lev 14:36	3548
afterward the *p* shall go in to	Lev 14:36	3548
Then the *p* shall go out of the	Lev 14:38	3548
the *p* shall come again the	Lev 14:39	3548
Then the *p* shall command that	Lev 14:40	3548
Then the *p* shall come and look, and	Lev 14:44	3548
if the *p* shall come in, and look	Lev 14:48	3548
then the *p* shall pronounce the	Lev 14:48	3548
and give them unto the *p*	Lev 15:14	3548
the *p* shall offer them, the one	Lev 15:15	3548
the *p* shall make an atonement for	Lev 15:15	3548
pigeons, and bring them unto the *p*	Lev 15:29	3548
the *p* shall offer the one for a	Lev 15:30	3548
the *p* shall make an atonement for	Lev 15:30	3548
the *p* make an atonement for you	Lev 16:30	
And the, *p*, whom he shall anoint,	Lev 16:32	3548
of the congregation, unto the *p*	Lev 17:5	3548
the *p* shall sprinkle the blood	Lev 17:6	3548
the *p* shall make an atonement for	Lev 19:22	3548
And the daughter of any *p*, if she	Lev 21:9	3548
is the high *p* among his brethren	Lev 21:10	3548
of the seed of Aaron the *p* shall	Lev 21:21	3548
a sojourner of the *p*, or an hired	Lev 22:10	3548
But if the *p* buy any soul with	Lev 22:11	3548
it unto the *p* with the holy thing	Lev 22:14	3548
of your harvest unto the *p*	Lev 23:10	3548
the sabbath the *p* shall wave it	Lev 23:11	3548
the *p* shall wave them with the	Lev 23:20	3548
be holy to the Lord for the *p*	Lev 23:20	3548
present himself before the *p*	Lev 27:8	3548
and the *p* shall value him	Lev 27:8	3548
that vowed shall the *p* value him	Lev 27:8	3548
present the beast before the *p*	Lev 27:11	3548
the *p* shall value it, whether it	Lev 27:12	3548
as thou valuest it, who art the *p*	Lev 27:12	3548
then the *p* shall estimate it,	Lev 27:14	3548
as the *p* shall estimate it, so	Lev 27:14	3548
then the *p* shall reckon unto him	Lev 27:18	3548
Then the *p* shall reckon unto him	Lev 27:23	3548
present them before Aaron the *p*	Num 3:6	3548
Eleazar the son of Aaron the *p*	Num 3:32	3548
the *p* pertaineth the oil for the	Num 4:16	3548
of Ithamar the son of Aaron the *p*	Num 4:28	3548
of Ithamar the son of Aaron the *p*	Num 4:33	3548
unto the Lord, even to the *p*	Num 5:8	3548
which they bring unto the *p*	Num 5:9	3548
whatsoever any man giveth the *p*	Num 5:10	3548
the man bring his wife unto the *p*	Num 5:15	3548
the *p* shall bring her near, and	Num 5:16	3548
the *p* shall take holy water in an	Num 5:17	3548
the tabernacle the *p* shall take	Num 5:17	3548
the *p* shall set the woman before	Num 5:18	3548
the *p* shall have in his hand the	Num 5:18	3548
the *p* shall charge her by an oath	Num 5:19	3548
Then the *p* shall charge the woman	Num 5:21	3548
the *p* shall say unto the woman,	Num 5:21	3548
the *p* shall write these curses in	Num 5:23	3548
Then the *p* shall take the	Num 5:25	3548
the *p* shall take an handful of	Num 5:26	3548
the *p* shall execute upon her all	Num 5:30	3548
or two young pigeons, to the *p*	Num 6:10	3548
the *p* shall offer the one for a	Num 6:11	3548
the *p* shall bring them before the	Num 6:16	3548
the *p* shall offer also his meat	Num 6:17	3548
the *p* shall take the sodden	Num 6:19	3548
the *p* shall wave them for a wave	Num 6:20	3548
this is holy for the *p*, with the	Num 6:20	3548
of Ithamar the son of Aaron the *p*	Num 7:8	3548
the *p* shall make an atonement for	Num 15:25	3548
the *p* shall make an atonement for	Num 15:28	3548
Eleazar the son of Aaron the *p*	Num 16:37	3548
Eleazar the *p* took the brasen	Num 16:39	3548
heave offering to Aaron the *p*	Num 18:28	3548
shall give her unto Eleazar the *p*	Num 19:3	3548
Eleazar the *p* shall take of her	Num 19:4	3548
the *p* shall take cedar wood, and	Num 19:6	3548
Then the *p* shall wash his clothes	Num 19:7	3548
the *p* shall be unclean until the	Num 19:7	3548
Eleazar, the son of Aaron the *p*	Num 25:7	3548
Eleazar, the son of Aaron the *p*	Num 25:11	3548
Eleazar the son of Aaron the *p*	Num 26:1	3548
Eleazar the *p* spake with them in	Num 26:3	3548
by Moses and Eleazar the *p*	Num 26:63	3548
Moses and Aaron the *p* numbered	Num 26:64	3548
Moses, and before Eleazar the *p*	Num 27:2	3548
And set him before Eleazar the *p*	Num 27:19	3548
shall stand before Eleazar the *p*	Num 27:21	3548
and set him before Eleazar the *p*	Num 27:22	3548
Phinehas the son of Eleazar the *p*	Num 31:6	3548
unto Moses, and Eleazar the *p*	Num 31:12	3548
And Moses, and Eleazar the *p*	Num 31:13	3548
Eleazar the *p* said unto the men	Num 31:21	3548
of beast, thou, and Eleazar the *p*	Num 31:26	3548
and give it unto Eleazar the *p*	Num 31:29	3548
Eleazar the *p* did as the Lord	Num 31:31	3548
offering, unto Eleazar the *p*	Num 31:41	3548
Eleazar the *p* took the gold of	Num 31:51	3548
Eleazar the *p* took the gold of	Num 31:54	3548
unto Moses, and to Eleazar the *p*	Num 32:2	3548
Moses commanded Eleazar the *p*	Num 32:28	3548
Aaron the *p* went up into mount	Num 33:38	3548
Eleazar the *p*, and Joshua the son	Num 34:17	3548
it unto the death of the high *p*	Num 35:25	3548
until the death of the high *p*	Num 35:28	3548
p the slayer shall return into	Num 35:28	3548
land, until the death of the *p*	Num 35:32	3548
will not hearken unto the *p* that	Deut 17:12	3548
give unto the *p* the shoulder	Deut 18:3	3548
that the *p* shall approach and	Deut 20:2	3548
thou shalt go unto the *p* that	Deut 26:3	3548
the *p* shall take the basket out	Deut 26:4	3548
of Canaan, which Eleazar the *p*	Josh 14:1	3548
came near before Eleazar the *p*	Josh 17:4	3548
inheritances, which Eleazar the *p*	Josh 19:51	3548
p that shall be in those days	Josh 20:6	3548
of the Levites unto Eleazar the *p*	Josh 21:1	3548
and the children of Aaron the *p*	Josh 21:4	3548
the *p* Hebron with her suburbs	Josh 21:13	3548
Phinehas the son of Eleazar the *p*	Josh 22:13	3548
And when Phinehas the *p*, and the	Josh 22:30	3548
the *p* said unto the children of	Josh 22:31	3548
Phinehas the son of Eleazar the *p*	Josh 22:32	3548
one of his sons, who became his *p*	Judg 17:5	3548
me, and be unto me a father and a *p*	Judg 17:10	3548
and the young man became his *p*	Judg 17:12	3548
seeing I have a Levite to my *p*	Judg 17:13	3548
and hath hired me, and I am his *p*	Judg 18:4	3548
the *p* said unto them, Go in peace	Judg 18:6	3548
the *p* stood in the entering of	Judg 18:17	3548
Then said the *p* unto them	Judg 18:18	3548
us, and be to us a father and a *p*	Judg 18:19	3548
be a *p* unto the house of one man	Judg 18:19	3548
or that thou be a *p* unto a tribe	Judg 18:19	3548
my gods which I made, and the *p*	Judg 18:24	3548
the *p* which he had, and came unto	Judg 18:27	3548
Now Eli the *p* sat upon a seat by	1Sa 1:9	3548
unto the Lord before Eli the *p*	1Sa 2:11	3548
brought up the *p* took for himself	1Sa 2:14	3548

Give flesh to roast for the *p*	1Sa 2:15	3548
the tribes of Israel to be my *p*	1Sa 2:28	3548
I will raise me up a faithful *p*	1Sa 2:35	3548
of Eli, the LORD's *p* in Shiloh	1Sa 14:3	3548
while Saul talked unto the *p*	1Sa 14:19	3548
and Saul said unto the *p*, Withdraw	1Sa 14:19	3548
Then said the *p*, Let us draw near	1Sa 14:36	3548
David to Nob to Ahimelech the *p*	1Sa 21:1	3548
David said unto Ahimelech the *p*	1Sa 21:2	3548
the *p* answered David, and said	1Sa 21:4	3548
And David answered the *p*, and said	1Sa 21:5	3548
So the *p* gave him hallowed bread	1Sa 21:6	3548
the *p* said, The sword of Goliath	1Sa 21:9	3548
king sent to call Ahimelech the *p*	1Sa 22:11	3548
and he said to Abiathar the *p*	1Sa 23:9	3548
And David said to Abiathar the *p*	1Sa 30:7	3548
king said also unto Zadok the *p*	2Sa 15:27	3548
Zeruiah, and with Abiathar the *p*	1Kin 1:7	3548
But Zadok the *p*, and Benaiah the	1Kin 1:8	3548
of the king, and Abiathar the *p*	1Kin 1:19	3548
of the host, and Abiathar the *p*	1Kin 1:25	3548
me thy servant, and Zadok the *p*	1Kin 1:26	3548
David said, Call me Zadok the *p*	1Kin 1:32	3548
And let Zadok the *p* and Nathan the	1Kin 1:34	3548
So Zadok the *p*, and Nathan the	1Kin 1:38	3548
Zadok the *p* took an horn of oil	1Kin 1:39	3548
the son of Abiathar the *p* came	1Kin 1:42	3548
hath sent with him Zadok the *p*	1Kin 1:44	3548
And Zadok the *p* and Nathan the	1Kin 1:45	3548
for him, and for Abiathar the *p*	1Kin 2:22	3548
unto Abiathar the *p* said the king	1Kin 2:26	3548
from being *p* unto the LORD	1Kin 2:27	3548
Zadok the *p* did the king put in	1Kin 2:35	3548
Azariah the son of Zadok the *p*	1Kin 4:2	3548
that Jehoiada the *p* commanded	2Kin 11:9	3548
and came to Jehoiada the *p*	2Kin 11:9	3548
the *p* give king David's spears	2Kin 11:10	3548
But Jehoiada the *p* commanded the	2Kin 11:15	3548
For the *p* had said, Let her not	2Kin 11:15	3548
slew Mattan the *p* of Baal before	2Kin 11:18	3548
the *p* appointed officers over the	2Kin 11:18	3548
Jehoiada the *p* instructed him	2Kin 12:2	3548
Jehoash called for Jehoiada the *p*	2Kin 12:7	3548
But Jehoiada the *p* took a chest	2Kin 12:9	3548
scribe and the high *p* came up	2Kin 12:10	3548
the *p* the fashion of the altar	2Kin 16:10	3548
Urijah the *p* built an altar	2Kin 16:11	3548
so Urijah the *p* made it against	2Kin 16:11	3548
king Ahaz commanded Urijah the *p*	2Kin 16:15	3548
Thus did Urijah the *p*, according	2Kin 16:16	3548
Go up to Hilkiah the high *p*	2Kin 22:4	3548
Hilkiah the high *p* said unto	2Kin 22:8	3548
Hilkiah the *p* hath delivered me a	2Kin 22:10	3548
the king commanded Hilkiah the *p*	2Kin 22:12	3548
So Hilkiah the *p*, and Ahikam, and	2Kin 22:14	3548
king commanded Hilkiah the high *p*	2Kin 23:4	3548
in the book that Hilkiah the *p*	2Kin 23:24	3548
guard took Seraiah the chief *p*	2Kin 25:18	3548
and Zephaniah the second *p*	2Kin 25:18	3548
And Zadok the *p*, and his brethren	1Chr 16:39	3548
and the princes, and Zadok the *p*	1Chr 24:6	3548
the son of Jehoiada, a chief *p*	1Chr 27:5	3548
chief governor, and Zadok to be *p*	1Chr 29:22	3548
the same may be a *p* of them that	2Chr 13:9	3548
true God, and without a teaching *p*	2Chr 15:3	3548
Amariah the chief *p* is over you	2Chr 19:11	3548
the wife of Jehoiada the *p*	2Chr 22:11	3548
that Jehoiada the *p* had commanded	2Chr 23:8	3548
for Jehoiada the *p* dismissed not	2Chr 23:8	3548
Moreover Jehoiada the *p* delivered	2Chr 23:9	3548
Then Jehoiada the *p* brought out	2Chr 23:14	3548
For the *p* said, Slay her not in	2Chr 23:14	3548
slew Mattan the *p* of Baal before	2Chr 23:17	3548
all the days of Jehoiada the *p*	2Chr 24:2	3548
the son of Jehoiada the *p*	2Chr 24:20	3548
of the sons of Jehoiada the *p*	2Chr 24:25	3548
Azariah the *p* went in after him,	2Chr 26:17	3548
And Azariah the chief *p*, and all	2Chr 26:20	3548
Azariah the chief *p* of the house	2Chr 31:10	3548
they came to Hilkiah the high *p*	2Chr 34:9	3548
Hilkiah the *p* found a book of the	2Chr 34:14	3548
Hilkiah the *p* hath given me a	2Chr 34:18	3548
till there stood up a *p* with Urim	Ezr 2:63	3548
the son of Aaron the chief *p*	Ezr 7:5	3548
Artaxerxes gave unto Ezra the *p*	Ezr 7:11	3548
king of kings, unto Ezra the *p*	Ezr 7:12	3549
river, that whatsoever Ezra the *p*	Ezr 7:21	3548
Meremoth the son of Uriah the *p*	Ezr 8:33	3548
And Ezra the *p* stood up, and said	Ezr 10:10	3548
And Ezra the *p*, with certain that	Ezr 10:16	3548
Then Eliashib the high *p* rose up	Neh 3:1	3548

the house of Eliashib the high *p*	Neh 3:20	3548
till there stood up a *p* with Urim	Neh 7:65	3548
Ezra the *p* brought the law before	Neh 8:2	3548
Ezra the *p* the scribe, and the	Neh 8:9	3548
the *p* the son of Aaron that shall be	Neh 10:38	3548
the governor, and of Ezra the *p*	Neh 12:26	3548
And before this, Eliashib the *p*	Neh 13:4	3548
the treasuries, Shelemiah the *p*	Neh 13:13	3548
the son of Eliashib the high *p*	Neh 13:28	3548
Thou art a *p* for ever after the	Ps 110:4	3548
witnesses to record, Uriah the *p*	Is 8:2	3548
as with the people, so with the *p*	Is 24:2	3548
the *p* and the prophet have erred	Is 28:7	3548
the *p* every one dealeth falsely	Jer 6:13	3548
the *p* every one dealeth falsely	Jer 8:10	3548
the *p* go about into a land that	Jer 14:18	3548
law shall not perish from the *p*	Jer 18:18	3548
Now Pashur the son of Immer the *p*	Jer 20:1	3548
the son of Maaseiah the *p*	Jer 21:1	3548
For both prophet and *p* are profane	Jer 23:11	3548
people, or the prophet, or a *p*	Jer 23:33	3548
And as for the prophet, and the *p*	Jer 23:34	3548
the son of Maaseiah the *p*	Jer 29:25	3548
The LORD hath made thee *p* in the	Jer 29:26	3548
in the stead of Jehoiada the *p*	Jer 29:26	3548
Zephaniah the *p* read this letter	Jer 29:29	3548
the *p* to the prophet Jeremiah	Jer 37:3	3548
guard took Seraiah the chief *p*	Jer 52:24	3548
and Zephaniah the second *p*	Jer 52:24	3548
of his anger the king and the *p*	Lam 2:6	3548
shall the *p* and the prophet be	Lam 2:20	3548
came expressly unto Ezekiel the *p*	Eze 1:3	3548
the law shall perish from the *p*	Eze 7:26	3548
to do the office of a *p* unto me	Eze 44:13	3547
Neither shall any *p* drink wine	Eze 44:21	3548
or a widow that had a *p* before	Eze 44:22	3548
the *p* the first of your dough	Eze 44:30	3548
the *p* shall take of the blood of	Eze 45:19	3548
as they that strive with the *p*	Hos 4:4	3548
that thou shalt be no *p* to me	Hos 4:6	3547
shall be, like people, like *p*	Hos 4:9	3548
Then Amaziah the *p* of Beth-el	Amos 7:10	3548
the son of Josedech, the high *p*	Hag 1:1	3548
the son of Josedech, the high *p*	Hag 1:12	3548
the son of Josedech, the high *p*	Hag 1:14	3548
the son of Josedech, the high *p*	Hag 2:2	3548
son of Josedech, the high *p*	Hag 2:4	3548
p standing before the angel of	Zec 3:1	3548
Hear now, O Joshua the high *p*	Zec 3:8	3548
the son of Josedech, the high *p*	Zec 6:11	3548
he shall be a *p* upon his throne	Zec 6:13	3548
go thy way, shew thyself to the *p*	Mt 8:4	2409
unto the palace of the high *p*	Mt 26:3	749
him away to Caiaphas the high *p*	Mt 26:57	749
And the high *p* arose, and said unto	Mt 26:62	749
And the high *p* answered and said	Mt 26:63	749
Then the high *p* rent his clothes,	Mt 26:65	749
go thy way, shew thyself to the *p*	Mk 1:44	2409
the days of Abiathar the high *p*	Mk 2:26	749
and staves, from the chief *p*	Mk 14:43	749
and smote a servant of the high *p*	Mk 14:47	749
they led Jesus away to the high *p*	Mk 14:53	749
into the palace of the high *p*	Mk 14:54	749
the high *p* stood up in the midst,	Mk 14:60	749
Again the high *p* asked him	Mk 14:61	749
Then the high *p* rent his clothes,	Mk 14:63	749
one of the maids of the high *p*	Mk 14:66	749
a certain *p* named Zacharias, of	Lk 1:5	2409
but go, and shew thyself to the *p*	Lk 5:14	2409
came down a certain *p* that way	Lk 10:31	2409
smote the servant of the high *p*	Lk 22:50	749
being the high *p* that same year	Jn 11:49	749
but being high *p* that year	Jn 11:51	749
was the high *p* that same year	Jn 18:13	749
was known unto the high *p*	Jn 18:15	749
into the palace of the high *p*	Jn 18:15	749
which was known unto the high *p*	Jn 18:16	749
The high *p* then asked Jesus of	Jn 18:19	749
Answerest thou the high *p* so	Jn 18:22	749
bound unto Caiaphas the high *p*	Jn 18:24	749
One of the servants of the high *p*	Jn 18:26	749
And Annas the high *p*, and Caiaphas,	Acts 4:6	749
were of the kindred of the high *p*	Acts 4:6	748
Then the high *p* rose up, and all	Acts 5:17	749
But the high *p* came, and they that	Acts 5:21	749
Now when the high *p* and the	Acts 5:24	749
and the high *p* asked them,	Acts 5:27	749
Then said the high *p*, Are these	Acts 7:1	749
of the Lord, went unto the high *p*	Acts 9:1	749
Then the *p* of Jupiter, which was	Acts 14:13	2409
As also the high *p* doth bear me	Acts 22:5	749

P

the high *p* Ananias commanded them	Acts 23:2	*749*
said, Revilest thou God's high *p*	Acts 23:4	*749*
brethren, that he was the high *p*	Acts 23:5	*749*
high *p* descended with the elders	Acts 24:1	*749*
Then the high *p* and the chief of	Acts 25:2	*749*
faithful high *p* in things	Heb 2:17	*749*
High *P* of our profession, Christ	Heb 3:1	*749*
then that we have a great high *p*	Heb 4:14	*749*
For we have not an high *p* which	Heb 4:15	*749*
For every high *p* taken from among	Heb 5:1	*749*
not himself to be made an high *p*	Heb 5:5	*749*
Thou art a *p* for ever after the	Heb 5:6	*2409*
Called of God an high *p* after the	Heb 5:10	*749*
made an high *p* for ever after the	Heb 6:20	*749*
p of the most high God, who met	Heb 7:1	*2409*
abideth a *p* continually	Heb 7:3	*2409*
need was there that another *p*	Heb 7:11	*2409*
there ariseth another *p*,	Heb 7:15	*2409*
Thou art a *p* for ever after the	Heb 7:17	*2409*
not without an oath he was made *p*	Heb 7:20	
Thou art a *p* for ever after the	Heb 7:21	*2409*
For such an high *p* became us	Heb 7:26	*749*
We have such an high *p*, who is	Heb 8:1	*749*
For every high *p* is ordained to	Heb 8:3	*749*
on earth, he should not be a *p*	Heb 8:4	*2409*
the high *p* alone once every year	Heb 9:7	*749*
an high *p* of good things to come	Heb 9:11	*749*
as the high *p* entereth into the	Heb 9:25	*749*
And every *p* standeth daily	Heb 10:11	*2409*
having an high *p* over the house	Heb 10:21	*2409*
sanctuary by the high *p* for sin	Heb 13:11	*749*

PRIESTHOOD

p throughout their generations	Ex 40:15	3550
and seek ye the *p* also	Num 16:10	3550
shall bear the iniquity of your *p*	Num 18:1	3550
the covenant of an everlasting *p*	Num 25:13	3550
for the *p* of the LORD is their	Josh 18:7	3550
they, as polluted, put from the *p*	Ezr 2:62	3550
they, as polluted, put from the *p*	Neh 7:64	3550
because they have defiled the *p*	Neh 13:29	3550
and the covenant of the *p*	Neh 13:29	3550
who receive the office of the *p*	Heb 7:5	*2405*
were by the Levitical *p*, (for	Heb 7:11	*2420*
For the *p* being changed, there is	Heb 7:12	*2420*
Moses spake nothing concerning *p*	Heb 7:14	*2420*
ever, hath an unchangeable *p*	Heb 7:24	*2420*
up a spiritual house, an holy *p*	1Pet 2:5	*2406*
a chosen generation, a royal *p*	1Pet 2:9	*2406*

PRIEST'S

minister unto me in the *p* office	Ex 28:1	3547
minister unto me in the *p* office	Ex 28:3	3547
minister unto me in the *p* office	Ex 28:4	3547
minister unto me in the *p* office	Ex 28:41	3547
minister unto me in the *p* office	Ex 29:1	3547
the *p* office shall be theirs for	Ex 29:9	3550
to minister to me in the *p* office	Ex 29:44	3547
minister unto me in the *p* office	Ex 30:30	3547
sons, to minister in the *p* office	Ex 31:10	3547
sons, to minister in the *p* office	Ex 35:19	3547
to minister in the *p* office	Ex 39:41	3547
minister unto me in the *p* office	Ex 40:13	3547
minister unto me in the *p* office	Ex 40:15	3547
and the remnant shall be the *p*	Lev 5:13	3548
shall be the *p* that offereth it	Lev 7:9	3548
it shall be the *p* that sprinkleth	Lev 7:14	3548
unto the LORD in the *p* office	Lev 7:35	3547
for as the sin offering is the *p*	Lev 14:13	3548
of the oil that is in the *p* hand	Lev 14:18	3548
rest of the oil that is in the *p*	Lev 14:29	3548
p office in his father's stead	Lev 16:32	3547
If the *p* daughter also be married	Lev 22:12	3548
But if the *p* daughter be a widow,	Lev 22:13	3548
possession thereof shall be the *p*	Lev 27:21	3548
to minister in the *p* office	Num 3:3	3547
Ithamar ministered in the *p*	Num 3:4	3547
they shall wait on their *p* office	Num 3:10	3550
p office for every thing of the	Num 18:7	3550
I have given your *p* office unto	Num 18:7	3550
in the *p* office in his stead	Deut 10:6	3547
this shall be the *p* due from the	Deut 18:3	3548
the *p* heart was glad, and he took	Judg 18:20	3548
the *p* custom with the people was,	1Sa 2:13	3548
the *p* servant came, while the	1Sa 2:13	3548
the *p* servant came, and said to	1Sa 2:15	3548
the *p* office in the temple that	1Chr 6:10	3547
and Ithamar executed the *p* office	1Chr 24:2	3547
the *p* office unto the LORD	2Chr 11:14	3547
the high *p* officer came and	2Chr 24:11	3548
of your oblations, shall be the *p*	Eze 44:30	3548
For the *p* lips should keep	Mal 2:7	3548
and struck a servant of the high *p*	Mt 26:51	*749*
afar off unto the high *p* palace	Mt 26:58	*749*
that while he executed the *p*	Lk 1:8	*2407*
to the custom of the *p* office	Lk 1:9	*2405*
brought him into the high *p* house	Lk 22:54	*749*
it, and smote the high *p* servant	Jn 18:10	*749*

PRIESTS

the land of the *p* bought he not	Gen 47:22	3548
for the *p* had a portion assigned	Gen 47:22	3548
except the land of the *p* only	Gen 47:26	3548
shall be unto me a kingdom of *p*	Ex 19:6	3548
And let the *p* also, which come	Ex 19:22	3548
but let not the *p* and the people	Ex 19:24	3548
and the *p*, Aaron's sons, shall	Lev 1:5	3548
And the *p*, Aaron's sons, shall lay	Lev 1:8	3548
and the *p*, Aaron's sons, shall	Lev 1:11	3548
bring it to Aaron's sons the *p*	Lev 2:2	3548
Aaron's sons the *p* shall sprinkle	Lev 3:2	3548
among the *p* shall eat thereof	Lev 6:29	3548
among the *p* shall eat thereof	Lev 7:6	3548
or unto one of his sons the *p*	Lev 13:2	3548
shall make an atonement for the *p*	Lev 16:33	3548
Speak unto the *p* the sons of	Lev 21:1	3548
the *p* which were anointed, whom	Num 3:3	3548
And the sons of Aaron, the *p*	Num 10:8	3548
shalt come unto the *p* the Levites	Deut 17:9	3548
which is before the *p* the Levites	Deut 17:18	3548
The *p* the Levites, and all the	Deut 18:1	3548
before the LORD, before the *p*	Deut 19:17	3548
the *p* the sons of Levi shall come	Deut 21:5	3548
the *p* the Levites shall teach you	Deut 24:8	3548
the *p* the Levites spake unto all	Deut 27:9	3548
it unto the *p* the sons of Levi	Deut 31:9	3548
the *p* the Levites bearing it,	Josh 3:3	3548
And Joshua spake unto the *p*	Josh 3:6	3548
thou shalt command the *p* that	Josh 3:8	3548
p that bear the ark of the LORD	Josh 3:13	3548
the *p* bearing the ark of the	Josh 3:14	3548
the feet of the *p* that bare the	Josh 3:15	3548
the *p* that bare the ark of the	Josh 3:17	3548
the *p* which bare the ark of the	Josh 4:9	3548
For the *p* which bare the ark	Josh 4:10	3548
of the LORD passed over, and the *p*	Josh 4:11	3548
Command the *p* that bear the ark	Josh 4:16	3548
Joshua therefore commanded the *p*	Josh 4:17	3548
when the *p* that bare the ark of	Josh 4:18	3548
seven *p* shall bear before the ark	Josh 6:4	3548
the *p* shall blow with the	Josh 6:4	3548
the son of Nun called the *p*	Josh 6:6	3548
let seven *p* bear seven trumpets	Josh 6:6	3548
that the seven *p* bearing the	Josh 6:8	3548
the *p* that blew with the trumpets	Josh 6:9	3548
the *p* going on, and blowing with	Josh 6:9	3548
the *p* took up the ark of the LORD	Josh 6:12	3548
seven *p* bearing seven trumpets of	Josh 6:13	
the *p* going on, and blowing with	Josh 6:13	3548
when the *p* blew with the trumpets	Josh 6:16	3548
when the *p* blew with the trumpets	Josh 6:20	3548
side before the *p* the Levites	Josh 8:33	3548
of the children of Aaron, the *p*	Josh 21:19	3548
his sons were *p* to the tribe of	Judg 18:30	3548
the *p* of the LORD, were there	1Sa 1:3	3548
Therefore neither the *p* of Dagon	1Sa 5:5	3548
the Philistines called for the *p*	1Sa 6:2	3548
house, the *p* that were in Nob	1Sa 22:11	3548
Turn, and slay the *p* of the LORD	1Sa 22:17	3548
to fall upon the *p* of the LORD	1Sa 22:17	3548
Turn thou, and fall upon the *p*	1Sa 22:18	3548
turned, and he fell upon the *p*	1Sa 22:18	3548
And Nob, the city of the *p*	1Sa 22:19	3548
that Saul had slain the LORD's *p*	1Sa 22:21	3548
the son of Abiathar, were the *p*	2Sa 8:17	3548
with thee Zadok and Abiathar the *p*	2Sa 15:35	3548
it to Zadok and Abiathar the *p*	2Sa 15:35	3548
unto Zadok and to Abiathar the *p*	2Sa 17:15	3548
to Zadok and to Abiathar the *p*	2Sa 19:11	3548
and Zadok and Abiathar were the *p*	2Sa 20:25	3548
and Zadok and Abiathar were the *p*	1Kin 4:4	3548
came, and the *p* took up the ark	1Kin 8:3	3548
tabernacle, even those did the *p*	1Kin 8:4	3548
the *p* brought in the ark of the	1Kin 8:6	3548
when the *p* were come out of the	1Kin 8:10	3548
So that the *p* could not stand to	1Kin 8:11	3548
made *p* of the lowest of the	1Kin 12:31	3548
he placed in Beth-el the *p* of the	1Kin 12:32	3548
p of the high places that burn	1Kin 13:2	3548
the people *p* of the high places	1Kin 13:33	3548
one of the *p* of the high places	1Kin 13:33	3548
men, and his kinsfolks, and his *p*	2Kin 10:11	3548
all his servants, and all his *p*	2Kin 10:19	3548

And Jehoash said to the *p*, All the	2Kin 12:4	3548
Let the *p* take it to them, every	2Kin 12:5	3548
year of king Jehoash the *p* had	2Kin 12:6	3548
the priest, and the other *p*	2Kin 12:7	3548
the *p* consented to receive no	2Kin 12:8	3548
the *p* that kept the door put	2Kin 12:9	3548
Carry thither one of the *p* whom	2Kin 17:27	3548
Then one of the *p* whom they had	2Kin 17:28	3548
of them *p* of the high places	2Kin 17:32	3548
scribe, and the elders of the *p*	2Kin 19:2	3548
of Jerusalem with him, and the *p*	2Kin 23:2	3548
the *p* of the second order, and the	2Kin 23:4	3548
And he put down the idolatrous *p*	2Kin 23:5	3548
he brought all the *p* out of the	2Kin 23:8	3548
where the *p* had burned incense	2Kin 23:8	3548
Nevertheless the *p* of the high	2Kin 23:9	3548
he slew all the *p* of the high	2Kin 23:20	3548
were, the Israelites, the *p*	1Chr 9:2	3548
And of the *p*; Jedaiah	1Chr 9:10	3548
some of the sons of the *p* made	1Chr 9:30	3548
and with them also to the *p*	1Chr 13:2	3548
for Zadok and Abiathar the *p*	1Chr 15:11	3548
So the *p* and the Levites	1Chr 15:14	3548
and Benaiah, and Eliezer, the *p*	1Chr 15:24	3548
Jahaziel the *p* with trumpets	1Chr 16:6	3548
the priest, and his brethren the *p*	1Chr 16:39	3548
the son of Abiathar, were the *p*	1Chr 18:16	3548
the princes of Israel, with the *p*	1Chr 23:2	3548
the chief of the fathers of the *p*	1Chr 24:6	3548
the chief of the fathers of the *p*	1Chr 24:31	3548
Also for the courses of the *p*	1Chr 28:13	3548
And, behold, the courses of the *p*	1Chr 28:21	3548
the sea was for the *p* to wash in	2Chr 4:6	3548
he made the court of the *p*	2Chr 4:9	3548
the tabernacle, these did the *p*	2Chr 5:5	3548
the *p* brought in the ark of the	2Chr 5:7	3548
when the *p* were come out of the	2Chr 5:11	3548
(for all the *p* that were present	2Chr 5:11	3548
twenty *p* sounding with trumpets	2Chr 5:12	3548
So that the *p* could not stand to	2Chr 5:14	3548
let thy *p*, O LORD God, be clothed	2Chr 6:41	3548
the *p* could not enter into the	2Chr 7:2	3548
the *p* waited on their offices	2Chr 7:6	3548
the *p* sounded trumpets before	2Chr 7:6	3548
courses of the *p* to their service	2Chr 8:14	3548
praise and minister before the *p*	2Chr 8:14	3548
of the king unto the *p* and Levites	2Chr 8:15	3548
And the *p* and the Levites that were	2Chr 11:13	3548
he ordained him *p* for the high	2Chr 11:15	3548
ye not cast out the *p* of the LORD	2Chr 13:9	3548
have made you *p* after the manner	2Chr 13:9	3548
and the *p*, which minister unto the	2Chr 13:10	3548
his *p* with sounding trumpets to	2Chr 13:12	3548
the *p* sounded with the trumpets	2Chr 13:14	3548
with them Elishama and Jehoram, *p*	2Chr 17:8	3548
set of the Levites, and of the *p*	2Chr 19:8	3548
entering on the sabbath, of the *p*	2Chr 23:4	3548
the house of the LORD, save the *p*	2Chr 23:6	3548
by the hand of the *p* the Levites	2Chr 23:18	3548
And he gathered together the *p*	2Chr 24:5	3548
with him fourscore *p* of the LORD	2Chr 26:17	3548
but to the *p* the sons of Aaron	2Chr 26:18	3548
and while he was wroth with the *p*	2Chr 26:19	3548
the *p* in the house of the LORD	2Chr 26:19	3548
the chief priest, and all the *p*	2Chr 26:20	3548
And he brought in the *p* and the	2Chr 29:4	3548
the *p* went into the inner part of	2Chr 29:16	3548
he commanded the *p* the sons of	2Chr 29:21	3548
the *p* received the blood, and	2Chr 29:22	3548
the *p* killed them, and they made	2Chr 29:24	3548
David, and the *p* with the trumpets	2Chr 29:26	3548
But the *p* were too few, so that	2Chr 29:34	3548
until the other *p* had sanctified	2Chr 29:34	3548
to sanctify themselves than the *p*	2Chr 29:34	3548
because the *p* had not sanctified	2Chr 30:3	3548
and the *p* and the Levites were	2Chr 30:15	3548
the *p* sprinkled the blood, which	2Chr 30:16	3548
the *p* praised the LORD day by day	2Chr 30:21	3548
a great number of *p* sanctified	2Chr 30:24	3548
congregation of Judah, with the *p*	2Chr 30:25	3548
Then the *p* the Levites arose and	2Chr 30:27	3548
appointed the courses of the *p*	2Chr 31:2	3548
according to his service, the *p*	2Chr 31:2	3548
to give the portion of the *p*	2Chr 31:4	3548
Hezekiah questioned with the *p*	2Chr 31:9	3548
Shecaniah, in the cities of the *p*	2Chr 31:15	3548
Both to the genealogy of the *p* by	2Chr 31:17	3548
Also of the sons of Aaron the *p*	2Chr 31:19	3548
to all the males among the *p*	2Chr 31:19	3548
bones of the *p* upon their altars	2Chr 34:5	3548
of Jerusalem, and the, *p*, and the	2Chr 34:30	3548
he set the *p* in their charges, and	2Chr 35:2	3548
unto the people, to the *p*	2Chr 35:8	3548
gave unto the *p* for the passover	2Chr 35:8	3548
the *p* stood in their place, and	2Chr 35:10	3548
the *p* sprinkled the blood from	2Chr 35:11	3548
for themselves, and for the *p*	2Chr 35:14	3548
because the *p* the sons of Aaron	2Chr 35:14	3548
for the *p* the sons of Aaron	2Chr 35:14	3548
passover as Josiah kept, and the *p*	2Chr 35:18	3548
Moreover all the chief of the *p*	2Chr 36:14	3548
of Judah and Benjamin, and the *p*	Ezr 1:5	3548
The *p*: the children of	Ezr 2:36	3548
And of the children of the *p*	Ezr 2:61	3548
So the *p*, and the Levites, and some	Ezr 2:70	3548
of Jozadak, and his brethren the *p*	Ezr 3:2	3548
remnant of their brethren the *p*	Ezr 3:8	3548
they set the *p* in their apparel	Ezr 3:10	3548
But many of the *p* and Levites and	Ezr 3:12	3548
of the *p* which are at Jerusalem	Ezr 6:9	3549
And the children of Israel, the *p*	Ezr 6:16	3549
they set the *p* in their divisions	Ezr 6:18	3549
For the *p* and the Levites were	Ezr 6:20	3548
and for their brethren the *p*	Ezr 6:20	3548
children of Israel, and of the *p*	Ezr 7:7	3548
the people of Israel, and of his *p*	Ezr 7:13	3549
of the people, and of the *p*	Ezr 7:16	3549
you, that touching any of the *p*	Ezr 7:24	3549
and I viewed the people, and the *p*	Ezr 8:15	3548
twelve of the chief of the *p*	Ezr 8:24	3548
them before the chief of the *p*	Ezr 8:29	3548
So took the *p* and the Levites the	Ezr 8:30	3548
The people of Israel, and the *p*	Ezr 9:1	3548
have we, our kings, and our *p*	Ezr 9:7	3548
arose Ezra, and made the chief *p*	Ezr 10:5	3548
among the sons of the *p* there	Ezr 10:18	3548
told it to the Jews, nor to the *p*	Neh 2:16	3548
rose up with his brethren the *p*	Neh 3:1	3548
And after him repaired the *p*	Neh 3:22	3548
the horse gate repaired the *p*	Neh 3:28	3548
Then I called the *p*, and took an	Neh 5:12	3548
The *p*: the children of	Neh 7:39	3548
And of the *p*: the children	Neh 7:63	3548
So the *p*, and the Levites, and the	Neh 7:73	3548
fathers of all the people, the *p*	Neh 8:13	3548
on our princes, and on our *p*	Neh 9:32	3548
our kings, our princes, our *p*	Neh 9:34	3548
and our princes, Levites, and *p*	Neh 9:38	3548
these were the *p*	Neh 10:8	3548
And the rest of the people, the *p*	Neh 10:28	3548
And we cast the lots among the *p*	Neh 10:34	3548
unto the *p* that minister in the	Neh 10:36	3548
of wine and of oil, unto the *p*	Neh 10:37	3548
the *p* that minister, and the	Neh 10:39	3548
cities, to wit, Israel, the *p*	Neh 11:3	3548
Of the *p*: Jedaiah	Neh 11:10	3548
the residue of Israel, of the *p*	Neh 11:20	3548
Now these are the *p* and the	Neh 12:1	3548
These were the chief of the *p*	Neh 12:7	3548
And in the days of Joiakim were *p*	Neh 12:12	3548
also the *p*, to the reign of	Neh 12:22	3548
And the *p* and the Levites purified	Neh 12:30	3548
And the *p*; Eliakim	Neh 12:41	3548
the portions of the law for the *p*	Neh 12:44	3548
for Judah rejoiced for the *p*	Neh 12:44	3548
and the offerings of the *p*	Neh 13:5	3548
and appointed the wards of the *p*	Neh 13:30	3548
Their *p* fell by the sword	Ps 78:64	3548
Moses and Aaron among his *p*	Ps 99:6	3548
Let thy *p* be clothed with	Ps 132:9	3548
also clothe her *p* with salvation	Ps 132:16	3548
the elders of the *p* covered with	Is 37:2	3548
shall be named the *P* of the LORD	Is 61:6	3548
And I will also take of them for *p*	Is 66:21	3548
of the *p* that were in Anathoth in	Jer 1:1	3548
thereof, against the *p* thereof	Jer 1:18	3548
The *p* said not, Where is the LORD	Jer 2:8	3548
kings, their princes, and their *p*	Jer 2:26	3548
the *p* shall be astonished, and the	Jer 4:9	3548
the *p* bear rule by their means	Jer 5:31	3548
princes, and the bones of the *p*	Jer 8:1	3548
sit upon David's throne, and the *p*	Jer 13:13	3548
and of the ancients of the *p*	Jer 19:1	3548
So the *p* and the prophets and all	Jer 26:7	3548
unto all the people, that the *p*	Jer 26:8	3548
Then spake the *p* and the prophets	Jer 26:11	3548
and all the people unto the *p*	Jer 26:16	3548
Also I spake to the *p* and to all	Jer 27:16	3548
LORD, in the presence of the *p*	Jer 28:1	3548
Hananiah in the presence of the *p*	Jer 28:5	3548
away captives, and to the *p*	Jer 29:1	3548
the priest, and to all the *p*	Jer 29:25	3548

the soul of the *p* with fatness	Jer 31:14	3548
kings, their princes, their *p*	Jer 32:32	3548
Neither shall the *p* the Levites	Jer 33:18	3548
and with the Levites the *p*	Jer 33:21	3548
Jerusalem, the eunuchs, and the *p*	Jer 34:19	3548
forth into captivity with his *p*	Jer 48:7	3548
shall go into captivity, and his *p*	Jer 49:3	3548
her *p* sigh, her virgins are	Lam 1:4	3548
my *p* and mine elders gave up the	Lam 1:19	3548
and the iniquities of her *p*	Lam 4:13	3548
not the persons of the *p*, they	Lam 4:16	3548
Her *p* have violated my law, and	Eze 22:26	3548
is toward the south, is for the *p*	Eze 40:45	3548
is toward the north is for the *p*	Eze 40:46	3548
where the *p* that approach unto	Eze 42:13	3548
When the *p* enter therein, then	Eze 42:14	3548
thou shalt give to the *p*	Eze 43:19	3548
the *p* shall cast salt upon them,	Eze 43:24	3548
the *p* shall make your burnt	Eze 43:27	3548
But the Levites, the sons	Eze 44:15	3548
The *p* shall not eat of any thing	Eze 44:31	3548
of the land shall be for the *p*	Eze 45:4	3548
the *p* shall prepare his burnt	Eze 46:2	3548
into the holy chambers of the *p*	Eze 46:19	3548
the *p* shall boil the trespass	Eze 46:20	3548
And for them, even for the *p*	Eze 48:10	3548
It shall be for the *p* that are	Eze 48:11	3548
the *p* the Levites shall have five	Eze 48:13	3548
Hear ye this, O *p*	Hos 5:1	3548
so the company of *p* murder in the	Hos 6:9	3548
the *p* thereof that rejoiced on it	Hos 10:5	3649
the *p*, the LORD's ministers,	Joel 1:9	3548
Gird yourselves, and lament, ye *p*	Joel 1:13	3548
Let the *p*, the ministers of the	Joel 2:17	3548
the *p* thereof teach for hire, and	Mic 3:11	3548
name of the Chemarims with the *p*	Zeph 1:4	3548
her *p* have polluted the sanctuary	Zeph 3:4	3548
Ask now the *p* concerning the law,	Hag 2:11	3548
the *p* answered and said, No	Hag 2:12	3548
the *p* answered and said, It shall	Hag 2:13	3548
to speak unto the *p* which were in	Zec 7:3	3548
people of the land, and to the *p*	Zec 7:5	3548
the LORD of hosts unto you, O *p*	Mal 1:6	3548
And now, O ye *p*, this commandment	Mal 2:1	3548
he had gathered all the chief *p*	Mt 2:4	749
were with him, but only for the *p*	Mt 12:4	2409
the *p* in the temple profane the	Mt 12:5	2409
things of the elders and chief *p*	Mt 16:21	749
be betrayed unto the chief *p*	Mt 20:18	749
come into the temple, the chief *p*	Mt 21:15	749
And when the chief *p* and Pharisees	Mt 21:23	749
assembled together the chief *p*	Mt 21:45	749
Iscariot, went unto the chief *p*	Mt 26:3	749
and staves, from the chief *p*	Mt 26:14	749
Now the chief *p*, and elders, and	Mt 26:47	749
morning was come, all the chief *p*	Mt 26:59	749
pieces of silver to the chief *p*	Mt 27:1	749
the chief *p* took the silver	Mt 27:3	749
he was accused of the chief *p*	Mt 27:6	749
But the chief *p* and elders	Mt 27:12	749
also the chief *p* mocking him	Mt 27:20	749
of the preparation, the chief *p*	Mt 27:41	749
shewed unto the chief *p* all the	Mt 27:62	749
not lawful to eat but for the *p*	Mt 28:11	749
of the elders, and of the chief *p*	Mk 2:26	2409
be delivered unto the chief *p*	Mk 8:31	749
chief *p* heard it, and sought how	Mk 10:33	749
there come to him the chief *p*	Mk 11:18	749
and the chief *p* and the scribes	Mk 11:27	749
the twelve, went unto the chief *p*	Mk 14:1	749
were assembled all the chief *p*	Mk 14:10	749
And the chief *p* and all the council	Mk 14:53	749
in the morning the chief *p* held a	Mk 14:55	749
the chief *p* accused him of many	Mk 15:1	749
p had delivered him for envy	Mk 15:3	749
But the chief *p* moved the people,	Mk 15:10	749
Likewise also the chief *p* mocking	Mk 15:11	749
and Caiaphas being the high *p*	Mk 15:31	749
lawful to eat but for the *p* alone	Lk 3:2	749
rejected of the elders and chief *p*	Lk 6:4	2409
Go shew yourselves unto the *p*	Lk 9:22	749
But the chief *p* and the scribes and	Lk 17:14	2409
preached the gospel, the chief *p*	Lk 19:47	749
And the chief *p* and the scribes the	Lk 20:1	749
And the chief *p* and scribes sought	Lk 20:19	749
way, and communed with the chief *p*	Lk 22:2	749
Then Jesus said unto the chief *p*	Lk 22:4	749
of the people and the chief *p*	Lk 22:52	749
Then said Pilate to the chief *p*	Lk 22:66	749
And the chief *p* and scribes stood	Lk 23:4	749
	Lk 23:10	749

had called together the chief *p*	Lk 23:13	749
them and of the chief *p* prevailed	Lk 23:23	749
And how the chief *p* and our rulers	Lk 24:20	749
of John, when the Jews sent *p*	Jn 1:19	2409
the chief *p* sent officers to take	Jn 7:32	749
came the officers to the chief *p*	Jn 7:45	749
Then gathered the chief *p*	Jn 11:47	749
Now both the chief *p* and the	Jn 11:57	749
But the chief *p* consulted that	Jn 12:10	749
men and officers from the chief *p*	Jn 18:3	749
the chief *p* have delivered thee	Jn 18:35	749
When the chief *p* therefore	Jn 19:6	749
The chief *p* answered, We have no	Jn 19:15	749
Then said the chief *p* of the Jews	Jn 19:21	749
they spake unto the people, the *p*	Acts 4:1	2409
and reported all that the chief *p*	Acts 4:23	749
the chief *p* heard these things,	Acts 5:24	749
a great company of the *p* were	Acts 6:7	2409
p to bind all that call on thy	Acts 9:14	749
bring them bound unto the chief *p*	Acts 9:21	749
Sceva, a Jew, and chief of the *p*	Acts 19:14	749
bands, and commanded the chief *p*	Acts 22:30	749
And they came to the chief *p*	Acts 23:14	749
I was at Jerusalem, the chief *p*	Acts 25:15	749
authority from the chief *p*	Acts 26:10	749
and commission from the chief *p*	Acts 26:12	749
(For those *p* were made without an	Heb 7:21	2409
And they truly were many *p*	Heb 7:23	2409
not daily, as those high *p*	Heb 7:27	749
men high *p* which have infirmity	Heb 7:28	749
seeing that there are *p* that	Heb 8:4	2409
the *p* went always into the first	Heb 9:6	2409
kings and *p* unto God and his Father	Rev 1:6	2409
made us unto our God kings and *p*	Rev 5:10	2409
power, but they shall be *p* of God	Rev 20:6	2409

PRIESTS'

place where the *p* feet stood firm	Josh 4:3	3548
the soles of the *p* feet were	Josh 4:18	3548
thee, into one of the *p* offices	1Sa 2:36	3548
it was the *p*	2Kin 12:16	3548
silver, and one hundred *p* garments	Ezr 2:69	3548
five hundred and thirty *p* garments	Neh 7:70	3548
and threescore and seven *p* garments	Neh 7:72	3548
certain of the *p* sons with	Neh 12:35	3548

PRINCE

thou art a mighty *p* among us	Gen 23:6	5387
for as a *p* hast thou power with	Gen 32:28	5387
p of the country, saw her, he	Gen 34:2	5387
And he said, Who made thee a *p*	Ex 2:14	8269
each *p* on his day, for the	Num 7:11	5387
of Zuar, *p* of Issachar, did offer	Num 7:18	5387
p of the children of Zebulun, did	Num 7:24	5387
p of the children of Reuben, did	Num 7:30	5387
p of the children of Simeon, did	Num 7:36	5387
p of the children of Gad, offered	Num 7:42	5387
p of the children of Ephraim,	Num 7:48	5387
p of the children of Manasseh	Num 7:54	5387
p of the children of Benjamin,	Num 7:60	5387
p of the children of Dan, offered	Num 7:66	5387
p of the children of Asher,	Num 7:72	5387
p of the children of Naphtali,	Num 7:78	5387
thyself altogether a *p* over us	Num 16:13	8323
him a rod apiece, for each *p* one	Num 17:6	5387
a *p* of a chief house among the	Num 25:14	5387
the daughter of a *p* of Midian	Num 25:18	5387
shall take one of every tribe	Num 34:18	5387
the *p* of the tribe of the	Num 34:22	5387
The *p* of the children of Joseph,	Num 34:23	5387
the *p* of the tribe of the	Num 34:24	5387
the *p* of the tribe of the	Num 34:25	5387
the *p* of the tribe of the	Num 34:26	5387
the *p* of the tribe of the	Num 34:27	5387
the *p* of the tribe of the	Num 34:28	5387
princes, of each chief house a *p*	Josh 22:14	5387
Know ye not that there is a *p*	2Sa 3:38	8269
but I will make him *p* all the	1Kin 11:34	5387
made thee *p* over my people Israel	1Kin 14:7	5057
made thee *p* over my people Israel	1Kin 16:2	5057
p of the children of Judah	1Chr 2:10	5387
he was *p* of the Reubenites	1Chr 5:6	5387
unto Sheshbazzar, the *p* of Judah	Ezr 1:8	5387
say, Where is the house of the *p*	Job 21:28	5081
as a *p* would I go near unto him	Job 31:37	5057
is the destruction of the *p*	Prov 14:28	7333
much less do lying lips a *p*	Prov 17:7	5081
will intreat the favour of the *p*	Prov 19:6	5081
the *p* whom thine eyes have seen	Prov 25:7	5081
long forbearing is a *p* persuaded	Prov 25:15	7101
The *p* that wanteth understanding	Prov 28:16	5057
Father, The *P* of Peace	Is 9:6	8269

a quiet *p*	Jer 51:59	8269
with	Eze 7:27	5387
rusalem	Eze 12:10	5387
hem shall	Eze 12:12	5387
p of Israel	Eze 21:25	5387
e *p* of Tyrus	Eze 28:2	5057
land of Egypt	Eze 30:13	5387
a *p* among them	Eze 34:24	5387
eir *p* for ever	Eze 37:25	5387
eshech and Tubal,	Eze 38:2	5387
eshech and Tubal	Eze 38:3	5387
eshech and Tubal	Eze 39:1	5387
	Eze 44:3	5387
in it to eat	Eze 44:3	5387
one side	Eze 45:7	5387
so in Israel	Eze 45:16	5387
himself	Eze 45:22	5387
way of	Eze 46:2	5387
ne *p*	Eze 46:4	5387
shall	Eze 46:8	5387
when	Eze 46:10	5387
e a	Eze 46:12	5387
	Eze 46:16	5387
	Eze 46:17	5387
	Eze 46:18	5387
ne *p*	Eze 48:21	5387
p	Eze 48:21	5387
the *p*	Eze 48:22	5387
eunuchs	Dan 1:7	8269
he might	Dan 1:8	8269
ne eunuchs	Dan 1:9	8269
chs said unto	Dan 1:10	8269
ne eunuchs had set	Dan 1:11	8269
he eunuchs brought	Dan 1:18	8269
n to the *p* of the host	Dan 8:11	8269
against the *P* of princes	Dan 8:25	8269
all be seven weeks	Dan 9:25	5057
ople of the *p* that shall	Dan 9:26	5057
the *p* of the kingdom of	Dan 10:13	8269
fight with the *p* of Persia	Dan 10:20	8269
the *p* of Grecia shall come	Dan 10:20	8269
these things, but Michael your *p*	Dan 10:21	8269
but a *p* for his own behalf shall	Dan 11:18	7101
also the *p* of the covenant	Dan 11:22	5057
the great *p* which standeth for	Dan 12:1	8269
without a king, and without a *p*	Hos 3:4	8269
the *p* asketh, and the judge asketh	Mic 7:3	8269
through the *p* of the devils	Mt 9:34	758
by Beelzebub the *p* of the devils	Mt 12:24	758
by the *p* of the devils casteth he	Mk 3:22	758
now shall the *p* of this world be	Jn 12:31	758
for the *p* of this world cometh,	Jn 14:30	758
because the *p* of this world is	Jn 16:11	758
And killed the *P* of life, whom God	Acts 3:15	747
with his right hand to be a *P*	Acts 5:31	747
according to the *p* of the power	Eph 2:2	758
the *p* of the kings of the earth	Rev 1:5	758

PRINCE'S

thy feet with shoes, O *p* daughter	Song 7:1	5081
it shall be the *p* part to give	Eze 45:17	5387
the midst of that which is the *p*	Eze 48:22	5387

PRINCES

The *p* also of Pharaoh saw her, and	Gen 12:15	8269
twelve *p* shall he beget, and I	Gen 17:20	5387
twelve *p* according to their	Gen 25:16	5387
p of the tribes of their fathers,	Num 1:16	5387
the *p* of Israel, being twelve men	Num 1:44	5387
That the *p* of Israel, heads of	Num 7:2	5387
who were the *p* of the tribes, and	Num 7:2	5387
a wagon for two of the *p*, and for	Num 7:3	5387
the *p* offered for dedicating of	Num 7:10	5387
even the *p* offered their offering	Num 7:10	5387
was anointed, by the *p* of Israel	Num 7:84	5387
but with one trumpet, then the *p*	Num 10:4	5387
fifty *p* of the assembly, famous	Num 16:2	5387
of all their *p* according to the	Num 17:2	5387
every one of their *p* gave him a	Num 17:6	5387
The *p* digged the well, the nobles	Num 21:18	8269
the *p* of Moab abode with Balaam	Num 22:8	8269
and said unto the *p* of Balak	Num 22:13	8269
the *p* of Moab rose up, and they	Num 22:14	8269
And Balak sent yet again	Num 22:15	8269
ass, and went with the *p* of Moab	Num 22:21	8269
Balaam went with the *p* of Balak	Num 22:35	8269
to the *p* that were with him	Num 22:40	8269
he, and all the *p* of Moab	Num 23:6	8269
and the *p* of Moab with him	Num 23:17	8269
the priest, and before the *p*	Num 27:2	5387
all the *p* of the congregation,	Num 31:13	5387
unto the *p* of the congregation,	Num 32:2	5387

before Moses, and before the *p*	Num 36:1	5387
the *p* of the congregation sware	Josh 9:15	5387
because the *p* of the congregation	Josh 9:18	5387
murmured against the *p*	Josh 9:18	5387
But all the *p* said unto all the	Josh 9:19	5387
the *p* said unto them, Let them	Josh 9:21	5387
as the *p* had promised them	Josh 9:21	5387
Moses smote with the *p* of Midian	Josh 13:21	5387
the son of Nun, and before the *p*	Josh 17:4	5387
And with him ten *p*, of each chief	Josh 22:14	5387
the *p* of the congregation and	Josh 22:30	5387
of Eleazar the priest, and the *p*	Josh 22:32	5387
give ear, O ye *p*	Judg 5:3	7336
the *p* of Issachar were with	Judg 5:15	8269
they took two *p* of the Midianites	Judg 7:25	8269
into your hands the *p* of Midian	Judg 8:3	8269
the *p* of Succoth said, Are the	Judg 8:6	8269
unto him the *p* of Succoth	Judg 8:14	8269
p of Gilead said one to another,	Judg 10:18	8269
the dunghill, to set them among *p*	1Sa 2:8	5081
Then the *p* of the Philistines	1Sa 18:30	8269
Then said the *p* of the	1Sa 29:3	8269
unto the *p* of the Philistines	1Sa 29:3	8269
the *p* of the Philistines were	1Sa 29:4	8269
the *p* of the Philistines said	1Sa 29:4	8269
notwithstanding the *p* of the	1Sa 29:9	8269
the *p* of the children of Ammon	2Sa 10:3	8269
regardest neither *p* nor servants	2Sa 19:6	8269
And these were the *p* which he had	1Kin 4:2	8269
of war, and his servants, and his *p*	1Kin 9:22	8269
men of the *p* of the provinces	1Kin 20:14	8269
men of the *p* of the provinces	1Kin 20:15	8269
the young men of the *p* of the	1Kin 20:17	8269
So these young men of the *p* of	1Kin 20:19	8269
as the manner was, and the *p*	2Kin 11:14	8269
mother, and his servants, and his *p*	2Kin 24:12	8269
away all Jerusalem, and all the *p*	2Kin 24:14	8269
names were *p* in their families	1Chr 4:38	5387
men of valour, chief of the *p*	1Chr 7:40	5387
But the *p* of the children of	1Chr 19:3	8269
David also commanded all the *p* of	1Chr 22:17	8269
together all the *p* of Israel	1Chr 23:2	8269
them before the king, and the *p*	1Chr 24:6	8269
These were the *p* of the tribes of	1Chr 27:22	8269
assembled all the *p* of Israel	1Chr 28:1	8269
the *p* of the tribes, and the	1Chr 28:1	8269
also the *p* and all the people will	1Chr 28:21	8269
p of the tribes of Israel, and the	1Chr 29:6	8269
And all the *p*, and the mighty men,	1Chr 29:24	8269
to the *p* of Judah, that were	2Chr 12:5	8269
Whereupon the *p* of Israel	2Chr 12:6	8269
of his reign he sent to his *p*	2Chr 17:7	8269
and divers also of the *p* of Israel	2Chr 21:4	8269
Jehoram went forth with his *p*	2Chr 21:9	8269
of Ahab, and found the *p* of Judah	2Chr 22:8	8269
at the entering in, and the *p*	2Chr 23:13	8269
And all the *p* and all the people	2Chr 24:10	8269
of Jehoiada came the *p* of Judah	2Chr 24:17	8269
destroyed all the *p* of the people	2Chr 24:23	8269
and the spoil before the *p*	2Chr 28:14	8269
house of the king, and of the *p*	2Chr 28:21	8269
the *p* commanded the Levites to	2Chr 29:30	8269
king had taken counsel, and his *p*	2Chr 30:2	8269
his *p* throughout all Israel and	2Chr 30:6	8269
of the king and of the *p*, by the	2Chr 30:12	8269
the *p* gave to the congregation a	2Chr 30:24	8269
the *p* came and saw the heaps, they	2Chr 31:8	8269
He took counsel with his *p*	2Chr 32:3	8269
ambassadors of the *p* of Babylon	2Chr 32:31	8269
his *p* gave willingly unto the	2Chr 35:8	8269
of the king, and of his *p*	2Chr 36:18	8269
and before all the king's mighty *p*	Ezr 7:28	8269
the *p* had appointed for the	Ezr 8:20	8269
the *p* came to me, saying, The	Ezr 9:1	8269
yea, the hand of the *p* and rulers	Ezr 9:2	8269
according to the counsel of the *p*	Ezr 10:8	8269
upon us, on our kings, on our *p*	Neh 9:32	8269
Neither have our kings, our *p*	Neh 9:34	8269
and our *p*, Levites, and priests,	Neh 9:38	8269
Then I brought up the *p* of Judah	Neh 12:31	8269
and half of the *p* of Judah	Neh 12:32	8269
he made a feast unto all his *p*	Est 1:3	8269
p of the provinces, being before	Est 1:3	8269
the people and the *p* her beauty	Est 1:11	8269
and Memucan, the seven *p* of Persia	Est 1:14	8269
answered before the king and the *p*	Est 1:16	8269
king only, but also to all the *p*	Est 1:16	8269
this day unto all the king's *p*	Est 1:18	8269
saying pleased the king and the *p*	Est 1:21	8269
made a great feast unto all his *p*	Est 2:18	8269
all the *p* that were with him	Est 3:1	8269

he had advanced him above the *p* .... Est 5:11   8269
of one of the king's most noble *p* .... Est 6:9   8269
Or with *p* that had gold, who .... Job 3:15   8269
He leadeth *p* away spoiled, and .... Job 12:19   3548
He poureth contempt upon *p* .... Job 12:21   5081
The *p* refrained talking, and laid .... Job 29:9   8269
and to *p*, Ye are ungodly .... Job 34:18   5081
accepteth not the persons of *p* .... Job 34:19   8269
mayest make *p* in all the earth .... Ps 45:16   8269
The *p* of the people are gathered .... Ps 47:9   5081
the *p* of Judah and their council, ... Ps 68:27   8269
the *p* of Zebulun .... Ps 68:27   8269
and the *p* of Naphtali .... Ps 68:27   8269
P shall come out of Egypt .... Ps 68:31   2831
He shall cut off the spirit of *p* .... Ps 76:12   5057
men, and fall like one of the *p* .... Ps 82:7   8269
yea, all their *p* as Zebah .... Ps 83:11   5257
To bind his *p* at his pleasure .... Ps 105:22   8269
He poureth contempt upon *p* .... Ps 107:40   5081
That he may set him with *p* .... Ps 113:8   5081
even with the *p* of his people .... Ps 113:8   5081
LORD than to put confidence in *p* .... Ps 118:9   5081
P also did sit and speak against .... Ps 119:23   8269
P have persecuted me without a .... Ps 119:161   8269
Put not your trust in *p*, nor in .....`....... Ps 146:3   5081
p, and all judges of the earth .... Ps 148:11   8269
kings reign, and *p* decree justice .... Prov 8:15   7336
By me *p* rule, and nobles, even all .... Prov 8:16   8269
good, nor to strike *p* for equity .... Prov 17:26   5081
for a servant to have rule over *p* .... Prov 19:10   8269
of a land many are the *p* thereof .... Prov 28:2   8269
nor for *p* strong drink .... Prov 31:4   7336
p walking as servants upon the .... Eccl 10:7   8269
and thy *p* eat in the morning .... Eccl 10:16   8269
thy *p* eat in due season, for .... Eccl 10:17   8269
Thy *p* are rebellious, and .... Is 1:23   8269
will give children to be their *p* .... Is 3:4   8269
of his people, and the *p* thereof .... Is 3:14   8269
Are not my *p* altogether kings .... Is 10:8   8269
Surely the *p* of Zoan are fools, ... Is 19:11   8269
The *p* of Zoan are become fools, ... Is 19:13   8269
the *p* of Noph are deceived .... Is 19:13   8269
arise, ye *p*, and anoint the shield .... Is 21:5   8269
city, whose merchants are *p* .... Is 23:8   8269
For his *p* were at Zoan, and his .... Is 30:4   8269
his *p* shall be afraid of the .... Is 31:9   8269
and *p* shall rule in judgment .... Is 32:1   8269
all her *p* shall be nothing .... Is 34:12   8269
That bringeth the *p* to nothing .... Is 40:23   7336
shall come upon *p* as upon morter .... Is 41:25   5461
profaned the *p* of the sanctuary .... Is 43:28   8269
p also shall worship, because of .... Is 49:7   8269
of Judah, against the *p* thereof .... Jer 1:18   8269
they, their kings, their *p* .... Jer 2:26   8269
perish, and the heart of the *p* .... Jer 4:9   8269
of Judah, and the bones of his *p* .... Jer 8:1   8269
p sitting upon the throne of .... Jer 17:25   8269
and on horses, they, and their *p* .... Jer 17:25   8269
and the *p* of Judah, with the .... Jer 24:1   8269
the king of Judah, and his *p* .... Jer 24:8   8269
the *p* thereof, to make them a .... Jer 25:18   8269
Egypt, and his servants, and his *p* .... Jer 25:19   8269
When the *p* of Judah heard these .... Jer 26:10   8269
and the prophets unto the *p* .... Jer 26:11   8269
spake Jeremiah unto all the *p* .... Jer 26:12   8269
Then said the *p* and all the people .... Jer 26:16   8269
all his mighty men, and all the *p* .... Jer 26:21   8269
the *p* of Judah and Jerusalem, and .... Jer 29:2   8269
anger, they, their kings, their *p* .... Jer 32:32   8269
Now when all the *p*, and all the .... Jer 34:10   8269
The *p* of Judah .... Jer 34:19   8269
the *p* of Jerusalem, the eunuchs, ... Jer 34:19   8269
his *p* will I give into the hand .... Jer 34:21   8269
which was by the chamber of the *p* .... Jer 35:4   8269
all the *p* sat there, even .... Jer 36:12   8269
the son of Hananiah, and all the *p* .... Jer 36:12   8269
Therefore all the *p* sent Jehudi .... Jer 36:14   8269
Then said the *p* unto Baruch .... Jer 36:19   8269
in the ears of all the *p* which .... Jer 36:21   8269
Jeremiah, and brought him to the *p* .... Jer 37:14   8269
Wherefore the *p* were wroth with .... Jer 37:15   8269
Therefore the *p* said unto the .... Jer 38:4   8269
unto the king of Babylon's *p* .... Jer 38:17   8269
forth to the king of Babylon's *p* .... Jer 38:18   8269
forth to the king of Babylon's *p* .... Jer 38:22   8269
But if the *p* hear that I have .... Jer 38:25   8269
Then came all the *p* unto Jeremiah .... Jer 38:27   8269
all the *p* of the king of Babylon .... Jer 39:3   8269
of the *p* of the king of Babylon .... Jer 39:3   8269
and all the king of Babylon's *p* .... Jer 39:13   7227
the *p* of the king, even ten men .... Jer 41:1   7227

our fathers, our kings, and our *p* ...... (torn)
fathers, your kings, and your *p* .... (torn)
his priests and his *p* together .... (torn)
and his priests and his *p* together .. (torn)
from thence the king and the *p* .... (torn)
of Babylon, and upon her *p* .... (torn)
And I will make drunk her *p* .... (torn)
also all the *p* of Judah in Riblah .... (torn)
her *p* are become like harts that .... (torn)
the kingdom and the *p* thereof .... (torn)
her *p* are among the Gentiles .... (torn)
P are hanged up by their hand .... Lam ... (torn)
son of Benaiah, *p* of the people .... Ez... (torn)
the *p* thereof, and led them with .... Ez... (torn)
a lamentation for the *p* of Israel .... Eze (torn)
shall be upon all the *p* of Israel .... Eze (torn)
the *p* of Israel, every one were .... Eze 2... (torn)
Her *p* in the midst thereof are .... Eze 2... (torn)
heads, all of them *p* to look to .... Eze 23... (torn)
Then all the *p* of the sea shall .... Eze 26:... (torn)
all the *p* of Kedar, they occupied .... Eze 27:2... (torn)
is Edom, her kings, and all her *p* .... Eze 32:2... (torn)
There be the *p* of the north .... Eze 32:30   8269
the blood of the *p* of the earth .... Eze 39:18   8269
my *p* shall no more oppress my .... Eze 45:8   8269
Let it suffice you, O *p* of Israel .... Eze 45:9   8269
of the king's seed, and of the *p* .... Dan 1:3   8269
sent to gather together the *p* .... Dan 3:2   8269
Then the *p*, the governors, and .... Dan 3:3   (torn)
And the *p*, governors, and captains, ... Dan 3:27   3... (torn)
that the king, and his *p*, his .... Dan 5:2   726... (torn)
and the king, and his *p*, his wives, ... Dan 5:3   7261 (torn)
kingdom an hundred and twenty *p* .... Dan 6:1   324
that the *p* might give accounts .... Dan 6:2   324
above the presidents and *p* .... Dan 6:3   324
p sought to find occasion against .... Dan 6:4   324
p assembled together to the king, ... Dan 6:6   324
kingdom, the governors, and the *p* .... Dan 6:7   324
stand up against the Prince of *p* .... Dan 8:25   8269
in thy name to our kings, our *p* .... Dan 9:6   8269
of face, to our kings, to our *p* .... Dan 9:8   8269
lo, Michael, one of the chief *p* .... Dan 10:13   8269
shall be strong, and one of his *p* .... Dan 11:5   8269
Egypt their gods, with their *p* .... Dan 11:8   5257
The *p* of Judah were like them .... Hos 5:10   8269
and the *p* with their lies .... Hos 7:3   8269
In the day of our king the *p* have .... Hos 7:5   8269
their *p* shall fall by the sword .... Hos 7:16   8269
they have made *p*, and I knew it .... Hos 8:4   8269
for the burden of the king of *p* .... Hos 8:10   8269
all their *p* are revolters .... Hos 9:15   8269
thou saidst, Give me a king and *p* .... Hos 13:10   8269
his *p* together, saith the LORD .... Amos 1:15   8269
slay all the *p* thereof with him .... Amos 2:3   8269
ye *p* of the house of Israel .... Mic 3:1   7101
p of the house of Israel, that .... Mic 3:9   7101
the *p* shall be a scorn unto them .... Hab 1:10   7336
that I will punish the *p* .... Zeph 1:8   8269
Her *p* within her are roaring .... Zeph 3:3   8269
not the least among the *p* of Juda .... Mt 2:6   2232
Ye know that the *p* of the .... Mt 20:25   758
nor of the *p* of this world, that 1Cor 2:6   758
Which none of the *p* of this world 1Cor 2:8   758

PRINCESS
p among the provinces, how is she ..... Lam 1:1   8282

PRINCESSES
And he had seven hundred wives, *p* 1Kin 11:3   8282

PRINCIPAL
Take thou also unto thee *p* spices .... Ex 30:23   7218
he shall even restore it in the *p* .... Lev 6:5   7218
his trespass with the *p* thereof .... Num 5:7   7218
the son of Nathan was *p* officer 1Kin 4:5   3548
the *p* scribe of the host, which 2Kin 25:19   8269
one *p* household being taken for 1Chr 24:6   1
even the *p* fathers over against 1Chr 24:31   7218
of Asaph, was the *p* to begin the .... Neh 11:17   7218
Wisdom is the *p* thing .... Prov 4:7   7225
broken down the *p* plants thereof .... Is 16:8   8291
cummin, and cast in the *p* wheat .... Is 28:25   7795
in the ashes, ye *p* of the flock .... Jer 25:34   117
nor the *p* of the flock to escape .... Jer 25:35   117
an howling of the *p* of the flock .... Jer 25:36   117
the *p* scribe of the host, who .... Jer 52:25   8269
seven shepherds, and eight *p* men .... Mic 5:5   5257
p men of the city, at .... Acts 25:23   3588,2596,1851,5607

PRINCIPALITIES
for your *p* shall come down, even .... Jer 13:18   4761
nor life, nor angels, nor *p* .... Rom 8:38   746
To the intent that now unto the *p* .... Eph 3:10   746

PRINCIPALITY

flesh and blood, but against *p*	Eph 6:12	746
be thrones, or dominions, or *p*	Col 1:16	746
And having spoiled *p* and powers, he	Col 2:15	746
them in mind to be subject to *p*	Titus 3:1	746

PRINCIPALITY

Far above all *p*, and power, and	Eph 1:21	746
him, which is the head of all *p*	Col 2:10	746

PRINCIPLES

the first *p* of the oracles of God	Heb 5:12	4747
Therefore leaving the *p* of the	Heb 6:1	746

PRINT

dead, nor *p* any marks upon you	Lev 19:28	5414
thou settest a *p* upon the heels	Job 13:27	2707
in his hands the *p* of the nails	Jn 20:25	5179
my finger into the *p* of the nails	Jn 20:25	5179

PRINTED

oh that they were *p* in a book	Job 19:23	2710

PRISCA *(pris'-cah)* See PRISCILLA. *Same as Priscilla.*

Salute *P* and Aquila, and the	2Ti 4:19	4251

PRISCILLA *(pris-sil'-lah)* See PRISCA. *Wife of Aquila and co-worker of Paul.*

come from Italy, with his wife *P*	Acts 18:2	4252
thence into Syria, and with him *P*	Acts 18:18	4252
P had heard, they took him unto	Acts 18:26	4252
Greet *P* and Aquila my helpers in	Rom 16:3	4252
P salute you much in the Lord,	1Cor 16:19	4252

PRISED

price that I was *p* at of them	Zec 11:13	3365

PRISON

took him, and put him into the *p*	Gen 39:20	1004,5470
and he was there in the *p*	Gen 39:20	1004,5470
the sight of the keeper of the *p*	Gen 39:21	1004,5470
the keeper of the *p* committed to	Gen 39:22	1004,5470
the prisoners that were in the *p*	Gen 39:22	1004,5470
The keeper of the *p* looked not to	Gen 39:23	1004,5470
captain of the guard, into the *p*	Gen 40:3	1004,5470
Egypt, which were bound in the *p*	Gen 40:5	1004,5470
brother, and ye shall be kept in *p*	Gen 42:16	
be bound in the house of your *p*	Gen 42:19	4929
and he did grind in the *p* house	Judg 16:21	631
for Samson out of the *p* house	Judg 16:25	631
king, Put this fellow in the *p*	1Kin 22:27	1004,3608
shut him up, and bound him in *p*	2Kin 17:4	1004,3608
Jehoiachin king of Judah out of *p*	2Kin 25:27	1004,3608
And changed his *p* garments	2Kin 25:29	3608
the seer, and put him in a *p* house	2Chr 16:10	4115
king, Put this fellow in the *p*	2Chr 18:26	1004,612
that was by the court of the *p*	Neh 3:25	4307
and they stood still in the *p* gate	Neh 12:39	4307
Bring my soul out of *p*, that I	Ps 142:7	4525
For out of *p* he cometh to reign	Eccl 4:14	1004,612
pit, and shall be shut up in the *p*	Is 24:22	4525
out the prisoners from the *p*	Is 42:7	4525
in darkness out of the *p* house	Is 42:7	3608
and they are hid in *p* houses	Is 42:22	3608
He was taken from *p* and from	Is 53:8	6115
the opening of the *p* to them that	Is 61:1	6495
that thou shouldest put him in *p*	Jer 29:26	4115
was shut up in the court of the *p*	Jer 32:2	4307
p according to the word of the	Jer 32:8	4307
that sat in the court of the *p*	Jer 32:12	4307
yet shut up in the court of the *p*	Jer 33:1	4307
for they had not put him into *p*	Jer 37:4	1004,3608
put him in *p* in the house of	Jer 37:15	1004,612
for they had made that the *p*	Jer 37:15	1004,3608
people, that ye have put me in *p*	Jer 37:18	1004,3608
Jeremiah into the court of the *p*	Jer 37:21	4307
remained in the court of the *p*	Jer 37:21	4307
that was in the court of the *p*	Jer 38:6	4307
remained in the court of the *p*	Jer 38:13	4307
abode in the court of the *p* until	Jer 38:28	4307
out of the court of the *p*	Jer 39:14	4307
was shut up in the court of the *p*	Jer 39:15	4307
put him in *p* till the day of his	Jer 52:11	1004,6486
and brought him forth out of *p*	Jer 52:31	1004,3608
And changed his *p* garments	Jer 52:33	3608
heard that John was cast into *p*	Mt 4:12	3860
officer, and thou be cast into *p*	Mt 5:25	5438
in the *p* the works of Christ	Mt 11:2	1201
put him in *p* for Herodias' sake,	Mt 14:3	5438
sent, and beheaded John in the *p*	Mt 14:10	5438
but went and cast him into *p*	Mt 18:30	5438
I was in *p*, and ye came unto me	Mt 25:36	5438
Or when saw we thee sick, or in *p*	Mt 25:39	5438
sick, and in *p*, and ye visited me	Mt 25:43	5438
or naked, or sick, or in *p*	Mt 25:44	5438
Now after that John was put in *p*	Mk 1:14	3860

bound him in *p* for Herodias' sake	Mk 6:17	5438
he went and beheaded him in the *p*	Mk 6:27	5438
all, that he shut up John in *p*	Lk 3:20	5438
and the officer cast thee into *p*	Lk 12:58	5438
to go with thee, both into *p*	Lk 22:33	5438
and for murder, was cast into *p*	Lk 23:19	5438
and murder was cast into *p*	Lk 23:25	5438
For John was not yet cast into *p*	Jn 3:24	5438
and put them in the common *p*	Acts 5:18	5084
Lord by night opened the *p* doors	Acts 5:19	5438
sent to the *p* to have them	Acts 5:21	1201
came, and found them not in the *p*	Acts 5:22	5438
The *p* truly found we shut with	Acts 5:23	1201
the men whom ye put in *p* are	Acts 5:25	5438
men and women committed them to *p*	Acts 8:3	5438
apprehended him, he put him in *p*	Acts 12:4	5438
Peter therefore was kept in *p*	Acts 12:5	5438
before the door kept the *p*	Acts 12:6	5438
him, and a light shined in the *p*	Acts 12:7	3612
Lord had brought him out of the *p*	Acts 12:17	5438
upon them, they cast them into *p*	Acts 16:23	5438
thrust them into the inner *p*	Acts 16:24	5438
foundations of the *p* were shaken	Acts 16:26	1201
the keeper of the *p* awaking out	Acts 16:27	1200
sleep, and seeing the *p* doors open	Acts 16:27	5438
the keeper of the *p* told this	Acts 16:36	1200
Romans, and have cast us into *p*	Acts 16:37	5438
And they went out of the *p*	Acts 16:40	5438
of the saints did I shut up in *p*	Acts 26:10	5438
and preached unto the spirits in *p*	1Pet 3:19	5438
shall cast some of you into *p*	Rev 2:10	5438
shall be loosed out of his *p*	Rev 20:7	5438

PRISONER

sighing of the *p* come before thee	Ps 79:11	616
To hear the groaning of the *p*	Ps 102:20	615
to release unto the people a *p*	Mt 27:15	1198
And they had then a notable *p*	Mt 27:16	1198
feast he released unto them one *p*	Mk 15:6	1198
Paul the *p* called me unto him, and	Acts 23:18	1198
to me unreasonable to send a *p*	Acts 25:27	1198
yet was I delivered *p* from	Acts 28:17	1198
the *p* of Jesus Christ for you	Eph 3:1	1198
the *p* of the Lord, beseech you	Eph 4:1	1198
of our Lord, nor of me his *p*	2Ti 1:8	1198
a *p* of Jesus Christ, and Timothy	Philem 1	1198
now also a *p* of Jesus Christ	Philem 9	1198

PRISONERS

where the king's *p* were bound	Gen 39:20	615
all the *p* that were in the prison	Gen 39:22	615
Israel, and took some of them *p*	Num 21:1	7628
There the *p* rest together	Job 3:18	615
the poor, and despiseth not his *p*	Ps 69:33	615
The LORD looseth the *p*	Ps 146:7	631
they shall bow down under the *p*	Is 10:4	616
opened not the house of his *p*	Is 14:17	615
Assyria lead away the Egyptians *p*	Is 20:4	7628
as *p* are gathered in the pit, and	Is 24:22	616
bring out the *p* from the prison	Is 42:7	616
That thou mayest say to the *p*	Is 49:9	631
his feet all the *p* of the earth	Lam 3:34	615
p out of the pit wherein is no	Zec 9:11	615
to the strong hold, ye *p* of hope	Zec 9:12	615
and the *p* heard them	Acts 16:25	1198
that the *p* had been fled	Acts 16:27	1198
certain other *p* unto one named	Acts 27:1	1202
counsel was to kill the *p*	Acts 27:42	1202
the *p* to the captain of the guard	Acts 28:16	1198

PRISONS

up to the synagogues, and into *p*	Lk 21:12	5438
and delivering into *p* both men	Acts 22:4	5438
in *p* more frequent, in deaths oft	2Cor 11:23	5438

PRIVATE

is of any *p* interpretation	2Pet 1:20	2398

PRIVATELY

the disciples came unto him *p*	Mt 24:3	2596,2398
into a desert place by ship *p*	Mk 6:32	2596,2398
house, his disciples asked him *p*	Mk 9:28	2596,2398
John and Andrew asked him *p*	Mk 13:3	2596,2398
went aside *p* into a desert place	Lk 9:10	2596,2398
him unto his disciples, and said *p*	Lk 10:23	2596,2398
hand, and went with him aside *p*	Acts 23:19	2596,2398
but *p* to them which were of	Gal 2:2	2596,2398

PRIVILY

sent messengers unto Abimelech *p*	Judg 9:31	8649
off the skirt of Saul's robe *p*	1Sa 24:4	3909
his eyes are *p* set against the	Ps 10:8	6845
that they may *p* shoot at the	Ps 11:2	652
net that they have laid *p* for me	Ps 31:4	2934

P

they commune of laying snares p .... Ps 64:5   2934
Whoso p slandereth his neighbour, ... Ps 101:5   5643
have they p laid a snare for me .... Ps 142:3   2934
let us lurk p for the innocent .... Prov 1:11
they lurk p for their own lives .... Prov 1:18
was minded to put her away p .... Mt 1:19   2977
when he had p called the wise men .... Mt 2:7   2977
and now do they thrust us out p .... Acts 16:37   2977
who came in p to spy out our .... Gal 2:4   3922
who p shall bring in damnable 2Pet 2:1   3918

PRIVY
or hath his p member cut off, ... Deut 23:1   8212
which thine heart is p to 1Kin 2:44   3045
entereth into their p chambers .... Eze 21:14   2314
his wife also being p to it .... Acts 5:2   4894

PRIZE
run all, but one receiveth the p 1Cor 9:24   1017
p of the high calling of God in .... Phil 3:14   1017

PROCEED
that p out of the candlestick .... Ex 25:35   3318
any word p out of your mouth .... Josh 6:10   3318
which shall p out of thy bowels, ... 2Sa 7:12   3318
but I will p no further .... Job 40:5   3254
I will p to do a marvellous work .... Is 29:14   3254
for a law shall p from me .... Is 51:4   3318
for they p from evil to evil, and .... Jer 9:3   3318
out of them shall p thanksgiving .... Jer 30:19   3318
their governor shall p from the .... Jer 30:21   3318
dignity shall p of themselves .... Hab 1:7   3318
But those things which p out of .... Mt 15:18   1607
out of the heart p evil thoughts .... Mt 15:19   1831
p evil thoughts, adulteries, ... Mk 7:21   1607
communication p out of your mouth ...... Eph 4:29   1607
But they shall p no further 2Ti 3:9   4298

PROCEEDED
then whatsoever p out of her lips .... Num 30:12   4161
which hath p out of your mouth .... Num 32:24   3318
which hath p out of thy mouth .... Judg 11:36   3318
Elihu also p, and said, ... Job 36:1   3254
words which p out of his mouth .... Lk 4:22   1607
for I p forth and came from God .... Jn 8:42   1831
he p further to take Peter also .... Acts 12:3   4369
And out of the throne p lightnings .... Rev 4:5   1607
which sword p out of his mouth .... Rev 19:21   1607

PROCEEDETH
The thing p from the LORD .... Gen 24:50   3318
to all that p out of his mouth .... Num 30:2   3318
but by every word that p out of .... Deut 8:3   4161
Wickedness p from the wicked 1Sa 24:13   3318
an error which p from the ruler .... Eccl 10:5   3318
mouth of the most High p not evil .... Lam 3:38   3318
therefore wrong judgment p .... Hab 1:4   3318
but by every word that p out of .... Mt 4:4   1607
which p from the Father, he shall .... Jn 15:26   1607
Out of the same mouth p blessing .... Jas 3:10   1831
fire p out of their mouth, and .... Rev 11:5   1607

PROCEEDING
p out of the throne of God and of .... Rev 22:1   1607

PROCESS
in p of time it came to pass, ... Gen 4:3   7093
in p of time the daughter of .... Gen 38:12   7235
And it came to pass in p of time .... Ex 2:23   7227
And it came to pass in p of time .... Judg 11:4
came to pass, that in p of time 2Chr 21:19

PROCHORUS (prok'-o-rus) A leader in the Jerusalem church.
the Holy Ghost, and Philip, and P .... Acts 6:5   4402

PROCLAIM
I will p the name of the LORD .... Ex 33:19   7121
which ye shall p to be holy .... Lev 23:2   7121
which ye shall p in their seasons .... Lev 23:4   7121
ye shall p on the selfsame day, ... Lev 23:21   7121
which ye shall p to be holy .... Lev 23:37   7121
p liberty throughout all the land .... Lev 25:10   7121
against it, then p peace unto it .... Deut 20:10   7121
p in the ears of the people, ... Judg 7:3   7121
P a fast, and set Naboth on high 1Kin 21:9   7121
P a solemn assembly for Baal 2Kin 10:20   6942
p in all their cities, and in .... Neh 8:15   5674
p before him, Thus shall it be .... Est 6:9   7121
Most men will p every one his own .... Prov 20:6   7121
to p liberty to the captives, and .... Is 61:1   7121
To p the acceptable year of the .... Is 61:2   7121
p these words toward the north, ... Jer 3:12   7121
p there this word, and say, Hear .... Jer 7:2   7121
P all these words in the cities .... Jer 11:6   7121

p there the words that I shall .... Jer 19:2   7121
Jerusalem, to p liberty unto them .... Jer 34:8   7121
I p a liberty for you, saith the .... Jer 34:17   7121
P ye this among the Gentiles .... Joel 3:9   7121
of thanksgiving with leaven, and p .... Amos 4:5   7121

PROCLAIMED
there, and p the name of the LORD .... Ex 34:5   7121
LORD passed by before him, and p .... Ex 34:6   7121
it to be p throughout the camp .... Ex 36:6   5674
They p a fast, and set Naboth on 1Kin 21:12   7121
And they p it 2Kin 10:20   7121
God p, who p these words 2Kin 23:16   7121
p these things that thou hast 2Kin 23:17   7121
p a fast throughout all Judah 2Chr 20:3   7121
Then I p a fast there, at the .... Ezr 8:21   7121
p before him, Thus shall it be .... Est 6:11   7121
the LORD hath p unto the end of .... Is 62:11   8085
that they p a fast before the .... Jer 36:9   7121
p a fast, and put on sackcloth, ... Jonah 3:5   7121
And he caused it to be p and .... Jonah 3:7   2199
shall be p upon the housetops .... Lk 12:3   2784

PROCLAIMETH
the heart of fools p foolishness .... Prov 12:23   7121

PROCLAIMING
in p liberty every man to his .... Jer 34:15   7121
in p liberty, every one to his .... Jer 34:17   7121
strong angel p with a loud voice .... Rev 5:2   2784

PROCLAMATION
and Aaron made p, and said, To .... Ex 32:5   7121
Asa made a p throughout all Judah 1Kin 15:22   8085
there went a p throughout the 1Kin 22:36   7440
they made a p through Judah and 2Chr 24:9   6963
to make p throughout all Israel 2Chr 30:5   5674,6963
that he made a p throughout all 2Chr 36:22   5674,6963
that he made a p throughout all .... Ezr 1:1   5674,6963
they made p throughout Judah .... Ezr 10:7   5674,6963
made a p concerning him, that he .... Dan 5:29   3745

PROCURE
Thus might we p great evil .... Jer 26:19   6213
the prosperity that I p unto it .... Jer 33:9   6213

PROCURED
Hast thou not p this unto thyself .... Jer 2:17   6213
thy doings have p these things .... Jer 4:18   6213

PROCURETH
diligently seeketh good p favour .... Prov 11:27   1245

PRODUCE
P your cause, saith the LORD .... Is 41:21   7126

PROFANE
neither shalt thou p the name of .... Lev 18:21   2490
neither shalt thou p the name of .... Lev 19:12   2490
sanctuary, and to p my holy name .... Lev 20:3   2490
among his people, to p himself .... Lev 21:4   2490
not p the name of their God .... Lev 21:6   2490
take a wife that is a whore, or p .... Lev 21:7   2491
if she p herself by playing the .... Lev 21:9   2490
nor p the sanctuary of his God .... Lev 21:12   2490
widow, or a divorced woman, or p .... Lev 21:14   2491
Neither shall he p his seed among .... Lev 21:15   2490
that he p not my sanctuaries .... Lev 21:23   2490
that they p not my holy name in .... Lev 22:2   2490
and die therefore, if they p it .... Lev 22:9   2490
they shall not p the holy things .... Lev 22:15   2490
Neither shall ye p my holy name .... Lev 22:32   2490
that ye do, and p the sabbath day .... Neh 13:17   2490
For both prophet and priest are p .... Jer 23:11   2610
p wicked prince of Israel, whose .... Eze 21:25   2491
difference between the holy and p .... Eze 22:26   2455
day into my sanctuary to p it .... Eze 23:39   2490
I will p my sanctuary, the .... Eze 24:21   2490
as p out of the mountain of God .... Eze 28:16   2490
the sanctuary and the p place .... Eze 42:20   2455
difference between the holy and p .... Eze 44:23   2455
shall be a p place for the city, ... Eze 48:15   2455
the same maid, to p my holy name .... Amos 2:7   2490
in the temple p the sabbath .... Mt 12:5   953
hath gone about to p the temple .... Acts 24:6   953
and for sinners, for unholy and p 1Ti 1:9   952
But refuse p and old wives' fables 1Ti 4:7   952
to thy trust, avoiding p and vain 1Ti 6:20   952
But shun p and vain babblings 2Ti 2:16   952
or p person, as Esau, who for one .... Heb 12:16   952

PROFANED
because he hath p the hallowed .... Lev 19:8   2490
thou hast p his crown by casting .... Ps 89:39   2490
Therefore I have p the princes of .... Is 43:28   2490
things, and hast p my sabbaths .... Eze 22:8   2490

law, and have *p* mine holy things............ Eze 22:26   2490
my sabbaths, and I am *p* among them .. Eze 22:26   2490
same day, and have *p* my sabbaths........ Eze 23:38   2490
my sanctuary, when it was *p* .... Eze 25:3   2490
they *p* my holy name, when they .... Eze 36:20   2490
of Israel had *p* among the heathen........ Eze 36:21   2490
which ye have *p* among the heathen ...... Eze 36:22   2490
which was *p* among the heathen, ... Eze 36:23   2490
which ye have *p* in the midst of .... Eze 36:23   2490
But ye have *p* it, in that ye say,............ Mal 1:12   2490
for Judah hath *p* the holiness of .... Mal 2:11   2490

PROFANENESS
is *p* gone forth into all the land.............. Jer 23:15   2613

PROFANETH
the whore, she *p* her father.................... Lev 21:9   2490

PROFANING
upon Israel by *p* the sabbath .... Neh 13:18   2490
by *p* the covenant of our fathers .... Mal 2:10   2490

PROFESS
I *p* this day unto the Lᴏʀᴅ thy .... Deut 26:3   5046
And then will I *p* unto them .... Mt 7:23   3670
They *p* that they know God.................... Titus 1:16   3670

PROFESSED
they glorify God for your *p*.............:....2Cor 9:13   3671
hast *p* a good profession before 1Ti 6:12   3670

PROFESSING
P themselves to be wise, they .... Rom 1:22   5335
But (which becometh women *p* 1Ti 2:10   1861
Which some *p* have erred...................... 1Ti 6:21   1861

PROFESSION
a good *p* before many witnesses............ 1Ti 6:12   3671
Apostle and High Priest of our *p* .... Heb 3:1   3671
of God, let us hold fast our *p* .... Heb 4:14   3671
Let us hold fast the *p* of our .... Heb 10:23   3671

PROFIT
what *p* shall this birthright do .... Gen 25:32
What *p* is it if we slay our .... Gen 37:26   1215
which cannot *p* nor deliver..................... 1Sa 12:21   3276
for the king's *p* to suffer them .... Est 3:8   7737
what *p* should we have, if we pray .... Job 21:15   3276
the strength of their hands *p* me .... Job 30:2
What *p* shall I have, if I be .... Job 35:3   3276
may *p* the son of man .... Job 35:8
What *p* is there in my blood, when .... Ps 30:9   1215
Treasures of wickedness *p* nothing .... Prov 10:2   3276
Riches *p* not in the day of wrath............ Prov 11:4   3276
In all labour there is *p* .... Prov 14:23   4195
What *p* hath a man of all his.................. Eccl 1:3   3504
there was no *p* under the sun................. Eccl 2:11   3504
What *p* hath he that worketh in .... Eccl 3:9   3504
Moreover the *p* of the earth is .... Eccl 5:9   3504
what *p* hath he that hath laboured .... Eccl 5:16   3504
by it there is *p* to them that see............. Eccl 7:11   3148
of a people that could not *p* them .... Is 30:5   3276
nor be an help nor *p* .... Is 30:5   3276
to a people that shall not *p* them........... Is 30:6   3276
delectable things shall not *p* .... Is 44:9   3276
if so be thou shalt be able to *p* .... Is 47:12   3276
thy God which teacheth thee to *p* .... Is 48:17   3276
for they shall not *p* thee........................ Is 57:12   3276
walked after things that do not *p* .... Jer 2:8   3276
glory for that which doth not *p* .... Jer 2:11   3276
in lying words, that cannot *p* .... Jer 7:8   3276
to pain, but shall not *p* .... Jer 12:13   3276
and things wherein there is no *p* .... Jer 16:19   3276
shall not *p* this people at all................... Jer 23:32   3276
what *p* is it that we have kept .... Mal 3:14   1215
For what shall it *p* a man...................... Mk 8:36   5623
or what *p* is there of .... Rom 3:1   5622
And this I speak for your own *p* 1Cor 7:35   4851
own *p*, but the *p* of many..................... 1Cor 10:33   4851
is given to every man to *p* withal 1Cor 12:7   4851
with tongues, what shall I *p* you 1Cor 14:6   5623
Christ shall *p* you nothing..................... Gal 5:2   5623
strive not about words to no *p* 2Ti 2:14   5539
the word preached did not *p* them.......... Heb 4:2   5623
but he for our *p*, that we might.............. Heb 12:10   4851
What doth it *p*, my brethren,................. Jas 2:14   3786
what doth it *p* .... Jas 2:16   3786

PROFITABLE
Can a man be *p* unto God, as he............ Job 22:2   5532
is wise may be *p* unto himself .... Job 22:2   5532
but wisdom is *p* to direct .... Eccl 10:10   3504
image that is *p* for nothing .... Is 44:10   3276
was marred, it was *p* for nothing............ Jer 13:7   6743
for it is *p* for thee that one of................. Mt 5:29   4851

for it is *p* for thee that one of .... Mt 5:30   4851
back nothing that was *p* unto you .... Acts 20:20   4851
godliness is *p* unto all things 1Ti 4:8   5624
is *p* for doctrine, for reproof, ... 2Ti 3:16   5624
for he is *p* to me for the 2Ti 4:11   2173
things are good and *p* unto men............. Titus 3:8   5624
unprofitable, but now *p* to thee.............. Philem 11   2173

PROFITED
which was right, and it *p* me not .... Job 33:27   7737
thou mightest be *p* by me .... Mt 15:5   5623
For what is a man *p*, if he shall .... Mt 16:26   5623
thou mightest be *p* by me .... Mk 7:11   5623
p in the Jews' religion above .... Gal 1:14   4298
which have not *p* them that have .... Heb 13:9   5623

PROFITETH
It *p* a man nothing that he should .... Job 34:9   5532
What *p* the graven image that the .... Hab 2:18   3276
the flesh *p* nothing .... Jn 6:63   5623
For circumcision verily *p* .... Rom 2:25   5623
have not charity, it *p* me nothing........... 1Cor 13:3   5623
For bodily exercise *p* little 1Ti 4:8   5624,2076

PROFITING
that thy *p* may appear to all................... 1Ti 4:15   4297

PROFOUND
revolters are *p* to make slaughter .... Hos 5:2   6009

PROGENITORS
above the blessings of my *p* unto .... Gen 49:26   2029

PROGNOSTICATORS
the stargazers, the monthly *p* .... Is 47:13   3045

PROLONG
ye shall not *p* your days upon it,........... Deut 4:26   748
that thou mayest *p* thy days upon .... Deut 4:40   748
that ye may *p* your days in the .... Deut 5:33   748
that ye may *p* your days in the .... Deut 11:9   748
to the end that he may *p* his days .... Deut 17:20   748
and that thou mayest *p* thy days .... Deut 22:7   748
that ye shall not *p* your days .... Deut 30:18   748
ye shall *p* your days in the land .... Deut 32:47   748
mine end, that I should *p* my life .... Job 6:11   748
neither shall he *p* the perfection .... Job 15:29   5186
Thou wilt *p* the king's life .... Ps 61:6   3254
covetousness shall *p* his days .... Prov 28:16   748
neither shall he *p* his days..................... Eccl 8:13   748
see his seed, he shall *p* his days .... Is 53:10   748

PROLONGED
that thy days may be *p*, and that .... Deut 5:16   748
and that thy days may be *p* .... Deut 6:2   748
the state thereof shall be *p* .... Prov 28:2   748
hundred times, and his days be *p*.......... Eccl 8:12   748
come, and her days shall not be *p* .... Is 13:22   4900
of Israel, saying, The days are *p*........... Eze 12:22   748
it shall be no more *p* .... Eze 12:25   4900
none of my words be *p* any more............ Eze 12:28   4900
their lives were *p* for a season .... Dan 7:12   754,3052

PROLONGETH
The fear of the Lᴏʀᴅ *p* days .... Prov 10:27   3254
that *p* his life in his wickedness............. Eccl 7:15   748

PROMISE
and ye shall know my breach of *p*.......... Num 14:34
failed one word of all his good *p* 1Kin 8:56   1697
let thy *p* unto David my father be.......... 2Chr 1:9   1697
should do according to this *p* .... Neh 5:12   1697
that performeth not this *p* .... Neh 5:13   1697
people did according to this *p* .... Neh 5:13   1697
doth his *p* fail for evermore .... Ps 77:8   562
For he remembered his holy *p*............... Ps 105:42   1697
I send the *p* of my Father upon .... Lk 24:49   1860
but wait for the *p* of the Father.............. Acts 1:4   1860
Father the *p* of the Holy Ghost .... Acts 2:33   1860
For the *p* is unto you, and to your.......... Acts 2:39   1860
when the time of the *p* drew nigh .... Acts 7:17   1860
p raised unto Israel a Saviour .... Acts 13:23   1860
how that the *p* which was made .... Acts 13:32   1860
ready, looking for a *p* from thee............. Acts 23:21   1860
p made of God unto our fathers .... Acts 26:6   1860
Unto which *p* our twelve tribes.............. Acts 26:7
For the *p*, that he should be the .... Rom 4:13   1860
the *p* made of none effect .... Rom 4:14   1860
to the end the *p* might be sure to .... Rom 4:16   1860
at the *p* of God through unbelief .... Rom 4:20   1860
but the children of the *p* are .... Rom 9:8   1860
For this is the word of *p*........................ Rom 9:9   1860
that we might receive the *p* of .... Gal 3:14   1860
should make the *p* of none effect .... Gal 3:17   1860
be of the law, it is no more of *p* .... Gal 3:18   1860
but God gave it to Abraham by *p*........... Gal 3:18   1860

P

come to whom the *p* was made	Gal 3:19	1861
that the *p* by faith of Jesus	Gal 3:22	1860
seed, and heirs according to the *p*	Gal 3:29	1860
but he of the freewoman was by *p*	Gal 4:23	1860
Isaac was, are the children of *p*	Gal 4:28	1860
sealed with that holy Spirit of *p*	Eph 1:13	1860
strangers from the covenants of *p*	Eph 2:12	1860
partakers of his *p* in Christ by	Eph 3:6	1860
is the first commandment with *p*	Eph 6:2	1860
having *p* of the life that now is,	1Ti 4:8	1860
according to the *p* of life which	2Ti 1:1	1860
a *p* being left us of entering	Heb 4:1	1860
For when God made *p* to Abraham	Heb 6:13	1861
endured, he obtained the *p*	Heb 6:15	1860
to shew unto the heirs of *p* the	Heb 6:17	1860
the *p* of eternal inheritance	Heb 9:15	1860
of God, ye might receive the *p*	Heb 10:36	1860
he sojourned in the land of *p*	Heb 11:9	1860
the heirs with him of the same *p*	Heb 11:9	1860
through faith, received not the *p*	Heb 11:39	1860
While they *p* them liberty, they	2Pet 2:19	1861
Where is the *p* of his coming	2Pet 3:4	1860
is not slack concerning his *p*	2Pet 3:9	1860
we, according to his *p*, look for	2Pet 3:13	1862
this is the *p* that he hath	1Jn 2:25	1860

PROMISED

give you, according as he hath *p*	Ex 12:25	1696
the place which the LORD hath *p*	Num 14:40	559
and bless you, as he hath *p* you	Deut 1:11	1696
God of thy fathers hath *p* thee	Deut 6:3	1696
into the land which he *p* them	Deut 9:28	1696
as the LORD thy God *p* him	Deut 10:9	1696
thy border, as he hath *p* thee	Deut 12:20	1696
God blesseth thee, as he *p* thee	Deut 15:6	1696
he *p* to give unto thy fathers	Deut 19:8	1696
which thou hast *p* with thy mouth	Deut 23:23	1696
people, as he hath *p* thee	Deut 26:18	1696
God of thy fathers hath *p* thee	Deut 27:3	1696
as the princes had *p* them	Josh 9:21	1696
unto your brethren, as he *p* them	Josh 22:4	1696
the LORD your God hath *p* unto you	Josh 23:5	1696
for you, as he hath *p* you	Josh 23:10	1696
which the LORD your God *p* you	Josh 23:15	1696
thou hast *p* this goodness unto	2Sa 7:28	1696
hath made me an house, as he *p*	1Kin 2:24	1696
gave Solomon wisdom, as he *p* him	1Kin 5:12	1696
throne of Israel, as the LORD *p*	1Kin 8:20	1696
according to all that he *p*	1Kin 8:56	1696
which he *p* by the hand of Moses	1Kin 8:56	1696
as I *p* to David thy father,	1Kin 9:5	1696
as he *p* him to give him alway a	2Kin 8:19	559
hast *p* this goodness unto thy	1Chr 17:26	1696
throne of Israel, as the LORD *p*	2Chr 6:10	1696
father that which thou hast *p* him	2Chr 6:15	1696
father that which thou hast *p* him	2Chr 6:16	1696
as he *p* to give a light to him and	2Chr 21:7	559
thou hadst *p* to their fathers	Neh 9:23	559
p to pay to the king's treasuries	Est 4:7	559
all the good that I have *p* them	Jer 32:42	1696
I have *p* unto the house of Israel	Jer 33:14	1696
Whereupon he *p* with an oath to	Mt 14:7	3670
were glad, and *p* to give him money	Mk 14:11	1861
the mercy *p* to our fathers	Lk 1:72	
And he *p*, and sought opportunity to	Lk 22:6	1843
yet he *p* that he would give it to	Acts 7:5	1861
(Which he had *p* afore by his	Rom 1:2	4279
persuaded that, what he had *p*	Rom 4:21	1861
lie, *p* before the world began	Titus 1:2	1861
(for he is faithful that *p*	Heb 10:23	1861
she judged him faithful who had *p*	Heb 11:11	1861
but now he hath *p*, saying, Yet	Heb 12:26	1861
which the Lord hath *p* to them	Jas 1:12	1861
he hath *p* to them that love him	Jas 2:5	1861
is the promise that he hath *p* us	1Jn 2:25	1861

PROMISEDST

David my father that thou *p* him	1Kin 8:24	1696
David my father that thou *p* him	1Kin 8:25	1696
p them that they should go in to	Neh 9:15	559

PROMISES

and the service of God, and the *p*	Rom 9:4	1860
to confirm the *p* made unto the	Rom 15:8	1860
For all the *p* of God in him are	2Cor 1:20	1860
therefore these *p* dearly beloved	2Cor 7:1	1860
and his seed were the *p* made	Gal 3:16	1860
the law then against the *p* of God	Gal 3:21	1860
faith and patience inherit the *p*	Heb 6:12	1860
and blessed him that had the *p*	Heb 7:6	1860
was established upon better *p*	Heb 8:6	1860
faith, not having received the *p*	Heb 11:13	1860

he that had received the *p*	Heb 11:17	1860
wrought righteousness, obtained *p*	Heb 11:33	1860
us exceeding great and precious *p*	2Pet 1:4	1862

PROMISING

his wicked way, by *p* him life	Eze 13:22	2421

PROMOTE

For I will *p* thee unto very great	Num 22:17	3513
able indeed to *p* thee to honour	Num 22:37	3513
I thought to *p* thee unto great	Num 24:11	3513
p Haman the son of Hammedatha the	Est 3:1	1431
Exalt her, and she shall *p* thee	Prov 4:8	7311

PROMOTED

go to be *p* over the trees	Judg 9:9	5128
go to be *p* over the trees	Judg 9:11	5128
go to be *p* over the trees	Judg 9:13	5128
things wherein the king had *p* him	Est 5:11	1431
Then the king *p* Shadrach, Meshach	Dan 3:30	6744

PROMOTION

For *p* cometh neither from the	Ps 75:6	7311
but shame shall be the *p* of fools	Prov 3:35	7311

PRONOUNCE

that a man shall *p* with an oath	Lev 5:4	981
look on him, and *p* him unclean	Lev 13:3	
the priest shall *p* him clean	Lev 13:6	
the priest shall *p* him unclean	Lev 13:8	
and the priest shall *p* him unclean	Lev 13:11	
he shall *p* him clean that hath	Lev 13:13	
raw flesh, and *p* him to be unclean	Lev 13:15	
then the priest shall *p* him clean	Lev 13:17	
the priest shall *p* him unclean	Lev 13:20	
the priest shall *p* him unclean	Lev 13:22	
and the priest shall *p* him clean	Lev 13:23	
the priest shall *p* him unclean	Lev 13:25	
the priest shall *p* him unclean	Lev 13:27	
and the priest shall *p* him unclean	Lev 13:28	
the priest shall *p* him unclean	Lev 13:30	
then the priest shall *p* him clean	Lev 13:34	
and the priest shall *p* him clean	Lev 13:37	
the priest shall *p* him utterly	Lev 13:44	
to *p* it clean, or to *p* it	Lev 13:59	
shall *p* him clean, and shall let	Lev 14:7	
priest shall *p* the house clean	Lev 14:48	
he could not frame to *p* it right	Judg 12:6	1696

PRONOUNCED

but that he *p* this prophecy	Neh 6:12	1696
hath *p* evil against thee, for the	Jer 11:17	1696
Wherefore hath the LORD *p* all	Jer 16:10	1696
nation, against whom I have *p*	Jer 18:8	1696
the evil that I have *p* against it	Jer 19:15	1696
words which I have *p* against it	Jer 25:13	1696
evil that he hath *p* against you	Jer 26:13	1696
evil which he had *p* against them	Jer 26:19	1696
for I have *p* the word, saith the	Jer 34:5	1696
evil that I have *p* against them	Jer 35:17	1696
LORD hath *p* against this people	Jer 36:7	1696
He *p* all these words unto me with	Jer 36:18	7126
evil that I have *p* against them	Jer 36:31	1691
The LORD thy God hath *p* this evil	Jer 40:2	1691

PRONOUNCING

p with his lips to do evil, or to	Lev 5:4	981

PROOF

that I might know the *p* of you	2Cor 2:9	1382
the *p* of your love, and of our	2Cor 8:24	1732
Since ye seek a *p* of Christ	2Cor 13:3	1382
But ye know the *p* of him, that,	Phil 2:22	1382
make full *p* of thy ministry	2Ti 4:5	4135

PROOFS

his passion by many infallible *p*	Acts 1:3	5039

PROPER

my God, I have of mine own *p* good	1Chr 29:3	5459
field is called in their *p* tongue	Acts 1:19	2398
every man hath his *p* gift of God	1Cor 7:7	2398
because they saw he was a *p* child	Heb 11:23	791

PROPHECIES

but whether there be *p*, they	1Cor 13:8	4394
according to the *p* which went	1Ti 1:18	4394

PROPHECY

in the *p* of Ahijah the Shilonite,	2Chr 9:29	5016
the *p* of Oded the prophet, he	2Chr 15:8	5016
he pronounced this *p* against me	Neh 6:12	5016
Agur the son of Jakeh, even the *p*	Prov 30:1	4853
the *p* that his mother taught him	Prov 31:1	4853
and to seal up the vision and *p*	Dan 9:24	5030
them is fulfilled the *p* of Esaias	Mt 13:14	4394
that is given to us, whether *p*	Rom 12:6	4394

to another p 1Cor 12:10   4394
And though I have the gift of p 1Cor 13:2   4394
thee, which was given thee by p 1Ti 4:14   4394
have also a more sure word of p 2Pet 1:19   4397
that no p of the scripture is of 2Pet 1:20   4394
For the p came not in old time by 2Pet 1:21   4394
that hear the words of this p .... Rev 1:3   4394
rain not in the days of their p .... Rev 11:6   4394
of Jesus is the spirit of p .... Rev 19:10   4394
the sayings of the p of this book .... Rev 22:7   4394
the sayings of the p of this book .... Rev 22:10   4394
the words of the p of this book .... Rev 22:18   4394
the words of the book of this p .... Rev 22:19   4394

PROPHESIED

spirit rested upon them, they p .... Num 11:25   5012
and they p in the camp .... Num 11:26   5012
came upon him, and he p among them .. 1Sa 10:10   5012
he p among the prophets, then the 1Sa 10:11   5012
he p in the midst of the house 1Sa 18:10   5012
of Saul, and they also p 1Sa 19:20   5012
messengers, and they p likewise 1Sa 19:21   5012
the third time, and they p also 1Sa 19:21   5012
him also, and he went on, and p 1Sa 19:23   5012
p before Samuel in like manner, ... 1Sa 19:24   5012
they p until the time of the 1Kin 18:29   5012
and all the prophets p before them 1Kin 22:10   5012
And all the prophets p so, saying, ... 1Kin 22:12   5012
which p according to the order of 1Chr 25:2   5012
who p with a harp, to give thanks 1Chr 25:3   5012
for he never p good unto me 2Chr 18:7   5012
and all the prophets p before them 2Chr 18:9   5012
And all the prophets p so, saying, ... 2Chr 18:11   5012
of Mareshah p against Jehoshaphat 2Chr 20:37   5012
p unto the Jews that were in .... Ezr 5:1   5013
me, and the prophets p by Baal .... Jer 2:8   5012
that Jeremiah p these things .... Jer 20:1   5012
friends, to whom thou hast p lies .... Jer 20:6   5012
they p in Baal, and caused my .... Jer 23:13   5012
not spoken to them, yet they p .... Jer 23:21   5012
which Jeremiah hath p against all .... Jer 25:13   5012
Why hast thou p in the name of .... Jer 26:9   5012
for he hath p against this city, ... Jer 26:11   5012
Micah the Morasthite p in the .... Jer 26:18   5012
that p in the name of the LORD .... Jer 26:20   5012
who p against this city and .... Jer 26:20   5012
thy words which thou hast p .... Jer 28:6   5012
before thee of old p both against .... Jer 28:8   5012
that Shemaiah hath p unto you .... Jer 29:31   5012
your prophets which p unto you .... Jer 37:19   5012
And it came to pass, when I p .... Eze 11:13   5012
So I p as I was commanded .... Eze 37:7   5012
and as I p, there was a noise, and .... Eze 37:7   5012
So I p as he commanded me, and the .... Eze 37:10   5012
which p in those days many years .... Eze 38:17   5012
one of his vision, when he hath p .... Zec 13:4   5012
Lord, have we not p in thy name .... Mt 7:22   4395
prophets and the law p until John .... Mt 11:13   4395
Well hath Esaias p of you .... Mk 7:6   4395
filled with the Holy Ghost, and p .... Lk 1:67   4395
he p that Jesus should die for .... Jn 11:51   4395
and they spake with tongues, and p ...... Acts 19:6   4395
tongues, but rather that ye p 1Cor 14:5   4395
who p of the grace that should 1Pet 1:10   4395
p of these, saying, Behold, the .... Jude 14   4395

PROPHESIETH

The prophet which p of peace .... Jer 28:9   5012
he p of the times that are far .... Eze 12:27   5012
thrust him through when he p .... Zec 13:3   5012
or p with her head uncovered 1Cor 11:5   4395
But he that p speaketh unto men 1Cor 14:3   4395
but he that p edifieth the church 1Cor 14:4   4395
for greater is he that p than he 1Cor 14:5   4395

PROPHESY

Eldad and Medad do p in the camp .... Num 11:27   5012
and they shall p 1Sa 10:5   5012
thee, and thou shalt p with them 1Sa 10:6   5012
for he doth not p good concerning 1Kin 22:8   5012
he would p no good concerning me 1Kin 22:18   5012
Jeduthun, who should p with harps 1Chr 25:1   5012
that he would not p good unto me 2Chr 18:17   5012
P not unto us right things, speak .... Is 30:10   2372
unto us smooth things, p deceits .... Is 30:10   2372
The prophets p falsely, and the .... Jer 5:31   5012
P not in the name of the LORD, ... Jer 11:21   5012
The prophets p lies in my name .... Jer 14:14   5012
they p unto you a false vision and .... Jer 14:14   5012
the prophets that p in my name .... Jer 14:15   5012
the people to whom they p shall .... Jer 14:16   5012
the LORD had sent him to p .... Jer 19:14   5012

of the prophets that p unto you .... Jer 23:16   5012
that p lies in my name, saying, I .... Jer 23:25   5012
heart of the prophets that p lies .... Jer 23:26   5012
against them that p false dreams .... Jer 23:32   5012
Therefore p thou against them all .... Jer 25:30   5012
sent me to p against this house .... Jer 26:12   5012
For they p a lie unto you, to .... Jer 27:10   5012
for they p a lie unto you .... Jer 27:14   5012
yet they p a lie in my name .... Jer 27:15   5012
and the prophets that p unto you .... Jer 27:15   5012
of your prophets that p unto you .... Jer 27:16   5012
for they p a lie unto you .... Jer 27:16   5012
For they p falsely unto you in my .... Jer 29:9   5012
which p a lie unto you in my name .... Jer 29:21   5012
up, saying, Wherefore dost thou p .... Jer 32:3   5012
and thou shalt p against it .... Eze 4:7   5012
of Israel, and p against them, ... Eze 6:2   5012
p against them, p, O son .... Eze 11:4   5012
p against the prophets of Israel .... Eze 13:2   5012
the prophets of Israel that p .... Eze 13:2   5012
that p out of their own hearts .... Eze 13:2   5012
which p concerning Jerusalem .... Eze 13:16   5012
which p out of their own heart .... Eze 13:17   5012
and p thou against them, ... Eze 13:17   5012
p against the forest of the south .... Eze 20:46   5012
p against the land of Israel, ... Eze 21:2   5012
Son of man, p, and say, Thus saith .... Eze 21:9   5012
Thou therefore, son of man, p .... Eze 21:14   5012
And thou, son of man, p and say, ... Eze 21:28   5012
the Ammonites, and p against them ...... Eze 25:2   5012
against Zidon, and p against it, ... Eze 28:21   5012
p against him, and against all .... Eze 29:2   5012
Son of man, p and say, Thus saith .... Eze 30:2   5012
p against the shepherds of Israel .... Eze 34:2   5012
the shepherds of Israel, p .... Eze 34:2   5012
mount Seir, and p against it, ... Eze 35:2   5012
p unto the mountains of Israel, ... Eze 36:1   5012
Therefore p and say, Thus saith .... Eze 36:3   5012
P therefore concerning the land .... Eze 36:6   5012
P upon these bones, and say unto .... Eze 37:4   5012
P unto the wind, p, son of .... Eze 37:9   5012
Therefore p and say unto them, ... Eze 37:12   5012
and Tubal, and p against him, ... Eze 38:2   5012
Therefore, son of man, p and say .... Eze 38:14   5012
p against Gog, and say, Thus saith .... Eze 39:1   5012
sons and your daughters shall p .... Joel 2:28   5012
the prophets, saying, P not .... Amos 2:12   5012
GOD hath spoken, who can but p .... Amos 3:8   5012
and there eat bread, and p there .... Amos 7:12   5012
But p not again any more at .... Amos 7:13   5012
me, Go, p unto my people Israel .... Amos 7:15   5012
P not against Israel, and drop not .... Amos 7:16   5012
P ye not, say they to them that .... Mic 2:6   5197
ye not, say they to them that p .... Mic 2:6   5197
they shall not p to them, that .... Mic 2:6   5197
I will p unto thee of wine and of .... Mic 2:11   5197
pass, that when any shall yet p .... Zec 13:3   5197
well did Esaias p of you .... Mt 15:7   4395
P unto us, thou Christ, Who is he .... Mt 26:68   4395
buffet him, and to say unto him, P .... Mk 14:65   4395
the face, and asked him, saying, P .... Lk 22:64   4395
sons and your daughters shall p .... Acts 2:17   4395
and they shall p .... Acts 2:18   4395
daughters, virgins, which did p .... Acts 21:9   4395
let us p according to the .... Rom 12:6   4395
we know in part, and we p in part 1Cor 13:9   4395
gifts, but rather that ye may p 1Cor 14:1   4395
But if all p, and there come in 1Cor 14:24   4395
For ye may all p one by one 1Cor 14:31   4395
Wherefore, brethren, covet to p 1Cor 14:39   4395
Thou must p again before many .... Rev 10:11   4395
they shall p a thousand two .... Rev 11:3   4395

PROPHESYING

And when he had made an end of p 1Sa 10:13   5012
saw the company of the prophets p 1Sa 19:20   5012
the p of Haggai the prophet .... Ezr 6:14   5017
Every man praying or p, having 1Cor 11:4   4395
or by knowledge, or by p 1Cor 14:6   4394
but p serveth not for them that 1Cor 14:22   4394

PROPHESYINGS

Despise not p 1Th 5:20   4394

PROPHET

for he is a p, and he shall pray .... Gen 20:7   5030
Aaron thy brother shall be thy p .... Ex 7:1   5030
If there be a p among you .... Num 12:6   5030
If there arise among you a p .... Deut 13:1   5030
hearken unto the words of that p .... Deut 13:3   5030
And that p, or that dreamer of .... Deut 13:5   5030
thee a P from the midst of thee .... Deut 18:15   5030

P

I will raise them up a *P* from	Deut 18:18	5030
But the *p*, which shall presume to	Deut 18:20	5030
other gods, even that *p* shall die	Deut 18:20	5030
When a *p* speaketh in the name of	Deut 18:22	5030
spoken, but the *p* hath spoken it	Deut 18:22	5030
there arose not a *p* since in	Deut 34:10	5030
That the LORD sent a *p* unto the	Judg 6:8	5030
established to be a *p* of the LORD	1Sa 3:20	5030
for he that is now called a *P* was	1Sa 9:9	5030
the *p* Gad said unto David, Abide	1Sa 22:5	5030
the king said unto Nathan the *p*	2Sa 7:2	5030
sent by the hand of Nathan the *p*	2Sa 12:25	5030
of the LORD came unto the *p* Gad	2Sa 24:11	5030
son of Jehoiada, and Nathan the *p*	1Kin 1:8	5030
But Nathan the *p*, and Benaiah, and	1Kin 1:10	5030
Nathan the *p* also came in	1Kin 1:22	5030
king, saying, Behold Nathan the *p*	1Kin 1:23	5030
Zadok the priest, and Nathan the *p*	1Kin 1:32	5030
Nathan the *p* anoint him there	1Kin 1:34	5030
Zadok the priest, and Nathan the *p*	1Kin 1:38	5030
Zadok the priest, and Nathan the *p*	1Kin 1:44	5030
Nathan the *p* have anointed him	1Kin 1:45	5030
that the *p* Ahijah the Shilonite	1Kin 11:29	5030
there dwelt an old *p* in Beth-el	1Kin 13:11	5030
I am a *p* also as thou art	1Kin 13:18	5030
unto the *p* that brought him back	1Kin 13:20	5030
for the *p* whom he had brought	1Kin 13:23	5030
in the city where the old *p* dwelt	1Kin 13:25	5030
when the *p* that brought him back	1Kin 13:26	5030
the *p* took up the carcase of the	1Kin 13:29	5030
the old *p* came to the city, to	1Kin 13:29	5030
behold, there is Ahijah the *p*	1Kin 14:2	5030
hand of his servant Ahijah the *p*	1Kin 14:18	5030
also by the hand of the *p* Jehu	1Kin 16:7	5030
against Baasha by Jehu the *p*	1Kin 16:12	5030
I only, remain a *p* of the LORD	1Kin 18:22	5030
that Elijah the *p* came near	1Kin 18:36	5030
thou anoint to be *p* in thy room	1Kin 19:16	5030
there came a *p* unto Ahab king of	1Kin 20:13	5030
the *p* came to the king of Israel,	1Kin 20:22	5030
So the *p* departed, and waited for	1Kin 20:38	5030
not here a *p* of the LORD besides	1Kin 22:7	5030
Is there not here a *p* of the LORD	2Kin 3:11	5030
with the *p* that is in Samaria	2Kin 5:3	5030
know that there is a *p* in Israel	2Kin 5:8	5030
if the *p* had bid thee do some	2Kin 5:13	5030
the *p* that is in Israel, telleth	2Kin 6:12	5030
Elisha the *p* called one of the	2Kin 9:1	5030
man, even the young man the *p*	2Kin 9:4	5030
Jonah, the son of Amittai, the *p*	2Kin 14:25	5030
to Isaiah the *p* the son of Amoz	2Kin 19:2	5030
the *p* Isaiah the son of Amoz came	2Kin 20:1	5030
Isaiah the *p* cried unto the LORD	2Kin 20:11	5030
Isaiah the *p* unto king Hezekiah	2Kin 20:14	5030
with the bones of the *p* that came	2Kin 23:18	5030
that David said to Nathan the *p*	1Chr 17:1	5030
and in the book of Nathan the *p*	1Chr 29:29	5030
in the book of Nathan the *p*	2Chr 9:29	5030
came Shemaiah the *p* to Rehoboam	2Chr 12:5	5030
in the book of Shemaiah the *p*	2Chr 12:15	5030
in the story of the *p* Iddo	2Chr 13:22	5030
and the prophecy of Oded the *p*	2Chr 15:8	5030
not here a *p* of the LORD besides	2Chr 18:6	5030
writing to him from Elijah the *p*	2Chr 21:12	5030
Amaziah, and he sent unto him a *p*	2Chr 25:15	5030
Then the *p* forbare, and said, I	2Chr 25:16	5030
first and last, did Isaiah the *p*	2Chr 26:22	5030
But a *p* of the LORD was there,	2Chr 28:9	5030
the king's seer, and Nathan the *p*	2Chr 29:25	5030
the *p* Isaiah the son of Amoz,	2Chr 30:20	5030
in the vision of Isaiah the *p*	2Chr 32:32	5030
from the days of Samuel the *p*	2Chr 35:18	5030
p speaking from the mouth of the	2Chr 36:12	5030
Then the prophets, Haggai the *p*	Ezr 5:1	5029
the prophesying of Haggai the *p*	Ezr 6:14	5029
when Nathan the *p* came unto him	Ps 51:*t*	5030
there is no more any *p*	Ps 74:9	5030
man of war, the judge, and the *p*	Is 3:2	5030
the *p* that teacheth lies, he is	Is 9:15	5030
the *p* have erred through strong	Is 28:7	5030
unto Isaiah the *p* the son of Amoz	Is 37:2	5030
Isaiah the *p* the son of Amoz came	Is 38:1	5030
Isaiah the *p* unto king Hezekiah	Is 39:3	5030
thee a *p* unto the nations	Jer 1:5	5030
from the *p* even unto the priest	Jer 6:13	5030
from the *p* even unto the priest	Jer 8:10	5030
yea, both the *p* and the priest go	Jer 14:18	5030
the wise, nor the word from the *p*	Jer 18:18	5030
Then Pashur smote Jeremiah the *p*	Jer 20:2	5030
For both *p* and priest are profane	Jer 23:11	5030
The *p* that hath a dream, let him	Jer 23:28	5030

And when this people, or the *p*	Jer 23:33	5030
And as for the *p*, and the priest,	Jer 23:34	5030
Thus shalt thou say to the *p*	Jer 23:37	5030
The which Jeremiah the *p* spake	Jer 25:2	5030
Hananiah the son of Azur the *p*	Jer 28:1	5030
p Jeremiah said unto the *p*	Jer 28:5	5030
Even the *p* Jeremiah said, Amen	Jer 28:6	5030
The *p* which prophesieth of peace,	Jer 28:9	5030
word of the *p* shall come to pass	Jer 28:9	5030
then shall the *p* be known	Jer 28:9	5030
Then Hananiah the *p* took the yoke	Jer 28:10	5030
from off the *p* Jeremiah's neck	Jer 28:10	5030
the *p* Jeremiah went his way	Jer 28:11	5030
the LORD came unto Jeremiah the *p*	Jer 28:12	5030
after that Hananiah the *p* had	Jer 28:12	5030
off the neck of the *p* Jeremiah	Jer 28:12	5030
Then said the *p* Jeremiah unto	Jer 28:15	5030
Jeremiah unto Hananiah the *p*	Jer 28:15	5030
So Hananiah the *p* died the same	Jer 28:17	5030
p sent from Jerusalem unto the	Jer 29:1	5030
is mad, and maketh himself a *p*	Jer 29:26	5012
which maketh himself a *p* to you	Jer 29:27	5012
in the ears of Jeremiah the *p*	Jer 29:29	5030
Jeremiah the *p* was shut up in the	Jer 32:2	5030
Then Jeremiah the *p* spake all	Jer 34:6	5030
that Jeremiah the *p* commanded him	Jer 36:8	5030
the scribe and Jeremiah the *p*	Jer 36:26	5030
which he spake by the *p* Jeremiah	Jer 37:2	5030
the priest to the *p* Jeremiah	Jer 37:3	5030
of the LORD unto the *p* Jeremiah	Jer 37:6	5030
and he took Jeremiah the *p*	Jer 37:13	5030
they have done to Jeremiah the *p*	Jer 38:9	5030
Jeremiah the *p* out of the dungeon	Jer 38:10	5030
took Jeremiah the *p* unto him into	Jer 38:14	5030
And said unto Jeremiah the *p*	Jer 42:2	5030
Jeremiah the *p* said unto them	Jer 42:4	5030
son of Shaphan, and Jeremiah the *p*	Jer 43:6	5030
The word that Jeremiah the *p*	Jer 45:1	5030
the *p* against the Gentiles	Jer 46:1	5030
the LORD spake to Jeremiah the *p*	Jer 46:13	5030
the *p* against the Philistines	Jer 47:1	5030
p against Elam in the beginning	Jer 49:34	5030
the Chaldeans by Jeremiah the *p*	Jer 50:1	5030
The word which Jeremiah the *p*	Jer 51:59	5030
the *p* be slain in the sanctuary	Lam 2:20	5030
there hath been a *p* among them	Eze 2:5	5030
shall they seek a vision of the *p*	Eze 7:26	5030
his face, and cometh to the *p*	Eze 14:4	5030
cometh to a *p* to enquire of him	Eze 14:7	5030
if the *p* be deceived when he hath	Eze 14:9	5030
I the LORD have deceived that *p*	Eze 14:9	5030
the punishment of the *p* shall be	Eze 14:10	5030
that a *p* hath been among them	Eze 33:33	5030
the LORD came unto Jeremiah the *p*	Dan 9:2	5030
the *p* also shall fall with thee	Hos 4:5	5030
the *p* is a fool, the spiritual	Hos 9:7	5030
but the *p* is a snare of a fowler	Hos 9:8	5030
by a *p* the LORD brought Israel	Hos 12:13	5030
Egypt, and by a *p* was he preserved	Hos 12:13	5030
and said to Amaziah, I was no *p*	Amos 7:14	5030
even be the *p* of this people	Mic 2:11	5197
which Habakkuk the *p* did see	Hab 1:1	5030
of Habakkuk the *p* upon Shigionoth	Hab 3:1	5030
the *p* unto Zerubbabel the son of	Hag 1:1	5030
word of the LORD by Haggai the *p*	Hag 1:3	5030
God, and the words of Haggai the *p*	Hag 1:12	5030
word of the LORD by the *p* Haggai	Hag 2:1	5030
word of the LORD by Haggai the *p*	Hag 2:10	5030
Berechiah, the son of Iddo the *p*	Zec 1:1	5030
Berechiah, the son of Iddo the *p*	Zec 1:7	5030
But he shall say, I am no *p*	Zec 13:5	5030
I will send you Elijah the *p*	Mal 4:5	5030
was spoken of the Lord by the *p*	Mt 1:22	4396
for thus it is written by the *p*	Mt 2:5	4396
was spoken of the Lord by the *p*	Mt 2:15	4396
which was spoken by Jeremy the *p*	Mt 2:17	4396
was spoken of by the *p* Esaias	Mt 3:3	4396
which was spoken by Esaias the *p*	Mt 4:14	4396
which was spoken by Esaias the *p*	Mt 8:17	4396
He that receiveth a *p* in the name	**Mt 10:41**	*4396*
of a *p* shall receive a prophet's	**Mt 10:41**	*4396*
for to see? A *p*?	**Mt 11:9**	*4396*
I say unto you, and more than a *p*	**Mt 11:9**	*4396*
which was spoken by Esaias the *p*	Mt 12:17	*4396*
it, but the sign of the *p* Jonas	**Mt 12:39**	*4396*
which was spoken by the *p*	Mt 13:35	*4396*
A *p* is not without honour, save	**Mt 13:57**	*4396*
because they counted him as a *p*	Mt 14:5	*4396*
it, but the sign of the *p* Jonas	**Mt 16:4**	*4396*
which was spoken by the *p*	Mt 21:4	*4396*
This is Jesus the *p* of Nazareth	Mt 21:11	*4396*

for all hold John as a *p*	Mt 21:26	4396
because they took him for a *p*	Mt 21:46	4396
spoken of by Daniel the *p*	Mt 24:15	4396
which was spoken by Jeremy the *p*	Mt 27:9	4396
which was spoken by the *p*	Mt 27:35	4396
A *p* is not without honour, but in	Mk 6:4	4396
And others said, That it is a *p*	Mk 6:15	4396
John, that he was a *p* indeed	Mk 11:32	4396
spoken of by Daniel the *p*	Mk 13:14	4396
be called the *p* of the Highest	Lk 1:76	4396
book of the words of Esaias the *p*	Lk 3:4	4396
unto him the book of the *p* Esaias	Lk 4:17	4396
No *p* is accepted in his own	Lk 4:24	4396
in the time of Eliseus the *p*	Lk 4:27	4396
That a great *p* is risen up among	Lk 7:16	4396
for to see? A *p*?	Lk 7:26	4396
unto you, and much more than a *p*	Lk 7:26	4396
a greater *p* than John the Baptist	Lk 7:28	4396
saying, This man, if he were a *p*	Lk 7:39	4396
it, but the sign of Jonas the *p*	Lk 11:29	4396
that a *p* perish out of Jerusalem	Lk 13:33	4396
be persuaded that John was a *p*	Lk 20:6	4396
which was a *p* mighty in deed and	Lk 24:19	4396
Art thou that *p*	Jn 1:21	4396
of the Lord, as said the *p* Esaias	Jn 1:23	4396
Christ, nor Elias, neither that *p*	Jn 1:25	4396
Sir, I perceive that thou art a *p*	Jn 4:19	4396
that a *p* hath no honour in his	Jn 4:44	4396
This is of a truth that *p* that	Jn 6:14	4396
said, Of a truth this is the *p*	Jn 7:40	4396
for out of Galilee ariseth no *p*	Jn 7:52	4396
He said, He is a *p*	Jn 9:17	4396
Esaias the *p* might be fulfilled	Jn 12:38	4396
which was spoken by the *p* Joel	Acts 2:16	4396
Therefore being a *p*, and knowing	Acts 2:30	4396
A *p* shall the Lord your God raise	Acts 3:22	4396
soul, which will not hear that *p*	Acts 3:23	4396
A *p* shall the Lord your God raise	Acts 7:37	4396
as saith the *p*,	Acts 7:48	4396
in his chariot read Esaias the *p*	Acts 8:28	4396
and heard him read the *p* Esaias	Acts 8:30	4396
thee, of whom speaketh the *p* this	Acts 8:34	4396
a certain sorcerer, a false *p*	Acts 13:6	5578
fifty years, until Samuel the *p*	Acts 13:20	4396
came down from Judaea a certain *p*	Acts 21:10	4396
by Esaias the *p* unto our fathers	Acts 28:25	4396
any man think himself to be a *p*	1Cor 14:37	4396
even a *p* of their own, said, The	Titus 1:12	4396
voice forbad the madness of the *p*	2Pet 2:16	4396
out of the mouth of the false *p*	Rev 16:13	5578
with him the false *p* that wrought	Rev 19:20	5578
the beast and the false *p* are	Rev 20:10	5578

PROPHETESS

And Miriam the *p*, the sister of	Ex 15:20	5031
And Deborah, a *p*, the wife of	Judg 4:4	5031
Asahiah, went unto Huldah the *p*	2Kin 22:14	5031
appointed, went to Huldah the *p*	2Chr 34:22	5031
on the *p* Noadiah, and the rest of	Neh 6:14	5031
And I went unto the *p*	Is 8:3	5031
And there was one Anna, a *p*	Lk 2:36	4398
which calleth herself a *p*	Rev 2:20	4398

PROPHET'S

prophet, neither was I an *p* son	Amos 7:14	5030
prophet shall receive a *p* reward	Mt 10:41	4396

PROPHETS

that all the Lord's people were *p*	Num 11:29	5030
thou shalt meet a company of *p*	1Sa 10:5	5030
behold, a company of *p* met him	1Sa 10:10	5030
behold, he prophesied among the *p*	1Sa 10:11	5030
Is Saul also among the *p*	1Sa 10:11	5030
proverb, Is Saul also among the *p*	1Sa 10:12	5030
the company of the *p* prophesying	1Sa 19:20	5030
say, Is Saul also among the *p*	1Sa 19:24	5030
by dreams, nor by Urim, nor by *p*	1Sa 28:6	5030
me no more, neither by *p*, nor by	1Sa 28:15	5030
Jezebel cut off the *p* of the Lord	1Kin 18:4	5030
that Obadiah took an hundred *p*	1Kin 18:4	5030
Jezebel slew the *p* of the Lord	1Kin 18:13	5030
the Lord's *p* by fifty in a cave	1Kin 18:13	5030
the *p* of Baal four hundred and	1Kin 18:19	5030
the *p* of the groves four hundred,	1Kin 18:19	5030
gathered the *p* together unto	1Kin 18:20	5030
but Baal's *p* are four hundred and	1Kin 18:22	5030
And Elijah said unto the *p* of Baal	1Kin 18:25	5030
unto them, Take the *p* of Baal	1Kin 18:40	5030
slain all the *p* with the sword	1Kin 19:1	5030
slain thy *p* with the sword	1Kin 19:10	5030
slain thy *p* with the sword	1Kin 19:14	5030
p said unto his neighbour in the	1Kin 20:35	5030

him that he was of the *p*	1Kin 20:41	5030
of Israel gathered the *p* together	1Kin 22:6	5030
all the *p* prophesied before them	1Kin 22:10	5030
all the *p* prophesied so, saying,	1Kin 22:12	5030
the words of the *p* declare good	1Kin 22:13	5030
spirit in the mouth of all his *p*	1Kin 22:22	5030
in the mouth of all these thy *p*	1Kin 22:23	5030
the sons of the *p* that were at	2Kin 2:3	5030
the sons of the *p* that were at	2Kin 2:5	5030
men of the sons of the *p* went	2Kin 2:7	5030
when the sons of the *p* which were	2Kin 2:15	5030
get thee to the *p* of thy father	2Kin 3:13	5030
and to the *p* of thy mother	2Kin 3:13	5030
of the sons of the *p* unto Elisha	2Kin 4:1	5030
the sons of the *p* were sitting	2Kin 4:38	5030
pottage for the sons of the *p*	2Kin 4:38	5030
young men of the sons of the *p*	2Kin 5:22	5030
the sons of the *p* said unto	2Kin 6:1	5030
one of the children of the *p*	2Kin 9:1	5030
the blood of the sons of the *p*	2Kin 9:7	5030
call unto me all the *p* of Baal	2Kin 10:19	5030
and against Judah, by all the *p*	2Kin 17:13	5030
sent to you by my servants the *p*	2Kin 17:13	5030
said by all his servants the *p*	2Kin 17:23	5030
Lord spake by his servants the *p*	2Kin 21:10	5030
him, and the priests, and the *p*	2Kin 23:2	5030
he spake by his servants the *p*	2Kin 24:2	5030
mine anointed, and do my *p* no harm	1Chr 16:22	5030
together of *p* four hundred men	2Chr 18:5	5030
all the *p* prophesied before them	2Chr 18:9	5030
all the *p* prophesied so, saying,	2Chr 18:11	5030
the words of the *p* declare good	2Chr 18:12	5030
spirit in the mouth of all his *p*	2Chr 18:21	5030
in the mouth of these thy *p*	2Chr 18:22	5030
believe his *p*, so shall ye	2Chr 20:20	5030
Yet he sent *p* to them, to bring	2Chr 24:19	5030
commandment of the Lord by his *p*	2Chr 29:25	5030
his words, and misused his *p*	2Chr 36:16	5030
Then the *p*, Haggai the prophet,	Ezr 5:1	5029
with them were the *p* of God	Ezr 5:2	5029
commanded by thy servants the *p*	Ezr 9:11	5030
thou hast also appointed *p* to	Neh 6:7	5030
Noadiah, and the rest of the *p*	Neh 6:14	5030
slew thy *p* which testified	Neh 9:26	5030
them by thy spirit in thy *p*	Neh 9:30	5030
and on our priests, and on our *p*	Neh 9:32	5030
mine anointed, and do my *p* no harm	Ps 105:15	5030
the *p* and your rulers, the seers	Is 29:10	5030
and to the *p*, Prophesy not unto us	Is 30:10	2374
the *p* prophesied by Baal, and	Jer 2:8	5030
and their priests, and their *p*	Jer 2:26	5030
own sword hath devoured your *p*	Jer 2:30	5030
astonished, and the *p* shall wonder	Jer 4:9	5030
the *p* shall become wind, and the	Jer 5:13	5030
The *p* prophesy falsely, and the	Jer 5:31	5030
unto you all my servants the *p*	Jer 7:25	5030
priests, and the bones of the *p*	Jer 8:1	5030
throne, and the priests, and the *p*	Jer 13:13	5030
the *p* say unto them, Ye shall not	Jer 14:13	5030
The *p* prophesy lies in my name	Jer 14:14	5030
the *p* that prophesy in my name	Jer 14:15	5030
famine shall those *p* be consumed	Jer 14:15	5030
me is broken because of the *p*	Jer 23:9	5030
seen folly in the *p* of Samaria	Jer 23:13	5030
I have seen also in the *p* of	Jer 23:14	5030
Lord of hosts concerning the *p*	Jer 23:15	5030
for from the *p* of Jerusalem is	Jer 23:15	5030
of the *p* that prophesy unto you	Jer 23:16	5030
I have not sent these *p*, yet they	Jer 23:21	5030
I have heard what the *p* said	Jer 23:25	5030
heart of the *p* that prophesy lies	Jer 23:26	5030
they are *p* of the deceit of their	Jer 23:26	5030
behold, I am against the *p*	Jer 23:30	5030
Behold, I am against the *p*	Jer 23:31	5030
unto you all his servants the *p*	Jer 25:4	5030
to the words of my servants the *p*	Jer 26:5	5030
So the priests and the *p* and all	Jer 26:7	5030
people, that the priests and the *p*	Jer 26:8	5030
the *p* unto the princes and to all	Jer 26:11	5030
unto the priests and the *p*	Jer 26:16	5030
hearken not ye to your *p*, nor to	Jer 27:9	5030
of the *p* that speak unto you	Jer 27:14	5030
the *p* that prophesy unto you	Jer 27:15	5030
of your *p* that prophesy unto you	Jer 27:16	5030
But if they be *p*, and if the word	Jer 27:18	5030
The *p* that have been before me and	Jer 28:8	5030
and to the priests, and to the *p*	Jer 29:1	5030
Let not your *p* and your diviners	Jer 29:8	5030
hath raised us up *p* in Babylon	Jer 29:15	5030
unto them by my servants the *p*	Jer 29:19	5030
their priests, and their *p*	Jer 32:32	5030

P

unto you all my servants the *p*	Jer 35:15	5030
Where are now your *p* which	Jer 37:19	5030
unto you all my servants the *p*	Jer 44:4	5030
her *p* also find no vision from	Lam 2:9	5030
Thy *p* have seen vain and foolish	Lam 2:14	5030
For the sins of her *p*, and the	Lam 4:13	5030
prophesy against the *p* of Israel	Eze 13:2	5030
Woe unto the foolish *p*, that	Eze 13:3	5030
thy *p* are like the foxes in the	Eze 13:4	5030
be upon the *p* that see vanity	Eze 13:9	5030
the *p* of Israel which prophesy	Eze 13:16	5030
of her *p* in the midst thereof	Eze 22:25	5030
her *p* have daubed them with	Eze 22:28	5030
by my servants the *p* of Israel	Eze 38:17	5030
hearkened unto thy servants the *p*	Dan 9:6	5030
before us by his servants the *p*	Dan 9:10	5030
have I hewed them by the *p*	Hos 6:5	5030
I have also spoken by the *p*	Hos 12:10	5030
by the ministry of the *p*	Hos 12:10	5030
And I raised up of your sons for *p*	Amos 2:11	5030
and commanded the *p*, saying	Amos 2:12	5030
secret unto his servants the *p*	Amos 3:7	5030
the *p* that make my people err	Mic 3:5	5030
the sun shall go down over the *p*	Mic 3:6	5030
the *p* thereof divine for money	Mic 3:11	5030
Her *p* are light and treacherous	Zeph 3:4	5030
unto whom the former *p* have cried	Zec 1:4	5030
and the *p*, do they live for ever	Zec 1:5	5030
I commanded my servants the *p*	Zec 1:6	5030
of the LORD of hosts, and to the *p*	Zec 7:3	5030
LORD hath cried by the former *p*	Zec 7:7	5030
in his spirit by the former *p*	Zec 7:12	5030
these words by the mouth of the *p*	Zec 8:9	5030
and also I will cause the *p*	Zec 13:2	5030
that the *p* shall be ashamed every	Zec 13:4	5030
which was spoken by the *p*	Mt 2:23	4396
they the *p* which were before you	Mt 5:12	4396
come to destroy the law, or the *p*	Mt 5:17	4396
for this is the law and the *p*	Mt 7:12	4396
Beware of false *p*, which come to	Mt 7:15	5578
For all the *p* and the law	Mt 11:13	4396
I say unto you, That many *p*	Mt 13:17	4396
others, Jeremias, or one of the *p*	Mt 16:14	4396
hang all the law and the *p*	Mt 22:40	4396
ye build the tombs of the *p*	Mt 23:29	4396
with them in the blood of the *p*	Mt 23:30	4396
of them which killed the *p*	Mt 23:31	4396
behold, I send unto you *p*	Mt 23:34	4396
thou that killest the *p*, and	Mt 23:37	4396
And many false *p* shall rise	Mt 24:11	5578
arise false Christs, and false *p*	Mt 24:24	5578
of the *p* might be fulfilled	Mt 26:56	4396
As it is written in the *p*	Mk 1:2	4396
is a prophet, or as one of the *p*	Mk 6:15	4396
and others, One of the *p*	Mk 8:28	4396
false *p* shall rise, and shall shew	Mk 13:22	5578
spake by the mouth of his holy *p*	Lk 1:70	4396
did their fathers unto the *p*	Lk 6:23	4396
did their fathers to the false *p*	Lk 6:26	5578
one of the old *p* was risen again	Lk 9:8	4396
one of the old *p* is risen again	Lk 9:19	4396
For I tell you, that many *p*	Lk 10:24	4396
ye build the sepulchres of the *p*	Lk 11:47	4396
wisdom of God, I will send them *p*	Lk 11:49	4396
That the blood of all the *p*	Lk 11:50	4396
and Isaac, and Jacob, and all the *p*	Lk 13:28	4396
Jerusalem, which killest the *p*	Lk 13:34	4396
The law and the *p* were until John	Lk 16:16	4396
him, They have Moses and the *p*	Lk 16:29	4396
If they hear not Moses and the *p*	Lk 16:31	4396
things that are written by the *p*	Lk 18:31	4396
all that the *p* have spoken	Lk 24:25	4396
beginning at Moses and all the *p*	Lk 24:27	4396
in the law of Moses, and in the *p*	Lk 24:44	4396
whom Moses in the law, and the *p*	Jn 1:45	4396
It is written in the *p*, And they	Jn 6:45	4396
Abraham is dead, and the *p*	Jn 8:52	4396
and the *p* are dead	Jn 8:53	4396
shewed by the mouth of all his *p*	Acts 3:18	4396
his holy *p* since the world began	Acts 3:21	4396
all the *p* from Samuel and those	Acts 3:24	4396
Ye are the children of the *p*	Acts 3:25	4396
is written in the book of the *p*	Acts 7:42	4396
Which of the *p* have not your	Acts 7:52	4396
To him give all the *p* witness	Acts 10:43	4396
in these days came *p* from	Acts 11:27	4396
that was at Antioch certain *p*	Acts 13:1	4396
the *p* the rulers of the synagogue	Acts 13:15	4396
nor yet the voices of the *p* which	Acts 13:27	4396
you, which is spoken of in the *p*	Acts 13:40	4396
to this agree the words of the *p*	Acts 15:15	4396

being *p* also themselves, exhorted	Acts 15:32	4396
written in the law and in the *p*	Acts 24:14	4396
things than those which the *p*	Acts 26:22	4396
Agrippa, believest thou the *p*	Acts 26:27	4396
the law of Moses, and out of the *p*	Acts 28:23	4396
by his *p* in the holy scriptures	Rom 1:2	4396
witnessed by the law and the *p*	Rom 3:21	4396
Lord, they have killed thy *p*	Rom 11:3	4396
and by the scriptures of the *p*	Rom 16:26	4397
first apostles, secondarily *p*	1Cor 12:28	4396
are all *p*?	1Cor 12:29	4396
Let the *p* speak two or three, and	1Cor 14:29	4396
the *p* are subject to the *p*	1Cor 14:32	4396
foundation of the apostles and *p*	Eph 2:20	4396
holy apostles and *p* by the Spirit	Eph 3:5	4396
and some, *p*	Eph 4:11	4396
the Lord Jesus, and their own *p*	1Th 2:15	4396
past unto the fathers by the *p*	Heb 1:1	4396
also, and Samuel, and of the *p*	Heb 11:32	4396
Take, my brethren, the *p*, who	Jas 5:10	4396
salvation the *p* have enquired	1Pet 1:10	4396
But there were false *p* also among	2Pet 2:1	5578
were spoken before by the holy *p*	2Pet 3:2	4396
because many false *p* are gone out	1Jn 4:1	5578
declared to his servants the *p*	Rev 10:7	4396
because these two *p* tormented	Rev 11:10	4396
reward unto thy servants the *p*	Rev 11:18	4396
shed the blood of saints and *p*	Rev 16:6	4396
heaven, and ye holy apostles and *p*	Rev 18:20	4396
in her was found the blood of *p*	Rev 18:24	4396
the Lord God of the holy *p* sent	Rev 22:6	4396
and of thy brethren the *p*	Rev 22:9	4396

PROPITIATION

be a *p* through faith in his blood	Rom 3:25	2435
And he is the *p* for our sins	1Jn 2:2	2434
his Son to be the *p* for our sins	1Jn 4:10	2434

PROPORTION

according to the *p* of every one	1Kin 7:36	4626
nor his power, nor his comely *p*	Job 41:12	6187
according to the *p* of faith	Rom 12:6	356

PROSELYTE

compass sea and land to make one *p*	Mt 23:15	4339
and Nicolas a *p* of Antioch	Acts 6:5	4339

PROSELYTES

and strangers of Rome, Jews and *p*	Acts 2:10	4339
religious *p* followed Paul and	Acts 13:43	4339

PROSPECT

their *p* was toward the south	Eze 40:44	6440
having the *p* toward the north	Eze 40:44	6440
whose *p* is toward the south, is	Eze 40:45	6440
the chamber whose *p* is toward the	Eze 40:46	6440
gate whose *p* is toward the east	Eze 42:15	6440
gate whose *p* is toward the east	Eze 43:4	6440

PROSPER

his angel with thee, and *p* thy way	Gen 24:40	6743
if now thou do *p* my way which I	Gen 24:42	6743
all that he did to *p* in his hand	Gen 39:3	6743
he did, the LORD made it to *p*	Gen 39:23	6743
but it shall not *p*	Num 14:41	6743
and thou shalt not *p* in thy ways	Deut 28:29	6743
that ye may *p* in all that ye do	Deut 29:9	7919
that thou mayest *p* whithersoever	Josh 1:7	7919
that thou mayest *p* in all that	1Kin 2:3	7919
Go up to Ramoth-gilead, and *p*	1Kin 22:12	6743
And he answered him, Go, and *p*	1Kin 22:15	6743
p thou, and build the house of the	1Chr 22:11	6743
Then shalt thou *p*, if thou takest	1Chr 22:13	6743
for ye shall not *p*	2Chr 13:12	6743
Go up to Ramoth-gilead, and *p*	2Chr 18:11	6743
And he said, Go ye up, and *p*	2Chr 18:14	6743
his prophets, so shall ye *p*	2Chr 20:20	6743
of the LORD, that ye cannot *p*	2Chr 24:20	6743
the LORD, God made him to *p*	2Chr 26:5	6743
and *p*, I pray thee, thy servant	Neh 1:11	6743
The God of heaven, he will *p* us	Neh 2:20	6743
The tabernacles of robbers *p*	Job 12:6	7951
and whatsoever he doeth shall *p*	Ps 1:3	6743
the ungodly, who *p* in the world	Ps 73:12	7951
they shall *p* that love thee	Ps 122:6	7951
covereth his sins shall not *p*	Prov 28:13	6743
thou knowest not whether shall *p*	Eccl 11:6	3787
of the LORD shall *p* in his hand	Is 53:10	6743
is formed against thee shall *p*	Is 54:17	6743
it shall *p* in the thing whereto I	Is 55:11	6743
and thou shalt not *p* in them	Jer 2:37	6743
of the fatherless, yet they *p*	Jer 5:28	6743
therefore they shall not *p*	Jer 10:21	7919
doth the way of the wicked *p*	Jer 12:1	6743

for they shall not *p*	Jer 20:11	7919
man that shall not *p* in his days	Jer 22:30	6743
for no man of his seed shall *p*	Jer 22:30	6743
and a King shall reign and *p*	Jer 23:5	7919
the Chaldeans, ye shall not *p*	Jer 32:5	6743
are the chief, her enemies *p*	Lam 1:5	7919
thou didst *p* into a kingdom	Eze 16:13	6743
Shall it *p*?	Eze 17:9	6743
behold, being planted, shall it *p*	Eze 17:10	6743
Shall he *p*?	Eze 17:15	6743
destroy wonderfully, and shall *p*	Dan 8:24	6743
cause craft to *p* in his hand	Dan 8:25	6743
but it shall not *p*	Dan 11:27	6743
shall *p* till the indignation be	Dan 11:36	6743
all things that thou mayest *p*	3Jn 2	2137

PROSPERED

seeing the LORD hath *p* my way	Gen 24:56	6743
hand of the children of Israel *p*	Judg 4:24	1980
the people did, and how the war *p*	2Sa 11:7	7965
he *p* whithersoever he went forth	2Kin 18:7	7919
instead of David his father, and *p*	1Chr 29:23	6743
So they built and *p*	2Chr 14:7	6743
did it with all his heart, and *p*	2Chr 31:21	6743
Hezekiah *p* in all his works	2Chr 32:30	6743
they *p* through the prophesying of	Ezr 6:14	6744
himself against him, and hath *p*	Job 9:4	7999
So this Daniel *p* in the reign of	Dan 6:28	6744
and it practised, and *p*	Dan 8:12	6743
him in store, as God hath *p* him	1Cor 16:2	2137

PROSPERETH

fast on, and *p* in their hands	Ezr 5:8	6744
because of him who *p* in his way	Ps 37:7	6743
whithersoever it turneth, it *p*	Prov 17:8	7919
be in health, even as thy soul *p*	3Jn 2	2137

PROSPERITY

nor their *p* all thy days for ever	Deut 23:6	2896
ye say to him that liveth in *p*	1Sa 25:6	
p exceedeth the fame which I	1Kin 10:7	2896
in *p* the destroyer shall come	Job 15:21	7965
they shall spend their days in *p*	Job 36:11	2896
in my *p* I said, I shall never be	Ps 30:6	7961
pleasure in the *p* of his servant	Ps 35:27	7965
when I saw the *p* of the wicked	Ps 73:3	7965
LORD, I beseech thee, send now *p*	Ps 118:25	6743
walls, and *p* within thy palaces	Ps 122:7	7962
the *p* of fools shall destroy them	Prov 1:32	7962
In the day of *p* be joyful	Eccl 7:14	2896
I spake unto thee in thy *p*	Jer 22:21	7962
for all the *p* that I procure unto	Jer 33:9	7965
I forgat *p*	Lam 3:17	2896
My cities through *p* shall yet be	Zec 1:17	2896
Jerusalem was inhabited and in *p*	Zec 7:7	7961

PROSPEROUS

had made his journey *p* or not	Gen 24:21	6743
with Joseph, and he was a *p* man	Gen 39:2	6743
then thou shalt make thy way *p*	Josh 1:8	6743
our way which we go shall be *p*	Judg 18:5	6743
habitation of thy righteousness *p*	Job 8:6	7999
him, and he shall make his way *p*	Is 48:15	6743
For the seed shall be *p*	Zec 8:12	7965
now at length I might have a *p*	Rom 1:10	2137

PROSPEROUSLY

in his own house, he *p* effected	2Chr 7:11	6743
majesty ride *p* because of truth	Ps 45:4	6743

PROSTITUTE

Do not *p* thy daughter, to cause	Lev 19:29	2490

PROTECTION

rise up and help you, and be your *p*	Deut 32:38	5643

PROTEST

The man did solemnly *p* unto us	Gen 43:3	5749
howbeit yet *p* solemnly unto them,	1Sa 8:9	5749
I *p* by your rejoicing which I	1Cor 15:31	3513

PROTESTED

p unto thee, saying, Know for a	1Kin 2:42	5749
For I earnestly *p* unto your	Jer 11:7	5749
angel of the LORD *p* unto Joshua	Zec 3:6	5749

PROTESTING

unto this day, rising early and *p*	Jer 11:7	5749

PROUD

the *p* helpers do stoop under him	Job 9:13	7293
he smiteth through the *p*	Job 26:12	7293
here shall thy *p* waves be stayed	Job 38:11	1347
and behold every one that is *p*	Job 40:11	1343
Look on every one that is *p*	Job 40:12	1343
the tongue that speaketh *p* things	Ps 12:3	1419

plentifully rewardeth the *p* doer	Ps 31:23	1346
trust, and respecteth not the *p*	Ps 40:4	7295
the *p* are risen against me, and	Ps 86:14	2086
render a reward to the *p*	Ps 94:2	1343
a *p* heart will not I suffer	Ps 101:5	7342
rebuked the *p* that are cursed	Ps 119:21	2086
The *p* have had me greatly in	Ps 119:51	2086
The *p* have forged a lie against	Ps 119:69	2086
Let the *p* be ashamed	Ps 119:78	2086
The *p* have digged pits for me,	Ps 119:85	2086
let not the *p* oppress me	Ps 119:122	2086
and with the contempt of the *p*	Ps 123:4	1349
Then the *p* waters had gone over	Ps 124:5	2121
but the *p* he knoweth afar off	Ps 138:6	1364
The *p* have hid a snare for me, and	Ps 140:5	1343
A *p* look, a lying tongue, and	Prov 6:17	7311
will destroy the house of the *p*	Prov 15:25	1343
Every one that is *p* in heart is	Prov 16:5	1362
to divide the spoil with the *p*	Prov 16:19	1343
a *p* heart, and the plowing of the	Prov 21:4	7342
P and haughty scorner is his name,	Prov 21:24	2086
who dealeth in *p* wrath	Prov 21:24	2087
He that is of a *p* heart stirreth	Prov 28:25	7342
is better than the *p* in spirit	Eccl 7:8	1362
shall be upon every one that is *p*	Is 2:12	1343
the arrogancy of the *p* to cease	Is 13:11	2086
he is very *p*	Is 16:6	1341
be not *p*	Jer 13:15	1341
son of Kareah, and all the *p* men	Jer 43:2	2086
(he is exceeding *p*) his loftiness	Jer 48:29	1343
she hath been *p* against the LORD	Jer 50:29	2102
I am against thee, O thou most *p*	Jer 50:31	2087
the most *p* shall stumble and fall,	Jer 50:32	2087
by wine, he is a *p* man, neither	Hab 2:5	3093
And now we call the *p* happy	Mal 3:15	2086
and all the *p*, yea, and all that do	Mal 4:1	2086
he hath scattered the *p* in the	Lk 1:51	5244
haters of God, despiteful, *p*	Rom 1:30	5244
He is *p*, knowing nothing, but	1Ti 6:4	5187
own selves, covetous, boasters, *p*	2Ti 3:2	5244
he saith, God resisteth the *p*	Jas 4:6	5244
for God resisteth the *p*, and	1Pet 5:5	5244

PROUDLY

they dealt *p* he was above them	Ex 18:11	2102
Talk no more so exceeding *p*	1Sa 2:3	1364
that they dealt *p* against them	Neh 9:10	2102
But they and our fathers dealt *p*	Neh 9:16	2102
yet they dealt *p*, and hearkened	Neh 9:29	2102
with their mouth they speak *p*	Ps 17:10	1348
which speak grievous things *p*	Ps 31:18	1346
himself *p* against the ancient	Is 3:5	7292
spoken *p* in the day of distress	Obad 12	1431

PROVE

rate every day, that I may *p* them	Ex 16:4	5254
for God is come to *p* you, and that	Ex 20:20	5254
to *p* thee, to know what was in	Deut 8:2	5254
thee, and that he might *p* thee	Deut 8:16	5254
one, whom thou didst *p* at Massah	Deut 33:8	5254
That through them I may *p* Israel	Judg 2:22	5254
to *p* Israel by them, even as many	Judg 3:1	5254
they were to *p* Israel by them, to	Judg 3:4	5254
let me *p*, I pray thee, but this	Judg 6:39	5254
she came to *p* him with hard	1Kin 10:1	5254
she came to *p* Solomon with hard	2Chr 9:1	5254
it shall also *p* me perverse	Job 9:20	
Examine me, O LORD, and *p* me	Ps 26:2	5254
I will *p* thee with mirth,	Eccl 2:1	
P thy servants, I beseech thee,	Dan 1:12	5254
p me now herewith, saith the LORD,	Mal 3:10	974
yoke of oxen, and I go to *p* them	Lk 14:19	1381
And this he said to *p* him	Jn 6:6	3985
Neither can they the things	Acts 24:13	3936
Paul, which they could not *p*	Acts 25:7	584
that ye may *p* what is that good,	Rom 12:2	1381
to *p* the sincerity of your love	2Cor 8:8	1381
p your own selves	2Cor 13:5	1381
But let every man *p* his own work	Gal 6:4	1381
P all things	1Th 5:21	1381

PROVED

Hereby ye shall be *p*	Gen 42:15	974
prison, that your words may be *p*	Gen 42:16	974
an ordinance, and there he *p* them	Ex 15:25	5254
for he had not *p* it	1Sa 17:39	5254
for I have not *p* them	1Sa 17:39	5254
Thou hast *p* mine heart	Ps 17:3	974
For thou, O God, hast *p* us	Ps 66:10	974
I *p* thee at the waters of Meribah	Ps 81:7	974
tempted me, *p* me, and saw my work	Ps 95:9	974
All this have I *p* by wisdom	Eccl 7:23	5254

P

this matter, and *p* them ten days .... Dan 1:14   5254
for we have before *p* both Jews .... Rom 3:9   *4256*
p diligent in many things 2Cor 8:22   *1381*
And let these also first be *p* 1Ti 3:10   *1381*
p me, and saw my works forty years...... Heb 3:9   *1381*

PROVENDER
p enough, and room to lodge in .... Gen 24:25   4554
p for the camels, and water to .... Gen 24:32   4554
sack to give his ass *p* in the inn .... Gen 42:27   4554
and he gave their asses *p* .... Gen 43:24   4554
is both straw and *p* for our asses .... Judg 19:19   4554
house, and gave *p* unto the asses .... Judg 19:21   1101
ear the ground shall eat clean *p* .... Is 30:24   1098

PROVERB
shalt become an astonishment, a *p* .... Deut 28:37   4912
Therefore it became a *p*, Is Saul 1Sa 10:12   4912
As saith the *p* of the ancients, ... 1Sa 24:13   4912
and Israel shall be a *p* and a 1Kin 9:7   4912
sight, and will make it to be a *p* 2Chr 7:20   4912
and I became a *p* to them .... Ps 69:11   4912
To understand a *p*, and the .... Prov 1:6   4912
p against the king of Babylon .... Is 14:4   4912
hurt, to be a reproach and a *p* .... Jer 24:9   4912
what is that *p* that ye have in .... Eze 12:22   4912
I will make this *p* to cease .... Eze 12:23   4912
no more use it as a *p* in Israel .... Eze 12:23   4911
and will make him a sign and a *p* .... Eze 14:8   4912
shall use this *p* against thee .... Eze 16:44   4911
that ye use this *p* concerning the .... Eze 18:2   4911
any more to use this *p* in Israel .... Eze 18:3   4911
a taunting *p* against him, and say, ... Hab 2:6   2420
Ye will surely say unto me this *p* .... Lk 4:23   *3850*
thou plainly, and speakest no *p* .... Jn 16:29   *3942*
unto them according to the true *p*.......... 2Pet 2:22   *3942*

PROVERBS
they that speak in *p* say, Come.............. Num 21:27   4911
And he spake three thousand *p* 1Kin 4:32   4912
The *P* of Solomon the son of David .... Prov 1:1   4912
The *p* of Solomon.................................. Prov 10:1   4912
These are also *p* of Solomon .... Prov 25:1   4912
out, and set in order many *p*.................. Eccl 12:9   4912
every one that useth *p* shall use .... Eze 16:44   4911
have I spoken unto you in *p* .... Jn 16:25   *3942*
shall no more speak unto you in *p*........ Jn 16:25   *3942*

PROVETH
for the Lᴏʀᴅ your God *p* you .... Deut 13:3   5254

PROVIDE
God will *p* himself a lamb for a .... Gen 22:8   7200
now when shall I *p* for mine own .... Gen 30:30   6213
Moreover thou shalt *p* out of all............. Ex 18:21   2372
P me now a man that can play well 1Sa 16:17   7200
whom David my father did *p*.................. 2Chr 2:7   3559
can he *p* flesh for his people .... Ps 78:20   3559
P neither gold, nor silver, nor .... Mt 10:9   *2532*
***p* yourselves bags which wax not** .... Lk 12:33   *4160*
p them beasts, that they may set .... Acts 23:24   *3936*
P things honest in the sight of .... Rom 12:17   *4306*
But if any *p* not for his own, and 1Ti 5:8   *4306*

PROVIDED
he *p* the first part for himself, ... Deut 33:21   7200
for I have *p* me a king among his 1Sa 16:1   7200
he had *p* the king of sustenance 2Sa 19:32
which *p* victuals for the king and 1Kin 4:7
those officers *p* victual for king 1Kin 4:27
Moreover he *p* him cities, and................ 2Chr 32:29   6213
corn, when thou hast so *p* for it .... Ps 65:9   3559
things be, which thou hast *p* .... Lk 12:20   *2090*
God having *p* some better thing .... Heb 11:40   *4265*

PROVIDENCE
done unto this nation by thy *p* .... Acts 24:2   *4307*

PROVIDETH
Who *p* for the raven his food .... Job 38:41   3559
P her meat in the summer, and .... Prov 6:8   3559

PROVIDING
P for honest things, not only in 2Cor 8:21   *4306*

PROVINCE
of the *p* that went up out of the .... Ezr 2:1   4082
that we went into the *p* of Judea .... Ezr 5:8   4083
that is in the *p* of the Medes .... Ezr 6:2   4082
find in all the *p* of Babylon .... Ezr 7:16   4082
in the *p* are in great affliction............... Neh 1:3   4082
These are the children of the *p* .... Neh 7:6   4082
of the *p* that dwelt in Jerusalem .... Neh 11:3   4082
into every *p* according to the .... Est 1:22   4082
governors that were over every *p*........... Est 3:12   4082
every *p* according to the writing............ Est 3:12   4082

to be given in every *p* was...................... Est 3:14   4082
And in every *p*, whithersoever the .... Est 4:3   4082
unto every *p* according to the .... Est 8:9   4082
p that would assault them, both .... Est 8:11   4082
to be given in every *p* was...................... Est 8:13   4082
And in every *p*, and in every city, ... Est 8:17   4082
generation, every family, every *p* .... Est 9:28   4082
of judgment and justice in a *p* .... Eccl 5:8   4082
ruler over the whole *p* of Babylon .... Dan 2:48   4083
the affairs of the *p* of Babylon .... Dan 2:49   4083
of Dura, in the *p* of Babylon .... Dan 3:1   4083
the affairs of the *p* of Babylon .... Dan 3:12   4083
and Abed-nego, in the *p* of Babylon .... Dan 3:30   4082
palace, which is in the *p* of Elam .... Dan 8:2   4082
upon the fattest places of the *p* .... Dan 11:24   4082
letter, he asked of what *p* he was........... Acts 23:34   *1885*
when Festus was come into the *p* .... Acts 25:1   *1885*

PROVINCES
young men of the princes of the *p* 1Kin 20:14   4082
young men of the princes of the *p* 1Kin 20:15   4082
princes of the *p* went out first 1Kin 20:17   4082
of the *p* came out of the city 1Kin 20:19   4082
city, and hurtful unto kings and *p* .... Ezr 4:15   4083
an hundred and seven and twenty *p* .... Est 1:1   4082
the nobles and princes of the *p* .... Est 1:3   4082
all the *p* of the king Ahasuerus .... Est 1:16   4082
letters into all the king's *p*..................... Est 1:22   4082
in all the *p* of his kingdom..................... Est 2:3   4082
and he made a release to the *p* .... Est 2:18   4082
in all the *p* of thy kingdom .... Est 3:8   4082
by posts into all the king's *p* .... Est 3:13   4082
and the people of the king's *p*................ Est 4:11   4082
which are in all the king's *p* .... Est 8:5   4082
rulers of the *p* which are from .... Est 8:9   4082
an hundred twenty and seven *p*.............. Est 8:9   4082
in all the *p* of king Ahasuerus .... Est 8:12   4082
all the *p* of the king Ahasuerus .... Est 9:2   4082
And all the rulers of the *p* .... Est 9:3   4082
went out throughout all the *p* .... Est 9:4   4082
done in the rest of the king's *p*............... Est 9:12   4082
p gathered themselves together............. Est 9:16   4082
all the *p* of the king Ahasuerus .... Est 9:20   4082
seven *p* of the kingdom of..................... Est 9:30   4082
treasure of kings and of the *p* .... Eccl 2:8   4082
nations, and princess among the *p*......... Lam 1:1   4082
him on every side from the *p*.................. Eze 19:8   4082
and all the rulers of the *p* .... Dan 3:2   4082
and all the rulers of the *p* .... Dan 3:3   4082

PROVING
p that this is very Christ .... Acts 9:22   *4822*
P what is acceptable unto the .... Eph 5:10   *1381*

PROVISION
and to give them *p* for the way .... Gen 42:25   6720
and gave them *p* for the way.................. Gen 45:21   6720
all the bread of their *p* was dry .... Josh 9:5   6718
our bread we took hot for our *p* .... Josh 9:12   6679
man his month in a year made *p* 1Kin 4:7   3557
Solomon's *p* for one day was 1Kin 4:22   3899
And he prepared great *p* for them.......... 2Kin 6:23   3740
for the which I have made *p* 1Chr 29:19   3559
I will abundantly bless her *p*.................. Ps 132:15   6718
them a daily *p* of the king's meat .... Dan 1:5   1697
make not *p* for the flesh, to .... Rom 13:14   *4307*

PROVOCATION
by his *p* wherewith he provoked 1Kin 15:30   3708
for the *p* wherewith thou hast 1Kin 21:22   3708
not mine eye continue in their *p* .... Job 17:2   4784
not your heart, as in the .... Ps 95:8   4808
been to me as a *p* of mine anger .... Jer 32:31   3708
presented the *p* of their offering .... Eze 20:28   3708
not your hearts, as in the *p* .... Heb 3:8   *3894*
not your hearts, as in the *p* .... Heb 3:15   *3894*

PROVOCATIONS
because of all the *p* that......................... 2Kin 23:26   3708
of Egypt, and had wrought great *p* .... Neh 9:18   5007
to thee, and they wrought great *p* .... Neh 9:26   5007

PROVOKE
him, and obey his voice, *p* him not........ Ex 23:21   4843
How long will this people *p* me .... Num 14:11   5006
Lᴏʀᴅ thy God, to *p* him to anger .... Deut 4:25
of the Lᴏʀᴅ, to *p* him to anger .... Deut 9:18
p me, and break my covenant .... Deut 31:20   5006
to *p* him to anger through the .... Deut 31:29
I will *p* them to anger with a .... Deut 32:21
to *p* me to anger, and hast cast me 1Kin 14:9
to *p* me to anger with their sins 1Kin 16:2
to *p* the Lᴏʀᴅ God of Israel to................. 1Kin 16:26
Ahab did more to *p* the Lᴏʀᴅ God 1Kin 16:33

things to *p* the LORD to anger	2Kin 17:11	
of the LORD, to *p* him to anger	2Kin 17:17	
of the LORD, to *p* him to anger	2Kin 21:6	
that they might *p* me to anger	2Kin 22:17	
had made to *p* the LORD to anger	2Kin 23:19	
of the LORD, to *p* him to anger	2Chr 33:6	
that they might *p* me to anger	2Chr 34:25	
they that *p* God are secure	Job 12:6	7264
How oft did they *p* him in the	Ps 78:40	4784
to *p* the eyes of his glory	Is 3:8	4784
gods, that they may *p* me to anger	Jer 7:18	
Do they *p* me to anger	Jer 7:19	
do they not *p* themselves to the	Jer 7:19	
p me to anger in offering incense	Jer 11:17	
p me not to anger with the works	Jer 25:6	
that ye might *p* me to anger with	Jer 25:7	
unto other gods, to *p* me to anger	Jer 32:29	
they have done to *p* me to anger	Jer 32:32	
have committed to *p* me to anger	Jer 44:3	
In that ye *p* me unto wrath with	Jer 44:8	
and have returned to *p* me to anger	Eze 8:17	
thy whoredoms, to *p* me to anger	Eze 16:26	
to *p* him to speak of many things	Lk 11:53	653
I will *p* you to jealousy by them	Rom 10:19	3863
for to *p* them to jealousy	Rom 11:11	3863
If by any means I may *p* to	Rom 11:14	3863
Do we *p* the Lord to jealousy	1Cor 10:22	3863
p not your children to wrath	Eph 6:4	3949
p not your children to anger,	Col 3:21	2042
some, when they had heard, did *p*	Heb 3:16	3893
one another to *p* unto love	Heb 10:24	3948

PROVOKED

any of them that *p* me see it	Num 14:23	5006
that these men have *p* the LORD	Num 16:30	5006
Also in Horeb ye *p* the LORD to	Deut 9:8	
ye *p* the LORD to wrath	Deut 9:22	
They *p* him to jealousy with	Deut 32:16	3707
abominations *p* they him to anger	Deut 32:16	
they have *p* me to anger with	Deut 32:21	
unto them, and *p* the LORD to anger	Judg 2:12	
And her adversary also *p* her sore	1Sa 1:6	3707
house of the LORD, so she *p* her	1Sa 1:7	3707
they *p* him to jealousy with their	1Kin 14:22	
p the LORD God of Israel to anger	1Kin 15:30	
wherewith thou hast *p* me to anger	1Kin 21:22	
p to anger the LORD God of Israel	1Kin 22:53	
have *p* me to anger, since the day	2Kin 21:15	
that Manasseh had *p* him withal	2Kin 23:26	3707
and *p* David to number Israel	1Chr 21:1	5496
p to anger the LORD God of his	2Chr 28:25	
p the God of heaven unto wrath	Ezr 5:12	7265
for they have *p* thee to anger	Neh 4:5	
p the most high God, and kept not	Ps 78:56	4784
For they *p* him to anger with	Ps 78:58	
but *p* him at the sea, even at the	Ps 106:7	4784
Thus they *p* him to anger with	Ps 106:29	
Because they *p* his spirit	Ps 106:33	4784
but they *p* him with their counsel	Ps 106:43	4784
they have *p* the Holy One of	Is 1:4	5006
Why have they *p* me to anger with	Jer 8:19	
p me to anger with the work of	Jer 32:30	
Ephraim *p* him to anger most	Hos 12:14	
when your fathers *p* me to wrath	Zec 8:14	
not her own, is not easily *p*	1Cor 13:5	3947
and your zeal hath *p* very many	2Cor 9:2	2042

PROVOKEDST

how thou *p* the LORD thy God to	Deut 9:7	

PROVOKETH

whoso *p* him to anger sinneth	Prov 20:2	5674
A people that *p* me to anger	Is 65:3	
of jealousy, which *p* to jealousy	Eze 8:3	

PROVOKING

because of the *p* of his sons	Deut 32:19	3707
their groves, *p* the LORD to anger	1Kin 14:15	
in *p* him to anger with the work	1Kin 16:7	
in *p* the LORD God of Israel to	1Kin 16:13	
sinned yet more against him by *p*	Ps 78:17	4784
p one another, envying one	Gal 5:26	4292

PRUDENCE

king a wise son, endued with *p*	2Chr 2:12	7922
I wisdom dwell with *p*, and find	Prov 8:12	6195
toward us in all wisdom and *p*	Eph 1:8	5428

PRUDENT

p in matters, and a comely person,	1Sa 16:18	995
but a *p* man covereth shame	Prov 12:16	6175
A *p* man concealeth knowledge	Prov 12:23	6175
Every *p* man dealeth with	Prov 13:16	6175
The wisdom of the *p* is to	Prov 14:8	6175

but the *p* man looketh well to his	Prov 14:15	6175
but the *p* are crowned with	Prov 14:18	6175
he that regardeth reproof is *p*	Prov 15:5	6191
wise in heart shall be called *p*	Prov 16:21	995
The heart of the *p* getteth	Prov 18:15	995
a *p* wife is from the LORD	Prov 19:14	7919
A *p* man foreseeth the evil, and	Prov 22:3	6175
A *p* man foreseeth the evil, and	Prov 27:12	6175
judge, and the prophet, and the *p*	Is 3:2	7080
own eyes, and *p* in their own sight	Is 5:21	995
for I am *p*	Is 10:13	995
of their *p* men shall be hid	Is 29:14	995
is counsel perished from the *p*	Jer 49:7	995
p, and he shall know them	Hos 14:9	995
Therefore the *p* shall keep	Amos 5:13	7919
these things from the wise and *p*	Mt 11:25	4908
these things from the wise and *p*	Lk 10:21	4908
country, Sergius Paulus, a *p* man	Acts 13:7	4908
the understanding of the *p*	1Cor 1:19	4908

PRUDENTLY

Behold, my servant shall deal *p*	Is 52:13	7919

PRUNE

years thou shalt *p* thy vineyard	Lev 25:3	2168
sow thy field, nor *p* thy vineyard	Lev 25:4	2168

PRUNED

it shall not be *p*, nor digged	Is 5:6	2167

PRUNINGHOOKS

and their spears into *p*	Is 2:4	4211
both cut off the sprigs with *p*	Is 18:5	4211
swords, and your *p* into spears	Joel 3:10	4211
and their spears into *p*	Mic 4:3	4211

PSALM

day David delivered first this *p*	1Chr 16:7	
A *P* of David, when he fled from	Ps 3:*t*	4210
on Neginoth, A *P* of David	Ps 4:*t*	4210
upon Nehiloth, A *P* of David	Ps 5:*t*	4210
upon Sheminith, A *P* of David	Ps 6:*t*	4210
upon Gittith, A *P* of David	Ps 8:*t*	4210
upon Muth-labben, A *P* of David	Ps 9:*t*	4210
the chief Musician, A *P* of David	Ps 11:*t*	
upon Sheminith, A *P* of David	Ps 12:*t*	4210
the chief Musician, A *P* of David	Ps 13:*t*	4210
the chief Musician, A *P* of David	Ps 14:*t*	
A *P* of David	Ps 15:*t*	4210
A *P* of David, the servant of the	Ps 18:*t*	4210
the chief Musician, A *P* of David	Ps 19:*t*	4210
the chief Musician, A *P* of David	Ps 20:*t*	4210
the chief Musician, A *P* of David	Ps 21:*t*	4210
Aijeleth Shahar, A *P* of David	Ps 22:*t*	4210
A *P* of David	Ps 23:*t*	4210
A *P* of David	Ps 24:*t*	
A *P* of David	Ps 25:*t*	
A *P* of David	Ps 26:*t*	
A *P* of David	Ps 27:*t*	
A *P* of David	Ps 28:*t*	
A *P* of David	Ps 29:*t*	4210
A *P* and Song at the dedication of	Ps 30:*t*	4210
the chief Musician, A *P* of David	Ps 31:*t*	4210
A *P* of David, A Maschil	Ps 32:*t*	
A *P* of David, when he changed his	Ps 34:*t*	
A *P* of David	Ps 35:*t*	
A *P* of David, the servant of the	Ps 36:*t*	
A *P* of David	Ps 37:*t*	
A *P* of David, to bring to	Ps 38:*t*	4210
even to Jeduthun, A *P* of David	Ps 39:*t*	4210
the chief Musician, A *P* of David	Ps 40:*t*	4210
the chief Musician, A *P* of David	Ps 41:*t*	4210
A *P* for the sons of Korah	Ps 47:*t*	4210
A Song and *P* for the sons of Korah	Ps 48:*t*	4210
A *P* for the sons of Korah	Ps 49:*t*	4210
A *P* of Asaph	Ps 50:*t*	4210
A *P* of David, when Nathan the	Ps 51:*t*	4210
A *P* of David, when Doeg the	Ps 52:*t*	
Mahalath, Maschil, A *P* of David	Ps 53:*t*	
A *P* of David, when the Ziphims	Ps 54:*t*	
Neginoth, Maschil, A *P* of David	Ps 55:*t*	
upon Neginah, A *P* of David	Ps 61:*t*	
to Jeduthun, A *P* of David	Ps 62:*t*	4210
A *P* of David, when he was in the	Ps 63:*t*	4210
the chief Musician, A *P* of David	Ps 64:*t*	4210
To the chief Musician, A *P*	Ps 65:*t*	4210
the chief Musician, A *P* or *P*	Ps 66:*t*	4210
Musician on Neginoth, A *P* or Song	Ps 67:*t*	4210
Musician, A *P* or Song of David	Ps 68:*t*	4210
upon Shoshannim, A *P* of David	Ps 69:*t*	
A *P* of David, to bring to	Ps 70:*t*	
A *P* for Solomon	Ps 72:*t*	4210
A *P* of Asaph	Ps 73:*t*	4210

P

Altaschith, A *P* or Song of Asaph	Ps 75:*t*	4210
on Neginoth, A *P* or Song of Asaph	Ps 76:*t*	4210
to Jeduthun, A *P* of Asaph	Ps 77:*t*	4210
A *P* of Asaph	Ps 79:*t*	4210
Shoshannim-Eduth, A *P* of Asaph	Ps 80:*t*	4210
upon Gittith, A *P* of Asaph	Ps 81:*t*	4210
Take a *p*, and bring hither the	Ps 81:2	2172
A *P* of Asaph	Ps 82:*t*	4210
A Song or *P* of Asaph	Ps 83:*t*	4210
A *P* for the sons of Korah	Ps 84:*t*	4210
A *P* for the sons of Korah	Ps 85:*t*	4210
A *P* or Song for the sons of Korah	Ps 87:*t*	4210
A Song or *P* for the sons of Korah	Ps 88:*t*	4210
A *P* or Song for the sabbath day	Ps 92:*t*	4210
A *P*.	Ps 98:*t*	4210
the harp, and the voice of a *p*	Ps 98:5	2172
A *P* of praise	Ps 100:*t*	4210
A *P* of David	Ps 101:*t*	4210
A *P* of David	Ps 103:*t*	
A Song or *P* of David	Ps 108:*t*	4210
the chief Musician, A *P* of David	Ps 109:*t*	4210
the chief Musician, A *P* of David	Ps 110:*t*	4210
A *P* of David	Ps 138:*t*	
the chief Musician, A *P* of David	Ps 139:*t*	4210
the chief Musician, A *P* of David	Ps 140:*t*	4210
A *P* of David	Ps 141:*t*	4210
A *P* of David	Ps 143:*t*	4210
A *P* of David	Ps 144:*t*	
David's *P* of praise	Ps 145:*t*	
is also written in the second *p*	Acts 13:33	5568
he saith also in another *p*	Acts 13:35	
every one of you hath a *p*	1Cor 14:26	5568

PSALMIST
Jacob, and the sweet *p* of Israel	2Sa 23:1	2158

PSALMS
sing *p* unto him, talk ye of all	1Chr 16:9	2167
a joyful noise unto him with *p*	Ps 95:2	2158
Sing unto him, sing *p* unto him	Ps 105:2	2167
himself saith in the book of *P*.	Lk 20:42	5568
and in the prophets, and in the *p*	Lk 24:44	5568
it is written in the book of *P*.	Acts 1:20	5568
Speaking to yourselves in *p*	Eph 5:19	5568
and admonishing one another in *p*	Col 3:16	5568
let him sing *p*.	Jas 5:13	5567

PSALTERIES
fir wood, even on harps, and on *p*	2Sa 6:5	5035
harps also and *p* for singers	1Kin 10:12	5035
singing, and with harps, and with *p*	1Chr 13:8	5035
with instruments of musick,	1Chr 15:16	5035
and Benaiah, with *p* on Alamoth	1Chr 15:20	5035
cymbals, making a noise with *p*	1Chr 15:28	5035
and Jeiel with *p* and with harps	1Chr 16:5	3627
prophesy with harps, with *p*	1Chr 25:1	5035
of the Lord, with cymbals, *p*	1Chr 25:6	5035
white linen, having cymbals and *p*	2Chr 5:12	5035
palace, and harps and *p* for singers	2Chr 9:11	5035
And they came to Jerusalem with *p*	2Chr 20:28	5035
of the Lord with cymbals, with *p*	2Chr 29:25	5035
and with singing, with cymbals, *p*	Neh 12:27	5035

PSALTERY
down from the high place with a *p*	1Sa 10:5	5035
sing unto him with the *p* and an	Ps 33:2	5035
awake, *p* and harp	Ps 57:8	5035
will also praise thee with the *p*	Ps 71:22	3627
the pleasant harp with the *p*	Ps 81:2	5035
of ten strings, and upon the *p*	Ps 92:3	5035
Awake, *p* and harp	Ps 108:2	5035
upon a *p* and an instrument of ten	Ps 144:9	5035
praise him with the *p* and harp	Ps 150:3	5035
cornet, flute, harp, sackbut, *p*	Dan 3:5	6460
cornet, flute, harp, sackbut, *p*	Dan 3:7	6460
cornet, flute, harp, sackbut, *p*	Dan 3:10	6460
cornet, flute, harp, sackbut, *p*	Dan 3:15	6460

PTOLEMAIS (*tol-e-ma'-is*) See Accho. *A seaport between Carmel and Tyre.*
course from Tyre, we came to *P*	Acts 21:7	4424

PUA (*pu'ah*) See Puah. *A son of Issachar.*
of *P*, the family of the Punites.	Num 26:23	6312

PUAH (*pu'-ah*) See Phuvah, Pua, Punites.
   1. Same as Pua.
sons of Issachar were, Tola, and *P*	1Chr 7:1	6312

   2. Father of Tola.
defend Israel Tola the son of *P*	Judg 10:1	6312

   3. A Hebrew midwife in Egypt.
and the name of the other *P*	Ex 1:15	6326

PUBLICAN
Thomas, and Matthew the *p*	Mt 10:3	5057
thee as an heathen man and a *p*	Mt 18:17	5057
things he went forth, and saw a *p*	Lk 5:27	5057
one a Pharisee, and the other a *p*	Lk 18:10	5057
adulterers, or even as this *p*	Lk 18:11	5057
And the *p*, standing afar off,	Lk 18:13	5057

PUBLICANS
do not even the *p* the same	Mt 5:46	5057
do not even the *p* so	Mt 5:47	5057
meat in the house, behold, many *p*	Mt 9:10	5057
Why eateth your Master with *p*	Mt 9:11	5057
and a winebibber, a friend of *p*	Mt 11:19	5057
Verily I say unto you, That the *p*	Mt 21:31	5057
but the *p* and the harlots believed	Mt 21:32	5057
sat at meat in his house, many *p*	Mk 2:15	5057
and Pharisees saw him eat with *p*	Mk 2:16	5057
that he eateth and drinketh with *p*	Mk 2:16	5057
Then came also *p* to be baptized	Lk 3:12	5057
and there was a great company of *p*	Lk 5:29	5057
Why do ye eat and drink with *p*	Lk 5:30	5057
people that heard him, and the *p*	Lk 7:29	5057
and a winebibber, a friend of *p*	Lk 7:34	5057
Then drew near unto him all the *p*	Lk 15:1	5057
which was the chief among the *p*	Lk 19:2	754

PUBLICK
willing to make her a *p* example	Mt 1:19	3856

PUBLICKLY
convinced the Jews, and that *p*	Acts 18:28	1219
shewed you, and have taught you *p*	Acts 20:20	1219

PUBLISH
Because I will *p* the name of the	Deut 32:3	7121
to *p* it in the house of their	1Sa 31:9	1319
p it not in the streets of	2Sa 1:20	1319
And that they should *p* and proclaim	Neh 8:15	8085
That I may *p* with the voice of	Ps 26:7	8085
ye in Judah, and *p* in Jerusalem	Jer 4:5	8085
p against Jerusalem, that	Jer 4:16	8085
Jacob, and *p* it in Judah, saying,	Jer 5:20	8085
p ye, praise ye, O Lord,	Jer 31:7	8085
p in Migdol, and *p* in Noph,	Jer 46:14	8085
ye among the nations, and *p*	Jer 50:2	8085
p, and conceal not	Jer 50:2	8085
P in the palaces at Ashdod, and in	Amos 3:9	8085
proclaim and *p* the free offerings	Amos 4:5	8085
went out, and began to *p* it much	Mk 1:45	2784
began to *p* in Decapolis how great	Mk 5:20	2784

PUBLISHED
be *p* throughout all his empire	Est 1:20	8085
that it should be *p* according to	Est 1:22	1696
province was *p* unto all people	Est 3:14	1540
province was *p* unto all people	Est 8:13	1540
the company of those that *p* it	Ps 68:11	1319
p through Nineveh by the decree	Jonah 3:7	559
the more a great deal they *p* it	Mk 7:36	2784
must first be *p* among all nations	Mk 13:10	2784
p throughout the whole city how	Lk 8:39	2784
which was *p* throughout all Judaea	Acts 10:37	1096
the word of the Lord was *p*	Acts 13:49	1308

PUBLISHETH
good tidings, that *p* peace	Is 52:7	8085
tidings of good, that *p* salvation	Is 52:7	8085
p affliction from mount Ephraim	Jer 4:15	8085
good tidings, that *p* peace	Nah 1:15	8085

PUBLIUS (*pub'-le-us*) *A chief man on Melita.*
of the island, whose name was *P*	Acts 28:7	4196
that the father of *P* lay sick of	Acts 28:8	4196

PUDENS (*pu'-denz*) *A Christian in Rome.*
Eubulus greeteth thee, and *P*	2Ti 4:21	4227

PUFFED
that no one of you be *p* up for	1Cor 4:6	5448
Now some are *p* up, as though I	1Cor 4:18	5448
the speech of them which are *p* up	1Cor 4:19	5448
And ye are *p* up, and have not	1Cor 5:2	5448
vaunteth not itself, is not *p* up	1Cor 13:4	5448
vainly *p* up by his fleshly mind,	Col 2:18	5448

PUFFETH
for all his enemies, he *p* at them	Ps 10:5	6315
in safety from him that *p* at him	Ps 12:5	6315
Knowledge *p* up, but charity	1Cor 8:1	5448

PUHITES (*pu'-hites*) *A family descended from Caleb.*
the Ithrites, and the *P*, and the	1Chr 2:53	6336

PUL (pul)
1. Same as Tiglath-pileser.

P the king of Assyria came	2Kin 15:19	6322
Menahem gave *P* a thousand talents	2Kin 15:19	6322
the spirit of *P* king of Assyria	1Chr 5:26	6322

2. A place near Libya.

unto the nations, to Tarshish, *P*	Is 66:19	6322

PULL

he could not *p* it in again to him	1Kin 13:4	7725
P me out of the net that they	Ps 31:4	3318
thy state shall he *p* thee down	Is 22:19	2040
to *p* down, and to destroy, and to	Jer 1:10	5422
p them out like sheep for the	Jer 12:3	5423
to *p* down, and to destroy it	Jer 18:7	5422
build them, and not *p* them down	Jer 24:6	2040
not *p* you down, and I will plant	Jer 42:10	2040
shall he not *p* up the roots	Eze 17:9	5423
ye *p* off the robe with the	Mic 2:8	6584
Let me *p* out the mote out of	Mt 7:4	*1544*
let me *p* out the mote that is in	Lk 6:42	*1544*
to *p* out the mote that is in thy	Lk 6:42	*1544*
I will *p* down my barns, and build	Lk 12:18	*2507*
will not straightway *p* him out on	Lk 14:5	*385*

PULLED

p her in unto him into the ark	Gen 8:9	4026
p Lot into the house to them, and	Gen 19:10	935
let timber be *p* down from his	Ezr 6:11	5256
aside my ways, and *p* me in pieces	Lam 3:11	6582
they shall no more be *p* up out of	Amos 9:15	5428
p away the shoulder, and stopped	Zec 7:11	5414
have been *p* in pieces of them	Acts 23:10	*1288*

PULLING

God to the *p* down of strong holds	2Cor 10:4	*2506*
with fear, *p* them out of the fire	Jude 23	*726*

PULPIT

the scribe stood upon a *p* of wood	Neh 8:4	4026

PULSE

beans, and lentiles, and parched *p*	2Sa 17:28	
and let them give us *p* to eat	Dan 1:12	2235
and gave them *p*	Dan 1:16	2235

PUNISH

then I will *p* you seven times	Lev 26:18	3256
will *p* you yet seven times for	Lev 26:24	5221
Also to *p* the just is not good,	Prov 17:26	6064
I will *p* the fruit of the stout	Is 10:12	6485
I will *p* the world for their evil	Is 13:11	6485
that the LORD shall *p* the host of	Is 24:21	6485
to *p* the inhabitants of the earth	Is 26:21	6485
strong sword shall *p* leviathan	Is 27:1	6485
that I will *p* all them which are	Jer 9:25	6485
of hosts, Behold, I will *p* them	Jer 11:22	6485
thou say when he shall *p* thee	Jer 13:21	6485
But I will *p* you according to the	Jer 21:14	6485
the LORD, I will even *p* that man	Jer 23:34	6485
that I will *p* the king of Babylon	Jer 25:12	6485
of Babylon, that nation will I *p*	Jer 27:8	6485
I will *p* Shemaiah the Nehelamite,	Jer 29:32	6485
I will *p* all that oppress them	Jer 30:20	6485
And I will *p* him and his seed and	Jer 36:31	6485
For I will *p* them that dwell in	Jer 44:13	6485
that I will *p* you in this place,	Jer 44:29	6485
I will *p* the multitude of No, and	Jer 46:25	6485
I will *p* the king of Babylon and	Jer 50:18	6485
I will *p* Bel in Babylon, and I	Jer 51:44	6485
I will *p* them for their ways, and	Hos 4:9	6485
I will not *p* your daughters when	Hos 4:14	6485
will *p* Jacob according to his	Hos 12:2	6485
therefore I will *p* you for all	Amos 3:2	6485
that I will *p* the princes	Zeph 1:8	6485
I *p* all those that leap on the	Zeph 1:9	6485
p the men that are settled on	Zeph 1:12	6485
As I thought to *p* you, when your	Zec 8:14	7489
nothing how they might *p* them	Acts 4:21	*2849*

PUNISHED

he shall be surely *p*	Ex 21:20	5358
a day or two, he shall not be *p*	Ex 21:21	5358
he shall be surely *p*, according	Ex 21:22	6064
p us less than our iniquities	Ezr 9:13	2820
an iniquity to be *p* by the judges	Job 31:11	
an iniquity to be *p* by the judge	Job 31:28	
When the scorner is *p*, the simple	Prov 21:11	6064
but the simple pass on, and are *p*	Prov 22:3	6064
but the simple pass on, and are *p*	Prov 27:12	6064
of Egypt, as I have *p* Jerusalem	Jer 44:13	6485
as I have *p* the king of Assyria	Jer 50:18	6485
be cut off, howsoever I *p* them	Zeph 3:7	6485
the shepherds, and I *p* the goats	Zec 10:3	6485

bound unto Jerusalem, for to be *p*	Acts 22:5	*5097*
I *p* them oft in every synagogue,	Acts 26:11	*5097*
Who shall be *p* with everlasting	2Th 1:9	*1349,5099*
unto the day of judgment to be *p*	2Pet 2:9	*2849*

PUNISHMENT

My *p* is greater than I can bear	Gen 4:13	5771
accept of the *p* of their iniquity	Lev 26:41	5771
accept of the *p* of their iniquity	Lev 26:43	5771
there shall no *p* happen to thee	1Sa 28:10	5771
a strange *p* to the workers of	Job 31:3	
man of great wrath shall suffer *p*	Prov 19:19	6066
a man for the *p* of his sins	Lam 3:39	2399
For the *p* of the iniquity of the	Lam 4:6	5771
than the *p* of the sin of Sodom	Lam 4:6	2403
The *p* of thine iniquity is	Lam 4:22	5771
bear the *p* of their iniquity	Eze 14:10	5771
the *p* of the prophet shall be	Eze 14:10	5771
p of him that seeketh unto him	Eze 14:10	5771
will not turn away the *p* thereof	Amos 1:3	
will not turn away the *p* thereof	Amos 1:6	
will not turn away the *p* thereof	Amos 1:9	
will not turn away the *p* thereof	Amos 1:11	
will not turn away the *p* thereof	Amos 1:13	
will not turn away the *p* thereof	Amos 2:1	
will not turn away the *p* thereof	Amos 2:4	
will not turn away the *p* thereof	Amos 2:6	
This shall be the *p* of Egypt	Zec 14:19	2403
the *p* of all nations that come	Zec 14:19	2403
shall go away into everlasting *p*	Mt 25:46	*2851*
to such a man is this *p*, which	2Cor 2:6	*2009*
Of how much sorer *p*, suppose ye,	Heb 10:29	*5098*
by him for the *p* of evildoers	1Pet 2:14	*1557*

PUNISHMENTS

wrath bringeth the *p* of the sword	Job 19:29	5771
the heathen, and *p* upon the people	Ps 149:7	5771

PUNITES (pu'-nites) *Descendents of Pua.*

of Pua, the family of the *P*	Num 26:23	6324

PUNON (pu'-non) *An Edomite city.*

from Zalmonah, and pitched in *P*	Num 33:42	6325
And they departed from *P*, and	Num 33:43	6325

PUR (pur) *See* PURIM. *Same as Purim.*

of king Ahasuerus, they cast *P*	Est 3:7	6332
to destroy them, and had cast *P*	Est 9:24	6332
days Purim after the name of *P*	Est 9:26	6332

PURAH *See* PHURAH.

PURCHASE

The *p* of the field and of the cave	Gen 49:32	4736
if a man *p* of the Levites, then	Lev 25:33	1350
So I took the evidence of the *p*	Jer 32:11	4736
I gave the evidence of the *p* unto	Jer 32:12	4736
that subscribed the book of the *p*	Jer 32:12	4736
evidences, this evidence of the *p*	Jer 32:14	4736
p unto Baruch the son of Neriah	Jer 32:16	4736
p to themselves a good degree	1Ti 3:13	*4046*

PURCHASED

Abraham *p* of the sons of Heth	Gen 25:10	7069
pass over, which thou hast *p*	Ex 15:16	7069
have I *p* to be my wife, to raise	Ruth 4:10	7069
which thou hast *p* of old	Ps 74:2	7069
which his right hand had *p*	Ps 78:54	7069
Now this man *p* a field with the	Acts 1:18	*2932*
gift of God may be *p* with money	Acts 8:20	*2932*
which he hath *p* with his own	Acts 20:28	*4046*
redemption of the *p* possession	Eph 1:14	*4047*

PURE

thou shalt overlay it with *p* gold	Ex 25:11	2889
shalt make a mercy seat of *p* gold	Ex 25:17	2889
thou shalt overlay it with *p* gold	Ex 25:24	2889
of *p* gold shalt thou make them	Ex 25:29	2889
make a candlestick of *p* gold	Ex 25:31	2889
be one beaten work of *p* gold	Ex 25:36	2889
thereof, shall be of *p* gold	Ex 25:38	2889
Of a talent of *p* gold shall he	Ex 25:39	2889
that they bring thee *p* oil olive	Ex 27:20	2134
two chains of *p* gold at the ends	Ex 28:14	2889
ends of wreathen work of *p* gold	Ex 28:22	2889
thou shalt make a plate of *p* gold	Ex 28:36	2889
thou shalt overlay it with *p* gold	Ex 30:3	2889
of *p* myrrh five hundred shekels	Ex 30:23	1865
sweet spices with *p* frankincense	Ex 30:34	2134
apothecary, tempered together, *p*	Ex 30:35	2889
the *p* candlestick with all his	Ex 31:8	2889
he overlaid it with *p* gold within	Ex 37:2	2889
he made the mercy seat of *p* gold	Ex 37:6	2889
And he overlaid it with *p* gold	Ex 37:11	2889
covers to cover withal, of *p* gold	Ex 37:16	2889

P

he made the candlestick of *p* gold	Ex 37:17	2889
it was one beaten work of *p* gold	Ex 37:22	2889
and his snuffdishes, of *p* gold	Ex 37:23	2889
Of a talent of *p* gold made he it,	Ex 37:24	2889
And he overlaid it with *p* gold	Ex 37:26	2889
the *p* incense of sweet spices,	Ex 37:29	2889
ends, of wreathen work of *p* gold	Ex 39:15	2889
And they made bells of *p* gold	Ex 39:25	2889
plate of the holy crown of *p* gold	Ex 39:30	2889
The *p* candlestick, with the lamps	Ex 39:37	2889
that they bring unto thee *p* oil	Lev 24:2	2134
the *p* candlestick before the LORD	Lev 24:4	2888
upon the *p* table before the LORD	Lev 24:6	2888
thou shalt put *p* frankincense	Lev 24:7	2134
drink the *p* blood of the grape	Deut 32:14	2561
With the *p* thou wilt shew thyself	2Sa 22:27	2889
thou wilt shew thyself *p*	2Sa 22:27	1305
and twenty measures of *p* oil	1Kin 5:11	3795
and he overlaid it with *p* gold	1Kin 6:20	5462
the house within with *p* gold	1Kin 6:21	5462
And the candlesticks of *p* gold	1Kin 7:49	5462
spoons, and the censers of *p* gold	1Kin 7:50	5462
forest of Lebanon were of *p* gold	1Kin 10:21	5462
Also *p* gold for the fleshhooks,	1Chr 28:17	2889
he overlaid it within with *p* gold	2Chr 3:4	2889
before the oracle, of *p* gold	2Chr 4:20	5462
spoons, and the censers, of *p* gold	2Chr 4:22	5462
ivory, and overlaid with *p* gold	2Chr 9:17	2889
forest of Lebanon were of *p* gold	2Chr 9:20	5462
they in order upon the *p* table	2Chr 13:11	2889
together, all of them were *p*	Ezr 6:20	2889
a man be more *p* than his maker	Job 4:17	2891
If thou wert *p* and upright	Job 8:6	2134
thou hast said, My doctrine is *p*	Job 11:4	2134
also my prayer is *p*	Job 16:17	2134
the stars are not *p* in his sight	Job 25:5	2141
shall it be valued with *p* gold	Job 28:19	2889
The words of the LORD are *p* words	Ps 12:6	2889
With the *p* thou wilt shew thyself	Ps 18:26	2889
thou wilt shew thyself *p*	Ps 18:26	1305
the commandment of the LORD is *p*	Ps 19:8	1249
a crown of *p* gold on his head	Ps 21:3	6337
hath clean hands, and a *p* heart	Ps 24:4	1249
Thy word is very *p*	Ps 119:140	6884
words of the *p* are pleasant words	Prov 15:26	2889
heart clean, I am *p* from my sin	Prov 20:9	2891
his doings, whether his work be *p*	Prov 20:11	2134
but as for the *p*, his work is	Prov 21:8	2134
Every word of God is *p*	Prov 30:5	6884
that are *p* in their own eyes	Prov 30:12	2889
hair of his head like the *p* wool	Dan 7:9	5343
Shall I count them *p* with the	Mic 6:11	2135
I turn to the people a *p* language	Zeph 3:9	1305
unto my name, and a *p* offering	Mal 1:11	2889
Blessed are the *p* in heart	Mt 5:8	2513
that I am *p* from the blood of all	Acts 20:26	2513
All things indeed are *p*	Rom 14:20	2513
are just, whatsoever things are *p*	Phil 4:8	53
is charity out of a *p* heart	1Ti 1:5	2513
of the faith in a *p* conscience	1Ti 3:9	2513
keep thyself *p*	1Ti 5:22	53
my forefathers with *p* conscience	2Ti 1:3	2513
call on the Lord out of a *p* heart	2Ti 2:22	2513
Unto the *p* all things are *p*	Titus 1:15	2513
and unbelieving is nothing *p*	Titus 1:15	2513
and our bodies washed with *p* water	Heb 10:22	2513
P religion and undefiled before	Jas 1:27	2513
that is from above is first *p*	Jas 3:17	53
another with a *p* heart fervently	1Pet 1:22	2513
p minds by way of remembrance	2Pet 3:1	1506
himself, even as he is *p*	1Jn 3:3	53
the seven plagues, clothed in *p*	Rev 15:6	2513
and the city was *p* gold, like unto	Rev 21:18	2513
the street of the city was *p* gold	Rev 21:21	2513
he shewed me a *p* river of water	Rev 22:1	2513

PURELY

p purge away thy dross, and take	Is 1:25	1252

PURENESS

delivered by the *p* of thine hands	Job 22:30	1252
He that loveth *p* of heart	Prov 22:11	2890
By *p*, by knowledge, by	2Cor 6:6	54

PURER

Her Nazarites were *p* than snow	Lam 4:7	2141
Thou art of *p* eyes than to behold	Hab 1:13	2889

PURGE

twelfth year he began to *p* Judah	2Chr 34:3	2891
P me with hyssop, and I shall be	Ps 51:7	2398
thou shalt *p* them away	Ps 65:3	3722
p away our sins, for thy name's	Ps 79:9	3722

purely *p* away thy dross, and take	Is 1:25	6884
I will *p* out from among you the	Eze 20:38	1305
thus shalt thou cleanse and *p* it	Eze 43:20	3722
Seven days shall they *p* the altar	Eze 43:26	3722
shall fall, to try them, and to *p*	Dan 11:35	1305
p them as gold and silver, that	Mal 3:3	2212
and he will throughly *p* his floor	Mt 3:12	1245
and he will throughly *p* his floor	Lk 3:17	1245
P out therefore the old leaven,	1Cor 5:7	1571
therefore *p* himself from these	2Ti 2:21	1571
p your conscience from dead works	Heb 9:14	2511

PURGED

of Eli's house shall not be *p*	1Sa 3:14	3722
his reign, when he had *p* the land	2Chr 34:8	2891
By mercy and truth iniquity is *p*	Prov 16:6	3722
shall have *p* the blood of	Is 4:4	1740
is taken away, and thy sin *p*	Is 6:7	3722
not be *p* from you till ye die	Is 22:14	3722
shall the iniquity of Jacob be *p*	Is 27:9	3722
because I have *p* thee	Eze 24:13	2891
and thou wast not *p*	Eze 24:13	2891
thou shalt not be *p* from thy	Eze 24:13	2891
when he had by himself *p* our sins.	Heb 1:3	4160,2512
are by the law *p* with blood	Heb 9:22	2511
once *p* should have had no more	Heb 10:2	2508
that he was *p* from his old sins	2Pet 1:9	2512

PURGETH

that beareth fruit, he *p* it	Jn 15:2	2508

PURGING

out into the draught, *p* all meats	Mk 7:19	2511

PURIFICATION

it is a *p* for sin	Num 19:9	2403
of the burnt heifer of *p* for sin	Num 19:17	2403
to the *p* of the sanctuary	2Chr 30:19	2893
their God, and the ward of the *p*	Neh 12:45	2893
their things for *p* be given them	Est 2:3	8562
gave her her things for *p*	Est 2:9	8562
when the days of her *p* according	Lk 2:22	2512
accomplishment of the days of *p*	Acts 21:26	49

PURIFICATIONS

the days of their *p* accomplished	Est 2:12	4795

PURIFIED

p the altar, and poured the blood	Lev 8:15	2398
And the Levites were *p*, and they	Num 8:21	2398
nevertheless it shall be *p* with	Num 31:23	2398
for she was *p* from her	2Sa 11:4	6942
and the Levites were *p* together	Ezr 6:20	2891
and the Levites *p* themselves	Neh 12:30	2891
p the people, and the gates, and	Neh 12:30	2891
a furnace of earth, *p* seven times	Ps 12:6	2891
Many shall be *p*, and made white,	Dan 12:10	1305
Asia found me *p* in the temple	Acts 24:18	48
heavens should be *p* with these	Heb 9:23	2511
Seeing ye have *p* your souls in	1Pet 1:22	48

PURIFIER

sit as a refiner and *p* of silver	Mal 3:3	2891

PURIFIETH

p not himself, defileth the	Num 19:13	2398
hath this hope in him *p* himself	1Jn 3:3	48

PURIFY

He shall *p* himself with it on the	Num 19:12	2398
but if he *p* not himself the third	Num 19:12	2398
seventh day he shall *p* himself	Num 19:19	2398
unclean, and shall not *p* himself	Num 19:20	2398
p both yourselves and your	Num 31:19	2398
p all your raiment, and all that	Num 31:20	2398
of breakings they *p* themselves	Job 41:25	2398
p themselves in the gardens	Is 66:17	2891
they purge the altar and *p* it	Eze 43:26	2891
he shall *p* the sons of Levi, and	Mal 3:3	2891
the passover, to *p* themselves	Jn 11:55	48
p thyself with them, and be at	Acts 21:24	48
p unto himself a peculiar people,	Titus 2:14	2511
p your hearts, ye double minded	Jas 4:8	48

PURIFYING

in the blood of her *p* three	Lev 12:4	2893
the days of her *p* be fulfilled	Lev 12:4	2892
in the blood of her *p* threescore	Lev 12:5	2893
the days of her *p* are fulfilled	Lev 12:6	2892
Sprinkle water of *p* upon them	Num 8:7	2403
in the *p* of all holy things, and	1Chr 23:28	2893
things for the *p* of the women	Est 2:12	8562
the manner of the *p* of the Jews	Jn 2:6	2512
disciples and the Jews about *p*	Jn 3:25	2512
and them, *p* their hearts by faith	Acts 15:9	2511

the next day *p* himself with them	Acts 21:26	48
sanctifieth to the *p* of the flesh	Heb 9:13	2514

PURIM (pu'-rim) See PUR. *A Jewish festival celebrating the deliverance from Haman.*

days *P* after the name of Pur	Est 9:26	6332
that these days of *P* should not	Est 9:28	6332
confirm this second letter of *P*	Est 9:29	6332
of *P* in their times appointed	Est 9:31	6332
confirmed these matters of *P*	Est 9:32	6332

PURITY

in spirit, in faith, in *p*	1Ti 4:12	47
younger as sisters, with all *p*	1Ti 5:2	47

PURLOINING

Not *p*, but shewing all good	Titus 2:10	3557

PURPLE

And blue, and *p*, and scarlet, and	Ex 25:4	713
fine twined linen, and blue, and *p*	Ex 26:1	713
shalt make a vail of blue, and *p*	Ex 26:31	713
door of the tent, of blue, and *p*	Ex 26:36	713
of twenty cubits, of blue, and *p*	Ex 27:16	713
shall take gold, and blue, and *p*	Ex 28:5	713
ephod of gold, of blue, and of *p*	Ex 28:6	713
even of gold, of blue, and *p*	Ex 28:8	713
of gold, of blue, and of *p*	Ex 28:15	713
pomegranates of blue, and of *p*	Ex 28:33	713
And blue, and *p*, and scarlet, and	Ex 35:6	713
with whom was found blue, and *p*	Ex 35:23	713
had spun, both of blue, and of *p*	Ex 35:25	713
the embroiderer, in blue, and in *p*	Ex 35:35	713
fine twined linen, and blue, and *p*	Ex 36:8	713
And he made a vail of blue, and *p*	Ex 36:35	713
the tabernacle door of blue, and *p*	Ex 36:37	713
was needlework, of blue, and *p*	Ex 38:18	713
an embroiderer in blue, and in *p*	Ex 38:23	713
And of the blue, and *p*, and scarlet,	Ex 39:1	713
the ephod of gold, blue, and *p*	Ex 39:2	713
work it in the blue, and in the *p*	Ex 39:3	713
of gold, blue, and *p*, and scarlet,	Ex 39:5	713
of gold, blue, and *p*, and scarlet,	Ex 39:8	713
robe pomegranates of blue, and *p*	Ex 39:24	713
fine twined linen, and blue, and *p*	Ex 39:29	713
and spread a *p* cloth thereon	Num 4:13	713
p raiment that was on the kings	Judg 8:26	713
and in brass, and in iron, and in *p*	2Chr 2:7	710
in stone, and in timber, in *p*	2Chr 2:14	713
And he made the vail of blue, and *p*	2Chr 3:14	713
p to silver rings and pillars of	Est 1:6	713
with a garment of fine linen and *p*	Est 8:15	713
her clothing is silk and *p*	Prov 31:22	713
of gold, the covering of it of *p*	Song 3:10	713
and the hair of thine head like *p*	Song 7:5	713
blue and *p* is their clothing	Jer 10:9	713
p from the isles of Elishah was	Eze 27:7	713
in thy fairs with emeralds, and *p*	Eze 27:16	713
And they clothed him with *p*	Mk 15:17	4209
him, they took off the *p* from him	Mk 15:20	4209
rich man, which was clothed in *p*	Lk 16:19	4209
head, and they put on him a *p* robe	Jn 19:2	4210
crown of thorns, and the *p* robe	Jn 19:5	4210
woman named Lydia, a seller of *p*	Acts 16:14	4211
And the woman was arrayed in *p*	Rev 17:4	4209
and of pearls, and fine linen, and *p*	Rev 18:12	4209
was clothed in fine linen, and *p*	Rev 18:16	4210

PURPOSE

some of the handfuls of *p* for her	Ruth 2:16	7997
I *p* to build an house unto the	1Kin 5:5	559
now ye *p* to keep under the	2Chr 28:10	559
them, to frustrate their *p*	Ezr 4:5	6098
which they had made for the *p*	Neh 8:4	1697
he may withdraw man from his *p*	Job 33:17	4639
Every *p* is established by counsel	Prov 20:18	4284
a time to every *p* under the	Eccl 3:1	2656
there is a time there for every *p*	Eccl 3:17	2656
Because to every *p* there is time	Eccl 8:6	2656
To what *p* is the multitude of	Is 1:11	
This is the *p* that is purposed	Is 14:26	6098
shall help in vain, and to no *p*	Is 30:7	7385
To what *p* cometh there to me	Jer 6:20	
which I *p* to do unto them because	Jer 26:3	2803
evil which I *p* to do unto them	Jer 36:3	2803
and hath conceived a *p* against you	Jer 49:30	4284
for every *p* of the LORD shall be	Jer 51:29	4284
that the *p* might not be changed	Dan 6:17	6640
saying, To what *p* is this waste	Mt 26:8	
that with *p* of heart they would	Acts 11:23	4286
appeared unto thee for this *p*	Acts 26:16	
that they had obtained their *p*	Acts 27:13	4286
save Paul, kept them from their *p*	Acts 27:43	1013

are the called according to his *p*	Rom 8:28	4286
that the *p* of God according to	Rom 9:11	4286
Even for this same *p* have I	Rom 9:17	
or the things that I *p*	2Cor 1:17	1011
do I *p* according to the flesh,	2Cor 1:17	1011
p of him who worketh all things	Eph 1:11	4286
According to the eternal *p* which	Eph 3:11	4286
have sent unto you for the same *p*	Eph 6:22	
have sent unto you for the same *p*	Col 4:8	
works, but according to his own *p*	2Ti 1:9	4286
my doctrine, manner of life, *p*	2Ti 3:10	4286
For this *p* the Son of God was	1Jn 3:8	

PURPOSED

that he was *p* to fight against	2Chr 32:2	6440
I am *p* that my mouth shall not	Ps 17:3	2161
who have *p* to overthrow my goings	Ps 140:4	2803
and as I have *p*, so shall it stand	Is 14:24	3289
that is *p* upon the whole earth	Is 14:26	3289
For the LORD of hosts hath	Is 14:27	3289
LORD of hosts hath *p* upon Egypt	Is 19:12	3289
The LORD of hosts hath *p* it	Is 23:9	3289
I have *p* it, I will also do it	Is 46:11	3335
I have spoken it, I have *p* it	Jer 4:28	2161
that he hath *p* against the	Jer 49:20	2803
that he hath *p* against the land	Jer 50:45	2803
The LORD hath *p* to destroy the	Lam 2:8	2803
But Daniel *p* in his heart that he	Dan 1:8	7760
Paul *p* in the spirit, when he had	Acts 19:21	5087
he *p* to return through Macedonia	Acts 20:3	1096,1106
oftentimes I *p* to come unto you	Rom 1:13	4388
which he hath *p* in himself	Eph 1:9	4388
he *p* in Christ Jesus our Lord	Eph 3:11	4160

PURPOSES

my *p* are broken off, even the	Job 17:11	2154
Without counsel *p* are	Prov 15:22	4284
shall be broken in the *p* thereof	Is 19:10	8356
and his *p*, that he hath purposed	Jer 49:20	4284
and his *p*, that he hath purposed	Jer 50:45	4284

PURPOSETH

according as he *p* in his heart	2Cor 9:7	4255

PURPOSING

comfort himself, *p* to kill thee	Gen 27:42	

PURSE

let us all have one *p*	Prov 1:14	3599
no bread, no money in their *p*	Mk 6:8	2223
Carry neither *p*, nor scrip, nor	Lk 10:4	905
them, When I sent you without *p*	Lk 22:35	905
them, But now, he that hath a *p*	Lk 22:36	905

PURSES

nor silver, nor brass in your *p*	Mt 10:9	2223

PURSUE

they did not *p* after the sons of	Gen 35:5	7291
The enemy said, I will *p*, I will	Ex 15:9	7291
avenger of the blood *p* the slayer	Deut 19:6	7291
they shall *p* thee until thou	Deut 28:22	7291
come upon thee, and shall *p* thee	Deut 28:45	7291
p after them quickly	Josh 2:5	7291
called together to *p* after them	Josh 8:16	7291
but *p* after your enemies, and	Josh 10:19	7291
the avenger of blood *p* after him	Josh 20:5	7291
after whom dost thou *p*	1Sa 24:14	7291
Yet a man is risen to *p* thee	1Sa 25:29	7291
my lord thus *p* after his servant	1Sa 26:18	7291
Shall I *p* after this troop	1Sa 30:8	7291
And he answered him, *P*	1Sa 30:8	7291
arise and *p* after David this night	2Sa 17:1	7291
p after him, lest he get him	2Sa 20:6	7291
to *p* after Sheba the son of	2Sa 20:7	7291
to *p* after Sheba the son of	2Sa 20:13	7291
thine enemies, while they *p* thee	2Sa 24:13	7291
wilt thou the dry stubble	Job 13:25	7291
they *p* my soul as the wind	Job 30:15	7291
seek peace, and *p* it	Ps 34:14	7291
shall they that you be swift	Is 30:16	7291
the sword shall *p* thee	Jer 48:2	3212
unto blood, and blood shall *p* thee	Eze 35:6	7291
blood, even blood shall *p* thee	Eze 35:6	7291
the enemy shall *p* him	Hos 8:3	7291
because he did *p* his brother with	Amos 1:11	7291
and darkness shall *p* his enemies	Nah 1:8	7291

PURSUED

and eighteen, and *p* them unto Dan	Gen 14:14	7291
p them unto Hobah, which is on	Gen 14:15	7291
p after him seven days' journey	Gen 31:23	7291
thou hast so hotly *p* after me	Gen 31:36	1814
he *p* after the children of Israel	Ex 14:8	7291
But the Egyptians *p* after them	Ex 14:9	7291

And the Egyptians *p*, and went in .... Ex 14:23 — 7291
overflow them as they *p* after you .... Deut 11:4 — 7291
the men *p* after them the way to .... Josh 2:7 — 7291
as soon as they which *p* after .... Josh 2:7 — 7291
they *p* after Joshua, and were .... Josh 8:16 — 7291
the city open, and *p* after Israel .... Josh 8:17 — 7291
the Egyptians *p* after your .... Josh 24:6 — 7291
they *p* after him, and caught him, ... Judg 1:6 — 7291
But Barak *p* after the chariots, ... Judg 4:16 — 7291
And, behold, as Barak *p* Sisera .... Judg 4:22 — 7291
and *p* after the Midianites.................. Judg 7:23 — 7291
p Midian, and brought the heads of ...... Judg 7:25 — 7291
he *p* after them, and took the two .... Judg 8:12 — 7291
p hard after them unto Gidom, and .... Judg 20:45 — 1692
p the Philistines, and smote them, ... 1Sa 7:11 — 7291
p the Philistines, until thou .... 1Sa 17:52 — 7291
that, he *p* after David in the .... 1Sa 23:25 — 7291
But David *p*, he and four hundred .... 1Sa 30:10 — 7291
And Asahel *p* after Abner .... 2Sa 2:19 — 7291
also and Abishai *p* after Abner.............. 2Sa 2:24 — 7291
p after Israel no more, neither .... 2Sa 2:28 — 7291
Abishai his brother *p* after Sheba .... 2Sa 20:10 — 7291
I have *p* mine enemies, and.................... 2Sa 22:38 — 7291
and Israel *p* him.................................. 1Kin 20:20 — 7291
of the Chaldees *p* after the king .... 2Kin 25:5 — 7291
Abijah *p* after Jeroboam, and took .... 2Chr 13:19 — 7291
were with him *p* them unto Gerar .... 2Chr 14:13 — 7291
I have *p* mine enemies, and.................... Ps 18:37 — 7291
He *p* them, and passed safely .... Is 41:3 — 7291
the Chaldeans' army *p* after them...... Jer 39:5 — 7291
of the Chaldeans *p* after the king.......... Jer 52:8 — 7291
they *p* us upon the mountains, ... Lam 4:19 — 1814

PURSUER
without strength before the *p*.................. Lam 1:6 — 7291

PURSUERS
the mountain, lest the *p* meet you .... Josh 2:16 — 7291
days, until the *p* be returned.................. Josh 2:16 — 7291
until the *p* were returned........................ Josh 2:22 — 7291
the *p* sought them throughout all .... Josh 2:22 — 7291
wilderness turned back upon the *p* .... Josh 8:20 — 7291

PURSUETH
and ye shall flee when none *p* you.......... Lev 26:17 — 7291
and they shall fall when none *p* .... Lev 26:36 — 7291
were before a sword, when none *p* .... Lev 26:37 — 7291
so he that *p* evil *p* it to.......................... Prov 11:19 — 7291
evil *p* it to his own death...................... Prov 11:19 — 7291
Evil *p* sinners.................................... Prov 13:21 — 7291
he *p* them with words, yet they .... Prov 19:7 — 7291
The wicked flee when no man *p* .... Prov 28:1 — 7291

PURSUING
were with him, faint, yet *p* them .... Judg 8:4 — 7291
I am *p* after Zebah and Zalmunna, ... Judg 8:5 — 7291
Saul returned from *p* after David .... 1Sa 23:28 — 7291
David and Joab came from *p* a troop..... 2Sa 3:22
returned from *p* after Israel .... 2Sa 18:16 — 7291
either he is talking, or he is *p* .... 1Kin 18:27 — 7873
that they turned back from *p* him, ... 1Kin 22:33 — 310
they turned back again from *p* him ...... 2Chr 18:32 — 310

PURTENANCE
his legs, and with the *p* thereof.............. Ex 12:9 — 7130

PUSH
to *p* with his horn in time past .... Ex 21:29 — 5056
If the ox shall *p* a manservant or .... Ex 21:32 — 5055
ox shall *p* in time past .... Ex 21:36 — 5056
with them he shall *p* the people .... Deut 33:17 — 5055
these shalt thou *p* the Syrians .... 1Kin 22:11 — 5055
With these thou shalt *p* Syria .... 2Chr 18:10 — 5055
they *p* away my feet, and they .... Job 30:12 — 7971
thee will we *p* down our enemies .... Ps 44:5 — 5055
the king of the south *p* at him .... Dan 11:40 — 5055

PUSHED
p all the diseased with your.................... Eze 34:21 — 5055

PUSHING
I saw the ram *p* westward, and.............. Dan 8:4 — 5055

PUT Also see APPENDIX. (put) See PHUT.
1. Descendant of Put 2.
P and Lubim were thy helpers................ Nah 3:9 — 6316
2. Son of Ham.
Cush, and Mizraim, *P*, and Canaan ...... 1Chr 1:8 — 6319

PUTEOLI (pu-te'-o-li) A seaport in Italy.
and we came the next day to *P* .... Acts 28:13 — 4223

PUTHITES See PUHITES.

PUTIEL (pu'-te-el) Father-in-law of Eleazar.
one of the daughters of *P* to wife............ Ex 6:25 — 6317

PUTRIFYING
wounds, and bruises, and *p* sores.......... Is 1:6 — 2961

PUTTEST See APPENDIX.

PUTTETH See APPENDIX.

PUTTING See APPENDIX.

PUVAH See PUA.

PUVVAH See PHUVAH.

PYGARG
deer, and the wild goat, and the *p* .... Deut 14:5 — 1787

PYRRHUS Not in KJV.

Q

QUAILS
pass, that at even the *q* came up............ Ex 16:13 — 7958
brought *q* from the sea, and let .... Num 11:31 — 7958
next day, and they gathered the *q* .... Num 11:32 — 7958
The people asked, and he brought *q* ...... Ps 105:40 — 7958

QUAKE
The earth shall *q* before them................ Joel 2:10 — 7264
The mountains *q* at him, and the .... Nah 1:5 — 7493
and the earth did *q*, and the rocks .... Mt 27:51 — 4579
said, I exceedingly fear and *q* .... Heb 12:21 — 1790

QUAKED
and the whole mount *q* greatly .... Ex 19:18 — 2729
also trembled, and the earth *q* .... 1Sa 14:15 — 7264

QUAKING
Son of man, eat thy bread with *q*.......... Eze 12:18 — 7494
but a great *q* fell upon them, so.............. Dan 10:7 — 2731

QUANTITY
the issue, all vessels of small *q* .... Is 22:24

QUARREL
shall avenge the *q* of my covenant .... Lev 26:25 — 5359
see how he seeketh a *q* against me........ 2Kin 5:7 — 579
Herodias had a *q* against him .... Mk 6:19 — 1758
if any man have a *q* against any .... Col 3:13 — 3437

QUARRIES
from the *q* that were by Gilgal................ Judg 3:19 — 6456
tarried, and passed beyond the *q* .... Judg 3:26 — 6456

QUARTER
all the people from every *q* .... Gen 19:4 — 7098
Then your south *q* shall be from............ Num 34:3 — 6285
their border in the north *q* was.............. Josh 15:5 — 6285

this was the west *q* .... Josh 18:14 — 6285
the south *q* was from the end of .... Josh 18:15 — 6285
shall wander every one to his *q* .... Is 47:15 — 5676
one for his gain, from his *q* .... Is 56:11 — 7098
and they came to him from every *q*........ Mk 1:45 — 3836

QUARTERS
seen with thee in all thy *q* .... Ex 13:7 — 1366
upon the four *q* of thy vesture................ Deut 22:12 — 3671
In four *q* were the porters,...................... 1Chr 9:24 — 7307
winds from the four *q* of heaven .... Jer 49:36 — 7098
house of Togarmah of the north *q* .... Eze 38:6 — 3411
as Peter passed throughout all *q* .... Acts 9:32
of the Jews which were in those *q* .... Acts 16:3 — 5117
In the same *q* were possessions of.......... Acts 28:7 — 5117
are in the four *q* of the earth .... Rev 20:8 — 1137

QUARTUS (quar'-tus) A Christian in Rome.
city saluteth you, and *Q* a brother .... Rom 16:23 — 2890

QUATERNIONS
delivered him to four *q* of .... Acts 12:4 — 5069

QUEEN
when the *q* of Sheba heard of the .... 1Kin 10:1 — 4436
when the *q* of Sheba had seen all.......... 1Kin 10:4 — 4436
of spices as these which the *q* of .... 1Kin 10:10 — 4436
the *q* of Sheba all her desire .... 1Kin 10:13 — 4436
the sister of Tahpenes the *q* .... 1Kin 11:19 — 1377
even her he removed from being *q* .... 1Kin 15:13 — 1377
the king and the children of the *q* .... 2Kin 10:13 — 1377
when the *q* of Sheba heard of the .... 2Chr 9:1 — 4436
when the *q* of Sheba had seen the.......... 2Chr 9:3 — 4436
the *q* of Sheba gave king Solomon .... 2Chr 9:9 — 4436
to the *q* of Sheba all her desire .... 2Chr 9:12 — 4436

king, he removed her from being *q*	2Chr 15:16	1377
(the *q* also sitting by him,) For	Neh 2:6	7694
Also Vashti the *q* made a feast	Est 1:9	4436
To bring Vashti the *q* before the	Est 1:11	4436
But the *q* Vashti refused to come	Est 1:12	4436
the *q* Vashti according to law	Est 1:15	4436
Vashti the *q* hath not done wrong	Est 1:16	4436
For this deed of the *q* shall come	Est 1:17	4436
the *q* to be brought in before him	Est 1:17	4436
have heard of the deed of the *q*	Est 1:18	4436
the king be *q* instead of Vashti	Est 2:4	4427
made her *q* instead of Vashti	Est 2:17	4427
who told it unto Esther the *q*	Est 2:22	4436
Then was the *q* exceedingly	Est 4:4	4436
the *q* standing in the court	Est 5:2	4436
her, What wilt thou, *q* Esther	Est 5:3	4436
Esther the *q* did let no man come	Est 5:12	4436
came to banquet with Esther the *q*	Est 7:1	4436
What is thy petition, *q* Esther	Est 7:2	4436
Then Esther the *q* answered	Est 7:3	4436
and said unto Esther the *q*	Est 7:5	4436
afraid before the king and the *q*	Est 7:6	4436
for his life to Esther the *q*	Est 7:7	4436
Will he force the *q* also before	Est 7:8	4436
the Jews' enemy unto Esther the *q*	Est 8:1	4436
Ahasuerus said unto Esther the *q*	Est 8:7	4436
the king said unto Esther the *q*	Est 9:12	4436
Then Esther the *q*, the daughter	Est 9:29	4436
Esther the *q* had enjoined them,	Est 9:31	4436
did stand the *q* in gold of Ophir	Ps 45:9	7694
to make cakes to the *q* of heaven	Jer 7:18	4446
Say unto the king and to the *q*	Jer 13:18	1377
that Jeconiah the king, and the *q*	Jer 29:2	1377
burn incense unto the *q* of heaven	Jer 44:17	4446
burn incense to the *q* of heaven	Jer 44:18	4446
burned incense to the *q* of heaven	Jer 44:19	4446
burn incense to the *q* of heaven	Jer 44:25	4446
Now the *q*, by reason of the words	Dan 5:10	4433
the *q* spake and said, O king, live	Dan 5:10	4433
The *q* of the south shall rise up	Mt 12:42	938
The *q* of the south shall rise up	Lk 11:31	938
under Candace *q* of the Ethiopians	Acts 8:27	938
she saith in her heart, I sit a *q*	Rev 18:7	938

QUEENS

There are threescore *q*, and	Song 6:8	4436
yea, the *q* and the concubines, and	Song 6:9	4436
their *q* thy nursing mothers	Is 49:23	8282

QUENCH

so they shall *q* my coal which is	2Sa 14:7	3518
that thou *q* not the light of	2Sa 21:17	3518
the wild asses *q* their thirst	Ps 104:11	7665
Many waters cannot *q* love	Song 8:7	3518
together, and none shall *q* them	Is 1:31	3518
the smoking flax shall he not *q*	Is 42:3	3518
burn that none can *q* it because	Jer 4:4	3518
fire, and burn that none can *q* it	Jer 21:12	3518
there be none to *q* it in Beth-el	Amos 5:6	3518
and smoking flax shall he not *q*	Mt 12:20	4570
to *q* all the fiery darts of the	Eph 6:16	4570
Q not the Spirit	1Th 5:19	4570

QUENCHED

unto the LORD, the fire was *q*	Num 11:2	8257
this place, and shall not be *q*	2Kin 22:17	3518
this place, and shall not be *q*	2Chr 34:25	3518
they are *q* as the fire of thorns	Ps 118:12	1846
It shall be not *q* night nor day	Is 34:10	3518
are extinct, they are *q* as tow	Is 43:17	3518
neither shall their fire be *q*	Is 66:24	3518
it shall burn, and shall not be *q*	Jer 7:20	3518
Jerusalem, and it shall not be *q*	Jer 17:27	3518
the flaming flame shall not be *q*	Eze 20:47	3518
it shall not be *q*	Eze 20:48	3518
the fire that never shall be *q*	Mk 9:43	762
dieth not, and the fire is not *q*	Mk 9:44	4570
the fire that never shall be *q*	Mk 9:45	762
dieth not, and the fire is not *q*	Mk 9:46	4570
dieth not, and the fire is not *q*	Mk 9:48	4570
Q the violence of fire, escaped	Heb 11:34	4570

QUESTION

which was a lawyer, asked him a *q*	Mt 22:35	
forth, and began to *q* with him	Mk 8:11	4802
the scribes, What *q* ye with them	Mk 9:16	4802
I will also ask of you one *q*	Mk 11:29	3056
after that durst ask him any *q*	Mk 12:34	
durst not ask him any *q* at all	Lk 20:40	
Then there arose a *q* between some	Jn 3:25	2214
apostles and elders about this *q*	Acts 15:2	2213
But if it be a *q* of words	Acts 18:15	2213
called in *q* for this day's uproar	Acts 19:40	1458

of the dead I am called in *q*	Acts 23:6	2919
I am called in *q* by you this day	Acts 24:21	2919
asking no *q* for conscience sake	1Cor 10:25	
asking no *q* for conscience sake	1Cor 10:27	

QUESTIONED

Then Hezekiah *q* with the priests	2Chr 31:9	1875
that they *q* among themselves	Mk 1:27	4802
Then he *q* with him in many words	Lk 23:9	1905

QUESTIONING

q one with another what the	Mk 9:10	4802
them, and the scribes *q* with them	Mk 9:14	4802

QUESTIONS

she came to prove him with hard *q*	1Kin 10:1	2420
And Solomon told her all her *q*	1Kin 10:3	1697
Solomon with hard *q* at Jerusalem	2Chr 9:1	2420
And Solomon told her all her *q*	2Chr 9:2	1697
that day forth ask him any more *q*	Mt 22:46	
hearing them, and asking them *q*	Lk 2:46	1905
to be accused of *q* of their law	Acts 23:29	2213
But had certain *q* against him of	Acts 25:19	2213
I doubted of such manner of *q*	Acts 25:20	2214
q which are among the Jews	Acts 26:3	2213
genealogies, which minister *q*	1Ti 1:4	2214
nothing, but doting about *q*	1Ti 6:4	2214
But foolish and unlearned *q* avoid	2Ti 2:23	2214
But avoid foolish *q*, and	Titus 3:9	2214

QUICK

there be *q* raw flesh in the	Lev 13:10	4241
the *q* flesh that burneth have a	Lev 13:24	4241
and they go down *q* into the pit	Num 16:30	2416
and let them go down *q* into hell	Ps 55:15	2416
Then they had swallowed us up *q*	Ps 124:3	2416
shall make him of *q* understanding	Is 11:3	
of God to be the Judge of the *q*	Acts 10:42	2198
Christ, who shall judge the *q*	2Ti 4:1	2198
For the word of God is *q*, and	Heb 4:12	2198
him that is ready to judge the *q*	1Pet 4:5	2198

QUICKEN

shalt *q* me again, and shalt bring	Ps 71:20	2421
q us, and we will call upon thy	Ps 80:18	2421
q thou me according to thy word	Ps 119:25	2421
and *q* thou me in thy way	Ps 119:37	2421
q me in thy righteousness	Ps 119:40	2421
Q me after thy lovingkindness	Ps 119:88	2421
q me, O LORD, according unto thy	Ps 119:107	2421
q me according to thy judgment	Ps 119:149	2421
q me according to thy word	Ps 119:154	2421
q me according to thy judgments	Ps 119:156	2421
q me, O LORD, according to thy	Ps 119:159	2421
Q me, O LORD, for thy name's sake	Ps 143:11	2421
also *q* your mortal bodies by his	Rom 8:11	2227

QUICKENED

for thy word hath *q* me	Ps 119:50	2421
for with them thou hast *q* me	Ps 119:93	2421
that which thou sowest is not *q*	1Cor 15:36	2227
And you hath he *q*, who were dead	Eph 2:1	
hath *q* us together with Christ,	Eph 2:5	4806
hath *q* us together with him,	Col 2:13	4806
in the flesh, but *q* by the Spirit	1Pet 3:18	2227

QUICKENETH

raiseth up the dead, and *q* them	Jn 5:21	2227
even so the Son *q* whom he will	Jn 5:21	2227
It is the spirit that *q*	Jn 6:63	2227
who *q* the dead, and calleth those	Rom 4:17	2227
who *q* all things, and before	1Ti 6:13	2227

QUICKENING

the last Adam was made a *q* spirit	1Cor 15:45	2227

QUICKLY

Make ready *q* three measures of	Gen 18:6	4116
it that thou hast found it so *q*	Gen 27:20	4116
aside *q* out of the way which I	Ex 32:8	4118
go *q* unto the congregation, and	Num 16:46	4120
drive them out, and destroy them *q*	Deut 9:3	4118
Arise, get thee down *q* from hence	Deut 9:12	4118
they are *q* turned aside out of	Deut 9:12	4118
ye had turned aside *q* out of the	Deut 9:16	4118
lest ye perish *q* from off the	Deut 11:17	4120
destroyed, and until thou perish *q*	Deut 28:20	4118
pursue after them *q*	Josh 2:5	4118
the ambush arose *q* out of their	Josh 8:19	4120
come up to us *q*, and save us, and	Josh 10:6	4120
ye shall perish *q* from off the	Josh 23:16	4120
they turned *q* out of the way	Judg 2:17	4118
days, then thou shalt go down *q*	1Sa 20:19	3966
Now therefore send *q*, and tell	2Sa 17:16	4120
but they went both of them away *q*	2Sa 17:18	4120

Arise, and pass *q* over the water	2Sa 17:21	4120
Come down *q*	2Kin 1:11	4120
Fetch *q* Micaiah the son of Imla	2Chr 18:8	4116
a threefold cord is not *q* broken	Eccl 4:12	4120
Agree with thine adversary *q*	Mt 5:25	5035
And go *q*, and tell his disciples	Mt 28:7	5035
And they departed *q* from the	Mt 28:8	5035
And they went out *q*, and fled from	Mk 16:8	5035
Go out *q* into the streets and	Lk 14:21	5030
him, Take thy bill, and sit down *q*	Lk 16:6	5030
as she heard that, she arose *q*	Jn 11:29	5035
unto him, That thou doest, do *q*	Jn 13:27	5032
raised him up, saying, Arise up *q*	Acts 12:7	1722,5034
get thee *q* out of Jerusalem	Acts 22:18	1722,5034
or else I will come unto thee *q*	Rev 2:5	5035
or else I will come unto thee *q*	Rev 2:16	5035
Behold, I come *q*	Rev 3:11	5035
behold, the third woe cometh *q*	Rev 11:14	5035
Behold, I come *q*	Rev 22:7	5035
And, behold, I come *q*	Rev 22:12	5035
things saith, Surely I come *q*	Rev 22:20	5035

QUICKSANDS
lest they should fall into the *q*	Acts 27:17	4950

QUIET
were *q* all the night, saying, In	Judg 16:2	2790
the manner of the Zidonians, *q*	Judg 18:7	8252
unto a people that were at *q*	Judg 18:27	8252
rejoiced, and the city was in *q*	2Kin 11:20	8252
good, and the land was wide, and *q*	1Chr 4:40	8252
his days the land was *q* ten years	2Chr 14:1	8252
and the kingdom was *q* before him	2Chr 14:5	8252
So the realm of Jehoshaphat was *q*	2Chr 20:30	8252
and the city was *q*, after that	2Chr 23:21	8252
I have lain still and been *q*	Job 3:13	8252
had I rest, neither was I *q*	Job 3:26	5117
being wholly at ease and *q*	Job 21:23	7961
them that are *q* in the land	Ps 35:20	7282
are they glad because they be *q*	Ps 107:30	8367
shall be *q* from fear of evil	Prov 1:33	7599
q more than the cry of him that	Eccl 9:17	5183
say unto him, Take heed, and be *q*	Is 7:4	8252
whole earth is at rest, and is *q*	Is 14:7	8252
dwellings, and in *q* resting places	Is 32:18	7600
see Jerusalem a *q* habitation	Is 33:20	7600
and shall be in rest, and be *q*	Jer 30:10	7599
how long will it be ere thou be *q*	Jer 47:6	8252
How can it be *q*, seeing the LORD	Jer 47:7	8252
it cannot be *q*	Jer 49:23	8252
And this Seraiah was a *q* prince	Jer 51:59	4496
depart from thee, and I will be *q*	Eze 16:42	8252
Though they be *q*, and likewise	Nah 1:12	8003
spoken against, ye ought to be *q*	Acts 19:36	2687

And that ye study to be *q*, and to	1Th 4:11	2270
that we may lead a *q* and peaceable	1Ti 2:2	2263
q spirit, which is in the sight	1Pet 3:4	2272

QUIETED
q myself, as a child that is	Ps 131:2	1826
toward the north country have *q*	Zec 6:8	5117

QUIETETH
when he *q* the earth by the south	Job 37:17	8252

QUIETLY
in the gate to speak with him *q*	2Sa 3:27	7987
q wait for the salvation of the	Lam 3:26	

QUIETNESS
the country was in *q* forty years	Judg 8:28	8252
q unto Israel in his days	1Chr 22:9	8253
he shall not feel *q* in his belly	Job 20:20	7961
When he giveth *q*, who then can	Job 34:29	8252
q therewith, than an house full	Prov 17:1	7962
Better is an handful with *q*	Eccl 4:6	5183
in *q* and in confidence shall be	Is 30:15	8252
and the effect of righteousness *q*	Is 32:17	8252
that by thee we enjoy great *q*	Acts 24:2	1515
Christ, that with *q* they work	2Th 3:12	2271

QUIRINIUS See CYRENIUS.

QUIT
then shall he that smote him be *q*	Ex 21:19	5352
the owner of the ox shall be *q*	Ex 21:28	5355
then we will be *q* of thine oath	Josh 2:20	5355
q yourselves like men, O ye	1Sa 4:9	1961
q yourselves like men, and fight	1Sa 4:9	
q you like men, be strong	1Cor 16:13	407

QUITE
hath *q* devoured also our money	Gen 31:15	
q break down their images	Ex 23:24	
thou shalt *q* take away their	Num 17:10	3615
q pluck down all their high	Num 33:52	
sent them away, and he is *q* gone	2Sa 3:24	
and is wisdom driven *q* from me	Job 6:13	5080
Thy bow was made *q* naked,	Hab 3:9	6181

QUIVER
I pray thee, thy weapons, thy *q*	Gen 27:3	8522
The *q* rattleth against him, the	Job 39:23	827
man that hath his *q* full of them	Ps 127:5	827
Elam bare the *q* with chariots of	Is 22:6	827
in his *q* hath he hid me	Is 49:2	827
Their *q* is as an open sepulchre,	Jer 5:16	827
of his *q* to enter into my reins	Lam 3:13	827

QUIVERED
my lips *q* at the voice	Hab 3:16	6750

R

RAAMA See RAAMAH.

RAAMAH (ra'-a-mah)
1. A son of Cush.
Seba, and Havilah, and Sabtah, and *R*	Gen 10:7	7484
and the sons of *R*	Gen 10:7	7484
Seba, and Havilah, and Sabta, and *R*	1Chr 1:9	7484
And the sons of *R*	1Chr 1:9	7484
2. A place in Arabia.
The merchants of Sheba and *R*	Eze 27:22	7484

RAAMIAH (ra-a-mi'-ah) A clan leader in exile.
Jeshua, Nehemiah, Azariah, *R*	Neh 7:7	7485

RAAMSES (ra-am'-seze) See RAMESES. An Egyptian city.
treasure cities, Pithom and *R*	Ex 1:11	7486

RABBAH (rab'-bah) See RABBATH.
1. An Ammonite city.
unto Aroer that is before *R*	Josh 13:25	7237
children of Ammon, and besieged *R*	2Sa 11:1	7237
Joab fought against *R* of the	2Sa 12:26	7237
and said, I have fought against *R*	2Sa 12:27	7237
the people together, and went to *R*	2Sa 12:29	7237
of *R* of the children of Ammon	2Sa 17:27	7237
of Ammon, and came and besieged *R*	1Chr 20:1	7237
And Joab smote *R*, and destroyed it	1Chr 20:1	7237
to be heard in *R* of the Ammonites	Jer 49:2	7237
cry, ye daughters of *R*, gird you	Jer 49:3	7237
I will make *R* a stable for camels	Eze 25:5	7237
kindle a fire in the wall of *R*	Amos 1:14	7237
2. A city in Judah.
which is Kirjath-jearim, and *R*	Josh 15:60	7237

RABBATH (rab'-bath) See RABBAH. Same as Rabbah 1.
is it not in *R* of the children of	Deut 3:11	7237
may come to *R* of the Ammonites	Eze 21:20	7237

RABBI (rab'-bi) See RABBONI. A Jewish title meaning "teacher."
and to be called of men, *R*, *R*	Mt 23:7	4461
But be not ye called *R*	Mt 23:8	4461
They said unto him, *R*, (which is	Jn 1:38	4461
answered and saith unto him, *R*	Jn 1:49	4461
by night, and said unto him, *R*	Jn 3:2	4461
unto John, and said unto him, *R*	Jn 3:26	4461
of the sea, they said unto him, *R*	Jn 6:25	4461

RABBITH (rab'-bith) A city in Issachar.
And *R*, and Kishion, and Abez,	Josh 19:20	7245

RABBONI (rab-bo'-ni) See RABBI. A Jewish title of respect.
herself, and saith unto him, *R*	Jn 20:16	4462

RAB-MAG A Babylonian prince.
Rab-saris, Nergal-sharezer, *R*	Jer 39:3	7248
Rab-saris, and Nergal-sharezer, *R*	Jer 39:13	7248

RAB-SARIS
1. A Babylonian prince.
Samgar-nebo, Sarsechim, *R*	Jer 39:3	7249
the guard sent, and Nebushasban, *R*	Jer 39:13	7249
2. An Assyrian officer.
king of Assyria sent Tartan and *R*	2Kin 18:17	7249

RAB-SHAKEH (rab'-sha-keh) See RABSHAKEH. An Assyrian officer.
R from Lachish to king Hezekiah	2Kin 18:17	7262
R said unto them, Speak ye now to	2Kin 18:19	7262

and Shebna, and Joah, unto *R* 2Kin 18:26   7262
But *R* said unto them, Hath my 2Kin 18:27   7262
Then *R* stood and cried with a loud 2Kin 18:28   7262
rent, and told him the words of *R* 2Kin 18:37   7262
God will hear all the words of *R* 2Kin 19:4   7262
So *R* returned, and found the king 2Kin 19:8   7262

RABSHAKEH *(rab'-sha-keh)* See Rab-shakeh. *Same as Rab-shakeh.*
the king of Assyria sent *R* from ....Is 36:2   7262
R said unto them, Say ye now to ....Is 36:4   7262
Eliakim and Shebna and Joah unto *R* ...Is 36:11   7262
But *R* said, Hath my master sent ....Is 36:12   7262
Then *R* stood, and cried with a..............Is 36:13   7262
rent, and told him the words of *R* ....Is 36:22   7262
thy God will hear the words of *R* ....Is 37:4   7262
So *R* returned, and found the king ....Is 37:8   7262

RACA *(ra'-cah)* *A Jewish term of disrespect.*
shall say to his brother, *R* ....Mt 5:22   4469

RACAL See Rachal.

RACE
as a strong man to run a *r* ....Ps 19:5   734
that the *r* is not to the swift, ...Eccl 9:11   4793
they which run in a *r* run all.................1Cor 9:24   4712
the *r* that is set before us ....Heb 12:1   73

RACHAB *(ra'kab)* See Rahab. *Same as Rahab; ancestor of Jesus.*
And Salmon begat Booz of *R* ....Mt 1:5   4477

RACHAL *(ra'-kal)* *A city in Judah.*
And to them which were in *R*.................1Sa 30:29   7403

RACHEL *(ra'-chel)* See Rachel's, Rahel. *Wife of Jacob.*
R his daughter cometh with the ....Gen 29:6   7354
R came with her father's sheep..............Gen 29:9   7354
when Jacob saw *R* the daughter of ....Gen 29:10   7354
And Jacob kissed *R*, and lifted up.........Gen 29:11   7354
Jacob told *R* that he was her ....Gen 29:12   7354
and the name of the younger was *R* ......Gen 29:16   7354
but *R* was beautiful and well ....Gen 29:17   7354
And Jacob loved *R* ....Gen 29:18   7354
years for *R* thy younger daughter ....Gen 29:18   7354
And Jacob served seven years for *R* ......Gen 29:20   7354
did not I serve with thee for *R* ....Gen 29:25   7354
he gave him *R* his daughter to ....Gen 29:28   7354
Laban gave to *R* his daughter................Gen 29:29   7354
And he went in also unto *R* ....Gen 29:30   7354
he loved also *R* more than Leah, ...Gen 29:30   7354
but *R* was barren ....Gen 29:31   7354
when *R* saw that she bare Jacob no ......Gen 30:1   7354
no children, *R* envied her sister ....Gen 30:1   7354
anger was kindled against *R* ....Gen 30:2   7354
R said, God hath judged me, and ....Gen 30:6   7354
R said, With great wrestlings ....Gen 30:8   7354
Then *R* said to Leah, Give me, I ....Gen 30:14   7354
R said, Therefore he shall lie ....Gen 30:15   7354
And God remembered *R*, and God ....Gen 30:22   7354
when *R* had born Joseph, that ....Gen 30:25   7354
And Jacob sent and called *R* ....Gen 31:4   7354
And *R* and Leah answered and said ......Gen 31:14   7354
R had stolen the images that were ....Gen 31:19   7354
knew not that *R* had stolen them ....Gen 31:32   7354
Now *R* had taken the images, and ....Gen 31:34   7354
the children unto Leah, and unto *R*.......Gen 33:1   7354
Leah and her children after, and *R*........Gen 33:2   7354
and after came Joseph near and *R*........Gen 33:7   7354
R travailed, and she had hard ....Gen 35:16   7354
R died, and was buried in the way.........Gen 35:19   7354
The sons of *R* ....Gen 35:24   7354
The sons of *R* Jacob's wife...................Gen 46:19   7354
These are the sons of *R*, which ....Gen 46:22   7354
Laban gave unto *R* his daughter ....Gen 46:25   7354
R died by me in the land of ....Gen 48:7   7354
is come into thine house like *R* ....Ruth 4:11   7354
R weeping for her children, and ....Mt 2:18   4478

RACHEL'S *(ra'-chelz)*
Bilhah *R* maid conceived again, and......Gen 30:7   7354
tent, and entered into *R* tent ....Gen 31:33   7354
pillar of *R* grave unto this day ....Gen 35:20   7354
And the sons of Bilhah, *R* handmaid ......Gen 35:25   7354
by *R* sepulchre in the border of 1Sa 10:2   7354

RADDAI *(rad'-dahee)* *Son of Jesse.*
the fourth, *R* the fifth, ...1Chr 2:14   7288

RAFTERS
house are cedar, and our *r* of fir ....Song 1:17   7351

RAGAU *(ra'-gaw)* See Reu. *Father of Saruch; ancestor of Jesus.*
of Saruch, which was the son of *R*..........Lk 3:35   4466

RAGE
So he turned and went away in a *r* 2Kin 5:12   2534
coming in, and thy *r* against me 2Kin 19:27   7264
Because thy *r* against me and thy 2Kin 19:28   7264
for he was in a *r* with him 2Chr 16:10   2197
ye have slain them in a *r* that 2Chr 28:9   2197
the ground with fierceness and *r* ....Job 39:24   7267
Cast abroad the *r* of thy wrath ....Job 40:11   5678
Why do the heathen *r*, and the ....Ps 2:1   7283
because of the *r* of mine enemies...........Ps 7:6   5678
For jealousy is the *r* of a man ....Prov 6:34   2534
man, whether he *r* or laugh.................Prov 29:9   7264
coming in, and thy *r* against me ....Is 37:28   7264
Because thy *r* against me, and thy ....Is 37:29   7264
and *r*, ye chariots.............................Jer 46:9   1984
Then Nebuchadnezzar in his *r* ....Dan 3:13   7266
sword for the *r* of their tongue ....Hos 7:16   2195
chariots shall *r* in the streets ....Nah 2:4   1984
hast said, Why did the heathen *r* ....Acts 4:25   5433

RAGED
The heathen *r*, the kingdoms were ....Ps 46:6   1993

RAGETH
but the fool *r*, and is confident ....Prov 14:16   5674

RAGGED
and into the tops of the *r* rocks ....Is 2:21

RAGING
Thou rulest the *r* of the sea ....Ps 89:9   1348
is a mocker, strong drink is *r* ....Prov 20:1   1993
and the sea ceased from her *r* ....Jonah 1:15   2197
the wind and the *r* of the water.............Lk 8:24   2830
R waves of the sea, foaming out ....Jude 13   66

RAGS
shall clothe a man with *r* ....Prov 23:21   7168
righteousnesses are as filthy *r* ....Is 64:6   899
old cast clouts and old rotten *r* ....Jer 38:11   4418
rotten *r* under thine armholes...............Jer 38:12   4418

RAGUEL *(ra-gu'-el)* *Father-in-law of Moses.*
the son of *R* the Midianite, ...Num 10:29   7467

RAHAB *(ra'-hab)* See Rachab.
  1. A Jericho woman who befriended the spies.
into an harlot's house, named *R* ....Josh 2:1   7343
the king of Jericho sent unto *R* ....Josh 2:3   7343
only *R* the harlot shall live, she ....Josh 6:17   7343
spies went in, and brought out *R* ....Josh 6:23   7343
Joshua saved *R* the harlot alive,............Josh 6:25   7343
By faith the harlot *R* perished ....Heb 11:31   4460
Likewise also was not *R* the ....Jas 2:25   4460
  2. A symbolic name for Egypt.
I will make mention of *R* and ....Ps 87:4   7294
Thou hast broken *R* in pieces ....Ps 89:10   7294
Art thou not it that hath cut *R*...............Is 51:9   7294

RAHAM *(ra'-ham)* *Son of Shema.*
And Shema begat *R*, the father of 1Chr 2:44   7357

RAHEL *(ra'-hel)* See Rachel. *Same as Rachel.*
R weeping for her children ....Jer 31:15   7354

RAIL
He wrote also letters to *r* on the 2Chr 32:17   2778

RAILED
and he *r* on them 1Sa 25:14   5860
And they that passed by *r* on him ....Mk 15:29   987
which were hanged *r* on him ....Lk 23:39   987

RAILER
covetous, or an idolater, or a *r*..............1Cor 5:11   3060

RAILING
evil for evil, or *r* for *r* 1Pet 3:9   3059
bring not *r* accusation against...............2Pet 2:11   989
bring against him a *r* accusation ....Jude 9   988

RAILINGS
whereof cometh envy, strife, *r* 1Ti 6:4   988

RAIMENT
silver, and jewels of gold, and *r* ....Gen 24:53   899
Rebekah took goodly *r* of her ....Gen 27:15   899
and he smelled the smell of his *r* ....Gen 27:27   899
me bread to eat, and *r* to put on, ...Gen 28:20   899
shaved himself, and changed his *r* ....Gen 41:14   8071
he gave each man changes of *r* ....Gen 45:22   8071
of silver, and five changes of *r*..............Gen 45:22   8071
silver, and jewels of gold, and *r*............Ex 3:22   8071
silver, and jewels of gold, and *r*............Ex 12:35   8071
her food, her *r*, and her duty of ....Ex 21:10   3682
for ox, for ass, for sheep, for *r* ....Ex 22:9   8008
take thy neighbour's *r* to pledge ....Ex 22:26   8008
only, it is his *r* for his skin ....Ex 22:27   8071
it be any vessel of wood, or *r* ....Lev 11:32   899

R

And purify all your r, and all that .... Num 31:20   899
Thy r waxed not old upon thee, ... Deut 8:4   8071
stranger, in giving him food and r .... Deut 10:18   8071
she shall put the r of her .... Deut 21:13   8071
and so shalt thou do with his r .... Deut 22:3   8071
that he may sleep in his own r .... Deut 24:13   8008
nor take a widow's r to pledge .... Deut 24:17   899
and with iron, and with very much r ...... Josh 22:8   8008
under his r upon his right thigh .... Judg 3:16   4055
purple r that was on the kings of .... Judg 8:26   899
put thy r upon thee, and get thee .... Ruth 3:3   8071
himself, and put on other r 1Sa 28:8   899
of gold, and ten changes of r 2Kin 5:5   899
thence silver, and gold, and r 2Kin 7:8   899
silver, and vessels of gold, and r 2Chr 9:24   8008
she sent r to clothe Mordecai, and .... Est 4:4   899
dust, and prepare r as the clay .... Job 27:16   4403
unto the king in r of needlework .... Ps 45:14   7553
as the r of those that are slain, ... Is 14:19   3830
and I will stain all my r .... Is 63:3   4403
thy r was of fine linen, and silk, ... Eze 16:13   4403
will clothe thee with change of r .... Zec 3:4   4254
John had his r of camel's hair .... Mt 3:4   1742
than meat, and the body than r .... Mt 6:25   1742
And why take ye thought for r .... Mt 6:28   1742
A man clothed in soft r .... Mt 11:8   2440
his r was white as the light .... Mt 17:2   2440
from him, and put his own r on him ...... Mt 27:31   2440
lightning, and his r white as snow .... Mt 28:3   1742
his r became shining, exceeding .... Mk 9:3   2440
A man clothed in soft r .... Lk 7:25   2440
his r was white and glistering .... Lk 9:29   2441
which stripped him of his r .... Lk 10:30   2441
meat, and the body is more than r ...... Lk 12:23   1742
And they parted his r, and cast .... Lk 23:34   2440
They parted my r among them .... Jn 19:24   2440
and blasphemed, he shook his r .... Acts 18:6   2440
kept the r of them that slew him .... Acts 22:20   2440
r let us be therewith content 1Ti 6:8   4629
come in also a poor man in vile r .... Jas 2:2   2066
same shall be clothed in white r .... Rev 3:5   2440
and white r, that thou mayest be .... Rev 3:18   2440
sitting, clothed in white r .... Rev 4:4   2440

RAIN

not caused it to r upon the earth .... Gen 2:5   4305
I will cause it to r upon the .... Gen 7:4   4305
the r was upon the earth forty .... Gen 7:12   1653
the r from heaven was restrained .... Gen 8:2   1653
it to r a very grievous hail .... Ex 9:18   4305
the r was not poured upon the .... Ex 9:33   4306
And when Pharaoh saw that the r .... Ex 9:34   4306
I will r bread from heaven for .... Ex 16:4   4305
I will give you r in due season .... Lev 26:4   1653
drinketh water of the r of heaven .... Deut 11:11   4306
That I will give you the r of .... Deut 11:14   4306
in his due season, the first r .... Deut 11:14   4456
and the latter r .... Deut 11:14   3138
up the heaven, that there be no r .... Deut 11:17   4306
the heaven to give the r unto thy .... Deut 28:12   4306
make the r of thy land powder .... Deut 28:24   4306
My doctrine shall drop as the r .... Deut 32:2   4306
as the small r upon the tender .... Deut 32:2   8164
and he shall send thunder and r 1Sa 12:17   4306
LORD sent thunder and r that day 1Sa 12:18   4306
be no dew, neither let there be r 2Sa 1:21   4306
earth by clear shining after r 2Sa 23:4   4306
is shut up, and there is no r 1Kin 8:35   4306
give r upon thy land, which thou 1Kin 8:36   4306
not be dew nor r these years 1Kin 17:1   4306
there had been no r in the land 1Kin 17:7   1653
the LORD sendeth r upon the earth 1Kin 17:14   1653
I will send r upon the earth 1Kin 18:1   4306
is a sound of abundance of r 1Kin 18:41   1653
down, that the r stop thee not 1Kin 18:44   1653
and wind, and there was a great r 1Kin 18:45   1653
see wind, neither shall ye see r 2Kin 3:17   1653
is shut up, and there is no r 2Chr 6:26   4306
send r upon thy land, which 2Chr 6:27   4306
shut up heaven that there be no r 2Chr 7:13   4306
this matter, and for the great .... Ezr 10:9   1653
many, and it is a time of much r .... Ezr 10:13   1653
Who giveth r upon the earth, and .... Job 5:10   4306
shall r it upon him while he is .... Job 20:23   4305
When he made a decree for the r .... Job 28:26   4306
they waited for me as for the r .... Job 29:23   4306
mouth wide as for the latter r .... Job 29:23   4456
they pour down r according to the .... Job 36:27   4306
likewise to the small r, and to .... Job 37:6   1653
to the great r of his strength .... Job 37:6   1653
To cause it to r on the earth .... Job 38:26   4305

Hath the r a father .... Job 38:28   4306
Upon the wicked he shall r snares .... Ps 11:6   4305
O God, didst send a plentiful r .... Ps 68:9   1653
down like r upon the mown grass .... Ps 72:6   4306
the r also filleth the pools .... Ps 84:6   4175
He gave them hail for r, and .... Ps 105:32   1653
he maketh lightnings for the r .... Ps 135:7   4306
who prepareth r for the earth .... Ps 147:8   4306
is as a cloud of the latter r .... Prov 16:15   4456
is like clouds and wind without r .... Prov 25:14   1653
The north wind driveth away r .... Prov 25:23   1653
as r in harvest, so honour is not .... Prov 26:1   1653
sweeping r which leaveth no food .... Prov 28:3   4306
If the clouds be full of r .... Eccl 11:3   1653
nor the clouds return after the r .... Eccl 12:2   1653
is past, the r is over and gone .... Song 2:11   1653
for a covert from storm and from r .... Is 4:6   4306
that they r no r upon it .... Is 5:6   4305
that they r no r upon it .... Is 5:6   4306
shall he give the r of thy seed .... Is 30:23   4306
an ash, and the r doth nourish it .... Is 44:14   1653
For as the r cometh down, and the .... Is 55:10   1653
and there hath been no latter r .... Jer 3:3   4456
the LORD our God, that giveth r .... Jer 5:24   1653
he maketh lightnings with r .... Jer 10:13   4306
for there was no r in the earth .... Jer 14:4   1653
of the Gentiles that can cause r .... Jer 14:22   1653
he maketh lightnings with r .... Jer 51:16   4306
is in the cloud in the day of r .... Eze 1:28   1653
I will r upon him, and upon his .... Eze 38:22   4305
are with him, and overflowing r .... Eze 38:22   1653
and he shall come unto us as the r .... Hos 6:3   1653
latter and former r unto the earth .... Hos 6:3   3384
come and r righteousness upon you ...... Hos 10:12   3384
given you the former r moderately .... Joel 2:23   4175
cause to come down for you the r .... Joel 2:23   1653
the former r, and the latter .... Joel 2:23   4175
the latter r in the first month .... Joel 2:23   4456
I have withholden the r from you .... Amos 4:7   1653
and I caused it to r upon one city .... Amos 4:7   4305
caused it not to r upon another .... Amos 4:7   4305
Ask ye of the LORD r in the time .... Zec 10:1   4306
in the time of the latter r .... Zec 10:1   4456
clouds, and give them showers of r ...... Zec 10:1   1653
even upon them shall be no r .... Zec 14:17   4306
up, and come not, that have no r .... Zec 14:18

sendeth r on the just and on the .... Mt 5:45   *1026*
the r descended, and the floods .... Mt 7:25   *1028*
the r descended, and the floods .... Mt 7:27   *1028*
gave us r from heaven, and .... Acts 14:17   *5205*
one, because of the present r .... Acts 28:2   *5205*
in the r that cometh oft upon it .... Heb 6:7   *5205*
he receive the early and latter r .... Jas 5:7   *5205*
earnestly that it might not r .... Jas 5:17   *1026*
again, and the heaven gave r .... Jas 5:18   *5205*
that it r not in the days of .... Rev 11:6   *1026,5205*

RAINBOW

there was a r round about the .... Rev 4:3   *2463*
a r was upon his head, and his .... Rev 10:1   *2463*

RAINED

Then the LORD r upon Sodom .... Gen 19:24   4305
the LORD r hail upon the land of .... Ex 9:23   4305
had r down manna upon them to eat ..... Ps 78:24   4305
He r flesh also upon them as dust .... Ps 78:27   4305
nor r upon in the day of .... Eze 22:24   1656
one piece was r upon, and the .... Amos 4:7   4305
piece whereupon it r not withered .... Amos 4:7   4305
Lot went out of Sodom it r fire .... Lk 17:29   *1026*
it r not on the earth by the .... Jas 5:17   *1026*

RAINY

dropping in a very r day and a .... Prov 27:15   5464

RAISE

her, and r up seed to thy brother .... Gen 38:8   6965
Thou shalt not r a false report .... Ex 23:1   5375
The LORD thy God will r up unto .... Deut 18:15   6965
I will r them up a Prophet from .... Deut 18:18   6965
r up unto his brother a name in .... Deut 25:7   6965
r thereon a great heap of stones, ... Josh 8:29   6965
to r up the name of the dead upon .... Ruth 4:5   6965
to r up the name of the dead upon .... Ruth 4:10   6965
I will r me up a faithful priest, ... 1Sa 2:35   6965
I will r up evil against thee out 2Sa 12:11   6965
to r him up from the earth 2Sa 12:17   6965
Moreover the LORD shall r him up 1Kin 14:14   6965
that I will r up thy seed after 1Chr 17:11   6965
who are ready to r up their .... Job 3:8   5782
r up their way against me, and .... Job 19:12   5549
they r up against me the ways of .... Job 30:12   5549
r me up, that I may requite them .... Ps 41:10   6965

shall *r* up a cry of destruction	Is 15:5	5782
I will *r* forts against thee	Is 29:3	6965
I will *r* up the decayed places	Is 44:26	6965
to *r* up the tribes of Jacob	Is 49:6	6965
thou shalt *r* up the foundations	Is 58:12	6965
they shall *r* up the former	Is 61:4	6965
that I will *r* unto David a	Jer 23:5	6965
whom I will *r* up unto them	Jer 30:9	6965
For, lo, I will *r* and cause to	Jer 50:9	5782
and fall, and none shall *r* him up	Jer 50:32	6965
I will *r* up against Babylon, and	Jer 51:1	5782
I will *r* up thy lovers against	Eze 23:22	5782
I will *r* up for them a plant of	Eze 34:29	6965
in the third day he will *r* us up	Hos 6:2	6965
I will *r* them out of the place	Joel 3:7	5782
there is none to *r* her up	Amos 5:2	6965
I will *r* up against you a nation,	Amos 6:14	6965
In that day will I *r* up the	Amos 9:11	6965
I will *r* up his ruins, and I will	Amos 9:11	6965
then shall we *r* against him seven	Mic 5:5	6965
and there are that *r* up strife	Hab 1:3	5375
I *r* up the Chaldeans, that bitter	Hab 1:6	6965
I will *r* up a shepherd in the	Zec 11:16	6965
to *r* up children unto Abraham	Mt 3:9	*1453*
r the dead, cast out devils	Mt 10:8	*1453*
r up seed unto his brother	Mt 22:24	*450*
r up seed unto his brother	Mk 12:19	*1817*
to *r* up children unto Abraham	Lk 3:8	*1453*
r up seed unto his brother	Lk 20:28	*1817*
and in three days I will *r* it up	Jn 2:19	*1453*
but should *r* it up again at the	Jn 6:39	*450*
I will *r* him up at the last day	Jn 6:40	*450*
I will *r* him up at the last day	Jn 6:44	*450*
I will *r* him up at the last day	Jn 6:54	*450*
he would *r* up Christ to sit on	Acts 2:30	*450*
r up unto you of your brethren	Acts 3:22	*450*
r up unto you of your brethren	Acts 7:37	*450*
you, that God should *r* the dead	Acts 26:8	*1453*
will also *r* up us by his own	1Cor 6:14	*1825*
Jesus shall *r* up us also by Jesus	2Cor 4:14	*1453*
that God was able to *r* him up	Heb 11:19	*1453*
sick, and the Lord shall *r* him up	Jas 5:15	*1453*

RAISED

for this cause have I *r* thee up	Ex 9:16	5975
whom he *r* up in their stead, them	Josh 5:7	6965
they *r* over him a great heap of	Josh 7:26	6965
Nevertheless the LORD *r* up judges	Judg 2:16	6965
when the LORD *r* them up judges,	Judg 2:18	6965
the LORD *r* up a deliverer to the	Judg 3:9	6965
the LORD *r* them up a deliverer,	Judg 3:15	6965
and the man who was *r* up on high	2Sa 23:1	6965
king Solomon *r* a levy out of all	1Kin 5:13	5927
of the levy which king Solomon *r*	1Kin 9:15	5927
r it up to the towers, and another	2Chr 32:5	5927
r it up a very great height, and	2Chr 33:14	1361
all them whose spirit God had *r*	Ezr 1:5	5782
nor be *r* out of their sleep	Job 14:12	5782
I *r* thee up under the apple tree	Song 8:5	5782
it hath *r* up from their thrones	Is 14:9	6965
they *r* up the palaces thereof	Is 23:13	6209
Who *r* up the righteous man from	Is 41:2	5782
I have *r* up one from the north,	Is 41:25	5782
I have *r* him up in righteousness,	Is 45:13	5782
a great nation shall be *r* from	Jer 6:22	5782
a great whirlwind shall be *r* up	Jer 25:32	5782
The LORD hath *r* up prophets in	Jer 29:15	6965
many kings shall be *r* up from the	Jer 50:41	5782
the LORD hath *r* up the spirit of	Jer 51:11	5782
it *r* up itself on one side, and it	Dan 7:5	6966
I *r* up of your sons for prophets,	Amos 2:11	6965
for he is *r* up out of his holy	Zec 2:13	5782
r up thy sons, O Zion, against	Zec 9:13	5782
Then Joseph being *r* from sleep	Mt 1:24	*1326*
the deaf hear, the dead are *r* up	Mt 11:5	*1453*
and be *r* again the third day	Mt 16:21	*1453*
the third day he shall be *r* again	Mt 17:23	*1453*
hath *r* up an horn of salvation	Lk 1:69	*1453*
the deaf hear, the dead are *r*	Lk 7:22	*1453*
be slain, and be *r* the third day	Lk 9:22	*1453*
Now that the dead are *r*, even	Lk 20:37	*1453*
dead, whom he *r* from the dead	Jn 12:1	*1453*
whom he had *r* from the dead	Jn 12:9	*1453*
r him from the dead, bare record	Jn 12:17	*1453*
Whom God hath *r* up, having loosed	Acts 2:24	*450*
This Jesus hath God *r* up, whereof	Acts 2:32	*450*
whom God hath *r* from the dead	Acts 3:15	*1453*
having *r* up his Son Jesus, sent	Acts 3:26	*450*
whom God *r* from the dead, even by	Acts 4:10	*1453*
The God of our fathers *r* up Jesus	Acts 5:30	*1453*
Him God *r* up the third day, and	Acts 10:40	*1453*

r him up, saying, Arise up	Acts 12:7	*1453*
he *r* up unto them David to be	Acts 13:22	*1453*
promise *r* unto Israel a Saviour	Acts 13:23	*1453*
But God *r* him from the dead	Acts 13:30	*1453*
in that he hath *r* up Jesus again	Acts 13:33	*450*
that he *r* him up from the dead	Acts 13:34	*450*
But he, whom God *r* again, saw no	Acts 13:37	*1453*
r persecution against Paul and	Acts 13:50	*1892*
in that he hath *r* him from the	Acts 17:31	*450*
if we believe on him that *r* up	Rom 4:24	*1453*
was *r* again for our justification	Rom 4:25	*1453*
that like as Christ was *r* up from	Rom 6:4	*1453*
Knowing that Christ being *r* from	Rom 6:9	*1453*
to him who is *r* from the dead,	Rom 7:4	*1453*
But if the Spirit of him that *r*	Rom 8:11	*1453*
he that *r* up Christ from the dead	Rom 8:11	*1453*
same purpose have I *r* thee up	Rom 9:17	*1825*
that God hath *r* him from the dead	Rom 10:9	*1453*
And God hath both *r* up the Lord	1Cor 6:14	*1453*
of God that he *r* up Christ	1Cor 15:15	*1453*
whom he *r* not up, if so be that	1Cor 15:15	*1453*
rise not, then is not Christ *r*	1Cor 15:16	*1453*
And if Christ be not *r*, your faith	1Cor 15:17	*1453*
will say, How are the dead *r* up	1Cor 15:35	*1453*
it is *r* in incorruption	1Cor 15:42	*1453*
it is *r* in glory	1Cor 15:43	*1453*
it is *r* in power	1Cor 15:43	*1453*
it is *r* a spiritual body	1Cor 15:44	*1453*
the dead shall be *r* incorruptible	1Cor 15:52	*1453*
Knowing that he which *r* up the	2Cor 4:14	*1453*
Father, who *r* him from the dead,	Gal 1:1	*1453*
when he *r* him from the dead, and	Eph 1:20	*1453*
hath *r* us up together, and made us	Eph 2:6	*4891*
who hath *r* him from the dead	Col 2:12	*1453*
whom he *r* from the dead, even	1Th 1:10	*1453*
r from the dead according to my	2Ti 2:8	*1453*
their dead *r* to life again	Heb 11:35	*386*
that *r* him up from the dead, and	1Pet 1:21	*1453*

RAISER

a *r* of taxes in the glory of the	Dan 11:20	5674

RAISETH

He *r* up the poor out of the dust,	1Sa 2:8	6965
When he *r* up himself, the mighty	Job 41:25	7613
r the stormy wind, which lifteth	Ps 107:25	5975
He *r* up the poor out of the dust,	Ps 113:7	6965
r up all those that be bowed down	Ps 145:14	2210
the LORD *r* them that are bowed	Ps 146:8	2210
For as the Father *r* up the dead	Jn 5:21	*1453*
but in God which *r* the dead	2Cor 1:9	*1453*

RAISING

who ceaseth from *r* after he hath	Hos 7:4	5872
neither *r* up the people, neither	Acts 24:12	*4160,1999*

RAISINS

corn, and an hundred clusters of *r*	1Sa 25:18	6778
of figs, and two clusters of *r*	1Sa 30:12	6778
bread, and an hundred bunches of *r*	2Sa 16:1	6778
cakes of figs, and bunches of *r*	1Chr 12:40	6778

RAKEM (ra'-kem) *Son of Sheresh.*

and his sons were Ulam and R	1Chr 7:16	7552

RAKKATH (rah'-kath) *A city in Naphtali.*

are Ziddim, Zer, and Hammath, *R*	Josh 19:35	7557

RAKKON (rak'-kon) *A city in Dan.*

And Me-jarkon, and *R*, with the	Josh 19:46	7542

RAM (ram)
1. *Father of Aminadab.*

And Hezron begat *R*	Ruth 4:19	7410
and *R* begat Amminadab	Ruth 4:19	7410
Jerahmeel, and *R*, and Chelubai	1Chr 2:9	7410
And *R* begat Amminadab	1Chr 2:10	7410

2. *Son of Jerahmeel.*

R, the firstborn, and Bunah, and	1Chr 2:25	7410
the sons of *R* the firstborn of	1Chr 2:27	7410

3. *Head of Elihu's family.*

the Buzite, of the kindred of *R*	Job 32:2	7410

4. *Male sheep.*

a *r* of three years old, and a	Gen 15:9	352
behold behind him a *r* caught in a	Gen 22:13	352
and Abraham went and took the *r*	Gen 22:13	352
Thou shalt also take one *r*	Ex 29:15	352
hands upon the head of the *r*	Ex 29:15	352
And thou shalt slay the *r*, and thou	Ex 29:16	352
And thou shalt cut the *r* in pieces	Ex 29:17	352
burn the whole *r* upon the altar	Ex 29:18	352
And thou shalt take the other *r*	Ex 29:19	352
hands upon the head of the *r*	Ex 29:19	352
Then shalt thou kill the *r*	Ex 29:20	352
thou shalt take of the *r* the fat	Ex 29:22	352

R

for it is a *r* of consecration	Ex 29:22	352
of the *r* of Aaron's consecration	Ex 29:26	352
of the *r* of the consecration,	Ex 29:27	352
take the *r* of the consecration	Ex 29:31	352
sons shall eat the flesh of the *r*	Ex 29:32	352
a *r* without blemish out of the	Lev 5:15	352
the *r* of the trespass offering	Lev 5:16	352
he shall bring a *r* without	Lev 5:18	352
a *r* without blemish out of the	Lev 6:6	352
he brought the *r* for the burnt	Lev 8:18	352
hands upon the head of the *r*	Lev 8:18	352
And he cut the *r* into pieces	Lev 8:20	352
burnt the whole *r* upon the altar	Lev 8:21	352
other ram, the *r* of consecration	Lev 8:22	352
hands upon the head of the *r*	Lev 8:22	352
for of the *r* of consecration it	Lev 8:29	352
a *r* for a burnt offering, without	Lev 9:2	352
a *r* for peace offerings, to	Lev 9:4	352
the *r* for a sacrifice of peace	Lev 9:18	352
fat of the bullock and of the *r*	Lev 9:19	352
and a *r* for a burnt offering	Lev 16:3	352
one *r* for a burnt offering	Lev 16:5	352
even a *r* for a trespass offering	Lev 19:21	352
an atonement for him with the *r*	Lev 19:22	352
beside the *r* of the atonement,	Num 5:8	352
one *r* without blemish for peace	Num 6:14	352
he shall offer the *r* for a	Num 6:17	352
take the sodden shoulder of the *r*	Num 6:19	352
One young bullock, one *r*, one	Num 7:15	352
One young bullock, one *r*, one	Num 7:21	352
One young bullock, one *r*, one	Num 7:27	352
One young bullock, one *r*, one	Num 7:33	352
One young bullock, one *r*, one	Num 7:39	352
One young bullock, one *r*, one	Num 7:45	352
One young bullock, one *r*, one	Num 7:51	352
One young bullock, one *r*, one	Num 7:57	352
One young bullock, one *r*, one	Num 7:63	352
One young bullock, one *r*, one	Num 7:69	352
One young bullock, one *r*, one	Num 7:75	352
One young bullock, one *r*, one	Num 7:81	352
Or for a *r*, thou shalt prepare	Num 15:6	352
for one bullock, or for one *r*	Num 15:11	352
on every altar a bullock and a *r*	Num 23:2	352
upon every altar a bullock and a *r*	Num 23:4	352
a bullock and a *r* on every altar	Num 23:14	352
a bullock and a *r* on every altar	Num 23:30	352
two young bullocks, and one *r*	Num 28:11	352
mingled with oil, for one *r*	Num 28:12	352
the third part of an hin unto a *r*	Num 28:14	352
two young bullocks, and one *r*	Num 28:19	352
and two tenth deals for a *r*	Num 28:20	352
two young bullocks, one *r*	Num 28:27	352
two tenth deals unto one *r*	Num 28:28	352
one young bullock, one *r*, and	Num 29:2	352
and two tenth deals for a *r*	Num 29:3	352
one young bullock, one *r*, and	Num 29:8	352
and two tenth deals to one *r*	Num 29:9	352
deals to each *r* of the two rams	Num 29:14	352
one bullock, one *r*, seven lambs	Num 29:36	352
for the bullock, for the *r*	Num 29:37	352
they offered a *r* of the flock for	Ezr 10:19	352
a *r* out of the flock without	Eze 43:23	352
a *r* out of the flock, without	Eze 43:25	352
a bullock, and an ephah for a *r*	Eze 45:24	352
blemish, and without blemish	Eze 46:4	352
shall be an ephah for a *r*	Eze 46:5	352
blemish, and six lambs, and a *r*	Eze 46:6	352
a bullock, and an ephah for a *r*	Eze 46:7	352
to a bullock, and an ephah to a *r*	Eze 46:11	352
the river a *r* which had two horns	Dan 8:3	352
I saw the *r* pushing westward, and	Dan 8:4	352
he came to the *r* that had two	Dan 8:6	352
I saw him come close unto the *r*	Dan 8:7	352
against him, and smote the *r*	Dan 8:7	352
in the *r* to stand before him	Dan 8:7	352
deliver the *r* out of his hand	Dan 8:7	352
The *r* which thou sawest having	Dan 8:20	352

RAMA (ra-mah) See RAMAH. *Same as Ramah 1.*
| In *R* was there a voice heard, | Mt 2:18 | 4471 |

RAMAH (ra'-mah) See RAMA, RAMATH.
1. A city in Benjamin.
Gibeon, and *R*, and Beeroth,	Josh 18:25	7414
palm tree of Deborah between *R*	Judg 4:5	7414
all night, in Gibeah, or in *R*	Judg 19:13	7414
went up against Judah, and built *R*	1Kin 15:17	7414
that he left off building of *R*	1Kin 15:21	7414
and they took away the stones of *R*	1Kin 15:22	7414
came up against Judah, and built *R*	2Chr 16:1	7414
that he left off building of *R*	2Chr 16:5	7414
they carried away the stones of *R*	2Chr 16:6	7414

The children of *R* and Gaba, six	Ezr 2:26	7414
The men of *R* and Gaba, six hundred	Neh 7:30	7414
Hazor, *R*, Gittaim,	Neh 11:33	7414
R is afraid	Is 10:29	7414
the guard had let him go from *R*	Jer 40:1	7414
in Gibeah, and the trumpet in *R*	Hos 5:8	7414

2. A city in Naphtali.
| And then the coast turneth to *R* | Josh 19:29 | 7414 |
| And Adamah, and *R*, and Hazor, | Josh 19:36 | 7414 |

3. A city in Ephraim.
and came to their house to *R*	1Sa 1:19	7414
And Elkanah went to *R* to his house	1Sa 2:11	7414
And his return was to *R*	1Sa 7:17	7414
and came to Samuel unto *R*	1Sa 8:4	7414
Then Samuel went to *R*	1Sa 15:34	7414
So Samuel rose up, and went to *R*	1Sa 16:13	7414
escaped, and came to Samuel to *R*	1Sa 19:18	7414
Behold, David is at Naioth in *R*	1Sa 19:19	7414
Then went he also to *R*, and came	1Sa 19:22	7414
Behold, they be at Naioth in *R*	1Sa 19:22	7414
And he went thither to Naioth in *R*	1Sa 19:23	7414
until he came to Naioth in *R*	1Sa 19:23	7414
And David fled from Naioth in *R*	1Sa 20:1	7414
abode in Gibeah under a tree in *R*	1Sa 22:6	7414
and buried him in his house at *R*	1Sa 25:1	7414
lamented him, and buried him in *R*	1Sa 28:3	7414
A voice was heard in *R*,	Jer 31:15	7414

4. A short form of Ramoth-Gilead.
| the Syrians had given him at *R* | 2Kin 8:29 | 7414 |
| wounds which were given him at *R* | 2Chr 22:6 | 7414 |

RAMATH (ra-math) *A city in Simeon.*
| to Baalath-beer, *R* of the south | Josh 19:8 | 7418 |

RAMATHAIM-ZOPHIM (ram-a-tha'-im-zo'-fim) *A city on Mt. Ephraim.*
| Now there was a certain man of *R* | 1Sa 1:1 | 7436 |

RAMATHITE (ra'-math-ite) *An inhabitant of Ramah 1.*
| the vineyards was Shimei the *R* | 1Chr 27:27 | 7435 |

RAMATH-LEHI (ra'-math-le'-hi) *A place in Judah.*
| his hand, and called that place *R* | Judg 15:17 | 7437 |

RAMATH MIZPAH See RAMATH-MIZPEH.

RAMATH-MIZPEH (ra'-math-miz'-peh) *A city in Gad.*
| And from Heshbon unto *R*, and | Josh 13:26 | 7434 |

RAMESES (ram'-e-seze) See RAAMSES. *A city in Goshen.*
of the land, in the land of *R*	Gen 47:11	7486
journeyed from *R* to Succoth	Ex 12:37	7486
from *R* in the first month	Num 33:3	7486
children of Israel removed from *R*	Num 33:5	7486

RAMIAH (ra'-mi-ah) *Married a foreigner while in exile.*
| *R*, and Jeziah, and Malchiah, and | Ezr 10:25 | 7422 |

RAMOTH (ra'-moth) See JARMUTH, RAMAH, RAMOTH-GILEAD, REMETH.
1. A Levitical city in Gad.
R in Gilead, of the Gadites	Deut 4:43	7216
R in Gilead out of the tribe of	Josh 20:8	7216
R in Gilead with her suburbs, to	Josh 21:38	7216
R in Gilead with her suburbs, and	1Chr 6:80	7216
2. A Levitical city in Issachar.
| *R* with her suburbs, and Anem with | 1Chr 6:73 | 7216 |
3. Married a foreigner in exile.
| and Adaiah, Jashub, and Sheal, and *R* | Ezr 10:29 | 3406 |
4. A city in Simeon.
| and to them which were in south *R* | 1Sa 30:27 | 7418 |
5. Same as Ramoth-gilead.
| Know ye that *R* in Gilead is ours, | 1Kin 22:3 | 7216 |

RAMOTH-GILEAD (ra'-moth-ghil'-e-ad) *A city in Gad.*
The son of Geber, in *R*	1Kin 4:13	7433
thou go with me to battle to *R*	1Kin 22:4	7433
Shall I go against *R* to battle	1Kin 22:6	7433
prophesied so, saying, Go up to *R*	1Kin 22:12	7433
shall we go against *R* to battle	1Kin 22:15	7433
that he may go up and fall at *R*	1Kin 22:20	7433
the king of Judah went up to *R*	1Kin 22:29	7433
against Hazael king of Syria in *R*	2Kin 8:28	7433
of oil in thine hand, and go to *R*	2Kin 9:1	7433
young man the prophet, went to *R*	2Kin 9:4	7433
(Now Joram had kept *R*, he and all	2Kin 9:14	7433
him to go up with him to *R*	2Chr 18:2	7433
Judah, Wilt thou go with me to *R*	2Chr 18:3	7433
them, Shall we go to *R* to battle	2Chr 18:5	7433
prophesied so, saying, Go up to *R*	2Chr 18:11	7433
shall we go to *R* to battle	2Chr 18:14	7433
that he may go up and fall at *R*	2Chr 18:19	7433
the king of Judah went up to *R*	2Chr 18:28	7433
against Hazael king of Syria at *R*	2Chr 22:5	7433

RAMOTH NEGEV See RAMOTH-GILEAD.

RAMPART
| therefore he made the *r* and the | Lam 2:8 | 2426 |
| whose *r* was the sea, and her wall | Nah 3:8 | 2426 |

RAM'S
| make a long blast with the *r* horn | Josh 6:5 | 3104 |

RAMS
the *r* which leaped upon the	Gen 31:10	6260
all the *r* which leap upon the	Gen 31:12	6260
the *r* of thy flock have I not	Gen 31:38	352
two hundred ewes, and twenty *r*	Gen 32:14	352
and two *r* without blemish,	Ex 29:1	352
with the bullock and the two *r*	Ex 29:3	352
and goats' hair, and red skins of *r*	Ex 35:23	352
for the sin offering, and two *r*	Lev 8:2	352
and one young bullock, and two *r*	Lev 23:18	352
peace offerings, two oxen, five *r*	Num 7:17	352
peace offerings, two oxen, five *r*	Num 7:23	352
peace offerings, two oxen, five *r*	Num 7:29	352
peace offerings, two oxen, five *r*	Num 7:35	352
peace offerings, two oxen, five *r*	Num 7:41	352
peace offerings, two oxen, five *r*	Num 7:47	352
peace offerings, two oxen, five *r*	Num 7:53	352
peace offerings, two oxen, five *r*	Num 7:59	352
peace offerings, two oxen, five *r*	Num 7:65	352
peace offerings, two oxen, five *r*	Num 7:71	352
peace offerings, two oxen, five *r*	Num 7:77	352
peace offerings, two oxen, five *r*	Num 7:83	352
the *r* twelve, the lambs of the	Num 7:87	352
the *r* sixty, the he goats sixty,	Num 7:88	352
me here seven oxen and seven *r*	Num 23:1	352
me here seven bullocks and seven *r*	Num 23:29	352
thirteen young bullocks, two *r*	Num 29:13	352
deals to each ram of the two *r*	Num 29:14	352
twelve young bullocks, two *r*	Num 29:17	352
for the bullocks, for the *r*	Num 29:18	352
third day eleven bullocks, two *r*	Num 29:20	352
for the bullocks, for the *r*	Num 29:21	352
fourth day ten bullocks, two *r*	Num 29:23	352
for the bullocks, for the *r*	Num 29:24	352
fifth day nine bullocks, two *r*	Num 29:26	352
for the bullocks, for the *r*	Num 29:27	352
sixth day eight bullocks, two *r*	Num 29:29	352
for the bullocks, for the *r*	Num 29:30	352
seventh day seven bullocks, two *r*	Num 29:32	352
for the bullocks, for the *r*	Num 29:33	352
r of the breed of Bashan, and	Deut 32:14	352
and to hearken than the fat of *r*	1Sa 15:22	352
lambs, and an hundred thousand *r*	2Kin 3:4	352
offered seven bullocks and seven *r*	1Chr 15:26	352
a thousand bullocks, a thousand *r*	1Chr 29:21	352
with a young bullock and seven *r*	2Chr 13:9	352
seven thousand and seven hundred *r*	2Chr 17:11	352
seven bullocks, and seven *r*	2Chr 29:21	352
when they had killed the *r*	2Chr 29:22	352
and ten bullocks, an hundred *r*	2Chr 29:32	352
of, both young bullocks, and *r*	Ezr 6:9	1798
hundred bullocks, two hundred *r*	Ezr 6:17	1798
with this money bullocks, *r*	Ezr 7:17	1798
for all Israel, ninety and six *r*	Ezr 8:35	352
you now seven bullocks and seven *r*	Job 42:8	352
fatlings, with the incense of *r*	Ps 66:15	352
The mountains skipped like *r*	Ps 114:4	352
mountains, that ye skipped like *r*	Ps 114:6	352
full of the burnt offerings of *r*	Is 1:11	352
with the fat of the kidneys of *r*	Is 34:6	352
the *r* of Nebaioth shall minister	Is 60:7	352
slaughter, like *r* with he goats	Jer 51:40	352
set battering *r* against it round	Eze 4:2	3733
battering *r* against the gates	Eze 21:22	3733
occupied with thee in lambs, and *r*	Eze 27:21	352
cattle and cattle, between the *r*	Eze 34:17	352
of the princes of the earth, of *r*	Eze 39:18	352
seven *r* without blemish daily the	Eze 45:23	352
be pleased with thousands of *r*	Mic 6:7	352

RAMS'
r skins dyed red, and badgers'	Ex 25:5	352
for the tent of *r* skins dyed red	Ex 26:14	352
r skins dyed red, and badgers'	Ex 35:7	352
for the tent of *r* skins dyed red	Ex 36:19	352
the covering of *r* skins dyed red	Ex 39:34	352
the ark seven trumpets of *r* horns	Josh 6:4	3104
of *r* horns before the ark of the	Josh 6:6	3104
bearing the seven trumpets of *r*	Josh 6:8	3104
bearing seven trumpets of *r* horns	Josh 6:13	3104

RAN
| he *r* to meet them from the tent | Gen 18:2 | 7323 |
| Abraham *r* unto the herd, and | Gen 18:7 | 7323 |

And the servant *r* to meet her	Gen 24:17	7323
r again unto the well to draw	Gen 24:20	7323
And the damsel *r*, and told them of	Gen 24:28	7323
Laban *r* out unto the man, unto	Gen 24:29	7323
and she *r* and told her father	Gen 29:12	7323
that he *r* to meet him, and	Gen 29:13	7323
Esau *r* to meet him, and embraced	Gen 33:4	7323
the fire *r* along upon the ground	Ex 9:23	1980
there *r* a young man, and told	Num 11:27	7323
and *r* into the midst of the	Num 16:47	7323
and they *r* unto the tent	Josh 7:22	7323
and they *r* as soon as he had	Josh 8:19	7323
and all the host *r*, and cried, and	Judg 7:21	7323
And Jotham *r* away, and fled, and	Judg 9:21	7323
the two other companies *r* upon	Judg 9:44	6584
And the woman made haste, and *r*	Judg 13:10	7323
he *r* unto Eli, and said, Here am I	1Sa 3:5	7323
there *r* a man of Benjamin out of	1Sa 4:12	7323
And they *r* and fetched him thence	1Sa 10:23	7323
r into the army, and came and	1Sa 17:22	7323
r toward the army to meet the	1Sa 17:48	7323
Therefore David *r*, and stood upon	1Sa 17:51	7323
And as the lad *r*, he shot an arrow	1Sa 20:36	7323
bowed himself unto Joab, and *r*	2Sa 18:21	7323
Then Ahimaaz *r* by the way of the	2Sa 18:23	7323
two of the servants of Shimei *r*	1Kin 2:39	1272
the water *r* round about the altar	1Kin 18:35	7323
r before Ahab to the entrance of	1Kin 18:46	7323
r after Elijah, and said, Let me,	1Kin 19:20	7323
the blood *r* out of the wound into	1Kin 22:35	3332
the brook that *r* through the	2Chr 32:4	7857
my sore *r* in the night, and ceased	Ps 77:2	5064
they *r* in the dry places like a	Ps 105:41	1980
that *r* down upon the beard, even	Ps 133:2	3331
sent these prophets, yet they *r*	Jer 23:21	7323
And the living creatures *r*	Eze 1:14	7519
there *r* out waters on the right	Eze 47:2	6379
r unto him in the fury of his	Dan 8:6	7323
the whole herd of swine *r*	Mt 8:32	3729
And straightway one of them *r*	Mt 27:48	5143
when he saw Jesus afar off, he *r*	Mk 5:6	5143
the herd *r* violently down a steep	Mk 5:13	3729
r afoot thither out of all cities	Mk 6:33	4936
r through that whole region round	Mk 6:55	4063
And one *r* and filled a spunge full	Mk 15:36	5143
the herd *r* violently down a steep	Lk 8:33	3729
saw him, and had compassion, and *r*	Lk 15:20	5143
he *r* before, and climbed up into a	Lk 19:4	4390
Peter, and *r* unto the sepulchre	Lk 24:12	5143
So they *r* both together	Jn 20:4	5143
all the people *r* together unto	Acts 3:11	4936
r upon him with one accord,	Acts 7:57	3729
Philip *r* thither to him, and heard	Acts 8:30	4370
the gate for gladness, but *r* in	Acts 12:14	1532
r in among the people, crying out	Acts 14:14	1530
moved, and the people *r* together	Acts 21:30	4890
centurions, and *r* down unto them	Acts 21:32	2701
seas met, they *r* the ship aground	Acts 27:41	2027
r greedily after the error of	Jude 11	1632

RANG
| shout, so that the earth *r* again | 1Sa 4:5 | 1949 |
| so that the city *r* again | 1Kin 1:45 | 1949 |

RANGE
| The *r* of the mountains is his | Job 39:8 | 3491 |

RANGES
or *r* for pots, they shall be	Lev 11:35	3600
and he that cometh within the *r*	2Kin 11:8	7713
Have her forth without the *r*	2Kin 11:15	7713
them, Have her forth of the *r*	2Chr 23:14	7713

RANGING
| As a roaring lion, and a *r* bear | Prov 28:15 | 8264 |

RANK
of corn came up upon one stalk, *r*	Gen 41:5	1277
thin ears devoured the seven *r*	Gen 41:7	1277
shall set forth in the second *r*	Num 2:16	
shall go forward in the third *r*	Num 2:24	
thousand, which could keep *r*	1Chr 12:33	5737
men of war, that could keep *r*	1Chr 12:38	4634

RANKS
was against light in three *r*	1Kin 7:4	6471
was against light in three *r*	1Kin 7:5	6471
and they shall not break their *r*	Joel 2:7	734
And they sat down in *r*, by	Mk 6:40	4237

RANSOM
then he shall give for the *r* of	Ex 21:30	6306
a *r* for his soul unto the LORD	Ex 30:12	3724
I have found a *r*	Job 33:24	3724

R

then a great *r* cannot deliver	Job 36:18	3724
nor give to God a *r* for him	Ps 49:7	3724
He will not regard any *r*	Prov 6:35	3724
The *r* of a man's life are his	Prov 13:8	3724
shall be a *r* for the righteous	Prov 21:18	3724
I gave Egypt for thy *r*, Ethiopia	Is 43:3	3724
I will *r* them from the power of	Hos 13:14	6299
and to give his life a *r* for many	Mt 20:28	*3083*
and to give his life a *r* for many	Mk 10:45	*3083*
Who gave himself a *r* for all	1Ti 2:6	*487*

RANSOMED

the *r* of the LORD shall return,	Is 35:10	6299
sea a way for the *r* to pass over	Is 51:10	1350
r him from the hand of him that	Jer 31:11	1350

RAPHA (ra'-fah) See BETH-RAPHA, REPHAIAH.
   1. Son of Benjamin.

Nohah the fourth, and *R* the fifth	1Chr 8:2	7498

   2. A member of Saul's family.

R was his son, Eleasah his son,	1Chr 8:37	7498

RAPHAIN See RAPHA.

RAPHU (ra'-fu) *A Benjamite spy sent to the Promised Land.*

of Benjamin, Palti the son of *R*	Num 13:9	7505

RARE

it is a *r* thing that the king	Dan 2:11	3358

RASE

R it, *r* it, even to the	Ps 137:7	6168

RASH

Be not *r* with thy mouth, and let	Eccl 5:2	926
The heart also of the *r* shall	Is 32:4	4116

RASHLY

to be quiet, and to do nothing *r*	Acts 19:36	*4312*

RASOR

like a sharp *r*, working	Ps 52:2	8593

RATE

and gather a certain *r* every day	Ex 16:4	1697
and mules, a *r* year by year	1Kin 10:25	1697
a daily *r* for every day, all the	2Kin 25:30	1697
Even after a certain *r* every day	2Chr 8:13	1697
and mules, a *r* year by year	2Chr 9:24	1697

RATHER See APPENDIX.

RATTLETH

The quiver *r* against him, the	Job 39:23	7439

RATTLING

the noise of the *r* of the wheels	Nah 3:2	7494

RAVEN

And he sent forth a *r*, which went	Gen 8:7	6158
Every *r* after his kind	Lev 11:15	6158
And every *r* after his kind,	Deut 14:14	6158
Who provideth for the *r* his food	Job 38:41	6158
locks are bushy, and black as a *r*	Song 5:11	6158
also and the *r* shall dwell in it	Is 34:11	6158

RAVENING

upon me with their mouths, as a *r*	Ps 22:13	2963
like a roaring lion *r* the prey	Eze 22:25	2963
are like wolves *r* the prey	Eze 22:27	2963
but inwardly they are *r* wolves	Mt 7:15	*727*
but your inward part is full of *r*	Lk 11:39	*724*

RAVENOUS

nor any *r* beast shall go up	Is 35:9	6530
Calling a *r* bird from the east,	Is 46:11	5861
unto the *r* birds of every sort	Eze 39:4	5861

RAVENS

the *r* to feed thee there	1Kin 17:4	6158
the *r* brought him bread and flesh	1Kin 17:6	6158
food, and to the young *r* which cry	Ps 147:9	6158
the *r* of the valley shall pick it	Prov 30:17	6158
Consider the *r*	Lk 12:24	*2876*

RAVIN

Benjamin shall *r* as a wolf	Gen 49:27	2963
with prey, and his dens with *r*	Nah 2:12	2966

RAVISHED

be thou *r* always with her love	Prov 5:19	7686
be *r* with a strange woman, and	Prov 5:20	7686
Thou hast *r* my heart, my sister,	Song 4:9	3823
thou hast *r* my heart with one of	Song 4:9	3823
be spoiled, and their wives *r*	Is 13:16	7693
They *r* the women in Zion, and the	Lam 5:11	6031
the houses rifled, and the women *r*	Zec 14:2	7693

RAW

Eat not of it *r*, nor sodden at	Ex 12:9	4995
there be quick *r* flesh in the	Lev 13:10	2416
But when *r* flesh appeareth in him	Lev 13:14	2416
the priest shall see the *r* flesh	Lev 13:15	2416
for the *r* flesh is unclean	Lev 13:15	2416
Or if the *r* flesh turn again, and	Lev 13:16	2416
have sodden flesh of thee, but *r*	1Sa 2:15	2416

RAZOR

shall no *r* come upon his head	Num 6:5	
no *r* shall come on his head	Judg 13:5	4177
hath not come a *r* upon mine head	Judg 16:17	4177
there shall no *r* come upon his	1Sa 1:11	4177
Lord shave with a *r* that is hired	Is 7:20	8593
knife, take thee a barber's *r*	Eze 5:1	8593

REACH See APPENDIX.

REACHED See APPENDIX.

REACHETH See APPENDIX.

REACHING See APPENDIX.

READ

r in the audience of the people	Ex 24:7	7121
he shall *r* therein all the days	Deut 17:19	7121
thou shalt *r* this law before all	Deut 31:11	7121
afterward he *r* all the words of	Josh 8:34	7121
which Joshua *r* not before all the	Josh 8:35	7121
king of Israel had *r* the letter	2Kin 5:7	7121
hand of the messengers, and *r* it	2Kin 19:14	7121
the book to Shaphan, and he *r* it	2Kin 22:8	7121
Shaphan *r* it before the king	2Kin 22:10	7121
which the king of Judah hath *r*	2Kin 22:16	7121
he *r* in their ears all the words	2Kin 23:2	7121
Shaphan *r* it before the king	2Chr 34:18	7121
have *r* before the king of Judah	2Chr 34:24	7121
he *r* in their ears all the words	2Chr 34:30	7121
us hath been plainly *r* before me	Ezr 4:18	7123
letter was *r* before Rehum	Ezr 4:23	7123
he *r* therein before the street	Neh 8:3	7121
So they *r* in the book in the law	Neh 8:8	7121
he *r* in the book of the law of	Neh 8:18	7121
r in the book of the law of the	Neh 9:3	7121
On that day they *r* in the book of	Neh 13:1	7121
they were *r* before the king	Est 6:1	7121
saying, *R* this, I pray thee	Is 29:11	7121
saying, *R* this, I pray thee	Is 29:12	7121
out of the book of the LORD, and *r*	Is 34:16	7121
hand of the messengers, and *r* it	Is 37:14	7121
Zephaniah the priest *r* this	Jer 29:29	7121
r in the roll, which thou hast	Jer 36:6	7121
also thou shalt *r* them in the	Jer 36:6	7121
Then *r* Baruch in the book the	Jer 36:10	7121
when Baruch *r* the book in the	Jer 36:13	7121
hast *r* in the ears of the people	Jer 36:14	7121
Sit down now, and *r* it in our ears	Jer 36:15	7121
So Baruch *r* it in their ears	Jer 36:15	7121
Jehudi *r* it in the ears of the	Jer 36:21	7121
Jehudi had *r* three or four leaves	Jer 36:23	7121
see, and shalt *r* all these words	Jer 51:61	7121
Whosoever shall *r* this writing	Dan 5:7	7123
but they could not *r* the writing	Dan 5:8	7123
that they should *r* this writing	Dan 5:15	7123
now if thou canst *r* the writing	Dan 5:16	7123
yet I will *r* the writing unto the	Dan 5:17	7123
Have ye not *r* what David did,	Mt 12:3	*314*
Or have ye not *r* in the law	Mt 12:5	*314*
and said unto them, Have ye not *r*	Mt 19:4	*314*
have ye never *r*, Out of the mouth	Mt 21:16	*314*
Did ye never *r* in the scriptures,	Mt 21:42	*314*
have ye not *r* that which was	Mt 22:31	*314*
Have ye never *r* what David did,	Mk 2:25	*314*
have ye not *r* this scripture	Mk 12:10	*314*
have ye not *r* in the book of	Mk 12:26	*314*
sabbath day, and stood up for to *r*	Lk 4:16	*314*
Have ye not *r* so much as this,	Lk 6:3	*314*
This title then *r* many of the	Jn 19:20	*314*
his chariot *r* Esaias the prophet	Acts 8:28	*314*
heard him *r* the prophet Esaias,	Acts 8:30	*314*
the scripture which he *r* was this	Acts 8:32	*314*
which are *r* every sabbath day	Acts 13:27	*314*
being *r* in the synagogues every	Acts 15:21	*314*
Which when they had *r*, they	Acts 15:31	*314*
the governor had *r* the letter	Acts 23:34	*314*
than what ye *r* or acknowledge	2Cor 1:13	*314*
our hearts, known and *r* of all men	2Cor 3:2	*314*
unto this day, when Moses is *r*	2Cor 3:15	*314*
Whereby, when ye *r*, ye may	Eph 3:4	*314*
when this epistle is *r* among you	Col 4:16	*314*
cause that it be *r* also in the	Col 4:16	*314*
that ye likewise *r* the epistle	Col 4:16	*314*

READEST

...ren	1Th 5:27	*314*
be r unto all the ho...ook	Rev 5:4	*314*
to r the book, neith...		
	Lk 10:26	*314*
...nat thou r	Acts 8:30	*314*

READETH

how r thou
Understand... un that r it .... Hab 2:2 7121
READETH
ace, (whoso r .... Mt 24:15 .... *314*
tables, th understand ... Mk 13:14 .... *314*
stand jr, and they .... Rev 1:3 .... *314*

not, l r of mind .... Acts 17:11 4288
Bles a r to will 2Cor 8:11 4288
RP revenge all 2Cor 10:6 2092

to understand the r	Neh 8:8	4744
the words of the	Jer 36:8	7121
an end of r this book	Jer 51:63	7121
of the law and the	Acts 13:15	320
the old testament	2Cor 3:14	320
e, give attendance to r	1Ti 4:13	320

quickly three measures of	Gen 18:6	4116
ome, and slay, and make r	Gen 43:16	3559
nade r the present against	Gen 43:25	3559
nd Joseph made r his chariot	Gen 46:29	631
he made r his chariot, and took	Ex 14:6	631
they be almost r to stone me	Ex 17:4	5750
be r against the third day	Ex 19:11	3559
Be r against the third day	Ex 19:15	3559
be r in the morning, and come up	Ex 34:2	3559
But we ourselves will go r armed	Num 32:17	2363
ye were r to go up into the hill	Deut 1:41	1951
A Syrian r to perish was my	Deut 26:5	
from the city, but be ye all r	Josh 8:4	3559
made a r kid, and unleavened cakes	Judg 6:19	
shall have made r a kid for thee	Judg 13:15	
of wine, and five sheep r dressed	1Sa 25:18	
Behold, thy servants are r to do	2Sa 15:15	
that thou hast no tidings r	2Sa 18:22	4672
was built of stone made r before	1Kin 6:7	8003
And Joram said, Make r	2Kin 9:21	631
And his chariot was made r	2Kin 9:21	631
that were r armed to the war	1Chr 12:23	
eight hundred, r armed to the war	1Chr 12:24	
had made r for the building	1Chr 28:2	3559
fourscore thousand r prepared for	2Chr 17:18	
they made a r for themselves	2Chr 35:14	3559
he was a r scribe in the law of	Ezr 7:6	4106
but thou art a God r to pardon	Neh 9:17	
they should be r against that day	Est 3:14	6264
that the Jews should be r against	Est 8:13	6264
who are r to raise up their	Job 3:8	6264
He that is r to slip with his	Job 12:5	3559
day of darkness is r at his hand	Job 15:23	3559
as a king r to the battle	Job 15:24	6264
which are r to become heaps	Job 15:28	6257
extinct, the graves are r for me	Job 17:1	
shall be r at his side	Job 18:12	3559
that was r to perish came upon me	Job 29:13	
it is r to burst like new bottles	Job 32:19	
hath bent his bow, and made it r	Ps 7:12	3559
they make r their arrow upon the	Ps 11:2	3559
when thou shalt make r thine	Ps 21:12	3559
For I am r to halt, and my sorrow	Ps 38:17	3559
tongue is the pen of a r writer	Ps 45:1	4106
Lord, art good, and r to forgive	Ps 86:5	
r to die from my youth up	Ps 88:15	
and those that are r to be slain	Prov 24:11	4131
unto him that is r to perish	Prov 31:6	
of God, and be more r to hear	Eccl 5:1	7138
were r to perish in the land of	Is 27:13	
be to you as a breach r to fall	Is 30:13	
shall be r to speak plainly	Is 32:4	4116
The LORD was r to save me	Is 38:20	
saying, It is r for the sodering	Is 41:7	2896
as if he were r to destroy	Is 51:13	3559
the trumpet, even to make all r	Eze 7:14	3559
Now if ye be r that at what time	Dan 3:15	6263
For they have made r their heart	Hos 7:6	7126
are killed, and all things are r	Mt 22:4	2092
to his servants, The wedding is r	Mt 22:8	2092
Therefore be ye also r	Mt 24:44	2092
they that were r went in with him	Mt 25:10	2092
and they made r the passover	Mt 26:19	2090
there make r for us	Mk 14:15	2090
and they made r the passover	Mk 14:16	2090
The spirit truly is r, but the	Mk 14:38	4289

to make r a people prepared for	Lk 1:17	2090
unto him, was sick, and r to die	Lk 7:2	3195
the Samaritans, to make r for him	Lk 9:52	2090
Be ye therefore r also	Lk 12:40	2092
for all things are now r	Lk 14:17	2092
Make r wherewith I may sup, and	Lk 17:8	2090
there make r	Lk 22:12	2090
and they made r the passover	Lk 22:13	2090
I am r to go with thee, both into	Lk 22:33	2092
but your time is alway r	Jn 7:6	2092
but while they made r, he fell	Acts 10:10	3903
r to depart on the morrow	Acts 20:7	3195
for I am r not to be bound only,	Acts 21:13	2093
he come near, are r to kill him	Acts 23:15	2092
and now are they r, looking for a	Acts 23:21	2092
Make r two hundred soldiers to go	Acts 23:23	2090
I am r to preach the gospel to	Rom 1:15	4289
and declaration of your r mind	2Cor 8:19	4288
that Achaia was r a year ago	2Cor 9:2	3903
that, as I said, ye may be r	2Cor 9:3	3903
before, that the same might be r	2Cor 9:5	2092
line of things made r to our hand	2Cor 10:16	2092
third time I am r to come to you	2Cor 12:14	2093
r to distribute, willing to	1Ti 6:18	2130
For I am now r to be offered, and	2Ti 4:6	4689
to be r to every good work,	Titus 3:1	2092
waxeth old is r to vanish away	Heb 8:13	*1451*
through faith unto salvation r to	1Pet 1:5	2092
be r always to give an answer to	1Pet 3:15	2092
him that is r to judge the quick	1Pet 4:5	2093
for filthy lucre, but of a r mind	1Pet 5:2	4289
which remain, that are r to die	Rev 3:2	3195
woman which was r to be delivered	Rev 12:4	3195
and his wife hath made herself r	Rev 19:7	2090

REAIA (re-ah'-yah) *Grandfather of Beerah.*
his son, R his son, Baal his son, ... 1Chr 5:5 ... 7211

REAIAH (re-ah'-yah) See REAIA.
   1. *Son of Shobal.*
R the son of Shobal begat Jahath .... 1Chr 4:2 ... 7211
   2. *A family of exiles.*
of Gahar, the children of R .... Ezr 2:47 ... 7211
The children of R, the children .... Neh 7:50 ... 7211

REALM

So the r of Jehoshaphat was quiet	2Chr 20:30	4438
his priests and Levites, in my r	Ezr 7:13	4437
wrath against the r of the king	Ezr 7:23	4437
that were in all his r	Dan 1:20	4438
to set him over the whole r	Dan 6:3	4437
king over the r of the Chaldeans	Dan 9:1	4438
up all against the r of Grecia	Dan 11:2	4438

REAP

when ye r the harvest of your	Lev 19:9	7114
thou shalt not wholly r the	Lev 19:9	
shall r the harvest thereof, then	Lev 23:10	7114
when ye r the harvest of your	Lev 23:22	7114
of thy harvest thou shalt not r	Lev 25:5	7114
neither r that which groweth of	Lev 25:11	7114
be on the field that they do r	Ruth 2:9	7114
to r his harvest, and to make his	1Sa 8:12	7114
and in the third year sow ye, and r	2Kin 19:29	7114
and sow wickedness, r the same	Job 4:8	7114
They r every one his corn in the	Job 24:6	7114
that sow in tears shall r in joy	Ps 126:5	7114
soweth iniquity shall r vanity	Prov 22:8	7114
regardeth the clouds shall not r	Eccl 11:4	7114
and in the third year sow ye, and r	Is 37:30	7114
sown wheat, but shall r thorns	Jer 12:13	7114
they shall r the whirlwind	Hos 8:7	7114
in righteousness, r in mercy	Hos 10:12	7114
shalt sow, but thou shalt not r	Mic 6:15	7114
they sow not, neither do they r	Mt 6:26	2325
that I r where I sowed not	Mt 25:26	2325
for they neither sow nor r	Lk 12:24	2325
I sent you to r that whereon ye	Jn 4:38	2325
if we shall r your carnal things	1Cor 9:11	2325
sparingly shall r also sparingly	2Cor 9:6	2325
shall r also bountifully	2Cor 9:6	2325
man soweth, that shall he also r	Gal 6:7	2325
shall of the flesh r corruption	Gal 6:8	2325
of the Spirit r life everlasting	Gal 6:8	2325
for in due season we shall r	Gal 6:9	2325
cloud, Thrust in thy sickle, and r	Rev 14:15	2325
the time is come for thee to r	Rev 14:15	2325

REAPED

wickedness, ye have r iniquity	Hos 10:13	7114
who have r down your fields	Jas 5:4	*270*
r are entered into the ears of	Jas 5:4	2325
and the earth was r	Rev 14:16	2325

R

REAPER
the plowman shall overtake the *r* .... Amos 9:13   7114

REAPERS
gleaned in the field after the *r* .... Ruth 2:3   7114
Beth-lehem, and said unto the *r* .... Ruth 2:4   7114
servant that was set over the *r* .... Ruth 2:5   7114
that was set over the *r* answered .... Ruth 2:6   7114
gather after the *r* among the .... Ruth 2:7   7114
And she sat beside the *r* .... Ruth 2:14   7114
went out to his father to the *r* 2Kin 4:18   7114
of harvest I will say to the *r* .... Mt 13:30   2327
and the *r* are the angels .... Mt 13:39   2327

REAPEST
corners of thy field when thou *r* .... Lev 23:22   7114
r that thou didst not sow .... Lk 19:21   2325

REAPETH
corn, and *r* the ears with his arm .... Is 17:5   7114
he that *r* receiveth wages, and .... Jn 4:36   2325
he that *r* may rejoice together .... Jn 4:36   2325
true, One soweth, and another *r* .... Jn 4:37   2325

REAPING
they of Beth-shemesh were *r* their 1Sa 6:13   7114
r where thou hast not sown, and .... Mt 25:24   2325
not down, and *r* that I did not sow .... Lk 19:22   2325

REAR
thou shalt *r* up the tabernacle .... Ex 26:30   6965
neither *r* you up a standing image .... Lev 26:1   6965
r an altar unto the LORD in the 2Sa 24:18   6965
wilt thou *r* it up in three days .... Jn 2:20   1453

REARED
that the tabernacle was *r* up .... Ex 40:17   6965
Moses *r* up the tabernacle, and .... Ex 40:18   6965
bars thereof, and *r* up his pillars .... Ex 40:18   6965
he *r* up the court round about the .... Ex 40:33   6965
was *r* up the cloud covered the .... Num 9:15   6965
r up for himself a pillar, which 2Sa 18:18   5324
he *r* up an altar for Baal in the 1Kin 16:32   6965
he *r* up altars for Baal, and made 2Kin 21:3   6965
he *r* up the pillars before the 2Chr 3:17   6965
he *r* up altars for Baalim, and 2Chr 33:3   6965

REASON
by *r* of that famine following .... Gen 41:31   6440
Canaan fainted by *r* of the famine .... Gen 47:13   6440
Israel sighed by *r* of the bondage .... Ex 2:23   4480
up unto God by *r* of the bondage .... Ex 2:23   4480
cry by *r* of their taskmasters .... Ex 3:7   6440
by *r* of the swarm of flies .... Ex 8:24   6440
be unclean by *r* of a dead body .... Num 9:10
given them by *r* of the anointing .... Num 18:8
ye shall bear no sin by *r* of it .... Num 18:32   5921
ye were afraid by *r* of the fire .... Deut 5:5   6440
that is not clean by *r* of .... Deut 23:10
old by *r* of the very long journey .... Josh 9:13
by *r* of them that oppressed them .... Judg 2:18
that I may *r* with you before the 1Sa 12:7   8199
this is the *r* of the levy which 1Kin 9:15   1697
his eyes were set by *r* of his age 1Kin 14:4
to minister by *r* of the cloud 2Chr 5:14   6440
by *r* of this great multitude 2Chr 20:15   6440
by *r* of the sickness day by day 2Chr 21:15   4480
fell out by *r* of his sickness 2Chr 21:19   5973
are blackish by *r* of the ice .... Job 6:16   4480
choose out my words to *r* with him ...... Job 9:14
and I desire to *r* with God .... Job 13:3   3198
Should he *r* with unprofitable .... Job 15:3   3198
eye also is dim by *r* of sorrow .... Job 17:7
by *r* of his highness I could not .... Job 31:23
By *r* of the multitude of .... Job 35:9
they cry out by *r* of the arm of .... Job 35:9
order our speech by *r* of darkness .... Job 37:19   6440
by *r* of breakings they purify .... Job 41:25
I have roared by *r* of the .... Ps 38:8
by *r* of the enemy and avenger .... Ps 44:16   6440
man that shouteth by *r* of wine .... Ps 78:65
eye mourneth by *r* of affliction .... Ps 88:9   4480
if by *r* of strength they be .... Ps 90:10
By *r* of the voice of my groaning .... Ps 102:5
will not plow by *r* of the cold .... Prov 20:4
seven men that can render a *r* .... Prov 26:16   2940
the *r* of things, and to know the .... Eccl 7:25   2808
let us *r* together, saith the LORD .... Is 1:18   3198
narrow by *r* of the inhabitants .... Is 49:19
of branches by *r* of many waters .... Eze 19:10
terrors by *r* of the sword shall .... Eze 21:12   413
By *r* of the abundance of his .... Eze 26:10
Tarshish was thy merchant by *r* of .... Eze 27:12
Syria was thy merchant by *r* of .... Eze 27:16

thy wisdom by *r* of thy brightness ....
same time my *r* returned unto me .... Eze 28:17
by *r* of the words of the king and .... Dan 4:36   5921
sacrifice by *r* of transgression 5:10   4486
I cried by *r* of mine affliction ....
by *r* of the multitude of men 12   6903
why *r* ye among yourselves, ... 12
Why *r* ye these things in your ....
it, he saith unto them, Why *r* ye ....
and the Pharisees began to *r* .... Lk
them, What *r* ye in your hearts .... Lk   1260
the sea arose by *r* of a great .... Jn 6:10
Because that by *r* of him many of .... Jn 12:1
It is not *r* that we should leave .... Acts 6:2
r would that I should bear with .... Acts 18:1
but by *r* of him who hath .... Rom 8:20
by *r* of the glory that excelleth 2Cor 3:10
by *r* hereof he ought, as for the .... Heb 5:3
even those who by *r* of use have .... Heb 5:14
to continue by *r* of death .... Heb 7:23
to every man that asketh you a *r* 1Pet 3:15   305
by *r* of whom the way of truth 2Pet 2:2   1223
by *r* of the other voices of the .... Rev 8:13   1537
by *r* of the smoke of the pit .... Rev 9:2   1537
in the sea by *r* of her costliness .... Rev 18:19   1537

REASONABLE
unto God, which is your *r* service .... Rom 12:1   3050

REASONED
they *r* among themselves, saying, ... Mt 16:7   1260
they *r* with themselves, saying, ... Mt 21:25   1260
that they so *r* within themselves .... Mk 2:8   1260
they *r* among themselves, saying, ... Mk 8:16   1260
they *r* with themselves, saying, ... Mk 11:31   3049
they *r* with themselves, saying, ... Lk 20:5   4817
they *r* among themselves, saying, ... Lk 20:14   1260
while they communed together and *r* .... Lk 24:15   4802
three sabbath days *r* with them .... Acts 17:2   1256
he *r* in the synagogue every .... Acts 18:4   1256
the synagogue, and *r* with the Jews ..... Acts 18:19   1256
as he *r* of righteousness, ... Acts 24:25   1256

REASONING
Hear now my *r*, and hearken to the ...... Job 13:6   8433
there, and *r* in their hearts, ... Mk 2:6   1260
and having heard them *r* together .... Mk 12:28   4802
Then there arose a *r* among them .... Lk 9:46   1261
had great *r* among themselves .... Acts 28:29   4803

REASONS
I gave ear to your *r*, whilst ye .... Job 32:11   8394
bring forth your strong *r* .... Is 41:21

REBA (re'-bah) A king of Midian.
and Rekem, and Zur, and Hur, and *R* ..... Num 31:8   7254
and Rekem, and Zur, and Hur, and *R* ..... Josh 13:21   7254

REBECCA (re-bek'-kah) See REBEKAH. Greek form of Rebekah.
but when *R* also had conceived by .... Rom 9:10   4479

REBEKAH (re-bek'-kah) See REBECCA, REBEKAH'S. Wife of Isaac.
And Bethuel begat *R* .... Gen 22:23   7259
R came out, who was born to .... Gen 24:15   7259
R had a brother, and his name was .... Gen 24:29   7259
heard the words of *R* his sister .... Gen 24:30   7259
R came forth with her pitcher on .... Gen 24:45   7259
R is before thee, take her, and go .... Gen 24:51   7259
and raiment, and gave them to *R* .... Gen 24:53   7259
And they called *R*, and said unto .... Gen 24:58   7259
And they sent away *R* their sister .... Gen 24:59   7259
And they blessed *R*, and said unto .... Gen 24:60   7259
R arose, and her damsels, and they ..... Gen 24:61   7259
and the servant took *R*, and went .... Gen 24:61   7259
R lifted up her eyes, and when she ...... Gen 24:64   7259
mother Sarah's tent, and took *R* .... Gen 24:67   7259
years old when he took *R* to wife .... Gen 25:20   7259
of him, and *R* his wife conceived .... Gen 25:21   7259
but *R* loved Jacob .... Gen 25:28   7259
of the place should kill me for *R* .... Gen 26:7   7259
was sporting with *R* his wife .... Gen 26:8   7259
grief of mind unto Isaac and to *R* .... Gen 26:35   7259
R heard when Isaac spake to Esau ...... Gen 27:5   7259
R spake unto Jacob her son, ... Gen 27:6   7259
And Jacob said to *R* his mother .... Gen 27:11   7259
R took goodly raiment of her .... Gen 27:15   7259
Esau her elder son were told to *R* .... Gen 27:42   7259
R said to Isaac, I am weary of my .... Gen 27:46   7259
the Syrian, the brother of *R* .... Gen 28:5   7259
they buried Isaac and *R* his wife .... Gen 49:31   7259

REBEKAH'S (re-bek'-kahz)
brother, and that he was *R* son	Gen 29:12	7259
But Deborah *R* nurse died, and she	Gen 35:8	7259

REBEL
Only *r* not ye against the LORD,	Num 14:9	4775
doth *r* against thy commandment	Josh 1:18	4784
that ye might *r* this day against	Josh 22:16	4775
seeing ye *r* to day against the	Josh 22:18	4775
but *r* not against the LORD	Josh 22:19	4775
nor *r* against us, in building you	Josh 22:19	4775
that we should *r* against the LORD	Josh 22:29	4775
not *r* against the commandment of	1Sa 12:14	4784
but *r* against the commandment of	1Sa 12:15	4784
will ye *r* against the king	Neh 2:19	4775
that thou and the Jews think to *r*	Neh 6:6	4775
of those that *r* against the light	Job 24:13	4775
But if ye refuse and *r*, ye shall	Is 1:20	4784
and wine, and they *r* against me	Hos 7:14	5493

REBELLED
and in the thirteenth year they *r*	Gen 14:4	4775
because ye *r* against my word at	Num 20:24	4784
For ye *r* against my commandment	Num 27:14	4784
but *r* against the commandment of	Deut 1:26	4784
but *r* against the commandment of	Deut 1:43	4784
then ye *r* against the commandment	Deut 9:23	4784
So Israel *r* against the house of	1Kin 12:19	6586
Then Moab *r* against Israel after	2Kin 1:1	6586
that the king of Moab *r* against	2Kin 3:5	6586
king of Moab hath *r* against me	2Kin 3:7	6586
he *r* against the king of Assyria,	2Kin 18:7	4775
then he turned and *r* against him	2Kin 24:1	4775
that Zedekiah *r* against the king	2Kin 24:20	4775
Israel *r* against the house of	2Chr 10:19	6856
up, and hath *r* against his lord	2Chr 13:6	4775
And he also *r* against king	2Chr 36:13	4775
r against thee, and cast thy law	Neh 9:26	4775
for they have *r* against thee	Ps 5:10	4784
they *r* not against his word	Ps 105:28	4784
Because they *r* against the words	Ps 107:11	4784
and they have *r* against me	Is 1:2	6586
But they *r*, and vexed his holy	Is 63:10	4784
that Zedekiah *r* against the king	Jer 52:3	4775
for I have *r* against his	Lam 1:18	4784
for I have grievously *r*	Lam 1:20	4784
We have transgressed and have *r*	Lam 3:42	4784
nation that hath *r* against me	Eze 2:3	4775
But he *r* against him in sending	Eze 17:15	4775
But they *r* against me, and would	Eze 20:8	4784
But the house of Israel *r* against	Eze 20:13	4784
the children *r* against me	Eze 20:21	4784
and have done wickedly, and have *r*	Dan 9:5	4775
though we have *r* against him	Dan 9:9	4775
for she hath *r* against her God	Hos 13:16	4784

REBELLEST
trust, that thou *r* against me	2Kin 18:20	4775
trust, that thou *r* against me	Is 36:5	4775

REBELLION
For I know thy *r*, and thy stiff	Deut 31:27	4805
if it be in *r*, or if in	Josh 22:22	4779
For *r* is as the sin of witchcraft	1Sa 15:23	4805
against kings, and that *r* and	Ezr 4:19	4776
in their *r* appointed a captain to	Neh 9:17	4805
For he addeth *r* unto his sin	Job 34:37	6588
An evil man seeketh only *r*	Prov 17:11	4805
hast taught *r* against the LORD	Jer 28:16	5627
he hath taught *r* against the LORD	Jer 29:32	5627

REBELLIOUS
ye have been *r* against the LORD	Deut 9:7	4784
Ye have been *r* against the LORD	Deut 9:24	4784
r son, which will not obey the	Deut 21:18	4784
This our son is stubborn and *r*	Deut 21:20	4784
ye have been *r* against the LORD	Deut 31:27	4784
Thou son of the perverse *r* woman	1Sa 20:30	4780
unto Jerusalem, building the *r*	Ezr 4:12	4779
know that this city is a *r* city	Ezr 4:15	4779
let not the *r* exalt themselves	Ps 66:7	5637
but the *r* dwell in a dry land	Ps 68:6	5637
yea, for the *r* also, that the	Ps 68:18	5637
a stubborn and *r* generation	Ps 78:8	4784
Thy princes are *r*, and companions	Is 1:23	5637
Woe to the *r* children, saith the	Is 30:1	5637
That this is a *r* people, lying,	Is 30:9	4805
opened mine ear, and I was not *r*	Is 50:5	4784
hands all the day unto a *r* people	Is 65:2	5637
she hath been *r* against me	Jer 4:17	4784
hath a revolting and a *r* heart	Jer 5:23	4784
to a *r* nation that hath rebelled	Eze 2:3	4775
forbear, (for they are a *r* house	Eze 2:5	4805

looks, though they be a *r* house	Eze 2:6	4805
for they are most *r*	Eze 2:7	4805
Be not thou *r* like that	Eze 2:8	4805
like that *r* house	Eze 2:8	4805
looks, though they be a *r* house	Eze 3:9	4805
for they are a *r* house	Eze 3:26	4805
for they are a *r* house	Eze 3:27	4805
in the midst of a *r* house	Eze 12:2	4805
for they are a *r* house	Eze 12:2	4805
though they be a *r* house	Eze 12:3	4805
the *r* house, said unto thee, What	Eze 12:9	4805
O *r* house, will I say the word,	Eze 12:25	4805
Say now to the *r* house, Know ye	Eze 17:12	4805
utter a parable unto the *r* house	Eze 24:3	4805
And thou shalt say to the *r*	Eze 44:6	4805

REBELS
be kept for a token against the *r*	Num 17:10	4805
he said unto them, Hear now, ye *r*	Num 20:10	4784
purge out from among you the *r*	Eze 20:38	4775

REBUKE
shalt in any wise *r* thy neighbour	Lev 19:17	3198
upon thee cursing, vexation, and *r*	Deut 28:20	4045
she may glean them, and *r* her not	Ruth 2:16	1605
day is a day of trouble, and of *r*	2Kin 19:3	8433
our fathers look thereon, and *r* it	1Chr 12:17	3198
r me not in thine anger, neither	Ps 6:1	3198
world were discovered at thy *r*	Ps 18:15	1606
O LORD, *r* me not in thy wrath	Ps 38:1	3198
R the company of spearmen, the	Ps 68:30	1605
At thy *r*, O God of Jacob, both	Ps 76:6	1606
at the *r* of thy countenance	Ps 80:16	1606
At thy *r* they fled	Ps 104:7	1606
r a wise man, and he will love	Prov 9:8	3198
but a scorner heareth not *r*	Prov 13:1	1606
but the poor heareth not *r*	Prov 13:8	1606
But to them that *r* him shall be	Prov 24:25	3198
Open *r* is better than secret love	Prov 27:5	8433
better to hear the *r* of the wise	Eccl 7:5	1606
nations, and shall *r* many people	Is 2:4	3198
but God shall *r* them, and they	Is 17:13	1605
the *r* of his people shall he take	Is 25:8	2781
shall flee at the *r* of one	Is 30:17	1606
at the *r* of five shall ye flee	Is 30:17	1606
day is a day of trouble, and of *r*	Is 37:3	8433
at my *r* I dry up the sea, I make	Is 50:2	1606
of the LORD, the *r* of thy God	Is 51:20	1606
be wroth with thee, nor *r* thee	Is 54:9	1605
his *r* with flames of fire	Is 66:15	1606
for thy sake I have suffered *r*	Jer 15:15	2781
shall be desolate in the day of *r*	Hos 5:9	8433
r strong nations afar off	Mic 4:3	3198
said unto Satan, The LORD *r* thee	Zec 3:2	1605
that hath chosen Jerusalem *r* thee	Zec 3:2	1605
I will *r* the devourer for your	Mal 3:11	1605
Peter took him, and began to *r* him	Mt 16:22	2008
Peter took him, and began to *r* him	Mk 8:32	2008
trespass against thee, *r* him	Lk 17:3	2008
unto him, Master, *r* thy disciples	Lk 19:39	2008
the sons of God, without *r*	Phil 2:15	298
R not an elder, but intreat him	1Ti 5:1	1969
Them that sin *r* before all	1Ti 5:20	1651
reprove, *r*, exhort with all	2Ti 4:2	1651
Wherefore *r* them sharply, that	Titus 1:13	1651
exhort, and *r* with all authority	Titus 2:15	1651
but said, The Lord *r* thee	Jude 9	2008
As many as I love, I *r* and chasten	Rev 3:19	1651

REBUKED
my hands, and *r* thee yesternight	Gen 31:42	3198
and his father *r* him, and said unto	Gen 37:10	1605
I *r* the nobles, and the rulers, and	Neh 5:7	7378
Thou hast *r* the heathen, thou	Ps 9:5	1605
He *r* the Red sea also, and it was	Ps 106:9	1605
Thou hast *r* the proud that are	Ps 119:21	1605
arose, and *r* the winds and the sea	Mt 8:26	2008
And Jesus *r* the devil	Mt 17:18	2008
and the disciples *r* them	Mt 19:13	2008
And the multitude *r* them, because	Mt 20:31	2008
And Jesus *r* him, saying, Hold thy	Mk 1:25	2008
r the wind, and said unto the sea,	Mk 4:39	2008
he *r* Peter, saying, Get thee	Mk 8:33	2008
he *r* the foul spirit, saying unto	Mk 9:25	2008
his disciples *r* those that	Mk 10:13	2008
And Jesus *r* him, saying, Hold thy	Lk 4:35	2008
he stood over her, and *r* the fever	Lk 4:39	2008
r the wind and the raging of the	Lk 8:24	2008
Jesus *r* the unclean spirit, and	Lk 9:42	2008
r them, and said, Ye know not what	Lk 9:55	2008
his disciples saw it, they *r* them	Lk 18:15	2008
And they which went before *r* him	Lk 18:39	2008

R

But the other answering *r* him	Lk 23:40	2008
nor faint when thou art *r* of him	Heb 12:5	1651
But was *r* for his iniquity	2Pet 2:16	2192,1649

REBUKER

I have been a *r* of them all	Hos 5:2	4148

REBUKES

When thou with *r* dost correct man	Ps 39:11	8433
anger and in fury and in furious *r*	Eze 5:15	8433
upon them with furious *r*	Eze 25:17	8433

REBUKETH

he that *r* a wicked man getteth	Prov 9:7	3198
He that *r* a man afterwards shall	Prov 28:23	3198
They hate him that *r* in the gate	Amos 5:10	3198
He *r* the sea, and maketh it dry,	Nah 1:4	1605

REBUKING

at the *r* of the LORD, at the	2Sa 22:16	1606
he *r* them suffered them not to	Lk 4:41	2008

RECALL

This I *r* to my mind, therefore	Lam 3:21	7725

RECEIPT

sitting at the *r* of custom	Mt 9:9	5058
sitting at the *r* of custom	Mk 2:14	5058
Levi, sitting at the *r* of custom	Lk 5:27	5058

RECEIVE

to *r* thy brother's blood from thy	Gen 4:11	3947
then *r* my present at my hand	Gen 33:10	3947
to *r* his pledge from the woman's	Gen 38:20	3947
make his pans to *r* his ashes	Ex 27:3	1878
thou shalt *r* them of their hands,	Ex 29:25	3947
which ye *r* of the children of	Num 18:28	3947
mount to *r* the tables of stone	Deut 9:9	3947
every one shall *r* of thy words	Deut 33:3	5375
which thou shalt *r* of their hands	1Sa 10:4	3947
Though I should *r* a thousand	2Sa 18:12	8254
there, and thou shalt *r* them	1Kin 5:9	5375
little to the burnt offerings	1Kin 8:64	3557
whom I stand, I will *r* none	2Kin 5:16	3947
Is it a time to *r* money	2Kin 5:26	3947
to *r* garments, and oliveyards, and	2Kin 5:26	3947
now therefore *r* no more money of	2Kin 12:7	3947
the priests consented to *r* no	2Kin 12:8	3947
not able to *r* the burnt offerings	2Chr 7:7	3557
shall we *r* good at the hand of	Job 2:10	6901
of God, and shall we not *r* evil	Job 2:10	6901
R, I pray thee, the law from his	Job 22:22	3947
they shall *r* of the Almighty	Job 27:13	3947
the LORD will *r* my prayer	Ps 6:9	3947
He shall *r* the blessing from the	Ps 24:5	5375
for he shall *r* me	Ps 49:15	3947
and afterward *r* me to glory	Ps 73:24	3947
When I shall *r* the congregation I	Ps 75:2	3947
To *r* the instruction of wisdom,	Prov 1:3	3947
My son, if thou wilt *r* my words	Prov 2:1	3947
Hear, O my son, and *r* my sayings,	Prov 4:10	3947
R my instruction, and not silver	Prov 8:10	3947
wise in heart will *r* commandments	Prov 10:8	3947
r instruction, that thou mayest	Prov 19:20	6901
Should I *r* comfort in these	Is 57:6	5162
they have refused to *r* correction	Jer 5:3	3947
let your ear *r* the word of his	Jer 9:20	3947
might not hear, nor *r* instruction	Jer 17:23	3947
not hearkened to *r* instruction	Jer 32:33	3947
Will ye not *r* instruction to	Jer 35:13	3947
speak unto thee *r* in thine heart	Eze 3:10	3947
when thou shalt *r* thy sisters	Eze 16:61	3947
that ye shall *r* no more reproach	Eze 36:30	3947
ye shall *r* of me gifts and rewards	Dan 2:6	6902
Ephraim shall *r* shame, and Israel	Hos 10:6	3947
all iniquity, and *r* us graciously	Hos 14:2	3947
he shall *r* of you his standing	Mic 1:11	3947
fear me, thou wilt *r* instruction	Zeph 3:7	3947
shall not be room enough to *r* it	Mal 3:10	3947
And whosoever shall not *r* you	Mt 10:14	1209
shall *r* a prophet's reward	Mt 10:41	2983
shall *r* a righteous man's reward	Mt 10:41	2983
The blind *r* their sight, and the	Mt 11:5	308
And if ye will *r* it, this is Elias	Mt 11:14	1209
whoso shall *r* one such little	Mt 18:5	1209
All men cannot *r* this saying	Mt 19:11	5562
He that is able to *r* it	Mt 19:12	5562
let him *r* it	Mt 19:12	5562
shall *r* an hundredfold, and shall	Mt 19:29	2983
is right, that shall ye *r*	Mt 20:7	2983
in prayer, believing, ye shall *r.*	Mt 21:22	2983
that they might *r* the fruits of	Mt 21:34	2983
therefore ye shall *r* the greater	Mt 23:14	2983
that there was no room to *r* them	Mk 2:2	5562

immediately *r* it with gladness	Mk 4:16	2983
r it, and bring forth fruit, some	Mk 4:20	3858
And whosoever shall not *r* you	Mk 6:11	1209
Whosoever shall *r* one of such	Mk 9:37	1209
and whosoever shall *r* me,	Mk 9:37	1209
Whosoever shall not *r* the kingdom	Mk 10:15	1209
But he shall *r* an hundredfold now	Mk 10:30	2983
Lord, that I might *r* my sight	Mk 10:51	308
ye pray, believe that ye *r* them	Mk 11:24	2983
servant, that he might *r* from the	Mk 12:2	2983
these shall *r* greater damnation	Mk 12:40	2983
lend to them of whom ye hope to *r*	Lk 6:34	618
to sinners, to *r* as much again	Lk 6:34	618
they hear, *r* the word with joy	Lk 8:13	1209
And whosoever will not *r* you	Lk 9:5	1209
Whosoever shall *r* this child in	Lk 9:48	1209
whosoever shall *r* me receiveth	Lk 9:48	1209
And they did not *r* him, because	Lk 9:53	1209
city ye enter, and they *r* you	Lk 10:8	1209
they *r* you not, go your ways out	Lk 10:10	1209
they may *r* me into their houses	Lk 16:4	1209
they may *r* you into everlasting	Lk 16:9	1209
Whosoever shall not *r* the kingdom	Lk 18:17	1209
Who shall not *r* manifold more in	Lk 18:30	618
said, Lord, that I may *r* my sight	Lk 18:41	308
Jesus said unto him, *R* thy sight	Lk 18:42	308
to *r* for himself a kingdom	Lk 19:12	2983
the same shall *r* greater	Lk 20:47	2983
for we *r* the due reward of our	Lk 23:41	618
and ye *r* not our witness	Jn 3:11	2983
and said, A man can *r* nothing	Jn 3:27	2983
But I *r* not testimony from man	Jn 5:34	2983
I *r* not honour from men	Jn 5:41	2983
my Father's name, and ye *r* me not	Jn 5:43	2983
in his own name, him ye will *r*	Jn 5:43	2983
which *r* honour one of another, and	Jn 5:44	2983
on the sabbath day *r* circumcision	Jn 7:23	2983
they that believe on him should *r*	Jn 7:39	2983
come again, and *r* you unto myself	Jn 14:3	3880
whom the world cannot *r,* because	Jn 14:17	2983
for he shall *r* of mine, and shall	Jn 16:14	2983
ask, and ye shall *r,* that your joy	Jn 16:24	2983
unto them, *R* ye the Holy Ghost	Jn 20:22	2983
But ye shall *r* power, after that	Acts 1:8	2983
ye shall *r* the gift of the Holy	Acts 2:38	2983
expecting to *r* something of them	Acts 3:5	2983
Whom the heaven must *r* until the	Acts 3:21	1209
saying, Lord Jesus, *r* my spirit	Acts 7:59	1209
that they might *r* the Holy Ghost	Acts 8:15	2983
hands, he may *r* the Holy Ghost	Acts 8:19	2983
on him, that he might *r* his sight	Acts 9:12	308
that thou mightest *r* thy sight	Acts 9:17	308
in him shall *r* remission of sins	Acts 10:43	2983
which are not lawful for us to *r*	Acts 16:21	3858
exhorting the disciples to *r* him	Acts 18:27	588
is more blessed to give than to *r*	Acts 20:35	2983
me, Brother Saul, *r* thy sight	Acts 22:13	308
for they will not *r* thy testimony	Acts 22:18	3858
that they may *r* forgiveness of	Acts 26:18	2983
they which *r* abundance of grace	Rom 5:17	2983
they that resist shall *r* to	Rom 13:2	2983
that is weak in the faith *r* ye	Rom 14:1	4355
Wherefore *r* ye one another, as	Rom 15:7	4355
That ye *r* her in the Lord, as	Rom 16:2	4327
every man shall *r* his own reward	1Cor 3:8	2983
thereupon, he shall *r* a reward	1Cor 3:14	2983
hast thou that thou didst not *r*	1Cor 4:7	2983
now if thou didst *r* it, why dost	1Cor 4:7	2983
that the church may *r* edifying	1Cor 14:5	2983
that every one may *r* the things	2Cor 5:10	2983
beseech you also that ye *r* not	2Cor 6:1	1209
and I will *r* you,	2Cor 6:17	1523
R us; we have wronged	2Cor 7:2	5562
that ye might *r* damage by us in	2Cor 7:9	2210
intreaty that we would *r* the gift	2Cor 8:4	1209
or if ye *r* another spirit, which	2Cor 11:4	2983
if otherwise, yet as a fool *r* me	2Cor 11:16	1209
that we might *r* the promise of	Gal 3:14	2983
that we might *r* the adoption of	Gal 4:5	618
the same shall he *r* of the Lord	Eph 6:8	2865
R him therefore in the Lord with	Phil 2:29	4327
that of the Lord ye shall *r* the	Col 3:24	618
r for the wrong which he hath	Col 3:25	2865
if he come unto you, *r* him	Col 4:10	1209
Against an elder *r* not an	1Ti 5:19	3858
thou therefore *r* him, that is,	Philem 12	4355
thou shouldest *r* him for ever	Philem 15	568
a partner, *r* him as myself	Philem 17	4355
of Levi, who *r* the office of the	Heb 7:5	2983
And here men that die *r* tithes	Heb 7:8	2983
might *r* the promise of eternal	Heb 9:15	2983

of God, ye might *r* the promise	Heb 10:36	2865
should after *r* for an inheritance	Heb 11:8	2983
he shall *r* any thing of the Lord	Jas 1:7	2983
he shall *r* the crown of life,	Jas 1:12	2983
r with meekness the engrafted	Jas 1:21	1209
knowing that we shall *r* the	Jas 3:1	2983
r not, because ye ask amiss, that	Jas 4:3	2983
until he *r* the early and latter	Jas 5:7	2983
ye shall *r* a crown of glory that	1Pet 5:4	2865
And shall *r* the reward of	2Pet 2:13	2865
we *r* of him, because we keep his	1Jn 3:22	2983
If we *r* the witness of men, the	1Jn 5:9	2983
but that we *r* a full reward	2Jn 8	618
r him not into your house,	2Jn 10	2983
We therefore ought to *r* such	3Jn 8	618
doth he himself *r* the brethren	3Jn 10	1926
to *r* glory and honour and power	Rev 4:11	2983
Lamb that was slain to *r* power	Rev 5:12	2983
to *r* a mark in their right hand,	Rev 13:16	1325
r his mark in his forehead, or in	Rev 14:9	2983
but *r* power as kings one hour	Rev 17:12	2983
that ye *r* not of her plagues	Rev 18:4	2983

RECEIVED

r in the same year an hundredfold	Gen 26:12	4672
he *r* them at their hand, and	Ex 32:4	3947
they *r* of Moses all the offering,	Ex 36:3	3947
after that let her be *r* in again	Num 12:14	622
I have *r* commandment to bless	Num 23:20	3947
fathers, have *r* their inheritance	Num 34:14	3947
Manasseh have *r* their inheritance	Num 34:14	3947
the half tribe have *r* their	Num 34:15	3947
of the tribe whereunto they are *r*	Num 36:3	1961
of the tribe whereunto they are *r*	Num 36:4	1961
and the Gadites have *r* their	Josh 13:8	3947
had not yet *r* their inheritance	Josh 18:2	2505
have *r* their inheritance beyond	Josh 18:7	3947
would not have *r* a burnt offering	Judg 13:23	3947
or of whose hand have I *r* any	1Sa 12:3	3947
So David *r* of her hand that which	1Sa 25:35	3947
the king's merchants *r* the linen	1Kin 10:28	3947
Hezekiah *r* the letter of the hand	2Kin 19:14	3947
Then David *r* them, and made them	1Chr 12:18	6901
the king's merchants *r* the linen	2Chr 1:16	3947
and it *r* and held three thousand	2Chr 4:5	2388
and the priests *r* the blood	2Chr 29:22	6901
which they *r* of the hand of the	2Chr 30:16	3947
but he *r* it not	Est 4:4	6901
mine ear *r* a little thereof	Job 4:12	3947
thou hast *r* gifts for men	Ps 68:18	3947
looked upon it, and *r* instruction	Prov 24:32	3947
Hezekiah *r* the letter from the	Is 37:14	3947
for she hath *r* of the Lord's hand	Is 40:2	3947
they *r* no correction	Jer 2:30	3947
that hath not *r* usury nor	Eze 18:17	3947
she *r* not correction	Zeph 3:2	3947
freely ye have *r*, freely give	Mt 10:8	2983
This is he which *r* seed by the	Mt 13:19	4687
But he that *r* the seed into stony	Mt 13:20	4687
He also that *r* seed among the	Mt 13:22	4687
But he that *r* seed into the good	Mt 13:23	4687
they that *r* tribute money came to	Mt 17:24	2983
hour, they *r* every man a penny	Mt 20:9	2983
that they should have *r* more	Mt 20:10	2983
they likewise *r* every man a penny	Mt 20:10	2983
And when they had *r* it, they	Mt 20:11	2983
and immediately their eyes *r* sight	Mt 20:34	308
Then he that had *r* the five	Mt 25:16	2983
And likewise he that had *r* two	Mt 25:17	
But he that had *r* one went	Mt 25:18	2983
so he that had *r* five talents	Mt 25:20	2983
also that had *r* two talents came	Mt 25:22	2983
Then he which had *r* the one	Mt 25:24	2983
should have *r* mine own with usury	Mt 25:27	2865
be, which they have *r* to hold	Mk 7:4	3880
And immediately he *r* his sight	Mk 10:52	308
but he *r* it not	Mk 15:23	2983
he was *r* up into heaven, and sat	Mk 16:19	353
for ye have *r* your consolation	Lk 6:24	568
returned, the people gladly *r* him	Lk 8:40	588
he *r* them, and spake unto them of	Lk 9:11	1209
was come that he should be *r* up	Lk 9:51	354
named Martha *r* him into her house	Lk 10:38	5264
calf, because he hath *r* him safe	Lk 15:27	618
And immediately he *r* his sight	Lk 18:43	308
and came down, and *r* him joyfully	Lk 19:6	5264
having *r* the kingdom, then he	Lk 19:15	2983
his own, and his own *r* him not	Jn 1:11	3880
But as many as *r* him, to them	Jn 1:12	2983
And of his fulness have all we *r*	Jn 1:16	2983
He that hath *r* his testimony hath	Jn 3:33	2983

Galilee, the Galilaeans *r* him	Jn 4:45	1209
willingly *r* him into the ship	Jn 6:21	2983
and I went and washed, and I *r* sight	Jn 9:11	308
asked him how he had *r* his sight	Jn 9:15	308
r his sight, until they called	Jn 9:18	308
of him that had *r* his sight	Jn 9:18	308
commandment have I *r* of my Father	Jn 10:18	2983
He then having *r* the sop went	Jn 13:30	2983
and they have *r* them, and have	Jn 17:8	2983
having *r* a band of men and	Jn 18:3	2983
Jesus therefore had *r* the vinegar	Jn 19:30	2983
a cloud *r* him out of their sight	Acts 1:9	5274
having *r* of the Father the	Acts 2:33	2983
Then they that gladly *r* his word	Acts 2:41	588
feet and ancle bones *r* strength	Acts 3:7	4732
who *r* the lively oracles to give	Acts 7:38	1209
Who have *r* the law by the	Acts 7:53	2983
Samaria had *r* the word of God	Acts 8:14	1209
on them, and they *r* the Holy Ghost	Acts 8:17	2983
r his sight forthwith, and arose,	Acts 9:18	308
And when he had *r* meat, he was	Acts 9:19	2983
the vessel was *r* up again into	Acts 10:16	353
which have *r* the Holy Ghost as	Acts 10:47	2983
had also *r* the word of God	Acts 11:1	1209
they were *r* of the church, and of	Acts 15:4	588
having *r* such a charge, thrust	Acts 16:24	
Whom Jason hath *r*	Acts 17:7	5264
in that they *r* the word with all	Acts 17:11	1209
Have ye *r* the Holy Ghost since ye	Acts 19:2	2983
which I have *r* of the Lord Jesus,	Acts 20:24	2983
the brethren *r* us gladly	Acts 21:17	1209
from whom also I *r* letters unto	Acts 22:5	1209
having *r* authority from the chief	Acts 26:10	2983
r us every one, because of the	Acts 28:2	4355
who *r* us, and lodged us three days	Acts 28:7	324
We neither *r* letters out of	Acts 28:21	1209
r all that came in unto him,	Acts 28:30	588
By whom we have *r* grace and	Rom 1:5	2983
he *r* the sign of circumcision, a	Rom 4:11	2983
whom we have now *r* the atonement	Rom 5:11	2983
For ye have not *r* the spirit of	Rom 8:15	2983
but ye have *r* the Spirit of	Rom 8:15	2983
for God hath *r* him	Rom 14:3	4355
as Christ also *r* us to the glory	Rom 15:7	4355
Now we have *r*, not the spirit of	1Cor 2:12	2983
glory, as if thou hadst not *r* it	1Cor 4:7	2983
For I have *r* of the Lord that	1Cor 11:23	3880
unto you, which also ye have *r*	1Cor 15:1	3880
first of all that which I also *r*	1Cor 15:3	3880
this ministry, as we have *r* mercy	2Cor 4:1	1653
with fear and trembling ye *r* him	2Cor 7:15	1209
spirit, which ye have not *r*	2Cor 11:4	2983
Of the Jews five times *r* I forty	2Cor 11:24	2983
unto you than that ye have *r*	Gal 1:9	3880
For I neither *r* it of man	Gal 1:12	3880
R ye the Spirit by the works of	Gal 3:2	2983
but *r* me as an angel of God, even	Gal 4:14	1209
which ye have both learned, and *r*	Phil 4:9	3880
having *r* of Epaphroditus the	Phil 4:18	1209
As ye have therefore *r* Christ	Col 2:6	3880
(touching whom ye *r* commandments	Col 4:10	2983
which thou hast *r* in the Lord	Col 4:17	3880
having *r* the word in much	1Th 1:6	1209
when ye *r* the word of God which	1Th 2:13	3880
ye *r* it not as the word of men,	1Th 2:13	1209
that as ye have *r* of us how ye	1Th 4:1	3880
because they *r* not the love of	2Th 2:10	1209
the tradition which he *r* of us	2Th 3:6	3880
on in the world, *r* up into glory	1Ti 3:16	353
which God hath created to be *r*	1Ti 4:3	3336
if it be *r* with thanksgiving	1Ti 4:4	2983
disobedience *r* a just recompence	Heb 2:2	2983
from them *r* tithes of Abraham	Heb 7:6	1183
for under it the people *r* the law	Heb 7:11	3549
have *r* the knowledge of the truth	Heb 10:26	2983
r strength to conceive seed	Heb 11:11	2983
not having *r* the promises, but	Heb 11:13	2983
he that had *r* the promises	Heb 11:17	324
whence also he *r* him in a figure	Heb 11:19	2865
when she had *r* the spies with	Heb 11:31	1209
Women *r* their dead raised to life	Heb 11:35	2983
through faith, *r* not the promise	Heb 11:39	2865
when she had *r* the messengers, and	Jas 2:25	5264
from your vain conversation *r* by	1Pet 1:18	
As every man hath *r* the gift	1Pet 4:10	2983
For he *r* from God the Father	2Pet 1:17	2983
ye have *r* of him abideth in you	1Jn 2:27	2983
as we have *r* a commandment from	2Jn 4	2983
even as I *r* of my Father	Rev 2:27	2983
therefore how thou hast *r*	Rev 3:3	2983
which have *r* no kingdom as yet	Rev 17:12	2983

R

that had *r* the mark of the beast .... Rev 19:20   2983
neither had *r* his mark upon their .... Rev 20:4

RECEIVEDST
in thy lifetime *r* thy good things .... Lk 16:25   618

RECEIVER
where is the *r*................................. Is 33:18   8254

RECEIVETH
is no man that *r* me to house .... Judg 19:18   622
or what *r* he of thine hand.................... Job 35:7   3947
is instructed, he *r* knowledge .... Prov 21:11   3947
but he that *r* gifts overthroweth............. Prov 29:4
LORD their God, nor *r* correction .... Jer 7:28   3947
or *r* it with good will at your .... Mal 2:13   3947
For every one that asketh *r* .... Mt 7:8   2983
He that *r* you *r* me, and he.................. Mt 10:40   1209
r me *r* him that sent me..................... Mt 10:40   1209
He that *r* a prophet in the name............... Mt 10:41   2983
he that *r* a righteous man in the .... Mt 10:41   2983
the word, and anon with joy *r* it .... Mt 13:20   2983
such little child in my name *r* me......... Mt 18:5   1209
of such children in my name, *r* me....... Mk 9:37   1209
r not me, but him that sent me .... Mk 9:37   1209
this child in my name *r* me .... Lk 9:48   1209
receive me *r* him that sent me .... Lk 9:48   1209
For every one that asketh *r* .... Lk 11:10   2983
saying, This man *r* sinners .... Lk 15:2   4327
and no man *r* his testimony .... Jn 3:32   2983
And he that reapeth *r* wages .... Jn 4:36   2983
r not my words, hath one that .... Jn 12:48   2983
r whomsoever I send *r* me .... Jn 13:20   2983
r me *r* him that sent me .... Jn 13:20   2983
But the natural man *r* not the................ 1Cor 2:14   1209
race run all, but one *r* the prize 1Cor 9:24   2983
is dressed, *r* blessing from God .... Heb 6:7   3335
but there he *r* them, of whom it.............. Heb 7:8
who *r* tithes, payed tithes in .... Heb 7:9   2983
and scourgeth every son whom he *r*...... Heb 12:6   3858
preeminence among them, *r* us not 3Jn 9   1926
man knoweth saving he that *r* it .... Rev 2:17   2983
whosoever *r* the mark of his name .... Rev 14:11   2983

RECEIVING
in not *r* at his hands that which 2Kin 5:20   3947
r a commandment unto Silas and .... Acts 17:15   2983
r in themselves that recompence .... Rom 1:27   618
what shall the *r* of them be .... Rom 11:15   4356
with me as concerning giving and *r* ..... Phil 4:15   3028
Wherefore we *r* a kingdom which........... Heb 12:28   3880
R the end of your faith, even the............. 1Pet 1:9   2865

RECHAB (re'-kab) See RECHABITES.
1. A son of Rimmon.
and the name of the other *R* 2Sa 4:2   7394
sons of Rimmon the Beerothite, *R* 2Sa 4:5   7394
and *R* and Baanah his brother 2Sa 4:6   7394
And David answered *R* and Baanah 2Sa 4:9   7394
2. Founder of the Rechabites.
the son of *R* coming to meet him 2Kin 10:15   7394
went, and Jehonadab the son of *R* 2Kin 10:23   7394
for Jonadab the son of *R* our .... Jer 35:6   7394
R our father in all that he hath............... Jer 35:8   7394
The words of Jonadab the son of *R*......... Jer 35:14   7394
R have performed the commandment .... Jer 35:16   7394
Jonadab the son of *R* shall not .... Jer 35:19   7394
3. A descendant of Hemath.
the father of the house of *R* 1Chr 2:55   7394
4. Father of Malchiah.
repaired Malchiah the son of *R* .... Neh 3:14   7394

RECHABITES (rek'-ab-ites) Descendants of Rechab 2.
Go unto the house of the *R* .... Jer 35:2   7397
sons, and the whole house of the *R* .... Jer 35:3   7397
house of the *R* pots full of wine .... Jer 35:5   7397
said unto the house of the *R* .... Jer 35:18   7397

RECHAH A family of Judah.
These are the men of *R*........................ 1Chr 4:12   7397

RECKON
he shall *r* with him that bought .... Lev 25:50   2803
then the priest shall *r* unto him .... Lev 27:18   2803
Then the priest shall *r* unto him .... Lev 27:23   2803
and by name ye shall *r* the.................... Num 4:32   6485
they shall *r* unto him seven days .... Eze 44:26   5608
And when he had begun to *r* .... Mt 18:24   4868
Likewise *r* ye also yourselves to .... Rom 6:11   3049
For I *r* that the sufferings of .... Rom 8:18   3049

RECKONED
offering shall be *r* unto you .... Num 18:27   2803
shall not be *r* among the nations .... Num 23:9   2803
Beeroth also was *r* to Benjamin............. 2Sa 4:2   2803

Moreover they *r* not with the men, ... 2Kin 12:15   2803
not to be *r* after the birthright 1Chr 5:1   3187
of their generations was *r* 1Chr 5:7   3187
All these were *r* by genealogies 1Chr 5:17   3187
r in all by their genealogies.................. 1Chr 7:5   3187
were *r* by their genealogies 1Chr 7:7   3187
all Israel were *r* by genealogies 1Chr 9:1   3187
These were *r* by their genealogy 1Chr 9:22   3187
to all that were *r* by genealogies............ 2Chr 31:19   3187
those that were *r* by genealogy .... Ezr 2:62   3187
with him were *r* by genealogy of............ Ezr 8:3   3187
that they might be *r* by genealogy .... Neh 7:5   3187
those that were *r* by genealogy .... Neh 7:64   3187
they cannot be *r* up in order unto .... Ps 40:5
I *r* till morning, that, as a lion .... Is 38:13   7737
he was *r* among the transgressors .... Lk 22:37   3049
is the reward not *r* of grace .... Rom 4:4   3049
for we say that faith was *r* to .... Rom 4:9   3049
How was it then *r* .... Rom 4:10   3049

RECKONETH
servants cometh, and *r* with them .. Mt 25:19   4868,3056

RECKONING
Howbeit there was no *r* made with 2Kin 22:7   2803
therefore they were in one *r*.................. 1Chr 23:11   6486

RECOMMENDED
from whence they had been *r* to .... Acts 14:26   3860
being *r* by the brethren unto the .... Acts 15:40   3860

RECOMPENCE
To me belongeth vengeance, and *r* .... Deut 32:35   8005
for vanity shall be his *r* .... Job 15:31   8545
with vengeance, even God with a *r* .... Is 35:4   1576
his adversaries, *r* to his enemies .... Is 59:18   1576
to the islands he will repay *r*................. Is 59:18   1576
that rendereth *r* to his enemies.............. Is 66:6   1576
he will render unto her a *r* .... Jer 51:6   1576
Render unto them a *r*, O LORD,.............. Lam 3:64   1576
are come, the days of *r* are come .... Hos 9:7   7966
will ye render me a *r*........................... Joel 3:4   1576
return your *r* upon your own head .... Joel 3:4   1576
will return your *r* upon your own .... Joel 3:7   1576
thee again, and a *r* be made thee .... Lk 14:12   468
receiving in themselves that *r* of .... Rom 1:27   489
stumblingblock, and a *r* unto them .... Rom 11:9   468
Now for a *r* in the same, (I speak........... 2Cor 6:13   489
received a just *r* of reward .... Heb 2:2   3405
which hath great *r* of reward .... Heb 10:35   3405
respect unto the *r* of the reward .... Heb 11:26   3405

RECOMPENCES
the year of *r* for the controversy .... Is 34:8   7966
for the LORD God of *r* shall .... Jer 51:56   1578

RECOMPENSE
he shall *r* his trespass with the .... Num 5:7   7725
no kinsman to *r* the trespass unto.......... Num 5:8   7725
The LORD *r* thy work, and a full .... Ruth 2:12   7999
why should the king *r* it me with 2Sa 19:36   1580
he will *r* it, whether thou refuse .... Job 34:33   7999
the *r* of a man's hands shall be .... Prov 12:14
Say not thou, I will *r* evil .... Prov 20:22   7999
will not keep silence, but will *r*.............. Is 65:6   7999
even *r* into their bosom, ... Is 65:6
first I will *r* their iniquity and .... Jer 16:18   7999
I will *r* them according to their .... Jer 25:14   7999
r her according to her work................... Jer 50:29   7999
will *r* upon thee all thine .... Eze 7:3   5414
but I will *r* thy ways upon thee,............. Eze 7:4   5414
will *r* thee for all thine .... Eze 7:8   5414
I will *r* thee according to thy .... Eze 7:9   5414
but I will *r* thy way upon their............... Eze 9:10   5414
I will *r* their way upon their own .... Eze 11:21   5414
therefore I also will *r* thy way .... Eze 16:43   5414
even it will I *r* upon his own .... Eze 17:19   5414
they shall *r* your lewdness upon .... Eze 23:49   5414
to his doings will he *r* him .... Hos 12:2   7725
and if ye *r* me, swiftly and .... Joel 3:4   1580
for they cannot *r* thee .... Lk 14:14   467
R to no man evil for evil .... Rom 12:17   591
God to *r* tribulation to them that 2Th 1:6   467
belongeth unto me, I will *r* .... Heb 10:30   467

RECOMPENSED
the trespass be *r* unto the LORD............ Num 5:8   7725
of my hands hath he *r* me 2Sa 22:21   7725
LORD hath *r* me according to my 2Sa 22:25   7725
of my hands hath he *r* me .... Ps 18:20   7725
the LORD *r* me according to my............. Ps 18:24   7725
righteous shall be *r* in the earth............ Prov 11:31   7999
Shall evil be *r* for good .... Jer 18:20   7999
own way have I *r* upon their heads .... Eze 22:31   5414

for thou shalt be *r* at the .... Lk 14:14   467
it shall be *r* unto him again .... Rom 11:35   467

RECOMPENSEST
r the iniquity of the fathers .... Jer 32:18   7999

RECOMPENSING
by *r* his way upon his own head 2Chr 6:23   5414

RECONCILE
of the congregation to *r* withal .... Lev 6:30   3722
he *r* himself unto his master 1Sa 29:4   7521
so shall ye *r* the house .... Eze 45:20   3722
that he might *r* both unto God in .... Eph 2:16   604
by him to *r* all things unto .... Col 1:20   604

RECONCILED
first be *r* to thy brother, and .... Mt 5:24   *1259*
we were *r* to God by the death of .... Rom 5:10   2644
of his Son, much more, being *r* .... Rom 5:10   2644
unmarried, or be *r* to her husband 1Cor 7:11   2644
who hath *r* us to himself by Jesus 2Cor 5:18   2644
in Christ's stead, be ye *r* to God 2Cor 5:20   2644
wicked works, yet now hath he *r* .... Col 1:21   604

RECONCILIATION
sanctified it, to make *r* upon it .... Lev 8:15   3722
they made *r* with their blood upon 2Chr 29:24   2398
to make *r* for them, saith the .... Eze 45:15   3722
to make *r* for the house of Israel .... Eze 45:17   3722
to make *r* for iniquity, and to .... Dan 9:24   3722
given to us the ministry of *r* 2Cor 5:18   2643
committed unto us the word of *r* 2Cor 5:19   2643
to make *r* for the sins of the .... Heb 2:17   2433

RECONCILING
made an end of *r* the holy place .... Lev 16:20   3722
of them be the *r* of the world .... Rom 11:15   2643
r the world unto himself, not 2Cor 5:19   2644

RECORD
in all places where I *r* my name I .... Ex 20:24   2142
earth to *r* this day against you, ... Deut 30:19   5749
heaven and earth to *r* against them .... Deut 31:28   5749
the ark of the LORD, and to *r* 1Chr 16:4   2142
and therein was a *r* thus written .... Ezr 6:2   1799
is in heaven, and my *r* is on high .... Job 16:19   7717
unto me faithful witnesses to *r* .... Is 8:2   5749
And this is the *r* of John, when .... Jn 1:19   *3141*
And John bare *r*, saying, I saw the .... Jn 1:32   *3140*
bare *r* that this is the Son of .... Jn 1:34   *3140*
him, Thou bearest *r* of thyself .... Jn 8:13   *3140*
thy *r* is not true .... Jn 8:13   *3141*
them, Though I bear *r* of myself .... Jn 8:14   *3140*
yet my *r* is true .... Jn 8:14   *3141*
raised him from the dead, bare *r* .... Jn 12:17   *3140*
And he that saw it bare *r*, and his .... Jn 19:35   *3140*
and his *r* is true .... Jn 19:35   *3141*
I take you to *r* this day, that I .... Acts 20:26   *3143*
For I bear them *r* that they have .... Rom 10:2   *3140*
I call God for a *r* upon my soul 2Cor 1:23   *3144*
For to their power, I bear *r* 2Cor 8:3   *3140*
for I bear you *r*, that, if it had .... Gal 4:15   *3140*
For God is my *r*, how greatly I .... Phil 1:8   *3144*
For I bear him *r*, that he hath a .... Col 4:13   *3140*
are three that bear *r* in heaven 1Jn 5:7   *3140*
the *r* that God gave of his Son 1Jn 5:10   *3141*
And this is the *r*, that God hath 1Jn 5:11   *3141*
yea, and we also bear *r* 3Jn 12   *3140*
and ye know that our *r* is true 3Jn 12   *3141*
Who bare *r* of the word of God, and ...... Rev 1:2   *3140*

RECORDED
were *r* chief of the fathers .... Neh 12:22   3789

RECORDER
the son of Ahilud was *r* 2Sa 8:16   2142
the son of Ahilud was *r* 2Sa 20:24   2142
the son of Ahilud, the *r* 1Kin 4:3   2142
and Joah the son of Asaph the *r* 2Kin 18:18   2142
and Joah the son of Asaph the *r* 2Kin 18:37   2142
Jehoshaphat the son of Ahilud, *r* 1Chr 18:15   2142
and Joah the son of Joahaz the *r* 2Chr 34:8   2142
and Joah, Asaph's son, the *r* .... Is 36:3   2142
and Joah, the son of Asaph, the *r* .... Is 36:22   2142

RECORDS
the book of the *r* of thy fathers .... Ezr 4:15   1799
thou find in the book of the *r* .... Ezr 4:15   1799
the book of *r* of the chronicles .... Est 6:1   2146

RECOUNT
He shall *r* his worthies .... Nah 2:5   2142

RECOVER
ye not *r* them within that time .... Judg 11:26   5337
them, and without fail *r* all 1Sa 30:8   5337

as he went to *r* his border at the 2Sa 8:3   7725
whether I shall *r* of this disease 2Kin 1:2   2421
for he would *r* him of his leprosy 2Kin 5:3   622
that thou mayest *r* him of his 2Kin 5:6   622
unto me to *r* a man of his leprosy 2Kin 5:7   622
over the place, and *r* the leper 2Kin 5:11   622
Shall I *r* of this disease 2Kin 8:8   2421
Shall I *r* of this disease 2Kin 8:9   2421
unto him, Thou mayest certainly *r* 2Kin 8:10   2421
me that thou shouldest surely *r* 2Kin 8:14   2421
Neither did Jeroboam *r* strength 2Chr 13:20   6113
that they could not *r* themselves 2Chr 14:13   4241
O spare me, that I may *r* strength .... Ps 39:13   1082
to *r* the remnant of his people .... Is 11:11   7069
so wilt thou *r* me, and make me to .... Is 38:16   2492
upon the boil, and he shall *r* .... Is 38:21   2421
will *r* my wool and my flax given .... Hos 2:9   5337
on the sick, and they shall *r* .... Mk 16:18   *2192,2573*
that they may *r* themselves out of 2Ti 2:26   *366*

RECOVERED
David *r* all that the Amalekites 1Sa 30:18   5337
David *r* all 1Sa 30:19   7725
ought of the spoil that we have *r* 1Sa 30:22   5337
him, and *r* the cities of Israel 2Kin 13:25   7725
how he *r* Damascus, and Hamath, ... 2Kin 14:28   7725
king of Syria *r* Elath to Syria 2Kin 16:6   7725
and laid it on the boil, and he *r* 2Kin 20:7   2421
sick, and was *r* of his sickness .... Is 38:9   2421
that he had been sick, and was *r* .... Is 39:1   2388
of the daughter of my people *r* .... Jer 8:22   5927
he had *r* from Ishmael the son of .... Jer 41:16   7725

RECOVERING
r of sight to the blind, to set .... Lk 4:18   *309*

RED *The sea dividing Egypt and Arabia.*
And the first came out *r*, all over .... Gen 25:25   132
thee, with that same *r* pottage .... Gen 25:30   122
His eyes shall be *r* with wine .... Gen 49:12   2447
and cast them into the *R* sea .... Ex 10:19   5488
of the wilderness of the *R* sea .... Ex 13:18   5488
also are drowned in the *R* sea .... Ex 15:4   5488
brought Israel from the *R* sea .... Ex 15:22   5488
R sea even unto the sea of the .... Ex 23:31   5488
And rams' skins dyed *r*, and .... Ex 25:5   119
the tent of rams' skins dyed *r* .... Ex 26:14   119
And rams' skins dyed *r*, and .... Ex 35:7   119
r skins of rams, and badgers' .... Ex 35:23   119
the tent of rams' skins dyed *r* .... Ex 36:19   119
covering of rams' skins dyed *r* .... Ex 39:34   119
by the way of the *R* sea .... Num 14:25   5488
thee a *r* heifer without spot .... Num 19:2   122
mount Hor by the way of the *R* sea .... Num 21:4   5488
LORD, What he did in the *R* sea .... Num 21:14   5492
Elim, and encamped by the *R* sea .... Num 33:10   5488
And they removed from the *R* sea .... Num 33:11   5488
the plain over against the *R* sea .... Deut 1:1   5489
by the way of the *R* sea .... Deut 1:40   5488
by the way of the *R* sea, as the .... Deut 2:1   5488
R sea to overflow them as they .... Deut 11:4   5488
up the water of the *R* sea for you .... Josh 2:10   5488
LORD your God did to the *R* sea .... Josh 4:23   5488
and horsemen unto the *R* sea .... Josh 24:6   5488
the wilderness unto the *R* sea .... Judg 11:16   5488
Eloth, on the shore of the *R* sea 1Kin 9:26   5488
on the other side as *r* as blood 2Kin 3:22   122
heardest their cry by the *R* sea .... Neh 9:9   5488
and silver, upon a pavement of *r* .... Est 1:6   923
there is a cup, and the wine is *r* .... Ps 75:8   2560
him at the sea, even at the *R* sea .... Ps 106:7   5488
He rebuked the *R* sea also .... Ps 106:9   5488
and terrible things by the *R* sea .... Ps 106:22   5488
divided the *R* sea into parts .... Ps 136:13   5488
Pharaoh and his host in the *R* sea .... Ps 136:15   5488
thou upon the wine when it is *r* .... Prov 23:31   119
though they be *r* like crimson .... Is 1:18   119
ye unto her, A vineyard of *r* wine .... Is 27:2   2561
art thou *r* in thine apparel .... Is 63:2   122
thereof was heard in the *R* sea .... Jer 49:21   5488
of his mighty men is made *r* .... Nah 2:3   119
a man riding upon a *r* horse .... Zec 1:8   122
and behind him were there *r* horses ...... Zec 1:8   122
the first chariot were *r* horses .... Zec 6:2   122
for the sky is *r* .... Mt 16:2   *4449*
for the sky is *r* and lowring .... Mt 16:3   *4449*
land of Egypt, and in the *R* sea .... Acts 7:36   *2281*
through the *R* sea as by dry land .... Heb 11:29   *2281*
went out another horse that was *r* .... Rev 6:4   *4450*
and behold a great *r* dragon .... Rev 12:3   *4450*

R

REDDISH

bright spot, white, and somewhat *r*	Lev 13:19	125
a white bright spot, somewhat *r*	Lev 13:24	125
or bald forehead, a white *r* sore	Lev 13:42	125
sore be white *r* in his bald head	Lev 13:43	125
be greenish or *r* in the garment	Lev 13:49	125
hollow strakes, greenish or *r*	Lev 14:37	125

REDEEM

I will *r* you with a stretched out	Ex 6:6	1350
an ass thou shalt *r* with a lamb	Ex 13:13	6299
and if thou wilt not *r* it, then	Ex 13:13	6299
among thy children shalt thou *r*	Ex 13:13	6299
the firstborn of my children I *r*	Ex 13:15	6299
an ass thou shalt *r* with a lamb	Ex 34:20	6299
and if thou *r* him not, then shalt	Ex 34:20	6299
of thy sons thou shalt *r*	Ex 34:20	6299
and if any of his kin come to *r* it	Lev 25:25	1350
then shall he *r* that which his	Lev 25:25	1350
And if the man have none to *r* it	Lev 25:26	1350
and himself be able to *r* it	Lev 25:26	1353
then he may *r* it within a whole	Lev 25:29	1353
within a full year may he *r* it	Lev 25:29	1353
may the Levites *r* at any time	Lev 25:32	1353
one of his brethren may *r* him	Lev 25:48	1350
or his uncle's son, may *r* him	Lev 25:49	1350
unto him of his family may *r* him	Lev 25:49	1350
if he be able, he may *r* himself	Lev 25:49	1353
But if he will at all *r* it	Lev 27:13	1350
sanctified it will *r* his house	Lev 27:15	1350
the field will in any wise *r* it	Lev 27:19	1350
And if he will not *r* the field	Lev 27:20	1350
then he shall *r* it according to	Lev 27:27	6299
will at all *r* ought of his tithes	Lev 27:31	1350
of man shalt thou surely *r*	Num 18:15	6299
of unclean beasts shalt thou *r*	Num 18:15	6299
from a month old shalt thou *r*	Num 18:16	6299
of a goat, thou shalt not *r*	Num 18:17	6299
If thou wilt *r*	Ruth 4:4	1350
r it: but if thou wilt	Ruth 4:4	6299
but if thou wilt not *r* it	Ruth 4:4	1350
there is none to *r* it beside thee	Ruth 4:4	1350
And he said, I will *r* it	Ruth 4:4	1350
I cannot *r* it for myself, lest I	Ruth 4:6	1350
r thou my right to thyself	Ruth 4:6	1350
for I cannot *r* it	Ruth 4:6	1350
whom God went to *r* for a people	2Sa 7:23	6299
whom God went to *r* to be his own	1Chr 17:21	6299
is it in our power to *r* them	Neh 5:5	
famine he shall *r* thee from death	Job 5:20	6299
R me from the hand of the mighty	Job 6:23	6299
R Israel, O God, out of all his	Ps 25:22	6299
r me, and be merciful unto me	Ps 26:11	6299
r us for thy mercies' sake	Ps 44:26	6299
can by any means *r* his brother	Ps 49:7	6299
But God will *r* my soul from the	Ps 49:15	6299
Draw nigh unto my soul, and *r* it	Ps 69:18	1350
He shall *r* their soul from deceit	Ps 72:14	1350
he shall *r* Israel from all his	Ps 130:8	6299
at all, that it cannot *r*	Is 50:2	6304
I will *r* thee out of the hand of	Jer 15:21	6299
I will *r* them from death	Hos 13:14	1350
there the Lord shall *r* thee from	Mic 4:10	1350
To *r* them that were under the law	Gal 4:5	1805
that he might *r* us from all	Titus 2:14	3084

REDEEMED

The angel which *r* me from all	Gen 48:16	1350
the people which thou hast *r*	Ex 15:13	1350
then shall he let her be *r*	Ex 21:8	6299
to an husband, and not at all *r*	Lev 19:20	6299
if it be not *r* within the space	Lev 25:30	1350
they may be *r*, and they shall go	Lev 25:31	1353
that he is sold he may be *r* again	Lev 25:48	1353
if he be not *r* in these years,	Lev 25:54	1350
man, it shall not be *r* any more	Lev 27:20	1350
or if it be not *r*, then it shall	Lev 27:27	1350
possession, shall be sold or *r*	Lev 27:28	1350
be devoted of men, shall be *r*	Lev 27:29	6299
it shall not be *r*	Lev 27:33	1350
are to be *r* of the two hundred	Num 3:46	6302
the odd number of them is to be *r*	Num 3:48	6302
them that were *r* by the Levites	Num 3:49	6306
of them that were *r* unto Aaron	Num 3:51	6306
those that are to be *r* from a	Num 18:16	6299
r you out of the house of bondmen	Deut 7:8	6299
which thou hast *r* through thy	Deut 9:26	6299
r you out of the house of bondage	Deut 13:5	6299
Egypt, and the Lord thy God *r* thee	Deut 15:15	6299
people Israel, whom thou hast *r*	Deut 21:8	6299
and the Lord thy God *r* thee thence	Deut 24:18	6299
who hath *r* my soul out of all	2Sa 4:9	6299

that hath *r* my soul out of all	1Kin 1:29	6299
whom thou hast *r* out of Egypt	1Chr 17:21	6299
whom thou hast *r* by thy great	Neh 1:10	6299
have *r* our brethren the Jews	Neh 5:8	7069
thou hast *r* me, O Lord God of	Ps 31:5	6299
and my soul, which thou hast *r*	Ps 71:23	6299
inheritance, which thou hast *r*	Ps 74:2	1350
hast with thine arm *r* thy people	Ps 77:15	1350
r them from the hand of the enemy	Ps 106:10	1350
Let the *r* of the Lord say so,	Ps 107:2	1350
whom he hath *r* from the hand of	Ps 107:2	1350
hath *r* us from our enemies	Ps 136:24	6561
Zion shall be *r* with judgment	Is 1:27	6299
who *r* Abraham, concerning the	Is 29:22	6299
but the *r* shall walk there	Is 35:9	1350
for I have *r* thee, I have called	Is 43:1	1350
for I have *r* thee	Is 44:22	1350
for the Lord hath *r* Jacob	Is 44:23	1350
The Lord hath *r* his servant Jacob	Is 48:20	1350
Therefore the *r* of the Lord shall	Is 51:11	6299
ye shall be *r* without money	Is 52:3	1350
his people, he hath *r* Jerusalem	Is 52:9	1350
holy people, The *r* of the Lord	Is 62:12	1350
and the year of my *r* is come	Is 63:4	1350
his love and in his pity he *r* them	Is 63:9	1350
For the Lord hath *r* Jacob	Jer 31:11	6299
thou hast *r* my life	Lam 3:58	1350
though I have *r* them, yet they	Hos 7:13	6299
r thee out of the house of	Mic 6:4	6299
for I have *r* them	Zec 10:8	6299
he hath visited and *r* his people,	Lk 1:68	4160,3085
he which should have *r* Israel	Lk 24:21	3084
Christ hath *r* us from the curse	Gal 3:13	1805
not *r* with corruptible things	1Pet 1:18	3084
hast *r* us to God by thy blood out	Rev 5:9	59
which were *r* from the earth	Rev 14:3	59
These were *r* from among men,	Rev 14:4	59

REDEEMEDST

which thou *r* to thee from Egypt,	2Sa 7:23	6299

REDEEMER

For I know that my *r* liveth	Job 19:25	1350
O Lord, my strength, and my *r*	Ps 19:14	1350
rock, and the high God their *r*	Ps 78:35	1350
For their *r* is mighty	Prov 23:11	1350
thee, saith the Lord, and thy *r*	Is 41:14	1350
Thus saith the Lord, your *r*	Is 43:14	1350
and his *r* the Lord of hosts	Is 44:6	1350
Thus saith the Lord, thy *r*	Is 44:24	1350
As for our *r*, the Lord of hosts	Is 47:4	1350
Thus saith the Lord, thy *R*	Is 48:17	1350
the *R* of Israel, and his Holy One,	Is 49:7	1350
the Lord am thy Saviour and thy *R*	Is 49:26	1350
thy *R* the Holy One of Israel	Is 54:5	1350
on thee, saith the Lord thy *R*	Is 54:8	1350
the *R* shall come to Zion, and unto	Is 59:20	1350
the Lord am thy Saviour and thy *R*	Is 60:16	1350
O Lord, art our father, our *r*	Is 63:16	1350
Their *R* is strong	Jer 50:34	1350

REDEEMETH

The Lord *r* the soul of his	Ps 34:22	6299
Who *r* thy life from destruction	Ps 103:4	1350

REDEEMING

time in Israel concerning *r*	Ruth 4:7	1353
R the time, because the days are	Eph 5:16	1805
them that are without, *r* the time	Col 4:5	1805

REDEMPTION

ye shall grant a *r* for the land	Lev 25:24	1353
give again the price of his *r* out	Lev 25:51	1353
give him again the price of his *r*	Lev 25:52	1353
Moses took the *r* money of them	Num 3:49	6306
(For the *r* of their soul is	Ps 49:8	6304
He sent *r* unto his people	Ps 111:9	6304
mercy, and with him is plenteous *r*	Ps 130:7	6304
for the right of *r* is thine to	Jer 32:7	1353
is thine, and the *r* is thine	Jer 32:8	1353
that looked for *r* in Jerusalem	Lk 2:38	3085
for your *r* draweth nigh	Lk 21:28	629
the *r* that is in Christ Jesus	Rom 3:24	629
to wit, the *r* of our body	Rom 8:23	629
and sanctification, and *r*	1Cor 1:30	629
In whom we have *r* through his	Eph 1:7	629
the *r* of the purchased possession	Eph 1:14	629
ye are sealed unto the day of *r*	Eph 4:30	629
In whom we have *r* through his	Col 1:14	629
having obtained eternal *r* for us	Heb 9:12	3085
for the *r* of the transgressions	Heb 9:15	629

REDNESS

who hath *r* of eyes	Prov 23:29	2498

REDOUND
of many *r* to the glory of God 2Cor 4:15   4052

REED
as a *r* is shaken in the water, and 1Kin 14:15   7070
upon the staff of this bruised *r* 2Kin 18:21   7070
trees, in the covert of the *r* .... Job 40:21   7070
in the staff of this broken *r* .... Is 36:6   7070
A bruised *r* shall he not break, ... Is 42:3   7070
staff of *r* to the house of Israel .... Eze 29:6   7070
in his hand, and a measuring *r* .... Eze 40:3   7070
in the man's hand a measuring *r* .... Eze 40:5   7070
breadth of the building, one *r* .... Eze 40:5   7070
and the height, one *r* .... Eze 40:5   7070
the gate, which was one *r* broad .... Eze 40:6   7070
the gate, which was one *r* broad .... Eze 40:6   7070
was one *r* long, and one *r* broad .... Eze 40:7   7070
of the gate within was one *r* .... Eze 40:7   7070
porch of the gate within, one *r* .... Eze 40:8   7070
were a full *r* of six great cubits .... Eze 41:8   7070
east side with the measuring *r* .... Eze 42:16   7070
with the measuring *r* round about .... Eze 42:16   7070
with the measuring *r* round about .... Eze 42:17   7070
reeds, with the measuring *r* .... Eze 42:18   7070
reeds with the measuring *r* .... Eze 42:19   7070
A *r* shaken with the wind .... Mt 11:7   2563
A bruised *r* shall he not break, ... Mt 12:20   2563
head, and a *r* in his right hand .... Mt 27:29   2563
they spit upon him, and took the *r* ...... Mt 27:30   2563
it with vinegar, and put it on a *r* .... Mt 27:48   2563
smote him on the head with a *r* .... Mk 15:19   2563
full of vinegar, and put it on a *r* .... Mk 15:36   2563
A *r* shaken with the wind .... Lk 7:24   2563
was given me a *r* like unto a rod .... Rev 11:1   2563
a golden *r* to measure the city .... Rev 21:15   2563
he measured the city with the *r* .... Rev 21:16   2563

REEDS
the *r* and flags shall wither .... Is 19:6   7070
The paper *r* by the brooks, by the .... Is 19:7
each lay, shall be grass with *r* .... Is 35:7   7070
the *r* they have burned with fire, ... Jer 51:32   98
measuring reed, five hundred *r* .... Eze 42:16   7070
the north side, five hundred *r* .... Eze 42:17   7070
the south side, five hundred *r* .... Eze 42:18   7070
measured five hundred *r* with the .... Eze 42:19   7070
round about, five hundred *r* long .... Eze 42:20
of five and twenty thousand *r* .... Eze 45:1
and twenty thousand *r* in breadth .... Eze 48:8

REEL
They *r* to and fro, and stagger like .... Ps 107:27   2287
The earth shall *r* to and fro like .... Is 24:20   5128

REELAIAH (re-el-ah'-yah) A clan leader with Zerubbabel.
Jeshua, Nehemiah, Seraiah, *R* .... Ezr 2:2   7480

REFINE
will *r* them as silver is refined, ... Zec 13:9   6884

REFINED
altar of incense *r* gold by weight 1Chr 28:18   2212
thousand talents of *r* silver 1Chr 29:4   2212
of wines on the lees well *r* .... Is 25:6   2212
Behold, I have *r* thee, but not .... Is 48:10   6884
will refine them as silver is *r* .... Zec 13:9   6884

REFINER
And he shall sit as a *r* and .... Mal 3:3   6884

REFINER'S
for he is like a *r* fire, and like .... Mal 3:2   6884

REFORMATION
on them until the time of *r* .... Heb 9:10   1357

REFORMED
if ye will not be *r* by me by .... Lev 26:23   3256

REFRAIN
Then Joseph could not *r* himself .... Gen 45:1   662
Therefore I will not *r* my mouth .... Job 7:11   2820
r thy foot from their path .... Prov 1:15   4513
a time to *r* from embracing .... Eccl 3:5   7368
for my praise will I *r* for thee .... Is 48:9   2413
Wilt thou *r* thyself for these .... Is 64:12   662
R thy voice from weeping, and .... Jer 31:16   4513
R from these men, and let them .... Acts 5:38   868
let him *r* his tongue from evil, ... 1Pet 3:10   3973

REFRAINED
r himself, and said, Set on bread .... Gen 43:31   662
Nevertheless Haman *r* himself .... Est 5:10   662
The princes *r* talking, and laid .... Job 29:9   6113
lo, I have not *r* my lips, O Lord, ... Ps 40:9   3607
I have *r* my feet from every evil .... Ps 119:101   3601

I have been still, and *r* myself .... Is 42:14   662
they have not *r* their feet .... Jer 14:10   2820

REFRAINETH
but he that *r* his lips is wise .... Prov 10:19   2820

REFRESH
r thyself, and I will give thee a 1Kin 13:7   5582
go unto his friends to *r* himself .... Acts 27:3   1958,5177
r my bowels in the Lord .... Philem 20   373

REFRESHED
and the stranger, may be *r* .... Ex 23:12   5314
seventh day he rested, and was *r* .... Ex 31:17   5314
so Saul was *r*, and was well, and 1Sa 16:23   7304
came weary, and *r* themselves there 2Sa 16:14   5314
I will speak, that I may be *r* .... Job 32:20   7304
will of God, and may with you be *r* .... Rom 15:32   4875
For they have *r* my spirit 1Cor 16:18   373
his spirit was *r* by you all 2Cor 7:13   373
for he oft *r* me, and was not 2Ti 1:16   404
of the saints are *r* by thee .... Philem 7   373

REFRESHETH
for he *r* the soul of his masters .... Prov 25:13   7725

REFRESHING
and this is the *r* .... Is 28:12   4774
when the times of *r* shall come .... Acts 3:19   403

REFUGE
there shall be six cities for *r* .... Num 35:6   4733
cities to be cities of *r* for you .... Num 35:11   4733
you cities for *r* from the avenger .... Num 35:12   4733
six cities shall ye have for *r* .... Num 35:13   4733
which shall be cities of *r* .... Num 35:14   4733
These six cities shall be a *r* .... Num 35:15   4733
restore him to the city of his *r* .... Num 35:25   4733
the border of the city of his *r* .... Num 35:26   4733
the borders of the city of his *r* .... Num 35:27   4733
his *r* until the death of the high .... Num 35:28   4733
that is fled to the city of his *r* .... Num 35:32   4733
The eternal God is thy *r*, and .... Deut 33:27   4585
Appoint out for you cities of *r* .... Josh 20:2   4733
they shall be your *r* from the .... Josh 20:3   4733
to be a city of *r* for the slayer .... Josh 21:13   4733
to be a city of *r* for the slayer .... Josh 21:21   4733
to be a city of *r* for the slayer .... Josh 21:27   4733
to be a city of *r* for the slayer .... Josh 21:32   4733
to be a city of *r* for the slayer .... Josh 21:38   4733
salvation, my high tower, and my *r* 2Sa 22:3   4498
namely, Hebron, the city of *r* 1Chr 6:57   4733
unto them, of the cities of *r* 1Chr 6:67   4733
will be a *r* for the oppressed .... Ps 9:9   4869
a *r* in times of trouble .... Ps 9:9   4869
poor, because the Lord is his *r* .... Ps 14:6   4268
God is our *r* and strength, a very .... Ps 46:1   4268
the God of Jacob is our *r* .... Ps 46:7   4869
the God of Jacob is our *r* .... Ps 46:11   4869
is known in her palaces for a *r* .... Ps 48:3   4869
of thy wings will I make my *r* .... Ps 57:1   2620
r in the day of my trouble .... Ps 59:16   4498
the rock of my strength, and my *r* .... Ps 62:7   4268
God is a *r* for us .... Ps 62:8   4268
but thou art my strong *r* .... Ps 71:7   4268
will say of the Lord, He is my *r* .... Ps 91:2   4268
hast made the Lord, which is my *r* .... Ps 91:9   4268
and my God is the rock of my *r* .... Ps 94:22   4268
hills are a *r* for the wild goats .... Ps 104:18   4268
r failed me .... Ps 142:4   4498
I said, Thou art my *r* and my .... Ps 142:5   4268
children shall have a place of *r* .... Prov 14:26   4268
the heat, and for a place of *r* .... Is 4:6   4268
a *r* from the storm, a shadow from .... Is 25:4   4268
for we have made lies our *r* .... Is 28:15   4268
shall sweep away the *r* of lies .... Is 28:17   4268
my *r* in the day of affliction, ... Jer 16:19   4498
who have fled for *r* to lay hold .... Heb 6:18   2703

REFUSE
if thou *r* to let him go, behold, ... Ex 4:23   3985
if thou *r* to let them go, behold, ... Ex 8:2   3986
For if thou *r* to let them go, and .... Ex 9:2   3986
How long wilt thou *r* to humble .... Ex 10:3   3985
if thou *r* to let my people go, ... Ex 10:4   3986
Moses, How long *r* ye to keep my .... Ex 16:28   3985
utterly *r* to give her unto him .... Ex 22:17   3985
every thing that was vile and *r* 1Sa 15:9   4549
recompense it, whether thou *r* .... Job 34:33   3988
and be wise, and *r* it not .... Prov 8:33   6544
because they *r* to do judgment .... Prov 21:7   3985
for his hands *r* to labour .... Prov 21:25   3985
But if ye *r* and rebel, ye shall be .... Is 1:20   3985
that he may know to *r* the evil .... Is 7:15   3988

R

child shall know to *r* the evil	Is 7:16	3988
fast deceit, they *r* to return	Jer 8:5	3985
through deceit they *r* to know me	Jer 9:6	3985
which *r* to hear my words, which	Jer 13:10	3987
if they *r* to take the cup at	Jer 25:28	3985
But if thou *r* to go forth	Jer 38:21	3986
r in the midst of the people	Lam 3:45	3973
yea, and sell the *r* of the wheat	Amos 8:6	4651
worthy of death, I *r* not to die	Acts 25:11	3868
But *r* profane and old wives'	1Ti 4:7	3868
But the younger widows *r*	1Ti 5:11	3868
See that ye *r* not him that	Heb 12:25	3868

REFUSED

but he *r* to be comforted	Gen 37:35	3985
But he *r*, and said unto his	Gen 39:8	3985
And his father *r*, and said, I know	Gen 48:19	3985
Thus Edom *r* to give Israel	Num 20:21	3985
Nevertheless the people *r* to obey	1Sa 8:19	3985
because I have *r* him	1Sa 16:7	3988
But he *r*, and said, I will not eat	1Sa 28:23	3985
Howbeit he *r* to turn aside	2Sa 2:23	3985
but he *r* to eat	2Sa 13:9	3985
And the man *r* to smite him	1Kin 20:35	3985
which he *r* to give thee for money	1Kin 21:15	3985
to take it; but he *r*	2Kin 5:16	3985
r to obey, neither were mindful	Neh 9:17	3985
But the queen Vashti *r* to come at	Est 1:12	3985
The things that my soul *r* to	Job 6:7	3985
my soul *r* to be comforted	Ps 77:2	3985
of God, and *r* to walk in his law	Ps 78:10	3985
Moreover he *r* the tabernacle of	Ps 78:67	3988
The stone which the builders *r* is	Ps 118:22	3988
Because I have called, and ye *r*	Prov 1:24	3985
a wife of youth, when thou wast *r*	Is 54:6	3988
but they have *r* to receive	Jer 5:3	3985
they have *r* to return	Jer 5:3	3985
which *r* to hear my words	Jer 11:10	3985
r to be comforted for her	Jer 31:15	3985
they *r* to let them go	Jer 50:33	3985
for they have *r* my judgments	Eze 5:6	3988
king, because they *r* to return	Hos 11:5	3985
But they *r* to hearken, and pulled	Zec 7:11	3985
This Moses whom they *r*, saying,	Acts 7:35	720
God is good, and nothing to be *r*	1Ti 4:4	579
r to be called the son of	Heb 11:24	720
not who *r* him that spake on earth	Heb 12:25	3868

REFUSEDST

forehead, thou *r* to be ashamed	Jer 3:3	3985

REFUSETH

he *r* to let the people go	Ex 7:14	3985
for the LORD *r* to give me leave	Num 22:13	3985
and said, Balaam *r* to come with us	Num 22:14	3985
My husband's brother *r* to raise	Deut 25:7	3985
but he that *r* reproof erreth	Prov 10:17	5800
be to him that *r* instruction	Prov 13:18	6544
He that *r* instruction despiseth	Prov 15:32	6544
Forasmuch as this people *r* the	Is 8:6	3988
incurable, which *r* to be healed	Jer 15:18	3985

REGARD

Also *r* not your stuff	Gen 45:20	5869,2437,5921
and let them not *r* vain words	Ex 5:9	8159
R not them that have familiar	Lev 19:31	6437
which shall not *r* the person of	Deut 28:50	5375
not, neither did she *r* it	1Sa 4:20	3820
r this man of Belial, even Nabal	1Sa 25:25	3820
r not this thing	2Sa 13:20	3820
were it not that I *r* the presence	2Kin 3:14	5375
let not God *r* it from above,	Job 3:4	1875
neither will the Almighty *r* it	Job 35:13	7789
Take heed, *r* not iniquity	Job 36:21	6437
Because they *r* not the works of	Ps 28:5	995
hated them that *r* lying vanities	Ps 31:6	8104
If I *r* iniquity in my heart, the	Ps 66:18	7200
shall the God of Jacob *r* it	Ps 94:7	995
He will *r* the prayer of the	Ps 102:17	6437
That thou mayest *r* discretion	Prov 5:2	8104
He will not *r* any ransom	Prov 6:35	5375,6440
that in *r* of the oath of God	Eccl 8:2	5921,1700
but they *r* not the work of the	Is 5:12	5027
them, which shall not *r* silver	Is 13:17	2803
he will no more *r* them	Lam 4:16	5027
Neither shall he *r* the God of his	Dan 11:37	995
desire of women, nor *r* any god	Dan 11:37	995
neither will I *r* the peace	Amos 5:22	5027
Behold ye among the heathen, and *r*	Hab 1:5	5027
will he *r* your persons	Mal 1:9	5375
Though I fear not God, nor *r* man	Lk 18:4	*1788*
And to him they had *r*, because	Acts 8:11	*4337*
day, to the Lord he doth not *r* it	Rom 14:6	*5426*

REGARDED

he that *r* not the word of the	Ex 9:21	3820
nor any to answer, nor any that *r*	1Kin 18:29	7182
hast *r* me according to the estate	1Chr 17:17	7200
Nevertheless he *r* their	Ps 106:44	7200
out my hand, and no man *r*	Prov 1:24	7181
men, O king, have not *r* thee	Dan 3:12	7761,2942
For he hath *r* the low estate of	Lk 1:48	*1914*
feared not God, neither *r* man	Lk 18:2	*1788*
I *r* them not, saith the Lord	Heb 8:9	*272*

REGARDEST

that thou *r* neither princes nor	2Sa 19:6	
I stand up, and thou *r* me not	Job 30:20	995
for thou *r* not the person of men	Mt 22:16	*991*
for thou *r* not the person of men,	Mk 12:14	*991*

REGARDETH

which *r* not persons, nor taketh	Deut 10:17	5375
nor *r* the rich more than the poor	Job 34:19	5234
neither *r* he the crying of the	Job 39:7	8085
A righteous man *r* the life of his	Prov 12:10	3045
but he that *r* reproof shall be	Prov 13:18	8104
but he that *r* reproof is prudent	Prov 15:5	8104
but the wicked *r* not to know it	Prov 29:7	995
that is higher than the highest *r*	Eccl 5:8	8104
he that *r* the clouds shall not	Eccl 11:4	7200
despised the cities, he *r* no man	Is 33:8	2803
r not thee, O king, nor the	Dan 6:13	7761,2942
insomuch that he *r* not the	Mal 2:13	6437
He that *r* the day, *r* it	Rom 14:6	5426
he that *r* not the day, to the	Rom 14:6	5426

REGARDING

perish for ever without any *r* it	Job 4:20	7760
not *r* his life, to supply your	Phil 2:30	*3851*

REGEM (re'-ghem) *A son of Jahdai.*

R, and Jotham, and Gesham, and	1Chr 2:47	7276

REGEM-MELECH (re'-ghem-me'-lek) *A messenger for Zechariah.*

the house of God Sherezer and *R*	Zec 7:2	7278

REGENERATION

in the *r* when the Son of man	Mt 19:28	*3824*
he saved us, by the washing of *r*	Titus 3:5	*3824*

REGION

all the *r* of Argob, the kingdom	Deut 3:4	2256
all the *r* of Argob, with all	Deut 3:13	2256
of Abinadab, in all the *r* of Dor	1Kin 4:11	5299
him also pertained the *r* of Argob	1Kin 4:13	2256
all the *r* on this side the river	1Kin 4:24	
all the *r* round about Jordan	Mt 3:5	4066
and to them which sat in the *r*	Mt 4:16	5561
all the *r* round about Galilee	Mk 1:28	4066
through that whole *r* round about	Mk 6:55	4066
of the *r* of Trachonitis, and	Lk 3:1	5561
him through all the *r* round about	Lk 4:14	4066
throughout all the *r* round about	Lk 7:17	4066
published throughout all the *r*	Acts 13:49	5561
unto the *r* that lieth round about	Acts 14:6	4066
the *r* of Galatia, and were	Acts 16:6	5561

REGIONS

abroad throughout the *r* of Judaea	Acts 8:1	5561
the gospel in the *r* beyond you	2Cor 10:16	
this boasting in the *r* of Achaia	2Cor 11:10	2825
I came into the *r* of Syria	Gal 1:21	2825

REGISTER

These sought their *r* among those	Ezr 2:62	3791
I found a *r* of the genealogy of	Neh 7:5	5612
These sought their *r* among those	Neh 7:64	3791

REHABIAH (re-hab-i'-ah) *A son of Eliezer.*

sons of Eliezer were, *R* the chief	1Chr 23:17	7345
but the sons of *R* were very many	1Chr 23:17	7345
Concerning *R*,	1Chr 24:21	7345
of the sons of *R*, the first was	1Chr 24:21	7345
R his son, and Jeshaiah his son,	1Chr 26:25	7345

REHEARSE

r it in the ears of Joshua	Ex 17:14	7760
there shall they *r* the righteous	Judg 5:11	8567

REHEARSED

he *r* them in the ears of the LORD	1Sa 8:21	1696
spake, they *r* them before Saul	1Sa 17:31	5046
But Peter *r* the matter from the	Acts 11:4	*756*
they *r* all that God had done with	Acts 14:27	*312*

REHOB (re'-hob)

1. A Levitical city in Asher.

from the wilderness of Zin unto *R*	Num 13:21	7340
and *R*, and Hammon, and	Josh 19:28	7340
Ummah also, and Aphek, and *R*	Josh 19:30	7340

REHOBOAM

suburbs ....Josh 21:31	7340
nor of R ....Judg 1:31	7340
of Helbah, nor of A nc of R 2Sa 10:8	7340
and the Syrians o'suburbs 1Chr 6:75	7340
suburbs, and R w'	
2. Father of P of R...............2Sa 8:3	7340
also Hadadeze son of R 2Sa 8:12	7340
the spoil of H	
...............Neh 10:11	7340
3. A Levit	

Micha, R, m) See ROBOAM. A son of
f Judah.

REHOBO

s stead 1Kin 11:43	7346
Solom m 1Kin 12:1	7346
R his s ake unto R 1Kin 12:3	7346
And P the old men 1Kin 12:6	7346
of Is third day 1Kin 12:12	7346
ver them 1Kin 12:17	7346
kinoram, who was 1Kin 12:18	7346
pede speed to 1Kin 12:18	7346
o Jerusalem, he 1Kin 12:21	7346
of Solomon, ...1Kin 12:21	7346
on of Solomon, ...1Kin 12:23	7346
Judah, and 1Kin 12:27	7346
of Judah 1Kin 12:27	7346
on reigned in 1Kin 14:21	7346
e years old when 1Kin 14:21	7346
ar of king R 1Kin 14:25	7346
eir stead brasen 1Kin 14:27	7346
e acts of R 1Kin 14:29	7346
r between R 1Kin 14:30	7346
athers, and was 1Kin 14:31	7346
ar between R 1Kin 15:6	7346
on was R, Abia his 1Chr 3:10	7346
d in his stead................2Chr 9:31	7346
Shechem 2Chr 10:1	7346
came and spake to R........2Chr 10:3	7346
counsel with the old 2Chr 10:6	7346
ne to R on the third day 2Chr 10:12	7346
orsook the counsel of the 2Chr 10:13	7346
h, R reigned over them 2Chr 10:17	7346
king R sent Hadoram that was 2Chr 10:18	7346
king R made speed to get him 2Chr 10:18	7346
hen R was come to Jerusalem, he 2Chr 11:1	7346
bring the kingdom again to R........2Chr 11:1	7346
Speak unto R the son of Solomon 2Chr 11:3	7346
R dwelt in Jerusalem, and built...............2Chr 11:5	7346
made R the son of Solomon strong,.....2Chr 11:17	7346
R took him Mahalath the daughter of 2Chr 11:18	7346
R loved Maachah the daughter of 2Chr 11:21	7346
R made Abijah the son of Maachah 2Chr 11:22	7346
when R had established the...................2Chr 12:1	7346
R Shishak king of Egypt came up 2Chr 12:2	7346
came Shemaiah the prophet to R 2Chr 12:5	7346
king R made shields of brass.................2Chr 12:10	7346
So king R strengthened himself in 2Chr 12:13	7346
for R was one and forty years old 2Chr 12:13	7346
Now the acts of R, first and last, ...2Chr 12:15	7346
And there were wars between R 2Chr 12:15	7346
R slept with his fathers, and was 2Chr 12:16	7346
against the son of Solomon 2Chr 13:7	7346
when R was young and tenderhearted ...2Chr 13:7	7346

REHOBOTH (re'-ho-both)
1. A city in Assyria.

and builded Nineveh, and the city R ......Gen 10:11	7344
Saul of R by the river reigned in ....Gen 36:37	7344
Shaul of R by the river reigned...............1Chr 1:48	7344

2. A well Isaac dug.

and he called the name of it R ....Gen 26:22	7344

REHOBOTH-BY-THE-WATER See REHOBOTH.

REHOBOTH-IR See REHOBOTH.

REHUM (re'-hum) See NEHUM.
1. A clan leader with Zerubbabel.

Bilshan, Mizpar, Bigvai, R...............Ezr 2:2	7348
Shechaniah, R, Meremoth, ...Neh 12:3	7348

2. An officer of King Artaxerxes.

R the chancellor and Shimshai the ....Ezr 4:8	7348
Then wrote R the chancellor, and ....Ezr 4:9	7348
an answer unto R the chancellor ....Ezr 4:17	7348
letter was read before R, and.................Ezr 4:23	7348

3. A Levite rebuilder of Jerusalem's wall.

the Levites, R the son of Bani ....Neh 3:17	7348

4. A renewer of the covenant.

R, Hashabnah, Maaseiah, ...Neh 10:25	7348

REI (re'-i) A friend of David.

the prophet, and Shimei, and R 1Kin 1:8	7472

REIGN

him, Shalt thou indeed r over us............Gen 37:8	4427
The LORD shall r for ever ....Ex 15:18	4427
that hate you shall r over you ....Lev 26:17	7287
thou shalt r over many nations, ...Deut 15:6	4910
but they shall not r over thee ....Deut 15:6	4910
r over you, or that one r ....Judg 9:2	4910
the olive tree, R thou over us ....Judg 9:8	4427
fig tree, Come thou, and r over us ....Judg 9:10	4427
the vine, Come thou, and r over us ....Judg 9:12	4427
bramble, Come thou, and r over us ....Judg 9:14	4427
me, that I should not r over them 1Sa 8:7	4427
the king that shall r over them 1Sa 8:9	4427
of the king that shall r over you............1Sa 8:11	4427
this same shall r over my people 1Sa 9:17	6113
that said, Shall Saul r over us 1Sa 11:12	4427
but a king shall r over us 1Sa 12:12	4427
when he began to r over Israel 2Sa 2:10	4427
that thou mayest r over all that 2Sa 3:21	4427
years old when he began to r..............2Sa 5:4	4427
the son of Haggith doth r 1Kin 1:11	4427
Solomon thy son shall r after me 1Kin 1:13	4427
why then doth Adonijah r 1Kin 1:13	4427
Solomon thy son shall r after me 1Kin 1:17	4427
said, Adonijah shall r after me 1Kin 1:24	4427
Solomon thy son shall r after me 1Kin 1:30	4427
faces on me, that I should r..................1Kin 2:15	4427
year of Solomon's r over Israel 1Kin 6:1	4427
thou shalt r according to all..................1Kin 11:37	4427
one years old when he began to r.........1Kin 14:21	4427
the son of Jeroboam began to r 1Kin 15:25	4427
to r over all Israel in Tirzah..................1Kin 15:33	4427
Baasha to r over Israel in Tirzah 1Kin 16:8	4427
came to pass, when he began to r.........1Kin 16:11	4427
did Zimri r seven days in Tirzah............1Kin 16:15	4427
Judah began Omri to r over Israel 1Kin 16:23	4427
the son of Omri to r over Israel 1Kin 16:29	4427
the son of Asa began to r 1Kin 22:41	4427
five years old when he began to r..........1Kin 22:42	4427
the son of Ahab began to r over 1Kin 22:51	4427
the son of Ahab began to r over 2Kin 3:1	4427
king of Judah began to r 2Kin 8:16	4427
old was he when he began to r 2Kin 8:17	4427
Jehoram king of Judah begin to r 2Kin 8:25	4427
was Ahaziah when he began to r 2Kin 8:26	4427
began Ahaziah to r over Judah 2Kin 9:29	4427
Athaliah did r over the land 2Kin 11:3	4427
was Jehoash when he began to r...........2Kin 11:21	4427
year of Jehu Jehoash began to r............2Kin 12:1	4427
began to r over Israel in Samaria 2Kin 13:1	4427
to r over Israel in Samaria 2Kin 13:10	4427
five years old when he began to r..........2Kin 14:2	4427
of Israel began to r in Samaria 2Kin 14:23	4427
son of Amaziah king of Judah to r 2Kin 15:1	4427
old was he when he began to r 2Kin 15:2	4427
r over Israel in Samaria six 2Kin 15:8	4427
of Jabesh began to r in the nine 2Kin 15:13	4427
the son of Gadi began to r over Israel 2Kin 15:17	4427
began to r over Israel in Samaria 2Kin 15:23	4427
began to r over Israel in Samaria 2Kin 15:27	4427
son of Uzziah king of Judah to r 2Kin 15:32	4427
old was he when he began to r 2Kin 15:33	4427
Jotham king of Judah began to r............2Kin 16:1	4427
old was Ahaz when he began to r 2Kin 16:2	4427
to r in Samaria over Israel nine 2Kin 17:1	4427
of Ahaz king of Judah began to r 2Kin 18:1	4427
old was he when he began to r 2Kin 18:2	4427
years old when he began to r 2Kin 21:1	4427
two years old when he began to r 2Kin 21:19	4427
years old when he began to r 2Kin 22:1	4427
years old when he began to r 2Kin 23:31	4427
that he might not r in Jerusalem 2Kin 23:33	4427
five years old when he began to r..........2Kin 23:36	4427
years old when he began to r;...............2Kin 24:8	4427
him in the eighth year of his r 2Kin 24:12	4427
one years old when he began to r 2Kin 24:18	4427
pass in the ninth year of his r 2Kin 25:1	4427
to r did lift up the head of 2Kin 25:27	4427
their cities unto the r of David 1Chr 4:31	4438
In the fortieth year of the r 1Chr 26:31	4438
With all his r and his might, and 1Chr 29:30	4438
and hast made me to r in his stead........2Chr 1:8	4427
in the fourth year of his r 2Chr 3:2	4438
years old when he began to r................2Chr 12:13	4427
began Abijah to r over Judah................2Chr 13:1	4427
fifteenth year of the r of Asa 2Chr 15:10	4438
and thirtieth year of the r of Asa............2Chr 15:19	4438
thirtieth year of the r of Asa 2Chr 16:1	4438
ninth year of his r was diseased 2Chr 16:12	4438
the one and fortieth year of his r 2Chr 16:13	4427
of his r he sent to his princes 2Chr 17:7	4427

R

REIGNED

five years old when he began to r	2Chr 20:31	4427
two years old when he began to r	2Chr 21:5	4427
old was he when he began to r	2Chr 21:20	4427
was Ahaziah when he began to r	2Chr 22:2	4427
Behold, the king's son shall r	2Chr 23:3	4427
years old when he began to r	2Chr 24:1	4427
five years old when he began to r	2Chr 25:1	4427
old was Uzziah when he began to r	2Chr 26:3	4427
five years old when he began to r	2Chr 27:1	4427
years old when he began to r	2Chr 27:8	4427
years old when he began to r	2Chr 28:1	4427
began to r when he was five	2Chr 29:1	4427
He in the first year of his r	2Chr 29:3	4427
in his r did cast away in his	2Chr 29:19	4438
years old when he began to r	2Chr 33:1	4427
years old when he began to r	2Chr 33:21	4427
years old when he began to r	2Chr 34:1	4427
For in the eighth year of his r	2Chr 34:3	4427
in the eighteenth year of his r	2Chr 34:8	4427
the r of Josiah was this passover	2Chr 35:19	4438
years old when he began to r	2Chr 36:2	4427
five years old when he began to r	2Chr 36:5	4427
years old when he began to r	2Chr 36:9	4427
years old when he began to r	2Chr 36:11	4427
his sons until the r of the	2Chr 36:20	4427
even until the r of Darius king	Ezr 4:5	4438
in the r of Ahasuerus, in the	Ezr 4:6	4438
in the beginning of his r	Ezr 4:6	4438
of the r of Darius king of Persia	Ezr 4:24	4437
year of the r of Darius the king	Ezr 6:15	4437
in the r of Artaxerxes king of	Ezr 7:1	4438
in the r of Artaxerxes the king	Ezr 8:1	4438
to the r of Darius the Persian	Neh 12:22	4438
In the third year of his r	Est 1:3	4427
in the seventh year of his r	Est 2:16	4438
That the hypocrite r not, lest	Job 34:30	4427
The LORD shall r for ever	Ps 146:10	4427
By me kings r, and princes decree	Prov 8:15	4427
For out of prison he cometh to r	Eccl 4:14	4427
of hosts shall r in mount Zion	Is 24:23	4427
a king shall r in righteousness,	Is 32:1	4427
in the thirteenth year of his r	Jer 1:2	4427
Shalt thou r, because thou	Jer 22:15	4427
Branch, and a King shall r	Jer 23:5	4427
In the beginning of the r of	Jer 26:1	4468
In the beginning of the r of	Jer 27:1	4467
in the beginning of the r of	Jer 28:1	4467
have a son to r upon his throne	Jer 33:21	4427
the r of Zedekiah king of Judah	Jer 49:34	4438
in the fourth year of his r	Jer 51:59	4427
years old when he began to r	Jer 52:1	4427
pass in the ninth year of his r	Jer 52:4	4427
of his r lifted up the head of	Jer 52:31	4438
In the third year of the r of	Dan 1:1	4438
year of the r of Nebuchadnezzar	Dan 2:1	4438
prospered in the r of Darius	Dan 6:28	4437
in the r of Cyrus the Persian	Dan 6:28	4437
In the third year of the r of	Dan 8:1	4438
In the first year of his r I	Dan 9:2	4427
the LORD shall r over them in	Mic 4:7	4427
he heard that Archelaus did r in	Mt 2:22	936
he shall r over the house of	Lk 1:33	936
year of the r of Tiberius Caesar	Lk 3:1	2231
not have this man to r over us	Lk 19:14	936
not that I should r over them	Lk 19:27	936
shall r in life by one, Jesus	Rom 5:17	936
even so might grace r through	Rom 5:21	936
therefore r in your mortal body	Rom 6:12	936
shall rise to r over the Gentiles	Rom 15:12	757
and I would to God ye did r	1Cor 4:8	936
that we also might r with you	1Cor 4:8	4821
For he must r, till he hath put	1Cor 15:25	936
suffer, we shall also r with him	2Ti 2:12	4821
and we shall r on the earth	Rev 5:10	936
and he shall r for ever and ever	Rev 11:15	936
shall r with him a thousand years	Rev 20:6	936
and they shall r for ever and ever	Rev 22:5	936

REIGNED

kings that r in the land of Edom	Gen 36:31	4427
before there r any king over the	Gen 36:31	4427
And Bela the son of Beor r in Edom	Gen 36:32	4427
of Zerah of Bozrah r in his stead	Gen 36:33	4427
the land of Temani r in his stead	Gen 36:34	4427
the field of Moab, r in his stead	Gen 36:35	4427
Samlah of Masrekah r in his stead	Gen 36:36	4427
by the river r in his stead	Gen 36:37	4427
the son of Achbor r in his stead	Gen 36:38	4427
died, and Hadar r in his stead	Gen 36:39	4427
r in mount Hermon, and in Salcah,	Josh 12:5	4910
which r in Heshbon, unto the	Josh 13:10	4427

which r in Ashtaroth and in Edre[i]		
which r in Heshbon, whom Moses		
king of Canaan, that r in Hazor	Josh 13:12	
When Abimelech had r thre years	Josh 13:21	4427
Saul r one year	Jdg 4:2	4427
when he had r two years over	?9:22	4427
reign over Israel, and r two years	?:1	7786
to reign, and he r forty years		4427
In Hebron he r over Judah seven		4427
and in Jerusalem he r thirty		4427
And David r over all Israel		4427
and Hanun his son r in his stead		4427
Saul, in whose stead thou hast r		4427
the days that David r over Israel		4427
seven years r he in Hebron, and	1K	
three years r he in Jerusalem	1Ki	
Solomon r over all kingdoms from	1Ki	
dwelt therein, and r in Damascus	1Kin	
abhorred Israel, and r over Syria	1Kin	
the time that Solomon r in	1Kin	
Rehoboam his son r in his stead	1Kin 1	
of Judah, Rehoboam r over them	1Kin 12	
how he warred, and how he r	1Kin 14:	
days which Jeroboam r were two	1Kin 14:	
and Nadab his son r in his stead	1Kin 14:21	
the son of Solomon r in Judah	1Kin 14:21	
he r seventeen years in Jerusalem	1Kin 14:21	
And Abijam his son r in his stead	1Kin 14:31	
son of Nebat r Abijam over Judah	1Kin 15:1	
Three years r he in Jerusalem	1Kin 15:2	
Asa his son r in his stead	1Kin 15:8	
king of Israel r Asa over Judah	1Kin 15:9	
one years r he in Jerusalem	1Kin 15:10	
his son r in his stead	1Kin 15:24	
Judah, and r over Israel two years	1Kin 15:25	
slay him, and r in his stead	1Kin 15:28	
And it came to pass, when he r	1Kin 15:29	
and Elah his son r in his stead	1Kin 16:6	4427
king of Judah, and r in his stead	1Kin 16:10	4427
so Tibni died, and Omri r	1Kin 16:22	4427
six years r he in Tirzah	1Kin 16:23	4427
and Ahab his son r in his stead	1Kin 16:28	4427
Ahab the son of Omri r over	1Kin 16:29	4427
and Ahaziah his son r in his stead	1Kin 22:40	4427
he r twenty and five years in	1Kin 22:42	4427
and Jehoram his son r in his stead	1Kin 22:50	4427
Judah, and r two years over Israel	1Kin 22:51	4427
Jehoram r in his stead in the	2Kin 1:17	4427
king of Judah, and r twelve years	2Kin 3:1	4427
that should have r in his stead	2Kin 3:27	4427
and Hazael r in his stead	2Kin 8:15	4427
he r eight years in Jerusalem	2Kin 8:17	4427
and Ahaziah his son r in his stead	2Kin 8:24	4427
he r one year in Jerusalem	2Kin 8:26	
Jehoahaz his son r in his stead	2Kin 10:35	4427
the time that Jehu r over Israel	2Kin 10:36	4427
forty years r he in Jerusalem	2Kin 12:1	4427
and Amaziah his son r in his stead	2Kin 12:21	4427
in Samaria, and r seventeen years	2Kin 13:1	
and Joash his son r in his stead	2Kin 13:9	4427
in Samaria, and r sixteen years	2Kin 13:10	
Ben-hadad his son r in his stead	2Kin 13:24	4427
r Amaziah the son of Joash king	2Kin 14:1	4427
r twenty and nine years in	2Kin 14:2	4427
Jeroboam his son r in his stead	2Kin 14:16	4427
Samaria, and r forty and one years	2Kin 14:23	
Zachariah his son r in his stead	2Kin 14:29	4427
he r two and fifty years in	2Kin 15:2	4427
and Jotham his son r in his stead	2Kin 15:7	4427
and slew him, and r in his stead	2Kin 15:10	4427
he r a full month in Samaria	2Kin 15:13	4427
and slew him, and r in his stead	2Kin 15:14	4427
Israel, and r ten years in Samaria	2Kin 15:17	
Pekahiah his son r in his stead	2Kin 15:22	4427
Israel in Samaria, and r two years	2Kin 15:23	
he killed him, and r in his room	2Kin 15:25	4427
in Samaria, and r twenty years	2Kin 15:27	
r in his stead, in the twentieth	2Kin 15:30	4427
he r sixteen years in Jerusalem	2Kin 15:33	4427
and Ahaz his son r in his stead	2Kin 15:38	4427
r sixteen years in Jerusalem, and	2Kin 16:2	4427
Hezekiah his son r in his stead	2Kin 16:20	4427
he r twenty and nine years in	2Kin 18:2	4427
his son r in his stead	2Kin 19:37	4427
Manasseh his son r in his stead	2Kin 20:21	4427
and r fifty and five years in	2Kin 21:1	4427
and Amon his son r in his stead	2Kin 21:18	4427
he r two years in Jerusalem	2Kin 21:19	4427
and Josiah his son r in his stead	2Kin 21:26	4427
he r thirty and one years in	2Kin 22:1	4427
he r three months in Jerusalem	2Kin 23:31	4427

REIGNEST

...ualem 2Kin 23:36	4427
he *r* eleven years in his stead 2Kin 24:6	4427
Jehoiachin his sore months 2Kin 24:8	4427
he *r* in Jerusalem...rusalem 2Kin 24:18	4427
he *r* eleven years...ngs that *r* in 1Chr 1:43	4427
Now these ar...*r* Israel 1Chr 1:43	4427
r over the ch...*r* in his stead 1Chr 1:44	4427
of Zerah o...n his stead 1Chr 1:45	4427
of the Ter...kah *r* in his stead 1Chr 1:46	4427
the field...is stead 1Chr 1:47	4427
Samla...r *r* in his stead 1Chr 1:49	4427
by th...d *r* in his stead 1Chr 1:50	4427
the...n years and six 1Chr 3:4	4427
...em he *r* thirty 1Chr 3:4	4427
...ver all Israel, and 1Chr 18:14	4427
...s son *r* in his stead 1Chr 19:1	4427
r over all Israel 1Chr 29:26	4427
at he *r* over Israel 1Chr 29:27	4427
...s *r* he in Hebron, and 1Chr 29:27	4427
...rs *r* he in Jerusalem 1Chr 29:27	4427
...mon his son *r* in his stead 1Chr 29:28	4427
...ation, and *r* over Israel 2Chr 1:13	4427
...r all the kings from the 2Chr 9:26	4910
...on *r* in Jerusalem over all 2Chr 9:30	4427
...oam his son *r* in his stead 2Chr 9:31	4427
...ah, Rehoboam *r* over them 2Chr 10:17	4427
...elf in Jerusalem, and *r*................... 2Chr 12:13	4427
...seventeen years in Jerusalem 2Chr 12:13	4427
and Abijah his son *r* in his stead 2Chr 12:16	4427
He *r* three years in Jerusalem 2Chr 13:2	4427
Asa his son *r* in his stead 2Chr 14:1	4427
his son *r* in his stead, and 2Chr 17:1	4427
And Jehoshaphat *r* over Judah 2Chr 20:31	4427
he *r* twenty and five years in 2Chr 20:31	4427
And Jehoram his son *r* in his stead 2Chr 21:1	4427
he *r* eight years in Jerusalem 2Chr 21:5	4427
he *r* in Jerusalem eight years, and 2Chr 21:20	4427
son of Jehoram king of Judah *r*............ 2Chr 22:1	4427
he *r* one year in Jerusalem 2Chr 22:2	4427
and Athaliah *r* over the land 2Chr 22:12	4427
he *r* forty years in Jerusalem 2Chr 24:1	4427
And Amaziah his son *r* in his stead 2Chr 24:27	4427
he *r* twenty and nine years in 2Chr 25:1	4427
he *r* fifty and two years in 2Chr 26:3	4427
and Jotham his son *r* in his stead 2Chr 26:23	4427
he *r* sixteen years in Jerusalem 2Chr 27:1	4427
r sixteen years in Jerusalem 2Chr 27:8	4427
and Ahaz his son *r* in his stead 2Chr 27:9	4427
he *r* sixteen years in Jerusalem 2Chr 28:1	4427
Hezekiah his son *r* in his stead 2Chr 28:27	4427
he *r* nine and twenty years in 2Chr 29:1	4427
Manasseh his son *r* in his stead 2Chr 32:33	4427
he *r* fifty and five years in 2Chr 33:1	4427
and Amon his son *r* in his stead 2Chr 33:20	4427
and *r* two years in Jerusalem................... 2Chr 33:21	4427
he *r* in Jerusalem one and thirty 2Chr 34:1	4427
he *r* three months in Jerusalem 2Chr 36:2	4427
he *r* eleven years in Jerusalem 2Chr 36:5	4427
Jehoiachin his son *r* in his stead 2Chr 36:8	4427
he *r* three months and ten days in 2Chr 36:9	4427
r eleven years in Jerusalem 2Chr 36:11	4427
(this is Ahasuerus which *r* from .... Est 1:1	4427
his son *r* in his stead......................... Is 37:38	4427
which *r* instead of Josiah his .... Jer 22:11	4427
r instead of Coniah the son of............... Jer 37:1	4427
he *r* eleven years in Jerusalem .... Jer 52:1	4427
death *r* from Adam to Moses .... Rom 5:14	936
one man's offence death *r* by one........... Rom 5:17	936
That as sin hath *r* unto death .... Rom 5:21	936
ye have *r* as kings without us 1Cor 4:8	936
thee thy great power, and hast *r*........... Rev 11:17	936
r with Christ a thousand years .... Rev 20:4	936

REIGNEST

come of thee, and thou *r* over all 1Chr 29:12	4910

REIGNETH

also the king that *r* over you 1Sa 12:14	4427
ye shall say, Absalom *r* in Hebron 2Sa 15:10	4427
And now, behold, Adonijah *r*.................. 1Kin 1:18	4427
say among the nations, The LORD *r* 1Chr 16:31	4427
God *r* over the heathen .... Ps 47:8	4427
The LORD *r*, he is clothed with .... Ps 93:1	4427
among the heathen that the LORD *r*........ Ps 96:10	4427
The LORD *r* .... Ps 97:1	4427
The LORD *r* .... Ps 99:1	4427
For a servant when he *r*........................... Prov 30:22	4427
that saith unto Zion, Thy God *r*............. Is 52:7	4427
which *r* over the kings of the .... Rev 17:18	2192,932
for the Lord God omnipotent *r*............... Rev 19:6	936

REIGNING

rejected him from *r* over Israel 1Sa 16:1	4427

REINS

about, he cleaveth my *r* asunder .... Job 16:13	3629
though my *r* be consumed within me ..... Job 19:27	3629
God trieth the hearts and *r* .... Ps 7:9	3629
my *r* also instruct me in the .... Ps 16:7	3629
try my *r* and my heart .... Ps 26:2	3629
grieved, and I was pricked in my *r*.......... Ps 73:21	3629
For thou hast possessed my *r* .... Ps 139:13	3629
my *r* shall rejoice, when thy lips .... Prov 23:16	3629
faithfulness the girdle of his *r*................ Is 11:5	2504
righteously, that triest the *r*................... Jer 11:20	3629
their mouth, and far from their *r* .... Jer 12:2	3629
search the heart, I try the *r*.................... Jer 17:10	3629
the righteous, and seest the *r*................. Jer 20:12	3629
of his quiver to enter into my *r* .... Lam 3:13	3629
I am he which searcheth the *r* .... Rev 2:23	3510

REJECT

knowledge, I will also *r* thee .... Hos 4:6	3988
sat with him, he would not *r* her .... Mk 6:26	114
Full well ye *r* the commandment of ...... Mk 7:9	114
the first and second admonition *r*........... Titus 3:10	3868

REJECTED

r thee, but they have *r* me...................... 1Sa 8:7	3988
And ye have this day *r* your God 1Sa 10:19	3988
Because thou hast *r* the word of 1Sa 15:23	3988
he hath also *r* thee from being................ 1Sa 15:23	3988
for thou hast *r* the word of the 1Sa 15:26	3988
the LORD hath *r* thee from being 1Sa 15:26	3988
seeing I have *r* him from reigning 1Sa 16:1	3988
they *r* his statutes, and his 2Kin 17:15	3988
the LORD *r* all the seed of Israel 2Kin 17:20	3988
He is despised and *r* of men .... Is 53:3	2310
the LORD hath *r* thy confidences .... Jer 2:37	3988
my words, nor to my law, but *r* it .... Jer 6:19	3988
because the LORD hath *r* them .... Jer 6:30	3988
for the LORD hath *r* and forsaken .... Jer 7:29	3988
they have *r* the word of the LORD .... Jer 8:9	3988
Hast thou utterly *r* Judah .... Jer 14:19	3988
But thou hast utterly *r* us .... Lam 5:22	3988
because thou hast *r* knowledge .... Hos 4:6	3988
The stone which the builders *r* .... Mt 21:42	593
be *r* of the elders, and of the .... Mk 8:31	593
r* is become the head of the.................... Mk 12:10	593
lawyers *r* the counsel of God .... Lk 7:30	114
be *r* of the elders and chief .... Lk 9:22	593
and be *r* of this generation .... Lk 17:25	593
The stone which the builders *r* .... Lk 20:17	593
my flesh ye despised not, nor *r*............... Gal 4:14	1609
beareth thorns and briers is *r* .... Heb 6:8	96
inherited the blessing, he was *r* .... Heb 12:17	593

REJECTETH

He that *r* me, and receiveth not my .... Jn 12:48	14

REJOICE

ye shall *r* before the LORD your .... Lev 23:40	8055
ye shall *r* in all that ye put..................... Deut 12:7	8055
ye shall *r* before the LORD your .... Deut 12:12	8055
thou shalt *r* before the LORD thy .... Deut 12:18	8055
the LORD thy God, and thou shalt *r* .... Deut 14:26	8055
thou shalt *r* before the LORD thy .... Deut 16:11	8055
thou shalt *r* in thy feast, thou,.............. Deut 16:14	8055
therefore thou shalt surely *r*.................. Deut 16:15	8055
thou shalt *r* in every good thing .... Deut 26:11	8056
r before the LORD thy God .... Deut 27:7	8055
so the LORD will *r* over you to................. Deut 28:63	7797
will again *r* over thee for good................ Deut 30:9	7797
R, O ye nations, with his people .... Deut 32:43	7442
And of Zebulun he said, *R*, Zebulun .... Deut 33:18	8055
then *r* ye in Abimelech............................ Judg 9:19	8055
and let him also *r* in you .... Judg 9:19	8055
unto Dagon their god, and to *r* .... Judg 16:23	8057
because I *r* in thy salvation..................... 1Sa 2:1	8055
thou sawest it, and didst *r* 1Sa 19:5	8055
daughters of the Philistines *r* 2Sa 1:20	8055
of them *r* that seek the LORD 1Chr 16:10	8055
be glad, and the earth *r* 1Chr 16:31	1523
let the fields *r*, and all that is 1Chr 16:32	5970
and let thy saints *r* in goodness 2Chr 6:41	8055
made them to *r* over their enemies........ 2Chr 20:27	8055
had made them *r* with great joy .... Neh 12:43	8055
Which *r* exceedingly, and are glad, ... Job 3:22	8055
be, and he shall not *r* therein .... Job 20:18	5965
r at the sound of the organ..................... Job 21:12	8055
with fear, and *r* with trembling .... Ps 2:11	1523
that put their trust in thee *r*................... Ps 5:11	8055
I will be glad and *r* in thee .... Ps 9:2	5970
I will *r* in thy salvation .... Ps 9:14	1523

R

that trouble me *r* when I am moved	Ps 13:4	1523
my heart shall *r* in thy salvation	Ps 13:5	1523
of his people, Jacob shall *r*	Ps 14:7	1523
We will *r* in thy salvation, and in	Ps 20:5	7442
salvation how greatly shall he *r*	Ps 21:1	1523
not made my foes to *r* over me	Ps 30:1	8055
I will be glad and *r* in thy mercy	Ps 31:7	8055
Be glad in the LORD, and *r*	Ps 32:11	1524
R in the LORD, O ye righteous	Ps 33:1	7442
For our heart shall *r* in him	Ps 33:21	8055
it shall *r* in his salvation	Ps 35:9	7797
mine enemies wrongfully *r* over me	Ps 35:19	8055
and let them not *r* over me	Ps 35:24	8055
together that *r* at mine hurt	Ps 35:26	8055
otherwise they should *r* over me	Ps 38:16	8056
Let all those that seek thee *r*	Ps 40:16	7797
Let mount Zion *r*, let the	Ps 48:11	8055
which thou hast broken may *r*	Ps 51:8	1523
of his people, Jacob shall *r*	Ps 53:6	1523
The righteous shall *r* when he	Ps 58:10	8055
I will *r*, I will divide Shechem,	Ps 60:6	5937
the shadow of thy wings will I *r*	Ps 63:7	7442
But the king shall *r* in God	Ps 63:11	8055
of the morning and evening to *r*	Ps 65:8	7442
the little hills *r* on every side	Ps 65:12	1524
there did we *r* in him	Ps 66:6	8055
let them *r* before God	Ps 68:3	5970
yea, let them exceedingly *r*	Ps 68:3	7797
by his name JAH, and *r* before him	Ps 68:4	5937
Let all those that seek thee *r*	Ps 70:4	7797
greatly when I sing unto thee	Ps 71:23	7442
that thy people may *r* in thee	Ps 85:6	8055
R the soul of thy servant	Ps 86:4	8055
and Hermon shall *r* in thy name	Ps 89:12	7442
thy name shall they *r* all the day	Ps 89:16	1523
hast made all his enemies to *r*	Ps 89:42	8055
that we may *r* and be glad all our	Ps 90:14	7442
Let the heavens *r*, and let the	Ps 96:11	8056
shall all the trees of the wood *r*	Ps 96:12	7442
let the earth *r*	Ps 97:1	1523
R in the LORD, ye righteous	Ps 97:12	8055
make a loud noise, and, and sing	Ps 98:4	7442
the LORD shall *r* in his works	Ps 104:31	8055
of them *r* that seek the LORD	Ps 105:3	8055
that I may *r* in the gladness of	Ps 106:5	8055
The righteous shall see it, and *r*	Ps 107:42	8055
I will *r*, I will divide Shechem,	Ps 108:7	5937
but let thy servant *r*	Ps 109:28	8055
we will *r* and be glad in it	Ps 118:24	1523
I *r* at thy word, as one that	Ps 119:162	7797
Let Israel *r* in him that made him	Ps 149:2	8055
Who *r* to do evil, and delight in	Prov 2:14	8056
r with the wife of thy youth	Prov 5:18	8055
heart be wise, my heart shall *r*	Prov 23:15	8055
Yea, my reins shall *r*, when thy	Prov 23:16	5937
of the righteous shall greatly *r*	Prov 23:24	1523
and she that bare thee shall *r*	Prov 23:25	1523
R not when thine enemy falleth,	Prov 24:17	8055
Ointment and perfume *r* the heart	Prov 27:9	8055
When righteous men do *r*, there is	Prov 28:12	5970
are in authority, the people *r*	Prov 29:2	8055
but the righteous doth sing and *r*	Prov 29:6	8055
she shall *r* in time to come	Prov 31:25	7832
good in them, but for a man to *r*	Eccl 3:12	8055
a man should *r* in his own works	Eccl 3:22	8055
come after shall not *r* in him	Eccl 4:16	8055
portion, and to *r* in his labour	Eccl 5:19	8055
live many years, and *r* in them all	Eccl 11:8	8055
R, O young man, in thy youth	Eccl 11:9	8055
r in thee, we will remember thy	Song 1:4	8055
r in Rezin and Remaliah's son	Is 8:6	4885
as men *r* when they divide the	Is 9:3	1523
even them that *r* in my highness	Is 13:3	5947
Yea, the fir trees *r* at thee	Is 14:8	8055
R not thou, whole Palestina,	Is 14:29	8055
And he said, Thou shalt no more *r*	Is 23:12	5937
the noise of them that *r* endeth	Is 24:8	5947
be glad and *r* in his salvation	Is 25:9	8055
the poor among men shall *r* in the	Is 29:19	1523
and the desert shall *r*, and blossom	Is 35:1	1523
r even with joy and singing	Is 35:2	1523
thou shalt *r* in the LORD, and	Is 41:16	1523
they shall *r* in their portion	Is 61:7	7442
I will greatly *r* in the LORD	Is 61:10	7797
so shall thy God *r* over thee	Is 62:5	7797
behold, my servants shall *r*	Is 65:13	8055
r for ever in that which I create	Is 65:18	1523
I will *r* in Jerusalem, and joy in	Is 65:19	1523
R ye with Jerusalem, and be glad	Is 66:10	8055
r for joy with her, all ye that	Is 66:10	7797
ye see this, your heart shall *r*	Is 66:14	7797

shall the virgin *r* in the dance	Jer 31:13	
make them *r* from their sorrow	Jer 31:13	
I will *r* over them to do them	Jer 31:13	8057
them drunken, that they may *r*	Jer 32:41	8057
caused thine enemy to *r* over thee	Lam 1:39	7797
R and be glad, O daughter of Edom,	Lam 4:21	5937
let not the buyer *r*, nor the	Eze 7:12	8055
As thou didst *r* at the	Eze 35:15	7797
R not, O Israel, for joy, as	Hos 9:1	8055
be glad and *r*	Joel 2:21	8057
Zion, and *r* in the LORD your God	Joel 2:23	8055
Ye which *r* in a thing of nought,	Amos 6:13	8055
R not against me, O mine enemy	Mic 7:8	8055
therefore they *r* and are glad	Hab 1:15	1523
Yet I will *r* in the LORD, I will	Hab 3:18	5937
of thee them that *r* in thy pride	Zeph 3:11	5947
r with all the heart, O daughter	Zeph 3:14	8055
he will *r* over thee with joy	Zeph 3:17	7797
Sing and *r*, O daughter of Zion	Zec 2:10	8055
for they shall *r*, and shall see	Zec 4:10	8056
R greatly, O daughter of Zion	Zec 9:9	1523
heart shall *r* as through wine	Zec 10:7	8055
their heart shall *r* in the LORD	Zec 10:7	1523
R, and be exceeding glad	Mt 5:12	5463
many shall *r* at his birth	Lk 1:14	5463
R ye in that day, and leap for joy	Lk 6:23	5463
Notwithstanding in this *r* not	Lk 10:20	5463
but rather *r*, because your names	Lk 10:20	5463
saying unto them, *R* with me	Lk 15:6	4796
together, saying, *R* with me	Lk 15:9	4796
of the disciples began to *r*	Lk 19:37	5463
and he that reapeth may *r* together	Jn 4:36	5463
for a season to *r* in his light	Jn 5:35	21
If ye loved me, ye would *r*	Jn 14:28	5463
and lament, but the world shall *r*	Jn 16:20	5463
you again, and your heart shall *r*	Jn 16:22	5463
Therefore did my heart *r*, and my	Acts 2:26	2165
r in hope of the glory of God	Rom 5:2	2744
R with them that do *r*	Rom 12:15	5463
And again he saith, *R*, ye Gentiles	Rom 15:10	2165
and they that *r*, as though they	1Cor 7:30	5463
all the members *r* with it	1Cor 12:26	4796
from them of whom I ought to *r*	2Cor 2:3	5463
Now I *r*, not that ye were made	2Cor 7:9	5463
I *r* therefore that I have	2Cor 7:16	5463
For it is written, *R*, thou barren	Gal 4:27	2165
do *r*, yea, and will *r*	Phil 1:18	5463
that I may *r* in the day of Christ	Phil 2:16	2745
faith, I joy, and *r* with you all	Phil 2:17	4796
also do ye joy, and *r* with me	Phil 2:18	4796
when ye see him again, ye may *r*	Phil 2:28	5463
my brethren, *r* in the Lord	Phil 3:1	5463
r in Christ Jesus, and have no	Phil 3:3	2744
R in the Lord alway	Phil 4:4	5463
and again I say, *R*	Phil 4:4	5463
Who now *r* in my sufferings for	Col 1:24	5463
R evermore	1Th 5:16	5463
degree in that he is exalted	Jas 1:9	2744
But now ye *r* in your boastings	Jas 4:16	2744
Wherein ye greatly *r*, though now	1Pet 1:6	21
ye *r* with joy unspeakable and full	1Pet 1:8	21
But *r*, inasmuch as ye are	1Pet 4:13	5463
upon the earth shall *r* over them	Rev 11:10	5463
Therefore *r*, ye heavens, and ye	Rev 12:12	2165
R over her, thou heaven, and ye	Rev 18:20	2165
Let us be glad and *r*, and give	Rev 19:7	21

REJOICED

Jethro *r* for all the goodness	Ex 18:9	2302
that as the LORD *r* over you to do	Deut 28:63	7797
good, as he *r* over thy fathers	Deut 30:9	7797
damsel saw him, he *r* to meet him	Judg 19:3	8055
and saw the ark, and *r* to see it	1Sa 6:13	8055
all the men of Israel *r* greatly	1Sa 11:15	8055
r with great joy, so that the	1Kin 1:40	8056
of Solomon, that he *r* greatly	1Kin 5:7	8055
and all the people of the land *r*	2Kin 11:14	8056
And all the people of the land *r*	2Kin 11:20	8055
Then the people *r*, for that they	1Chr 29:9	8055
the king also *r* with great joy	1Chr 29:9	8055
And all Judah *r* at the oath	2Chr 15:15	8055
and all the people of the land *r*	2Chr 23:13	8056
And all the people of the land *r*	2Chr 23:21	8055
the princes and all the people *r*	2Chr 24:10	8055
And Hezekiah *r*, and all the people,	2Chr 29:36	8055
Israel, and that dwelt in Judah, *r*	2Chr 30:25	8055
offered great sacrifices, and *r*	Neh 12:43	8055
the wives also and the children *r*	Neh 12:43	8055
for Judah *r* for the priests and	Neh 12:44	8057
and the city of Shushan *r* and was	Est 8:15	6670
If I *r* because my wealth was	Job 31:25	8055

REJOICEST

him .... Job 31:29	8055
r .... Ps 35:15	8055
If I r at the destr because .... Ps 97:8	1523
If I r at the destr adv .... Ps 119:14	7797
But in mine labour .... Eccl 2:10	8055
the daughters of th' nor r .... Jer 15:17	5937
I have r in the r .... Jer 50:11	5937
he espite .... Eze 25:6	8055
for my r on it .... Hos 10:5	1523
assembly were .... Obad 12	8055
ye w great joy .... Mt 2:10	5463
r in h my .... Lk 1:47	21
the r .... Lk 1:58	4796
spirit .... Lk 10:21	21
the .... Lk 13:17	5463
see my day .... Jn 8:56	21
r own hands .... Acts 7:41	2165
ation .... Acts 15:31	5463
hem, and r .... Acts 16:34	21
hey r not 1Cor 7:30	5463
.... 2Cor 7:7	5463
greatly, that .... Phil 4:10	5463
und of thy 2Jn 4	5463
en the 3Jn 3	5463

evil, then thou r .... Jer 11:15	5937

the LORD, mine horn 1Sa 2:1	5970
and r in his strength .... Job 39:21	7797
is glad, and my glory r .... Ps 16:9	1523
strong man to run a race .... Ps 19:5	7797
efore my heart greatly r .... Ps 28:7	5937
with the righteous, the city r .... Prov 11:10	5970
The light of the righteous .... Prov 13:9	8055
The light of the eyes r the heart .... Prov 15:30	8055
Whoso loveth wisdom r his father .... Prov 29:3	8055
and their pomp, and he that r .... Is 5:14	5938
the bridegroom r over the bride .... Is 62:5	4885
Thou meetest him that r and .... Is 64:5	7797
When the whole earth r, I will .... Eze 35:14	8055
he r more of that sheep, than of .... Mt 18:13	5463
him, r greatly because of the .... Jn 3:29	5463
R not in iniquity 1Cor 13:6	5463
but r in the truth 1Cor 13:6	4796
and mercy r against judgment .... Jas 2:13	2620

REJOICING

and they are come up from thence r 1Kin 1:45	8056
in the law of Moses, with r 2Chr 23:18	8057
with laughing, and thy lips with r .... Job 8:21	8643
the LORD are right, r the heart .... Ps 19:8	8055
and r shall they be brought .... Ps 45:15	1524
and declare his works with r .... Ps 107:22	7440
The voice of r and salvation is in .... Ps 118:15	7440
for they are the r of my heart .... Ps 119:111	8342
shall doubtless come again with r .... Ps 126:6	7440
his delight, r always before him .... Prov 8:30	7832
R in the habitable part of his .... Prov 8:31	7832
behold, I create Jerusalem a r .... Is 65:18	1525
me the joy and r of mine heart .... Jer 15:16	8057
their r was as to devour the poor .... Hab 3:14	5951
This is the r city that dwelt .... Zeph 2:15	5947
he layeth it on his shoulders, r .... Lk 15:5	5463
r that they were counted worthy .... Acts 5:41	5463
and he went on his way r .... Acts 8:39	5463
R in hope .... Rom 12:12	5463
I protest by your r which I have 1Cor 15:31	2746
For our r is this, the testimony 2Cor 1:12	2746
us in part, that we are your r 2Cor 1:14	2745
As sorrowful, yet alway r 2Cor 6:10	5463
shall he have r in himself alone .... Gal 6:4	2745
That your r may be more abundant .... Phil 1:26	2745
our hope, or joy, or crown of r 1Th 2:19	2746
the r of the hope firm unto the .... Heb 3:6	2745
all such r is evil .... Jas 4:16	2746

REKEM (re'-kem)

1. A prince of Midian.

namely, Evi, and R, and Zur, and Hur .... Num 31:8	7552
the princes of Midian, Evi, and R .... Josh 13:21	7552

2. A son of Hebron.

Korah, and Tappuah, and R, ... 1Chr 2:43	7552
and R begat Shammai 1Chr 2:44	7552

3. A city in Benjamin.

And R, and Irpeel, and Taralah, ... Josh 18:27	7552

RELEASE

seven years thou shalt make a r .... Deut 15:1	8059
And this is the manner of the r .... Deut 15:2	8059
unto his neighbour shall r it .... Deut 15:2	8058
because it is called the LORD's r .... Deut 15:2	8059

thy brother thine hand shall r .... Deut 15:3	8058
The seventh year, the year of r .... Deut 15:9	8059
in the solemnity of the year of r .... Deut 31:10	8059
he made a r to the provinces, and .... Est 2:18	2010
to r unto the people a prisoner .... Mt 27:15	630
Whom will ye that I r unto you .... Mt 27:17	630
twain will ye that I r unto you .... Mt 27:21	630
Will ye that I r unto you the .... Mk 15:9	630
rather r Barabbas unto them .... Mk 15:11	630
therefore chastise him, and r him .... Lk 23:16	630
(For of necessity he must r one .... Lk 23:17	630
this man, and r unto us Barabbas .... Lk 23:18	630
therefore, willing to r Jesus .... Lk 23:20	630
that I should r unto you one at .... Jn 18:39	630
will ye therefore that I r unto .... Jn 18:39	630
thee, and have power to r thee .... Jn 19:10	630
Pilate sought to r him .... Jn 19:12	630

RELEASED

Then r he Barabbas unto them .... Mt 27:26	630
Now at that feast he r unto them .... Mk 15:6	630
people, r Barabbas unto them, and .... Mk 15:15	630
he r unto them him that for .... Lk 23:25	630

RELIED

because they r upon the LORD God 2Chr 13:18	8172
Because thou hast r on the king 2Chr 16:7	8172
not r on the LORD thy God, ... 2Chr 16:7	8172

RELIEF

determined to send r unto the .... Acts 11:29	1248

RELIEVE

then thou shalt r him .... Lev 25:35	2388
r the oppressed, judge the .... Is 1:17	833
things for meat to r the soul .... Lam 1:11	7725
should r my soul is far from me .... Lam 1:16	7725
their meat to r their souls .... Lam 1:19	7725
have widows, let them r them 1Ti 5:16	1884
that it may r them that are 1Ti 5:16	1884

RELIEVED

if she have r the afflicted, if 1Ti 5:10	1884

RELIEVETH

he r the fatherless and widow .... Ps 146:9	5749

RELIGION

sect of our r I lived a Pharisee .... Acts 26:5	2356
in time past in the Jews' r .... Gal 1:13	2454
profited in the Jews' r above .... Gal 1:14	2454
own heart, this man's r is vain .... Jas 1:26	2356
Pure and undefiled before God and ..... Jas 1:27	2356

RELIGIOUS

r proselytes followed Paul and .... Acts 13:43	4576
If any man among you seem to be r .... Jas 1:26	2357

RELY

because thou didst r on the LORD 2Chr 16:8	8172

REMAIN

R a widow at thy father's house, ... Gen 38:11	3427
that they may r in the river only .... Ex 8:9	7604
they shall r in the river only .... Ex 8:11	7604
nothing of it r until the morning .... Ex 12:10	3498
my sacrifice r until the morning .... Ex 23:18	3885
r unto the morning, then thou .... Ex 29:34	3498
if ought r until the third day, ... Lev 19:6	3498
r in the hand of him that hath .... Lev 25:28	1961
if there r but few years unto the .... Lev 25:52	7604
according to the years that r .... Lev 27:18	3498
that those which ye let r of them .... Num 33:55	3498
of every city, we left none to r .... Deut 2:34	8300
r all night until the morning .... Deut 16:4	3885
And those which r shall hear .... Deut 19:20	7604
shall r in thine house, and bewail .... Deut 21:13	3427
His body shall not r all night .... Deut 21:23	3885
shall r in the land which Moses .... Josh 1:14	3427
neither did there r any more .... Josh 2:11	6965
they let none of them r or escape .... Josh 8:22	8300
which r until this very day .... Josh 10:27	
he let none r .... Josh 10:28	8300
he let none r in it .... Josh 10:30	8300
you by lot these nations that r .... Josh 23:4	7604
nations, these that r among you .... Josh 23:7	7604
even these that r among you .... Josh 23:12	7604
and why did Dan r in ships .... Judg 5:17	1481
we do for wives for them that r .... Judg 21:7	3498
we do for wives for them that r .... Judg 21:16	3498
shalt r by the stone Ezel 1Sa 20:19	3427
did Joab r there with all Israel 1Kin 11:16	3427
I only, r a prophet of the LORD 1Kin 18:22	3498
thee, five of the horses that r 2Kin 7:13	7604
for we r yet escaped, as it is .... Ezr 9:15	7604
the grave, and shall r in the tomb .... Job 21:32	8245

R

Those that *r* of him shall be .... Job 27:15   8300
into dens, and *r* in their places .... Job 37:8   7931
far off, and *r* in the wilderness .... Ps 55:7   3885
and the perfect shall *r* in it .... Prov 2:21   3498
the way of understanding shall *r* .... Prov 21:16   5117
As yet shall he *r* at Nob that day .... Is 10:32   5975
righteousness *r* in the fruitful .... Is 32:16   3427
that it may *r* in the house .... Is 44:13   3427
Which *r* among the graves, and .... Is 65:4   3427
shall *r* before me, saith the LORD .... Is 66:22   5975
so shall your seed and your name *r* ...... Is 66:22   5975
them that *r* of this evil family .... Jer 8:3   7604
which *r* in all the places whither .... Jer 8:3   7604
and this city shall *r* for ever .... Jer 17:25   3427
that *r* in this land, and them that .... Jer 24:8   7604
those will I let *r* still in their .... Jer 27:11   3241
the vessels that *r* in this city .... Jer 27:19   3498
that *r* in the house of the LORD .... Jer 27:21   3498
the palace shall *r* after the .... Jer 30:18   3427
men of war that *r* in this city .... Jer 38:4   7604
none of them shall *r* or escape .... Jer 42:17   8300
of Judah, to leave you none to *r* .... Jer 44:7   7611
sojourn there, shall escape or *r* .... Jer 44:14   8300
it off, that none shall *r* in it .... Jer 51:62   3427
none of them shall *r,* nor of .... Eze 7:11
they that *r* shall be scattered .... Eze 17:21   7604
all the fowls of the heaven *r* .... Eze 31:13   7931
of the heaven to *r* upon thee .... Eze 32:4   7931
that *r* upon the face of the earth .... Eze 39:14   3498
if there *r* ten men in one house, ... Amos 6:9   3498
that did *r* in the day of distress .... Obad 14   8300
it shall *r* in the midst of his .... Zec 5:4   3885
All the families that *r,* every .... Zec 12:14   7604
And in the same house *r,* eating and ..... Lk 10:7   *3306*
Gather up the fragments that *r* .... Jn 6:12   *4052*
you, that my joy might *r* in you .... Jn 15:11   *3306*
and that your fruit should *r* .... Jn 15:16   *3306*
that the bodies should not *r* upon .... Jn 19:31   *3306*
let her *r* unmarried, or be 1Cor 7:11   *3306*
greater part *r* unto this present 1Cor 15:6   *3306*
r unto the coming of the Lord 1Th 4:15   *4035*
r shall be caught up together 1Th 4:17   *4035*
which cannot be shaken may *r* .... Heb 12:27   *3306*
from the beginning shall *r* in you 1Jn 2:24   *3306*
and strengthen the things which *r* .... Rev 3:2   *3062*

REMAINDER

thou shalt burn the *r* with fire .... Ex 29:34   3498
the *r* thereof shall Aaron and his .... Lev 6:16   3498
also the *r* of it shall be eaten .... Lev 7:16   3498
But the *r* of the flesh of the .... Lev 7:17   3498
neither name nor *r* upon the earth 2Sa 14:7   7611
the *r* of wrath shalt thou .... Ps 76:10   7611

REMAINED

and Noah only *r* alive, and they .... Gen 7:23   7604
they that *r* fled to the mountain .... Gen 14:10   7604
there *r* not one .... Ex 8:31   7604
there *r* not any green thing in .... Ex 10:15   3498
there *r* not one locust in all the .... Ex 10:19   7604
there *r* not so much as one of .... Ex 14:28   7604
But there *r* two of the men in the .... Num 11:26   7604
Because he should have *r* in the .... Num 35:28   3427
their inheritance *r* in the tribe .... Num 36:12   1961
Bashan of the remnant of giants .... Deut 3:11   7604
ye shall have *r* long in the land, ... Deut 4:25   3462
that the rest which *r* of them .... Josh 10:20   8277
in Gath, and in Ashdod, there *r* .... Josh 11:22   7604
who *r* of the remnant of the .... Josh 13:12   7604
there *r* among the children of .... Josh 18:2   3498
the Levites which *r* of the .... Josh 21:20   3498
of the children of Kohath that *r* .... Josh 21:26   3498
and there *r* ten thousand .... Judg 7:3   7604
that they which *r* were scattered 1Sa 11:11   7604
r in a mountain in the wilderness 1Sa 23:14   3427
his men *r* in the sides of the 1Sa 24:3   3427
So Tamar *r* desolate in her 2Sa 13:20   3427
which *r* in the days of his father 1Kin 22:46   7604
So Jehu slew all that *r* of the 2Kin 10:11   7604
he slew all that *r* unto Ahab in 2Kin 10:17   7604
there *r* the grove also in Samaria 2Kin 13:6   5975
none *r,* save the poorest sort of 2Kin 24:14   7604
that *r* in the land of Judah 2Kin 25:22   7604
the ark of God *r* with the family 1Chr 13:14   3427
also my wisdom *r* with me .... Eccl 2:9   5975
cities *r* of the cities of Judah .... Jer 34:7   7604
there *r* but wounded men among .... Jer 37:10   7604
Jeremiah had *r* there many days .... Jer 37:16   3427
Thus Jeremiah *r* in the court of .... Jer 37:21   3427
Jeremiah *r* in the court of the .... Jer 38:13   3427
of the people that *r* in the city .... Jer 39:9   7604
the rest of the people that *r* .... Jer 39:9   7604

all the people that *r* in Mizpah ......
therefore his taste *r* in him ....
they have *r* in their holds ....
of the people that *r* in the city .... *'l:10*
LORD's anger none escaped nor *r* ....
r there astonished among them ....
there *r* no strength in me ....
I *r* there with the kings of ....
there *r* no strength in me ....
it would have *r* until this day ....
that *r* twelve baskets full ....
unto them, and *r* speechless ....
that *r* to them twelve baskets .... Lk 9:
five barley loaves, which *r* over .... Jn 6:1
Whiles it *r,* was it not thine own .... Acts 5
r unmoveable, but the hinder part .... Acts 27

REMAINEST

Thou, O LORD, *r* for ever .... Lam 5:19
but thou *r* .... Heb 1:11

REMAINETH

While the earth *r,* seedtime and .... Gen 8:22
which *r* unto you from the hail, ... Ex 10:5   7
that which *r* of it until the .... Ex 12:10   34
that which *r* over lay up for you .... Ex 16:23   575
the remnant that *r* of the .... Ex 26:12   5736
the tent, the half curtain that *r* .... Ex 26:12   5736
r in the length of the curtains .... Ex 26:13   5736
that which *r* of the flesh and of .... Lev 8:32   3498
Take the meat offering that *r* of .... Lev 10:12   3498
that *r* among them in the midst of .... Lev 16:16   7931
destroy him that *r* of the city .... Num 24:19   8300
of stones, that *r* unto this day .... Josh 8:29
there *r* yet very much land to be .... Josh 13:1   7604
This is the land that yet *r* .... Josh 13:2   7604
Then he made him that *r* have .... Judg 5:13   8300
which stone *r* unto this day in 1Sa 6:18
There *r* yet the youngest, and, ... 1Sa 16:11   7604
of the LORD *r* under curtains 1Chr 17:1
whosoever *r* in any place where he .... Ezr 1:4   7604
erred, mine error *r* with myself .... Job 19:4   3885
in your answers there *r* falsehood .... Job 21:34   7604
In his neck *r* strength, and sorrow .... Job 41:22   3885
he that *r* in Jerusalem, shall be' .... Is 4:3   3498
He that *r* in this city shall die .... Jer 38:2   3427
and Zidon every helper that *r* .... Jer 47:4   8300
and he that *r* and is besieged shall .... Eze 6:12   7604
Egypt, so my spirit *r* among you .... Hag 2:5   5975
but he that *r,* even he, shall be .... Zec 9:7   7604
therefore your sin *r* .... Jn 9:41   *3306*
it *r,* that both they that have 1Cor 7:29   *3588,3063*
more that which *r* is glorious 2Cor 3:11   *3306*
for until this day *r* the same 2Cor 3:14   *3306*
his righteousness *r* for ever 2Cor 9:9   *3306*
Seeing therefore it *r* that some .... Heb 4:6   *620*
There *r* therefore a rest to the .... Heb 4:9   *620*
there *r* no more sacrifice for .... Heb 10:26   *620*
for his seed *r* in him 1Jn 3:9   *3306*

REMAINING

r thereon, the children of Israel .... Num 9:22   7931
him until none was left to him *r* .... Deut 3:3   8300
until he had left him none *r* .... Josh 10:33   8300
he left none *r,* according to all .... Josh 10:37   8300
he left none *r* .... Josh 10:39   8300
he left none *r,* but utterly .... Josh 10:40   8300
them, until they left them none *r* .... Josh 11:8   8300
which were *r* of the families of .... Josh 21:40   3498
we should be destroyed from *r* in 2Sa 21:5   3320
priests, until he left him none *r* 2Kin 10:11   8300
who *r* in the chambers were free 1Chr 9:33
nor any *r* in his dwellings .... Job 18:19   8300
not be any *r* of the house of Esau .... Obad 18   8300
r on him, the same is he which .... Jn 1:33   *3306*

REMALIAH (rem-a-li'-ah) See REMALIAH'S. *Father of Pekah.*

But Pekah the son of *R,* a captain 2Kin 15:25   7425
R began to reign over Israel in 2Kin 15:27   7425
against Pekah the son of *R* 2Kin 15:30   7425
R king of Israel began Jotham the 2Kin 15:32   7425
of Syria, and Pekah the son of *R* 2Kin 15:37   7425
year of Pekah the son of *R* Ahaz 2Kin 16:1   7425
Pekah son of *R* king of Israel 2Kin 16:5   7425
For Pekah the son of *R* slew in 2Chr 28:6   7425
of Syria, and Pekah the son of *R* .... Is 7:1   7425
with Syria, and of the son of *R* .... Is 7:4   7425
Syria, Ephraim, and the son of *R* .... Is 7:5   7425

REMALIAH'S (rem-a-li'-ahs)

and the head of Samaria is *R* son .... Is 7:9   7425
and rejoice in Rezin and *R* son .... Is 8:6   7425

REMEDY

…s no r	2Chr 36:16	4832
…hout r	Prov 6:15	4832
…t without r	Prov 29:1	4832

REMEMBER

his people, th…
shall he be…
be destro… which is | Gen 9:15 | 2142
…rlasting | Gen 9:16 | 2142
…tler r Joseph | Gen 40:23 | 2142
…day | Gen 41:9 | 2142

REMEM…

I wi…h ye came out | Ex 13:3 | 2142
…th, to keep it | Ex 20:8 | 2142
…c, and Israel, thy | Ex 32:13 | 2142
…covenant with | Lev 26:42 | 2142
…h Abraham will I r | Lev 26:42 | 2142
…land | Lev 26:42 | 2142
…eir sakes r the | Lev 26:45 | 2142
…which we did eat | Num 11:5 | 2142
…andments of the | Num 15:39 | 2142
…r, and do all my | Num 15:40 | 2142
…ast a servant in the | Deut 5:15 | 2142
…ll r what the LORD | Deut 7:18 | 2142
…all the way which | Deut 8:2 | 2142
…alt r the LORD thy God | Deut 8:18 | 2142
…get not, how thou | Deut 9:7 | 2142
…ervants, Abraham, Isaac, | Deut 9:27 | 2142
…u shalt r that thou wast a | Deut 15:15 | 2142
…that thou mayest r the day when | Deut 16:3 | 2142
thou shalt r that thou wast a | Deut 16:12 | 2142
R what the LORD thy God did unto | Deut 24:9 | 2142
But thou shalt r that thou wast a | Deut 24:18 | 2142
thou shalt r that thou wast a | Deut 24:22 | 2142
R what Amalek did unto thee by | Deut 25:17 | 2142
R the days of old, consider the | Deut 32:7 | 2142
R the word which Moses the | Josh 1:13 | 2142
r also that I am your bone and | Judg 9:2 | 2142
r me, I pray thee, and strengthen | Judg 16:28 | 2142
r me, and not forget thine | 1Sa 1:11 | 2142
I r that which Amalek did to | 1Sa 15:2 | 6485
my lord, then r thine handmaid | 1Sa 25:31 | 2142
let the king r the LORD thy God, | 2Sa 14:11 | 2142
neither do thou r that which thy | 2Sa 19:19 | 2142
for r how that, when I and thou | 2Kin 9:25 | 2142
r now how I have walked before | 2Kin 20:3 | 2142
R his marvellous works that he | 1Chr 16:12 | 2142
r the mercies of David thy | 2Chr 6:42 | 2142
R, I beseech thee, the word that | Neh 1:8 | 2142
r the LORD, which is great and | Neh 4:14 | 2142
R me, O my God, concerning this, | Neh 13:14 | 2142
R me, O my God, concerning this, | Neh 13:22 | 2142
R them, O my God, because they | Neh 13:29 | 2142
R me, O my God, for good | Neh 13:31 | 2142
R, I pray thee, who ever perished | Job 4:7 | 2142
O r that my life is wind | Job 7:7 | 2142
R, I beseech thee, that thou hast | Job 10:9 | 2142
r it as waters that pass away | Job 11:16 | 2142
appoint me a set time, and r me | Job 14:13 | 2142
Even when I r I am afraid | Job 21:6 | 2142
R that thou magnify his work, | Job 36:24 | 2142
him, r the battle, do no more | Job 41:8 | 2142
R all thy offerings, and accept | Ps 20:3 | 2142
but we will r the name of the | Ps 20:7 | 2142
All the ends of the world shall | Ps 22:27 | 2142
R, O LORD, thy tender mercies and | Ps 25:6 | 2142
R not the sins of my youth, nor | Ps 25:7 | 2142
according to thy mercy r thou me | Ps 25:7 | 2142
When I r these things, I pour out | Ps 42:4 | 2142
therefore will I r thee from the | Ps 42:6 | 2142
When I r thee upon my bed, and | Ps 63:6 | 2142
R thy congregation, which thou | Ps 74:2 | 2142
R this, that the enemy hath | Ps 74:18 | 2142
r how the foolish man reproacheth | Ps 74:22 | 2142
but I will r the years of the | Ps 77:10 | 2142
I will r the works of the LORD | Ps 77:11 | 2142
surely I will r thy wonders of | Ps 77:11 | 2142
O r not against us former | Ps 79:8 | 2142
R how short my time is | Ps 89:47 | 2142
R, Lord, the reproach of thy | Ps 89:50 | 2142
to those that r his commandments | Ps 103:18 | 2142
R his marvellous works that he | Ps 105:5 | 2142
R me, O LORD, with the favour | Ps 106:4 | 2142
R the word unto thy servant, upon | Ps 119:49 | 2142
r David, and all his afflictions | Ps 132:1 | 2142
If I do not r thee, let my tongue | Ps 137:6 | 2142
R, O LORD, the children of Edom | Ps 137:7 | 2142
I r the days of old | Ps 143:5 | 2142
poverty, and r his misery no more | Prov 31:7 | 2142
not much r the days of his life | Eccl 5:20 | 2142
yet let him r the days of | Eccl 11:8 | 2142
R now thy Creator in the days of | Eccl 12:1 | 2142
we will r thy love more than wine | Song 1:4 | 2142

R now, O LORD, I beseech thee,	Is 38:3	2142
R ye not the former things,	Is 43:18	2142
own sake, and will not r thy sins	Is 43:25	2142
R these, O Jacob and Israel	Is 44:21	2142
R this, and shew yourselves men	Is 46:8	2142
R the former things of old	Is 46:9	2142
neither didst r the latter end of	Is 47:7	2142
shalt not r the reproach of thy	Is 54:4	2142
those that r thee in thy ways	Is 64:5	2142
neither r iniquity for ever	Is 64:9	2142
I r thee, the kindness of thy	Jer 2:2	2142
neither shall they r it	Jer 3:16	2142
he will now r their iniquity, and	Jer 14:10	2142
r, break not thy covenant with us	Jer 14:21	2142
r me, and visit me, and revenge me	Jer 15:15	2142
their children r their altars	Jer 17:2	2142
R that I stood before thee to	Jer 18:20	2142
him, I do earnestly r him still	Jer 31:20	2142
I will r their sin no more	Jer 31:34	2142
the land, did not the LORD r them	Jer 44:21	2142
r the LORD afar off, and let	Jer 51:50	2142
R, O LORD, what is come upon us	Lam 5:1	2142
r me among the nations whither	Eze 6:9	2142
Nevertheless I will r my covenant	Eze 16:60	2142
Then thou shalt r thy ways	Eze 16:61	2142
That thou mayest r, and be	Eze 16:63	2142
And there shall ye r your ways	Eze 20:43	2142
unto them, nor r Egypt any more	Eze 23:27	2142
Then shall ye r your own evil	Eze 36:31	2142
that I r all their wickedness	Hos 7:2	2142
now will he r their iniquity, and	Hos 8:13	2142
he will r their iniquity, he will	Hos 9:9	2142
r now what Balak king of Moab	Mic 6:5	2142
in wrath r mercy	Hab 3:2	2142
they shall r me in far countries	Zec 10:9	2142
R ye the law of Moses my servant,	Mal 4:4	2142
neither r the five loaves of the	Mt 16:9	*3421*
we r that that deceiver said,	Mt 27:63	*3415*
and do ye not r	Mk 8:18	*3421*
and to r his holy covenant	Lk 1:72	*3415*
r that thou in thy lifetime	Lk 16:25	*3415*
R Lot's wife	Lk 17:32	*3421*
r me when thou comest into thy	Lk 23:42	*3415*
r how he spake unto you when he	Lk 24:6	*3415*
R the word that I said unto you,	Jn 15:20	*3421*
ye may r that I told you of them	Jn 16:4	*3421*
Therefore watch, and r, that by	Acts 20:31	*3421*
to r the words of the Lord Jesus,	Acts 20:35	*3421*
that ye r me in all things, and	1Cor 11:2	*3415*
would that we should r the poor	Gal 2:10	*3421*
Wherefore r, that ye being in	Eph 2:11	*3421*
R my bonds	Col 4:18	*3421*
For ye r, brethren, our labour and	1Th 2:9	*3421*
R ye not, that, when I was yet	2Th 2:5	*3421*
R that Jesus Christ of the seed	2Ti 2:8	*3421*
their iniquities will I r no more	Heb 8:12	*3415*
and iniquities will I r no more	Heb 10:17	*3415*
R them that are in bonds, as	Heb 13:3	*3403*
R them which have the rule over	Heb 13:7	*3421*
I will r his deeds which he doeth	3Jn 10	*5279*
r ye the words which were spoken	Jude 17	*3415*
R therefore from whence thou art	Rev 2:5	*3421*
R therefore how thou hast	Rev 3:3	*3421*

REMEMBERED

God r Noah, and every living thing	Gen 8:1	2142
of the plain, that God r Abraham	Gen 19:29	2142
God r Rachel, and God hearkened to	Gen 30:22	2142
Joseph r the dreams which he	Gen 42:9	2142
God r his covenant with Abraham,	Ex 2:24	2142
and I have r my covenant	Ex 6:5	2142
ye shall be r before the LORD	Num 10:9	2142
Israel r not the LORD their God	Judg 8:34	2142
and the LORD r her	1Sa 1:19	2142
Thus Joash the king r not the	2Chr 24:22	2142
he r Vashti, and what she had done	Est 2:1	2142
And that these days should be r	Est 9:28	2142
he shall be no more r	Job 24:20	2142
name to be r in all generations	Ps 45:17	2142
I r God, and was troubled	Ps 77:3	2142
they r that God was their rock,	Ps 78:35	2142
For he r that they were but flesh	Ps 78:39	2142
They r not his hand, nor the day	Ps 78:42	2142
He hath r his mercy and his truth	Ps 98:3	2142
He hath r his covenant for ever,	Ps 105:8	2142
For he r his holy promise, and	Ps 105:42	2142
they r not the multitude of thy	Ps 106:7	2142
he r for them his covenant, and	Ps 106:45	2142
of his fathers be r with the LORD	Ps 109:14	2142
Because that he r not to shew	Ps 109:16	2142
made his wonderful works to be r	Ps 111:4	2143

R

I *r* thy judgments of old, O LORD .... Ps 119:52   2142
I have *r* thy name, O LORD, in the .... Ps 119:55   2142
Who *r* us in our low estate .... Ps 136:23   2142
yea, we wept, when we *r* Zion .... Ps 137:1   2142
yet no man *r* that same poor man .... Eccl 9:15   2142
many songs, that thou mayest be *r* ...... Is 23:16   2142
thou hast lied, and hast not *r* me .... Is 57:11   2142
Then he *r* the days of old, Moses, ... Is 63:11   2142
and the former shall not *r* .... Is 65:17   2142
that his name may be no more *r* .... Jer 11:19   2142
Jerusalem *r* in the days of her .... Lam 1:7   2142
r not his footstool in the day of .... Lam 2:1   2142
which he hath done shall not be *r* .... Eze 3:20   2142
hast not *r* the days of thy youth .... Eze 16:22   2142
hast not *r* the days of thy youth .... Eze 16:43   2142
have made your iniquity to be *r* .... Eze 21:24   2142
thou shalt be no more *r* .... Eze 21:32   2142
may not be *r* among the nations .... Eze 25:10   2142
righteousnesses shall not be *r* .... Eze 33:13   2142
shall no more be *r* by their name .... Hos 2:17   2142
r not the brotherly covenant .... Amos 1:9   2142
fainted within me I *r* the LORD .... Jonah 2:7   2142
land, and they shall no more be *r* .... Zec 13:2   2142
Peter *r* the word of Jesus, which .... Mt 26:75   3415
Peter *r* the word of the Lord, how .... Lk 22:61   5279
And *r* he .... Lk 24:8   3415
his disciples *r* that it was .... Jn 2:17   3415
his disciples *r* that he had said .... Jn 2:22   3415
then *r* they that these things .... Jn 12:16   3415
Then *r* I the word of the Lord, ... Acts 11:16   3415
God hath *r* her iniquities .... Rev 18:5   3421

REMEMBEREST

in the grave, whom thou *r* no more .... Ps 88:5   2142
there *r* that thy brother hath .... Mt 5:23   3415

REMEMBERETH

inquisition for blood, he *r* them .... Ps 9:12   2142
he *r* that we are dust .... Ps 103:14   2142
she *r* not her last end .... Lam 1:9   2142
she *r* no more the anguish, for .... Jn 16:21   3421
whilst he *r* the obedience of you 2Cor 7:15   363

REMEMBERING

R mine affliction and my misery, ... Lam 3:19   2142
R without ceasing your work of 1Th 1:3   3421

REMEMBRANCE

the *r* of Amalek from under heaven ..... Ex 17:14   2143
memorial, bringing iniquity to *r* .... Num 5:15   2142
the *r* of Amalek from under heaven ..... Deut 25:19   2143
I would make the *r* of them to .... Deut 32:26   2143
have no son to keep my name in *r* 2Sa 18:18   2142
come unto me to call my sin to *r* 1Kin 17:18   2142
His *r* shall perish from the earth .... Job 18:17   2143
in death there is no *r* of thee .... Ps 6:5   2143
thanks at the *r* of his holiness .... Ps 30:4   2143
to cut off the *r* of them from the .... Ps 34:16   2143
A Psalm of David, to bring to *r* .... Ps 38:t   2142
A Psalm of David, to bring to *r* .... Ps 70:t   2142
I call to *r* my song in the night .... Ps 77:6   2142
of Israel may be no more in *r* .... Ps 83:4   2142
thanks at the *r* of his holiness .... Ps 97:12   2143
thy *r* unto all generations .... Ps 102:12   2143
shall be in everlasting *r* .... Ps 112:6   2143
There is no *r* of former things .... Eccl 1:11   2146
neither shall there be any *r* of .... Eccl 1:11   2146
For there is no *r* of the wise .... Eccl 2:16   2146
to thy name, and to the *r* of thee .... Is 26:8   2143
Put me in *r* .... Is 43:26   2142
the posts hast thou set up thy *r* .... Is 57:8   2146
My soul hath them still in *r* .... Lam 3:20   2142
he will call to *r* the iniquity .... Eze 21:23   2142
I say, that ye are come to *r* .... Eze 21:24   2142
in calling to *r* the days of her .... Eze 23:19   2142
Thus thou calledst to *r* the .... Eze 23:21   6485
bringeth their iniquity to *r* .... Eze 29:16   2142
a book of *r* was written before .... Mal 3:16   2146
Peter calling to *r* saith unto him .... Mk 11:21   364
servant Israel, in *r* of his mercy .... Lk 1:54   3415
this do in *r* of me .... Lk 22:19   364
and bring all things to your *r* .... Jn 14:26   5279
are had in *r* in the sight of God .... Acts 10:31   3415
who shall bring you into *r* of my 1Cor 4:17   363
this do in *r* of me 1Cor 11:24   364
as oft as ye drink it, in *r* of me 1Cor 11:25   364
thank my God upon every *r* of you .... Phil 1:3   3417
that ye have good *r* of us always 1Ti 3:6   3417
the brethren in *r* of these things 1Ti 4:6   5294
r of thee in my prayers night 2Ti 1:3   3417
When I call to *r* the unfeigned 2Ti 1:5   5280
Wherefore I put thee in *r* that 2Ti 1:6   363
Of these things put them in *r* 2Ti 2:14   5279

a *r* again made of sins every year ..... **REMNANT**
But call to *r* the former days, in ....
you always in *r* of these things ....
stir you up by putting you in *r* ....
to have these things always in *r*   364
up your pure minds by way of *r*   363
I will therefore put you in *r* .... Jude   363
Babylon came in *r* before God .... Rev 79

REMEMBRANCES

Your *r* are like unto ashes, your .... Job 13:

REMETH (*re'-meth*) See RAMOTH, JARMUTH. *A Levi*
    city in Issachar.
And *R*, and En-gannim, ... Josh 19:21

REMISSION

shed for many for the *r* of sins .... Mt 26:28
of repentance for the *r* of sins .... Mk 1:4
his people by the *r* of their sins .... Lk 1:77   85
of repentance for the *r* of sins .... Lk 3:3   859
r of sins should be preached in .... Lk 24:47   859
of Jesus Christ for the *r* of sins .... Acts 2:38   859
in him shall receive *r* of sins .... Acts 10:43   859
for the *r* of sins that are past .... Rom 3:25   3929
without shedding of blood is no *r* .... Heb 9:22   859
Now where *r* of these is, there is .... Heb 10:18   859

REMIT

Whose soever sins ye *r*, they are .... Jn 20:23   863

REMITTED

ye remit, they are *r* unto them .... Jn 20:23   863

REMMON (*rem'-mon*) See RIMMON. *A city in Judah.*
Ain, *R*, and Ether, and Ashan .... Josh 19:7   7417

REMMON-METHOAR (*rem'-mon-meth'-o-ar*) *A city in*
    Zebulun.
and goeth out to *R* to Neah .... Josh 19:13   7417

REMNANT

the *r* that remaineth of the .... Ex 26:12   5629
the *r* of the meat offerings shall .... Lev 2:3   3498
the *r* shall be the priest's, as a .... Lev 5:13   3498
the *r* of the oil that is in the .... Lev 14:18   3498
remained of the *r* of giants .... Deut 3:11   3499
toward the *r* of his children .... Deut 28:54   3499
which was of the *r* of the giants .... Josh 12:4   3499
remained of the *r* of the giants .... Josh 13:12   3499
cleave unto the *r* of these .... Josh 23:12   3499
but of the *r* of the Amorites 2Sa 21:2   3499
to the *r* of the people, saying, ... 1Kin 12:23   3499
will take away the *r* of the house 1Kin 14:10   310
the *r* of the sodomites, which 1Kin 22:46   3499
prayer for the *r* that are left 2Kin 19:4   7611
the *r* that is escaped of the 2Kin 19:30   7604
of Jerusalem shall go forth a *r* 2Kin 19:31   7611
I will forsake the *r* of mine 2Kin 21:14   7611
with the *r* of the multitude, did 2Kin 25:11   3499
of the *r* of the sons of Kohath 1Chr 6:70   3498
and he will return to the *r* of you 2Chr 30:6   7604
and of all the *r* of Israel 2Chr 34:9   7611
the *r* of their brethren the .... Ezr 3:8   7605
God, to leave us a *r* to escape .... Ezr 9:8   7605
there should be no *r* nor escaping .... Ezr 9:14   7611
The *r* that are left of the .... Neh 1:3   7604
but the *r* of them the fire .... Job 22:20   3499
had left unto us a very small *r* .... Is 1:9   8300
that the *r* of Israel, and such as .... Is 10:20   7605
The *r* shall return, even the .... Is 10:21   7605
shall return, even the *r* of Jacob .... Is 10:21   7605
yet a *r* of them shall return .... Is 10:22   7605
to recover the *r* of his people .... Is 11:11   7605
highway for the *r* of his people .... Is 11:16   7605
off from Babylon the name, and *r* .... Is 14:22   7605
famine, and he shall slay thy *r* .... Is 14:30   7611
Moab, and upon the *r* of the land .... Is 15:9   7611
the *r* shall be very small and .... Is 16:14   7605
from Damascus, and the *r* of Syria .... Is 17:3   7605
thy prayer for the *r* that is left .... Is 37:4   7611
the *r* that is escaped of the .... Is 37:31   7604
of Jerusalem shall go forth a *r* .... Is 37:32   7611
all the *r* of the house of Israel, ... Is 46:3   7611
glean the *r* of Israel as a vine .... Jer 6:9   7611
And there shall be no *r* of them .... Jer 11:23   7611
it shall be well with thy *r* .... Jer 15:11   8293
I will gather the *r* of my flock .... Jer 23:3   7611
and Ekron, and the *r* of Ashdod, ... Jer 25:20   7611
save thy people, the *r* of Israel .... Jer 31:7   7611
away captive into Babylon the *r* .... Jer 39:9   3499
of Babylon had left a *r* of Judah .... Jer 40:11   7611
and the *r* in Judah perish .... Jer 40:15   7611
all the *r* of the people whom he .... Jer 41:16   7611
LORD thy God, even for all this *r* .... Jer 42:2   7611

word of the LORD, ye r of Judah	Jer 42:15	7611
concerning you, O ye r of Judah	Jer 42:19	7611
forces, took all the r of Judah	Jer 43:5	7611
And I will take the r of Judah	Jer 44:12	7611
So that none of the r of Judah	Jer 44:14	7611
all the r of Judah, that are gone	Jer 44:28	7611
the r of the country of Caphtor	Jer 47:4	7611
off with the r of their valley	Jer 47:5	7611
the whole r of thee will I	Eze 5:10	7611
Yet will I leave a r, that ye may	Eze 6:8	3498
a full end of the r of Israel	Eze 11:13	7611
therein shall be left a r that	Eze 14:22	6413
thy r shall fall by the sword	Eze 23:25	319
destroy the r of the sea coast	Eze 25:16	7611
in the r whom the LORD shall call	Joel 2:32	8300
the r of the Philistines shall	Amos 1:8	7611
be gracious unto the r of Joseph	Amos 5:15	7611
they may possess the r of Edom	Amos 9:12	7611
surely gather the r of Israel	Mic 2:12	7611
I will make her that halted a r	Mic 4:7	7611
then the r of his brethren shall	Mic 5:3	3499
the r of Jacob shall be in the	Mic 5:7	7611
the r of Jacob shall be among the	Mic 5:8	7611
of the r of his heritage	Mic 7:18	7611
all the r of the people shall	Hab 2:8	3499
I will cut off the r of Baal from	Zeph 1:4	7605
for the r of the house of Judah	Zeph 2:7	7611
the r of my people shall possess	Zeph 2:9	3499
The r of Israel shall not do	Zeph 3:13	7611
with all the r of the people,	Hag 1:12	7611
spirit of all the r of the people	Hag 1:14	7611
r of this people in these days	Zec 8:6	7611
I will cause the r of this people	Zec 8:12	7611
the r took his servants, and	Mt 22:6	3062
of the sea, a r shall be saved	Rom 9:27	2640
a r according to the election of	Rom 11:5	3005
the r were affrighted, and gave	Rev 11:13	3062
make war with the r of her seed	Rev 12:17	3062
the r were slain with the sword	Rev 19:21	3062

REMOVE

to r it from Ephraim's head unto	Gen 48:17	5493
of Israel r from tribe to tribe	Num 36:7	5437
Neither shall the inheritance r	Num 36:9	5437
Thou shalt not r thy neighbour's	Deut 19:14	5253
then ye shall r from your place,	Josh 3:3	5265
then would I r Abimelech	Judg 9:29	5493
So David would not r the ark of	2Sa 6:10	5493
I will r Judah also out of my	2Kin 23:27	5493
to r them out of his sight, for	2Kin 24:3	5493
Neither will I any more r the	2Chr 33:8	5493
Some r the landmarks	Job 24:2	5472
till I die I will not r mine	Job 27:5	5493
not the hand of the wicked r me	Ps 36:11	5110
R thy stroke away from me	Ps 39:10	5493
R from me reproach and contempt	Ps 119:22	1556
R from me the way of lying	Ps 119:29	5493
r thy foot from evil	Prov 4:27	5493
R thy way far from her, and come	Prov 5:8	7368
R not the ancient landmark, which	Prov 22:28	5253
R not the old landmark	Prov 23:10	5253
R far from me vanity and lies	Prov 30:8	7368
Therefore r sorrow from thy heart	Eccl 11:10	5493
the earth shall r out of her	Is 13:13	7493
from his place shall he not r	Is 46:7	4185
my sight, then shalt thou not r	Jer 4:1	5110
to r you far from your land	Jer 27:10	7368
that I should r it from before my	Jer 32:31	5493
they shall r, they shall depart,	Jer 50:3	5110
R out of the midst of Babylon, and	Jer 50:8	5110
and r by day in their sight	Eze 12:3	1540
thou shalt r from thy place to	Eze 12:3	1540
they shall r and go into captivity	Eze 12:11	5493
R the diadem, and take off the	Eze 21:26	5493
r violence and spoil, and execute	Eze 45:9	5493
were like them that r the bound	Hos 5:10	5253
But I will r far off from you the	Joel 2:20	7368
that ye might r them far from	Joel 3:6	7368
which ye shall not r your necks	Mic 2:3	4185
I will r the iniquity of that	Zec 3:9	4185
mountain shall r toward the north	Zec 14:4	4185
mountain, R hence to yonder place	Mt 17:20	3327
and it shall r	Mt 17:20	3327
be willing, r this cup from me	Lk 22:42	3911
so that I could r mountains	1Cor 13:2	3179
will r thy candlestick out of his	Rev 2:5	2795

REMOVED

Noah r the covering of the ark,	Gen 8:13	5493
he r from thence unto a mountain	Gen 12:8	6275
Then Abram r his tent, and came and	Gen 13:18	167
he r from thence, and digged	Gen 26:22	6275

he r that day the he goats that	Gen 30:35	5493
he r them to cities from one end	Gen 47:21	5674
he r the swarms of flies from	Ex 8:31	5493
went before the camp of Israel, r	Ex 14:19	5265
and when the people saw it, they r	Ex 20:18	5128
the people r from Hazeroth	Num 12:16	5265
From thence they r, and pitched in	Num 21:12	5265
From thence they r, and pitched on	Num 21:13	5265
children of Israel r from Rameses	Num 33:5	5265
they r from Etham, and turned	Num 33:7	5265
they r from Marah, and came unto	Num 33:9	5265
they r from Elim, and encamped by	Num 33:10	5265
they r from the Red sea, and	Num 33:11	5265
they r from Alush, and encamped at	Num 33:14	5265
they r from the desert of Sinai,	Num 33:16	5265
they r from Libnah, and pitched at	Num 33:21	5265
they r from mount Shapher, and	Num 33:24	5265
they r from Haradah, and pitched	Num 33:25	5265
they r from Makheloth, and	Num 33:26	5265
they r from Tarah, and pitched in	Num 33:28	5265
they r from Bene-jaakan, and	Num 33:32	5265
they r from Jotbathah, and	Num 33:34	5265
they r from Ezion-gaber, and	Num 33:36	5265
they r from Kadesh, and pitched in	Num 33:37	5265
they r from Dibon-gad, and	Num 33:46	5265
they r from Almon-diblathaim, and	Num 33:47	5265
shalt be r into all the kingdoms	Deut 28:25	2189
they r from Shittim, and came to	Josh 3:1	5265
when the people r from their	Josh 3:14	5265
why his hand is not r from you	1Sa 6:3	5493
Therefore Saul r him from him	1Sa 18:13	5493
he r Amasa out of the highway	2Sa 20:12	5437
When he was r out of the highway,	2Sa 20:13	3014
r all the idols that his fathers	1Kin 15:12	5493
even her he r from being queen,	1Kin 15:13	5493
But the high places were not r	1Kin 15:14	5493
that the high places were not r	2Kin 15:4	5493
the high places were not r	2Kin 15:35	5493
r the laver from off them	2Kin 16:17	5493
and r them out of his sight	2Kin 17:18	5493
Until the LORD r Israel out of	2Kin 17:23	5493
The nations which thou hast r	2Kin 17:26	1540
He r the high places, and brake	2Kin 18:4	5493
of my sight, as I have r Israel	2Kin 23:27	5493
Geba, and they r them to Manahath	1Chr 8:6	1540
he r them, and begat Uzza, and	1Chr 8:7	1540
he r her from being queen,	2Chr 15:16	5493
they r the burnt offerings, that	2Chr 35:12	5493
the rock is r out of his place	Job 14:18	6275
the rock be r out of his place	Job 18:4	6275
mine hope hath he r like a tree	Job 19:10	5265
Even so would he have r thee out	Job 36:16	5493
we fear, though the earth be r	Ps 46:2	4171
I r his shoulder from the burden	Ps 81:6	5493
the west, so far hath he r our	Ps 103:12	7368
that it should not be r for ever	Ps 104:5	4131
as mount Zion, which cannot be r	Ps 125:1	4131
The righteous shall never be r	Prov 10:30	4131
And the LORD have r men far away	Is 6:12	7368
I have r the bounds of the people	Is 10:13	5493
Madmenah is r	Is 10:31	5074
fastened in the sure place be r	Is 22:25	4185
shall be r like a cottage	Is 24:20	5110
thou hadst r it far unto all the	Is 26:15	7368
but have r their heart far from	Is 29:13	7368
be r into a corner any more	Is 30:20	3670
stakes thereof shall ever be r	Is 33:20	5265
is r from me as a shepherd's tent	Is 38:12	1556
shall depart, and the hills be r	Is 54:10	4131
the covenant of my peace be r	Is 54:10	4131
I will cause them to be r into	Jer 15:4	2189
I will deliver them to be r into	Jer 24:9	2189
will deliver them to be r to all	Jer 29:18	2189
I will make you to be r into all	Jer 34:17	2189
therefore she is r	Lam 1:8	5206
thou hast r my soul far off from	Lam 3:17	2186
streets, and their gold shall be r	Eze 7:19	5079
them, and will give them to be r	Eze 23:46	2189
as the uncleanness of a r woman	Eze 36:17	5079
stretched themselves shall be r	Amos 6:7	5493
how hath he r it from me	Mic 2:4	4185
day shall the decree be far r	Mic 7:11	
say unto this mountain, Be thou r	Mt 21:21	*142*
say unto this mountain, Be thou r	Mk 11:23	*142*
he r him into this land, wherein	Acts 7:4	3351
And when he had r him, he raised	Acts 13:22	3179
I marvel that ye are so soon r	Gal 1:6	3346

REMOVETH

Cursed be he that r his	Deut 27:17	5253
Which r the mountains, and they	Job 9:5	6275

R

He *r* away the speech of the	Job 12:20	5493
Whoso *r* stones shall be hurt	Eccl 10:9	5265
he *r* kings, and setteth up kings	Dan 2:21	5709

REMOVING

r from thence all the speckled and	Gen 30:32	5493
a captive, and *r* to and fro	Is 49:21	5493
of man, prepare thee stuff for *r*	Eze 12:3	1473
in their sight, as stuff for *r*	Eze 12:4	1473
signifieth the *r* of those things	Heb 12:27	3331

REMPHAN (rem'-fan) *An idol worshipped by Israel.*

Moloch, and the star of your god *R*	Acts 7:43	4481

REND

the hole, that it should not *r*	Ex 39:23	
heads, neither *r* your clothes	Lev 10:6	6533
then he shall *r* it out of the	Lev 13:56	7167
his head, nor *r* his clothes	Lev 21:10	6533
R your clothes, and gird you with	2Sa 3:31	7167
I will surely *r* the kingdom from	1Kin 11:11	7167
but I will *r* it out of the hand	1Kin 11:12	7167
Howbeit I will not *r* away all the	1Kin 11:13	7167
I will *r* the kingdom out of the	1Kin 11:31	7167
didst *r* thy clothes, and weep	2Chr 34:27	7167
A time to *r*, and a time to sew	Eccl 3:7	7167
that thou wouldest *r* the heavens	Is 64:1	7167
and a stormy wind shall *r* it	Eze 13:11	1234
I will even *r* it with a stormy	Eze 13:13	1234
break, and *r* all their shoulder	Eze 29:7	1234
will *r* the caul of their heart,	Hos 13:8	7167
r your heart, and not your	Joel 2:13	7167
feet, and turn again and *r* you	Mt 7:6	4486
among themselves, Let us not *r* it	Jn 19:24	4977

RENDER

which they shall *r* unto me	Num 18:9	7725
I will *r* vengeance to mine	Deut 32:41	7725
and will *r* vengeance to his	Deut 32:43	7725
did God *r* upon their heads	Judg 9:57	7725
The Lord *r* to every man his	1Sa 26:23	7725
r unto every man according unto	2Chr 6:30	5415
for he will *r* unto man his	Job 33:26	7725
work of a man shall he *r* unto him	Job 34:11	7999
r to them their desert	Ps 28:4	7725
They also that *r* evil for good	Ps 38:20	7999
I will *r* praises unto thee	Ps 56:12	7999
r unto our neighbours sevenfold	Ps 79:12	7725
r a reward to the proud	Ps 94:2	7725
What shall I *r* unto the Lord for	Ps 116:12	7725
shall not he *r* to every man	Prov 24:12	7725
I will *r* to the man according to	Prov 24:29	7725
seven men that can *r* a reason	Prov 26:16	7725
to *r* his anger with fury, and his	Is 66:15	7725
he will *r* unto her a recompence	Jer 51:6	7999
I will *r* unto Babylon and to all	Jer 51:24	7999
R unto them a recompence, O Lord,	Lam 3:64	7725
so will we *r* the calves of our	Hos 14:2	7999
will ye *r* me a recompence	Joel 3:4	7999
that I will *r* double unto thee	Zec 9:12	7999
which shall *r* him the fruits in	Mt 21:41	591
R therefore unto Caesar the	Mt 22:21	591
R to Caesar the things that are	Mk 12:17	591
R therefore unto Caesar the	Lk 20:25	591
Who will *r* to every man according	Rom 2:6	591
R therefore to all their dues	Rom 13:7	591
Let the husband *r* unto the wife	1Cor 7:3	591
can we *r* to God again for you	1Th 3:9	467
See that none *r* evil for evil	1Th 5:15	591

RENDERED

Thus God *r* the wickedness of	Judg 9:56	7725
r unto the king of Israel an	2Kin 3:4	7725
But Hezekiah *r* not again	2Chr 32:25	7725
a man's hands shall be *r* unto him	Prov 12:14	7725

RENDEREST

for thou *r* to every man according	Ps 62:12	7999

RENDERETH

a voice of the Lord that *r*	Is 66:6	7999

RENDERING

Not *r* evil for evil, or railing	1Pet 3:9	591

RENDING

r it in pieces, while there is	Ps 7:2	6561

RENEW

to Gilgal, and *r* the kingdom there	1Sa 11:14	2318
r a right spirit within me	Ps 51:10	2318
the Lord shall *r* their strength	Is 40:31	2498
let the people *r* their strength	Is 41:1	2498
r our days as of old	Lam 5:21	2318
to *r* them again unto repentance	Heb 6:6	340

RENEWED

r the altar of the Lord, that was	2Chr 15:8	2318
in me, and my bow was *r* in my hand	Job 29:20	2498
thy youth is *r* like the eagle's	Ps 103:5	2318
the inward man is *r* day by day	2Cor 4:16	341
be *r* in the spirit of your mind	Eph 4:23	365
which is *r* in knowledge after the	Col 3:10	341

RENEWEST

Thou *r* thy witnesses against me,	Job 10:17	2318
thou *r* the face of the earth	Ps 104:30	2318

RENEWING

transformed by the *r* of your mind	Rom 12:2	342
and *r* of the Holy Ghost	Titus 3:5	342

RENOUNCED

But have *r* the hidden things of	2Cor 4:2	550

RENOWN

men which were of old, men of *r*	Gen 6:4	8034
in the congregation, men of *r*	Num 16:2	8034
thy *r* went forth among the	Eze 16:14	8034
the harlot because of thy *r*	Eze 16:15	8034
raise up for them a plant of *r*	Eze 34:29	8034
it shall be to them a *r* the day	Eze 39:13	8034
hand, and hast gotten thee *r*	Dan 9:15	8034

RENOWNED

These were the *r* of the	Num 1:16	7121
of evildoers shall never be *r*	Is 14:20	7121
and rulers, great lords and *r*	Eze 23:23	7121
the *r* city, which wast strong in	Eze 26:17	1984

RENT

and he *r* his clothes	Gen 37:29	7167
is without doubt *r* in pieces	Gen 37:33	2963
Jacob *r* his clothes, and put	Gen 37:34	7167
Then they *r* their clothes, and	Gen 44:13	7167
of an habergeon, that it be not *r*	Ex 28:32	7167
plague is, his clothes shall be *r*	Lev 13:45	6533
the land, *r* their clothes	Num 14:6	7167
Joshua *r* his clothes, and fell to	Josh 7:6	7167
asses, and wine bottles, old, and *r*	Josh 9:4	1234
and, behold, they be *r*	Josh 9:13	1234
that he *r* his clothes, and said,	Judg 11:35	7167
he *r* him as he would have *r* a	Judg 14:6	8156
r him as he would have *r* a kid	Judg 14:6	8156
the same day with his clothes *r*	1Sa 4:12	7167
the skirt of his mantle, and it *r*	1Sa 15:27	7167
The Lord hath *r* the kingdom of	1Sa 15:28	7167
for the Lord hath *r* the kingdom	1Sa 28:17	7167
camp from Saul with his clothes *r*	2Sa 1:2	7167
hold on his clothes, and *r* them	2Sa 1:11	7167
r her garment of divers colours	2Sa 13:19	7167
stood by with their clothes *r*	2Sa 13:31	7167
came to meet him with his coat *r*	2Sa 15:32	7167
so that the earth *r* with the	1Kin 1:40	1234
on him, and *r* it in twelve pieces	1Kin 11:30	7167
Behold, the altar shall be *r*	1Kin 13:3	7167
The altar also was *r*, and the	1Kin 13:5	7167
r the kingdom away from the house	1Kin 14:8	7167
strong wind *r* the mountains, and	1Kin 19:11	6561
that he *r* his clothes, and put	1Kin 21:27	7167
clothes, and *r* them in two pieces	2Kin 2:12	7167
that he *r* his clothes, and said,	2Kin 5:7	7167
king of Israel had *r* his clothes	2Kin 5:8	7167
Wherefore hast thou *r* thy clothes	2Kin 5:8	7167
the woman, that he *r* his clothes	2Kin 6:30	7167
Athaliah *r* her clothes, and cried,	2Kin 11:14	7167
For he *r* Israel from the house of	2Kin 17:21	7167
to Hezekiah with their clothes *r*	2Kin 18:37	7167
that he *r* his clothes, and covered	2Kin 19:1	7167
of the law, that he *r* his clothes	2Kin 22:11	7167
hast *r* thy clothes, and wept	2Kin 22:19	7167
Then Athaliah *r* her clothes	2Chr 23:13	7167
of the law, that he *r* his clothes	2Chr 34:19	7167
I *r* my garment and my mantle, and	Ezr 9:3	7167
having *r* my garment and my mantle,	Ezr 9:5	7167
Mordecai *r* his clothes, and put on	Est 4:1	7167
r his mantle, and shaved his head,	Job 1:20	7167
they *r* every one his mantle, and	Job 2:12	7167
and the cloud is not *r* under them	Job 26:8	1234
and instead of a girdle a *r*	Is 3:24	5364
to Hezekiah with their clothes *r*	Is 36:22	7167
that he *r* his clothes, and covered	Is 37:1	7167
nor *r* their garments, neither the	Jer 36:24	7167
beards shaven, and their clothes *r*	Jer 41:5	7167
pain, and No shall be *r* asunder	Eze 30:16	1234
garment, and the *r* is made worse	Mt 9:16	4978
the high priest *r* his clothes	Mt 26:65	1284
the veil of the temple was *r* in	Mt 27:51	4977
earth did quake, and the rocks *r*	Mt 27:51	4977
the old, and the *r* is made worse	Mk 2:21	4978

r him sore, and came out of him	Mk 9:26	4682
the high priest *r* his clothes	Mk 14:63	1284
the veil of the temple was *r* in	Mk 15:38	4977
then both the new maketh a *r*	Lk 5:36	4977
of the temple was *r* in the midst	Lk 23:45	4977
they *r* their clothes, and ran in	Acts 14:14	1284
the magistrates *r* off their	Acts 16:22	4048

RENTEST

though thou *r* thy face with	Jer 4:30	7167

REPAID

to the righteous good shall be *r*	Prov 13:21	7999

REPAIR

let them *r* the breaches of the	2Kin 12:5	2388
Why *r* ye not the breaches of the	2Kin 12:7	2388
neither to *r* the breaches of the	2Kin 12:8	2388
hewed stone to *r* the breaches of	2Kin 12:12	2388
laid out for the house to *r* it	2Kin 12:12	2393
to *r* the breaches of the house,	2Kin 22:5	2388
and hewn stone to *r* the house	2Kin 22:6	2388
minded to *r* the house of the LORD	2Chr 24:4	2318
gather of all Israel money to *r*	2Chr 24:5	2388
carpenters to *r* the house of the	2Chr 24:12	2318
to *r* the house of the LORD his	2Chr 34:8	2388
in the house of the LORD, to *r*	2Chr 34:10	918
to *r* the desolations thereof, and	Ezr 9:9	5975
they shall *r* the waste cities,	Is 61:4	2318

REPAIRED

r the cities, and dwelt in them	Judg 21:23	1129
r the breaches of the city of	1Kin 11:27	5462
he *r* the altar of the LORD that	1Kin 18:30	7495
not *r* the breaches of the house	2Kin 12:6	2388
r therewith the house of the LORD	2Kin 12:14	2388
Joab *r* the rest of the city	1Chr 11:8	2421
the house of the LORD, and *r* them	2Chr 29:3	2388
r Millo in the city of David, and	2Chr 32:5	2388
he *r* the altar of the LORD, and	2Chr 33:16	1129
next unto them *r* Meremoth the son	Neh 3:4	2388
next unto them *r* Meshullam the	Neh 3:4	2388
next unto them *r* Zadok the son of	Neh 3:4	2388
And next unto them the Tekoites *r*	Neh 3:5	2388
Moreover the old gate *r* Jehoiada	Neh 3:6	2388
next unto them *r* Melatiah the	Neh 3:7	2388
Next unto him *r* Uzziel the son of	Neh 3:8	2388
Next unto him also *r* Hananiah the	Neh 3:8	2388
next unto them *r* Rephaiah the son	Neh 3:9	2388
next unto them *r* Jedaiah the son	Neh 3:10	2388
next unto him *r* Hattush the son	Neh 3:10	2388
r the other piece, and the tower	Neh 3:11	2388
next unto him *r* Shallum the son	Neh 3:12	2388
The valley gate *r* Hanun, and the	Neh 3:13	2388
But the dung gate *r* Malchiah the	Neh 3:14	2388
r Shallun the son of Colhozeh	Neh 3:15	2388
After him *r* Nehemiah the son of	Neh 3:16	2388
After him *r* the Levites, Rehum	Neh 3:17	2388
Next unto him *r* Hashabiah	Neh 3:17	2388
After him *r* their brethren, Bavai	Neh 3:18	2388
next to him *r* Ezer the son of	Neh 3:19	2388
earnestly *r* the other piece	Neh 3:20	2388
After him *r* Meremoth the son of	Neh 3:21	2388
after him *r* the priests, the men	Neh 3:22	2388
After him *r* Benjamin and Hashub	Neh 3:23	2388
After him *r* Azariah the son of	Neh 3:23	2388
After him *r* Binnui the son of	Neh 3:24	2388
them the Tekoites *r* another piece	Neh 3:27	2388
the horse gate *r* the priests	Neh 3:28	2388
After them *r* Zadok the son of	Neh 3:29	2388
After him *r* also Shemaiah the son	Neh 3:29	2388
After him *r* Hananiah the son of	Neh 3:30	2388
After him *r* Meshullam the son of	Neh 3:30	2388
After him *r* Malchiah the	Neh 3:31	2388
the sheep gate *r* the goldsmiths	Neh 3:32	2388

REPAIRER

The *r* of the breach, The restorer	Is 58:12	1443

REPAIRING

the *r* of the house of God, behold	2Chr 24:27	3247

REPAY

he will *r* him to his face	Deut 7:10	7999
who shall *r* him what he hath done	Job 21:31	7999
prevented me, that I should *r* him	Job 41:11	7999
deeds, accordingly he will *r*	Is 59:18	7999
the islands he will *r* recompence	Is 59:18	7999
when I come again, I will *r* thee	Lk 10:35	591
I will *r*, saith the Lord	Rom 12:19	457
with mine own hand, I will *r* it	Philem 19	661

REPAYETH

r them that hate him to their	Deut 7:10	7999

REPEATETH

but he that *r* a matter separateth	Prov 17:9	8138

REPENT

the people *r* when they see war	Ex 13:17	5162
r of this evil against thy people	Ex 32:12	5162
the son of man, that he should *r*	Num 23:19	5162
r himself for his servants, when	Deut 32:36	5162
of Israel will not lie nor *r*	1Sa 15:29	5162
he is not a man, that he should *r*	1Sa 15:29	5162
they were carried captives, and *r*	1Kin 8:47	7725
myself, and *r* in dust and ashes	Job 42:6	5162
let it *r* thee concerning thy	Ps 90:13	5162
LORD hath sworn, and will not *r*	Ps 110:4	5162
he will *r* himself concerning his	Ps 135:14	5162
I have purposed it, and will not *r*	Jer 4:28	5162
I will *r* of the evil that I	Jer 18:8	5162
voice, then I will *r* of the good	Jer 18:10	5162
that I may *r* me of the evil,	Jer 26:3	5162
the LORD will *r* him of the evil	Jer 26:13	5162
for I *r* me of the evil that I	Jer 42:10	5162
R, and turn yourselves from your	Eze 14:6	7725
R, and turn yourselves from all	Eze 18:30	7725
will I spare, neither will I *r*	Eze 24:14	5162
knoweth if he will return and *r*	Joel 2:14	5162
can tell if God will turn and *r*	Jonah 3:9	5162
And saying, *R* ye	Mt 3:2	3340
began to preach, and to say, *R*	Mt 4:17	3340
r ye, and believe the gospel	Mk 1:15	3340
and preached then men should *r*	Mk 6:12	3340
but, except ye *r*, ye shall all	Lk 13:3	3340
but, except ye *r*, ye shall all	Lk 13:5	3340
them from the dead, they will *r*	Lk 16:30	3340
and if he *r*, forgive him	Lk 17:3	3340
turn again to thee, saying, I *r*	Lk 17:4	3340
Then Peter said unto them, *R*.	Acts 2:38	3340
R ye therefore, and be converted	Acts 3:19	3340
R therefore of this thy	Acts 8:22	3340
all men every where to *r*	Acts 17:30	3340
the Gentiles, that they should *r*	Acts 26:20	3340
I do not *r*, though I did *r*	2Cor 7:8	3338
him, The Lord sware and will not *r*	Heb 7:21	3338
from whence thou art fallen, and *r*	Rev 2:5	3340
out of his place, except thou *r*	Rev 2:5	3340
R; or else I will	Rev 2:16	3340
her space to *r* of her fornication	Rev 2:21	3340
except they *r* of their deeds	Rev 2:22	3340
and heard, and hold fast, and *r*	Rev 3:3	3340
be zealous therefore, and *r*	Rev 3:19	3340

REPENTANCE

r shall be hid from mine eyes	Hos 13:14	5164
forth therefore fruits meet for *r*	Mt 3:8	3341
baptize you with water unto *r*	Mt 3:11	3341
the righteous, but sinners to *r*	Mt 9:13	3341
preach the baptism of *r* for the	Mk 1:4	3341
the righteous, but sinners to *r*	Mk 2:17	3341
preaching the baptism of *r* for	Lk 3:3	3341
therefore fruits worthy of *r*	Lk 3:8	3341
the righteous, but sinners to *r*	Lk 5:32	3341
just persons, which need no *r*	Lk 15:7	3341
And that *r* and remission of sins	Lk 24:47	3341
Saviour, for to give *r* to Israel	Acts 5:31	3341
the Gentiles granted *r* unto life	Acts 11:18	3341
his coming the baptism of *r* to	Acts 13:24	3341
baptized with the baptism of *r*	Acts 19:4	3341
r toward God, and faith toward our	Acts 20:21	3341
to God, and do works meet for *r*	Acts 26:20	3341
goodness of God leadeth thee to *r*	Rom 2:4	3341
and calling of God are without *r*	Rom 11:29	278
sorry, but that ye sorrowed to *r*	2Cor 7:9	3341
For godly sorrow worketh *r* to	2Cor 7:10	3341
r to the acknowledging of the	2Ti 2:25	3341
foundation of *r* from dead works	Heb 6:1	3341
away, to renew them again unto *r*	Heb 6:6	3341
for he found no place of *r*	Heb 12:17	3341
but that all should come to *r*	2Pet 3:9	3341

REPENTED

it *r* the LORD that he had made	Gen 6:6	5162
the LORD *r* of the evil which he	Ex 32:14	5162
for it *r* the LORD because of	Judg 2:18	5162
the children of Israel *r* them for	Judg 21:6	5162
the people *r* them for Benjamin,	Judg 21:15	5162
the LORD *r* that he had made Saul	1Sa 15:35	5162
the LORD *r* him of the evil, and	2Sa 24:16	5162
he *r* him of the evil, and said to	1Chr 21:15	5162
r according to the multitude of	Ps 106:45	5162
no man *r* him of his wickedness,	Jer 8:6	5162
the LORD overthrew, and *r* not	Jer 20:16	5162
the LORD *r* him of the evil which	Jer 26:19	5162
after that I was turned, I *r*	Jer 31:19	5162

R

The LORD r for this	Amos 7:3	5162
The LORD r for this	Amos 7:6	5162
God r of the evil, that he had	Jonah 3:10	5162
the LORD of hosts, and I r not	Zec 8:14	5162
were done, because they r not	Mt 11:20	3340
they would have r long ago in	Mt 11:21	3340
because they r at the preaching	Mt 12:41	3340
but afterward he r, and went	Mt 21:29	3338
r not afterward, that ye might	Mt 21:32	3338
r himself, and brought again the	Mt 27:3	3338
you, they had a great while ago r	Lk 10:13	3340
for they r at the preaching of	Lk 11:32	3340
to salvation not to be r of	2Cor 7:10	278
have not r of the uncleanness and	2Cor 12:21	3340
and she r not	Rev 2:21	3340
r not of the works of their hands	Rev 9:20	3340
Neither r they of their murders,	Rev 9:21	3340
they r not to give him glory	Rev 16:9	3340
sores, and r not of their deeds	Rev 16:11	3340

REPENTEST
kindness, and r thee of the evil	Jonah 4:2	5162

REPENTETH
for it r me that I have made them	Gen 6:7	5162
It r me that I have set up Saul	1Sa 15:11	5162
kindness, and r him of the evil	Joel 2:13	5162
in heaven over one sinner that r	Lk 15:7	3340
of God over one sinner that r	Lk 15:10	3340

REPENTING
I am weary with r	Jer 15:6	5162

REPENTINGS
my r are kindled together	Hos 11:8	5150

REPETITIONS
But when ye pray, use not vain r	Mt 6:7	945

REPHAEL (re'-fa-el) A sanctuary servant.
Othni, and R, and Obed, Elzabad,	1Chr 26:7	7501

REPHAH (re'-fah) A grandson of Ephraim.
R was his son, also Resheph, and	1Chr 7:25	7506

REPHAIAH (ref-a-i'-ah) See RAPHA, RHESA.
1. Head of a family.
the sons of R, the sons of Arnan,	1Chr 3:21	7509

2. A captain of Simeon.
Pelatiah, and Neariah, and R	1Chr 4:42	7509

3. A son of Tola.
Uzzi, and R, and Jeriel, and Jahmai,	1Chr 7:2	7509

4. Son of Binea.
R his son, Eleasah his son, Azel	1Chr 9:43	7509

5. A repairer of Jerusalem's wall.
them repaired R the son of Hur	Neh 3:9	7509

REPHAIM (re-fa'-im) See REPHAIMS. A valley near Jerusalem.
themselves in the valley of R	2Sa 5:18	7497
themselves in the valley of R	2Sa 5:22	7497
pitched in the valley of R	2Sa 23:13	7497
encamped in the valley of R	1Chr 11:15	7497
themselves in the valley of R	1Chr 14:9	7497
gathereth ears in the valley of R	Is 17:5	7497

REPHAIMS (re-fa'-ims) See REPHAIM. A tribe of Canaanites.
smote the R in Ashteroth Karnaim,	Gen 14:5	7497
and the Perizzites, and the R	Gen 15:20	7497

REPHAN See REMPHAN.

REPHIDIM (ref'-i-dim) An Israelite encampment in the wilderness.
of the LORD, and pitched in R	Ex 17:1	7508
and fought with Israel in R	Ex 17:8	7508
For they were departed from R	Ex 19:2	7508
from Alush, and encamped at R	Num 33:14	7508
And they departed from R, and	Num 33:15	7508

REPLENISH
r the earth, and subdue it	Gen 1:28	4390
and multiply, and r the earth	Gen 9:1	4390

REPLENISHED
because they be r from the east	Is 2:6	4390
that pass over the sea, have r	Is 23:2	4390
I have r every sorrowful soul	Jer 31:25	4390
I shall be r, now she is laid	Eze 26:2	4390
and thou wast r, and made very	Eze 27:25	4390

REPLIEST
who art thou that r against God	Rom 9:20	470

REPORT
unto his father their evil r	Gen 37:2	1681
Thou shalt not raise a false r	Ex 23:1	8088
they brought up an evil r of the	Num 13:32	1681

bring up the evil r upon the land	Num 14:37	1681
heaven, who shall hear r of thee	Deut 2:25	8088
for it is no good r that I hear	1Sa 2:24	8052
It was a true r that I heard in	1Kin 10:6	1697
It was a true r which I heard in	2Chr 9:5	1697
might have matter for an evil r	Neh 6:13	8034
a good r maketh the bones fat	Prov 15:30	8052
As at the r concerning Egypt, so	Is 23:5	8088
be sorely pained at the r of Tyre	Is 23:5	8088
vexation only to understand the r	Is 28:19	8052
Who hath believed our r	Is 53:1	8052
R, say they, and we will r it	Jer 20:10	5046
Babylon hath heard the r of them	Jer 50:43	8088
Lord, who hath believed our r	Jn 12:38	189
among you seven men of honest r	Acts 6:3	3140
of good r among all the nation of	Acts 10:22	3140
having a good r of all the Jews	Acts 22:12	3140
Lord, who hath believed our r	Rom 10:16	189
r that God is in you of a truth	1Cor 14:25	518
By honour and dishonour, by evil r	2Cor 6:8	1426
and good r: as deceivers	2Cor 6:8	2162
whatsoever things are of good r	Phil 4:8	2163
good r of them which are without	1Ti 3:7	3141
it the elders obtained a good r	Heb 11:2	3140
obtained a good r through faith	Heb 11:39	3140
Demetrius hath good r of all men	3Jn 12	3140

REPORTED
It is r among the heathen, and	Neh 6:6	8085
now shall it be r to the king	Neh 6:7	8085
Also they r his good deeds before	Neh 6:19	559
in their eyes, when it shall be r	Est 1:17	559
r the matter, saying, I have done	Eze 9:11	7725
this saying is commonly r among	Mt 28:15	1310
r all that the chief priests and	Acts 4:23	518
Which was well r of by the	Acts 16:2	3140
rather, (as we be slanderously r	Rom 3:8	987
It is r commonly that there is	1Cor 5:1	191
Well r of for good works	1Ti 5:10	3140
which are now r unto you by them	1Pet 1:12	312

REPROACH
and said, God hath taken away my r	Gen 30:23	2781
for that were a r unto us	Gen 34:14	2781
away the r of Egypt from off you	Josh 5:9	2781
among the sheaves, and r her not	Ruth 2:15	3637
lay it for a r upon all Israel	1Sa 11:2	2781
and taketh away the r from Israel	1Sa 17:26	2781
of my r from the hand of Nabal	1Sa 25:39	2781
hath sent to r the living God	2Kin 19:4	2778
hath sent him to r the living God	2Kin 19:16	2778
are in great affliction and r	Neh 1:3	2781
Jerusalem, that we be no more a r	Neh 2:17	2781
turn their r upon their own head,	Neh 4:4	2781
the r of the heathen our enemies	Neh 5:9	2781
evil report, that they might r me	Neh 6:13	2778
me, and plead against me my r	Job 19:5	2781
I have heard the check of my r	Job 20:3	3639
my heart shall not r me so long	Job 27:6	2778
nor taketh up a r against his	Ps 15:3	2781
a r of men, and despised of the	Ps 22:6	2781
I was a r among all mine enemies	Ps 31:11	2781
make me not the r of the foolish	Ps 39:8	2781
in my bones, mine enemies r me	Ps 42:10	2778
Thou makest us a r to our	Ps 44:13	2781
save me from the r of him that	Ps 57:3	2778
for thy sake I have borne r	Ps 69:7	2781
with fasting, that was to my r	Ps 69:10	2781
Thou hast known my r, and my shame	Ps 69:19	2781
R hath broken my heart	Ps 69:20	2781
let them be covered with r	Ps 71:13	2781
how long shall the adversary r	Ps 74:10	2778
he put them to a perpetual r	Ps 78:66	2781
We are become a r to our	Ps 79:4	2781
into their bosom their r,	Ps 79:12	2781
he is a r to his neighbours	Ps 89:41	2781
Lord, the r of thy servants	Ps 89:50	2781
the r of all the mighty people	Ps 89:50	
Mine enemies r me all the day	Ps 102:8	2778
I became also a r unto them	Ps 109:25	2781
Remove from me r and contempt	Ps 119:22	2781
Turn away my r which I fear	Ps 119:39	2781
his r shall not be wiped away	Prov 6:33	2781
but sin is a r to any people	Prov 14:34	2617
also contempt, and with ignominy r	Prov 18:3	2781
that causeth shame, and bringeth r	Prov 19:26	2659
yea, strife and r shall cease	Prov 22:10	7036
by thy name, to take away our r	Is 4:1	2781
profit, but a shame, and also a r	Is 30:5	2781
hath sent to r the living God	Is 37:4	2778
hath sent to r the living God	Is 37:17	2778
fear ye not the r of men, neither	Is 51:7	2781

shalt not remember the *r* of thy .... Is 54:4   2781
word of the LORD is unto them a *r* .... Jer 6:10   2781
of the LORD was made a *r* unto me .... Jer 20:8   2781
bring an everlasting *r* upon you .... Jer 23:40   2781
earth for their hurt, to be a *r* .... Jer 24:9   2781
and an hissing, and a *r*, among all........... Jer 29:18   2781
I did bear the *r* of my youth .... Jer 31:19   2781
astonishment, and a curse, and a *r* .... Jer 42:18   2781
a *r* among all the nations of the............. Jer 44:8   2781
astonishment, and a curse, and a *r* .... Jer 44:12   2781
shall become a desolation, a *r*.............. Jer 49:13   2781
because we have heard *r* .... Jer 51:51   2781
he is filled full with *r*............................... Lam 3:30   2781
Thou hast heard their *r*, O LORD, ... Lam 3:61   2781
consider, and behold our *r* .... Lam 5:1   2781
a *r* among the nations that are .... Eze 5:14   2781
So it shall be a *r* and a taunt, an .... Eze 5:15   2781
as at the time of thy *r* of the .... Eze 16:57   2781
Ammonites, and concerning their *r* .... Eze 21:28   2781
I made thee a *r* unto the heathen .... Eze 22:4   2781
bear the *r* of the people any more .... Eze 36:15   2781
r of famine among the heathen .... Eze 36:30   2781
thy people are become a *r* to all .... Dan 9:16   2781
the *r* offered by him to cease .... Dan 11:18   2781
without his own *r* he shall cause .... Dan 11:18   2781
his *r* shall his Lord return unto.............. Hos 12:14   2781
and give not thine heritage to *r* .... Joel 2:17   2781
make you a *r* among the heathen .... Joel 2:19   2781
ye shall bear the *r* of my people .... Mic 6:16   2781
I have heard the *r* of Moab .... Zeph 2:8   2781
to whom the *r* of it was a burden .... Zeph 3:18   2781
me, to take away my *r* among men .... Lk 1:25   3681
their company, and shall *r* you .... Lk 6:22   3679
I speak as concerning *r*, as 2Cor 11:21   819
lest he fall into *r* and the snare 1Ti 3:7   3680
we both labour and suffer *r*.................... 1Ti 4:10   3679
Esteeming the *r* of Christ greater .... Heb 11:26   3680
without the camp, bearing his *r* .... Heb 13:13   3680

REPROACHED

Whom hast thou *r* and blasphemed 2Kin 19:22   2778
messengers thou hast *r* the Lord 2Kin 19:23   2778
These ten times have ye *r* me................ Job 19:3   3637
For it was not an enemy that *r* me .... Ps 55:12   2778
that *r* thee are fallen upon me .... Ps 69:9   2778
this, that the enemy hath *r*.................... Ps 74:18   2778
wherewith they have *r* thee .... Ps 79:12   2778
Wherewith thine enemies have *r* .... Ps 89:51   2778
wherewith they have *r* the .... Ps 89:51   2778
Whom hast thou *r* and blasphemed .... Is 37:23   2778
thy servants hast thou *r* the Lord .... Is 37:24   2778
whereby they have *r* my people .... Zeph 2:8   2778
their pride, because they have *r*.............. Zeph 2:10   2778
of them that *r* thee fell on me .... Rom 15:3   3679
If ye be *r* for the name of Christ 1Pet 4:14   3679

REPROACHES

the *r* of them that reproached .... Ps 69:9   2781
to the curse, and Israel to *r*................... Is 43:28   1421
The *r* of them that reproached .... Rom 15:3   3679
pleasure in infirmities, in *r*.................... 2Cor 12:10   5196
were made a gazingstock both by *r* .... Heb 10:33   3680

REPROACHEST

thus saying thou *r* us also .... Lk 11:45   5195

REPROACHETH

a stranger, the same *r* the LORD .... Num 15:30   1442
For the voice of him that *r* .... Ps 44:16   2778
how the foolish man *r* thee daily .... Ps 74:22   2781
wherewith to answer him that *r* me .... Ps 119:42   2778
oppresseth the poor *r* his Maker .... Prov 14:31   2778
mocketh the poor *r* his Maker .... Prov 17:5   2778
that I may answer him that *r* me .... Prov 27:11   2778

REPROACHFULLY

have smitten me upon the cheek *r*.......... Job 16:10   2781
to the adversary to speak *r* 1Ti 5:14   5484,3059

REPROBATE

R silver shall men call them,.................. Jer 6:30   3988
God gave them over to a *r* mind .... Rom 1:28   96
minds, *r* concerning the faith 2Ti 3:8   96
and unto every good work *r* .... Titus 1:16   96

REPROBATES

Christ is in you, except ye be *r*............... 2Cor 13:5   96
ye shall know that we are not *r* 2Cor 13:6   96
is honest, though we be as *r*.................. 2Cor 13:7   96

REPROOF

and are astonished at his *r* .... Job 26:11   1606
Turn you at my *r* .... Prov 1:23   8433
my counsel, and would none of my *r* ...... Prov 1:25   8433
they despised all my *r* .... Prov 1:30   8433

and my heart despised *r* .... Prov 5:12   8433
but he that refuseth *r* erreth .... Prov 10:17   8433
but he that hateth *r* is brutish .... Prov 12:1   8433
regardeth *r* shall be honoured .... Prov 13:18   8433
he that regardeth *r* is prudent .... Prov 15:5   8433
and he that hateth *r* shall die .... Prov 15:10   8433
The ear that heareth the *r* of .... Prov 15:31   8433
but he that heareth *r* getteth .... Prov 15:32   8433
A *r* entereth more into a wise man .... Prov 17:10   1606
The rod and *r* give wisdom .... Prov 29:15   8433
is profitable for doctrine, for *r*............... 2Ti 3:16   1650

REPROOFS

not, and in whose mouth are no *r*........... Ps 38:14   8433
r of instruction are the way of .... Prov 6:23   8433

REPROVE

will *r* the words which the LORD............. 2Kin 19:4   3198
but what doth your arguing *r* .... Job 6:25   3198
Do ye imagine to *r* words, and the .... Job 6:26   3198
He will surely *r* you, if ye do.................. Job 13:10   3198
Will he *r* thee for fear of thee .... Job 22:4   3198
I will not *r* thee for thy.......................... Ps 50:8   3198
but I will *r* thee, and set them in .... Ps 50:21   3198
and let him *r* me .... Ps 141:5   3198
R not a scorner, lest he hate................. Prov 9:8   3198
r one that hath understanding, and .... Prov 19:25   3198
unto his words, lest he *r* thee .... Prov 30:6   3198
neither *r* after the hearing of................. Is 11:3   3198
r with equity for the meek of the .... Is 11:4   3198
will *r* the words which the LORD.............. Is 37:4   3198
and thy backslidings shall *r* thee........... Jer 2:19   3198
let no man strive, nor *r* another .... Hos 4:4   3198
he will *r* the world of sin, and of........... Jn 16:8   1651
of darkness, but rather *r* them .... Eph 5:11   1651
r, rebuke, exhort with all....................... 2Ti 4:2   1651

REPROVED

thus she was *r* .... Gen 20:16   3198
Abraham *r* Abimelech because of a .... Gen 21:25   3198
he *r* kings for their sakes,..................... 1Chr 16:21   3198
he *r* kings for their sakes...................... Ps 105:14   3198
that being often *r* hardeneth his .... Prov 29:1   8433
thou not *r* Jeremiah of Anathoth .... Jer 29:27   1605
what I shall answer when I am *r*............. Hab 2:1   8433
being *r* by him for Herodias his .... Lk 3:19   1651
light, lest his deeds should be *r*............. Jn 3:20   1651
But all things that are *r* are .... Eph 5:13   1651

REPROVER

so is a wise *r* upon an obedient .... Prov 25:12   3198
dumb, and shalt not be to them a *r* .... Eze 3:26   3198

REPROVETH

he that *r* God, let him answer it.............. Job 40:2   3198
He that *r* a scorner getteth to .... Prov 9:7   3256
scorner loveth not one that *r* him .... Prov 15:12   3198
snare for him that *r* in the gate .... Is 29:21   3198

REPUTATION

folly him that is in *r* for wisdom .... Eccl 10:1   3368
had in *r* among all the people, and .... Acts 5:34   5093
privately to them which were of *r* .... Gal 2:2   1380
But made himself of no *r*, and took .... Phil 2:7   2758
and hold such in *r*................................. Phil 2:29   1784

REPUTED

beasts, and *r* vile in your sight .... Job 18:3   2804
of the earth are *r* as nothing.................. Dan 4:35   2804

REQUEST

them, I would desire a *r* of you............... Judg 8:24   7596
perform the *r* of his handmaid 2Sa 14:15   1697
fulfilled the *r* of his servant 2Sa 14:22   1697
and the king granted him all his *r*........... Ezr 7:6   1246
me, For what dost thou make *r* .... Neh 2:4   1245
to make *r* before him for her .... Est 4:8   1245
and what is thy *r* .... Est 5:3   1246
and what is thy *r* .... Est 5:6   1246
and said, My petition and my *r* is........... Est 5:7   1246
my petition, and to perform my *r* .... Est 5:8   1246
and what is thy *r* .... Est 7:2   1246
my petition, and my people at my *r* .... Est 7:3   1246
Haman stood up to make *r* for his .... Est 7:7   1245
or what is thy *r* further .... Est 9:12   1246
Oh that I might have my *r* .... Job 6:8   7596
not withholden the *r* of his lips.............. Ps 21:2   782
And he gave them their *r*....................... Ps 106:15   7596
Making *r*, if by any means now at .... Rom 1:10   1189
for you all making *r* with joy.................. Phil 1:4   1162

REQUESTED

earrings that he *r* was a thousand .... Judg 8:26   7592
he *r* for himself that he might 1Kin 19:4   7592
God granted him that which he *r*............ 1Chr 4:10   7592

therefore he *r* of the prince of................Dan 1:8   1245
Then Daniel *r* of the king ....Dan 2:49   1156

REQUESTS
let your *r* be made known unto God.......Phil 4:6   *155*

REQUIRE
your blood of your lives will I *r* ....Gen 9:5   1875
hand of every beast will I *r* it ....Gen 9:5   1875
brother will I *r* the life of man.........Gen 9:5   1875
of my hand didst thou *r* it.................Gen 31:39   1245
of my hand shalt thou *r* him...........Gen 43:9   1245
doth the Lord thy God *r* of thee ....Deut 10:12   7592
in my name, I will *r* it of him.........Deut 18:19   1875
thy God will surely *r* it of thee ....Deut 23:21   1875
let the Lord himself *r* it ....Josh 22:23   1245
Let the Lord even *r* it at the...............1Sa 20:16   1245
but one thing I *r* of thee.................2Sa 3:13   7592
now *r* his blood of your hand 2Sa 4:11   1245
and whatsoever thou shalt *r* of me 2Sa 19:38   977
all times, as the matter shall *r*.............1Kin 8:59   3117
then doth my lord *r* this him.................1Chr 21:3   1245
The Lord look upon it, and *r* it 2Chr 24:22   1875
shall *r* of you, it be done ....Ezr 7:21   7593
For I was ashamed to *r* of the ....Ezr 8:22   7592
them, and will *r* nothing of them ....Neh 5:12   1245
in his heart, Thou wilt not *r* it ....Ps 10:13   1875
his blood will I *r* at thine hand ....Eze 3:18   1245
his blood will I *r* at thine hand ....Eze 3:20   1875
there will I *r* your offerings, and ....Eze 20:40   1875
but his blood will I *r* at the...............Eze 33:6   1875
his blood will I *r* at thine hand ....Eze 33:8   1245
I will *r* my flock at their hand, ...Eze 34:10   1875
and what doth the Lord *r* of thee ....Mic 6:8   1875
For the Jews *r* a sign, and the 1Cor 1:22   *154*
flower of her age, and need so *r*...........1Cor 7:36   *1096*

REQUIRED
behold, also his blood is *r*.......................Gen 42:22   1875
unto them such things as they *r* ....Ex 12:36
the king's business *r* haste 1Sa 21:8   1961
and when he *r*, they set bread 2Sa 12:20   7592
as every day's work *r*...........................1Chr 16:37   3117
as the duty of every day *r*.....................2Chr 8:14   3117
Why hast thou not *r* of the 2Chr 24:6   1875
as the duty of every day *r*.....................Ezr 3:4   3117
yet for all this *r* not I the ....Neh 5:18   1245
she *r* nothing but what Hegai the...........Est 2:15   1245
and sin offering hast thou not *r* ....Ps 40:6   7592
us away captive *r* of us a song ....Ps 137:3   7592
they that wasted us *r* of us mirth ....Ps 137:3
Two things have I *r* of thee ....Prov 30:7   7592
who hath *r* this at your hand, to ....Is 1:12   1245
may be *r* of this generation ....Lk 11:50   *1567*
It shall be *r* of this generation ....Lk 11:51   *1567*
night thy soul shall be *r* of thee ....Lk 12:20   *523*
is given, of him shall be much *r* ....Lk 12:48   *2212*
might have *r* mine own with usury ......Lk 19:23   *4238*
that it should be as they *r* ....Lk 23:24   *155*
Moreover it is *r* in stewards...................1Cor 4:2   *2212*

REQUIREST
I will do to thee all that thou *r*..............Ruth 3:11   559

REQUIRETH
and God *r* that which is past ....Eccl 3:15   1245
is a rare thing that the king *r* ....Dan 2:11   7593

REQUIRING
r that he might be crucified ....Lk 23:23   *154*

REQUITE
will certainly *r* us all the evil ....Gen 50:15   7725
Do ye thus *r* the Lord, O foolish ....Deut 32:6   1580
I also will *r* you this kindness, ...2Sa 2:6   6213
that the Lord will *r* me good for 2Sa 16:12   7725
I will *r* thee in this plat, saith.................2Kin 9:26   7999
and spite, to *r* it with thy hand ....Ps 10:14   5414
and raise me up, that I may *r* them.......Ps 41:10   7999
God of recompences shall surely *r* ....Jer 51:56   7999
at home, and to *r* their parents...............1Ti 5:4   *287,591*

REQUITED
as I have done, so God hath *r* me ....Judg 1:7   7999
he hath *r* me evil for good 1Sa 25:21   7725

REQUITING
by *r* the wicked, by recompensing 2Chr 6:23   7725

REREWARD
which was the *r* of all the camps ....Num 10:25   622
the *r* came after the ark, the ....Josh 6:9   622
but the *r* came after the ark of...............Josh 6:13   622
passed on in the *r* with Achish 1Sa 29:2   314
the God of Israel will be your *r*..............Is 52:12   622
glory of the Lord shall be thy *r*..............Is 58:8   622

RESCUE
and thou shalt have none to *r* them ....Deut 28:31   3467
r my soul from their destructions ....Ps 35:17   7725
take away, and none shall *r* him ....Hos 5:14   5337

RESCUED
So the people *r* Jonathan, that he..........1Sa 14:45   6299
and David *r* his two wives 1Sa 30:18   5337
r him, having understood that he ....Acts 23:27   *1807*

RESCUETH
He delivereth and *r*, and he worketh.......Dan 6:27   5338

RESEMBLANCE
This is their *r* through all the ....Zec 5:6   5869

RESEMBLE
and whereunto shall I *r* it ....Lk 13:18   *3666*

RESEMBLED
each one *r* the children of a king ....Judg 8:18   8389

RESEN (re'-zen) *A city between Nineveh and Calah.*
R between Nineveh and Calah ....Gen 10:12   7449

RESERVE
Will he *r* his anger for ever ....Jer 3:5   5201
for I will pardon them whom I *r*.............Jer 50:20   7604
to *r* the unjust unto the day of 2Pet 2:9   *5083*

RESERVED
Hast thou not *r* a blessing for me ....Gen 27:36   680
most holy things, *r* from the fire ....Num 18:9
because we *r* not to each man his ....Judg 21:22   3947
she had *r* after she was sufficed ....Ruth 2:18   3498
but *r* of them for an hundred 2Sa 8:4   3498
but *r* of them an hundred chariots 1Chr 18:4   3498
That the wicked is *r* to the day ....Job 21:30   2820
Which I have *r* against the time...........Job 38:23   2820
be *r* unto the hearing of Augustus.........Acts 25:21   *5083*
I have *r* to myself seven thousand ....Rom 11:4   *2641*
not away, *r* in heaven for you,..................1Pet 1:4   *5083*
darkness, to be *r* unto judgment 2Pet 2:4   *5083*
mist of darkness is *r* for ever 2Pet 2:17   *5083*
r unto fire against the day of 2Pet 3:7   *5083*
he hath *r* in everlasting chains ....Jude 6   *5083*
to whom is *r* the blackness of ....Jude 13   *5083*

RESERVETH
he *r* unto us the appointed weeks...........Jer 5:24   8104
he *r* wrath for his enemies......................Nah 1:2   5201

RESHEPH (re'-shef) *A son of Rephah.*
And Rephah was his son, also *R*.............1Chr 7:25   7566

RESIDUE
they shall eat the *r* of that ....Ex 10:5   3499
the *r* of the families of the sons 1Chr 6:66
the *r* of Israel, of the priests, ...Neh 11:20   7605
the *r* of the number of archers, ...Is 21:17   7605
unto the *r* of his people, ...Is 28:5   7605
am deprived of the *r* of my years............Is 38:10   3499
the *r* thereof he maketh a god,................Is 44:17   7611
shall I make the *r* thereof an.................Is 44:19   3499
the *r* of them that remain of this ....Jer 8:3   7611
the *r* of them will I deliver to..................Jer 15:9   7611
the *r* of Jerusalem, that remain ....Jer 24:8   7611
concerning the *r* of the vessels ....Jer 27:19   3499
the *r* of the elders which were ....Jer 29:1   3499
with all the *r* of the princes of ....Jer 39:3   7611
the *r* of the people that were in ....Jer 41:10   7611
the *r* of the people that remained ....Jer 52:15   3499
wilt thou destroy all the *r* of ....Eze 9:8   7611
thy *r* shall be devoured by the ....Eze 23:25   319
your feet the *r* of your pastures ....Eze 34:18   3499
ye must foul the *r* with your feet ....Eze 34:18   3498
unto the *r* of the heathen ....Eze 36:3   7611
derision to the *r* of the heathen ....Eze 36:4   7611
against the *r* of the heathen ....Eze 36:5   7611
the *r* in length over against the ....Eze 48:18   3498
the *r* shall be for the prince, on..............Eze 48:21   3498
stamped the *r* with the feet of it ....Dan 7:7   7606
stamped the *r* with his feet ....Dan 7:19   7606
the *r* of my people shall spoil ....Zeph 2:9   7611
to the *r* of the people, saying,................Hag 2:2   7611
But now I will not be unto the *r*.............Zec 8:11   7611
the *r* of the people shall not be ....Zec 14:2   3499
Yet had he the *r* of the spirit ....Mal 2:15   7605
they went and told it unto the *r*..............Mk 16:13   *3062*
That the *r* of men might seek..................Acts 15:17   *2645*

RESIST
at his right hand to *r* him ....Zec 3:1   7853
say unto you, That ye *r* not evil..................Mt 5:39   *436*
not be able to gainsay nor *r*...................Lk 21:15   *436*
were not able to *r* the wisdom ....Acts 6:10   *436*
ye do always *r* the Holy Ghost ....Acts 7:51   *496*

RESISTED

they that r shall re............ .... Rom 13:2 436
so do these also r........... .... 2Ti 3:8 436
R the devil, and ....lee from .... Jas 4:7 436
and he doth no.....faith, ... Jas 5:6 498
Whom r stedf.... .... 1Pet 5:9 436

RESISTED
For who ha... .... Rom 9:19 436
Ye have r.... .....blood .... Heb 12:4 478

RESIST....
...nce of God.......... Rom 13:2 498
...giveth grace .... Rom 13:2 436
Who.....and giveth .... Jas 4:6 498
the p........ .... 1Pet 5:5 498

Go...at, when I .... Lk 16:4 1097

Rither unto us .... Neh 4:20 6908
...ontinually r .... Ps 71:3 935
...im again .... Mk 10:1 4848
...e Jews always r .... Jn 18:20 4905

...their coasts 2Chr 11:13 3320
...ude r unto him .... Mk 2:13 2064
...and said, John .... Jn 10:41 2064
...s r thither with .... Jn 18:2 4863
which r thither .... Acts 16:13 4905

...ad r unto Abel .... Gen 4:4 8159
...ing he had not r .... Gen 4:5 8159
...ot r the person of .... Ex 2:25 3045
...not r the person of .... Lev 19:15 5375
...nave r unto you ....Lev 26:9 6437
...ou their offering .... Num 16:15 6437
...all not r persons in ....Deut 1:17 5234
...shalt not r persons, neither .... Deut 16:19 6437
...either doth God r any person 2Sa 14:14 5375
Yet have thou r unto the prayer 1Kin 8:28 6437
had r unto them, because of his 2Kin 13:23 6437
Have r therefore to the prayer of...........2Chr 6:19 6437
nor r of persons, nor taking of...............2Chr 19:7 4856
Have r unto the covenant ....Ps 74:20 5027
when I have r unto all thy ....Ps 119:6 5027
precepts, and have r unto thy ways.......Ps 119:15 5027
I will have r unto thy statutes ....Ps 119:117 8159
yet hath he r unto the lowly ....Ps 138:6 7200
to have r of persons in judgment ....Prov 24:23 5234
To have r of persons is not good ....Prov 28:21 5234
his eyes shall have r to the Holy ....Is 17:7 7200
neither shall r that which his ....Is 17:8 7200
neither had r unto him that...................Is 22:11 7200
For there is no r of persons with ....Rom 2:11 4382
glorious had no glory in this r.................2Cor 3:10 3313
neither is there r of persons ....Eph 6:9 3382
Not that I speak in r of want...................Phil 4:11 2596
or in r of an holyday, or of the ....Col 2:16 3313
and there is no r of persons ....Col 3:25 4382
for he had r unto the recompence...........Heb 11:26 578
Lord of glory, with r of persons ....Jas 2:1 4382
ye have r to him that weareth the ....Jas 2:3 1914
But if ye have r to persons ....Jas 2:9 4380
who without r of persons judgeth 1Pet 1:17 678

RESPECTED
they r not the persons of the ....Lam 4:16 5375

RESPECTER
that God is no r of persons....................Acts 10:34 4381

RESPECTETH
he r not any that are wise of ....Job 37:24 7200
r not the proud, nor such as turn ....Ps 40:4 6437

RESPITE
when Pharaoh saw that there was r........Ex 8:15 7309
unto him, Give us seven days' r 1Sa 11:3 7503

REST
But the dove found no r for the ....Gen 8:9 4494
r yourselves under the tree ....Gen 18:4 8172
Jacob fed the r of Laban's flocks............Gen 30:36 3498
And he saw that r was good....................Gen 49:15 4496
ye make them r from their burdens........Ex 5:5 7673
To morrow is the r of the holy ....Ex 16:23 7677
seventh year thou shalt let it r ....Ex 23:11 8058
on the seventh day thou shalt r..............Ex 23:12 7673
that thine ox and thine ass may r.........Ex 23:12 5117
names of the r on the other stone ....Ex 28:10 3498
the seventh is the sabbath of r..............Ex 31:15 7677
with thee, and I will give thee r ....Ex 33:14 5117
on the seventh day thou shalt r..............Ex 34:21 7673

time and in harvest thou shalt r ....Ex 34:21 7673
day, a sabbath of r to the LORD ....Ex 35:2 7677
the r of the blood shall be wrung...........Lev 5:9 7604
of the r of the oil that is in ....Lev 14:17 3499
the r of the oil that is in the ....Lev 14:29 3498
shall be a sabbath of r unto you ....Lev 16:31 7677
seventh day is the sabbath of r ....Lev 23:3 7677
shall be unto you a sabbath of r.............Lev 23:32 7677
be a sabbath of r unto the land ....Lev 25:4 7677
it is a year of r unto the land ....Lev 25:5 7677
even then shall the land r....................Lev 26:34 7673
as it lieth desolate it shall r.................Lev 26:35 7673
it did not r in your sabbaths.................Lev 26:35 7673
beside the r of them that were ....Num 31:8 7673
being the r of the prey which the...........Num 31:32 3499
the r of Gilead, and all Bashan, ...Deut 3:13 3499
have given r unto your brethren ....Deut 3:20 5117
maidservant may r as well as thou ....Deut 5:14 5117
ye are not as yet come to the r ....Deut 12:9 4496
when he giveth you r from all ....Deut 12:10 5117
r from all thine enemies round ....Deut 25:19 5117
shall the sole of thy foot have r.............Deut 28:65 4494
LORD your God hath given you r..............Josh 1:13 5117
LORD have given your brethren r............Josh 1:15 5117
shall r in the waters of Jordan................Josh 3:13 5117
that the r which remained of them ....Josh 10:20 8300
the r of the kingdom of Sihon ....Josh 13:27 3499
And the land had r from war ....Josh 14:15 8252
There was also a lot for the r of ....Josh 17:2 3498
the r of Manasseh's sons had the ....Josh 17:6 3498
the r of the children of Kohath ....Josh 21:5 3498
the r of the Levites, out of the ....Josh 21:34 3498
the LORD gave them r round about ....Josh 21:44 5117
hath given r unto your brethren ....Josh 22:4 5117
r unto Israel from all their ....Josh 23:1 5117
And the land had r forty years ....Judg 3:11 8252
the land had r fourscore years..............Judg 3:30 8252
And the land had r forty years ....Judg 5:31 8252
but all the r of the people bowed ....Judg 7:6 3499
he sent all the r of Israel every ....Judg 7:8
LORD grant you that ye may find r...........Ruth 1:9 4496
shall I not seek r for thee ....Ruth 3:1 4494
for the man will not be in r ....Ruth 3:18 8252
the r of the people he sent every 1Sa 13:2 3499
the r we have utterly destroyed 1Sa 15:15 3498
Let it r on the head of Joab, and 2Sa 3:29 2342
the LORD had given him r round 2Sa 7:1 5117
have caused thee to r from all 2Sa 7:11 5117
the r of the people he delivered..............2Sa 10:10 3499
the r of the people together 2Sa 12:28 3499
of the air to r on them by day 2Sa 21:10 5117
God hath given me r on every side 1Kin 5:4 5117
that hath given r unto his people...........1Kin 8:56 4496
the r of the acts of Solomon, and 1Kin 11:41 3499
the r of the acts of Jeroboam, ...1Kin 14:19 3499
Now the r of the acts of Rehoboam 1Kin 14:29 3499
Now the r of the acts of Abijam, ...1Kin 15:7 3499
The r of all the acts of Asa, and 1Kin 15:23 3499
Now the r of the acts of Nadab, ...1Kin 15:31 3499
Now the r of the acts of Baasha, ...1Kin 16:5 3499
Now the r of the acts of Elah, and 1Kin 16:14 3499
Now the r of the acts of Zimri, ...1Kin 16:20 3499
Now the r of the acts of Omri, ...1Kin 16:27 3499
But the r fled to Aphek, into the 1Kin 20:30 3498
Now the r of the acts of Ahab, and 1Kin 22:39 3499
Now the r of the acts of 1Kin 22:45 3499
Now the r of the acts of Ahaziah............2Kin 1:18 3499
spirit of Elijah doth r on Elisha...............2Kin 2:15 5117
thou and thy children of the r 2Kin 4:7 3498
the r of the acts of Joram, and 2Kin 8:23 3499
Now the r of the acts of Jehu, and 2Kin 10:34 3499
the r of the acts of Joash, and 2Kin 12:19 3499
Now the r of the acts of Jehoahaz 2Kin 13:9 3499
the r of the acts of Joash, and 2Kin 13:12 3499
Now the r of the acts of Jehoash 2Kin 14:15 3499
the r of the acts of Amaziah, are 2Kin 14:18 3499
Now the r of the acts of Jeroboam 2Kin 14:28 3499
the r of the acts of Azariah, and 2Kin 15:6 3499
Now the r of the acts of Zachariah, ...2Kin 15:11 3499
the r of the acts of Shallum, and 2Kin 15:15 3499
the r of the acts of Menahem, and 2Kin 15:21 3499
the r of the acts of Pekahiah, and 2Kin 15:26 3499
the r of the acts of Pekah, and 2Kin 15:31 3499
Now the r of the acts of Jotham, ...2Kin 15:36 3499
Now the r of the acts of Ahaz 2Kin 16:19 3499
the r of the acts of Hezekiah, and 2Kin 20:20 3499
Now the r of the acts of Manasseh.........2Kin 21:17 3499
Now the r of the acts of Amon 2Kin 21:25 3499
Now the r of the acts of Josiah,...............2Kin 23:28 3499
Now the r of the acts of 2Kin 24:5 3499
Now the r of the people that were...........2Kin 25:11 3499

R

And they smote the *r* of the	1Chr 4:43	7611
LORD, after that the ark had *r*	1Chr 6:31	4494
Unto the *r* of the children of	1Chr 6:77	3498
Joab repaired the *r* of the city	1Chr 11:8	7605
all the *r* also of Israel were of	1Chr 12:38	7611
the *r* that were chosen, who were	1Chr 16:41	7605
the *r* of the people he delivered	1Chr 19:11	3499
to thee, who shall be a man of *r*	1Chr 22:9	4496
I will give him *r* from all his	1Chr 22:9	5117
he not given you *r* on every side	1Chr 22:18	5117
hath given *r* unto his people	1Chr 23:25	3499
the *r* of the sons of Levi were	1Chr 24:20	3498
r for the ark of the covenant of	1Chr 28:2	4496
Now the *r* of the acts of Solomon,	2Chr 9:29	7605
the *r* of the acts of Abijah, and	2Chr 13:22	7605
for the land had *r*, and he had no	2Chr 14:6	8252
because the LORD had given him *r*	2Chr 14:6	5117
he hath given us *r* on every side	2Chr 14:7	5117
for we *r* on thee, and in thy name	2Chr 14:11	8172
the LORD gave them *r* round about	2Chr 15:15	5117
his God gave him *r* round about	2Chr 20:30	5117
Now the *r* of the acts of	2Chr 20:34	3499
they brought the *r* of the money	2Chr 24:14	7605
Now the *r* of the acts of Amaziah,	2Chr 25:26	3499
Now the *r* of the acts of Uzziah,	2Chr 26:22	3499
Now the *r* of the acts of Jotham,	2Chr 27:7	3499
Now the *r* of his acts and of all	2Chr 28:26	3499
Now the *r* of the acts of Hezekiah	2Chr 32:32	3499
Now the *r* of the acts of Manasseh	2Chr 33:18	3499
Now the *r* of the acts of Josiah,	2Chr 35:26	3499
Now the *r* of the acts of	2Chr 36:8	3499
the *r* of the chief of the fathers	Ezr 4:3	7605
the *r* of their companions, unto	Ezr 4:7	7605
the *r* of their companions	Ezr 4:9	7606
the *r* of the nations whom the	Ezr 4:10	7606
the *r* that are on this side the	Ezr 4:10	7606
to the *r* of their companions that	Ezr 4:17	7606
unto the *r* beyond the river,	Ezr 4:17	7606
the *r* of the children of the	Ezr 6:16	7606
to do with the *r* of the silver	Ezr 7:18	7606
nor to the *r* that did the work	Neh 2:16	3499
to the *r* of the people, Be not ye	Neh 4:14	3499
to the *r* of the people, The work	Neh 4:19	3499
the *r* of our enemies, heard that	Neh 6:1	3499
the *r* of the prophets, that would	Neh 6:14	3499
that which the *r* of the people	Neh 7:72	7611
But after they had *r*, they did	Neh 9:28	5117
the *r* of the people, the priests,	Neh 10:28	7605
the *r* of the people also cast	Neh 11:1	7605
in the *r* of the king's provinces	Est 9:12	7605
had *r* from their enemies, and slew	Est 9:16	5118
then had I been at *r*,	Job 3:13	5117
and there the weary be at *r*	Job 3:17	5117
There the prisoners *r* together	Job 3:18	7599
not in safety, neither had I *r*	Job 3:26	8252
thou shalt take thy *r* in safety	Job 11:18	7901
Turn from him, that he may *r*	Job 14:6	2308
when our *r* together is in the	Job 17:16	5183
and my sinews take no *r*	Job 30:17	7901
my flesh also shall *r* in hope	Ps 16:9	7931
leave the *r* of their substance to	Ps 17:14	3499
R in the LORD, and wait patiently	Ps 37:7	1826
neither is there any *r* in my	Ps 38:3	7965
then would I fly away, and be at *r*	Ps 55:6	7931
That thou mayest give him *r* from	Ps 94:13	8252
they should not enter into my *r*	Ps 95:11	4496
Return unto thy *r*, O my soul	Ps 116:7	4496
r upon the lot of the righteous	Ps 125:3	5117
Arise, O LORD, into thy *r*	Ps 132:8	4496
This is my *r* for ever	Ps 132:14	4496
neither will he *r* content	Prov 6:35	
he rage or laugh, there is no *r*	Prov 29:9	5183
thy son, and he shall give thee *r*	Prov 29:17	5117
heart taketh not *r* in the night	Eccl 2:23	
this hath more *r* than the other	Eccl 6:5	5183
makest thy flock to *r* at noon	Song 1:7	7257
shall *r* all of them in the	Is 7:19	5117
the *r* of the trees of his forest	Is 10:19	7605
of the LORD shall *r* upon him	Is 11:2	5117
and his *r* shall be glorious	Is 11:10	4496
shall give thee *r* from thy sorrow	Is 14:3	5117
The whole earth is at *r*, and is	Is 14:7	5117
said unto me, I will take my *r*	Is 18:4	8252
there also shalt thou have no *r*	Is 23:12	5117
shall the hand of the LORD *r*	Is 25:10	5117
This is the *r* wherewith ye may	Is 28:12	4496
ye may cause the weary to *r*	Is 28:12	5117
returning and *r* shall ye be saved	Is 30:15	5183
screech owl also shall *r* there	Is 34:14	7280
and find for herself a place of *r*	Is 34:14	4494
to *r* for a light of the people	Is 51:4	7280

they shall *r* in their beds, each	Is 57:2	
troubled sea, when it cannot *r*	Is 57:20	
for Jerusalem's sake I will not *r*	Is 62:1	
And give him no *r*, till he	Is 62:7	
of the LORD caused him to *r*	Is 63:14	5117
and where is the place of my *r*	Is 66:1	8252
ye shall find *r* for your souls	Jer 6:16	8252
shall return, and shall be in *r*	Jer 30:10	1824
when I went to cause him to *r*	Jer 31:2	5117
with the *r* of the people that	Jer 39:9	4496
in my sighing, and I find no *r*	Jer 45:3	4771
and Jacob shall return, and be in *r*	Jer 46:27	8252
up thyself into thy scabbard,	Jer 47:6	
that he may give *r* to the land	Jer 50:34	
and the *r* of the multitude	Jer 52:15	
the heathen, she findeth no *r*	Lam 1:3	
give thyself no *r*	Lam 2:18	
we labour, and have no *r*	Lam 5:5	
will cause my fury to *r* upon them	Eze 5:13	
I make my fury toward thee to *r*	Eze 16:42	
and I will cause my fury to *r*	Eze 21:17	
caused my fury to *r* upon thee	Eze 24:13	
I will go to them that are at *r*	Eze 38:11	
the blessing to *r* in thine house	Eze 44:30	
the *r* of the land shall they give	Eze 45:8	
As for the *r* of the tribes, from	Eze 48:23	
the *r* of the wise men of Babylon	Dan 2:18	
was at *r* in mine house, and	Dan 4:4	7954
As concerning the *r* of the beasts	Dan 7:12	7606
for thou shalt *r*, and stand in thy	Dan 12:13	5117
for this is not your *r*	Mic 2:10	4496
that I might *r* in the day of	Hab 3:16	5117
he will *r* in his love, he will	Zeph 3:17	2790
earth sitteth still, and is at *r*	Zec 1:11	8252
Damascus shall be the *r* thereof	Zec 9:1	4496
let the *r* eat every one the flesh	Zec 11:9	7604
heavy laden, and I will give you *r*	Mt 11:28	373
ye shall find *r* unto your souls	Mt 11:29	372
through dry places, seeking *r*	Mt 12:43	372
Sleep on now, and take your *r*	Mt 26:45	373
The *r* said, Let be, let us see	Mt 27:49	3062
into a desert place, and *r* a while	Mk 6:31	373
Sleep on now, and take your *r*	Mk 14:41	373
there, your peace shall *r* upon it	Lk 10:6	1879
through dry places, seeking *r*	Lk 11:24	372
why take ye thought for the *r*	Lk 12:26	3062
unto the eleven, and to all the *r*	Lk 24:9	3062
spoken of taking of *r* in sleep	Jn 11:13	2681
also my flesh shall *r* in hope	Acts 2:26	3062
to the *r* of the apostles, Men and	Acts 2:37	3062
of the *r* durst no man join	Acts 5:13	2663
or what is the place of my *r*	Acts 7:49	1515
churches *r* throughout all Judaea	Acts 9:31	3062
And the *r*, some on boards, and some	Acts 27:44	3062
it, and the *r* were blinded	Rom 11:7	3062
But to the *r* speak I, not the	1Cor 7:12	3062
the *r* will I set in order when I	1Cor 11:34	3062
I had no *r* in my spirit, because	2Cor 2:13	425
Macedonia, our flesh had no *r*	2Cor 7:5	425
the power of Christ may *r* upon me	2Cor 12:9	1981
to you who are troubled *r* with us	2Th 1:7	425
They shall not enter into my *r*	Heb 3:11	2663
they should not enter into his *r*	Heb 3:18	2663
left us of entering into his *r*	Heb 4:1	2663
have believed do enter into *r*	Heb 4:3	2663
if they shall enter into my *r*	Heb 4:3	2663
God did *r* the seventh day from	Heb 4:4	2664
If they shall enter into my *r*	Heb 4:5	2663
For if Jesus had given them *r*	Heb 4:8	2664
a *r* to the people of God	Heb 4:9	4520
For he that is entered into his *r*	Heb 4:10	2663
therefore to enter into that *r*	Heb 4:11	2663
he no longer should live the *r* of	1Pet 4:2	1954
unto the *r* in Thyatira, as many	Rev 2:24	3062
they *r* not day and night, saying,	Rev 4:8	2192,372
that they should *r* yet for a	Rev 6:11	373
the *r* of the men which were not	Rev 9:20	3062
they have no *r* day nor night, who	Rev 14:11	372
that they may *r* from their	Rev 14:13	373
But the *r* of the dead lived not	Rev 20:5	3062

RESTED

he *r* on the seventh day from all	Gen 2:2	7673
because that in it he had *r* from	Gen 2:3	7673
the ark *r* in the seventh month,	Gen 8:4	5117
r in all the coasts of Egypt	Ex 10:14	5117
So the people *r* on the seventh	Ex 16:30	7673
in them is, and *r* the seventh day	Ex 20:11	5117
earth, and on the seventh day he *r*	Ex 31:17	7673
tabernacle they *r* in their tents	Num 9:18	2583
of the LORD they *r* in the tents	Num 9:23	2583

the cloud r in the wilderness of	Num 10:12	7931
And when it r, he said, Return, O	Num 10:36	5117
that, when the spirit r upon them	Num 11:25	5117
and the spirit r upon them	Num 11:26	5117
And the land r from war	Josh 11:23	8252
they r on the house with timber	1Kin 6:10	270
the people r themselves upon the	2Chr 32:8	5564
fourteenth day of the same r they	Est 9:17	5118
fifteenth day of the same they r	Est 9:18	5118
the Jews r from their enemies	Est 9:22	5117
My bowels boiled, and r not	Job 30:27	1826
r the sabbath day according to	Lk 23:56	2270

RESTEST

r in the law, and makest thy boast	Rom 2:17	1879

RESTETH

him to be in safety, whereon he r	Job 24:23	8172
Wisdom r in the heart of him that	Prov 14:33	5117
for anger r in the bosom of fools	Eccl 7:9	5117
of glory and of God r upon you	1Pet 4:14	373

RESTING

to search out a r place for them	Num 10:33	4496
O Lord God, into thy r place	2Chr 6:41	5118
spoil not his r place	Prov 24:15	7258
dwellings, and in quiet r places	Is 32:18	4496

RESTINGPLACE

hill, they have forgotten their r	Jer 50:6	7258

RESTITUTION

for he should make full r	Ex 22:3	7999
his own vineyard, shall he make r	Ex 22:5	7999
the fire shall surely make r	Ex 22:6	7999
he shall make r unto the owner	Ex 22:12	7999
to his substance shall the r be	Job 20:18	8545
the times of r of all things	Acts 3:21	605

RESTORE

Now therefore r the man his wife	Gen 20:7	7725
and if thou r her not, know thou	Gen 20:7	7725
head, and r thee unto thy place	Gen 40:13	7725
to r every man's money into his	Gen 42:25	7725
he shall r five oxen for an ox,	Ex 22:1	7999
he shall r double	Ex 22:4	7999
that he shall r that which he	Lev 6:4	7725
he shall even r it in the	Lev 6:5	7999
killeth a beast, he shall r it	Lev 24:21	7999
r the overplus unto the man to	Lev 25:27	7725
if he be not able to r it to him	Lev 25:28	7725
the congregation shall r him to	Num 35:25	7725
thou shalt r it to him again	Deut 22:2	7725
now therefore r those lands again	Judg 11:13	7725
therefore I will r it unto thee	Judg 17:3	7725
and I will r it you	1Sa 12:3	7725
will r thee all the land of Saul	2Sa 9:7	7725
he shall r the lamb fourfold,	2Sa 12:6	7999
r me the kingdom of my father	2Sa 16:3	7725
took from thy father, I will r	1Kin 20:34	7725
R all that was hers, and all the	2Kin 8:6	7725
R, I pray you, to them, even this	Neh 5:11	7725
Then said they, We will r them	Neh 5:12	7725
and his hands shall r their goods	Job 20:10	7725
which he laboured for shall he r	Job 20:18	7725
R unto me the joy of thy	Ps 51:12	7725
he be found, he shall r sevenfold	Prov 6:31	7999
I will r thy judges as at the	Is 1:26	7725
for a spoil, and none saith, R	Is 42:22	7725
to r the preserved of Israel	Is 49:6	7725
r comforts unto him and to his	Is 57:18	7999
them up, and r them to this place	Jer 27:22	7725
For I will r health unto thee, and	Jer 30:17	5927
If the wicked r the pledge	Eze 33:15	7725
forth of the commandment to r	Dan 9:25	7725
I will r to you the years that	Joel 2:25	7999
shall first come, and r all things	Mt 17:11	600
accusation, I r him fourfold	Lk 19:8	591
wilt thou at this time r again	Acts 1:6	600
r such an one in the spirit of	Gal 6:1	2675

RESTORED

Abraham, and r him Sarah his wife	Gen 20:14	7725
he r the chief butler unto his	Gen 40:21	7725
me r unto mine office, and him	Gen 41:13	7725
unto his brethren, My money is r	Gen 42:28	7725
face, and shall not be r to thee	Deut 28:31	7725
when he had r the eleven hundred	Judg 17:3	7725
Yet he r the money unto his	Judg 17:4	7725
from Israel were r to Israel	1Sa 7:14	7725
that my hand may be r me again	1Kin 13:6	7725
the king's hand was r him again	1Kin 13:6	7725
woman, whose son he had r to life	2Kin 8:1	2421
how he had r a dead body to life	2Kin 8:5	2421

woman, whose son he had r to life	2Kin 8:5	2421
is her son, whom Elisha r to life	2Kin 8:5	2421
r it to Judah, after that the	2Kin 14:22	7725
He r the coast of Israel from the	2Kin 14:25	7725
which Huram had r to Solomon	2Chr 8:2	5414
r it to Judah, after that that	2Chr 26:2	7725
and brought unto Babylon, be r	Ezr 6:5	8421
then I r that which I took not	Ps 69:4	7725
but hath r to the debtor his	Eze 18:7	7725
hath not r the pledge, and hath	Eze 18:12	7725
and it was r whole, like as the	Mt 12:13	600
his hand was r whole as the other	Mk 3:5	600
and he was r, and saw every man	Mk 8:25	600
his hand was r whole as the other	Lk 6:10	600
that I may be r to you the sooner	Heb 13:19	600

RESTORER

be unto thee a r of thy life	Ruth 4:15	7725
The r of paths to dwell in	Is 58:12	7725

RESTORETH

He r my soul	Ps 23:3	7725
cometh first, and r all things	Mk 9:12	600

RESTRAIN

dost thou r wisdom to thyself	Job 15:8	1639
remainder of wrath shalt thou r	Ps 76:10	2296

RESTRAINED

and the rain from heaven was r	Gen 8:2	3607
now nothing will be r from them	Gen 11:6	1219
the Lord hath r me from bearing	Gen 16:2	6113
the people were r from bringing	Ex 36:6	3607
themselves vile, and he r them not	1Sa 3:13	3543
are they r	Is 63:15	662
I r the floods thereof, and the	Eze 31:15	4513
sayings scarce r they the people	Acts 14:18	2664

RESTRAINEST

off fear, and r prayer before God	Job 15:4	1639

RESTRAINT

for there is no r to the Lord to	1Sa 14:6	4622

RESTS

he made narrowed r round about	1Kin 6:6	

RESURRECTION

which say that there is no r	Mt 22:23	386
Therefore in the r whose wife	Mt 22:28	386
For in the r they neither marry,	Mt 22:30	386
But as touching the r of the dead	Mt 22:31	386
out of the graves after his r	Mt 27:53	1454
which say there is no r	Mk 12:18	386
In the r therefore, when they	Mk 12:23	386
recompensed at the r of the just	Lk 14:14	386
which deny that there is any r	Lk 20:27	386
Therefore in the r whose wife of	Lk 20:33	386
the r from the dead, neither	Lk 20:35	386
God, being the children of the r	Lk 20:36	386
done good, unto the r of life	Jn 5:29	386
evil, unto the r of damnation	Jn 5:29	386
again in the r at the last day	Jn 11:24	386
Jesus said unto her, I am the r	Jn 11:25	386
to be a witness with us of his r	Acts 1:22	386
before spake of the r of Christ	Acts 2:31	386
through Jesus the r from the dead	Acts 4:2	386
of the r of the Lord Jesus	Acts 4:33	386
unto them Jesus, and the r	Acts 17:18	386
they heard of the r of the dead	Acts 17:32	386
r of the dead I am called in	Acts 23:6	386
Sadducees say that there is no r	Acts 23:8	386
there shall be a r of the dead	Acts 24:15	386
Touching the r of the dead I am	Acts 24:21	386
holiness, by the r from the dead	Rom 1:4	386
be also in the likeness of his r	Rom 6:5	386
that there is no r of the dead	1Cor 15:12	386
But if there be no r of the dead	1Cor 15:13	386
man came also the r of the dead	1Cor 15:21	386
So also is the r of the dead	1Cor 15:42	386
know him, and the power of his r	Phil 3:10	386
attain unto the r of the dead	Phil 3:11	1815
saying that the r is past already	2Ti 2:18	386
of r of the dead, and of eternal	Heb 6:2	386
that they might obtain a better r	Heb 11:35	386
r of Jesus Christ from the dead	1Pet 1:3	386
by the r of Jesus Christ	1Pet 3:21	386
This is the first r	Rev 20:5	386
he that hath part in the first r	Rev 20:6	386

RETAIN

Dost thou still r thine integrity	Job 2:9	2388
me, Let thine heart r my words	Prov 4:4	8551
and strong men r riches	Prov 11:16	8551
over the spirit to r the spirit	Eccl 8:8	3607

R

but she shall not *r* the power of .... Dan 11:6 — 6113
and whose soever sins ye *r* .... Jn 20:23 — 2902
like to *r* God in their knowledge .... Rom 1:28 — 2192

RETAINED

r those three hundred men .... Judg 7:8 — 2388
law, the damsel's father, *r* him .... Judg 19:4 — 2388
corruption, and I *r* no strength .... Dan 10:8 — 6113
upon me, and I have *r* no strength .... Dan 10:16 — 6113
soever sins ye retain, they are *r* .... Jn 20:23 — 2902
Whom I would have *r* with me .... Philem 13 — 2722

RETAINETH

and happy is every one that *r* her .... Prov 3:18 — 8551
A gracious woman *r* honour .... Prov 11:16 — 8551
he *r* not his anger for ever, ... Mic 7:18 — 2388

RETIRE

r ye from him, that he may be .... 2Sa 11:15 — 7725
r, stay not .... Jer 4:6 — 5756

RETIRED

the men of Israel *r* in the battle .... Judg 20:39 — 2015
they *r* from the city, every man .... 2Sa 20:22 — 6327

RETURN

till thou *r* unto the ground .... Gen 3:19 — 7725
art, and unto dust shalt thou *r* .... Gen 3:19 — 7725
after his *r* from the slaughter of .... Gen 14:17 — 7725
R to thy mistress, and submit .... Gen 16:9 — 7725
I will certainly *r* unto thee .... Gen 18:10 — 7725
time appointed I will *r* unto thee .... Gen 18:14 — 7725
R unto the land of thy fathers, ... Gen 31:3 — 7725
r unto the land of thy kindred .... Gen 31:13 — 7725
R unto thy country, and to thy .... Gen 32:9 — 7725
r unto my brethren which are in .... Ex 4:18 — 7725
Moses in Midian, Go, *r* into Egypt. ...... Ex 4:19 — 7725
When thou goest to *r* into Egypt .... Ex 4:21 — 7725
they see war, and they *r* to Egypt .... Ex 13:17 — 7725
ye shall *r* every man unto his .... Lev 25:10 — 7725
ye shall *r* every man unto his .... Lev 25:10 — 7725
year of this jubile ye shall *r* .... Lev 25:13 — 7725
that he may *r* unto his possession .... Lev 25:27 — 7725
he shall *r* unto his possession .... Lev 25:28 — 7725
shall *r* unto his own family, and .... Lev 25:41 — 7725
of his fathers shall he *r* .... Lev 25:41 — 7725
of the jubile the field shall *r* .... Lev 27:24 — 7725
And when it rested, he said, *R* .... Num 10:36 — 7725
not better for us to *r* into Egypt .... Num 14:3 — 7725
a captain, and let us *r* into Egypt .... Num 14:4 — 7725
R unto Balak, and thus thou shalt .... Num 23:5 — 7725
We will not *r* unto our houses, ... Num 32:18 — 7725
then afterward ye shall *r* .... Num 32:22 — 7725
high priest the slayer shall *r* .... Num 35:28 — 7725
then shall ye *r* every man unto .... Deut 3:20 — 7725
cause the people to *r* to Egypt .... Deut 17:16 — 7725
henceforth *r* no more that way .... Deut 17:16 — 7725
r to his house, lest he die in .... Deut 20:5 — 7725
r unto his house, lest he die in .... Deut 20:6 — 7725
r unto his house, lest he die in .... Deut 20:7 — 7725
r unto his house, lest his .... Deut 20:8 — 7725
shalt *r* unto the LORD thy God, and .... Deut 30:2 — 7725
compassion upon thee, and will *r* .... Deut 30:3 — 7725
And thou shalt *r* and obey the voice ...... Deut 30:8 — 7725
then ye shall *r* unto the land of .... Josh 1:15 — 7725
then shall the slayer *r*, and come .... Josh 20:6 — 7725
therefore now *r* ye, and get you .... Josh 22:4 — 6437
R with much riches unto your .... Josh 22:8 — 7725
is fearful and afraid, let him *r* .... Judg 7:3 — 7725
when I *r* in peace from the .... Judg 11:31 — 7725
that she might *r* from the country .... Ruth 1:6 — 7725
way to *r* unto the land of Judah .... Ruth 1:7 — 7725
r each to her mother's house .... Ruth 1:8 — 7725
Surely we will *r* with thee unto .... Ruth 1:10 — 7725
r thou after thy sister in law .... Ruth 1:15 — 7725
or to *r* from following after thee .... Ruth 1:16 — 7725
but in any wise *r* him a trespass .... 1Sa 6:3 — 7725
offering which we shall *r* to him .... 1Sa 6:4 — 7725
which ye *r* him for a trespass .... 1Sa 6:8 — 7725
If ye do *r* unto the LORD with all .... 1Sa 7:3 — 7725
And his *r* was to Ramah .... 1Sa 7:17 — 8666
was with him, Come, and let us *r* .... 1Sa 9:5 — 7725
unto Saul, I will not *r* with thee .... 1Sa 15:26 — 7725
r, my son David .... 1Sa 26:21 — 7725
said unto him, Make this fellow *r* .... 1Sa 29:4 — 7725
Wherefore now *r*, and go in peace, ... 1Sa 29:7 — 7725
to *r* into the land of the .... 1Sa 29:11 — 7725
ere thou bid the people *r* from .... 2Sa 2:26 — 7725
Then said Abner unto him, Go, *r* .... 2Sa 3:16 — 7725
your beards be grown, and then *r* .... 2Sa 10:5 — 7725
to him, but he shall not *r* to me .... 2Sa 12:23 — 7725
r to thy place, and abide with the .... 2Sa 15:19 — 7725
r thou, and take back thy brethren .... 2Sa 15:20 — 7725

r into the city in peace, and your .... 2Sa 15:27 — 7725
But if thou *r* to the city .... 2Sa 15:34 — 7725
R thou, and all thy servants .... 2Sa 19:14 — 7725
I shall *r* to him that sent me .... 2Sa 24:13 — 7725
the LORD shall *r* his blood upon .... 1Kin 2:32 — 7725
therefore *r* upon the head of Joab .... 1Kin 2:33 — 7725
therefore the LORD shall *r* thy .... 1Kin 2:44 — 7725
so *r* unto thee with all their .... 1Kin 8:48 — 7725
r every man to his house .... 1Kin 12:24 — 7725
kingdom *r* to the house of David .... 1Kin 12:26 — 7725
And he said, I may not *r* with thee .... 1Kin 13:16 — 7725
r on thy way to the wilderness of .... 1Kin 19:15 — 7725
for at the *r* of the year the king .... 1Kin 20:22 — 8666
came to pass at the *r* of the year .... 1Kin 20:26 — 8666
let them *r* every man to his house .... 1Kin 22:17 — 7725
If thou *r* at all in peace, the .... 1Kin 22:28 — 7725
r from me .... 2Kin 18:14 — 7725
and shall *r* to his own land .... 2Kin 19:7 — 7725
he came, by the same shall he *r* .... 2Kin 19:33 — 7725
but let the shadow *r* backward ten .... 2Kin 20:10 — 7725
your beards be grown, and then *r* .... 1Chr 19:5 — 7725
and shall *r* and confess thy name, ... 2Chr 6:24 — 7725
If they *r* to thee with all their .... 2Chr 6:38 — 7725
ye me to *r* answer to this people .... 2Chr 10:6 — 7725
we may *r* answer to this people .... 2Chr 10:9 — 7725
r every man to his house .... 2Chr 11:4 — 7725
let them *r* therefore every man to .... 2Chr 18:16 — 7725
of affliction, until I *r* in peace .... 2Chr 18:26 — 7725
If thou certainly *r* in peace .... 2Chr 18:27 — 7725
he will *r* to the remnant of you, ... 2Chr 30:6 — 7725
face from you, if ye *r* unto him .... 2Chr 30:9 — 7725
and when wilt thou *r* .... Neh 2:6 — 7725
r unto us they will be upon you .... Neh 4:12 — 7725
a captain to *r* to their bondage .... Neh 9:17 — 7725
bade them *r* Mordecai this answer .... Est 4:15 — 7725
should *r* upon his own head, and .... Est 9:25 — 7725
womb, and naked shall I *r* thither .... Job 1:21 — 7725
R, I pray you, let it not be .... Job 6:29 — 7725
r again, my righteousness is in .... Job 6:29 — 7725
He shall *r* no more to his house, ... Job 7:10 — 7725
Before I go whence I shall not *r* .... Job 10:21 — 7725
that he shall *r* out of darkness .... Job 15:22 — 7725
go the way whence I shall not *r* .... Job 16:22 — 7725
But as for you all, do ye *r* .... Job 17:10 — 7725
If thou *r* to the Almighty, thou .... Job 22:23 — 7725
he shall *r* to the days of his .... Job 33:25 — 7725
that they *r* from iniquity .... Job 36:10 — 7725
they go forth, and *r* not unto them .... Job 39:4 — 7725
R, O LORD, deliver my soul .... Ps 6:4 — 7725
let them *r* and be ashamed suddenly ..... Ps 6:10 — 7725
sakes therefore *r* thou on high .... Ps 7:7 — 7725
shall *r* upon his own head .... Ps 7:16 — 7725
They *r* at evening .... Ps 59:6 — 7725
And at evening let them *r* .... Ps 59:14 — 7725
Therefore his people *r* hither .... Ps 73:10 — 7725
O let not the oppressed *r* ashamed .... Ps 74:21 — 7725
R, we beseech thee, O God of .... Ps 80:14 — 7725
and sayest, *R*, ye children of men .... Ps 90:3 — 7725
R, O LORD, how long .... Ps 90:13 — 7725
shall *r* unto righteousness .... Ps 94:15 — 7725
they die, and *r* to their dust .... Ps 104:29 — 7725
R unto thy rest, O my soul .... Ps 116:7 — 7725
None that go unto her *r* again .... Prov 2:19 — 7725
a stone, it will *r* upon him .... Prov 26:27 — 7725
rivers come, thither they *r* again .... Eccl 1:7 — 7725
naked shall he *r* to go as he came .... Eccl 5:15 — 7725
nor the clouds *r* after the rain .... Eccl 12:2 — 7725
Then shall the dust *r* to the .... Eccl 12:7 — 7725
the spirit shall *r* unto God who .... Eccl 12:7 — 7725
R, *r*, O Shulamite .... Song 6:13 — 7725
r, *r*, that we may look upon .... Song 6:13 — 7725
shall be a tenth, and it shall *r* .... Is 6:13 — 7725
The remnant shall *r*, even the .... Is 10:21 — 7725
yet a remnant of them shall *r* .... Is 10:22 — 7725
they shall *r* even to the LORD, and .... Is 19:22 — 7725
enquire ye: *r*, come .... Is 21:12 — 7725
the ransomed of the LORD shall *r* .... Is 35:10 — 7725
a rumour, and *r* to his own land .... Is 37:7 — 7725
he came, by the same shall he *r* .... Is 37:34 — 7725
r unto me .... Is 44:22 — 7725
in righteousness, and shall not *r* .... Is 45:23 — 7725
the redeemed of the LORD shall *r* .... Is 51:11 — 7725
let him *r* unto the LORD, and he .... Is 55:7 — 7725
it shall not *r* unto me void, ... Is 55:11 — 7725
R for thy servants' sake, the .... Is 63:17 — 7725
shall he *r* unto her again .... Jer 3:1 — 7725
yet *r* again to me, saith the LORD .... Jer 3:1 — 7725
words toward the north, and say, *R* .... Jer 3:12 — 7725
R, ye backsliding children, and I .... Jer 3:22 — 7725
If thou wilt *r*, O Israel, saith .... Jer 4:1 — 7725
Israel, saith the LORD, *r* unto me .... Jer 4:1 — 7725

RETURNED

they have refused to r .... Jer 5:3 — 7725
.... not r .... Jer 8:4 — 7725
shall he turn ut I will r .... Jer 8:5 — 7725
fast deceit, their ways .... Jer 12:15 — 7725
I have pluck thou r .... Jer 15:7 — 7725
since they .... Jer 15:19 — 7725
thus sai om his evil .... Jer 15:19 — 7725
let there em .... Jer 15:19 — 7725
.... r any more .... Jer 18:11 — 7725
r y desire to r .... Jer 22:10 — 7725
r ye ot r .... Jer 22:11 — 7725
fo om his .... Jer 22:27 — 7725
LORD shall not r .... Jer 22:27 — 7725
nto me with .... Jer 23:14 — 7725
r to this place .... Jer 23:20 — 7725
n to r to the .... Jer 24:7 — 7725
l r, and shall be in .... Jer 29:10 — 7725
RD shall not r .... Jer 30:3 — 7725
ny shall r thither .... Jer 30:10 — 7725
eir captivity to r .... Jer 30:24 — 7725
vity of Israel to r .... Jer 31:8 — 7725
se to r the .... Jer 32:44 — 7725
their captivity to r .... Jer 33:7 — 7725
had let go free, to r .... Jer 33:11 — 7725
their pleasure, to r .... Jer 33:26 — 7725
se them to r to this city .... Jer 34:11 — 7725
now every man from his evil .... Jer 34:16 — 7725
at they may r every man from .... Jer 34:22 — 7725
will r every one from his evil ...... Jer 35:15 — 7725
shall r Egypt into their own .... Jer 36:3 — 7725
that thou cause me not to r to .... Jer 36:7 — 7725
cause me to r to Jonathan's house .... Jer 37:7 — 7725
cause you to r to your own land ...... Jer 37:20 — 7725
that they should r into the land ..... Jer 38:26 — 7725
have a desire to r to dwell there .... Jer 42:12 — 7725
for none shall r but such as .... Jer 44:14 — 7725
that escape the sword shall r out .... Jer 44:14 — 7725
and Jacob shall r, and be in rest .... Jer 44:14 — 7725
none shall r in vain .... Jer 44:28 — 7725
shall not r to that which is sold .... Jer 46:27 — 7725
thereof, which shall not r .... Jer 50:9 — 7725
that he should not r from his .... Eze 7:13 — 7725
shall r to their former estate, ... Eze 7:13 — 7725
her daughters shall r to their .... Eze 13:22 — 7725
thy daughters shall r to your .... Eze 16:55 — 7725
that he should r from his ways .... Eze 16:55 — 7725
it shall not r any more .... Eze 16:55 — 7725
I cause it to r into his sheath ...... Eze 18:23 — 7725
will cause them to r into the .... Eze 21:5 — 7725
and thy cities shall not r .... Eze 21:30 — 7725
he shall not r by the way of the ..... Eze 29:14 — 7725
after, it shall r to the prince ...... Eze 35:9 — 3427
caused me to r to the brink of .... Eze 46:9 — 7725
now will I r to fight with the .... Eze 46:17 — 7725
shall r into his own land .... Eze 47:6 — 7725
then shall he r, and be stirred up ... Dan 10:20 — 7725
For the king of the north shall r .... Dan 11:9 — 7725
Then shall he r into his land .... Dan 11:10 — 7725
do exploits, and r to his own land ... Dan 11:13 — 7725
At the time appointed he shall r ..... Dan 11:28 — 7725
he shall be grieved, and r .... Dan 11:28 — 7725
he shall even r, and have .... Dan 11:29 — 7725
will go and r to my first husband .... Dan 11:30 — 7725
Therefore will I r, and take away .... Dan 11:30 — 7725
shall the children of Israel r .... Hos 2:7 — 7725
go and r to my place, till they ...... Hos 2:9 — 7725
Come, and let us r unto the LORD ..... Hos 3:5 — 7725
they do not r to the LORD their ...... Hos 5:15 — 7725
They r, but not to the most High ..... Hos 6:1 — 7725
they shall r to Egypt .... Hos 7:10 — 7725
but Ephraim shall r to Egypt .... Hos 7:16 — 7725
He shall not r into the land of ...... Hos 8:13 — 7725
king, because they refused to r ...... Hos 9:3 — 7725
I will not r to destroy Ephraim ...... Hos 11:5 — 7725
shall his Lord r unto him .... Hos 11:5 — 7725
O Israel, r unto the LORD thy God .... Hos 11:9 — 7725
dwell under his shadow shall r .... Hos 12:14 — 7725
Who knoweth if he will r and .... Hos 14:1 — 7725
speedily will I r your recompence .... Hos 14:7 — 7725
will r your recompence upon your ..... Joel 2:14 — 7725
thy reward shall r upon thine own .... Joel 3:4 — 7725
they shall r to the hire of an .... Joel 3:7 — 7725
r unto the children of Israel .... Obad 15 — 7725
are impoverished, but we will r ...... Mic 1:7 — 7725
R unto me, and I will r unto .... Mic 5:3 — 7725
But ye said, Wherein shall we r ...... Mal 1:4 — 7725
Then shall ye r, and discern .... Mal 3:7 — 7725
that they should not r to Herod ...... Mal 3:7 — 7725
worthy, let your peace r to you ..... Mal 3:18 — 7725
.... Mt 2:12 — 844
.... Mt 10:13 — 1994

I will r into my house from .... Mt 12:44 — 1994
field r back to take his clothes .... Mt 24:18 — 1994
R to thine own house, and shew how .... Lk 8:39 — 5290
I will r unto my house whence I .... Lk 11:24 — 5290
when he will r from the wedding .... Lk 12:36 — 360
let him likewise not r back .... Lk 17:31 — 1994
for himself a kingdom, and to r .... Lk 19:12 — 5290
now no more to r to corruption .... Acts 13:34 — 5290
After this I will r, and will .... Acts 15:16 — 390
but I will r again unto you, if .... Acts 18:21 — 344
Syria, he purposed to r through .... Acts 20:3 — 5290

RETURNED

the waters r from off the earth .... Gen 8:3 — 7725
she r unto him into the ark, for .... Gen 8:9 — 7725
which r not again unto him any .... Gen 8:12 — 7725
And they r, and came to En-mishpat, ... Gen 14:7 — 7725
and Abraham r unto his place .... Gen 18:33 — 7725
they r into the land of the .... Gen 21:32 — 7725
So Abraham r unto his young men, ... Gen 22:19 — 7725
departed, and r unto his place .... Gen 31:55 — 7725
And the messengers r to Jacob .... Gen 32:6 — 7725
So Esau r that day on his way .... Gen 33:16 — 7725
And Reuben r unto the pit .... Gen 37:29 — 7725
he r unto his brethren, and said, ... Gen 37:30 — 7725
he r to Judah, and said, I cannot .... Gen 38:22 — 7725
r to them again, and communed with ..... Gen 42:24 — 7725
now we had r this second time .... Gen 43:10 — 7725
Because of the money that was r .... Gen 43:18 — 7725
man his ass, and r to the city .... Gen 44:13 — 7725
Joseph r into Egypt, he, and his .... Gen 50:14 — 7725
r to Jethro his father in law, and .... Ex 4:18 — 7725
he r to the land of Egypt .... Ex 4:20 — 7725
Moses r unto the LORD, and said, ... Ex 5:22 — 7725
the sea r to his strength when .... Ex 14:27 — 7725
And the waters r, and covered the .... Ex 14:28 — 7725
Moses r the words of the people .... Ex 19:8 — 7725
Moses r unto the LORD, and said, ... Ex 32:31 — 7725
of the congregation r unto him .... Ex 34:31 — 7725
is r unto her father's house, as .... Lev 22:13 — 7725
they r from searching of the land .... Num 13:25 — 7725
sent to search the land, who r .... Num 14:36 — 7725
Aaron r unto Moses unto the door .... Num 16:50 — 7725
he r unto him and, lo, he stood by .... Num 23:6 — 7725
up, and went and r to his place .... Num 24:25 — 7725
And ye r and wept before the LORD .... Deut 1:45 — 7725
days, until the pursuers be r .... Josh 2:16 — 7725
days, until the pursuers were r .... Josh 2:22 — 7725
So the two men r, and descended .... Josh 2:23 — 7725
of Jordan r unto their place .... Josh 4:18 — 7725
the city once, and r into the camp .... Josh 6:14 — 7725
they r to Joshua, and said unto .... Josh 7:3 — 7725
that all the Israelites r unto Ai .... Josh 8:24 — 7725
And Joshua r, and all Israel with .... Josh 10:15 — 7725
all the people r to the camp to .... Josh 10:21 — 7725
And Joshua r, and all Israel with .... Josh 10:38 — 7725
And Joshua r, and all Israel with .... Josh 10:43 — 7725
and the half tribe of Manasseh r .... Josh 22:9 — 7725
r from the children of Reuben, and .... Josh 22:32 — 7725
the judge was dead, that they r .... Judg 2:19 — 7725
yea, she r answer to herself, ... Judg 5:29 — 7725
there r of the people twenty and .... Judg 7:3 — 7725
r into the host of Israel, and .... Judg 7:15 — 7725
Gideon the son of Joash r from .... Judg 8:13 — 7725
that she r unto her father, who .... Judg 11:39 — 7725
And after a time he r to take her .... Judg 14:8 — 7725
r unto their inheritance, and .... Judg 21:23 — 7725
So Naomi r, and Ruth the Moabitess ..... Ruth 1:22 — 7725
which r out of the country of .... Ruth 1:22 — 7725
worshipped before the LORD, and r .... 1Sa 1:19 — 7725
they r to Ekron the same day .... 1Sa 6:16 — 7725
r for a trespass offering unto .... 1Sa 6:17 — 7725
r from Saul to feed his father's .... 1Sa 17:15 — 7725
Israel r from chasing after the .... 1Sa 17:53 — 7725
as David r from the slaughter of .... 1Sa 17:57 — 7725
when David was r from the .... 1Sa 18:6 — 7725
Wherefore Saul r from pursuing .... 1Sa 23:28 — 7725
when Saul was r from following .... 1Sa 24:1 — 7725
for the LORD hath r the .... 1Sa 25:39 — 7725
his way, and Saul r to his place .... 1Sa 26:25 — 7725
the camels, and the apparel, and r .... 1Sa 27:9 — 7725
when David was r .... 2Sa 1:1 — 7725
and the sword of Saul r not empty .... 2Sa 1:22 — 7725
Joab r from following Abner .... 2Sa 2:30 — 7725
Go, return. And he r .... 2Sa 3:16 — 7725
And when Abner was r to Hebron .... 2Sa 3:27 — 7725
Then David r to bless his .... 2Sa 6:20 — 7725
David gat him a name when he r .... 2Sa 8:13 — 7725
So Joab r from the children of .... 2Sa 10:14 — 7725
and she r unto her house .... 2Sa 11:4 — 7725
all the people r unto Jerusalem .... 2Sa 12:31 — 7725

So Absalom *r* to his own house, and 2Sa 14:24 5437
The LORD hath *r* upon thee all the 2Sa 16:8 7725
whom thou seekest is as if all *r* 2Sa 17:3 7725
find them, they *r* to Jerusalem 2Sa 17:20 7725
the people *r* from pursuing after 2Sa 18:16 7725
So the king *r*, and came to Jordan 2Sa 19:15 7725
and he *r* unto his own place 2Sa 19:39 7725
Joab *r* to Jerusalem unto the king 2Sa 20:22 7725
the people *r* after him only to 2Sa 23:10 7725
r to depart, according to the 1Kin 12:24 7725
r not by the way that he came to 1Kin 13:10 7725
Jeroboam *r* not from his evil way 1Kin 13:33 7725
he *r* back from him, and took a 1Kin 19:21 7725
and from thence he *r* to Samaria 2Kin 2:25 7725
from him, and *r* to their own land 2Kin 3:27 7725
Then he *r*, and walked in the house 2Kin 4:35 7725
he *r* to the man of God, he and all 2Kin 5:15 7725
And the messengers *r*, and told the 2Kin 7:15 7725
that the woman *r* out of the land 2Kin 8:3 7725
But king Joram was *r* to be healed 2Kin 9:15 7725
and hostages, and *r* to Samaria 2Kin 14:14 7725
So Rab-shakeh *r*, and found the 2Kin 19:8 7725
of Assyria departed, and went and *r* 2Kin 19:36 7725
upon them, and *r* to Jerusalem 2Kin 23:20 7725
David *r* to bless his house 1Chr 16:43 5437
and all the people *r* to Jerusalem 1Chr 20:3 7725
it, that Jeroboam *r* out of Egypt 2Chr 10:2 7725
r from going against Jeroboam 2Chr 11:4 7725
in abundance, and *r* to Jerusalem 2Chr 14:15 7725
Judah *r* to his house in peace to 2Chr 19:1 7725
when they *r* to Jerusalem 2Chr 19:8 7725
Then they *r*, every man of Judah 2Chr 20:27 7725
he *r* to be healed in Jezreel 2Chr 22:6 7725
they *r* home in great anger 2Chr 25:10 7725
hostages also, and *r* to Samaria 2Chr 25:24 7725
then they *r* to Samaria 2Chr 28:15 7725
Then all the children of Israel *r* 2Chr 31:1 7725
So he *r* with shame of face to his 2Chr 32:21 7725
land of Israel, he *r* to Jerusalem 2Chr 34:7 7725
and they *r* to Jerusalem 2Chr 34:9 7725
then they *r* answer by letter ...... Ezr 5:5 8421
And thus they *r* us answer, saying, ... Ezr 5:11 8421
the gate of the valley, and so *r* ...... Neh 2:15 7725
that we *r* all of us to the wall, ... Neh 4:15 7725
yet when they *r*, and cried unto ...... Neh 9:28 7725
on the morrow she *r* into the ...... Est 2:14 7725
Then the king *r* out of the palace ...... Est 7:8 7725
my prayer *r* into mine own bosom ...... Ps 35:13 7725
and with Aram-zobah, when Joab *r* ...... Ps 60:*t* 7725
and they *r* and enquired early after ...... Ps 78:34 7725
So I *r*, and considered all the ...... Eccl 4:1 7725
Then I *r*, and I saw vanity under ...... Eccl 4:7 7725
I *r*, and saw under the sun, that ...... Eccl 9:11 7725
So Rabshakeh *r*, and found the king ...... Is 37:8 7725
of Assyria departed, and went and *r* ...... Is 37:37 7725
So the sun *r* ten degrees, by ...... Is 38:8 7725
But she *r* not ...... Jer 3:7 7725
they *r* with their vessels empty ...... Jer 14:3 7725
Even all the Jews *r* out of all ...... Jer 40:12 7725
from Mizpah cast about and *r* ...... Jer 41:14 7725
that were *r* from all nations, ... Jer 43:5 7725
r as the appearance of a flash of ...... Eze 1:14 7725
have *r* to provoke me to anger ...... Eze 8:17 7725
Now when I had *r*, behold, at the ...... Eze 47:7 7725
and mine understanding *r* unto me ...... Dan 4:34 7725
the same time my reason *r* unto me ...... Dan 4:36 7725
honour and brightness *r* unto me ...... Dan 4:36 7725
when I *r* the captivity of my ...... Hos 6:11 7725
yet have ye not *r* unto me ...... Amos 4:6 7725
yet have ye not *r* unto me ...... Amos 4:8 7725
yet have ye not *r* unto me ...... Amos 4:9 7725
yet have ye not *r* unto me ...... Amos 4:10 7725
yet have ye not *r* unto me ...... Amos 4:11 7725
and they *r* and said, Like as the ...... Zec 1:6 7725
I am *r* to Jerusalem with mercies ...... Zec 1:16 7725
that no man passed through nor *r* ...... Zec 7:14 7725
I am *r* unto Zion, and will dwell ...... Zec 8:3 7725
the morning as he *r* into the city ...... Mt 21:18 *1877*
And when he *r*, he found them ...... Mk 14:40 *5290*
months, and *r* to her own house ...... Lk 1:56 *5290*
And the shepherds *r*, glorifying and ...... Lk 2:20 *1994*
they *r* into Galilee, to their own ...... Lk 2:39 *5290*
had fulfilled the days, as they *r* ...... Lk 2:43 *5290*
of the Holy Ghost *r* from Jordan ...... Lk 4:1 *5290*
Jesus *r* in the power of the ...... Lk 4:14 *5290*
up into the ship, and *r* back again ...... Lk 8:37 *5290*
to pass, that, when Jesus was *r* ...... Lk 8:40 *5290*
And the apostles, when they were *r* ...... Lk 9:10 *5290*
the seventy *r* again with joy, ... Lk 10:17 *5290*
found that *r* to give glory to God ...... Lk 17:18 *5290*
came to pass, that when he was *r* ...... Lk 19:15 *1880*
done, smote their breasts, and *r* ......
And they *r*, and prepared spices and
r from the sepulchre, and told all ......
r to Jerusalem, and found the ......
r to Jerusalem with great joy ......
Then *r* they unto Jerusalem from ......
them not in the prison, they *r* ......
r to Jerusalem, and preached the ...... A
Saul *r* from Jerusalem, when they ...... Ac
from them *r* to Jerusalem ...... Act
they *r* again to Lystra, and to ...... Acts
and they *r* home again ...... Acts
go with him, and *r* to the castle ...... Acts 2
Arabia, and *r* again unto Damascus ...... Gal 1:1
have had opportunity to have *r* ...... Heb 11:1
but are now *r* unto the Shepherd 1Pet 2:25

RETURNETH
goeth forth, he *r* to his earth ...... Ps 146:4
As a dog *r* to his vomit ...... Prov 26:11
so a fool *r* to his folly ...... Prov 26:11 8
the wind *r* again according to his ...... Eccl 1:6 77
r not thither, but watereth the ...... Is 55:10 772
that passeth out and him that *r* ...... Eze 35:7 7725
by, and because of him that *r* ...... Zec 9:8 7725

RETURNING
In *r* and rest shall ye be saved ...... Is 30:15 7729
r to the house, found the servant ...... Lk 7:10 *5290*
Was *r*, and sitting in his chariot ...... Acts 8:28 *5290*
who met Abraham *r* from the ...... Heb 7:1 *5290*

REU *(re'-u)* See RAGAU. *Son of Peleg.*
lived thirty years, and begat *R* ...... Gen 11:18 7466
after he begat *R* two hundred ...... Gen 11:19 7466
R lived two and thirty years, and ...... Gen 11:20 7466
R lived after he begat Serug two ...... Gen 11:21 7466
Eber, Peleg, *R*, ... 1Chr 1:25 7466

REUBEN *(ru'-ben)* See REUBENITE.
1. *A son of Jacob and Leah.*
a son, and she called his name *R* ...... Gen 29:32 7205
R went in the days of wheat ...... Gen 30:14 7205
dwelt in that land, that *R* went ...... Gen 35:22 7205
R, Jacob's firstborn, and Simeon, ... Gen 35:23 7205
R heard it, and he delivered him ...... Gen 37:21 7205
R said unto them, Shed no blood, ... Gen 37:22 7205
And *R* returned unto the pit ...... Gen 37:29 7205
R answered them, saying, Spake I ...... Gen 42:22 7205
R spake unto his father, saying, ... Gen 42:37 7205
R, Jacob's firstborn ...... Gen 46:8 7205
And the sons of *R* ...... Gen 46:9 7205
as *R* and Simeon, they shall be ...... Gen 48:5 7205
R, thou art my firstborn, my ...... Gen 49:3 7205
R, Simeon, Levi, and Judah, ... Ex 1:2 7205
The sons of *R* the firstborn of ...... Ex 6:14 7205
these be the families of *R* ...... Ex 6:14 7205
And the children of *R*, Israel's ...... Num 1:20 7205
On, the son of Peleth, sons of *R* ...... Num 16:1 7205
R, the eldest son of Israel ...... Num 26:5 7205
the children of *R* ...... Num 26:5 7205
the sons of Eliab, the son of *R* ...... Deut 11:6 7205
the stone of Bohan the son of *R* ...... Josh 15:6 7205
the stone of Bohan the son of *R* ...... Josh 18:17 7205
R, Simeon, Levi, and Judah, ... 1Chr 2:1 7205
Now the sons of *R* the firstborn 1Chr 5:1 7205
of *R* the firstborn of Israel were 1Chr 5:3 7205
2. *Descendants of Reuben 1.*
of the tribe of *R* ...... Num 1:5 7205
of them, even of the tribe of *R* ...... Num 1:21 7205
of *R* according to their armies ...... Num 2:10 7205
of *R* shall be Elizur the son of ...... Num 2:10 7205
of *R* were an hundred thousand ...... Num 2:16 7205
prince of the children of *R* ...... Num 7:30 7205
the standard of the camp of *R* set ...... Num 10:18 7205
of the tribe of *R*, Shammua the ...... Num 13:4 7205
Now the children of *R* and the ...... Num 32:1 7205
of Gad and the children of *R* came ...... Num 32:2 7205
of Gad and to the children of *R* ...... Num 32:6 7205
the children of *R* spake unto ...... Num 32:25 7205
the children of *R* will pass with ...... Num 32:29 7205
Gad and the children of *R* answered ...... Num 32:31 7205
of Gad, and to the children of *R* ...... Num 32:33 7205
the children of *R* built Heshbon ...... Num 32:37 7205
the tribe of the children of *R* ...... Num 34:14 7206
R, Gad, and Asher, and Zebulun, Dan ...... Deut 27:13 7205
Let *R* live, and not die ...... Deut 33:6 7205
And the children of *R*, and the ...... Josh 4:12 7205
the tribe of the children of *R* ...... Josh 13:15 7205
of the children of *R* was Jordan ...... Josh 13:23 7205
of *R* after their families ...... Josh 13:23 7205
and Gad, and *R*, and half the tribe ...... Josh 18:7 7205
the plain out of the tribe of *R* ...... Josh 20:8 7205

REUBENITE

had out of the trib...	Bezer .... Josh 21:7	7205
And out of the ch...dren of R.........	...d the .... Josh 21:36	7205
And the childre...of R.............	...dren of R......... Josh 22:9	7205
land of Cana...of R.............	of R......... Josh 22:10	7205
say, Behold...and the	R............. Josh 22:11	7205
sent unto...n of R.............	ldren of R......... Josh 22:13	7205
they cam...ldren of R.............	and the .... Josh 22:15	7205
Then th...of R.............	Josh 22:21	7205
us and...ldren of R.............	n of R......... Josh 22:25	7205
the sai...and the	dren of R......... Josh 22:30	7205
sai...there were	of R......... Josh 22:31	7205
re...R there were	ldren of R......... Josh 22:32	7205
...he Gadites, and...	dren of R......... Josh 22:33	7205
...tribe of R.............	and the .... Josh 22:34	7205
...he tribe of R.............	there were .... Judg 5:15	7205
...rtion for R.............	R there were .... Judg 5:16	7205
...of R, from the	1Chr 5:18	7205
...gate of Judah,.............	1Chr 6:63	7205
...were sealed	1Chr 6:78	7205
	Eze 48:6	7205
	Eze 48:7	7205
	Eze 48:31	7205
	Rev 7:5	4502

(...ben-ite) See REUBENITES. *A descen-*
...n.

...Shiza the R 1Chr 11:42   7206

(...u'-ben-ites)

...amilies of the R .... Num 26:7	7206
...gave I unto the R .... Deut 3:12	7206
...s R and unto the Gadites .... Deut 3:16	7206
...n country, of the R............. Deut 4:43	7206
...inheritance unto the R .... Deut 29:8	7206
...o the R, and to the Gadites, ... Josh 1:12	7206
...r a possession unto the R............. Josh 12:6	7206
...ith whom the R and the Gadites ..... Josh 13:8	7206
Then Joshua called the R, and the .... Josh 22:1	7206
of Gilead, the Gadites, and the R 2Kin 10:33	7206
he was prince of the R 1Chr 5:6	7206
he carried them away, even the R......... 1Chr 5:26	7206
the Reubenite, a captain of the R 1Chr 11:42	7206
other side of Jordan, of the R 1Chr 12:37	7206
king David made rulers over the R 1Chr 26:32	7206
the ruler of the R was Eliezer 1Chr 27:16	7206

REUEL *(re-u'-el)* See DEUEL, JETHRO, RAGUEL.
  1. A son of Esau.

and Bashemath bare R............. Gen 36:4	7467
R the son of Bashemath the wife .... Gen 36:10	7467
And these are the sons of R .... Gen 36:13	7467
are the sons of R Esau's son .... Gen 36:17	7467
came of R in the land of Edom .... Gen 36:17	7467
Eliphaz, R, and Jeush, and Jaalam,........ 1Chr 1:35	7467
The sons of R............. 1Chr 1:37	7467

  2. Same as Jethro.
when they came to R their father .... Ex 2:18   7467
  3. Father of Eliasaph.
shall be Eliasaph the son of R .... Num 2:14   7467
  4. A Benjamite.
son of Shephatiah, the son of R 1Chr 9:8   7467

REUMAH *(re-u'-mah) Concubine of Nahor.*
his concubine, whose name was R .... Gen 22:24   7208

REVEAL

The heaven shall r his iniquity............. Job 20:27	1540
will r unto them the abundance of......... Jer 33:6	1540
seeing thou couldst r this secret .... Dan 2:47	1541
to whomsoever the Son will r him .... Mt 11:27	601
and he to whom the Son will r him ...... Lk 10:22	601
To r his Son in me, that I might .... Gal 1:16	601
God shall r even this unto you .... Phil 3:15	601

REVEALED

things which are r belong unto us .... Deut 29:29	1540
word of the LORD yet r unto him 1Sa 3:7	1540
for the LORD r himself to Samuel............. 1Sa 3:21	1540
hast r to thy servant, saying, I 2Sa 7:27	1540
it was r in mine ears by the LORD .... Is 22:14	1540
land of Chittim it is r to them .... Is 23:1	1540
the glory of the LORD shall be r............. Is 40:5	1540
to whom is the arm of the LORD r .... Is 53:1	1540
come, and my righteousness to be r....... Is 56:1	1540
for unto thee have I r my cause .... Jer 11:20	1540
Then was the secret r unto Daniel .... Dan 2:19	1541
this secret is not r to me for .... Dan 2:30	1541
Persia a thing was r unto Daniel .... Dan 10:1	1540
covered, that shall not be r.................. Mt 10:26	601
and hast r them unto babes.................. Mt 11:25	601
and blood hath not r it unto thee.......... Mt 16:17	601
it was r unto him by the Holy .... Lk 2:26	5537
thoughts of many hearts may be r .... Lk 2:35	601
and hast r them unto babes.................. Lk 10:21	601

covered, that shall not be r..................... Lk 12:2	601
the day when the Son of man is r ...... Lk 17:30	601
hath the arm of the Lord been r .... Jn 12:38	601
of God r from faith to faith .... Rom 1:17	601
God is r from heaven against all .... Rom 1:18	601
the glory which shall be r in us .... Rom 8:18	601
But God hath r them unto us by 1Cor 2:10	601
it, because it shall be r by fire................. 1Cor 3:13	601
If any thing be r to another that............. 1Cor 14:30	601
which should afterwards be r................... Gal 3:23	601
as it is now r unto his holy .... Eph 3:5	601
be r from heaven with his mighty 2Th 1:7	602
first, and that man of sin be r................... 2Th 2:3	601
that he might be r in his time 2Th 2:6	601
And then shall that Wicked be r 2Th 2:8	601
ready to be r in the last time 1Pet 1:5	601
Unto whom it was r, that not unto 1Pet 1:12	601
that, when his glory shall be r 1Pet 4:13	602
of the glory that shall be r..................... 1Pet 5:1	601

REVEALER
a r of secrets, seeing thou .... Dan 2:47   1541

REVEALETH

A talebearer r secrets .... Prov 11:13	1540
about as a talebearer r secrets .... Prov 20:19	1540
He r the deep and secret things............. Dan 2:22	1541
is a God in heaven that r secrets............. Dan 2:28	1541
he that r secrets maketh known to........ Dan 2:29	1541
but he r his secret unto his .... Amos 3:7	1540

REVELATION

r of the righteous judgment of .... Rom 2:5	602
according to the r of the mystery .... Rom 16:25	602
I shall speak to you either by r 1Cor 14:6	602
doctrine, hath a tongue, hath a r............. 1Cor 14:26	602
but by the r of Jesus Christ .... Gal 1:12	602
And I went up by r, and .... Gal 2:2	602
r in the knowledge of him........................ Eph 1:17	602
How that by r he made known unto .... Eph 3:3	602
unto you at the r of Jesus Christ 1Pet 1:13	602
The R of Jesus Christ, which God .... Rev 1:1	602

REVELATIONS

come to visions and r of the Lord 2Cor 12:1	602
through the abundance of the r 2Cor 12:7	602

REVELLINGS

Envyings, murders, drunkenness, ... Gal 5:21	2970
lusts, excess of wine, r 1Pet 4:3	2970

REVENGE

me, and r me of my persecutors .... Jer 15:15	5358
and we shall take our r on him .... Jer 20:10	5360
the Philistines have dealt by r............. Eze 25:15	5360
yea, what zeal, yea, what r 2Cor 7:11	1557
a readiness to r all disobedience 2Cor 10:6	1556

REVENGED
offended, and r himself upon them .... Eze 25:12   5358

REVENGER

The r of blood himself shall slay .... Num 35:19	1350
the r of blood shall slay the..................... Num 35:21	1350
the r of blood according to these .... Num 35:24	1350
out of the hand of the r of blood .... Num 35:25	1350
the r of blood find him without .... Num 35:27	1350
the r of blood kill the slayer .... Num 35:27	1350
a r to execute wrath upon him................. Rom 13:4	1558

REVENGERS
r of blood to destroy any more................. 2Sa 14:11   1350

REVENGES
the beginning of r upon the enemy .... Deut 32:42   6546

REVENGETH

God is jealous, and the LORD r............. Nah 1:2	5358
the LORD r, and is furious........................ Nah 1:2	5358

REVENGING
r of the blood of thy servants .... Ps 79:10   5360

REVENUE

shalt endamage the r of the kings .... Ezr 4:13	674
and my r than choice silver..................... Prov 8:19	8393
harvest of the river, is her r .... Is 23:3	8393

REVENUES

but in the r of the wicked is..................... Prov 15:6	8393
than great r without right .... Prov 16:8	8393
they shall be ashamed of your r .... Jer 12:13	8393

REVERENCE

my sabbaths, and r my sanctuary .... Lev 19:30	3372
my sabbaths, and r my sanctuary .... Lev 26:2	7812
he fell on his face, and did r 2Sa 9:6	7812
did r to the king, and said, Let 1Kin 1:31	7812
Mordecai bowed not, nor did him r .... Est 3:2	7812

R

Mordecai bowed not, nor did him *r* .... Est 3:5   7812
to be had in *r* of all them that .... Ps 89:7   3372
son, saying, They will *r* my son .... Mt 21:37   *1788*
them, saying, They will *r* my son .... Mk 12:6   *1788*
it may be they will *r* him when .... Lk 20:13   *1788*
wife see that she *r* her husband .... Eph 5:33   *5399*
corrected us, and we gave them *r* .... Heb 12:9   *1788*
may serve God acceptably with *r* .... Heb 12:28   *127*

REVERENCED
king's gate, bowed, and *r* Haman .... Est 3:2   7812

REVEREND
holy and *r* is his name .... Ps 111:9   3372

REVERSE
and I cannot *r* it .... Num 23:20   7725
let it be written to *r* the .... Est 8:5   7725
the king's ring, may no man *r* .... Est 8:8   7725

REVILE
Thou shalt not *r* the gods .... Ex 22:28   7043
are ye, when men shall *r* you .... Mt 5:11   *3679*

REVILED
And they that passed by *r* him .... Mt 27:39   *937*
were crucified with him *r* him .... Mk 15:32   *3679*
Then they *r* him, and said, Thou .... Jn 9:28   *3058*
being *r*, we bless 1Cor 4:12   *3058*
when he was *r*, *r* not again 1Pet 2:23   *486*

REVILERS
covetous, nor drunkards, nor *r* 1Cor 6:10   *3060*

REVILEST
by said, *R* thou God's high priest .... Acts 23:4   *3058*

REVILINGS
neither be ye afraid of their *r* .... Is 51:7   1421
the *r* of the children of Ammon, ... Zeph 2:8   1421

REVIVE
will they *r* the stones out of the .... Neh 4:2   2421
Wilt thou not *r* us again .... Ps 85:6   2421
midst of trouble, thou wilt *r* me .... Ps 138:7   2421
to *r* the spirit of the humble, and .... Is 57:15   2421
to *r* the heart of the contrite .... Is 57:15   2421
After two days will he *r* us .... Hos 6:2   2421
they shall *r* as the corn, and grow .... Hos 14:7   2421
r thy work in the midst of the .... Hab 3:2   2421

REVIVED
spirit of Jacob their father *r* .... Gen 45:27   2421
his spirit came again, and he *r* .... Judg 15:19   2421
came into him again, and he *r* 1Kin 17:22   2421
touched the bones of Elisha, he *r* 2Kin 13:21   2421
when the commandment came, sin *r* .... Rom 7:9   *326*
Christ both died, and rose, and *r* .... Rom 14:9   *326*

REVIVING
give us a little *r* in our bondage .... Ezr 9:8   4241
kings of Persia, to give us a *r* .... Ezr 9:9   4241

REVOLT
did Libnah *r* from under his hand 2Chr 21:10   6586
ye will *r* more and more .... Is 1:5   5627
our God, speaking oppression and *r* ...... Is 59:13   5627

REVOLTED
In his days Edom *r* from under the 2Kin 8:20   6586
Yet Edom *r* from under the hand of 2Kin 8:22   6586
Then Libnah *r* at the same time 2Kin 8:22   6586
In his days the Edomites *r* from 2Chr 21:8   6586
So the Edomites *r* from under the 2Chr 21:10   6586
children of Israel have deeply *r* .... Is 31:6   5627
they are *r* and gone .... Jer 5:23   5498

REVOLTERS
They are all grievous *r*, walking .... Jer 6:28   5637
the *r* are profound to make .... Hos 5:2   7846
all their princes are *r* .... Hos 9:15   5637

REVOLTING
But this people hath a *r* and a .... Jer 5:23   5637

REWARD
shield, and thy exceeding great *r* .... Gen 15:1   7939
for it is your *r* for your service .... Num 18:31   7939
not persons, nor taketh *r* .... Deut 10:17   7810
Cursed be he that taketh *r* to .... Deut 27:25   7810
and will *r* them that hate me .... Deut 32:41   7999
a full *r* be given thee of the .... Ruth 2:12   4909
wherefore the LORD *r* thee good 1Sa 24:19   7999
the LORD shall *r* the doer of evil 2Sa 3:39   7999
given him a *r* for his tidings 2Sa 4:10   1309
recompense it me with such a *r* 2Sa 19:36   1578
thyself, and I will give thee a *r* 1Kin 13:7   4991
Behold, I say, how they *r* us 2Chr 20:11   1580
Give a *r* for me of your substance .... Job 6:22   7809

looketh for the *r* of his work ....
nor taketh *r* against the innocent ....
keeping of them there is great *r* .... b 7:2
Let them be desolate for a *r* of 5
He shall *r* evil unto mine enemies 5
there is a *r* for the righteous   7810
for a *r* of their shame that say   6118
behold and see the *r* of the wicked   6118
render a *r* to the proud   7725
Let this be the *r* of mine Ps.529
and the fruit of the womb is his *r* .... Ps
righteousness shall be a sure *r* .... Pr
a *r* in the bosom strong wrath .... Pro
found it, then there shall be a *r* .... Prov
shall be no *r* to the evil man .... Prov
head, and the LORD shall *r* thee .... Prov .
have a good *r* for their labour .... Eccl 4:
neither have they any more a *r* .... Eccl 9:5
for the *r* of his hands shall be .... Is 3:11
Which justify the wicked for *r* .... Is 5:23
his *r* is with him, and his work .... Is 40:10
my captives, not for price nor *r* .... Is 45:13
his *r* is with him, and his work .... Is 62:11
guard gave him victuals and a *r* .... Jer 40:5
and in that thou givest a *r* .... Eze 16:34
and no *r* is given unto thee, ... Eze 16:34
ways, and *r* them their doings .... Hos 4:9   77
thou hast loved a *r* upon every .... Hos 9:1   86
thy *r* shall return upon thine own .... Obad 15   1576
The heads thereof judge for *r* .... Mic 3:11   7810
and the judge asketh for a *r* .... Mic 7:3   7966
for great is your *r* in heaven .... Mt 5:12   *3408*
which love you, what *r* have ye .... Mt 5:46   *3408*
otherwise ye have no *r* of your .... Mt 6:1   *3408*
I say unto you, They have their *r* .... Mt 6:2   *3408*
himself shall *r* thee openly .... Mt 6:4   *591*
I say unto you, They have their *r* .... Mt 6:5   *3408*
in secret shall *r* thee openly .... Mt 6:6   *591*
I say unto you, They have their *r* .... Mt 6:16   *3408*
in secret, shall *r* thee openly .... Mt 6:18   *591*
shall receive a prophet's *r* .... Mt 10:41   *3408*
shall receive a righteous man's *r* .... Mt 10:41   *3408*
he shall in no wise lose his *r* .... Mt 10:42   *3408*
then he shall *r* every man .... Mt 16:27   *591*
unto you, he shall not lose his *r* .... Mk 9:41   *3408*
your *r* is great in heaven .... Lk 6:23   *3408*
your *r* shall be great, and ye .... Lk 6:35   *3408*
we receive the due *r* of our deeds .... Lk 23:41   *514*
a field with the *r* of iniquity .... Acts 1:18   *3408*
is the *r* not reckoned of grace .... Rom 4:4   *3408*
own *r* according to his own labour 1Cor 3:8   *3408*
thereupon, he shall receive a *r* 1Cor 3:14   *3408*
this thing willingly, I have a *r* 1Cor 9:17   *3408*
What is my *r* then 1Cor 9:18   *3408*
of your *r* in a voluntary humility .... Col 2:18   *2603*
receive the *r* of the inheritance .... Col 3:24   *469*
The labourer is worthy of his *r* 1Ti 5:18   *3408*
the Lord *r* him according to his 2Ti 4:14   *591*
received a just recompence of *r* .... Heb 2:2   *3405*
which hath great recompence of *r* .... Heb 10:35   *3405*
unto the recompence of the *r* .... Heb 11:26   *3405*
And shall receive the *r* of 2Pet 2:13   *3408*
but that we receive a full *r* 2Jn 8   *3408*
after the error of Balaam for *r* .... Jude 11   *3408*
that thou shouldest give *r* unto .... Rev 11:18   *3408*
R her even as she rewarded you, ... Rev 18:6   *591*
my *r* is with me, to give every .... Rev 22:12   *3408*

REWARDED
Wherefore have ye *r* evil for good .... Gen 44:4   7999
for thou hast *r* me good, whereas 1Sa 24:17   1580
good, whereas I have *r* thee evil 1Sa 24:17   1580
The LORD *r* me according to my 2Sa 22:21   1580
for your work shall be *r* 2Chr 15:7   7939
If I have *r* evil unto him that .... Ps 7:4   1580
The LORD *r* me according to my .... Ps 18:20   1580
They *r* me evil for good to the .... Ps 35:12   7999
nor *r* us according to our .... Ps 103:10   1580
they have *r* me evil for good, and .... Ps 109:5   1580
the commandment shall be *r* .... Prov 13:13   7999
for they have *r* evil unto .... Is 3:9   1580
for thy work shall be *r*, saith .... Jer 31:16   7939
Reward her even as she *r* you .... Rev 18:6   *591*

REWARDER
that he is a *r* of them that .... Heb 11:6   *3406*

he *r* him, and he shall know it .... Job 21:19   7999
plentifully *r* the proud doer .... Ps 31:23   7999
that *r* thee as thou hast served .... Ps 137:8   7999
Whoso *r* evil for good, evil shall .... Prov 17:13   7725

REWARDS

r the fool .... Prov 26:10   7936
formed all things .... Prov 26:10   7936
and *r* transgresso...
their land .... Num 22:7
REWARDS
the *r* of divine ... after *r* .... Is 1:23   8021
gifts, and for me gifts and .... Dan 2:6   5023
ye shall r thy *r* to another .... Dan 5:17   5023
thyself, reat my lovers .... Hos 2:12   866
These fortress near Haran.
Haran, and *R*, and the ...2Kin 19:12   7530
Haran, and *R* .... Is 37:12   7530

REZE... n) Son of Ulla.
as aniel, and *R* 1Chr 7:39   7525

dah *R* the king of Syria 2Kin 15:37   7526
ng of Syria and Pekah son 2Kin 16:5   7526
me *R* king of Syria 2Kin 16:6   7526
tive to Kir, and slew *R* 2Kin 16:9   7526
e anger of *R* with Syria ....Is 7:4   7526
head of Damascus is *R* ....Is 7:8   7526
softly, and rejoice in *R* ....Is 8:6   7526
versaries of *R* against him ....Is 9:11   7526
A family of exiles.
children of *R*, the children..............Ezr 2:48   7526
Reaiah, the children of *R*........Neh 7:50   7526

REZON (re'-zon) An enemy of Solomon.
R the son of Eliadah, which fled 1Kin 11:23   7331

RHEGIUM (re'-je-um) A port of southern Italy.
fetched a compass, and came to *R* ....Acts 28:13   4484

RHESA (re'-sah) Son of Zorobabel; an ancestor of Jesus.
of Joanna, which was the son of *R* .. Lk 3:27   4488

RHODA (ro'-dah) A maiden in Mary's house.
a damsel came to hearken, named *R*.....Acts 12:13   4498

RHODES (rodes) A Mediterranean island.
Coos, and the day following unto *R* ....Acts 21:1

RIB
And the *r*, which the Lord God had........Gen 2:22   6763
spear smote him under the fifth *r*..........2Sa 2:23
smote him there under the fifth *r*...........2Sa 3:27
they smote him under the fifth *r*.............2Sa 4:6
him therewith in the fifth *r* 2Sa 20:10

RIBAI (rib'-ahee) Father of Ittai.
Ittai the son of *R* out of Gibeah 2Sa 23:29   7380
Ithai the son of *R* of Gibeah 1Chr 11:31   7380

RIBBAND
fringe of the borders a *r* of blue .... Num 15:38   6616

RIBLAH (rib'-lah) A city on the Orontes River.
shall go down from Shepham to *R* ....Num 34:11   7247
put him in bands at *R* in the land 2Kin 23:33   7247
up to the king of Babylon to *R* 2Kin 25:6   7247
them to the king of Babylon to *R* 2Kin 25:20   7247
slew them at *R* in the land of 2Kin 25:21   7247
king of Babylon to *R* in the land ....Jer 39:5   7247
of Zedekiah in *R* before his eyes ....Jer 39:6   7247
to *R* in the land of Hamath ....Jer 52:9   7247
all the princes of Judah in *R* ....Jer 52:10   7247
them to the king of Babylon to *R* ....Jer 52:26   7247
put them to death in *R* in the ....Jer 52:27   7247

RIBS
and he took one of his *r*, and ....Gen 2:21   6763
it had three *r* in the mouth of it ....Dan 7:5   6763

RICH
And Abram was very *r* in cattle.............Gen 13:2   3513
say, I have made Abram *r* ....Gen 14:23   6238
The *r* shall not give more, and the ....Ex 30:15   6223
or stranger wax *r* by thee ....Lev 25:47   5381
not young men, whether poor or *r* ....Ruth 3:10   6223
The Lord maketh poor, and maketh *r*....1Sa 2:7   6238
the one *r*, and the other poor 2Sa 12:1   6223
The *r* man had exceeding many 2Sa 12:2   6223
came a traveller unto the *r* man 2Sa 12:4   6223
He shall not be *r*, neither shall ....Job 15:29   6238
The *r* man shall lie down, but he ....Job 27:19   6223
nor regardeth the *r* more than the ....Job 34:19   7771
even the *r* among the people shall ....Ps 45:12   6223
Both low and high, *r* and poor,.............Ps 49:2   6223
thou afraid when one is made *r* ....Ps 49:16   6238
the hand of the diligent maketh *r* ....Prov 10:4   6238
The *r* man's wealth is his strong ....Prov 10:15   6223
blessing of the Lord, it maketh *r* ....Prov 10:22   6238
There is that maketh himself *r* ....Prov 13:7   6238
but the *r* hath many friends ....Prov 14:20   6223
The *r* man's wealth is his strong ....Prov 18:11   6223

but the *r* answereth roughly ....Prov 18:23   6223
loveth wine and oil shall not be *r* ....Prov 21:17   6238
The *r* and poor meet together ....Prov 22:2   6223
The *r* ruleth over the poor, and ....Prov 22:7   6223
and he that giveth to the *r* ....Prov 22:16   6223
Labour not to be *r* ....Prov 23:4   6238
in his ways, though he be *r* ....Prov 28:6   6223
The *r* man is wise in his own ....Prov 28:11   6223
to be *r* shall not be innocent ....Prov 28:20   6238
hasteth to be *r* hath an evil eye ....Prov 28:22   1952
but the abundance of the *r* will ....Eccl 5:12   6223
and the *r* sit in low place ....Eccl 10:6   6223
curse not the *r* in thy bedchamber ....Eccl 10:20   6223
and with the *r* in his death ....Is 53:9   6223
they are become great, and waxen *r* ......Jer 5:27   6238
let not the *r* man glory in his ....Jer 9:23   6223
work, and in chests of *r* apparel ....Eze 27:24
Ephraim said, Yet I am become *r* ....Hos 12:8   6238
For the *r* men thereof are full of ....Mic 6:12   6223
for I am *r*..Zec 11:5   6238
That a *r* man shall hardly enter ....Mt 19:23   4145
than for a *r* man to enter into...............Mt 19:24   4145
there came a *r* man of Arimathaea, ...Mt 27:57   4145
than for a *r* man to enter into...............Mk 10:25   4145
and many that were *r* cast in much......Mk 12:41   4145
the *r* he hath sent empty away ....Lk 1:53   4147
But woe unto you that are *r*...................Lk 6:24   4145
The ground of a certain *r* man ....Lk 12:16   4145
himself, and is not *r* toward God...........Lk 12:21   4147
thy kinsmen, nor thy *r* neighbours ....Lk 14:12   4145
There was a certain *r* man ....Lk 16:1   4145
There was a certain *r* man ....Lk 16:19   4145
which fell from the *r* man's table...........Lk 16:21   4145
the *r* man also died, and was ....Lk 16:22   4145
for he was very *r*................................Lk 18:23   4145
than for a *r* man to enter into...............Lk 18:25   4145
among the publicans, and he was *r* ......Lk 19:2   4145
saw the *r* men casting their gifts ....Lk 21:1   4145
is *r* unto all that call upon him ....Rom 10:12   4147
Now ye are full, now ye are *r* 1Cor 4:8   4147
as poor, yet making many *r* 2Cor 6:10   4148
Christ, that, though he was *r* 2Cor 8:9   4145
ye through his poverty might be *r* 2Cor 8:9   4147
who is *r* in mercy, for his great ....Eph 2:4   4145
will be *r* fall into temptation..................1Ti 6:9   4147
them that are *r* in this world 1Ti 6:17   4145
that they be *r* in good works,.................1Ti 6:18   4147
But the *r*, in that he is made low ....Jas 1:10   4145
so also shall the *r* man fade away ....Jas 1:11   4147
the poor of this world *r* in faith ....Jas 2:5   4145
Do not *r* men oppress you, and draw ......Jas 2:6   4145
ye *r* men, weep and howl for your ....Jas 5:1   4145
and poverty, (but thou art *r*)...................Rev 2:9   4145
Because thou sayest, I am *r*...................Rev 3:17   4145
the fire, that thou mayest be *r* ....Rev 3:18   4147
and the great men, and the *r* men ....Rev 6:15   4145
all, both small and great, *r*,...................Rev 13:16   4145
of the earth are waxed *r* through ....Rev 18:3   4147
things, which were made *r* by her..........Rev 18:15   4147
wherein were made *r* all that had..........Rev 18:19   4147

RICHER
shall be far *r* than they all ....Dan 11:2   6238

RICHES
For all the *r* which God hath ....Gen 31:16   6239
For their *r* were more than that ....Gen 36:7   7399
with much *r* unto your tents ....Josh 22:8   5233
king will enrich him with great *r*...........1Sa 17:25   6239
neither hast asked *r* for thyself 1Kin 3:11   6239
which thou hast not asked, both *r* 1Kin 3:13   6239
all the kings of the earth for *r* 1Kin 10:23   6239
Both *r* and honour come of thee, and 1Chr 29:12   6239
a good old age, full of days, *r* 1Chr 29:28   6239
heart, and thou hast not asked *r* 2Chr 1:11   6239
and I will give thee *r*, and wealth,.........2Chr 1:12   6239
all the kings of the earth in *r* 2Chr 9:22   6239
and he had *r* and honour in..................2Chr 17:5   6239
Now Jehoshaphat had *r* and honour 2Chr 18:1   6239
both *r* with the dead bodies 2Chr 20:25   7399
And Hezekiah had exceeding much *r* 2Chr 32:27   6239
When he shewed the *r* of his ....Est 1:4   6239
told them of the glory of his *r*................Est 5:11   6239
He hath swallowed down *r*, and he........Job 20:15   2428
Will he esteem thy *r*.............................Job 36:19   7769
better than the *r* of many wicked ....Ps 37:16   1995
he heapeth up *r*, and knoweth not ....Ps 39:6
in the multitude of their *r* ....Ps 49:6   6239
trusted in the abundance of his *r* ....Ps 52:7   6239
if *r* increase, set not your heart ....Ps 62:10   2428
they increase in *r* ....Ps 73:12   2428
the earth is full of thy *r* ....Ps 104:24   7075

Wealth and *r* shall be in his house	Ps 112:3	6239
testimonies, as much as in all *r*	Ps 119:14	1952
and in her left hand *r* and honour	Prov 3:16	6239
R and honour are with me	Prov 8:18	6239
yea, durable *r* and righteousness	Prov 8:18	1952
R profit not in the day of wrath	Prov 11:4	1952
and strong men retain *r*	Prov 11:16	6239
that trusteth in his *r* shall fall	Prov 11:28	6239
himself poor, yet hath great *r*	Prov 13:7	1952
ransom of a man's life are his *r*	Prov 13:8	6239
The crown of the wise is their *r*	Prov 14:24	6239
r are the inheritance of fathers	Prov 19:14	1952
rather to be chosen than great *r*	Prov 22:1	6239
and the fear of the LORD are *r*	Prov 22:4	6239
the poor to increase his *r*	Prov 22:16	
for *r* certainly make themselves	Prov 23:5	
with all precious and pleasant *r*	Prov 24:4	1952
For *r* are not for ever	Prov 27:24	2633
give me neither poverty nor *r*	Prov 30:8	6239
is his eye satisfied with *r*	Eccl 4:8	6239
r kept for the owners thereof to	Eccl 5:13	6239
But those *r* perish by evil	Eccl 5:14	6239
man also to whom God hath given *r*	Eccl 5:19	6239
A man to whom God hath given *r*	Eccl 6:2	6239
nor yet *r* to men of understanding	Eccl 9:11	6239
the *r* of Damascus and the spoil of	Is 8:4	2428
as a nest the *r* of the people	Is 10:14	2428
they will carry their *r* upon the	Is 30:6	2428
hidden *r* of secret places, that	Is 45:3	4301
shall eat the *r* of the Gentiles	Is 61:6	2428
not the rich man glory in his *r*	Jer 9:23	6239
so he that getteth *r*, and not by	Jer 17:11	6239
because the *r* that he hath gotten	Jer 48:36	3502
they shall make a spoil of thy *r*	Eze 26:12	2428
of the multitude of all kind of *r*	Eze 27:12	1952
for the multitude of all *r*	Eze 27:18	1952
Thy *r*, and thy fairs, thy	Eze 27:27	1952
earth with the multitude of thy *r*	Eze 27:33	6239
thou hast gotten thee *r*, and hast	Eze 28:4	2428
hast thou increased thy *r*	Eze 28:5	2428
is lifted up because of thy *r*	Eze 28:5	2428
by his strength through his *r* he	Dan 11:2	6239
with a great army and with much *r*	Dan 11:13	7399
them the prey, and spoil, and *r*	Dan 11:24	7399
return into his land with great *r*	Dan 11:28	7399
world, and the deceitfulness of *r*	Mt 13:22	4149
world, and the deceitfulness of *r*	Mk 4:19	4149
***r* enter into the kingdom of God**	Mk 10:23	5536
in *r* to enter into the kingdom of	Mk 10:24	5536
and are choked with cares and *r*	Lk 8:14	4149
commit to your trust the true *r*	Lk 16:11	
***r* enter into the kingdom of God**	Lk 18:24	5536
thou the *r* of his goodness	Rom 2:4	4149
that he might make known the *r* of	Rom 9:23	4149
of them be the *r* of the world	Rom 11:12	4149
of them the *r* of the Gentiles	Rom 11:12	4149
depth of the *r* both of the wisdom	Rom 11:33	4149
unto the *r* of their liberality	2Cor 8:2	4149
according to the *r* of his grace	Eph 1:7	4149
what the *r* of the glory of his	Eph 1:18	4149
he might shew the exceeding *r* of	Eph 2:7	4149
the unsearchable *r* of Christ	Eph 3:8	4149
according to the *r* of his glory	Eph 3:16	4149
to his *r* in glory by Christ Jesus	Phil 4:19	4149
r of the glory of this mystery	Col 1:27	4149
unto all *r* of the full assurance	Col 2:2	4149
nor trust in uncertain *r*	1Ti 6:17	4149
r than the treasures in Egypt	Heb 11:26	4149
Your *r* are corrupted, and your	Jas 5:2	4149
was slain to receive power, and *r*	Rev 5:12	4149
hour so great *r* is come to nought	Rev 18:17	4149

RICHLY

dwell in you *r* in all wisdom	Col 3:16	4146
who giveth us *r* all things to	1Ti 6:17	4146

RID

that he might *r* him out of their	Gen 37:22	5337
I will *r* you out of their bondage	Ex 6:6	5337
I will *r* evil beasts out of the	Lev 26:6	7673
r them out of the hand of the	Ps 82:4	5337
r me, and deliver me out of great	Ps 144:7	6475
R me, and deliver me from the hand	Ps 144:11	6475

RIDDANCE

thou shalt not make clean *r* of	Lev 23:22	3615
r of all them that dwell in the	Zeph 1:18	3617

RIDDEN

upon which thou hast *r* ever since	Num 22:30	7392

RIDDLE

I will now put forth a *r* unto you		
said unto him, Put forth thy *r*	Judg 14:12	2420
not in three days expound the *r*	Judg 14:13	2420
that he may declare unto us the *r*	Judg 14:13	2420
thou hast put forth a *r* unto the	Judg 14:14	2420
she told the *r* to the children of	Judg 14:15	2420
heifer, ye had not found out my *r*	Judg 14:18	2420
unto them which expounded the *r*	Judg 14:19	2420
Son of man, put forth a *r*	Eze 17:2	2420

RIDE

he made him to *r* in the second	Gen 41:43	
He made him *r* on the high places	Deut 32:13	
ye that *r* on white asses, ye that	Judg 5:10	
for the king's household to *r* on	2Sa 16:2	
me an ass, that I may *r* thereon	2Sa 19:26	
my son to *r* upon mine own mule	1Kin 1:33	
caused Solomon to *r* upon king	1Kin 1:38	7392
him to *r* upon the king's mule	1Kin 1:44	7392
So they made him *r* in his chariot	2Kin 10:16	7392
thou causest me to *r* upon it	Job 30:22	7392
in thy majesty *r* prosperously	Ps 45:4	7392
caused men to *r* over our heads	Ps 66:12	7392
and, We will *r* upon the swift	Is 30:16	7392
I will cause thee to *r* upon the	Is 58:14	7392
they *r* upon horses, set in array	Jer 6:23	7392
they shall *r* upon horses, every	Jer 50:42	7392
I will make Ephraim to *r*	Hos 10:11	7392
we will not *r* upon horses	Hos 14:3	7392
that thou didst *r* upon thine	Hab 3:8	7392
chariots, and those that *r* in them	Hag 2:22	7392

RIDER

so that his *r* shall fall backward	Gen 49:17	7392
his *r* hath he thrown into the sea	Ex 15:1	7392
his *r* hath he thrown into the sea	Ex 15:21	7392
she scorneth the horse and his *r*	Job 39:18	7392
in pieces the horse and his *r*	Jer 51:21	7392
in pieces the chariot and his *r*	Jer 51:21	7392
and his *r* with madness	Zec 12:4	7392

RIDERS

on thy part to set *r* upon them	2Kin 18:23	7392
r on mules, camels, and young	Est 8:10	7392
on thy part to set *r* upon them	Is 36:8	7392
their *r* shall come down, every	Hag 2:22	7392
them, and the *r* on horses shall be	Zec 10:5	7392

RIDETH

what saddle soever he *r* upon that	Lev 15:9	7392
who *r* upon the heaven in thy help	Deut 33:26	7392
and the horse that the king *r* upon	Est 6:8	7392
extol him that *r* upon the heavens	Ps 68:4	7392
To him that *r* upon the heavens of	Ps 68:33	7392
the LORD *r* upon a swift cloud, and	Is 19:1	7392
neither shall he that *r* the horse	Amos 2:15	7392

RIDGES

Thou waterest the *r* thereof	Ps 65:10	8525

RIDING

Now he was *r* upon his ass, and his	Num 22:22	7392
slack not thy *r* for me, except I	2Kin 4:24	7392
r in chariots and on horses, they,	Jer 17:25	7392
r in chariots and on horses, he	Jer 22:4	7392
young men, horsemen *r* upon horses	Eze 23:6	7392
horsemen *r* upon horses, all of	Eze 23:12	7392
all of them *r* upon horses	Eze 23:23	7392
thee, all of them *r* upon horses	Eze 38:15	7392
behold a man *r* upon a red horse	Zec 1:8	7392
r upon an ass, and upon a colt the	Zec 9:9	7392

RIE

wheat and the *r* were not smitten	Ex 9:32	3698
barley and the *r* in their place	Is 28:25	3698

RIFLED

shall be taken, and the houses *r*	Zec 14:2	8155

RIGHT

hand, then I will go to the *r*	Gen 13:9	3231
or if thou depart to the *r* hand	Gen 13:9	3225
the Judge of all the earth do *r*	Gen 18:25	4941
in the *r* way to take my master's	Gen 24:48	571
that I may turn to the *r* hand	Gen 24:49	3225
Ephraim in his *r* hand toward	Gen 48:13	3225
left hand toward Israel's *r* hand	Gen 48:13	3225
Israel stretched out his *r* hand	Gen 48:14	3225
saw that his father laid his *r*	Gen 48:17	3225
put thy *r* hand upon his head	Gen 48:18	3225
a wall unto them on their *r* hand	Ex 14:22	3225
a wall unto them on their *r* hand	Ex 14:29	3225
Thy *r* hand, O LORD, is become	Ex 15:6	3225
thy *r* hand, O LORD, hath dashed	Ex 15:6	3225

Thou stretchedst out thy *r* hand	Ex 15:12	3225
do that which is *r* in his sight	Ex 15:26	3477
the tip of the *r* ear of Aaron	Ex 29:20	
the tip of the *r* ear of his sons	Ex 29:20	3233
and upon the thumb of their *r* hand	Ex 29:20	3233
the great toe of their *r* foot	Ex 29:20	3233
is upon them, and the *r* shoulder	Ex 29:22	3233
the *r* shoulder shall ye give unto	Lev 7:32	3225
shall have the *r* shoulder for his	Lev 7:33	3225
it upon the tip of Aaron's *r* ear	Lev 8:23	3233
and upon the thumb of his *r* hand	Lev 8:23	3233
upon the great toe of his *r* foot	Lev 8:23	3233
blood upon the tip of their *r* ear	Lev 8:24	3233
upon the thumbs of their *r* hands	Lev 8:24	3233
the great toes of their *r* feet	Lev 8:24	3233
and their fat, and the *r* shoulder	Lev 8:25	3225
the fat, and upon the *r* shoulder	Lev 8:26	3225
the *r* shoulder Aaron waved for a	Lev 9:21	3225
of the *r* ear of him that is to be	Lev 14:14	3233
and upon the thumb of his *r* hand	Lev 14:14	3233
upon the great toe of his *r* foot	Lev 14:14	3233
the priest shall dip his *r* finger	Lev 14:16	3233
of the *r* ear of him that is to be	Lev 14:17	3233
and upon the thumb of his *r* hand	Lev 14:17	3233
upon the great toe of his *r* foot	Lev 14:17	3233
of the *r* ear of him that is to be	Lev 14:25	3233
and upon the thumb of his *r* hand	Lev 14:25	3233
upon the great toe of his *r* foot	Lev 14:25	3233
r finger some of the oil that is	Lev 14:27	3233
of the *r* ear of him that is to be	Lev 14:28	3233
and upon the thumb of his *r* hand	Lev 14:28	3233
upon the great toe of his *r* foot	Lev 14:28	3233
as the *r* shoulder are thine	Num 18:18	3225
to the *r* hand nor to the left	Num 20:17	3225
to the *r* hand or to the left	Num 22:26	3225
daughters of Zelophehad speak *r*	Num 27:7	3651
unto the *r* hand nor to the left	Deut 2:27	3225
to the *r* hand or to the left	Deut 5:32	3225
And thou shalt do that which is *r*	Deut 6:18	3477
whatsoever is *r* in his own eyes	Deut 12:8	3477
is *r* in the sight of the LORD	Deut 12:25	3477
r in the sight of the LORD thy	Deut 12:28	3477
to do that which is *r* in the eyes	Deut 13:18	3477
shall shew thee, to the *r* hand	Deut 17:11	3225
the commandment, to the *r* hand	Deut 17:20	3225
is *r* in the sight of the LORD	Deut 21:9	3477
the *r* of the firstborn is his	Deut 21:17	4941
thee this day, to the *r* hand	Deut 28:14	3225
without iniquity, just and *r* is he	Deut 32:4	3477
from his *r* hand went a fiery law	Deut 33:2	3225
it to the *r* hand or to the left	Josh 1:7	3225
passed over *r* against Jericho	Josh 3:16	
r unto thee to do unto us, do	Josh 9:25	3477
r hand unto the inhabitants of	Josh 17:7	3225
to the *r* hand or to the left	Josh 23:6	3225
his raiment upon his *r* thigh	Judg 3:16	3225
took the dagger from his *r* thigh	Judg 3:21	3225
her *r* hand to the workmen's	Judg 5:26	3225
in their *r* hands to blow withal	Judg 7:20	3225
could not frame to pronounce it *r*	Judg 12:6	3651
up, of the one with his *r* hand	Judg 16:29	3225
that which was *r* in his own eyes	Judg 17:6	3477
that which was *r* in his own eyes	Judg 21:25	3477
redeem thou my *r* to thyself	Ruth 4:6	1353
to the *r* hand or to the left	1Sa 6:12	3225
I may thrust out all your *r* eyes	1Sa 11:2	3225
teach you the good and the *r* way	1Sa 12:23	3477
the *r* hand nor to the left from	2Sa 2:19	3225
to thy *r* hand or to thy left	2Sa 2:21	3225
none can turn to the *r* hand or to	2Sa 14:19	3231
See, thy matters are good and *r*	2Sa 15:3	5228
the mighty men were on his *r* hand	2Sa 16:6	3225
What *r* therefore have I yet to	2Sa 19:28	6666
have also more *r* in David than ye	2Sa 19:43	3225
beard with the *r* hand to kiss him	2Sa 20:9	3225
on the *r* side of the city that	2Sa 24:5	3225
and she sat on his *r* hand	1Kin 2:19	3225
was in the *r* side of the house	1Kin 6:8	3233
and he set up the *r* pillar	1Kin 7:21	3225
bases on the *r* side of the house	1Kin 7:39	3225
he set the sea on the *r* side of	1Kin 7:39	3233
of pure gold, five on the *r* side	1Kin 7:49	3225
do that which is *r* in mine eyes	1Kin 11:33	3477
do that is *r* in my sight, to keep	1Kin 11:38	3477
only which was *r* in mine eyes	1Kin 14:8	3477
was *r* in the eyes of the LORD	1Kin 15:5	3477
Asa did that which was *r* in the	1Kin 15:11	3477
standing by him on his *r* hand	1Kin 22:19	3225
doing that which was *r* in the	1Kin 22:43	3477
and said to him, Is thine heart *r*	2Kin 10:15	3225
that which is *r* in mine eyes	2Kin 10:30	3225

from the *r* corner of the temple	2Kin 11:11	3233
Jehoash did that which was *r* in	2Kin 12:2	3477
on the *r* side as one cometh into	2Kin 12:9	3225
he did that which was *r* in the	2Kin 14:3	3477
he did that which was *r* in the	2Kin 15:3	3477
he did that which was *r* in the	2Kin 15:34	3477
did not that which was *r* in the	2Kin 16:2	3477
not *r* against the LORD their God	2Kin 17:9	3651
he did that which was *r* in the	2Kin 18:3	3477
he did that which was *r* in the	2Kin 22:2	3477
to the *r* hand or to the left	2Kin 22:2	3225
which were on the *r* hand of the	2Kin 23:13	3225
Asaph, who stood on his *r* hand	1Chr 6:39	3225
and could use both the *r* hand	1Chr 12:2	3231
for the thing was *r* in the eyes	1Chr 13:4	3477
the temple, one on the *r* hand	2Chr 3:17	3225
name of that on the *r* hand Jachin	2Chr 3:17	3227
lavers, and put five on the *r* hand	2Chr 4:6	3225
in the temple, five on the *r* hand	2Chr 4:7	3225
in the temple, five on the *r* side	2Chr 4:8	3225
sea on the *r* side of the east end	2Chr 4:10	3233
r in the eyes of the LORD his God	2Chr 14:2	3477
of heaven standing on his *r* hand	2Chr 18:18	3225
doing that which was *r* in the	2Chr 20:32	3477
from the *r* side of the temple to	2Chr 23:10	3233
Joash did that which was *r* in the	2Chr 24:2	3477
he did that which was *r* in the	2Chr 25:2	3477
he did that which was *r* in the	2Chr 26:4	3477
he did that which was *r* in the	2Chr 27:2	3477
was *r* in the sight of the LORD	2Chr 28:1	3477
he did that which was *r* in the :	2Chr 29:2	3477
wrought that which was good and *r*	2Chr 31:20	3477
he did that which was *r* in the	2Chr 34:2	3477
and declined neither to the *r* hand	2Chr 34:2	3225
to seek of him a *r* way for us	Ezr 8:21	3477
but ye have no portion, nor *r*	Neh 2:20	6666
and Maaseiah, on his *r* hand	Neh 8:4	3225
and gavest them *r* judgments	Neh 9:13	3477
for thou hast done *r*, but we have	Neh 9:33	571
whereof one went on the *r* hand	Neh 12:31	3225
the thing seem *r* before the king,	Est 8:5	3787
How forcible are *r* words	Job 6:25	3476
he hideth himself on the *r* hand	Job 23:9	3225
Upon my *r* hand rise the youth	Job 30:12	3225
and perverted that which was *r*	Job 33:27	3477
Should I lie against my *r*	Job 34:6	4941
even he that hateth *r* govern	Job 34:17	4941
will not lay upon man more than *r*	Job 34:23	4941
Thinkest thou this to be *r*	Job 35:2	4941
but giveth *r* to the poor	Job 36:6	4941
thine own *r* hand can save thee	Job 40:14	3225
spoken of me the thing that is *r*	Job 42:7	3559
spoken of me the thing which is *r*	Job 42:8	3559
For thou hast maintained my *r*	Ps 9:4	4941
satest in the throne judging *r*	Ps 9:4	6664
because he is at my *r* hand	Ps 16:8	3225
at thy *r* hand there are pleasures	Ps 16:11	3225
Hear the *r*, O LORD, attend unto	Ps 17:1	6664
O thou that savest by thy *r* hand	Ps 17:7	3225
thy *r* hand hath holden me up, and	Ps 18:35	3225
The statutes of the LORD are *r*	Ps 19:8	3477
the saving strength of his *r* hand	Ps 20:6	3225
thy *r* hand shall find out those	Ps 21:8	3225
their *r* hand is full of bribes	Ps 26:10	3225
For the word of the LORD is *r*	Ps 33:4	3477
but thy *r* hand, and thine arm, and	Ps 44:3	3225
thy *r* hand shall teach thee	Ps 45:4	3225
of thy kingdom is a *r* sceptre	Ps 45:6	4334
upon thy *r* hand did stand the	Ps 45:9	3225
shall help her, and that *r* early	Ps 46:5	6437
thy *r* hand is full of	Ps 48:10	3225
renew a *r* spirit within me	Ps 51:10	3559
save with thy *r* hand, and hear me	Ps 60:5	3225
thy *r* hand upholdeth me	Ps 63:8	3225
thou hast holden me by my *r* hand	Ps 73:23	3225
thou thy hand, even thy *r* hand	Ps 74:11	3225
of the *r* hand of the most High	Ps 77:10	3225
their heart was not *r* with him	Ps 78:37	3559
which his *r* hand had purchased	Ps 78:54	3225
which thy *r* hand hath planted	Ps 80:15	3225
be upon the man of thy *r* hand	Ps 80:17	3225
thy hand, and high is thy *r* hand	Ps 89:13	3225
sea, and his *r* hand in the rivers	Ps 89:25	3225
Thou hast set up the *r* hand of	Ps 89:42	3225
and ten thousand at thy *r* hand	Ps 91:7	3225
his *r* hand, and his holy arm, hath	Ps 98:1	3225
And he led them forth by the *r* way	Ps 107:7	3477
save with thy *r* hand, and answer	Ps 108:6	3225
and let Satan stand at his *r* hand	Ps 109:6	3225
stand at the *r* hand of the poor	Ps 109:31	3225
my Lord, Sit thou at my *r* hand	Ps 110:1	3225

R

The LORD at thy *r* hand shall	Ps 110:5	3225
the *r* hand of the LORD doeth	Ps 118:15	3225
The *r* hand of the LORD is exalted	Ps 118:16	3225
the *r* hand of the LORD doeth	Ps 118:16	3225
O LORD, that thy judgments are *r*	Ps 119:75	6664
concerning all things to be *r*	Ps 119:128	3474
LORD is thy shade upon thy *r* hand	Ps 121:5	3225
let my *r* hand forget her cunning	Ps 137:5	3225
and thy *r* hand shall save me	Ps 138:7	3225
me, and thy *r* hand shall hold me	Ps 139:10	3225
and that my soul knoweth *r* well	Ps 139:14	
afflicted, and the *r* of the poor	Ps 140:12	4941
I looked on my *r* hand, and beheld,	Ps 142:4	3225
their *r* hand is a *r* hand of	Ps 144:8	3225
their *r* hand is a *r* hand of	Ps 144:11	3225
Length of days is in her *r* hand	Prov 3:16	3225
I have led thee in *r* paths	Prov 4:11	3476
Let thine eyes look *r* on, and let	Prov 4:25	5227
Turn not to the *r* hand nor to the	Prov 4:27	3225
of my lips shall be *r* things	Prov 8:6	4339
r to them that find knowledge	Prov 8:9	3477
passengers who go *r* on their ways	Prov 9:15	3474
thoughts of the righteous are *r*	Prov 12:5	4941
of a fool is *r* in his own eyes	Prov 12:15	3477
a way which seemeth *r* unto a man	Prov 14:12	3477
than great revenues without *r*	Prov 16:8	4941
and they love him that speaketh *r*	Prov 16:13	3477
a way that seemeth *r* unto a man	Prov 16:25	3477
work be pure, and whether it be *r*	Prov 20:11	3477
way of a man is *r* in his own eyes	Prov 21:2	3477
as for the pure, his work is *r*	Prov 21:8	3477
when thy lips speak *r* things	Prov 23:16	4339
his lips that giveth a *r* answer	Prov 24:26	5228
and the ointment of his *r* hand	Prov 27:16	3225
all travail, and every *r* work	Eccl 4:4	3788
wise man's heart is at his *r* hand	Eccl 10:2	3225
his *r* hand doth embrace me	Song 2:6	3225
his *r* hand should embrace me	Song 8:3	3225
And he shall snatch on the *r* hand	Is 9:20	3225
to take away the *r* from the poor	Is 10:2	4941
Prophesy not unto us *r* things	Is 30:10	5229
in it, when ye turn to the *r* hand	Is 30:21	541
even when the needy speaketh *r*	Is 32:7	4941
the *r* hand of my righteousness	Is 41:10	3225
LORD thy God will hold thy *r* hand	Is 41:13	3225
Is there not a lie in my *r* hand	Is 44:20	3225
whose *r* hand I have holden, to	Is 45:1	3225
I declare things that are *r*	Is 45:19	4339
my hand hath spanned the	Is 48:13	3225
shalt break forth on the *r* hand	Is 54:3	3225
The LORD hath sworn by his *r* hand	Is 62:8	3225
That led them by the *r* hand of	Is 63:12	3225
a noble vine, wholly a *r* seed	Jer 2:21	571
the *r* of the needy do they not	Jer 5:28	4941
that getteth riches, and not by *r*	Jer 17:11	4941
out of my lips was *r* before thee	Jer 17:16	5227
were the signet upon my *r* hand	Jer 22:24	3225
is evil, and their force is not *r*	Jer 23:10	
for the *r* of redemption is thine	Jer 32:7	4941
for the *r* of inheritance is thine	Jer 32:8	4941
had done *r* in my sight, in	Jer 34:15	3477
be driven out every man *r* forth	Jer 49:5	6440
he hath drawn back his *r* hand	Lam 2:3	3225
he stood with his *r* hand as an	Lam 2:4	3225
To turn aside the *r* of a man	Lam 3:35	4941
the face of a lion, on the *r* side	Eze 1:10	3225
them, lie again on thy *r* side	Eze 4:6	6227
stood on the *r* side of the house	Eze 10:3	3225
that dwelleth at thy *r* hand	Eze 16:46	3225
and do that which is lawful and *r*	Eze 18:5	6666
done that which is lawful and *r*	Eze 18:19	6666
and do that which is lawful and *r*	Eze 18:21	6666
doeth that which is lawful and *r*	Eze 18:27	6666
or other, either on the *r* hand	Eze 21:16	3231
At his *r* hand was the divination	Eze 21:22	3225
more, until he come whose *r* it is	Eze 21:27	4941
and do that which is lawful and *r*	Eze 33:14	6666
done that which is lawful and *r*	Eze 33:16	6666
and do that which is lawful and *r*	Eze 33:19	6666
arrows to fall out of thy *r* hand	Eze 39:3	3225
from the *r* side of the house	Eze 47:1	3233
ran out waters on the *r* side	Eze 47:2	3233
river, when he held up his *r* hand	Dan 12:7	3225
for the ways of the LORD are *r*	Hos 14:9	3477
For they know not to do *r*	Amos 3:10	5229
the poor in the gate from their *r*	Amos 5:12	
discern between their *r* hand	Jonah 4:11	3225
the cup of the LORD's *r* hand	Hab 2:16	3225
at his *r* hand to resist him	Zec 3:1	3225
one upon the *r* side of the bowl,	Zec 4:3	3225
the *r* side of the candlestick	Zec 4:11	3225

upon his arm, and upon his *r* eye	Zec 11:17	3225
his *r* eye shall be utterly	Zec 11:17	3225
people round about, on the *r* hand	Zec 12:6	3225
aside the stranger from his *r*	Mal 3:5	3225
if thy *r* eye offend thee, pluck	Mt 5:29	1188
if thy *r* hand offend thee, cut it	Mt 5:30	1188
shall smite thee on thy *r* cheek	Mt 5:39	1188
hand know what thy *r* hand doeth	Mt 6:3	1188
whatsoever is *r* I will give you	Mt 20:4	1342
and whatsoever is *r*, that shall ye	Mt 20:7	1342
may sit, the one on thy *r* hand	Mt 20:21	1188
but to sit on my *r* hand, and on my	Mt 20:23	1188
my Lord, Sit thou on my *r* hand	Mt 22:44	1188
shall set the sheep on his *r* hand	Mt 25:33	1188
King say unto them on his *r* hand	Mt 25:34	1188
sitting on the *r* hand of power	Mt 26:64	1188
his head, and a reed in his *r* hand	Mt 27:29	1188
with him, one on the *r* hand	Mt 27:38	1188
and clothed, and in his *r* mind	Mk 5:15	4993
we may sit, one on thy *r* hand	Mk 10:37	1188
But to sit on my *r* hand and on my	Mk 10:40	1188
to my Lord, Sit thou on my *r* hand	Mk 12:36	1188
sitting on the *r* hand of power	Mk 14:62	1188
the one on his *r* hand, and the	Mk 15:27	1188
a young man sitting on the *r* side	Mk 16:5	1188
and sat on the *r* hand of God	Mk 16:19	1188
of the Lord standing on the *r*	Lk 1:11	1188
a man whose *r* hand was withered	Lk 6:6	1188
Jesus, clothed, and in his *r* mind	Lk 8:35	4993
unto him, Thou hast answered *r*	Lk 10:28	3723
yourselves judge ye not what is *r*	Lk 12:57	1342
my Lord, Sit thou on my *r* hand	Lk 20:42	1188
high priest, and cut off his *r* ear	Lk 22:50	1188
on the *r* hand of the power of God	Lk 22:69	1188
malefactors, one on the *r* hand	Lk 23:33	1188
servant, and cut off his *r* ear	Jn 18:10	1188
the net on the *r* side of the ship	Jn 21:6	1188
my face, for he is on my *r* hand	Acts 2:25	1188
by the *r* hand of God exalted	Acts 2:33	1188
my Lord, Sit thou on my *r* hand	Acts 2:34	1188
And he took him by the *r* hand	Acts 3:7	1188
Whether it be *r* in the sight of	Acts 4:19	1342
with his *r* hand to be a Prince	Acts 5:31	1188
standing on the *r* hand of God	Acts 7:55	1188
man standing on the *r* hand of God	Acts 7:56	1188
is not *r* in the sight of God	Acts 8:21	2117
to pervert the *r* ways of the Lord	Acts 13:10	2117
who is even at the *r* hand of God	Rom 8:34	1188
of righteousness on the *r* hand	2Cor 6:7	1188
to me and Barnabas the *r* hands of	Gal 2:9	1188
set him at his own *r* hand in the	Eph 1:20	1188
for this is *r*	Eph 6:1	1342
sitteth on the *r* hand of God	Col 3:1	1188
sat down on the *r* hand of the	Heb 1:3	1188
he at any times, Sit on my *r* hand	Heb 1:13	1188
who is set on the *r* hand of the	Heb 8:1	1188
sat down on the *r* hand of God	Heb 10:12	1188
is set down at the *r* hand of the	Heb 12:2	1188
whereof they have no *r* to eat	Heb 13:10	1849
and is on the *r* hand of God	1Pet 3:22	1188
Which have forsaken the *r* way	2Pet 2:15	2117
he had in his *r* hand seven stars	Rev 1:16	1188
he laid his *r* hand upon me,	Rev 1:17	1188
which thou sawest in my *r* hand	Rev 1:20	1188
the seven stars in his *r* hand	Rev 2:1	1188
I saw in the *r* hand of him that	Rev 5:1	1188
took the book out of the *r* hand	Rev 5:7	1188
he set his *r* foot upon the sea,	Rev 10:2	1188
to receive a mark in their *r* hand	Rev 13:16	1188
that they may have *r* to the tree	Rev 22:14	1849

RIGHTEOUS

for thee have I seen *r* before me	Gen 7:1	6662
destroy the *r* with the wicked	Gen 18:23	6662
there be fifty *r* within the city	Gen 18:24	6662
for the fifty *r* that are therein	Gen 18:24	6662
to slay the *r* with the wicked	Gen 18:25	6662
that the *r* should be as the	Gen 18:25	6662
in Sodom fifty *r* within the city	Gen 18:26	6662
shall lack five of the fifty *r*	Gen 18:28	6662
wilt thou slay also a *r* nation	Gen 20:4	6662
said, She hath been more *r* than I	Gen 38:26	6663
the LORD is *r*, and I and my people	Ex 9:27	6662
the innocent and *r* slay thou not	Ex 23:7	6662
and perverteth the words of the *r*	Ex 23:8	6662
Let me die the death of the *r*	Num 23:10	3477
judgments so *r* as all this law,	Deut 4:8	6662
and pervert the words of the *r*	Deut 16:19	6662
then they shall justify the *r*	Deut 25:1	6662
rehearse the *r* acts of the LORD	Judg 5:11	6666
even the *r* acts toward the	Judg 5:11	6666

of all the *r* acts of the ... than I	1Sa 12:7	6666
to David, Thou art ... me upon	1Sa 24:17	6662
a *r* person in his own ... *r*	2Sa 4:11	6662
who fell upon two ... *r* him	1Kin 2:32	6662
and justifying the ... giving	1Kin 8:32	6662
said to all the p ... *r*	2Kin 10:9	6662
and by justify ... ou art *r*	2Chr 6:23	6662
and they said ...	2Chr 12:6	6662
O Lᴏʀᴅ God ... off ... would	Ezr 9:15	6662
for thou art ... yet would	Neh 9:8	6662
or where ... wot lift	Job 4:7	6662
Whom, ... should be *r*	Job 9:15	6663
and if I ... in his way,	Job 10:15	6662
of a w ... thou art *r*	Job 15:14	6662
The *r* ... glad	Job 17:9	6662
to th ... pute with	Job 22:3	6663
The ... his own eyes	Job 22:19	6662
T ... am *r*	Job 23:7	3477
... vest thou	Job 32:1	6662
... ye *r*	Job 34:5	6663
... thou mayest be *r*	Job 35:7	6663
... n of the *r*	Job 36:7	6662
... the way of the *r*	Job 40:8	6663
... lt bless the *r*	Ps 1:5	6662
... th the hearts	Ps 1:6	6662
... *r*, and God is	Ps 5:12	6662
... at can the *r* do	Ps 7:9	6662
... the *r*	Ps 7:11	6662
... oveth	Ps 11:3	6662
... eneration of the *r*	Ps 11:5	6662
... ue and *r* altogether	Ps 11:7	6662
... iously against the *r*	Ps 14:5	6662
... nd rejoice, ye *r*	Ps 19:9	6663
... e Lᴏʀᴅ, O ye *r*	Ps 31:18	6662
... Lᴏʀᴅ are upon the *r*	Ps 32:11	6662
... y, and the Lᴏʀᴅ heareth,	Ps 33:1	6662
... are the afflictions of the *r*	Ps 34:15	6662
... nate the *r* shall be desolate	Ps 34:17	
... glad, that favour my *r* cause	Ps 34:19	6662
A little that a *r* man hath	Ps 34:21	6662
but the Lᴏʀᴅ upholdeth the *r*	Ps 35:27	6664
but the *r* sheweth mercy, and	Ps 37:16	6662
have I not seen the *r* forsaken	Ps 37:17	6662
The *r* shall inherit the land, and	Ps 37:21	6662
mouth of the *r* speaketh wisdom	Ps 37:25	6662
The wicked watcheth the *r*	Ps 37:29	6662
salvation of the *r* is of the Lᴏʀᴅ	Ps 37:30	6662
The *r* also shall see, and fear, and	Ps 37:32	6662
never suffer the *r* to be moved	Ps 37:39	6662
The *r* shall rejoice when he seeth	Ps 52:6	6662
there is a reward for the *r*	Ps 55:22	6662
The *r* shall be glad in the Lᴏʀᴅ,	Ps 58:10	6662
But let the *r* be glad	Ps 58:11	6662
and not be written with the *r*	Ps 64:10	6662
In his days shall the *r* flourish	Ps 69:28	6662
horns of the *r* shall be exalted	Ps 72:7	6662
The *r* shall flourish like the	Ps 75:10	6662
against the soul of the *r*	Ps 92:12	6662
Light is sown for the *r*, and	Ps 94:21	6662
Rejoice in the Lᴏʀᴅ, ye *r*	Ps 97:11	6662
The *r* shall see it, and rejoice	Ps 97:12	6662
and full of compassion, and *r*	Ps 107:42	3477
the *r* shall be in everlasting	Ps 112:4	6662
Gracious is the Lᴏʀᴅ, and *r*	Ps 112:6	6662
is in the tabernacles of the *r*	Ps 116:5	6662
into which the *r* shall enter	Ps 118:15	6662
have learned thy *r* judgments	Ps 118:20	6662
thee because of thy *r* judgments	Ps 119:7	6664
that I will keep thy *r* judgments	Ps 119:62	6664
R art thou, O Lᴏʀᴅ, and upright	Ps 119:106	6664
that thou hast commanded are *r*	Ps 119:137	3477
every one of thy *r* judgments	Ps 119:138	6664
thee because of thy *r* judgments	Ps 119:160	6664
not rest upon the lot of the *r*	Ps 119:164	6664
lest the *r* put forth their hands	Ps 125:3	6662
The Lᴏʀᴅ is *r*	Ps 125:3	6662
Surely the *r* shall give thanks	Ps 129:4	6662
Let the *r* smite me	Ps 140:13	6662
the *r* shall compass me about	Ps 141:5	6662
The Lᴏʀᴅ is *r* in all his ways, and	Ps 142:7	6662
the Lᴏʀᴅ loveth the *r*	Ps 145:17	6662
layeth up sound wisdom for the *r*	Ps 146:8	6662
men, and preserveth the paths of the *r*	Prov 2:7	3477
but his secret is with the *r*	Prov 2:20	6662
the soul of the *r* to famish	Prov 3:32	3477
The mouth of a *r* man is a well of	Prov 10:3	6662
labour of the *r* tendeth to life	Prov 10:11	6662
The lips of the *r* feed many	Prov 10:16	6662
desire of the *r* shall be granted	Prov 10:21	6662
	Prov 10:24	6662

but the *r* is an everlasting	Prov 10:25	6662
The hope of the *r* shall be	Prov 10:28	6662
The *r* shall never be removed	Prov 10:30	6662
The lips of the *r* know what is	Prov 10:32	6662
The *r* is delivered out of trouble	Prov 11:8	6662
When it goeth well with the *r*	Prov 11:10	6662
seed of the *r* shall be delivered	Prov 11:21	6662
The desire of the *r* is only good	Prov 11:23	6662
but the *r* shall flourish as a	Prov 11:28	6662
The fruit of the *r* is a tree of	Prov 11:30	6662
the *r* shall be recompensed in the	Prov 11:31	6662
root of the *r* shall not be moved	Prov 12:3	6662
The thoughts of the *r* are right	Prov 12:5	6662
the house of the *r* shall stand	Prov 12:7	6662
A *r* man regardeth the life of his	Prov 12:10	6662
the root of the *r* yieldeth fruit	Prov 12:12	6662
The *r* is more excellent than his	Prov 12:26	6662
A *r* man hateth lying	Prov 13:5	6662
The light of the *r* rejoiceth	Prov 13:9	6662
but to the *r* good shall be repaid	Prov 13:21	6662
The *r* eateth to the satisfying of	Prov 13:25	6662
but among the *r* there is favour	Prov 14:9	3477
the wicked at the gates of the *r*	Prov 14:19	6662
but the *r* hath hope in his death	Prov 14:32	6662
house of the *r* is much treasure	Prov 15:6	6662
the way of the *r* is made plain	Prov 15:19	3477
The heart of the *r* studieth to	Prov 15:28	6662
he heareth the prayer of the *r*	Prov 15:29	6662
R lips are the delight of kings	Prov 16:13	6664
to overthrow the *r* in judgment	Prov 18:5	6662
the *r* runneth into it, and is safe	Prov 18:10	6662
The *r* man wisely considereth the	Prov 21:12	6662
shall be a ransom for the *r*	Prov 21:18	6662
but the *r* giveth and spareth not	Prov 21:26	6662
The father of the *r* shall greatly	Prov 23:24	6662
against the dwelling of the *r*	Prov 24:15	6662
saith unto the wicked, Thou art *r*	Prov 24:24	6662
A *r* man falling down before the	Prov 25:26	6662
but the *r* are bold as a lion	Prov 28:1	6662
Whoso causeth the *r* to go astray	Prov 28:10	3477
When *r* men do rejoice, there is	Prov 28:12	6662
when they perish, the *r* increase	Prov 28:28	6662
When the *r* are in authority, the	Prov 29:2	6662
but the *r* doth sing and rejoice	Prov 29:6	6662
The *r* considereth the cause of	Prov 29:7	6662
but the *r* shall see their fall	Prov 29:16	6662
mine heart, God shall judge the *r*	Eccl 3:17	6662
Be not *r* over much	Eccl 7:16	6662
according to the work of the *r*	Eccl 8:14	6662
to declare all this, that the *r*	Eccl 9:1	6662
there is one event to the *r*	Eccl 9:2	6662
Say ye to the *r*, that it shall be	Is 3:10	6662
righteousness of the *r* from him	Is 5:23	6662
heard songs, even glory to the *r*	Is 24:16	6662
that the *r* nation which keepeth	Is 26:2	6662
raised up the *r* man from the east	Is 41:2	6664
that we may say, He is *r*	Is 41:26	6662
shall my *r* servant justify many	Is 53:11	6662
The *r* perisheth, and no man layeth	Is 57:1	6662
none considering that the *r* is	Is 57:1	6662
Thy people also shall be all *r*	Is 60:21	6662
R art thou, O Lᴏʀᴅ, when I plead	Jer 12:1	6662
Lᴏʀᴅ of hosts, that triest the *r*	Jer 20:12	6662
will raise unto David a *r* Branch	Jer 23:5	6662
The Lᴏʀᴅ is *r*	Lam 1:18	6662
When a *r* man doth turn from his	Eze 3:20	6662
if thou warn the *r* man	Eze 3:21	6662
that *r* sin not	Eze 3:21	6662
have made the heart of the *r* sad	Eze 13:22	6662
they are more *r* than thou	Eze 16:52	6663
of the *r* shall be upon him	Eze 18:20	6662
But when the *r* turneth away from	Eze 18:24	6662
When a *r* man turneth away from	Eze 18:26	6662
and will cut off from thee the *r*	Eze 21:3	6662
I will cut off from thee the *r*	Eze 21:4	6662
And the *r* men, they shall judge	Eze 23:45	6662
The righteousness of the *r* shall	Eze 33:12	6662
neither shall the *r* be able to	Eze 33:12	6662
When I shall say to the *r*	Eze 33:13	6662
When the *r* turneth from his	Eze 33:18	6662
for the Lᴏʀᴅ our God is *r* in all	Dan 9:14	6662
they sold the *r* for silver	Amos 2:6	6662
wicked doth compass about the *r*	Hab 1:4	6662
the man that is more *r* than he	Hab 1:13	6662
return, and discern between the *r*	Mal 3:18	6662
for I am not come to call the *r*	Mt 9:13	*1342*
he that receiveth a *r* man in the	Mt 10:41	*1342*
a *r* man shall receive a *r*	Mt 10:41	*1342*
r men have desired to see those	Mt 13:17	*1342*
Then shall the *r* shine forth as	Mt 13:43	*1342*
also outwardly appear *r* unto men	Mt 23:28	*1342*

R

garnish the sepulchres of the *r* .... Mt 23:29   *1342*
the *r* blood shed upon the earth .... Mt 23:35   *1342*
from the blood of *r* Abel unto the .... Mt 23:35   *1342*
Then shall the *r* answer him .... Mt 25:37   *1342*
but the *r* into life eternal .... Mt 25:46   *1342*
I came not to call the *r*, but .... Mk 2:17   *1342*
And they were both *r* before God .... Lk 1:6   *1342*
I came not to call the *r*, but .... Lk 5:32   *1342*
in themselves that they were *r* .... Lk 18:9   *1342*
Certainly this was a *r* man .... Lk 23:47   *1342*
appearance, but judge *r* judgment .... Jn 7:24   *1342*
O *r* Father, the world hath not .... Jn 17:25   *1342*
of the *r* judgment of God .... Rom 2:5   *1341*
As it is written, There is none .... Rom 3:10   *1342*
scarcely for a *r* man will one die .... Rom 5:7   *1342*
of one shall many be made .... Rom 5:19   *1342*
token of the *r* judgment of God 2Th 1:5   *1342*
Seeing it is a *r* thing with God 2Th 1:6   *1342*
the law is not made for a *r* man 1Ti 1:9   *1342*
the *r* judge, shall give me at 2Ti 4:8   *1342*
he obtained witness that he was *r* .... Heb 11:4   *1342*
prayer of a *r* man availeth much .... Jas 5:16   *1342*
eyes of the Lord are over the *r* 1Pet 3:12   *1342*
if the *r* scarcely be saved, where 1Pet 4:18   *1342*
(For that *r* man dwelling among 2Pet 2:8   *1342*
vexed his *r* soul from day to day 2Pet 2:8   *1342*
the Father, Jesus Christ the *r* 1Jn 2:1   *1342*
If ye know that he is *r*, ye know 1Jn 2:29   *1342*
he that doeth righteousness is *r* 1Jn 3:7   *1342*
even as he is *r* 1Jn 3:7   *1342*
were evil, and his brother's *r* 1Jn 3:12   *1342*
of the waters say, Thou art *r* .... Rev 16:5   *1342*
true and *r* are thy judgments .... Rev 16:7   *1342*
For true and *r* are his judgments .... Rev 19:2   *1342*
is *r*, let him be *r* still .... Rev 22:11   *1343*

RIGHTEOUSLY

judge *r* between every man and his .... Deut 1:16   6664
for thou shalt judge the people *r* .... Ps 67:4   4334
he shall judge the people *r* .... Ps 96:10   4339
Open thy mouth, judge *r*, and plead ...... Prov 31:9   6664
He that walketh *r*, and speaketh .... Is 33:15   6666
O Lord of hosts, that judgest *r* .... Jer 11:20   6664
lusts, we should live soberly, *r* .... Titus 2:12   *1346*
himself to him that judgeth *r* 1Pet 2:23   *1346*

RIGHTEOUSNESS

and he counted it to him for *r* .... Gen 15:6   6666
So shall my *r* answer for me in .... Gen 30:33   6666
but in *r* shalt thou judge thy .... Lev 19:15   6664
And it shall be our *r*, if we .... Deut 6:25   6666
For my *r* the Lord hath brought me .... Deut 9:4   6666
Not for thy *r*, or for the .... Deut 9:5   6666
good land to possess it for thy *r* .... Deut 9:6   6666
it shall be *r* unto thee before .... Deut 24:13   6666
they shall offer sacrifices of *r* .... Deut 33:19   6664
Lord render to every man his *r* 1Sa 26:23   6666
rewarded me according to my *r* 2Sa 22:21   6666
recompensed me according to my *r* 2Sa 22:25   6666
before thee in truth, and in *r* 1Kin 3:6   6666
to give him according to his *r* 1Kin 8:32   6666
by giving him according to his *r* 2Chr 6:23   6666
yea, return again, my *r* is in it .... Job 6:29   6664
habitation of thy *r* prosperous .... Job 8:6   6664
My *r* I hold fast, and will not let .... Job 27:6   6666
I put on *r*, and it clothed me .... Job 29:14   6664
for he will render unto man his *r* .... Job 33:26   6666
saidst, My *r* is more than God's .... Job 35:2   6664
thy *r* may profit the son of man .... Job 35:8   6666
and will ascribe *r* to my Maker .... Job 36:3   6664
me when I call, O God of my *r* .... Ps 4:1   6664
Offer the sacrifices of *r* .... Ps 4:5   6664
in thy *r* because of mine enemies .... Ps 5:8   6666
me, O Lord, according to my *r* .... Ps 7:8   6664
the Lord according to his *r* .... Ps 7:17   6664
And he shall judge the world in *r* .... Ps 9:8   6664
For the righteous Lord loveth *r* .... Ps 11:7   6666
walketh uprightly, and worketh *r* .... Ps 15:2   6664
me, I will behold thy face in *r* .... Ps 17:15   6664
rewarded me according to my *r* .... Ps 18:20   6664
recompensed me according to my *r* .... Ps 18:24   6664
shall declare his *r* unto a people .... Ps 22:31   6666
paths of *r* for his name's sake .... Ps 23:3   6664
r from the God of his salvation .... Ps 24:5   6666
deliver me in thy *r* .... Ps 31:1   6666
He loveth *r* and judgment .... Ps 33:5   6666
O Lord my God, according to thy *r* .... Ps 35:24   6664
And my tongue shall speak of thy *r* .... Ps 35:28   6666
Thy *r* is like the great mountains .... Ps 36:6   6666
thy *r* to the upright in heart .... Ps 36:10   6666
bring forth thy *r* as the light .... Ps 37:6   6664
I have preached *r* in the great .... Ps 40:9   6664

not hid thy *r* within my heart... .... Ps 40:10
because of truth and meekness .... Ps 45:4
Thou lovest *r*, and hatest .... Ps 45:7   6666
thy right hand is full of *r* .... Ps 48:10   6664
the heavens shall declare his *r* .... Ps 50:6   6664
tongue shall sing aloud of thy *r* .... Ps 51:14   6664
pleased with the sacrifices of *r* .... Ps   6664
and lying rather than to speak *r* .... Ps   6666
Do ye indeed speak *r*, O .... Ps   6664
things in *r* wilt thou answer us   6664
and let them not come into thy *r*   6666
Deliver me in thy *r*, and cause me   6664
My mouth shall shew forth thy *r*   6664
I will make mention of thy *r*   6666
Thy *r* also, O God, is very high   6666
talk of thy *r* all the day long .... Ps   6666
thy *r* unto the king's son .... Ps
He shall judge thy people with *r* .... Ps
people, and the little hills, by *r* .... Ps 7
r and peace have kissed each other ...... Ps 85
r shall look down from heaven .... Ps 85:
R shall go before him .... Ps 85:1
and thy *r* in the land of .... Ps 88:12
in thy *r* shall they be exalted .... Ps 89:16
But judgment shall return unto *r* .... Ps 94:15
he shall judge the world with *r* .... Ps 96:13
r and judgment are the habitation .... Ps 97:2
The heavens declare his *r* .... Ps 97:6
his *r* hath he openly shewed in .... Ps 98:2
with *r* shall he judge the world .... Ps 98:9
executest judgment and *r* in Jacob .... Ps 99:4   6
The Lord executeth *r* and judgment ...... Ps 103:6   66
his *r* unto children's children .... Ps 103:17   666
and he that doeth *r* at all times .... Ps 106:3   666
for *r* unto all generations for .... Ps 106:31   6666
and his *r* endureth for ever .... Ps 111:3   6666
and his *r* endureth for ever .... Ps 112:3   6666
his *r* endureth for ever .... Ps 112:9   6666
Open to me the gates of *r* .... Ps 118:19   6664
quicken me in thy *r* .... Ps 119:40   6666
and for the word of thy *r* .... Ps 119:123   6664
Thy *r* is an everlasting .... Ps 119:142   6666
r is an everlasting .... Ps 119:142   6666
The *r* of thy testimonies is .... Ps 119:144   6664
for all thy commandments are *r* .... Ps 119:172   6666
Let thy priests be clothed with *r* .... Ps 132:9   6664
answer me, and in thy *r* .... Ps 143:1   6666
goodness, and shall sing of thy *r* .... Ps 145:7   6666
Then shalt thou understand *r* .... Prov 2:9   6664
the words of my mouth are in *r* .... Prov 8:8   6664
yea, durable riches and *r* .... Prov 8:18   6666
I lead in the way of *r*, in the .... Prov 8:20   6666
but *r* delivereth from death .... Prov 10:2   6666
but *r* delivereth from death .... Prov 11:4   6666
The *r* of the perfect shall direct .... Prov 11:5   6666
The *r* of the upright shall .... Prov 11:6   6666
soweth *r* shall be a sure reward .... Prov 11:18   6666
As *r* tendeth to life .... Prov 11:19   6666
speaketh truth sheweth forth *r* .... Prov 12:17   6664
In the way of *r* is life .... Prov 12:28   6666
R keepeth him that is upright in .... Prov 13:6   6666
R exalteth a nation .... Prov 14:34   6666
loveth him that followeth after *r* .... Prov 15:9   6666
Better is a little with *r* than .... Prov 16:8   6666
the throne is established by *r* .... Prov 16:12   6664
if it be found in the way of *r* .... Prov 16:31   6666
He that followeth after *r* .... Prov 21:21   6666
and mercy findeth life, *r*, and .... Prov 21:21   6666
throne shall be established in *r* .... Prov 25:5   6664
and the place of *r*, that iniquity .... Eccl 3:16   6664
just man that perisheth in his *r* .... Eccl 7:15   6664
r lodged in it .... Is 1:21   6664
shalt be called, The city of *r* .... Is 1:26   6664
judgment, and her converts with *r* .... Is 1:27   6666
for *r*, but behold a cry .... Is 5:7   6664
is holy shall be sanctified in *r* .... Is 5:16   6666
take away the *r* of the righteous .... Is 5:23   6666
decreed shall overflow with *r* .... Is 10:22   6664
But with *r* shall he judge the .... Is 11:4   6664
r shall be the girdle of his .... Is 11:5   6664
and seeking judgment, and hasting *r* .... Is 16:5   6664
of the world will learn *r* .... Is 26:9   6664
wicked, yet will he not learn *r* .... Is 26:10   6664
to the line, and *r* to the plummet .... Is 28:17   6666
Behold, a king shall reign in *r* .... Is 32:1   6664
r remain in the fruitful field .... Is 32:16   6666
the work of *r* shall be peace .... Is 32:17   6666
and the effect of *r* quietness .... Is 32:17   6666
filled Zion with judgment and *r* .... Is 33:5   6666
thee with the right hand of my *r* .... Is 41:10   6664
I the Lord have called thee in *r* .... Is 42:6   6664

and let the skies pour down r	Is 45:8	6664
and let r spring up together	Is 45:8	6666
I have raised him up in r	Is 45:13	6664
I the LORD speak r, I declare	Is 45:19	6664
word is gone out of my mouth in r	Is 45:23	6666
one say, in the LORD have I r	Is 45:24	6666
stouthearted, that are far from r	Is 46:12	6666
I bring near my r	Is 46:13	6666
but not in truth, nor in r	Is 48:1	6666
thy r as the waves of the sea	Is 48:18	6666
to me, ye that follow after r	Is 51:1	6664
My r is near	Is 51:5	6664
my r shall not be abolished	Is 51:6	6666
Hearken unto me, ye that know r	Is 51:7	6664
but my r shall be for ever, and my	Is 51:8	6666
In r shalt thou be established	Is 54:14	6666
their r is of me, saith the LORD	Is 54:17	6666
to come, and my r to be revealed	Is 56:1	6666
I will declare thy r, and thy	Is 57:12	6666
my ways, as a nation that did r	Is 58:2	6666
thy r shall go before thee	Is 58:8	6664
and his r, it sustained him	Is 59:16	6666
For he put on r as a breastplate,	Is 59:17	6666
peace, and thine exactors r	Is 60:17	6666
they might be called trees of r	Is 61:3	6664
covered me with the robe of r	Is 61:10	6666
so the Lord GOD will cause r	Is 61:11	6666
until the r thereof go forth as	Is 62:1	6664
And the Gentiles shall see thy r	Is 62:2	6664
I that speak in r, mighty to save	Is 63:1	6666
him that rejoiceth and worketh r	Is 64:5	6664
in truth, in judgment, and in r	Jer 4:2	6666
lovingkindness, judgment, and r	Jer 9:24	6666
Execute ye judgment and r, and	Jer 22:3	6666
shall be called, THE LORD OUR R.	Jer 23:6	6664
Branch of r to grow up unto David	Jer 33:15	6666
execute judgment and r in the land	Jer 33:15	6666
shall be called, The LORD our r	Jer 33:16	6664
The LORD hath brought forth our r	Jer 51:10	6666
man doth turn from his r, and	Eze 3:20	6664
his r which he hath done shall	Eze 3:20	6666
but their own souls by their r	Eze 14:14	6666
their own souls by their r	Eze 14:20	6666
the r of the righteous shall be	Eze 18:20	6666
in his r that he hath done he	Eze 18:22	6666
righteous turneth away from his r	Eze 18:24	6666
All his r that he hath done shall	Eze 18:24	6666
man turneth away from his r	Eze 18:26	6666
The r of the righteous shall not	Eze 33:12	6666
be able to live for his r in the	Eze 33:12	
if he trust to his own r, and	Eze 33:13	6666
the righteous turneth from his r	Eze 33:18	6665
thee, and break off thy sins by r	Dan 4:27	6666
r belongeth unto thee, but unto	Dan 9:7	6666
O Lord, according to all thy r	Dan 9:16	6666
and to bring in everlasting r	Dan 9:24	6664
many to r as the stars for ever	Dan 12:3	6663
I will betroth thee unto me in r	Hos 2:19	6664
Sow to yourselves in r, reap in	Hos 10:12	6666
till he come and rain r upon you	Hos 10:12	6664
leave off r in the earth,	Amos 5:7	6666
waters, and r as a mighty stream	Amos 5:24	6666
and the fruit of r into hemlock	Amos 6:12	6666
ye may know the r of the LORD	Mic 6:5	6666
light, and I shall behold his r	Mic 7:9	6666
seek r, seek meekness	Zeph 2:3	6664
be their God, in truth and in r	Zec 8:8	6666
unto the LORD an offering in r	Mal 3:3	6666
fear my name shall the Sun of r	Mal 4:2	6666
it becometh us to fulfil all r	Mt 3:15	1343
which do hunger and thirst after r	Mt 5:6	1343
That except your r shall exceed	Mt 5:20	1343
shall exceed the r of the scribes	Mt 5:20	1343
the kingdom of God, and his r	Mt 6:33	1343
came unto you in the way of r	Mt 21:32	1343
r before him, all the days of our	Lk 1:75	1343
reprove the world of sin, and of r	Jn 16:8	1343
Of r, because I go to my Father,	Jn 16:10	1343
he that feareth him, and worketh r	Acts 10:35	1343
of the devil, thou enemy of all r	Acts 13:10	1343
in r by that man whom he hath	Acts 17:31	1343
And as he reasoned of r,	Acts 24:25	1343
For therein is the r of God	Rom 1:17	1343
keep the r of the law, shall not	Rom 2:26	1345
commend the r of God, what shall	Rom 3:5	1343
But now the r of God without the	Rom 3:21	1343
Even the r of God which is by	Rom 3:22	1343
blood, to declare his r for the	Rom 3:25	1343
I say, at this time his r	Rom 3:26	1343
and it was counted unto him for r	Rom 4:3	1343
his faith is counted for r	Rom 4:5	1343

whom God imputeth r without works	Rom 4:6	1343
was reckoned to Abraham for r	Rom 4:9	1343
a seal of the r of the faith	Rom 4:11	1343
that r might be imputed unto them	Rom 4:11	1343
law, but through the r of faith	Rom 4:13	1343
it was imputed to him for r	Rom 4:22	1343
of the gift of r shall reign in	Rom 5:17	1343
even so by the r of one the free	Rom 5:18	1345
r unto eternal life by Jesus	Rom 5:21	1343
as instruments of r unto God	Rom 6:13	1343
death, or of obedience unto r	Rom 6:16	1343
sin, ye became the servants of r	Rom 6:18	1343
servants to r unto holiness	Rom 6:19	1343
of sin, ye were free from r	Rom 6:20	1343
That the r of the law might be	Rom 8:4	1345
the Spirit is life because of r	Rom 8:10	1343
the work, and cut it short in r	Rom 9:28	1343
which followed not after r	Rom 9:30	1343
have attained to r	Rom 9:30	1343
even the r which is of faith	Rom 9:30	1343
which followed after the law of r	Rom 9:31	1343
hath not attained to the law of r	Rom 9:31	1343
they being ignorant of God's r	Rom 10:3	1343
about to establish their own r	Rom 10:3	1343
themselves unto the r of God	Rom 10:3	1343
is the end of the law for r to	Rom 10:4	1343
the r which is of the law	Rom 10:5	1343
But the r which is of faith	Rom 10:6	1343
the heart man believeth unto r	Rom 10:10	1343
but r, and peace, and joy in the	Rom 14:17	1343
God is made unto us wisdom, and r	1Cor 1:30	1343
Awake to r, and sin not	1Cor 15:34	1346
ministration of r exceed in glory	2Cor 3:9	1343
might be made the r of God in him	2Cor 5:21	1343
by the armour of r on the right	2Cor 6:7	1343
hath r with unrighteousness	2Cor 6:14	1343
his r remaineth for ever	2Cor 9:9	1343
and increase the fruits of your r	2Cor 9:10	1343
transformed as the ministers of r	2Cor 11:15	1343
for if r come by the law, then	Gal 2:21	1343
and it was accounted to him for r	Gal 3:6	1343
verily r should have been by the	Gal 3:21	1343
wait for the hope of r by faith	Gal 5:5	1343
which after God is created in r	Eph 4:24	1343
Spirit is in all goodness and r	Eph 5:9	1343
and having on the breastplate of r	Eph 6:14	1343
Being filled with the fruits of r	Phil 1:11	1343
touching the r which is in the	Phil 3:6	1343
in him, not having mine own r	Phil 3:9	1343
the r which is of God by faith	Phil 3:9	1343
and follow after r, godliness,	1Ti 6:11	1343
but follow r, faith, charity,	2Ti 2:22	1343
correction, for instruction in r	2Ti 3:16	1343
is laid up for me a crown of r	2Ti 4:8	1343
Not by works of r which we have	Titus 3:5	1343
a sceptre of r is the sceptre of	Heb 1:8	2118
Thou hast loved r, and hated	Heb 1:9	1343
is unskilful in the word of r	Heb 5:13	1343
being by interpretation King of r	Heb 7:2	1343
heir of the r which is by faith	Heb 11:7	1343
faith subdued kingdoms, wrought r	Heb 11:33	1343
r unto them which are exercised	Heb 12:11	1343
of man worketh not the r of God	Jas 1:20	1343
and it was imputed unto him for r	Jas 2:23	1343
the fruit of r is sown in peace	Jas 3:18	1343
dead to sins, should live unto r	1Pet 2:24	1343
with us through the r of God	2Pet 1:1	1343
eighth person, a preacher of r	2Pet 2:5	1343
not to have known the way of r	2Pet 2:21	1343
a new earth, wherein dwelleth r	2Pet 3:13	1343
one that doeth r is born of him	1Jn 2:29	1343
he that doeth r is righteous	1Jn 3:7	1343
doeth not r is not of God	1Jn 3:10	1343
the fine linen is the r of saints	Rev 19:8	1345
in r he doth judge and make war	Rev 19:11	1343

RIGHTEOUSNESS'

for thy r sake bring my soul out	Ps 143:11	6666
is well pleased for his r sake	Is 42:21	6664
which are persecuted for r sake.	Mt 5:10	1343
But and if ye suffer for r sake	1Pet 3:14	1343

RIGHTEOUSNESSES

all our r are as filthy rags	Is 64:6	6666
all his r shall not be remembered	Eze 33:13	6666
before thee for our r, but for	Dan 9:18	6666

RIGHTLY

he said, Is not he r named Jacob	Gen 27:36	3588
said unto him, Thou hast r judged	Lk 7:43	3723
that thou sayest and teachest r	Lk 20:21	3723
r dividing the word of truth	2Ti 2:15	3723

R

RIGOUR

of Israel to serve with *r*	Ex 1:13	6531
they made them serve, was with *r*	Ex 1:14	6531
shalt not rule over him with *r*	Lev 25:43	6531
not rule one over another with *r*	Lev 25:46	6531
rule with *r* over him in thy sight	Lev 25:53	6531

RIMMON (rim'-mon)
1. A city in Zebulun.

Lebaoth, and Shilhim, and Ain, and *R*	Josh 15:32	7417
R with her suburbs, Tabor with	1Chr 6:77	7417
from Geba to *R* south of Jerusalem	Zec 14:10	7417

2. A rock near Gibeah.

the wilderness unto the rock of *R*	Judg 20:45	7417
to the wilderness unto the rock *R*	Judg 20:47	7417
abode in the rock *R* four months	Judg 20:47	7417
Benjamin that were in the rock *R*	Judg 21:13	7417

3. Father of Baanah and Rechab.

the sons of *R* a Beerothite, of	2Sa 4:2	7417
the sons of *R* the Beerothite	2Sa 4:5	7417
the sons of *R* the Beerothite, and	2Sa 4:9	7417

4. A Syrian god.

the house of *R* to worship there	2Kin 5:18	7417
and I bow myself in the house of *R*	2Kin 5:18	7417
bow down myself in the house of *R*	2Kin 5:18	7417

5. A city in Simeon.

villages were, Etam, and Ain, *R*	1Chr 4:32	7417

RIMMONO See RIMMON.

RIMMON-PAREZ (rim'-mon-pa'-rez) An Israelite
encampment in the wilderness.

from Rithmah, and pitched at *R*	Num 33:19	7428
And they departed from *R*, and	Num 33:20	7428

RING

took off his *r* from his hand	Gen 41:42	2885
above the head of it unto one *r*	Ex 26:24	2885
at the head thereof, to one *r*	Ex 36:29	2885
the king took his *r* from his hand	Est 3:10	2885
and sealed with the king's *r*	Est 3:12	2885
And the king took off his *r*	Est 8:2	2885
and seal it with the king's *r*	Est 8:8	2885
name, and sealed with the king's *r*	Est 8:8	2885
and sealed it with the king's *r*	Est 8:10	2885
put a *r* on his hand, and shoes on	Lk 15:22	*1146*
your assembly a man with a gold *r*	Jas 2:2	5554

RINGLEADER

a *r* of the sect of the Nazarenes	Acts 24:5	4414

RINGS

shalt cast four *r* of gold for it	Ex 25:12	2885
two *r* shall be in the one side of	Ex 25:12	2885
two *r* in the other side of it	Ex 25:12	2885
the *r* by the sides of the ark	Ex 25:14	2885
shall be in the *r* of the ark	Ex 25:15	2885
shalt make for it four *r* of gold	Ex 25:26	2885
put the *r* in the four corners	Ex 25:26	2885
against the border shall the *r* be	Ex 25:27	2885
make their *r* of gold for places	Ex 26:29	2885
r in the four corners thereof	Ex 27:4	2885
staves shall be put into the *r*	Ex 27:7	2885
the breastplate two *r* of gold	Ex 28:23	2885
shalt put the two *r* on the two	Ex 28:23	2885
chains of gold in the two *r* which	Ex 28:24	2885
And thou shalt make two *r* of gold	Ex 28:26	2885
two other *r* of gold thou shalt	Ex 28:27	2885
bind the breastplate by the *r*	Ex 28:28	2885
the *r* of the ephod with a lace of	Ex 28:28	2885
two golden *r* shalt thou make to	Ex 30:4	2885
bracelets, and earrings, and *r*	Ex 35:22	2885
made their *r* of gold to be places	Ex 36:34	2885
And he cast for it four *r* of gold	Ex 37:3	2885
even two *r* upon the one side of	Ex 37:3	2885
two *r* upon the other side of it	Ex 37:3	2885
the *r* by the sides of the ark	Ex 37:5	2885
And he cast for it four *r* of gold	Ex 37:13	2885
put the *r* upon the four corners	Ex 37:13	2885
against the border were the *r*	Ex 37:14	2885
he made two *r* of gold for it	Ex 37:27	2885
he cast four *r* for the four ends	Ex 38:5	2885
the *r* on the sides of the altar	Ex 38:7	2885
two ouches of gold, and two gold *r*	Ex 39:16	2885
put the two *r* in the two ends of	Ex 39:16	2885
chains of gold in the two *r* on	Ex 39:17	2885
And they made two *r* of gold	Ex 39:19	2885
And they made two other golden *r*	Ex 39:20	2885
his *r* unto the *r* of the ephod	Ex 39:21	2885
of gold, chains, and bracelets, *r*	Num 31:50	2885
fine linen and purple to silver *r*	Est 1:6	1550
are as gold *r* set with the beryl	Song 5:14	1550
The *r*, and nose jewels,	Is 3:21	2885

As for their *r*, they were so high	Eze 1:18	1354
their *r* were full of eyes round	Eze 1:18	1354

RINGSTRAKED

that day the he goats that were *r*	Gen 30:35	6124
rods, and brought forth cattle *r*	Gen 30:39	6124
faces of the flocks toward the *r*	Gen 30:40	6124
thus, The *r* shall be thy hire	Gen 31:8	6124
then bare all the cattle *r*	Gen 31:8	6124
leaped upon the cattle were *r*	Gen 31:10	6124
which leap upon the cattle are *r*	Gen 31:12	6124

RINNAH (rin'-nah) A descendant of Caleb.

sons of Shimon were, Amnon, and *R*	1Chr 4:20	7441

RINSED

be both scoured, and *r* in water	Lev 6:28	7857
hath not *r* his hands in water, he	Lev 15:11	7857
of wood shall be *r* in water	Lev 15:12	7857

RIOT

not accused of *r* or unruly	Titus 1:6	*810*
with them to the same excess of *r*	1Pet 4:4	*810*
it pleasure to *r* in the daytime	2Pet 2:13	5172

RIOTING

not in *r* and drunkenness, not in	Rom 13:13	2970

RIOTOUS

among *r* eaters of flesh	Prov 23:20	2151
of *r* men shameth his father	Prov 28:7	2151
his substance with *r* living	Lk 15:13	*811*

RIP

r up their women with child	2Kin 8:12	1234

RIPE

thereof brought forth *r* grapes	Gen 40:10	1310
offer the first of thy *r* fruits	Ex 22:29	
whatsoever is first *r* in the land	Num 18:13	
like the figs that are first *r*	Jer 24:2	
the sickle, for the harvest is *r*	Joel 3:13	1310
for the harvest of the earth is *r*	Rev 14:15	3583
for her grapes are fully *r*	Rev 14:18	*187*

RIPENING

the sour grape is *r* in the flower	Is 18:5	1580

RIPHATH (ri'-fath) A son of Gomer.

Ashkenaz, and *R*, and Togarmah	Gen 10:3	7384
Ashchenaz, and *R*, and Togarmah	1Chr 1:6	7384

RIPPED

that were with child he *r* up	2Kin 15:16	1234
women with child shall be *r* up	Hos 13:16	1234
because they have *r* up the women	Amos 1:13	1234

RISE

your feet, and ye shall *r* up early	Gen 19:2	7925
that I cannot *r* up before thee	Gen 31:35	6965
R up early in the morning, and	Ex 8:20	7925
R up early in the morning, and	Ex 9:13	6965
R up, and get you forth from among	Ex 12:31	6965
If he *r* again, and walk abroad	Ex 21:19	6965
Thou shalt *r* up before the hoary	Lev 19:32	6965
R up, LORD, and let thine enemies	Num 10:35	6965
call thee, *r* up, and go with them	Num 22:20	6965
and said, *R* up, Balak, and hear	Num 23:18	6965
the people shall *r* up as a great	Num 23:24	6965
a Sceptre shall *r* out of Israel	Num 24:17	6965
Now *r* up, said I, and get you over	Deut 2:13	6965
R ye up, take your journey, and	Deut 2:24	6965
r up against him, and smite him	Deut 19:11	6965
One witness shall not *r* up	Deut 19:15	6965
If a false witness *r* up against	Deut 19:16	6965
r up against thee to be smitten	Deut 28:7	6965
that shall *r* up after you	Deut 29:22	6965
and this people will *r* up, and go a	Deut 31:16	6965
Let them *r* up and help you, and be	Deut 32:38	6965
loins of them that *r* against him	Deut 33:11	6965
hate him, that they *r* not again	Deut 33:11	6965
Then ye shall *r* up from the	Josh 8:7	6965
I will send them, and they shall *r*	Josh 18:4	6965
said, *R* thou, and fall upon us	Judg 8:21	6965
the sun is up, thou shalt *r* early	Judg 9:33	7925
with smoke *r* up out of the city	Judg 20:38	5927
him, that he should *r* against me	1Sa 22:13	6965
them not to *r* against Saul	1Sa 24:7	6965
Wherefore now *r* up early in the	1Sa 29:10	7925
the child was dead, thou didst *r*	2Sa 12:21	6965
all that *r* against thee to do	2Sa 18:32	6965
of Israel, which *r* up against me	2Kin 16:7	6965
And they said, Let us *r* up	Neh 2:18	6965
the earth shall *r* up against him	Job 20:27	6965
Upon my right hand *r* the youth	Job 30:12	6965
are they that *r* up against me	Ps 3:1	6965
from those that *r* up against them	Ps 17:7	6965

RISEN

them that they were not able to .... Ps 18:38   6965
above those that *r* up against r......... Ps 18:48   6965
though war should r against r .... Ps 27:3   6965
False witnesses did *r* up .... Ps 35:11   6965
down, and shall not be able .... Ps 36:12   6965
he lieth he shall *r* up no mo .... Ps 41:8   6965
them under that *r* up again .... Ps 44:5   6965
me from them that *r* up a .... Ps 59:1   6965
the tumult of those that .... Ps 74:23   6965
the wicked that *r* up age .... Ps 92:11   6965
Who will *r* up for me g .... Ps 94:16   6965
At midnight I will *r* t .... Ps 119:62   6965
It is vain for you to *r* .... Ps 127:2   6965
with those that *r* up .... Ps 139:21   8618
pits, that they *r* no is .... Ps 140:10   6965
their calamity sh .... Prov 24:22   6965
but when the wi .... Prov 28:12   6965
When the wicke .... Prov 28:28   6965
of the ruler *r* nd .... Eccl 10:4   5927
he shall *r* up le .... Eccl 12:4   6965
R up, my lo rly in .... Song 2:10   6965
I will *r* now ess .... Song 3:2   6965
Woe unto again .... Is 5:11   7925
that they ot *r* .... Is 14:21   6965
For I wi s in .... Is 14:22   6965
and i s at ease .... Is 24:20   6965
e ORD .... Is 26:14   6965
arth ll not *r* .... Is 28:21   6965
up, I *r* against .... Is 32:9   6965
Now curity .... Is 33:10   6965
dow the sword .... Is 43:17   6965
ever every man in .... Is 54:17   6965
sh he north, and .... Is 58:10   2224
r battle .... Jer 25:27   6965
y against me .... Jer 37:10   6965
he evil that I .... Jer 47:2   5927
not able to *r* up .... Jer 49:14   6965
ll *r* after them .... Jer 51:1   6965
re *r* .... Jer 51:64   6965
the house of .... Lam 1:14   6966
holly as a flood .... Dan 7:24   6965
d never *r* up again .... Amos 5:2   6965
wholly like a flood .... Amos 7:9   6965
against her in battle .... Amos 8:8   5927
up the second time .... Amos 8:14   6965
not *r* up suddenly that .... Amos 9:5   5927
at I *r* up to the prey .... Obad 1   6965
shall *r* up against the .... Nah 1:9   6965
his sun to *r* on the evil .... Hab 2:7   6965
ldren shall *r* up against .... Zeph 3:8   6965
r in judgment with this .... Zec 14:13   5927
the judgment with this .... Mt 5:45   393
the third day he shall *r* again .... Mt 10:21   1881
nation shall *r* against nation .... Mt 12:41   450
d many false prophets shall *r* .... Mt 12:42   1453
, let us be going .... Mt 20:19   450
After three days I will *r* again .... Mt 24:7   1453
if Satan *r* up against himself, and .... Mt 24:11   1453
r night and day, and the seed .... Mt 26:46   1453
killed, he shall *r* the third day .... Mt 27:63   1453
and the third day he shall *r* again .... Mk 3:26   450
unto him, Be of good comfort, *r* .... Mk 4:27   1453
therefore, when they shall *r* .... Mk 8:31   450
when they shall *r* from the dead .... Mk 9:31   450
as touching the dead, that they *r* .... Mk 10:34   450
For nation shall *r* against nation .... Mk 10:49   1453
children shall *r* up against their .... Mk 12:23   450
Christs and false prophets shall *r* .... Mk 12:25   450
R up, let us go .... Mk 12:26   1453
or to say, *R* up and walk .... Mk 13:8   1453
R up, and stand forth in the midst .... Mk 13:12   1881
I cannot *r* and give thee .... Mk 13:22   1453
unto you, Though he will not *r* .... Mk 14:42   1453
of his importunity he will *r* .... Lk 5:23   1453
The queen of the south shall *r* up .... Lk 6:8   1453
The men of Nineve shall *r* up in .... Lk 11:7   450
ye see a cloud *r* out of the west .... Lk 11:8   1453
and the third day he shall *r* again .... Lk 11:8   450
Nation shall *r* against nation, and .... Lk 11:31   1453
r and pray, lest ye enter into .... Lk 11:32   450
and the third day *r* again .... Lk 12:54   393
to *r* from the dead the third day .... Lk 18:33   450
Jesus saith unto him, *R*, take up .... Lk 21:10   1453
her, Thy brother shall *r* again .... Lk 22:46   450
I know that he shall *r* again in .... Lk 24:7   450
that he must *r* again from the .... Lk 24:46   450
of Jesus Christ of Nazareth *r* up .... Jn 5:8   1453
    Jn 11:23   450
    Jn 11:24   450
    Jn 20:9   450
    Acts 3:6   1453

And there came a voice to him, *R* .... Acts 10:13   450
But *r*, and stand upon thy feet .... Acts 26:16   450
first that should *r* from the dead .... Acts 26:23   386
he that shall *r* to reign over the .... Rom 15:12   450
up, if so be that the dead *r* not 1Cor 15:15   1453
For if the dead *r* not, then is 1Cor 15:16   1453
dead, if the dead *r* not at all 1Cor 15:29   1453
it me, if the dead *r* not 1Cor 15:32   1453
the dead in Christ shall *r* first 1Th 4:16   450
that another priest should *r* .... Heb 7:11   450
and the angel stood, saying, *R* .... Rev 11:1   1453
saw a beast *r* up out of the sea, ... Rev 13:1   305

RISEN

The sun was *r* upon the earth when .... Gen 19:23   3318
If the sun be *r* upon him, there .... Ex 22:3   2224
ye are *r* up in your fathers' .... Num 32:14   6965
ye are *r* up against my father's .... Judg 9:18   6965
And when she was *r* up to glean .... Ruth 2:15   6965
Yet a man is *r* to pursue thee, and 1Sa 25:29   6965
the whole family is *r* against 2Sa 14:7   6965
I am *r* up in the room of David my 1Kin 8:20   6965
of the man of God was *r* early 2Kin 6:15   6965
for I am *r* up in the room of 2Chr 6:10   6965
Solomon the son of David, is *r* up 2Chr 13:6   6965
Now when Jehoram was *r* up to the 2Chr 21:4   6965
but we are *r*, and stand upright .... Ps 20:8   6965
witnesses are *r* up against me .... Ps 27:12   6965
For strangers are *r* up against me .... Ps 54:3   6965
O God, the proud are *r* against me .... Ps 86:14   6965
glory of the LORD is *r* upon thee .... Is 60:1   2224
Violence is *r* up into a rod of .... Eze 7:11   6965
for the waters were *r*, waters to .... Eze 47:5   1342
my people is *r* up as an enemy .... Mic 2:8   6965
born of women there hath not *r* a .... Mt 11:11   1453
he is *r* from the dead .... Mt 14:2   1453
of man be *r* again from the dead .... Mt 17:9   450
But after I am *r* again, I will go .... Mt 26:32   1453
the people, He is *r* from the dead .... Mt 27:64   1453
for he is *r*, as he said .... Mt 28:6   1453
that he is *r* from the dead .... Mt 28:7   1453
the Baptist was *r* from the dead .... Mk 6:14   1453
he is *r* from the dead .... Mk 6:16   1453
Son of man were *r* from the dead .... Mk 9:9   450
But after that I am *r*, I will go .... Mk 14:28   1453
he is *r* .... Mk 16:6   1453
Now when Jesus was *r* early the .... Mk 16:9   450
which had seen him after he was *r* .... Mk 16:14   1453
a great prophet is *r* up among us .... Lk 7:16   1453
that John was *r* from the dead .... Lk 9:7   1453
of the old prophets was *r* again .... Lk 9:8   450
of the old prophets is *r* again .... Lk 9:19   450
the master of the house is *r* up .... Lk 13:25   1453
He is not here, but is *r* .... Lk 24:6   1453
Saying, The Lord is *r* indeed .... Lk 24:34   1453
therefore he was *r* from the dead .... Jn 2:22   1453
after that he was *r* from the dead .... Jn 21:14   1453
and *r* again from the dead .... Acts 17:3   450
died, yea rather, that is *r* again .... Rom 8:34   1453
of the dead, then is Christ not *r* 1Cor 15:13   1453
And if Christ be not *r*, then is 1Cor 15:14   1453
But now is Christ *r* from the dead 1Cor 15:20   1453
wherein also ye are *r* with him .... Col 2:12   4891
If ye then be *r* with Christ .... Col 3:1   4891
no sooner *r* with a burning heat .... Jas 1:11   393

RISEST

liest down, and when thou *r* up .... Deut 6:7   6965
liest down, and when thou *r* up .... Deut 11:19   6965

RISETH

for as when a man *r* against his .... Deut 22:26   6965
man before the LORD, that *r* up .... Josh 6:26   6965
of the morning, when the sun *r* 2Sa 23:4   2224
commandeth the sun, and it *r* not .... Job 9:7   2224
So man lieth down, and *r* not .... Job 14:12   6965
he *r* up, and no man is sure of .... Job 24:22   6965
he that *r* up against me as the .... Job 27:7   6965
then shall I do when God *r* up .... Job 31:14   6965
seven times, and *r* up again .... Prov 24:16   6965
She *r* also while it is yet night, ... Prov 31:15   6965
shalt not know from whence it *r* .... Is 47:11   7837
Egypt *r* up like a flood, and his .... Jer 46:8   5927
the daughter *r* up against her .... Mic 7:6   6965
He *r* from supper, and laid aside .... Jn 13:4   1453

RISING

have in the skin of his flesh a *r* .... Lev 13:2   7613
if the *r* be white in the skin, and .... Lev 13:10   7613
there be quick raw flesh in the *r* .... Lev 13:10   7613
of the boil there be a white *r* .... Lev 13:19   7613
it is a *r* of the burning, and the .... Lev 13:28   7613
if the *r* of the sore be white .... Lev 13:43   7613

R

And for a r, and for a scab, and for	Lev 14:56	7613
on the east side toward the r of	Num 2:3	4217
Jordan toward the r of the sun	Josh 12:1	4217
r up betimes, and sending	2Chr 36:15	7925
r of the morning till the stars	Neh 4:21	5927
my leanness r up in me beareth	Job 16:8	6965
r betimes for a prey	Job 24:5	7836
The murderer r with the light	Job 24:14	7925
called the earth from the r of	Ps 50:1	4217
From the r of the sun unto the	Ps 113:3	4217
r early in the morning, it shall	Prov 27:14	7925
against whom there is no r up	Prov 30:31	510
from the r of the sun shall he	Is 41:25	4217
may know from the r of the sun	Is 45:6	4217
his glory from the r of the sun	Is 59:19	4217
kings to the brightness of thy r	Is 60:3	2225
r up early and speaking, but ye	Jer 7:13	7925
daily r up early and sending them	Jer 7:25	7925
r early and protesting, saying,	Jer 11:7	7925
unto you, r early and speaking	Jer 25:3	7925
prophets, r early and sending them	Jer 25:4	7925
both r up early, and sending them,	Jer 26:5	7925
r up early and sending them	Jer 29:19	7925
r up early and teaching them, yet	Jer 32:33	7925
unto you, r early and speaking	Jer 35:14	7925
r up early and sending them,	Jer 35:15	7925
r early and sending them, saying,	Jer 44:4	7925
their sitting down, and their r up	Lam 3:63	7012
For from the r of the sun even	Mal 1:11	4217
r up a great while before day, he	Mk 1:35	450
the r from the dead should mean	Mk 9:10	305
the sepulchre at the r of the sun	Mk 16:2	393
r again of many in Israel	Lk 2:34	386

RISSAH (ris'-sah) *An Israelite encampment in the wilderness.*

from Libnah, and pitched at R	Num 33:21	7446
And they journeyed from R, and	Num 33:22	7446

RITES

according to all the r of it	Num 9:3	2708

RITHMAH (rith'-mah) *An Israelite encampment in the wilderness.*

from Hazeroth, and pitched in R	Num 33:18	7575
And they departed from R, and	Num 33:19	7575

RIVER

a r went out of Eden to water the	Gen 2:10	5104
the name of the second r is Gihon	Gen 2:13	5104
name of the third r is Hiddekel	Gen 2:14	5104
the fourth r is Euphrates	Gen 2:14	5104
from the r of Egypt unto the	Gen 15:18	5104
the great r, the r Euphrates	Gen 15:18	5104
he rose up, and passed over the r	Gen 31:21	5104
by the r reigned in his stead	Gen 36:37	5104
and, behold, he stood by the r	Gen 41:1	2975
of the r seven well favoured kine	Gen 41:2	2975
came up after them out of the r	Gen 41:3	2975
kine upon the brink of the r	Gen 41:3	2975
I stood upon the bank of the r	Gen 41:17	2975
came up out of the r seven kine	Gen 41:18	2975
is born ye shall cast into the r	Ex 1:22	2975
down to wash herself at the r	Ex 2:5	2975
shalt take of the water of the r	Ex 4:9	2975
which thou takest out of the r	Ex 4:9	2975
the waters which are in the r	Ex 7:17	2975
fish that is in the r shall die	Ex 7:18	2975
and the r shall stink	Ex 7:18	2975
to drink of the water of the r	Ex 7:18	2975
the waters that were in the r	Ex 7:20	2975
in the r were turned to blood	Ex 7:20	2975
the fish that was in the r died	Ex 7:21	2975
the r stank, and the Egyptians	Ex 7:21	2975
not drink of the water of the r	Ex 7:21	2975
about the r for water to drink	Ex 7:24	2975
not drink of the water of the r	Ex 7:24	2975
that the LORD had smitten the r	Ex 7:25	2975
the r shall bring forth frogs	Ex 8:3	2975
they may remain in the r only	Ex 8:9	2975
they shall remain in the r only	Ex 8:11	2975
rod, wherewith thou smotest the r	Ex 17:5	2975
and from the desert unto the r	Ex 23:31	5104
which is by the r of the land of	Num 22:5	5104
from Azmon unto the r of Egypt	Num 34:5	5158
and unto Lebanon, unto the great r	Deut 1:7	5104
the great, the r Euphrates	Deut 1:7	5104
journey, and pass over the r Arnon	Deut 2:24	5158
is by the brink of the r of Arnon	Deut 2:36	5158
and from the city that is by the r	Deut 2:36	5158
unto any place of the r Jabbok	Deut 2:37	5158
from the r of Arnon unto mount	Deut 3:8	5158
Aroer, which is by the r Arnon	Deut 3:12	5158

unto the r Arnon half t...		
the border even unto th valley	Deut 3:16	
is by the bank of the r Jabbok	Deut 3:16	5158
wilderness and Lebanon,	Deut 4:48	5158
the r Euphrates, even unt the r	Deut 11:24	5158
Lebanon even unto the gr	Deut 11:24	5158
the r Euphrates, all the lan	Deut 11:24	5104
from the r Arnon unto mou	Josh 1:4	5104
is upon the bank of the r Ar	Josh 1:4	5104
and from the middle of the r	Josh 12:2	5104
Gilead, even unto the r Jabbo	Josh 12:2	5158
is upon the bank of the r Arno	Josh 12:2	5158
that is in the midst of the r	Josh 12:2	5158
is on the bank of the r Arnon	Josh 13:9	5158
that is in the midst of the r	Josh 13:9	5158
and went out unto the r of Egypt	Josh 13:16	5158
is on the south side of the r	Josh 13:16	5158
her villages, unto the r of Egypt	Josh 15:4	5158
Tappuah westward unto the r Kan	:4	5158
r Kanah, southward of the r	:7	5158
was on the north side of the r	:7	5158
reached to the r that is before		5158
draw unto thee to the r Kishon		5158
the Gentiles unto the r of Kishon		5158
The r of Kishon swept them away,		158
that ancient r, the r Kishon		
his border at the r Euphrates		
Syrians that were beyond the r		
and we will draw it into the r		2...
in the midst of the r of Gad		2...
from the r unto the land of the		1K
all the region on this side the r		1K
all the kings on this side the r		1Kin
in of Hamath unto the r of Egypt		1Kin
shall scatter them beyond the r		1Kin
Aroer, which is by the r Arnon	2Kin	
and in Habor by the r of Gozan	2Kin 1	
and in Habor by the r of Gozan	2Kin 18	
of Assyria to the r Euphrates	2Kin 23	
the r of Egypt unto the	2Kin 24	
by the r reigned in his stead	1Chr 1:48	
wilderness from the r Euphrates	1Chr 5:9	
Habor, and Hara, and to the r Gozan	1Chr 5:26	
his dominion by the r Euphrates	1Chr 18:3	
Syrians that were beyond the r	1Chr 19:16	
in of Hamath unto the r of Egypt	2Chr 7:8	
the r even unto the land of the	2Chr 9:26	
rest that are on this side the r	Ezr 4:10	
the men on this side the r	Ezr 4:11	5
no portion on this side the r	Ezr 4:16	51
and unto the rest beyond the r	Ezr 4:17	51
over all countries beyond the r	Ezr 4:20	51
governor on this side the r	Ezr 5:3	5103
governor on this side the r	Ezr 5:6	5103
which were on this side the r	Ezr 5:6	5103
Tatnai, governor beyond the r	Ezr 6:6	5103
which are beyond the r, be ye	Ezr 6:6	5103
even of the tribute beyond the r	Ezr 6:8	5103
governor on this side the r	Ezr 6:13	5103
treasurers which are beyond the r	Ezr 7:21	5103
the people that are beyond the r	Ezr 7:25	5103
to the r than runneth to Ahava	Ezr 8:15	5104
at the r of Ahava, that we might	Ezr 8:21	5104
Then we departed from the r of	Ezr 8:31	5104
the governors on this side the r	Ezr 8:36	5104
me to the governors beyond the r	Neh 2:7	5104
to the governors beyond the r	Neh 2:9	5104
the governor on this side the r	Neh 3:7	5104
Behold, he drinketh up a r	Job 40:23	5104
drink of the r of thy pleasures	Ps 36:8	5158
There is a r, the streams whereof	Ps 46:4	5104
enricheth it with the r of God	Ps 65:9	5104
from the r unto the ends of the	Ps 72:8	5104
sea, and her branches unto the r	Ps 80:11	5104
ran in the dry places like a r	Ps 105:41	5104
namely, by them beyond the r	Is 7:20	5104
up upon them the waters of the r	Is 8:7	5104
he shake his hand over the r	Is 11:15	5104
the r shall be wasted and dried up	Is 19:5	5104
of Sihor, the harvest of the r	Is 23:3	2975
Pass through thy land as a r	Is 23:10	2975
of the r unto the stream of Egypt	Is 27:12	5104
then had thy peace been as a r	Is 48:18	5104
will extend peace to her like a r	Is 66:12	5104
to drink the waters of the r	Jer 2:18	5104
spreadeth out her roots by the r	Jer 17:8	3105
which was by the r Euphrates in	Jer 46:2	5104
the north by the r Euphrates	Jer 46:6	5104
north country by the r Euphrates	Jer 46:10	5104
let tears run down like a r day	Lam 2:18	5158
the captives by the r of Chebar	Eze 1:1	5104

RIVER'S

le r Chebar	Eze 1:3	5104
of the Chaldeans Chebir	Eze 3:15	5104
that dwelt by the r Chebar	Eze 3:23	5104
which I saw by r Chebar	Eze 10:15	5104
I saw by r of Chebar	Eze 10:20	5104
that I saw by r of Chebar	Eze 10:22	5104
God of Israeland I have made	Eze 29:3	2975
which I say have made it	Eze 29:9	2975
My r is my the r Chebar	Eze 43:3	5104
The r is ould not pass	Eze 47:5	5158
vision be passed over	Eze 47:6	5158
it was brink of the r	Eze 47:6	5158
it he r were very	Eze 47:7	5158
a r r the r cometh	Eze 47:9	5158
to e bank thereof,	Eze 47:12	5158
a r to the great sea	Eze 47:19	5158
i the great sea	Eze 48:28	5158
vas by the r of Ulai	Dan 8:2	180
efore the r a ram	Dan 8:3	180
anding before the r	Dan 8:6	180
side of the great r	Dan 10:4	5104
of the bank of the r	Dan 12:5	2975
e of the bank of the r	Dan 12:5	2975
he waters of the r	Dan 12:6	2975
the waters of the r	Dan 12:7	2975
of the wilderness	Amos 6:14	5158
fortress even to the r	Mic 7:12	5104
r even to the ends of	Zec 9:10	5104
s of the r shall dry up	Zec 10:11	2975
n the r of Jordan	Mk 1:5	4215
out of the city by a r side	Acts 16:13	4215
und in the great r Euphrates	Rev 9:14	4215
vial upon the great r Euphrates	Rev 16:12	4215
me a pure r of water of life	Rev 22:1	4215
of it, and on either side of the r	Rev 22:2	4215

RIVER'S

it in the flags by the r brink	Ex 2:3	2975
walked along by the r side	Ex 2:5	2975
by the r brink against he come	Ex 7:15	2975
forth, as gardens by the r side	Num 24:6	5104

RIVERS

upon their streams, upon their r	Ex 7:19	2975
rod over the streams, over the r	Ex 8:5	2975
waters, in the seas, and in the r	Lev 11:9	5158
scales in the seas, and in the r	Lev 11:10	5158
to Jotbath, a land of r of waters	Deut 10:7	5158
r of Damascus, better than all	2Kin 5:12	5104
up all the r of besieged places	2Kin 19:24	2975
He shall not see the r, the	Job 20:17	6390
He cutteth out r among the rocks	Job 28:10	2975
the rock poured me out r of oil	Job 29:6	6388
a tree planted by the r of water	Ps 1:3	6388
thou driedst up mighty r	Ps 74:15	5104
caused waters to run down like r	Ps 78:16	5104
And had turned their r into blood	Ps 78:44	2975
sea, and his right hand in the r	Ps 89:25	5104
He turneth r into a wilderness,	Ps 107:33	5104
R of waters run down mine eyes,	Ps 119:136	6388
By the r of Babylon, there we sat	Ps 137:1	5104
r of waters in the streets	Prov 5:16	6388
of the LORD, as the r of water	Prov 21:1	6388
All the r run into the sea	Eccl 1:7	5158
the place from whence the r come	Eccl 1:7	5158
eyes of doves by the r of waters	Song 5:12	650
uttermost part of the r of Egypt	Is 7:18	2975
which is beyond the r of Ethiopia	Is 18:1	5104
whose land the r have spoiled	Is 18:2	5104
whose land the r have spoiled	Is 18:7	5104
And they shall turn the r far away	Is 19:6	5104
and upon every high hill, r	Is 30:25	6388
as r of water in a dry ground,	Is 32:2	6388
be unto us a place of broad r	Is 33:21	5103
all the r of the besieged places	Is 37:25	2975
I will open r in high places, and	Is 41:18	5103
and I will make the r islands	Is 42:15	5103
and through the r, they shall not	Is 43:2	5103
wilderness, and r in the desert	Is 43:19	5103
r in the desert, to give drink to	Is 43:20	5103
Be dry, and I will dry up thy r	Is 44:27	5103
the thigh, pass over the r	Is 47:2	5103
I make the r a wilderness	Is 50:2	5103
the r of waters in a straight way	Jer 31:9	5158
whose waters are moved as the r	Jer 46:7	5104
his waters are moved like the r	Jer 46:8	5104
Mine eye runneth down with r of	Lam 3:48	6388
and to the hills, to the r	Eze 6:3	650
that lieth in the midst of his r	Eze 29:3	2975
of thy r to stick unto thy scales	Eze 29:4	2975
thee up out of the midst of thy r	Eze 29:4	2975
all the fish of thy r shall stick	Eze 29:4	2975

thee and all the fish of thy r	Eze 29:5	2975
am against thee, and against thy r	Eze 29:10	2975
And I will make the r dry, and sell	Eze 30:12	2975
set him up on high with her r	Eze 31:4	5104
sent out her little r unto all	Eze 31:4	8585
broken by all the r of the land	Eze 31:12	650
and thou camest forth with thy r	Eze 32:2	5104
thy feet, and fouledst their r	Eze 32:2	5104
the r shall be full of thee	Eze 32:6	650
cause their r to run like oil,	Eze 32:14	5104
the mountains of Israel by the r	Eze 34:13	650
in thy valleys, and in all thy r	Eze 35:8	650
and to the hills, to the r	Eze 36:4	650
and to the hills, to the r	Eze 36:6	650
whithersoever the r shall come	Eze 47:9	5158
for the r of waters are dried up,	Joel 1:20	650
all the r of Judah shall flow	Joel 3:18	650
or with ten thousands of r of oil	Mic 6:7	5158
it dry, and drieth up all the r	Nah 1:4	5104
gates of the r shall be opened	Nah 2:6	5104
No, that was situate among the r	Nah 3:8	2975
the LORD displeased against the r	Hab 3:8	5104
was thine anger against the r	Hab 3:8	5104
didst cleave the earth with r	Hab 3:9	5104
From beyond the r of Ethiopia my	Zeph 3:10	5104
shall flow r of living water	Jn 7:38	4215
fell upon the third part of the r	Rev 8:10	4215
poured out his vial upon the r	Rev 16:4	4215

RIZIA See REZIA.

RIZPAH (riz'-pah) A concubine of Saul.

had a concubine, whose name was R	2Sa 3:7	7532
sons of R the daughter of Aiah	2Sa 21:8	7532
R the daughter of Aiah took	2Sa 21:10	7532
David what R the daughter of Aiah	2Sa 21:11	7532

ROAD

Whither have ye made a r to day	1Sa 27:10	6584

ROAR

Let the sea r, and the fulness	1Chr 16:32	7481
Though the waters thereof r	Ps 46:3	1993
Thine enemies r in the midst of	Ps 74:4	7580
let the sea r, and the fulness	Ps 96:11	7580
Let the sea r, and the fulness	Ps 98:7	7481
The young lions r after their	Ps 104:21	7580
they shall r like young lions	Is 5:29	7580
yea, they shall r, and lay hold of	Is 5:29	5098
in that day they shall r against	Is 5:30	5098
he shall cry, yea, r	Is 42:13	6873
We r all like bears, and mourn	Is 59:11	1993
though they r, yet can they not	Jer 5:22	1993
The LORD shall r from on high	Jer 25:30	7580
he shall mightily r upon his	Jer 25:30	7580
the sea when the waves thereof r	Jer 31:35	1993
their voice shall r like the sea	Jer 50:42	1993
They shall r together like lions	Jer 51:38	7580
her waves do r like great waters	Jer 51:55	1993
he shall r like a lion	Hos 11:10	7580
when he shall r, then the	Hos 11:10	7580
The LORD also shall r out of Zion	Joel 3:16	7580
said, The LORD will r from Zion	Amos 1:2	7580
Will a lion r in the forest, when	Amos 3:4	7580

ROARED

a young lion r against him	Judg 14:5	7580
I have r by reason of the	Ps 38:8	7580
divided the sea, whose waves r	Is 51:15	1993
The young lions r upon him	Jer 2:15	7580
The lion hath r, who will not	Amos 3:8	7580

ROARETH

After it a voice r	Job 37:4	7580
their voice r like the sea	Jer 6:23	1993
a loud voice, as when a lion r	Rev 10:3	3455

ROARING

The r of the lion, and the voice	Job 4:10	7581
me, and from the words of my r	Ps 22:1	7581
mouths, as a ravening and a r lion	Ps 22:13	7580
old through my r all the day long	Ps 32:3	7581
wrath is as the r of a lion	Prov 19:12	5099
of a king is as the r of a lion	Prov 20:2	5099
As a r lion, and a ranging bear	Prov 28:15	5098
Their r shall be like a lion,	Is 5:29	7581
them like the r of the sea	Is 5:30	5100
and the young lion r on his prey	Is 31:4	1897
thereof, by the noise of his r	Eze 19:7	7581
like a r lion ravening the prey	Eze 22:25	7580
princes within her are r lions	Zeph 3:3	
a voice of the r of young lions	Zec 11:3	7581
the sea and the waves r	Lk 21:25	2278
adversary the devil, as a r lion	1Pet 5:8	5612

R

ROARINGS

my *r* are poured out like the	Job 3:24	7581

ROAST

r with fire, and unleavened bread	Ex 12:8	6748
all with water, but *r* with fire	Ex 12:9	6748
And thou shalt *r* and eat it in the	Deut 16:7	1310
Give flesh to *r* for the priest	1Sa 2:15	6740
he roasteth *r*, and is satisfied	Is 44:16	6748

ROASTED

they *r* the passover with fire	2Chr 35:13	1310
I have *r* flesh, and eaten it	Is 44:19	6740
the king of Babylon *r* in the fire	Jer 29:22	7033

ROASTETH

The slothful man *r* not that which	Prov 12:27	2760
he *r* roast, and is satisfied	Is 44:16	740

ROB

thy neighbour, neither *r* him	Lev 19:13	1497
which shall *r* you of your	Lev 26:22	7921
they *r* the threshingfloors	1Sa 23:1	8154
R not the poor, because he is	Prov 22:22	1497
that they may *r* the fatherless	Is 10:2	962
us, and the lot of them that *r* us	Is 17:14	962
r those that robbed them, saith	Eze 39:10	962
Will a man *r* God	Mal 3:8	6906

ROBBED

they *r* all that came along that	Judg 9:25	1497
as a bear *r* of her whelps in the	2Sa 17:8	7909
The bands of the wicked have *r* me	Ps 119:61	5749
Let a bear *r* of her whelps meet a	Prov 17:12	7909
have *r* their treasures, and I have	Is 10:13	8154
But this is a people *r* and spoiled	Is 42:22	962
and they shall be *r*	Jer 50:37	962
pledge, give again that he had *r*	Eze 33:15	5100
them, and rob those that *r* them	Eze 39:10	962
Yet ye have *r* me	Mal 3:8	6906
ye say, Wherein have we *r* thee	Mal 3:8	962
for ye have *r* me, even this whole	Mal 3:9	6906
I *r* other churches, taking wages	2Cor 11:8	4813

ROBBER

the *r* swalloweth up their	Job 5:5	6782
the *r* shall prevail against him	Job 18:9	6782
If he beget a son that is a *r*	Eze 18:10	6530
way, the same is a thief and a *r*	Jn 10:1	3027
Now Barabbas was a *r*	Jn 18:40	3027

ROBBERS

The tabernacles of *r* prosper	Job 12:6	7703
for a spoil, and Israel to the *r*	Is 42:24	962
become a den of *r* in your eyes	Jer 7:11	6530
for the *r* shall enter into it, and	Eze 7:22	6530
also the *r* of thy people shall	Dan 11:14	6530
as troops of *r* wait for a man, so	Hos 6:9	7703
the troop of *r* spoileth without	Hos 7:1	
if *r* by night, (how art thou cut	Obad 5	
came before me are thieves and *r*	Jn 10:8	3027
which are neither *r* of churches	Acts 19:37	2417
perils of waters, in perils of *r*	2Cor 11:26	3027

ROBBERY

and become not vain in *r*	Ps 62:10	1498
The *r* of the wicked shall destroy	Prov 21:7	7701
I hate *r* for burnt offering	Is 61:8	1498
used oppression, and exercised *r*	Eze 22:29	1498
up violence and *r* in their palaces	Amos 3:10	7701
it is all full of lies and *r*	Nah 3:1	6503
thought it not *r* to be equal with	Phil 2:6	725

ROBBETH

Whoso *r* his father or his mother,	Prov 28:24	1497

ROBE

breastplate, and an ephod, and a *r*	Ex 28:4	4598
thou shalt make the *r* of the	Ex 28:31	4598
upon the hem of the *r* round about	Ex 28:34	4598
the *r* of the ephod, and the ephod,	Ex 29:5	4598
he made the *r* of the ephod of	Ex 39:22	4598
was an hole in the midst of the *r*	Ex 39:23	4598
of the *r* pomegranates of blue	Ex 39:24	4598
upon the hem of the *r*, round	Ex 39:25	4598
the hem of the *r* to minister in	Ex 39:26	4598
girdle, and clothed him with the *r*	Lev 8:7	4598
of the *r* that was upon him	1Sa 18:4	4598
off the skirt of Saul's *r* privily	1Sa 24:4	4598
see the skirt of thy *r* in my hand	1Sa 24:11	4598
that I cut off the skirt of thy *r*	1Sa 24:11	4598
clothed with a *r* of fine linen	1Chr 15:27	4598
my judgment was as a *r* and a	Job 29:14	4598
And I will clothe him with thy *r*	Is 22:21	3301
me with the *r* of righteousness	Is 61:10	4598
throne, and he laid his *r* from him	Jonah 3:6	155

ye pull off the *r* with the		
him, and put on him a scarlet *r*	Mt 2:8	
him, they took the *r* off from him	Mt 27:28	145
servants, Bring forth the best *r*	Lk 7:31	5511
and arrayed him in a gorgeous *r*	Lk 7:31	5511
and they put on him a purple *r*	Jn 19:2	4749
crown of thorns, and the purple *r*	Jn 19:5	2066

ROBES

for with such *r* were the king's	2Sa 13:18	2440
his throne, having put on their *r*	1Kin 22:10	2440
but put thou on thy *r*	1Kin 22:30	
on his throne, clothed in their *r*	2Chr 18:9	
but put thou on thy *r*	2Chr 18:29	
thrones, and lay away their *r*	Eze 26:16	
which desire to walk in long *r*	Lk 20:46	
white *r* were given unto every one	Rev 6:11	
the Lamb, clothed with white *r*	Rev 7:9	
which are arrayed in white *r*	Rev 7:13	
and have washed their *r*, and made	Rev 7:14	

ROBOAM (ro-bo'-am) See REHOBOAM. *Same as Rehoboam; an ancestor of Jesus.*

And Solomon begat *R*	Mt 1:7	4497
and *R* begat Abia	Mt 1:7	44

ROCK

thee there upon the *r* in Horeb	Ex 17:6	6697
and thou shalt smite the *r*	Ex 17:6	6697
me, and thou shalt stand upon a *r*	Ex 33:21	6697
will put thee in a clift of the *r*	Ex 33:22	6697
ye unto the *r* before their eyes	Num 20:8	5553
forth to them water out of the *r*	Num 20:8	5553
together before the *r*, and he said	Num 20:10	5553
we fetch you water out of this *r*	Num 20:10	5553
with his rod he smote the *r* twice	Num 20:11	5553
and thou puttest thy nest in a *r*	Num 24:21	5553
forth water out of the *r* of flint	Deut 8:15	6697
He is the *R*, his work is perfect	Deut 32:4	6697
him to suck honey out of the *r*	Deut 32:13	5553
and oil out of the flinty *r*	Deut 32:13	6697
esteemed the *R* of his salvation	Deut 32:15	6697
Of the *R* that begat thee thou art	Deut 32:18	6697
except their *R* had sold them, and	Deut 32:30	6697
For their *r* is not as our *R*,	Deut 32:31	6697
their *r* in whom they trusted,	Deut 32:37	6697
going up to Akrabbim, from the *r*	Judg 1:36	5553
cakes, and lay them upon this *r*	Judg 6:20	5553
there rose up fire out of the *r*	Judg 6:21	6697
thy God upon the top of this *r*	Judg 6:26	4581
and they slew Oreb upon the *r* Oreb	Judg 7:25	6697
offered it upon a *r* unto the LORD	Judg 13:19	6697
and dwelt in the top of the *r* Etam	Judg 15:8	5553
went to the top of the *r* Etam	Judg 15:11	5553
and brought him up from the *r*	Judg 15:13	5553
wilderness unto the *r* of Rimmon	Judg 20:45	5553
the wilderness unto the *r* Rimmon	Judg 20:47	5553
abode in the *r* Rimmon four months	Judg 20:47	5553
that were in the *r* Rimmon	Judg 21:13	5553
is there any *r* like our God	1Sa 2:2	6697
was a sharp *r* on the one side	1Sa 14:4	5553
a sharp *r* on the other side	1Sa 14:4	5553
wherefore he came down into a *r*	1Sa 23:25	5553
and spread it for her upon the *r*	2Sa 21:10	6697
And he said, The LORD is my *r*	2Sa 22:2	5553
The God of my *r*	2Sa 22:3	6697
and who is a *r*, save our God	2Sa 22:32	6697
and blessed be my *r*	2Sa 22:47	6697
the God of the *r* of my salvation	2Sa 22:47	6697
the *R* of Israel spake to me, He	2Sa 23:3	6697
went down to the *r* to David	1Chr 11:15	6697
them unto the top of the *r*	2Chr 25:12	5553
them down from the top of the *r*	2Chr 25:12	5553
out of the *r* for their thirst	Neh 9:15	5553
the *r* is removed out of his place	Job 14:18	6697
shall the *r* be removed out of his	Job 18:4	6697
pen and lead in the *r* for ever	Job 19:24	6697
embrace the *r* for want of a	Job 24:8	6697
putteth forth his hand upon the *r*	Job 28:9	2496
the *r* poured me out rivers of oil	Job 29:6	6697
wild goats of the *r* bring forth	Job 39:1	5553
She dwelleth and abideth on the *r*	Job 39:28	5553
upon the crag of the *r*	Job 39:28	5553
The LORD is my *r*, and my fortress,	Ps 18:2	5553
or who is a *r* save our God	Ps 18:31	6697
and blessed be my *r*	Ps 18:46	6697
he shall set me up upon a *r*	Ps 27:5	6697
Unto thee will I cry, O LORD my *r*	Ps 28:1	6697
be thou my strong *r*, for an house	Ps 31:2	6697
For thou art my *r* and my fortress	Ps 31:3	5553
clay, and set my feet upon a *r*	Ps 40:2	5553
I will say unto God my *r*, Why	Ps 42:9	5553

ROCKS

...ter	Ps 61:2	6697
lead me to the r the...		
...lvation	Ps 62:2	6697
He only is my r a my		
...lvation	Ps 62:6	6697
He only is my r	Ps 62:7	6697
...r my r	Ps 71:3	5553
He only is my str t of the r	Ps 78:16	5553
the r of my c that the	Ps 78:20	6697
was their r	Ps 78:35	6697
to save me, str should I	Ps 81:16	6697
brought my salvation	Ps 89:26	6697
Behold, hay salvation	Ps 92:15	6697
remem f my refuge	Ps 94:22	6697
with Salvation	Ps 95:1	6697
my (the waters	Ps 105:41	6697
he into a	Ps 114:8	6697
...t upon a r	Prov 30:19	6697
...s of the r	Song 2:14	5553
...d hide thee in	Is 2:10	6697
...o both the	Is 8:14	6697
...r of Oreb	Is 10:26	6697
...f thy strength	Is 17:10	6697
...r himself in a r	Is 22:16	5553
...weary land	Is 32:2	5553
...nts of the r sing	Is 42:11	5553
...he r for them	Is 48:21	6697
...also, and the	Is 48:21	6697
...r whence ye are	Is 51:1	6697
...ces harder than a r	Jer 5:3	5553
...e in a hole of the r	Jer 13:4	
...rom the r of the field	Jer 18:14	6697
...e plain, saith the LORD	Jer 21:13	6697
...t breaketh the r in pieces	Jer 23:29	5553
...he cities, and dwell in	Jer 48:28	5553
dwellest in the clefts of the r	Jer 49:16	5553
she set it upon the top of a r	Eze 24:7	5553
set her blood upon the top of a r	Eze 24:8	5553
and make her like the top of a r	Eze 26:4	5553
make thee like the top of a r	Eze 26:14	5558
Shall horses run upon the r	Amos 6:12	5558
dwellest in the clefts of the r	Obad 3	5553
which built his house upon a r	Mt 7:24	4073
for it was founded upon a r	Mt 7:25	4073
upon this r I will build my	Mt 16:18	4073
which he had hewn out in the r	Mt 27:60	4073
which was hewn out of a r	Mk 15:46	4073
and laid the foundation on a r	Lk 6:48	4073
for it was founded upon a r	Lk 6:48	4073
And some fell upon a r	Lk 8:6	4073
They on the r are they, which,	Lk 8:13	4073
a stumblingstone and r of offence	Rom 9:33	4073
spiritual R that followed them	1Cor 10:4	4073
and that R was Christ	1Cor 10:4	4073
a r of offence, even to them	1Pet 2:8	4073

ROCKS

from the top of the r I see him	Num 23:9	6697
in caves, and in thickets, and in r	1Sa 13:6	5553
his men upon the r of the wild	1Sa 24:2	6697
in pieces the r before the LORD	1Kin 19:11	5553
He cutteth out rivers among the r	Job 28:10	6697
caves of the earth, and in the r	Job 30:6	3710
He clave the r in the wilderness,	Ps 78:15	6697
and the r for the conies	Ps 104:18	5553
make they their houses in the r	Prov 30:26	5553
shall go into the holes of the r	Is 2:19	6697
To go into the clefts of the r	Is 2:21	6697
and into the tops of the ragged r	Is 2:21	5553
valleys, and in the holes of the r	Is 7:19	5553
shall be the munitions of r	Is 33:16	5553
valleys under the clifts of the r	Is 57:5	5553
thickets, and climb up upon the r	Jer 4:29	3710
and out of the holes of the r	Jer 16:16	5553
and roll thee down from the r	Jer 51:25	5553
the r are thrown down by him	Nah 1:6	6697
earth did quake, and the r rent	Mt 27:51	4073
lest we should have fallen upon r	Acts 27:29	5138,5117
in the r of the mountains	Rev 6:15	4073
And said to the mountains and r	Rev 6:16	4073

ROD

And he said, A r	Ex 4:2	4294
it, and it became a r in his hand	Ex 4:4	4294
shalt take this r in thine hand	Ex 4:17	4294
Moses took the r of God in his	Ex 4:20	4294
shalt say unto Aaron, Take thy r	Ex 7:9	4294
cast down his r before Pharaoh	Ex 7:10	4294
they cast down every man his r	Ex 7:12	4294
but Aaron's r swallowed up their	Ex 7:12	4294
the r which was turned to a	Ex 7:15	4294
I will smite with the r that is	Ex 7:17	4294
Moses, Say unto Aaron, Take thy r	Ex 7:19	4294
and he lifted up the r, and smote	Ex 7:20	4294

hand with thy r over the streams	Ex 8:5	4294
Say unto Aaron, Stretch out thy r	Ex 8:16	4294
stretched out his hand with his r	Ex 8:17	4294
forth his r toward heaven	Ex 9:23	4294
his r over the land of Egypt	Ex 10:13	4294
But lift thou up thy r, and	Ex 14:16	4294
and thy r, wherewith thou smotest	Ex 17:5	4294
with the r of God in mine hand	Ex 17:9	4294
servant, or his maid, with a r	Ex 21:20	7626
of whatsoever passeth under the r	Lev 27:32	7626
take of every one of them a r	Num 17:2	4294
thou every man's name upon his r	Num 17:2	4294
Aaron's name upon the r of Levi	Num 17:3	4294
for one r shall be for the head	Num 17:3	4294
come to pass, that the man's r	Num 17:5	4294
their princes gave him a r apiece	Num 17:6	4294
the r of Aaron was among their	Num 17:6	4294
the r of Aaron for the house of	Num 17:8	4294
looked, and took every man his r	Num 17:9	4294
Bring Aaron's r again before the	Num 17:10	4294
Take the r, and gather thou the	Num 20:8	4294
Moses took the r from before the	Num 20:9	4294
with his r he smote the rock	Num 20:11	4294
end of the r that was in his hand	1Sa 14:27	4294
of the r that was in mine hand	1Sa 14:43	4294
chasten him with the r of men	2Sa 7:14	7626
Let him take his r away from me	Job 9:34	7626
neither is the r of God upon them	Job 21:9	7626
shalt break them with a r of iron	Ps 2:9	7626
thy r and thy staff they comfort	Ps 23:4	7626
the r of thine inheritance, which	Ps 74:2	7626
their transgression with the r	Ps 89:32	7626
The LORD shall send the r of thy	Ps 110:2	4294
For the r of the wicked shall not	Ps 125:3	7626
but a r is for the back of him	Prov 10:13	7626
that spareth his r hateth his son	Prov 13:24	7626
of the foolish is a r of pride	Prov 14:3	2415
the r of his anger shall fail	Prov 22:8	7626
but the r of correction shall	Prov 22:15	7626
if thou beatest him with the r	Prov 23:13	7626
Thou shalt beat him with the r	Prov 23:14	7626
ass, and a r for the fool's back	Prov 26:3	7626
The r and reproof give wisdom	Prov 29:15	7626
the r of his oppressor, as in the	Is 9:4	7626
the r of mine anger, and the staff	Is 10:5	7626
as if the r should shake itself	Is 10:15	7626
he shall smite thee with a r	Is 10:24	7626
as his r was upon the sea, so	Is 10:26	4294
a r out of the stem of Jesse	Is 11:1	2415
the earth with the r of his mouth	Is 11:4	7626
because the r of him that smote	Is 14:29	7626
a staff, and the cummin with a r	Is 28:27	7626
beaten down, which smote with a r	Is 30:31	7626
I see a r of an almond tree	Jer 1:11	4731
and Israel is the r of his	Jer 10:16	7626
staff broken, and the beautiful r	Jer 48:17	4731
and Israel is the r of his	Jer 51:19	7626
affliction by the r of his wrath	Lam 3:1	7626
the r hath blossomed, pride hath	Eze 7:10	4294
risen up into a r of wickedness	Eze 7:11	4294
gone out of a r of her branches	Eze 19:14	4294
strong r to be a sceptre to rule	Eze 19:14	4294
cause you to pass under the r	Eze 20:37	7626
it contemneth the r of my son	Eze 21:10	7626
if the sword contemn even the r	Eze 21:13	7626
of Israel with a r upon the cheek	Mic 5:1	7626
hear ye the r, and who hath	Mic 6:9	4294
Feed thy people with thy r	Mic 7:14	7626
shall I come unto you with a r	1Cor 4:21	4464
Aaron's r that budded, and the	Heb 9:4	4464
shall rule them with a r of iron	Rev 2:27	4464
was given me a reed like unto a r	Rev 11:1	4464
rule all nations with a r of iron	Rev 12:5	4464
shall rule them with a r of iron	Rev 19:15	4464

RODANIM See DODANIM.

RODE

they r upon the camels, and	Gen 24:61	7392
sons that r on thirty ass colts	Judg 10:4	7392
that r on threescore and ten ass	Judg 12:14	7392
as she r on the ass, that she	1Sa 25:20	7392
r upon an ass, with five damsels	1Sa 25:42	7392
which r upon camels, and fled	1Sa 30:17	7392
Absalom r upon a mule, and the	2Sa 18:9	7392
he r upon a cherub, and did fly	2Sa 22:11	7392
and he r thereon,	1Kin 13:13	7392
And Ahab r, and went to Jezreel	1Kin 18:45	7392
So Jehu r in a chariot, and went	2Kin 9:16	7392
thou r together after Ahab his	2Kin 9:25	7392
me, save the beast that I r upon	Neh 2:12	7392

R

So the posts that *r* upon mules .... Est 8:14   7392
he *r* upon a cherub, and did fly .... Ps 18:10   7392

RODS

Jacob took him *r* of green poplar, ... Gen 30:37   4731
white appear which was in the *r* .... Gen 30:37   4731
he set the *r* which he had pilled .... Gen 30:38   4731
the flocks conceived before the *r* .... Gen 30:39   4731
that Jacob laid the *r* before the .... Gen 30:41   4731
they might conceive among the *r* .... Gen 30:41   4731
Aaron's rod swallowed up their *r* .... Ex 7:12   4294
house of their fathers twelve *r* .... Num 17:2   4294
fathers' houses, even twelve *r* .... Num 17:6   4294
rod of Aaron was among their *r* .... Num 17:6   4294
Moses laid up the *r* before the .... Num 17:7   4294
Moses brought out all the *r* from .... Num 17:9   4294
she had strong *r* for the sceptres .... Eze 19:11   4294
her strong *r* were broken and .... Eze 19:12   4294
Thrice was I beaten with *r* 2Cor 11:25   4463

ROE

was as light of foot as a wild *r* 2Sa 2:18   6643
as the loving hind and pleasant *r* .... Prov 5:19   3280
Deliver thyself as a *r* from the .... Prov 6:5   6643
is like a *r* or a young hart .... Song 2:9   6643
be thou like a *r* or a young hart .... Song 2:17   6643
be thou like to a *r* or to a young .... Song 8:14   6643
And it shall be as the chased *r* .... Is 13:14   6643

ROEBUCK

may eat thereof, as of the *r* .... Deut 12:15   6643
Even as the *r* and the hart is .... Deut 12:22   6643
The hart, and the, *r*, and the fallow .... Deut 14:5   6643
shall eat it alike, as the *r* .... Deut 15:22   6643

ROEBUCKS

hundred sheep, beside harts, and *r* 1Kin 4:23   6643

ROES

swift as the *r* upon the mountains 1Chr 12:8   6643
daughters of Jerusalem, by the *r* .... Song 2:7   6643
daughters of Jerusalem, by the *r* .... Song 3:5   6643
like two young *r* that are twins .... Song 4:5   6646
like two young *r* that are twins .... Song 7:3   6646

ROGELIM (ro'-ghel-im) *A city in Gilead.*

and Barzillai the Gileadite of *R* 2Sa 17:27   7274
the Gileadite came down from *R* 2Sa 19:31   7274

ROHGAH (ro'-gah) *A son of Shamer.*

Ahi, and *R*, Jehubbah, and Aram 1Chr 7:34   7303

ROLL

till they *r* the stone from the .... Gen 29:8   1556
R great stones upon the mouth of .... Josh 10:18   1556
r a great stone unto me this day 1Sa 14:33   1556
in the province of the Medes, a *r* .... Ezr 6:2   4040
said unto me, Take thee a great *r* .... Is 8:1   1549
Take thee a *r* of a book, and write .... Jer 36:2   4039
unto him, upon a *r* of a book .... Jer 36:4   4039
go thou, and read in the *r* .... Jer 36:6   4039
Take in thine hand the *r* wherein .... Jer 36:14   4039
of Neriah took the *r* in his hand .... Jer 36:14   4039
but they laid up the *r* in the .... Jer 36:20   4039
king sent Jehudi to fetch the *r* .... Jer 36:21   4039
until all the *r* was consumed in .... Jer 36:23   4039
king that he would not burn the *r* .... Jer 36:25   4039
that the king had burned the *r* .... Jer 36:27   4039
Take thee again another *r* .... Jer 36:28   4039
words that were in the first *r* .... Jer 36:28   4039
Thou hast burned this *r*, saying, ... Jer 36:29   4039
Then took Jeremiah another *r* .... Jer 36:32   4039
r thee down from the rocks, and .... Jer 51:25   1556
a *r* of a book was therein .... Eze 2:9   4040
eat this *r*, and go speak unto the .... Eze 3:1   4040
and he caused me to eat that *r* .... Eze 3:2   4040
with this *r* that I give thee .... Eze 3:3   4040
of Aphrah *r* thyself in the dust .... Mic 1:10   6428
and looked, and behold a flying *r* .... Zec 5:1   4040
And I answered, I see a flying *r* .... Zec 5:2   4040
Who shall *r* us away the stone .... Mk 16:3   617

ROLLED

they *r* the stone from the well's .... Gen 29:3   1556
r the stone from the well's mouth .... Gen 29:10   1556
This day have I *r* away the .... Josh 5:9   1556
they *r* themselves upon me .... Job 30:14   1556
noise, and garments *r* in blood .... Is 9:5   1556
shall be *r* together as a scroll .... Is 34:4   1556
he *r* a great stone to the door of .... Mt 27:60   4351
r back the stone from the door, ... Mt 28:2   617
r a stone unto the door of the .... Mk 15:46   4351
saw that the stone *r* away .... Mk 16:4   617
they found the stone *r* away from .... Lk 24:2   617
as a scroll when it is *r* together .... Rev 6:14   1507

ROLLER

to put a *r* to bind it, to make it ......

ROLLETH

and he that *r* a stone, it will 30:21

ROLLING

like a *r* thing before the 2848

ROLLS

was made in the house of the *r* .... E 1556

ROMAMTI-EZER (romam'-ti-e'-zur) *A sanctu[...] servant.*

Hanani, Eliathah, Giddalti, and *R* 1Chr
The four and twentieth to *R* 1Chr

ROMAN (ro'-mun) *See* ROMANS. *A citizen of Rom[...]*

you to scourge a man that is a *R* .... Acts 22:[..]
for this man is a *R* .... Acts 22:2[.]
unto him, Tell me, art thou a *R* .... Acts 22:27
after he knew that he was a *R* .... Acts 22:29
having understood that he was a *R* .... Acts 23:27

ROMANS (ro'-muns)

the *R* shall come and take away .... Jn 11:48   45[..]
neither to observe, being *R* .... Acts 16:21   451[.]
us openly uncondemned, being *R* .... Acts 16:37   4514
when they heard that they were *R* .... Acts 16:38   4514
the *R* to deliver any man to die .... Acts 25:16   4514
Jerusalem into the hands of the *R* .... Acts 28:17   4514
Written to the *R* from Corinth .... Rom *s*   4514

ROME (rome) *See* ROMAN. *Administrative center of the Roman Empire.*

about Cyrene, and strangers of *R* .... Acts 2:10   4516
all Jews to depart from *R* .... Acts 18:2   4516
been there, I must also see *R* .... Acts 19:21   4516
must thou bear witness also at *R* .... Acts 23:11   4516
and so we went toward *R* .... Acts 28:14   4516
And when we came to *R*, the .... Acts 28:16   4516
To all that be in *R*, beloved of .... Rom 1:7   4516
gospel to you that are at *R* also .... Rom 1:15   4516
Unto the Galatians written from *R* .... Gal *s*   4516
Written from *R* unto the Ephesians .... Eph *s*   4516
from *R* by Epaphroditus .... Phil *s*   4516
Written from *R* to the Colossians .... Col *s*   4516
But, when he was in *R*, he sought 2Ti 1:17   4516
the Ephesians, was written from *R* .... 2Ti *s*   4516
Written from *R* to Philemon .... Philem *s*   4516

ROMPHA *See* REMPHAN.

ROOF

they under the shadow of my *r* .... Gen 19:8   6982
shalt make a battlement for thy *r* .... Deut 22:8   1406
them up to the *r* of the house .... Josh 2:6   1406
she had laid in order upon the *r* .... Josh 2:6   1406
she came up unto them upon the *r* .... Josh 2:8   1406
there were upon the *r* about three .... Judg 16:27   1406
walked upon the *r* of the king's 2Sa 11:2   1406
from the *r* he saw a woman washing 2Sa 11:2   1406
the *r* over the gate unto the wall 2Sa 18:24   1406
every one upon the *r* of his house .... Neh 8:16   1406
cleaved to the *r* of their mouth .... Job 29:10   2441
cleave to the *r* of my mouth .... Ps 137:6   2441
the *r* of thy mouth like the best .... Song 7:9   2441
to the *r* of his mouth for thirst .... Lam 4:4   2441
cleave to the *r* of thy mouth .... Eze 3:26   2441
r of one little chamber to the .... Eze 40:13   1406
chamber to the *r* of another .... Eze 40:13   1406
thou shouldest come under my *r* .... Mt 8:8   4721
they uncovered the *r* where he was .... Mk 2:4   4721
thou shouldest enter under my *r* .... Lk 7:6   4721

ROOFS

of all the houses upon whose *r* .... Jer 19:13   1406
upon whose *r* they have offered .... Jer 32:29   1406

ROOM

is there *r* in thy father's house .... Gen 24:23   4725
enough, and *r* to lodge in .... Gen 24:25   4725
the house, and *r* for the camels .... Gen 24:31   4725
now the LORD hath made *r* for us .... Gen 26:22   7337
me continually in the *r* of Joab 2Sa 19:13   8478
Jehoiada in his *r* over the host 1Kin 2:35   8478
the king put in the *r* of Abiathar 1Kin 2:35   8478
him king in the *r* of his father 1Kin 5:1   8478
will set upon thy throne in thy *r* 1Kin 5:5   8478
up in the *r* of David my father 1Kin 8:20   8478
anoint to be prophet in thy *r* 1Kin 19:16   8478
killed him, and reigned in his *r* 2Kin 15:25   8478
in the *r* of Josiah his father 2Kin 23:34   8478
up in the *r* of David my father 2Chr 6:10   8478
made him king in the *r* of his 2Chr 26:1   8478
hast set my feet in a large *r* .... Ps 31:8   4800

In right margin: **ROOM**

ROOMS

Thou preparedst b................Ps 80:9
im ....Prov 18:16   7337
it ....Mal 3:10
A man's gift make nem ....Mt 2:22   473
not be r of his ....Mk 2:2   5362
there was n hed ....Mk 14:15   508
in the r of his in ....Lk 2:7   5117
you a la to ....Lk 12:17
was no west r ....Lk 14:8   4411
becashed r ....Lk 14:9   5117
west r ....Lk 14:10   5117
there is r ......Lk 14:22   5117
.............Lk 22:12
st pper r ....Acts 1:13   5253
Felix' r ....Acts 24:27   1240
hen at 1Cor 14:16   5117

ark, and ....Gen 6:14   7064
n their r 1Kin 20:24   8478
ir r 1Chr 4:41   8478
r at feasts ....Mt 23:6   4411
easts ....Mk 12:39   4411
hief r ....Lk 14:7   4411
..................Lk 20:46   4411

eareth gall ....Deut 29:18   8328
against Amalek ....Judg 5:14   8328
rael out of this 1Kin 14:15   5428
ain take r downward 2Kin 19:30   8328
en the foolish taking r ....Job 5:3   8327
r thereof wax old in ....Job 14:8   8328
g the r of the matter is ....Job 19:28   8328
y r was spread out by the waters ......Job 29:19   8328
would r out all mine increase ....Job 31:12   8327
r thee out of the land of the ....Ps 52:5   8327
and didst cause it to take deep r ....Ps 80:9   8327
but the r of the righteous shall..............Prov 12:3   8328
but their r of the righteous ....Prov 12:12   8328
so their r shall be as rottenness ....Is 5:24   8328
day there shall be a r of Jesse ....Is 11:10   8327
for out of the serpent's r shall ....Is 14:29   8328
and I will kill thy r with famine ....Is 14:30   8328
them that come of Jacob to take r ....Is 27:6   8327
Judah shall again take r downward ......Is 37:31   8328
shall not take r in the earth ....Is 40:24   8327
as a r out of a dry ground ....Is 53:2   8328
to r out, and to pull down, and to ....Jer 1:10   5428
them, yea, they have taken r ....Jer 12:2   8327
for his r was by great waters.................Eze 31:7   8328
their r is dried up, they shall............Hos 9:16   8328
leave them neither r nor branch ....Mal 4:1   8328
is laid unto the r of the trees ....Mt 3:10   4491
and because they had no r, they ....Mt 13:6   4491
Yet hath he not r in himself ....Mt 13:21   4491
ye r up also the wheat with them ....Mt 13:29   1610
and because it had no r, it ....Mk 4:6   4491
have no r in themselves, and so ....Mk 4:17   4491
is laid unto the r of the trees ....Lk 3:9   4491
and these have no r, which for a ....Lk 8:13   4491
tree, Be thou plucked up by the r ....Lk 17:6   1610
if the r be holy, so are the ....Rom 11:16   4491
and with them partakest of the r...........Rom 11:17   4491
not the r, but the r thee ....Rom 11:18   4491
There shall be a r of Jesse ....Rom 15:12   4491
of money is the r of all evil 1Ti 6:10   4491
lest any r of bitterness ....Heb 12:15   4491
the R of David, hath prevailed to...........Rev 5:5   4491
I am the r and the offspring of ....Rev 22:16   4491

ROOTED

the LORD r them out of their land ....Deut 29:28   5428
shall be r out of his tabernacle ....Job 18:14   5423
yea, let my offspring be r out ....Job 31:8   8327
shall be r out of it ....Prov 2:22   5255
noonday, and Ekron shall be r up ....Zeph 2:4   6131
hath not planted, shall be r up.............Mt 15:13   1610
that ye, being r and grounded in ....Eph 3:17   4492
R and built up in him, and ....Col 2:7   4492

ROOTS

the r out of my land which I have 2Chr 7:20   5428
His r are wrapped about the heap, ...Job 8:17   8328
His r shall be dried up beneath, ...Job 18:16   8328
the mountains by the r......................Job 28:9   8328
and juniper r for their meat ....Job 30:4   8328
a Branch shall grow out of his r ....Is 11:1   8328
spreadeth out her r by the river............Jer 17:8   8328
the r thereof were under him.................Eze 17:6   8328
vine did bend her r toward him ....Eze 17:7   8328
he not pull up the r thereof ....Eze 17:9   8328
to pluck it up by the r thereof............Eze 17:9   8328

the stump of his r in the earth ....Dan 4:15   8330
of the r thereof in the earth ....Dan 4:23   8330
to leave the stump of the tree r.............Dan 4:26   8330
first horns plucked up by the r ....Dan 7:8   6132
her r shall one stand up in his ....Dan 11:7   8328
and cast forth his r as Lebanon ....Hos 14:5   8328
from above, and his r from beneath ....Amos 2:9   8328
the fig tree dried up from the r ....Mk 11:20   4491
twice dead, plucked up by the r ....Jude 12   1610

ROPE

and sin as it were with a cart r ....Is 5:18   5688

ROPES

new r that never were occupied ....Judg 16:11   5688
Delilah therefore took new r...................Judg 16:12   5688
all Israel bring r to that city 2Sa 17:13   2256
r upon our heads, and go out to 1Kin 20:31   2256
put r on their heads, and came to 1Kin 20:32   2256
cut off the r of the boat...........................Acts 27:32   4979

ROSE

that Cain r up against Abel his ....Gen 4:8   6965
the men r up from thence, and ....Gen 18:16   6965
Lot seeing them r up to meet them ....Gen 19:1   6965
Therefore Abimelech r early in ....Gen 20:8   7925
Abraham r up early in the morning ....Gen 21:14   7925
then Abimelech r up, and Phichol..........Gen 21:32   6965
Abraham r up early in the morning ....Gen 22:3   7925
r up, and went unto the place of ....Gen 22:3   6965
unto his young men, and they r up ....Gen 22:19   6965
they r up in the morning, and he ....Gen 24:54   6965
drink, and r up, and went his way ....Gen 25:34   6965
they r up betimes in the morning, ...Gen 26:31   7925
Jacob r up early in the morning, ...Gen 28:18   7925
Then Jacob r up, and set his sons ....Gen 31:17   6965
and he r up, and passed over the ....Gen 31:21   6965
early in the morning Laban r up ....Gen 31:55   7925
he r up that night, and took his ....Gen 32:22   6965
over Penuel the sun r upon him ....Gen 32:31   2224
his daughters r up to comfort him ....Gen 37:35   6965
r up, and went down to Egypt, and........Gen 43:15   6965
Jacob r up from Beer-sheba...................Gen 46:5   6965
neither r any from his place for ....Ex 10:23   6965
Pharaoh r up in the night, he, and..........Ex 12:30   6965
them that r up against thee ....Ex 15:7   6965
r up early in the morning, and ....Ex 24:4   7925
And Moses r up, and his minister..........Ex 24:13   6965
they r up early on the morrow, and ....Ex 32:6   7925
eat and to drink, and r up to play ....Ex 32:6   6965
that all the people r up ....Ex 33:8   6965
and all the people r up and ....Ex 33:10   6965
Moses r up early in the morning, ...Ex 34:4   7925
they r up early in the morning, ...Num 14:40   7925
they r up before Moses, with ....Num 16:2   6965
And Moses r up and went unto ....Num 16:25   6965
Balaam r up in the morning, and ....Num 22:13   6965
And the princes of Moab r up ....Num 22:14   6965
Balaam r up in the morning, and ....Num 22:21   6965
And Balaam r up, and went and ....Num 24:25   6965
saw it, he r up from among the ....Num 25:7   6965
and r up from Seir unto them ....Deut 33:2   2224
Joshua r early in the morning ....Josh 3:1   7925
r up upon an heap very far from ....Josh 3:16   6965
Joshua r early in the morning, and ....Josh 6:12   7925
that they r early about the ....Josh 6:15   7925
So Joshua r up early in the ....Josh 7:16   7925
Joshua r up early in the morning, ...Josh 8:10   7925
r up early, and the men of the ....Josh 8:14   7925
there r up fire out of the rock,................Judg 6:21   5927
for he r up early on the morrow, ...Judg 6:38   7925
r up early, and pitched beside the..........Judg 7:1   7925
And Abimelech r up, and all the ....Judg 9:34   6965
and Abimelech r up, and the people ....Judg 9:35   6965
he r up against them, and smote ....Judg 9:43   6965
morning, that he r up to depart ....Judg 19:5   6965
And when the man r up to depart ....Judg 19:7   6965
And when the man r up to depart ....Judg 19:9   6965
not tarry that night, but he r up ....Judg 19:10   6965
her lord r up in the morning, and ....Judg 19:27   6965
up upon an ass, and the man r up ....Judg 19:28   6965
And the men of Gibeah r against me .....Judg 20:5   6965
of Israel r up in the morning ....Judg 20:19   6965
of Israel r up out of their place ....Judg 20:33   6965
morrow, that the people r early..............Judg 21:4   7925
she r up before one could know ....Ruth 3:14   6965
So Hannah r up after they had 1Sa 1:9   6965
they r up in the morning early, ...1Sa 1:19   7925
when Samuel r early to meet Saul 1Sa 15:12   7925
So Samuel r up, and went to Ramah 1Sa 16:13   6965
David r up early in the morning, ...1Sa 17:20   7925
But Saul r up out of the cave, and 1Sa 24:7   6965

R

Then they *r* up, and went away that	1Sa 28:25	6965
his men *r* up early to depart in	1Sa 29:11	7925
Absalom *r* up early, and stood	2Sa 15:2	7925
all them that *r* up against thee	2Sa 18:31	6965
them that *r* up against me hast	2Sa 22:40	6965
above them that *r* up against me	2Sa 22:49	6965
r up, and went every man his way	1Kin 1:49	6965
the king *r* up to meet her, and	1Kin 2:19	6965
when I *r* in the morning to give	1Kin 3:21	6965
that Ahab *r* up to go down to the	1Kin 21:16	6965
they *r* up early in the morning,	2Kin 3:22	7925
of Israel, the Israelites *r* up	2Kin 3:24	6965
they *r* up in the twilight, to go	2Kin 7:5	6965
he *r* by night, and smote the	2Kin 8:21	6965
they *r* early in the morning, and	2Chr 20:20	7925
he *r* up by night, and smote the	2Chr 21:9	6965
the leprosy even *r* up in his	2Chr 26:19	2224
which were expressed by name *r* up	2Chr 28:15	6965
Then Hezekiah the king *r* early	2Chr 29:20	7925
Then *r* up the chief of the	Ezr 1:5	6965
Then *r* up Zerubbabel the son of	Ezr 5:2	6965
Then Ezra *r* up from before the	Ezr 10:6	6965
priest *r* up with his brethren the	Neh 3:1	6965
r up, and said unto the nobles, and	Neh 4:14	6965
r up early in the morning, and	Job 1:5	7925
me those that *r* up against me	Ps 18:39	6965
side, when men *r* up against us	Ps 124:2	6965
I am the *r* of Sharon, and the lily	Song 2:1	2261
I *r* up to open to my beloved	Song 5:5	6965
rejoice, and blossom as the *r*	Is 35:1	2261
Then *r* up certain of the elders	Jer 26:17	6965
of those that *r* up against me	Lam 3:62	6965
r up in haste, and spake, and said	Dan 3:24	6965
afterward I *r* up, and did the	Dan 8:27	6965
But Jonah *r* up to flee unto	Jonah 1:3	6965
when the morning *r* the next day	Jonah 1:5	5927
but they *r* early, and corrupted	Zeph 3:7	7925
he, casting away his garment, *r*	Mk 10:50	450
r up, and thrust him out of the	Lk 4:29	450
immediately he *r* up before them	Lk 5:25	450
left all, *r* up, and followed him	Lk 5:28	450
though one *r* from the dead	Lk 16:31	450
when he *r* up from prayer, and was	Lk 22:45	450
they *r* up the same hour, and	Lk 24:33	450
that she *r* up hastily and went out	Jn 11:31	450
Then the high priest *r* up	Acts 5:17	450
before these days *r* up Theudas	Acts 5:36	450
After this man *r* up Judas of	Acts 5:37	450
with him after he *r* from the dead	Acts 10:41	450
stood round about him, he *r* up	Acts 14:20	450
But there *r* up certain of the	Acts 15:5	1817
been much disputing, Peter *r* up	Acts 15:7	450
the multitude *r* up together	Acts 16:22	4911
he had thus spoken, the king *r* up	Acts 26:30	450
this end Christ both died, and *r*	Rom 14:9	450
to eat and drink, and *r* up to play	1Cor 10:7	450
that he *r* again the third day	1Cor 15:4	1453
preached that he *r* from the dead	1Cor 15:12	1453
which died for them, and *r* again	2Cor 5:15	1453
r again, even so them also which	1Th 4:14	450
her smoke *r* up for ever and ever	Rev 19:3	305

ROSH *(rosh) A son of Benjamin.*

Gera, and Naaman, Ehi, and *R*	Gen 46:21	7220

ROT

the LORD doth make thy thigh to *r*	Num 5:21	5307
belly to swell, and thy thigh to *r*	Num 5:22	5307
shall swell, and her thigh shall *r*	Num 5:27	5307
the name of the wicked shall *r*	Prov 10:7	7537
chooseth a tree that will not *r*	Is 40:20	7537

ROTTEN

as a *r* thing, consumeth, as a	Job 13:28	7538
iron as straw, and brass as *r* wood	Job 41:27	7538
old *r* rags, and let them down by	Jer 38:11	4418
r rags under thine armholes under	Jer 38:12	4418
The seed is *r* under their clods,	Joel 1:17	5685

ROTTENNESS

ashamed is as *r* in his bones	Prov 12:4	7538
but envy the *r* of the bones	Prov 14:30	7538
so their root shall be as *r*	Is 5:24	4716
and to the house of Judah as *r*	Hos 5:12	7538
r entered into my bones, and I	Hab 3:16	7538

ROUGH

down the heifer unto a *r* valley	Deut 21:4	386
he stayeth his *r* wind in the day	Is 27:8	7186
straight, and the *r* places plain	Is 40:4	7406
to come up as the *r* caterpillars	Jer 51:27	5569
the *r* goat is the king of Grecia	Dan 8:21	8163

they wear a *r* garment to deceiv		
the *r* ways shall be made smooth		

ROUGHLY

unto them, and spake *r* unto them		
lord of the land, spake *r* to us		
what if thy father answer thee *r*		
And the king answered the people *r*		
And the king answered them *r*		8181
but the rich answereth *r*		5138

ROUND

of Sodom, compassed the house *r*	Ge	
were in all the borders *r* about	Ge	
the cities that were *r* about them	Gen	
your sheaves stood *r* about	Gen	
which was *r* about every city,	Gen 4	
all the Egyptians digged *r* about	Ex 7:24	
the dew lay *r* about the host	Ex 16:13	
there lay a small *r* thing	Ex 16:14	
bounds unto the people *r* about	Ex 19:12	
upon it a crown of gold *r* about	Ex 25:11	
thereto a crown of gold *r* about	Ex 25:24	
border of an hand breadth *r* about	Ex 25:25	
to the border thereof *r* about	Ex 25:25	5
All the pillars *r* about the court	Ex 27:17	54
woven work *r* about the hole of it	Ex 28:32	543
scarlet, *r* about the hem thereof	Ex 28:33	5439
of gold between them *r* about	Ex 28:33	5439
upon the hem of the robe *r* about	Ex 28:34	5439
sprinkle it *r* about upon the	Ex 29:16	5439
the blood upon the altar *r* about	Ex 29:20	5439
and the sides thereof *r* about	Ex 30:3	5439
unto it a crown of gold *r* about	Ex 30:3	5439
a crown of gold to it *r* about	Ex 37:2	5439
thereunto a crown of gold *r* about	Ex 37:11	5439
border of an handbreadth *r* about	Ex 37:12	5439
for the border thereof *r* about	Ex 37:12	5439
it, and the sides thereof *r* about	Ex 37:26	5439
unto it a crown of gold *r* about	Ex 37:26	5439
All the hangings of the court *r*	Ex 38:16	5439
and of the court *r* about, were of	Ex 38:20	5439
the sockets of the court *r* about	Ex 38:31	5439
all the pins of the court *r* about	Ex 38:31	5439
with a band *r* about the hole,	Ex 39:23	5439
r about between the pomegranates	Ex 39:25	5439
r about the hem of the robe to	Ex 39:26	5439
shalt set up the court *r* about	Ex 40:8	5439
the court *r* about the tabernacle	Ex 40:33	5439
sprinkle the blood *r* about upon	Lev 1:5	5439
his blood *r* about upon the altar	Lev 1:11	5439
the blood upon the altar *r* about	Lev 3:2	5439
thereof *r* about upon the altar	Lev 3:8	5439
thereof upon the altar *r* about	Lev 3:13	5439
sprinkle *r* about upon the altar	Lev 7:2	5439
the altar *r* about with his finger	Lev 8:15	5439
the blood upon the altar *r* about	Lev 8:19	5439
the blood upon the altar *r* about	Lev 8:24	5439
which he sprinkled *r* about upon	Lev 9:12	5439
sprinkled upon the altar *r* about	Lev 9:18	5439
to be scraped within *r* about	Lev 14:41	5439
the horns of the altar *r* about	Lev 16:18	5439
Ye shall not *r* the corners of	Lev 19:27	5362
r about them shall be counted as	Lev 25:31	5439
the heathen that are *r* about you	Lev 25:44	5439
it, and shall encamp *r* about the	Num 1:50	5439
pitch *r* about the tabernacle of	Num 1:53	5439
and by the altar *r* about, and the	Num 3:26	5439
the pillars of the court *r* about	Num 3:37	5439
and by the altar *r* about, and their	Num 4:26	5439
the pillars of the court *r* about	Num 4:32	5439
set them *r* about the tabernacle	Num 11:24	5439
r about the camp, and as it were	Num 11:31	5439
for themselves *r* about the camp	Num 11:32	5439
all Israel that were *r* about them	Num 16:34	5439
lick up all that are *r* about us	Num 22:4	5439
the cities of the country *r* about	Num 32:33	5439
with the coasts thereof *r* about	Num 34:12	5439
for the cities *r* about	Num 35:2	5439
outward a thousand cubits *r* about	Num 35:4	5439
the people which are *r* about you	Deut 6:14	5439
from all your enemies *r* about	Deut 12:10	5439
the people which are *r* about you	Deut 13:7	5439
are *r* about him that is slain	Deut 21:2	5439
from all thine enemies *r* about	Deut 25:19	5439
war, and go about the city once	Josh 6:3	5362
hear of it, and shall environ us *r*	Josh 7:9	5921
Judah *r* about according to their	Josh 15:12	5439
by the coasts thereof *r* about	Josh 18:20	5439
that were *r* about these cities to	Josh 19:8	5439
the suburbs thereof *r* about it	Josh 21:11	5439
with their suburbs *r* about them	Josh 21:42	5439

the LORD gave them rest *r* about	Josh 21:44	5439
from all their enemies *r* about	Josh 23:1	5439
the people that were *r* about them	Judg 2:12	5439
hands of their enemies *r* about	Judg 2:14	5439
man in his place *r* about the camp	Judg 7:21	5439
Belial, beset the house *r* about	Judg 19:22	5437
beset the house *r* about upon me	Judg 20:5	5437
set liers in wait *r* about Gibeah	Judg 20:29	5439
inclosed the Benjamites *r* about	Judg 20:43	3803
the camp from the country *r* about	1Sa 14:21	5439
his men *r* about to take them	1Sa 23:26	
and the people pitched *r* about him	1Sa 26:5	5439
and the people lay *r* about him	1Sa 26:7	5439
land of the Philistines *r* about	1Sa 31:9	5439
David built *r* about from Millo and	2Sa 5:9	5439
rest *r* about from all his enemies	2Sa 7:1	5439
darkness pavilions *r* about him	2Sa 22:12	5439
and the wall of Jerusalem *r* about	1Kin 3:1	5439
peace on all sides *r* about him	1Kin 4:24	5439
fame was in all nations *r* about	1Kin 4:31	5439
house he built chambers *r* about	1Kin 6:5	5439
the walls of the house *r* about	1Kin 6:5	5439
and he made chambers *r* about	1Kin 6:5	5439
he made narrowed rests *r* about	1Kin 6:6	5439
all the walls of the house *r*	1Kin 6:29	4524
the great court *r* about was with	1Kin 7:12	5439
two rows *r* about upon the one	1Kin 7:18	5439
were two hundred in rows *r* about	1Kin 7:20	5439
it was *r* all about, and his height	1Kin 7:23	5696
cubits did compass it *r* about	1Kin 7:23	5439
under the brim of it *r* about	1Kin 7:24	5439
cubit, compassing the sea *r* about	1Kin 7:24	5439
but the mouth thereof was *r* after	1Kin 7:31	5696
their borders, foursquare, not *r*	1Kin 7:31	5696
a *r* compass of half a cubit high	1Kin 7:35	5696
every one, and additions *r* about	1Kin 7:36	5439
top of the throne was *r* behind	1Kin 10:19	5696
the water ran *r* about the altar	1Kin 18:35	5439
chariots of fire *r* about Elisha	2Kin 6:17	5439
ye shall compass the king *r* about	2Kin 11:8	5439
r about the king, from the right	2Kin 11:11	5439
heathen that were *r* about them	2Kin 17:15	5439
in the places *r* about Jerusalem	2Kin 23:5	4524
built forts against it *r* about	2Kin 25:1	5439
were against the city *r* about	2Kin 25:4	5439
the walls of Jerusalem *r* about	2Kin 25:10	5439
upon the chapiter *r* about	2Kin 25:17	5439
that were *r* about the same cities	1Chr 4:33	5439
and the suburbs thereof *r* about it	1Chr 6:55	5439
they lodged *r* about the house of	1Chr 9:27	5439
land of the Philistines *r* about	1Chr 10:9	5439
And he built the city *r* about	1Chr 11:8	5439
about, even from Millo *r* about	1Chr 11:8	5439
rest from all his enemies *r* about	1Chr 22:9	5439
and of all the chambers *r* about	1Chr 28:12	5439
r in compass, and five cubits the	2Chr 4:2	5696
cubits did compass it *r* about	2Chr 4:2	5439
which did compass it *r* about	2Chr 4:3	5439
cubit, compassing the sea *r* about	2Chr 4:3	5439
all the cities *r* about Gerar	2Chr 14:14	5439
the LORD gave them rest *r* about	2Chr 15:15	5439
the lands that were *r* about Judah	2Chr 17:10	5439
for his God gave him rest *r* about	2Chr 20:30	5439
shall compass the king *r* about	2Chr 23:7	5439
the temple, by the king *r* about	2Chr 23:10	5439
with their mattocks *r* about	2Chr 34:6	5439
plain country *r* about Jerusalem	Neh 12:28	5439
them villages *r* about Jerusalem	Neh 12:29	5439
and fashioned me together *r* about	Job 10:8	5439
His archers compass me *r* about	Job 16:13	5437
encamp *r* about my tabernacle	Job 19:12	5439
Therefore snares are *r* about thee	Job 22:10	5439
it is turned *r* about by his	Job 37:12	4524
his teeth are terrible *r* about	Job 41:14	5439
set themselves against me *r* about	Ps 3:6	5439
his pavilion *r* about him were	Ps 18:11	5439
bulls of Bashan have beset me *r*	Ps 22:12	3803
up above mine enemies *r* about me	Ps 27:6	5439
r about them that fear him	Ps 34:7	5439
to them that are *r* about us	Ps 44:13	5439
about Zion, and go *r* about her	Ps 48:12	5362
be very tempestuous *r* about him	Ps 50:3	5439
a dog, and go *r* about the city	Ps 59:6	5437
a dog, and go *r* about the city	Ps 59:14	5439
let all that be *r* about him bring	Ps 76:11	5439
r about their habitations	Ps 78:28	5439
shed like water *r* about Jerusalem	Ps 79:3	5439
to them that are *r* about us	Ps 79:4	5439
They came *r* about me daily like	Ps 88:17	5437
to thy faithfulness *r* about thee	Ps 89:8	5439
and darkness are *r* about him	Ps 97:2	5439
and burneth up his enemies *r* about	Ps 97:3	5439
mountains are *r* about Jerusalem	Ps 125:2	5439
so the LORD is *r* about his people	Ps 125:2	5439
olive plants *r* about thy table	Ps 128:3	5439
Thy navel is like a *r* goblet	Song 7:2	5469
their *r* tires like the moon,	Is 3:18	7720
For the cry is gone *r* about the	Is 15:8	5362
I will camp against thee *r* about	Is 29:3	1754
it hath set him on fire *r* about	Is 42:25	5439
Lift up thine eyes *r* about	Is 49:18	5439
Lift up thine eyes *r* about	Is 60:4	5439
all the walls thereof *r* about	Jer 1:15	5439
are they against her *r* about	Jer 4:17	5439
their tents against her *r* about	Jer 6:3	5439
the birds *r* about are against her	Jer 12:9	5439
devour all things *r* about it	Jer 21:14	5439
against all these nations *r* about	Jer 25:9	5439
for fear was *r* about, saith the	Jer 46:5	5439
sword shall devour *r* about thee	Jer 46:14	5439
in array against Babylon *r* about	Jer 50:14	5439
Shout against her *r* about	Jer 50:15	5439
the bow, camp against it *r* about	Jer 50:29	5439
it shall devour all *r* about him	Jer 50:32	5439
they shall be against her *r* about	Jer 51:2	5439
and built forts against it *r* about	Jer 52:4	5439
were by the city *r* about	Jer 52:7	5439
the walls of Jerusalem *r* about	Jer 52:14	5439
upon the chapiters *r* about	Jer 52:22	5439
network were an hundred *r* about	Jer 52:23	5439
adversaries should be *r* about him	Lam 1:17	5439
fire, which devoureth *r* about	Lam 2:3	5439
a solemn day my terrors *r* about	Lam 2:22	5439
full of eyes *r* about them four	Eze 1:18	5439
of fire *r* about within it	Eze 1:27	5439
and it had brightness *r* about	Eze 1:27	5439
of the brightness *r* about	Eze 1:28	5439
battering rams against it *r* about	Eze 4:2	5439
and countries that are *r* about her	Eze 5:5	5439
countries that are *r* about her	Eze 5:6	5439
the nations that are *r* about you	Eze 5:7	5439
the nations that are *r* about you	Eze 5:7	5439
fall by the sword *r* about thee	Eze 5:12	5439
the nations that are *r* about thee	Eze 5:14	5439
the nations that are *r* about thee	Eze 5:15	5439
your bones *r* about your altars	Eze 6:5	5439
their idols *r* about their altars	Eze 6:13	5439
pourtrayed upon the wall *r* about	Eze 8:10	5439
wheels, were full of eyes *r* about	Eze 10:12	5439
the heathen that are *r* about you	Eze 11:12	5439
gather them *r* about against thee	Eze 16:37	5439
and all that are *r* about her	Eze 16:57	5439
which despise thee *r* about	Eze 16:57	5439
and shield and helmet *r* about	Eze 23:24	5439
army were upon thy walls *r* about	Eze 27:11	5439
shields upon thy walls *r* about	Eze 27:11	5439
of all that are *r* about them	Eze 28:24	5439
that despise them *r* about them	Eze 28:26	5439
rivers running *r* about his plants	Eze 31:4	5439
her company is *r* about her grave	Eze 32:23	5439
her multitude *r* about her grave	Eze 32:24	5439
her graves are *r* about him	Eze 32:25	5439
her graves are *r* about him	Eze 32:26	5439
the places *r* about my hill a	Eze 34:26	5439
of the heathen that are *r* about	Eze 36:4	5439
Then the heathen that are left *r*	Eze 36:36	5439
caused me to pass by them *r* about	Eze 37:2	5439
the outside of the house *r* about	Eze 40:5	5439
of the court *r* about the gate	Eze 40:14	5439
posts within the gate *r* about	Eze 40:16	5439
and windows were *r* about inward	Eze 40:16	5439
made for the court *r* about	Eze 40:17	5439
and in the arches thereof *r* about	Eze 40:25	5439
and in the arches thereof *r* about	Eze 40:29	5439
the arches *r* about were five and	Eze 40:30	5439
and in the arches thereof *r* about	Eze 40:33	5439
and the windows to it *r* about	Eze 40:36	5439
an hand broad, fastened *r* about	Eze 40:43	5439
r about the house on every side	Eze 41:5	5439
for the side chambers *r* about	Eze 41:6	5439
still upward *r* about the house	Eze 41:7	5439
the height of the house *r* about	Eze 41:8	5439
r about the house on every side	Eze 41:10	5439
was left was five cubits *r* about	Eze 41:11	5439
was five cubits thick *r* about	Eze 41:12	5439
the galleries *r* about on their	Eze 41:16	5439
door, cieled with wood *r* about	Eze 41:16	5439
and by all the wall *r* about within	Eze 41:17	5439
through all the house *r* about	Eze 41:19	5439
the east, and measured it *r* about	Eze 42:15	5439
with the measuring reed *r* about	Eze 42:16	5439
with the measuring reed *r* about	Eze 42:17	5439

it had a wall r about, five	Eze 42:20	5439
the whole limit thereof r about	Eze 43:12	5439
thereof r about shall be a span	Eze 43:13	5439
and upon the border r about	Eze 43:20	5439
all the borders thereof r about	Eze 45:1	5439
in breadth, square r about	Eze 45:2	5439
fifty cubits r about for the	Eze 45:2	5439
a row of building r about in them	Eze 46:23	5439
r about them four, and it was made	Eze 46:23	5439
places under the rows r about	Eze 46:23	5439
It was r about eighteen thousand	Eze 48:35	5439
yourselves together r about	Joel 3:11	5439
to judge all the heathen r about	Joel 3:12	5439
shall be even r about the land	Amos 3:11	5439
the depth closed me r about	Jonah 2:5	5437
that had the waters r about it	Nah 3:8	5439
unto her a wall of fire r about	Zec 2:5	5439
and the cities thereof r about her	Zec 7:7	5439
unto all the people r about	Zec 12:2	5439
devour all the people r about	Zec 12:6	5439
heathen r about shall be gathered	Zec 14:14	5439
and all the region r about Jordan	Mt 3:5	4066
out into all that country r about	Mt 14:35	4066
a vineyard, and hedged it r about	Mt 21:33	
all the region r about Galilee	Mk 1:28	4066
when he had looked r about on	Mk 3:5	4017
he looked r about on them which	Mk 3:34	2943
he looked r about to see her that	Mk 5:32	4017
he went r about the villages,	Mk 6:6	2943
may go into the country r about	Mk 6:36	2943
through that whole region r about	Mk 6:55	4066
when they had looked r about	Mk 9:8	4017
And Jesus looked r about, and saith	Mk 10:23	4017
when he had looked r about upon	Mk 11:11	4017
on all that dwelt r about them	Lk 1:65	4039
of the Lord shone r about them	Lk 2:9	4034
through all the region r about	Lk 4:14	4066
place of the country r about	Lk 4:37	4066
looking r about upon them all, he	Lk 6:10	
throughout all the region r about	Lk 7:17	4066
r about besought him to depart	Lk 8:37	4066
into the towns and country r about	Lk 9:12	2943
about thee, and compass thee r	Lk 19:43	4033
Then came the Jews r about him	Jn 10:24	2944
the cities r about unto Jerusalem	Acts 5:16	4038
suddenly there shined r about him	Acts 9:3	4015
the region that lieth r about	Acts 14:6	4066
the disciples stood r about him	Acts 14:20	2944
heaven a great light r about me	Acts 22:6	4015
down from Jerusalem stood r about	Acts 25:7	4026
shining r about me and them which	Acts 26:13	4034
r about unto Illyricum, I have	Rom 15:19	2943
overlaid r about with gold	Heb 9:4	3840
was a rainbow r about the throne	Rev 4:3	2943
r about the throne were four and	Rev 4:4	2943
r about the throne, were four	Rev 4:6	2943
of many angels r about the throne	Rev 5:11	2943
angels stood r about the throne	Rev 7:11	2943

ROUSE

who shall r him up	Gen 49:9	6965

ROVERS

David against the band of the r	1Chr 12:21	

ROW

the first r shall be a sardius, a	Ex 28:17	2905
this shall be the first r	Ex 28:17	2905
the second r shall be an emerald,	Ex 28:18	2905
And the third r a ligure, an agate	Ex 28:19	2905
And the fourth r a beryl, and an	Ex 28:20	2905
the first r was a sardius, a	Ex 39:10	2905
this was the first r	Ex 39:10	2905
And the second r, an emerald, a	Ex 39:11	2905
And the third r, a ligure, an	Ex 39:12	2905
And the fourth r, a beryl, an onyx	Ex 39:13	2905
set them in two rows, six on a r	Lev 24:6	4635
put pure frankincense upon each r	Lev 24:7	4635
stone, and a r of cedar beams	1Kin 6:36	2905
five pillars, fifteen in a r	1Kin 7:3	2905
a r of cedar beams, both for the	1Kin 7:12	2905
stones, and a r of new timber	Ezr 6:4	5073
there was a r of building round	Eze 46:23	2905

ROWED

Nevertheless the men r hard to	Jonah 1:13	2864
So when they had r about five	Jn 6:19	1643

ROWERS

Thy r have brought thee into	Eze 27:26	7751

ROWING

And he saw them toiling in r	Mk 6:48	1643

ROWS

of stones, even four r of stones	Ex 28:17	2905
they set in it four r of stones	Ex 39:10	2905
And thou shalt set them in two r	Lev 24:6	4634
court with three r of hewed stone	1Kin 6:36	2905
upon four r of cedar pillars,	1Kin 7:2	2905
And there were windows in three r	1Kin 7:4	2905
was with three r of hewed stones	1Kin 7:12	2905
two r round about upon the one	1Kin 7:18	2905
were two hundred in r round about	1Kin 7:20	2905
the knops were cast in two r	1Kin 7:24	2905
even two r of pomegranates for	1Kin 7:42	2905
Two r of oxen were cast, when it	2Chr 4:3	2905
two r of pomegranates on each	2Chr 4:13	2905
With three r of great stones, and	Ezr 6:4	5073
are comely with r of jewels	Song 1:10	8447
places under the r round about	Eze 46:23	2918

ROYAL

fat, and he shall yield r dainties	Gen 49:20	4428
city, as one of the r cities	Josh 10:2	4467
dwell in the r city with thee	1Sa 27:5	4467
of Ammon, and took the r city	2Sa 12:26	4410
Solomon gave her of his r bounty	1Kin 10:13	4428
arose and destroyed all the seed r	2Kin 11:1	4467
son of Elishama, of the seed r	2Kin 25:25	4410
bestowed upon him such r majesty	1Chr 29:25	4438
the seed r of the house of Judah	2Chr 22:10	4467
r wine in abundance, according to	Est 1:7	4438
r house which belonged to king	Est 1:9	4438
before the king with the crown r	Est 1:11	4438
let there go a r commandment from	Est 1:19	4438
let the king give her r estate	Est 1:19	4438
his house r in the tenth month	Est 2:16	4438
so that he set the r crown upon	Est 2:17	4438
that Esther put on her r apparel	Est 5:1	4438
his r throne in her r house	Est 5:1	4438
Let the r apparel be brought	Est 6:8	4438
the crown r which is set upon his	Est 6:8	4438
of the king in r apparel of blue	Est 8:15	4438
a r diadem in the hand of thy God	Is 62:3	4410
son of Elishama, of the seed r	Jer 41:1	4410
spread his r pavilion over them	Jer 43:10	8237
together to establish a statute	Dan 6:7	4430
day Herod, arrayed in r apparel	Acts 12:21	937
If ye fulfil the r law according	Jas 2:8	937
a r priesthood, an holy nation, a	1Pet 2:9	934

RUBBING

and did eat, r them in their hands	Lk 6:1	5597

RUBBISH

heaps of the r which are burned	Neh 4:2	6083
is decayed, and there is much r	Neh 4:10	6083

RUBIES

the price of wisdom is above r	Job 28:18	6443
She is more precious than r	Prov 3:15	6443
For wisdom is better than r	Prov 8:11	6443
is gold, and a multitude of r	Prov 20:15	6443
for her price is far above r	Prov 31:10	6443
were more ruddy in body than r	Lam 4:7	6443

RUDDER

the sea, and loosed the r bands	Acts 27:40	4079

RUDDY

Now he was r, and withal of a	1Sa 16:12	132
for he was but a youth, and r	1Sa 17:42	132
My beloved is white and r, the	Song 5:10	132
they were more r in body than	Lam 4:7	119

RUDE

But though I be r in speech	2Cor 11:6	2399

RUDIMENTS

after the r of the world, and not	Col 2:8	4747
Christ from the r of the world	Col 2:20	4747

RUE

for ye tithe mint and r and all	Lk 11:42	4076

RUFUS (ru´-fus)
    1. Son of Simon the Cyrenian.

the father of Alexander and R	Mk 15:21	4504

    2. A Christian in Rome.

Salute R chosen in the Lord, and	Rom 16:13	4504

RUHAMAH (ru-ha´-mah) *A symbolic name of Israel.*

and to your sisters, R	Hos 2:1	7355

RUIN

But they were the r of him	2Chr 28:23	
brought his strong holds to r	Ps 89:40	4288
and who knoweth the r of them both	Prov 24:22	6365
and a flattering mouth worketh r	Prov 26:28	4072
let this r be under thy hand	Is 3:6	4384

and he brought it to r	Is 23:13	4654
of a defenced city a r	Is 25:2	4654
so iniquity shall not be your r	Eze 18:30	4383
of the seas in the day of thy r	Eze 27:27	4658
Upon his r shall all the fowls of	Eze 31:13	4658
the r of that house was great	Lk 6:49	*4485*

RUINED

For Jerusalem is r, and Judah is	Is 3:8	3782
r cities are become fenced, and	Eze 36:35	2040
I the LORD build the r places	Eze 36:36	2040

RUINOUS

waste fenced cities into r heaps	2Kin 19:25	5327
a city, and it shall be a r heap	Is 17:1	4654
defenced cities into r heaps	Is 37:26	5327

RUINS

faint, and their r be multiplied	Eze 21:15	4383
and I will raise up his r, and I	Amos 9:11	2034
I will build again the r thereof	Acts 15:16	2679

RULE

the greater light to r the day	Gen 1:16	4475
the lesser light to r the night	Gen 1:16	4475
to r over the day and over the	Gen 1:18	4910
husband, and he shall r over thee	Gen 3:16	4910
desire, and thou shalt r over him	Gen 4:7	4910
Thou shalt not r over him with	Lev 25:43	7287
ye shall not r one over another	Lev 25:46	7287
the other shall not r with rigour	Lev 25:53	7287
R thou over us, both thou, and thy	Judg 8:22	4910
unto them, I will not r over you	Judg 8:23	4910
neither shall my son r over you	Judg 8:23	4910
the LORD shall r over you	Judg 8:23	4910
which bare r over the people that	1Kin 9:23	7287
that had r over his chariots	1Kin 22:31	
that bare r over the people	2Chr 8:10	7287
servants bare r over the people	Neh 5:15	7980
should bear r in his own house	Est 1:22	8323
that the Jews had r over them	Est 9:1	7980
r thou in the midst of thine	Ps 110:2	7287
The sun to r by day	Ps 136:8	4475
The moon and stars to r by night	Ps 136:9	4475
By me princes r, and nobles, even	Prov 8:16	8323
hand of the diligent shall bear r	Prov 12:24	4910
A wise servant shall have r over	Prov 17:2	4910
a servant to have r over princes	Prov 19:10	4910
He that hath no r over his own	Prov 25:28	4623
but when the wicked beareth r	Prov 29:2	4910
yet shall he have r over all my	Eccl 2:19	7980
and babes shall r over them	Is 3:4	4910
oppressors, and women r over them	Is 3:12	4910
and they shall r over their	Is 14:2	7287
a fierce king shall r over them	Is 19:4	4910
that r this people which is in	Is 28:14	4910
and princes shall r in judgment	Is 32:1	8323
hand, and his arm shall r for him	Is 40:10	4910
him, and made him r over kings	Is 41:2	7287
carpenter stretcheth out his r	Is 44:13	4910
they that r over them make them	Is 52:5	4910
thou never barest r over them	Is 63:19	4910
the priests bear r by their means	Jer 5:31	7287
the sceptres of them that bare r	Eze 19:11	4910
strong rod to be a sceptre to r	Eze 19:14	4910
poured out, will I r over you	Eze 20:33	4427
shall no more r over the nations	Eze 29:15	7287
which shall bear r over all the	Dan 2:39	7981
have known that the heavens do r	Dan 4:26	7990
that shall r with great dominion,	Dan 11:3	4910
shall cause them to r over many	Dan 11:39	4910
the heathen should r over them	Joel 2:17	4910
and shall sit and r upon his throne	Zec 6:13	4910
that shall r my people Israel	Mt 2:6	*4165*
to r over the Gentiles exercise	Mk 10:42	*757*
when he shall have put down all r	1Cor 15:24	*746*
r which God hath distributed to	2Cor 10:13	*2583*
you according to our r abundantly	2Cor 10:15	*2583*
many as walk according to this r	Gal 6:16	*2583*
let us walk by the same r	Phil 3:16	*2583*
the peace of God r in your hearts	Col 3:15	*1018*
know not how to r his own house	1Ti 3:5	*4291*
Let the elders that r well be	1Ti 5:17	*4291*
them which have the r over you	Heb 13:7	*2233*
them that have the r over you	Heb 13:17	*2233*
all them that have the r over you	Heb 13:24	*2233*
he shall r them with a rod of	Rev 2:27	*4165*
who was to r all nations with a	Rev 12:5	*4165*
he shall r them with a rod of	Rev 19:15	*4165*

RULED

that r over all that he had, Put,	Gen 24:2	4910
thy word shall all my people be r	Gen 41:40	5401

r from Aroer, which is upon the	Josh 12:2	4910
in the days when the judges r	Ruth 1:1	8199
which r over the people that	1Kin 5:16	7287
that r throughout the house of	1Chr 26:6	4474
which have r over all countries	Ezr 4:20	7990
they that hated them r over them	Ps 106:41	4910
he that r the nations in anger,	Is 14:6	7287
Servants have r over us	Lam 5:8	4910
and with cruelty have ye r them	Eze 34:4	7287
high God r in the kingdom of men,	Dan 5:21	7990
to his dominion which he r	Dan 11:4	4910

RULER

he made him r over all the land	Gen 41:43	
he said to the r of his house	Gen 43:16	834,5921
a r throughout all the land of	Gen 45:8	4910
nor curse the r of thy people	Ex 22:28	5387
When a r hath sinned, and done	Lev 4:22	5387
a man, every one a r among them	Num 13:2	5387
when Zebul the r of the city	Judg 9:30	8269
have appointed thee r over Israel	1Sa 25:30	5057
to appoint me r over the people	2Sa 6:21	5057
to be r over my people, over	2Sa 7:8	5057
Jairite was a chief r about David	2Sa 20:26	
appointed him to be r over Israel	1Kin 1:35	5057
he made him r over all the charge	1Kin 11:28	6485
of Ahikam, the son of Shaphan, r	2Kin 25:22	6485
and of him came the chief r	1Chr 5:2	5057
the r of the house of God	1Chr 9:11	5057
was the r over them in time past	1Chr 9:20	5057
thou shalt be r over my people	1Chr 11:2	5057
be r over my people Israel	1Chr 17:7	5057
of Moses, was r of the treasures	1Chr 26:24	5057
his course was Mikloth also the r	1Chr 27:4	5057
the r of the Reubenites was	1Chr 27:16	5057
he hath chosen Judah to be the r	1Chr 28:4	5057
to be a r over my people Israel	2Chr 6:5	5057
fail thee a man to be r in Israel	2Chr 7:18	4910
to be r among his brethren	2Chr 11:22	5057
the r of the house of Judah, for	2Chr 19:11	5057
the scribe and Maaseiah the r	2Chr 26:11	7860
which Cononiah the Levite was r	2Chr 31:12	5057
Azariah the r of the house of God	2Chr 31:13	5057
the r of the half part of	Neh 3:9	8269
the r of the half part of	Neh 3:12	8269
the r of part of Beth-haccerem	Neh 3:14	8269
Colhozeh, the r of part of Mizpah	Neh 3:15	8269
the r of the half part of	Neh 3:16	8269
the r of the half part of Keilah,	Neh 3:17	8269
the r of the half part of Keilah	Neh 3:18	8269
the r of Mizpah, another piece	Neh 3:19	8269
Hananiah the r of the palace,	Neh 7:2	8269
was the r of the house of God	Neh 11:11	5057
is little Benjamin with their r	Ps 68:27	7287
even the r of the people, and let	Ps 105:20	4910
house, and r of all his substance	Ps 105:21	4910
having no guide, overseer, or r	Prov 6:7	4910
When thou sittest to eat with a r	Prov 23:1	4910
so is a wicked r over the poor	Prov 28:15	4910
If a r hearken to lies, all his	Prov 29:12	4910
of the r rise up against thee	Eccl 10:4	4910
error which proceedeth from the r	Eccl 10:5	7989
Thou hast clothing, be thou our r	Is 3:6	7101
make me not a r of the people	Is 3:7	7101
Send ye the lamb to the r of the	Is 16:1	4910
in the land, r against r	Jer 51:46	4910
there is no king, lord, nor r	Dan 2:10	7990
and hath made thee r over them all	Dan 2:38	7981
made him r over the whole	Dan 2:48	7981
be the third r in the kingdom	Dan 5:7	7981
be the third r in the kingdom	Dan 5:16	7981
be the third r in the kingdom	Dan 5:29	7990
unto me that is to be r in Israel	Mic 5:2	4910
things, that have no r over them	Hab 1:14	4910
behold, there came a certain r	Mt 9:18	*758*
hath made r over his household	Mt 24:45	*2525*
make him r over all his goods	Mt 24:47	*2525*
will make thee r over many things	Mt 25:21	*2525*
will make thee r over many things	Mt 25:23	*2525*
there came from the r of the	Mk 5:35	*752*
saith unto the r of the synagogue	Mk 5:36	*752*
house of the r of the synagogue	Mk 5:38	*752*
he was a r of the synagogue	Lk 8:41	*758*
the r of the synagogue's house	Lk 8:49	*752*
shall make r over his household	Lk 12:42	*2525*
make him r over all that he hath	Lk 12:44	*2525*
the r of the synagogue answered	Lk 13:14	*752*
And a certain r asked him, saying,	Lk 18:18	*758*
When the r of the feast had	Jn 2:9	*755*
named Nicodemus, a r of the Jews	Jn 3:1	*758*
away, saying, Who made thee a r	Acts 7:27	*758*

R

saying, Who made thee a *r* ....Acts 7:35   758
the same did God send to be a *r* ....Acts 7:35   758
the chief *r* of the synagogue, ...Acts 18:8   758
the chief *r* of the synagogue, and ....Acts 18:17   752
speak evil of the *r* of thy people ....Acts 23:5   758

RULER'S
Many seek the *r* favour ....Prov 29:26   4910
when Jesus came into the *r* house ....Mt 9:23   758

RULERS
then make them *r* over my cattle ....Gen 47:6   8269
all the *r* of the congregation ....Ex 16:22   5387
to be *r* of thousands ....Ex 18:21   8269
r of hundreds, *r* of fifties, ...Ex 18:21   8269
r of fifties, and *r* of tens ....Ex 18:21   8269
r of thousands ....Ex 18:25   8269
r of hundreds, *r* of fifties, ...Ex 18:25   8269
r of fifties, and *r* of tens ....Ex 18:25   8269
all the *r* of the congregation ....Ex 34:31   5387
the *r* brought onyx stones, and ....Ex 35:27   5387
and I will make them *r* over you ....Deut 1:13   7218
the Philistines are *r* over us ....Judg 15:11   4910
and David's sons were chief *r* 2Sa 8:18
r of his chariots, and his 1Kin 9:22   8269
unto the *r* of Jezreel, to the 2Kin 10:1   8269
fetched the *r* over hundreds, with 2Kin 11:4   8269
he took the *r* over hundreds, and 2Kin 11:19   8269
to the *r* of the people, Go, ...1Chr 21:2   8269
David made *r* over the Reubenites 1Chr 26:32   6485
All these were the *r* of the 1Chr 27:31   8269
with the *r* of the king's work, ...1Chr 29:6   8269
and gathered the *r* of the city 2Chr 29:20   8269
r of the house of God, gave unto 2Chr 35:8   5057
r hath been chief in this ....Ezr 9:2   5461
Let now our *r* of all the ....Ezr 10:14   8269
the *r* knew not whither I went, or ....Neh 2:16   5461
nor to the nobles, nor to the *r* ....Neh 2:16   5461
said unto the nobles, and to the *r* ....Neh 4:14   5461
the *r* were behind all the house ....Neh 4:16   8269
said unto the nobles, and to the *r* ....Neh 4:19   5461
and I rebuked the nobles, and the *r*......Neh 5:7   5461
hundred and fifty of the Jews and *r*......Neh 5:17   5461
together the nobles, and the *r* ....Neh 7:5   5461
the *r* of the people dwelt at ....Neh 11:1   8269
I, and the half of the *r* with me ....Neh 12:40   5461
Then contended I with the *r* ....Neh 13:11   5461
to the *r* of every people of every ....Est 3:12   8269
r of the provinces which are from ....Est 8:9   8269
all the *r* of the provinces, and ....Est 9:3   8269
the *r* take counsel together, ...Ps 2:2   7336
word of the LORD, ye *r* of Sodom ....Is 1:10   7101
wicked, and the sceptre of the *r* ....Is 14:5   4910
All thy *r* are fled together, they ....Is 22:3   7101
the prophets and your *r*, the seers ....Is 29:10   7218
abhorreth, to a servant of *r* ....Is 49:7   4910
to be *r* over the seed of Abraham ....Jer 33:26   4910
I break in pieces captains and *r* ....Jer 51:23   5461
thereof, and all the *r* thereof ....Jer 51:28   5461
wise men, her captains, and her *r* ....Jer 51:57   5461
clothed with blue, captains and *r* ....Eze 23:6   5461
r clothed most gorgeously, ...Eze 23:12   5461
young men, captains and *r*, great ....Eze 23:23   5461
all the *r* of the provinces, to ....Dan 3:2   7984
all the *r* of the provinces, were ....Dan 3:3   7984
her *r* with shame do love, Give ye ....Hos 4:18   4043
one of the *r* of the synagogue ....Mk 5:22   752
and ye shall be brought before *r* ......Mk 13:9   2232
kings and *r* for my name's sake ....Lk 21:12   2232
the chief priests and the *r* ....Lk 23:13   758
the *r* also with them derided him, ...Lk 23:35   758
our *r* delivered him to be ....Lk 24:20   758
Do the *r* know indeed that this is ....Jn 7:26   758
Have any of the *r* or of the ....Jn 7:48   758
chief *r* also many believed on him ....Jn 12:42   758
ye did it, as did also your *r* ....Acts 3:17   758
pass on the morrow, that their *r* ....Acts 4:5   758
Ye *r* of the people, and elders of ....Acts 4:8   758
the *r* were gathered together ....Acts 4:26   758
the prophets the *r* of the ....Acts 13:15   752
dwell at Jerusalem, and their *r* ....Acts 13:27   758
and also of the Jews with their *r* ....Acts 14:5   758
into the marketplace unto the *r* ....Acts 16:19   758
brethren unto the *r* of the city ....Acts 17:6   4178
the *r* of the city, when they ....Acts 17:8   4178
For *r* are not a terror to good ....Rom 13:3   758
against the *r* of the darkness of ....Eph 6:12   2888

RULEST
r not thou over all the kingdoms 2Chr 20:6   4910
Thou *r* the raging of the sea ....Ps 89:9   4910

RULETH
He that *r* over men must be just, ...2Sa 23:3   4910
let them know that God *r* in Jacob ....Ps 59:13   4910
He *r* by his power for ever ....Ps 66:7   4910
and his kingdom *r* over all ....Ps 103:19   4910
he that *r* his spirit than he that ....Prov 16:32   4910
The rich *r* over the poor, and the...........Prov 22:7   4910
r over another to his own hurt ....Eccl 8:9   7980
the cry of him that *r* among fools ....Eccl 9:17   4910
most High *r* in the kingdom of men ....Dan 4:17   7980
most High *r* in the kingdom of men ....Dan 4:25   7980
most High *r* in the kingdom of men ....Dan 4:32   7980
but Judah yet *r* with God, and is ....Hos 11:12   7300
he that *r*, with diligence ....Rom 12:8   4291
One that *r* well his own house, ...1Ti 3:4   4291

RULING
be just, *r* in the fear of God 2Sa 23:3   4910
of David, and *r* any more in Judah ....Jer 22:30   4910
r their children and their own 1Ti 3:12   4291

RUMAH *(ru'-mah)* See ARUMAH. *Home of Jehoiakim's mother.*
the daughter of Pedaiah of *R* 2Kin 23:36   7316

RUMBLING
at the *r* of his wheels, the ....Jer 47:3   1995

RUMOUR
upon him, and he shall hear a *r* 2Kin 19:7   8052
upon him, and he shall hear a *r* ....Is 37:7   8052
I have heard a *r* from the LORD.............Jer 49:14   8052
ye fear for the *r* that shall be ....Jer 51:46   8052
a *r* shall both come one year, and.........Jer 51:46   8052
in another year shall come a *r* ....Jer 51:46   8052
and *r* shall be upon *r* ....Eze 7:26   8052
We have heard a *r* from the LORD..........Obad 1   8052
And this *r* of him went forth ....Lk 7:17   3056

RUMOURS
shall hear of wars and *r* of wars ....Mt 24:6   189
r of wars, be ye not troubled ....Mk 13:7   189

RUMP
take the ram the fat and the *r* ....Ex 29:22   451
the fat thereof, and the whole *r* ....Lev 3:9   451
the *r*, and the fat that covereth ....Lev 7:3   451
And he took the fat, and the *r* ....Lev 8:25   451
the bullock and of the ram, the *r* ....Lev 9:19   451

RUN
whose branches *r* over the wall..............Gen 49:22   6805
his flesh *r* with his issue ....Lev 15:3   7325
or if it *r* beyond the time of her ....Lev 15:25   7325
lest angry fellows *r* upon thee ....Judg 18:25   6293
some shall *r* before his chariots 1Sa 8:11   7323
r to the camp to thy brethren 1Sa 17:17   7323
he might *r* to Beth-lehem his city 1Sa 20:6   7323
And he said unto his lad, *R* 1Sa 20:36   7323
and fifty men to *r* before him 2Sa 15:1   7323
the son of Zadok, Let me now *r* 2Sa 18:19   7323
I pray thee, also *r* after Cushi 2Sa 18:22   7323
Joab said, Wherefore wilt thou *r*............2Sa 18:22   7323
But howsoever, said he, let me *r* 2Sa 18:23   7323
And he said unto him, *R* 2Sa 18:23   7323
by thee I have *r* through a troop............2Sa 22:30   7323
and fifty men to *r* before him 1Kin 1:5   7323
that I may *r* to the man of God, ...2Kin 4:22   7323
R now, I pray thee, to meet her,.............2Kin 4:26   7323
I will *r* after him, and take 2Kin 5:20   7323
For the eyes of the LORD *r* to 2Chr 16:9   7751
by thee I have *r* through a troop ....Ps 18:29   7323
as a strong man to *r* a race...................Ps 19:5   7323
as waters which *r* continually ....Ps 58:7   1980
They *r* and prepare themselves ....Ps 59:4   7323
waters to *r* down like rivers ....Ps 78:16   3381
valleys, which *r* among the hills............Ps 104:10   1980
I will *r* the way of thy ....Ps 119:32   7323
Rivers of waters *r* down mine eyes ....Ps 119:136   3381
For their feet *r* to evil, and make ....Prov 1:16   7323
All the rivers *r* into the sea ....Eccl 1:7   1980
Draw me, we will *r* after thee ....Song 1:4   7323
of locusts shall he *r* upon them ....Is 33:4   8264
they shall *r*, and not be weary ....Is 40:31   7323
that knew not thee shall *r* unto ....Is 55:5   7323
Their feet *r* to evil, and they ....Is 59:7   7323
R ye to and fro through the...................Jer 5:1   7751
our eyes may *r* down with tears ....Jer 9:18   3381
If thou hast *r* with the footmen, ...Jer 12:5   7323
r down with tears, because the ....Jer 13:17   3381
Let mine eyes *r* down with tears ....Jer 14:17   3381
r to and fro by the hedges ....Jer 49:3   7751
suddenly make him *r* away from her ......Jer 49:19   7323
them suddenly *r* away from her ....Jer 50:44   7323

One post shall *r* to meet another,	Jer 51:31	7323
let tears *r* down like a river day	Lam 2:18	3381
neither shall thy tears *r* down	Eze 24:16	935
cause their rivers to *r* like oil	Eze 32:14	3212
many shall *r* to and fro, and	Dan 12:4	7751
and as horsemen, so shall they *r*	Joel 2:4	7323
They shall *r* like mighty men	Joel 2:7	7323
They shall *r* to and fro in the	Joel 2:9	8264
they shall *r* upon the wall, they	Joel 2:9	7323
But let judgment *r* down as waters	Amos 5:24	1556
Shall horses *r* upon the rock	Amos 6:12	7323
even to the east, they shall *r* to	Amos 8:12	7751
they shall *r* like the lightnings	Nah 2:4	7323
that he may *r* that readeth it	Hab 2:2	7323
ye *r* every man unto his own house	Hag 1:9	7323
And said unto him, R, speak to	Zec 2:4	7323
the eyes of the Lord, which *r* to	Zec 4:10	7751
did *r* to bring his disciples word	Mt 28:8	5143
they which *r* in a race *r* all	1Cor 9:24	5143
So *r*, that ye may obtain	1Cor 9:24	5143
I therefore so *r*, not as	1Cor 9:26	5143
any means I should *r*, or had *r*	Gal 2:2	5143
Ye did *r* well	Gal 5:7	5143
Christ, that I have not *r* in vain	Phil 2:16	5143
let us *r* with patience the race	Heb 12:1	5143
ye *r* not with them to the same	1Pet 4:4	4936

RUNNEST

and when thou *r*, thou shalt not	Prov 4:12	7323

RUNNETH

to the river than *r* to Ahava	Ezr 8:15	935
He *r* upon him, even on his neck,	Job 15:26	7323
he *r* upon me like a giant	Job 16:14	7323
my cup *r* over	Ps 23:5	7310
his word *r* very swiftly	Ps 147:15	7323
the righteous *r* into it, and is	Prov 18:10	7323
mine eye *r* down with water,	Lam 1:16	3381
Mine eye *r* down with rivers of	Lam 3:48	3381
bottles break, and the wine *r* out	Mt 9:17	1632
Then she *r*, and cometh to Simon	Jn 20:2	5143
that willeth, nor of him that *r*	Rom 9:16	5143

RUNNING

in an earthen vessel over *r* water	Lev 14:5	2416
that was killed over the *r* water	Lev 14:6	2416
in an earthen vessel over *r* water	Lev 14:50	2416
the slain bird, and in the *r* water	Lev 14:51	2416
of the bird, and with the *r* water	Lev 14:52	2416
When any man hath a *r* issue out	Lev 15:2	2100
and bathe his flesh in *r* water	Lev 15:13	2416
is a leper, or hath a *r* issue	Lev 22:4	2100
r water shall be put thereto in a	Num 19:17	2416
looked, and behold a man *r* alone	2Sa 18:24	7323
And the watchman saw another man *r*	2Sa 18:26	7323
said, Behold another man *r* alone	2Sa 18:26	7323
Me thinketh the *r* of the foremost	2Sa 18:27	4794

the *r* of Ahimaaz the son of Zadok	2Sa 18:27	4794
when Naaman saw him *r* after him	2Kin 5:21	7323
heard the noise of the people *r*	2Chr 23:12	7323
r waters out of thine own well	Prov 5:15	5140
that be swift in *r* to mischief	Prov 6:18	7323
as the *r* to and fro of locusts	Is 33:4	4944
rivers *r* round about his plants	Eze 31:4	1980
amazed, and *r* to him saluted him	Mk 9:15	4370
that the people came *r* together	Mk 9:25	1998
into the way, there came one *r*	Mk 10:17	4370
r over, shall men give into your	Lk 6:38	5240
r under a certain island which is	Acts 27:16	5295
of many horses *r* to battle	Rev 9:9	5143

RUSH

Can the *r* grow up without mire	Job 8:11	1573
Israel head and tail, branch and *r*	Is 9:14	100
The nations shall *r* like the	Is 17:13	7582
the head or tail, branch or *r*	Is 19:15	100

RUSHED

r forward, and stood in the	Judg 9:44	6584
in wait hasted, and *r* upon Gibeah	Judg 20:37	6584
they *r* with one accord into the	Acts 19:29	3729

RUSHES

shall be grass with reeds and *r*	Is 35:7	1573

RUSHETH

as the horse *r* into the battle	Jer 8:6	7857

RUSHING

to the *r* of nations	Is 17:12	7588
that make a *r* like the *r* of	Is 17:12	7582
rush like the *r* of many waters	Is 17:13	7588
at the *r* of his chariots, and at	Jer 47:3	7494
behind me a voice of a great *r*	Eze 3:12	7494
them, and a noise of a great *r*	Eze 3:13	7494
from heaven as of a *r* mighty wind	Acts 2:2	5342

RUST

r doth corrupt, and where thieves	Mt 6:19	1035
neither moth nor *r* doth corrupt	Mt 6:20	1035
the *r* of them shall be a witness	Jas 5:3	2447

RUTH *(rooth) Wife of Boaz; an ancestor of Jesus.*

Orpah, and the name of the other *R*	Ruth 1:4	7327
but *R* clave unto her	Ruth 1:14	7327
R said, Intreat me not to leave	Ruth 1:16	7327
R the Moabitess, her daughter in	Ruth 1:22	7327
R the Moabitess said unto Naomi,	Ruth 2:2	7327
Then said Boaz unto *R*, Hearest	Ruth 2:8	7327
R the Moabitess said, He said	Ruth 2:21	7327
Naomi said unto *R* her daughter in	Ruth 2:22	7327
answered, I am *R* thine handmaid	Ruth 3:9	7327
buy it also of *R* the Moabitess	Ruth 4:5	7327
Moreover *R* the Moabitess, the	Ruth 4:10	7327
So Boaz took *R*, and she was his	Ruth 4:13	7327
and Booz begat Obed of *R*	Mt 1:5	4503

S

SABACHTHANI

voice, saying, Eli, Eli, lama *s*	Mt 27:46	4518
voice, saying, Eloi, Eloi, lama *s*	Mk 15:34	4518

SABAOTH *(sab'-a-oth) Title meaning "Lord of Hosts."*

the Lord of *S* had left us a seed	Rom 9:29	4519
into the ears of the Lord of *S*	Jas 5:4	4519

SABBATH

rest of the holy *s* unto the Lord	Ex 16:23	7676
for to day is a *s* unto the Lord	Ex 16:25	7676
the seventh day, which is the *s*	Ex 16:26	7676
the Lord hath given you the *s*	Ex 16:29	7676
Remember the *s* day, to keep it	Ex 20:8	7676
day is the *s* of the Lord thy God	Ex 20:10	7676
the Lord blessed the *s* day	Ex 20:11	7676
Ye shall keep the *s* therefore	Ex 31:14	7676
in the seventh is the *s* of rest	Ex 31:15	7676
doeth any work in the *s* day	Ex 31:15	7676
of Israel shall keep the *s*	Ex 31:16	7676
to observe the *s* throughout their	Ex 31:16	7676
holy day, a *s* of rest to the Lord	Ex 35:2	7676
your habitations upon the *s* day	Ex 35:3	7676
It shall be a *s* of rest unto you,	Lev 16:31	7676
the seventh day is the *s* of rest	Lev 23:3	7676
it is the *s* of the Lord in all	Lev 23:3	7676
on the morrow after the *s* the	Lev 23:11	7676
you from the morrow after the *s*	Lev 23:15	7676
s shall ye number fifty days	Lev 23:16	7676
of the month, shall ye have a *s*	Lev 23:24	7677

It shall be unto you a *s* of rest	Lev 23:32	7676
even, shall ye celebrate your *s*	Lev 23:32	7676
on the first day shall be a *s*	Lev 23:39	7677
and on the eighth day shall be a *s*	Lev 23:39	7677
Every *s* he shall set it in order	Lev 24:8	7676
the land keep a *s* unto the Lord	Lev 25:2	7676
be a *s* of rest unto the land	Lev 25:4	7676
unto the land, a *s* for the Lord	Lev 25:4	7676
the *s* of the land shall be meat	Lev 25:6	7676
gathered sticks upon the *s* day	Num 15:32	7676
on the *s* day two lambs of the	Num 28:9	7676
is the burnt offering of every *s*	Num 28:10	7676
Keep the *s* day to sanctify it, as	Deut 5:12	7676
day is the *s* of the Lord thy God	Deut 5:14	7676
commanded thee to keep the *s* day	Deut 5:15	7676
it is neither new moon, nor *s*	2Kin 4:23	7676
of you that enter in on the *s*	2Kin 11:5	7676
of all you that go forth on the *s*	2Kin 11:7	7676
men that were to come in on the *s*	2Kin 11:9	7676
them that should go out on the *s*	2Kin 11:9	7676
the covert for the *s* that they	2Kin 16:18	7676
shewbread, to prepare it every *s*	1Chr 9:32	7676
part of you entering on the *s*	2Chr 23:4	7676
men that were to come in on the *s*	2Chr 23:8	7676
them that were to go out on the *s*	2Chr 23:8	7676
as she lay desolate she kept *s*	2Chr 36:21	7673
madest known unto them thy holy *s*	Neh 9:14	7676
any victuals on the *s* day to sell	Neh 10:31	7676
would not buy it of them on the *s*	Neh 10:31	7676

S

treading winepresses on the *s*	Neh 13:15	7676
into Jerusalem on the *s* day	Neh 13:15	7676
sold on the *s* unto the children	Neh 13:16	7676
that ye do, and profane the *s* day	Neh 13:17	7676
upon Israel by profaning the *s*	Neh 13:18	7676
began to be dark before the *s*	Neh 13:19	7676
not be opened till after the *s*	Neh 13:19	7676
burden be brought in on the *s* day	Neh 13:19	7676
forth came they no more on the *s*	Neh 13:21	7676
the gates, to sanctify the *s* day	Neh 13:22	7676
A Psalm or Song for the *s* day	Ps 92:*t*	7676
that keepeth the *s* from polluting	Is 56:2	7676
keepeth the *s* from polluting it	Is 56:6	7676
turn away thy foot from the *s*	Is 58:13	7676
call the *s* a delight, the holy of	Is 58:13	7676
from one *s* to another, shall all	Is 66:23	7676
and bear no burden on the *s* day	Jer 17:21	7676
out of your houses on the *s* day	Jer 17:22	7676
any work, but hallow ye the *s* day	Jer 17:22	7676
gates of this city on the *s* day	Jer 17:24	7676
but hallow the *s* day	Jer 17:24	7676
unto me to hallow the *s* day	Jer 17:27	7676
gates of Jerusalem on the *s* day	Jer 17:27	7676
but on the *s* it shall be opened,	Eze 46:1	7676
offer unto the LORD in the *s* day	Eze 46:4	7676
offerings, as he did on the *s* day	Eze 46:12	7676
and the *s*, that we may set forth	Amos 8:5	7676
on the *s* day through the corn	Mt 12:1	4521
not lawful to do upon the *s* day	Mt 12:2	4521
how that on the *s* days the	Mt 12:5	4521
in the temple profane the *s*	Mt 12:5	4521
of man is Lord even of the *s* day	Mt 12:8	4521
it lawful to heal on the *s* days	Mt 12:10	4521
it fall into a pit on the *s* day	Mt 12:11	4521
lawful to do well on the *s* days	Mt 12:12	4521
the winter, neither on the *s* day	Mt 24:20	4521
In the end of the *s*, as it began	Mt 28:1	4521
straightway on the *s* day he	Mk 1:21	4521
the corn fields on the *s* day	Mk 2:23	4521
why do they on the *s* day that	Mk 2:24	4521
The *s* was made for man	Mk 2:27	4521
and not man for the *s*	Mk 2:27	4521
Son of man is Lord also of the *s*	Mk 2:28	4521
he would heal him on the *s* day	Mk 3:2	4521
lawful to do good on the *s* days	Mk 3:4	4521
when the *s* day was come, he began	Mk 6:2	4521
that is, the day before the *s*	Mk 15:42	4315
And when the *s* was past, Mary	Mk 16:1	4521
into the synagogue on the *s* day	Lk 4:16	4521
and taught them on the *s* days	Lk 4:31	4521
on the second *s* after the first	Lk 6:1	4521
is not lawful to do on the *s* days	Lk 6:2	4521
Son of man is Lord also of the *s*	Lk 6:5	4521
it came to pass also on another *s*	Lk 6:6	4521
he would heal on the *s* day	Lk 6:7	4521
lawful on the *s* days to do good	Lk 6:9	4521
in one of the synagogues on the *s*	Lk 13:10	4521
Jesus had healed on the *s* day	Lk 13:14	4521
and be healed, and not on the *s* day	Lk 13:14	4521
s loose his ox or his ass from	Lk 13:15	4521
from this bond on the *s* day	Lk 13:16	4521
to eat bread on the *s* day	Lk 14:1	4521
Is it lawful to heal on the *s* day	Lk 14:3	4521
pull him out on the *s* day	Lk 14:5	4521
the preparation, and the *s* drew on	Lk 23:54	4521
rested the *s* day according to the	Lk 23:56	4521
and on the same day was the *s*	Jn 5:9	4521
that was cured, It is the *s* day	Jn 5:10	4521
done these things on the *s* day	Jn 5:16	4521
he not only had broken the *s*	Jn 5:18	4521
ye on the *s* day circumcise a man	Jn 7:22	4521
If a man on the *s* day receive	Jn 7:23	4521
man every whit whole on the *s* day	Jn 7:23	4521
it was the *s* day when Jesus made	Jn 9:14	4521
because he keepeth not the *s* day	Jn 9:16	4521
upon the cross on the *s* day	Jn 19:31	4521
(for that *s* day was an high day,)	Jn 19:31	4521
from Jerusalem a *s* day's journey	Acts 1:12	4521
into the synagogue on the *s* day	Acts 13:14	4521
which are read every *s* day	Acts 13:27	4521
be preached to them the next *s*	Acts 13:42	4521
the next *s* day came almost the	Acts 13:44	4521
in the synagogues every *s* day	Acts 15:21	4521
on the *s* we went out of the city	Acts 16:13	4521
three *s* days reasoned with them	Acts 17:2	4521
reasoned in the synagogue every *s*	Acts 18:4	4521
of the new moon, or of the *s* days	Col 2:16	4521

SABBATHS

Verily my *s* ye shall keep	Ex 31:13	7676
and his father, and keep my *s*	Lev 19:3	7676

Ye shall keep my *s*, and reverence	Lev 19:30	7676
seven *s* shall be complete	Lev 23:15	7676
Beside the *s* of the LORD, and	Lev 23:38	7676
number seven *s* of years unto thee	Lev 25:8	7676
the space of the seven *s* of years	Lev 25:8	7676
Ye shall keep my *s*, and reverence	Lev 26:2	7676
Then shall the land enjoy her *s*	Lev 26:34	7676
the land rest, and enjoy her *s*	Lev 26:34	7676
because it did not rest in your *s*	Lev 26:35	7676
of them, and shall enjoy her *s*	Lev 26:43	7676
sacrifices unto the LORD in the *s*	1Chr 23:31	7676
morning and evening, on the *s*	2Chr 2:4	7676
commandment of Moses, on the *s*	2Chr 8:13	7676
and the burnt offerings for the *s*	2Chr 31:3	7676
until the land had enjoyed her *s*	2Chr 36:21	7676
burnt offering, of the *s*, of the	Neh 10:33	7676
the new moons and *s*, the calling	Is 1:13	7676
unto the eunuchs that keep my *s*	Is 56:4	7676
saw her, and did mock at her *s*	Lam 1:7	4868
s to be forgotten in Zion, and	Lam 2:6	7676
Moreover also I gave them my *s*	Eze 20:12	7676
my *s* they greatly polluted	Eze 20:13	7676
in my statutes, but polluted my *s*	Eze 20:16	7676
And hallow my *s*	Eze 20:20	7676
they polluted my *s*	Eze 20:21	7676
my statutes, and had polluted my *s*	Eze 20:24	7676
things, and hast profaned my *s*	Eze 22:8	7676
and have hid their eyes from my *s*	Eze 22:26	7676
same day, and have profaned my *s*	Eze 23:38	7676
and they shall hallow my *s*	Eze 44:24	7676
and in the new moons, and in the *s*	Eze 45:17	7676
gate before the LORD in the *s*	Eze 46:3	7676
days, her new moons, and her *s*	Hos 2:11	7676

SABEANS (sab-e′-uns)
  1. Descendants of Sheba.

the *S* fell upon them, and took	Job 1:15	7614
and they shall sell them to the *S*	Joel 3:8	7615

  2. Descendants of Seba.

of Ethiopia and of the *S*, men of	Is 45:14	5436
brought *S* from the wilderness	Eze 23:42	5433

SABTA (sab′-tah) See SABTAH. *A son of Cush.*

Seba, and Havilah, and *S*, and Raamah	1Chr 1:9	5454

SABTAH (sab′-tah) See SABTA. *Same as Sabta.*

Seba, and Havilah, and *S*, and Raamah	Gen 10:7	5454

SABTECA See SABTECHAH.

SABTECHA (sab′-te-kah) See SABTECHAH. *A son of Cush.*

and Sabta, and Raamah, and *S*	1Chr 1:9	5455

SABTECHAH (sab′-te-kah) See SABTECHA. *Same as Sabtecha.*

and Sabtah, and Raamah, and *S*	Gen 10:7	5455

SACAR (sa′-kar) See SHARAR.
  1. Father of Ahiham.

Ahiam the son of *S* the Hararite	1Chr 11:35	7940

  2 A sanctuary servant.

S the fourth, and Nethaneel the	1Chr 26:4	7940

SACHIA See SHACHIA.

SACK

every man's money into his *s*	Gen 42:25	8242
as one of them opened his *s* to	Gen 42:27	8242
and, lo, it is even in my *s*	Gen 42:28	572
bundle of money was in his *s*	Gen 42:35	8242
money was in the mouth of his *s*	Gen 43:21	572
every man his *s* to the ground	Gen 44:11	572
and opened every man his *s*	Gen 44:11	572
the cup was found in Benjamin's *s*	Gen 44:12	572
wood, or raiment, or skin, or *s*	Lev 11:32	8242

SACKBUT

of the cornet, flute, harp, *s*	Dan 3:5	5443
of the cornet, flute, harp, *s*	Dan 3:7	5443
of the cornet, flute, harp, *s*	Dan 3:10	5443
of the cornet, flute, harp, *s*	Dan 3:15	5443

SACKCLOTH

put *s* upon his loins, and mourned	Gen 37:34	8242
your clothes, and gird you with *s*	2Sa 3:31	8242
the daughter of Aiah took *s*	2Sa 21:10	8242
put *s* on our loins, and ropes upon	1Kin 20:31	8242
So they girded *s* on their loins	1Kin 20:32	8242
put *s* upon his flesh, and fasted,	1Kin 21:27	8242
his flesh, and fasted, and lay in *s*	1Kin 21:27	8242
he had *s* within upon his flesh	2Kin 6:30	8242
and covered himself with *s*	2Kin 19:1	8242
of the priests, covered with *s*	2Kin 19:2	8242
of Israel, who were clothed in *s*	1Chr 21:16	8242
put on *s* with ashes, and went out	Est 4:1	8242

the king's gate clothed with *s*	Est 4:2	8242
and many lay in *s* and ashes	Est 4:3	8242
and to take away his *s* from him	Est 4:4	8242
I have sewed *s* upon my skin	Job 16:15	8242
thou hast put off my *s*, and girded	Ps 30:11	8242
they were sick, my clothing was *s*	Ps 35:13	8242
I made *s* also my garment	Ps 69:11	8242
of a stomacher a girding of *s*	Is 3:24	8242
they shall gird themselves with *s*	Is 15:3	8242
loose the *s* from off thy loins	Is 20:2	8242
to baldness, and to girding with *s*	Is 22:12	8242
bare, and gird *s* upon your loins	Is 32:11	8242
and covered himself with *s*	Is 37:1	8242
of the priests covered with *s*	Is 37:2	8242
and I make *s* their covering	Is 50:3	8242
head as a bulrush, and to spread *s*	Is 58:5	8242
For this gird you with *s*, lament	Jer 4:8	8242
of my people, gird thee with *s*	Jer 6:26	8242
be cuttings, and upon the loins *s*	Jer 48:37	8242
of Rabbah, gird you with *s*	Jer 49:3	8242
have girded themselves with *s*	Lam 2:10	8242
shall also gird themselves with *s*	Eze 7:18	8242
for thee, and gird them with *s*	Eze 27:31	8242
supplications, with fasting, and *s*	Dan 9:3	8242
like a virgin girded with *s* for	Joel 1:8	8242
come, lie all night in *s*, ye	Joel 1:13	8242
I will bring up *s* upon all loins	Amos 8:10	8242
and proclaimed a fast, and put on *s*	Jonah 3:5	8242
from him, and covered him with *s*	Jonah 3:6	8242
man and beast be covered with *s*	Jonah 3:8	8242
would have repented long ago in *s*	Mt 11:21	4526
while ago repented, sitting in *s*	Lk 10:13	4526
the sun became black as *s* of hair	Rev 6:12	4526
and threescore days, clothed in *s*	Rev 11:3	4526

SACKCLOTHES

assembled with fasting, and with *s*	Neh 9:1	8242

SACK'S

behold, it was in his *s* mouth	Gen 42:27	572
every man's money in his *s* mouth	Gen 44:1	572
in the *s* mouth of the youngest	Gen 44:2	572

SACKS

to fill their *s* with corn	Gen 42:25	3672
to pass as they emptied their *s*	Gen 42:35	8242
again in the mouth of your *s*	Gen 43:12	572
in our *s* at the first time are we	Gen 43:18	572
to the inn, that we opened our *s*	Gen 43:21	572
tell who put our money in our *s*	Gen 43:22	572
hath given you treasure in your *s*	Gen 43:23	572
Fill the men's *s* with food	Gen 44:1	572
took old *s* upon their asses, and	Josh 9:4	8242

SACKS'

which we found in our *s* mouths	Gen 44:8	572

SACRIFICE

Jacob offered *s* upon the mount	Gen 31:54	2077
that we may *s* to the LORD our God	Ex 3:18	2076
and *s* unto the LORD our God	Ex 5:3	2076
saying, Let us go and *s* to our God	Ex 5:8	2076
Let us go and do *s* to the LORD	Ex 5:17	2076
that they may do *s* unto the LORD	Ex 8:8	2076
s to your God in the land	Ex 8:25	2076
for we shall *s* the abomination of	Ex 8:26	2076
shall we *s* the abomination of the	Ex 8:26	2076
s to the LORD our God, as he	Ex 8:27	2076
that ye may *s* to the LORD your	Ex 8:28	2076
the people go to *s* to the LORD	Ex 8:29	2076
that we may *s* unto the LORD our	Ex 10:25	2077
It is the *s* of the LORD's	Ex 12:27	2077
therefore I *s* to the LORD all	Ex 13:15	2076
shalt *s* thereon thy burnt	Ex 20:24	2076
blood of my *s* with leavened bread	Ex 23:18	2077
of my *s* remain until the morning	Ex 23:18	2282
of the *s* of their peace offerings	Ex 29:28	2077
incense thereon, nor burnt *s*	Ex 30:9	
do *s* unto their gods, and one call	Ex 34:15	2076
call thee, and thou eat of his *s*	Ex 34:15	2077
the blood of my *s* with leaven	Ex 34:25	2077
neither shall the *s* of the feast	Ex 34:25	2077
offering be a burnt *s* of the herd	Lev 1:3	
all on the altar, to be a burnt *s*	Lev 1:9	
or of the goats, for a burnt *s*	Lev 1:10	
it is a burnt *s*, an offering made	Lev 1:13	
if the burnt *s* for his offering	Lev 1:14	
it is a burnt *s*, an offering made	Lev 1:17	
oblation be a *s* of peace offering	Lev 3:1	2077
he shall offer of the *s* of the	Lev 3:3	2077
it on the altar upon the burnt *s*	Lev 3:5	
if his offering for a *s* of peace	Lev 3:6	2077
he shall offer of the *s* of the	Lev 3:9	2077

of the *s* of peace offerings	Lev 4:10	2077
as the fat of the *s* of peace	Lev 4:26	2077
from off the *s* of peace offerings	Lev 4:31	2077
from the *s* of the peace offerings	Lev 4:35	2077
law of the *s* of peace offerings	Lev 7:11	2077
the *s* of thanksgiving unleavened	Lev 7:12	2077
leavened bread with the *s* of	Lev 7:13	2077
the flesh of the *s* of his peace	Lev 7:15	2077
But if the *s* of his offering be a	Lev 7:16	2077
same day that he offereth his *s*	Lev 7:16	2077
remainder of the flesh of the *s*	Lev 7:17	2077
if any of the flesh of the *s* of	Lev 7:18	2077
flesh of the *s* of peace offerings	Lev 7:20	2077
flesh of the *s* of peace offerings	Lev 7:21	2077
He that offereth the *s* of his	Lev 7:29	2077
of the *s* of his peace offerings	Lev 7:29	2077
of the *s* of the peace offerings	Lev 7:37	2077
it was a burnt *s* for a sweet	Lev 8:21	
offerings, to *s* before the LORD	Lev 9:4	2076
beside the burnt *s* of the morning	Lev 9:17	
and the ram for a *s* of peace	Lev 9:18	2077
offereth a burnt offering or *s*	Lev 17:8	2077
And if ye offer a *s* of peace	Lev 19:5	2077
whosoever offereth a *s* of peace	Lev 22:21	2077
when ye will offer a *s* of	Lev 22:29	2077
Then ye shall *s* one kid of the	Lev 23:19	6213
year for a *s* of peace offerings	Lev 23:19	2077
offering, and a meat offering, a *s*	Lev 23:37	2077
do not offer a *s* unto the LORD	Lev 27:11	7133
a *s* of peace offerings unto the	Num 6:17	2077
the *s* of the peace offerings	Num 6:18	2077
for a *s* of peace offerings, two	Num 7:17	2077
for a *s* of peace offerings, two	Num 7:23	2077
for a *s* of peace offerings, two	Num 7:29	2077
for a *s* of peace offerings, two	Num 7:35	2077
for a *s* of peace offerings, two	Num 7:41	2077
for a *s* of peace offerings, two	Num 7:47	2077
for a *s* of peace offerings, two	Num 7:53	2077
for a *s* of peace offerings, two	Num 7:59	2077
for a *s* of peace offerings, two	Num 7:65	2077
for a *s* of peace offerings, two	Num 7:71	2077
for a *s* of peace offerings, two	Num 7:77	2077
for a *s* of peace offerings, two	Num 7:83	2077
all the oxen for the *s* of the	Num 7:88	2077
or a *s* in performing a vow, or in	Num 15:3	2077
with the burnt offering or *s*	Num 15:5	2077
or for a *s* in performing a vow,	Num 15:8	2077
a *s* made by fire unto the LORD,	Num 15:25	
and, lo, he stood by his burnt *s*	Num 23:6	
a *s* made by fire unto the LORD	Num 28:6	
a *s* made by fire, of a sweet	Num 28:8	
a *s* made by fire unto the LORD	Num 28:13	
But ye shall offer a *s* made by	Num 28:19	
the meat of the *s* made by fire	Num 28:24	
a *s* made by fire unto the LORD	Num 29:6	
a *s* made by fire, of a sweet	Num 29:13	
a *s* made by fire, of a sweet	Num 29:36	
thou shalt not *s* it unto the LORD	Deut 15:21	2076
Thou shalt therefore *s* the	Deut 16:2	2076
Thou mayest not *s* the passover	Deut 16:5	2076
there thou shalt *s* the passover	Deut 16:6	2076
Thou shalt not *s* unto the LORD	Deut 17:1	2076
people, from them that offer a *s*	Deut 18:3	2077
whole burnt *s* upon thine altar	Deut 33:10	
not for burnt offering, nor for *s*	Josh 22:26	2077
offer a burnt *s* with the wood of	Judg 6:26	
a great *s* unto Dagon their god	Judg 16:23	2077
to *s* unto the LORD of hosts in	1Sa 1:3	2076
offer unto the LORD the yearly *s*	1Sa 1:21	2077
was, that, when any man offered *s*	1Sa 2:13	2077
her husband to offer the yearly *s*	1Sa 2:19	2077
Wherefore kick ye at my *s*	1Sa 2:29	2077
with *s* nor offering for ever	1Sa 3:14	2077
for there is a *s* of the people to	1Sa 9:12	2077
come, because he doth bless the *s*	1Sa 9:13	2077
and to *s* sacrifices of peace	1Sa 10:8	2076
to *s* unto the LORD thy God	1Sa 15:15	2076
to *s* unto the LORD thy God in	1Sa 15:21	2076
Behold, to obey is better than *s*	1Sa 15:22	2077
say, I am come to *s* to the LORD	1Sa 16:2	2076
And call Jesse to the *s*, and I will	1Sa 16:3	2077
I am come to *s* unto the LORD	1Sa 16:5	2076
and come with me to the *s*	1Sa 16:5	2077
his sons, and called them to the *s*	1Sa 16:5	2077
for there is a yearly *s* there for	1Sa 20:6	2077
our family hath a *s* in the city	1Sa 20:29	2077
behold, here be oxen for burnt *s*	2Sa 24:22	
king went to Gibeon to *s* there	1Kin 3:4	2076
offered *s* before the LORD	1Kin 8:62	2077
Solomon offered a *s* of peace	1Kin 8:63	2077
If this people go up to do *s* in	1Kin 12:27	2077

S

of the offering of the evening *s*	1Kin 18:29	4503
water, and pour it on the burnt *s*	1Kin 18:33	
of the offering of the evening *s*	1Kin 18:36	4503
fell, and consumed the burnt *s*	1Kin 18:38	
offering nor *s* unto other gods	2Kin 5:17	2077
I have a great *s* to do to Baal	2Kin 10:19	2077
as yet the people did *s* and burnt	2Kin 14:4	2076
offering, and the king's burnt *s*	2Kin 16:15	
and all the blood of the *s*	2Kin 16:15	2077
nor serve them, nor *s* to them	2Kin 17:35	2076
worship, and to him shall ye do *s*	2Kin 17:36	2076
save only to burn *s* before him	2Chr 2:6	
Solomon offered a *s* of twenty	2Chr 7:5	2077
place to myself for an house of *s*	2Chr 7:12	2077
to *s* unto the LORD God of their	2Chr 11:16	2076
them, therefore will I *s* to them	2Chr 28:23	2076
did *s* still in the high places	2Chr 33:17	2076
we do *s* unto him since the days	Ezr 4:2	2076
sat astonied until the evening *s*	Ezr 9:4	4503
at the evening *s* I arose up from	Ezr 9:5	4503
will they *s*	Neh 4:2	2076
offerings, and accept thy burnt *s*	Ps 20:3	
S and offering thou didst not	Ps 40:6	2077
have made a covenant with me by *s*	Ps 50:5	2077
For thou desirest not *s*	Ps 51:16	2077
I will freely *s* unto thee	Ps 54:6	2076
let them *s* the sacrifices of	Ps 107:22	2076
to thee the *s* of thanksgiving	Ps 116:17	2077
bind the *s* with cords, even unto	Ps 118:27	2282
up of my hands as the evening *s*	Ps 141:2	4503
The *s* of the wicked is an	Prov 15:8	2077
acceptable to the LORD than *s*	Prov 21:3	2077
The *s* of the wicked is	Prov 21:27	2077
hear, than to give the *s* of fools	Eccl 5:1	2077
LORD in that day, and shall do *s*	Is 19:21	2077
for the LORD hath a *s* in Bozrah	Is 34:6	2077
wentest thou up to offer *s*	Is 57:7	2077
of them that shall bring the *s* of	Jer 33:11	
offerings, and to do *s* continually	Jer 33:18	2077
a *s* in the north country by the	Jer 46:10	2077
every side to my *s*	Eze 39:17	2077
that I do *s* for you	Eze 39:17	2076
even a great *s* upon the mountains	Eze 39:17	2077
of my *s* which I have sacrificed	Eze 39:19	2076
slew the burnt offering and the *s*	Eze 40:42	2077
the *s* for the people, and they	Eze 44:11	2077
shall boil the *s* of the people	Eze 46:24	2077
by him the daily *s* was taken away	Dan 8:11	
s by reason of transgression	Dan 8:12	
the vision concerning the daily *s*	Dan 8:13	
of the week he shall cause the *s*	Dan 9:27	2077
and shall take away the daily *s*	Dan 11:31	
the daily *s* shall be taken away	Dan 12:11	
without a prince, and without a *s*	Hos 3:4	2077
They *s* upon the tops of the	Hos 4:13	2076
whores, and they *s* with harlots	Hos 4:14	2076
For I desired mercy, and not *s*	Hos 6:6	2077
They *s* flesh for the sacrifices	Hos 8:13	2076
they *s* bullocks in Gilgal	Hos 12:11	2076
the men that *s* kiss the calves	Hos 13:2	2076
offer a *s* of thanksgiving with	Amos 4:5	
offered a *s* unto the LORD, and	Jonah 1:16	2077
But I will *s* unto thee with the	Jonah 2:9	2076
Therefore they *s* unto their net	Hab 1:16	2076
for the LORD hath prepared a *s*	Zeph 1:7	2077
pass in the day of the LORD's *s*	Zeph 1:8	2077
and all they that *s* shall come	Zec 14:21	2076
And if ye offer the blind for *s*	Mal 1:8	2076
I will have mercy, and not *s*	Mt 9:13	2378
I will have mercy, and not *s*	Mt 12:7	2378
every *s* shall be salted with salt	Mk 9:49	2378
to offer a *s* according to that	Lk 2:24	2378
offered *s* unto the idol, and	Acts 7:41	2378
would have done *s* with the people	Acts 14:13	2380
they had not done *s* unto them	Acts 14:18	2380
ye present your bodies a living *s*	Rom 12:1	2378
that are offered in *s* unto idols	1Cor 8:4	1494
in *s* to idols is any thing	1Cor 10:19	1494
the things which the Gentiles *s*	1Cor 10:20	2380
they *s* to devils, and not to God	1Cor 10:20	2380
This is offered in *s* unto idols	1Cor 10:28	1494
a *s* to God for a sweetsmelling	Eph 5:2	2378
and if I be offered upon the *s*	Phil 2:17	2378
a *s* acceptable, wellpleasing to	Phil 4:18	2378
those high priests, to offer up *s*	Heb 7:27	2378
put away sin by the *s* of himself	Heb 9:26	2378
into the world, he saith, *S*	Heb 10:5	2378
Above when he said, *S* and offering	Heb 10:8	2378
offered one *s* for sins for ever	Heb 10:12	2378
remaineth no more *s* for sins	Heb 10:26	2378

God a more excellent *s* than Cain	Heb 11:4	2378
s of praise to God continually	Heb 13:15	2378

SACRIFICED

s peace offerings of oxen unto	Ex 24:5	2076
have *s* thereunto, and said, These	Ex 32:8	2076
They *s* unto devils, not to God	Deut 32:17	2076
the LORD, and *s* peace offerings	Josh 8:31	2076
they *s* there unto the LORD	Judg 2:5	2076
came, and said to the man that *s*	1Sa 2:15	2076
s sacrifices the same day unto	1Sa 6:15	2076
there they *s* sacrifices of peace	1Sa 11:15	2076
six paces, he *s* oxen and fatlings	2Sa 6:13	2076
Only the people *s* in high places	1Kin 3:2	2076
only he *s* and burnt incense in	1Kin 3:3	2076
incense and *s* unto their gods	1Kin 11:8	2076
the people still *s* and burnt	2Kin 12:3	2076
the people *s* and burnt incense	2Kin 15:4	2076
the people *s* and burned incense	2Kin 15:35	2076
And he *s* and burnt incense in the	2Kin 16:4	2076
which *s* for them in the houses of	2Kin 17:32	6213
the Jebusite, then he *s* there	1Chr 21:28	2076
they *s* sacrifices unto the LORD	1Chr 29:21	2076
s sheep and oxen, which could not	2Chr 5:6	2076
He *s* also and burnt incense in the	2Chr 28:4	2076
For he *s* unto the gods of	2Chr 28:23	2076
s thereon peace offerings and	2Chr 33:16	2076
for Amon *s* unto all the carved	2Chr 33:22	2076
of them that had *s* unto them	2Chr 34:4	2076
they *s* their sons and their	Ps 106:37	2076
whom they *s* unto the idols of	Ps 106:38	2076
these hast thou *s* unto them to be	Eze 16:20	2076
sacrifice which I have *s* for you	Eze 39:19	2076
they *s* unto Baalim, and burned	Hos 11:2	2076
Christ our passover is *s* for us	1Cor 5:7	2380
to eat things *s* unto idols	Rev 2:14	1494
and to eat things *s* unto idols	Rev 2:20	1494

SACRIFICEDST

which thou *s* the first day at	Deut 16:4	2076

SACRIFICES

offered *s* unto the God of his	Gen 46:1	2077
said, Thou must give us also *s*	Ex 10:25	2077
a burnt offering and *s* for God	Ex 18:12	2077
of the *s* of your peace offerings	Lev 7:32	2077
the *s* of their peace offerings	Lev 7:34	2077
of the *s* of the LORD made by fire	Lev 10:13	
the *s* of peace offerings of the	Lev 10:14	2077
of Israel may bring their *s*	Lev 17:5	2077
no more offer their *s* unto devils	Lev 17:7	2077
and over the *s* of your peace	Num 10:10	2077
people unto the *s* of their gods	Num 25:2	2077
and my bread for my *s* made by fire	Num 28:2	
your burnt offerings, and your *s*	Deut 12:6	2077
your burnt offerings, and your *s*	Deut 12:11	2077
the blood of thy *s* shall be	Deut 12:27	2077
Which did eat the fat of their *s*	Deut 32:38	2077
shall offer *s* of righteousness	Deut 33:19	2077
the *s* of the LORD God of Israel	Josh 13:14	
burnt offerings, and with our *s*	Josh 22:27	2077
for burnt offerings, nor for *s*	Josh 22:28	2077
for meat offerings, or for *s*	Josh 22:29	2077
sacrificed *s* the same day unto	1Sa 6:15	2077
to sacrifice *s* of peace offerings	1Sa 10:8	2077
there they sacrificed *s* of peace	1Sa 11:15	2077
delight in burnt offerings and *s*	1Sa 15:22	2077
from Giloh, while he offered *s*	2Sa 15:12	2077
And when they went in to offer *s*	2Kin 10:24	2077
and they offered burnt *s* and peace	1Chr 16:1	
to offer all burnt *s* unto the	1Chr 23:31	
they sacrificed *s* unto the LORD	1Chr 29:21	2077
s in abundance for all Israel	1Chr 29:21	2077
the burnt offering and the *s*	2Chr 7:1	2077
people offered *s* before the LORD	2Chr 7:4	2077
morning and every evening burnt *s*	2Chr 13:11	
the LORD, come near and bring *s*	2Chr 29:31	2077
And the congregation brought in *s*	2Chr 29:31	2077
the place where they offered *s*	Ezr 6:3	1685
That they may offer *s* of sweet	Ezr 6:10	
that day they offered great *s*	Neh 12:43	2077
Offer the *s* of righteousness, and	Ps 4:5	2077
offer in his tabernacle *s* of joy	Ps 27:6	2077
for thy *s* or thy burnt offerings	Ps 50:8	2077
The *s* of God are a broken spirit	Ps 51:17	2077
with the *s* of righteousness	Ps 51:19	2077
unto thee burnt *s* of fatlings	Ps 66:15	
and ate the *s* of the dead	Ps 106:28	2077
sacrifice the *s* of thanksgiving	Ps 107:22	2077
an house full of *s* with strife	Prov 17:1	2077
the multitude of your *s* unto me	Is 1:11	2077
let them kill *s*	Is 29:1	2282

SACRIFICETH

hast thou honoured me with thy s	Is 43:23	2077
filled me with the fat of thy s	Is 43:24	2077
their s shall be accepted upon	Is 56:7	2077
nor your s sweet unto me	Jer 6:20	2077
your burnt offerings unto your s	Jer 7:21	2077
concerning burnt offerings or s	Jer 7:22	2077
bringing burnt offerings, and s	Jer 17:26	2077
bringing s of praise, unto the	Jer 17:26	
and they offered there their s	Eze 20:28	2077
whereupon they slew their s	Eze 40:41	
be ashamed because of their s	Hos 4:19	2077
flesh for the s of mine offerings	Hos 8:13	2077
their s shall be unto them as the	Hos 9:4	2077
bring your s every morning, and	Amos 4:4	2077
Have ye offered unto me s	Amos 5:25	2077
all whole burnt offerings and s	Mk 12:33	2378
Pilate had mingled with their s	Lk 13:1	2378
s by the space of forty years in	Acts 7:42	2378
of the s partakers of the altar	1Cor 10:18	2378
offer both gifts and s for sins	Heb 5:1	2378
is ordained to offer gifts and s	Heb 8:3	2378
were offered both gifts and s	Heb 9:9	2378
with better s than these	Heb 9:23	2378
can never with those s which they	Heb 10:1	2378
But in those s there is a	Heb 10:3	
s for sin thou hast had no	Heb 10:6	
and offering oftentimes the same s	Heb 10:11	2378
for with such s God is well	Heb 13:16	2378
to offer up spiritual s,	1Pet 2:5	2378

SACRIFICE

He that s unto any god, save unto	Ex 22:20	2076
to him that s, and to him that	Eccl 9:2	2076
s, and to him that s not	Eccl 9:2	2076
that s in gardens, and burneth	Is 65:3	2076
he that s a lamb, as if he cut	Is 66:3	2076
s unto the Lord a corrupt thing	Mal 1:14	2076

SACRIFICING

s sheep and oxen, that could not	1Kin 8:5	2076
s unto the calves that he had	1Kin 12:32	2076

SACRILEGE

idols, dost thou commit s	Rom 2:22	2416

SAD

them, and, behold, they were s	Gen 40:6	2196
and her countenance was no more s	1Sa 1:18	
unto him, Why is thy spirit so s	1Kin 21:5	5620
been beforetime s in his presence	Neh 2:1	7451
unto me, Why is thy countenance s	Neh 2:2	7451
should not my countenance be s	Neh 2:3	7489
made the heart of the righteous s	Eze 13:22	3512
s, whom I have not made s	Eze 13:22	3510
hypocrites, of a s countenance	Mt 6:16	4659
he was s at that saying, and went	Mk 10:22	4768
to another, as ye walk, and are s	Lk 24:17	4659

SADDLE

what s soever he rideth upon that	Lev 15:9	4817
I will s me an ass, that I may	2Sa 19:26	2280
said unto his sons, S me the ass	1Kin 13:13	2280
to his sons, saying, S me the ass	1Kin 13:27	2280

SADDLED

s his ass, and took two of his	Gen 22:3	2280
s his ass, and went with the	Num 22:21	2280
there were with him two asses s	Judg 19:10	2280
met him, with a couple of asses s	2Sa 16:1	2280
he s his ass, and arose, and gat	2Sa 17:23	2280
s his ass, and went to Gath to	1Kin 2:40	2280
So they s him the ass	1Kin 13:13	2280
that he s for him the ass, to wit	1Kin 13:23	2280
And they s him	1Kin 13:27	2280
Then she s an ass, and said to her	2Kin 4:24	2280

SADDUCEES (sad'-du-sees) Members of a Jewish sect.

S come to his baptism, he said	Mt 3:7	4523
Pharisees also with the S came	Mt 16:1	4523
of the Pharisees and of the S	Mt 16:6	4523
of the Pharisees and of the S	Mt 16:11	4523
of the Pharisees and of the S	Mt 16:12	4523
The same day came to him the S	Mt 22:23	4523
that he had put the S to silence	Mt 22:34	4523
Then come unto him the S, which	Mk 12:18	4523
Then came to him certain of the S	Lk 20:27	4523
captain of the temple, and the S	Acts 4:1	4523
him, (which is the sect of the S	Acts 5:17	4523
that the one part were S, and the	Acts 23:6	4523
between the Pharisees and the S	Acts 23:7	4523
For the S say that there is no	Acts 23:8	4523

SADLY

Wherefore look ye so s to day	Gen 40:7	7451

SADNESS

for by the s of the countenance	Eccl 7:3	7455

SADOC (sa'-dok) Father of Achim; an ancestor of Jesus.

And Azor begat S	Mt 1:14	4524
and S begat Achim	Mt 1:14	

SAFE

on every side, and ye dwelled s	1Sa 12:11	983
said, Is the young man Absalom s	2Sa 18:29	7965
Cushi, Is the young man Absalom s	2Sa 18:32	7965
Their houses are s from fear	Job 21:9	7965
Hold thou me up, and I shall be s	Ps 119:117	3467
runneth into it, and is s	Prov 18:10	7682
his trust in the Lord shall be s	Prov 29:25	7682
prey, and shall carry it away s	Is 5:29	6403
and they shall be s in their land	Eze 34:27	983
because he hath received him s	Lk 15:27	5198
bring him s unto Felix the	Acts 23:24	1295
that they escaped all s to land	Acts 27:44	1295
not grievous, but for you it is s	Phil 3:1	809

SAFEGUARD

but with me thou shalt be in s	1Sa 22:23	4931

SAFELY

the full, and dwell in your land s	Lev 26:5	983
And Judah and Israel dwelt s	1Kin 4:25	983
And he led them on s, so that they	Ps 78:53	983
hearkeneth unto me shall dwell s	Prov 1:33	983
Then shalt thou walk in thy way s	Prov 3:23	983
her husband doth s trust in her	Prov 31:11	
He pursued them, and passed s	Is 41:3	7965
be saved, and Israel shall dwell s	Jer 23:6	983
and I will cause them to dwell s	Jer 32:37	983
saved, and Jerusalem shall dwell s	Jer 33:16	983
And they shall dwell s therein	Eze 28:26	983
they shall dwell s in the	Eze 34:25	983
but they shall dwell s, and none	Eze 34:28	983
and they shall dwell s all of them	Eze 38:8	983
that are at rest, that dwell s	Eze 38:11	983
my people of Israel dwelleth s	Eze 38:14	983
when they dwelt s in their land	Eze 39:26	983
and will make them to lie down s	Hos 2:18	983
Jerusalem shall be s inhabited	Zec 14:11	983
take him, and lead him away s	Mk 14:44	806
the jailer to keep them s	Acts 16:23	806

SAFETY

ye shall dwell in the land in s	Lev 25:18	983
your fill, and dwell therein in s	Lev 25:19	983
about, so that ye dwell in s	Deut 12:10	983
the Lord shall dwell in s by him	Deut 33:12	983
then shall dwell in s alone	Deut 33:28	983
I was not in s, neither had I	Job 3:26	7951
His children are far from s	Job 5:4	3468
which mourn may be exalted to s	Job 5:11	3468
and thou shalt take thy rest in s	Job 11:18	983
Though it be given him to be in s	Job 24:23	983
Lord, only makest me dwell in s	Ps 4:8	983
I will set him in s from him that	Ps 12:5	3468
An horse is a vain thing for s	Ps 33:17	8668
of counsellors there is s	Prov 11:14	8668
but s is of the Lord	Prov 21:31	8668
of counsellors there is s	Prov 24:6	8668
and the needy shall lie down in s	Is 14:30	983
truly found we shut with all s	Acts 5:23	803
when they shall say, Peace and s	1Th 5:3	803

SAFFRON

Spikenard and s	Song 4:14	3750

SAID See APPENDIX.

SAIDST See APPENDIX.

SAIL

mast, they could not spread the s	Is 33:23	5251
thou spreadest forth to be thy s	Eze 27:7	5251
as he was about to s into Syria	Acts 20:3	321
had determined to s by Ephesus	Acts 20:16	3896
that we should s into Italy	Acts 27:1	636
meaning to s by the coasts of	Acts 27:2	4126
into the quicksands, strake s	Acts 27:17	4632
thee all them that s with thee	Acts 27:24	4126

SAILED

But as they s he fell asleep	Lk 8:23	4126
and from thence they s to Cyprus	Acts 13:4	636
thence s to Antioch, from whence	Acts 14:26	636
took Mark, and s unto Cyprus	Acts 15:39	1602
s thence into Syria, and with him	Acts 18:18	1602
And he s from Ephesus	Acts 18:21	321
we s away from Philippi after the	Acts 20:6	1602
s unto Assos, there intending to	Acts 20:13	321
we s thence, and came the next day	Acts 20:15	636

S

s into Syria, and landed at Tyre	Acts 21:3	4126
we s under Cyprus, because the	Acts 27:4	5284
when we had s over the sea of	Acts 27:5	1277
when we had s slowly many days,	Acts 27:7	1020
we s under Crete, over against	Acts 27:7	5284
thence, they s close by Crete	Acts 27:13	3881

SAILING

finding a ship s over unto	Acts 21:2	1276
a ship of Alexandria s into Italy	Acts 27:6	4126
when s was now dangerous, because	Acts 27:9	4144

SAILORS

and all the company in ships, and s	Rev 18:17	3492

SAINT

camp, and Aaron the s of the LORD	Ps 106:16	6918
Then I heard one s speaking	Dan 8:13	6918
another s said unto that certain	Dan 8:13	6918
unto that certain s which spake	Dan 8:13	
Salute every s in Christ Jesus	Phil 4:21	40

SAINTS

he came with ten thousands of s	Deut 33:2	6944
all his s are in thy hand	Deut 33:3	6918
He will keep the feet of his s	1Sa 2:9	2623
let thy s rejoice in goodness	2Chr 6:41	2623
to which of the s wilt thou turn	Job 5:1	6918
he putteth no trust in his s	Job 15:15	6918
But the s that are in the	Ps 16:3	6918
O ye s of his, and give thanks at	Ps 30:4	2623
O love the LORD, all ye his s	Ps 31:23	2623
O fear the LORD, ye his s	Ps 34:9	6918
judgment, and forsaketh not his s	Ps 37:28	2623
Gather my s together unto me	Ps 50:5	2623
for it is good before thy s	Ps 52:9	2623
the flesh of thy s unto the	Ps 79:2	2623
unto his people, and to his s	Ps 85:8	2623
also in the congregation of the s	Ps 89:5	6918
feared in the assembly of his s	Ps 89:7	6918
he preserveth the souls of his s	Ps 97:10	2623
of the LORD is the death of his s	Ps 116:15	2623
and let thy s shout for joy	Ps 132:9	2623
her s shall shout aloud for joy	Ps 132:16	2623
and thy s shall bless thee	Ps 145:10	2623
people, the praise of all his s	Ps 148:14	2623
praise in the congregation of s	Ps 149:1	2623
Let the s be joyful in glory	Ps 149:5	2623
this honour have all his s	Ps 149:9	2623
and preserveth the way of his s	Prov 2:8	2623
But the s of the most High shall	Dan 7:18	6922
the same horn made war with the s	Dan 7:21	6922
given to the s of the most High	Dan 7:22	6922
that the s possessed the kingdom	Dan 7:22	6922
wear out the s of the most High	Dan 7:25	6922
people of the s of the most High	Dan 7:27	6922
God, and is faithful with the s	Hos 11:12	6918
come, and all the s with thee	Zec 14:5	6918
bodies of the s which slept arose	Mt 27:52	40
hath done to thy s at Jerusalem	Acts 9:13	40
to the s which dwelt at Lydda	Acts 9:32	40
up, and when he had called the s	Acts 9:41	40
many of the s did I shut up in	Acts 26:10	40
beloved of God, called to be s	Rom 1:7	40
s according to the will of God	Rom 8:27	40
to the necessity of s	Rom 12:13	40
Jerusalem to minister unto the s	Rom 15:25	40
the poor s which are at Jerusalem	Rom 15:26	40
may be accepted of the s	Rom 15:31	40
her in the Lord, as becometh s	Rom 16:2	40
all the s which are with them	Rom 16:15	40
in Christ Jesus, called to be s	1Cor 1:2	40
the unjust, and not before the s	1Cor 6:1	40
that the s shall judge the world	1Cor 6:2	40
as in all churches of the s	1Cor 14:33	40
the collection for the s, as I	1Cor 16:1	40
to the ministry of the s)	1Cor 16:15	40
with all the s which are in all	2Cor 1:1	40
of the ministering to the s	2Cor 8:4	40
touching the ministering to the s	2Cor 9:1	40
only supplieth the want of the s	2Cor 9:12	40
All the s salute you	2Cor 13:13	40
to the s which are at Ephesus, and	Eph 1:1	40
Jesus, and love unto all the s	Eph 1:15	40
glory of his inheritance in the s	Eph 1:18	40
but fellowcitizens with the s	Eph 2:19	40
am less than the least of all s	Eph 3:8	40
with all s what is the breadth	Eph 3:18	40
For the perfecting of the s	Eph 4:12	40
named among you, as becometh s	Eph 5:3	40
and supplication for all s	Eph 6:18	40
to all the s in Christ Jesus	Phil 1:1	40
All the s salute you, chiefly	Phil 4:22	40

To the s and faithful brethren in	Col 1:2	40
love which ye have to all the s	Col 1:4	40
the inheritance of the s in light	Col 1:12	40
but now is made manifest to his s	Col 1:26	40
Lord Jesus Christ with all his s	1Th 3:13	40
come to be glorified in his s	2Th 1:10	40
the Lord Jesus, and toward all s	Philem 5	40
of the s are refreshed by thee	Philem 7	40
that ye have ministered to the s	Heb 6:10	40
the rule over you, and all the s	Heb 13:24	40
was once delivered unto the s	Jude 3	40
with ten thousands of his s	Jude 14	40
which are the prayers of s	Rev 5:8	40
it with the prayers of all s upon	Rev 8:3	40
came with the prayers of the s	Rev 8:4	40
the prophets, and to the s	Rev 11:18	40
unto him to make war with the s	Rev 13:7	40
patience and the faith of the s	Rev 13:10	40
Here is the patience of the s	Rev 14:12	40
true are thy ways, thou King of s	Rev 15:3	40
For they have shed the blood of s	Rev 16:6	40
drunken with the blood of the s	Rev 17:6	40
the blood of prophets, and of s	Rev 18:24	40
linen is the righteousness of s	Rev 19:8	40
compassed the camp of the s about	Rev 20:9	40

SAINTS'

if she have washed the s feet	1Ti 5:10	40

SAITH See APPENDIX.

SAKE

cursed is the ground for thy s	Gen 3:17	5668
the ground any more for man's s	Gen 8:21	5668
it may be well with me for thy s	Gen 12:13	5668
he entreated Abram well for her s	Gen 12:16	5668
I will not do it for forty's s	Gen 18:29	5668
not destroy it for twenty's s	Gen 18:31	5668
I will not destroy it for ten's s	Gen 18:32	5668
they will slay me for my wife's s	Gen 20:11	1697
seed for my servant Abraham's s	Gen 26:24	5668
LORD hath blessed me for thy s	Gen 30:27	1558
Egyptian's house for Joseph's s	Gen 39:5	1558
to the Egyptians for Israel's s	Ex 18:8	182
let him go free for his eye's s	Ex 21:26	8478
let him go free for his tooth's s	Ex 21:27	8478
unto him, Enviest thou for my s	Num 11:29	
was zealous for my s among them	Num 25:11	7068
day of the plague for Peor's s	Num 25:18	1697
his people for his great name's s	1Sa 12:22	5668
to destroy the city for my s	1Sa 23:10	5668
kingdom for his people Israel's s	2Sa 5:12	5668
For thy word's s, and according to	2Sa 7:21	5668
him kindness for Jonathan's s	2Sa 9:1	5668
for Jonathan thy father's s	2Sa 9:7	5668
for my s with the young man	2Sa 18:5	
of a far country for thy name's s	1Kin 8:41	4616
do it for David thy father's s	1Kin 11:12	4616
thy son for David my servant's s	1Kin 11:13	4616
for Jerusalem's s which I have	1Kin 11:13	4616
tribe for my servant David's s	1Kin 11:32	4616
and for Jerusalem's s	1Kin 11:32	4616
his life for David my servant's s	1Kin 11:34	4616
Nevertheless for David's s did	1Kin 15:4	4616
Judah for David his servant's s	2Kin 8:19	4616
city, to save it, for mine own s	2Kin 19:34	4616
s, and for my servant David's s	2Kin 19:34	4616
defend this city for mine own s	2Kin 20:6	4616
and for my servant David's s	2Kin 20:6	4616
O LORD, for thy servant's s	1Chr 17:19	4616
country for thy great name's s	2Chr 6:32	4616
for thy great mercies' s thou	Neh 9:31	
the children's s of mine own body	Job 19:17	
oh save me for thy mercies' s	Ps 6:4	4616
of righteousness for his name's s	Ps 23:3	4616
thou me for thy goodness' s	Ps 25:7	4616
For thy name's s, O LORD, pardon	Ps 25:11	4616
for thy name's s lead me, and	Ps 31:3	4616
save me for thy mercies' s	Ps 31:16	
for thy s are we killed all the	Ps 44:22	
and redeem us for thy mercies' s	Ps 44:26	4616
GOD of hosts, be ashamed for my s	Ps 69:6	
seek thee be confounded for my s	Ps 69:6	
Because for thy s I have borne	Ps 69:7	4616
away our sins, for thy name's s	Ps 79:9	4616
he saved them for his name's s	Ps 106:8	4616
O GOD the Lord, for thy name's s	Ps 109:21	4616
thy mercy, and for thy truth's s	Ps 115:1	
For thy servant David's s turn	Ps 132:10	5668
me, O LORD, for thy name's s	Ps 143:11	
for thy righteousness' s bring my	Ps 143:11	
city to save it for mine own s	Is 37:35	

and for my servant David's *s*	Is 37:35	4616
pleased for his righteousness' *s*	Is 42:21	4616
For your *s* I have sent to Babylon	Is 43:14	4616
thy transgressions for mine own *s*	Is 43:25	4616
For Jacob my servant's *s*, and	Is 45:4	4616
For my name's *s* will I defer mine	Is 48:9	4616
own *s*, even for mine own *s*	Is 48:11	4616
against thee shall fall for thy *s*	Is 54:15	4616
For Zion's *s* will I not hold my	Is 62:1	4616
for Jerusalem's *s* I will not rest	Is 62:1	4616
Return for thy servants' *s*	Is 63:17	4616
that cast you out for my name's *s*	Is 66:5	4616
us, do thou it for thy name's *s*	Jer 14:7	4616
Do not abhor us, for thy name's *s*	Jer 14:21	4616
know that for thy *s* I have	Jer 15:15	
But I wrought for my name's *s*	Eze 20:9	4616
But I wrought for my name's *s*	Eze 20:14	4616
hand, and wrought for my name's *s*	Eze 20:22	4616
wrought with you for my name's *s*	Eze 20:44	4616
but for mine holy name's *s*	Eze 36:22	4616
is desolate, for the Lord's *s*	Dan 9:17	4616
defer not, for thine own *s*	Dan 9:19	4616
for I know that for my *s* this	Jonah 1:12	7945
for your *s* be plowed as a field	Mic 3:12	1558
persecuted for righteousness' *s*	Mt 5:10	1752
against you falsely, for my *s*	Mt 5:11	1752
governors and kings for my *s*	Mt 10:18	1752
hated of all men for my name's *s*	Mt 10:22	1752
his life for my *s* shall find it	Mt 10:39	1752
put him in prison for Herodias' *s*	Mt 14:3	
nevertheless for the oath's *s*	Mt 14:9	
his life for my *s* shall find it	Mt 16:25	1752
for the kingdom of heaven's *s*	Mt 19:12	
or lands, for my name's *s*	Mt 19:29	1752
of all nations for my name's *s*	Mt 24:9	
but for the elect's *s* those days	Mt 24:22	1752
ariseth for the word's *s*,	Mk 4:17	
him in prison for Herodias' *s*	Mk 6:17	
yet for his oath's *s*, and for	Mk 6:26	
shall lose his life for my *s*	Mk 8:35	1752
or children, or lands, for my *s*	Mk 10:29	1752
before rulers and kings for my *s*	Mk 13:9	1752
hated of all men for my name's *s*	Mk 13:13	
but for the elect's *s*, whom he	Mk 13:20	
as evil, for the Son of man's *s*	Lk 6:22	1752
will lose his life for my *s*	Lk 9:24	1752
for the kingdom of God's *s*	Lk 18:29	1752
kings and rulers for my name's *s*	Lk 21:12	1752
hated of all men for my name's *s*	Lk 21:17	
they came not for Jesus' *s* only	Jn 12:9	
I will lay down my life for thy *s*	Jn 13:37	
thou lay down thy life for my *s*	Jn 13:38	
believe me for the very works' *s*	Jn 14:11	
they do unto you for my name's *s*	Jn 15:21	
he must suffer for my name's *s*	Acts 9:16	
For which hope's *s*, king Agrippa,	Acts 26:7	
was not written for his *s* alone	Rom 4:23	
For thy *s* we are killed all the	Rom 8:36	1752
wrath, but also for conscience *s*	Rom 13:5	
for the Lord Jesus Christ's *s*	Rom 15:30	
We are fools for Christ's *s*	1Cor 4:10	
And this I do for the gospel's *s*	1Cor 9:23	
no question for conscience *s*	1Cor 10:25	
no question for conscience *s*	1Cor 10:27	
eat not for his *s* that shewed it	1Cor 10:28	
shewed it, and for conscience *s*	1Cor 10:28	
your servants for Jesus' *s*	2Cor 4:5	
delivered unto death for Jesus' *s*	2Cor 4:11	
in distresses for Christ's *s*	2Cor 12:10	
for Christ's *s* hath forgiven you	Eph 4:32	1722
him, but also to suffer for his *s*	Phil 1:29	
in my flesh for his body's *s*	Col 1:24	
For which things' *s* the wrath of	Col 3:6	
men we were among you for your *s*	1Th 1:5	
highly in love for their work's *s*	1Th 5:13	
a little wine for thy stomach's *s*	1Ti 5:23	
ought not, for filthy lucre's *s*	Titus 1:11	
Yet for love's *s* I rather beseech	Philem 9	
ordinance of man for the Lord's *s*	1Pet 2:13	
if ye suffer for righteousness' *s*	1Pet 3:14	
are forgiven you for his name's *s*	1Jn 2:12	
For the truth's *s*, which dwelleth	2Jn 2	
for his name's *s* they went forth	3Jn 7	
and for my name's *s* hast laboured	Rev 2:3	

SAKES

spare all the place for their *s*	Gen 18:26	5668
But I will for their *s* remember	Lev 26:45	
LORD was angry with me for your *s*	Deut 1:37	1558
LORD was wroth with me for your *s*	Deut 3:26	6616
LORD was angry with me for your *s*	Deut 4:21	1697

Be favourable unto them for our *s*	Judg 21:22	
s that the hand of the LORD is	Ruth 1:13	
he reproved kings for their *s*	1Chr 16:21	5921
for their *s* therefore return thou	Ps 7:7	5921
he reproved kings for their *s*	Ps 105:14	5921
went ill with Moses for their *s*	Ps 106:32	6616
For my brethren and companions' *s*	Ps 122:8	6616
so will I do for my servants' *s*	Is 65:8	6616
I do not this for your *s*, O house	Eze 36:22	6616
Not for your *s* do I this, saith	Eze 36:32	6616
but for their *s* that shall make	Dan 2:30	1701
rebuke the devourer for your *s*	Mal 3:11	
for their *s* which sat with him,	Mk 6:26	
I am glad for your *s* that I was	Jn 11:15	
not because of me, but for your *s*	Jn 12:30	
for their *s* I sanctify myself,	Jn 17:19	
they are enemies for your *s*	Rom 11:28	
are beloved for the fathers' *s*	Rom 11:28	
myself and to Apollos for your *s*	1Cor 4:6	
saith he it altogether for our *s*	1Cor 9:10	
For our *s*, no doubt, this is	1Cor 9:10	
for your *s* forgave I it in the	2Cor 2:10	
For all things are for your *s*	2Cor 4:15	
yet for your *s* he became poor,	2Cor 8:9	
we joy for your *s* before our God	1Th 3:9	
all things for the elect's *s*	2Ti 2:10	

SAKIA See SHACHIA.

SALA (*sa'-lah*) See SALAH. *Father of Heber; an ancestor of Jesus.*

of Heber, which was the son of S	Lk 3:35	4527

SALAH (*sa'-lah*) See SALA. *Son of Arphaxad.*

And Arphaxad begat S	Gen 10:24	7974
and S begat Eber	Gen 10:24	7974
five and thirty years, and begat S	Gen 11:12	7974
after he begat S four hundred	Gen 11:13	7974
S lived thirty years, and begat	Gen 11:14	7974
S lived after he begat Eber four	Gen 11:15	7974

SALAMIS (*sal'-a-mis*) *A city on Cyprus.*

And when they were at S, they	Acts 13:5	4529

SALATHIEL (*sa-la'-the-el*) See SHEALTIEL. *Descendant of Jehoiakim; an ancestor of Jesus.*

Assir, S his son,	1Chr 3:17	7597
to Babylon, Jechonias begat S	Mt 1:12	4528
and S begat Zorobabel	Mt 1:12	4528
Zorobabel, which was the son of S	Lk 3:27	4528

SALCAH (*sal'-kah*) See SALCHAH. *A city in Gad.*

reigned in mount Hermon, and in S	Josh 12:5	5548
Hermon, and all Bashan unto S	Josh 13:11	5548

SALCHAH (*sal'-kah*) See SALCAH. *Same as Salcah.*

all Gilead, and all Bashan, unto S	Deut 3:10	5548
in the land of Bashan unto S	1Chr 5:11	5548

SALE

count the years of the *s* thereof	Lev 25:27	4465
the price of his *s* shall be	Lev 25:50	4465
cometh the *s* of his patrimony	Deut 18:8	4465

SALECAH See SALCHAH.

SALEM (*sa'-lem*) See JERUSALEM. *The city of Melchizedek.*

king of S brought forth bread	Gen 14:18	8004
In S also is his tabernacle, and	Ps 76:2	8004
For this Melchisedec, king of S	Heb 7:1	4532
and after that also King of S	Heb 7:2	4532

SALIM (*sa'-lim*) *A city near Aenon.*

was baptizing in Aenon near to S	Jn 3:23	4530

SALLAI (*sal'-lahee*) See SALLU.
1. *An exile.*

And after him Gabbai, S, nine	Neh 11:8	5543

2. *A priest with Zerubbabel.*

Of S, Kallai	Neh 12:20	5543

SALLU (*sal'-lu*) See SALLAI. *A priest with Zerubbabel.*

S, Amok, Hilkiah, Jedaiah	Neh 12:7	5543
S the son of Meshullam, the son	1Chr 9:7	5543
S the son of Meshullam, the son	Neh 11:7	5543

SALMA (*sal'-mah*) See SALMON, ZALMA.
1. *Father of Boaz.*

And Nahshon begat S, and S	1Chr 2:11	8007

2. *A son of Caleb.*

begat Salma, and S begat Boaz,	1Chr 2:11	8007
S the father of Beth-lehem,	1Chr 2:51	8007
The sons of S	1Chr 2:54	8007

SALMI See SALMA.

S

SALMON (sal'-mon) See SALMA.
  1. Father of Boaz.

begat Nahshon, and Nahshon begat S ..	Ruth 4:20	8009
S begat Boaz, and Boaz begat Obed, ...	Ruth 4:21	8012
and Naasson begat S	Mt 1:4	4533
And S begat Booz of Rachab	Mt 1:5	4533
of Booz, which was the son of S	Lk 3:32	4533

  2. A mountain near Shechem.

in it, it was white as snow in S	Ps 68:14	6756

SALMONE (sal-mo'-ne) A promontory on Crete.

under Crete, over against S	Acts 27:7	4534

SALOME (sa-lo'-me) A woman follower of Jesus.

James the less and of Joses, and S	Mk 15:40	4539
and Mary the mother of James, and S ..	Mk 16:1	4539

SALT

of Siddim, which is the S Sea	Gen 14:3	4417
him, and she became a pillar of s	Gen 19:26	4417
offering shalt thou season with s	Lev 2:13	4417
s of the covenant of thy God to	Lev 2:13	4417
offerings thou shalt offer s	Lev 2:13	4417
it is a covenant of s for ever	Num 18:19	4417
coast of the s sea eastward	Num 34:3	4417
out of it shall be at the s sea	Num 34:12	4417
sea of the plain, even the s sea	Deut 3:17	4417
land thereof is brimstone, and s	Deut 29:23	4417
sea of the plain, even the s sea	Josh 3:16	4417
even the s sea on the east, the	Josh 12:3	4417
was from the shore of the s sea	Josh 15:2	4417
And the east border was the s sea	Josh 15:5	4417
And Nibshan, and the city of S	Josh 15:62	5898
were at the north bay of the s	Josh 18:19	4417
down the city, and sowed it with s	Judg 9:45	4417
of the Syrians in the valley of s	2Sa 8:13	4417
me a new cruse, and put s therein	2Kin 2:20	4417
waters, and cast the s in there	2Kin 2:21	4417
in the valley of s ten thousand	2Kin 14:7	4417
the valley of s eighteen thousand	1Chr 18:12	4417
and to his sons by a covenant of s	2Chr 13:5	4417
and went to the valley of s	2Chr 25:11	4417
of the God of heaven, wheat, s	Ezr 6:9	4416
s without prescribing how much	Ezr 7:22	4416
is unsavoury be eaten without s	Job 6:6	4417
the valley of s twelve thousand	Ps 60:t	4417
in the wilderness, in a s land	Jer 17:6	4420
priests shall cast s upon them	Eze 43:24	4417
they shall be given to s	Eze 47:11	4417
Ye are the s of the earth	Mt 5:13	217
but if the s have lost his savour	Mt 5:13	217
sacrifice shall be salted with s	Mk 9:49	251
S is good	Mk 9:50	217
but if the s have lost his s	Mk 9:50	217
Have s in yourselves, and have	Mk 9:50	217
S is good	Lk 14:34	217
but if the s have lost his savour	Lk 14:34	217
alway with grace, seasoned with s	Col 4:6	217
no fountain both yield s water	Jas 3:12	252

SALTED

thou wast not s at all, nor	Eze 16:4	4414
savour, wherewith shall it be s	Mt 5:13	233
every one shall be s with fire	Mk 9:49	233
sacrifice shall be s with salt	Mk 9:49	233

SALTNESS

but if the salt have lost his s	Mk 9:50	1096,358

SALTPITS

the breeding of nettles, and s	Zeph 2:9	4417

SALU (sa'-lu) Father of Zimri.

woman, was Zimri, the son of S	Num 25:14	5543

SALUTATION

what manner of s this should be	Lk 1:29	783
Elisabeth heard the s of Mary	Lk 1:41	783
of thy s sounded in mine ears	Lk 1:44	783
The s of me Paul with mine own	1Cor 16:21	783
The s by the hand of me Paul	Col 4:18	783
The s of Paul with mine own hand,	2Th 3:17	783

SALUTATIONS

love s in the marketplaces,	Mk 12:38	783

SALUTE

And they will s thee, and give thee	1Sa 10:4	7965
to meet him, that he might s him	1Sa 13:10	1288
of the wilderness to s our master	1Sa 25:14	1288
to s him, and to bless him,	2Sa 8:10	7592,7965
if thou meet any man, s him not	2Kin 4:29	1288
and if any s thee, answer him not	2Kin 4:29	1288
we go down to s the children of	2Kin 10:13	7965
if ye s your brethren only, what	Mt 5:47	782
when ye come into an house, s it	Mt 10:12	782

And began to s him, Hail, King of	Mk 15:18	782
and s no man by the way	Lk 10:4	782
came unto Caesarea to s Festus	Acts 25:13	782
S my wellbeloved Epaenetus, who	Rom 16:5	782
S Andronicus and Junia, my kinsmen	Rom 16:7	782
S Urbane, our helper in Christ,	Rom 16:9	782
S Apelles approved in Christ	Rom 16:10	782
S them which are of Aristobulus'	Rom 16:10	782
S Herodion my kinsman	Rom 16:11	782
S Tryphena and Tryphosa, who	Rom 16:12	782
S the beloved Persis, which	Rom 16:12	782
S Rufus chosen in the Lord, and	Rom 16:13	782
S Asyncritus, Phlegon, Hermas,	Rom 16:14	782
S Philologus, and Julia, Nereus,	Rom 16:15	782
S one another with an holy kiss	Rom 16:16	782
The churches of Christ s you	Rom 16:16	782
and Sosipater, my kinsmen, s you	Rom 16:21	782
this epistle, s you in the Lord	Rom 16:22	782
The churches of Asia s you	1Cor 16:19	782
Priscilla s you much in the Lord,	1Cor 16:19	782
All the saints s you	2Cor 13:13	782
S every saint in Christ Jesus	Phil 4:21	782
All the saints s you, chiefly	Phil 4:22	782
S the brethren which are in	Col 4:15	782
S Prisca and Aquila, and the	2Ti 4:19	782
All that are with me s thee	Titus 3:15	782
There s thee Epaphras, my	Philem 23	782
S all them that have the rule	Heb 13:24	782
They of Italy s you	Heb 13:24	782
Our friends s thee	3Jn 14	782

SALUTED

the house of Micah, and s him	Judg 18:15	7592,7965
and came and s his brethren	1Sa 17:22	7592,7965
near to the people, he s them	1Sa 30:21	7592,7965
he s him, and said to him, Is	2Kin 10:15	1288
amazed, and running to him s him	Mk 9:15	782
of Zacharias, and s Elisabeth	Lk 1:40	782
s the church, he went down to	Acts 18:22	782
s the brethren, and abode with	Acts 21:7	782
And when he had s them, he	Acts 21:19	782

SALUTETH

and of the whole church, s you	Rom 16:23	782
the chamberlain of the city s you	Rom 16:23	782
my fellowprisoner s you, and	Col 4:10	782
s you, always labouring fervently	Col 4:12	782
elected together with you, s you	1Pet 5:13	782

SALVATION

I have waited for thy s, O LORD	Gen 49:18	3444
see the s of the LORD, which he	Ex 14:13	3444
and song, and he is become my s	Ex 15:2	3444
esteemed the Rock of his s	Deut 32:15	3444
because I rejoice in thy s	1Sa 2:1	3444
the LORD hath wrought s in Israel	1Sa 11:13	8668
wrought this great s in Israel	1Sa 14:45	3444
wrought a great s for all Israel	1Sa 19:5	8668
is my shield, and the horn of my s	2Sa 22:3	3468
also given me the shield of thy s	2Sa 22:36	3468
be the God of the rock of my s	2Sa 22:47	3468
He is the tower of s for his king	2Sa 22:51	3444
for this is all my s, and all my	2Sa 23:5	3468
shew forth from day to day his s	1Chr 16:23	3444
say ye, Save us, O God of our s	1Chr 16:35	3468
O LORD God, be clothed with s	2Chr 6:41	8668
see the s of the LORD with you, O	2Chr 20:17	3444
He also shall be my s	Job 13:16	3444
S belongeth unto the LORD	Ps 3:8	3444
I will rejoice in thy s	Ps 9:14	3444
my heart shall rejoice in thy s	Ps 13:5	3444
Oh that the s of Israel were come	Ps 14:7	3444
my buckler, and the horn of my s	Ps 18:2	3468
also given me the shield of thy s	Ps 18:35	3468
and let the God of my s be exalted	Ps 18:46	3468
We will rejoice in thy s, and in	Ps 20:5	3444
in thy s how greatly shall he	Ps 21:1	3444
His glory is great in thy s	Ps 21:5	3444
from the God of his s	Ps 24:5	3468
for thou art the God of my s	Ps 25:5	3468
The LORD is my light and my s	Ps 27:1	3468
neither forsake me, O God of my s	Ps 27:9	3468
say unto my soul, I am thy s	Ps 35:3	3444
it shall rejoice in his s	Ps 35:9	3444
But the s of the righteous is of	Ps 37:39	8668
haste to help me, O Lord my s	Ps 38:22	8668
thy faithfulness and thy s	Ps 40:10	8668
as love thy s say continually	Ps 40:16	8668
aright will I shew the s of God	Ps 50:23	3468
Restore unto me the joy of thy s	Ps 51:12	3468
O God, thou God of my s	Ps 51:14	8668
Oh that the s of Israel were come	Ps 53:6	3444

from him cometh my s	Ps 62:1	3444
He only is my rock and my s	Ps 62:2	3444
He only is my rock and my s	Ps 62:6	3444
In God is my s and my glory	Ps 62:7	3468
thou answer us, O God of our s	Ps 65:5	3468
benefits, even the God of our s	Ps 68:19	3444
that is our God is the God of s	Ps 68:20	4190
hear me, in the truth of thy s	Ps 69:13	3468
let thy s, O God, set me up on	Ps 69:29	3444
as love thy s say continually	Ps 70:4	3444
and thy s all the day	Ps 71:15	8668
working s in the midst of the	Ps 74:12	3444
in God, and trusted not in his s	Ps 78:22	3444
Help us, O God of our s, for the	Ps 79:9	3468
Turn us, O God of our s, and cause	Ps 85:4	3468
mercy, O LORD, and grant us thy s	Ps 85:7	3468
Surely his s is nigh them that	Ps 85:9	3468
O lord God of my s, I have cried	Ps 88:1	3444
my God, and the rock of my s	Ps 89:26	3444
I satisfy him, and shew him my s	Ps 91:16	3444
joyful noise to the rock of our s	Ps 95:1	3468
shew forth his s from day to day	Ps 96:2	3444
The LORD hath made known his s	Ps 98:2	3444
earth have seen the s of our God	Ps 98:3	3444
O visit me with thy s	Ps 106:4	3444
I will take the cup of s, and call	Ps 116:13	3444
and song, and is become my s	Ps 118:14	3444
s is in the tabernacles of the	Ps 118:15	3444
hast heard me, and art become my s	Ps 118:21	3444
also unto me, O LORD, even thy s	Ps 119:41	8668
My soul fainteth for thy s	Ps 119:81	8668
Mine eyes fail for thy s, and for	Ps 119:123	3444
S is far from the wicked	Ps 119:155	3444
LORD, I have hoped for thy s	Ps 119:166	3444
I have longed for thy s, O LORD	Ps 119:174	3444
also clothe her priests with s	Ps 132:16	3468
the Lord, the strength of my s	Ps 140:7	3444
It is he that giveth s unto kings	Ps 144:10	8668
he will beautify the meek with s	Ps 149:4	3444
Behold, God is my s	Is 12:2	3444
he also is become my s	Is 12:2	3444
draw water out of the wells of s	Is 12:3	3444
hast forgotten the God of thy s	Is 17:10	3468
will be glad and rejoice in his s	Is 25:9	3444
s will God appoint for walls and	Is 26:1	3444
our s also in the time of trouble	Is 33:2	3444
of thy times, and strength of s	Is 33:6	3444
open, and let them bring forth s	Is 45:8	3468
in the LORD with an everlasting s	Is 45:17	8668
far off, and my s shall not tarry	Is 46:13	8668
I will place s in Zion for Israel	Is 46:13	8668
that thou mayest be my s unto the	Is 49:6	3444
in a day of s have I helped thee	Is 49:8	3444
my s is gone forth, and mine arms	Is 51:5	3468
but my s shall be for ever, and my	Is 51:6	3444
ever, and my s from generation to	Is 51:8	3444
of good, that publisheth s	Is 52:7	3444
earth shall see the s of our God	Is 52:10	3444
for my s is near to come, and my	Is 56:1	3444
for s, but it is far off from us	Is 59:11	3444
his arm brought s unto him	Is 59:16	3467
an helmet of s upon his head	Is 59:17	3444
but thou shalt call thy walls S	Is 60:18	3444
clothed me with the garments of s	Is 61:10	3468
the s thereof as a lamp that	Is 62:1	3444
of Zion, Behold, thy s cometh	Is 62:11	3468
mine own arm brought s unto me	Is 63:5	3467
Truly in vain is s hoped for from	Jer 3:23	
LORD our God is the s of Israel	Jer 3:23	8668
wait for the s of the LORD	Lam 3:26	8668
S is of the LORD	Jonah 2:9	3444
I will wait for the God of my s	Mic 7:7	3468
thine horses and thy chariots of s	Hab 3:8	3444
forth for the s of thy people	Hab 3:13	3468
even for s with thine anointed	Hab 3:13	3468
I will joy in the God of my s	Hab 3:18	3468
he is just, and having s	Zec 9:9	3467
hath raised up an horn of s for	Lk 1:69	4991
To give knowledge of s unto his	Lk 1:77	4991
For mine eyes have seen thy s	Lk 2:30	4992
all flesh shall see the s of God	Lk 3:6	4992
This day is s come to this house,	Lk 19:9	4991
for s is of the Jews	Jn 4:22	4991
Neither is there s in any other	Acts 4:12	4991
to you is the word of this s sent	Acts 13:26	4991
for s unto the ends of the earth	Acts 13:47	4991
which shew unto us the way of s	Acts 16:17	4991
that the s of God is sent unto	Acts 28:28	4992
s to every one that believeth	Rom 1:16	4991
mouth confession is made unto s	Rom 10:10	4991
fall s is come unto the Gentiles	Rom 11:11	4991

for now is our s nearer than when	Rom 13:11	4991
it is for your consolation and s	2Cor 1:6	4991
it is for your consolation and s	2Cor 1:6	4991
in the day of s have I succoured	2Cor 6:2	4991
behold, now is the day of s	2Cor 6:2	4991
to s not to be repented of	2Cor 7:10	4991
of truth, the gospel of your s	Eph 1:13	4991
And take the helmet of s, and the	Eph 6:17	4992
turn to my s through your prayer	Phil 1:19	4991
of perdition, but to you of s	Phil 1:28	4991
work out your own s with fear	Phil 2:12	4991
and for an helmet, the hope of s	1Th 5:8	4991
but to obtain s by our Lord Jesus	1Th 5:9	4991
the beginning chosen you to s	2Th 2:13	4991
s which is in Christ Jesus with	2Ti 2:10	4991
unto s through faith which is in	2Ti 3:15	4991
s hath appeared to all men	Titus 2:11	4992
for them who shall be heirs of s	Heb 1:14	4991
escape, if we neglect so great s	Heb 2:3	4991
s perfect through sufferings	Heb 2:10	4991
s unto all them that obey him	Heb 5:9	4991
you, and things that accompany s	Heb 6:9	4991
second time without sin unto s	Heb 9:28	4991
s ready to be revealed in the	1Pet 1:5	4991
faith, even the s of your souls	1Pet 1:9	4991
Of which s the prophets have	1Pet 1:10	4991
longsuffering of our Lord is s	2Pet 3:15	4991
to write unto you of the common s	Jude 3	4991
S to our God which sitteth upon	Rev 7:10	4991
saying in heaven, Now is come s	Rev 12:10	4991
S, and glory, and honour, and power,	Rev 19:1	4991

SAMARIA (sa-ma'-re-ah) See SAMARITAN.
1. A city in Ephraim.

he bought the hill S of Shemer	1Kin 16:24	8111
of Shemer, owner of the hill, S	1Kin 16:24	8111
his fathers, and was buried in S	1Kin 16:28	8111
reigned over Israel in S twenty	1Kin 16:29	8111
of Baal, which he had built in S	1Kin 16:32	8111
And there was a sore famine in S	1Kin 18:2	8111
and he went up and besieged S	1Kin 20:1	8111
if the dust of S shall suffice	1Kin 20:10	8111
There are men come out of S	1Kin 20:17	8111
Damascus, as my father made in S	1Kin 20:34	8111
heavy and displeased, and came to S	1Kin 20:43	8111
king of Israel, which is in S	1Kin 21:18	8111
in the entrance of the gate of S	1Kin 22:10	8111
king died, and was brought to S	1Kin 22:37	8111
and they buried the king in S	1Kin 22:37	8111
the chariot in the pool of S	1Kin 22:38	8111
in S the seventeenth year of	1Kin 22:51	8111
his upper chamber that was in S	2Kin 1:2	8111
and from thence he returned to S	2Kin 2:25	8111
in S the eighteenth year of	2Kin 3:1	8111
went out of S the same time	2Kin 3:6	8111
with the prophet that is in S	2Kin 5:3	8111
But he led them to S	2Kin 6:19	8111
pass, when they were come into S	2Kin 6:20	8111
they were in the midst of S	2Kin 6:20	8111
host, and went up, and besieged S	2Kin 6:24	8111
And there was a great famine in S	2Kin 6:25	8111
for a shekel, in the gate of S	2Kin 7:1	8111
about this time in the gate of S	2Kin 7:18	8111
And Ahab had seventy sons in S	2Kin 10:1	8111
Jehu wrote letters, and sent to S	2Kin 10:1	8111
arose and departed, and came to S	2Kin 10:12	8111
And when he came to S, he slew all	2Kin 10:17	8111
all that remained unto Ahab in S	2Kin 10:17	8111
and they buried him in S	2Kin 10:35	8111
over Israel in S was twenty	2Kin 10:36	8111
began to reign over Israel in S	2Kin 13:1	8111
remained the grove also in S	2Kin 13:6	8111
and they buried him in S	2Kin 13:9	8111
to reign over Israel in S	2Kin 13:10	8111
Joash was buried in S with the	2Kin 13:13	8111
and hostages, and returned to S	2Kin 14:14	8111
was buried in S with the kings of	2Kin 14:16	8111
of Israel began to reign in S	2Kin 14:23	8111
reign over Israel in S six months	2Kin 15:8	8111
and he reigned a full month in S	2Kin 15:13	8111
went up from Tirzah, and came to S	2Kin 15:14	8111
Shallum the son of Jabesh in S	2Kin 15:14	8111
Israel, and reigned ten years in S	2Kin 15:17	8111
began to reign over Israel in S	2Kin 15:23	8111
against him, and smote him in S	2Kin 15:25	8111
began to reign over Israel in S	2Kin 15:27	8111
reign in S over Israel nine years	2Kin 17:1	8111
all the land, and went up to S	2Kin 17:5	8111
Hoshea the king of Assyria took S	2Kin 17:6	8111
king of Assyria came up against S	2Kin 18:9	8111
king of Israel, S was taken	2Kin 18:10	8111

S

they delivered S out of mine hand	2Kin 18:34	8111
over Jerusalem the line of S	2Kin 21:13	8111
the entering in of the gate of S	2Chr 18:9	8111
caught him, (for he was hid in S	2Chr 22:9	8111
from S even unto Beth-horon, and	2Chr 25:13	8111
hostages also, and returned to S	2Chr 25:24	8111
them, and brought the spoil to S	2Chr 28:8	8111
before the host that came to S	2Chr 28:9	8111
then they returned to S	2Chr 28:15	8111
And the head of Ephraim is S	Is 7:9	8111
the head of S is Remaliah's son	Is 7:9	8111
the spoil of S shall be taken	Is 8:4	8111
Ephraim and the inhabitant of S	Is 9:9	8111
is not S as Damascus	Is 10:9	8111
excel them of Jerusalem and of S	Is 10:10	8111
I not, as I have done unto S	Is 10:11	8111
And thine elder sister is S	Eze 16:46	8111
Neither hath S committed half of	Eze 16:51	8111
daughters, and the captivity of S	Eze 16:53	8111
to their former estate, and S	Eze 16:55	8111
S is Aholah, and Jerusalem	Eze 23:4	8111
with the cup of thy sister S	Eze 23:33	8111
S shall become desolate	Hos 13:16	8111
dwell in S in the corner of a bed	Amos 3:12	8111
Judah, which he saw concerning S	Mic 1:1	8111
is it not S	Mic 1:5	8111
Therefore I will make S as an	Mic 1:6	8111
Philip went down to the city of S	Acts 8:5	4540
and bewitched the people of S	Acts 8:9	4540
S had received the word of God	Acts 8:14	4540

2. Territory of the northern tribes.

which are in the cities of S	1Kin 13:32	8111
by the palace of Ahab king of S	1Kin 21:1	8111
the messengers of the king of S	2Kin 1:3	8111
of S instead of the children of	2Kin 17:24	8111
and they possessed S, and dwelt in	2Kin 17:24	8111
and placed in the cities of S	2Kin 17:26	8111
they had carried away from S came	2Kin 17:28	8111
of the prophet that came out of S	2Kin 23:18	8111
that were in the cities of S	2Kin 23:19	8111
years he went down to Ahab to S	2Chr 18:2	8111
over, and set in the cities of S	Ezr 4:10	8115
their companions that dwell in S	Ezr 4:17	8115
his brethren and the army of S	Neh 4:2	8111
they delivered S out of my hand	Is 36:19	8111
seen folly in the prophets of S	Jer 23:13	8111
vines upon the mountains of S	Jer 31:5	8111
Shechem, from Shiloh, and from S	Jer 41:5	8111
and the wickedness of S	Hos 7:1	8111
Thy calf, O S, hath cast thee off	Hos 8:5	8111
but the calf of S shall be broken	Hos 8:6	8111
The inhabitants of S shall fear	Hos 10:5	8111
As for S, her king is cut off as	Hos 10:7	8111
upon the mountains of S, and	Amos 3:9	8111
that are in the mountain of S	Amos 4:1	8111
and trust in the mountain of S	Amos 6:1	8111
They that swear by the sin of S	Amos 8:14	8111
of Ephraim, and the fields of S	Obad 19	8111

3. District north of Judah.

he passed through the midst of S	Lk 17:11	4540
And he must needs go through S	Jn 4:4	4540
Then cometh he to a city of S	Jn 4:5	4540
cometh a woman of S to draw water	Jn 4:7	4540
saith the woman of S unto him	Jn 4:9	4540
of me, which am a woman of S	Jn 4:9	4540
and in all Judaea, and in S	Acts 1:8	4540
the regions of Judaea and S	Acts 8:1	4540
all Judaea and Galilee and S	Acts 9:31	4540
they passed through Phenice and S	Acts 15:3	4540

SAMARITAN (sa-mar'-i-tun) See SAMARITANS.
An inhabitant of Samaria.

But a certain S, as he journeyed,	Lk 10:33	4541
and he was a S	Lk 17:16	4541
Say we not well that thou art a S	Jn 8:48	4541

SAMARITANS (sa-mar'-i-tuns)

high places which the S had made	2Kin 17:29	8118
any city of the S enter ye not	Mt 10:5	4541
entered into a village of the S	Lk 9:52	4541
Jews have no dealings with the S	Jn 4:9	4541
many of the S of that city	Jn 4:39	4541
So when the S were come unto him,	Jn 4:40	4541
gospel in many villages of the S	Acts 8:25	4541

SAME See APPENDIX.

SAMGAR-NEBO (sam'-gar-ne'-bo) *A prince of Babylon.*

gate, even Nergal-sharezer, S	Jer 39:3	5562

SAMLAH (sam'-lah) *A king of Edom.*

S of Masrekah reigned in his	Gen 36:36	8072
S died, and Saul of Rehoboth by	Gen 36:37	8072

S of Masrekah reigned in his	1Chr 1:47	8072
when S was dead, Shaul of	1Chr 1:48	8072

SAMOS (sa'-mos) *An island in the Aegean Sea.*

and the next day we arrived at S	Acts 20:15	4544

SAMOTHRACE See SAMOTHRACIA.

SAMOTHRACIA (sam-o-thra'-she-ah) *An island in the Aegean Sea.*

came with a straight course to S	Acts 16:11	4543

SAMSON (sam'-sun) See SAMSON'S. *A judge of Israel.*

bare a son, and called his name S	Judg 13:24	8123
S went down to Timnath, and saw a	Judg 14:1	8123
S said unto his father, Get her	Judg 14:3	8123
Then went S down, and his father	Judg 14:5	8123
and she pleased S well	Judg 14:7	8123
and S made there a feast	Judg 14:10	8123
S said unto them, I will now put	Judg 14:12	8123
that S visited his wife with a	Judg 15:1	8123
S said concerning them, Now shall	Judg 15:3	8123
S went and caught three hundred	Judg 15:4	8123
And they answered, S, the son in	Judg 15:6	8123
S said unto them, Though ye have	Judg 15:7	8123
To bind S are we come up, to do	Judg 15:10	8123
of the rock Etam, and said to S	Judg 15:11	8123
S said unto them, Swear unto me,	Judg 15:12	8123
S said, With the jawbone of an	Judg 15:16	8123
Then went S to Gaza, and saw there	Judg 16:1	8123
Gazites, saying, S is come hither	Judg 16:2	8123
S lay till midnight, and arose at	Judg 16:3	8123
And Delilah said to S, Tell me, I	Judg 16:6	8123
S said unto her, If they bind me	Judg 16:7	8123
The Philistines be upon thee, S	Judg 16:9	8123
And Delilah said unto S, Behold,	Judg 16:10	8123
The Philistines be upon thee, S	Judg 16:12	8123
And Delilah said unto S, Hitherto	Judg 16:13	8123
The Philistines be upon thee, S	Judg 16:14	8123
The Philistines be upon thee, S	Judg 16:20	8123
Our god hath delivered S our	Judg 16:23	8123
merry, that they said, Call for S	Judg 16:25	8123
they called for S out of the	Judg 16:25	8123
S said unto the lad that held him	Judg 16:26	8123
that beheld while S made sport	Judg 16:27	8123
S called unto the LORD, and said,	Judg 16:28	8123
S took hold of the two middle	Judg 16:29	8123
S said, Let me die with the	Judg 16:30	8123
of Gedeon, and of Barak, and of S	Heb 11:32	4546

SAMSON'S (sam'-suns)

day, that they said unto S wife	Judg 14:15	8123
S wife wept before him, and said,	Judg 14:16	8123
But S wife was given to his	Judg 14:20	8123

SAMUEL (sam'-u-el) See SHEMUEL. *A priest and judge of Israel.*

bare a son, and called his name S	1Sa 1:20	8050
But S ministered before the LORD,	1Sa 2:18	8050
the child S grew before the LORD	1Sa 2:21	8050
And the child S grew on, and was in	1Sa 2:26	8050
the child S ministered unto the	1Sa 3:1	8050
was, and S was laid down to sleep	1Sa 3:3	8050
That the LORD called S	1Sa 3:4	8050
And the LORD called yet again, S	1Sa 3:6	8050
S arose and went to Eli, and said,	1Sa 3:6	8050
Now S did not yet know the LORD,	1Sa 3:7	8050
the LORD called S again the third	1Sa 3:8	8050
Therefore Eli said unto S	1Sa 3:9	8050
So S went and lay down in his	1Sa 3:9	8050
as at other times, S, S	1Sa 3:10	8050
Then S answered, Speak	1Sa 3:10	8050
And the LORD said to S, Behold, I	1Sa 3:11	8050
S lay until the morning, and	1Sa 3:15	8050
S feared to shew Eli the vision	1Sa 3:15	8050
Eli called S, and said, S	1Sa 3:16	8050
S told him every whit, and hid	1Sa 3:18	8050
S grew, and the LORD was with him,	1Sa 3:19	8050
even to Beer-sheba knew that S	1Sa 3:20	8050
to S in Shiloh by the word of the	1Sa 3:21	8050
the word of S came to all Israel	1Sa 4:1	8050
S spake unto all the house of	1Sa 7:3	8050
S said, Gather all Israel to	1Sa 7:5	8050
S judged the children of Israel	1Sa 7:6	8050
the children of Israel said to S	1Sa 7:8	8050
S took a sucking lamb, and offered	1Sa 7:9	8050
S cried unto the LORD for Israel	1Sa 7:9	8050
as S was offering up the burnt	1Sa 7:10	8050
Then S took a stone, and set it	1Sa 7:12	8050
the Philistines all the days of S	1Sa 7:13	8050
S judged Israel all the days of	1Sa 7:15	8050
when S was old, that he made his	1Sa 8:1	8050
and came to S unto Ramah,	1Sa 8:4	8050
But the thing displeased S	1Sa 8:6	8050

And S prayed unto the LORD	1Sa 8:6	8050
And the LORD said unto S, Hearken	1Sa 8:7	8050
S told all the words of the LORD	1Sa 8:10	8050
refused to obey the voice of S	1Sa 8:19	8050
S heard all the words of the	1Sa 8:21	8050
And the LORD said to S, Hearken	1Sa 8:22	8050
S said unto the men of Israel, Go	1Sa 8:22	8050
S came out against them, for to	1Sa 9:14	8050
Now the LORD had told S in his	1Sa 9:15	8050
when S saw Saul, the LORD said	1Sa 9:17	8050
Saul drew near to S in the gate	1Sa 9:18	8050
S answered Saul, and said, I am	1Sa 9:19	8050
S took Saul and his servant, and	1Sa 9:22	8050
S said unto the cook, Bring the	1Sa 9:23	8050
S said, Behold that which is left	1Sa 9:24	
So Saul did eat with S that day	1Sa 9:24	8050
S communed with Saul upon the top	1Sa 9:25	
that S called Saul to the top of	1Sa 9:26	8050
went out both of them, he and S	1Sa 9:26	8050
S said to Saul, Bid the servant	1Sa 9:27	8050
Then S took a vial of oil, and	1Sa 10:1	8050
had turned his back to go from S	1Sa 10:9	8050
they were no where, we came to S	1Sa 10:14	8050
I pray thee, what S said unto you	1Sa 10:15	8050
of the kingdom, whereof S spake	1Sa 10:16	8050
S called the people together unto	1Sa 10:17	8050
when S had caused all the tribes	1Sa 10:20	8050
S said to all the people, See ye	1Sa 10:24	8050
Then S told the people the manner	1Sa 10:25	8050
S sent all the people away, every	1Sa 10:25	8050
not forth after Saul and after S	1Sa 11:7	8050
And the people said unto S	1Sa 11:12	8050
Then said S to the people, Come,	1Sa 11:14	8050
S said unto all Israel, Behold, I	1Sa 12:1	8050
S said unto the people, It is the	1Sa 12:6	8050
and Bedan, and Jephthah, and S	1Sa 12:11	8050
So S called unto the LORD	1Sa 12:18	8050
greatly feared the LORD and S	1Sa 12:18	8050
And all the people said unto S	1Sa 12:19	8050
S said unto the people, Fear not	1Sa 12:20	8050
the set time that S had appointed	1Sa 13:8	8050
but S came not to Gilgal	1Sa 13:8	8050
burnt offering, behold, S came	1Sa 13:10	8050
S said, What hast thou done	1Sa 13:11	8050
S said to Saul, Thou hast done	1Sa 13:13	8050
S arose, and gat him up from	1Sa 13:15	8050
S also said unto Saul, The LORD	1Sa 15:1	8050
came the word of the LORD unto S	1Sa 15:10	8050
And it grieved S	1Sa 15:11	8050
when S rose early to meet Saul in	1Sa 15:12	8050
in the morning, it was told S	1Sa 15:12	8050
And S came to Saul	1Sa 15:13	8050
S said, What meaneth then this	1Sa 15:14	8050
Then S said unto Saul, Stay, and I	1Sa 15:16	8050
S said, When thou wast little in	1Sa 15:17	8050
And Saul said unto S, Yea, I have	1Sa 15:20	8050
S said, Hath the LORD as great	1Sa 15:22	8050
And Saul said unto S, I have	1Sa 15:24	8050
S said unto Saul, I will not	1Sa 15:26	8050
as S turned about to go away, he	1Sa 15:27	8050
S said unto him, The LORD hath	1Sa 15:28	8050
So S turned again after Saul	1Sa 15:31	8050
Then said S, Bring ye hither to	1Sa 15:32	8050
S said, As thy sword hath made	1Sa 15:33	8050
S hewed Agag in pieces before the	1Sa 15:33	8050
Then S went to Ramah	1Sa 15:34	8050
S came no more to see Saul until	1Sa 15:35	8050
nevertheless S mourned for Saul	1Sa 15:35	8050
And the LORD said unto S, How long	1Sa 16:1	8050
And S said, How can I go	1Sa 16:2	8050
S did that which the LORD spake,	1Sa 16:4	8050
But the LORD said unto S, Look	1Sa 16:7	8050
and made him pass before S	1Sa 16:8	8050
of his sons to pass before S	1Sa 16:10	8050
S said unto Jesse, The LORD hath	1Sa 16:10	8050
S said unto Jesse, Are here all	1Sa 16:11	8050
S said unto Jesse, Send and fetch	1Sa 16:11	8050
Then S took the horn of oil, and	1Sa 16:13	8050
So S rose up, and went to Ramah	1Sa 16:13	8050
came to S to Ramah, and told him	1Sa 19:18	8050
S went and dwelt in Naioth	1Sa 19:18	8050
S standing as appointed over them	1Sa 19:20	8050
and he asked and said, Where are S	1Sa 19:22	8050
before S in like manner, and lay	1Sa 19:24	8050
And S died	1Sa 25:1	8050
Now S was dead, and all Israel had	1Sa 28:3	8050
And he said, Bring me up S	1Sa 28:11	8050
And when the woman saw S, she	1Sa 28:12	8050
And Saul perceived that it was S	1Sa 28:14	8050
S said to Saul, Why hast thou	1Sa 28:15	8050
Then said S, Wherefore then dost	1Sa 28:16	8050

afraid, because of the words of S	1Sa 28:20	8050
And the sons of S	1Chr 6:28	8050
S the seer did ordain in their	1Chr 9:22	8050
to the word of the LORD by S	1Chr 11:3	8050
And all that S the seer, and Saul	1Chr 26:28	8050
written in the book of S the seer	1Chr 29:29	8050
from the days of S the prophet	2Chr 35:18	8050
S among them that call upon his	Ps 99:6	8050
S stood before me, yet my mind	Jer 15:1	8050
Yea, and all the prophets from S	Acts 3:24	4545
fifty years, until S the prophet	Acts 13:20	4545
of David also, and S, and of the	Heb 11:32	4545

SANBALLAT *(san-bal'-lat) An opponent of Nehemiah.*

When S the Horonite, and Tobiah	Neh 2:10	5571
But when S the Horonite, and	Neh 2:19	5571
that when S heard that we builded	Neh 4:1	5571
But it came to pass, that when S	Neh 4:7	5571
Now it came to pass, when S	Neh 6:1	5571
That S and Geshem sent unto me,	Neh 6:2	5571
Then sent S his servant unto me	Neh 6:5	5571
for Tobiah and S had hired him	Neh 6:12	5571
S according to these their works,	Neh 6:14	5571
was son in law to S the Horonite	Neh 13:28	5571

SANCTIFICATION

us wisdom, and righteousness, and s	1Cor 1:30	38
is the will of God, even your s	1Th 4:3	38
how to possess his vessel in s	1Th 4:4	38
salvation through s of the Spirit	2Th 2:13	38
through s of the Spirit, unto	1Pet 1:2	38

SANCTIFIED

blessed the seventh day, and s it	Gen 2:3	6942
unto the people, and s the people	Ex 19:14	6942
tabernacle shall be s by my glory	Ex 29:43	6942
all that was therein, and s them	Lev 8:10	6942
s it, to make reconciliation upon	Lev 8:15	6942
s Aaron, and his garments, and his	Lev 8:30	6942
I will be s in them that come	Lev 10:3	6942
if he that s it will redeem his	Lev 27:15	6942
if he that s the field will in	Lev 27:19	6942
s it, and all the instruments	Num 7:1	6942
and had anointed them, and s them	Num 7:1	6942
land of Egypt I s them for myself	Num 8:17	6942
the LORD, and he was s in them	Num 20:13	6942
because ye s me not in the midst	Deut 32:51	6942
s Eleazar his son to keep the ark	1Sa 7:1	6942
he s Jesse and his sons, and called	1Sa 16:5	6942
though it were s this day in the	1Sa 21:5	6942
the Levites s themselves to bring	1Chr 15:14	6942
priests that were present were s	2Chr 5:11	6942
s this house, that my name may be	2Chr 7:16	6942
house, which I have s for my name	2Chr 7:20	6942
s themselves, and came, according	2Chr 29:15	6942
so they s the house of the LORD	2Chr 29:17	6942
have we prepared and s, and,	2Chr 29:19	6942
other priests had s themselves	2Chr 29:34	6942
had not s themselves sufficiently	2Chr 30:3	6942
which he hath s for ever	2Chr 30:8	6942
s themselves, and brought in the	2Chr 30:15	6942
the congregation that were not s	2Chr 30:17	6942
number of priests s themselves	2Chr 30:24	6942
they s themselves in holiness	2Chr 31:18	6942
they s it, and set up the doors of	Neh 3:1	6942
unto the tower of Meah they s it	Neh 3:1	6942
they s holy things unto the	Neh 12:47	6942
the Levites s them unto the	Neh 12:47	6942
s them, and rose up early in the	Job 1:5	6942
holy shall be s in righteousness	Is 5:16	6942
I have commanded my s ones	Is 13:3	6942
forth out of the womb I s thee	Jer 1:5	6942
I will be s in you before the	Eze 20:41	6942
in her, and shall be s in her	Eze 28:22	6942
shall be s in them in the sight	Eze 28:25	6942
when I shall be s in you before	Eze 36:23	6942
me, when I shall be s in thee	Eze 38:16	6942
am s in them in the sight of many	Eze 39:27	6942
that are s of the sons of Zadok	Eze 48:11	6942
ye of him, whom the Father hath s	Jn 10:36	37
also might be s through the truth	Jn 17:19	37
among all them which are s	Acts 20:32	37
among them which are s by faith	Acts 26:18	37
being s by the Holy Ghost	Rom 15:16	37
them that are s in Christ Jesus	1Cor 1:2	37
but ye are washed, but ye are s	1Cor 6:11	37
husband is s by the wife, and the	1Cor 7:14	37
wife is s by the husband	1Cor 7:14	37
For it is s by the word of God and	1Ti 4:5	37
shall be a vessel unto honour, s	2Ti 2:21	37
they who are s are all of one	Heb 2:11	37
By the which will we are s	Heb 10:10	37

S

for ever them that are *s* .... Heb 10:14   37
the covenant, wherewith he was *s* .... Heb 10:29   37
to them that are *s* by God the .... Jude 1   37

SANCTIFIETH
or the temple that *s* the gold .... Mt 23:17   37
or the altar that *s* the gift .... Mt 23:19   37
For both he that *s* and they who .... Heb 2:11   37
s to the purifying of the flesh .... Heb 9:13   37

SANCTIFY
S unto me all the firstborn, ... Ex 13:2   6942
s them to day and to morrow, and .... Ex 19:10   6942
s themselves, lest the LORD break .... Ex 19:22   6942
bounds about the mount, and *s* it .... Ex 19:23   6942
s them, that they may minister .... Ex 28:41   6942
thou shalt *s* the breast of the .... Ex 29:27   6942
made, to consecrate and to *s* them......... Ex 29:33   6942
and thou shalt anoint it, to *s* it .... Ex 29:36   6942
atonement for the altar, and *s* it .... Ex 29:37   6942
I will *s* the tabernacle of the .... Ex 29:44   6942
I will *s* also both Aaron and his............. Ex 29:44   6942
And thou shalt *s* them, that they .... Ex 30:29   6942
I am the LORD that doth *s* you .... Ex 31:13   6942
all his vessels, and *s* the altar .... Ex 40:10   6942
the laver and his foot, and *s* it .... Ex 40:11   6942
garments, and anoint him, and *s* him .... Ex 40:13   6942
the laver and his foot, to *s* him .... Lev 8:11   6942
head, and anointed him, to *s* him .... Lev 8:12   6942
ye shall therefore *s* yourselves............... Lev 11:44   6942
S yourselves therefore, and be ye .... Lev 20:7   6942
I am the LORD which *s* you .... Lev 20:8   6942
Thou shalt *s* him therefore...................... Lev 21:8   6942
for I the LORD, which *s* you .... Lev 21:8   6942
for I the LORD do *s* him .... Lev 21:15   6942
for I the LORD do *s* them .... Lev 21:23   6942
I the LORD do *s* them............................... Lev 22:9   6942
for I the LORD do *s* them .... Lev 22:16   6942
when a man shall *s* his house to............ Lev 27:14   6942
if a man shall *s* unto the LORD .... Lev 27:16   6942
If he *s* his field from the year .... Lev 27:17   6942
But if he *s* his field after the .... Lev 27:18   6942
if a man *s* unto the LORD a field............ Lev 27:22   6942
firstling, no man shall *s* it .... Lev 27:26   6942
S yourselves against to morrow, ... Num 11:18   6942
to *s* me in the eyes of the .... Num 20:12   6942
to *s* me at the water before their .... Num 27:14   6942
Keep the sabbath day to *s* it................... Deut 5:12   6942
shalt *s* unto the LORD thy God .... Deut 15:19   6942
unto the people, *S* yourselves................. Josh 3:5   6942
s the people, and say, *S*......................... Josh 7:13   6942
s yourselves, and come with me to 1Sa 16:5   6942
s yourselves, both ye and your............... 1Chr 15:12   6942
that he should *s* the most holy 1Chr 23:13   6942
s now yourselves 2Chr 29:5   6942
s the house of the LORD God of 2Chr 29:5   6942
first day of the first month to *s* 2Chr 29:17   6942
to *s* themselves than the priests 2Chr 29:34   6942
clean, to *s* them unto the LORD 2Chr 30:17   6942
s yourselves, and prepare your............... 2Chr 35:6   6942
the gates, to *s* the sabbath day .... Neh 13:22   6942
S the LORD of hosts himself .... Is 8:13   6942
of him, they shall *s* my name .... Is 29:23   6942
s the Holy One of Jacob, and shall .... Is 29:23   6942
They that *s* themselves, and purify .... Is 66:17   6942
that I am the LORD that *s* them.............. Eze 20:12   6942
I will *s* my great name, which was .... Eze 36:23   6942
know that I the LORD do *s* Israel .... Eze 37:28   6942
I magnify myself, and *s* myself.............. Eze 38:23   6942
they shall not *s* the people with .... Eze 44:19   6942
the utter court, to *s* the people............... Eze 46:20   6942
S ye a fast, call a solemn........................ Joel 1:14   6942
s a fast, call a solemn assembly .... Joel 2:15   6942
s the congregation, assemble the............ Joel 2:16   6942
S them through thy truth .... Jn 17:17   37
And for their sakes I *s* myself .... Jn 17:19   37
That he might *s* and cleanse it................ Eph 5:26   37
very God of peace *s* you wholly 1Th 5:23   37
that he might *s* the people with .... Heb 13:12   37
But *s* the Lord God in your hearts.......... 1Pet 3:15   37

SANCTUARIES
that he profane not my *s* .... Lev 21:23   4720
bring your *s* unto desolation, and .... Lev 26:31   4720
into the *s* of the LORD's house................. Jer 51:51   4720
Thou hast defiled thy *s* by the................ Eze 28:18   4720
the *s* of Israel shall be laid .... Amos 7:9   4720

SANCTUARY
for thee to dwell in, in the *S* .... Ex 15:17   4720
And let them make me a *s* .... Ex 25:8   4720
shekel after the shekel of the *s*............... Ex 30:13   6944
after the shekel of the *s* .... Ex 30:24   6944

of work for the service of the *s* .... Ex 36:1   6944
the work of the service of the *s* .... Ex 36:3   6944
wrought all the work of the *s* .... Ex 36:4   6944
work for the offering of the *s* .... Ex 36:6   6944
after the shekel of the *s* .... Ex 38:24   6944
after the shekel of the *s* .... Ex 38:25   6944
shekel, after the shekel of the *s*.............. Ex 38:26   6944
were cast the sockets of the *s* .... Ex 38:27   6944
LORD, before the vail of the *s* .... Lev 4:6   6944
silver, after the shekel of the *s*............... Lev 5:15   6944
from before the *s* out of the camp .... Lev 10:4   6944
thing, nor come into the *s* .... Lev 12:4   4720
make an atonement for the holy *s* .... Lev 16:33   4720
my sabbaths, and reverence my *s* .... Lev 19:30   4720
seed unto Molech, to defile my *s* .... Lev 20:3   4720
Neither shall he go out of the *s* .... Lev 21:12   4720
nor profane the *s* of his God .... Lev 21:12   4720
my sabbaths, and reverence my *s* .... Lev 26:2   4720
silver, after the shekel of the *s*............... Lev 27:3   6944
according to the shekel of the *s* .... Lev 27:25   6944
keeping the charge of the *s* .... Num 3:28   6944
the vessels of the *s* wherewith .... Num 3:31   6944
that keep the charge of the *s*................... Num 3:32   6944
keeping the charge of the *s* for................ Num 3:38   4720
of the *s* shalt thou take them .... Num 3:47   6944
after the shekel of the *s* .... Num 3:50   6944
wherewith they minister in the *s*............ Num 4:12   6944
made an end of covering the *s* .... Num 4:15   6944
and all the vessels of the *s* .... Num 4:15   6944
of all that therein is, in the *s* .... Num 4:16   6944
because the service of the *s* .... Num 7:9   6944
after the shekel of the *s* .... Num 7:13   6944
after the shekel of the *s* .... Num 7:19   6944
after the shekel of the *s* .... Num 7:25   6944
after the shekel of the *s* .... Num 7:31   6944
after the shekel of the *s* .... Num 7:37   6944
after the shekel of the *s* .... Num 7:43   6944
after the shekel of the *s* .... Num 7:49   6944
after the shekel of the *s* .... Num 7:55   6944
after the shekel of the *s* .... Num 7:61   6944
after the shekel of the *s* .... Num 7:67   6944
after the shekel of the *s* .... Num 7:73   6944
after the shekel of the *s* .... Num 7:79   6944
after the shekel of the *s* .... Num 7:85   6944
apiece, after the shekel of the *s* .... Num 7:86   6944
of Israel come nigh unto the *s* .... Num 8:19   6944
set forward, bearing the *s* .... Num 10:21   4720
shall bear the iniquity of the *s* .... Num 18:1   4720
come nigh the vessels of the *s* .... Num 18:3   6944
ye shall keep the charge of the *s* .... Num 18:5   4720
after the shekel of the *s* .... Num 18:16   6944
he hath defiled the *s* of the LORD .... Num 19:20   4720
that was by the *s* of the LORD................. Josh 24:26   4720
and all the instruments of the *s* 1Chr 9:29   6944
build ye the *s* of the LORD God, ... 1Chr 22:19   4720
for the governors of the *s* 1Chr 24:5   6944
thee to build an house for the *s*.............. 1Chr 28:10   4720
have built thee a *s* therein for 2Chr 20:8   4720
go out of the *s* 2Chr 26:18   4720
for the kingdom, and for the *s* 2Chr 29:21   4720
the LORD, and enter into his *s*................. 2Chr 30:8   4720
to the purification of the *s* 2Chr 30:19   6944
the sword in the house of their *s*............ 2Chr 36:17   4720
where are the vessels of the *s* .... Neh 10:39   4720
Send thee help from the *s* .... Ps 20:2   6944
so as I have seen thee in the *s* .... Ps 63:2   6944
of my God, my King, in the *s* .... Ps 68:24   6944
Until I went into the *s* of God .... Ps 73:17   4720
enemy hath done wickedly in the *s*......... Ps 74:3   6944
They have cast fire into thy *s* .... Ps 74:7   4720
Thy way, O God, is in the *s*..................... Ps 77:13   6944
them to the border of his *s* .... Ps 78:54   6944
he built his *s* like high palaces,............. Ps 78:69   4720
strength and beauty are in his *s*.............. Ps 96:6   4720
down from the height of his *s* .... Ps 102:19   6944
Judah was his *s*, and Israel his .... Ps 114:2   6944
Lift up your hands in the *s* .... Ps 134:2   6944
Praise God in his *s* .... Ps 150:1   6944
And he shall be for a *s* .... Is 8:14   4720
he shall come to his *s* to pray .... Is 16:12   4720
profaned the princes of the *s*.................. Is 43:28   6944
to beautify the place of my *s*.................. Is 60:13   4720
have trodden down thy *s* .... Is 63:18   4720
beginning is the place of our *s* .... Jer 17:12   4720
the heathen entered into her *s* .... Lam 1:10   4720
his altar, he hath abhorred his *s*............ Lam 2:7   4720
be slain in the *s* of the Lord .... Lam 2:20   4720
the stones of the *s* are poured................ Lam 4:1   6944
because thou hast defiled my *s*............... Eze 5:11   4720
I should go far off from my *s* .... Eze 8:6   4720
and begin at my *s* .... Eze 9:6   4720

s in the countries where they	Eze 11:16	4720
have defiled my s in the same day	Eze 23:38	4720
same day into my s to profane it	Eze 23:39	4720
Behold, I will profane my s	Eze 24:21	4720
thou saidst, Aha, against my s	Eze 25:3	4720
will set my s in the midst of	Eze 37:26	4720
when my s shall be in the midst	Eze 37:28	4720
squared, and the face of the s	Eze 41:21	6944
the temple and the s had two doors	Eze 41:23	6944
make a separation between the s	Eze 42:20	6944
place of the house, without the s	Eze 43:21	4720
s which looketh toward the east	Eze 44:1	4720
with every going forth of the s	Eze 44:5	4720
have brought into my s strangers	Eze 44:7	4720
in flesh, to be in my s, to	Eze 44:7	4720
my charge in my s for yourselves	Eze 44:8	4720
in flesh, shall enter into my s	Eze 44:9	4720
they shall be ministers in my s	Eze 44:11	4720
that kept the charge of my s when	Eze 44:15	4720
They shall enter into my s	Eze 44:16	4720
the day that he goeth into the s	Eze 44:27	6944
inner court, to minister in the s	Eze 44:27	6944
for the s five hundred in length	Eze 45:2	6944
and in it shall be the s and the	Eze 45:3	4720
priests the ministers of the s	Eze 45:4	4720
and an holy place for the s	Eze 45:4	4720
without blemish, and cleanse the s	Eze 45:18	4720
they they issued out of the s	Eze 47:12	4720
the s shall be in the midst of it	Eze 48:8	4720
the s of the LORD shall be in the	Eze 48:10	4720
the s of the house shall be in	Eze 48:21	4720
the place of his s was cast down	Dan 8:11	4720
of desolation, to give both the s	Dan 8:13	6944
then shall the s be cleansed	Dan 8:14	6944
shine upon thy s that is desolate	Dan 9:17	4720
shall destroy the city and the s	Dan 9:26	6944
shall pollute the s of strength	Dan 11:31	4720
her priests have polluted the s	Zeph 3:4	6944
A minister of the s, and of the	Heb 8:2	39
of divine service, and a worldly s	Heb 9:1	39
which is called the s	Heb 9:2	39
the s by the high priest for sin	Heb 13:11	39

SAND

as the s which is upon the sea	Gen 22:17	2344
make thy seed as the s of the sea	Gen 32:12	2344
gathered corn as the s of the sea	Gen 41:49	2344
the Egyptian, and hid him in the s	Ex 2:12	2344
and of treasures hid in the s	Deut 33:19	2344
even as the s that is upon the	Josh 11:4	2344
as the s by the sea side for	Judg 7:12	2344
people as the s which is on the	1Sa 13:5	2344
as the s that is by the sea for	2Sa 17:11	2344
as the s which is by the sea in	1Kin 4:20	2344
even as the s that is on the sea	1Kin 4:29	2344
be heavier than the s of the sea	Job 6:3	2344
I shall multiply my days as the s	Job 29:18	2344
fowls like as the s of the sea	Ps 78:27	2344
are more in number than the s	Ps 139:18	2344
stone is heavy, and the s weighty	Prov 27:3	2344
Israel be as the s of the sea	Is 10:22	2344
Thy seed also had been as the s	Is 48:19	2344
which have placed the s for the	Jer 5:22	2344
to me above the s of the seas	Jer 15:8	2344
neither the s of the sea measured	Jer 33:22	2344
shall be as the s of the sea	Hos 1:10	2344
gather the captivity as the s	Hab 1:9	2344
which built his house upon the s	Mt 7:26	285
of Israel be as the s of the sea	Rom 9:27	285
as the s which is by the sea	Heb 11:12	285
And I stood upon the s of the sea	Rev 13:1	285
of whom is as the s of the sea	Rev 20:8	285

SANDALS

But be shod with s	Mk 6:9	4547
Gird thyself, and bind on thy s	Acts 12:8	4547

SANG

Then s Moses and the children of	Ex 15:1	7891
Then Israel s this song, Spring	Num 21:17	7891
Then s Deborah and Barak the son	Judg 5:1	7891
of whom they s one to another in	1Sa 29:5	6030
worshipped, and the singers s	2Chr 29:28	7891
they s praises with gladness, and	2Chr 29:30	
they s together by course in	Ezr 3:11	6030
And the singers s loud, with	Neh 12:42	7891
When the morning stars s together	Job 38:7	7442
which he s unto the LORD,	Ps 7:t	7891
they s his praise	Ps 106:12	7891
prayed, and s praises unto God	Acts 16:25	5214

SANK

they s into the bottom as a stone	Ex 15:5	3381
they s as lead in the mighty	Ex 15:10	6749

SANSANNAH (san-san'-nah) A city in Judah.

And Ziklag, and Madmannah, and S	Josh 15:31	5578

SAP

trees of the LORD are full of s	Ps 104:16	

SAPH (saf) See SIPHAI. A descendant of Rapha.

Sibbechai the Hushathite slew S	2Sa 21:18	5593

SAPHIR (sa'-fur) A city in Ephraim.

ye away, thou inhabitant of S	Mic 1:11	8208

SAPPHIRA (saf-fi'-rah) Wife of Ananias.

Ananias, with S his wife, sold a	Acts 5:1	4551

SAPPHIRE

it were a paved work of a s stone	Ex 24:10	5601
row shall be an emerald, a s	Ex 28:18	5601
the second row, an emerald, a s	Ex 39:11	5601
with the precious onyx, or the s	Job 28:16	5601
rubies, their polishing was of s	Lam 4:7	5601
as the appearance of a s stone	Eze 1:26	5601
over them as it were a s stone	Eze 10:1	5601
the onyx, and the jasper, the s	Eze 28:13	5601
the second, s	Rev 21:19	4552

SAPPHIRES

stones of it are the place of s	Job 28:6	5601
as bright ivory overlaid with s	Song 5:14	5601
and lay thy foundations with s	Is 54:11	5601

SARA (sa'-rah) See SARAH. Greek form of Sarah 1.

Through faith also S herself	Heb 11:11	4564

SARAH (sa'-rah) See SARA, SARAH'S, SARAI, SERAH.
1. Wife of Abraham.

Sarai, but S shall her name be	Gen 17:15	8283
and shall S, that is ninety years	Gen 17:17	8283
S thy wife shall bear thee a son	Gen 17:19	8283
which S shall bear unto thee at	Gen 17:21	8283
hastened into the tent unto S	Gen 18:6	8283
unto him, Where is S thy wife	Gen 18:9	8283
S thy wife shall have a son	Gen 18:10	8283
S heard it in the tent door,	Gen 18:10	8283
S were old and well stricken in	Gen 18:11	8283
it ceased to be with S after the	Gen 18:11	8283
Therefore S laughed within	Gen 18:12	8283
Abraham, Wherefore did S laugh	Gen 18:13	8283
of life, and S shall have a son	Gen 18:14	8283
Then S denied, saying, I laughed	Gen 18:15	8283
And Abraham said of S his wife	Gen 20:2	8283
king of Gerar sent, and took S	Gen 20:2	8283
and restored him S his wife	Gen 20:14	8283
unto S he said, Behold, I have	Gen 20:16	8283
because of S Abraham's wife	Gen 20:18	8283
the LORD visited S as he had said	Gen 21:1	8283
LORD did unto S as he had spoken	Gen 21:1	8283
For S conceived, and bare Abraham	Gen 21:2	8283
whom S bare to him, Isaac	Gen 21:3	8283
S said, God hath made me to laugh	Gen 21:6	8283
that S should have given children	Gen 21:7	8283
S saw the son of Hagar the	Gen 21:9	8283
in all that S hath said unto thee	Gen 21:12	8283
S was an hundred and seven and	Gen 23:1	8283
were the years of the life of S	Gen 23:1	8283
And S died in Kirjath-arba	Gen 23:2	8283
and Abraham came to mourn for S	Gen 23:2	8283
Abraham buried S his wife in the	Gen 23:19	8283
S my master's wife bare a son to	Gen 24:36	8283
was Abraham buried, and S his wife	Gen 25:10	8283
they buried Abraham and S his wife	Gen 49:31	8283
father, and unto S that bare you	Is 51:2	8283
I come, and S shall have a son	Rom 9:9	4564
Even as S obeyed Abraham, calling	1Pet 3:6	4564
2. A daughter of Asher.		
of the daughter of Asher was S	Num 26:46	8294

SARAH'S (sa'-rahs)

her into his mother S tent	Gen 24:67	8283
S handmaid, bare unto Abraham	Gen 25:12	8283
yet the deadness of S womb	Rom 4:19	4564

SARAI (sa'-rahee) See SARAH, SARAI'S. The original name of Sarah.

the name of Abram's wife was S	Gen 11:29	8297
But S was barren	Gen 11:30	8297
S his daughter in law, his son	Gen 11:31	8297
And Abram took S his wife, and Lot	Gen 12:5	8297
that he said unto S his wife	Gen 12:11	8297
plagues because of S Abram's wife	Gen 12:17	8297
Now S Abram's wife bare him no	Gen 16:1	8297
S said unto Abram, Behold now,	Gen 16:2	8297

S

Abram hearkened to the voice of *S*	Gen 16:2	8297
S Abram's wife took Hagar her	Gen 16:3	8297
S said unto Abram, My wrong be	Gen 16:5	8297
But Abram said unto *S*, Behold,	Gen 16:6	8297
when *S* dealt hardly with her, she	Gen 16:6	8297
from the face of my mistress *S*	Gen 16:8	8297
As for *S* thy wife, thou shalt not	Gen 17:15	8297
thou shalt not call her name *S*	Gen 17:15	8297

SARAI'S (sa'-rahees)
S maid, whence camest thou	Gen 16:8	8297

SARAPH (sa'-raf) *A descendant of Shelah.*
men of Chozeba, and Joash, and *S*	1Chr 4:22	8315

SARDINE
upon like a jasper and a *s* stone	Rev 4:3	4555

SARDIS (sar'-dis) *A city in Lydia in Asia Minor.*
and unto Thyatira, and unto *S*	Rev 1:11	4554
angel of the church in *S* write	Rev 3:1	4554
in *S* which have not defiled their	Rev 3:4	4554

SARDITES (sar'-dites) *Descendants of Sered.*
of Sered, the family of the *S*	Num 26:26	5625

SARDIUS
the first row shall be a *s*	Ex 28:17	124
the first row was a *s*, a topaz,	Ex 39:10	124
stone was thy covering, the *s*	Eze 28:13	124
the sixth, *s*	Rev 21:20	4556

SARDONYX
The fifth, *s*	Rev 21:20	4557

SAREPTA (sa-rep'-tah) See ZAREPHATH. *A city near Sidon.*
them was Elias sent, save unto *S*	Lk 4:26	4558

SARGON (sar'-gon) *An Assyrian king.*
(when *S* the king of Assyria sent	Is 20:1	5623

SARID (sa'-rid) *A city in Zebulun.*
of their inheritance was unto *S*	Josh 19:10	8301
turned from *S* eastward toward the	Josh 19:12	8301

SARON (sa'-ron) See SHARON. *The area between Joppa and Caesarea.*
S saw him, and turned to the Lord	Acts 9:35	4565

SARSECHIM (sar'-se-kim) *A prince of Babylon.*
Nergal-sharezer, Samgar-nebo, *S*	Jer 39:3	8310

SAR-SEKIM See SARSECHIM.

SARUCH (sa'-ruk) See SERUG. *Father of Nahor; an ancestor of Jesus.*
Which was the son of *S*, which was	Lk 3:35	4562

SAT
he *s* in the tent door in the heat	Gen 18:1	3427
Lot *s* in the gate of Sodom	Gen 19:1	3427
s her down over against him a	Gen 21:16	3427
she *s* over against him, and lift	Gen 21:16	3427
camel's furniture, and *s* upon them	Gen 31:34	3427
And they *s* down to eat bread	Gen 37:25	3427
s in an open place, which is by	Gen 38:14	3427
they *s* before him, the firstborn	Gen 43:33	3427
himself, and *s* upon the bed	Gen 48:2	3427
and he *s* down by a well	Ex 2:15	3427
that *s* on his throne unto the	Ex 12:29	3427
when we *s* by the flesh pots, and	Ex 16:3	3427
put it under him, and he *s* thereon	Ex 17:12	3427
that Moses *s* to judge the people	Ex 18:13	3427
the people *s* down to eat and to	Ex 32:6	3427
s that hath the issue shall wash	Lev 15:6	3427
she *s* upon shall wash his clothes	Lev 15:22	3427
and they *s* down at thy feet	Deut 33:3	8497
s under an oak which was in	Judg 6:11	3427
the woman as she *s* in the field	Judg 13:9	3427
And they *s* down, and did eat and	Judg 19:6	3427
he *s* him down in a street of the	Judg 19:15	3427
s there before the Lord, and	Judg 20:26	3427
And she *s* beside the reapers	Ruth 2:14	3427
to the gate, and *s* him down there	Ruth 4:1	3427
And he turned aside, and *s* down	Ruth 4:1	3427
And they *s* down	Ruth 4:2	3427
Now Eli the priest *s* upon a seat	1Sa 1:9	3427
Eli *s* upon a seat by the wayside	1Sa 4:13	3427
as he *s* in his house with his	1Sa 19:9	3427
the king *s* him down to eat meat	1Sa 20:24	3427
the king *s* upon his seat, as at	1Sa 20:25	3427
Abner *s* by Saul's side, and	1Sa 20:25	3427
from the earth, and *s* upon the bed	1Sa 28:23	3427
and they *s* down, the one on the	2Sa 2:13	3427
when the king *s* in his house	2Sa 7:1	3427
s before the Lord, and he said,	2Sa 7:18	3427
David *s* between the two gates	2Sa 18:24	3427
the king arose, and *s* in the gate	2Sa 19:8	3427

The Tachmonite that *s* in the seat	2Sa 23:8	3427
Then *s* Solomon upon the throne of	1Kin 2:12	3427
s down on his throne, and caused a	1Kin 2:19	3427
and she *s* on his right hand	1Kin 2:19	3427
as they *s* at the table, that the	1Kin 13:20	3427
as soon as he *s* on his throne	1Kin 16:11	3427
s down under a juniper tree	1Kin 19:4	3427
of Belial, and *s* before him	1Kin 21:13	3427
of Judah *s* each on his throne	1Kin 22:10	3427
he *s* on the top of an hill	2Kin 1:9	3427
he *s* on her knees till noon, and	2Kin 4:20	3427
But Elisha *s* in his house, and the	2Kin 6:32	3427
house, and the elders *s* with him	2Kin 6:32	3427
he *s* on the throne of the kings	2Kin 11:19	3427
Jeroboam *s* upon his throne	2Kin 13:13	3427
as David *s* in his house, that	1Chr 17:1	3427
s before the Lord, and said, Who	1Chr 17:16	3427
Then Solomon *s* on the throne of	1Chr 29:23	3427
Jehoshaphat king of Judah *s*	2Chr 18:9	3427
they *s* in a void place at the	2Chr 18:9	3427
of my beard, and *s* down astonied	Ezr 9:3	3427
I *s* astonied until the evening	Ezr 9:4	3427
all the people *s* in the street of	Ezr 10:9	3427
s down in the first day of the	Ezr 10:16	3427
heard these words, that I *s* down	Neh 1:4	3427
booths, and *s* under the booths	Neh 8:17	3427
when the king Ahasuerus *s* on the	Est 1:2	3427
which *s* the first in the kingdom	Est 1:14	3427
then Mordecai *s* in the king's	Est 2:19	3427
while Mordecai *s* in the king's	Est 2:21	3427
the king and Haman *s* down to drink	Est 3:15	3427
the king *s* upon his royal throne	Est 5:1	3427
he *s* down among the ashes	Job 2:8	3427
So they *s* down with him upon the	Job 2:13	3427
s chief, and dwelt as a king in	Job 29:25	3427
I have not *s* with vain persons,	Ps 26:4	3427
of Babylon, there we *s* down	Ps 137:1	3427
I *s* down under his shadow with	Song 2:3	3427
In the ways hast thou *s* for them	Jer 3:2	3427
I *s* not in the assembly of the	Jer 15:17	3427
I *s* alone because of thy hand	Jer 15:17	3427
s down in the entry of the new	Jer 26:10	3427
before all the Jews that *s* in the	Jer 32:12	3427
and, lo, all the princes *s* there	Jer 36:12	3427
Now the king *s* in the winterhouse	Jer 36:22	3427
s in the middle gate, even	Jer 39:3	3427
I *s* where they *s*, and remained	Eze 3:15	3427
of Chebar, and I *s* where they *s*	Eze 3:15	3427
as I *s* in mine house, and the	Eze 8:1	3427
the elders of Judah *s* before me	Eze 8:1	3427
there *s* women weeping for Tammuz	Eze 8:14	3427
of Israel unto me, and *s* before me	Eze 14:1	3427
of the Lord, and *s* before me	Eze 20:1	3427
but Daniel *s* in the gate of the	Dan 2:49	
him with sackcloth, and *s* in ashes	Jonah 3:6	3427
s on the east side of the city,	Jonah 4:5	3427
s under it in the shadow, till he	Jonah 4:5	3427
The people which *s* in darkness	Mt 4:16	2521
and to them which *s* in the region	Mt 4:16	2521
as Jesus *s* at meat in the house,	Mt 9:10	345
s down with him and his disciples	Mt 9:10	4873
the house, and *s* by the sea side	Mt 13:1	2521
so that he went into a ship, and *s*	Mt 13:2	2521
s **down, and gathered the good into**	Mt 13:48	2523
them which *s* with him at meat, he	Mt 14:9	4873
into a mountain, and *s* down there	Mt 15:29	2521
as he *s* upon the mount of Olives	Mt 24:3	2521
it on his head, as he *s* at meat	Mt 26:7	345
he *s* down with the twelve	Mt 26:20	345
I *s* daily with you teaching in	Mt 26:55	2516
s with the servants, to see the	Mt 26:58	2521
Now Peter *s* without in the palace	Mt 26:69	2521
stone from the door, and *s* upon it	Mt 28:2	2521
as Jesus *s* at meat in his house,	Mk 2:15	2621
sinners *s* also together with	Mk 2:15	4873
And the multitude *s* about him	Mk 3:32	2521
about on them which *s* about him	Mk 3:34	2521
into a ship, and *s* in the sea	Mk 4:1	2521
Herod and them that *s* with him	Mk 6:22	4873
for their sakes which *s* with him	Mk 6:26	4873
they *s* down in ranks, by hundreds	Mk 6:40	377
he *s* down, and called the twelve	Mk 9:35	2523
s by the highway side begging	Mk 10:46	2521
a colt tied, whereon never man *s*	Mk 11:2	2523
and he *s* upon him	Mk 11:7	2523
Jesus *s* over against the treasury	Mk 12:41	2523
as he *s* upon the mount of Olives	Mk 13:3	2521
as he *s* at meat, there came a	Mk 14:3	2621
And as they *s* and did eat, Jesus	Mk 14:18	345
he *s* with the servants, and warmed	Mk 14:54	4775
unto the eleven as they *s* at meat	Mk 16:14	345

s on the right hand of God	Mk 16:19	2523
again to the minister, and s down	Lk 4:20	2523
he s down, and taught the people	Lk 5:3	2523
of others that s down with them	Lk 5:29	2621
And he that was dead s up, and	Lk 7:15	339
house, and s down to meat	Lk 7:36	347
when she knew that Jesus s at	Lk 7:37	345
they that s at meat with him	Lk 7:49	4873
which also s at Jesus' feet, and	Lk 10:39	3869
and he went in, and s down to meat	Lk 11:37	377
when one of them that s at meat	Lk 14:15	4873
a certain blind man s by the way	Lk 18:35	2521
tied, whereon yet never man s	Lk 19:30	2523
he s down, and the twelve apostles	Lk 22:14	377
together, Peter s down among them	Lk 22:55	2521
beheld him as he s by the fire	Lk 22:56	2521
as he s at meat with him, he	Lk 24:30	2625
his journey, s thus on the well	Jn 4:6	2516
there he s with his disciples	Jn 6:3	2521
So the men s down, in number	Jn 6:10	377
he s down, and taught them	Jn 8:2	2523
said, Is not this he that s	Jn 9:8	2521
but Mary s still in the house	Jn 11:20	2516
them that s at the table with him	Jn 12:2	4873
had found a young ass, s thereon	Jn 12:14	2523
s down in the judgment seat in a	Jn 19:13	2523
fire, and it s upon each of them	Acts 2:3	2523
s for alms at the Beautiful gate	Acts 3:10	2521
all that s in the council,	Acts 6:15	2516
and when she saw Peter, she s up	Acts 9:40	339
s upon his throne, and made an	Acts 12:21	2523
on the sabbath day, s down	Acts 13:14	2523
there s a certain man at Lystra,	Acts 14:8	2521
we s down, and spake unto the	Acts 16:13	2523
there s in a window a certain	Acts 20:9	2521
morrow I s on the judgment seat	Acts 25:17	2523
Bernice, and they that s with them	Acts 26:30	4775
The people s down to eat and drink	1Cor 10:7	2523
s down on the right hand of the	Heb 1:3	2523
s down on the right hand of God	Heb 10:12	2523
in heaven, and one s on the throne	Rev 4:2	2521
he that s was to look upon like a	Rev 4:3	2521
to him that s on the throne	Rev 4:9	2521
before him that s on the throne	Rev 4:10	2521
s on the throne a book written	Rev 5:1	2521
of him that s upon the throne	Rev 5:7	2521
he that s on him had a bow	Rev 6:2	2521
power was given to him that s	Rev 6:4	2521
he that s on him had a pair of	Rev 6:5	2521
his name that s on him was Death,	Rev 6:8	2521
vision, and them that s on them	Rev 9:17	2521
which s before God on their seats	Rev 11:16	2521
upon the cloud one s like unto	Rev 14:14	2521
voice to him that s on the cloud	Rev 14:15	2521
he that s on the cloud thrust in	Rev 14:16	2521
God that s on the throne, saying,	Rev 19:4	2521
he that s upon him was called	Rev 19:11	2521
against him that s on the horse	Rev 19:19	2521
of him that s upon the horse	Rev 19:21	2521
they s upon them, and judgment was	Rev 20:4	2523
white horse, and him that s on it	Rev 20:11	2521
he that s upon the throne said,	Rev 21:5	2521

SATAN (sa'-tun) *The adversary.*

S stood up against Israel, and	1Chr 21:1	7854
LORD, and S came also among them	Job 1:6	7854
And the LORD said unto S, Whence	Job 1:7	7854
Then S answered the LORD, and said	Job 1:7	7854
And the LORD said unto S, Hast	Job 1:8	7854
Then S answered the LORD, and said	Job 1:9	7854
And the LORD said unto S, Behold,	Job 1:12	7854
So S went forth from the presence	Job 1:12	7854
S came also among them to present	Job 2:1	7854
And the LORD said unto S, From	Job 2:2	7854
S answered the LORD, and said,	Job 2:2	7854
And the LORD said unto S, Hast	Job 2:3	7854
S answered the LORD, and said,	Job 2:4	7854
And the LORD said unto S, Behold,	Job 2:6	7854
So went S forth from the presence	Job 2:7	7854
let S stand at his right hand	Ps 109:6	7854
S standing at his right hand to	Zec 3:1	7854
S, The LORD rebuke thee, O S	Zec 3:2	7854
Jesus unto him, Get thee hence, S	Mt 4:10	4567
And if S cast out S, he is	Mt 12:26	4567
unto Peter, Get thee behind me, S	Mt 16:23	4567
forty days, tempted of S	Mk 1:13	4567
How can S cast out S	Mk 3:23	4567
if S rise up against himself, and	Mk 3:26	4567
S cometh immediately, and taketh	Mk 4:15	4567
saying, Get thee behind me, S	Mk 8:33	4567
unto him, Get thee behind me, S	Lk 4:8	4567

I beheld S as lightning fall from	Lk 10:18	4567
If S also be divided against	Lk 11:18	4567
whom S hath bound, lo, these	Lk 13:16	4567
Then entered S into Judas	Lk 22:3	4567
S hath desired to have you, that	Lk 22:31	4567
after the sop S entered into him	Jn 13:27	4567
why hath S filled thine heart to	Acts 5:3	4567
and from the power of S unto God	Acts 26:18	4567
bruise S under your feet shortly	Rom 16:20	4567
unto S for the destruction of the	1Cor 5:5	4567
that S tempt you not for your	1Cor 7:5	4567
Lest S should get an advantage of	2Cor 2:11	4567
for S himself is transformed into	2Cor 11:14	4567
the messenger of S to buffet me	2Cor 12:7	4567
but S hindered us	1Th 2:18	4567
the working of S with all power	2Th 2:9	4567
whom I have delivered unto S	1Ti 1:20	4567
are already turned aside after S	1Ti 5:15	4567
not, but are the synagogue of S	Rev 2:9	4567
slain among you, where S dwelleth	Rev 2:13	4567
have not known the depths of S	Rev 2:24	4567
make them of the synagogue of S	Rev 3:9	4567
serpent, called the Devil, and S	Rev 12:9	4567
serpent, which is the Devil, and S	Rev 20:2	4567
S shall be loosed out of his	Rev 20:7	4567

SATAN'S (sa'-tuns)

dwellest, even where S seat is	Rev 2:13	4567

SATEST

thou s in the throne judging	Ps 9:4	3427
s upon a stately bed, and a table	Eze 23:41	3427

SATIATE

I will s the soul of the priests	Jer 31:14	7301
shall devour, and it shall be s	Jer 46:10	7646

SATIATED

For I have s the weary soul, and I	Jer 31:25	7301

SATISFACTION

Moreover ye shall take no s for	Num 35:31	3724
ye shall take no s for him that	Num 35:32	3724

SATISFIED

my lust shall be s upon them	Ex 15:9	4390
and ye shall eat, and not be s	Lev 26:26	7646
shall come, and shall eat and be s	Deut 14:29	7646
s with favour, and full with the	Deut 33:23	7649
God, and are not s with my flesh	Job 19:22	7646
shall not be s with bread	Job 27:14	7646
we cannot be s	Job 31:31	7646
I shall be s, when I awake, with	Ps 17:15	7646
The meek shall eat and be s	Ps 22:26	7646
They shall be abundantly s with	Ps 36:8	7301
days of famine they shall be s	Ps 37:19	7646
meat, and grudge if they be not s	Ps 59:15	7646
My soul shall be s as with marrow	Ps 63:5	7646
we shall be s with the goodness	Ps 65:4	7646
of the rock should I have s thee	Ps 81:16	7649
the earth is s with the fruit of	Ps 104:13	7646
his land shall be s with bread	Prov 12:11	7646
A man shall be s with good by the	Prov 12:14	7646
good man shall be s from himself	Prov 14:14	7646
A man's belly shall be s with the	Prov 18:20	7646
and he that hath it shall abide s	Prov 19:23	7649
and thou shalt be s with bread	Prov 20:13	7646
so the eyes of man are never s	Prov 27:20	7646
are three things that are never s	Prov 30:15	7646
the eye is not s with seeing	Eccl 1:8	7646
neither is his eye s with riches	Eccl 4:8	7646
silver shall not be s with silver	Eccl 5:10	7646
left hand, and they shall not be s	Is 9:20	7646
he roasteth roast, and is s	Is 44:16	7646
of his soul, and shall be s	Is 53:11	7646
be s with the breasts of her	Is 66:11	7646
shall be s with my goodness	Jer 31:14	7646
all that spoil her shall be s	Jer 50:10	7646
his soul shall be s upon mount	Jer 50:19	7646
the Assyrians, to be s with bread	Lam 5:6	7646
them, and yet couldest not be s	Eze 16:28	7646
and yet thou wast not s herewith	Eze 16:29	7646
oil, and ye shall be s therewith	Joel 2:19	7646
ye shall eat in plenty, and be s	Joel 2:26	7646
but they were not s	Amos 4:8	7646
Thou shalt eat, but not be s	Mic 6:14	7646
and is as death, and cannot be s	Hab 2:5	7646

SATISFIEST

s the desire of every living	Ps 145:16	7646

SATISFIETH

Who s thy mouth with good things	Ps 103:5	7646
For he s the longing soul, and	Ps 107:9	7646
your labour for that which s not	Is 55:2	7654

S

SATISFY

To *s* the desolate and waste ground	Job 38:27	7646
O *s* us early with thy mercy	Ps 90:14	7646
With long life will I *s* him	Ps 91:16	7646
I will *s* her poor with bread	Ps 132:15	7646
let her breasts *s* thee at all	Prov 5:19	7301
if he steal to *s* his soul when he	Prov 6:30	4390
hungry, and *s* the afflicted soul	Is 58:10	7646
s thy soul in drought, and make	Is 58:11	7646
they shall not *s* their souls	Eze 7:19	7646
From whence can a man *s* these men	Mk 8:4	5526

SATISFYING

eateth to the *s* of his soul	Prov 13:25	7648
any honour to the *s* of the flesh	Col 2:23	4140

SATISFIED

s them with the bread of heaven	Ps 105:40	7649

SATYR

the *s* shall cry to his fellow	Is 34:14	8163

SATYRS

there, and *s* shall dance there	Is 13:21	8163

SAUL (sawl) See PAUL, SAUL'S, SHAUL.
1. The first king of Israel.

And he had a son, whose name was *S*	1Sa 9:2	7586
And Kish said to *S* his son	1Sa 9:3	7586
S said to his servant that was	1Sa 9:5	7586
Then said *S* to his servant, But,	1Sa 9:7	7586
And the servant answered *S* again	1Sa 9:8	7586
Then said *S* to his servant, Well	1Sa 9:10	7586
in his ear a day before *S* came	1Sa 9:15	7586
And when Samuel saw *S*, the LORD	1Sa 9:17	7586
Then *S* drew near to Samuel in the	1Sa 9:18	7586
And Samuel answered *S*, and said, I	1Sa 9:19	7586
S answered and said, Am not I a	1Sa 9:21	7586
And Samuel took *S* and his servant,	1Sa 9:22	7586
was upon it, and set it before *S*	1Sa 9:24	7586
So *S* did eat with Samuel that day	1Sa 9:24	7586
Samuel communed with *S* upon the	1Sa 9:25	7586
that Samuel called *S* to the top	1Sa 9:26	7586
S arose, and they went out both of	1Sa 9:26	7586
end of the city, Samuel said to *S*	1Sa 9:27	7586
Is *S* also among the prophets	1Sa 10:11	7586
Is *S* also among the prophets	1Sa 10:12	7586
S said unto his uncle, He told us	1Sa 10:16	7586
S the son of Kish was taken	1Sa 10:21	7586
S also went home to Gibeah	1Sa 10:26	7586
the messengers to Gibeah of *S*	1Sa 11:4	7586
S came after the herd out of the	1Sa 11:5	7586
S said, What aileth the people	1Sa 11:5	7586
S when he heard those tidings	1Sa 11:6	7586
cometh not forth after *S* and after	1Sa 11:7	7586
that *S* put the people in three	1Sa 11:11	7586
that said, Shall *S* reign over us	1Sa 11:12	7586
S said, There shall not a man be	1Sa 11:13	7586
there they made *S* king before the	1Sa 11:15	7586
and there *S* and all the men of	1Sa 11:15	7586
S reigned one year	1Sa 13:1	7586
S chose him three thousand men of	1Sa 13:2	7586
thousand were with *S* in Michmash	1Sa 13:2	7586
S blew the trumpet throughout all	1Sa 13:3	7586
all Israel heard say that *S* had	1Sa 13:4	7586
called together after *S* to Gilgal	1Sa 13:4	7586
As for *S*, he was yet in Gilgal,	1Sa 13:7	7586
S said, Bring hither a burnt	1Sa 13:9	7586
S went out to meet him, that he	1Sa 13:10	7586
S said, Because I saw that the	1Sa 13:11	7586
And Samuel said to *S*, Thou hast	1Sa 13:13	7586
S numbered the people that were	1Sa 13:15	7586
And *S*, and Jonathan his son, and the	1Sa 13:16	7586
of the people that were with *S*	1Sa 13:22	7586
but with *S* and with Jonathan his	1Sa 13:22	7586
that Jonathan the son of *S* said	1Sa 14:1	7586
S tarried in the uttermost part	1Sa 14:2	7586
the watchmen of *S* in Gibeah of	1Sa 14:16	7586
Then said *S* unto the people that	1Sa 14:17	7586
S said unto Ahiah, Bring hither	1Sa 14:18	7586
while *S* talked unto the priest,	1Sa 14:19	7586
S said unto the priest, Withdraw	1Sa 14:19	7586
And *S* and all the people that were	1Sa 14:20	7586
the Israelites that were with *S*	1Sa 14:21	7586
for *S* had adjured the people,	1Sa 14:24	7586
Then they told *S*, saying, Behold,	1Sa 14:33	7586
S said, Disperse yourselves among	1Sa 14:34	7586
S built an altar unto the LORD	1Sa 14:35	7586
S said, Let us go down after the	1Sa 14:36	7586
S asked counsel of God, Shall I	1Sa 14:37	7586
S said, Draw ye near hither, all	1Sa 14:38	7586
And the people said unto *S*	1Sa 14:40	7586
Therefore *S* said unto the LORD	1Sa 14:41	7586

And *S* and Jonathan were taken	1Sa 14:41	7586
S said, Cast lots between me and	1Sa 14:42	7586
Then *S* said to Jonathan, Tell me	1Sa 14:43	7586
S answered, God do so and more	1Sa 14:44	7586
And the people said unto *S*	1Sa 14:45	7586
Then *S* went up from following the	1Sa 14:46	7586
So *S* took the kingdom over Israel	1Sa 14:47	7586
Now the sons of *S* were Jonathan	1Sa 14:49	7586
And Kish was the father of *S*	1Sa 14:51	7586
the Philistines all the days of *S*	1Sa 14:52	7586
when *S* saw any strong man, or any	1Sa 14:52	7586
Samuel also said unto *S*, The LORD	1Sa 15:1	7586
S gathered the people together,	1Sa 15:4	7586
S came to a city of Amalek, and	1Sa 15:5	7586
S said unto the Kenites, Go,	1Sa 15:6	7586
S smote the Amalekites from	1Sa 15:7	7586
But *S* and the people spared Agag,	1Sa 15:9	7586
that I have set up *S* to be king	1Sa 15:11	7586
early to meet *S* in the morning	1Sa 15:12	7586
S came to Carmel, and, behold, he	1Sa 15:12	7586
And Samuel came to *S*	1Sa 15:13	7586
S said unto him, Blessed be thou	1Sa 15:13	7586
S said, They have brought them	1Sa 15:15	7586
Then Samuel said unto *S*, Stay, and	1Sa 15:16	7586
S said unto Samuel, Yea, I have	1Sa 15:20	7586
S said unto Samuel, I have sinned	1Sa 15:24	7586
And Samuel said unto *S*, I will not	1Sa 15:26	7586
So Samuel turned again after *S*	1Sa 15:31	7586
and *S* worshipped the LORD	1Sa 15:31	7586
S went up to his house to Gibeah	1Sa 15:34	7586
up to his house to Gibeah of *S*	1Sa 15:34	7586
see *S* until the day of his death	1Sa 15:35	7586
nevertheless Samuel mourned for *S*	1Sa 15:35	7586
he had made *S* king over Israel	1Sa 15:35	7586
How long wilt thou mourn for *S*	1Sa 16:1	7586
if *S* hear it, he will kill me	1Sa 16:2	7586
of the LORD departed from *S*	1Sa 16:14	7586
S said unto his servants, Provide	1Sa 16:17	7586
Wherefore *S* sent messengers unto	1Sa 16:19	7586
sent them by David his son unto *S*	1Sa 16:20	7586
And David came to *S*, and stood	1Sa 16:21	7586
S sent to Jesse, saying, Let	1Sa 16:22	7586
evil spirit from God was upon *S*	1Sa 16:23	7586
so *S* was refreshed, and was well,	1Sa 16:23	7586
And *S* and the men of Israel were	1Sa 17:2	7586
a Philistine, and ye servants to *S*	1Sa 17:8	7586
When *S* and all Israel heard those	1Sa 17:11	7586
for an old man in the days of *S*	1Sa 17:12	7586
went and followed *S* to the battle	1Sa 17:13	7586
and the three eldest followed *S*	1Sa 17:14	7586
returned from *S* to feed his	1Sa 17:15	7586
Now *S*, and they, and all the men of	1Sa 17:19	7586
they rehearsed them before *S*	1Sa 17:31	7586
And David said to *S*, Let no man's	1Sa 17:32	7586
S said to David, Thou art not	1Sa 17:33	7586
And David said unto *S*, Thy servant	1Sa 17:34	7586
S said unto David, Go, and the	1Sa 17:37	7586
S armed David with his armour, and	1Sa 17:38	7586
And David said unto *S*, I cannot go	1Sa 17:39	7586
when *S* saw David go forth against	1Sa 17:55	7586
brought him before *S* with the	1Sa 17:57	7586
S said to him, Whose son art thou	1Sa 17:58	7586
made an end of speaking unto *S*	1Sa 18:1	7586
S took him that day, and would let	1Sa 18:2	7586
went out whithersoever *S* sent him	1Sa 18:5	7586
S set him over the men of war, and	1Sa 18:5	7586
and dancing, to meet king *S*	1Sa 18:6	7586
S hath slain his thousands, and	1Sa 18:7	7586
S was very wroth, and the saying	1Sa 18:8	7586
S eyed David from that day and	1Sa 18:9	7586
evil spirit from God came upon *S*	1Sa 18:10	7586
And *S* cast the javelin	1Sa 18:11	7586
S was afraid of David, because	1Sa 18:12	7586
with him, and was departed from *S*	1Sa 18:12	7586
Therefore *S* removed him from him,	1Sa 18:13	7586
Wherefore when *S* saw that he	1Sa 18:15	7586
S said to David, Behold my elder	1Sa 18:17	7586
For *S* said, Let not mine hand be	1Sa 18:17	7586
And David said unto *S*, Who am I	1Sa 18:18	7586
and they told *S*, and the thing	1Sa 18:20	7586
S said, I will give him her, that	1Sa 18:21	7586
Wherefore *S* said to David, Thou	1Sa 18:21	7586
S commanded his servants, saying,	1Sa 18:22	7586
And the servants of *S* told him	1Sa 18:24	7586
S said, Thus shall ye say to	1Sa 18:25	7586
But *S* thought to make David fall	1Sa 18:25	7586
S gave him Michal his daughter to	1Sa 18:27	7586
S saw and knew that the LORD was	1Sa 18:28	7586
S was yet the more afraid of	1Sa 18:29	7586
and *S* became David's enemy	1Sa 18:29	7586
wisely than all the servants of *S*	1Sa 18:30	7586

S spake to Jonathan his son, and	1Sa 19:1	7586
S my father seeketh to kill thee	1Sa 19:2	7586
good of David unto *S* his father	1Sa 19:4	7586
S hearkened unto the voice of	1Sa 19:6	7586
S sware, As the LORD liveth, he	1Sa 19:6	7586
And Jonathan brought David to *S*	1Sa 19:7	7586
spirit from the LORD was upon *S*	1Sa 19:9	7586
S sought to smite David even to	1Sa 19:10	7586
S also sent messengers unto	1Sa 19:11	7586
when *S* sent messengers to take	1Sa 19:14	7586
S sent the messengers again to	1Sa 19:15	7586
S said unto Michal, Why hast thou	1Sa 19:17	7586
And Michal answered *S*, He said	1Sa 19:17	7586
him all that *S* had done to him	1Sa 19:18	7586
And it was told *S*, saying, Behold,	1Sa 19:19	7586
S sent messengers to take David	1Sa 19:20	7586
God was upon the messengers of *S*	1Sa 19:20	7586
And when it was told *S*, he sent	1Sa 19:21	7586
S sent messengers again the third	1Sa 19:21	7586
Is *S* also among the prophets	1Sa 19:24	7586
Nevertheless *S* spake not any	1Sa 20:26	7586
S said unto Jonathan his son,	1Sa 20:27	7586
And Jonathan answered *S*, David	1Sa 20:28	7586
And Jonathan answered *S* his father	1Sa 20:32	7586
S cast a javelin at him to smite	1Sa 20:33	7586
servants of *S* was there that day	1Sa 21:7	7586
of the herdmen that belonged to *S*	1Sa 21:7	7586
and fled that day for fear of *S*	1Sa 21:10	7586
S hath slain his thousands, and	1Sa 21:11	7586
When *S* heard that David was	1Sa 22:6	7586
(now *S* abode in Gibeah under a	1Sa 22:6	7586
Then *S* said unto his servants	1Sa 22:7	7586
was set over the servants of *S*	1Sa 22:9	7586
S said, Hear now, thou son of	1Sa 22:12	7586
S said unto him, Why have ye	1Sa 22:13	7586
Abiathar shewed David that *S* had	1Sa 22:21	7586
that he would surely tell *S*	1Sa 22:22	7586
it was told *S* that David was come	1Sa 23:7	7586
S said, God hath delivered him	1Sa 23:7	7586
S called all the people together	1Sa 23:8	7586
David knew that *S* secretly	1Sa 23:9	7586
that *S* seeketh to come to Keilah	1Sa 23:10	7586
will *S* come down, as thy servant	1Sa 23:11	7586
me and my men into the hand of *S*	1Sa 23:12	7586
it was told *S* that David was	1Sa 23:13	7586
S sought him every day, but God	1Sa 23:14	7586
David saw that *S* was come out to	1Sa 23:15	7586
for the hand of *S* my father shall	1Sa 23:17	7586
that also *S* my father knoweth	1Sa 23:17	7586
up the Ziphites to *S* to Gibeah	1Sa 23:19	7586
S said, Blessed be ye of the LORD	1Sa 23:21	7586
arose, and went to Ziph before *S*	1Sa 23:24	7586
S also and his men went to seek	1Sa 23:25	7586
when *S* heard that, he pursued	1Sa 23:25	7586
S went on this side of the	1Sa 23:26	7586
haste to get away for fear of *S*	1Sa 23:26	7586
for *S* and his men compassed David	1Sa 23:26	7586
But there came a messenger unto *S*	1Sa 23:27	7586
Wherefore *S* returned from	1Sa 23:28	7586
to pass, when *S* was returned from	1Sa 24:1	7586
Then *S* took three thousand chosen	1Sa 24:2	7586
S went in to cover his feet	1Sa 24:3	7586
them not to rise against *S*	1Sa 24:7	7586
But *S* rose up out of the cave, and	1Sa 24:7	7586
out of the cave, and cried after *S*	1Sa 24:8	7586
when *S* looked behind him, David	1Sa 24:8	7586
And David said to *S*, Wherefore	1Sa 24:9	7586
words unto *S*, that *S* said	1Sa 24:16	7586
S lifted up his voice, and wept	1Sa 24:16	7586
And David sware unto *S*	1Sa 24:22	7586
And *S* went home	1Sa 24:22	7586
But *S* had given Michal his	1Sa 25:44	7586
Ziphites came unto *S* to Gibeah	1Sa 26:1	7586
Then *S* arose, and went down to the	1Sa 26:2	7586
S pitched in the hill of Hachilah	1Sa 26:3	7586
he saw that *S* came after him into	1Sa 26:3	7586
understood that *S* was come in	1Sa 26:4	7586
to the place where *S* had pitched	1Sa 26:5	7586
beheld the place where *S* lay	1Sa 26:5	7586
S lay in the trench, and the	1Sa 26:5	7586
go down with me to *S* to the camp	1Sa 26:6	7586
S lay sleeping within the trench,	1Sa 26:7	7586
S knew David's voice, and said, Is	1Sa 26:17	7586
Then said *S*, I have sinned	1Sa 26:21	7586
Then *S* said to David, Blessed be	1Sa 26:25	7586
way, and *S* returned to his place	1Sa 26:25	7586
perish one day by the hand of *S*	1Sa 27:1	7586
S shall despair of me, to seek me	1Sa 27:1	7586
it was told *S* that David was fled	1Sa 27:4	7586
S had put away those that had	1Sa 28:3	7586
S gathered all Israel together,	1Sa 28:4	7586
when *S* saw the host of the	1Sa 28:5	7586
when *S* enquired of the LORD, the	1Sa 28:6	7586
Then said *S* unto his servants,	1Sa 28:7	7586
S disguised himself, and put on	1Sa 28:8	7586
thou knowest what *S* hath done	1Sa 28:9	7586
S sware to her by the LORD,	1Sa 28:10	7586
and the woman spake to *S*, saying,	1Sa 28:12	7586
for thou art *S*	1Sa 28:12	7586
And the woman said unto *S*, I saw	1Sa 28:13	7586
S perceived that it was Samuel,	1Sa 28:14	7586
And Samuel said to *S*, Why hast	1Sa 28:15	7586
S answered, I am sore distressed	1Sa 28:15	7586
Then *S* fell straightway all along	1Sa 28:20	7586
And the woman came unto *S*, and saw	1Sa 28:21	7586
And she brought it before *S*	1Sa 28:25	7586
the servant of *S* the king of	1Sa 29:3	7586
S slew his thousands, and David	1Sa 29:5	7586
Philistines followed hard upon *S*	1Sa 31:2	7586
And the battle went sore against *S*	1Sa 31:3	7586
Then said *S* unto his armourbearer	1Sa 31:4	7586
Therefore *S* took a sword, and fell	1Sa 31:4	7586
armourbearer saw that *S* was dead	1Sa 31:5	7586
So *S* died, and his three sons, and	1Sa 31:6	7586
the men of Israel fled, and that *S*	1Sa 31:7	7586
the slain, that they found *S*	1Sa 31:8	7586
the Philistines had done to *S*	1Sa 31:11	7586
all night, and took the body of *S*	1Sa 31:12	7586
came to pass after the death of *S*	2Sa 1:1	7586
camp from *S* with his clothes rent	2Sa 1:2	7586
and *S* and Jonathan his son are dead	2Sa 1:4	7586
told him, How knowest thou that *S*	2Sa 1:5	7586
behold, *S* leaned upon his spear	2Sa 1:6	7586
wept, and fasted until even, for *S*	2Sa 1:12	7586
with this lamentation over *S*	2Sa 1:17	7586
vilely cast away, the shield of *S*	2Sa 1:21	7586
the sword of *S* returned not empty	2Sa 1:22	7586
S and Jonathan were lovely and	2Sa 1:23	7586
daughters of Israel, weep over *S*	2Sa 1:24	7586
were they that buried *S*	2Sa 2:4	7586
unto your lord, even unto *S*	2Sa 2:5	7586
for your master *S* is dead	2Sa 2:7	7586
took Ish-bosheth the son of *S*	2Sa 2:8	7586
of Ish-bosheth the son of *S*	2Sa 2:12	7586
to Ish-bosheth the son of *S*	2Sa 2:15	7586
long war between the house of *S*	2Sa 3:1	7586
and the house of *S* waxed weaker	2Sa 3:1	7586
was war between the house of *S*	2Sa 3:6	7586
himself strong for the house of *S*	2Sa 3:6	7586
S had a concubine, whose name was	2Sa 3:7	7586
unto the house of *S* thy father	2Sa 3:8	7586
the kingdom from the house of *S*	2Sa 3:10	7586
old when the tidings came of *S*	2Sa 4:4	7586
the son of *S* thine enemy, which	2Sa 4:8	7586
my lord the king this day of *S*	2Sa 4:8	7586
S is dead, thinking to have	2Sa 4:10	7586
when *S* was king over us, thou	2Sa 5:2	7586
of *S* came out to meet David	2Sa 6:20	7586
Michal the daughter of *S* had no	2Sa 6:23	7586
from him, as I took it from *S*	2Sa 7:15	7586
that is left of the house of *S*	2Sa 9:1	7586
there was of the house of *S* a	2Sa 9:2	7586
not yet any of the house of *S*	2Sa 9:3	7586
the son of Jonathan, the son of *S*	2Sa 9:6	7586
thee all the land of *S* thy father	2Sa 9:7	7586
son all that pertained to *S*	2Sa 9:9	7586
thee out of the hand of *S*	2Sa 12:7	7586
of the family of the house of *S*	2Sa 16:5	7586
all the blood of the house of *S*	2Sa 16:8	7586
the servant of the house of *S*	2Sa 19:17	7586
Mephibosheth the son of *S* came	2Sa 19:24	7586
And the LORD answered, It is for *S*	2Sa 21:1	7586
S sought to slay them in his zeal	2Sa 21:2	7586
will have no silver nor gold of *S*	2Sa 21:4	7586
up unto the LORD in Gibeah of *S*	2Sa 21:6	7586
the son of Jonathan the son of *S*	2Sa 21:7	7586
David and Jonathan the son of *S*	2Sa 21:7	7586
of Aiah, whom she bare unto *S*	2Sa 21:8	7586
sons of Michal the daughter of *S*	2Sa 21:8	7586
of Aiah, the concubine of *S*	2Sa 21:11	7586
David went and took the bones of *S*	2Sa 21:12	7586
Philistines had slain *S* in Gilboa	2Sa 21:12	7586
up from thence the bones of *S*	2Sa 21:13	7586
And the bones of *S* and Jonathan his	2Sa 21:14	7586
enemies, and out of the hand of *S*	2Sa 22:1	7586
in the days of *S* they made war	1Chr 5:10	7586
Ner begat Kish, and Kish begat *S*	1Chr 8:33	7586
S begat Jonathan, and Malchi-shua,	1Chr 8:33	7586
and Kish begat *S*	1Chr 9:39	7586
S begat Jonathan, and Malchi-shua,	1Chr 9:39	7586
Philistines followed hard after *S*	1Chr 10:2	7586
and Malchi-shua the sons of *S*	1Chr 10:2	7586

And the battle went sore against *S*	1Chr 10:3	7586
Then said *S* to his armourbearer,	1Chr 10:4	7586
So *S* took a sword, and fell upon	1Chr 10:4	7586
armourbearer saw that *S* was dead	1Chr 10:5	7586
So *S* died, and his three sons, and	1Chr 10:6	7586
saw that they fled, and that *S*	1Chr 10:7	7586
the slain, that they found *S*	1Chr 10:8	7586
the Philistines had done to *S*	1Chr 10:11	7586
men, and took away the body of *S*	1Chr 10:12	7586
So *S* died for his transgression	1Chr 10:13	7586
time past, even when *S* was king	1Chr 11:2	7586
because of *S* the son of Kish	1Chr 12:1	7586
Philistines against *S* to battle	1Chr 12:19	7586
He will fall to his master *S* to	1Chr 12:19	7586
to turn the kingdom of *S* to him	1Chr 12:23	7586
of Benjamin, the kindred of *S*	1Chr 12:29	7586
kept the ward of the house of *S*	1Chr 12:29	7586
not at it in the days of *S*	1Chr 13:3	7586
of *S* looking out at a window saw	1Chr 15:29	7586
S the son of Kish, and Abner the	1Chr 26:28	7586
enemies, and from the hand of *S*	Ps 18:*t*	7586
Doeg the Edomite came and told *S*	Ps 52:*t*	7586
the Ziphims came and said to *S*	Ps 54:*t*	7586
when he fled from *S* in the cave	Ps 57:*t*	7586
when *S* sent, and they watched the	Ps 59:*t*	7586
Gibeah of *S* is fled	Is 10:29	7586
gave unto them *S* the son of Cis	Acts 13:21	4569
2. *An Edomite king.*		
S of Rehoboth by the river	Gen 36:37	7586
S died, and Baal-hanan the son of	Gen 36:38	7586
3. *Original name of Paul.*		
man's feet, whose name was *S*	Acts 7:58	4569
S was consenting unto his death	Acts 8:1	4569
As for *S*, he made havock of the	Acts 8:3	4569
And *S*, yet breathing out	Acts 9:1	4569
a voice saying unto him, Saul, *S*	Acts 9:4	4569
And *S* arose from the earth	Acts 9:8	4569
house of Judas for one called *S*	Acts 9:11	4569
his hands on him said, Brother *S*	Acts 9:17	4569
Then was *S* certain days with the	Acts 9:19	4569
But *S* increased the more in	Acts 9:22	4569
their laying await was known of *S*	Acts 9:24	4569
when *S* was come to Jerusalem, he	Acts 9:26	4569
Barnabas to Tarsus, for to seek *S*	Acts 11:25	4569
by the hands of Barnabas and *S*	Acts 11:30	4569
S returned from Jerusalem, when	Acts 12:25	4569
up with Herod the tetrarch, and *S*	Acts 13:1	4569
S for the work whereunto I have	Acts 13:2	4569
who called for Barnabas and *S*	Acts 13:7	4569
Then *S*, (who also is called Paul,	Acts 13:9	4569
a voice saying unto me, Saul, *S*	Acts 22:7	4569
stood, and said unto me, Brother *S*	Acts 22:13	4569
in the Hebrew tongue, Saul, *S*	Acts 26:14	4569

SAUL'S *Refers to Saul 1.*

asses of Kish *S* father were lost	1Sa 9:3	7586
S uncle said unto him and to his	1Sa 10:14	7586
S uncle said, Tell me, I pray	1Sa 10:15	7586
the name of *S* wife was Ahinoam,	1Sa 14:50	7586
Abner, the son of Ner, *S* uncle	1Sa 14:50	7586
S servants said unto him, Behold	1Sa 16:15	7586
also in the sight of *S* servants	1Sa 18:5	7586
and there was a javelin in *S* hand	1Sa 18:10	7586
to pass at the time when Merab *S*	1Sa 18:19	7586
Michal *S* daughter loved David	1Sa 18:20	7586
S servants spake those words in	1Sa 18:23	7586
that Michal *S* daughter loved him	1Sa 18:28	7586
But Jonathan *S* son delighted much	1Sa 19:2	7586
he slipped away out of *S* presence	1Sa 19:10	7586
arose, and Abner sat by *S* side	1Sa 20:25	7586
Then *S* anger was kindled against	1Sa 20:30	7586
Jonathan *S* son arose, and went to	1Sa 23:16	7586
off the skirt of *S* robe privily	1Sa 24:4	7586
because he had cut off *S* skirt	1Sa 24:5	7586
the cruse of water from *S* bolster	1Sa 26:12	7586
Abinadab, and Melchi-shua, *S* sons	1Sa 31:2	7586
the son of Ner, captain of *S* host	2Sa 2:8	7586
Ish-bosheth was forty years	2Sa 2:10	7586
first bring Michal *S* daughter	2Sa 3:13	7586
messengers to Ish-bosheth *S* son	2Sa 3:14	7586
when *S* son heard that Abner was	2Sa 4:1	7586
S son had two men that were	2Sa 4:2	7586
S son, had a son that was lame of	2Sa 4:4	7586
Michal *S* daughter looked through	2Sa 6:16	7586
S servant, and said unto him, I	2Sa 9:9	7586
even of *S* brethren of Benjamin	1Chr 12:2	7586

SAVE

me, but they will *s* thee alive	Gen 12:12	2421
S only that which the young men	Gen 14:24	1107
s the bread which he did eat	Gen 39:6	3588,518
to *s* your lives by a great	Gen 45:7	2421

this day, to *s* much people alive	Gen 50:20	2421
every daughter ye shall *s* alive	Ex 1:22	2421
s that which every man must eat,	Ex 12:16	389
s unto the LORD only, he shall be	Ex 22:20	1115
s Caleb the son of Jephunneh, and	Num 14:30	3588,518
s Caleb the son of Jephunneh, and	Num 26:65	3588,518
S Caleb the son of Jephunneh the	Num 32:12	3588,518
S Caleb the son of Jephunneh	Deut 1:36	2108
S when there shall be no poor	Deut 15:4	657
against your enemies, to *s* you	Deut 20:4	3467
thou shalt *s* alive nothing that	Deut 20:16	2421
cried, and there was none to *s* her	Deut 22:27	3467
evermore, and no man shall *s* thee	Deut 28:29	3467
that ye will *s* alive my father,	Josh 2:13	2421
us quickly, and *s* us, and help us	Josh 10:6	3467
burned none of them, *s* Hazor only	Josh 11:13	2108
s the Hivites the inhabitants of	Josh 11:19	1115
s cities to dwell in, with their	Josh 14:4	3588,518
the LORD, (*s* us not this day,)	Josh 22:22	3467
thou shalt *s* Israel from the hand	Judg 6:14	3467
Lord, wherewith shall I *s* Israel	Judg 6:15	3467
will ye *s* him.	Judg 6:31	3467
If thou wilt *s* Israel by mine	Judg 6:36	3467
thou wilt *s* Israel by mine hand	Judg 6:37	3467
men that lapped will I *s* you	Judg 7:7	3467
This is nothing else *s* the sword	Judg 7:14	1115,518
it may *s* us out of the hand of	1Sa 4:3	3467
that he will *s* us out of the hand	1Sa 7:8	3467
that he may *s* my people out of	1Sa 9:16	3467
shouted, and said, God *s* the king	1Sa 10:24	2421
said, How shall this man *s* us	1Sa 10:27	3467
then, if there be no man to *s* us	1Sa 11:3	3467
the LORD to *s* by many or by few	1Sa 14:6	3467
If thou *s* not thy to night, to	1Sa 19:11	4422
for there is no other *s* that here	1Sa 21:9	2108
the Philistines, and *s* Keilah	1Sa 23:2	3467
s four hundred young men, which	1Sa 30:17	3588,518
s to every man his wife and his	1Sa 30:22	3588,518
s my people Israel out of the	2Sa 3:18	3467
s one little ewe lamb, which he	2Sa 12:3	3588,518
God *s* the king, God *s* the king	2Sa 16:16	2421
God *s* the king, God *s* the king	2Sa 16:16	2421
the afflicted people thou wilt *s*	2Sa 22:28	3467
For who is God, *s* the LORD	2Sa 22:32	1107
and who is a rock, *s* our God	2Sa 22:32	1107
looked, but there was none to *s*	2Sa 22:42	3467
that thou mayest *s* thine own life	1Kin 1:12	4422
him, and say, God *s* king Adonijah	1Kin 1:25	2421
and say, God *s* king Solomon	1Kin 1:34	2421
people said, God *s* king Solomon	1Kin 1:39	2421
the house, *s* we two in the house	1Kin 3:18	2108
the ark *s* the two tables of stone	1Kin 8:9	7535
s only in the matter of Uriah the	1Kin 15:5	3467
we may find grass to *s* the horses	1Kin 18:5	2421
peradventure he will *s* thy life	1Kin 20:31	2421
s only with the king of Israel	1Kin 22:31	3588,518
in the house, *s* a pot of oil	2Kin 4:2	3467
if they *s* us alive, we shall live	2Kin 7:4	2421
hands, and said, God *s* the king	2Kin 11:12	2421
S that the high places were not	2Kin 15:4	7535
s me out of the hand of the king	2Kin 16:7	3467
s thou us out of his hand, that	2Kin 19:19	3467
I will defend this city, to *s* it	2Kin 19:34	3467
s the poorest sort of the people	2Kin 24:14	2108
S us, O God of our salvation, and	1Chr 16:35	3467
s only to burn sacrifice before	2Chr 2:6	518
There was nothing in the ark *s*	2Chr 5:10	7535
s only with the king of Israel	2Chr 18:30	3588,518
s Jehoahaz, the youngest of his	2Chr 21:17	3467
s the priests, and they that	2Chr 23:6	3588,518
him, and said, God *s* the king	2Chr 23:11	2421
s the beast that I rode upon	Neh 2:12	3588,518
go into the temple to *s* his life	Neh 6:11	2425
but *s* his life	Job 2:6	8104
he shall not *s* of that which he	Job 20:20	4422
he shall *s* the humble person	Job 22:29	3467
thine own right hand can *s* thee	Job 40:14	3467
s me, O my God	Ps 3:7	3467
oh *s* me for thy mercies' sake	Ps 6:4	3467
s me from all them that persecute	Ps 7:1	3467
For thou wilt *s* the afflicted	Ps 18:27	3467
For who is God *s* the LORD	Ps 18:31	1107
or who is a rock *s* our God	Ps 18:31	2108
but there was none to *s* them	Ps 18:41	3467
S, LORD	Ps 20:9	3467
S me from the lion's mouth	Ps 22:21	3467
S thy people, and bless thine	Ps 28:9	3467
for an house of defence to *s* me	Ps 31:2	3467
s me for thy mercies' sake	Ps 31:16	3467
s them, because they trust in him	Ps 37:40	3467
neither did their own arm *s* them	Ps 44:3	3467

bow, neither shall my sword *s* me .... Ps 44:6 — 3467
S me, O God, by thy name, and .... Ps 54:1 — 3467
and the LORD shall *s* me .... Ps 55:16 — 3467
s me from the reproach of him................ Ps 57:3 — 3467
iniquity, and *s* me from bloody men .... Ps 59:2 — 3467
s with thy right hand, and hear ʀ e .... Ps 60:5 — 3467
S me, O God .... Ps 69:1 — 3467
For God will *s* Zion, and will .... Ps 69:35 — 3467
thine ear unto me, and *s* me.................. Ps 71:2 — 3467
hast given commandment to *s* me .... Ps 71:3 — 3467
he shall *s* the children of the ...... Ps 72:4 — 3467
shall *s* the souls of the needy .... Ps 72:13 — 3467
to *s* all the meek of the earth .... Ps 76:9 — 3467
up thy strength, and come and *s* us ...... Ps 80:2 — 3444
s thy servant that trusteth in .... Ps 86:2 — 3467
s the son of thine handmaid .... Ps 86:16 — 3467
S us, O LORD our God, and gathe ˙......... Ps 106:47 — 3467
s with thy right hand, and answeɪ .... Ps 108:6 — 3467
O *s* me according to thy mercy .... Ps 109:26 — 3467
to *s* him from those that condemn.......... Ps 109:31 — 3467
S now, I beseech thee, O LORD .... Ps 118:25 — 3467
I am thine, *s* me......................... Ps 119:94 — 3467
s me, and I shall keep thy.................. Ps 119:146 — 3467
and thy right hand shall *s* me .... Ps 138:7 — 3467
hear their cry, and will *s* them .... Ps 145:19 — 3467
on the LORD, and he shall *s* thee .... Prov 20:22 — 3467
waited for him, and he will *s* us .. .. Is 25:9 — 3467
he will *s* us.............................. Is 33:22 — 3467
he will come and *s* you.................... Is 35:4 — 3467
s us from his hand, that all the .... Is 37:20 — 3467
city to *s* it for mine own sake .... Is 37:35 — 3467
The LORD was ready to *s* me .... Is 38:20 — 3467
and pray unto a god that cannot ˂ .... Is 45:20 — 3467
nor *s* him out of his trouble .... Is 46:7 — 3467
s thee from these things that .... Is 47:13 — 3467
none shall *s* thee........................... Is 47:15 — 3467
thee, and I will *s* thy children............... Is 49:25 — 3467
not shortened, that it cannot *s* .... Is 59:1 — 3467
in righteousness, mighty to *s* ...... Is 63:1 — 3467
they will say, Arise, and *s* us .... Jer 2:27 — 3467
if they can *s* thee in the time of .... Jer 2:28 — 3467
but they shall not *s* them at all............... Jer 11:12 — 3467
as a mighty man that cannot *s* .... Jer 14:9 — 3467
for I am with thee to *s* thee .... Jer 15:20 — 3467
s me, and I shall be saved .... Jer 17:14 — 3467
I will *s* thee from afar, and thy .... Jer 30:10 — 3467
thee, saith the LORD, to *s* thee............... Jer 30:11 — 3467
s thy people, the remnant of.................. Jer 31:7 — 3467
for I am with you to *s* you .... Jer 42:11 — 3467
I will *s* you from afar off, and............... Jer 46:27 — 3467
s your lives, and be like the................... Jer 48:6 — 4422
for a nation that could not *s* us.. .... Lam 4:17 — 3467
his wicked way, to *s* his life .... Eze 3:18 — 2421
will ye *s* the souls alive that .... Eze 13:18 — 2421
to *s* the souls alive that should .... Eze 13:19 — 2421
he shall *s* his soul alive........................ Eze 18:27 — 2421
Therefore will I *s* my flock...................... Eze 34:22 — 3467
I will also *s* you from all your .... Eze 36:29 — 3467
but I will *s* them out of all .... Eze 37:23 — 3467
s of thee, O king, he shall be .... Dan 6:7 — 3861
s of thee, O king, shall be cast.............. Dan 6:12 — 3861
will *s* them by the LORD their God .... Hos 1:7 — 3467
will not *s* them by bow, nor by .... Hos 1:7 — 3467
that may *s* thee in all thy cities .... Hos 13:10 — 3467
Asshur shall not *s* us .... Hos 14:3 — 3467
of violence, and thou wilt not *s*............... Hab 1:2 — 3467
he will *s*, he will rejoice over .... Zeph 3:17 — 3467
I will *s* her that halteth, and............... Zeph 3:19 — 3467
I will *s* my people from the east............. Zec 8:7 — 3467
so will I *s* you, and ye shall be a............. Zec 8:13 — 3467
the LORD their God shall *s* them .... Zec 9:16 — 3467
I will *s* the house of Joseph, and . ... Zec 10:6 — 3467
The LORD also shall *s* the tents .... Zec 12:7 — 3467
for he shall *s* his people from .... Mt 1:21 — *4982*
and awoke him, saying, Lord, *s* us .... Mt 8:25 — *4982*
s the Son, and to whomsoever .... Mt 11:27 — *1508*
s in his own country, and in his .... Mt 13:57 — *1508*
he cried, saying, Lord, *s* me.................. Mt 14:30 — *4982*
For whosoever will s his life .... Mt 16:25 — *4982*
they saw no man, *s* Jesus only .... Mt 17:8 — *1508*
is come to s that which was lost .... Mt 18:11 — *4982*
s they to whom it is given .... Mt 19:11 — *235*
it in three days, *s* thyself .... Mt 27:40 — *4982*
himself he cannot *s*................................ Mt 27:42 — *4982*
whether Elias will come to *s* him .... Mt 27:49 — *4982*
to s life, or to kill .... Mk 3:4 — *4982*
s Peter, and James, and John the .... Mk 5:37 — *1508*
s that he laid his hands upon a.............. Mk 6:5 — *1508*
for their journey, *s* a staff only .... Mk 6:8 — *1508*
For whosoever will s his life .... Mk 8:35 — *4982*
the gospel's, the same shall s it............. Mk 8:35 — *4982*

s Jesus only with themselves .... Mk 9:8 — *235*
S thyself, and come down from the........ Mk 15:30 — *4982*
himself he cannot *s*................................ Mk 15:31 — *4982*
s unto Sarepta, a city of Sidon,............. Lk 4:26 — *1508*
to *s* life, or to destroy it......................... Lk 6:9 — *4982*
s Peter, and James, and John, and .... Lk 8:51 — *1508*
For whosoever will s his life .... Lk 9:24 — *4982*
for my sake, the same shall s it............. Lk 9:24 — *4982*
men's lives, but to s them .... Lk 9:56 — *4982*
glory to God, s this stranger .... Lk 17:18 — *1508*
seek to s his life shall lose it................. Lk 17:33 — *4982*
none is good, s one, that is, God............ Lk 18:19 — *1508*
seek and to s that which was lost .... Lk 19:10 — *4982*
let him *s* himself, if he be .... Lk 23:35 — *4982*
the king of the Jews, *s* thyself .... Lk 23:37 — *4982*
thou be Christ, *s* thyself and us............. Lk 23:39 — *4982*
there, *s* that one whereinto his .... Jn 6:22 — *1508*
s he which is of God, he hath .... Jn 6:46 — *1508*
Father, s me from this hour .... Jn 12:27 — *4982*
the world, but to s the world .... Jn 12:47 — *4982*
needeth not s to wash his feet .... Jn 13:10 — *2228*
S yourselves from this untoward .... Acts 2:40 — *4982*
S that the Holy Ghost witnesseth .... Acts 20:23 — *4133*
s only that they keep themselves .... Acts 21:25 — *1508*
the centurion, willing to *s* Paul............... Acts 27:43 — *1295*
my flesh, and might *s* some of them .... Rom 11:14 — *4982*
preaching to *s* them that believe .... 1Cor 1:21 — *4982*
s Jesus Christ, and him crucified .... 1Cor 2:2 — *1508*
s the spirit of man which is in................ 1Cor 5:5 — *1508*
whether thou shalt *s* thy husband .... 1Cor 7:16 — *4982*
whether thou shalt *s* thy wife .... 1Cor 7:16 — *4982*
that I might by all means *s* some .... 1Cor 9:22 — *4982*
received I forty stripes *s* one................. 2Cor 11:24 — *3844*
s James the Lord's brother .... Gal 1:19 — *1508*
s in the cross of our Lord Jesus .... Gal 6:14 — *1508*
came into the world to *s* sinners .... 1Ti 1:15 — *4982*
this thou shalt both *s* thyself.................. 1Ti 4:16 — *4982*
that was able to *s* him from death.......... Heb 5:7 — *4982*
Wherefore he is able also to *s*................ Heb 7:25 — *4982*
which is able to *s* your souls .... Jas 1:21 — *4982*
can faith *s* him .... Jas 2:14 — *4982*
is one lawgiver, who is able to *s* .... Jas 4:12 — *4982*
prayer of faith shall *s* the sick .... Jas 5:15 — *4982*
his way shall *s* a soul from death .... Jas 5:20 — *4982*
even baptism doth also now *s* us............ 1Pet 3:21 — *4982*
others *s* with fear, pulling them .... Jude 23 — *4982*
s he that had the mark, or the .... Rev 13:17 — *1508*

SAVED

they said, Thou hast *s* our lives .... Gen 47:25
but *s* the men children alive................... Ex 1:17 — 2421
have *s* the men children alive................. Ex 1:18 — 2421
Thus the LORD *s* Israel that day.............. Ex 14:30 — 3467
ye shall be *s* from your enemies .... Num 10:9 — 3467
I had slain thee, and *s* her alive............. Num 22:33 — 2421
Have ye *s* all the women alive................. Num 31:15 — 2421
O people *s* by the LORD, the.................... Deut 33:29 — 3467
Joshua *s* Rahab the harlot alive,............. Josh 6:25 — 2421
saying, Mine own hand hath *s* me .... Judg 7:2 — 3467
if ye had *s* them alive, I would .... Judg 8:19 — 2421
they had *s* alive of the women of............ Judg 21:14 — 2421
who himself *s* you out of all your .... 1Sa 10:19 — 3467
So the LORD *s* Israel that day................. 1Sa 14:23 — 3467
So David *s* the inhabitants of................. 1Sa 23:5 — 3467
David *s* neither man nor woman............. 1Sa 27:11 — 2421
which this day have *s* thy life................. 2Sa 19:5 — 4422
The king *s* us out of the hand of .... 2Sa 19:9 — 5337
so shall I be *s* from mine enemies .... 2Sa 22:4 — 3467
s himself there, not once nor .... 2Kin 6:10 — 8104
but he *s* them by the hand of .... 2Kin 14:27 — 3467
the LORD *s* them by a great .... 1Chr 11:14 — 3467
Thus the LORD *s* Hezekiah and the......... 2Chr 32:22 — 3467
who *s* them out of the hand of................ Neh 9:27 — 3467
so shall I be *s* from mine enemies.......... Ps 18:3 — 3467
There is no king *s* by the .... Ps 33:16 — 3467
s him out of all his troubles .... Ps 34:6 — 3467
But thou hast *s* us from our .... Ps 44:7 — 3467
and we shall be *s*........................... Ps 80:3 — 3467
and we shall be *s*........................... Ps 80:7 — 3467
and we shall be *s*........................... Ps 80:19 — 3467
Nevertheless he *s* them for his .... Ps 106:8 — 3467
he *s* them from the hand of him............. Ps 106:10 — 3467
he *s* them out of their distresses............. Ps 107:13 — 3467
walketh uprightly shall be *s* .... Prov 28:18 — 3467
returning and rest shall ye be *s*............. Is 30:15 — 3467
I have declared, and have *s*.................... Is 43:12 — 3467
But Israel shall be *s* in the LORD .... Is 45:17 — 3467
Look unto me, and be ye *s*, all the .... Is 45:22 — 3467
the angel of his presence *s* them .... Is 63:9 — 3467
is continuance, and we shall be *s* .... Is 64:5 — 3467
wickedness, that thou mayest be *s* .... Jer 4:14 — 3467

S

summer is ended, and we are not *s*	Jer 8:20	3467
save me, and I shall be *s*	Jer 17:14	3467
In his days Judah shall be *s*	Jer 23:6	3467
but he shall be *s* out of it	Jer 30:7	3467
In those days shall Judah be *s*	Jer 33:16	3467
endureth to the end shall be *s*	Mt 10:22	4982
amazed, saying, Who then can be *s*	Mt 19:25	4982
unto the end, the same shall be *s*	Mt 24:13	4982
there should no flesh be *s*	Mt 24:22	4982
He *s* others; himself he	Mt 27:42	4982
themselves, Who then can be *s*	Mk 10:26	4982
unto the end, the same shall be *s*	Mk 13:13	4982
those days, no flesh should be *s*	Mk 13:20	4982
with the scribes, He *s* others	Mk 15:31	4982
and is baptized shall be *s*	Mk 16:16	4982
we should be *s* from our enemies	Lk 1:71	4991
the woman, Thy faith hath *s* thee	Lk 7:50	4982
lest they should believe and be *s*	Lk 8:12	4982
Lord, are there few that be *s*	Lk 13:23	4982
heard it said, Who then can be *s*	Lk 18:26	4982
thy faith hath *s* thee	Lk 18:42	4982
derided him, saying, He *s* others	Lk 23:35	4982
the world through him might be *s*	Jn 3:17	4982
things I say, that ye might be *s*	Jn 5:34	4982
any man enter in, he shall be *s*	Jn 10:9	4982
the name of the Lord shall be *s*	Acts 2:21	4982
church daily such as should be *s*	Acts 2:47	4982
among men, whereby we must be *s*	Acts 4:12	4982
thou and all thy house shall be *s*	Acts 11:14	4982
manner of Moses, ye cannot be *s*	Acts 15:1	4982
Lord Jesus Christ we shall be *s*	Acts 15:11	4982
Sirs, what must I do to be *s*	Acts 16:30	4982
Jesus Christ, and thou shalt be *s*	Acts 16:31	4982
should be *s* was then taken away	Acts 27:20	4982
abide in the ship, ye cannot be *s*	Acts 27:31	4982
we shall be *s* from wrath through.....	Rom 5:9	4982
we shall be *s* by his life	Rom 5:10	4982
For we are *s* by hope	Rom 8:24	4982
of the sea, a remnant shall be *s*	Rom 9:27	4982
Israel is, that they might be *s*	Rom 10:1	4991
from the dead, thou shalt be *s*	Rom 10:9	4982
the name of the Lord shall be *s*	Rom 10:13	4982
And so all Israel shall be *s*	Rom 11:26	4982
but unto us which are *s* it is the	1Cor 1:18	4982
but he himself shall be *s*	1Cor 3:15	4982
that the spirit may be *s* in the	1Cor 5:5	4982
of many, that they may be *s*	1Cor 10:33	4982
By which also ye are *s*, if ye	1Cor 15:2	4982
of Christ, in them that are *s*	2Cor 2:15	4982
with Christ, (by grace ye are *s*	Eph 2:5	4982
by grace are ye *s* through faith	Eph 2:8	4982
the Gentiles that they might be *s*	1Th 2:16	4982
the truth, that they might be *s*	2Th 2:10	4982
Who will have all men to be *s*	1Ti 2:4	4982
she shall be *s* in childbearing	1Ti 2:15	4982
Who hath *s* us, and called us with	2Ti 1:9	4982
according to his mercy he *s* us	Titus 3:5	4982
is, eight souls were *s* by water	1Pet 3:20	1295
And if the righteous scarcely be *s*	1Pet 4:18	4982
but *s* Noah the eighth person, a	2Pet 2:5	5442
having *s* the people out of the	Jude 5	4982
s shall walk in the light of it	Rev 21:24	4982

SAVEST

thou *s* me from violence	2Sa 22:3	3467
how *s* thou the arm that hath no	Job 26:2	3467
O thou that *s* by thy right hand	Ps 17:7	3467

SAVETH

which *s* Israel, though it be in	1Sa 14:39	3467
that the Lord *s* not with sword	1Sa 17:47	3467
But he *s* the poor from the sword,	Job 5:15	3467
which *s* the upright in heart	Ps 7:10	3467
I that the Lord *s* his anointed	Ps 20:6	3467
s such as be of a contrite spirit	Ps 34:18	3467
he *s* them out of their distresses	Ps 107:19	3467

SAVING

hast shewed unto me in *s* my life	Gen 19:19	2421
s that every one put them off for	Neh 4:23	
the *s* strength of his right hand	Ps 20:6	3468
he is the *s* strength of his	Ps 28:8	3444
thy *s* health among all nations	Ps 67:2	3444
s the beholding of them with	Eccl 5:11	518
s that I will not utterly destroy	Amos 9:8	657
s for the cause of fornication,	Mt 5:32	3924
was cleansed, *s* Naaman the Syrian	Lk 4:27	1508
that believe to the *s* of the soul	Heb 10:39	4047
an ark to the *s* of his house	Heb 11:7	4991
knoweth *s* he that receiveth it	Rev 2:17	1508

SAVIOUR

my high tower, and my refuge, my *s*	2Sa 22:3	3467
(And the Lord gave Israel a *s*	2Kin 13:5	3467
They forgat God their *s*, which	Ps 106:21	3467
and he shall send them a *s*	Is 19:20	3467
the Holy One of Israel, thy *S*	Is 43:3	3467
and beside me there is no *s*	Is 43:11	3467
thyself, O God of Israel, the *S*	Is 45:15	3467
a just God and a *S*	Is 45:21	3467
know that I the Lord am thy *S*	Is 49:26	3467
know that I the Lord am thy *S*	Is 60:16	3467
so he was their *S*	Is 63:8	3467
the *s* thereof in time of trouble,	Jer 14:8	3467
for there is no *s* beside me	Hos 13:4	3467
spirit hath rejoiced in God my *S*	Lk 1:47	4990
this day in the city of David a *S*	Lk 2:11	4990
the Christ, the *S* of the world	Jn 4:42	4990
right hand to be a Prince and a *S*	Acts 5:31	4990
promise raised unto Israel a *S*	Acts 13:23	4990
and he is the *s* of the body	Eph 5:23	4990
whence also we look for the *S*	Phil 3:20	4990
by the commandment of God our *S*	1Ti 1:1	4990
in the sight of God our *S*	1Ti 2:3	4990
God, who is the *S* of all men	1Ti 4:10	4990
appearing of our *S* Jesus Christ	2Ti 1:10	4990
to the commandment of God our *S*	Titus 1:3	4990
and the Lord Jesus Christ our *S*	Titus 1:4	4990
of God our *S* in all things	Titus 2:10	4990
great God and our *S* Jesus Christ	Titus 2:13	4990
love of God our *S* toward man	Titus 3:4	4990
through Jesus Christ our *S*	Titus 3:6	4990
of God and our *S* Jesus Christ	2Pet 1:1	4990
of our Lord and *S* Jesus Christ	2Pet 1:11	4990
S Jesus Christ, they are again	2Pet 2:20	4990
us the apostles of the Lord and *S*	2Pet 3:2	4990
of our Lord and *S* Jesus Christ	2Pet 3:18	4990
the Son to be the *S* of the world	1Jn 4:14	4990
To the only wise God our *S*	Jude 25	4990

SAVIOURS

mercies thou gavest them *s*	Neh 9:27	3467
s shall come up on mount Zion to	Obad 21	3467

SAVOUR

And the Lord smelled a sweet *s*	Gen 8:21	7381
because ye have made our *s* to be	Ex 5:21	7381
it is a sweet *s*, an offering made	Ex 29:18	7381
for a sweet *s* before the Lord	Ex 29:25	7381
offering thereof, for a sweet *s*	Ex 29:41	7381
of a sweet *s* unto the Lord	Lev 1:9	7381
of a sweet *s* unto the Lord	Lev 1:13	7381
of a sweet *s* unto the Lord	Lev 1:17	7381
of a sweet *s* unto the Lord	Lev 2:2	7381
of a sweet *s* unto the Lord	Lev 2:9	7381
burnt on the altar for a sweet *s*	Lev 2:12	7381
of a sweet *s* unto the Lord	Lev 3:5	7381
made by fire for a sweet *s*	Lev 3:16	7381
altar for a sweet *s* unto the Lord	Lev 4:31	7381
it upon the altar for a sweet *s*	Lev 6:15	7381
offer for a sweet *s* unto the Lord	Lev 6:21	7381
a burnt sacrifice for a sweet *s*	Lev 8:21	7381
were consecrations for a sweet *s*	Lev 8:28	7381
fat for a sweet *s* unto the Lord	Lev 17:6	7381
fire unto the Lord for a sweet *s*	Lev 23:13	7381
by fire, of sweet *s* unto the Lord	Lev 23:18	7381
smell the *s* of your sweet odours	Lev 26:31	7381
to make a sweet *s* unto the Lord	Num 15:3	7381
for a sweet *s* unto the Lord	Num 15:7	7381
of a sweet *s* unto the Lord	Num 15:10	7381
of a sweet *s* unto the Lord	Num 15:13	7381
of a sweet *s* unto the Lord	Num 15:14	7381
for a sweet *s* unto the Lord, with	Num 15:24	7381
for a sweet *s* unto the Lord	Num 18:17	7381
by fire, for a sweet *s* unto me	Num 28:2	7381
in mount Sinai for a sweet *s*	Num 28:6	7381
of a sweet *s* unto the Lord	Num 28:8	7381
for a burnt offering of a sweet *s*	Num 28:13	7381
of a sweet *s* unto the Lord	Num 28:24	7381
for a sweet *s* unto the Lord	Num 28:27	7381
for a sweet *s* unto the Lord	Num 29:2	7381
unto their manner, for a sweet *s*	Num 29:6	7381
unto the Lord for a sweet *s*	Num 29:8	7381
of a sweet *s* unto the Lord	Num 29:13	7381
of a sweet *s* unto the Lord	Num 29:36	7381
to send forth a stinking *s*	Eccl 10:1	7381
Because of the *s* of thy good	Song 1:3	7381
offer sweet *s* to all their idols	Eze 6:13	7381
set it before them for a sweet *s*	Eze 16:19	7381
also they made their sweet *s*	Eze 20:28	7381
will accept you with your sweet *s*	Eze 20:41	7381
his ill *s* shall come up, because	Joel 2:20	6709
but if the salt have lost his *s*	Mt 5:13	3471

but if the salt have lost his *s* .... Lk 14:34   3471
maketh manifest the *s* of his 2Cor 2:14   3744
are unto God a sweet *s* of Christ 2Cor 2:15   2175
we are the *s* of death unto death 2Cor 2:16   3744
to the other the *s* of life unto 2Cor 2:16   3744
to God for a sweetsmelling *s* .... Eph 5:2   3744

SAVOUREST
for thou *s* not the things that be .... Mt 16:23   5426
for thou *s* not the things that be .... Mk 8:33   5426

SAVOURS
of sweet *s* unto the God of heaven .... Ezr 6:10   5208

SAVOURY
And make me *s* meat, such as I love ...... Gen 27:4   4303
me venison, and make me *s* meat .... Gen 27:7   4303
I will make them *s* meat for thy .... Gen 27:9   4303
and his mother made *s* meat .... Gen 27:14   4303
And she gave the *s* meat and the .... Gen 27:17   4303
And he also had made *s* meat .... Gen 27:31   4303

SAW See APPENDIX.

SAWED
s with saws, within and without, ... 1Kin 7:9   1641

SAWEST See APPENDIX.

SAWN
were stoned, they were *s* asunder .... Heb 11:37   4249

SAWS
were therein, and put them under *s* 2Sa 12:31   4050
of hewed stones, sawed with *s* 1Kin 7:9   4050
were in it, and cut them with *s* 1Chr 20:3   4050

SAY See APPENDIX.

SAYEST See APPENDIX.

SAYING See APPENDIX.

SAYINGS See APPENDIX.

SCAB
skin of his flesh a rising, a *s* .... Lev 13:2   5597
it is but a *s* .... Lev 13:6   4556
But if the *s* spread much abroad .... Lev 13:7   4556
the *s* spreadeth in the skin, then .... Lev 13:8   4556
And for a rising, and for a *s* .... Lev 14:56   5597
with the emerods, and with the *s* .... Deut 28:27   1618
the Lord will smite with a *s* the .... Is 3:17   5597

SCABBARD
put up thyself into thy *s* .... Jer 47:6   8593

SCABBED
in his eye, or be scurvy, or *s* .... Lev 21:20   3217
or having a wen, or scurvy, or *s* .... Lev 22:22   3217

SCAFFOLD
For Solomon had made a brasen *s* 2Chr 6:13   3595

SCALES
s in the waters, in the seas, and .... Lev 11:9   7193
s in the seas, and in the rivers, ... Lev 11:10   7193
hath no fins nor *s* in the waters .... Lev 11:12   7193
that have fins and *s* shall ye eat .... Deut 14:9   7193
hath not fins and *s* ye may not eat .... Deut 14:10   7193
His *s* are his pride, shut up .... Job 41:15   650,4043
and weighed the mountains in *s* .... Is 40:12   6425
of thy rivers to stick unto thy *s* .... Eze 29:4   7193
thy rivers shall stick unto thy *s* .... Eze 29:4   7193
from his eyes as it had been *s* .... Acts 9:18   3013

SCALETH
A wise man *s* the city of the .... Prov 21:22   5927

SCALL
it is a dry *s*, even a leprosy .... Lev 13:30   5424
look on the plague of the *s* .... Lev 13:31   5424
the plague of the *s* seven days .... Lev 13:31   5424
if the *s* spread not, and there be .... Lev 13:32   5424
the *s* be not in sight deeper than .... Lev 13:32   5424
but the *s* shall he not shave .... Lev 13:33   5424
that hath the *s* seven days more .... Lev 13:33   5424
the priest shall look on the *s* .... Lev 13:34   5424
if the *s* be not spread in the .... Lev 13:34   5424
But if the *s* spread much in the .... Lev 13:35   5424
if the *s* be spread in the skin, ... Lev 13:36   5424
But if the *s* be in his sight at a .... Lev 13:37   5424
the *s* is healed, he is clean .... Lev 13:37   5424
manner of plague of leprosy, and *s* .... Lev 14:54   5424

SCALP
the hairy *s* of such an one as .... Ps 68:21   6936

SCANT
the *s* measure that is abominable .... Mic 6:10   7332

SCAPEGOAT
LORD, and the other lot for the *s* .... Lev 16:8   5799
on which the lot fell to be the *s* .... Lev 16:10   5799
go for a *s* into the wilderness .... Lev 16:10   5799
for the *s* shall wash his clothes .... Lev 16:26   5799

SCARCE
Jacob was yet *s* gone out from the .... Gen 27:30
with these sayings *s* restrained .... Acts 14:18   3433
s were come over against Cnidus, ... Acts 27:7   3433

SCARCELY
For *s* for a righteous man will .... Rom 5:7   3433
And if the righteous *s* be saved 1Pet 4:18   3433

SCARCENESS
thou shalt eat bread without *s* .... Deut 8:9   4544

SCAREST
Then thou *s* me with dreams, and .... Job 7:14   2865

SCARLET
and bound upon his hand a *s* thread ..... Gen 38:28   8144
that had the *s* thread upon his .... Gen 38:30   8144
blue, and purple, and *s*, and fine ...... Ex 25:4   8144,8438
linen, and blue, and purple, and *s* ... Ex 26:1   8144,8438
a vail of blue, and purple, and *s* ...... Ex 26:31   8144,8438
tent, of blue, and purple, and *s* ...... Ex 26:36   8144,8438
cubits, of blue, and purple, and *s* ... Ex 27:16   8144,8438
gold, and blue, and purple, and *s* .... Ex 28:5   8144,8438
gold, of blue, and of purple, of *s* ..... Ex 28:6   8144,8438
of gold, of blue, and purple, and *s* .. Ex 28:8   8144,8438
of blue, and of purple, and of *s* ...... Ex 28:15   8144,8438
of blue, and of purple, and of *s* ...... Ex 28:33   8144,8438
blue, and purple, and *s*, and fine ..... Ex 35:6   8144,8438
was found blue, and purple, and *s* .. Ex 35:23   8144,8438
of blue, and of purple, and of *s* ...... Ex 35:25   8144,8438
in blue, and in purple, in *s* .... Ex 35:35   8144,8438
linen, and blue, and purple, and *s* ... Ex 36:8   8144,8438
a vail of blue, and purple, and *s* ...... Ex 36:35   8144,8438
door of blue, and purple, and *s* .... Ex 36:37   8144,8438
of blue, and purple, and *s* .... Ex 38:18   8144,8438
in blue, and in purple, and in *s* .... Ex 38:23   8144,8438
And of the blue, and purple, and *s* .. Ex 39:1   8144,8438
of gold, blue, and purple, and *s* ...... Ex 39:2   8144,8438
and in the purple, and in the *s* .... Ex 39:3   8144,8438
of gold, blue, and purple, and *s* ...... Ex 39:5   8144,8438
of gold, blue, and purple, and *s* ...... Ex 39:8   8144,8438
of blue, and purple, and *s*, and .... Ex 39:24   8144,8438
linen, and blue, and purple, and *s* ... Ex 39:29   8144,8438
and clean, and cedar wood, and *s* .. Lev 14:4   8144,8438
it, and the cedar wood, and the *s* ... Lev 14:6   8144,8438
two birds, and cedar wood, and *s* ... Lev 14:49   8144,8438
wood, and the hyssop, and the *s* ..... Lev 14:51   8144,8438
with the hyssop, and with the *s* ...... Lev 14:52   8144,8438
spread upon them a cloth of *s* .... Num 4:8   8144,8438
cedar wood, and hyssop, and *s* .... Num 19:6   8144,8438
thou shalt bind this line of *s* .... Josh 2:18   8144
she bound the *s* line in the .... Josh 2:21   8144
over Saul, who clothed you in *s* 2Sa 1:24   8144
her household are clothed with *s* .... Prov 31:21   8144
Thy lips are like a thread of *s* .... Song 4:3   8144
though your sins be as *s*, they .... Is 1:18   8144
brought up in *s* embrace dunghills .... Lam 4:5   8144
thereof, shall be clothed with *s* .... Dan 5:7   711
thou shalt be clothed with *s* .... Dan 5:16   711
and they clothed Daniel with *s* .... Dan 5:29   711
red, the valiant men are in *s* .... Nah 2:3   8529
him, and put on him a *s* robe .... Mt 27:28   2847
s wool, and hyssop, and sprinkled .... Heb 9:19   2847
woman sit upon a *s* coloured beast .... Rev 17:3   2847
s colour, and decked with gold and .... Rev 17:4   2847
linen, and purple, and silk, and *s* .... Rev 18:12   2847
in fine linen, and purple, and *s* .... Rev 18:16   2847

SCATTER
from thence did the LORD *s* them .... Gen 11:9   6327
in Jacob, and *s* them in Israel .... Gen 49:7   6327
I will *s* you among the heathen, ... Lev 26:33   2210
and *s* thou the fire yonder .... Num 16:37   2219
the LORD shall *s* you among the .... Deut 4:27   6327
the LORD shall *s* thee among all .... Deut 28:64   6327
I would *s* them into corners, I .... Deut 32:26   6284
shall *s* them beyond the river, ... 1Kin 14:15   2219
I will *s* you abroad among the .... Neh 1:8   6327
s them by thy power .... Ps 59:11   5128
s thou the people that delight in .... Ps 68:30   967
and to *s* them in the lands .... Ps 106:27   2219
Cast forth lightning, and *s* them .... Ps 144:6   6327
s the cummin, and cast in the .... Is 28:25   2236
and the whirlwind shall *s* them .... Is 41:16   6327
I will *s* them also among the .... Jer 9:16   6327
Therefore will I *s* them as the .... Jer 13:24   6327
I will *s* them as with an east .... Jer 18:17   6327

s the sheep of my pasture	Jer 23:1	6327
I will s into all winds them that	Jer 49:32	2219
will s them toward all those	Jer 49:36	2219
part thou shalt s in the wind	Eze 5:2	2219
thee will I s into all the winds	Eze 5:10	2219
I will s a third part into all	Eze 5:12	2219
I will s your bones round about	Eze 6:5	2219
and s them over the city	Eze 10:2	2236
I will s toward every wind all	Eze 12:14	2219
when I shall s them among the	Eze 12:15	6327
that I would s them among the	Eze 20:23	6327
I will s thee among the heathen,	Eze 22:15	6327
I will s the Egyptians among the	Eze 29:12	6327
I will s the Egyptians among the	Eze 30:23	6327
I will s the Egyptians among the	Eze 30:26	6327
off his leaves, and s his fruit	Dan 4:14	921
he shall s among them the prey,	Dan 11:24	967
to s the power of the holy people	Dan 12:7	5310
came out as a whirlwind to s me	Hab 3:14	6327
over the land of Judah to s it	Zec 1:21	2219

SCATTERED

lest we be s abroad upon the face	Gen 11:4	6327
So the LORD have them abroad from	Gen 11:8	6327
So the people were s abroad	Ex 5:12	6327
LORD, and let thine enemies be s	Num 10:35	6327
the LORD thy God hath s thee	Deut 30:3	6327
that they which remained were s	1Sa 11:11	6327
and the people were s from him	1Sa 13:8	6327
that the people were s from me	1Sa 13:11	5310
there s over the face of all the	2Sa 18:8	6327
And he sent out arrows, and s them	2Sa 22:15	6327
I saw all Israel s upon the hills	1Kin 22:17	6327
and all his army were s from him	2Kin 25:5	6327
all Israel s upon the mountains	2Chr 18:16	6327
is a certain people s abroad	Est 3:8	6340
stout lion's whelps are s abroad	Job 4:11	6504
brimstone shall be s upon his	Job 18:15	2219
he sent out his arrows, and s them	Ps 18:14	6327
hast s us among the heathen	Ps 44:11	2219
for God hath s the bones of him	Ps 53:5	6340
hast cast us off, thou hast s us	Ps 60:1	6555
God arise, let his enemies be s	Ps 68:1	6327
When the Almighty s kings in it	Ps 68:14	6566
thou hast s thine enemies with	Ps 89:10	6340
workers of iniquity shall be s	Ps 92:9	6504
Our bones are s at the grave's	Ps 141:7	6340
swift messengers, to a nation s	Is 18:2	4900
the LORD of hosts of a people s	Is 18:7	4900
up of thyself the nations were s	Is 33:3	5310
hast s thy ways to the strangers	Jer 3:13	6340
and all their flocks shall be s	Jer 10:21	6327
Ye have s my flock, and driven	Jer 23:2	6327
all nations whither I have s thee	Jer 30:11	6327
He that s Israel will gather him,	Jer 31:10	2219
gathered unto thee should be s	Jer 40:15	6327
Israel is a s sheep	Jer 50:17	6340
and all his army was s from him	Jer 52:8	6327
when ye shall be s through the	Eze 6:8	2219
although I have s them among the	Eze 11:16	6327
countries where ye have been s	Eze 11:17	6327
shall be s toward all winds	Eze 17:21	6566
of the countries wherein ye are s	Eze 20:34	6327
countries wherein ye have been s	Eze 20:41	6327
the people among whom they are s	Eze 28:25	6327
the people whither they were s	Eze 29:13	6327
And they were s, because there is	Eze 34:5	6327
of the field, when they were s	Eze 34:5	6327
my flock was s upon all the face	Eze 34:6	6327
he is among his sheep that are s	Eze 34:12	6566
they have been s in the cloudy	Eze 34:12	6327
horns, till ye have s them abroad	Eze 34:21	6327
I s them among the heathen, and	Eze 36:19	6327
that my people be not s every man	Eze 46:18	
whom they have s among the	Joel 3:2	6327
thy people is s upon the	Nah 3:18	6340
the everlasting mountains were s	Hab 3:6	6327
are the horns which have s Judah	Zec 1:19	2219
are the horns which have s Judah	Zec 1:21	2219
But I s them with a whirlwind	Zec 7:14	
shepherd, and the sheep shall be s	Zec 13:7	6327
were s abroad, as sheep having no	Mt 9:36	4496
of the flock shall be s abroad	Mt 26:31	1287
shepherd, and the sheep shall be s	Mk 14:27	1287
he hath s the proud in the	Lk 1:51	1287
of God that were s abroad	Jn 11:52	1287
is now come, that ye shall be s	Jn 16:32	4650
as many as obeyed him, were s	Acts 5:36	1262
they were all s abroad throughout	Acts 8:1	1289
were s abroad went every where	Acts 8:4	1289
Now they which were s abroad upon	Acts 11:19	1289

twelve tribes which are s abroad	Jas 1:1	1290
to the strangers s throughout	1Pet 1:1	1290

SCATTERETH

he s his bright cloud	Job 37:11	6327
which s the east wind upon the	Job 38:24	6327
he s the hoar frost like ashes	Ps 147:16	6340
There is that s, and yet	Prov 11:24	6340
in the throne of judgment s away	Prov 20:8	2219
A wise king s the wicked, and	Prov 20:26	2219
s abroad the inhabitants thereof	Is 24:1	6327
gathereth not with me s abroad	Mt 12:30	4650
he that gathereth not with me s	Lk 11:23	4650
catcheth them, and s the sheep	Jn 10:12	4650

SCATTERING

flame of a devouring fire, with s	Is 30:30	5311

SCENT

Yet through the s of water it	Job 14:9	7381
in him, and his s is not changed	Jer 48:11	7381
the s thereof shall be as the	Hos 14:7	2143

SCEPTRE

The s shall not depart from Judah	Gen 49:10	7626
a S shall rise out of Israel, and	Num 24:17	7626
king shall hold out the golden s	Est 4:11	8275
the golden s that was in his hand	Est 5:2	8275
near, and touched the top of the s	Est 5:2	8275
out the golden s toward Esther	Est 8:4	8275
the s of thy kingdom is a right	Ps 45:6	7626
of thy kingdom is a right s	Ps 45:6	7626
wicked, and the s of the rulers	Is 14:5	7626
no strong rod to be a s to rule	Eze 19:14	7626
him that holdeth the s from the	Amos 1:5	7626
that holdeth the s from Ashkelon	Amos 1:8	7626
the s of Egypt shall depart away	Zec 10:11	7626
a s of righteousness is the	Heb 1:8	4464
is the s of thy kingdom	Heb 1:8	4464

SCEPTRES

for the s of them that bare rule	Eze 19:11	7626

SCEVA (see'-vah) A Jewish priest at Ephesus.

And there were seven sons of one S	Acts 19:14	4630

SCHISM

there should be no s in the body	1Cor 12:25	4978

SCHOLAR

the great, the teacher as the s	1Chr 25:8	8527
doeth this, the master and the s	Mal 2:12	6030

SCHOOL

daily in the s of one Tyrannus	Acts 19:9	4981

SCHOOLMASTER

was our s to bring us unto Christ	Gal 3:24	3807
come, we are no longer under a s	Gal 3:25	3807

SCIENCE

in knowledge, and understanding s	Dan 1:4	4093
oppositions of s falsely so	1Ti 6:20	1108

SCOFF

they shall s at the kings, and the	Hab 1:10	7046

SCOFFERS

shall come in the last days s	2Pet 3:3	1703

SCORCH

given unto him to s men with fire	Rev 16:8	2739

SCORCHED

when the sun was up, they were s	Mt 13:6	2739
But when the sun was up, it was s	Mk 4:6	2739
men were s with great heat, and	Rev 16:9	2739

SCORN

thee, and laughed thee to s	2Kin 19:21	
but they laughed them to s	2Chr 30:10	
heard it, they laughed us to s	Neh 2:19	
he thought s to lay hands on	Est 3:6	959
just upright man is laughed to s	Job 12:4	
My friends s me	Job 16:20	3887
and the innocent laugh them to s	Job 22:19	
they that see me laugh me to s	Ps 22:7	
a reproach to our neighbours, a s	Ps 44:13	3933
a reproach to our neighbours, a s	Ps 79:4	3933
thee, and laughed thee to s	Is 37:22	
thou shalt be laughed to s	Eze 23:32	
princes shall be a s unto them	Hab 1:10	4890
And they laughed him to s	Mt 9:24	2606
And they laughed him to s	Mk 5:40	2606
And they laughed him to s, knowing	Lk 8:53	2606

SCORNER

He that reproveth a s getteth to	Prov 9:7	3887
Reprove not a s, lest he hate	Prov 9:8	3887
but a s heareth not rebuke	Prov 13:1	3887

A *s* seeketh wisdom, and findeth it	Prov 14:6	3887
A *s* loveth not one that reproveth	Prov 15:12	3887
Smite a *s*, and the simple will	Prov 19:25	3887
When the *s* is punished, the	Prov 21:11	3887
haughty *s* is his name, who	Prov 21:24	3887
Cast out the *s*, and contention	Prov 22:10	3887
the *s* is an abomination to men	Prov 24:9	3887
the *s* is consumed, and all that	Is 29:20	3887

SCORNERS

the *s* delight in their scorning,	Prov 1:22	3887
Surely he scorneth the *s*	Prov 3:34	3887
Judgments are prepared for *s*	Prov 19:29	3887
he stretched out his hand with *s*	Hos 7:5	3945

SCORNEST

but if thou *s*, thou alone shalt	Prov 9:12	3887
as an harlot, in that thou *s* hire	Eze 16:31	7046

SCORNETH

He *s* the multitude of the city,	Job 39:7	7832
she *s* the horse and his rider	Job 39:18	7832
Surely he *s* the scorners	Prov 3:34	3887
An ungodly witness *s* judgment	Prov 19:28	3887

SCORNFUL

nor sitteth in the seat of the *s*	Ps 1:1	3887
S men bring a city into a snare	Prov 29:8	3944
ye *s* men, that rule this people	Is 28:14	3944

SCORNING

Job, who drinketh up *s* like water	Job 34:7	3933
the *s* of those that are at ease	Ps 123:4	3933
the scorners delight in their *s*	Prov 1:22	3944

SCORPION

ask an egg, will he offer him a *s*	Lk 11:12	*4651*
torment was as the torment of a *s*	Rev 9:5	*4651*

SCORPION PASS See Maaleh-acrabbim.

SCORPIONS

wherein were fiery serpents, and *s*	Deut 8:15	6137
but I will chastise you with *s*	1Kin 12:11	6137
but I will chastise you with *s*	1Kin 12:14	6137
but I will chastise you with *s*	2Chr 10:11	6137
but I will chastise you with *s*	2Chr 10:14	6137
thee, and thou dost dwell among *s*	Eze 2:6	6137
power to tread on serpents and *s*	Lk 10:19	*4651*
as the *s* of the earth have power	Rev 9:3	*4651*
And they had tails like unto *s*	Rev 9:10	*4651*

SCOURED

a brasen pot, it shall be both *s*	Lev 6:28	4838

SCOURGE

be hid from the *s* of the tongue	Job 5:21	7752
If the *s* slay suddenly, he will	Job 9:23	7752
up a *s* for him according to the	Is 10:26	7752
overflowing *s* shall pass through	Is 28:15	7885
overflowing *s* shall pass through	Is 28:18	7752
and they will *s* you in their	Mt 10:17	*3164*
to the Gentiles to mock, and to *s*	Mt 20:19	*3164*
shall ye *s* in your synagogues	Mt 23:34	*3164*
shall mock him, and shall *s* him	Mk 10:34	*3164*
And they shall *s* him, and put him	Lk 18:33	*3164*
he had made a *s* of small cords	Jn 2:15	*5416*
you to *s* a man that is a Roman	Acts 22:25	*3147*

SCOURGED

she shall be *s*	Lev 19:20	1244
and when he had *s* Jesus, he	Mt 27:26	*5417*
Jesus, when he had *s* him, to be	Mk 15:15	*5417*
therefore took Jesus, and *s* him	Jn 19:1	*3146*

SCOURGES

s in your sides, and thorns in	Josh 23:13	7850

SCOURGETH

s every son whom he receiveth	Heb 12:6	*3146*

SCOURGING

that he should be examined by *s*	Acts 22:24	*3148*

SCOURGINGS

had trial of cruel mockings and *s*	Heb 11:36	*3148*

SCRABBLED

s on the doors of the gate, and	1Sa 21:13	8427

SCRAPE

pour out the dust that they *s* off	Lev 14:41	7096
a potsherd to *s* himself withal	Job 2:8	1623
I will also *s* her dust from her,	Eze 26:4	5500

SCRAPED

house to be *s* within round about	Lev 14:41	7106
and after he hath *s* the house	Lev 14:43	7096

SCREECH

the *s* owl also shall rest there,	Is 34:14	3917

SCRIBE

and Seraiah was the *s*	2Sa 8:17	5608
And Sheva was *s*	2Sa 20:25	5608
in the chest, that the king's *s*	2Kin 12:10	5608
the household, and Shebna the *s*	2Kin 18:18	5608
the household, and Shebna the *s*	2Kin 18:37	5608
the household, and Shebna the *s*	2Kin 19:2	5608
the son of Meshullam, the *s*	2Kin 22:3	5608
priest said unto Shaphan the *s*	2Kin 22:8	5608
Shaphan the *s* came to the king,	2Kin 22:9	5608
Shaphan the *s* shewed the king,	2Kin 22:10	5608
son of Michaiah, and Shaphan the *s*	2Kin 22:12	5608
and the principal *s* of the host	2Kin 25:19	5608
and Shavsha was *s*	1Chr 18:16	5608
the son of Nethaneel the *s*	1Chr 24:6	5608
a counsellor, a wise man, and a *s*	1Chr 27:32	5608
was much money, the king's *s*	2Chr 24:11	5608
by the hand of Jeiel the *s*	2Chr 26:11	5608
answered and said to Shaphan the *s*	2Chr 34:15	5608
Then Shaphan the *s* told the king	2Chr 34:18	5608
son of Micah, and Shaphan the *s*	2Chr 34:20	5608
Shimshai the *s* wrote a letter	Ezr 4:8	5613
the chancellor, and Shimshai the *s*	Ezr 4:9	5613
chancellor, and to Shimshai the *s*	Ezr 4:17	5613
before Rehum, and Shimshai the *s*	Ezr 4:23	5613
he was a ready *s* in the law of	Ezr 7:6	5608
gave unto Ezra the priest, the *s*	Ezr 7:11	5608
even a *s* of the words of the	Ezr 7:11	5608
a *s* of the law of the God of	Ezr 7:12	5613
the *s* of the law of the God of	Ezr 7:21	5613
they spake unto Ezra the *s* to	Neh 8:1	5608
Ezra the *s* stood upon a pulpit of	Neh 8:4	5608
and Ezra the priest the *s*	Neh 8:9	5608
and the Levites, unto Ezra the *s*	Neh 8:13	5608
and of Ezra the priest, the *s*	Neh 12:26	5608
of God, and Ezra the *s* before them	Neh 12:36	5608
the priest, and Zadok the *s*	Neh 13:13	5608
Where is the *s*	Is 33:18	5608
over the house, and Shebna the *s*	Is 36:3	5608
the household, and Shebna the *s*	Is 36:22	5608
the household, and Shebna the *s*	Is 37:2	5608
Gemariah the son of Shaphan the *s*	Jer 36:10	5608
sat there, even Elishama the *s*	Jer 36:20	5608
in the chamber of Elishama the *s*	Jer 36:20	5608
of Abdeel, to take Baruch the *s*	Jer 36:26	5608
roll, and gave it to Baruch the *s*	Jer 36:32	5608
in the house of Jonathan the *s*	Jer 37:15	5608
to the house of Jonathan the *s*	Jer 37:20	5608
and the principal *s* of the host	Jer 52:25	5608
And a certain *s* came, and said unto	Mt 8:19	*1122*
Therefore every *s* which is	Mt 13:52	*1122*
the *s* said unto him, Well, Master	Mk 12:32	*1122*
where is the *s*	1Cor 1:20	*1122*

SCRIBE'S

king's house, into the *s* chamber	Jer 36:12	5608
it out of Elishama the *s* chamber	Jer 36:21	5608

SCRIBES

and Ahiah, the sons of Shisha, *s*	1Kin 4:3	5608
the families of the *s* which dwelt	1Chr 2:55	5608
and of the Levites there were *s*	2Chr 34:13	5608
Then were the king's *s* called on	Est 3:12	5608
Then were the king's *s* called at	Est 8:9	5608
the pen of the *s* is in vain	Jer 8:8	5608
s of the people together, he	Mt 2:4	*1122*
exceed the righteousness of the *s*	Mt 5:20	*1122*
having authority, and not as the *s*	Mt 7:29	*1122*
certain of the *s* said within	Mt 9:3	*1122*
Then certain of the *s* and of the	Mt 12:38	*1122*
Then came to Jesus *s* and Pharisees	Mt 15:1	*1122*
the elders and chief priests and *s*	Mt 16:21	*1122*
Why then say the *s* that Elias	Mt 17:10	*1122*
the chief priests and unto the *s*	Mt 20:18	*1122*
s saw the wonderful things that	Mt 21:15	*1122*
Saying, The *s* and the Pharisees	Mt 23:2	*1122*
But woe unto you, *s* and Pharisees,	Mt 23:13	*1122*
Woe unto you, *s* and Pharisees,	Mt 23:14	*1122*
Woe unto you, *s* and Pharisees,	Mt 23:15	*1122*
Woe unto you, *s* and Pharisees,	Mt 23:23	*1122*
Woe unto you, *s* and Pharisees,	Mt 23:25	*1122*
Woe unto you, *s* and Pharisees,	Mt 23:27	*1122*
Woe unto you, *s* and Pharisees,	Mt 23:29	*1122*
you prophets, and wise men, and *s*	Mt 23:34	*1122*
the chief priests, and the *s*	Mt 26:3	*1122*
the high priest, where the *s*	Mt 26:57	*1122*
priests mocking him, with the *s*	Mt 27:41	*1122*
had authority, and not as the *s*	Mk 1:22	*1122*
certain of the *s* sitting there	Mk 2:6	*1122*
And when the *s* and Pharisees saw	Mk 2:16	*1122*
the *s* which came down from	Mk 3:22	*1122*
Pharisees, and certain of the *s*	Mk 7:1	*1122*

s asked him, Why walk not thy	Mk 7:5	*1122*
and of the chief priests, and s	Mk 8:31	*1122*
Why say the s that Elias must	Mk 9:11	*1122*
the s questioning with them	Mk 9:14	*1122*
And he asked the s, What question	Mk 9:16	*1122*
the chief priests, and unto the s	Mk 10:33	*1122*
And the s and chief priests heard	Mk 11:18	*1122*
him the chief priests, and the s	Mk 11:27	*1122*
And one of the s came, and having	Mk 12:28	*1122*
How say the s that Christ is the	Mk 12:35	*1122*
in his doctrine, Beware of the s	Mk 12:38	*1122*
the s sought how they might take	Mk 14:1	*1122*
from the chief priest and the s	Mk 14:43	*1122*
priests and the elders and the s	Mk 14:53	*1122*
consultation with the elders and s	Mk 15:1	*1122*
said among themselves with the s	Mk 15:31	*1122*
And the s and the Pharisees began	Lk 5:21	*1122*
But their s and Pharisees murmured	Lk 5:30	*1122*
And the s and Pharisees watched him	Lk 6:7	*1122*
the elders and chief priests and s	Lk 9:22	*1122*
Woe unto you, s and Pharisees,	Lk 11:44	*1122*
these things unto them, the s	Lk 11:53	*1122*
s murmured, saying, This man	Lk 15:2	*1122*
But the chief priests and the s	Lk 19:47	*1122*
the s came upon him with the	Lk 20:1	*1122*
the s the same hour sought to lay	Lk 20:19	*1122*
certain of the s answering said	Lk 20:39	*1122*
Beware of the s, which desire to	Lk 20:46	*1122*
s sought how they might kill him	Lk 22:2	*1122*
the s came together, and led him	Lk 22:66	*1122*
s stood and vehemently accused him	Lk 23:10	*1122*
And the s and Pharisees brought	Jn 8:3	*1122*
their rulers, and elders, and s	Acts 4:5	*1122*
people, and the elders, and the s	Acts 6:12	*1122*
the s that were of the Pharisees'	Acts 23:9	*1122*

SCRIP

bag which he had, even in a s	1Sa 17:40	3219
Nor s for your journey, neither	Mt 10:10	4082
no s, no bread, no money in their	Mk 6:8	4082
journey, neither staves, nor s	Lk 9:3	4082
Carry neither purse, nor s	Lk 10:4	4082
I sent you without purse, and s	Lk 22:35	4082
him take it, and likewise his s	Lk 22:36	4082

SCRIPTURE

which is noted in the s of truth	Dan 10:21	3791
And have ye not read this s	Mk 12:10	*1124*
the s was fulfilled, which saith,	Mk 15:28	*1124*
This day is this s fulfilled in	Lk 4:21	*1124*
and they believed the s, and the	Jn 2:22	*1124*
as the s hath said, out of his	Jn 7:38	*1124*
Hath not the s said, That Christ	Jn 7:42	*1124*
came, and the s cannot be broken	Jn 10:35	*1124*
but that the s may be fulfilled,	Jn 13:18	*1124*
that the s might be fulfilled	Jn 17:12	*1124*
that the s might be fulfilled,	Jn 19:24	*1124*
that the s might be fulfilled,	Jn 19:28	*1124*
that the s should be fulfilled, A	Jn 19:36	*1124*
And again another s saith, They	Jn 19:37	*1124*
For as yet they knew not the s	Jn 20:9	*1124*
this s must needs have been	Acts 1:16	*1124*
The place of the s which he read	Acts 8:32	*1124*
his mouth, and began at the same s	Acts 8:35	*1124*
For what saith the s	Rom 4:3	*1124*
For the s saith unto Pharaoh,	Rom 9:17	*1124*
For the s saith, Whosoever	Rom 10:11	*1124*
ye not what the s saith of Elias	Rom 11:2	*1124*
And the s, foreseeing that God	Gal 3:8	*1124*
But the s hath concluded all	Gal 3:22	*1124*
Nevertheless what saith the s	Gal 4:30	*1124*
For the s saith, Thou shalt not	1Ti 5:18	*1124*
All s is given by inspiration of	2Ti 3:16	*1124*
the royal law according to the s	Jas 2:8	*1124*
the s was fulfilled which saith,	Jas 2:23	*1124*
ye think that the s saith in vain	Jas 4:5	*1124*
also it is contained in the s	1Pet 2:6	*1124*
of the s is of any private	2Pet 1:20	*1124*

SCRIPTURES

them, Did ye never read in the s	Mt 21:42	*1124*
Ye do err, not knowing the s	Mt 22:29	*1124*
how then shall the s be fulfilled	Mt 26:54	*1124*
that the s of the prophets might	Mt 26:56	*1124*
err, because ye know not the s	Mk 12:24	*1124*
but the s must be fulfilled	Mk 14:49	*1124*
s the things concerning himself	Lk 24:27	*1124*
and while he opened to us the s	Lk 24:32	*1124*
that they might understand the s	Lk 24:45	*1124*
Search the s	Jn 5:39	*1124*
reasoned with them out of the s	Acts 17:2	*1124*
of mind, and searched the s daily	Acts 17:11	*1124*

eloquent man, and mighty in the s	Acts 18:24	*1124*
shewing by the s that Jesus was	Acts 18:28	*1124*
by his prophets in the holy s	Rom 1:2	*1124*
comfort of the s might have hope	Rom 15:4	*1124*
by the s of the prophets,	Rom 16:26	*1124*
for our sins according to the s	1Cor 15:3	*1124*
the third day according to the s	1Cor 15:4	*1124*
child thou hast known the holy s	2Ti 3:15	*1121*
as they do also the other s	2Pet 3:16	*1124*

SCROLL

shall be rolled together as a s	Is 34:4	5612
the heaven departed as a s when	Rev 6:14	975

SCUM

to the pot whose s is therein	Eze 24:6	2457
whose s is not gone out of it	Eze 24:6	2457
that the s of it may be consumed	Eze 24:11	2457
her great s went not forth out of	Eze 24:12	2457
her s shall be in the fire	Eze 24:12	2457

SCURVY

a blemish in his eye, or be s	Lev 21:20	1618
or maimed, or having a wen, or s	Lev 22:22	1618

SCYTHIAN (*sith'-e-un*) *A barbarous people north of the Black Sea.*

nor uncircumcision, Barbarian, S	Col 3:11	4658

SEA

dominion over the fish of the s	Gen 1:26	3220
dominion over the fish of the s	Gen 1:28	3220
and upon all the fishes of the s	Gen 9:2	3220
of Siddim, which is the Salt S	Gen 14:3	3220
sand which is upon the s shore	Gen 22:17	3220
thy seed as the sand of the s	Gen 32:12	3220
corn as the sand of the s	Gen 41:49	3220
shall dwell at the haven of the s	Gen 49:13	3220
and cast them into the s	Ex 10:19	3220
of the wilderness of the Red s	Ex 13:18	3220
between Migdol and the s, over	Ex 14:2	3220
it shall ye encamp by the s	Ex 14:2	3220
overtook them encamping by the s	Ex 14:9	3220
stretch out thine hand over the s	Ex 14:16	3220
ground through the midst of the s	Ex 14:16	3220
stretched out his hand over the s	Ex 14:21	3220
the LORD caused the s to go back	Ex 14:21	3220
night, and made the s dry land	Ex 14:21	3220
of the s upon the dry ground	Ex 14:22	3220
after them to the midst of the s	Ex 14:23	3220
Stretch out thine hand over the s	Ex 14:26	3220
forth his hand over the s	Ex 14:27	3220
the s returned to his strength	Ex 14:27	3220
Egyptians in the midst of the s	Ex 14:27	3220
that came into the s after them	Ex 14:28	3220
dry land in the midst of the s	Ex 14:29	3220
Egyptians dead upon the s shore	Ex 14:30	3220
rider hath he thrown into the s	Ex 15:1	3220
his host hath he cast into the s	Ex 15:4	3220
also are drowned in the Red s	Ex 15:4	3220
congealed in the heart of the s	Ex 15:8	3220
with thy wind, the s covered them	Ex 15:10	3220
and with his horsemen into the s	Ex 15:19	3220
the waters of the s upon them	Ex 15:19	3220
on dry land in the midst of the s	Ex 15:19	3220
rider hath he thrown into the s	Ex 15:21	3220
brought Israel from the Red s	Ex 15:22	3220
LORD made heaven and earth, the s	Ex 20:11	3220
Red s even unto the s of the	Ex 23:31	3220
or shall all the fish of the s be	Num 11:22	3220
and brought quails from the s	Num 11:31	3220
and the Canaanites dwell by the s	Num 13:29	3220
by the way of the Red s	Num 14:25	3220
mount Hor by the way of the Red s	Num 21:4	3220
LORD, What he did in the Red s	Num 21:14	3220
of the s into the wilderness	Num 33:8	3220
Elim, and encamped by the Red s	Num 33:10	3220
And they removed from the Red s	Num 33:11	3220
coast of the salt s eastward	Num 34:3	3220
out of it shall be at the s	Num 34:5	3220
have the great s for a border	Num 34:6	3220
from the great s ye shall point	Num 34:7	3220
of the s of Chinnereth eastward	Num 34:11	3220
out of it shall be at the salt s	Num 34:12	3220
the plain over against the Red s	Deut 1:1	3220
and in the south, and by the s side	Deut 1:7	3220
by the way of the Red s	Deut 1:40	3220
by the way of the Red s, as the	Deut 2:1	3220
s of the plain, even the salt s	Deut 3:17	3220
even unto the s of the plain	Deut 4:49	3220
Red s to overflow them as they	Deut 11:4	3220
uttermost s shall your coast be	Deut 11:24	3220
Neither is it beyond the s	Deut 30:13	3220

Who shall go over the s for us	Deut 30:13	3220
land of Judah, unto the utmost s	Deut 34:2	3220
unto the great s toward the going	Josh 1:4	3220
up the water of the Red s for you	Josh 2:10	3220
s of the plain, even the salt s	Josh 3:16	3220
LORD your God did to the Red s	Josh 4:23	3220
Canaanites, which were by the s	Josh 5:1	3220
the great s over against Lebanon	Josh 9:1	3220
is upon the s shore in multitude	Josh 11:4	3220
from the plain to the s of	Josh 12:3	3220
unto the s of the plain	Josh 12:3	3220
even the salt s on the east	Josh 12:3	3220
even unto the edge of the s of	Josh 13:27	3220
was from the shore of the salt s	Josh 15:2	3220
out of that coast were at the s	Josh 15:4	3220
And the east border was the salt s	Josh 15:5	3220
s at the uttermost part of Jordan	Josh 15:5	3220
out of the border were at the s	Josh 15:11	3220
west border was to the great s	Josh 15:12	3220
From Ekron even unto the s	Josh 15:46	3220
river of Egypt, and the great s	Josh 15:47	3220
goings out thereof are at the s	Josh 16:3	3220
the border went out toward the s	Josh 16:6	3220
goings out thereof were at the s	Josh 16:8	3220
the outgoings of it were at the s	Josh 17:9	3220
and the s is his border	Josh 17:10	3220
the corner of the s southward	Josh 18:14	3220
salt s at the south end of Jordan	Josh 18:19	3220
their border went up toward the s	Josh 19:11	3220
at the s from the coast to Achzib	Josh 19:29	3220
even unto the great s westward	Josh 23:4	3220
and ye came unto the s	Josh 24:6	3220
and horsemen unto the Red s	Josh 24:6	3220
and brought the s upon them	Josh 24:7	3220
Asher continued on the s shore	Judg 5:17	3220
sand by the s side for multitude	Judg 7:12	3220
the wilderness unto the Red s	Judg 11:16	3220
is on the s shore in multitude	1Sa 13:5	3220
that is by the s for multitude	2Sa 17:11	3220
And the channels of the s appeared	2Sa 22:16	3220
which is by the s in multitude	1Kin 4:20	3220
the sand that is on the s	1Kin 4:29	3220
them down from Lebanon unto the s	1Kin 5:9	3220
I will convey them by s in floats	1Kin 5:9	3220
And he made a molten s, ten cubits	1Kin 7:23	3220
compassing the s round about	1Kin 7:24	3220
the s was set above upon them, and	1Kin 7:25	3220
he set the s on the right side of	1Kin 7:39	3220
And one s, and twelve oxen under	1Kin 7:44	3220
s, and twelve oxen under the s	1Kin 7:44	3220
Eloth, on the shore of the Red s	1Kin 9:26	3220
that had knowledge of the s	1Kin 9:27	3220
For the king had at s a navy of	1Kin 10:22	3220
Go up now, look toward the s	1Kin 18:43	3220
a little cloud out of the s	1Kin 18:44	3220
of Hamath unto the s of the plain	2Kin 14:25	3220
took down the s from off the	2Kin 16:17	3220
the brasen s that was in the	2Kin 25:13	3220
The two pillars, one s, and the	2Kin 25:16	3220
Let the s roar, and the fulness	1Chr 16:32	3220
Solomon made the brasen s	1Chr 18:8	3220
to thee in flotes by s to Joppa	2Chr 2:16	3220
Also he made a molten s of ten	2Chr 4:2	3220
compassing the s round about	2Chr 4:3	3220
the s was set above upon them, and	2Chr 4:4	3220
but the s was for the priests to	2Chr 4:6	3220
he set the s on the right side of	2Chr 4:10	3220
One s, and twelve oxen under it	2Chr 4:15	3220
at the s side in the land of Edom	2Chr 8:17	3220
that had knowledge of the s	2Chr 8:18	3220
beyond the s on this side Syria	2Chr 20:2	3220
from Lebanon to the s of Joppa	Ezr 3:7	3220
heardest their cry by the Red s	Neh 9:9	3220
didst divide the s before them	Neh 9:11	3220
midst of the s on the dry land	Neh 9:11	3220
land, and upon the isles of the s	Est 10:1	3220
be heavier than the sand of the s	Job 6:3	3220
Am I a s, or a whale, that thou	Job 7:12	3220
treadeth upon the waves of the s	Job 9:8	3220
the earth, and broader than the s	Job 11:9	3220
the fishes of the s shall declare	Job 12:8	3220
As the waters fail from the s	Job 14:11	3220
He divideth the s with his power	Job 26:12	3220
the s saith, It is not with me	Job 28:14	3220
and covereth the bottom of the s	Job 36:30	3220
Or who shut up the s with doors	Job 38:8	3220
entered into the springs of the s	Job 38:16	3220
he maketh the s like a pot of	Job 41:31	3220
of the air, and the fish of the s	Ps 8:8	3220
of the s together as an heap	Ps 33:7	3220
carried into the midst of the s	Ps 46:2	3220

them that are afar off upon the s	Ps 65:5	3220
He turned the s into dry land	Ps 66:6	3220
again from the depths of the s	Ps 68:22	3220
have dominion also from s to s	Ps 72:8	3220
divide the s by thy strength	Ps 74:13	3220
Thy way is in the s, and thy path	Ps 77:19	3220
He divided the s, and caused them	Ps 78:13	3220
fowls like as the sand of the s	Ps 78:27	3220
but the s overwhelmed their	Ps 78:53	3220
sent out her boughs unto the s	Ps 80:11	3220
Thou rulest the raging of the s	Ps 89:9	3220
I will set his hand also in the s	Ps 89:25	3220
than the mighty waves of the s	Ps 93:4	3220
The s is his, and he made it	Ps 95:5	3220
let the s roar, and the fulness	Ps 96:11	3220
Let the s roar, and the fulness	Ps 98:7	3220
So is this great and wide s	Ps 104:25	3220
him at the s, even at the Red s	Ps 106:7	3220
He rebuked the Red s also	Ps 106:9	3220
and terrible things by the Red s	Ps 106:22	3220
that go down to the s in ships	Ps 107:23	3220
The s saw it, and fled	Ps 114:3	3220
What ailed thee, O thou s	Ps 114:5	3220
divided the Red s into parts	Ps 136:13	3220
Pharaoh and his host in the Red s	Ps 136:15	3220
in the uttermost parts of the s	Ps 139:9	3220
made heaven, and earth, the s	Ps 146:6	3220
When he gave to the s his decree	Prov 8:29	3220
lieth down in the midst of the s	Prov 23:34	3220
of a ship in the midst of the s	Prov 30:19	3220
All the rivers run into the s	Eccl 1:7	3220
yet the s is not full	Eccl 1:7	3220
them like the roaring of the s	Is 5:30	3220
afflict her by the way of the s	Is 9:1	3220
Israel be as the sand of the s	Is 10:22	3220
and as his rod was upon the s	Is 10:26	3220
LORD, as the waters cover the s	Is 11:9	3220
and from the islands of the s	Is 11:11	3220
the tongue of the Egyptian s	Is 11:15	3220
out, they are gone over the s	Is 16:8	3220
That sendeth ambassadors by the s	Is 18:2	3220
the waters shall fail from the s	Is 19:5	3220
The burden of the desert of the s	Is 21:1	3220
of Zidon, that pass over the s	Is 23:2	3220
for the s hath spoken, even the	Is 23:4	3220
even the strength of the s	Is 23:4	3220
stretched out his hand over the s	Is 23:11	3220
they shall cry aloud from the s	Is 24:14	3220
of Israel in the isles of the s	Is 24:15	3220
slay the dragon that is in the s	Is 27:1	3220
earth, ye that go down to the s	Is 42:10	3220
LORD, which maketh a way in the s	Is 43:16	3220
as the waves of the s	Is 48:18	3220
at my rebuke I dry up the s	Is 50:2	3220
not it which hath dried the s	Is 51:10	3220
hath made the depths of the s a	Is 51:10	3220
LORD thy God, that divided the s	Is 51:15	3220
wicked are like the troubled s	Is 57:20	3220
s shall be converted unto thee	Is 60:5	3220
s with the shepherd of his flock	Is 63:11	3220
of the s by a perpetual decree	Jer 5:22	3220
their voice roareth like the s	Jer 6:23	3220
the isles which are beyond the s	Jer 25:22	3220
the pillars, and concerning the s	Jer 27:19	3220
which divideth the s when the	Jer 31:35	3220
the sand of the s measured	Jer 33:22	3220
mountains, and as Carmel by the s	Jer 46:18	3220
Ashkelon, and against the s shore	Jer 47:7	3220
thy plants are gone over the s	Jer 48:32	3220
they reach even to the s of Jazer	Jer 48:32	3220
thereof was heard in the Red s	Jer 49:21	3220
there is sorrow on the s	Jer 49:23	3220
their voice shall roar like the s	Jer 50:42	3220
and I will dry up her s, and make	Jer 51:36	3220
The s is come up upon Babylon	Jer 51:42	3220
the brasen s that was in the	Jer 52:17	3220
The two pillars, one s, and twelve	Jer 52:20	3220
thy breach is great like the s	Lam 2:13	3220
Even the s monsters draw out the	Lam 4:3	
the remnant of the s coast	Eze 25:16	3220
as the s causeth his waves to	Eze 26:3	3220
of nets in the midst of the s	Eze 26:5	3220
the s shall come down from their	Eze 26:16	3220
city, which wast strong in the s	Eze 26:17	3220
in the s shall be troubled at thy	Eze 26:18	3220
art situate at the entry of the s	Eze 27:3	3220
all the ships of the s with their	Eze 27:9	3220
and all the pilots of the s	Eze 27:29	3220
destroyed in the midst of the s	Eze 27:32	3220
So that the fishes of the s	Eze 38:20	3220
passengers on the east of the s	Eze 39:11	3220

S

into the desert, and go into the *s*	Eze 47:8	3220
being brought forth into the *s*	Eze 47:8	3220
kinds, as the fish of the great *s*	Eze 47:10	3220
the north side, from the great *s*	Eze 47:15	3220
from the *s* shall be Hazar-enan	Eze 47:17	3220
from the border unto the east *s*	Eze 47:18	3220
Kadesh, the river to the great *s*	Eze 47:19	3220
be the great *s* from the border	Eze 47:20	3220
to the river toward the great *s*	Eze 48:28	3220
heaven strove upon the great *s*	Dan 7:2	3221
great beasts came up from the *s*	Dan 7:3	3221
shall be as the sand of the *s*	Hos 1:10	3220
the fishes of the *s* also shall be	Hos 4:3	3220
with his face toward the east *s*	Joel 2:20	3220
hinder part toward the utmost *s*	Joel 2:20	3220
calleth for the waters of the *s*	Amos 5:8	3220
they shall wander from *s* to *s*	Amos 8:12	3220
my sight in the bottom of the *s*	Amos 9:3	3220
calleth for the waters of the *s*	Amos 9:6	3220
sent out a great wind into the *s*	Jonah 1:4	3220
was a mighty tempest in the *s*	Jonah 1:4	3220
that were in the ship into the *s*	Jonah 1:5	3220
of heaven, which hath made the *s*	Jonah 1:9	3220
that the *s* may be calm unto us	Jonah 1:11	3220
for the *s* wrought, and was	Jonah 1:11	3220
up, and cast me forth into the *s*	Jonah 1:12	3220
so shall the *s* be calm unto you	Jonah 1:12	3220
for the *s* wrought, and was	Jonah 1:13	3220
and cast him forth into the *s*	Jonah 1:15	3220
the *s* ceased from her raging	Jonah 1:15	3220
from *s* to *s*, and from mountain	Mic 7:12	3220
sins into the depths of the *s*	Mic 7:19	3220
He rebuketh the *s*, and maketh it	Nah 1:4	3220
about it, whose rampart was the *s*	Nah 3:8	3220
and her wall was from the *s*	Nah 3:8	3220
makest men as the fishes of the *s*	Hab 1:14	3220
LORD, as the waters cover the *s*	Hab 2:14	3220
was thy wrath against the *s*	Hab 3:8	3220
through the *s* with thine horses	Hab 3:15	3220
heaven, and the fishes of the *s*	Zeph 1:3	3220
the inhabitants of the *s* coast	Zeph 2:5	3220
the *s* coast shall be dwellings and	Zeph 2:6	3220
heavens, and the earth, and the *s*	Hag 2:6	3220
he will smite her power in the *s*	Zec 9:4	3220
shall be from *s* even to *s*	Zec 9:10	3220
through the *s* with affliction	Zec 10:11	3220
and shall smite the waves in the *s*	Zec 10:11	3220
half of them toward the former *s*	Zec 14:8	3220
half of them toward the hinder *s*	Zec 14:8	3220
which is upon the *s* coast	Mt 4:13	3864
Nephthalim, by the way of the *s*	Mt 4:15	2281
walking by the *s* of Galilee	Mt 4:18	2281
brother, casting a net into the *s*	Mt 4:18	2281
arose a great tempest in the *s*	Mt 8:24	2281
and rebuked the winds and the *s*	Mt 8:26	2281
even the winds and the *s* obey him	Mt 8:27	2281
down a steep place into the *s*	Mt 8:32	2281
the house, and sat by the *s* side	Mt 13:1	2281
a net, that was cast into the *s*	Mt 13:47	2281
was now in the midst of the *s*	Mt 14:24	2281
went unto them, walking on the *s*	Mt 14:25	2281
saw him walking on the *s*, they	Mt 14:26	2281
came nigh unto the *s* of Galilee	Mt 15:29	2281
offend them, go thou to the *s*	Mt 17:27	2281
drowned in the depth of the *s*	Mt 18:6	2281
and be thou cast into the *s*	Mt 21:21	2281
for ye compass *s* and land to make	Mt 23:15	2281
as he walked by the *s* of Galilee	Mk 1:16	2281
brother casting a net into the *s*	Mk 1:16	2281
he went forth again by the *s* side	Mk 2:13	2281
with his disciples to the *s*	Mk 3:7	2281
again to teach by the *s* side	Mk 4:1	2281
into a ship, and sat in the *s*	Mk 4:1	2281
was by the *s* on the land	Mk 4:1	2281
the wind, and said unto the *s*	Mk 4:39	2281
even the wind and the *s* obey him	Mk 4:41	2281
over unto the other side of the *s*	Mk 5:1	2281
down a steep place into the *s*	Mk 5:13	2281
and were choked in the *s*	Mk 5:13	2281
and he was nigh unto the *s*	Mk 5:21	2281
ship was in the midst of the *s*	Mk 6:47	2281
unto them, walking upon the *s*	Mk 6:48	2281
they saw him walking upon the *s*	Mk 6:49	2281
he came unto the *s* of Galilee	Mk 7:31	2281
neck, and he were cast into the *s*	Mk 9:42	2281
and be thou cast into the *s*	Mk 11:23	2281
from the *s* coast of Tyre and Sidon	Lk 6:17	3882
his neck, and he cast into the *s*	Lk 17:2	2281
root, and be thou planted in the *s*	Lk 17:6	2281
the *s* and the waves roaring	Lk 21:25	2281
Jesus went over the *s* of Galilee	Jn 6:1	2281

which is the *s* of Tiberias	Jn 6:1	2281
disciples went down unto the *s*	Jn 6:16	2281
went over the *s* toward Capernaum	Jn 6:17	2281
the *s* arose by reason of a great	Jn 6:18	2281
they see Jesus walking on the *s*	Jn 6:19	2281
s saw that there was none other	Jn 6:22	2281
him on the other side of the *s*	Jn 6:25	2281
disciples at the *s* of Tiberias	Jn 21:1	2281
and did cast himself into the *s*	Jn 21:7	2281
made heaven, and earth, and the *s*	Acts 4:24	2281
land of Egypt, and in the Red *s*	Acts 7:36	2281
whose house is by the *s* side	Acts 10:6	2281
one Simon a tanner by the *s* side	Acts 10:32	2281
made heaven, and earth, and the *s*	Acts 14:15	2281
Paul to go as it were to the *s*	Acts 17:14	2281
had sailed over the *s* of Cilicia	Acts 27:5	3989
had let down the boat into the *s*	Acts 27:30	2281
and cast out the wheat into the *s*	Acts 27:38	2281
committed themselves unto the *s*	Acts 27:40	2281
cast themselves first into the *s*	Acts 27:43	2281
though he hath escaped the *s*	Acts 28:4	2281
of Israel be as the sand of the *s*	Rom 9:27	2281
and all passed through the *s*	1Cor 10:1	2281
Moses in the cloud and in the *s*	1Cor 10:2	2281
wilderness, in perils in the *s*	2Cor 11:26	2281
is by the *s* shore innumerable	Heb 11:12	2281
through the Red *s* as by dry land	Heb 11:29	2281
of the *s* driven with the wind	Jas 1:6	2281
serpents, and of things in the *s*	Jas 3:7	1724
Raging waves of the *s*, foaming	Jude 13	2281
a *s* of glass like unto crystal	Rev 4:6	2281
earth, and such as are in the *s*	Rev 5:13	2281
blow on the earth, nor on the *s*	Rev 7:1	2281
given to hurt the earth and the *s*	Rev 7:2	2281
Hurt not the earth, neither the *s*	Rev 7:3	2281
with fire was cast into the *s*	Rev 8:8	2281
third part of the *s* became blood	Rev 8:8	2281
the creatures which were in the *s*	Rev 8:9	2281
he set his right foot upon the *s*	Rev 10:2	2281
which I saw stand upon the *s*	Rev 10:5	2281
things that therein are, and the *s*	Rev 10:6	2281
angel which standeth upon the *s*	Rev 10:8	2281
of the earth and of the *s*	Rev 12:12	2281
And I stood upon the sand of the *s*	Rev 13:1	2281
saw a beast rise up out of the *s*	Rev 13:1	2281
made heaven, and earth, and the *s*	Rev 14:7	2281
I saw as it were a *s* of glass	Rev 15:2	2281
his name, stand on the *s* of glass	Rev 15:2	2281
poured out his vial upon the *s*	Rev 16:3	2281
every living soul died in the *s*	Rev 16:3	2281
sailors, and as many as trade by *s*	Rev 18:17	2281
the *s* by reason of her costliness	Rev 18:19	2281
millstone, and cast it into the *s*	Rev 18:21	2281
of whom is as the sand of the *s*	Rev 20:8	2281
the *s* gave up the dead which were	Rev 20:13	2281
and there was no more *s*	Rev 21:1	2281

SEAFARING

that wast inhabited of *s* men	Eze 26:17	3220

SEAL

name, and sealed them with his *s*	1Kin 21:8	2368
Levites, and priests, *s* unto it	Neh 9:38	2856
s it with the king's ring	Est 8:8	2856
It is turned as clay to the *s*	Job 38:14	2368
up together as with a close *s*	Job 41:15	2368
Set me as a *s* upon thine heart,	Song 8:6	2368
heart, as a *s* upon thine arm	Song 8:6	2368
s the law among my disciples	Is 8:16	2856
s them, and take witnesses in	Jer 32:44	2856
to *s* up the vision and prophecy,	Dan 9:24	2856
s the book, even to the time of	Dan 12:4	2856
set to his *s* that God is true	Jn 3:33	4972
a *s* of the righteousness of the	Rom 4:11	4973
for the *s* of mine apostleship are	1Cor 9:2	4973
God standeth sure, having this *s*	2Ti 2:19	4973
when he had opened the second *s*	Rev 6:3	4973
And when he had opened the third *s*	Rev 6:5	4973
when he had opened the fourth *s*	Rev 6:7	4973
And when he had opened the fifth *s*	Rev 6:9	4973
when he had opened the sixth *s*	Rev 6:12	4973
having the *s* of the living God	Rev 7:2	4973
when he had opened the seventh *s*	Rev 8:1	4973
the *s* of God in their foreheads	Rev 9:4	4973
S up those things which the seven	Rev 10:4	4972
set a *s* upon him, that he should	Rev 20:3	4972
S not the sayings of the prophecy	Rev 22:10	4972

SEALED

me, and *s* up among my treasures	Deut 32:34	2856
s them with his seal, and sent the	1Kin 21:8	2856
Now those that *s* were, Nehemiah,	Neh 10:1	2856

and *s* with the king's ring	Est 3:12	2856
s with the king's ring, may no	Est 8:8	2856
s it with the king's ring, and	Est 8:10	2856
My transgression is *s* up in a bag	Job 14:17	2856
a spring shut up, a fountain *s*	Song 4:12	2856
as the words of a book that is *s*	Is 29:11	2856
for it is *s*	Is 29:11	2856
s it, and took witnesses, and	Jer 32:10	2856
both that which was *s* according	Jer 32:11	2856
of the purchase, both which is *s*	Jer 32:14	2856
the king *s* it with his own signet	Dan 6:17	2857
s till the time of the end	Dan 12:9	2856
for him hath God the Father *s*	Jn 6:27	4972
have *s* to them this fruit, I will	Rom 15:28	4972
Who hath also *s* us, and given the	2Cor 1:22	4972
ye were *s* with that holy Spirit	Eph 1:13	4972
whereby ye are *s* unto the day of	Eph 4:30	4972
the backside, *s* with seven seals	Rev 5:1	2696
till we have *s* the servants of	Rev 7:3	4972
the number of them which were *s*	Rev 7:4	4972
and there were *s* an hundred	Rev 7:4	4972
of Juda were *s* twelve thousand	Rev 7:5	4972
of Reuben were *s* twelve thousand	Rev 7:5	4972
of Gad were *s* twelve thousand	Rev 7:5	4972
of Aser were *s* twelve thousand	Rev 7:6	4972
Nepthalim were *s* twelve thousand	Rev 7:6	4972
Manasses were *s* twelve thousand	Rev 7:6	4972
of Simeon were *s* twelve thousand	Rev 7:7	4972
of Levi were *s* twelve thousand	Rev 7:7	4972
Issachar were *s* twelve thousand	Rev 7:7	4972
of Zabulon were *s* twelve thousand	Rev 7:8	4972
of Joseph were *s* twelve thousand	Rev 7:8	4972
Benjamin were *s* twelve thousand	Rev 7:8	4972

SEALEST

Thou *s* up the sum, full of wisdom	Eze 28:12	2856

SEALETH

and *s* up the stars	Job 9:7	2856
of men, and *s* their instruction,	Job 33:16	2856
He *s* up the hand of every man	Job 37:7	2856

SEALING

s the stone, and setting a watch	Mt 27:66	4972

SEALS

the backside, sealed with seven *s*	Rev 5:1	4973
book, and to loose the *s* thereof	Rev 5:2	4973
and to loose the seven *s* thereof	Rev 5:5	4973
book, and to open the *s* thereof	Rev 5:9	4973
when the Lamb opened one of the *s*	Rev 6:1	4973

SEAM

now the coat was without *s*	Jn 19:23	729

SEARCH

He shall not *s* whether it be good	Lev 27:33	1239
to *s* out a resting place for them	Num 10:33	8446
that they may *s* the land of	Num 13:2	8446
which we have gone to *s* it	Num 13:32	8446
which we passed through to *s* it	Num 14:7	8446
which Moses sent to *s* the land	Num 14:36	8446
the men that went to *s* the land	Num 14:38	8446
they shall *s* us out the land, and	Deut 1:22	2658
to *s* you out a place to pitch	Deut 1:33	8446
shalt thou enquire, and make *s*	Deut 13:14	2713
of Israel to *s* out the country	Josh 2:2	2658
be come to *s* out all the country	Josh 2:3	2658
to spy out the land, and to *s* it	Judg 18:2	2713
said unto them, Go, *s* the land	Judg 18:2	2713
that I will *s* him out throughout	1Sa 23:23	2664
to *s* the city, and to spy it out,	2Sa 10:3	2713
they shall *s* thine house, and the	1Kin 20:6	2664
unto the worshippers of Baal, *S*	2Kin 10:23	2664
servants come unto thee for to *s*	1Chr 19:3	2713
That *s* may be made in the book of	Ezr 4:15	1240
s hath been made, and it is found	Ezr 4:19	1240
let there be *s* made in the king's	Ezr 5:17	1240
s was made in the house of the	Ezr 6:1	1240
thyself to the *s* of their fathers	Job 8:8	2714
it good that he should *s* you out	Job 13:9	2713
thou walked in the *s* of the depth	Job 38:16	2714
Shall not God *s* this out	Ps 44:21	2713
They *s* out iniquities	Ps 64:6	2664
they accomplish a diligent *s*	Ps 64:6	2665
and my spirit made diligent *s*	Ps 77:6	2664
S me, O God, and know my heart	Ps 139:23	2713
of kings is to *s* out a matter	Prov 25:2	2713
so for men to *s* their own glory	Prov 25:27	2714
s out by wisdom concerning all	Eccl 1:13	8446
mine heart to know, and to *s*	Eccl 7:25	8446
I have not found it by secret *s*	Jer 2:34	4290
I the Lord *s* the heart, I try the	Jer 17:10	2713
when ye shall *s* for me with all	Jer 29:13	1875

Let us *s* and try our ways, and turn	Lam 3:40	2664
none did *s* or seek after them	Eze 34:6	1875
did my shepherds *s* for my flock	Eze 34:8	1875
I, even I, will both *s* my sheep	Eze 34:11	1875
end of seven months shall they *s*	Eze 39:14	2713
in the top of Carmel, I will *s*	Amos 9:3	2664
that I will *s* Jerusalem with	Zeph 1:12	2664
s diligently for the young child	Mt 2:8	*1833*
S the scriptures	Jn 5:39	*2045*
S, and look	Jn 7:52	*2045*

SEARCHED

Laban *s* all the tent, but found	Gen 31:34	4959
And he *s*, but found not the images	Gen 31:35	2664
Whereas thou hast *s* all my stuff	Gen 31:37	4959
And he *s*, and began at the eldest,	Gen 44:12	2664
s the land from the wilderness of	Num 13:21	8446
of the land which they had *s* unto	Num 13:32	8446
were of them that *s* the land	Num 14:6	8446
the days in which ye *s* the land.	Num 14:34	8446
the valley of Eshcol, and *s* it out	Deut 1:24	7270
Lo this, we have *s* it, so it is	Job 5:27	2713
he prepared it, yea, and *s* it out	Job 28:27	2713
cause which I knew not I *s* out	Job 29:16	2713
whilst ye *s* out what to say	Job 32:11	2713
the number of his years be *s* out	Job 36:26	2714
O lord, thou hast *s* me, and known	Ps 139:1	2713
of the earth *s* out beneath	Jer 31:37	2713
the Lord, though it cannot be *s*	Jer 46:23	2713
How are the things of Esau *s* out	Obad 6	2664
s the scriptures daily, whether	Acts 17:11	*350*
s diligently, who prophesied of	1Pet 1:10	*1830*

SEARCHEST

mine iniquity, and *s* after my sin	Job 10:6	1875
s for her as for hid treasures	Prov 2:4	2664

SEARCHETH

for the Lord *s* all hearts	1Chr 28:9	1875
darkness, and *s* out all perfection	Job 28:3	2713
he *s* after every green thing	Job 39:8	1875
but his neighbour cometh and *s* him	Prov 18:17	2713
that hath understanding *s* him out	Prov 28:11	2713
he that *s* the hearts knoweth what	Rom 8:27	2045
for the Spirit *s* all things	1Cor 2:10	2045
that I am he which *s* the reins	Rev 2:23	2045

SEARCHING

they returned from *s* of the land	Num 13:25	8446
Canst thou by *s* find out God	Job 11:7	2714
s all the inward parts of the	Prov 20:27	2664
there is no *s* of his	Is 40:28	2714
S what, or what manner of time	1Pet 1:11	2045

SEARCHINGS

there were great *s* of heart	Judg 5:16	2714

SEARED

conscience *s* with a hot iron	1Ti 4:2	*2743*

SEAS

of the waters called he *S*	Gen 1:10	3220
and fill the waters in the *s*	Gen 1:22	3220
and scales in the waters, in the *s*	Lev 11:9	3220
have not fins and scales in the *s*	Lev 11:10	3220
suck of the abundance of the *s*	Deut 33:19	3220
things that are therein, the *s*	Neh 9:6	3220
through the paths of the *s*	Ps 8:8	3220
For he hath founded it upon the *s*	Ps 24:2	3220
Which stilleth the noise of the *s*	Ps 65:7	3220
heaven and earth praise him, the *s*	Ps 69:34	3220
in heaven, and in earth, in the *s*	Ps 135:6	3220
a noise like the noise of the *s*	Is 17:12	3220
to me above the sand of the *s*	Jer 15:8	3220
borders are in the midst of the *s*	Eze 27:4	3220
glorious in the midst of the *s*	Eze 27:25	3220
broken thee in the midst of the *s*	Eze 27:26	3220
of the *s* in the day of thy ruin	Eze 27:27	3220
thy wares went forth out of the *s*	Eze 27:33	3220
thou shalt be broken by the *s* in	Eze 27:34	3220
of God, in the midst of the *s*	Eze 28:2	3220
are slain in the midst of the *s*	Eze 28:8	3220
and thou art as a whale in the *s*	Eze 32:2	3220
of his palace between the *s* in	Dan 11:45	3220
the deep, in the midst of the *s*	Jonah 2:3	3220
into a place where two *s* met	Acts 27:41	*1337*

SEASON

and they continued a *s* in ward	Gen 40:4	3117
in his *s* from year to year	Ex 13:10	4150
offering shalt thou *s* with salt	Lev 2:13	4414
I will give you rain in due *s*	Lev 26:4	6256
the passover at his appointed *s*	Num 9:2	4150
shall keep it in his appointed *s*	Num 9:3	4150
s among the children of Israel	Num 9:7	4150

S

of the Lord in his appointed *s*	Num 9:13	4150
to offer unto me in their due *s*	Num 28:2	4150
rain of your land in his due *s*	Deut 11:14	6256
at the *s* that thou camest forth	Deut 16:6	4150
the rain unto thy land in his *s*	Deut 28:12	6256
dwelt in the wilderness a long *s*	Josh 24:7	3117
And he said, About this *s*,	2Kin 4:16	4150
bare a son at that *s* that Elisha	2Kin 4:17	4150
were at that *s* in the high place	1Chr 21:29	6256
Now for a long *s* Israel hath been	2Chr 15:3	3117
shock of corn cometh in in his *s*	Job 5:26	6256
are pierced in me in the night *s*	Job 30:17	
bring forth Mazzaroth in his *s*	Job 38:32	6256
bringeth forth his fruit in his *s*	Ps 1:3	6256
and in the night *s*, and am not	Ps 22:2	
give them their meat in due *s*	Ps 104:27	6256
givest them their meat in due *s*	Ps 145:15	6256
and a word spoken in due *s*	Prov 15:23	6256
To every thing there is a *s*	Eccl 3:1	2165
and thy princes eat in due *s*	Eccl 10:17	6256
a word in *s* to him that is weary	Is 50:4	
former and the latter, in his *s*	Jer 5:24	6256
not be day and night in their *s*	Jer 33:20	6256
the shower to come down in his *s*	Eze 34:26	6256
lives were prolonged for a *s*	Dan 7:12	2166
and my wine in the *s* thereof	Hos 2:9	4150
to give them meat in due *s*	Mt 24:45	2540
saltness, wherewith will ye *s* it	Mk 9:50	741
And at the *s* he sent to the	Mk 12:2	2540
shall be fulfilled in their *s*	Lk 1:20	2540
he departed from him for a *s*	Lk 4:13	2540
their portion of meat in due *s*	Lk 12:42	2540
that *s* some that told him of the	Lk 13:1	2540
at the *s* he sent a servant to the	Lk 20:10	2540
desirous to see him of a long *s*	Lk 23:8	
down at a certain *s* into the pool	Jn 5:4	2540
ye were willing for a *s* to	Jn 5:35	5610
blind, not seeing the sun for a *s*	Acts 13:11	2540
he himself stayed in Asia for a *s*	Acts 19:22	5550
when I have a convenient *s*	Acts 24:25	2540
sorry, though it were but for a *s*	2Cor 7:8	5610
for in due *s* we shall reap, if we	Gal 6:9	2540
be instant in *s*	2Ti 4:2	2121
out of *s*; reprove	2Ti 4:2	171
he therefore departed for a *s*	Philem 15	5610
the pleasures of sin for a *s*	Heb 11:25	4340
rejoice, though now for a *s*	1Pet 1:6	3641
should rest yet for a little *s*	Rev 6:11	5550
that he must be loosed a little *s*	Rev 20:3	5550

SEASONED

savour, wherewith shall it be *s*	Lk 14:34	741
s with salt, that ye may know how	Col 4:6	741

SEASONS

let them be for signs, and for *s*	Gen 1:14	4150
them judge the people at all *s*	Ex 18:22	6256
they judged the people at all *s*	Ex 18:26	6256
ye shall proclaim in their *s*	Lev 23:4	4150
also instruct me in the night *s*	Ps 16:7	
He appointed the moon for *s*	Ps 104:19	4150
And he changeth the times and the *s*	Dan 2:21	2166
render him the fruits in their *s*	Mt 21:41	2540
you to know the times or the *s*	Acts 1:7	2540
rain from heaven, and fruitful *s*	Acts 14:17	2540
I have been with you at all *s*	Acts 20:18	5550
But of the times and the *s*	1Th 5:1	2540

SEAT

shalt make a mercy *s* of pure gold	Ex 25:17	
in the two ends of the mercy *s*	Ex 25:18	
even of the mercy *s* shall ye make	Ex 25:19	
the mercy *s* with their wings	Ex 25:20	
toward the mercy *s* shall the	Ex 25:20	
the mercy *s* above upon the ark	Ex 25:21	
with thee from above the mercy *s*	Ex 25:22	
thou shalt put the mercy *s* upon	Ex 26:34	
before the mercy *s* that is over	Ex 30:6	
the mercy *s* that is thereupon, and	Ex 31:7	
staves thereof, with the mercy *s*	Ex 35:12	
he made the mercy *s* of pure gold	Ex 37:6	
on the two ends of the mercy *s*	Ex 37:7	
out of the mercy *s* made he the	Ex 37:8	
with their wings over the mercy *s*	Ex 37:9	
staves thereof, and the mercy *s*	Ex 39:35	
put the mercy *s* above upon the	Ex 40:20	
the vail before the mercy *s*	Lev 16:2	
in the cloud upon the mercy *s*	Lev 16:2	
s that is upon the testimony	Lev 16:13	
finger upon the mercy *s* eastward	Lev 16:14	
before the mercy *s* shall he	Lev 16:14	
and sprinkle it upon the mercy *s*	Lev 16:15	

and before the mercy *s*	Lev 16:15	
mercy *s* that was upon the ark of	Num 7:89	
And he arose out of his *s*	Judg 3:20	3678
Now Eli the priest sat upon a *s*	1Sa 1:9	3678
Eli sat upon a *s* by the wayside	1Sa 4:13	3678
that he fell from off the *s*	1Sa 4:18	3678
because thy *s* will be empty	1Sa 20:18	4186
And the king sat upon his *s*	1Sa 20:25	4186
times, even upon a *s* by the wall	1Sa 20:25	4186
The Tachmonite that sat in the *s*	2Sa 23:8	7674
caused a *s* to be set for the	1Kin 2:19	3678
either side on the place of the *s*	1Kin 10:19	7675
and of the place of the mercy *s*	1Chr 28:11	
set his *s* above all the princes	Est 3:1	3678
that I might come even to his *s*	Job 23:3	8499
I prepared my *s* in the street	Job 29:7	4186
sitteth in the *s* of the scornful	Ps 1:1	
on a *s* in the high places of the	Prov 9:14	3678
where was the *s* of the image of	Eze 8:3	4186
I am a God, I sit in the *s* of God	Eze 28:2	4186
cause the *s* of violence to come	Amos 6:3	7675
and the Pharisees sit in Moses' *s*	Mt 23:2	2515
he was set down on the judgment *s*	Mt 27:19	968
sat down in the judgment *s* in a	Jn 19:13	968
and brought him to the judgment *s*	Acts 18:12	968
he drave them from the judgment *s*	Acts 18:16	968
and beat him before the judgment *s*	Acts 18:17	968
day sitting on the judgment *s*	Acts 25:6	968
I stand at Caesar's judgment *s*	Acts 25:10	968
morrow I sat on the judgment *s*	Acts 25:17	968
before the judgment *s* of Christ	Rom 14:10	968
before the judgment *s* of Christ	2Cor 5:10	968
dwellest, even where Satan's *s* is	Rev 2:13	2362
gave him his power, and his *s*	Rev 13:2	2362
his vial upon the *s* of the beast	Rev 16:10	2362

SEATED

portion of the lawgiver, was he *s*	Deut 33:21	5603

SEATS

the *s* of them that sold doves,	Mt 21:12	2515
the chief *s* in the synagogues,	Mt 23:6	4410
the *s* of them that sold doves	Mk 11:15	2515
the chief *s* in the synagogues, and	Mk 12:39	4410
put down the mighty from their *s*	Lk 1:52	2362
the uppermost *s* in the synagogues	Lk 11:43	4410
the highest *s* in the synagogues,	Lk 20:46	4410
and draw you before the judgment *s*	Jas 2:6	
the throne were four and twenty *s*	Rev 4:4	2362
upon the *s* I saw four and twenty	Rev 4:4	2362
which sat before God on their *s*	Rev 11:16	2362

SEATWARD

even to the mercy *s* were the	Ex 37:9	

SEBA *(se'-bah)* See SABEANS, SHEBA.
   1. A son of Cush.

S, and Havilah, and Sabtah, and	Gen 10:7	5434
S, and Havilah, and Sabta, and	1Chr 1:9	5434

   2. The land.

of Sheba and *S* shall offer gifts	Ps 72:10	5434
ransom, Ethiopia and *S* for thee	Is 43:3	5434

SEBAM See SHEBAM.

SEBAT *(se'-bat) The eleventh month of the Hebrew year.*

month, which is the month *S*	Zec 1:7	7627

SECACAH *(se-ca'-cah) A village in Judah.*

Beth-arabah, Middin, and *S*	Josh 15:61	5527

SECHU *(se'-ku) A city in Benjamin.*

came to a great well that is in *S*	1Sa 19:22	7906

SECOND

and the morning were the *s* day	Gen 1:8	8145
the name of the *s* river is Gihon	Gen 2:13	8145
with lower, *s*, and third stories	Gen 6:16	8145
of Noah's life, in the *s* month	Gen 7:11	8145
And in the *s* month, on the seven	Gen 8:14	8145
Abraham out of heaven the *s* time	Gen 22:15	8145
again, and bare Jacob a *s* son	Gen 30:7	8145
Leah's maid bare Jacob a *s* son	Gen 30:12	8145
And so commanded he the *s*, and the	Gen 32:19	8145
And he slept and dreamed the *s* time	Gen 41:5	8145
in the *s* chariot which he had	Gen 41:43	4932
the name of the *s* called he	Gen 41:52	8145
now we had returned this *s* time	Gen 43:10	
they came unto him the *s* year	Gen 47:18	8145
And when he went out the *s* day	Ex 2:13	8145
on the fifteenth day of the *s*	Ex 16:1	8145
curtain, in the coupling of the *s*	Ex 26:4	8145
that is in the coupling of the *s*	Ex 26:5	8145
the curtain which coupleth the *s*	Ex 26:10	8145
for the *s* side of the tabernacle	Ex 26:20	8145

the *s* row shall be an emerald, a	Ex 28:18	8145
curtain, in the coupling of the *s*	Ex 36:11	8145
was in the coupling of the *s*	Ex 36:12	8145
the curtain which coupleth the *s*	Ex 36:17	8145
And the *s* row, an emerald, a	Ex 39:11	8145
in the first month in the *s* year	Ex 40:17	8145
he shall offer the *s* for a burnt	Lev 5:10	8145
it shall be washed the *s* time	Lev 13:58	8145
on the first day of the *s* month	Num 1:1	8145
in the *s* year after they were	Num 1:1	8145
on the first day of the *s* month	Num 1:18	8145
shall set forth in the *s* rank	Num 2:16	8145
On the *s* day Nethaneel the son of	Num 7:18	8145
in the first month of the *s* year	Num 9:1	8145
The fourteenth day of the *s* month	Num 9:11	8145
When ye blow an alarm the *s* time	Num 10:6	8145
the *s* month, in the *s* year	Num 10:11	8145
on the *s* day ye shall offer	Num 29:17	8145
the children of Israel the *s* time	Josh 5:2	8145
the *s* day they compassed the city	Josh 6:14	8145
which took it on the *s* day	Josh 10:32	8145
the *s* lot came forth to Simeon,	Josh 19:1	8145
even the *s* bullock of seven years	Judg 6:25	8145
place, and take the *s* bullock	Judg 6:26	8145
the *s* bullock was offered upon	Judg 6:28	8145
children of Benjamin the *s* day	Judg 20:24	8145
them out of Gibeah the *s* day	Judg 20:25	8145
and the name of his *s*, Abiah	1Sa 8:2	4932
which was the *s* day of the month,	1Sa 20:27	8145
no meat the *s* day of the month	1Sa 20:34	8145
I will not smite him the *s* time	1Sa 26:8	8138
And his *s*, Chileab, of Abigail the	2Sa 3:3	4932
and when he sent again the *s* time	2Sa 14:29	8145
month Zif, which is the *s* month	1Kin 6:1	8145
appeared to Solomon the *s* time	1Kin 9:2	8145
the *s* year of Asa king of Judah	1Kin 15:25	8147
And he said, Do it the *s* time	1Kin 18:34	8138
And they did it the *s* time	1Kin 18:34	8138
of the LORD came again the *s* time	1Kin 19:7	8145
the *s* year of Jehoram the son of	2Kin 1:17	8147
Then he sent out a *s* on horseback	2Kin 9:19	8145
wrote a letter the *s* time to them	2Kin 10:6	8145
In the *s* year of Joash son of	2Kin 14:1	8147
In the *s* year of Pekah the son of	2Kin 15:32	8147
and in the *s* year that which	2Kin 19:29	8145
and the priests of the *s* order	2Kin 23:4	4932
like unto these had the *s* pillar	2Kin 25:17	8145
priest, and Zephaniah the *s* priest	2Kin 25:18	4932
Eliab, and Abinadab the *s*, and	1Chr 2:13	8145
the *s* Daniel, of Abigail the	1Chr 3:1	8145
the *s* Jehoiakim, the third	1Chr 3:15	8145
the name of the *s* was Zelophehad	1Chr 7:15	8145
Bela his firstborn, Ashbel the *s*	1Chr 8:1	8145
Ulam his firstborn, Jehush the *s*	1Chr 8:39	8145
Ezer the first, Obadiah the *s*	1Chr 12:9	8145
their brethren of the *s* degree	1Chr 15:18	4932
was the chief, and Zizah the *s*	1Chr 23:11	8145
Jeriah the first, Amariah the *s*	1Chr 23:19	8145
Micah the first, and Jesiah the *s*	1Chr 23:20	8145
to Jehoiarib, the *s* to Jedaiah,	1Chr 24:7	8145
Jeriah the first, Amariah the *s*	1Chr 24:23	8145
the *s* to Gedaliah, who with his	1Chr 25:9	8145
the firstborn, Jediael the *s*	1Chr 26:2	8145
the firstborn, Jehozabad the *s*	1Chr 26:4	8145
Hilkiah the *s*, Tebaliah the third	1Chr 26:11	8145
over the course of the *s* month	1Chr 27:4	8145
the son of David king the *s* time	1Chr 29:22	8145
in the *s* day of the month	2Chr 3:2	8145
pay unto him, both the *s* year	2Chr 27:5	8145
keep the passover in the *s* month	2Chr 30:2	8145
unleavened bread in the *s* month	2Chr 30:13	8145
the fourteenth day of the *s* month	2Chr 30:15	8145
put him in the *s* chariot that he	2Chr 35:24	4932
basons of a *s* sort four hundred	Ezr 1:10	4932
Now in the *s* year of their coming	Ezr 3:8	8145
God at Jerusalem, in the *s* month	Ezr 3:8	8145
So it ceased unto the *s* year of	Ezr 4:24	8648
on the *s* day were gathered	Neh 8:13	8145
son of Senuah was *s* over the city	Neh 11:9	4932
Bakbukiah the *s* among his	Neh 11:17	4932
into the *s* house of the women	Est 2:14	8145
were gathered together the *s* time	Est 2:19	8145
the *s* day at the banquet of wine	Est 7:2	8145
to confirm this *s* letter of Purim	Est 9:29	8145
and the name of the *s*, Kezia	Job 42:14	8145
is one alone, and there is not a *s*	Eccl 4:8	8145
with the *s* child that shall stand	Eccl 4:15	8145
shall set his hand again the *s*	Is 11:11	8145
the *s* year that which springeth	Is 37:30	8145
the LORD came unto me the *s* time	Jer 1:13	8145
the LORD came unto me the *s* time	Jer 13:3	8145

came unto Jeremiah the *s* time	Jer 33:1	8145
it came to pass the *s* day after	Jer 41:4	8145
The *s* pillar also and the	Jer 52:22	8145
priest, and Zephaniah the *s* priest	Jer 52:24	4932
the *s* face was the face of a man,	Eze 10:14	8145
on the *s* day thou shalt offer a	Eze 43:22	8145
in the *s* year of the reign of	Dan 2:1	8147
And behold another beast, a *s*	Dan 7:5	8578
LORD came unto Jonah the *s* time	Jonah 3:1	8145
shall not rise up the *s* time	Nah 1:9	
gate, and an howling from the *s*	Zeph 1:10	4932
In the *s* year of Darius the king,	Hag 1:1	8147
in the *s* year of Darius the king	Hag 1:15	8147
in the *s* year of Darius, came the	Hag 2:10	8147
in the *s* year of Darius, came the	Zec 1:1	8147
in the *s* year of Darius, came the	Zec 1:7	8147
in the *s* chariot black horses	Zec 6:2	8145
And he came to the *s*, and said	Mt 21:30	*1208*
Likewise the *s* also, and the third	Mt 22:26	*1208*
the *s* is like unto it, Thou shalt	Mt 22:39	*1208*
He went away again the *s* time	Mt 26:42	*1208*
the *s* took her, and died, neither	Mk 12:21	*1208*
the *s* is like, namely this, Thou	Mk 12:31	*1208*
And the *s* time the cock crew	Mk 14:72	*1208*
it came to pass on the *s* sabbath	Lk 6:1	*1207*
if he shall come in the *s* watch	Lk 12:38	*1208*
the *s* came, saying, Lord, thy	Lk 19:18	*1208*
the *s* took her to wife, and he	Lk 20:30	*1208*
can he enter the *s* time into his	Jn 3:4	*1208*
This is again the *s* miracle that	Jn 4:54	*1208*
He saith to him again the *s* time	Jn 21:16	*1208*
at the *s* time Joseph was made	Acts 7:13	*1208*
spake unto him again the *s* time	Acts 10:15	*1208*
the *s* ward, they came unto the	Acts 12:10	*1208*
it is also written in the *s* psalm	Acts 13:33	*1208*
the *s* man is the Lord from heaven	1Cor 15:47	*1208*
that ye might have a *s* benefit	2Cor 1:15	*1208*
as if I were present, the *s* time	2Cor 13:2	*1208*
The *s* epistle to the Corinthians	2Cor *s*	*1208*
The *s* epistle to the	2Th *s*	*1208*
The *s* epistle unto Timotheus,	2Ti *s*	*1208*
brought before Nero the *s* time	2Ti *s*	*1208*
the first and *s* admonition reject	Titus 3:10	*1208*
place have been sought for the *s*	Heb 8:7	*1208*
And after the *s* veil, the	Heb 9:3	*1208*
But into the *s* went the high	Heb 9:7	*1208*
for him shall he appear the *s*	Heb 9:28	*1208*
that he may establish the *s*	Heb 10:9	*1208*
This *s* epistle, beloved, I now	2Pet 3:1	*1208*
shall not be hurt of the *s* death	Rev 2:11	*1208*
the *s* beast like a calf, and the	Rev 4:7	*1208*
And when he had opened the *s* seal	Rev 6:3	*1208*
I heard the *s* beast say	Rev 6:3	*1208*
the *s* angel sounded, and as it	Rev 8:8	*1208*
The *s* woe is past	Rev 11:14	*1208*
the *s* angel poured out his vial	Rev 16:3	*1208*
on such the *s* death hath no power	Rev 20:6	*1208*
This is the *s* death	Rev 20:14	*1208*
which is the *s* death	Rev 21:8	*1208*
the *s*, sapphire	Rev 21:19	*1208*

SECONDARILY
s prophets, thirdly teachers,	1Cor 12:28	*1208*

SECRET
soul, come not thou into their *s*	Gen 49:6	5475
and putteth it in a *s* place	Deut 27:15	5643
The *s* things belong unto the LORD	Deut 29:29	5641
I have a *s* errand unto thee, O	Judg 3:19	5643
after my name, seeing it is *s*	Judg 13:18	6383
they had emerods in their *s* parts	1Sa 5:9	8368
morning, and abide in a *s* place	1Sa 19:2	5643
that thou wouldest keep me *s*	Job 14:13	5641
Hast thou heard the *s* of God	Job 15:8	5475
is there any *s* thing with thee	Job 15:11	328
shall be hid in his *s* places	Job 20:26	6845
when the *s* of God was upon my	Job 29:4	5475
and bind their faces in *s*	Job 40:13	2934
in the *s* places doth he murder	Ps 10:8	4565
a young lion lurking in *s* places	Ps 17:12	4565
He made darkness his *s* place	Ps 18:11	5643
cleanse thou me from *s* faults	Ps 19:12	5641
The *s* of the LORD is with them	Ps 25:14	5475
in the *s* of his tabernacle shall	Ps 27:5	5643
Thou shalt hide them in the *s* of	Ps 31:20	5643
Hide me from the *s* counsel of the	Ps 64:2	5475
may shoot in *s* at the perfect	Ps 64:4	4565
thee in the *s* place of thunder	Ps 81:7	5643
our *s* sins in the light of thy	Ps 90:8	5956
He that dwelleth in the *s* place	Ps 91:1	5643
from thee, when I was made in *s*	Ps 139:15	5643
but his *s* is with the righteous	Prov 3:32	5475

S

and bread eaten in *s* is pleasant	Prov 9:17	5643
A gift in *s* pacifieth anger	Prov 21:14	5643
and discover not a *s* to another	Prov 25:9	5475
Open rebuke is better than *s* love	Prov 27:5	5641
into judgment, with every *s* thing	Eccl 12:14	5956
in the *s* places of the stairs,	Song 2:14	5643
LORD will discover their *s* parts	Is 3:17	6596
and hidden riches of *s* places	Is 45:3	4565
I have not spoken in *s*, in a dark	Is 45:19	5643
spoken in *s* from the beginning	Is 48:16	5643
I have not found it by *s* search	Jer 2:34	5643
weep in *s* places for your pride	Jer 13:17	4565
Can any hide himself in *s* places	Jer 23:24	4565
I have uncovered his *s* places	Jer 49:10	4565
in wait, and as a lion in *s* places	Lam 3:10	4565
and they shall pollute my *s* place	Eze 7:22	6845
there is no *s* that they can hide	Eze 28:3	5640
God of heaven concerning this *s*	Dan 2:18	7328
Then was the *s* revealed unto	Dan 2:19	7328
He revealeth the deep and *s* things	Dan 2:22	5642
The *s* which the king hath	Dan 2:27	7328
this *s* is not revealed to me for	Dan 2:30	7328
seeing thou couldest reveal this *s*	Dan 2:47	7328
no *s* troubleth thee, tell me the	Dan 4:9	7328
but he revealeth his *s* unto his	Amos 3:7	5475
That thine alms may be in *s*	Mt 6:4	2927
in *s* himself shall reward thee	Mt 6:4	2927
pray to thy Father which is in *s*	Mt 6:6	2927
in *s* shall reward thee openly	Mt 6:6	2927
but unto thy Father which is in *s*	Mt 6:18	2927
and thy Father, which seeth in *s*	Mt 6:18	2927
kept *s* from the foundation of the	Mt 13:35	2928
behold, he is in the *s* chambers	Mt 24:26	5009
neither was any thing kept *s*	Mk 4:22	614
For nothing is *s*, that shall not	Lk 8:17	2927
a candle, putteth it in a *s* place	Lk 11:33	2926
no man that doeth any thing in *s*	Jn 7:4	2927
not openly, but as it were in *s*	Jn 7:10	2927
and in *s* have I said nothing	Jn 18:20	2927
which was kept *s* since the world	Rom 16:25	4601
which are done of them in *s*	Eph 5:12	2931

SECRETLY

Wherefore didst thou flee away *s*	Gen 31:27	2244
as thine own soul, entice thee *s*	Deut 13:6	5643
he that smiteth his neighbour *s*	Deut 27:24	5643
want of all things *s* in the siege	Deut 28:57	5643
out of Shittim two men to spy *s*	Josh 2:1	2791
saying, Commune with David *s*	1Sa 18:22	3909
David knew that Saul *s* practised	1Sa 23:9	2790
For thou didst it *s*	2Sa 12:12	5643
did *s* those things that were not	2Kin 17:9	2644
Now a thing was *s* brought to me	Job 4:12	1589
if ye do *s* accept persons	Job 13:10	5643
And my heart hath been *s* enticed	Job 31:27	5643
He lieth in wait as a lion in	Ps 10:9	4565
thou shalt keep them *s* in a	Ps 31:20	6845
the king asked him *s* in his house	Jer 37:17	5643
the king sware *s* unto Jeremiah	Jer 38:16	5643
spake to Gedaliah in Mizpah *s*	Jer 40:15	5643
was as to devour the poor *s*	Hab 3:14	4565
way, and called Mary her sister *s*	Jn 11:28	2977
but *s* for fear of the Jews,	Jn 19:38	2928

SECRETS

her hand, and taketh him by the *s*	Deut 25:11	4016
would shew thee the *s* of wisdom	Job 11:6	8587
for he knoweth the *s* of the heart	Ps 44:21	8587
A talebearer revealeth *s*	Prov 11:13	5475
about as a talebearer revealeth *s*	Prov 20:19	5475
a God in heaven that revealeth *s*	Dan 2:28	7328
he that revealeth *s* maketh known	Dan 2:29	7328
LORD of kings, and a revealer of *s*	Dan 2:47	7328
the *s* of men by Jesus Christ	Rom 2:16	2927
thus are the *s* of his heart made	1Cor 14:25	2927

SECT

(which is the *s* of the Sadducees,	Acts 5:17	139
there rose up certain of the *s* of	Acts 15:5	139
of the *s* of the Nazarenes	Acts 24:5	139
s of our religion I lived a	Acts 26:5	139
for as concerning this *s*, we know	Acts 28:22	139

SECU See SECHU.

SECUNDUS (*se-cun'-dus*) A Christian in Thessalonica.
Thessalonians, Aristarchus and *S*	Acts 20:4	4580

SECURE

for the host was *s*	Judg 8:11	983
of the Zidonians, quiet and *s*	Judg 18:7	982
go, ye shall come unto a people *s*	Judg 18:10	982
a people that were at quiet and *s*	Judg 18:27	982
And thou shalt be *s*, because there	Job 11:18	982

and they that provoke God are *s*	Job 12:6	987
we will persuade him, and *s* you	Mt 28:14	4160,275

SECURELY

seeing he dwelleth *s* by thee	Prov 3:29	983
pass by *s* as men averse from war	Mic 2:8	983

SECURITY

And when they had taken *s* of Jason	Acts 17:9	2425

SEDITION

that they have moved *s* within the	Ezr 4:15	849
and *s* have been made therein	Ezr 4:19	849
for a certain *s* made in the city	Lk 23:19	4714
released unto them him that for *s*	Lk 23:25	4714
a mover of *s* among all the Jews	Acts 24:5	4714

SEDITIONS

emulations, wrath, strife, *s*	Gal 5:20	1370

SEDUCE

shall shew signs and wonders, to *s*	Mk 13:22	635
you concerning them that *s* you	1Jn 2:26	4105
to *s* my servants to commit	Rev 2:20	4105

SEDUCED

Manasseh *s* them to do more evil	2Kin 21:9	8582
they have also *s* Egypt, even they	Is 19:13	8582
because they have *s* my people	Eze 13:10	2937

SEDUCERS

s shall wax worse and worse,	2Ti 3:13	1114

SEDUCETH

but the way of the wicked *s* them	Prov 12:26	8582

SEDUCING

faith, giving heed to *s* spirits	1Ti 4:1	4108

SEE See APPENDIX.

SEED

forth grass, the herb yielding *s*	Gen 1:11	2233
whose *s* is in itself, upon the	Gen 1:11	2233
herb yielding *s* after his kind,	Gen 1:12	2233
whose *s* was in itself, after his	Gen 1:12	2233
given you every herb bearing *s*	Gen 1:29	2233
is the fruit of a tree yielding *s*	Gen 1:29	2233
and between thy *s* and her *s*	Gen 3:15	2233
me another *s* instead of Abel	Gen 4:25	2233
to keep *s* alive upon the face of	Gen 7:3	2233
you, and with your *s* after you	Gen 9:9	2233
Unto thy *s* will I give this land	Gen 12:7	2233
I give it, and to thy *s* for ever	Gen 13:15	2233
I will make thy *s* as the dust of	Gen 13:16	2233
then shall thy *s* also be numbered	Gen 13:16	2233
to me thou hast given no *s*	Gen 15:3	2233
said unto him, So shall thy *s* be	Gen 15:5	2233
Know of a surety that thy *s* shall	Gen 15:13	2233
Unto thy *s* have I given this land	Gen 15:18	2233
I will multiply thy *s* exceedingly	Gen 16:10	2233
thy *s* after thee in their	Gen 17:7	2233
unto thee, and to thy *s* after thee	Gen 17:7	2233
to thy *s* after thee, the land	Gen 17:8	2233
thy *s* after thee in their	Gen 17:9	2233
me and you and thy *s* after thee	Gen 17:10	2233
stranger, which is not of thy *s*	Gen 17:12	2233
covenant, and with his *s* after him	Gen 17:19	2233
we may preserve *s* of our father	Gen 19:32	2233
we may preserve *s* of our father	Gen 19:34	2233
in Isaac shall thy *s* be called	Gen 21:12	2233
a nation, because he is thy *s*	Gen 21:13	2233
thy *s* as the stars of the heaven	Gen 22:17	2233
thy *s* shall possess the gate of	Gen 22:17	2233
in thy *s* shall all the nations of	Gen 22:18	2233
Unto thy *s* will I give this land	Gen 24:7	2233
let thy *s* possess the gate of	Gen 24:60	2233
for unto thee, and unto thy *s*	Gen 26:3	2233
I will make thy *s* to multiply as	Gen 26:4	2233
will give unto thy *s* all these	Gen 26:4	2233
in thy *s* shall all the nations of	Gen 26:4	2233
multiply thy *s* for my servant	Gen 26:24	2233
to thee, and to thy *s* with thee	Gen 28:4	2233
thee will I give it, and to thy *s*	Gen 28:13	2233
thy *s* shall be as the dust of the	Gen 28:14	2233
in thy *s* shall all the families	Gen 28:14	2233
make thy *s* as the sand of the sea	Gen 32:12	2233
to thy *s* after thee will I give	Gen 35:12	2233
raise up *s* to thy brother	Gen 38:8	2233
knew that the *s* should not be his	Gen 38:9	2233
he should give *s* to his brother	Gen 38:9	2233
Jacob, and all his *s* with him	Gen 46:6	2233
all his *s* brought he with him	Gen 46:7	2233
and give us *s*, that we may live,	Gen 47:19	2233
lo, here is *s* for you, and ye	Gen 47:23	2233
for *s* of the field, and for your	Gen 47:24	2233

will give this land to thy *s*	Gen 48:4	2233
lo, God hath shewed me also thy *s*	Gen 48:11	2233
his *s* shall become a multitude of	Gen 48:19	2233
and it was like coriander *s*	Ex 16:31	2233
ever unto him and his *s* after him	Ex 28:43	2233
to his *s* throughout their	Ex 30:21	2233
I will multiply your *s* as the	Ex 32:13	2233
spoken of will I give unto your *s*	Ex 32:13	2233
Unto thy *s* will I give it	Ex 33:1	2233
any sowing *s* which is to be sown	Lev 11:37	2233
if any water be put upon the *s*	Lev 11:38	2233
If a woman have conceived *s*	Lev 12:2	2233
if any man's *s* of copulation go	Lev 15:16	2233
whereon is the *s* of copulation	Lev 15:17	2233
shall lie with *s* of copulation	Lev 15:18	2233
of him whose *s* goeth from him, and	Lev 15:32	2233
thou shalt not let any of thy *s*	Lev 18:21	2233
not sow thy field with mingled *s*	Lev 19:19	
giveth any of his *s* unto Molech	Lev 20:2	2233
hath given of his *s* unto Molech	Lev 20:3	2233
he giveth of his *s* unto Molech	Lev 20:4	2233
he profane his *s* among his people	Lev 21:15	2233
Whosoever he be of thy *s* in their	Lev 21:17	2233
s of Aaron the priest shall come	Lev 21:21	2233
all your *s* among your generations	Lev 22:3	2233
of the *s* of Aaron is a leper	Lev 22:4	2233
or a man whose *s* goeth from him	Lev 22:4	
and ye shall sow your *s* in vain	Lev 26:16	2233
be according to the *s* thereof	Lev 27:16	2233
a homer of barley *s* shall be	Lev 27:16	2233
whether of the *s* of the land	Lev 27:30	2233
be free, and shall conceive *s*	Num 5:28	2233
And the manna was as coriander *s*	Num 11:7	2233
and his *s* shall possess it	Num 14:24	2233
which is not of the *s* of Aaron	Num 16:40	2233
unto thee and to thy *s* with thee	Num 18:19	2233
it is no place of, or of figs,	Num 20:5	2233
his *s* shall be in many waters, and	Num 24:7	2233
his *s* after him, even the	Num 25:13	2233
them and to their *s* after them	Deut 1:8	2233
he chose their *s* after them	Deut 4:37	2233
and he chose their *s* after them	Deut 10:15	2233
to give unto them and to their *s*	Deut 11:9	2233
out, where thou sowedst thy *s*	Deut 11:10	2233
tithe all the increase of thy *s*	Deut 14:22	2233
of thy *s* which thou hast sown	Deut 22:9	2233
carry much *s* out into the field	Deut 28:38	2233
a wonder, and upon thy *s* for ever	Deut 28:46	2233
and the plagues of thy *s*, even	Deut 28:59	2233
heart, and the heart of thy *s*	Deut 30:6	2233
that both thou and thy *s* may live	Deut 30:19	2233
out of the mouths of their *s*	Deut 31:21	2233
saying, I will give it unto thy *s*	Deut 5 1:4	2233
of Canaan, and multiplied his *s*	Josh 24:3	2233
of the *s* which the LORD shall	Ruth 4:12	2233
The LORD give thee *s* of this	1Sa 2:20	2233
he will take the tenth of your *s*	1Sa 8:15	2233
between my *s* and thy *s* for ever	1Sa 20:42	2233
wilt not cut off my *s* after me	1Sa 24:21	2233
this day of Saul, and of his *s*	2Sa 4:8	2233
I will set up thy *s* after thee	2Sa 7:12	2233
David, and to his *s* for evermore	2Sa 22:51	2233
upon the head of his *s* for ever	1Kin 2:33	2233
but upon David, and upon his *s*	1Kin 2:33	2233
he was of the king's *s* in Edom	1Kin 11:14	2233
for this afflict the *s* of David	1Kin 11:39	2233
would contain two measures of *s*	1Kin 18:32	2233
unto thee, and unto thy *s* for ever	2Kin 5:27	2233
and destroyed all the *s* royal	2Kin 11:1	2233
LORD rejected all the *s* of Israel	2Kin 17:20	2233
son of Elishama, of the *s* royal	2Kin 25:25	2233
O ye *s* of Israel his servant, ye	1Chr 16:13	2233
I will raise up thy *s* after thee	1Chr 17:11	2233
gavest it to the *s* of Abraham thy	2Chr 20:7	2233
destroyed all the *s* royal of the	2Chr 22:10	2233
their father's house, and their *s*	Ezr 2:59	2233
so that the holy *s* have mingled	Ezr 9:2	2233
their father's house, nor their *s*	Neh 7:61	2233
the *s* of Israel separated	Neh 9:2	2233
to give it, I say, to his *s*	Neh 9:8	2233
Mordecai be of the *s* of the Jews	Est 6:13	2233
took upon them, and upon their *s*	Est 9:27	2233
of them perish from their *s*	Est 9:28	2233
for themselves and for their *s*	Est 9:31	2233
and speaking peace to all his *s*	Est 10:3	2233
also that thy *s* shall be great	Job 5:25	2233
Their *s* is established in their	Job 21:8	2233
that he will bring home thy *s*	Job 39:12	2233
David, and to his *s* for evermore	Ps 18:50	2233
their *s* from among the children	Ps 21:10	2233
all ye the *s* of Jacob, glorify	Ps 22:23	2233

fear him, all ye the *s* of Israel	Ps 22:23	2233
A *s* shall serve him	Ps 22:30	2233
his *s* shall inherit the earth	Ps 25:13	2233
forsaken, nor his *s* begging bread	Ps 37:25	2233
and his *s* is blessed	Ps 37:26	2233
but the *s* of the wicked shall be	Ps 37:28	2233
The *s* also of his servants shall	Ps 69:36	2233
Thy *s* will I establish for ever,	Ps 89:4	2233
His *s* also will I make to endure	Ps 89:29	2233
His *s* endure for ever, and	Ps 89:36	2233
their *s* shall be established	Ps 102:28	2233
O ye *s* of Abraham his servant, ye	Ps 105:6	2233
To overthrow their *s* also among	Ps 106:27	2233
His *s* shall be mighty upon earth	Ps 112:2	2233
and weepeth, bearing precious *s*	Ps 126:6	2233
but the *s* of the righteous shall	Prov 11:21	2233
In the morning sow thy *s*, and in	Eccl 11:6	2233
a *s* of evildoers, children that	Is 1:4	2233
the *s* of an homer shall yield an	Is 5:10	2233
so the holy *s* shall be the	Is 6:13	2233
the *s* of evildoers shall never be	Is 14:20	2233
shalt thou make thy *s* to flourish	Is 17:11	2233
And by great waters the *s* of Sihor	Is 23:3	2233
shall he give the rain of thy *s*	Is 30:23	2233
the *s* of Abraham my friend	Is 41:8	2233
I will bring thy *s* from the east	Is 43:5	2233
I will pour my spirit upon thy *s*	Is 44:3	2233
I said not unto the *s* of Jacob	Is 45:19	2233
all the *s* of Israel be justified	Is 45:25	2233
Thy *s* also had been as the sand,	Is 48:19	2233
for sin, he shall see his *s*	Is 53:10	2233
thy *s* shall inherit the Gentiles,	Is 54:3	2233
that it may give *s* to the sower	Is 55:10	2233
the *s* of the adulterer and the	Is 57:3	2233
transgression, a *s* of falsehood,	Is 57:4	2233
nor out of the mouth of thy *s*	Is 59:21	2233
out of the mouth of thy seed's *s*	Is 59:21	2233
their *s* shall be known among the	Is 61:9	2233
that they are the *s* which the	Is 61:9	2233
will bring forth a *s* out of Jacob	Is 65:9	2233
for they are the *s* of the blessed	Is 65:23	2233
saith the LORD, so shall your *s*	Is 66:22	2233
a noble vine, wholly a right *s*	Jer 2:21	2233
even the whole *s* of Ephraim	Jer 7:15	2233
are they cast out, he and his *s*	Jer 22:28	2233
for no man of his *s* shall prosper	Jer 22:30	2233
which led the *s* of the house of	Jer 23:8	2233
Shemaiah the Nehelamite, and his *s*	Jer 29:32	2233
thy *s* from the land of their	Jer 30:10	2233
house of Judah with the *s* of man	Jer 31:27	2233
of man, and with the *s* of beast	Jer 31:27	2233
then the *s* of Israel also shall	Jer 31:36	2233
the *s* of Israel for all that they	Jer 31:37	2233
the *s* of David my servant	Jer 33:22	2233
will I cast away the *s* of Jacob	Jer 33:26	2233
s to be rulers over the *s* of	Jer 33:26	2233
be rulers over the *s* of Abraham	Jer 33:26	2233
shall ye build house, nor sow *s*	Jer 35:7	2233
we vineyard, nor field, nor *s*	Jer 35:9	2233
And I will punish him and his *s*	Jer 36:31	2233
son of Elishama, of the *s* royal	Jer 41:1	2233
thy *s* from the land of their	Jer 46:27	2233
his *s* is spoiled, and his brethren	Jer 49:10	2233
He took also of the *s* of the land	Eze 17:5	2233
And hath taken of the king's *s*	Eze 17:13	2233
unto the *s* of the house of Jacob,	Eze 20:5	2233
Levites that be of the *s* of Zadok	Eze 43:19	2233
of the *s* of the house of Israel	Eze 44:22	2233
of Israel, and of the king's *s*	Dan 1:3	2233
themselves with the *s* of men	Dan 2:43	2234
of the *s* of the Medes, which was	Dan 9:1	2233
The *s* is rotten under their clods	Joel 1:17	6507
of grapes him that soweth *s*	Amos 9:13	2233
Is the *s* yet in the barn	Hag 2:19	2233
For the *s* shall be prosperous	Zec 8:12	2233
Behold, I will corrupt your *s*	Mal 2:3	2233
That he might seek a godly *s*	Mal 2:15	2233
which received *s* by the way side	Mt 13:19	4687
received the *s* into stony places	Mt 13:20	4687
He also that received *s* among the	Mt 13:22	4687
But he that received *s* into the	Mt 13:23	4687
which sowed good *s* in his field	Mt 13:24	4690
not thou sow good *s* in thy field	Mt 13:27	4690
is like to a grain of mustard *s*	Mt 13:31	
the good *s* is the Son of man	Mt 13:37	4690
the good *s* are the children of	Mt 13:38	4690
faith as a grain of mustard *s*	Mt 17:20	
raise up *s* unto his brother	Mt 22:24	4690
man should cast *s* into the ground	Mk 4:26	4703
the *s* should spring and grow up,	Mk 4:27	4703
It is like a grain of mustard *s*	Mk 4:31	4690

raise up s unto his brother	Mk 12:19	4690
took a wife, and dying left no s	Mk 12:20	4690
and died, neither left he any s	Mk 12:21	4690
the seven had her, and left no s	Mk 12:22	4690
to Abraham, and to his s for ever	Lk 1:55	4690
A sower went out to sow his s	Lk 8:5	4703
The s is the word of God	Lk 8:11	4703
It is like a grain of mustard s	Lk 13:19	
had faith as a grain of mustard s	Lk 17:6	
raise up s unto his brother	Lk 20:28	4690
Christ cometh of the s of David	Jn 7:42	4690
answered him, We be Abraham's s	Jn 8:33	4690
I know that ye are Abraham's s	Jn 8:37	4690
in thy s shall all the kindreds	Acts 3:25	4690
to his s after him, when as yet	Acts 7:5	4690
That his s should sojourn in a	Acts 7:6	4690
Of this man's s hath God	Acts 13:23	4690
which was made of the s of David	Rom 1:3	4690
was not to Abraham, or to his s	Rom 4:13	4690
might be sure to all the s	Rom 4:16	4690
was spoken, So shall thy s be	Rom 4:18	4690
because they are the s of Abraham	Rom 9:7	4690
In Isaac shall thy s be called	Rom 9:7	4690
the promise are counted for the s	Rom 9:8	4690
Lord of Sabaoth had left us a s	Rom 9:29	4690
of the s of Abraham, of the tribe	Rom 11:1	4690
him, and to every s his own body	1Cor 15:38	4690
Now he that ministereth s to the	2Cor 9:10	4690
food, and multiply your s sown	2Cor 9:10	4703
Are they the s of Abraham	2Cor 11:22	4690
his s were the promises made	Gal 3:16	4690
but as of one, And to thy s	Gal 3:16	4690
till the s should come to whom	Gal 3:19	4690
Christ's, then are ye Abraham's s	Gal 3:29	4690
that Jesus Christ of the s of	2Ti 2:8	4690
he took on him the s of Abraham	Heb 2:16	4690
received strength to conceive s	Heb 11:11	4690
in Isaac shall thy s be called	Heb 11:18	4690
born again, not of corruptible s	1Pet 1:23	4701
for his s remaineth in him	1Jn 3:9	4690
war with the remnant of her s	Rev 12:17	4690

SEED'S

out of the mouth of thy s seed	Is 59:21	2233

SEEDS

sow thy vineyard with divers s	Deut 22:9	
some s fell by the way side, and	Mt 13:4	
indeed is the least of all s	Mt 13:32	4690
all the s that be in the earth	Mk 4:31	4690
He saith not, And to s, as of many	Gal 3:16	4690

SEEDTIME

While the earth remaineth, s	Gen 8:22	2233

SEEING See APPENDIX.

SEEK

And he said, I s my brethren	Gen 37:16	1245
that he may s occasion against us	Gen 43:18	1556
shall not s for yellow hair	Lev 13:36	1239
neither s after wizards, to be	Lev 19:31	1245
that ye s not after your own	Num 15:39	8446
and s ye the priesthood also	Num 16:10	1245
to s for enchantments, but he set	Num 24:1	7125
thou shalt s the LORD thy God	Deut 4:29	1245
if thou s him with all thy heart	Deut 4:29	1875
unto his habitation shall ye s	Deut 12:5	1875
thee until thy brother s after it	Deut 22:2	1875
Thou shalt not s their peace nor	Deut 23:6	1875
shall I not s rest for thee, that	Ruth 3:1	1245
thee, and arise, go s the asses	1Sa 9:3	1245
which thou wentest to s are found	1Sa 10:2	1245
And he said, To s the asses	1Sa 10:14	1245
to s out a man, who is a cunning	1Sa 16:16	1245
Saul was come out to s his life	1Sa 23:15	1245
also and his men went to s him	1Sa 23:25	1245
of all Israel, and went to s David	1Sa 24:2	1245
they that s evil to my lord, be	1Sa 25:26	1245
to pursue thee, and to s thy soul	1Sa 25:29	1245
to s David in the wilderness of	1Sa 26:2	1245
of Israel is come out to s a flea	1Sa 26:20	1245
to s me any more in any coast of	1Sa 27:1	1245
S me a woman that hath a familiar	1Sa 28:7	1245
Philistines came up to s David	2Sa 5:17	1245
Gath to Achish to s his servants	1Kin 2:40	1245
my lord hath not sent to s thee	1Kin 18:10	1245
they s my life, to take it away	1Kin 19:10	1245
they s my life, to take it away	1Kin 19:14	1245
go, we pray thee, and s thy master	2Kin 2:16	1245
bring you to the man whom ye s	2Kin 6:19	1245
to s pasture for their flocks	1Chr 4:39	1245
Philistines went up to s David	1Chr 14:8	1245

of them rejoice that s the LORD	1Chr 16:10	1245
S the LORD and his strength	1Chr 16:11	1875
s his face continually	1Chr 16:11	1245
your soul to s the LORD your God	1Chr 22:19	1875
s for all the commandments of the	1Chr 28:8	1875
if thou s him, he will be found	1Chr 28:9	1875
s my face, and turn from their	2Chr 7:14	1245
such as set their hearts to s the	2Chr 11:16	1245
not his heart to s the LORD	2Chr 12:14	1875
commanded Judah to s the LORD God	2Chr 14:4	1875
and if ye s him, he will be found	2Chr 15:2	1875
s the LORD God of their fathers	2Chr 15:12	1875
That whosoever would not s the	2Chr 15:13	1875
prepared thine heart to s God	2Chr 19:3	1875
and set himself to s the LORD	2Chr 20:3	1875
of Judah they came to s the LORD	2Chr 20:4	1245
That prepareth his heart to s God	2Chr 30:19	1875
to s his God, he did it with all	2Chr 31:21	1875
he began to s after the God of	2Chr 34:3	1875
for we s your God, as ye do	Ezr 4:2	1875
to s the LORD God of Israel, did	Ezr 6:21	1875
heart to s the law of the LORD	Ezr 7:10	1875
to s of him a right way for us	Ezr 8:21	1245
upon all them for good that s him	Ezr 8:22	1245
nor s their peace or their wealth	Ezr 9:12	1875
that there was come a man to s	Neh 2:10	1245
I would s unto God, and unto God	Job 5:8	1875
thou shalt s me in the morning	Job 7:21	7836
thou wouldest s unto God betimes	Job 8:5	7836
shall s to please the poor	Job 20:10	
love vanity, and s after leasing	Ps 4:2	1245
not forsaken them that s thee	Ps 9:10	1875
countenance, will not s after God	Ps 10:4	1875
s out his wickedness till thou	Ps 10:15	1875
any that did understand, and s God	Ps 14:2	1875
shall praise the LORD that s him	Ps 22:26	1875
the generation of them that s him	Ps 24:6	1875
him, that s thy face, O Jacob	Ps 24:6	1245
of the LORD, that will I s after	Ps 27:4	1245
When thou saidst, S ye my face	Ps 27:8	1245
thee, Thy face, LORD, will I s	Ps 27:8	1245
but they that s the LORD shall	Ps 34:10	1875
s peace, and pursue it	Ps 34:14	1245
put to shame that s after my soul	Ps 35:4	1245
They also that s after my life	Ps 38:12	1245
they that s my hurt speak	Ps 38:12	1875
confounded together that s after	Ps 40:14	1245
Let all those that s thee rejoice	Ps 40:16	1245
did understand, that did s God	Ps 53:2	1875
oppressors s after my soul	Ps 54:3	1245
early will I s thee	Ps 63:1	7836
But those that s my soul, to	Ps 63:9	1245
let not those that s thee be	Ps 69:6	1875
your heart shall live that s God	Ps 69:32	1875
confounded that s after my soul	Ps 70:2	1245
Let all those that s thee rejoice	Ps 70:4	1245
and dishonour that s my hurt	Ps 71:13	1245
unto shame, that s my hurt	Ps 71:24	1245
that they may s thy name, O LORD	Ps 83:16	1245
prey, and s their meat from God	Ps 104:21	1245
of them rejoice that s the LORD	Ps 105:3	1245
S the LORD, and his strength	Ps 105:4	1875
s his face evermore	Ps 105:4	1245
let them s their bread also out	Ps 109:10	1875
that s him with the whole heart	Ps 119:2	1875
for I s thy precepts	Ps 119:45	1245
for they s not thy statutes	Ps 119:155	1875
s thy servant	Ps 119:176	1245
LORD our God I will s thy good	Ps 122:9	1245
they shall s me early, but they	Prov 1:28	7836
thee, diligently to s thy face	Prov 7:15	7836
those that s me early shall find	Prov 8:17	7836
to and fro of them that s death	Prov 21:6	1245
they that go to s mixed wine	Prov 23:30	2713
I will s it yet again	Prov 23:35	1245
but they that s the LORD	Prov 28:5	1245
but the just s his soul	Prov 29:10	1245
Many s the ruler's favour	Prov 29:26	1245
And I gave my heart to s and search	Eccl 1:13	1875
to s out wisdom, and the reason of	Eccl 7:25	1245
though a man labour to s it out	Eccl 8:17	1245
I will s him whom my soul loveth	Song 3:2	1245
that we may s him with thee	Song 6:1	1245
s judgment, relieve the oppressed	Is 1:17	1875
S unto them that have familiar	Is 8:19	1875
not a people s unto their God	Is 8:19	1875
neither do they s the LORD of	Is 9:13	1875
to it shall the Gentiles s	Is 11:10	1875
they shall s to the idols, and to	Is 19:3	1875
within me will I s thee early	Is 26:9	7836
Woe unto them that s deep to hide	Is 29:15	

One of Israel, neither *s* the LORD	Is 31:1	1875
S ye out of the book of the LORD,	Is 34:16	1875
Thou shalt *s* them, and shalt not	Is 41:12	1245
When the poor and needy *s* water	Is 41:17	1245
seed of Jacob, *S* ye me in vain	Is 45:19	1245
righteousness, ye that *s* the LORD	Is 51:1	1245
S ye the LORD while he may be	Is 55:6	1875
Yet they *s* me daily, and delight	Is 58:2	1875
all they that *s* her will not	Jer 2:24	1245
trimmest thou thy way to *s* love	Jer 2:33	1245
thee, they will *s* thy life	Jer 4:30	1245
s in the broad places thereof, if	Jer 5:1	1245
that *s* thy life, saying, Prophesy	Jer 11:21	1245
hands of them that *s* their lives	Jer 19:7	1245
they that *s* their lives, shall	Jer 19:9	1245
hand of those that *s* their life	Jer 21:7	1245
the hand of them that *s* thy life	Jer 22:25	1245
s the peace of the city whither I	Jer 29:7	1875
And ye shall *s* me, and find me,	Jer 29:13	1245
they *s* thee not	Jer 30:14	1875
hand of them that *s* their life	Jer 34:20	1245
hand of them that *s* their life	Jer 34:21	1245
hand of these men that *s* thy life	Jer 38:16	1245
the hand of them that *s* his life	Jer 44:30	1245
s them not	Jer 45:5	1245
hand of those that *s* their lives	Jer 46:26	1245
and before them that *s* their life	Jer 49:37	1245
shall go, and *s* the LORD their God	Jer 50:4	1245
All her people sigh, they *s* bread	Lam 1:11	1245
and they shall *s* peace, and there	Eze 7:25	1245
then shall they *s* a vision of the	Eze 7:26	1245
none did search or *s* after them	Eze 34:6	1245
search my sheep, and *s* them out	Eze 34:11	1239
so will I *s* out my sheep, and will	Eze 34:12	1239
I will *s* that which was lost, and	Eze 34:16	1245
to *s* by prayer and supplications,	Dan 9:3	1245
and she shall *s* them, but shall	Hos 2:7	1245
s the LORD their God, and David	Hos 3:5	1245
and with their herds to *s* the LORD	Hos 5:6	1245
their offence, and will *s* my face	Hos 5:15	1245
affliction they will *s* me early	Hos 5:15	7836
their God, nor *s* him for all this	Hos 7:10	1245
for it is time to *s* the LORD	Hos 10:12	1875
S ye me, and ye shall live	Amos 5:4	1875
But *s* not Beth-el, nor enter into	Amos 5:5	1875
S the LORD, and ye shall live	Amos 5:6	1875
S him that maketh the seven stars	Amos 5:8	
S good, and not evil, that ye may	Amos 5:14	1875
fro to *s* the word of the LORD, and	Amos 8:12	1245
whence shall I *s* comforters for	Nah 3:7	1245
thou also shalt *s* strength	Nah 3:11	1245
S ye the LORD, all ye meek of the	Zeph 2:3	1245
s righteousness, *s* meekness	Zeph 2:3	1245
LORD, and to *s* the LORD of hosts	Zec 8:21	1245
strong nations shall come to *s*	Zec 8:22	1245
neither shall *s* the young one	Zec 11:16	1245
that I will *s* to destroy all the	Zec 12:9	1245
they should *s* the law at his	Mal 2:7	1245
That he might *s* a godly seed	Mal 2:15	1245
and the Lord, whom ye *s*, shall	Mal 3:1	1245
for Herod will *s* the young child	Mt 2:13	2212
these things do the Gentiles *s*	Mt 6:32	1934
But *s* ye first the kingdom of God	Mt 6:33	2212
s, and ye shall find	Mt 7:7	2212
for I know that ye *s* Jesus	Mt 28:5	2212
said unto him, All men *s* for thee	Mk 1:37	2212
thy brethren without *s* for thee	Mk 3:32	2212
this generation *s* after a sign	Mk 8:12	1934
Ye *s* Jesus of Nazareth, which was	Mk 16:6	2212
s, and ye shall find	Lk 11:9	2212
they *s* a sign	Lk 11:29	1934
s not ye what ye shall eat, or	Lk 12:29	2212
the nations of the world *s* after	Lk 12:30	1934
But rather *s* ye the kingdom of	Lk 12:31	2212
will *s* to enter in, and shall not	Lk 13:24	2212
s diligently till the find it	Lk 15:8	2212
Whosoever shall *s* to save his	Lk 17:33	2212
For the Son of man is come to *s*	Lk 19:10	2212
Why *s* ye the living among the	Lk 24:5	2212
and saith unto them, What *s* ye	Jn 1:38	2212
because I *s* not mine own will,	Jn 5:30	2212
s not the honour that cometh from	Jn 5:44	2212
verily, I say unto you, Ye *s* me	Jn 6:26	2212
not this he, whom they *s* to kill	Jn 7:25	2212
Ye shall *s* me, and shall not find	Jn 7:34	2212
this that he said, Ye shall *s* me	Jn 7:36	2212
I go my way, and ye shall *s* me	Jn 8:21	2212
but ye *s* to kill me, because my	Jn 8:37	2212
But now ye *s* to kill me, a man	Jn 8:40	2212
And I *s* not mine own glory	Jn 8:50	2212
Ye shall *s* me	Jn 13:33	2212

and said unto them, Whom *s* ye	Jn 18:4	2212
asked he them again, Whom *s* ye	Jn 18:7	2212
if therefore ye *s* me, let these	Jn 18:8	2212
him, Behold, three men *s* thee	Acts 10:19	2212
said, Behold, I am he whom ye *s*	Acts 10:21	2212
Barnabas to Tarsus, for to *s* Saul	Acts 11:25	327
of men might *s* after the Lord	Acts 15:17	1567
That they should *s* the Lord	Acts 17:27	2212
in well doing *s* for glory	Rom 2:7	2212
am left alone, and they *s* my life	Rom 11:3	2212
the Greeks *s* after wisdom	1Cor 1:22	2212
s not to be loosed	1Cor 7:27	2212
s not a wife	1Cor 7:27	2212
Let no man *s* his own, but every	1Cor 10:24	2212
s that ye may excel to the	1Cor 14:12	2212
for I *s* not yours, but you	2Cor 12:14	2212
Since ye *s* a proof of Christ	2Cor 13:3	2212
or do I *s* to please men	Gal 1:10	2212
while we *s* to be justified by	Gal 2:17	2212
For all *s* their own, not the	Phil 2:21	2212
s those things which are above,	Col 3:1	2212
of them that diligently *s* him	Heb 11:6	1567
plainly that they *s* a country	Heb 11:14	1934
city, but we *s* one to come	Heb 13:14	1934
let him *s* peace, and ensue it	1Pet 3:11	2212
in those days shall men *s* death	Rev 9:6	2212

SEEKEST

asked him, saying, What *s* thou	Gen 37:15	1245
shew thee the man whom thou *s*	Judg 4:22	1245
the man whom thou *s* is as if all	2Sa 17:3	1245
thou *s* to destroy a city and a	2Sa 20:19	1245
thou *s* to go to thine own country	1Kin 11:22	1245
If thou *s* her as silver, and	Prov 2:4	1245
s thou great things for thyself	Jer 45:5	1245
yet no man said, What *s* thou	Jn 4:27	2212
whom *s* thou	Jn 20:15	2212

SEEKETH

Saul my father *s* to kill thee	1Sa 19:2	1245
thy father, that he *s* my life	1Sa 20:1	1245
for he that *s* my life *s* thy	1Sa 22:23	1245
that *s* my life *s* thy life	1Sa 22:23	1245
that Saul *s* to come to Keilah	1Sa 23:10	1245
saying, Behold, David *s* thy hurt	1Sa 24:9	1245
forth of my bowels, *s* my life	2Sa 16:11	1245
and see how this man *s* mischief	1Kin 20:7	1245
see how he *s* a quarrel against me	2Kin 5:7	579
From thence she *s* the prey	Job 39:29	2658
the righteous, and *s* to slay him	Ps 37:32	1245
He that diligently *s* good	Prov 11:27	7836
but he that *s* mischief, it shall	Prov 11:27	1875
A scorner *s* wisdom, and findeth it	Prov 14:6	1245
hath understanding *s* knowledge	Prov 15:14	1245
covereth a transgression *s* love	Prov 17:9	1245
An evil man *s* only rebellion	Prov 17:11	1245
exalteth his gate *s* destruction	Prov 17:19	1245
man, having separated himself, *s*	Prov 18:1	1245
the ear of the wise *s* knowledge	Prov 18:15	1245
She *s* wool, and flax, and worketh	Prov 31:13	1875
Which yet my soul *s*, but I find	Eccl 7:28	1245
he *s* unto him a cunning workman	Is 40:20	1245
judgment, that *s* the truth	Jer 5:1	1245
This is Zion, whom no man *s* after	Jer 30:17	1875
for this man *s* not the welfare of	Jer 38:4	1875
for him, to the soul that *s* him	Lam 3:25	1875
punishment of them that *s* unto him	Eze 14:10	1875
As a shepherd *s* out his flock in	Eze 34:12	1243
and he that *s* findeth	Mt 7:8	2212
generation *s* after a sign	Mt 12:39	1934
generation *s* after a sign	Mt 16:4	1934
s that which is gone astray	Mt 18:12	2212
and he that *s* findeth	Lk 11:10	2212
for the Father *s* such to worship	Jn 4:23	2212
he himself *s* to be known openly	Jn 7:4	2212
of himself *s* his own glory	Jn 7:18	2212
but he that *s* his glory that sent	Jn 7:18	2212
there is one that *s* and judgeth	Jn 8:50	2212
there is none that *s* after God	Rom 3:11	1567
not obtained that which he *s* for	Rom 11:7	1934
s not her own, is not easily	1Cor 13:5	2212

SEEKING

s the wealth of his people, and	Est 10:3	1875
and *s* judgment, and hasting	Is 16:5	1875
places, *s* rest, and findeth none	Mt 12:43	2212
a merchant man, *s* goodly pearls	Mt 13:45	2212
s of him a sign from heaven,	Mk 8:11	2212
back again to Jerusalem, *s* him	Lk 2:45	2212
through dry places, *s* rest	Lk 11:24	2212
s to catch something out of his	Lk 11:54	2212
I come *s* fruit on this fig tree	Lk 13:7	2212

S

and came to Capernaum, *s* for Jesus ..... Jn 6:24 *2212*
s to turn away the deputy from ..... Acts 13:8 *2212*
he went about *s* some to lead him ..... Acts 13:11 *2212*
not *s* mine own profit, but the 1Cor 10:33 *2212*
about, *s* whom he may devour 1Pet 5:8 *2212*

SEEM See APPENDIX.

SEEMED See APPENDIX.

SEEMETH See APPENDIX.

SEEMLY See APPENDIX.

SEEN
for thee have I *s* righteous ..... Gen 7:1 7200
were the tops of the mountains *s* ..... Gen 8:5 7200
the bow shall be *s* in the cloud ..... Gen 9:14 7200
mount of the LORD it shall be *s* ..... Gen 22:14 7200
for I have *s* all that Laban doeth ..... Gen 31:12 7200
God hath *s* mine affliction and the ..... Gen 31:42 7200
for I have *s* God face to face, and ..... Gen 32:30 7200
for therefore I have *s* thy face ..... Gen 33:10 7200
as though I had *s* the face of God ..... Gen 33:10 7200
Egypt, and of all that ye have *s* ..... Gen 45:13 7200
me die, since I have *s* thy face ..... Gen 46:30 7200
I have surely *s* the affliction of ..... Ex 3:7 7200
I have also *s* the oppression ..... Ex 3:9 7200
s that which is done to you in ..... Ex 3:16
nor thy fathers' fathers have *s* ..... Ex 10:6 7200
no leavened bread be *s* with thee ..... Ex 13:7 7200
s with thee in all thy quarters ..... Ex 13:7 7200
Egyptians whom ye have *s* to day ..... Ex 14:13 7200
Ye have *s* what I did unto the ..... Ex 19:4 7200
Ye have *s* that I have talked with ..... Ex 20:22 7200
I have *s* this people, and, behold, ... Ex 32:9 7200
but my face shall not be *s* ..... Ex 33:23 7200
thee, neither let any man be *s* ..... Ex 34:3 7200
whether he hath *s* or known of it ..... Lev 5:1 7200
after that he hath been *s* of the ..... Lev 13:7 7200
he shall be *s* of the priest again ..... Lev 13:7 7200
that thou LORD art *s* face to face ..... Num 14:14 7200
those men which have *s* my glory ..... Num 14:22 7200
neither hath he *s* perverseness in ..... Num 23:21 7200
And when thou hast *s* it, thou also ..... Num 27:13 7200
moreover we have *s* the sons of ..... Deut 1:28 7200
where thou hast *s* how that the ..... Deut 1:31 7200
Thine eyes have *s* all that the ..... Deut 3:21 7200
Your eyes have *s* what the LORD ..... Deut 4:3 7200
things which thine eyes have *s* ..... Deut 4:9 7200
we have *s* this day that God doth ..... Deut 5:24 7200
I have *s* this people, and, behold, ... Deut 9:13 7200
things, which thine eyes have *s* ..... Deut 10:21 7200
which have not *s* the chastisement ..... Deut 11:2 7200
But your eyes have *s* all the ..... Deut 11:7 7200
s with thee in all thy coast ..... Deut 16:4 7200
blood, neither have our eyes *s* it ..... Deut 21:7 7200
Ye have *s* all that the LORD did ..... Deut 29:2 7200
which thine eyes have *s*, the ..... Deut 29:3 7200
ye have *s* their abominations, and ..... Deut 29:17 7200
to his mother, I have not *s* him ..... Deut 33:9 7200
ye have *s* all that the LORD your ..... Josh 23:3 7200
your eyes have *s* what I have done ..... Josh 24:7 7200
who had *s* all the great works of ..... Judg 2:7 7200
was there a shield or spear *s* ..... Judg 5:8 7200
for because I have *s* an angel of ..... Judg 6:22 7200
with him, What ye have *s* me do ..... Judg 9:48 7200
surely die, because we have *s* God ..... Judg 13:22 7200
I have *s* a woman in Timnath of ..... Judg 14:2 7200
for we have *s* the land, and, ... Judg 18:9 7200
s from the day that the children ..... Judg 19:30 7200
lords of the Philistines had *s* it 1Sa 6:16 7200
I have *s* a son of Jesse the 1Sa 16:18 7200
Have ye *s* this man that is come 1Sa 17:25 7200
haunt is, and who hath *s* him there 1Sa 23:22 7200
this day thine eyes have *s* how 1Sa 24:10 7200
not be *s* to come into the city 2Sa 17:17 7200
Go tell the king what thou hast *s* 2Sa 18:21 7200
he was *s* upon the wings of the 2Sa 22:11 7200
there was no stone *s* 1Kin 6:18 7200
the ends of the staves were *s* out 1Kin 8:8 7200
and they were not *s* without 1Kin 8:8 7200
Sheba had *s* all Solomon's wisdom 1Kin 10:4 7200
I came, and mine eyes had *s* it 1Kin 10:7 7200
trees, nor were *s* unto this day 1Kin 10:12 7200
For his sons had *s* what way the 1Kin 13:12 7200
Hast thou *s* all this great 1Kin 20:13 7200
Surely I have *s* yesterday the 2Kin 9:26 7200
thy prayer, I have *s* thy tears 2Kin 20:5 7200
What have they *s* in thine house 2Kin 20:15 7200
are in mine house have they *s* 2Kin 20:15 7200
him at Megiddo, when he had *s* him 2Kin 23:29 7200
now have I *s* with joy thy people, ... 1Chr 29:17 7200
the ends of the staves were *s* 2Chr 5:9 7200
but they were not *s* without 2Chr 5:9 7200
Sheba had *s* the wisdom of Solomon 2Chr 9:3 7200
I came, and mine eyes had *s* it 2Chr 9:6 7200
there were none such *s* before in 2Chr 9:11 7200
that had *s* the first house, when ..... Ezr 3:12 7200
they had *s* concerning this matter ..... Est 9:26 7200
Even as I have *s*, they that plow ..... Job 4:8 7200
I have *s* the foolish taking root ..... Job 5:3 7200
hath *s* me shall see me no more ..... Job 7:8 7210
him, saying, I have not *s* thee ..... Job 8:18 7200
up the ghost, and no eye had *s* me ..... Job 10:18 7200
Lo, mine eye hath *s* all this ..... Job 13:1 7200
which I have *s* I will declare ..... Job 15:17 2372
they which have *s* him shall say ..... Job 20:7 7200
all ye yourselves have *s* it ..... Job 27:12 2372
the vulture's eye hath not *s* ..... Job 28:7 7805
If I have *s* any perish for want ..... Job 31:19 7200
away, that it cannot be *s* ..... Job 33:21 7210
bones that were not *s* stick out ..... Job 33:21 7200
or hast thou *s* the doors of the ..... Job 38:17 7200
or hast thou *s* the treasures of ..... Job 38:22 7200
Thou hast *s* it ..... Ps 10:14 7200
the channels of waters were *s* ..... Ps 18:15 7200
said, Aha, aha, our eye hath *s* it ..... Ps 35:21 7200
This thou hast *s*, O LORD ..... Ps 35:22 7200
yet have I not *s* the righteous ..... Ps 37:25 7200
I have *s* the wicked in great ..... Ps 37:35 7200
so have we *s* in the city of the ..... Ps 48:8 7200
mine eye hath *s* his desire upon ..... Ps 54:7 7200
for I have *s* violence and strife ..... Ps 55:9 7200
so as I have *s* thee in the ..... Ps 63:2 2372
They have *s* thy goings, O God ..... Ps 68:24 7200
the years wherein we have *s* evil ..... Ps 90:15 7200
have *s* the salvation of our God ..... Ps 98:3 7200
I have *s* an end of all perfection ..... Ps 119:96 7200
the prince whom thine eyes have *s* ..... Prov 25:7 7200
I have *s* all the works that are ..... Eccl 1:14 7200
I have *s* the travail, which God ..... Eccl 3:10 7200
who hath not *s* the evil work that ..... Eccl 4:3 7200
evil which I have *s* under the sun ..... Eccl 5:13 7200
Behold that which I have *s* ..... Eccl 5:18 7200
evil which I have *s* under the sun ..... Eccl 6:1 7200
Moreover he hath not *s* the sun ..... Eccl 6:5 7200
twice told, yet hath he *s* no good ..... Eccl 6:6 7200
All things have I *s* in the days ..... Eccl 7:15 7200
All this have I *s*, and applied my ..... Eccl 8:9 7200
have I *s* also under the sun ..... Eccl 9:13 7200
evil which I have *s* under the sun ..... Eccl 10:5 7200
I have *s* servants upon horses, and ..... Eccl 10:7 7200
for mine eyes have *s* the King ..... Is 6:5 7200
in darkness have *s* a great light ..... Is 9:2 7200
when it is *s* that Moab is weary ..... Is 16:12 7200
Ye have *s* also the breaches of ..... Is 22:9 7200
thy prayer, I have *s* thy tears ..... Is 38:5 7200
What have they *s* in thine house ..... Is 39:4 7200
that is in mine house have they *s* ..... Is 39:4 7200
Aha, I am warm, I have *s* the fire ..... Is 44:16 7200
yea, thy shame shall be *s* ..... Is 47:3 7200
I have *s* his ways, and will heal ..... Is 57:18 7200
and his glory shall be *s* upon thee ..... Is 60:2 7200
the ear, neither hath the eye *s* ..... Is 64:4 7200
who hath *s* such things ..... Is 66:8 7200
my fame, neither have *s* my glory ..... Is 66:19 7200
LORD unto me, Thou hast well *s* ..... Jer 1:12 7200
the king, Hast thou *s* that which ..... Jer 3:6 7200
Behold, even I have *s* it, saith ..... Jer 7:11 7200
thou hast *s* me, and tried mine ..... Jer 12:3 7200
I have *s* thine adulteries, and thy ..... Jer 13:27 7200
I have *s* folly in the prophets of ..... Jer 23:13 7200
I have *s* also in the prophets of ..... Jer 23:14 7200
Ye have *s* all the evil that I ..... Jer 44:2 7200
Wherefore have I *s* them dismayed ..... Jer 46:5 7200
because they have *s* her nakedness ..... Lam 1:8 7200
for she hath *s* that the heathen ..... Lam 1:10 7200
Thy prophets have *s* vain and ..... Lam 2:14 2372
but have *s* for thee false burdens ..... Lam 2:14 2372
we have found, we have *s* it ..... Lam 2:16 7200
I am the man that hath *s* ..... Lam 3:1 7200
O LORD, thou hast *s* my wrong ..... Lam 3:59 7200
Thou hast *s* all their vengeance ..... Lam 3:60 7200
hast thou *s* what the ancients of ..... Eze 8:12 7200
said he unto me, Hast thou *s* this ..... Eze 8:15 7200
he said unto me, Hast thou *s* this ..... Eze 8:17 7200
that I had *s* went up from me ..... Eze 11:24 7200
own spirit, and have *s* nothing ..... Eze 13:3 7200
They have *s* vanity and lying ..... Eze 13:6 2372
Have ye not *s* a vain vision, and ..... Eze 13:7 2372
s lies, therefore, behold, I am ..... Eze 13:8 2372
me, Son of man, hast thou *s* this ..... Eze 47:6 7200
unto me the dream which I have *s* ..... Dan 2:26 2370

visions of my dream that I have s	Dan 4:9	2370
I king Nebuchadnezzar have s	Dan 4:18	2370
which I had s standing before the	Dan 8:6	7200
had s the vision, and sought for	Dan 8:15	7200
whom I had s in the vision at the	Dan 9:21	7200
I have s an horrible thing in the	Hos 6:10	7200
for now have I s with mine eyes	Zec 9:8	7200
And the LORD shall be s over them	Zec 9:14	7200
and the diviners have s a lie	Zec 10:2	2372
for we have s his star in the	Mt 2:2	1492
alms before men, to be s of them	Mt 6:1	2300
that they may be s of men	Mt 6:5	5316
It was never so s in Israel	Mt 9:33	5316
which ye see, and have not s them	Mt 13:17	1492
and ye, when ye had s it, repented	Mt 21:32	1492
works they do for to be s of men	Mt 23:5	2300
till they have s the kingdom of	Mk 9:1	1492
no man what things they had s	Mk 9:9	1492
was alive, and had been s of her	Mk 16:11	2300
had s him after he was risen	Mk 16:14	2300
he had s a vision in the temple	Lk 1:22	3708
And when they had s it, they made	Lk 2:17	1492
things that they had heard and s	Lk 2:20	1492
before he had s the Lord's Christ	Lk 2:26	1492
mine eyes have s thy salvation	Lk 2:30	1492
We have s strange things to day	Lk 5:26	1492
tell John what things ye have s	Lk 7:22	1492
of those things which they had s	Lk 9:36	3708
which ye see, and have not s them	Lk 10:24	1492
the mighty works that they had s	Lk 19:37	1492
he hoped to have s some miracle	Lk 23:8	1492
had also s a vision of angels	Lk 24:23	3708
supposed that they had s a spirit	Lk 24:37	2334
No man hath s God at any time	Jn 1:18	3708
know, and testify that we have s	Jn 3:11	3708
And what he hath s and heard, that	Jn 3:32	3708
having s all the things that he	Jn 4:45	3708
at any time, nor s his shape	Jn 5:37	3708
when they had s the miracle that	Jn 6:14	1492
unto you, That ye also have s me	Jn 6:36	3708
that any man hath s the Father	Jn 6:46	3708
is of God, he hath s the Father	Jn 6:46	3708
which I have s with my Father	Jn 8:38	3708
which ye have s with your father	Jn 8:38	3708
years old, and hast thou s Abraham	Jn 8:57	3708
had s him that he was blind	Jn 9:8	2334
unto him, Thou hast both s him	Jn 9:37	3708
had s the things which Jesus did,	Jn 11:45	2300
ye know him, and have s him	Jn 14:7	3708
hath s me hath s the Father	Jn 14:9	3708
but now have they both s and hated	Jn 15:24	3708
disciples that she had s the Lord	Jn 20:18	3708
said unto him, We have s the Lord	Jn 20:25	3708
Thomas, because thou hast s me	Jn 20:29	3708
blessed are they that have not s	Jn 20:29	1492
being s of them forty days, and	Acts 1:3	3700
as ye have s him go into heaven	Acts 1:11	2300
speak the things which we have s	Acts 4:20	1492
I have s, I have s the	Acts 7:34	1492
to the fashion that he had s	Acts 7:44	3708
hath s in a vision a man named	Acts 9:12	1492
how he had s the Lord in the way	Acts 9:27	1492
vision which he had s should mean	Acts 10:17	1492
he had s an angel in his house	Acts 11:13	1492
had s the grace of God, was glad,	Acts 11:23	1492
he was s many days of them which	Acts 13:31	3700
And after he had s the vision	Acts 16:10	1492
and when they had s the brethren	Acts 16:40	1492
(For they had s before with him	Acts 21:29	4308
unto all men of what thou hast s	Acts 22:15	3708
of these things which thou hast s	Acts 26:16	1492
of the world are clearly s	Rom 1:20	2529
but hope that is s is not hope	Rom 8:24	991
as it is written, Eye hath not s	1Cor 2:9	1492
have I not s Jesus Christ our	1Cor 9:1	3708
And that he was s of Cephas	1Cor 15:5	3700
he was s of above five hundred	1Cor 15:6	3700
After that, he was s of James	1Cor 15:7	3700
last of all he was s of me also	1Cor 15:8	3700
not at the things which are s	2Cor 4:18	991
but at the things which are not s	2Cor 4:18	991
things which are s are temporal	2Cor 4:18	991
which are not s are eternal	2Cor 4:18	991
and heard, and in me, do	Phil 4:9	1492
have not s my face in the flesh	Col 2:1	3708
those things which he hath not s	Col 2:18	3708
s of angels, preached unto the	1Ti 3:16	3700
whom no man hath s, nor can see	1Ti 6:16	1492
for, the evidence of things not s	Heb 11:1	991
so that things which are s were	Heb 11:3	991
of God of things not s as yet	Heb 11:7	991

but having s them afar off, and	Heb 11:13	1492
have s the end of the Lord	Jas 5:11	1492
Whom having not s, ye love	1Pet 1:8	1492
which we have s with our eyes	1Jn 1:1	3708
was manifested, and we have s it	1Jn 1:2	3708
That which we have s and heard	1Jn 1:3	3708
whosoever sinneth hath not s him	1Jn 3:6	3708
No man hath s God at any time	1Jn 4:12	2300
And we have s and do testify that	1Jn 4:14	2300
not his brother whom he hath s	1Jn 4:20	3708
he love God whom he hath not s	1Jn 4:20	3708
he that doeth evil hath not s God	3Jn 11	3780
the things which thou hast s	Rev 1:19	1492
there was s in his temple the ark	Rev 11:19	3700
And when I had heard and s, I fell	Rev 22:8	991

SEER

Come, and let us go to the s	1Sa 9:9	7200
Prophet was beforetime called a S	1Sa 9:9	7200
and said unto them, Is the s here	1Sa 9:11	7200
Saul, and said, I am the s	1Sa 9:19	7200
the priest, Art not thou a s	2Sa 15:27	7200
unto the prophet Gad, David's s	2Sa 24:11	2374
Samuel the s did ordain in their	1Chr 9:22	7200
LORD spake unto Gad, David's s	1Chr 21:9	2374
the king's s in the words of God	1Chr 25:5	2374
And all that Samuel the s, and Saul	1Chr 26:28	7200
in the book of Samuel the s	1Chr 29:29	7200
and in the book of Gad the s	1Chr 29:29	2374
in the visions of Iddo the s	2Chr 9:29	2374
and of Iddo the s concerning	2Chr 12:15	2374
at that time Hanani the s came to	2Chr 16:7	7200
Then Asa was wroth with the s	2Chr 16:10	7200
Hanani the s went out to meet him	2Chr 19:2	2374
of David, and of Gad the king's s	2Chr 29:25	2374
words of David, and of Asaph the s	2Chr 29:30	2374
Heman, and Jeduthun the king's s	2Chr 35:15	2374
Amaziah said unto Amos, O thou s	Amos 7:12	2374

SEER'S

I pray thee, where the s house is	1Sa 9:18	7200

SEERS

all the prophets, and by all the s	2Kin 17:13	2374
the words of the s that spake to	2Chr 33:18	2374
among the sayings of the s	2Chr 33:19	2374
rulers, the s hath he covered	Is 29:10	2374
Which say to the s, See not	Is 30:10	7200
Then shall the s be ashamed	Mic 3:7	2374

SEEST See APPENDIX.

SEETH See APPENDIX.

SEETHE

to day, and s that ye will s	Ex 16:23	1310
Thou shalt not s a kid in his	Ex 23:19	1310
s his flesh in the holy place	Ex 29:31	1310
Thou shalt not s a kid in his	Ex 34:26	1310
Thou shalt not s a kid in his	Deut 14:21	1310
s pottage for the sons of the	2Kin 4:38	1310
let them s the bones of it	Eze 24:5	1310
and take of them, and s therein	Zec 14:21	1310

SEETHING

came, while the flesh was in s	1Sa 2:13	1310
as out of a s pot or caldron	Job 41:20	5301
and I said, I see a s pot	Jer 1:13	5301

SEGUB (se'-gub)
1. A son of Hiel.

thereof in his youngest son S	1Kin 16:34	7687

2. A son of Hezron.

and she bare him S	1Chr 2:21	7687
S begat Jair, who had three and	1Chr 2:22	7687

SEIR (se'-ur)
1. A region south of the Dead Sea.

And the Horites in their mount S	Gen 14:6	8165
his brother unto the land of S	Gen 32:3	8165
until I come unto my lord unto S	Gen 33:14	8165
that day on his way unto S	Gen 33:16	8165
Thus dwelt Esau in mount S	Gen 36:8	8165
father of the Edomites in mount S	Gen 36:9	8165
the children of S in the land of	Gen 36:21	8165
their dukes in the land of S	Gen 36:30	8165
S also shall be a possession for	Num 24:18	8165
way of mount S unto Kadesh-barnea	Deut 1:2	8165
as bees do, and destroyed you in S	Deut 1:44	8165
we compassed mount S many days	Deut 2:1	8165
of Esau, which dwell in S	Deut 2:4	8165
S unto Esau for a possession	Deut 2:5	8165
of Esau, which dwelt in S	Deut 2:8	8165
Horims also dwelt in S beforetime	Deut 2:12	8165
of Esau, which dwelt in S	Deut 2:22	8165

S

children of Esau which dwell in S .... Deut 2:29   8165
and rose up from S unto them .... Deut 33:2   8165
mount Halak, that goeth up to S .... Josh 11:17   8165
mount Halak, that goeth up to S .... Josh 12:7   8165
from Baalah westward unto mount S ..... Josh 15:10   8165
and I gave unto Esau mount S .... Josh 24:4   8165
LORD, when thou wentest out of S .... Judg 5:4   8165
five hundred men, went to mount S 1Chr 4:42   8165
of Ammon and Moab and mount S 2Chr 20:10   8165
of Ammon, Moab, and mount S 2Chr 20:22   8165
the inhabitants of mount S 2Chr 20:23   8165
an end of the inhabitants of S 2Chr 20:23   8165
of the children of S ten thousand 2Chr 25:11   8165
the gods of the children of S.................. 2Chr 25:14   8165
He calleth to me out of S .... Is 21:11   8165
S do say, Behold, the house of .... Eze 25:8   8165
man, set thy face against mount S .... Eze 35:2   8165
Behold, O mount S, I am against........... Eze 35:3   8165
will I make mount S most desolate .... Eze 35:7   8165
thou shalt be desolate, O mount S .... Eze 35:15   8165
  2. *Grandfather of Hori.*
are the sons of S the Horite.................... Gen 36:20   8165
And the sons of S 1Chr 1:38   8165

SEIRAH See SEIRAH.

SEIRATH *(se'-ur-ath) A city in Ephraim.*
the quarries, and escaped unto S .... Judg 3:26   8167

SEIZE
the ambush, and s upon the city .... Josh 8:7   3423
night, let darkness s upon it.................. Job 3:6   3947
Let death s upon them, and let .... Ps 55:15   3451
let us s on his inheritance.................... Mt 21:38   2722

SEIZED
to flee, and fear hath s on her................ Jer 49:24   2388

SELA *(se'-lah) See* SELAH. *Same as Selah 1.*
the land from S to the wilderness .... Is 16:1   5554

SELAH *(se'-lah) See* JOKTHEEL, SELA.
  1. *Capital of Edom.*
took S by war, and called the name........ 2Kin 14:7   5554
  2. *A musical notation.*
no help for him in God. S .... Ps 3:2   5542
me out of his holy hill. S .... Ps 3:4   5542
blessing is upon thy people. S................ Ps 3:8   5542
vanity, and seek after leasing? S .... Ps 4:2   5542
your bed, and be still. S .... Ps 4:4   5542
mine honour in the dust. S .... Ps 7:5   5542
his own hands. Higgaion. S................... Ps 9:16   5542
themselves to be but men. S .... Ps 9:20   5542
accept thy burnt sacrifice; S .... Ps 20:3   5542
the request of his lips. S........................ Ps 21:2   5542
thy face, O Jacob. S .... Ps 24:6   5542
he is the King of glory. S....................... Ps 24:10   5542
the drought of summer. S .... Ps 32:4   5542
the iniquity of my sin. S........................ Ps 32:5   5542
songs of deliverance. S .... Ps 32:7   5542
state is altogether vanity. S .... Ps 39:5   5542
every man is vanity. S........................... Ps 39:11   5542
thy name for ever. S .... Ps 44:8   5542
with the swelling thereof. S .... Ps 46:3   5542
Jacob is our refuge. S .... Ps 46:7   5542
Jacob is our refuge. S .... Ps 46:11   5542
Jacob whom he loved. S........................ Ps 47:4   5542
establish it for ever. S........................... Ps 48:8   5542
approve their sayings. S .... Ps 49:13   5542
he shall receive me. S .... Ps 49:15   5542
God is judge himself. S.......................... Ps 50:6   5542
to speak righteousness. S....................... Ps 52:3   5542
land of the living. S .... Ps 52:5   5542
set God before them. S .... Ps 54:3   5542
remain in the wilderness. S.................... Ps 55:7   5542
that abideth of old. S .... Ps 55:19   5542
swallow me up. S................................... Ps 57:3   5542
are fallen themselves. S......................... Ps 57:6   5542
wicked transgressors. S .... Ps 59:5   5542
ends of the earth. S .... Ps 59:13   5542
because of the truth. S........................... Ps 60:4   5542
the covert of thy wings. S...................... Ps 61:4   5542
but they curse inwardly. S...................... Ps 62:4   5542
is a refuge for us. S .... Ps 62:8   5542
sing to thy name. S .... Ps 66:4   5542
exalt themselves. S................................ Ps 66:7   5542
offer bullocks with goats. S .... Ps 66:15   5542
face to shine upon us; S......................... Ps 67:1   5542
the nations upon earth. S....................... Ps 67:4   5542
through the wilderness. S .... Ps 68:7   5542
the God of our salvation. S..................... Ps 68:19   5542
praises unto the Lord. S .... Ps 68:32   5542
up the pillars of it. S .... Ps 75:3   5542
sword, and the battle. S......................... Ps 76:3   5542

the meek of the earth. S .... Ps 76:9   5542
was overwhelmed. S.............................. Ps 77:3   5542
up his tender mercies? S........................ Ps 77:9   5542
of Jacob and Joseph. S .... Ps 77:15   5542
the waters of Meribah. S .... Ps 81:7   5542
persons of the wicked? S .... Ps 82:2   5542
the children of Lot. S............................ Ps 83:8   5542
be still praising thee. S.......................... Ps 84:4   5542
O God of Jacob. S .... Ps 84:8   5542
covered all their sin. S .... Ps 85:2   5542
O city of God. S.................................... Ps 87:3   5542
man was born there. S........................... Ps 87:6   5542
me with all thy waves. S........................ Ps 88:7   5542
dead arise and praise thee? S................. Ps 88:10   5542
throne to all generations. S .... Ps 89:4   5542
witness in heaven. S.............................. Ps 89:37   5542
him with shame. S .... Ps 89:45   5542
hand of the grave? S .... Ps 89:48   5542
is under their lips. S.............................. Ps 140:3   5542
have set gins for me. S........................... Ps 140:5   5542
they exalt themselves. S .... Ps 140:8   5542
as a thirsty land. S................................ Ps 143:6   5542
from mount Paran. S .... Hab 3:3   5542
even thy word. S................................... Hab 3:9   5542
foundation unto the neck. S.................... Hab 3:13   5542

SELA-HAMMAHLEKOTH *(se'-lah-ham-mah'-le-koth) A*
  hill in the wilderness of Maon.
they called that place S.......................... 1Sa 23:28   5555

SELED *(se'-led) A descendant of Jerahmeel.*
S, and Appaim: but S died...................... 1Chr 2:30   5540

SELEUCIA *(sel-u-si'-ah) A city in Syria.*
the Holy Ghost, departed unto S .... Acts 13:4   *4581*

SELF See APPENDIX.

SELFSAME
In the s day entered Noah, and....... Gen 7:13   2088,6106
of their foreskin in the s day .... Gen 17:23   2088,6106
In the s day was Abraham .... Gen 17:26   2088,6106
for in this s day have I brought....... Ex 12:17   2088,6106
even the s day it came to pass, ... Ex 12:41   2088,6106
And it came to pass the s day .... Ex 12:51   2088,6106
until the s day that ye have .... Lev 23:14   2088,6106
And ye shall proclaim on the s day Lev 23:21   2088,6106
LORD spake unto Moses that s day . Deut 32:48   2088,6106
and parched corn in the s day .... Josh 5:11   2088,6106
in the s day the hand of the LORD ... Eze 40:1   2088,6106
servant was healed in the s hour .... Mt 8:13   1565
the s Spirit, dividing to every 1Cor 12:11   846
wrought us for the s thing is God ... 2Cor 5:5   846,5124
For behold this s thing, that ye 2Cor 7:11   *846*

SELFWILL
in their s they digged down a................. Gen 49:6   7522

SELFWILLED
not s, not soon angry, not given .... Titus 1:7   *829*
Presumptuous are they, s, they 2Pet 2:10   *829*

SELL
S me this day thy birthright.................... Gen 25:31   4376
let us s him to the Ishmeelites, ... Gen 37:27   4376
if a man s his daughter to be a.............. Ex 21:7   4376
to s her unto a strange nation he........... Ex 21:8   4376
then they shall s the live ox.................. Ex 21:35   4376
or a sheep, and kill it, or s it .... Ex 22:1   4376
And if thou s ought unto thy .... Lev 25:14   4376
the fruits he shall s unto thee .... Lev 25:15   4376
of the fruits doth he s unto thee............ Lev 25:16   4376
if a man s a dwelling house in a .... Lev 25:29   4376
s himself unto the stranger or................ Lev 25:47   4376
Thou shalt s me meat for money, ... Deut 2:28   7666
or thou mayest s it unto an alien .... Deut 14:21   4376
but thou shalt not s her at all................ Deut 21:14   4376
for the LORD shall s Sisera into .... Judg 4:9   4376
which did s himself to work 1Kin 21:25   4376
s the oil, and pay thy debt, and............. 2Kin 4:7   4376
will ye even s your brethren .... Neh 5:8   4376
victuals on the sabbath day to s .... Neh 10:31   4376
Buy the truth, and s it not .... Prov 23:23   4376
s the land into the hand of the .... Eze 30:12   4376
And they shall not s of it .... Eze 48:14   4376
I will s your sons and your.................... Joel 3:7   4376
they shall s them to the Sabeans,.......... Joel 3:8   4376
moon be gone, that we may s corn .... Amos 8:5   7666
s the refuse of the wheat .... Amos 8:6   7666
and they that s them say, Blessed .... Zec 11:5   4376
s that thou hast, and give to the............ Mt 19:21   *4453*
but go ye rather to them that s............. Mt 25:9   *4453*
s whatsoever thou hast, and give .... Mk 10:21   *4453*
S that ye have, and give alms .... Lk 12:33   *4453*
s all that thou hast, and .... Lk 18:22   *4453*

let him *s* his garment, and buy one	Lk 22:36	4453
there a year, and buy and *s*	Jas 4:13	1710
And that no man might buy or *s*	Rev 13:17	4453

SELLER

as with the buyer, so with the *s*	Is 24:2	4376
buyer rejoice, nor the *s* mourn	Eze 7:12	4376
For the *s* shall not return to	Eze 7:13	4376
a *s* of purple, of the city of	Acts 16:14	4211

SELLERS

s of all kind of ware lodged	Neh 13:20	4376

SELLEST

Thou *s* thy people for nought, and	Ps 44:12	4376

SELLETH

s him, or if he be found in his	Ex 21:16	4376
merchandise of him, or *s* him	Deut 24:7	4376
s a parcel of land, which was our	Ruth 4:3	4376
be upon the head of him that *s* it	Prov 11:26	7666
She maketh fine linen, and *s* it	Prov 31:24	4376
that *s* nations through her	Nah 3:4	4376
s all that he hath, and buyeth	Mt 13:44	4453

SELVEDGE

from the *s* in the coupling	Ex 26:4	7098
from the *s* in the coupling	Ex 36:11	7098

SELVES

know of your own *s* that summer is	Lk 21:30	1438
of your own *s* shall men arise	Acts 20:30	846
gave their own *s* to the Lord	2Cor 8:5	1438
prove your own *s*	2Cor 13:5	1438
Know ye not your own *s*, how that	2Cor 13:5	1438
shall be lovers of their own *s*	2Ti 3:2	5367
only, deceiving your own *s*	Jas 1:22	846

SEM *(sem)* See SHEM. *Greek form of Shem.*

Arphaxad, which was the son of *S*	Lk 3:36	4590

SEMACHIAH *(sem-a-ki'-ah) A sanctuary servant.*

were strong men, Elihu, and *S*	1Chr 26:7	5565

SEMEI *(sem'-e-i)* See SHEMAIAH. *A son of Joseph; an ancestor of Jesus.*

which was the son of *S*, which	Lk 3:26	4584

SEMEIN See SEMEI.

SENAAH *(sen'-a-ah)* See HASSENAAH. *A city in Judah.*

The children of *S*, three thousand	Ezr 2:35	5570
The children of *S*, three thousand	Neh 7:38	5570

SENATE

all the *s* of the children of	Acts 5:21	1087

SENATORS

and teach his *s* wisdom	Ps 105:22	2205

SEND

he shall *s* his angel before thee,	Gen 24:7	7971
s me good speed this day, and shew	Gen 24:12	7136
will *s* his angel with thee, and	Gen 24:40	7971
he said, *S* me away unto my master	Gen 24:54	7971
s me away that I may go to my	Gen 24:56	7971
then I will *s*, and fetch thee from	Gen 27:45	7971
S me away, that I may go unto	Gen 30:25	7971
come, and I will *s* thee unto them	Gen 37:13	7971
I will *s* thee a kid from the	Gen 38:17	7971
give me a pledge, till thou *s* it	Gen 38:17	7971
S one of you, and let him fetch	Gen 42:16	7971
If thou wilt *s* our brother with	Gen 43:4	7971
But if thou wilt not *s* him	Gen 43:5	7971
S the lad with me, and we will	Gen 43:8	7971
that he may *s* away your other	Gen 43:14	7971
for God did *s* me before you to	Gen 45:5	7971
I will *s* thee unto Pharaoh, that	Ex 3:10	7971
And he said, O my Lord, *s*, I pray	Ex 4:13	7971
the hand of him whom thou wilt *s*	Ex 4:13	7971
that he *s* the children of Israel	Ex 7:2	7971
I will *s* swarms of flies upon	Ex 8:21	7971
For I will at this time *s* all my	Ex 9:14	7971
S therefore now, and gather thy	Ex 9:19	7971
that they might *s* them out of the	Ex 12:33	7971
I *s* an Angel before thee, to keep	Ex 23:20	7971
I will *s* my fear before thee, and	Ex 23:27	7971
I will *s* hornets before thee,	Ex 23:28	7971
I will *s* an angel before thee	Ex 33:2	7971
me know whom thou wilt *s* with me	Ex 33:12	7971
shall *s* him away by the hand of a	Lev 16:21	7971
I will also *s* wild beasts among	Lev 26:22	7971
I will *s* the pestilence among you	Lev 26:25	7971
are left alive of you I will *s* a	Lev 26:36	935
S thou men, that they may search	Num 13:2	7971
of their fathers shall ye *s* a man	Num 13:2	7971
Did I not earnestly *s* unto thee	Num 22:37	7971
of Israel, shall ye *s* to the war	Num 31:4	7971

We will *s* men before us, and they	Deut 1:22	7971
God will *s* the hornet among them	Deut 7:20	7971
I will *s* grass in thy fields for	Deut 11:15	5414
the elders of his city shall *s*	Deut 19:12	7971
hand, and *s* her out of his house	Deut 24:1	7971
The LORD shall *s* upon thee	Deut 28:20	7971
the LORD shall *s* against thee	Deut 28:48	7971
I will also *s* the teeth of beasts	Deut 32:24	7971
and I will *s* them, and they shall	Josh 18:4	7971
thou didst *s* come again unto us	Judg 13:8	7971
S away the ark of the God of	1Sa 5:11	7971
we shall *s* it to his place	1Sa 6:2	7971
If ye *s* away the ark of the God	1Sa 6:3	7971
the God of Israel, *s* it not empty	1Sa 6:3	7971
s it away, that it may go	1Sa 6:8	7971
s thee a man out of the land of	1Sa 9:16	7971
Up, that I may *s* thee away	1Sa 9:26	7971
that we may *s* messengers unto all	1Sa 11:3	7971
the LORD, and he shall *s* thunder	1Sa 12:17	5414
I will *s* thee to Jesse the	1Sa 16:1	7971
And Samuel said unto Jesse, *S*	1Sa 16:11	7971
S me David thy son, which is with	1Sa 16:19	7971
I then *s* not unto thee, and shew	1Sa 20:12	7971
s thee away, that thou mayest go	1Sa 20:13	7971
And, behold, I will *s* a lad	1Sa 20:21	7971
Wherefore now *s* and fetch him unto	1Sa 20:31	7971
the business whereabout I *s* thee	1Sa 21:2	7971
men of my lord, whom thou didst *s*	1Sa 25:25	7971
saying, *S* me Uriah the Hittite	2Sa 11:6	7971
that I may *s* thee to the king, to	2Sa 14:32	7971
by them ye shall *s* unto me every	2Sa 15:36	7971
Now therefore *s* quickly, and tell	2Sa 17:16	7971
whithersoever thou shalt *s* them	1Kin 8:44	7971
I will *s* rain upon the earth	1Kin 18:1	5414
Now therefore *s*, and gather to me	1Kin 18:19	7971
Yet I will *s* my servants unto	1Kin 20:6	7971
All that thou didst *s* for to thy	1Kin 20:9	7971
I will *s* thee away with this	1Kin 20:34	7971
And he said, Ye shall not *s*	2Kin 2:16	7971
till he was ashamed, he said, *S*	2Kin 2:17	7971
S me, I pray thee, one of the	2Kin 4:22	7971
I will *s* a letter unto the king	2Kin 5:5	7971
that this man doth *s* unto me to	2Kin 5:7	7971
and spy where he is, that I may *s*	2Kin 6:13	7971
and let us *s* and see	2Kin 7:13	7971
s to meet them, and let him say,	2Kin 9:17	7971
s against Judah Rezin the king of	2Kin 15:37	7971
I will *s* a blast upon him, and he	2Kin 19:7	5414
let us *s* abroad unto our brethren	1Chr 13:2	7971
didst *s* him cedars to build him	2Chr 2:3	7971
S me now therefore a man cunning	2Chr 2:7	7971
S me also cedar trees, fir trees,	2Chr 2:8	7971
let him *s* unto his servants	2Chr 2:15	7971
s rain upon thy land, which thou	2Chr 6:27	5414
by the way that thou shalt *s* them	2Chr 6:34	7971
or if I *s* pestilence among my	2Chr 7:13	7971
At that time did king Ahaz *s* unto	2Chr 28:16	7971
s his servants to Jerusalem	2Chr 32:9	7971
let the king *s* his pleasure to us	Ezr 5:17	7972
thou wouldest *s* me unto Judah	Neh 2:5	7971
So it pleased the king to *s* me	Neh 2:6	7971
s portions unto them for whom	Neh 8:10	7971
to *s* portions, and to make great	Neh 8:12	7971
They *s* forth their little ones	Job 21:11	7971
Canst thou *s* lightnings, that	Job 38:35	7971
S thee help from the sanctuary,	Ps 20:2	7971
O *s* out thy light and thy truth	Ps 43:3	7971
He shall *s* from heaven, and save	Ps 57:3	7971
God shall *s* forth his mercy and	Ps 57:3	7971
didst *s* a plentiful rain, whereby	Ps 68:9	5130
he doth *s* out his voice, and that	Ps 68:33	5414
The LORD shall *s* the rod of thy	Ps 110:2	7971
I beseech thee, *s* now prosperity	Ps 118:25	
S thine hand from above	Ps 144:7	7971
the sluggard to them that *s* him	Prov 10:26	7971
of truth to them that *s* unto thee	Prov 22:21	7971
messenger to them that *s* him	Prov 25:13	7971
to *s* forth a stinking savour	Eccl 10:1	5042
the Lord, saying, Whom shall I *s*	Is 6:8	7971
Here am I; *s* me	Is 6:8	7971
I will *s* him against an	Is 10:6	7971
s among his fat ones leanness	Is 10:16	7971
S ye the lamb to the ruler of the	Is 16:1	7971
he shall *s* them a saviour, and a	Is 19:20	7971
that *s* forth thither the feet of	Is 32:20	7971
I will *s* a blast upon him, and he	Is 37:7	7971
didst *s* thy messengers far off,	Is 57:9	7971
I will *s* those that escape of	Is 66:19	7971
go to all that I shall *s* thee	Jer 1:7	7971
s unto Kedar, and consider	Jer 2:10	7971
I will *s* serpents, cockatrices,	Jer 8:17	7971

I will *s* a sword after them, till .... Jer 9:16   7971
s for cunning women, that they .... Jer 9:17   7971
I will *s* for many fishers, saith .... Jer 16:16   7971
after will I *s* for many hunters, ... Jer 16:16   7971
I will *s* the sword, the famine, ... Jer 24:10   7971
Behold, I will *s* and take all the .... Jer 25:9   7971
all the nations, to whom I *s* thee .... Jer 25:15   7971
sword that I will *s* among them .... Jer 25:16   7971
sword which I will *s* among you .... Jer 25:27   7971
s them to the king of Edom, and to .... Jer 27:3   7971
I will *s* upon them the sword, the .... Jer 29:17   7971
S to all them of the captivity, ... Jer 29:31   7971
LORD thy God shall *s* thee to us .... Jer 42:5   7971
LORD our God, to whom we *s* thee .... Jer 42:6   7971
Behold, I will *s* and take .... Jer 43:10   7971
that I will *s* unto him wanderers, ... Jer 48:12   7971
I will *s* the sword after them, ... Jer 49:37   7971
will *s* unto Babylon fanners, that .... Jer 51:2   7971
I *s* thee to the children of .... Eze 2:3   7971
I do *s* thee unto them .... Eze 2:4   7971
When I shall *s* upon them the evil .... Eze 5:16   7971
which I will *s* to destroy you .... Eze 5:16   7971
So will I *s* upon you famine and .... Eze 5:17   7971
I will *s* mine anger upon thee, and .... Eze 7:3   7971
will *s* famine upon it, and will .... Eze 14:13   7971
Or if I *s* a pestilence into that .... Eze 14:19   7971
How much more when I *s* my four .... Eze 14:21   7971
For I will *s* into her pestilence, ... Eze 28:23   7971
I will *s* a fire on Magog, and .... Eze 39:6   7971
but I will *s* a fire upon his .... Hos 8:14   7971
I will *s* you corn, and wine, and .... Joel 2:19   7971
But I will *s* a fire into the .... Amos 1:4   7971
But I will *s* a fire on the wall .... Amos 1:7   7971
But I will *s* a fire on the wall .... Amos 1:10   7971
But I will *s* a fire upon Teman, ... Amos 1:12   7971
But I will *s* a fire upon Moab, and .... Amos 2:2   7971
But I will *s* a fire upon Judah, ... Amos 2:5   7971
that I will *s* a famine in the .... Amos 8:11   7971
I will even *s* a curse upon you, ... Mal 2:2   7971
I will *s* my messenger, and he .... Mal 3:1   7971
I will *s* you Elijah the prophet .... Mal 4:5   7971
that he will *s* forth labourers .... Mt 9:38   1544
I *s* you forth as sheep in the .... Mt 10:16   649
I am come to *s* peace on earth .... Mt 10:34   906
I came not to *s* peace, but a .... Mt 10:34   906
I *s* my messenger before thy face, ... Mt 11:10   649
till he have sent judgment unto .... Mt 12:20   1544
of man shall *s* forth his angels .... Mt 13:41   649
s the multitude away, that they .... Mt 14:15   630
besought him, saying, *S* her away .... Mt 15:23   630
I will not *s* them away fasting, ... Mt 15:32   630
and straightway he will *s* them .... Mt 21:3   649
I *s* unto you prophets, and wise .... Mt 23:34   649
he shall *s* his angels with a .... Mt 24:31   649
I *s* my messenger before thy face, ... Mk 1:2   649
that he might *s* them forth to .... Mk 3:14   649
him much that he would not *s* them ...... Mk 5:10   649
S us into the swine, that we may .... Mk 5:12   3992
began to *s* them forth by two and .... Mk 6:7   649
S them away, that they may go .... Mk 6:36   630
if I *s* them away fasting to their .... Mk 8:3   630
straightway he will *s* him hither .... Mk 11:3   649
they *s* unto him certain of the .... Mk 12:13   649
And then shall he *s* his angels .... Mk 13:27   649
I *s* my messenger before thy face, ... Lk 7:27   649
S the multitude away, that they .... Lk 9:12   630
that he would *s* forth labourers .... Lk 10:2   1544
I *s* you forth as lambs among .... Lk 10:3   649
I will *s* them prophets and .... Lk 11:49   649
I am come to *s* fire on the earth .... Lk 12:49   906
s Lazarus, that he may dip the .... Lk 16:24   3992
that thou wouldest *s* him to my .... Lk 16:27   3992
I will *s* my beloved son .... Lk 20:13   3992
I *s* the promise of my Father upon ...... Lk 24:49   649
whomsoever I *s* receiveth me .... Jn 13:20   3992
whom the Father will *s* in my name ...... Jn 14:26   3992
whom I will *s* unto you from the .... Jn 15:26   3992
I depart, I will *s* him unto you .... Jn 16:7   3992
believed that thou didst *s* me .... Jn 17:8   649
hath sent me, even so *s* I you .... Jn 20:21   3992
he shall *s* Jesus Christ, which .... Acts 3:20   649
come, I will *s* thee into Egypt .... Acts 7:34   649
the same did God *s* to be a ruler .... Acts 7:35   649
now *s* men to Joppa, and call for .... Acts 10:5   3992
to *s* for thee into his house .... Acts 10:22   3343
S therefore to Joppa, and call .... Acts 10:32   3992
S men to Joppa, and call for Simon .... Acts 11:13   3992
determined to *s* relief unto the .... Acts 11:29   3992
to *s* chosen men of their own .... Acts 15:22   3992
brethren *s* greeting unto the .... Acts 15:23   649
to *s* chosen men unto you with our .... Acts 15:25   3992

for I will *s* thee far hence unto .... Acts 22:21   *1821*
that he would *s* for him to .... Acts 25:3   *3343*
kept till I might *s* him to Caesar .... Acts 25:21   *3992*
I have determined to *s* him .... Acts 25:25   *3992*
me unreasonable to *s* a prisoner .... Acts 25:27   *3992*
Gentiles, unto whom now I *s* thee .... Acts 26:17   *649*
them will I *s* to bring your 1Cor 16:3   *3992*
to *s* Timotheus shortly unto you .... Phil 2:19   *3992*
therefore I hope to *s* presently .... Phil 2:23   *3992*
to *s* to you Epaphroditus, my .... Phil 2:25   *3992*
God shall *s* them strong delusion 2Th 2:11   *3992*
When I shall *s* Artemas unto thee, ... Titus 3:12   *3992*
Doth a fountain *s* forth at the .... Jas 3:11   *1032*
s it unto the seven churches .... Rev 1:11   *3992*
shall *s* gifts one to another .... Rev 11:10   *3992*

SENDEST
when thou *s* him out free from .... Deut 15:13   7971
when thou *s* him away free from .... Deut 15:18   7971
do, and whithersoever thou *s* us .... Josh 1:16   7971
that thou *s* to enquire of 2Kin 1:6   7971
his countenance, and *s* him away .... Job 14:20   7971
Thou *s* forth thy spirit, they are .... Ps 104:30   7971

SENDETH
hand, and *s* her out of his house .... Deut 24:3   7971
the LORD *s* rain upon the earth 1Kin 17:14   5414
and *s* waters upon the fields .... Job 5:10   7971
also he *s* them out, and they .... Job 12:15   7971
He *s* the springs into the valleys .... Ps 104:10   7971
He *s* forth his commandment upon .... Ps 147:15   7971
He *s* out his word, and melteth .... Ps 147:18   7971
He that *s* a message by the hand .... Prov 26:6   7971
my spikenard *s* forth the smell .... Song 1:12   5414
That *s* ambassadors by the sea, ... Is 18:2   7971
s rain on the just and on the .... Mt 5:45   *1026*
he *s* forth two of his disciples, ... Mk 11:1   *649*
he *s* forth two of his disciples, ... Mk 14:13   *649*
he *s* an ambassage, and desireth .... Lk 14:32   *649*
governor Felix *s* greeting .... Acts 23:26   *649*

SENDING
this evil in *s* me away is greater 2Sa 13:16   7971
rising up betimes, and *s* 2Chr 36:15   7971
of *s* portions one to another .... Est 9:19   4916
of *s* portions one to another, and .... Est 9:22   4916
by *s* evil angels among them .... Ps 78:49   4917
shall be for the *s* forth of oxen .... Is 7:25   4916
daily rising up early and *s* them .... Jer 7:25   7971
prophets, rising early and *s* them .... Jer 25:4   7971
s them, but ye have not hearkened .... Jer 26:5   7971
rising up early and *s* them .... Jer 29:19   7971
s them, saying, Return ye now .... Jer 35:15   7971
s them, saying, Oh, do not this .... Jer 44:4   7971
in *s* his ambassadors into Egypt .... Eze 17:15   7971
God *s* his own Son in the likeness .... Rom 8:3   *3992*

SENEH *(se'-neh) A rock in Benjamin.*
Bozez, and the name of the other *S* 1Sa 14:4   5573

SENIR *(se'-nur) See* SHENIR. *A mountain between Amana and Hermon.*
from Bashan unto Baal-hermon and *S* ... 1Chr 5:23   8149
thy ship boards of fir trees of *S* .... Eze 27:5   8149

SENNACHERIB *(sen-nak'-er-ib) An Assyrian king.*
year of king Hezekiah did *S* king 2Kin 18:13   5576
and hear the words of *S*, which 2Kin 19:16   5576
S king of Assyria I have heard 2Kin 19:20   5576
So *S* king of Assyria departed, and 2Kin 19:36   5576
S king of Assyria came, and 2Chr 32:1   5576
when Hezekiah saw that *S* was come 2Chr 32:2   5576
After this did *S* king of Assyria 2Chr 32:9   5576
Thus saith *S* king of Assyria, ... 2Chr 32:10   5576
the hand of *S* the king of Assyria 2Chr 32:22   5576
that *S* king of Assyria came up .... Is 36:1   5576
and hear all the words of *S* .... Is 37:17   5576
to me against *S* king of Assyria .... Is 37:21   5576
So *S* king of Assyria departed, and .... Is 37:37   5576

SENSE
of God distinctly, and gave the *s* .... Neh 8:8   7922

SENSES
s exercised to discern both good .... Heb 5:14   *145*

SENSUAL
not from above, but is earthly, *s* .... Jas 3:15   *5591*
they who separate themselves, *s* .... Jude 19   *5591*

SENT See APPENDIX.

SENTENCE
shall shew thee the *s* of judgment .... Deut 17:9   1697
thou shalt do according to the *s* .... Deut 17:10   1697
According to the *s* of the law .... Deut 17:11   6310

the *s* which they shall shew thee	Deut 17:11	1697
Let my *s* come forth from thy	Ps 17:2	4941
A divine *s* is in the lips of the	Prov 16:10	7081
Because *s* against an evil work is	Eccl 8:11	6599
also will I give *s* against them	Jer 4:12	4941
Pilate gave *s* that it should be	Lk 23:24	1948
Wherefore my *s* is, that we	Acts 15:19	2919
But we had the *s* of death in	2Cor 1:9	610

SENTENCES

of dreams, and shewing of hard *s*	Dan 5:12	280
and understanding dark *s*, shall	Dan 8:23	2420

SENTEST

thou *s* forth thy wrath, which	Ex 15:7	7971
unto the land whither thou *s* us	Num 13:27	7971
messengers which thou *s* unto me	Num 24:12	7971
the things which thou *s* to me for	1Kin 5:8	7971

SENUAH (*sen'-u-ah*) See HASSENUAH. *Father of Judah.*

Judah the son of *S* was second	Neh 11:9	5574

SEORIM (*se-o'-rim*) *A sanctuary servant.*

third to Harim, the fourth to *S*	1Chr 24:8	8188

SEPARATE

s thyself, I pray thee, from me	Gen 13:9	6504
And Jacob did *s* the lambs, and set	Gen 30:40	6504
him that was *s* from his brethren	Gen 49:26	5139
Thus shall ye *s* the children of	Lev 15:31	5144
that they *s* themselves from the	Lev 22:2	5144
s themselves to vow a vow of a	Num 6:2	6381
to *s* themselves unto the LORD	Num 6:2	5144
He shall *s* himself from wine and	Num 6:3	5144
Thus shalt thou *s* the Levites	Num 8:14	914
S yourselves from among this	Num 16:21	914
Thou shalt *s* three cities for	Deut 19:2	914
Thou shalt *s* three cities for	Deut 19:7	914
the LORD shall *s* him unto evil	Deut 29:21	914
the *s* cities for the children of	Josh 16:9	3995
For thou didst *s* them from among	1Kin 8:53	914
s yourselves from the people of	Ezr 10:11	914
to *s* himself thence in the midst	Jer 37:12	2505
the *s* place at the end toward the	Eze 41:12	1508
the *s* place, and the building,	Eze 41:13	1508
of the *s* place toward the east,	Eze 41:14	1508
the *s* place which was behind it	Eze 41:15	1508
that was over against the *s* place	Eze 42:1	1508
east, over against the *s* place	Eze 42:10	1508
which are before the *s* place	Eze 42:13	1508
he shall *s* them one from another,	Mt 25:32	873
when they shall *s* you from their	Lk 6:22	873
S me Barnabas and Saul for the	Acts 13:2	873
Who shall *s* us from the love of	Rom 8:35	5562
shall be able to *s* us from the	Rom 8:39	5562
out from among them, and be ye *s*	2Cor 6:17	873
s from sinners, and made higher	Heb 7:26	5562
These be they who *s* themselves	Jude 19	873

SEPARATED

they *s* themselves the one from	Gen 13:11	6504
after that Lot was *s* from him	Gen 13:14	6504
people shall be *s* from thy bowels	Gen 25:23	6504
so shall we be *s*, I and thy people	Ex 33:16	6395
which have *s* you from other	Lev 20:24	914
which I have *s* from you as	Lev 20:25	914
that the God of Israel hath *s* you	Num 16:9	914
time the LORD *s* the tribe of Levi	Deut 10:8	914
when he *s* the sons of Adam, he	Deut 32:8	6504
him that was *s* from his brethren	Deut 33:16	5139
of the Gadites there *s* themselves	1Chr 12:8	914
and Aaron was *s*, that he should	1Chr 23:13	914
the captains of the host *s* to the	1Chr 25:1	914
Then Amaziah *s* them, to wit, the	2Chr 25:10	914
all such as had *s* themselves unto	Ezr 6:21	6395
Then I *s* twelve of the chief of	Ezr 8:24	914
have not *s* themselves from the	Ezr 9:1	914
himself *s* from the congregation	Ezr 10:8	914
of them by their names, were *s*	Ezr 10:16	914
we are *s* upon the wall, one far	Neh 4:19	6504
the seed of Israel *s* themselves	Neh 9:2	914
all they that had *s* themselves	Neh 10:28	914
that they *s* from Israel all the	Neh 13:3	914
having *s* himself, seeketh and	Prov 18:1	6504
but the poor is *s* from his	Prov 19:4	6504
hath utterly *s* me from his people	Is 56:3	914
iniquities have *s* between you	Is 59:2	914
for themselves are *s* with whores	Hos 4:14	6504
s themselves unto that shame	Hos 9:10	5144
s the disciples, disputing daily	Acts 19:9	873
s unto the gospel of God,	Rom 1:1	873
who *s* me from my mother's womb,	Gal 1:15	873
s himself, fearing them which	Gal 2:12	873

SEPARATETH

in the which he *s* himself unto	Num 6:5	5144
All the days that he *s* himself	Num 6:6	5144
a whisperer *s* chief friends	Prov 16:28	6504
repeateth a matter *s* very friends	Prov 17:9	6504
which *s* himself from me, and	Eze 14:7	5144

SEPARATING

s myself, as I have done these so	Zec 7:3	5144

SEPARATION

according to the days of the *s*	Lev 12:2	5079
be unclean two weeks, as in her *s*	Lev 12:5	5079
upon in her *s* shall be unclean	Lev 15:20	5079
days out of the time of her *s*	Lev 15:25	5079
it run beyond the time of her *s*	Lev 15:25	5079
shall be as the days of her *s*	Lev 15:25	5079
be unto her as the bed of her *s*	Lev 15:26	5079
as the uncleanness of her *s*	Lev 15:26	5079
All the days of his *s* shall he	Num 6:4	5145
s there shall no razor come upon	Num 6:5	5145
All the days of his *s* he is holy	Num 6:8	5145
unto the LORD the days of his *s*	Num 6:12	5145
lost, because his *s* was defiled	Num 6:12	5145
the days of his *s* are fulfilled	Num 6:13	5145
shall shave the head of his *s* at	Num 6:18	5145
the hair of the head of his *s*	Num 6:18	5145
after the hair of his *s* is shaven	Num 6:19	5145
offering unto the LORD for his *s*	Num 6:21	5145
he must do after the law of his *s*	Num 6:21	5145
of Israel for a water of *s*	Num 19:9	5079
because the water of *s* was not	Num 19:13	5079
the water of *s* hath not been	Num 19:20	5079
water of *s* shall wash his clothes	Num 19:21	5079
of *s* shall be unclean until even	Num 19:21	5079
be purified with the water of *s*	Num 31:23	5079
to make a *s* between the sanctuary	Eze 42:20	914

SEPHAR (*se'-far*) *A mountain in Arabia.*

as thou goest unto *S* a mount of	Gen 10:30	5611

SEPHARAD (*sef-a-rad*) *A city in Media.*

of Jerusalem, which is in *S*	Obad 20	5614

SEPHARVAIM (*sef-ar-va'-im*) See SEPHARVITES. *A city in Mesopotamia.*

Ava, and from Hamath, and from *S*	2Kin 17:24	5617
and Anammelech, the gods of *S*	2Kin 17:31	5617
where are the gods of *S*, Hena, and	2Kin 18:34	5617
and the king of the city of *S*	2Kin 19:13	5617
where are the gods of *S*	Is 36:19	5617
and the king of the city of *S*	Is 37:13	5617

SEPHARVITES (*sef-ar-vites*) *Inhabitants of Sepharvaim.*

the *S* burnt their children in	2Kin 17:31	5616

SEPULCHRE

us shall withhold from thee his *s*	Gen 23:6	6913
knoweth of his *s* unto this day	Deut 34:6	6900
was buried in the *s* of Joash his	Judg 8:32	6913
s in the border of Benjamin at	1Sa 10:2	6900
buried him in the *s* of his father	2Sa 2:32	6913
buried it in the *s* of Abner in	2Sa 4:12	6913
was buried in the *s* of his father	2Sa 17:23	6913
in the *s* of Kish his father	2Sa 21:14	6913
come unto the *s* of thy fathers	1Kin 13:22	6913
then bury me in the *s* wherein the	1Kin 13:31	6913
buried him in his *s* with his	2Kin 9:28	6900
cast the man into the *s* of Elisha	2Kin 13:21	6913
he was buried in his *s* in the	2Kin 21:26	6900
It is the *s* of the man of God,	2Kin 23:17	6913
and buried him in his own *s*	2Kin 23:30	6900
their throat is an open *s*	Ps 5:9	6913
thou hast hewed thee out a *s* here	Is 22:16	6913
that heweth him out an *s* on high	Is 22:16	6913
Their quiver is as an open *s*	Jer 5:16	6913
great stone to the door of the *s*	Mt 27:60	3419
Mary, sitting over against the *s*	Mt 27:61	5028
Command therefore that the *s* be	Mt 27:64	5028
So they went, and made the *s* sure	Mt 27:66	5028
and the other Mary to see the *s*	Mt 28:1	5028
quickly from the *s* with fear	Mt 28:8	3419
laid him in a *s* which was hewn	Mk 15:46	3419
a stone unto the door of the *s*	Mk 15:46	3419
they came unto the *s* at the	Mk 16:2	3419
the stone from the door of the *s*	Mk 16:3	3419
And entering into the *s*, they saw	Mk 16:5	3419
out quickly, and fled from the *s*	Mk 16:8	3419
laid it in a *s* that was hewn in	Lk 23:53	3418
followed after, and beheld the *s*	Lk 23:55	3419
the morning, they came unto the *s*	Lk 24:1	3418
the stone rolled away from the *s*	Lk 24:2	3419
And returned from the *s*, and told	Lk 24:9	3419

S

arose Peter, and ran unto the *s* .... Lk 24:12   *3419*
which were early at the *s* .... Lk 24:22   *3419*
which were with us went to the *s* .... Lk 24:24   *3419*
and in the garden a new *s*, wherein ...... Jn 19:41   *3419*
for the *s* was nigh at hand .... Jn 19:42   *3419*
when it was yet dark, unto the *s* .... Jn 20:1   *3419*
the stone taken away from the *s* .... Jn 20:1   *3419*
taken away the Lord out of the *s* .... Jn 20:2   *3419*
other disciple, and came to the *s* .... Jn 20:3   *3419*
Peter, and came first to the *s* .... Jn 20:4   *3419*
following him, and went into the *s* .... Jn 20:6   *3419*
which came first to the *s* .... Jn 20:8   *3419*
stood without at the *s* weeping .... Jn 20:11   *3419*
down, and looked into the *s* .... Jn 20:11   *3419*
his *s* is with us unto this day .... Acts 2:29   *3418*
laid in the *s* that Abraham bought ...... Acts 7:16   *3418*
from the tree, and laid him in a *s* ...... Acts 13:29   *3419*
Their throat is an open *s* .... Rom 3:13   *5028*

SEPULCHRES
the choice of our *s* bury thy dead ...... Gen 23:6   *6913*
he spied the *s* that were there in 2Kin 23:16   *6913*
and took the bones out of the *s* 2Kin 23:16   *6913*
And they buried him in his own *s* 2Chr 16:14   *6913*
but not in the *s* of the kings 2Chr 21:20   *6913*
him not in the *s* of the kings 2Chr 24:25   *6913*
into the *s* of the kings of Israel 2Chr 28:27   *6913*
of the *s* of the sons of David 2Chr 32:33   *6913*
in one of the *s* of his fathers 2Chr 35:24   *6913*
city, the place of my fathers' *s* .... Neh 2:3   *6913*
unto the city of my fathers' *s* .... Neh 2:5   *6913*
place over against the *s* of David .... Neh 3:16   *6913*
for ye are like unto whited *s* .... Mt 23:27   *5028*
garnish them, and the *s* of the righteous, ... Mt 23:29   *3419*
ye build the *s* of the prophets .... Lk 11:47   *3419*
killed them, and ye build their *s* .... Lk 11:48   *3419*

SERAH *(se'·rah)* See SARAH. *A daughter of Asher.*
and Beriah, and *S* their sister .... Gen 46:17   *8294*
and Beriah, and *S* their sister 1Chr 7:30   *8294*

SERAIAH *(se·ra·i'·ah)* See SHAVSHA.
  1. David's scribe.
and *S* was the scribe 2Sa 8:17   *8304*
  2. High priest in Zedekiah's time.
the guard took *S* the chief priest 2Kin 25:18   *8304*
And Azariah begat *S*, and Seraiah 1Chr 6:14   *8304*
Seraiah, and *S* begat Jehozadak, ... 1Chr 6:14   *8304*
king of Persia, Ezra the son of *S* .... Ezr 7:1   *8304*
the guard took *S* the chief priest .... Jer 52:24   *8304*
  3. Son of Tanhumeth.
S the son of Tanhumeth the 2Kin 25:23   *8304*
S the son of Tanhumeth, and the .... Jer 40:8   *8304*
  4. A son of Kenaz.
Othniel, and *S* 1Chr 4:13   *8304*
S begat Joab, the father of the 1Chr 4:14   *8304*
  5. Son of Asiel.
the son of Josibiah, the son of *S* 1Chr 4:35   *8304*
  6. A priest with Zerubbabel.
Jeshua, Nehemiah, *S*, Reelaiah, ... Ezr 2:2   *8304*
S, Azariah, Jeremiah, ... Neh 10:2   *8304*
S, Jeremiah, Ezra, ... Neh 12:1   *8304*
of *S*, Meraiah .... Neh 12:12   *8304*
  7. An exile.
S the son of Hilkiah, the son of .... Neh 11:11   *8304*
  8. Son of Azriel.
S the son of Azriel, and Shelemiah .... Jer 36:26   *8304*
  9. Son of Neriah.
commanded *S* the son of Neriah .... Jer 51:59   *8304*
this *S* was a quiet prince .... Jer 51:59   *8304*
And Jeremiah said to *S*, When thou ...... Jer 51:61   *8304*

SERAPHIMS
Above it stood the *s* .... Is 6:2   *8314*
Then flew one of the *s* unto me .... Is 6:6   *8314*

SERED *(se'·red)* See SARDITES. *A son of Zebulun.*
S, and Elon, and Jahleel .... Gen 46:14   *5624*
of *S*, the family of the Sardites .... Num 26:26   *5624*

SEREDITES See SARDITES.

SERGIUS *(sur'·je·us)* *Roman governor of Cyprus.*
country, *S* Paulus, a prudent man .... Acts 13:7   *4588*

SERJEANTS
day, the magistrates sent the *s* .... Acts 16:35   *4465*
the *s* told these words unto the .... Acts 16:38   *4465*

SERPENT
Now the *s* was more subtil than .... Gen 3:1   *5175*
And the woman said unto the *s* .... Gen 3:2   *5175*
the *s* said unto the woman, Ye .... Gen 3:4   *5175*
The *s* beguiled me, and I did eat .... Gen 3:13   *5175*
And the LORD God said unto the *s* .... Gen 3:14   *5175*

Dan shall be a *s* by the way .... Gen 49:17   *5175*
on the ground, and it became a *s* .... Ex 4:3   *5175*
Pharaoh, and it shall become a *s* .... Ex 7:9   *8577*
his servants, and it became a *s* .... Ex 7:10   *8577*
a *s* shalt thou take in thine hand .... Ex 7:15   *5175*
unto Moses, Make thee a fiery *s* .... Num 21:8   *8314*
And Moses made a *s* of brass .... Num 21:9   *5175*
that if a *s* had bitten any man, ... Num 21:9   *5175*
when he beheld the *s* of brass .... Num 21:9   *5175*
the brasen *s* that Moses had made 2Kin 18:4   *5175*
hand hath formed the crooked *s* .... Job 26:13   *5175*
poison is like the poison of a *s* .... Ps 58:4   *5175*
sharpened their tongues like a *s* .... Ps 140:3   *5175*
At the last it biteth like a *s* .... Prov 23:32   *5175*
the way of a *s* upon a rock .... Prov 30:19   *5175*
an hedge, a *s* shall bite him .... Eccl 10:8   *5175*
Surely the *s* will bite without .... Eccl 10:11   *5175*
fruit shall be a fiery flying *s* .... Is 14:29   *8314*
punish leviathan the piercing *s* .... Is 27:1   *5175*
even leviathan that crooked *s* .... Is 27:1   *5175*
lion, the viper and fiery flying *s* .... Is 30:6   *8314*
voice thereof shall go like a *s* .... Jer 46:22   *5175*
hand on the wall, and a *s* bit him .... Amos 5:19   *5175*
sea, thence will I command the *s* .... Amos 9:3   *5175*
They shall lick the dust like a *s* .... Mic 7:17   *5175*
ask a fish, will he give him a *s* .... **Mt 7:10**   *3789*
will he for a fish give him a *s* .... **Lk 11:11**   *3789*
lifted up the *s* in the wilderness .... **Jn 3:14**   *3789*
as the *s* beguiled Eve through his 2Cor 11:3   *3789*
dragon was cast out, that old *s* .... Rev 12:9   *3789*
a time, from the face of the *s* .... Rev 12:14   *3789*
the *s* cast out of his mouth water .... Rev 12:15   *3789*
hold on the dragon, that old *s* .... Rev 20:2   *3789*

SERPENT'S
for out of the *s* root shall come .... Is 14:29   *5175*
and dust shall be the *s* meat .... Is 65:25   *5175*

SERPENTS
man his rod, and they became *s* .... Ex 7:12   *8577*
sent fiery *s* among the people .... Num 21:6   *5175*
that he take away the *s* from us .... Num 21:7   *5175*
wilderness, wherein were fiery *s* .... Deut 8:15   *5175*
with the poison of *s* of the dust .... Deut 32:24   *2119*
For, behold, I will send *s* .... Jer 8:17   *5175*
be ye therefore wise as *s* .... **Mt 10:16**   *3789*
Ye *s*, ye generation of vipers, ... **Mt 23:33**   *3789*
They shall take up *s* .... **Mk 16:18**   *3789*
give unto you power to tread on *s* .... **Lk 10:19**   *3789*
tempted, and were destroyed of *s* 1Cor 10:9   *3789*
of beasts, and of birds, and of *s* .... Jas 3:7   *2062*
for their tails were like unto *s* .... Rev 9:19   *3789*

SERUG *(se'·rug)* See SARUCH. *Father of Nahor.*
two and thirty years, and begat *S* .... Gen 11:20   *8286*
after he begat *S* two hundred .... Gen 11:21   *8286*
S lived thirty years, and begat .... Gen 11:22   *8286*
S lived after he begat Nahor two .... Gen 11:23   *8286*
S, Nahor, Terah, ... 1Chr 1:26   *8286*

SERVANT
a *s* of servants shall he be unto .... Gen 9:25   *5650*
and Canaan shall be his *s* .... Gen 9:26   *5650*
and Canaan shall be his *s* .... Gen 9:27   *5650*
not away, I pray thee, from thy *s* .... Gen 18:3   *5650*
therefore are ye come to your *s* .... Gen 18:5   *5650*
thy *s* hath found grace in thy .... Gen 19:19   *5650*
unto his eldest *s* of his house .... Gen 24:2   *5650*
the *s* said unto him, Peradventure .... Gen 24:5   *5650*
the *s* put his hand under the .... Gen 24:9   *5650*
the *s* took ten camels of the .... Gen 24:10   *5650*
hast appointed for thy *s* Isaac .... Gen 24:14   *5650*
the *s* ran to meet her, and said, ... Gen 24:17   *5650*
And he said, I am Abraham's *s* .... Gen 24:34   *5650*
when Abraham's *s* heard their .... Gen 24:52   *5650*
the *s* brought forth jewels of .... Gen 24:53   *5650*
and her nurse, and Abraham's *s* .... Gen 24:59   *5650*
the *s* took Rebekah, and went to .... Gen 24:61   *5650*
For she had said unto the *s* .... Gen 24:65   *5650*
the *s* had said, It is my master .... Gen 24:65   *5650*
the *s* told Isaac all things that .... Gen 24:66   *5650*
thy seed for my *s* Abraham's sake .... Gen 26:24   *5650*
Thy *s* Jacob saith thus, I have .... Gen 32:4   *5650*
which thou hast shewed unto thy *s* .... Gen 32:10   *5650*
shalt say, They be thy *s* Jacob's .... Gen 32:18   *5650*
Behold, thy *s* Jacob is behind us .... Gen 32:20   *5650*
God hath graciously given thy *s* .... Gen 33:5   *5650*
pray thee, pass over before his *s* .... Gen 33:14   *5650*
these words, saying, The Hebrew *s* .... Gen 39:17   *5650*
After this manner did thy *s* to me .... Gen 39:19   *5650*
s to the captain of the guard .... Gen 41:12   *5650*
Thy *s* our father is in good .... Gen 43:28   *5650*
whom it is found shall be my *s* .... Gen 44:10   *5650*

cup is found, he shall be my *s*	Gen 44:17	5650
and said, Oh my lord, let thy *s*	Gen 44:18	5650
thine anger burn against thy *s*	Gen 44:18	5650
we came up unto thy *s* my father	Gen 44:24	5650
thy *s* my father said unto us, Ye	Gen 44:27	5650
when I come to thy *s* my father	Gen 44:30	5650
down the gray hairs of thy *s* our	Gen 44:31	5650
For thy *s* became surety for the	Gen 44:32	5650
let thy *s* abide instead of the	Gen 44:33	5650
bear, and became a *s* unto tribute	Gen 49:15	5647
since thou hast spoken unto thy *s*	Ex 4:10	5650
But every man's *s* that is bought	Ex 12:44	5650
an hired *s* shall not eat thereof	Ex 12:45	7916
believed the LORD, and his *s* Moses	Ex 14:31	5650
If thou buy an Hebrew *s*, six	Ex 21:2	5650
if the *s* shall plainly say, I	Ex 21:5	5650
And if a man smite his *s*, or his	Ex 21:20	5650
if a man smite the eye of his *s*	Ex 21:26	5650
but his *s* Joshua, the son of Nun,	Ex 33:11	8334
of the priest, or an hired *s*	Lev 22:10	7916
for thee, and for thy *s*, and for	Lev 25:6	5650
for thy maid, and for thy hired *s*	Lev 25:6	7916
But as an hired *s*, and as a	Lev 25:40	7916
an hired *s* shall it be with him	Lev 25:50	7916
as a yearly hired *s* shall he be	Lev 25:53	7916
hast thou afflicted thy *s*	Num 11:11	5650
the *s* of Moses, one of his young	Num 11:28	8334
My *s* Moses is not so, who is	Num 12:7	5650
to speak against my *s* Moses	Num 12:8	5650
But my *s* Caleb, because he had	Num 14:24	5650
begun to shew thy *s* thy greatness	Deut 3:24	5650
wast a *s* in the land of Egypt	Deut 5:15	5650
and he shall be thy *s* for ever	Deut 15:17	5650
worth a double hired *s* to thee	Deut 15:18	7916
the *s* which is escaped from his	Deut 23:15	5650
oppress an hired *s* that is poor	Deut 24:14	7916
So Moses the *s* of the LORD died	Deut 34:5	5650
the *s* of the LORD it came to pass	Josh 1:1	5650
Moses my *s* is dead	Josh 1:2	5650
which Moses my *s* commanded thee	Josh 1:7	5650
the word which Moses the *s* of the	Josh 1:13	5650
which Moses the LORD's *s* gave you	Josh 1:15	5650
What saith my lord unto his *s*	Josh 5:14	5650
As Moses the *s* of the LORD	Josh 8:31	5650
as Moses the *s* of the LORD had	Josh 8:33	5650
s Moses to give you all the land	Josh 9:24	5650
as Moses the *s* of the LORD	Josh 11:12	5650
As the LORD commanded Moses his *s*	Josh 11:15	5650
Them did Moses the *s* of the LORD	Josh 12:6	5650
Moses the *s* of the LORD gave it	Josh 12:6	5650
even as Moses the *s* of the LORD	Josh 13:8	5650
the *s* of the LORD sent me from	Josh 14:7	5650
which Moses the *s* of the LORD	Josh 18:7	5650
the *s* of the LORD commanded you	Josh 22:2	5650
which Moses the *s* of the LORD	Josh 22:4	5650
which Moses the *s* of the LORD	Josh 22:5	5650
the *s* of the LORD, died, being an	Josh 24:29	5650
the *s* of the LORD, died, being an	Judg 2:8	5650
Phurah thy *s* down to the host	Judg 7:10	5288
went he down with Phurah his *s*	Judg 7:11	5288
into the hand of thy *s*	Judg 15:18	5650
her again, having his *s* with him	Judg 19:3	5288
he, and his concubine, and his *s*	Judg 19:9	5288
the *s* said unto his master, Come,	Judg 19:11	5288
And he said unto his *s*, Come, and	Judg 19:13	5288
Then said Boaz unto his *s* that	Ruth 2:5	5288
the *s* that was set over the	Ruth 2:6	5288
sacrifice, the priest's *s* came	1Sa 2:13	5288
the fat, the priest's *s* came	1Sa 2:15	5288
for thy *s* heareth	1Sa 3:9	5650
for thy *s* heareth	1Sa 3:10	5650
Saul said to his *s* that was with	1Sa 9:5	5288
Then said Saul to his *s*, But,	1Sa 9:7	5288
the *s* answered Saul again, and	1Sa 9:8	5288
Then said Saul to his *s*, Well	1Sa 9:10	5288
And Samuel took Saul and his *s*	1Sa 9:22	5288
Bid the *s* pass on before us, (and	1Sa 9:27	5288
uncle said unto him and to his *s*	1Sa 10:14	5288
thy *s* will go and fight with this	1Sa 17:32	5650
Thy *s* kept his father's sheep, and	1Sa 17:34	5650
Thy *s* slew both the lion and the	1Sa 17:36	5650
I am the son of thy *s* Jesse the	1Sa 17:58	5650
not the king sin against his *s*	1Sa 19:4	5650
thy *s* shall have peace	1Sa 20:7	5650
thou shalt deal kindly with thy *s*	1Sa 20:8	5650
for thou hast brought thy *s* into	1Sa 20:8	5650
hath stirred up my *s* against me	1Sa 22:8	5650
king impute any thing unto his *s*	1Sa 22:15	5650
for thy *s* knew nothing of all	1Sa 22:15	5650
thy *s* hath certainly heard that	1Sa 23:10	5650
come down, as thy *s* hath heard	1Sa 23:11	5650
I beseech thee, tell thy *s*	1Sa 23:11	5650
and hath kept his *s* from evil	1Sa 25:39	5650
be a *s* to wash the feet of the	1Sa 25:41	5650
my lord thus pursue after his *s*	1Sa 26:18	5650
the king hear the words of his *s*	1Sa 26:19	5650
for why should thy *s* dwell in the	1Sa 27:5	5650
he shall be my *s* for ever	1Sa 27:12	5650
thou shalt know what thy *s* can do	1Sa 28:2	5650
the *s* of Saul the king of Israel,	1Sa 29:3	5650
thy *s* so long as I have been with	1Sa 29:8	5650
man of Egypt, *s* to an Amalekite	1Sa 30:13	5650
By the hand of my *s* David I will	2Sa 3:18	5650
Go and tell my *s* David, Thus saith	2Sa 7:5	5650
so shalt thou say unto my *s* David	2Sa 7:8	5650
for thou, Lord GOD, knowest thy *s*	2Sa 7:20	5650
things, to make thy *s* know them	2Sa 7:21	5650
thou hast spoken concerning thy *s*	2Sa 7:25	5650
let the house of thy *s* David be	2Sa 7:26	5650
of Israel, hast revealed to thy *s*	2Sa 7:27	5650
therefore hath thy *s* found in his	2Sa 7:27	5650
promised this goodness unto thy *s*	2Sa 7:28	5650
thee to bless the house of thy *s*	2Sa 7:29	5650
of thy *s* be blessed for ever	2Sa 7:29	5650
of Saul a *s* whose name was Ziba	2Sa 9:2	5650
And he said, Thy *s* is he	2Sa 9:2	5650
And he answered, Behold thy *s*	2Sa 9:6	5650
himself, and said, What is thy *s*	2Sa 9:8	5650
the king called to Ziba, Saul's *s*	2Sa 9:9	5288
his *s*, so shall thy *s* do	2Sa 9:11	5650
Thy *s* Uriah the Hittite is dead	2Sa 11:21	5650
thy *s* Uriah the Hittite is dead	2Sa 11:24	5650
Then he called his *s* that	2Sa 13:17	5650
Then his *s* brought her out, and	2Sa 13:18	8334
now, thy *s* hath sheepshearers	2Sa 13:24	5650
and his servants go with thy *s*	2Sa 13:24	5650
as thy *s* said, so it is	2Sa 13:35	5650
for thy *s* Joab, he bade me, and he	2Sa 14:19	5650
hath thy *s* Joab done this thing	2Sa 14:20	5650
Today thy *s* knoweth that I have	2Sa 14:22	5650
fulfilled the request of his *s*	2Sa 14:22	5650
Thy *s* is of one of the tribes of	2Sa 15:2	5650
For thy *s* vowed a vow while I	2Sa 15:8	5650
even there also will thy *s* be	2Sa 15:21	5650
say unto Absalom, I will be thy *s*	2Sa 15:34	5650
have been thy father's *s* hitherto	2Sa 15:34	5650
so will I now also be thy *s*	2Sa 15:34	5650
Ziba the *s* of Mephibosheth met	2Sa 16:1	5288
the king's *s*, and me thy *s*	2Sa 18:29	5650
Ziba the *s* of the house of Saul,	2Sa 19:17	5288
s did perversely the day that my	2Sa 19:19	5650
For thy *s* doth know that I have	2Sa 19:20	5650
My lord, O king, my *s* deceived me	2Sa 19:26	5650
for thy *s* said, I will saddle me	2Sa 19:26	5650
because thy *s* is lame	2Sa 19:26	5650
thy *s* unto my lord the king	2Sa 19:27	5650
yet didst thou set thy *s* among	2Sa 19:28	5650
can thy *s* taste what I eat or	2Sa 19:35	5650
wherefore then should thy *s* be	2Sa 19:35	5650
Thy *s* will go a little way over	2Sa 19:36	5650
Let thy *s*, I pray thee, turn back	2Sa 19:37	5650
But behold thy *s* Chimham	2Sa 19:37	5650
take away the iniquity of thy *s*	2Sa 24:10	5650
is my lord the king come to his *s*	2Sa 24:21	5650
but Solomon thy *s* hath he not	1Kin 1:19	5650
But me, even me thy *s*, and Zadok	1Kin 1:26	5650
thy *s* Solomon, hath he not called	1Kin 1:26	5650
hast not shewed it unto thy *s*	1Kin 1:27	5650
not slay his *s* with the sword	1Kin 1:51	5650
king hath said, so will thy *s* do	1Kin 2:38	5650
Thou hast shewed unto thy *s* David	1Kin 3:6	5650
thou hast made thy *s* king instead	1Kin 3:7	5650
thy *s* is in the midst of thy	1Kin 3:8	5650
Give therefore thy *s* an	1Kin 3:9	5650
Who hast kept with thy *s* David my	1Kin 8:24	5650
keep with thy *s* David my father	1Kin 8:25	5650
unto thy *s* David my father	1Kin 8:26	5650
respect unto the prayer of thy *s*	1Kin 8:28	5650
which thy *s* prayeth before thee	1Kin 8:28	5650
unto the prayer which thy *s* shall	1Kin 8:29	5650
thou to the supplication of thy *s*	1Kin 8:30	5650
unto the supplication of thy *s*	1Kin 8:52	5650
by the hand of Moses thy *s*	1Kin 8:53	5650
by the hand of Moses his *s*	1Kin 8:56	5650
he maintain the cause of his *s*	1Kin 8:59	5650
the LORD had done for David his *s*	1Kin 8:66	5650
thee, and will give it to thy *s*	1Kin 11:11	5650
Ephrathite of Zereda, Solomon's *s*	1Kin 11:26	5650
one tribe for my *s* David's sake	1Kin 11:32	5650
that David my *s* may have a light	1Kin 11:36	5650
commandments, as David my *s* did	1Kin 11:38	5650
If thou wilt be a *s* unto this	1Kin 12:7	5650

S

thou hast not been as my s David	1Kin 14:8	5650
hand of his s Ahijah the prophet	1Kin 14:18	5650
by his s Ahijah the Shilonite	1Kin 15:29	5650
his s Zimri, captain of half his	1Kin 16:9	5650
thy s into the hand of Ahab	1Kin 18:9	5650
but I thy s fear the LORD from my	1Kin 18:12	5650
God in Israel, and that I am thy s	1Kin 18:36	5650
And said to his s, Go up now, look	1Kin 18:43	5288
to Judah, and left his s there	1Kin 19:3	5288
to thy s at the first I will do	1Kin 20:9	5650
Thy s Ben-hadad saith, I pray	1Kin 20:32	5650
Thy s went out into the midst of	1Kin 20:39	5650
as thy s was busy here and there,	1Kin 20:40	5650
saying, Thy s my husband is dead	2Kin 4:1	5650
that thy s did fear the LORD	2Kin 4:1	5650
And he said to Gehazi his s	2Kin 4:12	5288
saddled an ass, and said to her s	2Kin 4:24	5288
off, that he said to Gehazi his s	2Kin 4:25	5288
and he said unto his s, Set on the	2Kin 4:38	5288
sent Naaman my s to thee, that	2Kin 5:6	5650
thee, take a blessing of thy s	2Kin 5:15	5650
be given to thy s two mules'	2Kin 5:17	5650
for thy s will henceforth offer	2Kin 5:17	5650
this thing the LORD pardon thy s	2Kin 5:18	5650
LORD pardon thy s in this thing	2Kin 5:18	5650
the s of Elisha the man of God,	2Kin 5:20	5288
And he said, Thy s went no whither	2Kin 5:25	5650
when the s of the man of God was	2Kin 6:15	8334
his s said unto him, Alas, my	2Kin 6:15	5288
Gehazi the s of the man of God	2Kin 8:4	5288
said, But what, is thy s a dog	2Kin 8:13	5650
by his s Elijah the Tishbite	2Kin 9:36	5650
which he spake by his s Elijah	2Kin 10:10	5650
spake by the hand of his s Jonah	2Kin 14:25	5650
of Assyria, saying, I am thy s	2Kin 16:7	5650
and Hoshea became his s, and gave	2Kin 17:3	5650
all that Moses the s of the LORD	2Kin 18:12	5650
sake, and for my s David's sake	2Kin 19:34	5650
sake, and for my s David's sake	2Kin 20:6	5650
that my s Moses commanded them	2Kin 21:8	5650
Asahiah a s of the king's, saying	2Kin 22:12	5650
became his s three years	2Kin 24:1	5650
a s of the king of Babylon, unto	2Kin 25:8	5650
And Sheshan had a s, an Egyptian,	1Chr 2:34	5650
daughter to Jarha his s to wife	1Chr 2:35	5650
Moses the s of God had commanded	1Chr 6:49	5650
O ye seed of Israel his s	1Chr 16:13	5650
Go and tell David my s, Thus saith	1Chr 17:4	5650
shalt thou say unto my s David	1Chr 17:7	5650
to thee for the honour of thy s	1Chr 17:18	5650
for thou knowest thy s	1Chr 17:18	5650
thou hast spoken concerning thy s	1Chr 17:23	5650
thy s be established before thee	1Chr 17:24	5650
hast told thy s that thou wilt	1Chr 17:25	5650
therefore thy s hath found in his	1Chr 17:25	5650
promised this goodness unto thy s	1Chr 17:26	5650
thee to bless the house of thy s	1Chr 17:27	5650
do away the iniquity of thy s	1Chr 21:8	5650
which Moses the s of the LORD had	2Chr 1:3	5650
Thou which hast kept with thy s	2Chr 6:15	5650
keep with thy s David my father	2Chr 6:16	5650
thou hast spoken unto thy s David	2Chr 6:17	5650
therefore to the prayer of thy s	2Chr 6:19	5650
which thy s prayeth before thee	2Chr 6:19	5650
thy s prayeth toward this place	2Chr 6:20	5650
unto the supplications of thy s	2Chr 6:21	5650
the mercies of David thy s	2Chr 6:42	5650
the s of Solomon the son of David	2Chr 13:6	5650
of Moses the s of the LORD	2Chr 24:6	5650
the collection that Moses the s	2Chr 24:9	5650
God, and against his s Hezekiah	2Chr 32:16	5650
Asaiah a s of the king's, saying	2Chr 34:20	5650
mayest hear the prayer of thy s	Neh 1:6	5650
thou commandedst thy s Moses	Neh 1:7	5650
that thou commandedst thy s Moses	Neh 1:8	5650
attentive to the prayer of thy s	Neh 1:11	5650
thy s this day, and grant him	Neh 1:11	5650
if thy s have found favour in thy	Neh 2:5	5650
the Horonite, and Tobiah the s	Neh 2:10	5650
the Horonite, and Tobiah the s	Neh 2:19	5650
with his s lodge within Jerusalem	Neh 4:22	5650
Then sent Sanballat his s unto me	Neh 6:5	5650
laws, by the hand of Moses thy s	Neh 9:14	5650
was given by Moses the s of God	Neh 10:29	5650
Hast thou considered my s Job	Job 1:8	5650
Hast thou considered my s Job	Job 2:3	5650
the s is free from his master	Job 3:19	5650
As a s earnestly desireth the	Job 7:2	5650
I called my s, and he gave me no	Job 19:16	5650
thou take him for a s for ever	Job 41:4	5650
that is right, as my s Job hath	Job 42:7	5650

and seven rams, and go to my s Job	Job 42:8	5650
my s Job shall pray for you	Job 42:8	5650
which is right, like my s Job	Job 42:8	5650
the s of the LORD, who spake unto	Ps 18:t	5650
Moreover by them is thy s warned	Ps 19:11	5650
Keep back thy s also from	Ps 19:13	5650
put not thy s away in anger	Ps 27:9	5650
Make thy face to shine upon thy s	Ps 31:16	5650
in the prosperity of his s	Ps 35:27	5650
Psalm of David, the s of the LORD	Ps 36:t	5650
And hide not thy face from thy s	Ps 69:17	5650
He chose David also his s	Ps 78:70	5650
save thy s that trusteth in thee	Ps 86:2	5650
Rejoice the soul of thy s	Ps 86:4	5650
give thy strength unto thy s	Ps 86:16	5650
I have sworn unto David my s	Ps 89:3	5650
I have found David my s	Ps 89:20	5650
made void the covenant of thy s	Ps 89:39	5650
O ye seed of Abraham his s	Ps 105:6	5650
even Joseph, who was sold for a s	Ps 105:17	5650
He sent Moses his s	Ps 105:26	5650
holy promise, and Abraham his s	Ps 105:42	5650
but let thy s rejoice	Ps 109:28	5650
O LORD, truly I am thy s	Ps 116:16	5650
I am thy s, and the son of thine	Ps 116:16	5650
Deal bountifully with thy s	Ps 119:17	5650
but thy s did meditate in thy	Ps 119:23	5650
Stablish thy word unto thy s	Ps 119:38	5650
Remember the word unto thy s	Ps 119:49	5650
Thou hast dealt well with thy s	Ps 119:65	5650
according to thy word unto thy s	Ps 119:76	5650
How many are the days of thy s	Ps 119:84	5650
Be surety for thy s for good	Ps 119:122	5650
Deal with thy s according unto	Ps 119:124	5650
I am thy s	Ps 119:125	5650
Make thy face to shine upon thy s	Ps 119:135	5650
therefore thy s loveth it	Ps 119:140	5650
seek thy s	Ps 119:176	5650
For thy s David's sake turn not	Ps 132:10	5650
an heritage unto Israel his s	Ps 136:22	5650
not into judgment with thy s	Ps 143:2	5650
for I am thy s	Ps 143:12	5650
his s from the hurtful sword	Ps 144:10	5650
the fool shall be s to the wise	Prov 11:29	5650
He that is despised, and hath a s	Prov 12:9	5650
king's favour is toward a wise s	Prov 14:35	5650
A wise s shall have rule over a	Prov 17:2	5650
much less for a s to have rule	Prov 19:10	5650
the borrower is s to the lender	Prov 22:7	5650
A s will not be corrected by	Prov 29:19	5650
his s from a child shall have him	Prov 29:21	5650
Accuse not a s unto his master,	Prov 30:10	5650
For a s when he reigneth	Prov 30:22	5650
lest thou hear thy s curse thee	Eccl 7:21	5650
Like as my s Isaiah hath walked	Is 20:3	5650
that I will call my s Eliakim the	Is 22:20	5650
as with the s, so with his master	Is 24:2	5650
sake, and for my s David's sake	Is 37:35	5650
But thou, Israel, art my s	Is 41:8	5650
and said unto thee, Thou art my s	Is 41:9	5650
Behold my s, whom I uphold	Is 42:1	5650
Who is blind, but my s	Is 42:19	5650
perfect, and blind as the LORD'S s	Is 42:19	5650
LORD, and my s whom I have chosen	Is 43:10	5650
Yet now hear, O Jacob my s	Is 44:1	5650
Fear not, O Jacob, my s	Is 44:2	5650
for thou art my s	Is 44:21	5650
thou art my s	Is 44:21	5650
That confirmeth the word of his s	Is 44:26	5650
LORD hath redeemed his s Jacob	Is 48:20	5650
And said unto me, Thou art my s	Is 49:3	5650
me from the womb to be his s	Is 49:5	5650
s to raise up the tribes of Jacob	Is 49:6	5650
to a s of rulers, Kings shall see	Is 49:7	5650
that obeyeth the voice of his s	Is 50:10	5650
my s shall deal prudently, he	Is 52:13	5650
shall my righteous s justify many	Is 53:11	5650
Is Israel a s	Jer 2:14	5650
the king of Babylon, my s	Jer 25:9	5650
the king of Babylon, my s	Jer 27:6	5650
O my s Jacob, saith the LORD	Jer 30:10	5650
be broken with David my s	Jer 33:21	5650
I multiply the seed of David my s	Jer 33:22	5650
the seed of Jacob, and David my s	Jer 33:26	5650
name, and caused every man his s	Jer 34:16	5650
the king of Babylon, my s	Jer 43:10	5650
O my s Jacob, and be not dismayed,	Jer 46:28	5650
Fear thou not, O Jacob my s	Jer 46:28	5650
that I have given to my s Jacob	Eze 28:25	5650
shall feed them, even my s David	Eze 34:23	5650
my s David a prince among them	Eze 34:24	5650

David my *s* shall be king over	Eze 37:24	5650
that I have given unto Jacob my *s*	Eze 37:25	5650
my *s* David shall be their prince	Eze 37:25	5650
s of the living God, is thy God,	Dan 6:20	5649
in the law of Moses the *s* of God	Dan 9:11	5650
our God, hear the prayer of thy *s*	Dan 9:17	5650
For how can the *s* of this my lord	Dan 10:17	5650
I take thee, O Zerubbabel, my *s*	Hag 2:23	5650
will bring forth my *s* the BRANCH	Zec 3:8	5650
his father, and a *s* his master	Mal 1:6	5650
Remember ye the law of Moses my *s*	Mal 4:4	5650
my *s* lieth at home sick of the	Mt 8:6	3816
only, and my *s* shall be healed	Mt 8:8	3816
and to my *s*, Do this, and he doeth	Mt 8:9	1401
his *s* was healed in the selfsame	Mt 8:13	3816
master, nor the *s* above his lord	Mt 10:24	1401
his master, and the *s* as his lord	Mt 10:25	1401
Behold my *s*, whom I have chosen	Mt 12:18	3816
The *s* therefore fell down, and	Mt 18:26	1401
Then the lord of that *s* was moved	Mt 18:27	1401
But the same *s* went out, and found	Mt 18:28	1401
said unto him, O thou wicked	Mt 18:32	1401
among you, let him be your *s*	Mt 20:27	1401
among you shall be your *s*	Mt 23:11	1249
Who then is a faithful and wise *s*	Mt 24:45	1401
Blessed is that *s*, whom his lord	Mt 24:46	1401
if that evil *s* shall say in his	Mt 24:48	1401
The lord of that *s* shall come in	Mt 24:50	1401
done, thou good and faithful *s*	Mt 25:21	1401
Well done, good and faithful *s*	Mt 25:23	1401
him, Thou wicked and slothful *s*	Mt 25:26	1401
***s* into outer darkness**	Mt 25:30	1401
struck a *s* of the high priest's,	Mt 26:51	1401
shall be last of all, and *s* of all	Mk 9:35	1249
the chiefest, shall be *s* of all	Mk 10:44	1401
he sent to the husbandmen a *s*	Mk 12:2	1401
again he sent unto them another *s*	Mk 12:4	1401
smote a *s* of the high priest, and	Mk 14:47	1401
He hath holpen his *s* Israel	Lk 1:54	3816
us in the house of his *s* David	Lk 1:69	3816
thou thy *s* depart in peace	Lk 2:29	1401
And a certain centurion's *s*	Lk 7:2	1401
that he would come and heal his *s*	Lk 7:3	1401
a word, and my *s* shall be healed	Lk 7:7	3816
and to my *s*, Do this, and he doeth	Lk 7:8	1401
found the *s* whole that had been	Lk 7:10	1401
Blessed is that *s*, whom his lord	Lk 12:43	1401
if thy *s* say in his heart, My	Lk 12:45	1401
The lord of that *s* will come in a	Lk 12:46	1401
And that *s*, which knew his lord's	Lk 12:47	1401
sent his *s* at supper time to say	Lk 14:17	1401
So that *s* came, and shewed his	Lk 14:21	1401
house being angry said to his *s*	Lk 14:21	1401
the *s* said, Lord, it is done as	Lk 14:22	1401
And the lord said unto the *s*.	Lk 14:23	1401
No *s* can serve two masters	Lk 16:13	3610
having a *s* plowing or feeding	Lk 17:7	1401
Doth he thank that *s* because he	Lk 17:9	1401
said unto him, Well, thou good	Lk 19:17	1401
will I judge thee, thou wicked *s*	Lk 19:22	1401
he sent a *s* to the husbandmen	Lk 20:10	1401
And again he sent another *s*	Lk 20:11	1401
smote the *s* of the high priest	Lk 22:50	1401
committeth sin is the *s* of sin	Jn 8:34	1401
the *s* abideth not in the house	Jn 8:35	1401
I am, there shall also my *s* be	Jn 12:26	1249
The *s* is not greater than his	Jn 13:16	1401
for the *s* knoweth not what his	Jn 15:15	1401
The *s* is not greater than his	Jn 15:20	1401
it, and smote the high priest's *s*	Jn 18:10	1401
mouth of thy *s* David hast said	Acts 4:25	3816
a *s* of Jesus Christ, called to be	Rom 1:1	1401
thou that judgest another man's *s*	Rom 14:4	3610
which is a *s* of the church which	Rom 16:1	1248
sent by Phebe *s* of the church at	Rom *s*	1248
Art thou called being a *s*	1Cor 7:21	1401
is called in the Lord, being a *s*	1Cor 7:22	1401
called, being free, is Christ's *s*	1Cor 7:22	1401
yet have I made myself a *s* unto all	1Cor 9:19	1402
I should not be the *s* of Christ	Gal 1:10	1401
child, differeth nothing from a *s*	Gal 4:1	1401
Wherefore thou art no more a *s*	Gal 4:7	1401
and took upon him the form of a *s*	Phil 2:7	1401
a *s* of Christ, saluteth you,	Col 4:12	1401
the *s* of the Lord must not strive	2Ti 2:24	1401
a *s* of God, and an apostle of	Titus 1:1	1401
Not now as a *s*, but above a	Philem 16	1401
now as a *s*, but above a *s*	Philem 16	1401
to Philemon, by Onesimus, a *s*	Philem *s*	3610
faithful in all his house, as a *s*	Heb 3:5	2324
a *s* of God and of the Lord Jesus	Jas 1:1	1401

Simon Peter, a *s* and an apostle of	2Pet 1:1	*1401*
the *s* of Jesus Christ, and brother	Jude 1	*1401*
it by his angel unto his *s* John	Rev 1:1	*1401*
the song of Moses the *s* of God	Rev 15:3	*1401*

SERVANT'S

in, I pray you, into your *s* house	Gen 19:2	5650
thou hast spoken also of thy *s*	2Sa 7:19	5650
to thy son for David my *s* sake	1Kin 11:13	5650
of his life for David my *s* sake	1Kin 11:34	5650
Judah for David his *s* sake	2Kin 8:19	5650
thou hast also spoken of thy *s*	1Chr 17:17	5650
O Lord, for thy *s* sake, and	1Chr 17:19	5650
For Jacob my *s* sake, and Israel	Is 45:4	5650
The *s* name was Malchus	Jn 18:10	*1401*

SERVANTS

a servant of *s* shall he be unto	Gen 9:25	5650
captive, he armed his trained *s*	Gen 14:14	
himself against them, he and his *s*	Gen 14:15	5650
the morning, and called all his *s*	Gen 20:8	5650
which Abimelech's *s* had violently	Gen 21:25	5650
of herds, and great store of *s*	Gen 26:14	5657
s had digged in the days of	Gen 26:15	5650
Isaac's *s* digged in the valley,	Gen 26:19	5650
and there Isaac's *s* digged a well	Gen 26:25	5650
the same day, that Isaac's *s* came	Gen 26:32	5650
have I given to him for *s*	Gen 27:37	5650
them into the hand of his *s*	Gen 32:16	5650
and said unto his *s*, Pass over	Gen 32:16	5650
he made a feast unto all his *s*	Gen 40:20	5650
and of the chief baker among his *s*	Gen 40:20	5650
Pharaoh was wroth with his *s*	Gen 41:10	5650
and in the eyes of all his *s*	Gen 41:37	5650
And Pharaoh said unto his *s*	Gen 41:38	5650
but to buy food are thy *s* come	Gen 42:10	5650
are true men, thy *s* are no spies	Gen 42:11	5650
Thy *s* are twelve brethren, the	Gen 42:13	5650
God forbid that thy *s* should do	Gen 44:7	5650
whomsoever of thy *s* it be found	Gen 44:9	5650
found out the iniquity of thy *s*	Gen 44:16	5650
behold, we are my lord's *s*	Gen 44:16	5650
My lord asked his *s*, saying, Have	Gen 44:19	5650
And thou saidst unto thy *s*	Gen 44:21	5650
And thou saidst unto thy *s*	Gen 44:23	5650
thy *s* shall bring down the gray	Gen 44:31	5650
it pleased Pharaoh well, and his *s*	Gen 45:16	5650
Thy *s* are shepherds, both we, and	Gen 47:3	5650
for thy *s* have no pasture for	Gen 47:4	5650
let thy *s* dwell in the land of	Gen 47:4	5650
our land will be *s* unto Pharaoh	Gen 47:19	5650
lord, and we will be Pharaoh's *s*	Gen 47:25	5650
Joseph commanded his *s* the	Gen 50:2	5650
him went up all the *s* of Pharaoh	Gen 50:7	5650
of the *s* of the God of thy father	Gen 50:17	5650
and they said, Behold, we be thy *s*	Gen 50:18	5650
dealest thou thus with thy *s*	Ex 5:15	5650
is no straw given unto thy *s*	Ex 5:16	5650
and, behold, thy *s* are beaten	Ex 5:16	5650
Pharaoh, and in the eyes of his *s*	Ex 5:21	5650
before Pharaoh, and before his *s*	Ex 7:10	5650
Pharaoh, and in the sight of his *s*	Ex 7:20	5650
bed, and into the house of thy *s*	Ex 8:3	5650
thy people, and upon all thy *s*	Ex 8:4	5650
I intreat for thee, and for thy *s*	Ex 8:9	5650
and from thy houses, and from thy *s*	Ex 8:11	5650
of flies upon thee, and upon thy *s*	Ex 8:21	5650
depart from Pharaoh, from his *s*	Ex 8:29	5650
of flies from Pharaoh, from his *s*	Ex 8:31	5650
upon thine heart, and upon thy *s*	Ex 9:14	5650
s of Pharaoh made his *s*	Ex 9:20	5650
the word of the Lord left his *s*	Ex 9:21	5650
But as for thee and thy *s*, I know	Ex 9:30	5650
hardened his heart, he and his *s*	Ex 9:34	5650
his heart, and the heart of his *s*	Ex 10:1	5650
and the houses of all thy *s*	Ex 10:6	5650
Pharaoh's *s* said unto him, How	Ex 10:7	5650
in the sight of Pharaoh's *s*	Ex 11:3	5650
all these thy *s* shall come down	Ex 11:8	5650
up in the night, he, and all his *s*	Ex 12:30	5650
of his *s* was turned against the	Ex 14:5	5650
Abraham, Isaac, and Israel, thy *s*	Ex 32:13	5650
For they are my *s*, which I	Lev 25:42	5650
me the children of Israel are *s*	Lev 25:55	5650
they are my *s* whom I brought	Lev 25:55	5650
and said unto the *s* of Balak	Num 22:18	5650
ass, and his two *s* were with him	Num 22:22	5288
Thy *s* have taken the sum of the	Num 31:49	5650
for cattle, and thy *s* have cattle	Num 32:4	5650
given unto thy *s* for a possession	Num 32:5	5650
saying, Thy *s* will do as my lord	Num 32:25	5650
But thy *s* will pass over, every	Num 32:27	5650

S

As the LORD hath said unto thy s	Num 32:31	5650	all his s stood by with their	2Sa 13:31	5650
Remember thy s, Abraham, Isaac,	Deut 9:27	5650	also and all his s wept very sore	2Sa 13:36	5650
unto Pharaoh, and unto all his s	Deut 29:2	5650	Therefore he said unto his s	2Sa 14:30	5650
and repent himself for his s	Deut 32:36	5650	Absalom's s set the field on fire	2Sa 14:30	5650
he will avenge the blood of his s	Deut 32:43	5650	Wherefore have thy s set my field	2Sa 14:31	5650
Egypt to Pharaoh, and to all his s	Deut 34:11	5650	David said unto all his s that	2Sa 15:14	5650
said unto Joshua, We are thy s	Josh 9:8	5650	the king's s said unto the king,	2Sa 15:15	5650
From a very far country thy s are	Josh 9:9	5650	thy s are ready to do whatsoever	2Sa 15:15	5650
and say unto them, We are your s	Josh 9:11	5650	all his s passed on beside him	2Sa 15:18	5650
it was certainly told thy s	Josh 9:24	5650	at all the s of king David	2Sa 16:6	5650
Slack not thy hand from thy s	Josh 10:6	5650	said to Abishai, and to all his s	2Sa 16:11	5650
When he was gone out, his s came	Judg 3:24	5650	when Absalom's s came to the	2Sa 17:20	5650
Then Gideon took ten men of his s	Judg 6:27	5650	were slain before the s of David	2Sa 18:7	5650
the young man which is with thy s	Judg 19:19	5650	And Absalom met the s of David	2Sa 18:9	5650
that ye be not s unto the Hebrews	1Sa 4:9	5647	this day the faces of all thy s	2Sa 19:5	5650
of them, and give them to his s	1Sa 8:14	5650	regardest neither princes nor s	2Sa 19:6	5650
give to his officers, and to his s	1Sa 8:15	5650	and speak comfortably unto thy s	2Sa 19:7	5650
and ye shall be his s	1Sa 8:17	5650	king, Return thou, and all thy s	2Sa 19:14	5650
Take now one of the s with thee	1Sa 9:3	5650	sons and his twenty s with him	2Sa 19:17	5650
Pray for thy s unto the LORD thy	1Sa 12:19	5650	take thou thy lord's s, and pursue	2Sa 20:6	5650
Saul's s said unto him, Behold	1Sa 16:15	5650	his s with him, and fought against	2Sa 21:15	5650
Let our lord now command thy s	1Sa 16:16	5650	of David, and by the hand of his s	2Sa 21:22	5650
And Saul said unto his s, Provide	1Sa 16:17	5650	his s coming on toward him	2Sa 24:20	5650
Then answered one of the s	1Sa 16:18	5288	Wherefore his s said unto him	1Kin 1:2	5650
I a Philistine, and ye s to Saul	1Sa 17:8	5650	all the men of Judah the king's s	1Kin 1:9	5650
kill me, then will we be your s	1Sa 17:9	5650	Take with you the s of your lord	1Kin 1:33	5650
kill him, then shall ye be our s	1Sa 17:9	5650	moreover the king's s came to	1Kin 1:47	5650
and also in the sight of Saul's s	1Sa 18:5	5650	that two of the s of Shimei ran	1Kin 2:39	5650
And Saul commanded his s, saying,	1Sa 18:22	5650	saying, Behold, thy s be in Gath	1Kin 2:39	5650
in thee, and all his s love thee	1Sa 18:22	5650	to Gath to Achish to seek his s	1Kin 2:40	5650
Saul's s spake those words in the	1Sa 18:23	5650	went, and brought his s from Gath	1Kin 2:40	5650
the s of Saul told him, saying,	1Sa 18:24	5650	and made a feast to all his s	1Kin 3:15	5650
when his s told David these words	1Sa 18:26	5650	of Tyre sent his s unto Solomon	1Kin 5:1	5650
wisely than all the s of Saul	1Sa 18:30	5650	my s shall be with thy s	1Kin 5:6	5650
Jonathan his son, and to all his s	1Sa 19:1	5650	thy s according to all that thou	1Kin 5:6	5650
and I have appointed my s to such	1Sa 21:2	5288	My s shall bring them down from	1Kin 5:9	5650
Now a certain man of the s of	1Sa 21:7	5650	mercy with thy s that walk before	1Kin 8:23	5650
the s of Achish said unto him, Is	1Sa 21:11	5650	in heaven, and do, and judge thy s	1Kin 8:32	5650
Then said Achish unto his s	1Sa 21:14	5650	and forgive the sin of thy s	1Kin 8:36	5650
all his s were standing about him	1Sa 22:6	5650	they were men of war, and his s	1Kin 9:22	5650
unto his s that stood about him	1Sa 22:7	5650	And Hiram sent in the navy his s	1Kin 9:27	5650
which was set over the s of Saul	1Sa 22:9	5650	of the sea, with the s of Solomon	1Kin 9:27	5650
faithful among all thy s as David	1Sa 22:14	5650	table, and the sitting of his s	1Kin 10:5	5650
But the s of the king would not	1Sa 22:17	5650	thy men, happy are these thy s	1Kin 10:8	5650
stayed his s with these words	1Sa 24:7	582	to her own country, she and her s	1Kin 10:13	5650
cometh to thine hand unto thy s	1Sa 25:8	5650	of his father's s with him	1Kin 11:17	5650
And Nabal answered David's s	1Sa 25:10	5650	then they will be thy s for ever	1Kin 12:7	5650
there be many s now a days that	1Sa 25:10	5650	them into the hand of his s	1Kin 15:18	5650
And she said unto her s, Go on	1Sa 25:19	5288	Yet I will send my s unto thee to	1Kin 20:6	5650
when the s of David were come to	1Sa 25:40	5650	house, and the houses of thy s	1Kin 20:6	5650
wash the feet of the s of my lord	1Sa 25:41	5650	that he said unto his s, Set	1Kin 20:12	5650
Then said Saul unto his s	1Sa 28:7	5650	the s of the king of Syria said	1Kin 20:23	5650
his s said to him, Behold, there	1Sa 28:7	5650	his s said unto him, Behold now,	1Kin 20:31	5650
But his s, together with the	1Sa 28:23	5650	king of Israel said unto his s	1Kin 22:3	5650
it before Saul, and before his s	1Sa 28:25	5650	Let my s go with thy s in	1Kin 22:49	5650
s that are come with thee	1Sa 29:10	5650	and the life of these fifty thy s	2Kin 1:13	5650
the s of Ish-bosheth the son of	2Sa 2:12	5650	be with thy s fifty strong men	2Kin 2:16	5650
the s of David, went out, and met	2Sa 2:13	5650	the king of Israel's s answered	2Kin 3:11	5650
Saul, and twelve of the s of David	2Sa 2:15	5650	his s came near, and spake unto	2Kin 5:13	5650
of Israel, before the s of David	2Sa 2:17	5650	and laid them upon two of his s	2Kin 5:23	5288
lacked of David's s nineteen men	2Sa 2:30	5650	I pray thee, and go with thy s	2Kin 6:3	5650
But the s of David had smitten of	2Sa 2:31	5650	and took counsel with his s	2Kin 6:8	5650
the s of David and Joab came from	2Sa 3:22	5650	and he called his s, and said unto	2Kin 6:11	5650
And the king said unto his s	2Sa 3:38	5650	And one of his s said, None, my	2Kin 6:12	5650
eyes of the handmaids of his s	2Sa 6:20	5650	in the night, and said unto his s	2Kin 7:12	5650
so the Moabites became David's s	2Sa 8:2	5650	And one of his s answered and said,	2Kin 7:13	5650
and the Syrians became s to David	2Sa 8:6	5650	the blood of my s the prophets	2Kin 9:7	5650
that were on the s of Hadadezer	2Sa 8:7	5650	blood of all the s of the LORD	2Kin 9:7	5650
all they of Edom became David's s	2Sa 8:14	5650	came forth to the s of his lord	2Kin 9:11	5650
therefore, and thy sons, and thy s	2Sa 9:10	5650	his s carried him in a chariot to	2Kin 9:28	5650
Ziba had fifteen sons and twenty s	2Sa 9:10	5650	to Jehu, saying, We are thy s	2Kin 10:5	5650
of Ziba were s unto Mephibosheth	2Sa 9:12	5650	the prophets of Baal, all his s	2Kin 10:19	5647
the hand of his s for his father	2Sa 10:2	5650	you none of the s of the LORD	2Kin 10:23	5650
David's s came into the land of	2Sa 10:2	5650	his s arose, and made a conspiracy	2Kin 12:20	5650
David rather sent his s unto thee	2Sa 10:3	5650	the son of Shomer, his s, smote	2Kin 12:21	5650
Wherefore Hanun took David's s	2Sa 10:4	5650	that he slew his s which had	2Kin 14:5	5650
when all the kings that were s to	2Sa 10:19	5650	sent to you by my s the prophets	2Kin 17:13	5650
his s with him, and all Israel	2Sa 11:1	5650	said by all his s the prophets	2Kin 17:23	5650
house with all the s of his lord	2Sa 11:9	5650	of the least of my master's s	2Kin 18:24	5650
the s of my lord, are encamped in	2Sa 11:11	5650	to thy s in the Syrian language	2Kin 18:26	5650
on his bed with the s of his lord	2Sa 11:13	5650	So the s of king Hezekiah came to	2Kin 19:5	5650
of the people of the s of David	2Sa 11:17	5650	with which the s of the king of	2Kin 19:6	5288
shot from off the wall upon thy s	2Sa 11:24	5650	LORD spake by his s the prophets	2Kin 21:10	5650
and some of the king's s be dead	2Sa 11:24	5650	the s of Amon conspired against	2Kin 21:23	5650
the s of David feared to tell him	2Sa 12:18	5650	Thy s have gathered the money	2Kin 22:9	5650
David saw that his s whispered	2Sa 12:19	5650	his s carried him in a chariot	2Kin 23:30	5650
therefore David said unto his s	2Sa 12:19	5650	he spake by his s the prophets	2Kin 24:2	5650
Then said his s unto him, What	2Sa 12:21	5650	At that time the s of	2Kin 24:10	5650
his s go with thy servant	2Sa 13:24	5650	the city, and his s did besiege it	2Kin 24:11	5650
Now Absalom had commanded his s	2Sa 13:28	5288	he, and his mother, and his s	2Kin 24:12	5650
the s of Absalom did unto Amnon	2Sa 13:29	5288	not to be the s of the Chaldees	2Kin 25:24	5650

and the Moabites became David's *s*	1Chr 18:2	5650
and the Syrians became David's *s*	1Chr 18:6	5650
that were on the *s* of Hadarezer	1Chr 18:7	5650
all the Edomites became David's *s*	1Chr 18:13	5650
So the *s* of David came into the	1Chr 19:2	5650
are not his *s* come unto thee for	1Chr 19:3	5650
Wherefore Hanun took David's *s*	1Chr 19:4	5650
when the *s* of Hadarezer saw that	1Chr 19:19	5650
peace with David, and became his *s*	1Chr 19:19	5647
of David, and by the hand of his *s*	1Chr 20:8	5650
are they not all my lord's *s*	1Chr 21:3	5650
for I know that thy *s* can skill	2Chr 2:8	5650
my *s* shall be with thy *s*,	2Chr 2:8	5650
And, behold, I will give to thy *s*	2Chr 2:10	5650
of, let him send unto his *s*	2Chr 2:15	5650
and shewest mercy unto thy *s*	2Chr 6:14	5650
heaven, and do, and judge thy *s*	2Chr 6:23	5650
and forgive the sin of thy *s*	2Chr 6:27	5650
Solomon make no *s* for his work	2Chr 8:9	5650
him by the hands of his *s* ships	2Chr 8:18	5650
s that had knowledge of the sea	2Chr 8:18	5650
they went with the *s* of Solomon	2Chr 8:18	5650
table, and the sitting of his *s*	2Chr 9:4	5650
thy men, and happy are these thy *s*	2Chr 9:7	5650
the *s* also of Huram, and the	2Chr 9:10	5650
the *s* of Solomon, which brought	2Chr 9:10	5650
to her own land, she and her *s*	2Chr 9:12	5650
to Tarshish with the *s* of Huram	2Chr 9:21	5650
them, they will be thy *s* for ever	2Chr 10:7	5650
Nevertheless they shall be his *s*	2Chr 12:8	5650
his own *s* conspired against him	2Chr 24:25	5650
that he slew his *s* that had	2Chr 25:3	5650
Assyria send his *s* to Jerusalem	2Chr 32:9	5650
his *s* spake yet more against the	2Chr 32:16	5650
his *s* conspired against him, and	2Chr 33:24	5650
All that was committed to thy *s*	2Chr 34:16	5650
and the king said to his *s*	2Chr 35:23	5650
His *s* therefore took him out of	2Chr 35:24	5650
where they were *s* to him and his	2Chr 36:20	5650
The children of Solomon's *s*	Ezr 2:55	5650
and the children of Solomon's *s*	Ezr 2:58	5650
Beside their *s* and their maids, of	Ezr 2:65	5650
Thy *s* the men on this side the	Ezr 4:11	5649
We are the *s* of the God of heaven	Ezr 5:11	5649
commanded by thy *s* the prophets	Ezr 9:11	5650
for the children of Israel thy *s*	Neh 1:6	5650
Now these are thy *s* and thy people	Neh 1:10	5650
and to the prayer of thy *s*	Neh 1:11	5650
therefore we his *s* will arise	Neh 2:20	5650
half of my *s* wrought in the work	Neh 4:16	5288
I, nor my brethren, nor my *s*	Neh 4:23	5288
our sons and our daughters to be *s*	Neh 5:5	5650
likewise, and my brethren, and my *s*	Neh 5:10	5288
even their *s* bare rule over the	Neh 5:15	5288
all my *s* were gathered thither	Neh 5:16	5288
The children of Solomon's *s*	Neh 7:57	5650
and the children of Solomon's *s*	Neh 7:60	5650
upon Pharaoh, and on all his *s*	Neh 9:10	5650
we are *s* this day, and for the	Neh 9:36	5650
thereof, behold, we are *s* in it	Neh 9:36	5650
and the children of Solomon's *s*	Neh 11:3	5650
some of my *s* set I at the gates,	Neh 13:19	5288
unto all his princes and his *s*	Est 1:3	5650
Then said the king's *s* that	Est 2:2	5288
unto all his princes and his *s*	Est 2:18	5650
And all the king's *s*, that were in	Est 3:2	5650
Then the king's *s*, which were in	Est 3:3	5650
All the king's *s*, and the people	Est 4:11	5650
the princes and *s* of the king	Est 5:11	5650
Then said the king's *s* that	Est 6:3	5288
the king's *s* said unto him,	Est 6:5	5288
they have slain the *s* with the	Job 1:15	5288
burned up the sheep, and the *s*	Job 1:16	5288
slain the *s* with the edge of the	Job 1:17	5288
Behold, he put no trust in his *s*	Job 4:18	5650
LORD redeemeth the soul of his *s*	Ps 34:22	5650
also of his *s* shall inherit it	Ps 69:36	5650
The dead bodies of thy *s* have	Ps 79:2	5650
the blood of thy *s* which is shed	Ps 79:10	5650
Lord, the reproach of thy *s*	Ps 89:50	5650
it repent thee concerning thy *s*	Ps 90:13	5650
Let thy work appear unto thy *s*	Ps 90:16	5650
For thy *s* take pleasure in her	Ps 102:14	5650
children of thy *s* shall continue	Ps 102:28	5650
to deal subtilly with his *s*	Ps 105:25	5650
O ye *s* of the LORD, praise the	Ps 113:1	5650
for all are thy *s*	Ps 119:91	5650
as the eyes of *s* look unto the	Ps 123:2	5650
all ye *s* of the LORD, which by	Ps 134:1	5650
praise him, O ye *s* of the LORD	Ps 135:1	5650
upon Pharaoh, and upon all his *s*	Ps 135:9	5650

repent himself concerning his *s*	Ps 135:14	5650
to lies, all his *s* are wicked	Prov 29:12	8334
I got me *s* and maidens, and had	Eccl 2:7	5650
and had *s* born in my house	Eccl 2:7	
I have seen *s* upon horses	Eccl 10:7	5650
walking as *s* upon the earth	Eccl 10:7	5650
in the land of the LORD for *s*	Is 14:2	5650
of the least of my master's *s*	Is 36:9	5650
unto thy *s* in the Syrian language	Is 36:11	5650
So the *s* of king Hezekiah came to	Is 37:5	5650
wherewith the *s* of the king of	Is 37:6	5288
By thy *s* hast thou reproached the	Is 37:24	5650
the heritage of the *s* of the LORD	Is 54:17	5650
the name of the LORD, to be his *s*	Is 56:6	5650
it, and my *s* shall dwell there	Is 65:9	5650
my *s* shall eat, but ye shall be	Is 65:13	5650
my *s* shall drink, but ye shall be	Is 65:13	5650
my *s* shall rejoice, but ye shall	Is 65:13	5650
my *s* shall sing for joy of heart,	Is 65:14	5650
call his *s* by another name	Is 65:15	5650
LORD shall be known toward his *s*	Is 66:14	5650
unto you all my *s* the prophets	Jer 7:25	5650
Zedekiah king of Judah, and his *s*	Jer 21:7	5650
throne of David, thou, and thy *s*	Jer 22:2	5650
and on horses, he, and his *s*	Jer 22:4	5650
unto you all his *s* the prophets	Jer 25:4	5650
Pharaoh king of Egypt, and his *s*	Jer 25:19	5650
to the words of my *s* the prophets	Jer 26:5	5650
unto them by my *s* the prophets	Jer 29:19	5650
they turned, and caused the *s*	Jer 34:11	5650
them into subjection for *s*	Jer 34:11	5650
subjection, to be unto you for *s*	Jer 34:16	5650
unto you all my *s* the prophets	Jer 35:15	5650
nor any of his *s* that heard all	Jer 36:24	5650
seed and his *s* for their iniquity	Jer 36:31	5650
But neither he, nor his *s*	Jer 37:2	5650
against thee, or against thy *s*	Jer 37:18	5650
unto you all my *s* the prophets	Jer 44:4	5650
and into the hand of his *s*	Jer 46:26	5650
S have ruled over us	Lam 5:8	5650
by my *s* the prophets of Israel	Eze 38:17	5650
his inheritance to one of his *s*	Eze 46:17	5650
Prove thy *s*, I beseech thee, ten	Dan 1:12	5650
and as thou seest, deal with thy *s*	Dan 1:13	5650
tell thy *s* the dream, and we will	Dan 2:4	5649
Let the king tell his *s* the dream	Dan 2:7	5649
ye *s* of the most high God, come	Dan 3:26	5649
delivered his *s* that trusted in	Dan 3:28	5649
hearkened unto thy *s* the prophets	Dan 9:6	5650
before us by his *s* the prophets	Dan 9:10	5650
And also upon the *s* and upon the	Joel 2:29	5650
secret unto his *s* the prophets	Amos 3:7	5650
thee out of the house of *s*	Mic 6:4	5650
I commanded my *s* the prophets	Zec 1:6	5650
they shall be a spoil to their *s*	Zec 2:9	5647
So the *s* of the householder came	Mt 13:27	*1401*
The *s* said unto him, Wilt thou	Mt 13:28	*1401*
And said unto his *s*, This is John	Mt 14:2	*1401*
which would take account of his *s*	Mt 18:23	*1401*
he sent his *s* to the husbandmen,	Mt 21:34	*1401*
And the husbandmen took his *s*	Mt 21:35	*1401*
he sent other *s* more than the	Mt 21:36	*1401*
sent forth his *s* to call them	Mt 22:3	*1401*
Again, he sent forth other *s*	Mt 22:4	*1401*
And the remnant took his *s*	Mt 22:6	*1401*
Then saith he to his *s*, The	Mt 22:8	*1401*
So those *s* went out into the	Mt 22:10	*1401*
Then said the king to the *s*	Mt 22:13	*1401*
far country, who called his own *s*	Mt 25:14	*1401*
time the lord of those *s* cometh	Mt 25:19	*1401*
and went in, and sat with the *s*	Mt 26:58	5257
in the ship with the hired *s*	Mk 1:20	*341*
house, and gave authority to his *s*	Mk 13:34	*1401*
and he sat with the *s*, and warmed	Mk 14:54	5257
the *s* did strike him with the	Mk 14:65	5257
Blessed are those *s*, whom the	Lk 12:37	*1401*
find them so, blessed are those *s*	Lk 12:38	*1401*
How many hired *s* of my father's	Lk 15:17	*3407*
make me as one of thy hired *s*	Lk 15:19	*3407*
But the father said to his *s*	Lk 15:22	*1401*
And he called one of the *s*	Lk 15:26	*3816*
you, say, We are unprofitable *s*	Lk 17:10	*1401*
And he called his ten *s*, and	Lk 19:13	*1401*
these *s* to be called unto him	Lk 19:15	*1401*
His mother saith unto the *s*	Jn 2:5	*1249*
(but the *s* which drew the water	Jn 2:9	*1249*
his *s* met him, and told him,	Jn 4:51	*1401*
Henceforth I call you not *s*	Jn 15:15	*1401*
And the *s* and officers stood there,	Jn 18:18	*1401*
One of the *s* of the high priest,	Jn 18:26	*1401*
this world, then would my *s* fight	Jn 18:36	5257

And on my *s* and on my handmaidens ...	Acts 2:18	1401
and grant unto thy *s*, that with	Acts 4:29	1401
he called two of his household *s*	Acts 10:7	
These men are the *s* of the most	Acts 16:17	1401
ye yield yourselves *s* to obey	Rom 6:16	1401
his *s* ye are to whom ye obey	Rom 6:16	1401
that ye were the *s* of sin	Rom 6:17	1401
ye became the *s* of righteousness	Rom 6:18	1402
your members *s* to uncleanness	Rom 6:19	1401
s to righteousness unto holiness	Rom 6:19	1401
For when ye were the *s* of sin	Rom 6:20	1401
free from sin, and become *s* to God	Rom 6:22	1402
be not ye the *s* of men	1Cor 7:23	1401
ourselves your *s* for Jesus' sake	2Cor 4:5	1401
S, be obedient to them that are	Eph 6:5	1401
but as the *s* of Christ, doing the	Eph 6:6	1401
the *s* of Jesus Christ, to all the	Phil 1:1	1401
S, obey in all things your	Col 3:22	1401
give unto your *s* that which is	Col 4:1	1401
Let as many *s* as are under the	1Ti 6:1	1401
Exhort *s* to be obedient unto	Titus 2:9	1401
but as the *s* of God	1Pet 2:16	1401
S, be subject to your masters	1Pet 2:18	3610
are the *s* of corruption	2Pet 2:19	1401
to shew unto his *s* things which	Rev 1:1	1401
teach and to seduce my *s* to commit	Rev 2:20	1401
till we have sealed the *s* of our	Rev 7:3	1401
declared to his *s* the prophets	Rev 10:7	1401
reward unto thy *s* the prophets	Rev 11:18	1401
the blood of his *s* at her hand	Rev 19:2	1401
Praise our God, all ye his *s*	Rev 19:5	1401
and his *s* shall serve him	Rev 22:3	1401
s the things which must shortly	Rev 22:6	1401

SERVANTS'

Thy *s* trade hath been about	Gen 46:34	5650
of Pharaoh, and into his *s* houses	Ex 8:24	5650
Return for thy *s* sake, the tribes	Is 63:17	5650
so will I do for my *s* sakes	Is 65:8	5650

SERVE

is not theirs, and shall *s* them	Gen 15:13	5647
that nation, whom they shall *s*	Gen 15:14	5647
and the elder shall *s* the younger	Gen 25:23	5647
Let people *s* thee, and nations bow	Gen 27:29	5647
thou live, and shalt *s* thy brother	Gen 27:40	5647
thou therefore *s* me for nought	Gen 29:15	5647
I will *s* thee seven years for	Gen 29:18	5647
did not I *s* with thee for Rachel	Gen 29:25	5647
the service which thou shalt *s*	Gen 29:27	5647
of Israel to *s* with rigour	Ex 1:13	5647
service, wherein they made them *s*	Ex 1:14	5647
ye shall *s* God upon this mountain	Ex 3:12	5647
Let my son go, that he may *s* me	Ex 4:23	5647
that they may *s* me in the	Ex 7:16	5647
my people go, that they may *s* me	Ex 8:1	5647
my people go, that they may *s* me	Ex 8:20	5647
my people go, that they may *s* me	Ex 9:1	5647
my people go, that they may *s* me	Ex 9:13	5647
my people go, that they may *s* me	Ex 10:3	5647
that they may *s* the LORD their	Ex 10:7	5647
them, Go, *s* the LORD your God	Ex 10:8	5647
ye that are men, and *s* the LORD	Ex 10:11	5647
Moses, and said, Go ye, *s* the LORD	Ex 10:24	5647
we take to *s* the LORD our God	Ex 10:26	5647
not with what we must *s* the LORD	Ex 10:26	5647
s the LORD, as ye have said	Ex 12:31	5647
that we may *s* the Egyptians	Ex 14:12	5647
better for us to *s* the Egyptians	Ex 14:12	5647
down thyself to them, nor *s* them	Ex 20:5	5647
servant, six years he shall *s*	Ex 21:2	5647
and he shall *s* him for ever	Ex 21:6	5647
nor *s* them, nor do after their	Ex 23:24	5647
ye shall *s* the LORD your God, and	Ex 23:25	5647
for if thou *s* their gods, it will	Ex 23:33	5647
compel him to *s* as a bondservant	Lev 25:39	5656
shall *s* thee unto the year of	Lev 25:40	5647
families of the Gershonites, to *s*	Num 4:24	5647
so shall they *s*	Num 4:26	5647
thereof, and shall *s* no more	Num 8:25	5647
and ye shall *s*	Num 18:7	5647
for their service which they *s*	Num 18:21	5647
s them, which the LORD thy God	Deut 4:19	5647
And there ye shall *s* gods, the	Deut 4:28	5647
thyself unto them, nor *s* them	Deut 5:9	5647
s him, and shalt swear by his name	Deut 6:13	5647
me, that they may *s* other gods	Deut 7:4	5647
neither shalt thou *s* their gods	Deut 7:16	5647
s them, and worship them, I	Deut 8:19	5647
to *s* the LORD thy God with all	Deut 10:12	5647
him shalt thou *s*, and to him shalt	Deut 10:20	5647
to *s* him with all your heart and	Deut 11:13	5647

s other gods, and worship them	Deut 11:16	5647
did these nations *s* their gods	Deut 12:30	5647
hast not known, and let us *s* them	Deut 13:2	5647
obey his voice, and ye shall *s* him	Deut 13:4	5647
s other gods, which thou hast not	Deut 13:6	5647
s other gods, which ye have not	Deut 13:13	5647
unto thee, and *s* thee six years	Deut 15:12	5647
unto thee, and they shall *s* thee	Deut 20:11	5647
to go after other gods to *s* them	Deut 28:14	5647
and there shalt thou *s* other gods	Deut 28:36	5647
Therefore shalt thou *s* thine	Deut 28:48	5647
and there thou shalt *s* other gods	Deut 28:64	5647
s the gods of these nations	Deut 29:18	5647
and worship other gods, and *s* them	Deut 30:17	5647
s them, and provoke me, and break	Deut 31:20	5647
unto this day, and *s* under tribute	Josh 16:10	5647
to *s* him with all your heart and	Josh 22:5	5647
to swear by them, neither *s* them	Josh 23:7	5647
s him in sincerity and in truth	Josh 24:14	5647
and *s* ye the LORD	Josh 24:14	5647
seem evil unto you to *s* the LORD	Josh 24:15	5647
you this day whom ye will *s*	Josh 24:15	5647
and my house, we will *s* the LORD	Josh 24:15	5647
forsake the LORD, to *s* other gods	Josh 24:16	5647
therefore will we also *s* the LORD	Josh 24:18	5647
the people, Ye cannot *s* the LORD	Josh 24:19	5647
s strange gods, then he will turn	Josh 24:20	5647
but we will *s* the LORD	Josh 24:21	5647
chosen you the LORD, to *s* him	Josh 24:22	5647
The LORD our God will we *s*	Josh 24:24	5647
in following other gods to *s* them	Judg 2:19	5647
is Shechem, that we should *s* him	Judg 9:28	5647
s the men of Hamor the father of	Judg 9:28	5647
for why should we *s* him	Judg 9:28	5647
Abimelech, that we should *s* him	Judg 9:38	5647
unto the LORD, and *s* him only	1Sa 7:3	5647
that thou do as occasion *s* thee	1Sa 10:7	5647
with us, and we will *s* thee	1Sa 11:1	5647
of our enemies, and we will *s* thee	1Sa 12:10	5647
s him, and obey his voice, and not	1Sa 12:14	5647
but *s* the LORD with all your	1Sa 12:20	5647
s him in truth with all your	1Sa 12:24	5647
shall ye be our servants, and *s* us	1Sa 17:9	5647
LORD, saying, Go, *s* other gods	1Sa 26:19	5647
Jerusalem, then I will *s* the LORD	2Sa 15:8	5647
And again, whom should I *s*	2Sa 16:19	5647
should I not *s* in the presence of	2Sa 16:19	5647
which I knew not shall *s* me	2Sa 22:44	5647
s other gods, and worship them	1Kin 9:6	5647
us, lighter, and we will *s* thee	1Kin 12:4	5647
people this day, and wilt *s* them	1Kin 12:7	5647
but Jehu shall *s* him much	2Kin 10:18	5647
nor *s* them, nor sacrifice to them	2Kin 17:35	5647
land, and *s* the king of Babylon	2Kin 25:24	5647
s him with a perfect heart and	1Chr 28:9	5647
s other gods, and worship them	2Chr 7:19	5647
he put upon us, and we will *s* thee	2Chr 10:4	5647
to *s* him, and that ye should	2Chr 29:11	8334
s the LORD your God, that the	2Chr 30:8	5647
commanded Judah to *s* the LORD God	2Chr 33:16	5647
that were present in Israel to *s*	2Chr 34:33	5647
even to *s* the LORD their God	2Chr 34:33	5647
s now the LORD your God, and his	2Chr 35:3	5647
Almighty, that we should *s* him	Job 21:15	5647
s him, they shall spend their	Job 36:11	5647
the unicorn be willing to *s* thee	Job 39:9	5647
S the LORD with fear, and rejoice	Ps 2:11	5647
whom I have not known shall *s* me	Ps 18:43	5647
A seed shall *s* him	Ps 22:30	5647
all nations shall *s* him	Ps 72:11	5647
be all they that *s* graven images	Ps 97:7	5647
S the LORD with gladness	Ps 100:2	5647
in a perfect way, he shall *s* me	Ps 101:6	8334
and the kingdoms, to *s* the LORD	Ps 102:22	5647
wherein thou wast made to *s*	Is 14:3	5647
shall *s* with the Assyrians	Is 19:23	5647
caused thee to *s* with an offering	Is 43:23	5647
hast made me to *s* with thy sins	Is 43:24	5647
to *s* him, and to love the name of	Is 56:6	8334
that will not *s* thee shall perish	Is 60:12	5647
so shall ye *s* strangers in a land	Jer 5:19	5647
went after other gods to *s* them	Jer 11:10	5647
to *s* them, and to worship them,	Jer 13:10	5647
there shall ye *s* other gods day	Jer 16:13	5647
I will cause thee to *s* thine	Jer 17:4	5647
go not after other gods to *s* them	Jer 25:6	5647
these nations shall *s* the king of	Jer 25:11	5647
great kings shall *s* themselves of	Jer 25:14	5647
field have I given also to *s* him	Jer 27:6	5647
And all nations shall *s* him	Jer 27:7	5647
kings shall *s* themselves of him	Jer 27:7	5647

kingdom which will not s the same	Jer 27:8	5647
Ye shall not s the king of	Jer 27:9	5647
s him, those will I let remain	Jer 27:11	5647
s him and his people, and live	Jer 27:12	5647
will not s the king of Babylon	Jer 27:13	5647
Ye shall not s the king of	Jer 27:14	5647
s the king of Babylon, and live	Jer 27:17	5647
that they may s Nebuchadnezzar	Jer 28:14	5647
and they shall s him	Jer 28:14	5647
shall no more s themselves of him	Jer 30:8	5647
But they shall s the LORD their	Jer 30:9	5647
none should s himself of them	Jer 34:9	5647
that none should s themselves of	Jer 34:10	5647
go not after other gods to s them	Jer 35:15	5647
Fear not to s the Chaldeans	Jer 40:9	5647
s the king of Babylon, and it	Jer 40:9	5647
at Mizpah to s the Chaldeans	Jer 40:10	5975,6440
to s other gods, whom they knew	Jer 44:3	5647
the countries, to s wood and stone	Eze 20:32	8334
s ye every one his idols, and	Eze 20:39	5647
all of them in the land, s me	Eze 20:40	5647
s a great service against Tyrus	Eze 29:18	5647
food unto them that s the city	Eze 48:18	5647
they that s the city shall s	Eze 48:19	5647
they s not thy gods, nor worship	Dan 3:12	6399
and Abed-nego, do not ye s my gods	Dan 3:14	6399
our God whom we s is able to	Dan 3:17	6399
king, that we will not s thy gods	Dan 3:18	6399
might not s nor worship any god	Dan 3:28	6399
and languages, should s him	Dan 7:14	6399
kingdom, and all dominions shall s	Dan 7:27	6399
to s him with one consent	Zeph 3:9	5647
Ye have said, It is vain to s God	Mal 3:14	5647
thy God, and him only shalt thou s	Mt 4:10	*3000*
No man can s two masters	Mt 6:24	*1398*
Ye cannot s God and mammon	Mt 6:24	*1398*
enemies might s him without fear	Lk 1:74	*3000*
thy God, and him only shalt thou s	Lk 4:8	*3000*
my sister hath left me to s alone	Lk 10:40	*1247*
and will come forth and s them	Lk 12:37	*1247*
Lo, these many years do I s thee	Lk 15:29	*1398*
No servant can s two masters	Lk 16:13	*1398*
Ye cannot s God and mammon	Lk 16:13	*1398*
s me, till I have eaten and	Lk 17:8	*1247*
that is chief, as he that doth s	Lk 22:26	*1247*
If any man s me, let him follow	Jn 12:26	*1247*
if any man s me, him will my	Jn 12:26	*1247*
the word of God, and s tables	Acts 6:2	*1247*
come forth, and s me in this place	Acts 7:7	*3000*
of God, whose I am, and whom I s	Acts 27:23	*3000*
whom I s with my spirit in the	Rom 1:9	*3000*
henceforth we should not s sin	Rom 6:6	*1398*
that we should s in newness of	Rom 7:6	*1398*
mind I myself s the law of God	Rom 7:25	*1398*
The elder shall s the younger	Rom 9:12	*1398*
For they that are such s not our	Rom 16:18	*1398*
flesh, but by love s one another	Gal 5:13	*1398*
for ye s the Lord Christ	Col 3:24	*1398*
to God from idols to s the living	1Th 1:9	*1398*
whom I s from my forefathers with	2Ti 1:3	*3000*
Who s unto the example and shadow	Heb 8:5	*3000*
dead works to s the living God	Heb 9:14	*3000*
whereby we may s God acceptably	Heb 12:28	*3000*
to eat which s the tabernacle	Heb 13:10	*3000*
s him day and night in his temple	Rev 7:15	*3000*
and his servants shall s him	Rev 22:3	*3000*

SERVED

Twelve years they s Chedorlaomer	Gen 14:4	5647
Jacob s seven years for Rachel	Gen 29:20	5647
s with him yet seven other years	Gen 29:30	5647
children, for whom I have s thee	Gen 30:26	5647
Thou knowest how I have s thee	Gen 30:29	5647
all my power I have s your father	Gen 31:6	5647
I s thee fourteen years for thy	Gen 31:41	5647
grace in his sight, and he s him	Gen 39:4	8334
Joseph with them, and he s them	Gen 40:4	8334
ye shall possess s their gods	Deut 12:2	5647
s other gods, and worshipped them	Deut 17:3	5647
s other gods, and worshipped them	Deut 29:26	5647
s other gods, and bowed yourselves	Josh 23:16	5647
and they s other gods	Josh 24:2	5647
the gods which your fathers s on	Josh 24:14	5647
the gods which your fathers s	Josh 24:15	5647
Israel s the LORD all the days of	Josh 24:31	5647
the people s the LORD all the	Judg 2:7	5647
sight of the LORD, and s Baalim	Judg 2:11	5647
the LORD, and s Baal and Ashtaroth	Judg 2:13	5647
to their sons, and s their gods	Judg 3:6	5647
God, and s Baalim and the groves	Judg 3:7	5647
and the children of Israel s	Judg 3:8	5647

So the children of Israel s Eglon	Judg 3:14	5647
unto him, Why hast thou s us thus	Judg 8:1	6213
s Baalim, and Ashtaroth, and the	Judg 10:6	5647
and forsook the LORD, and s not him	Judg 10:6	5647
our God, and also s Baalim	Judg 10:10	5647
have forsaken me, and s other gods	Judg 10:13	5647
from among them, and s the LORD	Judg 10:16	5647
and Ashtaroth, and s the LORD only	1Sa 7:4	5647
s other gods, so do they also	1Sa 8:8	5647
have s Baalim and Ashtaroth	1Sa 12:10	5647
made peace with Israel, and s them	2Sa 10:19	5647
as I have s in thy father's	2Sa 16:19	5647
s Solomon all the days of his	1Kin 4:21	5647
have worshipped them, and s them	1Kin 9:9	5647
s Baal, and worshipped him	1Kin 16:31	5647
For he s Baal, and worshipped him,	1Kin 22:53	5647
unto them, Ahab s Baal a little	2Kin 10:18	5647
For they s idols, whereof the	2Kin 17:12	5647
all the host of heaven, and s Baal	2Kin 17:16	5647
s their own gods, after the	2Kin 17:33	5647
s their graven images, both their	2Kin 17:41	5647
the king of Assyria, and s him not	2Kin 18:7	5647
all the host of heaven, and s them	2Kin 21:3	5647
s the idols that his father	2Kin 21:21	5647
the idols that his father s	2Kin 21:21	5647
and told David how the men were s	1Chr 19:5	
their officers that s the king in	1Chr 27:1	8334
and worshipped them, and s them	2Chr 7:22	5647
fathers, and s groves and idols	2Chr 24:18	5647
all the host of heaven, and s them	2Chr 33:3	5647
his father had made, and s them	2Chr 33:22	5647
For they have not s thee in their	Neh 9:35	5647
the seven chamberlains that s in	Est 1:10	8334
And they s their idols	Ps 106:36	5647
rewardeth thee as thou hast s us	Ps 137:8	1580
king himself is s by the field	Eccl 5:9	5647
s strange gods in your land, so	Jer 5:19	5647
have loved, and whom they have s	Jer 8:2	5647
after other gods, and have s them	Jer 16:11	5647
worshipped other gods, and s them	Jer 22:9	5647
when he hath s thee six years,	Jer 34:14	5647
which s the king of Babylon, into	Jer 52:12	5975,6440
service that he had s against it	Eze 29:18	5647
labour wherewith he s against it	Eze 29:20	5647
those that s themselves of them	Eze 34:27	5647
Israel s for a wife, and for a	Hos 12:12	5647
but s God with fastings and	Lk 2:37	*3000*
and Martha s	Jn 12:2	*1247*
after he had s his own generation	Acts 13:36	*5256*
s the creature more than the	Rom 1:25	*3000*
he hath s with me in the gospel	Phil 2:22	*1398*

SERVEDST

Because thou s not the LORD thy	Deut 28:47	5647

SERVEST

Thy God whom thou s continually	Dan 6:16	6399
whom thou s continually, able to	Dan 6:20	6399

SERVETH

thereof, and all that s thereto	Num 3:36	5656
spareth his own son that s him	Mal 3:17	5647
s God and him that s him not	Mal 3:18	5647
sitteth at meat, or he that s	Lk 22:27	*1247*
but I am among you as he that s	Lk 22:27	*1247*
s Christ is acceptable to God	Rom 14:18	*1398*
but prophesying s not for them	1Cor 14:22	
Wherefore then s the law	Gal 3:19	

SERVICE

give thee this also for the s	Gen 29:27	5656
for thou knowest my s which I	Gen 30:26	5656
in all manner of s in the field	Ex 1:14	5656
all their s, wherein they made	Ex 1:14	5656
that ye shall keep this s	Ex 12:25	5656
unto you, What mean ye by this s	Ex 12:26	5656
shalt keep this s in this month	Ex 13:5	5656
tabernacle in all the s thereof	Ex 27:19	5656
the s of the tabernacle of the	Ex 30:16	5656
And the cloths of s, and the holy	Ex 31:10	8278
The cloths of s, to do s in	Ex 35:19	8278
to do s in the holy place, the	Ex 35:19	8334
congregation, and for all his s	Ex 35:21	5656
wood for any work of the s	Ex 35:24	5656
work for the s of the sanctuary	Ex 36:1	5656
work for the s of the sanctuary	Ex 36:3	5656
than enough for the s of the work	Ex 36:5	5656
for the s of the Levites, by the	Ex 38:21	5656
and scarlet, they made cloths of s	Ex 39:1	8278
to do s in the holy place, and	Ex 39:1	8334
of the s of the tabernacle	Ex 39:40	5656
The cloths of s to do	Ex 39:41	8278
to do s in the holy place	Ex 39:41	8334

S

to do the *s* of the tabernacle.................Num 3:7	5656
to do the *s* of the tabernacle.................Num 3:8	5656
cords of it for all the *s* thereof...............Num 3:26	5656
the hanging, and all the *s* thereof..........Num 3:31	5656
This shall be the *s* of the sons................Num 4:4	5656
appoint them every one to his *s*............Num 4:19	5656
that enter in to perform the *s*................Num 4:23	5656
This is the *s* of the families of..............Num 4:24	5656
and all the instruments of their *s*.........Num 4:26	5656
his sons shall be all the *s* of.................Num 4:27	5656
their burdens, and in all their *s*............Num 4:27	5656
This is the *s* of the families of..............Num 4:28	5656
one that entereth into the *s*..................Num 4:30	6635
according to all their *s* in the...............Num 4:31	5656
instruments, and with all their *s*...........Num 4:32	5656
This is the *s* of the families of..............Num 4:33	5656
Merari, according to all their *s*.............Num 4:33	5656
one that entereth into the *s*..................Num 4:35	6635
all that might do *s* in the.......................Num 4:37	5647
one that entereth into the *s*..................Num 4:39	6635
of all that might do *s* in the..................Num 4:41	5647
one that entereth into the *s*..................Num 4:43	6635
came to do the *s* of the ministry...........Num 4:47	5656
the *s* of the burden in the......................Num 4:47	5656
every one according to his *s*..................Num 4:49	5656
do the *s* of the tabernacle of the...........Num 7:5	5656
to every man according to his *s*.............Num 7:5	5656
of Gershon, according to their *s*............Num 7:7	5656
of Merari, according unto their *s*...........Num 7:8	5656
because the *s* of the sanctuary...............Num 7:9	5656
may execute the *s* of the LORD..............Num 8:11	5656
do the *s* of the tabernacle of the...........Num 8:15	5647
to do the *s* of the children of.................Num 8:19	5656
their *s* in the tabernacle of the..............Num 8:22	5656
the *s* of the tabernacle of the................Num 8:24	5656
cease waiting upon the *s* thereof...........Num 8:25	5656
keep the charge, and shall do no *s*........Num 8:26	5656
s of the tabernacle of the LORD.............Num 16:9	5656
for all the *s* of the tabernacle................Num 18:4	5656
to do the *s* of the tabernacle of.............Num 18:6	5656
office unto you as a *s* of gift..................Num 18:7	5656
for their *s* which they serve,..................Num 18:21	5656
even the *s* of the tabernacle of..............Num 18:21	5656
do the *s* of the tabernacle of the...........Num 18:23	5656
your *s* in the tabernacle of the...............Num 18:31	5656
that we might do the *s* of the................Josh 22:27	5656
thou the grievous *s* of thy father...........1Kin 12:4	5656
the *s* of song in the house of the...........1Chr 6:31	3027
appointed unto all manner of *s* of.........1Chr 6:48	5656
work of the *s* of the house of God.........1Chr 9:13	5656
were over the work of the *s*...................1Chr 9:19	5656
the *s* of the house of the LORD..............1Chr 23:24	5656
vessels of it for the *s* thereof................1Chr 23:26	5656
the *s* of the house of the LORD..............1Chr 23:28	5656
the work of the *s* of the house of..........1Chr 23:28	5656
in the *s* of the house of the LORD..........1Chr 23:32	5656
to their offices in their *s*.......................1Chr 24:3	5656
s to come into the house of the.............1Chr 24:19	5656
to the *s* of the sons of Asaph................1Chr 25:1	5656
workmen according to their *s* was.........1Chr 25:1	5656
for the *s* of the house of God,...............1Chr 25:6	5656
able men for strength for the *s*.............1Chr 26:8	5656
the LORD, and in the *s* of the king.........1Chr 26:30	5656
for all the work of the *s* of the..............1Chr 28:13	5656
for all the vessels of *s* in the.................1Chr 28:13	5656
instruments of all manner of *s*..............1Chr 28:14	5656
instruments of every kind of *s*...............1Chr 28:14	5656
the *s* of the house of the LORD..............1Chr 28:20	5656
for all the *s* of the house of God...........1Chr 28:21	5656
skilful man, for any manner of *s*............1Chr 28:21	5656
his *s* this day unto the LORD...................1Chr 29:5	3027
gave for the *s* of the house of...............1Chr 29:7	5656
courses of the priests to their *s*............2Chr 8:14	5656
that they may know my *s*, and the.........2Chr 12:8	5656
the *s* of the kingdoms of the.................2Chr 12:8	5656
of the *s* of the house of the LORD..........2Chr 24:12	5656
So the *s* of the house of the LORD..........2Chr 29:35	5656
every man according to his *s*.................2Chr 31:2	5656
his daily portion for their *s* in..............2Chr 31:16	5656
in the *s* of the house of God..................2Chr 31:21	5656
the work in any manner of *s*..................2Chr 34:13	5656
encouraged them to the *s* of the...........2Chr 35:2	5656
So the *s* was prepared, and the.............2Chr 35:10	5656
might not depart from their *s*................2Chr 35:15	5656
So all the *s* of the LORD was...................2Chr 35:16	5656
their courses, for the *s* of God...............Ezr 6:18	5673
for the *s* of the house of thy God..........Ezr 7:19	6402
for the *s* of the Levites, two..................Ezr 8:20	5656
for the *s* of the house of our God..........Neh 10:32	5656
cattle, and herb for the *s* of man...........Ps 104:14	5656
his neighbour's *s* without wages............Jer 22:13	5647

to serve a great *s* against Tyrus.............Eze 29:18	5656
for the *s* that he had served....................Eze 29:18	5656
the house, for all the *s* thereof...............Eze 44:14	5656
will think that he doeth God *s*..............Jn 16:2	2999
the *s* of God, and the promises...............Rom 9:4	2999
God, which is your reasonable *s*..............Rom 12:1	2999
that my *s* which I have for......................Rom 15:31	1248
s not only supplieth the want of..............2Cor 9:12	3009
taking wages of them, to do you *s*...........2Cor 11:8	1248
ye did *s* unto them which by...................Gal 4:8	1398
With good will doing *s*, as to the............Eph 6:7	1398
s of your faith, I joy, and.......................Phil 2:17	3009
supply your lack of *s* toward me............Phil 2:30	3009
but rather do them *s*, because................1Ti 6:2	1398
had also ordinances of divine *s*..............Heb 9:1	2999
accomplishing the *s* of God.....................Heb 9:6	2999
make him that did the *s* perfect..............Heb 9:9	3000
know thy works, and charity, and *s*.......Rev 2:19	1248

SERVILE

ye shall do no *s* work therein.................Lev 23:7	5656
ye shall do no *s* work therein.................Lev 23:8	5656
ye shall do no *s* work therein.................Lev 23:21	5656
Ye shall do no *s* work therein.................Lev 23:25	5656
ye shall do no *s* work therein.................Lev 23:35	5656
and ye shall do no *s* work therein...........Lev 23:36	5656
do no manner of *s* work therein.............Num 28:18	5656
ye shall do no *s* work.............................Num 28:25	5656
ye shall do no *s* work.............................Num 28:26	5656
ye shall do no *s* work.............................Num 29:1	5656
ye shall do no *s* work, and ye................Num 29:12	5656
ye shall do no *s* work therein.................Num 29:35	5656

SERVING

we have let Israel go from *s* us.............Ex 14:5	5647
to thee, in *s* thee six years....................Deut 15:18	5647
Martha was cumbered about much *s*.....Lk 10:40	1248
S the Lord with all humility of................Acts 20:19	1398
tribes, instantly *s* God day....................Acts 26:7	3000
fervent in spirit; *s* the Lord....................Rom 12:11	1398
s divers lusts and pleasures,.................Titus 3:3	1398

SERVITOR

his *s* said, What, should I set.................2Kin 4:43	8334

SERVITUDE

the grievous *s* of thy father....................2Chr 10:4	5656
affliction, and because of great *s*...........Lam 1:3	5656

SET See APPENDIX.

SETH *(seth)* See SHETH. *A son of Adam and Eve.*

bare a son, and called his name *S*.........Gen 4:25	8352
And to *S*, to him also there was..............Gen 4:26	8352
and called his name *S*............................Gen 5:3	8352
S were eight hundred years....................Gen 5:4	8352
S lived an hundred and five years,.........Gen 5:6	8352
S lived after he begat Enos eight............Gen 5:7	8352
all the days of *S* were nine.....................Gen 5:8	8352
of Enos, which was the son of *S*.............Lk 3:38	4589

SETHUR *(se'-thur) A spy sent to the Promised Land.*

of Asher, *S* the son of Michael.................Num 13:13	5639

SETTER

He seemeth to be a *s* forth of.................Acts 17:18	2604

SETTEST

thou *s* thine hand to in the land.............Deut 23:20	4916
all that thou *s* thine hand unto...............Deut 28:8	4916
in all that thou *s* thine hand..................Deut 28:20	4916
that thou *s* a watch over me..................Job 7:12	7760
thou *s* a print upon the heels of.............Job 13:27	7760
thou *s* a crown of pure gold on..............Ps 21:3	7896
s me before thy face for ever..................Ps 41:12	5324

SETTETH

And when the tabernacle *s* forward.......Num 1:51	5265
And when the camp *s* forward................Num 4:5	5265
is poor, and *s* his heart upon it..............Deut 24:15	5375
Cursed be he that *s* light by his..............Deut 27:16	7034
and *s* me upon my high places...............2Sa 22:34	5975
He *s* an end to darkness, and.................Job 28:3	7760
feet, and *s* me upon my high places.......Ps 18:33	5975
he *s* himself in a way that is not............Ps 36:4	3320
his strength *s* fast the mountains..........Ps 65:6	3559
God *s* the solitary in families.................Ps 68:6	3427
putteth down one, and *s* up another......Ps 75:7	7311
as the flame *s* the mountains on............Ps 83:14	3857
Yet *s* he the poor on high from...............Ps 107:41	
lay wait, as he that *s* snares..................Jer 5:26	7918
of Neriah *s* thee on against us................Jer 43:3	5496
that *s* up his idols in his heart................Eze 14:4	5927
s up his idols in his heart, and...............Eze 14:7	5927
he removeth kings, and *s* up kings.........Dan 2:21	6966
s up over it the basest of men...............Dan 4:17	6966

s him on a pinnacle of the temple........... Mt 4:5 — 2476
but s it on a candlestick, that .... Lk 8:16 — *2007*
s on fire the course of nature .... Jas 3:6 — 5394

SETTING See APPENDIX.

SETTINGS See APPENDIX.

SETTLE
But I will s him in mine house and .... 1Chr 17:14 — 5975
I will s you after your old........................ Eze 36:11 — 3427
the lower s shall be two cubits .... Eze 43:14 — 5835
from the lesser s even to the .... Eze 43:14 — 5835
greater s shall be four cubits .... Eze 43:14 — 5835
the s shall be fourteen cubits .... Eze 43:17 — 5835
and on the four corners of the s .... Eze 43:20 — 5835
corners of the s of the altar .... Eze 45:19 — 5835
S it therefore in your hearts, ... Lk 21:14 — *5087*
stablish, strengthen, s you..................... 1Pet 5:10 — 2311

SETTLED
a s place for thee to abide in.................. 1Kin 8:13 — 4349
he s his countenance stedfastly,............. 2Kin 8:11 — 5975
O LORD, thy word is s in heaven .... Ps 119:89 — 5324
Before the mountains were s .... Prov 8:25 — 2883
he hath s on his lees, and hath .... Jer 48:11 — 8252
the men that are s on their lees .... Zeph 1:12 — 7087
in the faith grounded and s .... Col 1:23 — *1476*

SETTLEST
thou s the furrows thereof .... Ps 65:10 — 5181

SEVEN
s years, and begat sons and................... Gen 5:7 — 7651
and s years, and begat Lamech .... Gen 5:25 — 7651
he begat Lamech s hundred eighty .... Gen 5:26 — 7651
s hundred seventy and s years................ Gen 5:31 — 7651
For yet s days, and I will cause .... Gen 7:4 — 7651
And it came to pass after s days .... Gen 7:10 — 7651
And he stayed yet other s days .... Gen 8:10 — 7651
And he stayed yet other s days .... Gen 8:12 — 7651
And in the second month, on the s .... Gen 8:14 — 7651
s years, and begat sons and................... Gen 11:21 — 7651
Abraham set s ewe lambs of the............. Gen 21:28 — 7651
What mean these s ewe lambs which .... Gen 21:29 — 7651
For these s ewe lambs shalt thou .... Gen 21:30 — 7651
And Sarah was an hundred and s.......... Gen 23:1 — 7651
an hundred and thirty and s years........ Gen 25:17 — 7651
I will serve thee s years for .... Gen 29:18 — 7651
Jacob served s years for Rachel .... Gen 29:20 — 7651
serve with me yet s other years .... Gen 29:27 — 7651
served with him yet s other years .... Gen 29:30 — 7651
pursued after him s days' journey .... Gen 31:23 — 7651
himself to the ground s times................. Gen 33:3 — 7651
of the river s well favoured kine............. Gen 41:2 — 7651
s other kine came up after them............. Gen 41:3 — 7651
did eat up the s well favoured .... Gen 41:4 — 7651
s ears of corn came up upon one........... Gen 41:5 — 7651
s thin ears and blasted with the............. Gen 41:6 — 7651
the s thin ears devoured the .... Gen 41:7 — 7651
thin ears devoured the s rank................. Gen 41:7 — 7651
came up out of the river s kine .... Gen 41:18 — 7651
s other kine came up after them,........... Gen 41:19 — 7651
did eat up the first s fat kine .... Gen 41:20 — 7651
s ears came up in one stalk, full .... Gen 41:22 — 7651
s ears, withered, thin, and .... Gen 41:23 — 7651
ears devoured the s good ears .... Gen 41:24 — 7651
The s good kine are s years .... Gen 41:26 — 7651
the s good ears are s years .... Gen 41:26 — 7651
the s thin and ill favoured kine .... Gen 41:27 — 7651
came up after them are s years............. Gen 41:27 — 7651
the s empty ears blasted with the .... Gen 41:27 — 7651
wind shall be s years of famine .... Gen 41:27 — 7651
there come s years of great .... Gen 41:29 — 7651
after them s years of famine .... Gen 41:30 — 7651
of Egypt in the s plenteous years........... Gen 41:34 — 7651
against the s years of famine .... Gen 41:36 — 7651
in the s plenteous years the................... Gen 41:47 — 7651
up all the food of the s years................. Gen 41:48 — 7651
the s years of plenteousness,................. Gen 41:53 — 7651
the s years of dearth began to .... Gen 41:54 — 7651
all the souls were s................................ Gen 46:25 — 7651
was an hundred forty and s years .... Gen 47:28 — 7651
a mourning for his father s days .... Gen 50:10 — 7651
priest of Midian had s daughters........... Ex 2:16 — 7651
were an hundred thirty and s years....... Ex 6:16 — 7651
an hundred and thirty and s years........ Ex 6:20 — 7651
s days were fulfilled, after that .... Ex 7:25 — 7651
S days shall ye eat unleavened............... Ex 12:15 — 7651
S days shall there be no leaven.............. Ex 12:19 — 7651
S days thou shalt eat unleavened .... Ex 13:6 — 7651
bread shall be eaten s days.................... Ex 13:7 — 7651
s days it shall be with his dam .... Ex 22:30 — 7651
shalt eat unleavened bread s days .... Ex 23:15 — 7651

shalt make the s lamps thereof............... Ex 25:37 — 7651
stead shall put them on s days .... Ex 29:30 — 7651
s days shalt thou consecrate them .... Ex 29:35 — 7651
S days thou shalt make an..................... Ex 29:37 — 7651
S days thou shalt eat unleavened .... Ex 34:18 — 7651
And he made his s lamps, and his......... Ex 37:23 — 7651
s hundred and thirty shekels, ... Ex 38:24 — 7651
talents, and a thousand s hundred .... Ex 38:25 — 7651
of the thousand s hundred seventy .... Ex 38:28 — 7651
the blood s times before the LORD........... Lev 4:6 — 7651
sprinkle it s times before the................. Lev 4:17 — 7651
thereof upon the altar s times .... Lev 8:11 — 7651
of the congregation in s days .... Lev 8:33 — 7651
for s days shall he consecrate .... Lev 8:33 — 7651
congregation day and night s days......... Lev 8:35 — 7651
then she shall be unclean s days .... Lev 12:2 — 7651
him that hath the plague s days............. Lev 13:4 — 7651
shall shut him up s days more .... Lev 13:5 — 7651
priest shall shut him up s days .... Lev 13:21 — 7651
priest shall shut him up s days .... Lev 13:26 — 7651
the plague of the scall s days .... Lev 13:31 — 7651
that hath the scall s days more.............. Lev 13:33 — 7651
up it that hath the plague s days........... Lev 13:50 — 7651
he shall shut it up s days more .... Lev 13:54 — 7651
cleansed from the leprosy s times .... Lev 14:7 — 7651
abroad out of his tent s days.................. Lev 14:8 — 7651
finger s times before the LORD................ Lev 14:16 — 7651
left hand s times before the LORD .... Lev 14:27 — 7651
and shut up the house s days................. Lev 14:38 — 7651
and sprinkle the house s times .... Lev 14:51 — 7651
himself s days for his cleansing.............. Lev 15:13 — 7651
she shall be put apart s days .... Lev 15:19 — 7651
him, he shall be unclean s days .... Lev 15:24 — 7651
shall number to herself s days .... Lev 15:28 — 7651
the blood with his finger s times .... Lev 16:14 — 7651
upon it with his finger s times............... Lev 16:19 — 7651
then it shall be s days under the............ Lev 22:27 — 7651
s days ye must eat unleavened .... Lev 23:6 — 7651
made by fire unto the LORD s days .... Lev 23:8 — 7651
s sabbaths shall be complete .... Lev 23:15 — 7651
s lambs without blemish of the .... Lev 23:18 — 7651
for s days unto the LORD .... Lev 23:34 — 7651
S days ye shall offer an offering............. Lev 23:36 — 7651
keep a feast unto the LORD s days .... Lev 23:39 — 7651
before the LORD your God s days .... Lev 23:40 — 7651
unto the LORD s days in the year .... Lev 23:41 — 7651
Ye shall dwell in booths s days .... Lev 23:42 — 7651
thou shalt number s sabbaths of............ Lev 25:8 — 7651
unto thee, s times s years .... Lev 25:8 — 7651
the space of the s sabbaths of................ Lev 25:8 — 7651
then I will punish you s times .... Lev 26:18 — 7651
I will bring s times more plagues .... Lev 26:21 — 7651
you yet s times for your sins .... Lev 26:24 — 7651
will chastise you s times for .... Lev 26:28 — 7651
s thousand and four hundred .... Num 1:31 — 7651
and two thousand and s hundred .... Num 1:39 — 7651
s thousand and four hundred .... Num 2:8 — 7651
and two thousand and s hundred .... Num 2:26 — 7651
s thousand and six hundred .... Num 2:31 — 7651
numbered of them were s thousand........ Num 3:22 — 7651
were two thousand s hundred .... Num 4:36 — 7651
the s lamps shall give light over .... Num 8:2 — 7651
should she not be ashamed s days .... Num 12:14 — 7651
be shut out from the camp s days......... Num 12:14 — 7651
was shut out from the camp s days .... Num 12:15 — 7651
(Now Hebron was built s years.............. Num 13:22 — 7651
s hundred, beside them that died .... Num 16:49 — 7651
of the congregation s times .... Num 19:4 — 7651
any man shall be unclean s days .... Num 19:11 — 7651
the tent, shall be unclean s days........... Num 19:14 — 7651
a grave, shall be unclean s days .... Num 19:16 — 7651
Balak, Build me here s altars .... Num 23:1 — 7651
me here s oxen and s rams.................... Num 23:1 — 7651
him, I have prepared s altars .... Num 23:4 — 7651
built s altars, and offered a .... Num 23:14 — 7651
Balak, Build me here s altars .... Num 23:29 — 7651
me here s bullocks and s rams .... Num 23:29 — 7651
thousand and s hundred and thirty .... Num 26:7 — 7651
and two thousand and s hundred .... Num 26:34 — 7651
thousand and a thousand s hundred ...... Num 26:51 — 7651
s lambs of the first year without .... Num 28:11 — 7651
s days shall unleavened bread be........... Num 28:17 — 7651
s lambs of the first year........................ Num 28:19 — 7651
lamb, throughout the s lambs .... Num 28:21 — 7651
daily, throughout the s days .... Num 28:24 — 7651
s lambs of the first year........................ Num 28:27 — 7651
one lamb, throughout the s lambs .... Num 28:29 — 7651
s lambs of the first year without .... Num 29:2 — 7651
one lamb, throughout the s lambs .... Num 29:4 — 7651
s lambs of the first year........................ Num 29:8 — 7651
one lamb, throughout the s lambs .... Num 29:10 — 7651

S

keep a feast unto the LORD *s* days	Num 29:12	7651
And on the seventh day *s* bullocks	Num 29:32	7651
s lambs of the first year without	Num 29:36	7651
ye abide without the camp *s* days	Num 31:19	7651
three hundred thousand and *s*	Num 31:36	7651
s thousand and five hundred sheep,	Num 31:43	7651
was sixteen thousand *s* hundred	Num 31:52	7651
s nations greater and mightier	Deut 7:1	7651
At the end of every *s* years thou	Deut 15:1	7651
s days shalt thou eat unleavened	Deut 16:3	7651
with thee in all thy coast *s* days	Deut 16:4	7651
S weeks shalt thou number unto	Deut 16:9	7651
begin to number the *s* weeks from	Deut 16:9	7651
the feast of tabernacles *s* days	Deut 16:13	7651
S days shalt thou keep a solemn	Deut 16:15	7651
way, and flee before thee *s* ways	Deut 28:7	7651
them, and flee *s* ways before them	Deut 28:25	7651
At the end of every *s* years	Deut 31:10	7651
s priests shall bear before the	Josh 6:4	7651
the ark *s* trumpets of rams' horns	Josh 6:4	7651
ye shall compass the city *s* times	Josh 6:4	7651
let *s* priests bear *s* trumpets	Josh 6:6	7651
the *s* priests bearing the *s*	Josh 6:8	7651
s priests bearing *s* trumpets	Josh 6:13	7651
after the same manner *s* times	Josh 6:15	7651
they compassed the city *s* times	Josh 6:15	7651
the children of Israel *s* tribes	Josh 18:2	7651
they shall divide it into *s* parts	Josh 18:5	7651
describe the land into *s* parts	Josh 18:6	7651
by cities into *s* parts in a book	Josh 18:9	7651
into the hand of Midian *s* years	Judg 6:1	7651
the second bullock of *s* years old	Judg 6:25	7651
s hundred shekels of gold	Judg 8:26	7651
And he judged Israel *s* years	Judg 12:9	7651
me within the *s* days of the feast	Judg 14:12	7651
And she wept before him the *s* days	Judg 14:17	7651
If they bind me with *s* green	Judg 16:7	7651
Philistines brought up to her *s*	Judg 16:8	7651
If thou weavest the *s* locks of my	Judg 16:13	7651
shave off the *s* locks of his head	Judg 16:19	7651
numbered *s* hundred chosen men	Judg 20:15	7651
all this people there were *s*	Judg 20:16	7651
is better to thee than *s* sons	Ruth 4:15	7651
so that the barren hath born *s*	1Sa 2:5	7651
of the Philistines *s* months	1Sa 6:1	7651
s days shalt thou tarry, till I	1Sa 10:8	7651
Give us *s* days' respite, that we	1Sa 11:3	7651
And he tarried *s* days, according	1Sa 13:8	7651
Jesse made *s* of his sons to pass	1Sa 16:10	7651
tree at Jabesh, and fasted *s* days	1Sa 31:13	7651
the house of Judah was *s* years	2Sa 2:11	7651
he reigned over Judah *s* years	2Sa 5:5	7651
s hundred horsemen, and twenty	2Sa 8:4	7651
David slew the men of *s* hundred	2Sa 10:18	7651
Let *s* men of his sons be	2Sa 21:6	7651
and they fell all *s* together	2Sa 21:9	7651
thirty and *s* in all	2Sa 23:39	7651
Shall *s* years of famine come unto	2Sa 24:13	7651
s years reigned he in Hebron, and	1Kin 2:11	7651
and the third was *s* cubits broad	1Kin 6:6	7651
So was he *s* years in building it	1Kin 6:38	7651
s for the one chapiter	1Kin 7:17	7651
and *s* for the other chapiter	1Kin 7:17	7651
s days and *s* days, even	1Kin 8:65	7651
And he had *s* hundred wives,	1Kin 11:3	7651
did Zimri reign *s* days in Tirzah	1Kin 16:15	7651
And he said, Go again *s* times	1Kin 18:43	7651
have left me *s* thousand in Israel	1Kin 19:18	7651
of Israel, being *s* thousand	1Kin 20:15	7651
one over against the other *s* days	1Kin 20:29	7651
s thousand of the men that were	1Kin 20:30	7651
a compass of *s* days' journey	2Kin 3:9	7651
he took with him *s* hundred men	2Kin 3:26	7651
and the child sneezed *s* times	2Kin 4:35	7651
Go and wash in Jordan *s* times	2Kin 5:10	7651
dipped himself *s* times in Jordan,	2Kin 5:14	7651
also come upon the land *s* years	2Kin 8:1	7651
land of the Philistines *s* years	2Kin 8:2	7651
came to pass at the *s* years' end	2Kin 8:3	7651
S years old was Jehoash when he	2Kin 11:21	7651
even *s* thousand, and craftsmen and	2Kin 24:16	7651
And it came to pass in the *s*	2Kin 25:27	7651
in the twelfth month, on the *s*	2Kin 25:27	7651
and there he reigned *s* years	1Chr 3:4	7651
Johanan, and Dalaiah, and Anani, *s*	1Chr 3:24	7651
and Jachan, and Zia, and Heber, *s*	1Chr 5:13	7651
four and forty thousand *s* hundred	1Chr 5:18	7651
fourscore and *s* thousand	1Chr 7:5	7651
and *s* hundred and threescore	1Chr 9:13	7651
were to come after *s* days from	1Chr 9:25	7651
oak in Jabesh, and fasted *s* days	1Chr 10:12	7651
s thousand and one hundred	1Chr 12:25	7651
were three thousand and *s* hundred	1Chr 12:27	7651
and spear thirty and *s* thousand	1Chr 12:34	7651
offered *s* bullocks and *s* rams	1Chr 15:26	7651
s thousand horsemen, and twenty	1Chr 18:4	7651
David slew of the Syrians *s*	1Chr 19:18	7651
s hundred, were officers among	1Chr 26:30	7651
s hundred chief fathers, whom	1Chr 26:32	7651
s thousand talents of refined	1Chr 29:4	7651
s years reigned he in Hebron, and	1Chr 29:27	7651
Solomon kept the feast *s* days	2Chr 7:8	7651
dedication of the altar *s* days	2Chr 7:9	7651
s days, and the feast *s* days	2Chr 7:9	7651
s rams, the same may be a priest	2Chr 13:9	7651
s hundred oxen and *s* thousand	2Chr 15:11	7651
s thousand and *s* hundred rams,	2Chr 17:11	7651
s thousand and *s* hundred he	2Chr 17:11	7651
Joash was *s* years old when he	2Chr 24:1	7651
s thousand and five hundred, that	2Chr 26:13	7651
And they brought *s* bullocks	2Chr 29:21	7651
s rams, and *s* lambs	2Chr 29:21	7651
s he goats, for a sin offering	2Chr 29:21	7651
bread *s* days with great gladness	2Chr 30:21	7651
eat throughout the feast *s* days	2Chr 30:22	7651
took counsel to keep other *s* days	2Chr 30:23	7651
they kept other *s* days with	2Chr 30:23	7651
bullocks and *s* thousand sheep	2Chr 30:24	7651
feast of unleavened bread *s* days	2Chr 35:17	7651
s hundred seventy and five	Ezr 2:5	7651
Zaccai, *s* hundred and threescore	Ezr 2:9	7651
s hundred and forty and three	Ezr 2:25	7651
and Ono, *s* hundred twenty and five	Ezr 2:33	7651
a thousand two hundred forty and *s*	Ezr 2:38	7651
of whom there were *s* thousand	Ezr 2:65	7651
three hundred thirty and *s*	Ezr 2:65	7651
horses were *s* hundred thirty	Ezr 2:66	7651
asses, six thousand *s* hundred	Ezr 2:67	7651
unleavened bread *s* days with joy	Ezr 6:22	7651
of his *s* counsellors, to enquire	Ezr 7:14	7655
s lambs, twelve he goats for a	Ezr 8:35	7651
Zaccai, *s* hundred and threescore	Neh 7:14	7651
six hundred threescore and *s*	Neh 7:18	7651
two thousand threescore and *s*	Neh 7:19	7651
Beeroth, *s* hundred forty and three	Neh 7:29	7651
and Ono, *s* hundred twenty and one	Neh 7:37	7651
a thousand two hundred forty and *s*	Neh 7:41	7651
of whom there were *s* thousand	Neh 7:67	7651
three hundred thirty and *s*	Neh 7:67	7651
horses, *s* hundred thirty and six	Neh 7:68	7651
six thousand *s* hundred and twenty	Neh 7:69	7651
threescore and *s* priests' garments	Neh 7:72	7651
And they kept the feast *s* days	Neh 8:18	7651
Ethiopia, over an hundred and *s*	Est 1:1	7651
s days, in the court of the	Est 1:5	7651
the *s* chamberlains that served in	Est 1:10	7651
the *s* princes of Persia and Media,	Est 1:14	7651
s maidens, which were meet to be	Est 2:9	7651
s provinces, unto every province	Est 8:9	7651
s provinces of the kingdom of	Est 9:30	7651
there were born unto him *s* sons	Job 1:2	7651
also was *s* thousand sheep	Job 1:3	7651
with him upon the ground *s* days	Job 2:13	7651
s nights, and none spake a word	Job 2:13	7651
in *s* there shall no evil touch	Job 5:19	7651
take unto you now *s* bullocks	Job 42:8	7651
s rams, and go to my servant Job,	Job 42:8	7651
He had also *s* sons and three	Job 42:13	7658
of earth, purified *s* times	Ps 12:6	7659
S times a day do I praise thee	Ps 119:164	7651
s are an abomination unto him	Prov 6:16	7651
she hath hewn out her *s* pillars	Prov 9:1	7651
For a just man falleth *s* times	Prov 24:16	7651
s men that can render a reason	Prov 26:16	7651
for there are *s* abominations in	Prov 26:25	7651
Give a portion to *s*, and also to	Eccl 11:2	7651
in that day *s* women shall take	Is 4:1	7651
shall smite it in the *s* streams	Is 11:15	7651
sevenfold, as the light of *s* days	Is 30:26	7651
She that hath borne *s* languisheth	Jer 15:9	7651
At the end of *s* years let ye go	Jer 34:14	7651
s men of them that were near the	Jer 52:25	7651
of the Jews *s* hundred forty	Jer 52:30	7651
And it came to pass in the *s*	Jer 52:31	7651
astonished among them *s* days	Eze 3:15	7651
came to pass at the end of *s* days	Eze 3:16	7651
And it came to pass in the *s*	Eze 29:17	7651
shall burn them with fire *s* years	Eze 39:9	7651
s months shall the house of	Eze 39:12	7651
after the end of *s* months shall	Eze 39:14	7651
they went up unto it by *s* steps	Eze 40:22	7651
there were *s* steps to go up to it	Eze 40:26	7651

the breadth of the door, *s* cubits	Eze 41:3	7651
S days shalt thou prepare every	Eze 43:25	7651
S days shall they purge the altar	Eze 43:26	7651
they shall reckon unto him *s* days	Eze 44:26	7651
the passover, a feast of *s* days	Eze 45:21	7651
s days of the feast he shall	Eze 45:23	7651
s bullocks and *s* rams without	Eze 45:23	7651
s rams without blemish daily the	Eze 45:23	7651
without blemish daily the *s* days	Eze 45:23	7651
like in the feast of the *s* days	Eze 45:25	7651
should heat the furnace one *s*	Dan 3:19	7655
let *s* times pass over him	Dan 4:16	7655
till *s* times pass over him	Dan 4:23	7655
s times shall pass over thee,	Dan 4:25	7655
s times pass over him,	Dan 4:32	7655
the Prince shall be *s* weeks	Dan 9:25	7651
Seek him that maketh the *s* stars	Amos 5:8	3598
we raise against him *s* shepherds	Mic 5:5	7651
upon one stone shall be *s* eyes	Zec 3:9	7651
his *s* lamps thereon	Zec 4:2	7651
and *s* pipes to the *s* lamps	Zec 4:2	7651
hand of Zerubbabel with those *s*	Zec 4:10	7651
taketh with himself *s* other	Mt 12:45	2033
And they said, *S*, and a few little	Mt 15:34	2033
And he took the *s* loaves and the	Mt 15:36	2033
meat that was left *s* baskets full	Mt 15:37	2033
Neither the *s* loaves of the four	Mt 16:10	2033
till *s* times	Mt 18:21	2034
say not unto thee, Until *s* times	Mt 18:22	2034
but, Until seventy times *s*	Mt 18:22	2033
Now there were with us *s* brethren	Mt 22:25	2033
whose wife shall she be of the *s*	Mt 22:28	2033
And they said, *S*	Mk 8:5	2033
and he took the *s* loaves, and gave	Mk 8:6	2033
meat that was left *s* baskets	Mk 8:8	2033
when the *s* among four thousand,	Mk 8:20	2033
And they said, *S*	Mk 8:20	2033
Now there were *s* brethren	Mk 12:20	2033
the *s* had her, and left no seed	Mk 12:22	2033
for the *s* had her to wife	Mk 12:23	2033
out of whom he had cast *s* devils	Mk 16:9	2033
s years from her virginity	Lk 2:36	2033
out of whom went *s* devils	Lk 8:2	2033
taketh to him *s* other spirits	Lk 11:26	2033
against thee *s* times in a day	Lk 17:4	2034
s times in a day turn again to	Lk 17:4	2034
There were therefore *s* brethren	Lk 20:29	2033
and in like manner the *s* also	Lk 20:31	2033
for *s* had her to wife	Lk 20:33	2033
among you *s* men of honest report	Acts 6:3	2033
when he had destroyed *s* nations	Acts 13:19	2033
there were *s* sons of one Sceva, a	Acts 19:14	2033
where we abode *s* days	Acts 20:6	2033
we tarried there *s* days	Acts 21:4	2033
which was one of the *s*	Acts 21:8	2033
when the *s* days were almost ended	Acts 21:27	2033
desired to tarry with them *s* days	Acts 28:14	2033
reserved to myself *s* thousand men	Rom 11:4	2035
they were compassed about *s* days	Heb 11:30	2033
John to the *s* churches which are	Rev 1:4	2033
from the *s* Spirits which are	Rev 1:4	2033
send it unto the *s* churches which	Rev 1:11	2033
I saw *s* golden candlesticks	Rev 1:12	2033
And in the midst of the *s*	Rev 1:13	2033
he had in his right hand *s* stars	Rev 1:16	2033
The mystery of the *s* stars which	Rev 1:20	2033
the *s* golden candlesticks	Rev 1:20	2033
The *s* stars are the angels of the	Rev 1:20	2033
are the angels of the *s* churches	Rev 1:20	2033
the *s* candlesticks which thou	Rev 1:20	2033
thou sawest are the *s* churches	Rev 1:20	2033
the *s* stars in his right hand	Rev 2:1	2033
of the *s* golden candlesticks	Rev 2:1	2033
he that hath the *s* Spirits of God	Rev 3:1	2033
Spirits of God, and the *s* stars	Rev 3:1	2033
there were *s* lamps of fire	Rev 4:5	2033
which are the *s* Spirits of God	Rev 4:5	2033
the backside, sealed with *s* seals	Rev 5:1	2033
to loose the *s* seals thereof	Rev 5:5	2033
it had been slain, having *s* horns	Rev 5:6	2033
horns and *s* eyes, which are	Rev 5:6	2033
which are the *s* Spirits of God	Rev 5:6	2033
I saw the *s* angels which stood	Rev 8:2	2033
and to them were given *s* trumpets	Rev 8:2	2033
the *s* angels which had the *s*	Rev 8:6	2033
s thunders uttered their voices	Rev 10:3	2033
when the *s* thunders had uttered	Rev 10:4	2033
which the *s* thunders uttered	Rev 10:4	2033
were slain of men *s* thousand	Rev 11:13	2033
great red dragon, having *s* heads	Rev 12:3	2033
horns, and *s* crowns upon his heads	Rev 12:3	2033

up out of the sea, having *s* heads	Rev 13:1	2033
s angels having the *s* last	Rev 15:1	2033
the *s* angels came out of the	Rev 15:6	2033
the temple, having the *s* plagues	Rev 15:6	2033
gave unto the *s* angels *s*	Rev 15:7	2033
till the *s* plagues of the *s*	Rev 15:8	2033
the temple saying to the *s* angels	Rev 16:1	2033
there came one of the *s* angels	Rev 17:1	2033
angels which had the *s* vials	Rev 17:1	2033
of blasphemy, having *s* heads	Rev 17:3	2033
her, which hath the *s* heads	Rev 17:7	2033
The *s* heads are *s* mountains,	Rev 17:9	2033
And there are *s* kings	Rev 17:10	2033
he is the eighth, and is of the *s*	Rev 17:11	2033
the *s* angels which had the	Rev 21:9	2033
s vials full of the last	Rev 21:9	2033

SEVENFOLD

vengeance shall be taken on him *s*	Gen 4:15	7659
If Cain shall be avenged *s*	Gen 4:24	7659
truly Lamech seventy and *s*	Gen 4:24	7659
render unto our neighbours *s* into	Ps 79:12	7659
he be found, he shall restore *s*	Prov 6:31	7659
the light of the sun shall be *s*	Is 30:26	7659

SEVENS

thou shalt take to thee by *s*	Gen 7:2	7651
Of fowls also of the air by *s*	Gen 7:3	7651

SEVENTEEN

being *s* years old, was feeding	Gen 37:2	7651,6240
in the land of Egypt *s* years	Gen 47:28	7651,6240
thereof, even threescore and *s* men	Judg 8:14	7657,7651
he reigned *s* years in Jerusalem,	1Kin 14:21	7651,6240
in Samaria, and reigned *s* years	2Kin 13:1	7651,6240
were *s* thousand and two hundred	1Chr 7:11	7651,6240
he reigned *s* years in Jerusalem,	2Chr 12:13	7651,6240
of Harim, a thousand and *s*	Ezr 2:39	7651,6240
of Harim, a thousand and *s*	Neh 7:42	7651,6240
money, even *s* shekels of silver	Jer 32:9	7651,6240

SEVENTEENTH

the *s* day of the month, the same	Gen 7:11	7651,6240
on the *s* day of the month, upon	Gen 8:4	7651,6240
over Israel in Samaria the *s* year	1Kin 22:51	7651,6240
In the *s* year of Pekah the son of	2Kin 16:1	7651,6240
The *s* to Hezir, the eighteenth to	1Chr 24:15	7651,6240
The *s* to Joshbekashah, he, his	1Chr 25:24	7651,6240

SEVENTH

on the *s* day God ended his work	Gen 2:2	7637
he rested on the *s* day from all	Gen 2:2	7637
And God blessed the *s* day, and	Gen 2:3	7637
And the ark rested in the *s* month	Gen 8:4	7637
the first day until the *s* day	Ex 12:15	7637
in the *s* day there shall be an	Ex 12:16	7637
in the *s* day shall be a feast to	Ex 13:6	7637
but on the *s* day, which is the	Ex 16:26	7637
people on the *s* day for to gather	Ex 16:27	7637
go out of his place on the *s* day	Ex 16:29	7637
So the people rested on the *s* day	Ex 16:30	7637
But the *s* day is the sabbath of	Ex 20:10	7637
in them is, and rested the *s* day	Ex 20:11	7637
in the *s* he shall go out free for	Ex 21:2	7637
But the *s* year thou shalt let it	Ex 23:11	7637
on the *s* day thou shalt rest	Ex 23:12	7637
the *s* day he called unto Moses	Ex 24:16	7637
but in the *s* is the sabbath of	Ex 31:15	7637
on the *s* day he rested, and was	Ex 31:17	7637
but on the *s* day thou shalt rest	Ex 34:21	7637
but on the *s* day there shall be	Ex 35:2	7637
shall look on him the *s* day	Lev 13:5	7637
shall look on him again the *s* day	Lev 13:6	7637
shall look upon him the *s* day	Lev 13:27	7637
in the *s* day the priest shall	Lev 13:32	7637
in the *s* day the priest shall	Lev 13:34	7637
look on the plague on the *s* day	Lev 13:51	7637
But it shall be on the *s* day	Lev 14:9	7637
priest shall come again the *s* day	Lev 14:39	7637
that in the *s* month, on the tenth	Lev 16:29	7637
but the *s* day is the sabbath of	Lev 23:3	7637
in the *s* day is an holy	Lev 23:8	7637
s sabbath shall ye number fifty	Lev 23:16	7637
of Israel, saying, In the *s* month	Lev 23:24	7637
s month there shall be a day of	Lev 23:27	7637
The fifteenth day of this *s* month	Lev 23:34	7637
the fifteenth day of the *s* month	Lev 23:39	7637
shall celebrate it in the *s* month	Lev 23:41	7637
But in the *s* year shall be a	Lev 25:4	7637
on the tenth day of the *s* month	Lev 25:9	7637
say, What shall we eat the *s* year	Lev 25:20	7637
on the *s* day shall he shave it	Num 6:9	7637
On the *s* day Elishama the son of	Num 7:48	7637

S

on the *s* day he shall be clean	Num 19:12	7637
then the *s* day he shall not be	Num 19:12	7637
on the third day, and on the *s* day	Num 19:19	7637
on the *s* day he shall purify	Num 19:19	7637
on the *s* day ye shall have an	Num 28:25	7637
And in the *s* month, on the first	Num 29:1	7637
this *s* month an holy convocation	Num 29:7	7637
the *s* month ye shall have an holy	Num 29:12	7637
on the *s* day seven bullocks, two	Num 29:32	7637
on the third day, and on the *s* day	Num 31:19	7637
wash your clothes on the *s* day	Num 31:24	7637
But the *s* day is the sabbath of	Deut 5:14	7637
The *s* year, the year of release,	Deut 15:9	7637
then in the *s* year thou shalt let	Deut 15:12	7637
on the *s* day shall be a solemn	Deut 16:8	7637
the *s* day ye shall compass the	Josh 6:4	7637
And it came to pass on the *s* day	Josh 6:15	7637
And it came to pass at the *s* time	Josh 6:16	7637
the *s* lot came out for the tribe	Josh 19:40	7637
And it came to pass on the *s* day	Judg 14:15	7637
and it came to pass on the *s* day	Judg 14:17	7637
s day before the sun went down	Judg 14:18	7637
And it came to pass on the *s* day	2Sa 12:18	7637
Ethanim, which is the *s* month	1Kin 8:2	7637
s year of Asa king of Judah, and	1Kin 16:10	7651
s year of Asa king of Judah did	1Kin 16:15	7651
And it came to pass at the *s* time	1Kin 18:44	7637
that in the *s* day the battle was	1Kin 20:29	7637
the *s* year Jehoiada sent and	2Kin 11:4	7637
In the *s* year of Jehu Jehoash	2Kin 12:1	7651
s year of Joash king of Judah	2Kin 13:10	7651
s year of Jeroboam king of Israel	2Kin 15:1	7651
which was the *s* year of Hoshea	2Kin 18:9	7651
on the *s* day of the month, which	2Kin 25:8	7651
it came to pass in the *s* month	2Kin 25:25	7637
Ozem the sixth, David the *s*	1Chr 2:15	7637
Attai the sixth, Eliel the *s*	1Chr 12:11	7637
The *s* to Hakkoz, the eighth to	1Chr 24:10	7637
The *s* to Jesharelah, he, his sons	1Chr 25:14	7637
the sixth, Elioenai the *s*	1Chr 26:3	7637
Ammiel the sixth, Issachar the *s*	1Chr 26:5	7637
The *s* captain for the *s*	1Chr 27:10	7637
feast which was in the *s* month	2Chr 5:3	7637
twentieth day of the *s* month he	2Chr 7:10	7637
And in the *s* year Jehoiada	2Chr 23:1	7637
and finished them in the *s* month	2Chr 31:7	7637
when the *s* month was come, and the	Ezr 3:1	7637
From the first day of the *s* month	Ezr 3:6	7637
in the *s* year of Artaxerxes the	Ezr 7:7	7651
was in the *s* year of the king	Ezr 7:8	7637
when the *s* month came, the	Neh 7:73	7637
upon the first day of the *s* month	Neh 8:2	7637
in the feast of the *s* month	Neh 8:14	7637
and that we would leave the *s* year	Neh 10:31	7637
On the *s* day, when the heart of	Est 1:10	7637
in the *s* year of his reign	Est 2:16	7651
died the same year in the *s* month	Jer 28:17	7637
it came to pass in the *s* month	Jer 41:1	7637
in the *s* year three thousand Jews	Jer 52:28	7651
And it came to pass in the *s* year	Eze 20:1	7637
in the *s* day of the month, that	Eze 30:20	7651
so thou shalt do the *s* day of the	Eze 45:20	7651
In the *s* month, in the fifteenth	Eze 45:25	7651
In the *s* month, in the one and	Hag 2:1	7637
s month, even those seventy years	Zec 7:5	7637
the fifth, and the fast of the *s*	Zec 8:19	7637
also, and the third, unto the *s*	Mt 22:26	2035
Yesterday at the *s* hour the fever	Jn 4:52	1442
place of the *s* day on this wise	Heb 4:4	1442
God did rest the *s* day from all	Heb 4:4	1442
the *s* from Adam, prophesied of	Jude 14	1442
And when he had opened the *s* seal	Rev 8:1	1442
days of the voice of the *s* angel	Rev 10:7	1442
And the *s* angel sounded	Rev 11:15	1442
the *s* angel poured out his vial	Rev 16:17	1442
the *s*, chrysolite	Rev 21:20	1442

SEVENTY

avenged sevenfold, truly Lamech *s*	Gen 4:24	7657
And Cainan lived *s* years, and begat	Gen 5:12	7657
of Lamech were seven hundred *s*	Gen 5:31	7657
And Terah lived *s* years, and begat	Gen 11:26	7657
and Abram was *s* and five years old	Gen 12:4	7657
the loins of Jacob were *s* souls	Ex 1:5	7657
s of the elders of Israel	Ex 24:1	7657
s of the elders of Israel	Ex 24:9	7657
of the thousand seven hundred *s*	Ex 38:28	7657
of the offering was *s* talents	Ex 38:29	7657
one silver bowl of *s* shekels	Num 7:13	7657
one silver bowl of *s* shekels	Num 7:19	7657
one silver bowl of *s* shekels	Num 7:25	7657

one silver bowl of *s* shekels	Num 7:31	7657
one silver bowl of *s* shekels	Num 7:37	7657
a silver bowl of *s* shekels	Num 7:43	7657
one silver bowl of *s* shekels	Num 7:49	7657
one silver bowl of *s* shekels	Num 7:55	7657
one silver bowl of *s* shekels	Num 7:61	7657
one silver bowl of *s* shekels	Num 7:67	7657
one silver bowl of *s* shekels	Num 7:73	7657
one silver bowl of *s* shekels	Num 7:79	7657
and thirty shekels, each bowl *s*	Num 7:85	7657
Gather unto me *s* men of the	Num 11:16	7657
gathered the *s* men of the elders	Num 11:24	7657
him, and gave it unto the *s* elders	Num 11:25	7657
s thousand and five thousand sheep	Num 31:32	7657
father, in slaying his *s* brethren	Judg 9:56	7657
even to Beer-sheba *s* thousand men	2Sa 24:15	7657
Ahab had *s* sons in Samaria	2Kin 10:1	7657
being *s* persons, were with the	2Kin 10:6	7657
slew *s* persons, and put their	2Kin 10:7	7657
fell of Israel *s* thousand men	1Chr 21:14	7657
Parosh, two thousand an hundred *s*	Ezr 2:3	7657
of Shephatiah, three hundred *s*	Ezr 2:4	7657
children of Arah, seven hundred *s*	Ezr 2:5	7657
house of Jeshua, nine hundred *s*	Ezr 2:36	7657
of the children of Hodaviah, *s*	Ezr 2:40	7657
of Athaliah, and with him *s* males	Ezr 8:7	7657
and Zabbud, and with them *s* males	Ezr 8:14	7657
all Israel, ninety and six rams, *s*	Ezr 8:35	7657
Parosh, two thousand an hundred *s*	Neh 7:8	7657
of Shephatiah, three hundred *s*	Neh 7:9	7657
house of Jeshua, nine hundred *s*	Neh 7:39	7657
and of the children of Hodevah, *s*	Neh 7:43	7657
kept the gates, were an hundred *s*	Neh 11:19	7657
enemies, and slew of their foes *s*	Est 9:16	7657
Tyre shall be forgotten *s* years	Is 23:15	7657
after the end of *s* years shall	Is 23:15	7657
to pass after the end of *s* years	Is 23:17	7657
serve the king of Babylon *s* years	Jer 25:11	7657
when *s* years are accomplished,	Jer 25:12	7657
the LORD, That after *s* years be	Jer 29:10	7657
there stood before them *s* men of	Eze 8:11	7657
the west was *s* cubits broad	Eze 41:12	7657
that he would accomplish *s* years	Dan 9:2	7657
S weeks are determined upon thy	Dan 9:24	7657
seventh month, even those *s* years	Zec 7:5	7657
but, Until *s* times seven	Mt 18:22	1441
the Lord appointed other *s* also	Lk 10:1	1440
the *s* returned again with joy,	Lk 10:17	1440

SEVER

I will *s* in that day the land of	Ex 8:22	6395
the LORD shall *s* between the	Ex 9:4	6395
they shall *s* out men of continual	Eze 39:14	914
s the wicked from among the just,	Mt 13:49	873

SEVERAL See APPENDIX.

SEVERALLY

to every man *s* as he will	1Cor 12:11	2398

SEVERED

have *s* you from other people,	Lev 20:26	914
Then Moses *s* three cities on this	Deut 4:41	914
had *s* himself from the Kenites,	Judg 4:11	6504

SEVERITY

the goodness and *s* of God	Rom 11:22	663
on them which fell, *s*	Rom 11:22	663

SEW

A time to rend, and a time to *s*	Eccl 3:7	8609
Woe to the women that *s* pillows	Eze 13:18	8609

SEWED

they *s* fig leaves together, and	Gen 3:7	8609
I have *s* sackcloth upon my skin,	Job 16:15	8609

SEWEST

a bag, and thou *s* up mine iniquity	Job 14:17	2950

SEWETH

No man also *s* a piece of new	Mk 2:21	1976

SHAALABBIN (sha-al-ab'-bin) See SHAALBIM. *A city in Dan.*

And S, and Ajalon, and Jethlah,	Josh 19:42	8169

SHAALBIM (sha-al'-bim) See SHAALABBIN, SHAALBO-NITE. *Same as Shaalabbin.*

mount Heres in Aijalon, and in S	Judg 1:35	8169
son of Dekar, in Makaz, and in S	1Kin 4:9	8169

SHAALBON See SHAALBONITE.

SHAALBONITE (sha-al'-bo-nite) *A native of Shaal-abbin.*

Eliahba the S, of the sons of	2Sa 23:32	8170
the Baharumite, Eliahba the S	1Chr 11:33	8170

SHAALIM See SHALIM.

SHAAPH (sha'-af) A son of Jahdai.
Gesham, and Pelet, and Ephah, and S ...1Chr 2:47   8174
She bare also S the father of.................1Chr 2:49   8174

SHAARAIM (sha-a-ra'-im) See SHARAIM, SHARUHEN. A city in Judah.
fell down by the way to S.......................1Sa 17:52   8189
and at Beth-birei, and at S 1Chr 4:31   8189

SHAASHGAZ (sha-ash'-gaz) A servant of King Ahasuerus.
of the women, to the custody of S ....Est 2:14   8190

SHABBETHAI (shab'-be-thahee)
   1. A Levite who dealt with the foreign wife problem.
and S the Levite helped them ....Ezr 10:15   7678
   2. A Levite who aided Ezra.
and Sherebiah, Jamin, Akkub, S............Neh 8:7   7678
   3. A family of exiles.
And S and Jozabad, of the chief of ....Neh 11:16   7678

SHACHIA (sha-ki'-ah) A son of Shaharaim.
And Jeuz, and, S, and Mirma.................1Chr 8:10   7634

SHADE
the LORD is thy s upon thy right ....Ps 121:5   6783

SHADOW
came they under the s of my roof ....Gen 19:8   6738
come and put your trust in my s ....Judg 9:15   6738
Thou seest the s of the mountains ....Judg 9:36   6738
shall the s go forward ten....................2Kin 20:9   6738
for the s to go down ten degrees............2Kin 20:10   6738
but let the s return backward ten.........2Kin 20:10   6738
he brought the s ten degrees................2Kin 20:11   6738
our days on the earth are as a s...........1Chr 29:15   6738
and the s of death stain it ....Job 3:5   6757
servant earnestly desireth the s...........Job 7:2   6738
our days upon earth are a s..................Job 8:9   6738
of darkness and the s of death..............Job 10:21   6757
of the s of death, without any...............Job 10:22   6738
out to light the s of death ....Job 12:22   6757
he fleeth also as a s, and.....................Job 14:2   6738
on my eyelids is the s of death ....Job 16:16   6757
and all my members are as a s...............Job 17:7   6738
is to them even as the s of death ....Job 24:17   6757
in the terrors of the s of death ....Job 24:17   6757
of darkness, and the s of death ....Job 28:3   6757
nor s of death, where the workers..........Job 34:22   6757
seen the doors of the s of death ....Job 38:17   6757
trees cover him with their s ....Job 40:22   6752
hide me under the s of thy wings ....Ps 17:8   6738
the valley of the s of death ....Ps 23:4   6757
trust under the s of thy wings ....Ps 36:7   6738
and covered us with the s of death ....Ps 44:19   6757
in the s of thy wings will I make............Ps 57:1   6738
therefore in the s of thy wings...............Ps 63:7   6738
were covered with the s of it..................Ps 80:10   6738
abide under the s of the Almighty ....Ps 91:1   6738
days are like a s that declineth..............Ps 102:11   6738
in the s of death, being bound in ....Ps 107:10   6757
the s of death, and brake their...............Ps 107:14   6738
gone like the s when it declineth............Ps 109:23   6738
days are as a s that passeth away.........Ps 144:4   6738
life which he spendeth as a s ....Eccl 6:12   6738
his days, which are as a s ....Eccl 8:13   6738
under his s with great delight ....Song 2:3   6738
shall be a tabernacle for a s in ....Is 4:6   6738
in the land of the s of death ....Is 9:2   6757
make thy s as the night in the ....Is 16:3   6738
a s from the heat, when the blast ....Is 25:4   6738
the heat with the s of a cloud ....Is 25:5   6738
and to trust in the s of Egypt ....Is 30:2   6738
the trust in the s of Egypt your..............Is 30:3   6738
as the s of a great rock in a ....Is 32:2   6738
and hatch, and gather under her s ....Is 34:15   6738
bring again the s of the degrees............Is 38:8   6738
in the s of his hand hath he hid ....Is 49:2   6738
thee in the s of mine hand....................Is 51:16   6738
of the s of death, through a land ....Jer 2:6   6757
he turn it into the s of death ....Jer 13:16   6757
They that fled stood under the s............Jer 48:45   6738
Under his s we shall live among ....Lam 4:20   6738
in the s of the branches thereof............Eze 17:23   6738
under his s dwelt all great...................Eze 31:6   6738
earth are gone down from his s ....Eze 31:12   6738
that dwelt under his s in the.................Eze 31:17   6738
of the field had s under it......................Dan 4:12   2927
because the s thereof is good ....Hos 4:13   6738
dwell under his s shall return ....Hos 14:7   6738
turneth the s of death into the ....Amos 5:8   6757
a booth, and sat under it in the s...........Jonah 4:5   6738

it might be a s over his head..................Jonah 4:6   6738
s of death light is sprung up ....Mt 4:16   4639
air may lodge under the s of it ....Mk 4:32   4639
in the s of death, to guide our ....Lk 1:79   4639
that at the least the s of Peter................Acts 5:15   4639
Which are a s of things to come............Col 2:17   4639
s of heavenly things, as Moses...............Heb 8:5   4639
For the law having a s of good ....Heb 10:1   4639
neither s of turning ....Jas 1:17   644

SHADOWING
Woe to the land s with wings ....Is 18:1   6767
fair branches, and with a s shroud ....Eze 31:3   6751
of glory s the mercyseat ....Heb 9:5   2683

SHADOWS
the s flee away, turn, my beloved.........Song 2:17   6752
the s flee away, I will get me to.............Song 4:6   6752
for the s of the evening are....................Jer 6:4   6752

SHADRACH (sha'-drak) See HANANIAH. A companion of Daniel.
and to Hananiah, of S..........................Dan 1:7   7714
of the king, and he set S, Meshach........Dan 2:49   7715
of the province of Babylon, S.................Dan 3:12   7715
rage and fury commanded to bring S....Dan 3:13   7715
said unto them, Is it true, O S...............Dan 3:14   7715
S, Meshach, and Abed-nego, ...Dan 3:16   7715
his visage was changed against S..........Dan 3:19   7715
that were in his army to bind S.............Dan 3:20   7715
slew those men that took up S...............Dan 3:22   7715
And these three men, S, Meshach, ...Dan 3:23   7715
furnace, and spake, and said, S............Dan 3:26   7715
Then S, Meshach, and Abed-nego,.........Dan 3:26   7715
and said, Blessed be the God of S ....Dan 3:28   7715
thing amiss against the God of S ....Dan 3:29   7715
Then the king promoted S, Meshach......Dan 3:30   7715

SHADY
He lieth under the s trees ....Job 40:21   6628
The s trees cover him with their ....Job 40:22   6628

SHAFT
his s, and his branches, his bowls..........Ex 25:31   3409
his s, and his branch, his bowls,............Ex 37:17   3409
beaten gold, unto the s thereof..............Num 8:4   3409
hid me, and made me a polished s ....Is 49:2   2671

SHAGE (sha'-ghe) A "mighty man" of David.
the son of S the Hararite 1Chr 11:34   7681

SHAGEE See SHAGE.

SHAGEH See SHAGE.

SHAHAR (sha'-har) A musical notation.
chief Musician upon Aijeleth S ....Ps 22:t   7837

SHAHARAIM (sha-ha-ra'-im) A Benjamite from Moab.
S begat children in the country 1Chr 8:8   7842

SHAHAZIMAH (sha-haz'-i-mah) A city in Issachar.
the coast reacheth to Tabor, and S ....Josh 19:22   7831

SHAHAZUMAH See SHAHAZIMAH.

SHAKE
other times before, and s myself ....Judg 16:20   5287
So God s out every man from his ....Neh 5:13   5287
which made all my bones to s.................Job 4:14   6342
He shall s off his unripe grape................Job 15:33   2554
you, and s mine head at you ....Job 16:4   5128
the lip, they s the head, saying,..............Ps 22:7   5128
though the mountains s with the ....Ps 46:3   7493
make their loins continually to s...........Ps 69:23   4571
thereof shall s like Lebanon ....Ps 72:16   7493
ariseth to s terribly the earth................Is 2:19   6206
ariseth to s terribly the earth................Is 2:21   6206
as if the rod should s itself ....Is 10:15   5130
he shall s his hand against the ....Is 10:32   5130
he s his hand over the river ....Is 11:15   5130
s the hand, that they may go into ....Is 13:2   5130
Therefore I will s the heavens ....Is 13:13   7264
to tremble, that did s kingdoms ....Is 14:16   7493
the foundations of the earth do s ....Is 24:18   7493
Carmel s off their fruits ....Is 33:9   5287
S thyself from the dust ....Is 52:2   5287
all my bones s..................................Jer 23:9   7363
thy walls shall s at the noise of.............Eze 26:10   7493
Shall not the isles s at the ....Eze 26:15   7493
The suburbs shall s at the sound ....Eze 27:28   7493
I made the nations to s at the ....Eze 31:16   7493
shall s at my presence, and the ....Eze 38:20   7493
s off his leaves, and scatter his..............Dan 4:14   5426
the heavens and the earth shall s..........Joel 3:16   7493
of the door, that the posts may s...........Amos 9:1   7493
I will s the heavens, and the.................Hag 2:6   7493
I will s all nations, and the...................Hag 2:7   7493

S

I will s the heavens and the earth .... Hag 2:21	7493
I will s mine hand upon them, and .... Zec 2:9	5130
s off the dust of your feet .... Mt 10:14	1621
for fear of him the keepers did s .... Mt 28:4	4579
s off the dust under your feet .... Mk 6:11	1621
that house, and could not s it .... Lk 6:48	4531
s off the very dust from your .... Lk 9:5	660
Yet once more I s not the earth .... Heb 12:26	4579

SHAKED
looked upon me they s their heads .... Ps 109:25	5128

SHAKEN
the sound of a s leaf shall chase .... Lev 26:36	5086
as a reed is s in the water 1Kin 14:15	5110
Jerusalem hath s her head at thee 2Kin 19:21	5128
promise, even thus be he s out .... Neh 5:13	5287
s me to pieces, and set me up for .... Job 16:12	6327
the wicked might be s out of it .... Job 38:13	5287
also of the hills moved and were s .... Ps 18:7	1607
Jerusalem hath s her head at thee .... Is 37:22	5128
the fir trees shall be terribly s .... Nah 2:3	7477
if they be s, they shall even .... Nah 3:12	5128
A reed s with the wind .... Mt 11:7	4531
powers of the heavens shall be s .... Mt 24:29	4531
that are in heaven shall be s .... Mk 13:25	4531
s together, and running over, ... Lk 6:38	4531
A reed s with the wind .... Lk 7:24	4531
the powers of heaven shall be s .... Lk 21:26	4531
the place was s where they were .... Acts 4:31	4531
foundations of the prison were s .... Acts 16:26	4531
That ye be not soon s in mind 2Th 2:2	4531
of those things that are s .... Heb 12:27	4531
which cannot be s may remain .... Heb 12:27	4531
when she is s of a mighty wind .... Rev 6:13	4579

SHAKETH
Which s the earth out of her .... Job 9:6	7264
of the LORD s the wilderness .... Ps 29:8	2342
the LORD s the wilderness of .... Ps 29:8	2342
thereof; for it s .... Ps 60:2	4131
itself against him that s it .... Is 10:15	5130
LORD of hosts, which he s over it .... Is 19:16	5130
that s his hands from holding of .... Is 33:15	5287

SHAKING
he laugheth at the s of a spear .... Job 41:29	7494
a s of the head among the people .... Ps 44:14	4493
as the s of an olive tree, two or .... Is 17:6	5363
fear because of the s of the hand .... Is 19:16	8573
be as the s of an olive tree .... Is 24:13	5363
in battles of s will he fight .... Is 30:32	8573
there was a noise, and behold a s .... Eze 37:7	7494
a great s in the land of Israel .... Eze 38:19	7494

SHALEM *(sha'-lem) A city in Ephraim.*
And Jacob came to S, a city of .... Gen 33:18	8003

SHALIM *(sha'-lim) A district in Dan.*
they passed through the land of S 1Sa 9:4	8171

SHALISHA *(shal'-i-shah) A district in Ephraim.*
and passed through the land of S 1Sa 9:4	8031

SHALISHAH See SHALISHA.

SHALL See APPENDIX.

SHALLECHETH *(shal'-le-keth) A gate of the First Temple.*
forth westward, with the gate S 1Chr 26:16	7996

SHALLIM See SHALIM.

SHALLUM *(shal'-lum) See JEHOAHAZ, MESHELEMIAH, SHILLEM.*
1. A king of Israel.
S the son of Jabesh conspired 2Kin 15:10	7967
S the son of Jabesh began to 2Kin 15:13	7967
smote S the son of Jabesh in 2Kin 15:14	7967
And the rest of the acts of S 2Kin 15:15	7967

2. Husband of Huldah.
the wife of S the son of Tikvah, ... 2Kin 22:14	7967
the wife of S the son of Tikvath, ... 2Chr 34:22	7967

3. A descendant of Jerahmeel.
begat Sisamai, and Sisamai begat S 1Chr 2:40	7967
S begat Jekamiah, and Jekamiah 1Chr 2:41	7967

4. A son of King Josiah.
the third Zedekiah, the fourth S 1Chr 3:15	7967
thus saith the LORD touching S .... Jer 22:11	7967

5. Grandson of Simeon.
S his son, Mibsam his son, Mishma 1Chr 4:25	7967

6. Father of Hilkiah.
begat Zadok, and Zadok begat S 1Chr 6:12	7967
S begat Hilkiah, and Hilkiah begat 1Chr 6:13	7967
The son of S, the son of Zadok, ... Ezr 7:2	7967

7. Son of Naphtali.
Jahziel, and Guni, and Jezer, and S 1Chr 7:13	7967

8. A family of exiles.
And the porters were, S, and Akkub, ... 1Chr 9:17	7967
S was the chief 1Chr 9:17	7967
S the son of Kore, the son of 1Chr 9:19	7967
the firstborn of S the Korahite 1Chr 9:31	7967
the children of S, the children .... Ezr 2:42	7967
the children of S, the children .... Neh 7:45	7967

9. Father of Jehizkiah.
and Jehizkiah the son of S 2Chr 28:12	7967

10. A gatekeeper who married a foreigner.
S, and Telem, and Uri .... Ezr 10:24	7967

11. A son of Bani who married a foreigner.
S, Amariah, and Joseph .... Ezr 10:42	7967

12. A rebuilder of Jerusalem's wall.
repaired S the son of Halohesh .... Neh 3:12	7967

13. Father of Hanameel.
Hanameel the son of S thine uncle .... Jer 32:7	7967

14. Father of Maaseiah.
chamber of Maaseiah the son of S .... Jer 35:4	7967

SHALLUN *(shal'-lun) A rebuilder of Jerusalem's wall.*
repaired S the son of Colhozeh .... Neh 3:15	7968

SHALMAI *(shal'-mahee) A family of exiles.*
of Hagab, the children of S .... Ezr 2:46	8073
of Hagaba, the children of S .... Neh 7:48	8014

SHALMAN *(shal'-man) See SHALMANESER. A king of Assyria.*
as S spoiled Beth-arbel in the .... Hos 10:14	8020

SHALMANESER *(shal-man-e'-zer) See SHALMAN. A king of Assyria.*
him came up S king of Assyria 2Kin 17:3	8022
that S king of Assyria came up 2Kin 18:9	8022

SHALT See APPENDIX.

SHAMA *(sha'-mah) A "mighty man" of David.*
Uzzia the Ashterathite, S 1Chr 11:44	8091

SHAMARIAH *Son of Rehoboam.*
Jeush, and S, and Zaham 2Chr 11:19	

SHAMBLES
Whatsoever is sold in the s 1Cor 10:25	3111

SHAME
unto their s among their enemies .... Ex 32:25	8103
might put them to s in any thing .... Judg 18:7	3637
because his father had done him s 1Sa 20:34	3637
whither there shall I cause my s to go ... 2Sa 13:13	2781
So he returned with s of face to 2Chr 32:21	1322
hate their own and be clothed with s .... Job 8:22	1322
long will ye turn my glory into s .... Ps 4:2	3639
put to s that seek after my soul .... Ps 35:4	3637
let them be clothed with s .... Ps 35:26	1322
put to s that wish me evil .... Ps 40:14	3637
of their s that say unto me .... Ps 40:15	1322
hast put them to s that hated us .... Ps 44:7	954
hast cast off, and put us to s .... Ps 44:9	3637
the s of my face hath covered me, ... Ps 44:15	1322
thou hast put them to s, because .... Ps 53:5	954
s hath covered my face .... Ps 69:7	3639
hast known my reproach, and my s ...... Ps 69:19	1322
for a reward of their s that say .... Ps 70:3	1322
for they are brought unto s .... Ps 71:24	2659
Fill their faces with s .... Ps 83:16	7036
yea, let them be put to s .... Ps 83:17	2659
thou hast covered him with s .... Ps 89:45	955
adversaries be clothed with s .... Ps 109:29	3639
O LORD, put me not to s .... Ps 119:31	954
His enemies will I clothe with s .... Ps 132:18	1322
but s shall be the promotion of .... Prov 3:35	7036
a scorner getteth to himself s .... Prov 9:7	7036
harvest is a son that causeth s .... Prov 10:5	954
When pride cometh, then cometh s .... Prov 11:2	7036
but a prudent man covereth s .... Prov 12:16	7036
man is loathsome, and cometh to s .... Prov 13:5	2659
s shall be to him that refuseth .... Prov 13:18	7036
is against him that causeth s .... Prov 14:35	954
rule over a son that causeth s .... Prov 17:2	954
it, it is folly and s unto him .... Prov 18:13	3639
mother, is a son that causeth s .... Prov 19:26	954
thy neighbour hath put thee to s .... Prov 25:8	3637
he that heareth it put thee to s .... Prov 25:10	2616
himself bringeth his mother to s .... Prov 29:15	954
uncovered, to the s of Egypt .... Is 20:4	6172
be the s of thy lord's house .... Is 22:18	7036
the strength of Pharaoh be your s .... Is 30:3	1322
be an help nor profit, but a s .... Is 30:5	1322
yea, thy s shall be seen .... Is 47:3	2781
I hid not my face from s and .... Is 50:6	3639

for thou shalt not be put to *s*	Is 54:4	2659
shalt forget the *s* of thy youth	Is 54:4	1322
For your *s* ye shall have double	Is 61:7	1322
For *s* hath devoured the labour of	Jer 3:24	1322
We lie down in our *s*, and our	Jer 3:25	1322
thy face, that thy *s* may appear	Jer 13:26	7036
my days should be consumed with *s*	Jer 20:18	1322
upon you, and a perpetual *s*	Jer 23:40	3640
The nations have heard of thy *s*	Jer 46:12	7036
hath Moab turned the back with *s*	Jer 48:39	954
s hath covered our faces	Jer 51:51	3639
s shall be upon all faces, and	Eze 7:18	955
bear thine own *s* for thy sins	Eze 16:52	3639
confounded also, and bear thy *s*	Eze 16:52	3639
That thou mayest bear thine own *s*	Eze 16:54	3639
mouth any more because of thy *s*	Eze 16:63	3639
yet have they borne their *s* with	Eze 32:24	3639
yet have they borne their *s* with	Eze 32:25	3639
bear their *s* with them that go	Eze 32:30	3639
neither bear the *s* of the heathen	Eze 34:29	3639
have borne the *s* of the heathen	Eze 36:6	3639
you, they shall bear their *s*	Eze 36:7	3639
the *s* of the heathen any more	Eze 36:15	3639
that they have borne their *s*	Eze 39:26	3639
but they shall bear their *s*	Eze 44:13	3639
to everlasting life, and some to *s*	Dan 12:2	2781
will I change their glory into *s*	Hos 4:7	7036
her rulers with *s* do love	Hos 4:18	7036
separated themselves unto that *s*	Hos 9:10	1322
Ephraim shall receive *s*, and	Hos 10:6	1317
brother Jacob *s* shall cover thee	Obad 10	955
of Saphir, having thy *s* naked	Mic 1:11	1322
them, that they shall not take *s*	Mic 2:6	3639
s shall cover her which said unto	Mic 7:10	955
nakedness, and the kingdoms thy *s*	Nah 3:5	7036
Thou hast consulted *s* to thy	Hab 2:10	1322
Thou art filled with *s* for glory	Hab 2:16	7036
but the unjust knoweth no *s*	Zeph 3:5	1322
where they have been put to *s*	Zeph 3:19	1322
thou begin with *s* to take the	Lk 14:9	152
worthy to suffer *s* for his name	Acts 5:41	818
I write not these things to *s* you	1Cor 4:14	1788
I speak to your *s*	1Cor 6:5	1791
but if it be a *s* for a woman to	1Cor 11:6	149
long hair, it is a *s* unto him	1Cor 11:14	819
of God, and *s* them that have not	1Cor 11:22	2617
for it is a *s* for women to speak	1Cor 14:35	149
I speak this to your *s*	1Cor 15:34	1791
For it is a *s* even to speak of	Eph 5:12	149
and whose glory is in their *s*	Phil 3:19	152
afresh, and put him to an open *s*	Heb 6:6	3856
the cross, despising the *s*	Heb 12:2	152
the sea, foaming out their own *s*	Jude 13	152
that the *s* of thy nakedness do	Rev 3:18	152
he walk naked, and they see his *s*	Rev 16:15	808

SHAMED (sha'-med) *A son of Elpaal.*

her take it to her, lest we be *s*	Gen 38:23	937
said Thou hast *s* this day the	2Sa 19:5	3001
Eber, and Misham, and *S*, who built	1Chr 8:12	8106
Ye have *s* the counsel of the poor	Ps 14:6	954

SHAMEFACEDNESS

in modest apparel, with *s*	1Ti 2:9	127

SHAMEFUL

ye set up altars to that *s* thing	Jer 11:13	1322
s spewing shall be on thy glory	Hab 2:16	7022

SHAMEFULLY

that conceived them hath done *s*	Hos 2:5	3001
head, and sent him away *s* handled	Mk 12:4	821
beat him also, and entreated him *s*	Lk 20:11	818
were *s* entreated, as ye know, at	1Th 2:2	5195

SHAMELESSLY

vain fellows *s* uncovereth himself	2Sa 6:20	1540

SHAMER (sha'-mur) See SHOMER.
1. *Son of Mahli.*

the son of Bani, the son of *S*	1Chr 6:46	8106
2. *Son of Heber.*		
And the sons of *S*	1Chr 7:34	8106

SHAMETH

of riotous men *s* his father	Prov 28:7	3637

SHAMGAR (sham'-gar) *A judge of Israel.*

after him was *S* the son of Anath,	Judg 3:31	8044
In the days of *S* the son of Anath	Judg 5:6	8044

SHAMHUTH (sham'-huth) See SHAMMOTH. *A captain in David's army.*

fifth month was *S* the Izrahite	1Chr 27:8	8049

SHAMIR (sha'-mur)
1. *A city in Judah.*

And in the mountains, *S*, and Jattir	Josh 15:48	8069
2. *A city near Mt. Ephraim.*		
he dwelt in *S* in mount Ephraim	Judg 10:1	8069
and died, and was buried in *S*	Judg 10:2	8069
3. *Son of Micah the Levite.*		
the sons of Michah; *S*	1Chr 24:24	8053

SHAMLAI See SAMLAH.

SHAMMA (sham'-mah) See SHAMMAH. *A son of Zophah.*

Bezer, and Hod, and *S*, and Shilshah,	1Chr 7:37	8037

SHAMMAH (sham'-mah) See SHAMMA, SHAMMOTH, SHIMEA, SHIMMA.
1. *A son of Reuel.*

Nahath, and Zerah, *S*, and Mizzah	Gen 36:13	8048
duke Nahath, duke Zerah, duke *S*	Gen 36:17	8048
Nahath, Zerah, *S*, and Mizzah	1Chr 1:37	8048
2. *A son of Jesse.*		
Then Jesse made *S* to pass by	1Sa 16:9	8048
unto him Abinadab, and the third *S*	1Sa 17:13	8048
3. *A "mighty man" of David.*		
after him was *S* the son of Agee	2Sa 23:11	8048
4. *A Hararite "mighty man" of David.*		
S the Hararite, Ahiam the son of	2Sa 23:33	8048
5. *A Harodite "mighty man" of David.*		
S the Harodite, Elika the	2Sa 23:25	8048

SHAMMAI (sham'-mahee)
1. *A son of Onan.*

And the sons of Onam were, *S*	1Chr 2:28	8060
And the sons of *S*	1Chr 2:28	8060
the sons of Jada the brother of *S*	1Chr 2:32	8060
2. *Father of Maon.*		
and Rekem begat *S*	1Chr 2:44	8060
And the son of *S* was Maon	1Chr 2:45	8060
3. *A descendant of Caleb.*		
and she bare Miriam, and *S*, and	1Chr 4:17	8060

SHAMMOTH (sham'-moth) See SHAMMAH, SHAMHUTH. *A "mighty man" of David.*

S the Harorite, Helez the	1Chr 11:27	8054

SHAMMUA (sham-mu'-ah) See SHAMMUAH, SHEMAIH, SHIMEA.
1. *A spy sent to the Promised Land.*

of Reuben, *S* the son of Zaccur	Num 13:4	8051
2. *A son of David.*		
S, and Shobab, Nathan, and Solomon,	1Chr 14:4	8051
3. *A family of exiles.*		
brethren, and Abda the son of *S*	Neh 11:17	8051
4. *A priest with Zerubbabel.*		
Of Bilgah, *S*	Neh 12:18	8051

SHAMMUAH (sham-mu'-ah) See SHAMMUA. *Same as Shammua 2.*

S, and Shobab, and Nathan, and	2Sa 5:14	8051

SHAMSHERAI (sham'-she-rahee) *A son of Jeroham.*

And *S*, and Shehariah, and Athaliah,	1Chr 8:26	8125

SHAPE

a bodily *s* like a dove upon him	Lk 3:22	1491
voice at any time, nor seen his *s*	Jn 5:37	1491

SHAPEN

Behold, I was *s* in iniquity	Ps 51:5	2342

SHAPES

the *s* of the locusts were like	Rev 9:7	3667

SHAPHAM (sha'-fam) *A Gadite chief.*

S the next, and Jaanai, and Shaphat	1Chr 5:12	8223

SHAPHAN (sha'-fan)
1. *A scribe in Josiah's time.*

king sent *S* the son of Azaliah	2Kin 22:3	8227
priest said unto *S* the scribe	2Kin 22:8	8227
And Hilkiah gave the book to *S*	2Kin 22:8	8227
S the scribe came to the king, and	2Kin 22:9	8227
S the scribe shewed the king,	2Kin 22:10	8227
S read it before the king	2Kin 22:10	8227
S the scribe, and Asahiah a	2Kin 22:12	8227
and Ahikam, and Achbor, and *S*	2Kin 22:14	8227
he sent *S* the son of Azaliah, and	2Chr 34:8	8227
said to *S* the scribe, I have	2Chr 34:15	8227
Hilkiah delivered the book to *S*	2Chr 34:15	8227
S carried the book to the king,	2Chr 34:16	8227
Then *S* the scribe told the king,	2Chr 34:18	8227
S read it before the king	2Chr 34:18	8227
S the scribe, and Asaiah a servant	2Chr 34:20	8227
Gemariah the son of *S* the scribe	Jer 36:10	8227
the son of Gemariah, the son of *S*	Jer 36:11	8227
Achbor, and Gemariah the son of *S*	Jer 36:12	8227

S

2. *Father of Ahikam.*
priest, and Ahikam the son of S 2Kin 22:12   8227
the son of Ahikam, the son of S 2Kin 25:22   8227
Hilkiah, and Ahikam the son of S 2Chr 34:20   8227
the son of S was with Jeremiah ....Jer 26:24   8227
the son of Ahikam the son of S ....Jer 39:14   8227
the son of Ahikam the son of S ....Jer 40:5   8227
the son of S sware unto them...................Jer 40:9   8227
the son of Ahikam the son of S ....Jer 40:11   8227
the son of S with the sword ....Jer 41:2   8227
the son of Ahikam the son of S ....Jer 43:6   8227
3. *Messenger for Jeremiah.*
the hand of Elasah the son of S ....Jer 29:3   8227
4. *Father of Jaazaniah.*
them stood Jaazaniah the son of S ....Eze 8:11   8227

SHAPHAT (sha'-fat)
1. *A spy sent to the Promised Land.*
of Simeon, S the son of Hori....................Num 13:5   8202
2. *Father of Elisha the prophet.*
and Elisha the son of S of.......................1Kin 19:16   8202
and found Elisha the son of S 1Kin 19:19   8202
said, Here is Elisha the son of S 2Kin 3:11   8202
of S shall stand on him this day 2Kin 6:31   8202
3. *A grandson of Shechaniah.*
and Bariah, and Neariah, and S.............1Chr 3:22   8202
4. *A chief Gadite.*
next, and Jaanai, and S in Bashan.........1Chr 5:12   8202
5. *A shepherd of David's herds.*
valleys was S the son of Adlai.................1Chr 27:29   8202

SHAPHER (sha'-fur) *An Israelite encampment in the wilderness.*
Kehelathah, and pitched in mount S ......Num 33:23   8234
And they removed from mount S ....Num 33:24   8234

SHAPHIR See SHAPHER.

SHARAI (sha'-rahee) *Married a foreigner in exile.*
Machnadebai, Shashai, S, ...Ezr 10:40   8298

SHARAIM (sha-ra'-im) See SHAARAIM. *Same as Shaaraim.*
And S, and Adithaim, and Gederah, and Josh 15:36   8189

SHARAR (sha'-rar) See SARAR. *A "mighty man" of David.*
Ahiam the son of S the Hararite............2Sa 23:33   8325

SHARE
to sharpen every man his s 1Sa 13:20   4282

SHAREZER (sha-re'-zur) See SHEREZER. *Son of Sennacherib.*
S his sons smote him with the 2Kin 19:37   8272
S his sons smote him with the ....Is 37:38   8272

SHARON (sha'-run) See SARON, SHARONITE.
1. *A plain of Ephraim.*
in S was Shitrai the Sharonite 1Chr 27:29   8289
I am the rose of S, and the lily ....Song 2:1   8289
S is like a wilderness ....Is 33:9   8289
it, the excellency of Carmel and S ....Is 35:2   8289
S shall be a fold of flocks, and ....Is 65:10   8289
2. *A plain or city in Gad.*
towns, and in all the suburbs of S 1Chr 5:16   8289

SHARONITE (sha'-run-ite) *An inhabitant of Sharon 1.*
fed in Sharon was Shitrai the S 1Chr 27:29   8290

SHARP
Then Zipporah took a s stone ....Ex 4:25   6864
unto Joshua, Make thee s knives............Josh 5:2   6697
And Joshua made him s knives ....Josh 5:3   6697
there was a s rock on the one 1Sa 14:4   8127
a s rock on the other side 1Sa 14:4   8127
S stones are under him............................Job 41:30   2303
he spreadeth s pointed things.................Job 41:30   2742
Thine arrows are s in the heart ....Ps 45:5   8150
like a s rasor, working..............................Ps 52:2   3913
arrows, and their tongue a s sword ....Ps 57:4   2299
S arrows of the mighty, with ....Ps 120:4   8150
wormwood, s as a twoedged sword ....Prov 5:4   2299
a maul, and a sword, and a s arrow ....Prov 25:18   8150
Whose arrows are s, and all their ....Is 5:28   8150
Behold, I will make thee a new s ....Is 41:15   2742
hath made my mouth like a s sword ......Is 49:2   2299
son of man, take thee a s knife ....Eze 5:1   2299
contention was so s between them ....Acts 15:39
his mouth went a s twoedged sword.......Rev 1:16   3691
hath the s sword with two edges ....Rev 2:12   *3691*
crown, and in his hand a s sickle............Rev 14:14   *3691*
heaven, he also having a s sickle...........Rev 14:17   *3691*
cry to him that had the s sickle ....Rev 14:18   *3691*
saying, Thrust in thy s sickle ....Rev 14:18   *3691*
out of his mouth goeth a s sword...........Rev 19:15   *3691*

SHARPEN
to s every man his share, and his 1Sa 13:20   3913
for the axes, and to s the goads 1Sa 13:21   5324

SHARPENED
They have s their tongues like a ....Ps 140:3   8150
Say, A sword, a sword is s ....Eze 21:9   2300
It is s to make a sore slaughter...............Eze 21:10   2300
this sword is s, and it is ....Eze 21:11   2300

SHARPENETH
mine enemy s his eyes upon me ....Job 16:9   3913
Iron s iron ....Prov 27:17   2300
so a man s the countenance of his ....Prov 27:17   2300

SHARPER
upright is s than a thorn hedge ....Mic 7:4
s than any twoedged sword,...................Heb 4:12   *5114*

SHARPLY
And they did chide with him s ....Judg 8:1   2394
Wherefore rebuke them s, that ....Titus 1:13   *664*

SHARPNESS
lest being present I should use s............2Cor 13:10   *664*

SHARUHEN (sha-ru'-hen) See SHAARAIM, SHILHIM. *A city in Simeon.*
And Beth-lebaoth, and S........................Josh 19:6   8287

SHASHAI (sha'-shahee) *Married a foreigner in exile.*
Machnadebai, S, Sharai, ...Ezr 10:40   8343

SHASHAK (sha'-shak) *A son of Elpaal.*
And Ahio, S, and Jeremoth,....................1Chr 8:14   8349
and Penuel, the sons of S........................1Chr 8:25   8349

SHAUL (sha'-ul) See SAUL, SHAULITES.
1. *A son of Simeon.*
S the son of a Canaanitish woman........Gen 46:10   7586
S the son of a Canaanitish woman........Ex 6:15   7586
of S, the family of the Shaulites ....Num 26:13   7586
and Jamin, Jarib, Zerah, and S............1Chr 4:24   7586
2. *A king of Edom.*
S of Rehoboth by the river......................1Chr 1:48   7586
when S was dead, Baal-hanan the..........1Chr 1:49   7586
3. *Son of Kohath.*
son, Uzziah his son, and S his son 1Chr 6:24   7586

SHAULITES (sha'-ul-ites) *Descendants of Shaul 1.*
of Shaul, the family of the S ....Num 26:13   7587

SHAVE
but the scall shall he not s ....Lev 13:33   1548
s off all his hair, and wash......................Lev 14:8   1548
that he shall s all his hair off ....Lev 14:9   1548
even all his hair he shall s off ....Lev 14:9   1548
neither shall they s off the ....Lev 21:5   1548
then he shall s his head in the ....Num 6:9   1548
on the seventh day shall he s it...............Num 6:9   1548
the Nazarite shall s the head of.............Num 6:18   1548
let them s all their flesh, and ....Num 8:7   5674,8593
and she shall s her head, and pare........Deut 21:12   1548
she caused him to s off the seven ....Judg 16:19   1548
Lord s with a razor that is hired ....Is 7:20   1548
Neither shall they s their heads ....Eze 44:20   1548
them, that they may s their heads........Acts 21:24   *3587*

SHAVED
he s himself, and changed his.................Gen 41:14   1548
s off the one half of their 2Sa 10:4   1548
s them, and cut off their garments 1Chr 19:4   1548
s his head, and fell down upon the ....Job 1:20   1494

SHAVEH (sha'-veh) *A valley near Aenon.*
Ham, and the Emims in S Kiriathaim....Gen 14:5   7741
were with him, at the valley of S............Gen 14:17   7740

SHAVEN
He shall be s, but the scall ....Lev 13:33   1548
the hair of his separation is s.................Num 6:19   1548
if I be s, then my strength will.............Judg 16:17   1548
to grow again after he was s ....Judg 16:22   1548
men, having their beards s......................Jer 41:5   1548
is even all one as if she were s 1Cor 11:5   *3587*
for a woman to be shorn or s 1Cor 11:6   *3587*

SHAVSHA (shav'-shah) See SERAIAH, SHEVA, SHISHA. *David's scribe.*
and S was scribe 1Chr 18:16   7798

SHE See APPENDIX.

SHEAF
my s arose, and also stood upright ....Gen 37:7   485
about, and made obeisance to my s ....Gen 37:7   485
then ye shall bring a s of the ....Lev 23:10   6016
shall wave the s before the LORD...........Lev 23:11   6016
s an he lamb without blemish of.............Lev 23:12   6016
the s of the wave offering.......................Lev 23:15   6016

and hast forgot a *s* in the field	Deut 24:19	6016
take away the *s* from the hungry	Job 24:10	6016
and like a torch of fire in a *s*	Zec 12:6	5995

SHEAL (she'-al) *Married a foreigner in exile.*
Malluch, and Adaiah, Jashub, and *S*	Ezr 10:29	7594

SHEALTIEL (she-al'-te-el) See SALATHIEL. *Father of Ze-rubbabel.*
and Zerubbabel the son of *S*	Ezr 3:2	7597
began Zerubbabel the son of *S*	Ezr 3:8	7597
rose up Zerubbabel the son of *S*	Ezr 5:2	7597
up with Zerubbabel the son of *S*	Neh 12:1	7597
unto Zerubbabel the son of *S*	Hag 1:1	7597
Then Zerubbabel the son of *S*	Hag 1:12	7597
spirit of Zerubbabel the son of *S*	Hag 1:14	7597
now to Zerubbabel the son of *S*	Hag 2:2	7597
my servant, the son of *S*	Hag 2:23	7597

SHEAR
And Laban went to *s* his sheep	Gen 31:19	1494
up to Timnath to *s* his sheep	Gen 38:13	1494
nor *s* the firstling of thy sheep	Deut 15:19	1494
that Nabal did *s* his sheep	1Sa 25:4	1494

SHEARER
and like a lamb dumb before his *s*	Acts 8:32	2751

SHEARERS
now I have heard that thou hast *s*	1Sa 25:7	1494
flesh that I have killed for my *s*	1Sa 25:11	1494
as a sheep before her *s* is dumb	Is 53:7	1494

SHEARIAH (she-a-ri'-ah) *Son of Azel.*
Bocheru, and Ishmael, and *S*	1Chr 8:38	8187
Bocheru, and Ishmael, and *S*	1Chr 9:44	8187

SHEARING
he was *s* his sheep in Carmel	1Sa 25:2	1494
he was at the *s* house in the way	2Kin 10:12	1044,7462
them at the pit of the *s* house	2Kin 10:14	1044

SHEAR-JASHUB (she'-ar-ja'-shub) *Symbolic name of a son of Isaiah.*
S thy son, at the end of the	Is 7:3	7610

SHEATH
and drew it out of the *s* thereof	1Sa 17:51	8593
upon his loins in the *s* thereof	2Sa 20:8	8593
sword again into the *s* thereof	1Chr 21:27	5084
draw forth my sword out of his *s*	Eze 21:3	8593
his *s* against all flesh from the	Eze 21:4	8593
drawn forth my sword out of his *s*	Eze 21:5	8593
I cause it to return into his *s*	Eze 21:30	8593
Put up thy sword into the *s*	Jn 18:11	2336

SHEAVES
we were binding *s* in the field	Gen 37:7	485
your *s* stood round about, and made	Gen 37:7	485
after the reapers among the *s*	Ruth 2:7	6016
Let her glean even among the *s*	Ruth 2:15	6016
on the sabbath, and bringing in *s*	Neh 13:15	6194
bringing his *s* with him	Ps 126:6	485
nor he that bindeth *s* his bosom	Ps 129:7	
cart is pressed that is full of *s*	Amos 2:13	5995
them as the *s* into the floor	Mic 4:12	5995

SHEBA (she'-bah) See BATH-SHEBA, BEERSHEBA, SHEBAH.
1. Son of Raamah.
Raamah; *S*, and Dedan	Gen 10:7	7614
Raamah; *S*, and Dedan	1Chr 1:9	7614
2. Son of Yoktan.
And Obal, and Abimael, and *S*	Gen 10:28	7614
And Ebal, and Abimael, and *S*	1Chr 1:22	7614
3. Son of Yokshan.
And Jokshan begat *S*, and Dedan	Gen 25:3	7614
Jokshan; *S*, and Dedan	1Chr 1:32	7614
4. A region in southwestern Arabia.
when the queen of *S* heard of the	1Kin 10:1	7614
when the queen of *S* had seen all	1Kin 10:4	7614
queen of *S* gave to king Solomon	1Kin 10:10	7614
the queen of *S* all her desire	1Kin 10:13	7614
when the queen of *S* heard of the	2Chr 9:1	7614
when the queen of *S* had seen the	2Chr 9:3	7614
the queen of *S* gave king Solomon	2Chr 9:9	7614
to the queen of *S* all her desire	2Chr 9:12	7614
companies of *S* waited for them	Job 6:19	7614
the kings of *S* and Seba shall	Ps 72:10	7614
shall be given of the gold of *S*	Ps 72:15	7614
all they from *S* shall come	Is 60:6	7614
cometh there to me incense from *S*	Jer 6:20	7614
The merchants of *S* and Raamah,	Eze 27:22	7614
and Eden, the merchants of *S*	Eze 27:23	7614
S, and Dedan, and the merchants of	Eze 38:13	7614
5. A city in Simeon.
inheritance Beer-sheba, or *S*	Josh 19:2	7652

6. A son of Bichri.
a man of Belial, whose name was *S*	2Sa 20:1	7652
followed *S* the son of Bichri	2Sa 20:2	7652
Now shall *S* the son of Bichri do	2Sa 20:6	7652
to pursue after *S* the son of	2Sa 20:7	7652
pursued after *S* the son of Bichri	2Sa 20:10	7652
to pursue after *S* the son of	2Sa 20:13	7652
S the son of Bichri by name, hath	2Sa 20:21	7652
the head of *S* the son of Bichri	2Sa 20:22	7652
7. A chief Gadite.
were, Michael, and Meshullam, and *S*	1Chr 5:13	7652

SHEBAH (she'-bah) See SHEBA. *A well at Beersheba.*
And he called it *S*	Gen 26:33	7656

SHEBAM (she'-bam) See SHIBMAH. *A city in Reuben.*
and Heshbon, and Elealeh, and *S*	Num 32:3	7643

SHEBANIAH (sheb-a-ni'-ah) See SHECHANIAH.
1. A priest who moved the Ark.
And *S*, and Jehoshaphat, and	1Chr 15:24	7645
2. A Levite who aided Ezra.
Jeshua, and Bani, Kadmiel, *S*	Neh 9:4	7645
Hashabniah, Sherebiah, Hodijah, *S*	Neh 9:5	7645
And their brethren, *S*, Hodijah,	Neh 10:10	7645
3. A priest who renewed the covenant.
Hattush, *S*, Malluch,	Neh 10:4	7645
of *S*, Joseph	Neh 12:14	7645
4. A Levite who renewed the covenant.
Zaccur, Sherebiah, *S*,	Neh 10:12	7645

SHEBARIM (sheb-a-rim) *A place near Jericho.*
from before the gate even unto *S*	Josh 7:5	7671

SHEBAT See SEBAT.

SHEBER (she'-bur) *A son of Caleb.*
Caleb's concubine, bare *S*	1Chr 2:48	7669

SHEBNA (sheb'-nah)
1. King Hezekiah's scribe.
S the scribe, and Joah the son of	2Kin 18:18	7644
Eliakim the son of Hilkiah, and *S*	2Kin 18:26	7644
S the scribe, and Joah the son of	2Kin 18:37	7644
S the scribe, and the elders of	2Kin 19:2	7644
S the scribe, and Joah, Asaph's	Is 36:3	7644
Then said Eliakim and *S* and Joah	Is 36:11	7644
S the scribe, and Joah, the son of	Is 36:22	7644
S the scribe, and the elders of	Is 37:2	7644
2. An unspecified treasurer.
unto this treasurer, even unto *S*	Is 22:15	7644

SHEBNAH See SHEBNA.

SHEBUEL (she-bu'-el) See SHUBAEL.
1. A son of Gershom.
sons of Gershom, *S* was the chief	1Chr 23:16	7619
S the son of Gershom, the son of	1Chr 26:24	7619
2. A son of Haman.
Bukkiah, Mattaniah, Uzziel, *S*	1Chr 25:4	7619

SHECANIAH (shek-a-ni'-ah) See SHEBANIAH, SHECHANIAH.
1. A priest in David's time.
ninth to Jeshua, the tenth to *S*	1Chr 24:11	7935
2. A priest in Hezekiah's time.
and Shemaiah, Amariah, and *S*	2Chr 31:15	7935

SHECHANIAH (shek-a-ni'-ah) See SHEBANIAH, SHECANIAH.
1. Head of a Davidic family.
sons of Obadiah, the sons of *S*	1Chr 3:21	7935
And the sons of *S*	1Chr 3:22	7935
2. A family of exiles.
Of the sons of *S*, of the sons of	Ezr 8:3	7935
3. Another family of exiles.
Of the sons of *S*	Ezr 8:5	7935
4. Married a foreigner in exile.
S the son of Jehiel, one of the	Ezr 10:2	7935
5. Father of Shemaiah.
also Shemaiah the son of *S*	Neh 3:29	7935
6. Son of Arah.
son in law of *S* the son of Arah	Neh 6:18	7935
7. A priest with Zerubbabel.
S, Rehum, Meremoth,	Neh 12:3	7935

SHECHEM (she'-kem) See SHECHEMITES, SHECHEM'S, SICHEM, SYCHEM.
1. A Levitical city near Mt. Ephraim.
Jacob came to Shalem, a city of *S*	Gen 33:18	7927
them under the oak which was by *S*	Gen 35:4	7927
to feed their father's flock in *S*	Gen 37:12	7927
thy brethren feed the flock in *S*	Gen 37:13	7927
vale of Hebron, and he came to *S*	Gen 37:14	7927
Michmethah, that lieth before *S*	Josh 17:7	7927
and *S* in mount Ephraim, and	Josh 20:7	7927
For they gave them *S* with her	Josh 21:21	7927

S

all the tribes of Israel to *S*	Josh 24:1	7927
a statute and an ordinance in *S*	Josh 24:25	7927
And his concubine that was in *S*	Judg 8:31	7927
to *S* unto his mother's brethren	Judg 9:1	7927
in the ears of all the men of *S*	Judg 9:2	7927
all the men of *S* all these words	Judg 9:3	7927
all the men of *S* gathered	Judg 9:6	7927
plain of the pillar that was in *S*	Judg 9:6	7927
Hearken unto me, ye men of *S*	Judg 9:7	7927
king over the men of *S*, because	Judg 9:18	7927
Abimelech, and devour the men of *S*	Judg 9:20	7927
fire come out from the men of *S*	Judg 9:20	7927
between Abimelech and the men of *S*	Judg 9:23	7927
the men of *S* dealt treacherously	Judg 9:23	7927
and upon the men of *S*, which aided	Judg 9:24	7927
the men of *S* set liers in wait	Judg 9:25	7927
his brethren, and went over to *S*	Judg 9:26	7927
the men of *S* put their confidence	Judg 9:26	7927
Ebed and his brethren be come to *S*	Judg 9:31	7927
wait against *S* in four companies	Judg 9:34	7927
Gaal went out before the men of *S*	Judg 9:39	7927
that they should not dwell in *S*	Judg 9:41	7927
men of the tower of *S* heard that	Judg 9:46	7927
tower of *S* were gathered together	Judg 9:47	7927
men of the tower of *S* died also	Judg 9:49	7927
all the evil of the men of *S* did	Judg 9:57	7927
that goeth up from Beth-el to *S*	Judg 21:19	7927
And Rehoboam went to *S*	1Kin 12:1	7927
were come to *S* to make him king	1Kin 12:1	7927
Jeroboam built *S* in mount Ephraim	1Kin 12:25	7927
S in mount Ephraim with her	1Chr 6:67	7927
S also and the towns thereof, unto	1Chr 7:28	7927
And Rehoboam went to *S*	2Chr 10:1	7927
for to *S* were all Israel come to	2Chr 10:1	7927
I will rejoice, I will divide *S*	Ps 60:6	7927
I will rejoice, I will divide *S*	Ps 108:7	7927
That there came certain from *S*	Jer 41:5	7927

    2. *Son of Hamor.*

when *S* the son of Hamor the	Gen 34:2	7928
S spake unto his father Hamor,	Gen 34:4	7928
Hamor the father of *S* went out	Gen 34:6	7928
The soul of my son *S* longeth for	Gen 34:8	7928
S said unto her father and unto	Gen 34:11	7928
And the sons of Jacob answered *S*	Gen 34:13	7928
pleased Hamor, and *S* Hamor's son	Gen 34:18	7928
S his son came unto the gate of	Gen 34:20	7928
unto *S* his son hearkened all that	Gen 34:24	7928
S his son with the edge of the	Gen 34:26	7928
up out of Egypt, buried they in *S*	Josh 24:32	7928
S for an hundred pieces of silver	Josh 24:32	7928
Who is Abimelech, and who is *S*	Judg 9:28	7928
the men of Hamor the father of *S*	Judg 9:28	7928

    3. *Son of Gilead.*

and of *S*, the family of the	Num 26:31	7928
Asriel, and for the children of *S*	Josh 17:2	7928

    4. *A son of Shemidah.*

of Shemidah were, Ahian, and *S*	1Chr 7:19	7928

SHECHEMITES *(she'-kem-ites) Descendants of Shechem.*

of Shechem, the family of the *S*	Num 26:31	7930

SHECHEM'S *(she'-kems) Refers to Shechem 2.*

S father, for an hundred pieces	Gen 33:19	7927
and took Dinah out of *S* house	Gen 34:26	7927

SHED

by man shall his blood be *s*	Gen 9:6	8210
S no blood, but cast him into	Gen 37:22	8210
there shall no blood be *s* for him	Ex 22:2	
there shall be blood *s* for him	Ex 22:3	
he hath *s* blood	Lev 17:4	8210
of the blood that is *s* therein	Num 35:33	8210
but by the blood of him that *s* it	Num 35:33	8210
blood be not *s* in thy land	Deut 19:10	8210
Our hands have not *s* this blood	Deut 21:7	8210
thee from coming to *s* blood	1Sa 25:26	
that thou hast *s* blood causeless	1Sa 25:31	8210
this day from coming to *s* blood,	1Sa 25:33	
s out his bowels to the ground,	2Sa 20:10	8210
s the blood of war in peace, and	1Kin 2:5	7760
the innocent blood, which Joab *s*	1Kin 2:31	8210
Moreover Manasseh *s* innocent	2Kin 21:16	8210
for the innocent blood that he *s*	2Kin 24:4	8210
Thou hast *s* blood abundantly, and	1Chr 22:8	8210
because thou hast *s* much blood	1Chr 22:8	8210
a man of war, and hast *s* blood	1Chr 28:3	8210
Their blood have they *s* like	Ps 79:3	8210
blood of thy servants which is *s*	Ps 79:10	8210
s innocent blood, even the blood	Ps 106:38	8210
to evil, and make haste to *s* blood	Prov 1:16	8210
hands that *s* innocent blood,	Prov 6:17	8210

make haste to *s* innocent blood	Is 59:7	8210
s not innocent blood in this	Jer 7:6	8210
neither *s* innocent blood in this	Jer 22:3	8210
for to *s* innocent blood, and for	Jer 22:17	8210
that have *s* the blood of the just	Lam 4:13	8210
wedlock and *s* blood are judged	Eze 16:38	8210
in thy blood that thou hast *s*	Eze 22:4	8210
in thee to their power to *s* blood	Eze 22:6	8210
men that carry tales to *s* blood	Eze 22:9	8210
have they taken gifts to *s* blood	Eze 22:12	8210
to *s* blood, and to destroy souls,	Eze 22:27	8210
the manner of women that *s* blood	Eze 23:45	8210
toward your idols, and *s* blood	Eze 33:25	8210
hast *s* the blood of the children	Eze 35:5	5064
that they had *s* upon the land	Eze 36:18	8210
because they have *s* innocent	Joel 3:19	8210
righteous blood *s* upon the earth	Mt 23:35	*1632*
which is *s* for many for the	Mt 26:28	*1632*
testament, which is *s* for many	Mk 14:24	*1632*
which was *s* from the foundation	Lk 11:50	*1632*
in my blood, which is *s* for you	Lk 22:20	*1632*
he hath *s* forth this, which ye	Acts 2:33	*1632*
blood of thy martyr Stephen was *s*	Acts 22:20	*1632*
Their feet are swift to *s* blood	Rom 3:15	*1632*
because the love of God is *s*	Rom 5:5	*1632*
Which he *s* on us abundantly	Titus 3:6	*1632*
For they have *s* the blood of	Rev 16:6	*1632*

SHEDDER

a *s* of blood, and that doeth the	Eze 18:10	8210

SHEDDETH

Whoso *s* man's blood, by man shall	Gen 9:6	8210
The city *s* blood in the midst of	Eze 22:3	8210

SHEDDING

and without *s* of blood is no	Heb 9:22	*130*

SHEDEUR *(shed'-e-ur) A Reubenite who counted the people.*

Elizur the son of *S*	Num 1:5	7707
shall be Elizur the son of *S*	Num 2:10	7707
fourth day Elizur the son of *S*	Num 7:30	7707
offering of Elizur the son of *S*.	Num 7:35	7707
his host was Elizur the son of *S*	Num 10:18	7707

SHEEP

And Abel was a keeper of *s*	Gen 4:2	6629
and he had *s*, and oxen, and he asses	Gen 12:16	6629
And Abimelech took *s*, and oxen, and	Gen 20:14	6629
And Abraham took *s* and oxen, and	Gen 21:27	6629
three flocks of *s* lying by it	Gen 29:2	6629
well's mouth, and watered the *s*	Gen 29:3	6629
his daughter cometh with the *s*	Gen 29:6	6629
water ye the *s*, and go and feed	Gen 29:7	6629
then we water the *s*	Gen 29:8	6629
Rachel came with her father's *s*	Gen 29:9	6629
the *s* of Laban his mother's	Gen 29:10	6629
all the brown cattle among the *s*	Gen 30:32	3775
the goats, and brown among the *s*	Gen 30:33	3775
it, and all the brown among the *s*	Gen 30:35	3775
And Laban went to shear his *s*	Gen 31:19	6629
They took their *s*, and their oxen,	Gen 34:28	6629
up to Timnah to shear his *s*	Gen 38:13	6629
upon the oxen, and upon the *s*	Ex 9:3	6629
ye shall take it out from the *s*	Ex 12:5	3532
and thy peace offerings, thy *s*	Ex 20:24	6629
a man shall steal an ox, or a *s*	Ex 22:1	7716
for an ox, and four *s* for a *s*	Ex 22:1	6629
whether it be ox, or ass, or *s*	Ex 22:4	7716
it be for ox, for ass, for *s*	Ex 22:9	7716
an ass, or an ox, or a *s*, or any	Ex 22:10	7716
do with thine oxen, and with thy *s*	Ex 22:30	6629
among thy cattle, whether ox or *s*	Ex 34:19	7716
of the flocks, namely, of the *s*	Lev 1:10	3775
no manner of fat, of ox, or of *s*	Lev 7:23	3775
blemish, of the beeves, of the *s*	Lev 22:19	3775
freewill offering in beeves or *s*	Lev 22:21	6629
When a bullock, or a *s*, or a goat	Lev 22:27	3775
whether it be ox, or *s*	Lev 27:26	7716
of a cow, or the firstling of a *s*	Num 18:17	3775
And Balak offered oxen and *s*	Num 22:40	6629
of the LORD be not as *s* which	Num 27:17	6629
and of the asses, and of the *s*	Num 31:28	6629
thousand and five thousand *s*	Num 31:32	6629
thirty thousand and five hundred *s*	Num 31:36	6629
tribute of the *s* was six hundred	Num 31:37	6629
seven thousand and five hundred *s*	Num 31:43	6629
little ones, and folds for your *s*	Num 32:24	6792
and folds of *s*	Num 32:36	6629
thy kine, and the flocks of thy *s*	Deut 7:13	6629
the ox, the *s*, and the goat,	Deut 14:4	3775
lusteth after, for oxen, or for *s*	Deut 14:26	6629

nor shear the firstling of thy s	Deut 15:19	6629
LORD thy God any bullock, or s	Deut 17:1	7716
sacrifice, whether it be ox or s	Deut 18:3	7716
the first of the fleece of thy s	Deut 18:4	6629
brother's ox or his s go astray	Deut 22:1	7716
thy kine, and the flocks of thy s	Deut 28:4	6629
thy kine, and the flocks of thy s	Deut 28:18	6629
thy s shall be given unto thine	Deut 28:31	6629
of thy kine, or flocks of thy s	Deut 28:51	6629
Butter of kine, and milk of s	Deut 32:14	6629
woman, young and old, and ox, and s	Josh 6:21	7716
his oxen, and his asses, and his s	Josh 7:24	6629
sustenance for Israel, neither s	Judg 6:4	7716
He will take the tenth of your s	1Sa 8:17	6629
flew upon the spoil, and took s	1Sa 14:32	6629
man his ox, and every man his s	1Sa 14:34	7716
infant and suckling, ox and s	1Sa 15:3	7716
spared Agag, and the best of the s	1Sa 15:9	6629
bleating of the s in mine ears	1Sa 15:14	6629
people spared the best of the s	1Sa 15:15	6629
the people took of the spoil, s	1Sa 15:21	6629
and, behold, he keepeth the s	1Sa 16:11	6629
thy son, which is with the s	1Sa 16:19	6629
feed his father's s at Beth-lehem	1Sa 17:15	6629
left the s with a keeper, and took	1Sa 17:20	6629
those few s in the wilderness	1Sa 17:28	6629
Thy servant kept his father's s	1Sa 17:34	6629
and oxen, and asses, and s, with	1Sa 22:19	7716
great, and he had three thousand s	1Sa 25:2	6629
he was shearing his s in Carmel	1Sa 25:2	6629
that Nabal did shear his s	1Sa 25:4	6629
we were with them keeping the s	1Sa 25:16	6629
five s ready dressed, and five	1Sa 25:18	6629
woman alive, and took away the s	1Sa 27:9	6629
sheepcote, from following the s	2Sa 7:8	6629
And honey, and butter, and s	2Sa 17:29	6629
but these s, what have they done	2Sa 24:17	6629
And Adonijah slew s and oxen and fat	1Kin 1:9	6629
s in abundance, and hath called	1Kin 1:19	6629
s in abundance, and hath called	1Kin 1:25	6629
of the pastures, and an hundred s	1Kin 4:23	6629
him before the ark, sacrificing s	1Kin 8:5	6629
an hundred and twenty thousand s	1Kin 8:63	6629
as s that have not a shepherd	1Kin 22:17	6629
and oliveyards, and vineyards, and s	2Kin 5:26	6629
of s two hundred and fifty	1Chr 5:21	6629
and oil, and oxen, and s abundantly	1Chr 12:40	6629
even from following the s	1Chr 17:7	6629
but as for these s, what have	1Chr 21:17	6629
him before the ark, sacrificed s	2Chr 5:6	6629
an hundred and twenty thousand s	2Chr 7:5	6629
of cattle, and carried away s	2Chr 14:15	6629
hundred oxen and seven thousand s	2Chr 15:11	6629
And Ahab killed s and oxen for him	2Chr 18:2	6629
as s that have no shepherd	2Chr 18:16	6629
hundred oxen and three thousand s	2Chr 29:33	6629
bullocks and seven thousand s	2Chr 30:24	6629
bullocks and ten thousand s	2Chr 30:24	6629
brought in the tithe of oxen and s	2Chr 31:6	6629
and they builded the s gate	Neh 3:1	6629
s gate repaired the goldsmiths	Neh 3:32	6629
daily was one ox and six choice s	Neh 5:18	6629
of Meah, even unto the s gate	Neh 12:39	6629
also was seven thousand s	Job 1:3	6629
heaven, and hath burned up the s	Job 1:16	6629
warmed with the fleece of my s	Job 31:20	3532
for he had fourteen thousand s	Job 42:12	6629
All s and oxen, yea, and the beasts	Ps 8:7	6792
us like s appointed for meat	Ps 44:11	6629
counted as s for the slaughter	Ps 44:22	6629
Like s they are laid in the grave	Ps 49:14	6629
against the s of thy pasture	Ps 74:1	6629
his own people to go forth like s	Ps 78:52	6629
s of thy pasture will give thee	Ps 79:13	6629
his pasture, and the s of his hand	Ps 95:7	6629
people, and the s of his pasture	Ps 100:3	6629
I have gone astray like a lost s	Ps 119:176	6629
that our s may bring forth	Ps 144:13	6629
a flock of s that are even shorn	Song 4:2	
Thy teeth are as a flock of s	Song 6:6	7353
nourish a young cow, and two s	Is 7:21	6629
as a s that no man taketh up	Is 13:14	6629
slaying oxen, and killing s	Is 22:13	6629
All we like s have gone astray	Is 53:6	6629
as a s before her shearers is	Is 53:7	7353
them out like s for the slaughter	Jer 12:3	6629
scatter the s of my pasture	Jer 23:1	6629
My people hath been lost s	Jer 50:6	6629
Israel is a scattered s	Jer 50:17	7716
My s wandered through all the	Eze 34:6	6629
I, even I, will both search my s	Eze 34:11	6629

is among his s that are scattered	Eze 34:12	6629
so will I seek out my s, and will	Eze 34:12	6629
a wife, and for a wife he kept s	Hos 12:12	
the flocks of s are made desolate	Joel 1:18	6629
them together as the s of Bozrah	Mic 2:12	6629
young lion among the flocks of s	Mic 5:8	6629
and the s shall be scattered	Zec 13:7	6629
abroad, as s having no shepherd	Mt 9:36	4263
the lost s of the house of Israel	Mt 10:6	4263
I send you forth as s in the	Mt 10:16	4263
among you, that shall have one s	Mt 12:11	4263
then is a man better than a s	Mt 12:12	4263
the lost s of the house of Israel	Mt 15:24	4263
if a man have an hundred s	Mt 18:12	4263
you, he rejoiceth more of that s	Mt 18:13	4263
divideth his s from the goats	Mt 25:32	4263
he shall set the s on his right	Mt 25:33	4263
the s of the flock shall be	Mt 26:31	4263
because they were as s not having	Mk 6:34	4263
and the s shall be scattered	Mk 14:27	4263
man of you, having an hundred s	Lk 15:4	4263
I have found my s which was lost	Lk 15:6	4263
temple those that sold oxen and s	Jn 2:14	4263
all out of the temple, and the s	Jn 2:15	4263
Jerusalem by the s market a pool	Jn 5:2	4262
the door is the shepherd of the s	Jn 10:2	4263
and the s hear his voice	Jn 10:3	4263
and he calleth his own s by name	Jn 10:3	4263
when he putteth forth his own s	Jn 10:4	4263
before them, and the s follow him	Jn 10:4	4263
unto you, I am the door of the s	Jn 10:7	4263
but the s did not hear them	Jn 10:8	4263
giveth his life for the s	Jn 10:11	4263
shepherd, whose own the s are not	Jn 10:12	4263
the wolf coming, and leaveth the s	Jn 10:12	4263
them, and scattereth the s	Jn 10:12	4263
hireling, and careth not for the s	Jn 10:13	4263
the good shepherd, and know my s	Jn 10:14	
and I lay down my life for the s	Jn 10:15	4263
other s I have, which are not of	Jn 10:16	4263
not, because ye are not of my s	Jn 10:26	4263
My s hear my voice, and I know	Jn 10:27	4263
He saith unto him, Feed my s	Jn 21:16	4263
Jesus saith unto him, Feed my s	Jn 21:17	4263
this, He was led as a s to the	Acts 8:32	4263
accounted as s for the slaughter	Rom 8:36	4263
that great shepherd of the s	Heb 13:20	4263
For ye were as s going astray	1Pet 2:25	4263
flour, and wheat, and beasts, and s	Rev 18:13	4263

SHEEPCOTE

of hosts, I took thee from the s	2Sa 7:8	5116
of hosts, I took thee from the s	1Chr 17:7	5116

SHEEPCOTES

And he came to the s by the way	1Sa 24:3	1448,6629

SHEEPFOLD

not by the door into the s	Jn 10:1	*833,4263*

SHEEPFOLDS

We will build s here for our	Num 32:16	1488,6629
Why abodest thou among the s	Judg 5:16	4942
servant, and took him from the s	Ps 78:70	4356,6629

SHEEPMASTER

And Mesha king of Moab was a s	2Kin 3:4	5349

SHEEP'S

which come to you in s clothing	Mt 7:15	*4263*

SHEEPSHEARERS

and went up unto his s to Timnath	Gen 38:12	1494,6629
that Absalom had s in Baal-hazor	2Sa 13:23	1494
Behold now, thy servant hath s	2Sa 13:24	1494

SHEEPSKINS

they wandered about in s and	Heb 11:37	*3374*

SHEERAH See SHERAH.

SHEET

as it had been a great s knit at	Acts 10:11	3607
descend, as it had been a great s	Acts 11:5	3607

SHEETS

then I will give you thirty s	Judg 14:12	5466
then shall ye give me thirty s	Judg 14:13	5466

SHEHARIAH (she-ha-ri'-ah) A son of Jeroham.

And Shamsherai, and S, and Athaliah,	1Chr 8:26	7841

SHEKEL

golden earring of half a s weight	Gen 24:22	1235
half a s after the s of the	Ex 30:13	8255
(a s is twenty gerahs	Ex 30:13	8255
an half s shall be the offering	Ex 30:13	8255
shall not give less than half a s	Ex 30:15	8255

S

after the *s* of the sanctuary, and .... Ex 30:24   8255
after the *s* of the sanctuary .... Ex 38:24   8255
after the *s* of the sanctuary .... Ex 38:25   8255
for every man, that is, half a *s* .... Ex 38:26   8255
after the *s* of the sanctuary, for .... Ex 38:26   8255
after the *s* of the sanctuary, for .... Lev 5:15   8255
after the *s* of the sanctuary .... Lev 27:3   8255
to the *s* of the sanctuary .... Lev 27:25   8255
twenty gerahs shall be the *s* .... Lev 27:25   8255
after the *s* of the sanctuary .... Num 3:47   8255
(the *s* is twenty gerahs .... Num 3:47   8255
after the *s* of the sanctuary .... Num 3:50   8255
after the *s* of the sanctuary .... Num 7:13   8255
after the *s* of the sanctuary .... Num 7:19   8255
after the *s* of the sanctuary .... Num 7:25   8255
after the *s* of the sanctuary .... Num 7:31   8255
after the *s* of the sanctuary .... Num 7:37   8255
after the *s* of the sanctuary .... Num 7:43   8255
after the *s* of the sanctuary .... Num 7:49   8255
after the *s* of the sanctuary .... Num 7:55   8255
after the *s* of the sanctuary .... Num 7:61   8255
after the *s* of the sanctuary .... Num 7:67   8255
after the *s* of the sanctuary .... Num 7:73   8255
after the *s* of the sanctuary .... Num 7:79   8255
after the *s* of the sanctuary .... Num 7:85   8255
after the *s* of the sanctuary, ... Num 7:86   8255
after the *s* of the sanctuary, ... Num 18:16   8255
the fourth part of a *s* of silver 1Sa 9:8   8255
of fine flour be sold for a *s* 2Kin 7:1   8255
and two measures of barley for a *s* 2Kin 7:1   8255
of fine flour was sold for a *s* 2Kin 7:16   8255
and two measures of barley for a *s* 2Kin 7:16   8255
Two measures of barley for a *s* 2Kin 7:18   8255
a measure of fine flour for a *s* 2Kin 7:18   8255
s for the service of the house of .... Neh 10:32   8255
the *s* shall be twenty gerahs .... Eze 45:12   8255
the *s* great, and falsifying the .... Amos 8:5   8255

SHEKELS

is worth four hundred *s* of silver .... Gen 23:15   8255
of Heth, four hundred *s* of silver .... Gen 23:16   8255
her hands of ten *s* weight of gold .... Gen 24:22   8255
their master thirty *s* of silver .... Ex 21:32   8255
of pure myrrh five hundred *s* .... Ex 30:23
much, even two hundred and fifty *s* ...... Ex 30:23
calamus two hundred and fifty *s* .... Ex 30:23
And of cassia five hundred *s* .... Ex 30:24
and seven hundred and thirty *s* .... Ex 38:24   8255
and threescore and fifteen *s* .... Ex 38:25   8255
five *s* he made hooks for the .... Ex 38:28
and two thousand and four hundred *s* ... Ex 38:29   8255
thy estimation by *s* of silver .... Lev 5:15   8255
shall be fifty *s* of silver .... Lev 27:3   8255
thy estimation shall be thirty *s* .... Lev 27:4   8255
shall be of the male twenty *s* .... Lev 27:5   8255
and for the female ten *s* .... Lev 27:5   8255
be of the male five *s* of silver .... Lev 27:6   8255
shall be three *s* of silver .... Lev 27:6   8255
thy estimation shall be fifteen *s* .... Lev 27:7   8255
and for the female ten *s* .... Lev 27:7   8255
be valued at fifty *s* of silver .... Lev 27:16   8255
take five *s* apiece by the poll .... Num 3:47   8255
hundred and threescore and five *s* .... Num 7:13
was an hundred and thirty *s* .... Num 7:13
one silver bowl of seventy *s* .... Num 7:13
One spoon of ten *s* of gold .... Num 7:14
was an hundred and thirty *s* .... Num 7:19
one silver bowl of seventy *s* .... Num 7:19   8255
One spoon of gold of ten *s* .... Num 7:20
was an hundred and thirty *s* .... Num 7:25
one silver bowl of seventy *s* .... Num 7:25   8255
One golden spoon of ten *s* .... Num 7:26
weight of an hundred and thirty *s* .... Num 7:31
one silver bowl of seventy *s* .... Num 7:31   8255
One golden spoon of ten *s* .... Num 7:32
was an hundred and thirty *s* .... Num 7:37
one silver bowl of seventy *s* .... Num 7:37   8255
One golden spoon of ten *s* .... Num 7:38
weight of an hundred and thirty *s* .... Num 7:43
a silver bowl of seventy *s* .... Num 7:43   8255
One golden spoon of ten *s* .... Num 7:44
was an hundred and thirty *s* .... Num 7:49
one silver bowl of seventy *s* .... Num 7:49   8255
One golden spoon of ten *s* .... Num 7:50
weight of an hundred and thirty *s* .... Num 7:55
one silver bowl of seventy *s* .... Num 7:55   8255
One golden spoon of ten *s* .... Num 7:56
was an hundred and thirty *s* .... Num 7:61
one silver bowl of seventy *s* .... Num 7:61   8255
One golden spoon of ten *s* .... Num 7:62
was an hundred and thirty *s* .... Num 7:67

one silver bowl of seventy *s* .... Num 7:67   8255
One golden spoon of ten *s* .... Num 7:68
was an hundred and thirty *s* .... Num 7:73
one silver bowl of seventy *s* .... Num 7:73   8255
One golden spoon of ten *s* .... Num 7:74
was an hundred and thirty *s* .... Num 7:79
one silver bowl of seventy *s* .... Num 7:79   8255
One golden spoon of ten *s* .... Num 7:80
weighing an hundred and thirty *s* .... Num 7:85
two thousand and four hundred *s* .... Num 7:85
of incense, weighing ten *s* apiece........... Num 7:86
spoons was an hundred and twenty *s* .... Num 7:86
for the money of five *s*, after .... Num 18:16   8255
thousand seven hundred and fifty *s* ...... Num 31:52   8255
him in an hundred *s* of silver .... Deut 22:19
damsel's father fifty *s* of silver .... Deut 22:29
and two hundred *s* of silver .... Josh 7:21   8255
a wedge of gold of fifty *s* weight .... Josh 7:21   8255
and seven hundred *s* of gold.................... Judg 8:26
The eleven hundred *s* of silver .... Judg 17:2
hundred *s* of silver to his mother .... Judg 17:3
took two hundred *s* of silver .... Judg 17:4
I will give thee ten *s* of silver .... Judg 17:10
coat was five thousand *s* of brass 1Sa 17:5   8255
weighed six hundred *s* of iron 1Sa 17:7   8255
hundred *s* after the king's weight 2Sa 14:26   8255
have given thee ten *s* of silver 2Sa 18:11
thousand *s* of silver in mine hand.......... 2Sa 18:12
hundred *s* of brass in weight.................. 2Sa 21:16
and the oxen for fifty *s* of silver 2Sa 24:24   8255
six hundred *s* of gold went to one 1Kin 10:16
Egypt for six hundred *s* of silver........... 1Kin 10:29
of each man fifty *s* of silver.................... 2Kin 15:20   8255
six hundred *s* of gold by weight 1Chr 21:25   8255
for six hundred *s* of silver 2Chr 1:17
of the nails was fifty *s* of gold 2Chr 3:9   8255
six hundred *s* of beaten gold went 2Chr 9:15
three hundred *s* of gold went to 2Chr 9:16
and wine, beside forty *s* of silver .... Neh 5:15   8255
money, even seventeen *s* of silver .... Jer 32:9   8255
be by weight, twenty *s* a day .... Eze 4:10   8255
twenty *s*, five and twenty .... Eze 45:12   8255
five and twenty *s*, fifteen *s* .... Eze 45:12   8255

SHELAH *(she'-lah)* See SALAH, SHELANITES.
1. Son of Judah.
and called his name *S* .... Gen 38:5   7956
house, till *S* my son be grown .... Gen 38:11   7956
for she saw that *S* was grown .... Gen 38:14   7956
that I gave her not to *S* my son .... Gen 38:26   7956
Er, and Onan, and *S*, and Pharez, and ... Gen 46:12   7956
of *S*, the family of the .... Num 26:20   7956
Er, and Onan, and *S*............................... 1Chr 2:3   7956
The sons of *S* the son of Judah 1Chr 4:21   7956
2. Son of Arphaxad.
And Arphaxad begat *S*, and Shelah....... 1Chr 1:18   7974
begat Shelah, and *S* begat Eber 1Chr 1:18   7956
Shem, Arphaxad, *S*, ... 1Chr 1:24   7956

SHELANITE See SHELANITES.

SHELANITES *(she'-lan-ites)* Descendants of Shelah.
of Shelah, the family of the *S* .... Num 26:20   8024

SHELEMIAH *(shel-e-mi'-ah)* See MESHELEMIAH,
SHALLUM.
1. A sanctuary servant.
And the lot eastward fell to *S* 1Chr 26:14   8018
2. A son of Bani who married a foreigner.
And *S*, and Nathan, and Adaiah,........... Ezr 10:39   8018
3. Another son of Bani.
Azareel, and *S*, Shemariah, ... Ezr 10:41   8018
4. Father of Hananiah.
repaired Hananiah the son of *S*............. Neh 3:30   8018
5. A treasury servant.
S the priest, and Zadok the scribe.......... Neh 13:13   8018
6. Son of Cushi.
son of Nethaniah, the son of *S* .... Jer 36:14   8018
7. Son of Abdeel.
S the son of Abdeel, to take.................... Jer 36:26   8018
8. Father of Jehucal.
king sent Jehucal the son of *S*................ Jer 37:3   8018
of Pashur, and Jucal the son of *S* .... Jer 38:1   8018
9. Father of Irijah.
name was Irijah, the son of *S*.................. Jer 37:13   8018

SHELEPH *(she'-lef)* A son of Joktan.
And Joktan begat Almodad, and *S*......... Gen 10:26   8026
And Joktan begat Almodad, and *S*......... 1Chr 1:20   8026

SHELESH *(she'-lesh)* A son of Helem.
Zophah, and Imna, and *S*, and Amal 1Chr 7:35   8028

SHELOMI (shel'-o-mi) *Father of Ahihud.*
of Asher, Ahihud the son of S .... Num 34:27   8015

SHELOMITH (shel'-o-mith)
  1. Daughter of Debri.
(and his mother's name was S .... Lev 24:11   8019
  2. Daughter of Zerubbabel.
and Hananiah, and S their sister 1Chr 3:19   8019
  3. A son of Shimei.
S, and Haziel, and Haran, three 1Chr 23:9   8013
  4. A son of Izhar.
S the chief 1Chr 23:18   8013
  5. A descendant of Eliezer.
and Zichri his son, and S his son 1Chr 26:25   8013
Which S and his brethren were over 1Chr 26:26   8013
thing, it was under the hand of S 1Chr 26:28   8019
  6. A child of King Rehoboam.
Abijah, and Attai, and Ziza, and S 2Chr 11:20   8019
  7. A family of exiles.
And of the sons of S .... Ezr 8:10   8019

SHELOMOTH (shel'-o-moth) See SHELOMITH. *A descendant of Izhar.*
S: of the sons of S 1Chr 24:22   8013

SHELTER
embrace the rock for want of a s .... Job 24:8   4268
For thou hast been a s for me .... Ps 61:3   4268

SHELUMIEL
S the son of Zurishaddai .... Num 1:6   8017
shall be S the son of Zurishaddai .... Num 2:12   8017
On the fifth day S the son of .... Num 7:36   8017
of S the son of Zurishaddai .... Num 7:41   8017
was S the son of Zurishaddai .... Num 10:19   8017

SHEM (shem) See SEM. *A son of Noah.*
and Noah begat S, Ham, and Japheth ... Gen 5:32   8035
And Noah begat three sons, S .... Gen 6:10   8035
selfsame day entered Noah, and S .... Gen 7:13   8035
went forth of the ark, were S .... Gen 9:18   8035
And S and Japheth took a garment, ... Gen 9:23   8035
Blessed be the LORD God of S .... Gen 9:26   8035
he shall dwell in the tents of S .... Gen 9:27   8035
of the sons of Noah, S, Ham, and .... Gen 10:1   8035
Unto S also, the father of all .... Gen 10:21   8035
The children of S .... Gen 10:22   8035
These are the sons of S, after................. Gen 10:31   8035
These are the generations of S............... Gen 11:10   8035
S was an hundred years old, and............ Gen 11:10   8035
S lived after he begat Arphaxad............. Gen 11:11   8035
Noah, S, Ham, and Japheth 1Chr 1:4   8035
The sons of S 1Chr 1:17   8035
S, Arphaxad, Shelah, ... 1Chr 1:24   8035

SHEMA (she'-mah) See SHEMAIAH, SHIMHI.
  1. A city in Judah.
Amam, and S, and Moladah,................... Josh 15:26   8087
  2. A son of Hebron.
Korah, and Tappuah, and Rekem, and S 1Chr 2:43   8087
S begat Raham, the father of 1Chr 2:44   8087
  3. Father of Azaz.
the son of Azaz, the son of S 1Chr 5:8   8087
  4. A Benjamite Chief.
Beriah also, and S, who were heads....... 1Chr 8:13   8087
  5. A priest who aided Ezra.
beside him stood Mattithiah, and S .... Neh 8:4   8087

SHEMAAH (shem'-a-ah) *Father of two warriors in David's army.*
the sons of S the Gibeathite 1Chr 12:3   8094

SHEMAIAH (shem-a-i'-ah) See SHAMMUA, SHEMA, SHIMEI, SIMEI.
  1. A prophet in King Rehoboam's time.
of God came unto S the man of God 1Kin 12:22   8098
the LORD came to S the man of God....... 2Chr 11:2   8098
Then came S the prophet to 2Chr 12:5   8098
the word of the LORD came to S 2Chr 12:7   8098
in the book of S the prophet.................... 2Chr 12:15   8098
  2. Son of Shechaniah.
S: and the sons of Shemaiah 1Chr 3:22   8098
  3. Father of Shimri.
the son of Shimri, the son of S 1Chr 4:37   8098
  4. Son of Joel.
S his son, Gog his son, Shimei 1Chr 5:4   8098
  5. Son of Hasshub.
S the son of Hasshub, the son of 1Chr 9:14   8098
S the son of Hashub, the son of.............. Neh 11:15   8098
  6. Father of Obadiah.
And Obadiah the son of S, the son 1Chr 9:16   8098
  7. A priest who moved the Ark.
S the chief, and his brethren two 1Chr 15:8   8098
for Uriel, Asaiah, and Joel, S................... 1Chr 15:11   8098

  8. Son of Nathaneel.
S the son of Nethaneel the scribe 1Chr 24:6   8098
  9. A sanctuary servant.
S the firstborn, Jehozabad the................ 1Chr 26:4   8098
Also unto S his son were sons................. 1Chr 26:6   8098
The sons of S 1Chr 26:7   8098
  10. A Levite teacher of the people.
with them he sent Levites, even S........... 2Chr 17:8   8098
  11. A Levite who cleansed the temple.
S, and Uzziel 2Chr 29:14   8098
  12. A Levite in Hezekiah's time.
and Miniamin, and Jeshua, and S 2Chr 31:15   8098
  13. A Levite in Josiah's time.
Conaniah also, and S and Nethaneel, ... 2Chr 35:9   8098
  14. A family of exiles.
are these, Eliphelet, Jeiel, and S .... Ezr 8:13   8098
  15. A messenger of Ezra.
I for Eliezer, for Ariel, for S .... Ezr 8:16   8098
  16. A priest who married a foreigner.
Maaseiah, and Elijah, and S................... Ezr 10:21   8098
  17. A son of Harim.
Eliezer, Ishijah, Malchiah, S................... Ezr 10:31   8098
  18. A rebuilder of Jerusalem's wall.
also S the son of Shechaniah .... Neh 3:29   8098
  19. Son of Delaiah.
I came unto the house of S the .... Neh 6:10   8098
  20. A priest who renewed the covenant.
Maaziah, Bilgai, S.................................... Neh 10:8   8098
S, and Joiarib, Jedaiah, ... Neh 12:6   8098
of S, Jehonathan..................................... Neh 12:18   8098
Judah, and Benjamin, and S, and .... Neh 12:34   8098
the son of Jonathan, the son of S........... Neh 12:35   8098
  21. A priest who dedicated the wall.
And his brethren, S, and Azarael, ... Neh 12:36   8098
  22. A priest who gave thanks at the wall.
And Maaseiah, and S, and Eleazar, and Neh 12:42   8098
  23. Father of Urijah.
the son of S of Kirjath-jearim .... Jer 26:20   8098
  24. A false prophet.
also speak to S the Nehelamite .... Jer 29:24   8098
LORD concerning S the Nehelamite .... Jer 29:31   8098
Because that S hath prophesied .... Jer 29:31   8098
I will punish S the Nehelamite,............... Jer 29:32   8098
  25. Father of Delaiah.
scribe, and Delaiah the son of S............. Jer 36:12   8098

SHEMARIAH (shem-a-ri'-ah)
  1. A warrior in David's army.
and Jerimoth, and Bealiah, and S 1Chr 12:5   8114
  2. Married a foreigner in exile.
Benjamin, Malluch, and S .... Ezr 10:32   8114
  3. Married a foreigner in exile.
Azareel, and Shelemiah, S...................... Ezr 10:41   8114

SHEMEBER (shem-e'-ber) *King of Zeboim.*
S king of Zeboiim, and the king of......... Gen 14:2   8038

SHEMED See SHAMED.

SHEMER (she'-mur) *Owner of a hill, later the site of Samaria.*
of S for two talents of silver.................... 1Kin 16:24   8106
he built, after the name of S 1Kin 16:24   8106

SHEMIDA (shem-i'-dah) See SHEMIDAH. *Son of Gilead.*
And of S, the family of the .... Num 26:32   8061
Hepher, and for the children of S............ Josh 17:2   8061

SHEMIDAH (shem-i'-dah) See SHEMIDA, SHEMIDAITES. *Same as Shemida.*
And the sons of S were, Ahian, and........ 1Chr 7:19   8061

SHEMIDAITES (shem'-i-dah-ites) *Descendants of Shemida.*
of Shemida, the family of the S .... Num 26:32   8062

SHEMINITH (shem'-i-nith) *A musical notation.*
with harps on the S to excel.................... 1Chr 15:21   8067
chief Musician on Neginoth upon S .... Ps 6:t   8067
To the chief Musician upon S.................. Ps 12:t   8067

SHEMIRAMOTH (she-mir'-a-moth)
  1. A priest who moved the Ark.
Zechariah, Ben, and Jaaziel, and S 1Chr 15:18   8070
And Zechariah, and Aziel, and S............. 1Chr 15:20   8070
to him Zechariah, Jeiel, and S 1Chr 16:5   8070
  2. A Levite in Jehoshaphat's time.
and Zebadiah, and Asahel, and S........... 2Chr 17:8   8070

SHEMUEL (shem-u-'el) See SAMUEL.
  1. A Simeonite prince.
of Simeon, S the son of Ammihud.......... Num 34:20   8050
  2. Another name for Samuel the prophet.
the son of Joel, the son of S 1Chr 6:33   8050
  3. Head of a family in Issachar.
and Jahmai, and Jibsam, and S 1Chr 7:2   8050

S

SHEN *(shen) A place in Benjamin.*
and set it between Mizpeh and *S* 1Sa 7:12   8129

SHENAZAR *(she-na'-zar) Descendant of King Jehoi-*
akim.
Malchiram also, and Pedaiah, and *S* 1Chr 3:18   8137

SHENAZZAR See SHENAZAR.

SHENIR *(she'-nur) See SENIR, SION. A mountain be-*
tween Amana and Hermon.
and the Amorites call it *S* .... Deut 3:9   8149
top of Amana, from the top of *S* .... Song 4:8   8149

SHEOL See HELL.

SHEPHAM *(she'-fam) See SHIPMITE. A place east of the*
Sea of Cinneroth.
east border from Hazar-enan to *S* .... Num 34:10   8221
shall go down from *S* to Riblah .... Num 34:11   8221

SHEPHATIAH *(shef-a-ti'-ah)*
1. A son of David.
and the fifth, *S* the son of Abital 2Sa 3:4   8203
The fifth, *S* of Abital 1Chr 3:3   8203
Michri, and Meshullam the son of *S* 1Chr 9:8   8203
2. A warrior in David's army.
and Shemariah, and *S* the Haruphite, .. 1Chr 12:5   8203
3. A Simeonite prince.
Simeonites, *S* the son of Maachah 1Chr 27:16   8203
4. A son of King Jehoshaphat.
and Azariah, and Michael, and *S* 2Chr 21:2   8203
5. A family of exiles with Zerubbabel.
The children of *S*, three hundred .... Ezr 2:4   8203
The children of *S*, three hundred .... Neh 7:9   8203
6. Descendants of a servant of Solomon.
The children of *S*, the children .... Ezr 2:57   8203
The children of *S*, the children .... Neh 7:59   8203
7. A family of exiles with Ezra.
And of the sons of *S* .... Ezr 8:8   8203
8. A family of exiles who resettled in Jerusalem.
the son of Amariah, the son of *S* .... Neh 11:4   8203
9. A prince of Judah.
Then *S* the son of Mattan, and .... Jer 38:1   8203

SHEPHELAH See PLAIN.

SHEPHER See SHAPHER.

SHEPHERD
for every *s* is an abomination ...... Gen 46:34   7462,6629
(from thence is the *s*, the stone .... Gen 49:24   7462
be not as sheep which have no *s* .... Num 27:17   7462
hills, as sheep that have not a *s* 1Kin 22:17   7462
as sheep that have no *s* 2Chr 18:16   7462
The LORD is my *s* .... Ps 23:1   7462
O *S* of Israel, thou that leadest .... Ps 80:1   7462
which are given from one *s* .... Eccl 12:11   7462
He shall feed his flock like a *s* .... Is 40:11   7462
That saith of Cyrus, He is my *s* .... Is 44:28   7462
the sea with the *s* of his flock .... Is 63:11   7462
keep him, as a *s* doth his flock .... Jer 31:10   7462
as a *s* putteth on his garment .... Jer 43:12   7462
who is that *s* that will stand .... Jer 49:19   7462
who is that *s* that will stand .... Jer 50:44   7462
break in pieces with thee the *s* .... Jer 51:23   7462
scattered, because there is no *s* .... Eze 34:5   7462
the field, because there was no *s* .... Eze 34:8   7462
As a *s* seeketh out his flock in .... Eze 34:12   7462
And I will set up one *s* over them .... Eze 34:23   7462
feed them, and he shall be their *s* .... Eze 34:23   7462
and they all shall have one *s* .... Eze 37:24   7462
As the *s* taketh out of the mouth .... Amos 3:12   7462
troubled, because there was no *s* .... Zec 10:2   7462
the instruments of a foolish *s* .... Zec 11:15   7462
I will raise up a *s* in the land .... Zec 11:16   7462
Woe to the idol *s* that leaveth .... Zec 11:17   7473
Awake, O sword, against my *s* .... Zec 13:7   7462
smite the *s*, and the sheep shall .... Zec 13:7   7462
abroad, as sheep having no *s* .... Mt 9:36   4166
as a *s* divideth his sheep from .... Mt 25:32   4166
it is written, I will smite the *s* .... Mt 26:31   4166
they were as sheep not having a *s* .... Mk 6:34   4166
it is written, I will smite the *s* .... Mk 14:27   4166
by the door is the *s* of the sheep .... Jn 10:2   4166
I am the good *s* .... Jn 10:11   4166
the good *s* giveth his life for .... Jn 10:11   4166
that is an hireling, and not the *s* .... Jn 10:12   4166
I am the good *s*, and know my sheep ...... Jn 10:14   4166
there shall be one fold, and one *s* .... Jn 10:16   4166
that great *s* of the sheep, ... Heb 13:20   4166
but are now returned unto the *S* 1Pet 2:25   4166
And when the chief *S* shall appear 1Pet 5:4   750

SHEPHERD'S
put them in a *s* bag which he had, ... 1Sa 17:40   7462
and is removed from me as a *s* tent .... Is 38:12   7473

SHEPHERDS
And the men are *s*, for their trade .. Gen 46:32   7462,6629
unto Pharaoh, Thy servants are *s* ... Gen 47:3   7462,6629
the *s* came and drove them away .... Ex 2:17   7462
us out of the hand of the *s* .... Ex 2:19   7462
now thy *s* which were with us, we 1Sa 25:7   7462
neither shall the *s* make their .... Is 13:20   7462
when a multitude of *s* is called .... Is 31:4   7462
they are *s* that cannot understand .... Is 56:11   7462
The *s* with their flocks shall .... Jer 6:3   7462
I will set up *s* over them which .... Jer 23:4   7462
Howl, ye *s*, and cry .... Jer 25:34   7462
the *s* shall have no way to flee, ... Jer 25:35   7462
A voice of the cry of the *s* .... Jer 25:36   7462
shall be an habitation of *s* .... Jer 33:12   7462
their *s* have caused them to go .... Jer 50:6   7462
prophesy against the *s* of Israel .... Eze 34:2   7462
saith the Lord GOD unto the *s* .... Eze 34:2   7462
Woe be to the *s* of Israel that do .... Eze 34:2   7462
should not the *s* feed the flocks .... Eze 34:2   7462
Therefore, ye *s*, hear the word of .... Eze 34:7   7462
neither did my *s* search for my .... Eze 34:8   7462
but the *s* fed themselves, and fed .... Eze 34:8   7462
Therefore, O ye *s*, hear the word .... Eze 34:9   7462
Behold, I am against the *s* .... Eze 34:10   7462
neither shall the *s* feed .... Eze 34:10   7462
habitations of the *s* shall mourn .... Amos 1:2   7462
we raise against him seven *s* .... Mic 5:5   7462
Thy *s* slumber, O king of Assyria .... Nah 3:18   7462
be dwellings and cottages for *s* .... Zeph 2:6   7462
anger was kindled against the *s* .... Zec 10:3   7462
a voice of the howling of the *s* .... Zec 11:3   7462
their own *s* pity them not .... Zec 11:5   7462
Three *s* also I cut off in one .... Zec 11:8   7462
country *s* abiding in the field .... Lk 2:8   4166
the *s* said one to another, Let us .... Lk 2:15   4166
which were told them by the *s* .... Lk 2:18   4166
the *s* returned, glorifying and .... Lk 2:20   4166

SHEPHERDS'
feed thy kids beside the *s* tents .... Song 1:8   7462

SHEPHI *(she'-fi) See SHEPHO. A son of Shobal.*
Alian, and Manahath, and Ebal, *S* 1Chr 1:40   8195

SHEPHO *(she'-fo) See SHEPHI. Same as Shephi.*
Alvan, and Manahath, and Ebal, *S* .... Gen 36:23   8195

SHEPHUPHAM See SHUPHAM.

SHEPHUPHAN *(shef-u-fan) See SHUPHAM, SHUPPIM. A*
son of Bela.
And Gera, and *S*, and Huram 1Chr 8:5   8197

SHERAH *(she'-rah) Daughter of Beriah.*
(And his daughter was *S*, who built 1Chr 7:24   7609

SHERD
a *s* to take fire from the hearth .... Is 30:14   2789

SHERDS
and thou shalt break the *s* thereof .... Eze 23:34   2789

SHEREBIAH *(sher-e-bi'-ah)*
1. A family of exiles.
and *S*, with his sons and his .... Ezr 8:18   8274
of the chief of the priests, *S* .... Ezr 8:24   8274
Also Jeshua, and Bani, and *S* .... Neh 8:7   8274
Kadmiel, Shebaniah, Bunni, *S* .... Neh 9:4   8274
and Kadmiel, Bani, Hashabniah, *S* .... Neh 9:5   8274
2. A Levite who renewed the covenant.
Zaccur, *S*, Shebaniah, ... Neh 10:12   8274
Jeshua, Binnui, Kadmiel, *S* .... Neh 12:8   8274
Hashabiah, *S*, and Jeshua the son .... Neh 12:24   8274

SHERESH *(she'-resh) Son of Machir.*
and the name of his brother was *S* 1Chr 7:16   8329

SHEREZER *(she-re'-zur) See SHAREZER. A messenger in*
Zechariah's time.
had sent unto the house of God *S* .... Zec 7:2   8272

SHERIFFS
the counsellors, the *s*, and all .... Dan 3:2   8614
the counsellors, the *s*, and all .... Dan 3:3   8614

SHESHACH *(she'-shak) See BABYLON. Another name*
for Babylon.
the king of *S* shall drink after .... Jer 25:26   8347
How is *S* taken .... Jer 51:41   8347

SHESHAI *(she'-shahee) A son of Anak.*
where Ahiman, *S*, and Talmai, the .... Num 13:22   8344
thence the three sons of Anak, *S* .... Josh 15:14   8344
and they slew *S*, and Ahiman, and .... Judg 1:10   8344

SHESHAK See SHESHACH.

SHESHAN (she'-shan) *A descendant of Jerahmeel.*
S. And the children of S 1Chr 2:31   8348
Now S had no sons, but daughters 1Chr 2:34   8348
S had a servant, an Egyptian, ... 1Chr 2:34   8348
S gave his daughter to Jarha his 1Chr 2:35   8348

SHESHBAZZAR (shesh-baz'-zur) See ZERUBBABEL.
Same as Zerubbabel.
and numbered them unto S, the .... Ezr 1:8   8339
All these did S bring up with .... Ezr 1:11   8339
unto one, whose name was S .... Ezr 5:14   8339
Then came the same S, and laid the ..... Ezr 5:16   8339

SHETH (sheth) See SETH.
   1. A Moabite chief.
and destroy all the children of S .... Num 24:17   8352
   2. Same as Seth.
Adam, S, Enosh, ... 1Chr 1:1   8352

SHETHAR (she'-thar) *A prince of Media and Persia.*
the next unto him was Carshena, S........ Est 1:14   8369

SHETHAR-BOZENAI See SHETHAR-BOZNAI.

SHETHAR-BOZNAI (she'-thar-boz'-nahee) *A Persian official.*
on this side the river, and S .... Ezr 5:3   8370
on this side the river, and S .... Ezr 5:6   8370
governor beyond the river, S .... Ezr 6:6   8370
on this side the river, S .... Ezr 6:13   8370

SHETHER BAZNAI See SHETHAR BOZNAI.

SHEVA (she'-vah) See SHAVSHA.
   1. David's scribe.
And S was scribe................................... 2Sa 20:25   7724
   2. Son of Maachah.
S the father of Machbenah, and the 1Chr 2:49   7724

SHEW

unto a land that I will s thee .... Gen 12:1   7200
which thou shalt s unto me .... Gen 20:13   6213
s kindness unto my master Abraham .... Gen 24:12   6213
s kindness, I pray thee, unto me, ... Gen 40:14   6213
s Pharaoh, and say unto him, My .... Gen 46:31   5046
you, saying, S a miracle for you............. Ex 7:9   5414
for to s in thee my power .... Ex 9:16   7200
that I might s these my signs .... Ex 10:1   7896
thou shalt s thy son in that day,............. Ex 13:8   5046
which he will s to you to day .... Ex 14:13   6213
shalt s them the way wherein they .... Ex 18:20   3045
According to all that I s thee .... Ex 25:9   7200
s me now thy way, that I may know ...... Ex 33:13   3045
I beseech thee, s me thy glory .... Ex 33:18   7200
s mercy on whom I will s mercy .... Ex 33:19   7200
the LORD will s who are his .... Num 16:5   3045
to s you by what way ye should go .... Deut 1:33   7200
thou hast begun to s thy servant .... Deut 3:24   7200
to s you the word of the LORD................ Deut 5:5   5046
with them, nor s mercy unto them .... Deut 7:2
s thee mercy, and have compassion ...... Deut 13:17   5414
they shall s thee the sentence of .... Deut 17:9   5046
LORD shall choose shall s thee .... Deut 17:10   5046
sentence which they shall s thee............ Deut 17:11   5046
nor s favour to the young...................... Deut 28:50
ask thy father, and he will s thee .... Deut 32:7   5046
that ye will also s kindness unto............. Josh 2:12   6213
that he would not s them the land .... Josh 5:6   7200
S us, we pray thee, the entrance .... Judg 1:24   7200
the city, and we will s thee mercy .... Judg 1:24   6213
I will s thee the man whom thou .... Judg 4:22   7200
then s me a sign that thou .... Judg 6:17   6213
Samuel feared to s Eli the vision 1Sa 3:15   5046
s them the manner of the king 1Sa 8:9   5046
peradventure he can s us our way.......... 1Sa 9:6   5046
that I may s thee the word of God 1Sa 9:27   8085
s thee what thou shalt do 1Sa 10:8   3045
to us, and we will s you a thing 1Sa 14:12   3045
I will s thee what thou shalt do.............. 1Sa 16:3   3045
small, but that he will s it me................. 1Sa 20:2   1540
send not unto thee, and s it thee 1Sa 20:12   1540
thee evil, then I will s it thee 1Sa 20:13   1540
s me the kindness of the LORD 1Sa 20:14   6213
he fled, and did not s it to me................ 1Sa 22:17   1540
young men, and they will s thee 1Sa 25:8   5046
And now the LORD s kindness 2Sa 2:6   6213
which against Judah do s kindness........ 2Sa 3:8   6213
that I may s him kindness for 2Sa 9:1   6213
that I may s the kindness of God............ 2Sa 9:3   6213
for I will surely s kindness 2Sa 9:7   6213
I will s kindness unto Hanun the 2Sa 10:2   6213
s me both it, and his habitation 2Sa 15:25   7200
thou wilt s thyself merciful.................... 2Sa 22:26

man thou wilt s thyself upright............... 2Sa 22:26
the pure thou wilt s thyself pure 2Sa 22:27
thou wilt s thyself unsavoury 2Sa 22:27
If he will s himself a worthy man 1Kin 1:52
therefore, and s thyself a man 1Kin 2:2
But s kindness unto the sons of 1Kin 2:7   6213
saying, Go, s thyself unto Ahab.............. 1Kin 18:1   7200
Elijah went to s himself unto.................. 1Kin 18:2   7200
I will surely s myself unto him............... 1Kin 18:15   7200
Will ye not s me which of us is 2Kin 6:11   5046
I will now s you what the Syrians 2Kin 7:12   5046
s forth from day to day his 1Chr 16:23   1319
I will s kindness unto Hanun the 1Chr 19:2   6213
to s himself strong in the behalf 2Chr 16:9
but they could not s their...................... Ezr 2:59   5046
but they could not s their...................... Neh 7:61   5046
to s them light, and the way .... Neh 9:19
to s the people and the princes .... Est 1:11   7200
her that she should not s it .... Est 2:10   5046
to s it unto Esther, and to .... Est 4:8   7200
s me wherefore thou contendest .... Job 10:2   3045
that he would s thee the secrets .... Job 11:6   5046
I will s thee, hear me .... Job 15:17   2331
durst not s you mine opinion................. Job 32:6   2331
I also will s mine opinion...................... Job 32:10   2331
I also will s mine opinion...................... Job 32:17   2331
to s unto man his uprightness .... Job 33:23   5046
I will s thee that I have yet to .... Job 36:2   2331
that say, Who will s us any good............ Ps 4:6   7200
I will s forth all thy marvellous.............. Ps 9:1   5608
That I may s forth all thy praise............. Ps 9:14   5608
Thou wilt s me the path of life .... Ps 16:11   3045
S thy marvellous lovingkindness, ... Ps 17:7
thou wilt s thyself merciful .... Ps 18:25
man thou wilt s thyself upright............... Ps 18:25
the pure thou wilt s thyself pure .... Ps 18:26
thou wilt s thyself froward.................... Ps 18:26
S me thy ways, O LORD .... Ps 25:4   3045
he will s them his covenant .... Ps 25:14   3045
every man walketh in a vain s............... Ps 39:6   6754
will I s the salvation of God .... Ps 50:23   7200
my mouth shall s forth thy praise .... Ps 51:15   5046
My mouth shall s forth thy.................... Ps 71:15   5608
we will s forth thy praise to all .... Ps 79:13   5608
S us thy mercy, O LORD, and grant......... Ps 85:7   7200
S me a token for good........................... Ps 86:17   6213
Wilt thou s wonders to the dead .... Ps 88:10   6213
him, and s him my salvation.................. Ps 91:16   7200
To s forth thy lovingkindness in .... Ps 92:2   5046
To s that the LORD is upright.................. Ps 92:15   5046
vengeance belongeth, s thyself .... Ps 94:1   3313
s forth his salvation from day to .... Ps 96:2   1319
who can s forth all his praise................. Ps 106:2   8085
that he remembered not to s mercy........ Ps 109:16   6213
friends must s himself friendly............... Prov 18:24
The s of their countenance doth .... Is 3:9   1971
formed them will s them no favour .... Is 27:11
shall s the lighting down of his .... Is 30:30   7200
forth, and s us what shall happen .... Is 41:22   5046
let them s the former things, ... Is 41:22   5046
S the things that are to come................. Is 41:23   5046
this, and s us former things.................... Is 43:9   8085
they shall s forth my praise .... Is 43:21   5608
shall come, let them s unto them .... Is 44:7   5046
this, and s yourselves men .... Is 46:8
thou didst s them no mercy .... Is 47:6   7760
are in darkness, S yourselves .... Is 49:9   1540
s my people their transgression,............ Is 58:1   5046
they shall s forth the praises of .... Is 60:6   1319
when thou shalt s this people all .... Jer 16:10   5046
where I will not s you favour .... Jer 16:13   5414
I will s them the back, and not .... Jer 18:17   7200
s thee great and mighty things, ... Jer 33:3   5046
That the LORD thy God may s us .... Jer 42:3   5046
I will s mercies unto you, that .... Jer 42:12   5414
are cruel, and will not s mercy .... Jer 50:42
to s the king of Babylon that his .... Jer 51:31   5046
yea, thou shalt s her all her .... Eze 22:2   3045
with their mouth they s much love .... Eze 33:31   6213
Wilt thou not s us what thou .... Eze 37:18   5046
upon all that I shall s thee .... Eze 40:4   7200
for to the intent that I might s................ Eze 40:4   7200
s the house to the house of .... Eze 43:10   5046
s them the form of the house, and .... Eze 43:11   3045
for to s the king his dreams .... Dan 2:2   5046
we will s the interpretation .... Dan 2:4   2324
But if ye s the dream, and the .... Dan 2:6   2324
therefore s me the dream, and the .... Dan 2:6   2324
we will s the interpretation of................ Dan 2:7   2324
I shall know that ye can s me the........... Dan 2:9   2324
that can s the king's matter .... Dan 2:10   2324

S

that can *s* before the king	Dan 2:11	2324
that he would *s* the king the	Dan 2:16	2324
I will *s* unto the king the	Dan 2:24	2324
the soothsayers, unto the king	Dan 2:27	2324
I thought it good to *s* the signs	Dan 4:2	2324
s me the interpretation thereof,	Dan 5:7	2324
he will *s* the interpretation	Dan 5:12	5046
but they could not *s* the	Dan 5:15	2324
forth, and I am come to *s* thee	Dan 9:23	5046
But I will *s* thee that which is	Dan 10:21	5046
now will I *s* thee the truth	Dan 11:2	5046
I will *s* wonders in the heavens	Joel 2:30	5414
I *s* unto him marvellous things	Mic 7:15	7200
face, and I will *s* the nations thy	Nah 3:5	7200
Why dost thou *s* me iniquity	Hab 1:3	7200
I will *s* thee what these be	Zec 1:9	7200
s mercy and compassions every man	Zec 7:9	6213
s thyself to the priest, and offer	Mt 8:4	1166
s John again those things which	Mt 11:4	518
he shall *s* judgment to the	Mt 12:18	518
do *s* forth themselves in him	Mt 14:2	1754
would *s* them a sign from heaven	Mt 16:1	1925
Jesus to *s* unto his disciples	Mt 16:21	1166
S me the tribute money	Mt 22:19	1925
disciples came in him for to *s*	Mt 24:1	1925
shall *s* great signs and wonders	Mt 24:24	1325
s thyself to the priest, and offer	Mk 1:44	1166
do *s* forth themselves in him	Mk 6:14	1754
shall rise, and shall *s* signs	Mk 13:22	1325
he will *s* you a large upper room	Mk 14:15	1166
to *s* thee these glad tidings	Lk 1:19	2097
s thyself to the priest, and offer	Lk 5:14	1166
I will *s* you to whom he is like	Lk 6:47	5263
s how great things God hath done	Lk 8:39	1334
Go *s* yourselves unto the priests	Lk 17:14	1925
S me a penny	Lk 20:24	1925
for a *s* make long prayers	Lk 20:47	4392
he shall *s* you a large upper room	Lk 22:12	1166
he will *s* him greater works than	Jn 5:20	1166
things, *s* thyself to the world	Jn 7:4	5319
where he were, he should *s* it	Jn 11:57	3377
s us the Father, and it sufficeth	Jn 14:8	1166
sayest thou then, *S* us the Father	Jn 14:9	1166
he will *s* you things to come	Jn 16:13	312
of mine, and shall *s* it unto you	Jn 16:14	312
of mine, and shall *s* it unto you	Jn 16:15	312
but I shall *s* you plainly of the	Jn 16:25	312
s whether of these two thou hast	Acts 1:24	322
I will *s* wonders in heaven above,	Acts 2:19	1325
the land which I shall *s* thee	Acts 7:3	1166
For I will *s* him how great things	Acts 9:16	5263
Go *s* these things unto James, and	Acts 12:17	518
which *s* unto us the way of	Acts 16:17	2605
willing to *s* the Jews a pleasure,	Acts 24:27	2698
should *s* light unto the people,	Acts 26:23	2605
Which is the work of the law	Rom 2:15	1731
that I might *s* my power in thee,	Rom 9:17	1731
if God, willing to *s* his wrath	Rom 9:22	1731
ye do *s* the Lord's death till he	1Cor 11:26	2605
yet *s* I unto you a more excellent	1Cor 12:31	1166
Behold, I *s* you a mystery	1Cor 15:51	3004
Wherefore *s* ye to them, and before	2Cor 8:24	1731
to make a fair *s* in the flesh	Gal 6:12	2146
s the exceeding riches of his	Eph 2:7	1731
he made a *s* of them openly,	Col 2:15	1165
a *s* of wisdom in will worship	Col 2:23	3056
For they themselves *s* of us what	1Th 1:9	518
might *s* forth all longsuffering	1Ti 1:16	1731
learn first to *s* piety at home	1Ti 5:4	2151
Which in his times he shall *s*	1Ti 6:15	1166
Study to *s* thyself approved unto	2Ti 2:15	3936
s the same diligence to the full	Heb 6:11	1731
willing more abundantly to *s* unto	Heb 6:17	1925
s me thy faith without thy works,	Jas 2:18	1166
I will *s* thee my faith by my	Jas 2:18	1166
let him *s* out of a good	Jas 3:13	1166
that ye should *s* forth the	1Pet 2:9	1804
s unto you that eternal life,	1Jn 1:2	518
to *s* unto his servants things	Rev 1:1	1166
I will *s* thee things which must	Rev 4:1	1166
I will *s* unto thee the judgment	Rev 17:1	1166
I will *s* thee the bride, the	Rev 21:9	1166
to *s* unto his servants the things	Rev 22:6	1166

SHEWBREAD

upon the table *s* before me alway	Ex 25:30	3899,6440
and all his vessels, and the *s*	Ex 35:13	3899,6440
all the vessels thereof, and the *s*	Ex 39:36	3899,6440
upon the table of *s* they shall	Num 4:7	6440
was no bread there but the *s*	1Sa 21:6	3899,6440
of gold, whereupon the *s* was	1Kin 7:48	3899,6440

the Kohathites, were over the *s*	1Chr 9:32	3899,4635
Both for the *s*, and for the fine	1Chr 23:29	3899,4635
he gave gold for the tables of *s*	1Chr 28:16	4635
incense, and for the continual *s*	2Chr 2:4	4635
the tables whereon the *s* was set	2Chr 4:19	3899,6440
the *s* also set they in order upon	2Chr 13:11	3899,4635
the *s* table, with all the vessels	2Chr 29:18	4635
For the *s*, and for the continual	Neh 10:33	3899,4635
house of God, and did eat the *s*	Mt 12:4	740,4286
the high priest, and did eat the *s*	Mk 2:26	740,4286
of God, and did take and eat the *s*	Lk 6:4	740,4286
and the table, and the *s*	Heb 9:2	4286,740

SHEWED

which thou hast *s* unto me in	Gen 19:19	6213
hast *s* kindness unto my master	Gen 24:14	6213
which thou hast *s* unto thy	Gen 32:10	6213
s him mercy, and gave him favour	Gen 39:21	5186
God hath *s* Pharaoh what he is	Gen 41:25	5046
as God hath *s* thee all this	Gen 41:39	3045
God hath *s* me also thy seed	Gen 48:11	7200
the LORD *s* him a tree, which when	Ex 15:25	3384
which was *s* thee in the mount	Ex 25:40	7200
which was *s* thee in the mount	Ex 26:30	7200
as it was *s* thee in the mount, so	Ex 27:8	7200
reddish, and it be *s* to the priest	Lev 13:19	7200
shall be *s* unto the priest	Lev 13:49	7200
mind of the LORD might be *s* them	Lev 24:12	6567
which the LORD had *s* Moses	Num 8:4	7200
s them the fruit of the land	Num 13:26	7200
signs which I have *s* among them	Num 14:11	6213
Unto thee it was *s*, that thou	Deut 4:35	7200
upon earth he *s* thee his great	Deut 4:36	7200
LORD our God hath *s* us his glory	Deut 5:24	7200
And the LORD *s* signs and wonders,	Deut 6:22	5414
the LORD *s* him all the land of	Deut 34:1	7200
s in the sight of all Israel	Deut 34:12	6213
LORD, since I have *s* you kindness	Josh 2:12	6213
when he *s* them the entrance into	Judg 1:25	7200
they *s* Sisera that Barak the son	Judg 4:12	5046
Neither *s* they kindness to the	Judg 8:35	6213
which he had *s* unto Israel	Judg 8:35	6213
s her husband, and said unto him,	Judg 13:10	5046
he have *s* us all these things	Judg 13:23	7200
for he hath *s* me all his heart	Judg 16:18	5046
unto her, It hath fully been *s* me	Ruth 2:11	5046
she *s* her mother in law with whom	Ruth 2:19	5046
for thou hast *s* more kindness in	Ruth 3:10	3190
s it to the men of Jabesh	1Sa 11:9	5046
for ye *s* kindness to all the	1Sa 15:6	6213
Jonathan *s* him all those things	1Sa 19:7	5046
Abiathar *s* David that Saul had	1Sa 22:21	5046
thou hast *s* this day how that	1Sa 24:18	5046
that ye have *s* this kindness unto	2Sa 2:5	6213
as his father *s* kindness unto me	2Sa 10:2	6213
s David all that Joab had sent	2Sa 11:22	5046
thou hast not *s* it unto thy	1Kin 1:27	3045
Thou hast *s* unto thy servant	1Kin 3:6	6213
he did, and his might that he *s*	1Kin 16:27	6213
and his might that he *s*, and how	1Kin 22:45	6213
And he *s* him the place	2Kin 6:6	7200
howbeit the LORD hath *s* me that	2Kin 8:10	7200
The LORD hath *s* me that thou	2Kin 8:13	7200
LORD, and *s* them the king's son	2Kin 11:4	7200
s them all the house of his	2Kin 20:13	7200
that Hezekiah *s* them not	2Kin 20:13	7200
treasures that I have not *s* them	2Kin 20:15	7200
And Shaphan the scribe *s* the king	2Kin 22:10	7200
his father *s* kindness to me	1Chr 19:2	6213
Thou hast *s* great mercy unto	2Chr 1:8	6213
that the LORD had *s* unto David	2Chr 7:10	6213
hath been *s* from the LORD our God	Ezr 9:8	
When he *s* the riches of his	Est 1:4	7200
Esther had not *s* her people nor	Est 2:10	5046
Esther had not yet *s* her kindred	Est 2:20	5046
for they had *s* him the people of	Est 3:6	5046
pity should be *s* from his friend	Job 6:14	
for he hath *s* me his marvellous	Ps 31:21	
Thou hast *s* thy people hard	Ps 60:3	
until I have *s* thy strength unto	Ps 71:18	5046
Thou, which hast *s* me great	Ps 71:20	7200
and his wonders that he had *s* them	Ps 78:11	7200
s in the sight of the heathen	Ps 98:2	1540
They *s* his signs among them, and	Ps 105:27	7760
He hath *s* his people the power of	Ps 111:6	5046
the LORD, which hath *s* us light	Ps 118:27	
I *s* before him my trouble	Ps 142:2	5046
his wickedness shall be *s* before	Prov 26:26	1540
wherein I have *s* myself wise	Eccl 2:19	
Let favour be *s* to the wicked	Is 26:10	
s them the house of his precious	Is 39:2	7200

that Hezekiah *s* them not	Is 39:2	7200
treasures that I have not *s* them	Is 39:4	7200
s to him the way of understanding	Is 40:14	3045
and have saved, and I have *s*	Is 43:12	8085
out of my mouth, and I *s* them	Is 48:3	8085
it came to pass I *s* it thee	Is 48:5	8085
I have *s* thee new things from	Is 48:6	8085
The Lord *s* me, and, behold, two	Jer 24:1	7200
the word that the Lord hath *s* me	Jer 38:21	7200
the things that the Lord had *s* me	Eze 11:25	7200
s them my judgments, which if a	Eze 20:11	3045
neither have they *s* difference	Eze 22:26	3045
Thus hath the Lord God *s* unto me	Amos 7:1	7200
Thus hath the Lord God *s* unto me	Amos 7:4	7200
Thus he *s* me	Amos 7:7	7200
Thus hath the Lord God *s* unto me	Amos 8:1	7200
He hath *s* thee, O man, what is	Mic 6:8	5046
the Lord *s* me four carpenters	Zec 1:20	7200
he *s* me Joshua the high priest	Zec 3:1	7200
s unto the chief priests all the	Mt 28:11	518
He hath *s* strength with his arm	Lk 1:51	4160
Lord had *s* great mercy upon her	Lk 1:58	3170
s unto him all the kingdoms of	Lk 4:5	1166
the disciples of John *s* him of	Lk 7:18	518
he said, He that *s* mercy on him	Lk 10:37	4160
came, and *s* his lord these things	Lk 14:21	518
even Moses *s* at the bush, when he	Lk 20:37	3377
he *s* them his hands and his feet	Lk 24:40	1925
works have I *s* you from my Father	Jn 10:32	1166
he *s* unto them his hands and his	Jn 20:20	1166
After these things Jesus *s*	Jn 21:1	5319
and on this wise *s* he himself	Jn 21:1	5319
Jesus *s* himself to his disciples	Jn 21:14	5319
To whom also he *s* himself alive	Acts 1:3	3936
which God before had *s* by the	Acts 3:18	4293
this miracle of healing was *s*	Acts 4:22	1096
the next day he *s* himself unto	Acts 7:26	3700
out, after that he had *s* wonders	Acts 7:36	4160
they have slain them which *s*	Acts 7:52	4293
but God hath *s* me that I should	Acts 10:28	1166
up the third day, and *s* him	Acts 10:40	1325,1717,1096
he *s* us how he had seen an angel	Acts 11:13	518
and confessed, and *s* their deeds	Acts 19:18	312
unto you, but have *s* you, and have	Acts 20:20	312
I have *s* you all things, how that	Acts 20:35	5268
thou hast *s* these things to me	Acts 23:22	1718
But *s* first unto them of Damascus	Acts 26:20	518
the barbarous people *s* us no	Acts 28:2	3930
came *s* or spake any harm of thee	Acts 28:21	518
for God hath *s* it unto them	Rom 1:19	5319
eat not for his sake that *s* it	1Cor 10:28	3377
which ye have *s* toward his name	Heb 6:10	1731
pattern *s* to thee in the mount	Heb 8:5	1166
mercy, that hath *s* no mercy	Jas 2:13	4160
our Lord Jesus Christ hath *s* me	2Pet 1:14	1213
s me that great city, the holy	Rev 21:10	1166
he *s* me a pure river of water of	Rev 22:1	1166
the angel which *s* me these things	Rev 22:8	1166

SHEWEDST

s signs and wonders upon Pharaoh,	Neh 9:10	5414
then thou *s* me their doings	Jer 11:18	7200

SHEWEST

s mercy unto thy servants, that	2Chr 6:14	
again thou *s* thyself marvellous	Job 10:16	
Thou *s* lovingkindness unto	Jer 32:18	6213
What sign *s* thou unto us, seeing	Jn 2:18	1166
unto him, What sign *s* thou then	Jn 6:30	4160

SHEWETH

is about to do he *s* unto Pharaoh	Gen 41:28	7200
whatsoever he *s* me I will tell	Num 23:3	7200
there is none that *s* me that my	1Sa 22:8	1540,241
or *s* unto me that my son hath	1Sa 22:8	1540,241
s mercy to his anointed, unto	2Sa 22:51	6213
Then he *s* them their work, and	Job 36:9	5046
The noise thereof *s* concerning it	Job 36:33	5046
s mercy to his anointed, to David	Ps 18:50	6213
and the firmament *s* his handywork	Ps 19:1	5046
and night unto night *s* knowledge	Ps 19:2	2331
but the righteous *s* mercy	Ps 37:21	
A good man *s* favour, and lendeth	Ps 112:5	
He *s* his word unto Jacob, his	Ps 147:19	5046
truth *s* forth righteousness	Prov 12:17	5046
and the tender grass *s* itself	Prov 27:25	7200
yea, there is none that *s*	Is 41:26	5046
s him all the kingdoms of the	Mt 4:8	1166
s* him all things that himself	Jn 5:20	1166
runneth, but of God that *s* mercy	Rom 9:16	1658
he that *s* mercy, with	Rom 12:8	1658

SHEWING

s mercy unto thousands of them	Ex 20:6	6213
s mercy unto thousands of them	Deut 5:10	6213
s to the generation to come the	Ps 78:4	5608
s himself through the lattice	Song 2:9	6692
iniquities by *s* mercy to the poor	Dan 4:27	
and *s* of hard sentences, and	Dan 5:12	263
till the day of his *s* unto Israel	Lk 1:80	323
s the glad tidings of the kingdom	Lk 8:1	
s the coats and garments which	Acts 9:39	1925
s by the scriptures that Jesus	Acts 18:28	1925
of God, *s* himself that he is God	2Th 2:4	584
In all things *s* thyself a pattern	Titus 2:7	3930
in doctrine *s* uncorruptness,	Titus 2:7	
but *s* all good fidelity	Titus 2:10	1731
s all meekness unto all men	Titus 3:2	1731

SHIBAH See Shebah.

SHIBBOLETH (*shib'-bo-leth*) See Sibboleth. *Password that distinguished Gileadites from Ephraimites.*

said they unto him, Say now *S*	Judg 12:6	7641

SHIBMAH (*shib'-mah*) See Shebam, Sibmah. *A city in Reuben.*

(their names being changed,) and *S*	Num 32:38	7643

SHICRON (*shi'-cron*) *A city in Judah.*

and the border was drawn to *S*	Josh 15:11	7942

SHIELD

I am thy *s*, and thy exceeding	Gen 15:1	4043
the *s* of thy help, and who is the	Deut 33:29	4043
was there a *s* or spear seen among	Judg 5:8	4043
one bearing a *s* went before him	1Sa 17:7	6793
that bare the *s* went before him	1Sa 17:41	6793
and with a spear, and with a *s*	1Sa 17:45	3591
for there the *s* of the mighty is	2Sa 1:21	4043
the *s* of Saul, as though he had	2Sa 1:21	4043
he is my *s*, and the horn of my	2Sa 22:3	4043
given me the *s* of thy salvation	2Sa 22:36	4043
three pound of gold went to one *s*	1Kin 10:17	4043
there, nor come before it with *s*	2Kin 19:32	4043
the battle, that could handle *s*	1Chr 12:8	6793
The children of Judah that bare *s*	1Chr 12:24	6793
captains, and with them with *s*	1Chr 12:34	6793
shekels of gold went to one *s*	2Chr 9:16	4043
bow and *s* two hundred thousand	2Chr 17:17	4043
war, that could handle spear and *s*	2Chr 25:5	6793
the glittering spear and the *s*	Job 39:23	3591
But thou, O Lord, art a *s* for me	Ps 3:3	4043
wilt thou compass him as with a *s*	Ps 5:12	6793
given me the *s* of thy salvation	Ps 18:35	4043
The Lord is my strength and my *s*	Ps 28:7	4043
he is our help and our *s*	Ps 33:20	4043
Take hold of *s* and buckler, and	Ps 35:2	4043
and bring them down, O Lord our *s*	Ps 59:11	4043
he the arrows of the bow, the *s*	Ps 76:3	4043
Behold, O God our *s*, and look upon	Ps 84:9	4043
For the Lord God is a sun and *s*	Ps 84:11	4043
his truth shall be thy *s* and	Ps 91:4	6793
he is their help and their *s*	Ps 115:9	4043
he is their help and their *s*	Ps 115:10	4043
he is their help and their *s*	Ps 115:11	4043
Thou art my hiding place and my *s*	Ps 119:114	4043
my *s*, and he in whom I trust	Ps 144:2	4043
he is a *s* unto them that put	Prov 30:5	4043
ye princes, and anoint the *s*	Is 21:5	4043
horsemen, and Kir uncovered the *s*	Is 22:6	4043
Order ye the buckler and *s*	Jer 46:3	6793
and the Libyans, that handle the *s*	Jer 46:9	4043
set against thee buckler and *s*	Eze 23:24	4043
they hanged the *s* and helmet in	Eze 27:10	4043
all of them with *s* and helmet	Eze 38:5	4043
The *s* of his mighty men is made	Nah 2:3	4043
Above all, taking the *s* of faith	Eph 6:16	2375

SHIELDS

David took the *s* of gold that	2Sa 8:7	7982
three hundred *s* of beaten gold	1Kin 10:17	4043
he took away all the *s* of gold	1Kin 14:26	4043
made in their stead brasen *s*	1Kin 14:27	4043
give king David's spears and *s*	2Kin 11:10	7982
David took the *s* of gold that	1Chr 18:7	7982
three hundred *s* made he of beaten	2Chr 9:16	4043
And in every several city he put *s*	2Chr 11:12	6793
he carried away also the *s* of	2Chr 12:9	4043
king Rehoboam made *s* of brass	2Chr 12:10	4043
and out of Benjamin, that bare *s*	2Chr 14:8	4043
spears, and bucklers, and *s*	2Chr 23:9	7982
them throughout all the host *s*	2Chr 26:14	4043
and made darts and *s* in abundance	2Chr 32:5	4043
stones, and for spices, and for *s*	2Chr 32:27	4043
them held both the spears, the *s*	Neh 4:16	4043

S

for the *s* of the earth belong .... Ps 47:9   4043
bucklers, all *s* of mighty men .... Song 4:4   7982
there, nor come before it with *s*. .... Is 37:33   4043
gather the *s*. .... Jer 51:11   7982
they hanged their *s* upon thy .... Eze 27:11   7982
great company with bucklers and *s*. .... Eze 38:4   4043
and burn the weapons, both the *s* .... Eze 39:9   4043

SHIGGAION (*shig-gah'-yon*) See SHIGIONOTH. *A musical notation.*
S of David, which he sang unto .... Ps 7:t   7692

SHIGIONOTH (*shig-i'-o-noth*) See SHIGGAION. *A musical notation.*
of Habakkuk the prophet upon *S* .... Hab 3:1   7692

SHIHON (*shi'-hon*) *A city in Issachar.*
Haphraim, and *S*, and Anaharath, ... Josh 19:19   7866

SHIHOR (*shi'-hor*) See SHIHOR-LIBNATH. *Same as Sihor.*
from *S* of Egypt even unto the 1Chr 13:5   7883

SHIHOR-LIBNATH (*shi'-hor-lib'-nath*) *A small river in Asher.*
to Carmel westward, and to *S* .... Josh 19:26   7884

SHIKKERON See SHICRON.

SHILHI (*shil'-hi*) *Father of Azubah.*
name was Azubah the daughter of *S* 1Kin 22:42   7977
name was Azubah the daughter of *S* 2Chr 20:31   7977

SHILHIM (*shil'-him*) See SHAARAIM, SHARUHEN. *A city in Judah.*
And Lebaoth, and *S*, and Ain, and .... Josh 15:32   7978

SHILLEM (*shil'-lem*) See SHALLUM, SHILLEMITES. *A son of Naphtali.*
Jahzeel, and Guni, and Jezer, and *S* .... Gen 46:24   8006
of *S*, the family of the .... Num 26:49   8006

SHILLEMITES (*shil'-lem-ites*) *Descendants of Shillem.*
of Shillem, the family of the *S* .... Num 26:49   8016

SHILOAH (*shi-lo'-ah*) See SILOAH, SILOAM. *A fountain in Jerusalem.*
the waters of *S* that go softly .... Is 8:6   7975

SHILOH (*shi'-loh*) See SHILONITE.
1. Symbolic name for the Ruler from Judah.
between his feet, until *S* come .... Gen 49:10   7886
2. A city in Ephraim.
of Israel assembled together at *S* .... Josh 18:1   7887
lots for you before the LORD in *S* .... Josh 18:8   7887
again to Joshua to the host at *S* .... Josh 18:9   7887
for them in *S* before the LORD .... Josh 18:10   7887
by lot in *S* before the LORD .... Josh 19:51   7887
them at *S* in the land of Canaan .... Josh 21:2   7887
the children of Israel out of *S*. .... Josh 22:9   7887
gathered themselves together at *S* .... Josh 22:12   7887
that the house of God was in *S* .... Judg 18:31   7887
brought them unto the camp to *S* .... Judg 21:12   7887
S yearly in a place which is on .... Judg 21:19   7887
if the daughters of *S* come out to .... Judg 21:21   7887
his wife of the daughters of *S* .... Judg 21:21   7887
unto the LORD of hosts in *S* 1Sa 1:3   7887
rose up after they had eaten in *S* 1Sa 1:9   7887
unto the house of the LORD in *S* 1Sa 1:24   7887
So they did in *S* unto all the 1Sa 2:14   7887
And the LORD appeared again in *S* 1Sa 3:21   7887
in *S* by the word of the LORD 1Sa 3:21   7887
of the LORD out of *S* unto us 1Sa 4:3   7887
So the people sent to *S*, that 1Sa 4:4   7887
came to *S* the same day with his 1Sa 4:12   7887
of Eli, the LORD's priest in *S* 1Sa 14:3   7887
concerning the house of Eli in *S* 1Kin 2:27   7887
and get thee to *S*. 1Kin 14:2   7887
did so, and arose, and went to *S* 1Kin 14:4   7887
he forsook the tabernacle of *S* .... Ps 78:60   7887
now unto my place which was in *S* .... Jer 7:12   7887
your fathers, as I have done to *S* .... Jer 7:14   7887
will I make this house like *S* .... Jer 26:6   7887
This house shall be like *S* .... Jer 26:9   7887
came certain from Shechem, from *S* ...... Jer 41:5   7887

SHILONI (*shi-lo'-ni*) See SHILONITE. *Father of Zechariah.*
son of Zechariah, the son of *S* .... Neh 11:5   8023

SHILONITE (*shi'-lon-ite*) See SHILONI, SHILONITES. *An inhabitant of Shiloh.*
Ahijah the *S* found him in the way 1Kin 11:29   7888
the LORD spake by Ahijah the *S*. 1Kin 12:15   7888
spake by his servant Ahijah the *S* 1Kin 15:29   7888
in the prophecy of Ahijah the *S* 2Chr 9:29   7888
S to Jeroboam the son of Nebat 2Chr 10:15   7888

SHILONITES (*shi'-lon-ites*)
And of the *S* 1Chr 9:5   7888

SHILSHAH (*shil'-shah*) *Son of Zophah.*
Bezer, and Hod, and Shamma, and *S* 1Chr 7:37   8030

SHIMEA (*shim'e-ah*) See SHAMMAH, SHAMMUA, SHAMMUAH, SHIMEAH, SHIMEATHITES, SHIMMA.
1. David's brother.
Jonathan the son of *S* David's 1Chr 20:7   8092
2. A son of David.
S, and Shobab, and Nathan, and 1Chr 3:5   8092
3. Father of Haggiah.
S his son, Haggiah his son, ... 1Chr 6:30   8092
4. Father of Berachiah.
son of Berachiah, the son of *S* 1Chr 6:39   8092

SHIMEAH (*shim'-e-ah*) See SHIMEA, SHIMEAM.
1. Same as Shimea 1.
the son of *S* David's brother 2Sa 13:3   8093
the son of *S* David's brother, ... 2Sa 13:32   8093
Jonathan the son of *S* the brother 2Sa 21:21   8092
2. A relative of King Saul.
And Mikloth begat *S* 1Chr 8:32   8039

SHIMEAM (*shim'-e-am*) See SHIMEA. *Son of Mikloth.*
And Mikloth begat *S* 1Chr 9:38   8043

SHIMEATH (*shim'-e-ath*) *Mother of Jozachar.*
For Jozachar the son of *S* 2Kin 12:21   8100
Zabad the son of *S* an Ammonitess 2Chr 24:26   8100

SHIMEATHITES (*shim'-e-ath-ites*) *A family of scribes.*
the Tirathites, the *S*, and 1Chr 2:55   8101

SHIMEI (*shim'-e-i*) See SHEMAIAH, SHIMHI, SHIMI, SHIMITES.
1. A son of Gershon.
families; Libni, and *S* .... Num 3:18   8096
Gershom; Libni, and *S* 1Chr 6:17   8096
the son of Zimmah, the son of *S* 1Chr 6:42   8096
Gershonites were, Laadan, and *S* 1Chr 23:7   8096
And the sons of *S* were, Jahath, ... 1Chr 23:10   8096
These four were the sons of *S* 1Chr 23:10   8096
2. A son of Gera.
house of Saul, whose name was *S* 2Sa 16:5   8096
thus said *S* when he cursed, Come 2Sa 16:7   8096
S went along on the hill's side 2Sa 16:13   8096
S the son of Gera, a Benjamite, ... 2Sa 19:16   8096
S the son of Gera fell down 2Sa 19:18   8096
Shall not *S* be put to death for 2Sa 19:21   8096
Therefore the king said unto *S* 2Sa 19:23   8096
hast with thee *S* the son of Gera 1Kin 2:8   8096
And the king sent and called for *S* 1Kin 2:36   8096
S said unto the king, The saying 1Kin 2:38   8096
S dwelt in Jerusalem many days 1Kin 2:38   8096
of *S* ran away unto Achish son of 1Kin 2:39   8096
And they told *S*, saying, Behold, ... 1Kin 2:39   8096
S arose, and saddled his ass, and 1Kin 2:40   8096
S went, and brought his servants 1Kin 2:40   8096
it was told Solomon that *S* had 1Kin 2:41   8096
And the king sent and called for *S* 1Kin 2:42   8096
The king said moreover to *S* 1Kin 2:44   8096
3. An officer of David.
and Nathan the prophet, and *S* 1Kin 1:8   8096
4. An officer of Solomon.
S the son of Elah, in Benjamin 1Kin 4:18   8096
5. A descendant of King Jehoiakim.
of Pedaiah were, Zerubbabel, and *S* 1Chr 3:19   8096
6. Son of Zacchur.
son, Zacchur his son, *S* his son 1Chr 4:26   8096
S had sixteen sons and six 1Chr 4:27   8096
7. Son of Gog.
his son, Gog his son, *S* his son, ... 1Chr 5:4   8096
8. Son of Libni.
his son, *S* his son, Uzza his son, ... 1Chr 6:29   8096
9. A Levite of the Laadan family.
The sons of *S* 1Chr 23:9   8096
10. A sanctuary servant.
The tenth to *S*, he, his sons, and 1Chr 25:17   8096
11. A vineyard keeper.
the vineyards was *S* the Ramathite 1Chr 27:27   8096
12. A Levite who cleansed the Temple.
Jehiel, and *S* 2Chr 29:14   8096
13. A Temple servant in Hezekiah's time.
S his brother was the next 2Chr 31:12   8096
S his brother, at the commandment 2Chr 31:13   8096
14. A Levite who married a foreigner.
Jozabad, and *S*, and Kelaiah, (the .... Ezr 10:23   8096
15. A Hashumite who married a foreigner.
Jeremai, Manasseh, and *S* .... Ezr 10:33   8096
16. A Banite who married a foreigner.
And Bani, and Binnui, *S*, ... Ezr 10:38   8096
17. Grandfather of Mordecai.
the son of Jair, the son of *S* .... Est 2:5   8096
18. A representative of the Gershonites.
the family of *S* apart, and their .... Zec 12:13   8097

SHIMEITES See SHIMITES.

SHIMEON (shim'-e-on) See SIMEON. *A member of the Harim family.*
Ishijah, Malchiah, Shemaiah, S .... Ezr 10:31   8095

SHIMHI (shim'-hi) See SHEMA, SHIMEI. *Father of a chief family in Judah.*
and Shimrath, the sons of S 1Chr 8:21   8096

SHIMI (shi'-mi) See SHIMEI, SHIMITES. *Same as Shimei 1.*
Libni, and S, according to their .... Ex 6:17   8096

SHIMITES (shi'-mites) *Descendants of Shimei 1.*
Libnites, and the family of the S .... Num 3:21   8097

SHIMMA (shim'-mah) See SHAMMAH. *Same as Shamma.*
the second, and S the third, ... 1Chr 2:13   8092

SHIMON (shi'-mon) *A descendant of Caleb.*
And the sons of S were, Amnon, and 1Chr 4:20   7889

SHIMRATH (shim'-rath) *A son of Shimri.*
And Adaiah, and Beraiah, and S 1Chr 8:21   8119

SHIMRI (shim'-ri) See SIMRI.
1. *Head of a family in Simeon.*
the son of Jedaiah, the son of S 1Chr 4:37   8113
2. *Father of Jediaiah.*
Jediael the son of S, and Joha his 1Chr 11:45   8113
3. *A Levite who cleansed the Temple.*
S, and Jeiel 2Chr 29:13   8113

SHIMRITH (shim'-rith) See SHOMER. *Mother of Jehozabad.*
the son of S a Moabitess 2Chr 24:26   8116

SHIMROM (shim'-rom) See SHIMRON. *A son of Issachar.*
were, Tola, and Puah, Jashub, and S ... 1Chr 7:1   8110

SHIMRON (shim'-ron) See SHIMROM, SHIMRONITES. *Same as Shimron.*
Tola, and Phuvah, and Job, and S .... Gen 46:13   8110
of S, the family of the .... Num 26:24   8110
of Madon, and to the king of S .... Josh 11:1   8110
And Kattath, and Nahallal, and S .... Josh 19:15   8110

SHIMRONITE See SHIMRONITES.

SHIMRONITES (shim'-ron-ites) *Descendants of Shimrom.*
of Shimron, the family of the S .... Num 26:24   8117

SHIMRON-MERON (shim'-ron-me'-ron) *A city in Galilee.*
The king of S, one .... Josh 12:20   8112

SHIMSHAI (shim'-shahee) *An opponent of Nehemiah.*
S the scribe wrote a letter .... Ezr 4:8   8124
S the scribe, and the rest of .... Ezr 4:9   8124
to S the scribe, and to the rest .... Ezr 4:17   8124
S the scribe, and their companions .... Ezr 4:23   8124

SHINAB (shi'-nab) *King of Admah.*
S king of Admah, and Shemeber king .... Gen 14:2   8134

SHINAR (shi'-nar) *A nation in Babylonia.*
and Calneh, in the land of S .... Gen 10:10   8152
found a plain in the land of S .... Gen 11:2   8152
in the days of Amraphel king of S .... Gen 14:1   8152
of nations, and Amraphel king of S .... Gen 14:9   8152
Cush, and from Elam, and from S .... Is 11:11   8152
land of S to the house of his god .... Dan 1:2   8152
it an house in the land of S .... Zec 5:11   8152

SHINE
LORD make his face s upon thee .... Num 6:25   215
neither let the light s upon it .... Job 3:4   3313
s upon the counsel of the wicked .... Job 10:3   3313
thou shalt s forth, thou shalt be .... Job 11:17   5774
the spark of his fire shall not s .... Job 18:5   5050
the light shall s upon thy ways .... Job 22:28   5050
commandeth it not to s by the .... Job 36:32
the light of his cloud to s .... Job 37:15   3313
By his neesings a light doth s .... Job 41:18   1984
He maketh a path to s after him .... Job 41:32   215
thy face to s upon thy servant................ Ps 31:16   215
and cause his face to s upon us .... Ps 67:1   215
between the cherubims, s forth .... Ps 80:1   3313
O God, and cause thy face to s .... Ps 80:3   215
of hosts, and cause thy face to s .... Ps 80:7   215
God of hosts, cause thy face to s .... Ps 80:19   215
man, and oil to make his face to s........ Ps 104:15   6670
thy face to s upon thy servant................ Ps 119:135   215
man's wisdom maketh his face to s .... Eccl 8:1   215
shall not cause her light to s .... Is 13:10   5050
Arise, s; for thy light .... Is 60:1   215

They are waxen fat, they s...................... Jer 5:28   6245
cause thy face to s upon thy .... Dan 9:17   215
they that be wise shall s as the.............. Dan 12:3   2094
Let your light so s before men .... Mt 5:16   2989
Then shall the righteous s forth .... Mt 13:43   1584
and his face did s as the sun .... Mt 17:2   2989
image of God, should s unto them 2Cor 4:4   826
the light to s out of darkness 2Cor 4:6   2989
among whom ye s as lights in the .... Phil 2:15   5316
shall s no more at all in thee.................. Rev 18:23   5316
neither of the moon, to s in it .... Rev 21:23   5316

SHINED
he s forth from mount Paran, and.......... Deut 33:2   3313
When his candle s upon my head .... Job 29:3   1984
If I beheld the sun when it s.................... Job 31:26   1984
perfection of beauty, God hath s .... Ps 50:2   3313
death, upon them hath the light s .... Is 9:2   5050
the earth s with his glory .... Eze 43:2   215
suddenly there s round about him .... Acts 9:3   4015
him, and a light s in the prison .... Acts 12:7   2989
hath s in our hearts, to give the............ 2Cor 4:6   2989

SHINETH
even to the moon, and it s not .... Job 25:5   166
but the night s as the day...................... Ps 139:12   215
as the shining light, that s more .... Prov 4:18   215
the east, and s even unto the west .... Mt 24:27   5316
s unto the other part under .... Lk 17:24   2989
And the light s in darkness .... Jn 1:5   5316
a light that s in a dark place 2Pet 1:19   5316
is past, and the true light now s 1Jn 2:8   5316
was as the sun s in his strength .... Rev 1:16   5316

SHINING
the earth by clear s after rain................ 2Sa 23:4   5051
of the just is as the s light .... Prov 4:18   5051
the s of a flaming fire by night .... Is 4:5   5051
the stars shall withdraw their s .... Joel 2:10   5051
the stars shall withdraw their s .... Joel 3:15   5051
at the s of thy glittering spear .... Hab 3:11   5051
And his raiment became s,...................... Mk 9:3   4744
as when the bright s of a candle .... Lk 11:36   796
men stood by them in s garments .... Lk 24:4   797
He was a burning and a s light............ Jn 5:35   5316
s round about me and them which .... Acts 26:13   4034

SHION See SHIHON.

SHIP
the way of a s in the midst of .... Prov 30:19   591
shall gallant s pass thereby .... Is 33:21   6716
They have made all thy s boards............ Eze 27:5
he found a s going to Tarshish .... Jonah 1:3   591
so that the s was like to be.................... Jonah 1:4   591
that were in the s into the sea................ Jonah 1:5   591
gone down into the sides of the s .... Jonah 1:5   5600
in a s with Zebedee their father, ... Mt 4:21   4143
And they immediately left the s .... Mt 4:22   4143
And when he was entered into a s.......... Mt 8:23   4143
insomuch that the s was covered............ Mt 8:24   4143
And he entered into a s, and passed ...... Mt 9:1   4143
him, so that he went into a s .... Mt 13:2   4143
he departed thence by s into a .... Mt 14:13   4143
his disciples to get into a s .... Mt 14:22   4143
But the s was now in the midst of.......... Mt 14:24   4143
Peter was come down out of the s.......... Mt 14:29   4143
And when they were come into the s ...... Mt 14:32   4143
Then they that were in the s came .... Mt 14:33   4143
away the multitude, and took s .... Mt 15:39   4143
were in the s mending their nets .... Mk 1:19   4143
in the s with the hired servants .... Mk 1:20   4143
that a small s should wait on him.......... Mk 3:9   4142
so that he entered into a s...................... Mk 4:1   4143
took him even as he was in the s .... Mk 4:36   4143
and the waves beat into the s.................. Mk 4:37   4143
was in the hinder part of the s .... Mk 4:38
And when he was come out of the s ...... Mk 5:2   4143
And when he was come into the s .... Mk 5:18   4143
again by s unto the other side................ Mk 5:21   4143
a desert place by s privately .... Mk 6:32   4143
his disciples to get into the s.................. Mk 6:45   4143
the s was in the midst of the sea .... Mk 6:47   4143
he went up unto them into the s .... Mk 6:51   4143
when they were come out of the s.......... Mk 6:54   4143
into a s with his disciples .... Mk 8:10   4143
entering into the s again........................ Mk 8:13   4143
neither had they in the s with .... Mk 8:14   4143
and taught the people out of the s .... Lk 5:3   4143
which were in the other s .... Lk 5:7   4143
went into a s with his disciples.............. Lk 8:22   4143
and he went up into the s, and.............. Lk 8:37   4143
And entered into a s, and went over ...... Jn 6:17   4143

S

sea, and drawing nigh unto the *s*	Jn 6:19	4143
willingly received him into the *s*	Jn 6:21	4143
immediately the *s* was at the land	Jn 6:21	4143
and entered into a *s* immediately	Jn 21:3	4143
net on the right side of the *s*	Jn 21:6	4143
disciples came in a little *s*	Jn 21:8	4142
And we went before to *s*, and sailed	Acts 20:13	4143
they accompanied him unto the *s*	Acts 20:38	4143
finding a *s* sailing over unto	Acts 21:2	4143
for there the *s* was to unlade her	Acts 21:3	4143
leave one of another, we took *s*	Acts 21:6	4143
entering into a *s* of Adramyttium	Acts 27:2	4143
a *s* of Alexandria sailing into	Acts 27:6	4143
not only of the lading and *s*	Acts 27:10	4143
the master and the owner of the *s*	Acts 27:11	3490
when the *s* was caught, and could	Acts 27:15	4143
used helps, undergirding the *s*	Acts 27:17	4143
the next day they lightened the *s*	Acts 27:18	
own hands the tackling of the *s*	Acts 27:19	4143
life among you, but of the *s*	Acts 27:22	4143
were about to flee out of the *s*	Acts 27:30	4143
Except these abide in the *s*	Acts 27:31	4143
we were in all in the *s* two	Acts 27:37	4143
enough, they lightened the *s*	Acts 27:38	4143
were possible, to thrust in the *s*	Acts 27:39	4143
seas met, they ran the *s* aground	Acts 27:41	3491
and some on broken pieces of the *s*	Acts 27:44	4143
we departed in a *s* of Alexandria	Acts 28:11	4143

SHIPHI (shi'-fi) *Father of Ziza.*
And Ziza the son of *S*, the son of	1Chr 4:37	8230

SHIPHMITE (shif'-mite) *Family name of Zabdi.*
the wine cellars was Zabdi the *S*	1Chr 27:27	8225

SHIPHRAH (shif'-rah) *A Hebrew midwife in Egypt.*
which the name of the one was *S*	Ex 1:15	8236

SHIPHTAN (shif'-tan) *Father of Kemuel.*
of Ephraim, Kemuel the son of *S*	Num 34:24	8204

SHIPMASTER
So the *s* came to him, and said	Jonah 1:6	7227,2259
And every *s*, and all the company in	Rev 18:17	2942

SHIPMEN
s that had knowledge of the sea,	1Kin 9:27	582,591
about midnight the *s* deemed that	Acts 27:27	3492
as the *s* were about to flee out	Acts 27:30	3492

SHIPPING
his disciples, they also took *s*	Jn 6:24	4143

SHIPS
and he shall be for an haven of *s*	Gen 49:13	591
s shall come come from the coast	Num 24:24	6716
thee into Egypt again with *s*	Deut 28:68	591
and why did Dan remain in *s*	Judg 5:17	591
made a navy of *s* in Ezion-gaber	1Kin 9:26	
Jehoshaphat made *s* of Tharshish	1Kin 22:48	591
for the *s* were broken at	1Kin 22:48	591
go with thy servants in the *s*	1Kin 22:49	591
by the hands of his servants *s*	2Chr 8:18	591
For the king's *s* went to Tarshish	2Chr 9:21	591
the *s* of Tarshish bringing gold	2Chr 9:21	591
him to make *s* to go to Tarshish	2Chr 20:36	591
they made *s* in Ezion-gaber	2Chr 20:36	591
the *s* were broken, that they were	2Chr 20:37	591
are passed away as the swift *s*	Job 9:26	591
Thou breakest the *s* of Tarshish	Ps 48:7	591
There go the *s*	Ps 104:26	591
They that go down to the sea in *s*	Ps 107:23	591
She is like the merchants' *s*	Prov 31:14	591
And upon all the *s* of Tarshish	Is 2:16	591
Howl, ye *s* of Tarshish	Is 23:1	591
Howl, ye *s* of Tarshish	Is 23:14	591
Chaldeans, whose cry is in the *s*	Is 43:14	591
the *s* of Tarshish first, to bring	Is 60:9	591
all the *s* of the sea with their	Eze 27:9	591
The *s* of Tarshish did sing of	Eze 27:25	591
sea, shall come down from their *s*	Eze 27:29	591
messengers go forth from me in *s*	Eze 30:9	6716
For the *s* of Chittim shall come	Dan 11:30	6716
and with horsemen, and with many *s*	Dan 11:40	591
were also with him other little *s*	Mk 4:36	4142
saw two *s* standing by the lake	Lk 5:2	4143
And he entered into one of the *s*	Lk 5:3	4143
they came, and filled both the *s*	Lk 5:7	4143
they had brought their *s* to land	Lk 5:11	4143
Behold also the *s*, which though	Jas 3:4	4143
part of the *s* were destroyed	Rev 8:9	4143
and all the company in *s*, and	Rev 18:17	4143
had *s* in the sea by reason of her	Rev 18:19	4143

SHIPWRECK
was I stoned, thrice I suffered *s*	2Cor 11:25	3489
away concerning faith have made *s*	1Ti 1:19	3489

SHISHA (shi'-shah) *See* SHAVSHA. *Father of Elihoreph and Ahiah.*
Elihoreph and Ahiah, the sons of *S*	1Kin 4:3	7894

SHISHAK (shi'-shak) *A king of Egypt.*
unto *S* king of Egypt, and was in	1Kin 11:40	7895
that *S* king of Egypt came up	1Kin 14:25	7895
S king of Egypt came up against	2Chr 12:2	7895
to Jerusalem because of *S*	2Chr 12:5	7895
I also left you in the hand of *S*	2Chr 12:5	7895
upon Jerusalem by the hand of *S*	2Chr 12:7	7895
So *S* king of Egypt came up	2Chr 12:9	7895

SHITRAI (shit'-ra-i) *A herdsman in David's court.*
fed in Sharon was *S* the Sharonite	1Chr 27:29	7861

SHITTAH
the *s* tree, and the myrtle, and the	Is 41:19	7848

SHITTIM (shit'-tim) *A place in Moab.*
and badgers' skins, and *s* wood,	Ex 25:5	7848
they shall make an ark of *s* wood	Ex 25:10	7848
thou shalt make staves of *s* wood	Ex 25:13	7848
shalt also make a table of *s* wood	Ex 25:23	7848
shalt make the staves of *s* wood	Ex 25:28	7848
tabernacle of *s* wood standing up	Ex 26:15	7848
And thou shalt make bars of *s* wood	Ex 26:26	7848
of *s* wood overlaid with gold	Ex 26:32	7848
hanging five pillars of *s* wood	Ex 26:37	7848
shalt make an altar of *s* wood	Ex 27:1	7848
for the altar, staves of *s* wood	Ex 27:6	7848
of *s* wood shalt thou make it	Ex 30:1	7848
shalt make the staves of *s* wood	Ex 30:5	7848
and badgers' skins, and *s* wood,	Ex 35:7	7848
with whom was found *s* wood for	Ex 35:24	7848
for the tabernacle of *s* wood	Ex 36:20	7848
And he made bars of *s* wood	Ex 36:31	7848
thereunto four pillars of *s* wood	Ex 36:36	7848
Bezaleel made the ark of *s* wood	Ex 37:1	7848
And he made staves of *s* wood	Ex 37:4	7848
And he made the table of *s* wood	Ex 37:10	7848
And he made the staves of *s* wood	Ex 37:15	7848
made the incense altar of *s* wood	Ex 37:25	7848
And he made the staves of *s* wood	Ex 37:28	7848
altar of burnt offering of *s* wood	Ex 38:1	7848
And he made the staves of *s* wood	Ex 38:6	7848
And Israel abode in *S*, and the	Num 25:1	7851
And I made an ark of *s* wood	Deut 10:3	7848
out of *S* two men to spy secretly	Josh 2:1	7851
and they removed from *S*, and came	Josh 3:1	7851
and shall water the valley of *S*	Joel 3:18	7851
answered him from *S* unto Gilgal	Mic 6:5	7851

SHIVERS
potter shall they be broken to *s*	Rev 2:27	4937

SHIZA (shi'-zah) *A "mighty man" of David.*
Adina the son of *S* the Reubenite	1Chr 11:42	7877

SHOA (sho'-ah) *A tribal enemy of Israel.*
and all the Chaldeans, Pekod, and *S*	Eze 23:23	7772

SHOBAB (sho'-bab)
1. A son of David.
Shammuah, and *S*, and Nathan, and	2Sa 5:14	7727
Shimea, and *S*, and Nathan, and	1Chr 3:5	7727
and *S*, Nathan, and Solomon	1Chr 14:4	7727
2. A son of Caleb.
Jesher, and *S*, and Ardon	1Chr 2:18	7727

SHOBACH (sho'-bak) *See* SHOPHACH. *A Syrian defeated by David.*
S the captain of the host of	2Sa 10:16	7731
smote *S* the captain of their host	2Sa 10:18	7731

SHOBAI (sho'-bahee) *A family of exiles.*
of Hatita, the children of *S*	Ezr 2:42	7630
of Hatita, the children of *S*	Neh 7:45	7630

SHOBAL (sho'-bal)
1. A son of Seir.
Lotan, and *S*, and Zibeon, and Anah,	Gen 36:20	7732
And the children of *S* were these	Gen 36:23	7732
duke Lotan, duke *S*, duke Zibeon,	Gen 36:29	7732
Lotan, and *S*, and Zibeon, and Anah,	1Chr 1:38	7732
The sons of *S*	1Chr 1:40	7732
2. A son of Caleb.
S the father of Kirjath-jearim,	1Chr 2:50	7732
S the father of Kirjath-jearim	1Chr 2:52	7732
3. A son of Judah.
Hezron, and Carmi, and Hur, and *S*	1Chr 4:1	7732
Reaiah the son of *S* begat Jahath	1Chr 4:2	7732

SHOBEK
(sho'-bek) A clan leader who renewed the covenant.
Hallohesh, Pileha, S, ... Neh 10:24   7733

SHOBI
(sho'-bi) A son of Nahash.
that S the son of Nahash of 2Sa 17:27   7629

SHOCHO
(sho'-ko) See CHOCHO. *A city in Judah.*
S with the villages thereof, and 2Chr 28:18   7755

SHOCHOH
(sho'-ko) See SHOCHO, SHOCO, SOCHOH, SOCO, SOCOH. *Same as Shocho.*
and were gathered together at S 1Sa 17:1   7755
to Judah, and pitched between S 1Sa 17:1   7755

SHOCK
like as a s of corn cometh in in .... Job 5:26   1430

SHOCKS
and burnt up both the s, and also .... Judg 15:5   1430

SHOCO
(sho'-ko) See SHOCHOH. *Same as Shocho.*
And Beth-zur, and S, and Adullam, ... 2Chr 11:7   7755

SHOD
s them, and gave them to eat and to 2Chr 28:15   5274
s thee with badgers' skin, and I .... Eze 16:10   5274
But be s with sandals .... Mk 6:9   5265
your feet s with the preparation .... Eph 6:15   5265

SHOE
loose his s from off his foot, and .... Deut 25:9   5275
of him that hath his s loosed.................. Deut 25:10   5275
thy s is not waxen old upon thy .... Deut 29:5   5275
Loose thy s from off thy foot .... Josh 5:15   5275
a man plucked off his s, and gave .... Ruth 4:7   5275
So he drew off his s .... Ruth 4:8   5275
over Edom will I cast out my s .... Ps 60:8   5275
over Edom will I cast out my s .... Ps 108:9   5275
put off thy s from thy foot .... Is 20:2   5275

SHOELATCHET
take from a thread even to a s .... Gen 14:23   8288,5275

SHOE'S
whose s latchet I am not worthy .... Jn 1:27   5266

SHOES
put off thy s from off thy feet, ... Ex 3:5   5275
your s on your feet, and your .... Ex 12:11   5275
Thy s shall be iron and brass .... Deut 33:25   4515
And old s and clouted upon their .... Josh 9:5   5275
our s are become old by reason of .... Josh 9:13   5275
in his s that were on his feet 1Kin 2:5   5275
How beautiful are thy feet with s .... Song 7:1   5275
the latchet of their s be broken .... Is 5:27   5275
put on thy s upon thy feet, and .... Eze 24:17   5275
heads, and your s upon your feet........... Eze 24:23   5275
and the poor for a pair of s .... Amos 2:6   5275
and the needy for a pair of s .... Amos 8:6   5275
whose s I am not worthy to bear .... Mt 3:11   5266
neither two coats, neither s .... Mt 10:10   5266
the latchet of whose s I am not .... Mk 1:7   5266
the latchet of whose s I am not .... Lk 3:16   5266
neither purse, nor scrip, nor s .... Lk 10:4   5266
on his hand, and s on his feet .... Lk 15:22   5266
you without purse, and scrip, and s . Lk 22:35   5266
Put off thy s from thy feet .... Acts 7:33   5266
whose s off his feet I am not .... Acts 13:25   5266

SHOHAM
(sho'-ham) A Merarite.
Beno, and S, and Zaccur, and Ibri 1Chr 24:27   7719

SHOMER
(sho'-mur) See SHAMER, SHIMRITH.
1. Same as Shimrith.
and Jehozabad the son of S 2Kin 12:21   7763
2. Son of Heber.
And Heber begat Japhlet, and S 1Chr 7:32   7763

SHONE
face s while he talked with him .... Ex 34:29   7160
behold, the skin of his face s .... Ex 34:30   7160
that the skin of Moses' face s................. Ex 34:35   7160
the sun s upon the water, and the 2Kin 3:22   2224
of the Lord s round about them .... Lk 2:9   4034
suddenly there s from heaven a .... Acts 22:6   4015
the day s not for a third part of .... Rev 8:12   5316

SHOOK
for the oxen s it...................................... 2Sa 6:6   8058
Then the earth s and trembled 2Sa 22:8   1607
foundations of heaven moved and s 2Sa 22:8   1607
Also I s my lap, and said, So God .... Neh 5:13   5287
Then the earth s and trembled .... Ps 18:7   1607
The earth s, the heavens also .... Ps 68:8   7493
the earth trembled and s .... Ps 77:18   7493
over the sea, he s the kingdoms .... Is 23:11   7264
But they s off the dust of their .... Acts 13:51   1621
he s his raiment, and said unto .... Acts 18:6   1621

he s off the beast into the fire, ... Acts 28:5   660
Whose voice then s the earth .... Heb 12:26   4531

SHOOT
he made the middle bar to s .... Ex 36:33   1272
I will s three arrows on the side 1Sa 20:20   3384
find out now the arrows which I s 1Sa 20:36   3384
that they would s from the wall.............. 2Sa 11:20   3384
Then Elisha said, S 2Kin 13:17   3384
nor s an arrow there, nor come 2Kin 19:32   3384
to s with bow, and skilful in war,........... 1Chr 5:18   1869
to s arrows and great stones.................. 2Chr 26:15   3384
that they may privily s at the .... Ps 11:2   3384
they s out the lip, they shake .... Ps 22:7   6362
bendeth his bow to s his arrows .... Ps 58:7   3384
bend their bows to s their arrows .... Ps 64:3
That they may s in secret at the .... Ps 64:4   3384
suddenly do they s at him .... Ps 64:4   3384
But God shall s at them with an............ Ps 64:7   3384
s out thine arrows, and destroy .... Ps 144:6   7971
nor s an arrow there, nor come .... Is 37:33
s at her, spare no arrows .... Jer 50:14   3034
neither s up their top among the............ Eze 31:14   5414
ye shall s forth your branches, ... Eze 36:8   5414
When they now s forth, ye see and ... Lk 21:30   4261

SHOOTERS
the s shot from off the wall upon 2Sa 11:24   3384

SHOOTETH
his branch s forth in his garden .... Job 8:16   3318
In measure, when it s forth .... Is 27:8   7971
herbs, and s out great branches .... Mk 4:32   4160

SHOOTING
s arrows out of a bow, even of................ 1Chr 12:2
of the s up of the latter growth .... Amos 7:1   5927

SHOPHACH
(sho'-fak) See SHOBACH. *Same as Shoback.*
S the captain of the host of 1Chr 19:16   7780
killed S the captain of the host 1Chr 19:18   7780

SHOPHAN
(sho'-fan) See ZAPHON. *A city in Gad.*
And Atroth, S, and Jaazer, and.............. Num 32:35   5855

SHORE
the sand which is upon the sea s............ Gen 22:17   8193
the Egyptians dead upon the sea s .... Ex 14:30   8193
is upon the sea s in multitude .... Josh 11:4   8193
was from the s of the salt sea .... Josh 15:2   7097
Asher continued on the sea s .... Judg 5:17   2348
is on the sea s in multitude 1Sa 13:5   8193
as the sand that is on the sea s 1Kin 4:29   8193
on the s of the Red sea, in the............... 1Kin 9:26   8193
Ashkelon, and against the sea s .... Jer 47:7   2348
whole multitude stood on the s .... Mt 13:2   123
when it was full, they drew to s .... Mt 13:48   123
of Gennesaret, and drew to the s........... Mk 6:53   4358
now come, Jesus stood on the s .... Jn 21:4   123
and we kneeled down on the s .... Acts 21:5   123
a certain creek with a s, into .... Acts 27:39   123
to the wind, and made toward s.............. Acts 27:40   123
which is by the sea s innumerable......... Heb 11:12   5491

SHORN
a flock of sheep that are even s .... Song 4:2   7094
having s his head in Cenchrea............... Acts 18:18   2751
be not covered, let her also be s 1Cor 11:6   2751
for a woman to be s or shaven 1Cor 11:6   2751

SHORT
Moses, Is the LORD's hand waxed s .... Num 11:23   7114
the LORD began to cut Israel s 2Kin 10:32
the light is s because of .... Job 17:12   7138
the triumphing of the wicked is s........... Job 20:5   7138
Remember how s my time is .... Ps 89:47   2465
come s of the glory of God...................... Rom 3:23   5302
cut it s in righteousness......................... Rom 9:28   4932
because a s work will the Lord .... Rom 9:28   4932
I say, brethren, the time is s 1Cor 7:29   4958
from you for a s time in presence 1Th 2:17   5610
you should seem to come s of it .... Heb 4:1   5302
knoweth that he hath but a s time .... Rev 12:12   3641
he must continue a s space .... Rev 17:10   3641

SHORTENED
The days of his youth hast thou s .... Ps 89:45   7114
he s my days... Ps 102:23   7114
years of the wicked shall be s .... Prov 10:27   7114
Is my hand s at all, that it...................... Is 50:2   7114
Behold, the LORD's hand is not s .... Is 59:1   7114
And except those days should be s .... Mt 24:22   2856
sake those days shall be s .... Mt 24:22   2856
that the Lord had s those days .... Mk 13:20   2856
hath chosen, he hath s the days ...... Mk 13:20   2856

S

SHORTER

For the bed is *s* than that a man	Is 28:20	7114
Now the upper chambers were *s*	Eze 42:5	7114

SHORTLY

God will *s* bring it to pass	Gen 41:32	4116
s be brought again from Babylon	Jer 27:16	4120
Now will I *s* pour out my fury	Eze 7:8	7138
he himself *s* depart *s* thither	Acts 25:4	1722,5034
bruise Satan under your feet *s*	Rom 16:20	1722,5034
But I will come to you *s*, if the	1Cor 4:19	5030
to send Timotheus *s* unto you	Phil 2:19	5030
that I also myself shall come *s*	Phil 2:24	5030
thee, hoping to come unto thee *s*	1Ti 3:14	5032
thy diligence to come *s* unto me	2Ti 4:9	5030
with whom, if he come *s*, I will	Heb 13:23	5032
Knowing that *s* I must put off	2Pet 1:14	5031
But I trust I shall *s* see thee	3Jn 14	2112
things which must *s* come to pass	Rev 1:1	1722,5034
the things which must *s* be done	Rev 22:6	1722,5034

SHOSHANNIM (sho-shan'-nim) A musical notation.

To the chief Musician upon *S*:	Ps 45:*t*	7799
To the chief Musician upon *S*	Ps 69:*t*	7799

SHOSHANNIM-EDUTH (sho-shan'-nim-e'-duth) A musical notation.

To the chief Musician upon *S*	Ps 80:*t*	7802

SHOT

budded, and her blossoms *s* forth	Gen 40:10	5927
him, and *s* at him, and hated him	Gen 49:23	7232
surely be stoned, or *s* through	Ex 19:13	3384
We have *s* at them	Num 21:30	3384
thereof, as though I *s* at a mark	1Sa 20:20	7971
lad ran, he *s* an arrow beyond him	1Sa 20:36	3384
of the arrow which Jonathan had *s*	1Sa 20:37	3384
the shooters *s* from off the wall	2Sa 11:24	3384
said, Shoot. And he *s*	2Kin 13:17	3384
the archers *s* at king Josiah	2Chr 35:23	3384
and he *s* out lightnings, and	Ps 18:14	7232
Their tongue is as an arrow *s* out	Jer 9:8	7819
forth branches, and *s* forth sprigs	Eze 17:6	7971
s forth her branches toward him,	Eze 17:7	7971
of waters, when he *s* forth	Eze 31:5	7971
he hath *s* up his top among the	Eze 31:10	7971

SHOULD

not good that the man *s* be alone	Gen 2:18
lest any finding him *s* kill him	Gen 4:15
the righteous be as the wicked	Gen 18:25
that Sarah *s* have given children	Gen 21:7
If it be your mind that I *s* bury	Gen 23:8
the place *s* kill me for Rebekah	Gen 26:7
why *s* I be deprived also of you	Gen 27:45
the cattle *s* be gathered together	Gen 29:7
than that I *s* give her to another	Gen 29:19
that they *s* conceive when they	Gen 30:38
if men *s* overdrive them one day,	Gen 33:13
S he deal with our sister as with	Gen 34:31
knew that the seed *s* not be his	Gen 38:9
lest that he *s* give seed to his	Gen 38:9
they *s* put me into the dungeon	Gen 40:15
heard that they *s* eat bread there	Gen 43:25
s do according to this thing	Gen 44:7
how then *s* we steal out of thy	Gen 44:8
said, God forbid that I *s* do so	Gen 44:17
for if he *s* leave his father, his	Gen 44:22
for why *s* we die in thy presence	Gen 47:15
that Pharaoh *s* have the fifth	Gen 47:26
that I *s* go unto Pharaoh	Ex 3:11
that I *s* bring forth the children	Ex 3:11
that I *s* obey his voice to let	Ex 5:2
than that we *s* die in the	Ex 14:12
for he *s* make full restitution	Ex 22:3
Wherefore *s* the Egyptians speak,	Ex 32:12
hath commanded, that ye *s* do them	Ex 35:1
that they *s* be stones for a	Ex 39:7
the hole, that it *s* not rend	Ex 39:23
things which *s* not be done	Lev 4:13
things which *s* not be done	Lev 4:22
the Lord commanded that ye *s* do	Lev 9:6
ye *s* indeed have eaten it in the	Lev 10:18
s it have been accepted in the	Lev 10:19
that ye *s* be defiled thereby	Lev 11:43
other people, that ye *s* be mine	Lev 20:26
that they *s* bring forth him that	Lev 24:23
that ye *s* not be their bondmen	Lev 26:13
which *s* be the Lord's firstling,	Lev 27:26
unto them was that they *s* bear	Num 7:9
that they *s* keep the passover	Num 9:4
Whence *s* I have flesh to give	Num 11:13
s she not be ashamed seven days	Num 12:14

wives and our children *s* be a prey	Num 14:3
ones, which ye said *s* be a prey	Num 14:31
declared what *s* be done to him	Num 15:34
that we and our cattle *s* die there	Num 20:4
God is not a man, that he *s* lie	Num 23:19
the son of man, that he *s* repent	Num 23:19
Why *s* the name of our father be	Num 27:4
that they *s* not go into the land	Num 32:9
Because he *s* have remained in the	Num 35:28
that he *s* come again to dwell in	Num 35:32
time all the things which ye *s* do	Deut 1:18
to shew you by what way ye *s* go	Deut 1:33
ones, which ye said *s* be a prey	Deut 1:39
that ye *s* do so in the land	Deut 4:5
sware that I *s* not go over Jordan	Deut 4:21
that I *s* not go in unto that good	Deut 4:21
which *s* kill his neighbour	Deut 4:42
Now therefore why *s* we die	Deut 5:25
the end that he *s* multiply horses	Deut 17:16
so *s* ye sin against the Lord your	Deut 20:18
if he *s* exceed, and beat him above	Deut 25:3
then thy brother *s* seem vile unto	Deut 25:3
Lest there *s* be among you man, or	Deut 29:18
lest there *s* be among you a root	Deut 29:18
lest their adversaries *s* behave	Deut 32:27
strangely, and lest they *s* say	Deut 32:27
How *s* one chase a thousand, and	Deut 32:30
Joshua commanded that they *s* take	Josh 8:29
that they *s* bless the people of	Josh 8:33
in the place which he *s* choose	Josh 9:27
that they *s* come against Israel	Josh 11:20
when they *s* so say to us or to	Josh 22:28
God forbid that we *s* rebel	Josh 22:29
forbid that we *s* forsake the Lord	Josh 24:16
that we *s* give bread unto thine	Judg 8:6
that we *s* give bread unto thy men	Judg 8:15
S I leave my fatness, wherewith	Judg 9:9
S I forsake my sweetness, and my	Judg 9:11
S I leave my wine, which cheereth	Judg 9:13
is Shechem, that we *s* serve him	Judg 9:28
for why *s* we serve him	Judg 9:28
is Abimelech, that we *s* serve him	Judg 9:38
that they *s* not dwell in Shechem	Judg 9:41
that they *s* make a great flame	Judg 20:38
that there *s* be to day one tribe	Judg 21:3
at this time, that ye *s* be guilty	Judg 21:22
If I *s* say, I have hope	Ruth 1:12
if I *s* have an husband also to	Ruth 1:12
to night, and *s* also bear sons	Ruth 1:12
s walk before me for ever	1Sa 2:30
that I *s* not reign over them	1Sa 8:7
can shew us our way that we *s* go	1Sa 9:6
if the man *s* yet come thither	1Sa 10:22
for then *s* ye go after vain	1Sa 12:21
God forbid that I *s* sin against	1Sa 12:23
s have been utterly destroyed	1Sa 15:21
he is not a man, that he *s* repent	1Sa 15:29
that he *s* defy the armies of the	1Sa 17:26
that I *s* be son in law to the	1Sa 18:18
s have been given to David	1Sa 18:19
servants, that they *s* kill David	1Sa 19:1
why *s* I kill thee	1Sa 19:17
why *s* my father hide this thing	1Sa 20:2
I *s* not fail to sit with the king	1Sa 20:5
that he *s* rise against me, to lie	1Sa 22:13
The Lord forbid that I *s* do this	1Sa 24:6
The Lord forbid that I *s* stretch	1Sa 26:11
better for me than that I *s*	1Sa 27:1
for why *s* thy servant dwell in	1Sa 27:5
Lest they *s* tell on us, saying,	1Sa 27:11
for wherewith *s* he reconcile	1Sa 29:4
s it not be with the heads of	1Sa 29:4
wherefore *s* I smite thee to the	2Sa 2:22
how then *s* I hold up my face to	2Sa 2:22
he is dead, wherefore *s* I fast	2Sa 12:23
unto him, Why *s* he go with thee	2Sa 13:26
s I this day make thee go up and	2Sa 15:20
Why *s* this dead dog curse my lord	2Sa 16:9
And again, whom *s* I serve	2Sa 16:19
s I not serve in the presence of	2Sa 16:19
Though I *s* receive a thousand	2Sa 18:12
Otherwise I *s* have wrought	2Sa 18:13
that the king *s* take it to his	2Sa 19:19
that ye *s* this day be adversaries	2Sa 19:22
that I *s* go up with the king unto	2Sa 19:34
wherefore then *s* thy servant be	2Sa 19:35
why *s* the king recompense it me	2Sa 19:36
that our advice *s* not be first	2Sa 19:43
that I *s* swallow up or destroy	2Sa 20:20
s be destroyed from remaining in	2Sa 21:5
from me, O Lord, that I *s* do this	2Sa 23:17

who *s* sit on the throne of my 1Kin 1:27
of David drew nigh that he *s* die 1Kin 2:1
their faces on me, that I *s* reign 1Kin 2:15
that the beams *s* not be fastened 1Kin 6:6
the good way wherein they *s* walk 1Kin 8:36
that he *s* not go after other gods 1Kin 11:10
which told me that I *s* be king 1Kin 14:2
that I *s* give the inheritance of 1Kin 21:3
that *s* have reigned in his stead 2Kin 3:27
s I set this before an hundred 2Kin 4:43
what *s* I wait for the LORD any 2Kin 6:33
if the LORD *s* make windows in 2Kin 7:19
that he *s* do this great thing 2Kin 8:13
with them that *s* go out on the 2Kin 11:9
that they *s* be the LORD's people 2Kin 11:17
that they *s* not do like them 2Kin 17:15
them how they *s* fear the LORD 2Kin 17:28
that the LORD *s* deliver Jerusalem 2Kin 18:35
that they *s* become a desolation 2Kin 22:19
that they *s* bring them in and out 1Chr 9:28
it me, that I *s* do this thing 1Chr 11:19
for those that *s* make a sound 1Chr 16:42
people, that they *s* be plagued 1Chr 21:17
say to David, that David *s* go up 1Chr 21:18
that he *s* sanctify the most holy 1Chr 23:13
that they *s* keep the charge of 1Chr 23:32
who *s* prophesy with harps, with 1Chr 25:1
that we *s* be able to offer so 1Chr 29:14
that I *s* build him an house, save 2Chr 2:6
that they *s* burn after the manner 2Chr 4:20
the good way, wherein they *s* walk 2Chr 6:27
God of Israel *s* be put to death 2Chr 15:13
that *s* praise the beauty of 2Chr 20:21
that they *s* be the LORD's people 2Chr 23:16
unclean in any thing *s* enter in 2Chr 23:19
that they *s* not go with him to 2Chr 25:13
that ye *s* minister unto him, and 2Chr 29:11
the sin offering *s* be made for 2Chr 29:24
that they *s* come to the house of 2Chr 30:1
that they *s* come to keep the 2Chr 30:5
Why *s* the kings of Assyria come, ... 2Chr 32:4
that your God *s* be able to 2Chr 32:14
that they *s* not eat of the most .... Ezr 2:63
why *s* damage grow to the hurt of .... Ezr 4:22
for why *s* there be wrath against .... Ezr 7:23
them what they *s* say unto Iddo .... Ezr 8:17
that they *s* bring unto us .... Ezr 8:17
S we again break thy commandments ... Ezr 9:14
so that there *s* be no remnant nor .... Ezr 9:14
to swear that they *s* do according .... Ezr 10:5
that they *s* gather themselves .... Ezr 10:7
all his substance *s* be forfeited .... Ezr 10:8
why *s* not my countenance be sad, ... Neh 2:3
that they *s* do according to this .... Neh 5:12
why *s* the work cease, whilst I .... Neh 6:3
And I said, *S* such a man as I flee .... Neh 6:11
that I *s* be afraid, and do so, and .... Neh 6:13
that they *s* not eat of the most .... Neh 7:65
that the children of Israel *s* .... Neh 8:14
And that they *s* publish and .... Neh 8:15
in the way wherein they *s* go .... Neh 9:12
promisedst them that they *s* go in .... Neh 9:15
and the way wherein they *s* go .... Neh 9:19
that they *s* go in to possess it .... Neh 9:23
that we *s* bring the firstfruits .... Neh 10:37
portion *s* be for the singers .... Neh 11:23
the Moabite *s* not come into the .... Neh 13:1
them, that he *s* curse them .... Neh 13:2
that the gates *s* be shut, and .... Neh 13:19
charged that they *s* not be opened .... Neh 13:19
that there *s* no burden be brought .... Neh 13:19
that they *s* cleanse themselves .... Neh 13:22
and that they *s* come .... Neh 13:22
that they *s* do according to every .... Est 1:8
that every man *s* bear rule in his .... Est 1:22
that it *s* be published according .... Est 1:22
her that she *s* not shew it .... Est 2:10
did, and what *s* become of her .... Est 2:11
that they *s* be ready against that .... Est 3:14
that she *s* go in unto the king .... Est 4:8
that the Jews *s* be ready against .... Est 8:13
that they *s* keep the fourteenth .... Est 9:21
that they *s* make them days of .... Est 9:22
s return upon his own head, and .... Est 9:25
his sons *s* be hanged on the .... Est 9:25
unto them, so as it *s* not fail .... Est 9:27
that these days *s* be remembered .... Est 9:28
that these days of Purim *s* not .... Est 9:28
or why the breasts that I *s* suck .... Job 3:12
For now *s* I have lain still and .... Job 3:13
and been quiet, I *s* have slept .... Job 3:13

Then *s* I yet have comfort .... Job 6:10
is my strength, that I *s* hope .... Job 6:11
end, that I *s* prolong my life .... Job 6:11
pity *s* be shewed from his friend .... Job 6:14
thy latter end *s* greatly increase .... Job 8:7
but how *s* man be just with God .... Job 9:2
that I *s* answer him .... Job 9:32
we *s* come together in judgment .... Job 9:32
I *s* have been as though I had not .... Job 10:19
I *s* have been carried from the .... Job 10:19
S not the multitude of words be .... Job 11:2
s a man full of talk be justified .... Job 11:2
S thy lies make men hold their .... Job 11:3
and it *s* be your wisdom .... Job 13:5
it good that he *s* search you out .... Job 13:9
S a wise man utter vain knowledge .... Job 15:2
S he reason with unprofitable .... Job 15:3
What is man, that he *s* be clean .... Job 15:14
a woman, that he *s* be righteous .... Job 15:14
of my lips *s* asswage your grief .... Job 16:5
But ye *s* say, Why persecute we .... Job 19:28
why *s* not my spirit be troubled .... Job 21:4
the Almighty, that we *s* serve him .... Job 21:15
and what profit *s* we have, if we .... Job 21:15
so I *s* be delivered for ever from .... Job 23:7
God forbid that I *s* justify you .... Job 27:5
why then *s* I think upon a maid .... Job 31:1
for I *s* have denied the God that .... Job 31:28
Days *s* speak, and multitude of .... Job 32:7
multitude of years *s* teach wisdom .... Job 32:7
Lest ye *s* say, We have found out .... Job 32:13
S I lie against my right .... Job 34:6
he *s* delight himself with God .... Job 34:9
from God, that he *s* do wickedness .... Job 34:10
that he *s* commit iniquity .... Job 34:10
that he *s* enter into judgment .... Job 34:23
S it be according to thy mind .... Job 34:33
that which *s* be set on thy table .... Job 36:16
on thy table *s* be full of fatness .... Job 36:16
prevented me, that I *s* repay him .... Job 41:11
Though an host *s* encamp against .... Ps 27:3
though war *s* rise against me, in .... Ps 27:3
that I *s* not go down to the pit .... Ps 30:3
otherwise they *s* rejoice over me .... Ps 38:16
Wherefore *s* I fear in the days of .... Ps 49:5
That he *s* still live for ever, and .... Ps 49:9
that which *s* have been for their .... Ps 69:22
I *s* offend against the generation .... Ps 73:15
that they *s* make them known to .... Ps 78:5
even the children which *s* be born .... Ps 78:6
who *s* arise and declare them to .... Ps 78:6
Wherefore *s* the heathen say, ... Ps 79:10
I *s* soon have subdued their .... Ps 81:14
The haters of the LORD *s* have .... Ps 81:15
but their time *s* have endured for .... Ps 81:15
He *s* have fed them also with the *S* ...... Ps 81:16
the rock *s* I have satisfied thee .... Ps 81:16
they *s* not enter into my rest .... Ps 95:11
that it *s* not be removed for ever .... Ps 104:5
his wrath, lest he *s* destroy them .... Ps 106:23
Wherefore *s* the heathen say, ... Ps 115:2
I *s* then have perished in mine .... Ps 119:92
If I *s* count them, they are more .... Ps 139:18
to know the way wherein I *s* walk .... Ps 143:8
that the waters *s* not pass his .... Prov 8:29
up a child in the way he *s* go .... Prov 22:6
why *s* he take away thy bed from .... Prov 22:27
which they *s* do under the heaven .... Eccl 2:3
because I *s* leave it unto the man .... Eccl 2:18
for a man, than that he *s* eat .... Eccl 2:24
that he *s* make his soul enjoy .... Eccl 2:24
And also that every man *s* eat .... Eccl 3:13
that men *s* fear before him .... Eccl 3:14
than that a man *s* rejoice in his .... Eccl 3:22
wherefore *s* God be angry at thy .... Eccl 5:6
to the end that man *s* find .... Eccl 7:14
for why *s* I be as one that .... Song 1:7
when I *s* find thee without, I .... Song 8:1
yea, I *s* not be despised .... Song 8:1
His left hand *s* be under my head, ... Song 8:3
and his right hand *s* embrace me .... Song 8:3
Why *s* ye be stricken any more .... Is 1:5
we *s* have been as Sodom .... Is 1:9
we *s* have been like unto Gomorrah ...... Is 1:9
he looked that it *s* bring forth .... Is 5:2
that it *s* bring forth grapes .... Is 5:4
instructed me that I *s* not walk .... Is 8:11
s not a people seek unto their .... Is 8:19
as if the rod *s* shake itself .... Is 10:15
as if the staff *s* lift up itself .... Is 10:15
that the LORD *s* deliver Jerusalem .... Is 36:20

nails, that it *s* not be moved	Is 41:7
for how *s* my name be polluted	Is 48:11
his name *s* not have been cut off	Is 48:19
that she *s* not have compassion on	Is 49:15
that I *s* know how to speak a word	Is 50:4
that he *s* not die in the pit	Is 51:14
nor that his bread *s* fail	Is 51:14
is no beauty that we *s* desire him	Is 53:2
Noah *s* no more go over the earth	Is 54:9
S I receive comfort in these	Is 57:6
for the spirit *s* fail before me	Is 57:16
that they *s* not stumble	Is 63:13
thy sons and thy daughters *s* eat	Jer 5:17
that my days *s* be consumed with	Jer 20:18
then they *s* have turned them from	Jer 23:22
s ye be utterly unpunished	Jer 25:29
that they *s* not give him into the	Jer 26:24
that I *s* drive you out	Jer 27:10
drive you out, and ye *s* perish	Jer 27:10
wherefore *s* this city be laid	Jer 27:17
that ye *s* be officers in the	Jer 29:26
that I *s* remove it from before my	Jer 32:31
that they *s* do this abomination,	Jer 32:35
night, and that there *s* not be day	Jer 33:20
that he *s* not have a son to reign	Jer 33:21
that they *s* be no more a nation	Jer 33:24
That every man *s* let his	Jer 34:9
that none *s* serve himself of them	Jer 34:9
every one *s* let his manservant	Jer 34:10
that none *s* serve themselves of	Jer 34:10
yet *s* they rise up every man in	Jer 37:10
the king commanded that they *s*	Jer 37:21
that they *s* give him daily a	Jer 37:21
Shaphan, that he *s* carry him home	Jer 39:14
wherefore *s* he slay thee, that	Jer 40:15
gathered unto thee *s* be scattered	Jer 40:15
that they *s* return into the land	Jer 44:14
king of Babylon *s* come and smite	Jer 46:13
Though Babylon *s* mount up to	Jer 51:53
though she *s* fortify the height	Jer 51:53
the evil that *s* come upon Babylon	Jer 51:60
thou didst command that they *s*	Lam 1:10
because the comforter that *s*	Lam 1:16
adversaries *s* be round about him	Lam 1:17
It is good that a man *s* both hope	Lam 3:26
that our prayer *s* not pass	Lam 3:44
the enemy *s* have entered into the	Lam 4:12
that I *s* go far off from my	Eze 8:6
to slay the souls that *s* not die	Eze 13:19
the souls alive that *s* not live	Eze 13:19
that he *s* not return from his	Eze 13:22
s I be enquired of at all by them	Eze 14:3
they *s* deliver but their own	Eze 14:14
at all that the wicked *s* die	Eze 18:23
not that he *s* return from his	Eze 18:23
that his voice *s* no more be heard	Eze 19:9
that it *s* not be polluted before	Eze 20:9
that it *s* not be polluted before	Eze 20:14
that it *s* not be polluted in the	Eze 20:22
judgments whereby they *s* not live	Eze 20:25
s we then make mirth	Eze 21:10
that *s* make up the hedge, and	Eze 22:30
the land, that I *s* not destroy it	Eze 22:30
a rock, that it *s* not be covered	Eze 24:8
away in them, how *s* we then live	Eze 33:10
s not the shepherds feed the	Eze 34:2
that he *s* bring certain of the	Dan 1:3
for why *s* he see your faces worse	Dan 1:10
and the wine that they *s* drink	Dan 1:16
king had said he *s* bring them in	Dan 1:18
that the wise men *s* be slain	Dan 2:13
his fellows *s* not perish with the	Dan 2:18
what *s* come to pass hereafter	Dan 2:29
that they *s* offer an oblation	Dan 2:46
that he *s* be cast into the midst	Dan 3:11
commanded that they *s* heat the	Dan 3:19
that they *s* read this writing, and	Dan 5:15
that he *s* be the third ruler in	Dan 5:29
which *s* be over the whole kingdom	Dan 6:1
the king *s* have no damage	Dan 6:2
commanded that they *s* take Daniel	Dan 6:23
and languages, *s* serve him	Dan 7:14
what then *s* a king do to us	Hos 10:3
my desire that I *s* chastise them	Hos 10:10
for he *s* not stay long in the	Hos 13:13
that the heathen *s* rule over them	Joel 2:17
wherefore *s* they say among the	Joel 2:17
s not I spare Nineveh, that great	Jonah 4:11
that I *s* make thee a desolation,	Mic 6:16
their dwelling *s* not be cut off	Zeph 3:7
that the LORD's house *s* be built	Hag 1:2

S I weep in the fifth month,	Zec 7:3
S ye not hear the words which the	Zec 7:7
their ears, that they *s* not hear	Zec 7:11
lest they *s* hear the law, and the	Zec 7:12
s it also be marvellous in mine	Zec 8:6
s I accept this of your hand	Mal 1:13
priest's lips *s* keep knowledge	Mal 2:7
they *s* seek the law at his mouth	Mal 2:7
of them where Christ *s* be born	Mt 2:4
that they *s* not return to Herod	Mt 2:12
that one of thy members *s* perish	Mt 5:29
whole body *s* be cast into hell	Mt 5:29
that one of thy members *s* perish	Mt 5:30
whole body *s* be cast into hell	Mt 5:30
ye would that men *s* do to you	Mt 7:12
unto him, Art thou he that *s* come	Mt 11:3
that they *s* not make him known	Mt 12:16
time they *s* see with their eyes	Mt 13:15
***s* understand with their heart, and**	Mt 13:15
***s* be converted, and I *s* heal**	Mt 13:15
Whence *s* we have so much bread in	Mt 15:33
that ye *s* beware of the leaven of	Mt 16:11
he his disciples that they *s* tell	Mt 16:20
lest we *s* offend them, go thou to	Mt 17:27
one of these little ones *s* perish	Mt 18:14
prison, till he *s* pay the debt	Mt 18:30
till he *s* pay all that was due	Mt 18:34
that he *s* put his hands on them,	Mt 19:13
that they *s* have received more	Mt 20:10
because they *s* hold their peace	Mt 20:31
except those days *s* be shortened	Mt 24:22
there *s* no flesh be saved	Mt 24:22
then at my coming I *s* have	Mt 25:27
Though I *s* die with thee, yet	Mt 26:35
that they *s* ask Barabbas, and	Mt 27:20
that a small ship *s* wait on him	Mk 3:9
multitude, lest they *s* throng him	Mk 3:9
that they *s* not make him known	Mk 3:12
that they *s* be with him, and that	Mk 3:14
at any time they *s* be converted	Mk 4:12
their sins *s* be forgiven them	Mk 4:12
secret, but that it *s* come abroad	Mk 4:22
as if a man *s* cast seed into the	Mk 4:26
***s* sleep, and rise night and day**	Mk 4:27
and the seed *s* spring	Mk 4:27
straitly that no man *s* know it	Mk 5:43
something *s* be given her to eat	Mk 5:43
commanded them that they *s* take	Mk 6:8
and preached that men *s* repent	Mk 6:12
them that they *s* tell no man	Mk 7:36
that they *s* tell no man of him	Mk 8:30
he charged them that they *s* tell	Mk 9:9
the rising from the dead *s* mean	Mk 9:10
that they *s* cast him out	Mk 9:18
would not that any man *s* know it	Mk 9:30
themselves, who *s* be the greatest	Mk 9:34
to him, that he *s* touch them	Mk 10:13
what things *s* happen unto him	Mk 10:32
What would ye that I *s* do for you	Mk 10:36
him that he *s* hold his peace	Mk 10:48
wilt thou that I *s* do unto thee	Mk 10:51
s carry any vessel through the	Mk 11:16
that his brother *s* take his wife	Mk 12:19
those days, no flesh *s* be saved	Mk 13:20
If I *s* die with thee, I will not	Mk 14:31
that he *s* rather release Barabbas	Mk 15:11
upon them, what every man *s* take	Mk 15:24
manner of salutation this *s* be	Lk 1:29
mother of my Lord *s* come to me	Lk 1:43
time came that she *s* be delivered	Lk 1:57
That we *s* be saved from our	Lk 1:71
that all the world *s* be taxed	Lk 2:1
that she *s* be delivered	Lk 2:6
that he *s* not see death, before	Lk 2:26
that he *s* not depart from them	Lk 4:42
the other ship, that they *s* come	Lk 5:7
as ye would that men *s* do to you	Lk 6:31
was worthy for whom he *s* do this	Lk 7:4
saying, Art thou he that *s* come	Lk 7:19
saying, Art thou he that *s* come	Lk 7:20
their hearts, lest they *s* believe	Lk 8:12
they *s* tell no man what was done	Lk 8:56
except we *s* go and buy meat for	Lk 9:13
he *s* accomplish at Jerusalem	Lk 9:31
them, which of them *s* be greatest	Lk 9:46
was come that he *s* be received up	Lk 9:51
It was meet that we *s* make merry	Lk 15:32
than that he *s* offend one of	Lk 17:2
and it *s* obey you	Lk 17:6
when the kingdom of God *s* come	Lk 17:20
him, that he *s* hold his peace	Lk 18:39

1163

3195

1163

3195

of God s immediately appear .... Lk 19:11	3195
not that I s reign over them .... Lk 19:27	
if these s hold their peace, the .... Lk 19:40	
that they s give him of the fruit .... Lk 20:10	
which s feign themselves just men .... Lk 20:20	
that his brother s take his wife .... Lk 20:28	
them it was that s do this thing .... Lk 22:23	3195
which of them s be accounted the .... Lk 22:24	
that it s be as they required .... Lk 23:24	
holden that they s not know him......... Lk 24:16	
he which s have redeemed Israel .... Lk 24:21	3195
remission of sins s be preached .... Lk 24:47	
but that he s be made manifest to........ Jn 1:31	
not that any s testify of man .... Jn 2:25	
believeth in him s not perish .... Jn 3:15	
believeth in him s not perish .... Jn 3:16	
lest his deeds s be reproved .... Jn 3:20	
That all men s honour the Son,............. Jn 5:23	
that s come into the world .... Jn 6:14	
he hath given me I s lose nothing........ Jn 6:39	
but s raise it up again at the .... Jn 6:39	
believed not, and who s betray him....... Jn 6:64	
for he it was that s betray him............. Jn 6:71	3195
the law of Moses s not be broken .... Jn 7:23	
that believe on him s receive .... Jn 7:39	3195
us, that such s be stoned .... Jn 8:5	
ye s have known my Father also .... Jn 8:19	
and if I s say, I know him not, I .... Jn 8:55	
of God s be made manifest in him........ Jn 9:3	
he s be put out of the synagogue........... Jn 9:22	
ye were blind, ye s have no sin .... Jn 9:41	
which s come into the world .... Jn 11:27	
even this man s not have died .... Jn 11:37	
that one man s die for the people .... Jn 11:50	
that Jesus s die for that nation .... Jn 11:51	3195
but that also he s gather .... Jn 11:52	
he s shew it, that they might .... Jn 11:57	
Simon's son, which s betray him,........... Jn 12:4	3195
the Son of man s be glorified................ Jn 12:23	
signifying what death he s die .... Jn 12:33	3195
that they s not see with their .... Jn 12:40	
and be converted, and I s heal them ...... Jn 12:40	
lest they s be put out of the.................... Jn 12:42	
on me s not abide in darkness................ Jn 12:46	
I s say, and what I s speak.................... Jn 12:49	
s depart out of this world unto .... Jn 13:1	
For he knew who s betray him .... Jn 13:11	
that ye s do as I have done to .... Jn 13:15	
that he s ask who it s be of.................. Jn 13:24	
that he s give something to the............. Jn 13:29	
ye s have known my Father also .... Jn 14:7	
and ordained you, that ye s go .... Jn 15:16	
and that your fruit s remain .... Jn 15:16	
that ye s not be offended .... Jn 16:1	
not that any man s ask thee .... Jn 16:30	
that he s give eternal life to as............. Jn 17:2	
all things that s come upon him .... Jn 18:4	
that one man s die for the people .... Jn 18:14	
hall, lest they s be defiled .... Jn 18:28	
signifying what death he s die .... Jn 18:32	3195
that I s not be delivered to the............... Jn 18:36	
that I s bear witness unto the .... Jn 18:37	
that I s release unto you one at .... Jn 18:39	
that the bodies s not remain upon .... Jn 19:31	
that the scripture s be fulfilled .... Jn 19:36	
by what death he s glorify God............... Jn 21:19	
that that disciple s not die..................... Jn 21:23	
if they s be written every one, I............. Jn 21:25	
the books that s be written .... Jn 21:25	
commanded them that they s not .... Acts 1:4	
that he s be holden of it .... Acts 2:24	
right hand, that I s not be moved .... Acts 2:25	
church daily such as s be saved .... Acts 2:47	
prophets, that Christ s suffer .... Acts 3:18	
lest they s have been stoned .... Acts 5:26	
that ye s not teach in this name .... Acts 5:28	
they commanded that they s not .... Acts 5:40	
that we s leave the word of God............. Acts 6:2	
That his seed s sojourn in a .... Acts 7:6	
that they s bring them into.................... Acts 7:6	
that he s make it according to .... Acts 7:44	
can I, except some man s guide me .... Acts 8:31	
vision which he had seen s mean .... Acts 10:17	
I s not call any man common or .... Acts 10:28	
that these s not be baptized,.................. Acts 10:47	
that he s go as far as Antioch .... Acts 11:22	
by the Spirit that there s be .... Acts 11:28	3195
that they s be put to death .... Acts 12:19	
they Pilate that he s be slain................. Acts 13:28	
s first have been spoken to you............. Acts 13:46	
preach unto you that ye s turn .... Acts 14:15	

s go up to Jerusalem unto the................ Acts 15:2	
s hear the word of the gospel................ Acts 15:7	
That they s seek the Lord, if.................. Acts 17:27	
would that I s bear with you................. Acts 18:14	
that they s believe on him which .... Acts 19:4	
on him which s come after him............. Acts 19:4	
great goddess Diana s be despised .... Acts 19:27	
her magnificence s be destroyed .... Acts 19:27	3195
that they s see his face no more .... Acts 20:38	3195
that he s not go up to Jerusalem .... Acts 21:4	
disciple, with whom we s lodge .... Acts 21:16	
until that an offering s be .... Acts 21:26	
for it is not fit that he s live .... Acts 22:22	
bade that he s be examined by .... Acts 22:24	
him which s have examined him .... Acts 22:29	3195
fearing lest Paul s have been .... Acts 23:10	
s have been killed of them..................... Acts 23:27	3195
that he s forbid none of his .... Acts 24:23	
He hoped also that money s have .... Acts 24:26	
that Paul s be kept at Caesarea,............ Acts 25:4	
Why s it be thought a thing .... Acts 26:8	
that God s raise the dead....................... Acts 26:8	
the Gentiles, that they s repent .... Acts 26:20	
prophets and Moses did say s come .... Acts 26:22	3195
That Christ s suffer, and that he .... Acts 26:23	
that he s be the first that..................... Acts 26:23	
first that s rise from the dead .... Acts 26:23	
s shew light unto the people, and .... Acts 26:23	3195
that we s sail into Italy .... Acts 27:1	
fearing lest they s fall into the .... Acts 27:17	
all hope that we s be saved was .... Acts 27:20	
ye s have hearkened unto me, and .... Acts 27:21	1163
Then fearing lest we s have .... Acts 27:29	
lest any of them s swim out.................. Acts 27:42	
that they which could swim s cast......... Acts 27:43	
looked when he s have swollen............... Acts 28:6	3195
lest they s see with their eyes,.............. Acts 28:27	
s be converted, and I s heal................... Acts 28:27	
that preachest a man s not steal .... Rom 2:21	
a man s not commit adultery .... Rom 2:22	
that he s be the heir of the .... Rom 4:13	
even so we also s walk in newness .... Rom 6:4	
henceforth we s not serve sin .... Rom 6:6	
that ye s obey it in the lusts................. Rom 6:12	
that ye s be married to another, ... Rom 7:4	
that we s bring forth fruit unto .... Rom 7:4	
that we s serve in newness of .... Rom 7:6	
what we s pray for as we ought .... Rom 8:26	
slumber, eyes that they s not see .... Rom 11:8	
and ears that they s not hear .... Rom 11:8	
they stumbled that they s fall .... Rom 11:11	
that ye s be ignorant of this .... Rom 11:25	
lest ye s be wise in your own .... Rom 11:25	
That I s be the minister of Jesus........... Rom 15:16	
lest I s build upon another man's........... Rom 15:20	
Lest any s say that I had........................ 1Cor 1:15	
Christ s be made of none effect 1Cor 1:17	
That no flesh s glory in his................... 1Cor 1:29	
That your faith s not stand in 1Cor 2:5	
thing that I s be judged of you.............. 1Cor 4:3	
that one s have his father's wife 1Cor 5:1	
he that ploweth s plow in hope............. 1Cor 9:10	3784
in hope s be partaker of his hope 1Cor 9:10	
lest we s hinder the gospel of................ 1Cor 9:12	
the gospel s live of the gospel 1Cor 9:14	
that it s be so done unto me 1Cor 9:15	
than that any man s make my 1Cor 9:15	
others, I myself s be a castaway 1Cor 9:27	
I would not that ye s be ignorant 1Cor 10:1	
to the intent we s not lust after 1Cor 10:6	
I would not that ye s have 1Cor 10:20	
ourselves, we s not be judged 1Cor 11:31	
that we s not be condemned with........... 1Cor 11:32	
That there s be no schism in the........... 1Cor 12:25	
but that the members s have the 1Cor 12:25	
that we s not trust in ourselves, ... 2Cor 1:9	
that with me there s be yea yea............. 2Cor 1:17	
I s have sorrow from them of whom 2Cor 2:3	
not that ye s be grieved, but.................. 2Cor 2:4	
lest perhaps such a one s be 2Cor 2:7	
Lest Satan s get an advantage of........... 2Cor 2:11	
image of God, s shine unto them 2Cor 4:4	
that they which live s not 2Cor 5:15	
that no man s blame us in this 2Cor 8:20	
lest our boasting of you s be in 2Cor 9:3	
ye s be ashamed in this same 2Cor 9:4	
For though I s boast somewhat 2Cor 10:8	
destruction, I s not be ashamed............. 2Cor 10:8	
so your minds s be corrupted from 2Cor 11:3	
lest any man s think of me above 2Cor 12:6	
lest I s be exalted above measure........... 2Cor 12:7	

lest I *s* be exalted above measure...........2Cor 12:7
not that we *s* appear approved, ...2Cor 13:7
but that ye *s* do that which is.................2Cor 13:7
being present I *s* use sharpness 2Cor 13:10
I *s* not be the servant of Christ ....Gal 1:10
lest by any means I *s* run ....Gal 2:2
that we *s* go unto the heathen, and ....Gal 2:9
would that we *s* remember the poor ....Gal 2:10
that ye *s* not obey the truth,.................Gal 3:1
that it *s* make the promise of ....Gal 3:17
till the seed *s* come to whom the ....Gal 3:19
s have been by the law ....Gal 3:21
which *s* afterwards be revealed ....Gal 3:23   3195
you that ye *s* not obey the truth.............Gal 5:7
only lest they *s* suffer ....Gal 6:12
But God forbid that I *s* glory ....Gal 6:14
of the world, that we *s* be holy ....Eph 1:4
That we *s* be to the praise of his............Eph 1:12
of works, lest any man *s* boast ....Eph 2:9
ordained that we *s* walk in them ....Eph 2:10
the Gentiles *s* be fellowheirs.................Eph 3:6
that I *s* preach among the ....Eph 3:8
but that it *s* be holy and without.............Eph 5:27
But I would ye *s* understand ....Phil 1:12
name of Jesus every knee *s* bow ....Phil 2:10
that every tongue *s* confess that ....Phil 2:11
lest I *s* have sorrow upon sorrow ....Phil 2:27
that in him *s* all fulness dwell ....Col 1:19
lest any man *s* beguile you with ....Col 2:4
That no man *s* be moved by these 1Th 3:4
that we *s* suffer tribulation 1Th 3:4   3195
that ye *s* abstain from.............................1Th 4:3
That every one of you *s* know how 1Th 4:4
that that day *s* overtake you as a 1Th 5:4
we *s* live together with him 1Th 5:10
that they *s* believe a lie 2Th 2:11
would not work, neither *s* he eat 2Th 3:10
s hereafter believe on him to 1Ti 1:16   3195
we *s* live soberly, righteously, ...Titus 2:12
we *s* be made heirs according to ....Titus 3:7
that thy benefit *s* not be as it ....Philem 14
at any time we *s* let them slip ....Heb 2:1
God *s* taste death for every man ....Heb 2:9
they *s* not enter into his rest...................Heb 3:18
any of you *s* seem to come short...........Heb 4:1
priest *s* rise after the order of ....Heb 7:11
he *s* not be a priest, seeing that.............Heb 8:4
then *s* no place have been sought...........Heb 8:7
heavens *s* be purified with these ....Heb 9:23
Nor yet that he *s* offer himself ....Heb 9:25
the worshippers once purged *s* ....Heb 10:2
of goats *s* take away sins........................Heb 10:4
that he *s* not see death ....Heb 11:5
which he *s* after receive for an..............Heb 11:8   3195
the firstborn *s* touch them ....Heb 11:28
without us *s* not be made perfect ....Heb 11:40
heard intreated that the word *s* ....Heb 12:19
of truth, that we *s* be a kind of..............Jas 1:18
of the grace that *s* come unto you 1Pet 1:10
and the glory that *s* follow 1Pet 1:11
that ye *s* shew forth the praises.............1Pet 2:9
that ye *s* follow his steps........................1Pet 2:21
s live unto righteousness 1Pet 2:24
that ye *s* inherit a blessing 1Pet 3:9
That he no longer *s* live the rest 1Pet 4:2
those that after *s* live ungodly 2Pet 2:6   3195
not willing that any *s* perish 2Pet 3:9
but that all *s* come to repentance 2Pet 3:9
that we *s* be called the sons of 1Jn 3:1
that we *s* love one another.....................1Jn 3:11
That we *s* believe on the name of 1Jn 3:23
ye have heard that it *s* come 1Jn 4:3
the beginning, ye *s* walk in it 2Jn 6
exhort you that ye *s* earnestly................Jude 3
s be mockers in the last time ....Jude 18
who *s* walk after their own ....Jude 18
that they *s* kill one another ....Rev 6:4
that they *s* rest yet for a little ....Rev 6:11
that *s* be killed as they were, ...Rev 6:11   3195
as they were, *s* be fulfilled.....................Rev 6:11
that the wind *s* not blow on the ....Rev 7:1
that he *s* offer it with the ....Rev 8:3
s not hurt the grass of the earth ....Rev 9:4
given that they *s* not kill them ....Rev 9:5
but that they *s* be tormented five...........Rev 9:5
that they *s* not worship devils, ...Rev 9:20
that there *s* be time no longer ....Rev 10:6
the mystery of God *s* be finished ....Rev 10:7
the dead, that they *s* be judged ....Rev 11:18
that they *s* feed her there a ....Rev 12:6
that they *s* make an image to the..........Rev 13:14

image of the beast *s* both speak.............Rev 13:15
image of the beast *s* be killed ....Rev 13:15
she *s* be arrayed in fine linen.................Rev 19:8
that with it he *s* smite the......................Rev 19:15
that he *s* deceive the nations no ....Rev 20:3
the thousand years *s* be fulfilled............Rev 20:3

SHOULDER
unto Hagar, putting it on her *s*..............Gen 21:14   7926
with her pitcher upon her *s* ....Gen 24:15   7926
forth with her pitcher on her *s* ....Gen 24:45   7926
let down her pitcher from her *s* ....Gen 24:46
and bowed his *s* to bear, and became ....Gen 49:15   7926
that is upon them, and the right *s* ....Ex 29:22   7785
the *s* of the heave offering,....................Ex 29:27   7785
the right *s* shall ye give unto.................Lev 7:32   7785
have the right *s* for his part ....Lev 7:33   7785
the heave *s* have I taken of the ....Lev 7:34   7785
and their fat, and the right *s* ....Lev 8:25   7785
on the fat, and upon the right *s* ....Lev 8:26   7785
the right *s* Aaron waved for a ....Lev 9:21   7785
heave *s* shall ye eat in a clean ....Lev 10:14   7785
The heave *s* and the wave breast...........Lev 10:15   7785
take the sodden *s* of the ram.................Num 6:19   2220
with the wave breast and heave *s*..........Num 6:20   7785
and as the right *s* are thine....................Num 18:18   7785
shall give unto the priest the *s* ....Deut 18:3   2220
man of you a stone upon his *s* ....Josh 4:5   7926
and took it, and laid it on his *s* ....Judg 9:48   7926
And the cook took up the *s* 1Sa 9:24   7785
) and withdrew the *s*, and hardened ......Neh 9:29   3802
let mine arm fall from my *s* blade ....Job 31:22   7929
Surely I would take it upon my *s* ....Job 31:36   7926
I removed his *s* from the burden............Ps 81:6   7926
his burden, and the staff of his *s* ....Is 9:4   7926
government shall be upon his *s* ....Is 9:6   7926
be taken away from off thy *s* ....Is 10:27   7926
of David will I lay upon his *s* ....Is 22:22   7926
They bear him upon the *s*, they ....Is 46:7   3802
bare it upon my *s* in their sight ....Eze 12:7   3802
bear upon his *s* in the twilight ....Eze 12:12   3802
good piece, the thigh, and the *s*............Eze 24:4   3802
didst break, and rend all their *s* ....Eze 29:7   3802
made bald, and every *s* was peeled ....Eze 29:18   3802
have thrust with side and with *s*............Eze 34:21   3802
to hearken, and pulled away the *s* ....Zec 7:11   3802

SHOULDERPIECES
It shall have the two *s* thereof ....Ex 28:7   3802
put them on the *s* of the ephod ....Ex 28:25   3802
They made *s* for it, to couple it..............Ex 39:4   3802
and put them on the *s* of the ephod ....Ex 39:18   3802

SHOULDERS
and laid it upon both their *s*.................Gen 9:23   7926
up in their clothes upon their *s* ....Ex 12:34   7926
the *s* of the ephod for stones of ....Ex 28:12   3802
upon his two *s* for a memorial ....Ex 28:12   3802
he put them on the *s* of the ephod ....Ex 39:7   3802
they should bear upon their *s* ....Num 7:9   3802
and he shall dwell between his *s* ....Deut 33:12   3802
and all, and put them upon his *s*...........Judg 16:3   3802
from his *s* and upward he was 1Sa 9:2   7926
than any of the people from his *s* 1Sa 10:23   7926
a target of brass between his *s*..............1Sa 17:6   3802
their *s* with the staves thereon 1Chr 15:15   3802
shall not be a burden upon your *s*..........2Chr 35:3   3802
But they shall fly upon the *s* of ....Is 11:14   3802
burden depart from off their *s* ....Is 14:25   7926
riches upon the *s* of young asses ....Is 30:6   3802
shall be carried upon their *s* ....Is 49:22   3802
shalt thou bear it upon thy *s*.................Eze 12:6   3802
be borne, and lay them on men's *s*.....Mt 23:4   5606
found it, he layeth it on his *s* ....Lk 15:5   5606

SHOULDEST
thee that thou *s* not eat ....Gen 3:11
that is thine, lest thou *s* say ....Gen 14:23
thou *s* have brought guiltiness ....Gen 26:10
s therefore serve me for.........................Gen 29:15
that thou *s* say unto me, Carry ....Num 11:12
s be driven to worship them, and ....Deut 4:19
thee, and that thou *s* keep all his...........Deut 26:18
That thou *s* enter into covenant ....Deut 29:12
is not in heaven, that thou *s* say ....Deut 30:12
beyond the sea, that thou *s* say ....Deut 30:13
Israel, and *s* thou possess it ....Judg 11:23
that thou *s* take knowledge of me,..........Ruth 2:10
for why *s* thou bring me to thy................1Sa 20:8
that thou *s* look upon such a dead 2Sa 9:8
that thou *s* tell them who shall 1Kin 1:20
me that thou *s* surely recover 2Kin 8:14
Thou *s* have smitten five or six 2Kin 13:19

for why s thou meddle to thy hurt	2Kin 14:10	
to thy hurt, that thou s fall	2Kin 14:10	
that thou s be to lay waste	2Kin 19:25	
that thou s be ruler over my	1Chr 17:7	
S thou help the ungodly, and love	2Chr 19:2	
why s thou be smitten	2Chr 25:16	
why s thou meddle to thine hurt,	2Chr 25:19	
to thine hurt, that thou s fall	2Chr 25:19	
is man, that thou s magnify him	Job 7:17	
that thou s set thine heart upon	Job 7:17	
that thou s visit him every	Job 7:18	
unto thee that thou s oppress	Job 10:3	
that thou s despise the work of	Job 10:3	
That thou s take it to the bound	Job 38:20	
that thou s know the paths to the	Job 38:20	
or that thou s take my covenant	Ps 50:16	
s mark iniquities, O Lord, who	Ps 130:3	
Lest thou s ponder the path of	Prov 5:6	
than that thou s put lower in	Prov 25:7	
Though thou s bray a fool in a	Prov 27:22	
Better is it that thou s not vow	Eccl 5:5	
than that thou s vow	Eccl 5:5	
why s thou destroy thyself	Eccl 7:16	
why s thou die before thy time	Eccl 7:17	
that thou s take hold of this	Eccl 7:18	
that thou s be to lay waste	Is 37:26	
lest thou s say, Mine idol hath	Is 48:5	
lest thou s say, Behold, I knew	Is 48:7	
thee by the way that thou s go	Is 48:17	
s be my servant to raise up the	Is 49:6	
that thou s be afraid of a man	Is 51:12	
why s thou be as a stranger in	Jer 14:8	
Why s thou be as a man astonied	Jer 14:9	
that thou s put him in prison, and	Jer 29:26	
though thou s make thy nest as	Jer 49:16	
But thou s not have looked on the	Obad 12	
neither s thou have rejoiced over	Obad 12	
neither s thou have spoken	Obad 12	
Thou s not have entered into the	Obad 13	
thou s not have looked on their	Obad 13	
Neither s thou have stood in the	Obad 14	
neither s thou have delivered up	Obad 14	
that thou s come under my roof	Mt 8:8	
S not thou also have had	Mt 18:33	
we would that thou s do for us	Mk 10:35	
that thou s enter under my roof	Lk 7:6	
thou s see the glory of God	Jn 11:40	
I pray not that thou s take them	Jn 17:15	
but that thou s keep them from	Jn 17:15	
that thou s be for salvation unto	Acts 13:47	
that thou s know his will, and see	Acts 22:14	
s hear the voice of his mouth	Acts 22:14	
that thou s set in order the	Titus 1:5	
that thou s receive him for ever	Philem 15	
that thou s give reward unto thy	Rev 11:18	
s destroy them which destroy the	Rev 11:18	

SHOUT

voice of them that s for mastery	Ex 32:18	6030
the s of a king is among them	Num 23:21	8643
people shall s with a great s	Josh 6:5	7321
people shall s with a great s	Josh 6:5	8643
people, saying, Ye shall not s	Josh 6:10	7321
mouth, until the day I bid you s	Josh 6:10	7321
then shall ye s	Josh 6:10	7321
Joshua said unto the people, S	Josh 6:16	7321
the people shouted with a great s	Josh 6:20	8643
all Israel shouted with a great s	1Sa 4:5	8643
heard the noise of the s, they	1Sa 4:6	8643
s in the camp of the Hebrews	1Sa 4:6	8643
Then the men of Judah gave a s	2Chr 13:15	7321
the people shouted with a great s	Ezr 3:11	8643
s of joy from the noise of the	Ezr 3:13	8643
the people shouted with a loud s	Ezr 3:13	8643
let them ever s for joy, because	Ps 5:11	7442
s for joy, all ye that are	Ps 32:11	7442
Let them s for joy, and be glad,	Ps 35:27	7442
s unto God with the voice of	Ps 47:1	7321
God is gone up with a s, the Lord	Ps 47:5	8643
they s for joy, they also sing	Ps 65:13	7321
and let thy saints s for joy	Ps 132:9	7442
her saints shall s aloud for joy	Ps 132:16	7442
Cry out and s, thou inhabitant of	Is 12:6	7442
let them s from the top of the	Is 42:11	6681
s, ye lower parts of the earth	Is 44:23	7321
he shall give a s, as they that	Jer 25:30	
s among the chief of the nations	Jer 31:7	6670
S against her round about	Jer 50:15	7321
shall lift up a s against thee	Jer 51:14	1959
Also when I cry and s, he shutteth	Lam 3:8	7768
s, O Israel	Zeph 3:14	7321

s, O daughter of Jerusalem	Zec 9:9	7321
And the people gave a s, saying,	Acts 12:22	2019
descend from heaven with a s	1Th 4:16	2752

SHOUTED

the noise of the people as they s	Ex 32:17	7452
when all the people saw, they s	Lev 9:24	7442
So the people s when the priests	Josh 6:20	7321
the people s with a great shout,	Josh 6:20	7321
the Philistines s against him	Judg 15:14	7321
all Israel s with a great shout,	1Sa 4:5	7321
And all the people s, and said, God	1Sa 10:24	7321
to the fight, and s for the battle	1Sa 17:20	7321
of Israel and of Judah arose, and s	1Sa 17:52	7321
and as the men of Judah s, it came	2Chr 13:15	7321
all the people s with a great	Ezr 3:11	7321
and many s aloud for joy	Ezr 3:12	8643
for the people s with a loud	Ezr 3:13	7321
and all the sons of God s for joy	Job 38:7	7321

SHOUTETH

man that s by reason of wine	Ps 78:65	7442

SHOUTING

up the ark of the Lord with s	2Sa 6:15	8643
the covenant of the Lord with s	1Chr 15:28	8643
Lord with a loud voice, and with s	2Chr 15:14	8643
thunder of the captains, and the s	Job 39:25	8643
the wicked perish, there is s	Prov 11:10	7440
for the s for thy summer fruits	Is 16:9	1959
singing, neither shall there be s	Is 16:10	7321
made their vintage s to cease	Is 16:10	1959
the morning, and the s at noontide	Jer 20:16	8643
none shall tread with s	Jer 48:33	1959
their s shall be no s	Jer 48:33	1959
to lift up the voice with s	Eze 21:22	8643
with s in the day of battle, with	Amos 1:14	8643
shall die with tumult, with s	Amos 2:2	8643

SHOUTINGS

the headstone thereof with s	Zec 4:7	8663

SHOVEL

hath been winnowed with the s	Is 30:24	7371

SHOVELS

to receive his ashes, and his s	Ex 27:3	3257
of the altar, the pots, and the s	Ex 38:3	3257
censers, the fleshhooks, and the s	Num 4:14	3257
Hiram made the lavers, and the s	1Kin 7:40	3257
And the pots, and the s, and the	1Kin 7:45	3257
And the pots, and the s, and the	2Kin 25:14	3257
And Huram made the pots, and the s	2Chr 4:11	3257
The pots also, and the s, and the	2Chr 4:16	3257
The caldrons also, and the s	Jer 52:18	3257

SHOWER

there shall be an overflowing s	Eze 13:11	1653
be an overflowing s in mine anger	Eze 13:13	1653
I will cause the s to come down	Eze 34:26	1653
ye say, There cometh a s	Lk 12:54	3655

SHOWERS

herb, and as the s upon the grass	Deut 32:2	7241
wet with the s of the mountains	Job 24:8	2230
thou makest it soft with s	Ps 65:10	7241
as s that water the earth	Ps 72:6	7241
Therefore the s have been	Jer 3:3	7241
or can the heavens give s	Jer 14:22	7241
there shall be s of blessing	Eze 34:26	1653
as the s upon the grass, that	Mic 5:7	7241
clouds, and give them s of rain	Zec 10:1	1653

SHRANK

eat not of the sinew which s	Gen 32:32	5384
Jacob's thigh in the sinew that s	Gen 32:32	5384

SHRED

s them into the pot of pottage	2Kin 4:39	6398

SHRINES

which made silver s for Diana	Acts 19:24	3485

SHROUD

branches, and with a shadowing s	Eze 31:3	2793

SHRUBS

cast the child under one of the s	Gen 21:15	7880

SHUA (shu'-ah) See SHUAH.
1. Daughter of Judah.

the daughter of S the Canaanitess	1Chr 2:3	7770

2. Daughter of Heber.

and Hotham, and S their sister	1Chr 7:32	7774

SHUAH (shu'-ah)
1. A son of Abraham.

and Midian, and Ishbak, and S	Gen 25:2	7744
and Midian, and Ishbak, and S	1Chr 1:32	7744

S

SHUAL

2. *Same as Shua 1.*
Canaanite, whose name was *S* .... Gen 38:2   7770
daughter of *S* Judah's wife died .... Gen 38:12   7770
3. *A descendant of Caleb.*
the brother of *S* begat Mehir 1Chr 4:11   7746

SHUAL *(shu'-al)*
1. *A district in Benjamin.*
to Ophrah, unto the land of *S* 1Sa 13:17   7777
2. *Son of Zophah.*
Suah, and Harnepher, and *S*, and Beri ... 1Chr 7:36   7777

SHUBAEL *(shu'-ba-el)* See SHEBUEL.
1. *Son of Amram.*
sons of Amram; *S* 1Chr 24:20   2619
of the sons of *S* 1Chr 24:20   2619
2. *A sanctuary servant.*
The thirteenth to *S*, he, his sons 1Chr 25:20   2619

SHUHAH Seè SHUAH.

SHUHAM *(shu'-ham)* See HUSHIM, SHUHAMITES. *A son of Dan.*
of *S*, the family of the .... Num 26:42   7748

SHUHAMITES *(shu'-ham-ites) Descendants of Shuham.*
of Shuham, the family of the *S* .... Num 26:42   7749
All the families of the *S* .... Num 26:43   7749

SHUHITE *(shu'-hite) A descendant of Shuah.*
the Temanite, and Bildad the *S* .... Job 2:11   7747
Then answered Bildad the *S* .... Job 8:1   7747
Then answered Bildad the *S* .... Job 18:1   7747
Then answered Bildad the *S* .... Job 25:1   7747
the Temanite and Bildad the *S* .... Job 42:9   7747

SHULAMITE *(shu'-lam-ite) An inhabitant of Shulam.*
Return, return, O *S* .... Song 6:13   7759
What will ye see in the *S* .... Song 6:13   7759

SHULAMMITE See SHULAMITE.

SHUMATHITES *(shu'-math-ites) Descendants of Shobal.*
and the Puhites, and the *S* 1Chr 2:53   8126

SHUN
But *s* profane and vain babblings 2Ti 2:16   4026

SHUNAMMITE *(shu'-nam-mite) An inhabitant of Shunem.*
of Israel, and found Abishag a *S* 1Kin 1:3   7767
Abishag the *S* ministered unto the 1Kin 1:15   7767
he give me Abishag the *S* to wife 1Kin 2:17   7767
Let Abishag the *S* be given to 1Kin 2:21   7767
ask Abishag the *S* for Adonijah 1Kin 2:22   7767
Gehazi his servant, Call this *S* 2Kin 4:12   7767
servant, Behold, yonder is that *S* 2Kin 4:25   7767
Gehazi, and said, Call this *S* 2Kin 4:36   7767

SHUNEM *(shu'-nem)* See SHUNAMMITE. *A city in Issachar.*
Jezreel, and Chesulloth, and *S* .... Josh 19:18   7766
together, and came and pitched in *S* 1Sa 28:4   7766
on a day, that Elisha passed to *S* 2Kin 4:8   7766

SHUNI *(shu'-ni)* See SHUNITES. *A son of Gad.*
Ziphion, and Haggi, *S*, and Ezbon, ... Gen 46:16   7764
of *S*, the family of the Shunites .... Num 26:15   7764

SHUNITES *(shu'-nites) Descendants of Shuni.*
of Shuni, the family of the *S* .... Num 26:15   7765

SHUNNED
For I have not *s* to declare unto .... Acts 20:27   5288

SHUPHAM *(shu'-fam)* See SHEPHUPHAN, SHUPHAMITES. *A son of Benjamin.*
Of *S*, the family of the .... Num 26:39   8197

SHUPHAMITES *(shu'-fam-ites) Descendants of Shupham.*
Of Shupham, the family of the *S* .... Num 26:39   7781

SHUPPIM *(shup'-pim)* See MUPPIM, SHEPHUPHAN.
1. *A Benjamite.*
S also, and Huppim, the children 1Chr 7:12   8206
to wife the sister of Huppim and *S* 1Chr 7:15   8206
2. *A Levite gatekeeper.*
To *S* and Hosah the lot came forth 1Chr 26:16   8206

SHUR *(shur) A wilderness east of Egypt.*
by the fountain in the way to *S* .... Gen 16:7   7793
and dwelled between Kadesh and *S* .... Gen 20:1   7793
And they dwelt from Havilah unto *S* ...... Gen 25:18   7793
went out into the wilderness of *S* .... Ex 15:22   7793
Havilah until thou comest to *S* 1Sa 15:7   7793
of the land, as thou goest to *S* 1Sa 27:8   7793

SHUSHAN *(shu'-shan)* See SHOSHANNIM. *Capital of Persia.*
year, as I was in *S* the palace .... Neh 1:1   7800
which was in *S* the palace .... Est 1:2   7800
that were present in *S* the palace .... Est 1:5   7800
young virgins unto *S* the palace .... Est 2:3   7800
Now in *S* the palace there was a .... Est 2:5   7800
together unto *S* the palace .... Est 2:8   7800
decree was given in *S* the palace .... Est 3:15   7800
but the city *S* was perplexed .... Est 3:15   7800
was given at *S* to destroy them .... Est 4:8   7800
the Jews that are present in *S* .... Est 4:16   7800
decree was given at *S* the palace .... Est 8:14   7800
and the city of *S* rejoiced .... Est 8:15   7800
in *S* the palace the Jews slew and .... Est 9:6   7800
of those that were slain in *S* the .... Est 9:11   7800
five hundred men in *S* the palace .... Est 9:12   7800
to the Jews which are in *S* to do .... Est 9:13   7800
and the decree was given at *S* .... Est 9:14   7800
For the Jews that were in *S* .... Est 9:15   7800
and slew three hundred men at *S* .... Est 9:15   7800
at *S* assembled together on the .... Est 9:18   7800
that I was at *S* in the palace .... Dan 8:2   7800

SHUSHAN-EDUTH *(shu'-shan-e'-duth)*
To the chief Musician upon *S* .... Ps 60:t   7802

SHUT

and the LORD *s* him in .... Gen 7:16   5462
them, and *s* the door after him, ... Gen 19:6   5462
house to them, and *s* to the door .... Gen 19:10   5462
the wilderness hath *s* them in .... Ex 14:3   5462
then the priest shall *s* up him .... Lev 13:4   5462
then the priest shall *s* him up .... Lev 13:5   5462
unclean, and shall not *s* him up .... Lev 13:11   5462
priest shall *s* him up seven days .... Lev 13:21   5462
priest shall *s* him up seven days .... Lev 13:26   5462
then the priest shall *s* him up .... Lev 13:31   5462
the priest shall *s* up him that .... Lev 13:33   5462
s up it that hath the plague .... Lev 13:50   5462
he shall *s* it up seven days more .... Lev 13:54   5462
s up the house seven days .... Lev 14:38   5462
s up shall be unclean until the .... Lev 14:46   5462
let her be *s* out from the camp .... Num 12:14   5462
Miriam was *s* out from the camp .... Num 12:15   5462
he *s* up the heaven, that there be .... Deut 11:17   6113
nor *s* thine hand from thy poor .... Deut 15:7   7092
them, and the LORD had *s* them up .... Deut 32:30   5462
is gone, and there is none *s* up .... Deut 32:36   6113
were gone out, they *s* the gate .... Josh 2:7   5462
Now Jericho was straitly *s* up .... Josh 6:1   5462
s the doors of the parlour upon .... Judg 3:23   5462
s it to them, and gat them up to .... Judg 9:51   5462
but the LORD had *s* up her womb 1Sa 1:5   5462
the LORD had *s* up her womb 1Sa 1:6   5462
s up their calves at home 1Sa 6:10   3607
for he is *s* in, by entering into 1Sa 23:7   5462
So they were *s* up unto the day of 2Sa 20:3   6887
When heaven is *s* up, and there is 1Kin 8:35   6113
the wall, and him that is *s* up 1Kin 14:10   6113
the wall, and him that is *s* up 1Kin 21:21   6113
thou shalt *s* the door upon thee 2Kin 4:4   5462
s the door upon her and upon her 2Kin 4:5   5462
s the door upon him, and went out 2Kin 4:21   5462
s the door upon them twain, and 2Kin 4:33   5462
s the door, and hold him fast at 2Kin 6:32   5462
the wall, and him that is *s* up 2Kin 9:8   6113
for there was not any *s* up 2Kin 14:26   6113
the king of Assyria *s* him up 2Kin 17:4   6113
When the heaven is *s* up, and there 2Chr 6:26   6113
If I *s* up heaven that there be no 2Chr 7:13   6113
s up the doors of the house of 2Chr 28:24   5462
Also they have *s* up the doors of 2Chr 29:7   5462
son of Mehetabel, who was *s* up .... Neh 6:10   6113
let us *s* the doors of the temple .... Neh 6:10   5462
let them *s* the doors, and bar them .... Neh 7:3   1479
that the gates should be *s* .... Neh 13:19   5462
Because it is not up the doors of .... Job 3:10   5462
s up, or gather together, then .... Job 11:10   5462
Or who *s* up the sea with doors, ... Job 38:8   5526
s up together as with a close .... Job 41:15   5462
hast not *s* me up into the hand of .... Ps 31:8   5462
let not the pit *s* her mouth upon .... Ps 69:15   332
hath he in anger *s* up his tender .... Ps 77:9   7092
I am *s* up, and I cannot come forth .... Ps 88:8   3607
doors shall be *s* in the streets .... Eccl 12:4   5462
a spring *s* up, a fountain sealed .... Song 4:12   5274
their ears heavy, and *s* their eyes .... Is 6:10   8173
so he shall open, and none shall *s* .... Is 22:22   5462
and he shall *s*, and none shall open ...... Is 22:22   5462
every house is *s* up, that no man .... Is 24:10   5462
shall be *s* up in the prison, and .... Is 24:22   5462

and *s* thy doors about thee	Is 26:20	5462
for he hath *s* their eyes, that	Is 44:18	2902
and the gates shall not be *s*	Is 45:1	5462
the kings shall *s* their mouths at	Is 52:15	7092
they shall not be *s* day nor night	Is 60:11	5462
to bring forth, and *s* the womb	Is 66:9	6113
cities of the south shall be *s* up	Jer 13:19	5462
a burning fire *s* up in my bones	Jer 20:9	6113
Jeremiah the prophet was *s* up in	Jer 32:2	3607
king of Judah had *s* him up	Jer 32:3	3607
while he was yet *s* up in the	Jer 33:1	6113
Baruch, saying, I am *s* up	Jer 36:5	6113
while he was *s* up in the court of	Jer 39:15	6113
s thyself within thine house	Eze 3:24	5462
and it was *s*	Eze 44:1	5462
This gate being *s*, it shall	Eze 44:2	5462
in by it, therefore it shall be *s*	Eze 44:2	5462
shall be *s* the six working days	Eze 46:1	5462
shall not be *s* until the evening	Eze 46:2	5462
going forth one shall *s* the gate	Eze 46:12	5462
hath *s* the lions' mouths, that	Dan 6:22	5463
wherefore *s* thou up the vision	Dan 8:26	5640
s up the words, and seal the book,	Dan 12:4	5640
that would *s* the doors for nought	Mal 1:10	5462
and when thou hast *s* thy door	Mt 6:6	2808
for ye *s* up the kingdom of heaven	Mt 23:13	2808
and the door was *s*	Mt 25:10	2808
that he *s* up John in prison	Lk 3:20	2623
the heaven was *s* up three years	Lk 4:25	2808
the door is now *s*, and my children	Lk 11:7	2808
hath *s* to the door, and ye begin	Lk 13:25	608
when the doors were *s* where the	Jn 20:19	2808
came Jesus, the doors being *s*	Jn 20:26	2808
truly found we *s* with all safety	Acts 5:23	2808
and forthwith the doors were *s*	Acts 21:30	2808
the saints did I *s* up in prison	Acts 26:10	2623
s up unto the faith which should	Gal 3:23	4788
an open door, and no man can *s* it	Rev 3:8	2808
These have power to *s* heaven	Rev 11:6	2808
s him up, and set a seal upon him,	Rev 20:3	2808
it shall not be *s* at all by day	Rev 21:25	2808

SHUTHALHITES (shu'-thal-hites) *Descendants of Shu-thelah.*

of Shuthelah, the family of the *S*	Num 26:35	8364

SHUTHELAH (shu'-the-lah) See SHUTHALHITES.
1. A son of Ephraim.

of *S*, the family of the	Num 26:35	7803
And these are the sons of *S*	Num 26:36	7803
S, and Bered his son, and Tahath	1Chr 7:20	7803

2. Son of Zabad.

S his son, and Ezer, and Elead,	1Chr 7:21	7803

SHUTHELAHITES See SHUTHALHITES.

SHUTTETH

he *s* up a man, and there can be no	Job 12:14	5462
He *s* his eyes to devise froward	Prov 16:30	6095
he that *s* his lips is esteemed a	Prov 17:28	331
s his eyes from seeing evil	Is 33:15	6105
cry and shout, he *s* out my prayer	Lam 3:8	5640
s up his bowels of compassion	1Jn 3:17	2808
he that openeth, and no man *s*	Rev 3:7	2808
and *s*, and no man openeth	Rev 3:7	2808

SHUTTING

about the time of *s* of the gate	Josh 2:5	5462

SHUTTLE

are swifter than a weaver's *s*	Job 7:6	708

SIA (si'-ah) See SIAHA. *A family of exiles.*

of Keros, the children of *S*	Neh 7:47	5517

SIAHA (si'-a-hah) See SIA. *Same as Sia.*

of Keros, the children of *S*	Ezr 2:44	5517

SIBBECAI (sib'-be-cahee) See SIBBECHAI. *A "mighty man" of David.*

S the Hushathite, Ilai the	1Chr 11:29	5444
eighth month was *S* the Hushathite	1Chr 27:11	5444

SIBBECHAI (sib'-be-kahee) See SIBBECAI. *Same as Sib-becai.*

then *S* the Hushathite slew Saph,	2Sa 21:18	5444
at which time *S* the Hushathite	1Chr 20:4	5444

SIBBOLETH (sib'-bo-leth) See SHIBBOLETH. *The Ephra-imite pronunciation of Shibboleth.*

and he said *S*	Judg 12:6	5451

SIBMAH (sib'-mah) *A city in Reuben.*

And Kirjathaim, and *S*, and	Josh 13:19	7643
languish, and the vine of *S*	Is 16:8	7643
weeping of Jazer the vine of *S*	Is 16:9	7643
O vine of *S*, I will weep for thee	Jer 48:32	7643

SIBRAIM (sib'-ra-im) *A city in Syria between Damas-cus and Hamath.*

Hamath, Berothah, *S*, which is	Eze 47:16	5453

SICHEM (si'-kem) See SHECHEM, SYCHEM. *A place on the plain of Moreh.*

the land unto the place of *S*	Gen 12:6	7927

SICK

Joseph, Behold, thy father is *s*	Gen 48:1	2470
of her that is *s* of her flowers	Lev 15:33	1739
to take David, she said, He is *s*	1Sa 19:14	2470
because three days agone I fell *s*	1Sa 30:13	2470
bare unto David, and it was very *s*	2Sa 12:15	605
that he fell *s* for his sister	2Sa 13:2	2470
on thy bed, and make thyself *s*	2Sa 13:5	2470
Amnon lay down, and made himself *s*	2Sa 13:6	2470
Abijah the son of Jeroboam fell *s*	1Kin 14:1	2470
for he is *s*	1Kin 14:5	2470
the mistress of the house, fell *s*	1Kin 17:17	2470
that was in Samaria, and was *s*	2Kin 1:2	2470
Ben-hadad the king of Syria was *s*	2Kin 8:7	2470
Ahab in Jezreel, because he was *s*	2Kin 8:29	2470
Now Elisha was fallen *s* of his	2Kin 13:14	2470
days was Hezekiah *s* unto death	2Kin 20:1	2470
heard that Hezekiah had been *s*	2Kin 20:12	2470
Ahab at Jezreel, because he was *s*	2Chr 22:6	2470
days Hezekiah was *s* to the death	2Chr 32:24	2470
sad, seeing thou art not *s*	Neh 2:2	2470
But as for me, when they were *s*	Ps 35:13	2470
Hope deferred maketh the heart *s*	Prov 13:12	2470
shalt thou say, and I was not *s*	Prov 23:35	2470
for I am *s* of love	Song 2:5	2470
ye tell him, that I am *s* of love	Song 5:8	2470
the whole head is *s*, and the whole	Is 1:5	2483
inhabitant shall not say, I am *s*	Is 33:24	2470
days was Hezekiah *s* unto death	Is 38:1	2470
king of Judah, when he had been *s*	Is 38:9	2470
he had heard that he had been *s*	Is 39:1	2470
them that are *s* with famine	Jer 14:18	8463
have ye healed that which was *s*	Eze 34:4	2470
will strengthen that which was *s*	Eze 34:16	2470
fainted, and was *s* certain days	Dan 8:27	2470
made him *s* with bottles of wine	Hos 7:5	2470
I make thee *s* in smiting thee	Mic 6:13	2470
and if ye offer the lame and *s*	Mal 1:8	2470
was torn, and the lame, and the *s*	Mal 1:13	2470
they brought unto him all *s*	Mt 4:24	2192,2560
lieth at home *s* of the palsy	Mt 8:6	3885
mother laid, and *s* of a fever	Mt 8:14	4445
word, and healed all that were *s*	Mt 8:16	2192,2560
to him a man *s* of the palsy	Mt 9:2	3885
said unto the *s* of the palsy	Mt 9:2	3885
saith he to the *s* of the palsy	Mt 9:6	3885
a physician, but they that are *s*	Mt 9:12	2192,2560
Heal the *s*, cleanse the lepers,	Mt 10:8	770
toward them, and he healed their *s*	Mt 14:14	732
I was *s*, and ye visited me	Mt 25:36	770
Or when saw we thee *s*, or in	Mt 25:39	772
***s*, and in prison, and ye visited me**	Mt 25:43	772
or a stranger, or naked, or *s*	Mt 25:44	772
wife's mother lay *s* of a fever	Mk 1:30	4445
that were of divers diseases	Mk 1:34	2192,2560
him, bringing one *s* of the palsy	Mk 2:3	3885
wherein the *s* of the palsy lay	Mk 2:4	3885
he said unto the *s* of the palsy	Mk 2:5	3885
to say to the *s* of the palsy	Mk 2:9	3885
(he saith to the *s* of the palsy	Mk 2:10	3885
physician, but they that are *s*	Mk 2:17	2192,2560
laid his hands upon a few *s* folk	Mk 6:5	732
with oil many that were *s*	Mk 6:13	732
about in beds those that were *s*	Mk 6:55	2192,2560
they laid the *s* in the streets,	Mk 6:56	770
they shall lay hands on the *s*	Mk 16:18	732
all they that had any *s* with	Lk 4:40	770
(he said unto the *s* of the palsy	Lk 5:24	3885
but they that are *s*	Lk 5:31	2192,2560
who was dear unto him, was *s*	Lk 7:2	2192,2560
the servant whole that had been *s*	Lk 7:10	770
kingdom of God, and to heal the *s*	Lk 9:2	770
heal the *s* that are therein, and	Lk 10:9	772
whose son was *s* at Capernaum	Jn 4:46	770
Now a certain man was *s*, named	Jn 11:1	770
hair, whose brother Lazarus was *s*	Jn 11:2	770
behold, he whom thou lovest is *s*	Jn 11:3	770
had heard therefore that he was *s*	Jn 11:6	770
forth the *s* into the streets	Acts 5:15	772
unto Jerusalem, bringing *s* folks	Acts 5:16	772
years, and was *s* of the palsy	Acts 9:33	3885
in those days, that she was *s*	Acts 9:37	770
the *s* handkerchiefs or aprons	Acts 19:12	770
of Publius lay *s* of a fever	Acts 28:8	

S

ye had heard that he had been *s*	Phil 2:26	770
indeed he was *s* nigh unto death	Phil 2:27	770
have I left at Miletum *s*	2Ti 4:20	770
Is any *s* among you	Jas 5:14	770
prayer of faith shall save the *s*	Jas 5:15	2577

SICKLE

to put the *s* to the corn	Deut 16:9	2770
but thou shalt not move a *s* unto	Deut 23:25	2770
him that handleth the *s* in the	Jer 50:16	4038
Put ye in the *s*, for the harvest	Joel 3:13	4038
immediately he putteth in the *s*	Mk 4:29	*1407*
crown, and in his hand a sharp *s*	Rev 14:14	*1407*
sat on the cloud, Thrust in thy *s*	Rev 14:15	*1407*
thrust in his *s* on the earth	Rev 14:16	*1407*
heaven, he also having a sharp *s*	Rev 14:17	*1407*
cry to him that had the sharp *s*	Rev 14:18	*1407*
saying, Thrust in thy sharp *s*	Rev 14:18	*1407*
thrust in his *s* into the earth	Rev 14:19	*1407*

SICKLY

s among you, and many sleep	1Cor 11:30	732

SICKNESS

I will take *s* away from the midst	Ex 23:25	4245
lie with a woman having her *s*	Lev 20:18	1739
will take away from thee all *s*	Deut 7:15	2483
Also every *s*, and every plague,	Deut 28:61	2483
plague, whatsoever *s* there be	1Kin 8:37	4245
his *s* was so sore, that there was	1Kin 17:17	2483
sick of his *s* whereof he died	2Kin 13:14	2483
sore or whatsoever *s* there be	2Chr 6:28	4245
thou shalt have great *s* by	2Chr 21:15	2483
out by reason of the *s* day by day	2Chr 21:15	2483
fell out by reason of his *s*	2Chr 21:19	2483
wilt make all his bed in his *s*	Ps 41:3	2483
much sorrow and wrath with his *s*	Eccl 5:17	2483
sick, and was recovered of his *s*	Is 38:9	2483
he will cut me off with pining *s*	Is 38:12	
When Ephraim saw his *s*, and Judah	Hos 5:13	2483
and healing all manner of *s*	Mt 4:23	*3554*
the kingdom, and healing every *s*	Mt 9:35	*3554*
out, and to heal all manner of *s*	Mt 10:1	*3554*
This *s* is not unto death, but for	Jn 11:4	*769*

SICKNESSES

and of long continuance, and sore *s*	Deut 28:59	2483
the *s* which the LORD hath laid	Deut 29:22	8463
our infirmities, and bare our *s*	Mt 8:17	*3554*
And to have power to heal *s*	Mk 3:15	*3554*

SIDDIM (sid´-dim) *Area of Sodom and Gomorrah*

joined together in the vale of *S*	Gen 14:3	7708
battle with them in the vale of *S*	Gen 14:8	7708
the vale of *S* was full of	Gen 14:10	7708

SIDE

shalt thou set in the *s* thereof	Gen 6:16	6654
that was openly by the way *s*	Gen 38:21	
walked along by the river's *s*	Ex 2:5	3027
and strike it on the two *s* posts	Ex 12:7	
the two *s* posts with the blood	Ex 12:22	
the lintel, and on the two *s* posts	Ex 12:23	
his hands, the one on the one *s*	Ex 17:12	
and the other on the other *s*	Ex 17:12	
rings shall be in the one *s* of it	Ex 25:12	6753
and two rings in the other *s* of it	Ex 25:12	6753
the candlestick out of the one *s*	Ex 25:32	6654
candlestick out of the other *s*	Ex 25:32	6654
And a cubit on the one *s*	Ex 26:13	
a cubit on the other *s* of that	Ex 26:13	
on this *s* and on that *s*	Ex 26:13	
boards on the south *s* southward	Ex 26:18	6285
And for the second *s* of the	Ex 26:20	6763
s there shall be twenty boards	Ex 26:20	6285
of the one *s* of the tabernacle	Ex 26:26	6763
of the other *s* of the tabernacle	Ex 26:27	6763
boards of the *s* of the tabernacle	Ex 26:27	6763
s of the tabernacle toward the	Ex 26:35	6763
put the table on the north *s*	Ex 26:35	6763
for the south *s* southward there	Ex 27:9	6285
an hundred cubits long for one *s*	Ex 27:9	
likewise for the north *s* in	Ex 27:11	6285
of the court on the west *s* shall	Ex 27:12	6285
of the court on the east *s*	Ex 27:13	6285
The hangings of one *s* of the gate	Ex 27:14	3802
on the other *s* shall be hangings	Ex 27:15	3802
which is in the *s* of the ephod	Ex 28:26	5676
on the one *s* and on the other were	Ex 32:15	
and said, Who is on the LORD's *s*	Ex 32:26	
Put every man his sword by his *s*	Ex 32:27	3409
uttermost *s* of another curtain	Ex 36:11	8193
boards for the south *s* southward	Ex 36:23	6285
for the other *s* of the tabernacle	Ex 36:25	6763

of the one *s* of the tabernacle	Ex 36:31	6763
of the other *s* of the tabernacle	Ex 36:32	6763
two rings upon the one *s* of it	Ex 37:3	6763
two rings upon the other *s* of it	Ex 37:3	6763
One cherub on the end on this *s*	Ex 37:8	
cherub on the other end on that *s*	Ex 37:8	
out of the one *s* thereof, and	Ex 37:18	6654
out of the other *s* thereof	Ex 37:18	6654
on the south *s* southward the	Ex 38:9	6285
for the north *s* the hangings were	Ex 38:11	6285
for the west *s* were hangings of	Ex 38:12	6285
for the east *s* eastward fifty	Ex 38:13	6285
The hangings of the one *s* of the	Ex 38:14	3802
for the other *s* of the court gate	Ex 38:15	3802
which was on the *s* of the ephod	Ex 39:19	5676
upon the *s* of the tabernacle	Ex 40:22	3409
on the *s* of the tabernacle	Ex 40:24	3409
he shall kill it on the *s* of the	Lev 1:11	3409
wrung out at the *s* of the altar	Lev 1:15	7023
offering upon the *s* of the altar	Lev 5:9	7023
on the east *s* toward the rising	Num 2:3	6924
On the south *s* shall be the	Num 2:10	
On the west *s* shall be the	Num 2:18	
be on the north's by their armies	Num 2:25	
the *s* of the tabernacle southward	Num 3:29	3409
these shall pitch on the *s* of the	Num 3:35	3409
south *s* shall take their journey	Num 10:6	
it were a day's journey on this *s*	Num 11:31	3541
a day's journey on the other *s*	Num 11:31	3541
Dathan, and Abiram, on every *s*	Num 16:27	5439
pitched on the other *s* of Arnon	Num 21:13	5676
Moab on this *s* Jordan by Jericho	Num 22:1	5676
on this *s*, and a wall on that *s*	Num 22:24	
as gardens by the river's *s*	Num 24:6	
with them on yonder *s* Jordan	Num 32:19	5676
to us on this *s* Jordan eastward	Num 32:19	5676
on this *s* Jordan may be ours	Num 32:32	5676
to Riblah, on the east *s* of Ain	Num 34:11	6924
shall reach unto the *s* of the sea	Num 34:11	3802
their inheritance on this *s*	Num 34:15	5676
on the east *s* two thousand cubits	Num 35:5	6285
on the south *s* two thousand	Num 35:5	6285
on the west *s* two thousand cubits	Num 35:5	6285
on the north *s* two thousand	Num 35:5	6285
three cities in this *s* Jordan	Num 35:14	5676
this *s* Jordan in the wilderness	Deut 1:1	5676
On this *s* Jordan, in the land of	Deut 1:5	5676
and in the south, and by the sea *s*	Deut 1:7	2348
land that was on this *s* Jordan	Deut 3:8	5676
ask from the one *s* of heaven unto	Deut 4:32	7097
s Jordan toward the sunrising	Deut 4:41	5676
On this *s* Jordan, in the valley	Deut 4:46	5676
which were on this *s* Jordan	Deut 4:47	5676
plain on this *s* Jordan eastward	Deut 4:49	5676
they not on the other *s* Jordan	Deut 11:30	5676
put it in the *s* of the ark of the	Deut 31:26	6654
Moses gave you on this *s* Jordan	Josh 1:14	5676
s Jordan toward the sunrising	Josh 1:15	5676
that were on the other *s* Jordan	Josh 2:10	5676
which were on the *s* of Jordan	Josh 5:1	5676
on the east *s* of Beth-el	Josh 7:2	
and dwelt on the other *s* Jordan	Josh 7:7	5676
and Ai, on the west *s* of Ai	Josh 8:9	
and pitched on the north *s* of Ai	Josh 8:11	
and Ai, on the west *s* of the city	Josh 8:12	
on this *s*, and some on that *s*	Josh 8:22	
judges, stood on this *s* the ark	Josh 8:33	
on that *s* before the priests the	Josh 8:33	
kings which were on this *s* Jordan	Josh 9:1	5676
their land on the other *s* Jordan	Josh 12:1	5676
on this *s* Jordan on the west	Josh 12:7	5676
on the other *s* Jordan eastward	Josh 13:27	5676
of Moab, on the other *s* Jordan	Josh 13:32	5676
half tribe on the other *s* Jordan	Josh 14:3	5676
to the south *s* to Maaleh-acrabbim	Josh 15:3	
on the south *s* unto Kadesh-barnea	Josh 15:3	
is on the south *s* of the river	Josh 15:7	
unto the south *s* of the Jebusite	Josh 15:8	3802
along unto the *s* of mount Jearim	Josh 15:10	3802
which is Chesalon, on the north *s*	Josh 15:10	
out unto the *s* of Ekron northward	Josh 15:11	3802
on the east *s* was Ataroth-addar	Josh 16:5	
sea to Michmethah on the north *s*	Josh 16:6	
which were on the other *s* Jordan	Josh 17:5	5676
was on the north *s* of the river	Josh 17:9	
on the north *s* was from Jordan	Josh 18:12	6285
the border went up to the *s* of	Josh 18:12	3802
of Jericho on the north *s*	Josh 18:12	
toward Luz, to the *s* of Luz	Josh 18:13	3802
south *s* of the nether Beth-horon	Josh 18:13	
to the *s* of Jebusi on the south,	Josh 18:16	3802

passed along toward the *s* over	Josh 18:18	3802
to the *s* of Beth-hoglah northward	Josh 18:19	3802
the border of it on the east *s*	Josh 18:20	6285
it on the north *s* to Hannathon	Josh 19:14	
toward the north *s* of Beth-emek	Josh 19:27	
to Zebulun on the south *s*	Josh 19:34	
reacheth to Asher on the west *s*	Josh 19:34	
on the other *s* Jordan by Jericho	Josh 20:8	5676
gave you on the other *s* Jordan	Josh 22:4	5676
on this *s* Jordan westward	Josh 22:7	5676
other *s* of the flood in old time	Josh 24:2	5676
from the other *s* of the flood	Josh 24:3	5676
which dwelt on the other *s* Jordan	Josh 24:8	5676
on the other *s* of the flood	Josh 24:14	5676
were on the other *s* of the flood	Josh 24:15	5676
on the north *s* of the hill of	Josh 24:30	
on the north *s* of the hill Gaash	Judg 2:9	
were on the north *s* of them	Judg 7:1	
sand by the sea *s* for multitude	Judg 7:12	8193
also on every *s* of all the camp	Judg 7:18	5439
to Gideon on the other *s* Jordan	Judg 7:25	5676
of all their enemies on every *s*	Judg 8:34	5439
other *s* Jordan in the land of the	Judg 10:8	5676
came by the east *s* of the land of	Judg 11:18	
pitched on the other *s* of Arnon	Judg 11:18	5676
on the *s* of mount Ephraim	Judg 19:1	3411
toward the *s* of mount Ephraim	Judg 19:18	3411
is on the north *s* of Beth-el	Judg 21:19	
on the east *s* of the highway that	Judg 21:19	
backward by the *s* of the gate	1Sa 4:18	3027
in a coffer by the *s* thereof	1Sa 6:8	6654
hand of your enemies on every *s*	1Sa 12:11	5439
garrison, that is on the other *s*	1Sa 14:1	5676
was a sharp rock on the one *s*	1Sa 14:4	5676
and a sharp rock on the other *s*	1Sa 14:4	5676
unto all Israel, Be ye on one *s*	1Sa 14:40	5676
my son will be on the other *s*	1Sa 14:40	5676
all his enemies on every *s*	1Sa 14:47	5439
stood on a mountain on the one *s*	1Sa 17:3	
on a mountain on the other *s*	1Sa 17:3	
three arrows on the *s* thereof	1Sa 20:20	6654
the arrows are on this *s* of thee	1Sa 20:21	
arose, and Abner sat by Saul's *s*	1Sa 20:25	6654
went on this *s* of the mountain	1Sa 23:26	6654
his men on that *s* of the mountain	1Sa 23:26	6654
David went over to the other *s*	1Sa 26:13	5676
were on the other *s* of the valley	1Sa 31:7	5676
that were on the other *s* Jordan	1Sa 31:7	5676
the one on the one *s* of the pool	2Sa 2:13	
other on the other *s* of the pool	2Sa 2:13	
his sword in his fellow's *s*	2Sa 2:16	6654
the way of the hill *s* behind him	2Sa 13:34	6654
on the hill's *s* over against him	2Sa 16:13	6763
And the king stood by the gate *s*	2Sa 18:4	3027
on the right *s* of the city that	2Sa 24:5	3225
the region on this *s* the river	1Kin 4:24	5676
all the kings on this *s* the river	1Kin 4:24	5676
which were about him on every *s*	1Kin 5:3	
God hath given me rest on every *s*	1Kin 5:4	5439
was in the right *s* of the house	1Kin 6:8	3802
s posts were a fifth part of the	1Kin 6:31	
one *s* of the floor to the other	1Kin 7:7	
at the *s* of every addition	1Kin 7:30	5676
bases on the right *s* of the house	1Kin 7:39	3802
five on the left *s* of the house	1Kin 7:39	3802
s of the house eastward over	1Kin 7:39	3802
of pure gold, five on the right *s*	1Kin 7:49	
either *s* on the place of the seat	1Kin 10:19	
lions stood there on the one *s*	1Kin 10:20	
on the other *s* as red as blood	2Kin 3:22	5048
window, and said, Who is on my *s*	2Kin 9:32	
on the right *s* as one cometh into	2Kin 12:9	3225
it on the north *s* of the altar	2Kin 16:14	3409
unto the east *s* of the valley	1Chr 4:39	4217
on the other *s* Jordan by Jericho,	1Chr 6:78	5676
on the east *s* of Jordan	1Chr 6:78	4217
Thine are we, David, and on thy *s*	1Chr 12:18	
And on the other *s* of Jordan	1Chr 12:37	5676
he not given you rest on every *s*	1Chr 22:18	5439
this *s* Jordan westward in all the	1Chr 26:30	5676
the temple, five on the right *s*	2Chr 4:8	
on the right *s* of the east end	2Chr 4:10	3802
at the sea *s* in the land of Edom	2Chr 8:17	8193
stays on each *s* of the sitting	2Chr 9:18	
lions stood there on the one *s*	2Chr 9:19	
having Judah and Benjamin on his *s*	2Chr 11:12	
he hath given us rest on every *s*	2Chr 14:7	5439
beyond the sea on this *s* Syria	2Chr 20:2	
from the right *s* of the temple to	2Chr 23:10	3802
to the left *s* of the temple	2Chr 23:10	3802
other, and guided them on every *s*	2Chr 32:22	5439
the west *s* of the city of David	2Chr 32:30	
of David, on the west *s* of Gihon	2Chr 33:14	
rest that are on this *s* the river	Ezr 4:10	5675
the men on this *s* the river	Ezr 4:11	5675
no portion on this *s* the river	Ezr 4:16	5675
governor on this *s* the river	Ezr 5:3	5675
governor on this *s* the river	Ezr 5:6	5675
which were on this *s* the river	Ezr 5:6	5675
governor on this *s* the river	Ezr 6:13	5675
the governors on this *s* the river	Ezr 8:36	5676
the governor on this *s* the river	Neh 3:7	5676
one had his sword girded by his *s*	Neh 4:18	4975
about all that he hath on every *s*	Job 1:10	5439
shall make him afraid on every *s*	Job 18:11	5439
shall be ready at his *s*	Job 18:12	6763
He hath destroyed me on every *s*	Job 19:10	5439
The wicked walk on every *s*	Ps 12:8	5439
fear was on every *s*	Ps 31:13	5439
little hills rejoice on every *s*	Ps 65:12	2296
and comfort me on every *s*	Ps 71:21	5437
A thousand shall fall at thy *s*	Ps 91:7	6654
The LORD is on my *s*	Ps 118:6	
been the LORD who was on our *s*	Ps 124:1	
been the LORD who was on our *s*	Ps 124:2	
on the *s* of their oppressors	Eccl 4:1	3027
shall be nursed at thy *s*	Is 60:4	6654
the enemy and fear is on every *s*	Jer 6:25	5439
defaming of many, fear on every *s*	Jer 20:10	5439
cry unto them, Fear is on every *s*	Jer 49:29	5439
ninety and six pomegranates on a *s*	Jer 52:23	7307
face of a lion, on the right *s*	Eze 1:10	3225
the face of an ox on the left *s*	Eze 1:10	8040
had two, which covered on this *s*	Eze 1:23	
had two, which covered on that *s*	Eze 1:23	
Lie thou also upon thy left *s*	Eze 4:4	6654
them, lie again on thy right *s*	Eze 4:6	6654
turn thee from one *s* to another	Eze 4:8	6654
that thou shalt lie upon thy *s*	Eze 4:9	6654
with a writer's inkhorn by his *s*	Eze 9:2	4975
had the writer's inkhorn by his *s*	Eze 9:3	4975
which had the inkhorn by his *s*	Eze 9:11	4975
stood on the right *s* of the house	Eze 10:3	3225
is on the east *s* of the city	Eze 11:23	6954
thee on every *s* for thy whoredom	Eze 16:33	5439
him on every *s* from the provinces	Eze 19:8	5439
them against thee on every *s*	Eze 23:22	5439
I will open the *s* of Moab from	Eze 25:9	3802
by the sword upon her on every *s*	Eze 28:23	5439
Because ye have thrust with *s*	Eze 34:21	6654
and swallowed you up on every *s*	Eze 36:3	5439
and will gather them on every *s*	Eze 37:21	5439
every *s* to my sacrifice that I do	Eze 39:17	5439
on this *s*, and three on that *s*	Eze 40:10	6311
measure on this *s* and on that *s*	Eze 40:10	
chambers was one cubit on this *s*	Eze 40:12	
the space was one cubit on that *s*	Eze 40:12	
were six cubits on this *s*	Eze 40:12	
and six cubits on that *s*	Eze 40:12	
the pavement by the *s* of the	Eze 40:18	3802
on this *s* and three on that *s*	Eze 40:21	
this *s*, and another on that *s*	Eze 40:26	
on this *s*, and on that *s*	Eze 40:34	
on this *s*, and on that *s*	Eze 40:37	
gate were two tables on this *s*	Eze 40:39	
and two tables on that *s*	Eze 40:39	
at the *s* without, as one goeth up	Eze 40:40	3802
and on the other *s*, which was at	Eze 40:40	3802
Four tables were on this *s*	Eze 40:41	3802
that *s*, by the *s* of the gate	Eze 40:41	3802
which, was at the *s* of the north	Eze 40:44	3802
one at the *s* of the east gate	Eze 40:44	3802
the porch, five cubits on this *s*	Eze 40:48	
and five cubits on that *s*	Eze 40:48	
gate was three cubits on this *s*	Eze 40:48	
and three cubits on that *s*	Eze 40:48	
this *s*, and another on that *s*	Eze 40:49	
six cubits broad on the one *s*	Eze 41:1	6311
six cubits broad on the other *s*	Eze 41:1	
were five cubits on the one *s*	Eze 41:2	
and five cubits on the other *s*	Eze 41:2	
and the breadth of every *s* chamber	Eze 41:5	6763
round about the house on every *s*	Eze 41:5	5439
the *s* chambers were three, one	Eze 41:6	6763
for the *s* chambers round about	Eze 41:6	6763
still upward to the *s* chambers	Eze 41:7	6763
the foundations of the *s* chambers	Eze 41:8	6763
was for the *s* chamber without	Eze 41:9	6763
the *s* chambers that were within	Eze 41:9	6763
round about the house on every *s*	Eze 41:10	5439
the doors of the *s* chambers were	Eze 41:11	6763
on the one *s* and on the other *s*	Eze 41:15	

S

toward the palm tree on the one *s* .... Eze 41:19
the palm tree on the other *s* .... Eze 41:19
on the one *s* and on the other *s* .... Eze 41:26
upon the *s* chambers of the house, ... Eze 41:26 6763
was the entry on the east *s* .... Eze 42:9 6921
He measured the east *s* with the .... Eze 42:16 7307
He measured the north *s*, five .... Eze 42:17 7307
He measured the south *s*, five .... Eze 42:18 7307
He turned about to the west *s* .... Eze 42:19 7307
be for the prince on the one *s* .... Eze 45:7
on the other *s* of the oblation of .... Eze 45:7
city, from the west *s* westward .... Eze 45:7 6285
and from the east *s* eastward .... Eze 45:7 6285
which was at the *s* of the gate .... Eze 46:19 6285
from the right *s* of the house .... Eze 47:1
at the south *s* of the altar .... Eze 47:1
ran out waters on the right *s* .... Eze 47:2 3802
were very many trees on the one *s* .... Eze 47:7
on this *s* and on that *s* .... Eze 47:12
of the land toward the north *s* .... Eze 47:15 6285
And this is the north *s* .... Eze 47:17 6285
the east *s* ye shall measure from .... Eze 47:18 6285
And this is the east *s* .... Eze 47:18 6285
And the south *s* southward, from .... Eze 47:19 6285
And this is the south *s* southward .... Eze 47:19 6285
The west *s* also shall be the .... Eze 47:20 6285
This is the west *s* .... Eze 47:20 6285
the east *s* unto the west *s* .... Eze 48:2 6285
east *s* even unto the west *s* .... Eze 48:3 6285
the east *s* unto the west *s* .... Eze 48:4 6285
the east *s* unto the west *s* .... Eze 48:5 6285
east *s* even unto the west *s* .... Eze 48:6 6285
the east *s* unto the west *s* .... Eze 48:7 6285
the east *s* unto the west *s* .... Eze 48:8 6285
the east *s* unto the west *s* .... Eze 48:8 6285
the north *s* four thousand and five .... Eze 48:16 6285
the south *s* four thousand and five .... Eze 48:16 6285
on the east *s* four thousand and .... Eze 48:16 6285
the west *s* four thousand and five .... Eze 48:16 6285
be for the prince, on the one *s* .... Eze 48:21 6285
the east *s* unto the west *s* .... Eze 48:23 6285
the east *s* unto the west *s* .... Eze 48:24 6285
the east *s* unto the west *s* .... Eze 48:25 6285
the east *s* unto the west *s* .... Eze 48:26 6285
the east *s* unto the west *s* .... Eze 48:27 6285
of Gad, at the south *s* southward .... Eze 48:28 6285
out of the city on the north *s* .... Eze 48:30 6285
at the east *s* four thousand and .... Eze 48:32 6285
at the south *s* four thousand and .... Eze 48:33 6285
At the west *s* four thousand and .... Eze 48:34 6285
and it raised up itself on one *s* .... Dan 7:5 7859
as I was by the *s* of the great .... Dan 10:4 3027
but she shall not stand on his *s* .... Dan 11:17
the one on this *s* of the bank of .... Dan 12:5
the other on that *s* of the bank .... Dan 12:5
that thou stoodest on the other *s* .... Obad 11 5048
and sat on the east *s* of the city .... Jonah 4:5 6924
one upon the right *s* of the bowl .... Zec 4:3
the other upon the left *s* thereof .... Zec 4:3
the right *s* of the candlestick .... Zec 4:11
and upon the left *s* thereof .... Zec 4:11
off as on this *s* according to it .... Zec 5:3
off as on that *s* according to it .... Zec 5:3
to depart unto the other *s* .... Mt 8:18 *4008*
other *s* into the country of the .... Mt 8:28 *4008*
of the house, and sat by the sea *s* .... Mt 13:1 *3844*
some seeds fell by the way *s* .... Mt 13:4 *3844*
which received seed by the way *s* ...... Mt 13:19 *3844*
to go before him unto the other *s* .... Mt 14:22 *4008*
were come to the other *s*, they .... Mt 16:5 *4008*
blind men sitting by the way *s* .... Mt 20:30 *3844*
he went forth again by the sea *s* .... Mk 2:13 *3844*
began again to teach by the sea *s* .... Mk 4:1 *3844*
he sowed, some fell by the way *s* ...... Mk 4:4 *3844*
And these are they by the way *s* .... Mk 4:15 *3844*
Let us pass over unto the other *s* ...... Mk 4:35 *4008*
over unto the other *s* of the sea .... Mk 5:1 *4008*
again by ship unto the other *s* .... Mk 5:21 *4008*
to go to the other *s* before unto .... Mk 6:45 *4008*
again departed to the other *s* .... Mk 8:13 *4008*
Judaea by the farther *s* of Jordan .... Mk 10:1 *4008*
sat by the highway *s* begging .... Mk 10:46 *3844*
young man sitting on the right *s* .... Mk 16:5 *1188*
right *s* of the altar of incense .... Lk 1:11 *1188*
he sowed, some fell by the way *s* ...... Lk 8:5 *3844*
Those by the way *s* are they that .... Lk 8:12 *3844*
over unto the other *s* of the lake .... Lk 8:22 *4008*
him, he passed by on the other *s* .... Lk 10:31 *492*
him, and passed by on the other *s* .... Lk 10:32 *492*
man sat by the way *s* begging .... Lk 18:35 *3844*
round, and keep thee in on every *s* .... Lk 19:43 *3840*

s of the sea saw that there was .... Jn 6:22 *4008*
him on the other *s* of the sea .... Jn 6:25 *4008*
others with him, on either *s* one .... Jn 19:18 *1782*
with a spear pierced his *s* .... Jn 19:34 *4125*
unto them his hands and his *s* .... Jn 20:20 *4125*
and thrust my hand into his *s* .... Jn 20:25 *4125*
thy hand, and thrust it into my *s* .... Jn 20:27 *4125*
net on the right *s* of the ship .... Jn 21:6 *3313*
whose house is by the sea *s* .... Acts 10:6 *3844*
one Simon a tanner by the sea *s* .... Acts 10:32 *3844*
and he smote Peter on the *s* .... Acts 12:7 *4125*
went out of the city by a river *s* .... Acts 16:13 *3844*
We are troubled on every *s* 2Cor 4:8
but we were troubled on every *s* 2Cor 7:5
on either *s* of the river, was.................... Rev 22:2 *1782*

SIDES

the rings by the *s* of the ark .... Ex 25:14 6763
shall come out of the *s* of it .... Ex 25:32 6654
it shall hang over the *s* of the .... Ex 26:13 6654
for the *s* of the tabernacle .... Ex 26:22 3411
of the tabernacle in the two *s* .... Ex 26:23 3411
for the two *s* westward .... Ex 26:27 3411
be upon the two *s* of the altar .... Ex 27:7 6763
the two *s* of the ephod underneath .... Ex 28:27 3802
the *s* thereof round about, and the .... Ex 30:3 7023
upon the two *s* of it shalt thou .... Ex 30:4 6654
were written on both their *s* .... Ex 32:15 5676
for the *s* of the tabernacle .... Ex 36:27 3411
of the tabernacle in the two *s* .... Ex 36:28 3411
the tabernacle for the *s* westward .... Ex 36:32 3411
the rings by the *s* of the ark .... Ex 37:5 6763
going out of the *s* thereof .... Ex 37:18 6654
the *s* thereof round about, and the .... Ex 37:26 7023
of it, upon the two *s* thereof .... Ex 37:27 6654
the rings on the *s* of the altar .... Ex 38:7 6763
put them on the two *s* of the .... Ex 39:20 3802
in your eyes, and thorns in your *s* .... Num 33:55 6654
unto you, and scourges in your *s* .... Josh 23:13 6654
they shall be as thorns in your *s* .... Judg 2:3 6654
colours of needlework on both *s* .... Judg 5:30
men remained in the *s* of the cave 1Sa 24:3 3411
peace on all *s* round about him 1Kin 4:24 5676
cubits on the *s* of the house 1Kin 6:16 3411
to the *s* of Lebanon, and will cut........... 2Kin 19:23 3411
on the *s* of the north, the city .... Ps 48:2 3411
vine by the *s* of thine house................... Ps 128:3 3411
in the *s* of the north .... Is 14:13 3411
down to hell, to the *s* of the pit.............. Is 14:15 3411
mountains, to the *s* of Lebanon .... Is 37:24 3411
ye shall be borne upon her *s* .... Is 66:12 6654
be raised from the *s* of the earth .... Jer 6:22 3411
nest in the *s* of the hole's mouth .... Jer 48:28 5676
their calamity from all *s* thereof .... Jer 49:32 5676
under their wings on their four *s* .... Eze 1:8 7253
went, they went upon their four *s* .... Eze 1:17 7253
went, they went upon their four *s* .... Eze 10:11 7253
are set in the *s* of the pit .... Eze 32:23 3411
the *s* of the door were five .... Eze 41:2 3802
on the *s* of the porch, and upon .... Eze 41:26 3802
He measured it by the four *s* .... Eze 42:20 7307
was a place on the two *s* westward .... Eze 46:19 3411
for these are his *s* east and west .... Eze 48:1 6285
him that is by the *s* of the house............ Amos 6:10 3411
gone down into the *s* of the ship .... Jonah 1:5 3411

SIDON (si'-don) See SIDONIANS, ZIDON.
 1. Son of Canaan.
Canaan begat *S* his firstborn, and... Gen 10:15 6721
 2. Phoenician city north of Tyre.
of the Canaanites was from *S* .... Gen 10:19 6721
you, had been done in Tyre and *S* .... Mt 11:21 *4605*
***S* at the day of judgment, than** .... Mt 11:22 *4605*
into the coasts of Tyre and *S* .... Mt 15:21 *4605*
and they about Tyre and *S*, a great .... Mk 3:8 *4605*
into the borders of Tyre and *S* .... Mk 7:24 *4605*
from the coasts of Tyre and *S* .... Mk 7:31 *4605*
save unto Sarepta, a city of *S* .... Lk 4:26 *4605*
from the sea coast of Tyre and *S* .... Lk 6:17 *4605*
works had been done in Tyre and *S* ..... Lk 10:13 *4605*
***S* at the judgment, than for you** .... Lk 10:14 *4605*
displeased with them of Tyre and *S* .... Acts 12:20 *4605*
And the next day we touched at *S* .... Acts 27:3 *4605*

SIDONIANS (si-do'-ne-uns) See ZIDONIANS. *Inhabitants of Sidon.*
(Which Hermon the *S* call Sirion .... Deut 3:9 6722
and Mearah that is beside the *S*........... Josh 13:4 6722
Misrephoth-maim, and all the *S* .... Josh 13:6 6722
and all the Canaanites, and the *S*........ Judg 3:3 6722
to hew timber like unto the *S* 1Kin 5:6 6722

SIEGE

life) to employ them in the *s*	Deut 20:19	4692
thy God hath given thee, in the *s*	Deut 28:53	4692
he hath nothing left him in the *s*	Deut 28:55	4692
of all things secretly in the *s*	Deut 28:57	4692
and all Israel laid *s* to Gibbethon	1Kin 15:27	6696
he himself laid *s* against Lachish	2Chr 32:9	
ye abide in the *s* in Jerusalem	2Chr 32:10	4692
will lay *s* against thee with a	Is 29:3	6696
the flesh of his friend in the *s*	Jer 19:9	4692
lay *s* against it, and build a fort	Eze 4:2	4692
and thou shalt lay *s* against it	Eze 4:3	6696
face toward the *s* of Jerusalem	Eze 4:7	4692
thou hast ended the days of thy *s*	Eze 4:8	4692
the days of the *s* are fulfilled	Eze 5:2	4692
he hath laid *s* against us	Mic 5:1	4692
Draw thee waters for the *s*	Nah 3:14	4692
be in the *s* both against Judah	Zec 12:2	4692

SIEVE

the nations with the *s* of vanity	Is 30:28	5299
like as corn is sifted in a *s*	Amos 9:9	3531

SIFT

to *s* the nations with the sieve	Is 30:28	5130
I will *s* the house of Israel	Amos 9:9	5128
that he may *s* you as wheat	Lk 22:31	*4617*

SIFTED

like as corn is *s* in a sieve	Amos 9:9	5128

SIGH

all the merryhearted do *s*	Is 24:7	584
her priests *s*, her virgins are	Lam 1:4	584
All her people *s*, they seek bread	Lam 1:11	584
They have heard that I *s*	Lam 1:21	584
the foreheads of the men that *s*	Eze 9:4	584
S therefore, thou son of man	Eze 21:6	584
with bitterness *s* before their	Eze 21:6	584

SIGHED

the children of Israel *s* by	Ex 2:23	584
And looking up to heaven, he *s*	Mk 7:34	4727
he *s* deeply in his spirit, and	Mk 8:12	389

SIGHEST

say unto thee, Wherefore *s* thou	Eze 21:7	584

SIGHETH

yea, she *s*, and turneth backward	Lam 1:8	584

SIGHING

For my *s* cometh before I eat, and	Job 3:24	585
for the *s* of the needy, now will	Ps 12:5	603
with grief, and my years with *s*	Ps 31:10	585
Let the *s* of the prisoner come	Ps 79:11	603
all the *s* thereof have I made to	Is 21:2	585
and sorrow and *s* shall flee away	Is 35:10	585
I fainted in my *s*, and I find no	Jer 45:3	585

SIGHS

for my *s* are many, and my heart is	Lam 1:22	585

SIGHT

tree that is pleasant to the *s*	Gen 2:9	4758
now I have found favour in thy *s*	Gen 18:3	5869
servant hath found grace in thy *s*	Gen 19:19	5869
in Abraham's *s* because of his son	Gen 21:11	5869
in thy *s* because of the lad	Gen 21:12	5869
I may bury my dead out of my *s*	Gen 23:4	6440
I should bury my dead out of my *s*	Gen 23:8	6440
that I may find grace in thy *s*	Gen 32:5	5869
to find grace in the *s* of my lord	Gen 33:8	5869
now I have found grace in thy *s*	Gen 33:10	5869
me find grace in the *s* of my lord	Gen 33:15	5869
was wicked in the *s* of the LORD	Gen 38:7	5869
And Joseph found grace in his *s*	Gen 39:4	5869
gave him favour in the *s* of the	Gen 39:21	5869
ought left in the *s* of my lord	Gen 47:18	6440
us find grace in the *s* of my lord	Gen 47:25	5869
now I have found grace in thy *s*	Gen 47:29	5869
turn aside, and see this great *s*	Ex 3:3	4758
favour in the *s* of the Egyptians	Ex 3:21	5869
the signs in the *s* of the people	Ex 4:30	5869
in the *s* of Pharaoh, and in the	Ex 7:20	5869
and in the *s* of his servants	Ex 7:20	5869
the heaven in the *s* of Pharaoh	Ex 9:8	5869
favour in the *s* of the Egyptians	Ex 11:3	5869
in the *s* of Pharaoh's servants,	Ex 11:3	5869
and in the *s* of the people	Ex 11:3	5869
favour in the *s* of the Egyptians	Ex 12:36	5869
do that which is right in his *s*	Ex 15:26	5869
Moses did so in the *s* of the	Ex 17:6	5869
s of all the people upon mount	Ex 19:11	5869
the *s* of the glory of the LORD	Ex 24:17	4758
hast also found grace in my *s*	Ex 33:12	5869

if I have found grace in thy *s*	Ex 33:13	5869
that I may find grace in thy *s*	Ex 33:13	5869
people have found grace in thy *s*	Ex 33:16	5869
for thou hast found grace in my *s*	Ex 33:17	5869
now I have found grace in thy *s*	Ex 34:9	5869
in the *s* of all the house of	Ex 40:38	5869
accepted in the *s* of the LORD	Lev 10:19	5869
the plague in *s* be deeper than	Lev 13:3	4758
in *s* be not deeper than the skin,	Lev 13:4	4758
the plague in his *s* be at a stay	Lev 13:5	5869
it be in *s* lower than the skin,	Lev 13:20	4758
it be in *s* deeper than the skin	Lev 13:25	4758
if it be in *s* deeper than the	Lev 13:30	4758
it be not in *s* deeper than the	Lev 13:31	4758
the scall be not in *s* deeper than	Lev 13:32	4758
nor be in *s* deeper than the skin	Lev 13:34	4758
the scall be in his *s* at a stay	Lev 13:37	5869
which in *s* are lower than the	Lev 14:37	4758
cut off in the *s* of their people	Lev 20:17	5869
with rigour over him in thy *s*	Lev 25:53	5869
of Egypt in the *s* of the heathen	Lev 26:45	5869
in the *s* of Aaron their father	Num 3:4	6440
have I not found favour in thy *s*	Num 11:11	5869
if I have found favour in thy *s*	Num 11:15	5869
were in our own *s* as grasshoppers	Num 13:33	5869
and so we were in their *s*	Num 13:33	5869
shall burn the heifer in his *s*	Num 19:5	5869
in the *s* of all the congregation	Num 20:27	5869
woman in the *s* of Moses, and in	Num 25:6	5869
in the *s* of all the congregation	Num 25:6	5869
and give him a charge in their *s*	Num 27:19	5869
if we have found grace in thy *s*	Num 32:5	5869
done evil in the *s* of the LORD	Num 32:13	5869
in the *s* of all the Egyptians	Num 33:3	5869
in the *s* of the nations, which	Deut 4:6	5869
evil in the *s* of the LORD thy God	Deut 4:25	5869
brought thee out in his *s* with	Deut 4:37	6440
and good in the *s* of the LORD	Deut 6:18	5869
wickedly in the *s* of the LORD	Deut 9:18	5869
is right in the *s* of the LORD	Deut 12:25	5869
right in the *s* of the LORD thy	Deut 12:28	5869
in the *s* of the LORD thy God	Deut 17:2	5869
is right in the *s* of the LORD	Deut 21:9	5869
s of thine eyes which thou shalt	Deut 28:34	4758
for the *s* of thine eyes which	Deut 28:67	4758
unto him in the *s* of all Israel	Deut 31:7	5869
will do evil in the *s* of the LORD	Deut 31:29	5869
shewed in the *s* of all Israel	Deut 34:12	5869
thee in the *s* of all Israel	Josh 3:7	5869
Joshua in the *s* of all Israel	Josh 4:14	5869
and he said in the *s* of Israel	Josh 10:12	5869
and drive them from out of your *s*	Josh 23:5	6440
did those great signs in our *s*	Josh 24:17	5869
did evil in the *s* of the LORD	Judg 2:11	5869
did evil in the *s* of the LORD	Judg 3:7	5869
evil again in the *s* of the LORD	Judg 3:12	5869
done evil in the *s* of the LORD	Judg 3:12	5869
did evil in the *s* of the LORD	Judg 4:1	5869
did evil in the *s* of the LORD	Judg 6:1	5869
now I have found grace in thy *s*	Judg 6:17	5869
of the LORD departed out of his *s*	Judg 6:21	5869
evil again in the *s* of the LORD	Judg 10:6	5869
evil again in the *s* of the LORD	Judg 13:1	5869
him in whose *s* I shall find grace	Ruth 2:2	5869
said, Let me find favour in thy *s*	Ruth 2:13	5869
handmaid find grace in thy *s*	1Sa 1:18	5869
ye have done in the *s* of the LORD	1Sa 12:17	5869
thou wast little in thine own *s*	1Sa 15:17	5869
didst evil in the *s* of the LORD	1Sa 15:19	5869
for he hath found favour in my *s*	1Sa 16:22	5869
in the *s* of all the people	1Sa 18:5	5869
also in the *s* of Saul's servants	1Sa 18:5	5869
me in the host is good in my *s*	1Sa 29:6	5869
I know that thou art good in my *s*	1Sa 29:9	5869
and will be base in mine own *s*	2Sa 6:22	5869
all thine enemies out of thy *s*	2Sa 7:9	6440
was yet a small thing in thy *s*	2Sa 7:19	5869
of the LORD, to do evil in his *s*	2Sa 12:9	5869
thy wives in the *s* of this sun	2Sa 12:11	5869
meat, and dress the meat in my *s*	2Sa 13:5	5869
make me a couple of cakes in my *s*	2Sa 13:6	5869
it, and made cakes in his *s*	2Sa 13:8	5869
that I have found grace in thy *s*	2Sa 14:22	5869
that I may find grace in thy *s*	2Sa 16:4	5869
concubines in the *s* of all Israel	2Sa 16:22	5869
to my cleanness in his eye *s*	2Sa 22:25	5869
s to sit on the throne of Israel	1Kin 8:25	6440
my name, will I cast out of my *s*	1Kin 9:7	6440
did evil in the *s* of the LORD	1Kin 11:6	5869
great favour in the *s* of Pharaoh	1Kin 11:19	5869
ways, and do that is right in my *s*	1Kin 11:38	5869

S

did evil in the s of the LORD	1Kin 14:22	5869
he did evil in the s of the LORD	1Kin 15:26	5869
he did evil in the s of the LORD	1Kin 15:34	5869
that he did in the s of the LORD	1Kin 16:7	5869
doing evil in the s of the LORD	1Kin 16:19	5869
s of the LORD above all that were	1Kin 16:30	5869
to work evil in the s of the LORD	1Kin 21:20	5869
wickedness in the s of the LORD	1Kin 21:25	5869
he did evil in the s of the LORD	1Kin 22:52	5869
servants, be precious in thy s	2Kin 1:13	5869
my life now be precious in thy s	2Kin 1:14	5869
wrought evil in the s of the LORD	2Kin 3:2	5869
light thing in the s of the LORD	2Kin 3:18	5869
he did evil in the s of the LORD	2Kin 8:18	5869
and did evil in the s of the LORD	2Kin 8:27	5869
in the s of the LORD all his days	2Kin 12:2	5869
was evil in the s of the LORD	2Kin 13:2	5869
was evil in the s of the LORD	2Kin 13:11	5869
was right in the s of the LORD	2Kin 14:3	5869
was evil in the s of the LORD	2Kin 14:24	5869
was right in the s of the LORD	2Kin 15:3	5869
was evil in the s of the LORD	2Kin 15:9	5869
was evil in the s of the LORD	2Kin 15:18	5869
was evil in the s of the LORD	2Kin 15:24	5869
was evil in the s of the LORD	2Kin 15:28	5869
was right in the s of the LORD	2Kin 15:34	5869
in the s of the LORD his God	2Kin 16:2	5869
was evil in the s of the LORD	2Kin 17:2	5869
to do evil in the s of the LORD	2Kin 17:17	5869
and removed them out of his s	2Kin 17:18	6440
he had cast them out of his s	2Kin 17:20	6440
LORD removed Israel out of his s	2Kin 17:23	6440
was right in the s of the LORD	2Kin 18:3	5869
done that which is good in thy s	2Kin 20:3	5869
was evil in the s of the LORD	2Kin 21:2	5869
wickedness in the s of the LORD	2Kin 21:6	5869
done that which was evil in my s	2Kin 21:15	5869
was evil in the s of the LORD	2Kin 21:16	5869
was evil in the s of the LORD	2Kin 21:20	5869
was right in the s of the LORD	2Kin 22:2	5869
remove Judah also out of my s	2Kin 23:27	6440
was evil in the s of the LORD	2Kin 23:32	5869
was evil in the s of the LORD	2Kin 23:37	5869
to remove them out of his s	2Kin 24:3	6440
was evil in the s of the LORD	2Kin 24:9	5869
was evil in the s of the LORD	2Kin 24:19	5869
was evil in the s of the LORD	1Chr 2:3	5869
do that which is good in his s	1Chr 19:13	5869
much blood upon the earth in my s	1Chr 22:8	6440
in the s of all Israel the	1Chr 28:8	5869
in the s of all Israel, and	1Chr 29:25	5869
in my s to sit upon the throne of	2Chr 6:16	6440
my name, will I cast out of my s	2Chr 7:20	5869
was right in the s of the LORD	2Chr 20:32	5869
Wherefore he did evil in the s of	2Chr 22:4	5869
the s of the LORD all the days of	2Chr 24:2	5869
was right in the s of the LORD	2Chr 25:2	5869
was right in the s of the LORD	2Chr 26:4	5869
was right in the s of the LORD	2Chr 27:2	5869
was right in the s of the LORD	2Chr 28:1	5869
was right in the s of the LORD	2Chr 29:2	5869
s of all nations from thenceforth	2Chr 32:23	5869
was evil in the s of the LORD	2Chr 33:2	5869
much evil in the s of the LORD	2Chr 33:6	5869
was evil in the s of the LORD	2Chr 33:22	5869
was right in the s of the LORD	2Chr 34:2	5869
evil in the s of the LORD his God	2Chr 36:5	5869
was evil in the s of the LORD	2Chr 36:9	5869
evil in the s of the LORD his God	2Chr 36:12	5869
in the s of the kings of Persia	Ezr 9:9	6440
him mercy in the s of this man	Neh 1:11	6440
have found favour in thy s	Neh 2:5	6440
the book in the s of all people	Neh 8:5	5869
s of all them that looked upon	Est 2:15	5869
favour in his s more than all the	Est 2:17	6440
that she obtained favour in his s	Est 5:2	5869
found favour in the s of the king	Est 5:8	5869
If I have found favour in thy s	Est 7:3	5869
if I have found favour in thy s	Est 8:5	5869
heavens are not clean in his s	Job 15:15	5869
beasts, and reputed vile in your s	Job 18:3	5869
I am an alien in their s	Job 19:15	5869
established in their s with them	Job 21:8	6440
the stars are not pure in his s	Job 25:5	5869
men in the open s of others	Job 34:26	7200
be cast down even at the s of him	Job 41:9	4758
foolish shall not stand in thy s	Ps 5:5	5869
the heathen be judged in thy s	Ps 9:19	6440
are far above out of his s	Ps 10:5	5048
my heart, be acceptable in thy s	Ps 19:14	6440
and done this evil in thy s	Ps 51:4	5869
shall their blood be in his s	Ps 72:14	5869
who may stand in thy s when once	Ps 76:7	6440
did he in the s of their fathers	Ps 78:12	5048
s by the revenging of the blood	Ps 79:10	5869
For a thousand years in thy s are	Ps 90:4	5869
shewed in the s of the heathen	Ps 98:2	5869
lies shall not tarry in my s	Ps 101:7	5869
Precious in the s of the LORD is	Ps 116:15	5869
for in thy s shall no man living	Ps 143:2	6440
is spread in the s of any bird	Prov 1:17	5869
understanding in the s of God	Prov 3:4	5869
beloved in the s of my mother	Prov 4:3	6440
man that is good in his s wisdom	Eccl 2:26	6440
Better is the s of the eyes than	Eccl 6:9	4758
Be not hasty to go out of his s	Eccl 8:3	6440
heart, and in the s of thine eyes	Eccl 11:9	4758
eyes, and prudent in their own s	Is 5:21	6440
not judge after the s of his eyes	Is 11:3	4758
so have we been in thy s, O LORD	Is 26:17	6440
done that which is good in thy s	Is 38:3	5869
Since thou wast precious in my s	Is 43:4	5869
thine abominations out of my s	Jer 4:1	6440
And I will cast you out of my s	Jer 7:15	6440
of Judah have done evil in my s	Jer 7:30	5869
cast them out of my s, and let	Jer 15:1	6440
If it do evil in my s, that it	Jer 18:10	5869
blot out their sin from thy s	Jer 18:23	5869
s of the men that go with thee	Jer 19:10	5869
in the s of Hanameel mine uncle's	Jer 32:12	5869
turned, and had done right in my s	Jer 34:15	5869
in the s of the men of Judah	Jer 43:9	5869
they have done in Zion in your s	Jer 51:24	5869
cometh out of man, in their s	Eze 4:12	5869
of thee in the s of the nations	Eze 5:8	5869
in the s of all that pass by	Eze 5:14	5869
And he went in in my s	Eze 10:2	5869
mounted up from the earth in my s	Eze 10:19	5869
and remove by day in their s	Eze 12:3	5869
place to another place in their s	Eze 12:3	5869
forth thy stuff by day in their s	Eze 12:4	5869
shalt go forth at even in their s	Eze 12:4	5869
thou through the wall in their s	Eze 12:5	5869
In their s shalt thou bear it	Eze 12:6	5869
it upon my shoulder in their s	Eze 12:7	5869
upon thee in the s of many women	Eze 16:41	5869
in whose s I made myself known	Eze 20:9	5869
in whose s I brought them out	Eze 20:14	5869
polluted in the s of the heathen	Eze 20:22	5869
in whose s I brought them forth	Eze 20:22	5869
lothe yourselves in your own s	Eze 20:43	6440
as a false divination in their s	Eze 21:23	5869
thyself in the s of the heathen	Eze 22:16	5869
s of all them that behold thee	Eze 28:18	5869
in them in the s of the heathen	Eze 28:25	5869
in your own s for your iniquities	Eze 36:31	6440
in the s of all that passed by	Eze 36:34	5869
in them in the s of many nations	Eze 39:27	5869
and write it in their s, that they	Eze 43:11	5869
the s thereof to the end of all	Dan 4:11	2379
the s thereof to all the earth	Dan 4:20	2379
away her whoredoms out of her s	Hos 2:2	6440
lewdness in the s of her lovers	Hos 2:10	5869
us up, and we shall live in his s	Hos 6:2	6440
my s in the bottom of the sea	Amos 9:3	5869
I said, I am cast out of thy s	Jonah 2:4	5869
evil is good in the s of the LORD	Mal 2:17	5869
The blind receive their s	Mt 11:5	308
for so it seemed good in thy s	Mt 11:26	1715
immediately their eyes received s	Mt 20:34	308
Lord, that I might receive my s	Mk 10:51	308
And immediately he received his s	Mk 10:52	308
be great in the s of the Lord	Lk 1:15	1799
and recovering of s to the blind	Lk 4:18	309
many that were blind he gave s	Lk 7:21	991
for so it seemed good in thy s	Lk 10:21	1715
against heaven, and in thy s	Lk 15:21	1799
is abomination in the s of God	Lk 16:15	1799
Lord, that I may receive my s	Lk 18:41	308
said unto him, Receive thy s	Lk 18:42	308
And immediately he received his s	Lk 18:43	308
that came together to that s	Lk 23:48	2335
and he vanished out of their s	Lk 24:31	
I went and washed, and I received s	Jn 9:11	308
him how he had received his s	Jn 9:15	308
had been blind, and received his s	Jn 9:18	308
of him that had received his s	Jn 9:18	308
cloud received him out of their s	Acts 1:9	3788
Whether it be right in the s of	Acts 4:19	1799
wisdom in the s of Pharaoh king	Acts 7:10	1726
saw it, he wondered at the s	Acts 7:31	3705
is not right in the s of God	Acts 8:21	1799

And he was three days without *s* .... Acts 9:9   *991*
him, that he might receive his *s* .... Acts 9:12   *308*
that thou mightest receive thy *s* .... Acts 9:17   *308*
and he received *s* forthwith.................... Acts 9:18   *308*
in remembrance in the *s* of God .... Acts 10:31   *1799*
me, Brother Saul, receive thy *s* .... Acts 22:13   *308*
no flesh be justified in his *s* .... Rom 3:20   *1799*
things honest in the *s* of all men .... Rom 12:17   *1799*
in the *s* of God speak we in 2Cor 2:17   *2714*
man's conscience in the *s* of God 2Cor 4:2   *1799*
(For we walk by faith, not by *s* 2Cor 5:7   *1491*
s of God might appear unto you 2Cor 7:12   *1799*
not only in the *s* of the Lord 2Cor 8:21   *1799*
but also in the *s* of men 2Cor 8:21   *1799*
by the law in the *s* of God...................... Gal 3:11   *3844*
and unreproveable in his *s* .... Col 1:22   *2714*
Jesus Christ, in the *s* of God 1Th 1:3   *1715*
acceptable in the *s* of God our 1Ti 2:3   *1799*
give thee charge in the *s* of God 1Ti 6:13   *1799*
that is not manifest in his *s* .... Heb 4:13   *1799*
And so terrible was the *s*, that .... Heb 12:21   *5324*
which is wellpleasing in his *s* .... Heb 13:21   *1799*
yourselves in the *s* of the Lord .... Jas 4:10   *1799*
which is in the *s* of God of great 1Pet 3:4   *1799*
things that are pleasing in his *s* 1Jn 3:22   *1799*
in *s* like unto an emerald .... Rev 4:3   *3706*
on the earth in the *s* of men .... Rev 13:13   *1799*
power to do in the *s* of the beast .... Rev 13:14   *1799*

SIGHTS
and fearful *s* **and great signs shall** .... Lk 21:11   *5400*

SIGN
to the voice of the first *s* .... Ex 4:8   *226*
believe the voice of the latter *s* .... Ex 4:8   *226*
to morrow shall this *s* be .... Ex 8:23   *226*
it shall be for a *s* unto thee .... Ex 13:9   *226*
for it is a *s* between me and you .... Ex 31:13   *226*
It is a *s* between me and the .... Ex 31:17   *226*
they shall be a *s* unto the .... Num 16:38   *226*
and they became a *s* .... Num 26:10   *5251*
bind them for a *s* upon thine hand .... Deut 6:8   *226*
bind them for a *s* upon your hand .... Deut 11:18   *226*
and giveth thee a *s* or a wonder............. Deut 13:1   *226*
the *s* or the wonder come to pass,........... Deut 13:2   *226*
they shall be upon thee for a *s*............... Deut 28:46   *226*
That this may be a *s* among you .... Josh 4:6   *226*
then shew me a *s* that thou .... Judg 6:17   *226*
s between the men of Israel .... Judg 20:38
And this shall be a *s* unto thee 1Sa 2:34   *226*
and this shall be a *s* unto us 1Sa 14:10   *226*
he gave a *s* the same day, saying,........... 1Kin 13:3   *4159*
This is the *s* which the LORD hath 1Kin 13:3   *4159*
according to the *s* which the man 1Kin 13:5   *4159*
And this shall be a *s* unto thee 2Kin 19:29   *226*
What shall be the *s* that the LORD 2Kin 20:8   *226*
This *s* shalt thou have of the 2Kin 20:9   *226*
unto him, and he gave him a *s* 2Chr 32:24   *4159*
Ask thee a *s* of the LORD thy God .... Is 7:11   *226*
Lord himself shall give you a *s* .... Is 7:14   *226*
And it shall be for a *s* and for a .... Is 19:20   *226*
and barefoot three years for a *s* .... Is 20:3   *226*
And this shall be a *s* unto thee .... Is 37:30   *226*
this shall be a *s* unto thee from .... Is 38:7   *226*
What is the *s* that I shall go up............... Is 38:22   *226*
for an everlasting *s* that shall .... Is 55:13   *226*
And I will set a *s* among them .... Is 66:19   *226*
Tekoa, and set up a *s* of fire in............... Jer 6:1   *4864*
And this shall be a *s* unto you .... Jer 44:29   *226*
This shall be a *s* to the house of .... Eze 4:3   *226*
for a *s* unto the house of Israel .... Eze 12:6   *4159*
Say, I am your *s*.................................... Eze 12:11   *4159*
that man, and will make him a *s*............. Eze 14:8   *226*
to be a *s* between me and them, ... Eze 20:12   *226*
and they shall be a *s* between me........... Eze 20:20   *226*
Thus Ezekiel is unto you a *s* .... Eze 24:24   *4159*
and thou shalt be a *s* unto them .... Eze 24:27   *4159*
then shall he set up a *s* by it .... Eze 39:15   *6725*
s the writing, that it be not..................... Dan 6:8   *7560*
we would see a *s* from thee..................... Mt 12:38   *4592*
generation seeketh after a *s*.................. Mt 12:39   *4592*
there shall no *s* **be given to it** .... Mt 12:39   *4592*
but the *s* **of the prophet Jonas**............. Mt 12:39   *4592*
would shew them a *s* from heaven .... Mt 16:1   *4592*
generation seeketh after a *s*.................. Mt 16:4   *4592*
there shall no *s* **be given unto it** .... Mt 16:4   *4592*
but the *s* **of the prophet Jonas**............. Mt 16:4   *4592*
what shall be the *s* of thy coming........... Mt 24:3   *4592*
then shall appear the *s* **of the**............. Mt 24:30   *4592*
that betrayed him gave them a *s*............. Mt 26:48   *4592*
seeking of him a *s* from heaven .... Mk 8:11   *4592*
this generation seek after a *s* .... Mk 8:12   *4592*

There shall no *s* **be given unto**............... Mk 8:12   *4592*
what shall be the *s* when all .... Mk 13:4   *4592*
And this shall be a *s* unto you .... Lk 2:12   *4592*
for a *s* which shall be spoken................. Lk 2:34   *4592*
sought of him a *s* from heaven .... Lk 11:16   *4592*
they seek a *s*...................................... Lk 11:29   *4592*
and there shall no *s* **be given it** .... Lk 11:29   *4592*
but the *s* **of Jonas the prophet**............. Lk 11:29   *4592*
Jonas was a *s* **unto the Ninevites** .... Lk 11:30   *4592*
what *s* will there be when these.............. Lk 21:7   *4592*
What *s* shewest thou unto us,................. Jn 2:18   *4592*
What *s* shewest thou then, that we........ Jn 6:30   *4592*
whose *s* was Castor and Pollux............... Acts 28:11   *3902*
he received the *s* of circumcision........... Rom 4:11   *4592*
For the Jews require a *s*, and the 1Cor 1:22   *4592*
Wherefore tongues are for a *s* 1Cor 14:22   *4592*
And I saw another *s* in heaven............... Rev 15:1   *4592*

SIGNED
king Darius *s* the writing .... Dan 6:9   *7560*
knew that the writing was *s* .... Dan 6:10   *7560*
Hast thou not *s* a decree, that................. Dan 6:12   *7560*
nor the decree that thou hast *s*............... Dan 6:13   *7560*

SIGNET
And she said, Thy *s*, and thy .... Gen 38:18   *2368*
pray thee, whose are these, the *s*........... Gen 38:25   *2858*
stone, like the engravings of a *s* .... Ex 28:11   *2368*
names, like the engravings of a *s* .... Ex 28:21   *2368*
it, like the engravings of a *s* .... Ex 28:36   *2368*
names, like the engravings of a *s* .... Ex 39:14   *2368*
like to the engravings of a *s* .... Ex 39:30   *2368*
were the *s* upon my right hand .... Jer 22:24   *2368*
the king sealed it with his own *s*............. Dan 6:17   *5824*
and with the *s* of his lords .... Dan 6:17   *5824*
LORD, and will make thee as a *s* .... Hag 2:23   *2368*

SIGNETS
as *s* are graven, with the names .... Ex 39:6   *2368*

SIGNIFICATION
and none of them is without *s* 1Cor 14:10   *880*

SIGNIFIED
s by the Spirit that there should .... Acts 11:28   *4591*
s it by his angel unto his .... Rev 1:1   *4591*

SIGNIFIETH
s the removing of those things .... Heb 12:27   *1213*

SIGNIFY
to *s* the accomplishment of the .... Acts 21:26   *1229*
s to the chief captain that he .... Acts 23:15   *1718*
not withal to *s* the crimes laid .... Acts 25:27   *4591*
of Christ which was in them did *s* 1Pet 1:11   *1213*

SIGNIFYING
s what death he should die..................... Jn 12:33   *4591*
s what death he should die..................... Jn 18:32   *4591*
s by what death he should glorify........... Jn 21:19   *4591*
The Holy Ghost this *s*, that the .... Heb 9:8   *1213*

SIGNS
and let them be for *s*, and for.................. Gen 1:14   *226*
will not believe also these two *s*.............. Ex 4:9   *226*
hand, wherewith thou shalt do *s* .... Ex 4:17   *226*
all the *s* which he had commanded .... Ex 4:28   *226*
did the *s* in the sight of the .... Ex 4:30   *226*
Pharaoh's heart, and multiply my *s*........ Ex 7:3   *226*
might shew these my *s* before him .... Ex 10:1   *226*
my *s* which I have done among them .... Ex 10:2   *226*
for all the *s* which I have shewed........... Num 14:11   *226*
nation, by temptations, by *s* .... Deut 4:34   *226*
And the LORD shewed *s* and wonders,... Deut 6:22   *226*
which thine eyes saw, and the *s* .... Deut 7:19   *226*
great terribleness, and with *s*................. Deut 26:8   *226*
which thine eyes have seen, the *s* .... Deut 29:3   *226*
In all the *s* and the wonders, ... Deut 34:11   *226*
did those great *s* in our sight .... Josh 24:17   *226*
when these *s* are come unto thee,........... 1Sa 10:7   *226*
all those *s* came to pass that day 1Sa 10:9   *226*
And shewedst *s* and wonders upon........ Neh 9:10   *226*
they set up their ensigns for *s*............... Ps 74:4   *226*
We see not our *s* .... Ps 74:9   *226*
How he had wrought his *s* in Egypt .... Ps 78:43   *226*
They shewed his *s* among them .... Ps 105:27   *226*
the LORD hath given me are for *s*........... Is 8:18   *226*
not dismayed at the *s* of heaven .... Jer 10:2   *226*
Which hast set *s* and wonders in........... Jer 32:20   *226*
out of the land of Egypt with *s*............... Jer 32:21   *226*
I thought it good to shew the *s* .... Dan 4:2   *852*
How great are his *s* .... Dan 4:3   *852*
and rescueth, and he worketh *s*............. Dan 6:27   *852*
ye not discern the *s* of the times .... Mt 16:3   *4592*
prophets, and shall shew great *s*........... Mt 24:24   *4592*

S

shall rise, and shall shew *s*	Mk 13:22	4592
these *s* shall follow them that	Mk 16:17	4592
the word with *s* following	Mk 16:20	4592
they made *s* to his father, how he	Lk 1:62	1770
great *s* shall there be from	Lk 21:11	4591
And there shall be *s* in the sun	Lk 21:25	4591
Jesus unto him, Except ye see *s*	Jn 4:48	4591
many other *s* truly did Jesus in	Jn 20:30	4591
above, and *s* in the earth beneath	Acts 2:19	4591
you by miracles and wonders and *s*	Acts 2:22	4591
s were done by the apostles	Acts 2:43	4591
and that *s* and wonders may be done	Acts 4:30	4591
hands of the apostles were many *s*	Acts 5:12	4591
s in the land of Egypt, and in the	Acts 7:36	4591
the miracles and *s* which were done	Acts 8:13	4591
word of his grace, and granted *s*	Acts 14:3	4591
Through mighty *s* and wonders, by	Rom 15:19	4591
Truly the *s* of an apostle were	2Cor 12:12	4591
among you in all patience, in *s*	2Cor 12:12	4591
of Satan with all power and *s*	2Th 2:9	4591
bearing them witness, both with *s*	Heb 2:4	4591

SIHON (si'-hon) *An Amorite king.*

unto *S* king of the Amorites	Num 21:21	5511
S would not suffer Israel to pass	Num 21:23	5511
but *S* gathered all his people	Num 21:23	5511
of *S* the king of the Amorites	Num 21:26	5511
let the city of *S* be built	Num 21:27	5511
a flame from the city of *S*	Num 21:28	5511
into captivity unto *S* king of the	Num 21:29	5511
didst unto *S* king of the Amorites	Num 21:34	5511
the kingdom of *S* king of the	Num 32:33	5511
After he had slain *S* the king of	Deut 1:4	5511
into thine hand *S* the Amorite	Deut 2:24	5511
S king of Heshbon with words of	Deut 2:26	5511
But *S* king of Heshbon would not	Deut 2:30	5511
Behold, I have begun to give *S*	Deut 2:31	5511
Then *S* came out against us, he and	Deut 2:32	5511
didst unto *S* king of the Amorites	Deut 3:2	5511
as we did unto *S* king of Heshbon,	Deut 3:6	5511
in the land of *S* king of the	Deut 4:46	5511
S the king of Heshbon, and Og the	Deut 29:7	5511
shall do unto them as he did to *S*	Deut 31:4	5511
were on the other side Jordan, *S*	Josh 2:10	5511
to *S* king of Heshbon, and to Og	Josh 9:10	5511
S king of the Amorites, who dwelt	Josh 12:2	5511
the border of *S* king of Heshbon	Josh 12:5	5511
all the cities of *S* king of the	Josh 13:10	5511
all the kingdom of *S* king of the	Josh 13:21	5511
and Reba, which were dukes of *S*	Josh 13:21	5511
the kingdom of *S* king of Heshbon	Josh 13:27	5511
unto *S* king of the Amorites	Judg 11:19	5511
But *S* trusted not Israel to pass	Judg 11:20	5511
but *S* gathered all his people	Judg 11:20	5511
LORD God of Israel delivered *S*	Judg 11:21	5511
in the country of *S* king of the	1Kin 4:19	5511
so they possessed the land of *S*	Neh 9:22	5511
S king of the Amorites, and Og	Ps 135:11	5511
S king of the Amorites	Ps 136:19	5511
and a flame from the midst of *S*	Jer 48:45	5511

SIHOR (si'-hor) See SHIHOR. *A river in southern Canaan.*

From *S*, which is before Egypt,	Josh 13:3	7883
And by great waters the seed of *S*	Is 23:3	7883
Egypt, to drink the waters of *S*	Jer 2:18	7883

SIKKUTH See MOLOCH.

SILAS (si'-las) See SILVANUS. *A co-worker with Paul.*

Judas surnamed Barsabas, and *S*	Acts 15:22	4609
We have sent therefore Judas and *S*	Acts 15:27	4609
And Judas and *S*, being prophets	Acts 15:32	4609
it pleased *S* to abide there still	Acts 15:34	4609
And Paul chose *S*, and departed,	Acts 15:40	4609
was gone, they caught Paul and *S*	Acts 16:19	4609
S prayed, and sang praises unto	Acts 16:25	4609
and fell down before Paul and *S*	Acts 16:29	4609
and consorted with Paul and *S*	Acts 17:4	4609
Paul and *S* by night unto Berea	Acts 17:10	4609
but *S* and Timotheus abode there	Acts 17:14	4609
and receiving a commandment unto *S*	Acts 17:15	4609
And when *S* and Timotheus were come	Acts 18:5	4609

SILENCE

who said, Keep *s*	Judg 3:19	2013
was before mine eyes, there was *s*	Job 4:16	1827
waited, and kept *s* at my counsel	Job 29:21	1826
terrify me, that I kept *s*	Job 31:34	1826
Let the lying lips be put to *s*	Ps 31:18	481
When I kept *s*, my bones waxed old	Ps 32:3	2790
keep not *s*	Ps 35:22	2790
I was dumb with *s*, I held my	Ps 39:2	1747

shall come, and shall not keep *s*	Ps 50:3	2790
hast thou done, and I kept *s*	Ps 50:21	2790
Keep not thou *s*, O God	Ps 83:1	1824
my soul had almost dwelt in *s*	Ps 94:17	1745
neither any that go down into *s*	Ps 115:17	1745
a time to keep *s*, and a time to	Eccl 3:7	2814
is laid waste, and brought to *s*	Is 15:1	1820
is laid waste, and brought to *s*	Is 15:1	
Keep *s* before me, O islands	Is 41:1	2790
mention of the LORD, keep not *s*	Is 62:6	1824
I will not keep *s*, but will	Is 65:6	2814
the LORD our God hath put us to *s*	Jer 8:14	1826
sit upon the ground, and keep *s*	Lam 2:10	1826
He sitteth alone and keepeth *s*	Lam 3:28	1826
prudent shall keep *s* in that time	Amos 5:13	1826
they shall cast them forth with *s*	Amos 8:3	2013
all the earth keep *s* before him	Hab 2:20	2013
he had put the Sadducees to *s*	Mt 22:34	5392
Then all the multitude kept *s*	Acts 15:12	4601
And when there was made a great *s*	Acts 21:40	4602
to them, they kept the more *s*	Acts 22:2	4602
let him keep *s* in the church	1Cor 14:28	4601
your women keep *s* in the churches	1Cor 14:34	4601
learn in *s* with all subjection	1Ti 2:11	2271
over the man, but to be in *s*	1Ti 2:12	2271
to *s* the ignorance of foolish men	1Pet 2:15	5392
there was *s* in heaven about the	Rev 8:1	4602

SILENT

the wicked shall be *s* in darkness	1Sa 2:9	1826
in the night season, and am not *s*	Ps 22:2	1947
be not *s* to me	Ps 28:1	2790
lest, if thou be *s* to me, I	Ps 28:1	2790
sing praise to thee, and not be *s*	Ps 30:12	1826
let them be *s* in the grave	Ps 31:17	1826
Sit thou *s*, and get thee into	Is 47:5	1748
cities, and let us be *s* there	Jer 8:14	1826
Be *s*, O all flesh, before the	Zec 2:13	2013

SILK

her clothing is *s* and purple	Prov 31:22	8336
linen, and I covered thee with *s*	Eze 16:10	4897
raiment was of fine linen, and *s*	Eze 16:13	4897
and fine linen, and purple, and *s*	Rev 18:12	2596

SILLA (sil'-lah) *A place near Jerusalem.*

of Millo, which goeth down to *S*	2Kin 12:20	5538

SILLY

man, and envy slayeth the *s* one	Job 5:2	6601
is like a *s* dove without heart	Hos 7:11	6601
lead captive *s* women laden with	2Ti 3:6	1133

SILOAH (si-lo'-ah) See SHILOAH, SILOAM. *Same as Siloam.*

pool of *S* by the king's garden	Neh 3:15	7975

SILOAM (si'-lo-am) See SHILOAH. *A pool south of Jerusalem.*

upon whom the tower in *S* fell	Lk 13:4	4611
him, Go, wash in the pool of *S*	Jn 9:7	4611
said unto me, Go to the pool of *S*	Jn 9:11	4611

SILVANUS (sil-va'-nus) See SILAS.
    1. A co-worker with Paul.

among you by us, even by me and *S*	2Cor 1:19	4610
Paul, and *S*, and Timotheus, unto	1Th 1:1	4610
Paul, and *S*, and Timotheus, unto	2Th 1:1	4610

    2. A messenger for Peter.

By *S*, a faithful brother unto you	1Pet 5:12	4610

SILVER

was very rich in cattle, in *s*	Gen 13:2	3701
brother a thousand pieces of *s*	Gen 20:16	3701
worth four hundred shekels of *s*	Gen 23:15	3701
Abraham weighed to Ephron the *s*	Gen 23:16	3701
Heth, four hundred shekels of *s*	Gen 23:16	3701
given him flocks, and herds, and *s*	Gen 24:35	3701
servant brought forth jewels of *s*	Gen 24:53	3701
for twenty pieces of *s*	Gen 37:28	3701
And put my cup, the *s* cup, in the	Gen 44:2	3701
out of thy lord's house *s* or gold	Gen 44:8	3701
he gave three hundred pieces of *s*	Gen 45:22	3701
in her house, jewels of *s*	Ex 3:22	3701
of her neighbour, jewels of *s*	Ex 11:2	3701
of the Egyptians jewels of *s*	Ex 12:35	3701
shall not make with me gods of *s*	Ex 20:23	3701
their master thirty shekels of *s*	Ex 21:32	3701
gold, and *s*, and brass,	Ex 25:3	3701
of *s* under the twenty boards,	Ex 26:19	3701
And their forty sockets of *s*	Ex 26:21	3701
boards, and their sockets of *s*	Ex 26:25	3701
gold, upon the four sockets of *s*	Ex 26:32	3701
and their fillets shall be of *s*	Ex 27:10	3701
the pillars and their fillets of *s*	Ex 27:11	3701

court shall be filleted with s	Ex 27:17	3701
their hooks shall be of s	Ex 27:17	3701
works, to work in gold, and in s	Ex 31:4	3701
gold, and s, and brass,	Ex 35:5	3701
that did offer an offering of s	Ex 35:24	3701
works, to work in gold, and in s	Ex 35:32	3701
forty sockets of s he made under	Ex 36:24	3701
And their forty sockets of s	Ex 36:26	3701
sockets were sixteen sockets of s	Ex 36:30	3701
cast for them four sockets of s	Ex 36:36	3701
and their fillets were of s	Ex 38:10	3701
the pillars and their fillets of s	Ex 38:11	3701
the pillars and their fillets of s	Ex 38:12	3701
the pillars and their fillets of s	Ex 38:17	3701
of their chapiters of s	Ex 38:17	3701
of the court were filleted with s	Ex 38:17	3701
their hooks of s, and the	Ex 38:19	3701
chapiters and their fillets of s	Ex 38:19	3701
the s of them that were numbered	Ex 38:25	3701
of the hundred talents of s were	Ex 38:27	3701
thy estimation by shekels of s	Lev 5:15	3701
shall be fifty shekels of s	Lev 27:3	3701
be of the male five shekels of s	Lev 27:6	3701
shall be three shekels of s	Lev 27:6	3701
be valued at fifty shekels of s	Lev 27:16	3701
And his offering was one s charger	Num 7:13	3701
one s bowl of seventy shekels,	Num 7:13	3701
for his offering one s charger	Num 7:19	3701
one s bowl of seventy shekels,	Num 7:19	3701
His offering was one s charger	Num 7:25	3701
one s bowl of seventy shekels,	Num 7:25	3701
His offering was one s charger of	Num 7:31	3701
one s bowl of seventy shekels,	Num 7:31	3701
His offering was one s charger	Num 7:37	3701
one s bowl of seventy shekels,	Num 7:37	3701
His offering was one s charger of	Num 7:43	3701
a s bowl of seventy shekels,	Num 7:43	3701
His offering was one s charger	Num 7:49	3701
one s bowl of seventy shekels,	Num 7:49	3701
His offering was one s charger of	Num 7:55	3701
one s bowl of seventy shekels,	Num 7:55	3701
His offering was one s charger	Num 7:61	3701
one s bowl of seventy shekels,	Num 7:61	3701
His offering was one s charger	Num 7:67	3701
one s bowl of seventy shekels,	Num 7:67	3701
His offering was one s charger	Num 7:73	3701
one s bowl of seventy shekels,	Num 7:73	3701
His offering was one s charger	Num 7:79	3701
one s bowl of seventy shekels,	Num 7:79	3701
of s, twelve s bowls	Num 7:84	3701
Each charger of s weighing an	Num 7:85	3701
all the s vessels weighed two	Num 7:85	3701
Make thee two trumpets of s	Num 10:2	3701
would give me his house full of s	Num 22:18	3701
would give me his house full of s	Num 24:13	3701
Only the gold, and the s, the	Num 31:22	3701
the s or gold that is on them	Deut 7:25	3701
and thy flocks multiply, and thy s	Deut 8:13	3701
he greatly multiply to himself s	Deut 17:17	3701
him in an hundred shekels of s	Deut 22:19	3701
father fifty shekels of s	Deut 22:29	3701
and their idols, wood and stone, s	Deut 29:17	3701
But all the s, and gold, and	Josh 6:19	3701
only the s, and the gold, and the	Josh 6:24	3701
and two hundred shekels of s	Josh 7:21	3701
of my tent, and the s under it	Josh 7:21	3701
in his tent, and the s under it	Josh 7:22	3701
Achan the son of Zerah, and the s	Josh 7:24	3701
and with very much cattle, with s	Josh 22:8	3701
for an hundred pieces of s	Josh 24:32	7192
ten pieces of s out of the house	Judg 9:4	3701
of us eleven hundred pieces of s	Judg 16:5	3701
of s that were taken from thee	Judg 17:2	3701
ears, behold, the s is with me	Judg 17:2	3701
shekels of s to his mother	Judg 17:3	3701
I had wholly dedicated the s unto	Judg 17:3	3701
took two hundred shekels of s	Judg 17:4	3701
thee ten shekels of s by the year	Judg 17:10	3701
and crouch to him for a piece of s	1Sa 2:36	3701
the fourth part of a shekel of s	1Sa 9:8	3701
brought with him vessels of s	2Sa 8:10	3701
unto the LORD, with the s	2Sa 8:11	3701
have given thee ten shekels of s	2Sa 18:11	3701
shekels of s in mine hand	2Sa 18:12	3701
We will have no s nor gold of	2Sa 21:4	3701
the oxen for fifty shekels of s	2Sa 24:24	3701
even the s, and the gold, and the	1Kin 7:51	3701
none were of s	1Kin 10:21	3701
of Tharshish, bringing gold, and s	1Kin 10:22	3701
man his present, vessels of s	1Kin 10:25	3701
And the king made s to be in	1Kin 10:27	3701
for six hundred shekels of s	1Kin 10:29	3701
into the house of the LORD, s	1Kin 15:15	3701
Then Asa took all the s and the	1Kin 15:18	3701
sent unto thee a present of s	1Kin 15:19	3701
of Shemer for two talents of s	1Kin 16:24	3701
Thy s and thy gold is mine	1Kin 20:3	3701
Thou shalt deliver me thy s	1Kin 20:5	3701
and for my children, and for my s	1Kin 20:7	3701
else thou shalt pay a talent of s	1Kin 20:39	3701
and took with him ten talents of s	2Kin 5:5	3701
them, I pray thee, a talent of s	2Kin 5:22	3701
two talents of s in two bags	2Kin 5:23	3701
sold for fourscore pieces of s	2Kin 6:25	3701
dove's dung for five pieces of s	2Kin 6:25	3701
eat and drink, and carried thence s	2Kin 7:8	3701
the house of the LORD bowls of s	2Kin 12:13	3701
vessels of gold, or vessels of s	2Kin 12:13	3701
And he took all the gold and s	2Kin 14:14	3701
gave Pul a thousand talents of s	2Kin 15:19	3701
of each man fifty shekels of s	2Kin 15:20	3701
And Ahaz took the s and gold that	2Kin 16:8	3701
Judah three hundred talents of s	2Kin 18:14	3701
Hezekiah gave him all the s that	2Kin 18:15	3701
of his precious things, the s	2Kin 20:13	3701
that he may sum the s which is	2Kin 22:4	3701
of an hundred talents of s	2Kin 23:33	3701
And Jehoiakim gave the s and the	2Kin 23:35	3701
he exacted the s and the gold of	2Kin 23:35	3701
gold, in gold, and of s, in s	2Kin 25:15	3701
manner of vessels of gold and s	1Chr 18:10	3701
unto the LORD, with the s	1Chr 18:11	3701
of s to hire them chariots	1Chr 19:6	3701
a thousand thousand talents of s	1Chr 22:14	3701
Of the gold, the s, and the brass,	1Chr 22:16	3701
s also for all instruments of	1Chr 28:14	3701
all instruments of s by weight	1Chr 28:14	3701
the candlesticks of s by weight	1Chr 28:15	3701
s for the tables of s	1Chr 28:16	3701
likewise s by weight for every	1Chr 28:17	3701
by weight for every bason of s	1Chr 28:17	3701
the s for things of s, and	1Chr 29:2	3701
own proper good, of gold and s	1Chr 29:3	3701
thousand talents of refined s	1Chr 29:4	3701
and the s for things of s	1Chr 29:5	3701
of s ten thousand talents, and of	1Chr 29:7	3701
And the king made s and gold at	2Chr 1:15	3701
for six hundred shekels of s	2Chr 1:17	3701
cunning to work in gold, and in s	2Chr 2:7	3701
skilful to work in gold, and in s	2Chr 2:14	3701
and the s, and the gold, and all the	2Chr 5:1	3701
brought gold and s to Solomon	2Chr 9:14	3701
none were of s	2Chr 9:20	3701
of Tarshish bringing gold, and s	2Chr 9:21	3701
man his present, vessels of s	2Chr 9:24	3701
the king made s in Jerusalem as	2Chr 9:27	3701
that he himself had dedicated, s	2Chr 15:18	3701
Then Asa brought out s and gold	2Chr 16:2	3701
behold, I have sent thee s	2Chr 16:3	3701
presents, and tribute	2Chr 17:11	3701
father gave them great gifts of s	2Chr 21:3	3701
spoons, and vessels of gold and s	2Chr 24:14	3701
for an hundred talents of s	2Chr 25:6	3701
same year an hundred talents of s	2Chr 27:5	3701
he made himself treasuries for s	2Chr 32:27	3701
land in an hundred talents of s	2Chr 36:3	3701
men of his place help him with s	Ezr 1:4	3701
their hands with vessels of s	Ezr 1:6	3701
of gold, a thousand chargers of s	Ezr 1:9	3701
s basons of a second sort four	Ezr 1:10	3701
of s were five thousand and four	Ezr 1:11	3701
gold, and five thousand pound of s	Ezr 2:69	3701
s of the house of God, which	Ezr 5:14	3702
s vessels of the house of God,	Ezr 6:5	3702
And to carry the s and gold, which	Ezr 7:15	3702
And all the s and gold that thou	Ezr 7:16	3702
to do with the rest of the s	Ezr 7:18	3702
Unto an hundred talents of s	Ezr 7:22	3702
And weighed unto them the s	Ezr 8:25	3701
six hundred and fifty talents of s	Ezr 8:26	3701
s vessels an hundred talents, and	Ezr 8:26	3701
and the s and the gold are a	Ezr 8:28	3701
the Levites the weight of the s	Ezr 8:30	3701
Now on the fourth day was the s	Ezr 8:33	3701
wine, beside forty shekels of s	Neh 5:15	3701
and two hundred pounds of s	Neh 7:71	3701
gold, and two thousand pounds of s	Neh 7:72	3701
fine linen and purple to s rings	Est 1:6	3701
the beds were of gold and s	Est 1:6	3701
pay ten thousand talents of s to	Est 3:9	3701
The s is given to thee, the	Est 3:11	3701
who filled their houses with s	Job 3:15	3701

S

and thou shalt have plenty of *s*	Job 22:25	3701
Though he heap up *s* as the dust	Job 27:16	3701
the innocent shall divide the *s*	Job 27:17	3701
Surely there is a vein for the *s*	Job 28:1	3701
neither shall *s* be weighed for	Job 28:15	3701
as *s* tried in a furnace of earth,	Ps 12:6	3701
thou hast tried us, as *s* is tried	Ps 66:10	3701
wings of a dove covered with *s*	Ps 68:13	3701
submit himself with pieces of *s*	Ps 68:30	3701
He brought them forth also with *s*	Ps 105:37	3701
Their idols are *s* and gold, the	Ps 115:4	3701
me than thousands of gold and *s*	Ps 119:72	3701
The idols of the heathen are *s*	Ps 135:15	3701
If thou seekest her as *s*, and	Prov 2:4	3701
better than the merchandise of *s*	Prov 3:14	3701
Receive my instruction, and not *s*	Prov 8:10	3701
and my revenue than choice *s*	Prov 8:19	3701
tongue of the just is as choice *s*	Prov 10:20	3701
rather to be chosen than *s*	Prov 16:16	3701
The fining pot is for *s*, and the	Prov 17:3	3701
and loving favour rather than *s*	Prov 22:1	3701
Take away the dross from the *s*	Prov 25:4	3701
apples of gold in pictures of *s*	Prov 25:11	3701
a potsherd covered with *s* dross	Prov 26:23	3701
As the fining pot for *s*, and the	Prov 27:21	3701
I gathered me also *s* and gold, and	Eccl 2:8	3701
He that loveth *s* shall not be	Eccl 5:10	3701
shall not be satisfied with *s*	Eccl 5:10	3701
Or ever the *s* cord be loosed, or	Eccl 12:6	3701
borders of gold with studs of *s*	Song 1:11	3701
He made the pillars thereof of *s*	Song 3:10	3701
will build upon her a palace of *s*	Song 8:9	3701
to bring a thousand pieces of *s*	Song 8:11	3701
Thy *s* is become dross, thy wine	Is 1:22	3701
Their land also is full of *s*	Is 2:7	3701
a man shall cast his idols of *s*	Is 2:20	3701
them, which shall not regard *s*	Is 13:17	3701
of thy graven images of *s*	Is 30:22	3701
shall cast away his idols of *s*	Is 31:7	3701
of his precious things, the *s*	Is 39:2	3701
with gold, and casteth *s* chains	Is 40:19	3701
weigh *s* in the balance, and hire a	Is 46:6	3701
have refined thee, but not with *s*	Is 48:10	3701
bring thy sons from far, their *s*	Is 60:9	3701
gold, and for iron I will bring *s*	Is 60:17	3701
Reprobate *s* shall men call them,	Jer 6:30	3701
They deck it with *s* and with gold	Jer 10:4	3701
S spread into plates is brought	Jer 10:9	3701
even seventeen shekels of *s*	Jer 32:9	3701
and that which was of *s* in *s*	Jer 52:19	3701
shall cast their *s* in the streets	Eze 7:19	3701
their *s* and their gold shall not	Eze 7:19	3701
wast thou decked with gold and *s*	Eze 16:13	3701
fair jewels of my gold and of my *s*	Eze 16:17	3701
they are even the dross of *s*	Eze 22:18	3701
As they gather *s*, and brass, and	Eze 22:20	3701
As *s* is melted in the midst of	Eze 22:22	3701
with *s*, iron, tin, and lead, they	Eze 27:12	3701
gold and *s* into thy treasures	Eze 28:4	3701
to carry away *s* and gold, to take	Eze 38:13	3701
gold, his breast and his arms of *s*	Dan 2:32	3702
iron, the clay, the brass, the *s*	Dan 2:35	3702
iron, the brass, the clay, the *s*	Dan 2:45	3702
s vessels which his father	Dan 5:2	3702
praised the gods of gold, and of *s*	Dan 5:4	3702
thou hast praised the gods of *s*	Dan 5:23	3702
with their precious vessels of *s*	Dan 11:8	3701
shall he honour with gold, and *s*	Dan 11:38	3701
the treasures of gold and of *s*	Dan 11:43	3701
wine, and oil, and multiplied her *s*	Hos 2:8	3701
her to me for fifteen pieces of *s*	Hos 3:2	3701
of their *s* and their gold have	Hos 8:4	3701
the pleasant places for their *s*	Hos 9:6	3701
them molten images of their *s*	Hos 13:2	3701
Because ye have taken my *s*	Joel 3:5	3701
they sold the righteous for *s*	Amos 2:6	3701
That we may buy the poor for *s*	Amos 8:6	3701
Take ye the spoil of *s*, take the	Nah 2:9	3701
it is laid over with gold and *s*	Hab 2:19	3701
all they that bear *s* are cut off	Zeph 1:11	3701
Neither their *s* nor their gold	Zeph 1:18	3701
The *s* is mine, and the gold is	Hag 2:8	3701
Then take *s* and gold, and make	Zec 6:11	3701
heaped up *s* as the dust, and fine	Zec 9:3	3701
for my price thirty pieces of *s*	Zec 11:12	3701
And I took the thirty pieces of *s*	Zec 11:13	3701
will refine them as *s* is refined	Zec 13:9	3701
be gathered together, gold, and *s*	Zec 14:14	3701
sit as a refiner and purifier of *s*	Mal 3:3	3701
Levi, and purge them as gold and *s*	Mal 3:3	3701
Provide neither gold, nor *s*	Mt 10:9	696

with him for thirty pieces of *s*	Mt 26:15	694
pieces of *s* to the chief priests	Mt 27:3	694
the pieces of *s* in the temple	Mt 27:5	694
chief priests took the *s* pieces	Mt 27:6	694
they took the thirty pieces of *s*	Mt 27:9	694
what woman having ten pieces of *s*	Lk 15:8	1406
Then Peter said, *S* and gold have I	Acts 3:6	694
Godhead is like unto gold, or *s*	Acts 17:29	696
it fifty thousand pieces of *s*	Acts 19:19	694
which made *s* shrines for Diana,	Acts 19:24	693
I have coveted no man's *s*	Acts 20:33	694
upon this foundation gold, *s*	1Cor 3:12	696
not only vessels of gold and of *s*	2Ti 2:20	693
Your gold and *s* is cankered	Jas 5:3	696
with corruptible things, as *s*	1Pet 1:18	694
devils, and idols of gold, and *s*	Rev 9:20	693
The merchandise of gold, and *s*	Rev 18:12	696

SILVERLINGS

a thousand vines at a thousand *s*	Is 7:23	3701

SILVERSMITH

certain man named Demetrius, a *s*	Acts 19:24	695

SIMEON *(sim'-e-un)* See SHIMEON, SIMEONITES, SIMON.
1. A son of Jacob.

and she called his name *S*	Gen 29:33	8095
that two of the sons of Jacob, *S*	Gen 34:25	8095
And Jacob said to *S* and Levi, Ye	Gen 34:30	8095
Reuben, Jacob's firstborn, and *S*	Gen 35:23	8095
with them, and took from them *S*	Gen 42:24	8095
S is not, and ye will take	Gen 42:36	8095
he brought *S* out unto them	Gen 43:23	8095
And the sons of *S*	Gen 46:10	8095
as Reuben and *S*, they shall be	Gen 48:5	8095
S and Levi are brethren	Gen 49:5	8095
Reuben, *S*, Levi, and Judah,	Ex 1:2	8095
And the sons of *S*	Ex 6:15	8095
these are the families of *S*	Ex 6:15	8095

2. Descendants of Simeon 1 and their land.

Of *S*	Num 1:6	8095
Of the children of *S*, by their	Num 1:22	8095
of them, even of the tribe of *S*	Num 1:23	8095
by him shall be the tribe of *S*	Num 2:12	8095
S shall be Shelumiel the son of	Num 2:12	8095
prince of the children of *S*	Num 7:36	8095
of *S* was Shelumiel the son of	Num 10:19	8095
Of the tribe of *S*, Shaphat the	Num 13:5	8095
The sons of *S* after their	Num 26:12	8095
of the tribe of the children of *S*	Num 34:20	8095
S, and Levi, and Judah, and Issachar	Deut 27:12	8095
And the second lot came forth to *S*	Josh 19:1	8095
of *S* according to their families	Josh 19:1	8095
of *S* according to their families	Josh 19:8	8095
inheritance of the children of *S*	Josh 19:9	8095
therefore the children of *S* had	Josh 19:9	8095
Judah, and out of the tribe of *S*	Josh 21:4	8099
of the tribe of the children of *S*	Josh 21:9	8095
And Judah said unto *S* his brother	Judg 1:3	8095
So *S* went with him	Judg 1:3	8095
And Judah went with *S* his brother	Judg 1:17	8095
Reuben, *S*, Levi, and Judah,	1Chr 2:1	8095
The sons of *S* were, Nemuel, and	1Chr 4:24	8095
of them, even of the sons of *S*	1Chr 4:42	8095
of the tribe of the children of *S*	1Chr 6:65	8095
Of the children of *S*, mighty men	1Chr 12:25	8095
Ephraim and Manasseh, and out of *S*	2Chr 15:9	8095
of Manasseh, and Ephraim, and *S*	2Chr 34:6	8095
west side, *S* shall have a portion	Eze 48:24	8095
And by the border of *S*, from the	Eze 48:25	8095
one gate of *S*, one gate of	Eze 48:33	8095
Of the tribe of *S* were sealed	Rev 7:7	4826

3. A devout man who blessed Jesus.

in Jerusalem, whose name was *S*	Lk 2:25	4826
S blessed them, and said unto Mary	Lk 2:34	4826

4. Father of Levi; an ancestor of Jesus.

Which was the son of *S*, which was	Lk 3:30	4826

5. A prophet of Antioch.

S that was called Niger, and	Acts 13:1	4826

6. Same as Simon Peter.

S hath declared how God at the	Acts 15:14	4826

SIMEONITES *(sim'-e-un-ites)* Descendants of Simeon 1.

of a chief house among the *S*	Num 25:14	8099
These are the families of the *S*	Num 26:14	8099
of the *S*, Shephatiah the son of	1Chr 27:16	8099

SIMILITUDE

the *s* of the LORD shall he behold	Num 12:8	8544
voice of the words, but saw no *s*	Deut 4:12	8544
for ye saw no manner of *s* on the	Deut 4:15	8544
the *s* of any figure, the likeness	Deut 4:16	8544
And under it was the *s* of oxen	2Chr 4:3	1823

the s of an ox that eateth grass	Ps 106:20	8403
polished after the s of a palace	Ps 144:12	8403
one like the s of the sons of men	Dan 10:16	1823
the s of Adam's transgression	Rom 5:14	3667
for that after the s of	Heb 7:15	3665
which are made after the s of God	Jas 3:9	3669

SIMILITUDES

multiplied visions, and used s	Hos 12:10	1819

SIMON (si'mun) See BAR-JONA, NIGER, PETER, SIMEON,
SIMON'S, ZELOTES.
1. Same as Peter.

S called Peter, and Andrew his	Mt 4:18	4613
The first, S, who is called Peter	Mt 10:2	4613
S Peter answered and said, Thou	Mt 16:16	4613
him, Blessed art thou, S Bar-jona	Mt 16:17	4613
saying, What thinkest thou, S	Mt 17:25	4613
by the sea of Galilee, he saw	Mk 1:16	4613
they entered into the house of S	Mk 1:29	4613
And S and they that were with him	Mk 1:36	4613
And S he surnamed Peter	Mk 3:16	4613
sleeping, and saith unto Peter, S	Mk 14:37	4613
had left speaking, he said unto S	Lk 5:4	4613
S answering said unto him, Master	Lk 5:5	4613
When S Peter saw it, he fell down	Lk 5:8	4613
which were partners with S	Lk 5:10	4613
And Jesus said unto S, Fear not	Lk 5:10	4613
S, (whom he also named Peter,) and	Lk 6:14	4613
And the Lord said, S, S	Lk 22:31	4613
indeed, and hath appeared to S	Lk 24:34	4613
was Andrew, S Peter's brother	Jn 1:40	4613
first findeth his own brother S	Jn 1:41	4613
Thou art S the son of Jona	Jn 1:42	4613
S Peter's brother, saith unto him	Jn 6:8	4613
Then S Peter answered him, Lord,	Jn 6:68	4613
Then cometh he to S Peter	Jn 13:6	4613
S Peter saith unto him, Lord, not	Jn 13:9	4613
S Peter therefore beckoned to him	Jn 13:24	4613
S Peter said unto him, Lord,	Jn 13:36	4613
Then S Peter having a sword drew	Jn 18:10	4613
S Peter followed Jesus, and so did	Jn 18:15	4613
S Peter stood and warmed himself	Jn 18:25	4613
she runneth, and cometh to S Peter	Jn 20:2	4613
Then cometh S Peter following him	Jn 20:6	4613
There were together S Peter	Jn 21:2	4613
S Peter saith unto them, I go a	Jn 21:3	4613
Now when S Peter heard that it	Jn 21:7	4613
S Peter went up, and drew the net	Jn 21:11	4613
Jesus saith to S Peter, S	Jn 21:15	4613
to him again the second time, S	Jn 21:16	4613
saith unto him the third time, S	Jn 21:17	4613
men to Joppa, and call for one S	Acts 10:5	4613
And called, and asked whether S	Acts 10:18	4613
to Joppa, and call hither S	Acts 10:32	4613
Send men to Joppa, and call for S	Acts 11:13	4613
S Peter, a servant and an apostle	2Pet 1:1	4613

2. A Canaanite disciple of Jesus.

S the Canaanite, and Judas	Mt 10:4	4613
and Thaddaeus, and S the Canaanite,	Mk 3:18	4613
of Alphaeus, and S called Zelotes,	Lk 6:15	4613
S Zelotes, and Judas the brother	Acts 1:13	4613

3. A brother of Jesus.

brethren, James, and Joses, and S	Mt 13:55	4613
James, and Joses, and of Juda, and S	Mk 6:3	4613

4. A leper in Bethany.

in the house of S the leper	Mt 26:6	4613
in the house of S the leper	Mk 14:3	4613

5. A Cyrenian who bore Jesus' cross.

found a man of Cyrene, S by name	Mt 27:32	4613
And they compel one S a Cyrenian	Mk 15:21	4613
away, they laid hold upon one S	Lk 23:26	4613

6. A Pharisee.

Jesus answering said unto him, S	Lk 7:40	4613
S answered and said, I suppose	Lk 7:43	4613
to the woman, and said unto S	Lk 7:44	4613

7. Father of Judas Iscariot.

of Judas Iscariot the son of S	Jn 6:71	4613
to Judas Iscariot, the son of S	Jn 13:26	4613

8. A Samaritan sorcerer.

there was a certain man, called S	Acts 8:9	4613
Then S himself believed also	Acts 8:13	4613
when S saw that through laying on	Acts 8:18	4613
Then answered S, and said, Pray ye	Acts 8:24	4613

9. A tanner at Joppa.

days in Joppa with one S a tanner	Acts 9:43	4613
He lodgeth with one S a tanner	Acts 10:6	4613
of one S a tanner by the sea side	Acts 10:32	4613

SIMON'S (si'-muns)
1. Refers to Simon 1.

But S wife's mother lay sick of a	Mk 1:30	4613
and entered into S house	Lk 4:38	4613
S wife's mother was taken with a	Lk 4:38	4613
one of the ships, which was S	Lk 5:3	4613

2. Refers to Simon 7.

S son, which should betray him,	Jn 12:4	4613
Iscariot, S son, to betray him	Jn 13:2	4613

3. Refers to Simon 9.

had made enquiry for S house	Acts 10:17	4613

SIMPLE

LORD is sure, making wise the s	Ps 19:7	6612
The LORD preserveth the s	Ps 116:6	6612
giveth understanding unto the s	Ps 119:130	6612
To give subtilty to the s	Prov 1:4	6612
How long, ye s ones, will ye love	Prov 1:22	6612
away of the s shall slay them	Prov 1:32	6612
And beheld among the s ones	Prov 7:7	6612
O ye s, understand wisdom	Prov 8:5	6612
Whoso is s, let him turn in	Prov 9:4	6612
she is s, and knoweth nothing	Prov 9:13	6615
Whoso is s, let him turn in	Prov 9:16	6612
The s believeth every word	Prov 14:15	6612
The s inherit folly	Prov 14:18	6612
a scorner, and the s will beware	Prov 19:25	6612
is punished, the s is made wise	Prov 21:11	6612
but the s pass on, and are	Prov 22:3	6612
but the s pass on, and are	Prov 27:12	6612
that erreth, and for him that is s	Eze 45:20	6612
deceive the hearts of the s	Rom 16:18	172
is good, and s concerning evil	Rom 16:19	185

SIMPLICITY

and they went in their s, and they	2Sa 15:11	8537
ye simple ones, will ye love s	Prov 1:22	6612
that giveth, let him do it with s	Rom 12:8	572
of our conscience, that in s	2Cor 1:12	572
from the s that is in Christ	2Cor 11:3	572

SIMRI (sim'-ri) See SHIMRI. *A sanctuary servant.*

S the chief, (for though he was	1Chr 26:10	8113

SIN (sin)
1. A transgression.

not well, s lieth at the door	Gen 4:7	2403
because their s is very grievous	Gen 18:20	2403
on me and on my kingdom a great s	Gen 20:9	2401
what is my s, that thou hast so	Gen 31:36	2403
wickedness, and s against God	Gen 39:9	2398
Do not s against the child	Gen 42:22	2398
of thy brethren, and their s	Gen 50:17	2403
my s only this once, and intreat	Ex 10:17	2403
before your faces, that ye s not	Ex 20:20	2398
lest they make thee s against me	Ex 23:33	2398
it is a s offering	Ex 29:14	2403
for a s offering for atonement	Ex 29:36	2403
of the s offering of atonements	Ex 30:10	2403
brought so great a s upon them	Ex 32:21	2401
people, Ye have sinned a great s	Ex 32:30	2401
make an atonement for your s	Ex 32:30	2403
this people have sinned a great s	Ex 32:31	2401
now, if thou wilt forgive their s	Ex 32:32	2403
I will visit their s upon them	Ex 32:34	2403
iniquity and transgression and s	Ex 34:7	2402
and pardon our iniquity and our s	Ex 34:9	2403
If a soul shall s through	Lev 4:2	2398
do s according to the	Lev 4:3	2398
according to the s of the people	Lev 4:3	819
then let him bring for his s	Lev 4:3	2403
unto the LORD for a s offering	Lev 4:3	2403
of the bullock for the s offering	Lev 4:8	2403
of Israel sin through ignorance	Lev 4:13	7686
When the s, which they have	Lev 4:14	2403
offer a young bullock for the s	Lev 4:14	2403
with the bullock for a s offering	Lev 4:20	2403
it is a s offering for the	Lev 4:21	2403
Or if his s, wherein he hath	Lev 4:23	2403
it is a s offering	Lev 4:24	2403
of the s offering with his finger	Lev 4:25	2403
for him as concerning his s	Lev 4:26	2403
common people s through ignorance	Lev 4:27	2398
Or if his s, which he hath sinned	Lev 4:28	2403
for his s which he hath sinned	Lev 4:28	2403
upon the head of the s offering	Lev 4:29	2403
slay the s offering in the place	Lev 4:29	2403
he bring a lamb for a s offering	Lev 4:32	2403
upon the head of the s offering	Lev 4:33	2403
slay it for a s offering in the	Lev 4:33	2403
of the s offering with his finger	Lev 4:34	2403
for his s that he hath committed	Lev 4:35	2403
And if a soul s, and hear the voice	Lev 5:1	2398

S

for his *s* which he hath sinned	Lev 5:6	2403
of the goats, for a *s* offering	Lev 5:6	2403
for him concerning his *s*	Lev 5:6	2403
one for a *s* offering, and the	Lev 5:7	2403
which is for the *s* offering first	Lev 5:8	2403
sprinkle of the blood of the *s*	Lev 5:9	2403
it is a *s* offering	Lev 5:9	2403
for his *s* which he hath sinned	Lev 5:10	2403
of fine flour for a *s* offering	Lev 5:11	2403
for it is a *s* offering	Lev 5:11	2403
it is a *s* offering	Lev 5:12	2403
for him as touching his *s* that he	Lev 5:13	2403
s through ignorance, in the holy	Lev 5:15	2398
And if a soul *s*, and commit any of	Lev 5:17	2398
If a soul *s*, and commit a trespass	Lev 6:2	2398
most holy, as is the *s* offering	Lev 6:17	2403
This is the law of the *s* offering	Lev 6:25	2403
offering is killed shall the *s*	Lev 6:25	2403
offereth it for *s* shall eat it	Lev 6:26	2398
no *s* offering, whereof any of the	Lev 6:30	2403
As the *s* offering is, so is the	Lev 7:7	2403
of the *s* offering, and of the	Lev 7:37	2403
and a bullock for the *s* offering	Lev 8:2	2403
the bullock for the *s* offering	Lev 8:14	2403
of the bullock for the *s* offering	Lev 8:14	2403
a young calf for a *s* offering	Lev 9:2	2403
kid of the goats for a *s* offering	Lev 9:3	2403
altar, and offer thy *s* offering	Lev 9:7	2403
slew the calf of the *s* offering	Lev 9:8	2403
above the liver of the *s* offering	Lev 9:10	2403
which was the *s* offering for the	Lev 9:15	2403
and slew it, and offered it for *s*	Lev 9:15	2403
from offering of the *s* offering	Lev 9:22	2403
sought the goat of the *s* offering	Lev 10:16	2403
the *s* offering in the holy place	Lev 10:17	2403
they offered their *s* offering	Lev 10:19	2403
I had eaten the *s* offering to day	Lev 10:19	2403
for a *s* offering, unto the door	Lev 12:6	2403
and the other for a *s* offering	Lev 12:8	2403
he shall kill the *s* offering	Lev 14:13	2403
for as the *s* offering is the	Lev 14:13	2403
priest shall offer the *s* offering	Lev 14:19	2403
and the one shall be a *s* offering	Lev 14:22	2403
to get, the one for a *s* offering	Lev 14:31	2403
them, the one for a *s* offering	Lev 15:15	2403
offer the one for a *s* offering	Lev 15:30	2403
a young bullock for a *s* offering	Lev 16:3	2403
of the goats for a *s* offering	Lev 16:5	2403
his bullock of the *s* offering	Lev 16:6	2403
and offer him for a *s* offering	Lev 16:9	2403
the bullock of the *s* offering	Lev 16:11	2403
s offering which is for himself	Lev 16:11	2403
kill the goat of the *s* offering	Lev 16:15	2403
the fat of the *s* offering shall	Lev 16:25	2403
And the bullock for the *s* offering	Lev 16:27	2403
and the goat for the *s* offering	Lev 16:27	2403
and not suffer *s* upon him	Lev 19:17	2399
LORD for his *s* which he hath done	Lev 19:22	2403
the *s* which he hath done shall be	Lev 19:22	2403
they shall bear their *s*	Lev 20:20	2399
lest they bear *s* for it, and die	Lev 22:9	2399
kid of the goats for a *s* offering	Lev 23:19	2403
curseth his God shall bear his *s*	Lev 24:15	2399
commit any *s* that men commit	Num 5:6	2403
their *s* which they have done	Num 5:7	2403
offer the one for a *s* offering	Num 6:11	2403
without blemish for a *s* offering	Num 6:14	2403
and shall offer his *s* offering	Num 6:16	2403
kid of the goats for a *s* offering	Num 7:16	2403
kid of the goats for a *s* offering	Num 7:22	2403
kid of the goats for a *s* offering	Num 7:28	2403
kid of the goats for a *s* offering	Num 7:34	2403
kid of the goats for a *s* offering	Num 7:40	2403
kid of the goats for a *s* offering	Num 7:46	2403
kid of the goats for a *s* offering	Num 7:52	2403
kid of the goats for a *s* offering	Num 7:58	2403
kid of the goats for a *s* offering	Num 7:64	2403
kid of the goats for a *s* offering	Num 7:70	2403
kid of the goats for a *s* offering	Num 7:76	2403
kid of the goats for a *s* offering	Num 7:82	2403
the goats for *s* offering twelve	Num 7:87	2403
shalt thou take for a *s* offering	Num 8:8	2403
offer the one for a *s* offering	Num 8:12	2403
season, that man shall bear his *s*	Num 9:13	2399
thee, lay not the *s* upon us	Num 12:11	2403
kid of the goats for a *s* offering	Num 15:24	2403
their *s* offering before the LORD,	Num 15:25	2403
if any soul *s* through ignorance,	Num 15:27	2398
the first year for a *s* offering	Num 15:27	2403
of all flesh, shall one man *s*	Num 16:22	2398
every *s* offering of theirs, and	Num 18:9	2403
congregation, lest they bear *s*	Num 18:22	2399
shall bear no *s* by reason of it	Num 18:32	2399
it is a purification for *s*	Num 19:9	2403
heifer of purification for *s*	Num 19:17	2403
but died in his own *s*, and had no	Num 27:3	2399
one kid of the goats for a *s*	Num 28:15	2403
And one goat for a *s* offering	Num 28:22	2403
kid of the goats for a *s* offering	Num 29:5	2403
kid of the goats for a *s* offering	Num 29:11	2403
beside the *s* offering of	Num 29:11	2403
kid of the goats for a *s* offering	Num 29:16	2403
kid of the goats for a *s* offering	Num 29:19	2403
And one goat for a *s* offering	Num 29:22	2403
kid of the goats for a *s* offering	Num 29:25	2403
And one goat for a *s* offering	Num 29:28	2403
And one goat for a *s* offering	Num 29:31	2403
And one goat for a *s* offering	Num 29:34	2403
And one goat for a *s* offering	Num 29:38	2403
be sure your *s* will find you out	Num 32:23	2403
And I took your *s*, the calf which	Deut 9:21	2403
their wickedness, nor to their *s*	Deut 9:27	2403
thee, and it be *s* unto thee	Deut 15:9	2399
for any iniquity, or for any *s*	Deut 19:15	2403
in any *s* that he sinneth	Deut 19:15	2399
so should ye *s* against the LORD	Deut 20:18	2398
committed a *s* worthy of death	Deut 21:22	2399
the damsel no *s* worthy of death	Deut 22:26	2399
and it would be *s* in thee	Deut 23:21	2399
to vow, it shall be no *s* in thee	Deut 23:22	2399
shalt not cause the land to *s*	Deut 24:4	2398
the LORD, and it be *s* unto thee	Deut 24:15	2399
be put to death for his own *s*	Deut 24:16	2399
Wherefore the *s* of the young men	1Sa 2:17	2403
If one man *s* against another, the	1Sa 2:25	2398
but if a man *s* against the LORD,	1Sa 2:25	2398
God forbid that I should *s*	1Sa 12:23	2398
the people *s* against the LORD, in	1Sa 14:33	2398
s not against the LORD in eating	1Sa 14:34	2398
see wherein this *s* hath been this	1Sa 14:38	2403
is as the *s* of witchcraft	1Sa 15:23	2403
I pray thee, pardon my *s*	1Sa 15:25	2403
Let not the king *s* against his	1Sa 19:4	2398
thou *s* against innocent blood	1Sa 19:5	2398
what is my *s* before thy father,	1Sa 20:1	2403
The LORD also hath put away thy *s*	2Sa 12:13	2403
forgive the *s* of thy people	1Kin 8:34	2403
thy name, and turn from their *s*	1Kin 8:35	2403
forgive the *s* of thy servants, and	1Kin 8:36	2403
If they *s* against thee, (for	1Kin 8:46	2398
And this thing became a *s*	1Kin 12:30	2403
this thing became *s* unto the	1Kin 13:34	2403
the sins of Jeroboam, who did *s*	1Kin 14:16	2398
and who made Israel to *s*	1Kin 14:16	2398
in his *s* wherewith he made Israel	1Kin 15:26	2403
wherewith he made Israel to *s*	1Kin 15:26	2398
sinned, and which he made Israel *s*	1Kin 15:30	2398
in his *s* wherewith he made Israel	1Kin 15:34	2403
wherewith he made Israel to *s*	1Kin 15:34	2398
hast made my people Israel to *s*	1Kin 16:2	2398
and by which they made Israel to *s*	1Kin 16:13	2398
in his *s* which he did, to make	1Kin 16:19	2403
which he did, to make Israel to *s*	1Kin 16:19	2398
in his *s* wherewith he made Israel	1Kin 16:26	2403
wherewith he made Israel to *s*	1Kin 16:26	2398
me to call my *s* to remembrance	1Kin 17:18	5771
me to anger, and made Israel to *s*	1Kin 21:22	2398
of Nebat, who made Israel to *s*	1Kin 22:52	2398
of Nebat, which made Israel to *s*	2Kin 3:3	2398
of Nebat, who made Israel to *s*	2Kin 10:29	2398
Jeroboam, which made Israel to *s*	2Kin 10:31	2398
s money was not brought into the	2Kin 12:16	
of Nebat, which made Israel to *s*	2Kin 13:2	2398
of Jeroboam, who made Israel *s*	2Kin 13:6	2398
son of Nebat, who made Israel *s*	2Kin 13:11	2398
be put to death for his own *s*	2Kin 14:6	2399
of Nebat, who made Israel to *s*	2Kin 14:24	2398
of Nebat, who made Israel to *s*	2Kin 15:9	2398
of Nebat, who made Israel to *s*	2Kin 15:18	2398
of Nebat, who made Israel to *s*	2Kin 15:24	2398
of Nebat, who made Israel to *s*	2Kin 15:28	2398
LORD, and made them *s*	2Kin 17:21	2398
a great *s*	2Kin 17:21	2401
Judah also to *s* with his idols	2Kin 21:11	2398
beside his *s* wherewith he made	2Kin 21:16	2403
wherewith he made Judah to *s*	2Kin 21:16	2398
his *s* that he sinned, are they	2Kin 21:17	2403
of Nebat, who made Israel to *s*	2Kin 23:15	2398
If a man *s* against his neighbour,	2Chr 6:22	2398
forgive the *s* of thy people	2Chr 6:25	2403
thy name, and turn from their *s*	2Chr 6:26	2403
forgive the *s* of thy servants, and	2Chr 6:27	2403

If they *s* against thee, (for	2Chr 6:36	2398
heaven, and will forgive their *s*	2Chr 7:14	2403
every man shall die for his own *s*	2Chr 25:4	2399
for a *s* offering for the kingdom,	2Chr 29:21	2403
the *s* offering before the king	2Chr 29:23	2403
the *s* offering should be made for	2Chr 29:24	2403
intreated of him, and all his *s*	2Chr 33:19	2403
for a *s* offering for all Israel,	Ezr 6:17	2409
twelve he goats for a *s* offering	Ezr 8:35	2403
let not their *s* be blotted out	Neh 4:5	2403
should be afraid, and do so, and *s*	Neh 6:13	2398
for the *s* offerings to make an	Neh 10:33	2403
king of Israel *s* by these things	Neh 13:26	2398
did outlandish women cause to *s*	Neh 13:26	2398
this did not Job *s* with his lips	Job 2:10	2398
thy habitation, and shalt not *s*	Job 5:24	2403
iniquity, and searchest after my *s*	Job 10:6	2403
If I *s*, then thou markest me, and	Job 10:14	2398
to know my transgression and my *s*	Job 13:23	2403
dost thou not watch over my *s*	Job 14:16	2403
are full of the *s* of his youth	Job 20:11	
have I suffered my mouth to *s* by	Job 31:30	2398
he addeth rebellion unto his *s*	Job 34:37	2403
have, if I be cleansed from my *s*	Job 35:3	2403
Stand in awe, and *s* not	Ps 4:4	2398
is forgiven, whose *s* is covered	Ps 32:1	2401
I acknowledged my *s* unto thee	Ps 32:5	2403
forgavest the iniquity of my *s*	Ps 32:5	2403
rest in my bones because of my *s*	Ps 38:3	2403
I will be sorry for my *s*	Ps 38:18	2403
that I *s* not with my tongue	Ps 39:1	2398
s offering hast thou not required	Ps 40:6	2401
iniquity, and cleanse me from my *s*	Ps 51:2	2403
and my *s* is ever before me	Ps 51:3	2403
in *s* did my mother conceive me	Ps 51:5	2399
my transgression, nor for my *s*	Ps 59:3	2403
For the *s* of their mouth and the	Ps 59:12	2403
thou hast covered all their *s*	Ps 85:2	2403
and let his prayer become *s*	Ps 109:7	2401
let not the *s* of his mother be	Ps 109:14	2403
that I might not *s* against thee	Ps 119:11	2398
the fruit of the wicked to *s*	Prov 10:16	2403
of words there wanteth not *s*	Prov 10:19	6588
Fools make a mock at *s*	Prov 14:9	817
but *s* is a reproach to any people	Prov 14:34	2403
heart clean, I am pure from my *s*	Prov 20:9	2403
the plowing of the wicked, is *s*	Prov 21:4	2403
The thought of foolishness is *s*	Prov 24:9	2403
thy mouth to cause thy flesh to *s*	Eccl 5:6	2398
and they declare their *s* as Sodom	Is 3:9	2403
s as it were with a cart rope	Is 5:18	2402
is taken away, and thy *s* purged	Is 6:7	2403
all the fruit to take away his *s*	Is 27:9	2403
that they may add *s* to *s*	Is 30:1	2403
hands have made unto you for a *s*	Is 31:7	2399
make his soul an offering for *s*	Is 53:10	817
and he bare the *s* of many, and made	Is 53:12	2399
or what is our *s* that we have	Jer 16:10	2403
their iniquity and their *s* double	Jer 16:18	2403
The *s* of Judah is written with a	Jer 17:1	2403
spoil, and thy high places for *s*	Jer 17:3	2403
blot out their *s* from thy sight	Jer 18:23	2403
I will remember their *s* no more	Jer 31:34	2403
abomination, to cause Judah to *s*	Jer 32:35	2398
forgive their iniquity and their *s*	Jer 36:3	2403
their land was filled with *s*	Jer 51:5	817
the punishment of the *s* of Sodom	Lam 4:6	
warning, he shall die in his *s*	Eze 3:20	2403
s not, and he doth not *s*	Eze 3:21	2398
in his *s* that he hath sinned, in	Eze 18:24	2403
if he turn from his *s*, and do that	Eze 33:14	2403
the *s* offering and the trespass	Eze 40:39	2403
the *s* offering, and the trespass	Eze 42:13	2403
a young bullock for a *s* offering	Eze 43:19	2403
bullock also of the *s* offering	Eze 43:21	2403
without blemish for a *s* offering	Eze 43:22	2403
every day a goat for a *s* offering	Eze 43:25	2403
he shall offer his *s* offering	Eze 44:27	2403
the *s* offering, and the trespass	Eze 44:29	2403
he shall prepare the *s* offering	Eze 45:17	2403
of the blood of the *s* offering	Eze 45:19	2403
land a bullock for a *s* offering	Eze 45:22	2403
the goats daily for a *s* offering	Eze 45:23	2403
days, according to the *s* offering	Eze 45:25	2403
the *s* offering, where they shall	Eze 46:20	2403
and praying, and confessing my *s*	Dan 9:20	2403
the *s* of my people Israel, and	Dan 9:20	2403
They eat up the *s* of my people	Hos 4:8	2403
hath made many altars to *s*	Hos 8:11	2398
altars shall be unto him to *s*	Hos 8:11	2398
the *s* of Israel, shall be	Hos 10:8	2403

none iniquity in me that were *s*	Hos 12:8	2399
And now they *s* more and more, and	Hos 13:2	2398
his *s* is hid	Hos 13:12	2403
that swear by the *s* of Samaria	Amos 8:14	819
of the *s* to the daughter of Zion	Mic 1:13	2403
transgression, and to Israel his *s*	Mic 3:8	2403
of my body for the *s* of my soul	Mic 6:7	2403
inhabitants of Jerusalem for *s*	Zec 13:1	2403
I say unto you, All manner of *s*	Mt 12:31	266
oft shall my brother *s* against me	Mt 18:21	264
taketh away the *s* of the world	Jn 1:29	266
***s* no more, lest a worse thing**	Jn 5:14	264
He that is without *s* among you	Jn 8:7	361
go, and *s* no more	Jn 8:11	264
Whosoever committeth *s* is the	Jn 8:34	266
is the servant of *s*	Jn 8:34	266
Which of you convinceth me of *s*	Jn 8:46	266
him, saying, Master, who did *s*	Jn 9:2	264
were blind, ye should have no *s*	Jn 9:41	266
therefore your *s* remaineth	Jn 9:41	266
unto them, they had not had *s*	Jn 15:22	266
they have no cloke for their *s*	Jn 15:22	266
other man did, they had not had *s*	Jn 15:24	266
he will reprove the world of *s*	Jn 16:8	266
Of *s*, because they believe not on	Jn 16:9	266
me unto thee hath the greater *s*	Jn 19:11	266
lay not this *s* to their charge	Acts 7:60	266
that they are all under *s*	Rom 3:9	266
by the law is the knowledge of *s*	Rom 3:20	266
whom the Lord will not impute *s*	Rom 4:8	266
as by one man *s* entered into the	Rom 5:12	266
into the world, and death by *s*	Rom 5:12	266
until the law *s* was in the world	Rom 5:13	266
but *s* is not imputed when there	Rom 5:13	266
But where *s* abounded, grace did	Rom 5:20	266
That as *s* hath reigned unto death	Rom 5:21	266
Shall we continue in *s*, that	Rom 6:1	266
How shall we, that are dead to *s*	Rom 6:2	266
that the body of *s* might be	Rom 6:6	266
henceforth we should not serve *s*	Rom 6:6	266
he that is dead is freed from *s*	Rom 6:7	266
that he died, he died unto *s* once	Rom 6:10	266
to be dead indeed unto *s*, but	Rom 6:11	266
Let not *s* therefore reign in your	Rom 6:12	266
of unrighteousness unto *s*	Rom 6:13	266
For *s* shall not have dominion	Rom 6:14	266
shall we *s*, because we are not	Rom 6:15	264
whether of *s* unto death, or of	Rom 6:16	266
that ye were the servants of *s*	Rom 6:17	266
Being then made free from *s*	Rom 6:18	266
when ye were the servants of *s*	Rom 6:20	266
But now being made free from *s*	Rom 6:22	266
For the wages of *s* is death	Rom 6:23	266
Is the law *s*	Rom 7:7	266
Nay, I had not known *s*, but by	Rom 7:7	266
But *s*, taking occasion by the	Rom 7:8	266
For without the law *s* was dead	Rom 7:8	266
came, *s* revived, and I died	Rom 7:9	266
For *s*, taking occasion by the	Rom 7:11	266
But *s*, that it might appear *s*,	Rom 7:13	266
that *s* by the commandment might	Rom 7:13	266
but I am carnal, sold under *s*	Rom 7:14	266
but *s* that dwelleth in me	Rom 7:17	266
but *s* that dwelleth in me	Rom 7:20	266
law of *s* which is in my members	Rom 7:23	266
but with the flesh the law of *s*	Rom 7:25	266
made me free from the law of *s*	Rom 8:2	266
for *s*, condemned *s* in the flesh	Rom 8:3	266
the body is dead because of *s*	Rom 8:10	266
whatsoever is not of faith is *s*	Rom 14:23	266
Every *s* that a man doeth is	1Cor 6:18	265
But when ye *s* so against the	1Cor 8:12	264
conscience, ye *s* against Christ	1Cor 8:12	264
Awake to righteousness, and *s* not	1Cor 15:34	264
The sting of death is *s*	1Cor 15:56	266
and the strength of *s* is the law	1Cor 15:56	266
to be *s* for us, who knew no *s*	2Cor 5:21	266
Christ the minister of *s*	Gal 2:17	266
hath concluded all under *s*	Gal 3:22	266
Be ye angry, and *s* not	Eph 4:26	266
and that man of *s* be revealed	2Th 2:3	266
Them that *s* rebuke before all,	1Ti 5:20	264
through the deceitfulness of *s*	Heb 3:13	266
like as we are, yet without *s*	Heb 4:15	266
s by the sacrifice of himself	Heb 9:26	266
time without *s* unto salvation	Heb 9:28	266
sacrifices for *s* thou hast had no	Heb 10:6	266
offering for *s* thou wouldest not,	Heb 10:8	266
there is no more offering for *s*	Heb 10:18	266
For if we *s* wilfully after that	Heb 10:26	264
the pleasures of *s* for a season	Heb 11:25	266

S

the *s* which doth so easily beset	Heb 12:1	*266*
unto blood, striving against *s*	Heb 12:4	*266*
by the high priest for *s*, are	Heb 13:11	*266*
conceived, it bringeth forth *s*	Jas 1:15	*266*
and *s*, when it is finished,	Jas 1:15	*266*
respect to persons, ye commit *s*	Jas 2:9	*266*
and doeth it not, to him it is *s*	Jas 4:17	*266*
Who did no *s*, neither was guile	1Pet 2:22	*266*
in the flesh hath ceased from *s*	1Pet 4:1	*266*
and that cannot cease from *s*	2Pet 2:14	*266*
his Son cleanseth us from all *s*	1Jn 1:7	*266*
If we say that we have no *s*	1Jn 1:8	*266*
write I unto you, that ye *s* not	1Jn 2:1	*264*
And if any man *s*, we have an	1Jn 2:1	*264*
Whosoever committeth *s*	1Jn 3:4	*266*
for *s* is the transgression of the	1Jn 3:4	*266*
and in him is no *s*	1Jn 3:5	*266*
that committeth *s* is of the devil	1Jn 3:8	*266*
is born of God doth not commit *s*	1Jn 3:9	*266*
and he cannot *s*, because he is	1Jn 3:9	*264*
s a *s* which is not unto death	1Jn 5:16	*264*
for them that *s* not unto death	1Jn 5:16	*264*
There is a *s* unto death	1Jn 5:16	*266*
All unrighteousness is *s*	1Jn 5:17	*266*
there is a *s* not unto death	1Jn 5:17	*266*

2. Eastern border of Egypt.

And I will pour my fury upon *S*	Eze 30:15	*5512*
S shall have great pain, and No	Eze 30:16	*5512*

3. Desert between Elim and Sinai.

came unto the wilderness of *S*	Ex 16:1	*5512*
from the wilderness of *S*, after	Ex 17:1	*5512*
encamped in the wilderness of *S*	Num 33:11	*5512*
out of the wilderness of *S*	Num 33:12	*5512*

SINA (si'-nah) See SINAI. *Greek form of Sinai.*

him in the wilderness of mount *S*	Acts 7:30	*4614*
which spake to him in the mount *S*	Acts 7:38	*4614*

SINAI (si'-nahee) See HOREB, SINA. *Mountainous district in the southern Sinai peninsula.*

Sin, which is between Elim and *S*	Ex 16:1	*5514*
they into the wilderness of *S*	Ex 19:1	*5514*
and were come to the desert of *S*	Ex 19:2	*5514*
of all the people upon mount *S*	Ex 19:11	*5514*
mount *S* was altogether on a smoke	Ex 19:18	*5514*
the LORD came down upon mount *S*	Ex 19:20	*5514*
people cannot come up to mount *S*	Ex 19:23	*5514*
of the LORD abode upon mount *S*	Ex 24:16	*5514*
communing with him upon mount *S*	Ex 31:18	*5514*
up in the morning unto mount *S*	Ex 34:2	*5514*
morning, and went up unto mount *S*	Ex 34:4	*5514*
mount *S* with the two tables of	Ex 34:29	*5514*
had spoken with him in mount *S*	Ex 34:32	*5514*
LORD commanded Moses in mount *S*	Lev 7:38	*5514*
the LORD, in the wilderness of *S*	Lev 7:38	*5514*
LORD spake unto Moses in mount *S*	Lev 25:1	*5514*
in mount *S* by the hand of Moses	Lev 26:46	*5514*
the children of Israel in mount *S*	Lev 27:34	*5514*
unto Moses in the wilderness of *S*	Num 1:1	*5514*
them in the wilderness of *S*	Num 1:19	*5514*
LORD spake with Moses in mount *S*	Num 3:1	*5514*
the LORD, in the wilderness of *S*	Num 3:4	*5514*
unto Moses in the wilderness of *S*	Num 3:14	*5514*
unto Moses in the wilderness of *S*	Num 9:1	*5514*
at even in the wilderness of *S*	Num 9:5	*5514*
out of the wilderness of *S*	Num 10:12	*5514*
of Israel in the wilderness of *S*	Num 26:64	*5514*
in mount *S* for a sweet savour	Num 28:6	*5514*
and pitched in the wilderness of *S*	Num 33:15	*5514*
they removed from the desert of *S*	Num 33:16	*5514*
And he said, The LORD came from *S*	Deut 33:2	*5514*
even that *S* from before the LORD	Judg 5:5	*5514*
camest down also upon mount *S*	Neh 9:13	*5514*
even *S* itself was moved at the	Ps 68:8	*5514*
the Lord is among them, as in *S*	Ps 68:17	*5514*
the one from the mount *S*, which	Gal 4:24	*4614*
this Agar is mount *S* in Arabia	Gal 4:25	*4614*

SINCE

hath blessed thee *s* my coming	Gen 30:30	
and I saw him not *s*	Gen 44:28	*2008*
s I have seen thy face, because	Gen 46:30	*310*
nor *s* thou hast spoken unto thy	Ex 4:10	*227*
For *s* I came to Pharaoh to speak	Ex 5:23	*4480*
s the foundation thereof even	Ex 9:18	*4480*
of Egypt *s* it became a nation	Ex 9:24	*4480*
s the day that they were upon the	Ex 10:6	*4480*
ever *s* I was thine unto this day	Num 22:30	*5750*
s the day that God created man	Deut 4:32	*4480*
s in Israel like unto Moses	Deut 34:10	*5750*
s I have shewed you kindness,	Josh 2:12	*3588*
even *s* the LORD spake this word	Josh 14:10	*227*

law *s* the death of thine husband	Ruth 2:11	*310*
s the day that I brought them up	1Sa 8:8	
it been kept for thee *s* I said	1Sa 9:24	
s I came out, and the vessels of	1Sa 21:5	
I have found no fault in him *s* he	1Sa 29:3	
s the day of thy coming unto me	1Sa 29:6	
I have not dwelt in any house *s*	2Sa 7:6	
as *s* the time that I commanded	2Sa 7:11	*4480*
S the day that I brought forth my	1Kin 8:16	*4480*
all the fruits of the field *s* the	2Kin 8:6	
s the day their fathers came	2Kin 21:15	*4480*
house *s* the day that I brought up	1Chr 17:5	*4480*
s the time that I commanded	1Chr 17:10	
S the day that I brought forth my	2Chr 6:5	*4480*
for *s* the time of Solomon the son	2Chr 30:26	
S the people began to bring the	2Chr 31:10	
we do sacrifice unto him *s* the	Ezr 4:2	
s that time even until now hath	Ezr 5:16	*4481*
S the days of our fathers have we	Ezr 9:7	
for *s* the days of Jeshua the son	Neh 8:17	
s the time of the kings of	Neh 9:32	
s man was placed upon earth,	Job 20:4	*4480*
commanded the morning *s* thy days	Job 38:12	
S thou art laid down, no feller	Is 14:8	*227*
concerning Moab *s* that time	Is 16:13	
S thou wast precious in my sight,	Is 43:4	
s I appointed the ancient people	Is 44:7	
For *s* the beginning of the world	Is 64:4	
S the day that your fathers came	Jer 7:25	*4480*
s they return not from their ways	Jer 15:7	
For *s* I spake, I cried out, I	Jer 20:8	*1767*
But *s* ye say, The burden of the	Jer 23:38	*518*
for *s* I spake against him, I do	Jer 31:20	*1767*
But *s* we left off to burn incense	Jer 44:18	*4480,227*
for *s* thou spakest of him, thou	Jer 48:27	*1767*
such as never was *s* there was a	Dan 12:1	
S those days were, when one came	Hag 2:16	
such as was not *s* the beginning	Mt 24:21	*575*
is it ago *s* this came unto him	Mk 9:21	*5613*
which have been *s* the world began	Lk 1:70	*575*
but this woman *s* the time I came	Lk 7:45	*575*
s that time the kingdom of God is	Lk 16:16	*575*
day *s* these things were done	Lk 24:21	*575*
S the world began was it not	Jn 9:32	*1537*
holy prophets *s* the world began	Acts 3:21	*575*
the Holy Ghost *s* ye believed	Acts 19:2	
s I went up to Jerusalem for to	Acts 24:11	*575,3739*
was kept secret *s* the world began	Rom 16:25	
For *s* by man came death, by man	1Cor 15:21	*1894*
S ye seek a proof of Christ	2Cor 13:3	*1893*
S we heard of your faith in	Col 1:4	
s the day ye heard of it, and knew	Col 1:6	*575*
s the day we heard it, do not	Col 1:9	*575*
of the oath, which was *s* the law	Heb 7:28	*3326*
s the foundation of the world	Heb 9:26	*575*
for *s* the fathers fell asleep,	2Pet 3:4	*575,3739*
such as was not *s* men were upon	Rev 16:18	*575,3739*

SINCERE

that ye may be *s* and without	Phil 1:10	*1506*
desire the *s* milk of the word,	1Pet 2:2	*97*

SINCERELY

if ye have done truly and *s*	Judg 9:16	*8549*
s with Jerubbaal and with his	Judg 9:19	*8549*
Christ of contention, not *s*	Phil 1:16	*55*

SINCERITY

fear the LORD, and serve him in *s*	Josh 24:14	*8549*
with the unleavened bread of *s*	1Cor 5:8	*1505*
that in simplicity and godly *s*	2Cor 1:12	*1505*
but as of *s*, but as of God, in	2Cor 2:17	*1505*
and to prove the *s* of your love	2Cor 8:8	*1103*
love our Lord Jesus Christ in *s*	Eph 6:24	*861*
shewing uncorruptness, gravity, *s*	Titus 2:7	*861*

SINEW

eat not of the *s* which shrank	Gen 32:32	*1517*
thigh in the *s* that shrank	Gen 32:32	*1517*
and thy neck is an iron *s*	Is 48:4	*1517*

SINEWS

and hast fenced me with bones and *s*	Job 10:11	*1517*
and my *s* take no rest	Job 30:17	*6207*
the *s* of his stones are wrapped	Job 40:17	*1517*
And I will lay *s* upon you, and will	Eze 37:6	*1517*
And when I beheld, lo, the *s*	Eze 37:8	*1517*

SINFUL

stead, an increase of *s* men	Num 32:14	*2400*
Ah *s* nation, a people laden with	Is 1:4	*2398*
Lord GOD be upon the *s* kingdom	Amos 9:8	*2401*
this adulterous and *s* generation	Mk 8:38	*268*
for I am a *s* man, O Lord	Lk 5:8	*268*

delivered into the hands of *s* men	Lk 24:7	268
might become exceeding *s*	Rom 7:13	268
Son in the likeness of *s* flesh	Rom 8:3	266

SING

I will *s* unto the LORD, for he	Ex 15:1	7891
S ye to the LORD, for he hath	Ex 15:21	7891
noise of them that *s* do I hear	Ex 32:18	6031
s ye unto it	Num 21:17	6030
I, even I, will *s* unto the LORD	Judg 5:3	7891
I will *s* praise to the LORD God	Judg 5:3	2167
did they not *s* one to another of	1Sa 21:11	6030
S unto him, *s* psalms unto him	1Chr 16:9	7891
S unto the LORD, all the earth	1Chr 16:23	7891
shall the trees of the wood *s* out	1Chr 16:33	7442
And when they began to *s* and to	2Chr 20:22	7440
and such as taught to *s* praise	2Chr 23:13	1984
commanded the Levites to *s* praise	2Chr 29:30	1984
the widow's heart to *s* for joy	Job 29:13	7442
will *s* praise to the name of the	Ps 7:17	
I will *s* praise to thy name, O	Ps 9:2	
S praises to the LORD, which	Ps 9:11	
I will *s* unto the LORD, because	Ps 13:6	7891
and *s* praises unto thy name	Ps 18:49	
so will we *s* and praise thy power	Ps 21:13	7891
I will *s*, yea	Ps 27:6	7891
I will *s* praises unto the LORD	Ps 27:6	2167
S unto the LORD, O ye saints of	Ps 30:4	2167
my glory may *s* praise to thee	Ps 30:12	2167
s unto him with the psaltery and	Ps 33:2	2167
S unto him a new song	Ps 33:3	7891
S praises to God, *s* praises	Ps 47:6	2167
s praises unto our King, *s*	Ps 47:6	2167
s ye praises with understanding	Ps 47:7	2167
my tongue shall *s* aloud of thy	Ps 51:14	7442
I will *s* and give praise	Ps 57:7	7891
I will *s* unto thee among the	Ps 57:9	2167
But I will *s* of thy power	Ps 59:16	7891
I will *s* aloud of thy mercy in	Ps 59:16	7442
thee, O my strength, will I *s*	Ps 59:17	2167
So will I *s* praise unto thy name	Ps 61:8	2167
they shout for joy, they also *s*	Ps 65:13	7891
S forth the honour of his name	Ps 66:2	2167
thee, and shall *s* unto thee	Ps 66:4	2167
they shall *s* to thy name	Ps 66:4	2167
the nations be glad and *s* for joy	Ps 67:4	7442
S unto God	Ps 68:4	7891
s praises to his name	Ps 68:4	2167
S unto God, ye kingdoms of the	Ps 68:32	7891
O *s* praises unto the Lord	Ps 68:32	2167
unto thee will I *s* with the harp	Ps 71:22	2167
rejoice when I *s* unto thee	Ps 71:23	2167
I will *s* praises to the God of	Ps 75:9	
S aloud unto God our strength	Ps 81:1	7442
I will *s* of the mercies of the	Ps 89:1	7891
to *s* praises unto thy name, O	Ps 92:1	2167
O come, let us *s* unto the LORD	Ps 95:1	7442
O *s* unto the LORD a new song	Ps 96:1	7891
s unto the LORD, all the earth	Ps 96:1	7891
S unto the LORD, bless his name	Ps 96:2	7891
O *s* unto the LORD a new song	Ps 98:1	7891
noise, and rejoice, and *s* praise	Ps 98:4	2167
S unto the LORD with the harp	Ps 98:5	2167
I will *s* of mercy and judgment	Ps 101:1	7891
unto thee, O LORD, will I *s*	Ps 101:1	2167
which *s* among the branches	Ps 104:12	5414,6963
I will *s* unto the LORD as long as	Ps 104:33	7891
I will *s* praise to my God while I	Ps 104:33	2167
S unto him	Ps 105:2	7891
s psalms unto him	Ps 105:2	2167
I will *s* and give praise, even	Ps 108:1	7891
I will *s* praises unto thee among	Ps 108:3	2167
s praises unto his name	Ps 135:3	2167
S us one of the songs of Zion	Ps 137:3	7891
How shall we *s* the LORD's song in	Ps 137:4	7891
gods will I *s* praise unto thee	Ps 138:1	2167
they shall *s* in the ways of the	Ps 138:5	7891
I will *s* a new song unto thee, O	Ps 144:9	7891
will I *s* praises unto thee	Ps 144:9	2167
shall *s* of thy righteousness	Ps 145:7	7442
I will *s* praises unto my God	Ps 146:2	2167
for it is good to *s* praises unto	Ps 147:1	2167
S unto the LORD with thanksgiving	Ps 147:7	6030
s praise upon the harp unto our	Ps 147:7	2167
S unto the LORD a new song, and	Ps 149:1	7891
let them *s* praises unto him with	Ps 149:3	2167
let them *s* aloud upon their beds	Ps 149:5	7442
but the righteous doth *s* and	Prov 29:6	7442
Now will I *s* to my wellbeloved a	Is 5:1	7891
S unto the LORD	Is 12:5	2167
years shall Tyre *s* as an harlot	Is 23:15	7892

s many songs, that thou mayest be	Is 23:16	
they shall *s* for the majesty of	Is 24:14	7442
Awake and *s*, ye that dwell in dust	Is 26:19	7442
In that day *s* ye unto her	Is 27:2	6031
hart, and the tongue of the dumb *s*	Is 35:6	7442
therefore we will *s* my songs to	Is 38:20	
S unto the LORD a new song, and	Is 42:10	7891
let the inhabitants of the rock *s*	Is 42:11	7442
S, O ye heavens	Is 44:23	7442
S, O heavens	Is 49:13	7442
the voice together shall they *s*	Is 52:8	7442
s together, ye waste places of	Is 52:9	7442
S, O barren, thou that didst not	Is 54:1	7442
servants shall *s* for joy of heart	Is 65:14	7442
S unto the LORD, praise ye the	Jer 20:13	7891
S with gladness for Jacob, and	Jer 31:7	7442
s in the height of Zion, and shall	Jer 31:12	7442
is therein, shall *s* for Babylon	Jer 51:48	7442
did *s* of thee in thy market	Eze 27:25	7788
and she shall *s* there, as in the	Hos 2:15	6030
voice shall *s* in the windows	Zeph 2:14	7891
S, O daughter of Zion	Zeph 3:14	7442
S and rejoice, O daughter of Zion	Zec 2:10	7442
the Gentiles, and *s* unto thy name	Rom 15:9	5567
I will *s* with the spirit	1Cor 14:15	5567
I will *s* with the understanding	1Cor 14:15	5567
church will I *s* praise unto thee	Heb 2:12	5214
let him *s* psalms	Jas 5:13	5567
they *s* the song of Moses the	Rev 15:3	103

SINGED

nor was an hair of their head *s*	Dan 3:27	2761

SINGER

Heman a *s*, the son of Joel, the	1Chr 6:33	7891
To the chief *s* on my stringed	Hab 3:19	5329

SINGERS

harps also and psalteries for *s*	1Kin 10:12	7891
And these are the *s*, chief of the	1Chr 9:33	7891
their brethren to be the *s* with	1Chr 15:16	7891
So the *s*, Heman, Asaph, and Ethan,	1Chr 15:19	7891
that bare the ark, and the *s*	1Chr 15:27	7891
the master of the song with the *s*	1Chr 15:27	7891
Also the Levites which were the *s*	2Chr 5:12	7891
s were as one, to make one sound	2Chr 5:13	7891
and harps and psalteries for *s*	2Chr 9:11	7891
he appointed *s* unto the LORD, and	2Chr 20:21	7891
also the *s* with instruments of	2Chr 23:13	7891
the *s* sang, and the trumpeters	2Chr 29:28	7892
the *s* the sons of Asaph were in	2Chr 35:15	7891
The *s*: the children of Asaph	Ezr 2:41	7891
and some of the people, and the *s*	Ezr 2:70	7891
priests, and the Levites, and the *s*	Ezr 7:7	7891
any of the priests and Levites, *s*	Ezr 7:24	2171
Of the *s* also	Ezr 10:24	7891
doors, and the porters and the *s*	Neh 7:1	7891
The *s*: the children of Asaph	Neh 7:44	7891
Levites, and the porters, and the *s*	Neh 7:73	7891
the Levites, the porters, the *s*	Neh 10:28	7891
and the porters, and the *s*	Neh 10:39	7891
the *s* were over the business of	Neh 11:22	7891
portion should be for the *s*	Neh 11:23	7891
the sons of the *s* gathered	Neh 12:28	7891
for the *s* had builded them	Neh 12:29	7891
the *s* sang loud, with Jezrahiah	Neh 12:42	7891
And both the *s* and the porters kept	Neh 12:45	7891
of old there were chief of the *s*	Neh 12:46	7891
gave the portions of the *s*	Neh 12:47	7891
be given to the Levites, and the *s*	Neh 13:5	7891
for the Levites and the *s*, that	Neh 13:10	7891
The *s* went before, the players on	Ps 68:25	7891
As well the *s* as the players on	Ps 87:7	7891
I gat me men *s* and women *s*	Eccl 2:8	7891
of the *s* in the inner court	Eze 40:44	7891

SINGETH

so is he that *s* songs to an heavy	Prov 25:20	7891

SINGING

out of all cities of Israel, *s*	1Sa 18:6	7891
voice of *s* men and *s* women	2Sa 19:35	7891
of the congregation with *s*	1Chr 6:32	7892
with all their might, and with *s*	1Chr 13:8	7892
Moses, with rejoicing and with *s*	2Chr 23:18	7892
s with loud instruments unto the	2Chr 30:21	
and all the *s* men and the *s*	2Chr 35:25	7891
hundred *s* men and *s* women	Ezr 2:65	7891
and five *s* men and *s* women	Neh 7:67	7891
with thanksgivings, and with *s*	Neh 12:27	7892
come before his presence with *s*	Ps 100:2	7445
laughter, and our tongue with *s*	Ps 126:2	7440
the time of the *s* of birds is	Song 2:12	2158

S

they break forth into s	Is 14:7	7440
the vineyards there shall be no s	Is 16:10	7442
and rejoice even with joy and s	Is 35:2	7442
break forth into s, ye mountains,	Is 44:23	7440
with a voice of s declare ye	Is 48:20	7440
and break forth into s, O	Is 49:13	7440
return, and come with s unto Zion	Is 51:11	7440
break forth into s, and cry aloud,	Is 54:1	7440
break forth before you into s	Is 55:12	7440
he will joy over thee with s	Zeph 3:17	7440
and hymns and spiritual songs, s	Eph 5:19	103
s with grace in your hearts to	Col 3:16	103

SINGLE
| if therefore thine eye be s | Mt 6:22 | 573 |
| therefore when thine eye is s | Lk 11:34 | 573 |

SINGLENESS
meat with gladness and s of heart,	Acts 2:46	858
in s of your heart, as unto	Eph 6:5	572
but in s of heart, fearing God	Col 3:22	572

SINGULAR
| When a man shall make a s vow | Lev 27:2 | 6381 |

SINIM (si'-nim) An unspecified people.
| and these from the land of S | Is 49:12 | 5515 |

SINITE (si'-nite) A tribe of Canaanites.
| Hivite, and the Arkite, and the S | Gen 10:17 | 5513 |
| Hivite, and the Arkite, and the S | 1Chr 1:15 | 5513 |

SINK
I s in deep mire, where there is	Ps 69:2	2883
out of the mire, and let me not s	Ps 69:14	2883
shalt say, Thus shall Babylon s	Jer 51:64	8257
and beginning to s, he cried,	Mt 14:30	2670
ships, so that they began to s	Lk 5:7	1036
Let these sayings s down into	Lk 9:44	5087

SINNED
unto them, I have s this time	Ex 9:27	2398
he s yet more, and hardened his	Ex 9:34	2398
I have s against the LORD your	Ex 10:16	2398
the people, Ye have s a great sin	Ex 32:30	2398
this people have s a great sin	Ex 32:31	2398
Whosoever hath s against me	Ex 32:33	2398
for his sin, which he hath s	Lev 4:3	2398
sin, which they have s against it	Lev 4:14	2398
When a ruler hath s, and done	Lev 4:22	2398
Or if his sin, wherein he hath s	Lev 4:23	2398
Or if his sin, which he hath s	Lev 4:28	2398
for his sin which he hath s	Lev 4:28	2398
that he hath s in that thing	Lev 5:5	2398
LORD for his sin which he hath s	Lev 5:6	2398
him for his sin which he hath s	Lev 5:10	2398
then he that s shall bring for	Lev 5:11	2398
that he hath s in one of these	Lev 5:13	2398
it shall be, because he hath s	Lev 6:4	2398
him, for that he s by the dead	Num 6:11	2398
foolishly, and wherein we have s	Num 12:11	2398
for we have s	Num 14:40	2398
came to Moses, and said, We have s	Num 21:7	2398
the angel of the LORD, I have s	Num 22:34	2398
ye have s against the LORD	Num 32:23	2398
We have s against the LORD, we	Deut 1:41	2398
ye had s against the LORD your	Deut 9:16	2398
of all your sins which ye s	Deut 9:18	2398
Israel hath s, and they have also	Josh 7:11	2398
Indeed I have s against the LORD	Josh 7:20	2398
We have s against thee, both	Judg 10:10	2398
said unto the LORD, We have s	Judg 10:15	2398
I have not s against thee	Judg 11:27	2398
We have s against the LORD	1Sa 7:6	2398
unto the LORD, and said, We have s	1Sa 12:10	2398
Saul said unto Samuel, I have s	1Sa 15:24	2398
Then he said, I have s	1Sa 15:30	2398
he hath not s against thee	1Sa 19:4	2398
I have not s against thee	1Sa 24:11	2398
Then said Saul, I have s	1Sa 26:21	2398
I have s against the LORD	2Sa 12:13	2398
servant doth know that I have s	2Sa 19:20	2398
I have s greatly in that I have	2Sa 24:10	2398
the people, and said, Lo, I have s	2Sa 24:17	2398
because they have s against thee	1Kin 8:33	2398
because they have s against thee	1Kin 8:35	2398
them captives, saying, We have s	1Kin 8:47	2398
people that have s against thee	1Kin 8:50	2398
the sins of Jeroboam which he s	1Kin 15:30	2398
of Elah his son, by which they s	1Kin 16:13	2398
For his sins which he s in doing	1Kin 16:19	2398
And he said, What have I s	1Kin 18:9	2398
had s against the LORD their God	2Kin 17:7	2398
that he did, and his sin that he s	2Kin 21:17	2398

I have s greatly, because I have	1Chr 21:8	2398
even I it is that have s and done	1Chr 21:17	2398
because they have s against thee	2Chr 6:24	2398
because they have s against thee	2Chr 6:26	2398
captivity, saying, We have s	2Chr 6:37	2398
people which have s against thee	2Chr 6:39	2398
which we have s against thee	Neh 1:6	2398
I and my father's house have s	Neh 1:6	2398
but s against thy judgments,	Neh 9:29	2398
It may be that my sons have s	Job 1:5	2398
In all this Job s not, nor	Job 1:22	2398
I have s	Job 7:20	2398
thy children have s against him	Job 8:4	2398
doth the grave those which have s	Job 24:19	2398
upon men, and if any say, I have s	Job 33:27	2398
for I have s against thee	Ps 41:4	2398
Against thee, thee only, have I s	Ps 51:4	2398
they s yet more against him by	Ps 78:17	2398
For all this they s still	Ps 78:32	2398
We have s with our fathers, we	Ps 106:6	2398
LORD, he against whom we have s	Is 42:24	2398
Thy first father hath s, and thy	Is 43:27	2398
for we have s	Is 64:5	2398
because thou sayest, I have not s	Jer 2:35	2398
for we have s against the LORD	Jer 3:25	2398
because we have s against the	Jer 8:14	2398
we have s against thee	Jer 14:7	2398
for we have s against thee	Jer 14:20	2398
whereby they have s against me	Jer 33:8	2398
iniquities, whereby they have s	Jer 33:8	2398
because ye have s against the	Jer 40:3	2398
because ye have s against the	Jer 44:23	2398
they have s against the LORD	Jer 50:7	2398
for she hath s against the LORD	Jer 50:14	2398
Jerusalem hath grievously s	Lam 1:8	2398
Our fathers have s, and are not	Lam 5:7	2398
woe unto us, that we have s	Lam 5:16	2398
and in his sin that he hath s	Eze 18:24	2398
with violence, and thou hast s	Eze 28:16	2398
wherein they have s, and will	Eze 37:23	2398
We have s, and have committed	Dan 9:5	2398
because we have s against thee	Dan 9:8	2398
because we have s against the	Dan 9:11	2398
we have s, we have done wickedly	Dan 9:15	2398
increased, so they s against me	Hos 4:7	2398
thou hast s from the days of	Hos 10:9	2398
because I have s against him	Mic 7:9	2398
and hast s against thy soul	Hab 2:10	2398
they have s against the LORD	Zeph 1:17	2398
I have s in that I have betrayed	Mt 27:4	264
I have s against heaven, and	Lk 15:18	264
I have s against heaven, and in	Lk 15:21	264
answered, Neither hath this man s	Jn 9:3	264
For as many as have s without law	Rom 2:12	264
as many as have s in the law	Rom 2:12	264
For all have s, and come short of	Rom 3:23	264
upon all men, for that all have s	Rom 5:12	264
even over them that had not s	Rom 5:14	264
And not as it was by one that s	Rom 5:16	264
and if thou marry, thou hast not s	1Cor 7:28	264
if a virgin marry, she hath not s	1Cor 7:28	264
bewail many which have s already	2Cor 12:21	4258
to them which heretofore have s	2Cor 13:2	4258
was it not with them that had s	Heb 3:17	264
God spared not the angels that s	2Pet 2:4	264
If we say that we have not s	1Jn 1:10	264

SINNER
much more the wicked and the s	Prov 11:31	2398
but wickedness overthroweth the s	Prov 13:6	2403
the wealth of the s is laid up	Prov 13:22	2398
but to the s he giveth travail,	Eccl 2:26	2398
but the s shall be taken by her	Eccl 7:26	2398
Though a s do evil an hundred	Eccl 8:12	2398
as is the good, so is the s	Eccl 9:2	2398
but one s destroyeth much good	Eccl 9:18	2398
but the s being an hundred years	Is 65:20	2398
woman in the city, which was a s	Lk 7:37	268
for she is a s	Lk 7:39	268
heaven over one s that repenteth	Lk 15:7	268
of God over one s that repenteth	Lk 15:10	268
saying, God be merciful to me a s	Lk 18:13	268
be guest with a man that is a s	Lk 19:7	268
man that is a s do such miracles	Jn 9:16	268
we know that this man is a s	Jn 9:24	268
and said, Whether he be a s or no	Jn 9:25	268
why yet am I also judged as a s	Rom 3:7	268
that he which converteth the s	Jas 5:20	268
shall the ungodly and the s appear	1Pet 4:18	268

SINNERS

s before the LORD exceedingly	Gen 13:13	2400
The censers of these *s* against	Num 16:38	2400
destroy the *s* the Amalekites	1Sa 15:18	2400
nor standeth in the way of *s*	Ps 1:1	2400
nor *s* in the congregation of the	Ps 1:5	2400
will he teach *s* in the way	Ps 25:8	2400
Gather not my soul with *s*	Ps 26:9	2400
s shall be converted unto thee	Ps 51:13	2400
Let the *s* be consumed out of the	Ps 104:35	2400
if *s* entice thee, consent thou	Prov 1:10	2400
Evil pursueth *s*	Prov 13:21	2400
Let not thine heart envy *s*	Prov 23:17	2400
of the *s* shall be together, and	Is 1:28	2400
destroy the *s* thereof out of it	Is 13:9	2400
The *s* in Zion are afraid	Is 33:14	2400
All the *s* of my people shall die	Amos 9:10	2400
s came and sat down with him and	Mt 9:10	268
your Master with publicans and *s*	Mt 9:11	268
righteous, but *s* to repentance	Mt 9:13	268
a friend of publicans and *s*	Mt 11:19	268
is betrayed into the hands of *s*	Mt 26:45	268
s sat also together with Jesus and	Mk 2:15	268
saw him eat with publicans and s	Mk 2:16	268
and drinketh with publicans and s	Mk 2:16	268
righteous, but *s* to repentance	Mk 2:17	268
is betrayed into the hands of *s*	Mk 14:41	268
eat and drink with publicans and *s*	Lk 5:30	268
righteous, but *s* to repentance	Lk 5:32	268
for *s* also love those that love	Lk 6:32	268
for *s* also do even the same	Lk 6:33	268
for *s* also lend to *s*	Lk 6:34	268
a friend of publicans and *s*	Lk 7:34	268
were *s* above all the Galilaeans	Lk 13:2	268
think ye that they were *s* above	Lk 13:4	3781
publicans and *s* for to hear him	Lk 15:1	268
saying, This man receiveth *s*	Lk 15:2	268
we know that God heareth not *s*	Jn 9:31	268
us, in that, while we were yet *s*	Rom 5:8	268
disobedience many were made *s*	Rom 5:19	268
nature, and not *s* of the Gentiles,	Gal 2:15	268
we ourselves also are found *s*	Gal 2:17	268
for the ungodly and for *s*	1Ti 1:9	268
came into the world to save *s*	1Ti 1:15	268
undefiled, separate from *s*	Heb 7:26	268
of *s* against himself, lest ye be	Heb 12:3	268
Cleanse your hands, ye *s*	Jas 4:8	268
ungodly *s* have spoken against him	Jude 15	268

SINNEST

If thou *s*, what doest thou	Job 35:6	2398

SINNETH

for the soul that *s* ignorantly	Num 15:28	7683
when he *s* by ignorance before the	Num 15:28	2398
for him that *s* through ignorance	Num 15:29	6213
for any sin, in any sin that he *s*	Deut 19:15	2398
(for there is no man that *s* not	1Kin 8:46	2398
(for there is no man which *s* not	2Chr 6:36	2398
But he that *s* against me wrongeth	Prov 8:36	2398
He that despiseth his neighbour *s*	Prov 14:21	2398
he that hasteth with his feet *s*	Prov 19:2	2398
to anger *s* against his own soul	Prov 20:2	2398
earth, that doeth good, and *s* not	Eccl 7:20	2398
when the land *s* against me by	Eze 14:13	2398
the soul that *s*, it shall die	Eze 18:4	2398
The soul that *s*, it shall die	Eze 18:20	2398
in the day that he *s*	Eze 33:12	2398
s against his own body	1Cor 6:18	264
let him do what he will, he *s* not	1Cor 7:36	264
that is such is subverted, and *s*	Titus 3:11	264
Whosoever abideth in him *s* not	1Jn 3:6	264
whosoever *s* hath not seen him,	1Jn 3:6	264
for the devil *s* from the	1Jn 3:8	264
whosoever is born of God *s* not	1Jn 5:18	264

SINNING

withheld thee from *s* against me	Gen 20:6	2398
these that a man doeth, *s* therein	Lev 6:3	2398

SINS

transgressions in all their *s*	Lev 16:16	2403
transgressions in all their *s*	Lev 16:21	2403
from all your *s* before the LORD	Lev 16:30	2403
for all their *s* once a year	Lev 16:34	2403
you seven times more for your *s*	Lev 26:18	2403
upon you according to your *s*	Lev 26:21	2403
you yet seven times for your *s*	Lev 26:24	2403
you seven times for your *s*	Lev 26:28	2403
ye be consumed in all their *s*	Num 16:26	2403
of all your *s* which ye sinned	Deut 9:18	2403
your transgressions nor your *s*	Josh 24:19	2403
added unto all our *s* this evil	1Sa 12:19	2403

up because of the *s* of Jeroboam	1Kin 14:16	2403
their *s* which they had committed	1Kin 14:22	2403
walked in all the *s* of his father	1Kin 15:3	2403
Because of the *s* of Jeroboam	1Kin 15:30	2403
provoke me to anger with their *s*	1Kin 16:2	2403
For all the *s* of Baasha, and the	1Kin 16:13	2403
the *s* of Elah his son, by which	1Kin 16:13	2403
For his *s* which he sinned in	1Kin 16:19	2403
s of Jeroboam the son of Nebat	1Kin 16:31	2403
he cleaved unto the *s* of Jeroboam	2Kin 3:3	2403
Howbeit from the *s* of Jeroboam	2Kin 10:29	2399
not from the *s* of Jeroboam	2Kin 10:31	2403
followed the *s* of Jeroboam the	2Kin 13:2	2403
the *s* of the house of Jeroboam	2Kin 13:6	2403
s of Jeroboam the son of Nebat	2Kin 13:11	2403
s of Jeroboam the son of Nebat	2Kin 14:24	2403
he departed not from the *s* of	2Kin 15:9	2403
not all his days from the *s* of	2Kin 15:18	2403
he departed not from the *s* of	2Kin 15:24	2403
he departed not from the *s* of	2Kin 15:28	2403
the *s* of Jeroboam which he did	2Kin 17:22	2403
for the *s* of Manasseh, according	2Kin 24:3	2403
s against the LORD your God	2Chr 28:10	819
ye intend to add more to our *s*	2Chr 28:13	2403
confess the *s* of the children of	Neh 1:6	2403
and stood and confessed their *s*	Neh 9:2	2403
hast set over us because of our *s*	Neh 9:37	2403
How many are mine iniquities and *s*	Job 13:23	2403
servant also from presumptuous *s*	Ps 19:13	
Remember not the *s* of my youth	Ps 25:7	2403
and forgive all my *s*	Ps 25:18	2403
Hide thy face from my *s*, and blot	Ps 51:9	2399
my *s* are not hid from thee	Ps 69:5	819
deliver us, and purge away our *s*	Ps 79:9	2403
our secret *s* in the light of thy	Ps 90:8	
not dealt with us after our *s*	Ps 103:10	2399
be holden with the cords of his *s*	Prov 5:22	2403
but love covereth all *s*	Prov 10:12	6588
covereth his *s* shall not prosper	Prov 28:13	6588
though your *s* be as scarlet, they	Is 1:18	2399
cast all my *s* behind thy back	Is 38:17	2399
LORD's hand double for all her *s*	Is 40:2	2403
hast made me to serve with thy *s*	Is 43:24	2403
sake, and will not remember thy *s*	Is 43:25	2403
and, as a cloud, thy *s*	Is 44:22	2403
and the house of Jacob their *s*	Is 58:1	2403
your *s* have hid his face from you	Is 59:2	2403
thee, and our *s* testify against us	Is 59:12	2403
your *s* have withholden good	Jer 5:25	2403
their iniquity, and visit their *s*	Jer 14:10	2403
price, and that for all thy *s*	Jer 15:13	2403
because thy *s* were increased	Jer 30:14	2403
because thy *s* were increased, I	Jer 30:15	2403
the *s* of Judah, and they shall not	Jer 50:20	2403
a man for the punishment of his *s*	Lam 3:39	2399
For the *s* of her prophets, and the	Lam 4:13	2403
he will discover thy *s*	Lam 4:22	2403
Samaria committed half of thy *s*	Eze 16:51	2403
bear thine own shame for thy *s*	Eze 16:52	2403
his father's *s* which he hath done	Eze 18:14	2403
all his *s* that he hath committed	Eze 18:21	2403
all your doings your *s* do appear	Eze 21:24	2403
ye shall bear the *s* of your idols	Eze 23:49	2399
our *s* be upon us, and we pine away	Eze 33:10	2403
None of his *s* that he hath	Eze 33:16	2403
break off thy *s* by righteousness,	Dan 4:27	2408
because for our *s*, and for the	Dan 9:16	2399
and to make an end of *s*, and to	Dan 9:24	2403
their iniquity, and visit their *s*	Hos 8:13	2403
iniquity, he will visit their *s*	Hos 9:9	2403
transgressions and your mighty *s*	Amos 5:12	2403
for the *s* of the house of Israel	Mic 1:5	2403
thee desolate because of thy *s*	Mic 6:13	2403
thou wilt cast all their *s* into	Mic 7:19	2403
save his people from their *s*	Mt 1:21	266
him in Jordan, confessing their *s*	Mt 3:6	266
thy *s* be forgiven thee	Mt 9:2	266
to say, Thy *s* be forgiven thee	Mt 9:5	266
hath power on earth to forgive *s*	Mt 9:6	266
for many for the remission of *s*	Mt 26:28	266
repentance for the remission of *s*	Mk 1:4	266
of Jordan, confessing their *s*	Mk 1:5	266
Son, thy *s* be forgiven thee	Mk 2:5	266
who can forgive *s* but God only	Mk 2:7	266
the palsy, Thy *s* be forgiven thee	Mk 2:9	266
hath power on earth to forgive *s*	Mk 2:10	266
All *s* shall be forgiven unto the	Mk 3:28	265
their *s* should be forgiven them	Mk 4:12	265
by the remission of their *s*	Lk 1:77	266
repentance for the remission of *s*	Lk 3:3	266
him, Man, thy *s* are forgiven thee	Lk 5:20	266

S

Who can forgive s, but God alone	Lk 5:21	266
to say, Thy s be forgiven thee	Lk 5:23	266
power upon earth to forgive s	Lk 5:24	266
Wherefore I say unto thee, Her s	Lk 7:47	266
said unto her, Thy s are forgiven	Lk 7:48	266
Who is this that forgiveth s also	Lk 7:49	266
And forgive us our s	Lk 11:4	266
remission of s should be preached	Lk 24:47	266
seek me, and shall die in your s	Jn 8:21	266
you, that ye shall die in your s	Jn 8:24	266
I am he, ye shall die in your s	Jn 8:24	266
Thou wast altogether born in s	Jn 9:34	266
Whose soever s ye remit, they are	Jn 20:23	266
and whose soever s ye retain	Jn 20:23	266
Christ for the remission of s	Acts 2:38	266
that your s may be blotted out,	Acts 3:19	266
to Israel, and forgiveness of s	Acts 5:31	266
him shall receive remission of s	Acts 10:43	266
unto you the forgiveness of s	Acts 13:38	266
be baptized, and wash away thy s	Acts 22:16	266
they may receive forgiveness of s	Acts 26:18	266
the remission of s that are past	Rom 3:25	265
forgiven, and whose s are covered	Rom 4:7	266
in the flesh, the motions of s	Rom 7:5	266
when I shall take away their s	Rom 11:27	266
our s according to the scriptures	1Cor 15:3	266
ye are yet in your s	1Cor 15:17	266
Who gave himself for our s	Gal 1:4	266
his blood, the forgiveness of s	Eph 1:7	3900
who were dead in trespasses and s	Eph 2:1	266
Even when we were dead in s	Eph 2:5	3900
blood, even the forgiveness of s	Col 1:14	266
body of the s of the flesh by the	Col 2:11	266
And you, being dead in your s	Col 2:13	3900
saved, to fill up their s alway	1Th 2:16	266
be partaker of other men's s	1Ti 5:22	266
Some men's s are open beforehand,	1Ti 5:24	266
captive silly women laden with s	2Ti 3:6	266
he had by himself purged our s	Heb 1:3	266
for the s of the people	Heb 2:17	266
both gifts and sacrifices for s	Heb 5:1	266
also for himself, to offer for s	Heb 5:3	266
up sacrifice, first for his own s	Heb 7:27	266
their unrighteousness, and their s	Heb 8:12	266
offered to bear the s of many	Heb 9:28	266
have had no more conscience of s	Heb 10:2	266
again made of s every year	Heb 10:3	266
and of goats should take away s	Heb 10:4	266
which can never take away s	Heb 10:11	266
one sacrifice for s for ever	Heb 10:12	266
And their s and iniquities will I	Heb 10:17	266
remaineth no more sacrifice for s	Heb 10:26	266
and if he have committed s	Jas 5:15	266
and shall hide a multitude of s	Jas 5:20	266
Who his own self bare our s in	1Pet 2:24	266
tree, that we, being dead to s	1Pet 2:24	266
also hath once suffered for s	1Pet 3:18	266
shall cover the multitude of s	1Pet 4:8	266
that he was purged from his old s	2Pet 1:9	266
If we confess our s, he is	1Jn 1:9	266
and just to forgive us our s	1Jn 1:9	266
he is the propitiation for our s	1Jn 2:2	266
but also for the s of the whole	1Jn 2:2	
because your s are forgiven you	1Jn 2:12	266
was manifested to take away our s	1Jn 3:5	266
to be the propitiation for our s	1Jn 4:10	266
us from our s in his own blood	Rev 1:5	266
that ye be not partakers of her s	Rev 18:4	266
For her s have reached unto	Rev 18:5	266

SION (si'-on) See SHENIR, SIRION, ZION.
 1. The peak of Mount Hermon.

even unto mount S which is Hermon	Deut 4:48	7865

 2. A district of Jerusalem.

waiteth for thee, O God in S	Ps 65:1	6726
Tell ye the daughter of S	Mt 21:5	4622
Fear not, daughter of S	Jn 12:15	4622
I lay in S a stumblingstone and	Rom 9:33	4622
shall come out of S the Deliverer	Rom 11:26	4622
But ye are come unto mount S	Heb 12:22	4622
I lay in S a chief corner stone,	1Pet 2:6	4622
lo, a Lamb stood on the mount S	Rev 14:1	4622

SIPHMOTH (sif'-moth) A city in Judah.

Aroer, and to them which were in S	1Sa 30:28	8224

SIPPAI (sip'-pahee) See SAPH. Son of Rapha.

Sibbechai the Hushathite slew S	1Chr 20:4	5598

SIR

And said, O s, we came indeed down	Gen 43:20	113
came and said unto him, S, didst	Mt 13:27	2962
And he answered and said, I go s	Mt 21:30	2962

Saying, S, we remember that that	Mt 27:63	2962
The woman saith unto him, S	Jn 4:11	2962
The woman saith unto him, S	Jn 4:15	2962
The woman saith unto him, S	Jn 4:19	2962
The nobleman saith unto him, S	Jn 4:49	2962
The impotent man answered him, S	Jn 5:7	2962
and desired him, saying, S	Jn 12:21	2962
the gardener, saith unto him, S	Jn 20:15	2962
And I said unto him, S, thou	Rev 7:14	2962

SIRAH (si'-rah) A well near Hebron.

him again from the well of S	2Sa 3:26	5626

SIRION (sir'-e-on) See HERMON. A Sidonian name for
    Mount Hermon.

Which Hermon the Sidonians call S	Deut 3:9	8304
Lebanon and S like a young unicorn	Ps 29:6	8304

SIRS

set them at one again, saying, S	Acts 7:26	435
And saying, S, why do ye these	Acts 14:15	435
And brought them out, and said, S	Acts 16:30	2962
of like occupation, and said, S	Acts 19:25	435
And said unto them, S, I perceive	Acts 27:10	435
in the midst of them, and said, S	Acts 27:21	435
Wherefore, s, be of good cheer	Acts 27:25	435

SISAMAI (sis'-a-mahee) Son of Eleasah.

And Eleasah begat S	1Chr 2:40	5581
and S begat Shallum	1Chr 2:40	5581

SISERA (sis'-e-rah)
 1. A captain in the Canaanite army.

the captain of whose host was S	Judg 4:2	5516
unto thee to the river Kishon, S	Judg 4:7	5516
for the LORD shall sell S into	Judg 4:9	5516
they shewed S that Barak the son	Judg 4:12	5516
S gathered together all his	Judg 4:13	5516
hath delivered S into thine hand	Judg 4:14	5516
And the LORD discomfited S	Judg 4:15	5516
so that S lighted down off his	Judg 4:15	5516
all the host of S fell upon the	Judg 4:16	5516
Howbeit S fled away on his feet	Judg 4:17	5516
And Jael went out to meet S	Judg 4:18	5516
And, behold, as Barak pursued S	Judg 4:22	5516
S lay dead, and the nail was in	Judg 4:22	5516
in their courses fought against S	Judg 5:20	5516
and with the hammer she smote S	Judg 5:26	5516
The mother of S looked out at a	Judg 5:28	5516
to S a prey of divers colours, a	Judg 5:30	5516
he sold them into the hand of S	1Sa 12:9	5516
as to S, as to Jabin, at the	Ps 83:9	5516

 2. A family of exiles.

of Barkos, the children of S	Ezr 2:53	5516
of Barkos, the children of S	Neh 7:55	5516

SISMAI See SISAMAI.

SISTER

the s of Tubal-cain was Naamah	Gen 4:22	269
Say, I pray thee, thou art my s	Gen 12:13	269
Why saidst thou, She is my s	Gen 12:19	269
of Sarah his wife, She is my s	Gen 20:2	269
Said he not unto me, She is my s	Gen 20:5	269
And yet indeed she is my s	Gen 20:12	269
heard the words of Rebekah his s	Gen 24:30	269
And they sent away Rebekah their s	Gen 24:59	269
and said unto her, Thou art our s	Gen 24:60	269
the s to Laban the Syrian	Gen 25:20	269
and he said, She is my s	Gen 26:7	269
and how saidst thou, She is my s	Gen 26:9	269
the s of Nebajoth, to be his wife	Gen 28:9	269
no children, Rachel envied her s	Gen 30:1	269
have I wrestled with my s	Gen 30:8	269
he had defiled Dinah their s	Gen 34:13	269
to give our s to one that is	Gen 34:14	269
because they had defiled their s	Gen 34:27	269
deal with our s as with an harlot	Gen 34:31	269
Ishmael's daughter, s of Nebajoth	Gen 36:3	269
and Lotan's s was Timna	Gen 36:22	269
Isui, and Beriah, and Serah their s	Gen 46:17	269
his s stood afar off, to wit what	Ex 2:4	269
Then said his s to Pharaoh's	Ex 2:7	269
Jochebed his father's s to wife	Ex 6:20	1733
Amminadab, s of Naashon, to wife	Ex 6:23	269
the s of Aaron, took a timbrel in	Ex 15:20	269
The nakedness of thy s, the	Lev 18:9	269
of thy father, she is thy s	Lev 18:11	269
the nakedness of thy father's s	Lev 18:12	269
the nakedness of thy mother's s	Lev 18:13	269
shalt thou take a wife to her s	Lev 18:18	269
And if a man shall take his s	Lev 20:17	269
the nakedness of thy mother's s	Lev 20:19	269
nor of thy father's s	Lev 20:19	269

for his *s* a virgin, that is nigh.................. Lev 21:3   269
for his brother, or for his *s* .... Num 6:7   269
of a prince of Midian, their *s* .... Num 25:18   269
Aaron and Moses, and Miriam their *s* .. Num 26:59   269
be he that lieth with his *s* .... Deut 27:22   269
not her younger *s* fairer than she........... Judg 15:2   269
thy *s* in law is gone back unto .... Ruth 1:15   2994
return thou after thy *s* in law .... Ruth 1:15   2994
the son of David had a fair *s* 2Sa 13:1   269
that he fell sick for his *s* Tamar 2Sa 13:2   269
Tamar, my brother Absalom's *s* 2Sa 13:4   269
let my *s* Tamar come, and give me 2Sa 13:5   269
I pray thee, let Tamar my *s* come 2Sa 13:6   269
unto her, Come lie with me, my *s* 2Sa 13:11   269
but hold now thy peace, my *s* 2Sa 13:20   269
because he had forced his *s* Tamar 2Sa 13:22   269
day that he forced his *s* Tamar 2Sa 13:32   269
s to Zeruiah Joab's mother 2Sa 17:25   269
him to wife the *s* of his own wife 1Kin 11:19   269
the *s* of Tahpenes the queen 1Kin 11:19   269
the *s* of Tahpenes bare him 1Kin 11:20   269
s of Ahaziah, took Joash the son 2Kin 11:2   269
and Timna was Lotan's *s* 1Chr 1:39   269
the concubines, and Tamar their *s* 1Chr 3:9   269
and Hananiah, and Shelomith their *s* 1Chr 3:19   269
name of their *s* was Hazelelponi 1Chr 4:3   269
of his wife Hodiah the *s* of Naham 1Chr 4:19   269
took to wife the *s* of Huppim 1Chr 7:15   269
his *s* Hammoleketh bare Ishod, and 1Chr 7:18   269
and Beriah, and Serah their *s* 1Chr 7:30   269
and Hotham, and Shua their *s* 1Chr 7:32   269
(for she was the *s* of Ahaziah 2Chr 22:11   269
worm, Thou art my mother, and my *s* .... Job 17:14   269
Say unto wisdom, Thou art my *s* .... Prov 7:4   269
Thou hast ravished my heart, my *s* .... Song 4:9   269
How fair is thy love, my *s* .... Song 4:10   269
A garden inclosed is my *s* .... Song 4:12   269
I am come into my garden, my *s* .... Song 5:1   269
saying, Open to me, my *s* .... Song 5:2   269
We have a little *s*, and she hath .... Song 8:8   269
what shall we do for our *s* in the .... Song 8:8   269
And her treacherous *s* Judah saw it .... Jer 3:7   269
treacherous *s* Judah feared not .... Jer 3:8   269
for all this her treacherous *s* .... Jer 3:10   269
my brother! or, Ah *s*! .... Jer 22:18   269
thou art the *s* of thy sisters, ... Eze 16:45   269
And thine elder *s* is Samaria .... Eze 16:46   269
and thy younger *s*, that dwelleth .... Eze 16:46   269
Sodom thy *s* hath not done, she .... Eze 16:48   269
was the iniquity of thy *s* Sodom .... Eze 16:49   269
For thy *s* Sodom was not mentioned ...... Eze 16:56   269
in thee hath humbled her *s* .... Eze 22:11   269
the elder, and Aholibah her *s* .... Eze 23:4   269
when her *s* Aholibah saw this, she .... Eze 23:11   269
more than her *s* in her whoredoms .... Eze 23:11   269
my mind was alienated from her *s* .... Eze 23:18   269
hast walked in the way of thy *s* .... Eze 23:31   269
with the cup of thy *s* Samaria .... Eze 23:33   269
or for *s* that hath had no husband.......... Eze 44:25   269
the same is my brother, and *s* .... Mt 12:50   79
the same is my brother, and my *s* ...... Mk 3:35   79
she had a *s* called Mary, which .... Lk 10:39   79
dost thou not care that my *s* hath .... Lk 10:40   79
the town of Mary and her *s* Martha .... Jn 11:1   79
Now Jesus loved Martha, and her *s* .... Jn 11:5   79
and called Mary her *s* secretly .... Jn 11:28   79
the *s* of him that was dead, saith........... Jn 11:39   79
his mother, and his mother's *s* .... Jn 19:25   79
I commend unto you Phebe our *s* .... Rom 16:1   79
and Julia, Nereus, and his *s* .... Rom 16:15   79
A brother or a *s* is not under 1Cor 7:15   79
we not power to lead about a *s* 1Cor 9:5   79
If a brother or *s* be naked .... Jas 2:15   79
of thy elect *s* greet thee 2Jn 13   79

SISTER'S

and bracelets upon his *s* hands .... Gen 24:30   269
the tidings of Jacob his *s* son .... Gen 29:13   269
he hath uncovered his *s* nakedness .... Lev 20:17   269
Shuppim, whose *s* name was Maachah . 1Chr 7:15   269
shalt drink of thy *s* cup deep................. Eze 23:32   269
when Paul's *s* son heard of their .... Acts 23:16   79
s son to Barnabas, (touching whom........ Col 4:10   431

SISTERS

mother, and my brethren, and my *s* .... Josh 2:13   269
Whose *s* were Zeruiah, and Abigail 1Chr 2:16   269
called for their three *s* to eat .... Job 1:4   269
all his brethren, and all his *s* .... Job 42:11   269
and thou art the sister of thy *s*.............. Eze 16:45   269
hast justified thy *s* in all thine .... Eze 16:51   269
also, which hast judged thy *s*................ Eze 16:52   269

in that thou hast justified thy *s* .... Eze 16:52   269
When thy *s*, Sodom and her .... Eze 16:55   269
when thou shalt receive thy *s* .... Eze 16:61   269
and to your *s*, Ruhamah........................ Hos 2:1   269
And his *s*, are they not all with.............. Mt 13:56   79
houses, or brethren, or *s*.................... Mt 19:29   79
are not his *s* here with us .... Mk 6:3   79
left house, or brethren, or *s*............... Mk 10:29   79
time, houses, and brethren, and *s* ..... Mk 10:30   79
and children, and brethren, and *s* ...... Lk 14:26   79
Therefore his *s* sent unto him .... Jn 11:3   79
the younger as *s*, with all purity 1Ti 5:2   79

SIT

arise, I pray thee, *s* and eat of .... Gen 27:19   3427
go to war, and shall ye *s* here .... Num 32:6   3427
ye that *s* in judgment, and walk by........ Judg 5:10   3427
S still, my daughter, until thou .... Ruth 3:18   3427
turn aside, *s* down here......................... Ruth 4:1   3427
the city, and said, *S* ye down here......... Ruth 4:2   3427
made them *s* in the chiefest place 1Sa 9:22   5414
for we will not *s* down till he 1Sa 16:11   5437
I should not fail to *s* with the 1Sa 20:5   3427
the king doth *s* in the gate 2Sa 19:8   3427
he shall *s* upon my throne 1Kin 1:13   3427
he shall *s* upon my throne 1Kin 1:17   3427
s on the throne of my lord the 1Kin 1:20   3427
he shall *s* upon my throne 1Kin 1:24   3427
who should *s* on the throne of my 1Kin 1:27   3427
he shall *s* upon my throne in my 1Kin 1:30   3427
he may come and *s* upon my throne....... 1Kin 1:35   3427
one to *s* on my throne this day 1Kin 1:48   3427
him a son to *s* on his throne 1Kin 3:6   3427
s on the throne of Israel, as the 1Kin 8:20   3427
to *s* on the throne of Israel 1Kin 8:25   3427
Why *s* we here until we die 2Kin 7:3   3427
if we *s* still here, we die also................. 2Kin 7:4   3427
shall *s* on the throne of Israel 2Kin 10:30   3427
Thy sons shall *s* on the throne of 2Kin 15:12   3427
me to the men which *s* on the wall 2Kin 18:27   3427
hath chosen Solomon my son to *s*.......... 1Chr 28:5   3427
to *s* upon the throne of Israel 2Chr 6:16   3427
will not *s* with the wicked...................... Ps 26:5   3427
They that *s* in the gate speak .... Ps 69:12   3427
Such as *s* in darkness and in the........... Ps 107:10   3427
S thou at my right hand, until I .... Ps 110:1   3427
Princes also did *s* and speak................. Ps 119:23   3427
to *s* up late, to eat the bread of.............. Ps 127:2   3427
their children shall also *s* upon.............. Ps 132:12   3427
and the rich *s* in low place .... Eccl 10:6   3427
desolate shall *s* upon the ground .... Is 3:26   3427
I will also upon the mount of................... Is 14:13   3427
he shall *s* upon it in truth in .... Is 16:5   3427
Their strength is to *s* still .... Is 30:7   7674
to the men that *s* upon the wall .... Is 36:12   3427
them that *s* in darkness out of............... Is 42:7   3427
s in the dust, O virgin daughter .... Is 47:1   3427
of Babylon, *s* on the ground................... Is 47:1   3427
S thou silent, and get thee into .... Is 47:5   3427
I shall not *s* as a widow, neither .... Is 47:8   3427
warm at, nor fire to *s* before it .... Is 47:14   3427
arise, and *s* down, O Jerusalem .... Is 52:2   3427
Why do we *s* still .... Jer 8:14   3427
kings that *s* upon David's throne .... Jer 13:13   3427
queen, Humble yourselves, *s* down......... Jer 13:18   3427
to *s* with them to eat and to drink.......... Jer 16:8   3427
s upon the throne of the house of .... Jer 33:17   3427
S down now, and read it in our .... Jer 36:15   3427
He shall have none to *s* upon the........... Jer 36:30   3427
from thy glory, and *s* in thirst .... Jer 48:18   3427
How doth the city *s* solitary .... Lam 1:1   3427
of Zion *s* upon the ground .... Lam 2:10   3427
they shall *s* upon the ground, and .... Eze 26:16   3427
I *s* in the seat of God, in the.................. Eze 28:2   3427
they *s* before thee as my people,........... Eze 33:31   3427
he shall *s* in it to eat bread .... Eze 44:3   3427
and the Ancient of days did *s* .... Dan 7:9   3488
But the judgment shall *s*, and they .... Dan 7:26   3488
for there will I *s* to judge all .... Joel 3:12   3427
But they shall *s* every man under .... Mic 4:4   3427
when I *s* in darkness, the LORD .... Mic 7:8   3427
and thy fellows that *s* before thee .... Zec 3:8   3427
shall bear the glory, and shall *s*............. Zec 6:13   3427
he shall *s* as a refiner and .... Mal 3:3   3427
shall *s* down with Abraham, and .... Mt 8:11   347
multitude to *s* down on the grass........... Mt 14:19   347
multitude to *s* down on the ground .... Mt 15:35   377
when the Son of man shall *s* in .... Mt 19:28   2523
ye also shall *s* upon twelve .... Mt 19:28   2523
that these my two sons may *s*............... Mt 20:21   2523
but to *s* on my right hand, and on ...... Mt 20:23   2523

S

S thou on my right hand, till I .... Mt 22:44   2521
the Pharisees *s* in Moses' seat .... Mt 23:2   2523
then shall he *s* upon the throne .... Mt 25:31   2523
S ye here, while I go and pray .... Mt 26:36   2523
all *s* down by companies upon the .... Mk 6:39   347
people to *s* down on the ground .... Mk 8:6   377
him, Grant unto us that we may *s* .... Mk 10:37   2523
But to *s* on my right hand and on .... Mk 10:40   2523
S thou on my right hand, till I .... Mk 12:36   2521
S ye here, while I shall pray .... Mk 14:32   2523
light to them that *s* in darkness .... Lk 1:79   2521
Make them *s* down by fifties in a .... Lk 9:14   2625
did so, and made them all *s* down .... Lk 9:15   347
and make them to *s* down to meat .... Lk 12:37   347
shall *s* down in the kingdom of .... Lk 13:29   347
s not down in the highest room .... Lk 14:8   2625
s down in the lowest room .... Lk 14:10   377
of them that *s* at meat with thee .... Lk 14:10   4873
s down quickly, and write fifty .... Lk 16:6   2523
the field, Go and *s* down to meat .... Lk 17:7   377
my Lord, *S* thou on my right hand, ... Lk 20:42   2521
s on thrones judging the twelve .... Lk 22:30   2523
s on the right hand of the power .... Lk 22:69   2521
Jesus said, Make the men *s* down .... Jn 6:10   377
up Christ to *s* on his throne .... Acts 2:30   2523
my Lord, *S* thou on my right hand .... Acts 2:34   2521
he would come up and *s* with him .... Acts 8:31   2523
s at meat in the idol's temple 1Cor 8:10   2621
made us *s* together in heavenly .... Eph 2:6   4776
S on my right hand, until I make .... Heb 1:13   2521
S thou here in a good place .... Jas 2:3   2521
or *s* here under my footstool .... Jas 2:3   2521
I grant to *s* with me in my throne .... Rev 3:21   2523
I saw a woman *s* upon a scarlet .... Rev 17:3   2521
I *s* a queen, and am no widow, and .... Rev 18:7   2521
horses, and of them that *s* on them .... Rev 19:18   2521

SITH *See also* SINCE.
s thou hast not hated blood, even .... Eze 35:6   518

SITHRI See ZITHRI.

SITNAH *(sit'-nah) A well near Gerar.*
and he called the name of it *S* .... Gen 26:21   7856

SITTEST
why *s* thou thyself alone, and all .... Ex 18:14   3427
them when thou *s* in thine house .... Deut 6:7   3427
them when thou *s* in thine house .... Deut 11:19   3427
Thou *s* and speakest against thy .... Ps 50:20   3427
When thou *s* to eat with a ruler, ... Prov 23:1   3427
that *s* upon the throne of David, ... Jer 22:2   3427
for *s* thou to judge me after the .... Acts 23:3   2521

SITTETH
of Pharaoh that *s* upon his throne .... Ex 11:5   3427
and every thing, whereon he *s* .... Lev 15:4   3427
he that *s* on any thing whereon he .... Lev 15:6   3427
that she *s* upon shall be unclean .... Lev 15:20   3427
or on any thing whereon she *s* .... Lev 15:23   3427
whatsoever she *s* upon shall be .... Lev 15:26   3427
when he *s* upon the throne of his .... Deut 17:18   3427
also Solomon *s* on the throne of 1Kin 1:46   3427
that *s* in the king's gate .... Est 6:10   3427
nor *s* in the seat of the scornful .... Ps 1:1   3427
He that *s* in the heavens shall .... Ps 2:4   3427
He is in the lurking places of the .... Ps 10:8   3427
The LORD *s* upon the flood .... Ps 29:10   3427
yea, the LORD *s* King for ever .... Ps 29:10   3427
God *s* upon the throne of his .... Ps 47:8   3427
he *s* between the cherubims .... Ps 99:1   3427
For she *s* at the door of her .... Prov 9:14   3427
A king that *s* in the throne of .... Prov 20:8   3427
when he *s* among the elders of the .... Prov 31:23   3427
While the king *s* at his table .... Song 1:12
to him that *s* in judgment .... Is 28:6   3427
It is he that *s* upon the circle .... Is 40:22   3427
As the partridge *s* on eggs .... Jer 17:11   1716
that *s* upon the throne of David .... Jer 29:16   3427
He *s* alone and keepeth silence, ... Lam 3:28   3427
and, behold, all the earth *s* still .... Zec 1:11   3427
this is a woman that *s* in the .... Zec 5:7   3427
of God, and by him that *s* thereon .... Mt 23:22   2521
s not down first, and counteth the .... Lk 14:28   2523
s not down first, and consulteth .... Lk 14:31   2523
is greater, he that *s* at meat .... Lk 22:27   345
is not he that *s* at meat .... Lk 22:27   345
be revealed to another that *s* by 1Cor 14:30   2521
where Christ *s* on the right hand .... Col 3:1   2521
so that he as God *s* in the temple 2Th 2:4   2523
unto him that *s* upon the throne .... Rev 5:13   2521
face of him that *s* on the throne .... Rev 6:16   2521
our God which *s* upon the throne .... Rev 7:10   2521

he that *s* on the throne shall .... Rev 7:15   2521
whore that *s* upon many waters .... Rev 17:1   2521
mountains, on which the woman *s* .... Rev 17:9   2521
thou sawest, where the whore *s* .... Rev 17:15   2521

SITTING
the dam *s* upon the young, or upon .... Deut 22:6   7257
he was *s* in a summer parlour, ... Judg 3:20   3427
the *s* of his servants, and the 1Kin 10:5   4186
God, and found him *s* under an oak 1Kin 13:14   3427
I saw the LORD *s* on his throne 1Kin 22:19   3427
of the prophets were *s* before him 2Kin 4:38   3427
the captains of the host were *s* 2Kin 9:5   3427
the *s* of his servants, and the 2Chr 9:4   4186
stays on each side of the *s* place 2Chr 9:18   3427
I saw the LORD *s* upon his throne, ... 2Chr 18:18   3427
unto me, (the queen also *s* by him .... Neh 2:6   3427
the Jew *s* at the king's gate .... Est 5:13   3427
saw also the Lord *s* upon a throne .... Is 6:1   3427
princes *s* upon the throne of .... Jer 17:25   3427
kings *s* upon the throne of David .... Jer 22:4   3427
s upon the throne of David, and .... Jer 22:30   3427
the king then *s* in the gate of .... Jer 38:7   3427
Behold their *s* down, and their .... Lam 3:63   3427
s at the receipt of custom .... Mt 9:9   2521
unto children *s* in the markets .... Mt 11:16   2521
two blind men *s* by the way side, ... Mt 20:30   2521
s upon an ass, and a colt the foal .... Mt 21:5   1910
man *s* on the right hand of power .... Mt 26:64   2521
s down they watched him there .... Mt 27:36   2521
s over against the sepulchre .... Mt 27:61   2521
certain of the scribes *s* there .... Mk 2:6   2521
s at the receipt of custom .... Mk 2:14   2521
the devil, and had the legion, *s* .... Mk 5:15   2521
man *s* on the right hand of power .... Mk 14:62   2521
a young man *s* on the right side .... Mk 16:5   2521
s in the midst of the doctors, ... Lk 2:46   2516
and doctors of the law *s* by .... Lk 5:17   2521
s at the receipt of custom .... Lk 5:27   2521
children *s* in the marketplace .... Lk 7:32   2521
s at the feet of Jesus, clothed, ... Lk 8:35   2521
repented, *s* in sackcloth and ashes .... Lk 10:13   2521
doves, and the changers of money *s* ...... Jn 2:14   2521
King cometh, *s* on an ass's colt .... Jn 12:15   2521
And seeth two angels in white *s* .... Jn 20:12   2516
all the house where they were *s* .... Acts 2:2   2521
s in his chariot read Esaias the .... Acts 8:28   2521
the next day *s* on the judgment .... Acts 25:6   2523
I saw four and twenty elders *s* .... Rev 4:4   2521

SITUATE
The forefront of the one was *s* 1Sa 14:5   4690
O thou that art *s* at the entry of .... Eze 27:3   3427
that was *s* among the rivers, that .... Nah 3:8   3427

SITUATION
the *s* of this city is pleasant, ... 2Kin 2:19   4186
Beautiful for *s*, the joy of the .... Ps 48:2   5131

SIVAN *(si'-van) Third month of the Hebrew year.*
third month, that is, the month *S* .... Est 8:9   5510

SIX
Noah was *s* hundred years old when ..... Gen 7:6   8337
In the *s* hundredth year of Noah's .... Gen 7:11   8337
came to pass in the *s* hundredth .... Gen 8:13   8337
s years old, when Hagar bare .... Gen 16:16   8337
because I have born him *s* sons .... Gen 30:20   8337
and *s* years for thy cattle .... Gen 31:41   8337
the souls were threescore and *s* .... Gen 46:26   8337
about *s* hundred thousand on foot .... Ex 12:37   8337
he took *s* hundred chosen chariots .... Ex 14:7   8337
S days ye shall gather it .... Ex 16:26   8337
S days shalt thou labour, and do .... Ex 20:9   8337
For in *s* days the LORD made .... Ex 20:11   8337
servant, *s* years he shall serve .... Ex 21:2   8337
s years thou shalt sow thy land, ... Ex 23:10   8337
S days thou shalt do thy work, and .... Ex 23:12   8337
and the cloud covered it *s* days .... Ex 24:16   8337
s branches shall come out of the .... Ex 25:32   8337
so in the *s* branches that come .... Ex 25:33   8337
according to the *s* branches that .... Ex 25:35   8337
s curtains by themselves, and .... Ex 26:9   8337
westward thou shalt make *s* boards .... Ex 26:22   8337
S of their names on one stone, and .... Ex 28:10   8337
the other *s* names of the rest on .... Ex 28:10   8337
S days may work be done .... Ex 31:15   8337
for in *s* days the LORD made .... Ex 31:17   8337
S days thou shalt work, but on .... Ex 34:21   8337
S days shall work be done, but on .... Ex 35:2   8337
and *s* curtains by themselves .... Ex 36:16   8337
westward he made *s* boards .... Ex 36:27   8337
s branches going out of the sides .... Ex 37:18   8337

so throughout the *s* branches	Ex 37:19	8337
according to the *s* branches going	Ex 37:21	8337
for *s* hundred thousand and three	Ex 38:26	8337
purifying threescore and *s* days	Lev 12:5	8337
S days shall work be done	Lev 23:3	8337
s on a row, upon the pure table	Lev 24:6	8337
S years thou shalt sow thy field,	Lev 25:3	8337
s years thou shalt prune thy	Lev 25:3	8337
s thousand and five hundred	Num 1:21	8337
forty and five thousand *s* hundred	Num 1:25	8337
and fourteen thousand and *s* hundred	Num 1:27	8337
numbered were *s* hundred thousand	Num 1:46	8337
and fourteen thousand and *s* hundred	Num 2:4	8337
s thousand and four hundred,	Num 2:9	8337
s thousand and five hundred	Num 2:11	8337
thousand and *s* hundred and fifty	Num 2:15	8337
and seven thousand and *s* hundred	Num 2:31	8337
hosts were *s* hundred thousand	Num 2:32	8337
s hundred, keeping the charge of	Num 3:28	8337
were *s* thousand and two hundred	Num 3:34	8337
thousand and *s* hundred and thirty	Num 4:40	8337
s covered wagons, and twelve oxen	Num 7:3	8337
are *s* hundred thousand footmen	Num 11:21	8337
and five thousand and *s* hundred	Num 26:41	8337
s hundred thousand and a thousand	Num 26:51	8337
was *s* hundred thousand and seventy	Num 31:32	8337
of the sheep was *s* hundred	Num 31:37	8337
beeves were thirty and *s* thousand	Num 31:38	8337
And thirty and *s* thousand beeves,	Num 31:44	8337
shall be *s* cities for refuge	Num 35:6	8337
cities which ye shall give *s*	Num 35:13	8337
These *s* cities shall be a refuge,	Num 35:15	8337
S days thou shalt labour, and do	Deut 5:13	8337
unto thee, and serve thee *s* years	Deut 15:12	8337
to thee, in serving thee *s* years	Deut 15:18	8337
S days thou shalt eat unleavened	Deut 16:8	8337
Thus shalt thou do *s* days	Josh 6:3	8337
so they did *s* days	Josh 6:14	8337
of them about thirty and *s* men	Josh 7:5	8337
s cities with their villages	Josh 15:59	8337
s cities with their villages	Josh 15:62	8337
s hundred men with an ox goad	Judg 3:31	8337
And Jephthah judged Israel *s* years	Judg 12:7	8337
s hundred men appointed with	Judg 18:11	8337
the *s* hundred men appointed with	Judg 18:16	8337
entering of the gate with the *s*	Judg 18:17	8337
s thousand men that drew sword,	Judg 20:15	8337
But *s* hundred men turned and fled	Judg 20:47	8337
he measured *s* measures of barley,	Ruth 3:15	8337
These *s* measures of barley gave	Ruth 3:17	8337
s thousand horsemen, and people as	1Sa 13:5	8337
with him, about *s* hundred men	1Sa 13:15	8337
with him were about *s* hundred men	1Sa 14:2	8337
Gath, whose height was *s* cubits	1Sa 17:4	8337
weighed *s* hundred shekels of iron	1Sa 17:7	8337
men, which were about *s* hundred	1Sa 23:13	8337
he passed over with the *s* hundred	1Sa 27:2	8337
the *s* hundred men that were with	1Sa 30:9	8337
Judah was seven years and *s* months	2Sa 2:11	8337
Judah seven years and *s* months	2Sa 5:5	8337
ark of the LORD had gone *s* paces	2Sa 6:13	8337
s hundred men which came after	2Sa 15:18	8337
that had on every hand *s* fingers	2Sa 21:20	8337
fingers, and on every foot *s* toes	2Sa 21:20	8337
and the middle was *s* cubits over	1Kin 6:6	8337
one year was *s* hundred threescore	1Kin 10:14	8337
threescore and *s* talents of gold,	1Kin 10:14	8337
s hundred shekels of gold went to	1Kin 10:16	8337
The throne had *s* steps, and the	1Kin 10:19	8337
and on the other upon the *s* steps	1Kin 10:20	8337
went out of Egypt for *s* hundred	1Kin 10:29	8337
(For *s* months did Joab remain	1Kin 11:16	8337
s years reigned he in Tirzah	1Kin 16:23	8337
s thousand pieces of gold, and ten	2Kin 5:5	8337
in the house of the LORD *s* years	2Kin 11:3	8337
have smitten five or *s* times	2Kin 13:19	8337
over Israel in Samaria *s* months	2Kin 15:8	8337
These *s* were born unto him in	1Chr 3:4	8337
reigned seven years and *s* months	1Chr 3:4	8337
Bariah, and Neariah, and Shaphat, *s*	1Chr 3:22	8337
had sixteen sons and *s* daughters	1Chr 4:27	8337
and twenty thousand and *s* hundred	1Chr 7:2	8337
were bands of soldiers for war, *s*	1Chr 7:4	8337
was twenty and *s* thousand men	1Chr 7:40	8337
And Azel had *s* sons, whose names	1Chr 8:38	8337
brethren, *s* hundred and ninety	1Chr 9:6	8337
nine hundred and fifty and *s*	1Chr 9:9	8337
And Azel had *s* sons, whose names	1Chr 9:44	8337
shield and spear were *s* thousand	1Chr 12:24	8337
Levi four thousand and *s* hundred	1Chr 12:26	8337
and eight thousand and *s* hundred	1Chr 12:35	8337

s on each hand, and *s* on each	1Chr 20:6	8337
s hundred shekels of gold by	1Chr 21:25	8337
s thousand were officers and	1Chr 23:4	8337
Hashabiah, and Mattithiah, *s*	1Chr 25:3	8337
Eastward were *s* Levites,	1Chr 26:17	8337
for *s* hundred shekels of silver	2Chr 1:17	8337
s hundred to oversee them	2Chr 2:2	8337
and three thousand and *s* hundred	2Chr 2:17	8337
s hundred overseers to set the	2Chr 2:18	8337
amounting to *s* hundred talents	2Chr 3:8	8337
Solomon in one year was *s* hundred	2Chr 9:13	8337
threescore and *s* talents of gold	2Chr 9:13	8337
s hundred shekels of beaten gold	2Chr 9:15	8337
there were *s* steps to the throne,	2Chr 9:18	8337
and on the other upon the *s* steps	2Chr 9:19	8337
In the *s* and thirtieth year of the	2Chr 16:1	8337
hid in the house of God *s* years	2Chr 22:12	8337
were two thousand and *s* hundred	2Chr 26:12	8337
things were *s* hundred oxen	2Chr 29:33	8337
s hundred small cattle, and three	2Chr 35:8	8337
of Bani, *s* hundred forty and two	Ezr 2:10	8337
s hundred twenty and three	Ezr 2:11	8337
Adonikam, *s* hundred sixty and *s*	Ezr 2:13	8337
Bigvai, two thousand fifty and *s*	Ezr 2:14	8337
The men of Netophah, fifty and *s*	Ezr 2:22	8337
and Gaba, *s* hundred twenty and one	Ezr 2:26	8337
of Magbish, an hundred fifty and *s*	Ezr 2:30	8337
thousand and *s* hundred and thirty	Ezr 2:35	8337
of Nekoda, *s* hundred fifty and two	Ezr 2:60	8337
were seven hundred thirty and *s*	Ezr 2:66	8337
s thousand seven hundred and	Ezr 2:67	8337
weighed unto their hand *s* hundred	Ezr 8:26	8337
s rams, seventy and seven lambs,	Ezr 8:35	8337
was one ox and *s* choice sheep	Neh 5:18	8337
of Arah, *s* hundred fifty and two	Neh 7:10	8337
Binnui, *s* hundred forty and eight	Neh 7:15	8337
s hundred twenty and eight	Neh 7:16	8337
s hundred threescore and seven	Neh 7:18	8337
of Adin, *s* hundred fifty and five	Neh 7:20	8337
and Gaba, *s* hundred twenty and one	Neh 7:30	8337
of Nekoda, *s* hundred forty and two	Neh 7:62	8337
horses, seven hundred thirty and *s*	Neh 7:68	8337
s thousand seven hundred and	Neh 7:69	8337
s months with oil of myrrh, and	Est 2:12	8337
s months with sweet odours, and	Est 2:12	8337
shall deliver thee in *s* troubles	Job 5:19	8337
s thousand camels, and a thousand	Job 42:12	8337
These *s* things doth the LORD hate	Prov 6:16	8337
each one had *s* wings	Is 6:2	8337
when he hath served thee *s* years	Jer 34:14	8337
and *s* pomegranates on a side	Jer 52:23	8337
were four thousand and *s* hundred	Jer 52:30	8337
s men came from the way of the	Eze 9:2	8337
of *s* cubits long by the cubit	Eze 40:5	8337
were *s* cubits on this side	Eze 40:12	8337
and *s* cubits on that side	Eze 40:12	8337
s cubits broad on the one side,	Eze 41:1	8337
s cubits broad on the other side,	Eze 41:1	8337
and the door, *s* cubits	Eze 41:3	8337
the wall of the house, *s* cubits	Eze 41:5	8337
a full reed of *s* great cubits	Eze 41:8	8337
shall be shut the *s* working days	Eze 46:1	8337
shall be *s* lambs without blemish	Eze 46:4	8337
blemish, and *s* lambs, and a ram	Eze 46:6	8337
and the breadth thereof *s* cubits	Dan 3:1	8353
after *s* days Jesus taketh Peter,	Mt 17:1	1803
after *s* days Jesus taketh with	Mk 9:2	1803
s months, when great famine was	Lk 4:25	1803
There are *s* days in which men	Lk 13:14	1803
set there *s* waterpots of stone	Jn 2:6	1803
s years was this temple in	Jn 2:20	1803
Then Jesus *s* days before the	Jn 12:1	1803
Moreover these *s* brethren	Acts 11:12	1803
s months, teaching the word of	Acts 18:11	1803
space of three years and *s* months	Jas 5:17	1803
each of them *s* wings about him	Rev 4:8	1803
is *s* hundred threescore and *s*	Rev 13:18	5516
a thousand and *s* hundred furlongs	Rev 14:20	1812

SIXSCORE

to the king *s* talents of gold	1Kin 9:14	3967,6242
are more than *s* thousand	Jonah 4:11	8147,6240,7239

SIXTEEN

she bare unto Jacob, even *s* souls	Gen 46:18	8337,6240
sockets of silver, *s* sockets	Ex 26:25	8337,6240
sockets were *s* sockets of silver	Ex 36:30	8337,6240
s thousand and five hundred	Num 26:22	8337,6240
And the persons were *s* thousand	Num 31:40	8337,6240
And *s* thousand persons	Num 31:46	8337,6240
was *s* thousand seven hundred	Num 31:52	8337,6240
s cities with their villages	Josh 15:41	8337,6240

S

_s_ cities with their villages	Josh 19:22	8337,6240
in Samaria, and reigned _s_ years	2Kin 13:10	8337,6240
Azariah, which was _s_ years old	2Kin 14:21	8337,6240
_S_ years old was he when he began	2Kin 15:2	8337,6240
he reigned _s_ years in Jerusalem	2Kin 15:33	8337,6240
reigned _s_ years in Jerusalem, and	2Kin 16:2	8337,6240
And Shimei had _s_ sons and six	1Chr 4:27	8337,6240
the sons of Eleazar there were _s_	1Chr 24:4	8337,6240
and two sons, and _s_ daughters	2Chr 13:21	8337,6240
was _s_ years old, and made him	2Chr 26:1	8337,6240
_S_ years old was Uzziah when he	2Chr 26:3	8337,6240
he reigned _s_ years in Jerusalem	2Chr 27:1	8337,6240
reigned _s_ years in Jerusalem	2Chr 27:8	8337,6240
he reigned _s_ years in Jerusalem	2Chr 28:1	8337,6240
two hundred threescore and _s_	Acts 27:37	1440,1803

SIXTEENTH

to Bilgah, the _s_ to Immer,	1Chr 24:14	8337,6240
The _s_ to Hananiah, he, his sons,	1Chr 25:23	8337,6240
in the _s_ day of the first month	2Chr 29:17	8337,6240

SIXTH

and the morning were the _s_ day	Gen 1:31	8345
again, and bare Jacob the _s_ son	Gen 30:19	8345
that on the _s_ day they shall	Ex 16:5	8345
that on the _s_ day they gathered	Ex 16:22	8345
the _s_ day the bread of two days	Ex 16:29	8345
shalt double the _s_ curtain in the	Ex 26:9	8345
blessing upon you in the _s_ year	Lev 25:21	8345
On the _s_ day Eliasaph the son of	Num 7:42	8345
on the _s_ day eight bullocks, two	Num 29:29	8345
The _s_ lot came out to the	Josh 19:32	8345
And the _s_, Ithream, by Eglah	2Sa 3:5	8345
_s_ year of Asa king of Judah began	1Kin 16:8	8337
even in the _s_ year of Hezekiah,	2Kin 18:10	8337
Ozem the _s_, David the seventh	1Chr 2:15	8345
the _s_, Ithream by Eglah his wife	1Chr 3:3	8345
Attai the _s_, Eliel the seventh,	1Chr 12:11	8345
to Malchijah, the _s_ to Mijamin,	1Chr 24:9	8345
The _s_ to Bukkiah, he, his sons,	1Chr 25:13	8345
Elam the fifth, Jehohanan the _s_	1Chr 26:3	8345
Ammiel the _s_, Issachar the	1Chr 26:5	8345
The _s_ captain for the _s_ month	1Chr 27:9	8345
which was in the _s_ year of the	Ezr 6:15	8353
Hanun the _s_ son of Zalaph,	Neh 3:30	8345
by measure, the _s_ part of an hin	Eze 4:11	8345
in the _s_ year, in the _s_ month	Eze 8:1	8345
and leave but the _s_ part of thee	Eze 39:2	8338
the _s_ part of an ephah of an	Eze 45:13	8345
ye shall give the _s_ part of an	Eze 45:13	8341
the _s_ part of an ephah, and the	Eze 46:14	8345
Darius the king, in the _s_ month	Hag 1:1	8345
and twentieth day of the _s_ month	Hag 1:15	8345
Again he went out about the _s_	Mt 20:5	1623
Now from the _s_ hour there was	Mt 27:45	1623
when the _s_ hour was come, there	Mk 15:33	1623
in the _s_ month the angel Gabriel	Lk 1:26	1623
this is the _s_ month with her, who	Lk 1:36	1623
And it was about the _s_ hour	Lk 23:44	1623
and it was about the _s_ hour	Jn 4:6	1623
the passover, and about the _s_ hour	Jn 19:14	1623
housetop to pray about the _s_ hour	Acts 10:9	1623
when he had opened the _s_ seal	Rev 6:12	1623
the _s_ angel sounded, and I heard a	Rev 9:13	1623
Saying to the _s_ angel which had	Rev 9:14	1623
the _s_ angel poured out his vial	Rev 16:12	1623
the _s_, sardius	Rev 21:20	1623

SIXTY

And Mahalaleel lived _s_ and five	Gen 5:15	8346
And Jared lived an hundred a _s_	Gen 5:18	8346
days of Jared were nine hundred _s_	Gen 5:20	8346
And Enoch lived _s_ and five years,	Gen 5:21	8346
of Enoch were three hundred _s_	Gen 5:23	8346
of Methuselah were nine hundred _s_	Gen 5:27	8346
years old even unto _s_ years old	Lev 27:3	8346
And if it be from _s_ years old	Lev 27:7	8346
the rams _s_, the he goats _s_	Num 7:88	8346
the lambs of the first year _s_	Num 7:88	8346
of Adonikam, six hundred _s_	Ezr 2:13	8346
some an hundredfold, some _s_	Mt 13:23	1835
forth, some thirty, and some _s_	Mk 4:8	1835
fruit, some thirtyfold, some _s_	Mk 4:20	1835

SIXTYFOLD

some an hundredfold, some _s_	Mt 13:8	1835

SIYON See SION.

SIZE

the curtains were all of one _s_	Ex 36:9	4060
the eleven curtains were of one _s_	Ex 36:15	4060
were of one measure and one _s_	1Kin 6:25	7095

casting, one measure, and one _s_	1Kin 7:37	7095
and for all manner of measure and _s_	1Chr 23:29	4060

SKIES

waters, and thick clouds of the _s_	2Sa 22:12	7834
waters and thick clouds of the _s_	Ps 18:11	7834
the _s_ sent out a sound	Ps 77:17	7834
let the _s_ pour down righteousness	Is 45:8	7834
and is lifted up even to the _s_	Jer 51:9	7834

SKILFUL

_s_ in war, were four and forty	1Chr 5:18	3925
about the song, because he was _s_	1Chr 15:22	995
workmanship every willing _s_ man	1Chr 28:21	2451
_s_ to work in gold, and in silver,	2Chr 2:14	3045
of brutish men, and _s_ to destroy	Eze 21:31	2796
_s_ in all wisdom, and cunning in	Dan 1:4	7919
such as are _s_ of lamentation to	Amos 5:16	3045

SKILFULLY

play _s_ with a loud noise	Ps 33:3	3190

SKILFULNESS

guided them by the _s_ of his hands	Ps 78:72	8394

SKILL

can _s_ to hew timber like unto the	1Kin 5:6	3045
that can _s_ to grave with the	2Chr 2:7	3045
can _s_ to cut timber in Lebanon	2Chr 2:8	3045
all that could _s_ of instruments	2Chr 34:12	995
nor yet favour to men of _s_	Eccl 9:11	3045
_s_ in all learning and wisdom	Dan 1:17	7919
am now come forth to give thee _s_	Dan 9:22	7919

SKIN

only, it is his raiment for his _s_	Ex 22:27	5785
flesh of the bullock, and his _s_	Ex 29:14	5785
the _s_ of his face shone while he	Ex 34:29	5785
behold, the _s_ of his face shone	Ex 34:30	5785
that the _s_ of Moses' face shone	Ex 34:35	5785
the _s_ of the bullock, and all his	Lev 4:11	5785
shall have to himself the _s_ of	Lev 7:8	5785
vessel of wood, or raiment, or _s_	Lev 11:32	5785
in the _s_ of his flesh a rising	Lev 13:2	5785
it be in the _s_ of his flesh like	Lev 13:2	5785
the plague in the _s_ of the flesh	Lev 13:3	5785
be deeper than the _s_ of his flesh	Lev 13:3	5785
be white in the _s_ of his flesh	Lev 13:4	5785
in sight not deeper than the _s_	Lev 13:4	5785
and the plague spread not in the _s_	Lev 13:5	5785
and the plague spread not in the _s_	Lev 13:6	5785
scab spread much abroad in the _s_	Lev 13:7	5785
the scab spreadeth in the _s_	Lev 13:8	5785
if the rising be white in the _s_	Lev 13:10	5785
old leprosy in the _s_ of his flesh	Lev 13:11	5785
leprosy break out abroad in the _s_	Lev 13:12	5785
the leprosy cover all the _s_ of	Lev 13:12	5785
in which, even in the _s_ thereof	Lev 13:18	5785
it be in sight lower than the _s_	Lev 13:20	5785
and if it be not lower than the _s_	Lev 13:21	5785
if it spread much abroad in the _s_	Lev 13:22	5785
in the _s_ whereof there is a hot	Lev 13:24	5785
it be in sight deeper than the _s_	Lev 13:25	5785
it be no lower than the other _s_	Lev 13:26	5785
it be spread much abroad in the _s_	Lev 13:27	5785
his place, and spread not in the _s_	Lev 13:28	5785
it be in sight deeper than the _s_	Lev 13:30	5785
be not in sight deeper than the _s_	Lev 13:31	5785
be not in sight deeper than the _s_	Lev 13:32	5785
the scall be not spread in the _s_	Lev 13:34	5785
nor be in sight deeper than the _s_	Lev 13:34	5785
much in the _s_ after his cleansing	Lev 13:35	5785
if the scall be spread in the _s_	Lev 13:36	5785
the _s_ of their flesh bright spots	Lev 13:38	5785
if the bright spots in the _s_ of	Lev 13:39	5785
spot that growth in the _s_	Lev 13:39	5785
appeareth in the _s_ of the flesh	Lev 13:43	5785
a _s_, or in any thing made of _s_	Lev 13:48	5785
in the garment, or in the _s_	Lev 13:49	5785
in the woof, or in any thing of _s_	Lev 13:49	5785
warp, or in the woof, or in a _s_	Lev 13:51	5785
or in any work that is made of _s_	Lev 13:51	5785
or in linen, or any thing of _s_	Lev 13:52	5785
in the woof, or in any thing of _s_	Lev 13:53	5785
of the garment, or out of the _s_	Lev 13:56	5785
in the woof, or in any thing of _s_	Lev 13:57	5785
or whatsoever thing of _s_ it be	Lev 13:58	5785
And every garment, and every _s_	Lev 15:17	5785
her _s_, and her flesh, and her blood	Num 19:5	5785
_S_ for _s_, yea, all that a man	Job 2:4	5785
my _s_ is broken, and become	Job 7:5	5785
Thou hast clothed me with _s_	Job 10:11	5785
I have sewed sackcloth upon my _s_	Job 16:15	1539
devour the strength of his _s_	Job 18:13	5785

My bone cleaveth to my *s* and to my	Job 19:20	5785
am escaped with the *s* of my teeth	Job 19:20	5785
though after my *s* worms destroy	Job 19:26	5785
My *s* is black upon me, and my	Job 30:30	5785
thou fill his *s* with barbed irons	Job 41:7	5785
groaning my bones cleave to my *s*	Ps 102:5	1320
Can the Ethiopian change his *s*	Jer 13:23	5785
My flesh and my *s* hath he made old	Lam 3:4	5785
their *s* cleaveth to their bones	Lam 4:8	5785
Our *s* was black like an oven	Lam 5:10	5785
and shod them with badgers' *s*	Eze 16:10	5785
upon you, and cover you with *s*	Eze 37:6	5785
them, and the *s* covered them above	Eze 37:8	5785
pluck off their *s* from off them	Mic 3:2	5785
flay their *s* from off them	Mic 3:3	5785
a girdle of a *s* about his loins	Mk 1:6	1193

SKINS

did the Lord God make coats of *s*	Gen 3:21	5785
she put the *s* of the kids of the	Gen 27:16	5785
s dyed red, and badgers' *s*	Ex 25:5	5785
for the tent of rams' *s* dyed red	Ex 26:14	5785
and a covering above of badgers' *s*	Ex 26:14	5785
s dyed red, and badgers' *s*	Ex 35:7	5785
red *s* of rams, and badgers' *s*	Ex 35:23	5785
for the tent of rams' *s* dyed red	Ex 36:19	5785
covering of badgers' *s* above that	Ex 36:19	5785
the covering of rams' *s* dyed red	Ex 39:34	5785
and the covering of badgers' *s*	Ex 39:34	5785
warp, or woof, or any thing of *s*	Lev 13:59	5785
shall burn in the fire their *s*	Lev 16:27	5785
the covering of badgers' *s*	Num 4:6	5785
with a covering of badgers' *s*	Num 4:8	5785
within a covering of badgers' *s*	Num 4:10	5785
it with a covering of badgers' *s*	Num 4:11	5785
with a covering of badgers' *s*	Num 4:12	5785
upon it a covering of badgers' *s*	Num 4:14	5785
badgers' *s* that is above upon it	Num 4:25	5785
raiment, and all that is made of *s*	Num 31:20	5785

SKIP

maketh them also to *s* like a calf	Ps 29:6	7540

SKIPPED

The mountains *s* like rams	Ps 114:4	7540
Ye mountains, that ye *s* like rams	Ps 114:6	7540

SKIPPEDST

spakest of him, thou *s* for joy	Jer 48:27	5110

SKIPPING

the mountains, *s* upon the hills	Song 2:8	7092

SKIRT

wife, nor discover his father's *s*	Deut 22:30	3671
he uncovereth his father's *s*	Deut 27:20	3671
thy *s* over thine handmaid	Ruth 3:9	3671
hold upon the *s* of his mantle	1Sa 15:27	3671
cut off the *s* of Saul's robe	1Sa 24:4	3671
because he had cut off Saul's *s*	1Sa 24:5	3671
see the *s* of thy robe in my hand	1Sa 24:11	3671
that I cut off the *s* of thy robe	1Sa 24:11	3671
and I spread my *s* over thee	Eze 16:8	3671
flesh in the *s* of his garment	Hag 2:12	3671
with his *s* do touch bread, or	Hag 2:12	3671
of the *s* of him that is a Jew	Zec 8:23	3671

SKIRTS

down to the *s* of his garments	Ps 133:2	6310
Also in thy *s* is found the blood	Jer 2:34	3671
iniquity are thy *s* discovered	Jer 13:22	7757
I discover thy *s* upon thy face	Jer 13:26	7757
Her filthiness is in her *s*	Lam 1:9	7757
in number, and bind them in thy *s*	Eze 5:3	3671
will discover thy *s* upon thy face	Nah 3:5	7757

SKULL

head, and all to brake his *s*	Judg 9:53	1538
found no more of her than the *s*	2Kin 9:35	1538
that is to say, a place of a *s*	Mt 27:33	2898
interpreted, The place of a *s*	Mk 15:22	2898
a place called the place of a *s*	Jn 19:17	2898

SKY

and in his excellency on the *s*	Deut 33:26	7834
thou with him spread out the *s*	Job 37:18	7834
for the *s* is red	Mt 16:2	3772
for the *s* is red and lowring	Mt 16:3	3772
ye can discern the face of the *s*	Mt 16:3	3772
ye can discern the face of the *s*	Lk 12:56	3772
the stars of the *s* in multitude	Heb 11:12	3772

SLACK

he will not be *s* to him that	Deut 7:10	309
God, thou shalt not *s* to pay it	Deut 23:21	309
S not thy hand from thy servants	Josh 10:6	7503

How long are ye *s* to go to	Josh 18:3	7503
s not thy riding for me, except I	2Kin 4:24	6113
poor that dealeth with a *s* hand	Prov 10:4	7423
to Zion, Let not thine hands be *s*	Zeph 3:16	7503
The Lord is not *s* concerning his	2Pet 3:9	*1019*

SLACKED

Therefore the law is *s*, and	Hab 1:4	6313

SLACKNESS

his promise, as some men count *s*	2Pet 3:9	*1022*

SLAIN

for I have *s* a man to my wounding	Gen 4:23	2026
The sons of Jacob came upon the *s*	Gen 34:27	2491
them in the blood of the *s* bird	Lev 14:51	7819
ye shall be *s* before your enemies	Lev 26:17	5062
flocks and the herds be *s* for them	Num 11:22	7819
therefore he hath *s* them in the	Num 14:16	7819
whosoever toucheth one that is *s*	Num 19:16	2491
him that touched a bone, or one *s*	Num 19:18	2491
me, surely now also I had *s* thee	Num 22:33	2026
prey, and drink the blood of the *s*	Num 23:24	2491
name of the Israelite that was *s*	Num 25:14	5221
even that was *s* with the	Num 25:14	5221
woman that was *s* was Cozbi	Num 25:15	5221
which was *s* in the day of the	Num 25:18	5221
the rest of them that were *s*	Num 31:8	2491
and whosoever hath touched any *s*	Num 31:19	2491
After he had *s* Sihon the king of	Deut 1:4	5221
If one be found *s* in the land	Deut 21:1	2491
and it be not known who hath *s* him	Deut 21:1	2491
are round about him that is *s*	Deut 21:2	2491
city which is next unto the *s* man	Deut 21:3	2491
that are next unto the *s* man	Deut 21:6	2491
ox shall be *s* before thine eyes	Deut 28:31	2873
and that with the blood of the *s*	Deut 32:42	2491
them up all *s* before Israel	Josh 11:6	2491
among them that were *s* by them	Josh 13:22	2491
have *s* his sons, threescore and	Judg 9:18	2026
of an ass have I *s* a thousand men	Judg 15:16	5221
husband of the woman that was *s*	Judg 20:4	7523
by night, and thought to have *s* me	Judg 20:5	2026
Eli, Hophni and Phinehas, were *s*	1Sa 4:11	4191
Saul hath *s* his thousands, and	1Sa 18:7	5221
Lord liveth, he shall not be *s*	1Sa 19:6	4191
night, to morrow thou shalt be *s*	1Sa 19:11	4191
unto him, Wherefore shall he be *s*	1Sa 20:32	4191
Saul hath *s* his thousands, and	1Sa 21:11	5221
Saul had *s* the Lord's priests	1Sa 22:21	2026
fell down *s* in mount Gilboa	1Sa 31:1	2491
Philistines came to strip the *s*	1Sa 31:8	2491
I have *s* the Lord's anointed	2Sa 1:16	4191
Israel is *s* upon thy high places	2Sa 1:19	2491
From the blood of the *s*, from the	2Sa 1:22	2491
thou wast *s* in thine high places	2Sa 1:25	2491
because he had *s* their brother	2Sa 3:30	4191
more, when wicked men have *s* a	2Sa 4:11	2026
hast *s* him with the sword of the	2Sa 12:9	2026
Absalom hath *s* all the king's	2Sa 13:30	5221
s all the young men the king's	2Sa 13:32	4191
s before the servants of David	2Sa 18:7	5062
Philistines had *s* Saul in Gilboa	2Sa 21:12	5221
sword, thought to have *s* David	2Sa 21:16	5221
And he hath *s* oxen and fat cattle	1Kin 1:19	2076
down this day, and hath *s* oxen	1Kin 1:25	2076
s the Canaanites that dwelt in	1Kin 9:16	2026
host was gone up to bury the *s*	1Kin 11:15	2491
s him, according to the word of	1Kin 13:26	4191
and hath also *s* the king	1Kin 16:16	5221
withal how he had *s* all the	1Kin 19:1	2026
s thy prophets with the sword	1Kin 19:10	2026
s thy prophets with the sword	1Kin 19:14	2026
the kings are surely *s*, and they	2Kin 3:23	2717
the king's sons which were *s*	2Kin 11:2	4191
Athaliah, so that he was not *s*	2Kin 11:2	4191
within the ranges, let him be *s*	2Kin 11:8	4191
Let her not be *s* in the house of	2Kin 11:15	4191
and there was she *s*	2Kin 11:16	4191
which had *s* the king his father	2Kin 14:5	4191
For there fell down many *s*	1Chr 5:22	2491
fell down *s* in mount Gilboa	1Chr 10:1	2491
Philistines came to strip the *s*	1Chr 10:8	2491
hundred *s* by him at one time	1Chr 11:11	2491
so there fell down *s* of Israel	2Chr 13:17	2491
also hast *s* thy brethren of thy	2Chr 21:13	2026
to the camp had *s* all the eldest	2Chr 22:1	2026
and when they had *s* him, they	2Chr 22:9	4191
among the king's sons that were *s*	2Chr 22:11	4191
let him be *s* with the sword	2Chr 23:14	4191
after that they had *s* Athaliah	2Chr 23:21	4191
ye have *s* them in a rage that	2Chr 28:9	2026

S

people, to be destroyed, to be s............... Est 7:4 — 2026
were s in Shushan the palace was......... Est 9:11 — 2026
Esther the queen, The Jews have s....... Est 9:12 — 2026
they have s the servants with the .... Job 1:15 — 5221
s the servants with the edge of .... Job 1:17 — 5221
and where the s are, there is she .... Job 39:30 — 2491
ye shall be s all of you .... Ps 62:3 — 7523
like the s that lie in the grave, ... Ps 88:5 — 2491
Rahab in pieces, as one that is s .... Ps 89:10 — 2491
strong men have been s by her .... Prov 7:26 — 2026
I shall be s in the streets .... Prov 22:13 — 7523
and those that are ready to be s......... Prov 24:11 — 2027
and they shall fall under the s................. Is 10:4 — 2026
the raiment of those that are s.............. Is 14:19 — 2026
thy land, and s thy people .... Is 14:20 — 2026
thy s men are not s with the................... Is 22:2 — 2491
and shall no more cover her s .... Is 26:21 — 2026
or is he s according to the .... Is 27:7 — 2026
of them that are s by him .... Is 27:7 — 2026
Their s also shall be cast out, ... Is 34:3 — 2491
the s of the Lord shall be many............. Is 66:16 — 2491
night for the s of the daughter .... Jer 9:1 — 2491
then behold the s with the sword .... Jer 14:18 — 2491
men be s by the sword in battle .... Jer 18:21 — 5221
the s of the Lord shall be at.................... Jer 25:33 — 2491
whom I have s in mine anger and in ...... Jer 33:5 — 5221
day after he had s Gedaliah.................... Jer 41:4 — 4191
whom he had s because of Gedaliah...... Jer 41:9 — 5221
filled it with them that were s .... Jer 41:9 — 2491
after that he had s Gedaliah the .... Jer 41:16 — 5221
the son of Nethaniah had s .... Jer 41:18 — 5221
Thus the s shall fall in the land .... Jer 51:4 — 2491
all her s shall fall in the midst .... Jer 51:47 — 2491
caused the s of Israel to fall .... Jer 51:49 — 2491
shall fall the s of all the earth .... Jer 51:49 — 2491
the prophet be s in the sanctuary.......... Lam 2:20 — 2026
thou hast s them in the day of .... Lam 2:21 — 2026
thou hast s, thou hast not pitied .... Lam 3:43 — 2026
They that be s with the sword are .... Lam 4:9 — 2491
than they that be s with hunger .... Lam 4:9 — 2491
down your s men before your idols .... Eze 6:4 — 2491
the s shall fall in the midst of .... Eze 6:7 — 2491
when their s men shall be among .... Eze 6:13 — 2491
and fill the courts with the s .... Eze 9:7 — 2491
multiplied your s in this city .... Eze 11:6 — 2491
the streets thereof with the s .... Eze 11:6 — 2491
Your s whom ye have laid in the .... Eze 11:7 — 2491
That thou hast s my children .... Eze 16:21 — 7819
third time, the sword of the s .... Eze 21:14 — 2491
sword of the great men that are s.......... Eze 21:14 — 2491
upon the necks of them that are s .... Eze 21:29 — 2491
For when they had s their......................... Eze 23:39 — 7819
the field shall be s by the sword............ Eze 26:6 — 2026
are s in the midst of the seas .... Eze 28:8 — 2491
when the s shall fall in Egypt, ... Eze 30:4 — 2491
and fill the land with the s .... Eze 30:11 — 2491
them that be s with the sword .... Eze 31:17 — 2491
with them that be s by the sword .... Eze 31:18 — 2491
of them that are s by the sword .... Eze 32:20 — 2491
lie uncircumcised, s by the sword .... Eze 32:21 — 2491
all of them s, fallen by the .... Eze 32:22 — 2491
all of them s, fallen by the .... Eze 32:23 — 2491
about her grave, all of them s .... Eze 32:24 — 2491
of the s with all her multitude .... Eze 32:25 — 2491
uncircumcised, s by the sword .... Eze 32:25 — 2491
in the midst of them that be s................ Eze 32:25 — 2491
s by the sword, though they.................... Eze 32:26 — 2490
them that are s with the sword .... Eze 32:28 — 2491
by them that were s by the sword .... Eze 32:29 — 2491
which are gone down with the s .... Eze 32:30 — 2491
with them that be s by the sword .... Eze 32:30 — 2491
and all his army s by the sword............. Eze 32:31 — 2491
them that are s with the sword .... Eze 32:32 — 2491
fill his mountains with his s men .... Eze 35:8 — 2491
fall that are s with the sword .... Eze 35:8 — 2491
O breath, and breathe upon these s...... Eze 37:9 — 2026
that the wise men should be s .... Dan 2:13 — 6992
Daniel and his fellows to be s .... Dan 2:13 — 6992
the king of the Chaldeans s................... Dan 5:30 — 6992
beheld even till the beast was s .... Dan 7:11 — 6992
and many shall fall down s..................... Dan 11:26 — 2491
I have s them by the words of my .... Hos 6:5 — 2026
young men have I s with the sword .... Amos 4:10 — 2026
and there is a multitude of s.................. Nah 3:3 — 2491
also, ye shall be s by my sword............. Zeph 2:12 — 2491
chief priests and scribes, and be s ...... Lk 9:22 — 615
wicked hands have crucified and s........ Acts 2:23 — 337
who was s; and all................................... Acts 5:36 — 337
have ye offered to me s beasts .... Acts 7:42 — 4968
they have s them which shewed............ Acts 7:52 — 615
they Pilate that he should be s.............. Acts 13:28 — 337

eat nothing until we have s Paul........... Acts 23:14 — 615
having s the enmity thereby................... Eph 2:16 — 615
were s with the sword............... Heb 11:37 — 1722,5408,599
who was s among you, where Satan ...... Rev 2:13 — 615
stood a Lamb as it had been s .... Rev 5:6 — 4969
for thou wast s, and hast redeemed ..... Rev 5:9 — 4969
Lamb that was s to receive power .... Rev 5:12 — 4969
that were s for the word of God .... Rev 6:9 — 4969
were s of men seven thousand.............. Rev 11:13 — 615
Lamb s from the foundation of the .... Rev 13:8 — 4969
of all that were s upon the earth .... Rev 18:24 — 4969
the remnant were s with the sword .... Rev 19:21 — 615

SLANDER
by bringing up a s upon the land .... Num 14:36 — 1681
For I have heard the s of many .... Ps 31:13 — 1681
lips, and he that uttereth a s.................. Prov 10:18 — 1681

SLANDERED
he hath s thy servant unto my .... 2Sa 19:27 — 7270

SLANDERERS
must their wives be grave, not s .... 1Ti 3:11 — 1228

SLANDEREST
thou s thine own mother's son......... Ps 50:20 — 5414,1848

SLANDERETH
Whoso privily s his neighbour .... Ps 101:5 — 3960

SLANDEROUSLY
not rather, (as we be s reported............. Rom 3:8 — 987

SLANDERS
revolters, walking with s .... Jer 6:28 — 7400
every neighbour will walk with s .... Jer 9:4 — 7400

SLANG
s it, and smote the Philistine in............. 1Sa 17:49 — 7049

SLAUGHTER
return from the s of Chedorlaomer .... Gen 14:17 — 5221
them with a great s at Gibeon .... Josh 10:10 — 4347
slaying them with a very great s .... Josh 10:20 — 4347
vineyards, with a very great s................ Judg 11:33 — 4347
them hip and thigh with a great s.......... Judg 15:8 — 4347
and there was a very great s .... 1Sa 4:10 — 4347
also a great s among the people .... 1Sa 4:17 — 4046
many of the people with a great s .... 1Sa 6:19 — 4347
And that first s, which Jonathan .... 1Sa 14:14 — 4347
greater s among the Philistines .... 1Sa 14:30 — 4347
from the s of the Philistine .... 1Sa 17:57 — 5221
from the s of the Philistine .... 1Sa 18:6 — 5221
and slew them with a great s .... 1Sa 19:8 — 4347
and smote them with a great s .... 1Sa 23:5 — 4347
from the s of the Amalekites .... 2Sa 1:1 — 5221
There is a s among the people .... 2Sa 17:9 — 4046
there was there a great s that .... 2Sa 18:7 — 4046
slew the Syrians with a great s .... 1Kin 20:21 — 4347
people slew them with a great s .... 2Chr 13:17 — 4347
come from the s of the Edomites............ 2Chr 25:14 — 5221
who smote him with a great s................ 2Chr 28:5 — 4347
the stroke of the sword, and s .... Est 9:5 — 2027
we are counted as sheep for the s........ Ps 44:22 — 2878
as an ox goeth to the s, or as a.............. Prov 7:22 — 2875
for him according to the s of .... Is 10:26 — 4347
Prepare s for his children for.................. Is 14:21 — 4293
s of them that are slain by him .... Is 27:7 — 2027
waters in the day of the great s .... Is 30:25 — 2027
he hath delivered them to the s .... Is 34:2 — 2875
a great s in the land of Idumea............. Is 34:6 — 2875
he is brought as a lamb to the s .... Is 53:7 — 2875
and ye shall all bow down to the s .... Is 65:12 — 2875
of Hinnom, but the valley of s .... Jer 7:32 — 2028
or an ox that is brought to the s .... Jer 11:19 — 2873
them out like sheep for the s .... Jer 12:3 — 2873
and prepare them for the day of s .... Jer 12:3 — 2028
of Hinnom, but The valley of s .... Jer 19:6 — 2028
for the days of your s and of your .... Jer 25:34 — 2873
young men are gone down to the s .... Jer 48:15 — 2875
let them go down to the s .... Jer 50:27 — 2875
them down like lambs to the s .... Jer 51:40 — 2873
every man a s weapon in his hand .... Eze 9:2 — 4660
It is sharpened to make a sore .... Eze 21:10 — 2873
it is wrapped up for the s .... Eze 21:15 — 2875
to open the mouth in the s...................... Eze 21:22 — 7524
for the s it is furbished, to .... Eze 21:28 — 2875
when the s is made in the midst .... Eze 26:15 — 2027
revolters are profound to make s .... Hos 5:2 — 7819
mount of Esau may be cut off by s .... Obad 9 — 6993
Feed the flock of the s .... Zec 11:4 — 2028
And I will feed the flock of s .... Zec 11:7 — 2028
He was led as a sheep to the s .... Acts 8:32 — 4967
s against the disciples of the................. Acts 9:1 — 5408
are accounted as sheep for the s .... Rom 8:36 — 4967

SLAVE

returning from the *s* of the kings	Heb 7:1	2871
your hearts, as in a day of *s*	Jas 5:5	4967

SLAVE

is he a homeborn *s*	Jer 2:14	

SLAVES

and horses, and chariots, and *s*	Rev 18:13	4983

SLAY

one that findeth me shall *s* me	Gen 4:14	2026
to *s* the righteous with the	Gen 18:25	4191
wilt thou *s* also a righteous	Gen 20:4	2026
they will *s* me for my wife's sake	Gen 20:11	2026
and took the knife to *s* his son	Gen 22:10	7819
then will I *s* my brother Jacob	Gen 27:41	2026
together against me, and *s* me	Gen 34:30	5221
conspired against him to *s* him	Gen 37:18	4191
now therefore, and let us *s* him	Gen 37:20	2026
profit is it if we *s* our brother	Gen 37:26	2026
S my two sons, if I bring him not	Gen 42:37	4191
house, Bring these men home, and *s*	Gen 43:16	2875
this thing, he sought to *s* Moses	Ex 2:15	2026
I will *s* thy son, even thy	Ex 4:23	2026
put a sword in their hand to *s* us	Ex 5:21	2026
neighbour, to *s* him with guile	Ex 21:14	2026
innocent and righteous *s* thou not	Ex 23:7	2026
And thou shalt *s* the ram, and thou	Ex 29:16	7819
to *s* them in the mountains, and to	Ex 32:12	2026
s every man his brother, and every	Ex 32:27	2026
s the sin offering in the place	Lev 4:29	7819
s it for a sin offering in the	Lev 4:33	7819
he shall *s* the lamb in the place	Lev 14:13	7819
and ye shall *s* the beast	Lev 20:15	2026
one shall *s* her before his face	Num 19:3	7819
S ye every one his men that were	Num 25:5	2026
himself shall *s* the murderer	Num 35:19	4191
he meeteth him, he shall *s* him	Num 35:19	4191
of blood shall *s* the murderer	Num 35:21	4191
out to *s* them in the wilderness	Deut 9:28	4191
because the way is long, and *s* him	Deut 19:6	5221
reward to *s* an innocent person	Deut 27:25	5221
did the children of Israel *s* with	Josh 13:22	2026
them alive, I would not *s* you	Judg 8:19	2026
his firstborn, Up, and *s* them	Judg 8:20	2026
s me, that men say not of me, A	Judg 9:54	4191
because the LORD would *s* them	1Sa 2:25	4191
the God of Israel to us, to *s* us	1Sa 5:10	4191
his own place, that it *s* us not	1Sa 5:11	4191
his sheep, and *s* them here, and eat	1Sa 14:34	7819
but *s* both man and woman, infant	1Sa 15:3	4191
to *s* David without a cause	1Sa 19:5	4191
him, and to *s* him in the morning	1Sa 19:11	4191
me in the bed, that I may *s* him	1Sa 19:15	4191
be in me iniquity, *s* me thyself	1Sa 20:8	4191
of his father to *s* David	1Sa 20:33	4191
s the priests of the LORD	1Sa 22:17	4191
I pray thee, upon me, and *s* me	2Sa 1:9	4191
king to *s* Abner the son of Ner	2Sa 3:37	4191
Saul sought to *s* them in his zeal	2Sa 21:2	5221
not *s* thy servant with the sword	1Kin 1:51	4191
living child, and in no wise *s* it	1Kin 3:26	4191
living child, and in no wise *s* it	1Kin 3:27	4191
king of Judah did Baasha *s* him	1Kin 15:28	4191
to remembrance, and to *s* my son	1Kin 17:18	4191
into the hand of Ahab, to *s* me	1Kin 18:9	4191
cannot find thee, he shall *s* me	1Kin 18:12	2026
and he shall *s* me	1Kin 18:14	2026
the sword of Hazael shall Jehu *s*	1Kin 19:17	4191
the sword of Jehu shall Elisha *s*	1Kin 19:17	4191
from me, a lion shall *s* thee	1Kin 20:36	5221
men wilt thou *s* with the sword	2Kin 8:12	2026
to the captains, Go in, and *s* them	2Kin 10:25	5221
them, and, behold, they *s* them	2Kin 17:26	4191
of mount Seir, utterly to *s*	2Chr 20:23	2763
S her not in the house of the	2Chr 23:14	4191
s them, and cause the work to	Neh 4:11	2026
for they will come to *s* thee	Neh 6:10	2026
night will they come to *s* thee	Neh 6:10	2026
for their life, to destroy, to *s*	Est 8:11	2026
If the scourge *s* suddenly	Job 9:23	4191
Though he *s* me, yet will I trust	Job 13:15	6991
the viper's tongue shall *s* him	Job 20:16	2026
Evil shall *s* the wicked	Ps 34:21	4191
to *s* such as be of upright	Ps 37:14	2873
righteous, and seeketh to *s* him	Ps 37:32	4191
S them not, lest my people forget	Ps 59:11	2026
They *s* the widow and the stranger	Ps 94:6	2026
that he might even *s* the broken	Ps 109:16	4191
Surely thou wilt *s* the wicked	Ps 139:19	6991
away of the simple shall *s* them	Prov 1:32	2026
of his lips shall he *s* the wicked	Is 11:4	4191

famine, and he shall *s* thy remnant	Is 14:30	2026
he shall *s* the dragon that is in	Is 27:1	2026
for the Lord GOD shall *s* thee	Is 65:15	4191
out of the forest shall *s* them	Jer 5:6	5221
the sword to *s*, and the dogs to	Jer 15:3	2026
their counsel against me to *s* me	Jer 18:23	1194
shall *s* them with the sword	Jer 20:4	5221
he shall *s* them before your eyes	Jer 29:21	5221
the son of Nethaniah to *s* thee	Jer 40:14	5221,5315
I will *s* Ishmael the son of	Jer 40:15	5221
wherefore should he *s* thee	Jer 40:15	5221
that said unto Ishmael, *S* us not	Jer 41:8	4191
S all her bullocks	Jer 50:27	2717
S utterly old and young, both	Eze 9:6	2026
to *s* the souls that should not	Eze 13:19	4191
they shall *s* their sons and their	Eze 23:47	4191
He shall *s* with the sword thy	Eze 26:8	4191
he shall *s* thy people by the	Eze 26:11	4191
to *s* thereon the burnt offering	Eze 40:39	7819
they shall *s* the burnt offering	Eze 44:11	7819
to *s* the wise men of Babylon	Dan 2:14	6992
a dry land, and *s* her with thirst	Hos 2:3	4191
yet will I *s* even the beloved	Hos 9:16	4191
will *s* all the princes thereof	Amos 2:3	2026
I will *s* the last of them with	Amos 9:1	2026
the sword, and it shall *s* them	Amos 9:4	2026
continually to *s* the nations	Hab 1:17	2026
Whose possessors *s* them, and hold	Zec 11:5	2026
and some of them they shall *s*	Lk 11:49	*615*
bring hither, and *s* them before me	Lk 19:27	*2695*
Jesus, and sought to *s* him	Jn 5:16	*615*
heart, and took counsel to *s* them	Acts 5:33	*337*
but they went about to *s* him	Acts 9:29	*337*
s and eat	Acts 11:7	*2380*
for to *s* the third part of men	Rev 9:15	*615*

SLAYER

that the *s* may flee thither	Num 35:11	7523
shall judge between the *s*	Num 35:24	5221
congregation shall deliver the *s*	Num 35:25	7523
But if the *s* shall at any time	Num 35:26	7523
the revenger of blood kill the *s*	Num 35:27	7523
death of the high priest the *s*	Num 35:28	7523
That the *s* might flee thither	Deut 4:42	7523
that every *s* may flee thither	Deut 19:3	7523
And this is the case of the *s*	Deut 19:4	7523
avenger of the blood pursue the *s*	Deut 19:6	7523
That the *s* that killeth any	Josh 20:3	7523
deliver the *s* up into his hand	Josh 20:5	7523
then shall the *s* return, and come	Josh 20:6	7523
to be a city of refuge for the *s*	Josh 21:13	7523
to be a city of refuge for the *s*	Josh 21:21	7523
to be a city of refuge for the *s*	Josh 21:27	7523
to be a city of refuge for the *s*	Josh 21:32	7523
to be a city of refuge for the *s*	Josh 21:38	7523
to give it into the hand of the *s*	Eze 21:11	2026

SLAYETH

him, Therefore whosoever *s* Cain	Gen 4:15	2026
s him, even so is this matter	Deut 22:26	7523,5315
man, and envy *s* the silly one	Job 5:2	4191
yet say before him that *s* thee	Eze 28:9	2026
in the hand of him that *s* thee	Eze 28:9	2490

SLAYING

of *s* all the inhabitants of Ai in	Josh 8:24	2026
end of *s* them with a very great	Josh 10:20	5221
in *s* his seventy brethren	Judg 9:56	2026
with whom I sojourn, by *s* her son	1Kin 17:20	4191
s oxen, and killing sheep, eating	Is 22:13	2026
s the children in the valleys	Is 57:5	7819
to pass, while they were *s* them	Eze 9:8	5221

SLEEP

caused a deep *s* to fall upon Adam	Gen 2:21	3462
down, a deep *s* fell upon Abram	Gen 15:12	8639
and lay down in that place to *s*	Gen 28:11	7901
And Jacob awaked out of his *s*	Gen 28:16	8142
my *s* departed from mine eyes	Gen 31:40	8142
wherein shall he *s*	Ex 22:27	7901
thou shalt not *s* with his pledge	Deut 24:12	7901
that he may *s* in his own raiment	Deut 24:13	7901
thou shalt *s* with thy fathers	Deut 31:16	7901
And he awaked out of his *s*	Judg 16:14	3462
she made him *s* upon her knees	Judg 16:19	3462
And he awoke out of his *s*, and said	Judg 16:20	8142
was, and Samuel was laid down to *s*	1Sa 3:3	
because a deep *s* from the LORD	1Sa 26:12	8639
thou shalt *s* with thy fathers, I	2Sa 7:12	7901
the king shall *s* with his fathers	1Kin 1:21	7901
that night could not the king *s*	Est 6:1	8142
when deep *s* falleth on men	Job 4:13	8639
for now shall I *s* in the dust	Job 7:21	7901

S

nor be raised out of their *s*	Job 14:12	8142
when deep *s* falleth upon men, in	Job 33:15	
both lay me down in peace, and *s*	Ps 4:8	3462
lest I *s* the *s* of death	Ps 13:3	3462
spoiled, they have slept their *s*	Ps 76:5	8142
and horse are cast into a dead *s*	Ps 76:6	7290
the Lord awaked as one out of *s*	Ps 78:65	3463
they are as a *s*	Ps 90:5	8142
shall neither slumber nor *s*	Ps 121:4	3462
for so he giveth his beloved *s*	Ps 127:2	8142
I will not give *s* to mine eyes	Ps 132:4	8142
lie down, and thy *s* shall be sweet	Prov 3:24	8142
For they *s* not, except they have	Prov 4:16	3462
their *s* is taken away, unless	Prov 4:16	8142
Give not *s* to thine eyes, nor	Prov 6:4	8142
How long wilt thou *s*, O sluggard	Prov 6:9	7901
when wilt thou arise out of thy *s*	Prov 6:9	8142
Yet a little *s*, a little slumber,	Prov 6:10	8142
little folding of the hands to *s*	Prov 6:10	7901
casteth into a deep *s*	Prov 19:15	3462
Love not *s*, lest thou come to	Prov 20:13	8142
Yet a little *s*, a little slumber,	Prov 24:33	8142
little folding of the hands to *s*	Prov 24:33	7901
The *s* of a labouring man is sweet	Eccl 5:12	8142
the rich will not suffer him to *s*	Eccl 5:12	3462
nor night seeth *s* with his eyes	Eccl 8:16	8142
I *s*, but my heart waketh	Song 5:2	3463
none shall slumber nor *s*	Is 5:27	3463
out upon you the spirit of deep *s*	Is 29:10	8639
and my *s* was sweet unto me	Jer 31:26	8142
they may rejoice, and *s*	Jer 51:39	3462
a perpetual *s*, and not wake	Jer 51:39	8142
they shall *s* a perpetual *s*,	Jer 51:57	3462
and they shall *s* a perpetual *s*	Jer 51:57	8142
the wilderness, and *s* in the woods	Eze 34:25	3462
troubled, and his *s* brake from him	Dan 2:1	8142
and his *s* went from him	Dan 6:18	8139
I was in a deep *s* on my face	Dan 8:18	7290
then was I in a deep *s* on my face	Dan 10:9	7290
many of them that *s* in the dust	Dan 12:2	3463
man that is wakened out of his *s*	Zec 4:1	8142
s did as the angel of the Lord	Mt 1:24	5258
S on now, and take your rest	Mt 26:45	2518
And should *s*, and rise night and day	Mk 4:27	2518
S on now, and take your rest	Mk 14:41	2518
were with him were heavy with *s*	Lk 9:32	5258
And said unto them, Why *s* ye	Lk 22:46	2518
go, that I may awake him out of *s*	Jn 11:11	1852
said his disciples, Lord, if he *s*	Jn 11:12	2837
had spoken of taking of rest in *s*	Jn 11:13	5258
by the will of God, fell on *s*	Acts 13:36	2837
the prison awaking out of his *s*	Acts 16:27	1853
being fallen into a deep *s*	Acts 20:9	5258
preaching, he sunk down with *s*	Acts 20:9	5258
it is high time to awake out of *s*	Rom 13:11	5258
and sickly among you, and many *s*	1Cor 11:30	2837
We shall not all *s*, but we shall	1Cor 15:51	2837
even so them which *s* in	1Th 4:14	2837
Therefore let us not *s*, as do	1Th 5:6	2518
they that *s* *s* in the night	1Th 5:7	2518
us, that, whether we wake or *s*	1Th 5:10	2518

SLEEPER

unto him, What meanest thou, O *s*	Jonah 1:6	7290

SLEEPEST

Awake, why *s* thou, O Lord	Ps 44:23	3462
when thou *s*, it shall keep thee	Prov 6:22	7901
saith unto Peter, Simon, *s* thou	Mk 14:37	2518
he saith, Awake thou that *s*	Eph 5:14	2518

SLEEPETH

a journey, or peradventure he *s*	1Kin 18:27	3463
but he that *s* in harvest is a son	Prov 10:5	7290
their baker *s* all the night	Hos 7:6	3463
for the maid is not dead, but *s*	Mt 9:24	2518
the damsel is not dead, but *s*	Mk 5:39	2518
she is not dead, but *s*	Lk 8:52	2518
unto them, Our friend Lazarus *s*	Jn 11:11	2837

SLEEPING

Saul lay *s* within the trench, and	1Sa 26:7	3463
s, lying down, loving to slumber	Is 56:10	1957
coming suddenly he find you *s*	Mk 13:36	2518
And he cometh, and findeth them *s*	Mk 14:37	2518
he found them *s* for sorrow	Lk 22:45	2837
Peter was *s* between two soldiers	Acts 12:6	2837

SLEIGHT

wind of doctrine, by the *s* of men	Eph 4:14	2940

SLEPT

sleep to fall upon Adam, and he *s*	Gen 2:21	3462
And he *s* and dreamed the second	Gen 41:5	3462

But Uriah *s* at the door of the	2Sa 11:9	7901
So David *s* with his fathers, and	1Kin 2:10	7901
beside me, while thine handmaid *s*	1Kin 3:20	3463
that David *s* with his fathers	1Kin 11:21	7901
Solomon *s* with his fathers, and	1Kin 11:43	7901
he *s* with his fathers, and Nadab	1Kin 14:20	7901
Rehoboam *s* with his fathers, and	1Kin 14:31	7901
Abijam *s* with his fathers	1Kin 15:8	7901
Asa *s* with his fathers, and was	1Kin 15:24	7901
So Baasha *s* with his fathers, and	1Kin 16:6	7901
So Omri *s* with his fathers, and	1Kin 16:28	7901
s under a juniper tree, behold,	1Kin 19:5	3462
So Ahab *s* with his fathers	1Kin 22:40	7901
Jehoshaphat *s* with his fathers,	1Kin 22:50	7901
Joram *s* with his fathers, and was	2Kin 8:24	7901
And Jehu *s* with his fathers	2Kin 10:35	7901
Jehoahaz *s* with his fathers	2Kin 13:9	7901
And Joash *s* with his fathers	2Kin 13:13	7901
Jehoash *s* with his fathers, and	2Kin 14:16	7901
that the king *s* with his fathers	2Kin 14:22	7901
Jeroboam *s* with his fathers, even	2Kin 14:29	7901
So Azariah *s* with his fathers	2Kin 15:7	7901
Menahem *s* with his fathers	2Kin 15:22	7901
Jotham *s* with his fathers, and was	2Kin 15:38	7901
Ahaz *s* with his fathers, and was	2Kin 16:20	7901
Hezekiah *s* with his fathers	2Kin 20:21	7901
Manasseh *s* with his fathers, and	2Kin 21:18	7901
So Jehoiakim *s* with his fathers	2Kin 24:6	7901
Solomon *s* with his fathers, and he	2Chr 9:31	7901
Rehoboam *s* with his fathers, and	2Chr 12:16	7901
So Abijah *s* with his fathers, and	2Chr 14:1	7901
Asa *s* with his fathers, and died	2Chr 16:13	7901
Now Jehoshaphat *s* with his	2Chr 21:1	7901
that the king *s* with his fathers	2Chr 26:2	7901
So Uzziah *s* with his fathers, and	2Chr 26:23	7901
Jotham *s* with his fathers, and	2Chr 27:9	7901
Ahaz *s* with his fathers, and they	2Chr 28:27	7901
Hezekiah *s* with his fathers, and	2Chr 32:33	7901
So Manasseh *s* with his fathers,	2Chr 33:20	7901
and been quiet, I should have *s*	Job 3:13	3462
I laid me down and *s*	Ps 3:5	3462
spoiled, they have slept their sleep	Ps 76:5	5123
But while men *s*, his enemy came	Mt 13:25	2518
tarried, they all slumbered and *s*	Mt 25:5	2518
of the saints which *s* arose	Mt 27:52	2837
and stole him away while we *s*	Mt 28:13	2837
the firstfruits of them that *s*	1Cor 15:20	2837

SLEW

Abel his brother, and *s* him	Gen 4:8	2026
seed instead of Abel, whom Cain *s*	Gen 4:25	2026
city boldly, and *s* all the males	Gen 34:25	2026
they *s* Hamor and Shechem his son	Gen 34:26	2026
and the Lord *s* him	Gen 38:7	4191
wherefore he *s* him also	Gen 38:10	4191
for in their anger they *s* a man	Gen 49:6	2026
he *s* the Egyptian, and hid him in	Ex 2:12	5221
that the Lord *s* all the firstborn	Ex 13:15	2026
And he *s* it	Lev 8:15	7819
And he *s* it	Lev 8:23	7819
s the calf of the sin offering,	Lev 9:8	7819
And he *s* the burnt offering	Lev 9:12	7819
s it, and offered it for sin, as	Lev 9:15	7819
He *s* also the bullock and the ram	Lev 9:18	7819
and they *s* all the males	Num 31:7	2026
they *s* the kings of Midian	Num 31:8	2026
son of Beor they *s* with the sword	Num 31:8	2026
turned again, and *s* the men of Ai	Josh 8:21	5221
of Israel, that they *s* them not	Josh 9:26	2026
s them with a great slaughter at	Josh 10:10	5221
of Israel *s* with the sword	Josh 10:11	2026
s them, and hanged them on five	Josh 10:26	4191
he took, and smote them, and *s* them	Josh 11:17	4191
they *s* of them in Bezek ten	Judg 1:4	5221
they *s* the Canaanites and the	Judg 1:5	5221
they *s* Sheshai, and Ahiman, and	Judg 1:10	5221
they *s* the Canaanites that	Judg 1:17	5221
they *s* of Moab at that time about	Judg 3:29	5221
which *s* of the Philistines six	Judg 3:31	5221
they *s* Oreb upon the rock Oreb,	Judg 7:25	2026
Zeeb they *s* at the winepress of	Judg 7:25	2026
Penuel, and *s* the men of the city	Judg 8:17	2026
men were they whom ye *s* at Tabor	Judg 8:18	2026
s Zebah and Zalmunna,	Judg 8:21	2026
s his brethren the sons of	Judg 9:5	2026
their brother, which *s* them	Judg 9:24	2026
were in the fields, and *s* them	Judg 9:44	5221
s the people that was therein, and	Judg 9:45	2026
men say not of me, A woman *s* him	Judg 9:54	2026
s him at the passages of Jordan	Judg 12:6	7819
s thirty men of them, and took	Judg 14:19	5221

s a thousand men therewith .... Judg 15:15   5221
our country, which *s* many of us .... Judg 16:24   2491
So the dead which he *s* at his .... Judg 16:30   4191
than they which he *s* in his life .... Judg 16:30   4191
s two thousand men of them .... Judg 20:45   5221
they *s* a bullock, and brought the 1Sa 1:25   7819
they *s* of the army in the field 1Sa 4:2   5221
s the Ammonites until the heat of........... 1Sa 11:11   5221
and his armourbearer *s* after him 1Sa 14:13   4191
calves, and *s* them on the ground 1Sa 14:32   7819
him that night, and *s* them there 1Sa 14:34   7819
his beard, and smote him, and *s* him ... 1Sa 17:35   4191
Thy servant *s* both the lion and 1Sa 17:36   5221
and smote the Philistine, and *s* him 1Sa 17:50   4191
s him, and cut off his head 1Sa 17:51   4191
s of the Philistines two hundred............ 1Sa 18:27   5221
s the Philistine, and the LORD................ 1Sa 19:5   5221
s them with a great slaughter 1Sa 19:8   5221
s on that day fourscore and five 1Sa 22:18   4191
Saul *s* his thousands, and David............ 1Sa 29:5   5221
they *s* not any, either great or 1Sa 30:2   4191
and the Philistines *s* Jonathan 1Sa 31:2   5221
s him, because I was sure that he 2Sa 1:10   4191
and Abishai his brother *s* Abner 2Sa 3:30   2026
s him, and beheaded him, and took 2Sa 4:7   4191
s him in Ziklag, who thought that 2Sa 4:10   2026
his young men, and they *s* them 2Sa 4:12   2026
David *s* of the Syrians two and.............. 2Sa 8:5   5221
David *s* the men of seven hundred......... 2Sa 10:18   2126
the one smote the other, and *s* him 2Sa 14:6   4191
the life of his brother whom he *s* 2Sa 14:7   2026
about and Absalom, and *s* him 2Sa 18:15   4191
because he *s* the Gibeonites.................... 2Sa 21:1   4191
Sibbechai the Hushathite *s* Saph 2Sa 21:18   5221
s the brother of Goliath the 2Sa 21:19   5221
the brother of David *s* him 2Sa 21:21   5221
hundred, whom he *s* at one time 2Sa 23:8   2491
defended it, and *s* the Philistines 2Sa 23:12   5221
s them, and had the name among 2Sa 23:18   2491
he *s* two lionlike men of Moab 2Sa 23:20   5221
s a lion in the midst of a pit in 2Sa 23:20   5221
he *s* an Egyptian, a goodly man 2Sa 23:21   2026
hand, and *s* him with his own spear 2Sa 23:21   5221
And Adonijah *s* sheep and oxen and 1Kin 1:9   2076
the son of Jether, whom he *s* 1Kin 2:5   2026
s them with the sword, my father 1Kin 2:32   2026
up, and fell upon him, and *s* him 1Kin 2:34   4191
when David *s* them of Zobah 1Kin 11:24   2026
lion met him by the way, and *s* him 1Kin 13:24   4191
that he *s* all the house of Baasha 1Kin 16:11   5221
s the prophets of the LORD..................... 1Kin 18:13   2026
the brook Kishon, and *s* them there 1Kin 18:40   7819
s them, and boiled their flesh 1Kin 19:21   2076
And they *s* every one his man 1Kin 20:20   5221
s the Syrians with a great...................... 1Kin 20:21   5221
the children of Israel *s* of the 1Kin 20:29   5221
him, a lion found him, and *s* him 1Kin 20:36   5221
Had Zimri peace, who *s* his master........ 2Kin 9:31   2026
s seventy persons, and put their 2Kin 10:7   7819
against my master, and *s* him................ 2Kin 10:9   2026
but who *s* all these 2Kin 10:9   5221
So Jehu *s* all that remained of 2Kin 10:11   5221
s them at the pit of the shearing 2Kin 10:14   7819
he *s* all that remained unto Ahab........... 2Kin 10:17   5221
s Mattan the priest of Baal 2Kin 11:18   2026
they *s* Athaliah with the sword 2Kin 11:20   4191
s Joash in the house of Millo,................ 2Kin 12:20   5221
that he *s* his servants which had 2Kin 14:5   5221
of the murderers he *s* not....................... 2Kin 14:6   4191
He *s* of Edom in the valley of................. 2Kin 14:7   5221
him to Lachish, and *s* him there 2Kin 14:19   4191
s him, and reigned in his stead.............. 2Kin 15:10   4191
s him, and reigned in his stead.............. 2Kin 15:14   4191
s him, and reigned in his stead,............ 2Kin 15:30   4191
of it captive to Kir, and *s* Rezin........... 2Kin 16:9   4191
among them, which *s* some of them 2Kin 17:25   2026
s the king in his own house 2Kin 21:23   4191
the people of the land *s* all them........... 2Kin 21:24   5221
he *s* all the priests of the high............... 2Kin 23:20   2076
he *s* him at Megiddo, when he had 2Kin 23:29   4191
they *s* the sons of Zedekiah 2Kin 25:7   7819
s them at Riblah in the land of 2Kin 25:21   4191
and he *s* him 1Chr 2:3   4191
that were born in that land *s* 1Chr 7:21   2026
and the Philistines *s* Jonathan 1Chr 10:2   5221
therefore he *s* him, and turned the 1Chr 10:14   4191
it, and *s* the Philistines 1Chr 11:14   5221
he *s* them, and had a name among 1Chr 11:20   2490
he *s* two lionlike men of Moab 1Chr 11:22   5221
s a lion in a pit in a snowy day 1Chr 11:22   5221
he *s* an Egyptian, a man of great 1Chr 11:23   5221

hand, and *s* him with his own spear 1Chr 11:23   2026
David *s* of the Syrians two and.............. 1Chr 18:5   5221
Abishai the son Zeruiah *s* of the 1Chr 18:12   5221
David *s* of the Syrians seven 1Chr 19:18   2026
Sibbechai the Hushathite *s* Sippai 1Chr 20:4   5221
Elhanan the son of Jair *s* Lahmi............ 1Chr 20:5   5221
of Shimea David's brother *s* him........... 1Chr 20:7   5221
his people *s* them with a great............... 2Chr 13:17   5221
s all his brethren with the sword 2Chr 21:4   2026
ministered to Ahaziah, he *s* them.......... 2Chr 22:8   2026
Athaliah, so that she *s* him not.............. 2Chr 22:11   4191
king's house, they *s* her there................ 2Chr 23:15   4191
s Mattan the priest of Baal 2Chr 23:17   2026
had done to him, but *s* his son 2Chr 24:22   5221
s him on his bed, and he died 2Chr 24:25   2026
that he *s* his servants that had 2Chr 25:3   2026
But he *s* not their children, but 2Chr 25:4   4191
Lachish after him, and *s* him there........ 2Chr 25:27   4191
of Remaliah *s* in Judah an hundred....... 2Chr 28:6   2026
s Maaseiah the king's son, and............. 2Chr 28:7   2026
bowels *s* him there with the sword 2Chr 32:21   5307
him, and *s* him in his own house 2Chr 33:24   4191
But the people of the land *s* all 2Chr 33:25   5221
who *s* their young men with the............ 2Chr 36:17   2026
s thy prophets which testified .... Neh 9:26   2026
in Shushan the palace the Jews *s*........... Est 9:6   2026
the enemy of the Jews, *s* they .... Est 9:10   2026
s three hundred men at Shushan .... Est 9:15   2026
s of their foes seventy and five .... Est 9:16   2026
s the fattest of them, and smote........... Ps 78:31   2026
When he *s* them, then they sought........ Ps 78:34   2026
into blood, and *s* their fish.................... Ps 105:29   4191
great nations, and *s* mighty kings......... Ps 135:10   2026
And *s* famous kings................................. Ps 136:18   2026
killeth an ox is as if he *s* a man........... Is 66:3   5221
Because he *s* me not from the womb ..... Jer 20:17   4191
who *s* him with the sword, and cast ..... Jer 26:23   5221
Then the king of Babylon *s* the .... Jer 39:6   7819
Babylon *s* all the nobles of Judah .... Jer 39:6   7819
s him, whom the king of Babylon .... Jer 41:2   4191
Ishmael also *s* all the Jews that............ Jer 41:3   5221
the son of Nethaniah *s* them .... Jer 41:7   7819
s them not among their brethren .... Jer 41:8   4191
the king of Babylon *s* the sons of .... Jer 52:10   7819
he *s* also all the princes of.................... Jer 52:10   7819
s all that were pleasant to the.............. Lam 2:4   2026
they went forth, and *s* in the city .... Eze 9:7   5221
and *s* her with the sword .... Eze 23:10
whereupon they *s* their sacrifices .... Eze 40:41   7819
they *s* the burnt offering .... Eze 40:42   7819
the flame of the fire *s* those men .... Dan 3:22   6992
whom he would he *s* .... Dan 5:19   6992
s all the children that were in .... Mt 2:16   337
him out of the vineyard, and *s* him ... Mt 21:39   *615*
them spitefully, and *s* them .... Mt 22:6   *615*
whom ye *s* between the temple and ... Mt 23:35   *5407*
s them, think ye that they were** .... Lk 13:4   *615*
raised up Jesus, whom ye *s*................... Acts 5:30   *1315*
whom they *s* and hanged on a tree .... Acts 10:39   337
the raiment of them that *s* him .... Acts 22:20   337
deceived me, and by it *s* me .... Rom 7:11   *615*
that wicked one, and *s* his brother 1Jn 3:12   *4969*
And wherefore *s* he him......................... 1Jn 3:12   *4969*

SLEWEST
whom thou *s* in the valley of Elah 1Sa 21:9   5221

SLIDDEN
is this people of Jerusalem *s* .... Jer 8:5   7725

SLIDE
their foot shall *s* in due time .... Deut 32:35   4131
therefore I shall not *s* .... Ps 26:1   4571
none of his steps shall *s* .... Ps 37:31   4571

SLIDETH
For Israel *s* back as a .... Hos 4:16   5637

SLIGHTLY
of the daughter of my people *s* .... Jer 6:14   7043
of the daughter of my people *s* .... Jer 8:11   7043

SLIME
stone, and *s* had they for morter .... Gen 11:3   2564
of bulrushes, and daubed it with *s*......... Ex 2:3   2564

SLIMEPITS
the vale of Siddim was full of *s* .... Gen 14:10   2564

SLING
every one could *s* stones at an .... Judg 20:16   7049
and his *s* was in his hand 1Sa 17:40   7050
over the Philistine with a *s* 1Sa 17:50   7050
enemies, them shall he *s* out 1Sa 25:29   7049
as out of the middle of a *s* 1Sa 25:29   7050

S

As he that bindeth a stone in a s	Prov 26:8	4773
I will s out the inhabitants of	Jer 10:18	7049
devour, and subdue with s stones	Zec 9:15	7050

SLINGERS

howbeit the s went about it, and	2Kin 3:25	7051

SLINGS

and bows, and s to cast stones	2Chr 26:14	7050

SLINGSTONES

s are turned with him into	Job 41:28	68,7050

SLIP

so that my feet did not s	2Sa 22:37	4571
He that is ready to s with his	Job 12:5	4571
paths, that my footsteps s not	Ps 17:5	4131
under me, that my feet did not s	Ps 18:36	4571
at any time we should let them s	Heb 2:1	3901

SLIPPED

but he s away out of Saul's	1Sa 19:10	6362
my steps had well nigh s	Ps 73:2	8210

SLIPPERY

Let their way be dark and s	Ps 35:6	2519
thou didst set them in s places	Ps 73:18	2513
them as s ways in the darkness	Jer 23:12	2519

SLIPPETH

the head s from the helve, and	Deut 19:5	5394
when my foot s, they magnify	Ps 38:16	4131
When I said, My foot s	Ps 94:18	4131

SLIPS

and shalt set it with strange s	Is 17:10	2156

SLIVER

And he took all the gold and the s	2Chr 25:24	

SLOTHFUL

be not s to go, and to enter to	Judg 18:9	6101
but the s shall be under tribute	Prov 12:24	7423
The s man roasteth not that which	Prov 12:27	7423
The way of the s man is as an	Prov 15:19	6102
He also that is s in his work is	Prov 18:9	7503
A s man hideth his hand in his	Prov 19:24	6102
The desire of the s killeth him	Prov 21:25	6102
The s man saith, There is a lion	Prov 22:13	6102
I went by the field of the s	Prov 24:30	6102
The s man saith, There is a lion	Prov 26:13	6102
so doth the s upon his bed	Prov 26:14	6102
The s hideth his hand in his	Prov 26:15	6102
s servant, thou knewest that I	Mt 25:26	3636
Not s in business	Rom 12:11	3636
That ye be not s, but followers	Heb 6:12	3576

SLOTHFULNESS

S casteth into a deep sleep	Prov 19:15	6103
By much s the building decayeth	Eccl 10:18	6103

SLOW

but I am s of speech	Ex 4:10	3515
and of a s tongue	Ex 4:10	750
s to anger, and of great kindness,	Neh 9:17	750
s to anger, and plenteous in mercy	Ps 103:8	750
s to anger, and of great mercy	Ps 145:8	750
He that is s to wrath is of great	Prov 14:29	750
but he that is s to anger	Prov 15:18	750
He that is s to anger is better	Prov 16:32	750
s to anger, and of great kindness,	Joel 2:13	750
s to anger, and of great kindness,	Jonah 4:2	750
The LORD is s to anger, and great	Nah 1:3	750
s of heart to believe all that	Lk 24:25	1021
liars, evil beasts, s bellies	Titus 1:12	692
s to speak, s to wrath	Jas 1:19	1021

SLOWLY

And when we had sailed s many days	Acts 27:7	1020

SLUGGARD

Go to the ant, thou s	Prov 6:6	6102
How long wilt thou sleep, O s	Prov 6:9	6102
so is the s to them that send him	Prov 10:26	6102
The soul of the s desireth	Prov 13:4	6102
The s will not plow by reason of	Prov 20:4	6102
The s is wiser in his own conceit	Prov 26:16	6102

SLUICES

purposes thereof, all that make s	Is 19:10	7938

SLUMBER

he that keepeth thee will not s	Ps 121:3	5123
Israel shall neither s nor sleep	Ps 121:4	5123
mine eyes, or s to mine eyelids,	Ps 132:4	8572
eyes, nor s to thine eyelids	Prov 6:4	8572
Yet a little sleep, a little s	Prov 6:10	8572
Yet a little sleep, a little s	Prov 24:33	8572
none shall s nor sleep	Is 5:27	5123

sleeping, lying down, loving to s	Is 56:10	5123
Thy shepherds s, O king of	Nah 3:18	5123
hath given them the spirit of s	Rom 11:8	2659

SLUMBERED

bridegroom tarried, they all s	Mt 25:5	3573

SLUMBERETH

not, and their damnation s not	2Pet 2:3	3573

SLUMBERINGS

upon men, in s upon the bed	Job 33:15	8572

SMALL

the house with blindness, both s	Gen 19:11	6996
Is it a s matter that thou hast	Gen 30:15	4592
it shall become s dust in all the	Ex 9:9	
there lay a s round thing	Ex 16:14	1851
as s as the hoar frost on the	Ex 16:14	1851
but every s matter they shall	Ex 18:22	6996
but every s matter they judged	Ex 18:26	6996
thou shalt beat some of it very s	Ex 30:36	1854
full of sweet incense beaten s	Lev 16:12	1851
Seemeth it but a s thing unto you	Num 16:9	4592
Is it a s thing that thou hast	Num 16:13	4592
took the s towns thereof, and	Num 32:41	
hear the s as well as the great	Deut 1:17	6996
stamped it, and ground it very s	Deut 9:21	3190
even until it was as s as dust	Deut 9:21	1854
divers weights, a great and a s	Deut 25:13	6996
divers measures, a great and a s	Deut 25:14	6996
as the s rain upon the tender	Deut 32:2	
smote the men of the city, both s	1Sa 5:9	6996
will do nothing either great or s	1Sa 20:2	6996
slew not any, either great or s	1Sa 30:2	6996
neither s nor great, neither sons	1Sa 30:19	6996
this was yet a s thing in thy	2Sa 7:19	6994
be not one s stone found there	2Sa 17:13	1571
Then did I beat them as s as the	2Sa 22:43	
I desire one s petition of thee	1Kin 2:20	6996
and after the fire a still s voice	1Kin 19:12	1851
Fight neither with s nor great	1Kin 22:31	6996
their inhabitants were of s power	2Kin 19:26	7116
and all the people, both s	2Kin 23:2	6996
Kidron, and stamped it s to powder	2Kin 23:6	1854
place, and stamped it s to powder	2Kin 23:15	1854
And all the people, both s	2Kin 25:26	6996
yet this was a s thing in thine	1Chr 17:17	6994
as well the s as the great, the	1Chr 25:8	6996
as well the s as the great,	1Chr 26:13	6996
whether s or great, whether man	2Chr 15:13	6996
Fight ye not with s or great	2Chr 18:30	6996
came with a s company of men	2Chr 24:24	4705
as well to the great as to the s	2Chr 31:15	6996
and all the people, great and s	2Chr 34:30	6996
thousand and six hundred s cattle	2Chr 35:8	
offerings five thousand s cattle	2Chr 35:9	
of the house of God, great and s	2Chr 36:18	6996
the palace, both unto great and s	Est 1:5	6996
honour, both to great and s	Est 1:20	6996
The s and great are there	Job 3:19	6996
Though thy beginning was s	Job 8:7	4705
consolations of God s with thee	Job 15:11	4592
For he maketh s the drops of	Job 36:27	1639
likewise to the s rain, and to the	Job 37:6	
Then did I beat them s as the	Ps 18:42	
creeping innumerable, both s	Ps 104:25	6996
them that fear the LORD, both s	Ps 115:13	6996
I am s and despised	Ps 119:141	6810
of adversity, thy strength is s	Prov 24:10	6862
s cattle above all that were in	Eccl 2:7	
had left unto us a very s remnant	Is 1:9	4592
Is it a s thing for you to weary	Is 7:13	4592
and the remnant shall be very s	Is 16:14	4213
issue, all vessels of s quantity	Is 22:24	6996
strangers shall be like s dust	Is 29:5	1851
their inhabitants were of s power	Is 37:27	7116
are counted as the s dust of the	Is 40:15	
the mountains, and beat them s	Is 41:15	1854
Thou hast not brought me the s	Is 43:23	
For a s moment have I forsaken	Is 54:7	6996
and a s one a strong nation	Is 60:22	6810
the s shall die in this land	Jer 16:6	6996
them, and they shall not be s	Jer 30:19	6819
Yet a s number that escape the	Jer 44:28	4962
I will make thee s among the	Jer 49:15	6996
this of thy whoredoms a s matter	Eze 16:20	4592
Seemeth it a s thing unto you to	Eze 34:18	4592
become strong with a s people	Dan 11:23	4592
for he is s	Amos 7:2	6996
for he is s	Amos 7:5	6996
forth wheat, making the ephah s	Amos 8:5	6994
I have made thee s among the	Obad 2	6996

hath despised the day of *s* things	Zec 4:10	6996
that a *s* ship should wait on him	Mk 3:9	4142
And they had a few *s* fishes	Mk 8:7	2485
he had made a scourge of *s* cords	Jn 2:15	4979
barley loaves, and two *s* fishes	Jn 6:9	3795
there was no *s* stir among the	Acts 12:18	3641
and Barnabas had no *s* dissension	Acts 15:2	3641
arose no *s* stir about that way	Acts 19:23	3641
brought no *s* gain unto the	Acts 19:24	3641
this day, witnessing both to *s*	Acts 26:22	3398
no *s* tempest lay on us, all hope	Acts 27:20	3641
But with me it is a very *s* thing	1Cor 4:3	1646
turned about with a very *s* helm	Jas 3:4	1646
and them that fear thy name, *s*	Rev 11:18	3398
And he causeth all, both *s*	Rev 13:16	3398
and ye that fear him, both *s*	Rev 19:5	3398
men, both free and bond, both *s*	Rev 19:18	3398
And I saw the dead, *s* and great,	Rev 20:12	3398

SMALLEST

of the *s* of the tribes of Israel	1Sa 9:21	6996
unworthy to judge the *s* matters	1Cor 6:2	1646

SMART

for a stranger shall *s* for it	Prov 11:15	7321,7451

SMELL

he smelled the *s* of his raiment	Gen 27:27	7381
the *s* of my son is as the *s*	Gen 27:27	7381
to *s* thereto, shall even be cut	Ex 30:38	7306
I will not *s* the savour of your	Lev 26:31	7306
see, nor hear, nor eat, nor *s*	Deut 4:28	7306
All thy garments *s* of myrrh	Ps 45:8	
noses have they, but they *s* not	Ps 115:6	7306
sendeth forth the *s* thereof	Song 1:12	7381
the tender grape give a good *s*	Song 2:13	7381
the *s* of thine ointments than all	Song 4:10	7381
the *s* of thy garments is like the	Song 4:11	7381
garments is like the *s* of Lebanon	Song 4:11	7381
the *s* of thy nose like apples	Song 7:8	7381
The mandrakes give a *s*, and at our	Song 7:13	7381
of sweet *s* there shall be stink	Is 3:24	1314
nor the *s* of fire had passed on	Dan 3:27	7382
olive tree, and his *s* as Lebanon	Hos 14:6	7381
I will not *s* in your solemn	Amos 5:21	7306
from you, an odour of a sweet *s*	Phil 4:18	2175

SMELLED

the LORD *s* a sweet savour	Gen 8:21	7306
he *s* the smell of his raiment, and	Gen 27:27	7306

SMELLETH

he *s* the battle afar off, the	Job 39:25	7306

SMELLING

and my fingers with sweet *s* myrrh	Song 5:5	5674
lilies, dropping sweet *s* myrrh	Song 5:13	5674
were hearing, where were the *s*	1Cor 12:17	3750

SMITE

neither will I again *s* any more	Gen 8:21	5221
s it, then the other company	Gen 32:8	5221
s me, and the mother with the	Gen 32:11	5221
s Egypt with all my wonders which	Ex 3:20	5221
I will *s* with the rod that is in	Ex 7:17	5221
I will *s* all thy borders with	Ex 8:2	5062
s the dust of the land, that it	Ex 8:16	5221
out my hand, that I may *s* thee	Ex 9:15	5221
will *s* all the firstborn in the	Ex 12:12	5221
when I *s* the land of Egypt	Ex 12:13	5221
pass through to *s* the Egyptians	Ex 12:23	5062
come in unto your houses to *s* you	Ex 12:23	5062
and thou shalt *s* the rock, and	Ex 17:6	5221
one another with a stone, or	Ex 21:18	5221
if a man *s* his servant, or his	Ex 21:20	5221
if a man *s* the eye of his servant	Ex 21:26	5221
if he *s* out his manservant's	Ex 21:27	5307
I will *s* them with the pestilence	Num 14:12	5221
shall prevail, that we may *s* them	Num 22:6	5221
shall *s* the corners of Moab, and	Num 24:17	4272
Vex the Midianites, and *s* them	Num 25:17	5221
if he *s* him with an instrument of	Num 35:16	5221
if he *s* him with throwing a stone	Num 35:17	5221
Or if he *s* him with an hand	Num 35:18	5221
Or in enmity *s* him with his hand,	Num 35:21	5221
thou shalt *s* them, and utterly	Deut 7:2	5221
Thou shalt surely *s* the	Deut 13:15	5221
s him mortally that he die, and	Deut 19:11	5221
thou shalt *s* every male thereof	Deut 20:13	5221
The LORD shall *s* thee with a	Deut 28:22	5221
The LORD will *s* thee with the	Deut 28:27	5221
The LORD shall *s* thee with	Deut 28:28	5221
The LORD shall *s* thee in the	Deut 28:35	5221
s through the loins of them that	Deut 33:11	4272

three thousand men go up and *s* Ai	Josh 7:3	6221
and help me, that we may *s* Gibeon	Josh 10:4	6221
and *s* the hindmost of them	Josh 10:19	5221
LORD and the children of Israel *s*	Josh 12:6	5221
for these did Moses *s*, and cast	Josh 13:12	5221
thou shalt *s* the Midianites as	Judg 6:16	5221
and they began to *s* of the people	Judg 20:31	5221
the battle, Benjamin began to *s*	Judg 20:39	5221
Go and *s* the inhabitants of	Judg 21:10	5221
s Amalek, and utterly destroy all	1Sa 15:3	5221
and I will *s* thee, and take thine	1Sa 17:46	5221
I will *s* David even to the wall	1Sa 18:11	5221
Saul sought to *s* David even to	1Sa 19:10	5221
cast a javelin at him to *s* him	1Sa 20:33	5221
Shall I go and *s* these Philistines	1Sa 23:2	5221
s the Philistines, and save Keilah	1Sa 23:2	5221
now therefore let me *s* him	1Sa 26:8	5221
I will not *s* him the second time	1Sa 26:8	5221
LORD liveth, the LORD shall *s* him	1Sa 26:10	5062
should I *s* thee to the ground	2Sa 2:22	5221
to *s* the host of the Philistines	2Sa 5:24	5221
and when I say unto you, *S* Amnon	2Sa 13:28	5221
s the city with the edge of the	2Sa 15:14	5221
and I will *s* the king only	2Sa 17:2	5221
why didst thou not *s* him there to	2Sa 18:11	5221
For the LORD shall *s* Israel	1Kin 14:15	5221
of the LORD, *S* me, I pray thee	1Kin 20:35	5221
And the man refused to *s* him	1Kin 20:35	5221
man, and said, *S* me, I pray thee	1Kin 20:37	5221
ye shall *s* every fenced city, and	2Kin 3:19	5221
S this people, I pray thee, with	2Kin 6:18	5221
them, My father, shall I *s* them	2Kin 6:21	5221
shall I *s* them	2Kin 6:21	5221
answered, Thou shalt not *s* them	2Kin 6:22	5221
wouldest thou *s* those whom thou	2Kin 6:22	5221
thou shalt *s* the house of Ahab	2Kin 9:7	5221
S him also in the chariot	2Kin 9:27	5221
for thou shalt *s* the Syrians in	2Kin 13:17	5221
king of Israel, *S* upon the ground	2Kin 13:18	5221
now thou shalt *s* Syria but thrice	2Kin 13:19	5221
to *s* the host of the Philistines	1Chr 14:15	5221
plague will the LORD *s* thy people	2Chr 21:14	5062
The sun shall not *s* thee by day	Ps 121:6	5221
Let the righteous *s* me	Ps 141:5	1986
S a scorner, and the simple will	Prov 19:25	5221
Therefore the Lord will *s* with a	Is 3:17	5596
he shall *s* thee with a rod, and	Is 10:24	5221
he shall *s* the earth with the rod	Is 11:4	5221
shall *s* it in the seven streams,	Is 11:15	5221
And the LORD shall *s* Egypt	Is 19:22	5062
he shall *s* and heal it	Is 19:22	5062
shall the heat nor sun *s* them	Is 49:10	5221
to *s* with the fist of wickedness	Is 58:4	5221
let us *s* him with the tongue, and	Jer 18:18	5221
I will *s* the inhabitants of this	Jer 21:6	5221
he shall *s* them with the edge of	Jer 21:7	5221
he shall *s* the land of Egypt, and	Jer 43:11	5221
come and *s* the land of Egypt	Jer 46:13	5221
king of Babylon shall *s*, thus	Jer 49:28	5221
part, and *s* about it with a knife	Eze 5:2	5221
S with thine hand, and stamp with	Eze 6:11	5221
after him through the city, and *s*	Eze 9:5	5221
s therefore upon thy thigh	Eze 21:12	5606
s thine hands together, and let	Eze 21:14	5221
I will also *s* mine hands together	Eze 21:17	5221
when I shall *s* all them that	Eze 32:15	5221
I will *s* thy bow out of thy left	Eze 39:3	5221
I will *s* the winter house with	Amos 3:15	5221
he will *s* the great house with	Amos 6:11	5221
S the lintel of the door, that	Amos 9:1	5221
they shall *s* the judge of Israel	Mic 5:1	5221
melteth, and the knees *s* together	Nah 2:10	6375
he will *s* her power in the sea	Zec 9:4	5221
shall *s* the waves in the sea, and	Zec 10:11	5221
and they shall *s* the land, and out	Zec 11:6	3807
I will *s* every horse with	Zec 12:4	5221
will *s* every horse of the people	Zec 12:4	5221
s the shepherd, and the sheep	Zec 13:7	5221
plague wherewith the LORD will *s*	Zec 14:12	5062
wherewith the LORD will *s* the	Zec 14:18	5062
come and smite the earth with a curse	Mal 4:6	5221
but whosoever shall *s* thee on thy	Mt 5:39	4474
And shall begin to *s* his	Mt 24:49	5180
I will *s* the shepherd, and the	Mt 26:31	3960
I will *s* the shepherd, and the	Mk 14:27	3960
shall we *s* with the sword	Lk 22:49	3960
by him to *s* him on the mouth	Acts 23:2	5180
Paul unto him, God shall *s* thee	Acts 23:3	5180
if a man *s* you on the face	2Cor 11:20	1194
to *s* the earth with all plagues,	Rev 11:6	3960

S

with it he should *s* the nations .... Rev 19:15   *3960*

SMITERS
I gave my back to the *s*, and my .... Is 50:6   5221

SMITEST
Wherefore *s* thou thy fellow .... Ex 2:13   5221
but if well, why *s* thou me .... Jn 18:23   *1194*

SMITETH
He that *s* a man, so that he die, ... Ex 21:12   5221
he that *s* his father, or his .... Ex 21:15   5221
out of the hand of him that *s* him .... Deut 25:11   5221
Cursed be he that *s* his neighbour .... Deut 27:24   5221
He that *s* Kirjath-sepher, and .... Josh 15:16   5221
He that *s* Kirjath-sepher, and .... Judg 1:12   5221
s the Jebusites, and the lame and 2Sa 5:8   5221
Whosoever *s* the Jebusites first 1Chr 11:6   5221
he *s* through the proud .... Job 26:12   4272
turneth not unto him that *s* them .... Is 9:13   5221
his cheek to him that *s* him .... Lam 3:30   5221
know that I am the LORD that *s* .... Eze 7:9   5221
unto him that *s* thee on the one .... Lk 6:29   *5180*

SMITH
Now there was no *s* found 1Sa 13:19   2796
The *s* with the tongs both worketh . Is 44:12   2796,1270
I have created the *s* that bloweth .... Is 54:16   2796

SMITHS
and all the craftsmen and *s* 2Kin 24:14   4525
s a thousand, all that were 2Kin 24:16   4525
Judah, with the carpenters and *s* .... Jer 24:1   4525
and the carpenters, and the *s* .... Jer 29:2   4525

SMITING
he spied an Egyptian *s* an Hebrew .... Ex 2:11   5221
a name when he returned from *s* of 2Sa 8:13   5221
so that in he wounded him 1Kin 20:37   5221
they went forward *s* the Moabites 2Kin 3:24   5221
will I make thee sick in *s* thee .... Mic 6:13   5221

SMITTEN
that the LORD had *s* the river .... Ex 7:25   5221
And the flax and the barley was *s* .... Ex 9:31   5221
the wheat and the rie were not *s* .... Ex 9:32   5221
be *s* that he die, there shall no .... Ex 22:2   5221
that ye be not *s* before your .... Num 14:42   5062
that thou hast *s* me these three .... Num 22:28   5221
Wherefore hast thou *s* thine ass .... Num 22:32   5221
which the LORD had *s* among them .... Num 33:4   5221
lest ye be *s* before your enemies .... Deut 1:42   5062
thee to be *s* before thy face .... Deut 28:7   5062
thee to be *s* before thine enemies .... Deut 28:25   5062
s it with the edge of the sword, ... Judg 1:8   5221
They are *s* down before us, as at .... Judg 20:32   5062
of Benjamin saw that they were *s* .... Judg 20:36   5062
Surely they are *s* down before us .... Judg 20:39   5062
battle, Israel was *s* before the 1Sa 4:2   5062
the LORD *s* us to day before the 1Sa 4:3   5062
fought, and Israel was *s*, and they 1Sa 4:10   5062
died not were *s* with the emerods 1Sa 5:12   5221
because the LORD had *s* many of 1Sa 6:19   5221
they were *s* before Israel 1Sa 7:10   5062
s a garrison of the Philistines 1Sa 13:4   5221
s Ziklag, and burned it with fire 1Sa 30:1   5221
of David had *s* of Benjamin 2Sa 2:31   5221
had *s* all the host of Hadadezer 2Sa 8:9   5221
against Hadadezer, and *s* him 2Sa 8:10   5221
that they were *s* before Israel 2Sa 10:15   5062
that they were *s* before Israel 2Sa 10:19   5062
ye from him, that he may be *s* 2Sa 11:15   5221
Israel be *s* down before the enemy 1Kin 8:33   5062
after he had *s* every male in Edom 1Kin 11:15   5221
and when he also had *s* the waters 2Kin 2:14   5221
slain, and they have *s* one another 2Kin 3:23   5221
have *s* five or six times 2Kin 13:19   5221
then hadst thou *s* Syria till thou 2Kin 13:19   5221
Thou hast indeed *s* Edom, and thine 2Kin 14:10   5221
of Hamath heard how David had *s* 1Chr 18:9   5221
against Hadarezer, and *s* him 1Chr 18:10   5221
and they were *s* 2Chr 20:22   5062
why shouldest thou be *s* 2Chr 25:16   5221
Lo, thou hast *s* the Edomites 2Chr 25:19   5221
out, because the LORD had *s* him 2Chr 26:20   5060
s Judah, and carried away captives 2Chr 28:17   5221
they have *s* me upon the cheek .... Job 16:10   5221
for thou hast *s* all mine enemies .... Ps 3:7   5221
persecute whom thou hast *s* .... Ps 69:26   5221
My heart is *s*, and withered like .... Ps 102:4   5221
he hath *s* my life down to the .... Ps 143:3   1792
hand against them, and hath *s* them ..... Is 5:25   5221
the gate is *s* with destruction .... Is 24:12   3807
Hath he *s* him, as he smote those .... Is 27:7   5221

stricken, *s* of God, and afflicted .... Is 53:4   5221
In vain have I *s* your children .... Jer 2:30   5221
why hast thou *s* us, and there is .... Jer 14:19   5221
For though ye had *s* the whole .... Jer 37:10   5221
therefore I have *s* mine hand at .... Eze 22:13   5221
unto me, saying, The city is *s* .... Eze 33:21   5221
year after that the city was *s* .... Eze 40:1   5221
he hath *s*, and he will bind us up .... Hos 6:1   5221
Ephraim is *s*, their root is dried .... Hos 9:16   5221
I have *s* you with blasting and .... Amos 4:9   5221
me to be *s* contrary to the law .... Acts 23:3   *5180*
the third part of the sun was *s* .... Rev 8:12   *4141*

SMOKE
the *s* of the country went up as .... Gen 19:28   7008
went up as the *s* of a furnace .... Gen 19:28   7008
mount Sinai was altogether on a *s* .... Ex 19:18   6225
the *s* thereof ascended as the .... Ex 19:18   6227
ascended as the *s* of a furnace .... Ex 19:18   6227
jealousy shall *s* against that man .... Deut 29:20   6225
the *s* of the city ascended up to .... Josh 8:20   6227
that the *s* of the city ascended, ... Josh 8:21   6227
with *s* rise up out of the city .... Judg 20:38   6227
of the city with a pillar of *s* .... Judg 20:40   6227
There went up a *s* out of his 2Sa 22:9   6227
Out of his nostrils goeth *s* .... Job 41:20   6227
There went up a *s* out of his .... Ps 18:8   6227
into *s* shall they consume away .... Ps 37:20   6227
As *s* is driven away, so drive .... Ps 68:2   6227
why doth thine anger *s* against .... Ps 74:1   6225
For my days are consumed like *s* .... Ps 102:3   6227
he toucheth the hills, and they *s* .... Ps 104:32   6225
am become like a bottle in the *s* .... Ps 119:83   7008
the mountains, and they shall *s* .... Ps 144:5   6225
as *s* to the eyes, so is the .... Prov 10:26   6227
the wilderness like pillars of *s* .... Song 3:6   6227
s by day, and the shining of a .... Is 4:5   6227
and the house was filled with *s* .... Is 6:4   6227
mount up like the lifting up of *s* .... Is 9:18   6227
shall come from the north a *s* .... Is 14:31   6227
the *s* thereof shall go up for .... Is 34:10   6227
heavens shall vanish away like *s* .... Is 51:6   6227
These are a *s* in my nose, a fire .... Is 65:5   6227
as the *s* out of the chimney .... Hos 13:3   6227
blood, and fire, and pillars of *s* .... Joel 2:30   6227
I will burn her chariots in the *s* .... Nah 2:13   6227
blood, and fire, and vapour of *s* .... Acts 2:19   2586
the *s* of the incense, which came .... Rev 8:4   2586
there arose a *s* out of the pit, ... Rev 9:2   2586
as the *s* of a great furnace .... Rev 9:2   2586
by reason of the *s* of the pit .... Rev 9:2   2586
there came out of the *s* locusts .... Rev 9:3   2586
of their mouths issued fire and *s* .... Rev 9:17   2586
killed, by the fire, and by the *s* .... Rev 9:18   2586
the *s* of their torment ascendeth .... Rev 14:11   2586
with *s* from the glory of God .... Rev 15:8   2586
shall see the *s* of her burning .... Rev 18:9   2586
they saw the *s* of her burning .... Rev 18:18   2586
her *s* rose up for ever and ever .... Rev 19:3   2586

SMOKING
it was dark, behold a *s* furnace .... Gen 15:17   6227
of the trumpet, and the mountain *s* .... Ex 20:18   6226
two tails of these *s* firebrands .... Is 7:4   6226
the *s* flax shall he not quench .... Is 42:3   3544
s flax shall he not quench, till .... Mt 12:20   *5187*

SMOOTH
is a hairy man, and I am a *s* man .... Gen 27:11   2509
hands, and upon the *s* of his neck .... Gen 27:16   2513
chose him five *s* stones out of 1Sa 17:40   2512
things, speak unto us *s* things .... Is 30:10   2513
Among the *s* stones of the stream .... Is 57:6   2511
and the rough ways shall be made *s* ..... Lk 3:5   *3006*

SMOOTHER
of his mouth were *s* than butter .... Ps 55:21   2505
and her mouth is *s* than oil .... Prov 5:3   2513

SMOOTHETH
he that *s* with the hammer him .... Is 41:7   2505

SMOTE
s the Rephaims in Ashteroth .... Gen 14:5   5221
and *s* all the country of the .... Gen 14:7   5221
s them, and pursued them unto .... Gen 14:15   5221
they *s* the men that were at the .... Gen 19:11   5221
who *s* Midian in the field of Moab .... Gen 36:35   5221
s the waters that were in the .... Ex 7:20   5221
s the dust of the earth, and it .... Ex 8:17   5221
the hail *s* throughout all the .... Ex 9:25   5221
the hail *s* every herb of the .... Ex 9:25   5221
when he *s* the Egyptians, and .... Ex 12:27   5062

that at midnight the LORD *s* all	Ex 12:29	5221
then shall he that *s* him be quit	Ex 21:19	5221
for on the day that I *s* all the	Num 3:13	5221
on the day that I *s* every	Num 8:17	5221
the LORD *s* the people with a very	Num 11:33	5221
s them, and discomfited them, even	Num 14:45	5221
with his rod he *s* the rock twice	Num 20:11	5221
Israel *s* him with the edge of the	Num 21:24	5221
So they *s* him, and his sons, and	Num 21:35	5221
Balaam *s* the ass, to turn her	Num 22:23	5221
and he *s* her again	Num 22:25	5221
he *s* the ass with a staff	Num 22:27	5221
and he *s* his hands together	Num 24:10	5606
LORD *s* before the congregation of	Num 32:4	5221
he that *s* him shall surely be put	Num 35:21	5221
we *s* him, and his sons, and all his	Deut 2:33	5221
we *s* him until none was left to	Deut 3:3	5221
Moses and the children of Israel *s*	Deut 4:46	5221
s the hindmost of thee, even all	Deut 25:18	5221
us unto battle, and we *s* them	Deut 29:7	5221
the men of Ai *s* of them about	Josh 7:5	5221
and *s* them in the going down	Josh 7:5	5221
and they *s* them, so that they let	Josh 8:22	5221
s it with the edge of the sword	Josh 8:24	5221
the children of Israel *s* them not	Josh 9:18	5221
s them to Azekah, and unto	Josh 10:10	5221
And afterward Joshua *s* them	Josh 10:26	5221
s it with the edge of the sword,	Josh 10:28	5221
he *s* it with the edge of the	Josh 10:30	5221
s it with the edge of the sword,	Josh 10:32	5221
and Joshua *s* him and his people,	Josh 10:33	5221
s it with the edge of the sword,	Josh 10:35	5221
s it with the edge of the sword,	Josh 10:37	5221
they *s* them with the edge of the	Josh 10:39	5221
So Joshua *s* all the country of	Josh 10:40	5221
Joshua *s* them from Kadesh-barnea	Josh 10:41	5221
who *s* them, and chased them unto	Josh 11:8	5221
and they *s* them, until they left	Josh 11:8	5221
s the king thereof with the sword	Josh 11:10	5221
they *s* all the souls that were	Josh 11:11	5221
s them with the edge of the sword	Josh 11:12	5221
but every man they *s* with the	Josh 11:14	5221
he took, and *s* them, and slew them	Josh 11:17	5221
which the children of Israel *s*	Josh 12:1	5221
the children of Israel *s* on this	Josh 12:7	5221
whom Moses *s* with the princes of	Josh 13:21	5221
s it with the edge of the sword,	Josh 19:47	5221
because he *s* his neighbour	Josh 20:5	5221
they *s* the city with the edge of	Judg 1:25	5221
s Israel, and possessed the city	Judg 3:13	5221
s the nail into his temples, and	Judg 4:21	5221
and with the hammer she *s* Sisera	Judg 5:26	1986
she *s* off his head, when she had	Judg 5:26	4277
s it that it fell, and overturned	Judg 7:13	5221
Nobah and Jogbehah, and *s* the host	Judg 8:11	5221
rose up against them, and *s* them	Judg 9:43	5221
hand of Israel, and they *s* them	Judg 11:21	5221
he *s* them from Aroer, even till	Judg 11:33	5221
and the men of Gilead *s* Ephraim	Judg 12:4	5221
he *s* them hip and thigh with a	Judg 15:8	5221
they *s* them with the edge of the	Judg 18:27	5221
the LORD *s* Benjamin before Israel	Judg 20:35	5062
s all the city with the edge of	Judg 20:37	5221
s them with the edge of the sword	Judg 20:48	5221
these are the Gods that *s* the	1Sa 4:8	5221
s them with emerods, even Ashdod	1Sa 5:6	5221
he *s* the men of the city, both	1Sa 5:9	5221
that it is not his hand that *s* us	1Sa 6:9	5060
he *s* the men of Beth-shemesh,	1Sa 6:19	5221
even he *s* of the people fifty	1Sa 6:19	5221
s them, until they came under	1Sa 7:11	5221
Jonathan *s* the garrison of the	1Sa 13:3	5221
they *s* the Philistines that day	1Sa 14:31	5221
s the Amalekites, and delivered	1Sa 14:48	5221
Saul *s* the Amalekites from	1Sa 15:7	5221
s him, and delivered it out of his	1Sa 17:35	5221
his beard, and *s* him, and slew him	1Sa 17:35	5221
s the Philistine in his forehead,	1Sa 17:49	5221
s the Philistine, and slew him	1Sa 17:50	5221
he *s* the javelin into the wall	1Sa 19:10	5221
s he with the edge of the sword,	1Sa 22:19	5221
s them with a great slaughter	1Sa 23:5	5221
that David's heart *s* him	1Sa 24:5	5221
days after, that the LORD *s* Nabal	1Sa 25:38	5062
David *s* the land, and left neither	1Sa 27:9	5221
David *s* them from the twilight	1Sa 30:17	5221
And he *s* him that he died	2Sa 1:15	5221
spear *s* him under the fifth rib	2Sa 2:23	5221
s him there under the fifth rib,	2Sa 3:27	5221
they *s* him under the fifth rib	2Sa 4:6	5221
in his bedchamber, and they *s* him	2Sa 4:7	5221
David *s* them there, and said, The	2Sa 5:20	5221
s the Philistines from Geba until	2Sa 5:25	5221
God *s* him there for his error	2Sa 6:7	5221
that David *s* the Philistines, and	2Sa 8:1	5221
he *s* Moab, and measured them with	2Sa 8:2	5221
David *s* also Hadadezer, the son	2Sa 8:3	5221
s Shobach the captain of their	2Sa 10:18	5221
Who *s* Abimelech the son of	2Sa 11:21	5221
them, but the one *s* the other	2Sa 14:6	5221
Deliver him that *s* his brother	2Sa 14:7	5221
about and *s* Absalom, and slew him	2Sa 18:15	5221
so he *s* him therewith in the	2Sa 20:10	5221
s the Philistine, and killed him	2Sa 21:17	5221
s the Philistines until his hand	2Sa 23:10	5221
David's heart *s* him after that he	2Sa 24:10	5221
saw the angel that *s* the people	2Sa 24:17	5221
of Israel, and *s* Ijon, and Dan, and	1Kin 15:20	5221
Baasha *s* him at Gibbethon, which	1Kin 15:27	5221
that he *s* all the house of	1Kin 15:29	5221
s him, and killed him, in the	1Kin 16:10	5221
s the horses and chariots, and slew	1Kin 20:21	5221
And the man *s* him, so that in	1Kin 20:37	5221
s Micaiah on the cheek, and said,	1Kin 22:24	5221
s the king of Israel between the	1Kin 22:34	5221
s the waters, and they were	2Kin 2:8	5221
s the waters, and said, Where is	2Kin 2:14	5221
s the Moabites, so that they fled	2Kin 3:24	5221
slingers went about it, and *s* it	2Kin 3:25	5221
And he *s* them with blindness	2Kin 6:18	5221
s the Edomites which compassed	2Kin 8:21	5221
s Jehoram between his arms, and	2Kin 9:24	5221
they *s* them with the edge of the	2Kin 10:25	5221
Hazael *s* them in all the coasts	2Kin 10:32	5221
his servants, *s* him, and he died	2Kin 12:21	5221
And he *s* thrice, and stayed	2Kin 13:18	5221
And the LORD *s* the king, so that	2Kin 15:5	5221
s him before the people, and slew	2Kin 15:10	5221
s Shallum the son of Jabesh in	2Kin 15:14	5221
Then Menahem *s* Tiphsah, and all	2Kin 15:16	5221
not to him, therefore he *s* it	2Kin 15:16	5221
s him in Samaria, in the palace	2Kin 15:25	5221
s him, and slew him, and reigned in	2Kin 15:30	5221
He *s* the Philistines, even unto	2Kin 18:8	5221
s in the camp of the Assyrians an	2Kin 19:35	5221
Sharezer his sons *s* him with the	2Kin 19:37	5221
And the king of Babylon *s* them	2Kin 25:21	5221
s Gedaliah, that he died, and the	2Kin 25:25	5221
which *s* Midian in the field of	1Chr 1:46	5221
s their tents, and the habitations	1Chr 4:41	5221
they *s* the rest of the Amalekites	1Chr 4:43	5221
he *s* him, because he put his hand	1Chr 13:10	5221
and David *s* them there	1Chr 14:11	5221
and they *s* the host of the	1Chr 14:16	5221
that David *s* the Philistines, and	1Chr 18:1	5221
And he *s* Moab	1Chr 18:2	5221
David *s* Hadarezer king of Zobah	1Chr 18:3	5221
Joab *s* Rabbah, and destroyed it	1Chr 20:1	5221
therefore he *s* Israel	1Chr 21:7	5221
came to pass, that God *s* Jeroboam	2Chr 13:15	5062
So the LORD *s* the Ethiopians	2Chr 14:12	5062
they *s* all the cities round about	2Chr 14:14	5221
They *s* also the tents of cattle,	2Chr 14:15	5221
and they *s* Ijon, and Dan, and	2Chr 16:4	5221
s Micaiah upon the cheek, and said	2Chr 18:23	5221
s the king of Israel between the	2Chr 18:33	5221
s the Edomites which compassed	2Chr 21:9	5221
after all this the LORD *s* him in	2Chr 21:18	5062
and the Syrians *s* Joram	2Chr 22:5	5221
s of the children of Seir ten	2Chr 25:11	5221
s three thousand of them, and took	2Chr 25:13	5221
and they *s* him, and carried away a	2Chr 28:5	5221
who *s* him with a great slaughter	2Chr 28:5	5221
the gods of Damascus, which *s* him	2Chr 28:23	5221
s certain of them, and plucked off	Neh 13:25	5221
Thus the Jews *s* all their enemies	Est 9:5	5221
s the four corners of the house,	Job 1:19	5060
s Job with sore boils from the	Job 2:7	5221
s of Edom in the valley of salt	Ps 60:t	5221
he *s* the rock, that the waters	Ps 78:20	5221
s down the chosen men of Israel	Ps 78:31	3766
s all the firstborn in Egypt	Ps 78:51	5221
he *s* his enemies in the hinder	Ps 78:66	5221
He *s* their vines also and their	Ps 105:33	5221
He *s* also all the firstborn in	Ps 105:36	5221
Who *s* the firstborn of Egypt,	Ps 135:8	5221
Who *s* great nations, and slew	Ps 135:10	5221
To him that *s* Egypt in their	Ps 136:10	5221
To him which *s* great kings	Ps 136:17	5221
the city found me, they *s* me	Song 5:7	5221

S

again stay upon him that *s* them	Is 10:20	5221
He who *s* the people in wrath with	Is 14:6	5221
rod of him that *s* thee is broken	Is 14:29	5221
as he *s* those that	Is 27:7	4347
those that *s* him	Is 27:7	5221
beaten down, which *s* with a rod	Is 30:31	5221
s in the camp of the Assyrians an	Is 37:36	5221
Sharezer his sons *s* him with the	Is 37:38	5221
the hammer him that *s* the anvil	Is 41:7	1986
was I wroth, and *s* him	Is 57:17	5221
for in my wrath I *s* thee, but in	Is 60:10	5221
Then Pashur *s* Jeremiah the	Jer 20:2	5221
was instructed, I *s* upon my thigh	Jer 31:19	5606
s him, and put him in prison in	Jer 37:15	5221
s Gedaliah the son of Ahikam the	Jer 41:2	5221
Nebuchadrezzar king of Babylon *s*	Jer 46:2	5221
before that Pharaoh *s* Gaza	Jer 47:1	5221
And the king of Babylon *s* them	Jer 52:27	5221
which *s* the image upon his feet	Dan 2:34	4223
the stone that *s* the image became	Dan 2:35	4223
his knees *s* one against another	Dan 5:6	5368
s the ram, and brake his two horns	Dan 8:7	5221
it *s* the gourd that it withered	Jonah 4:7	5221
I *s* you with blasting and with	Hag 2:17	5221
high priest's, and *s* off his ear	Mt 26:51	851
others *s* him with the palms of	Mt 26:67	4474
Christ, Who is he that *s* thee	Mt 26:68	3817
the reed, and *s* him on the head	Mt 27:30	5180
s a servant of the high priest,	Mk 14:47	3817
they *s* him on the head with a	Mk 15:19	5180
but *s* upon his breast, saying,	Lk 18:13	5180
one of them *s* the servant of the	Lk 22:50	3960
held Jesus mocked him, and *s* him	Lk 22:63	1194
Prophesy, who is it that *s* thee	Lk 22:64	3817
s their breasts, and returned	Lk 23:48	5180
s the high priest's servant, and	Jn 18:10	3817
they *s* him with their hands	Jn 19:3	1325,4475
was oppressed, and *s* the Egyptian	Acts 7:24	3960
he *s* Peter on the side, and raised	Acts 12:7	3960
the angel of the Lord *s* him	Acts 12:23	3960

SMOTEST
rod, wherewith thou *s* the river	Ex 17:5	5221

SMYRNA (smir'-na) A City of Ionia in Asia Minor.
unto Ephesus, and unto S, and unto	Rev 1:11	4667
angel of the church in S write	Rev 2:8	4668

SNAIL
and the lizard, and the *s*, and the	Lev 11:30	2546
As a *s* which melteth, let every	Ps 58:8	7642

SNARE
shall this man be a *s* unto us	Ex 10:7	4170
it will surely be a *s* unto thee	Ex 23:33	4170
lest it be for a *s* in the midst	Ex 34:12	4170
for that will be a *s* unto thee	Deut 7:16	4170
their gods shall be a *s* unto you	Judg 2:3	4170
thing became a *s* unto Gideon	Judg 8:27	4170
her, that she may be a *s* to him	1Sa 18:21	4170
then layest thou a *s* for my life	1Sa 28:9	5367
own feet, and he walketh upon a *s*	Job 18:8	7639
The *s* is laid for him in the	Job 18:10	2256
table become a *s* before them	Ps 69:22	6341
thee from the *s* of the fowler	Ps 91:3	6341
which were a *s* unto them	Ps 106:36	4170
The wicked have laid a *s* for me	Ps 119:110	6341
bird out of the *s* of the fowlers	Ps 124:7	6341
the *s* is broken, and we are	Ps 124:7	6341
The proud have hid a *s* for me	Ps 140:5	6341
have they privily laid a *s* for me	Ps 142:3	6341
as a bird hasteth to the *s*	Prov 7:23	6341
and his lips are the *s* of his soul	Prov 18:7	4170
It is a *s* to the man who	Prov 20:25	4170
his ways, and get a *s* to thy soul	Prov 22:25	4170
of an evil man there is a *s*	Prov 29:6	4170
men bring a city into a *s*	Prov 29:8	6315
The fear of man bringeth a *s*	Prov 29:25	4170
birds that are caught in the *s*	Eccl 9:12	6341
for a *s* to the inhabitants of	Is 8:14	4170
Fear, and the pit, and the *s*	Is 24:17	6341
the pit shall be taken in the *s*	Is 24:18	6341
lay a *s* for him that reproveth in	Is 29:21	6983
Fear, and the pit, and the *s*	Jer 48:43	6341
the pit shall be taken in the *s*	Jer 48:44	6341
I have laid a *s* for thee, and thou	Jer 50:24	3369
a *s* is come upon us, desolation	Lam 3:47	6354
him, and he shall be taken in my *s*	Eze 12:13	4686
him, and he shall be taken in my *s*	Eze 17:20	4686
ye have been a *s* on Mizpah	Hos 5:1	6341
but the prophet is a *s* of a	Hos 9:8	6341

a bird fall in a *s* upon the earth	Amos 3:5	6341
one take up a *s* from the earth	Amos 3:5	6341
For as a *s* shall it come on all	Lk 21:35	3803
Let their table be made a *s*	Rom 11:9	3803
not that I may cast a *s* upon you	1Cor 7:35	1029
reproach and the *s* of the devil	1Ti 3:7	3803
rich fall into temptation and a *s*	1Ti 6:9	3803
out of the *s* of the devil	2Ti 2:26	3803

SNARED
unto thee, lest thou be *s* therein	Deut 7:25	3369
thou be not *s* by following them	Deut 12:30	5367
the wicked is *s* in the work of	Ps 9:16	5367
Thou art *s* with the words of thy	Prov 6:2	3369
The wicked is *s* by the	Prov 12:13	4170
the sons of men *s* in an evil time	Eccl 9:12	3369
and fall, and be broken, and be *s*	Is 8:15	3369
fall backward, and be broken, and *s*	Is 28:13	3369
they are all of them *s* in holes	Is 42:22	6351

SNARES
but they shall be *s* and traps unto	Josh 23:13	6341
the *s* of death prevented me	2Sa 22:6	4170
Therefore *s* are round about thee,	Job 22:10	6341
his nose pierceth through *s*	Job 40:24	4170
Upon the wicked he shall rain *s*	Ps 11:6	6341
the *s* of death prevented me	Ps 18:5	4170
seek after my life lay *s* for me	Ps 38:12	5367
they commune of laying *s* privily	Ps 64:5	4170
Keep me from the *s* which they	Ps 141:9	6341
to depart from the *s* of death	Prov 13:14	4170
to depart from the *s* of death	Prov 14:27	4170
s are in the way of the froward	Prov 22:5	6341
death the woman, whose heart is *s*	Eccl 7:26	4685
lay wait, as he that setteth *s*	Jer 5:26	3353
to take me, and hid *s* for my feet	Jer 18:22	6341

SNATCH
he shall *s* on the right hand, and	Is 9:20	1504

SNEEZED
the child *s* seven times, and the	2Kin 4:35	2237

SNORTING
The *s* of his horses was heard	Jer 8:16	5170

SNOUT
As a jewel of gold in a swine's *s*	Prov 11:22	639

SNOW
behold, his hand was leprous as *s*	Ex 4:6	7950
Miriam became leprous, white as *s*	Num 12:10	7950
the midst of a pit in time of *s*	2Sa 23:20	7950
presence a leper as white as *s*	2Kin 5:27	7950
the ice, and wherein the *s* is hid	Job 6:16	7950
If I wash myself with *s* water	Job 9:30	7950
and heat consume the *s* waters	Job 24:19	7950
For he saith to the *s*, Be thou on	Job 37:6	7950
into the treasures of the *s*	Job 38:22	7950
me, and I shall be whiter than *s*	Ps 51:7	7950
it, it was white as *s* in Salmon	Ps 68:14	7949
He giveth *s* like wool	Ps 147:16	7950
Fire, and hail; *s*, and vapours	Ps 148:8	7950
As the cold of *s* in the time of	Prov 25:13	7950
As *s* in summer, and as rain in	Prov 26:1	7950
afraid of the *s* for her household	Prov 31:21	7950
they shall be as white as *s*	Is 1:18	7950
the *s* from heaven, and returneth	Is 55:10	7950
Will a man leave the *s* of Lebanon	Jer 18:14	7950
Her Nazarites were purer than *s*	Lam 4:7	7950
sit, whose garment was white as *s*	Dan 7:9	8517
and his raiment white as *s*	Mt 28:3	5510
shining, exceeding white as *s*	Mk 9:3	5510
white like wool, as white as *s*	Rev 1:14	5510

SNOWY
slew a lion in a pit in a *s* day	1Chr 11:22	7950

SNUFFDISHES
the *s* thereof, shall be of pure	Ex 25:38	4289
lamps, and his snuffers, and his *s*	Ex 37:23	4289
his lamps, and his tongs, and his *s*	Num 4:9	4289

SNUFFED
they *s* up the wind like dragons	Jer 14:6	7602
and ye have *s* at it, saith the	Mal 1:13	5301

SNUFFERS
he made his seven lamps, and his *s*	Ex 37:23	4457
And the bowls, and the *s*, and the	1Kin 7:50	4212
of the LORD bowls of silver, *s*	2Kin 12:13	4212
pots, and the shovels, and the *s*	2Kin 25:14	4212
And the *s*, and the basons, and the	2Chr 4:22	4212
also, and the shovels, and the *s*	Jer 52:18	4212

SNUFFETH
that *s* up the wind at her	Jer 2:24	7602

SO (so) *Also see* APPENDIX.		
A king of Egypt.		
messengers to *S* king of Egypt	2Kin 17:4	5471

SOAKED
their land shall be *s* with blood	Is 34:7	7301

SOBER
or whether we be *s*, it is for	2Cor 5:13	4993
but let us watch and be *s*	1Th 5:6	3525
let us, who are of the day, be *s*	1Th 5:8	3525
husband of one wife, vigilant, *s*	1Ti 3:2	4998
wives be grave, not slanderers, *s*	1Ti 3:11	3524
a lover of good men, *s*, just	Titus 1:8	4998
That the aged men be *s*, grave	Titus 2:2	3524
may teach the young women to be *s*	Titus 2:4	4994
likewise exhort to be *s* minded	Titus 2:6	4993
up the loins of your mind, be *s*	1Pet 1:13	3525
be ye therefore *s*, and watch unto	1Pet 4:7	4993
Be *s*, be vigilant	1Pet 5:8	3525

SOBERLY
but to think *s*, according as God	Rom 12:3	1519,4993
worldly lusts, we should live *s*	Titus 2:12	4996

SOBERNESS
forth the words of truth and *s*	Acts 26:25	4997

SOBRIETY
apparel, with shamefacedness and *s*	1Ti 2:9	4997
and charity and holiness with *s*	1Ti 2:15	4997

SOCHO (so'-ko) See SOCHOH. *A son of Heber.*
Gedor, and Heber the father of *S*	1Chr 4:18	7755

SOCHOH (so'-ko) See SHOCHOH, SOCHO, SOCOH. *A city in Judah near Adullam.*
to him pertained *S*, and all the	1Kin 4:10	7755

SOCKET
hundred talents, a talent for a *s*	Ex 38:27	134

SOCKETS
thou shalt make forty *s* of silver	Ex 26:19	134
two *s* under one board for his two	Ex 26:19	134
two *s* under another board for his	Ex 26:19	134
And their forty *s* of silver	Ex 26:21	134
two *s* under one board	Ex 26:21	134
two *s* under another board	Ex 26:21	134
s of silver, sixteen *s*	Ex 26:25	134
two *s* under one board	Ex 26:25	134
two *s* under another board	Ex 26:25	134
gold, upon the *s* of silver	Ex 26:32	134
cast five *s* of brass for them	Ex 26:37	134
their twenty *s* shall be of brass	Ex 27:10	134
and their twenty *s* of brass	Ex 27:11	134
their pillars ten, and their *s* ten	Ex 27:12	134
pillars three, and their *s* three	Ex 27:14	134
pillars three, and their *s* three	Ex 27:15	134
shall be four, and their *s* four	Ex 27:16	134
be of silver, and their *s* of brass	Ex 27:17	134
twined linen, and their *s* of brass	Ex 27:18	134
his bars, his pillars, and his *s*	Ex 35:11	134
court, his pillars, and their *s*	Ex 35:17	134
forty *s* of silver he made under	Ex 36:24	134
two *s* under one board for his two	Ex 36:24	134
two *s* under another board for his	Ex 36:24	134
And their forty *s* of silver	Ex 36:26	134
two *s* under one board	Ex 36:26	134
two *s* under another board	Ex 36:26	134
s were sixteen *s* of silver	Ex 36:30	134
under every board two *s*	Ex 36:30	134
he cast for them four *s* of silver	Ex 36:36	134
but their five *s* were of brass	Ex 36:38	134
twenty, and their brasen *s* twenty	Ex 38:10	134
and their *s* of brass twenty	Ex 38:11	134
their pillars ten, and their *s* ten	Ex 38:12	134
pillars three, and their *s* three	Ex 38:14	134
pillars three, and their *s* three	Ex 38:15	134
the *s* for the pillars were of	Ex 38:17	134
four, and their *s* of brass four	Ex 38:19	134
were cast the *s* of the sanctuary	Ex 38:27	134
and the *s* of the vail	Ex 38:27	134
an hundred *s* of the hundred	Ex 38:27	134
therewith he made the *s* to the	Ex 38:30	134
the *s* of the court round about	Ex 38:31	134
the *s* of the court gate, and all	Ex 38:31	134
bars, and his pillars, and his *s*	Ex 39:33	134
the court, his pillars, and his *s*	Ex 39:40	134
the tabernacle, and fastened his *s*	Ex 40:18	134
the *s* thereof, and all the vessels	Num 3:36	134
the court round about, and their *s*	Num 3:37	134
pillars thereof, and *s* thereof	Num 4:31	134
the court round about, and their *s*	Num 4:32	134
marble, set upon *s* of fine gold	Song 5:15	134

SOCOH (so'-ko) See SOCHOH.		
1. Same as Sochoh.		
Jarmuth, and Adullam, *S*, and Azekah	Josh 15:35	7755
2. A city in the hill country of Judah.		
Shamir, and Jattir, and *S*,	Josh 15:48	7755

SOD
And Jacob *s* pottage	Gen 25:29	2102
holy offerings *s* they in pots	2Chr 35:13	1310

SODDEN
nor *s* at all with water, but	Ex 12:9	1310
wherein it is *s* shall be broken	Lev 6:28	1310
if it be *s* in a brasen pot, it	Lev 6:28	1310
take the *s* shoulder of the ram	Num 6:19	1311
he will not take *s* flesh of thee	1Sa 2:15	1310
women have *s* their own children	Lam 4:10	1310

SODERING
saying, It is ready for the *s*	Is 41:7	1694

SODI (so'-di) *A spy sent to the Promised Land.*
of Zebulun, Gaddiel the son of *S*	Num 13:10	5476

SODOM (sod'-om) See SODOMA, SODOMITE. *A city on the Salt Sea.*
as thou goest, unto *S*, and	Gen 10:19	5467
before the LORD destroyed *S*	Gen 13:10	5467
and pitched his tent toward *S*	Gen 13:12	5467
But the men of *S* were wicked	Gen 13:13	5467
made war with Bera king of *S*	Gen 14:2	5467
And there went out the king of *S*	Gen 14:8	5467
and the kings of *S* and Gomorrah	Gen 14:10	5467
And they took all the goods of *S*	Gen 14:11	5467
brother's son, who dwelt in *S*	Gen 14:12	5467
the king of *S* went out to meet	Gen 14:17	5467
the king of *S* said unto Abram	Gen 14:21	5467
And Abram said to the king of *S*	Gen 14:22	5467
from thence, and looked toward *S*	Gen 18:16	5467
LORD said, Because the cry of *S*	Gen 18:20	5467
from thence, and went toward *S*	Gen 18:22	5467
If I find in *S* fifty righteous	Gen 18:26	5467
came two angels to *S* at even	Gen 19:1	5467
and Lot sat in the gate of *S*	Gen 19:1	5467
of the city, even the men of *S*	Gen 19:4	5467
Then the LORD rained upon *S*	Gen 19:24	5467
he looked toward *S* and Gomorrah	Gen 19:28	5467
therein, like the overthrow of *S*	Deut 29:23	5467
their vine is of the vine of *S*	Deut 32:32	5467
remnant, we should have been as *S*	Is 1:9	5467
word of the LORD, ye rulers of *S*	Is 1:10	5467
and they declare their sin as *S*	Is 3:9	5467
shall be as when God overthrew *S*	Is 13:19	5467
they are all of them unto me as *S*	Jer 23:14	5467
As in the overthrow of *S* and	Jer 49:18	5467
As God overthrew *S* and Gomorrah	Jer 50:40	5467
the punishment of the sin of *S*	Lam 4:6	5467
dwelleth at thy right hand, is *S*	Eze 16:46	5467
S thy sister hath not done, she	Eze 16:48	5467
was the iniquity of thy sister *S*	Eze 16:49	5467
captivity, the captivity of *S*	Eze 16:53	5467
When thy sisters, *S* and her	Eze 16:55	5467
For thy sister *S* was not	Eze 16:56	5467
some of you, as God overthrew *S*	Amos 4:11	5467
Israel, Surely Moab shall be as *S*	Zeph 2:9	5467
more tolerable for the land of *S*	Mt 10:15	4670
done it, had been done in *S*	Mt 11:23	4670
land of *S* in the day of judgment	Mt 11:24	4670
It shall be more tolerable for *S*	Mk 6:11	4670
more tolerable in that day for *S*	Lk 10:12	4670
Lot went out of *S* it rained fire	Lk 17:29	4670
And turning the cities of *S*	2Pet 2:6	4670
Even as *S* and Gomorrha, and the	Jude 7	4670
which spiritually is called *S*	Rev 11:8	4670

SODOMA (sod'-o-mah) See SODOM. *Greek form of Sodom.*
left us a seed, we had been as *S*	Rom 9:29	4670

SODOMITE
nor a *s* of the sons of Israel	Deut 23:17	6945

SODOMITES
And there were also *s* in the land	1Kin 14:24	6945
took away the *s* out of the land	1Kin 15:12	6945
And the remnant of the *s*, which	1Kin 22:46	6945

SOEVER
what saddle *s* he rideth upon that	Lev 15:9	834
What man *s* there be of the house	Lev 17:3	
What man *s* of the seed of Aaron	Lev 22:4	
What thing *s* I command you,	Deut 12:32	834
that what thing *s* thou shalt hear	2Sa 15:35	834
the people, how many *s* they be	2Sa 24:3	
supplication *s* be made by any man	1Kin 8:38	834

S

s shall be made of any man	2Chr 6:29	834
what cause *s* shall come to you of	2Chr 19:10	
wherewith *s* they shall blaspheme	Mk 3:28	3745,302
In what place *s* ye enter into a	Mk 6:10	*1437*
unto you, What things *s* ye desire	Mk 11:24	3745,302
for what things *s* he doeth	Jn 5:19	*302*
Whose *s* sins ye remit, they are	Jn 20:23	*302*
whose *s* sins ye retain, they are	Jn 20:23	*302*
that which things *s* the law saith	Rom 3:19	*1437*

SOFT

For God maketh my heart *s*	Job 23:16	7401
will he speak *s* words unto thee	Job 41:3	7390
thou makest it *s* with showers	Ps 65:10	4127
A *s* answer turneth away wrath	Prov 15:1	7390
a *s* tongue breaketh the bone	Prov 25:15	7390
A man clothed in *s* raiment	Mt 11:8	*3120*
they that wear *s* clothing are in	Mt 11:8	*3120*
A man clothed in *s* raiment	Lk 7:25	*3120*

SOFTER

his words were *s* than oil	Ps 55:21	7401

SOFTLY

and I will lead on *s*, according as	Gen 33:14	328
went *s* unto him, and smote the	Judg 4:21	3814
and she came *s*, and uncovered his	Ruth 3:7	3909
and lay in sackcloth, and went *s*	1Kin 21:27	328
the waters of Shiloah that go *s*	Is 8:6	328
I shall go *s* all my years in the	Is 38:15	
And when the south wind blew *s*	Acts 27:13	5285

SOIL

in a good *s* by great waters	Eze 17:8	7704

SOJOURN

went down into Egypt to *s* there	Gen 12:10	1481
This one fellow came in to *s*	Gen 19:9	1481
S in this land, and I will be with	Gen 26:3	1481
For to *s* in the land are we come	Gen 47:4	1481
when a stranger shall *s* with thee	Ex 12:48	1481
the strangers which *s* among you	Lev 17:8	1481
of the strangers that *s* among you	Lev 17:10	1481
of the strangers that *s* among you	Lev 17:13	1481
if a stranger *s* with thee in your	Lev 19:33	1481
of the strangers that *s* in Israel	Lev 20:2	1481
the strangers that do *s* among you	Lev 25:45	1481
if a stranger shall *s* among you	Num 9:14	1481
And if a stranger *s* with you	Num 15:14	1481
to *s* where he could find a place	Judg 17:8	1481
I go to *s* where I may find a	Judg 17:9	1481
went to *s* in the country of Moab	Ruth 1:1	1481
evil upon the widow with whom I *s*	1Kin 17:20	1481
s wheresoever thou canst *s*	2Kin 8:1	1481
that I *s* in Mesech, that I dwell	Ps 120:5	1481
shall carry her afar off to *s*	Is 23:7	1481
aforetime into Egypt to *s* there	Is 52:4	1481
into Egypt, and go to *s* there	Jer 42:15	1481
faces to go into Egypt to *s* there	Jer 42:17	1481
whither ye desire to go and to *s*	Jer 42:22	1481
say, Go not into Egypt to *s* there	Jer 43:2	1481
into the land of Egypt to *s* there	Jer 44:12	1481
into the land of Egypt to *s* there	Jer 44:14	1481
into the land of Egypt to *s* there	Jer 44:28	1481
They shall no more *s* there	Lam 4:15	1481
out of the country where they *s*	Eze 20:38	4033
to the strangers that *s* among you	Eze 47:22	1481
seed should *s* in a strange land	Acts 7:6	1510,3941

SOJOURNED

Kadesh and Shur, and *s* in Gerar	Gen 20:1	1481
to the land wherein thou hast *s*	Gen 21:23	1481
Abraham *s* in the Philistines'	Gen 21:34	1481
I have *s* with Laban, and stayed	Gen 32:4	1481
Hebron, where Abraham and Isaac *s*	Gen 35:27	1481
out of all Israel, where he *s*	Deut 18:6	1481
s there with a few, and became	Deut 26:5	1481
who was a Levite, and he *s* there	Judg 17:7	1481
and he *s* in Gibeah	Judg 19:16	1481
s in the land of the Philistines	2Kin 8:2	1481
Jacob *s* in the land of Ham	Ps 105:23	1481
By faith he *s* in the land of	Heb 11:9	3939

SOJOURNER

I am a stranger and a *s* with you	Gen 23:4	8453
a *s* of the priest, or an hired	Lev 22:10	8453
though he be a stranger, or a *s*	Lev 25:35	8453
as an hired servant, and as a *s*	Lev 25:40	8453
if a *s* or stranger wax rich by	Lev 25:47	1616
unto the stranger or *s* by thee	Lev 25:47	8453
stranger, and for the *s* among them	Num 35:15	8453
I am a stranger with thee, and a *s*	Ps 39:12	8453

SOJOURNERS

for ye are strangers and *s* with me	Lev 25:23	8453
were *s* there until this day	2Sa 4:3	1481
are strangers before thee, and *s*	1Chr 29:15	8453

SOJOURNETH

of her that *s* in her house,	Ex 3:22	1481
the stranger that *s* among you	Ex 12:49	1481
or a stranger that *s* among you	Lev 16:29	1481
that *s* among you eat blood	Lev 17:12	1481
nor any stranger that *s* among you	Lev 18:26	1481
for thy stranger that *s* with thee	Lev 25:6	1481
for the stranger that *s* with you	Num 15:15	1481
for the stranger that *s* with you	Num 15:16	1481
and the stranger that *s* among them	Num 15:26	1481
the stranger that *s* among them	Num 15:29	1481
the stranger that *s* among them	Num 19:10	1481
the stranger that *s* among them	Josh 20:9	1481
remaineth in any place where he *s*	Ezr 1:4	1481
of the stranger that *s* in Israel	Eze 14:7	1481
that in what tribe the stranger *s*	Eze 47:23	1481

SOJOURNING

Now the *s* of the children of	Ex 12:40	4186
s on the side of mount Ephraim	Judg 19:1	1481
the time of your *s* here in fear	1Pet 1:17	*3940*

SOLACE

let us *s* ourselves with loves	Prov 7:18	5965

SOLD

he *s* his birthright unto Jacob	Gen 25:33	4376
for he hath *s* us, and hath quite	Gen 31:15	4376
s Joseph to the Ishmeelites for	Gen 37:28	4376
the Midianites *s* him into Egypt	Gen 37:36	4376
and *s* unto the Egyptians	Gen 41:56	7666
he it was that *s* to all the	Gen 42:6	7666
brother, whom ye *s* into Egypt	Gen 45:4	4376
yourselves, that ye *s* me hither	Gen 45:5	4376
for the Egyptians *s* every man his	Gen 47:20	4376
wherefore they *s* not their lands	Gen 47:22	4376
then he shall be *s* for his theft	Ex 22:3	4376
The land shall not be *s* for ever	Lev 25:23	4376
poor, and hath *s* away some of his	Lev 25:25	4376
redeem that which his brother *s*	Lev 25:25	4465
unto the man to whom he *s* it	Lev 25:27	4376
then that which is *s* shall remain	Lev 25:28	4465
within a whole year after it is *s*	Lev 25:29	4465
then the house that was *s*	Lev 25:33	4465
of their cities may not be *s*	Lev 25:34	4376
be waxen poor, and be *s* unto thee	Lev 25:39	4376
they shall not be *s* as bondmen	Lev 25:42	4376
After that he is *s* he may be	Lev 25:48	4376
him from the year that he was *s*	Lev 25:50	4376
or if he have *s* the field to	Lev 27:20	4376
then it shall be *s* according to	Lev 27:27	4376
shall be *s* or redeemed	Lev 27:28	4376
be *s* unto thee, and serve thee six	Deut 15:12	4376
there ye shall be *s* unto your	Deut 28:68	4376
except their Rock had *s* them	Deut 32:30	4376
he *s* them into the hands of their	Judg 2:14	4376
he *s* them into the hand of	Judg 3:8	4376
the LORD *s* them into the hand of	Judg 4:2	4376
he *s* them into the hands of the	Judg 10:7	4376
he *s* them into the hand of Sisera	1Sa 12:9	4376
because thou hast *s* thyself to	1Kin 21:20	4376
until an ass's head was *s* for	2Kin 6:25	
of fine flour be *s* for a shekel	2Kin 7:1	
of fine flour was *s* for a shekel	2Kin 7:16	
s themselves to do evil in the	2Kin 17:17	4376
which were *s* unto the heathen	Neh 5:8	4376
or shall they be *s* unto us	Neh 5:8	4376
the day wherein they *s* victuals	Neh 13:15	4376
s on the sabbath unto the	Neh 13:16	4376
For we are *s*, I and my people, to	Est 7:4	4376
But if we had been *s* for bondmen	Est 7:4	4376
Joseph, who was *s* for a servant	Ps 105:17	4376
is it to whom I have *s* you	Is 50:1	4376
iniquities have ye *s* yourselves	Is 50:1	4376
Ye have *s* yourselves for nought	Is 52:3	4376
which hath been *s* unto thee	Jer 34:14	4376
our wood is *s* unto us	Lam 5:4	935,4242
not return to that which is *s*	Eze 7:13	4465
s a girl for wine, that they	Joel 3:3	4376
have ye *s* unto the Grecians	Joel 3:6	4376
the place whither ye have *s* them	Joel 3:6	4376
because they *s* the righteous for	Amos 2:6	4376
not two sparrows *s* for a farthing	Mt 10:29	*4453*
all that he had, and bought it	Mt 13:46	*4097*
his lord commanded him to be *s*	Mt 18:25	*4097*
God, and cast out all them that *s*	Mt 21:12	*4453*
and the seats of them that *s* doves	Mt 21:12	*4453*
might have been *s* for much	Mt 26:9	*4097*

and began to cast out them that *s*	Mk 11:15	4453
and the seats of them that *s* doves	Mk 11:15	4453
For it might have been *s* for more	Mk 14:5	4097
five sparrows *s* for two farthings	Lk 12:6	4453
they drank, they bought, they *s*	Lk 17:28	4453
to cast out them that *s* therein	Lk 19:45	4453
in the temple those that *s* oxen	Jn 2:14	4453
And said unto them that *s* doves	Jn 2:16	4453
s for three hundred pence	Jn 12:5	4097
s their possessions and goods, and	Acts 2:45	4097
of lands or houses *s* them	Acts 4:34	4453
prices of the things that were *s*	Acts 4:34	4097
s it, and brought the money, and	Acts 4:37	4453
his wife, *s* a possession,	Acts 5:1	4453
and after it was *s*, was it not in	Acts 5:4	4097
Tell me whether ye *s* the land for	Acts 5:8	591
with envy, *s* Joseph into Egypt	Acts 7:9	591
but I am carnal, *s* under sin	Rom 7:14	4097
Whatsoever is *s* in the shambles,	1Cor 10:25	4453
morsel of meat *s* his birthright	Heb 12:16	591

SOLDIER

four parts, to every *s* a part	Jn 19:23	4757
a devout *s* of them that waited on	Acts 10:7	4757
by himself with a *s* that kept him	Acts 28:16	4757
companion in labour, and fellow *s*	Phil 2:25	
as a good *s* of Jesus Christ	2Ti 2:3	4757
him who hath chosen him to be a *s*	2Ti 2:4	4758

SOLDIERS

fathers, were bands of *s* for war	1Chr 7:4	6635
thousand and two hundred *s*	1Chr 7:11	
But the *s* of the army which	2Chr 25:13	1121
require of the king a band of *s*	Ezr 8:22	2428
therefore the armed *s* of Moab	Is 15:4	2502
authority, having *s* under me	Mt 8:9	4757
Then the *s* of the governor took	Mt 27:27	4757
unto him the whole band of *s*	Mt 27:27	
they gave large money unto the *s*	Mt 28:12	4757
the *s* led him away into the hall,	Mk 15:16	4757
the *s* likewise demanded of him,	Lk 3:14	4754
authority, having under me *s*	Lk 7:8	4757
the *s* also mocked him, coming to	Lk 23:36	4757
the *s* platted a crown of thorns,	Jn 19:2	4757
Then the *s*, when they had	Jn 19:23	4757
These things therefore the *s* did	Jn 19:24	4757
Then came the *s*, and brake the	Jn 19:32	4757
But one of the *s* with a spear	Jn 19:34	4757
four quaternions of *s* to keep him	Acts 12:4	4757
Peter was sleeping between two *s*	Acts 12:6	4757
was no small stir among the *s*	Acts 12:18	4757
Who immediately took *s* and	Acts 21:32	4757
saw the chief captain and the *s*	Acts 21:32	4757
that he was borne of the *s* for	Acts 21:35	4757
them, commanded the *s* to go down	Acts 23:10	4753
two hundred *s* to go to Caesarea	Acts 23:23	4757
Then the *s*, as it was commanded	Acts 23:31	4757
said to the centurion and to the *s*	Acts 27:31	4757
Then the *s* cut off the ropes of	Acts 27:32	4757

SOLDIERS'

the *s* counsel was to kill the	Acts 27:42	4757

SOLE

no rest for the *s* of her foot	Gen 8:9	3709
from the *s* of thy foot unto the	Deut 28:35	3709
would not adventure to set the *s*	Deut 28:56	3709
neither shall the *s* of thy foot	Deut 28:65	3709
Every place that the *s* of your	Josh 1:3	3709
from the *s* of his foot even to	2Sa 14:25	3709
with the *s* of my feet have I	2Kin 19:24	3709
the *s* of his foot unto his crown	Job 2:7	3709
From the *s* of the foot even unto	Is 1:6	3709
with the *s* of my feet have I	Is 37:25	3709
the *s* of their feet was like the	Eze 1:7	3709
was like the *s* of a calf's foot	Eze 1:7	3709

SOLEMN

it is a *s* assembly	Lev 23:36	6116
your gladness, and in your *s* days	Num 10:10	4150
offering, or in your *s* feasts	Num 15:3	4150
day ye shall have a *s* assembly	Num 29:35	6116
a *s* assembly to the LORD thy God	Deut 16:8	6116
Seven days shalt thou keep a *s*	Deut 16:15	2287
Proclaim a *s* assembly for Baal	2Kin 10:20	6116
on the *s* feasts of the LORD our	2Chr 2:4	4150
eighth day they made a *s* assembly	2Chr 7:9	6116
the new moons, and on the *s* feasts	2Chr 8:13	4150
the eighth day was a *s* assembly	Neh 8:18	6116
appointed, on our *s* feast day	Ps 81:3	2282
upon the harp with a *s* sound	Ps 92:3	
is iniquity, even the *s* meeting	Is 1:13	6116
because none come to the *s* feasts	Lam 1:4	4150

the LORD hath caused the *s* feasts	Lam 2:6	4150
LORD, as in the day of a *s* feast	Lam 2:7	4150
Thou hast called as in a *s* day my	Lam 2:22	4150
of Jerusalem in her *s* feasts	Eze 36:38	4150
before the LORD in the *s* feasts	Eze 46:9	4150
her sabbaths, and all her *s* feasts	Hos 2:11	4150
What will ye do in the *s* day	Hos 9:5	4150
as in the days of the *s* feast	Hos 12:9	4150
call a *s* assembly, gather the	Joel 1:14	6116
a fast, call a *s* assembly	Joel 2:15	6116
not smell in your *s* assemblies	Amos 5:21	6116
O Judah, keep thy *s* feasts	Nah 1:15	2282
are sorrowful for the *s* assembly	Zeph 3:18	4150
even the dung of your *s* feasts	Mal 2:3	2282

SOLEMNITIES

Look upon Zion, the city of our *s*	Is 33:20	4150
in all *s* of the house of Israel	Eze 45:17	4150
in the *s* the meat offering shall	Eze 46:11	4150

SOLEMNITY

in the *s* of the year of release,	Deut 31:10	4150
the night when a holy *s* is kept	Is 30:29	2282

SOLEMNLY

The man did *s* protest unto us,	Gen 43:3	5749
howbeit yet protest *s* unto them	1Sa 8:9	5749

SOLES

Every place whereon the *s* of your	Deut 11:24	3709
as soon as the *s* of the feet of	Josh 3:13	3709
the *s* of the priests' feet were	Josh 4:18	3709
put them under the *s* of his feet	1Kin 5:3	3709
down at the *s* of thy feet	Is 60:14	3709
and the place of the *s* of my feet	Eze 43:7	3709
they shall be ashes under the *s*	Mal 4:3	3709

SOLITARILY

which dwell *s* in the wood	Mic 7:14	910

SOLITARY

Lo, let that night be *s*	Job 3:7	1565
For want and famine they were *s*	Job 30:3	1565
God setteth the *s* in families	Ps 68:6	3173
in the wilderness in a *s* way	Ps 107:4	3452
the *s* place shall be glad for	Is 35:1	6723
How doth the city sit *s*, that was	Lam 1:1	910
out, and departed into a *s* place	Mk 1:35	*2048*

SOLOMON (*sol'-o-mun*) See JEDIDIAH, SOLOMON'S. *Son of David; king of Israel.*

and Shobab, and Nathan, and *S*	2Sa 5:14	8010
a son, and he called his name *S*	2Sa 12:24	8010
S his brother, he called not	1Kin 1:10	8010
unto Bath-sheba the mother of *S*	1Kin 1:11	8010
life, and the life of thy son *S*	1Kin 1:12	8010
Assuredly *S* thy son shall reign	1Kin 1:13	8010
Assuredly *S* thy son shall reign	1Kin 1:17	8010
but *S* thy servant hath he not	1Kin 1:19	8010
my son *S* shall be counted	1Kin 1:21	8010
son of Jehoiada, and thy servant *S*	1Kin 1:26	8010
Assuredly *S* thy son shall reign	1Kin 1:30	8010
cause *S* my son to ride upon mine	1Kin 1:33	8010
trumpet, and say, God save king *S*	1Kin 1:34	8010
the king, even so be he with *S*	1Kin 1:37	8010
caused *S* to ride upon king	1Kin 1:38	8010
of the tabernacle, and anointed *S*	1Kin 1:39	8010
the people said, God save king *S*	1Kin 1:39	8010
lord king David hath made *S* king	1Kin 1:43	8010
also *S* sitteth on the throne of	1Kin 1:46	8010
name of *S* better than thy name	1Kin 1:47	8010
And Adonijah feared because of *S*	1Kin 1:50	8010
And it was told *S*, saying, Behold,	1Kin 1:51	8010
Behold, Adonijah feareth king *S*	1Kin 1:51	8010
Let king *S* swear unto me to day	1Kin 1:51	8010
S said, If he will shew himself a	1Kin 1:52	8010
So king *S* sent, and they brought	1Kin 1:53	8010
came and bowed himself to king *S*	1Kin 1:53	8010
S said unto him, Go to thine	1Kin 1:53	8010
and he charged *S* his son, saying,	1Kin 2:1	8010
Then sat *S* upon the throne of	1Kin 2:12	8010
to Bath-sheba the mother of *S*	1Kin 2:13	8010
unto *S* the king, (for he will not	1Kin 2:17	8010
therefore unto king *S*	1Kin 2:19	8010
king *S* answered and said unto his	1Kin 2:22	8010
Then king *S* sware by the LORD,	1Kin 2:23	8010
king *S* sent by the hand of	1Kin 2:25	8010
So *S* thrust out Abiathar from	1Kin 2:27	8010
it was told king *S* that Joab was	1Kin 2:29	8010
Then *S* sent Benaiah the son of	1Kin 2:29	8010
it was told *S* that Shimei had	1Kin 2:41	8010
king *S* shall be blessed, and the	1Kin 2:45	8010
was established in the hand of *S*	1Kin 2:46	8010
S made affinity with Pharaoh king	1Kin 3:1	8010

S

S loved the LORD, walking in the	1Kin 3:3	8010
did S offer upon that altar	1Kin 3:4	8010
appeared to S in a dream by night	1Kin 3:5	8010
S said, Thou hast shewed unto thy	1Kin 3:6	8010
that S had asked this thing	1Kin 3:10	8010
And S awoke	1Kin 3:15	8010
So king S was king over all	1Kin 4:1	8010
S had twelve officers over all	1Kin 4:7	8010
Taphath the daughter of S to wife	1Kin 4:11	8010
Basmath the daughter of S to wife	1Kin 4:15	8010
S reigned over all kingdoms from	1Kin 4:21	8010
served S all the days of his life	1Kin 4:21	8010
to Beer-sheba, all the days of S	1Kin 4:25	8010
S had forty thousand stalls of	1Kin 4:26	8010
provided victual for king S	1Kin 4:27	8010
And God gave S wisdom and	1Kin 4:29	8010
people to hear the wisdom of S	1Kin 4:34	8010
of Tyre sent his servants unto S	1Kin 5:1	8010
And S sent to Hiram, saying,	1Kin 5:2	8010
when Hiram heard the words of S	1Kin 5:7	8010
And Hiram sent to S, saying, I	1Kin 5:8	8010
So Hiram gave S cedar trees	1Kin 5:10	8010
S gave Hiram twenty thousand	1Kin 5:11	8010
thus gave to Hiram year by year	1Kin 5:11	8010
And the LORD gave S wisdom	1Kin 5:12	8010
was peace between Hiram and S	1Kin 5:12	8010
king S raised a levy out of all	1Kin 5:13	8010
S had threescore and ten thousand	1Kin 5:15	8010
which king S built for the LORD	1Kin 6:2	8010
And the word of the LORD came to S	1Kin 6:11	8010
So S built the house, and finished	1Kin 6:14	8010
So S overlaid the house within	1Kin 6:21	8010
But S was building his own house	1Kin 7:1	8010
S made also an house for	1Kin 7:8	8010
And king S sent and fetched Hiram	1Kin 7:13	8010
And he came to king S, and wrought	1Kin 7:14	8010
king S for the house of the LORD	1Kin 7:40	8010
which Hiram made to king S for	1Kin 7:45	8010
S left all the vessels unweighed,	1Kin 7:47	8010
S made all the vessels that	1Kin 7:48	8010
ended all the work that king S	1Kin 7:51	8010
S brought in the things which	1Kin 7:51	8010
Then S assembled the elders of	1Kin 8:1	8010
unto king S in Jerusalem, that	1Kin 8:1	8010
king S at the feast in the month	1Kin 8:2	8010
And king S, and all the	1Kin 8:5	8010
Then spake S, The LORD said that	1Kin 8:12	8010
S stood before the altar of the	1Kin 8:22	8010
that when S had made an end of	1Kin 8:54	8010
S offered a sacrifice of peace	1Kin 8:63	8010
And at that time S held a feast	1Kin 8:65	8010
when S had finished the building	1Kin 9:1	8010
appeared to S the second time	1Kin 9:2	8010
when S had built the two houses,	1Kin 9:10	8010
had furnished S with cedar trees	1Kin 9:11	8010
that then king S gave Hiram	1Kin 9:11	8010
the cities which S had given him	1Kin 9:12	8010
of the levy which king S raised	1Kin 9:15	8010
S built Gezer, and Beth-horon the	1Kin 9:17	8010
the cities of store that S had	1Kin 9:19	8010
that which S desired to build in	1Kin 9:19	8010
upon those did S levy a tribute	1Kin 9:21	8010
of Israel did S make no bondmen	1Kin 9:22	8010
house which S had built for her	1Kin 9:24	8010
year did S offer burnt offerings	1Kin 9:25	8010
king S made a navy of ships in	1Kin 9:26	8010
the sea, with the servants of S	1Kin 9:27	8010
talents, and brought it to king S	1Kin 9:28	8010
of Sheba heard of the fame of S	1Kin 10:1	8010
and when she was come to S	1Kin 10:2	8010
S told her all her questions	1Kin 10:3	8010
the queen of Sheba gave to king S	1Kin 10:10	8010
king S gave unto the queen of	1Kin 10:13	8010
beside that which S gave her of	1Kin 10:13	8010
to S in one year was six hundred	1Kin 10:14	8010
king S made two hundred targets	1Kin 10:16	8010
accounted of in the days of S	1Kin 10:21	8010
So king S exceeded all the kings	1Kin 10:23	8010
And all the earth sought to S	1Kin 10:24	8010
S gathered together chariots and	1Kin 10:26	8010
S had horses brought out of Egypt	1Kin 10:28	8010
But king S loved many strange	1Kin 11:1	8010
S clave unto these in love	1Kin 11:2	8010
when S was old, that his wives	1Kin 11:4	8010
For S went after Ashtoreth the	1Kin 11:5	8010
S did evil in the sight of the	1Kin 11:6	8010
Then did S build an high place	1Kin 11:7	8010
And the LORD was angry with S	1Kin 11:9	8010
Wherefore the LORD said unto S	1Kin 11:11	8010
stirred up an adversary unto S	1Kin 11:14	8010
to Israel all the days of S	1Kin 11:25	8010
S built Millo, and repaired the	1Kin 11:27	8010
S seeing the young man that he	1Kin 11:28	8010
the kingdom out of the hand of S	1Kin 11:31	8010
S sought therefore to kill	1Kin 11:40	8010
was in Egypt until the death of S	1Kin 11:40	8010
And the rest of the acts of S	1Kin 11:41	8010
in the book of the acts of S	1Kin 11:41	8010
the time that S reigned in	1Kin 11:42	8010
S slept with his fathers, and was	1Kin 11:43	8010
fled from the presence of king S	1Kin 12:2	8010
that stood before S his father	1Kin 12:6	8010
again to Rehoboam the son of S	1Kin 12:21	8010
Speak unto Rehoboam, the son of S	1Kin 12:23	8010
the son of S reigned in Judah	1Kin 14:21	8010
shields of gold which S had made	1Kin 14:26	8010
to S his son, In this house, and	2Kin 21:7	8010
which S the king of Israel had	2Kin 23:13	8010
all the vessels of gold which S	2Kin 24:13	8010
the bases which S had made for	2Kin 25:16	8010
and Shobab, and Nathan, and S	1Chr 3:5	8010
temple that S built in Jerusalem	1Chr 6:10	8010
until S had built the house of	1Chr 6:32	8010
and Shobab, Nathan, and S	1Chr 14:4	8010
wherewith S made the brasen sea,	1Chr 18:8	8010
S my son is young and tender, and	1Chr 22:5	8010
Then he called for S his son	1Chr 22:6	8010
And David said to S, My son, as	1Chr 22:7	8010
for his name shall be S, and I	1Chr 22:9	8010
of Israel to help S his son	1Chr 22:17	8010
he made S his son king over	1Chr 23:1	8010
he hath chosen S my son to sit	1Chr 28:5	8010
S thy son, he shall build my	1Chr 28:6	8010
S my son, know thou the God of	1Chr 28:9	8010
Then David gave to S his son the	1Chr 28:11	8010
And David said to S his son	1Chr 28:20	8010
S my son, whom alone God hath	1Chr 29:1	8010
give unto S my son a perfect	1Chr 29:19	8010
they made S the son of David king	1Chr 29:22	8010
Then S sat on the throne of the	1Chr 29:23	8010
themselves unto S the king	1Chr 29:24	8010
the LORD magnified S exceedingly	1Chr 29:25	8010
S his son reigned in his stead	1Chr 29:28	8010
And S the son of David was	2Chr 1:1	8010
Then S spake unto all Israel, to	2Chr 1:2	8010
So S, and all the congregation	2Chr 1:3	8010
and S and the congregation sought	2Chr 1:5	8010
S went up thither to the brasen	2Chr 1:6	8010
that night did God appear unto S	2Chr 1:7	8010
S said unto God, Thou hast shewed	2Chr 1:8	8010
And God said to S, Because this	2Chr 1:11	8010
Then S came from his journey to	2Chr 1:13	8010
S gathered chariots and horsemen	2Chr 1:14	8010
S had horses brought out of Egypt	2Chr 1:16	8010
S determined to build an house	2Chr 2:1	8010
S told out threescore and ten	2Chr 2:2	8010
S sent to Huram the king of Tyre,	2Chr 2:3	8010
in writing, which he sent to S	2Chr 2:11	8010
S numbered all the strangers that	2Chr 2:17	8010
Then S began to build the house	2Chr 3:1	8010
these are the things wherein S	2Chr 3:3	8010
for king S for the house of God	2Chr 4:11	8010
S for the house of the LORD of	2Chr 4:16	8010
Thus made S all these vessels in	2Chr 4:18	8010
S made all the vessels that were	2Chr 4:19	8010
Thus all the work that S made for	2Chr 5:1	8010
S brought in all the things that	2Chr 5:1	8010
Then S assembled the elders of	2Chr 5:2	8010
Also king S, and all the	2Chr 5:6	8010
Then said S, The LORD hath said	2Chr 6:1	8010
For S had made a brasen scaffold,	2Chr 6:13	8010
Now when S had made an end of	2Chr 7:1	8010
king S offered a sacrifice of	2Chr 7:5	8010
Moreover S hallowed the middle of	2Chr 7:7	8010
which S had made was not able to	2Chr 7:7	8010
Also at the same time S kept the	2Chr 7:8	8010
had shewed unto David, and to S	2Chr 7:10	8010
Thus S finished the house of the	2Chr 7:11	8010
the LORD appeared to S by night	2Chr 7:12	8010
wherein S had built the house of	2Chr 8:1	8010
which Huram had restored to S	2Chr 8:2	8010
S built them, and caused the	2Chr 8:2	8010
S went to Hamath-zobah, and	2Chr 8:3	8010
all the store cities that S had	2Chr 8:6	8010
all that S desired to build in	2Chr 8:6	8010
them did S make to pay tribute	2Chr 8:8	8010
S make no servants for his work	2Chr 8:9	8010
S brought up the daughter of	2Chr 8:11	8010
Then S offered burnt offerings	2Chr 8:12	8010
Now all the work of S was	2Chr 8:16	8010
Then went to Ezion-geber, and to	2Chr 8:17	8010
with the servants of S to Ophir	2Chr 8:18	8010

gold, and brought them to king *S*	2Chr 8:18	8010
of Sheba heard of the fame of *S*	2Chr 9:1	8010
she came to prove *S* with hard	2Chr 9:1	8010
and when she was come to *S*	2Chr 9:1	8010
S told her all her questions	2Chr 9:2	8010
hid from *S* which he told her not	2Chr 9:2	8010
of Sheba had seen the wisdom of *S*	2Chr 9:3	8010
as the queen of Sheba gave king *S*	2Chr 9:9	8010
of Huram, and the servants of *S*	2Chr 9:10	8010
king *S* gave to the queen of Sheba	2Chr 9:12	8010
to *S* in one year was six hundred	2Chr 9:13	8010
brought gold and silver to *S*	2Chr 9:14	8010
king *S* made two hundred targets	2Chr 9:15	8010
vessels of king *S* were of gold	2Chr 9:20	8010
accounted of in the days of *S*	2Chr 9:20	8010
king *S* passed all the kings of	2Chr 9:22	8010
earth sought the presence of *S*	2Chr 9:23	8010
S had four thousand stalls for	2Chr 9:25	8010
they brought unto *S* horses out of	2Chr 9:28	8010
Now the rest of the acts of *S*	2Chr 9:29	8010
S reigned in Jerusalem over all	2Chr 9:30	8010
S slept with his fathers, and he	2Chr 9:31	8010
from the presence of *S* the king	2Chr 10:2	8010
S his father while he yet lived	2Chr 10:6	8010
Speak unto Rehoboam the son of *S*	2Chr 11:3	8010
made Rehoboam the son of *S* strong	2Chr 11:17	8010
walked in the way of David and *S*	2Chr 11:17	8010
shields of gold which *S* had made	2Chr 12:9	8010
the servant of *S* the son of David	2Chr 13:6	8010
against Rehoboam the son of *S*	2Chr 13:7	8010
for since the time of *S* the son	2Chr 30:26	8010
to *S* his son, In this house, and	2Chr 33:7	8010
S the son of David king of Israel	2Chr 35:3	8010
to the writing of *S* his son	2Chr 35:4	8010
of David, and of *S* his son	Neh 12:45	8010
Did not *S* king of Israel sin by	Neh 13:26	8010
A Psalm for *S*	Ps 72:*t*	8010
A Song of degrees for *S*	Ps 127:*t*	8010
The Proverbs of *S* the son of	Prov 1:1	8010
The proverbs of *S*	Prov 10:1	8010
These are also proverbs of *S*	Prov 25:1	8010
of Kedar, as the curtains of *S*	Song 1:5	8010
King *S* made himself a chariot of	Song 3:9	8010
behold king *S* with the crown	Song 3:11	8010
S had a vineyard at Baal-hamon	Song 8:11	8010
thou, O *S*, must have a thousand	Song 8:12	8010
which king *S* had made in the	Jer 52:20	8010
David the king begat *S* of her	Mt 1:6	4672
And *S* begat Roboam	Mt 1:7	4672
That even *S* in all his glory was	Mt 6:29	4672
the earth to hear the wisdom of *S*.	Mt 12:42	4672
behold, a greater than *S* is here	Mt 12:42	4672
the earth to hear the wisdom of *S*	Lk 11:31	4672
behold, a greater than *S* is here	Lk 11:31	4672
that *S* in all his glory was not	Lk 12:27	4672
But *S* built him an house	Acts 7:47	4672

SOLOMON'S (sol'-o-muns)

S provision for one day was	1Kin 4:22	8010
all that came unto king *S* table	1Kin 4:27	8010
S wisdom excelled the wisdom of	1Kin 4:30	8010
Beside the chief of *S* officers	1Kin 5:16	8010
S builders and Hiram's builders	1Kin 5:18	8010
year of *S* reign over Israel	1Kin 6:1	8010
all *S* desire which he was pleased	1Kin 9:1	8010
present unto his daughter, *S* wife	1Kin 9:16	8010
officers that were over *S* work	1Kin 9:23	8010
of Sheba had seen all *S* wisdom	1Kin 10:4	8010
all king *S* drinking vessels were	1Kin 10:21	8010
S servant, whose mother's name	1Kin 11:26	8010
S son was Rehoboam, Abia his son,	1Chr 3:10	8010
all that came into *S* heart to	2Chr 7:11	8010
were the chief of king *S* officers	2Chr 8:10	8010
The children of *S* servants	Ezr 2:55	8010
and the children of *S* servants	Ezr 2:58	8010
The children of *S* servants	Neh 7:57	8010
and the children of *S* servants	Neh 7:60	8010
and the children of *S* servants	Neh 11:3	8010
The song of songs, which is *S*	Song 1:1	8010
Behold his bed, which is *S*	Song 3:7	8010
walked in the temple in *S* porch	Jn 10:23	4672
in the porch that is called *S*	Acts 3:11	4672
all with one accord in *S* porch	Acts 5:12	4672

SOME See APPENDIX.

SOMEBODY See APPENDIX.

SOMETHING See APPENDIX.

SOMETIME See APPENDIX.

SOMETIMES

s were far off are made nigh by	Eph 2:13	4218
For ye were *s* darkness, but now	Eph 5:8	4218
we ourselves also were *s* foolish	Titus 3:3	4218

SOMEWHAT See APPENDIX.

SON

the city, after the name of his *s*	Gen 4:17	1121
and she bare a *s*, and called his	Gen 4:25	1121
to him also there was born a *s*	Gen 4:26	1121
begat a *s* in his own likeness,	Gen 5:3	
eighty and two years, and begat a *s*	Gen 5:28	1121
his younger *s* had done unto him	Gen 9:24	1121
And Terah took Abram his *s*	Gen 11:31	1121
Lot the *s* of Haran his son's *s*,	Gen 11:31	1121
in law, his *s* Abram's wife	Gen 11:31	
his wife, and Lot his brother's *s*	Gen 12:5	1121
took Lot, Abram's brother's *s*	Gen 14:12	1121
art with child, and shalt bear a *s*.	Gen 16:11	1121
And Hagar bare Abram a *s*	Gen 16:15	1121
her, and give thee a *s* also of her	Gen 16:16	1121
wife shall bear thee a *s* indeed	Gen 17:19	1121
And Abraham took Ishmael his *s*	Gen 17:23	1121
Ishmael his *s* was thirteen years	Gen 17:25	1121
circumcised, and Ishmael his *s*	Gen 17:26	1121
lo, Sarah thy wife shall have a *s*	Gen 18:10	1121
of life, and Sarah shall have a *s*.	Gen 18:14	1121
s in law, and thy sons, and thy	Gen 19:12	1121
And the firstborn bare a *s*	Gen 19:37	1121
And the younger, she also bare a *s*	Gen 19:38	1121
bare Abraham a *s* in his old age	Gen 21:2	1121
of his *s* that was born unto him	Gen 21:3	1121
Abraham circumcised his *s* Isaac	Gen 21:4	1121
when his *s* Isaac was born unto	Gen 21:5	1121
have born him a *s* in his old age	Gen 21:7	1121
Sarah saw the *s* of Hagar the	Gen 21:9	1121
Cast out this bondwoman and her *s*	Gen 21:10	1121
for the *s* of this bondwoman shall	Gen 21:10	1121
shall not be heir with my *s*	Gen 21:10	
Abraham's sight because of his *s*	Gen 21:11	1121
also of the *s* of the bondwoman	Gen 21:13	1121
with my *s*, nor with my son's *s*	Gen 21:23	5220
And he said, Take now thy *s*	Gen 22:2	1121
thine only *s* Isaac	Gen 22:2	
men with him, and Isaac his *s*	Gen 22:3	1121
and laid it upon Isaac his *s*	Gen 22:6	1121
and he said, Here am I, my *s*	Gen 22:7	1121
And Abraham said, My *s*, God will	Gen 22:8	1121
in order, and bound Isaac his *s*	Gen 22:9	1121
and took the knife to slay his *s*	Gen 22:10	1121
thou hast not withheld thy *s*	Gen 22:12	1121
thine only *s* from me	Gen 22:12	
offering in the stead of his *s*	Gen 22:13	1121
thing, and hast not withheld thy *s*	Gen 22:16	1121
thine only *s*	Gen 22:16	
for me to Ephron the *s* of Zohar	Gen 23:8	1121
unto my *s* of the daughters of the	Gen 24:3	1121
and take a wife unto my *s* Isaac	Gen 24:4	1121
must I needs bring thy *s* again	Gen 24:5	1121
thou bring not my *s* thither again	Gen 24:6	1121
take a wife unto my *s* from thence	Gen 24:7	1121
only bring not my *s* thither again	Gen 24:8	1121
s of Milcah, the wife of Nahor,	Gen 24:15	1121
of Bethuel the *s* of Milcah	Gen 24:24	1121
a *s* to my master when she was old	Gen 24:36	1121
to my *s* of the daughters of the	Gen 24:37	1121
kindred, and take a wife unto my *s*	Gen 24:38	1121
a wife for my *s* of my kindred	Gen 24:40	1121
appointed out for my master's *s*	Gen 24:44	1121
daughter of Bethuel, Nahor's *s*	Gen 24:47	1121
brother's daughter unto his *s*	Gen 24:48	1121
sent them away from Isaac his *s*	Gen 25:6	1121
Ephron the *s* of Zohar the Hittite	Gen 25:9	1121
that God blessed his *s* Isaac	Gen 25:11	1121
of Ishmael, Abraham's *s*, whom	Gen 25:12	1121
generations of Isaac, Abraham's *s*	Gen 25:19	1121
see, he called Esau his eldest *s*	Gen 27:1	1121
and said unto him, My *s*	Gen 27:1	1121
when Isaac spake to Esau his *s*	Gen 27:5	1121
And Rebekah spake unto Jacob her *s*	Gen 27:6	1121
Now therefore, my *s*, obey my	Gen 27:8	1121
him, Upon me be thy curse, my *s*	Gen 27:13	1121
raiment of her eldest *s* Esau	Gen 27:15	1121
put them upon Jacob her younger *s*	Gen 27:15	1121
into the hand of her *s* Jacob	Gen 27:17	1121
who art thou, my *s*	Gen 27:18	1121
And Isaac said unto his *s*, How is	Gen 27:20	1121
hast found it so quickly, my *s*	Gen 27:20	1121
thee, that I may feel thee, my *s*	Gen 27:21	1121
thou be my very *s* Esau or not	Gen 27:21	1121
he said, Art thou my very *s* Esau	Gen 27:24	1121

Come near now, and kiss me, my *s*	Gen 27:26	1121
the smell of my *s* is as the smell	Gen 27:27	1121
And he said, I am thy *s*, thy	Gen 27:32	1121
shall I do now unto thee, my *s*	Gen 27:37	1121
her elder *s* were told to Rebekah	Gen 27:42	1121
and called Jacob her younger *s*	Gen 27:42	1121
Now therefore, my *s*, obey my	Gen 27:43	1121
s of Bethuel the Syrian, the	Gen 28:5	1121
daughter of Ishmael Abraham's *s*	Gen 28:9	1121
Know ye Laban the *s* of Nahor	Gen 29:5	1121
and that he was Rebekah's *s*	Gen 29:12	1121
tidings of Jacob his sister's *s*	Gen 29:13	1121
And Leah conceived, and bare a *s*	Gen 29:32	1121
she conceived again, and bare a *s*	Gen 29:33	1121
therefore given me this *s* also	Gen 29:33	1121
she conceived again, and bare a *s*	Gen 29:34	1121
she conceived again, and bare a *s*	Gen 29:35	1121
conceived, and bare Jacob a *s*	Gen 30:5	1121
my voice, and hath given me a *s*	Gen 30:6	1121
again, and bare Jacob a second *s*	Gen 30:7	1121
Zilpah Leah's maid bare Jacob a *s*	Gen 30:10	1121
Leah's maid bare Jacob a second *s*	Gen 30:12	1121
and bare Jacob the fifth *s*	Gen 30:17	1121
again, and bare Jacob the sixth *s*	Gen 30:19	1121
And she conceived, and bare a *s*	Gen 30:23	1121
LORD shall add to me another *s*	Gen 30:24	1121
when Shechem the *s* of Hamor the	Gen 34:2	1121
The soul of my *s* Shechem longeth	Gen 34:8	1121
Hamor, and Shechem Hamor's *s*	Gen 34:18	1121
Shechem his *s* came unto the gate	Gen 34:20	1121
unto Shechem his *s* hearkened all	Gen 34:24	1121
Shechem his *s* with the edge of	Gen 34:26	1121
thou shalt have this *s* also	Gen 35:17	1121
Eliphaz the *s* of Adah the wife of	Gen 36:10	1121
Reuel the *s* of Bashemath the wife	Gen 36:10	1121
was concubine to Eliphaz Esau's *s*	Gen 36:12	1121
Eliphaz the firstborn *s* of Esau	Gen 36:15	1121
are the sons of Reuel Esau's *s*	Gen 36:17	1121
Bela the *s* of Beor reigned in	Gen 36:32	1121
Jobab the *s* of Zerah of Bozrah	Gen 36:33	1121
died, and Hadad the *s* of Bedad	Gen 36:35	1121
Baal-hanan the *s* of Achbor	Gen 36:38	1121
Baal-hanan the *s* of Achbor died	Gen 36:39	1121
he was the *s* of his old age	Gen 37:3	1121
and mourned for his *s* many days	Gen 37:34	1121
into the grave unto my *s* mourning	Gen 37:35	1121
And she conceived, and bare a *s*	Gen 38:3	1121
she conceived again, and bare a *s*	Gen 38:4	1121
yet again conceived, and bare a *s*	Gen 38:5	1121
house, till Shelah my *s* be grown	Gen 38:11	1121
I gave her not to Shelah my *s*	Gen 38:26	1121
My *s* shall not go down with you	Gen 42:38	1121
brother Benjamin, his mother's *s*	Gen 43:29	1121
God be gracious unto thee, my *s*	Gen 43:29	1121
unto him, Thus saith thy *s* Joseph	Gen 45:9	1121
Joseph my *s* is yet alive	Gen 45:28	1121
Shaul the *s* of a Canaanitish	Gen 46:10	1121
and he called his *s* Joseph	Gen 47:29	1121
thy *s* Joseph cometh unto thee	Gen 48:2	1121
refused, and said, I know it, my *s*	Gen 48:19	1121
from the prey, my *s*, thou art	Gen 49:9	1121
the *s* of Manasseh were brought up	Gen 50:23	1121
if it be a *s*, then ye shall kill	Ex 1:16	1121
Every *s* that is born ye shall	Ex 1:22	1121
the woman conceived, and bare a *s*	Ex 2:2	1121
daughter, and he became her *s*	Ex 2:10	1121
And she bare him a *s*, and he called	Ex 2:22	1121
saith the LORD, Israel is my *s*	Ex 4:22	1121
And I say unto thee, Let my *s* go	Ex 4:23	1121
him go, behold, I will slay thy *s*	Ex 4:23	1121
and cut off the foreskin of her *s*	Ex 4:25	1121
Shaul the *s* of a Canaanitish	Ex 6:15	1121
Eleazar Aaron's *s* took him one of	Ex 6:25	1121
of thy *s*, and of thy son's *s*	Ex 10:2	1121
thou shalt shew thy *s* in that day	Ex 13:8	1121
it shall be when thy *s* asketh	Ex 13:14	1121
not do any work, thou, nor thy *s*	Ex 20:10	1121
he have betrothed her unto his *s*	Ex 21:9	1121
Whether it have gored a *s*	Ex 21:31	1121
the *s* of thy handmaid, and the	Ex 23:12	1121
that *s* that is priest in his	Ex 29:30	1121
by name Bezaleel the *s* of Uri	Ex 31:2	1121
the *s* of Hur, of the tribe of	Ex 31:2	1121
the *s* of Ahisamach, of the tribe	Ex 31:6	1121
LORD, even every man upon his *s*	Ex 32:29	1121
the *s* of Nun, a young man,	Ex 33:11	1121
by name Bezaleel the *s* of Uri	Ex 35:30	1121
the *s* of Hur, of the tribe of	Ex 35:30	1121
the *s* of Ahisamach, of the tribe	Ex 35:34	1121
of Ithamar, *s* to Aaron the priest	Ex 38:21	1121
And Bezaleel the *s* of Uri	Ex 38:22	1121

the *s* of Hur, of the tribe of	Ex 38:22	1121
s of Ahisamach, of the tribe of	Ex 38:23	1121
purifying are fulfilled, for a *s*	Lev 12:6	1121
and for his father, and for his *s*	Lev 21:2	1121
the *s* of an Israelitish woman,	Lev 24:10	1121
this *s* of the Israelitish woman	Lev 24:10	1121
the Israelitish woman's *s*	Lev 24:11	1121
his uncle, or his uncle's *s*	Lev 25:49	1121
Elizur the *s* of Shedeur	Num 1:5	1121
Shelumiel the *s* of Zurishaddai	Num 1:6	1121
Nahshon the *s* of Amminadab	Num 1:7	1121
Nethaneel the *s* of Zuar	Num 1:8	1121
Eliab the *s* of Helon	Num 1:9	1121
Elishama the *s* of Ammihud	Num 1:10	1121
Gamaliel the *s* of Pedahzur	Num 1:10	1121
Abidan the *s* of Gideoni	Num 1:11	1121
Ahiezer the *s* of Ammishaddai	Num 1:12	1121
Pagiel the *s* of Ocran	Num 1:13	1121
Eliasaph the *s* of Deuel	Num 1:14	1121
Ahira the *s* of Enan	Num 1:15	1121
of Reuben, Israel's eldest *s*	Num 1:20	1121
Nahshon the *s* of Amminadab shall	Num 2:3	1121
Nethaneel the *s* of Zuar shall be	Num 2:5	1121
Eliab the *s* of Helon shall be	Num 2:7	1121
shall be Elizur the *s* of Shedeur	Num 2:10	1121
be Shelumiel the *s* of Zurishaddai	Num 2:12	1121
shall be Eliasaph the *s* of Reuel	Num 2:14	1121
be Elishama the *s* of Ammihud	Num 2:18	1121
be Gamaliel the *s* of Pedahzur	Num 2:20	1121
shall be Abidan the *s* of Gideoni	Num 2:22	1121
be Ahiezer the *s* of Ammishaddai	Num 2:25	1121
shall be Pagiel the *s* of Ocran	Num 2:27	1121
shall be Ahira the *s* of Enan	Num 2:29	1121
shall be Eliasaph the *s* of Lael	Num 3:24	1121
be Elizaphan the *s* of Uzziel	Num 3:30	1121
Eleazar the *s* of Aaron the priest	Num 3:32	1121
was Zuriel the *s* of Abihail	Num 3:35	1121
to the office of Eleazar the *s* of	Num 4:16	1121
Ithamar the *s* of Aaron the priest	Num 4:28	1121
Ithamar the *s* of Aaron the priest	Num 4:33	1121
Ithamar the *s* of Aaron the priest	Num 7:8	1121
was Nahshon the *s* of Amminadab	Num 7:12	1121
of Nahshon the *s* of Amminadab	Num 7:17	1121
day Nethaneel the *s* of Zuar	Num 7:18	1121
of Nethaneel the *s* of Zuar	Num 7:23	1121
third day Eliab the *s* of Helon	Num 7:24	1121
offering of Eliab the *s* of Helon	Num 7:29	1121
day Elizur the *s* of Shedeur	Num 7:30	1121
of Elizur the *s* of Shedeur	Num 7:35	1121
Shelumiel the *s* of Zurishaddai	Num 7:36	1121
of Shelumiel the *s* of Zurishaddai	Num 7:41	1121
sixth day Eliasaph the *s* of Deuel	Num 7:42	1121
of Eliasaph the *s* of Deuel	Num 7:47	1121
day Elishama the *s* of Ammihud	Num 7:48	1121
of Elishama the *s* of Ammihud	Num 7:53	1121
Gamaliel the *s* of Pedahzur	Num 7:54	1121
of Gamaliel the *s* of Pedahzur	Num 7:59	1121
ninth day Abidan the *s* of Gideoni	Num 7:60	1121
of Abidan the *s* of Gideoni	Num 7:65	1121
day Ahiezer the *s* of Ammishaddai	Num 7:66	1121
of Ahiezer the *s* of Ammishaddai	Num 7:71	1121
day Pagiel the *s* of Ocran	Num 7:72	1121
offering of Pagiel the *s* of Ocran	Num 7:77	1121
twelfth day Ahira the *s* of Enan	Num 7:78	1121
offering of Ahira the *s* of Enan	Num 7:83	1121
was Nahshon the *s* of Amminadab	Num 10:14	1121
was Nethaneel the *s* of Zuar	Num 10:15	1121
Zebulun was Eliab the *s* of Helon	Num 10:16	1121
host was Elizur the *s* of Shedeur	Num 10:18	1121
Shelumiel the *s* of Zurishaddai	Num 10:19	1121
Gad was Eliasaph the *s* of Deuel	Num 10:20	1121
was Elishama the *s* of Ammihud	Num 10:22	1121
was Gamaliel the *s* of Pedahzur	Num 10:23	1121
was Abidan the *s* of Gideoni	Num 10:24	1121
was Ahiezer the *s* of Ammishaddai	Num 10:25	1121
Asher was Pagiel the *s* of Ocran	Num 10:26	1121
Naphtali was Ahira the *s* of Enan	Num 10:27	1121
the *s* of Raguel the Midianite,	Num 10:29	1121
And Joshua the *s* of Nun, the	Num 11:28	1121
Reuben, Shammua the *s* of Zaccur	Num 13:4	1121
of Simeon, Shaphat the *s* of Hori	Num 13:5	1121
Judah, Caleb the *s* of Jephunneh	Num 13:6	1121
of Issachar, Igal the *s* of Joseph	Num 13:7	1121
of Ephraim, Oshea the *s* of Nun	Num 13:8	1121
of Benjamin, Palti the *s* of Raphu	Num 13:9	1121
of Zebulun, Gaddiel the *s* of Sodi	Num 13:10	1121
of Manasseh, Gaddi the *s* of Susi	Num 13:11	1121
of Dan, Ammiel the *s* of Gemalli	Num 13:12	1121
of Asher, Sethur the *s* of Michael	Num 13:13	1121
Naphtali, Nahbi the *s* of Vophsi	Num 13:14	1121
of Gad, Geuel the *s* of Machi	Num 13:15	1121

S

the LORD from my hand for my s	Judg 17:3	1121
the s of Gershom	Judg 18:30	1121
the s of Manasseh, he and his sons	Judg 18:30	1121
father said unto his s in law	Judg 19:5	2860
the s of Eleazar	Judg 20:28	1121
the s of Aaron, stood before it	Judg 20:28	1121
her conception, and she bare a s	Ruth 4:13	1121
There is a s born to Naomi	Ruth 4:17	1121
the s of Jeroham	1Sa 1:1	1121
the s of Elihu, the s of Tohu,	1Sa 1:1	1121
the s of Zuph, an Ephrathite	1Sa 1:1	1121
had conceived, that she bare a s	1Sa 1:20	1121
gave her s suck until she weaned	1Sa 1:23	1121
he answered, I called not, my s	1Sa 3:6	1121
Samuel, and said, Samuel, my s	1Sa 3:16	1121
he said, What is there done, my s	1Sa 4:16	1121
for thou hast born a s	1Sa 4:20	1121
sanctified Eleazar his s to keep	1Sa 7:1	1121
the s of Abiel, the s of Zeror,	1Sa 9:1	1121
the s of Bechorath	1Sa 9:1	1121
the s of Aphiah, a Benjamite, a	1Sa 9:1	1121
And he had a s, whose name was	1Sa 9:2	1121
And Kish said to Saul his s	1Sa 9:3	1121
saying, What shall I do for my s	1Sa 10:2	1121
that is come unto the s of Kish	1Sa 10:11	1121
Saul the s of Kish was taken	1Sa 10:21	1121
And Saul, and Jonathan his s	1Sa 13:16	1121
Jonathan his s was there found	1Sa 13:22	1121
that Jonathan the s of Saul said	1Sa 14:1	1121
the s of Ahitub, I-chabod's	1Sa 14:3	1121
the s of Phinehas, the s of Eli	1Sa 14:3	1121
though it be in Jonathan my s	1Sa 14:39	1121
Jonathan my s will be on the	1Sa 14:40	1121
lots between me and Jonathan my s	1Sa 14:42	1121
the s of Ner, Saul's uncle	1Sa 14:50	1121
of Abner was the s of Abiel	1Sa 14:51	1121
I have seen a s of Jesse the	1Sa 16:18	1121
and said, Send me David thy s	1Sa 16:19	1121
them by David his s unto Saul	1Sa 16:20	1121
Now David was the s of that	1Sa 17:12	1121
And Jesse said unto David his s	1Sa 17:17	1121
Abner, whose s is this youth	1Sa 17:55	1121
thou whose s the stripling is	1Sa 17:56	1121
Whose s art thou, thou young man	1Sa 17:58	1121
I am the s of thy servant Jesse	1Sa 17:58	1121
that I should be s in law to the	1Sa 18:18	2860
Thou shalt this day be my s in	1Sa 18:21	2859
therefore be the king's s in law	1Sa 18:22	2859
thing to be a king's s in law	1Sa 18:23	2859
well to be the king's s in law	1Sa 18:26	2859
he might be the king's s in law	1Sa 18:27	2859
And Saul spake to Jonathan his s	1Sa 19:1	1121
But Saul's s delighted	1Sa 19:2	1121
and Saul said unto Jonathan his s	1Sa 20:27	1121
cometh not the s of Jesse to meat	1Sa 20:27	1121
Thou s of the perverse rebellious	1Sa 20:30	1121
know that thou hast chosen the s	1Sa 20:30	1121
For as long as the s of Jesse	1Sa 20:31	1121
will the s of Jesse give every	1Sa 22:7	1121
s hath made a league with the s	1Sa 22:8	1121
my s hath stirred up my servant	1Sa 22:8	1121
I saw the s of Jesse coming to	1Sa 22:9	1121
Nob, to Ahimelech the s of Ahitub	1Sa 22:9	1121
the s of Ahitub, and all his	1Sa 22:11	1121
said, Hear now, thou s of Ahitub	1Sa 22:12	1121
the s of Jesse, in that thou hast	1Sa 22:13	1121
which is the king's s in law	1Sa 22:14	2860
sons of Ahimelech the s of Ahitub	1Sa 22:20	1121
when Abiathar the s of Ahimelech	1Sa 23:6	1121
And Jonathan Saul's s arose	1Sa 23:16	1121
Is this thy voice, my s David	1Sa 24:16	1121
thy servants, and to thy s David	1Sa 25:8	1121
and who is the s of Jesse	1Sa 25:10	1121
for he is such a s of Belial	1Sa 25:17	1121
wife, to Phalti the s of Laish	1Sa 25:44	1121
Saul lay, and Abner the s of Ner	1Sa 26:5	1121
and to Abishai the s of Zeruiah	1Sa 26:6	1121
people, and to Abner the s of Ner	1Sa 26:14	1121
Is this thy voice, my s David	1Sa 26:17	1121
return, my s David	1Sa 26:21	1121
Blessed be thou, my s David	1Sa 26:25	1121
the s of Maoch, king of Gath	1Sa 27:2	1121
the priest, Ahimelech's s	1Sa 30:7	1121
Jonathan his s are dead also	2Sa 1:4	1121
Saul and Jonathan his s be dead	2Sa 1:5	1121
for Saul, and for Jonathan his s	2Sa 1:12	1121
I am the s of a stranger, an	2Sa 1:13	1121
over Saul and over Jonathan his s	2Sa 1:17	1121
But Abner the s of Ner, captain	2Sa 2:8	1121
took Ish-bosheth the s of Saul	2Sa 2:8	1121
Ish-bosheth Saul's s was forty	2Sa 2:10	1121
And Abner the s of Ner, and the	2Sa 2:12	1121
of Ish-bosheth the s of Saul	2Sa 2:12	1121
Joab the s of Zeruiah, and the	2Sa 2:13	1121
to Ish-bosheth the s of Saul	2Sa 2:15	1121
Absalom the s of Maacah the	2Sa 3:3	1121
fourth, Adonijah the s of Haggith	2Sa 3:4	1121
fifth, Shephatiah the s of Abital	2Sa 3:4	1121
to Ish-bosheth Saul's s, saying,	2Sa 3:14	1121
even from Phaltiel the s of Laish	2Sa 3:15	1121
Abner the s of Ner came to the	2Sa 3:23	1121
Thou knowest Abner the s of Ner	2Sa 3:25	1121
the blood of Abner the s of Ner	2Sa 3:28	1121
king to slay Abner the s of Ner	2Sa 3:37	1121
when Saul's s heard that Abner	2Sa 4:1	1121
Saul's s had two men that were	2Sa 4:2	1121
And Jonathan, Saul's s, had a s	2Sa 4:4	1121
the s of Saul thine enemy	2Sa 4:8	1121
his father, and he shall be my s	2Sa 7:14	1121
the s of Rehob, king of Zobah, as	2Sa 8:3	1121
sent Joram his s unto king David	2Sa 8:10	1121
s of Rehob, king of Zobah	2Sa 8:12	1121
Joab the s of Zeruiah was over	2Sa 8:16	1121
Jehoshaphat the s of Ahilud was	2Sa 8:16	1121
And Zadok the s of Ahitub, and	2Sa 8:17	1121
and Ahimelech the s of Abiathar	2Sa 8:17	1121
Benaiah the s of Jehoiada was	2Sa 8:18	1121
the king, Jonathan hath yet a s	2Sa 9:3	1121
the s of Ammiel, in Lo-debar	2Sa 9:4	1121
the s of Ammiel, from Lo-debar	2Sa 9:5	1121
the s of Jonathan	2Sa 9:6	1121
the s of Saul, was come unto	2Sa 9:6	1121
s all that pertained to Saul	2Sa 9:9	1121
that thy master's s may have food	2Sa 9:10	1121
s shall eat bread alway at my	2Sa 9:10	1121
And Mephibosheth had a young s	2Sa 9:12	1121
Hanun his s reigned in his stead	2Sa 10:1	1121
unto Hanun the s of Nahash	2Sa 10:2	1121
Abimelech the s of Jerubbesheth	2Sa 11:21	1121
became his wife, and bare him a s	2Sa 11:27	1121
and she bare a s, and he called his	2Sa 12:24	1121
that Absalom the s of David had a	2Sa 13:1	1121
Amnon the s of David loved her	2Sa 13:1	1121
the s of Shimeah David's brother	2Sa 13:3	1121
Why art thou, being the king's s	2Sa 13:4	1121
king said to Absalom, Nay, my s	2Sa 13:25	1121
the s of Shimeah David's brother,	2Sa 13:32	1121
the s of Ammihud, king of Geshur	2Sa 13:37	1121
David mourned for his s every day	2Sa 13:37	1121
Now Joab the s of Zeruiah	2Sa 14:1	1121
any more, lest they destroy my s	2Sa 14:11	1121
hair of thy s fall to the earth	2Sa 14:11	1121
me and my s together out of the	2Sa 14:16	1121
two sons with you, Ahimaaz thy s	2Sa 15:27	1121
and Jonathan the s of Abiathar	2Sa 15:27	1121
their two sons, Ahimaaz Zadok's s	2Sa 15:36	
and Jonathan Abiathar's s	2Sa 15:36	
said, And where is thy master's s	2Sa 16:3	1121
name was Shimei, the s of Gera	2Sa 16:5	1121
into the hand of Absalom thy s	2Sa 16:8	1121
Then said Abishai the s of	2Sa 16:9	1121
to all his servants, Behold, my s	2Sa 16:11	1121
serve in the presence of his s	2Sa 16:19	1121
which Amasa was a man's s	2Sa 17:25	1121
that Shobi the s of Nahash of	2Sa 17:27	1121
Machir the s of Ammiel of	2Sa 17:27	1121
hand of Abishai the s of Zeruiah	2Sa 18:2	1121
mine hand against the king's s	2Sa 18:12	1121
I have no s to keep my name in	2Sa 18:18	1121
Then said Ahimaaz the s of Zadok	2Sa 18:19	1121
because the king's s is dead	2Sa 18:20	1121
Then said Ahimaaz the s of Zadok	2Sa 18:22	1121
Wherefore wilt thou run, my s	2Sa 18:22	1121
running of Ahimaaz the s of Zadok	2Sa 18:27	1121
O my s Absalom, my s, my s	2Sa 18:33	1121
for thee, O Absalom, my s, my s	2Sa 18:33	1121
the king was grieved for his s	2Sa 19:2	1121
O my s Absalom	2Sa 19:4	1121
O Absalom, my s, my s	2Sa 19:4	1121
And Shimei the s of Gera, a	2Sa 19:16	1121
Shimei the s of Gera fell down	2Sa 19:18	1121
But Abishai the s of Zeruiah	2Sa 19:21	1121
Mephibosheth the s of Saul came	2Sa 19:24	1121
the s of Bichri, a Benjamite	2Sa 20:1	1121
we inheritance in the s of Jesse	2Sa 20:1	1121
and followed Sheba the s of Bichri	2Sa 20:2	1121
Now shall Sheba the s of Bichri	2Sa 20:6	1121
after Sheba the s of Bichri	2Sa 20:7	1121
after Sheba the s of Bichri	2Sa 20:10	1121
after Sheba the s of Bichri	2Sa 20:13	1121
Sheba the s of Bichri by name,	2Sa 20:21	1121
the head of Sheba the s of Bichri	2Sa 20:22	1121

Benaiah the *s* of Jehoiada was	2Sa 20:23	1121
Jehoshaphat the *s* of Ahilud was	2Sa 20:24	1121
the *s* of Jonathan the *s* of Saul	2Sa 21:7	1121
David and Jonathan the *s* of Saul	2Sa 21:7	1121
s of Barzillai the Meholathite	2Sa 21:8	1121
the bones of Jonathan his *s* from	2Sa 21:12	1121
and the bones of Jonathan his *s*	2Sa 21:13	1121
Jonathan his *s* buried they in the	2Sa 21:14	1121
But Abishai the *s* of Zeruiah	2Sa 21:17	1121
Elhanan the *s* of Jaare-oregim	2Sa 21:19	1121
Jonathan the *s* of Shimeah the	2Sa 21:21	1121
David the *s* of Jesse said, and the	2Sa 23:1	1121
Eleazar the *s* of Dodo the Ahohite	2Sa 23:9	1121
the *s* of Agee the Hararite	2Sa 23:11	1121
the *s* of Zeruiah, was chief among	2Sa 23:18	1121
And Benaiah the *s* of Jehoiada	2Sa 23:20	1121
the *s* of a valiant man, of	2Sa 23:20	1121
did Benaiah the *s* of Jehoiada	2Sa 23:22	1121
Elhanan the *s* of Dodo of	2Sa 23:24	1121
Ira the *s* of Ikkesh the Tekoite,	2Sa 23:26	1121
Heleb the *s* of Baanah, a	2Sa 23:29	1121
Ittai the *s* of Ribai out of	2Sa 23:29	1121
Ahiam the *s* of Sharar the	2Sa 23:33	1121
Eliphelet the *s* of Ahasbai	2Sa 23:34	1121
the *s* of the Maachathite, Eliam	2Sa 23:34	1121
Eliam the *s* of Ahithophel the	2Sa 23:34	1121
Igal the *s* of Nathan of Zobah,	2Sa 23:36	1121
to Joab the *s* of Zeruiah,	2Sa 23:37	1121
Then Adonijah the *s* of Haggith	1Kin 1:5	1121
with Joab the *s* of Zeruiah	1Kin 1:7	1121
and Benaiah the *s* of Jehoiada	1Kin 1:8	1121
the *s* of Haggith doth reign	1Kin 1:11	1121
and the life of thy *s* Solomon	1Kin 1:12	1121
thy *s* shall reign after me	1Kin 1:13	1121
thy *s* shall reign after me	1Kin 1:17	1121
my *s* Solomon shall be counted	1Kin 1:21	1121
and Benaiah the *s* of Jehoiada	1Kin 1:26	1121
thy *s* shall reign after me	1Kin 1:30	1121
and Benaiah the *s* of Jehoiada	1Kin 1:32	1121
cause Solomon my *s* to ride upon	1Kin 1:33	1121
Benaiah the *s* of Jehoiada	1Kin 1:36	1121
and Benaiah the *s* of Jehoiada	1Kin 1:38	1121
Jonathan the *s* of Abiathar the	1Kin 1:42	1121
and Benaiah the *s* of Jehoiada	1Kin 1:44	1121
and he charged Solomon his *s*	1Kin 2:1	1121
Joab the *s* of Zeruiah did to me	1Kin 2:5	1121
Israel, unto Abner the *s* of Ner	1Kin 2:5	1121
and unto Amasa the *s* of Jether	1Kin 2:5	1121
with thee Shimei the *s* of Gera	1Kin 2:8	1121
Adonijah the *s* of Haggith came to	1Kin 2:13	1121
and for Joab the *s* of Zeruiah	1Kin 2:22	1121
hand of Benaiah the *s* of Jehoiada	1Kin 2:25	1121
sent Benaiah the *s* of Jehoiada	1Kin 2:29	1121
to wit, Abner the *s* of Ner	1Kin 2:32	1121
Israel, and Amasa the *s* of Jether	1Kin 2:32	1121
So Benaiah the *s* of Jehoiada went	1Kin 2:34	1121
the king put Benaiah the *s* of	1Kin 2:35	1121
Achish *s* of Maachah king of Gath	1Kin 2:39	1121
Benaiah the *s* of Jehoiada	1Kin 2:46	1121
him a *s* to sit on his throne	1Kin 3:6	1121
took my *s* from beside me, while	1Kin 3:20	1121
morning, behold, it was not my *s*	1Kin 3:21	1121
is my *s*, and the dead is thy *s*	1Kin 3:22	1121
is thy *s*, and the living is my *s*	1Kin 3:22	1121
This is my *s* that liveth, and thy	1Kin 3:23	1121
that liveth, and thy *s* is the dead	1Kin 3:23	1121
but thy *s* is the dead, and my *s*	1Kin 3:23	1121
for her bowels yearned upon her *s*	1Kin 3:26	1121
Azariah the *s* of Zadok the priest	1Kin 4:2	1121
Jehoshaphat the *s* of Ahilud	1Kin 4:3	1121
Benaiah the *s* of Jehoiada was	1Kin 4:4	1121
Azariah the *s* of Nathan was over	1Kin 4:5	1121
Zabud the *s* of Nathan was	1Kin 4:5	1121
Adoniram the *s* of Abda was over	1Kin 4:6	1121
The *s* of Hur, in mount Ephraim	1Kin 4:8	1133
The *s* of Dekar, in Makaz, and in	1Kin 4:9	1128
The *s* of Hesed, in Aruboth	1Kin 4:10	1136
The *s* of Abinadab, in all the	1Kin 4:11	1125
Baana the *s* of Ahilud	1Kin 4:12	1121
The *s* of Geber, in Ramoth-gilead	1Kin 4:13	1127
towns of Jair the *s* of Manasseh	1Kin 4:13	1121
Ahinadab the *s* of Iddo had	1Kin 4:14	1121
Baanah the *s* of Hushai was in	1Kin 4:16	1121
Jehoshaphat the *s* of Paruah	1Kin 4:17	1121
Shimei the *s* of Elah, in Benjamin	1Kin 4:18	1121
Geber the *s* of Uri was in the	1Kin 4:19	1121
David my father, saying, Thy *s*	1Kin 5:5	1121
a wise *s* over this great people	1Kin 5:7	1121
He was a widow's *s* of the tribe	1Kin 7:14	1121
but thy *s* that shall come forth	1Kin 8:19	1121
rend it out of the hand of thy *s*	1Kin 11:12	1121

thy *s* for David my servant's sake	1Kin 11:13	1121
Tahpenes bare him Genubath his *s*	1Kin 11:20	1121
Rezon the *s* of Eliadah, which	1Kin 11:23	1121
And Jeroboam the *s* of Nebat	1Kin 11:26	1121
unto his *s* will I give one tribe,	1Kin 11:36	1121
Rehoboam his *s* reigned in his	1Kin 11:43	1121
when Rehoboam the *s* of Nebat	1Kin 12:2	1121
unto Jeroboam the *s* of Nebat	1Kin 12:15	1121
we inheritance in the *s* of Jesse	1Kin 12:16	1121
to Rehoboam the *s* of Solomon	1Kin 12:21	1121
the *s* of Solomon, king of Judah,	1Kin 12:23	1121
the *s* of Jeroboam fell sick	1Kin 14:1	1121
to ask a thing of thee for her *s*	1Kin 14:5	1121
Nadab his *s* reigned in his stead	1Kin 14:20	1121
Rehoboam the *s* of Solomon reigned	1Kin 14:21	1121
Abijam his *s* reigned in his stead	1Kin 14:31	1121
year of king Jeroboam the *s* of	1Kin 15:1	1121
to set up his *s* after him	1Kin 15:4	1121
Asa his *s* reigned in his stead	1Kin 15:8	1121
the *s* of Tabrimon	1Kin 15:18	1121
the *s* of Hezion, king of Syria,	1Kin 15:18	1121
Jehoshaphat his *s* reigned in his	1Kin 15:24	1121
Nadab the *s* of Jeroboam began to	1Kin 15:25	1121
And Baasha the *s* of Ahijah	1Kin 15:27	1121
the *s* of Ahijah to reign over all	1Kin 15:33	1121
the *s* of Hanani against Baasha	1Kin 16:1	1121
house of Jeroboam the *s* of Nebat	1Kin 16:3	1121
Elah his *s* reigned in his stead	1Kin 16:6	1121
hand of the prophet Jehu the *s* of	1Kin 16:7	1121
king of Judah began Elah the *s* of	1Kin 16:8	1121
Baasha, and the sins of Elah his *s*	1Kin 16:13	1121
followed Tibni the *s* of Ginath	1Kin 16:21	1121
followed Tibni the *s* of Ginath	1Kin 16:22	1121
way of Jeroboam the *s* of Nebat	1Kin 16:26	1121
Ahab his *s* reigned in his stead	1Kin 16:28	1121
s of Omri to reign over Israel	1Kin 16:29	1121
Ahab the *s* of Omri reigned over	1Kin 16:29	1121
Ahab the *s* of Omri did evil in	1Kin 16:30	1121
sins of Jeroboam the *s* of Nebat	1Kin 16:31	1121
thereof in his youngest *s* Segub	1Kin 16:34	
he spake by Joshua the *s* of Nun	1Kin 16:34	1121
go in and dress it for me and my *s*	1Kin 17:12	1121
after make for thee and for thy *s*	1Kin 17:13	1121
that the *s* of the woman, the	1Kin 17:17	1121
to remembrance, and to slay my *s*	1Kin 17:18	1121
he said unto her, Give me thy *s*	1Kin 17:19	1121
whom I sojourn, by slaying her *s*	1Kin 17:20	1121
and Elijah said, See, thy *s* liveth	1Kin 17:23	1121
Jehu the *s* of Nimshi shalt thou	1Kin 19:16	1121
Elisha the *s* of Shaphat of	1Kin 19:16	1121
and found Elisha the *s* of Shaphat	1Kin 19:19	1121
house of Jeroboam the *s* of Nebat	1Kin 21:22	1121
house of Baasha the *s* of Ahijah	1Kin 21:22	1121
one man, Micaiah the *s* of Imlah	1Kin 22:8	1121
hither Micaiah the *s* of Imlah	1Kin 22:9	1121
Zedekiah the *s* of Chenaanah made	1Kin 22:11	1121
But Zedekiah the *s* of Chenaanah	1Kin 22:24	1121
city, and to Joash the king's *s*	1Kin 22:26	1121
Ahaziah his *s* reigned in his	1Kin 22:40	1121
Jehoshaphat the *s* of Asa began to	1Kin 22:41	1121
Then said Ahaziah the *s* of Ahab	1Kin 22:49	1121
Jehoram his *s* reigned in his	1Kin 22:50	1121
Ahaziah the *s* of Ahab began to	1Kin 22:51	1121
way of Jeroboam the *s* of Nebat	1Kin 22:52	1121
s of Jehoshaphat king of Judah	2Kin 1:17	1121
because he had no *s*	2Kin 1:17	1121
Now Jehoram the *s* of Ahab began	2Kin 3:1	1121
sins of Jeroboam the *s* of Nebat	2Kin 3:3	1121
Here is Elisha the *s* of Shaphat	2Kin 3:11	1121
Then he took his eldest *s* that	2Kin 3:27	1121
full, that she said unto her *s*	2Kin 4:6	1121
of life, thou shalt embrace a *s*	2Kin 4:16	1121
bare a *s* at that season that	2Kin 4:17	1121
said, Did I desire a *s* of my lord	2Kin 4:28	1121
unto him, he said, Take up thy *s*	2Kin 4:36	1121
to the ground, and took up her *s*	2Kin 4:37	1121
woman said unto me, Give thy *s*	2Kin 6:28	1121
and we will eat my *s* to morrow	2Kin 6:28	1121
So we boiled my *s*, and did eat him	2Kin 6:29	1121
her on the next day, Give thy *s*	2Kin 6:29	1121
and she hath hid her *s*	2Kin 6:29	1121
if the head of Elisha the *s* of	2Kin 6:31	1121
See ye how this *s* of a murderer	2Kin 6:32	1121
whose *s* he had restored to life,	2Kin 8:1	1121
whose *s* he had restored to life,	2Kin 8:5	1121
is the woman, and this is her *s*	2Kin 8:5	1121
Thy *s* Ben-hadad king of Syria	2Kin 8:9	1121
the *s* of Ahab king of Israel	2Kin 8:16	1121
Jehoram the *s* of Jehoshaphat king	2Kin 8:16	1121
Ahaziah his *s* reigned in his	2Kin 8:24	1121
the *s* of Ahab king of Israel did	2Kin 8:25	1121

S

s of Jehoram king of Judah begin	2Kin 8:25	1121
for he was the s in law of the	2Kin 8:27	2860
he went with Joram the s of Ahab	2Kin 8:28	1121
Ahaziah the s of Jehoram king of	2Kin 8:29	1121
Joram the s of Ahab in Jezreel	2Kin 8:29	1121
Jehu the s of Jehoshaphat	2Kin 9:2	1121
Jehoshaphat the s of Nimshi	2Kin 9:2	1121
house of Jeroboam the s of Nebat	2Kin 9:9	1121
house of Baasha the s of Ahijah	2Kin 9:9	1121
So Jehu the s of Jehoshaphat the	2Kin 9:14	1121
the s of Nimshi conspired against	2Kin 9:14	1121
driving of Jehu the s of Nimshi	2Kin 9:20	1121
s of Ahab began Ahaziah to reign	2Kin 9:29	1121
he lighted on Jehonadab the s of	2Kin 10:15	1121
and Jehonadab the s of Rechab	2Kin 10:23	1121
sins of Jeroboam the s of Nebat	2Kin 10:29	1121
Jehoahaz his s reigned in his	2Kin 10:35	1121
Ahaziah saw that her s was dead	2Kin 11:1	1121
took Joash the s of Ahaziah	2Kin 11:2	1121
LORD, and shewed them the king's s	2Kin 11:4	1121
And he brought forth the king's s	2Kin 11:12	1121
For Jozachar the s of Shimeath	2Kin 12:21	1121
and Jehozabad the s of Shomer	2Kin 12:21	1121
Amaziah his s reigned in his	2Kin 12:21	1121
the s of Ahaziah king of Judah	2Kin 13:1	1121
king of Judah Jehoahaz the s of	2Kin 13:1	1121
sins of Jeroboam the s of Nebat	2Kin 13:2	1121
hand of Ben-hadad the s of Hazael	2Kin 13:3	1121
Joash his s reigned in his stead	2Kin 13:9	1121
the s of Jehoahaz to reign over	2Kin 13:10	1121
sins of Jeroboam the s of Nebat	2Kin 13:11	1121
Ben-hadad his s reigned in his	2Kin 13:24	1121
Jehoash the s of Jehoahaz took	2Kin 13:25	1121
the s of Hazael the cities	2Kin 13:25	1121
s of Jehoahaz king of Israel	2Kin 14:1	1121
the s of Joash king of Judah	2Kin 14:1	1121
the s of Jehoahaz s of Jehu	2Kin 14:8	1121
Give thy daughter to my s to wife	2Kin 14:9	1121
s of Jehoash the s of Ahaziah	2Kin 14:13	1121
Jeroboam his s reigned in his	2Kin 14:16	1121
Amaziah the s of Joash king of	2Kin 14:17	1121
s of Jehoahaz king of Israel	2Kin 14:17	1121
fifteenth year of Amaziah the s	2Kin 14:23	1121
king of Judah Jeroboam the s of	2Kin 14:23	1121
sins of Jeroboam the s of Nebat	2Kin 14:24	1121
the s of Amittai, the prophet,	2Kin 14:25	1121
hand of Jeroboam the s of Joash	2Kin 14:27	1121
Zachariah his s reigned in his	2Kin 14:29	1121
s of Amaziah king of Judah to	2Kin 15:1	1121
Jotham the king's s was over the	2Kin 15:5	1121
Jotham his s reigned in his stead	2Kin 15:7	1121
s of Jeroboam reign over Israel	2Kin 15:8	1121
sins of Jeroboam the s of Nebat	2Kin 15:9	1121
Shallum the s of Jabesh conspired	2Kin 15:10	1121
Shallum the s of Jabesh began to	2Kin 15:13	1121
For Menahem the s of Gadi went up	2Kin 15:14	1121
smote Shallum the s of Jabesh in	2Kin 15:14	1121
s of Gadi to reign over Israel	2Kin 15:17	1121
sins of Jeroboam the s of Nebat	2Kin 15:18	1121
Pekahiah his s reigned in his	2Kin 15:22	1121
king of Judah Pekahiah the s of	2Kin 15:23	1121
sins of Jeroboam the s of Nebat	2Kin 15:24	1121
But Pekah the s of Remaliah	2Kin 15:25	1121
s of Remaliah began to reign over	2Kin 15:27	1121
sins of Jeroboam the s of Nebat	2Kin 15:28	1121
Hoshea the s of Elah made a	2Kin 15:30	1121
against Pekah the s of Remaliah	2Kin 15:30	1121
year of Jotham the s of Uzziah	2Kin 15:30	1121
the s of Remaliah king of Israel	2Kin 15:32	1121
the s of Uzziah king of Judah to	2Kin 15:32	1121
Syria, and Pekah the s of Remaliah	2Kin 15:37	1121
Ahaz his s reigned in his stead	2Kin 15:38	1121
the s of Remaliah	2Kin 16:1	1121
Ahaz the s of Jotham	2Kin 16:1	1121
made his s to pass through the	2Kin 16:3	1121
Pekah s of Remaliah king of	2Kin 16:5	1121
saying, I am thy servant and thy s	2Kin 16:7	1121
Hezekiah his s reigned in his	2Kin 16:20	1121
the s of Elah to reign in Samaria	2Kin 17:1	1121
made Jeroboam the s of Nebat king	2Kin 17:21	1121
Hoshea s of Elah king of Israel	2Kin 18:1	1121
that Hezekiah the s of Ahaz king	2Kin 18:1	1121
Hoshea s of Elah king of Israel	2Kin 18:9	1121
to them Eliakim the s of Hilkiah	2Kin 18:18	1121
Joah the s of Asaph the recorder	2Kin 18:18	1121
said Eliakim the s of Hilkiah	2Kin 18:26	1121
came Eliakim the s of Hilkiah	2Kin 18:37	1121
Joah the s of Asaph the recorder,	2Kin 18:37	1121
Isaiah the prophet the s of Amoz	2Kin 19:2	1121
Then Isaiah the s of Amoz sent to	2Kin 19:20	1121
Esar-haddon his s reigned in his	2Kin 19:37	1121

Isaiah the s of Amoz came to him	2Kin 20:1	1121
the s of Baladan, king of Babylon	2Kin 20:12	1121
Manasseh his s reigned in his	2Kin 20:21	1121
he made his s pass through the	2Kin 21:6	1121
to David, and to Solomon his s	2Kin 21:7	1121
Amon his s reigned in his stead	2Kin 21:18	1121
Josiah his s king in his stead	2Kin 21:24	1121
Josiah his s reigned in his stead	2Kin 21:26	1121
sent Shaphan the s of Azaliah	2Kin 22:3	1121
the s of Meshullam, the scribe,	2Kin 22:3	1121
and Ahikam the s of Shaphan	2Kin 22:12	1121
Achbor the s of Michaiah, and	2Kin 22:12	1121
wife of Shallum the s of Tikvah	2Kin 22:14	1121
the s of Harhas, keeper of the	2Kin 22:14	1121
that no man might make his s or	2Kin 23:10	1121
which Jeroboam the s of Nebat	2Kin 23:15	1121
took Jehoahaz the s of Josiah	2Kin 23:30	1121
s of Josiah king in the room of	2Kin 23:34	1121
Jehoiachin his s reigned in his	2Kin 24:6	1121
he made Gedaliah the s of Ahikam	2Kin 25:22	1121
Ahikam, the s of Shaphan, ruler	2Kin 25:22	1121
even Ishmael the s of Nethaniah	2Kin 25:23	1121
and Johanan the s of Careah	2Kin 25:23	1121
Seraiah the s of Tanhumeth the	2Kin 25:23	1121
Jaazaniah the s of a Maachathite,	2Kin 25:23	1121
that Ishmael the s of Nethaniah	2Kin 25:25	1121
the s of Elishama, of the seed	2Kin 25:25	1121
Bela the s of Beor	1Chr 1:43	1121
Jobab the s of Zerah of Bozrah	1Chr 1:44	1121
was dead, Hadad the s of Bedad	1Chr 1:46	1121
Baal-hanan the s of Achbor	1Chr 1:49	1121
Caleb the s of Hezron begat	1Chr 2:18	1121
the s of Shammai was Maon	1Chr 2:45	1121
the sons of Caleb the s of Hur	1Chr 2:50	1121
Absalom the s of Maachah the	1Chr 3:2	1121
fourth, Adonijah the s of Haggith	1Chr 3:2	1121
s was Rehoboam, Abia his s	1Chr 3:10	1121
Asa his s, Jehoshaphat his s	1Chr 3:10	1121
Joram his s, Ahaziah his s	1Chr 3:11	1121
Joash his s	1Chr 3:11	1121
Amaziah his s	1Chr 3:12	1121
Azariah his s	1Chr 3:12	1121
Jotham his s	1Chr 3:12	1121
Ahaz his s	1Chr 3:13	1121
Hezekiah his s	1Chr 3:13	1121
Manasseh his s	1Chr 3:13	1121
Amon his s, Josiah his s	1Chr 3:14	1121
Jeconiah his s, Zedekiah his s	1Chr 3:16	1121
Assir, Salathiel his s,	1Chr 3:17	1121
Reaiah the s of Shobal begat	1Chr 4:2	1121
of Aharhel the s of Harum	1Chr 4:8	1121
sons of Caleb the s of Jephunneh	1Chr 4:15	1121
of Shelah the s of Judah were	1Chr 4:21	1121
Shallum his s, Mibsam his s,	1Chr 4:25	1121
Mishma his s	1Chr 4:25	1121
Hamuel his s, Zacchur his s	1Chr 4:26	1121
Shimei his s	1Chr 4:26	1121
and Joshah the s of Amaziah	1Chr 4:34	1121
Jehu the s of Josibiah	1Chr 4:35	1121
s of Seraiah, the s of Asiel,	1Chr 4:35	1121
Ziza the s of Shiphi	1Chr 4:37	1121
the s of Allon	1Chr 4:37	1121
the s of Jedaiah	1Chr 4:37	1121
s of Shimri, the s of Shemaiah	1Chr 4:37	1121
sons of Joseph the s of Israel	1Chr 5:1	1121
Shemaiah his s, Gog his s,	1Chr 5:4	1121
Shimei his s	1Chr 5:4	1121
Micah his s, Reaia his s	1Chr 5:5	1121
Baal his s	1Chr 5:5	1121
Beerah his s, whom	1Chr 5:6	1121
And Bela the s of Azaz	1Chr 5:8	1121
the s of Shema, the s of Joel,	1Chr 5:8	1121
children of Abihail the s of Huri	1Chr 5:14	1121
the s of Jaroah	1Chr 5:14	1121
the s of Gilead	1Chr 5:14	1121
the s of Michael	1Chr 5:14	1121
the s of Jeshishai	1Chr 5:14	1121
the s of Jahdo, the s of Buz	1Chr 5:14	1121
Ahi the s of Abdiel	1Chr 5:15	1121
the s of Guni, chief of the house	1Chr 5:15	1121
Libni his s, Jahath his s	1Chr 6:20	1121
Zimmah his s	1Chr 6:20	1121
Joah his s, Iddo his s, Zerah	1Chr 6:21	1121
Zerah his s, Jeaterai his s	1Chr 6:21	1121
Amminadab his s, Korah his s	1Chr 6:22	1121
Assir his s	1Chr 6:22	1121
Elkanah his s	1Chr 6:23	1121
Ebiasaph his s, and Assir his s	1Chr 6:23	1121
Tahath his s, Uriel his s	1Chr 6:24	1121
Uzziah his s, and Shaul his s	1Chr 6:24	1121
Zophai his s, and Nahath his s,	1Chr 6:26	1121

Eliab his s, Jeroham his s	1Chr 6:27	1121
Elkanah his s	1Chr 6:27	1121
Mahli, Libni his s, Shimei his s	1Chr 6:29	1121
s, Shimei his s, Uzza his s	1Chr 6:29	1121
Shimea his s, Haggiah his s	1Chr 6:30	1121
Asaiah his s	1Chr 6:30	1121
the s of Joel, the s of Shemuel	1Chr 6:33	1121
The s of Elkanah	1Chr 6:34	1121
the s of Jeroham	1Chr 6:34	1121
the s of Eliel, the s of Toah,	1Chr 6:34	1121
The s of Zuph, the s of Elkanah	1Chr 6:35	1121
s of Mahath, the s of Amasai,	1Chr 6:35	1121
The s of Elkanah, the s of Joel	1Chr 6:36	1121
of Azariah, the s of Zephaniah,	1Chr 6:36	1121
The s of Tahath, the s of Assir	1Chr 6:37	1121
s of Ebiasaph, the s of Korah,	1Chr 6:37	1121
The s of Izhar, the s of Kohath	1Chr 6:38	1121
the s of Levi, the s of Israel	1Chr 6:38	1121
even Asaph the s of Berachiah	1Chr 6:39	1121
of Berachiah, the s of Shimea,	1Chr 6:39	1121
The s of Michael	1Chr 6:40	1121
the s of Baaseiah	1Chr 6:40	1121
the s of Malchiah	1Chr 6:40	1121
The s of Ethni, the s of Zerah,	1Chr 6:41	1121
the s of Adaiah	1Chr 6:41	1121
The s of Ethan, the s of Zimmah	1Chr 6:42	1121
the s of Shimei	1Chr 6:42	1121
The s of Jahath	1Chr 6:43	1121
the s of Gershom, the s of Levi	1Chr 6:43	1121
Ethan the s of Kishi	1Chr 6:44	1121
the s of Abdi, the s of Malluch	1Chr 6:44	1121
The s of Hashabiah	1Chr 6:45	1121
s of Amaziah, the s of Hilkiah,	1Chr 6:45	1121
The s of Amzi, the s of Bani,	1Chr 6:46	1121
the s of Shamer	1Chr 6:46	1121
The s of Mahli, the s of Mushi,	1Chr 6:47	1121
the s of Merari, the s of Levi	1Chr 6:47	1121
Eleazar his s, Phinehas his s	1Chr 6:50	1121
Abishua his s	1Chr 6:50	1121
Bukki his s, Uzzi his s	1Chr 6:51	1121
Zerahiah his s	1Chr 6:51	1121
Meraioth his s, Amariah his s	1Chr 6:52	1121
Ahitub his s	1Chr 6:52	1121
Zadok his s, Ahimaaz his s	1Chr 6:53	1121
gave to Caleb the s of Jephunneh	1Chr 6:56	1121
the wife of Machir bare a s	1Chr 7:16	1121
s of Machir, the s of Manasseh	1Chr 7:17	1121
and Bered his s, and Tahath his s	1Chr 7:20	1121
Eladah his s, and Tahath his s	1Chr 7:20	1121
Zabad his s, and Shuthelah his s	1Chr 7:21	1121
wife, she conceived, and bare a s	1Chr 7:23	1121
And Rephah was his s, also Resheph	1Chr 7:25	1121
and Telah his s, and Tahan his s	1Chr 7:25	1121
Laadan his s, Ammihud his s,	1Chr 7:26	1121
Laadan his s, Ammihud his s	1Chr 7:26	1121
Elishama his s	1Chr 7:26	1121
Non his s, Jehoshuah his s	1Chr 7:27	1121
of Joseph the s of Israel	1Chr 7:29	1121
And his firstborn s Abdon, and Zur,	1Chr 8:30	1121
the s of Jonathan was Merib-baal	1Chr 8:34	1121
Rapha was his s, Eleasah his s,	1Chr 8:37	1121
Azel his s	1Chr 8:37	1121
Uthai the s of Ammihud	1Chr 9:4	1121
the s of Omri, the s of Imri,	1Chr 9:4	1121
the s of Bani, the children of	1Chr 9:4	1121
children of Pharez the s of Judah	1Chr 9:4	1121
Sallu the s of Meshullam	1Chr 9:7	1121
the s of Hodaviah	1Chr 9:7	1121
of Hodaviah, the s of Hasenuah,	1Chr 9:7	1121
And Ibneiah the s of Jeroham	1Chr 9:8	1121
of Jeroham, and Elah the s of Uzzi	1Chr 9:8	1121
the s of Michri, and Meshullam the	1Chr 9:8	1121
and Meshullam the s of Shephatiah	1Chr 9:8	1121
s of Reuel, the s of Ibnijah	1Chr 9:8	1121
And Azariah the s of Hilkiah	1Chr 9:11	1121
the s of Meshullam	1Chr 9:11	1121
the s of Zadok	1Chr 9:11	1121
the s of Meraioth	1Chr 9:11	1121
the s of Ahitub, the ruler of the	1Chr 9:11	1121
And Adaiah the s of Jeroham	1Chr 9:12	1121
the s of Pashur	1Chr 9:12	1121
the s of Malchijah	1Chr 9:12	1121
and Maasiai the s of Adiel	1Chr 9:12	1121
the s of Jahzerah	1Chr 9:12	1121
the s of Meshullam	1Chr 9:12	1121
the s of Meshillemith	1Chr 9:12	1121
of Meshillemith, the s of Immer	1Chr 9:12	1121
Shemaiah the s of Hasshub	1Chr 9:14	1121
the s of Azrikam	1Chr 9:14	1121
the s of Hashabiah, of the sons	1Chr 9:14	1121
and Mattaniah the s of Micah	1Chr 9:15	1121
the s of Zichri, the s of Asaph	1Chr 9:15	1121
And Obadiah the s of Shemaiah	1Chr 9:16	1121
the s of Galal	1Chr 9:16	1121
the s of Jeduthun, and Berechiah	1Chr 9:16	1121
and Berechiah the s of Asa	1Chr 9:16	1121
the s of Elkanah, that dwelt in	1Chr 9:16	1121
And Shallum the s of Kore	1Chr 9:19	1121
the s of Ebiasaph	1Chr 9:19	1121
the s of Korah, and his brethren,	1Chr 9:19	1121
Phinehas the s of Eleazar was the	1Chr 9:20	1121
Zechariah the s of Meshelemiah	1Chr 9:21	1121
And his firstborn s Abdon, then	1Chr 9:36	1121
the s of Jonathan was Merib-baal	1Chr 9:40	1121
Rephaiah his s, Eleasah his s	1Chr 9:43	1121
Azel his s	1Chr 9:43	1121
kingdom unto David the s of Jesse	1Chr 10:14	1121
So Joab the s of Zeruiah went	1Chr 11:6	1121
him was Eleazar the s of Dodo	1Chr 11:12	1121
Benaiah the s of Jehoiada	1Chr 11:22	1121
the s of a valiant man of Kabzeel	1Chr 11:22	1121
did Benaiah the s of Jehoiada	1Chr 11:24	1121
of Joab, Elhanan the s of Dodo of	1Chr 11:26	1121
Ira the s of Ikkesh the Tekoite,	1Chr 11:28	1121
Heled the s of Baanah the	1Chr 11:30	1121
Ithai the s of Ribai of Gibeah,	1Chr 11:31	1121
Jonathan the s of Shage the	1Chr 11:34	1121
Ahiam the s of Sacar the Hararite	1Chr 11:35	1121
the Hararite, Eliphal the s of Ur	1Chr 11:35	1121
Carmelite, Naarai the s of Ezbai	1Chr 11:37	1121
Nathan, Mibhar the s of Haggeri	1Chr 11:38	1121
of Joab the s of Zeruiah,	1Chr 11:39	1121
the Hittite, Zabad the s of Ahlai	1Chr 11:41	1121
Adina the s of Shiza the	1Chr 11:42	1121
Hanan the s of Maachah, and	1Chr 11:43	1121
Jediael the s of Shimri, and Joha	1Chr 11:45	1121
because of Saul the s of Kish	1Chr 12:1	1121
and on thy side, thou s of Jesse	1Chr 12:18	1121
appointed Heman the s of Joel	1Chr 15:17	1121
Asaph the s of Berechiah	1Chr 15:17	1121
brethren, Ethan the s of Kushaiah	1Chr 15:17	1121
Obed-edom also the s of Jeduthun	1Chr 16:38	1121
his father, and he shall be my s	1Chr 17:13	1121
sent Hadoram his s to king David	1Chr 18:10	1121
Abishai the s Zeruiah slew of the	1Chr 18:12	1121
Joab the s of Zeruiah was over	1Chr 18:15	1121
and Jehoshaphat the s of Ahilud,	1Chr 18:15	1121
And Zadok the s of Ahitub, and	1Chr 18:16	1121
and Abimelech the s of Abiathar,	1Chr 18:16	1121
Benaiah the s of Jehoiada was	1Chr 18:17	1121
his s reigned in his stead	1Chr 19:1	1121
unto Hanun the s of Nahash	1Chr 19:2	1121
Elhanan the s of Jair slew Lahmi	1Chr 20:5	1121
and he also was the s of the giant	1Chr 20:6	3025
Jonathan the s of Shimea David's	1Chr 20:7	1121
David said, Solomon my s is young	1Chr 22:5	1121
Then he called for Solomon his s	1Chr 22:6	1121
And David said to Solomon, My s	1Chr 22:7	1121
a s shall be born to thee, who	1Chr 22:9	1121
and he shall be my s, and I will be	1Chr 22:10	1121
Now, my s, the LORD be with thee	1Chr 22:11	1121
of Israel to help Solomon his s	1Chr 22:17	1121
Solomon his s king over Israel	1Chr 23:1	1121
Shemaiah the s of Nethaneel the	1Chr 24:6	1121
and Ahimelech the s of Abiathar	1Chr 24:6	1121
the s of Kish was Jerahmeel	1Chr 24:29	1121
was Meshelemiah the s of Kore	1Chr 26:1	1121
Shemaiah his s were sons born	1Chr 26:6	1121
Then for Zechariah his s, a wise	1Chr 26:14	1121
And Shebuel the s of Gershom	1Chr 26:24	1121
the s of Moses, was ruler of the	1Chr 26:24	1121
Rehabiah his s	1Chr 26:25	1121
and Jeshaiah his s	1Chr 26:25	1121
and Joram his s, and Zichri his s	1Chr 26:25	1121
and Shelomith his s	1Chr 26:25	1121
the seer, and Saul the s of Kish	1Chr 26:28	1121
of Kish, and Abner the s of Ner	1Chr 26:28	1121
Joab the s of Zeruiah, had	1Chr 26:28	1121
was Jashobeam the s of Zabdiel	1Chr 27:2	1121
was Benaiah the s of Jehoiada	1Chr 27:5	1121
in his course was Ammizabad his s	1Chr 27:6	1121
Joab, and Zebadiah his s after him	1Chr 27:7	1121
Ira the s of Ikkesh the Tekoite	1Chr 27:9	1121
was Eliezer the s of Zichri	1Chr 27:16	1121
Shephatiah the s of Maachah	1Chr 27:16	1121
Hashabiah the s of Kemuel	1Chr 27:17	1121
Issachar, Omri the s of Michael	1Chr 27:18	1121
Ishmaiah the s of Obadiah	1Chr 27:19	1121
Jerimoth the s of Azriel	1Chr 27:19	1121
Ephraim, Hoshea the s of Azaziah	1Chr 27:20	1121
Manasseh, Joel the s of Pedaiah	1Chr 27:20	1121
Gilead, Iddo the s of Zechariah	1Chr 27:21	1121

S

Benjamin, Jaasiel the *s* of Abner	1Chr 27:21	1121
Of Dan, Azareel the *s* of Jeroham	1Chr 27:22	1121
Joab the *s* of Zeruiah began to	1Chr 27:24	1121
was Azmaveth the *s* of Adiel	1Chr 27:25	1121
was Jehonathan the *s* of Uzziah	1Chr 27:25	1121
ground was Ezri the *s* of Chelub	1Chr 27:26	1121
was Shaphat the *s* of Adlai	1Chr 27:29	1121
Jehiel the *s* of Hachmoni was with	1Chr 27:32	1121
was Jehoiada the *s* of Benaiah	1Chr 27:34	1121
he hath chosen Solomon my *s* to	1Chr 28:5	1121
And he said unto me, Solomon thy *s*	1Chr 28:6	1121
for I have chosen him to be my *s*	1Chr 28:6	1121
And thou, Solomon my *s*, know thou	1Chr 28:9	1121
his *s* the pattern of the porch	1Chr 28:11	1121
And David said to Solomon his *s*	1Chr 28:20	1121
the congregation, Solomon my *s*	1Chr 29:1	1121
unto Solomon my *s* a perfect heart	1Chr 29:19	1121
they made Solomon the *s* of David	1Chr 29:22	1121
Thus David the *s* of Jesse reigned	1Chr 29:26	1121
Solomon his *s* reigned in his	1Chr 29:28	1121
Solomon the *s* of David was	2Chr 1:1	1121
altar, that Bezaleel the *s* of Uri	2Chr 1:5	1121
the *s* of Hur, had made, he put	2Chr 1:5	1121
given to Solomon the king a wise *s*	2Chr 2:12	1121
The *s* of a woman of the daughters	2Chr 2:14	1121
but thy *s* which shall come forth	2Chr 6:9	1121
against Jeroboam *s* of Nebat	2Chr 9:29	1121
Rehoboam his *s* reigned in his	2Chr 9:31	1121
when Jeroboam the *s* of Nebat	2Chr 10:2	1121
to Jeroboam the *s* of Nebat	2Chr 10:15	1121
inheritance in the *s* of Jesse	2Chr 10:16	1121
unto Rehoboam the *s* of Solomon	2Chr 11:3	1121
Rehoboam the *s* of Solomon strong	2Chr 11:17	1121
Jerimoth the *s* of David to wife	2Chr 11:18	1121
daughter of Eliab the *s* of Jesse	2Chr 11:18	1121
Abijah the *s* of Maachah the chief	2Chr 11:22	1121
Abijah his *s* reigned in his stead	2Chr 12:16	1121
Yet Jeroboam the *s* of Nebat	2Chr 13:6	1121
servant of Solomon the *s* of David	2Chr 13:6	1121
against Rehoboam the *s* of Solomon	2Chr 13:7	1121
Asa his *s* reigned in his stead	2Chr 14:1	1121
came upon Azariah the *s* of Oded	2Chr 15:1	1121
Jehoshaphat his *s* reigned in his	2Chr 17:1	1121
him was Amasiah the *s* of Zichri	2Chr 17:16	1121
the same is Micaiah the *s* of Imla	2Chr 18:7	1121
quickly Micaiah the *s* of Imla	2Chr 18:8	1121
Zedekiah the *s* of Chenaanah had	2Chr 18:10	1121
Then Zedekiah the *s* of Chenaanah	2Chr 18:23	1121
city, and to Joash the king's *s*	2Chr 18:25	1121
Jehu the *s* of Hanani the seer	2Chr 19:2	1121
and Zebadiah the *s* of Ishmael	2Chr 19:11	1121
upon Jahaziel the *s* of Zechariah	2Chr 20:14	1121
the *s* of Benaiah	2Chr 20:14	1121
the *s* of Jeiel	2Chr 20:14	1121
the *s* of Mattaniah	2Chr 20:14	1121
the book of Jehu the *s* of Hanani	2Chr 20:34	1121
Then Eliezer the *s* of Dodavah of	2Chr 20:37	1121
Jehoram his *s* reigned in his	2Chr 21:1	1121
that there was never a *s* left him	2Chr 21:17	1121
his youngest *s* king in his stead	2Chr 22:1	1121
So Ahaziah the *s* of Jehoram king	2Chr 22:1	1121
went with Jehoram the *s* of Ahab	2Chr 22:5	1121
Azariah the *s* of Jehoram king of	2Chr 22:6	1121
Jehoram the *s* of Ahab at Jezreel	2Chr 22:6	1121
against Jehu the *s* of Nimshi	2Chr 22:7	1121
he is the *s* of Jehoshaphat, who	2Chr 22:9	1121
Ahaziah saw that her *s* was dead	2Chr 22:10	1121
king, took Joash the *s* of Ahaziah	2Chr 22:11	1121
Azariah the *s* of Jeroham	2Chr 23:1	1121
Ishmael the *s* of Jehohanan	2Chr 23:1	1121
and Azariah the *s* of Obed	2Chr 23:1	1121
Obed, and Maaseiah the *s* of Adaiah	2Chr 23:1	1121
and Elishaphat the *s* of Zichri	2Chr 23:1	1121
the king's *s* shall reign, as the	2Chr 23:3	1121
they brought out the king's *s*	2Chr 23:11	1121
the *s* of Jehoiada the priest	2Chr 24:20	1121
had done to him, but slew his *s*	2Chr 24:22	1121
Zabad the *s* of Shimeath an	2Chr 24:26	1121
Jehozabad the *s* of Shimrith a	2Chr 24:26	1121
Amaziah his *s* reigned in his	2Chr 24:27	1121
the *s* of Jehoahaz	2Chr 25:17	1121
the *s* of Jehu, king of Israel	2Chr 25:17	1121
Give thy daughter to my *s* to wife	2Chr 25:18	1121
the *s* of Joash	2Chr 25:23	1121
the *s* of Jehoahaz	2Chr 25:23	1121
Amaziah the *s* of Joash king of	2Chr 25:25	1121
s of Jehoahaz king of Israel	2Chr 25:25	1121
Jotham his *s* was over the king's	2Chr 26:21	1121
the prophet, the *s* of Amoz, write	2Chr 26:22	1121
Jotham his *s* reigned in his stead	2Chr 26:23	1121
Ahaz his *s* reigned in his stead	2Chr 27:9	1121

in the valley of the *s* of Hinnom	2Chr 28:3	1121
For Pekah the *s* of Remaliah slew	2Chr 28:6	1121
slew Maaseiah the king's *s*	2Chr 28:7	1121
Ephraim, Azariah the *s* of Johanan	2Chr 28:12	1121
Berechiah the *s* of Meshillemoth	2Chr 28:12	1121
and Jehizkiah the *s* of Shallum	2Chr 28:12	1121
Shallum, and Amasa the *s* of Hadlai	2Chr 28:12	1121
Hezekiah his *s* reigned in his	2Chr 28:27	1121
arose, Mahath the *s* of Amasai	2Chr 29:12	1121
Joel the *s* of Azariah, of the	2Chr 29:12	1121
of Merari, Kish the *s* of Abdi	2Chr 29:12	1121
Azariah the *s* of Jehalelel	2Chr 29:12	1121
Joah the *s* of Zimmah, and Eden the	2Chr 29:12	1121
of Zimmah, and Eden the *s* of Joah	2Chr 29:12	1121
s of David king of Israel there	2Chr 30:26	1121
Kore the *s* of Imnah the Levite,	2Chr 31:14	1121
the prophet Isaiah the *s* of Amoz	2Chr 32:20	1121
the *s* of Amoz, and in the book of	2Chr 32:32	1121
Manasseh his *s* reigned in his	2Chr 32:33	1121
in the valley of the *s* of Hinnom	2Chr 33:6	1121
said to David and to Solomon his *s*	2Chr 33:7	1121
Amon his *s* reigned in his stead	2Chr 33:20	1121
Josiah his *s* king in his stead	2Chr 33:25	1121
he sent Shaphan the *s* of Azaliah	2Chr 34:8	1121
Joah the *s* of Joahaz the recorder	2Chr 34:8	1121
and Ahikam the *s* of Shaphan	2Chr 34:20	1121
Shaphan, and Abdon the *s* of Micah	2Chr 34:20	1121
wife of Shallum the *s* of Tikvath	2Chr 34:22	1121
the *s* of Hasrah, keeper of the	2Chr 34:22	1121
the *s* of David king of Israel did	2Chr 35:3	1121
to the writing of Solomon his *s*	2Chr 35:4	1121
took Jehoahaz the *s* of Josiah	2Chr 36:1	1121
Jehoiachin his *s* reigned in his	2Chr 36:8	1121
stood up Jeshua the *s* of Jozadak	Ezr 3:2	1121
and Zerubbabel the *s* of Shealtiel	Ezr 3:2	1121
Zerubbabel the *s* of Shealtiel	Ezr 3:8	1121
and Jeshua the *s* of Jozadak	Ezr 3:8	1121
and Zechariah the *s* of Iddo	Ezr 5:1	1247
up Zerubbabel the *s* of Shealtiel	Ezr 5:2	1247
and Jeshua the *s* of Jozadak	Ezr 5:2	1247
and Zechariah the *s* of Iddo	Ezr 6:14	1247
Ezra the *s* of Seraiah	Ezr 7:1	1121
s of Azariah, the *s* of Hilkiah,	Ezr 7:1	1121
The *s* of Shallum	Ezr 7:2	1121
the *s* of Zadok, the *s* of Ahitub	Ezr 7:2	1121
The *s* of Amariah	Ezr 7:3	1121
the *s* of Azariah	Ezr 7:3	1121
the *s* of Meraioth	Ezr 7:3	1121
The *s* of Zerahiah	Ezr 7:4	1121
the *s* of Uzzi, the *s* of Bukki,	Ezr 7:4	1121
The *s* of Abishua	Ezr 7:5	1121
the *s* of Phinehas	Ezr 7:5	1121
the *s* of Eleazar	Ezr 7:5	1121
the *s* of Aaron the chief priest	Ezr 7:5	1121
Elihoenai the *s* of Zerahiah	Ezr 8:4	1121
the *s* of Jahaziel, and with him	Ezr 8:5	1121
Ebed the *s* of Jonathan, and with	Ezr 8:6	1121
Jeshaiah the *s* of Athaliah	Ezr 8:7	1121
Zebadiah the *s* of Michael	Ezr 8:8	1121
Obadiah the *s* of Jehiel, and with	Ezr 8:9	1121
the *s* of Josiphiah, and with him	Ezr 8:10	1121
Zechariah the *s* of Bebai, and with	Ezr 8:11	1121
Johanan the *s* of Hakkatan	Ezr 8:12	1121
the *s* of Levi, the *s* of Israel	Ezr 8:18	1121
the *s* of Uriah the priest	Ezr 8:33	1121
him was Eleazar the *s* of Phinehas	Ezr 8:33	1121
them was Jozabad the *s* of Jeshua	Ezr 8:33	1121
and Noadiah the *s* of Binnui	Ezr 8:33	1121
And Shechaniah the *s* of Jehiel	Ezr 10:2	1121
of Johanan the *s* of Eliashib	Ezr 10:6	1121
Only Jonathan the *s* of Asahel	Ezr 10:15	1121
Jahaziah the *s* of Tikvah were	Ezr 10:15	1121
sons of Jeshua the *s* of Jozadak	Ezr 10:18	1121
of Nehemiah the *s* of Hachaliah	Neh 1:1	1121
them builded Zaccur the *s* of Imri	Neh 3:2	1121
the *s* of Urijah, the *s* of Koz	Neh 3:4	1121
Meshullam the *s* of Berechiah	Neh 3:4	1121
Berechiah, the *s* of Meshezabeel	Neh 3:4	1121
repaired Zadok the *s* of Baana	Neh 3:4	1121
repaired Jehoiada the *s* of Paseah	Neh 3:6	1121
and Meshullam the *s* of Besodeiah	Neh 3:6	1121
repaired Uzziel the *s* of Harhaiah	Neh 3:8	1121
the *s* of one of the apothecaries	Neh 3:8	1121
repaired Rephaiah the *s* of Hur	Neh 3:9	1121
Jedaiah the *s* of Harumaph	Neh 3:10	1121
Hattush the *s* of Hashabniah	Neh 3:10	1121
Malchijah the *s* of Harim, and	Neh 3:11	1121
Hashub the *s* of Pahath-moab,	Neh 3:11	1121
Shallum the *s* of Halohesh	Neh 3:12	1121
repaired Malchiah the *s* of Rechab	Neh 3:14	1121
Shallun the *s* of Colhozeh	Neh 3:15	1121

repaired Nehemiah the s of Azbuk	Neh 3:16	1121
the Levites, Rehum the s of Bani	Neh 3:17	1121
Bavai the s of Henadad, the ruler	Neh 3:18	1121
him repaired Ezer the s of Jeshua	Neh 3:19	1121
After him Baruch the s of Zabbai	Neh 3:20	1121
the s of Urijah the s of Koz	Neh 3:21	1121
s of Maaseiah the s of Ananiah	Neh 3:23	1121
the s of Henadad another piece	Neh 3:24	1121
Palal the s of Uzai, over against	Neh 3:25	1121
After him Pedaiah the s of Parosh	Neh 3:25	1121
After them repaired Zadok the s	Neh 3:29	1121
also Shemaiah the s of Shechaniah	Neh 3:29	1121
Hananiah the s of Shelemiah	Neh 3:30	1121
and Hanun the sixth s of Zalaph	Neh 3:30	1121
him repaired Meshullam the s of	Neh 3:30	1121
Malchiah the goldsmith's s unto	Neh 3:31	1121
the s of Delaiah	Neh 6:10	1121
of Delaiah the s of Mehetabeel	Neh 6:10	1121
because he was the s in law of	Neh 6:18	2860
law of Shechaniah the s of Arah	Neh 6:18	1121
his s Johanan had taken the	Neh 6:18	1121
of Meshullam the s of Berechiah	Neh 6:18	1121
s of Nun unto that day had not	Neh 8:17	1121
the s of Hachaliah, and Zidkijah	Neh 10:1	1121
both Jeshua the s of Azaniah	Neh 10:9	1121
the priest the s of Aaron shall	Neh 10:38	1121
Athaiah the s of Uzziah	Neh 11:4	1121
the s of Zechariah	Neh 11:4	1121
the s of Amariah	Neh 11:4	1121
the s of Shephatiah	Neh 11:4	1121
the s of Mahalaleel, of the	Neh 11:4	1121
And Maaseiah the s of Baruch	Neh 11:5	1121
the s of Colhozeh	Neh 11:5	1121
the s of Hazaiah	Neh 11:5	1121
the s of Adaiah	Neh 11:5	1121
the s of Joiarib	Neh 11:5	1121
the s of Zechariah	Neh 11:5	1121
of Zechariah, the s of Shiloni	Neh 11:5	1121
Sallu the s of Meshullam	Neh 11:7	1121
the s of Joed, the s of Pedaiah	Neh 11:7	1121
the s of Pedaiah, the s of	Neh 11:7	1121
the s of Kolaiah	Neh 11:7	1121
the s of Maaseiah	Neh 11:7	1121
the s of Ithiel, the s of	Neh 11:7	1121
s of Ithiel, the s of Jesaiah	Neh 11:7	1121
Joel the s of Zichri was their	Neh 11:9	1121
Judah the s of Senuah was second	Neh 11:9	1121
Jedaiah the s of Joiarib, Jachin	Neh 11:10	1121
Seraiah the s of Hilkiah	Neh 11:11	1121
the s of Meshullam	Neh 11:11	1121
the s of Zadok	Neh 11:11	1121
the s of Meraioth	Neh 11:11	1121
the s of Ahitub, was the ruler of	Neh 11:11	1121
and Adaiah the s of Jeroham	Neh 11:12	1121
the s of Pelaliah	Neh 11:12	1121
the s of Amzi	Neh 11:12	1121
the s of Zechariah	Neh 11:12	1121
s of Pashur, the s of Malchiah,	Neh 11:12	1121
and Amashai the s of Azareel	Neh 11:13	1121
the s of Ahasai	Neh 11:13	1121
the s of Meshillemoth	Neh 11:13	1121
the s of Immer	Neh 11:13	1121
the s of one of the great men	Neh 11:14	1121
Shemaiah the s of Hashub	Neh 11:15	1121
the s of Azrikam	Neh 11:15	1121
the s of Hashabiah	Neh 11:15	1121
the s of Bunni	Neh 11:15	1121
And Mattaniah the s of Micha	Neh 11:17	1121
the s of Zabdi, the s of Asaph,	Neh 11:17	1121
Abda the s of Shammua	Neh 11:17	1121
the s of Galal, the s of	Neh 11:17	1121
s of Galal, the s of Jeduthun	Neh 11:17	1121
Jerusalem was Uzzi the s of Bani	Neh 11:22	1121
the s of Hashabiah	Neh 11:22	1121
s of Mattaniah, the s of Micha	Neh 11:22	1121
Pethahiah the s of Meshezabeel,	Neh 11:24	1121
children of Zerah the s of Judah	Neh 11:24	1121
Zerubbabel the s of Shealtiel	Neh 12:1	1121
days of Johanan the s of Eliashib	Neh 12:23	1121
and Jeshua the s of Kadmiel	Neh 12:24	1121
days of Joiakim the s of Jeshua	Neh 12:26	1121
the s of Jozadak, and in the days	Neh 12:26	1121
Zechariah the s of Jonathan	Neh 12:35	1121
the s of Shemaiah	Neh 12:35	1121
the s of Mattaniah	Neh 12:35	1121
the s of Michaiah	Neh 12:35	1121
the s of Zaccur, the s of Asaph	Neh 12:35	1121
of David, and of Solomon his s	Neh 12:45	1121
s of Zaccur, the s of Mattaniah	Neh 13:13	1121
the s of Eliashib the high priest	Neh 13:28	1121
was s in law to Sanballat the	Neh 13:28	2860

the s of Jair, the s of Shimei,	Est 2:5	1121
the s of Kish, a Benjamite	Est 2:5	1121
the s of Hammedatha the Agagite	Est 3:1	1121
gave it unto Haman the s of	Est 3:10	1121
the s of Hammedatha the Agagite	Est 8:5	1121
sons of Haman the s of Hammedatha	Est 9:10	1121
Because Haman the s of Hammedatha	Est 9:24	1121
He shall neither have s nor	Job 18:19	5209
the s of man, which is a worm	Job 25:6	1121
the s of Barachel the Buzite	Job 32:2	1121
Elihu the s of Barachel the	Job 32:6	1121
may profit the s of man	Job 35:8	1121
hath said unto me, Thou art my S	Ps 2:7	1121
Kiss the S, lest he be angry, and	Ps 2:12	1248
when he fled from Absalom his s	Ps 3:t	1121
the s of man, that thou visitest	Ps 8:4	1121
slanderest thine own mother's s	Ps 50:20	1121
righteousness unto the king's s	Ps 72:1	1121
of David the s of Jesse are ended	Ps 72:20	1121
upon the s of man whom thou	Ps 80:17	1121
save the s of thine handmaid	Ps 86:16	1121
nor the s of wickedness afflict	Ps 89:22	1121
and the s of thine handmaid	Ps 116:16	1121
or the s of man, that thou makest	Ps 144:3	1121
in princes, nor in the s of man	Ps 146:3	1121
of Solomon the s of David	Prov 1:1	1121
My s, hear the instruction of thy	Prov 1:8	1121
My s, if sinners entice thee,	Prov 1:10	1121
My s, walk not thou in the way	Prov 1:15	1121
My s, if thou wilt receive my	Prov 2:1	1121
My s, forget not my law	Prov 3:1	1121
My s, despise not the chastening	Prov 3:11	1121
even as a father the s in whom he	Prov 3:12	1121
My s, let not them depart from	Prov 3:21	1121
For I was my father's s, tender	Prov 4:3	1121
Hear, O my s, and receive my	Prov 4:10	1121
My s, attend to my words	Prov 4:20	1121
My s, attend unto my wisdom, and	Prov 5:1	1121
And why wilt thou, my s, be	Prov 5:20	1121
My s, if thou be surety for thy	Prov 6:1	1121
Do this now, my s, and deliver	Prov 6:3	1121
My s, keep thy father's	Prov 6:20	1121
My s, keep my words, and lay up my	Prov 7:1	1121
A wise s maketh a glad father	Prov 10:1	1121
but a foolish s is the heaviness	Prov 10:1	1121
gathereth in summer is a wise s	Prov 10:5	1121
harvest is a s that causeth shame	Prov 10:5	1121
A wise s heareth his father's	Prov 13:1	1121
that spareth his rod hateth his s	Prov 13:24	1121
A wise s maketh a glad father	Prov 15:20	1121
rule over a s that causeth shame	Prov 17:2	1121
A foolish s is a grief to his	Prov 17:25	1121
A foolish s is the calamity of	Prov 19:13	1121
Chasten thy s while there is hope	Prov 19:18	1121
is a s that causeth shame, and	Prov 19:26	1121
Cease, my s, to hear the	Prov 19:27	1121
My s, if thine heart be wise, my	Prov 23:15	1121
Hear thou, my s, and be wise, and	Prov 23:19	1121
My s, give me thine heart, and let	Prov 23:26	1121
My s, eat thou honey, because it	Prov 24:13	1121
My s, fear thou the LORD and the	Prov 24:21	1121
My s, be wise, and make my heart	Prov 27:11	1121
Whoso keepeth the law is a wise s	Prov 28:7	1121
Correct thy s, and he shall give	Prov 29:17	1121
him become his s at the length	Prov 29:21	4497
The words of Agur the s of Jakeh	Prov 30:1	1121
What, my s	Prov 31:2	1248
and what, the s of my womb	Prov 31:2	1248
and what, the s of my vows	Prov 31:2	1248
the s of David, king in Jerusalem	Eccl 1:1	1121
and he begetteth a s, and there is	Eccl 5:14	1121
when thy king is the s of nobles	Eccl 10:17	1121
And further, by these, my s	Eccl 12:12	1121
vision of Isaiah the s of Amoz	Is 1:1	1121
The word that Isaiah the s of	Is 2:1	1121
the days of Ahaz the s of Jotham	Is 7:1	1121
the s of Uzziah, king of Judah,	Is 7:1	1121
Pekah the s of Remaliah, king of	Is 7:1	1121
Ahaz, thou, and Shear-jashub thy s	Is 7:3	1121
Syria, and of the s of Remaliah	Is 7:4	1121
the s of Remaliah, have taken	Is 7:5	1121
midst of it, even the s of Tabeal	Is 7:6	1121
head of Samaria is Remaliah's s	Is 7:9	1121
shall conceive, and bear a s	Is 7:14	1121
Zechariah the s of Jeberechiah	Is 8:2	1121
and she conceived, and bare a s	Is 8:3	1121
rejoice in Rezin and Remaliah's s	Is 8:6	1121
is born, unto us a s is given	Is 9:6	1121
Isaiah the s of Amoz did see	Is 13:1	1121
O Lucifer, s of the morning	Is 14:12	1121
the name, and remnant, and s	Is 14:22	5209

I am the *s* of the wise	Is 19:11	1121	
the wise, the *s* of ancient kings	Is 19:11	1121	
the LORD by Isaiah the *s* of Amoz	Is 20:2	1121	
servant Eliakim the *s* of Hilkiah	Is 22:20	1121	
unto him Eliakim, Hilkiah's *s*	Is 36:3	1121	
the scribe, and Joah, Asaph's *s*	Is 36:3	1121	
the *s* of Hilkiah, that was over	Is 36:22	1121	
the *s* of Asaph, the recorder, to	Is 36:22	1121	
Isaiah the prophet the *s* of Amoz	Is 37:2	1121	
Then Isaiah the *s* of Amoz sent	Is 37:21	1121	
Esar-haddon his *s* reigned in his	Is 37:38	1121	
the *s* of Amoz came unto him	Is 38:1	1121	
the *s* of Baladan, king of Babylon	Is 39:1	1121	
compassion on the *s* of her womb	Is 49:15	1121	
of the *s* of man which shall be	Is 51:12	1121	
the *s* of man that layeth hold on	Is 56:2	1121	
Neither let the *s* of the stranger	Is 56:3	1121	
of Jeremiah the *s* of Hilkiah	Jer 1:1	1121	
the *s* of Amon king of Judah	Jer 1:2	1121	
the *s* of Josiah king of Judah	Jer 1:3	1121	
the *s* of Josiah king of Judah	Jer 1:3	1121	
thee mourning, as for an only *s*	Jer 6:26	3173	
in the valley of the *s* of Hinnom	Jer 7:31	1121	
nor the valley of the *s* of Hinnom	Jer 7:32	1121	
because of Manasseh the *s* of	Jer 15:4	1121	
the valley of the *s* of Hinnom	Jer 19:2	1121	
nor The valley of the *s* of Hinnom	Jer 19:6	1121	
Now Pashur the *s* of Immer the	Jer 20:1	1121	
unto him Pashur the *s* of Melchiah	Jer 21:1	1121	
Zephaniah the *s* of Maaseiah the	Jer 21:1	1121	
the *s* of Josiah king of Judah	Jer 22:11	1121	
the *s* of Josiah king of Judah	Jer 22:18	1121	
though Coniah the *s* of Jehoiakim	Jer 22:24	1121	
away captive Jeconiah the *s* of	Jer 24:1	1121	
the *s* of Josiah king of Judah	Jer 25:1	1121	
the *s* of Amon king of Judah	Jer 25:3	1121	
s of Josiah king of Judah came	Jer 26:1	1121	
Urijah the *s* of Shemaiah of	Jer 26:20	1121	
namely, Elnathan the *s* of Achbor	Jer 26:22	1121	
the hand of Ahikam the *s* of	Jer 26:24	1121	
s of Josiah king of Judah came	Jer 27:1	1121	
him, and his *s*, and his son's *s*	Jer 27:7	1121	
away captive Jeconiah the *s* of	Jer 27:20	1121	
that Hananiah the *s* of Azur the	Jer 28:1	1121	
the *s* of Jehoiakim king of Judah	Jer 28:4	1121	
hand of Elasah the *s* of Shaphan	Jer 29:3	1121	
and Gemariah the *s* of Hilkiah	Jer 29:3	1121	
Israel, of Ahab the *s* of Kolaiah	Jer 29:21	1121	
and of Zedekiah the *s* of Maaseiah	Jer 29:21	1121	
to Zephaniah the *s* of Maaseiah	Jer 29:25	1121	
Is Ephraim my dear *s*	Jer 31:20	1121	
Hanameel the *s* of Shallum thine	Jer 32:7	1121	
So Hanameel mine uncle's *s* came	Jer 32:8	1121	
field of Hanameel my uncle's *s*	Jer 32:9	1121	
unto Baruch the *s* of Neriah	Jer 32:12	1121	
the *s* of Maaseiah, in the sight	Jer 32:12	1121	
sight of Hanameel mine uncle's *s*	Jer 32:12		
unto Baruch the *s* of Neriah	Jer 32:16	1121	
in the valley of the *s* of Hinnom	Jer 32:35	1121	
have a *s* to reign upon his throne	Jer 33:21	1121	
the *s* of Josiah king of Judah	Jer 35:1	1121	
took Jaazaniah the *s* of Jeremiah	Jer 35:3	1121	
the *s* of Habaziniah, and his	Jer 35:3	1121	
the *s* of Igdaliah, a man of God,	Jer 35:4	1121	
of Maaseiah the *s* of Shallum	Jer 35:4	1121	
for Jonadab the *s* of Rechab our	Jer 35:6	1121	
the *s* of Rechab our father in all	Jer 35:8	1121	
words of Jonadab the *s* of Rechab	Jer 35:14	1121	
s of Rechab have performed the	Jer 35:16	1121	
Jonadab the *s* of Rechab shall not	Jer 35:19	1121	
the *s* of Josiah king of Judah	Jer 36:1	1121	
called Baruch the *s* of Neriah	Jer 36:4	1121	
Baruch the *s* of Neriah did	Jer 36:8	1121	
the *s* of Josiah king of Judah	Jer 36:9	1121	
the *s* of Shaphan the scribe	Jer 36:10	1121	
When Michaiah the *s* of Gemariah	Jer 36:11	1121	
the *s* of Shaphan, had heard out	Jer 36:11	1121	
and Delaiah the *s* of Shemaiah	Jer 36:12	1121	
and Elnathan the *s* of Achbor	Jer 36:12	1121	
and Gemariah the *s* of Shaphan	Jer 36:12	1121	
and Zedekiah the *s* of Hananiah	Jer 36:12	1121	
sent Jehudi the *s* of Nethaniah	Jer 36:14	1121	
the *s* of Shelemiah	Jer 36:14	1121	
the *s* of Cushi, unto Baruch	Jer 36:14	1121	
So Baruch the *s* of Neriah took	Jer 36:14	1121	
Jerahmeel the *s* of Hammelech	Jer 36:26	1121	
and Seraiah the *s* of Azriel	Jer 36:26	1121	
and Shelemiah the *s* of Abdeel	Jer 36:26	1121	
the scribe, the *s* of Neriah	Jer 36:32	1121	
king Zedekiah the *s* of Josiah	Jer 37:1	1121	
of Coniah the *s* of Jehoiakim	Jer 37:1	1121	
sent Jehucal the *s* of Shelemiah	Jer 37:3	1121	
Zephaniah the *s* of Maaseiah the	Jer 37:3	1121	
the *s* of Shelemiah	Jer 37:13	1121	
the *s* of Hananiah	Jer 37:13	1121	
Then Shephatiah the *s* of Mattan	Jer 38:1	1121	
and Gedaliah the *s* of Pashur	Jer 38:1	1121	
Jucal the *s* of Shelemiah, and	Jer 38:1	1121	
Pashur the *s* of Malchiah, heard	Jer 38:1	1121	
of Malchiah the *s* of Hammelech	Jer 38:6	1121	
s of Ahikam the *s* of Shaphan	Jer 39:14	1121	
s of Ahikam the *s* of Shaphan	Jer 40:5	1121	
the *s* of Ahikam to Mizpah	Jer 40:6	1121	
Babylon had made Gedaliah the *s*	Jer 40:7	1121	
even Ishmael the *s* of Nethaniah	Jer 40:8	1121	
Seraiah the *s* of Tanhumeth, and	Jer 40:8	1121	
Jezaniah the *s* of a Maachathite,	Jer 40:8	1121	
Gedaliah the *s* of Ahikam	Jer 40:9	1121	
the *s* of Shaphan sware unto them	Jer 40:9	1121	
s of Ahikam the *s* of Shaphan	Jer 40:11	1121	
Moreover Johanan the *s* of Kareah	Jer 40:13	1121	
the *s* of Nethaniah to slay thee	Jer 40:14	1121	
But Gedaliah the *s* of Ahikam	Jer 40:14	1121	
Then Johanan the *s* of Kareah	Jer 40:15	1121	
slay Ishmael the *s* of Nethaniah	Jer 40:15	1121	
But Gedaliah the *s* of Ahikam said	Jer 40:16	1121	
said unto Johanan the *s* of Kareah	Jer 40:16	1121	
that Ishmael the *s* of Nethaniah	Jer 41:1	1121	
of Nethaniah the *s* of Elishama	Jer 41:1	1121	
the *s* of Ahikam to Mizpah	Jer 41:1	1121	
arose Ishmael the *s* of Nethaniah	Jer 41:2	1121	
smote Gedaliah the *s* of Ahikam	Jer 41:2	1121	
the *s* of Shaphan with the sword	Jer 41:2	1121	
Ishmael the *s* of Nethaniah went	Jer 41:6	1121	
Come to Gedaliah the *s* of Ahikam	Jer 41:6	1121	
that Ishmael the *s* of Nethaniah	Jer 41:7	1121	
Ishmael the *s* of Nethaniah filled	Jer 41:9	1121	
to Gedaliah the *s* of Ahikam	Jer 41:10	1121	
Ishmael the *s* of Nethaniah	Jer 41:10	1121	
But when Johanan the *s* of Kareah	Jer 41:11	1121	
the *s* of Nethaniah had done	Jer 41:11	1121	
with Ishmael the *s* of Nethaniah	Jer 41:12	1121	
saw Johanan the *s* of Kareah	Jer 41:13	1121	
went unto Johanan the *s* of Kareah	Jer 41:14	1121	
But Ishmael the *s* of Nethaniah	Jer 41:15	1121	
Then took Johanan the *s* of Kareah	Jer 41:16	1121	
from Ishmael the *s* of Nethaniah	Jer 41:16	1121	
slain Gedaliah the *s* of Ahikam	Jer 41:16	1121	
of them, because Ishmael the *s* of	Jer 41:18	1121	
slain Gedaliah the *s* of Ahikam	Jer 41:18	1121	
and Johanan the *s* of Kareah	Jer 42:1	1121	
and Jezaniah the *s* of Hoshaiah	Jer 42:1	1121	
called he Johanan the *s* of Kareah	Jer 42:8	1121	
spake Azariah the *s* of Hoshaiah	Jer 43:2	1121	
and Johanan the *s* of Kareah	Jer 43:2	1121	
But Baruch the *s* of Neriah	Jer 43:3	1121	
So Johanan the *s* of Kareah	Jer 43:4	1121	
But Johanan the *s* of Kareah	Jer 43:5	1121	
s of Ahikam the *s* of Shaphan	Jer 43:6	1121	
and Baruch the *s* of Neriah	Jer 43:6	1121	
spake unto Baruch the *s* of Neriah	Jer 45:1	1121	
the *s* of Josiah king of Judah	Jer 45:1	1121	
the *s* of Josiah king of Judah	Jer 46:2	1121	
neither shall a *s* of man dwell in	Jer 49:18	1121	
nor any *s* of man dwell in it	Jer 49:33	1121	
neither shall any *s* of man dwell	Jer 50:40	1121	
neither doth any *s* of man pass	Jer 51:43	1121	
commanded Seraiah the *s* of Neriah	Jer 51:59	1121	
the *s* of Maaseiah, when he went	Jer 51:59	1121	
the *s* of Buzi, in the land of the	Eze 1:3	1121	
S of man, stand upon thy feet, and	Eze 2:1	1121	
S of man, I send thee to the	Eze 2:3	1121	
s of man, be not afraid of them,	Eze 2:6	1121	
s of man, hear what I say unto	Eze 2:8	1121	
S of man, eat that thou findest	Eze 3:1	1121	
S of man, cause thy belly to eat,	Eze 3:3	1121	
S of man, go, get thee unto the	Eze 3:4	1121	
S of man, all my words that I	Eze 3:10	1121	
S of man, I have made thee a	Eze 3:17	1121	
O *s* of man, behold, they shall	Eze 3:25	1121	
s of man, take thee a tile, and	Eze 4:1	1121	
S of man, behold, I will break	Eze 4:16	1121	
s of man, take thee a sharp knife	Eze 5:1	1121	
S of man, set thy face toward the	Eze 6:2	1121	
thou *s* of man, thus saith the	Eze 7:2	1121	
S of man, lift up thine eyes now	Eze 8:5	1121	
S of man, seest thou what they do	Eze 8:6	1121	
S of man, dig now in the wall	Eze 8:8	1121	
stood Jaazaniah the *s* of Shaphan	Eze 8:11	1121	
S of man, hast thou seen what the	Eze 8:12	1121	
Hast thou seen this, *O* *s* of man	Eze 8:15	1121	
Hast thou seen this, *O* *s* of man	Eze 8:17	1121	

I saw Jaazaniah the *s* of Azur	Eze 11:1	1121
and Pelatiah the *s* of Benaiah	Eze 11:1	1121
S of man, these are the men that	Eze 11:2	1121
them, prophesy, O *s* of man	Eze 11:4	1121
Pelatiah the *s* of Benaiah died	Eze 11:13	1121
S of man, thy brethren, even thy	Eze 11:15	1121
S of man, thou dwellest in the	Eze 12:2	1121
thou *s* of man, prepare thee stuff	Eze 12:3	1121
S of man, hath not the house of	Eze 12:9	1121
S of man, eat thy bread with	Eze 12:18	1121
S of man, what is that proverb	Eze 12:22	1121
S of man, behold, they of the	Eze 12:27	1121
S of man, prophesy against the	Eze 13:2	1121
thou *s* of man, set thy face	Eze 13:17	1121
S of man, these men have set up	Eze 14:3	1121
S of man, when the land sinneth	Eze 14:13	1121
deliver neither *s* nor daughter	Eze 14:20	1121
S of man, What is the vine tree	Eze 15:2	1121
S of man, cause Jerusalem to know	Eze 16:2	1121
S of man, put forth a riddle, and	Eze 17:2	1121
so also the soul of the *s* is mine	Eze 18:4	1121
If he beget a *s* that is a robber,	Eze 18:10	1121
Now, lo, if he beget a *s*, that	Eze 18:14	1121
doth not the *s* bear the iniquity	Eze 18:19	1121
When the *s* hath done that which	Eze 18:19	1121
The *s* shall not bear the iniquity	Eze 18:20	1121
father bear the iniquity of the *s*	Eze 18:20	1121
S of man, speak unto the elders	Eze 20:3	1121
s of man, wilt thou judge them	Eze 20:4	1121
s of man, speak unto the house of	Eze 20:27	1121
S of man, set thy face toward the	Eze 20:46	1121
S of man, set thy face toward	Eze 21:2	1121
thou *s* of man, with the breaking	Eze 21:6	1121
S of man, prophesy, and say, Thus	Eze 21:9	1121
it contemneth the rod of my *s*	Eze 21:10	1121
Cry and howl, *s* of man	Eze 21:12	1121
s of man, prophesy, and smite	Eze 21:14	1121
thou *s* of man, appoint thee two	Eze 21:19	1121
s of man, prophesy and say, Thus	Eze 21:28	1121
thou *s* of man, wilt thou judge,	Eze 22:2	1121
S of man, the house of Israel is	Eze 22:18	1121
S of man, say unto her, Thou art	Eze 22:24	1121
S of man, there were two women,	Eze 23:2	1121
S of man, wilt thou judge Aholah	Eze 23:36	1121
S of man, write thee the name of	Eze 24:2	1121
S of man, behold, I take away	Eze 24:16	1121
thou *s* of man, shall it not be in	Eze 24:25	1121
S of man, set thy face against	Eze 25:2	1121
S of man, because that Tyrus hath	Eze 26:2	1121
Now, thou *s* of man, take up a	Eze 27:2	1121
S of man, say unto the prince of	Eze 28:2	1121
S of man, take up a lamentation	Eze 28:12	1121
S of man, set thy face against	Eze 28:21	1121
S of man, set thy face against	Eze 29:2	1121
S of man, Nebuchadrezzar king of	Eze 29:18	1121
S of man, prophesy and say, Thus	Eze 30:2	1121
S of man, I have broken the arm	Eze 30:21	1121
S of man, speak unto Pharaoh king	Eze 31:2	1121
S of man, take up a lamentation	Eze 32:2	1121
S of man, wail for the multitude	Eze 32:18	1121
S of man, speak to the children	Eze 33:2	1121
O *s* of man, I have set thee a	Eze 33:7	1121
Therefore, O thou *s* of man	Eze 33:10	1121
thou *s* of man, say unto the	Eze 33:12	1121
S of man, they that inhabit those	Eze 33:24	1121
thou *s* of man, the children of	Eze 33:30	1121
S of man, prophesy against the	Eze 34:2	1121
S of man, set thy face against	Eze 35:2	1121
thou *s* of man, prophesy unto the	Eze 36:1	1121
S of man, when the house of	Eze 36:17	1121
S of man, can these bones live	Eze 37:3	1121
s of man, and say to the wind,	Eze 37:9	1121
S of man, these bones are the	Eze 37:11	1121
thou *s* of man, take thee one	Eze 37:16	1121
S of man, set thy face against	Eze 38:2	1121
s of man, prophesy and say unto	Eze 38:14	1121
thou *s* of man, prophesy against	Eze 39:1	1121
thou *s* of man, thus saith the	Eze 39:17	1121
S of man, behold with thine eyes,	Eze 40:4	1121
S of man, the place of my throne,	Eze 43:7	1121
Thou *s* of man, shew the house to	Eze 43:10	1121
S of man, thus saith the Lord GOD	Eze 43:18	1121
S of man, mark well, and behold	Eze 44:5	1121
father, or for mother, or for *s*	Eze 44:25	1121
S of man, hast thou seen this	Eze 47:6	1121
the fourth is like the *S* of God	Dan 3:25	1247
And thou his *s*, O Belshazzar, hast	Dan 5:22	1247
one like the *s* of man came with	Dan 7:13	1247
unto me, Understand, O *s* of man	Dan 8:17	1121
year of Darius the *s* of Ahasuerus	Dan 9:1	1121
the *s* of Beeri, in the days of	Hos 1:1	1121

days of Jeroboam the *s* of Joash	Hos 1:1	1121
which conceived, and bare him a *s*	Hos 1:3	1121
she conceived, and bare a *s*	Hos 1:8	1121
him, and called my *s* out of Egypt	Hos 11:1	1121
he is an unwise *s*	Hos 13:13	1121
came to Joel the *s* of Pethuel	Joel 1:1	1121
the *s* of Joash king of Israel	Amos 1:1	1121
neither was I an prophet's *s*	Amos 7:14	1121
it as the mourning of an only *s*	Amos 8:10	
came unto Jonah the *s* of Amittai	Jonah 1:1	1121
what Balaam the *s* of Beor	Mic 6:5	1121
For the *s* dishonoureth the father	Mic 7:6	1121
unto Zephaniah the *s* of Cushi	Zeph 1:1	1121
the *s* of Gedaliah	Zeph 1:1	1121
the *s* of Amariah	Zeph 1:1	1121
the *s* of Hizkiah	Zeph 1:1	1121
the days of Josiah the *s* of Amon	Zeph 1:1	1121
Zerubbabel the *s* of Shealtiel	Hag 1:1	1121
and to Joshua the *s* of Josedech	Hag 1:1	1121
Zerubbabel the *s* of Shealtiel	Hag 1:12	1121
Joshua the *s* of Josedech, the	Hag 1:12	1121
of Zerubbabel the *s* of Shealtiel	Hag 1:14	1121
of Joshua the *s* of Josedech	Hag 1:14	1121
to Zerubbabel the *s* of Shealtiel	Hag 2:2	1121
and to Joshua the *s* of Josedech	Hag 2:2	1121
s of Josedech, the high priest	Hag 2:4	1121
the *s* of Shealtiel, saith the	Hag 2:23	1121
the *s* of Berechiah	Zec 1:1	1121
the *s* of Iddo the prophet, saying,	Zec 1:1	1121
the *s* of Berechiah	Zec 1:7	1121
the *s* of Iddo the prophet, saying,	Zec 1:7	1121
of Josiah the *s* of Zephaniah	Zec 6:10	1121
head of Joshua the *s* of Josedech	Zec 6:11	1121
to Hen the *s* of Zephaniah, for a	Zec 6:14	1121
as one mourneth for his only *s*	Zec 12:10	
A *s* honoureth his father, and a	Mal 1:6	1121
his own *s* that serveth him	Mal 3:17	1121
s of David, the *s* of Abraham	Mt 1:1	5207
thou *s* of David, fear not to take	Mt 1:20	5207
And she shall bring forth a *s*	Mt 1:21	5207
child, and shall bring forth a *s*	Mt 1:23	5207
had brought forth her firstborn *s*	Mt 1:25	5207
Out of Egypt have I called my *s*	Mt 2:15	5207
saying, This is my beloved *S*	Mt 3:17	5207
he said, If thou be the *S* of God	Mt 4:3	5207
unto him, If thou be the *S* of God	Mt 4:6	5207
James the *s* of Zebedee, and John	Mt 4:21	
of you, whom if his *s* ask bread	Mt 7:9	5207
but the *S* of man hath not where	Mt 8:20	5207
with thee, Jesus, thou *S* of God	Mt 8:29	5207
S, be of good cheer	Mt 9:2	5048
S of man hath power on earth to	Mt 9:6	5207
Thou *s* of David, have mercy on us	Mt 9:27	5207
James the *s* of Zebedee, and John	Mt 10:2	
James the *s* of Alphaeus, and	Mt 10:3	
till the S of man be come	Mt 10:23	5207
he that loveth *s* or daughter more	Mt 10:37	5207
The S of man came eating and	Mt 11:19	5207
and no man knoweth the S, but the	Mt 11:27	5207
any man the Father, save the S	Mt 11:27	5207
whomsoever the S will reveal him	Mt 11:27	5207
For the S of man is Lord even of	Mt 12:8	5207
said, Is not this the *s* of David?	Mt 12:23	5207
a word against the S of man	Mt 12:32	5207
so shall the S of man be three	Mt 12:40	5207
the good seed is the S of man	Mt 13:37	5207
The S of man shall send forth his	Mt 13:41	5207
Is not this the carpenter's *s*	Mt 13:55	5207
Of a truth thou art the *S* of God	Mt 14:33	5207
on me, O Lord, thou *s* of David	Mt 15:22	5207
do men say that I the S of man am	Mt 16:13	5207
Christ, the *S* of the living God	Mt 16:16	5207
For the S of man shall come in	Mt 16:27	5207
till they see the S of man coming	Mt 16:28	5207
which said, This is my beloved *S*	Mt 17:5	5207
until the S of man be risen again	Mt 17:9	5207
also the S of man suffer of them	Mt 17:12	5207
Lord, have mercy on my *s*	Mt 17:15	5207
The S of man shall be betrayed	Mt 17:22	5207
For the S of man is come to save	Mt 18:11	5207
in the regeneration when the S of	Mt 19:28	5207
the S of man shall be betrayed	Mt 20:18	5207
Even as the S of man came not to	Mt 20:28	5207
on us, O Lord, thou *s* of David	Mt 20:30	5207
on us, O Lord, thou *s* of David	Mt 20:31	5207
saying, Hosanna to the *s* of David	Mt 21:9	5207
saying, Hosanna to the *s* of David	Mt 21:15	5207
he came to the first, and said, *S*	Mt 21:28	5043
of all he sent unto them his *s*	Mt 21:37	5207
saying, They will reverence my s	Mt 21:37	5207
But when the husbandmen saw the s	Mt 21:38	5207

which made a marriage for his *s*	Mt 22:2	5207
whose *s* is he	Mt 22:42	5207
They say unto him, The *s* of David	Mt 22:42	
how is he his *s*	Mt 22:45	5207
blood of Zacharias *s* of Barachias	Mt 23:35	5207
the coming of the *S* of man be	Mt 24:27	5207
sign of the *S* of man in heaven	Mt 24:30	5207
they shall see the *S* of man	Mt 24:30	5207
the coming of the *S* of man be	Mt 24:37	5207
the coming of the *S* of man be	Mt 24:39	5207
ye think not the *S* of man cometh	Mt 24:44	5207
hour wherein the *S* of man cometh	Mt 25:13	5207
When the *S* of man shall come in	Mt 25:31	5207
the *S* of man is betrayed to be	Mt 26:2	5207
The *S* of man goeth as it is	Mt 26:24	5207
by whom the *S* of man is betrayed	Mt 26:24	5207
the *S* of man is betrayed into the	Mt 26:45	5207
thou be the Christ, the *S* of God	Mt 26:63	5207
Hereafter shall ye see the *S* of	Mt 26:64	5207
If thou be the *S* of God, come	Mt 27:40	5207
for he said, I am the *S* of God	Mt 27:43	5207
Truly this was the *S* of God	Mt 27:54	5207
name of the Father, and of the *S*	Mt 28:19	5207
of Jesus Christ, the *S* of God	Mk 1:1	5207
saying, Thou art my beloved *S*	Mk 1:11	5207
he saw James the *s* of Zebedee	Mk 1:19	
unto the sick of the palsy, *S*	Mk 2:5	5043
S of man hath power on earth to	Mk 2:10	5207
he saw Levi the *s* of Alphaeus	Mk 2:14	
Therefore the *S* of man is Lord	Mk 2:28	5207
saying, Thou art the *S* of God	Mk 3:11	5207
James the *s* of Zebedee, and John	Mk 3:17	
James the *s* of Alphaeus, and	Mk 3:18	
thou *S* of the most high God	Mk 5:7	
the *s* of Mary, the brother of	Mk 6:3	
that the *S* of man must suffer	Mk 8:31	
shall the *S* of man be ashamed	Mk 8:38	
saying, This is my beloved *S*	Mk 9:7	
till the *S* of man were risen from	Mk 9:9	
how it is written of the *S* of man	Mk 9:12	
I have brought unto thee my *s*	Mk 9:17	
The *S* of man is delivered into	Mk 9:31	
the *S* of man shall be delivered	Mk 10:33	
For even the *S* of man came not to	Mk 10:45	
the *s* of Timaeus, sat by the	Mk 10:46	
thou *s* of David, have mercy on me	Mk 10:47	
Thou *s* of David, have mercy on me	Mk 10:48	
Having yet therefore one *s*	Mk 12:6	
saying, They will reverence my *s*	Mk 12:6	
that Christ is the *s* of David	Mk 12:35	
and whence is he then his *s*	Mk 12:37	
to death, and the father the *s*	Mk 13:12	5043
then shall they see the *S* of man	Mk 13:26	5207
are in heaven, neither the *S*	Mk 13:32	5207
For the *S* of man is as a man	Mk 13:34	
The *S* of man indeed goeth, as it	Mk 14:21	5207
by whom the *S* of man is betrayed	Mk 14:21	5207
the *S* of man is betrayed into the	Mk 14:41	5207
the Christ, the *S* of the Blessed	Mk 14:61	5207
ye shall see the *S* of man sitting	Mk 14:62	5207
Truly this man was the *S* of God	Mk 15:39	5207
Elisabeth shall bear thee a *s*	Lk 1:13	5207
in thy womb, and bring forth a *s*	Lk 1:31	5207
be called the *S* of the Highest	Lk 1:32	5207
thee shall be called the *S* of God	Lk 1:35	5207
also conceived a *s* in her old age	Lk 1:36	5207
and she brought forth a *s*	Lk 1:57	5207
she brought forth her firstborn *s*	Lk 2:7	5207
and his mother said unto him, *S*	Lk 2:48	5043
s of Zacharias in the wilderness	Lk 3:2	5207
which said, Thou art my beloved *S*	Lk 3:22	5207
(as was supposed) the *s* of Joseph	Lk 3:23	5207
Joseph, which was the *s* of Heli	Lk 3:23	
Which was the *s* of Matthat	Lk 3:24	
Matthat, which was the *s* of Levi	Lk 3:24	
Levi, which was the *s* of Melchi	Lk 3:24	
Melchi, which was the *s* of Janna	Lk 3:24	
Janna, which was the *s* of Joseph	Lk 3:24	
Which was the *s* of Mattathias	Lk 3:25	
which was the *s* of Amos, which	Lk 3:25	
of Amos, which was the *s* of Naum	Lk 3:25	
of Naum, which was the *s* of Esli	Lk 3:25	
of Esli, which was the *s* of Nagge	Lk 3:25	
Which was the *s* of Maath, which	Lk 3:26	
which was the *s* of Mattathias	Lk 3:26	
which was the *s* of Semei	Lk 3:26	
Semei, which was the *s* of Joseph	Lk 3:26	
Joseph, which was the *s* of Juda	Lk 3:26	
Which was the *s* of Joanna	Lk 3:27	
Joanna, which was the *s* of Rhesa	Lk 3:27	
which was the *s* of Zorobabel	Lk 3:27	

which was the *s* of Salathiel	Lk 3:27	
which was the *s* of Neri,	Lk 3:27	
Which was the *s* of Melchi	Lk 3:28	
Melchi, which was the *s* of Addi	Lk 3:28	
of Addi, which was the *s* of Cosam	Lk 3:28	
Cosam, which was the *s* of Elmodam	Lk 3:28	
of Elmodam, which was the *s* of Er	Lk 3:28	
Which was the *s* of Jose, which	Lk 3:29	
Jose, which was the *s* of Eliezer	Lk 3:29	
Eliezer, which was the *s* of Jorim	Lk 3:29	
Jorim, which was the *s* of Matthat	Lk 3:29	
Matthat, which was the *s* of Levi	Lk 3:29	
Which was the *s* of Simeon	Lk 3:30	
Simeon, which was the *s* of Juda	Lk 3:30	
Juda, which was the *s* of Joseph	Lk 3:30	
Joseph, which was the *s* of Jonan	Lk 3:30	
Jonan, which was the *s* of Eliakim	Lk 3:30	
Which was the *s* of Melea, which	Lk 3:31	
Melea, which was the *s* of Menan	Lk 3:31	
which was the *s* of Mattatha	Lk 3:31	
which was the *s* of Nathan	Lk 3:31	
Nathan, which was the *s* of David	Lk 3:31	
Which was the *s* of Jesse, which	Lk 3:32	
of Jesse, which was the *s* of Obed	Lk 3:32	
of Obed, which was the *s* of Booz	Lk 3:32	
Booz, which was the *s* of Salmon	Lk 3:32	
which was the *s* of Naasson	Lk 3:32	
Which was the *s* of Aminadab	Lk 3:33	
Aminadab, which was the *s* of Aram	Lk 3:33	
of Aram, which was the *s* of Esrom	Lk 3:33	
Esrom, which was the *s* of Phares	Lk 3:33	
Phares, which was the *s* of Juda	Lk 3:33	
Which was the *s* of Jacob, which	Lk 3:34	
Jacob, which was the *s* of Isaac	Lk 3:34	
Isaac, which was the *s* of Abraham	Lk 3:34	
Abraham, which was the *s* of Thara	Lk 3:34	
Thara, which was the *s* of Nachor	Lk 3:34	
Which was the *s* of Saruch	Lk 3:35	
Saruch, which was the *s* of Ragau	Lk 3:35	
Ragau, which was the *s* of Phalec	Lk 3:35	
Phalec, which was the *s* of Heber	Lk 3:35	
of Heber, which was the *s* of Sala	Lk 3:35	
Which was the *s* of Arphaxad	Lk 3:36	
which was the *s* of Arphaxad	Lk 3:36	
Arphaxad, which was the *s* of Sem	Lk 3:36	
of Sem, which was the *s* of Noe	Lk 3:36	
of Noe, which was the *s* of Lamech	Lk 3:36	
Which was the *s* of Mathusala	Lk 3:37	
which was the *s* of Enoch	Lk 3:37	
Enoch, which was the *s* of Jared	Lk 3:37	
which was the *s* of Maleleel	Lk 3:37	
which was the *s* of Cainan	Lk 3:37	
Which was the *s* of Enos, which	Lk 3:38	
of Enos, which was the *s* of Seth	Lk 3:38	
of Seth, which was the *s* of Adam	Lk 3:38	
of Adam, which was the *s* of God	Lk 3:38	
unto him, If thou be the *S* of God	Lk 4:3	5207
unto him, If thou be the *S* of God	Lk 4:9	5207
they said, Is not this Joseph's *s*	Lk 4:22	5207
Thou art Christ the *S* of God	Lk 4:41	5207
But that ye may know that the *S*	Lk 5:24	5207
That the *S* of man is Lord also of	Lk 6:5	5207
James the *s* of Alphaeus, and Simon	Lk 6:15	
as evil, for the *S* of man's sake	Lk 6:22	5207
the only *s* of his mother, and she	Lk 7:12	5207
The *S* of man is come eating and	Lk 7:34	5207
Jesus, thou *S* of God most high	Lk 8:28	5207
The *S* of man must suffer many	Lk 9:22	5207
of him shall the *S* of man be	Lk 9:26	5207
saying, This is my beloved *S*	Lk 9:35	5207
I beseech thee, look upon my *s*	Lk 9:38	5207
Bring thy *s* hither	Lk 9:41	5207
for the *S* of man shall be	Lk 9:44	5207
For the *S* of man is not come to	Lk 9:56	5207
but the *S* of man hath not where	Lk 9:58	5207
if the *s* of peace be there, your	Lk 10:6	5207
and no man knoweth who the *S* is	Lk 10:22	5207
and who the Father is, but the *S*	Lk 10:22	5207
he to whom the *S* will reveal him	Lk 10:22	5207
If a *s* shall ask bread of any of	Lk 11:11	5207
so shall also the *S* of man be to	Lk 11:30	5207
him shall the *S* of man also	Lk 12:8	5207
speak a word against the *S* of man	Lk 12:10	5207
for the *S* of man cometh at an	Lk 12:40	5207
shall be divided against the *s*	Lk 12:53	5207
and the *s* against the father	Lk 12:53	5207
younger *s* gathered all together	Lk 15:13	5207
no more worthy to be called thy *s*	Lk 15:19	5207
the *s* said unto him, Father, I	Lk 15:21	5207
no more worthy to be called thy *s*	Lk 15:21	5207
For this my *s* was dead, and is	Lk 15:24	5207

Now his elder *s* was in the field	Lk 15:25	5207
as soon as this thy *s* was come	Lk 15:30	5207
And he said unto him, S, thou art	Lk 15:31	5043
But Abraham said, S, remember	Lk 16:25	5043
one of the days of the S of man	Lk 17:22	5207
so shall also the S of man be in	Lk 17:24	5207
also in the days of the S of man	Lk 17:26	5207
day when the S of man is revealed	Lk 17:30	5207
when the S of man cometh, shall	Lk 18:8	5207
S of man shall be accomplished	Lk 18:31	5207
thou *s* of David, have mercy on me	Lk 18:38	5207
Thou *s* of David, have mercy on me	Lk 18:39	5207
as he also is a *s* of Abraham	Lk 19:9	5207
For the S of man is come to seek	Lk 19:10	5207
I will send my beloved *s*	Lk 20:13	5207
say they that Christ is David's *s*	Lk 20:41	5207
him Lord, how is he then his *s*	Lk 20:44	5207
then shall they see the S of man	Lk 21:27	5207
and to stand before the S of man	Lk 21:36	5207
truly the S of man goeth, as it	Lk 22:22	5207
thou the S of man with a kiss	Lk 22:48	5207
Hereafter shall the S of man sit	Lk 22:69	5207
all, Art thou then the S of God	Lk 22:70	5207
The S of man must be delivered	Lk 24:7	5207
the only begotten S, which is in	Jn 1:18	5207
record that this is the S of God	Jn 1:34	5207
Thou art Simon the *s* of Jona	Jn 1:42	5207
of Nazareth, the *s* of Joseph	Jn 1:45	5207
him, Rabbi, thou art the S of God	Jn 1:49	5207
and descending upon the S of man	Jn 1:51	5207
even the S of man which is in	Jn 3:13	5207
even so must the S of man be	Jn 3:14	5207
that he gave his only begotten S	Jn 3:16	5207
For God sent not his S into the	Jn 3:17	5207
of the only begotten S of God	Jn 3:18	5207
The Father loveth the S, and hath	Jn 3:35	5207
on the S hath everlasting life	Jn 3:36	5207
not the S shall not see life	Jn 3:36	5207
that Jacob gave to his *s* Joseph	Jn 4:5	5207
whose *s* was sick at Capernaum	Jn 4:46	5207
he would come down, and heal his *s*	Jn 4:47	5207
thy *s* liveth	Jn 4:50	5207
and told him, saying, Thy *s* liveth	Jn 4:51	3816
Jesus said unto him, Thy *s* liveth	Jn 4:53	5207
The S can do nothing of himself,	Jn 5:19	5207
these also doeth the S likewise	Jn 5:19	5207
For the Father loveth the S	Jn 5:20	5207
even so the S quickeneth whom he	Jn 5:21	5207
committed all judgment unto the S	Jn 5:22	5207
That all men should honour the S	Jn 5:23	5207
He that honoureth not the S	Jn 5:23	5207
hear the voice of the S of God	Jn 5:25	5207
to the S to have life in himself	Jn 5:26	5207
also, because he is the S of man	Jn 5:27	5207
which the S of man shall give	Jn 6:27	5207
that every one which seeth the S	Jn 6:40	5207
the *s* of Joseph, whose father and	Jn 6:42	5207
ye eat the flesh of the S of man	Jn 6:53	5207
if ye shall see the S of man	Jn 6:62	5207
Christ, the S of the living God	Jn 6:69	5207
of Judas Iscariot the *s* of Simon	Jn 6:71	
ye have lifted up the S of man	Jn 8:28	5207
but the S abideth ever	Jn 8:35	5207
If the S therefore shall make you	Jn 8:36	5207
them, saying, This your *s*	Jn 9:19	5207
said, We know that this is our *s*	Jn 9:20	5207
Dost thou believe on the S of God	Jn 9:35	5207
because I said, I am the S of God	Jn 10:36	5207
that the S of God might be	Jn 11:4	5207
the S of God, which should come	Jn 11:27	5207
Judas Iscariot, Simon's *s*	Jn 12:4	
that the S of man should be	Jn 12:23	5207
The S of man must be lifted up	Jn 12:34	5207
who is this S of man	Jn 12:34	5207
of Judas Iscariot, Simon's *s*	Jn 13:2	
to Judas Iscariot, the *s* of Simon	Jn 13:26	
Now is the S of man glorified, and	Jn 13:31	5207
Father may be glorified in the S	Jn 14:13	5207
glorify thy S, that thy S also	Jn 17:1	5207
is lost, but the *s* of perdition	Jn 17:12	5207
he made himself the S of God	Jn 19:7	5207
his mother, Woman, behold thy *s*	Jn 19:26	5207
Jesus is the Christ, the S of God	Jn 20:31	5207
s of Jonas, lovest thou me more	Jn 21:15	
s of Jonas, lovest thou me	Jn 21:16	
s of Jonas, lovest thou me	Jn 21:17	
James the *s* of Alphaeus, and Simon	Acts 1:13	
hath glorified his S Jesus	Acts 3:13	3816
God, having raised up his S Jesus	Acts 3:26	3816
The *s* of consolation,) a Levite,	Acts 4:36	5207
and nourished him for her own *s*	Acts 7:21	5207

the S of man standing on the	Acts 7:56	5207
that Jesus Christ is the S of God	Acts 8:37	5207
that he is the S of God	Acts 9:20	5207
gave unto them Saul the *s* of Cis	Acts 13:21	5207
I have found David the *s* of Jesse	Acts 13:22	5207
the second psalm, Thou art my S	Acts 13:33	5207
the *s* of a certain woman, which	Acts 16:1	5207
a Pharisee, the *s* of a Pharisee	Acts 23:6	5207
when Paul's sister's *s* heard of	Acts 23:16	5207
Concerning his S Jesus Christ our	Rom 1:3	5207
to be the S of God with power	Rom 1:4	5207
my spirit in the gospel of his S	Rom 1:9	5207
to God by the death of his S	Rom 5:10	5207
God sending his own S in the	Rom 8:3	5207
conformed to the image of his S	Rom 8:29	5207
He that spared not his own S	Rom 8:32	5207
I come, and Sarah shall have a *s*	Rom 9:9	5207
of his S Jesus Christ our Lord	1Cor 1:9	5207
Timotheus, who is my beloved *s*	1Cor 4:17	5043
then shall the S also himself be	1Cor 15:28	5207
For the S of God, Jesus Christ,	2Cor 1:19	5207
To reveal his S in me, that I	Gal 1:16	5207
live by the faith of the S of God	Gal 2:20	5207
was come, God sent forth his S	Gal 4:4	5207
Spirit of his S into your hearts	Gal 4:6	5207
art no more a servant, but a *s*	Gal 4:7	5207
and if a *s*, then an heir of God	Gal 4:7	5207
Cast out the bondwoman and her *s*	Gal 4:30	5207
for the *s* of the bondwoman shall	Gal 4:30	5207
heir with the *s* of the free woman	Gal 4:30	5207
of the knowledge of the S of God	Eph 4:13	5207
as a *s* with the father, he hath	Phil 2:22	5043
us into the kingdom of his dear S	Col 1:13	5207
sister's *s* to Barnabas, (touching	Col 4:10	431
And to wait for his S from heaven	1Th 1:10	5207
be revealed, the *s* of perdition	2Th 2:3	5207
Timothy, my own *s* in the faith	1Ti 1:2	5043
s Timothy, according to the	1Ti 1:18	5043
To Timothy, my dearly beloved *s*	2Ti 1:2	5043
Thou therefore, my *s*, be strong	2Ti 2:1	5043
mine own *s* after the common faith	Titus 1:4	5043
I beseech thee for my *s* Onesimus	Philem 10	5043
last days spoken unto us by his S	Heb 1:2	5207
he at any time, Thou art my S	Heb 1:5	5207
Father, and he shall be to me a S	Heb 1:5	5207
But unto the S he saith, Thy	Heb 1:8	5207
or the *s* of man, that thou	Heb 2:6	5207
But Christ as a *s* over his own	Heb 3:6	5207
the heavens, Jesus the S of God	Heb 4:14	5207
that said unto him, Thou art my S	Heb 5:5	5207
Though he were a S, yet learned	Heb 5:8	5207
to themselves the S of God afresh	Heb 6:6	5207
but made like unto the S of God	Heb 7:3	5207
was since the law, maketh the S	Heb 7:28	5207
trodden under foot the S of God	Heb 10:29	5207
offered up his only begotten *s*	Heb 11:17	5207
the *s* of Pharaoh's daughter	Heb 11:24	5207
unto you as unto children, My *s*	Heb 12:5	5207
scourgeth every *s* whom he	Heb 12:6	5207
for what *s* is he whom the father	Heb 12:7	5207
Isaac his *s* upon the altar	Jas 2:21	5207
and so doth Marcus my *s*	1Pet 5:13	5207
glory, This is my beloved S	2Pet 1:17	5207
the way of Balaam the *s* of Bosor	2Pet 2:15	5207
and with his S Jesus Christ	1Jn 1:3	
his S cleanseth us from all sin	1Jn 1:7	5207
that denieth the Father and the S	1Jn 2:22	5207
Whosoever denieth the S, the same	1Jn 2:23	5207
the S hath the Father also	1Jn 2:23	5207
ye also shall continue in the S	1Jn 2:24	5207
For this purpose the S of God was	1Jn 3:8	5207
on the name of his S Jesus Christ	1Jn 3:23	5207
only begotten S into the world	1Jn 4:9	5207
sent his S to be the propitiation	1Jn 4:10	5207
that the Father sent the S to be	1Jn 4:14	5207
that Jesus is the S of God	1Jn 4:15	5207
that Jesus is the S of God	1Jn 5:5	5207
which he hath testified of his S	1Jn 5:9	5207
He that believeth on the S of God	1Jn 5:10	5207
the record that God gave of his S	1Jn 5:10	5207
life, and this life is in his S	1Jn 5:11	5207
He that hath the S hath life	1Jn 5:12	5207
not the S of God hath not life	1Jn 5:12	5207
on the name of the S of God	1Jn 5:13	5207
on the name of the S of God	1Jn 5:13	5207
we know that the S of God is come	1Jn 5:20	5207
even in his S Jesus Christ	1Jn 5:20	5207
the S of the Father, in truth and	2Jn 3	5207
he hath both the Father and the S	2Jn 9	5207
one like unto the S of man	Rev 1:13	5207
These things saith the S of God	Rev 2:18	5207

S

SONG

one sat like unto the *S* of man	Rev 14:14	5207
be his God, and he shall be my *s*	Rev 21:7	5207

SONG

of Israel this *s* unto the LORD	Ex 15:1	7892
The LORD is my strength and *s*	Ex 15:2	2176
Then Israel sang this *s*, Spring	Num 21:17	7892
therefore write ye this *s* for you	Deut 31:19	7892
that this *s* may be a witness for	Deut 31:19	7892
that this *s* shall testify against	Deut 31:21	7892
wrote this *s* the same day	Deut 31:22	7892
of Israel the words of this *s*	Deut 31:30	7892
this *s* in the ears of the people	Deut 32:44	7892
awake, awake, utter a *s*	Judg 5:12	7892
unto the LORD the words of this *s*	2Sa 22:1	7892
of *s* in the house of the LORD	1Chr 6:31	7892
chief of the Levites, was for *s*	1Chr 15:22	4853
he instructed about the *s*	1Chr 15:22	4853
master of the *s* with the singers	1Chr 15:27	4853
for *s* in the house of the LORD	1Chr 25:6	7892
the *s* of the LORD began also with	2Chr 29:27	7892
And now am I their *s*, yea, I am	Job 30:9	5058
this *s* in the day that the LORD	Ps 18:*t*	7892
with my *s* will I praise him	Ps 28:7	7892
S at the dedication of the house	Ps 30:*t*	7892
Sing unto him a new *s*	Ps 33:3	7892
he hath put a new *s* in my mouth	Ps 40:3	7892
the night his *s* shall be with me	Ps 42:8	7892
of Korah, A Maschil, A *S* of loves	Ps 45:*t*	7892
sons of Korah, A *S* upon Alamoth	Ps 46:*t*	7892
A *S* and Psalm for the sons of	Ps 48:*t*	7892
Musician, A Psalm and *S* of David	Ps 65:*t*	7892
the chief Musician, A *S* or Psalm	Ps 66:*t*	7892
on Neginoth, A Psalm or *S*	Ps 67:*t*	7892
Musician, A Psalm or *S* of David	Ps 68:*t*	7892
I was the *s* of the drunkards	Ps 69:12	5058
praise the name of God with a *s*	Ps 69:30	7892
Altaschith, A Psalm or *S* of Asaph	Ps 75:*t*	7892
Neginoth, A Psalm or *S* of Asaph	Ps 76:*t*	7892
to remembrance my *s* in the night	Ps 77:6	5058
A *S* or Psalm of Asaph	Ps 83:*t*	7892
A Psalm or *S* for the sons of	Ps 87:*t*	7892
A *S* or Psalm for the sons of	Ps 88:*t*	7892
A Psalm or *S* for the sabbath day	Ps 92:*t*	7892
O sing unto the LORD a new *s*	Ps 96:1	7892
O sing unto the LORD a new *s*	Ps 98:1	7892
A *S* or Psalm of David	Ps 108:*t*	7892
The LORD is my strength and *s*	Ps 118:14	2176
A *S* of degrees	Ps 120:*t*	7892
A *S* of degrees	Ps 121:*t*	7892
A *S* of degrees of David	Ps 122:*t*	7892
A *S* of degrees	Ps 123:*t*	7892
A *S* of degrees of David	Ps 124:*t*	7892
A *S* of degrees	Ps 125:*t*	7892
A *S* of degrees	Ps 126:*t*	7892
A *S* of degrees for Solomon	Ps 127:*t*	7892
A *S* of degrees	Ps 128:*t*	7892
A *S* of degrees	Ps 129:*t*	7892
A *S* of degrees	Ps 130:*t*	7892
A *S* of degrees of David	Ps 131:*t*	7892
A *S* of degrees	Ps 132:*t*	7892
A *S* of degrees of David	Ps 133:*t*	7892
A *S* of degrees	Ps 134:*t*	7892
away captive required of us a *s*	Ps 137:3	7892
the LORD's *s* in a strange land	Ps 137:4	7892
I will sing a new *s* unto thee	Ps 144:9	7892
Sing unto the LORD a new *s*	Ps 149:1	7892
for a man to hear the *s* of fools	Eccl 7:5	7892
The *s* of songs, which is	Song 1:1	7892
a *s* of my beloved touching his	Is 5:1	7892
JEHOVAH is my strength and my *s*	Is 12:2	2176
shall not drink wine with a *s*	Is 24:9	7892
In that day shall this *s* be sung	Is 26:1	7892
Ye shall have a *s*, as in the	Is 30:29	7892
Sing unto the LORD a new *s*	Is 42:10	7892
and their *s* all the day	Lam 3:14	5058
s of one that hath a pleasant	Eze 33:32	7892
And they sung a new *s*, saying	Rev 5:9	5603
it were a new *s* before the throne	Rev 14:3	5603
learn that *s* but the hundred	Rev 14:3	5603
they sing the *s* of Moses the	Rev 15:3	5603
the *s* of the Lamb, saying, Great	Rev 15:3	5603

SONGS

thee away with mirth, and with *s*	Gen 31:27	7892
his *s* were a thousand and five	1Kin 4:32	7892
instructed in the *s* of the LORD	1Chr 25:7	7892
s of praise and thanksgiving unto	Neh 12:46	7892
who giveth *s* in the night	Job 35:10	2158
me about with *s* of deliverance	Ps 32:7	7438
Thy statutes have been my *s* in	Ps 119:54	2158
Sing us one of the *s* of Zion	Ps 137:3	7892

that singeth *s* to an heavy heart	Prov 25:20	7892
The song of *s*, which is Solomon's	Song 1:1	7892
make sweet melody, sing many *s*	Is 23:16	7892
part of the earth have we heard *s*	Is 24:16	2158
return, and come to Zion with *s*	Is 35:10	7440
therefore we will sing my *s* to	Is 38:20	5058
cause the noise of thy *s* to cease	Eze 26:13	7892
away from me the noise of thy *s*	Amos 5:23	7892
the *s* of the temple shall be	Amos 8:3	7892
all your *s* into lamentation	Amos 8:10	7892
in psalms and hymns and spiritual *s*	Eph 5:19	5603
in psalms and hymns and spiritual *s*	Col 3:16	5603

SON'S See APPENDIX.

SONS See APPENDIX.

SONS' See APPENDIX.

SOON

as *s* as he had left communing	Gen 18:33	834
as *s* as Isaac had made an end of	Gen 27:30	834
As *s* as the morning was light,	Gen 44:3	
it that ye are come so *s* to day	Ex 2:18	4116
As *s* as I am gone out of the city	Ex 9:29	
as *s* as he came nigh unto the	Ex 32:19	834
that ye shall *s* utterly perish	Deut 4:26	4116
as *s* as they which pursued after	Josh 2:7	834
as *s* as we had heard these things	Josh 2:11	
as *s* as the soles of the feet of	Josh 3:13	
they ran as *s* as he had stretched	Josh 8:19	
as *s* as the sun was down, Joshua	Josh 8:29	
as *s* as Gideon was dead, that the	Judg 8:33	834
as *s* as the sun is up, thou shalt	Judg 9:33	
As *s* as ye be come into the city,	1Sa 9:13	
that as *s* as he had made an end	1Sa 13:10	
as *s* as the lad was gone, David	1Sa 20:41	
as *s* as ye be up early in the	1Sa 29:10	
as *s* as David had made an end of	2Sa 6:18	
as *s* as he had made an end of	2Sa 13:36	
As *s* as ye hear the sound of the	2Sa 15:10	
as *s* as they hear, they shall be	2Sa 22:45	
as *s* as he sat on his throne,	1Kin 16:11	
as *s* as I am gone from thee, that	1Kin 18:12	
as *s* as thou art departed from me	1Kin 20:36	
as *s* as he was departed from him,	1Kin 20:36	
Now as *s* as this letter cometh to	2Kin 10:2	
as *s* as he had made an end of	2Kin 10:25	
as *s* as the kingdom was confirmed	2Kin 14:5	834
as *s* as the commandment came	2Chr 31:5	
my maker would *s* take me away	Job 32:22	4592
As *s* as they hear of me, they	Ps 18:44	
For they shall *s* be cut down like	Ps 37:2	4120
go astray as *s* as they be born	Ps 58:3	
Ethiopia shall *s* stretch out her	Ps 68:31	7323
I should *s* have subdued their	Ps 81:14	4592
for it is *s* cut off, and we fly	Ps 90:10	2440
They *s* forgat his works	Ps 106:13	4116
He that is *s* angry dealeth	Prov 14:17	7116
for as *s* as Zion travailed, she	Is 66:8	1571
as *s* as she saw them with her	Eze 23:16	4758
How *s* is the fig tree withered	Mt 21:20	3916
And as *s* as he had spoken,	Mk 1:42	
As *s* as Jesus heard the word that	Mk 5:36	2112
as *s* as ye be entered into it, ye	Mk 11:2	2112
as *s* as he was come, he goeth	Mk 14:45	
that, as *s* as the days of his	Lk 1:23	
For, lo, as *s* as the voice of thy	Lk 1:44	
as *s* as it was sprung up, it	Lk 8:6	
But as *s* as this thy son was come	Lk 15:30	3753
as *s* as it was day, the elders of	Lk 22:66	
as *s* as he knew that he belonged	Lk 23:7	
as *s* as she heard that Jesus was	Jn 11:20	
As *s* as she heard that, she arose	Jn 11:29	
but as *s* as Jesus is delivered of	Jn 16:21	3752
As *s* then as he had said unto	Jn 18:6	
As *s* then as they were come to	Jn 21:9	
as *s* as I was sent for	Acts 10:29	
Now as *s* as it was day, there was	Acts 12:18	1096
I marvel that ye are so *s* removed	Gal 1:6	5030
so *s* as I shall see how it will	Phil 2:23	
That ye be not *s* shaken in mind	2Th 2:2	5030
not *s* angry, not given to wine,	Titus 1:7	3711
as *s* as I had eaten it, my belly	Rev 10:10	3753
her child as *s* as it was born	Rev 12:4	3752

SOONER

I may be restored to you the *s*	Heb 13:19	5032
For the sun is no *s* risen with a	Jas 1:11	

SOOTHSAYER

also the son of Beor, the *s*	Josh 13:22	7080

SOOTHSAYERS

are s like the Philistines, and	Is 2:6	6049
astrologers, the magicians, the s	Dan 2:27	1505
the Chaldeans, and the s	Dan 4:7	1505
the Chaldeans, and the s	Dan 5:7	1505
astrologers, Chaldeans, and s	Dan 5:11	1505
and thou shalt have no more s	Mic 5:12	6049

SOOTHSAYING

her masters much gain by s	Acts 16:16	*3132*

SOP

it is, to whom I shall give a s	Jn 13:26	*5596*
And when he had dipped the s	Jn 13:26	*5596*
after the s Satan entered into	Jn 13:27	*5596*
the s went immediately out	Jn 13:30	*5596*

SOPATER (so'-pa-ter) See SOSIPATER. *A Christian from Berea.*

him into Asia S of Berea	Acts 20:4	*4986*

SOPE

with nitre, and take thee much s	Jer 2:22	1287
fire, and like fullers' s	Mal 3:2	1287

SOPHERETH (so-fe'-reth) *A family of exiles.*

of Sotai, the children of S	Ezr 2:55	5618
of Sotai, the children of S	Neh 7:57	5618

SORCERER

Paphos, they found a certain s	Acts 13:6	*3097*
But Elymas the s (for so is his	Acts 13:8	*3097*

SORCERERS

also called the wise men and the s	Ex 7:11	3784
to your enchanters, nor to your s	Jer 27:9	3786
and the astrologers, and the s	Dan 2:2	3784
be a swift witness against the s	Mal 3:5	3784
murderers, and whoremongers, and s	Rev 21:8	5332
For without are dogs, and s	Rev 22:15	5333

SORCERESS

near hither, ye sons of the s	Is 57:3	6049

SORCERIES

for the multitude of thy s	Is 47:9	3785
and with the multitude of thy s	Is 47:12	3785
time he had bewitched them with s	Acts 8:11	3095
of their murders, nor of their s	Rev 9:21	5331
for by thy s were all nations	Rev 18:23	5331

SORCERY

in the same city used s, and	Acts 8:9	3096

SORE

And they pressed s upon the man	Gen 19:9	3966
and the men were s afraid	Gen 20:8	3966
because thou s longedst after thy	Gen 31:30	
the third day, when they were s	Gen 34:25	3510
the famine waxed s in the land of	Gen 41:56	2388
the famine was so s in all lands	Gen 41:57	2388
And the famine was s in the land	Gen 43:1	3515
for the famine is s in the land	Gen 47:4	3515
for the famine was very s	Gen 47:13	3515
a great and very s lamentation	Gen 50:10	3515
and they were s afraid	Ex 14:10	3966
bald forehead, a white reddish s	Lev 13:42	5061
if the rising of the s be white	Lev 13:43	5061
Moab was s afraid of the people,	Num 22:3	3966
signs and wonders, great and s	Deut 6:22	7451
with a s botch that cannot be	Deut 28:35	7451
and s sicknesses, and of long	Deut 28:59	7451
therefore we were s afraid of our	Josh 9:24	3966
so that Israel was s distressed	Judg 10:9	3966
her, because she lay s upon him	Judg 14:17	
he was s athirst, and called on	Judg 15:18	3966
all Israel, and the battle was s	Judg 20:34	3513
lifted up their voices, and wept s	Judg 21:2	
her adversary also provoked her s	1Sa 1:6	3708
prayed unto the LORD, and wept s	1Sa 1:10	
for his hand is s upon us	1Sa 5:7	7185
there was s war against the	1Sa 14:52	2389
fled from him, and were s afraid	1Sa 17:24	3966
was s afraid of Achish the king	1Sa 21:12	3966
Saul answered, I am s distressed	1Sa 28:15	3966
was s afraid, because of the	1Sa 28:20	3966
and saw that he was s troubled	1Sa 28:21	3966
And the battle went s against Saul	1Sa 31:3	3513
he was s wounded of the archers	1Sa 31:3	3966
for he was s afraid	1Sa 31:4	3966
was a very s battle that day	2Sa 2:17	7188
and all his servants wept very s	2Sa 13:36	1419
and his sickness was so s, that	1Kin 17:17	2389
there was a s famine in Samaria	1Kin 18:2	2389
that the battle was too s for him	2Kin 3:26	2388
was s troubled for this thing	2Kin 6:11	

And Hezekiah wept s	2Kin 20:3	1419
And the battle went s against Saul	1Chr 10:3	3513
for he was s afraid	1Chr 10:4	3966
whatsoever s or whatsoever	2Chr 6:28	5061
every one shall know his own s	2Chr 6:29	5061
so he died of s diseases	2Chr 21:19	7451
transgressed s against the LORD	2Chr 28:19	
for I am s wounded	2Chr 35:23	3966
for the people wept very s	Ezr 10:1	
Then I was s afraid,	Neh 2:2	7235
And it grieved me s	Neh 13:8	3966
smote Job with s boils from the	Job 2:7	7451
For he maketh s, and bindeth up	Job 5:18	3510
and vex them in his s displeasure	Ps 2:5	
My soul is also s vexed	Ps 6:3	3966
enemies be ashamed and s vexed	Ps 6:10	3966
in me, and thy hand presseth me s	Ps 38:2	5704,3966
I am feeble and s broken	Ps 38:8	
my friends stand aloof from my s	Ps 38:11	5061
Though thou hast s broken us in	Ps 44:19	
My heart is s pained within me	Ps 55:4	
s troubles, shalt quicken me	Ps 71:20	7451
my s ran in the night, and ceased	Ps 77:2	3027
Thou hast thrust s at me that I	Ps 118:13	
The LORD hath chastened me s	Ps 118:18	
this s travail hath God given to	Eccl 1:13	7451
vanity, yea, it is a s travail	Eccl 4:8	7451
There is s evil which I have	Eccl 5:13	2470
And this also is a s evil, that in	Eccl 5:16	2470
In that day the LORD with his s	Is 27:1	7186
And Hezekiah wept s	Is 38:3	1419
like bears, and mourn s like doves	Is 59:11	
Be not wroth very s, O LORD,	Is 64:9	3966
thy peace, and afflict us very s	Is 64:12	3966
and mine eye shall weep s, and run	Jer 13:17	
but weep s for him that goeth	Jer 22:10	
Your mother shall be s confounded	Jer 50:12	3966
the famine was s in the city	Jer 52:6	2388
She weepeth s in the night, and	Lam 1:2	
Mine enemies chased me s, like a	Lam 3:52	
four s judgments upon Jerusalem	Eze 14:21	7451
sharpened to make a s slaughter	Eze 21:10	
and their kings shall be s afraid	Eze 27:35	8178
was s displeased with himself, and	Dan 6:14	7690
you, even with a s destruction	Mic 2:10	4834
The LORD hath been s displeased	Zec 1:2	
I am very s displeased with the	Zec 1:15	
on their face, and were s afraid	Mt 17:6	4970
for he is lunatick, and s vexed	Mt 17:15	2560
they were s displeased	Mt 21:15	23
they were s amazed in themselves	Mk 6:51	3029
for they were s afraid	Mk 9:6	1630
the spirit cried, and rent him s	Mk 9:26	4183
and John, and began to be s amazed	Mk 14:33	1568
and they were s afraid	Lk 2:9	3173
And they all wept s, and fell on	Acts 20:37	2425
grievous s upon the men which had	Rev 16:2	1668

SOREK (so'-rek) *A valley between Ashkelon and Gaza.*

loved a woman in the valley of S	Judg 16:4	7796

SORELY

The archers have s grieved him	Gen 49:23	4843
so shall they be s pained at the	Is 23:5	

SORER

Of how much s punishment, suppose	Heb 10:29	*5501*

SORES

and bruises, and putrifying s	Is 1:6	4347
was laid at his gate, full of s	Lk 16:20	*1669*
the dogs came and licked his s	Lk 16:21	*1668*
because of their pains and their s	Rev 16:11	*1668*

SORROW

I will greatly multiply thy s	Gen 3:16	6093
in s thou shalt bring forth	Gen 3:16	6089
in s shalt thou eat of it all the	Gen 3:17	6093
my gray hairs with s to the grave	Gen 42:38	3015
my gray hairs with s to the grave	Gen 44:29	7451
our father with s to the grave	Gen 44:31	3015
s shall take hold on the	Ex 15:14	2427
the eyes, and cause s of heart	Lev 26:16	1727
and failing of eyes, and s of mind	Deut 28:65	1671
saying, Because I bare him with s	1Chr 4:9	6090
is nothing else but s of heart	Neh 2:2	7455
turned unto them from s to joy	Est 9:22	3015
womb, nor hid s from mine eyes	Job 3:10	5999
yea, I would harden myself in s	Job 6:10	2427
eye also is dim by reason of s	Job 17:7	3708
s is turned into joy before him	Job 41:22	1670
having s in my heart daily	Ps 13:2	3015
my s is continually before me	Ps 38:17	4341

and my *s* was stirred .... Ps 39:2   3511
also and *s* are in the midst of it .... Ps 55:10   5999
yet is their strength labour and *s* .... Ps 90:10   205
oppression, affliction, and *s* .... Ps 107:39   3015
I found trouble and *s* .... Ps 116:3   3015
winketh with the eye causeth *s* .... Prov 10:10   6094
rich, and he addeth no *s* with it .... Prov 10:22   6089
but by *s* of the heart the spirit .... Prov 15:13   6094
a fool doeth it to his *s* .... Prov 17:21   8424
who hath *s* .... Prov 23:29   17
increaseth knowledge increaseth *s* .... Eccl 1:18   4341
in darkness, and he hath much *s* .... Eccl 5:17   3708
S is better than laughter......................... Eccl 7:3   3708
Therefore remove *s* from thy heart .... Eccl 11:10   3708
the land, behold darkness and *s* .... Is 5:30   6862
shall give thee rest from thy *s* .... Is 14:3   6090
day of grief and of desperate *s* .... Is 17:11   3511
and there shall be heaviness and *s* .... Is 29:2   592
obtain joy and gladness, and *s* .... Is 35:10   3015
ye shall lie down in *s* .... Is 50:11   4620
and *s* and mourning shall flee away .... Is 51:11   3015
but ye shall cry for *s* of heart .... Is 65:14   3511
I would comfort myself against *s* .... Jer 8:18   3015
of the womb to see labour and *s* .... Jer 20:18   3015
thy *s* is incurable for the....................... Jer 30:15   4341
they shall not *s* any more at all .... Jer 31:12   1669
and make them rejoice from their *s* .... Jer 31:13   3015
the LORD hath added grief to my *s* .... Jer 45:3   4341
there is *s* on the sea .... Jer 49:23   1674
And the land shall tremble and *s* .... Jer 51:29   2342
be any *s* like unto my *s* .... Lam 1:12   4341
you, all people, and behold my *s* .... Lam 1:18   4341
Give them *s* of heart, thy curse............. Lam 3:65   4044
be filled with drunkenness and *s* .... Eze 23:33   3015
they shall *s* a little for the...................... Hos 8:10   2490
he found them sleeping for *s* .... Lk 22:45   3077
you, *s* hath filled your heart .... Jn 16:6   3077
but your *s* shall be turned into............. Jn 16:20   3077
when she is in travail hath *s* .... Jn 16:21   3077
And ye now therefore have *s* .... Jn 16:22   3077
and continual *s* in my heart .... Rom 9:2   3601
I should have *s* from them of whom 2Cor 2:3   3077
be swallowed up with overmuch *s*.......... 2Cor 2:7   3077
For godly *s* worketh repentance to......... 2Cor 7:10   3077
but the *s* of the world worketh 2Cor 7:10   3077
lest I should have *s* upon *s* .... Phil 2:27   3077
which are asleep, that ye *s* not 1Th 4:13   3076
so much torment and *s* give her .... Rev 18:7   3997
and am no widow, and shall see no *s* ..... Rev 18:7   3997
shall be no more death, neither *s*........... Rev 21:4   3997

SORROWED
but that ye *s* to repentance.................... 2Cor 7:9   3076
that ye *s* after a godly sort, ... 2Cor 7:11   3076

SORROWETH
s for you, saying, What shall I 1Sa 10:2   1672

SORROWFUL
lord, I am a woman of a *s* spirit............... 1Sa 1:15   7186
refused to touch are as my *s* meat .... Job 6:7   1741
But I am poor and *s*................................. Ps 69:29   3510
Even in laughter the heart is *s*................ Prov 14:13   3510
I have replenished every *s* soul .... Jer 31:25   1669
are *s* for the solemn assembly................ Zeph 3:18   3013
also shall see it, and be very *s* .... Zec 9:5   2342
heard that saying, he went away *s*......... Mt 19:22   3076
And they were exceeding *s*, and............. Mt 26:22   3076
sons of Zebedee, and began to be *s*....... Mt 26:37   3076
unto them, My soul is exceeding *s* .... Mt 26:38   4036
And they began to be *s*, and to say .... Mk 14:19   3076
My soul is exceeding *s* unto death....... Mk 14:34   4036
when he heard this, he was very *s* .... Lk 18:23   4036
when Jesus saw that he was very *s* .... Lk 18:24   4036
and ye shall be *s*, but your sorrow ...... Jn 16:20   3076
As *s*, yet alway rejoicing 2Cor 6:10   3076
and that I may be the less *s* .... Phil 2:28   253

SORROWING
father and I have sought thee *s* .... Lk 2:48   3600
S most of all for the words which .... Acts 20:38   3600

SORROWS
for I know their *s*..................................... Ex 3:7   4341
The *s* of hell compassed me about......... 2Sa 22:6   2256
I am afraid of all my *s*, I know................. Job 9:28   6094
God distributeth *s* in his anger............... Job 21:17   2256
young ones, they cast out their *s* .... Job 39:3   2256
Their *s* shall be multiplied that............... Ps 16:4   6094
The *s* of death compassed me, and........ Ps 18:4   2256
The *s* of hell compassed me about......... Ps 18:5   2256
Many *s* shall be to the wicked................ Ps 32:10   4341
The *s* of death compassed me, and........ Ps 116:3   2256

up late, to eat the bread of *s* .... Ps 127:2   6089
For all his days are *s*, and his .... Eccl 2:23   4341
s shall take hold of them .... Is 13:8   2256
a man of *s*, and acquainted with .... Is 53:3   4341
our griefs, and carried our *s* .... Is 53:4   4341
shall not *s* take thee, as a woman .... Jer 13:21   2256
s have taken her, as a woman in............ Jer 49:24   2256
by the vision my *s* are turned................. Dan 10:16   6735
The *s* of a travailing woman shall .... Hos 13:13   2256
All these are the beginning of *s*.......... Mt 24:8   5604
these are the beginnings of *s* .... Mk 13:8   5604
themselves through with many *s*........... 1Ti 6:10   3601

SORRY
is none of you that is *s* for me 1Sa 22:8   2470
neither be ye *s* .... Neh 8:10   6087
I will be *s* for my sin .... Ps 38:18   1672
who shall be *s* for thee .... Is 51:19   5110
And the king was *s*................................. Mt 14:9   3076
And they were exceeding *s* .... Mt 17:23   3076
what was done, they were very *s* .... Mt 18:31   3076
And the king was exceeding *s* .... Mk 6:26   4036
For if I make you *s*, who is he 2Cor 2:2   3076
the same which is made *s* by me 2Cor 2:2   3076
though I made you *s* with a letter........... 2Cor 7:8   3076
the same epistle hath made you *s* 2Cor 7:8   3076
rejoice, not that ye were made *s* 2Cor 7:9   3076
for ye were made *s* after a godly............ 2Cor 7:9   3076

SORT
two of every *s* shalt thou bring............... Gen 6:19
two of every *s* shall come unto .... Gen 6:20
his kind, every bird of every *s* .... Gen 7:14   3671
save the poorest *s* of the people 2Kin 24:14
by lot, one *s* with another 1Chr 24:5
offer so willingly after this *s* 1Chr 29:14
time in such *s* as it was written 2Chr 30:5
basons of a second *s* four hundred .... Ezr 1:10
to Artaxerxes the king in this *s* .... Ezr 4:8   3660
unto me four times after this *s* .... Neh 6:4   1697
with the men of the common *s* were ...... Eze 23:42
the ravenous birds of every *s* .... Eze 39:4   3671
of every *s* of your oblations,................... Eze 44:30
the children which are of your *s* .... Dan 1:10   1524
God that can deliver after this *s* .... Dan 3:29
lewd fellows of the baser *s* .... Acts 17:5
more boldly unto you in some *s*............... Rom 15:15   *3313*
every man's work of what *s* it is............. 1Cor 3:13   *3697*
that ye sorrowed after a godly *s* 2Cor 7:11
For of this *s* are they which.................... 2Ti 3:6
on their journey after a godly *s*.............. 3Jn 6   *516*

SORTS
not wear a garment of divers *s* .... Deut 22:11
ten days store of all *s* of wine................. Neh 5:18
He sent divers *s* of flies among .... Ps 78:45
and there came divers *s* of flies .... Ps 105:31
instruments, and that of all *s* .... Eccl 2:8
thy merchants in all *s* of things .... Eze 27:24   4360
them clothed with all *s* of armour .... Eze 38:4   4358

SOSIPATER (so-sip'-a-tur) See SOPATER. *A relative of Paul.*
and Lucius, and Jason, and *S*................. Rom 16:21   4989

SOSTHENES (sos'-the-neze)
1. Chief ruler of a synagogue in Corinth.
Then all the Greeks took *S*..................... Acts 18:17   4988
2. A co-worker with Paul.
will of God, and *S* our brother, ... 1Cor 1:1   4988

SOTAI (so'-tahee) *A family of Temple servants.*
the children of *S*, the children .... Ezr 2:55   5479
the children of *S*, the children .... Neh 7:57   5479

SOTTISH
they are *s* children, and they have......... Jer 4:22   5530

SOUGHT See APPENDIX.

SOUL
and man became a living *s* .... Gen 2:7   5315
my *s* shall live because of thee............... Gen 12:13   5315
that *s* shall be cut off from his................ Gen 17:14   5315
and my *s* shall live .... Gen 19:20   5315
that my *s* may bless thee before I........... Gen 27:4   5315
venison, that thy *s* may bless me............ Gen 27:19   5315
venison, that my *s* may bless thee.......... Gen 27:25   5315
venison, that my *s* may bless me .... Gen 27:31   5315
his *s* clave unto Dinah the .... Gen 34:3   5315
The *s* of my son Shechem longeth .... Gen 34:8   5315
as her *s* was in departing, (for............... Gen 35:18   5315
that we saw the anguish of his *s*............ Gen 42:21   5315
O my *s*, come not thou into their .... Gen 49:6   5315
that *s* shall be cut off from .... Ex 12:15   5315

even that *s* shall be cut off from	Ex 12:19	5315
a ransom for his *s* unto the LORD	Ex 30:12	5315
that *s* shall be cut off from	Ex 31:14	5315
saying, If a *s* shall sin through	Lev 4:2	5315
And if a *s* sin, and hear the voice	Lev 5:1	5315
Or if a *s* touch any unclean thing	Lev 5:2	5315
Or if a *s* swear, pronouncing with	Lev 5:4	5315
If a *s* commit a trespass, and sin	Lev 5:15	5315
And if a *s* sin, and commit any of	Lev 5:17	5315
If a *s* sin, and commit a trespass	Lev 6:2	5315
the *s* that eateth of it shall	Lev 7:18	5315
But the *s* that eateth of the	Lev 7:20	5315
even that *s* shall be cut off from	Lev 7:20	5315
Moreover the *s* that shall touch	Lev 7:21	5315
even that *s* shall be cut off from	Lev 7:21	5315
even the *s* that eateth it shall	Lev 7:25	5315
Whatsoever *s* it be that eateth	Lev 7:27	5315
even that *s* shall be cut off from	Lev 7:27	5315
against that *s* that eateth blood	Lev 17:10	5315
maketh an atonement for the *s*	Lev 17:11	5315
No *s* of you shall eat blood	Lev 17:12	5315
every *s* that eateth that which	Lev 17:15	5315
that *s* shall be cut off from	Lev 19:8	5315
the *s* that turneth after such as	Lev 20:6	5315
even set my face against that *s*	Lev 20:6	5315
that *s* shall be cut off from my	Lev 22:3	5315
The *s* which hath touched any such	Lev 22:6	5315
priest buy any *s* with his money	Lev 22:11	5315
For whatsoever *s* it be that shall	Lev 23:29	5315
whatsoever *s* it be that doeth any	Lev 23:30	5315
the same *s* will I destroy from	Lev 23:30	5315
and my *s* shall not abhor you	Lev 26:11	5315
or if your *s* abhor my judgments	Lev 26:15	5315
idols, and my *s* shall abhor you	Lev 26:30	5315
because their *s* abhorred my	Lev 26:43	5315
even the same *s* shall be cut off	Num 9:13	5315
But now our *s* is dried away	Num 11:6	5315
if any *s* sin through ignorance	Num 15:27	5315
for the *s* that sinneth ignorantly	Num 15:28	5315
But the *s* that doeth ought	Num 15:30	5315
that *s* shall be cut off from	Num 15:30	5315
that *s* shall utterly be cut off	Num 15:31	5315
that *s* shall be cut off from	Num 19:13	5315
that *s* shall be cut off from	Num 19:20	5315
the *s* that toucheth it shall be	Num 19:22	5315
the *s* of the people was much	Num 21:4	5315
our *s* loatheth this light bread	Num 21:5	5315
an oath to bind his *s* with a bond	Num 30:2	5315
wherewith she hath bound her *s*	Num 30:4	5315
she hath bound her *s* shall stand	Num 30:4	5315
wherewith she hath bound her *s*	Num 30:5	5315
lips, wherewith she bound her *s*	Num 30:6	5315
she bound her *s* shall stand	Num 30:7	5315
lips, wherewith she bound her *s*	Num 30:8	5315
or bound her *s* by a bond with an	Num 30:10	5315
she bound her *s* shall stand	Num 30:11	5315
or concerning the bond of her *s*	Num 30:12	5315
binding oath to afflict the *s*	Num 30:13	5315
one *s* of five hundred, both of	Num 31:28	5315
keep thy *s* diligently, lest thou	Deut 4:9	5315
all thy heart and with all thy *s*	Deut 4:29	5315
thine heart, and with all thy *s*	Deut 6:5	5315
all thy heart and with all thy *s*	Deut 10:12	5315
all your heart and with all your *s*	Deut 11:13	5315
words in your heart and in your *s*	Deut 11:18	5315
whatsoever thy *s* lusteth after	Deut 12:15	5315
because thy *s* longeth to eat	Deut 12:20	5315
whatsoever thy *s* lusteth after	Deut 12:20	5315
whatsoever thy *s* lusteth after	Deut 12:21	5315
all your heart and with all your *s*	Deut 13:3	5315
friend, which is as thine own *s*	Deut 13:6	5315
whatsoever thy *s* lusteth after	Deut 14:26	5315
or for whatsoever thy *s* desireth	Deut 14:26	5315
thine heart, and with all thy *s*	Deut 26:16	5315
thine heart, and with all thy *s*	Deut 30:2	5315
thine heart, and with all thy *s*	Deut 30:6	5315
thine heart, and with all thy *s*	Deut 30:10	5315
all your heart and with all your *s*	Josh 22:5	5315
O my *s*, thou hast trodden down	Judg 5:21	5315
his *s* was grieved for the misery	Judg 10:16	5315
so that his *s* was vexed unto	Judg 16:16	5315
And she was in bitterness of *s*	1Sa 1:10	5315
poured out my *s* before the LORD	1Sa 1:15	5315
said, Oh my lord, as thy *s* liveth	1Sa 1:26	5315
take as much as thy *s* desireth	1Sa 2:16	5315
And Abner said, As thy *s* liveth	1Sa 17:55	5315
that the *s* of Jonathan was knit	1Sa 18:1	5315
was knit with the *s* of David	1Sa 18:1	5315
Jonathan loved him as his own *s*	1Sa 18:1	5315
because he loved him as his own *s*	1Sa 18:3	5315
LORD liveth, and as thy *s* liveth	1Sa 20:3	5315
David, Whatsoever thy *s* desireth	1Sa 20:4	5315
loved him as he loved his own *s*	1Sa 20:17	5315
the desire of thy *s* to come down	1Sa 23:20	5315
yet thou huntest my *s* to take it	1Sa 24:11	5315
LORD liveth, and as thy *s* liveth	1Sa 25:26	5315
to pursue thee, and to seek thy *s*	1Sa 25:29	5315
but the *s* of my lord shall be	1Sa 25:29	5315
because my *s* was precious in	1Sa 26:21	5315
because the *s* of all the people	1Sa 30:6	5315
my *s* out of all adversity	2Sa 4:9	5315
that are hated of David's *s*	2Sa 5:8	5315
thou livest, and as thy *s* liveth	2Sa 11:11	5315
the *s* of king David longed to go	2Sa 13:39	5315
answered and said, As thy *s* liveth	2Sa 14:19	
redeemed my *s* out of all distress	1Kin 1:29	5315
their heart and with all their *s*	1Kin 2:4	5315
their heart, and with all their *s*	1Kin 8:48	5315
to all that thy *s* desireth	1Kin 11:37	5315
let this child's *s* come into him	1Kin 17:21	5315
the *s* of the child came into him	1Kin 17:22	5315
LORD liveth, and as thy *s* liveth	2Kin 2:2	5315
LORD liveth, and as thy *s* liveth	2Kin 2:4	5315
LORD liveth, and as thy *s* liveth	2Kin 2:6	5315
for her *s* is vexed within her	2Kin 4:27	5315
LORD liveth, and as thy *s* liveth	2Kin 4:30	5315
all their heart and all their *s*	2Kin 23:3	5315
all his heart, and with all his *s*	2Kin 23:25	5315
your *s* to seek the LORD your God	1Chr 22:19	5315
with all their *s* in the land of	2Chr 6:38	5315
their heart and with all their *s*	2Chr 15:12	5315
all his heart, and with all his *s*	2Chr 34:31	5315
and life unto the bitter in *s*	Job 3:20	5315
The things that my *s* refused to	Job 6:7	5315
in the bitterness of my *s*	Job 7:11	5315
So that my *s* chooseth strangling	Job 7:15	5315
yet would I not know my *s*	Job 9:21	5315
My *s* is weary of my life	Job 10:1	5315
speak in the bitterness of my *s*	Job 10:1	5315
In whose hand is the *s* of every	Job 12:10	5315
his *s* within him shall mourn	Job 14:22	5315
if your *s* were in my soul's stead	Job 16:4	5315
How long will ye vex my *s*	Job 19:2	5315
dieth in the bitterness of his *s*	Job 21:25	5315
And what his *s* desireth, even that	Job 23:13	5315
the *s* of the wounded crieth out	Job 24:12	5315
the Almighty, who hath vexed my *s*	Job 27:2	5315
when God taketh away his *s*	Job 27:8	5315
they pursue my *s* as the wind	Job 30:15	5082
now my *s* is poured out upon me	Job 30:16	5315
was not my *s* grieved for the poor	Job 30:25	5315
sin by wishing a curse to his *s*	Job 31:30	5315
keepeth back his *s* from the pit	Job 33:18	5315
bread, and his *s* dainty meat	Job 33:20	5315
his *s* draweth near unto the grave	Job 33:22	5315
He will deliver his *s* from going	Job 33:28	5315
To bring back his *s* from the pit	Job 33:30	5315
Many there be which say of my *s*	Ps 3:2	5315
My *s* is also sore vexed	Ps 6:3	5315
Return, O LORD, deliver my *s*	Ps 6:4	5315
Lest he tear my *s* like a lion	Ps 7:2	5315
Let the enemy persecute my *s*	Ps 7:5	5315
how say ye to my *s*, Flee as a	Ps 11:1	5315
that loveth violence his *s* hateth	Ps 11:5	5315
long shall I take counsel in my *s*	Ps 13:2	5315
O my *s*, thou hast said unto the	Ps 16:2	5315
thou wilt not leave my *s* in hell	Ps 16:10	5315
deliver my *s* from the wicked	Ps 17:13	5315
LORD is perfect, converting the *s*	Ps 19:7	5315
Deliver my *s* from the sword	Ps 22:20	5315
and none can keep alive his own *s*	Ps 22:29	5315
He restoreth my *s*	Ps 23:3	5315
not lifted up his *s* unto vanity	Ps 24:4	5315
thee, O LORD, do I lift up my *s*	Ps 25:1	5315
His *s* shall dwell at ease	Ps 25:13	5315
O keep my *s*, and deliver me	Ps 25:20	5315
Gather not my *s* with sinners	Ps 26:9	5315
brought up my *s* from the grave	Ps 30:3	5315
hast known my *s* in adversities	Ps 31:7	5315
is consumed with grief, yea, my *s*	Ps 31:9	5315
To deliver their *s* from death	Ps 33:19	5315
Our *s* waiteth for the LORD	Ps 33:20	5315
My *s* shall make her boast in the	Ps 34:2	5315
redeemeth the *s* of his servants	Ps 34:22	5315
say unto my *s*, I am thy salvation	Ps 35:3	5315
put to shame that seek after my *s*	Ps 35:4	5315
cause their *s* have digged for my	Ps 35:7	5315
my *s* shall be joyful in the LORD	Ps 35:9	5315
for good to the spoiling of my *s*	Ps 35:12	5315
I humbled my *s* with fasting	Ps 35:13	5315
rescue my *s* from their	Ps 35:17	5315
seek after my *s* to destroy it	Ps 40:14	5315

heal my *s* .... Ps 41:4   5315
so panteth my *s* after thee .... Ps 42:1   5315
My *s* thirsteth for God, for the .... Ps 42:2   5315
things, I pour out my *s* in me .... Ps 42:4   5315
Why art thou cast down, O my *s* .... Ps 42:5   5315
my *s* is cast down within me .... Ps 42:6   5315
Why art thou cast down, O my *s* .... Ps 42:11   5315
Why art thou cast down, O my *s* .... Ps 43:5   5315
For our *s* is bowed down to the .... Ps 44:25   5315
redemption of their *s* is precious .... Ps 49:8   5315
But God will redeem my *s* from the ...... Ps 49:15   5315
while he lived he blessed his *s* .... Ps 49:18   5315
me, and oppressors seek after my *s* ..... Ps 54:3   5315
is with them that uphold my *s* .... Ps 54:4   5315
He hath delivered my *s* in peace .... Ps 55:18   5315
my steps, when they wait for my *s* .... Ps 56:6   5315
hast delivered my *s* from death .... Ps 56:13   5315
for my *s* trusteth in thee .... Ps 57:1   5315
My *s* is among lions .... Ps 57:4   5315
my *s* is bowed down .... Ps 57:6   5315
lo, they lie in wait for my *s* .... Ps 59:3   5315
Truly my *s* waiteth upon God .... Ps 62:1   5315
My *s*, wait thou only upon God .... Ps 62:5   5315
my *s* thirsteth for thee, my flesh .... Ps 63:1   5315
My *s* shall be satisfied as with .... Ps 63:5   5315
My *s* followeth hard after thee .... Ps 63:8   5315
But those that seek my *s*, to .... Ps 63:9   5315
Which holdeth our *s* in life .... Ps 66:9   5315
what he hath done for my *s* .... Ps 66:16   5315
the waters are come in unto my *s* .... Ps 69:1   5315
and chastened my *s* with fasting .... Ps 69:10   5315
Draw nigh unto my *s*, and redeem it ..... Ps 69:18   5315
confounded that seek after my *s* .... Ps 70:2   5315
for my *s* take counsel together .... Ps 71:10   5315
that are adversaries to my *s* .... Ps 71:13   5315
and my *s*, which thou hast redeemed .... Ps 71:23   5315
shall redeem their *s* from deceit .... Ps 72:14   5315
O deliver not the *s* of thy .... Ps 74:19   5315
my *s* refused to be comforted .... Ps 77:2   5315
he spared not their *s* from death .... Ps 78:50   5315
My *s* longeth, yea, even fainteth .... Ps 84:2   5315
Preserve my *s* .... Ps 86:2   5315
Rejoice *s* of thy servant .... Ps 86:4   5315
thee, O Lord, do I lift up my *s* .... Ps 86:4   5315
my *s* from the lowest hell .... Ps 86:13   5315
men have sought after my *s* .... Ps 86:14   5315
For my *s* is full of troubles .... Ps 88:3   5315
Lord, why castest thou off my *s* .... Ps 88:14   5315
shall he deliver his *s* from the .... Ps 89:48   5315
my *s* had almost dwelt in silence .... Ps 94:17   5315
me thy comforts delight my *s* .... Ps 94:19   5315
against the *s* of the righteous .... Ps 94:21   5315
Bless the Lord, O my *s* .... Ps 103:1   5315
Bless the Lord, O my *s*, and forget .... Ps 103:2   5315
bless the Lord, O my *s* .... Ps 103:22   5315
Bless the Lord, O my *s* .... Ps 104:1   5315
Bless thou the Lord, O my *s* .... Ps 104:35   5315
but sent leanness into their *s* .... Ps 106:15   5315
thirsty, their *s* fainted in them .... Ps 107:5   5315
For he satisfieth the longing *s* .... Ps 107:9   5315
the hungry *s* with goodness .... Ps 107:9   5315
Their *s* abhorreth all manner of .... Ps 107:18   5315
their *s* is melted because of .... Ps 107:26   5315
them that speak evil against my *s* .... Ps 109:20   5315
him from those that condemn his *s* .... Ps 109:31   5315
I beseech thee, deliver my *s* .... Ps 116:4   5315
Return unto thy rest, O my *s* .... Ps 116:7   5315
hast delivered my *s* from death .... Ps 116:8   5315
My *s* breaketh for the longing .... Ps 119:20   5315
My *s* cleaveth unto the dust .... Ps 119:25   5315
My *s* melteth for heaviness .... Ps 119:28   5315
My *s* fainteth for thy salvation .... Ps 119:81   5315
My *s* is continually in my hand .... Ps 119:109   5315
therefore doth my *s* keep them .... Ps 119:129   5315
My *s* hath kept thy testimonies .... Ps 119:167   5315
Let my *s* live, and it shall praise .... Ps 119:175   5315
Deliver my *s*, O Lord, from lying .... Ps 120:2   5315
My *s* hath long dwelt with him .... Ps 120:6   5315
he shall preserve thy *s* .... Ps 121:7   5315
Our *s* is exceedingly filled with .... Ps 123:4   5315
the stream had gone over our *s* .... Ps 124:4   5315
proud waters had gone over our *s* .... Ps 124:5   5315
Our *s* is escaped as a bird out of .... Ps 124:7   5315
my *s* doth wait, and in his word do .... Ps 130:5   5315
My *s* waiteth for the Lord more .... Ps 130:6   5315
my *s* is even as a weaned child .... Ps 131:2   5315
me with strength in my *s* .... Ps 138:3   5315
that my *s* knoweth right well .... Ps 139:14   5315
leave not my *s* destitute .... Ps 141:8   5315
no man cared for my *s* .... Ps 142:4   5315
Bring my *s* out of prison, that I .... Ps 142:7   5315

the enemy hath persecuted my *s* .... Ps 143:3   5315
my *s* thirsteth after thee, as a .... Ps 143:6   5315
for I lift up my *s* unto thee .... Ps 143:8   5315
sake bring my *s* out of trouble .... Ps 143:11   5315
all them that afflict my *s* .... Ps 143:12   5315
Praise the Lord, O my *s* .... Ps 146:1   5315
knowledge is pleasant unto thy *s* .... Prov 2:10   5315
So shall they be life unto thy *s* .... Prov 3:22   5315
satisfy his *s* when he is hungry .... Prov 6:30   5315
doeth it destroyeth his own *s* .... Prov 6:32   5315
against me wrongeth his own *s* .... Prov 8:36   5315
the *s* of the righteous to famish .... Prov 10:3   5315
man doeth good to his own *s* .... Prov 11:17   5315
The liberal *s* shall be made fat .... Prov 11:25   5315
but the *s* of the transgressors .... Prov 13:2   5315
The *s* of the sluggard desireth, ... Prov 13:4   5315
but the *s* of the diligent shall .... Prov 13:4   5315
accomplished is sweet to the *s* .... Prov 13:19   5315
eateth to the satisfying of his *s* .... Prov 13:25   5315
instruction despiseth his own *s* .... Prov 15:32   5315
keepeth his way preserveth his *s* .... Prov 16:17   5315
as an honeycomb, sweet to the *s* .... Prov 16:24   5315
his lips are the snare of his *s* .... Prov 18:7   5315
that the *s* be without knowledge, ... Prov 19:2   5315
getteth wisdom loveth his own *s* .... Prov 19:8   5315
an idle *s* shall suffer hunger .... Prov 19:15   5315
the commandment keepeth his own *s* .... Prov 19:16   5315
let not thy *s* spare for his .... Prov 19:18   5315
anger sinneth against his own *s* .... Prov 20:2   5315
The *s* of the wicked desireth evil .... Prov 21:10   5315
keepeth his *s* from troubles .... Prov 21:23   5315
he that doth keep his *s* shall be .... Prov 22:5   5315
spoil the *s* of those that spoiled .... Prov 22:23   5315
his ways, and get a snare to thy *s* .... Prov 22:25   5315
and shalt deliver his *s* from hell .... Prov 23:14   5315
and he that keepeth thy *s*, doth .... Prov 24:12   5315
knowledge of wisdom be unto thy *s* ...... Prov 24:14   5315
refresheth the *s* of his masters .... Prov 25:13   5315
As cold waters to a thirsty *s* .... Prov 25:25   5315
The full *s* loatheth an honeycomb .... Prov 27:7   5315
but to the hungry *s* every bitter .... Prov 27:7   5315
but the just seek his *s* .... Prov 29:10   5315
he shall give delight unto thy *s* .... Prov 29:17   5315
with a thief hateth his own *s* .... Prov 29:24   5315
that he should make his *s* enjoy .... Eccl 2:24   5315
I labour, and bereave my *s* of good .... Eccl 4:8   5315
for his *s* of all that he desireth .... Eccl 6:2   5315
his *s* be not filled with good, and .... Eccl 6:3   5315
Which yet my *s* seeketh, but I .... Eccl 7:28   5315
Tell me, O thou whom my *s* loveth .... Song 1:7   5315
bed I sought him whom my *s* loveth ...... Song 3:1   5315
I will seek him whom my *s* loveth .... Song 3:2   5315
said, Saw ye him whom my *s* loveth ...... Song 3:3   5315
but I found him whom my *s* loveth .... Song 3:4   5315
my *s* failed when he spake .... Song 5:6   5315
my *s* made me like the chariots of .... Song 6:12   5315
your appointed feasts my *s* hateth .... Is 1:14   5315
Woe unto their *s* .... Is 3:9   5315
and of his fruitful field, both *s* .... Is 10:18   5315
desire of our *s* is to thy name .... Is 26:8   5315
With my *s* have I desired thee in .... Is 26:9   5315
but he awaketh, and his *s* is empty .... Is 29:8   5315
is faint, and his *s* hath appetite .... Is 29:8   5315
to make empty the *s* of the hungry .... Is 32:6   5315
years in the bitterness of my *s* .... Is 38:15   5315
but thou hast in love to my *s* .... Is 38:17   5315
elect, in whom my *s* delighteth .... Is 42:1   5315
that he cannot deliver his *s* .... Is 44:20   5315
which have said to thy *s*, Bow .... Is 51:23   5315
make his *s* an offering for sin .... Is 53:10   5310
shall see of the travail of his *s* .... Is 53:11   5315
hath poured out his *s* unto death .... Is 53:12   5315
let your *s* delight itself in .... Is 55:2   5315
hear, and your *s* shall live .... Is 55:3   5315
wherefore have we afflicted our *s* .... Is 58:3   5315
a day for a man to afflict his *s* .... Is 58:5   5315
thou draw out thy *s* to the hungry .... Is 58:10   5315
and satisfy the afflicted *s* .... Is 58:10   5315
and satisfy thy *s* in drought .... Is 58:11   5315
my *s* shall be joyful in my God .... Is 61:10   5315
their *s* delighteth in their .... Is 66:3   5315
the sword reacheth unto the *s* .... Jer 4:10   5315
because thou hast heard, O my *s* .... Jer 4:19   5315
for my *s* is wearied because of .... Jer 4:31   5315
shall not my *s* be avenged on such .... Jer 5:9   5315
shall not my *s* be avenged on such .... Jer 5:29   5315
lest my *s* depart from thee .... Jer 6:8   5315
shall not my *s* be avenged on such .... Jer 9:9   5315
my *s* into the hand of her enemies .... Jer 12:7   5315
my *s* shall weep in secret places .... Jer 13:17   5315
hath thy *s* lothed Zion .... Jer 14:19   5315

they have digged a pit for my *s* .... Jer 18:20 — 5315
for he hath delivered the *s* of .... Jer 20:13 — 5315
their *s* shall be as a watered .... Jer 31:12 — 5315
I will satiate the *s* of the .... Jer 31:14 — 5315
For I have satiated the weary *s* .... Jer 31:25 — 5315
replenished every sorrowful *s* .... Jer 31:25 — 5315
my whole heart and with my whole *s* .... Jer 32:41 — 5315
LORD liveth, that made us this *s* .... Jer 38:16 — 5315
then thy *s* shall live, and this .... Jer 38:17 — 5315
unto thee, and thy *s* shall live .... Jer 38:20 — 5315
his *s* shall be satisfied upon .... Jer 50:19 — 5315
and deliver every man his *s* .... Jer 51:6 — 5315
deliver ye every man his *s* from .... Jer 51:45 — 5315
things for meat to relieve the *s* .... Lam 1:11 — 5315
relieve my *s* is far from me .... Lam 1:16 — 5315
when their *s* was poured out into .... Lam 2:12 — 5315
removed my *s* far off from peace .... Lam 3:17 — 5315
My *s* hath them still in .... Lam 3:20 — 5315
LORD is my portion, saith my *s* .... Lam 3:24 — 5315
to the *s* that seeketh him....................... Lam 3:25 — 5315
hast pleaded the causes of my *s* .... Lam 3:58 — 5315
but thou hast delivered thy *s* .... Eze 3:19 — 5315
also thou hast delivered thy *s* .... Eze 3:21 — 5315
my *s* hath not been polluted................... Eze 4:14 — 5315
as the *s* of the father, so also .... Eze 18:4 — 5315
so also the *s* of the son is mine .... Eze 18:4 — 5315
the *s* that sinneth, it shall die .... Eze 18:4 — 5315
The *s* that sinneth, it shall die .... Eze 18:20 — 5315
right, he shall save his *s* alive .... Eze 18:27 — 5315
and that which your *s* pitieth................ Eze 24:21 — 5315
warning shall deliver his *s* .... Eze 33:5 — 5315
but thou hast delivered thy *s* .... Eze 33:9 — 5315
for their bread for their *s* shall .... Hos 9:4 — 5315
compassed me about, even to the *s* ...... Jonah 2:5 — 5315
When my *s* fainted within me I .... Jonah 2:7 — 5315
of my body for the sin of my *s* .... Mic 6:7 — 5315
my *s* desired the firstripe fruit............. Mic 7:1 — 5315
his *s* which is lifted up is not .... Hab 2:4 — 5315
and hast sinned against thy *s*................ Hab 2:10 — 5315
my *s* lothed them................................... Zec 11:8 — 5315
and their *s* also abhorred me................. Zec 11:8 — 5315
but are not able to kill the *s* .... Mt 10:28 — 5590
which is able to destroy both *s*........... Mt 10:28 — 5590
in whom my *s* is well pleased................ Mt 12:18 — 5590
whole world, and lose his own *s* .... Mt 16:26 — 5590
a man give in exchange for his *s* .... Mt 16:26 — 5590
all thy heart, and with all thy *s* .... Mt 22:37 — 5590
My *s* is exceeding sorrowful, even ...... Mt 26:38 — 5590
whole world, and lose his own *s* .... Mk 8:36 — 5590
a man give in exchange for his *s*........ Mk 8:37 — 5590
all thy heart, and with all thy *s* .... Mk 12:30 — 5590
understanding, and with all the *s* .... Mk 12:33 — 5590
My *s* is exceeding sorrowful unto .... Mk 14:34 — 5590
My *s* doth magnify the Lord,.................. Lk 1:46 — 5590
pierce through thy own *s* also................ Lk 2:35 — 5590
all thy heart, and with all thy *s* .... Lk 10:27 — 5590
And I will say to my *s*, *S*, thou .... Lk 12:19 — 5590
And I will say to my *s*, *S* .... Lk 12:19 — 5590
this night thy *s* shall be .... Lk 12:20 — 5590
Now is my *s* troubled .... Jn 12:27 — 5590
thou wilt not leave my *s* in hell .... Acts 2:27 — 5590
that his *s* was not left in hell, ... Acts 2:31 — 5590
And fear came upon every *s*................... Acts 2:43 — 5590
shall come to pass, that every *s* .... Acts 3:23 — 5590
were of one heart and of one *s* .... Acts 4:32 — 5590
upon every *s* of man that doeth .... Rom 2:9 — 5590
Let every *s* be subject unto the .... Rom 13:1 — 5590
man Adam was made a living *s*.............. 1Cor 15:45 — 5590
I call God for a record upon my *s*.......... 2Cor 1:23 — 5590
I pray God your whole spirit and *s*......... 1Th 5:23 — 5590
even to the dividing asunder of *s* .... Heb 4:12 — 5590
we have as an anchor of the *s*................ Heb 6:19 — 5590
my *s* shall have no pleasure in .... Heb 10:38 — 5590
believe to the saving of the *s* .... Heb 10:39 — 5590
his way shall save a *s* from death.......... Jas 5:20 — 5590
lusts, which war against the *s* .... 1Pet 2:11 — 5590
vexed his righteous *s* from day to .... 2Pet 2:8 — 5590
health, even as thy *s* prospereth .... 3Jn 2 — 5590
every living *s* died in the sea .... Rev 16:3 — 5590
the fruits that thy *s* lusted..................... Rev 18:14 — 5590

SOUL'S
if your soul were in my *s* stead .... Job 16:4 — 5315

SOULS
the *s* that they had gotten in.................. Gen 12:5 — 5315
all the *s* of his sons and his .... Gen 46:15 — 5315
bare unto Jacob, even sixteen *s*............. Gen 46:18 — 5315
all the *s* were fourteen .... Gen 46:22 — 5315
all the *s* were seven................................ Gen 46:25 — 5315
All the *s* that came with Jacob .... Gen 46:26 — 5315
all the *s* were threescore and six .... Gen 46:26 — 5315

born him in Egypt, were two *s* .... Gen 46:27 — 5315
all the *s* of the house of Jacob, ... Gen 46:27 — 5315
all the *s* that came out of the .... Ex 1:5 — 5315
the loins of Jacob were seventy *s* .... Ex 1:5 — 5315
according to the number of the *s* .... Ex 12:4 — 5315
to make an atonement for your *s* .... Ex 30:15 — 5315
to make an atonement for your *s* .... Ex 30:16 — 5315
month, ye shall afflict your *s* .... Lev 16:29 — 5315
you, and ye shall afflict your *s* .... Lev 16:31 — 5315
to make an atonement for your *s* .... Lev 17:11 — 5315
even the *s* that commit them shall .... Lev 18:29 — 5315
make your *s* abominable by beast.......... Lev 20:25 — 5315
and ye shall afflict your *s* .... Lev 23:27 — 5315
rest, and ye shall afflict your *s*.............. Lev 23:32 — 5315
these sinners against their own *s* .... Num 16:38 — 5315
and ye shall afflict your *s* .... Num 29:7 — 5315
wherewith they have bound their *s* .... Num 30:9 — 5315
for our *s* before the LORD .... Num 31:50 — 5315
all the *s* that were therein .... Josh 10:28 — 5315
all the *s* that were therein .... Josh 10:30 — 5315
all the *s* that were therein, ... Josh 10:32 — 5315
all the *s* that were therein he .... Josh 10:35 — 5315
all the *s* that were therein .... Josh 10:37 — 5315
all the *s* that were therein .... Josh 10:37 — 5315
all the *s* that were therein .... Josh 10:39 — 5315
they smote all the *s* that were .... Josh 11:11 — 5315
all your hearts and in all your *s* .... Josh 23:14 — 5315
the *s* of thine enemies, them................... 1Sa 25:29 — 5315
and shall save the *s* of the needy .... Ps 72:13 — 5315
he preserveth the *s* of his saints .... Ps 97:10 — 5315
and he that winneth *s* is wise .... Prov 11:30 — 5315
A true witness delivereth *s*.................... Prov 14:25 — 5315
me, and the *s* which I have made .... Is 57:16 — 5397
of the *s* of the poor innocents .... Jer 2:34 — 5315
and ye shall find rest for your *s* .... Jer 6:16 — 5315
procure great evil against our *s* .... Jer 26:19 — 5315
ye this great evil against your *s* .... Jer 44:7 — 5315
their meat to relieve their *s* .... Lam 1:19 — 5315
they shall not satisfy their *s* .... Eze 7:19 — 5315
head of every stature to hunt *s* .... Eze 13:18 — 5315
Will ye hunt the *s* of my people .... Eze 13:18 — 5315
will ye save the *s* alive that .... Eze 13:18 — 5315
to slay the *s* that should not die .... Eze 13:19 — 5315
to save the *s* alive that should.............. Eze 13:19 — 5315
there hunt the *s* to make them fly .... Eze 13:20 — 5315
your arms, and will let the *s* go .... Eze 13:20 — 5315
even the *s* that ye hunt to make .... Eze 13:20 — 5315
own *s* by their righteousness................ Eze 14:14 — 5315
own *s* by their righteousness................ Eze 14:20 — 5315
Behold, all *s* are mine .... Eze 18:4 — 5315
they have devoured *s* .... Eze 22:25 — 5315
to shed blood, and to destroy *s* .... Eze 22:27 — 5315
and ye shall find rest unto your *s* .... Mt 11:29 — 5590
your patience possess ye your *s*............ Lk 21:19 — 5590
unto them about three thousand *s* .... Acts 2:41 — 5590
kindred, threescore and fifteen *s* .... Acts 7:14 — 5590
Confirming the *s* of the disciples .... Acts 14:22 — 5590
you with words, subverting your *s* .... Acts 15:24 — 5590
hundred threescore and sixteen *s* .... Acts 27:37 — 5590
of God only, but also our own *s* .... 1Th 5:23 — 5590
for they watch for your *s* .... Heb 13:17 — 5590
which is able to save your *s* .... Jas 1:21 — 5590
even the salvation of your *s*................... 1Pet 1:9 — 5590
s in obeying the truth through............... 1Pet 1:22 — 5590
the Shepherd and Bishop of your *s* .... 1Pet 2:25 — 5590
eight *s* are saved by water .... 1Pet 3:20 — 5590
of their *s* to him in well doing .... 1Pet 4:19 — 5590
beguiling unstable *s*............................... 2Pet 2:14 — 5590
I saw under the altar the *s* of .... Rev 6:9 — 5590
chariots, and slaves, and *s* of men .... Rev 18:13 — 5590
I saw the *s* of them that were .... Rev 20:4 — 5590

SOUND
his *s* shall be heard when he.................. Ex 28:35 — 6963
the trumpet of the jubile to *s* on............ Lev 25:9 — 5674
s throughout all your land .... Lev 25:9 — 5674
the *s* of a shaken leaf shall.................... Lev 26:36 — 6963
blow, but ye shall not *s* an alarm........... Num 10:7 — 7321
when ye hear the *s* of the trumpet......... Josh 6:5 — 6963
people heard the *s* of the trumpet.......... Josh 6:20 — 6963
when thou hearest the *s* of a .... 2Sa 5:24 — 6963
with the *s* of the trumpet...................... 2Sa 6:15 — 6963
as ye hear the *s* of the trumpet .... 2Sa 15:10 — 6963
the earth rent with the *s* of them........... 1Kin 1:40 — 6963
Joab heard the *s* of the trumpet .... 1Kin 1:41 — 6963
Ahijah heard the *s* of her feet .... 1Kin 14:6 — 6963
for there is a *s* of abundance of............ 1Kin 18:41 — 6963
is not the *s* of his master's feet............ 2Kin 6:32 — 6963
when thou shalt hear a *s* of going .... 1Chr 14:15 — 6963
were appointed to *s* with cymbals .... 1Chr 15:19 — 8085
with *s* of the cornet, and with .... 1Chr 15:28 — 6963

but Asaph made a *s* with cymbals	1Chr 16:5	8085
for those that should make a *s*	1Chr 16:42	8085
to make one *s* to be heard in	2Chr 5:13	6963
ye hear the *s* of the trumpet	Neh 4:20	6963
A dreadful *s* is in his ears	Job 15:21	6963
and rejoice at the *s* of the organ	Job 21:12	6963
the *s* that goeth out of his mouth	Job 37:2	1899
that it is the *s* of the trumpet	Job 39:24	6963
the LORD with the *s* of a trumpet	Ps 47:5	6963
the skies sent out a *s*	Ps 77:17	6963
the people that know the joyful *s*	Ps 89:15	8643
upon the harp with a solemn *s*	Ps 92:3	1902
s of cornet make a joyful noise	Ps 98:6	6963
Let my heart be *s* in thy statutes	Ps 119:80	8549
him with the *s* of the trumpet	Ps 150:3	8629
He layeth up *s* wisdom for the	Prov 2:7	8454
keep *s* wisdom and discretion	Prov 3:21	8454
Counsel is mine, and *s* wisdom	Prov 8:14	8454
A *s* heart is the life of the	Prov 14:30	4832
when the *s* of the grinding is low	Eccl 12:4	6963
shall *s* like an harp for Moab	Is 16:11	1993
the *s* of the trumpet, the alarm	Jer 4:19	6963
hear the *s* of the trumpet	Jer 4:21	6963
Hearken to the *s* of the trumpet	Jer 6:17	6963
s of the neighing of his strong	Jer 8:16	6963
the *s* of the millstones, and the	Jer 25:10	6963
nor hear the *s* of the trumpet	Jer 42:14	6963
heart shall *s* for Moab like pipes	Jer 48:36	1993
mine heart shall *s* like pipes for	Jer 48:36	1993
A *s* of battle is in the land, and	Jer 50:22	6963
A *s* of a cry cometh from Babylon,	Jer 51:54	6963
the *s* of the cherubims' wings was	Eze 10:5	6963
the *s* of thy harps shall be no	Eze 26:13	6963
isles shake at the *s* of thy fall	Eze 26:15	6963
at the *s* of the cry of thy pilots	Eze 27:28	6963
to shake at the *s* of his fall	Eze 31:16	6963
heareth the *s* of the trumpet	Eze 33:4	6963
He heard the *s* of the trumpet, and	Eze 33:5	6963
time ye hear the *s* of the cornet	Dan 3:5	7032
people heard the *s* of the cornet	Dan 3:7	7032
shall hear the *s* of the cornet	Dan 3:10	7032
time ye hear the *s* of the cornet	Dan 3:15	7032
s an alarm in my holy mountain	Joel 2:1	7321
with the *s* of the trumpet	Amos 2:2	6963
That chant to the *s* of the viol	Amos 6:5	6310
do not *s* a trumpet before thee,	Mt 6:2	4537
with a great *s* of a trumpet	Mt 24:31	5456
he hath received him safe and *s*	Lk 15:27	5198
and thou hearest the *s* thereof	Jn 3:8	5456
suddenly there came a *s* from	Acts 2:2	2279
their *s* went into all the earth,	Rom 10:18	5353
even things without life giving *s*	1Cor 14:7	5456
the trumpet give an uncertain *s*	1Cor 14:8	5456
for the trumpet shall *s*, and the	1Cor 15:52	4537
that is contrary to *s* doctrine	1Ti 1:10	5198
power, and of love, and of a *s* mind	2Ti 1:7	4995
Hold fast the form of *s* words	2Ti 1:13	5198
they will not endure *s* doctrine	2Ti 4:3	5198
that he may be able by *s* doctrine	Titus 1:9	5198
that they may be *s* in the faith	Titus 1:13	5198
things which become *s* doctrine	Titus 2:1	5198
s in faith, in charity, in	Titus 2:2	5198
S speech, that cannot be	Titus 2:8	5199
the *s* of a trumpet, and the voice	Heb 12:19	2279
his voice as the *s* of many waters	Rev 1:15	5456
trumpets prepared themselves to *s*	Rev 8:6	4537
three angels, which are yet to *s*	Rev 8:13	4537
the *s* of their wings was as the	Rev 9:9	5456
the *s* of chariots of many horses	Rev 9:9	5456
angel, when he shall begin to *s*	Rev 10:7	4537
the *s* of a millstone shall be	Rev 18:22	5456

SOUNDED

the voice of the trumpet *s* long	Ex 19:19	
when I have *s* my father about to	1Sa 20:12	2713
the priests *s* trumpets before	2Chr 7:6	2690
the priests with the trumpets	2Chr 13:14	2690
s with trumpets, also the singers	2Chr 23:13	8628
singers sang, and the trumpeters *s*	2Chr 29:28	2690
he that *s* the trumpet was by me	Neh 4:18	8628
of thy salutation *s* in mine ears	Lk 1:44	1096
And *s*, and found it twenty fathoms	Acts 27:28	1001
they *s* again, and found it fifteen	Acts 27:28	1001
For from you *s* out the word of	1Th 1:8	1837
The first angel *s*, and there	Rev 8:7	4537
And the second angel *s*, and as it	Rev 8:8	4537
And the third angel *s*, and there	Rev 8:10	4537
And the fourth angel *s*, and the	Rev 8:12	4537
And the fifth angel *s*, and I saw a	Rev 9:1	4537
And the sixth angel *s*, and I heard	Rev 9:13	4537
And the seventh angel *s*	Rev 11:15	4537

SOUNDETH

when the trumpet *s* long, they	Ex 19:13	

SOUNDING

psalteries and harps and cymbals, *s*	1Chr 15:16	8085
and twenty priests *s* with trumpets	2Chr 5:12	2690
his priests with *s* trumpets to	2Chr 13:12	8643
him upon the high *s* cymbals	Ps 150:5	8643
the *s* of thy bowels and of thy	Is 63:15	1995
not the *s* again of the mountains	Eze 7:7	1906
charity, I am become as *s* brass	1Cor 13:1	2278

SOUNDNESS

There is no *s* in my flesh because	Ps 38:3	4974
and there is no *s* in my flesh	Ps 38:7	4974
unto the head there is no *s* in it	Is 1:6	4974
s in the presence of you all	Acts 3:16	3647

SOUNDS

they give a distinction in the *s*	1Cor 14:7	5353

SOUR

the *s* grape is ripening in the	Is 18:5	1155
The fathers have eaten a *s* grape	Jer 31:29	1155
every man that eateth the *s* grape	Jer 31:30	1155
The fathers have eaten *s* grapes	Eze 18:2	1155
Their drink is *s*	Hos 4:18	5493

SOUTH

going on still toward the *s*	Gen 12:9	5045
had, and Lot with him, into the *s*	Gen 13:1	5045
from the *s* even to Beth-el	Gen 13:3	5045
from thence toward the *s* country	Gen 20:1	5045
for he dwelt in the *s* country	Gen 24:62	5045
and to the north, and to the *s*	Gen 28:14	5045
boards on the *s* side southward	Ex 26:18	5045
of the tabernacle toward the *s*	Ex 26:35	8486
for the *s* side southward there	Ex 27:9	5045
boards for the *s* side southward	Ex 36:23	5045
on the *s* side southward the	Ex 38:9	5045
On the *s* side shall be the	Num 2:10	8486
s side shall take their journey	Num 10:6	8486
And they ascended by the *s*	Num 13:22	5045
dwell in the land of the *s*	Num 13:29	5045
Canaanite, which dwelt in the *s*	Num 21:1	5045
which dwelt in the *s* in the land	Num 33:40	5045
Then your *s* quarter shall be from	Num 34:3	5045
your *s* border shall be the	Num 34:3	5045
the *s* to the ascent of Akrabbim	Num 34:4	5045
be from the *s* to Kadesh-barnea	Num 34:4	5045
on the *s* side two thousand cubits	Num 35:5	5045
and in the vale, and in the *s*	Deut 1:7	5045
possess thou the west and the *s*	Deut 33:23	1864
And the *s*, and the plain of the	Deut 34:3	5045
country of the hills, and of the *s*	Josh 10:40	5045
and of the plains *s* of Chinneroth	Josh 11:2	5045
the hills, and all the *s* country	Josh 11:16	5045
and from the *s*, under	Josh 12:3	8486
wilderness, and in the *s* country	Josh 12:8	5045
From the *s*, all the land of the	Josh 13:4	8486
the uttermost part of the *s* coast	Josh 15:1	5045
their *s* border was from the shore	Josh 15:2	5045
it went out to the *s* side to	Josh 15:3	5045
ascended up on the *s* side unto	Josh 15:3	5045
this shall be your *s* coast	Josh 15:4	5045
which is on the *s* side of the	Josh 15:7	5045
unto the *s* side of the Jebusite	Josh 15:8	5045
for thou hast given me a *s* land	Josh 15:19	5045
abide in their coast on the *s*	Josh 18:5	5045
s side of the nether Beth-horon	Josh 18:13	5045
the *s* quarter was from the end of	Josh 18:15	5045
to the side of Jebusi on the *s*	Josh 18:16	5045
salt sea at the *s* end of Jordan	Josh 18:19	5045
this was the *s* coast	Josh 18:19	5045
to Baalath-beer, Ramath of the *s*	Josh 19:8	5045
reacheth to Zebulun on the *s* side	Josh 19:34	5045
in the mountain, and in the *s*	Judg 1:9	5045
for thou hast given me a *s* land	Judg 1:15	5045
which lieth in the *s* of Arad	Judg 1:16	5045
Shechem, and on the *s* of Lebonah	Judg 21:19	5045
arose out of a place toward the *s*	1Sa 20:41	5045
which is on the *s* of Jeshimon	1Sa 23:19	3225
in the plain on the *s* of Jeshimon	1Sa 23:24	3225
said, Against the *s* of Judah	1Sa 27:10	5045
of Judah, and against the *s* of the	1Sa 27:10	5045
against the *s* of the Kenites	1Sa 27:10	5045
the Amalekites had invaded the *s*	1Sa 30:1	5045
upon the *s* of the Cherethites	1Sa 30:14	5045
to Judah, and upon the *s* of Caleb	1Sa 30:14	5045
and to them which were in *s* Ramoth	1Sa 30:27	5045
they went out to the *s* of Judah	2Sa 24:7	5045
and three looking toward the *s*	1Kin 7:25	5045
house eastward over against the *s*	1Kin 7:39	5045

the east, west, north, and *s*	1Chr 9:24	5045
and three looking toward the *s*	2Chr 4:4	5045
the east end, over against the *s*	2Chr 4:10	5045
of the *s* of Judah, and had taken	2Chr 28:18	5045
and the chambers of the *s*	Job 9:9	8486
Out of the *s* cometh the whirlwind	Job 37:9	2315
quieteth the earth by the *s* wind	Job 37:17	1864
and stretch her wings toward the *s*	Job 39:26	8486
nor from the west, nor from the *s*	Ps 75:6	4057
power he brought in the *s* wind	Ps 78:26	8486
the *s* thou hast created them	Ps 89:12	3225
from the north, and from the *s*	Ps 107:3	3220
O Lord, as the streams in the *s*	Ps 126:4	5045
The wind goeth toward the *s*	Eccl 1:6	1864
and if the tree fall toward the *s*	Eccl 11:3	1864
and come, thou *s*	Song 4:16	8486
whirlwinds in the *s* pass through	Is 21:1	5045
The burden of the beasts of the *s*	Is 30:6	5045
and to the *s*, Keep not back	Is 43:6	8486
cities of the *s* shall be shut up	Jer 13:19	5045
from the mountains, and from the *s*	Jer 17:26	5045
valley, and in the cities of the *s*	Jer 32:44	5045
vale, and in the cities of the *s*	Jer 33:13	5045
of man, set thy face toward the *s*	Eze 20:46	8486
and drop thy word toward the *s*	Eze 20:46	1864
against the forest of the *s* field	Eze 20:46	5045
And say to the forest of the *s*	Eze 20:47	5045
all faces from the *s* to the north	Eze 20:47	5045
all flesh from the *s* to the north	Eze 21:4	5045
as the frame of a city on the *s*	Eze 40:2	5045
that he brought me toward the *s*	Eze 40:24	1864
and behold a gate toward the *s*	Eze 40:24	1864
in the inner court toward the *s*	Eze 40:27	1864
toward the *s* an hundred cubits	Eze 40:27	1864
to the inner court by the *s* gate	Eze 40:28	1864
he measured the *s* gate according	Eze 40:28	1864
their prospect was toward the *s*	Eze 40:44	1864
whose prospect is toward the *s*	Eze 40:45	1864
and another door toward the *s*	Eze 41:11	1864
s was a door in the head of the	Eze 42:12	1864
the *s* chambers, which are before	Eze 42:13	1864
He measured the *s* side, five	Eze 42:18	1864
go out by the way of the *s* gate	Eze 46:9	5045
s gate shall go forth by the way	Eze 46:9	5045
at the *s* side of the altar	Eze 47:1	5045
the *s* side southward, from Tamar	Eze 47:19	5045
this is the *s* side southward	Eze 47:19	8486
in breadth, and toward the *s* five	Eze 48:10	5045
the *s* side four thousand and five	Eze 48:16	5045
toward the *s* two hundred and fifty	Eze 48:17	5045
at the *s* side southward, the	Eze 48:28	5045
at the *s* side four thousand and	Eze 48:33	5045
exceeding great, toward the *s*	Dan 8:9	5045
the king of the *s* shall be strong	Dan 11:5	5045
s shall come to the king of the	Dan 11:6	5045
So the king of the *s* shall come	Dan 11:9	5045
the king of the *s* shall be moved	Dan 11:11	5045
up against the king of the *s*	Dan 11:14	5045
the arms of the *s* shall not	Dan 11:15	5045
king of the *s* with a great army	Dan 11:25	5045
the king of the *s* shall be	Dan 11:25	5045
return, and come toward the *s*	Dan 11:29	5045
the king of the *s* push at him	Dan 11:40	5045
they of the *s* shall possess the	Obad 19	5045
shall possess the cities of the *s*	Obad 20	5045
go forth toward the *s* country	Zec 6:6	8486
her, when men inhabited the *s*	Zec 7:7	5045
shall go with whirlwinds of the *s*	Zec 9:14	8486
north, and half of it toward the *s*	Zec 14:4	5045
Geba to Rimmon *s* of Jerusalem	Zec 14:10	5045
The queen of the *s* shall rise up	Mt 12:42	3558
The queen of the *s* shall rise up	Lk 11:31	3558
And when ye see the *s* wind blow	Lk 12:55	3558
and from the north, and from the *s*	Lk 13:29	3558
go toward the *s* unto the way that	Acts 8:26	3314
Crete, and lieth toward the *s* west	Acts 27:12	3047
when the *s* wind blew softly	Acts 27:13	3558
and after one day the *s* wind blew	Acts 28:13	3558
on the *s* three gates	Rev 21:13	3558

SOUTHWARD

where thou art northward, and *s*	Gen 13:14	5045
twenty boards on the south side *s*	Ex 26:18	8486
for the south side *s* there shall	Ex 27:9	8486
boards for the south side *s*	Ex 36:23	8486
on the south side *s* the hangings	Ex 38:9	8486
on the side of the tabernacle *s*	Ex 40:24	5045
on the side of the tabernacle *s*	Num 3:29	8486
unto them, Get you this way *s*	Num 13:17	5045
eyes westward, and northward, and *s*	Deut 3:27	8486
s was the uttermost part of the	Josh 15:1	8486

sea, from the bay that looketh *s*	Josh 15:2	5045
the coast of Edom *s* were Kabzeel	Josh 15:21	5045
the river Kanah, *s* of the river	Josh 17:9	5045
S it was Ephraim's, and northward	Josh 17:10	5045
side of Luz, which is Beth-el, *s*	Josh 18:13	5045
compassed the corner of the sea *s*	Josh 18:14	5045
that lieth before Beth-horon *s*	Josh 18:14	5045
the other *s* over against Gibeah	1Sa 14:5	5045
To Obed-edom *s*	1Chr 26:15	5045
s four a day, and toward Asuppim	1Chr 26:17	5045
And the south side *s*, from Tamar	Eze 47:19	5045
And this is the south side *s*	Eze 47:19	5045
of Gad, at the south side *s*	Eze 48:28	5045
westward, and northward, and *s*	Dan 8:4	5045

SOW

for you, and ye shall *s* the land	Gen 47:23	2232
six years thou shalt *s* thy land	Ex 23:10	2232
thou shalt not *s* thy field with	Lev 19:19	2232
Six years thou shalt *s* thy field	Lev 25:3	2232
thou shalt neither *s* thy field	Lev 25:4	2232
ye shall not *s*, neither reap that	Lev 25:11	2232
behold, we shall not *s*, nor	Lev 25:20	2232
ye shall *s* the eighth year, and	Lev 25:22	2232
ye shall *s* your seed in vain, for	Lev 26:16	2232
Thou shalt not *s* thy vineyard	Deut 22:9	2232
and in the third year *s* ye	2Kin 19:29	2232
s wickedness, reap the same	Job 4:8	2232
Then let me *s*, and let another eat	Job 31:8	2232
s the fields, and plant vineyards,	Ps 107:37	2232
They that *s* in tears shall reap	Ps 126:5	2232
observeth the wind shall not *s*	Eccl 11:4	2232
In the morning *s* thy seed	Eccl 11:6	2232
the plowman plow all day to *s*	Is 28:24	2232
that thou shalt *s* the ground	Is 30:23	2232
are ye that *s* beside all waters	Is 32:20	2232
and in the third year *s* ye	Is 37:30	2232
ground, and *s* not among thorns	Jer 4:3	2232
that I will *s* the house of Israel	Jer 31:27	2232
nor *s* seed, nor plant vineyard,	Jer 35:7	2232
I will *s* her unto me in the earth	Hos 2:23	2232
S to yourselves in righteousness,	Hos 10:12	2232
Thou shalt *s*, but thou shalt not	Mic 6:15	2232
I will *s* them among the people	Zec 10:9	2232
for they *s* not, neither do they	Mt 6:26	4687
Behold, a sower went forth to *s*	Mt 13:3	4687
didst not thou *s* good seed in thy	Mt 13:27	4687
there went out a sower to *s*	Mk 4:3	4687
A sower went out to *s* his seed	Lk 8:5	4687
for they neither *s* nor reap	Lk 12:24	4687
and reapest that thou didst not *s*	Lk 19:21	4687
down, and reaping that I did not *s*	Lk 19:22	4687
the *s* that was washed to her	2Pet 2:22	5300

SOWED

Then Isaac *s* in that land, and	Gen 26:12	2232
down the city, and *s* it with salt	Judg 9:45	2232
And when he *s*, some seeds fell by	Mt 13:4	4687
which *s* good seed in his field	Mt 13:24	4687
s tares among the wheat, and went	Mt 13:25	4687
a man took, and *s* in his field	Mt 13:31	4687
The enemy that *s* them is the	Mt 13:39	4687
knewest that I reap where I *s* not	Mt 25:26	4687
And it came to pass, as he *s*	Mk 4:4	4687
and as he *s*, some fell by the way	Lk 8:5	4687

SOWEDST

came out, where thou *s* thy seed	Deut 11:10	2232

SOWER

that it may give seed to the *s*	Is 55:10	2232
Cut off the *s* from Babylon, and	Jer 50:16	2232
Behold, a *s* went forth to sow	Mt 13:3	4687
ye therefore the parable of the *s*	Mt 13:18	4687
Behold, there went out a *s* to sow	Mk 4:3	4687
The *s* soweth the word	Mk 4:14	4687
A *s* went out to sow his seed	Lk 8:5	4687
s both minister bread for your	2Cor 9:10	4687

SOWEST

fool, that which thou *s* is not	1Cor 15:36	4687
And that which thou *s*	1Cor 15:37	4687
thou *s* not that body that shall	1Cor 15:37	4687

SOWETH

he *s* discord	Prov 6:14	7971
he that *s* discord among brethren	Prov 6:19	7971
but to him that *s* righteousness	Prov 11:18	2232
A froward man *s* strife	Prov 16:28	7971
He that *s* iniquity shall reap	Prov 22:8	2232
treader of grapes him that *s* seed	Amos 9:13	4900
He that *s* the good seed is the	Mt 13:37	4687
The sower *s* the word	Mk 4:14	4687
that both he that *s* and he that	Jn 4:36	4687

S

herein is that saying true, One *s* .... Jn 4:37   4687
He which *s* sparingly shall reap 2Cor 9:6   4687
he which *s* bountifully shall reap 2Cor 9:6   4687
for whatsoever a man *s*, that .... Gal 6:7   4687
For he that *s* to his flesh shall .... Gal 6:8   4687
but he that *s* to the Spirit shall .... Gal 6:8   4687

SOWING
any *s* seed which is to be sown .... Lev 11:37   2221
shall reach unto the *s* time .... Lev 26:5   2233

SOWN
which thou hast *s* in the field .... Ex 23:16   2232
any sowing seed which is to be *s* .... Lev 11:37   2232
which is neither eared nor *s* .... Deut 21:4   2232
of thy seed which thou hast *s* .... Deut 22:9   2232
and burning, that it is not *s* .... Deut 29:23   2232
And so it was, when Israel had *s* .... Judg 6:3   2232
Light is *s* for the righteous, and .... Ps 97:11   2232
every thing *s* by the brooks, ... Is 19:7   4218
yea, they shall not be *s* .... Is 40:24   2232
that are *s* in it to spring forth .... Is 61:11   2221
in a land that was not *s* .... Jer 2:2   2232
They have *s* wheat, but shall reap .... Jer 12:13   2232
you, and ye shall be tilled and *s* .... Eze 36:9   2232
For they have *s* the wind, and they .... Hos 8:7   2232
that no more of thy name be *s* .... Nah 1:14   2232
Ye have *s* much, and bring in .... Hag 1:6   2232
that which was *s* in his heart .... Mt 13:19   *4687*
reaping where thou hast not *s* .... Mt 25:24   *4687*
the way side, where the word is *s* .... Mk 4:15   *4687*
word that was *s* in their hearts .... Mk 4:15   *4687*
which are *s* on stony ground .... Mk 4:16   *4687*
are they which are *s* among thorns .... Mk 4:18   *4687*
they which are *s* on good ground .... Mk 4:20   *4687*
when it is *s* in the earth, is .... Mk 4:31   *4687*
But when it is *s*, it groweth up, ... Mk 4:32   *4687*
If we have *s* unto you spiritual 1Cor 9:11   *4687*
It is *s* in corruption 1Cor 15:42   *4687*
It is *s* in dishonour 1Cor 15:43   *4687*
it is *s* in weakness 1Cor 15:43   *4687*
It is *s* a natural body 1Cor 15:44   *4687*
food, and multiply your seed *s* 2Cor 9:10
is *s* in peace of them that make .... Jas 3:18   *4687*

SPACE
abode with him the *s* of a month .... Gen 29:14   3117
put a *s* betwixt drove and drove .... Gen 32:16   7305
the *s* of the seven sabbaths of .... Lev 25:8   3117
within the *s* of a full year .... Lev 25:30   4390
the *s* in which we came from .... Deut 2:14   3117
there shall be a *s* between you .... Josh 3:4   7350
a great *s* being between them 1Sa 26:13   4725
now for a little *s* grace hath .... Ezr 9:8   7281
within the *s* of two full years .... Jer 28:11   5750
The *s* also before the little .... Eze 40:12   1366
the *s* was one cubit on that side .... Eze 40:12   1366
about the *s* of one hour after .... Lk 22:59   *1339*
it was about the *s* of three hours .... Acts 5:7   *1292*
put the apostles forth a little *s* .... Acts 5:34   *1024*
sacrifices by the *s* of forty .... Acts 7:42
about the *s* of four hundred .... Acts 13:20
Benjamin, by the *s* of forty years .... Acts 13:21
after they had tarried there a *s* .... Acts 15:33   *5550*
boldly for the *s* of three months .... Acts 19:8   *1909*
continued by the *s* of two years .... Acts 19:10   *1909*
the *s* of two hours cried out .... Acts 19:34   *1909*
that by the *s* of three years I .... Acts 20:31   *4158*
the earth by the *s* of three years .... Jas 5:17
I gave her *s* to repent of her .... Rev 2:21   *5550*
about the *s* of half an hour .... Rev 8:1
by the *s* of a thousand and six .... Rev 14:20   575
he must continue a short *s* .... Rev 17:10

SPAIN (*spane*) *Land at the western extremity of the Mediterranean Sea.*
I take my journey into *S*, I will .... Rom 15:24   *4681*
fruit, I will come by you into *S* .... Rom 15:28   *4681*

SPAKE See APPENDIX.

SPAKEST See APPENDIX.

SPAN
a *s* shall be the length thereof, ... Ex 28:16   2239
a *s* shall be the breadth thereof .... Ex 28:16   2239
a *s* was the length thereof, and a .... Ex 39:9   2239
a *s* the breadth thereof, being .... Ex 39:9   2239
height was six cubits and a *s* 1Sa 17:4   2239
and meted out heaven with the *s* .... Is 40:12   2239
fruit, and children of a *s* long .... Lam 2:20   2949
thereof round about shall be a *s* .... Eze 43:13   2239

SPANNED
my right hand hath *s* the heavens .... Is 48:13   2946

SPARE
not *s* the place for the fifty .... Gen 18:24   5375
then I will *s* all the place for .... Gen 18:26   5375
pity him, neither shalt thou *s* .... Deut 13:8   2550
The Lord will not *s* him, but then .... Deut 29:20   5545
all that they have, and *s* them not 1Sa 15:3   2550
s me according to the greatness .... Neh 13:22   2347
let him not *s* .... Job 6:10   2550
my reins asunder, and doth not *s* .... Job 16:13   2550
Though he *s* it, and forsake it not .... Job 20:13   2550
God shall cast upon him, and not *s* .... Job 27:22   2550
me, and *s* not to spit in my face .... Job 30:10   2820
O *s* me, that I may recover .... Ps 39:13   8159
He shall *s* the poor and needy, and .... Ps 72:13   2347
therefore he will not *s* in the .... Prov 6:34   2550
let not thy soul *s* for his crying .... Prov 19:18   5375
no man shall *s* his brother .... Is 9:19   2550
their eye shall not *s* children .... Is 13:18   2347
he shall not *s* .... Is 30:14   2550
s not, lengthen thy cords, and .... Is 54:2   2820
s not, lift up thy voice like a .... Is 58:1   2820
I will not pity, nor *s*, nor have .... Jer 13:14   2347
he shall not *s* them, neither have .... Jer 21:7   2347
bow, shoot at her, *s* no arrows .... Jer 50:14   2550
and *s* ye not her young men .... Jer 51:3   2550
neither shall mine eye *s*, neither .... Eze 5:11   2347
And mine eye shall not *s* thee .... Eze 7:4   2347
And mine eye shall not *s*, neither .... Eze 7:9   2347
mine eye shall not *s*, neither .... Eze 8:18   2347
let not your eye *s*, neither have .... Eze 9:5   2347
for me also, mine eye shall not *s* .... Eze 9:10   2347
not go back, neither will I *s* .... Eze 24:14   2347
S thy people, O Lord, and give not .... Joel 2:17   2347
And should not I *s* Nineveh .... Jonah 4:11   2347
not *s* continually to slay the .... Hab 1:17   2550
and I will *s* them, as a man .... Mal 3:17   2550
have bread enough and to *s* .... Lk 15:17   *4052*
take heed lest he also *s* not thee .... Rom 11:21   *5339*
but I *s* you 1Cor 7:28   *5339*
that to *s* you I came not as yet 2Cor 1:23   *5339*
if I come again, I will not *s* 2Cor 13:2   *5339*

SPARED
But Saul and the people *s* Agag 1Sa 15:9   2550
for the people *s* the best of the 1Sa 15:15   2550
but mine eye *s* thee 1Sa 24:10   2347
he *s* to take their own flock and 2Sa 12:4   2550
But the king *s* Mephibosheth 2Sa 21:7   2550
my master hath *s* Naaman this 2Kin 5:20   2820
he *s* not their soul from death, ... Ps 78:50   2820
Nevertheless mine eye *s* them from .... Eze 20:17   2347
He that *s* not his own Son, but .... Rom 8:32   *5339*
For if God *s* not the natural .... Rom 11:21   *5339*
For if God *s* not the angels that 2Pet 2:4   *5339*
s not the old world, but saved 2Pet 2:5   *5339*

SPARETH
He that *s* his rod hateth his son .... Prov 13:24   2820
that hath knowledge *s* his words .... Prov 17:27   2820
but the righteous giveth and *s* not .... Prov 21:26   2820
as a man *s* his own son that .... Mal 3:17   2550

SPARING
in among you, not *s* the flock .... Acts 20:29   *5339*

SPARINGLY
He which soweth *s* shall reap also 2Cor 9:6   *5340*
shall reap also *s* 2Cor 9:6   *5340*

SPARK
the *s* of his fire shall not shine .... Job 18:5   7632
as tow, and the maker of it as a *s* .... Is 1:31   5213

SPARKLED
they *s* like the colour of .... Eze 1:7   5340

SPARKS
unto trouble, as the *s* fly upward .... Job 5:7   1121,7565
lamps, and *s* of fire leap out .... Job 41:19   3590
compass yourselves about with *s* .... Is 50:11   2131
in the *s* that ye have kindled .... Is 50:11   2131

SPARROW
the *s* hath found an house, and the .... Ps 84:3   6833
am as a *s* alone upon the house .... Ps 102:7   6833

SPARROWS
Are not two *s* sold for a farthing .... Mt 10:29   *4765*
ye are of more value than many *s* .... Mt 10:31   *4765*
Are not five *s* sold for two .... Lk 12:6   *4765*
ye are of more value than many *s* .... Lk 12:7   *4765*

SPAT
he *s* on the ground, and made clay .... Jn 9:6   *4429*

SPEAK See APPENDIX.

SPEAKER

Let not an evil *s* be established	Ps 140:11	376,3956
because he was the chief *s*	Acts 14:12	3056

SPEAKEST See APPENDIX.

SPEAKETH See APPENDIX.

SPEAKING See APPENDIX.

SPEAKINGS

and envies, and all evil *s*	1Pet 2:1	2636

SPEAR

Stretch out the *s* that is in thy	Josh 8:18	3591
Joshua stretched out the *s* that..............	Josh 8:18	3591
wherewith he stretched out the *s*	Josh 8:26	3591
was there a shield or *s* seen	Judg 5:8	7420
there was neither sword nor *s*	1Sa 13:22	2595
the staff of his *s* was like a	1Sa 17:7	2595
to me with a sword, and with a *s*	1Sa 17:45	2595
LORD saveth not with sword and *s*	1Sa 17:47	2595
here under thine hand *s* or sword	1Sa 21:8	2595
having his *s* in his hand, and all	1Sa 22:6	2595
his *s* stuck in the ground at his	1Sa 26:7	2595
with the *s* even to the earth at	1Sa 26:8	2595
take thou now the *s* that is at	1Sa 26:11	2595
So David took the *s* and the cruse	1Sa 26:12	2595
And now see where the king's *s* is	1Sa 26:16	2595
and said, Behold the king's *s*	1Sa 26:22	2595
behold, Saul leaned upon his *s*	2Sa 1:6	2595
with the hinder end of the *s*	2Sa 2:23	2595
that the *s* came out behind him	2Sa 2:23	2595
the weight of whose *s* weighed.............	2Sa 21:16	7013
the staff of whose *s* was like a	2Sa 21:19	2595
with iron and the staff of a *s*	2Sa 23:7	2595
he lift up his *s* against eight	2Sa 23:8	
he lifted up his *s* against three	2Sa 23:18	2595
the Egyptian had a *s* in his hand	2Sa 23:21	2595
and plucked the *s* out of the	2Sa 23:21	2595
hand, and slew him with his own *s*	2Sa 23:21	2595
he lifted up his *s* against three	1Chr 11:11	2595
for lifting up his *s* against	1Chr 11:20	2595
hand was a *s* like a weaver's beam.......	1Chr 11:23	2595
and plucked the *s* out of the	1Chr 11:23	2595
hand, and slew him with his own *s*.......	1Chr 11:23	2595
s were six thousand and eight...............	1Chr 12:24	7420
s thirty and seven thousand...................	1Chr 12:34	2595
whose *s* staff was like a weaver's........	1Chr 20:5	2595
forth to war, that could handle *s*	2Chr 25:5	7420
against him, the glittering *s*	Job 39:23	2595
the *s*, the dart, nor the	Job 41:26	2595
he laugheth at the shaking of a *s*	Job 41:29	3591
Draw out also the *s*, and stop the	Ps 35:3	2595
bow, and cutteth the *s* in sunder...........	Ps 46:9	2595
They shall lay hold on bow and *s*...........	Jer 6:23	3591
bright sword and the glittering *s*	Nah 3:3	2595
the shining of thy glittering *s*	Hab 3:11	2595
with a *s* pierced his side	Jn 19:34	3057

SPEARMEN

Rebuke the company of *s*, the	Ps 68:30	7070
s two hundred, at the third hour	Acts 23:23	1187

SPEAR'S

his *s* head weighed six hundred..............	1Sa 17:7	2595

SPEARS

the Hebrews make them swords or *s*......	1Sa 13:19	2595
the priest give king David's *s*	2Kin 11:10	2595
several city he put shields and *s*	2Chr 11:12	7420
of men that bare targets and *s*	2Chr 14:8	7420
to the captains of hundreds *s*.................	2Chr 23:9	2595
all the host shields, and *s*	2Chr 26:14	7420
with their swords, their *s*	Neh 4:13	7420
half of them held both the *s*	Neh 4:16	7420
half of them held the *s* from the.............	Neh 4:21	7420
or his head with fish *s*	Job 41:7	6767
sons of men, whose teeth are *s*	Ps 57:4	2595
their *s* into pruninghooks	Is 2:4	2595
furbish the *s*, and put on the	Jer 46:4	7420
and the handstaves, and the *s*	Eze 39:9	7420
and your pruninghooks into *s*	Joel 3:10	7420
their *s* into pruninghooks	Mic 4:3	2595

SPECIAL

to be a *s* people unto himself	Deut 7:6	5459
God wrought *s* miracles by the		
....	Acts 19:11	3756,3858,5177

SPECIALLY

S the day that thou stoodest	Deut 4:10	
s before thee, O king Agrippa,...............	Acts 26:26	3122
all men, *s* of those that believe...............	1Ti 4:10	3122
s for those of his own house, he	1Ti 5:8	3122

s they of the circumcision........................	Titus 1:10	3122
s to me, but how much more unto	Philem 16	3122

SPECKLED

removing from thence all the *s*	Gen 30:32	5348
the spotted and *s* among the goats	Gen 30:32	5348
every one that is not *s* and	Gen 30:33	5348
and all the she goats that were *s*	Gen 30:35	5348
forth cattle ringstraked, *s*......................	Gen 30:39	5348
thus, The *s* shall be thy wages	Gen 31:8	5348
then all the cattle bare *s*	Gen 31:8	5348
the cattle were ringstraked, *s*	Gen 31:10	5348
the cattle are ringstraked, *s*	Gen 31:12	5348
heritage is unto me as a *s* bird..............	Jer 12:9	6641
him were there red horses, *s*..................	Zec 1:8	8320

SPECTACLE

we are made a *s* unto the world.............	1Cor 4:9	2302

SPED

Have they not *s*.....................................	Judg 5:30	4672

SPEECH

of Lamech, hearken unto my *s*................	Gen 4:23	565
was of one language, and of one *s*	Gen 11:1	1697
not understand one another's *s*	Gen 11:7	8193
but I am slow of *s*, and of a slow	Ex 4:10	6310
give occasions of *s* against her	Deut 22:14	1697
given occasions of *s* against her	Deut 22:17	1697
my *s* shall distil as the dew, as	Deut 32:2	565
To fetch about this form of *s*	2Sa 14:20	1697
seeing the *s* of all Israel is....................	2Sa 19:11	1697
the *s* pleased the Lord, that	1Kin 3:10	1697
s unto the people of Jerusalem	2Chr 32:18	3066
spake half in the *s* of Ashdod.................	Neh 13:24	3066
removeth away the *s* of the trusty	Job 12:20	8193
Hear diligently my *s*, and my	Job 13:17	4405
Hear diligently my *s*, and let this...........	Job 21:2	4405
liar, and make my *s* nothing worth.........	Job 24:25	4405
and my *s* dropped upon them	Job 29:22	4405
order our *s* by reason of darkness	Job 37:19	
thine ear unto me, and hear my *s*	Ps 17:6	565
Day unto day uttereth *s*, and night........	Ps 19:2	562
There is no *s* nor language, where..........	Ps 19:3	562
With her much fair *s* she caused	Prov 7:21	3948
Excellent *s* becometh not a fool	Prov 17:7	8193
of scarlet, and thy *s* is comely	Song 4:3	4057
hearken, and hear my *s*........................	Is 28:23	565
thy *s* shall be low out of the	Is 29:4	565
thy *s* shall whisper out of the	Is 29:4	565
give ear unto my *s*	Is 32:9	565
a people of a deeper *s* than thou	Is 33:19	8193
use this *s* in the land of Judah	Jer 31:23	1697
of the Almighty, the voice of *s*	Eze 1:24	1999
sent to a people of a strange *s*	Eze 3:5	8193
Not to many people of a strange *s*.........	Eze 3:6	8193
O LORD, I have heard thy *s*.....................	Hab 3:2	8088
for thy *s* bewrayeth thee	Mt 26:73	2981
and had an impediment in his *s*	Mk 7:32	3424
and thy *s* agreeth thereto	Mk 14:70	2981
Why do ye not understand my *s*.........	Jn 8:43	2981
saying in the *s* of Lycaonia....................	Acts 14:11	3072
continued his *s* until midnight	Acts 20:7	3056
with excellency of *s* or of wisdom	1Cor 2:1	3056
And my *s* and my preaching was not.....	1Cor 2:4	3056
not the *s* of them which are...................	1Cor 4:19	3056
hope, we use great plainness of *s*	2Cor 3:12	
is my boldness of *s* toward you	2Cor 7:4	
is weak, and his *s* contemptible	2Cor 10:10	3056
But though I be rude in *s*	2Cor 11:6	3056
Let your *s* be alway with grace,.............	Col 4:6	3056
Sound *s*, that cannot be condemned	Titus 2:8	3056

SPEECHES

even apparently, and not in dark *s*	Num 12:8	2420
the *s* of one that is desperate, ...	Job 6:26	561
or with *s* wherewith he can do no	Job 15:3	4405
will I answer him with your *s*	Job 32:14	561
Job, I pray thee, hear my *s*	Job 33:1	4405
fair *s* deceive the hearts of the..............	Rom 16:18	2129
of all their hard *s* which ungodly...........	Jude 15	

SPEECHLESS

And he was *s*	Mt 22:12	5392
beckoned unto them, and remained *s*	Lk 1:22	2974
which journeyed with him stood *s*	Acts 9:7	1769

SPEED

thee, send me good *s* this day	Gen 24:12	7136
cried after the lad, Make *s*	1Sa 20:38	4120
make *s* to depart, lest he	2Sa 15:14	4116
s to get him up to his chariot................	1Kin 12:18	553
But king Rehoboam made *s* to get	2Chr 10:18	553
let it be done with *s*.............................	Ezr 6:12	629

S

That say, Let him make s, and	Is 5:19	4116
they shall come with s swiftly	Is 5:26	4120
for to come to him with all s	Acts 17:15	5613,5033
your house, neither bid him God s	2Jn 10	5463
For he that biddeth him God s is	2Jn 11	5463

SPEEDILY

Then they s took down every man	Gen 44:11	4116
for me than that I should s	1Sa 27:1	4422
the wilderness, but s pass over	2Sa 17:16	5674
divided them s among all the	2Chr 35:13	
the king had sent, so they did s	Ezr 6:13	629
That thou mayest buy s with this	Ezr 7:17	629
require of you, it be done s	Ezr 7:21	629
judgment be executed s upon him	Ezr 7:26	629
he s gave her her things for	Est 2:9	926
deliver me s	Ps 31:2	4120
hear me s	Ps 69:17	4118
thy tender mercies s prevent us	Ps 79:8	4118
the day when I call answer me s	Ps 102:2	4118
Hear me s, O Lord	Ps 143:7	4118
an evil work is not executed s	Eccl 8:11	4120
thine health shall spring forth s	Is 58:8	4120
s will I return your recompence	Joel 3:4	4120
Let us go s to pray before the	Zec 8:21	1980
you that he will avenge them s	Lk 18:8	1722,5034

SPEEDY

for he shall make even a s	Zeph 1:18	926

SPEND

I will s mine arrows upon them	Deut 32:23	3615
They s their days in wealth, and	Job 21:13	3615
they shall s their days in	Job 36:11	3615
we s our years as a tale that is	Ps 90:9	3615
Wherefore do ye s money for that	Is 55:2	8254
he would not s the time in Asia	Acts 20:16	5551
And I will very gladly s and be	2Cor 12:15	1159

SPENDEST

and whatsoever thou s more	Lk 10:35	4325

SPENDETH

but a foolish man s it up	Prov 21:20	1104
with harlots s his substance	Prov 29:3	6
vain life which he s as a shadow	Eccl 6:12	6213

SPENT

And the water was s in the bottle	Gen 21:15	3615
my lord, how that our money is s	Gen 47:18	8552
your strength shall be s in vain	Lev 26:20	8552
were by Jebus, the day was far s	Judg 19:11	7286
for the bread is s in our vessels	1Sa 9:7	235
shuttle, and are s without hope	Job 7:6	3615
For my life is s with grief	Ps 31:10	3615
I have s my strength for nought,	Is 49:4	3615
all the bread in the city were s	Jer 37:21	8552
had s all that she had, and was	Mk 5:26	1159
And when the day was now far s	Mk 6:35	
which had s all her living upon	Lk 8:43	4321
And when he had s all, there arose	Lk 15:14	1159
evening, and the day is far s	Lk 24:29	2827
s their time in nothing else	Acts 17:21	2119
after he had s some time there,	Acts 18:23	4160
Now when much time was s, and when	Acts 27:9	1230
The night is far s, the day is at	Rom 13:12	4298
very gladly spend and be s for you	2Cor 12:15	1550

SPEWING

shameful s shall be on thy glory	Hab 2:16	7022

SPICE

And s, and oil for the light, and	Ex 35:28	1314
the traffick of the s merchants	1Kin 10:15	7402
neither was there any such s as	2Chr 9:9	1314
have gathered my myrrh with my s	Song 5:1	1313
s it well, and let the bones out	Eze 24:10	7543

SPICED

of s wine of the juice of my	Song 8:2	7544

SPICERY

with their camels bearing s	Gen 37:25	5219

SPICES

little balm, and a little honey, s	Gen 43:11	5219
s for anointing oil, and for sweet	Ex 25:6	1314
s of pure myrrh five hundred	Ex 30:23	1314
Moses, Take unto thee sweet s	Ex 30:34	5561
these sweet s with pure	Ex 30:34	5561
s for anointing oil, and for the	Ex 35:8	1314
and the pure incense of sweet s	Ex 37:29	5561
train, with camels that bare s	1Kin 10:2	1314
of s very great store, and	1Kin 10:10	1314
of s as these which the queen of	1Kin 10:10	1314
and garments, and armour, and s	1Kin 10:25	1314

the silver, and the gold, and the s	2Kin 20:13	1314
and the frankincense, and the s	1Chr 9:29	1314
made the ointment of the s	1Chr 9:30	1314
company, and camels that bare s	2Chr 9:1	1314
of s great abundance, and precious	2Chr 9:9	1314
gold, and raiment, harness, and s	2Chr 9:24	1314
divers kinds of s prepared by the	2Chr 16:14	
and for precious stones, and for s	2Chr 32:27	1314
of thine ointments than all s	Song 4:10	1314
and aloes, with all the chief s	Song 4:14	1314
that the s thereof may flow out	Song 4:16	1314
His cheeks are as a bed of s	Song 5:13	1314
into his garden, to the beds of s	Song 6:2	1314
hart upon the mountains of s	Song 8:14	1314
the silver, and the gold, and the s	Is 39:2	1314
in thy fairs with chief of all s	Eze 27:22	1314
and Salome, had bought sweet s	Mk 16:1	759
And they returned, and prepared s	Lk 23:56	759
bringing the s which they had	Lk 24:1	759
it in linen clothes with the s	Jn 19:40	759

SPIDER

The s taketh hold with her hands,	Prov 30:28	8079

SPIDER'S

and whose trust shall be a s web	Job 8:14	5908
eggs, and weave the s web	Is 59:5	5908

SPIED

he s an Egyptian smiting an	Ex 2:11	7200
men that had s out the country	Josh 6:22	7270
he s the company of Jehu as he	2Kin 9:17	7200
behold, they s a band of men	2Kin 13:21	7200
he s the sepulchres that were	2Kin 23:16	7200
that were s in the land of Judah	2Kin 23:24	7200

SPIES

them, and said unto them, Ye are s	Gen 42:9	7270
true men, thy servants are no s	Gen 42:11	7270
spake unto you, saying, Ye are s	Gen 42:14	7270
life of Pharaoh surely ye are s	Gen 42:16	7270
took us for s of the country	Gen 42:30	7270
we are no s	Gen 42:31	7270
shall I know that ye are no s	Gen 42:34	7270
Israel came by the way of the s	Num 21:1	871
the young men that were s went in	Josh 6:23	7270
the s saw a man come forth out of	Judg 1:24	8104
David therefore sent out s	1Sa 26:4	7270
But Absalom sent s throughout all	2Sa 15:10	7270
they watched him, and sent forth s	Lk 20:20	1455
she had received the s with peace	Heb 11:31	2685

SPIKENARD

my s sendeth forth the smell	Song 1:12	5373
camphire, with s,	Song 4:13	5373
S and saffron	Song 4:14	5373
of ointment of s very precious	Mk 14:3	3487,4101
Mary a pound of ointment of s	Jn 12:3	3487,4101

SPILLED

that he s it on the ground, lest	Gen 38:9	7843
the bottles, and the wine is s	Mk 2:22	1632
will burst the bottles, and be s	Lk 5:37	1632

SPILT

are as water s on the ground,	2Sa 14:14	5064

SPIN

hearted did s with their hands	Ex 35:25	2901
they toil not, neither do they s	Mt 6:28	3514
they toil not, they s not	Lk 12:27	3514

SPINDLE

She layeth her hands to the s	Prov 31:19	3601

SPIRIT

the S of God moved upon the face	Gen 1:2	7307
My s shall not always strive with	Gen 6:3	7307
morning that his s was troubled	Gen 41:8	7307
is, a man in whom the S of God is	Gen 41:38	7307
the s of Jacob their father	Gen 45:27	7307
not unto Moses for anguish of s	Ex 6:9	7307
have filled with the s of wisdom	Ex 28:3	7307
have filled him with the s of God	Ex 31:3	7307
every one whom his s made willing	Ex 35:21	7307
hath filled him with the s of God	Ex 35:31	7307
or woman that hath a familiar s	Lev 20:27	178
the s of jealousy come upon him,	Num 5:14	7307
or if the s of jealousy come upon	Num 5:14	7307
Or when the s of jealousy cometh	Num 5:30	7307
take of the s which is upon thee	Num 11:17	7307
took of the s that was upon him,	Num 11:25	7307
when the s rested upon them, they	Num 11:25	7307
and the s rested upon them	Num 11:26	7307
Lord would put his s upon them,	Num 11:29	7307
because he had another s with him	Num 14:24	7307

the *s* of God came upon him	Num 24:2	7307
of Nun, a man in whom is the *s*	Num 27:18	7307
the LORD thy God hardened his *s*	Deut 2:30	7307
Nun was full of the *s* of wisdom	Deut 34:9	7307
was there *s* in them any more	Josh 5:1	7307
the *s* of the LORD came upon him,	Judg 3:10	7307
But the *S* of the LORD came upon	Judg 6:34	7307
sent an evil *s* between Abimelech	Judg 9:23	7307
Then the *S* of the LORD came upon	Judg 11:29	7307
the *S* of the LORD began to move	Judg 13:25	7307
the *S* of the LORD came mightily	Judg 14:6	7307
the *s* of the LORD came upon him,	Judg 14:19	7307
the *S* of the LORD came mightily	Judg 15:14	7307
his *s* came again, and he revived	Judg 15:19	7307
I am a woman of a sorrowful *s*	1Sa 1:15	7307
the *S* of the LORD will come upon	1Sa 10:6	7307
the *S* of God came upon him, and he	1Sa 10:10	7307
the *S* of God came upon Saul when	1Sa 11:6	7307
the *S* of the LORD came upon David	1Sa 16:13	7307
But the *S* of the LORD departed	1Sa 16:14	7307
an evil *s* from God troubled	1Sa 16:14	7307
an evil *s* from God troubleth thee	1Sa 16:15	7307
when the evil *s* from God is upon	1Sa 16:16	7307
when the evil *s* from God was upon	1Sa 16:23	7307
the evil *s* departed from him	1Sa 16:23	7307
that the evil *s* from God came	1Sa 18:10	7307
the evil *s* from the LORD was upon	1Sa 19:9	7307
the *S* of God was upon the	1Sa 19:20	7307
the *S* of God was upon him also,	1Sa 19:23	7307
me a woman that hath a familiar *s*	1Sa 28:7	178
that hath a familiar *s* at En-dor	1Sa 28:7	178
divine unto me by the familiar *s*	1Sa 28:8	178
eaten, his *s* came again to him	1Sa 30:12	7307
The *S* of the LORD spake by me, and	2Sa 23:2	7307
there was no more *s* in her	1Kin 10:5	7307
that the *S* of the LORD shall	1Kin 18:12	7307
unto him, Why is thy *s* so sad	1Kin 21:5	7307
And there came forth a *s*, and stood	1Kin 22:21	7307
I will be a lying *s* in the mouth	1Kin 22:22	7307
the LORD hath put a lying *s* in	1Kin 22:23	7307
Which way went the *S* of the LORD	1Kin 22:24	7307
portion of thy *s* be upon me	2Kin 2:9	7307
The *s* of Elijah doth rest on	2Kin 2:15	7307
lest peradventure the *S* of the	2Kin 2:16	7307
up the *s* of Pul king of Assyria	1Chr 5:26	7307
the *s* of Tilgath-pilneser king of	1Chr 5:26	7307
of one that had a familiar *s*	1Chr 10:13	178
Then the *s* came upon Amasai, who	1Chr 12:18	7307
of all that he had by the *s*	1Chr 28:12	7307
there was no more *s* in her	2Chr 9:4	7307
the *S* of God came upon Azariah	2Chr 15:1	7307
Then there came out a *s*, and stood	2Chr 18:20	7307
be a lying *s* in the mouth of all	2Chr 18:21	7307
lying *s* in the mouth of these thy	2Chr 18:22	7307
Which way went the *S* of the LORD	2Chr 18:23	7307
came the *S* of the LORD in the	2Chr 20:14	7307
Jehoram the *s* of the Philistines	2Chr 21:16	7307
the *S* of God came upon Zechariah	2Chr 24:20	7307
and dealt with a familiar *s*	2Chr 33:6	178
up the *s* of Cyrus king of Persia	2Chr 36:22	7307
up the *s* of Cyrus king of Persia	Ezr 1:1	7307
all them whose *s* God had raised	Ezr 1:5	7307
also thy good *s* to instruct them	Neh 9:20	7307
them by thy *s* in thy prophets	Neh 9:30	7307
Then a *s* passed before my face	Job 4:15	7307
poison whereof drinketh up my *s*	Job 6:4	7307
will speak in the anguish of my *s*	Job 7:11	7307
visitation hath preserved my *s*	Job 10:12	7307
thou turnest thy *s* against God	Job 15:13	7307
the *s* of my understanding causeth	Job 20:3	7307
why should not my *s* be troubled	Job 21:4	7307
and whose *s* came from thee	Job 26:4	5397
By his *s* he hath garnished the	Job 26:13	7307
the *s* of God is in my nostrils	Job 27:3	7307
But there is a *s* in man	Job 32:8	7307
the *s* within me constraineth me	Job 32:18	7307
The *s* of God hath made me, and the	Job 33:4	7307
if he gather unto himself his *s*	Job 34:14	7307
Into thine hand I commit my *s*	Ps 31:5	7307
in whose *s* there is no guile	Ps 32:2	7307
saveth such as be of a contrite *s*	Ps 34:18	7307
and renew a right *s* within me	Ps 51:10	7307
and take not thy holy *s* from me	Ps 51:11	7307
and uphold me with thy free *s*	Ps 51:12	7307
sacrifices of God are a broken *s*	Ps 51:17	7307
He shall cut off the *s* of princes	Ps 76:12	7307
and my *s* was overwhelmed	Ps 77:3	7307
my *s* made diligent search	Ps 77:6	7307
whose *s* was not stedfast with God	Ps 78:8	7307
Thou sendest forth thy *s*, they	Ps 104:30	7307
Because they provoked his *s*	Ps 106:33	7307
Whither shall I go from thy *s*	Ps 139:7	7307
When my *s* was overwhelmed within	Ps 142:3	7307
Therefore is my *s* overwhelmed	Ps 143:4	7307
my *s* faileth	Ps 143:7	7307
thy *s* is good	Ps 143:10	7307
I will pour out my *s* unto you	Prov 1:23	7307
faithful *s* concealeth the matter	Prov 11:13	7307
that is hasty of *s* exalteth folly	Prov 14:29	7307
therein is a breach in the *s*	Prov 15:4	7307
of the heart the *s* is broken	Prov 15:13	7307
an haughty *s* before a fall	Prov 16:18	7307
be of an humble *s* with the lowly	Prov 16:19	7307
he that ruleth his *s* than he that	Prov 16:32	7307
but a broken *s* drieth the bones	Prov 17:22	7307
is of an excellent *s*	Prov 17:27	7307
The *s* of a man will sustain his	Prov 18:14	7307
but a wounded *s* who can bear	Prov 18:14	7307
The *s* of man is the candle of the	Prov 20:27	5397
s is like a city that is broken	Prov 25:28	7307
shall uphold the humble in *s*	Prov 29:23	7307
all is vanity and vexation of *s*	Eccl 1:14	7307
that this also is vexation of *s*	Eccl 1:17	7307
all was vanity and vexation of *s*	Eccl 2:11	7307
all is vanity and vexation of *s*	Eccl 2:17	7307
also is vanity and vexation of *s*	Eccl 2:26	7307
Who knoweth the *s* of man that	Eccl 3:21	7307
the *s* of the beast that goeth	Eccl 3:21	7307
is also vanity and vexation of *s*	Eccl 4:4	7307
with travail and vexation of *s*	Eccl 4:6	7307
also is vanity and vexation of *s*	Eccl 4:16	7307
is also vanity and vexation of *s*	Eccl 6:9	7307
the patient in *s* is better than	Eccl 7:8	7307
is better than the proud in *s*	Eccl 7:8	7307
Be not hasty in thy *s* to be angry	Eccl 7:9	7307
over the *s* to retain the *s*	Eccl 8:8	7307
If the *s* of the ruler rise up	Eccl 10:4	7307
not what is the way of the *s*	Eccl 11:5	7307
the *s* shall return unto God who	Eccl 12:7	7307
thereof by the *s* of judgment	Is 4:4	7307
and by the *s* of burning	Is 4:4	7307
the *s* of the LORD shall rest upon	Is 11:2	7307
the *s* of wisdom and understanding,	Is 11:2	7307
the *s* of counsel and might	Is 11:2	7307
the *s* of knowledge and of the fear	Is 11:2	7307
the *s* of Egypt shall fail in the	Is 19:3	7307
a perverse *s* in the midst thereof	Is 19:14	7307
with my *s* within me will I seek	Is 26:9	7307
for a *s* of judgment to him that	Is 28:6	7307
as of one that hath a familiar *s*	Is 29:4	178
out upon you the *s* of deep sleep	Is 29:10	7307
They also that erred in *s* shall	Is 29:24	7307
with a covering, but not of my *s*	Is 30:1	7307
and their horses flesh, and not *s*	Is 31:3	7307
Until the *s* be poured upon us	Is 32:15	7307
his *s* it hath gathered them	Is 34:16	7307
these things is the life of my *s*	Is 38:16	7307
because the *s* of the LORD bloweth	Is 40:7	7307
hath directed the *S* of the LORD	Is 40:13	7307
I have put my *s* upon him	Is 42:1	7307
s to them that walk therein	Is 42:5	7307
I will pour my *s* upon thy seed	Is 44:3	7307
and now the Lord GOD, and his *S*	Is 48:16	7307
a woman forsaken and grieved in *s*	Is 54:6	7307
that is of a contrite and humble *s*	Is 57:15	7307
to revive the *s* of the humble	Is 57:15	7307
for the *s* should fail before me,	Is 57:16	7307
the *S* of the LORD shall lift up a	Is 59:19	7307
My *s* that is upon thee, and my	Is 59:21	7307
The *S* of the Lord GOD is upon me	Is 61:1	7307
of praise for the *s* of heaviness	Is 61:3	7307
rebelled, and vexed his holy *S*	Is 63:10	7307
he that put his holy *S* within him	Is 63:11	7307
the *S* of the LORD caused him to	Is 63:14	7307
and shall howl for vexation of *s*	Is 65:14	7307
that is poor and of a contrite *s*	Is 66:2	7307
the *s* of the kings of the Medes	Jer 51:11	7307
whither the *s* was to go, they	Eze 1:12	7307
Whithersoever the *s* was to go	Eze 1:20	7307
went, thither was their *s* to go	Eze 1:20	7307
for the *s* of the living creature	Eze 1:20	7307
for the *s* of the living creature	Eze 1:21	7307
the *s* entered into me when he	Eze 2:2	7307
Then the *s* took me up, and I heard	Eze 3:12	7307
So the *s* lifted me up, and took me	Eze 3:14	7307
bitterness, in the heat of my *s*	Eze 3:14	7307
Then the *s* entered into me, and	Eze 3:24	7307
the *s* lifted me up between the	Eze 8:3	7307
for the *s* of the living creature	Eze 10:17	7307
Moreover the *s* lifted me up	Eze 11:1	7307
the *S* of the LORD fell upon me,	Eze 11:5	7307
and I will put a new *s* within you	Eze 11:19	7307

S

Afterwards the *s* took me up	Eze 11:24	7307
by the *S* of God into Chaldea	Eze 11:24	7307
prophets, that follow their own *s*	Eze 13:3	7307
make you a new heart and a new *s*	Eze 18:31	7307
every *s* shall faint, and all knees	Eze 21:7	7307
a new *s* will I put within you	Eze 36:26	7307
And I will put my *s* within you	Eze 36:27	7307
me out in the *s* of the LORD	Eze 37:1	7307
And shall put my *s* in you, and ye	Eze 37:14	7307
out my *s* upon the house of Israel	Eze 39:29	7307
So the *s* took me up, and brought	Eze 43:5	7307
wherewith his *s* was troubled	Dan 2:1	7307
my *s* was troubled to know the	Dan 2:3	7307
in whom is the *s* of the holy gods	Dan 4:8	7308
because I know that the *s* of the	Dan 4:9	7308
for the *s* of the holy gods is in	Dan 4:18	7308
in whom is the *s* of the holy gods	Dan 5:11	7308
Forasmuch as an excellent *s*	Dan 5:12	7308
that the *s* of the gods is in thee	Dan 5:14	7308
because an excellent *s* was in him	Dan 6:3	7308
in my *s* in the midst of my body	Dan 7:15	7308
for the *s* of whoredoms hath	Hos 4:12	7307
for the *s* of whoredoms is in the	Hos 5:4	7307
will pour out my *s* upon all flesh	Joel 2:28	7307
those days will I pour out my *s*	Joel 2:29	7307
is the *s* of the LORD straitened	Mic 2:7	7307
If a man walking in the *s*	Mic 2:11	7307
of power by the *s* of the LORD	Mic 3:8	7307
the LORD stirred up the *s* of	Hag 1:14	7307
the *s* of Joshua the son of	Hag 1:14	7307
the *s* of all the remnant of the	Hag 1:14	7307
so my *s* remaineth among you	Hag 2:5	7307
might, nor by power, but by my *s*	Zec 4:6	7307
quieted my *s* in the north country	Zec 6:8	7307
in his *s* by the former prophets	Zec 7:12	7307
formeth the *s* of man within him	Zec 12:1	7307
Jerusalem, the *s* of grace and of	Zec 12:10	7307
the unclean *s* to pass out of the	Zec 13:2	7307
Yet had he the residue of the *s*	Mal 2:15	7307
Therefore take heed to your *s*	Mal 2:15	7307
therefore take heed to your *s*	Mal 2:16	7307
he saw the *S* of God descending	Mt 3:16	4151
the *s* into the wilderness to be	Mt 4:1	4151
Blessed are the poor in *s*	Mt 5:3	4151
but the *S* of your Father which	Mt 10:20	4151
I will put my *S* upon him, and he	Mt 12:18	4151
I cast out devils by the *S* of God	Mt 12:28	4151
When the unclean *s* is gone out of	Mt 12:43	4151
were troubled, saying, It is a *s*	Mt 14:26	4151
doth David in *s* call him Lord	Mt 22:43	4151
the *s* indeed is willing, but the	Mt 26:41	4151
the *S* like a dove descending upon	Mk 1:10	4151
immediately the *s* driveth him	Mk 1:12	4151
synagogue a man with an unclean *s*	Mk 1:23	4151
when the unclean *s* had torn him	Mk 1:26	4151
when Jesus perceived in his *s*	Mk 2:8	4151
they said, He hath an unclean *s*	Mk 3:30	4151
the tombs a man with an unclean *s*	Mk 5:2	4151
out of the man, thou unclean *s*	Mk 5:8	4151
they supposed it had been a *s*	Mk 6:49	5326
young daughter had an unclean *s*	Mk 7:25	4151
And he sighed deeply in his *s*	Mk 8:12	4151
thee my son, which hath a dumb *s*	Mk 9:17	4151
him, straightway the *s* tare him	Mk 9:20	4151
together, he rebuked the foul *s*	Mk 9:25	4151
unto him, Thou dumb and deaf *s*	Mk 9:25	4151
the *s* cried, and rent him sore, and	Mk 9:26	
The *s* truly is ready, but the	Mk 14:38	4151
he shall go before him in the *s*	Lk 1:17	4151
my *s* hath rejoiced in God my	Lk 1:47	4151
child grew, and waxed strong in *s*	Lk 1:80	4151
he came by the *S* into the temple	Lk 2:27	4151
child grew, and waxed strong in *s*	Lk 2:40	4151
was led by the *S* into the	Lk 4:1	4151
the power of the *S* into Galilee	Lk 4:14	4151
The *S* of the Lord is upon me,	Lk 4:18	4151
which had a *s* of an unclean devil	Lk 4:33	4151
unclean *s* to come out of the man	Lk 8:29	4151
her *s* came again, and she arose	Lk 8:55	4151
a *s* taketh him, and he suddenly	Lk 9:39	4151
And Jesus rebuked the unclean *s*	Lk 9:42	4151
not what manner of *s* ye are of	Lk 9:55	4151
In that hour Jesus rejoiced in *s*	Lk 10:21	4151
the Holy *S* to them that ask him	Lk 11:13	4151
When the unclean *s* is gone out of	Lk 11:24	4151
a *s* of infirmity eighteen years	Lk 13:11	4151
into thy hands I commend my *s*	Lk 23:46	4151
supposed that they had seen a *s*	Lk 24:37	4151
for a *s* hath not flesh and bones,	Lk 24:39	4151
I saw the *S* descending from	Jn 1:32	4151
thou shalt see the *S* descending	Jn 1:33	4151

man be born of water and of the *S*	Jn 3:5	4151
which is born of the *S* is *s*	Jn 3:6	4151
every one that is born of the *S*	Jn 3:8	4151
not the *S* by measure unto him	Jn 3:34	4151
shall worship the Father in *s*	Jn 4:23	4151
God is a *S*	Jn 4:24	4151
worship him must worship him in *s*	Jn 4:24	4151
It is the *s* that quickeneth	Jn 6:63	4151
that I speak unto you, they are *s*	Jn 6:63	4151
(But this spake he of the *S*	Jn 7:39	4151
with her, he groaned in the *s*	Jn 11:33	4151
thus said, he was troubled in *s*	Jn 13:21	4151
Even the *S* of truth	Jn 14:17	4151
the Father, even the *S* of truth	Jn 15:26	4151
the *S* of truth, is come, he will	Jn 16:13	4151
as the *S* gave them utterance	Acts 2:4	4151
pour out of my *S* upon all flesh	Acts 2:17	4151
pour out in those days of my *S*	Acts 2:18	4151
to tempt the *S* of the Lord	Acts 5:9	4151
wisdom and the *s* by which he spake	Acts 6:10	4151
saying, Lord Jesus, receive my *s*	Acts 7:59	4151
Then the *S* said unto Philip, Go	Acts 8:29	4151
the *S* of the Lord caught away	Acts 8:39	4151
the *S* said unto him, Behold,	Acts 10:19	4151
the *S* bade me go with them,	Acts 11:12	4151
signified by the *S* that there	Acts 11:28	4151
but the *S* suffered them not	Acts 16:7	4151
with a *s* of divination met us	Acts 16:16	4151
grieved, turned and said to the *s*	Acts 16:18	4151
his *s* was stirred in him, when he	Acts 17:16	4151
Paul was pressed in the *s*	Acts 18:5	4151
and being fervent in the *s*	Acts 18:25	4151
And the evil *s* answered and said,	Acts 19:15	4151
the evil *s* was leaped on them	Acts 19:16	4151
ended, Paul purposed in the *s*	Acts 19:21	4151
go bound in the *s* unto Jerusalem	Acts 20:22	4151
who said to Paul through the *S*	Acts 21:4	4151
neither angel, nor *s*	Acts 23:8	4151
but if a *s* or an angel hath	Acts 23:9	4151
according to the *s* of holiness	Rom 1:4	4151
whom I serve with my *s* in the	Rom 1:9	4151
is that of the heart, in the *s*	Rom 2:29	4151
we should serve in newness of *s*	Rom 7:6	4151
after the flesh, but after the *S*	Rom 8:1	4151
For the law of the *S* of life	Rom 8:2	4151
after the flesh, but after the *S*	Rom 8:4	4151
the *S* the things of the *S*	Rom 8:5	4151
not in the flesh, but in the *S*	Rom 8:9	4151
if so be that the *S* of God dwell	Rom 8:9	4151
any man have not the *S* of Christ	Rom 8:9	4151
but the *S* is life because of	Rom 8:10	4151
But if the *S* of him that raised	Rom 8:11	4151
by his *S* that dwelleth in you	Rom 8:11	4151
but if ye through the *S* do	Rom 8:13	4151
many as are led by the *S* of God	Rom 8:14	4151
the *s* of bondage again to fear	Rom 8:15	4151
have received the *S* of adoption	Rom 8:15	4151
The *S* itself beareth witness with	Rom 8:16	4151
itself beareth witness with our *s*	Rom 8:16	4151
have the firstfruits of the *S*	Rom 8:23	4151
Likewise the *S* also helpeth our	Rom 8:26	4151
but the *S* itself maketh	Rom 8:26	4151
knoweth what is the mind of the *S*	Rom 8:27	4151
hath given them the *s* of slumber	Rom 11:8	4151
fervent in *s*	Rom 12:11	4151
by the power of the *S* of God	Rom 15:19	4151
sake, and for the love of the *S*	Rom 15:30	4151
but in demonstration of the *S*	1Cor 2:4	4151
revealed them unto us by his *S*	1Cor 2:10	4151
for the *S* searcheth all things,	1Cor 2:10	4151
save the *s* of man which is in him	1Cor 2:11	4151
knoweth no man, but the *S* of God	1Cor 2:11	4151
not the *s* of the world	1Cor 2:12	4151
but the *s* which is of God	1Cor 2:12	4151
not the things of the *S* of God	1Cor 2:14	4151
that the *S* of God dwelleth in you	1Cor 3:16	4151
in love, and in the *s* of meekness	1Cor 4:21	4151
absent in body, but present in *s*	1Cor 5:3	4151
ye are gathered together, and my *s*	1Cor 5:4	4151
that the *s* may be saved in the	1Cor 5:5	4151
Jesus, and by the *S* of our God	1Cor 6:11	4151
is joined unto the Lord is one *s*	1Cor 6:17	4151
God in your body, and in your *s*	1Cor 6:20	4151
may be holy both in body and in *s*	1Cor 7:34	4151
also that I have the *S* of God	1Cor 7:40	4151
that no man speaking by the *S* of	1Cor 12:3	4151
of gifts, but the same *S*	1Cor 12:4	4151
But the manifestation of the *S* is	1Cor 12:7	4151
given by the *S* the word of wisdom	1Cor 12:8	4151
word of knowledge by the same *S*	1Cor 12:8	4151
To another faith by the same *S*	1Cor 12:9	4151

gifts of healing by the same *S*	1Cor 12:9	4151
that one and the selfsame *S*	1Cor 12:11	4151
For by one *S* are we all baptized	1Cor 12:13	4151
been all made to drink into one *S*	1Cor 12:13	4151
howbeit in the *s* he speaketh	1Cor 14:2	4151
tongue, my *s* prayeth, but my	1Cor 14:14	4151
I will pray with the *s*, and I will	1Cor 14:15	4151
I will sing with the *s*, and I will	1Cor 14:15	4151
when thou shalt bless with the *s*	1Cor 14:16	4151
last Adam was made a quickening *s*	1Cor 15:45	4151
For they have refreshed my *s*	1Cor 16:18	4151
earnest of the *S* in our hearts	2Cor 1:22	4151
I had no rest in my *s*, because I	2Cor 2:13	4151
but with the *S* of the living God	2Cor 3:3	4151
not of the letter, but of the *s*	2Cor 3:6	4151
killeth, but the *s* giveth life	2Cor 3:6	4151
of the *s* be rather glorious	2Cor 3:8	4151
Now the Lord is that *S*	2Cor 3:17	4151
where the *S* of the Lord is, there	2Cor 3:17	4151
even as by the *S* of the Lord	2Cor 3:18	4151
We having the same *s* of faith	2Cor 4:13	4151
unto us the earnest of the *S*	2Cor 5:5	4151
all filthiness of the flesh and *s*	2Cor 7:1	4151
because his *s* was refreshed by	2Cor 7:13	4151
or if ye receive another *s*	2Cor 11:4	4151
walked we not in the same *s*	2Cor 12:18	4151
Received ye the *S* by the works of	Gal 3:2	4151
having begun in the *S*, are ye now	Gal 3:3	4151
that ministereth to you the *S*	Gal 3:5	4151
promise of the *S* through faith	Gal 3:14	4151
God hath sent forth the *S* of his	Gal 4:6	4151
him that was born after the *S*	Gal 4:29	4151
For we through the *S* wait for the	Gal 5:5	4151
This I say then, Walk in the *S*	Gal 5:16	4151
the flesh lusteth against the *S*	Gal 5:17	4151
and the *S* against the flesh	Gal 5:17	4151
But if ye be led of the *S*	Gal 5:18	4151
But the fruit of the *S* is love	Gal 5:22	4151
If we live in the *S*, let us also	Gal 5:25	4151
let us also walk in the *S*	Gal 5:25	4151
such an one in the *s* of meekness	Gal 6:1	4151
but he that soweth to the *S* shall	Gal 6:8	4151
of the *S* reap life everlasting	Gal 6:8	4151
Lord Jesus Christ be with your *s*	Gal 6:18	4151
with that holy *S* of promise	Eph 1:13	4151
may give unto you the *s* of wisdom	Eph 1:17	4151
the *s* that now worketh in the	Eph 2:2	4151
access by one *S* unto the Father	Eph 2:18	4151
habitation of God through the *S*	Eph 2:22	4151
apostles and prophets by the *S*	Eph 3:5	4151
might by his *S* in the inner man	Eph 3:16	4151
of the *S* in the bond of peace	Eph 4:3	4151
There is one body, and one *S*	Eph 4:4	4151
be renewed in the *s* of your mind	Eph 4:23	4151
And grieve not the holy *S* of God	Eph 4:30	4151
fruit of the *S* is in all goodness	Eph 5:9	4151
but be filled with the *S*	Eph 5:18	4151
salvation, and the sword of the *S*	Eph 6:17	4151
prayer and supplication in the *S*	Eph 6:18	4151
supply of the *S* of Jesus Christ	Phil 1:19	4151
that ye stand fast in one *s*	Phil 1:27	4151
love, if any fellowship of the *S*	Phil 2:1	4151
which worship God in the *s*	Phil 3:3	4151
unto us your love in the *S*	Col 1:8	4151
flesh, yet am I with you in the *s*	Col 2:5	4151
also given unto us his holy *S*	1Th 4:8	4151
Quench not the *S*	1Th 5:19	4151
and I pray God your whole *s*	1Th 5:23	4151
or be troubled, neither by *s*	2Th 2:2	4151
consume with the *s* of his mouth	2Th 2:8	4151
through sanctification of the *S*	2Th 2:13	4151
in the flesh, justified in the *S*	1Ti 3:16	4151
Now the *S* speaketh expressly,	1Ti 4:1	4151
in conversation, in charity, in *s*	1Ti 4:12	4151
hath not given us the *s* of fear	2Ti 1:7	4151
Lord Jesus Christ be with thy *s*	2Ti 4:22	4151
Lord Jesus Christ be with your *s*	Philem 25	4151
the dividing asunder of soul and *s*	Heb 4:12	4151
who through the eternal *S* offered	Heb 9:14	4151
done despite unto the *S* of grace	Heb 10:29	4151
as the body without the *s* is dead	Jas 2:26	4151
The *s* that dwelleth in us lusteth	Jas 4:5	4151
through sanctification of the *S*	1Pet 1:2	4151
or what manner of time the *S* of	1Pet 1:11	4151
the *S* unto unfeigned love of the	1Pet 1:22	4151
the ornament of a meek and quiet *s*	1Pet 3:4	4151
the flesh, but quickened by the *S*	1Pet 3:18	4151
live according to God in the *s*	1Pet 4:6	4151
for the *s* of glory and of God	1Pet 4:14	4151
by the *S* which he hath given us	1Jn 3:24	4151
Beloved, believe not every *s*	1Jn 4:1	4151

Hereby know ye the *S* of God	1Jn 4:2	4151
Every *s* that confesseth that	1Jn 4:2	4151
every *s* that confesseth not that	1Jn 4:3	4151
this is that *s* of antichrist	1Jn 4:3	4151
Hereby know we the *s* of truth	1Jn 4:6	4151
of truth, and the *s* of error	1Jn 4:6	4151
because he hath given us of his *S*	1Jn 4:13	4151
it is the *S* that beareth witness,	1Jn 5:6	4151
witness, because the *S* is truth	1Jn 5:6	4151
that bear witness in earth, the *s*	1Jn 5:8	4151
sensual, having not the *S*	Jude 19	4151
I was in the *S* on the Lord's day,	Rev 1:10	4151
let him hear what the *S* saith	Rev 2:7	4151
let him hear what the *S* saith	Rev 2:11	4151
let him hear what the *S* saith	Rev 2:17	4151
let him hear what the *S* saith	Rev 2:29	4151
let him hear what the *S* saith	Rev 3:6	4151
let him hear what the *S* saith	Rev 3:13	4151
let him hear what the *S* saith	Rev 3:22	4151
And immediately I was in the *s*	Rev 4:2	4151
an half the *s* of life from God	Rev 11:11	4151
Yea, saith the *S*, that they may	Rev 14:13	4151
away in the *s* into the wilderness	Rev 17:3	4151
and the hold of every foul *s*	Rev 18:2	4151
of Jesus is the *s* of prophecy	Rev 19:10	4151
me away in the *s* to a great	Rev 21:10	4151
And the *S* and the bride say, Come	Rev 22:17	4151

SPIRITS

not them that have familiar *s*	Lev 19:31	178
after such as have familiar *s*	Lev 20:6	178
the God of the *s* of all flesh	Num 16:22	7307
the God of the *s* of all flesh	Num 27:16	7307
or a consulter with familiar *s*	Deut 18:11	178
away those that had familiar *s*	1Sa 28:3	178
off those that have familiar *s*	1Sa 28:9	178
and dealt with familiar *s*	2Kin 21:6	178
the workers with familiar *s*	2Kin 23:24	178
Who maketh his angels *s*	Ps 104:4	7307
but the LORD weigheth the *s*	Prov 16:2	7307
unto them that have familiar *s*	Is 8:19	178
and to them that have familiar *s*	Is 19:3	178
are the four *s* of the heavens	Zec 6:5	7307
he cast out the *s* with his word	Mt 8:16	4151
gave them power against unclean *s*	Mt 10:1	4151
other *s* more wicked than himself	Mt 12:45	4151
commandeth he even the unclean *s*	Mk 1:27	4151
And unclean *s*, when they saw him,	Mk 3:11	4151
And the unclean *s* went out	Mk 5:13	4151
and gave them power over unclean *s*	Mk 6:7	4151
power he commandeth the unclean *s*	Lk 4:36	4151
that were vexed with unclean *s*	Lk 6:18	4151
and plagues, and of evil *s*	Lk 7:21	4151
which had been healed of evil *s*	Lk 8:2	4151
that the *s* are subject unto you	Lk 10:20	4151
other *s* more wicked than himself	Lk 11:26	4151
which were vexed with unclean *s*	Acts 5:16	4151
For unclean *s*, crying with loud	Acts 8:7	4151
the evil *s* went out of them	Acts 19:12	4151
evil *s* the name of the Lord Jesus	Acts 19:13	4151
to another discerning of *s*	1Cor 12:10	4151
the *s* of the prophets are subject	1Cor 14:32	4151
faith, giving heed to seducing *s*	1Ti 4:1	4151
he saith, Who maketh his angels *s*	Heb 1:7	4151
Are they not all ministering *s*	Heb 1:14	4151
subjection unto the Father of *s*	Heb 12:9	4151
to the *s* of just men made perfect	Heb 12:23	4151
and preached unto the *s* in prison	1Pet 3:19	4151
but try the *s* whether they are of	1Jn 4:1	4151
from the seven *S* which are before	Rev 1:4	4151
he that hath the seven *S* of God	Rev 3:1	4151
which are the seven *S* of God	Rev 4:5	4151
which are the seven *S* of God sent	Rev 5:6	4151
I saw three unclean *s* like frogs	Rev 16:13	4151
For they are the *s* of devils	Rev 16:14	4151

SPIRITUAL

the *s* man is mad, for the	Hos 9:7	7307
I may impart unto you some *s* gift	Rom 1:11	4152
For we know that the law is *s*	Rom 7:14	4152
made partakers of their *s* things	Rom 15:27	4152
comparing *s* things with *s*	1Cor 2:13	4152
But he that is *s* judgeth all	1Cor 2:15	4152
not speak unto you as unto *s*	1Cor 3:1	4152
If we have sown unto you *s* things	1Cor 9:11	4152
And did all eat the same *s* meat	1Cor 10:3	4152
And did all drink the same *s* drink	1Cor 10:4	4152
for they drank of that *s* Rock	1Cor 10:4	4152
Now concerning *s* gifts, brethren,	1Cor 12:1	4152
after charity, and desire *s* gifts	1Cor 14:1	4152
as ye are zealous of *s* gifts	1Cor 14:12	4151
himself to be a prophet, or *s*	1Cor 14:37	4152

S

it is raised a *s* body	1Cor 15:44	4152
body, and there is a *s* body	1Cor 15:44	4152
that was not first which is *s*	1Cor 15:46	4152
and afterward that which is *s*	1Cor 15:46	4152
in a fault, ye which are *s*	Gal 6:1	4152
who hath blessed us with all *s*	Eph 1:3	4152
s songs, singing and making melody	Eph 5:19	4152
against *s* wickedness in high	Eph 6:12	4152
in all wisdom and *s* understanding	Col 1:9	4152
s songs, singing with grace in	Col 3:16	4152
stones, are built up a *s* house	1Pet 2:5	4152
to offer up *s* sacrifices	1Pet 2:5	4152

SPIRITUALLY

but to be *s* minded is life and	Rom 8:6	3588,4151
because they are *s* discerned	1Cor 2:14	4153
which *s* is called Sodom and Egypt,	Rev 11:8	4153

SPIT

issue *s* upon him that is clean	Lev 15:8	7556
her father had but *s* in her face	Num 12:14	3417
s in his face, and shall answer and	Deut 25:9	3417
me, and spare not to *s* in my face	Job 30:10	7536
Then did they *s* in his face	Mt 26:67	1716
they *s* upon him, and took the reed	Mt 27:30	1716
fingers into his ears, and he *s*	Mk 7:33	4429
and when he had *s* on his eyes	Mk 8:23	4429
shall *s* upon him, and shall kill	Mk 10:34	1716
And some began to *s* on him	Mk 14:65	1716
did *s* upon him, and bowing their	Mk 15:19	1716

SPITE

for thou beholdest mischief and *s*	Ps 10:14	3708

SPITEFULLY

his servants, and entreated them *s*	Mt 22:6	5195
s entreated, and spitted on	Lk 18:32	5195

SPITTED

and spitefully entreated, and *s* on	Lk 18:32	1716

SPITTING

I hid not my face from shame and *s*	Is 50:6	7536

SPITTLE

let his *s* fall down upon his	1Sa 21:13	7388
me alone till I swallow down my *s*	Job 7:19	7536
the ground, and made clay of the *s*	Jn 9:6	4427

SPOIL

and at night he shall divide the *s*	Gen 49:27	7998
and ye shall *s* the Egyptians	Ex 3:22	5337
overtake, I will divide the *s*	Ex 15:9	7998
took the *s* of all their cattle,	Num 31:9	962
And they took all the *s*, and all	Num 31:11	7998
captives, and the prey, and the *s*	Num 31:12	7998
(For the men of war had taken *s*	Num 31:53	962
the *s* of the cities which we took	Deut 2:35	7998
the *s* of the cities, we took for	Deut 3:7	7998
thou shalt gather all the *s* of it	Deut 13:16	7998
all the *s* thereof every whit, for	Deut 13:16	7998
the city, even all the *s* thereof	Deut 20:14	7998
shalt eat the *s* of thine enemies	Deut 20:14	7998
only the *s* thereof, and the cattle	Josh 8:2	7998
the *s* of that city Israel took	Josh 8:27	7998
all the *s* of these cities, and the	Josh 11:14	7998
divide the *s* of your enemies with	Josh 22:8	7998
the necks of them that take the *s*	Judg 5:30	7998
men of them, and took their *s*	Judg 14:19	2488
the *s* of their enemies which they	1Sa 14:30	7998
And the people flew upon the *s*	1Sa 14:32	7998
s them until the morning light,	1Sa 14:36	962
LORD, but didst fly upon the *s*	1Sa 15:19	7998
But the people took of the *s*	1Sa 15:21	7998
because of all the great *s* that	1Sa 30:16	7998
sons nor daughters, neither *s*	1Sa 30:19	7998
and said, This is David's *s*	1Sa 30:20	7998
of the *s* that we have recovered	1Sa 30:22	7998
he sent of the *s* unto the elders	1Sa 30:26	7998
the *s* of the enemies of the LORD	1Sa 30:26	7998
and brought in a great *s* with them	2Sa 3:22	7998
of the *s* of Hadadezer, son of	2Sa 8:12	7998
he brought forth the *s* of the	2Sa 12:30	7998
returned after him only to *s*	2Sa 23:10	6584
now therefore, Moab, to the *s*	2Kin 3:23	7998
prey and a *s* to all their enemies	2Kin 21:14	4933
exceeding much *s* out of the city	1Chr 20:2	7998
and they carried away very much *s*	2Chr 14:13	7998
was exceeding much *s* in them	2Chr 14:14	961
of the *s* which they had brought,	2Chr 15:11	7998
came to take away the *s* of them	2Chr 20:25	7998
three days in gathering of the *s*	2Chr 20:25	7998
sent all the *s* of them unto the	2Chr 24:23	7998
thousand of them, and took much *s*	2Chr 25:13	961
took also away much *s* from them	2Chr 28:8	7998

and brought the *s* to Samaria	2Chr 28:8	7998
the *s* before the princes and all	2Chr 28:14	961
with the *s* clothed all that were	2Chr 28:15	7998
sword, to captivity, and to a *s*	Ezr 9:7	961
to take the *s* of them for a prey	Est 3:13	7998
to take the *s* of them for a prey,	Est 8:11	7998
but on the *s* laid they not their	Est 9:10	961
plucked the *s* out of his teeth	Job 29:17	2964
which hate us *s* for themselves	Ps 44:10	8154
tarried at home divided the *s*	Ps 68:12	7998
All that pass by the way *s* him	Ps 89:41	8155
and let the strangers *s* his labour	Ps 109:11	962
word, as one that findeth great *s*	Ps 119:162	7998
we shall fill our houses with *s*	Prov 1:13	7998
to divide the *s* with the proud	Prov 16:19	7998
s the soul of those that spoiled	Prov 22:23	6906
s not his resting place	Prov 24:15	7703
that he shall have no need of *s*	Prov 31:11	7998
little foxes, that *s* the vines	Song 2:15	2254
the *s* of the poor is in your	Is 3:14	1500
the *s* of Samaria shall be taken	Is 8:4	7998
rejoice when they divide the *s*	Is 9:3	7998
give him a charge, to take the *s*	Is 10:6	7998
they shall *s* them of the east	Is 11:14	962
is the portion of them that *s* us	Is 17:14	8154
when thou shalt cease to *s*	Is 33:1	7703
your *s* shall be gathered like the	Is 33:4	7998
is the prey of a great *s* divided	Is 33:23	7998
for a *s*, and none saith, Restore	Is 42:22	4933
Who gave Jacob for a *s*, and Israel	Is 42:24	4882
divide the *s* with the strong	Is 53:12	7998
wolf of the evenings shall *s* them	Jer 5:6	7703
violence and *s* is heard in her	Jer 6:7	7701
I give to the *s* without price	Jer 15:13	957
and all thy treasures to the *s*	Jer 17:3	957
their enemies, which shall *s* them	Jer 20:5	962
cried out, I cried violence and *s*	Jer 20:8	7701
they that *s* thee shall be a	Jer 30:16	7701
thee shall be a *s*	Jer 30:16	4933
cometh to *s* all the Philistines	Jer 47:4	7703
the LORD will *s* the Philistines	Jer 47:4	7703
Kedar, and *s* the men of the east	Jer 49:28	7703
the multitude of their cattle a *s*	Jer 49:32	7998
And Chaldea shall be a *s*	Jer 50:10	7998
all that *s* her shall be satisfied,	Jer 50:10	7998
the wicked of the earth for a *s*	Eze 7:21	7998
through the land, and they *s* it	Eze 14:15	7921
thee for a *s* to the heathen	Eze 25:7	957
shall become a *s* to the nations	Eze 26:5	957
they shall make a *s* of thy riches	Eze 26:12	7997
take her multitude, and take her *s*	Eze 29:19	7997
they shall *s* the pomp of Egypt,	Eze 32:12	7703
To take a *s*, and to take a prey	Eze 38:12	7998
thee, Art thou come to take a *s*	Eze 38:13	7998
and goods, to take a great *s*	Eze 38:13	7998
they shall *s* those that spoiled	Eze 39:10	7997
remove violence and *s*, and execute	Eze 45:9	7701
scatter among them the prey, and *s*	Dan 11:24	7998
by flame, by captivity, and by *s*	Dan 11:33	961
altars, he shall *s* their images	Hos 10:2	7703
he shall *s* the treasure of all	Hos 13:15	8154
Take ye the *s* of silver, take the	Nah 2:9	962
of silver, take the *s* of gold	Nah 2:9	7997
of the people shall *s* thee	Hab 2:8	7701
the *s* of beasts, which made them	Hab 2:17	962
residue of my people shall *s* them	Zeph 2:9	7998
they shall be a *s* to their	Zec 2:9	7998
thy *s* shall be divided in the	Zec 14:1	7998
s his goods, except he first bind	Mt 12:29	*1283*
and then he will *s* his house	Mt 12:29	*1283*
s his goods, except he will first	Mk 3:27	*1283*
and then he will *s* his house	Mk 3:27	*1283*
Beware lest any man *s* you through	Col 2:8	4812

SPOILED

s the city, because they had	Gen 34:27	962
s even all that was in the house	Gen 34:29	962
And they *s* the Egyptians	Ex 12:36	5337
s evermore, and no man shall save	Deut 28:29	1497
the hands of spoilers that *s* them	Judg 2:14	8155
of the hand of those that *s* them	Judg 2:16	8154
of the hands of them that *s* them	1Sa 14:48	8154
and they *s* their tents	1Sa 17:53	8155
s the tents of the Syrians	2Kin 7:16	962
and they *s* all the cities	2Chr 14:14	962
He leadeth counsellors away *s*	Job 12:17	7758
He leadeth princes away *s*	Job 12:19	7758
The stouthearted are *s*, they have	Ps 76:5	7997
the soul of those that *s* them	Prov 22:23	6906
their houses shall be *s*, and their	Is 13:16	8155
whose land the rivers have *s*	Is 18:2	958

whose land the rivers have s .... Is 18:7   958
be utterly emptied, and utterly s .... Is 24:3   962
that spoilest, and thou wast not s .... Is 33:1   7703
cease to spoil, thou shalt be s .... Is 33:1   7703
But this is a people robbed and s .... Is 42:22   8154
why is he s .... Jer 2:14   957
for we are s .... Jer 4:13   7703
for the whole land is s .... Jer 4:20   7703
suddenly are my tents s, and my .... Jer 4:20   7703
And when thou art s, what wilt .... Jer 4:30   7703
heard out of Zion, How are we s .... Jer 9:19   7703
My tabernacle is s, and all my .... Jer 10:20   7703
deliver him that is s out of the .... Jer 21:12   1497
deliver the s out of the hand of .... Jer 22:3   1497
for the LORD hath s their pasture .... Jer 25:36   7703
for it is s .... Jer 48:1   7703
Moab is s, and gone up out of her .... Jer 48:15   7703
ye it in Arnon, that Moab is s .... Jer 48:20   7703
Howl, O Heshbon, for Ai is s .... Jer 49:3   7703
his seed is s, and his brethren, ... Jer 49:10   7703
Because the LORD hath s Babylon .... Jer 51:55   7703
hath s none by violence, hath.................. Eze 18:7   1497
hath s by violence, hath not .... Eze 18:12   1497
neither hath s by violence...................... Eze 18:16   1497
s his brother by violence, and did .... Eze 18:18   1497
will give them to be removed and s .... Eze 23:46   957
shall spoil those that s them .... Eze 39:10   7997
and all thy fortresses shall be s .... Hos 10:14   7703
as Shalman s Beth-arbel in the .... Hos 10:14   7701
thee, and thy palaces shall be s.............. Amos 3:11   962
the s against the strong, so that .... Amos 5:9   7701
so that the s shall come against .... Amos 5:9   7701
and say, We be utterly s .... Mic 2:4   7703
Because thou hast s many nations .... Hab 2:8   7997
me unto the nations which s you .... Zec 2:8   7997
because the mighty are s .... Zec 11:2   7703
for their glory is s .... Zec 11:3   7703
for the pride of Jordan is s...................... Zec 11:3   7703
having s principalities and powers .... Col 2:15   554

SPOILER
to them from the face of the s .... Is 16:4   7703
the s ceaseth, the oppressors are .... Is 16:4   7701
treacherously, and the s spoileth .... Is 21:2   7703
for the s shall suddenly come.................. Jer 6:26   7703
of the young men a s at noonday .... Jer 15:8   7703
the s shall come upon every city, ... Jer 48:8   7703
for the s of Moab shall come upon .... Jer 48:18   7703
the s is fallen upon thy summer .... Jer 48:32   7703
Because the s is come upon her, ... Jer 51:56   7703

SPOILERS
the hands of s that spoiled them .... Judg 2:14   8154
the s came out of the camp of the.......... 1Sa 13:17   7843
the garrison, and the s, they also 1Sa 14:15   7843
delivered them into the hand of s 2Kin 17:20   8154
The s are come upon all high.................. Jer 12:12   7703
for the s shall come unto her .... Jer 51:48   7703
yet from me shall s come unto her .... Jer 51:53   7703

SPOILEST
Woe to thee that s, and thou wast .... Is 33:1   7703

SPOILETH
and the needy from him that s him .... Ps 35:10   1497
treacherously, and the spoiler s .... Is 21:2   7703
and the troop of robbers s without........ Hos 7:1   6584
the cankerworm s, and fleeth away .... Nah 3:16   6584

SPOILING
evil for good to the s of my soul.............. Ps 35:12   7908
because of the s of the daughter .... Is 22:4   7701
crying shall be from Horonaim, s............ Jer 48:3   7701
for s and violence are before me .... Hab 1:3   7701
took joyfully the s of your goods .... Heb 10:34   724

SPOILS
When I saw among the s a goodly .... Josh 7:21   7998
Out of the s won in battles did................ 1Chr 26:27   7998
with the s of their hands........................ Is 25:11   698
he trusted, and divideth his s .... Lk 11:22   *4661*
Abraham gave the tenth of the s .... Heb 7:4   205

SPOKEN
as the LORD had s unto him .... Gen 12:4   1696
that which he hath s of him .... Gen 18:19   1696
city, for the which thou hast s .... Gen 19:21   1696
LORD did unto Sarah as he had s............ Gen 21:1   1696
time of which God had s to him.............. Gen 21:2   1696
son's wife, as the LORD hath s .... Gen 24:51   1696
that which I have s to thee of.................. Gen 28:15   1696
thing which I have s unto Pharaoh.......... Gen 41:28   1696
to the word that Joseph had s .... Gen 44:2   1696
thou hast s unto thy servant .... Ex 4:10   1696

which the LORD had s unto Moses .... Ex 4:30   1696
as the LORD had s unto Moses .... Ex 9:12   1696
as the LORD had s by Moses .... Ex 9:35   1696
And Moses said, Thou hast s well.......... Ex 10:29   1696
that the LORD hath s we will do .... Ex 19:8   1696
all this land that I have s of .... Ex 32:13   559
place of which I have s unto thee .... Ex 32:34   1696
this thing also that thou hast s .... Ex 33:17   1696
all that the LORD had s with him .... Ex 34:32   1696
statutes which the LORD hath s................ Lev 10:11   1696
For the LORD had s unto Moses................ Num 1:48   1696
for the LORD hath s good .... Num 10:29   1696
the LORD indeed s only by Moses............ Num 12:2   1696
hath he not s also by us.......................... Num 12:2   1696
great, according as thou hast s .... Num 14:17   1696
as ye have s in mine ears, so .... Num 14:28   1696
which the LORD hath s unto Moses........ Num 15:22   1696
for we have s against the LORD, ... Num 21:7   1696
And Balak did as Balaam had s .... Num 23:2   1696
unto him, What hath the LORD s .... Num 23:17   1696
thou hast s is good for us to do.............. Deut 1:14   1696
which they have s unto thee .... Deut 5:28   1696
well said all that they have s.................. Deut 5:28   1696
before thee, as the LORD hath s.............. Deut 6:19   1696
because he hath s to turn you.................. Deut 13:5   1696
They have well s that which they............ Deut 18:17   1696
that which they have s.............................. Deut 18:17
word which the LORD hath not s .... Deut 18:21   1696
thing which the LORD hath not s............ Deut 18:22   1696
prophet hath s it presumptuously.......... Deut 18:22   1696
the LORD thy God, as he hath s.............. Deut 26:19   1696
when Joshua had s unto the people........ Josh 6:8   559
had s unto the house of Israel................ Josh 21:45   1696
for that thou hast s friendly.................... Ruth 2:13   1696
and grief have I s hitherto 1Sa 1:16   1696
I have s concerning his house 1Sa 3:12   1696
matter which thou and I have s of 1Sa 20:23   1696
that he hath s concerning thee 1Sa 25:30   1696
God liveth, unless thou hadst s.............. 2Sa 2:27   1696
for the LORD hath s of David 2Sa 3:18   559
maidservants which thou hast s of 2Sa 6:22   559
but thou hast s also of thy 2Sa 7:19   1696
hast s concerning thy servant 2Sa 7:25   1696
for thou, O Lord GOD, hast s it 2Sa 7:29   1696
that my lord the king hath s 2Sa 14:19   1696
Ahithophel hath s after this 2Sa 17:6   1696
if Adonijah have not s this word 1Kin 2:23   1696
this people, who have s to me 1Kin 12:9   1696
is the sign which the LORD hath s............ 1Kin 13:3   1696
which he had s unto the king.................. 1Kin 13:11   1696
for the LORD hath s it 1Kin 14:11   1696
answered and said, It is well s 1Kin 18:24   1697
the Jezreelite had s to him 1Kin 21:4   1696
the LORD hath s evil concerning.............. 1Kin 22:23   1696
peace, the LORD hath s not by me 1Kin 22:28   1696
of the LORD which Elijah had s 2Kin 1:17   1696
thou be s for to the king 2Kin 4:13   1696
the man of God had s to the king.......... 2Kin 7:18   1696
the LORD hath s concerning him 2Kin 19:21   1696
will do the thing that he hath s.............. 2Kin 20:9   1696
of the LORD which thou hast s 2Kin 20:19   1696
for thou hast also s of thy 1Chr 17:17   1696
hast s concerning thy servant 1Chr 17:23   1696
the wine, which my lord hath s of.......... 2Chr 2:15   559
performed his word that he hath s 2Chr 6:10   1696
which thou hast s unto thy...................... 2Chr 6:17   1696
this people, which have s to me 2Chr 10:9   1696
the LORD hath s evil against thee 2Chr 18:22   1696
then hath not the LORD s by me 2Chr 18:27   1696
that the word of the LORD s by 2Chr 36:22   1696
because we had s unto the king.............. Ezr 8:22   559
words that he had s unto me .... Neh 2:18   559
fail of all that thou hast s .... Est 6:10   1696
who had s good for the king.................... Est 7:9   1696
and after that I have s, mock on .... Job 21:3   1696
Elihu had waited till Job had s .... Job 32:4   1697
my tongue hath s in my mouth................ Job 33:2   1696
thou hast s in mine hearing.................... Job 33:8   559
Job hath s without knowledge, and........ Job 34:35   1696
Once have I s.. Job 40:5   1696
LORD had s these words unto Job .... Job 42:7   1696
for ye have not s of me the thing .... Job 42:7   1696
in that ye have not s of me the .... Job 42:8   1696
mighty God, even the LORD, hath s........ Ps 50:1   1696
God hath s in his holiness .... Ps 60:6   1696
God hath s once .... Ps 62:11   1696
have uttered, and my mouth hath s .... Ps 66:14   1696
Glorious things are s of thee .... Ps 87:3   1696
God hath s in his holiness .... Ps 108:7   1696
they have s against me with a .... Ps 109:2   1696
I believed, therefore have I s .... Ps 116:10   1696

S

a word *s* in due season, how good	Prov 15:23	
A word fitly *s* is like apples of	Prov 25:11	1696
no heed unto all words that are *s*	Eccl 7:21	1696
the day when she shall be *s* for	Song 8:8	1696
for the LORD hath *s*, I have	Is 1:2	1696
the mouth of the LORD hath *s* it	Is 1:20	1696
is the word that the LORD hath *s*	Is 16:13	1696
But now the LORD hath *s*, saying,	Is 16:14	1696
the LORD God of Israel hath *s* it	Is 21:17	1696
for the LORD hath *s* it	Is 22:25	1696
for the sea hath *s*, even the	Is 23:4	559
for the LORD hath *s* this word	Is 24:3	1696
for the LORD hath *s* it	Is 25:8	1696
For thus hath the LORD *s* unto me	Is 31:4	559
the LORD hath *s* concerning him	Is 37:22	1696
will do this thing that he hath *s*	Is 38:7	1696
He hath both *s* unto me, and	Is 38:15	559
of the LORD which thou hast *s*	Is 39:8	1696
the mouth of the LORD hath *s* it	Is 40:5	1696
I have not *s* in secret, in a dark	Is 45:19	1696
yea, I have *s* it, I will also	Is 46:11	1696
I, even I, have *s*	Is 48:15	1696
I have not *s* in secret from the	Is 48:16	1696
the mouth of the LORD hath *s* it	Is 58:14	1696
your lips have *s* lies, your	Is 59:3	1696
Behold, thou hast *s* and done evil	Jer 3:5	1696
because I have *s* it, I have	Jer 4:28	1696
whom the mouth of the LORD hath *s*	Jer 9:12	1696
for the LORD hath *s*	Jer 13:15	1696
I have not *s* to them, yet they	Jer 23:21	1696
and, What hath the LORD *s*	Jer 23:35	1696
and, What hath the LORD *s*	Jer 23:37	1696
I have *s* unto you, rising early	Jer 25:3	1696
for he hath *s* to us in the name	Jer 26:16	1696
as the LORD hath *s* against the	Jer 27:13	1696
have *s* lying words in my name,	Jer 29:23	1696
that I have *s* unto thee in a book	Jer 30:2	1696
what thou hast *s* is come to pass	Jer 32:24	1696
thou not what this people have *s*	Jer 33:24	1696
notwithstanding I have *s* unto you	Jer 35:14	1696
because I have *s* unto them	Jer 35:17	1696
I have *s* unto thee against Israel	Jer 36:2	1696
the LORD, which he had *s* unto him	Jer 36:4	1696
had *s* unto all the people	Jer 38:1	1696
As for the word that thou hast *s*	Jer 44:16	1696
have both *s* with your mouths	Jer 44:25	1696
be destroyed, as the LORD hath *s*	Jer 48:8	559
thou hast *s* against this place,	Jer 51:62	1696
I the LORD have *s* it in my zeal	Eze 5:13	1696
I the LORD have *s* it	Eze 5:15	1696
I the LORD have *s* it	Eze 5:17	1696
word which I have *s* shall be done	Eze 12:28	1696
have ye not *s* a lying divination,	Eze 13:7	1696
albeit I have not *s*	Eze 13:7	559
Because ye have *s* vanity, and seen	Eze 13:8	1696
deceived when he hath *s* a thing	Eze 14:9	1696
know that I the LORD have *s* it	Eze 17:21	1696
I the LORD have *s* and have done it	Eze 17:24	1696
for I the LORD have *s* it	Eze 21:32	1696
I the LORD have *s* it, and will do	Eze 22:14	1696
GOD, when the LORD hath not *s*	Eze 22:28	1696
for I have *s* it, saith the Lord	Eze 23:34	1696
I the LORD have *s* it	Eze 24:14	1696
for I have *s* it, saith the Lord	Eze 26:5	1696
for I the LORD have *s* it, saith	Eze 26:14	1696
for I have *s* it, saith the Lord	Eze 28:10	1696
I the LORD have *s* it	Eze 30:12	1696
I the LORD have *s* it	Eze 34:24	1696
s against the mountains of Israel	Eze 35:12	559
I *s* against the residue of the	Eze 36:5	1696
I have *s* in my jealousy and in my	Eze 36:6	1696
I the LORD have *s* it, and I will	Eze 36:36	1696
ye know that I the LORD have *s* it	Eze 37:14	1696
Art thou he of whom I have *s* in	Eze 38:17	1696
in the fire of my wrath have I *s*	Eze 38:19	1696
for I have *s* it, saith the Lord	Eze 39:5	1696
this is the day whereof I have *s*	Eze 39:8	1696
Nebuchadnezzar, to thee it is *s*	Dan 4:31	560
when he had *s* this word unto me,	Dan 10:11	1696
when he had *s* such words unto me,	Dan 10:15	1696
And when he had *s* unto me, I was	Dan 10:19	1696
yet they have *s* lies against me	Hos 7:13	1696
They have *s* words, swearing	Hos 10:4	1696
I have also *s* by the prophets, and	Hos 12:10	1696
for the LORD hath *s* it	Joel 3:8	1696
that the LORD hath *s* against you	Amos 3:1	1696
the Lord GOD hath *s*, who can but	Amos 3:8	1696
shall be with you, as ye have *s*	Amos 5:14	559
neither shouldest thou have *s*	Obad 12	6310
for the LORD hath *s* it	Obad 18	1696
of the LORD of hosts hath *s* it	Mic 4:4	1696
inhabitants thereof have *s* lies	Mic 6:12	1696
For the idols have *s* vanity	Zec 10:2	1696
What have we *s* so much against	Mal 3:13	1696
was *s* of the Lord by the prophet	Mt 1:22	4483
was *s* of the Lord by the prophet	Mt 2:15	4483
which was *s* by Jeremy the prophet	Mt 2:17	4483
which was *s* by the prophets	Mt 2:23	4483
For this is he that was *s* of by	Mt 3:3	4483
which was *s* by Esaias the prophet	Mt 4:14	4483
which was *s* by Esaias the prophet	Mt 8:17	4483
which was *s* by Esaias the prophet	Mt 12:17	4483
which was *s* by the prophet	Mt 13:35	4483
which was *s* by the prophet	Mt 21:4	4483
that which was *s* unto you by God	Mt 22:31	4483
s of by Daniel the prophet, stand	Mt 24:15	4483
saying, He hath *s* blasphemy	Mt 26:65	987
which was *s* by Jeremy the prophet	Mt 27:9	4483
which was *s* by the prophet	Mt 27:35	4483
And as soon as he had *s*,	Mk 1:42	2036
Jesus heard the word that was *s*	Mk 5:36	2980
he had *s* the parable against them	Mk 12:12	2036
s of by Daniel the prophet,	Mk 13:14	4483
be *s* of for a memorial of her	Mk 14:9	2980
after the Lord had *s* unto them	Mk 16:19	2980
those things which were *s* of him	Lk 2:33	2980
a sign which shall be *s* against	Lk 2:34	483
Therefore whatsoever ye have *s* in	Lk 12:3	2036
that which ye have *s* in the ear	Lk 12:3	2980
knew they the things which were *s*	Lk 18:34	3004
And when he had thus *s*, he went	Lk 19:28	2036
had *s* this parable against them	Lk 20:19	2036
all that the prophets have *s*	Lk 24:25	2980
And when he had thus *s*, he shewed	Lk 24:40	2036
word that Jesus had *s* unto him	Jn 4:50	2036
When he had thus *s*, he spat on	Jn 9:6	2036
had *s* of taking of rest in sleep	Jn 11:13	3004
And when he thus had *s*, he cried	Jn 11:43	2036
the word that I have *s*, the same	Jn 12:48	2980
For I have not *s* of myself	Jn 12:49	2980
These things have I *s* unto you	Jn 14:25	2980
the word which I have *s* unto you	Jn 15:3	2980
These things have I *s* unto you	Jn 15:11	2980
s unto them, they had not had sin	Jn 15:22	2980
These things have I *s* unto you	Jn 16:1	2980
These things have I *s* unto you in	Jn 16:25	2980
These things I have *s* unto you	Jn 16:33	2980
When Jesus had *s* these words	Jn 18:1	2036
And when he had thus *s*, one of the	Jn 18:22	2036
answered him, If I have *s* evil	Jn 18:23	2980
that he had *s* these things unto	Jn 20:18	2036
And when he had *s* this, he saith	Jn 21:19	2036
when he had *s* these things, while	Acts 1:9	2036
which was *s* by the prophet Joel	Acts 2:16	2046
which God hath *s* by the mouth of	Acts 3:21	2980
follow after, as many as have *s*	Acts 3:24	2980
which ye have *s* come upon me	Acts 8:24	2046
the way, and that he had *s* to him	Acts 9:27	2980
which is *s* of in the prophets	Acts 13:40	2046
those things which were *s* by Paul	Acts 13:45	3004
should first have been *s* to you	Acts 13:46	2980
the things which were *s* of Paul	Acts 16:14	2980
these things cannot be *s* against	Acts 19:36	369
And when he had thus *s*, he	Acts 19:41	2036
And when he had thus *s*, he kneeled	Acts 20:36	2036
spirit or an angel hath *s* to him	Acts 23:9	2980
And when he had thus *s*, the king	Acts 26:30	2036
those things which were *s* by Paul	Acts 27:11	3004
And when he had thus *s*, he took	Acts 27:35	2036
that every where it is *s* against	Acts 28:22	483
believed the things which were *s*	Acts 28:24	3004
after that Paul had *s* one word	Acts 28:25	2980
you all, that your faith is *s* of	Rom 1:8	2605
according to that which was *s*	Rom 4:18	2046
not then your good be evil *s* of	Rom 14:16	987
written, To whom he was not *s* of	Rom 15:21	312
why am I evil *s* of for that for	1Cor 10:30	987
how shall it be known what is *s*	1Cor 14:9	2980
I believed, and therefore have I *s*	2Cor 4:13	2980
last days *s* unto us by his Son	Heb 1:2	2980
For if the word *s* by angels was	Heb 2:2	2980
first began to be *s* by the Lord	Heb 2:3	2980
things which were to be *s* after	Heb 3:5	2980
afterward have *s* of another day	Heb 4:8	2980
are *s* pertaineth to another tribe	Heb 7:13	3004
which we have *s* this is the sum	Heb 8:1	3004
For when Moses had *s* every	Heb 9:19	2980
should not be *s* to them any more	Heb 12:19	4369
who have *s* unto you the word of	Heb 13:7	2980
who have *s* in the name of the	Jas 5:10	2980
on their part he is evil *s* of	1Pet 4:14	987
way of truth shall be evil *s* of	2Pet 2:2	987

s before by the holy prophets	2Pet 3:2	4280
sinners have *s* against him	Jude 15	2980
ye the words which were *s* before	Jude 17	4280

SPOKES
and their felloes, and their *s*	1Kin 7:33	2840

SPOKESMAN
he shall be thy *s* unto the people	Ex 4:16	1696

SPOON
One *s* of ten shekels of gold,	Num 7:14	3709
One *s* of gold of ten shekels,	Num 7:20	3709
One golden *s* of ten shekels, full	Num 7:26	3709
One golden *s* of ten shekels, full	Num 7:32	3709
One golden *s* of ten shekels, full	Num 7:38	3709
One golden *s* of ten shekels, full	Num 7:44	3709
One golden *s* of ten shekels, full	Num 7:50	3709
One golden *s* of ten shekels, full	Num 7:56	3709
One golden *s* of ten shekels, full	Num 7:62	3709
One golden *s* of ten shekels, full	Num 7:68	3709
One golden *s* of ten shekels, full	Num 7:74	3709
One golden *s* of ten shekels, full	Num 7:80	3709

SPOONS
s thereof, and covers thereof, and	Ex 25:29	3709
the table, his dishes, and his *s*	Ex 37:16	3709
put thereon the dishes, and the *s*	Num 4:7	3709
silver bowls, twelve *s* of gold	Num 7:84	3709
The golden *s* were twelve, full of	Num 7:86	3709
the gold of the *s* was an hundred	Num 7:86	3709
snuffers, and the basons, and the *s*	1Kin 7:50	3709
and the snuffers, and the *s*	2Kin 25:14	3709
snuffers, and the basons, and the *s*	2Chr 4:22	3709
and to offer withal, and *s*	2Chr 24:14	3709
snuffers, and the bowls, and the *s*	Jer 52:18	3709
and the candlesticks, and the *s*	Jer 52:19	3709

SPORT
for Samson, that he may make us *s*	Judg 16:25	7832
and he made them *s*	Judg 16:25	6711
that beheld while Samson made *s*	Judg 16:27	7832
It is as *s* to a fool to do	Prov 10:23	7814
and saith, Am not I in *s*	Prov 26:19	7832
Against whom do ye *s* yourselves	Is 57:4	6026

SPORTING
Isaac was *s* with Rebekah his wife	Gen 26:8	6711
s themselves with their own	2Pet 2:13	1792

SPOT
a rising, a scab, or bright *s*	Lev 13:2	934
If the bright *s* be white in the	Lev 13:4	934
be a white rising, or a bright *s*	Lev 13:19	934
if the bright *s* stay in his place	Lev 13:23	934
burneth have a white bright *s*	Lev 13:24	934
in the bright *s* be turned white	Lev 13:25	934
be no white hair in the bright *s*	Lev 13:26	934
if the bright *s* stay in his place	Lev 13:28	934
it is a freckled *s* that groweth	Lev 13:39	933
and for a scab, and for a bright *s*	Lev 14:56	934
bring thee a red heifer without *s*	Num 19:2	8549
first year without *s* day by day	Num 28:3	8549
lambs of the first year without *s*	Num 28:9	8549
lambs of the first year without *s*	Num 28:11	8549
lambs of the first year without *s*	Num 29:17	8549
lambs of the first year without *s*	Num 29:26	8549
their *s* is not the *s* of his	Deut 32:5	3971
is not the *s* of his children	Deut 32:5	3971
thou lift up thy face without *s*	Job 11:15	3971
there is no *s* in thee	Song 4:7	3971
a glorious church, not having *s*	Eph 5:27	4696
keep this commandment without *s*	1Ti 6:14	784
offered himself without *s* to God	Heb 9:14	299
lamb without blemish and without *s*	1Pet 1:19	784
found of him in peace, without *s*	2Pet 3:14	784

SPOTS
bright *s*, even white bright *s*	Lev 13:38	934
if the bright *s* in the skin of	Lev 13:39	934
his skin, or the leopard his *s*	Jer 13:23	2272
S they are and blemishes, sporting	2Pet 2:13	4696
These are *s* in your feasts of	Jude 12	4694

SPOTTED
s cattle, and all the brown cattle	Gen 30:32	2921
cattle among the sheep, and the *s*	Gen 30:32	2921
s among the goats, and brown among	Gen 30:33	2921
goats that were ringstraked and *s*	Gen 30:35	2921
she goats that were speckled and *s*	Gen 30:35	2921
ringstraked, speckled, and *s*	Gen 30:39	2921
even the garment *s* by the flesh	Jude 23	4695

SPOUSE
Come with me from Lebanon, my *s*	Song 4:8	3618
my heart, my sister, my *s*	Song 4:9	3618

fair is thy love, my sister, my *s*	Song 4:10	3618
Thy lips, O my *s*, drop as the	Song 4:11	3618
inclosed is my sister, my *s*	Song 4:12	3618
into my garden, my sister, my *s*	Song 5:1	3618

SPOUSES
your *s* shall commit adultery	Hos 4:13	3618
nor your *s* when they commit	Hos 4:14	3618

SPRANG
and immediately it *s* up, because	Mk 4:5	*1816*
and did yield fruit that *s* up	Mk 4:8	*305*
and the thorns *s* up with it	Lk 8:7	*4855*
ground, and *s* up, and bare fruit an	Lk 8:8	*5453*
s in, and came trembling, and fell	Acts 16:29	*1530*
that our Lord *s* out of Juda	Heb 7:14	*393*
Therefore *s* there even of one, and	Heb 11:12	*1080*

SPREAD
of the Canaanites *s* abroad	Gen 10:18	6327
thou shalt *s* abroad to the west,	Gen 28:14	6555
a field, where he had *s* his tent	Gen 33:19	5186
s his tent beyond the tower of	Gen 35:21	5186
I will *s* abroad my hands unto the	Ex 9:29	6566
s abroad his hands unto the LORD	Ex 9:33	6566
the cherubims *s* out their wings	Ex 37:9	6566
he *s* abroad the tent over the	Ex 40:19	6566
the plague *s* not in the skin	Lev 13:5	6581
the plague *s* not in the skin, the	Lev 13:6	6581
But if the scab *s* much abroad in	Lev 13:7	6581
if it *s* much abroad in the skin,	Lev 13:22	6581
s not, it is a burning boil	Lev 13:23	6581
if it be *s* much abroad in the	Lev 13:27	6581
s not in the skin, but it be	Lev 13:28	6581
and, behold, if the scall *s* not	Lev 13:32	6581
if the scall be not *s* in the skin	Lev 13:34	6581
But if the scall *s* much in the	Lev 13:35	6581
if the scall be *s* in the skin	Lev 13:36	6581
if the plague be *s* in the garment	Lev 13:51	6581
plague be not *s* in the garment	Lev 13:53	6581
colour, and the plague be not *s*	Lev 13:55	6581
if the plague be *s* in the walls	Lev 14:39	6581
if the plague be *s* in the house	Lev 14:44	6581
plague hath not *s* in the house	Lev 14:48	6581
shall *s* over it a cloth wholly of	Num 4:6	6566
they shall *s* a cloth of blue	Num 4:7	6566
they shall *s* upon them a cloth of	Num 4:8	6566
they shall *s* a cloth of blue	Num 4:11	6566
and *s* a purple cloth thereon	Num 4:13	6566
they shall *s* upon it a covering	Num 4:14	6566
they *s* them all abroad for	Num 11:32	7849
As the valleys are they *s* forth	Num 24:6	5186
they shall *s* the cloth before the	Deut 22:17	6566
they *s* a garment, and did cast	Judg 8:25	6566
in Judah, and *s* themselves in Lehi	Judg 15:9	5203
s therefore thy skirt over thine	Ruth 3:9	6566
they were *s* abroad upon all the	1Sa 30:16	5203
s themselves in the valley of	2Sa 5:18	5203
s themselves in the valley of	2Sa 5:22	5203
So they *s* Absalom a tent upon the	2Sa 16:22	5186
s a covering over the well's	2Sa 17:19	6566
mouth, and *s* ground corn thereon	2Sa 17:19	7849
s it for her upon the rock, from	2Sa 21:10	5186
the street, and did *s* them abroad	2Sa 22:43	7554
s gold upon the cherubims, and	1Kin 6:32	7286
For the cherubims *s* forth their	1Kin 8:7	6566
s forth his hands toward heaven	1Kin 8:22	6566
s forth his hands toward this	1Kin 8:38	6566
with his hands *s* up to heaven	1Kin 8:54	6566
s it on his face, so that he died	2Kin 8:15	6566
the LORD, and *s* it before the LORD	2Kin 19:14	6566
s themselves in the valley of	1Chr 14:9	6584
the Philistines yet again *s*	1Chr 14:13	6584
that *s* out their wings, and	1Chr 28:18	6566
The wings of these cherubims *s*	2Chr 3:13	6566
For the cherubims *s* forth their	2Chr 5:8	6566
of Israel, and *s* forth his hands	2Chr 6:12	6566
s forth his hands toward heaven,	2Chr 6:13	6566
shall *s* forth his hands in this	2Chr 6:29	6566
his name *s* abroad even to the	2Chr 26:8	3212
And his name *s* far abroad	2Chr 26:15	3318
s out my hands unto the LORD my	Ezr 9:5	6566
My root was *s* out by the waters,	Job 29:19	6605
Hast thou with him *s* out the sky	Job 37:18	7554
He *s* a cloud for a covering	Ps 105:39	6566
they have *s* a net by the wayside	Ps 140:5	6566
net is *s* in the sight of any bird	Prov 1:17	2219
when ye *s* forth your hands, I	Is 1:15	6566
the worm is *s* under thee, and the	Is 14:11	3331
they that *s* nets upon the waters	Is 19:8	6566
vail that is *s* over all nations	Is 25:7	5259
he shall *s* forth his hands in the	Is 25:11	6566

S

mast, they could not *s* the sail	Is 33:23	6566
the LORD, and *s* it before the LORD	Is 37:14	6566
he that *s* forth the earth, and	Is 42:5	7554
to *s* sackcloth and ashes under him	Is 58:5	3331
I have *s* out my hands all the day	Is 65:2	6566
they shall *s* them before the sun,	Jer 8:2	7849
Silver *s* into plates is brought	Jer 10:9	7554
he shall *s* his royal pavilion	Jer 43:10	5186
shall *s* his wings over Moab	Jer 48:40	6566
eagle, and *s* his wings over Bozrah	Jer 49:22	6566
The adversary hath *s* out his hand	Lam 1:10	6566
he hath *s* a net for my feet, he	Lam 1:13	6566
And he *s* it before me	Eze 2:10	6566
My net also will I *s* upon him	Eze 12:13	6566
I *s* my skirt over thee, and	Eze 16:8	6566
I will *s* my net upon him, and he	Eze 17:20	6566
and *s* their net over him	Eze 19:8	6566
shalt be a place to *s* nets upon	Eze 26:14	4894
I will therefore *s* out my net	Eze 32:3	6566
shall be a place to *s* forth nets	Eze 47:10	4894
on Mizpah, and a net *s* upon Tabor	Hos 5:1	6566
I will *s* my net upon them	Hos 7:12	6566
His branches shall *s*, and his	Hos 14:6	3212
as the morning *s* upon the	Joel 2:2	6566
their horsemen shall *s* themselves	Hab 1:8	6335
prosperity shall yet be *s* abroad	Zec 1:17	6327
for I have *s* you abroad as the	Zec 2:6	6566
s dung upon your faces, even the	Mal 2:3	2219
s abroad his fame in all that	Mt 9:31	1310
a very great multitude *s* their	Mt 21:8	4766
immediately his fame *s* abroad	Mk 1:28	1831
(for his name was *s* abroad	Mk 6:14	4766
many *s* their garments in the way	Mk 11:8	4766
they *s* their clothes in the way	Lk 19:36	5291
But that it *s* no further among	Acts 4:17	1268
faith to God-ward is *s* abroad	1Th 1:8	1831

SPREADEST
which thou *s* forth to be thy sail	Eze 27:7	4666

SPREADETH
the scab *s* in the skin, then the	Lev 13:8	6581
s abroad her wings, taketh them,	Deut 32:11	6566
Which alone *s* out the heavens, and	Job 9:8	5186
throne, and *s* his cloud upon it	Job 26:9	6576
he *s* his light upon it, and	Job 36:30	6566
he *s* sharp pointed things upon	Job 41:30	7502
neighbour *s* a net for his feet	Prov 29:5	6566
as he that swimmeth *s* forth his	Is 25:11	6566
the goldsmith *s* it over with gold	Is 40:19	7554
s them out as a tent to dwell in	Is 40:22	4969
that *s* abroad the earth by myself	Is 44:24	7554
that *s* her hands, saying, Woe is	Jer 4:31	6566
that *s* out her roots by the river	Jer 17:8	7971
Zion *s* forth her hands, and there	Lam 1:17	6566

SPREADING
it is a *s* plague	Lev 13:57	6524
s himself like a green bay tree	Ps 37:35	6168
became a *s* vine of low stature,	Eze 17:6	5628
It shall be a place for the *s* of	Eze 26:5	4894

SPREADINGS
understand the *s* of the clouds	Job 36:29	4666

SPRIGS
cut off the *s* with pruninghooks	Is 18:5	2150
forth branches, and shot forth *s*	Eze 17:6	6288

SPRING
sang this song, *S* up, O well	Num 21:17	5927
depths that *s* out of valleys and	Deut 8:7	3318
and when the day began to *s*	Judg 19:25	5927
to pass about the *s* of the day	1Sa 9:26	5927
forth unto the *s* of the waters	2Kin 2:21	4161
doth trouble *s* out of the ground	Job 5:6	6779
bud of the tender herb to *s* forth	Job 38:27	6779
Truth shall *s* out of the earth	Ps 85:11	6779
When the wicked *s* as the grass	Ps 92:7	6524
troubled fountain, and a corrupt *s*	Prov 25:26	4726
a *s* shut up, a fountain sealed	Song 4:12	1530
before they *s* forth I tell you of	Is 42:9	6779
now it shall *s* forth	Is 43:19	6779
they shall *s* up as among the	Is 44:4	6779
let righteousness *s* up together	Is 45:8	6779
health shall *s* forth speedily	Is 58:8	6779
like a *s* of water, whose waters	Is 58:11	4161
that are sown in it to *s* forth	Is 61:11	6779
praise to *s* forth before all the	Is 61:11	6779
wither in all the leaves of her *s*	Eze 17:9	6780
his *s* shall become dry, and his	Hos 13:15	4726
pastures of the wilderness do *s*	Joel 2:22	1876
and day, and the seed should *s*	Mk 4:27	985

SPRINGETH
the hyssop that *s* out of the wall	1Kin 4:33	3318
year that which *s* of the same	2Kin 19:29	7823
year that which *s* of the same	Is 37:30	7823
thus judgment *s* up as hemlock in	Hos 10:4	6524

SPRINGING
and found there a well of *s* water	Gen 26:19	2416
as the tender grass *s* out of the	2Sa 23:4	
thou blessest the *s* thereof	Ps 65:10	6780
water *s* up into everlasting life	Jn 4:14	*242*
of bitterness *s* up trouble you	Heb 12:15	5453

SPRINGS
the plain, under the *s* of Pisgah	Deut 4:49	794
and of the vale, and of the *s*	Josh 10:40	794
and in the plains, and in the *s*	Josh 12:8	794
give me also *s* of water	Josh 15:19	1543
upper *s*, and the nether *s*	Josh 15:19	1543
give me also *s* of water	Judg 1:15	1543
the upper *s* and the nether *s*	Judg 1:15	1543
entered into the *s* of the sea	Job 38:16	5033
all my *s* are in thee	Ps 87:7	4599
He sendeth the *s* into the valleys	Ps 104:10	4599
and the thirsty land *s* of water	Is 35:7	4002
water, and the dry land *s* of water	Is 41:18	4161
even by the *s* of water shall he	Is 49:10	4002
dry up her sea, and make her *s* dry	Jer 51:36	4726

SPRINKLE
let Moses *s* it toward the heaven	Ex 9:8	2236
s it round about upon the altar	Ex 29:16	2236
s the blood upon the altar round	Ex 29:20	2236
s it upon Aaron, and upon his	Ex 29:21	5137
s the blood round about upon the	Lev 1:5	2236
shall *s* his blood round about	Lev 1:11	2236
s the blood upon the altar round	Lev 3:2	2236
Aaron's sons shall *s* the blood	Lev 3:8	2236
the sons of Aaron shall *s* the	Lev 3:13	2236
s of the blood seven times before	Lev 4:6	5137
s it seven times before the LORD,	Lev 4:17	5137
he shall *s* of the blood of the	Lev 5:9	5137
he *s* round about upon the altar	Lev 7:2	2236
he shall *s* upon him that is to be	Lev 14:7	5137
shall *s* of the oil with his	Lev 14:16	5137
the priest shall *s* with his right	Lev 14:27	5137
water, and the house seven times	Lev 14:51	5137
s it with his finger upon the	Lev 16:14	5137
he *s* of the blood with his finger	Lev 16:14	5137
s it upon the mercy seat, and	Lev 16:15	5137
he shall *s* of the blood upon it	Lev 16:19	5137
the priest shall *s* the blood upon	Lev 17:6	2236
S water of purifying upon them,	Num 8:7	5137
thou shalt *s* blood upon the	Num 18:17	2236
s of her blood directly before	Num 19:4	5137
s it upon the tent, and upon all	Num 19:18	5137
the clean person shall *s* upon the	Num 19:19	5137
s upon it all the blood of the	2Kin 16:15	2236
So shall he *s* many nations	Is 52:15	5137
Then will I *s* clean water upon	Eze 36:25	2236
thereon, and to *s* blood thereon	Eze 43:18	2236

SPRINKLED
Moses *s* it up toward heaven	Ex 9:10	2236
of the blood he *s* on the altar	Ex 24:6	2236
s it on the people, and said,	Ex 24:8	2236
when there is *s* of the blood	Lev 6:27	5137
it was *s* in the holy place	Lev 6:27	5137
he *s* thereof upon the altar seven	Lev 8:11	5137
Moses *s* the blood upon the altar	Lev 8:19	2236
Moses *s* the blood upon the altar	Lev 8:24	2236
s it upon Aaron, and upon his	Lev 8:30	5137
which he *s* round about upon the	Lev 9:12	2236
which he *s* upon the altar round	Lev 9:18	2236
of separation was not *s* upon him	Num 19:13	2236
hath not been *s* upon him	Num 19:20	2236
of her blood was *s* on the wall	2Kin 9:33	5137
and *s* the blood of his peace	2Kin 16:13	2236
the blood, and *s* it on the altar	2Chr 29:22	2236
they *s* the blood upon the altar	2Chr 29:22	2236
they *s* the blood upon the altar	2Chr 29:22	2236
the priests *s* the blood, which	2Chr 30:16	2236
the priests *s* the blood from	2Chr 35:11	2236
s dust upon their heads toward	Job 2:12	2236
blood shall be *s* upon my garments	Is 63:3	5137
s both the book, and all the	Heb 9:19	4472
Moreover he *s* with blood both the	Heb 9:21	4472
having our hearts *s* from an evil	Heb 10:22	4472

SPRINKLETH
that *s* the blood of the peace	Lev 7:14	2236
that he that *s* the water of	Num 19:21	5137

SPRINKLING

ashes of an heifer *s* the unclean	Heb 9:13	4472
the *s* of blood, lest he that	Heb 11:28	4378
covenant, and to the blood of *s*	Heb 12:24	4473
s of the blood of Jesus Christ	1Pet 1:2	4473

SPROUT

be cut down, that it will *s* again	Job 14:7	2498

SPRUNG

the east wind *s* up after them	Gen 41:6	6779
the east wind, *s* up after them	Gen 41:23	6779
it is a leprosy *s* up in his bald	Lev 13:42	6524
and shadow of death light is *s* up	Mt 4:16	393
and forthwith they *s* up, because	Mt 13:5	1816
and the thorns *s* up, and choked	Mt 13:7	305
But when the blade *s* up	Mt 13:26	985
and as soon as it was *s* up	Lk 8:6	5453

SPUE

That the land *s* not you out also,	Lev 18:28	6958
to dwell therein, *s* you not out	Lev 20:22	6958
Drink ye, and be drunken, and *s*	Jer 25:27	7006
I will *s* thee out of my mouth	Rev 3:16	1692

SPUED

as it *s* out the nations that were	Lev 18:28	6958

SPUN

and brought that which they had *s*	Ex 35:25	4299
them up in wisdom *s* goats' hair	Ex 35:26	2901

SPUNGE

one of them ran, and took a *s*	Mt 27:48	4699
filled a *s* full of vinegar, and	Mk 15:36	4699
and they filled a *s* with vinegar	Jn 19:29	4699

SPY

Moses sent to *s* out the land	Num 13:16	8446
Moses sent them to *s* out the land	Num 13:17	8446
And Moses sent to *s* out Jaazer	Num 21:32	7270
of Shittim two men to *s* secretly	Josh 2:1	7270
Joshua sent to *s* out Jericho	Josh 6:25	7270
to *s* out the land, and to search	Judg 18:2	7270
to *s* out the country of Laish	Judg 18:14	7270
went to *s* out the land went up	Judg 18:17	7270
to *s* it out, and to overthrow it	2Sa 10:3	7270
s where he is, that I may send and	2Kin 6:13	7200
overthrow, and to *s* out the land	1Chr 19:3	7200
who came in privily to *s* out our	Gal 2:4	2684

SQUARE

And all the doors and posts were *s*	1Kin 7:5	7251
s in the four squares thereof	Eze 43:16	7251
hundred in breadth, *s* round about	Eze 45:2	7251

SQUARED

The posts of the temple were *s*	Eze 41:21	7251

SQUARES

square in the four *s* thereof	Eze 43:16	7253
broad in the four *s* thereof	Eze 43:17	7253

STABILITY

shall be the *s* of thy times	Is 33:6	530

STABLE

the world also shall be *s*	1Chr 16:30	3559
I will make Rabbah a *s* for camels	Eze 25:5	5116

STABLISH

I will *s* the throne of his	2Sa 7:13	3559
I will *s* his throne for ever	1Chr 17:12	3559
as he went to *s* his dominion by	1Chr 18:3	5324
Then will I *s* the throne of thy	2Chr 7:18	6965
To *s* this among them, that they	Est 9:21	6965
S thy word unto thy servant, who	Ps 119:38	6965
to *s* you according to my gospel	Rom 16:25	4741
To the end he may *s* your hearts	1Th 3:13	4741
s you in every good word and work	2Th 2:17	4741
Lord is faithful, who shall *s* you	2Th 3:3	4741
s your hearts	Jas 5:8	4741
a while, make you perfect, *s*	1Pet 5:10	4741

STABLISHED

Therefore the LORD *s* the kingdom	2Chr 17:5	3559
the world also is *s*, that it	Ps 93:1	3559
He hath also *s* them for ever and	Ps 148:6	5975
s in the faith, as ye have been	Col 2:7	950

STABLISHETH

blood, and *s* a city by iniquity	Hab 2:12	3559
Now he which *s* us with you in	2Cor 1:21	950

STACHYS (*sta'-kis*) *A Christian in Rome.*

helper in Christ, and *S* my beloved	Rom 16:9	4720

STACKS

in thorns, so that the *s* of corn	Ex 22:6	1430

STACTE

Take unto thee sweet spices, *s*	Ex 30:34	5198

STAFF

for with my *s* I passed over this	Gen 32:10	4731
thy *s* that is in thine hand	Gen 38:18	4294
the signet, and bracelets, and *s*	Gen 38:25	4294
your feet, and your *s* in your hand	Ex 12:11	4731
again, and walk abroad upon his *s*	Ex 21:19	4938
I have broken the *s* of your bread	Lev 26:26	4294
they bare it between two upon a *s*	Num 13:23	4132
and he smote the ass with a *s*	Num 22:27	4731
end of the *s* that was in his hand	Judg 6:21	4938
the *s* of his spear was like a	1Sa 17:7	2671
And he took his *s* in his hand	1Sa 17:40	4731
a leper, or that leaneth on a *s*	2Sa 3:29	6418
the *s* of whose spear was like a	2Sa 21:19	6086
with iron and the *s* of a spear	2Sa 23:7	6086
but he went down to him with a *s*	2Sa 23:21	7626
take my *s* in thine hand, and go	2Kin 4:29	4938
lay my *s* upon the face of the	2Kin 4:29	4938
laid the *s* upon the face of the	2Kin 4:31	4938
upon the *s* of this bruised reed	2Kin 18:21	4938
and he went down to him with a *s*	1Chr 11:23	7626
whose spear *s* was like a weaver's	1Chr 20:5	6086
thy rod and thy *s* they comfort me	Ps 23:4	4938
he brake the whole *s* of bread	Ps 105:16	4294
and from Judah the stay and the *s*	Is 3:1	4938
the *s* of his shoulder, the rod of	Is 9:4	4294
the *s* in their hand is mine	Is 10:5	4294
or as if the *s* should lift up	Is 10:15	4294
shall lift up his *s* against thee	Is 10:24	4294
hath broken the *s* of the wicked	Is 14:5	4294
fitches are beaten out with a *s*	Is 28:27	4294
where the grounded *s* shall pass	Is 30:32	4294
in the *s* of this broken reed	Is 36:6	4938
say, How is the strong *s* broken	Jer 48:17	4294
I will break the *s* of bread in	Eze 4:16	4294
and will break your *s* of bread	Eze 5:16	4294
will break the *s* of the bread	Eze 14:13	4294
because they have been a *s* of	Eze 29:6	4938
their *s* declareth unto them	Hos 4:12	4731
every man with his *s* in his hand	Zec 8:4	4938
And I took my *s*, even Beauty, and	Zec 11:10	4731
Then I cut asunder mine other *s*	Zec 11:14	4731
for their journey, save a *s* only	Mk 6:8	4464
leaning upon the top of his *s*	Heb 11:21	4464

STAGGER

he maketh them to *s* like a	Job 12:25	8582
s like a drunken man, and are at	Ps 107:27	5128
they *s*, but not with strong drink	Is 29:9	5128

STAGGERED

He *s* not at the promise of God	Rom 4:20	1252

STAGGERETH

as a drunken man *s* in his vomit	Is 19:14	8582

STAIN

and the shadow of death *s* it	Job 3:5	1350
to *s* the pride of all glory, and	Is 23:9	2490
and I will *s* all my raiment	Is 63:3	1351

STAIRS

winding *s* into the middle chamber	1Kin 6:8	3883
it under him on the top of the *s*	2Kin 9:13	4609
unto the *s* that go down from the	Neh 3:15	4609
Then stood up upon the *s*, of the	Neh 9:4	4608
they went up by the *s* of the city	Neh 12:37	4609
in the secret places of the *s*	Song 2:14	4095
east, and went up the *s* thereof	Eze 40:6	4609
his *s* shall look toward the east	Eze 43:17	4609
And when he came upon the *s*	Acts 21:35	304
him licence, Paul stood on the *s*	Acts 21:40	304

STAKES

not one of the *s* thereof shall	Is 33:20	3489
thy cords, and strengthen thy *s*	Is 54:2	3489

STALK

ears of corn came up upon one *s*	Gen 41:5	7070
seven ears came up in one *s*	Gen 41:22	7070
it hath no *s*	Hos 8:7	7054

STALKS

and hid them with the *s* of flax	Josh 2:6	6086

STALL

calves out of the midst of the *s*	Amos 6:4	4770
and grow up as calves of the *s*	Mal 4:2	4770
his ox or his ass from the *s*	Lk 13:15	5336

STALLED

herbs where love is, than a *s* ox	Prov 15:17	75

S

STALLS

s of horses for his chariots	1Kin 4:26	723
had four thousand *s* for horses	2Chr 9:25	723
s for all manner of beasts, and	2Chr 32:28	723
there shall be no herd in the *s*	Hab 3:17	7517

STAMMERERS

the tongue of the *s* shall be	Is 32:4	5926

STAMMERING

For with *s* lips and another tongue	Is 28:11	3934
of a *s* tongue, that thou canst	Is 33:19	3932

STAMP

I did *s* them as the mire of the	2Sa 22:43	1854
s with thy foot, and say, Alas for	Eze 6:11	7554

STAMPED

s it, and ground it very small,	Deut 9:21	3807
s it small to powder, and cast the	2Kin 23:6	1854
s it small to powder, and burned	2Kin 23:15	1854
s it, and burnt it at the brook	2Chr 15:16	1854
s with the feet, and rejoiced in	Eze 25:6	7554
s the residue with the feet of it	Dan 7:7	7512
s the residue with his feet	Dan 7:19	7512
down to the ground, and *s* upon him	Dan 8:7	7429
to the ground, and *s* upon them	Dan 8:10	7429

STAMPING

At the noise of the *s* of the	Jer 47:3	8161

STANCHED

immediately her issue of blood *s*	Lk 8:44	2476

STAND

And they said, *S* back	Gen 19:9	5066
I *s* here by the well of water	Gen 24:13	5324
Behold, I *s* by the well of water	Gen 24:43	5324
thou shalt *s* by the river's brink	Ex 7:15	5324
the morning, and *s* before Pharaoh	Ex 8:20	3320
the magicians could not *s* before	Ex 9:11	5975
s before Pharaoh, and say unto him	Ex 9:13	3320
s still, and see the salvation of	Ex 14:13	3320
I will *s* before thee there upon	Ex 17:6	5975
to morrow I will *s* on the top of	Ex 17:9	5324
all the people *s* by thee from	Ex 18:14	5324
pillar *s* at the tabernacle door	Ex 33:10	5975
me, and thou shalt *s* upon a rock	Ex 33:21	5324
neither shall any woman *s* before	Lev 18:23	5975
neither shalt thou *s* against the	Lev 19:16	5975
no power to *s* before your enemies	Lev 26:37	8617
shall estimate it, so shall it *s*	Lev 27:14	6965
to thy estimation it shall *s*	Lev 27:17	6965
of the men that shall *s* with you	Num 1:5	5975
S still, and I will hear what the	Num 9:8	5975
that they may *s* there with thee	Num 11:16	3320
to *s* before the congregation to	Num 16:9	5975
S by thy burnt offering, and I	Num 23:3	3320
S here by thy burnt offering,	Num 23:15	3320
he shall *s* before Eleazar the	Num 27:21	5975
then all her vows shall *s*	Num 30:4	6965
she hath bound her soul shall *s*	Num 30:4	6965
she hath bound her soul, shall *s*	Num 30:5	6965
then her vows shall *s*, and her	Num 30:7	6965
she bound her soul shall *s*	Num 30:7	6965
their souls, shall *s* against her	Num 30:9	6965
then all her vows shall *s*	Num 30:11	6965
she bound her soul shall *s*	Num 30:11	6965
the bond of her soul, shall not *s*	Num 30:12	6965
die not, until he *s* before the	Num 35:12	5975
s thou here by me, and I will	Deut 5:31	5975
no man be able to *s* before thee	Deut 7:24	3320
Who can *s* before the children of	Deut 9:2	3320
to *s* before the LORD to minister	Deut 10:8	5975
no man be able to *s* before you	Deut 11:25	3320
to *s* to minister in the name of	Deut 18:5	5975
which *s* there before the LORD	Deut 18:7	5975
shall *s* before the LORD, before	Deut 19:17	5975
Thou shalt *s* abroad, and the man	Deut 24:11	5975
and if he *s* to it, and say, I like	Deut 25:8	5975
These shall *s* upon mount Gerizim	Deut 27:12	5975
these shall *s* upon mount Ebal to	Deut 27:13	5975
Ye *s* this day all of you before	Deut 29:10	5324
shall not any man be able to *s*	Josh 1:5	3320
ye shall *s* still in Jordan	Josh 3:8	5975
they shall *s* upon an heap	Josh 3:13	5975
could not *s* before their enemies	Josh 7:12	6965
thou canst not *s* before thine	Josh 7:13	6965
not a man of them *s* before thee	Josh 10:8	5975
Sun, *s* thou still upon Gibeon	Josh 10:12	1826
s at the entering of the gate of	Josh 20:4	5975
that city, until he *s* before the	Josh 20:6	5975
to *s* before you unto this day	Josh 23:9	5975
any longer *s* before their enemies	Judg 2:14	5975

S in the door of the tent, and it	Judg 4:20	5975
Who is able to *s* before this holy	1Sa 6:20	5975
but *s* thou still a while, that I	1Sa 9:27	5975
Now therefore *s* still, that I may	1Sa 12:7	3320
Now therefore *s* and see this great	1Sa 12:16	3320
then we will *s* still in our place	1Sa 14:9	5975
David, I pray thee, *s* before me	1Sa 16:22	5975
s beside my father in the field	1Sa 19:3	5975
He said unto me again, *S*, I pray	2Sa 1:9	5975
unto him, Turn aside, and *s* here	2Sa 18:30	3320
let her *s* before the king, and let	1Kin 1:2	5975
not *s* to minister because of the	1Kin 8:11	5975
which *s* continually before thee,	1Kin 10:8	5975
of Israel liveth, before whom I *s*	1Kin 17:1	5975
of hosts liveth, before whom I *s*	1Kin 18:15	5975
s upon the mount before the LORD	1Kin 19:11	5975
of hosts liveth, before whom I *s*	2Kin 3:14	5975
will surely come out to me, and *s*	2Kin 5:11	5975
the LORD liveth, before whom I *s*	2Kin 5:16	5975
Shaphat shall *s* on him this day	2Kin 6:31	5975
how then shall we *s*	2Kin 10:4	5975
of the LORD *s* between the earth	1Chr 21:16	5975
to *s* every morning to thank and	1Chr 23:30	5975
s to minister by reason of the	2Chr 5:14	5975
which *s* continually before thee,	2Chr 9:7	5975
we *s* before this house, and in thy	2Chr 20:9	5975
s ye still, and see the salvation	2Chr 20:17	5975
hath chosen you to *s* before him	2Chr 29:11	5975
Jerusalem and Benjamin to *s* to it	2Chr 34:32	5975
s in the holy place according to	2Chr 35:5	5975
for we cannot *s* before thee	Ezr 9:15	5975
and we are not able to *s* without	Ezr 10:13	5975
rulers of all the congregation *s*	Ezr 10:14	5975
and while they *s* by, let them shut	Neh 7:3	5975
S up and bless the LORD your God	Neh 9:5	6965
Mordecai's matters would *s*	Est 3:4	5975
to *s* for their life, to destroy,	Est 8:11	5975
his house, but it shall not *s*	Job 8:15	5975
that he shall *s* at the latter day	Job 19:25	6965
I *s* up, and thou regardest me not	Job 30:20	5975
words in order before me, *s* up	Job 33:5	3320
s still, and consider the wondrous	Job 37:14	5975
and they *s* as a garment	Job 38:14	3320
who then is able to *s* before me	Job 41:10	3320
shall not *s* in the judgment	Ps 1:5	6965
S in awe, and sin not	Ps 4:4	
foolish shall not *s* in thy sight	Ps 5:5	3320
but we are risen, and *s* upright	Ps 20:8	5749
or who shall *s* in his holy place	Ps 24:3	6965
hast made my mountain to *s* strong	Ps 30:7	5975
of the world *s* in awe of him	Ps 33:8	1481
and buckler, and *s* up for mine help	Ps 35:2	6965
my friends *s* aloof from my sore	Ps 38:11	5975
and my kinsmen *s* afar off	Ps 38:11	5975
upon thy right hand did *s* the	Ps 45:9	5324
Their eyes *s* out with fatness	Ps 73:7	3318
who may *s* in thy sight when once	Ps 76:7	5975
made the waters to *s* as an heap	Ps 78:13	5324
my covenant shall *s* fast with him	Ps 89:28	539
not made him to *s* in the battle	Ps 89:43	6965
or who will *s* up for me against	Ps 94:16	5975
let Satan *s* at his right hand	Ps 109:6	5975
For he shall *s* at the right hand	Ps 109:31	5975
They *s* fast for ever and ever, and	Ps 111:8	5564
Our feet shall *s* within thy gates	Ps 122:2	5975
iniquities, O Lord, who shall *s*	Ps 130:3	5975
which by night *s* in the house of	Ps 134:1	5975
Ye that *s* in the house of the	Ps 135:2	5975
who can *s* before his cold	Ps 147:17	5975
house of the righteous shall *s*	Prov 12:7	5975
counsel of the LORD, that shall *s*	Prov 19:21	6965
he shall *s* before kings	Prov 22:29	3320
he shall not *s* before mean men	Prov 22:29	3320
s not in the place of great men	Prov 25:6	5975
but who is able to *s* before envy	Prov 27:4	5975
that shall *s* up in his stead	Eccl 4:15	5975
s not in an evil thing	Eccl 8:3	5975
the Lord GOD, It shall not *s*	Is 7:7	6965
speak the word, and it shall not *s*	Is 8:10	6965
which shall *s* for an ensign of	Is 11:10	5975
as I have purposed, so shall it *s*	Is 14:24	6965
My lord, I *s* continually upon the	Is 21:8	5975
groves and images shall not *s* up	Is 27:9	6965
agreement with hell shall not *s*	Is 28:18	6965
and by liberal things shall he *s*	Is 32:8	6965
word of our God shall *s* for ever	Is 40:8	6965
gathered together, let them *s* up	Is 44:11	5975
done, saying, My counsel shall *s*	Is 46:10	6965
S now with thine enchantments, and	Is 47:12	5975
s up, and save thee from these	Is 47:13	5975
unto them, they *s* up together	Is 48:13	5975

let us s together	Is 50:8	5975
s up, O Jerusalem, which hast	Is 51:17	6965
And strangers shall s and feed your	Is 61:5	5975
S by thyself, come not near to me	Is 65:5	7126
S ye in the ways, and see, and ask	Jer 6:16	5975
S in the gate of the LORD's house	Jer 7:2	5975
s before me in this house, which	Jer 7:10	5975
asses did s in the high places	Jer 14:6	5975
again, and thou shalt s before me	Jer 15:19	5975
s in the gate of the children of	Jer 17:19	5975
S in the court of the LORD's	Jer 26:2	5975
a man to s before me for ever	Jer 35:19	5975
shall know whose words shall s	Jer 44:28	6965
surely s against you for evil	Jer 44:29	6965
s forth with your helmets	Jer 46:4	3320
say ye, S fast, and prepare thee	Jer 46:14	3320
they did not s, because the day	Jer 46:21	5975
of Aroer, s by the way, and espy	Jer 48:19	5975
shepherd that will s before me	Jer 49:19	5975
shepherd that will s before me	Jer 50:44	5975
the sword, go away, s not still	Jer 51:50	5975
s upon thy feet, and I will speak	Eze 2:1	5975
for the house of Israel to s in	Eze 13:5	5975
of his covenant it might s	Eze 17:14	5975
s in the gap before me for the	Eze 22:30	5975
they shall s upon the land	Eze 27:29	5975
all their loins to be at a s	Eze 29:7	5976
their trees s up in their height	Eze 31:14	5975
Ye s upon your sword, ye work	Eze 33:26	5975
they shall s before them to	Eze 44:11	5975
they shall s before me to offer	Eze 44:15	5975
they shall s in judgment	Eze 44:24	5975
shall s by the post of the gate,	Eze 46:2	5975
that the fishers shall s upon it	Eze 47:10	5975
in them to s in the king's palace	Dan 1:4	5975
they might s before the king	Dan 1:5	5975
kingdoms, and it shall s for ever	Dan 2:44	6966
made s upon the feet as a man, and	Dan 7:4	6966
that no beasts might s before him	Dan 8:4	5975
power in the ram to s before him	Dan 8:7	5975
four kingdoms shall s up out of	Dan 8:22	5975
dark sentences, shall s up	Dan 8:23	5975
he shall also s up against the	Dan 8:25	5975
I speak unto thee, and s upright	Dan 10:11	5975
there shall s up yet three kings	Dan 11:2	5975
And a mighty king shall s up	Dan 11:3	5975
And when he shall s up, his	Dan 11:4	5975
neither shall he s, nor his arm	Dan 11:6	5975
shall one s up in his estate	Dan 11:7	5975
many s up against the king of the	Dan 11:14	5975
will, and none shall s before him	Dan 11:16	5975
he shall s in the glorious land,	Dan 11:16	5975
but she shall not s on his side	Dan 11:17	5975
Then shall s up in his estate a	Dan 11:20	5975
estate shall s up a vile person	Dan 11:21	5975
but he shall not s	Dan 11:25	5975
arms shall s on his part, and they	Dan 11:31	5975
at that time shall Michael s up	Dan 12:1	5975
s in thy lot at the end of the	Dan 12:13	5975
Neither shall he s that handleth	Amos 2:15	5975
And he shall s and feed in the	Mic 5:4	5975
Who can s before his indignation	Nah 1:6	5975
S, s, shall they cry	Nah 2:8	5975
I will s upon my watch, and set me	Hab 2:1	5975
to walk among these that s by	Zec 3:7	5975
that s by the Lord of the whole	Zec 4:14	5975
his feet shall s in that day upon	Zec 14:4	5975
away while they s upon their feet	Zec 14:12	5975
who shall s when he appeareth	Mal 3:2	5975
against itself shall not s	Mt 12:25	2476
how shall then his kingdom s	Mt 12:26	2476
mother and thy brethren s without	Mt 12:47	2476
Why s ye here all the day idle	Mt 20:6	2476
s in the holy place, (whoso	Mt 24:15	2476
had the withered hand, S forth	Mk 3:3	1453
itself, that kingdom cannot s	Mk 3:24	2476
itself, that house cannot s	Mk 3:25	2476
and be divided, he cannot s	Mk 3:26	2476
there be some of them that s here	Mk 9:1	2476
And when ye s praying, forgive, if	Mk 11:25	4739
that s in the presence of God	Lk 1:19	3936
Rise up, and s forth in the midst	Lk 6:8	2476
mother and thy brethren s without	Lk 8:20	2476
himself, how shall his kingdom s	Lk 11:18	2476
door, and ye begin to s without	Lk 13:25	2476
to s before the Son of man	Lk 21:36	2476
the people which s by I said it	Jn 11:42	4026
why s ye gazing up into heaven	Acts 1:11	2476
this man s here before you whole	Acts 4:10	3936
Go, s and speak in the temple to	Acts 5:20	2476
commanded the chariot to s still	Acts 8:38	2476

Peter took him up, saying, S up	Acts 10:26	450
loud voice, S upright on thy feet	Acts 14:10	450
I s at Caesar's judgment seat	Acts 25:10	2476
And now I s and am judged for the	Acts 26:6	2476
But rise, and s upon thy feet	Acts 26:16	2476
into this grace wherein we s	Rom 5:2	2476
God according to election might s	Rom 9:11	3306
for God is able to make him s	Rom 14:4	2476
for we shall all s before the	Rom 14:10	3936
should not s in the wisdom of men	1Cor 2:5	1510
ye have received, and wherein ye s	1Cor 15:1	2476
why s we in jeopardy every hour	1Cor 15:30	
s fast in the faith, quit you	1Cor 16:13	4739
for by faith ye s	2Cor 1:24	2476
for I s in doubt of you	Gal 4:20	639
S fast therefore in the liberty	Gal 5:1	4739
that ye may be able to s against	Eph 6:11	2476
day, and having done all, to s	Eph 6:13	2476
S therefore, having your loins	Eph 6:14	2476
that ye s fast in one spirit,	Phil 1:27	4739
so s fast in the Lord, my dearly	Phil 4:1	4739
in prayers, that ye may s perfect	Col 4:12	2476
we live, if ye s fast in the Lord	1Th 3:8	4739
s fast, and hold the traditions	2Th 2:15	4739
S thou there, or sit here under	Jas 2:3	2476
true grace of God wherein ye s	1Pet 5:12	2476
I s at the door, and knock	Rev 3:20	2476
and who shall be able to s	Rev 6:17	2476
angel which I saw s upon the sea	Rev 10:5	2476
s on the sea of glass, having the	Rev 15:2	2476
shall s afar off for the fear of	Rev 18:15	2476
small and great, s before God	Rev 20:12	2476

STANDARD

camp, and every man by his own s	Num 1:52	1714
Israel shall pitch by his own s	Num 2:2	1714
the s of the camp of Judah pitch	Num 2:3	1714
On the south side shall be the s	Num 2:10	1714
be the s of the camp of Ephraim	Num 2:18	1714
The s of the camp of Dan shall be	Num 2:25	1714
In the first place went the s of	Num 10:14	1714
the s of the camp of Reuben set	Num 10:18	1714
the s of the camp of the children	Num 10:22	1714
the s of the camp of the children	Num 10:25	1714
set up my s to the people	Is 49:22	5251
shall lift up a s against him	Is 59:19	5127
lift up a s for the people	Is 62:10	5251
Set up the s toward Zion	Jer 4:6	5251
How long shall I see the s	Jer 4:21	5251
and publish, and set up a s	Jer 50:2	5251
Set up the s upon the walls of	Jer 51:12	5251
Set ye up a s in the land	Jer 51:27	5251

STANDARD-BEARER

shall be as when a s fainteth	Is 10:18	5264

STANDARDS

every man in his place by their s	Num 2:17	1714
shall go hindmost with their s	Num 2:31	1714
so they pitched by their s	Num 2:34	1714

STANDEST

wherefore s thou without	Gen 24:31	5975
whereon thou s is holy ground	Ex 3:5	5975
the place whereon thou s is holy	Josh 5:15	5975
Why s thou afar off, O LORD	Ps 10:1	5975
place where thou s is holy ground	Acts 7:33	2476
broken off, and thou s by faith	Rom 11:20	2476

STANDETH

and that thy cloud s over them	Num 14:14	5975
which s before thee, he shall go	Deut 1:38	5975
s to minister there before the	Deut 17:12	5975
But with him that s here with us	Deut 29:15	5975
the pillars whereupon the house s	Judg 16:26	3559
him, Behold, Haman s in the court	Est 6:5	5975
the king, s in the house of Haman	Est 7:9	5975
nor s in the way of sinners, nor	Ps 1:1	5975
My foot s in an even place	Ps 26:12	5975
counsel of the LORD s for ever	Ps 33:11	5975
God s in the congregation of the	Ps 82:1	5324
but my heart s in awe of thy word	Ps 119:161	5975
She is in the top of high places,	Prov 8:2	5324
he s behind our wall, he looketh	Song 2:9	5975
The LORD s up to plead	Is 3:13	5324
and s to judge the people	Is 3:13	5975
and set him in his place, and he s	Is 46:7	5975
backward, and justice s afar off	Is 59:14	5975
the great prince which s for the	Dan 12:1	5975
nor feed that that s still	Zec 11:16	5324
but there s one among you, whom	Jn 1:26	2476
friend of the bridegroom, which s	Jn 3:29	2476
to his own master he s or falleth	Rom 14:4	4739

S

Nevertheless he that *s* stedfast 1Cor 7:37   2476
eat no flesh while the world *s* 1Cor 8:13
he *s* take heed lest he fall 1Cor 10:12   2476
the foundation of God *s* sure 2Ti 2:19   2476
every priest *s* daily ministering.............. Heb 10:11   2476
the judge *s* before the door .... Jas 5:9   2476
of the angel which *s* upon the sea .... Rev 10:8   2476

STANDING

the stacks of corn, or the *s* corn .... Ex 22:6   7054
tabernacle of shittim wood *s* up .... Ex 26:15   5975
tabernacle of shittim wood *s* up.............. Ex 36:20   5975
neither rear you up a *s* image.................. Lev 26:1   4676
angel of the LORD *s* in the way .... Num 22:23   5324
angel of the LORD *s* in the way .... Num 22:31   5324
into the *s* corn of thy neighbour.............. Deut 23:25   7054
unto thy neighbour's *s* corn .... Deut 23:25   7054
the *s* corn of the Philistines.................... Judg 15:5   7054
the shocks, and also the *s* corn.............. Judg 15:5   7054
Samuel *s* as appointed over them,.......... 1Sa 19:20   5975
all his servants were *s* about him 1Sa 22:6   5324
the lion *s* by the carcase.......................... 1Kin 13:25   5975
the lion *s* by the carcase.......................... 1Kin 13:28   5975
all the host of heaven *s* by him 1Kin 22:19   5975
and two lions by the stays 2Chr 9:18   5975
of heaven *s* on his right hand 2Chr 18:18   5975
Esther the queen *s* in the court................ Est 5:2   5975
in deep mire, where there is no *s* .... Ps 69:2   4613
the wilderness into a *s* water .... Ps 107:35   98
turned the rock into a *s* water .... Ps 114:8   98
I had seen *s* before the river.................... Dan 8:6   5975
I saw the Lord *s* upon the altar.............. Amos 9:1   5324
he shall receive of you his *s* .... Mic 1:11   5979
thy *s* images out of the midst of.............. Mic 5:13   4676
me Joshua the high priest *s* .... Zec 3:1   5975
Satan *s* at his right hand to .... Zec 3:1   5975
which go forth from *s* before the.............. Zec 6:5   3320
love to pray *s* in the synagogues.......... Mt 6:5   2476
unto you, There be some *s* here.............. Mt 16:28   2476
hour, and saw others *s* idle in the.......... Mt 20:3   2476
went out, and found others *s* idle .... Mt 20:6   2476
s without, sent unto him, calling .... Mk 3:31   2476
s where it ought not, (let him.................. Mk 13:14   2476
unto him an angel of the Lord *s*.............. Lk 1:11   2476
And saw two ships *s* by the lake.............. Lk 5:2   2476
of a truth, there be some *s* here .... Lk 9:27   2476
s afar off, would not lift up so .... Lk 18:13   2476
and the woman *s* in the midst .... Jn 8:9   2476
his mother, and the disciple *s* by .... Jn 19:26   3936
herself back, and saw Jesus *s* .... Jn 20:14   2476
s up with the eleven, lifted up .... Acts 2:14   2476
man which was healed *s* with them .... Acts 4:14   2476
the keepers *s* without before the .... Acts 5:23   2476
put in prison are *s* in the temple............ Acts 5:25   2476
Jesus *s* on the right hand of God, ... Acts 7:55   2476
the Son of man *s* on the right .... Acts 7:56   2476
Stephen was shed, I also was *s* by .... Acts 22:20   2186
voice, that I cried *s* among them .... Acts 24:21   2476
as the first tabernacle was yet *s*... Heb 9:8   2192,4174
the earth *s* out of the water and 2Pet 3:5   4921
s on the four corners of the .... Rev 7:1   2476
the two candlesticks *s* before the............ Rev 11:4   2476
S afar off for the fear of her .... Rev 18:10   2476
And I saw an angel *s* in the sun .... Rev 19:17   2476

STANK

and the river *s*, and the Egyptians .... Ex 7:21   887
and the land *s*.. Ex 8:14   887
morning, and it bred worms, and *s*........ Ex 16:20   887
saw that they *s* before David.................. 2Sa 10:6   887

STAR

there shall come a *S* out of Jacob .... Num 24:17   3556
the *s* of your god, which ye made .... Amos 5:26   3556
we have seen his *s* in the east.................. Mt 2:2   792
what time the *s* appeared........................ Mt 2:7   792
and, lo, the *s*, which they saw in .... Mt 2:9   792
When they saw the *s*, they .... Mt 2:10   792
the *s* of your god Remphan, ... Acts 7:43   798
for one *s* differeth from another 1Cor 15:41   792
differeth from another *s* in glory 1Cor 15:41   792
the day *s* arise in your hearts.................. 2Pet 1:19   5459
And I will give him the morning *s*.......... Rev 2:28   792
there fell a great *s* from heaven .... Rev 8:10   792
the name of the *s* is called........................ Rev 8:11   792
I saw a *s* fall from heaven unto .... Rev 9:1   792
David, and the bright and morning *s* .... Rev 22:16   792

STARE

they look and *s* upon me.......................... Ps 22:17   7200

STARGAZERS

Let now the astrologers, the *s* .... Is 47:13   2374,3556

STARS

he made the *s* also .... Gen 1:16   3556
now toward heaven, and tell the *s* .... Gen 15:5   3556
thy seed as the *s* of the heaven.............. Gen 22:17   3556
to multiply as the *s* of heaven .... Gen 26:4   3556
the eleven *s* made obeisance to me .... Gen 37:9   3556
your seed as the *s* of heaven .... Ex 32:13   3556
ye are this day as the *s* of .... Deut 1:10   3556
the sun, and the moon, and the *s*.......... Deut 4:19   3556
as the *s* of heaven for multitude.............. Deut 10:22   3556
whereas ye were as the *s* of.................... Deut 28:62   3556
the *s* in their courses fought.................... Judg 5:20   3556
like to the *s* of the heavens 1Chr 27:23   3556
the morning till the *s* appeared .... Neh 4:21   3556
thou as the *s* of heaven, and.................. Neh 9:23   3556
Let the *s* of the twilight thereof.............. Job 3:9   3556
and sealeth up the *s*................................ Job 9:7   3556
and behold the height of the *s* .... Job 22:12   3556
the *s* are not pure in his sight .... Job 25:5   3556
When the morning *s* sang together .... Job 38:7   3556
of thy fingers, the moon and the *s* .... Ps 8:3   3556
The moon and *s* to rule by night............ Ps 136:9   3556
He telleth the number of the *s*................ Ps 147:4   3556
praise him, all ye *s* of light.................... Ps 148:3   3556
the light, or the moon, or the *s*.............. Eccl 12:2   3556
For the *s* of heaven and the .... Is 13:10   3556
my throne above the *s* of God .... Is 14:13   3556
of the *s* for a light by night, ... Jer 31:35   3556
and make the *s* thereof dark.................... Eze 32:7   3556
of the *s* to the ground, and .... Dan 8:10   3556
righteousness as the *s* for ever................ Dan 12:3   3556
the *s* shall withdraw their........................ Joel 2:10   3556
the *s* shall withdraw their........................ Joel 3:15   3556
Seek him that maketh the seven *s* .... Amos 5:8   3598
thou set thy nest among the *s* .... Obad 4   3556
merchants above the *s* of heaven .... Nah 3:16   3556
the *s* shall fall from heaven, and.......... Mt 24:29   792
the *s* of heaven shall fall, and .... Mk 13:25   792
sun, and in the moon, and in the *s* ...... Lk 21:25   798
when neither sun nor *s* in many .... Acts 27:20   798
moon, and another glory of the *s* 1Cor 15:41   792
so many as the *s* of the sky in .... Heb 11:12   798
wandering *s*, to whom is reserved.......... Jude 13   792
he had in his right hand seven *s*............ Rev 1:16   792
The mystery of the seven *s* which .... Rev 1:20   792
The seven *s* are the angels of the .... Rev 1:20   792
the seven *s* in his right hand .... Rev 2:1   792
Spirits of God, and the seven *s* .... Rev 3:1   792
the *s* of heaven fell unto the .... Rev 6:13   792
moon, and the third part of the *s* .... Rev 8:12   792
upon her head a crown of twelve *s* .... Rev 12:1   792
the third part of the *s* of heaven .... Rev 12:4   792

STATE

man asked us straitly of our *s* .... Gen 43:7
set the house of God in his *s* 2Chr 24:13   4971
according to the *s* of the king .... Est 1:7   3027
according to the *s* of the king .... Est 2:18   3027
his best *s* is altogether vanity .... Ps 39:5   5324
to know the *s* of thy flocks.................... Prov 27:23   6440
knowledge the *s* thereof shall be .... Prov 28:2   3651
from thy *s* shall he pull thee.................. Is 22:19   4612
the last *s* of that man is worse.............. Mt 12:45
the last *s* of that man is worse .... Lk 11:26
good comfort, when I know your *s*.. Phil 2:19   3588,4012
will naturally care for your *s*.......... Phil 2:20   3588,4012
learned, in whatsoever *s* I am .... Phil 4:11
All my *s* shall Tychicus declare ...... Col 4:7   3588,2596

STATELY

And satest upon a *s* bed, and a .... Eze 23:41   3520

STATION

And I will drive thee from thy *s* .... Is 22:19   4673

STATURE

we saw in it are men of a great *s*.......... Num 13:32   4060
or on the height of his *s* 1Sa 16:7   6967
Gath, where was a man of great *s*.......... 2Sa 21:20   4055
an Egyptian, a man of great *s* 1Chr 11:23   4060
Gath, where was a man of great *s* 1Chr 20:6   4060
This thy *s* is like to a palm tree .... Song 7:7   6967
the high ones of *s* shall be hewn .... Is 10:33   6967
and of the Sabeans, men of *s* .... Is 45:14   4060
the head of every *s* to hunt souls .... Eze 13:18   6967
became a spreading vine of low *s*.......... Eze 17:6   6967
her *s* was exalted among the thick .... Eze 19:11   6967
shadowing shroud, and of an high *s*...... Eze 31:3   6967
can add one cubit unto his *s* .... Mt 6:27   2244
And Jesus increased in wisdom and *s*... Lk 2:52   2244
can add to his *s* one cubit .... Lk 12:25   2244
press, because he was little of *s*............ Lk 19:3   2244
unto the measure of the *s* of the .... Eph 4:13   2244

STATUTE

there he made for them a *s*	Ex 15:25	2706
it shall be a *s* for ever unto	Ex 27:21	2708
it shall be a *s* for ever unto him	Ex 28:43	2708
shall be theirs for a perpetual *s*	Ex 29:9	2708
his sons' by a *s* for ever from	Ex 29:28	2706
it shall be a *s* for ever to them,	Ex 30:21	2706
It shall be a perpetual *s* for	Lev 3:17	2708
It shall be a *s* for ever in your	Lev 6:18	2706
it is a *s* for ever unto the Lord	Lev 6:22	2706
unto his sons by a *s* for ever	Lev 7:34	2706
by a *s* for ever throughout their	Lev 7:36	2708
it shall be a *s* for ever	Lev 10:9	2708
sons' with thee, by a *s* for ever	Lev 10:15	2706
this shall be a *s* for ever unto	Lev 16:29	2708
your souls, by a *s* for ever	Lev 16:31	2708
be an everlasting *s* unto you	Lev 16:34	2708
This shall be a *s* for ever unto	Lev 17:7	2708
it shall be a *s* for ever	Lev 23:14	2708
it shall be a *s* for ever in all	Lev 23:21	2708
it shall be a *s* for ever in your	Lev 23:31	2708
It shall be a *s* for ever in your	Lev 23:41	2708
it shall be a *s* for ever in your	Lev 24:3	2708
made by fire by a perpetual *s*	Lev 24:9	2706
with thee, by a *s* for ever	Num 18:11	2706
with thee, by a *s* for ever	Num 18:19	2706
it shall be a *s* for ever	Num 18:23	2708
among them, for a *s* for ever	Num 19:10	2708
shall be a perpetual *s* unto them	Num 19:21	2708
of Israel a *s* of judgment	Num 27:11	2708
So these things shall be for a *s*	Num 35:29	2708
people that day, and set them a *s*	Josh 24:25	2706
day forward, that he made it a *s*	1Sa 30:25	2706
For this was a *s* for Israel	Ps 81:4	2706
together to establish a royal *s*	Dan 6:7	7010
That no decree nor *s* which the	Dan 6:15	7010

STATUTES

my charge, my commandments, my *s*	Gen 26:5	2708
commandments, and keep all his *s*	Ex 15:26	2706
I do make them know the *s* of God	Ex 18:16	2706
the children of Israel all the *s*	Lev 10:11	2706
Ye shall therefore keep my *s*	Lev 18:5	2708
Ye shall therefore keep my *s*	Lev 18:26	2708
Ye shall keep my *s*	Lev 19:19	2708
shall ye observe all my *s*	Lev 19:37	2708
And ye shall keep my *s*, and do them	Lev 20:8	2708
Ye shall therefore keep all my *s*	Lev 20:22	2708
Wherefore ye shall do my *s*	Lev 25:18	2708
If ye walk in my *s*, and keep my	Lev 26:3	2708
And if ye shall despise my *s*	Lev 26:15	2708
because their soul abhorred my *s*	Lev 26:43	2708
These are the *s* and judgments and	Lev 26:46	2708
These are the *s*, which the Lord	Num 30:16	2706
hearken, O Israel, unto the *s*	Deut 4:1	2706
Behold, I have taught you *s*	Deut 4:5	2706
which shall hear all these *s*	Deut 4:6	2706
is there so great, that hath *s*	Deut 4:8	2706
me at that time to teach you *s*	Deut 4:14	2706
Thou shalt keep therefore his *s*	Deut 4:40	2706
are the testimonies, and the *s*	Deut 4:45	2706
unto them, Hear, O Israel, the *s*	Deut 5:1	2706
all the commandments, and the *s*	Deut 5:31	2706
these are the commandments, the *s*	Deut 6:1	2706
Lord thy God, to keep all his *s*	Deut 6:2	2708
God, and his testimonies, and his *s*	Deut 6:17	2706
mean the testimonies, and the *s*	Deut 6:20	2706
commanded us to do all these *s*	Deut 6:24	2706
keep the commandments, and the *s*	Deut 7:11	2706
and his judgments, and his *s*	Deut 8:11	2708
of the Lord, and his *s*, which I	Deut 10:13	2708
God, and keep his charge, and his *s*	Deut 11:1	2708
ye shall observe to do all the *s*	Deut 11:32	2706
These are the *s* and judgments,	Deut 12:1	2706
thou shalt observe and do these *s*	Deut 16:12	2706
the words of this law and these *s*	Deut 17:19	2706
hath commanded thee to do these *s*	Deut 26:16	2706
in his ways, and to keep his *s*	Deut 26:17	2706
and do his commandments and his *s*	Deut 27:10	2706
his *s* which I command thee this	Deut 28:15	2708
his *s* which he commanded thee	Deut 28:45	2708
his *s* which are written in this	Deut 30:10	2708
to keep his commandments and his *s*	Deut 30:16	2708
and as for his *s*, I did not depart	2Sa 22:23	2706
walk in his ways, to keep his *s*	1Kin 2:3	2708
walking in the *s* of David his	1Kin 3:3	2708
walk in my ways, to keep my *s*	1Kin 3:14	2706
if thou wilt walk in my *s*	1Kin 6:12	2708
keep his commandments, and his *s*	1Kin 8:58	2706
Lord our God, to walk in his *s*	1Kin 8:61	2708
commanded thee, and wilt keep my *s*	1Kin 9:4	2706
my *s* which I have set before you,	1Kin 9:6	2708
hast not kept my covenant and my *s*	1Kin 11:11	2708
in mine eyes, and to keep my *s*	1Kin 11:33	2708
he kept my commandments and my *s*	1Kin 11:34	2708
right in my sight, to keep my *s*	1Kin 11:38	2708
walked in the *s* of the heathen,	2Kin 17:8	2708
keep my commandments and my *s*	2Kin 17:13	2708
And they rejected his *s*, and his	2Kin 17:15	2706
but walked in the *s* of Israel	2Kin 17:19	2708
neither do they after their *s*	2Kin 17:34	2708
And the *s*, and the ordinances, and	2Kin 17:37	2708
his *s* with all their heart and all	2Kin 23:3	2708
thou takest heed to fulfil the *s*	1Chr 22:13	2706
thy testimonies, and thy *s*	1Chr 29:19	2708
thee, and shalt observe my *s*	2Chr 7:17	2708
if ye turn away, and forsake my *s*	2Chr 7:19	2708
between law and commandment, *s*	2Chr 19:10	2706
to the whole law and the *s*	2Chr 33:8	2706
and his testimonies, and his *s*	2Chr 34:31	2706
to do it, and to teach in Israel *s*	Ezr 7:10	2706
the Lord, and of his *s* to Israel	Ezr 7:11	2706
kept the commandments, nor the *s*	Neh 1:7	2706
judgments, and true laws, good *s*	Neh 9:13	2706
and commandedst them precepts, *s*	Neh 9:14	2706
Lord, and his judgments and his *s*	Neh 10:29	2706
I did not put away his *s* from me	Ps 18:22	2708
The *s* of the Lord are right,	Ps 19:8	6490
hast thou to do to declare my *s*	Ps 50:16	2706
If they break my *s*, and keep not	Ps 89:31	2708
That they might observe his *s*	Ps 105:45	2706
ways were directed to keep thy *s*	Ps 119:5	2706
I will keep thy *s*	Ps 119:8	2706
teach me thy *s*	Ps 119:12	2706
I will delight myself in thy *s*	Ps 119:16	2708
thy servant did meditate in thy *s*	Ps 119:23	2706
teach me thy *s*	Ps 119:26	2706
me, O Lord, the way of thy *s*	Ps 119:33	2706
and I will meditate in thy *s*	Ps 119:48	2706
Thy *s* have been my songs in the	Ps 119:54	2706
teach me thy *s*	Ps 119:64	2706
teach me thy *s*	Ps 119:68	2706
that I might learn thy *s*	Ps 119:71	2706
Let my heart be sound in thy *s*	Ps 119:80	2706
yet do I not forget thy *s*	Ps 119:83	2706
mine heart to perform thy *s* alway	Ps 119:112	2706
respect unto thy *s* continually	Ps 119:117	2706
down all them that err from thy *s*	Ps 119:118	2706
unto thy mercy, and teach me thy *s*	Ps 119:124	2706
and teach me thy *s*	Ps 119:135	2706
I will keep thy *s*	Ps 119:145	2706
for they seek not thy *s*	Ps 119:155	2706
when thou hast taught me thy *s*	Ps 119:171	2706
his word unto Jacob, his *s*	Ps 147:19	2706
nor walked in my law, nor in my *s*	Jer 44:10	2708
walked in my law, nor in his *s*	Jer 44:23	2708
my *s* more than the countries that	Eze 5:6	2708
have refused my judgments and my *s*	Eze 5:6	2708
you, and have not walked in my *s*	Eze 5:7	2708
for ye have not walked in my *s*	Eze 11:12	2706
That they may walk in my *s*	Eze 11:20	2708
Hath walked in my *s*, and hath kept	Eze 18:9	2708
my judgments, hath walked in my *s*	Eze 18:17	2708
and right, and hath kept all my *s*	Eze 18:19	2708
hath committed, and keep all my *s*	Eze 18:21	2708
And I gave them my *s*, and shewed	Eze 20:11	2708
they walked not in my *s*, and they	Eze 20:13	2708
judgments, and walked not in my *s*	Eze 20:16	2708
ye not in the *s* of your fathers	Eze 20:18	2708
walk in my *s*, and keep my	Eze 20:19	2708
they walked not in my *s*, neither	Eze 20:21	2708
judgments, but had despised my *s*	Eze 20:24	2708
them also *s* that were not good	Eze 20:25	2706
had robbed, walk in the *s* of life	Eze 33:15	2708
you, and cause you to walk in my *s*	Eze 36:27	2706
in my judgments, and observe my *s*	Eze 37:24	2708
my *s* in all mine assemblies	Eze 44:24	2708
For the *s* of Omri are kept, and	Mic 6:16	2708
But my words and my *s*, which I	Zec 1:6	2706
Horeb for all Israel, with the *s*	Mal 4:4	2706

STAVES

thou shalt make *s* of shittim wood	Ex 25:13	905
thou shalt put the *s* into the	Ex 25:14	905
The *s* shall be in the rings of	Ex 25:15	905
places of the *s* to bear the table	Ex 25:27	905
shalt make the *s* of shittim wood	Ex 25:28	905
thou shalt make *s* for the altar	Ex 27:6	905
s of shittim wood, and overlay	Ex 27:6	905
the *s* shall be put into the rings	Ex 27:7	905
the *s* shall be upon the two sides	Ex 27:7	905
for the *s* to bear it withal	Ex 30:4	905

shalt make the *s* of shittim wood	Ex 30:5	905
the *s* thereof, with the mercy	Ex 35:12	905
The table, and his *s*, and all his	Ex 35:13	905
And the incense altar, and his *s*	Ex 35:15	905
with his brasen grate, his *s*	Ex 35:16	905
he made *s* of shittim wood, and	Ex 37:4	905
he put the *s* into the rings by	Ex 37:5	905
for the *s* to bear the table	Ex 37:14	905
he made the *s* of shittim wood, and	Ex 37:15	905
for the *s* to bear it withal	Ex 37:27	905
he made the *s* of shittim wood, and	Ex 37:28	905
of brass, to be places for the *s*	Ex 38:5	905
he made the *s* of shittim wood, and	Ex 38:6	905
he put the *s* into the rings on	Ex 38:7	905
the *s* thereof, and the mercy seat,	Ex 39:35	905
and his grate of brass, his *s*	Ex 39:39	905
set the *s* on the ark, and put the	Ex 40:20	905
and shall put in the *s* thereof	Num 4:6	905
and shall put in the *s* thereof	Num 4:8	905
and shall put to the *s* thereof	Num 4:11	905
skins, and put the *s* thereof	Num 4:14	905
of the lawgiver, with their *s*	Num 21:18	4938
that thou comest to me with *s*	1Sa 17:43	4731
the ark and the *s* thereof above	1Kin 8:7	905
And they drew out the *s*, that the	1Kin 8:8	905
that the ends of the *s* were seen	1Kin 8:8	905
shoulders with the *s* thereon	1Chr 15:15	4133
the ark and the *s* thereof above	2Chr 5:8	905
And they drew out the *s* of the ark	2Chr 5:9	905
that the ends of the *s* were seen	2Chr 5:9	905
his *s* the head of his villages	Hab 3:14	4294
And I took unto me two *s*	Zec 11:7	4731
coats, neither shoes, nor yet *s*	Mt 10:10	4464
great multitude with swords and *s*	Mt 26:47	3586
with swords and *s* for to take me	Mt 26:55	3586
great multitude with swords and *s*	Mk 14:43	3586
with swords and with *s* to take me	Mk 14:48	3586
for your journey, neither *s*	Lk 9:3	4464
against a thief, with swords and *s*	Lk 22:52	3586

STAY See APPENDIX.

STAYED See APPENDIX.

STAYETH

he *s* his rough wind in the day of	Is 27:8	1898

STAYS

there were *s* on either side on	1Kin 10:19	3027
and two lions stood beside the *s*	1Kin 10:19	3027
s on each side of the sitting	2Chr 9:18	3027
and two lions standing by the *s*	2Chr 9:18	3027

STEAD See APPENDIX.

STEADS

in their *s* until the captivity	1Chr 5:22	8478

STEADY

his hands were *s* until the going	Ex 17:12	530

STEAL

away secretly, and *s* away from me	Gen 31:27	1589
how then should we *s* out of thy	Gen 44:8	1589
Thou shalt not *s*	Ex 20:15	1589
If a man shall *s* an ox, or a	Ex 22:1	1589
Ye shall not *s*, neither deal	Lev 19:11	1589
Neither shalt thou *s*	Deut 5:19	1589
as people being ashamed *s* away	2Sa 19:3	1589
if he *s* to satisfy his soul when	Prov 6:30	1589
or lest I be poor, and *s*, and take	Prov 30:9	1589
Will ye *s*, murder, and commit	Jer 7:9	1589
that *s* my words every one from	Jer 23:30	1589
where thieves break through and *s*	Mt 6:19	2813
do not break through nor *s*	Mt 6:20	2813
commit adultery, Thou shalt not *s*	Mt 19:18	2813
s him away, and say unto the	Mt 27:64	2813
adultery, Do not kill, Do not *s*	Mk 10:19	2813
adultery, Do not kill, Do not *s*	Lk 18:20	2813
thief cometh not, but for to *s*	Jn 10:10	2813
man should not *s*, dost thou *s*	Rom 2:21	2813
shalt not kill, Thou shalt not *s*	Rom 13:9	2813
Let him that stole *s* no more	Eph 4:28	2813

STEALETH

And he that *s* a man, and selleth	Ex 21:16	1589
a tempest *s* him away in the night	Job 27:20	1589
for every one that *s* shall be cut	Zec 5:3	1589

STEALING

If a man be found *s* any of his	Deut 24:7	1589
and lying, and killing, and *s*	Hos 4:2	1589

STEALTH

them by *s* that day into the city	2Sa 19:3	1589

STEDFAST

yea, thou shalt be *s*, and shalt	Job 11:15	3332
whose spirit was not *s* with God	Ps 78:8	539
were they *s* in his covenant	Ps 78:37	539
s for ever, and his kingdom that	Dan 6:26	7011
he that standeth *s* in his heart	1Cor 7:37	1476
my beloved brethren, be ye *s*	1Cor 15:58	1476
And our hope of you is *s*, knowing,	2Cor 1:7	949
the word spoken by angels was *s*	Heb 2:2	949
of our confidence *s* unto the end	Heb 3:14	949
of the soul, both sure and *s*	Heb 6:19	949
Whom resist *s* in the faith,	1Pet 5:9	4731

STEDFASTLY

she was *s* minded to go with her	Ruth 1:18	553
And he settled his countenance *s*	2Kin 8:11	7760
he *s* set his face to go to	Lk 9:51	4741
while they looked *s* toward heaven	Acts 1:10	816
they continued *s* in the apostles'	Acts 2:42	4342
in the council, looking *s* on him	Acts 6:15	816
looked up *s* into heaven, and saw	Acts 7:55	816
who *s* beholding him, and	Acts 14:9	816
s behold the face of Moses for	2Cor 3:7	816
children of Israel could not *s*	2Cor 3:13	816

STEDFASTNESS

the *s* of your faith in Christ	Col 2:5	4733
the wicked, fall from your own *s*	2Pet 3:17	4740

STEEL

so that a bow of *s* is broken by	2Sa 22:35	5154
the bow of *s* shall strike him	Job 20:24	5154
so that a bow of *s* is broken by	Ps 18:34	5154
break the northern iron and the *s*	Jer 15:12	5178

STEEP

the *s* places shall fall, and every	Eze 38:20	4095
that are poured down a *s* place	Mic 1:4	4174
down a *s* place into the sea	Mt 8:32	2911
down a *s* place into the sea	Mk 5:13	2911
down a *s* place into the lake	Lk 8:33	2911

STEM

forth a rod out of the *s* of Jesse	Is 11:1	1503

STEP

there is but a *s* between me	1Sa 20:3	6587
If my *s* hath turned out of the	Job 31:7	838

STEPHANAS (stef'-a-nas) *A convert of Paul from Achaia.*

baptized also the household of S	1Cor 1:16	4734
brethren, (ye know the house of S	1Cor 16:15	4734
I am glad of the coming of S	1Cor 16:17	4734

STEPHANUS

was written from Philippi by S	1Cor *s*	4734

STEPHEN (ste'-ven) *A leader of the Jerusalem church.*

and they chose S, a man full of	Acts 6:5	4736
And S, full of faith and power, did	Acts 6:8	4736
and of Asia, disputing with S	Acts 6:9	4736
And they stoned S, calling upon	Acts 7:59	4736
men carried S to his burial	Acts 8:2	4736
S travelled as far as Phenice	Acts 11:19	4736
blood of thy martyr S was shed	Acts 22:20	4736

STEPPED

the troubling of the water *s* in	Jn 5:4	1684

STEPPETH

coming, another *s* down before me	Jn 5:7	2597

STEPS

thou go up by *s* unto mine altar	Ex 20:26	4609
Thou hast enlarged my *s* under me	2Sa 22:37	6806
The throne had six *s*, and the top	1Kin 10:19	4609
and on the other upon the six *s*	1Kin 10:20	4609
And there were six *s* to the throne	2Chr 9:18	4609
and on the other upon the six *s*	2Chr 9:19	4609
For now thou numberest my *s*	Job 14:16	6806
The *s* of his strength shall be	Job 18:7	838
My foot hath held his *s*, his way	Job 23:11	838
When I washed my *s* with butter	Job 29:6	1978
he see my ways, and count all my *s*	Job 31:4	6806
unto him the number of my *s*	Job 31:37	6806
have now compassed us in our *s*	Ps 17:11	838
Thou hast enlarged my *s* under me	Ps 18:36	6806
The *s* of a good man are ordered	Ps 37:23	4703
none of his *s* shall slide	Ps 37:31	838
neither have our *s* declined from	Ps 44:18	838
hide themselves, they mark my *s*	Ps 56:6	6119
They have prepared a net for my *s*	Ps 57:6	6471
my *s* had well nigh slipped	Ps 73:2	838
shall set us in the way of his *s*	Ps 85:13	6471
Order my *s* in thy word	Ps 119:133	6471
thy *s* shall not be straitened	Prov 4:12	6806

her *s* take hold on hell .... Prov 5:5 — 6806
but the LORD directeth his *s* .... Prov 16:9 — 6806
the poor, and the *s* of the needy .... Is 26:6 — 6471
man that walketh to direct his *s* .... Jer 10:23 — 6806
They hunt our *s*, that we cannot .... Lam 4:18 — 6806
they went up unto it by seven *s* .... Eze 40:22 — 4609
there were seven *s* to go up to it .... Eze 40:26 — 4609
and the going up to it had eight *s* .... Eze 40:31 — 4609
and the going up to it had eight *s* .... Eze 40:34 — 4609
and the going up to it had eight *s* .... Eze 40:37 — 4609
he brought me by the *s* whereby .... Eze 40:49 — 4609
the Ethiopians shall be at his *s* .... Dan 11:43 — 4703
but who also walk in the *s* of .... Rom 4:12 — 2487
walked we not in the same *s* .... 2Cor 12:18 — 2487
that ye should follow his *s* .... 1Pet 2:21 — 2487

STERN
cast four anchors out of the *s* .... Acts 27:29 — 4403

STEWARD
the *s* of my house is this Eliezer ..... Gen 15:2 — 1121,4943
near to the *s* of Joseph's house Gen 43:19 — 376,834,5921
he commanded the *s* of his house ... Gen 44:1 — 834,5921
far off, Joseph said unto his *s* .... Gen 44:4 — 834,5921
of Arza *s* of his house in Tirzah ...... 1Kin 16:9 — 834,5921
of the vineyard saith unto his *s* .... Mt 20:8 — 2012
the wife of Chuza Herod's *s* .... Lk 8:3 — 2012
then is that faithful and wise *s* .... Lk 12:42 — 3623
a certain rich man, which had a *s* ...... Lk 16:1 — 3623
for thou mayest be no longer *s* .... Lk 16:2 — 3621
Then the *s* said within himself, ... Lk 16:3 — 3622
the lord commended the unjust *s* ...... Lk 16:8 — 3622
be blameless, as the *s* of God .... Titus 1:7 — 3622

STEWARDS
the *s* over all the substance and .... 1Chr 28:1 — 8269
s of the mysteries of God .... 1Cor 4:1 — 3623
Moreover it is required in *s* .... 1Cor 4:2 — 3623
as good *s* of the manifold grace .... 1Pet 4:10 — 3623

STEWARDSHIP
give an account of thy *s* .... Lk 16:2 — 3622
my lord taketh away from me the *s* .... Lk 16:3 — 3622
that, when I am put out of the *s* .... Lk 16:4 — 3622

STICK
And he cut down a *s*, and cast it in .... 2Kin 6:6 — 6086
bones that were not seen *s* out .... Job 33:21 — 8205
they *s* together, that they cannot .... Job 41:17 — 3920
For thine arrows *s* fast in me .... Ps 38:2 — 5181
withered, it is become like a *s* .... Lam 4:8 — 6086
thy rivers to *s* unto thy scales .... Eze 29:4 — 1692
rivers shall *s* unto thy scales .... Eze 29:4 — 1692
thou son of man, take thee one *s* .... Eze 37:16 — 6086
then take another *s*, and write .... Eze 37:16 — 6086
the *s* of Ephraim, and for all the .... Eze 37:16 — 6086
them one to another into one *s* .... Eze 37:17 — 6086
I will take the *s* of Joseph .... Eze 37:19 — 6086
him, even with the *s* of Judah .... Eze 37:19 — 6086
of Judah, and make them one *s* .... Eze 37:19 — 6086

STICKETH
that *s* closer than a brother .... Prov 18:24 — 1695

STICKS
gathered *s* upon the sabbath day .... Num 15:32 — 6086
s brought him unto Moses and Aaron.... Num 15:33 — 6086
woman was there gathering of *s* .... 1Kin 17:10 — 6086
and, behold, I am gathering two *s* .... 1Kin 17:12 — 6086
the *s* whereon thou writest shall .... Eze 37:20 — 6086
Paul had gathered a bundle of *s* .... Acts 28:3 — 5484

STIFF
know thy rebellion, and thy *s* neck .... Deut 31:27 — 7186
speak not with a *s* neck .... Ps 75:5 — 6277
their ear, but made their neck *s* .... Jer 17:23 — 7185

STIFFENED
but he *s* his neck, and hardened .... 2Chr 36:13 — 7185

STIFFHEARTED
they are impudent children and *s* ... Eze 2:4 — 2389,3820

STIFFNECKED
and, behold, it is a *s* people .... Ex 32:9 — 7186,6203
for thou art a *s* people .... Ex 33:3 — 7186,6203
of Israel, Ye are a *s* people .... Ex 33:5 — 7186,6203
for it is a *s* people............................. Ex 34:9 — 7186,6203
for thou art a *s* people .... Deut 9:6 — 7186,6203
and, behold, it is a *s* people .... Deut 9:13 — 7186,6203
of your heart, and be no more *s* .... Deut 10:16 — 7185,6203
Now be ye not *s*, as your fathers ..... 2Chr 30:8 — 7185,6203
Ye *s* and uncircumcised in heart and ..... Acts 7:51 — 4644

STILL
going on *s* toward the south .... Gen 12:9 — 5265
but they were *s* ill favoured .... Gen 41:21

let them go, and wilt hold them *s* .... Ex 9:2
the people, Fear ye not, stand *s* .... Ex 14:13
arm they shall be as *s* as a stone .... Ex 15:16 — 1826
thou shalt let it rest and lie *s* .... Ex 23:11
if it appear *s* in the garment, ... Lev 13:57 — 5750
And Moses said unto them, Stand *s* ...... Num 9:8
went to search the land, lived *s* .... Num 14:38
ye shall stand *s* in Jordan...................... Josh 3:8
Sun, stand thou *s* upon Gibeon .... Josh 10:12 — 1826
And the sun stood *s*, and the moon ...... Josh 10:13 — 1826
So the sun stood *s* in the midst............. Josh 10:13
that stood *s* in their strength .... Josh 11:13
therefore he blessed you *s* .... Josh 24:10
and are ye *s*... Judg 18:9 — 2814
Then said she, Sit *s*, my daughter .... Ruth 3:18
on,) but stand thou *s* a while 1Sa 9:27
Now therefore stand *s*, that I may 1Sa 12:7
But if ye shall *s* do wickedly................... 1Sa 12:25
then we will stand *s* in our place 1Sa 14:9
things, and also shalt *s* prevail 1Sa 26:25
Asahel fell down and died stood *s* 2Sa 2:23
and all the people stood *s*...................... 2Sa 2:28
But David tarried *s* at Jerusalem 2Sa 11:1
good for me to have been there *s*........... 2Sa 14:32
forth, and cursed *s* as he came............. 2Sa 16:5
And he turned aside, and stood *s* 2Sa 18:30
saw that all the people stood *s* 2Sa 20:12
one that came by him stood *s* 2Sa 20:12
and after the fire a *s* small voice .... 1Kin 19:12 — 1827
in Gilead is ours, and we be *s* 1Kin 22:3
came to pass, as they *s* went on............. 2Kin 2:11
and if we sit *s* here, we die also 2Kin 7:4
the people *s* sacrificed and burnt .... 2Kin 12:3 — 5750
burnt incense *s* on the high .... 2Kin 15:4 — 5750
burned incense *s* in the high .... 2Kin 15:35 — 5750
set yourselves, stand ye *s* 2Chr 20:17
no power to keep *s* the kingdom 2Chr 22:9
sacrifice *s* in the high places................... 2Chr 33:17 — 5750
they stood *s* in the prison gate .... Neh 12:39
s he holdeth fast his integrity, ... Job 2:3 — 5750
him, Dost thou *s* retain thine .... Job 2:9 — 5750
For now should I have lain *s*................... Job 3:13
It stood *s*, but I could not........................ Job 4:16
but keep it *s* within his mouth .... Job 20:13
(for they spake not, but stood *s* .... Job 32:16 — 5975
stand *s*, and consider the wondrous .... Job 37:14 — 5975
own heart upon your bed, and be *s* .... Ps 4:4 — 1826
that thou mightest *s* the enemy .... Ps 8:2 — 7673
he leadeth me beside the *s* waters .... Ps 23:2 — 4496
Be *s*, and know that I am God .... Ps 46:10 — 7503
That he should *s* live for ever .... Ps 49:9 — 5750
as goeth on *s* in his trespasses .... Ps 68:21
the earth feared, and was *s* .... Ps 76:8 — 8252
For all this they sinned *s* .... Ps 78:32 — 5750
hold not thy peace, and be not *s* .... Ps 83:1 — 8252
they will be *s* praising thee .... Ps 84:4 — 5750
They shall *s* bring forth fruit in .... Ps 92:14 — 5750
so that the waves thereof are *s* .... Ps 107:29 — 2814
when I awake, I am *s* with thee .... Ps 139:18 — 5750
he *s* taught the people knowledge .... Eccl 12:9 — 5750
but his hand is stretched out *s*............... Is 5:25 — 5750
but his hand is stretched out *s*............... Is 9:12 — 5750
but his hand is stretched out *s*............... Is 9:17 — 5750
but his hand is stretched out *s*............... Is 9:21 — 5750
but his hand is stretched out *s*............... Is 10:4 — 5750
Be *s*, ye inhabitants of the isle .... Is 23:2 — 1826
this, Their strength is to sit *s* .... Is 30:7 — 7673
I have been *s*, and refrained.................. Is 42:14 — 2790
Why do we sit *s*....................................... Jer 8:14
They say *s* unto them that despise .... Jer 23:17
I let remain *s* in their own land .... Jer 27:11
I do earnestly remember him *s* .... Jer 31:20 — 5750
If ye will *s* abide in this land, ... Jer 42:10
into thy scabbard, rest, and be *s* .... Jer 47:6 — 1826
the sword, go away, stand not *s* .... Jer 51:50 — 5975
soul hath them *s* in remembrance .... Lam 3:20
the children of thy people *s* are............. Eze 33:30
a winding about *s* upward to the .... Eze 41:7
s upward round about the house .... Eze 41:7
breadth of the house was *s* upward....... Eze 41:7
moon stood *s* in their habitation............. Hab 3:11
behold, all the earth sitteth *s* .... Zec 1:11
nor feed that that standeth *s* .... Zec 11:16
And Jesus stood *s*, and called them, ... Mt 20:32 — 2476
and said unto the sea, Peace, be *s* .... Mk 4:39 — 5392
And Jesus stood *s*, and commanded ...... Mk 10:49 — 2476
and they that bare him stood *s* .... Lk 7:14 — 2476
unto them, he abode *s* in Galilee .... Jn 7:9
he abode two days *s* in the same .... Jn 11:6
but Mary sat *s* in the house .... Jn 11:20
commanded the chariot to stand *s* .... Acts 8:38 — 2476

S

it pleased Silas to abide there *s*	Acts 15:34	
Silas and Timotheus abode there *s*	Acts 17:14	
if they abide not *s* in unbelief	Rom 11:23	
thee to abide *s* at Ephesus	1Ti 1:3	4357
is unjust, let him be unjust *s*	Rev 22:11	2089
is filthy, let him be filthy *s*	Rev 22:11	2089
righteous, let him be righteous *s*	Rev 22:11	2089
that is holy, let him be holy *s*	Rev 22:11	2089

STILLED

Caleb *s* the people before Moses,	Num 13:30	2013
So the Levites *s* all the people	Neh 8:11	2814

STILLEST

waves thereof arise, thou *s* them	Ps 89:9	7623

STILLETH

Which *s* the noise of the seas,	Ps 65:7	7623

STING

O death, where is thy *s*	1Cor 15:55	2759
The *s* of death is sin	1Cor 15:56	2759

STINGETH

a serpent, and *s* like an adder	Prov 23:32	6567

STINGS

there were *s* in their tails	Rev 9:10	2759

STINK

to *s* among the inhabitants of the	Gen 34:30	887
shall die, and the river shall *s*	Ex 7:18	887
and it did not *s*, neither was	Ex 16:24	887
My wounds *s* and are corrupt	Ps 38:5	887
of sweet smell there shall be *s*	Is 3:24	4716
their *s* shall come up out of	Is 34:3	889
his *s* shall come up, and his ill	Joel 2:20	889
I have made the *s* of your camps	Amos 4:10	889

STINKETH

their fish *s*, because there is no	Is 50:2	887
unto him, Lord, by this time he *s*	Jn 11:39	3605

STINKING

to send forth a *s* savour	Eccl 10:1	887

STIR

who shall *s* him up	Num 24:9	6965
the innocent shall *s* up himself	Job 17:8	5782
is so fierce that dare *s* him up	Job 41:10	5782
S up thyself, and awake to my	Ps 35:23	5782
did not *s* up all his wrath	Ps 78:38	5782
Manasseh *s* up thy strength, and	Ps 80:2	5782
but grievous words *s* up anger	Prov 15:1	5927
of the field, that ye *s* not up	Song 2:7	5782
of the field, that ye *s* not up	Song 3:5	5782
of Jerusalem, that ye *s* not up	Song 8:4	5782
the LORD of hosts shall *s* up a	Is 10:26	5782
I will *s* up the Medes against	Is 13:17	5782
he shall *s* up jealousy like a man	Is 42:13	5782
s up all against the realm of	Dan 11:2	5782
he shall *s* up his power and his	Dan 11:25	5782
was no small *s* among the soldiers	Acts 12:18	5017
arose no small *s* about that way	Acts 19:23	5017
that thou *s* up the gift of God	2Ti 1:6	329
to *s* you up by putting you in	2Pet 1:13	1326
in both which I *s* up your pure	2Pet 3:1	1326

STIRRED

every one whose heart *s* him up	Ex 35:21	5375
all the women whose heart *s* them	Ex 35:26	5375
even every one whose heart *s* him	Ex 36:2	5375
hath *s* up my servant against me	1Sa 22:8	6965
If the LORD have *s* thee up	1Sa 26:19	5496
the LORD *s* up an adversary unto	1Kin 11:14	6965
God *s* him up another adversary,	1Kin 11:23	6965
LORD, whom Jezebel his wife *s* up	1Kin 21:25	5496
the God of Israel *s* up the spirit	1Chr 5:26	5782
Moreover the LORD *s* up against	2Chr 21:16	5782
the LORD *s* up the spirit of Cyrus	2Chr 36:22	5782
the LORD *s* up the spirit of Cyrus	Ezr 1:1	5782
and my sorrow was *s*	Ps 39:2	5916
But his sons shall be *s* up	Dan 11:10	1624
then shall he return, and be *s* up	Dan 11:10	1624
s up to battle with a very great	Dan 11:25	1624
the LORD *s* up the spirit of	Hag 1:14	5782
they *s* up the people, and the	Acts 6:12	4787
But the Jews *s* up the devout and	Acts 13:50	3951
Jews *s* up the Gentiles, and made	Acts 14:2	1892
thither also, and *s* up the people	Acts 17:13	4531
Athens, his spirit was *s* in him	Acts 17:16	3947
s up all the people, and laid	Acts 21:27	4797

STIRRETH

As an eagle *s* up her nest	Deut 32:11	5782
Hatred *s* up strifes	Prov 10:12	5782
A wrathful man *s* up strife	Prov 15:18	1624

is of a proud heart *s* up strife	Prov 28:25	1624
An angry man *s* up strife, and a	Prov 29:22	1624
it *s* up the dead for thee, even	Is 14:9	5782
that *s* up himself to take hold of	Is 64:7	5782
He *s* up the people, teaching	Lk 23:5	*383*

STIRS

Thou that art full of *s*, a	Is 22:2	8663

STOCK

or to the *s* of the stranger's	Lev 25:47	6133
the *s* thereof die in the ground	Job 14:8	1503
their *s* shall not take root in	Is 40:24	1503
I fall down to the *s* of a tree	Is 44:19	944
Saying to a *s*, Thou art my father	Jer 2:27	6086
the *s* is a doctrine of vanities	Jer 10:8	6086
children of the *s* of Abraham	Acts 13:26	*1085*
of the *s* of Israel, of the tribe	Phil 3:5	*1085*

STOCKS

puttest my feet also in the *s*	Job 13:27	5465
He putteth my feet in the *s*	Job 33:11	5465
a fool to the correction of the *s*	Prov 7:22	5914
adultery with stones and with *s*	Jer 3:9	6086
put him in the *s* that were in the	Jer 20:2	4115
forth Jeremiah out of the *s*	Jer 20:3	4115
put him in prison, and in the *s*	Jer 29:26	6729
My people ask counsel at their *s*	Hos 4:12	6086
and made their feet fast in the *s*	Acts 16:24	*3586*

STOIC See STOICKS.

STOICKS (sto'-ics) *A sect of Greek philosophers.*

of the Epicureans, and of the *S*	Acts 17:18	*4770*

STOLE

Jacob *s* away unawares to Laban	Gen 31:20	1589
so Absalom *s* the hearts of the	2Sa 15:6	1589
s him from among the king's sons	2Kin 11:2	1589
s him from among the king's sons	2Chr 22:11	1589
s him away while we slept	Mt 28:13	*2813*
Let him that *s* steal no more	Eph 4:28	*2813*

STOLEN

that shall be counted *s* with me	Gen 30:33	1589
Rachel had *s* the images that were	Gen 31:19	1589
that thou hast *s* away unawares to	Gen 31:26	1589
yet wherefore hast thou *s* my gods	Gen 31:30	1589
knew not that Rachel had *s* them	Gen 31:32	1589
s by day, or *s* by night	Gen 31:39	1589
For indeed I was *s* away out of	Gen 40:15	1589
it be *s* out of the man's house	Ex 22:7	1589
And if it be *s* from him, he shall	Ex 22:12	1589
accursed thing, and have also *s*	Josh 7:11	1589
the men of Judah *s* thee away	2Sa 19:41	1589
which had *s* them from the street	2Sa 21:12	1589
S waters are sweet, and bread	Prov 9:17	1589
not have *s* till they had enough	Obad 5	1589

STOMACHER

instead of a *s* a girding of	Is 3:24	6614

STOMACH'S

use a little wine for thy *s* sake	1Ti 5:23	*4751*

STONE

there is bdellium and the onyx *s*	Gen 2:12	68
And they had brick for *s*, and slime	Gen 11:3	68
took the *s* that he had put for	Gen 28:18	68
And this *s*, which I have set for a	Gen 28:22	68
a great *s* was upon the well's	Gen 29:2	68
they rolled the *s* from the well's	Gen 29:3	68
put the *s* again upon the well's	Gen 29:3	68
till they roll the *s* from the	Gen 29:8	68
rolled the *s* from the well's	Gen 29:10	68
And Jacob took a *s*, and set it up	Gen 31:45	68
with him, even a pillar of *s*	Gen 35:14	68
is the shepherd, the *s* of Israel	Gen 49:24	68
Then Zipporah took a sharp *s*	Ex 4:25	6697
of wood, and in vessels of *s*	Ex 7:19	68
their eyes, and will they not *s* us	Ex 8:26	5619
they sank into the bottom as a *s*	Ex 15:5	68
arm they shall be as still as a *s*	Ex 15:16	68
they be almost ready to *s* me	Ex 17:4	5619
and they took a *s*, and put it under	Ex 17:12	68
thou wilt make me an altar of *s*	Ex 20:25	68
thou shalt not build it of hewn *s*	Ex 20:25	
and one smite another with a *s*	Ex 21:18	68
were a paved work of a sapphire *s*	Ex 24:10	
and I will give thee tables of *s*	Ex 24:12	68
Six of their names on one *s*	Ex 28:10	68
names of the rest on the other *s*	Ex 28:10	68
With the work of an engraver in *s*	Ex 28:11	68
tables of testimony, tables of *s*	Ex 31:18	68
tables of *s* like unto the first	Ex 34:1	68
tables of *s* like unto the first	Ex 34:4	68

in his hand the two tables of *s*	Ex 34:4	68
the land shall *s* him with stones	Lev 20:2	7275
they shall *s* them with stones	Lev 20:27	7275
and let all the congregation *s* him	Lev 24:14	7275
shall certainly *s* him	Lev 24:16	7275
of the camp, and *s* him with stones	Lev 24:23	7275
up any image of *s* in your land	Lev 26:1	68
bade *s* them with stones	Num 14:10	7275
all the congregation shall *s* him	Num 15:35	7275
if he smite him with throwing a *s*	Num 35:17	68
Or with any *s*, wherewith a man	Num 35:23	68
wrote them upon two tables of *s*	Deut 4:13	68
work of men's hands, wood and *s*	Deut 4:28	68
he wrote them in two tables of *s*	Deut 5:22	68
mount to receive the tables of *s*	Deut 9:9	68
s written with the finger of God	Deut 9:10	68
LORD gave me the two tables of *s*	Deut 9:11	68
tables of *s* like unto the first	Deut 10:1	68
tables of *s* like unto the first	Deut 10:3	68
thou shalt *s* him with stones,	Deut 13:10	5619
shalt *s* them with stones, till	Deut 17:5	5619
his city shall *s* him with stones	Deut 21:21	7275
the men of her city shall *s* her	Deut 22:21	5619
ye shall *s* them with stones that	Deut 22:24	5619
thou serve other gods, wood and *s*	Deut 28:36	68
have known, even wood and *s*	Deut 28:64	68
and their idols, wood and *s*	Deut 29:17	68
man of you a *s* upon his shoulder	Josh 4:5	68
the border went up to the *s* of	Josh 15:6	68
descended to the *s* of Bohan the	Josh 18:17	68
the law of God, and took a great *s*	Josh 24:26	68
this *s* shall be a witness unto us	Josh 24:27	68
and ten persons, upon one *s*	Judg 9:5	68
and ten persons, upon one *s*	Judg 9:18	68
there, where there was a great *s*	1Sa 6:14	68
were, and put them on the great *s*	1Sa 6:15	68
even unto the great *s* of Abel	1Sa 6:18	68
which *s* remaineth unto this day	1Sa 6:18	68
Then Samuel took a *s*, and set it	1Sa 7:12	68
roll a great *s* unto me this day	1Sa 14:33	68
in his bag, and took thence a *s*	1Sa 17:49	68
that the *s* sunk into his forehead	1Sa 17:49	68
with a sling and with a *s*, and	1Sa 17:50	68
and shalt remain by the *s* Ezel	1Sa 20:19	68
within him, and he became as a *s*	1Sa 25:37	68
be not one small *s* found there	2Sa 17:13	6872
at the great *s* which is in Gibeon	2Sa 20:8	68
fat cattle by the *s* of Zoheleth	1Kin 1:9	68
was built of *s* made ready before	1Kin 6:7	68
there was no *s* seen	1Kin 6:18	68
court with three rows of hewed *s*	1Kin 6:36	1496
the ark save the two tables of *s*	1Kin 8:9	68
out, and *s* him, that he may die	1Kin 21:10	5619
of land cast every man his *s*	2Kin 3:25	68
And to masons, and hewers of *s*	2Kin 12:12	68
hewed *s* to repair the breaches of	2Kin 12:12	68
work of men's hands, wood and *s*	2Kin 19:18	68
hewn *s* to repair the house	2Kin 22:6	68
timber also and *s* have I prepared	1Chr 22:14	68
abundance, hewers and workers of *s*	1Chr 22:15	68
silver, in brass, in iron, in *s*	2Chr 2:14	68
gave they it, to buy hewn *s*	2Chr 34:11	68
even break down their *s* wall	Neh 4:3	68
as a *s* into the mighty waters	Neh 9:11	68
and brass is molten out of the *s*	Job 28:2	68
or who laid the corner *s* thereof	Job 38:6	68
The waters are hid as with a *s*	Job 38:30	68
His heart is as firm as a *s*	Job 41:24	68
thou dash thy foot against a *s*	Ps 91:12	68
The *s* which the builders refused	Ps 118:22	68
become the head *s* of the corner	Ps 118:22	68
A gift is as a precious *s* in the	Prov 17:8	68
the *s* wall thereof was broken	Prov 24:31	68
As he that bindeth a *s* in a sling	Prov 26:8	68
and he that rolleth a *s*, it will	Prov 26:27	68
A *s* is heavy, and the sand weighty	Prov 27:3	68
but for a *s* of stumbling and for a	Is 8:14	68
a foundation a *s*, a tried *s*	Is 28:16	68
a precious corner *s*	Is 28:16	68
work of men's hands, wood and *s*	Is 37:19	68
and to a *s*, Thou hast brought me	Jer 2:27	68
not take of thee a *s* for a corner	Jer 51:26	68
a corner, nor a *s* for foundations	Jer 51:26	68
that thou shalt bind a *s* to it	Jer 51:63	68
hath inclosed my ways with hewn *s*	Lam 3:9	1496
the dungeon, and cast a *s* upon me	Lam 3:53	68
as the appearance of a sapphire *s*	Eze 1:26	68
over them as it were a sapphire *s*	Eze 10:1	68
was as the colour of a beryl *s*	Eze 10:9	68
they shall *s* thee with stones, and	Eze 16:40	7275
the countries, to serve wood and *s*	Eze 20:32	68

company shall *s* them with stones	Eze 23:47	7275
every precious *s* was thy covering	Eze 28:13	68
of hewn *s* for the burnt offering	Eze 40:42	68
Thou sawest till that a *s* was cut	Dan 2:34	69
the *s* that smote the image became	Dan 2:35	69
as thou sawest that the *s* was cut	Dan 2:45	69
brass, of iron, of wood, and of *s*	Dan 5:4	69
gold, of brass, iron, wood, and *s*	Dan 5:23	69
a *s* was brought, and laid upon the	Dan 6:17	69
ye have built houses of hewn *s*	Amos 5:11	1496
For the *s* shall cry out of the	Hab 2:11	68
to the dumb *s*, Arise, it shall	Hab 2:19	68
from before a *s* was laid upon a	Hag 2:15	68
a *s* in the temple of the LORD	Hag 2:15	68
For behold the *s* that I have laid	Zec 3:9	68
upon one *s* shall be seven eyes	Zec 3:9	68
made their hearts as an adamant *s*	Zec 7:12	8068
a burdensome *s* for all people	Zec 12:3	68
thou dash thy foot against a *s*	Mt 4:6	3037
ask bread, will he give him a *s*	Mt 7:9	3037
The *s* which the builders rejected	Mt 21:42	3037
fall on this *s* shall be broken	Mt 21:44	3037
be left here one *s* upon another	Mt 24:2	3037
he rolled a great *s* to the door	Mt 27:60	3037
the sepulchre sure, sealing the *s*	Mt 27:66	3037
rolled back the *s* from the door	Mt 28:2	3037
The *s* which the builders rejected	Mk 12:10	3037
not be left one *s* upon another	Mk 13:2	3037
rolled a *s* unto the door of the	Mk 15:46	3037
Who shall roll us away the *s* from	Mk 16:3	3037
saw that the *s* was rolled away	Mk 16:4	3037
command this *s* that it be made	Lk 4:3	3037
thou dash thy foot against a *s*	Lk 4:11	3037
is a father, will he give him a *s*	Lk 11:11	3037
leave in thee one *s* upon another	Lk 19:44	3037
all the people will *s* us	Lk 20:6	2642
The *s* which the builders rejected	Lk 20:17	3037
fall upon that *s* shall be broken	Lk 20:18	3037
not be left one *s* upon another	Lk 21:6	3037
in a sepulchre that was hewn in *s*	Lk 23:53	2991
they found the *s* rolled away from	Lk 24:2	3037
which is by interpretation, A *s*	Jn 1:42	4074
were set there six waterpots of *s*	Jn 2:6	3035
let him first cast a *s* at her	Jn 8:7	3037
took up stones again to *s* him	Jn 10:31	3034
which of those works do ye *s* me	Jn 10:32	3034
For a good work we *s* thee not	Jn 10:33	3034
the Jews of late sought to *s* thee	Jn 11:8	3034
It was a cave, and a *s* lay upon it	Jn 11:38	3037
Jesus said, Take ye away the *s*	Jn 11:39	3037
Then they took away the *s* from	Jn 11:41	3037
seeth the *s* taken away from the	Jn 20:1	3037
This is the *s* which was set at	Acts 4:11	3037
them despitefully, and to *s* them,	Acts 14:5	3036
like unto gold, or silver, or *s*	Acts 17:29	3037
not in tables of *s*, but in	2Cor 3:3	3035
himself being the chief corner *s*	Eph 2:20	
whom coming, as unto a living *s*	1Pet 2:4	3037
I lay in Sion a chief corner *s*	1Pet 2:6	3037
the *s* which the builders	1Pet 2:7	3037
a *s* of stumbling, and a rock of	1Pet 2:8	3037
manna, and will give him a white *s*	Rev 2:17	5586
in the *s* a new name written,	Rev 2:17	5586
upon like a jasper and a sardine *s*	Rev 4:3	3037
gold, and silver, and brass, and *s*	Rev 9:20	3035
every *s* about the weight of a	Rev 16:21	
up a *s* like a great millstone	Rev 18:21	3037
was like unto a *s* most precious	Rev 21:11	3037
precious, even like a jasper *s*	Rev 21:11	3037

STONED

it, but he shall surely be *s*	Ex 19:13	5619
then the ox shall be surely *s*	Ex 21:28	5619
the ox shall be *s*, and his owner	Ex 21:29	5619
of silver, and the ox shall be *s*	Ex 21:32	5619
s him with stones, and he died	Num 15:36	7275
all Israel *s* him with stones, and	Josh 7:25	5619
after they had *s* them with stones	Josh 7:25	7275
all Israel *s* him with stones,	1Kin 12:18	7275
s him with stones, that he died	1Kin 21:13	5619
to Jezebel, saying, Naboth is *s*	1Kin 21:14	5619
Jezebel heard that Naboth was *s*	1Kin 21:15	5619
of Israel *s* him with stones	2Chr 10:18	7275
him, and *s* him with stones at the	2Chr 24:21	7275
and killed another, and *s* another	Mt 21:35	3036
us, that such should be *s*	Jn 8:5	3036
lest they should have been *s*	Acts 5:26	3034
him out of the city, and *s* him	Acts 7:58	3036
they *s* Stephen, calling upon God,	Acts 7:59	3036
the people, and, having *s* Paul	Acts 14:19	3034
I beaten with rods, once was I *s*	2Cor 11:25	3034

They were s, they were sawn	Heb 11:37	3034
touch the mountain, it shall be s	Heb 12:20	3036

STONE'S

from them about a s cast, and	Lk 22:41	3037

STONES

and he took of the s of that place	Gen 28:11	68
said unto his brethren, Gather s	Gen 31:46	68
and they took s, and made an heap	Gen 31:46	68
Onyx s, and s to be set in	Ex 25:7	68
And thou shalt take two onyx s	Ex 28:9	68
shalt thou engrave the two s with	Ex 28:11	68
thou shalt put the two s upon the	Ex 28:12	68
s of memorial unto the children	Ex 28:12	68
shalt set in it settings of s	Ex 28:17	68
even four rows of s	Ex 28:17	68
the s shall be with the names of	Ex 28:21	68
And in cutting of s, to set them,	Ex 31:5	68
And onyx s, and s to be set	Ex 35:9	68
And the rulers brought onyx s	Ex 35:27	68
s to be set, for the ephod, and	Ex 35:27	68
And in the cutting of s, to set	Ex 35:33	68
they wrought onyx s inclosed in	Ex 39:6	68
that they should be s for a	Ex 39:7	68
And they set in it four rows of s	Ex 39:10	68
the s were according to the names	Ex 39:14	68
away the s in which the plague is	Lev 14:40	68
And they shall take other s	Lev 14:42	68
put them in the place of those s	Lev 14:42	68
that he hath taken away the s	Lev 14:43	68
the s of it, and the timber	Lev 14:45	68
the land shall stone him with s	Lev 20:2	68
they shall stone them with s	Lev 20:27	68
or scabbed, or hath his s broken	Lev 21:20	810
of the camp, and stone him with s	Lev 24:23	68
bade stone them with s	Num 14:10	68
stone him s without the camp	Num 15:35	68
the camp, and stoned him with s	Num 15:36	68
a land whose s are iron, and out	Deut 8:9	68
And thou shalt stone him with s	Deut 13:10	68
woman, and shalt stone them with s	Deut 17:5	68
his city shall stone him with s	Deut 21:21	68
stone her with s that she die	Deut 22:21	68
stone them with s that they die	Deut 22:24	68
He that is wounded in the s	Deut 23:1	
thou shalt set thee up great s	Deut 27:2	68
that ye shall set up these s	Deut 27:4	68
the Lord thy God, an altar of s	Deut 27:5	68
of the Lord thy God of whole s	Deut 27:6	68
thou shalt write upon the s all	Deut 27:8	68
feet stood firm, twelve s	Josh 4:3	68
saying, What mean ye by these s	Josh 4:6	68
these s shall be for a memorial	Josh 4:7	68
took up twelve s out of the midst	Josh 4:8	68
Joshua set up twelve s in the	Josh 4:9	68
And those twelve s, which they	Josh 4:20	68
come, saying, What mean these s	Josh 4:21	68
And all Israel stoned him with s	Josh 7:25	68
after they had stoned them with s	Josh 7:25	68
a great heap of s unto this day	Josh 7:26	68
raise thereon a great heap of s	Josh 8:29	68
law of Moses, an altar of whole s	Josh 8:31	68
he wrote there upon the s a copy	Josh 8:32	68
s from heaven upon them unto	Josh 10:11	68
Roll great s upon the mouth of	Josh 10:18	68
laid great s in the cave's mouth,	Josh 10:27	68
could sling s at an hair breadth	Judg 20:16	68
five smooth s out of the brook	1Sa 17:40	68
of gold with the precious s	2Sa 12:30	68
he cast s at David, and at all the	2Sa 16:6	68
threw s at him, and cast dust	2Sa 16:13	68
a very great heap of s upon him	2Sa 18:17	68
s, costly s, and hewed s	1Kin 5:17	68
timber and s to build the house	1Kin 5:18	68
All these were of costly s	1Kin 7:9	68
to the measures of hewed s	1Kin 7:9	1496
of costly s, even great s	1Kin 7:10	68
s of ten cubits, and s of	1Kin 7:10	68
And above were costly s, after the	1Kin 7:11	68
after the measures of hewed s	1Kin 7:11	1496
was with three rows of hewed s	1Kin 7:12	1496
and very much gold, and precious s	1Kin 10:2	68
very great store, and precious s	1Kin 10:10	68
of almug trees, and precious s	1Kin 10:11	68
silver to be in Jerusalem as s	1Kin 10:27	68
and all Israel stoned him with s	1Kin 12:18	68
and they took away the s of Ramah	1Kin 15:22	68
And Elijah took twelve s,	1Kin 18:31	68
with the s he built an altar in	1Kin 18:32	68
sacrifice, and the wood, and the s	1Kin 18:38	68
of the city, and stoned him with s	1Kin 21:13	68

every good piece of land with s	2Kin 3:19	68
left they the s thereof	2Kin 3:25	68
and put it upon a pavement of s	2Kin 16:17	68
hand and the left in hurling s	1Chr 12:2	68
and there were precious s in it	1Chr 20:2	68
s to build the house of God	1Chr 22:2	68
onyx s, and s to be set,	1Chr 29:2	68
to be set, glistering s	1Chr 29:2	68
and all manner of precious s	1Chr 29:2	68
s, and marble s in abundance	1Chr 29:2	68
they with whom precious s were	1Chr 29:8	68
at Jerusalem as plenteous as s	2Chr 1:15	68
house with precious s for beauty	2Chr 3:6	68
gold in abundance, and precious s	2Chr 9:1	68
great abundance, and precious s	2Chr 9:9	68
brought algum trees and precious s	2Chr 9:10	68
made silver in Jerusalem as s	2Chr 9:27	68
of Israel stoned him with s	2Chr 10:18	68
they carried away the s of Ramah	2Chr 16:6	68
him, and stoned him with s at the	2Chr 24:21	68
and bows, and slings to cast s	2Chr 26:14	68
to shoot arrows and great s withal	2Chr 26:15	68
and for gold, and for precious s	2Chr 32:27	68
which is builded with great s	Ezr 5:8	69
With three rows of great s	Ezr 6:4	69
will they revive the s out of the	Neh 4:2	68
in league with the s of the field	Job 5:23	68
Is my strength the strength of s	Job 6:12	68
the heap, and seeth the place of s	Job 8:17	68
The waters wear the s	Job 14:19	68
of Ophir as the s of the brooks	Job 22:24	6697
the s of darkness, and the shadow	Job 28:3	68
The s of it are the place of	Job 28:6	68
the sinews of his s are wrapped	Job 40:17	6344
Sharp s are under him	Job 41:30	2789
his thick clouds passed, hail s	Ps 18:12	68
hail s and coals of fire	Ps 18:13	
servants take pleasure in her s	Ps 102:14	68
thy little ones against the s	Ps 137:9	5553
our daughters may be as corner s	Ps 144:12	2106
A time to cast away s, and a time	Eccl 3:5	68
and a time to gather s together	Eccl 3:5	68
Whoso removeth s shall be hurt	Eccl 10:9	68
it, and gathered out the s thereof	Is 5:2	5619
but we will build with hewn s	Is 9:10	1496
that go down to the s of the pit	Is 14:19	68
when he maketh all the s of the	Is 27:9	68
confusion, and the s of emptiness	Is 34:11	68
I will lay thy s with fair colors	Is 54:11	68
and all thy borders of pleasant s	Is 54:12	68
Among the smooth s of the stream	Is 57:6	
and for wood brass, and for s iron	Is 60:17	68
gather out the s	Is 62:10	68
and committed adultery with s	Jer 3:9	68
Take great s in thine hand, and	Jer 43:9	68
upon these s that I have hid	Jer 43:10	68
broken my teeth with gravel s	Lam 3:16	2687
the s of the sanctuary are poured	Lam 4:1	68
and they shall stone thee with s	Eze 16:40	68
company shall stone them with s	Eze 23:47	68
and they shall lay thy s and thy	Eze 26:12	68
spices, and with all precious s	Eze 27:22	68
in the midst of the s of fire	Eze 28:14	68
from the midst of the s of fire	Eze 28:16	68
and silver, and with precious s	Dan 11:38	68
I will pour down the s thereof	Mic 1:6	68
timber thereof and the s thereof	Zec 5:4	68
devour, and subdue with sling s	Zec 9:15	68
they shall be as the s of a crown	Zec 9:16	68
these s to raise up children unto	Mt 3:9	3037
that these s be made bread	Mt 4:3	3037
crying, and cutting himself with s	Mk 5:5	3037
and at him they cast s, and wounded	Mk 12:4	3036
him, Master, see what manner of s	Mk 13:1	3037
these s to raise up children unto	Lk 3:8	3037
the s would immediately cry out	Lk 19:40	3037
how it was adorned with goodly s	Lk 21:5	3037
took they up s to cast at him	Jn 8:59	3037
Jews took up s again to stone him	Jn 10:31	3037
gold, silver, precious s, wood,	1Cor 3:12	3037
death, written and engraven in s	2Cor 3:7	3037
Ye also, as lively s, are built	1Pet 2:5	3037
and decked with gold and precious s	Rev 17:4	3037
of gold, and silver, and precious s	Rev 18:12	3037
decked with gold, and precious s	Rev 18:16	3037
with all manner of precious s	Rev 21:19	3037

STONESQUARERS

builders did hew them, and the s	1Kin 5:18	1382

STONEST

s them which are sent unto thee,	Mt 23:37	3036
s them that are sent unto thee	Lk 13:34	3036

STONING

for the people spake of *s* him	1Sa 30:6	5619

STONY

judges are overthrown in *s* places	Ps 141:6	5553
I will take the *s* heart out of	Eze 11:19	68
I will take away the *s* heart out	Eze 36:26	68
Some fell upon *s* places, where	Mt 13:5	4075
received the seed into *s* places	Mt 13:20	4075
And some fell on *s* ground, where	Mk 4:5	4075
which are sown on *s* ground	Mk 4:16	4075

STOOD

and, lo, three men *s* by him	Gen 18:2	5324
he *s* by them under the tree, and	Gen 18:8	5975
but Abraham *s* yet before the LORD	Gen 18:22	5975
place where he *s* before the LORD	Gen 19:27	5975
Abraham *s* up from before his dead	Gen 23:3	6965
Abraham *s* up, and bowed himself	Gen 23:7	6965
he *s* by the camels at the well	Gen 24:30	5975
And, behold, the LORD *s* above it	Gen 28:13	5324
my sheaf arose, and also *s* upright	Gen 37:7	5324
your sheaves *s* round about	Gen 37:7	
and, behold, he *s* by the river	Gen 41:1	5975
s by the other kine upon the	Gen 41:3	5975
I *s* upon the bank of the river	Gen 41:17	5975
he *s* before Pharaoh king of Egypt	Gen 41:46	5975
down to Egypt, and *s* before Joseph	Gen 43:15	5975
before all them that *s* by him	Gen 45:1	5324
there *s* no man with him, while	Gen 45:1	5975
And his sister *s* afar off, to wit	Ex 2:4	3320
but Moses *s* up and helped them, and	Ex 2:17	6965
who *s* in the way, as they came	Ex 5:20	5324
the furnace, and *s* before Pharaoh	Ex 9:10	5975
their face, and *s* behind them	Ex 14:19	5975
the floods *s* upright as an heap	Ex 15:8	5324
the people *s* by Moses from the	Ex 18:13	5975
they *s* at the nether part of the	Ex 19:17	3320
it, they removed, and *s* afar off	Ex 20:18	5975
And the people *s* afar off, and	Ex 20:21	5975
Then Moses *s* in the gate of the	Ex 32:26	5975
s every man at his tent door, and	Ex 33:8	5324
s at the door of the tabernacle,	Ex 33:9	5975
s with him there, and proclaimed	Ex 34:5	3320
drew near and *s* before the LORD	Lev 9:5	5975
the people *s* up all that day, and	Num 11:32	6965
s in the door of the tabernacle,	Num 12:5	5975
s in the door of the tabernacle,	Num 16:18	5975
s in the door of their tents, and	Num 16:27	5324
he *s* between the dead and the	Num 16:48	5975
the angel of the LORD *s* in the	Num 22:22	3320
But the angel of the LORD *s* in a	Num 22:24	5975
s in a narrow place, where was no	Num 22:26	5975
he *s* by his burnt sacrifice, he,	Num 23:6	5324
he *s* by his burnt offering, and	Num 23:17	5324
they *s* before Moses, and before	Num 27:2	5975
came near and *s* under the mountain	Deut 4:11	5975
(I *s* between the LORD and you at	Deut 5:5	5975
the pillar of the cloud *s* over	Deut 31:15	5975
which came down from above *s*	Josh 3:16	5975
s firm on dry ground in the midst	Josh 3:17	5975
where the priests' feet *s* firm	Josh 4:3	4673
bare the ark of the covenant *s*	Josh 4:9	4673
the ark *s* in the midst of Jordan	Josh 4:10	5975
there *s* a man over against him	Josh 5:13	5975
s on this side the ark and on that	Josh 8:33	5975
And the sun *s* still, and the moon	Josh 10:13	1826
So the sun *s* still in the midst	Josh 10:13	5975
that *s* still in their strength	Josh 11:13	5975
of blood, until he *s* before the	Josh 20:9	5975
there *s* not a man of all their	Josh 21:44	5975
all that *s* by him went out from	Judg 3:19	5975
said unto all that *s* against him	Judg 6:31	5975
they *s* every man in his place	Judg 7:21	5975
s in the top of mount Gerizim, and	Judg 9:7	5975
s in the entering of the gate of	Judg 9:35	5975
s in the entering of the gate of	Judg 9:44	5975
pillars upon which the house *s*	Judg 16:29	3559
s by the entering of the gate	Judg 18:16	5324
the priest *s* in the entering of	Judg 18:17	5324
s before the LORD in those days,)	Judg 20:28	5975
am the woman that *s* by thee here	1Sa 1:26	5324
And the LORD came, and *s*, and called	1Sa 3:10	3320
women that *s* by her said unto her	1Sa 4:20	5324
s there, where there was a great	1Sa 6:14	5975
when he *s* among the people, he	1Sa 10:23	3320
came to Saul, and *s* before him	1Sa 16:21	5975
the Philistines *s* on a mountain	1Sa 17:3	5975
Israel *s* on a mountain on the	1Sa 17:3	5975
And he *s* and cried unto the armies	1Sa 17:8	5975
spake to the men that *s* by him	1Sa 17:26	5975
s upon the Philistine, and took	1Sa 17:51	5975
his servants that *s* about him	1Sa 22:7	5324
unto the footmen that *s* about him	1Sa 22:17	5324
s on the top of an hill afar off	1Sa 26:13	5975
So I *s* upon him, and slew him,	2Sa 1:10	5975
Asahel fell down and died *s* still	2Sa 2:23	5975
troop, and *s* on the top of an hill	2Sa 2:25	5975
and all the people *s* still	2Sa 2:28	5975
all his servants *s* by with their	2Sa 13:31	5324
s beside the way of the gate	2Sa 15:2	5975
the king *s* by the gate side, and	2Sa 18:4	5975
And he turned aside, and *s* still	2Sa 18:30	5975
And one of Joab's men *s* by him	2Sa 20:11	5975
saw that all the people *s* still	2Sa 20:12	5975
one that came by him *s* still	2Sa 20:12	5975
the city, and it *s* in the trench	2Sa 20:15	5975
But he *s* in the midst of the	2Sa 23:12	3320
presence, and *s* before the king	1Kin 1:28	5975
s before the ark of the covenant	1Kin 3:15	5975
unto the king, and *s* before him	1Kin 3:16	5975
It *s* upon twelve oxen, three	1Kin 7:25	5975
all the congregation of Israel *s*	1Kin 8:14	5975
Solomon *s* before the altar of the	1Kin 8:22	5975
And he *s*, and blessed all the	1Kin 8:55	5975
two lions *s* beside the stays	1Kin 10:19	5975
twelve lions *s* there on the one	1Kin 10:20	5975
that *s* before Solomon his father	1Kin 12:6	5975
with him, and which *s* before him	1Kin 12:8	5975
Jeroboam *s* by the altar to burn	1Kin 13:1	5975
in the way, and the ass *s* by it	1Kin 13:24	5975
the lion also *s* by the carcase	1Kin 13:24	5975
s in the entering in of the cave	1Kin 19:13	5975
s before the LORD, and said, I	1Kin 22:21	5975
went, and *s* to view afar off	2Kin 2:7	5975
and they two *s* by Jordan	2Kin 2:7	5975
back, and *s* by the bank of Jordan	2Kin 2:13	5975
and upward, and *s* in the border	2Kin 3:21	5975
had called her, she *s* before him	2Kin 4:12	5975
had called her, she *s* in the door	2Kin 4:15	5975
s at the door of the house of	2Kin 5:9	5975
company, and came, and *s* before him	2Kin 5:15	5975
went in, and *s* before his master	2Kin 5:25	5975
s before him, and said, Thy son	2Kin 8:9	5975
there *s* a watchman on the tower	2Kin 9:17	5975
two kings *s* not before him	2Kin 10:4	5975
morning, that he went out, and *s*	2Kin 10:9	5975
And the guard, every man with	2Kin 11:11	5975
the king *s* by a pillar, as the	2Kin 11:14	5975
he revived, and *s* up on his feet	2Kin 13:21	6965
s by the conduit of the upper	2Kin 18:17	5975
Then Rab-shakeh *s* and cried with a	2Kin 18:28	5975
the king *s* by a pillar, and made a	2Kin 23:3	5975
all the people *s* to the covenant	2Kin 23:3	5975
who *s* on his right hand, even	1Chr 6:39	5975
sons of Merari *s* on the left hand	1Chr 6:44	
Satan *s* up against Israel, and	1Chr 21:1	5975
the angel of the LORD *s* by the	1Chr 21:15	5975
David the king *s* up upon his feet	1Chr 28:2	6965
they *s* on their feet, and their	2Chr 3:13	5975
It *s* upon twelve oxen, three	2Chr 4:4	5975
s at the east end of the altar,	2Chr 5:12	5975
all the congregation of Israel *s*	2Chr 6:3	5975
he *s* before the altar of the LORD	2Chr 6:12	5975
and upon it he *s*, and kneeled down	2Chr 6:13	5975
before them, and all Israel *s*	2Chr 7:6	5975
twelve lions *s* there on the one	2Chr 9:19	5975
with the old men that had *s*	2Chr 10:6	5975
up with him, that *s* before him	2Chr 10:8	5975
Abijah *s* up upon mount Zemaraim,	2Chr 13:4	6965
s before the LORD, and said, I	2Chr 18:20	5975
Jehoshaphat *s* in the congregation	2Chr 20:5	5975
all Judah *s* before the LORD, with	2Chr 20:13	5975
s up to praise the LORD God of	2Chr 20:19	6965
as they went forth, Jehoshaphat *s*	2Chr 20:20	5975
Moab *s* up against the inhabitants	2Chr 20:23	5975
the king *s* at his pillar at the	2Chr 23:13	5975
which *s* above the people, and said	2Chr 24:20	5975
s up against them that came from	2Chr 28:12	6965
And the Levites *s* with the	2Chr 29:26	5975
they *s* in their place after their	2Chr 30:16	5975
the king *s* in his place, and made	2Chr 34:31	5975
the priests *s* in their place, and	2Chr 35:10	5975
till there *s* up a priest with	Ezr 2:63	5975
Then *s* up Jeshua the son of	Ezr 3:2	6965
Then *s* Jeshua with his sons and	Ezr 3:9	5975
And Ezra the priest *s* up, and said	Ezr 10:10	6965
till there *s* up a priest with	Neh 7:65	5975
Ezra the scribe *s* upon a pulpit	Neh 8:4	5975

S

and beside him *s* Mattithiah	Neh 8:4	5975
he opened it, all the people *s* up	Neh 8:5	5975
the people *s* in their place	Neh 8:7	
from all strangers, and *s* and	Neh 9:2	5975
they *s* up in their place, and read	Neh 9:3	6965
Then *s* up upon the stairs, of the	Neh 9:4	6965
they *s* still in the prison gate	Neh 12:39	
So *s* the two companies of them	Neh 12:40	5975
s in the inner court of the	Est 5:1	5975
the king's gate, that he *s* not up	Est 5:9	6965
Haman *s* up to make request for	Est 7:7	5975
arose, and *s* before the king,	Est 8:4	5975
s for their lives, and had rest	Est 9:16	5975
the hair of my flesh *s* up	Job 4:15	5568
It *s* still, but I could not	Job 4:16	5975
and the aged arose, and *s* up	Job 29:8	5975
I *s* up, and I cried in the	Job 30:28	6965
but *s* still, and answered no more	Job 32:16	5975
he commanded, and it *s* fast	Ps 33:9	5975
the waters *s* above the mountains	Ps 104:6	5975
chosen *s* before him in the breach	Ps 106:23	5975
Then *s* up Phinehas, and executed	Ps 106:30	5975
Above it *s* the seraphims	Is 6:2	5975
he *s* by the conduit of the upper	Is 36:2	5975
Then Rabshakeh *s*, and cried with a	Is 36:13	5975
Samuel *s* before me, yet my mind	Jer 15:1	5975
Remember that I *s* before thee to	Jer 18:20	5975
he *s* in the court of the LORD's	Jer 19:14	5975
For who hath *s* in the counsel of	Jer 23:18	5975
But if they had *s* in my counsel	Jer 23:22	5975
that *s* in the house of the LORD	Jer 28:5	5975
princes which *s* beside the king	Jer 36:21	5975
gods, and all the women that *s* by	Jer 44:15	5975
they *s* not, because the LORD did	Jer 46:15	5975
They that fled *s* under the shadow	Jer 48:45	5975
he *s* with his right hand as an	Lam 2:4	5324
and when those *s*, these *s*	Eze 1:21	5975
when they *s*, they let down their	Eze 1:24	5975
was over their heads, when they *s*	Eze 1:25	5975
the glory of the LORD *s* there	Eze 3:23	5975
there *s* before them seventy men	Eze 8:11	5975
in the midst of them *s* Jaazaniah	Eze 8:11	5975
s beside the brasen altar	Eze 9:2	5975
Now the cherubims *s* on the right	Eze 10:3	5975
s over the threshold of the house	Eze 10:4	
went in, and *s* beside the wheels	Eze 10:6	5975
When they *s*, these *s*	Eze 10:17	5975
house, and *s* over the cherubims	Eze 10:18	5975
every one *s* at the door of the	Eze 10:19	5975
s upon the mountain which is on	Eze 11:23	5975
For the king of Babylon *s* at the	Eze 21:21	5975
and *s* up upon their feet, an	Eze 37:10	5975
and he *s* in the gate	Eze 40:3	5975
and the man *s* by me	Eze 43:6	5975
of the house *s* toward the east	Eze 47:1	
therefore *s* they before the king	Dan 1:19	5975
So they came and *s* before the king	Dan 2:2	5975
was excellent, *s* before thee	Dan 2:31	6966
they *s* before the image that	Dan 3:3	6966
times ten thousand *s* before him	Dan 7:10	6966
near unto one of them that *s* by	Dan 7:16	6966
there *s* before the river a ram	Dan 8:3	5975
behold, there *s* before me as the	Dan 8:15	5975
So he came near where I *s*	Dan 8:17	5977
broken, whereas four *s* up for it	Dan 8:22	5975
this word unto me, I *s* trembling	Dan 10:11	5975
and said unto him that *s* before me	Dan 10:16	5975
s to confirm and to strengthen him	Dan 11:1	5975
there *s* other two, the one on	Dan 12:5	5975
there they *s*	Hos 10:9	5975
the Lord *s* upon a wall made by a	Amos 7:7	5324
thou have *s* in the crossway	Obad 14	5975
He *s*, and measured the earth	Hab 3:6	5975
moon *s* still in their habitation	Hab 3:11	5975
he *s* among the myrtle trees that	Zec 1:8	5975
the man that *s* among the myrtle	Zec 1:10	5975
that *s* among the myrtle trees	Zec 1:11	5975
garments, and *s* before the angel	Zec 3:3	5975
unto those that *s* before him	Zec 3:4	5975
And the angel of the LORD *s* by	Zec 3:5	5975
s over where the young child was	Mt 2:9	2476
mother and his brethren *s* without	Mt 12:46	2476
whole multitude *s* on the shore	Mt 13:2	2476
And Jesus *s* still, and called them,	Mt 20:32	2476
came unto him they that *s* by	Mt 26:73	2476
Jesus *s* before the governor	Mt 27:11	2476
Some of them that *s* there	Mt 27:47	2476
And Jesus *s* still, and commanded	Mk 10:49	2476
them that *s* there said unto them	Mk 11:5	2476
of them that *s* by drew a sword	Mk 14:47	3936
the high priest *s* up in the midst	Mk 14:60	450

and began to say to them that *s* by	Mk 14:69	3936
they that *s* by said again to	Mk 14:70	3936
And some of them that *s* by	Mk 15:35	3936
which *s* over against him, saw	Mk 15:39	3936
sabbath day, and *s* up for to read	Lk 4:16	450
he *s* over her, and rebuked the	Lk 4:39	2186
he *s* by the lake of Gennesaret,	Lk 5:1	2476
And he arose and *s* forth	Lk 6:8	2476
s in the plain, and the company of	Lk 6:17	2476
and they that bare him *s* still	Lk 7:14	2476
s at his feet behind him weeping,	Lk 7:38	2476
and the two men that *s* with him	Lk 9:32	4921
And, behold, a certain lawyer *s* up	Lk 10:25	450
were lepers, which *s* afar off	Lk 17:12	2476
The Pharisee *s* and prayed thus	Lk 18:11	2476
And Jesus *s*, and commanded him to	Lk 18:40	2476
And Zacchaeus *s*, and said unto the	Lk 19:8	2476
And he said unto them that *s* by	Lk 19:24	3936
And the chief priests and scribes *s*	Lk 23:10	2476
And the people *s* beholding	Lk 23:35	2476
s afar off, beholding these	Lk 23:49	2476
two men *s* by them in shining	Lk 24:4	2186
Jesus himself *s* in the midst of	Lk 24:36	2476
Again the next day after John *s*	Jn 1:35	2476
when the people which *s* on the	Jn 6:22	2476
great day of the feast, Jesus *s*	Jn 7:37	2476
as they *s* in the temple, What	Jn 11:56	2476
The people therefore, that *s* by	Jn 12:29	2476
which betrayed him, *s* with them	Jn 18:5	2476
But Peter *s* at the door without	Jn 18:16	2476
the servants and officers *s* there	Jn 18:18	2476
Peter *s* with them, and warmed	Jn 18:18	2476
one of the officers which *s* by	Jn 18:22	3936
And Simon Peter *s* and warmed	Jn 18:25	2476
Now there *s* by the cross of Jesus	Jn 19:25	2476
But Mary *s* without at the	Jn 20:11	2476
s in the midst, and saith unto	Jn 20:19	2476
***s* in the midst, and said, Peace be**	Jn 20:26	2476
now come, Jesus *s* on the shore	Jn 21:4	2476
two men *s* by them in white	Acts 1:10	3936
in those days Peter *s* up in the	Acts 1:15	450
And he leaping up *s*, and walked, and	Acts 3:8	2476
The kings of the earth *s* up	Acts 4:26	3936
Then *s* there up one in the	Acts 5:34	450
journeyed with him *s* speechless	Acts 9:7	2476
all the widows *s* by him weeping	Acts 9:39	3936
house, and *s* before the gate,	Acts 10:17	2186
a man *s* before me in bright	Acts 10:30	2476
an angel in his house, which *s*	Acts 11:13	2476
there *s* up one of them named	Acts 11:28	450
told how Peter *s* before the gate	Acts 12:14	2476
Then Paul *s* up, and beckoning with	Acts 13:16	450
the disciples *s* round about him	Acts 14:20	2944
There *s* a man of Macedonia, and	Acts 16:9	2476
Then Paul *s* in the midst of Mars'	Acts 17:22	2476
Paul *s* on the stairs, and beckoned	Acts 21:40	2476
Came unto me, and *s*, and said unto	Acts 22:13	2186
said unto the centurion that *s* by	Acts 22:25	2476
that *s* by him to smite him on the	Acts 23:2	3936
And they that *s* by said, Revilest	Acts 23:4	3936
night following the Lord *s* by him	Acts 23:11	2186
while I *s* before the council,	Acts 24:20	2476
down from Jerusalem *s* round about	Acts 25:7	4026
whom when the accusers *s* up	Acts 25:18	2476
Paul *s* forth in the midst of them	Acts 27:21	2476
For there *s* by me this night the	Acts 27:23	3936
my first answer no man *s* with me	2Ti 4:16	4836
the Lord *s* with me, and	2Ti 4:17	3936
Which *s* only in meats and drinks,	Heb 9:10	
s a Lamb as it had been slain,	Rev 5:6	2476
s before the throne, and before	Rev 7:9	2476
all the angels *s* round about the	Rev 7:11	2476
seven angels which *s* before God	Rev 8:2	2476
s at the altar, having a golden	Rev 8:3	2476
and the angel, saying, Rise, and	Rev 11:1	2476
them, and they *s* upon their feet	Rev 11:11	2476
the dragon *s* before the woman	Rev 12:4	2476
I *s* upon the sand of the sea, and	Rev 13:1	2476
a Lamb *s* on the mount Sion, and	Rev 14:1	2476
many as trade by sea, *s* afar off,	Rev 18:17	2476

STOODEST

that thou *s* in the way against me	Num 22:34	5324
thou *s* before the LORD thy God in	Deut 4:10	5975
day that thou *s* on the other side	Obad 11	5975

STOOL

there a bed, and a table, and a *s*	2Kin 4:10	3678

STOOLS

women, and see them upon the *s*	Ex 1:16	70

STOOP

the proud helpers do *s* under him	Job 9:13	7817
in the heart of man maketh it *s*	Prov 12:25	7812
They *s*, they bow down together	Is 46:2	7164
shoes I am not worthy to *s* down	Mk 1:7	2955

STOOPED

he *s* down, he couched as a lion,	Gen 49:9	3766
David *s* with his face to the	1Sa 24:8	6915
he *s* with his face to the ground,	1Sa 28:14	6915
old man, or him that *s* for age	2Chr 36:17	3486
But Jesus *s* down, and with his	Jn 8:6	2955
And again he *s* down, and wrote on	Jn 8:8	2955
she *s* down, and looked into the	Jn 20:11	3879

STOOPETH

Bel boweth down, Nebo *s*, their	Is 46:1	7164

STOOPING

s down, he beheld the linen	Lk 24:12	3879
he *s* down, and looking in, saw the	Jn 20:5	3879

STOP

down, that the rain *s* thee not	1Kin 18:44	6113
s all wells of water, and mar	2Kin 3:19	5640
his mighty men to *s* the waters of	2Chr 32:3	5640
s the way against them that	Ps 35:3	5462
and all iniquity shall *s* her mouth	Ps 107:42	7092
it shall *s* the noses of the	Eze 39:11	2629
no man shall *s* me of this	2Cor 11:10	5420

STOPPED

and the windows of heaven were *s*	Gen 8:2	5534
the Philistines had *s* them	Gen 26:15	5640
for the Philistines had *s* them	Gen 26:18	5640
or his flesh be *s* from his issue	Lev 15:3	2856
they *s* all the wells of water, and	2Kin 3:25	5640
who *s* all the fountains, and the	2Chr 32:4	5640
This same Hezekiah also *s* the	2Chr 32:30	5640
that the breaches began to be *s*	Neh 4:7	5640
them that speak lies shall be *s*	Ps 63:11	5534
And that the passages are *s*	Jer 51:32	8610
s their ears, that they should	Zec 7:11	3513
s their ears, and ran upon him	Acts 7:57	4912
that every mouth may be *s*	Rom 3:19	5420
Whose mouths must be *s*, who	Titus 1:11	1998
promises, *s* the mouths of lions,	Heb 11:33	5420

STOPPETH

hope, and iniquity *s* her mouth	Job 5:16	7092
the deaf adder that *s* her ear	Ps 58:4	331
Whoso *s* his ears at the cry of	Prov 21:13	331
that *s* his ears from hearing of	Is 33:15	331

STORE

of herds, and great *s* of servants	Gen 26:14	
that food shall be for *s* to the	Gen 41:36	6487
come in ye shall eat of the old *s*	Lev 25:22	
And ye shall eat old *s*, and bring	Lev 26:10	3462
shall be thy basket and thy *s*	Deut 28:5	4863
shall be thy basket and thy *s*	Deut 28:17	4863
Is not this laid up in *s* with me	Deut 32:34	
the cities of *s* that Solomon had	1Kin 9:19	4543
gold, and of spices very great *s*	1Kin 10:10	
have laid up in *s* this day	2Kin 20:17	686
all this *s* that we have prepared	1Chr 29:16	1995
wilderness, and all the *s* cities	2Chr 8:4	4543
all the *s* cities that Solomon had	2Chr 8:6	4543
s of victual, and of oil and wine	2Chr 11:11	214
all the *s* cities of Naphtali	2Chr 16:4	4543
in Judah castles, and cities of *s*	2Chr 17:12	4543
which is left is this great *s*	2Chr 31:10	1995
once in ten days *s* of all sorts	Neh 5:18	7235
full, affording all manner of *s*	Ps 144:13	
have laid up in *s* until this day	Is 39:6	686
who *s* up violence and robbery in	Amos 3:10	686
for there is none end of the *s*	Nah 2:9	8498
every one of you lay by him in *s*	1Cor 16:2	2343
Laying up in *s* for themselves a	1Ti 6:19	597
by the same word are kept in *s*	2Pet 3:7	2343

STOREHOUSE

ye all the tithes into the *s*	Mal 3:10	214
which neither have *s* nor barn	Lk 12:24	5009

STOREHOUSES

And Joseph opened all the *s*	Gen 41:56	834
the blessing upon thee in thy *s*	Deut 28:8	618
over the *s* in the fields, in the	1Chr 27:25	214
S also for the increase of corn,	2Chr 32:28	4543
he layeth up the depth in *s*	Ps 33:7	214
the utmost border, open her *s*	Jer 50:26	3965

STORIES

third *s* shalt thou make it	Gen 6:16	
round about on their three *s*	Eze 41:16	

against gallery in three *s*	Eze 42:3	
For they were in three *s*, but had	Eze 42:6	
that buildeth his *s* in the heaven	Amos 9:6	4609

STORK

And the *s*, the heron after her	Lev 11:19	2624
And the *s*, and the heron after her	Deut 14:18	2624
as for the *s*, the fir trees are	Ps 104:17	2624
the *s* in the heaven knoweth her	Jer 8:7	2624
had wings like the wings of a *s*	Zec 5:9	2624

STORM

as chaff that the *s* carrieth away	Job 21:18	5492
as a *s* hurleth him out of his	Job 27:21	
hasten my escape from the windy *s*	Ps 55:8	5584
and make them afraid with thy *s*	Ps 83:15	5492
He maketh the *s* a calm, so that	Ps 107:29	5591
of refuge, and for a covert from *s*	Is 4:6	2230
his distress, a refuge from the *s*	Is 25:4	2230
ones is as a *s* against the wall	Is 25:4	2230
tempest of hail and a destroying *s*	Is 28:2	8178
and great noise, with *s* and	Is 29:6	5492
shalt ascend and come like a *s*	Eze 38:9	7722
way in the whirlwind and in the *s*	Nah 1:3	8183
And there arose a great *s* of wind	Mk 4:37	2978
there came down a *s* of wind on	Lk 8:23	2978

STORMY

commandeth, and raiseth the *s* wind	Ps 107:25	5591
s wind fulfilling his word	Ps 148:8	5591
and a *s* wind shall rend it	Eze 13:11	5591
rend it with a *s* wind in my fury	Eze 13:13	5591

STORY

are written in the *s* of the	2Chr 13:22	4097
they are written in the *s* of the	2Chr 24:27	4097

STOUT

the *s* lion's whelps are scattered	Job 4:11	
s heart of the king of Assyria	Is 10:12	1433
look was more *s* than his fellows	Dan 7:20	7229
Your words have been *s* against me	Mal 3:13	2388

STOUTHEARTED

The *s* are spoiled, they have	Ps 76:5	47,3820
Hearken unto me, ye *s*, that are	Is 46:12	47,3820

STOUTNESS

say in the pride and *s* of heart,	Is 9:9	1433

STRAIGHT

ascend up every man *s* before him	Josh 6:5	
every man *s* before him, and they	Josh 6:20	
the kine took the *s* way to the	1Sa 6:12	3474
brought it *s* down to the west	2Chr 32:30	3474
make thy way *s* before my face	Ps 5:8	3474
thine eyelids look *s* before thee	Prov 4:25	3474
which is crooked cannot be made *s*	Eccl 1:15	8626
for who can make that *s*, which he	Eccl 7:13	8626
make *s* in the desert a highway	Is 40:3	3474
and the crooked shall be made *s*	Is 40:4	4334
before them, and crooked things *s*	Is 42:16	4334
and make the crooked places *s*	Is 45:2	4334
the rivers of waters in a *s* way	Jer 31:9	3474
And their feet were *s* feet	Eze 1:7	3474
they went every one *s* forward	Eze 1:9	5676
And they went every one *s* forward	Eze 1:12	5676
the firmament were their wings *s*	Eze 1:23	3474
they went every one *s* forward	Eze 10:22	5676
way of the Lord, make his paths *s*	Mt 3:3	2117
way of the Lord, make his paths *s*	Mk 1:3	2117
way of the Lord, make his paths *s*	Lk 3:4	2117
and the crooked shall be made *s*	Lk 3:5	2117
and immediately she was made *s*	Lk 13:13	461
Make *s* the way of the Lord, as	Jn 1:23	2116
into the street which is called *S*	Acts 9:11	2117
we came with a *s* course to	Acts 16:11	2113
we came with a *s* course unto Coos	Acts 21:1	2113
make *s* paths for your feet, lest	Heb 12:13	3717

STRAIGHTWAY

the city, ye shall *s* find him	1Sa 9:13	3651
Then Saul fell *s* all along on the	1Sa 28:20	4116
He goeth after her *s*, as an ox	Prov 7:22	6597
s there remained no strength in	Dan 10:17	6258
went up *s* out of the water	Mt 3:16	2117
they *s* left their nets, and	Mt 4:20	2112
And *s* Jesus constrained his	Mt 14:22	2112
But *s* Jesus spake unto them,	Mt 14:27	2112
s ye shall find an ass tied, and a	Mt 21:2	2112
and *s* he will send them	Mt 21:3	2112
and *s* took his journey	Mt 25:15	2112
s one of them ran, and took a	Mt 27:48	2112
s coming up out of the water, he	Mk 1:10	2112
s they forsook their nets, and	Mk 1:18	2112

S

And *s* he called them .... Mk 1:20 | 2112
s on the sabbath day he entered .... Mk 1:21 | 2112
s many were gathered together, ... Mk 2:2 | 2112
s took counsel with the Herodians .... Mk 3:6 | 2112
s the fountain of her blood was .... Mk 5:29 | 2112
s the damsel arose, and walked............... Mk 5:42 | 2112
she came in *s* with haste unto the .... Mk 6:25 | 2112
s he constrained his disciples to .... Mk 6:45 | 2112
out of the ship, *s* they knew him, ... Mk 6:54 | 2112
s his ears were opened, and the.............. Mk 7:35 | 2112
s he entered into a ship with his .... Mk 8:10 | 2112
s all the people, when they .... Mk 9:15 | 2112
he saw him, *s* the spirit tare him .... Mk 9:20 | 2112
s the father of the child cried .... Mk 9:24 | 2112
s he will send him hither .... Mk 11:3 | 2112
as he came, he goeth *s* to him .... Mk 14:45 | 2112
s in the morning the chief .... Mk 15:1 | 2112
drunk old wine s desireth new .... Lk 5:39 | 2112
spirit came again, and she arose *s*.......... Lk 8:55 | 3916
s ye say, There cometh a shower .... Lk 12:54 | 2112
will not s pull him out on the .... Lk 14:5 | 2112
himself, and shall s glorify him .... Jn 13:32 | 2117
Then fell she down *s* at his feet............... Acts 5:10 | 3916
s he preached Christ in the .... Acts 9:20 | 2112
and was baptized, he and all his, *s* .... Acts 16:33 | 3916
Then *s* they departed from him................ Acts 22:29 | 2112
I sent *s* to thee, and gave ya .... Acts 23:30 | 1824
s forgetteth what manner of man .... Jas 1:24 | 2112

STRAIN
which s at a gnat, and swallow a .... Mt 23:24 | 1368

STRAIT
Israel saw that they were in a *s*.............. 1Sa 13:6 | 6887
said unto Gad, I am in a great *s*............. 2Sa 24:14 | 6887
dwell with thee is too *s* for us................ 2Kin 6:1 | 6862
said unto Gad, I am in a great *s*............. 1Chr 21:13 | 6887
out of the *s* into a broad place .... Job 36:16 | 6862
ears, The place is too *s* for me .... Is 49:20 | 6862
Enter ye in at the s gate .... Mt 7:13 | 4728
Because s is the gate, and narrow .... Mt 7:14 | 4728
Strive to enter in at the s gate .... Lk 13:24 | 4728
For I am in a *s* betwixt two .... Phil 1:23 | 4912

STRAITEN
seek their lives, shall *s* them................... Jer 19:9 | 6693

STRAITENED
steps of his strength shall be *s*............... Job 18:7 | 3334
and the breadth of the waters is *s* .... Job 37:10 | 4164
goest, thy steps shall not be *s* .... Prov 4:12 | 3334
was *s* more than the lowest .... Eze 42:6 | 680
is the spirit of the LORD *s*...................... Mic 2:7 | 7114
and how am I s till it be .... Lk 12:50 | 4912
Ye are not *s* in us, but ye are .... 2Cor 6:12 | 4729
but ye are *s* in your own bowels .... 2Cor 6:12 | 4729

STRAITENETH
the nations, and *s* them again .... Job 12:23 | 5148

STRAITEST
that after the most *s* sect of our.............. Acts 26:5 | 196

STRAITLY
The man asked us *s* of our state............. Gen 43:7 |
for he had *s* sworn the children............... Ex 13:19 |
Now Jericho was *s* shut up because .... Josh 6:1 |
Thy father *s* charged the people .... 1Sa 14:28 |
Jesus s charged them, saying, See .... Mt 9:30 |
he *s* charged him, and forthwith............. Mk 1:43 |
he *s* charged them that they .... Mk 3:12 | 4183
he charged them *s* that no man .... Mk 5:43 | 4183
he *s* charged them, and commanded ..... Lk 9:21 |
let us *s* threaten them, that they............. Acts 4:17 | 547
Did not we *s* command you that ye .... Acts 5:28 |

STRAITNESS
thee, in the siege, and in the *s* .... Deut 28:53 | 4689
him in the siege, and in the *s*................. Deut 28:55 | 4689
things secretly in the siege and *s* .... Deut 28:57 | 4689
broad place, where there is no *s* .... Job 36:16 | 4164
of his friend in the siege and *s*............... Jer 19:9 | 4689

STRAITS
his sufficiency he shall be in *s* .... Job 20:22 | 3334
overtook her between the *s*..................... Lam 1:3 | 4712

STRAKE
s sail, and so were driven .... Acts 27:17 | 5465

STRAKES
and pilled white *s* in them .... Gen 30:37 | 6479
walls of the house with hollow *s*............. Lev 14:37 | 8258

STRANGE
Put away the *s* gods that are .... Gen 35:2 | 5236
they gave unto Jacob all the *s*............... Gen 35:4 | 5236

but made himself *s* unto them .... Gen 42:7 | 5234
have been a stranger in a *s* land .... Ex 2:22 | 5237
I have been an alien in a *s* land............. Ex 18:3 | 5237
to sell her unto a *s* nation he.................. Ex 21:8 | 5237
shall offer no *s* incense thereon............. Ex 30:9 | 2114
offered *s* fire before the LORD, ... Lev 10:1 | 2114
when they offered *s* fire before.............. Num 3:4 | 2114
when they offered *s* fire before .... Num 26:61 | 2114
and there was no *s* god with him .... Deut 32:12 | 5236
him to jealousy with *s* gods.................... Deut 32:16 | 2114
forsake the *s* gods, and serve *s* gods ... Josh 24:20 | 5236
the *s* gods which are among you, ... Josh 24:23 | 5236
they put away the *s* gods from .... Judg 10:16 | 5236
for thou art the son of a *s* woman.......... Judg 11:2 | 312
hearts, then put away the *s* gods .... 1Sa 7:3 | 5236
king Solomon loved many *s* women .... 1Kin 11:1 | 5237
did he for all his *s* wives .... 1Kin 11:8 | 5237
drunk *s* waters, and with the sole.......... 2Kin 19:24 | 2114
away the altars of the *s* gods................. 2Chr 14:3 | 5236
And he took away the *s* gods................. 2Chr 33:15 | 5236
have taken *s* wives of the people .... Ezr 10:2 | 5237
and have taken *s* wives, to .... Ezr 10:10 | 5237
of the land, and from the *s* wives .... Ezr 10:11 | 5237
s wives in our cities come at .... Ezr 10:14 | 5237
s wives by the first day of the .... Ezr 10:17 | 5237
were found that had taken *s* wives .... Ezr 10:18 | 5237
All these had taken *s* wives................... Ezr 10:44 | 5237
our God in marrying *s* wives .... Neh 13:27 | 5237
that ye make yourselves *s* to me .... Job 19:3 | 1970
My breath is *s* to my wife....................... Job 19:17 | 2114
a *s* punishment to the workers of........... Job 31:3 | 5235
out our hands to a *s* god........................ Ps 44:20 | 2114
There shall no *s* god be in thee .... Ps 81:9 | 2114
shalt thou worship any *s* god .... Ps 81:9 | 5236
Jacob from a people of *s* language .... Ps 114:1 | 3937
sing the LORD's song in a *s* land .... Ps 137:4 | 5236
from the hand of *s* children .... Ps 144:7 | 5236
me from the hand of *s* children .... Ps 144:11 | 2114
To deliver thee from the *s* woman .... Prov 2:16 | 2114
For the lips of a *s* woman drop as.......... Prov 5:3 | 2114
son, be ravished with a *s* woman.......... Prov 5:20 | 2114
of the tongue of a *s* woman .... Prov 6:24 | 5237
may keep thee from the *s* woman .... Prov 7:5 | 2114
a pledge of him for a *s* woman .... Prov 20:16 | 5237
The way of man is froward and *s*........... Prov 21:8 | 2114
The mouth of *s* women is a deep........... Prov 22:14 | 2114
a *s* woman is a narrow pit...................... Prov 23:27 | 5237
Thine eyes shall behold *s* women .... Prov 23:33 | 2114
a pledge of him for a *s* woman .... Prov 27:13 | 5237
and shalt set it with *s* slips.................... Is 17:10 | 2114
he may do his work, his *s* work.............. Is 28:21 | 2114
bring to pass his act, his *s* act .... Is 28:21 | 5237
when there was no *s* god among you...... Is 43:12 | 2114
plant of a *s* vine unto me .... Jer 2:21 | 5237
served *s* gods in your land, so............... Jer 5:19 | 5236
graven images, and with *s* vanities .... Jer 8:19 | 5236
sent to a people of a *s* speech .... Eze 3:5 | 6012
Not to many people of a *s* speech.......... Eze 3:6 | 6012
most strong holds with a *s* god .... Dan 11:39 | 5236
for they have begotten *s* children........... Hos 5:7 | 2114
they were counted as a *s* thing .... Hos 8:12 | 2114
as are clothed with *s* apparel................ Zeph 1:8 | 5237
married the daughter of a *s* god .... Mal 2:11 | 5236
We have seen *s* things to day................ Lk 5:26 | 3861
seed should sojourn in a *s* land .... Acts 7:6 | 245
to be a setter forth of *s* gods .... Acts 17:18 | 3581
certain *s* things to our ears .... Acts 17:20 | 3579
them even unto *s* cities .... Acts 26:11 | 1854
of promise, as in a *s* country.................. Heb 11:9 | 245
about with divers and *s* doctrines .... Heb 13:9 | 3581
Wherein they think it *s* that ye .... 1Pet 4:4 | 3579
think it not *s* concerning the .... 1Pet 4:12 | 3579
as though some *s* thing happened .... 1Pet 4:12 | 3581
and going after *s* flesh, are set .... Jude 7 | 2087

STRANGELY
should behave themselves *s* .... Deut 32:27 | 5234

STRANGER
a *s* in a land that is not theirs............... Gen 15:13 | 1616
the land wherein thou art a *s*................. Gen 17:8 | 4033
or bought with money of any *s* .... Gen 17:12 | 1121,5235
and bought with money of the *s*...... Gen 17:27 | 1121,5235
I am a *s* and a sojourner with you.......... Gen 23:4 | 1616
the land wherein thou art a *s* .... Gen 28:4 | 4033
land wherein his father was a *s* .... Gen 37:1 | 4033
I have been a *s* in a strange land .... Ex 2:22 | 1616
of Israel, whether he be a *s* .... Ex 12:19 | 1616
There shall no *s* eat thereof............ Ex 12:43 | 1121,5235
when a *s* shall sojourn with thee, ... Ex 12:48 | 1616
unto the *s* that sojourneth among.......... Ex 12:49 | 1616
nor thy *s* that is within thy .... Ex 20:10 | 1616

Thou shalt neither vex a *s*	Ex 22:21	1616
Also thou shalt not oppress a *s*	Ex 23:9	1616
for ye know the heart of a *s*	Ex 23:9	1616
the son of thy handmaid, and the *s*	Ex 23:12	1616
but a *s* shall not eat thereof,	Ex 29:33	2114
putteth any of it upon a *s*	Ex 30:33	2114
or a *s* that sojourneth among you	Lev 16:29	1616
blood, neither shall any *s* that	Lev 17:12	1616
one of your own country, or a *s*	Lev 17:15	1616
nor any *s* that sojourneth among	Lev 18:26	1616
leave them for the poor and *s*	Lev 19:10	1616
if a *s* sojourn with thee in your	Lev 19:33	1616
But the *s* that dwelleth with you	Lev 19:34	1616
There shall no *s* eat of the holy	Lev 22:10	2114
daughter also be married unto a *s*.	Lev 22:12	376,2114
but there shall no *s* eat thereof	Lev 22:13	2114
them unto the poor, and to the *s*	Lev 23:22	1616
as well the *s*, as he that is born	Lev 24:16	1616
manner of law, as well for the *s*	Lev 24:22	1616
for thy *s* that sojourneth with	Lev 25:6	8453
yea, though he be a *s*, or a	Lev 25:35	1616
a sojourner or *s* wax rich by thee	Lev 25:47	8453
unto the *s* or sojourner by thee	Lev 25:47	1616
the *s* that cometh nigh shall be	Num 1:51	2114
the *s* that cometh nigh shall be	Num 3:10	2114
the *s* that cometh nigh shall be	Num 3:38	2114
if a *s* shall sojourn among you,	Num 9:14	1616
one ordinance, both for the *s*	Num 9:14	1616
if a *s* sojourn with you, or	Num 15:14	1616
also for the *s* that sojourneth	Num 15:15	1616
so shall the *s* be before the L ORD	Num 15:15	1616
for the *s* that sojourneth with	Num 15:16	1616
the *s* that sojourneth among them	Num 15:26	1616
for the *s* that sojourneth among	Num 15:29	1616
he be born in the land, or a *s*	Num 15:30	1616
the children of Israel, that no *s*	Num 16:40	376,2114
a *s* shall not come nigh unto you	Num 18:4	2114
the *s* that cometh nigh shall be	Num 18:7	2114
unto the *s* that sojourneth among	Num 19:10	1616
children of Israel, and for the *s*	Num 35:15	1616
and the *s* that is with him	Deut 1:16	1616
nor thy *s* that is within thy	Deut 5:14	1616
and widow, and loveth the *s*	Deut 10:18	1616
Love ye therefore the *s*	Deut 10:19	1616
unto the *s* that is in thy gates	Deut 14:21	1616
inheritance with thee,) and the *s*	Deut 14:29	1616
is within thy gates, and the *s*	Deut 16:11	1616
maidservant, and the Levite, the *s*	Deut 16:14	1616
thou mayest not set a *s* over thee	Deut 17:15	376,5237
because thou wast a *s* in his land	Deut 23:7	1616
Unto a *s* thou mayest lend upon	Deut 23:20	5237
not pervert the judgment of the *s*	Deut 24:17	1616
it shall be for the *s*, for the	Deut 24:19	1616
it shall be for the *s*, for the	Deut 24:20	1616
it shall be for the *s*, for the	Deut 24:21	1616
shall not marry without unto a *s*	Deut 25:5	376,2114
and the *s* that is among you	Deut 26:11	1616
given it unto the Levite, the *s*	Deut 26:12	1616
unto the Levite, and unto the *s*	Deut 26:13	1616
perverteth the judgment of the *s*	Deut 27:19	1616
The *s* that is within thee shall	Deut 28:43	1616
thy *s* that is in thy camp, from	Deut 29:11	1616
the *s* that shall come from a far	Deut 29:22	5237
thy *s* that is within thy gates,	Deut 31:12	1616
of the L ORD, as well the *s*	Josh 8:33	1616
for the *s* that sojourneth among	Josh 20:9	1616
aside hither into the city of a *s*	Judg 19:12	5237
knowledge of me, seeing I am a *s*	Ruth 2:10	5237
he answered, I am the son of a *s*	2Sa 1:13	376,1616
for thou art a *s*, and also an	2Sa 15:19	5237
there was no *s* with us in the	1Kin 3:18	2114
Moreover concerning a *s*, that is	1Kin 8:41	5237
that the *s* calleth to thee for	1Kin 8:43	5237
Moreover concerning the *s*	2Chr 6:32	5237
that the *s* calleth to thee for	2Chr 6:33	5237
given, and no *s* passed among them	Job 15:19	2114
and my maids, count me for a *s*	Job 19:15	2114
The *s* did not lodge in the street	Job 31:32	1616
for I am a *s* with thee, and a	Ps 39:12	1616
I am become a *s* unto my brethren,	Ps 69:8	2114
They slay the widow and the *s*	Ps 94:6	1616
I am a *s* in the earth.	Ps 119:19	1616
even from the *s* which flattereth	Prov 2:16	5237
labours be in the house of a *s*	Prov 5:10	5237
and embrace the bosom of a *s*	Prov 5:20	5237
hast stricken thy hand with a *s*	Prov 6:1	2114
from the *s* which flattereth with	Prov 7:5	5237
surety for a *s* shall smart for it	Prov 11:15	2114
a *s* doth not intermeddle with his	Prov 14:10	2114
garment that is surety for a *s*	Prov 20:16	2114
a *s*, and not thine own lips	Prov 27:2	5237

garment that is surety for a *s*	Prov 27:13	2114
to eat thereof, but a *s* eateth it	Eccl 6:2	376,5237
Neither let the son of the *s*	Is 56:3	5236
Also the sons of the, *s* that join	Is 56:6	5236
the sons of the *s* shall not drink	Is 62:8	5236
If ye oppress not the *s*, the	Jer 7:6	1616
thou be as a *s* in the land	Jer 14:8	1616
no wrong, do no violence to the *s*	Jer 22:3	1616
or of the *s* that sojourneth in	Eze 14:7	1616
dealt by oppression with the *s*	Eze 22:7	1616
have oppressed the *s* wrongfully	Eze 22:29	1616
No *s*, uncircumcised in heart, nor	Eze 44:9	1121,5236
of any *s* that is among the	Eze 44:9	1121,5236
in what tribe the *s* sojourneth	Eze 47:23	1616
in the day that he became a *s*	Obad 12	5235
widow, nor the fatherless, the *s*	Zec 7:10	1616
turn aside the *s* from his right	Mal 3:5	1616
I was a *s*, and ye took me in	Mt 25:35	*3581*
When saw we thee a *s*, and took	Mt 25:38	*3581*
I was a *s*, and ye took me not in	Mt 25:43	*3581*
an hungred, or athirst, or a *s*	Mt 25:44	*3581*
to give glory to God, save this *s*	Lk 17:18	*241*
Art thou only a *s* in Jerusalem	Lk 24:18	*3939*
a *s* will they not follow, but	Jn 10:5	*245*
was a *s* in the land of Madian,	Acts 7:29	*3941*

STRANGER'S

Neither from a *s* hand shall ye	Lev 22:25	1121,5236
or to the stock of the *s* family	Lev 25:47	1616

STRANGERS

Are we not counted of him *s*	Gen 31:15	5237
the land wherein they were *s*	Gen 36:7	4033
pilgrimage, wherein they were *s*	Ex 6:4	1481
for ye were *s* in the land of	Ex 22:21	1616
seeing ye were *s* in the land of	Ex 23:9	1616
or of the *s* which sojourn among	Lev 17:8	1616
or of the *s* that sojourn among	Lev 17:10	1616
or of the *s* that sojourn among	Lev 17:13	1616
for ye were *s* in the land of	Lev 19:34	1616
or of the *s* that sojourn in	Lev 20:2	1616
of Israel, or of the *s* in Israel	Lev 22:18	1616
for ye are *s* and sojourners with	Lev 25:23	1616
the *s* that do sojourn among you	Lev 25:45	8453
for ye were *s* in the land of	Deut 10:19	1616
or of thy *s* that are in thy land	Deut 24:14	1616
the gods of the *s* of the land	Deut 31:16	5236
the *s* that were conversant among	Josh 8:35	1616
S shall submit themselves unto me	2Sa 22:45	1121,5236
S shall fade away, and they shall	2Sa 22:46	1121,5236
but few, even a few, and *s* in it	1Chr 16:19	1481
to gather together the *s* that	1Chr 22:2	1616
For we are *s* before thee, and	1Chr 29:15	1616
Solomon numbered all the *s* that	2Chr 2:17	582,1616
the *s* with them out of Ephraim and	2Chr 15:9	1481
the *s* that came out of the land	2Chr 30:25	1616
separated themselves from all *s*	Neh 9:2	1121,5236
Thus cleansed I them from all *s*	Neh 13:30	5236
the *s* shall submit themselves	Ps 18:44	1121,5236
The *s* shall fade away, and be	Ps 18:45	1121,5236
For *s* are risen up against me, and	Ps 54:3	2114
yea, very few, and *s* in it	Ps 105:12	1481
let the *s* spoil his labour	Ps 109:11	2114
The L ORD preserveth the *s*	Ps 146:9	1616
Lest *s* be filled with thy wealth	Prov 5:10	2114
s devour it in your presence, and	Is 1:7	2114
is desolate, as overthrown by *s*	Is 1:7	2114
themselves in the children of *s*	Is 2:6	5237
of the fat ones shall *s* eat	Is 5:17	1481
the *s* shall be joined with them,	Is 14:1	1616
a palace of *s* to be no city	Is 25:2	2114
shalt bring down the noise of *s*	Is 25:5	2114
of thy *s* shall be like small dust	Is 29:5	2114
the sons of *s* shall build up thy	Is 60:10	5236
s shall stand and feed your flocks	Is 61:5	2114
for I have loved *s*, and after them	Jer 2:25	2114
to the *s* under every green tree	Jer 3:13	2114
so shall ye serve *s* in a land	Jer 5:19	2114
s shall no more serve themselves	Jer 30:8	2114
days in the land where ye be *s*	Jer 35:7	1481
for *s* are come into the	Jer 51:51	2114
Our inheritance is turned to *s*	Lam 5:2	2114
the hands of the *s* for a prey	Eze 7:21	2114
deliver you into the hands of *s*	Eze 11:9	2114
which taketh *s* instead of her	Eze 16:32	2114
I will bring *s* upon thee, the	Eze 28:7	2114
uncircumcised by the hand of *s*	Eze 28:10	2114
that is therein, by the hand of *s*	Eze 30:12	2114
And *s*, the terrible of the nations	Eze 31:12	2114
have brought into my sanctuary *s*	Eze 44:7	1121,5236
to the *s* that sojourn among you,	Eze 47:22	1616
S have devoured his strength, and	Hos 7:9	2114

S

the *s* shall swallow it up	Hos 8:7	2114
there shall no *s* pass through her	Joel 3:17	2114
in the day that the *s* carried	Obad 11	2114
of their own children, or of *s*	Mt 17:25	245
Peter saith unto him, Of *s*	Mt 17:26	245
the potter's field, to bury *s* in	Mt 27:7	3581
for they know not the voice of *s*	Jn 10:5	245
s of Rome, Jews and proselytes,	Acts 2:10	1927
dwelt as *s* in the land of Egypt	Acts 13:17	1722,3940
s which were there spent their	Acts 17:21	3581
s from the covenants of promise,	Eph 2:12	3581
Now therefore ye are no more *s*	Eph 2:19	3581
up children, if she have lodged *s*	1Ti 5:10	3580
and confessed that they were *s*	Heb 11:13	3581
Be not forgetful to entertain *s*	Heb 13:2	5381
to the *s* scattered throughout	1Pet 1:1	3927
beloved, I beseech you as *s*	1Pet 2:11	3941
doest to the brethren, and to *s*	3Jn 5	3581

STRANGERS'

thine own, and not *s* with thee	Prov 5:17	2114

STRANGLED

s for his lionesses, and filled	Nah 2:12	2614
fornication, and from things *s*	Acts 15:20	4156
and from blood, and from things *s*	Acts 15:29	4156
idols, and from blood, and from *s*	Acts 21:25	4156

STRANGLING

So that my soul chooseth *s*	Job 7:15	4267

STRAW

moreover unto him, We have both *s*	Gen 24:25	8401
he ungirded his camels, and gave *s*	Gen 24:32	8401
give the people *s* to make brick	Ex 5:7	8401
go and gather *s* for themselves	Ex 5:7	8401
Pharaoh, I will not give you *s*	Ex 5:10	8401
get you *s* where ye can find it	Ex 5:11	8401
to gather stubble instead of *s*	Ex 5:12	8401
daily tasks, as when there was *s*	Ex 5:13	8401
There is no *s* given unto thy	Ex 5:16	8401
for there shall no *s* be given you	Ex 5:18	8401
Yet there is both *s* and provender	Judg 19:19	8401
s for the horses and dromedaries	1Kin 4:28	8401
He esteemeth iron as *s*, and brass	Job 41:27	8401
the lion shall eat *s* like the ox	Is 11:7	8401
even as *s* is trodden down for the	Is 25:10	4963
lion shall eat *s* like the bullock	Is 65:25	8401

STRAWED

s it upon the water, and made the	Ex 32:20	2219
the trees, and *s* them in the way	Mt 21:8	4766
gathering where thou hast not *s*	Mt 25:24	1287
not, and gather where I have not *s*	Mt 25:26	1287
the trees, and *s* them in the way	Mk 11:8	4766

STREAM

at the *s* of the brooks that goeth	Num 21:15	793
as the *s* of brooks they pass away	Job 6:15	650
the *s* had gone over our soul	Ps 124:4	5158
of the river unto the *s* of Egypt	Is 27:12	5158
his breath, as an overflowing *s*	Is 30:28	5158
like a *s* of brimstone, doth	Is 30:33	5158
stones of the *s*	Is 57:6	5158
of the Gentiles like a flowing *s*	Is 66:12	5158
A fiery *s* issued and came forth	Dan 7:10	5103
and righteousness as a mighty *s*	Amos 5:24	5158
the *s* beat vehemently upon that	Lk 6:48	4215
against which the *s* did beat	Lk 6:49	4215

STREAMS

the waters of Egypt, upon their *s*	Ex 7:19	5104
hand with thy rod over the *s*	Ex 8:5	5104
the *s* whereof shall make glad the	Ps 46:4	6388
He brought *s* also out of the rock	Ps 78:16	5140
gushed out, and the *s* overflowed	Ps 78:20	5158
O LORD, as the *s* in the south	Ps 126:4	650
living waters, and *s* from Lebanon	Song 4:15	5140
and shall smite it in the seven *s*	Is 11:15	5158
s of waters in the day of the	Is 30:25	2988
us a place of broad rivers and *s*	Is 33:21	2975
the *s* thereof shall be turned	Is 34:9	5158
break out, and *s* in the desert	Is 35:6	5158

STREET

we will abide in the *s* all night	Gen 19:2	7339
into the midst of the *s* thereof	Deut 13:16	7339
the doors of thy house into the *s*	Josh 2:19	2351
sat him down in a *s* of the city	Judg 19:15	7339
man in the *s* of the city	Judg 19:17	7339
only lodge not in the *s*	Judg 19:20	7339
them from the *s* of Beth-shan	2Sa 21:12	7339
stamp them as the mire of the *s*	2Sa 22:43	2351
them together into the east *s*	2Chr 29:4	7339
in the *s* of the gate of the city	2Chr 32:6	7339

sat in the *s* of the house of God	Ezr 10:9	7339
together as one man into the *s*	Neh 8:1	7339
he read therein before the *s* that	Neh 8:3	7339
in the *s* of the water gate, and in	Neh 8:16	7339
in the *s* of the gate of Ephraim	Neh 8:16	7339
Mordecai unto the *s* of the city	Est 4:6	7339
through the *s* of the city	Est 6:9	7339
through the *s* of the city	Est 6:11	7339
and he shall have no name in the *s*	Job 18:17	2351,6440
when I prepared my seat in the *s*	Job 29:7	7339
stranger did not lodge in the *s*	Job 31:32	2351
through the *s* near her corner	Prov 7:8	7784
his voice to be heard in the *s*	Is 42:2	2351
body as the ground, and as the *s*	Is 51:23	2351
for truth is fallen in the *s*	Is 59:14	7339
of bread out of the bakers' *s*	Jer 37:21	2351
for hunger in the top of every *s*	Lam 2:19	2351
poured out in the top of every *s*	Lam 4:1	2351
thee an high place in every *s*	Eze 16:24	7339
thine high place in every *s*	Eze 16:31	7339
pestilence, and blood into her *s*	Eze 28:23	7339
the *s* shall be built again, and	Dan 9:25	7339
go into the *s* which is called	Acts 9:11	4505
out, and passed on through one *s*	Acts 12:10	4505
lie in the *s* of the great city	Rev 11:8	4113
the *s* of the city was pure gold,	Rev 21:21	4113
In the midst of the *s* of it	Rev 22:2	4113

STREETS

it not in the *s* of Askelon	2Sa 1:20	2351
thou shalt make *s* for thee in	1Kin 20:34	2351
them out as the dirt in the *s*	Ps 18:42	2351
and guile depart not from her *s*	Ps 55:11	7339
and ten thousands in our *s*	Ps 144:13	2351
there be no complaining in our *s*	Ps 144:14	7339
she uttereth her voice in the *s*	Prov 1:20	7339
and rivers of waters in the *s*	Prov 5:16	7339
Now is she without, now in the *s*	Prov 7:12	2351
I shall be slain in the *s*	Prov 22:13	7339
a lion is in the *s*	Prov 26:13	7339
the doors shall be shut in the *s*	Eccl 12:4	7784
and the mourners go about the *s*	Eccl 12:5	7784
and go about the city in the *s*	Song 3:2	7784
were torn in the midst of the *s*	Is 5:25	2351
them down like the mire of the *s*	Is 10:6	2351
In their *s* they shall gird	Is 15:3	2351
of their houses, and in their *s*	Is 15:3	7339
is a crying for wine in the *s*	Is 24:11	2351
they lie at the head of all the *s*	Is 51:20	2351
and fro through the *s* of Jerusalem	Jer 5:1	2351
of Judah and in the *s* of Jerusalem	Jer 7:17	2351
from the *s* of Jerusalem, the	Jer 7:34	2351
and the young men from the *s*	Jer 9:21	7339
in the *s* of Jerusalem, saying,	Jer 11:6	2351
the *s* of Jerusalem have ye set up	Jer 11:13	2351
shall be cast out in the *s* of	Jer 14:16	2351
in the *s* of Jerusalem, that are	Jer 33:10	2351
of Judah and in the *s* of Jerusalem	Jer 44:6	2351
Judah, and in the *s* of Jerusalem	Jer 44:9	2351
Judah, and in the *s* of Jerusalem	Jer 44:17	2351
in the *s* of Jerusalem, ye, and	Jer 44:21	2351
of Moab, and in the *s* thereof	Jer 48:38	7339
her young men shall fall in her *s*	Jer 49:26	7339
shall her young men fall in the *s*	Jer 50:30	7339
that are thrust through in her *s*	Jer 51:4	2351
swoon in the *s* of the city	Lam 2:11	7339
the wounded in the *s* of the city	Lam 2:12	7339
old lie on the ground in the *s*	Lam 2:21	2351
delicately are desolate in the *s*	Lam 4:5	2351
they are not known in the *s*	Lam 4:8	2351
wandered as blind men in the *s*	Lam 4:14	2351
steps, that we cannot go in our *s*	Lam 4:18	7339
shall cast their silver in the *s*	Eze 7:19	2351
ye have filled the *s* thereof with	Eze 11:6	2351
shall he tread down all thy *s*	Eze 26:11	2351
Wailing shall be in all *s*	Amos 5:16	7339
trodden down as the mire of the *s*	Mic 7:10	2351
The chariots shall rage in the *s*	Nah 2:4	2351
in pieces at the top of all the *s*	Nah 3:10	2351
I made their *s* waste, that none	Zeph 3:6	2351
women dwell in the *s* of Jerusalem	Zec 8:4	7339
the *s* of the city shall be full	Zec 8:5	7339
and girls playing in the *s* thereof	Zec 8:5	7339
and fine gold as the mire of the *s*	Zec 9:3	2351
the mire of the *s* in the battle	Zec 10:5	2351
do in the synagogues and in the *s*	Mt 6:2	4505
and in the corners of the *s*	Mt 6:5	4113
any man hear his voice in the *s*	Mt 12:19	4113
they laid the sick in the *s*	Mk 6:56	58
ways out into the *s* of the same	Lk 10:10	4113
and thou hast taught in our *s*	Lk 13:26	4113

Go out quickly into the *s*	Lk 14:21	4113
brought forth the sick into the *s*	Acts 5:15	4113

STRENGTH

henceforth yield unto thee her *s*	Gen 4:12	3581
might, and the beginning of my *s*	Gen 49:3	202
But his bow abode in *s*, and the	Gen 49:24	386
for by *s* of hand the LORD brought	Ex 13:3	2392
By *s* of hand the LORD brought us	Ex 13:14	2392
for by *s* of hand the LORD brought	Ex 13:16	2392
the sea returned to his *s* when	Ex 14:27	386
The LORD is my *s* and song, and he	Ex 15:2	5797
in thy *s* unto thy holy habitation	Ex 15:13	5797
your *s* shall be spent in vain	Lev 26:20	3581
as it were the *s* of a unicorn	Num 23:22	8443
as it were the *s* of a unicorn	Num 24:8	8443
for he is the beginning of his *s*	Deut 21:17	202
and as thy days, so shall thy *s* be	Deut 33:25	1679
that stood still in their *s*	Josh 11:13	8510
as my *s* was then, even so is my	Josh 14:11	3581
was then, even so is my *s* now	Josh 14:11	3581
my soul, thou hast trodden down *s*	Judg 5:21	5797
for as the man is, so is his *s*	Judg 8:21	1369
and see wherein his great *s* lieth	Judg 16:5	3581
thee, wherein thy great *s* lieth	Judg 16:6	3581
So his *s* was not known	Judg 16:9	3581
told me wherein thy great *s* lieth	Judg 16:15	3581
then my *s* will go from me, and I	Judg 16:17	3581
him, and his *s* went from him	Judg 16:19	3581
that stumbled are girded with *s*	1Sa 2:4	2428
for by *s* shall no man prevail	1Sa 2:9	3581
and he shall give *s* unto his king	1Sa 2:10	5797
also the *S* of Israel will not lie	1Sa 15:29	5331
and there was no *s* in him	1Sa 28:20	3581
and eat, that thou mayest have *s*	1Sa 28:22	3581
God is my *s* and power	2Sa 22:33	4581
hast girded me with *s* to battle	2Sa 22:40	2428
went in the *s* of that meat forty	1Kin 19:8	3581
Jehu drew a bow with his full *s*	2Kin 9:24	3027
I have counsel and *s* for the war	2Kin 18:20	1369
there is not *s* to bring forth	2Kin 19:3	3581
Seek the LORD and his *s*, seek his	1Chr 16:11	5797
s and gladness are in his place	1Chr 16:27	5797
give unto the LORD glory and *s*	1Chr 16:28	5797
able men for *s* for the service,	1Chr 26:8	3581
make great, and to give *s* unto all	1Chr 29:12	2388
place, thou, and the ark of thy *s*	2Chr 6:41	5797
s again in the days of Abijah	2Chr 13:20	3581
The *s* of the bearers of burdens	Neh 4:10	3581
for the joy of the LORD is your *s*	Neh 8:10	4581
What is my *s*, that I should hope	Job 6:11	3581
Is my *s* the *s* of stones	Job 6:12	3581
is wise in heart, and mighty in *s*	Job 9:4	3581
If I speak of *s*, lo, he is strong	Job 9:19	3581
With him is wisdom and *s*, he hath	Job 12:13	1369
With him is *s* and wisdom	Job 12:16	5797
and weakeneth the *s* of the mighty	Job 12:21	4206
The steps of his *s* shall be	Job 18:7	202
His *s* shall be hungerbitten, and	Job 18:12	202
It shall devour the *s* of his skin	Job 18:13	905
of death shall devour his *s*	Job 18:13	905
One dieth in his full *s*, being	Job 21:23	6106
but he would put *s* in me	Job 23:6	
thou the arm that hath no *s*	Job 26:2	5797
whereto might the *s* of their	Job 30:2	3581
he is mighty in *s* and wisdom	Job 36:5	3581
not gold, nor all the forces of *s*	Job 36:19	3581
and to the great rain of his *s*	Job 37:6	5797
trust him, because his *s* is great	Job 39:11	3581
Hath thou given the horse *s*	Job 39:19	1369
the valley, and rejoiceth in his *s*	Job 39:21	3581
his *s* is in his loins, and his	Job 40:16	3581
In his neck remaineth *s*, and	Job 41:22	5797
s because of thine enemies	Ps 8:2	5797
I will love thee, O LORD, my *s*	Ps 18:1	2391
my God, my *s*, in whom I will	Ps 18:2	6697
It is God that girdeth me with *s*	Ps 18:32	2428
girded me with *s* unto the battle	Ps 18:39	2428
in thy sight, O LORD, my *s*	Ps 19:14	6697
the saving *s* of his right hand	Ps 20:6	1369
The king shall joy in thy *s*	Ps 21:1	5797
exalted, LORD, in thine own *s*	Ps 21:13	5797
My *s* is dried up like a potsherd	Ps 22:15	3581
O my *s*, haste thee to help me	Ps 22:19	360
the LORD is the *s* of my life	Ps 27:1	4581
The LORD is my *s* and my shield	Ps 28:7	5797
The LORD is their *s*, and he is the	Ps 28:8	5797
is the saving *s* of his anointed	Ps 28:8	4581
give unto the LORD glory and *s*	Ps 29:1	5797
LORD will give *s* unto his people	Ps 29:11	5797
for thou art my *s*	Ps 31:4	4581

my *s* faileth because of mine	Ps 31:10	3581
man is not delivered by much *s*	Ps 33:16	3581
he deliver any by his great *s*	Ps 33:17	2428
he is their *s* in the time of	Ps 37:39	4581
My heart panteth, my *s* faileth me	Ps 38:10	3581
O spare me, that I may recover *s*	Ps 39:13	1082
For thou art the God of my *s*	Ps 43:2	4581
God is our refuge and *s*, a very	Ps 46:1	5797
the man that made not God his *s*	Ps 52:7	4581
by thy name, and judge me by thy *s*	Ps 54:1	1369
Because of his *s* will I wait upon	Ps 59:9	5797
Unto thee, O my *s*, will I sing	Ps 59:17	5797
also is the *s* of mine head	Ps 60:7	4581
the rock of my *s*, and my refuge,	Ps 62:7	5797
Which by his *s* setteth fast the	Ps 65:6	3581
Thy God hath commanded thy *s*	Ps 68:28	5797
Ascribe ye *s* unto God	Ps 68:34	5797
Israel, and his *s* is in the clouds	Ps 68:34	5797
God of Israel is he that giveth *s*	Ps 68:35	5797
forsake me not when my *s* faileth	Ps 71:9	3581
will go in the *s* of the Lord GOD	Ps 71:16	1369
shewed thy *s* unto this generation	Ps 71:18	2220
but their *s* is firm	Ps 73:4	193
but God is the *s* of my heart	Ps 73:26	6697
didst divide the sea by thy *s*	Ps 74:13	5797
declared thy *s* among the people	Ps 77:14	5797
the praises of the LORD, and his *s*	Ps 78:4	5807
the chief of their *s* in the	Ps 78:51	202
delivered his *s* into captivity,	Ps 78:61	5797
and Manasseh stir up thy *s*	Ps 80:2	1369
Sing aloud unto God our *s*	Ps 81:1	5797
is the man whose *s* is in thee	Ps 84:5	5797
They go from *s* to *s*	Ps 84:7	2428
give thy *s* unto thy servant, and	Ps 86:16	5797
I am as a man that hath no *s*	Ps 88:4	353
For thou art the glory of their *s*	Ps 89:17	5797
if by reason of *s* they be	Ps 90:10	1369
years, yet is their *s* labour	Ps 90:10	7296
the LORD is clothed with *s*	Ps 93:1	5797
the *s* of the hills is his also	Ps 95:4	8443
s and beauty are in his sanctuary	Ps 96:6	5797
give unto the LORD glory and *s*	Ps 96:7	5797
The king's *s* also loveth judgment	Ps 99:4	5797
He weakened my *s* in the way	Ps 102:23	3581
ye his angels, that excel in *s*	Ps 103:20	3581
Seek the LORD, and his *s*	Ps 105:4	5797
land, the chief of all their *s*	Ps 105:36	202
also is the *s* of mine head	Ps 108:8	4581
send the rod of thy *s* out of Zion	Ps 110:2	5797
The LORD is my *s* and song, and is	Ps 118:14	5797
thou, and the ark of thy *s*	Ps 132:8	5797
me with *s* in my soul	Ps 138:3	5797
the *s* of my salvation, thou hast	Ps 140:7	5797
Blessed be the LORD my *s*, which	Ps 144:1	6697
not in the *s* of the horse	Ps 147:10	1369
I have *s*	Prov 8:14	1369
of the LORD is *s* to the upright	Prov 10:29	4581
increase is by the *s* of the ox	Prov 14:4	3581
The glory of young men is their *s*	Prov 20:29	3581
casteth down the *s* of the	Prov 21:22	5797
a man of knowledge increaseth *s*	Prov 24:5	3581
day of adversity, thy *s* is small	Prov 24:10	3581
Give not thy *s* unto women	Prov 31:3	2428
She girdeth her loins with *s*	Prov 31:17	5797
S and honour are her clothing	Prov 31:25	5797
said I, Wisdom is better than *s*	Eccl 9:16	1369
edge, then must he put to more *s*	Eccl 10:10	2428
princes eat in due season, for *s*	Eccl 10:17	1369
men of *s* to mingle strong drink	Is 5:22	2428
By the *s* of my hand I have done	Is 10:13	3581
for the LORD JEHOVAH is my *s*	Is 12:2	5797
been mindful of the rock of thy *s*	Is 17:10	4581
even the *s* of the sea, saying, I	Is 23:4	4581
there is no more *s*	Is 23:10	4206
for your *s* is laid waste	Is 23:14	4581
thou hast been a *s* to the poor	Is 25:4	4581
a *s* to the needy in his distress,	Is 25:4	4581
the LORD JEHOVAH is everlasting *s*	Is 26:4	6697
Or let him take hold of my *s*	Is 27:5	4581
for *s* to them that turn the	Is 28:6	1369
themselves in the *s* of Pharaoh	Is 30:2	4581
Therefore shall the *s* of Pharaoh	Is 30:3	4581
this, Their *s* is to sit still	Is 30:7	7293
and in confidence shall be your *s*	Is 30:15	1369
of times, and *s* of salvation	Is 33:6	2633
I have counsel and *s* for war	Is 36:5	1369
there is not *s* to bring forth	Is 37:3	3581
tidings, lift up thy voice with *s*	Is 40:9	3581
have no might he increaseth *s*	Is 40:29	6109
upon the LORD shall renew their *s*	Is 40:31	3581
and let the people renew their *s*	Is 41:1	3581

S

of his anger, and the *s* of battle	Is 42:25	5807
worketh it with the *s* of his arms	Is 44:12	3581
he is hungry, and his *s* faileth	Is 44:12	3581
LORD have I righteousness and *s*	Is 45:24	5797
I have spent my *s* for nought	Is 49:4	3581
the LORD, and my God shall be my *s*...	Is 49:5	5797
Awake, awake, put on *s*, O arm of	Is 51:9	5797
put on thy *s*, O Zion	Is 52:1	5797
hand, and by the arm of his *s*	Is 62:8	5797
in the greatness of his *s*	Is 63:1	3581
bring down their *s* to the earth	Is 63:6	5332
where is thy zeal and thy *s*	Is 63:15	1369
O LORD, my *s*, and my fortress, and	Jer 16:19	5797
deliver all the *s* of this city	Jer 20:5	2633
fortify the height of her *s*	Jer 51:53	5797
gone without *s* before the pursuer	Lam 1:6	3581
he hath made my *s* to fall	Lam 1:14	3581
And I said, My *s* and my hope is	Lam 3:18	5331
the excellency of your *s*	Eze 24:21	5797
day when I take from them their *s*	Eze 24:25	4581
my fury upon Sin, the *s* of Egypt	Eze 30:15	4581
the pomp of her *s* shall cease in	Eze 30:18	5797
and the pomp of her *s* shall cease	Eze 33:28	5797
given thee a kingdom, power, and *s* ...	Dan 2:37	8632
be in it of the *s* of the iron	Dan 2:41	5326
and there remained no *s* in me	Dan 10:8	3581
corruption, and I retained no *s*	Dan 10:8	3581
upon me, and I have retained no *s*	Dan 10:16	3581
there remained no *s* in me	Dan 10:17	3581
by his *s* through his riches he	Dan 11:2	2394
shall there be any *s* to withstand	Dan 11:15	3581
with the *s* of his whole kingdom	Dan 11:17	8633
shall pollute the sanctuary of *s*	Dan 11:31	4581
Strangers have devoured his *s*	Hos 7:9	3581
by his *s* he had power with God	Hos 12:3	202
tree and the vine do yield their *s*	Joel 2:22	2428
the *s* of the children of Israel	Joel 3:16	4581
shall bring down thy *s* from thee	Amos 3:11	5797
taken to us horns by our own *s*	Amos 6:13	2392
and feed in the *s* of the LORD	Mic 5:4	5797
Ethiopia and Egypt were her *s*	Nah 3:9	6109
shalt seek *s* because of the enemy	Nah 3:11	4581
The LORD God is my *s*, and he will	Hab 3:19	2428
I will destroy the *s* of the	Hag 2:22	2392
of Jerusalem shall be my *s* in the	Zec 12:5	556
all thy mind, and with all thy *s*	Mk 12:30	2479
all the soul, and with all the *s*	Mk 12:33	2479
He hath shewed *s* with his arm	Lk 1:51	2904
all thy soul, and with all thy *s*	Lk 10:27	2479
feet and ancle bones received *s*	Acts 3:7	4732
But Saul increased the more in *s*...	Acts 9:22	1743
For when we were yet without *s*	Rom 5:6	772
and the *s* of sin is the law	1Cor 15:56	1411
pressed out of measure, above *s*	2Cor 1:8	1411
for my *s* is made perfect in	2Cor 12:9	1411
otherwise it is of no *s* at all	Heb 9:17	2480
received *s* to conceive seed	Heb 11:11	1411
was as the sun shineth in his *s*	Rev 1:16	1411
for thou hast a little *s*, and hast	Rev 3:8	1411
power, and riches, and wisdom, and *s*	Rev 5:12	2479
Now is come salvation, and *s*	Rev 12:10	1411
their power and *s* unto the beast	Rev 17:13	1849

STRENGTHEN

and encourage him, and *s* him	Deut 3:28	553
s me, I pray thee, only this once	Judg 16:28	2388
s thyself, and mark, and see what	1Kin 20:22	2388
to *s* their hands in the work of	Ezr 6:22	2388
Now therefore, O God, *s* my hands	Neh 6:9	2388
But I would *s* you with my mouth,	Job 16:5	553
sanctuary, and *s* thee out of Zion	Ps 20:2	5582
and he shall *s* thine heart	Ps 27:14	553
he shall *s* your heart, all ye	Ps 31:24	553
The LORD will *s* him upon the bed	Ps 41:3	5582
s, O God, that which thou hast	Ps 68:28	5810
mine arm also shall *s* him	Ps 89:21	553
s thou me according unto thy word	Ps 119:28	6965
s him with thy girdle, and I will	Is 22:21	2388
to *s* themselves in the strength	Is 30:2	5810
they could not well *s* their mast	Is 33:23	2388
S ye the weak hands, and confirm	Is 35:3	2388
I will *s* thee	Is 41:10	553
thy cords, and *s* thy stakes	Is 54:2	2388
they *s* also the hands of	Jer 23:14	2388
neither shall any *s* himself in	Eze 7:13	2388
neither did she *s* the hand of the	Eze 16:49	2388
I will *s* the arms of the king of	Eze 30:24	2388
But I will *s* the arms of the king	Eze 30:25	2388
will *s* that which was sick	Eze 34:16	2388
I, stood to confirm and to *s* him	Dan 11:1	4581
the strong shall not *s* his force	Amos 2:14	553

I will *s* the house of Judah, and I	Zec 10:6	1396
I will *s* them in the LORD	Zec 10:12	1396
art converted, *s* thy brethren	Lk 22:32	4741
make you perfect, stablish, *s*	1Pet 5:10	4599
s the things which remain, that	Rev 3:2	4741

STRENGTHENED

Israel *s* himself, and sat upon the	Gen 48:2	2388
the LORD *s* Eglon the king of Moab	Judg 3:12	2388
be *s* to go down unto the host	Judg 7:11	2388
the wood, and *s* his hand in God	1Sa 23:16	2388
Therefore now let your hands be *s*	2Sa 2:7	2388
who *s* themselves with him in his	1Chr 11:10	2388
son of David was *s* in his kingdom	2Chr 1:1	2388
So they *s* the kingdom of Judah,	2Chr 11:17	2388
had *s* himself, he forsook the law	2Chr 12:1	2394
So king Rehoboam *s* himself in	2Chr 12:13	2388
have *s* themselves against	2Chr 13:7	553
and *s* himself against Israel	2Chr 17:1	2388
he *s* himself, and slew all his	2Chr 21:4	2388
seventh year Jehoiada *s* himself	2Chr 23:1	2388
of God in his state, and *s* it	2Chr 24:13	553
And Amaziah *s* himself, and led	2Chr 25:11	2388
for he *s* himself exceedingly	2Chr 26:8	2388
and distressed him, but *s* him not	2Chr 28:20	2388
Also he *s* himself, and built up	2Chr 32:5	2388
s their hands with vessels of	Ezr 1:6	2388
I was *s* as the hand of the LORD	Ezr 7:28	2388
So they *s* their hands for this	Neh 2:18	2388
thou hast *s* the weak hands	Job 4:3	2388
thou hast *s* the feeble knees	Job 4:4	553
s himself in his wickedness	Ps 52:7	5810
For he hath *s* the bars of thy	Ps 147:13	2388
when he *s* the fountains of the	Prov 8:28	5810
s the hands of the wicked, that	Eze 13:22	2388
The diseased have ye not *s*	Eze 34:4	2388
appearance of a man, and he *s* me	Dan 10:18	2388
he had spoken unto me, I was *s*	Dan 10:19	2388
for thou hast *s* me	Dan 10:19	2388
he that *s* her in these times	Dan 11:6	2388
but he shall not be *s* by it	Dan 11:12	5810
s their arms, yet do they imagine	Hos 7:15	2388
he had received meat, he was *s*	Acts 9:19	1765
to be *s* with might by his Spirit	Eph 3:16	2901
S with all might, according to	Col 1:11	1412
the Lord stood with me, and *s* me	2Ti 4:17	1743

STRENGTHENEDST

s me with strength in my soul	Ps 138:3	7292

STRENGTHENETH

s himself against the Almighty	Job 15:25	1396
and bread which *s* man's heart	Ps 104:15	5582
with strength, and *s* her arms	Prov 31:17	553
Wisdom *s* the wise more than ten	Eccl 7:19	5810
which he *s* for himself among the	Is 44:14	553
That *s* the spoiled against the	Amos 5:9	1082
things through Christ which *s* me	Phil 4:13	1743

STRENGTHENING

angel unto him from heaven, *s* him	Lk 22:43	1765
in order, *s* all the disciples	Acts 18:23	1991

STRETCH

I will *s* out my hand, and smite	Ex 3:20	7971
when I *s* forth mine hand upon	Ex 7:5	5186
s out thine hand upon the waters	Ex 7:19	5186
S forth thine hand with thy rod	Ex 8:5	5186
S out thy rod, and smite the dust	Ex 8:16	5186
For now I will *s* out my hand	Ex 9:15	7971
S forth thine hand toward heaven,	Ex 9:22	5186
S out thine hand over the land of	Ex 10:12	5186
S out thine hand toward heaven,	Ex 10:21	5186
s out thine hand over the sea, and	Ex 14:16	5186
S out thine hand over the sea,	Ex 14:26	5186
the cherubim shall *s* forth their	Ex 25:20	6566
S out the spear that is in thy	Josh 8:18	5186
to *s* forth mine hand against him,	1Sa 24:6	7971
for who can *s* forth his hand	1Sa 26:9	7971
s forth mine hand against the	1Sa 26:11	7971
but I would not *s* forth mine hand	1Sa 26:23	7971
How wast thou not afraid to *s*	2Sa 1:14	7971
I will *s* over Jerusalem the line	2Kin 21:13	5186
s out thine hands toward him	Job 11:13	6566
Howbeit he will not *s* out his	Job 30:24	7971
s her wings toward the south	Job 39:26	6566
Ethiopia shall soon *s* out her	Ps 68:31	7323
thou shalt *s* forth thine hand	Ps 138:7	7971
I *s* forth my hands unto thee	Ps 143:6	6566
that a man can *s* himself on it	Is 28:20	8311
the LORD shall *s* out his hand	Is 31:3	5186
he shall *s* out upon it the line	Is 34:11	5186
let them *s* forth the curtains of	Is 54:2	5186

for I will *s* out my hand upon the	Jer 6:12	5186
there is none to *s* forth my tent	Jer 10:20	5186
therefore will I *s* out my hand	Jer 15:6	5186
I will *s* out mine hand upon thee,	Jer 51:25	5186
So will I *s* out my hand upon them	Eze 6:14	5186
I will *s* out my hand upon him, and	Eze 14:9	5186
then will I *s* out mine hand upon	Eze 14:13	5186
therefore I will *s* out mine hand	Eze 25:7	5186
I will also *s* out mine hand upon	Eze 25:13	5186
I will *s* out mine hand upon the	Eze 25:16	5186
he shall *s* it out upon the land	Eze 30:25	5186
I will *s* out mine hand against	Eze 35:3	5186
He shall *s* forth his hand against	Dan 11:42	7971
s themselves upon their couches	Amos 6:4	5628
I will also *s* out mine hand upon	Zeph 1:4	5186
he will *s* out his hand against	Zeph 2:13	5186
he to the man, S forth thine hand	Mt 12:13	*1614*
unto the man, S forth thine hand	Mk 3:5	*1614*
unto the man, S forth thy hand	Lk 6:10	*1614*
thou shalt s forth thy hands, and	Jn 21:18	*1614*
For we *s* not ourselves beyond our	2Cor 10:14	5239

STRETCHED

Abraham *s* forth his hand, and took	Gen 22:10	7971
Israel *s* his right hand, and	Gen 48:14	7971
will redeem you with a *s* out arm	Ex 6:6	5186
Aaron *s* out his hand over the	Ex 8:6	5186
for Aaron *s* out his hand with his	Ex 8:17	5186
Moses *s* forth his rod toward	Ex 9:23	5186
Moses *s* forth his rod over the	Ex 10:13	5186
Moses *s* forth his hand toward	Ex 10:22	5186
Moses *s* out his hand over the sea	Ex 14:21	5186
Moses *s* forth his hand over the	Ex 14:27	5186
by a *s* out arm, and by great	Deut 4:34	5186
a mighty hand and by a *s* out arm	Deut 5:15	5186
the *s* out arm, whereby the LORD	Deut 7:19	5186
mighty power and by thy *s* out arm	Deut 9:29	5186
mighty hand, and his *s* out arm,	Deut 11:2	5186
Joshua *s* out the spear that he	Josh 8:18	5186
as soon as he had *s* out his hand	Josh 8:19	5186
wherewith he had *s* out the spear,	Josh 8:26	5186
when the angel *s* out his hand	2Sa 24:16	7971
they *s* forth the wings of the	1Kin 6:27	6566
strong hand, and of thy *s* out arm	1Kin 8:42	5186
he *s* himself upon the child three	1Kin 17:21	4058
he *s* himself upon the child	2Kin 4:34	1457
and went up, and *s* himself upon him	2Kin 4:35	1457
a *s* out arm, him shall ye fear,	2Kin 17:36	5186
in his hand *s* out over Jerusalem	1Chr 21:16	5186
thy mighty hand, and thy *s* out arm	2Chr 6:32	5186
or who hath *s* the line upon it	Job 38:5	5186
or *s* out our hands to a strange	Ps 44:20	6566
I have *s* out my hands unto thee	Ps 88:9	7849
To him that *s* out the earth above	Ps 136:6	7554
strong hand, and with a *s* out arm	Ps 136:12	5186
I have *s* out my hand, and no man	Prov 1:24	5186
walk with *s* forth necks and wanton	Is 3:16	5186
he hath *s* forth his hand against	Is 5:25	5186
away, but his hand is *s* out still	Is 5:25	5186
away, but his hand is *s* out still	Is 9:12	5186
away, but his hand is *s* out still	Is 9:17	5186
away, but his hand is *s* out still	Is 9:21	5186
away, but his hand is *s* out still	Is 10:4	5186
is *s* out upon all the nations	Is 14:26	5186
and his hand is *s* out, and who	Is 14:27	5186
her branches are *s* out, they are	Is 16:8	5203
He *s* out his hand over the sea,	Is 23:11	5186
the heavens, and *s* them out	Is 42:5	5186
have *s* out the heavens, and all	Is 45:12	5186
that hath *s* forth the heavens, and	Is 51:13	5186
shadows of the evening are *s* out	Jer 6:4	5186
hath *s* out the heavens by his	Jer 10:12	5186
s out arm, and there is nothing	Jer 32:17	5186
with a *s* out arm, and with great	Jer 32:21	5186
hath *s* out the heaven by his	Jer 51:15	5186
he hath *s* out a line, he hath not	Lam 2:8	5186
and their wings were *s* upward	Eze 1:11	6504
s forth over their heads above	Eze 1:22	5186
one cherub *s* forth his hand from	Eze 10:7	7971
therefore I have *s* out my hand	Eze 16:27	5186
with a *s* out arm, and with fury	Eze 20:33	5186
with a *s* out arm, and with fury	Eze 20:34	5186
he *s* out his hand with scorners	Hos 7:5	4900
the banquet of them that *s*	Amos 6:7	5628
a line shall be *s* forth upon	Zec 1:16	5186
And he *s* it forth	Mt 12:13	*1614*
he *s* forth his hand toward his	Mt 12:49	*1614*
Jesus *s* forth his hand, and caught	Mt 14:31	*1614*
were with Jesus *s* out his hand	Mt 26:51	*1614*
And he *s* it out	Mk 3:5	*1614*
ye *s* forth no hands against me	Lk 22:53	*1614*

s forth his hands to vex certain	Acts 12:1	*1911*
Then Paul *s* forth the hand, and	Acts 26:1	*1614*
All day long I have *s* forth my	Rom 10:21	*1600*

STRETCHEDST

Thou *s* out thy right hand, the	Ex 15:12	5186

STRETCHEST

who *s* out the heavens like a	Ps 104:2	5186

STRETCHETH

For he *s* out his hand against God	Job 15:25	5186
He *s* out the north over the empty	Job 26:7	5186
She *s* out her hand to the poor	Prov 31:20	6566
that *s* out the heavens as a	Is 40:22	5186
The carpenter *s* out his rule	Is 44:13	5186
that *s* forth the heavens alone	Is 44:24	5186
which *s* forth the heavens, and	Zec 12:1	5186

STRETCHING

the *s* out of his wings shall fill	Is 8:8	4298
By *s* forth thine hand to heal	Acts 4:30	*1614*

STRICKEN

Sarah were old and well *s* in age	Gen 18:11	935
Abraham was old, and well *s* in age	Gen 24:1	935
Now Joshua was old and *s* in years	Josh 13:1	935
s in years, and there remaineth	Josh 13:1	935
that Joshua waxed old and *s* in age	Josh 23:1	935
unto them, I am old and *s* in age	Josh 23:2	935
pierced and *s* through his temples	Judg 5:26	2498
king David was old and *s* in years	1Kin 1:1	935
if thou hast *s* thy hand with a	Prov 6:1	8628
They have *s* me, shalt thou say,	Prov 23:35	5221
Why should ye be *s* any more	Is 1:5	5221
surely they are *s*	Is 16:7	5218
yet we did esteem him *s*, smitten	Is 53:4	5060
of my people was he *s*	Is 53:8	5061
thou hast *s* them, but they have	Jer 5:3	5221
s through for want of the fruits	Lam 4:9	1856
both were now well *s* in years	Lk 1:7	*4260*
man, and my wife well *s* in years	Lk 1:18	*4260*

STRIFE

there was a *s* between the herdmen	Gen 13:7	7379
said unto Lot, Let there be no *s*	Gen 13:8	4808
in the *s* of the congregation, to	Num 27:14	4808
and your burden, and your *s*	Deut 1:12	7379
my people were at great *s* with	Judg 12:2	7379
And all the people were at *s*	2Sa 19:9	1777
a pavilion from the *s* of tongues	Ps 31:20	7379
seen violence and *s* in the city	Ps 55:9	7379
Thou makest us a *s* unto our	Ps 80:6	4066
him also at the waters of *s*	Ps 106:32	4808
A wrathful man stirreth up *s*	Prov 15:18	4066
that is slow to anger appeaseth *s*	Prov 15:18	7379
A froward man soweth *s*	Prov 16:28	4066
house full of sacrifices with *s*	Prov 17:1	7379
The beginning of *s* is as when one	Prov 17:14	4066
transgression that loveth *s*	Prov 17:19	4683
honour for a man to cease from *s*	Prov 20:3	7379
yea, *s* and reproach shall cease	Prov 22:10	1779
meddleth with *s* belonging not to	Prov 26:17	7379
is no talebearer, the *s* ceaseth	Prov 26:20	4066
is a contentious man to kindle *s*	Prov 26:21	7379
is of a proud heart stirreth up *s*	Prov 28:25	4066
An angry man stirreth up *s*	Prov 29:22	4066
forcing of wrath bringeth forth *s*	Prov 30:33	7379
Behold, ye fast for *s* and debate,	Is 58:4	7379
thou hast borne me a man of *s*	Jer 15:10	7379
even to the waters of *s* in Kadesh	Eze 47:19	4808
unto the waters of *s* in Kadesh	Eze 48:28	4808
and there are that raise up *s*	Hab 1:3	7379
And there was also a *s* among them	Lk 22:24	*5379*
and wantonness, not in *s* and	Rom 13:13	*2054*
there is among you envying, and *s*	1Cor 3:3	*2054*
variance, emulations, wrath, *s*	Gal 5:20	*2052*
preach Christ even of envy and *s*	Phil 1:15	*2054*
be done through *s* or vainglory	Phil 2:3	*2052*
of words, whereof cometh envy, *s*	1Ti 6:4	*2054*
is to them an end of all *s*	Heb 6:16	*485*
s in your hearts, glory not, and	Jas 3:14	*2052*
s is, there is confusion and every	Jas 3:16	*2052*

STRIFES

Hatred stirreth up *s*	Prov 10:12	4090
be debates, envyings, wraths, *s*	2Cor 12:20	*2052*
s of words, whereof cometh envy,	1Ti 6:4	*3055*
knowing that they do gender *s*	2Ti 2:23	*3163*

STRIKE

s it on the two side posts and on	Ex 12:7	5414
s the lintel and the two side	Ex 12:22	5060
shall *s* off the heifer's neck	Deut 21:4	
s his hand over the place, and	2Kin 5:11	5130

S

is he that will s hands with me .... Job 17:3   8628
bow of steel shall s him through .... Job 20:24   2498
LORD at thy right hand shall s .... Ps 110:5   4272
Till a dart s through his liver .... Prov 7:23   6398
nor to s princes for equity .... Prov 17:26   5221
not thou one of them that s hands .... Prov 22:26   8628
Thou didst s through with his .... Hab 3:14   5344
the servants did s him with the.............. Mk 14:65   *906*

STRIKER
Not given to wine, no s, not 1Ti 3:3   *4131*
angry, not given to wine, no s .... Titus 1:7   *4131*

STRIKETH
He s them as wicked men in the............ Job 34:26   5606
man void of understanding s hands ...... Prov 17:18   8628
of a scorpion, when he s a man .... Rev 9:5   *3817*

STRING
make ready their arrow upon the s....... Ps 11:2   3499
the s of his tongue was loosed, ... Mk 7:35   *1199*

STRINGED
praise him with s instruments .... Ps 150:4   4482
we will sing my songs to the s .... Is 38:20   5058
chief singer on my s instruments .... Hab 3:19   5058

STRINGS
thy s against the face of them................ Ps 21:12   4340
and an instrument of ten s .... Ps 33:2
Upon an instrument of ten s .... Ps 92:3
an instrument of ten s will I .... Ps 144:9

STRIP
s Aaron of his garments, and put .... Num 20:26   6584
Philistines came to s the slain 1Sa 31:8   6584
Philistines came to s the slain 1Chr 10:8   6584
s you, and make you bare, and gird .... Is 32:11   6584
they shall s thee also of thy................... Eze 16:39   6584
They shall also s thee out of thy .... Eze 23:26   6584
Lest I s her naked, and set her as .... Hos 2:3   6584

STRIPE
wound for wound, s for s .... Ex 21:25   2250

STRIPES
Forty s he may give him, and not .... Deut 25:3   5221
beat him above these with many s........ Deut 25:3   4347
with the s of the children of men 2Sa 7:14   5061
the rod, and their iniquity with s .... Ps 89:32   5061
man than an hundred s into a fool .... Prov 17:10   5221
and s for the back of fools .... Prov 19:29   4112
so do s the inward parts of the .... Prov 20:30   4347
and with his s we are healed .... Is 53:5   2250
will, shall be beaten with many s .... Lk 12:47
and did commit things worthy of s....... Lk 12:48   *4127*
shall be beaten with few s .... Lk 12:48   *4127*
they had laid many s upon them .... Acts 16:23   *4127*
of the night, and washed their s .... Acts 16:33   *4127*
In s, in imprisonments, in 2Cor 6:5   *4127*
in s above measure, in prisons 2Cor 11:23   *4127*
times received forty s save one............. 2Cor 11:24   *4127*
by whose s ye were healed 1Pet 2:24   *3468*

STRIPLING
Enquire thou whose son the s is 1Sa 17:56   5958

STRIPPED
And the children of Israel s.................... Ex 33:6   5337
Moses s Aaron of his garments, and ..... Num 20:28   6584
Jonathan s himself of the robe 1Sa 18:4   6584
s off his armour, and sent into................ 1Sa 31:9   6584
And when they had s him, they took 1Chr 10:9   6584
which they s off for themselves, ... 2Chr 20:25   5337
He hath s me of my glory, and .... Job 19:9   6584
s the naked of their clothing,.................. Job 22:6   6584
I will wail and howl, I will go s .... Mic 1:8   7758
And they s him, and put on him a .... Mt 27:28   *1562*
which s him of his raiment, and .... Lk 10:30   *1562*

STRIPT
that they s Joseph out of his................... Gen 37:23   6584
he s off his clothes also, and 1Sa 19:24

STRIVE
shall not always s with man................... Gen 6:3   1777
Gerar did s with Isaac's herdmen .... Gen 26:20   7378
if men s together, and one smite .... Ex 21:18   7378
If men s, and hurt a woman with .... Ex 21:22   5327
When men s together one with .... Deut 25:11   5327
with whom thou didst s at the................. Deut 33:8   7378
did he ever s against Israel, or .... Judg 11:25   7378
Why dost thou s against him .... Job 33:13   7378
O LORD, with them that s with me .... Ps 35:1   3401
S not with a man without cause, ... Prov 3:30   7378
Go not forth hastily to s......................... Prov 25:8   7378
they that s with thee shall .... Is 41:11   7379

Let the potsherd s with the .... Is 45:9
Yet let no man s, nor reprove .... Hos 4:4   7378
as they that s with the priest .... Hos 4:4   7378
He shall not s, nor cry............................ Mt 12:19   *2051*
S to enter in at the strait gate .... Lk 13:24   *75*
that ye s together with me in .... Rom 15:30   *4865*
And if a man also s for masteries........... 2Ti 2:5   *118*
not crowned, except he s lawfully 2Ti 2:5   *118*
s not about words to no profit 2Ti 2:14   *3054*
servant of the Lord must not s 2Ti 2:24   *3164*

STRIVED
so have I s to preach the gospel, ... Rom 15:20   *5389*

STRIVEN
thou hast s against the LORD .... Jer 50:24   1624

STRIVETH
unto him that s with his Maker .... Is 45:9   7378
every man that s for the mastery 1Cor 9:25   *75*

STRIVING
with one mind s together for the............ Phil 1:27   *4866*
s according to his working, which .... Col 1:29   *75*
unto blood, s against sin .... Heb 12:4   *464*

STRIVINGS
me from the s of my people 2Sa 22:44   7379
me from the s of the people .... Ps 18:43   7379
contentions, and s about the law .... Titus 3:9   *3163*

STROKE
and plea, and between s and s .... Deut 17:8   5061
his hand fetcheth a s with the................ Deut 19:5
controversy and every s be tried............ Deut 21:5   5061
enemies with the s of the sword .... Est 9:5   4347
my s is heavier than my groaning .... Job 23:2   3027
lest he take thee away with his s .... Job 36:18   5607
Remove thy s away from me .... Ps 39:10   5061
in wrath with a continual s .... Is 14:6   4347
healeth the s of their wound.................. Is 30:26   4273
the desire of thine eyes with a s .... Eze 24:16   4046

STROKES
and his mouth calleth for s.................... Prov 18:6   4112

STRONG
Issachar is a s ass couching down .... Gen 49:14   1634
s by the hands of the mighty God.......... Gen 49:24   6339
for with a s hand shall he let................. Ex 6:1   2389
with a s hand shall he drive them .... Ex 6:1   2389
LORD turned a mighty s west wind .... Ex 10:19   2389
for with a s hand hath the LORD .... Ex 13:9   2389
by a s east wind all that night .... Ex 14:21   5794
Do not drink wine nor s drink .... Lev 10:9
s drink, and shall drink no .... Num 6:3
of wine, or vinegar of s drink .... Num 6:3
whether they be s or weak .... Num 13:18   2389
whether in tents, or in s holds................ Num 13:19   4013
be s that dwell in the land...................... Num 13:28   5794
much people, and with a s hand .... Num 20:20   2389
of the children of Ammon was s.............. Num 21:24   5794
S is thy dwellingplace, and thou .... Num 24:21   386
s wine to be poured unto the LORD .... Num 28:7
was not one city too s for us .... Deut 2:36   7682
you this day, that ye may be s................ Deut 11:8   2388
or for wine, or for s drink .... Deut 14:26
have ye drunk wine or s drink .... Deut 29:6
Be s and of a good courage, fear .... Deut 31:6   2388
in the sight of all Israel, Be s.................. Deut 31:7   2388
of Nun a charge, and said, Be s.............. Deut 31:23   2388
Be s and of a good courage .... Josh 1:6   2388
Only be thou s and very courageous ...... Josh 1:7   2388
Be s and of a good courage .... Josh 1:9   2388
only be s and of a good courage .... Josh 1:18   2388
Fear not, nor be dismayed, be s .... Josh 10:25   2388
As yet I am as s this day as I .... Josh 14:11   2389
children of Israel were waxen s.............. Josh 17:13   2388
chariots, and though they be s............... Josh 17:18   2388
to Ramah, and to the s city Tyre............ Josh 19:29   4013
before you great nations and s.............. Josh 23:9   '6099
came to pass, when Israel was s .... Judg 1:28   2388
mountains, and caves, and s holds .... Judg 6:2   4679
But there was a s tower within .... Judg 9:51   5797
and drink not wine nor s drink .... Judg 13:4
and now drink no wine nor s drink .... Judg 13:7
let her drink wine or s drink .... Judg 13:14
out of the s came forth sweetness .... Judg 14:14   5794
saw that they were too s for him .... Judg 18:26   2389
drunken neither wine nor s drink 1Sa 1:15
Be s, and quit yourselves like men 1Sa 4:9   2388
and when Saul saw any s man 1Sa 14:52   1368
in the wilderness in s holds 1Sa 23:14   4679
with us in s holds in the wood 1Sa 23:19   4679
dwelt in s holds at En-gedi..................... 1Sa 23:29   4679

himself s for the house of Saul..............2Sa 3:6	2388
David took the s hold of Zion..................2Sa 5:7	4686
If the Syrians be too s for me..................2Sa 10:11	2388
of Ammon be too s for thee....................2Sa 10:11	2388
battle more s against the city.................2Sa 11:25	2388
And the conspiracy was s......................2Sa 15:12	533
of all that are with thee be s..................2Sa 16:21	2388
He delivered me from my s enemy.........2Sa 22:18	5794
for they were too s for me.....................2Sa 22:18	553
came to the s hold of Tyre, and to..........2Sa 24:7	4013
be thou s therefore, and shew................1Kin 2:2	2388
thy great name, and of thy s hand.........1Kin 8:42	2389
s wind rent the mountains, and..............1Kin 19:11	2389
be with thy servants fifty s men.............2Kin 2:16	2428
their s holds wilt thou set on.................2Kin 8:12	4013
a thousand, all that were s....................2Kin 24:16	1368
If the Syrians be too s for me................1Chr 19:12	2388
of Ammon be too s for thee...................1Chr 19:12	2388
be s, and of good courage.....................1Chr 22:13	2388
whose brethren were s men...................1Chr 26:7	2428
sons and brethren, s men, eighteen.......1Chr 26:9	2428
be s, and do it....................................1Chr 28:10	2388
said to Solomon his son, Be s................1Chr 28:20	2388
And he fortified the s holds...................2Chr 11:11	4694
spears, and made them exceeding s......2Chr 11:12	2388
Rehoboam the son of Solomon s...........2Chr 11:17	559
Be ye s therefore, and let not...............2Chr 15:7	2388
to shew himself s in the behalf..............2Chr 16:9	2388
go, do it, be s for the battle..................2Chr 25:8	2388
helped, till he was s............................2Chr 26:15	2388
But when he was s, his heart was..........2Chr 26:16	2394
Be s and courageous, be not afraid........2Chr 32:7	2388
that ye may be s, and eat the good.......Ezr 9:12	2388
thy great power, and by thy s hand.......Neh 1:10	2389
And they took s cities, and a fat...........Neh 9:25	1219
of thy mouth be like a s wind................Job 8:2	3524
I speak of strength, lo, he is s...............Job 9:19	533
with thy s hand thou opposest..............Job 30:21	6108
of his bones with s pain.......................Job 33:19	386
spread out the sky, which is s...............Job 37:18	2389
crag of the rock, and the s place...........Job 39:28	4686
bones are as s pieces of brass...............Job 40:18	650
the poor may fall by his s ones.............Ps 10:10	6099
He delivered me from my s enemy.........Ps 18:17	5794
for they were too s for me....................Ps 18:17	553
rejoiceth as a s man to run a.................Ps 19:5	1368
s bulls of Bashan have beset me............Ps 22:12	47
The LORD s and mighty, the LORD..........Ps 24:8	5808
hast made my mountain to stand s........Ps 30:7	5797
be thou my s rock, for an house............Ps 31:2	4581
marvellous kindness in a s city..............Ps 31:21	4692
from him that is too s for me.................Ps 35:10	2389
enemies are lively, and they are s..........Ps 38:19	6105
Who will bring me into the s city...........Ps 60:9	4692
me, and a s tower from the enemy.........Ps 61:3	5797
Be thou my s habitation,......................Ps 71:3	6697
but thou art my s refuge......................Ps 71:7	5797
that thou madest s for thyself...............Ps 80:15	553
whom thou madest s for thyself.............Ps 80:17	553
who is a s LORD like unto thee...............Ps 89:8	2626
thine enemies with thy s arm.................Ps 89:10	5797
s is thy hand, and high is thy................Ps 89:13	5810
hast brought his s holds to ruin.............Ps 89:40	4013
Who will bring me into the s city...........Ps 108:10	4013
With a s hand, and with a.....................Ps 136:12	2389
That our oxen may be s to labour..........Ps 144:14	
many s men have been slain by her.......Prov 7:26	6099
rich man's wealth is his s city...............Prov 10:15	5797
and s men retain riches.......................Prov 11:16	6184
fear of the LORD is s confidence............Prov 14:26	5797
The name of the LORD is a s tower.........Prov 18:10	5797
rich man's wealth is his s city...............Prov 18:11	5797
is harder to be won than a s city............Prov 18:19	5797
is a mocker, s drink is raging.................Prov 20:1	
and a reward in the bosom s wrath........Prov 21:14	5794
A wise man is s...................................Prov 24:5	5797
The ants are a people not s...................Prov 30:25	5794
nor for princes s drink.........................Prov 31:4	
Give s drink unto him that is..................Prov 31:6	
swift, nor the battle to the s.................Eccl 9:11	1368
the s men shall bow themselves,............Eccl 12:3	2428
for love is s as death...........................Song 8:6	5794
the s shall be as tow, and the...............Is 1:31	2634
that they may follow s drink..................Is 5:11	
men of strength to mingle s drink..........Is 5:22	
them the waters of the river, s..............Is 8:7	6099
spake thus to me with a s hand.............Is 8:11	2393
In that day shall his s cities be.............Is 17:9	4581
to destroy the s holds thereof...............Is 23:11	4581
s drink shall be bitter to them...............Is 24:9	
shall the s people glorify thee...............Is 25:3	5794

We have a s city.................................Is 26:1	5797
s sword shall punish leviathan...............Is 27:1	2389
s one, which as a tempest of hail...........Is 28:2	533
through s drink are out of the...............Is 28:7	
have erred through s drink....................Is 28:7	
out of the way through s drink...............Is 28:7	
lest your bands be made s....................Is 28:22	2388
stagger, but not with s drink.................Is 29:9	
horsemen, because they are very s........Is 31:1	6105
pass over to his s hold for fear..............Is 31:9	5553
that are of a fearful heart, Be s.............Is 35:4	2388
Lord GOD will come with s hand............Is 40:10	2389
might, for that he is s in power..............Is 40:26	533
bring forth your s reasons.....................Is 41:21	6110
shall divide the spoil with the s............Is 53:12	6099
will fill ourselves with s drink...............Is 56:12	
and a small one a s nation....................Is 60:22	6099
of the neighing of his s ones.................Jer 8:16	47
outstretched hand and with a s arm......Jer 21:5	2389
and with wonders, and with a s hand....Jer 32:21	2389
of the hoofs of his s horses...................Jer 47:3	47
are mighty and s men for the war..........Jer 48:14	2428
How is the s staff broken, and the.........Jer 48:17	5797
and he shall destroy thy s holds............Jer 48:18	4013
the s holds are surprised, and the..........Jer 48:41	4679
against the habitation of the s..............Jer 49:19	386
Their Redeemer is s.............................Jer 50:34	2389
unto the habitation of the s..................Jer 50:44	386
of Babylon, make the watch s................Jer 51:12	2388
thrown down in his wrath the s.............Lam 2:2	4013
he hath destroyed his s holds...............Lam 2:5	4013
thy face s against their faces.................Eze 3:8	2389
thy forehead s against their...................Eze 3:8	2389
hand of the LORD was s upon me............Eze 3:14	2388
make the pomp of the s to cease..........Eze 7:24	5794
she had s rods for the sceptres.............Eze 19:11	5797
her s rods were broken and...................Eze 19:12	5797
so that she hath no s rod to be a...........Eze 19:14	5797
endure, or can thine hands be s............Eze 22:14	2388
thy s garrisons shall go down to............Eze 26:11	5797
city, which wast s in the sea.................Eze 26:17	2389
to make it s to hold the sword..............Eze 30:21	2388
and will break his arms, the s...............Eze 30:22	2389
The s among the mighty shall...............Eze 32:21	410
I will destroy the fat and the s..............Eze 34:16	2389
fourth kingdom shall be s as iron..........Dan 2:40	8624
so the kingdom shall be partly s............Dan 2:42	8624
The tree grew, and was s, and the........Dan 4:11	8631
thou sawest, which grew, and was s......Dan 4:20	8631
king, that art grown and become s.........Dan 4:22	8631
and terrible, and s exceedingly..............Dan 7:7	8624
and when he was s, the great horn........Dan 8:8	6105
unto thee, be s, yea, be s.....................Dan 10:19	2388
the king of the south shall be s.............Dan 11:5	2388
and he shall be s above him..................Dan 11:5	2388
shall become s with a small..................Dan 11:23	6105
his devices against the s holds..............Dan 11:24	4013
that do know their God shall be s..........Dan 11:32	2388
most s holds with a strange god............Dan 11:39	4581
nation is come up upon my land, s........Joel 1:6	6099
a great people and a s..........................Joel 2:2	6099
as a s people set in battle array............Joel 2:5	6099
for he is s that executeth his................Joel 2:11	6099
let the weak say, I am s.......................Joel 3:10	1368
cedars, and he was s as the oaks..........Amos 2:9	2364
the s shall not strengthen his................Amos 2:14	2389
the spoiled against the s.......................Amos 5:9	5794
unto the wine and of s drink.................Mic 2:11	7941
rebuke s nations afar off.......................Mic 4:3	6099
that was cast far off a s nation.............Mic 4:7	6099
the s hold of the daughter of................Mic 4:8	6076
and throw down all thy s holds..............Mic 5:11	4013
ye s foundations of the earth................Mic 6:2	386
a s hold in the day of trouble................Nah 1:7	4581
watch the way, make thy loins s............Nah 2:1	2388
All thy s holds shall be like fig...............Nah 3:12	4013
the siege, fortify thy s holds.................Nah 3:14	4013
the morter, make s the brickkiln............Nah 3:14	2388
they shall deride thy s holds..................Hab 1:10	4013
Yet now be s, O Zerubbabel, saith.........Hag 2:4	2388
and be s, O Joshua, son of....................Hag 2:4	2388
and be s, all ye people of the................Hag 2:4	2388
Let your hands be s, ye that hear..........Zec 8:9	2388
fear not, but let your hands be s...........Zec 8:13	2388
s nations shall come to seek the............Zec 8:22	6099
Tyrus did build herself a s hold.............Zec 9:3	4692
Turn you to the s hold, ye.....................Zec 9:12	1225
one enter into a s man's house.........Mt 12:29	*2478*
except he first bind the s man...........Mt 12:29	*2478*
can enter into a s man's house..........Mk 3:27	*2478*
he will first bind the s man...............Mk 3:27	*2478*

drink neither wine nor *s* drink	Lk 1:15	4608
waxed *s* in spirit, and was in the	Lk 1:80	2901
waxed *s* in spirit, filled with	Lk 2:40	2901
When a *s* man armed keepeth his	Lk 11:21	2478
in his name hath made this man *s*	Acts 3:16	4732
but was *s* in faith, giving glory	Rom 4:20	1743
We then that are *s* ought to bear	Rom 15:1	1415
we are weak, but ye are *s*	1Cor 4:10	2478
faith, quit you like men, be *s*	1Cor 16:13	2901
to the pulling down of *s* holds	2Cor 10:4	3794
for when I am weak, then am I *s*	2Cor 12:10	1415
when we are weak, and ye are *s*	2Cor 13:9	1415
be *s* in the Lord, and in the power	Eph 6:10	1743
God shall send them *s* delusion	2Th 2:11	1753
be *s* in the grace that is in	2Ti 2:1	1743
and supplications with *s* crying	Heb 5:7	2478
need of milk, and not of *s* meat	Heb 5:12	4731
But *s* meat belongeth to them that	Heb 5:14	4731
we might have a *s* consolation	Heb 6:18	2478
out of weakness were made *s*	Heb 11:34	1743
you, young men, because ye are *s*	1Jn 2:14	2478
I saw a *s* angel proclaiming with	Rev 5:2	2478
he cried mightily with a *s* voice	Rev 18:2	3173
for *s* is the Lord God who judgeth	Rev 18:8	2478

STRONGER

shall be *s* than the other people	Gen 25:23	553
whensoever the *s* cattle did	Gen 30:41	7194
were Laban's, and the *s* Jacob's	Gen 30:42	7194
for they are *s* than we	Num 13:31	2389
And what is *s* than a lion	Judg 14:18	5794
eagles, they were *s* than lions	2Sa 1:23	1396
but David waxed *s* and *s*, and	2Sa 3:1	2390
being *s* than she, forced her, and	2Sa 13:14	2388
therefore they were *s* than we	1Kin 20:23	2388
and surely we shall be *s* than they	1Kin 20:23	2388
and surely we shall be *s* than they	1Kin 20:25	2388
hands shall be *s* and *s*	Job 17:9	555
made them *s* than their enemies	Ps 105:24	6105
for they are *s* than I	Ps 142:6	553
thou art *s* than I, and hast	Jer 20:7	2388
hand of him that was *s* than he	Jer 31:11	2388
But when a *s* than he shall come	Lk 11:22	2478
the weakness of God is *s* than men	1Cor 1:25	2478
are we *s* than he	1Cor 10:22	2478

STRONGEST

A lion which is *s* among beasts	Prov 30:30	1368

STRONGLY

the foundations thereof be *s* laid	Ezr 6:3	

STROVE

because they *s* with him	Gen 26:20	6229
another well, and *s* for that also	Gen 26:21	7378
and for that they *s* not	Gen 26:22	7378
two men of the Hebrews *s* together	Ex 2:13	5327
a man of Israel *s* together in the	Lev 24:10	5327
of Israel *s* with the Lord	Num 20:13	7378
who *s* against Moses and against	Num 26:9	5327
when they *s* against the Lord	Num 26:9	5327
they two *s* together in the field	2Sa 14:6	5327
when he *s* with Aram-naharaim and	Ps 60:*t*	5327
the heaven *s* upon the great sea	Dan 7:2	1519
Jews therefore *s* among themselves	Jn 6:52	3164
himself unto them as they *s*	Acts 7:26	3164
the Pharisees' part arose, and *s*	Acts 23:9	1264

STROWED

s it upon the graves of them that	2Chr 34:4	2236

STRUCK

he *s* it into the pan, or kettle	1Sa 2:14	5221
the Lord *s* the child that Uriah's	2Sa 12:15	5062
to the ground, and *s* him not again	2Sa 20:10	8138
and the Lord *s* him, and he died	2Chr 13:20	5062
s a servant of the high priest's	Mt 26:51	3960
they *s* him on the face, and asked	Lk 22:64	5180
of the officers which stood by *s*	Jn 18:22	1325,4475

STRUGGLED

the children *s* together within	Gen 25:22	7533

STUBBLE

to gather *s* instead of straw	Ex 5:12	7179
wrath, which consumed them as *s*	Ex 15:7	7179
and wilt thou pursue the dry *s*	Job 13:25	7179
They are as *s* before the wind, and	Job 21:18	8401
are turned with him into *s*	Job 41:28	7179
Darts are counted as *s*	Job 41:29	7179
as the *s* before the wind	Ps 83:13	7179
as the fire devoureth the *s*	Is 5:24	7179
chaff, ye shall bring forth *s*	Is 33:11	7179
shall take them away as *s*	Is 40:24	7179
sword, and as driven *s* to his bow	Is 41:2	7179

Behold, they shall be as *s*	Is 47:14	7179
will I scatter them as the *s* that	Jer 13:24	7179
of fire that devoureth the *s*	Joel 2:5	7179
flame, and the house of Esau for *s*	Obad 18	7179
shall be devoured as *s* fully dry	Nah 1:10	7179
all that do wickedly, shall be *s*	Mal 4:1	7179
precious stones, wood, hay, *s*	1Cor 3:12	2562

STUBBORN

If a man have a *s* and rebellious	Deut 21:18	5637
of his city, This our son is *s*	Deut 21:20	5637
own doings, nor from their *s* way	Judg 2:19	7186
not be as their fathers, a *s*	Ps 78:8	5637
(She is loud and *s*	Prov 7:11	5637

STUBBORNNESS

not unto the *s* of this people	Deut 9:27	7190
s is as iniquity and idolatry	1Sa 15:23	6484

STUCK

his spear *s* in the ground at his	1Sa 26:7	4600
I have *s* unto thy testimonies	Ps 119:31	1692
and the forepart *s* fast, and	Acts 27:41	2043

STUDIETH

of the righteous *s* to answer	Prov 15:28	1897
For their heart *s* destruction	Prov 24:2	1897

STUDS

borders of gold with *s* of silver	Song 1:11	5351

STUDY

much *s* is a weariness of the	Eccl 12:12	3854
that ye *s* to be quiet, and to do	1Th 4:11	5389
S to shew thyself approved unto	2Ti 2:15	4704

STUFF

thou hast searched all my *s*	Gen 31:37	3627
thou found of all thy household *s*	Gen 31:37	3627
Also regard not your *s*	Gen 45:20	3627
his neighbour money or *s* to keep	Ex 22:7	3627
For the *s* they had was sufficient	Ex 36:7	4399
put it even among their own *s*	Josh 7:11	3627
he hath hid himself among the *s*	1Sa 10:22	3627
and two hundred abode by the *s*	1Sa 25:13	3627
part be that tarrieth by the *s*	1Sa 30:24	3627
s of Tobiah out of the chamber	Neh 13:8	3627
man, prepare thee *s* for removing	Eze 12:3	3627
forth thy *s* by day in their sight	Eze 12:4	3627
in their sight, as *s* for removing	Eze 12:4	3627
I brought forth my *s* by day	Eze 12:7	3627
as *s* for captivity, and in the	Eze 12:7	3627
his *s* in the house, let him not	Lk 17:31	4632

STUMBLE

safely, and thy foot shall not *s*	Prov 3:23	5062
thou runnest, thou shalt not *s*	Prov 4:12	3782
they know not at what they *s*	Prov 4:19	3782
shall be weary nor *s* among them	Is 5:27	3782
And many among them shall *s*	Is 8:15	3782
err in vision, they *s* in judgment	Is 28:7	6328
we *s* at noonday as in the night	Is 59:10	3782
that they should not *s*	Is 63:13	3782
before your feet *s* upon the dark	Jer 13:16	5062
they have caused them to *s* in	Jer 18:15	3782
therefore my persecutors shall *s*	Jer 20:11	3782
way, wherein they shall not *s*	Jer 31:9	3782
they shall *s*, and fall toward the	Jer 46:6	3782
And the most proud shall *s*	Jer 50:32	3782
but he shall *s* and fall, and not be	Dan 11:19	3782
they shall *s* in their walk	Nah 2:5	3782
they *s* upon their corpses	Nah 3:3	3782
have caused many to *s* at the law	Mal 2:8	3782
even to them which *s* at the word	1Pet 2:8	4350

STUMBLED

they that *s* are girded with	1Sa 2:4	3782
for the oxen *s*	1Chr 13:9	8058
me to eat up my flesh, they *s*	Ps 27:2	3782
man hath *s* against the mighty	Jer 46:12	3782
For they *s* at that stumblingstone	Rom 9:32	4350
Have they *s* that they should fall	Rom 11:11	4417

STUMBLETH

not thine heart be glad when he *s*	Prov 24:17	3782
he *s* not, because he seeth the	Jn 11:9	4350
if a man walk in the night, he *s*	Jn 11:10	4350
any thing whereby thy brother *s*	Rom 14:21	4350

STUMBLING

but for a stone of *s* and for a	Is 8:14	5063
And a stone of *s*, and a rock of	1Pet 2:8	
is none occasion of *s* in him	1Jn 2:10	4625

STUMBLINGBLOCK

nor put a *s* before the blind, but	Lev 19:14	4383
take up the *s* out of the way of	Is 57:14	4383

I lay a *s* before him, he shall .... Eze 3:20   4383
it is the *s* of their iniquity .... Eze 7:19   4383
put the *s* of their iniquity .... Eze 14:3   4383
putteth the *s* of his iniquity .... Eze 14:4   4383
putteth the *s* of his iniquity .... Eze 14:7   4383
made a snare, and a trap, and a *s* .... Rom 11:9   4625
that no man put a *s* or an .... Rom 14:13   4348
crucified, unto the Jews a *s* 1Cor 1:23   4625
become a *s* to them that are weak 1Cor 8:9   4348
who taught Balac to cast a *s* .... Rev 2:14   4625

STUMBLINGBLOCKS
I will lay *s* before this people, ... Jer 6:21   4383
the sea, and the *s* with the wicked .... Zeph 1:3   4384

STUMBLINGSTONE
For they stumbled at that *s* .... Rom 9:32   3037,4348
Behold, I lay in Sion a *s* .... Rom 9:33   3037,4348

STUMP
only the *s* of Dagon was left to 1Sa 5:4
Nevertheless leave the *s* of his .... Dan 4:15   6136
yet leave the *s* of the roots .... Dan 4:23   6136
to leave the *s* of the tree roots .... Dan 4:26   6136

SUAH (*su'-ah*) *Son of Zophah.*
S, and Harnepher, and Shual, and 1Chr 7:36   5477

SUBDUE
and replenish the earth, and *s* it .... Gen 1:28   3533
Moreover I will *s* all thine 1Chr 17:10   3665
He shall *s* the people under us, ... Ps 47:3   1696
holden, to *s* nations before him .... Is 45:1   7286
first, and he shall *s* three kings .... Dan 7:24   8214
he will *s* our iniquities............................ Mic 7:19   3533
devour, and *s* with sling stones .... Zec 9:15   3533
even to *s* all things unto himself .... Phil 3:21   5293

SUBDUED
the land be *s* before the LORD................. Num 32:22   3533
and the land shall be *s* before you .... Num 32:29   3533
war with thee, until it be *s*...................... Deut 20:20   3381
And the land was *s* before them .... Josh 18:1   3533
So Moab was *s* that day under the .... Judg 3:30   3665
So God *s* on that day Jabin the .... Judg 4:23   3665
Thus was Midian *s* before the .... Judg 8:28   3665
s before the children of Israel.................. Judg 11:33   3665
So the Philistines were *s* 1Sa 7:13   3665
smote the Philistines, and *s* them 2Sa 8:1   3665
of all nations which he *s* 2Sa 8:11   3533
against me hast thou *s* under me 2Sa 22:40   3766
s them, and took Gath and her towns 1Chr 18:1   3665
and they were *s* 1Chr 20:4   3665
the land is *s* before the LORD, and......... 1Chr 22:18   3533
thou hast *s* under me those that .... Ps 18:39   3766
should soon have *s* their enemies .... Ps 81:14   3665
all things shall be *s* unto him.................. 1Cor 15:28   5293
Who through faith *s* kingdoms .... Heb 11:33   2610

SUBDUEDST
land, and thou *s* before them the .... Neh 9:24   3665

SUBDUETH
me, and *s* the people under me .... Ps 18:47   1696
who *s* my people under me....................... Ps 144:2   7286
in pieces and *s* all things .... Dan 2:40   2827

SUBJECT
to Nazareth, and was *s* unto them .... Lk 2:51   5293
even the devils are *s* unto us.................. Lk 10:17   5293
that the spirits are *s* unto you.............. Lk 10:20   5293
for it is not *s* to the law of God............... Rom 8:7   5293
the creature was made *s* to vanity .... Rom 8:20   5293
Let every soul be *s* unto the .... Rom 13:1   5293
Wherefore ye must needs be *s* .... Rom 13:5   5293
prophets are *s* to the prophets 1Cor 14:32   5293
be *s* unto him that put all things 1Cor 15:28   5293
as the church is *s* unto Christ............... Eph 5:24   5293
world, are ye *s* to ordinances, ... Col 2:20   1379
in mind to be *s* to principalities .... Titus 3:1   5293
all their lifetime to *s* to bondage .... Heb 2:15   1777
Elias was a man *s* to like...................... Jas 5:17   3663
be *s* to your masters with all.................. 1Pet 2:18   5293
and powers being made *s* unto him........ 1Pet 3:22   5293
all of you be *s* one to another, ... 1Pet 5:5   5293

SUBJECTED
him who hath *s* the same in hope .... Rom 8:20   5293

SUBJECTION
brought into *s* under their hand............. Ps 106:42   3665
brought them into *s* for servants............ Jer 34:11   3533
to return, and brought them into *s* .... Jer 34:16   3533
under my body, and bring it into *s* 1Cor 9:27   1396
s into the gospel of Christ 2Cor 9:13   5292
To whom we gave place by *s* .... Gal 2:5   5292

woman learn in silence with all *s* 1Ti 2:11   5292
children in *s* with all gravity 1Ti 3:4   5292
he not put in *s* the world to come .... Heb 2:5   5293
all things in *s* under his feet................... Heb 2:8   5293
in that he put all in *s* under him............. Heb 2:8   5293
in *s* unto the Father of spirits .... Heb 12:9   5293
be in *s* to your own husbands 1Pet 3:1   5293
being in *s* unto their own........................ 1Pet 3:5   5293

SUBMIT
s thyself under her hands .... Gen 16:9   6031
Strangers shall *s* themselves unto 2Sa 22:45   3584
shall *s* themselves unto me .... Ps 18:44   3584
enemies *s* themselves unto thee.............. Ps 66:3   3584
till every one *s* himself with .... Ps 68:30   7511
That ye *s* yourselves unto such, ... 1Cor 16:16   5293
s yourselves unto your own .... Eph 5:22   5293
s yourselves unto your own .... Col 3:18   5293
rule over you, and *s* yourselves .... Heb 13:17   5226
S yourselves therefore to God .... Jas 4:7   5293
S yourselves to every ordinance 1Pet 2:13   5293
s yourselves unto the elder 1Pet 5:5   5293

SUBMITTED
s themselves unto Solomon the 1Chr 29:24   5414,3027
should have *s* themselves unto him .... Ps 81:15   3584
have not *s* themselves unto the.............. Rom 10:3   5293

SUBMITTING
S yourselves one to another in .... Eph 5:21   5293

SUBORNED
Then they *s* men, which said, We........... Acts 6:11   5260

SUBSCRIBE
another shall *s* with his hand................. Is 44:5   3789
s evidences, and seal them, and............. Jer 32:44   3789

SUBSCRIBED
I *s* the evidence, and sealed it, ... Jer 32:10   3789
that *s* the book of the purchase .... Jer 32:12   3789

SUBSTANCE
every living *s* that I have made.............. Gen 7:4   3351
every living *s* was destroyed .... Gen 7:23   3351
all their *s* that they had .... Gen 12:5   7399
for their *s* was great, so that .... Gen 13:6   7399
shall they come out with great *s* .... Gen 15:14   7399
Shall not their cattle and their *s* .... Gen 34:23   7075
and all his beasts, and all his *s* .... Gen 36:6   7075
all the *s* that was in their .... Deut 11:6   3351
Bless, LORD, his *s*, and accept the .... Deut 33:11   3428
for their cattle and for their *s* .... Josh 14:4   7075
of the *s* which was king David's............. 1Chr 27:31   7399
and the stewards over all the *s* 1Chr 28:1   7399
carried away all the *s* that was............... 2Chr 21:17   7399
of his *s* for the burnt offerings 2Chr 31:3   7399
for God had given him *s* very much 2Chr 32:29   7399
these were of the king's............................ 2Chr 35:7   7399
our little ones, and for all our *s*............. Ezr 8:21   7399
all his *s* should be forfeited, and .... Ezr 10:8   7399
His *s* also was seven thousand .... Job 1:3   4735
his *s* is increased in the land .... Job 1:10   4735
the robber swalloweth up their *s*............. Job 5:5   2428
Give a reward for me of your *s* .... Job 6:22   3581
neither shall his *s* continue.................... Job 15:29   2428
according to his *s* shall the .... Job 20:18   2428
Whereas our *s* is not cut down, ... Job 22:20   7009
ride upon it, and dissolvest my *s* .... Job 30:22   7738
rest of their *s* to their babes .... Ps 17:14
his house, and ruler of all his *s* .... Ps 105:21   7075
My *s* was not hid from thee, when .... Ps 139:15   6108
Thine eyes did see my *s*, yet................... Ps 139:16   1564
We shall find all precious *s* .... Prov 1:13   1952
Honour the LORD with thy *s*................... Prov 3:9   1952
shall give all the *s* of his house .... Prov 6:31   1952
those that love me to inherit *s* .... Prov 8:21   3426
casteth away the *s* of the wicked .... Prov 10:3   1942
but the *s* of a diligent man is .... Prov 12:27   1952
and unjust gain increaseth his *s* .... Prov 28:8   1952
with harlots spendeth his *s* .... Prov 29:3   1952
all the *s* of his house for love .... Song 8:7   1952
whose *s* is in them, when they .... Is 6:13   4678
holy seed shall be the *s* thereof............. Is 6:13   4678
Thy *s* and thy treasures will I............... Jer 15:13   2428
in the field, I will give thy *s* .... Jer 17:3   2428
rich, I have found me out *s* .... Hos 12:8   202
s in the day of their calamity .... Obad 13   2428
their *s* unto the Lord of the .... Mic 4:13   2428
ministered unto him of their *s*................ Lk 8:3   5224
there wasted his *s* with riotous.............. Lk 15:13   3776
heaven a better and an enduring *s*......... Heb 10:34   5223
Now faith is the *s* of things .... Heb 11:1   5287

S

SUBTIL

Now the serpent was more *s* than	Gen 3:1	6175
and Jonadab was a very *s* man	2Sa 13:3	2450
of an harlot, and *s* of heart	Prov 7:10	5341

SUBTILLY

is told me that he dealeth very *s*	1Sa 23:22	6191
to deal *s* with his servants	Ps 105:25	5230
The same dealt *s* with our kindred	Acts 7:19	*2686*

SUBTILTY

he said, Thy brother came with *s*	Gen 27:35	4820
But Jehu did it in *s*, to the	2Kin 10:19	6122
To give *s* to the simple, to the	Prov 1:4	6195
that they might take Jesus by *s*	Mt 26:4	*1388*
And said, O full of all *s* and all	Acts 13:10	*1388*
beguiled Eve through his *s*	2Cor 11:3	*3834*

SUBURBS

But the field of the *s* of their	Lev 25:34	4054
give also unto the Levites *s* for	Num 35:2	4054
the *s* of them shall be for their	Num 35:3	4054
the *s* of the cities, which ye	Num 35:4	4054
be to them the *s* of the cities	Num 35:5	4054
them shall ye give with their *s*	Num 35:7	4054
with their *s* for their cattle and	Josh 14:4	4054
with the *s* thereof for our cattle	Josh 21:2	4054
the LORD, these cities and their *s*	Josh 21:3	4054
Levites these cities with their *s*	Josh 21:8	4054
with the *s* thereof round about it	Josh 21:11	4054
the priest Hebron with her *s*	Josh 21:13	4054
and Libnah with her *s*,	Josh 21:13	4054
And Jattir with her *s*, and Eshtemoa	Josh 21:14	4054
and Eshtemoa with her *s*	Josh 21:14	4054
And Holon with her *s*, and Debir	Josh 21:15	4054
and Debir with her *s*	Josh 21:15	4054
And Ain with her *s*, and Juttah with	Josh 21:16	4054
and Juttah with her *s*	Josh 21:16	4054
and Beth-shemesh with her *s*	Josh 21:16	4054
of Benjamin, Gibeon with her *s*	Josh 21:17	4054
Geba with her *s*	Josh 21:17	4054
Anathoth with her *s*, and Almon	Josh 21:18	4054
and Almon with her *s*	Josh 21:18	4054
were thirteen cities with their *s*	Josh 21:19	4054
with her *s* in mount Ephraim	Josh 21:21	4054
and Gezer with her *s*,	Josh 21:21	4054
And Kibzaim with her *s*, and	Josh 21:22	4054
and Beth-horon with her *s*	Josh 21:22	4054
tribe of Dan, Eltekeh with her *s*	Josh 21:23	4054
Gibbethon with her *s*	Josh 21:23	4054
Aijalon with her *s*, Gath-rimmon	Josh 21:24	4054
Gath-rimmon with her *s*	Josh 21:24	4054
of Manasseh, Tanach with her *s*	Josh 21:25	4054
and Gath-rimmon with her *s*	Josh 21:25	4054
their *s* for the families of the	Josh 21:26	4054
gave Golan in Bashan with her *s*	Josh 21:27	4054
and Beesh-terah with her *s*	Josh 21:27	4054
of Issachar, Kishon with her *s*	Josh 21:28	4054
Dabareh with her *s*	Josh 21:28	4054
Jarmuth with her *s*, En-gannim	Josh 21:29	4054
En-gannim with her *s*	Josh 21:29	4054
tribe of Asher, Mishal with her *s*	Josh 21:30	4054
Abdon with her *s*	Josh 21:30	4054
Helkath with her *s*, and Rehob with	Josh 21:31	4054
Rehob with her *s*	Josh 21:31	4054
Kedesh in Galilee with her *s*	Josh 21:32	4054
and Hammoth-dor with her *s*	Josh 21:32	4054
and Kartan with her *s*	Josh 21:32	4054
were thirteen cities with their *s*	Josh 21:33	4054
of Zebulun, Jokneam with her *s*	Josh 21:34	4054
and Kartah with her *s*	Josh 21:34	4054
Dimnah with her *s*, Nahalal with	Josh 21:35	4054
her *s*, Nahalal with her *s*	Josh 21:35	4054
tribe of Reuben, Bezer with her *s*	Josh 21:36	
and Jahazah with her *s*	Josh 21:36	
Kedemoth with her *s*, and Mephaath	Josh 21:37	
and Mephaath with her *s*	Josh 21:37	
Gad, Ramoth in Gilead with her *s*	Josh 21:38	4054
and Mahanaim with her *s*	Josh 21:38	4054
Heshbon with her *s*, Jazer with	Josh 21:39	4054
Jazer with her *s*	Josh 21:39	4054
and eight cities with their *s*	Josh 21:41	4054
one with their *s* round about them	Josh 21:42	4054
chamberlain, which was in the	2Kin 23:11	6503
towns, and in all the *s* of Sharon	1Chr 5:16	4054
the *s* thereof round about it	1Chr 6:55	4054
of refuge, and Libnah with her *s*	1Chr 6:57	4054
Jattir, and Eshtemoa, with their *s*	1Chr 6:57	4054
And Hilen with her *s*, Debir with	1Chr 6:58	4054
Debir with her *s*	1Chr 6:58	4054
And Ashan with her *s*, and	1Chr 6:59	4054
and Beth-shemesh with her *s*	1Chr 6:59	4054

Geba with her *s*	1Chr 6:60	4054
and Alemeth with her *s*	1Chr 6:60	4054
and Anathoth with her *s*	1Chr 6:60	4054
Levites these cities with their *s*	1Chr 6:64	4054
in mount Ephraim with her *s*	1Chr 6:67	4054
they gave also Gezer with her *s*	1Chr 6:67	4054
And Jokmeam with her *s*, and	1Chr 6:68	4054
and Beth-horon with her *s*	1Chr 6:68	4054
And Aijalon with her *s*, and	1Chr 6:69	4054
and Gath-rimmon with her *s*	1Chr 6:69	4054
Aner with her *s*, and Bileam with	1Chr 6:70	4054
and Bileam with her *s*	1Chr 6:70	4054
Golan in Bashan with her *s*	1Chr 6:71	4054
and Ashtaroth with her *s*	1Chr 6:71	4054
Kedesh with her *s*	1Chr 6:72	4054
Daberath with her *s*	1Chr 6:72	4054
And Ramoth with her *s*	1Chr 6:73	4054
and Anem with her *s*	1Chr 6:73	4054
Mashal with her *s*	1Chr 6:74	4054
and Abdon with her *s*	1Chr 6:74	4054
And Hukok with her *s*	1Chr 6:75	4054
and Rehob with her *s*	1Chr 6:75	4054
Kedesh in Galilee with her *s*	1Chr 6:76	4054
and Hammon with her *s*	1Chr 6:76	4054
and Kirjathaim with her *s*	1Chr 6:76	4054
of Zebulun, Rimmon with her *s*	1Chr 6:77	4054
Tabor with her *s*	1Chr 6:77	4054
in the wilderness with her *s*	1Chr 6:78	4054
and Jahzah with her *s*	1Chr 6:78	4054
Kedemoth also with her *s*, and	1Chr 6:79	4054
and Mephaath with her *s*	1Chr 6:79	4054
Ramoth in Gilead with her *s*	1Chr 6:80	4054
and Mahanaim with her *s*	1Chr 6:80	4054
And Heshbon with her *s*, and Jazer	1Chr 6:81	4054
and Jazer with her *s*	1Chr 6:81	4054
which are in their cities and *s*	1Chr 13:2	4054
For the Levites left their *s*	2Chr 11:14	4054
fields of the *s* of their cities	2Chr 31:19	4054
The *s* shall shake at the sound of	Eze 27:28	4054
round about for the *s* thereof	Eze 45:2	4054
the city, for dwelling, and for *s*	Eze 48:15	4054
the *s* of the city shall be toward	Eze 48:17	4054

SUBVERT

To *s* a man in his cause, the Lord	Lam 3:36	5791
who *s* whole houses, teaching	Titus 1:11	*396*

SUBVERTED

Knowing that he that is such is *s*	Titus 3:11	*1612*

SUBVERTING

s your souls, saying, Ye must be	Acts 15:24	*384*
but to the *s* of the hearers	2Ti 2:14	*2692*

SUCATHITES See SUCHATHITES.

SUCCEED

which she beareth shall *s* in the	Deut 25:6	6965

SUCCEEDED

but the children of Esau *s* them	Deut 2:12	3423
and they *s* them, and dwelt in their	Deut 2:21	3423
and they *s* them, and dwelt in their	Deut 2:22	3423

SUCCEEDEST

to possess them, and thou *s* them	Deut 12:29	3423
God giveth thee, and thou *s* them	Deut 19:1	3423

SUCCESS

and then thou shalt have good *s*	Josh 1:8	7919

SUCCOTH (*suc'-coth*)

1. A place east of the Jordan.

And Jacob journeyed to *S*, and built	Gen 33:17	5523
the name of the place is called *S*	Gen 33:17	5523

2. An Israelite encampment in the wilderness.

journeyed from Rameses to *S*	Ex 12:37	5523
And they took their journey from *S*	Ex 13:20	5523
from Rameses, and pitched in *S*	Num 33:5	5523
And they departed from *S*, and	Num 33:6	5523

3. A place in Gad.

Beth-aram, and Beth-nimrah, and *S*	Josh 13:27	5523
And he said unto the men of *S*	Judg 8:5	5523
And the princes of *S* said, Are the	Judg 8:6	5523
as the men of *S* had answered him	Judg 8:8	5523
a young man of the men of *S*	Judg 8:14	5523
unto him the princes of *S*	Judg 8:14	5523
And he came unto the men of *S*	Judg 8:15	5523
with them he taught the men of *S*	Judg 8:16	5523

4. A city in Ephraim.

in the clay ground between *S*	1Kin 7:46	5523
in the clay ground between *S*	2Chr 4:17	5523
and mete out the valley of *S*	Ps 60:6	5523
and mete out the valley of *S*	Ps 108:7	5523

SUCCOTH-BENOTH (suc'-coth-be'-noth) A Babylonian god.

And the men of Babylon made S	2Kin 17:30	5524

SUCCOUR

came to s Hadadezer king of Zobah	2Sa 8:5	5826
that thou s us out of the city	2Sa 18:3	5826
he is able to s them that are	Heb 2:18	997

SUCCOURED

Abishai the son of Zeruiah s him	2Sa 21:17	5826
day of salvation have I s thee	2Cor 6:2	997

SUCCOURER

for she hath been a s of many	Rom 16:2	4368

SUCH See APPENDIX.

SUCHATHITES (soo'-kath-ites) A family of scribes.

the Shimeathites, and S	1Chr 2:55	7756

SUCK

should have given children s	Gen 21:7	3243
he made him to s honey out of the	Deut 32:13	3243
for they shall s of the abundance	Deut 33:19	3243
gave her son s until she weaned	1Sa 1:23	3243
in the morning to give my child s	1Kin 3:21	3243
why the breasts that I should s	Job 3:12	3243
He shall s the poison of asps	Job 20:16	3243
Her young ones also s up blood	Job 39:30	5966
Thou shalt also s the milk of the	Is 60:16	3243
shalt s the breast of kings	Is 60:16	3243
That ye may s, and be satisfied	Is 66:11	3243
then shall ye s, ye shall be	Is 66:12	3243
they give s to their young ones	Lam 4:3	3243
s it out, and thou shalt break the	Eze 23:34	4680
and those that s the breasts	Joel 2:16	3243
to them that give s in those days	Mt 24:19	2337
to them that give s in those days	Mk 13:17	2337
child, and to them that give s	Lk 21:23	2337
and the paps which never gave s	Lk 23:29	2337

SUCKED

that s the breasts of my mother	Song 8:1	3243
and the paps which thou hast s	Lk 11:27	2337

SUCKING

father beareth the s child	Num 11:12	3243
And Samuel took a s lamb, and	1Sa 7:9	2461
the s child shall play on the	Is 11:8	3243
Can a woman forget her s child	Is 49:15	5764
The tongue of the s child	Lam 4:4	3243

SUCKLING

the s also with the man of gray	Deut 32:25	3243
both man and woman, infant and s	1Sa 15:3	3243
man and woman, child and s	Jer 44:7	3243

SUCKLINGS

both men and women, children and s	1Sa 22:19	3243
s hast thou ordained strength	Ps 8:2	3243
the s swoon in the streets of the	Lam 2:11	3243
s thou hast perfected praise	Mt 21:16	2337

SUDDEN

thee, and s fear troubleth thee	Job 22:10	6597
Be not afraid of s fear, neither	Prov 3:25	6597
then s destruction cometh upon	1Th 5:3	160

SUDDENLY

And if any man die very s by him	Num 6:9	6597
And the LORD spake s unto Moses	Num 12:4	6597
if he thrust him s without enmity	Num 35:22	6621
against you, and destroy thee s	Deut 7:4	4118
Joshua therefore came unto them s	Josh 10:9	6597
them by the waters of Merom s	Josh 11:7	6597
to depart, lest he overtake us s	2Sa 15:14	4116
for the thing was done s	2Chr 29:36	6597
but s I cursed his habitation	Job 5:3	6597
If the scourge slay s, he will	Job 9:23	6597
let them return and be ashamed s	Ps 6:10	7281
s do they shoot at him, and fear	Ps 64:4	6597
s shall they be wounded	Ps 64:7	6597
shall his calamity come s	Prov 6:15	6597
s shall he be broken without	Prov 6:15	6621
For their calamity shall rise s	Prov 24:22	6597
shall s be destroyed, and that	Prov 29:1	6621
time, when it falleth s upon them	Eccl 9:12	6597
yea, it shall be at an instant s	Is 29:5	6597
breaking cometh s at an instant	Is 30:13	6597
desolation shall come upon thee s	Is 47:11	6597
I did them s, and they came to	Is 48:3	6597
s are my tents spoiled, and my	Jer 4:20	6597
the spoiler shall s come upon us	Jer 6:26	6597
have caused him to fall upon it s	Jer 15:8	6597
shalt bring a troop s upon them	Jer 18:22	6597
but I will s make him run away	Jer 49:19	7280

make them s run away from her	Jer 50:44	7280
Babylon is s fallen and destroyed	Jer 51:8	6597
rise up s that shall bite thee	Hab 2:7	6621
shall s come to his temple, even	Mal 3:1	6597
And s, when they had looked round	Mk 9:8	1819
Lest coming s he find you	Mk 13:36	1810
s there was with the angel a	Lk 2:13	1810
taketh him, and he s crieth out	Lk 9:39	1810
s there came a sound from heaven	Acts 2:2	869
s there shined round about him a	Acts 9:3	1810
s there was a great earthquake,	Acts 16:26	869
s there shone from heaven a great	Acts 22:6	1810
swollen, or fallen down dead	Acts 28:6	869
Lay hands s on no man, neither be	1Ti 5:22	5030

SUE

if any man will s thee at the law	Mt 5:40	2919

SUFFER

will not s the destroyer to come	Ex 12:23	5414
Thou shalt not s a witch to live	Ex 22:18	
neither shalt thou s the salt of	Lev 2:13	
neighbour, and not s sin upon him	Lev 19:17	5375
Or s them to bear the iniquity of	Lev 22:16	5375
Sihon would not s Israel to pass	Num 21:23	5414
s them not to enter into their	Josh 10:19	5414
for they would not s them to come	Judg 1:34	5414
father would not s him to go in	Judg 15:1	5414
S me that I may feel the pillars	Judg 16:26	3240
that thou wouldest not s the	2Sa 14:11	
that he might not s any to go out	1Kin 15:17	5414
for the king's profit to s them	Est 3:8	3240
He will not s me to take my	Job 9:18	5414
S me that I may speak	Job 21:3	5375
their winepresses, and s thirst	Job 24:11	
S me a little, and I will shew	Job 36:2	3803
which I s of them that hate me	Ps 9:13	
neither wilt thou s thine Holy	Ps 16:10	5414
young lions do lack, and s hunger	Ps 34:10	
he shall never s the righteous to	Ps 55:22	5414
while I s thy terrors I am	Ps 88:15	5375
nor s my faithfulness to fail	Ps 89:33	
and a proud heart will not I s	Ps 101:5	3201
He will not s thy foot to be	Ps 121:3	5414
The LORD will not s the soul of	Prov 10:3	
and an idle soul shall s hunger	Prov 19:15	
of great wrath shall s punishment	Prov 19:19	5375
S not thy mouth to cause thy	Eccl 5:6	5414
the rich will not s him to sleep	Eccl 5:12	3240
nor s their locks to grow long	Eze 44:20	
said unto him, S it to be so now	Mt 3:15	863
s me first to go and bury my	Mt 8:21	2010
s us to go away into the herd of	Mt 8:31	2010
s many things of the elders and	Mt 16:21	3958
also the Son of man s of them	Mt 17:12	3958
how long shall I s you	Mt 17:17	430
S little children, and forbid them	Mt 19:14	863
neither s ye them that are	Mt 23:13	863
ye s him no more to do ought for	Mk 7:12	863
the Son of man must s many things	Mk 8:31	3958
man, that he must s many things	Mk 9:12	3958
how long shall I s you	Mk 9:19	430
S the little children to come	Mk 10:14	863
would not s that any man should	Mk 11:16	863
would s them to enter into them	Lk 8:32	2010
The Son of man must s many things	Lk 9:22	3958
shall I be with you, and s you	Lk 9:41	430
s me first to go and bury my	Lk 9:59	2010
But first must he s many things	Lk 17:25	3958
S little children to come unto me	Lk 18:16	863
this passover with you before I s	Lk 22:15	3958
answered and said, S ye thus far	Lk 22:51	1439
and thus it behoved Christ to s	Lk 24:46	3958
neither wilt thou s thine Holy	Acts 2:27	1325
prophets, that Christ should s	Acts 3:18	3958
worthy to s shame for his name	Acts 5:41	818
And seeing one of them s wrong	Acts 7:24	
he must s for my name's sake	Acts 9:16	3958
Thou shalt not s thine Holy One	Acts 13:35	1325
s me to speak unto the people	Acts 21:39	2010
That Christ should s, and that he	Acts 26:23	3805
if so be that we s with him	Rom 8:17	4841
shall be burned, he shall s loss	1Cor 3:15	2210
being persecuted, we s it	1Cor 4:12	430
why do ye not rather s yourselves	1Cor 6:7	
but s all things, lest we should	1Cor 9:12	4722
who will not s you to be tempted	1Cor 10:13	1439
And whether one member s, all the	1Cor 12:26	3958
s, all the members s with it	1Cor 12:26	4841
same sufferings which we also s	2Cor 1:6	3958
For ye s fools gladly, seeing ye	2Cor 11:19	430
For ye s, if a man bring you into	2Cor 11:20	430

why do I yet *s* persecution	Gal 5:11	1377
only lest they should *s*	Gal 6:12	1377
but also to *s* for his sake	Phil 1:29	3958
both to abound and to *s* need	Phil 4:12	5302
that we should *s* tribulation	1Th 3:4	
of God, for which ye also *s*	2Th 1:5	
But I *s* not a woman to teach, nor	1Ti 2:12	2010
s reproach, because we trust in	1Ti 4:10	
which cause I also *s* these things	2Ti 1:12	3958
Wherein I *s* trouble, as an evil	2Ti 2:9	2553
If we *s*, we shall also reign with	2Ti 2:12	5278
Christ Jesus shall *s* persecution	2Ti 3:12	1377
Choosing rather to *s* affliction	Heb 11:25	4778
and them which *s* adversity	Heb 13:3	2558
s the word of exhortation	Heb 13:22	430
s for it, ye take it patiently,	1Pet 2:20	3958
if ye *s* for righteousness' sake,	1Pet 3:14	3958
that ye *s* for well doing, than	1Pet 3:17	3958
let none of you *s* as a murderer	1Pet 4:15	3958
Yet if any man *s* as a Christian	1Pet 4:16	
Wherefore let them that *s*	1Pet 4:19	3958
those things which thou shalt *s*	Rev 2:10	3958
shall not *s* their dead bodies to	Rev 11:9	863

SUFFERED

therefore *s* I thee not to touch	Gen 20:6	5414
but God *s* him not to hurt me	Gen 31:7	5414
hast not *s* me to kiss my sons and	Gen 31:28	5203
s thee to hunger, and fed thee	Deut 8:3	
thy God hath not *s* thee so to do	Deut 18:14	5414
Moab, and *s* not a man to pass over	Judg 3:28	5414
s them not to rise against Saul	1Sa 24:7	5414
s neither the birds of the air to	2Sa 21:10	5414
He *s* no man to do them wrong	1Chr 16:21	3240
(Neither have I *s* my mouth to sin	Job 31:30	5414
He *s* no man to do them wrong	Ps 105:14	3240
that for thy sake I have *s* rebuke	Jer 15:15	5375
Then he *s* him	Mt 3:15	863
s you to put away your wives	Mt 19:8	2010
would not have *s* his house to be	Mt 24:43	1439
for I have *s* many things this day	Mt 27:19	3958
s not the devils to speak,	Mk 1:34	863
Howbeit Jesus *s* him not, but	Mk 5:19	863
had *s* many things of many	Mk 5:26	3958
he *s* no man to follow him, save	Mk 5:37	863
Moses *s* to write a bill of	Mk 10:4	2010
he rebuking them *s* them not to	Lk 4:41	1439
And he *s* them	Lk 8:32	2010
he *s* no man to go in, save Peter,	Lk 8:51	863
not have *s* his house to be broken	Lk 12:39	863
because Jesus *s* such things	Lk 13:2	3958
not Christ to have *s* these things	Lk 24:26	3958
years *s* he their manners in the	Acts 13:18	5159
Who in times past *s* all nations	Acts 14:16	1439
but the Spirit *s* them not	Acts 16:7	1439
that Christ must needs have *s*	Acts 17:3	3958
people, the disciples *s* him not	Acts 19:30	1439
but Paul was *s* to dwell by	Acts 28:16	2010
nor for his cause that *s* wrong	2Cor 7:12	
thrice I *s* shipwreck, a night and	2Cor 11:25	
Have ye *s* so many things in vain	Gal 3:4	3958
for whom I have *s* the loss of all	Phil 3:8	2210
even after that we had *s* before	1Th 2:2	4310
for ye also have *s* like things of	1Th 2:14	3958
he himself hath *s* being tempted	Heb 2:18	3958
by the things which he *s*	Heb 5:8	3958
because they were not *s* to	Heb 7:23	2967
s since the foundation of the	Heb 9:26	3958
his own blood, *s* without the gate	Heb 13:12	3958
because Christ also *s* for us	1Pet 2:21	3958
when he *s*, he threatened not	1Pet 2:23	3958
Christ also hath once *s* for sins	1Pet 3:18	3958
Christ hath *s* for us in the flesh	1Pet 4:1	3958
for he that hath *s* in the flesh	1Pet 4:1	3958
after that ye have *s* a while	1Pet 5:10	3958

SUFFEREST

because thou *s* that woman Jezebel	Rev 2:20	1439

SUFFERETH

s not our feet to be moved	Ps 66:9	5414
s not their cattle to decrease.	Ps 107:38	
the kingdom of heaven *s* violence	Mt 11:12	971
sea, yet vengeance *s* not to live	Acts 28:4	1439
Charity *s* long, and is kind	1Cor 13:4	3114

SUFFERING

against Cnidus, the wind not *s* us	Acts 27:7	4330
the angels for the *s* of death	Heb 2:9	3804
for an example of *s* of affliction	Jas 5:10	2552
God endure grief, *s* wrongfully	1Pet 2:19	3958
s the vengeance of eternal fire	Jude 7	5254

SUFFERINGS

For I reckon that the *s* of this	Rom 8:18	3804
For as the *s* of Christ abound in	2Cor 1:5	3804
the same *s* which we also suffer	2Cor 1:6	3804
that as ye are partakers of the *s*	2Cor 1:7	3804
and the fellowship of his *s*	Phil 3:10	3804
Who now rejoice in my *s* for you	Col 1:24	3804
their salvation perfect through *s*	Heb 2:10	3804
beforehand the *s* of Christ	1Pet 1:11	3804
as ye are partakers of Christ's *s*	1Pet 4:13	3804
and a witness of the *s* of Christ	1Pet 5:1	3804

SUFFICE

be slain for them, to *s* them	Num 11:22	4672
together for them, to *s* them	Num 11:22	4672
LORD said unto me, Let it *s* thee	Deut 3:26	7227
if the dust of Samaria shall *s*	1Kin 20:10	5606
Israel, let it *s* you of all your	Eze 44:6	7227
Let it *s* you, O princes of Israel	Eze 45:9	7227
the time past of our life may *s*	1Pet 4:3	713

SUFFICED

and yet so they *s* them not	Judg 21:14	4672
corn, and she did eat, and was *s*	Ruth 2:14	7646
she had reserved after she was *s*	Ruth 2:18	7648

SUFFICETH

shew us the Father, and it *s* us	Jn 14:8	714

SUFFICIENCY

In the fulness of his *s* he shall	Job 20:22	5607
but our *s* is of God	2Cor 3:5	2426
always having all *s* in all things	2Cor 9:8	841

SUFFICIENT

For the stuff they had was *s* for	Ex 36:7	1767
surely lend him *s* for his need	Deut 15:8	1767
let his hands be *s* for him	Deut 33:7	7227
eat so much as is *s* for thee	Prov 25:16	1767
And Lebanon is not *s* to burn	Is 40:16	1767
thereof *s* for a burnt offering	Is 40:16	1767
S unto the day is the evil	Mt 6:34	713
whether he have *s* to finish it	Lk 14:28	
of bread is not *s* for them	Jn 6:7	714
S to such a man is this	2Cor 2:6	2425
who is *s* for these things	2Cor 2:16	2425
Not that we are *s* of ourselves to	2Cor 3:5	2425
unto me, My grace is *s* for thee	2Cor 12:9	714

SUFFICIENTLY

had not sanctified themselves *s*	2Chr 30:3	4078
dwell before the LORD, to eat *s*	Is 23:18	7654

SUIT

a *s* of apparel, and thy victuals	Judg 17:10	6187
any *s* or cause might come unto me	2Sa 15:4	7379
yea, many shall make *s* unto thee	Job 11:19	2470

SUITS

The changeable *s* of apparel	Is 3:22	

SUKKIIMS (suk'-ke-ims) An Egyptian tribe.

the Lubim, the *S*, and the	2Chr 12:3	5525

SUM

there be laid on him a *s* of money	Ex 21:30	3724
When thou takest the *s* of the	Ex 30:12	7218
This is the *s* of the tabernacle,	Ex 38:21	6485
Take ye the *s* of all the	Num 1:2	7218
neither take the *s* of them among	Num 1:49	7218
Take the *s* of the sons of Kohath	Num 4:2	7218
Take also the *s* of the sons of	Num 4:22	7218
Take the *s* of all the	Num 26:2	7218
Take the *s* of the people, from	Num 26:4	
Take the *s* of the prey that was	Num 31:26	7218
the *s* of the men of war which are	Num 31:49	7218
Joab gave up the *s* of the number	2Sa 24:9	4557
that he may *s* the silver which is	2Kin 22:4	8552
Joab gave the *s* of the number of	1Chr 21:5	4557
of the *s* of the money that Haman	Est 4:7	6575
How great is the *s* of them	Ps 139:17	7218
Thou sealest up the *s*, full of	Eze 28:12	8508
told the *s* of the matters	Dan 7:1	7217
that Abraham bought for a *s* of	Acts 7:16	5092
With a great *s* obtained I this	Acts 22:28	2774
we have spoken this is the *s*	Heb 8:1	2774

SUMMER

and harvest, and cold and heat, and *s*	Gen 8:22	7019
and he was sitting in a *s* parlour	Judg 3:20	4747
his feet in his *s* chamber	Judg 3:24	4747
and an hundred of *s* fruits	2Sa 16:1	7019
s fruit for the young men to eat	2Sa 16:2	7019
is turned unto the drought of *s*	Ps 32:4	7019
thou hast made *s* and winter	Ps 74:17	7019
Provideth her meat in the *s*	Prov 6:8	7019

that gathereth in s is a wise son	Prov 10:5	7019
As snow in s, and as rain in	Prov 26:1	7019
they prepare their meat in the s	Prov 30:25	7019
for the shouting for thy s fruits	Is 16:9	7019
and the fowls shall s upon them	Is 18:6	6972
as the hasty fruit before the s	Is 28:4	7019
the s is ended, and we are not	Jer 8:20	7019
s fruits, and oil, and put them in	Jer 40:10	7019
wine and s fruits very much	Jer 40:12	7019
is fallen upon thy s fruits	Jer 48:32	7019
chaff of the s threshingfloors	Dan 2:35	7007
the winter house with the s house	Amos 3:15	7019
and behold a basket of s fruit	Amos 8:1	7019
And I said, A basket of s fruit	Amos 8:2	7019
they have gathered the s fruits	Mic 7:1	7019
in s and in winter shall it be	Zec 14:8	7019
leaves, ye know that s is nigh	Mt 24:32	2330
leaves, ye know that s is near	Mk 13:28	2330
selves that s is now nigh at hand	Lk 21:30	2330

SUMPTUOUSLY

fine linen, and fared s every day	Lk 16:19	2983

SUN

when the s was going down, a deep	Gen 15:12	8121
when the s went down, and it was	Gen 15:17	8121
The s was risen upon the earth	Gen 19:23	8121
all night, because the s was set	Gen 28:11	8121
over Penuel the s rose upon him	Gen 32:31	8121
and, behold, the s and the moon and	Gen 37:9	8121
when the s waxed hot, it melted	Ex 16:21	8121
until the going down of the s	Ex 17:12	8121
If the s be risen upon him, there	Ex 22:3	8121
unto him by that the s goeth down	Ex 22:26	8121
And when the s is down, he shall	Lev 22:7	8121
s shall they of the standard of	Num 2:3	
up before the LORD against the s	Num 25:4	8121
heaven, and when thou seest the s	Deut 4:19	8121
by the way where the s goeth down	Deut 11:30	8121
even, at the going down of the s	Deut 16:6	8121
and worshipped them, either the s	Deut 17:3	8121
and when the s is down, he shall	Deut 23:11	8121
again when the s goeth down	Deut 24:13	8121
shall the s go down upon it	Deut 24:15	8121
fruits brought forth by the s	Deut 33:14	8121
toward the going down of the s	Josh 1:4	8121
and as soon as the s was down	Josh 8:29	8121
he said in the sight of Israel, S	Josh 10:12	8121
the s stood still, and the moon	Josh 10:13	8121
So the s stood still in the midst	Josh 10:13	8121
time of the going down of the s	Josh 10:27	8121
Jordan toward the rising of the s	Josh 12:1	8121
the s when he goeth forth in his	Judg 5:31	8121
from battle before the s was up	Judg 8:13	2775
morning, as soon as the s is up	Judg 9:33	8121
day before the s went down	Judg 14:18	2775
the s went down upon them when	Judg 19:14	8121
morrow, by that time the s be hot	1Sa 11:9	8121
the s went down when they were	2Sa 2:24	8121
or ought else, till the s be down	2Sa 3:35	8121
thy wives in the sight of this s	2Sa 12:11	8121
all Israel, and before the s	2Sa 12:12	8121
of the morning, when the s riseth	2Sa 23:4	8121
about the going down of the s	1Kin 22:36	8121
the s shone upon the water, and	2Kin 3:22	8121
incense unto Baal, to the s	2Kin 23:5	8121
kings of Judah had given to the s	2Kin 23:11	8121
the chariots of the s with fire	2Kin 23:11	8121
time of the s going down he died	2Chr 18:34	8121
be opened until the s be hot	Neh 7:3	8121
He is green before the s, and his	Job 8:16	8121
Which commandeth the s, and it	Job 9:7	2775
I went mourning without the s	Job 30:28	2535
If I beheld the s when it shined	Job 31:26	216
he set a tabernacle for the s	Ps 19:4	8121
the s unto the going down thereof	Ps 50:1	8121
that they may not see the s	Ps 58:8	8121
shall fear thee as long as the s	Ps 72:5	8121
be continued as long as the s	Ps 72:17	8121
hast prepared the light and the s	Ps 74:16	8121
For the LORD God is a s and shield	Ps 84:11	8121
and his throne as the s before me	Ps 89:36	8121
the s knoweth his going down	Ps 104:19	8121
The s ariseth, they gather	Ps 104:22	8121
From the rising of the s unto the	Ps 113:3	8121
The s shall not smite thee by day	Ps 121:6	8121
The s to rule by day	Ps 136:8	8121
Praise ye him, s and moon	Ps 148:3	8121
which he taketh under the s	Eccl 1:3	8121
The s also ariseth	Eccl 1:5	8121
the s goeth down, and hasteth to	Eccl 1:5	8121
there is no new thing under the s	Eccl 1:9	8121

works that are done under the s	Eccl 1:14	8121
there was no profit under the s	Eccl 2:11	8121
under the s is grievous unto me	Eccl 2:17	8121
which I had taken under the s	Eccl 2:18	8121
shewed myself wise under the s	Eccl 2:19	8121
labour which I took under the s	Eccl 2:20	8121
he hath laboured under the s	Eccl 2:22	8121
under the s the place of judgment	Eccl 3:16	8121
that are done under the s	Eccl 4:1	8121
work that is done under the s	Eccl 4:3	8121
and I saw vanity under the s	Eccl 4:7	8121
the living which walk under the s	Eccl 4:15	8121
which I have seen under the s	Eccl 5:13	8121
the s all the days of his life	Eccl 5:18	8121
which I have seen under the s	Eccl 6:1	8121
Moreover he hath not seen the s	Eccl 6:5	8121
shall be after him under the s	Eccl 6:12	8121
is profit to them that see the s	Eccl 7:11	8121
work that is done under the s	Eccl 8:9	8121
hath no better thing under the s	Eccl 8:15	8121
which God giveth him under the s	Eccl 8:15	8121
the work that is done under the s	Eccl 8:17	8121
things that are done under the s	Eccl 9:3	8121
thing that is done under the s	Eccl 9:6	8121
he hath given thee under the s	Eccl 9:9	8121
which thou takest under the s	Eccl 9:9	8121
I returned, and saw under the s	Eccl 9:11	8121
have I seen also under the s	Eccl 9:13	8121
which I have seen under the s	Eccl 10:5	8121
is for the eyes to behold the s	Eccl 11:7	8121
While the s, or the light, or the	Eccl 12:2	8121
because the s hath looked upon me	Song 1:6	2535
fair as the moon, clear as the s	Song 6:10	2535
the s shall be darkened in his	Is 13:10	8121
the s ashamed, when the LORD of	Is 24:23	2535
shall be as the light of the s	Is 30:26	2535
the light of the s shall be	Is 30:26	8121
gone down in the s dial of Ahaz	Is 38:8	8121
So the s returned ten degrees, by	Is 38:8	8121
from the rising of the s shall he	Is 41:25	8121
may know from the rising of the s	Is 45:6	8121
shall the heat nor s smite them	Is 49:10	8121
glory from the rising of the s	Is 59:19	8121
The s shall be no more thy light	Is 60:19	8121
Thy s shall no more go down	Is 60:20	8121
shall spread them before the s	Jer 8:2	8121
her s is gone down while it was	Jer 15:9	8121
which giveth the s for a light by	Jer 31:35	8121
worshipped the s toward the east	Eze 8:16	8121
I will cover the s with a cloud	Eze 32:7	8121
down of the s to deliver him	Dan 6:14	8122
the s and the moon shall be dark,	Joel 2:10	8121
The s shall be turned into	Joel 2:31	8121
The s and the moon shall be	Joel 3:15	8121
cause the s to go down at noon	Amos 8:9	8121
when the s did arise, that God	Jonah 4:8	8121
the s beat upon the head of Jonah	Jonah 4:8	8121
the s shall go down over the	Mic 3:6	8121
but when the s ariseth they flee	Nah 3:17	8121
The s and moon stood still in	Hab 3:11	8121
For from the rising of the s even	Mal 1:11	8121
the S of righteousness arise with	Mal 4:2	8121
for he maketh his s to rise on	Mt 5:45	2246
And when the s was up, they were	Mt 13:6	2246
righteous shine forth as the s in	Mt 13:43	2246
and his face did shine as the s	Mt 17:2	2246
days shall the s be darkened	Mt 24:29	2246
And at even, when the s did set	Mk 1:32	2246
But when the s was up, it was	Mk 4:6	2246
the s shall be darkened, and the	Mk 13:24	2246
sepulchre at the rising of the s	Mk 16:2	2246
Now when the s was setting	Lk 4:40	2246
And there shall be signs in the s	Lk 21:25	2246
the s was darkened, and the veil	Lk 23:45	2246
The s shall be turned into	Acts 2:20	2246
not seeing the s for a season	Acts 13:11	2246
above the brightness of the s	Acts 26:13	2246
when neither s nor stars in many	Acts 27:20	2246
There is one glory of the s	1Cor 15:41	2246
let not the s go down upon your	Eph 4:26	2246
For the s is no sooner risen with	Jas 1:11	2246
as the s shineth in his strength	Rev 1:16	2246
the s became black as sackcloth	Rev 6:12	2246
neither shall the s light on them	Rev 7:16	2246
third part of the s was smitten	Rev 8:12	2246
and the s and the air were darkened	Rev 9:2	2246
and his face was as it were the s	Rev 10:1	2246
a woman clothed with the s	Rev 12:1	2246
poured out his vial upon the s	Rev 16:8	2246
I saw an angel standing in the s	Rev 19:17	2246

S

And the city had no need of the *s* .... Rev 21:23   2246
no candle, neither light of the *s* .... Rev 22:5   2246

SUNDER
bow, and cutteth the spear in *s* .... Ps 46:9
death, and brake their bands in *s* .... Ps 107:14
and cut the bars of iron in *s* .... Ps 107:16
chalkstones that are beaten in *s* .... Is 27:9
cut in *s* the bars of iron .... Is 45:2
and will burst thy bonds in *s* .... Nah 1:13
not aware, and will cut him in *s* .... Lk 12:46

SUNDERED
together, that they cannot be *s* .... Job 41:17   6504

SUNDRY
God, who at *s* times and in divers .... Heb 1:1   4181

SUNG
song be *s* in the land of Judah .... Is 26:1   7891
And when they had *s* an hymn .... Mt 26:30   5214
And when they had *s* an hymn .... Mk 14:26   5214
they *s* a new song, saying, Thou .... Rev 5:9   103
they *s* as it were a new song.................. Rev 14:3   103

SUNK
that the stone *s* into his 1Sa 17:49   2883
and he *s* down in his chariot 2Kin 9:24   3766
The heathen are *s* down in the pit .... Ps 9:15   2883
so Jeremiah *s* in the mire .... Jer 38:6   2883
thy feet are *s* in the mire .... Jer 38:22   2883
Her gates are *s* into the ground .... Lam 2:9   2883
he *s* down with sleep, and fell .... Acts 20:9   2702

SUNRISING
is before Moab, toward the *s* .... Num 21:11   4217,8121
Jericho eastward, toward the *s* .... Num 34:15   4217
on this side Jordan toward the *s* ..... Deut 4:41   4217,8121
on this side Jordan toward the *s* ..... Deut 4:47   4217,8121
on this side Jordan toward the *s* ..... Josh 1:15   4217,8121
and all Lebanon, toward the *s* .... Josh 13:5   4217,8121
toward the *s* unto the border of....... Josh 19:12   4217,8121
toward the *s* to Beth-dagon .... Josh 19:27   4217,8121
to Judah upon Jordan toward the *s* Josh 19:34   4217,8121
over against Gibeah toward the *s*... Judg 20:43   4217,8121

SUP
their faces shall *s* up as the .... Hab 1:9   4041
him, Make ready wherewith I may *s* ..... Lk 17:8   1172
will *s* with him, and he with me .... Rev 3:20   1172

SUPERFLUITY
s of naughtiness, and receive with.......... Jas 1:21   4050

SUPERFLUOUS
hath a flat nose, or any thing............... Lev 21:18   8311
thing *s* or lacking in his parts................ Lev 22:23   8311
it is *s* for me to write to you 2Cor 9:1   4053

SUPERSCRIPTION
them, Whose is this image and *s* ...... Mt 22:20   1923
them, Whose is this image and *s* .... Mk 12:16   1923
the *s* of his accusation was.................... Mk 15:26   1923
Whose image and *s* hath it .... Lk 20:24   1923
a *s* also was written over him in .... Lk 23:38   1923

SUPERSTITION
against him of their own *s* .... Acts 25:19   1175

SUPERSTITIOUS
that in all things ye are too *s*................. Acts 17:22   1174

SUPPED
he took the cup, when he had *s* 1Cor 11:25   1172

SUPPER
birthday made a *s* to his lords .... Mk 6:21   1173
When thou makest a dinner or a *s*...... Lk 14:12   1173
him, A certain man made a great *s* .... Lk 14:16   1173
sent his servant at *s* time to say .... Lk 14:17   1173
were bidden shall taste of my *s* .... Lk 14:24   1173
Likewise also the cup after *s* .... Lk 22:20   1172
There they made him a *s*........................ Jn 12:2   1173
s being ended, the devil having.............. Jn 13:2   1173
He riseth from *s*, and laid aside .... Jn 13:4   1173
also leaned on his breast at *s* .... Jn 21:20   1173
this is not to eat the Lord's *s*,................ 1Cor 11:20   1173
one taketh before other his own *s*.......... 1Cor 11:21   1173
unto the marriage *s* of the Lamb .... Rev 19:9   1173
unto the *s* of the great God .... Rev 19:17   1173

SUPPLANT
for every brother will utterly *s* .... Jer 9:4   6117

SUPPLANTED
for he hath *s* me these two times........... Gen 27:36   6117

SUPPLE
thou washed in water to *s* thee .... Eze 16:4   4935

SUPPLIANTS
the rivers of Ethiopia my *s* .... Zeph 3:10   6282

SUPPLICATION
I have not made *s* unto the LORD 1Sa 13:12   2420
of thy servant, and to his *s* 1Kin 8:28   8467
thou to the *s* of thy servant 1Kin 8:30   8467
make *s* unto thee in this house 1Kin 8:33   2603
s soever be made by any man, or 1Kin 8:38   8467
in heaven their prayer and their *s* 1Kin 8:45   8467
make *s* unto thee in the land of 1Kin 8:47   2603
their *s* in heaven thy dwelling 1Kin 8:49   8467
be open unto the *s* of thy servant 1Kin 8:52   8467
unto the *s* of thy people Israel,.............. 1Kin 8:52   8467
s unto the LORD, he arose from 1Kin 8:54   8467
I have made *s* before the LORD 1Kin 8:59   2603
I have heard thy prayer and thy *s* 1Kin 9:3   8467
of thy servant, and to his *s* 2Chr 6:19   8467
make *s* before thee in this house 2Chr 6:24   2603
Then what prayer or what *s* soever 2Chr 6:29   8467
heavens their prayer and their *s* 2Chr 6:35   8467
intreated of him, and heard his *s*........... 2Chr 33:13   8467
to make *s* unto him, and to make .... Est 4:8   2603
make thy *s* to the Almighty .... Job 8:5   2603
but I would make *s* to my judge............. Job 9:15   2603
The LORD hath heard my *s* .... Ps 6:9   8467
and unto the LORD I made *s* .... Ps 30:8   2603
and hide not thyself from my *s* .... Ps 55:1   8467
Let my *s* come before thee .... Ps 119:170   8467
unto the LORD did I make my *s* .... Ps 142:1   2603
thee, they shall make *s* unto thee .... Is 45:14   6419
present their *s* before the LORD .... Jer 36:7   8467
let my *s*, I pray thee, be .... Jer 37:20   8467
I presented my *s* before the king,........... Jer 38:26   8467
our *s* be accepted before thee, and .... Jer 42:2   8467
me to present your *s* before him .... Jer 42:9   8467
and making *s* before his God .... Dan 6:11   2604
presenting my *s* before the LORD .... Dan 9:20   8467
he wept, and made *s* unto him............... Hos 12:4   2603
with one accord in prayer and *s* .... Acts 1:14   1162
s in the Spirit, and watching .... Eph 6:18   1162
perseverance and *s* for all saints .... Eph 6:18   1162
s with thanksgiving let your .... Phil 4:6   1162

SUPPLICATIONS
unto the *s* of thy servant 2Chr 6:21   8469
place, their prayer and their *s*................ 2Chr 6:39   8467
Will he make many *s* unto thee .... Job 41:3   8469
Hear the voice of my *s*, when I............... Ps 28:2   8469
he hath heard the voice of my *s* .... Ps 28:6   8469
of my *s* when I cried unto thee .... Ps 31:22   8469
and attend to the voice of my *s* .... Ps 86:6   8469
he hath heard my voice and my *s* .... Ps 116:1   8469
be attentive to the voice of my *s* .... Ps 130:2   8469
hear the voice of my *s*, O LORD .... Ps 140:6   8469
prayer, O LORD, give ear to my *s* .... Ps 143:1   8469
s of the children of Israel........................ Jer 3:21   8469
and with *s* will I lead them .... Jer 31:9   8469
Lord God, to seek by prayer and *s* .... Dan 9:3   8469
prayer of thy servant, and his *s* .... Dan 9:17   8469
present our *s* before thee for our .... Dan 9:18   8469
At the beginning of thy *s* the .... Dan 9:23   8469
the spirit of grace and of *s* .... Zec 12:10   8469
therefore, that, first of all, *s*.................. 1Ti 2:1   1162
in God, and continueth in *s* 1Ti 5:5   1162
s with strong crying and tears................ Heb 5:7   2428

SUPPLIED
lacking on your part they have *s* 1Cor 16:17   378
which came from Macedonia *s* 2Cor 11:9   4322

SUPPLIETH
not only *s* the want of the saints 2Cor 9:12   4322
by that which every joint *s* .... Eph 4:16   2024

SUPPLY
may be a *s* for their want 2Cor 8:14
also may be a *s* for your want................ 2Cor 8:14
the *s* of the Spirit of Jesus .... Phil 1:19   2024
to *s* your lack of service toward .... Phil 2:30   378
But my God shall *s* all your need .... Phil 4:19   4137

SUPPORT
labouring ye ought to *s* the weak .... Acts 20:35   482
s the weak, be patient toward all........... 1Th 5:14   472

SUPPOSE
Let not my lord *s* that they have............ 2Sa 13:32   559
I *s* that he, to whom he forgave............. Lk 7:43   5274
S ye that I am come to give peace .... Lk 12:51   1380
S ye that these Galilaeans were .... Lk 13:2   1380
I *s* that even the world itself................... Jn 21:25   3633
these are not drunken, as ye *s* .... Acts 2:15   5274
I *s* therefore that this is good 1Cor 7:26   3543

For I *s* I was not a whit behind	2Cor 11:5	3049
s ye, shall he be thought worthy,	Heb 10:29	1380
faithful brother unto you, as I *s*	1Pet 5:12	3049

SUPPOSED

they *s* that they should have	Mt 20:10	3543
they *s* it had been a spirit, and	Mk 6:49	1380
being (as was *s*) the son of	Lk 3:23	3543
s that they had seen a spirit	Lk 24:37	1380
For he *s* his brethren would have	Acts 7:25	3543
whom they *s* that Paul had brought	Acts 21:29	3543
accusation of such things as I *s*	Acts 25:18	5282
Yet I *s* it necessary to send to	Phil 2:25	2233

SUPPOSING

s him to have been in the company	Lk 2:44	3543
s him to be the gardener, saith	Jn 20:15	1380
of the city, *s* he had been dead	Acts 14:19	3543
s that the prisoners had been	Acts 16:27	3543
s that they had obtained their	Acts 27:13	1380
s to add affliction to my bonds	Phil 1:16	3633
truth, *s* that gain is godliness	1Ti 6:5	3543

SUPREME

whether it be to the king, as *s*	1Pet 2:13	5242

SUR (sur) *A gate of the Temple.*

part shall be at the gate of S	2Kin 11:6	5495

SURE

borders round about, were made *s*	Gen 23:17	6965
were made *s* unto Abraham for a	Gen 23:20	6965
I am *s* that the king of Egypt	Ex 3:19	3045
be *s* your sin will find you out	Num 32:23	3045
Only be *s* that thou eat not the	Deut 12:23	2388
and I will build him a *s* house	1Sa 2:35	539
then be *s* that evil is determined	1Sa 20:7	3045
certainly make my lord a *s* house	1Sa 25:28	539
because I was *s* that he could not	2Sa 1:10	3045
ordered in all things, and *s*	2Sa 23:5	8104
thee, and build thee a *s* house	1Kin 11:38	539
of all this we make a *s* covenant	Neh 9:38	548
riseth up, and no man is *s* of life	Job 24:22	539
the testimony of the LORD is *s*	Ps 19:7	539
Thy testimonies are very *s*	Ps 93:5	539
all his commandments are *s*	Ps 111:7	539
thyself, and make *s* thy friend	Prov 6:3	7292
and he that hateth suretiship is *s*	Prov 11:15	982
righteousness shall be a *s* reward	Prov 11:18	571
fasten him as a nail in a *s* place	Is 22:23	539
in the *s* place be removed	Is 22:25	539
corner stone, a *s* foundation	Is 28:16	3245
in *s* dwellings, and in quiet	Is 32:18	4009
his waters shall be *s*	Is 33:16	539
even the *s* mercies of David	Is 55:3	539
and the interpretation thereof *s*	Dan 2:45	546
thy kingdom shall be *s* unto thee	Dan 4:26	7011
be made *s* until the third day	Mt 27:64	805
your way, make it as *s* as ye can	Mt 27:65	805
went, and made the sepulchre *s*	Mt 27:66	805
notwithstanding be ye *s* of this	Lk 10:11	1097
are *s* that thou art that Christ,	Jn 6:69	1097
Now are we *s* that thou knowest	Jn 16:30	1492
give you the *s* mercies of David	Acts 13:34	4103
But we are *s* that the judgment of	Rom 2:2	1492
might be *s* to all the seed	Rom 4:16	949
And I am *s* that, when I come unto	Rom 15:29	1492
the foundation of God standeth *s*	2Ti 2:19	4731
as an anchor of the soul, both *s*	Heb 6:19	804
make your calling and election *s*	2Pet 1:10	949
also a more *s* word of prophecy	2Pet 1:19	949

SURELY See APPENDIX.

SURETIES

or of them that are *s* for debts	Prov 22:26	6148

SURETISHIP

and he that hateth *s* is sure	Prov 11:15	8628

SURETY

Know of a *s* that thy seed shall	Gen 15:13	3045
Shall I of a *s* bear a child	Gen 18:13	552
Behold, of a *s* she is thy wife	Gen 26:9	389
I will be *s* for him	Gen 43:9	6148
For thy servant became *s* for the	Gen 44:32	6148
down now, put me in a *s* with thee	Job 17:3	6148
Be *s* for thy servant for good	Ps 119:122	6148
if thou be *s* for thy friend, if	Prov 6:1	6148
He that is *s* for a stranger shall	Prov 11:15	6148
becometh *s* in the presence of his	Prov 17:18	6161
garment that is *s* for a stranger	Prov 20:16	6148
garment that is *s* for a stranger	Prov 27:13	6148
he said, Now I know of a *s*	Acts 12:11	230
made a *s* of a better testament	Heb 7:22	1450

SURFEITING

your hearts be overcharged with *s*	Lk 21:34	2897

SURMISINGS

envy, strife, railings, evil *s*	1Ti 6:4	5283

SURNAME

s himself by the name of Israel	Is 44:5	3655
Lebbaeus, whose *s* was Thaddaeus	Mt 10:3	1941
for one Simon, whose *s* is Peter	Acts 10:5	1941
hither Simon, whose *s* is Peter	Acts 10:32	1941
call for Simon, whose *s* is Peter	Acts 11:13	1941
mother of John, whose *s* was Mark	Acts 12:12	1941
with them John, whose *s* was Mark	Acts 12:25	1941
with them John, whose *s* was Mark	Acts 15:37	2564

SURNAMED

I have *s* thee, though thou hast	Is 45:4	3655
And Simon he *s* Peter	Mk 3:16	2007,3686
he *s* them Boanerges, which is,	Mk 3:17	2007,3686
Satan into Judas *s* Iscariot	Lk 22:3	1941
called Barsabas, who was *s* Justus	Acts 1:23	1941
by the apostles was *s* Barnabas	Acts 4:36	1941
whether Simon, which was *s* Peter	Acts 10:18	1941
Judas *s* Barsabas, and Silas, chief	Acts 15:22	1941

SURPRISED

fearfulness hath *s* the hypocrites	Is 33:14	270
taken, and the strong holds are *s*	Jer 48:41	8610
the praise of the whole earth *s*	Jer 51:41	8610

SUSA See SHUSHAN, SUSANCHITES.

SUSANCHITES (su'-san-kites) *Resettled foreigners in Israel.*

the Babylonians, the S, the	Ezr 4:9	7801

SUSANNA (su'-zan'-nah) *A woman follower of Jesus.*

of Chuza Herod's steward, and S	Lk 8:3	4677

SUSI (su'-si) *Father of Gaddi.*

of Manasseh, Gaddi the son of S	Num 13:11	5485

SUSTAIN

a widow woman there to *s* thee	1Kin 17:9	3557
thou *s* them in the wilderness	Neh 9:21	3557
upon the LORD, and he shall *s* thee	Ps 55:22	3557
of a man will *s* his infirmity	Prov 18:14	3557

SUSTAINED

and with corn and wine have I *s* him	Gen 27:37	5564
for the LORD *s* me	Ps 3:5	5564
and his righteousness, it *s* him	Is 59:16	5564

SUSTENANCE

left no *s* for Israel, neither	Judg 6:4	4241
of *s* while he lay at Mahanaim	2Sa 19:32	3557
and our fathers found no *s*	Acts 7:11	5527

SWADDLED

those that I have *s* and brought up	Lam 2:22	2946
not salted at all, nor *s* at all	Eze 16:4	2853

SWADDLING

son, and wrapped him in *s* clothes	Lk 2:7	4683
the babe wrapped in *s* clothes	Lk 2:12	4683

SWADDLINGBAND

and thick darkness a *s* for it	Job 38:9	2854

SWALLOW

and *s* them up, with all that	Num 16:30	1104
said, Lest the earth *s* us up also	Num 16:34	1104
why wilt thou *s* up the	2Sa 20:19	1104
me, that I should *s* up or destroy	2Sa 20:20	1104
me alone till I *s* down my spittle	Job 7:19	1104
restore, and shall not *s* it down	Job 20:18	1104
the LORD shall *s* them up in his	Ps 21:9	1104
for man would *s* me up	Ps 56:1	7602
Mine enemies would daily *s* me up	Ps 56:2	7602
of him that would *s* me up	Ps 57:3	7602
me, neither let the deep *s* me up	Ps 69:15	1104
the *s* a nest for herself, where	Ps 84:3	1866
Let us *s* them up alive as the	Prov 1:12	1104
as the *s* by flying, so the curse	Prov 26:2	1866
lips of a fool will *s* up himself	Eccl 10:12	1104
He will *s* up death in victory	Is 25:8	1104
Like a crane or a *s*, so did I	Is 38:14	5693
the *s* observe the time of their	Jer 8:7	5693
the strangers shall *s* it up	Hos 8:7	1104
O ye that *s* up them selves, even to	Amos 8:4	7602
shall drink, and they shall *s* down	Obad 16	3886
a great fish to *s* up Jonah	Jonah 1:17	1104
strain at a gnat, and *s* a camel	Mt 23:24	2666

SWALLOWED

but Aaron's rod *s* up their rods	Ex 7:12	1104
thy right hand, the earth *s* them	Ex 15:12	1104
s them up, and their houses, and	Num 16:32	1104

S

s them up together with Korah,	Num 26:10	1104
s them up, and their households,	Deut 11:6	1104
lest the king be *s* up, and all the	2Sa 17:16	1104
therefore my words are *s* up	Job 6:3	3886
He hath *s* down riches, and he	Job 20:15	1104
speak, surely he shall be *s* up	Job 37:20	1104
them not say, We have *s* him up	Ps 35:25	1104
s up Dathan, and covered the	Ps 106:17	1104
Then they had *s* us up quick	Ps 124:3	1104
they are *s* up of wine, they are	Is 28:7	1104
they that *s* thee up shall be far	Is 49:19	1104
he hath *s* me up like a dragon, he	Jer 51:34	1104
his mouth that which he hath *s* up	Jer 51:44	1105
The Lord hath *s* up all the	Lam 2:2	1104
he hath *s* up Israel, he hath	Lam 2:5	1104
he hath *s* up all her palaces	Lam 2:5	1104
they say, We have *s* her up	Lam 2:16	1104
s you up on every side, that ye	Eze 36:3	7602
Israel is *s* up	Hos 8:8	1104
written, Death is *s* up in victory	1Cor 15:54	2666
be *s* up with overmuch sorrow	2Cor 2:7	2666
mortality might be *s* up of life	2Cor 5:4	2666
s up the flood which the dragon	Rev 12:16	2666

SWALLOWETH

the robber *s* up their substance	Job 5:5	7602
He *s* the ground with fierceness	Job 39:24	1572

SWAN

And the *s*, and the pelican, and the	Lev 11:18	8580
owl, and the great owl, and the *s*	Deut 14:16	8580

SWARE

because there they *s* both of them	Gen 21:31	7650
that *s* unto me, saying, Unto thy	Gen 24:7	7650
s to him concerning that matter	Gen 24:9	7650
and he *s* unto him	Gen 25:33	7650
which I *s* unto Abraham thy father	Gen 26:3	7650
the morning, and *s* one to another	Gen 26:31	7650
Jacob *s* by the fear of his father	Gen 31:53	7650
And he *s* unto him	Gen 47:31	7650
the land which he *s* to Abraham	Gen 50:24	7650
which he *s* unto thy fathers to	Ex 13:5	7650
as he *s* unto thee and to thy	Ex 13:11	7650
the land which I *s* unto Abraham	Ex 33:1	7650
the land which he *s* unto them	Num 14:16	7650
land which I *s* unto their fathers	Num 14:23	7650
concerning which I *s* to make you	Num 14:30	5375
kindled the same time, and he *s*	Num 32:10	7650
the land which I *s* unto Abraham	Num 32:11	7650
the LORD *s* unto your fathers	Deut 1:8	7650
of your words, and was wroth, and *s*	Deut 1:34	7650
which I *s* to give unto your	Deut 1:35	7650
the host, as the LORD *s* unto them	Deut 2:14	7650
s that I should not go over	Deut 4:21	7650
thy fathers which he *s* unto them	Deut 4:31	7650
land which he *s* unto thy fathers	Deut 6:10	7650
which the LORD *s* unto thy fathers	Deut 6:18	7650
land which he *s* unto our fathers	Deut 6:23	7650
mercy which he *s* unto thy fathers	Deut 7:12	7650
in the land which he *s* unto thy	Deut 7:13	7650
the LORD *s* unto your fathers	Deut 8:1	7650
which he *s* unto thy fathers	Deut 8:18	7650
which the LORD *s* unto thy fathers	Deut 9:5	7650
which I *s* unto their fathers to	Deut 10:11	7650
which the LORD *s* unto your	Deut 11:9	7650
in the land which the LORD *s* unto	Deut 11:21	7650
s unto our fathers for to give us	Deut 26:3	7650
in the land which the LORD *s* unto	Deut 28:11	7650
which the LORD *s* unto thy fathers	Deut 30:20	7650
land which I *s* unto their fathers	Deut 31:20	7650
them into the land which I *s*	Deut 31:21	7650
into the land which I *s* unto them	Deut 31:23	7650
the land which I *s* unto Abraham	Deut 34:4	7650
which I *s* unto their fathers to	Josh 1:6	7650
unto whom the LORD *s* that he	Josh 5:6	7650
which the LORD *s* unto them	Josh 5:6	7650
that she hath, as ye *s* unto her	Josh 6:22	7650
of the congregation *s* unto them	Josh 9:15	7650
of the oath which we *s* unto them	Josh 9:20	7650
Moses *s* on that day, saying,	Josh 14:9	7650
he *s* to give unto their fathers	Josh 21:43	7650
all that he *s* unto their fathers	Josh 21:44	7650
land which I *s* unto your fathers	Judg 2:1	7650
and Saul *s*, As the LORD liveth, he	1Sa 19:6	7650
David *s* moreover, and said, Thy	1Sa 20:3	7650
And David *s* unto Saul	1Sa 24:22	7650
Saul *s* to her by the LORD, saying	1Sa 28:10	7650
while it was yet day, David *s*	2Sa 3:35	7650
And the king *s* unto him	2Sa 19:23	7650
Then the men of David *s* unto him	2Sa 21:17	7650
And the king *s*, and said, As the	1Kin 1:29	7650

Even as I *s* unto thee by the LORD	1Kin 1:30	7650
I *s* to him by the LORD, saying, I	1Kin 2:8	7650
Then king Solomon *s* by the LORD	1Kin 2:23	7650
And Gedaliah *s* to them, and to	2Kin 25:24	7650
they *s* unto the LORD with a loud	2Chr 15:14	7650
And they *s*	Ezr 10:5	7650
Unto whom I *s* in my wrath that	Ps 95:11	7650
How he *s* unto the LORD, and vowed	Ps 132:2	7650
So Zedekiah the king *s* secretly	Jer 38:16	7650
the son of Shaphan *s* unto them	Jer 40:9	7650
I *s* unto thee, and entered into a	Eze 16:8	7650
s by him that liveth for ever	Dan 12:7	7650
he *s* unto her, Whatsoever thou	Mk 6:23	3660
The oath which he *s* to our father	Lk 1:73	3660
So I *s* in my wrath, They shall	Heb 3:11	3660
to whom *s* he that they should not	Heb 3:18	3660
by no greater, he *s* by himself,	Heb 6:13	3660
that said unto him, The Lord *s*	Heb 7:21	3660
s by him that liveth for ever and	Rev 10:6	3660

SWAREST

to whom thou *s* by thine own self,	Ex 32:13	7650
which thou *s* unto their fathers	Num 11:12	7650
as thou *s* unto our fathers, a	Deut 26:15	7650
thou *s* by the LORD thy God unto	1Kin 1:17	7650
which thou *s* unto David in thy	Ps 89:49	7650

SWARM

there came a grievous *s* of flies	Ex 8:24	6157
by reason of the *s* of flies	Ex 8:24	6157
and, behold, there was a *s* of bees	Judg 14:8	5712

SWARMS

I will send *s* of flies upon thee,	Ex 8:21	6157
shall be full of *s* of flies	Ex 8:21	6157
that no *s* of flies shall be there	Ex 8:22	6157
the *s* of flies may depart from	Ex 8:29	6157
he removed the *s* of flies from	Ex 8:31	6157

SWEAR

Now therefore *s* unto me here by	Gen 21:23	7650
And Abraham said, I will *s*	Gen 21:24	7650
And I will make thee *s* by the LORD	Gen 24:3	7650
And my master made me *s*, saying,	Gen 24:37	7650
And Jacob said, *S* to me this day	Gen 25:33	7650
And he said, *S* unto me	Gen 47:31	7650
My father made me *s*, saying, Lo,	Gen 50:5	7650
according as he made thee *s*	Gen 50:6	7650
I did *s* to give it to Abraham	Ex 6:8	5375
Or if a soul *s*, pronouncing with	Lev 5:4	7650
ye shall not *s* by my name falsely	Lev 19:12	7650
or *s* an oath to bind his soul	Num 30:2	7650
serve him, and shalt *s* by his name	Deut 6:13	7650
thou cleave, and *s* by his name	Deut 10:20	7650
s unto me by the LORD, since I	Josh 2:12	7650
oath which thou hast made us *s*	Josh 2:17	7650
oath which thou hast made us to *s*	Josh 2:20	7650
gods, nor cause to *s* by them	Josh 23:7	7650
S unto me, that ye will not fall	Judg 15:12	7650
Jonathan caused David to *s* again	1Sa 20:17	7650
S now therefore unto me by the	1Sa 24:21	7650
S unto me by God, that thou wilt	1Sa 30:15	7650
for I *s* by the LORD, if thou go	2Sa 19:7	7650
s unto thine handmaid, saying,	1Kin 1:13	7650
Let king Solomon *s* unto me to day	1Kin 1:51	7650
I not make thee to *s* by the LORD	1Kin 2:42	7650
laid upon him to cause him to *s*	1Kin 8:31	422
be laid upon him to make him *s*	2Chr 6:22	422
who had made him *s* by God	2Chr 36:13	7650
Israel, to *s* that they should do	Ezr 10:5	7650
their hair, and made them *s* by God	Neh 13:25	7650
In that day shall he *s*, saying, I	Is 3:7	5375
Canaan, and *s* to the LORD of hosts	Is 19:18	7650
shall bow, every tongue shall *s*	Is 45:23	7650
which *s* by the name of the LORD,	Is 48:1	7650
earth shall *s* by the God of truth	Is 65:16	7650
And thou shalt *s*, The LORD liveth,	Jer 4:2	7650
surely they *s* falsely	Jer 5:2	7650
s falsely, and burn incense unto	Jer 7:9	7650
to *s* by my name, The LORD liveth	Jer 12:16	7650
taught my people to *s* by Baal	Jer 12:16	7650
I *s* by myself, saith the LORD,	Jer 22:5	7650
which thou didst *s* to their	Jer 32:22	7650
go ye up to Beth-aven, nor *s*	Hos 4:15	7650
They that *s* by the sin of Samaria	Amos 8:14	7650
that *s* by the LORD	Zeph 1:5	7650
and that *s* by Malcham	Zeph 1:5	7650
But I say unto you, *S* not at all	Mt 5:34	3660
Neither shalt thou *s* by thy head	Mt 5:36	3660
Whosoever shall *s* by the temple	Mt 23:16	3660
but whosoever shall *s* by the gold	Mt 23:16	3660
Whosoever shall *s* by the altar	Mt 23:18	3660
therefore shall *s* by the altar	Mt 23:20	3660

whoso shall s by the temple,	Mt 23:21	3660
And he that shall s by heaven	Mt 23:22	3660
Then began he to curse and to s	Mt 26:74	3660
But he began to curse and to s	Mk 14:71	3660
because he could s by no greater	Heb 6:13	3660
For men verily s by the greater	Heb 6:16	3660
s not, neither by heaven, neither	Jas 5:12	3660

SWEARERS

adulterers, and against false s	Mal 3:5	7650

SWEARETH

lieth concerning it, and s falsely	Lev 6:3	7650
He that s to his own hurt, and	Ps 15:4	7650
every one that s by him shall	Ps 63:11	7650
and he that s, as he that feareth	Eccl 9:2	7650
he that s in the earth shall	Is 65:16	7650
every one that s shall be cut off	Zec 5:3	7650
of him that s falsely by my name	Zec 5:4	7650
but whosoever s by the gift that	Mt 23:18	3660
s by it, and by all things thereon	Mt 23:20	3660
s by it, and by him that dwelleth	Mt 23:21	3660
s by the throne of God, and by him	Mt 23:22	3660

SWEARING

soul sin, and hear the voice of s	Lev 5:1	423
for because of s the land	Jer 23:10	423
By s, and lying, and killing, and	Hos 4:2	422
s falsely in making a covenant	Hos 10:4	422

SWEAT

In the s of thy face shalt thou	Gen 3:19	2188
with any thing that causeth s	Eze 44:18	3154
his s was as it were great drops	Lk 22:44	2402

SWEEP

I will s it with the besom of	Is 14:23	2894
the hail shall s away the refuge	Is 28:17	3261
s the house, and seek diligently	Lk 15:8	4563

SWEEPING

a s rain which leaveth no food	Prov 28:3	5502

SWEET

And the LORD smelled a s savour	Gen 8:21	5207
waters, the waters were made s	Ex 15:25	4985
anointing oil, and for s incense,	Ex 25:6	5561
it is a s savour, an offering	Ex 29:18	5207
for a s savour before the LORD	Ex 29:25	5207
for a s savour, an offering made	Ex 29:41	5207
thereon s incense every morning	Ex 30:7	5561
of s cinnamon half so much, even	Ex 30:23	1314
of s calamus two hundred and fifty	Ex 30:23	1314
Moses, Take unto thee s spices	Ex 30:34	5561
these s spices with pure	Ex 30:34	5561
s incense for the holy place	Ex 31:11	5561
oil, and for the s incense	Ex 35:8	5561
the s incense, and the hanging for	Ex 35:15	5561
oil, and for the s incense	Ex 35:28	5561
and the pure incense of s spices	Ex 37:29	5561
the s incense, and the hanging for	Ex 39:38	5561
he burnt s incense thereon	Ex 40:27	5561
of a s savour unto the LORD	Lev 1:9	5207
of a s savour unto the LORD	Lev 1:13	5207
of a s savour unto the LORD	Lev 1:17	5207
of a s savour unto the LORD	Lev 2:2	5207
of a s savour unto the LORD	Lev 2:9	5207
burnt on the altar for a s savour	Lev 2:12	5207
of a s savour unto the LORD	Lev 3:5	5207
made by fire for a s savour	Lev 3:16	5207
of s incense before the LORD	Lev 4:7	5561
for a s savour unto the LORD	Lev 4:31	5207
it upon the altar for a s savour	Lev 6:15	5207
for a s savour unto the LORD	Lev 6:21	5207
a burnt sacrifice for a s savour	Lev 8:21	5207
were consecrations for a s savour	Lev 8:28	5207
his hands full of s incense	Lev 16:12	5561
burn the fat for a s savour unto	Lev 17:6	5207
fire unto the LORD for a s savour	Lev 23:13	5207
of s savour unto the LORD	Lev 23:18	5207
smell the savour of your s odours	Lev 26:31	5207
the s incense, and the daily meat	Num 4:16	5561
to make a s savour unto the LORD,	Num 15:3	5207
for a s savour unto the LORD	Num 15:7	5207
of a s savour unto the LORD	Num 15:10	5207
of a s savour unto the LORD	Num 15:13	5207
of a s savour unto the LORD	Num 15:14	5207
for a s savour unto the LORD,	Num 15:24	5207
for a s savour unto the LORD	Num 18:17	5207
for a s savour unto me, shall ye	Num 28:2	5207
in mount Sinai for a s savour	Num 28:6	5207
of a s savour unto the LORD	Num 28:8	5207
a burnt offering of a s savour	Num 28:13	5207
of a s savour unto the LORD	Num 28:24	5207

for a s savour unto the LORD	Num 28:27	5207
for a s savour unto the LORD	Num 29:2	5207
for a s savour, a sacrifice made	Num 29:6	5207
unto the LORD for a s savour	Num 29:8	5207
of a s savour unto the LORD	Num 29:13	5207
of a s savour unto the LORD	Num 29:36	5207
the s psalmist of Israel, said,	2Sa 23:1	5273
and to burn before him s incense	2Chr 2:4	5561
burnt sacrifices and s incense	2Chr 13:11	5561
which was filled with s odours	2Chr 16:14	1314
they may offer sacrifices of s	Ezr 6:10	5208
way, eat the fat, and drink the s	Neh 8:10	4477
and six months with s odours	Est 2:12	1314
wickedness be s in his mouth	Job 20:12	4985
of the valley shall be s unto him	Job 21:33	4985
Canst thou bind the s influences	Job 38:31	4575
We took s counsel together, and	Ps 55:14	4985
My meditation of him shall be s	Ps 104:34	6148
How s are thy words unto my taste	Ps 119:103	4452
for they are s	Ps 141:6	5276
lie down, and thy sleep shall be s	Prov 3:24	6148
Stolen waters are s, and bread	Prov 9:17	4985
accomplished is s to the soul	Prov 13:19	6148
s to the soul, and health to the	Prov 16:24	4966
Bread of deceit is s to a man	Prov 20:17	6149
vomit up, and lose thy s words	Prov 23:8	5273
which is s to thy taste	Prov 24:13	4966
soul every bitter thing is s	Prov 27:7	4966
The sleep of a labouring man is s	Eccl 5:12	4966
Truly the light is s, and a	Eccl 11:7	4966
and his fruit was s to my taste	Song 2:3	4966
for s is thy voice, and thy	Song 2:14	6149
my fingers with s smelling myrrh	Song 5:5	5674
as a bed of spices, as s flowers	Song 5:13	4840
dropping s smelling myrrh	Song 5:13	5674
His mouth is most s	Song 5:16	4477
that instead of s smell there	Is 3:24	1314
bitter for s, and s for bitter	Is 5:20	4966
make s melody, sing many songs,	Is 23:16	3190
bought me no s cane with money	Is 43:24	7070
their own blood, as with s wine	Is 49:26	6071
the s cane from a far country	Jer 6:20	2896
nor your sacrifices s unto me	Jer 6:20	6148
and my sleep was s unto me	Jer 31:26	6148
offer s savour to all their idols	Eze 6:13	5207
set it before them for a s savour	Eze 16:19	5207
also they made their s savour	Eze 20:28	5207
accept you with your s savour	Eze 20:41	5207
an oblation and s odours unto him	Dan 2:46	5208
the mountains shall drop s wine	Amos 9:13	6071
s wine, but shalt not drink wine	Mic 6:15	8492
and Salome, had bought s spices	Mk 16:1	
are unto God a s savour of Christ	2Cor 2:15	2175
from you, an odour of a s smell	Phil 4:18	2175
forth at the same place s water	Jas 3:11	1099
shall be in thy mouth s as honey	Rev 10:9	1099
and it was in my mouth s as honey	Rev 10:10	1099

SWEETER

went down, What is s than honey	Judg 14:18	4966
s also than honey and the	Ps 19:10	4966
yea, s than honey to my mouth	Ps 119:103	

SWEETLY

the worm shall feed s on him	Job 24:20	4988
for my beloved, that goeth down s	Song 7:9	4339

SWEETNESS

unto them, Should I forsake my s	Judg 9:11	4987
and out of the strong came forth s	Judg 14:14	4966
the s of the lips increaseth	Prov 16:21	4986
so doth the s of a man's friend	Prov 27:9	4986
it was in my mouth as honey for s	Eze 3:3	4966

SWEETSMELLING

a sacrifice to God for a s savour	Eph 5:2	2175

SWELL

thigh to rot, and thy belly to s	Num 5:21	6639
bowels, to make thy belly to s	Num 5:22	6638
bitter, and her belly shall s	Num 5:27	6638
upon thee, neither did thy foot s	Deut 8:4	1216

SWELLED

not old, and their feet s not	Neh 9:21	1216

SWELLING

shake with the s thereof	Ps 46:3	1346
s out in a high wall, whose	Is 30:13	1158
wilt thou do in the s of Jordan	Jer 12:5	1347
from the s of Jordan against the	Jer 49:19	1347
come up like a lion from the s of	Jer 50:44	1347
speak great s words of vanity	2Pet 2:18	5246
mouth speaketh great s words	Jude 16	5246

S

SWELLINGS
backbitings, whisperings, s 2Cor 12:20   5450

SWEPT
The river of Kishon s them away .... Judg 5:21   1640
Why are thy valiant men s away .... Jer 46:15   5502
is come, he findeth it empty, s .... Mt 12:44   4563
when he cometh, he findeth it s .... Lk 11:25   4563

SWERVED
From which some having s have 1Ti 1:6   795

SWIFT
earth, as s as the eagle flieth .... Deut 28:49
were as s as the roes upon the 1Chr 12:8   4116
are passed away as the s ships .... Job 9:26   16
He is s as the waters .... Job 24:18   7031
feet that be s in running to .... Prov 6:18   4116
that the race is not to the s .... Eccl 9:11   7031
ye s messengers, to a nation .... Is 18:2   7031
the Lord rideth upon a s cloud .... Is 19:1   7031
and, We will ride upon the s .... Is 30:16   7031
shall they that pursue you be s .... Is 30:16   7043
upon s beasts, to my holy .... Is 66:20   3753
thou art a s dromedary traversing .... Jer 2:23   7031
Let not the s flee away, nor the .... Jer 46:6   7031
flight should perish from the s .... Amos 2:14   7031
he that is s of foot shall not .... Amos 2:15   7031
bind the chariot to the s beast .... Mic 1:13   7409
I will be a s witness against the .... Mal 3:5   4116
Their feet are s to shed blood .... Rom 3:15   3691
let every man be s to hear .... Jas 1:19   5036
upon themselves s destruction 2Pet 2:1   5031

SWIFTER
they were s than eagles, they 2Sa 1:23   7043
My days are s than a weaver's .... Job 7:6   7043
Now my days are s than a post .... Job 9:25   7043
his horses are s than eagles .... Jer 4:13   7043
Our persecutors are s than the .... Lam 4:19   7031
also are s than the leopards .... Hab 1:8   7043

SWIFTLY
his word runneth very s .... Ps 147:15   4120
they shall come with speed s .... Is 5:26   7031
beginning, being caused to fly s .... Dan 9:21   3288
and if ye recompense me, s .... Joel 3:4   7031

SWIM
and the iron did s 2Kin 6:6   6687
all the night make I my bed to s .... Ps 6:6   7811
spreadeth forth his hands to s .... Is 25:11   7811
waters were risen, waters to s in .... Eze 47:5   7813
lest any of them should s out .... Acts 27:42   1579
s should cast themselves first .... Acts 27:43   2860

SWIMMEST
thy blood the land wherein thou s .... Eze 32:6   6824

SWIMMETH
as he that s spreadeth forth his .... Is 25:11   7811

SWINE
And the s, though he divide the .... Lev 11:7   2386
And the s, because it divideth the .... Deut 14:8   2386
cast ye your pearls before s .... Mt 7:6   5519
them an herd of many s feeding .... Mt 8:30   5519
us to go away into the herd of s .... Mt 8:31   5519
out, they went into the herd of s .... Mt 8:32   5519
the whole herd of s ran violently .... Mt 8:32   5519
a great herd of s feeding .... Mk 5:11   5519
him, saying, Send us into the s .... Mk 5:12   5519
went out, and entered into the s .... Mk 5:13   5519
And they that fed the s fled .... Mk 5:14   5519
devil, and also concerning the s .... Mk 5:16   5519
of many s feeding on the mountain .... Lk 8:32   5519
of the man, and entered into the s .... Lk 8:33   5519
him into his fields to feed s .... Lk 15:15   5519
with the husks that the s did eat .... Lk 15:16   5519

SWINE'S
As a jewel of gold in a s snout .... Prov 11:22   2386
the monuments, which eat s flesh .... Is 65:4   2386
as if he offered s blood .... Is 66:3   2386
tree in the midst, eating s flesh .... Is 66:17   2386

SWOLLEN
they looked when he should have s .... Acts 28:6   4092

SWOON
the sucklings s in the streets of .... Lam 2:11   5848

SWOONED
when they s as the wounded in the .... Lam 2:12   5848

SWORD
a flaming s which turned every .... Gen 3:24   2719
by thy s shalt thou live, and .... Gen 27:40   2719

as captives taken with the s .... Gen 31:26   2719
brethren, took each man his s .... Gen 34:25   2719
his son with the edge of the s .... Gen 34:26   2719
the hand of the Amorite with my s .... Gen 48:22   2719
us with pestilence, or with the s .... Ex 5:3   2719
to put a s in their hand to slay .... Ex 5:21   2719
I will draw my s, my hand shall .... Ex 15:9   2719
his people with the edge of the s .... Ex 17:13   2719
me from the s of Pharaoh .... Ex 18:4   2719
and I will kill you with the s .... Ex 22:24   2719
Put every man his s by his side .... Ex 32:27   2719
neither shall the s go through .... Lev 26:6   2719
shall fall before you by the s .... Lev 26:7   2719
shall fall before you by the s .... Lev 26:8   2719
And I will bring a s upon you .... Lev 26:25   2719
and will draw out a s after you .... Lev 26:33   2719
shall flee, as fleeing from a s .... Lev 26:36   2719
another, as it were before a s .... Lev 26:37   2719
unto this land, to fall by the s .... Num 14:3   2719
you, and ye shall fall by the s .... Num 14:43   2719
slain with a s in the open fields .... Num 19:16   2719
come out against thee with the s .... Num 20:18   2719
smote him with the edge of the s .... Num 21:24   2719
way, and his s drawn in his hand .... Num 22:23   2719
would there were a s in mine hand .... Num 22:29   2719
way, and his s drawn in his hand .... Num 22:31   2719
son of Beor they slew with the s .... Num 31:8   2719
that city with the edge of the s .... Deut 13:15   2719
thereof, with the edge of the s .... Deut 13:15   2719
thereof with the edge of the s .... Deut 20:13   2719
an extreme burning, and with the s ...... Deut 28:22   2719
The s without, and terror within, ... Deut 32:25   2719
If I whet my glittering s .... Deut 32:41   2719
blood, and my s shall devour flesh .... Deut 32:42   2719
who is the s of thy excellency .... Deut 33:29   2719
him with his s drawn in his hand .... Josh 5:13   2719
and ass, with the edge of the s .... Josh 6:21   2719
all fallen on the edge of the s .... Josh 8:24   2719
smote it with the edge of the s .... Josh 8:24   2719
of Israel slew with the s .... Josh 10:11   2719
smote it with the edge of the s .... Josh 10:28   2719
smote it with the edge of the s .... Josh 10:30   2719
smote it with the edge of the s .... Josh 10:32   2719
smote it with the edge of the s .... Josh 10:35   2719
smote it with the edge of the s .... Josh 10:37   2719
smote them with the edge of the s .... Josh 10:39   2719
smote the king thereof with the s .... Josh 11:10   2719
therein with the edge of the s .... Josh 11:11   2719
smote them with the edge of the s .... Josh 11:12   2719
they smote with the edge of the s .... Josh 11:14   2719
of Israel slay with the s among .... Josh 13:22   2719
smote it with the edge of the s .... Josh 19:47   2719
but not with thy s, nor with thy .... Josh 24:12   2719
smitten it with the edge of the s .... Judg 1:8   2719
the city with the edge of the s .... Judg 1:25   2719
the edge of the s before Barak .... Judg 4:15   2719
fell upon the edge of the s .... Judg 4:16   2719
the s of Gideon the son of Joash .... Judg 7:14   2719
The s of the Lord, and of Gideon .... Judg 7:18   2719
The s of the Lord, and of Gideon .... Judg 7:20   2719
every man's s against his fellow .... Judg 7:22   2719
twenty thousand men that drew s .... Judg 8:10   2719
But the youth drew not his s .... Judg 8:20   2719
and said unto him, Draw thy s .... Judg 9:54   2719
smote them with the edge of the s .... Judg 18:27   2719
thousand footmen that drew s .... Judg 20:2   2719
and six thousand men that drew s .... Judg 20:15   2719
hundred thousand men that drew s .... Judg 20:17   2719
all these drew the s .... Judg 20:25   2719
all these drew the s .... Judg 20:35   2719
the city with the edge of the s .... Judg 20:37   2719
five thousand men that drew the s .... Judg 20:46   2719
smote them with the edge of the s .... Judg 20:48   2719
with the edge of the s, with the .... Judg 21:10   2719
that there was neither s nor 1Sa 13:22   2719
every man's s was against his 1Sa 14:20   2719
the people with the edge of the s 1Sa 15:8   2719
said, As thy s hath made women 1Sa 15:33   2719
girded his s upon his armour 1Sa 17:39   2719
Thou comest to me with a s 1Sa 17:45   2719
that the Lord saveth not with s 1Sa 17:47   2719
but there was no s in the hand of 1Sa 17:50   2719
the Philistine, and took his s 1Sa 17:51   2719
and his garments, even to his s 1Sa 18:4   2719
here under thine hand spear or s 1Sa 21:8   2719
my s nor my weapons with me 1Sa 21:8   2719
The s of Goliath the Philistine, ... 1Sa 21:9   2719
gave him the s of Goliath the 1Sa 22:10   2719
thou hast given him bread, and a s 1Sa 22:13   2719
smote he with the edge of the s 1Sa 22:19   2719
and sheep, with the edge of the s 1Sa 22:19   2719

men, Gird ye on every man his *s*	1Sa 25:13	2719
And they girded on every man his *s*	1Sa 25:13	2719
and David also girded on his *s*	1Sa 25:13	2719
unto his armourbearer, Draw thy *s*	1Sa 31:4	2719
Therefore Saul took a *s*, and fell	1Sa 31:4	2719
dead, he fell likewise upon his *s*	1Sa 31:5	2719
because they were fallen by the *s*	2Sa 1:12	2719
the *s* of Saul returned not empty	2Sa 1:22	2719
thrust his *s* in his fellow's side	2Sa 2:16	2719
Shall the *s* devour for ever	2Sa 2:26	2719
a staff, or that falleth on the *s*	2Sa 3:29	2719
for the *s* devoureth one as well	2Sa 11:25	2719
Uriah the Hittite with the *s*	2Sa 12:9	2719
hast slain him with the *s* of the	2Sa 12:9	2719
Now therefore the *s* shall never	2Sa 12:10	2719
the city with the edge of the *s*	2Sa 15:14	2719
that day than the *s* devoured	2Sa 18:8	2719
upon it a girdle with a *s*	2Sa 20:8	2719
to the *s* that was in Joab's hand	2Sa 20:10	2719
he being girded with a new *s*	2Sa 21:16	2719
and his hand clave unto the *s*	2Sa 23:10	2719
valiant men that drew the *s*	2Sa 24:9	2719
not slay his servant with the *s*	1Kin 1:51	2719
not put thee to death with the *s*	1Kin 2:8	2719
than he, and slew them with the *s*	1Kin 2:32	2719
And the king said, Bring me a *s*	1Kin 3:24	2719
they brought a *s* before the king	1Kin 3:24	2719
slain all the prophets with the *s*	1Kin 19:1	2719
and slain thy prophets with the *s*	1Kin 19:10	2719
and slain thy prophets with the *s*	1Kin 19:14	2719
the *s* of Hazael shall Jehu slay	1Kin 19:17	2719
the *s* of Jehu shall Elisha slay	1Kin 19:17	2719
hast taken captive with thy *s*	2Kin 6:22	2719
men wilt thou slay with the *s*	2Kin 8:12	2719
smote them with the edge of the *s*	2Kin 10:25	2719
followeth her kill with the *s*	2Kin 11:15	2719
the *s* beside the king's house	2Kin 11:20	2719
to fall by the *s* in his own land	2Kin 19:7	2719
his sons smote him with the *s*	2Kin 19:37	2719
men able to bear buckler and *s*	1Chr 5:18	2719
to his armourbearer, Draw thy *s*	1Chr 10:4	2719
So Saul took a *s*, and fell upon it	1Chr 10:4	2719
dead, he fell likewise on the *s*	1Chr 10:5	2719
hundred thousand men that drew *s*	1Chr 21:5	2719
and ten thousand men that drew *s*	1Chr 21:5	2719
while that the *s* of thine enemies	1Chr 21:12	2719
else three days the *s* of the Lord	1Chr 21:12	2719
having a drawn *s* in his hand	1Chr 21:16	2719
he put up his *s* again into the	1Chr 21:27	2719
of the *s* of the angel of the Lord	1Chr 21:30	2719
evil cometh upon us, as the *s*	2Chr 20:9	2719
slew all his brethren with the *s*	2Chr 21:4	2719
her, let him be slain with the *s*	2Chr 23:14	2719
had slain Athaliah with the *s*	2Chr 23:21	2719
our fathers have fallen by the *s*	2Chr 29:9	2719
bowels slew him there with the *s*	2Chr 32:21	2719
slew their young men with the *s*	2Chr 36:17	2719
the *s* carried he away to Babylon	2Chr 36:20	2719
the kings of the lands, to the *s*	Ezr 9:7	2719
every one had his *s* girded by his	Neh 4:18	2719
enemies with the stroke of the *s*	Est 9:5	2719
servants with the edge of the *s*	Job 1:15	2719
servants with the edge of the *s*	Job 1:17	2719
But he saveth the poor from the *s*	Job 5:15	2719
and in war from the power of the *s*	Job 5:20	2719
and he is waited for of the *s*	Job 15:22	2719
Be ye afraid of the *s*	Job 19:29	2719
bringeth the punishments of the *s*	Job 19:29	2719
the glittering *s* cometh out of	Job 20:25	1300
be multiplied, it is for the *s*	Job 27:14	2719
his life from perishing by the *s*	Job 33:18	7973
not, they shall perish by the *s*	Job 36:12	7973
turneth he back from the *s*	Job 39:22	2719
make his *s* to approach unto him	Job 40:19	2719
The *s* of him that layeth at him	Job 41:26	2719
he turn not, he will whet his *s*	Ps 7:12	2719
from the wicked, which is thy *s*	Ps 17:13	2719
Deliver my soul from the *s*	Ps 22:20	2719
The wicked have drawn out the *s*	Ps 37:14	2719
Their *s* shall enter into their	Ps 37:15	2719
As with a *s* in my bones, mine	Ps 42:10	7524
land in possession by their own *s*	Ps 44:3	2719
bow, neither shall my *s* save me	Ps 44:6	2719
Gird thy *s* upon thy thigh, O most	Ps 45:3	2719
arrows, and their tongue a sharp *s*	Ps 57:4	2719
They shall fall by the *s*	Ps 63:10	2719
Who whet their tongue like a *s*	Ps 64:3	2719
of the bow, the shield, and the *s*	Ps 76:3	2719
his people over also unto the *s*	Ps 78:62	2719
Their priests fell by the *s*	Ps 78:64	2719
also turned the edge of his *s*	Ps 89:43	2719
his servant from the hurtful *s*	Ps 144:10	2719
a twoedged *s* in their hand	Ps 149:6	2719
wormwood, sharp as a twoedged *s*	Prov 5:4	2719
like the piercings of a *s*	Prov 12:18	2719
his neighbour is a maul, and a *s*	Prov 25:18	2719
every man hath his *s* upon his	Song 3:8	2719
ye shall be devoured with the *s*	Is 1:20	2719
not lift up *s* against nation	Is 2:4	2719
Thy men shall fall by the *s*	Is 3:25	2719
unto them shall fall by the *s*	Is 13:15	2719
slain, thrust through with a *s*	Is 14:19	2719
from the swords, from the drawn *s*	Is 21:15	2719
men are not slain with the *s*	Is 22:2	2719
strong *s* shall punish leviathan	Is 27:1	2719
the Assyrian fall with the *s*	Is 31:8	2719
and the *s*, not of a mean man,	Is 31:8	2719
but he shall flee from the *s*	Is 31:8	2719
For my *s* shall be bathed in	Is 34:5	2719
The *s* of the Lord is filled with	Is 34:6	2719
to fall by the *s* in his own land	Is 37:7	2719
his sons smote him with the *s*	Is 37:38	2719
he gave them as the dust to his *s*	Is 41:2	2719
hath made my mouth like a sharp *s*	Is 49:2	2719
and the famine, and the *s*	Is 51:19	2719
will I number you to the *s*	Is 65:12	2719
by his *s* will the Lord plead with	Is 66:16	2719
your own *s* hath devoured your	Jer 2:30	2719
whereas the *s* reacheth unto the	Jer 4:10	2719
neither shall we see *s* nor famine	Jer 5:12	2719
thou trustedst, with the *s*	Jer 5:17	2719
for the *s* of the enemy and fear is	Jer 6:25	2719
and I will send a *s* after them	Jer 9:16	2719
the young men shall die by the *s*	Jer 11:22	2719
for the *s* of the Lord shall	Jer 12:12	2719
but I will consume them by the *s*	Jer 14:12	2719
unto them, Ye shall not see the *s*	Jer 14:13	2719
I sent them not, yet they say, S	Jer 14:15	2719
By *s* and famine shall those	Jer 14:15	2719
because of the famine and the *s*	Jer 14:16	2719
then behold the slain with the *s*	Jer 14:18	2719
as are for the *s*, to the *s*	Jer 15:2	2719
the *s* to slay, and the dogs to	Jer 15:3	2719
to the *s* before their enemies	Jer 15:9	2719
they shall be consumed by the *s*	Jer 16:4	2719
their blood by the force of the *s*	Jer 18:21	2719
men be slain by the *s* in battle	Jer 18:21	2719
by the *s* before their enemies	Jer 19:7	2719
fall by the *s* of their enemies	Jer 20:4	2719
and shall slay them with the *s*	Jer 20:4	2719
from the pestilence, from the *s*	Jer 21:7	2719
smite them with the edge of the *s*	Jer 21:7	2719
in this city shall die by the *s*	Jer 21:9	2719
And I will send the *s*, the famine,	Jer 24:10	2719
because of the *s* that I will send	Jer 25:16	2719
because of the *s* which I will	Jer 25:27	2719
for I will call for a *s* upon all	Jer 25:29	2719
them that are wicked to the *s*	Jer 25:31	2719
who slew him with the *s*, and cast	Jer 26:23	2719
saith the Lord, with the *s*	Jer 27:8	2719
die, thou and thy people, by the *s*	Jer 27:13	2719
I will send upon them the *s*	Jer 29:17	2719
I will persecute them with the *s*	Jer 29:18	2719
s found grace in the wilderness	Jer 31:2	2719
against it, because of the *s*	Jer 32:24	2719
of the king of Babylon by the *s*	Jer 32:36	2719
down by the mounts, and by the *s*	Jer 33:4	2719
thee, Thou shalt not die by the *s*	Jer 34:4	2719
for you, saith the Lord, to the *s*	Jer 34:17	2719
in this city shall die by the *s*	Jer 38:2	2719
and thou shalt not fall by the *s*	Jer 39:18	2719
the son of Shaphan with the *s*	Jer 41:2	2719
it shall come to pass, that the *s*	Jer 42:16	2719
they shall die by the *s*, by the	Jer 42:17	2719
that ye shall die by the *s*	Jer 42:22	2719
as are for the *s* to the *s*	Jer 43:11	2719
shall even be consumed by the *s*	Jer 44:12	2719
even unto the greatest, by the *s*	Jer 44:12	2719
have punished Jerusalem, by the *s*	Jer 44:13	2719
and have been consumed by the *s*	Jer 44:18	2719
Egypt shall be consumed by the *s*	Jer 44:27	2719
a small number that escape the *s*	Jer 44:28	2719
the *s* shall devour, and it shall	Jer 46:10	2719
for the *s* shall devour round	Jer 46:14	2719
nativity, from the oppressing *s*	Jer 46:16	2719
O thou *s* of the Lord, how long	Jer 47:6	2719
the *s* shall pursue thee	Jer 48:2	2719
keepeth back his *s* from blood	Jer 48:10	2719
and I will send the *s* after them	Jer 49:37	2719
for fear of the oppressing *s* they	Jer 50:16	2719
A *s* is upon the Chaldeans, saith	Jer 50:35	2719
A *s* is upon the liars	Jer 50:36	2719

S

a s is upon her mighty men.................... Jer 50:36	2719
A s is upon their horses, and upon......... Jer 50:37	2719
a s is upon her treasures.................... Jer 50:37	2719
Ye that have escaped the s.................... Jer 51:50	2719
abroad the s bereaveth, at home........... Lam 1:20	2719
my young men are fallen by the s.......... Lam 2:21	2719
They that be slain with the s are.......... Lam 4:9	2719
of the s of the wilderness.................... Lam 5:9	2719
and I will draw out a s after them......... Eze 5:2	2719
fall by the s round about thee................ Eze 5:12	2719
and I will draw out a s after them......... Eze 5:12	2719
and I will bring the s upon thee............. Eze 5:17	2719
even I, will bring a s upon you.............. Eze 6:3	2719
escape the s among the nations............. Eze 6:8	2719
for they shall fall by the s.................... Eze 6:11	2719
that is near shall fall by the s.............. Eze 6:12	2719
The s-is without, and the.................... Eze 7:15	2719
in the field shall die with the s............. Eze 7:15	2719
Ye have feared the s.......................... Eze 11:8	2719
and I will bring a s upon you............... Eze 11:8	2719
Ye shall fall by the s.......................... Eze 11:10	2719
I will draw out the s after them............ Eze 12:14	2719
a few men of them from the s............... Eze 12:16	2719
a s upon that land, and say, S.............. Eze 14:17	2719
judgments upon Jerusalem, the s.......... Eze 14:21	2719
all his bands shall fall by the s............ Eze 17:21	2719
draw forth my s out of his sheath......... Eze 21:3	2719
therefore shall my s go forth out.......... Eze 21:4	2719
forth my s out of his sheath................ Eze 21:5	2719
Say, A s, a s is sharpened,.................. Eze 21:9	2719
this s is sharpened, and it is................ Eze 21:11	2719
of the s shall be upon my people .... Eze 21:12	2719
what if the s contemn even the............. Eze 21:13	2719
let the s be doubled the third.............. Eze 21:14	2719
third time, the s of the slain................ Eze 21:14	2719
it is the s of the great men that............ Eze 21:14	2719
of the s against all their gates............. Eze 21:15	2719
that the s of the king of Babylon.......... Eze 21:19	2719
that the s may come to Rabbath of........ Eze 21:20	2719
thou, The s, the s is drawn.................. Eze 21:28	2719
daughters, and slew her with the s........ Eze 23:10	2719
thy remnant shall fall by the s.............. Eze 23:25	2719
ye have left shall fall by the s.............. Eze 24:21	2719
they of Dedan shall fall by the s........... Eze 25:13	2719
the field shall be slain by the s............. Eze 26:6	2719
He shall slay with the s thy.................. Eze 26:8	2719
he shall slay thy people by the s........... Eze 26:11	2719
by the s upon her on every side............ Eze 28:23	2719
I will bring a s upon thee.................... Eze 29:8	2719
the s shall come upon Egypt, and.......... Eze 30:4	2719
shall fall with them by the s................ Eze 30:5	2719
shall they fall in it by the s................. Eze 30:6	2719
of Pi-beseth shall fall by the s............. Eze 30:17	2719
to make it strong to hold the s............. Eze 30:21	2719
I will cause the s to fall out of............. Eze 30:22	2719
Babylon, and put my s in his hand........ Eze 30:24	2719
when I shall put my s into the.............. Eze 30:25	2719
them that be slain with the s............... Eze 31:17	2719
with them that be slain by the s........... Eze 31:18	2719
I shall brandish my s before them......... Eze 32:10	2719
The s of the king of Babylon................ Eze 32:11	2719
of them that are slain by the s............. Eze 32:20	2719
she is delivered to the s...................... Eze 32:20	2719
lie uncircumcised, slain by the s........... Eze 32:21	2719
of them slain, fallen by the s............... Eze 32:22	2719
of them slain, fallen by the s............... Eze 32:23	2719
of them slain, fallen by the s............... Eze 32:24	2719
uncircumcised, slain by the s............... Eze 32:25	2719
uncircumcised, slain by the s............... Eze 32:26	2719
them that are slain with the s.............. Eze 32:28	2719
by them that were slain by the s........... Eze 32:29	2719
with them that be slain by the s........... Eze 32:30	2719
and all his army slain by the s............. Eze 32:31	2719
them that are slain with the s.............. Eze 32:32	2719
When I bring the s upon a land............. Eze 33:2	2719
he seeth the s come upon the land........ Eze 33:3	2719
if the s come, and take him away,......... Eze 33:4	2719
if the watchman see the s come............ Eze 33:6	2719
if the s come, and take any person....... Eze 33:6	2719
Ye stand upon your s, ye work.............. Eze 33:26	2719
in the wastes shall fall by the s............ Eze 33:27	2719
s in the time of their calamity.............. Eze 35:5	2719
fall that are slain with the s................ Eze 35:8	2719
that is brought back from the s............. Eze 38:8	2719
I will call for a s against him............... Eze 38:21	2719
every man's s shall be against.............. Eze 38:21	2719
so fell they all by the s...................... Eze 39:23	2719
yet they shall fall by the s.................. Dan 11:33	2719
not save them by bow, nor by s............ Hos 1:7	2719
and I will break the bow and the s........ Hos 2:18	2719
s for the rage of their tongue.............. Hos 7:16	2719

the s shall abide on his cities,.............. Hos 11:6	2719
they shall fall by the s....................... Hos 13:16	2719
and when they fall upon the s.............. Joel 2:8	7973
did pursue his brother with the s.......... Amos 1:11	2719
young men have I slain with the s......... Amos 4:10	2719
the house of Jeroboam by the s............. Amos 7:9	2719
Jeroboam shall die by the s................. Amos 7:11	2719
thy daughters shall fall by the s........... Amos 7:17	2719
slay the last of them with the s............ Amos 9:1	2719
thence will I command the s................. Amos 9:4	2719
of my people shall die by the s............. Amos 9:10	2719
not lift up a s against nation............... Mic 4:3	2719
the land of Assyria with the s.............. Mic 5:6	2719
will I give up to the s......................... Mic 6:14	2719
the s shall devour thy young................ Nah 2:13	2719
lifteth up both the bright s.................. Nah 3:3	2719
the s shall cut thee off, it.................... Nah 3:15	2719
also, ye shall be slain by my s.............. Zeph 2:12	2719
every one by the s of his brother.......... Hag 2:22	2719
thee as the s of a mighty man.............. Zec 9:13	2719
the s shall be upon his arm, and.......... Zec 11:17	2719
Awake, O s, against my shepherd,......... Zec 13:7	2719
I came not to send peace, but a s...... Mt 10:34	3162
out his hand, and drew his s................ Mt 26:51	3162
Put up again thy s into his place....... Mt 26:52	3162
the s shall perish with the s............. Mt 26:52	3162
of them that stood by drew a s............. Mk 14:47	3162
a s shall pierce through thy own........... Lk 2:35	4501
shall fall by the edge of the s.......... Lk 21:24	3162
and he that hath no s, let him.......... Lk 22:36	3162
Lord, shall we smite with the s............. Lk 22:49	3162
Simon Peter having a s drew it............. Jn 18:10	3162
Put up thy s into the sheath............. Jn 18:11	3162
the brother of John with the s.............. Acts 12:2	3162
doors open, he drew out his s............... Acts 16:27	3162
or nakedness, or peril, or s.................. Rom 8:35	3162
for he beareth not the s in vain............ Rom 13:4	3162
the s of the Spirit, which is the............ Eph 6:17	3162
and sharper than any twoedged s.......... Heb 4:12	3162
fire, escaped the edge of the s.............. Heb 11:34	3162
tempted, were slain with the s............. Heb 11:37	3162
his mouth went a sharp twoedged s...... Rev 1:16	4501
hath the sharp s with two edges....... Rev 2:12	4501
them with the s of my mouth........... Rev 2:16	4501
was given unto him a great s............... Rev 6:4	3162
part of the earth, to kill with s............. Rev 6:8	4501
he that killeth with the s must............. Rev 13:10	3162
must be killed with the s.................... Rev 13:10	3162
beast, which had the wound by a s........ Rev 13:14	3162
out of his mouth goeth a sharp s.......... Rev 19:15	4501
s of him that sat upon the horse.......... Rev 19:21	4501
which s proceeded out of his............... Rev 19:21	

SWORDS

the Hebrews make them s or spears...... 1Sa 13:19	2719
him seven hundred men that drew s...... 2Kin 3:26	2719
after their families with their s............ Neh 4:13	2719
than oil, yet were they drawn s............. Ps 55:21	6609
s are in their lips............................. Ps 59:7	2719
generation, whose teeth are as s.......... Prov 30:14	2719
They all hold s, being expert in............ Song 3:8	2719
beat their s into plowshares................ Is 2:4	2719
For they fled from the s, from.............. Is 21:15	2719
thrust thee through with their s........... Eze 16:40	2719
and dispatch them with their s............. Eze 23:47	2719
they shall draw their s against............. Eze 28:7	2719
shall draw their s against Egypt........... Eze 30:11	2719
By the s of the mighty will I................. Eze 32:12	2719
laid their s under their heads.............. Eze 32:27	2719
shields, all of them handling s............. Eze 38:4	2719
Beat your plowshares into s................. Joel 3:10	2719
beat their s into plowshares................ Mic 4:3	2719
with him a great multitude with s......... Mt 26:47	3162
out as against a thief with s............ Mt 26:55	3162
with him a great multitude with s......... Mk 14:43	3162
out, as against a thief, with s.......... Mk 14:48	3162
Lord, behold, here are two s................ Lk 22:38	3162
out, as against a thief, with s.......... Lk 22:52	3162

SWORN

And said, By myself have I s................ Gen 22:16	7650
for he had straitly s the..................... Ex 13:19	7650
Because the LORD hath s ....Ex 17:16	3027,5920,3676
about which he hath s falsely............... Lev 6:5	7650
which he had s unto your fathers.......... Deut 7:8	7650
as he hath s unto thy fathers............... Deut 13:17	7650
as he hath s unto thy fathers, and........ Deut 19:8	7650
himself, as he hath s unto thee............ Deut 28:9	7650
as he hath s unto thy fathers, to.......... Deut 29:13	7650
the land which the LORD hath s............ Deut 31:7	7650
s unto them by the LORD God of........... Josh 9:18	7650

We have s unto them by the LORD .... Josh 9:19	7650
and as the LORD had s unto them .... Judg 2:15	7650
the men of Israel had s in Mizpeh .... Judg 21:1	7650
seeing we have s by the LORD that .... Judg 21:7	7650
for the children of Israel have s .... Judg 21:18	7650
therefore I have s unto the house 1Sa 3:14	7650
forasmuch as we have s both of us 1Sa 20:42	7650
as the LORD hath s to David 2Sa 3:9	7650
of Israel had s unto them 2Sa 21:2	7650
for they had s with all their 2Chr 15:15	7650
were many in Judah s unto him ...... Neh 6:18	1167,7621
which thou hadst s to give them .... Neh 9:15	5375
unto vanity, nor s deceitfully .... Ps 24:4	7650
I have s unto David my servant, ... Ps 89:3	7650
Once have I s by my holiness that .... Ps 89:35	7650
mad against me are s against me .... Ps 102:8	7650
The LORD hath s, and will not .... Ps 110:4	7650
I have s, and I will perform it, ... Ps 119:106	7650
The LORD hath s in truth unto .... Ps 132:11	7650
The LORD of hosts hath s, saying, ... Is 14:24	7650
I have s by myself, the word is .... Is 45:23	7650
for as I have s that the waters .... Is 54:9	7650
so have I s that I would not be .... Is 54:9	7650
The LORD hath s by his right hand .... Is 62:8	7650
s by them that are no gods.................... Jer 5:7	7650
which I have s unto your fathers............ Jer 11:5	7650
I have s by my great name, saith .... Jer 44:26	7650
For I have s by myself, saith the .... Jer 49:13	7650
LORD of hosts hath s by himself .... Jer 51:14	7650
sight, to them that have s oaths .... Eze 21:23	7650
Lord GOD hath s by his holiness .... Amos 4:2	7650
The Lord GOD hath s by himself .... Amos 6:8	7650
The LORD hath s by the excellency .... Amos 8:7	7650
which thou hast s unto our.................... Mic 7:20	7650
God had s with an oath to him .... Acts 2:30	3660
nigh, which God had s to Abraham .... Acts 7:17	3660
As I have s in my wrath, if they .... Heb 4:3	3660

SYCAMINE

ye might say unto this s tree .... Lk 17:6	4807

SYCHAR (si'-kar) See SHECHEM. *A city in Samaria.*

of Samaria, which is called S .... Jn 4:5	4965

SYCHEM (si'-kem) See SHECHEM. *Same as Shechem.*

And were carried over into S .... Acts 7:16	4966
the sons of Emmor the father of S .... Acts 7:16	4966

SYCOMORE

the s trees that are in the vale 1Kin 10:27	8256
the s trees that were in the low 1Chr 27:28	8256
cedar trees made he as the s 2Chr 1:15	8256
the s trees that are in the low 2Chr 9:27	8256
hail, and their s trees with frost .... Ps 78:47	8256
herdman, and a gatherer of s fruit .... Amos 7:14	8256
up into a s tree to see him.................... Lk 19:4	4809

SYCOMORES

the s are cut down, but we will .... Is 9:10	8256

SYENE (si-e'-ne) *An Egyptian city.*

from the tower of S even unto the .... Eze 29:10	5482
from the tower of S shall they .... Eze 30:6	5482

SYNAGOGUE

thence, he went into their s .... Mt 12:9	4864
he taught them in their s .... Mt 13:54	4864
sabbath day he entered into the s.......... Mk 1:21	4864
there was in their s a man with .... Mk 1:23	4864
when they were come out of the s .... Mk 1:29	4864
And he entered again into the s.............. Mk 3:1	4864
cometh one of the rulers of the s............ Mk 5:22	752
he saith unto the ruler of the s.............. Mk 5:36	752
the house of the ruler of the s .... Mk 5:38	752
come, he began to teach in the s .... Mk 6:2	4864
he went into the s on the sabbath .... Lk 4:16	4864
in the s were fastened on him .... Lk 4:20	4864
And all they in the s, when they .... Lk 4:28	4864
in the s there was a man, which .... Lk 4:33	4864
And he arose out of the s, and .... Lk 4:38	4864
that he entered into the s .... Lk 6:6	4864
nation, and he hath built us a s .... Lk 7:5	4864
and he was a ruler of the s .... Lk 8:41	4864
the ruler of the s answered with .... Lk 13:14	752
These things said he in the s.................. Jn 6:59	4864
he should be put out of the s .... Jn 9:22	656
they should be put out of the s.............. Jn 12:42	656
I ever taught in the s, and in the .... Jn 18:20	4864
Then there arose certain of the s .... Acts 6:9	4864
is called the s of the Libertines .... Acts 6:9	4864
went into the s on the sabbath .... Acts 13:14	4864
rulers of the s sent unto them .... Acts 13:15	752
the Jews were gone out of the s.............. Acts 13:42	4864

together into the s of the Jews .... Acts 14:1	4864
where was a s of the Jews .... Acts 17:1	4864
went into the s of the Jews.................... Acts 17:10	4864
he in the s with the Jews .... Acts 17:17	4864
reasoned in the s every sabbath .... Acts 18:4	4864
whose house joined hard to the s .... Acts 18:7	4864
Crispus, the chief ruler of the s.............. Acts 18:8	752
the chief ruler of the s.......................... Acts 18:17	752
but he himself entered into the s .... Acts 18:19	4864
he began to speak boldly in the s .... Acts 18:26	4864
And he went into the s, and spake .... Acts 19:8	4864
beat in every s them that .... Acts 22:19	4864
And I punished them oft in every s .... Acts 26:11	4864
are not, but are the s of Satan .... Rev 2:9	4864
will make them of the s of Satan .... Rev 3:9	4864

SYNAGOGUE'S

of the s house certain which said............ Mk 5:35	752
one from the ruler of the s house .... Lk 8:49	752

SYNAGOGUES

up all the s of God in the land .... Ps 74:8	4150
all Galilee, teaching in their s................ Mt 4:23	4864
as the hypocrites do in the s .... Mt 6:2	4864
love to pray standing in the s .... Mt 6:5	4864
and villages, teaching in their s .... Mt 9:35	4864
they will scourge you in their s .... Mt 10:17	4864
and the chief seats in the s .... Mt 23:6	4864
them shall ye scourge in your s .... Mt 23:34	4864
he preached in their s throughout .... Mk 1:39	4864
And the chief seats in the s.................... Mk 12:39	4864
in the s ye shall be beaten .... Mk 13:9	4864
And he taught in their s, being .... Lk 4:15	4864
he preached in the s of Galilee .... Lk 4:44	4864
love the uppermost seats in the s .... Lk 11:43	4864
And when they bring you unto the s .... Lk 12:11	4864
in one of the s on the sabbath .... Lk 13:10	4864
and the highest seats in the s................ Lk 20:46	4864
you, delivering you up to the s .... Lk 21:12	4864
They shall put you out of the s .... Jn 16:2	656
him letters to Damascus to the s .... Acts 9:2	4864
he preached Christ in the s .... Acts 9:20	4864
word of God in the s of the Jews .... Acts 13:5	4864
read in the s every sabbath day............ Acts 15:21	4864
up the people, neither in the s .... Acts 24:12	4864

SYNTYCHE (sin'-ti-ke) *A Christian at Philippi.*

I beseech Euodias, and beseech S.......... Phil 4:2	4941

SYRACUSE (sir'-a-cuse) *A city on Sicily.*

And landing at S, we tarried there .... Acts 28:12	4946

SYRIA (sir'-e-ah) See ARAM, SYRIA-DAMASCUS, SYRIA-MAACHAH, SYRIAN. *Nation·north of Israel.*

and Ashtaroth, and the gods of S .... Judg 10:6	758
put garrisons in S of Damascus 2Sa 8:6	758
Of S, and of Moab, and of the 2Sa 8:12	758
vow while I abode at Geshur in S 2Sa 15:8	758
Hittites, and for the kings of S 1Kin 10:29	758
Israel, and reigned over S 1Kin 11:25	758
the son of Hezion, king of S.................... 1Kin 15:18	758
anoint Hazael to be king over S 1Kin 19:15	758
Ben-hadad the king of S gathered 1Kin 20:1	758
Ben-hadad the king of S escaped 1Kin 20:20	758
of S will come up against thee 1Kin 20:22	758
of the king of S said unto him 1Kin 20:23	758
three years without war between S........ 1Kin 22:1	758
out of the hand of the king of S 1Kin 22:3	758
But the king of S commanded his 1Kin 22:31	758
of the host of the king of S 2Kin 5:1	758
LORD had given deliverance unto S 2Kin 5:1	758
And the king of S said, Go to, go, ... 2Kin 5:5	758
Then the king of S warred against 2Kin 6:8	758
the heart of the king of S was 2Kin 6:11	758
So the bands of S came no more 2Kin 6:23	758
king of S gathered all his host 2Kin 6:24	758
uttermost part of the camp of S............ 2Kin 7:5	758
Ben-hadad the king of S was sick 2Kin 8:7	758
king of S hath sent me to thee 2Kin 8:9	758
me that thou shalt be king over S 2Kin 8:13	758
Hazael king of S in Ramoth-gilead........ 2Kin 8:28	758
fought against Hazael king of S 2Kin 8:29	758
because of Hazael king of S.................... 2Kin 9:14	758
he fought with Hazael king of S 2Kin 9:15	758
Then Hazael king of S went up 2Kin 12:17	758
and sent it to Hazael king of S 2Kin 12:18	758
into the hand of Hazael king of S 2Kin 13:3	758
the king of S oppressed them................ 2Kin 13:4	758
for the king of S had destroyed.............. 2Kin 13:7	758
the arrow of deliverance from S.............. 2Kin 13:17	758
then hadst thou smitten S till................ 2Kin 13:19	758
now thou shalt smite S but thrice 2Kin 13:19	758

S

But Hazael king of *S* oppressed	2Kin 13:22	758
So Hazael king of *S* died	2Kin 13:24	758
against Judah Rezin the king of *S*	2Kin 15:37	758
Then Rezin king of *S* and Pekah son	2Kin 16:5	758
of *S* recovered Elath to *S*	2Kin 16:6	758
out of the hand of the king of *S*	2Kin 16:7	758
Hittites, and for the kings of *S*	2Chr 1:17	758
and sent to Ben-hadad king of *S*	2Chr 16:2	758
thou hast relied on the king of *S*	2Chr 16:7	758
of *S* escaped out of thine hand	2Chr 16:7	758
push *S* until they be consumed	2Chr 18:10	758
Now the king of *S* had commanded	2Chr 18:30	758
beyond the sea on this side *S*	2Chr 20:2	758
Hazael king of *S* at Ramoth-gilead	2Chr 22:5	758
he fought with Hazael king of *S*	2Chr 22:6	758
that the host of *S* came up	2Chr 24:23	758
into the hand of the king of *S*	2Chr 28:5	758
gods of the kings of *S* help them	2Chr 28:23	758
Judah, that Rezin the king of *S*	Is 7:1	758
S is confederate with Ephraim	Is 7:2	758
the fierce anger of Rezin with *S*	Is 7:4	758
Because *S*, Ephraim, and the son of	Is 7:5	758
For the head of *S* is Damascus	Is 7:8	758
Damascus, and the remnant of *S*	Is 17:3	758
reproach of the daughters of *S*	Eze 16:57	758
S was thy merchant by reason of	Eze 27:16	758
Jacob fled into the country of *S*	Hos 12:12	758
the people of *S* shall go into	Amos 1:5	758
And his fame went throughout all *S*	Mt 4:24	4947
when Cyrenius was governor of *S*	Lk 2:2	4947
of the Gentiles in Antioch and *S*	Acts 15:23	4947
And he went through *S* and Cilicia,	Acts 15:41	4947
brethren, and sailed thence into *S*	Acts 18:18	4947
as he was about to sail into *S*	Acts 20:3	4947
the left hand, and sailed into *S*	Acts 21:3	4947
I came into the regions of *S*	Gal 1:21	4947

SYRIACK *(sir'-e-ak)* See SYRIAN. *Language of the Syrians.*

the Chaldeans to the king in *S*	Dan 2:4	762

SYRIA-DAMASCUS *(sir'-e-ah-da-mas'-cus)* See SYRIA, DAMASCUS. *Same as Damascus.*

Then David put garrisons in *S*	1Chr 18:6	758,1834

SYRIA-MAACHAH *(sir'-e-ah-ma-a-kah)* A Syrian city-state.

out of Mesopotamia, and out of *S*	1Chr 19:6	758

SYRIAN *(sir'-e-un)* See ARAMITES, SYRIANS, SYROPHENICIAN.
  1. *An inhabitant of Syria.*

of Bethuel the *S* of Padan-aram	Gen 25:20	761
the sister to Laban the *S*	Gen 25:20	761
unto Laban, son of Bethuel the *S*	Gen 28:5	761
away unawares to Laban the *S*	Gen 31:20	761
Laban the *S* in a dream by night	Gen 31:24	761
A *S* ready to perish was my father	Deut 26:5	761
master hath spared Naaman this *S*	2Kin 5:20	761
was cleansed, saving Naaman the *S*	Lk 4:27	4948

  2. *The language of Syria.*

to thy servants in the *S* language	2Kin 18:26	762
was written in the *S* tongue	Ezr 4:7	762
and interpreted in the *S* tongue	Ezr 4:7	762
thy servants in the *S* language	Is 36:11	762

SYRIANS

when the *S* of Damascus came to	2Sa 8:5	758
of Zobah, David slew of the *S* two	2Sa 8:5	758
the *S* became servants to David,	2Sa 8:6	758
of the *S* in the valley of salt	2Sa 8:13	758
hired the *S* of Beth-rehob, and the	2Sa 10:6	758
the *S* of Zoba, twenty thousand	2Sa 10:6	758
the *S* of Zoba, and of Rehob, and	2Sa 10:8	758
put them in array against the *S*	2Sa 10:9	758
If the *S* be too strong for me,	2Sa 10:11	758
unto the battle against the *S*	2Sa 10:13	758
of Ammon saw that the *S* were fled	2Sa 10:14	758
when the *S* saw that they were	2Sa 10:15	758
brought out the *S* that were	2Sa 10:16	758
the *S* set themselves in array	2Sa 10:17	758
And the *S* fled before Israel	2Sa 10:18	758
seven hundred chariots of the *S*	2Sa 10:18	758
So the *S* feared to help the	2Sa 10:19	758
and the *S* fled	1Kin 20:20	758
slew the *S* with a great slaughter	1Kin 20:21	758
that Ben-hadad numbered the *S*	1Kin 20:26	758
but the *S* filled the country	1Kin 20:27	758
the LORD, Because the *S* have said	1Kin 20:28	758
S an hundred thousand footmen in	1Kin 20:29	758
With these shalt thou push the *S*	1Kin 22:11	758
up in his chariot against the *S*	1Kin 22:35	758
the *S* had gone out by companies,	2Kin 5:2	758
for thither the *S* are come down	2Kin 6:9	758
us fall unto the host of the *S*	2Kin 7:4	758
to go unto the camp of the *S*	2Kin 7:5	758
the *S* to hear a noise of chariots	2Kin 7:6	758
We came to the camp of the *S*	2Kin 7:10	758
you what the *S* have done to us	2Kin 7:12	758
king sent after the host of the *S*	2Kin 7:14	758
which the *S* had cast away in	2Kin 7:15	758
and spoiled the tents of the *S*	2Kin 7:16	758
and the *S* wounded Joram	2Kin 8:28	761
the *S* had given him at Ramah	2Kin 8:29	761
wounds which the *S* had given him	2Kin 9:15	761
out from under the hand of the *S*	2Kin 13:5	758
thou shalt smite the *S* in Aphek	2Kin 13:17	758
the *S* came to Elath, and dwelt	2Kin 16:6	758
the Chaldees, and bands of the *S*	2Kin 24:2	758
when the *S* of Damascus came to	1Chr 18:5	758
of Zobah, David slew of the *S* two	1Chr 18:5	758
the *S* became David's servants, and	1Chr 18:6	758
put them in array against the *S*	1Chr 19:10	758
If the *S* be too strong for me,	1Chr 19:12	758
nigh before the *S* unto the battle	1Chr 19:14	758
of Ammon saw that the *S* were fled	1Chr 19:15	758
when the *S* saw that they were put	1Chr 19:16	758
drew forth the *S* that were beyond	1Chr 19:16	758
the battle in array against the *S*	1Chr 19:17	758
But the *S* fled before Israel	1Chr 19:18	758
David slew of the *S* seven	1Chr 19:18	758
neither would the *S* help the	1Chr 19:19	758
against the *S* until the even	2Chr 18:34	758
and the *S* smote Joram	2Chr 22:5	761
For the army of the *S* came with a	2Chr 24:24	758
The *S* before, and the Philistines	Is 9:12	758
and for fear of the army of the *S*	Jer 35:11	758
from Caphtor, and the *S* from Kir	Amos 9:7	758

SYROPHENICIAN *(sy'-ro-fe-ne'-she-un)* A citizen of Phenicia in Syria.

woman was a Greek, a *S* by nation	Mk 7:26	4949

SYRTIS See QUICKSANDS.

T

TAANACH *(ta'-a-nak)* See TANACH. *A Levitical city in Manasseh.*

The king of *T*, one	Josh 12:21	8590
towns, and the inhabitants of *T*	Josh 17:11	8590
of Beth-shean and her towns, nor *T*	Judg 1:27	8590
in *T* by the waters of Megiddo	Judg 5:19	8590
to him pertained *T* and Megiddo, and	1Kin 4:12	8590
Beth-shean and her towns, *T*	1Chr 7:29	8590

TAANATH-SHILOH *(ta'-a-nath-shi'-lo)* A city on the border of Benjamin.

border went about eastward unto *T*	Josh 16:6	8387

TABALIAH See TEBALIAH.

TABBAOTH *(tab'-ba-oth)* A family of exiles.

of Hasupha, the children of *T*	Ezr 2:43	2884
of Hashupha, the children of *T*	Neh 7:46	2884

TABBATH *(tab'-bath)* A city in Issachar.

border of Abel-meholah, unto *T*	Judg 7:22	2888

TABEAL *(tab'-e-al)* See TABEEL. *Father of a would-be king of Israel.*

midst of it, even the son of *T*	Is 7:6	2870

TABEEL *(tab'-e-el)* See TABEAL. *A Persian official in Samaria.*

wrote Bishlam, Mithredath, *T*	Ezr 4:7	2870

TABERAH *(tab'-e-rah)* A place in the wilderness of Paran.

he called the name of the place *T*	Num 11:3	8404
And at *T*, and at Massah, and at	Deut 9:22	8404

TABERING

of doves, *t* upon their breasts	Nah 2:7	8608

TABERNACLE

thee, after the pattern of the *t*	Ex 25:9	4908
the *t* with ten curtains of fine	Ex 26:1	4908
and it shall be one *t*	Ex 26:6	4908
hair to be a covering upon the *t*	Ex 26:7	4908
curtain in the forefront of the *t*	Ex 26:9	168
hang over the backside of the *t*	Ex 26:12	4908
the sides of the *t* on this side	Ex 26:13	4908
the *t* of shittim wood standing up	Ex 26:15	4908
make for all the boards of the *t*	Ex 26:17	4908
shalt make the boards for the *t*	Ex 26:18	4908
for the second side of the *t* on	Ex 26:20	4908
for the sides of the *t* westward	Ex 26:22	4908
corners of the *t* in the two sides	Ex 26:23	4908
boards of the one side of the *t*	Ex 26:26	4908
boards of the other side of the *t*	Ex 26:27	4908
the boards of the side of the *t*	Ex 26:27	4908
And thou shalt rear up the *t*	Ex 26:30	4908
side of the *t* toward the south	Ex 26:35	4908
shalt make the court of the *t*	Ex 27:9	4908
All the vessels of the *t* in all	Ex 27:19	4908
In the *t* of the congregation	Ex 27:21	168
in unto the *t* of the congregation	Ex 28:43	168
door of the *t* of the congregation	Ex 29:4	168
before the *t* of the congregation	Ex 29:10	168
by the door of the *t* of the	Ex 29:11	168
when he cometh into the *t* of the	Ex 29:30	168
by the door of the *t* of the	Ex 29:32	168
t of the congregation before the	Ex 29:42	168
the *t* shall be sanctified by my	Ex 29:43	
the *t* of the congregation	Ex 29:44	168
of the *t* of the congregation	Ex 30:16	168
between the *t* of the congregation	Ex 30:18	168
go into the *t* of the congregation	Ex 30:20	168
thou shalt anoint *t* of the	Ex 30:26	168
in the *t* of the congregation	Ex 30:36	168
The *t* of the congregation, and the	Ex 31:7	168
and all the furniture of the *t*	Ex 31:7	168
And Moses took the *t*, and pitched	Ex 33:7	168
camp, and called it the *T* of the	Ex 33:7	168
unto the *t* of the congregation	Ex 33:7	168
when Moses went out unto the *t*	Ex 33:8	168
until he was gone into the *t*	Ex 33:8	168
pass, as Moses entered into the *t*	Ex 33:9	168
and stood at the door of the *t*	Ex 33:9	168
cloudy pillar stand at the *t* door	Ex 33:10	168
man, departed not out of the *t*	Ex 33:11	168
The *t*, his tent, and his covering,	Ex 35:11	4908
door at the entering in of the *t*	Ex 35:15	4908
The pins of the *t*, and the pins of	Ex 35:18	4908
work of the *t* of the congregation	Ex 35:21	168
the *t* made ten curtains of fine	Ex 36:8	4908
so it became one *t*	Ex 36:13	4908
hair for the tent over the *t*	Ex 36:14	4908
boards for the *t* of shittim wood	Ex 36:20	4908
make for all the boards of the *t*	Ex 36:22	4908
And he made boards for the *t*	Ex 36:23	4908
And for the other side of the *t*	Ex 36:25	4908
for the sides of the *t* westward	Ex 36:27	4908
corners of the *t* in the two sides	Ex 36:28	4908
boards of the one side of the *t*	Ex 36:31	4908
boards of the other side of the *t*	Ex 36:32	4908
of the *t* for the sides westward	Ex 36:32	4908
an hanging for the *t* door of blue	Ex 36:37	168
door of the *t* of the congregation	Ex 38:8	168
And all the pins of the *t*, and of	Ex 38:20	4908
This is the sum of the *t*, even of	Ex 38:21	4908
even of the *t* of testimony, as it	Ex 38:21	4908
door of the *t* of the congregation	Ex 38:30	168
gate, and all the pins of the *t*	Ex 38:31	4908
Thus was all the work of the *t* of	Ex 39:32	4908
And they brought the *t* unto Moses	Ex 39:33	4908
and the hanging for the *t* door	Ex 39:38	168
vessels of the service of the *t*	Ex 39:40	4908
month shalt thou set up the *t* of	Ex 40:2	4908
the hanging of the door to the *t*	Ex 40:5	4908
t of the tent of the congregation	Ex 40:6	4908
anointing oil, and anoint the *t*	Ex 40:9	4908
door of the *t* of the congregation	Ex 40:12	168
month, that the *t* was reared up	Ex 40:17	4908
And Moses reared up the *t*, and	Ex 40:18	4908
spread abroad the tent over the *t*	Ex 40:19	4908
And he brought the ark into the *t*	Ex 40:21	4908
upon the side of the *t* northward	Ex 40:22	4908
on the side of the *t* southward	Ex 40:24	4908
the hanging at the door of the *t*	Ex 40:28	4908
offering by the door of the *t* of	Ex 40:29	4908
up the court round about the *t*	Ex 40:33	4908
glory of the Lord filled the *t*	Ex 40:34	4908
glory of the Lord filled the *t*	Ex 40:35	4908
was taken up from over the *t*	Ex 40:36	4908

of the Lord was upon the *t* by day	Ex 40:38	4908
out of the *t* of the congregation	Lev 1:1	168
will at the door of the *t* of the	Lev 1:3	168
door of the *t* of the congregation	Lev 1:5	168
door of the *t* of the congregation	Lev 3:2	168
kill it before the *t* of the	Lev 3:8	168
kill it before the *t* of the	Lev 3:13	168
bullock unto the door of the *t* of	Lev 4:4	168
and bring it to the *t* of the	Lev 4:5	168
Lord, which is in the *t* of the	Lev 4:7	168
door of the *t* of the congregation	Lev 4:7	168
before the *t* of the congregation	Lev 4:14	168
to the *t* of the congregation	Lev 4:16	168
the Lord, that is in the *t* of the	Lev 4:18	168
door of the *t* of the congregation	Lev 4:18	168
in the court of the *t* of the	Lev 6:16	168
of the *t* of the congregation	Lev 6:26	168
into the *t* of the congregation to	Lev 6:30	168
door of the *t* of the congregation	Lev 8:3	168
door of the *t* of the congregation	Lev 8:4	168
anointing oil, and anointed the *t*	Lev 8:10	4908
door of the *t* of the congregation	Lev 8:31	168
t of the congregation in seven	Lev 8:33	168
of the *t* of the congregation day	Lev 8:35	168
before the *t* of the congregation	Lev 9:5	168
into the *t* of the congregation	Lev 9:23	168
door of the *t* of the congregation	Lev 10:7	168
go into the *t* of the congregation	Lev 10:9	168
door of the *t* of the congregation	Lev 12:6	168
at the door of the *t* of the	Lev 14:11	168
door of the *t* of the congregation	Lev 14:23	168
door of the *t* of the congregation	Lev 15:14	168
to the door of the *t* of the	Lev 15:29	168
defile my *t* that is among them	Lev 15:31	4908
door of the *t* of the congregation	Lev 16:7	168
do for the *t* of the congregation	Lev 16:16	168
the *t* of the congregation when he	Lev 16:17	168
the *t* of the congregation, and the	Lev 16:20	168
into the *t* of the congregation	Lev 16:23	168
for the *t* of the congregation	Lev 16:33	168
door of the *t* of the congregation	Lev 17:4	168
the Lord before the *t* of the Lord	Lev 17:4	4908
door of the *t* of the congregation	Lev 17:5	168
door of the *t* of the congregation	Lev 17:6	168
door of the *t* of the congregation	Lev 17:9	168
door of the *t* of the congregation	Lev 19:21	168
in the *t* of the congregation,	Lev 24:3	168
And I will set my *t* among you	Lev 26:11	4908
in the *t* of the congregation, on	Num 1:1	168
Levites over the *t* of testimony	Num 1:50	4908
they shall bear the *t*, and all the	Num 1:50	4908
and shall encamp round about the *t*	Num 1:50	4908
when the *t* setteth forward, the	Num 1:51	4908
when the *t* is to be pitched, the	Num 1:51	4908
round about the *t* of testimony	Num 1:53	4908
the charge of the *t* of testimony	Num 1:53	4908
far off about the *t* of the	Num 2:2	168
Then the *t* of the congregation	Num 2:17	168
before the *t* of the congregation	Num 3:7	168
to do the service of the *t*	Num 3:7	4908
of the *t* of the congregation	Num 3:8	168
to do the service of the *t*	Num 3:8	4908
shall pitch behind the *t* westward	Num 3:23	4908
t of the congregation shall be	Num 3:25	168
the congregation shall be the *t*	Num 3:25	4908
door of the *t* of the congregation	Num 3:25	168
of the court, which is by the *t*	Num 3:26	4908
on the side of the *t* southward	Num 3:29	4908
on the side of the *t* northward	Num 3:35	4908
shall be the boards of the *t*	Num 3:36	4908
before the *t* toward the east	Num 3:38	4908
even before the *t* of the	Num 3:38	168
work in the *t* of the congregation	Num 4:3	168
in the *t* of the congregation	Num 4:4	168
in the *t* of the congregation	Num 4:15	168
and the oversight of all the *t*	Num 4:16	4908
work in the *t* of the congregation	Num 4:23	168
shall bear the curtains of the *t*	Num 4:25	4908
the *t* of the congregation, his	Num 4:25	168
door of the *t* of the congregation	Num 4:25	168
of the court, which is by the *t*	Num 4:26	4908
in the *t* of the congregation	Num 4:28	168
work in the *t* of the congregation	Num 4:30	168
in the *t* of the congregation	Num 4:31	168
the boards of the *t*, and the bars	Num 4:31	4908
in the *t* of the congregation,	Num 4:33	168
work in the *t* of the congregation	Num 4:35	168
in the *t* of the congregation	Num 4:37	168
work in the *t* of the congregation	Num 4:39	168
in the *t* of the congregation	Num 4:41	168
work in the *t* of the congregation	Num 4:43	168

T

in the *t* of the congregation	Num 4:47	168
of the *t* the priest shall take	Num 5:17	4908
to the door of the *t* of the	Num 6:10	168
door of the *t* of the congregation	Num 6:13	168
door of the *t* of the congregation	Num 6:18	168
that Moses had fully set up the *t*	Num 7:1	4908
and they brought them before the *t*	Num 7:3	4908
of the *t* of the congregation	Num 7:5	168
t of the congregation to speak	Num 7:89	168
before the *t* of the congregation	Num 8:9	168
of the *t* of the congregation	Num 8:15	168
in the *t* of the congregation	Num 8:19	168
the *t* of the congregation before	Num 8:22	168
of the *t* of the congregation	Num 8:24	168
in the *t* of the congregation	Num 8:26	168
on the day that the *t* was reared	Num 9:15	4908
reared up the cloud covered the *t*	Num 9:15	4908
at even there was upon the *t* as	Num 9:15	4908
the cloud was taken up from the *t*	Num 9:17	168
the *t* they rested in their tents	Num 9:18	4908
tarried long upon the *t* many days	Num 9:19	4908
cloud was a few days upon the *t*	Num 9:20	4908
that the cloud tarried upon the *t*	Num 9:22	4908
door of the *t* of the congregation	Num 10:3	168
from off the *t* of the testimony	Num 10:11	4908
And the *t* was taken down	Num 10:17	4908
Merari set forward, bearing the *t*	Num 10:17	4908
set up the *t* against they came	Num 10:21	4908
unto the *t* of the congregation	Num 11:16	168
and set them round about the *t*	Num 11:24	168
but went not out unto the *t*	Num 11:26	168
unto the *t* of the congregation	Num 12:4	168
and stood in the door of the *t*	Num 12:5	168
the cloud departed from off the *t*	Num 12:10	168
of the LORD appeared in the *t* of	Num 14:10	168
the service of the *t* of the LORD	Num 16:9	4908
stood in the door of the *t* of the	Num 16:18	168
door of the *t* of the congregation	Num 16:19	168
you up from about the *t* of Korah	Num 16:24	4908
they gat up from the *t* of Korah	Num 16:27	4908
toward the *t* of the congregation	Num 16:42	168
before the *t* of the congregation	Num 16:43	168
door of the *t* of the congregation	Num 16:50	168
thou shalt lay them up in the *t*	Num 17:4	168
the LORD in the *t* of witness	Num 17:7	168
Moses went into the *t* of witness	Num 17:8	168
unto the *t* of the LORD shall die	Num 17:13	4908
minister before the *t* of witness	Num 18:2	168
and the charge of all the *t*	Num 18:3	168
of the *t* of the congregation	Num 18:4	168
for all the service of the *t*	Num 18:4	168
of the *t* of the congregation	Num 18:6	168
of the *t* of the congregation	Num 18:21	168
nigh the *t* of the congregation	Num 18:22	168
of the *t* of the congregation	Num 18:23	168
in the *t* of the congregation	Num 18:31	168
her blood directly before the *t*	Num 19:4	168
defileth the *t* of the LORD	Num 19:13	4908
door of the *t* of the congregation	Num 20:6	168
door of the *t* of the congregation	Num 25:6	168
by the door of the *t* of the	Num 27:2	168
the charge of the *t* of the LORD	Num 31:30	4908
the charge of the *t* of the LORD	Num 31:47	4908
it into the *t* of the congregation	Num 31:54	168
in the *t* of the congregation	Deut 31:14	168
in the *t* of the congregation	Deut 31:14	168
in the *t* in a pillar of a cloud	Deut 31:15	168
stood over the door of the *t*	Deut 31:15	168
set up the *t* of the congregation	Josh 18:1	168
at the door of the *t* of the	Josh 19:51	168
wherein the LORD's *t* dwelleth	Josh 22:19	4908
LORD our God that is before his *t*	Josh 22:29	4908
door of the *t* of the congregation	1Sa 2:22	168
in the midst of the *t* that David	2Sa 6:17	168
have walked in a tent and in a *t*	2Sa 7:6	4908
took an horn of oil out of the *t*	1Kin 1:39	168
Joab fled unto the *t* of the LORD	1Kin 2:28	168
was fled unto the *t* of the LORD	1Kin 2:29	168
Benaiah came to the *t* of the LORD	1Kin 2:30	168
the *t* of the congregation, and all	1Kin 8:4	168
holy vessels that were in the *t*	1Kin 8:4	168
of the *t* of the congregation with	1Chr 6:32	168
of the *t* of the house of God	1Chr 6:48	4908
keepers of the gates of the *t*	1Chr 9:19	168
door of the *t* of the congregation	1Chr 9:21	168
LORD, namely, the house of the *t*	1Chr 9:23	168
before the *t* of the LORD in the	1Chr 16:39	4908
to tent, and from one *t* to another	1Chr 17:5	168
For the *t* of the LORD, which	1Chr 21:29	4908
they shall no more carry the *t*	1Chr 23:26	4908
of the *t* of the congregation	1Chr 23:32	168

for there was the *t* of the	2Chr 1:3	168
he put before the *t* of the LORD	2Chr 1:5	4908
which was at the *t* of the	2Chr 1:6	168
from before the *t* of the	2Chr 1:13	168
the *t* of the congregation, and all	2Chr 5:5	168
holy vessels that were in the *t*	2Chr 5:5	168
of Israel, for the *t* of witness	2Chr 24:6	168
know that thy *t* shall be in peace	Job 5:24	168
The light shall be dark in his *t*	Job 18:6	168
shall be rooted out of his *t*	Job 18:14	168
It shall dwell in his *t*, because	Job 18:15	168
me, and encamp round about my *t*	Job 19:12	168
with him that is left in his *t*	Job 20:26	168
the secret of God was upon my *t*	Job 29:4	168
If the men of my *t* said not	Job 31:31	168
the clouds, or the noise of his *t*	Job 36:29	5521
Lord, who shall abide in thy *t*	Ps 15:1	168
them hath he set a *t* for the sun	Ps 19:4	168
secret of his *t* shall he hide me	Ps 27:5	168
offer in his *t* sacrifices of joy	Ps 27:6	168
I will abide in thy *t* for ever	Ps 61:4	168
In Salem also is his *t*, and his	Ps 76:2	5520
that he forsook the *t* of Shiloh	Ps 78:60	4908
he refused the *t* of Joseph	Ps 78:67	168
not come into the *t* of my house	Ps 132:3	168
but the *t* of the upright shall	Prov 14:11	168
there shall be a *t* for a shadow	Is 4:6	5521
it in truth in the *t* of David	Is 16:5	168
a *t* that shall not be taken down	Is 33:20	168
My *t* is spoiled, and all my cords	Jer 10:20	168
in the *t* of the daughter of Zion	Lam 2:4	168
hath violently taken away his *t*	Lam 2:6	7900
My *t* also shall be with them	Eze 37:27	4908
which was the breadth of the *t*	Eze 41:1	168
have borne the *t* of your Moloch	Amos 5:26	5522
up the *t* of David that is fallen	Amos 9:11	5521
Yea, ye took up the *t* of Moloch	Acts 7:43	4633
Our fathers had the *t* of witness	Acts 7:44	4633
desired to find a *t* for the God	Acts 7:46	4638
will build again the *t* of David	Acts 15:16	4633
house of this *t* were dissolved	2Cor 5:1	4636
we that are in this *t* do groan	2Cor 5:4	4636
the sanctuary, and of the true *t*	Heb 8:2	4633
when he was about to make the *t*	Heb 8:5	4633
For there was a *t* made	Heb 9:2	4633
the *t* which is called the Holiest	Heb 9:3	4633
went always into the first *t*	Heb 9:6	4633
as the first *t* was yet standing	Heb 9:8	4633
by a greater and more perfect *t*	Heb 9:11	4633
sprinkled with blood both the *t*	Heb 9:21	4633
no right to eat which serve the *t*	Heb 13:10	4633
meet, as long as I am in this *t*	2Pet 1:13	4638
shortly I must put off this my *t*	2Pet 1:14	4638
to blaspheme his name, and his *t*	Rev 13:6	4633
the temple of the *t* of the	Rev 15:5	4633
the *t* of God is with men, and he	Rev 21:3	4633

TABERNACLES

month shall be the feast of *t* for	Lev 23:34	5521
are thy tents, O Jacob, and thy *t*	Num 24:5	4908
observe the feast of *t* seven days	Deut 16:13	5521
of weeks, and in the feast of *t*	Deut 16:16	5521
of release, in the feast of *t*	Deut 31:10	5521
of weeks, and in the feast of *t*	2Chr 8:13	5521
They kept also the feast of *t*	Ezr 3:4	5521
let not wickedness dwell in thy *t*	Job 11:14	168
The *t* of robbers prosper, and they	Job 12:6	168
shall consume the *t* of bribery	Job 15:34	168
put away iniquity far from thy *t*	Job 22:23	168
unto thy holy hill, and to thy *t*	Ps 43:3	4908
place of the *t* of the most High	Ps 46:4	4908
of their strength in the *t* of Ham	Ps 78:51	168
The *t* of Edom, and the Ishmaelites	Ps 83:6	168
How amiable are thy *t*, O LORD of	Ps 84:1	4908
is in the *t* of the righteous	Ps 118:15	168
We will go into his *t*	Ps 132:7	4908
he shall plant the *t* of his	Dan 11:45	168
thorns be in their *t*	Hos 9:6	168
will yet make thee to dwell in *t*	Hos 12:9	168
hosts, and to keep the feast of *t*	Zec 14:16	5521
not up to keep the feast of *t*	Zec 14:18	5521
not up to keep the feast of *t*	Zec 14:19	5521
scholar, out of the *t* of Jacob	Mal 2:12	168
wilt, let us make here three *t*	Mt 17:4	4633
and let us make three *t*	Mk 9:5	4633
and let us make three *t*	Lk 9:33	4633
the Jews' feast of *t* was at hand	Jn 7:2	4634
country, dwelling in *t* with Isaac	Heb 11:9	4633

TABITHA (tab'-ith-ah) *Woman raised from the dead by Peter.*
Joppa a certain disciple named *T* .... Acts 9:36 — 5000
turning him to the body said, *T* .... Acts 9:40 — 5000

TABLE
also make a *t* of shittim wood .... Ex 25:23 — 7979
of the staves to bear the *t* .... Ex 25:27 — 7979
that the *t* may be borne with them ...... Ex 25:28 — 7979
thou shalt set upon the *t* .... Ex 25:30 — 7979
shalt set the *t* without the vail .... Ex 26:35 — 7979
candlestick over against the *t* on .... Ex 26:35 — 7979
shalt put the *t* on the north side .... Ex 26:35 — 7979
And the *t* and all his vessels, and .... Ex 30:27 — 7979
The *t*, and his staves, and all his .... Ex 31:8 — 7979
The *t*, and his staves, and all his .... Ex 35:13 — 7979
he made the *t* of shittim wood .... Ex 37:10 — 7979
for the staves to bear the *t* .... Ex 37:14 — 7979
them with gold, to bear the *t* .... Ex 37:15 — 7979
the vessels which were upon the *t* .... Ex 37:16 — 7979
The *t*, and all the vessels thereof .... Ex 39:36 — 7979
And thou shalt bring in the *t* .... Ex 40:4 — 7979
he put the *t* in the tent of the .... Ex 40:22 — 7979
congregation, over against the *t* .... Ex 40:24 — 7979
upon the pure *t* before the LORD .... Lev 24:6 — 7979
charge shall be the ark, and the *t* ...... Num 3:31 — 7979
upon the *t* of shewbread they .... Num 4:7 — 7979
gathered their meat under my *t* .... Judg 1:7 — 7979
he cometh not unto the king's *t* .... 1Sa 20:29 — 7979
arose from the *t* in fierce anger .... 1Sa 20:34 — 7979
eat bread at my *t* continually .... 2Sa 9:7 — 7979
son shall eat bread alway at my *t* .... 2Sa 9:10 — 7979
the king, he shall eat at my *t* .... 2Sa 9:11 — 7979
eat continually at the king's *t* .... 2Sa 9:13 — 7979
them that did eat at thine own *t* .... 2Sa 19:28 — 7979
be of those that eat at thy *t* .... 1Kin 2:7 — 7979
that came unto king Solomon's *t* .... 1Kin 4:27 — 7979
the *t* of gold, whereupon the .... 1Kin 7:48 — 7979
And the meat of his *t*, and the .... 1Kin 10:5 — 7979
to pass, as they sat at the *t* .... 1Kin 13:20 — 7979
hundred, which eat at Jezebel's *t* .... 1Kin 18:19 — 7979
set for him there a bed, and a *t* .... 2Kin 4:10 — 7979
tables of shewbread, for every *t* .... 1Chr 28:16 — 7979
And the meat of his *t*, and the .... 2Chr 9:4 — 7979
set they in order upon the pure *t* .... 2Chr 13:11 — 7979
thereof, and the shewbread *t* .... 2Chr 29:18 — 7979
there were at my *t* an hundred .... Neh 5:17 — 7979
thy *t* should be full of fatness .... Job 36:16 — 7979
Thou preparest a *t* before me in .... Ps 23:5 — 7979
Let their *t* become a snare before .... Ps 69:22 — 7979
God furnish a *t* in the wilderness .... Ps 78:19 — 7979
olive plants round about thy *t* .... Ps 128:3 — 7979
them upon the *t* of thine heart .... Prov 3:3 — 3871
them upon the *t* of thine heart .... Prov 7:3 — 3871
she hath also furnished her *t* .... Prov 9:2 — 7979
While the king sitteth at his *t* .... Song 1:12 — 4524
Prepare the *t*, watch in the .... Is 21:5 — 7979
go, write it before them in a *t* .... Is 30:8 — 3871
that prepare a *t* for that troop .... Is 65:11 — 7979
graven upon the *t* of their heart .... Jer 17:1 — 3871
a *t* prepared before it, whereupon ...... Eze 23:41 — 7979
be filled at my *t* with horses .... Eze 39:20 — 7979
This is the *t* that is before the .... Eze 41:22 — 7979
and they shall come near to my *t* .... Eze 44:16 — 7979
and they shall speak lies at one *t* .... Dan 11:27 — 7979
The *t* of the LORD is contemptible .... Mal 1:7 — 7979
The *t* of the LORD is polluted .... Mal 1:12 — 7979
which fall from their masters' *t* .... Mt 15:27 — 5132
yet the dogs under the *t* eat of .... Mk 7:28 — 5132
And he asked for a writing *t* .... Lk 1:63 — 4093
which fell from the rich man's *t* .... Lk 16:21 — 5132
betrayeth me is with me on the *t* .... Lk 22:21 — 5132
drink at my *t* in my kingdom, and .... Lk 22:30 — 5132
them that sat at the *t* with him .... Jn 12:2 — 7979
Now no man at the *t* knew for what ...... Jn 13:28 — 345
Let their *t* be made a snare, and a ...... Rom 11:9 — 5132
be partakers of the Lord's *t* .... 1Cor 10:21 — 5132
and of the *t* of devils .... 1Cor 10:21 — 5132
was the candlestick, and the *t* .... Heb 9:2 — 5132

TABLES
and I will give thee *t* of stone .... Ex 24:12 — 3871
two *t* of testimony, *t* of .... Ex 31:18 — 3871
t of stone, written with the .... Ex 31:18 — 3871
the two *t* of the testimony were .... Ex 32:15 — 3871
the *t* were written on both their .... Ex 32:15 — 3871
the *t* were the work of God, and .... Ex 32:16 — 3871
writing of God, graven upon the *t* .... Ex 32:16 — 3871
he cast the *t* out of his hands, ... Ex 32:19 — 3871
Hew thee two *t* of stone like unto .... Ex 34:1 — 3871
I will write upon these *t* the .... Ex 34:1 — 3871
words that were in the first *t* .... Ex 34:1 — 3871

he hewed two *t* of stone like unto .... Ex 34:4 — 3871
in his hand the two *t* of stone .... Ex 34:4 — 3871
he wrote upon the *t* the words of .... Ex 34:28 — 3871
two *t* of testimony in Moses' hand .... Ex 34:29 — 3871
he wrote them upon two *t* of stone ...... Deut 4:13 — 3871
he wrote them in two *t* of stone .... Deut 5:22 — 3871
mount to receive the *t* of stone .... Deut 9:9 — 3871
even the *t* of the covenant which .... Deut 9:9 — 3871
two *t* of stone written with the .... Deut 9:10 — 3871
LORD gave me the two *t* of stone .... Deut 9:11 — 3871
even the *t* of the covenant .... Deut 9:11 — 3871
the two *t* of the covenant were in .... Deut 9:15 — 3871
And I took the two *t*, and cast them ...... Deut 9:17 — 3871
Hew thee two *t* of stone like unto .... Deut 10:1 — 3871
I will write on the *t* the words .... Deut 10:2 — 3871
in the first *t* which thou brakest .... Deut 10:2 — 3871
hewed two *t* of stone like unto .... Deut 10:3 — 3871
having the two *t* in mine hand .... Deut 10:3 — 3871
And he wrote on the *t*, according .... Deut 10:4 — 3871
put the *t* in the ark which I had .... Deut 10:5 — 3871
the ark save the two *t* of stone .... 1Kin 8:9 — 3871
gave gold for the *t* of shewbread .... 1Chr 28:16 — 7979
silver for the *t* of silver .... 1Chr 28:16 — 7979
He made also ten *t*, and placed .... 2Chr 4:8 — 7979
the *t* whereon the shewbread was .... 2Chr 4:19 — 7979
two *t* which Moses put therein at .... 2Chr 5:10 — 3871
For all *t* are full of vomit and .... Is 28:8 — 7979
the gate were two *t* on this side .... Eze 40:39 — 7979
two *t* on that side, to slay .... Eze 40:39 — 7979
of the north gate, were two *t* .... Eze 40:40 — 7979
the porch of the gate, were two *t* .... Eze 40:40 — 7979
Four *t* were on this side, and four ...... Eze 40:41 — 7979
four *t* on that side, by the side .... Eze 40:41 — 7979
eight *t*, whereupon they slew .... Eze 40:41 — 7979
the four *t* were of hewn stone for .... Eze 40:42 — 7979
upon the *t* was the flesh of the .... Eze 40:43 — 7979
vision, and make it plain upon *t* .... Hab 2:2 — 3871
temple, and overthrew the *t* of the ...... Mt 21:12 — 5132
and pots, brasen vessels, and of *t* .... Mk 7:4 — 2825
temple, and overthrew the *t* of the ...... Mk 11:15 — 5132
money, and overthrew the *t* .... Jn 2:15 — 5132
leave the word of God, and serve *t* ...... Acts 6:2 — 5132
not in *t* of stone, but in fleshly .... 2Cor 3:3 — 4109
but in fleshly *t* of the heart .... 2Cor 3:3 — 4109
budded, and the *t* of the covenant ...... Heb 9:4 — 4109

TABLETS
and earrings, and rings, and *t* .... Ex 35:22 — 3558
bracelets, rings, earrings, and *t* .... Num 31:50 — 3558
legs, and the headbands, and the *t*. Is 3:20 — 1004,5315

TABOR (ta'-bor)
  1. A mountain in Issachar and Zebulun.
And the coast reacheth to *T* .... Josh 19:22 — 8396
saying, Go and draw toward mount *T* .... Judg 4:6 — 8396
of Abinoam was gone up to mount *T* ...... Judg 4:12 — 8396
So Barak went down from mount *T* .... Judg 4:14 — 8396
men were they whom ye slew at *T* .... Judg 8:18 — 8396
T and Hermon shall rejoice in thy .... Ps 89:12 — 8396
hosts, Surely as *T* is among the .... Jer 46:18 — 8396
on Mizpah, and a net spread upon *T* ..... Hos 5:1 — 8396
  2. A plain in Benjamin.
thou shalt come to the plain of *T* .... 1Sa 10:3 — 8396
  3. A Levitical city in Zebulun.
her suburbs, *T* with her suburbs .... 1Chr 6:77 — 8396

TABRET
with mirth, and with songs, with *t* .... Gen 31:27 — 8596
place with a psaltery, and a *t* .... 1Sa 10:5 — 8596
and aforetime I was as a *t* .... Job 17:6 — 8611
And the harp, and the viol, the *t* .... Is 5:12 — 8596

TABRETS
to meet king Saul, with *t* .... 1Sa 18:6 — 8596
The mirth of *t* ceaseth, the noise .... Is 24:8 — 8596
lay upon him, it shall be with *t* .... Is 30:32 — 8596
shalt again be adorned with thy *t* .... Jer 31:4 — 8596
the workmanship of thy *t* and of .... Eze 28:13 — 8596

TABRIMMON See TABRIMON.

TABRIMON (tab'-rim-on) *Father of Ben-hadad, king of Syria.*
them to Ben-hadad, the son of *T* .... 1Kin 15:18 — 2886

TACHES
thou shalt make fifty *t* of gold .... Ex 26:6 — 7165
the curtains together with the *t* .... Ex 26:6 — 7165
thou shalt make fifty *t* of brass .... Ex 26:11 — 7165
put the *t* into the loops, and .... Ex 26:11 — 7165
hang up the vail under the *t* .... Ex 26:33 — 7165
his tent, and his covering, his *t* .... Ex 35:11 — 7165
And he made fifty *t* of gold .... Ex 36:13 — 7165
one unto another with the *t* .... Ex 36:13 — 7165

T

he made fifty *t* of brass to	Ex 36:18	7165
tent, and all his furniture, his *t*	Ex 39:33	7165

TACHMONITE (tak'-mun-ite) See HACHMONITE. *Family name of a "mighty man" of David.*

The *T* that sat in the seat, chief	2Sa 23:8	8461

TACKLING

our own hands the *t* of the ship	Acts 27:19	*4631*

TACKLINGS

Thy *t* are loosed	Is 33:23	2256

TADMOR (tad'-mor) *A city rebuilt by Solomon.*

T in the wilderness, in the land,	1Kin 9:18	8412
he built *T* in the wilderness, and	2Chr 8:4	8412

TAHAN (ta'-han) See TAHANITES.
1. A son of Ephraim.

of *T,* the family of the Tahanites	Num 26:35	8465

2. A descendant of Ephraim.

and Telah his son, and *T* his son,	1Chr 7:25	8465

TAHANITES (ta'-han-ites) *Descendants of Tahan 1.*

of Tahan, the family of the *T*	Num 26:35	8470

TAHAPANES (ta-hap'-a-neze) See TAHAPANHES. *A city in Egypt.*

T have broken the crown of thy	Jer 2:16	8471

TAHASH See THAHASH.

TAHATH (ta'-hath)
1. An Israelite encampment in the wilderness.

from Makheloth, and encamped at *T*	Num 33:26	8480
And they departed from *T,* and	Num 33:27	8480

2. Father of Uriel.

T his son, Uriel his son, Uzziah	1Chr 6:24	8480
The son of *T,* the son of Assir,	1Chr 6:37	8480

3. Father of Eladah.

T his son, and Eladah his son, and	1Chr 7:20	8480

4. Son of Eladah.

and Eladah his son, and *T* his son,	1Chr 7:20	8480

TAHCHEMONITE See TACHMONITE.

TAHKEMONITE See TACHMONITE.

TAHPANHES (tah'-pan-heze) See TAHAPANES, TAHPE-NES, TEHAPHNEHES. *Same as Tahaphnes.*

thus came they even to *T*	Jer 43:7	8471
of the LORD unto Jeremiah in *T*	Jer 43:8	8471
the entry of Pharaoh's house in *T*	Jer 43:9	8471
which dwell at Migdol, and at *T*	Jer 44:1	8471
and publish in Noph and in *T*	Jer 46:14	8471

TAHPENES (tah'-pe-neze) See TAHPANHES. *Queen of a pharaoh.*

wife, the sister of *T* the queen	1Kin 11:19	8472
the sister of *T* bare him Genubath	1Kin 11:20	8472
whom *T* weaned in Pharaoh's house	1Kin 11:20	8472

TAHREA (tah'-re-ah) See TAREA. *Son of Micah.*

were, Pithon, and Melech, and *T*	1Chr 9:41	8475

TAHTIM-HODSHI (tah'-tim-hod'-shi) *A district north of Gilead in Bashan.*

to Gilead, and to the land of *T*	2Sa 24:6	8483

TAIL

thine hand, and take it by the *t*	Ex 4:4	2180
make thee the head, and not the *t*	Deut 28:13	2180
the head, and thou shalt be the *t*	Deut 28:44	2180
firebrands, and turned *t* to *t*	Judg 15:4	2180
He moveth his *t* like a cedar	Job 40:17	2180
cut off from Israel head and *t*	Is 9:14	2180
that teacheth lies, he is the *t*	Is 9:15	2180
for Egypt, which the head or *t*	Is 19:15	2180
his *t* drew the third part of the	Rev 12:4	3769

TAILS

in the midst between two *t*	Judg 15:4	2180
two *t* of these smoking firebrands	Is 7:4	2180
they had *t* like unto scorpions,	Rev 9:10	3769
and there were stings in their *t*	Rev 9:10	3769
is in their mouth, and in their *t*	Rev 9:19	3769
for their *t* were like unto	Rev 9:19	3769

TAKE See APPENDIX.

TAKEN See APPENDIX.

TAKER

as with the *t* of usury, so with	Is 24:2	

TAKEST

the water which thou *t* out of the	Ex 4:9	3947
When thou *t* the sum of the	Ex 30:12	5375
the journey that thou *t* shall not	Judg 4:9	1980
if thou *t* heed to fulfil the	1Chr 22:13	8104
thou *t* away their breath, they	Ps 104:29	622
that thou *t* knowledge of him	Ps 144:3	3947

labour which thou *t* under the sun	Eccl 9:9	6001
our soul, and thou *t* no knowledge	Is 58:3	
thou *t* up that thou layedst not	Lk 19:21	*142*

TAKETH See APPENDIX.

TAKING See APPENDIX.

TALE

the *t* of the bricks, which they	Ex 5:8	4971
shall ye deliver the *t* of bricks	Ex 5:18	8506
gave them in full *t* to the king	1Sa 18:27	
should bring them in and out by *t*	1Chr 9:28	4557
our years as a *t* that is told	Ps 90:9	1899

TALEBEARER

down as a *t* among thy people	Lev 19:16	7400
A *t* revealeth secrets	Prov 11:13	1980,7400
The words of a *t* are as wounds	Prov 18:8	5372
about as a *t* revealeth secrets	Prov 20:19	7400
so where there is no *t,* the	Prov 26:20	5372
The words of a *t* are as wounds	Prov 26:22	5372

TALENT

Of a *t* of pure gold shall he make	Ex 25:39	3603
Of a *t* of pure gold made he it,	Ex 37:24	3603
hundred talents, a *t* for a socket	Ex 38:27	3603
the weight whereof was a *t* of	2Sa 12:30	3603
else thou shalt pay a *t* of silver	1Kin 20:39	3603
a *t* of silver, and two changes of	2Kin 5:22	3603
talents of silver, and a *t* of gold	2Kin 23:33	3603
and found it to weigh a *t* of gold	1Chr 20:2	3603
talents of silver and a *t* of gold	2Chr 36:3	3603
there was lifted up a *t* of lead	Zec 5:7	3603
which had received the one *t* came	Mt 25:24	*5007*
and went and hid thy *t* in the earth.	Mt 25:25	*5007*
Take therefore the *t* from him	Mt 25:28	*5007*
stone about the weight of a *t*	Rev 16:21	*5006*

TALENTS

offering, was twenty and nine *t*	Ex 38:24	3603
the congregation was an hundred *t*	Ex 38:25	3603
of the hundred *t* of silver were	Ex 38:27	3603
hundred sockets of the hundred *t*	Ex 38:27	3603
of the offering was seventy *t*	Ex 38:29	3603
to the king sixscore *t* of gold	1Kin 9:14	3603
gold, four hundred and twenty *t*	1Kin 9:28	3603
twenty *t* of gold, and of spices	1Kin 10:10	3603
threescore and six *t* of gold,	1Kin 10:14	3603
of Shemer for two *t* of silver	1Kin 16:24	3603
and took with him ten *t* of silver	2Kin 5:5	3603
said, Be content, take two *t*	2Kin 5:23	3603
bound two *t* of silver in two bags	2Kin 5:23	3603
gave Pul a thousand *t* of silver	2Kin 15:19	3603
Judah three hundred *t* of silver	2Kin 18:14	3603
of silver and thirty *t* of gold	2Kin 18:14	3603
tribute of an hundred *t* of silver	2Kin 23:33	3603
of Ammon sent a thousand *t* of	1Chr 19:6	3603
an hundred thousand *t* of gold	1Chr 22:14	3603
a thousand thousand *t* of silver	1Chr 22:14	3603
Even three thousand *t* of gold	1Chr 29:4	3603
seven thousand *t* of refined	1Chr 29:4	3603
of God of gold five thousand *t*	1Chr 29:7	3603
and of silver ten thousand *t*	1Chr 29:7	3603
and of brass eighteen thousand *t*	1Chr 29:7	3603
and one hundred thousand *t* of iron	1Chr 29:7	3603
gold, amounting to six hundred *t*	2Chr 3:8	3603
fifty *t* of gold, and brought them	2Chr 8:18	3603
twenty *t* of gold, and of spices	2Chr 9:9	3603
and threescore and six *t* of gold	2Chr 9:13	3603
Israel for an hundred *t* of silver	2Chr 25:6	3603
shall we do for the hundred *t*	2Chr 25:9	3603
same year an hundred *t* of silver	2Chr 27:5	3603
land in an hundred *t* of silver	2Chr 36:3	3603
Unto an hundred *t* of silver	Ezr 7:22	3604
fifty *t* of silver, and silver	Ezr 8:26	3603
and silver vessels an hundred *t*	Ezr 8:26	3603
and of gold an hundred *t*	Ezr 8:26	3603
I will pay ten thousand *t* of	Est 3:9	3603
which owed him ten thousand *t*	Mt 18:24	*5007*
And unto one he gave five *t*	Mt 25:15	*5007*
that had received the five *t* went	Mt 25:16	*5007*
same, and made them other five *t*	Mt 25:16	*5007*
he that had received five *t* came	Mt 25:20	*5007*
came and brought other five *t*	Mt 25:20	*5007*
thou deliveredst unto me five *t*	Mt 25:20	*5007*
gained beside them five *t* more	Mt 25:20	*5007*
also that had received two *t* came	Mt 25:22	*5007*
thou deliveredst unto me two *t*	Mt 25:22	*5007*
gained two other *t* beside them	Mt 25:22	*5007*
give it unto him which hath ten *t*	Mt 25:28	*5007*

TALES

men that carry *t* to shed blood	Eze 22:9	7400
words seemed to them as idle *t*	Lk 24:11	3026

TALITHA *(tal'-ith-ah) Aramaic for damsel.*

hand, and said unto her, *T* cumi	Mk 5:41	5008

TALK See APPENDIX.

TALKED See APPENDIX.

TALKERS

ye are taken up in the lips of *t*	Eze 36:3	3956
there are many unruly and vain *t*	Titus 1:10	3151

TALKEST

me a sign that thou *t* with me	Judg 6:17	1696
while thou yet *t* there with the	1Kin 1:14	1696
or, Why *t* thou with her	Jn 4:27	2980

TALKETH

and his tongue *t* of judgment	Ps 37:30	1696
him, and it is he that *t* with thee	Jn 9:37	2980

TALKING See APPENDIX.

TALL

a people great, and many, and *t*	Deut 2:10	7311
A people great, and many, and *t*	Deut 2:21	7311
A people great and *t*, the children	Deut 9:2	7311
will cut down the *t* cedar trees	2Kin 19:23	6967
cut down the *t* cedars thereof	Is 37:24	6967

TALLER

people is greater and *t* than we	Deut 1:28	7311

TALMAI *(tal'-mahee)*
1. A son of Anak.

where Ahiman, Sheshai, and *T*	Num 13:22	8526
of Anak, Sheshai, and Ahiman, and *T*	Josh 15:14	8526
slew Sheshai, and Ahiman, and *T*	Judg 1:10	8526

2. A king of Geshur.

the daughter of *T* king of Geshur	2Sa 3:3	8526
But Absalom fled, and went to *T*	2Sa 13:37	8526
the daughter of *T* king of Geshur	1Chr 3:2	8526

TALMON *(tal'-mon) A Levite in Jerusalem.*

were, Shallum, and Akkub, and *T*	1Chr 9:17	2929
of Ater, the children of *T*	Ezr 2:42	2929
of Ater, the children of *T*	Neh 7:45	2929
Moreover the porters, Akkub, *T*	Neh 11:19	2929
Bakbukiah, Obadiah, Meshullam, *T*	Neh 12:25	2929

TAMAH *(ta'-mah) See* THAMAH. *A family of exiles.*

of Sisera, the children of *T*	Neh 7:55	8547

TAMAR *(ta'-mar) See* THAMAR.
1. Wife of Er.

his firstborn, whose name was *T*	Gen 38:6	8559
Then said Judah to *T* his daughter	Gen 38:11	8559
T went and dwelt in her father's	Gen 38:11	8559
And it was told *T*, saying, Behold	Gen 38:13	8559
T thy daughter in law hath played	Gen 38:24	8559
whom *T* bare unto Judah, of the	Ruth 4:12	8559
T his daughter in law bare him	1Chr 2:4	8559

2. A daughter of David.

a fair sister, whose name was *T*	2Sa 13:1	8559
he fell sick for his sister *T*	2Sa 13:2	8559
And Amnon said unto him, I love *T*	2Sa 13:4	8559
I pray thee, let my sister *T* come	2Sa 13:5	8559
let *T* my sister come, and make me	2Sa 13:6	8559
Then David sent home to *T*	2Sa 13:7	8559
So *T* went to her brother Amnon's	2Sa 13:8	8559
And Amnon said unto *T*, Bring the	2Sa 13:10	8559
T took the cakes which she had	2Sa 13:10	8559
T put ashes on her head, and rent	2Sa 13:19	8559
So *T* remained desolate in her	2Sa 13:20	8559
he had forced his sister *T*	2Sa 13:22	8559
day that he forced his sister *T*	2Sa 13:32	8559
the concubines, and *T* their sister	1Chr 3:9	8559

3. A daughter of Absalom.

and one daughter, whose name was *T*	2Sa 14:27	8559

4. A city in Judah.

from *T* even to the waters of	Eze 47:19	8559
T unto the waters of strife in	Eze 48:28	8559

TAME

neither could any man *t* him	Mk 5:4	1150
But the tongue can no man *t*	Jas 3:8	1150

TAMED

and of things in the sea, is *t*	Jas 3:7	1150
and hath been *t* of mankind	Jas 3:7	1150

TAMMUZ *(tam'-muz) A Syrian god.*

there sat women weeping for *T*	Eze 8:14	8542

TANACH *(ta'-nak) See* TAANACH. *Same as Taanach.*

Manasseh, *T* with her suburbs, and	Josh 21:25	8590

TANHUMETH *(tan'-hu-meth) Father of Seraiah.*

the son of *T* the Netophathite	2Kin 25:23	8576
Kareah, and Seraiah the son of *T*	Jer 40:8	8576

TANNER

days in Joppa with one Simon a *t*	Acts 9:43	1033
He lodgeth with one Simon a *t*	Acts 10:6	1033
of one Simon a *t* by the sea side	Acts 10:32	1033

TAPESTRY

decked my bed with coverings of *t*	Prov 7:16	
She maketh herself coverings of *t*	Prov 31:22	

TAPHATH *(ta'-fath) A daughter of Solomon.*

which had *T* the daughter of	1Kin 4:11	2955

TAPPUAH *(tap'-pu-ah)*
1. A city in Judah.

The king of *T*, one	Josh 12:17	8599
And Zanoah, and En-gannim, *T*	Josh 15:34	8599

2. A city in Ephraim.

The border went out from *T*	Josh 16:8	8599
Now Manasseh had the land of *T*	Josh 17:8	8599
but *T* on the border of Manasseh	Josh 17:8	8599

3. A son of Hebron.

Korah, and *T*, and Rekem, and Shema	1Chr 2:43	8599

TARAH *(ta'-rah) An Israelite encampment in the wilderness.*

from Tahath, and pitched at *T*	Num 33:27	8646
And they removed from *T*, and	Num 33:28	8646

TARALAH *(tar'-a-lah) A city in Benjamin.*

And Rekem, and Irpeel, and *T*	Josh 18:27	8634

TARE

t his garments, and lay on the	2Sa 13:31	7167
t forty and two children of them	2Kin 2:24	1234
him, straightway the spirit *t* him	Mk 9:20	4682
devil threw him down, and *t* him	Lk 9:42	4952

TAREA *(ta'-re-ah) See* TAHREA. *A son of Micah.*

were, Pithon, and Melech, and *T*	1Chr 8:35	8390

TARES

sowed *t* among the wheat, and went	Mt 13:25	2215
fruit, then appeared the *t* also	Mt 13:26	2215
from whence then hath it *t*	Mt 13:27	2215
lest while ye gather up the *t*	Mt 13:29	2215
Gather ye together first the *t*	Mt 13:30	2215
the parable of the *t* of the field	Mt 13:36	2215
but the *t* are the children of the	Mt 13:38	2215
As therefore the *t* are gathered	Mt 13:40	2215

TARGET

legs, and a *t* of brass between his	1Sa 17:6	3591
shekels of gold went to one *t*	1Kin 10:16	6793
of beaten gold went to one *t*	2Chr 9:15	6793

TARGETS

made two hundred *t* of beaten gold	1Kin 10:16	6793
made two hundred *t* of beaten gold	2Chr 9:15	6793
had an army of men that bare *t*	2Chr 14:8	6793

TARPELITES *(tar'-pel-ites) Foreigners resettled in Israel.*

the Apharsathchites, the *T*	Ezr 4:9	2967

TARRIED

were with him, and *t* all night	Gen 24:54	3885
t there all night, because the	Gen 28:11	3885
and *t* all night in the mount	Gen 31:54	3885
when the cloud *t* long upon the	Num 9:19	748
that the cloud *t* upon the	Num 9:22	748
they *t* till they were ashamed	Judg 3:25	2342
And Ehud escaped while they *t*	Judg 3:26	4102
they *t* until afternoon, and they	Judg 19:8	4102
that she *t* a little in the house	Ruth 2:7	3427
he *t* seven days, according to the	1Sa 13:8	3176
Saul *t* in the uttermost part of	1Sa 14:2	3427
But David *t* still at Jerusalem	2Sa 11:1	3427
t in a place that was far off	2Sa 15:17	5975
and they *t* there	2Sa 15:29	3427
but he *t* longer than the set time	2Sa 20:5	3186
(for he *t* at Jericho,) he said	2Kin 2:18	3427
But David *t* at Jerusalem	1Chr 20:1	3427
she that *t* at home divided the	Ps 68:12	5116
While the bridegroom *t*, they all	Mt 25:5	5549
marvelled that he *t* so long in	Lk 1:21	5549
the child Jesus *t* behind in	Lk 2:43	5278
there he *t* with them, and baptized	Jn 3:22	1304
that he *t* many days in Joppa with	Acts 9:43	3306
And after they had *t* there a space	Acts 15:33	4160
Paul after this *t* there yet a	Acts 18:18	4357
going before *t* for us at Troas	Acts 20:5	3306
at Samos, and *t* at Trogyllium	Acts 20:15	3306
disciples, we *t* there seven days	Acts 21:4	1961
as we *t* there many days, there	Acts 21:10	1961
when he had *t* among them more	Acts 25:6	1304

T

the fourteenth day that ye have t........... Acts 27:33   4328
Syracuse, we t there three days............. Acts 28:12   1961

TARRIEST
And now why t thou................................. Acts 22:16   3195

TARRIETH
his part be that t by the stuff 1Sa 30:24   3427
that t not for man, nor waiteth .... Mic 5:7   6960

TARRY
t all night, and wash your feet, ... Gen 19:2   3885
t with him a few days, until thy .... Gen 27:44   3427
found favour in thine eyes, t .... Gen 30:27   3427
come down unto me, t not .... Gen 45:9   5975
out of Egypt, and could not t .... Ex 12:39   4102
T ye here for us, until we come .... Ex 24:14   3427
shall t abroad out of his tent................. Lev 14:8   3427
t ye also here this night, that I .... Num 22:19   3427
Why t the wheels of his chariots .... Judg 5:28   309
I will t until thou come again .... Judg 6:18   3427
t all night, and let thine heart .... Judg 19:6   3885
evening, I pray you t all night .... Judg 19:9   3885
the man would not t that night .... Judg 19:10   3885
Would ye t for them till they .... Ruth 1:13   7663
T this night, and it shall be in .... Ruth 3:13   3885
t until thou have weaned him 1Sa 1:23   3427
seven days shalt thou t, till I 1Sa 10:8   3176
unto us, T until we come to you 1Sa 14:9   1826
T at Jericho until your beards be........... 2Sa 10:5   3427
T here to day also, and to morrow 2Sa 11:12   3427
I will t in the plain of the 2Sa 15:28   4102
I may not t thus with thee 2Sa 18:14   3176
there will not t one with thee 2Sa 19:7   3885
unto Elisha, T here, I pray thee 2Kin 2:2   3427
him, Elisha, t here, I pray thee............. 2Kin 2:4   3427
And Elijah said unto him, T 2Kin 2:6   3427
if we t till the morning light,............... 2Kin 7:9   2442
open the door, and flee, and t not 2Kin 9:3   2442
glory of this, and t at home 2Kin 14:10   3427
T at Jericho until your beards be........... 1Chr 19:5   3427
lies shall not t in my sight..................... Ps 101:7   3559
They that t long at the wine .... Prov 23:30   309
off, and my salvation shall not t .... Is 46:13   309
turneth aside to t for a night................. Jer 14:8   3885
though it t, wait for it .... Hab 2:3   4102
will surely come, it will not t .... Hab 2:3   309
t ye here, and watch with me .... Mt 26:38   3306
t ye here, and watch .... Mk 14:34   3306
And he went in to t with them .... Lk 24:29   3306
but t ye in the city of Jerusalem .... Lk 24:49   2523
him that he would t with them .... Jn 4:40   3306
If I will that he t till I come .... Jn 21:22   3306
If I will that he t till I come .... Jn 21:23   3306
prayed they him to t certain days........... Acts 10:48   1961
him to t longer time with them .... Acts 18:20   3306
were desired to t with them seven .... Acts 28:14   1961
to eat, t one for another 1Cor 11:33   1551
but I trust to t a while with you 1Cor 16:7   1961
But I will t at Ephesus until 1Cor 16:8   1961
But if I t long, that thou mayest 1Ti 3:15   1019
come will come, and will not t................ Heb 10:37   5549

TARRYING
make no t, O my God .... Ps 40:17   309
O LORD, make no t .... Ps 70:5   309

TARSHISH (tar'-shish) See THARSHISH.
1. A son of Javan.
Elishah, and T, Kittim, and Dodanim ..... Gen 10:4   8659
Elishah, and T, Kittim, and Dodanim 1Chr 1:7   8659
2. Spain.
to T with the servants of Huram 2Chr 9:21   8659
came the ships of T bringing gold 2Chr 9:21   8659
with him to make ships to go to T........... 2Chr 20:36   8659
they were not able to go to T 2Chr 20:37   8659
the ships of T with an east wind............. Ps 48:7   8659
The kings of T and of the isles .... Ps 72:10   8659
And upon all the ships of T .... Is 2:16   8659
Howl, ye ships of T................................. Is 23:1   8659
Pass ye over to T .... Is 23:6   8659
land as a river, O daughter of T............. Is 23:10   8659
Howl, ye ships of T................................. Is 23:14   8659
for me, and the ships of T first .... Is 60:9   8659
of them unto the nations, to T .... Is 66:19   8659
into plates is brought from T .... Jer 10:9   8659
T was thy merchant by reason of .... Eze 27:12   8659
The ships of T did sing of thee .... Eze 27:25   8659
and Dedan, and the merchants of T .... Eze 38:13   8659
T from the presence of the LORD .... Jonah 1:3   8659
and he found a ship going to T .... Jonah 1:3   8659
to go with them unto T from the............. Jonah 1:3   8659
Therefore I fled before unto T .... Jonah 4:2   8659

3. A prince of Persia.
was Carshena, Shethar, Admatha, T ...... Est 1:14   8659

TARSHISHAH See TARSHISH.

TARSUS (tar'-sus) *Capital of Roman province of Cilicia.*
Judas for one called Saul, of T .... Acts 9:11   5018
Caesarea, and sent him forth to T........... Acts 9:30   5019
Then departed Barnabas to T................. Acts 11:25   5019
I am a man which am a Jew of T .... Acts 21:39   5018
a man which am a Jew, born in T .... Acts 22:3   5019

TARTAK (tar'-tak) *A god of the Avites.*
And the Avites made Nibhaz and T 2Kin 17:31   8662

TARTAN (tar'-tan) *The commander of the Assyrian army.*
And the king of Assyria sent T 2Kin 18:17   8661
the year that T came unto Ashdod......... Is 20:1   8661

TASK
have ye not fulfilled your t in .... Ex 5:14   2706
from your bricks of your daily t .... Ex 5:19   1697

TASKMASTERS
they did set over them t to...................... Ex 1:11
their cry by reason of their t .... Ex 3:7   5065
the same day the t of the people .... Ex 5:6   5065
the t of the people went out, and........... Ex 5:10   5065
the t hasted them, saying, Fulfil .... Ex 5:13   5065
which Pharaoh's t had set over............... Ex 5:14   5065

TASKS
Fulfil your works, your daily t .... Ex 5:13   1697

TASTE
the t of it was like wafers made .... Ex 16:31   2940
the t of it was as the .... Num 11:8   2940
of it was as the t of fresh oil................... Num 11:8   2940
I did but t a little honey with 1Sa 14:43   2938
if I t bread, or ought else, till 2Sa 3:35   2938
can thy servant t what I eat or 2Sa 19:35   2938
or is there any t in the white of.............. Job 6:6   2940
cannot my t discern perverse................... Job 6:30   2441
and the mouth t his meat .... Job 12:11   2938
O t and see that the LORD is good .... Ps 34:8   2938
How sweet are thy words unto my t ...... Ps 119:103   2441
which is sweet to thy t .... Prov 24:13   2441
and his fruit was sweet to my t.............. Song 2:3   2441
therefore his t remained in him, ... Jer 48:11   2940
herd nor flock, t any thing...................... Jonah 3:7   2938
here, which shall not t of death .... Mt 16:28   1089
here, which shall not t of death .... Mk 9:1   1089
here, which shall not t of death .... Lk 9:27   1089
were bidden shall t of my supper .... Lk 14:24   1089
saying, he shall never t of death .... Jn 8:52   1089
t not... Col 2:21   1089
God should t death for every man .... Heb 2:9   1089

TASTED
So none of the people t any food............ 1Sa 14:24   2938
because I t a little of this........................ 1Sa 14:29   2938
Belshazzar, whiles he t the wine............ Dan 5:2   2942
and when he had t thereof, he................ Mt 27:34   1089
t the water that was made wine .... Jn 2:9   1089
have t of the heavenly gift, and............. Heb 6:4   1089
have t the good word of God, and........... Heb 6:5   1089
If so be ye have t that the Lord.............. 1Pet 2:3   1089

TASTETH
trieth words, as the mouth t meat .... Job 34:3   2938

TATNAI (tat'-nahee) *Persian governor of Samaria.*
At the same time came to them T .... Ezr 5:3   8674
The copy of the letter that T................... Ezr 5:6   8674
Now therefore, T, governor beyond .... Ezr 6:6   8674
Then T, governor on this side the .... Ezr 6:13   8674

TATTENAI See TATNAI.

TATTLERS
but t also and busybodies, ... 1Ti 5:13   5397

TAUGHT
Behold, I have t you statutes and .... Deut 4:5   3925
t it the children of Israel .... Deut 31:22   3925
with them he t the men of Succoth .... Judg 8:16   3045
t them how they should fear the 2Kin 17:28   3384
when thou hast t them the good 2Chr 6:27   3384
they t in Judah, and had the book 2Chr 17:9   3925
cities of Judah, and t the people 2Chr 17:9   3925
and such as t to sing praise 2Chr 23:13   3045
unto all the Levites that t the 2Chr 30:22   7919
the Levites that t all Israel 2Chr 35:3   4000
and the Levites that t the people .... Neh 8:9   995
thou hast t me from my youth .... Ps 71:17   3925
for thou hast t me................................... Ps 119:102   3384
when thou hast t me thy statutes .... Ps 119:171   3925

He *t* me also, and said unto me,.............. Prov 4:4 — 3384
I have *t* thee in the way of .... Prov 4:11 — 3384
prophecy that his mother *t* him .... Prov 31:1 — 3256
he still *t* the people knowledge............... Eccl 12:9 — 3925
me is *t* by the precept of men .... Is 29:13 — 3925
being his counsellor hath *t* him .... Is 40:13 — 3045
t him in the path of judgment, and .... Is 40:14 — 3925
t him knowledge, and shewed to him ..... Is 40:14 — 3925
children shall be *t* of the LORD .... Is 54:13 — 3928
also *t* the wicked ones thy ways .... Jer 2:33 — 3925
they have *t* their tongue to speak .... Jer 9:5 — 3925
which their fathers *t* them .... Jer 9:14 — 3925
as they *t* my people to swear by .... Jer 12:16 — 3925
for thou hast *t* them to be....................... Jer 13:21 — 3925
because thou hast *t* rebellion .... Jer 28:16 — 1696
because he hath *t* rebellion .... Jer 29:32 — 1696
though I *t* them, rising up early .... Jer 32:33 — 3256
that all women may be *t* not to do .... Eze 23:48 — 3256
Ephraim is as an heifer that is *t* .... Hos 10:11 — 3925
I *t* Ephraim also to go, taking............... Hos 11:3 — 8637
for man *t* me to keep cattle from .... Zec 13:5
his mouth, and *t* them, saying,............... Mt 5:2 — 1321
For he *t* them as one having .... Mt 7:29 — 2258,1321
he *t* them in their synagogue, ... Mt 13:54 — 1321
the money, and did as they were *t*.......... Mt 28:15 — 1321
entered into the synagogue, and *t* .... Mk 1:21 — 1321
for he *t* them as one that had........ Mk 1:22 — 2258,1321
resorted unto him, and he *t* them......... Mk 2:13 — 1321
he *t* them many things by parables....... Mk 4:2 — 1321
they had done, and what they had *t* ...... Mk 6:30 — 1321
For he *t* his disciples, and said.............. Mk 9:31 — 1321
as he was wont, he *t* them again .... Mk 10:1 — 1321
And he *t*, saying unto them, Is it............. Mk 11:17 — 1321
while he *t* in the temple, How say .... Mk 12:35 — 1321
he *t* in their synagogues, being .... Lk 4:15 — 1321
t them on the sabbath days............. Lk 4:31 — 2258,1321
t the people out of the ship................ Lk 5:3 — 1321
entered into the synagogue and *t*......... Lk 6:6 — 1321
as John also *t* his disciples.................. Lk 11:1 — 1321
thou hast *t* in our streets........................ Lk 13:26 — 1321
And he *t* daily in the temple .... Lk 19:47 — 2258,1321
as he *t* the people in the temple, ... Lk 21:37 — 1321
And they shall be all *t* of God .... Jn 6:45 — 1318
synagogue, as he *t* in Capernaum .... Jn 6:59 — 1321
went up into the temple, and *t* .... Jn 7:14 — 1321
cried Jesus in the temple as he *t* .... Jn 7:28 — 1321
and he sat down, and *t* them.................. Jn 8:2 — 1321
treasury, as he *t* in the temple .... Jn 8:20 — 1321
but as my Father hath *t* me .... Jn 8:28 — 1321
I ever *t* in the synagogue, and in.......... Jn 18:20 — 1321
grieved that they *t* the people .... Acts 4:2 — 1321
temple early in the morning, and *t* .... Acts 5:21 — 1321
with the church, and *t* much people ...... Acts 11:26 — 1321
had *t* many, they returned again .... Acts 14:21 — 3100
down from Judaea *t* the brethren .... Acts 15:1 — 1321
t diligently the things of the .... Acts 18:25 — 1321
have *t* you publickly, and from .... Acts 20:20 — 1321
t according to the perfect manner .... Acts 22:3 — 3811
it of man, neither was I *t* it .... Gal 1:12 — 1321
Let him that is *t* in the word .... Gal 6:6 — 2727
heard him, and have been *t* by him....... Eph 4:21 — 1321
in the faith, as ye have been *t* .... Col 2:7 — 1321
for ye yourselves are *t* of God to............ 1Th 4:9 — 2312
traditions which ye have been *t* .... 2Th 2:15 — 1321
faithful word as he hath been *t*............. Titus 1:9 — 1322
no lie, and even as it hath *t* you............ 1Jn 2:27 — 1321
of Balaam, who *t* Balac to cast a .... Rev 2:14 — 1321

TAUNT

be a reproach and a proverb, a *t* .... Jer 24:9 — 8148
So it shall be a reproach and a *t* .... Eze 5:15 — 1422

TAUNTING

a *t* proverb against him, and say, ... Hab 2:6 — 4426

TAVERNS

as Appii forum, and The three *t* .... Acts 28:15 — 4999

TAXATION

of every one according to his *t*...............2Kin 23:35 — 6187

TAXED

but he *t* the land to give the ....2Kin 23:35 — 6186
that all the world should be *t* .... Lk 2:1 — 582
And all went to be *t*, every one.............. Lk 2:3 — 582
To be *t* with Mary his espoused............. Lk 2:5 — 582

TAXES

of *t* in the glory of the kingdom.............. Dan 11:20 — 5065

TAXING

this *t* was first made when.................... Lk 2:2 — 583
of Galilee in the days of the *t* .... Acts 5:37 — 583

TEACH

t thee what thou shalt say .... Ex 4:12 — 3384
will *t* you what ye shall do..................... Ex 4:15 — 3384
thou shalt *t* them ordinances and .... Ex 18:20 — 2094
that thou mayest *t* them .... Ex 24:12 — 3384
put in his heart that he may *t*................ Ex 35:34 — 3384
that ye may *t* the children of .... Lev 10:11 — 3384
To *t* when it is unclean, and when .... Lev 14:57 — 3384
unto the judgments, which I *t* you .... Deut 4:1 — 3925
but *t* them thy sons, and thy sons'......... Deut 4:9 — 3045
that they may *t* their children .... Deut 4:10 — 3925
me at that time to *t* you statutes .... Deut 4:14 — 3925
which thou shalt *t* them, that................ Deut 5:31 — 3925
LORD your God commanded to *t* you...... Deut 6:1 — 3925
thou shalt *t* them diligently unto........... Deut 6:7 — 8150
ye shall *t* them your children, ... Deut 11:19 — 3925
the law which they shall *t* thee .... Deut 17:11 — 3384
That they *t* you not to do after.............. Deut 20:18 — 3925
priests the Levites shall *t* you .... Deut 24:8 — 3384
t it the children of Israel .... Deut 31:19 — 3925
They shall *t* Jacob thy judgments, ... Deut 33:10 — 3384
to *t* them war, at the least such .... Judg 3:2 — 3925
t us what we shall do unto the .... Judg 13:8 — 3384
but I will *t* you the good and the.......... 1Sa 12:23 — 3384
(Also he bade them *t* the children ....2Sa 1:18 — 3925
that thou *t* them the good way .... 1Kin 8:36 — 3384
let him *t* them the manner of the..........2Kin 17:27 — 3384
to *t* in the cities of Judah ....2Chr 17:7 — 3925
to *t* in Israel statutes and .... Ezr 7:10 — 3925
t ye them that know them not .... Ezr 7:25 — 3046
T me, and I will hold my tongue .... Job 6:24 — 3384
Shall not they *t* thee, and tell................ Job 8:10 — 3384
the beasts, and they shall *t* thee .... Job 12:7 — 3384
to the earth, and it shall *t* thee .... Job 12:8 — 3384
Shall any *t* God knowledge................... Job 21:22 — 3925
I will *t* you by the hand of God .... Job 27:11 — 3384
of years should *t* wisdom .... Job 32:7 — 3045
peace, and I shall *t* thee wisdom .... Job 33:33 — 502
That which I see not *t* thou me .... Job 34:32 — 3384
T us what we shall say unto him .... Job 37:19 — 3045
t me thy paths .... Ps 25:4 — 3925
Lead me in thy truth, and *t* me .... Ps 25:5 — 3925
therefore will he *t* sinners in................. Ps 25:8 — 3384
and the meek will he *t* his way .... Ps 25:9 — 3925
him shall he *t* in the way that he .... Ps 25:12 — 3384
T me thy way, O LORD, and lead me ...... Ps 27:11 — 3384
t thee in the way which thou .... Ps 32:8 — 3384
I will *t* you the fear of the LORD .... Ps 34:11 — 3925
hand shall *t* thee terrible things .... Ps 45:4 — 3384
Then will I *t* transgressors thy .... Ps 51:13 — 3925
Michtam of David, to *t* .... Ps 60:t — 3925
T me thy way, O LORD .... Ps 86:11 — 3384
So *t* us to number our days, that .... Ps 90:12 — 3045
and *t* his senators wisdom .... Ps 105:22
t me thy statutes .... Ps 119:12 — 3925
t me thy statutes .... Ps 119:26 — 3925
T me, O LORD, the way of thy .... Ps 119:33 — 3384
t me thy statutes .... Ps 119:64 — 3925
T me good judgment and knowledge ...... Ps 119:66 — 3925
t me thy statutes .... Ps 119:68 — 3925
O LORD, and *t* me thy judgments .... Ps 119:108 — 3925
thy mercy, and *t* me thy statutes .... Ps 119:124 — 3925
and *t* me thy statutes .... Ps 119:135 — 3925
my testimony that I shall *t* them .... Ps 132:12 — 3925
T me to do thy will .... Ps 143:10 — 3925
t a just man, and he will increase .... Prov 9:9 — 3045
he will *t* us of his ways, and we............ Is 2:3 — 3384
Whom shall he *t* knowledge.................. Is 28:9 — 3384
him to discretion, and doth *t* him .... Is 28:26 — 3384
t your daughters wailing, and .... Jer 9:20 — 3925
they shall *t* no more every man .... Jer 31:34 — 3925
they shall *t* my people the .... Eze 44:23 — 3384
and whom they might *t* the learning ...... Dan 1:4 — 3925
and the priests thereof *t* for hire .... Mic 3:11 — 3384
he will *t* us of his ways, and we............ Mic 4:2 — 3384
the dumb stone, Arise, it shall *t* .... Hab 2:19 — 3384
shall *t* men so, he shall be .... Mt 5:19 — 1321
t them, the same shall be called .... Mt 5:19 — 1321
he departed thence to *t* and to .... Mt 11:1 — 1321
t all nations, baptizing them in .... Mt 28:19 — 3100
began again to *t* by the sea side .... Mk 4:1 — 1321
he began to *t* in the synagogue .... Mk 6:2 — 1321
he began to *t* them many things .... Mk 6:34 — 1321
And he began to *t* them, that the .... Mk 8:31 — 1321
t us to pray, as John also taught .... Lk 11:1 — 1321
For the Holy Ghost shall *t* you in .... Lk 12:12 — 1321
the Gentiles, and *t* the Gentiles .... Jn 7:35 — 1321
born in sins, and dost thou *t* us .... Jn 9:34 — 1321
he shall *t* you all things, and .... Jn 14:26 — 1321
that Jesus began both to do and *t*......... Acts 1:1 — 1321
at all nor *t* in the name of Jesus .... Acts 4:18 — 1321

T

that ye should not *t* in this name .... Acts 5:28   *1321*
every house, they ceased not to *t* .... Acts 5:42   *1321*
t customs, which are not lawful .... Acts 16:21   *2605*
as I *t* every where in every 1Cor 4:17   *1321*
Doth not even nature itself *t* you 1Cor 11:14   *1321*
by my voice I might *t* others also 1Cor 14:19   *2727*
that they *t* no other doctrine 1Ti 1:3   *2085*
But I suffer not a woman to *t* 1Ti 2:12   *1321*
given to hospitality, apt to *t* 1Ti 3:2   *1317*
These things command and *t* 1Ti 4:11   *1321*
These things *t* and exhort 1Ti 6:2   *1321*
If any man *t* otherwise, and 1Ti 6:3   *2085*
shall be able to *t* others also 2Ti 2:2   *1321*
be gentle unto all men, apt to *t* 2Ti 2:24   *1317*
That they may *t* the young women .... Titus 2:4   *4994*
ye have need that one *t* you again .... Heb 5:12   *1321*
they shall not *t* every man his .... Heb 8:11   *1321*
and ye need not that any man *t* you 1Jn 2:27   *1321*
herself a prophetess, to *t* .... Rev 2:20   *1321*

TEACHER
the great, the *t* as the scholar 1Chr 25:8   *995*
a *t* of lies, that the maker of .... Hab 2:18   *3384*
that thou art a *t* come from God .... Jn 3:2   *1320*
a *t* of babes, which hast the form .... Rom 2:20   *1320*
a *t* of the Gentiles in faith and 1Ti 2:7   *1320*
apostle, and a *t* of the Gentiles 2Ti 1:11   *1320*

TEACHERS
more understanding than all my *t* .... Ps 119:99   *3925*
have not obeyed the voice of my *t* .... Prov 5:13   *3384*
yet shall not thy *t* be removed .... Is 30:20   *3384*
but thine eyes shall see thy *t* .... Is 30:20   *3384*
thy *t* have transgressed against .... Is 43:27   *3887*
at Antioch certain prophets and *t* .... Acts 13:1   *1320*
secondarily prophets, thirdly *t* 1Cor 12:28   *1320*
are all *t*? 1Cor 12:29   *1320*
and some, pastors and *t* .... Eph 4:11   *1320*
Desiring to be *t* of the law 1Ti 1:7   *3547*
shall they heap to themselves *t* 2Ti 4:3   *1320*
to much wine, *t* of good things .... Titus 2:3   *2567*
for the time ye ought to be *t* .... Heb 5:12   *1320*
there shall be false *t* among you 2Pet 2:1   *5572*

TEACHEST
O Lᴏʀᴅ, and *t* him out of thy law .... Ps 94:12   *3925*
t the way of God in truth, ... Mt 22:16   *1321*
but *t* the way of God in truth .... Mk 12:14   *1321*
t rightly, neither acceptest thou .... Lk 20:21   *1321*
but *t* the way of God truly .... Lk 20:21   *1321*
that thou *t* all the Jews which .... Acts 21:21   *1321*
Thou therefore which *t* another .... Rom 2:21   *1321*
t thou not thyself? .... Rom 2:21   *1321*

TEACHETH
He *t* my hands to war 2Sa 22:35   *3925*
Who *t* us more than the beasts of .... Job 35:11   *502*
who *t* like him .... Job 36:22   *3384*
He *t* my hands to war, so that a .... Ps 18:34   *3925*
he that *t* man knowledge, shall .... Ps 94:10   *3925*
which *t* my hands to war, and my .... Ps 144:1   *3925*
his feet, he *t* with his fingers .... Prov 6:13   *3384*
The heart of the wise *t* his mouth .... Prov 16:23   *7919*
and the prophet that *t* lies .... Is 9:15   *3384*
thy God which *t* thee to profit .... Is 48:17   *3925*
that *t* all men every where .... Acts 21:28   *1321*
or he that *t*, on teaching .... Rom 12:7   *1321*
in the words which man's wisdom *t* 1Cor 2:13   *1318*
but which the Holy Ghost *t* 1Cor 2:13   *1318*
him that *t* in all good things .... Gal 6:6   *2727*
anointing *t* you of all things 1Jn 2:27   *1321*

TEACHING
true God, and without a *t* priest 2Chr 15:3   *3384*
t them, they have them not .... Jer 32:33   *3925*
t in their synagogues, and .... Mt 4:23   *1321*
t in their synagogues, and .... Mt 9:35   *1321*
t for doctrines the commandments ...... Mt 15:9   *1321*
people came unto him as he was *t* .... Mt 21:23   *1321*
daily with you *t* in the temple .... Mt 26:55   *1321*
T them to observe all things .... Mt 28:20   *1321*
went round about the villages, *t* .... Mk 6:6   *1321*
t for doctrines the commandments .... Mk 7:7   *1321*
daily with you in the temple *t* .... Mk 14:49   *1321*
on a certain day, as he was *t* .... Lk 5:17   *1321*
he was *t* in one of the synagogues .... Lk 13:10   *1321*
through the cities and villages, *t* .... Lk 13:22   *1321*
day time he was *t* in the temple .... Lk 21:37   *1321*
t throughout all Jewry, beginning .... Lk 23:5   *1321*
in the temple, and *t* the people .... Acts 5:25   *1321*
Barnabas continued in Antioch, *t* .... Acts 15:35   *1321*
t the word of God among them .... Acts 18:11   *1321*
t those things which concern the .... Acts 28:31   *1321*

or he that teacheth, on *t* .... Rom 12:7   *1319*
t every man in all wisdom .... Col 1:28   *1321*
t and admonishing one another in .... Col 3:16   *1321*
t things which they ought not, ... Titus 1:11   *1321*
T us that, denying ungodliness and ...... Titus 2:12   *3811*

TEAR
then I will *t* your flesh with the .... Judg 8:7   *1758*
Lest he *t* my soul like a lion, ... Ps 7:2   *2963*
they did *t* me, and ceased not .... Ps 35:15   *7167*
lest I *t* you in pieces, and there .... Ps 50:22   *2963*
sword to slay, and the dogs to *t* .... Jer 15:3   *5498*
Neither shall men *t* themselves .... Jer 16:7   *6536*
I will *t* them from your arms, and .... Eze 13:20   *7167*
Your kerchiefs also will I *t* .... Eze 13:21   *7167*
I, even I, will *t* and go away .... Hos 5:14   *2963*
the wild beast shall *t* them .... Hos 13:8   *1234*
and his anger did *t* perpetually .... Amos 1:11   *2963*
The lion did *t* in pieces enough .... Nah 2:12   *2963*
fat, and their claws in pieces .... Zec 11:16   *6561*

TEARETH
t the arm with the crown of the .... Deut 33:20   *2963*
He *t* me in his wrath, who hateth .... Job 16:9   *2963*
He *t* himself in his anger .... Job 18:4   *2963*
t in pieces, and none can deliver .... Mic 5:8   *2963*
he taketh him, he *t* him .... Mk 9:18   *4486*
it *t* him that he foameth again, ... Lk 9:39   *4682*

TEARS
thy prayer, I have seen thy *t* 2Kin 20:5   *1832*
besought him with *t* to put away .... Est 8:3   *1058*
mine eye poureth out *t* unto God .... Job 16:20
I water my couch with my *t* .... Ps 6:6   *1832*
hold not thy peace at my *t* .... Ps 39:12   *1832*
My *t* have been my meat day and .... Ps 42:3   *1832*
put thou my *t* into thy bottle .... Ps 56:8   *1832*
feedest them with the bread of *t* .... Ps 80:5   *1832*
givest them *t* to drink in great .... Ps 80:5   *1832*
soul from death, mine eyes from *t* .... Ps 116:8   *1832*
They that sow in *t* shall reap in .... Ps 126:5   *1832*
behold the *t* of such as were .... Eccl 4:1   *1832*
I will water thee with my *t* .... Is 16:9   *1832*
wipe away *t* from off all faces .... Is 25:8   *1832*
thy prayer, I have seen thy *t* .... Is 38:5   *1832*
and mine eyes a fountain of *t* .... Jer 9:1   *1832*
that our eyes may run down with *t* .... Jer 9:18   *1832*
weep sore, and run down with *t* .... Jer 13:17   *1832*
mine eyes run down with *t* night .... Jer 14:17   *1832*
weeping, and thine eyes from *t* .... Jer 31:16   *1832*
night, and her *t* are on her cheeks .... Lam 1:2   *1832*
Mine eyes do fail with *t*, my .... Lam 2:11   *1832*
let *t* run down like a river day .... Lam 2:18   *1832*
neither shall thy *t* run down .... Eze 24:16   *1832*
the altar of the Lᴏʀᴅ with *t* .... Mal 2:13   *1832*
child cried out, and said with *t* .... Mk 9:24   *1144*
and began to wash his feet with *t* .... Lk 7:38   *1144*
she hath washed my feet with *t* .... Lk 7:44   *1144*
humility of mind, and with many *t* .... Acts 20:19   *1144*
every one night and day with *t* .... Acts 20:31   *1144*
I wrote unto you with many *t* 2Cor 2:4   *1144*
see thee, being mindful of thy *t* 2Ti 1:4   *1144*
t unto him that was able to save .... Heb 5:7   *1144*
he sought it carefully with *t* .... Heb 12:17   *1144*
wipe away all *t* from their eyes .... Rev 7:17   *1144*
wipe away all *t* from their eyes .... Rev 21:4   *1144*

TEATS
They shall lament for the *t* .... Is 32:12   *7699*
bruised the *t* of their virginity .... Eze 23:3   *1717*
youth, in bruising thy *t* by the .... Eze 23:21   *1717*

TEBAH *(te′-bah) A son of Nahor.*
name was Reumah, she bare also *T* ...... Gen 22:24   *2875*

TEBALIAH *(teb-a-li′-ah) A sanctuary servant.*
T the third, Zechariah the fourth 1Chr 26:11   *2882*

TEBETH *(te′-beth) Tenth month of the Hebrew year.*
tenth month, which is the month *T* .... Est 2:16   *2887*

TEDIOUS
that I be not further *t* unto thee .... Acts 24:4   *1465*

TEETH
wine, and his *t* white with milk .... Gen 49:12   *8127*
the flesh was yet between their *t* .... Num 11:33   *8127*
send the *t* of beasts upon them .... Deut 32:24   *8127*
fleshhook of three *t* in his hand 1Sa 2:13   *8127*
the *t* of the young lions, are .... Job 4:10   *8127*
do I take my flesh in my *t* .... Job 13:14   *8127*
he gnasheth upon me with his *t* .... Job 16:9   *8127*
am escaped with the skin of my *t* .... Job 19:20   *8127*
and plucked the spoil out of his *t* .... Job 29:17   *8127*
his *t* are terrible round about .... Job 41:14   *8127*

hast broken the *t* of the ungodly	Ps 3:7	8127
they gnashed upon me with their *t*	Ps 35:16	8127
and gnasheth upon him with his *t*	Ps 37:12	8127
whose *t* are spears and arrows, and	Ps 57:4	8127
Break their *t*, O God, in their	Ps 58:6	8127
the great *t* of the young lions	Ps 58:6	4973
he shall gnash with his *t*	Ps 112:10	8127
not given us as a prey to their *t*	Ps 124:6	8127
As vinegar to the *t*, and as smoke	Prov 10:26	8127
whose *t* are as swords, and their	Prov 30:14	8127
swords, and their jaw *t* as knives	Prov 30:14	4973
Thy *t* are like a flock of sheep	Song 4:2	8127
Thy *t* are as a flock of sheep	Song 6:6	8127
threshing instrument having *t*	Is 41:15	6374
the children's *t* are set on edge	Jer 31:29	8127
his *t* shall be set on edge	Jer 31:30	8127
they hiss and gnash the *t*	Lam 2:16	8127
broken my *t* with gravel stones	Lam 3:16	8127
the children's *t* are set on edge	Eze 18:2	8127
mouth of it between the *t* of it	Dan 7:5	8128
and it had great iron *t*	Dan 7:7	8128
whose *t* were of iron, and his	Dan 7:19	8128
whose *t* are the	Joel 1:6	8127
are the *t* of a lion	Joel 1:6	8127
hath the cheek *t* of a great lion	Joel 1:6	4973
cleanness of *t* in all your cities	Amos 4:6	8127
err, that bite with their *t*	Mic 3:5	8127
abominations from between his *t*	Zec 9:7	8127
shall be weeping and gnashing of *t*	Mt 8:12	3599
shall be wailing and gnashing of *t*	Mt 13:42	3599
shall be wailing and gnashing of *t*	Mt 13:50	3599
shall be weeping and gnashing of *t*	Mt 22:13	3599
shall be weeping and gnashing of *t*	Mt 24:51	3599
shall be weeping and gnashing of *t*	Mt 25:30	3599
with him, cast the same in his *t*	Mt 27:44	3679
foameth, and gnasheth with his *t*	Mk 9:18	3599
shall be weeping and gnashing of *t*	Lk 13:28	3599
they gnashed on him with their *t*	Acts 7:54	3599
their *t* were as the	Rev 9:8	3599
were as the *t* of lions	Rev 9:8	3599

TEHAPHNEHES (te-haf'-ne-heze) *Same as Tahpanhes.*
At *T* also the day shall be	Eze 30:18	8471

TEHINNAH (te-hin'-nah) *A descendant of Judah.*
T the father of Ir-nahash	1Chr 4:12	8468

TEIL
as a *t* tree, and as an oak, whose	Is 6:13	424

TEKEL (te'-kel) *Part of the "handwriting of the wall."*
that was written, MENE, MENE, *T*	Dan 5:25	8625
T; Thou art weighed	Dan 5:27	8625

TEKOA (te'-ko-ah) *See Tekoah, Tekoite.*
1. Son of Ashur.
bare him Ashur the father of *T*	1Chr 2:24	8620
the father of *T* had two wives	1Chr 4:5	8620
2. A city in Judah.
even Beth-lehem, and Etam, and *T*	2Chr 11:6	8620
forth into the wilderness of *T*	2Chr 20:20	8620
and blow the trumpet in *T*	Jer 6:1	8620
who was among the herdmen of *T*	Amos 1:1	8620

TEKOAH (te'-ko-ah) *See Tekoa. Same as Tekoa 2.*
And Joab sent to *T*, and fetched	2Sa 14:2	8620
the woman of *T* spake to the king	2Sa 14:4	8621
the woman of *T* said unto the king	2Sa 14:9	8621

TEKOITE (te'-ko-ite) *See Tekoites. An inhabitant of Tekoa.*
Ira the son of Ikkesh the *T*	2Sa 23:26	8621
Ira the son of Ikkesh the *T*	1Chr 11:28	8621
was Ira the son of Ikkesh the *T*	1Chr 27:9	8621

TEKOITES (te'-ko-ites)
And next unto them the *T* repaired	Neh 3:5	8621
After them the *T* repaired another	Neh 3:27	8621

TEL-ABIB (tel-a'-bib) *Town on the River Chebar.*
to them of the captivity at *T*	Eze 3:15	8512

TELAH (te'-lah) *Father of Tahan.*
T his son, and Tahan his son,	1Chr 7:25	8520

TELAIM (tel'-a-im) *See Telem. A place in Judah.*
together, and numbered them in *T*	1Sa 15:4	2923

TELASSAR (te-las'-sar) *See Thelasar. A city in Mesopotamia.*
children of Eden which were in *T*	Is 37:12	8515

TEL AVIV *See Tel-abib.*

TELEM (te'-lem) *See Telaim.*
1. A city in Judah.
Ziph, and *T*, and Bealoth,	Josh 15:24	2928

2. Married a foreigner in exile.
Shallum, and *T*, and Uri	Ezr 10:24	2928

TEL-HARESHA (tel-ha-re'-sha) *See Tel-harsa. A Babylonian settlement of exiles.*
went up also from Tel-melah, *T*	Neh 7:61	8521

TEL-HARSA (tel'-har-sah) *See Tel-haresha. Same as Tel-haresha.*
which went up from Tel-melah, *T*	Ezr 2:59	8521

TELL *See APPENDIX.*

TELLEST
Thou *t* my wanderings	Ps 56:8	5608

TELLETH
Also the LORD *t* thee that he will	2Sa 7:11	5046
t the king of Israel the words	2Kin 6:12	5046
when he goeth abroad, he *t* it	Ps 41:6	1696
he that *t* lies shall not tarry in	Ps 101:7	1696
He *t* the number of the stars	Ps 147:4	4487
the hands of him that *t* them	Jer 33:13	4487
Philip cometh and *t* Andrew	Jn 12:22	3004

TELLING *See APPENDIX.*

TEL-MELAH (tel-me'-lah) *A place where the exiles lived.*
were they which went up from *T*	Ezr 2:59	8528
they which went up also from *T*	Neh 7:61	8528

TEMA (te'-mah)
1. A son of Ishmael.
Hadar, and *T*, Jetur, Naphish, and	Gen 25:15	8485
and Dumah, Massa, Hadad, and *T*	1Chr 1:30	8485
T brought water to him that was	Is 21:14	8485
Dedan, and *T*, and Buz, and all that	Jer 25:23	8485
2. A city in northern Arabia.
The troops of *T* looked, the	Job 6:19	8485

TEMAH *See Thamah.*

TEMAN (te'-man) *See Temanite.*
1. A son of Eliphaz.
And the sons of Eliphaz were *T*	Gen 36:11	8487
duke *T*, duke Omar, duke Zepho,	Gen 36:15	8487
Duke Kenaz, duke *T*, duke Mibzar,	Gen 36:42	8487
T, and Omar, Zephi, and Gatam,	1Chr 1:36	8487
Duke Kenaz, duke *T*, duke Mibzar,	1Chr 1:53	8487
2. A race and district of Edom.
Is wisdom no more in *T*	Jer 49:7	8487
against the inhabitants of *T*	Jer 49:20	8487
and I will make it desolate from *T*	Eze 25:13	8487
But I will send a fire upon *T*	Amos 1:12	8487
And thy mighty men, O *T*, shall be	Obad 9	8487
God came from *T*, and the Holy One	Hab 3:3	8487

TEMANI (te'-ma-ni) *See Temanite. A son of Ashur.*
land of *T* reigned in his stead	Gen 36:34	8489

TEMANITE (te'-man-ite) *See Temani, Temanites. An inhabitant of Teman 2.*
Eliphaz the *T*, and Bildad the	Job 2:11	8489
Then Eliphaz the *T* answered	Job 4:1	8489
Then answered Eliphaz the *T*	Job 15:1	8489
Then Eliphaz the *T* answered	Job 22:1	8489
the LORD said to Eliphaz the *T*	Job 42:7	8489
So Eliphaz the *T* and Bildad the	Job 42:9	8489

TEMANITES (te'-man-ites)
of the *T* reigned in his stead	1Chr 1:45	8489

TEMENI (tem'-e-ni) *A descendant of Caleb.*
bare him Ahuzam, and Hepher, and *T*	1Chr 4:6	8488

TEMPER
of oil, to *t* with the fine flour	Eze 46:14	7450

TEMPERANCE
he reasoned of righteousness, *t*	Acts 24:25	1466
Meekness, *t*	Gal 5:23	1466
And to knowledge *t*	2Pet 1:6	1466
and to *t* patience	2Pet 1:6	1466

TEMPERATE
the mastery is *t* in all things	1Cor 9:25	1467
of good men, sober, just, holy, *t*	Titus 1:8	1468
the aged men be sober, grave, *t*	Titus 2:2	4998

TEMPERED
and cakes unleavened *t* with oil	Ex 29:2	1101
t together, pure and holy	Ex 30:35	4414
but God hath *t* the body together,	1Cor 12:24	4786

TEMPEST
For he breaketh me with a *t*	Job 9:17	8183
a *t* stealeth him away in the	Job 27:20	5492
and brimstone, and an horrible *t*	Ps 11:6	7307
escape from the windy storm and *t*	Ps 55:8	5591
So persecute them with thy *t*	Ps 83:15	5591
strong one, which as a *t* of hail	Is 28:2	2230

T

and great noise, with storm and *t* .... Is 29:6   5591
fire, with scattering, and *t* .... Is 30:30   2230
the wind, and a covert from the *t* .... Is 32:2   2230
O thou afflicted, tossed with *t* .... Is 54:11   5590
with a *t* in the day of the .... Amos 1:14   5591
there was a mighty *t* in the sea .... Jonah 1:4   5591
my sake this great *t* is upon you .... Jonah 1:12   5591
there arose a great *t* in the sea .... Mt 8:24   4578
being exceedingly tossed with a *t* .... Acts 27:18   5492
no small *t* lay on us, all hope .... Acts 27:20   5494
unto blackness, and darkness, and *t* ..... Heb 12:18   2366
clouds that are carried with a *t* 2Pet 2:17   2978

TEMPESTUOUS

shall be very *t* round about him .... Ps 50:3   8175
for the sea wrought, and was *t* .... Jonah 1:11   5490
wrought, and was *t* against them .... Jonah 1:13   5490
there arose against it a *t* wind............. Acts 27:14   5189

TEMPLE

by a post of the *t* of the LORD 1Sa 1:9   1964
God went out in the *t* of the LORD 1Sa 3:3   1964
he did hear my voice out of his *t* 2Sa 22:7   1964
porch before the *t* of the house 1Kin 6:3   1964
house round about, both of the *t* 1Kin 6:5   1964
the *t* before it, was forty cubits 1Kin 6:17   1964
door of the *t* posts of olive tree 1Kin 6:33   1964
the pillars in the porch of the *t* 1Kin 7:21   1964
of the house, to wit, of the *t* 1Kin 7:50   1964
that were in the *t* of the LORD................ 2Kin 11:10   1004
the *t* to the left corner of the 2Kin 11:11   1004
to the left corner of the 2Kin 11:11   1004
along by the altar and the *t*.................... 2Kin 11:11   1004
the people into the *t* of the LORD 2Kin 11:13   1004
the doors of the *t* of the LORD 2Kin 18:16   1964
to bring forth out of the *t* of 2Kin 23:4   1964
had made in the *t* of the LORD................ 2Kin 24:13   1964
the priest's office in the *t* that 1Chr 6:10   1004
his head in the *t* of Dagon 1Chr 10:10   1004
up the pillars before the *t*...................... 2Chr 3:17   1964
their form, and set them in the *t* 2Chr 4:7   1964
tables, and placed them in the *t* 2Chr 4:8   1964
the doors of the house of the *t*.............. 2Chr 4:22   1964
from the right side of the *t* to 2Chr 23:10   1004
to the left side of the *t* 2Chr 23:10   1004
along by the altar and the *t* 2Chr 23:10   1004
went into the *t* of the LORD to 2Chr 26:16   1964
not into the *t* of the LORD 2Chr 27:2   1964
that they found in the *t* of the 2Chr 29:16   1964
when Josiah had prepared the *t* 2Chr 35:20   1004
and put them in his *t* at Babylon 2Chr 36:7   1964
But the foundation of the *t* of .... Ezr 3:6   1964
foundation of the *t* of the LORD .... Ezr 3:10   1964
the *t* unto the LORD God of Israel .... Ezr 4:1   1964
of the *t* that was in Jerusalem................ Ezr 5:14   1965
them into the *t* of Babylon .... Ezr 5:14   1965
king take out of the *t* of Babylon .... Ezr 5:14   1965
carry them into the *t* that is in .... Ezr 5:15   1965
of the *t* which is at Jerusalem .... Ezr 6:5   1965
unto the *t* which is at Jerusalem............ Ezr 6:5   1965
in the house of God, within the *t* .... Neh 6:10   1964
and let us shut the doors of the *t* .... Neh 6:10   1964
go into the *t* to save his life .... Neh 6:11   1964
will I worship toward thy holy *t* .... Ps 5:7   1964
The LORD is in his holy *t* .... Ps 11:4   1964
he heard my voice out of his *t*................ Ps 18:6   1964
the LORD, and to enquire in his *t* .... Ps 27:4   1964
in his *t* doth every one speak of.............. Ps 29:9   1964
O God, in the midst of thy *t* .... Ps 48:9   1964
of thy house, even of thy holy *t* .... Ps 65:4   1964
Because of thy *t* at Jerusalem .... Ps 68:29   1964
thy holy *t* have they defiled .... Ps 79:1   1964
I will worship toward thy holy *t* .... Ps 138:2   1964
up, and his train filled the *t* .... Is 6:1   1964
and to the *t*, Thy foundation shall .... Is 44:28   1964
from the city, a voice from the *t* .... Is 66:6   1964
The *t* of the LORD .... Jer 7:4   1964
The *t* of the LORD .... Jer 7:4   1964
The *t* of the LORD, are these .... Jer 7:4   1964
were set before the *t* of the LORD .... Jer 24:1   1964
our God, the vengeance of his *t* .... Jer 50:28   1964
the LORD, the vengeance of his *t*............ Jer 51:11   1964
at the door of the *t* of the LORD .... Eze 8:16   1964
backs toward the *t* of the LORD .... Eze 8:16   1964
Afterward he brought me to the *t* .... Eze 41:1   1964
twenty cubits, before the *t* .... Eze 41:4   1964
hundred cubits, with the inner *t*............ Eze 41:15   1964
made, and on the wall of the *t* .... Eze 41:20   1964
The posts of the *t* were squared............ Eze 41:21   1964
And the *t* and the sanctuary had two .... Eze 41:23   1964
on them, on the doors of the *t* .... Eze 41:25   1964
before the *t* were an hundred .... Eze 42:8   1964

had taken out of the *t* which was............ Dan 5:2   1965
that were taken out of the *t* of................ Dan 5:3   1965
the songs of the *t* shall be .... Amos 8:3   1964
will look again toward thy holy *t* .... Jonah 2:4   1964
in unto thee, into thine holy *t* .... Jonah 2:7   1964
you, the Lord from his holy *t* .... Mic 1:2   1964
But the LORD is in his holy *t* .... Hab 2:20   1964
upon a stone in the *t* of the LORD .... Hag 2:15   1964
of the LORD's *t* was laid, ... Hag 2:18   1964
he shall build the *t* of the LORD .... Zec 6:12   1964
he shall build the *t* of the LORD .... Zec 6:13   1964
a memorial in the *t* of the LORD .... Zec 6:14   1964
and build in the *t* of the LORD................ Zec 6:15   1964
that the *t* might be built .... Zec 8:9   1964
shall suddenly come to his *t* .... Mal 3:1   1964
him on a pinnacle of the *t* .... Mt 4:5   2411
in the *t* profane the sabbath .... Mt 12:5   2411
place is one greater than the *t* .... Mt 12:6   2411
And Jesus went into the *t* of God .... Mt 21:12   2411
them that sold and bought in the *t* .... Mt 21:12   2411
and the lame came to him in the *t* .... Mt 21:14   2411
and the children crying in the *t* .... Mt 21:15   2411
And when he was come into the *t*............ Mt 21:23   2411
Whosoever shall swear by the *t* .... Mt 23:16   3485
shall swear by the gold of the *t* .... Mt 23:16   3485
or the *t* that sanctifieth the .... Mt 23:17   3485
And whoso shall swear by the *t* .... Mt 23:21   3485
whom ye slew between the *t* .... Mt 23:35   3485
went out, and departed from the *t* .... Mt 24:1   2411
shew him the buildings of the *t*.............. Mt 24:1   2411
daily with you teaching in the *t* .... Mt 26:55   2411
I am able to destroy the *t* of God .... Mt 26:61   3485
the pieces of silver in the *t* .... Mt 27:5   3485
Thou that destroyest the *t* .... Mt 27:40   3485
the veil of the *t* was rent in.................... Mt 27:51   3485
into Jerusalem, and into the *t* .... Mk 11:11   2411
and Jesus went into the *t*, and .... Mk 11:15   2411
them that sold and bought in the *t* .... Mk 11:15   2411
carry any vessel through the *t* .... Mk 11:16   2411
and as he was walking in the *t* .... Mk 11:27   2411
and said, while he taught in the *t* .... Mk 12:35   2411
And as he went out of the *t* .... Mk 13:1   2411
of Olives over against the *t* .... Mk 13:3   2411
daily with you in the *t* teaching............ Mk 14:49   2411
I will destroy this *t* that is .... Mk 14:58   3485
Ah, thou that destroyest the *t* .... Mk 15:29   3485
the veil of the *t* was rent in.................... Mk 15:38   3485
he went into the *t* of the Lord .... Lk 1:9   3485
that he tarried so long in the *t*................ Lk 1:21   3485
he had seen a vision in the *t* .... Lk 1:22   3485
he came by the Spirit into the *t* .... Lk 2:27   2411
which departed not from the *t* .... Lk 2:37   2411
days they found him in the *t* .... Lk 2:46   2411
and set him on a pinnacle of the *t*.......... Lk 4:9   2411
between the altar and the *t* .... Lk 11:51   3624
men went up into the *t* to pray .... Lk 18:10   2411
And he went into the *t*, and began .... Lk 19:45   2411
And he taught daily in the *t* .... Lk 19:47   2411
as he taught the people in the *t* .... Lk 20:1   2411
And as some spake of the *t* .... Lk 21:5   2411
day time he was teaching in the *t*.......... Lk 21:37   2411
in the morning to him in the *t* .... Lk 21:38   2411
priests, and captains of the *t* .... Lk 22:52   2411
I was daily with you in the *t* .... Lk 22:53   2411
the veil of the *t* was rent in the .... Lk 23:45   3485
And were continually in the *t* .... Lk 24:53   2411
found in the *t* those that sold .... Jn 2:14   2411
he drove them all out of the *t* .... Jn 2:15   2411
and said unto them, Destroy this *t*...... Jn 2:19   3485
six years was this *t* in building .... Jn 2:20   3485
But he spake of the *t* of his body .... Jn 2:21   3485
Jesus findeth him in the *t* .... Jn 5:14   2411
feast Jesus went up into the *t* .... Jn 7:14   2411
cried Jesus in the *t* as he taught .... Jn 7:28   2411
morning he came again into the *t* .... Jn 8:2   2411
treasury, as he taught in the *t* .... Jn 8:20   2411
hid himself, and went out of the *t* .... Jn 8:59   2411
in the *t* in Solomon's porch .... Jn 10:23   2411
as they stood in the *t*, What.................... Jn 11:56   2411
in the synagogue, and in the *t* .... Jn 18:20   2411
daily with one accord in the *t* .... Acts 2:46   2411
into the *t* at the hour of prayer .... Acts 3:1   2411
the *t* which is called Beautiful .... Acts 3:2   2411
of them that entered into the *t* .... Acts 3:2   2411
to go into the *t* asked an alms .... Acts 3:3   2411
and entered with them into the *t* .... Acts 3:8   2411
at the Beautiful gate of the *t* .... Acts 3:10   2411
priests, and the captain of the *t* .... Acts 4:1   2411
speak in the *t* to the people all .... Acts 5:20   2411
into the *t* early in the morning .... Acts 5:21   2411
priest and the captain of the *t* .... Acts 5:24   2411

in prison are standing in the *t*	Acts 5:25	2411
And daily in the *t*, and in every	Acts 5:42	2411
but also that the *t* of the great	Acts 19:27	2411
with them entered into the *t*	Acts 21:26	2411
Asia, when they saw him in the *t*	Acts 21:27	2411
brought Greeks also into the *t*	Acts 21:28	2411
that Paul had brought into the *t*	Acts 21:29	2411
Paul, and drew him out of the *t*	Acts 21:30	2411
even while I prayed in the *t*	Acts 22:17	2411
hath gone about to profane the *t*	Acts 24:6	2411
in the *t* disputing with any man	Acts 24:12	2411
Asia found me purified in the *t*	Acts 24:18	2411
the Jews, neither against the *t*	Acts 25:8	2411
the Jews caught me in the *t*	Acts 26:21	2411
ye not that ye are the *t* of God	1Cor 3:16	3485
If any man defile the *t* of God	1Cor 3:17	3485
for the *t* of God is holy, which	1Cor 3:17	3485
of God is holy, which *t* ye are	1Cor 3:17	3485
ye not that your body is the *t* of	1Cor 6:19	3485
sit at meat in the idol's *t*	1Cor 8:10	
live of the things of the *t*	1Cor 9:13	2411
hath the *t* of God with idols	2Cor 6:16	3485
for ye are the *t* of the living	2Cor 6:16	3485
unto an holy *t* in the Lord	Eph 2:21	3485
he as God sitteth in the *t* of God	2Th 2:4	3485
make a pillar in the *t* of my God	Rev 3:12	3485
serve him day and night in his *t*	Rev 7:15	3485
Rise, and measure the *t* of God	Rev 11:1	3485
which is without the *t* leave out	Rev 11:2	3485
the *t* of God was opened in heaven	Rev 11:19	3485
there was seen in his *t* the ark	Rev 11:19	3485
another angel came out of the *t*	Rev 14:15	3485
out of the *t* which is in heaven	Rev 14:17	3485
the *t* of the tabernacle of the	Rev 15:5	3485
seven angels came out of the *t*	Rev 15:6	3485
the *t* was filled with smoke from	Rev 15:8	3485
man was able to enter into the *t*	Rev 15:8	3485
the *t* saying to the seven angels	Rev 16:1	3485
voice out of the *t* of heaven	Rev 16:17	3485
And I saw no *t* therein	Rev 21:22	3485
and the Lamb are the *t* of it	Rev 21:22	3485

TEMPLES

him, and smote the nail into his *t*	Judg 4:21	7451
dead, and the nail was in his *t*	Judg 4:22	7451
pierced and stricken through his *t*	Judg 5:26	7451
thy *t* are like a piece of a	Song 4:3	7451
are thy *t* within thy locks	Song 6:7	7451
his Maker, and buildeth *t*	Hos 8:14	1964
have carried into your *t* my	Joel 3:5	1964
dwelleth not in *t* made with hands	Acts 7:48	3485
dwelleth not in *t* made with hands	Acts 17:24	3485

TEMPORAL

the things which are seen are *t*	2Cor 4:18	4340

TEMPT

things, that God did *t* Abraham	Gen 22:1	5254
wherefore do ye *t* the LORD	Ex 17:2	5254
Ye shall not *t* the LORD your God,	Deut 6:16	5254
ask, neither will I *t* the LORD	Is 7:12	5254
yea, they that *t* God are even	Mal 3:15	974
Thou shalt not *t* the Lord thy God	Mt 4:7	1598
Why *t* ye me, ye hypocrites	Mt 22:18	3985
said unto them, Why *t* ye me	Mk 12:15	3985
Thou shalt not *t* the Lord thy God	Lk 4:12	1598
and said unto them, Why *t* ye me	Lk 20:23	3985
to *t* the Spirit of the Lord	Acts 5:9	3985
Now therefore why *t* ye God	Acts 15:10	3985
that Satan *t* you not for your	1Cor 7:5	3985
Neither let us *t* Christ, as some	1Cor 10:9	1598

TEMPTATION

as in the day of *t* in the	Ps 95:8	4531
And lead us not into *t*, but	Mt 6:13	3986
and pray, that ye enter not into *t*	Mt 26:41	3986
ye and pray, lest ye enter into *t*	Mk 14:38	3986
the devil had ended all the *t*	Lk 4:13	3986
and in time of *t* fall away	Lk 8:13	3986
And lead us not into *t*	Lk 11:4	3986
Pray that ye enter not into *t*	Lk 22:40	3986
and pray, lest ye enter into *t*	Lk 22:46	3986
There hath no *t* taken you but	1Cor 10:13	3986
but will with the *t* also make a	1Cor 10:13	3986
my *t* which was in my flesh ye	Gal 4:14	3986
that will be rich fall into *t*	1Ti 6:9	3986
in the day of *t* in the wilderness	Heb 3:8	3986
is the man that endureth *t*	Jas 1:12	3986
will keep thee from the hour of *t*	Rev 3:10	3986

TEMPTATIONS

the midst of another nation, by *t*	Deut 4:34	4531
The great *t* which thine eyes saw,	Deut 7:19	4531

The great *t* which thine eyes have	Deut 29:3	4531
have continued with me in my *t*	Lk 22:28	3986
of mind, and with many tears, and *t*	Acts 20:19	3986
joy when ye fall into divers *t*	Jas 1:2	3986
in heaviness through manifold *t*	1Pet 1:6	3986
how to deliver the godly out of *t*	2Pet 2:9	3986

TEMPTED

and because they *t* the LORD	Ex 17:7	5254
have *t* me now these ten times, and	Num 14:22	5254
your God, as ye *t* him in Massah	Deut 6:16	5254
they *t* God in their heart to	Ps 78:18	5254
t God, and limited the Holy One of	Ps 78:41	5254
Yet they *t* and provoked the most	Ps 78:56	5254
When your fathers *t* me, proved me	Ps 95:9	5254
and *t* God in the desert	Ps 106:14	5254
wilderness to be *t* of the devil	Mt 4:1	3985
wilderness forty days, *t* of Satan	Mk 1:13	3985
Being forty days *t* of the devil	Lk 4:2	3985
t him, saying, Master, what shall	Lk 10:25	1598
Christ, as some of them also *t*	1Cor 10:9	3985
to be *t* above that ye are able	1Cor 10:13	3985
thyself, lest thou also be *t*	Gal 6:1	3985
some means the tempter have *t* you	1Th 3:5	3985
he himself hath suffered being *t*	Heb 2:18	3985
able to succour them that are *t*	Heb 2:18	3985
When your fathers *t* me, proved me	Heb 3:9	3985
in all points *t* like as we are	Heb 4:15	3985
they were sawn asunder, were *t*	Heb 11:37	3985
when he is *t*, I am *t* of God	Jas 1:13	3985
for God cannot be *t* with evil	Jas 1:13	551
But every man is *t*, when he is	Jas 1:14	3985

TEMPTER

when the *t* came to him, he said,	Mt 4:3	3985
some means the *t* have tempted you	1Th 3:5	3985

TEMPTETH

with evil, neither *t* he any man	Jas 1:13	3985

TEMPTING

t desired him that he would shew	Mt 16:1	3985
t him, and saying unto him, Is it	Mt 19:3	3985
him a question, *t* him, and saying,	Mt 22:35	3985
of him a sign from heaven, *t* him	Mk 8:11	3985
put away his wife? *t* him	Mk 10:2	3985
t him, sought of him a sign from	Lk 11:16	3985
t him, that they might have to	Jn 8:6	3985

TEN

were nine hundred and *t* years	Gen 5:14	6235
after Abram had dwelt *t* years in	Gen 16:3	6235
Peradventure *t* shall be found	Gen 18:32	6235
the servant took *t* camels of the	Gen 24:10	6235
hands of *t* shekels weight of gold	Gen 24:22	6235
us a few days, at the least *t*	Gen 24:55	6218
me, and changed my wages *t* times	Gen 31:7	6235
hast changed my wages *t* times	Gen 31:41	6235
t bulls, twenty she asses	Gen 32:15	6235
twenty she asses, and *t* foals	Gen 32:15	6235
Joseph's *t* brethren went down to	Gen 42:3	6235
t asses laden with the good	Gen 45:23	6235
t she asses laden with corn and	Gen 45:23	6235
into Egypt, were threescore and *t*	Gen 46:27	
for him threescore and *t* days	Gen 50:3	
lived an hundred and *t* years	Gen 50:22	6235
being an hundred and *t* years old	Gen 50:26	6235
and threescore and *t* palm trees	Ex 15:27	
t curtains of fine twined linen	Ex 26:1	6235
T cubits shall be the length of a	Ex 26:16	6235
pillars *t*, and their sockets *t*	Ex 27:12	6235
the covenant, the *t* commandments	Ex 34:28	6235
t curtains of fine twined linen	Ex 36:8	6235
length of a board was *t* cubits	Ex 36:21	6235
pillars *t*, and their sockets *t*	Ex 38:12	6235
shall put *t* thousand to flight	Lev 26:8	7233
t women shall bake your bread in	Lev 26:26	6235
and for the female *t* shekels	Lev 27:5	6235
and for the female *t* shekels	Lev 27:7	6235
One spoon of *t* shekels of gold,	Num 7:14	6235
One spoon of gold of *t* shekels	Num 7:20	6235
One golden spoon of *t* shekels	Num 7:26	6235
One golden spoon of *t* shekels	Num 7:32	6235
One golden spoon of *t* shekels	Num 7:38	6235
One golden spoon of *t* shekels	Num 7:44	6235
One golden spoon of *t* shekels	Num 7:50	6235
One golden spoon of *t* shekels	Num 7:56	6235
One golden spoon of *t* shekels	Num 7:62	6235
One golden spoon of *t* shekels	Num 7:68	6235
One golden spoon of *t* shekels	Num 7:74	6235
One golden spoon of *t* shekels	Num 7:80	6235
weighing *t* shekels apiece, after	Num 7:86	6235
nor five days, neither *t* days	Num 11:19	6235

gathered least gathered *t* homers	Num 11:32	6235
have tempted me now these *t* times	Num 14:22	6235
And on the fourth day *t* bullocks	Num 29:23	6235
and threescore and *t* palm trees	Num 33:9	
to perform, even *t* commandments	Deut 4:13	6235
the *t* commandments, which the	Deut 10:4	6235
with threescore and *t* persons	Deut 10:22	
two put *t* thousand to flight,	Deut 32:30	7233
he came with *t* thousands of	Deut 33:2	7233
they are the *t* thousands of	Deut 33:17	7233
t cities with their villages	Josh 15:57	6235
there fell *t* portions to Manasseh	Josh 17:5	6235
half tribe of Manasseh, *t* cities	Josh 21:5	6235
All the cities were *t* with their	Josh 21:26	6235
And with him *t* princes, of each	Josh 22:14	6235
being an hundred and *t* years old	Josh 24:29	6235
of them in Bezek *t* thousand men	Judg 1:4	6235
t kings, having their thumbs and	Judg 1:7	
being an hundred and *t* years old	Judg 2:8	6235
at that time about *t* thousand men	Judg 3:29	6235
take with thee *t* thousand men of	Judg 4:6	6235
he went up with *t* thousand men at	Judg 4:10	6235
and *t* thousand men after him	Judg 4:14	6235
Then Gideon took *t* men of his	Judg 6:27	6235
and there remained *t* thousand	Judg 7:3	6235
t sons of his body begotten	Judg 8:30	
t persons, reign over you, or	Judg 9:2	
t pieces of silver out of the	Judg 9:4	
t persons, upon one stone	Judg 9:5	
t persons, upon one stone, and	Judg 9:18	
t sons of Jerubbaal might come,	Judg 9:24	
and he judged Israel *t* years	Judg 12:11	6235
rode on threescore and *t* ass colts	Judg 12:14	
I will give thee *t* shekels of	Judg 17:10	6235
we will take *t* men of an hundred	Judg 20:10	6235
and a thousand out of *t* thousand	Judg 20:10	7233
there came against Gibeah *t*	Judg 20:34	6235
they dwelled there about *t* years	Ruth 1:4	6235
he took *t* men of the elders of	Ruth 4:2	6235
not I better to thee than *t* sons	1Sa 1:8	6235
thousand and threescore and *t* men	1Sa 6:19	
and *t* thousand men of Judah	1Sa 15:4	6235
these *t* loaves, and run to the	1Sa 17:17	6235
carry these *t* cheeses unto the	1Sa 17:18	6235
and David his *t* thousands.	1Sa 18:7	7233
ascribed unto David *t* thousands	1Sa 18:8	7233
and David his *t* thousands	1Sa 21:11	7233
And David sent out *t* young men	1Sa 25:5	6235
came to pass about *t* days after	1Sa 25:38	6235
and David his *t* thousands	1Sa 29:5	7233
And the king left *t* women, which	2Sa 15:16	6235
thou art worth *t* thousand of us	2Sa 18:3	6235
given thee *t* shekels of silver	2Sa 18:11	6235
t young men that bare Joab's	2Sa 18:15	6235
We have *t* parts in the king, and	2Sa 19:43	6235
the king took the *t* women his	2Sa 20:3	6235
T fat oxen, and twenty oxen out of	1Kin 4:23	6235
t thousand a month by courses	1Kin 5:14	6235
t thousand that bare burdens, and	1Kin 5:15	
t cubits was the breadth thereof	1Kin 6:3	6235
of olive tree, each *t* cubits high	1Kin 6:23	6235
part of the other were *t* cubits	1Kin 6:24	6235
And the other cherub was *t* cubits	1Kin 6:25	6235
of the one cherub was *t* cubits	1Kin 6:26	6235
great stones, stones of *t* cubits	1Kin 7:10	6235
t cubits from the one brim to the	1Kin 7:23	6235
t in a cubit, compassing the sea	1Kin 7:24	6235
And he made *t* bases of brass.	1Kin 7:27	6235
this manner he made the *t* bases	1Kin 7:37	6235
Then made he *t* lavers of brass	1Kin 7:38	6235
one of the *t* bases one laver	1Kin 7:38	6235
bases, and *t* lavers on the bases	1Kin 7:43	6235
to Jeroboam, Take thee *t* pieces	1Kin 11:31	6235
will give *t* tribes to thee	1Kin 11:31	6235
give it unto thee, even *t* tribes	1Kin 11:35	6235
And take with thee *t* loaves	1Kin 14:3	6235
took with him *t* talents of silver	2Kin 5:5	6235
of gold, and *t* changes of raiment	2Kin 5:5	6235
t chariots, and *t* thousand	2Kin 13:7	
in the valley of salt *t* thousand	2Kin 14:7	6235
reigned *t* years in Samaria	2Kin 15:17	6235
t degrees, or go back *t* degrees	2Kin 20:9	6235
the shadow to go down *t* degrees	2Kin 20:10	6235
shadow return backward *t* degrees	2Kin 20:10	6235
the shadow *t* degrees backward	2Kin 20:11	6235
even *t* thousand captives, and all	2Kin 24:14	6235
t men with him, and smote Gedaliah	2Kin 25:25	6235
of Manasseh, by lot, *t* cities	1Chr 6:61	6235
t thousand men that drew sword	1Chr 21:5	
t thousand drams, and of silver	1Chr 29:7	7239
of silver *t* thousand talents, and	1Chr 29:7	6235

t thousand men to bear burdens,	2Chr 2:2	
t thousand of them to be bearers	2Chr 2:18	
t cubits the height thereof	2Chr 4:1	6235
sea of *t* cubits from brim to brim	2Chr 4:2	6235
t in a cubit, compassing the sea	2Chr 4:3	6235
He made also *t* lavers, and put	2Chr 4:6	6235
he made *t* candlesticks of gold	2Chr 4:7	6235
He made also *t* tables, and placed	2Chr 4:8	6235
days the land was quiet *t* years	2Chr 14:1	6235
the children of Seir *t* thousand	2Chr 25:11	6235
other *t* thousand left alive did	2Chr 25:12	6235
t thousand measures of wheat	2Chr 27:5	6235
and *t* thousand of barley	2Chr 27:5	6235
t bullocks, an hundred rams, and	2Chr 29:32	6235
bullocks and *t* thousand sheep	2Chr 30:24	6235
months and *t* days in Jerusalem	2Chr 36:9	6235
to fulfil threescore and *t* years	2Chr 36:21	
a second sort four hundred and *t*	Ezr 1:10	6235
and with him an hundred and *t* males	Ezr 8:12	6235
t of their brethren with them,	Ezr 8:24	6235
came, they said unto us *t* times	Neh 4:12	6235
once in *t* days store of all sorts	Neh 5:18	6235
to bring one of *t* to dwell in	Neh 11:1	6235
I will pay *t* thousand talents of	Est 3:9	6235
The *t* sons of Haman the son of	Est 9:10	6235
palace, and the *t* sons of Haman	Est 9:12	6235
let Haman's *t* sons be hanged upon	Est 9:13	6235
and they hanged Haman's *t* sons	Est 9:14	6235
These *t* times have ye reproached	Job 19:3	6235
afraid of *t* thousands of people	Ps 3:6	7233
and an instrument of *t* strings	Ps 33:2	6218
years are threescore years and *t*	Ps 90:10	
t thousand at thy right hand	Ps 91:7	7233
Upon an instrument of *t* strings	Ps 92:3	6218
an instrument of *t* strings will I	Ps 144:9	6218
t thousands in our streets	Ps 144:13	7231
the wise more than *t* mighty men	Eccl 7:19	6235
the chiefest among *t* thousand	Song 5:10	7233
t acres of vineyard shall yield	Is 5:10	6235
dial of Ahaz, *t* degrees backward	Is 38:8	6235
So the sun returned *t* degrees	Is 38:8	6235
even *t* men with him, came unto	Jer 41:1	6235
the *t* men that were with him, and	Jer 41:2	6235
But *t* men were found among them	Jer 41:8	6235
And it came to pass after *t* days	Jer 42:7	6235
the entry of the gate, *t* cubits	Eze 40:11	6235
breadth of the door was *t* cubits	Eze 41:2	6235
a walk of *t* cubits breadth inward	Eze 42:4	6235
the breadth shall be *t* thousand	Eze 45:1	6235
and the breadth of *t* thousand	Eze 45:3	6235
the *t* thousand of breadth, shall	Eze 45:5	6235
cor, which is an homer of *t* baths	Eze 45:14	6235
for *t* baths are an homer	Eze 45:14	6235
and of *t* thousand in breadth	Eze 48:9	6235
toward the west *t* thousand in	Eze 48:10	6235
toward the east *t* thousand in	Eze 48:10	6235
length, and *t* thousand in breadth	Eze 48:13	6235
and the breadth *t* thousand	Eze 48:13	6235
shall be *t* thousand eastward	Eze 48:18	6235
and *t* thousand westward	Eze 48:18	6235
servants, I beseech thee, *t* days	Dan 1:12	6235
matter, and proved them *t* days	Dan 1:14	6235
at the end of *t* days their	Dan 1:15	6235
he found them *t* times better than	Dan 1:20	6235
and it had *t* horns	Dan 7:7	6236
unto him, and *t* thousand times	Dan 7:10	7240
t thousand stood before him	Dan 7:10	7240
of the *t* horns that were in his	Dan 7:20	6236
the *t* horns out of this kingdom	Dan 7:24	6236
are *t* kings that shall arise	Dan 7:24	6236
shall cast down many *t* thousands	Dan 11:12	7239
forth by an hundred shall leave *t*	Amos 5:3	6235
if there remain *t* men in one	Amos 6:9	6235
or with *t* thousands of rivers of	Mic 6:7	7233
twenty measures, there were but *t*	Hag 2:16	6235
these threescore and *t* years	Zec 1:12	
and the breadth thereof *t* cubits	Zec 5:2	6235
that *t* men shall take hold out of	Zec 8:23	6235
which owed him *t* thousand talents	Mt 18:24	3463
And when the *t* heard it, they were	Mt 20:24	1176
heaven be likened unto *t* virgins	Mt 25:1	1176
it unto him which hath *t* talents	Mt 25:28	1176
And when the *t* heard it, they	Mk 10:41	1176
whether he be able with *t*	Lk 14:31	1176
woman having *t* pieces of silver	Lk 15:8	1176
there met him *t* men that were	Lk 17:12	1176
said, Were there not *t* cleansed	Lk 17:17	1176
And he called his *t* servants	Lk 19:13	1176
and delivered them *t* pounds	Lk 19:13	1176
thy pound hath gained *t* pounds	Lk 19:16	1176
have thou authority over *t* cities	Lk 19:17	1176

give it to him that hath *t* pounds	Lk 19:24	*1176*
unto him, Lord, he hath *t* pounds	Lk 19:25	*1176*
and horsemen threescore and *t*	Acts 23:23	
among them more than *t* days	Acts 25:6	*1176*
For though ye have *t* thousand	1Cor 4:15	*3463*
than *t* thousand words in an	1Cor 14:19	*3463*
the Lord cometh with *t* thousands	Jude 14	*3461*
ye shall have tribulation *t* days	Rev 2:10	*1176*
the number of them was *t* thousand	Rev 5:11	*3461*
thousand times *t* thousand	Rev 5:11	*3461*
t horns, and seven crowns upon his	Rev 12:3	*1176*
t horns, and upon his horns	Rev 13:1	*1176*
and upon his horns *t* crowns	Rev 13:1	*1176*
having seven heads and *t* horns	Rev 17:3	*1176*
hath the seven heads and *t* horns	Rev 17:7	*1176*
the *t* horns which thou sawest are	Rev 17:12	*1176*
which thou sawest are *t* kings	Rev 17:12	*1176*
the *t* horns which thou sawest	Rev 17:16	*1176*

TEND

diligent *t* only to plenteousness	Prov 21:5	

TENDER

unto the herd, and fetch a calf *t*	Gen 18:7	7390
Leah was *t* eyed	Gen 29:17	7390
knoweth that the children are *t*	Gen 33:13	7390
that the man that is *t* among you	Deut 28:54	7390
The *t* and delicate woman among you	Deut 28:56	7390
as the small rain upon the *t* herb	Deut 32:2	
as the *t* grass springing out of	2Sa 23:4	
Because thine heart was *t*	2Kin 22:19	7401
Solomon my son is young and *t*	1Chr 22:5	7390
hath chosen, is yet young and *t*	1Chr 29:1	7390
Because thine heart was *t*	2Chr 34:27	7401
that the *t* branch thereof will	Job 14:7	3127
bud of the *t* herb to spring forth	Job 38:27	
O Lord, thy *t* mercies and thy	Ps 25:6	
not thou thy *t* mercies from me	Ps 40:11	
of thy *t* mercies blot out my	Ps 51:1	
to the multitude of thy *t* mercies	Ps 69:16	
he in anger shut up his *t* mercies	Ps 77:9	
let thy *t* mercies speedily	Ps 79:8	
with lovingkindness and *t* mercies	Ps 103:4	
Let thy *t* mercies come unto me,	Ps 119:77	
Great are thy *t* mercies, O Lord	Ps 119:156	
his *t* mercies are over all his	Ps 145:9	
For I was my father's son, *t*	Prov 4:3	7390
but the *t* mercies of the wicked	Prov 12:10	
the *t* grass sheweth itself, and	Prov 27:25	
the vines with the *t* grape give a	Song 2:13	
for our vines have *t* grapes	Song 2:15	
whether the *t* grape appear, and	Song 7:12	
thou shalt no more be called *t*	Is 47:1	7390
grow up before him as a *t* plant	Is 53:2	3126
top of his young twigs a *t* one	Eze 17:22	7390
t love with the prince of the	Dan 1:9	
in the *t* grass of the field	Dan 4:15	
in the *t* grass of the field	Dan 4:23	
When his branch is yet *t*, and	Mt 24:32	*527*
When her branch is yet *t*, and	Mk 13:28	*527*
Through the *t* mercy of our God	Lk 1:78	*4698*
is very pitiful, and of *t* mercy	Jas 5:11	*3629*

TENDERHEARTED

when Rehoboam was young and *t*	2Chr 13:7	7390,3824
And be ye kind one to another, *t*	Eph 4:32	*2155*

TENDERNESS

the ground for delicateness and *t*	Deut 28:56	7391

TENDETH

labour of the righteous *t* to life	Prov 10:16	
As righteousness *t* to life	Prov 11:19	
than is meet, but it *t* to poverty	Prov 11:24	
talk of the lips *t* only to penury	Prov 14:23	
The fear of the Lord *t* to life	Prov 19:23	

TENONS

Two *t* shall there be in one board	Ex 26:17	3027
under one board for his two *t*	Ex 26:19	3027
under another board for his two *t*	Ex 26:19	3027
One board had two *t*, equally	Ex 36:22	3027
under one board for his two *t*	Ex 36:24	3027
under another board for his two *t*	Ex 36:24	3027

TENOR

according to the *t* of these words	Gen 43:7	6310
for after the *t* of these words I	Ex 34:27	6310

TEN'S

I will not destroy it for *t* sake	Gen 18:32	6235

TENS

rulers of fifties, and rulers of *t*	Ex 18:21	6235
rulers of fifties, and rulers of *t*	Ex 18:25	6235
over fifties, and captains over *t*	Deut 1:15	6235

TENT

and he was uncovered within his *t*	Gen 9:21	168
east of Beth-el, and pitched his *t*	Gen 12:8	168
unto the place where his *t* had	Gen 13:3	168
pitched his *t* toward Sodom	Gen 13:12	167
Then Abram removed his *t*, and came	Gen 13:18	167
he sat in the *t* door in the heat	Gen 18:1	168
ran to meet them from the *t* door	Gen 18:2	168
hastened into the *t* unto Sarah	Gen 18:6	168
And he said, Behold, in the *t*	Gen 18:9	168
And Sarah heard it in the *t* door	Gen 18:10	168
her into his mother Sarah's *t*	Gen 24:67	168
pitched his *t* in the valley of	Gen 26:17	
the Lord, and pitched his *t* there	Gen 26:25	168
had pitched his *t* in the mount	Gen 31:25	168
Jacob's *t*, and into Leah's *t*	Gen 31:33	168
Then went he out of Leah's *t*	Gen 31:33	168
and entered into Rachel's *t*	Gen 31:33	168
And Laban searched all the *t*	Gen 31:34	168
pitched it before the city	Gen 33:18	
field, where he had spread his *t*	Gen 33:19	168
spread his *t* beyond the tower of	Gen 35:21	168
and they came into the *t*	Ex 18:7	168
loops, and couple the *t* together	Ex 26:11	168
of the curtains of the *t*, the	Ex 26:12	168
length of the curtains of the *t*	Ex 26:13	168
for the *t* of rams' skins dyed red	Ex 26:14	168
an hanging for the door of the *t*	Ex 26:36	168
and stood every man at his *t* door	Ex 33:8	168
every man in his *t* door	Ex 33:10	168
The tabernacle, his *t*, and his	Ex 35:11	168
for the *t* over the tabernacle	Ex 36:14	168
of brass to couple the *t* together	Ex 36:18	168
for the *t* of rams' skins dyed red	Ex 36:19	168
t of the congregation finished	Ex 39:32	168
the tabernacle unto Moses, the *t*	Ex 39:33	168
for the *t* of the congregation,	Ex 39:40	168
of the *t* of the congregation	Ex 40:2	168
of the *t* of the congregation	Ex 40:6	168
between the *t* of the congregation	Ex 40:7	168
abroad the *t* over the tabernacle	Ex 40:19	168
covering of the *t* above upon it	Ex 40:19	168
in the *t* of the congregation	Ex 40:22	168
in the *t* of the congregation	Ex 40:24	168
t of the congregation before the	Ex 40:26	168
of the *t* of the congregation	Ex 40:29	168
between the *t* of the congregation	Ex 40:30	168
into the *t* of the congregation	Ex 40:32	168
covered the *t* of the congregation	Ex 40:34	168
into the *t* of the congregation	Ex 40:35	168
abroad out of his *t* seven days	Lev 14:8	168
shall be the tabernacle, and the *t*	Num 3:25	168
namely, the *t* of the testimony	Num 9:15	168
every man in the door of his *t*	Num 11:10	168
the law, when a man dieth in a *t*	Num 19:14	168
all that come into the *t*, and all	Num 19:14	168
and all that is in the *t*	Num 19:14	168
water, and sprinkle it upon the *t*	Num 19:18	168
the man of Israel into the *t*	Num 25:8	6898
in the earth in the midst of my *t*	Josh 7:21	168
and they ran unto the *t*	Josh 7:22	168
and, behold, it was hid in his *t*	Josh 7:22	168
them out of the midst of the *t*	Josh 7:23	168
his asses, and his sheep, and his *t*	Josh 7:24	168
pitched his *t* unto the plain of	Judg 4:11	168
fled away on his feet to the *t* of	Judg 4:17	168
had turned in unto her into the *t*	Judg 4:18	168
her, Stand in the door of the *t*	Judg 4:20	168
Heber's wife took a nail of the *t*	Judg 4:21	168
And when he came into her *t*	Judg 4:22	
shall she be above women in the *t*	Judg 5:24	168
of Israel every man unto his *t*	Judg 7:8	168
host of Midian, and came unto a *t*	Judg 7:13	168
it, that the *t* lay along	Judg 7:13	168
We will not any of us go to his *t*	Judg 20:8	168
and they fled every man into his *t*	1Sa 4:10	168
people he sent every man to his *t*	1Sa 13:2	168
but he put his armour in his *t*	1Sa 17:54	168
this day, but have walked in a *t*	2Sa 7:6	168
So they spread Absalom a *t* upon	2Sa 16:22	168
Israel every man to his *t*	2Sa 17:8	168
had fled every man to his *t*	2Sa 19:8	168
from the city, every man to his *t*	2Sa 20:22	168
of the camp, they went into one *t*	2Kin 7:8	168
again, and entered into another *t*	2Kin 7:8	168
ark of God, and pitched for it a *t*	1Chr 15:1	168
set it in the midst of the *t* that	1Chr 16:1	168
but have gone from *t* to *t*	1Chr 17:5	168
pitched a *t* for it at Jerusalem	2Chr 1:4	168
and they fled every man to his *t*	2Chr 25:22	168
the *t* which he placed among men	Ps 78:60	168

shall the Arabian pitch *t* there	Is 13:20	167
removed from me as a shepherd's *t*	Is 38:12	168
them out as a *t* to dwell in	Is 40:22	168
Enlarge the place of thy *t*	Is 54:2	168
to stretch forth my *t* any more	Jer 10:20	168
they rise up every man in his *t*	Jer 37:10	168

TENTH

continually until the *t* month	Gen 8:5	6224
in the *t* month, on the first day	Gen 8:5	6224
will surely give the *t* unto thee	Gen 28:22	6237
In the *t* day of this month they	Ex 12:3	6218
an omer is the *t* part of an ephah	Ex 16:36	6224
with the one lamb a *t* deal of	Ex 29:40	6241
bring for his offering the *t* part	Lev 5:11	6224
the *t* part of an ephah of fine	Lev 6:20	6224
three *t* deals of fine flour for a	Lev 14:10	6241
one *t* deal of fine flour mingled	Lev 14:21	6241
on the *t* day of the month, ye	Lev 16:29	6218
two *t* deals of fine flour mingled	Lev 23:13	6241
two wave loaves of two *t* deals	Lev 23:17	6241
Also on the *t* day of this seventh	Lev 23:27	6218
two *t* deals shall be in one cake	Lev 24:5	6241
on the *t* day of the seventh month	Lev 25:9	6218
the *t* shall be holy unto the LORD	Lev 27:32	6224
the *t* part of an ephah of barley	Num 5:15	6224
On the *t* day Ahiezer the son of	Num 7:66	6224
t deal of flour mingled with the	Num 15:4	6241
t deals of flour mingled with the	Num 15:6	6241
a meat offering of three *t* deals	Num 15:9	6241
t in Israel for an inheritance	Num 18:21	4643
even a *t* part of the tithe	Num 18:26	4643
a *t* part of an ephah of flour for	Num 28:5	6224
two *t* deals of flour for a meat	Num 28:9	6241
three *t* deals of flour for a meat	Num 28:12	6241
two *t* deals of flour for a meat	Num 28:12	6241
a several *t* deal of flour mingled	Num 28:13	6241
three *t* deals shall ye offer for	Num 28:20	6241
bullock, and two *t* deals for a ram	Num 28:20	6241
A several *t* deal shalt thou offer	Num 28:21	6241
three *t* deals unto one bullock,	Num 28:28	6241
two *t* deals unto one ram,	Num 28:28	6241
A several *t* deal unto one lamb,	Num 28:29	6241
three *t* deals for a bullock	Num 29:3	6241
and two *t* deals for a ram,	Num 29:3	6241
And one *t* deal for one lamb,	Num 29:4	6241
ye shall have on the *t* day of	Num 29:7	6218
three *t* deals to a bullock	Num 29:9	6241
and two *t* deals to one ram,	Num 29:9	6241
A several *t* deal for one lamb,	Num 29:10	6241
three *t* deals unto every bullock	Num 29:14	6241
two *t* deals to each ram of the	Num 29:14	6241
a several *t* deal to each lamb of	Num 29:15	6241
even to his *t* generation shall he	Deut 23:2	6224
even to their *t* generation shall	Deut 23:3	6224
on the *t* day of the first month	Josh 4:19	6218
he will take the *t* of your seed	1Sa 8:15	6237
He will take the *t* of your sheep	1Sa 8:17	6237
year of his reign, in the *t* month	2Kin 25:1	6218
in the *t* day of the month, that	2Kin 25:1	6218
Jeremiah, to Machbanai the	1Chr 12:13	6224
to Jeshua, the *t* to Shecaniah,	1Chr 24:11	6224
The *t* to Shimei, he, his sons, and	1Chr 25:17	6224
The *t* captain for the *t* month	1Chr 27:13	6224
the *t* month to examine the matter	Ezr 10:16	6224
his house royal in the *t* month	Est 2:16	6224
But yet in it shall be a *t*	Is 6:13	6224
Jeremiah from the LORD in the *t*	Jer 32:1	6224
king of Judah, in the *t* month	Jer 39:1	6224
year of his reign, in the *t* month	Jer 52:4	6224
in the *t* day of the month, that	Jer 52:4	6218
in the *t* day of the month, which	Jer 52:12	6218
the *t* day of the month, that	Eze 20:1	6218
in the ninth year, in the *t* month	Eze 24:1	6224
in the *t* day of the month, the	Eze 24:1	6218
In the *t* year, in the *t* month	Eze 29:1	6224
of our captivity, in the *t* month	Eze 33:21	6224
in the *t* day of the month, in the	Eze 40:1	6218
contain the *t* part of an homer	Eze 45:11	4643
the ephah the *t* part of an homer	Eze 45:11	6224
ye shall offer the *t* part of a	Eze 45:14	4643
the seventh, and the fast of the *t*	Zec 8:19	6224
for it was about the *t* hour	Jn 1:39	1182
also Abraham gave a *t* part of all	Heb 7:2	1181
Abraham gave the *t* of the spoils	Heb 7:4	1181
the *t* part of the city fell, and	Rev 11:13	1182
the *t*, a chrysoprasus	Rev 21:20	1182

TENTMAKERS

by their occupation they were *t*	Acts 18:3	4635

TENTS

the father of such as dwell in *t*	Gen 4:20	168
he shall dwell in the *t* of Shem	Gen 9:27	168
Abram, had flocks, and herds, and *t*	Gen 13:5	168
was a plain man, dwelling in *t*	Gen 25:27	168
and into the two maidservants' *t*	Gen 31:33	168
man for them which are in his *t*	Ex 16:16	168
of Israel shall pitch their *t*	Num 1:52	
of Israel pitched their *t*	Num 9:17	
tabernacle they rested in their *t*	Num 9:18	
of the LORD they abode in their *t*	Num 9:20	
of Israel abode in their *t*	Num 9:22	
of the LORD they rested in the *t*	Num 9:23	
that they dwell in, whether in *t*	Num 13:19	4264
from the *t* of these wicked men,	Num 16:26	168
and stood in the door of their *t*	Num 16:27	168
his *t* according to their tribes	Num 24:2	
How goodly are thy *t*, O Jacob, and	Num 24:5	168
And ye murmured in your *t*, and said	Deut 1:27	168
out a place to pitch your *t* in	Deut 1:33	
them, Get you into your *t* again	Deut 5:30	168
and their households, and their *t*	Deut 11:6	168
in the morning, and go unto thy *t*	Deut 16:7	168
and, Issachar, in thy *t*	Deut 33:18	168
the people removed from their *t*	Josh 3:14	168
return ye, and get you unto your *t*	Josh 22:4	168
and they went unto their *t*	Josh 22:6	168
sent them away also unto their *t*	Josh 22:7	168
with much riches unto your *t*	Josh 22:8	168
up with their cattle and their *t*	Judg 6:5	168
dwelt in *t* on the east of Nobah	Judg 8:11	168
and they spoiled their *t*	1Sa 17:53	4264
and Israel, and Judah, abide in *t*	2Sa 11:11	5521
every man to his *t*, O Israel	2Sa 20:1	168
king, and went unto their *t* joyful	1Kin 8:66	168
to your *t*, O Israel	1Kin 12:16	168
So Israel departed unto their *t*	1Kin 12:16	168
in the twilight, and left their *t*	2Kin 7:7	168
asses tied, and the *t* as they were	2Kin 7:10	168
spoiled the *t* of the Syrians	2Kin 7:16	4264
and the people fled into their *t*	2Kin 8:21	168
of Israel dwelt in their *t*	2Kin 13:5	168
and they fled every man to his *t*	2Kin 14:12	168
king of Judah, and smote their *t*	1Chr 4:41	168
they dwelt in their *t* throughout	1Chr 5:10	168
sent the people away into their *t*	2Chr 7:10	168
every man to your *t*, O Israel, and	2Chr 10:16	168
So all Israel went to their *t*	2Chr 10:16	168
They smote also the *t* of cattle	2Chr 14:15	168
in the gates of the *t* of the LORD	2Chr 31:2	4264
and there abode we in *t* three days	Ezr 8:15	2583
and let none dwell in their *t*	Ps 69:25	168
of Israel to dwell in their *t*	Ps 78:55	168
to dwell in the *t* of wickedness	Ps 84:10	168
But murmured in their *t*, and	Ps 106:25	168
that I dwell in the *t* of Kedar	Ps 120:5	168
as the *t* of Kedar, as the	Song 1:5	168
thy kids beside the shepherds' *t*	Song 1:8	4908
suddenly are my *t* spoiled	Jer 4:20	168
they shall pitch their *t* against	Jer 6:3	168
again the captivity of Jacob's *t*	Jer 30:18	168
all your days ye shall dwell in *t*	Jer 35:7	168
But we have dwelt in *t*, and have	Jer 35:10	168
Their *t* and their flocks shall	Jer 49:29	168
I saw the *t* of Cushan in	Hab 3:7	168
shall save the *t* of Judah first	Zec 12:7	168
beasts that shall be in these *t*	Zec 14:15	4264

TERAH *(te'-rah)* See THARA. *Father of Abraham.*

nine and twenty years, and begat *T*	Gen 11:24	8646
lived after he begat *T* an hundred	Gen 11:25	8646
T lived seventy years, and begat	Gen 11:26	8646
these are the generations of *T*	Gen 11:27	8646
T begat Abram, Nahor, and Haran	Gen 11:27	8646
T in the land of his nativity	Gen 11:28	8646
T took Abram his son, and Lot the	Gen 11:31	8646
the days of *T* were two hundred and	Gen 11:32	8646
and *T* died in Haran	Gen 11:32	8646
of the flood in old time, even *T*	Josh 24:2	8646
Serug, Nahor, *T*,	1Chr 1:26	8646

TERAPHIM

of gods, and made an ephod, and *t*	Judg 17:5	8655
is in these houses an ephod, and *t*	Judg 18:14	8655
image, and the ephod, and the *t*	Judg 18:17	8655
carved image, the ephod, and the *t*	Judg 18:18	8655
and he took the ephod, and the *t*	Judg 18:20	8655
and without an ephod, and without *t*	Hos 3:4	8655

TERESH *(te'-resh) A servant of King Ahasuerus.*

king's chamberlains, Bigthan and *T*	Est 2:21	8657
had told of Bigthana and *T*	Est 6:2	8657

TERMED

Thou shalt no more be t Forsaken	Is 62:4	559
thy land any more be t Desolate	Is 62:4	559

TERRACES

trees t to the house of the LORD	2Chr 9:11	4546

TERRESTRIAL

celestial bodies, and bodies t	1Cor 15:40	*1919*
and the glory of the t is another	1Cor 15:40	*1919*

TERRIBLE

for it is a t thing that I will	Ex 34:10	3372
t wilderness, which ye saw by the	Deut 1:19	3372
is among you, a mighty God and t	Deut 7:21	3372
t wilderness, wherein were fiery	Deut 8:15	3372
a great God, a mighty, and a t	Deut 10:17	3372
t things, which thine eyes have	Deut 10:21	3372
of an angel of God, very t	Judg 13:6	3372
to do for you great things and t	2Sa 7:23	3372
t God, that keepeth covenant and	Neh 1:5	3372
the LORD, which is great and t	Neh 4:14	3372
great, the mighty, and the t God	Neh 9:32	3372
with God is t majesty	Job 37:22	3372
the glory of his nostrils is t	Job 39:20	367
his teeth are t round about	Job 41:14	367
hand shall teach thee t things	Ps 45:4	3372
For the LORD most high is t	Ps 47:2	3372
By t things in righteousness wilt	Ps 65:5	3372
How t art thou in thy works	Ps 66:3	3372
he is t in his doing toward the	Ps 66:5	3372
thou art t out of thy holy places	Ps 68:35	3372
he is t to the kings of the earth	Ps 76:12	3372
them praise thy great and t name	Ps 99:3	3372
Ham, and t things by the Red sea	Ps 106:22	3372
speak of the might of thy t acts	Ps 145:6	3372
t as an army with banners	Song 6:4	366
t as an army with banners	Song 6:10	366
lay low the haughtiness of the t	Is 13:11	6184
peeled, to a people t from their	Is 18:2	3372
from a people t from their	Is 18:7	3372
from the desert, from a t land	Is 21:1	3372
the city of the t nations shall	Is 25:3	6184
when the blast of the t ones is	Is 25:4	6184
the branch of the t ones shall be	Is 25:5	6184
the multitude of the t ones shall	Is 29:5	6184
For the t one is brought to	Is 29:20	6184
the prey of the t shall be	Is 49:25	6184
When thou didst t things which we	Is 64:3	3372
thee out of the hand of the t	Jer 15:21	6184
LORD is with me as a mighty t one	Jer 20:11	6184
an oven because of the t famine	Lam 5:10	2152
as the colour of the t crystal	Eze 1:22	3372
upon thee, the t of the nations	Eze 28:7	6184
the t of the nations, shall be	Eze 30:11	6184
the t of the nations, have cut	Eze 31:12	6184
the t of the nations, all of them	Eze 32:12	6184
and the form thereof was t	Dan 2:31	1763
a fourth beast, dreadful and t	Dan 7:7	574
of the LORD is great and very t	Joel 2:11	3372
the t day of the LORD come	Joel 2:31	3372
They are t and dreadful	Hab 1:7	366
The LORD will be t unto them	Zeph 2:11	3372
so t was the sight, that Moses	Heb 12:21	5398

TERRIBLENESS

outstretched arm, and with great t	Deut 26:8	4172
thee a name of greatness and t	1Chr 17:21	3372
Thy t hath deceived thee, and the	Jer 49:16	8606

TERRIBLY

he ariseth to shake t the earth	Is 2:19	6206
he ariseth to shake t the earth	Is 2:21	6206
the fir trees shall be t shaken	Nah 2:3	6206

TERRIFIED

neither be ye t because of them	Deut 20:3	6206
of wars and commotions, be not t	Lk 21:9	4422
But they were t and affrighted, and	Lk 24:37	4422
in nothing t by your adversaries	Phil 1:28	4426

TERRIFIEST

dreams, and t me through visions	Job 7:14	1204

TERRIFY

let the blackness of the day t it	Job 3:5	1204
from me, and let not his fear t me	Job 9:34	1204
did the contempt of families t me	Job 31:34	2865
as if I would t you by letters	2Cor 10:9	*1629*

TERROR

the t of God was upon the cities	Gen 35:5	2847
I will even appoint over you t	Lev 26:16	928
t within, shall destroy both the	Deut 32:25	367
in all the great t which Moses	Deut 34:12	4172

that your t is fallen upon us, and	Josh 2:9	367
from God was a t to me, and by	Job 31:23	6343
my t shall not make thee afraid,	Job 33:7	367
not be afraid for the t by night	Ps 91:5	6343
hosts, shall lop the bough with t	Is 10:33	4637
of Judah shall be a t unto Egypt	Is 19:17	2283
Thine heart shall meditate t	Is 33:18	367
and from t	Is 54:14	4288
Be not a t unto me	Jer 17:17	4288
I will make thee a t to thyself	Jer 20:4	4032
out arm, and with great t	Jer 32:21	4172
which cause their t to be on all	Eze 26:17	2851
I will make thee a t, and thou	Eze 26:21	1091
thou shalt be a t, and never shalt	Eze 27:36	1091
thou shalt be a t, and never shalt	Eze 28:19	1091
which caused t in the land of the	Eze 32:23	2851
which caused their t in the land	Eze 32:24	2851
though their t was caused in the	Eze 32:25	2851
though they caused their t in the	Eze 32:26	2851
though they were the t of the	Eze 32:27	2851
with their t they are ashamed of	Eze 32:30	2851
For I have caused my t in the	Eze 32:32	2851
rulers are not a t to good works	Rom 13:3	5401
therefore the t of the Lord	2Cor 5:11	5401
and be not afraid of their t	1Pet 3:14	5401

TERRORS

stretched out arm, and by great t	Deut 4:34	4172
the t of God do set themselves in	Job 6:4	1161
T shall make him afraid on every	Job 18:11	1091
shall bring him to the king of t	Job 18:14	1091
t are upon him	Job 20:25	367
they are in the t of the shadow	Job 24:17	1091
T take hold on him as waters, a	Job 27:20	1091
T are turned upon me	Job 30:15	1091
the t of death are fallen upon me	Ps 55:4	367
they are utterly consumed with t	Ps 73:19	1091
I suffer thy t I am distracted	Ps 88:15	367
thy t have cut me off	Ps 88:16	1161
it suddenly, and t upon the city	Jer 15:8	928
in a solemn day my t round about	Lam 2:22	4032
t by reason of the sword shall be	Eze 21:12	4048

TERTIUS *(tur'-she-us) An assistant of Paul.*

I T, who wrote this epistle,	Rom 16:22	5060

TERTULLUS *(tur-tul'-lus) An orator who opposed Paul.*

and with a certain orator named T	Acts 24:1	5061
T began to accuse him, saying,	Acts 24:2	5061

TESTAMENT

For this is my blood of the new t	Mt 26:28	*1242*
This is my blood of the new t	Mk 14:24	*1242*
This cup is the new t in my blood	Lk 22:20	*1242*
This cup is the new t in my blood	1Cor 11:25	*1242*
us able ministers of the new t	2Cor 3:6	*1242*
away in the reading of the old t	2Cor 3:14	*1242*
Jesus made a surety of a better t	Heb 7:22	*1242*
he is the mediator of the new t	Heb 9:15	*1242*
that were under the first t	Heb 9:15	*1242*
For where a t is, there must also	Heb 9:16	*1242*
For a t is of force after men are	Heb 9:17	*1242*
t was dedicated without blood	Heb 9:18	
This is the blood of the t which	Heb 9:20	*1248*
in his temple the ark of his t	Rev 11:19	*1248*

TESTATOR

necessity be the death of the t	Heb 9:16	*1303*
at all while the t liveth	Heb 9:17	*1303*

TESTIFIED

and it hath been t to his owner	Ex 21:29	5749
hath t falsely against his	Deut 19:18	6030
seeing the LORD hath t against me	Ruth 1:21	6030
for thy mouth hath t against thee	2Sa 1:16	6030
Yet the LORD t against Israel, and	2Kin 17:13	5749
which he t against them	2Kin 17:15	5749
and they t against them	2Chr 24:19	5749
slew thy prophets which t against	Neh 9:26	5749
I t against them in the day	Neh 13:15	5749
Then I t against them, and said	Neh 13:21	5749
the saying of the woman, which t	Jn 4:39	3140
For Jesus himself t, that a	Jn 4:44	3140
he was troubled in spirit, and t	Jn 13:21	3140
And they, when they had t and	Acts 8:25	1263
t to the Jews that Jesus was	Acts 18:5	1263
for as thou hast t of me in	Acts 23:11	1263
t the kingdom of God, persuading	Acts 28:23	1263
because we have t of God that he	1Cor 15:15	3140
we also have forewarned you and t	1Th 4:6	1263
for all, to be t in due time	1Ti 2:6	3142
But one in a certain place t	Heb 2:6	1263
signify, when it t beforehand the	1Pet 1:11	4303

T

of God which he hath *t* of his Son	1Jn 5:9	3140
t of the truth that is in thee,	3Jn 3	3140

TESTIFIEDST

t against them, that thou	Neh 9:29	5749
t against them by thy spirit in	Neh 9:30	5749

TESTIFIETH

the pride of Israel *t* to his face	Hos 7:10	6030
he hath seen and heard, that he *t*	Jn 3:32	3140
disciple which *t* of these things	Jn 21:24	3140
For he *t*, Thou art a priest for	Heb 7:17	3140
He which *t* these things saith,	Rev 22:20	3140

TESTIFY

but one witness shall not *t*	Num 35:30	6030
I *t* against you this day that ye	Deut 8:19	5749
rise up against any man to *t*	Deut 19:16	6030
that this song shall *t* against	Deut 31:21	6030
which I *t* among you this day	Deut 32:46	5749
thou didst *t* against them	Neh 9:34	5749
thine own lips *t* against thee	Job 15:6	6030
Israel, and I will *t* against thee	Ps 50:7	5749
my people, and I will *t* unto thee	Ps 81:8	5749
thee, and our sins *t* against us	Is 59:12	6030
our iniquities *t* against us	Jer 14:7	6030
of Israel doth *t* to his face	Hos 5:5	5749
t in the house of Jacob, saith	Amos 3:13	5749
t against me	Mic 6:3	6030
that he may *t* unto them, lest	Lk 16:28	1263
not that any should *t* of man	Jn 2:25	3140
do know, and *t* that we have seen	Jn 3:11	3140
and they are they which *t* of me	Jn 5:39	3140
me it hateth, because I *t* of it	Jn 7:7	3140
from the Father, he shall *t* of me	Jn 15:26	3140
And with many other words did he *t*	Acts 2:40	1263
to *t* that it is he which was	Acts 10:42	1263
to *t* the gospel of the grace of	Acts 20:24	1263
the beginning, if they would *t*	Acts 26:5	3140
For I *t* again to every man that	Gal 5:3	3143
t in the Lord, that ye henceforth	Eph 4:17	3143
do *t* that the Father sent the Son	1Jn 4:14	3140
to *t* unto you these things in the	Rev 22:16	3140
For I *t* unto every man that	Rev 22:18	4828

TESTIFYING

T both to the Jews, and also to	Acts 20:21	1263
was righteous, God *t* of his gifts	Heb 11:4	3140
t that this is the true grace of	1Pet 5:12	1957

TESTIMONIES

These are the *t*, and the statutes,	Deut 4:45	5713
of the LORD your God, and his *t*	Deut 6:17	5713
to come, saying, What mean the *t*	Deut 6:20	5713
and his judgments, and his *t*	1Kin 2:3	5715
his *t* which he testified against	2Kin 17:15	5715
to keep his commandments and his *t*	2Chr 23:3	5715
to keep thy commandments, thy *t*	1Chr 29:19	5715
keep his commandments, and his *t*	2Chr 34:31	5715
unto thy commandments and thy *t*	Neh 9:34	5715
as keep his covenant and his *t*	Ps 25:10	5713
most high God, and kept not his *t*	Ps 78:56	5713
Thy *t* are very sure	Ps 93:5	5713
they kept his *t*, and the ordinance	Ps 99:7	5713
Blessed are they that keep his *t*	Ps 119:2	5713
have rejoiced in the way of thy *t*	Ps 119:14	5715
for I have kept thy *t*	Ps 119:22	5713
Thy *t* also are my delight, and my	Ps 119:24	5713
I have stuck unto thy *t*	Ps 119:31	5715
Incline my heart unto thy *t*	Ps 119:36	5715
speak of thy *t* also before kings	Ps 119:46	5713
and turned my feet unto thy *t*	Ps 119:59	5713
and those that have known thy *t*	Ps 119:79	5713
but I will consider thy *t*	Ps 119:95	5713
for thy *t* are my meditation	Ps 119:99	5715
Thy *t* have I taken as an heritage	Ps 119:111	5713
therefore I love thy *t*	Ps 119:119	5713
that I may know thy *t*	Ps 119:125	5713
Thy *t* are wonderful	Ps 119:129	5715
Thy *t* that thou hast commanded	Ps 119:138	5713
of thy *t* is everlasting	Ps 119:144	5715
save me, and I shall keep thy *t*	Ps 119:146	5713
Concerning thy *t*, I have known of	Ps 119:152	5713
yet do I not decline from thy *t*	Ps 119:157	5715
My soul hath kept thy *t*	Ps 119:167	5713
I have kept thy precepts and thy *t*	Ps 119:168	5713
nor in his statutes, nor in his *t*	Jer 44:23	5715

TESTIMONY

so Aaron laid it up before the *T*	Ex 16:34	5715
ark the *t* which I shall give thee	Ex 25:16	5715
put the *t* that I shall give thee	Ex 25:21	5715
which are upon the ark of the *t*	Ex 25:22	5715
within the vail the ark of the *t*	Ex 26:33	5715

of the *t* in the most holy place	Ex 26:34	5715
the vail, which is before the *t*	Ex 27:21	5715
vail that is by the ark of the *t*	Ex 30:6	5715
the mercy seat that is over the *t*	Ex 30:6	5715
therewith, and the ark of the *t*	Ex 30:26	5715
put it before the *t* in the	Ex 30:36	5715
congregation, and the ark of the *t*	Ex 31:7	5715
upon mount Sinai, two tables of *t*	Ex 31:18	5715
tables of the *t* were in his hand	Ex 32:15	5715
two tables of *t* in Moses' hand	Ex 34:29	5715
even of the tabernacle of *t*	Ex 38:21	5715
The ark of the *t*, and the staves	Ex 39:35	5715
put therein the ark of the *t*	Ex 40:3	5715
incense before the ark of the *t*	Ex 40:5	5715
put the *t* into the ark, and set	Ex 40:20	5715
and covered the ark of the *t*	Ex 40:21	5715
the mercy seat that is upon the *t*	Lev 16:13	5715
Without the vail of the *t*	Lev 24:3	5715
Levites over the tabernacle of *t*	Num 1:50	5715
round about the tabernacle of *t*	Num 1:53	5715
the charge of the tabernacle of *t*	Num 1:53	5715
and cover the ark of *t* with it	Num 4:5	5715
seat that was upon the ark of *t*	Num 7:89	5715
namely, the tent of the *t*	Num 9:15	5715
from off the tabernacle of the *t*	Num 10:11	5715
of the congregation before the *t*	Num 17:4	5715
Aaron's rod again before the *t*	Num 17:10	5715
that bear the ark of the *t*	Josh 4:16	5715
and this was a *t* in Israel	Ruth 4:7	8584
crown upon him, and gave him the *t*	2Kin 11:12	5715
him the crown, and gave him the *t*	2Chr 23:11	5715
the *t* of the LORD is sure, making	Ps 19:7	5715
For he established a *t* in Jacob	Ps 78:5	5715
he ordained in Joseph for a *t*	Ps 81:5	5715
shall I keep the *t* of thy mouth	Ps 119:88	5715
unto the *t* of Israel, to give	Ps 122:4	5715
my *t* that I shall teach them,	Ps 132:12	5713
Bind up the *t*, seal the law among	Is 8:16	8584
To the law and to the *t*	Is 8:20	8584
commanded, for a *t* unto them	Mt 8:4	3142
for a *t* against them and the	Mt 10:18	3142
commanded, for a *t* unto them	Mk 1:44	3142
your feet for a *t* against them	Mk 6:11	3142
for my sake, for a *t* against them	Mk 13:9	3142
commanded, for a *t* unto them	Lk 5:14	3142
your feet for a *t* against them	Lk 9:5	3142
And it shall turn to you for a *t*	Lk 21:13	3142
and no man receiveth his *t*	Jn 3:32	3141
He that hath received his *t* hath	Jn 3:33	3141
But I receive not *t* from man	Jn 5:34	3141
that the *t* of two men is true	Jn 8:17	3141
and we know that his *t* is true	Jn 21:24	3141
to whom also he gave *t*, and said,	Acts 13:22	3140
which gave *t* unto the word of his	Acts 14:3	3140
not receive thy *t* concerning me	Acts 22:18	3141
Even as the *t* of Christ was	1Cor 1:6	3142
declaring unto you the *t* of God	1Cor 2:1	3142
the *t* of our conscience, that in	2Cor 1:12	3142
them that believe (because our *t*	2Th 1:10	3142
ashamed of the *t* of our Lord	2Ti 1:8	3142
for a *t* of those things which	Heb 3:5	3142
his translation he had this *t*	Heb 11:5	3140
of the *t* of Jesus Christ, and of	Rev 1:2	3141
for the *t* of Jesus Christ	Rev 1:9	3141
for the *t* which they held	Rev 6:9	3141
they shall have finished their *t*	Rev 11:7	3141
Lamb, and by the word of their *t*	Rev 12:11	3141
have the *t* of Jesus Christ	Rev 12:17	3141
of the *t* in heaven was opened	Rev 15:5	3142
brethren that have the *t* of Jesus	Rev 19:10	3141
for the *t* of Jesus is the spirit	Rev 19:10	3141

TETRARCH

At that time Herod the *t* heard of	Mt 14:1	5076
and Herod being *t* of Galilee	Lk 3:1	5075
his brother Philip *t* of Ituraea	Lk 3:1	5075
and Lysanias the *t* of Abilene	Lk 3:1	5075
But Herod the *t*, being reproved	Lk 3:19	5076
Now Herod the *t* heard of all that	Lk 9:7	5076
been brought up with Herod the *t*	Acts 13:1	5076

THADDAEUS (thad-de'-us) See JUDE, LEBBAEUS. *A disciple of Jesus.*

and Lebbaeus, whose surname was *T*	Mt 10:3	2280
James the son of Alphaeus, and *T*	Mk 3:18	2280

THAHASH (tha'-hash) *A son of Reumah.*

bare also Tebah, and Gaham, and *T*	Gen 22:24	8477

THAMAH (tha'-mah) See TAMAH. *A family of exiles.*

of Sisera, the children of *T*	Ezr 2:53	8547

THAMAR (tha'-mar) See TAMAR. *Mother of Phares and*
  Zara; ancestor of Jesus.
  Judas begat Phares and Zara of *T* .... Mt 1:3   2283

THAN See APPENDIX.

THANK

the LORD, and to record, and to *t* 1Chr 16:4	3034
delivered first this psalm to *t* 1Chr 16:7	3034
And to stand every morning to *t* 1Chr 23:30	3034
we *t* thee, and praise thy glorious 1Chr 29:13	3034
t offerings into the house of the 2Chr 29:31	8426
in sacrifices and *t* offerings 2Chr 29:31	8426
t offerings, and commanded Judah 2Chr 33:16	8426
I *t* thee, and praise thee, O thou .... Dan 2:23	3029
I *t* thee, O Father, Lord of .... Mt 11:25	1843
which love you, what *t* have ye .... Lk 6:32	5485
do good to you, what *t* have ye .... Lk 6:33	5485
hope to receive, what *t* have ye .... Lk 6:34	5485
I *t* thee, O Father, Lord of .... Lk 10:21	1843
Doth he *t* that servant because he . Lk 17:9	2192,5485
I *t* thee, that I am not as other .... Lk 18:11	2168
I *t* thee that thou hast heard me .... Jn 11:41	2168
I *t* my God through Jesus Christ .... Rom 1:8	2168
I *t* God through Jesus Christ our .... Rom 7:25	2168
I *t* my God always on your behalf, ... 1Cor 1:4	2168
I *t* God that I baptized none of 1Cor 1:14	2168
I *t* my God, I speak with tongues 1Cor 14:18	2168
I *t* my God upon every remembrance .... Phil 1:3	2168
For this cause also I *t* we God 1Th 2:13	2168
We are bound to *t* God always for 2Th 1:3	2168
I *t* Christ Jesus our Lord, who 1Ti 1:12	2192,5485
I *t* God, whom I serve from my 2Ti 1:3	2192,5485
I *t* my God, making mention of .... Philem 4	2168

THANKED

and bowed himself, and *t* the king 2Sa 14:22	1288
he *t* God, and took courage .... Acts 28:15	2168
But God be *t*, that ye were the .... Rom 6:17	5485

THANKFUL

be *t* unto him, and bless his name .... Ps 100:4	3034
him not as God, neither were *t* .... Rom 1:21	2168
and be ye *t* .... Col 3:15	2170

THANKFULNESS

most noble Felix, with all *t* .... Acts 24:3   2169

THANKING

heard in praising and *t* the LORD 2Chr 5:13   3034

THANKS

Therefore I will give *t* unto thee 2Sa 22:50	3034
Give *t* unto the LORD, call upon 1Chr 16:8	3034
O give *t* unto the LORD 1Chr 16:34	3034
we may give *t* to thy holy name 1Chr 16:35	3034
to give *t* to the LORD, because 1Chr 16:41	3034
prophesied with a harp, to give *t* 1Chr 25:3	3034
to minister, and to give *t* 2Chr 31:2	3034
and giving *t* unto the LORD .... Ezr 3:11	3034
them, to praise and to give *t* .... Neh 12:24	3034
companies of them that gave *t* .... Neh 12:31	8426
gave *t* went over against them .... Neh 12:38	8426
that gave *t* in the house of God .... Neh 12:40	8426
the grave who shall give thee *t* .... Ps 6:5	3034
Therefore will I give *t* unto thee .... Ps 18:49	3034
give *t* at the remembrance of his .... Ps 30:4	3034
I will give *t* unto thee for ever .... Ps 30:12	3034
I will give thee *t* in the great .... Ps 35:18	3034
Unto thee, O God, do we give *t* .... Ps 75:1	3034
unto thee do we give *t* .... Ps 75:1	3034
pasture will give thee *t* for ever .... Ps 79:13	3034
thing to give *t* unto the LORD .... Ps 92:1	3034
give *t* at the remembrance of his .... Ps 97:12	3034
O give *t* unto the LORD .... Ps 105:1	3034
O give *t* unto the LORD .... Ps 106:1	3034
to give *t* unto thy holy name, and .... Ps 106:47	3034
O give *t* unto the LORD, for he is .... Ps 107:1	3034
O give *t* unto the LORD .... Ps 118:1	3034
O give *t* unto the LORD .... Ps 118:29	3034
give *t* unto thee because of thy .... Ps 119:62	3034
to give *t* unto the name of the .... Ps 122:4	3034
O Give *t* unto the LORD .... Ps 136:1	3034
O give *t* unto the God of gods .... Ps 136:2	3034
O give *t* to the Lord of lords .... Ps 136:3	3034
O give *t* unto the God of heaven .... Ps 136:26	3034
shall give *t* unto thy name .... Ps 140:13	3034
gave *t* before his God, as he did .... Dan 6:10	3029
loaves and the fishes, and gave *t* .... Mt 15:36	2168
And he took the cup, and gave *t* .... Mt 26:27	2168
took the seven loaves, and gave *t* .... Mk 8:6	2168
the cup, and when he had given *t* .... Mk 14:23	2168
gave *t* likewise unto the Lord .... Lk 2:38	437
face at his feet, giving *t* .... Lk 17:16	2168
And he took the cup, and gave *t* .... Lk 22:17	2168
And he took bread, and gave *t* .... Lk 22:19	2168
and when he had given *t*, he .... Jn 6:11	2168
after that the Lord had given *t*, ... Jn 6:23	2168
gave *t* to God in presence of them .... Acts 27:35	2168
to the Lord, for he giveth God *t* .... Rom 14:6	2168
he eateth not, and giveth God *t* .... Rom 14:6	2168
unto whom not only I give *t* .... Rom 16:4	2168
of for that for which I give *t* 1Cor 10:30	2168
And when he had given *t*, he brake 1Cor 11:24	2168
say Amen at thy giving of *t* 1Cor 14:16	2169
For thou verily givest *t* well 1Cor 14:17	2168
But to God, which giveth us 1Cor 15:57	5485
t may be given by many on our 2Cor 1:11	2168
Now *t* be unto God, which always 2Cor 2:14	5485
But *t* be to God, which put the 2Cor 8:16	5485
T be unto God for his unspeakable 2Cor 9:15	5485
Cease not to give *t* for you .... Eph 1:16	2168
but rather giving of *t* .... Eph 5:4	2169
Giving *t* always for all things .... Eph 5:20	2168
We give *t* to God and the Father of .... Col 1:3	2168
Giving *t* unto the Father, which .... Col 1:12	2168
the Lord Jesus, giving *t* to God .... Col 3:17	2168
We give *t* to God always for you 1Th 1:2	2168
For what *t* can we render to God 1Th 3:9	2169
In every thing give *t* 1Th 5:18	2168
to give *t* alway to God for you 2Th 2:13	2168
intercessions, and giving of *t* 1Ti 2:1	2169
of our lips giving *t* to his name .... Heb 13:15	3670
t to him that sat on the throne, ... Rev 4:9	2169
Saying, We give thee *t*, O Lord .... Rev 11:17	2168

THANKSGIVING

If he offer it for a *t*, then he .... Lev 7:12	8426
offer with the sacrifice of *t* .... Lev 7:12	8426
of *t* of his peace offerings .... Lev 7:13	8426
of his peace offerings for *t* .... Lev 7:15	8426
a sacrifice of *t* unto the LORD .... Lev 22:29	8426
to begin the *t* in prayer .... Neh 11:17	3034
Mattaniah, which was over the *t* .... Neh 12:8	1960
and songs of praise and *t* unto God ...... Neh 12:46	
I may publish with the voice of *t* .... Ps 26:7	3034
Offer unto God *t* .... Ps 50:14	8426
song, and will magnify him with *t* .... Ps 69:30	8426
come before his presence with *t* .... Ps 95:2	8426
Enter into his gates with *t* .... Ps 100:4	8426
sacrifice the sacrifices of *t* .... Ps 107:22	8426
offer to thee the sacrifice of *t* .... Ps 116:17	8426
Sing unto the LORD with *t* .... Ps 147:7	8426
shall be found therein, *t* .... Is 51:3	8426
And out of them shall proceed *t* .... Jer 30:19	8426
a sacrifice of *t* with leaven .... Amos 4:5	8426
unto thee with the voice of *t* .... Jonah 2:9	8426
grace might through the *t* of many 2Cor 4:15	2169
which causeth through us *t* to God 2Cor 9:11	2169
supplication with *t* let your .... Phil 4:6	2169
taught, abounding therein with *t* .... Col 2:7	2169
and watch in the same with *t* .... Col 4:2	2169
with *t* of them which believe 1Ti 4:3	2169
refused, if it be received with *t* 1Ti 4:4	2169
and glory, and wisdom, and *t* .... Rev 7:12	2169

THANKSGIVINGS

with gladness, both with *t* .... Neh 12:27	8426
abundant also by many *t* unto God 2Cor 9:12	2169

THANKWORTHY

For this is *t*, if a man for 1Pet 2:19   5485

THARA (tha'-rah) See TERAH. *Greek form of Terah.*
  Abraham, which was the son of *T* .... Lk 3:34   2291

THARSHISH (thar'-shish) See TARSHISH.
  1. Ships fitted for long voyages.

navy of *T* with the navy of Hiram 1Kin 10:22	8659
in three years came the navy of *T* 1Kin 10:22	8659
of *T* to go to Ophir for gold 1Kin 22:48	8659

  2. Son of Bilhan.
  and Chenaanah, and Zethan, and *T* 1Chr 7:10   8659

THAT See APPENDIX.

THE See APPENDIX.

THEATRE

rushed with one accord into the *t* .... Acts 19:29	2302
not adventure himself into the *t* .... Acts 19:31	2302

THEBES See THEBEZ.

THEBEZ (the'-bez) *A city in Ephraim.*

Then went Abimelech to *T*, and .... Judg 9:50	8405
to *T*, and encamped against *T* .... Judg 9:50	8405
from the wall, that he died in *T* 2Sa 11:21	8405

THEE See APPENDIX.

T

THEE-WARD
works have been to *t* very good 1Sa 19:4

THEFT
then he shall be sold for his *t* .... Ex 22:3   1591
If the *t* be certainly found in .... Ex 22:4   1591

THEFTS
adulteries, fornications, *t* .... Mt 15:19   2829
T, covetousness, wickedness, ... Mk 7:22   2829
their fornication, nor of their *t* .... Rev 9:21   2804

THEIR See APPENDIX.

THEIR'S
thing in Israel shall be *t* .... Eze 44:29   1992

THEIRS See APPENDIX.

THELASAR (the-la'-sar) See TELASSAR. *Same as Telassar.*
children of Eden which were in *T* 2Kin 19:12   8515

THEM See APPENDIX.

THEMSELVES See APPENDIX.

THEN See APPENDIX.

THENCE
from *t* it was parted, and became .... Gen 2:10   8033
t upon the face of all the earth .... Gen 11:8   8033
from *t* did the LORD scatter them .... Gen 11:9   8033
he removed from *t* unto a mountain ...... Gen 12:8   8033
And the men rose up from *t* .... Gen 18:16   8033
the men turned their faces from *t* .... Gen 18:22   8033
Abraham journeyed from *t* toward .... Gen 20:1   8033
take a wife unto my son from *t* .... Gen 24:7   8033
And Isaac departed *t*, and pitched .... Gen 26:17   8033
And he removed from *t*, and digged ...... Gen 26:22   8033
he went up from *t* to Beer-sheba .... Gen 26:23   8033
fetch me from *t* two good kids of .... Gen 27:9   8033
I will send, and fetch thee from *t* .... Gen 27:45   8033
take thee a wife from *t* of the .... Gen 28:2   8033
to take him a wife from *t* .... Gen 28:6   8033
removing from *t* all the speckled .... Gen 30:32   8033
thither, and buy for us from *t* .... Gen 42:2   8033
with the corn, and departed *t* .... Gen 42:26   8033
(from *t* is the shepherd, the .... Gen 49:24   8033
cut down from *t* a branch with one .... Num 13:23   8033
of Israel cut down from *t* .... Num 13:24   8033
From *t* they removed, and pitched .... Num 21:12   8033
From *t* they removed, and pitched .... Num 21:13   8033
And from *t* they went to Beer .... Num 21:16   8033
that *t* he might see the utmost .... Num 22:41   8033
and curse me them from *t* .... Num 23:13   8033
thou mayest curse me them from *t* .... Num 23:27   8033
But if from *t* thou shalt seek the .... Deut 4:29   8033
thee out *t* through a mighty hand .... Deut 5:15   8033
And he brought us out from *t* .... Deut 6:23   8033
From *t* they journeyed unto .... Deut 10:7   8033
city shall send and fetch him *t* .... Deut 19:12   8033
house, if any man fall from *t* .... Deut 22:8
the LORD thy God redeemed thee *t* .... Deut 24:18   8033
from *t* will the LORD thy God .... Deut 30:4   8033
from *t* will he fetch thee .... Deut 30:4   8033
house, and bring out *t* the woman .... Josh 6:22   8033
From *t* it passed toward Azmon, and ..... Josh 15:4
Caleb drove *t* the three sons of .... Josh 15:14   8033
he went up *t* to the inhabitants .... Josh 15:15   8033
went over from *t* toward Luz .... Josh 18:13   8033
And the border was drawn *t* .... Josh 18:14
from *t* passeth on along on the .... Josh 19:13   8033
and goeth out from *t* to Hukkok .... Josh 19:34   8033
from *t* he went against the .... Judg 1:11   8033
he expelled *t* the three sons of .... Judg 1:20   8033
And he went up *t* to Penuel .... Judg 8:8   8033
there went from *t* of the family .... Judg 18:11   8033
they passed *t* unto mount Ephraim, ... Judg 18:13   8033
from *t* am I .... Judg 19:18   8033
of Israel departed *t* at that time .... Judg 21:24   8033
they went out from *t* every man to .... Judg 21:24   8033
that they might bring from *t* the 1Sa 4:4   8033
shalt thou go on forward from *t* 1Sa 10:3   8033
And they ran and fetched him *t* 1Sa 10:23   8033
took *t* a stone, and slang it, and 1Sa 17:49   8033
David therefore departed *t* 1Sa 22:1   8033
David went *t* to Mizpeh of Moab 1Sa 22:3   8033
And David went up from *t*, and dwelt ... 1Sa 23:29   8033
to bring up from *t* the ark of God 2Sa 6:2   8033
fetched *t* a wise woman, and said 2Sa 14:2   8033
t came out a man of the family of 2Sa 16:5   8033
up from *t* the bones of Saul 2Sa 21:13   8033
they are come up from *t* rejoicing 1Kin 1:45   8033
and go not forth *t* any whither 1Kin 2:36   8033
to Ophir, and fetched from *t* gold 1Kin 9:28   8033

and went out from *t*, and built 1Kin 12:25   8033
So he departed *t*, and found Elisha 1Kin 19:19   8033
there shall not be from *t* any 2Kin 2:21   8033
And he went up from *t* unto Beth-el 2Kin 2:23   8033
he went from *t* to mount Carmel, ... 2Kin 2:25   8033
from *t* he returned to Samaria 2Kin 2:25   8033
take *t* every man a beam, and let 2Kin 6:2   8033
eat and drink, and carried *t* silver.......... 2Kin 7:8   8033
another tent, and carried *t* also 2Kin 7:8   8033
And when he was departed *t* 2Kin 10:15   8033
priests whom ye brought from *t* 2Kin 17:27   8033
whom they carried away from *t* 2Kin 17:33   8033
down, and brake them down from *t* 2Kin 23:12   8033
And he carried out *t* all the.................... 2Kin 24:13   8033
to bring up *t* the ark of God the 1Chr 13:6   8033
took *t* four hundred and fifty.................. 2Chr 8:18   8033
and they thrust him out from *t* 2Chr 26:20   8033
the river, ye far from *t* .... Ezr 6:6   8536
yet will I gather them from *t* .... Neh 1:9   8033
From *t* she seeketh the prey, and........... Job 39:29   8033
ye, depart ye, go ye out from *t* .... Is 52:11   8033
be no more *t* an infant of days .... Is 65:20   8033
out *t* shall be torn in pieces.................... Jer 5:6   2007
and take the girdle from *t* .... Jer 13:6   8033
hand, yet would I pluck thee *t* .... Jer 22:24   8033
shall cause to cease from *t* man .... Jer 36:29
to separate himself *t* in the .... Jer 37:12   8033
took *t* old cast clouts and old .... Jer 38:11   8033
he shall go forth from *t* in peace .... Jer 43:12   8033
I will bring thee down from *t* .... Jer 49:16   8033
and will destroy from *t* the king .... Jer 49:38   8033
from *t* she shall be taken........................ Jer 50:9   8033
the abominations thereof from *t* .... Eze 11:18
give her her vineyards from *t* .... Hos 2:15   8033
from *t* go ye to Hamath the great........... Amos 6:2   8033
t shall mine hand take them .... Amos 9:2   8033
heaven, *t* will I bring them down .... Amos 9:2   8033
I will search and take them out *t* .... Amos 9:3   8033
t will I command the serpent, and .... Amos 9:3   8033
t will I command the sword, and it .... Amos 9:4   8033
t will I bring thee down, saith .... Obad 4   8033
And going on from *t*, he saw other .... Mt 4:21   1564
Thou shalt by no means come out *t* .... Mt 5:26   1564
And as Jesus passed forth from *t* .... Mt 9:9   1564
And when Jesus departed *t*, two .... Mt 9:27   1564
and there abide till ye go *t* .... Mt 10:11   1564
disciples, he departed *t* to teach .... Mt 11:1   1564
And when he was departed *t* .... Mt 12:9   1564
it, he withdrew himself from *t* .... Mt 12:15   1564
these parables, he departed *t* .... Mt 13:53   1564
he departed *t* by ship into a .... Mt 14:13   1564
Then Jesus went *t*, and departed .... Mt 15:21   1564
And Jesus departed from *t*, and came.... Mt 15:29   1564
his hands on them, and departed *t* .... Mt 19:15   1564
he had gone a little farther *t* .... Mk 1:19   1564
And he went out from *t*, and came .... Mk 6:1   1564
nor hear you, when ye depart *t* .... Mk 6:11   1564
from *t* he arose, and went into the......... Mk 7:24   1564
And they departed *t*, and passed........... Mk 9:30   1564
And he arose from *t*, and cometh .... Mk 10:1   1564
into, there abide, and *t* depart .... Lk 9:4   1564
thee, thou shalt not depart *t* .... Lk 12:59   1564
to us, that would come from *t* .... Lk 16:26   1564
Now after two days he departed *t* .... Jn 4:43   1564
but went *t* unto a country near to.......... Jn 11:54   1564
and from *t*, when his father was .... Acts 7:4   1564
from *t* they sailed to Cyprus .... Acts 13:4   1564
t sailed to Antioch, from whence .... Acts 14:26   1564
from *t* to Philippi, which is the .... Acts 16:12   1564
And he departed *t*, and entered into...... Acts 18:7   1564
sailed *t* into Syria, and with him .... Acts 18:18
And we sailed *t*, and came the next....... Acts 20:15   1564
Rhodes, and from *t* unto Patara............. Acts 21:1   1564
And when we had launched from *t* .... Acts 27:4   1564
part advised to depart *t* also .... Acts 27:12   1564
obtained their purpose, loosing *t*........... Acts 27:13   1564
from *t* we fetched a compass, and .... Acts 28:13   3606
And from *t*, when the brethren .... Acts 28:15   1564
I went from *t* into Macedonia................. 2Cor 2:13

THENCEFORTH
t it shall be accepted for an .... Lev 22:27   1973
the sight of all nations from *t* 2Chr 32:23   310,3651
it is *t* good for nothing, but to .... Mt 5:13   2089
from *t* Pilate sought to release .... Jn 19:12   1537,5127

THEOPHILUS (the-of'-il-us) *To whom the gospel of Luke and the Acts of the Apostles are addressed.*
thee in order, most excellent *T* .... Lk 1:3   2321
former treatise have I made, O *T* .... Acts 1:1   2321

THERE See APPENDIX.

THEREABOUT
as they were much perplexed *t* .... Lk 24:4   *4012,5127*

THEREAT
wash their hands and their feet *t* .... Ex 30:19
their hands and their feet *t* .... Ex 40:31
and many there be which go in it ... Mt 7:13   *1223,846*

THEREBY See APPENDIX.

THEREFORE See APPENDIX.

THEREFROM
that ye turn not aside *t* to the .... Josh 23:6
he departed not *t* 2Kin 3:3
he departed not *t* 2Kin 13:2

THEREIN See APPENDIX.

THEREINTO
that are in the countries enter *t* ...... Lk 21:21   *1519,846*

THEREOF See APPENDIX.

THEREON See APPENDIX.

THEREOUT
he shall take *t* his handful of .... Lev 2:2   *8033*
in the jaw, and there came water *t* .... Judg 15:19

THERETO See APPENDIX.

THEREUNTO
it, and have sacrificed *t*, and said .... Ex 32:8
he made *t* four pillars of shittim .... Ex 36:36
made *t* a crown of gold round .... Ex 37:11
Also he made *t* a border of an .... Ex 37:12
and unto all the places nigh *t* .... Deut 1:7
t with all perseverance .... Eph 6:18   *1519,846,5124*
know that we are appointed *t* 1Th 3:3   *1519,5124*
make the comers *t* perfect .... Heb 10:1   *4334*
knowing that ye are *t* called 1Pet 3:9   *1519,5124*

THEREUPON See APPENDIX.

THEREWITH
corn, or the field, be consumed *t* .... Ex 22:6
tabernacle of the congregation *t* .... Ex 30:26
t he made the sockets to the door .... Ex 38:30
maketh atonement *t* shall have it .... Lev 7:7
the ephod, and bound it unto him *t* .... Lev 8:7
goeth from him, and is defiled *t* .... Lev 15:32
any beast to defile thyself *t* .... Lev 18:23
shall not eat to defile himself *t* .... Lev 22:8
shalt thou eat unleavened bread *t* .... Deut 16:3   *5921*
thyself abroad, thou shalt dig *t* .... Deut 23:13
took it, and slew a thousand men *t* .... Judg 15:15
took new ropes, and bound him *t* .... Judg 16:12
any bribe to blind mine eyes *t* 1Sa 12:3
slew him, and cut off his head *t* 1Sa 17:51
thy sword, and thrust me through *t* 1Sa 31:4
so he smote him *t* in the fifth 2Sa 20:10
I have *t* sent Naaman my servant 2Kin 5:6
repaired *t* the house of the Lord............. 2Kin 12:14
thy sword, and thrust me through *t* 1Chr 10:4
I made, said David, to praise *t* 1Chr 23:5
and he built *t* Geba and Mizpah............. 2Chr 16:6
than great treasure and trouble *t* .... Prov 15:16
is, than a stalled ox and hatred *t* .... Prov 15:17
is a dry morsel, and quietness *t* .... Prov 17:1
for thee, lest thou be filled *t* .... Prov 25:16
the sons of man to be exercised *t* .... Eccl 1:13
to water *t* the wood that bringeth .... Eccl 2:6
removeth stones shall be hurt *t* .... Eccl 10:9
itself against him that heweth *t* .... Is 10:15
and thou shalt prepare thy bread *t* .... Eze 4:15   *5921*
oil, and ye shall be satisfied *t* .... Joel 2:19   *854*
state I am, *t* to be content .... Phil 4:11
and raiment let us be *t* content 1Ti 6:8   *5125*
T bless we God, even the Father ..... Jas 3:9   *1722,846*
t curse we men, which are made ... Jas 3:9   *1722,846*
and not content *t*, neither doth he ... 3Jn 10   *1909,5125*

THESE See APPENDIX.

THESSALONIANS (*thes-sa-lo'-ne-uns*) *The inhabitants of Thessalonica.*
and of the *T*, Aristarchus and.................. Acts 20:4   *2331*
unto the church of the *T* which is 1Th 1:1   *2331*
the *T* was written from Athens............... 1Th s   *2331*
church of the *T* in God our Father 2Th 1:1   *2331*
to the *T* was written from Athens........... 2Th s   *2331*

THESSALONICA (*thes-sa-lo-ni'-cah*) *A city in Macedonia.*
and Apollonia, they came to *T* .... Acts 17:1   *2332*
were more noble than those in *T* .... Acts 17:11   *2332*
But when the Jews of *T* had .... Acts 17:13   *2332*
Aristarchus, a Macedonian of *T* .... Acts 27:2   *2331*

For even in *T* ye sent once and............... Phil 4:16   *2332*
world, and is departed unto *T* 2Ti 4:10   *2332*

THEUDAS (*thew'-das*) *A false Jewish Messiah.*
For before these days rose up *T* .... Acts 5:36   *2333*

THEY See APPENDIX.

THICK
there was a *t* darkness in all the .... Ex 10:22   *653*
Lo, I come unto thee in a *t* cloud .... Ex 19:9   *5645*
a *t* cloud upon the mount, and the .... Ex 19:16   *3515*
unto the *t* darkness where God was ...... Ex 20:21
trees, and the boughs of *t* trees .... Lev 23:40   *5687*
darkness, clouds, and *t* darkness........... Deut 4:11
of the *t* darkness, with a great............... Deut 5:22
art waxen fat, thou art grown *t*............... Deut 32:15   *5666*
under the *t* boughs of a great oak 2Sa 18:9
waters, and *t* clouds of the skies 2Sa 22:12
the *t* beam were before them 1Kin 7:6
And it was an hand breadth *t* 1Kin 7:26   *5672*
he would dwell in the *t* darkness 1Kin 8:12
morrow, that he took a *t* cloth 2Kin 8:15
he would dwell in the *t* darkness 2Chr 6:1
branches, and branches of *t* trees.......... Neh 8:15   *5687*
upon the *t* bosses of his bucklers........... Job 15:26   *5672*
T clouds are a covering to him,.............. Job 22:14
up the waters in his *t* clouds .... Job 26:8
watering he wearieth the *t* cloud .... Job 37:11
t darkness a swaddlingband for it .... Job 38:9
waters and *t* clouds of the skies .... Ps 18:11
before him his *t* clouds passed.............. Ps 18:12
lifted up axes upon the *t* trees .... Ps 74:5   *5441*
as a *t* cloud, thy transgressions, ... Is 44:22
green tree, and under every *t* oak .... Eze 6:13   *5687*
a *t* cloud of incense went up .... Eze 8:11   *6282*
was exalted among the *t* branches .... Eze 19:11   *5688*
high hill, and all the *t* trees................... Eze 20:28   *5687*
and his top was among the *t* boughs....... Eze 31:3   *5688*
up his top among the *t* boughs .... Eze 31:10   *5688*
up their top among the *t* boughs .... Eze 31:14   *5688*
was five cubits *t* round about................. Eze 41:12   *7341*
there were *t* planks upon the face .... Eze 41:25   *5645*
of the house, and *t* planks .... Eze 41:26
of *t* darkness, as the morning .... Joel 2:2
that ladeth himself with *t* clay .... Hab 2:6
a day of clouds and *t* darkness, ... Zeph 1:15
people were gathered *t* together .... Lk 11:29

THICKER
shall be *t* than my father's loins 1Kin 12:10   *5666*
shall be *t* than my father's loins 2Chr 10:10   *5666*

THICKET
a ram caught in a *t* by his horns .... Gen 22:13   *5442*
The lion is come up from his *t*................ Jer 4:7   *5441*

THICKETS
hide themselves in caves, and in *t* 1Sa 13:6   *2337*
kindle in the *t* of the forest .... Is 9:18   *5442*
he shall cut down the *t* of the .... Is 10:34   *5442*
they shall go into *t*, and climb up .... Jer 4:29   *5645*

THICKNESS
the *t* of it was an handbreadth,.............. 2Chr 4:5   *5672*
the *t* thereof was four fingers .... Jer 52:21   *5672*
The *t* of the wall, which was for .... Eze 41:9   *7341*
The chambers were in the *t* of the .... Eze 42:10   *7341*

THIEF
If a *t* be found breaking up, and .... Ex 22:2   *1590*
if the *t* be found, let him pay .... Ex 22:7   *1590*
If the *t* be not found, then the .... Ex 22:8   *1590*
then that *t* shall die................................ Deut 24:7   *1590*
needy, and in the night is as a *t*.............. Job 24:14   *1590*
cried after them as after a *t* .... Job 30:5   *1590*
When thou sawest a *t*, then thou .... Ps 50:18   *1590*
Men do not despise a *t*, if he .... Prov 6:30   *1590*
with a *t* hateth his own soul................... Prov 29:24   *1590*
As the *t* is ashamed when he is .... Jer 2:26   *1590*
the *t* cometh in, and the troop of .... Hos 7:1   *1590*
enter in at the windows like a *t*............. Joel 2:9   *1590*
enter into the house of the *t* .... Zec 5:4   *1590*
in what watch the *t* would come .... Mt 24:43   *2812*
out as against a *t* with swords............. Mt 26:55   *3027*
Are ye come out, as against a *t* .... Mk 14:48   *3027*
where no *t* approacheth, neither .... Lk 12:33   *2812*
known what hour the *t* would come ..... Lk 12:39   *2812*
Be ye come out, as against a *t* .... Lk 22:52   *3027*
some other way, the same is a *t* .... Jn 10:1   *2812*
The *t* cometh not, but for to .... Jn 10:10   *2812*
but because he was a *t*, and had .... Jn 12:6   *2812*
so cometh as a *t* in the night 1Th 5:2   *2812*
day should overtake you as a *t* 1Th 5:4   *2812*
suffer as a murderer, or as a *t*............... 1Pet 4:15   *2812*

T

THIEVES

will come as a *t* in the night	2Pet 3:10	2812
watch, I will come on thee as a *t*	Rev 3:3	2812
Behold, I come as a *t*	Rev 16:15	2812

THIEVES

rebellious, and companions of *t*	Is 1:23	1590
was he found among *t*	Jer 48:27	1590
if *t* by night, they will destroy	Jer 49:9	1590
If *t* came to thee, if robbers by	Obad 5	1590
where *t* break through and steal	Mt 6:19	2812
where *t* do not break through nor	Mt 6:20	2812
but ye have made it a den of *t*	Mt 21:13	3027
there two *t* crucified with him	Mt 27:38	3027
The *t* also, which were crucified	Mt 27:44	3027
but ye have made it a den of *t*	Mk 11:17	3027
And with him they crucify two *t*	Mk 15:27	3027
to Jericho, and fell among *t*	Lk 10:30	3027
unto him that fell among the *t*	Lk 10:36	3027
but ye have made it a den of *t*	Lk 19:46	3027
that ever came before me are *t*	Jn 10:8	2812
Nor *t*, nor covetous, nor	1Cor 6:10	2812

THIGH

I pray thee, thy hand under my *t*	Gen 24:2	3409
under the *t* of Abraham his master	Gen 24:9	3409
he touched the hollow of his *t*	Gen 32:25	3409
of Jacob's *t* was out of joint	Gen 32:25	3409
upon him, and he halted upon his *t*	Gen 32:31	3409
which is upon the hollow of the *t*	Gen 32:32	3409
t in the sinew that shrank	Gen 32:32	3409
I pray thee, thy hand under my *t*	Gen 47:29	3409
the LORD doth make thy *t* to rot	Num 5:21	3409
belly to swell, and thy *t* to rot	Num 5:22	3409
shall swell, and her *t* shall rot	Num 5:27	3409
his raiment upon his right *t*	Judg 3:16	3409
took the dagger from his right *t*	Judg 3:21	3409
hip and *t* with a great slaughter	Judg 15:8	3409
Gird thy sword upon thy *t*	Ps 45:3	3409
man hath his sword upon his *t*	Song 3:8	3409
make bare the leg, uncover the *t*	Is 47:2	7785
was instructed, I smote upon my *t*	Jer 31:19	3409
smite therefore upon thy *t*	Eze 21:12	3409
it, even every good piece, the *t*	Eze 24:4	3409
on his *t* a name written, KING OF	Rev 19:16	3382

THIGHS

even unto the *t* they shall reach	Ex 28:42	3409
joints of thy *t* are like jewels	Song 7:1	3409
his belly and his *t* of brass,	Dan 2:32	3410

THIMNATHAH (thim'-nath-ah) See TIMNAH. *A city in Dan.*

And Elon, and *T*, and Ekron,	Josh 19:43	8553

THIN

And, behold, seven *t* ears and	Gen 41:6	1851
the seven *t* ears devoured the	Gen 41:7	1851
behold, seven ears, withered, *t*	Gen 41:23	1851
the *t* ears devoured the seven	Gen 41:24	1851
And the seven *t* and ill favoured	Gen 41:27	7534
did beat the gold into *t* plates	Ex 39:3	
and there be in it a yellow *t* hair	Lev 13:30	1851
certain additions made of *t* work	1Kin 7:29	4174
glory of Jacob shall be made *t*	Is 17:4	1809

THINE See APPENDIX.

THING See APPENDIX.

THINGS See APPENDIX.

THINGS'

For which *t* sake the wrath of God	Col 3:6	

THINK

But *t* on me when it shall be well	Gen 40:14	2142
them marry to whom they *t* best	Num 36:6	5869
to *t* that all the king's sons are	2Sa 13:33	559
now ye *t* to withstand the kingdom	2Chr 13:8	559
T upon me, my God, for good,	Neh 5:19	2142
that thou and the Jews *t* to rebel	Neh 6:6	2803
t thou upon Tobiah and Sanballat	Neh 6:14	2142
T not with thyself that thou	Est 4:13	1819
why then should I *t* upon a maid	Job 31:1	995
one would *t* the deep to be hoary	Job 41:32	2803
though a wise man *t* to know it	Eccl 8:17	559
so, neither doth his heart *t* so	Is 10:7	2803
Which *t* to cause my people to	Jer 23:27	2803
the thoughts that I *t* toward you	Jer 29:11	2803
thou shalt *t* an evil thought	Eze 38:10	2803
t to change times and laws	Dan 7:25	5452
if so be that God will *t* upon us	Jonah 1:6	6245
And I said unto them, If ye *t* good	Zec 11:12	5869
t not to say within yourselves,	Mt 3:9	1380
T not that I am come to destroy	Mt 5:17	3543
for they *t* that they shall be	Mt 6:7	1380

Wherefore *t* ye evil in your	Mt 9:4	1760
T not that I am come to send	Mt 10:34	3543
How *t* ye?	Mt 18:12	1380
But what *t* ye	Mt 21:28	1380
Saying, What *t* ye of Christ	Mt 22:42	1380
as ye *t* not the Son of man cometh	Mt 24:44	1380
What *t* ye?	Mt 26:66	1380
what *t* ye?	Mk 14:64	5316
cometh at an hour when ye *t* not	Lk 12:40	1380
t ye that they were sinners above	Lk 13:4	1380
for in them ye *t* ye have eternal	Jn 5:39	1380
Do not *t* that I will accuse you	Jn 5:45	1380
stood in the temple, What *t* ye	Jn 11:56	1380
will *t* that he doeth God service	Jn 16:2	1380
he said, Whom *t* ye that I am	Acts 13:25	5282
we ought not to *t* that the	Acts 17:29	3543
I *t* myself happy, king Agrippa,	Acts 26:2	2233
not to *t* of himself more highly	Rom 12:3	5252
more highly than he ought to *t*	Rom 12:3	5426
but to *t* soberly, according as	Rom 12:3	5426
to *t* of men above that which is	1Cor 4:6	5426
For I *t* that God hath set forth	1Cor 4:9	1380
But if any man *t* that he behaveth	1Cor 7:36	3543
I *t* also that I have the Spirit	1Cor 7:40	1380
if any man *t* that he knoweth any	1Cor 8:2	1380
which we *t* to be less honourable,	1Cor 12:23	1380
If any man *t* himself to be a	1Cor 14:37	1380
to *t* any thing as of ourselves	2Cor 3:5	3049
wherewith I *t* to be bold against	2Cor 10:2	3049
which *t* of us as if we walked	2Cor 10:2	3049
let him of himself *t* this again	2Cor 10:7	3049
Let such an one *t* this, that,	2Cor 10:11	1380
say again, Let no man *t* me a fool	2Cor 11:16	1380
lest any man should *t* of me above	2Cor 12:6	3049
t ye that we excuse ourselves	2Cor 12:19	1380
For if a man *t* himself to be	Gal 6:3	1380
above all that we ask or *t*	Eph 3:20	3539
meet for me to *t* this of you all	Phil 1:7	5426
be any praise, *t* on these things	Phil 4:8	3049
For let not that man *t* that he	Jas 1:7	3633
Do ye *t* that the scripture saith	Jas 4:5	1380
Wherein they *t* it strange that ye	1Pet 4:4	
t it not strange concerning the	1Pet 4:12	
I *t* it meet, as long as I am in	2Pet 1:13	2233

THINKEST

T thou that David doth honour thy	2Sa 10:3	5869
T thou that David doth honour thy	1Chr 19:3	5869
T thou this to be right, that	Job 35:2	2803
him, saying, What *t* thou, Simon	Mt 17:25	1380
Tell us therefore, What *t* thou	Mt 22:17	1380
T thou that I cannot now pray to	Mt 26:53	1380
t thou, was neighbour unto him	Lk 10:36	1380
to hear of thee what thou *t*	Acts 28:22	5426
t thou this, O man, that judgest	Rom 2:3	3049

THINKETH

Me *t* the running of the foremost	2Sa 18:27	7200
yet the Lord *t* upon me	Ps 40:17	2803
For as he *t* in his heart, so is	Prov 23:7	8176
Wherefore let him that *t* he	1Cor 10:12	1380
is not easily provoked, *t* no evil	1Cor 13:5	3049
If any other man *t* that he hath	Phil 3:4	1380

THINKING

t to have brought good tidings, I	2Sa 4:10	1931,1961
t, David cannot come in	2Sa 5:6	559

THIRD

and the morning were the *t* day	Gen 1:13	7992
the name of the *t* river is	Gen 2:14	7992
t stories shalt thou make it	Gen 6:16	7992
Then on the *t* day Abraham lifted	Gen 22:4	7992
on the *t* day that Jacob was fled	Gen 31:22	7992
commanded he the second, and the *t*	Gen 32:19	7992
And it came to pass on the *t* day	Gen 34:25	7992
And it came to pass the *t* day	Gen 40:20	7992
Joseph said unto them the *t* day	Gen 42:18	7992
children of the *t* generation	Gen 50:23	8029
In the *t* month, when the children	Ex 19:1	7992
And be ready against the *t* day	Ex 19:11	7992
for the *t* day the LORD will come	Ex 19:11	7992
Be ready against the *t* day	Ex 19:15	7969
pass on the *t* day in the morning	Ex 19:16	7992
upon the children unto the *t*	Ex 20:5	8029
the *t* row a ligure, an agate, and	Ex 28:19	7992
children's children, unto the *t*	Ex 34:7	8029
And the *t* row, a ligure, an agate,	Ex 39:12	7992
t day shall be burnt with fire	Lev 7:17	7992
be eaten at all on the *t* day	Lev 7:18	7992
if ought remain until the *t* day	Lev 19:6	7992
it be eaten at all on the *t* day	Lev 19:7	7992
shall go forward in the *t* rank	Num 2:24	7992

On the *t* day Eliab the son of	Num 7:24	7992
upon the children unto the *t*	Num 14:18	8029
with the *t* part of an hin of oil	Num 15:6	7992
the *t* part of an hin of wine	Num 15:7	7992
himself with it on the *t* day	Num 19:12	7992
he purify not himself the *t* day	Num 19:12	7992
upon the unclean on the *t* day	Num 19:19	7992
the *t* part of an hin unto a ram,	Num 28:14	7992
on the *t* day eleven bullocks, two	Num 29:20	7992
and your captives on the *t* day	Num 31:19	7992
upon the children unto the *t*	Deut 5:9	8029
of the LORD in their *t* generation	Deut 23:8	7992
of thine increase the *t* year	Deut 26:12	7992
unto their cities on the *t* day	Josh 9:17	7992
the *t* lot came up for the	Josh 19:10	7992
children of Benjamin on the *t* day	Judg 20:30	7992
called Samuel again the *t* time	1Sa 3:8	7992
him Abinadab, and the *t* Shammah	1Sa 17:13	7992
sent messengers again the *t* time	1Sa 19:21	7992
the field unto the *t* day at even	1Sa 20:5	7992
to morrow any time, or the *t* day	1Sa 20:12	7992
were come to Ziklag on the *t* day	1Sa 30:1	7992
It came to pass on the *t* day	2Sa 1:2	7992
and the *t*, Absalom the son of	2Sa 3:3	7992
David sent forth a *t* part of the	2Sa 18:2	7992
a *t* part under the hand of	2Sa 18:2	7992
a *t* part under the hand of Ittai	2Sa 18:2	7992
it came to pass the *t* day after	1Kin 3:18	7992
the *t* was seven cubits broad	1Kin 6:6	7992
and out of the middle into the *t*	1Kin 6:8	7992
people came to Rehoboam the *t* day	1Kin 12:12	7992
Come to me again the *t* day	1Kin 12:12	7992
Even in the *t* year of Asa king of	1Kin 15:28	7969
In the *t* year of Asa king of	1Kin 15:33	7969
LORD came to Elijah in the *t* year	1Kin 18:1	7992
And he said, Do it the *t* time	1Kin 18:34	8027
And they did it the *t* time	1Kin 18:34	8027
And it came to pass in the *t* year	1Kin 22:2	7992
of the *t* fifty with his fifty	2Kin 1:13	7992
the *t* captain of fifty went up,	2Kin 1:13	7992
A *t* part of you that enter in on	2Kin 11:5	7992
a *t* part shall be at the gate of	2Kin 11:6	7992
a *t* part at the gate behind the	2Kin 11:6	7992
Now it came to pass in the *t* year	2Kin 18:1	7969
in the *t* year sow ye, and reap, and	2Kin 19:29	7992
on the *t* day thou shalt go up	2Kin 20:5	7992
the house of the LORD the *t* day	2Kin 20:8	7992
the second, and Shimma the *t*	1Chr 2:13	7992
The *t*, Absalom the son of Maachah	1Chr 3:2	7992
the *t* Zedekiah, the fourth	1Chr 3:15	7992
the second, and Aharah the *t*	1Chr 8:1	7992
the second, and Eliphelet the *t*	1Chr 8:39	7992
Obadiah the second, Eliab the *t*	1Chr 12:9	7992
the second, Jahaziel the *t*	1Chr 23:19	7992
The *t* to Harim, the fourth to	1Chr 24:8	7992
the second, Jahaziel the *t*	1Chr 24:23	7992
The *t* to Zaccur, he, his sons, and	1Chr 25:10	7992
the second, Zebadiah the *t*	1Chr 26:2	7992
Jehozabad the second, Joah the *t*	1Chr 26:4	7992
the second, Tebaliah the *t*	1Chr 26:11	7992
The *t* captain of the host for the	1Chr 27:5	7992
captain of the host for the *t*	1Chr 27:5	7992
came to Rehoboam on the *t* day	2Chr 10:12	7992
Come again to me on the *t* day	2Chr 10:12	7992
at Jerusalem in the *t* month	2Chr 15:10	7992
Also in the *t* year of his reign	2Chr 17:7	7969
A *t* part of you entering on the	2Chr 23:4	7992
a *t* part shall be at the king's	2Chr 23:5	7992
a *t* part at the gate of the	2Chr 23:5	7992
both the second year, and the *t*	2Chr 27:5	7992
In the *t* month they began to lay	2Chr 31:7	7992
on the *t* day of the month Adar	Ezr 6:15	8531
the *t* part of a shekel for the	Neh 10:32	7992
In the *t* year of his reign, he	Est 1:3	7969
Now it came to pass on the *t* day	Est 5:1	7992
at that time in the *t* month	Est 8:9	7992
and the name of the *t*	Job 42:14	7992
shall Israel be the *t* with Egypt	Is 19:24	7992
in the *t* year sow ye, and reap, and	Is 37:30	7992
t entry that is in the house of	Jer 38:14	7992
Thou shalt burn with fire a *t*	Eze 5:2	7992
and thou shalt take a *t* part	Eze 5:2	7992
a *t* part thou shalt scatter in	Eze 5:2	7992
A *t* part of thee shall die with	Eze 5:12	7992
a *t* part shall fall by the sword	Eze 5:12	7992
I will scatter a *t* part into all	Eze 5:12	7992
the *t* the face of a lion, and the	Eze 10:14	7992
the sword be doubled the *t* time	Eze 21:14	7992
the eleventh year, in the *t* month	Eze 31:1	7992
the *t* part of an hin of oil, to	Eze 46:14	7992
In the *t* year of the reign of	Dan 1:1	7969

another *t* kingdom of brass, which	Dan 2:39	8523
shall be the *t* ruler in the	Dan 5:7	8523
shalt be the *t* ruler in the	Dan 5:16	8531
be the *t* ruler in the kingdom	Dan 5:29	8531
In the *t* year of the reign of	Dan 8:1	7969
In the *t* year of Cyrus king of	Dan 10:1	7969
in the *t* day he will raise us up,	Hos 6:2	7992
in the *t* chariot white horses	Zec 6:3	7992
but the *t* shall be left therein	Zec 13:8	7992
I will bring the *t* part through	Zec 13:9	7992
and be raised again the *t* day	Mt 16:21	5154
the *t* day he shall be raised	Mt 17:23	5154
And he went out about the *t* hour	Mt 20:3	5154
the *t* day he shall rise again	Mt 20:19	5154
the second also, and the *t*	Mt 22:26	5154
away again, and prayed the *t* time	Mt 26:44	5154
be made sure until the *t* day	Mt 27:64	5154
killed, he shall rise the *t* day	Mk 9:31	5154
the *t* day he shall rise again	Mk 10:34	5154
and the *t* likewise	Mk 12:21	5154
And he cometh the *t* time, and saith	Mk 14:41	5154
And it was the *t* hour, and they	Mk 15:25	5154
be slain, and be raised the *t* day	Lk 9:22	5154
watch, or come in the *t* watch	Lk 12:38	5154
the *t* day I shall be perfected	Lk 13:32	5154
the *t* day he shall rise again	Lk 18:33	5154
And again he sent a *t*	Lk 20:12	5154
And the *t* took her	Lk 20:31	5154
And he said unto them the *t* time	Lk 23:22	5154
and the *t* day rise again	Lk 24:7	5154
to day is the *t* day since these	Lk 24:21	5154
to rise from the dead the *t* day	Lk 24:46	5154
the *t* day there was a marriage in	Jn 2:1	5154
This is now the *t* time that Jesus	Jn 21:14	5154
He saith unto him the *t* time	Jn 21:17	5154
he said unto him the *t* time	Jn 21:17	5154
it is but the *t* hour of the day	Acts 2:15	5154
Him God raised up the *t* day	Acts 10:40	5154
and fell down from the *t* loft	Acts 20:9	5152
at the *t* hour of the night	Acts 23:23	5154
the *t* day we cast out with our	Acts 27:19	5154
that he rose again the *t* day	1Cor 15:4	5154
an one caught up to the *t* heaven	2Cor 12:2	5154
the *t* time I am ready to come to	2Cor 12:14	5154
This is the *t* time I am coming to	2Cor 13:1	5154
the *t* beast had a face as a man,	Rev 4:7	5154
And when he had opened the *t* seal	Rev 6:5	5154
I heard the *t* beast say	Rev 6:5	5154
the *t* part of trees was burnt up,	Rev 8:7	5154
the *t* part of the sea became	Rev 8:8	5154
the *t* part of the creatures which	Rev 8:9	5154
the *t* part of the ships were	Rev 8:9	5154
the *t* angel sounded, and there	Rev 8:10	5154
it fell upon the *t* part of the	Rev 8:10	5154
the *t* part of the waters became	Rev 8:11	5154
the *t* part of the sun was smitten	Rev 8:12	5154
the *t* part of the moon, and the	Rev 8:12	5154
moon, and the *t* part of the stars	Rev 8:12	5154
so as the *t* part of them was	Rev 8:12	5154
day shone not for a *t* part of it	Rev 8:12	5154
for to slay the *t* part of men	Rev 9:15	5154
was the *t* part of men killed	Rev 9:18	5154
behold, the *t* woe cometh quickly	Rev 11:14	5154
his tail drew the *t* part of the	Rev 12:4	5154
the *t* angel followed them, saying	Rev 14:9	5154
the *t* angel poured out his vial	Rev 16:4	5154
the *t*, a chalcedony	Rev 21:19	5154

THIRDLY

t teachers, after that miracles,	1Cor 12:28	5154

THIRST

our children and our cattle with *t*	Ex 17:3	6772
against thee, in hunger, and in *t*	Deut 28:48	6772
heart, to add drunkenness to *t*	Deut 29:19	6771
and now shall I die for *t*, and fall	Judg 15:18	6772
to die by famine and by *t*, saying,	2Chr 32:11	6772
them out of the rock for their *t*	Neh 9:15	6772
and gavest them water for their *t*	Neh 9:20	6772
their winepresses, and suffer *t*	Job 24:11	6770
in my *t* they gave me vinegar to	Ps 69:21	6772
the wild asses quench their *t*	Ps 104:11	6772
their multitude dried up with *t*	Is 5:13	6772
and their tongue faileth for *t*	Is 41:17	6772
They shall not hunger nor *t*	Is 49:10	6770
there is no water, and dieth for *t*	Is 50:2	6772
unshod, and thy throat from *t*	Jer 2:25	6773
down from thy glory, and sit in *t*	Jer 48:18	6772
to the roof of his mouth for *t*	Lam 4:4	6772
a dry land, and slay her with *t*	Hos 2:3	6772
nor a *t* for water, but of hearing	Amos 8:11	6772
virgins and young men faint for *t*	Amos 8:13	6772

T

hunger and *t* after righteousness	Mt 5:6	1372
of this water shall *t* again	Jn 4:13	1372
I shall give him shall never *t*	Jn 4:14	1372
give me this water, that I *t* not	Jn 4:15	1372
believeth on me shall never *t*	Jn 6:35	1372
and cried, saying, If any man *t*	Jn 7:37	1372
might be fulfilled, saith, I *t*	Jn 19:28	1372
if he *t*, give him drink	Rom 12:20	1372
present hour we both hunger, and *t*	1Cor 4:11	1372
watchings often, in hunger and *t*	2Cor 11:27	1373
no more, neither *t* any more	Rev 7:16	1372

THIRSTED

the people *t* there for water	Ex 17:3	6770
they *t* not when he led them	Is 48:21	6770

THIRSTETH

My soul *t* for God, for the living	Ps 42:2	6770
my soul *t* for thee, my flesh	Ps 63:1	6770
my soul *t* after thee, as a	Ps 143:6	
Ho, every one that *t*, come ye to	Is 55:1	6771

THIRSTY

for I am *t*	Judg 4:19	6770
people is hungry, and weary, and *t*	2Sa 17:29	6771
t land, where no water is	Ps 63:1	
Hungry and *t*, their soul fainted	Ps 107:5	6771
thirsteth after thee, as a *t* land	Ps 143:6	
and if he be *t*, give him water to	Prov 25:21	6771
As cold waters to a *t* soul	Prov 25:25	
brought water to him that was *t*	Is 21:14	6771
or as when a *t* man dreameth	Is 29:8	
cause the drink of the *t* to fail	Is 32:6	6771
the *t* land springs of water	Is 35:7	6774
pour water upon him that is *t*	Is 44:3	6771
shall drink, but ye shall be *t*	Is 65:13	6770
wilderness, in a dry and *t* ground	Eze 19:13	6772
I was *t*, and ye gave me drink	Mt 25:35	1372
or *t*, and gave thee drink	Mt 25:37	1372
I was *t*, and ye gave me no drink	Mt 25:42	1372

THIRTEEN

Ishmael his son was *t* years old	Gen 17:25	7969,6240
two hundred and threescore and *t*	Num 3:43	7969
t of the firstborn of the	Num 3:46	7969
t young bullocks, two rams, and	Num 29:13	7969,6240
every bullock of the *t* bullocks	Num 29:14	7969,6240
t cities and their villages	Josh 19:6	7969,6240
the tribe of Benjamin, *t* cities	Josh 21:4	7969,6240
of Manasseh in Bashan, *t* cities	Josh 21:6	7969,6240
were *t* cities with their suburbs	Josh 21:19	7969,6240
to their families were *t* cities	Josh 21:33	7969,6240
building his own house *t* years	1Kin 7:1	7969,6240
their families were *t* cities	1Chr 6:60	7969,6240
of Manasseh in Bashan, *t* cities	1Chr 6:62	7969,6240
sons and brethren of Hosah were *t*	1Chr 26:11	7969,6240
the length of the gate, *t* cubits	Eze 40:11	7969,6240

THIRTEENTH

in the *t* year they rebelled	Gen 14:4	7969,6240
The *t* to Huppah, the fourteenth	1Chr 24:13	7969,6240
The *t* to Shubael, he, his sons,	1Chr 25:20	7969,6240
on the *t* day of the first month	Est 3:12	7969,6240
even upon the *t* day of the	Est 3:13	7969,6240
upon the *t* day of the twelfth	Est 8:12	7969,6240
on the *t* day of the same, when	Est 9:1	7969,6240
On the *t* day of the month Adar	Est 9:17	7969,6240
together on the *t* day thereof	Est 9:18	7969,6240
in the *t* year of his reign	Jer 1:2	7969,6240
From the *t* year of Josiah the son	Jer 25:3	7969,6240

THIRTIETH

t year of Uzziah king of Judah	2Kin 15:13	7970
t year of Azariah king of Judah	2Kin 15:17	7970
t year of the captivity of	2Kin 25:27	7970
t year of the reign of Asa	2Chr 15:19	7970
t year of the reign of Asa Baasha	2Chr 16:1	7970
t year of Artaxerxes the king,	Neh 5:14	7970
t year of Artaxerxes king of	Neh 13:6	7970
t year of the captivity of	Jer 52:31	7970
Now it came to pass in the *t* year	Eze 1:1	7970

THIRTY

t years, and begat a son in his	Gen 5:3	7970
were nine hundred and *t* years	Gen 5:5	7970
t years, and begat sons and	Gen 5:16	7970
and the height of it *t* cubits	Gen 6:15	7970
five and *t* years, and begat Salah	Gen 11:12	7970
And Salah lived *t* years, and begat	Gen 11:14	7970
four and *t* years, and begat Peleg	Gen 11:16	7970
t years, and begat sons and	Gen 11:17	7970
And Peleg lived *t* years, and begat	Gen 11:18	7970
two and *t* years, and begat Serug	Gen 11:20	7970
And Serug lived *t* years, and begat	Gen 11:22	7970

there shall *t* be found there	Gen 18:30	7970
will not do it, if I find *t* there	Gen 18:30	7970
life of Ishmael, an hundred and *t*	Gen 25:17	7970
T milch camels with their colts,	Gen 32:15	7970
Joseph was *t* years old when he	Gen 41:46	7970
his sons and his daughters were *t*	Gen 46:15	7970
are an hundred and *t* years	Gen 47:9	7970
life of Levi were an hundred *t*	Ex 6:16	7970
life of Kohath were an hundred *t*	Ex 6:18	7970
of Amram were an hundred and *t*	Ex 6:20	7970
was four hundred and *t* years	Ex 12:40	7970
t years, even the selfsame day it	Ex 12:41	7970
their master *t* shekels of silver	Ex 21:32	7970
of one curtain shall be *t* cubits	Ex 26:8	7970
of one curtain was *t* cubits	Ex 36:15	7970
t shekels, after the shekel of	Ex 38:24	7970
of her purifying three and *t* days	Lev 12:4	7970
thy estimation shall be *t* shekels	Lev 27:4	7970
of the tribe of Manasseh, were *t*	Num 1:35	7970
of the tribe of Benjamin, were *t*	Num 1:37	7970
were numbered of them, were *t*	Num 2:21	7970
were numbered of them, were *t*	Num 2:23	7970
From *t* years old and upward even	Num 4:3	7970
From *t* years old and upward until	Num 4:23	7970
From *t* years old and upward even	Num 4:30	7970
From *t* years old and upward even	Num 4:35	7970
From *t* years old and upward even	Num 4:39	7970
two thousand and six hundred and *t*	Num 4:40	7970
From *t* years old and upward even	Num 4:43	7970
From *t* years old and upward even	Num 4:47	7970
t shekels, one silver bowl of	Num 7:13	7970
t shekels, one silver bowl of	Num 7:19	7970
t shekels, one silver bowl of	Num 7:25	7970
t shekels, one silver bowl of	Num 7:31	7970
t shekels, one silver bowl of	Num 7:37	7970
t shekels, a silver bowl of	Num 7:43	7970
t shekels, one silver bowl of	Num 7:49	7970
t shekels, one silver bowl of	Num 7:55	7970
t shekels, one silver bowl of	Num 7:61	7970
t shekels, one silver bowl of	Num 7:67	7970
t shekels, one silver bowl of	Num 7:73	7970
t shekels, one silver bowl of	Num 7:79	7970
t shekels, each bowl seventy	Num 7:85	7970
they mourned for Aaron *t* days	Num 20:29	7970
thousand and seven hundred and *t*	Num 26:7	7970
that were numbered of them, *t*	Num 26:37	7970
and a thousand seven hundred and *t*	Num 26:51	7970
And *t* and two thousand persons in	Num 31:35	7970
t thousand and five hundred sheep	Num 31:36	7970
And the beeves were *t* and six	Num 31:38	7970
And the asses were *t* thousand	Num 31:39	7970
of which the LORD's tribute was *t*	Num 31:40	7970
t thousand and seven thousand and	Num 31:43	7970
And *t* and six thousand beeves,	Num 31:44	7970
t thousand asses and five hundred,	Num 31:45	7970
come over the brook Zered, was *t*	Deut 2:14	7970
in the plains of Moab *t* days	Deut 34:8	7970
men of Ai smote of them about *t*	Josh 7:5	7970
Joshua chose out *t* thousand	Josh 8:3	7970
all the kings *t* and one	Josh 12:24	7970
he had *t* sons that rode	Judg 10:4	7970
sons that rode on *t* ass colts	Judg 10:4	7970
ass colts, and they had *t* cities	Judg 10:4	7970
And he had *t* sons	Judg 12:9	7970
t daughters, whom he sent abroad,	Judg 12:9	7970
took in *t* daughters from abroad	Judg 12:9	7970
sons and *t* nephews, that rode on	Judg 12:14	7970
that they brought *t* companions to	Judg 14:11	7970
then I will give you *t* sheets	Judg 14:12	7970
sheets and *t* change of garments	Judg 14:12	7970
then shall ye give me *t* sheets	Judg 14:13	7970
sheets and *t* change of garments,	Judg 14:13	7970
slew *t* men of them, and took their	Judg 14:19	7970
the field, about *t* men of Israel	Judg 20:31	7970
the men of Israel about *t* persons	Judg 20:39	7970
fell of Israel *t* thousand footmen	1Sa 4:10	7970
which were about *t* persons	1Sa 9:22	7970
and the men of Judah *t* thousand	1Sa 11:8	7970
t thousand chariots, and six	1Sa 13:5	7970
David was *t* years old when he	2Sa 5:4	7970
and in Jerusalem he reigned *t*	2Sa 5:5	7970
chosen men of Israel, *t* thousand	2Sa 6:1	7970
three of the *t* chief went down,	2Sa 23:13	7970
He was more honourable than the *t*	2Sa 23:23	7970
brother of Joab was one of the *t*	2Sa 23:24	7970
t and seven in all	2Sa 23:39	7970
years reigned he in Hebron, and *t*	1Kin 2:11	7970
day was *t* measures of fine flour	1Kin 4:22	7970
and the levy was *t* thousand men	1Kin 5:13	7970
and the height thereof *t* cubits	1Kin 6:2	7970
and the height thereof *t* cubits	1Kin 7:2	7970

and the breadth thereof *t* cubits	1Kin 7:6	7970
a line of *t* cubits did compass it	1Kin 7:23	7970
In the *t* and first year of Asa	1Kin 16:23	7970
And in the *t* and eighth year of Asa	1Kin 16:29	7970
and there were *t* and two kings with	1Kin 20:1	7970
and they were two hundred and *t* two	1Kin 20:15	7970
pavilions, he and the kings, the *t*	1Kin 20:16	7970
the king of Syria commanded his *t*	1Kin 22:31	7970
Jehoshaphat was *t* and five years	1Kin 22:42	7970
T and two years old was he when he	2Kin 8:17	7970
In the *t* and seventh year of Joash	2Kin 13:10	7970
In the *t* and eighth year of	2Kin 15:8	7970
of silver and *t* talents of gold	2Kin 18:14	7970
began to reign, and he reigned *t*	2Kin 22:1	7970
and in Jerusalem he reigned *t*	1Chr 3:4	7970
for war, six and *t* thousand men	1Chr 7:4	7970
twenty and two thousand and *t*	1Chr 7:7	7970
Now three of the *t* captains went	1Chr 11:15	7970
he was honourable among the *t*	1Chr 11:25	7970
of the Reubenites, and *t* with him	1Chr 11:42	7970
among the *t*, and over the *t*	1Chr 12:4	7970
with them with shield and spear *t*	1Chr 12:34	7970
and his brethren an hundred and *t*	1Chr 15:7	7970
So they hired *t* and two thousand	1Chr 19:7	7970
numbered from the age of *t* years	1Chr 23:3	7970
by their polls, man by man, was *t*	1Chr 23:3	7970
among the *t*, and above the *t*	1Chr 27:6	7970
years reigned he in Hebron, and *t*	1Chr 29:27	7970
before the house two pillars of *t*	2Chr 3:15	7970
a line of *t* cubits did compass it	2Chr 4:2	7970
And Asa in the *t* and ninth year of	2Chr 16:12	7970
he was *t* and five years old when	2Chr 20:31	7970
Jehoram was *t* and two years old	2Chr 21:5	7970
T and two years old was he when he	2Chr 21:20	7970
t years old was he when he died	2Chr 24:15	7970
in Jerusalem one and *t* years	2Chr 34:1	7970
to the number of *t* thousand	2Chr 35:7	7970
t chargers of gold, a thousand	Ezr 1:9	7970
T basons of gold, silver basons	Ezr 1:10	7970
thousand and six hundred and *t*	Ezr 2:35	7970
of Shobai, in all an hundred *t*	Ezr 2:42	7970
seven thousand three hundred *t*	Ezr 2:65	7970
Their horses were seven hundred *t*	Ezr 2:66	7970
Their camels, four hundred *t*	Ezr 2:67	7970
three thousand nine hundred and *t*	Neh 7:38	7970
children of Shobai, an hundred *t*	Neh 7:45	7970
seven thousand three hundred *t*	Neh 7:67	7970
Their horses, seven hundred *t*	Neh 7:68	7970
Their camels, four hundred *t*	Neh 7:69	7970
hundred and *t* priests' garments	Neh 7:70	7970
in unto the king these *t* days	Est 4:11	7970
Take from hence *t* men with thee	Jer 38:10	7970
from Jerusalem eight hundred *t*	Jer 52:29	7970
t chambers were upon the pavement	Eze 40:17	7970
one over another, and *t* in order	Eze 41:6	7970
of forty cubits long and *t* broad	Eze 46:22	7970
of any God or man for *t* days	Dan 6:7	8533
of any God or man within *t* days	Dan 6:12	8533
three hundred and five and *t* days	Dan 12:12	7970
for my price *t* pieces of silver	Zec 11:12	7970
I took the *t* pieces of silver, and	Zec 11:13	7970
hundredfold, some sixty, some *t*	Mt 13:23	5144
with him for *t* pieces of silver	Mt 26:15	5144
brought again the *t* pieces of	Mt 27:3	5144
they took the *t* pieces of silver,	Mt 27:9	5144
and brought forth, some *t*, and some	Mk 4:8	5144
began to be about *t* years of age	Lk 3:23	5144
there, which had an infirmity *t*	Jn 5:5	5144
five and twenty or *t* furlongs	Jn 6:19	5144
t years after, cannot disannul,	Gal 3:17	5144

THIRTYFOLD

some sixtyfold, some *t*	Mt 13:8	5144
it, and bring forth fruit, some *t*	Mk 4:20	5144

THIS See APPENDIX.

THISTLE

The *t* that was in Lebanon sent to	2Kin 14:9	2336
in Lebanon, and trode down the *t*	2Kin 14:9	2336
The *t* that was in Lebanon sent to	2Chr 25:18	2336
in Lebanon, and trode down the *t*	2Chr 25:18	2336
the *t* shall come up on their	Hos 10:8	1863

THISTLES

t shall it bring forth to thee	Gen 3:18	1863
Let *t* grow instead of wheat, and	Job 31:40	2336
grapes of thorns, or figs of *t*	Mt 7:16	5146

THITHER

Oh, let me escape *t*, (is it not a	Gen 19:20	
Haste thee, escape *t*	Gen 19:22	
do any thing till thou be come *t*	Gen 19:22	

thou bring not my son *t* again	Gen 24:6	
only bring not my son *t* again	Gen 24:8	8033
t were all the flocks gathered	Gen 29:3	8033
which had brought him down *t*	Gen 39:1	8033
get you down *t*, and buy for us	Gen 42:2	8033
serve the LORD, until we come *t*	Ex 10:26	8033
that thou mayest bring in *t*	Ex 26:33	8033
the manslayer, that he may flee *t*	Num 35:6	8033
that the slayer may flee *t*	Num 35:11	8033
any person unawares may flee *t*	Num 35:15	8033
Thou also shalt not go in *t*	Deut 1:37	8033
before thee, he shall go in *t*	Deut 1:38	8033
good and evil, they shall go in *t*	Deut 1:39	8033
That the slayer might flee *t*	Deut 4:42	8033
ye seek, and *t* thou shalt come	Deut 12:5	8033
t ye shall bring your burnt	Deut 12:6	8033
t shall ye bring all that I	Deut 12:11	8033
that every slayer may flee *t*	Deut 19:3	8033
of the slayer, which shall flee *t*	Deut 19:4	8033
but thou shalt not go *t* unto the	Deut 32:52	8033
but thou shalt not go over *t*	Deut 34:4	8033
not all the people to labour *t*	Josh 7:3	8033
So there went up *t* of the people	Josh 7:4	8033
and unwittingly may flee *t*	Josh 20:3	8033
person at unawares might flee *t*	Josh 20:9	8033
all Israel went *t* a whoring after	Judg 8:27	8033
t fled all the men and women, and	Judg 9:51	8033
and they turned in *t*, and said unto	Judg 18:3	8033
the land went up, and came in *t*	Judg 18:17	8033
And they turned aside *t*, to go in	Judg 18:15	8033
the congregation sent *t* twelve	Judg 21:10	8033
all the Israelites that came *t*	1Sa 2:14	8033
ark of the God of Israel about *t*	1Sa 5:8	
now let us go *t*	1Sa 9:6	
when thou art come *t* to the city	1Sa 10:5	8033
And when they came *t* to the hill	1Sa 10:10	8033
if the man should yet come *t*	1Sa 10:22	1988
he went *t* to Naioth in Ramah	1Sa 19:23	8033
heard it, they went down *t* to him	1Sa 22:1	8033
Abiathar brought *t* the ephod to	1Sa 30:7	
So David went up *t*, and his two	2Sa 2:2	8033
they came *t* into the midst of the	2Sa 4:6	
ready before it was brought *t*	1Kin 6:7	
he came *t* unto a cave, and lodged	1Kin 19:9	8033
and they were divided hither and *t*	2Kin 2:8	2008
waters, they parted hither and *t*	2Kin 2:14	2008
by, he turned in *t* to eat bread	2Kin 4:8	8033
to us, that he shall turn in *t*	2Kin 4:10	8033
it fell on a day, that he came *t*	2Kin 4:11	8033
cut down a stick, and cast it in *t*	2Kin 6:6	8033
for *t* the Syrians are come down	2Kin 6:9	8033
Therefore sent he *t* horses	2Kin 6:14	8033
And when thou comest *t*, look out	2Kin 9:2	8033
Carry *t* one of the priests whom	2Kin 17:27	8033
Solomon went up *t* to the brasen	2Chr 1:6	8033
and when he came *t*, he did eat no	Ezr 10:6	8033
the trumpet, resort ye *t* unto us	Neh 4:20	8033
were gathered *t* unto the work	Neh 5:16	8033
t brought I again the vessels of	Neh 13:9	8033
womb, and naked shall I return *t*	Job 1:21	8033
they came *t*, and were ashamed	Job 6:20	5704
rivers come, *t* they return again	Eccl 1:7	8033
and with bows shall men come *t*	Is 7:24	8033
not come *t* the fear of briers	Is 7:25	8033
that send forth *t* the feet of the	Is 32:20	
from heaven, and returneth not *t*	Is 55:10	8033
even *t* wentest thou up to offer	Is 57:7	8033
He shall not return *t* any more	Jer 22:11	8033
return, *t* shall they not return	Jer 22:27	8033
a great company shall return *t*	Jer 31:8	2008
convenient for thee to go, *t* go	Jer 40:4	8033
went, *t* was their spirit to go	Eze 1:20	8033
And they shall come *t*, and they	Eze 11:18	8033
was upon me, and brought me, *t*	Eze 40:1	8033
And he brought me *t*, and, behold,	Eze 40:3	8033
because these waters shall come *t*	Eze 47:9	
t cause thy mighty ones to come	Joel 3:11	
Herod, he was afraid to go *t*	Mt 2:22	1563
ran afoot out of all cities, and	Mk 6:33	1563
t will the eagles be gathered	Lk 17:37	1563
poor widow casting in *t* two mites	Lk 21:2	1563
and where I am, *t* ye cannot come	Jn 7:34	
and where I am, *t* ye cannot come	Jn 7:36	
and goest thou *t* again	Jn 11:8	1563
resorted *t* with his disciples	Jn 18:2	1563
cometh *t* with lanterns and torches	Jn 18:3	1563
And Philip ran *t* to him, and heard	Acts 8:30	4370
there came *t* certain Jews from	Acts 14:19	1904
unto the women which resorted *t*	Acts 16:13	
who coming *t* went into the	Acts 17:10	3854

T

Paul at Berea, they came *t* also .... Acts 17:13   *1563*
he himself would depart shortly *t* .... Acts 25:4

THITHERWARD
And they turned *t*, and came to the .... Judg 18:15   8033
way to Zion with their faces *t* .... Jer 50:5   2008
to be brought on my way *t* by you .... Rom 15:24   *1563*

THOMAS *(tom'-us)* See DIDYMUS. *One of the twelve
   apostles.*
T, and Matthew the publican .... Mt 10:3   *2381*
and Bartholomew, and Matthew, and *T*.. Mk 3:18   *2381*
Matthew and *T*, James the son of .... Lk 6:15   *2381*
Then said *T*, which is called .... Jn 11:16   *2381*
T saith unto him, Lord, we know .... Jn 14:5   *2381*
But *T*, one of the twelve, called .... Jn 20:24   *2381*
were within, and *T* with them .... Jn 20:26   *2381*
Then saith he to *T*, Reach hither .... Jn 20:27   *2381*
T answered and said unto him, My .... Jn 20:28   *2381*
Jesus saith unto him, *T*, because .... Jn 20:29   *2381*
T called Didymus, and Nathanael of...... Jn 21:2   *2381*
and John, and Andrew, Philip, and *T*...... Acts 1:13   *2381*

THONGS
And as they bound him with *t* .... Acts 22:25   *2438*

THORN
or bore his jaw through with a *t* .... Job 41:2   2336
As a *t* goeth up into the hand of .... Prov 26:9   2336
Instead of the *t* shall come .... Is 55:13   5285
nor any grieving *t* of all that .... Eze 28:24   6975
the *t* and the thistle shall come .... Hos 10:8   6975
upright is sharper than a *t* hedge .... Mic 7:4   4534
was given to me a *t* in the flesh 2Cor 12:7   *4647*

THORNS
T also and thistles shall it bring .... Gen 3:18   6975
If fire break out, and catch in *t*............... Ex 22:6   6975
t in your sides, and shall vex you .... Num 33:55   6975
t in your eyes, until ye perish .... Josh 23:13   6975
they shall be as *t* in your sides .... Judg 2:3
with the *t* of the wilderness .... Judg 8:7   6975
t of the wilderness and briers, and .... Judg 8:16   6975
be all of them as *t* thrust away 2Sa 23:6   6975
which took Manasseh among the *t* 2Chr 33:11   2336
and taketh it even out of the *t* .... Job 5:5   6791
Before their pots can feel the *t* .... Ps 58:9   329
are quenched as the fire of *t* .... Ps 118:12   6975
slothful man is as an hedge of *t* .... Prov 15:19   2312
T and snares are in the way of the .... Prov 22:5   6791
lo, it was all grown over with *t*.............. Prov 24:31   7063
as the crackling of *t* under a pot .... Eccl 7:6   5518
As the lily among *t*, so is my .... Song 2:2   2336
there shall come up briers and *t*............ Is 5:6   7898
holes of the rocks, and upon all *t* .... Is 7:19   5285
it shall even be for briers and *t*............... Is 7:23   7898
the land shall become briers and *t* .... Is 7:24   7898
thither the fear of briers and *t* .... Is 7:25   7898
it shall devour the briers and *t* .... Is 9:18   7898
and it shall burn and devour his *t* .... Is 10:17   7898
briers and *t* against me in battle .... Is 27:4   7898
land of my people shall come up *t* .... Is 32:13   6975
as *t* cut up shall they be burned .... Is 33:12   6975
t shall come up in her palaces, ... Is 34:13   5518
fallow ground, and sow not among *t* ...... Jer 4:3   6975
have sown wheat, but shall reap *t*......... Jer 12:13   6975
t be with thee, and thou dost .... Eze 2:6   5544
I will hedge up thy way with *t* .... Hos 2:6   5518
t shall be in their tabernacles .... Hos 9:6   2336
they be folden together as *t* .... Nah 1:10   5518
Do men gather grapes of *t* .... Mt 7:16   *173*
And some fell among *t* .... Mt 13:7   *173*
the *t* sprung up, and choked them .... Mt 13:7   *173*
the *t* is he that heareth the word .... Mt 13:22   *173*
they had platted a crown of *t*................. Mt 27:29   *173*
And some fell among *t*, and the .... Mk 4:7   *173*
the *t* grew up, and choked it, and .... Mk 4:7   *173*
are they which are sown among *t*.......... Mk 4:18   *173*
purple, and platted a crown of *t* .... Mk 15:17   *174*
For of *t* men do not gather figs, ... Lk 6:44   *173*
And some fell among *t* .... Lk 8:7   *173*
the *t* sprang up with it, and .... Lk 8:7   *173*
that which fell among *t* are they............ Lk 8:14   *173*
the soldiers platted a crown of *t* .... Jn 19:2   *173*
forth, wearing the crown of *t*................. Jn 19:5   *174*
But that which beareth *t* and................. Heb 6:8   *173*

THOROUGHLY
and shall cause him to be *t* healed........ Ex 21:19   7495
his images brake they in pieces *t* 2Kin 11:18   3190

THOSE See APPENDIX.

THOU See APPENDIX.

THOUGH See APPENDIX.

THOUGHT
And Abraham said, Because I *t* .... Gen 20:11   559
saw her, he *t* her to be an harlot .... Gen 38:15   2803
I had not *t* to see thy face .... Gen 48:11   6419
as for you, ye *t* evil against me .... Gen 50:20   2803
which he *t* to do unto his people .... Ex 32:14   1696
I *t* to promote thee unto great................ Num 24:11   559
unto you, as I *t* to do unto them............ Num 33:56   1819
be not a *t* in thy wicked heart............... Deut 15:9   1697
as he had *t* to have done unto his .... Deut 19:19   2161
I verily *t* that thou hadst .... Judg 15:2   559
by night, and *t* to have slain me .... Judg 20:5   1819
I *t* to advertise thee, saying, ... Ruth 4:4   559
therefore Eli *t* she had been 1Sa 1:13   2803
for the asses, and take *t* for us............... 1Sa 9:5   1672
But Saul *t* to make David fall by 1Sa 18:25   2803
for he *t*, Something hath befallen 1Sa 20:26   559
who *t* that I would have given him 2Sa 4:10
Amnon *t* it hard for him to do any........ 2Sa 13:2   5869
Wherefore then hast thou *t* such a 2Sa 14:13   2803
and to do what he *t* good....................... 2Sa 18:27   5869
new sword, *t* to have slain David 2Sa 21:16   559
went away, and said, Behold, I *t* 2Kin 5:11   559
for he *t* to make him king...................... 2Chr 11:22
t to win them for himself....................... 2Chr 32:1   559
But they *t* to do me mischief .... Neh 6:2   2803
he *t* scorn to lay hands on .... Est 3:6   5869
Now Haman *t* in his heart, To whom..... Est 6:6   559
in the *t* of him that is at ease .... Job 12:5   6248
that no *t* can be withholden from .... Job 42:2   4209
We have *t* of thy lovingkindness, ... Ps 48:9   1819
Their inward *t* is, that their .... Ps 49:11
both the inward *t* of every one of .... Ps 64:6
When I *t* to know this, it was too........... Ps 73:16   2803
I *t* on my ways, and turned my feet........ Ps 119:59   2803
thou understandest my *t* afar off .... Ps 139:2   7454
The *t* of foolishness is sin .... Prov 24:9   2154
thyself, or if thou hast *t* evil .... Prov 30:32   2161
not the king, no not in thy *t*................... Eccl 10:20   4093
sworn, saying, Surely as I have *t* .... Is 14:24   1819
the evil that I *t* to do unto them .... Jer 18:8   2803
and thou shalt think an evil *t*................. Eze 38:10   4284
I *t* it good to shew the signs and..... Dan 4:2   8232,6925
the king *t* to set him over the .... Dan 6:3   6246
declareth unto man what is his *t*............ Amos 4:13   7807
the LORD of hosts *t* to do unto us .... Zec 1:6   2161
As I *t* to punish you, when your............. Zec 8:14   2161
So again have I *t* in these days............... Zec 8:15   2161
the LORD, and that *t* upon his name ...... Mal 3:16   2803
But while he *t* on these things, ... Mt 1:20   *1760*
Take no *t* for your life, what ye .... Mt 6:25   *3309*
Which of you by taking *t* can add ...... Mt 6:27   *3309*
And why take ye *t* for raiment .... Mt 6:28   *3309*
Therefore take no *t*, saying, What .... Mt 6:31   *3309*
therefore no *t* for the morrow .... Mt 6:34   *3309*
take *t* for the things of itself .... Mt 6:34   *3309*
take no *t* how or what ye shall .... Mt 10:19   *3309*
take no *t* beforehand what ye .... Mk 13:11   *4305*
And when he *t* thereon, he wept........... Mk 14:72   *1911*
Wherefore neither *t* I myself .... Lk 7:7
perceiving the *t* of their heart .... Lk 9:47   *1261*
take ye no *t* how or what thing ye ...... Lk 12:11   *3309*
he *t* within himself, saying, What .... Lk 12:17   *1260*
Take no *t* for your life, what ye .... Lk 12:22   *3309*
which of you with taking *t* can .... Lk 12:25   *3309*
why take ye *t* for the rest .... Lk 12:26   *3309*
because they *t* that the kingdom .... Lk 19:11   *1380*
but they *t* that he had spoken of............ Jn 11:13   *1380*
For some of them *t*, because Judas .... Jn 13:29   *1380*
because thou hast *t* that the gift............ Acts 8:20   *3543*
if perhaps the *t* of thine heart .... Acts 8:22   *1963*
While Peter *t* on the vision, the............. Acts 10:19   *1760*
but *t* he saw a vision .... Acts 12:9   *1380*
But Paul *t* not good to take him .... Acts 15:38
Why should it be *t* a thing..................... Acts 26:8   *2919*
I verily *t* with myself, that I.................... Acts 26:9   *1380*
as a child, I *t* as a child 1Cor 13:11   *3049*
Therefore I *t* it necessary to 2Cor 9:5   *2233*
t to the obedience of Christ 2Cor 10:5   *3540*
t it not robbery to be equal with .... Phil 2:6   *2233*
we *t* it good to be left at Athens............ 1Th 3:1   *2106*
suppose ye, shall he be *t* worthy............ Heb 10:29

THOUGHTEST
thou *t* that I was altogether such .... Ps 50:21   1819

THOUGHTS
the *t* of his heart was only evil .... Gen 6:5   4284
there were great *t* of heart .... Judg 5:15   2711
all the imaginations of the *t* 1Chr 28:9   4284
the *t* of the heart of thy people............... 1Chr 29:18   4284
In *t* from the visions of the .... Job 4:13   5587

off, even the *t* of my heart	Job 17:11	4180
Therefore do my *t* cause me to	Job 20:2	5587
Behold, I know your *t*, and the	Job 21:27	4284
God is not in all his *t*	Ps 10:4	4209
the *t* of his heart to do	Ps 33:11	4284
thy *t* which are to us-ward	Ps 40:5	4284
all their *t* are against me for	Ps 56:5	4284
and thy *t* are very deep	Ps 92:5	4284
The LORD knoweth the *t* of man	Ps 94:11	4284
In the multitude of my *t* within	Ps 94:19	8312
I hate vain *t*	Ps 119:113	5588
precious also are thy *t* unto me	Ps 139:17	7454
try me, and know my *t*	Ps 139:23	8312
in that very day his *t* perish	Ps 146:4	6250
The *t* of the righteous are right	Prov 12:5	4284
The *t* of the wicked are an	Prov 15:26	4284
thy *t* shall be established	Prov 16:3	4284
The *t* of the diligent tend only	Prov 21:5	4284
way, and the unrighteous man his *t*	Is 55:7	4284
For my *t* are not your *t*,	Is 55:8	4284
ways, and my *t* than your *t*	Is 55:9	4284
their *t* are *t* of iniquity	Is 59:7	4284
was not good, after their own *t*	Is 65:2	4284
For I know their works and their *t*	Is 66:18	4284
thy vain *t* lodge within thee	Jer 4:14	4284
people, even the fruit of their *t*	Jer 6:19	4284
have performed the *t* of his heart	Jer 23:20	4209
For I know the *t* that I think	Jer 29:11	4284
of peace, and not of evil, to	Jer 29:11	4284
thy *t* came into thy mind upon thy	Dan 2:29	7476
mightest know the *t* of thy heart	Dan 2:30	7476
the *t* upon my bed and the visions	Dan 4:5	2031
one hour, and his *t* troubled him	Dan 4:19	7476
his *t* troubled him, so that the	Dan 5:6	7476
let not thy *t* trouble thee, nor	Dan 5:10	7476
they know not the *t* of the LORD	Mic 4:12	4284
And Jesus knowing their *t* said	Mt 9:4	1761
And Jesus knew their *t*, and said	Mt 12:25	1761
out of the heart proceed evil *t*	Mt 15:19	1261
the heart of men, proceed evil *t*	Mk 7:21	1261
that the *t* of many hearts may be	Lk 2:35	1261
But when Jesus perceived their *t*	Lk 5:22	1261
But he knew their *t*, and said to	Lk 6:8	1261
But he, knowing their *t*, said	Lk 11:17	1270
why do *t* arise in your hearts	Lk 24:38	1261
their *t* the mean while accusing	Rom 2:15	3053
Lord knoweth the *t* of the wise	1Cor 3:20	1261
and is a discerner of the *t*	Heb 4:12	1761
and are become judges of evil *t*	Jas 2:4	1261

THOUSAND

thy brother a *t* pieces of silver	Gen 20:16	505
about six hundred *t* on foot that	Ex 12:37	505
people that day about three *t* men	Ex 32:28	505
a *t* seven hundred and threescore	Ex 38:25	505
six hundred *t* and three	Ex 38:26	505
of the *t* seven hundred seventy and	Ex 38:28	505
was seventy talents, and two *t*	Ex 38:29	505
of you shall put ten *t* to flight	Lev 26:8	7233
of Reuben, were forty and six *t*	Num 1:21	505
of Simeon, were fifty and nine *t*	Num 1:23	505
five *t* six hundred and fifty	Num 1:25	505
were threescore and fourteen *t*	Num 1:27	505
of Issachar, were fifty and four *t*	Num 1:29	505
of Zebulun, were fifty and seven *t*	Num 1:31	505
tribe of Ephraim, were forty *t*	Num 1:33	505
of Manasseh, were thirty and two *t*	Num 1:35	505
Benjamin, were thirty and five *t*	Num 1:37	505
of Dan, were threescore and two *t*	Num 1:39	505
of Asher, were forty and one *t*	Num 1:41	505
Naphtali, were fifty and three *t*	Num 1:43	505
were numbered were six hundred *t*	Num 1:46	505
six hundred *t* and three	Num 1:46	505
were threescore and fourteen *t*	Num 2:4	505
thereof, were fifty and four *t*	Num 2:6	505
thereof, were fifty and seven *t*	Num 2:8	505
camp of Judah were an hundred *t*	Num 2:9	505
and fourscore *t* and six *t*	Num 2:9	505
thereof, were forty and six *t*	Num 2:11	505
of them, were fifty and nine *t*	Num 2:13	505
of them, were forty and five *t*	Num 2:15	505
camp of Reuben were an hundred *t*	Num 2:16	505
t and fifty and one *t*	Num 2:16	505
numbered of them, were forty *t*	Num 2:19	505
of them, were thirty and two *t*	Num 2:21	505
of them, were thirty and five *t*	Num 2:23	505
an hundred *t* and eight *t*	Num 2:24	505
of them, were threescore and two *t*	Num 2:26	505
of them, were forty and one *t*	Num 2:28	505
of them, were fifty and three *t*	Num 2:30	505
the camp of Dan were an hundred *t*	Num 2:31	505

and fifty and seven *t*	Num 2:31	505
six hundred *t* and three *t*	Num 2:32	505
numbered of them were seven *t*	Num 3:22	505
month old and upward, were eight *t*	Num 3:28	505
a month old and upward, were six *t*	Num 3:34	505
and upward, were twenty and two *t*	Num 3:39	505
two *t* two hundred and threescore	Num 3:43	505
a *t* three hundred and threescore	Num 3:50	505
families were two *t* seven hundred	Num 4:36	505
of their fathers, were two *t*	Num 4:40	505
their families, were three *t*	Num 4:44	505
numbered of them, were eight *t*	Num 4:48	505
the silver vessels weighed two *t*	Num 7:85	505
I am, are six hundred *t* footmen	Num 11:21	505
in the plague were fourteen *t*	Num 16:49	505
the plague were twenty and four *t*	Num 25:9	505
of them were forty and three *t*	Num 26:7	505
the Simeonites, twenty and two *t*	Num 26:14	505
were numbered of them, forty *t*	Num 26:18	505
of them, threescore and sixteen *t*	Num 26:22	505
of them, threescore and four *t*	Num 26:25	505
numbered of them, threescore *t*	Num 26:27	505
numbered of them, fifty and two *t*	Num 26:34	505
numbered of them, thirty and two *t*	Num 26:37	505
of them were forty and five *t*	Num 26:41	505
them, were threescore and four *t*	Num 26:43	505
who were fifty and three *t*	Num 26:47	505
of them were forty and five *t*	Num 26:50	505
children of Israel, six hundred *t*	Num 26:51	505
a *t* seven hundred and thirty	Num 26:51	505
of them were twenty and three *t*	Num 26:62	505
Of every tribe a *t*, throughout	Num 31:4	505
a *t* of every tribe, twelve	Num 31:5	505
tribe, twelve *t* armed for war	Num 31:5	505
a *t* of every tribe, them and	Num 31:6	505
war had caught, was six hundred *t*	Num 31:32	505
seventy *t* and five *t* sheep,	Num 31:32	505
And threescore and twelve *t* beeves	Num 31:33	505
And threescore and one *t* asses,	Num 31:34	505
two *t* persons in all, of women	Num 31:35	505
was in number three hundred *t*	Num 31:36	505
and seven and thirty *t*	Num 31:36	505
the beeves were thirty and six *t*	Num 31:38	505
And the asses were thirty *t*	Num 31:39	505
And the persons were sixteen *t*	Num 31:40	505
congregation was three hundred *t*	Num 31:43	505
and thirty *t* and seven *t*	Num 31:43	505
And thirty and six *t* beeves,	Num 31:44	505
And thirty *t* asses and five hundred	Num 31:45	505
And sixteen *t* persons	Num 31:46	505
was sixteen *t* seven hundred and	Num 31:52	505
outward a *t* cubits round about	Num 35:4	505
on the east side two *t* cubits	Num 35:5	505
and on the south side two *t* cubits	Num 35:5	505
and on the west side two *t* cubits	Num 35:5	505
and on the north side two *t* cubits	Num 35:5	505
a *t* times so many more as ye are	Deut 1:11	505
commandments to a *t* generations	Deut 7:9	505
How should one chase a *t*, and two	Deut 32:30	505
and two put ten *t* to flight	Deut 32:30	505
about two *t* cubits by measure	Josh 3:4	505
About forty *t* prepared for war	Josh 4:13	505
about two or three *t* men go up	Josh 7:3	505
of the people about three *t* men	Josh 7:4	505
out thirty *t* mighty men of valour	Josh 8:3	505
And he took about five *t* men	Josh 8:12	505
of men and women, were twelve *t*	Josh 8:25	505
One man of you shall chase a *t*	Josh 23:10	505
slew of them in Bezek ten *t* men	Judg 1:4	505
Moab at that time about ten *t* men	Judg 3:29	505
take with thee ten *t* men of the	Judg 4:6	505
up with ten *t* men at his feet	Judg 4:10	505
Tabor, and ten *t* men after him	Judg 4:14	505
seen among forty *t* in Israel	Judg 5:8	505
of the people twenty and two *t*	Judg 7:3	505
and there remained ten *t*	Judg 7:3	505
with them, about fifteen *t* men	Judg 8:10	505
twenty *t* men that drew sword	Judg 8:10	505
that he requested was a *t*	Judg 8:26	505
Shechem died also, about a *t* men	Judg 9:49	505
of the Ephraimites forty and two *t*	Judg 12:6	505
Then three *t* men of Judah went to	Judg 15:11	505
it, and slew a *t* men therewith	Judg 15:15	505
of an ass have I slain a *t* men	Judg 15:16	505
upon the roof about three *t* men	Judg 16:27	505
four hundred *t* footmen that drew	Judg 20:2	505
of Israel, and an hundred of a *t*	Judg 20:10	505
and a *t* out of ten *t*	Judg 20:10	7233
six *t* men that drew sword, beside	Judg 20:15	505
hundred *t* men that drew sword	Judg 20:17	505
that day twenty and two *t* men	Judg 20:21	505

T

of Israel again eighteen *t* men	Judg 20:25	505
t chosen men out of all Israel	Judg 20:34	505
that day twenty and five *t*	Judg 20:35	505
fell of Benjamin eighteen *t* men	Judg 20:44	505
them in the highways five *t* men	Judg 20:45	505
Gidom, and slew two *t* men of them	Judg 20:45	505
five *t* men that drew the sword	Judg 20:46	505
sent thither twelve *t* men of the	Judg 21:10	505
in the field about four *t* men	1Sa 4:2	505
fell of Israel thirty *t* footmen	1Sa 4:10	505
he smote of the people fifty *t*	1Sa 6:19	505
of Israel were three hundred *t*	1Sa 11:8	505
and the men of Judah thirty *t*	1Sa 11:8	505
chose him three *t* men of Israel	1Sa 13:2	505
whereof two *t* were with Saul in	1Sa 13:2	505
a *t* were with Jonathan in Gibeah	1Sa 13:2	505
thirty *t* chariots, and six	1Sa 13:5	505
six *t* horsemen, and people as the	1Sa 13:5	505
in Telaim, two hundred *t* footmen	1Sa 15:4	505
footmen, and ten *t* men of Judah	1Sa 15:4	505
coat was five *t* shekels of brass	1Sa 17:5	505
unto the captain of their *t*	1Sa 17:18	505
and made him his captain over a *t*	1Sa 18:13	505
Then Saul took three *t* chosen men	1Sa 24:2	505
great, and he had three *t* sheep	1Sa 25:2	505
sheep, and a *t* goats	1Sa 25:2	505
having three *t* chosen men of	1Sa 26:2	505
chosen men of Israel, thirty *t*	2Sa 6:1	505
David took from him a *t* chariots	2Sa 8:4	505
horsemen, and twenty *t* footmen	2Sa 8:4	505
the Syrians two and twenty *t* men	2Sa 8:5	505
of salt, being eighteen *t* men	2Sa 8:13	505
twenty *t* footmen, and of king	2Sa 10:6	505
and of king Maacah a *t* men	2Sa 10:6	505
and of Ish-tob twelve *t* men	2Sa 10:6	505
forty *t* horsemen, and smote	2Sa 10:18	505
me now choose out twelve *t* men	2Sa 17:1	505
now thou art worth ten *t* of us	2Sa 18:3	505
that day of twenty *t* men	2Sa 18:7	505
Though I should receive a *t*	2Sa 18:12	505
there were a *t* men of Benjamin	2Sa 19:17	505
were in Israel eight hundred *t*	2Sa 24:9	505
of Judah were five hundred *t* men	2Sa 24:9	505
even to Beer-sheba seventy *t* men	2Sa 24:15	505
a *t* burnt offerings did Solomon	1Kin 3:4	505
Solomon had forty *t* stalls of	1Kin 4:26	505
chariots, and twelve *t* horsemen	1Kin 4:26	505
And he spake three *t* proverbs	1Kin 4:32	505
and his songs were a *t* and five	1Kin 4:32	505
Solomon gave Hiram twenty *t*	1Kin 5:11	505
and the levy was thirty *t* men	1Kin 5:13	505
Lebanon, ten *t* a month by courses	1Kin 5:14	505
ten *t* that bare burdens, and	1Kin 5:15	505
fourscore *t* hewers in the	1Kin 5:15	505
which were over the work, three *t*	1Kin 5:16	505
it contained two *t* baths	1Kin 7:26	505
the LORD, two and twenty *t* oxen	1Kin 8:63	505
and an hundred and twenty *t* sheep	1Kin 8:63	505
and he had a *t* and four hundred	1Kin 10:26	505
twelve *t* horsemen, whom he	1Kin 10:26	505
fourscore *t* chosen men, which	1Kin 12:21	505
I have left me seven *t* in Israel	1Kin 19:18	505
children of Israel, being seven *t*	1Kin 20:15	505
an hundred *t* footmen in one day	1Kin 20:29	505
seven *t* of the men that were left	1Kin 20:30	505
king of Israel an hundred *t* lambs	2Kin 3:4	505
lambs, and an hundred *t* rams	2Kin 3:4	505
six *t* pieces of gold, and ten	2Kin 5:5	505
and ten chariots, and ten *t* footmen	2Kin 13:7	505
Edom in the valley of salt ten *t*	2Kin 14:7	505
gave Pul a *t* talents of silver	2Kin 15:19	505
I will deliver thee two *t* horses	2Kin 18:23	505
an hundred fourscore and five *t*	2Kin 19:35	505
of valour, even ten *t* captives	2Kin 24:14	505
the men of might, even seven *t*	2Kin 24:16	505
and craftsmen and smiths a *t*	2Kin 24:16	505
four and forty *t* seven hundred and	1Chr 5:18	505
of their camels fifty *t*, and of	1Chr 5:21	505
fifty *t*, and of asses two *t*	1Chr 5:21	505
and of men an hundred *t*	1Chr 5:21	505
the days of David two and twenty *t*	1Chr 7:2	505
for war, six and thirty *t* men	1Chr 7:4	505
genealogies fourscore and seven *t*	1Chr 7:5	505
their genealogies twenty and two *t*	1Chr 7:7	505
men of valour, was twenty *t*	1Chr 7:9	505
men of valour, were seventeen *t*	1Chr 7:11	505
to battle was twenty and six *t* men	1Chr 7:40	505
the house of their fathers, a *t*	1Chr 9:13	505
hundred, and the greatest over a *t*	1Chr 12:14	505
bare shield and spear were six *t*	1Chr 12:24	505
of valour for the war, seven *t*	1Chr 12:25	505
Of the children of Levi four *t*	1Chr 12:26	505
and with him were three *t*	1Chr 12:27	505
the kindred of Saul, three *t*	1Chr 12:29	505
the children of Ephraim twenty *t*	1Chr 12:30	505
half tribe of Manasseh eighteen *t*	1Chr 12:31	505
all instruments of war, fifty *t*	1Chr 12:33	505
And of Naphtali a *t* captains	1Chr 12:34	505
shield and spear thirty and seven *t*	1Chr 12:34	505
expert in war twenty and eight *t*	1Chr 12:35	505
to battle, expert in war, forty *t*	1Chr 12:36	505
battle, an hundred and twenty *t*	1Chr 12:37	505
he commanded to a *t* generations	1Chr 16:15	505
David took from him a *t* chariots	1Chr 18:4	505
seven *t* horsemen, and twenty	1Chr 18:4	505
horsemen, and twenty *t* footmen	1Chr 18:4	505
the Syrians two and twenty *t* men	1Chr 18:5	505
in the valley of salt eighteen *t*	1Chr 18:12	505
the children of Ammon sent a *t*	1Chr 19:6	505
two *t* chariots, and the king of	1Chr 19:7	505
t men which fought in chariots	1Chr 19:18	505
forty *t* footmen, and killed	1Chr 19:18	505
they of Israel were a *t* *t*	1Chr 21:5	505
an hundred *t* men that drew sword	1Chr 21:5	505
ten *t* men that drew sword	1Chr 21:5	505
fell of Israel seventy *t* men	1Chr 21:14	505
LORD an hundred *t* talents of gold	1Chr 22:14	505
a *t* *t* talents of silver	1Chr 22:14	505
man by man, was thirty and eight *t*	1Chr 23:3	505
four *t* were to set forward the	1Chr 23:4	505
six *t* were officers and judges	1Chr 23:4	505
Moreover four *t* were porters	1Chr 23:5	505
four *t* praised the LORD with the	1Chr 23:5	505
his brethren, men of valour, a *t*	1Chr 26:30	505
men of valour, were two *t*	1Chr 26:32	505
course were twenty and four *t*	1Chr 27:1	505
his course were twenty and four *t*	1Chr 27:2	505
likewise were twenty and four *t*	1Chr 27:4	505
his course were twenty and four *t*	1Chr 27:5	505
his course were twenty and four *t*	1Chr 27:7	505
his course were twenty and four *t*	1Chr 27:8	505
his course were twenty and four *t*	1Chr 27:9	505
his course were twenty and four *t*	1Chr 27:10	505
his course were twenty and four *t*	1Chr 27:11	505
his course were twenty and four *t*	1Chr 27:12	505
his course were twenty and four *t*	1Chr 27:13	505
his course were twenty and four *t*	1Chr 27:14	505
his course were twenty and four *t*	1Chr 27:15	505
Even three *t* talents of gold, of	1Chr 29:4	505
seven *t* talents of refined silver	1Chr 29:4	505
of God of gold five *t* talents	1Chr 29:7	505
ten *t* drams, and of silver ten	1Chr 29:7	7239
drams, and of silver ten *t* talents	1Chr 29:7	505
and of brass eighteen *t* talents	1Chr 29:7	7239,505
one hundred *t* talents of iron	1Chr 29:7	505
even a *t* bullocks, a *t*	1Chr 29:21	505
a *t* rams, and a *t* lambs	1Chr 29:21	505
offered a *t* burnt offerings upon	2Chr 1:6	505
and he had a *t* and four hundred	2Chr 1:14	505
twelve *t* horsemen, which he	2Chr 1:14	505
ten *t* men to bear burdens, and	2Chr 2:2	505
fourscore *t* to hew in the	2Chr 2:2	505
hew in the mountain, and three *t*	2Chr 2:2	505
twenty *t* measures of beaten wheat	2Chr 2:10	505
twenty *t* measures of barley, and	2Chr 2:10	505
twenty *t* baths of wine, and twenty	2Chr 2:10	505
of wine, and twenty *t* baths of oil	2Chr 2:10	505
and fifty *t* and three *t*	2Chr 2:17	505
ten *t* of them to be bearers of	2Chr 2:18	505
fourscore *t* to be hewers in the	2Chr 2:18	505
in the mountain, and three *t*	2Chr 2:18	505
it received and held three *t* baths	2Chr 4:5	505
two *t* oxen, and an hundred and	2Chr 7:5	505
and an hundred and twenty *t* sheep	2Chr 7:5	505
Solomon had four *t* stalls for	2Chr 9:25	505
and chariots, and twelve *t* horsemen	2Chr 9:25	505
fourscore *t* chosen men, which	2Chr 11:1	505
and threescore *t* horsemen	2Chr 12:3	505
even four hundred *t* chosen men	2Chr 13:3	505
with eight hundred *t* chosen men	2Chr 13:3	505
Israel five hundred *t* chosen men	2Chr 13:17	505
out of Judah three hundred *t*	2Chr 14:8	505
bows, two hundred and fourscore *t*	2Chr 14:8	505
with an host of a *t* *t*	2Chr 14:9	505
hundred oxen and seven *t* sheep	2Chr 15:11	505
brought him flocks, seven *t*	2Chr 17:11	505
and seven hundred rams, and seven *t*	2Chr 17:11	505
men of valour three hundred *t*	2Chr 17:14	505
him two hundred and fourscore *t*	2Chr 17:15	505
hundred *t* mighty men of valour	2Chr 17:16	505
with bow and shield two hundred *t*	2Chr 17:17	505
fourscore *t* ready prepared for	2Chr 17:18	505

T

and Satan, and bound him a *t* years ...... Rev 20:2   5507
till the *t* years should be .... Rev 20:3   5507
and reigned with Christ a *t* years .... Rev 20:4   5507
until the *t* years were finished .... Rev 20:5   5507
and shall reign with him a *t* years .... Rev 20:6   5507
when the *t* years are expired, ... Rev 20:7   5507
with the reed, twelve *t* furlongs .... Rev 21:16   5505

THOUSANDS

thou the mother of *t* of millions .... Gen 24:60   505
such over them, to be rulers of *t* .... Ex 18:21   505
over the people, rulers of *t* .... Ex 18:25   505
shewing mercy unto *t* of them that .... Ex 20:6   505
Keeping mercy for *t*, forgiving .... Ex 34:7   505
fathers, heads of *t* in Israel .... Num 1:16   505
are heads of the *t* of Israel .... Num 10:4   505
O LORD, unto the many *t* of Israel .... Num 10:36   505
delivered out of the *t* of Israel .... Num 31:5   505
host, with the captains over *t* .... Num 31:14   505
which were over *t* of the host .... Num 31:48   505
of the host, the captains of *t* .... Num 31:48   505
to the LORD, of the captains of *t* .... Num 31:52   505
the gold of the captains of *t* .... Num 31:54   505
heads over you, captains over *t* .... Deut 1:15   505
shewing mercy unto *t* of them that .... Deut 5:10   505
and he came with ten *t* of saints .... Deut 33:2   7233
and they are the ten *t* of Ephraim .... Deut 33:17   7233
and they are the *t* of Manasseh .... Deut 33:17   505
fathers among the *t* of Israel .... Josh 22:14   505
unto the heads of the *t* of Israel .... Josh 22:21   505
heads of the *t* of Israel which .... Josh 22:30   505
will appoint him captains over *t* 1Sa 8:12   505
LORD by your tribes, and by your *t* 1Sa 10:19   505
his *t*, and David his ten *t* 1Sa 18:7   505
have ascribed unto David ten *t* 1Sa 18:8   7233
and to me they have ascribed but *t* 1Sa 18:8   505
saying, Saul hath slain his *t* 1Sa 21:11   505
and David his ten *t* 1Sa 21:11   7233
and make you all captains of *t* 1Sa 22:7   505
out throughout all the *t* of Judah 1Sa 23:23   505
passed on by hundreds, and by *t* 1Sa 29:2   505
dances, saying, Saul slew his *t* 1Sa 29:5   7233
and David his ten *t* 1Sa 29:5   505
with him, and set captains of *t* 2Sa 18:1   505
came out by hundreds and by *t* 2Sa 18:4   505
captains of the *t* that were of 1Chr 12:20   505
consulted with the captains of *t* 1Chr 13:1   505
of Israel, and the captains over *t* 1Chr 15:25   505
fathers, the captains over *t* 1Chr 26:26   505
chief fathers and captains of *t* 1Chr 27:1   505
and the captains over the *t* 1Chr 28:1   505
of Israel, and the captains of *t* 1Chr 29:6   505
all Israel, to the captains of *t* 2Chr 1:2   505
Of Judah, the captains of *t* 2Chr 17:14   505
and made them captains over *t* 2Chr 25:5   505
not be afraid of ten *t* of people .... Ps 3:6   7233
twenty thousand, even *t* of angels .... Ps 68:17   505
is better unto me than *t* of gold.............. Ps 119:72   505
that our sheep may bring forth *t* .... Ps 144:13   503
and ten *t* in our streets.......................... Ps 144:13   7232
shewest lovingkindness unto *t* .... Jer 32:18   505
thousand *t* ministered unto him,............. Dan 7:10   506
and he shall cast down many ten *t*........ Dan 11:12   7239
be little among the *t* of Judah .... Mic 5:2   505
LORD be pleased with *t* of rams .... Mic 6:7   505
or with ten *t* of rivers of oil.................... Mic 6:7   7233
how many *t* of Jews there are .... Acts 21:20   3461
cometh with ten *t* of his saints .... Jude 14   3461
ten thousand, and *t* of *t*....................... Rev 5:11   5505

THREAD

from a *t* even to a shoelatchet................ Gen 14:23   2339
bound upon his hand a scarlet *t* .... Gen 38:28
had the scarlet *t* upon his hand.............. Gen 38:30
t in the window which thou didst .... Josh 2:18   2339
as a *t* of tow is broken when it .... Judg 16:9   6616
them from off his arms like a *t* .... Judg 16:12   2339
Thy lips are like a *t* of scarlet .... Song 4:3   2339

THREATEN

people, let us straitly *t* them .... Acts 4:17   546

THREATENED

So when they had further *t* them............ Acts 4:21   4324
when he suffered, he *t* not 1Pet 2:23   546

THREATENING

things unto them, forbearing *t*................ Eph 6:9   547

THREATENINGS

And now, Lord, behold their *t*.................. Acts 4:29   547
And Saul, yet breathing out *t*.................. Acts 9:1   547

THREE

begat Methuselah *t* hundred years .... Gen 5:22   7969
of Enoch were *t* hundred sixty .... Gen 5:23   7969
And Noah begat *t* sons, Shem, Ham, ... Gen 6:10   7969
the ark shall be *t* hundred cubits .... Gen 6:15   7969
the *t* wives of his sons with them .... Gen 7:13   7969
These are the *t* sons of Noah .... Gen 9:19   7969
lived after the flood *t* hundred .... Gen 9:28   7969
t years, and begat sons and .... Gen 11:13   7969
t years, and begat sons and .... Gen 11:15   7969
t hundred and eighteen, and pursued .... Gen 14:14   7969
Take me an heifer of *t* years old .... Gen 15:9   8027
old, and a she goat of *t* years old .... Gen 15:9   8027
a ram of *t* years old, and a .... Gen 15:9   8027
and, lo, *t* men stood by him .... Gen 18:2   7969
Make ready quickly *t* measures of .... Gen 18:6   7969
there were *t* flocks of sheep .... Gen 29:2   7969
because I have born him *t* sons .... Gen 29:34   7969
he set *t* days' journey betwixt .... Gen 30:36   7969
came to pass about *t* months after .... Gen 38:24   7969
And in the vine were *t* branches .... Gen 40:10   7969
The *t* branches are *t* days .... Gen 40:12   7969
Yet within *t* days shall Pharaoh .... Gen 40:13   7969
I had *t* white baskets on my head .... Gen 40:16   7969
The *t* baskets are *t* days .... Gen 40:18   7969
Yet within *t* days shall Pharaoh .... Gen 40:19   7969
all together into ward *t* days .... Gen 42:17   7969
but to Benjamin he gave *t* hundred .... Gen 45:22   7969
and his daughters were thirty and *t* .... Gen 46:15   7969
child, she hid him *t* months .... Ex 2:2   7969
thee, *t* days' journey into the .... Ex 3:18   7969
t days' journey into the desert, ... Ex 5:3   7969
were an hundred thirty and *t* years .... Ex 6:18   7969
t years old, when they spake unto .... Ex 7:7   7969
We will go *t* days' journey into .... Ex 8:27   7969
in all the land of Egypt *t* days................ Ex 10:22   7969
any from his place for *t* days .... Ex 10:23   7969
and they went *t* days in the .... Ex 15:22   7969
And if he do not these *t* unto her .... Ex 21:11   7969
T times thou shalt keep a feast .... Ex 23:14   7969
T times in the year all thy males .... Ex 23:17   7969
t branches of the candlestick out .... Ex 25:32   7969
t branches of the candlestick out .... Ex 25:32   7969
T bowls made like unto almonds, ... Ex 25:33   7969
t bowls made like almonds in the .... Ex 25:33   7969
height thereof shall be *t* cubits .... Ex 27:1   7969
pillars *t*, and their sockets *t* .... Ex 27:14   7969
pillars *t*, and their sockets *t* .... Ex 27:15   7969
that day about *t* thousand men............... Ex 32:28   7969
t branches of the candlestick out .... Ex 37:18   7969
t branches of the candlestick out .... Ex 37:18   7969
T bowls made after the fashion of .... Ex 37:19   7969
t bowls made like almonds in................ Ex 37:19   7969
t cubits the height thereof...................... Ex 38:1   7969
pillars *t*, and their sockets *t* .... Ex 38:14   7969
pillars *t*, and their sockets *t* .... Ex 38:15   7969
t thousand and five hundred and............ Ex 38:26   7969
in the blood of her purifying *t* .... Lev 12:4   7969
t tenth deals of fine flour for a .... Lev 14:10   7969
t years shall it be as .... Lev 19:23   7969
bring forth fruit for *t* years .... Lev 25:21   7969
shall be *t* shekels of silver .... Lev 27:6   7969
and nine thousand and *t* hundred .... Num 1:23   7969
t thousand and four hundred .... Num 1:43   7969
t thousand and five hundred and............ Num 1:46   7969
and nine thousand and *t* hundred .... Num 2:13   7969
t thousand and four hundred .... Num 2:30   7969
t thousand and four hundred and........... Num 2:32   7969
a thousand *t* hundred and .... Num 3:50   7969
were *t* thousand and two hundred .... Num 4:44   7969
mount of the LORD's journey .... Num 10:33   7969
them in the *t* days' journey .... Num 10:33   7969
Come out ye *t* unto the tabernacle .... Num 12:4   7969
And they *t* came out .... Num 12:4   7969
of *t* tenth deals of flour mingled............. Num 15:9   7969
hast smitten me these *t* times .... Num 22:28   7969
smitten thine ass these *t* times .... Num 22:32   7969
and turned from me these *t* times .... Num 22:33   7969
blessed them these *t* times .... Num 24:10   7969
t thousand and seven hundred and .... Num 26:7   7969
and four thousand and *t* hundred .... Num 26:25   7969
t thousand and four hundred .... Num 26:47   7969
t thousand, all males from a .... Num 26:62   7969
t tenth deals of flour for a meat .... Num 28:12   7969
t tenth deals shall ye offer for .... Num 28:20   7969
t tenth deals unto one bullock, ... Num 28:28   7969
t tenth deals for a bullock, and .... Num 29:3   7969
t tenth deals to a bullock, and .... Num 29:9   7969
t tenth deals unto every bullock............ Num 29:14   7969
was in number *t* hundred thousand........ Num 31:36   7969
was *t* hundred thousand and thirty .... Num 31:43   7969

went *t* days' journey in the	Num 33:8	7969
t years old when he died in mount	Num 33:39	7969
Ye shall give *t* cities on this	Num 35:14	7969
t cities shall ye give in the	Num 35:14	7969
Then Moses severed *t* cities on	Deut 4:41	7969
At the end of *t* years thou shalt	Deut 14:28	7969
T times in a year shall all thy	Deut 16:16	7969
or *t* witnesses, shall he that is	Deut 17:6	7969
Thou shalt separate *t* cities for	Deut 19:2	7969
into *t* parts, that every slayer	Deut 19:3	8027
shalt separate *t* cities for thee	Deut 19:7	7969
then shalt thou add *t* cities more	Deut 19:9	7969
more for thee, beside these *t*	Deut 19:9	7969
or at the mouth of *t* witnesses	Deut 19:15	7969
for within *t* days ye shall pass	Josh 1:11	7969
and hide yourselves there *t* days	Josh 2:16	7969
mountain, and abode there *t* days	Josh 2:22	7969
And it came to pass after *t* days	Josh 3:2	7969
about two or *t* thousand men go up	Josh 7:3	7969
the people about *t* thousand men	Josh 7:4	7969
of *t* days after they had made a	Josh 9:16	7969
drove thence the *t* sons of Anak	Josh 15:14	7969
and her towns, even *t* countries	Josh 17:11	7969
among you *t* men for each tribe	Josh 18:4	7969
with her suburbs; *t* cities	Josh 21:32	7969
thence the *t* sons of Anak	Judg 1:20	7969
their mouth, were *t* hundred men	Judg 7:6	7969
By the *t* hundred men that lapped	Judg 7:7	7969
and retained those *t* hundred men	Judg 7:8	7969
he divided the *t* hundred men into	Judg 7:16	7969
hundred men into *t* companies	Judg 7:16	7969
the *t* companies blew the trumpets	Judg 7:20	7969
the *t* hundred blew the trumpets,	Judg 7:22	7969
the *t* hundred men that were with	Judg 8:4	7969
had reigned *t* years over Israel	Judg 9:22	7969
and divided them into *t* companies	Judg 9:43	7969
t years, and died, and was buried	Judg 10:2	7969
coasts of Arnon, *t* hundred years	Judg 11:26	7969
they could not in *t* days expound	Judg 14:14	7969
caught *t* hundred foxes, and took	Judg 15:4	7969
Then *t* thousand men of Judah went	Judg 15:11	7969
thou hast mocked me these *t* times	Judg 16:15	7969
the roof about *t* thousand men	Judg 16:27	7969
and he abode with him *t* days	Judg 19:4	7969
with *t* bullocks, and one ephah of	1Sa 1:24	7969
fleshhook of *t* teeth in his hand	1Sa 2:13	7969
she conceived, and bare *t* sons	1Sa 2:21	7969
asses that were lost *t* days ago	1Sa 9:20	7969
there shall meet thee *t* men going	1Sa 10:3	7969
to Beth-el, one carrying *t* kids	1Sa 10:3	7969
carrying *t* loaves of bread	1Sa 10:3	7969
of Israel were *t* hundred thousand	1Sa 11:8	7969
put the people in *t* companies	1Sa 11:11	7969
Saul chose him *t* thousand men of	1Sa 13:2	7969
of the Philistines in *t* companies	1Sa 13:17	7969
the *t* eldest sons of Jesse went	1Sa 17:13	7969
the names of his *t* sons that went	1Sa 17:13	7969
the *t* eldest followed Saul	1Sa 17:14	7969
And when thou hast stayed *t* days	1Sa 20:19	8027
I will shoot *t* arrows on the side	1Sa 20:20	7969
ground, and bowed himself *t* times	1Sa 20:41	7969
kept from us about these *t* days	1Sa 21:5	8032
Then Saul took *t* thousand chosen	1Sa 24:2	7969
he had *t* thousand sheep, and a	1Sa 25:2	7969
having *t* thousand chosen men of	1Sa 26:2	7969
any water, *t* days and *t* nights	1Sa 30:12	7969
because *t* days agone I fell sick	1Sa 30:13	7969
his *t* sons, and his armourbearer,	1Sa 31:6	7969
his *t* sons fallen in mount Gilboa	1Sa 31:8	7969
there were *t* sons of Zeruiah	2Sa 2:18	7969
of Abner's fame, so that *t* hundred	2Sa 2:31	7969
t years over all Israel and Judah	2Sa 5:5	7969
of Obed-edom the Gittite *t* months	2Sa 6:11	7969
to Geshur, and was there *t* years	2Sa 13:38	7969
Absalom there were born *t* sons	2Sa 14:27	7969
he took *t* darts in his hand, and	2Sa 18:14	7969
me the men of Judah within *t* days	2Sa 20:4	7969
in the days of David *t* years	2Sa 21:1	7969
t hundred shekels of brass in	2Sa 21:16	7969
one of the *t* mighty men with	2Sa 23:9	7969
t of the thirty chief went down,	2Sa 23:13	7991
the *t* mighty men brake through	2Sa 23:16	7969
things did these *t* mighty men	2Sa 23:17	7969
son of Zeruiah, was chief among *t*	2Sa 23:18	7992
up his spear against *t* hundred	2Sa 23:18	7969
them, and had the name among *t*	2Sa 23:18	7969
Was he not most honourable of *t*	2Sa 23:19	7969
he attained not unto the first *t*	2Sa 23:19	7969
had the name among *t* mighty men	2Sa 23:22	7969
he attained not to the first *t*	2Sa 23:23	7969
the LORD, I offer thee *t* things	2Sa 24:12	7969
or wilt thou flee *t* months before	2Sa 24:13	7969
or that there be *t* days'	2Sa 24:13	7969
t years reigned he in Jerusalem	1Kin 2:11	7969
to pass at the end of *t* years	1Kin 2:39	7969
he spake *t* thousand proverbs	1Kin 4:32	7969
t thousand and *t* hundred,	1Kin 5:16	7969
court with *t* rows of hewed stone	1Kin 6:36	7969
And there were windows in *t* rows	1Kin 7:4	7969
was against light in *t* ranks	1Kin 7:4	7969
was against light in *t* ranks	1Kin 7:5	7969
was with *t* rows of hewed stones	1Kin 7:12	7969
t looking toward the north, and	1Kin 7:25	7969
t looking toward the west, and	1Kin 7:25	7969
t looking toward the south, and	1Kin 7:25	7969
t looking toward the east	1Kin 7:25	7969
t cubits the height of it	1Kin 7:27	7969
t times in a year did Solomon	1Kin 9:25	7969
he made *t* hundred shields of	1Kin 10:17	7969
t pound of gold went to one	1Kin 10:17	7969
once in *t* years came the navy of	1Kin 10:22	7969
and *t* hundred concubines	1Kin 11:3	7969
unto them, Depart yet for *t* days	1Kin 12:5	7969
T years reigned he in Jerusalem	1Kin 15:2	7969
himself upon the child *t* times	1Kin 17:21	7969
they continued *t* years without	1Kin 22:1	7969
and they sought *t* days, but found	2Kin 2:17	7969
called these *t* kings together	2Kin 3:10	7969
called these *t* kings together	2Kin 3:13	7969
out to him two or *t* eunuchs	2Kin 9:32	7969
But it was so, that in the *t*	2Kin 12:6	7969
In the *t* and twentieth year of	2Kin 13:1	7969
T times did Joash beat him, and	2Kin 13:25	7969
Samaria, and besieged it *t* years	2Kin 17:5	7969
at the end of *t* years they took	2Kin 18:10	7969
Judah *t* hundred talents of silver	2Kin 18:14	7969
t years old when he began to	2Kin 23:31	7969
he reigned *t* months in Jerusalem	2Kin 23:31	7969
became his servant *t* years	2Kin 24:1	7969
he reigned in Jerusalem *t* months	2Kin 24:8	7969
height of the chapiter *t* cubits	2Kin 25:17	7969
the *t* keepers of the door	2Kin 25:18	7969
which *t* were born unto him of the	1Chr 2:3	7969
Abishai, and Joab, and Asahel, *t*	1Chr 2:16	7969
And Segub begat Jair, who had *t*	1Chr 2:22	7969
he reigned thirty and *t* years	1Chr 3:4	7969
and Hezekiah, and Azrikam, *t*	1Chr 3:23	7969
Bela, and Becher, and Jediael, *t*	1Chr 7:6	7969
his *t* sons, and all his house died	1Chr 10:6	7969
t hundred slain by him at one	1Chr 11:11	7969
who was one of the *t* mighties	1Chr 11:12	7969
Now *t* of the thirty captains went	1Chr 11:15	7969
the *t* brake through the host of	1Chr 11:18	7969
things did these *t* mightiest	1Chr 11:19	7969
of Joab, he was chief of the *t*	1Chr 11:20	7969
up his spear against *t* hundred	1Chr 11:20	7969
them, and had a name among the *t*	1Chr 11:20	7969
Of the *t*, he was more honourable	1Chr 11:21	7969
he attained not to the first *t*	1Chr 11:21	7969
had the name among the *t* mighties	1Chr 11:24	7969
but attained not to the first *t*	1Chr 11:25	7969
and with him were *t* thousand	1Chr 12:27	7969
the kindred of Saul, *t* thousand	1Chr 12:29	7969
there they were with David *t* days	1Chr 12:39	7969
Obed-edom in his house *t* months	1Chr 13:14	7969
the LORD, I offer thee *t* things	1Chr 21:10	7969
Either *t* years' famine	1Chr 21:12	7969
or *t* months to be destroyed	1Chr 21:12	7969
or else *t* days the sword of the	1Chr 21:12	7969
was Jehiel, and Zetham, and Joel, *t*	1Chr 23:8	7969
Shelomith, and Haziel, and Haran, *t*	1Chr 23:9	7969
Mahli, and Eder, and Jeremoth, *t*	1Chr 23:23	7969
The *t* and twentieth to Delaiah,	1Chr 24:18	7969
fourteen sons and *t* daughters	1Chr 25:5	7969
The *t* and twentieth to Mahazioth,	1Chr 25:30	7969
Even *t* thousand talents of gold,	1Chr 29:4	7969
t years reigned he in Jerusalem	1Chr 29:27	7969
t thousand and six hundred to	2Chr 2:2	7969
t thousand and six hundred	2Chr 2:17	7969
t thousand and six hundred	2Chr 2:18	7969
t looking toward the north, and	2Chr 4:4	7969
t looking toward the west, and	2Chr 4:4	7969
t looking toward the south, and	2Chr 4:4	7969
t looking toward the east	2Chr 4:4	7969
received and held *t* thousand baths	2Chr 4:5	7969
t cubits high, and had set it in	2Chr 6:13	7969
And on the *t* and twentieth day of	2Chr 7:10	7969
t times in the year, even in the	2Chr 8:13	7969
t hundred shields made he of	2Chr 9:16	7969
t hundred shekels of gold went to	2Chr 9:16	7969
every *t* years once came the ships	2Chr 9:21	7969
Come again unto me after *t* days	2Chr 10:5	7969

T

son of Solomon strong, *t* years	2Chr 11:17	7969
for *t* years they walked in the	2Chr 11:17	7969
He reigned *t* years in Jerusalem	2Chr 13:2	7969
out of Judah *t* hundred thousand	2Chr 14:8	7969
thousand, and *t* hundred chariots	2Chr 14:9	7969
men of valour *t* hundred thousand	2Chr 17:14	7969
they were *t* days in gathering of	2Chr 20:25	7969
found them *t* hundred thousand	2Chr 25:5	7969
smote *t* thousand of them, and took	2Chr 25:13	7969
t hundred thousand and seven	2Chr 26:13	7969
hundred oxen and *t* thousand sheep	2Chr 29:33	7969
from *t* years old and upward, even	2Chr 31:16	7969
thousand, and *t* thousand bullocks	2Chr 35:7	7969
small cattle, and *t* hundred oxen	2Chr 35:8	7969
t years old when he began to	2Chr 36:2	7969
he reigned *t* months in Jerusalem	2Chr 36:2	7969
to reign, and he reigned *t* months	2Chr 36:9	7969
t hundred seventy and two	Ezr 2:4	7969
of Bebai, six hundred twenty and *t*	Ezr 2:11	7969
Bezai, *t* hundred twenty and *t*	Ezr 2:17	7969
Hashum, two hundred twenty and *t*	Ezr 2:19	7969
an hundred twenty and *t*	Ezr 2:21	7969
seven hundred and forty and *t*	Ezr 2:25	7969
and Ai, two hundred twenty and *t*	Ezr 2:28	7969
of Harim, *t* hundred and twenty	Ezr 2:32	7969
Jericho, *t* hundred forty and five	Ezr 2:34	7969
t thousand and six hundred and	Ezr 2:35	7969
Jeshua, nine hundred seventy and *t*	Ezr 2:36	7969
were *t* hundred ninety and two	Ezr 2:58	7969
forty and two thousand *t* hundred	Ezr 2:64	7969
seven thousand *t* hundred thirty	Ezr 2:65	7969
With *t* rows of great stones, and a	Ezr 6:4	8532
and with him *t* hundred males	Ezr 8:5	7969
and there abode we in tents *t* days	Ezr 8:15	7969
Jerusalem, and abode there *t* days	Ezr 8:32	7969
would not come within *t* days	Ezr 10:8	7969
unto Jerusalem within *t* days	Ezr 10:9	7969
to Jerusalem, and was there *t* days	Neh 2:11	7969
t hundred seventy and two	Neh 7:9	7969
two thousand *t* hundred twenty and	Neh 7:17	7969
t hundred twenty and eight	Neh 7:22	7969
Bezai, *t* hundred twenty and four	Neh 7:23	7969
Beeroth, seven hundred forty and *t*	Neh 7:29	7969
and Ai, an hundred twenty and *t*	Neh 7:32	7969
of Harim, *t* hundred and twenty	Neh 7:35	7969
Jericho, *t* hundred forty and five	Neh 7:36	7969
t thousand nine hundred and thirty	Neh 7:38	7969
Jeshua, nine hundred seventy and *t*	Neh 7:39	7969
were *t* hundred ninety and two	Neh 7:60	7969
forty and two thousand *t* hundred	Neh 7:66	7969
seven thousand *t* hundred thirty	Neh 7:67	7969
and neither eat nor drink *t* days	Est 4:16	7969
is, the month Sivan, on the *t*	Est 8:9	7969
slew *t* hundred men at Shushan	Est 9:15	7969
him seven sons and *t* daughters	Job 1:2	7969
t thousand camels, and five	Job 1:3	7969
called for their *t* sisters to eat	Job 1:4	7969
The Chaldeans made out *t* bands	Job 1:17	7969
Now when Job's *t* friends heard of	Job 2:11	7969
So these *t* men ceased to answer	Job 32:1	7969
Also against his *t* friends was	Job 32:3	7969
in the mouth of these *t* men	Job 32:5	7969
also seven sons and *t* daughters	Job 42:13	7969
There are *t* things that are never	Prov 30:15	7969
There be *t* things which are too	Prov 30:18	7969
For *t* things the earth is	Prov 30:21	7969
There be *t* things which go well,	Prov 30:29	7969
Zoar, an heifer of *t* years old	Is 15:5	7992
spoken, saying, Within *t* years	Is 16:14	7969
two or *t* berries in the top of	Is 17:6	7969
barefoot *t* years for a sign and	Is 20:3	7969
even unto this day, that is the *t*	Jer 25:3	7969
Jehudi had read *t* or four leaves	Jer 36:23	7969
as an heifer of *t* years old	Jer 48:34	7992
the *t* keepers of the door	Jer 52:24	7969
year *t* thousand Jews and *t*	Jer 52:28	7969
In the *t* and twentieth year of	Jer 52:30	7969
days, *t* hundred and ninety days	Eze 4:5	7969
t hundred and ninety days shalt	Eze 4:9	7969
Though these *t* men, Noah, Daniel,	Eze 14:14	7969
Though these *t* men were in it, as	Eze 14:16	7969
Though these *t* men were in it, as	Eze 14:18	7969
gate eastward were *t* on this side	Eze 40:10	7969
on this side, and *t* on that side	Eze 40:10	7969
they *t* were of one measure	Eze 40:10	7969
thereof were *t* on this side	Eze 40:21	7969
on this side and *t* on that side	Eze 40:21	7969
gate was *t* cubits on this side	Eze 40:48	7969
side, and *t* cubits on that side	Eze 40:48	7969
And the side chambers were *t*	Eze 41:6	7969
round about on their *t* stories	Eze 41:16	7969
altar of wood was *t* cubits high	Eze 41:22	7969
against gallery in *t* stories	Eze 42:3	7992
For they were in *t* stories	Eze 42:6	8027
t gates northward	Eze 48:31	7969
five hundred: and *t* gates	Eze 48:32	7969
hundred measures: and *t* gates	Eze 48:33	7969
five hundred, with their *t* gates	Eze 48:34	7969
so nourishing them *t* years	Dan 1:5	7969
And these *t* men, Shadrach, Meshach,	Dan 3:23	8532
Did not we cast *t* men bound into	Dan 3:24	8532
And over these *t* presidents	Dan 6:2	8532
upon his knees *t* times a day	Dan 6:10	8532
maketh his petition *t* times a day	Dan 6:13	8532
it had *t* ribs in the mouth of it	Dan 7:5	8532
before whom there were *t* of the	Dan 7:8	8532
came up, and before whom *t* fell	Dan 7:20	8532
first, and he shall subdue *t* kings	Dan 7:24	8532
two thousand and *t* hundred days	Dan 8:14	7969
Daniel was mourning *t* full weeks	Dan 10:2	7969
till *t* whole weeks were fulfilled	Dan 10:3	7969
stand up yet *t* kings in Persia	Dan 11:2	7969
cometh to the thousand *t* hundred	Dan 12:12	7969
For *t* transgressions of Damascus,	Amos 1:3	7969
For *t* transgressions of Gaza, and	Amos 1:6	7969
For *t* transgressions of Tyrus, and	Amos 1:9	7969
For *t* transgressions of Edom, and	Amos 1:11	7969
For *t* transgressions of the	Amos 1:13	7969
For *t* transgressions of Moab, and	Amos 2:1	7969
For *t* transgressions of Judah, and	Amos 2:4	7969
For *t* transgressions of Israel,	Amos 2:6	7969
and your tithes after *t* years	Amos 4:4	7969
when there were yet *t* months to	Amos 4:7	7969
So two or *t* cities wandered unto	Amos 4:8	7969
the fish *t* days and *t* nights	Jonah 1:17	7969
great city of *t* days' journey	Jonah 3:3	7969
T shepherds also I cut off in one	Zec 11:8	7969
For as Jonas was *t* days	Mt 12:40	5140
t nights in the whale's belly	Mt 12:40	5140
so shall the Son of man be *t* days	Mt 12:40	5140
t nights in the heart of the	Mt 12:40	5140
hid in *t* measures of meal, till	Mt 13:33	5140
they continue with me now *t* days	Mt 15:32	5140
let us make here *t* tabernacles	Mt 17:4	5140
or *t* witnesses every word may be	Mt 18:16	5140
For where two or *t* are gathered	Mt 18:20	5140
of God, and to build it in *t* days	Mt 26:61	5140
temple, and buildest it in *t* days	Mt 27:40	5140
After *t* days I will rise again	Mt 27:63	5140
they have now been with me *t* days	Mk 8:2	5140
and after *t* days rise again	Mk 8:31	5140
and let us make *t* tabernacles	Mk 9:5	5140
for more than *t* hundred pence	Mk 14:5	5145
within *t* days I will build	Mk 14:58	5140
temple, and buildest it in *t* days	Mk 15:29	5140
abode with her about *t* months	Lk 1:56	5140
that after *t* days they found him	Lk 2:46	5140
the heaven was shut up *t* years	Lk 4:25	5140
and let us make *t* tabernacles	Lk 9:33	5140
Which now of these *t*, thinkest	Lk 10:36	5140
him, Friend, lend me *t* loaves	Lk 11:5	5140
t against two, and two against	Lk 12:52	5140
against two, and two against *t*	Lk 12:52	5140
these *t* years I come seeking	Lk 13:7	5140
hid in *t* measures of meal, till	Lk 13:21	5140
two or *t* firkins apiece	Jn 2:6	5140
in *t* days I will raise it up	Jn 2:19	5140
and wilt thou rear it up in *t* days	Jn 2:20	5140
ointment sold for *t* hundred pence	Jn 12:5	5145
fishes, an hundred and fifty and *t*	Jn 21:11	5140
unto them about *t* thousand souls	Acts 2:41	5153
about the space of *t* hours after	Acts 5:7	5140
up in his father's house *t* months	Acts 7:20	5140
he was *t* days without sight, and	Acts 9:9	5140
unto him, Behold, *t* men seek thee	Acts 10:19	5140
And this was done *t* times	Acts 11:10	5151
immediately there were *t* men	Acts 11:11	5140
t sabbath days reasoned with them	Acts 17:2	5140
boldly for the space of *t* months	Acts 19:8	5140
And there abode *t* months	Acts 20:3	5140
that by the space of *t* years I	Acts 20:31	5148
after *t* days he ascended from	Acts 25:1	5140
lodged us *t* days courteously	Acts 28:7	5140
after *t* months we departed in a	Acts 28:11	5140
Syracuse, we tarried there *t* days	Acts 28:12	5140
as Appii forum, and The *t* taverns	Acts 28:15	5140
that after *t* days Paul called the	Acts 28:17	5140
committed, and fell in one day *t*	1Cor 10:8	5140
faith, hope, charity, these *t*	1Cor 13:13	5140
it be by two, or at the most by *t*	1Cor 14:27	5140
Let the prophets speak two or *t*	1Cor 14:29	5140
In the mouth of two or *t*	2Cor 13:1	5140

Then after *t* years I went up to	Gal 1:18	5140
but before two or *t* witnesses	1Ti 5:19	5140
mercy under two or *t* witnesses	Heb 10:28	5140
was hid *t* months of his parents,	Heb 11:23	5150
the earth by the space of *t* years	Jas 5:17	5140
For there are *t* that bear record	1Jn 5:7	5140
and these *t* are one	1Jn 5:7	5140
there are *t* that bear witness in	1Jn 5:8	5140
and these *t* agree in one	1Jn 5:8	5140
t measures of barley for a penny	Rev 6:6	5140
of the trumpet of the *t* angels	Rev 8:13	5140
By these *t* was the third part of	Rev 9:18	5140
see their dead bodies *t* days	Rev 11:9	5140
And after *t* days and an half the	Rev 11:11	5140
I saw *t* unclean spirits like	Rev 16:13	5140
city was divided into *t* parts	Rev 16:19	5140
On the east *t* gates	Rev 21:13	5140
on the north *t* gates	Rev 21:13	5140
on the south *t* gates	Rev 21:13	5140
and on the west *t* gates	Rev 21:13	5140

THREEFOLD

a *t* cord is not quickly broken	Eccl 4:12	8027

THREESCORE

life which he lived, an hundred *t*	Gen 25:7	7657
Isaac was *t* years old when she	Gen 25:26	8346
sons' wives, all the souls were *t*	Gen 46:26	8346
which came into Egypt, were *t*	Gen 46:27	7657
the Egyptians mourned for him *t*	Gen 50:3	7657
were twelve wells of water, and *t*	Ex 15:27	7657
and a thousand seven hundred and *t*	Ex 38:25	7657
in the blood of her purifying *t*	Lev 12:5	8346
of the tribe of Judah, were *t*	Num 1:27	7657
even of the tribe of Dan, were *t*	Num 1:39	8346
were numbered of them, were *t*	Num 2:4	7657
were numbered of them, were *t*	Num 2:26	8346
and two thousand two hundred and *t*	Num 3:43	7657
redeemed of the two hundred and *t*	Num 3:46	7657
a thousand three hundred and *t*	Num 3:50	8346
that were numbered of them, *t*	Num 26:22	7657
that were numbered of them, *t*	Num 26:25	8346
t thousand and five hundred	Num 26:27	8346
were numbered of them, were *t*	Num 26:43	8346
And *t* and twelve thousand beeves,	Num 31:33	7657
And *t* and one thousand asses,	Num 31:34	8346
of the sheep were six hundred and *t*	Num 31:37	7657
of which the LORD's tribute was *t*	Num 31:38	8346
of which the LORD's tribute was *t*	Num 31:39	8346
twelve fountains of water, and *t*	Num 33:9	7657
t cities, all the region of Argob	Deut 3:4	8346
went down into Egypt with *t*	Deut 10:22	7657
which are in Bashan, *t* cities,	Josh 13:30	8346
And Adoni-bezek said, *T* and ten	Judg 1:7	7657
and the elders thereof, even *t*	Judg 8:14	7657
And Gideon had *t* and ten sons of	Judg 8:30	7657
sons of Jerubbaal, which are *t*	Judg 9:2	7657
And they gave him *t* and ten pieces	Judg 9:4	7657
the sons of Jerubbaal, being *t*	Judg 9:5	7657
day, and have slain his sons, *t*	Judg 9:18	7657
That the cruelty done to the *t*	Judg 9:24	7657
and thirty nephews, that rode on *t*	Judg 12:14	7657
of the people fifty thousand and *t*	1Sa 6:19	7657
that three hundred and *t* men died	2Sa 2:31	8346
t great cities with walls and	1Kin 4:13	8346
flour, and *t* measures of meal,	1Kin 4:22	8346
And Solomon had *t* and ten thousand	1Kin 5:15	7657
the length thereof was *t* cubits	1Kin 6:2	8346
in one year was six hundred *t*	1Kin 10:14	8346
t men of the people of the land	2Kin 25:19	8346
married when he was *t* years old	1Chr 2:21	8346
the towns thereof, even *t* cities	1Chr 2:23	8346
forty thousand seven hundred and *t*	1Chr 5:18	7657
a thousand and seven hundred and *t*	1Chr 9:13	8346
Obed-edom with their brethren, *t*	1Chr 16:38	8346
and Judah was four hundred *t*	1Chr 21:5	7657
strength for the service, were *t*	1Chr 26:8	8346
And Solomon told out *t* and ten	2Chr 2:2	7657
And he set *t* and ten thousand of	2Chr 2:18	7657
the first measure was *t* cubits	2Chr 3:3	8346
in one year was six hundred and *t*	2Chr 9:13	8346
eighteen wives, and *t* concubines	2Chr 11:21	8346
and eight sons, and *t* daughters	2Chr 11:21	8346
chariots, and *t* thousand horsemen	2Chr 12:3	8346
the congregation brought, was *t*	2Chr 29:32	7657
she kept sabbath, to fulfil *t*	2Chr 36:21	7657
of Zaccai, seven hundred and *t*	Ezr 2:9	8346
two thousand three hundred and *t*	Ezr 2:64	8346
unto the treasure of the work *t*	Ezr 2:69	7239
the height thereof *t* cubits	Ezr 6:3	8361
and the breadth thereof *t* cubits	Ezr 6:3	8361
and with him an hundred and *t* males	Ezr 8:10	8346

and Shemaiah, and with them *t* males	Ezr 8:13	8346
of Zaccai, seven hundred and *t*	Neh 7:14	8346
of Adonikam, six hundred *t*	Neh 7:18	8346
of Bigvai, two thousand *t*	Neh 7:19	8346
two thousand three hundred and *t*	Neh 7:66	8346
thousand pounds of silver, and *t*	Neh 7:72	8346
at Jerusalem were four hundred *t*	Neh 11:6	8346
The days of our years are *t* years	Ps 90:10	7657
t valiant men are about it, of	Song 3:7	7657
There are *t* queens, and fourscore	Song 6:8	7657
and within *t* and five years shall	Is 7:8	7657
t men of the people of the land,	Jer 52:25	7657
He made also posts of *t* cubits	Eze 40:14	7657
gold, whose height was *t* cubits	Dan 3:1	8361
took the kingdom, being about *t*	Dan 5:31	8361
Prince shall be seven weeks, and *t*	Dan 9:25	8346
And after *t* and two weeks shall	Dan 9:26	8346
thou hast had indignation these *t*	Zec 1:12	7657
from Jerusalem about *t* furlongs	Lk 24:13	1835
to him, and all his kindred, *t*	Acts 7:14	1440
to go to Caesarea, and horsemen *t*	Acts 23:23	1440
in all in the ship two hundred *t*	Acts 27:37	1440
into the number under *t* years old	1Ti 5:9	1835
t days, clothed in sackcloth	Rev 11:3	1835
a thousand two hundred and *t* days	Rev 12:6	1835
and his number is six hundred *t*	Rev 13:18	5516

THRESH

thou shalt *t* the mountains, and	Is 41:15	1758
it is time to *t* her	Jer 51:33	1869
Arise and *t*, O daughter of Zion	Mic 4:13	1758
thou didst *t* the heathen in anger	Hab 3:12	1758

THRESHED

his son Gideon *t* wheat by the	Judg 6:11	2251
For the fitches are not *t* with a	Is 28:27	1758
because they have *t* Gilead with	Amos 1:3	1758

THRESHETH

that he that *t* in hope should be	1Cor 9:10	248

THRESHING

your *t* shall reach unto the	Lev 26:5	1786
and *t* instruments and other	2Sa 24:22	4173
had made them like the dust by *t*	2Kin 13:7	1758
Now Ornan was *t* wheat	1Chr 21:20	1758
the *t* instruments for wood, and	1Chr 21:23	4173
O my *t*, and the corn of my floor	Is 21:10	4098
not threshed with a *t* instrument	Is 28:27	2742
because he will not ever be *t* it	Is 28:28	1758
sharp *t* instrument having teeth	Is 41:15	4173
Gilead with *t* instruments of iron	Amos 1:3	2742

THRESHINGFLOOR

And they came to the *t* of Atad	Gen 50:10	1637
ye do the heave offering of the *t*	Num 15:20	1637
though it were the corn of the *t*	Num 18:27	1637
Levites as the increase of the *t*	Num 18:30	1637
barley to night in the *t*	Ruth 3:2	1637
And when they came to Nachon's *t*	2Sa 6:6	1637
in the *t* of Araunah the Jebusite	2Sa 24:18	1637
David said, To buy the *t* of thee	2Sa 24:21	1637
So David bought the *t* and the oxen	2Sa 24:24	1637
they came unto the *t* of Chidon	1Chr 13:9	1637
by the *t* of Ornan the Jebusite	1Chr 21:15	1637
in the *t* of Ornan the Jebusite	1Chr 21:18	1637
saw David, and went out of the *t*	1Chr 21:21	1637
Grant me the place of this *t*	1Chr 21:22	1637
in the *t* of Ornan the Jebusite	1Chr 21:28	1637
in the *t* of Ornan the Jebusite	2Chr 3:1	1637
daughter of Babylon is like a *t*	Jer 51:33	1637

THRESHINGFLOORS

against Keilah, and they rob the *t*	1Sa 23:1	1637
like the chaff of the summer *t*	Dan 2:35	147

THRESHINGPLACE

by the *t* of Araunah the Jebusite	2Sa 24:16	1637

THRESHOLD

and her hands were upon the *t*	Judg 19:27	5592
his hands were cut off upon the *t*	1Sa 5:4	4670
tread on the *t* of Dagon in Ashdod	1Sa 5:5	4670
she came to the *t* of the door	1Kin 14:17	5592
he was, to the *t* of the house	Eze 9:3	4670
and stood over the *t* of the house	Eze 10:4	4670
from off the *t* of the house	Eze 10:18	4670
and measured the *t* of the gate	Eze 40:6	5592
the other *t* of the gate, which	Eze 40:6	5592
the *t* of the gate by the porch of	Eze 40:7	5592
of their *t* by my thresholds	Eze 43:8	5592
worship at the *t* of the gate	Eze 46:2	4670
under the *t* of the house eastward	Eze 47:1	4670
all those that leap on the *t*	Zeph 1:9	4670

T

THRESHOLDS

the ward at the *t* of the gates	Neh 12:25	624
of their threshold by my *t*	Eze 43:8	5592
desolation shall be in the *t*	Zeph 2:14	5592

THREW

t stones at him, and cast dust	2Sa 16:13	5619
So they *t* her down	2Kin 9:33	8058
t down the high places and the	2Chr 31:1	5422
she *t* in two mites, which make a	Mk 12:42	906
a coming, the devil *t* him down	Lk 9:42	4952
clothes, and *t* dust into the air,	Acts 22:23	906

THREWEST

persecutors thou *t* into the deeps	Neh 9:11	7993

THRICE

T in the year shall all your men	Ex 34:23	7969,6471
the LORD thy God in the year	Ex 34:24	7969,6471
And he smote *t*, and stayed	2Kin 13:18	7969,6471
now thou shalt smite Syria but *t*	2Kin 13:19	7969,6471
cock crow, thou shalt deny me *t*	Mt 26:34	5151
cock crow, thou shalt deny me *t*	Mt 26:75	5151
crow twice, thou shalt deny me *t*	Mk 14:30	5151
crow twice, thou shalt deny me *t*	Mk 14:72	5151
before that thou shalt *t* deny	Lk 22:34	5151
cock crow, thou shalt deny me *t*	Lk 22:61	5151
crow, till thou hast denied me *t*	Jn 13:38	5151
This was done *t*	Acts 10:16	5151
T was I beaten with rods, once	2Cor 11:25	5151
t I suffered shipwreck, a night	2Cor 11:25	5151
this thing I besought the Lord *t*	2Cor 12:8	5151

THROAT

their *t* is an open sepulchre	Ps 5:9	1627
my *t* is dried	Ps 69:3	1627
speak they through their *t*	Ps 115:7	1627
And put a knife to thy *t*, if thou	Prov 23:2	3930
unshod, and thy *t* from thirst	Jer 2:25	1627
on him, and took him by the *t*	Mt 18:28	4155
Their *t* is an open sepulchre	Rom 3:13	2995

THRONE

only in the *t* will I be greater	Gen 41:40	3678
Pharaoh that sitteth upon his *t*	Ex 11:5	3678
his *t* unto the firstborn of the	Ex 12:29	3678
sitteth upon the *t* of his kingdom	Deut 17:18	3678
make them inherit the *t* of glory	1Sa 2:8	3678
to set up the *t* of David over	2Sa 3:10	3678
I will stablish the *t* of his	2Sa 7:13	3678
thy *t* shall be established for	2Sa 7:16	3678
and the king and his *t* be guiltless	2Sa 14:9	3678
me, and he shall sit upon my *t*	1Kin 1:13	3678
me, and he shall sit upon my *t*	1Kin 1:17	3678
t of my lord the king after him	1Kin 1:20	3678
me, and he shall sit upon my *t*	1Kin 1:24	3678
who should sit on the *t* of my	1Kin 1:27	3678
shall sit upon my *t* in my stead	1Kin 1:30	3678
that he may come and sit upon my *t*	1Kin 1:35	3678
make his *t* greater than the	1Kin 1:37	3678
than the *t* of my lord king David	1Kin 1:37	3678
sitteth on the *t* of the kingdom	1Kin 1:46	3678
his *t* greater than thy *t*	1Kin 1:47	3678
given one to sit on my *t* this day	1Kin 1:48	3678
said he) a man on the *t* of Israel	1Kin 2:4	3678
upon the *t* of David his father	1Kin 2:12	3678
unto her, and sat down on his *t*	1Kin 2:19	3678
set me on the *t* of David my	1Kin 2:24	3678
and upon his house, and upon his *t*	1Kin 2:33	3678
and the *t* of David shall be	1Kin 2:45	3678
given him a son to sit on his *t*	1Kin 3:6	3678
I will set upon thy *t* in thy room	1Kin 5:5	3678
for the *t* where he might judge	1Kin 7:7	3678
father, and sit on the *t* of Israel	1Kin 8:20	3678
sight to sit on the *t* of Israel	1Kin 8:25	3678
Then I will establish the *t* of	1Kin 9:5	3678
thee a man upon the *t* of Israel	1Kin 9:5	3678
to set thee on the *t* of Israel	1Kin 10:9	3678
the king made a great *t* of ivory	1Kin 10:18	3678
The *t* had six steps, and the top	1Kin 10:19	3678
the top of the *t* was round behind	1Kin 10:19	3678
reign, as soon as he sat on his *t*	1Kin 16:11	3678
king of Judah sat each on his *t*	1Kin 22:10	3678
I saw the LORD sitting on his *t*	1Kin 22:19	3678
and set him on his father's *t*	2Kin 10:3	3678
shall sit on the *t* of Israel	2Kin 10:30	3678
And he sat on the *t* of the kings	2Kin 11:19	3678
and Jeroboam sat upon his *t*	2Kin 13:13	3678
the *t* of Israel unto the fourth	2Kin 15:12	3678
set his *t* above the *t* of the	2Kin 25:28	3678
and I will stablish his *t* for ever	1Chr 17:12	3678
his *t* shall be established for	1Chr 17:14	3678
I will establish the *t* of his	1Chr 22:10	3678
Solomon my son to sit upon the *t*	1Chr 28:5	3678
Then Solomon sat on the *t* of the	1Chr 29:23	3678
and am set on the *t* of Israel	2Chr 6:10	3678
sight to sit upon the *t* of Israel	2Chr 6:16	3678
I stablish the *t* of thy kingdom	2Chr 7:18	3678
in thee to set thee on his *t*	2Chr 9:8	3678
the king made a great *t* of ivory	2Chr 9:17	3678
And there were six steps to the *t*	2Chr 9:18	3678
which were fastened to the *t*	2Chr 9:18	3678
Judah sat either of them on his *t*	2Chr 18:9	3678
I saw the LORD sitting upon his *t*	2Chr 18:18	3678
king upon the *t* of the kingdom	2Chr 23:20	3678
unto the *t* of the governor on	Neh 3:7	3678
sat on the *t* of his kingdom	Est 1:2	3678
his royal *t* in the royal house	Est 5:1	3678
He holdeth back the face of his *t*	Job 26:9	3678
but with kings are they on the *t*	Job 36:7	3678
satest in the *t* judging right	Ps 9:4	3678
hath prepared his *t* for judgment	Ps 9:7	3678
the LORD's *t* is in heaven	Ps 11:4	3678
Thy *t*, O God, is for ever and ever	Ps 45:6	3678
upon the *t* of his holiness	Ps 47:8	3678
build up thy *t* to all generations	Ps 89:4	3678
are the habitation of thy *t*	Ps 89:14	3678
his *t* as the days of heaven	Ps 89:29	3678
his *t* as the sun before me	Ps 89:36	3678
cast his *t* down to the ground	Ps 89:44	3678
Thy *t* is established of old	Ps 93:2	3678
Shall the *t* of iniquity have	Ps 94:20	3678
are the habitation of his *t*	Ps 97:2	3678
prepared his *t* in the heavens	Ps 103:19	3678
of thy body will I set upon thy *t*	Ps 132:11	3678
also sit upon thy *t* for evermore	Ps 132:12	3678
for the *t* is established by	Prov 16:12	3678
A king that sitteth in the *t* of	Prov 20:8	3678
his *t* is upholden by mercy	Prov 20:28	3678
his *t* shall be established in	Prov 25:5	3678
his *t* shall be established for	Prov 29:14	3678
also the Lord sitting upon a *t*	Is 6:1	3678
be no end, upon the *t* of David	Is 9:7	3678
I will exalt my *t* above the stars	Is 14:13	3678
mercy shall the *t* be established	Is 16:5	3678
glorious *t* to his father's house	Is 22:23	3678
there is no *t*, O daughter of the	Is 47:1	3678
the LORD, The heaven is my *t*	Is 66:1	3678
they shall set every one his *t* at	Jer 1:15	3678
call Jerusalem the *t* of the LORD	Jer 3:17	3678
the kings that sit upon David's *t*	Jer 13:13	3678
not disgrace the *t* of thy glory	Jer 14:21	3678
A glorious high *t* from the	Jer 17:12	3678
sitting upon the *t* of David	Jer 17:25	3678
that sittest upon the *t* of David	Jer 22:2	3678
kings sitting upon the *t* of David	Jer 22:4	3678
sitting upon the *t* of David	Jer 22:30	3678
that sitteth upon the *t* of David	Jer 29:16	3678
upon the *t* of the house of Israel	Jer 33:17	3678
have a son to reign upon his *t*	Jer 33:21	3678
none to sit upon the *t* of David	Jer 36:30	3678
will set his *t* upon these stones	Jer 43:10	3678
And I will set my *t* in Elam	Jer 49:38	3678
set his *t* above the *t* of the	Jer 52:32	3678
thy *t* from generation to	Lam 5:19	3678
heads was the likeness of a *t*	Eze 1:26	3678
of the *t* was the likeness as the	Eze 1:26	3678
appearance of the likeness of a *t*	Eze 10:1	3678
me, Son of man, the place of my *t*	Eze 43:7	3678
he was deposed from his kingly *t*	Dan 5:20	3764
his *t* was like the fiery flame,	Dan 7:9	3764
Nineveh, and he arose from his *t*	Jonah 3:6	3678
will overthrow the *t* of kingdoms	Hag 2:22	3678
and shall sit and rule upon his *t*	Zec 6:13	3678
he shall be a priest upon his *t*	Zec 6:13	3678
for it is God's *t*	Mt 5:34	2362
shall sit in the *t* of his glory	Mt 19:28	2362
heaven, sweareth by the *t* of God	Mt 23:22	2362
he sit upon the *t* of his glory	Mt 25:31	2362
him the *t* of his father David	Lk 1:32	2362
raise up Christ to sit on his *t*	Acts 2:30	2362
Heaven is my *t*, and earth is my	Acts 7:49	2362
in royal apparel, sat upon his *t*	Acts 12:21	968
But unto the Son he saith, Thy *t*	Heb 1:8	2362
come boldly unto the *t* of grace	Heb 4:16	2362
t of the Majesty in the heavens	Heb 8:1	2362
at the right hand of the *t* of God	Heb 12:2	2362
Spirits which are before his *t*	Rev 1:4	2362
I grant to sit with me in my *t*	Rev 3:21	2362
set down with my Father in his *t*	Rev 3:21	2362
a *t* was set in heaven, and one sat	Rev 4:2	2362
in heaven, and one sat on the *t*	Rev 4:2	2362
was a rainbow round about the *t*	Rev 4:3	2362
And round about the *t* were four	Rev 4:4	2362

out of the *t* proceeded lightnings	Rev 4:5	2362
of fire burning before the *t*	Rev 4:5	2362
before the *t* there was a sea of	Rev 4:6	2362
and in the midst of the *t*, and	Rev 4:6	2362
and round about the *t*	Rev 4:6	2362
thanks to him that sat on the *t*	Rev 4:9	2362
down before him that sat on the *t*	Rev 4:10	2362
and cast their crowns before the *t*	Rev 4:10	2362
on the *t* a book written within	Rev 5:1	2362
and, lo, in the midst of the *t*	Rev 5:6	2362
hand of him that sat upon the *t*	Rev 5:7	2362
of many angels round about the *t*	Rev 5:11	2362
unto him that sitteth upon the *t*	Rev 5:13	2362
face of him that sitteth on the *t*	Rev 6:16	2362
and tongues, stood before the *t*	Rev 7:9	2362
our God which sitteth upon the *t*	Rev 7:10	2362
angels stood round about the *t*	Rev 7:11	2362
fell before the *t* on their faces	Rev 7:11	2362
are they before the *t* of God	Rev 7:15	2362
on the *t* shall dwell among them	Rev 7:15	2362
midst of the *t* shall feed them	Rev 7:17	2362
altar which was before the *t*	Rev 8:3	2362
caught up unto God, and to his *t*	Rev 12:5	2362
it were a new song before the *t*	Rev 14:3	2362
without fault before the *t* of God	Rev 14:5	2362
the temple of heaven, from the *t*	Rev 16:17	2362
worshipped God that sat on the *t*	Rev 19:4	2362
And a voice came out of the *t*	Rev 19:5	2362
And I saw a great white *t*, and him	Rev 20:11	2362
And he that sat upon the *t* said	Rev 21:5	2362
proceeding out of the *t* of God	Rev 22:1	2362
but the *t* of God and of the Lamb	Rev 22:3	2362

THRONES

For there are set *t* of judgment	Ps 122:5	3678
the *t* of the house of David	Ps 122:5	3678
t all the kings of the nations	Is 14:9	3678
sea shall come down from their *t*	Eze 26:16	3678
beheld till the *t* were cast down	Dan 7:9	3764
ye also shall sit upon twelve *t*	Mt 19:28	2362
sit on *t* judging the twelve	Lk 22:30	2362
and invisible, whether they be *t*	Col 1:16	2362
And I saw *t*, and they sat upon them	Rev 20:4	2362

THRONG

multitude, lest they should *t* him	Mk 3:9	2346
Master, the multitude *t* thee	Lk 8:45	4912

THRONGED

people followed him, and *t* him	Mk 5:24	4918
But as he went the people *t* him	Lk 8:42	4846

THRONGING

Thou seest the multitude *t* thee	Mk 5:31	4918

THROUGH See APPENDIX.

THROUGHLY

let us make brick, and burn them *t*	Gen 11:3	
O that my grief were *t* weighed	Job 6:2	
Wash me *t* from mine iniquity, and	Ps 51:2	7235
They shall *t* glean the remnant of	Jer 6:9	
For if ye *t* amend your ways and	Jer 7:5	
if ye *t* execute judgment between	Jer 7:5	
he shall *t* plead their cause,	Jer 50:34	
I *t* washed away thy blood from	Eze 16:9	
he will *t* purge his floor, and	Mt 3:12	1245
he will *t* purge his floor, and	Lk 3:17	1245
but we have been *t* made manifest	2Cor 11:6	1722,3956
t furnished unto all good works	2Ti 3:17	1822

THROUGHOUT See APPENDIX.

THROW

ye shall *t* down their altars	Judg 2:2	5422
t down the altar of Baal that thy	Judg 6:25	2040
battered the wall, to *t* it down	2Sa 20:15	5307
And he said, *T* her down	2Kin 9:33	8058
to *t* down, to build, and to plant	Jer 1:10	2040
to *t* down, and to destroy, and to	Jer 31:28	2040
they shall *t* down thine eminent	Eze 16:39	2040
t down all thy strong holds	Mic 5:11	2040
shall build, but I will *t* down	Mal 1:4	2040

THROWING

And if he smite him with *t* a stone	Num 35:17	3027

THROWN

his rider hath he *t* into the sea	Ex 15:1	7411
his rider hath he *t* into the sea	Ex 15:21	
because he hath *t* down his altar	Judg 6:32	5422
his head shall be *t* to thee over	2Sa 20:21	7993
t down thine altars, and slain thy	1Kin 19:10	2040
t down thine altars, and slain thy	1Kin 19:14	2040
nor *t* down any more for ever	Jer 31:40	2040
which are *t* down by the mounts,	Jer 33:4	5422

are fallen, her walls are *t* down	Jer 50:15	2040
he hath *t* down in his wrath the	Lam 2:2	2040
he hath *t* down, and hath not	Lam 2:17	2040
I will leave thee *t* into the	Eze 29:5	
and the mountains shall be *t* down	Eze 38:20	2040
and the rocks are *t* down by him	Nah 1:6	5422
another, that shall not be *t* down	Mt 24:2	2647
another, that shall not be *t* down	Mk 13:2	2647
the devil had *t* him in the midst	Lk 4:35	4496
another, that shall not be *t* down	Lk 21:6	2647
that great city Babylon be *t* down	Rev 18:21	906

THRUST

he shall surely *t* you out hence	Ex 11:1	1644
because they were *t* out of Egypt	Ex 12:39	1644
she *t* herself unto the wall, and	Num 22:25	3905
t both of them through, the man	Num 25:8	1856
But if he *t* him of hatred, or	Num 35:20	1920
But if he *t* him suddenly without	Num 35:22	1920
to *t* thee out of the way which	Deut 13:5	5080
because he hath sought to *t* thee	Deut 13:10	5080
t it through his ear unto the	Deut 15:17	5414
he shall *t* out the enemy from	Deut 33:27	1644
thigh, and *t* it into his belly	Judg 3:21	8628
t the fleece together, and wringed	Judg 6:38	2115
Zebul *t* out Gaal and his brethren,	Judg 9:41	1644
And his young man *t* him through	Judg 9:54	1856
they *t* out Jephthah, and said unto	Judg 11:2	1644
that I may *t* out all your right	1Sa 11:2	5365
sword, and *t* me through therewith	1Sa 31:4	1856
t me through, and abuse me	1Sa 31:4	1856
t his sword in his fellow's side	2Sa 2:16	
t them through the heart of	2Sa 18:14	8628
be all of them as thorns *t* away	2Sa 23:6	5074
So Solomon *t* out Abiathar from	1Kin 2:27	1644
Gehazi came near to *t* her away	2Kin 4:27	1920
sword, and *t* me through therewith	1Chr 10:4	1856
they *t* him out from thence	2Chr 26:20	926
Thou hast *t* sore at me that I	Ps 118:13	1760
that is found shall be *t* through	Is 13:15	1856
t through with a sword, that go	Is 14:19	2944
they that are *t* through in her	Jer 51:4	1856
t thee through with their swords	Eze 16:40	1333
Because ye have *t* with side	Eze 34:21	1920
to *t* them out of their possession	Eze 46:18	3238
Neither shall one *t* another	Joel 2:8	1766
t him through when he prophesieth	Zec 13:3	1856
t him out of the city, and led him	Lk 4:29	1544
prayed him that he would *t* out a	Lk 5:3	1877
heaven, shalt be *t* down to hell	Lk 10:15	2601
of God, and you yourselves *t* out	Lk 13:28	1544
t my hand into his side, I will	Jn 20:25	906
thy hand, and *t* it into my side	Jn 20:27	906
his neighbour wrong *t* him away	Acts 7:27	683
but *t* him from them, and in their	Acts 7:39	683
t them into the inner prison, and	Acts 16:24	906
now do they *t* us out privily	Acts 16:37	1544
were possible, to *t* in the ship	Acts 27:39	1856
stoned, or *t* through with a dart	Heb 12:20	2700
cloud, *T* in thy sickle, and reap	Rev 14:15	3992
he that sat on the cloud *t* in his	Rev 14:16	906
T in thy sharp sickle, and gather	Rev 14:18	3992
the angel *t* in his sickle into	Rev 14:19	906

THRUSTETH

God *t* him down, not man	Job 32:13	5086

THUMB

upon the *t* of their right hand,	Ex 29:20	931
upon the *t* of his right hand, and	Lev 8:23	931
upon the *t* of his right hand, and	Lev 14:14	931
upon the *t* of his right hand, and	Lev 14:17	931
upon the *t* of his right hand, and	Lev 14:25	931
upon the *t* of his right hand, and	Lev 14:28	931

THUMBS

upon the *t* of their right hands,	Lev 8:24	931
and caught him, and cut off his *t*	Judg 1:6	931,3027
and ten kings, having their *t*	Judg 1:7	931,3027

THUMMIM (thum'-mim) *A symbolic object in the High Priest's breastplate.*

of judgment the Urim and the *T*	Ex 28:30	8550
the breastplate the Urim and the *T*	Lev 8:8	8550
And of Levi he said, Let thy *T*	Deut 33:8	8550
up a priest with Urim and with *T*	Ezr 2:63	8550
stood up a priest with Urim and *T*	Neh 7:65	8550

THUNDER

and the Lord sent *t* and hail, and	Ex 9:23	6963
the *t* shall cease, neither shall	Ex 9:29	6963
of heaven shall he *t* upon them	1Sa 2:10	7481
a great *t* on that day upon the	1Sa 7:10	6963
unto the Lord, and he shall send *t*	1Sa 12:17	6963

T

and the L<small>ORD</small> sent *t* and rain that 1Sa 12:18   6963
but the *t* of his power who can .... Job 26:14   7482
a way for the lightning of the *t*. .... Job 28:26   6963
or a way for the lightning of *t* .... Job 38:25   6963
hast thou clothed his neck with *t* .... Job 39:19   7483
the *t* of the captains, and the .... Job 39:25   7482
or canst thou *t* with a voice like .... Job 40:9   7481
The voice of thy *t* was in the .... Ps 77:18   7482
thee in the secret place of *t* .... Ps 81:7   7482
voice of thy *t* they hasted away .... Ps 104:7   7482
of the L<small>ORD</small> of hosts with *t*. .... Is 29:6   7482
which is, The sons of *t* .... Mk 3:17   1027
heard, as it were the noise of *t* .... Rev 6:1   1027
and as the voice of a great *t* .... Rev 14:2   1027

THUNDERBOLTS
hail, and their flocks to hot *t* .... Ps 78:48   7565

THUNDERED
but the L<small>ORD</small> *t* with a great 1Sa 7:10   7481
The L<small>ORD</small> *t* from heaven, and the 2Sa 22:14   7481
The L<small>ORD</small> also *t* in the heavens, ... Ps 18:13   7481
by, and heard it, said that it *t* .... Jn 12:29   1027,1096

THUNDERETH
he *t* with the voice of his .... Job 37:4   7481
God *t* marvellously with his voice .... Job 37:5   7481
the God of glory *t* .... Ps 29:3   7481

THUNDERINGS
that there be no more mighty *t* .... Ex 9:28   6963
And all the people saw the *t* .... Ex 20:18   6963
throne proceeded lightnings and *t* .... Rev 4:5   1027
and there were voices, and *t* .... Rev 8:5   1027
were lightnings, and voices, and *t* .... Rev 11:19   1027
and as the voice of mighty *t* .... Rev 19:6   1027

THUNDERS
and the *t* and hail ceased, and the .... Ex 9:33   6963
the *t* were ceased, he sinned yet .... Ex 9:34   6963
in the morning, that there were *t* .... Ex 19:16   6963
seven *t* uttered their voices .... Rev 10:3   1027
when the seven *t* had uttered .... Rev 10:4   1027
things which the seven *t* uttered .... Rev 10:4   1027
And there were voices, and *t* .... Rev 16:18   1027

THUS See APPENDIX.

THY See APPENDIX.

THYATIRA (thi-a-ti'-rah) *A city in Lydia in Asia Minor.*
of purple, of the city of *T* .... Acts 16:14   2363
and unto Pergamos, and unto *T* .... Rev 1:11   2363
angel of the church in *T* write .... Rev 2:18   2363
you I say, and unto the rest in *T* .... Rev 2:24   2363

THYINE
all *t* wood, and all manner vessels .... Rev 18:12   2367

THYSELF
separate *t*, I pray thee, from me .... Gen 13:9
persons, and take the goods to *t* .... Gen 14:21
and submit *t* under her hands .... Gen 16:9
keep that thou hast unto *t* .... Gen 33:9
exaltest thou *t* against my people .... Ex 9:17
thou refuse to humble *t* before me .... Ex 10:3
Get thee from me, take heed to *t* .... Ex 10:28
why sittest thou *t* alone, and all .... Ex 18:14   859
not able to perform it *t* alone .... Ex 18:18
so shall it be easier for *t* .... Ex 18:22
Thou shalt not bow down *t* to them .... Ex 20:5
present *t* there to me in the top .... Ex 34:2
Take heed to *t*, lest thou make a .... Ex 34:12
and make an atonement for *t* .... Lev 9:7
wife, to defile *t* with her .... Lev 18:20
any beast to defile *t* therewith .... Lev 18:23
shalt love thy neighbour as *t* .... Lev 19:18
you, and thou shalt love him as *t* .... Lev 19:34
that thou bear it not *t* alone .... Num 11:17
except thou make *t* altogether a .... Num 16:13
Only take heed to *t*, and keep thy .... Deut 4:9
shalt not bow down *t* unto them .... Deut 5:9
greater and mightier than *t* .... Deut 9:1
Take heed to *t* that thou offer .... Deut 12:13
Take heed to *t* that thou forsake .... Deut 12:19
Take heed to *t* that thou be not .... Deut 12:30
thereof, shalt thou take unto *t* .... Deut 20:14
go astray, and hide *t* from them .... Deut 22:1
thou mayest not hide *t* .... Deut 22:3
by the way, and hide *t* from them .... Deut 22:4
wherewith thou coverest *t* .... Deut 22:12
be, when thou wilt ease *t* abroad .... Deut 23:13
shalt not anoint *t* with the oil .... Deut 28:40
cut down for *t* there in the land .... Josh 17:15
Wash *t* therefore, and anoint thee, ... Ruth 3:3
but make not *t* known unto the man ...... Ruth 3:3

redeem thou my right to *t* .... Ruth 4:6
take heed to *t* until the morning, ... 1Sa 19:2
in a secret place, and hide *t* 1Sa 19:2
be in me iniquity, slay me *t* 1Sa 20:8   859
t when the business was in hand 1Sa 20:19
from avenging *t* with thine own 1Sa 25:26
that then thou shalt bestir *t* 2Sa 5:24
to *t* thy people Israel to be a 2Sa 7:24
down on thy bed, and make *t* sick 2Sa 13:5
feign *t* to be a mourner, and put 2Sa 14:2
apparel, and anoint not *t* with oil 2Sa 14:2
thou *t* wouldest have set *t* 2Sa 18:13   859
wouldest have set *t* against me 2Sa 18:13
thou wilt shew *t* merciful 2Sa 22:26
man thou wilt shew *t* upright 2Sa 22:26
the pure thou wilt shew *t* pure 2Sa 22:27
thou wilt shew *t* unsavoury 2Sa 22:27
strong therefore, and shew *t* a man 1Kin 2:2
and whithersoever thou turnest *t* 1Kin 2:3
and hast not asked for *t* long life 1Kin 3:11
neither hast asked riches for *t* 1Kin 3:11
but hast asked for *t* 1Kin 3:11
Come home with me, and refresh *t* 1Kin 13:7
Arise, I pray thee, and disguise *t* 1Kin 14:2
why feignest thou *t* to be another 1Kin 14:6
hide *t* by the brook Cherith, that 1Kin 17:3
saying, Go, shew *t* unto Ahab 1Kin 18:1
said unto him, Go, strengthen *t* 1Kin 20:22
t hast decided it 1Kin 20:40
because thou hast sold *t* to work 1Kin 21:20
into an inner chamber to hide *t* 1Kin 22:25
hast humbled *t* before the L<small>ORD</small> 2Kin 22:19
Now therefore advise *t* what word 1Chr 21:12
asked wisdom and knowledge for *t* 2Chr 1:11
into an inner chamber to hide *t* 2Chr 18:24
thou hast joined *t* with Ahaziah 2Chr 20:37
house, which were better than *t* 2Chr 21:13
and thou didst humble *t* before God 2Chr 34:27
thereof, and humbledst *t* before me 2Chr 34:27
Think not with *t* that thou shalt .... Est 4:13   5315
prepare *t* to the search of their .... Job 8:8
thou shewest *t* marvellous upon me .... Job 10:16
and dost thou restrain wisdom to *t* .... Job 15:8   413
Acquaint now *t* with him, and be at ...... Job 22:21
hand thou opposest *t* against me .... Job 30:21
Deck *t* now with majesty and .... Job 40:10
array *t* with glory and beauty .... Job 40:10
lift up *t* because of the rage of .... Ps 7:6
why hidest thou *t* in times of .... Ps 10:1
thou wilt shew *t* merciful .... Ps 18:25
man thou wilt shew *t* upright .... Ps 18:25
the pure thou wilt shew *t* pure .... Ps 18:26
froward thou wilt shew *t* froward .... Ps 18:26
Stir up *t*, and awake to my .... Ps 35:23
Fret not *t* because of evildoers, ... Ps 37:1
Delight *t* also in the L<small>ORD</small> .... Ps 37:4
fret not *t* because of him who .... Ps 37:7
fret not *t* in any wise to do evil .... Ps 37:8
thee, when thou doest well to *t* .... Ps 49:18
I was altogether such an one as *t* .... Ps 50:21
Why boastest thou *t* in mischief .... Ps 52:1
hide not *t* from my supplication .... Ps 55:1
O turn *t* to us again .... Ps 60:1
that thou madest strong for *t* .... Ps 80:15
man whom thou madest strong for *t* ...... Ps 80:17
thou hast turned *t* from the .... Ps 85:3
wilt thou hide *t* for ever .... Ps 89:46
whom vengeance belongeth, shew *t* .... Ps 94:1
Lift up *t*, thou judge of the .... Ps 94:2
Who coverest *t* with light as with .... Ps 104:2
Do this now, my son, and deliver *t* .... Prov 6:3
go, humble *t*, and make sure thy .... Prov 6:3
Deliver *t* as a roe from the hand .... Prov 6:5
be wise, thou shalt be wise for *t* .... Prov 9:12
Fret not *t* because of evil men, ... Prov 24:19
and make it fit for *t* in the field .... Prov 24:27
Put not forth *t* in the presence .... Prov 25:6
Boast not *t* of to morrow .... Prov 27:1
done foolishly in lifting up *t* .... Prov 30:32
neither make *t* over wise .... Eccl 7:16
why shouldest thou destroy *t* .... Eccl 7:16
t likewise hast cursed others .... Eccl 7:22   859
hide *t* as it were for a little .... Is 26:20
at the lifting up of *t* the .... Is 33:3
thou art a God that hidest *t* .... Is 45:15
Shake *t* from the dust .... Is 52:2
loose *t* from the bands of thy .... Is 52:2
discovered *t* to another than me .... Is 57:8
didst debase *t* even unto hell .... Is 57:9
that thou hide not *t* from thine .... Is 58:7
shalt thou delight *t* in the L<small>ORD</small> .... Is 58:14

to make *t* a glorious name...................... Is 63:14
thou refrain *t* for these things............... Is 64:12
Which say, Stand by *t*, come not............ Is 65:5
thou not procured this unto *t*................. Jer 2:17
thou clothest *t* with crimson............... Jer 4:30
in vain shalt thou make *t* fair.............. Jer 4:30
sackcloth, and wallow *t* in ashes .... Jer 6:26
And thou, even *t*, shalt..................... Jer 17:4
I will make thee a terror to *t*............... Jer 20:4
because thou closest *t* in cedar.............. Jer 22:15
buy it for *t*................................. Jer 32:8
seekest thou great things for *t*.............. Jer 45:5
furnish *t* to go into captivity .... Jer 46:19
how long wilt thou cut *t* .... Jer 47:5
put up *t* into thy scabbard, rest, ... Jer 47:6
give *t* no rest............................... Lam 2:18
Thou hast covered *t* with a cloud........... Lam 3:44
be drunken, and shalt make *t* naked ..... Lam 4:21
shut *t* within thine house .... Eze 3:24
madest to *t* images of men, and............. Eze 16:17
hast defiled *t* in thine idols................. Eze 22:4
in *t* in the sight of the heathen.............. Eze 22:16
for whom thou didst wash *t*................. Eze 23:40
deckedst *t* with ornaments, ... Eze 23:40
thou hast lifted up *t* in height .... Eze 31:10
thou prepared, and prepare for *t*........... Eze 38:7
the king, Let thy gifts be to *t*............... Dan 5:17
But hast lifted up *t* against the .... Dan 5:23
to chasten *t* before thy God, thy .... Dan 10:12
O Israel, thou hast destroyed *t*.............. Hos 13:9
Though thou exalt *t* as the eagle .... Obad 4
of Aphrah roll *t* in the dust................. Mic 1:10
Now gather *t* in troops, O.................. Mic 5:1
make *t* many as the cankerworm, ... Nah 3:15
make *t* many as the locusts................. Nah 3:15
Deliver *t*, O Zion, that dwellest .... Zec 2:7
be the Son of God, cast *t* down............. Mt 4:6   4572
time, Thou shalt not forswear *t*.......... Mt 5:33
shew *t* to the priest, and offer............ Mt 8:4   4572
shalt love thy neighbour as *t*............. Mt 19:19   4572
shalt love thy neighbour as *t*............. Mt 22:39   4572
buildest it in three days, save *t* .... Mt 27:40   4572
shew *t* to the priest, and offer............ Mk 1:44   4572
shalt love thy neighbour as *t*............. Mk 12:31   4572
Save *t*, and come down from the .... Mk 15:30   4572
of God, cast *t* down from hence .... Lk 4:9   4572
this proverb, Physician, heal *t*........... Lk 4:23   4572
shew *t* to the priest, and offer............ Lk 5:14   4572
when thou *t* beholdest not the............ Lk 6:42   846
unto him, Lord, trouble not *t* .... Lk 7:6
and thy neighbour as *t*..................... Lk 10:27   4572
wherewith I may sup, and gird *t*.......... Lk 17:8
be the king of the Jews, save *t*............. Lk 23:37   4572
saying, If thou be Christ, save *t*............ Lk 23:39   4572
What sayest thou of *t* .... Jn 1:22
these things, shew *t* to the world .... Jn 7:4   4572
him, Thou bearest record of *t* .... Jn 8:13   4572
whom makest thou *t* .... Jn 8:53   4572
thou, being a man, makest *t* God .... Jn 10:33   4572
that thou wilt manifest *t* unto us .... Jn 14:22   4572
him, Sayest thou this thing of *t*.......... Jn 18:34   1438
thou wast young, thou girdedst *t*.......... Jn 21:18   4572
near, and join *t* to this chariot.............. Acts 8:29
the angel said unto him, Gird *t*............. Acts 12:8
loud voice, saying, Do *t* no harm .... Acts 16:28   4572
purify with them, and be at .... Acts 21:24
but that thou *t* also walkest .... Acts 21:24   846
by examining of whom *t* mayest .... Acts 24:8   846
Thou art permitted to speak for *t*........... Acts 26:1   4572
voice, Paul, thou art beside *t* .... Acts 26:24
another, thou condemnest *t* .... Rom 2:1   4572
heart treasurest up unto *t* wrath............ Rom 2:5   4572
art confident that thou *t* art a .... Rom 2:19   4572
another, teachest thou not *t*................. Rom 2:21   4572
shalt love thy neighbour as *t*............. Rom 13:9   1438
have it to *t* before God .... Rom 14:22   4572
shalt love thy neighbour as *t*............. Gal 5:14   1438
considering *t*, lest thou also be .... Gal 6:1   4572
to behave *t* in the house of God 1Ti 3:15
exercise *t* rather unto godliness............ 1Ti 4:7   4572
give *t* wholly to them 1Ti 4:15
Take heed unto *t*, and unto the 1Ti 4:16
doing this thou shalt both save *t* 1Ti 4:16   4572
keep *t* pure................................. 1Ti 5:22   4572
from such withdraw *t* 1Ti 6:5
Study to shew *t* approved unto God 2Ti 2:15   4572
In all things shewing *t* a pattern .... Titus 2:7   4572
shalt love thy neighbour as *t*............. Jas 2:8   4572

TIARAS See Hoods.

TIBERIAS *(ti-be'-re-as) A city on the Sea of Galilee.*
of Galilee, which is the sea of *T*............. Jn 6:1   5085
there came other boats from *T* .... Jn 6:23   5085
to the disciples at the sea of *T* .... Jn 21:1   5085

TIBERIUS *(ti-be'-re-us)* See Caesar. *A Roman emperor.*
year of the reign of *T* Caesar .... Lk 3:1   5086

TIBHATH *(tib'-hath) A city in Aram Zobah.*
Likewise from *T*, and from Chun, ... 1Chr 18:8   2880

TIBNI *(tib'-ni) Son of Ginath.*
followed *T* the son of Ginath 1Kin 16:21   8402
that followed *T* the son of Ginath 1Kin 16:22   8402
so *T* died, and Omri reigned 1Kin 16:22   8402

TIDAL *(ti'-dal) A king of Goyim.*
of Elam, and *T* king of nations.............. Gen 14:1   8413
with *T* king of nations, and .... Gen 14:9   8413

TIDINGS
when Laban heard the *t* of Jacob .... Gen 29:13   8088
the people heard these evil *t* .... Ex 33:4   1697
when she heard the *t* that the ark 1Sa 4:19   8052
told the *t* in the ears of the 1Sa 11:4   1697
they told him the *t* of the men of 1Sa 11:5   1697
upon Saul when he heard those *t* 1Sa 11:6   1697
woman alive, to bring *t* to Gath 1Sa 27:11
years old when the *t* came of Saul.......... 2Sa 4:4   8052
thinking to have brought good *t* 2Sa 4:10   1319
have given him a reward for his *t*........... 2Sa 4:10   1309
that *t* came to David, saying,............... 2Sa 13:30   8052
me now run, and bear the king *t* 2Sa 18:19   1319
Thou shalt not bear *t* this day.............. 2Sa 18:20   1309
but thou shalt bear *t* another day........... 2Sa 18:20   1319
but this day thou shalt bear no *t* 2Sa 18:20   1319
seeing that thou hast no *t* ready............. 2Sa 18:22   1309
be alone, there is *t* in his mouth............. 2Sa 18:25   1309
the king said, He also bringeth *t* 2Sa 18:26   1319
a good man, and cometh with good *t*..... 2Sa 18:27   1309
and Cushi said, *T*, my lord the 2Sa 18:31   1319
a valiant man, and bringest good *t* 1Kin 1:42   1319
Then *t* came to Joab 1Kin 2:28   8052
I am sent to thee with heavy *t* 1Kin 14:6
this day is a day of good *t* 2Kin 7:9   1309
to carry *t* unto their idols, and 1Chr 10:9   1319
He shall not be afraid of evil *t* .... Ps 112:7   8052
O Zion, that bringest good *t*................. Is 40:9   1319
O Jerusalem, that bringest good *t*........... Is 40:9   1319
one that bringeth good *t*.................... Is 41:27   1319
feet of him that bringeth good *t*............. Is 52:7   1319
that bringeth good *t* of good .... Is 52:7   1319
me to preach good *t* unto the meek......... Is 61:1   1319
man who brought *t* to my father............ Jer 20:15   1319
Jerusalem heard *t* of them .... Jer 37:5   8088
for they have heard evil *t*................... Jer 49:23   8052
that thou shalt answer, For the *t* .... Eze 21:7   8052
But *t* out of the east and out of.............. Dan 11:44   8052
feet of him that bringeth good *t*............. Nah 1:15   1319
and to shew these these glad *t* .... Lk 1:19   2097
I bring you good *t* of great joy .... Lk 2:10   2097
shewing the glad *t* of the kingdom .... Lk 8:1   2097
Then *t* of these things came unto .... Acts 11:22   3056
And we declare unto you glad *t* .... Acts 13:32   2097
t came unto the chief captain of .... Acts 21:31   5334
bring glad *t* of good things................. Rom 10:15   2097
brought us good *t* of your faith 1Th 3:6   2097

TIE
t the kine to the cart, and bring............ 1Sa 6:7   631
heart, and *t* them about thy neck .... Prov 6:21   6029

TIED
they *t* unto it a lace of blue, to .... Ex 39:31   5414
t them to the cart, and shut up.............. 1Sa 6:10   631
voice of man, but horses *t* 2Kin 7:10   631
man, but horses *t*, and asses *t* 2Kin 7:10   631
ye shall find an ass *t*, and a colt .... Mt 21:2   1210
into it, ye shall find a colt *t*................. Mk 11:2   1210
found the colt *t* by the door .... Mk 11:4   1210
entering ye shall find a colt *t* .... Lk 19:30   1210

TIGLATH-PILESER *(tig'-lath-pi-le'-zur)* See Tilgath-
PILNESER. *An Assyrian king.*
of Israel came *T* king of Assyria............. 2Kin 15:29   8407
messengers to *T* king of Assyria............ 2Kin 16:7   8407
to meet *T* king of Assyria.................... 2Kin 16:10   8407

TIGRIS See Hiddekel.

TIKVAH *(tik'-vah)* See Tikvath.
  1. Father-in-law of Huldah.
the wife of Shallum the son of *T* 2Kin 22:14   8616
  2. Father of Jahaziah.
Jahaziah the son of *T* were .... Ezr 10:15   8616

T

TIKVATH (tik'-vath) See TIKVAH. Same as Tikvah 1.
the wife of Shallum the son of T	2Chr 34:22	8616

TIL
t the Assyrian founded it for	Is 23:13	

TILE
also, son of man, take thee a t	Eze 4:1	3843

TILGATH-PILNESER (til'-gath-pil-ne'-zur) See TIGLATH-PILESER. Same as Tiglath-pileser.
whom T king of Assyria carried	1Chr 5:6	8407
the spirit of T king of Assyria,	1Chr 5:26	8407
T king of Assyria came unto him,	2Chr 28:20	8407

TILING
let him down through the t with	Lk 5:19	2766

TILL See APPENDIX.

TILLAGE
did the work of the field for t	1Chr 27:26	5656
tithes in all the cities of our t	Neh 10:37	5656
Much food is in the t of the poor	Prov 13:23	5215

TILLED
turn unto you, and ye shall be t	Eze 36:9	5647
And the desolate land shall be t	Eze 36:34	5647

TILLER
but Cain was a t of the ground	Gen 4:2	5647

TILLEST
When thou t the ground, it shall	Gen 4:12	5647

TILLETH
He that t his land shall be	Prov 12:11	5647
He that t his land shall have	Prov 28:19	5647

TILON (ti'-lon) A descendant of Judah.
and Rinnah, Ben-hanan, and T	1Chr 4:20	8436

TIMAEUS (ti-me'-us) See BARTIMAEUS. Father of Bartimaeus.
blind Bartimaeus, the son of T	Mk 10:46	5090

TIMBER
to set them, and in carving of t	Ex 31:5	6086
the t thereof, and all the morter	Lev 14:45	6086
to hew t like unto the Sidonians	1Kin 5:6	6086
thy desire concerning t of cedar	1Kin 5:8	6086
of cedar, and concerning t of fir	1Kin 5:8	6086
so they prepared t and stones to	1Kin 5:18	6086
on the house with t of cedar	1Kin 6:10	6086
the t thereof, wherewith Baasha	1Kin 15:22	6086
and hewers of stone, and to buy t	2Kin 12:12	6086
builders, and masons, and to buy t	2Kin 22:6	6086
t of cedars, with masons and	1Chr 14:1	6086
t also and stone have I prepared	1Chr 22:14	6086
hewers and workers of stone and t	1Chr 22:15	6086
can skill to cut t in Lebanon	2Chr 2:8	6086
Even to prepare me t in abundance	2Chr 2:9	6086
servants, the hewers that cut t	2Chr 2:10	6086
brass, in iron, in stone, and in t	2Chr 2:14	6086
the t thereof, wherewith Baasha	2Chr 16:6	6086
t for couplings, and to floor the	2Chr 34:11	6086
t is laid in the walls, and this	Ezr 5:8	636
great stones, and a row of new t	Ezr 6:4	636
let t be pulled down from his	Ezr 6:11	636
that he may give me t to make	Neh 2:8	6086
shall lay thy stones and thy t	Eze 26:12	6086
beam out of the t shall answer it	Hab 2:11	6086
consume it with the t thereof	Zec 5:4	6086

TIMBREL
of Aaron, took a t in her hand	Ex 15:20	8596
They take the t and harp, and	Job 21:12	8596
a psalm, and bring hither the t	Ps 81:2	8596
sing praises unto him with the t	Ps 149:3	8596
Praise him with the t and dance	Ps 150:4	8596

TIMBRELS
women went out after her with t	Ex 15:20	8596
came out to meet him with t	Judg 11:34	8596
harps, and on psalteries, and on t	2Sa 6:5	8596
and with psalteries, and with t	1Chr 13:8	8596
were the damsels playing with t	Ps 68:25	8608

TIME See APPENDIX.

TIMES See APPENDIX.

TIMNA (tim'-nah) See TIMNATH.
1. Concubine of Eliphaz.
T was concubine to Eliphaz Esau's	Gen 36:12	8555
2. Daughter of Seir
and Lotan's sister was T	Gen 36:22	8555
and T was Lotan's sister	1Chr 1:39	8555
3. A son of Eliphaz.
Zephi, and Gatam, Kenaz, and T	1Chr 1:36	8555

TIMNAH (tim'-nah) See TIMNA, TIMNATH.
1. A chief of Edom.
duke T, duke Alvah, duke Jetheth,	Gen 36:40	8555
duke T, duke Aliah, duke Jetheth,	1Chr 1:51	8555
2. A city in Judah.
Cain, Gibeah, and T	Josh 15:57	8553
3. A city in Dan.
Beth-shemesh, and passed on to T	Josh 15:10	8553
T with the villages thereof,	2Chr 28:18	8553

TIMNATH (tim'-nath) See THIMNATHAH, TIMNAH.
1. Same as Timnah 2.
up unto his sheepshearers to T	Gen 38:12	8553
goeth up to T to shear his sheep	Gen 38:13	8553
place, which is by the way to T	Gen 38:14	8553
2. Same as Timnah 3.
And Samson went down to T, and saw	Judg 14:1	8553
saw a woman in T of the daughters	Judg 14:1	8553
I have seen a woman in T of the	Judg 14:2	8553
and his father and his mother, to T	Judg 14:5	8553
and came to the vineyards of T	Judg 14:5	8553

TIMNATH-HERES (tim'-nath-he'-rez) See TIMNATH-SERAH. Land near Mount Ephraim.
border of his inheritance in	Judg 2:9	8556

TIMNATH-SERAH (tim'-nath-se'-rah) See TIMNATH-HERES. Same as Timnath-heres.
he asked, even T in mount Ephraim	Josh 19:50	8556
border of his inheritance in T	Josh 24:30	8556

TIMNITE (tim'-nite) An inhabitant of Timnah.
Samson, the son in law of the T	Judg 15:6	8554

TIMON (ti'-mon) A leader in the Jerusalem church.
and Prochorus, and Nicanor, and T	Acts 6:5	5096

TIMOTHEOUS
and Fortunatus, and Achaicus, and T	1Cor s	5095

TIMOTHEUS (tim-o'-the-us) See TIMOTHY. Same as Timothy.
disciple was there, named T	Acts 16:1	5095
but Silas and T abode there still	Acts 17:14	5095
T for to come to him with all	Acts 17:15	5095
T were come from Macedonia, Paul	Acts 18:5	5095
them that ministered unto him, T	Acts 19:22	5095
and Gaius of Derbe, and T	Acts 20:4	5095
T my workfellow, and Lucius, and	Rom 16:21	5095
this cause have I sent unto you T	1Cor 4:17	5095
Now if T come, see that he may be	1Cor 16:10	5095
us, even by me and Silvanus and T	2Cor 1:19	5095
Paul and T, the servants of Jesus	Phil 1:1	5095
Jesus to send T shortly unto you	Phil 2:19	5095
will of God, and T our brother,	Col 1:1	5095
Paul, and Silvanus, and T, unto the	1Th 1:1	5095
And sent T, our brother, and	1Th 3:2	5095
But now when T came from you unto	1Th 3:6	5095
Paul, and Silvanus, and T, unto the	2Th 1:1	5095
The second epistle unto T	2Ti s	5095

TIMOTHY (tim'-o-thy) See TIMOTHEUS. A co-worker with Paul.
T our brother, unto the church of	2Cor 1:1	5095
Unto T, my own son in the faith	1Ti 1:2	5095
charge I commit unto thee, son T	1Ti 1:18	5095
O T, keep that which is committed	1Ti 6:20	5095
The first to T was written from	1Ti s	5095
To T, my dearly beloved son	2Ti 1:2	5095
T our brother, unto Philemon our	Philem 1	5095
our brother T is set at liberty	Heb 13:23	5095
to the Hebrews from Italy by T	Heb s	5095

TIN
the brass, the iron, the t	Num 31:22	913
thy dross, and take away all thy t	Is 1:25	913
all they are brass, and t, and iron	Eze 22:18	913
and brass, and iron, and lead, and t	Eze 22:20	913
with silver, iron, t, and lead,	Eze 27:12	913

TINGLE
every one that heareth it shall t	1Sa 3:11	6750
of it, both his ears shall t	2Kin 21:12	6750
heareth, his ears shall t	Jer 19:3	6750

TINKLING
making a t with their feet	Is 3:16	5913
t ornaments about their feet	Is 3:18	
as sounding brass, or a t cymbal	1Cor 13:1	214

TIP
put it upon the t of the right	Ex 29:20	8571
upon the t of the right ear of	Ex 29:20	8571
put it upon the t of Aaron's	Lev 8:23	8571
upon the t of their right ear	Lev 8:24	8571
priest shall put it upon the t of	Lev 14:14	8571
shall the priest put the t	Lev 14:17	8571

put it upon the *t* of the right .... Lev 14:25   8571
that is in his hand upon the *t* of .... Lev 14:28   8571
that he may dip the *t* of his .... Lk 16:24   206

TIPHSAH *(tif'-sah)*
    1. A city on the Euphrates River.
from *T* even to Azzah, over all 1Kin 4:24   8607
    2. A city in Judah.
Then Menahem smote *T*, and all that 2Kin 15:16   8607

TIRAS *(Ti'-ras) A son of Japheth.*
Javan, and Tubal, and Meshech, and *T* .. Gen 10:2   8493
Javan, and Tubal, and Meshech, and *T* .. 1Chr 1:5   8493

TIRATHITES *(ti'-rath-ites) A family of scribes.*
the *T*, the Shimeathites, and 1Chr 2:55   8654

TIRE
bind the *t* of thine head upon .... Eze 24:17   6287

TIRED
t her head, and looked out at a 2Kin 9:30   3190

TIRES
their round *t* like the moon, ... Is 3:18   7720
your *t* shall be upon your heads, ... Eze 24:23   6287

TIRHAKAH *(tur-ha'-kah) A king of Ethiopia.*
heard say of *T* king of Ethiopia 2Kin 19:9   8640
say concerning *T* king of Ethiopia .... Is 37:9   8640

TIRHANAH *(tur-ha'-nah) A son of Caleb.*
concubine, bare Sheber, and *T* 1Chr 2:48   8647

TIRIA *(tir'-e-ah) A descendant of Judah.*
Ziph, and Ziphah, *T*, and Asareel 1Chr 4:16   8493

TIRSHATHA *(tur'-sha-thah) Persian governors of*
    Judah.
the *T* said unto them, that they .... Ezr 2:63   8660
the *T* said unto them, that they .... Neh 7:65   8660
The *T* gave to the treasure a .... Neh 7:70   8660
And Nehemiah, which is the *T*. .... Neh 8:9   8660
that sealed were, Nehemiah, the *T* .... Neh 10:1   8660

TIRZAH *(tur'-zah)*
    1. A daughter of Zelophehad.
and Noah, Hoglah, Milcah, and *T* .... Num 26:33   8656
Noah, and Hoglah, and Milcah, and *T*... Num 27:1   8656
For Mahlah, *T*, and Hoglah, and .... Num 36:11   8656
and Noah, Hoglah, Milcah, and *T* .... Josh 17:3   8656
    2. A city in Ephraim.
The king of *T*, one .... Josh 12:24   8656
arose, and departed, and came to *T*....... 1Kin 14:17   8656
building of Ramah, and dwelt in *T* 1Kin 15:21   8656
to reign over all Israel in *T* 1Kin 15:33   8656
his fathers, and was buried in *T* 1Kin 16:6   8656
Baasha to reign over Israel in *T* 1Kin 16:8   8656
against him, as he was in *T* 1Kin 16:9   8656
of Arza steward of his house in *T* 1Kin 16:9   8656
did Zimri reign seven days in *T* 1Kin 16:15   8656
with him, and they besieged *T* 1Kin 16:17   8656
six years reigned he in *T* 1Kin 16:23   8656
the son of Gadi went up from *T* 2Kin 15:14   8656
and the coasts thereof from *T* 2Kin 15:16   8656
art beautiful, O my love, as *T* .... Song 6:4   8656

TISHBE See TISHBITE.

TISHBITE *(tish'-bite) An inhabitant of Tishbeh.*
And Elijah the *T*, who was of the 1Kin 17:1   8664
of the LORD came to Elijah the *T* 1Kin 21:17   8664
of the LORD came to Elijah the *T* 1Kin 21:28   8664
of the LORD said to Elijah the *T* 2Kin 1:3   8664
And he said, It is Elijah the *T*.............. 2Kin 1:8   8664
spake by his servant Elijah the *T* 2Kin 9:36   8664

TITHE
all the *t* of the land, whether of.............. Lev 27:30   4643
And concerning the *t* of the herd .... Lev 27:32   4643
LORD, even a tenth part of the *t* .... Num 18:26   4643
thy gates the *t* of thy corn .... Deut 12:17   4643
Thou shalt truly *t* all the .... Deut 14:22   6237
the *t* of thy corn, of thy wine, ... Deut 14:23   4643
thou shalt bring forth all the *t* .... Deut 14:28   4643
the *t* of all things brought they 2Chr 31:5   4643
also brought in the *t* of oxen 2Chr 31:6   4643
the *t* of holy things which were 2Chr 31:6   4643
the Levites shall bring up the *t*.............. Neh 10:38   4643
all Judah the *t* of the corn .... Neh 13:12   4643
for ye pay *t* of mint and anise and........ Mt 23:23   586
for ye *t* mint and rue and all .... Lk 11:42   586

TITHES
And he gave him *t* of all .... Gen 14:20   4643
will at all redeem ought of his *t* .... Lev 27:31   4643
But the *t* of the children of .... Num 18:24   4643
the *t* which I have given you from .... Num 18:26   4643
unto the LORD of all your *t*................... Num 18:28   4643

and your sacrifices, and your *t* .... Deut 12:6   4643
and your sacrifices, your *t* .... Deut 12:11   4643
the *t* of thine increase the third .... Deut 26:12   4643
brought in the offerings and the *t*......... 2Chr 31:12   4643
the *t* of our ground unto the .... Neh 10:37   4643
the *t* in all the cities of our .... Neh 10:37   6237
Levites, when the Levites take *t*............. Neh 10:38   6237
the *t* unto the house of our God .... Neh 10:38   4643
for the firstfruits, and for the *t* .... Neh 12:44   4643
the *t* of the corn, the new wine, ... Neh 13:5   4643
and your *t* after three years .... Amos 4:4   4643
In *t* and offerings .... Mal 3:8   4643
Bring ye all the *t* into the .... Mal 3:10   4643
I give *t* of all that I possess .... Lk 18:12   586
have a commandment to take *t* of .... Heb 7:5   586
from them received *t* of Abraham .... Heb 7:6   1183
And here men that die receive *t*............. Heb 7:8   1181
say, Levi also, who receiveth *t* .... Heb 7:9   1183
payed *t* in Abraham .... Heb 7:9   1183

TITHING
end of *t* all the tithes of thine .... Deut 26:12   6237
year, which is the year of *t* .... Deut 26:12   4643

TITIUS See JUSTUS.

TITIUS JUSTUS See JUSTUS.

TITLE
What *t* is that that I see 2Kin 23:17   6725
And Pilate wrote a *t*, and put it on .... Jn 19:19   5102
This *t* then read many of the Jews .... Jn 19:20   5102

TITLES
let me give flattering *t* unto man .... Job 32:21
I know not to give flattering *t* .... Job 32:22

TITTLE
one jot or one *t* shall in no wise .... Mt 5:18   2762
than one *t* of the law to fail .... Lk 16:17   2762

TITUS *(ti'-tus) A co-worker with Paul.*
because I found not *T* my brother 2Cor 2:13   5103
comforted us by the coming of *T* 2Cor 7:6   5103
more joyed we for the joy of *T* 2Cor 7:13   5103
boasting, which I made before *T* 2Cor 7:14   5103
Insomuch that we desired *T* 2Cor 8:6   5103
care into the heart of *T* for you 2Cor 8:16   5103
Whether any do enquire of *T* 2Cor 8:23   5103
I desired *T*, and with him I sent a 2Cor 12:18   5103
Did *T* make a gain of you 2Cor 12:18   5103
a city of Macedonia, by *T* .... 2Cor s   5103
Barnabas, and took *T* with me also .... Gal 2:1   5103
But neither *T*, who was with me, ... Gal 2:3   5103
to Galatia, *T* unto Dalmatia 2Ti 4:10   5103
To *T*, mine own son after the .... Titus 1:4   5103
It was written to *T*, ordained the .... Titus s   5103

TIZITE *(ti'-zite) Family name of Joha.*
and Joha his brother, the *T*.................... 1Chr 11:45   8491

TO See APPENDIX.

TOAH *(to'-ah) See NAHATH, TOHU. An ancestor of*
    Samuel.
the son of Eliel, the son of *T* 1Chr 6:34   8430

TOB *(tob) A district in Syria.*
and dwelt in the land of *T*...................... Judg 11:3   2897
Jephthah out of the land of *T* .... Judg 11:5   2897

TOB-ADONIJAH *(tob'-ad-o-ni-jah) A Levite messenger*
    of King Jehoshaphat.
and Adonijah, and Tobijah, and *T* 2Chr 17:8   2899

TOBIAH *(to-bi'-ah) See TOBIJAH.*
    1. A family of exiles.
of Delaiah, the children of *T*................... Ezr 2:60   2900
of Delaiah, the children of *T*................... Neh 7:62   2900
    2. An Ammonite who opposed Nehemiah.
T the servant, the Ammonite, ... Neh 2:10   2900
T the servant, the Ammonite, and .... Neh 2:19   2900
Now *T* the Ammonite was by him, and .. Neh 4:3   2900
pass, that when Sanballat, and *T*........... Neh 4:7   2900
to pass, when Sanballat, and *T* .... Neh 6:1   2900
for *T* and Sanballat had hired him .... Neh 6:12   2900
My God, think thou upon *T*................... Neh 6:14   2900
of Judah sent many letters unto *T*.......... Neh 6:17   2900
the letters of *T* came unto them .... Neh 6:17   2900
T sent letters to put me in fear .... Neh 6:19   2900
of our God, was allied unto *T* .... Neh 13:4   2900
the evil that Eliashib did for *T* .... Neh 13:7   2900
stuff of *T* out of the chamber .... Neh 13:8   2900

TOBIJAH *(to-bi'-jah) See TOBIAH.*
    1. A Levite messenger of King Jehoshaphat.
and Jehonathan, and Adonijah, and *T*.... 2Chr 17:8   2900

T

2. A clan leader of exiles.
captivity, even of Heldai, of *T* .... Zec 6:10   2900
crowns shall be to Helem, and to *T* .... Zec 6:14   2900

TOCHEN *(to'-ken) A city in Simeon.*
were, Etam, and Ain, Rimmon, and *T* 1Chr 4:32   8507

TODAY
glorious was the king of Israel *t* 2Sa 6:20
T thy servant knoweth that I have 2Sa 14:22
T shall the house of Israel 2Sa 16:3

TOE
upon the great *t* of their right .... Ex 29:20   931
upon the great *t* of his right .... Lev 8:23   931
upon the great *t* of his right .... Lev 14:14   931
upon the great *t* of his right .... Lev 14:17   931
upon the great *t* of his right .... Lev 14:25   931
upon the great *t* of his right .... Lev 14:28   931

TOES
upon the great *t* of their right .... Lev 8:24   931
cut off his thumbs and his great *t* .. Judg 1:6   931,7272
thumbs and their great *t* cut off ..... Judg 1:7   931,7272
fingers, and on every foot six *t* 2Sa 21:20   676
t were four and twenty, six on 1Chr 20:6   676
whereas thou sawest the feet and *t* .... Dan 2:41   677
as the *t* of the feet were part of .... Dan 2:42   677

TOGARMAH *(to-gar'-mah) A son of Gomer.*
Ashkenaz, and Riphath, and *T* .... Gen 10:3   8425
Ashchenaz, and Riphath, and *T*............. 1Chr 1:6   8425
They of the house of *T* traded in .... Eze 27:14   8425
the house of *T* of the north .... Eze 38:6   8425

TOGETHER See APPENDIX.

TOHU *(to'-hu)* See NAHATH, TOAH. *An ancestor of Samuel.*
the son of Elihu, the son of *T* 1Sa 1:1   8459

TOI *(to'-i)* See TOU. *King of Hamath.*
When *T* king of Hamath heard that....... 2Sa 8:9   8583
Then *T* sent Joram his son unto............. 2Sa 8:10   8583
for Hadadezer had wars with *T*............. 2Sa 8:10   8583

TOIL
t of our hands, because of the .... Gen 5:29   6093
he, hath made me forget all my *t* .... Gen 41:51   5999
they *t* not, neither do they spin.............. Mt 6:28   2872
they *t* not, they spin not .... Lk 12:27   2872

TOILED
we have *t* all the night, and have .... Lk 5:5   2872

TOILING
And he saw them *t* in rowing .... Mk 6:48   928

TOKEN
This is the *t* of the covenant .... Gen 9:12   226
it shall be for a *t* of a covenant .... Gen 9:13   226
This is the *t* of the covenant, ... Gen 9:17   226
it shall be a *t* for a covenant .... Gen 17:11   226
and this shall be a *t* unto thee .... Ex 3:12   226
a *t* upon the houses where ye are .... Ex 12:13   226
shall be for a *t* upon thine hand .... Ex 13:16   226
to be kept for a *t* against the .... Num 17:10   226
house, and give me a true *t* .... Josh 2:12   226
Shew me a *t* for good .... Ps 86:17   226
betrayed him had given them a *t* .... Mk 14:44   4953
to them an evident *t* of perdition............ Phil 1:28   1732
Which is a manifest *t* of the................... 2Th 1:5   1730
which is the *t* in every epistle................. 2Th 3:17   4592

TOKENS
bring forth the *t* of the damsel's .... Deut 22:15
yet these are the *t* of my........................ Deut 22:17
the *t* of virginity be not found .... Deut 22:20
and do ye not know their *t* .... Job 21:29   226
parts are afraid at thy *t*......................... Ps 65:8   226
Who sent *t* and wonders into the .... Ps 135:9   226
frustrateth the *t* of the liars .... Is 44:25   226

TOKHATH See TIKVATH.

TOLA *(to'-lah)* See TOLAITES.
1. A son of Issachar.
T, and Phuvah, and Job, and Shimron.... Gen 46:13   8439
of *T*, the family of the Tolaites .... Num 26:23   8439
Now the sons of Issachar were, *T* 1Chr 7:1   8439
And the sons of *T* 1Chr 7:2   8439
father's house, to wit, of *T*.................... 1Chr 7:2   8439
2. A judge of Israel.
defend Israel *T* the son of Puah .... Judg 10:1   8439

TOLAD *(to'-lad)* See EL-TOLAD. *A city in Simeon.*
And at Bilhah, and at Ezem, and at *T* ... 1Chr 4:29   8434

TOLAITES *(to'-lah-ites) Descendants of Tola.*
of Tola, the family of the *T*...................... Num 26:23   8440

TOLD See APPENDIX.

TOLERABLE
It shall be more *t* for the land .... Mt 10:15   *414*
you, It shall be more *t* for Tyre .... Mt 11:22   *414*
That it shall be more *t* for the................ Mt 11:24   *414*
you, It shall be more *t* for Sodom .... Mk 6:11   *414*
be more *t* in that day for Sodom .... Lk 10:12   *414*
But it shall be more *t* for Tyre .... Lk 10:14   *414*

TOLL
again, then will they not pay *t* .... Ezr 4:13   4061
and *t*, tribute, and custom, was............. Ezr 4:20   4061
shall not be lawful to impose *t*............... Ezr 7:24   4061

TOMB
grave, and shall remain in the *t*............. Job 21:32   1430
And laid it in his own new *t* .... Mt 27:60   *3419*
up his corpse, and laid it in a *t* .... Mk 6:29   *3419*

TOMBS
with devils, coming out of the *t* .... Mt 8:28   *3419*
ye build the *t* of the prophets................. Mt 23:29   5028
there met him out of the *t* a man........... Mk 5:2   *3419*
Who had his dwelling among the *t*......... Mk 5:3   *3419*
was in the mountains, and in the *t* .... Mk 5:5   *3418*
abode in any house, but in the *t* .... Lk 8:27   *3418*

TONGS
the *t* thereof, and the snuffdishes .... Ex 25:38   4457
the light, and his lamps, and his *t* .... Num 4:9   4457
and the lamps, and the *t* of gold, ... 1Kin 7:49   4457
flowers, and the lamps, and the *t* 2Chr 4:21   4457
with the *t* from off the altar................... Is 6:6   4457
The smith with the *t* both worketh .... Is 44:12   4621

TONGUE
every one after his *t*, after .... Gen 10:5   3956
am slow of speech, and of a slow *t* .... Ex 4:10   3956
Israel shall not a dog move his *t* .... Ex 11:7   3956
a nation whose *t* thou shalt not .... Deut 28:49   3956
none moved his *t* against any of .... Josh 10:21   3956
lappeth of the water with his *t* .... Judg 7:5   3956
by me, and his word was in my *t* 2Sa 23:2   3956
was written in the Syrian *t* .... Ezr 4:7   762
and interpreted in the Syrian *t* .... Ezr 4:7   762
and bondwomen, I had held my *t* .... Est 7:4   2790
be hid from the scourge of the *t*............. Job 5:21   3956
Teach me, and I will hold my *t* .... Job 6:24   2790
Is there iniquity in my *t*......................... Job 6:30   3956
for now, if I hold my *t*, I shall .... Job 13:19   2790
thou choosest the *t* of the crafty .... Job 15:5   3956
though he hide it under his *t* .... Job 20:12   3956
the viper's *t* shall slay him .... Job 20:16   3956
wickedness, nor my *t* utter deceit.......... Job 27:4   3956
their *t* cleaved to the roof of................... Job 29:10   3956
my *t* hath spoken in my mouth.............. Job 33:2   3956
or his *t* with a cord which thou............. Job 41:1   3956
they flatter with their *t* .... Ps 5:9   3956
under his *t* is mischief and vanity.......... Ps 10:7   3956
the *t* that speaketh proud things .... Ps 12:3   3956
With our *t* will we prevail...................... Ps 12:4   3956
He that backbiteth not with his *t* .... Ps 15:3   3956
and my *t* cleaveth to my jaws .... Ps 22:15   3956
Keep thy *t* from evil, and thy lips .... Ps 34:13   3956
And my *t* shall speak of thy .... Ps 35:28   3956
his *t* talketh of judgment .... Ps 37:30   3956
my ways, that I sin not with my *t* .... Ps 39:1   3956
then spake I with my *t*,......................... Ps 39:3   3956
my *t* is the pen of a ready writer .... Ps 45:1   3956
to evil, and thy *t* frameth deceit............ Ps 50:19   3956
my *t* shall sing aloud of thy .... Ps 51:14   3956
Thy *t* deviseth mischiefs .... Ps 52:2   3956
words, O thou deceitful *t* .... Ps 52:4   3956
arrows, and their *t* a sharp sword .... Ps 57:4   3956
Who whet their *t* like a sword............... Ps 64:3   3956
own *t* to fall upon themselves .... Ps 64:8   3956
and he was extolled with my *t* .... Ps 66:17   3956
the *t* of thy dogs in the same................. Ps 68:23   3956
My *t* also shall talk of thy .... Ps 71:24   3956
their *t* walketh through the earth........... Ps 73:9   3956
spoken against me with a lying *t* .... Ps 109:2   3956
My *t* shall speak of thy word .... Ps 119:172   3956
lying lips, and from a deceitful *t*............ Ps 120:2   3956
be done unto thee, thou false *t* .... Ps 120:3   3956
laughter, and our *t* with singing .... Ps 126:2   3956
let my *t* cleave to the roof of my .... Ps 137:6   3956
For there is not a word in my *t* .... Ps 139:4   3956
A proud look, a lying *t*, and hands........ Prov 6:17   3956
of the *t* of a strange woman .... Prov 6:24   3956
The *t* of the just is as choice.................. Prov 10:20   3956
but the froward *t* shall be cut .... Prov 10:31   3956
but the *t* of the wise is health................ Prov 12:18   3956
but a lying *t* is but for a moment .... Prov 12:19   3956

The *t* of the wise useth knowledge .... Prov 15:2   3956
A wholesome *t* is a tree of life .... Prov 15:4   3956
in man, and the answer of the *t* .... Prov 16:1   3956
a liar giveth ear to a naughty *t* .... Prov 17:4   3956
perverse *t* falleth into mischief .... Prov 17:20   3956
and life are in the power of the *t* .... Prov 18:21   3956
a lying *t* is a vanity tossed to .... Prov 21:6   3956
his *t* keepeth his soul from .... Prov 21:23   3956
a soft *t* breaketh the bone .... Prov 25:15   3956
angry countenance a backbiting *t* .... Prov 25:23   3956
A lying *t* hateth those that are .... Prov 26:28   3956
he that flattereth with the *t* .... Prov 28:23   3956
in her *t* is the law of kindness .... Prov 31:26   3956
honey and milk are under thy *t* .... Song 4:11   3956
because their *t* and their doings .... Is 3:8   3956
destroy the *t* of the Egyptian sea .... Is 11:15   3956
another *t* will he speak to this .... Is 28:11   3956
his *t* as a devouring fire .... Is 30:27   3956
the *t* of the stammerers shall be .... Is 32:4   3956
of a stammering *t*, that thou .... Is 33:19   3956
hart, and the *t* of the dumb sing .... Is 35:6   3956
their *t* faileth for thirst, I the .... Is 41:17   3956
shall bow, every *t* shall swear .... Is 45:23   3956
given me the *t* of the learned .... Is 50:4   3956
every *t* that shall rise against .... Is 54:17   3956
a wide mouth, and draw out the *t* .... Is 57:4   3956
your *t* hath muttered perverseness .... Is 59:3   3956
have taught their *t* to speak lies .... Jer 9:5   3956
Their *t* is as an arrow shot out .... Jer 9:8   3956
and let us smite him with the *t* .... Jer 18:18   3956
The *t* of the sucking child .... Lam 4:4   3956
I will make thy *t* cleave to the.............. Eze 3:26   3956
and the *t* of the Chaldeans .... Dan 1:4   3956
the sword for the rage of their *t* .... Hos 7:16   3956
Then shall he say, Hold thy *t* .... Amos 6:10   2013
their *t* is deceitful in their...................... Mic 6:12   3956
holdest thy *t* when the wicked................. Hab 1:13   2790
t be found in their mouth...................... Zeph 3:13   3956
their *t* shall consume away in .... Zec 14:12   3956
and he spit, and touched his *t* .... Mk 7:33   1100
and the string of his *t* was loosed .... Mk 7:35   1100
his *t* loosed, and he spake, and............. Lk 1:64   1100
his finger in water, and cool my *t* .... Lk 16:24   1100
called in the Hebrew *t* Bethesda............. Jn 5:2   1447
field is called in their proper *t*............... Acts 1:19   1258
hear we every man in our own *t*............. Acts 2:8   1258
heart rejoice, and my *t* was glad .... Acts 2:26   1100
spake unto them in the Hebrew *t* .... Acts 21:40   1258
he spake in the Hebrew *t* to them......... Acts 22:2   1258
me, and saying in the Hebrew *t*............ Acts 26:14   1258
every *t* shall confess to God .... Rom 14:11   1100
unknown *t* speaketh not unto men 1Cor 14:2   1100
in an unknown *t* edifieth himself............ 1Cor 14:4   1100
except ye utter by *t* words 1Cor 14:9   1100
t pray that he may interpret................... 1Cor 14:13   1100
For if I pray in an unknown *t* 1Cor 14:14   1100
thousand words in an unknown *t* 1Cor 14:19   1100
psalm, hath a doctrine, hath a *t* 1Cor 14:26   1100
If any man speak in an unknown *t* 1Cor 14:27   1100
that every *t* should confess that .... Phil 2:11   1100
religious, and bridleth not his *t*.............. Jas 1:26   1100
Even so the *t* is a little member,............. Jas 3:5   1100
the *t* is a fire, a world of .... Jas 3:6   1100
so is the *t* among our members,............. Jas 3:6   1100
But the *t* can no man tame .... Jas 3:8   1100
let him refrain his *t* from evil 1Pet 3:10   1100
us not love in word, neither in *t* 1Jn 3:18   1100
blood out of every kindred, and *t*........... Rev 5:9   1100
name in the Hebrew *t* is Abaddon .... Rev 9:11   1447
but in the Greek *t* hath his name........... Rev 9:11   1447
to every nation, and kindred, and *t* .... Rev 14:6   1100
called in the Hebrew *t* Armageddon ...... Rev 16:16   1447

TONGUES

their families, after their *t* .... Gen 10:20   3956
their families, after their *t* .... Gen 10:31   3956
a pavilion from the strife of *t* .... Ps 31:20   3956
O Lord, and divide their *t* .... Ps 55:9   3956
they lied unto him with their *t* .... Ps 78:36   3956
sharpened their *t* like a serpent............. Ps 140:3   3956
I will gather all nations and *t*................. Is 66:18   3956
they bend their *t* like their bow............. Jer 9:3   3956
saith the LORD, that use their *t* .... Jer 23:31   3956
they shall speak with new *t* .... Mk 16:17   1100
them cloven *t* like as of fire .... Acts 2:3   1100
and began to speak with other *t* .... Acts 2:4   1100
our *t* the wonderful works of God .... Acts 2:11   1100
For they heard them speak with *t* .... Acts 10:46   1100
and they spake with *t*, and .... Acts 19:6   1100
with their *t* they have used.................... Rom 3:13   1100
to another divers kinds of *t* 1Cor 12:10   1100

another the interpretation of *t*................. 1Cor 12:10   *1100*
governments, diversities of *t*.................. 1Cor 12:28   *1100*
do all speak with *t* 1Cor 12:30   *1100*
Though I speak with the *t* of men........... 1Cor 13:1   *1100*
whether there be *t*, they shall................ 1Cor 13:8   *1100*
I would that ye all spake with *t* 1Cor 14:5   *1100*
than he that speaketh with *t*.................. 1Cor 14:5   *1100*
I come unto you speaking with *t* 1Cor 14:6   *1100*
I speak with *t* more than ye all.............. 1Cor 14:18   *1100*
is written, With men of other *t* 1Cor 14:21   *2084*
Wherefore *t* are for a sign, not.............. 1Cor 14:22   *1100*
one place, and all speak with *t* 1Cor 14:23   *1100*
and forbid not to speak with *t*................ 1Cor 14:39   *1100*
and kindreds, and people, and *t* .... Rev 7:9   *1100*
many peoples, and nations, and *t* .... Rev 10:11   *1100*
of the people and kindreds and *t* .... Rev 11:9   *1100*
given him over all kindreds, and *t* .... Rev 13:7   *1100*
and they gnawed their *t* for pain .... Rev 16:10   *1100*
and multitudes, and nations, and *t* .... Rev 17:15   *1100*

TOO See APPENDIX.

TOOK See APPENDIX.

TOOKEST

though thou *t* vengeance of their .... Ps 99:8
t thy broidered garments, and .... Eze 16:18   3947

TOOL

for if thou lift up thy *t* upon it .... Ex 20:25   2719
and fashioned it with a graving *t*........... Ex 32:4
not lift up any iron *t* upon them .... Deut 27:5
any *t* of iron heard in the house.............. 1Kin 6:7   3627

TOOTH

Eye for eye, *t* for *t*, hand .... Ex 21:24   8127
he smite out his manservant's *t* .... Ex 21:27   8127
or his maidservant's *t* .... Ex 21:27   8127
breach, eye for eye, *t* for *t*...................... Lev 24:20   8127
life, eye for eye, *t* for *t* .... Deut 19:21   8127
of trouble is like a broken *t* .... Prov 25:19   8127
for an eye, and a *t* for a *t*.................... Mt 5:38   *3599*

TOOTH'S

let him go free for his *t* sake .... Ex 21:27   8127

TOP

whose *t* may reach unto heaven .... Gen 11:4   7218
the *t* of it reached to heaven .... Gen 28:12   7218
and poured oil upon the *t* of it .... Gen 28:18   7218
to morrow I will stand on the *t* .... Ex 17:9   7218
Hur went up to the *t* of the hill .... Ex 17:10   7218
Sinai, on the *t* of the mount .... Ex 19:20   7218
Moses up to the *t* of the mount .... Ex 19:20   7218
was like devouring fire on the *t*.............. Ex 24:17   7218
shall be an hole in the *t* of it .... Ex 28:32   7218
the *t* thereof, and the sides .... Ex 30:3   1406
there to me in the *t* of the mount .... Ex 34:2   7218
with pure gold, both the *t* of it .... Ex 37:26   1406
up into the *t* of the mountain .... Num 14:40   7218
presumed to go up unto the hill *t* .... Num 14:44   7218
died from the *t* of the mount .... Num 20:28   7218
to the *t* of Pisgah, which looketh .... Num 21:20   7218
For from the *t* of the rocks I see............ Num 23:9   7218
to the *t* of Pisgah, and built .... Num 23:14   7218
brought Balaam unto the *t* of Peor .... Num 23:28   7218
Get thee up into the *t* of Pisgah .... Deut 3:27   7218
thy foot unto the *t* of thy head .... Deut 28:35   6936
upon the *t* of the head of him .... Deut 33:16   6936
to the *t* of Pisgah, that is over .... Deut 34:1   7218
the border went up to the *t* of .... Josh 15:8   7218
t of the hill unto the fountain .... Josh 15:9   7218
thy God upon the *t* of this rock.............. Judg 6:26   7218
stood in the *t* of mount Gerizim,............ Judg 9:7   7218
for him in the *t* of the mountains .... Judg 9:25   7218
down from the *t* of the mountains .... Judg 9:36   7218
gat them up to the *t* of the tower .... Judg 9:51   1406
dwelt in the *t* of the rock Etam .... Judg 15:8   5585
went to the *t* of the rock Etam .... Judg 15:11   5585
carried them up to the *t* of an .... Judg 16:3   7218
with Saul upon the *t* of the house 1Sa 9:25   1406
called Saul to the *t* of the house 1Sa 9:26   1406
stood on the *t* of an hill afar 1Sa 26:13   7218
and stood on the *t* of an hill 2Sa 2:25   7218
was come to the *t* of the mount 2Sa 15:32   7218
a little past the *t* of the hill.................. 2Sa 16:1   7218
a tent upon the *t* of the house 2Sa 16:22   1406
were upon the *t* of the pillars 1Kin 7:17   7218
chapiters that were upon the *t*................ 1Kin 7:18   7218
the *t* of the pillars were of lily 1Kin 7:19   7218
upon the *t* of the pillars was 1Kin 7:22   7218
in the *t* of the base was there a............. 1Kin 7:35   7218
on the *t* of the base the ledges 1Kin 7:35   7218
were on the *t* of the two pillars 1Kin 7:41   7218

T

were upon the *t* of the pillars 1Kin 7:41   7218
the *t* of the throne was round 1Kin 10:19   7218
Elijah went up to the *t* of Carmel 1Kin 18:42   7218
he sat on the *t* of an hill 2Kin 1:9   7218
under him on the *t* of the stairs 2Kin 9:13   1634
the altars that were on the *t* of 2Kin 23:12   1406
the chapiter that was on the *t* of 2Chr 3:15   7218
were on the *t* of the two pillars 2Chr 4:12   7218
were on the *t* of the pillars 2Chr 4:12   7218
them unto the *t* of the rock 2Chr 25:12   7218
them down from the *t* of the rock 2Chr 25:12   7218
touched the *t* of the sceptre .... Est 5:2   7218
earth upon the *t* of the mountains .... Ps 72:16   7218
a sparrow alone upon the house *t* .... Ps 102:7   1406
standeth in the *t* of high places .... Prov 8:2   7218
that lieth upon the *t* of a mast .... Prov 23:34   7218
look from the *t* of Amana, from .... Song 4:8   7218
from the *t* of Shenir and Hermon, ... Song 4:8   7218
in the *t* of the mountains .... Is 2:2   7218
in the *t* of the uppermost bough .... Is 17:6   7218
a beacon upon the *t* of a mountain .... Is 30:17   7218
shout from the *t* of the mountains .... Is 42:11   7218
hunger in the *t* of every street .... Lam 2:19   7218
out in the *t* of every street .... Lam 4:1   7218
off the *t* of his young twigs .... Eze 17:4   7218
I will crop off from the *t* of his .... Eze 17:22   7218
she set it upon the *t* of a rock .... Eze 24:7   6706
her blood upon the *t* of a rock .... Eze 24:8   6706
and make her like the *t* of a rock .... Eze 26:4   6706
make thee like the *t* of a rock .... Eze 26:14   6706
his *t* was among the thick boughs .... Eze 31:3   6788
he hath shot up his *t* among the .... Eze 31:10   6788
up their *t* among the thick boughs .... Eze 31:14   6788
Upon the *t* of the mountain the .... Eze 43:12   7218
the *t* of Carmel shall wither .... Amos 1:2   7218
themselves in the *t* of Carmel .... Amos 9:3   7218
in the *t* of the mountains .... Mic 4:1   7218
at the *t* of all the streets .... Nah 3:10   7218
with a bowl upon the *t* of it .... Zec 4:2   7218
which are upon the *t* thereof .... Zec 4:2   7218
in twain from the *t* to the bottom .... Mt 27:51   509
in twain from the *t* to the bottom .... Mk 15:38   509
seam, woven from the *t* throughout .... Jn 19:23   509
leaning upon the *t* of his staff .... Heb 11:21   206

TOPAZ
first row shall be a sardius, a *t* .... Ex 28:17   6357
the first row was a sardius, a *t* .... Ex 39:10   6357
The *t* of Ethiopia shall not equal .... Job 28:19   6357
was thy covering, the sardius, *t* .... Eze 28:13   6357
the ninth, a *t* .... Rev 21:20   5116

TOPHEL (*to'-fel*) *A place in the Sinai wilderness.*
the Red sea, between Paran, and *T* .... Deut 1:1   8603

TOPHET (*to'-fet*) *See* TOPHETH. *A place in the valley of Hinnom.*
For *T* is ordained of old .... Is 30:33   8613
have built the high places of *T* .... Jer 7:31   8612
that it shall no more be called *T* .... Jer 7:32   8612
for they shall bury in *T*, till .... Jer 7:32   8612
place shall no more be called *T* .... Jer 19:6   8612
and they shall bury them in *T* .... Jer 19:11   8612
and even make this city as *T* .... Jer 19:12   8612
be defiled as the place of *T* .... Jer 19:13   8612
Then came Jeremiah from *T* .... Jer 19:14   8612

TOPHETH (*to'-feth*) *See* TOPHET. *Same as Tophet.*
And he defiled *T*, which is in the 2Kin 23:10   8612

TOPS
were the *t* of the mountains seen .... Gen 8:5   7218
in the *t* of the mulberry trees 2Sa 5:24   7218
to set upon the *t* of the pillars 1Kin 7:16   7218
herb, as the grass on the house *t* 2Kin 19:26   1406
in the *t* of the mulberry trees 1Chr 14:15   7218
cut off as the *t* of the ears of .... Job 24:24   7218
into the *t* of the ragged rocks, ... Is 2:21   5585
on the *t* of their houses, and in .... Is 15:3   1406
in all the *t* of the mountains, and .... Eze 6:13   7218
upon the *t* of the mountains .... Hos 4:13   7218
t of mountains shall they leap .... Joel 2:5   7218

TORCH
like a *t* of fire in a sheaf .... Zec 12:6   3940

TORCHES
t in the day of his preparation .... Nah 2:3   6393
they shall seem like *t*, they .... Nah 2:4   3940
cometh thither with lanterns and *t* .... Jn 18:3   2985

TORMENT
hither to *t* us before the time .... Mt 8:29   928
thee by God, that thou *t* me not .... Mk 5:7   928
I beseech thee, *t* me not .... Lk 8:28   928

also come into this place of *t* .... Lk 16:28   931
because fear hath *t* 1Jn 4:18   2851
their *t* was as the *t* of a .... Rev 9:5   929
was as the *t* of a scorpion .... Rev 9:5   929
the smoke of their *t* ascendeth up .... Rev 14:11   929
and lived deliciously, so much *t* .... Rev 18:7   929
afar off for the fear of her *t* .... Rev 18:10   929
afar off for the fear of her *t* .... Rev 18:15   929

TORMENTED
sick of the palsy, grievously *t* .... Mt 8:6   928
for I am *t* in this flame .... Lk 16:24   3600
he is comforted, and thou art *t* .... Lk 16:25   3600
being destitute, afflicted, *t* .... Heb 11:37   2558
that they should be *t* five months .... Rev 9:5   928
because these two prophets *t* them .... Rev 11:10   928
and he shall be *t* with fire .... Rev 14:10   928
prophet are, and shall be *t* day .... Rev 20:10   928

TORMENTORS
wroth, and delivered him to the *t* .... Mt 18:34   930

TORMENTS
taken with divers diseases and *t* .... Mt 4:24   931
he lift up his eyes, being in *t* .... Lk 16:23   931

TORN
That which was *t* of beasts I .... Gen 31:39   2966
I said, Surely he is *t* in pieces .... Gen 44:28   2963
If it be *t* in pieces, then let .... Ex 22:13   2963
not make good that which was *t* .... Ex 22:13   2966
that is *t* of beasts in the field .... Ex 22:31   2966
of that which is *t* with beasts .... Lev 7:24   2966
or that which was *t* with beasts .... Lev 17:15   2966
or is *t* with beasts, he shall not............ Lev 22:8   2966
unto the lion, which hath *t* him 1Kin 13:26   7665
eaten the carcase, nor *t* the ass............ 1Kin 13:28   7665
their carcases were *t* in the.................. Is 5:25   5478
out thence shall be *t* in pieces.............. Jer 5:6   2963
of itself, or is *t* in pieces...................... Eze 4:14   2966
that is dead of itself, or *t* .... Eze 44:31   2966
for he hath *t*, and he will heal us .... Hos 6:1   2963
and ye brought that which was *t* .... Mal 1:13   1497
when the unclean spirit had *t* him .... Mk 1:26   4682

TORTOISE
mouse, and the *t* after his kind, ... Lev 11:29   6632

TORTURED
and others were *t*, not accepting............ Heb 11:35   5178

TOSS
t thee like a ball into a large.................. Is 22:18   6802
the waves thereof *t* themselves .... Jer 5:22   1607

TOSSED
I am *t* up and down as the locust .... Ps 109:23   5287
a lying tongue, a vanity *t* to .... Prov 21:6   5086
t with tempest, and not comforted,........ Is 54:11
midst of the sea, *t* with waves .... Mt 14:24   928
exceedingly *t* with a tempest .... Acts 27:18   5492
t to and fro, and carried about .... Eph 4:14   2831
the sea driven with the wind and *t*........ Jas 1:6   4494

TOSSINGS
and I am full of *t* to and fro unto .... Job 7:4   5076

TOTTERING
wall shall ye be, and as a *t* fence .... Ps 62:3   1760

TOU (*to'-u*) *See* TOI. *Same as Toi.*
Now when *T* king of Hamath heard 1Chr 18:9   8583
(for Hadarezer had war with *T* 1Chr 18:10   8583

TOUCH
eat of it, neither shall ye *t* it .... Gen 3:3   5060
suffered I thee not to *t* her...................... Gen 20:6   5060
the mount, or *t* the border of it.............. Ex 19:12   5060
There shall not an hand *t* it .... Ex 19:13   5060
Or if a soul *t* any unclean thing,............ Lev 5:2   5060
Or if he *t* the uncleanness of man .... Lev 5:3   5060
Whatsoever shall *t* the flesh .... Lev 6:27   5060
that shall *t* any unclean thing................ Lev 7:21   5060
and their carcase shall ye not *t* .... Lev 11:8   5060
whosoever doth *t* them, when they .... Lev 11:31   5060
she shall *t* no hallowed thing, ... Lev 12:4   5060
they shall not *t* any holy thing .... Num 4:15   5060
t nothing of theirs, lest ye be................ Num 16:26   5060
flesh, nor *t* their dead carcase .... Deut 14:8   5060
now therefore we may not *t* them .... Josh 9:19   5060
men that they shall not *t* thee .... Ruth 2:9   5060
he shall not *t* thee any more 2Sa 14:10   5060
Beware that none *t* the young man 2Sa 18:12
But the man that shall *t* them 2Sa 23:7   5060
T not mine anointed, and do my 1Chr 16:22   5060
t all that he hath, and he will.............. Job 1:11   5060
t his bone and his flesh, and he .... Job 2:5   5060

seven there shall no evil *t* thee............Job 5:19	5060
to *t* are as my sorrowful meat............Job 6:7	5060
T not mine anointed, and do my............Ps 105:15	5060
t the mountains, and they shall............Ps 144:5	5060
from thence, *t* no unclean thing............Is 52:11	5060
that *t* the inheritance which I............Jer 12:14	5060
men could not *t* their garments............Lam 4:14	5060
depart, depart, *t* not............Lam 4:15	5060
and with his skirt do *t* bread............Hag 2:12	5060
by a dead body *t* any of these............Hag 2:13	5060
If I may but *t* his garment............Mt 9:21	680
only *t* the hem of his garment............Mt 14:36	680
pressed upon him for to *t* him............Mk 3:10	680
If I may *t* but his clothes, I............Mk 5:28	680
t if it were but the border of............Mk 6:56	680
him, and besought him to *t* him............Mk 8:22	680
to him, that he should *t* them............Mk 10:13	680
whole multitude sought to *t* him............Lk 6:19	680
ye yourselves *t* not the burdens............Lk 11:46	4379
infants, that he would *t* them............Lk 18:15	680
Jesus saith unto her, *T* me not............Jn 20:17	680
good for a man not to *t* a woman............1Cor 7:1	680
Lord, and *t* not the unclean thing............2Cor 6:17	680
T not; taste not............Col 2:21	680
the firstborn should *t* them............Heb 11:28	2345
so much as a beast the mountain............Heb 12:20	2345

TOUCHED

us no hurt, as we have not *t* thee............Gen 26:29	5060
he *t* the hollow of his thigh............Gen 32:25	5060
because he *t* the hollow of............Gen 32:32	5060
The soul which hath *t* any such............Lev 22:6	5060
there, and upon him that *t* a bone............Num 19:18	5060
and whosoever hath *t* any slain............Num 31:19	5060
t the flesh and the unleavened............Judg 6:21	5060
of men, whose hearts God had *t*............1Sa 10:26	5060
wing of the one *t* the one wall............1Kin 6:27	5060
the other cherub *t* the other wall............1Kin 6:27	5060
their wings *t* one another in the............1Kin 6:27	5060
tree, behold, then an angel *t* him............1Kin 19:5	5060
t him, and said, Arise and eat............1Kin 19:7	5060
t the bones of Elisha, he revived............2Kin 13:21	5060
near, and *t* the top of the sceptre............Est 5:2	5060
for the hand of God hath *t* me............Job 19:21	5060
and said, Lo, this hath *t* thy lips............Is 6:7	5060
put forth his hand, and *t* my mouth............Jer 1:9	5060
creatures that *t* one another............Eze 3:13	5401
whole earth, and *t* not the ground............Dan 8:5	5060
but he *t* me, and set me upright............Dan 8:18	5060
t me about the time of the............Dan 9:21	5060
And, behold, an hand *t* me, which............Dan 10:10	5060
of the sons of men *t* my lips............Dan 10:16	5060
t me one like the appearance of a............Dan 10:18	5060
hand, and *t* him, saying, I will............Mt 8:3	680
he *t* her hand, and the fever left............Mt 8:15	680
him, and the hem of his garment............Mt 9:20	680
Then *t* he their eyes, saying,............Mt 9:29	680
as many as *t* were made perfectly............Mt 14:36	680
t them, and said, Arise, and be not............Mt 17:7	680
on them, and *t* their eyes............Mt 20:34	680
t him, and saith unto him, I will............Mk 1:41	680
press behind, and *t* his garment............Mk 5:27	680
press, and said, Who *t* my clothes............Mk 5:30	680
thee, and sayest thou, Who *t* me............Mk 5:31	680
as many as *t* him were made whole............Mk 6:56	680
ears, and he spit, and *t* his tongue............Mk 7:33	680
hand, and *t* him, saying, I will............Lk 5:13	680
And he came and *t* the bier............Lk 7:14	680
t the border of his garment............Lk 8:44	680
And Jesus said, Who *t* me............Lk 8:45	680
thee, and sayest thou, Who *t* me............Lk 8:45	680
And Jesus said, Somebody hath *t* me............Lk 8:46	680
for what cause she had *t* him............Lk 8:47	680
he *t* his ear, and healed him............Lk 22:51	680
And the next day we *t* at Sidon............Acts 27:3	2609
be *t* with the feeling of our............Heb 4:15	4834
unto the mount that might be *t*............Heb 12:18	5584

TOUCHETH

He that *t* this man or his wife............Gen 26:11	5060
whosoever *t* the mount shall be............Ex 19:12	5060
whatsoever *t* the altar shall be............Ex 29:37	5060
whatsoever *t* them shall be holy............Ex 30:29	5060
every one that *t* them shall be............Lev 6:18	5060
the flesh that *t* any unclean............Lev 7:19	5060
whosoever *t* the carcase of them............Lev 11:24	5060
every one that *t* them shall be............Lev 11:26	5060
whoso *t* their carcase shall be............Lev 11:27	5060
but that which *t* their carcase............Lev 11:36	5060
he that *t* the carcase thereof............Lev 11:39	5060
whosoever *t* his bed shall wash............Lev 15:5	5060
he that *t* the flesh of him that............Lev 15:7	5060

whosoever *t* any thing that was............Lev 15:10	5060
whomsoever he *t* that hath the............Lev 15:11	5060
that he *t* which hath the issue,............Lev 15:12	5060
whosoever *t* her shall be unclean............Lev 15:19	5060
whosoever *t* her bed shall wash............Lev 15:21	5060
whosoever *t* any thing that she............Lev 15:22	5060
whereon she sitteth, when he *t*............Lev 15:23	5060
whosoever *t* those things shall be............Lev 15:27	5060
whoso *t* any thing that is unclean............Lev 22:4	5060
Or whosoever *t* any creeping thing............Lev 22:5	5060
He that *t* the dead body of any............Num 19:11	5060
Whosoever *t* the dead body of any............Num 19:13	5060
whosoever *t* one that is slain............Num 19:16	5060
he that *t* the water of separation............Num 19:21	5060
unclean person *t* shall be unclean............Num 19:22	5060
the soul that *t* it shall be............Num 19:22	5060
tow is broken when it *t* the fire............Judg 16:9	7306
it *t* thee, and thou art troubled............Job 4:5	5060
he *t* the hills, and they smoke............Ps 104:32	5060
whosoever *t* her shall not be............Prov 6:29	5060
wither, when the east wind *t* it............Eze 17:10	5060
they break out, and blood *t* blood............Hos 4:2	5060
of hosts is he that *t* the land............Amos 9:5	5060
for he that *t* you............Zec 2:8	5060
you *t* the apple of his eye............Zec 2:8	5060
of woman this is that *t* him............Lk 7:39	680
and that wicked one *t* him not............1Jn 5:18	680

TOUCHING

as *t* thee, doth comfort himself,............Gen 27:42	
make an atonement for him as *t*............Lev 5:13	413
unto the Levites *t* their charge............Num 8:26	
as *t* the matter which thou and I............1Sa 20:23	
As *t* the words which thou hast............2Kin 22:18	
that *t* any of the priests and............Ezr 7:24	
T the Almighty, we cannot find............Job 37:23	
which I have made *t* the king............Ps 45:1	
song of my beloved *t* his vineyard............Is 5:1	
them *t* all their wickedness............Jer 1:16	5921
t the house of the king of Judah,............Jer 21:11	
For thus saith the LORD *t* Shallum............Jer 22:11	413
for the vision is *t* the whole............Eze 7:13	413
t any thing that they shall ask............Mt 18:19	4012
But as *t* the resurrection of the............Mt 22:31	4012
as *t* the dead, that they rise............Mk 12:26	4012
t those things whereof ye accuse............Lk 23:14	
ye intend to do as *t* these men............Acts 5:35	1909
As *t* the Gentiles which believe,............Acts 21:25	4012
T the resurrection of the dead I............Acts 24:21	4012
t all the things whereof I am............Acts 26:2	4012
but as *t* the election, they are............Rom 11:28	2596
Now as *t* things offered unto............1Cor 8:1	4012
As *t* our brother Apollos, I............1Cor 16:12	4012
For as *t* the ministering to the............2Cor 9:1	4012
as *t* the law, a Pharisee............Phil 3:5	2596
t the righteousness which is in............Phil 3:6	2596
(*t* whom ye received commandments............Col 4:10	4012
But as *t* brotherly love ye need............1Th 4:9	4012
have confidence in the Lord *t* you............2Th 3:4	1909

TOW

as a thread of *t* is broken when............Judg 16:9	5296
And the strong shall be as *t*............Is 1:31	5296
extinct, they are quenched as *t*............Is 43:17	6594

TOWARD See APPENDIX.

TOWEL

and took a *t*, and girded himself............Jn 13:4	3012
to wipe them with the *t* wherewith............Jn 13:5	3012

TOWER

to, let us build us a city and a *t*............Gen 11:4	4026
down to see the city and the *t*............Gen 11:5	4026
his tent beyond the *t* of Edar............Gen 35:21	4026
peace, I will break down this *t*............Judg 8:9	4026
And he beat down the *t* of Penuel............Judg 8:17	4026
of the *t* of Shechem heard that............Judg 9:46	4026
that all the men of the *t* of............Judg 9:47	4026
men of the *t* of Shechem died also............Judg 9:49	4026
was a strong *t* within the city............Judg 9:51	4026
gat them up to the top of the *t*............Judg 9:51	4026
And Abimelech came unto the *t*............Judg 9:52	4026
of the *t* to burn it with fire............Judg 9:52	4026
horn of my salvation, my high *t*............2Sa 22:3	4869
He is the *t* of salvation for his............2Sa 22:51	1431
And when he came to the *t*, he took............2Kin 5:24	6076
a watchman on the *t* in Jezreel............2Kin 9:17	4026
from the *t* of the watchmen to the............2Kin 17:9	4026
from the *t* of the watchmen to the............2Kin 18:8	4026
the watch *t* in the wilderness............2Chr 20:24	
even unto the *t* of Meah they............Neh 3:1	4026
it, unto the *t* of Hananeel............Neh 3:1	4026

T

piece, and the *t* of the furnaces	Neh 3:11	4026
the *t* which lieth out from the	Neh 3:25	4026
the east, and the *t* that lieth out	Neh 3:26	4026
the great *t* that lieth out	Neh 3:27	4026
from beyond the *t* of the furnaces	Neh 12:38	4026
the *t* of Hananeel	Neh 12:39	4026
the *t* of Meah, even unto the	Neh 12:39	4026
of my salvation, and my high *t*	Ps 18:2	4869
a strong *t* from the enemy	Ps 61:3	4026
my high *t*, and my deliverer	Ps 144:2	4869
name of the LORD is a strong *t*	Prov 18:10	4026
Thy neck is like the *t* of David	Song 4:4	4026
Thy neck is as a *t* of ivory	Song 7:4	4026
thy nose is as the *t* of Lebanon	Song 7:4	4026
And upon every high *t*, and upon	Is 2:15	4026
built a *t* in the midst of it, and	Is 5:2	4026
I have set thee for a *t* and a	Jer 6:27	969
t of Hananeel unto the gate of	Jer 31:38	4026
from the *t* of Syene even unto the	Eze 29:10	4024
from the *t* of Syene shall they	Eze 30:6	4024
O *t* of the flock, the strong hold	Mic 4:8	4026
my watch, and set me upon the *t*...........	Hab 2:1	4692
from the *t* of Hananeel unto the	Zec 14:10	4026
a winepress in it, and built a *t*	Mt 21:33	4444
for the winefat, and built a *t*	Mk 12:1	4444
upon whom the *t* in Siloam fell,.........	Lk 13:4	4444
of you, intending to build a *t*	Lk 14:28	4444

TOWERS

and make about them walls, and *t*........	2Chr 14:7	4026
Moreover Uzziah built *t* in	2Chr 26:9	4026
Also he built *t* in the desert	2Chr 26:10	4026
by cunning men, to be on the *t*	2Chr 26:15	4026
the forests he built castles and *t*	2Chr 27:4	4026
broken, and raised it up to the *t*	2Chr 32:5	4026
tell the *t* thereof	Ps 48:12	4026
I am a wall, and my breasts like *t*.........	Song 8:10	4026
they set up the *t* thereof	Is 23:13	971
great slaughter, when the *t* fall	Is 30:25	4026
t shall be for dens for ever, a	Is 32:14	975
where is he that counted the *t*	Is 33:18	4026
of Tyrus, and break down her *t*	Eze 26:4	4026
axes he shall break down thy *t*	Eze 26:9	4026
and the Gammadims were in thy *t*.........	Eze 27:11	4026
cities, and against the high *t*	Zeph 1:16	6438
their *t* are desolate...............................	Zeph 3:6	6438

TOWN

for her house was upon the *t* wall	Josh 2:15	7023
the elders of the *t* trembled at	1Sa 16:4	7023
entering into a *t* that hath gates	1Sa 23:7	5892
a place in some *t* in the country	1Sa 27:5	5892
him that buildeth a *t* with blood	Hab 2:12	5892
city or *t* ye shall enter, enquire	Mt 10:11	2968
the hand, and led him out of the *t*	Mk 8:23	2968
saying, Neither go into the *t*	Mk 8:26	2968
nor tell it to any in the *t*	Mk 8:26	2968
come out of every *t* of Galilee................	Lk 5:17	2968
out of the *t* of Bethlehem, where	Jn 7:42	2968
the *t* of Mary and her sister	Jn 11:1	2968
Jesus was not yet come into the *t*	Jn 11:30	2968

TOWNCLERK

when the *t* had appeased the................	Acts 19:35	1122

TOWNS

these are their names, by their *t*	Gen 25:16	2691
went and took the small *t* thereof	Num 32:41	2333
beside unwalled *t* a great many	Deut 3:5	5892
of Bashan, and all the *t* of Jair	Josh 13:30	2333
Ekron, with her *t* and her villages	Josh 15:45	1323
Ashdod with her *t* and her villages	Josh 15:47	1323
her villages, Gaza with her *t*	Josh 15:47	1323
and in Asher Beth-shean and her *t*.......	Josh 17:11	1323
and Ibleam and her *t*	Josh 17:11	1323
the inhabitants of Dor and her *t*	Josh 17:11	1323
inhabitants of En-dor and her *t*.............	Josh 17:11	1323
inhabitants of Taanach and her *t*..........	Josh 17:11	1323
inhabitants of Megiddo and her *t*	Josh 17:11	1323
who are of Beth-shean and her *t*...........	Josh 17:16	1323
of Beth-shean and her *t*, nor	Judg 1:27	1323
nor Taanach and her *t*	Judg 1:27	1323
the inhabitants of Dor and her *t*	Judg 1:27	1323
inhabitants of Ibleam and her *t*	Judg 1:27	1323
inhabitants of Megiddo and her *t*	Judg 1:27	1323
Israel taken in Heshbon and her *t*	Judg 11:26	1323
and in Aroer and her *t*...........................	Judg 11:26	1323
to him pertained the *t* of Jair	1Kin 4:13	2333
and Aram, with *t*, even threescore	1Chr 2:23	2333
the *t* thereof, even threescore	1Chr 2:23	1323
in Gilead in Bashan, and in her *t*	1Chr 5:16	1323
the *t* thereof, and eastward Naaran	1Chr 7:28	1323
Gezer, with the *t* thereof	1Chr 7:28	1323

unto Gaza and the *t* thereof..................	1Chr 7:28	1323
of Manasseh, Beth-shean and her *t*.......	1Chr 7:29	
Taanach and her *t*	1Chr 7:29	
Megiddo and her *t*.................................	1Chr 7:29	
Dor and her *t*	1Chr 7:29	
Ono, and Lod, with the *t* thereof...........	1Chr 8:12	1323
her *t* out of the hand of the	1Chr 18:1	1323
him, Beth-el with the *t* thereof	2Chr 13:19	1323
and Jeshanah with the *t* thereof	2Chr 13:19	1323
and Ephrain with the *t* thereof..............	2Chr 13:19	1323
that dwelt in the unwalled *t*	Est 9:19	5892
upon all her *t* all the evil that	Jer 19:15	5892
t without walls for the multitude	Zec 2:4	6519
them, Let us go into the next *t*...........	Mk 1:38	2969
into the *t* of Caesarea Philippi	Mk 8:27	2968
departed, and went through the *t*	Lk 9:6	2968
away, that they may go into the *t*..........	Lk 9:12	2968

TRACHONITIS (*trak-o-ni'-tis*) *A rocky district east of the Jordan.*

of Ituraea and of the region of *T*...........	Lk 3:1	5139

TRADE

dwell and *t* ye therein, and get you.......	Gen 34:10	5503
dwell in the land, and *t* therein.............	Gen 34:21	5503
for their *t* hath been to feed	Gen 46:32	582
Thy servants' *t* hath been about	Gen 46:34	582
sailors, and as many as *t* by sea	Rev 18:17	2038

TRADED

tin, and lead, they *t* in thy fairs	Eze 27:12	5414
they *t* the persons of men and..............	Eze 27:13	5414
t in thy fairs with horses	Eze 27:14	5414
they *t* in thy market wheat of	Eze 27:17	5414
***t* with the same, and made them**..........	Mt 25:16	2038

TRADING

much every man had gained by *t*	Lk 19:15	1281

TRADITION

transgress the *t* of the elders	Mt 15:2	3862
the commandment of God by your *t*......	Mt 15:3	3862
of God of none effect by your *t*	Mt 15:6	3862
holding the *t* of the elders	Mk 7:3	3862
according to the *t* of the elders	Mk 7:5	3862
of God, ye hold the *t* of men	Mk 7:8	3862
God, that ye may keep your own *t*	Mk 7:9	3862
God of none effect through your *t*	Mk 7:13	3862
vain deceit, after the *t* of men	Col 2:8	3862
not after the *t* which he received	2Th 3:6	3862
received by *t* from your fathers..............	1Pet 1:18	3862

TRADITIONS

zealous of the *t* of my fathers	Gal 1:14	3862
hold the *t* which ye have been	2Th 2:15	3862

TRAFFICK

and ye shall *t* in the land......................	Gen 42:34	5503
of the *t* of the spice merchants, ...	1Kin 10:15	4536
and carried it into a land of *t*................	Eze 17:4	3667
by thy *t* hast thou increased thy	Eze 28:5	7404
by the iniquity of thy *t*	Eze 28:18	7404

TRAFFICKERS

whose *t* are the honourable of the	Is 23:8	3669

TRAIN

to Jerusalem with a very great *t*...........	1Kin 10:2	2428
T up a child in the way he should	Prov 22:6	2596
up, and his *t* filled the temple	Is 6:1	7757

TRAINED

captive, he armed his *t* servants...........	Gen 14:14	2593

TRAITOR

Iscariot, which also was the *t*	Lk 6:16	4273

TRAITORS

T, heady, highminded, lovers of	2Ti 3:4	4273

TRAMPLE

dragon shalt thou *t* under feet	Ps 91:13	7429
mine anger, and *t* them in my fury	Is 63:3	7429
lest they *t* them under their feet..........	Mt 7:6	2662

TRANCE

of the Almighty, falling into a *t*	Num 24:4	
of the Almighty, falling into a *t*	Num 24:16	
they made ready, he fell into a *t*	Acts 10:10	1611
in a *t* I saw a vision, A certain	Acts 11:5	1611
in the temple, I was in a *t*.....................	Acts 22:17	1611

TRANQUILITY

it may be a lengthening of thy *t*............	Dan 4:27	7963

TRANSFERRED

I have in a figure *t* to myself................	1Cor 4:6	3345

TRANSFIGURED

And was *t* before them............................Mt 17:2   3339
and he was *t* before them ....Mk 9:2   3339

TRANSFORMED

but be ye *t* by the renewing of................Rom 12:2   3339
for Satan himself is *t* into an 2Cor 11:14   3345
also be *t* as the ministers of 2Cor 11:15   3345

TRANSFORMING

t themselves into the apostles of 2Cor 11:13   3345

TRANSGRESS

Wherefore now do ye *t* the ....Num 14:41   5674
ye make the LORD's people to *t* 1Sa 2:24   5674
Why *t* ye the commandments of the.......2Chr 24:20   5674
servant Moses, saying, If ye *t*.................Neh 1:8   4603
to *t* against our God in marrying ....Neh 13:27   4603
that my mouth shall not *t*.....................Ps 17:3   5674
be ashamed which *t* without cause ....Ps 25:3   898
a piece of bread that man will *t* ....Prov 28:21   6586
and thou saidst, I will not *t* ....Jer 2:20   5647
rebels, and them that *t* against me ....Eze 20:38   6586
Come to Beth-el, and *t* ....Amos 4:4   6586
Why do thy disciples *t* the......................Mt 15:2   3845
Why do ye also *t* the commandment .... Mt 15:3   3845
and circumcision dost *t* the law ....Rom 2:27   3848

TRANSGRESSED

I have not *t* thy commandments, ...Deut 26:13   5674
they have also *t* my covenant ....Josh 7:11   5674
because he hath *t* the covenant of.........Josh 7:15   5674
When ye have *t* the covenant of ....Josh 23:16   5674
t my covenant which I commanded ....Judg 2:20   5674
And he said, Ye have *t* 1Sa 14:33   898
for I have *t* the commandment of 1Sa 15:24   5674
wherein they have *t* against thee...........1Kin 8:50   6586
but *t* his covenant, and all that...............2Kin 18:12   5674
who *t* in the thing accursed 1Chr 2:7   4603
they *t* against the God of their...............1Chr 5:25   4603
they had *t* against the LORD,...................2Chr 12:2   4603
for he *t* against the LORD his God........2Chr 26:16   4603
naked, and *t* sore against the LORD......2Chr 28:19   4603
t very much after all the 2Chr 36:14   4603
up, and said unto them, Ye have *t* ....Ezr 10:10   4603
many that have *t* in this thing ....Ezr 10:13   6586
because they have *t* the laws ....Is 24:5   5674
and thy teachers have *t* against me ......Is 43:27   6586
of the men that have *t* against me ....Is 66:24   6586
the pastors also *t* against me ....Jer 2:8   6586
ye all have *t* against me, saith ....Jer 2:29   6586
that thou hast *t* against the LORD........Jer 3:13   6586
and whereby they have *t* against me......Jer 33:8   6586
the men that have *t* my covenant ....Jer 34:18   5674
We have *t* and have rebelled..................Lam 3:42   6586
their fathers have *t* against me ....Eze 2:3   6586
transgressions, whereby ye have *t*.........Eze 18:31   6586
Yea, all Israel have *t* thy law.................Dan 9:11   5674
they like men have *t* the covenant ....Hos 6:7   5674
because they have *t* against me..............Hos 7:13   6586
because they have *t* my covenant..........Hos 8:1   5674
wherein thou hast *t* against me ....Zeph 3:11   6586
neither *t* I at any time thy.....................Lk 15:29   3928

TRANSGRESSEST

Why *t* thou the king's commandment .... Est 3:3   5674

TRANSGRESSETH

his mouth *t* not in judgment....................Prov 16:10   4603
Yea also, because he *t* by wine ....Hab 2:5   898
committeth sin *t* also the law...............1Jn 3:4   458,4160
Whosoever *t*, and abideth not in.............2Jn 9   3845

TRANSGRESSING

LORD thy God, in *t* his covenant,............Deut 17:2   5674
In *t* and lying against the LORD,.............Is 59:13   6586

TRANSGRESSION

forgiving iniquity and *t* and sin, ...Ex 34:7   6588
mercy, forgiving iniquity and *t*................Num 14:18   6588
or if in *t* against the LORD, ...Josh 22:22   4604
neither evil nor *t* in mine hand...............1Sa 24:11   6588
away to Babylon for their *t* 1Chr 9:1   4604
So Saul died for his *t* which he 1Chr 10:13   4604
his reign did cast away in his *t* 2Chr 29:19   4604
because of the *t* of those that................Ezr 9:4   4604
t of them that had been carried..............Ezr 10:6   4604
And why dost thou not pardon my *t*.......Job 7:21   6588
have cast them away for their *t* ....Job 8:4   6588
make me to know my *t* and my sin ....Job 13:23   6588
My *t* is sealed up in a bag, and.............Job 14:17   6588
I am clean without *t*, I am.....................Job 33:9   6588
my wound is incurable without *t* ....Job 34:6   6588
be innocent from the great *t* ....Ps 19:13   6588
Blessed is he whose *t* is forgiven ....Ps 32:1   6588

The *t* of the wicked saith within ....Ps 36:1   6588
not for my *t*, nor for my sin, O ....Ps 59:3   6588
will I visit their *t* with the rod ....Ps 89:32   6588
Fools, because of their *t* ....Ps 107:17   6588
is snared by the *t* of his lips...................Prov 12:13   6588
He that covereth a *t* seeketh love ....Prov 17:9   6588
He loveth *t* that loveth strife ....Prov 17:19   6588
it is his glory to pass over a *t*.................Prov 19:11   6588
For the *t* of a land many are the ....Prov 28:2   6588
his mother, and saith, It is no *t* ....Prov 28:24   6588
In the *t* of an evil man there is ....Prov 29:6   6588
are multiplied, *t* increaseth ....Prov 29:16   6588
and a furious man aboundeth in *t*..........Prov 29:22   6588
the *t* thereof shall be heavy upon ....Is 24:20   6588
for the *t* of my people was he ....Is 53:8   6588
are ye not children of *t*, a seed ....Is 57:4   6588
and shew my people their *t* ....Is 58:1   6588
them that turn from *t* in Jacob ....Is 59:20   6588
deliver him in the day of his *t* ....Eze 33:12   6588
daily sacrifice by reason of *t*..................Dan 8:12   6588
the *t* of desolation, to give both ....Dan 8:13   6588
thy holy city, to finish the *t* ....Dan 9:24   6588
at Gilgal multiply *t* ....Amos 4:4   6586
For the *t* of Jacob is all this,.................Mic 1:5   6588
What is the *t* of Jacob..............................Mic 1:5   6588
to declare unto Jacob his *t* ....Mic 3:8   6588
I give my firstborn for my *t*....................Mic 6:7   6588
passeth by the *t* of the remnant............Mic 7:18   6588
from which Judas by *t* fell ....Acts 1:25   3845
where no law is, there is no *t* ....Rom 4:15   3847
after the similitude of Adam's *t*.............Rom 5:14   3847
woman being deceived was in the *t*........1Ti 2:14   3847
angels was stedfast, and every *t*............Heb 2:2   3847
for sin is the *t* of the law.......................1Jn 3:4   458

TRANSGRESSIONS

for he will not pardon your *t* ....Ex 23:21   6588
because of their *t* in all their.................Lev 16:16   6588
all their *t* in all their sins,.....................Lev 16:21   6588
not forgive your *t* nor your sins ....Josh 24:19   6588
all their *t* wherein they have 1Kin 8:50   6588
If I covered my *t* as Adam.......................Job 31:33   6588
or if thy *t* be multiplied, what ....Job 35:6   6588
their *t* that they have exceeded ....Job 36:9   6588
out in the multitude of their *t* ....Ps 5:10   6588
the sins of my youth, nor my *t* ....Ps 25:7   6588
I will confess my *t* unto the LORD ....Ps 32:5   6588
Deliver me from all my *t* ....Ps 39:8   6588
thy tender mercies blot out my *t* ....Ps 51:1   6588
For I acknowledge my *t* ....Ps 51:3   6588
as for our *t*, thou shalt purge ....Ps 65:3   6588
far hath he removed our *t* from us ....Ps 103:12   6588
out thy *t* for mine own sake ....Is 43:25   6588
out, as a thick cloud, thy *t* ....Is 44:22   6588
for your *t* is your mother put ....Is 50:1   6588
But he was wounded for our *t* ....Is 53:5   6588
For our *t* are multiplied before ....Is 59:12   6588
for our *t* are with us ....Is 59:12   6588
because their *t* are many, and ....Jer 5:6   6588
her for the multitude of her *t* ....Lam 1:5   6588
The yoke of my *t* is bound by his ....Lam 1:14   6588
hast done unto me for all my *t* ....Lam 1:22   6588
any more with all their *t*........................Eze 14:11   6588
All his *t* that he hath committed,...........Eze 18:22   6588
all his *t* that he hath committed ....Eze 18:28   6588
turn yourselves from all your *t* ....Eze 18:30   6588
Cast away from you all your *t* ....Eze 18:31   6588
in that your *t* are discovered, so ....Eze 21:24   6588
Thus ye speak, saying, If our *t* ....Eze 33:10   6588
things, nor with any of their *t* ....Eze 37:23   6588
according to their *t* have I done ....Eze 39:24   6588
For three *t* of Damascus, and for ....Amos 1:3   6588
For three *t* of Gaza, and for four,...........Amos 1:6   6588
For three *t* of Tyrus, and for four ....Amos 1:9   6588
For three *t* of Edom, and for four,..........Amos 1:11   6588
For three *t* of the children of ....Amos 1:13   6588
For three *t* of Moab, and for four,...........Amos 2:1   6588
For three *t* of Judah, and for four...........Amos 2:4   6588
For three *t* of Israel, and for ....Amos 2:6   6588
t of Israel upon him I will also...............Amos 3:14   6588
For I know your manifold *t* ....Amos 5:12   6588
for the *t* of Israel were found in.............Mic 1:13   6588
It was added because of the *t* ....Gal 3:19   3847
the *t* that were under the first ....Heb 9:15   3847

TRANSGRESSOR

and the *t* for the upright.........................Prov 21:18   898
overthroweth the words of the *t* ....Prov 22:12   898
and wast called a *t* from the womb ....Is 48:8   6586
I destroyed, I make myself a *t* ....Gal 2:18   3848
thou art become a *t* of the law ....Jas 2:11   3848

TRANSGRESSORS

But the *t* shall be destroyed	Ps 37:38	6586
Then will I teach *t* thy ways	Ps 51:13	6586
be not merciful to any wicked *t*	Ps 59:5	898
I beheld the *t*, and was grieved	Ps 119:158	898
the *t* shall be rooted out of it	Prov 2:22	898
of *t* shall destroy them	Prov 11:3	898
but *t* shall be taken in their own	Prov 11:6	898
soul of the *t* shall eat violence	Prov 13:2	898
but the way of *t* is hard	Prov 13:15	898
and increaseth the *t* among men	Prov 23:28	898
the fool, and rewardeth *t*	Prov 26:10	5674
And the destruction of the *t*	Is 1:28	6586
bring it again to mind, O ye *t*	Is 46:8	6586
and he was numbered with the *t*	Is 53:12	6586
and made intercession for the *t*	Is 53:12	6586
when the *t* are come to the full,	Dan 8:23	6586
but the *t* shall fall therein	Hos 14:9	6586
And he was numbered with the *t*	Mk 15:28	459
And he was reckoned among the *t*	Lk 22:37	459
and are convinced of the law as *t*	Jas 2:9	3848

TRANSLATE

To *t* the kingdom from the house	2Sa 3:10	5674

TRANSLATED

hath *t* us into the kingdom of his	Col 1:13	3179
By faith Enoch was *t* that he	Heb 11:5	3346
not found, because God had *t* him	Heb 11:5	3346

TRANSLATION

for before his *t* he had this	Heb 11:5	3331

TRANSPARENT

was pure gold, as it were *t* glass	Rev 21:21	1307

TRAP

ground, and a *t* for him in the way	Job 18:10	4434
their welfare, let it become a *t*	Ps 69:22	4170
they set a *t*, they catch men	Jer 5:26	4889
table be made a snare, and a *t*	Rom 11:9	2339

TRAPS

t unto you, and scourges in your	Josh 23:13	4170

TRAVAIL

came to pass in the time of her *t*	Gen 38:27	3205
all the *t* that had come upon them	Ex 18:8	8513
and pain, as of a woman in *t*	Ps 48:6	3205
this sore *t* hath God given to the	Eccl 1:13	6045
days are sorrows, and his *t* grief	Eccl 2:23	6045
but to the sinner he giveth *t*	Eccl 2:26	6045
I have seen the *t*, which God hath	Eccl 3:10	6045
Again, I considered all *t*	Eccl 4:4	5999
than both the hands full with *t*	Eccl 4:6	5999
also vanity, yea, it is a sore *t*	Eccl 4:8	6045
But those riches perish by evil *t*	Eccl 5:14	6045
I *t* not, nor bring forth children	Is 23:4	2342
He shall see of the *t* of his soul	Is 53:11	5999
thou that didst not *t* with child	Is 54:1	2342
heard a voice as of a woman in *t*	Jer 4:31	2470
us, and pain, as of a woman in *t*	Jer 6:24	3205
take thee, as a woman in *t*	Jer 13:21	3205
thee, the pain as of a woman in *t*	Jer 22:23	3205
whether a man doth *t* with child	Jer 30:6	3205
on his loins, as a woman in *t*	Jer 30:6	3205
have taken her, as a woman in *t*	Jer 49:24	3205
him, and pangs as of a woman in *t*	Jer 50:43	3205
have taken thee as a woman in *t*	Mic 4:9	3205
of Zion, like a woman in *t*	Mic 4:10	3205
when she is in *t* hath sorrow	Jn 16:21	5088
of whom I *t* in birth again until	Gal 4:19	5605
brethren, our labour and *t*	1Th 2:9	3449
as *t* upon a woman with child	1Th 5:3	5604
t night and day, that we might not	2Th 3:8	3449

TRAVAILED

and Rachel *t*, and she had hard	Gen 35:16	3205
And it came to pass, when she *t*	Gen 38:28	3205
were dead, she bowed herself and *t*	1Sa 4:19	3205
Before she *t*, she brought forth	Is 66:7	2342
for as soon as Zion *t*, she	Is 66:8	2342

TRAVAILEST

forth and cry, thou that *t* not	Gal 4:27	5605

TRAVAILETH

The wicked man *t* with pain all	Job 15:20	2342
he *t* with iniquity, and hath	Ps 7:14	2254
be in pain as a woman that *t*	Is 13:8	3205
as the pangs of a woman that *t*	Is 21:3	3205
her that *t* with child together	Jer 31:8	3205
she which *t* hath brought forth	Mic 5:3	3205
t in pain together until now	Rom 8:22	4944

TRAVAILING

now will I cry like a *t* woman	Is 42:14	3205
The sorrows of a *t* woman shall	Hos 13:13	3205
t in birth, and pained to be	Rev 12:2	5605

TRAVEL

Thou knowest all the *t* that hath	Num 20:14	8513
and compassed me with gall and *t*	Lam 3:5	8513
Macedonia, Paul's companions in *t*	Acts 19:29	4898
to *t* with us with this grace	2Cor 8:19	4898

TRAVELERS

the *t* walked through byways	Judg 5:6	

TRAVELLED

about Stephen *t* as far as Phenice	Acts 11:19	1330

TRAVELLER

there came a *t* unto the rich man,	2Sa 12:4	1982
but I opened my doors to the *t*	Job 31:32	734

TRAVELLETH

thy poverty come as one that *t*	Prov 6:11	1980
thy poverty come as one that *t*	Prov 24:34	1980

TRAVELLING

O ye *t* companies of Dedanim	Is 21:13	736
t in the greatness of his	Is 63:1	6808
is as a man *t* into a far country	Mt 25:14	589

TRAVERSING

art a swift dromedary *t* her ways	Jer 2:23	8308

TREACHEROUS

the *t* dealer dealeth	Is 21:2	898
the *t* dealers have dealt	Is 24:16	898
the *t* dealers have dealt very	Is 24:16	898
her *t* sister Judah saw it	Jer 3:7	901
yet her *t* sister Judah feared not	Jer 3:8	898
yet for all this her *t* sister	Jer 3:10	901
herself more than Judah	Jer 3:11	898
adulterers, an assembly of *t* men	Jer 9:2	898
prophets are light and *t* persons	Zeph 3:4	900

TREACHEROUSLY

of Shechem dealt *t* with Abimelech	Judg 9:23	898
the treacherous dealer dealeth *t*	Is 21:2	898
treacherous dealers have dealt *t*	Is 24:16	898
dealers have dealt very *t*	Is 24:16	898
and dealest *t*, and they dealt not	Is 33:1	898
and they dealt not *t* with thee	Is 33:1	898
thou shalt make an end to deal *t*	Is 33:1	898
they shall deal *t* with thee	Is 33:1	898
that thou wouldest deal very *t*	Is 48:8	898
Surely as a wife *t* departeth from	Jer 3:20	898
so have ye dealt *t* with me	Jer 3:20	898
have dealt very *t* against me	Jer 5:11	898
all they happy that deal very *t*	Jer 12:1	898
even they have dealt *t* with thee	Jer 12:6	898
her friends have dealt *t* with her	Lam 1:2	898
They have dealt *t* against the	Hos 5:7	898
have they dealt *t* against me	Hos 6:7	898
thou upon them that deal *t*	Hab 1:13	898
why do we deal *t* every man	Mal 2:10	898
Judah hath dealt *t*, and an	Mal 2:11	898
against whom thou hast dealt *t*	Mal 2:14	898
let none deal *t* against the wife	Mal 2:15	898
your spirit, that ye deal not *t*	Mal 2:16	898

TREACHERY

and said to Ahaziah, There is *t*	2Kin 9:23	4820

TREAD

your feet shall *t* shall be yours	Deut 11:24	1869
all the land that ye shall *t* upon	Deut 11:25	1869
thou shalt *t* upon their high	Deut 33:29	1869
sole of your foot shall *t* upon	Josh 1:3	1869
t on the threshold of Dagon in	1Sa 5:5	1869
t their winepresses, and suffer	Job 24:11	1869
t down the wicked in their place	Job 40:12	1915
let him *t* down my life upon the	Ps 7:5	7429
through thy name will we *t* them	Ps 44:5	947
is that shall *t* down our enemies	Ps 60:12	947
Thou shalt *t* upon the lion and	Ps 91:13	1869
is that shall *t* down our enemies	Ps 108:13	947
this at your hand, to *t* my courts	Is 1:12	7429
to *t* them down like the mire of	Is 10:6	7760,4823
my mountains *t* him under foot	Is 14:25	947
the treaders shall *t* out no wine	Is 16:10	1869
The foot shall *t* it down, even	Is 26:6	7429
for I will *t* them in mine anger,	Is 63:3	1869
I will *t* down the people in mine	Is 63:6	947
shout, as they that *t* the grapes	Jer 25:30	1869
none shall *t* with shouting	Jer 48:33	1869
shall he *t* down all thy streets	Eze 26:11	7429
but ye must *t* down with your feet	Eze 34:18	7429

shall *t* it down, and break it in	Dan 7:23	1759
and loveth to *t* out the corn	Hos 10:11	1758
t upon the high places of the	Mic 1:3	1869
when he shall *t* in our palaces,	Mic 5:5	1869
thou shalt *t* the olives, but thou	Mic 6:15	1869
t the morter, make strong the	Nah 3:14	7429
which *t* down their enemies in the	Zec 10:5	947
ye shall *t* down the wicked	Mal 4:3	6072
unto you power to *t* on serpents	Lk 10:19	3961
shall they *t* under foot forty	Rev 11:2	3961

TREADER

the *t* of grapes him that soweth	Amos 9:13	1869

TREADERS

the *t* shall tread out no wine in	Is 16:10	1869

TREADETH

the ox when he *t* out the corn	Deut 25:4	1758
t upon the waves of the sea	Job 9:8	1869
morter, and as the potter *t* clay	Is 41:25	7429
like him that *t* in the winefat	Is 63:2	1869
t upon the high places of the	Amos 4:13	1869
when he *t* within our borders	Mic 5:6	1869
if he go through, both *t* down	Mic 5:8	7429
of the ox that *t* out the corn	1Cor 9:9	248
muzzle the ox that *t* out the corn	1Ti 5:18	248
he *t* the winepress of the	Rev 19:15	3961

TREADING

some *t* winepresses on the sabbath	Neh 13:15	1869
for the *t* of lesser cattle	Is 7:25	4823
of *t* down, and of perplexity by	Is 22:5	4001
as your *t* is upon the poor	Amos 5:11	1318

TREASON

his *t* that he wrought, are they	1Kin 16:20	7195
rent her clothes, and cried, *T*	2Kin 11:14	7195
her clothes, and cried, *T, T*	2Kin 11:14	7195
rent her clothes, and said, *T*	2Chr 23:13	7195
her clothes, and said, *T, T*	2Chr 23:13	7195

TREASURE

hath given you *t* in your sacks	Gen 43:23	4301
they built for Pharaoh *t* cities	Ex 1:11	4543
t unto me above all people	Ex 19:5	
shall open unto thee his good *t*	Deut 28:12	214
to the *t* of the house of the LORD	1Chr 29:8	214
unto the *t* of the work threescore	Ezr 2:69	214
search made in the king's *t* house	Ezr 5:17	1596
it out of the king's *t* house	Ezr 7:20	1596
to the *t* a thousand drams of gold	Neh 7:71	214
of the fathers gave to the *t* of	Neh 7:71	214
to the chambers, into the *t* house	Neh 10:38	214
belly thou fillest with thy hid *t*	Ps 17:14	
and Israel for his peculiar *t*	Ps 135:4	
house of the righteous is much *t*	Prov 15:6	2633
the fear of the LORD than great *t*	Prov 15:16	214
There is *t* to be desired and oil	Prov 21:20	214
gold, and the peculiar *t* of kings	Eccl 2:8	
the fear of the LORD is his *t*	Is 33:6	214
they have taken the *t* and precious	Eze 22:25	2633
into the *t* house of his god	Dan 1:2	214
he shall spoil the *t* of all	Hos 13:15	214
For where your *t* is, there	Mt 6:21	2344
A good man out of the good *t* of	Mt 12:35	2344
evil *t* bringeth forth evil things	Mt 12:35	2344
is like unto *t* hid in a field	Mt 13:44	2344
forth out of his *t* things new	Mt 13:52	2344
and thou shalt have *t* in heaven	Mt 19:21	2344
and thou shalt have *t* in heaven	Mk 10:21	2344
A good man out of the good *t* of	Lk 6:45	2344
t of his heart bringeth forth	Lk 6:45	2344
he that layeth up *t* for himself	Lk 12:21	2343
a *t* in the heavens that faileth	Lk 12:33	2344
For where your *t* is, there will	Lk 12:34	2344
and thou shalt have *t* in heaven	Lk 18:22	2344
who had the charge of all her *t*	Acts 8:27	1047
But we have this *t* in earthen	2Cor 4:7	2344
Ye have heaped *t* together for the	Jas 5:3	2343

TREASURED

it shall not be *t* nor laid up	Is 23:18	686

TREASURER

by the hand of Mithredath the *t*	Ezr 1:8	1489
hosts, Go, get thee unto this *t*	Is 22:15	5532

TREASURERS

the *t* which are beyond the river	Ezr 7:21	1490
I made *t* over the treasuries,	Neh 13:13	686
the captains, the judges, the *t*	Dan 3:2	1411
and captains, the judges, the *t*	Dan 3:3	1411

TREASURES

with me, and sealed up among my *t*	Deut 32:34	214
the seas, and of *t* hid in the sand	Deut 33:19	8226
did he put among the *t* of the	1Kin 7:51	214
he took away the *t* of the house	1Kin 14:26	214
the *t* of the king's house	1Kin 14:26	214
in the *t* of the house of the LORD	1Kin 15:18	214
the *t* of the king's house, and	1Kin 15:18	214
in the *t* of the house of the LORD	2Kin 12:18	214
in the *t* of the king's house, and	2Kin 14:14	214
in the *t* of the king's house, and	2Kin 16:8	214
in the *t* of the king's house	2Kin 18:15	214
and all that was found in his *t*	2Kin 20:13	214
there is nothing among my *t* that	2Kin 20:15	214
the *t* of the house of the LORD	2Kin 24:13	214
the *t* of the king's house, and cut	2Kin 24:13	214
over the *t* of the house of God	1Chr 26:20	214
over the *t* of the dedicated	1Chr 26:20	214
which were over the *t* of the	1Chr 26:22	214
son of Moses, was ruler of the *t*	1Chr 26:24	214
all the *t* of the dedicated things	1Chr 26:26	214
over the king's *t* was Azmaveth	1Chr 27:25	214
put he among the *t* of the house	2Chr 5:1	214
any matter, or concerning the *t*	2Chr 8:15	214
took away the *t* of the house of	2Chr 12:9	214
the *t* of the king's house	2Chr 12:9	214
gold out of the *t* of the house of	2Chr 16:2	214
the *t* of the king's house, the	2Chr 25:24	214
the *t* of the house of the LORD,	2Chr 36:18	214
the *t* of the king, and of his	2Chr 36:18	214
where the *t* were laid up in	Ezr 6:1	1596
over the chambers for the *t*	Neh 12:44	214
and dig for it more than for hid *t*	Job 3:21	4301
entered into the *t* of the snow	Job 38:22	214
hast thou seen the *t* of the hail	Job 38:22	214
and searchest for her as for hid *t*	Prov 2:4	4301
and I will fill their *t*	Prov 8:21	214
T of wickedness profit nothing	Prov 10:2	214
The getting of *t* by a lying	Prov 21:6	214
is there any end of their *t*	Is 2:7	214
people, and have robbed their *t*	Is 10:13	6259
their *t* upon the bunches of	Is 30:6	214
and all that was found in his *t*	Is 39:2	214
there is nothing among my *t* that	Is 39:4	214
will give thee the *t* of darkness	Is 45:3	214
forth the wind out of his *t*	Jer 10:13	214
thy *t* will I give to the spoil	Jer 15:13	214
all thy *t* to the spoil, and thy	Jer 17:3	214
all the *t* of the kings of Judah	Jer 20:5	214
for we have *t* in the field, of	Jer 41:8	4301
trusted in thy works and in thy *t*	Jer 48:7	214
that trusted in her *t*, saying,	Jer 49:4	214
a sword is upon her *t*	Jer 50:37	214
upon many waters, abundant in *t*	Jer 51:13	214
forth the wind out of his *t*	Jer 51:16	214
gotten gold and silver into thy *t*	Eze 28:4	214
have power over the *t* of gold	Dan 11:43	4362
Are there yet the *t* of wickedness	Mic 6:10	214
and when they had opened their *t*	Mt 2:11	2344
up for yourselves *t* upon earth	Mt 6:19	2344
lay up for yourselves *t* in heaven	Mt 6:20	2344
whom are hid all the *t* of wisdom	Col 2:3	2344
riches than the *t* in Egypt	Heb 11:26	2344

TREASUREST

impenitent heart *t* up unto	Rom 2:5	2343

TREASURIES

chambers and *t* of the house of God	1Chr 9:26	214
of the *t* thereof, and of the upper	1Chr 28:11	1597
of the *t* of the house of God, and	1Chr 28:12	214
of the *t* of the dedicated things	1Chr 28:12	214
and he made himself *t* for silver	2Chr 32:27	214
new wine and the oil unto the *t*	Neh 13:12	214
And I made treasurers over the *t*	Neh 13:13	214
to bring it into the king's *t*	Est 3:9	1595
pay to the king's *t* for the Jews	Est 4:7	1595
he bringeth the wind out of his *t*	Ps 135:7	214

TREASURY

shall come into the *t* of the LORD	Josh 6:19	214
they put into the *t* of the house	Josh 6:24	214
the house of the king under the *t*	Jer 38:11	214
lawful for to put them into the *t*	Mt 27:6	2878
And Jesus sat over against the *t*	Mk 12:41	1049
the people cast money into the *t*	Mk 12:41	1049
they which have cast into the *t*	Mk 12:43	1049
casting their gifts into the *t*	Lk 21:1	1049
These words spake Jesus in the *t*	Jn 8:20	1049

TREATISE

The former *t* have I made, O	Acts 1:1	3056

TREE

the fruit *t* yielding fruit after	Gen 1:11	6086
the *t* yielding fruit, whose seed	Gen 1:12	6086
face of all the earth, and every *t*	Gen 1:29	6086
is the fruit of a *t* yielding seed	Gen 1:29	6086
t that is pleasant to the sight	Gen 2:9	6086
the *t* of life also in the midst	Gen 2:9	6086
the *t* of knowledge of good and	Gen 2:9	6086
Of every *t* of the garden thou	Gen 2:16	6086
But of the *t* of the knowledge of	Gen 2:17	6086
not eat of every *t* of the garden	Gen 3:1	6086
But of the fruit of the *t* which	Gen 3:3	6086
saw that the *t* was good for food	Gen 3:6	6086
a *t* to be desired to make one	Gen 3:6	6086
Hast thou eaten of the *t*, whereof	Gen 3:11	6086
be with me, she gave me of the *t*	Gen 3:12	6086
thy wife, and hast eaten of the *t*	Gen 3:17	6086
and take also of the *t* of life	Gen 3:22	6086
to keep the way of the *t* of life	Gen 3:24	6086
and rest yourselves under the *t*	Gen 18:4	6086
and he stood by them under the *t*	Gen 18:8	6086
and of the hazel and chesnut *t*	Gen 30:37	
thee, and shall hang thee on a *t*	Gen 40:19	6086
brake every *t* of the field	Ex 9:25	6086
shall eat every *t* which groweth	Ex 10:5	6086
and the LORD shewed him a *t*	Ex 15:25	6086
land, or of the fruit of the *t*	Lev 27:30	6086
that is made of the vine *t*	Num 6:4	
the hills, and under every green *t*	Deut 12:2	6086
with the axe to cut down the *t*	Deut 19:5	6086
not cut them down (for the *t* of	Deut 20:19	6086
to death, and thou hang him on a *t*	Deut 21:22	6086
not remain all night upon the *t*	Deut 21:23	6086
before thee in the way in any *t*	Deut 22:6	6086
When thou beatest thine olive *t*	Deut 24:20	
he hanged on a *t* until eventide	Josh 8:29	6086
take his carcase down from the *t*	Josh 8:29	6086
palm *t* of Deborah between Ramah	Judg 4:5	
and they said unto the olive *t*	Judg 9:8	
But the olive *t* said unto them,	Judg 9:9	
And the trees said to the fig *t*	Judg 9:10	6086
But the fig *t* said unto them,	Judg 9:11	6086
pomegranate *t* which is in Migron	1Sa 14:2	
in Gibeah under a *t* in Ramah	1Sa 22:6	815
buried them under a *t* at Jabesh	1Sa 31:13	815
under his vine and under his fig *t*	1Kin 4:25	
from the cedar *t* that is in	1Kin 4:33	6086
he made two cherubims of olive *t*	1Kin 6:23	6086
oracle he made doors of olive *t*	1Kin 6:31	6086
two doors also were of olive *t*	1Kin 6:32	6086
of the temple posts of olive *t*	1Kin 6:33	6086
And the two doors were of fir *t*	1Kin 6:34	6086
high hill, and under every green *t*	1Kin 14:23	6086
and sat down under a juniper *t*	1Kin 19:4	
he lay and slept under a juniper *t*	1Kin 19:5	
city, and shall fell every good *t*	2Kin 3:19	6086
the hills, and under every green *t*	2Kin 16:4	6086
high hill, and under every green *t*	2Kin 17:10	6086
vine, and every one of his fig *t*	2Kin 18:31	
house he cieled with fir *t*	2Chr 3:5	6086
the hills, and under every green *t*	2Chr 28:4	6086
they were both hanged on a *t*	Est 2:23	6086
For there is hope of a *t*, if it	Job 14:7	6086
hope hath he removed like a *t*	Job 19:10	6086
wickedness shall be broken as a *t*	Job 24:20	6086
he shall be like a *t* planted by	Ps 1:3	6086
himself like a green bay *t*	Ps 37:35	
green olive *t* in the house of God	Ps 52:8	
shall flourish like the palm *t*	Ps 92:12	
She is a *t* of life to them that	Prov 3:18	6086
of the righteous is a *t* of life	Prov 11:30	6086
desire cometh, it is a *t* of life	Prov 13:12	6086
A wholesome tongue is a *t* of life	Prov 15:4	
Whoso keepeth the fig *t* shall eat	Prov 27:18	
if the *t* fall toward the south,	Eccl 11:3	6086
in the place where the *t* falleth	Eccl 11:3	6086
the almond *t* shall flourish, and	Eccl 12:5	
As the apple *t* among the trees of	Song 2:3	6086
The fig *t* putteth forth her green	Song 2:13	
thy stature is like to a palm *t*	Song 7:7	
said, I will go up to the palm *t*	Song 7:8	
raised thee up under the apple *t*	Song 8:5	
as a teil *t*, and as an oak, whose	Is 6:13	
it, as the shaking of an olive *t*	Is 17:6	
be as the shaking of an olive *t*	Is 24:13	
as a falling fig from the fig *t*	Is 34:4	
vine, and every one of his fig *t*	Is 36:16	
chooseth a *t* that will not rot	Is 40:20	6086
the cedar, the shittah *t*, and the	Is 41:19	6086
t, and the myrtle, and the oil *t*	Is 41:19	6086
will set in the desert the fir *t*	Is 41:19	

the pine, and the box *t* together	Is 41:19	
I fall down to the stock of a *t*	Is 44:19	6086
O forest, and every *t* therein	Is 44:23	6086
the thorn shall come up the fir *t*	Is 55:13	
brier shall come up the myrtle *t*	Is 55:13	
eunuch say, Behold, I am a dry *t*	Is 56:3	6086
with idols under every green *t*	Is 57:5	6086
shall come unto thee, the fir *t*	Is 60:13	
thee, the fir *t*, the pine *t*	Is 60:13	
for as the days of a *t* are the	Is 65:22	6086
gardens behind one *t* in the midst	Is 66:17	
said, I see a rod of an almond *t*	Jer 1:11	
every green *t* thou wanderest	Jer 2:20	6086
mountain and under every green *t*	Jer 3:6	6086
the strangers under every green *t*	Jer 3:13	6086
the vine, nor figs on the fig *t*	Jer 8:13	
one cutteth a *t* out of the forest	Jer 10:3	6086
They are upright as the palm *t*	Jer 10:5	
called thy name, A green olive *t*	Jer 11:16	
Let us destroy the *t* with the	Jer 11:19	6086
For he shall be as a *t* planted by	Jer 17:8	6086
mountains, and under every green *t*	Eze 6:13	6086
is the vine *t* more than any *t*	Eze 15:2	6086
As the vine *t* among the trees of	Eze 15:6	6086
waters, and set it as a willow *t*	Eze 17:5	
LORD have brought down the high *t*	Eze 17:24	6086
have exalted the low *t*	Eze 17:24	6086
t, have dried up the green *t*	Eze 17:24	6086
have made the dry *t* to flourish	Eze 17:24	6086
devour every green *t* in thee	Eze 20:47	6086
and every dry *t*	Eze 20:47	6086
the rod of my son, as every *t*	Eze 21:10	6086
nor any *t* in the garden of God	Eze 31:8	6086
the *t* of the field shall yield	Eze 34:27	6086
will multiply the fruit of the *t*	Eze 36:30	6086
so that a palm *t* was between a	Eze 41:18	
toward the palm *t* on the one side	Eze 41:19	
the palm *t* on the other side	Eze 41:19	
behold a *t* in the midst of the	Dan 4:10	363
The *t* grew, and was strong, and the	Dan 4:11	363
and said thus, Hew down the *t*	Dan 4:14	363
The *t* that thou sawest, which	Dan 4:20	363
heaven, and saying, Hew the *t* down	Dan 4:23	363
to leave the stump of the *t* roots	Dan 4:26	363
in the fig *t* at her first time	Hos 9:10	
beauty shall be as the olive *t*	Hos 14:6	
I am like a green fir *t*	Hos 14:8	
my vine waste, and barked my fig *t*	Joel 1:7	
up, and the fig *t* languisheth	Joel 1:12	
pomegranate *t*, the palm *t* also	Joel 1:12	
also, and the apple *t*	Joel 1:12	
for the *t* beareth her fruit, the	Joel 2:22	
beareth her fruit, the fig *t*	Joel 2:22	6086
under his vine and under his fig *t*	Mic 4:4	
Although the fig *t* shall not	Hab 3:17	
as yet the vine, and the fig *t*	Hag 2:19	
the pomegranate, and the olive *t*	Hag 2:19	6086
under the vine and under the fig *t*	Zec 3:10	
Howl, fir *t*	Zec 11:2	
therefore every *t* which bringeth	Mt 3:10	1186
Even so every good *t* bringeth	Mt 7:17	1186
but a corrupt *t* bringeth forth	Mt 7:17	1186
A good *t* cannot bring forth evil	Mt 7:18	1186
neither can a corrupt *t* bring	Mt 7:18	1186
Every *t* that bringeth not forth	Mt 7:19	1186
Either make the *t* good, and his	Mt 12:33	1186
or else make the *t* corrupt	Mt 12:33	1186
for the *t* is known by his fruit	Mt 12:33	1186
among herbs, and becometh a *t*	Mt 13:32	1186
And when he saw a fig *t* in the way	Mt 21:19	4808
presently the fig *t* withered away	Mt 21:19	4808
soon is the fig *t* withered away	Mt 21:20	4808
this which is done to the fig *t*	Mt 21:21	4808
Now learn a parable of the fig *t*	Mt 24:32	4808
seeing a fig *t* afar off having	Mk 11:13	4808
they saw the fig *t* dried up from	Mk 11:20	4808
the fig *t* which thou cursedst is	Mk 11:21	4808
Now learn a parable of the fig *t*	Mk 13:28	4808
every *t* therefore which bringeth	Lk 3:9	1186
For a good *t* bringeth not forth	Lk 6:43	1186
corrupt *t* bring forth good fruit	Lk 6:43	1186
For every *t* is known by his own	Lk 6:44	1186
a fig *t* planted in his vineyard	Lk 13:6	4808
come seeking fruit on this fig *t*	Lk 13:7	4808
and it grew, and waxed a great *t*	Lk 13:19	1186
ye might say unto this sycamine *t*	Lk 17:6	
up into a sycomore *t* to see him	Lk 19:4	4809
Behold the fig *t*, and all the	Lk 21:29	4808
they do these things in a green *t*	Lk 23:31	3586
when thou wast under the fig *t*	Jn 1:48	4808
thee, I saw thee under the fig *t*	Jn 1:50	4808

whom ye slew and hanged on a *t*	Acts 5:30	3586
whom they slew and hanged on a *t*	Acts 10:39	3586
they took him down from the *t*	Acts 13:29	3586
and thou, being a wild olive *t*	Rom 11:17	65
root and fatness of the olive *t*	Rom 11:17	
olive *t* which is wild by nature	Rom 11:24	65
to nature into a good olive *t*	Rom 11:24	2565
be graffed into their own olive *t*	Rom 11:24	
is every one that hangeth on a *t*	Gal 3:13	3586
Can the fig *t*, my brethren, bear	Jas 3:12	4808
our sins in his own body on the *t*	1Pet 2:24	3586
I give to eat of the *t* of life	Rev 2:7	3586
even as a fig *t* casteth her	Rev 6:13	4808
nor on the sea, nor on any *t*	Rev 7:1	1186
any green thing, neither any *t*	Rev 9:4	1186
river, was there the *t* of life	Rev 22:2	3586
the leaves of the *t* were for the	Rev 22:2	3586
may have right to the *t* of life	Rev 22:14	3586

TREES

the fruit of the *t* of the garden	Gen 3:2	6086
God amongst the *t* of the garden	Gen 3:8	6086
all the *t* that were in the field,	Gen 23:17	6086
all the fruit of the *t* which the	Ex 10:15	6086
not any green thing in the *t*	Ex 10:15	6086
and threescore and ten palm *t*	Ex 15:27	
planted all manner of *t* for food	Lev 19:23	6086
first day the boughs of goodly *t*	Lev 23:40	6086
branches of palm *t*	Lev 23:40	
and the boughs of thick *t*	Lev 23:40	
the *t* of the field shall yield	Lev 26:4	6086
neither shall the *t* of the land	Lev 26:20	6086
as the *t* of lign aloes which the	Num 24:6	
as cedar *t* beside the waters	Num 24:6	
and threescore and ten palm *t*	Num 33:9	
not, vineyards and olive *t*	Deut 6:11	
and barley, and vines, and fig *t*	Deut 8:8	
not plant thee a grove of any *t*	Deut 16:21	6086
the *t* thereof by forcing an ax	Deut 20:19	6086
Only the *t* which thou knowest	Deut 20:20	6086
that they be not *t* for meat	Deut 20:20	6086
Thou shalt have olive *t*	Deut 28:40	
All thy *t* and fruit of thy land	Deut 28:42	6086
of Jericho, the city of palm *t*	Deut 34:3	
them, and hanged them on five *t*	Josh 10:26	6086
upon the *t* until the evening	Josh 10:26	6086
and they took them down off the *t*	Josh 10:27	6086
t with the children of Judah into	Judg 1:16	
and possessed the city of palm *t*	Judg 3:13	
The *t* went forth on a time to	Judg 9:8	6086
and go to be promoted over the *t*	Judg 9:9	6086
the *t* said to the fig tree, Come	Judg 9:10	6086
and go to be promoted over the *t*	Judg 9:11	6086
Then said the *t* unto the vine	Judg 9:12	6086
and go to be promoted over the *t*	Judg 9:13	6086
said all the *t* unto the bramble	Judg 9:14	6086
And the bramble said unto the *t*	Judg 9:15	6086
and cut down a bough from the *t*	Judg 9:48	6086
messengers to David, and cedar *t*	2Sa 5:11	6086
them over against the mulberry *t*	2Sa 5:23	
in the tops of the mulberry *t*	2Sa 5:24	
And he spake of *t*, from the cedar	1Kin 4:33	6086
hew me cedar *t* out of Lebanon	1Kin 5:6	
So Hiram gave Solomon cedar *t*	1Kin 5:10	6086
fir *t* according to all his desire	1Kin 5:10	6086
figures of cherubims and palm *t*	1Kin 6:29	
carvings of cherubims and palm *t*	1Kin 6:32	
the cherubims, and upon the palm *t*	1Kin 6:32	
thereon cherubims and palm *t*	1Kin 6:35	
cherubims, lions, and palm *t*	1Kin 7:36	
Solomon with cedar *t* and fir *t*	1Kin 9:11	6086
Ophir great plenty of almug *t*	1Kin 10:11	6086
the king made of the almug *t*	1Kin 10:12	6086
there came no such almug *t*	1Kin 10:12	6086
sycomore *t* that are in the vale	1Kin 10:27	
water, and felled all the good *t*	2Kin 3:25	6086
cut down the tall cedar *t* thereof	2Kin 19:23	
and the choice fir *t* thereof	2Kin 19:23	
them over against the mulberry *t*	1Chr 14:14	
in the tops of the mulberry *t*	1Chr 14:15	
Then shall the *t* of the wood sing	1Chr 16:33	6086
Also cedar *t* in abundance	1Chr 22:4	6086
And over the olive *t* and the	1Chr 27:28	
the sycomore *t* that were in the	1Chr 27:28	
cedar *t* made he as the sycomore	2Chr 1:15	
t that are in the vale for	2Chr 1:15	
Send me also cedar *t*	2Chr 2:8	6086
fir *t*, and algum *t*	2Chr 2:8	
fine gold, and set thereon palm *t*	2Chr 3:5	
gold from Ophir, brought algum *t*	2Chr 9:10	6086
the king made of the algum *t*	2Chr 9:11	6086

cedar *t* made he as the sycomore	2Chr 9:27	
t that are in the low plains in	2Chr 9:27	
to Jericho, the city of palm *t*	2Chr 28:15	
to bring cedar *t* from Lebanon to	Ezr 3:7	6086
branches, and branches of thick *t*	Neh 8:15	6086
and fruit *t* in abundance	Neh 9:25	6086
firstfruits of all fruit of all *t*	Neh 10:35	6086
and the fruit of all manner of *t*	Neh 10:37	6086
He lieth under the shady *t*	Job 40:21	
The shady *t* cover him with their	Job 40:22	
lifted up axes upon the thick *t*	Ps 74:5	6086
and their sycomore *t* with frost	Ps 78:47	
then shall all the *t* of the wood	Ps 96:12	6086
The *t* of the LORD are full of sap	Ps 104:16	6086
stork, the fir *t* are her house	Ps 104:17	
their vines also and their fig *t*	Ps 105:33	
brake the *t* of their coasts	Ps 105:33	6086
fruitful *t*, and all cedars	Ps 148:9	6086
I planted *t* in them of all kind	Eccl 2:5	6086
the wood that bringeth forth *t*	Eccl 2:6	6086
tree among the *t* of the wood	Song 2:3	6086
with all *t* of frankincense	Song 4:14	6086
as the *t* of the wood are moved	Is 7:2	6086
the rest of the *t* of his forest	Is 10:19	6086
the fir *t* rejoice at thee, and the	Is 14:8	
and the choice fir *t* thereof	Is 37:24	
himself among the *t* of the forest	Is 44:14	6086
all the *t* of the field shall clap	Is 55:12	6086
be called *t* of righteousness	Is 61:3	352
eat up thy vines and thy fig *t*	Jer 5:17	
LORD of hosts said, Hew ye down *t*	Jer 6:6	6097
upon the *t* of the field, and upon	Jer 7:20	6086
the green *t* upon the high hills	Jer 17:2	6086
is among the *t* of the forest	Eze 15:2	6086
tree among the *t* of the forest	Eze 15:6	6086
all the *t* of the field shall know	Eze 17:24	6086
high hill, and all the thick *t*	Eze 20:28	6086
thy ship boards of fir *t* of Senir	Eze 27:5	
unto all the *t* of the field	Eze 31:4	6086
above all the *t* of the field	Eze 31:5	6086
the fir *t* were not like his	Eze 31:8	
the chesnut *t* were not like his	Eze 31:8	
so that all the *t* of Eden	Eze 31:9	6086
t by the waters exalt themselves	Eze 31:14	6086
neither their *t* stand up in their	Eze 31:14	352
all the *t* of the field fainted	Eze 31:15	6086
and all the *t* of Eden, the choice	Eze 31:16	6086
in greatness among the *t* of Eden	Eze 31:18	6086
t of Eden unto the nether parts	Eze 31:18	6086
and upon each post were palm *t*	Eze 40:16	
and their arches, and their palm *t*	Eze 40:22	
and it had palm *t*, one on this	Eze 40:26	
palm *t* were upon the posts	Eze 40:31	
palm *t* were upon the posts	Eze 40:34	
palm *t* were upon the posts	Eze 40:37	
was made with cherubims and palm *t*	Eze 41:18	
were cherubims and palm *t* made	Eze 41:20	
the temple, cherubims and palm *t*	Eze 41:25	
palm *t* on the one side and on the	Eze 41:26	
were very many *t* on the one side	Eze 47:7	6086
side, shall grow all *t* for meat	Eze 47:12	6086
destroy their vines and her fig *t*	Hos 2:12	
tree, even all the *t* of the field	Joel 1:12	6086
burned all the *t* of the field	Joel 1:19	6086
and your vineyards and your fig *t*	Amos 4:9	
and your olive *t* increased	Amos 4:9	
the fir *t* shall be terribly	Nah 2:3	
fig *t* with the firstripe figs	Nah 3:12	
myrtle *t* that were in the bottom	Zec 1:8	
stood among the myrtle *t* answered	Zec 1:10	
that stood among the myrtle *t*	Zec 1:11	
And two olive *t* by it, one upon	Zec 4:3	
What are these two olive *t* upon	Zec 4:11	
ax is laid unto the root of the *t*	Mt 3:10	1186
cut down branches from the *t*	Mt 21:8	1186
up, and said, I see men as *t*	Mk 8:24	1186
cut down branches off the *t*	Mk 11:8	1186
is laid unto the root of the *t*	Lk 3:9	1186
Behold the fig tree, and all the	Lk 21:29	1186
Took branches of palm *t*, and went	Jn 12:13	
t whose fruit withereth, without	Jude 12	1186
earth, neither the sea, nor the *t*	Rev 7:3	1186
the third part of *t* was burnt up	Rev 8:7	1186
These are the two olive *t*	Rev 11:4	

TREMBLE

hear report of thee, and shall *t*	Deut 2:25	7264
faint, fear not, and do not *t*	Deut 20:3	2648
lord, and of those that *t* at the	Ezr 10:3	2730
place, and the pillars thereof *t*	Job 9:6	6426
The pillars of heaven *t*, and are	Job 26:11	7322

Thou hast made the earth to *t* .... Ps 60:2   7493
let the people *t* .... Ps 99:1   7264
T, thou earth, at the presence of .... Ps 114:7   2342
the keepers of the house shall *t* .... Eccl 12:3   2111
and the hills did *t*, and their .... Is 5:25   7264
the man that made the earth to *t* .... Is 14:16   7264
T, ye women that are at ease .... Is 32:11   2729
the nations may *t* at thy presence .... Is 64:2   7264
the LORD, ye that *t* at his word .... Is 66:5   2730
will ye not *t* at my presence, ... Jer 5:22   2342
at his wrath the earth shall *t* .... Jer 10:10   7493
t for all the goodness and for all .... Jer 33:9   7264
And the land shall *t* and sorrow .... Jer 51:29   7493
shall *t* at every moment, and be .... Eze 26:16   2729
Now shall the isles *t* in the day .... Eze 26:18   2729
they shall *t* at every moment, ... Eze 32:10   2729
dominion of my kingdom men *t* .... Dan 6:26   2112
children shall *t* from the west .... Hos 11:10   2729
They shall *t* as a bird out of .... Hos 11:11   2729
all the inhabitants of the land *t* .... Joel 2:1   7264
the heavens shall *t* .... Joel 2:10   7493
Shall not the land *t* for this .... Amos 8:8   7264
of the land of Midian did *t* .... Hab 3:7   7264
the devils also believe, and *t* .... Jas 2:19   *5425*

TREMBLED
Isaac *t* very exceedingly, and said .... Gen 27:33   2729
the people that was in the camp *t* .... Ex 19:16   2729
of the field of Edom, the earth *t* .... Judg 5:4   7493
for his heart *t* for the ark of 1Sa 4:13   2730
and the spoilers, they also *t* 1Sa 14:15   2729
of the town *t* at his coming 1Sa 16:4   2729
afraid, and his heart greatly *t* 1Sa 28:5   2729
Then the earth shook and *t* 2Sa 22:8   7493
unto me every one that *t* at the .... Ezr 9:4   2730
Then the earth shook and *t* .... Ps 18:7   7493
the earth *t* and shook .... Ps 77:18   7264
the earth saw, and *t* .... Ps 97:4   2342
the mountains, and, lo, they *t* .... Jer 4:24   7493
the whole land *t* at the sound of .... Jer 8:16   7493
people, nations, and languages, *t* .... Dan 5:19   2112
The mountains saw thee, and they *t* ..... Hab 3:10   2342
When I heard, my belly *t* .... Hab 3:16   7364
I *t* in myself, that I might rest .... Hab 3:16   7264
for they *t* and were amazed .... Mk 16:8   *2192,5156*
Then Moses *t*, and durst not .... Acts 7:32   *1790,1096*
and judgment to come, Felix *t* .... Acts 24:25   *1719,1096*

TREMBLETH
At this also my heart *t*, and is .... Job 37:1   2729
He looketh on the earth, and it *t* .... Ps 104:32   7460
My flesh *t* for fear of thee..................... Ps 119:120   5568
contrite spirit, and *t* at my word .... Is 66:2   2730

TREMBLING
t shall take hold upon them.................... Ex 15:15   7460
shall give thee there a *t* heart .... Deut 28:65   7268
and all the people followed him *t* 1Sa 13:7   2729
there was *t* in the host, in the 1Sa 14:15   2731
so it was a very great *t* 1Sa 14:15   2731
t because of this matter, and for .... Ezr 10:9   7460
Fear came upon me, and *t*, which .... Job 4:14   7460
t taketh hold on my flesh....................... Job 21:6   6427
LORD with fear, and rejoice with *t* .... Ps 2:11   7460
t are come upon me, and horror .... Ps 55:5   7460
drunken the dregs of the cup of *t* .... Is 51:17   8653
out of thine hand the cup of *t* .... Is 51:22   8653
We have heard a voice of *t* .... Jer 30:5   2731
and drink thy water with *t* .... Eze 12:18   7269
shall clothe themselves with *t* .... Eze 26:16   2731
this word unto me, I stood *t* .... Dan 10:11   7460
When Ephraim spake *t*, he exalted .... Hos 13:1   7578
I will make Jerusalem a cup of *t* .... Zec 12:2   7478
But the woman fearing and *t* .... Mk 5:33   *5141*
that she was not hid, she came *t* .... Lk 8:47   *5141*
And he *t* and astonished said, Lord, ... Acts 9:6   *5141*
a light, and sprang in, and came *t*.. Acts 16:29   *1096,1790*
and in fear, and in much *t* 1Cor 2:3   *5156*
with fear and *t* ye received him 2Cor 7:15   *5156*
to the flesh, with fear and *t*................... Eph 6:5   *5156*
your own salvation with fear and *t*........ Phil 2:12   *5156*

TRENCH
and he came to the *t*, as the host........... 1Sa 17:20   4570
and Saul lay in the *t*, and the.................. 1Sa 26:5   4570
Saul lay sleeping within the *t*.................. 1Sa 26:7   4570
the city, and it stood in the *t* 2Sa 20:15   2426
he made a *t* about the altar, as 1Kin 18:32   8585
he filled the *t* also with water 1Kin 18:35   8565
up the water that was in the *t* 1Kin 18:38   8565
enemies shall cast a *t* about thee........... Lk 19:43   *5482*

TRESPASS
and said to Laban, What is my *t* .... Gen 31:36   6588
the *t* of thy brethren, and their .... Gen 50:17   6588
forgive the *t* of the servants of .... Gen 50:17   6588
For all manner of *t*, whether it .... Ex 22:9   6588
he shall bring his *t* offering .... Lev 5:6   817
then he shall bring for his *t*.................... Lev 5:7   817
If a soul commit a *t*, and sin .... Lev 5:15   4604
his *t* unto the LORD a ram without.......... Lev 5:15   817
the sanctuary, for a *t* offering................ Lev 5:15   817
with the ram of the *t* offering .... Lev 5:16   817
for a *t* offering, unto the priest.............. Lev 5:18   817
It is a *t* offering .... Lev 5:19   817
commit a *t* against the LORD, and .... Lev 6:2   4604
in the day of his *t* offering .... Lev 6:5   819
he shall bring his *t* offering .... Lev 6:6   817
for a *t* offering, unto the priest .... Lev 6:6   817
offering, and as the *t* offering .... Lev 6:17   817
this is the law of the *t* offering .... Lev 7:1   817
shall they kill the *t* offering .... Lev 7:2   817
it is a *t* offering .... Lev 7:5   817
offering is, so is the *t* offering .... Lev 7:7   817
of the *t* offering, and of the .... Lev 7:37   817
and offer him for a *t* offering .... Lev 14:12   817
priest's, so is the *t* offering .... Lev 14:13   817
of the blood of the *t* offering .... Lev 14:14   817
upon the blood of the *t* offering .... Lev 14:17   817
lamb for a *t* offering to be waved .... Lev 14:21   817
take the lamb of the *t* offering............... Lev 14:24   817
kill the lamb of the *t* offering................. Lev 14:25   817
of the blood of the *t* offering .... Lev 14:25   817
of the blood of the *t* offering .... Lev 14:28   817
he shall bring his *t* offering .... Lev 19:21   817
even a ram for a *t* offering .... Lev 19:21   817
for him with the ram of the *t*................. Lev 19:22   817
them to bear the iniquity of *t* .... Lev 22:16   819
fathers, with their *t* which they .... Lev 26:40   4604
to do a *t* against the LORD, and.............. Num 5:6   4604
he shall recompense his *t* with .... Num 5:7   817
kinsman to recompense the *t* unto .... Num 5:8   817
let the *t* be recompensed unto the .... Num 5:8   817
aside, and commit a *t* against him,......... Num 5:12   4604
have done *t* against her husband,........... Num 5:27   4604
the first year for a *t* offering.................. Num 6:12   817
every *t* offering of theirs, which .... Num 18:9   817
to commit *t* against the LORD in .... Num 31:16   4604
a *t* in the accursed thing .... Josh 7:1   4604
What *t* is this that ye have..................... Josh 22:16   4604
commit a *t* in the accursed thing .... Josh 22:20   4604
committed this *t* against the LORD .... Josh 22:31   4604
any wise return him a *t* offering 1Sa 6:3   817
What shall be the *t* offering.................... 1Sa 6:4   817
ye return him for a *t* offering 1Sa 6:8   817
for a *t* offering unto the LORD 1Sa 6:17   817
forgive the *t* of thine handmaid 1Sa 25:28   6588
If any man *t* against his.......................... 1Kin 8:31   2398
The *t* money and sin money was not 2Kin 12:16   817
will he be a cause of *t* to Israel.............. 1Chr 21:3   819
that they *t* not against the LORD............. 2Chr 19:10   816
this do, and ye shall not *t* 2Chr 19:10   816
and Jerusalem for this their *t* 2Chr 24:18   819
add more to our sins and to our *t*........... 2Chr 28:13   819
for our *t* is great, and there is 2Chr 28:13   819
he *t* yet more against the LORD............... 2Chr 28:22   4603
of him, and all his sin, and his *t* 2Chr 33:19   4604
rulers hath been chief in this *t*.............. Ezr 9:2   4604
our *t* is grown up unto the...................... Ezr 9:6   819
been in a great *t* unto this day .... Ezr 9:7   819
evil deeds, and for our great *t* .... Ezr 9:13   819
to increase the *t* of Israel .... Ezr 10:10   819
a ram of the flock for their *t* .... Ezr 10:19   819
because they have committed a *t* .... Eze 15:8   4604
plead with him there for his *t*................. Eze 17:20   4604
in his *t* that he hath trespassed,............ Eze 18:24   4604
have committed a *t* against me .... Eze 20:27   4604
sin offering and the *t* offering................ Eze 40:39   817
sin offering, and the *t* offering .... Eze 42:13   817
sin offering, and the *t* offering .... Eze 44:29   817
priests shall boil the *t* offering .... Eze 46:20   817
because of their *t* that they have .... Dan 9:7   4604
thy brother shall *t* against thee .... Mt 18:15   *264*
If thy brother *t* against thee .... Lk 17:3   *264*
if he *t* against thee seven times .... Lk 17:4   *264*

TRESPASSED
hath certainly *t* against the LORD .... Lev 5:19   816
trespass which they *t* against me .... Lev 26:40   4604
unto him against whom he hath *t* .... Num 5:7   816
Because ye *t* against me among the .... Deut 32:51   4603
for thou hast *t*...................................... 2Chr 26:18   4603
For our fathers have *t*, and done 2Chr 29:6   4603

which *t* against the Lᴏʀᴅ God of	2Chr 30:7	4603
but Amon *t* more and more	2Chr 33:23	819
We have *t* against our God, and	Ezr 10:2	4603
that he hath *t* against me	Eze 17:20	4604
in his trespass that he hath *t*	Eze 18:24	4604
because they *t* against me	Eze 39:23	4603
whereby they have *t* against me	Eze 39:26	4603
that they have *t* against thee	Dan 9:7	4603
my covenant, and *t* against my law	Hos 8:1	

TRESPASSES

we are before thee in our *t*	Ezr 9:15	819
an one as goeth on still in his *t*	Ps 68:21	817
all their *t* whereby they have	Eze 39:26	4604
For if ye forgive men their *t*	Mt 6:14	*3900*
But if ye forgive not men their *t*	Mt 6:15	*3900*
will your Father forgive your *t*	Mt 6:15	*3900*
not every one his brother their *t*	Mt 18:35	*3900*
in heaven may forgive you your *t*	Mk 11:25	*3900*
which is in heaven forgive your *t*	Mk 11:26	*3900*
not imputing their *t* unto them	2Cor 5:19	*3900*
he quickened, who were dead in *t*	Eph 2:1	*3900*
him, having forgiven you all *t*	Col 2:13	*3900*

TRESPASSING

that he hath done in *t* therein	Lev 6:7	819
against me by *t* grievously	Eze 14:13	4603

TRIAL

laugh at the *t* of the innocent	Job 9:23	4531
Because it is a *t*, and what if the	Eze 21:13	974
How that in a great *t* of	2Cor 8:2	*1382*
others had *t* of cruel mockings and	Heb 11:36	*3984*
That the *t* of your faith, being	1Pet 1:7	*1383*
the fiery *t* which is to try you	1Pet 4:12	

TRIBE

the son of Hur, of the *t* of Judah	Ex 31:2	4294
son of Ahisamach, of the *t* of Dan	Ex 31:6	4294
the son of Hur, of the *t* of Judah	Ex 35:30	4294
son of Ahisamach, of the *t* of Dan	Ex 35:34	4294
of the *t* of Judah, made all that	Ex 38:22	4294
son of Ahisamach, of the *t* of Dan	Ex 38:23	4294
of Dibri, of the *t* of Dan	Lev 24:11	4294
there shall be a man of every *t*	Num 1:4	4294
of the *t* of Reuben	Num 1:5	
of them, even of the *t* of Reuben	Num 1:21	4294
of them, even of the *t* of Simeon	Num 1:23	4294
of them, even of the *t* of Gad	Num 1:25	4294
of them, even of the *t* of Judah	Num 1:27	4294
them, even of the *t* of Issachar	Num 1:29	4294
of them, even of the *t* of Zebulun	Num 1:31	4294
of them, even of the *t* of Ephraim	Num 1:33	4294
them, even of the *t* of Manasseh	Num 1:35	4294
them, even of the *t* of Benjamin	Num 1:37	4294
of them, even of the *t* of Dan	Num 1:39	4294
of them, even of the *t* of Asher	Num 1:41	4294
them, even of the *t* of Naphtali	Num 1:43	4294
the *t* of their fathers were not	Num 1:47	4294
shalt not number the *t* of Levi	Num 1:49	4294
him shall be the *t* of Issachar	Num 2:5	4294
Then the *t* of Zebulun	Num 2:7	4294
by him shall be the *t* of Simeon	Num 2:12	4294
Then the *t* of Gad	Num 2:14	4294
by him shall be the *t* of Manasseh	Num 2:20	4294
Then the *t* of Benjamin	Num 2:22	4294
by him shall be the *t* of Asher	Num 2:27	4294
Then the *t* of Naphtali	Num 2:29	4294
Bring the *t* of Levi near, and	Num 3:6	4294
Cut ye not off the *t* of the	Num 4:18	7626
of Amminadab, of the *t* of Judah	Num 7:12	4294
over the host of the *t* of the	Num 10:15	4294
over the host of the *t* of the	Num 10:16	4294
over the host of the *t* of the	Num 10:19	4294
over the host of the *t* of the	Num 10:20	4294
over the host of the *t* of the	Num 10:23	4294
over the host of the *t* of the	Num 10:24	4294
over the host of the *t* of the	Num 10:26	4294
over the host of the *t* of the	Num 10:27	4294
of every *t* of their fathers shall	Num 13:2	4294
of the *t* of Reuben, Shammua the	Num 13:4	4294
Of the *t* of Simeon, Shaphat the	Num 13:5	4294
Of the *t* of Judah, Caleb the son	Num 13:6	4294
Of the *t* of Issachar, Igal the	Num 13:7	4294
Of the *t* of Ephraim, Oshea the	Num 13:8	4294
Of the *t* of Benjamin, Palti the	Num 13:9	4294
Of the *t* of Zebulun, Gaddiel the	Num 13:10	4294
Of the *t* of Joseph, namely, of	Num 13:11	4294
of the *t* of Manasseh, Gaddi the	Num 13:11	4294
Of the *t* of Dan, Ammiel the son	Num 13:12	4294
Of the *t* of Asher, Sethur the son	Num 13:13	4294
Of the *t* of Naphtali, Nahbi the	Num 13:14	4294
Of the *t* of Gad, Geuel the son of	Num 13:15	4294

brethren also of the *t* of Levi	Num 18:2	4294
the *t* of thy father, bring thou	Num 18:2	7626
Of every *t* a thousand, throughout	Num 31:4	4294
of Israel, a thousand of every *t*	Num 31:5	4294
to the war, a thousand of every *t*	Num 31:6	4294
unto half the *t* of Manasseh the	Num 32:33	7626
the nine tribes, and to the half *t*	Num 34:13	4294
For the *t* of the children of	Num 34:14	4294
the *t* of the children of Gad	Num 34:14	4294
half the *t* of Manasseh have	Num 34:14	4294
the half *t* have received their	Num 34:15	4294
shall take one prince of every *t*	Num 34:18	4294
Of the *t* of Judah, Caleb the son	Num 34:19	4294
of the *t* of the children of	Num 34:20	4294
Of the *t* of Benjamin, Elidad the	Num 34:21	4294
the prince of the *t* of the	Num 34:22	4294
for the *t* of the children of	Num 34:23	4294
the prince of the *t* of the	Num 34:24	4294
the prince of the *t* of the	Num 34:25	4294
the prince of the *t* of the	Num 34:26	4294
the prince of the *t* of the	Num 34:27	4294
the prince of the *t* of the	Num 34:28	4294
the *t* whereunto they are received	Num 36:3	4294
the *t* whereunto they are received	Num 36:4	4294
of the *t* of our fathers	Num 36:4	4294
The *t* of the sons of Joseph hath	Num 36:5	4294
only to the family of the *t* of	Num 36:6	4294
of Israel remove from *t* to *t*	Num 36:7	4294
of the *t* of his fathers	Num 36:7	4294
an inheritance in any *t* of the	Num 36:8	4294
the family of the *t* of her father	Num 36:8	4294
from one *t* to another *t*	Num 36:9	4294
inheritance remained in the *t* of	Num 36:12	4294
twelve men of you, one of a *t*	Deut 1:23	7626
I unto the half *t* of Manasseh	Deut 3:13	7626
the Lᴏʀᴅ separated the *t* of Levi	Deut 10:8	7626
the Levites, and all the *t* of Levi	Deut 18:1	7626
and to the half *t* of Manasseh	Deut 29:8	7626
man, or woman, or family, or *t*	Deut 29:18	7626
and to half the *t* of Manasseh	Josh 1:12	7626
of Israel, out of every *t* a man	Josh 3:12	4294
the people, out of every *t* a man	Josh 4:2	7626
of Israel, out of every *t* a man	Josh 4:4	4294
half the *t* of Manasseh, passed	Josh 4:12	7626
of the *t* of Judah, took of the	Josh 7:1	4294
that the *t* which the Lᴏʀᴅ taketh	Josh 7:14	7626
and the *t* of Judah was taken	Josh 7:16	4294
of the *t* of Judah, was taken	Josh 7:18	4294
and the half *t* of Manasseh	Josh 12:6	7626
and the half *t* of Manasseh,	Josh 13:7	7626
Only unto the *t* of Levi he gave	Josh 13:14	7626
Moses gave unto the *t* of the	Josh 13:15	4294
inheritance unto the *t* of Gad	Josh 13:24	4294
unto the half *t* of Manasseh	Josh 13:29	7626
t of the children of Manasseh by	Josh 13:29	4294
But unto the *t* of Levi Moses gave	Josh 13:33	7626
nine tribes, and for the half *t*	Josh 14:2	4294
an half *t* on the other side	Josh 14:3	4294
the *t* of the children of Judah by	Josh 15:1	4294
of the *t* of the children of Judah	Josh 15:20	4294
the uttermost cities of the *t* of	Josh 15:21	4294
t of the children of Ephraim by	Josh 16:8	4294
also a lot for the *t* of Manasseh	Josh 17:1	4294
among you three men for each *t*	Josh 18:4	7626
half the *t* of Manasseh, have	Josh 18:7	7626
the lot of the *t* of the children	Josh 18:11	4294
Now the cities of the *t* of the	Josh 18:21	4294
even for the *t* of the children of	Josh 19:1	4294
the *t* of the children of Simeon	Josh 19:8	4294
the *t* of the children of Issachar	Josh 19:23	4294
the *t* of the children of Asher	Josh 19:24	4294
of the *t* of the children of Asher	Josh 19:31	4294
the *t* of the children of Naphtali	Josh 19:39	4294
for the *t* of the children of Dan	Josh 19:40	4294
of the *t* of the children of Dan	Josh 19:48	4294
the plain out of the *t* of Reuben	Josh 20:8	4294
in Gilead out of the *t* of Gad	Josh 20:8	4294
Bashan out of the *t* of Manasseh	Josh 20:8	4294
had by lot out of the *t* of Judah	Josh 21:4	4294
Judah, and out of the *t* of Simeon	Josh 21:4	4294
out of the *t* of Benjamin,	Josh 21:4	4294
the families of the *t* of Ephraim	Josh 21:5	4294
Ephraim, and out of the *t* of Dan	Josh 21:5	4294
and out of the half *t* of Manasseh	Josh 21:5	4294
the families of the *t* of Issachar	Josh 21:6	4294
and out of the *t* of Asher	Josh 21:6	4294
out of the *t* of Naphtali, and out	Josh 21:6	4294
out of the half *t* of Manasseh in	Josh 21:6	4294
had out of the *t* of Reuben	Josh 21:7	4294
of Reuben, and out of the *t* of Gad	Josh 21:7	4294
Gad, and out of the *t* of Zebulun	Josh 21:7	4294

T

they gave out of the *t* of the	Josh 21:9	4294
out of the *t* of the children of	Josh 21:9	4294
out of the *t* of Benjamin, Gibeon	Josh 21:17	4294
their lot out of the *t* of Ephraim	Josh 21:20	4294
And out of the *t* of Dan, Eltekeh	Josh 21:23	4294
And out of the half *t* of Manasseh	Josh 21:25	4294
out of the other half *t* of	Josh 21:27	4294
out of the *t* of Issachar, Kishon	Josh 21:28	4294
And out of the *t* of Asher, Mishal	Josh 21:30	4294
out of the *t* of Naphtali, Kedesh	Josh 21:32	4294
Levites, out of the *t* of Zebulun	Josh 21:34	4294
And out of the *t* of Reuben	Josh 21:36	
And out of the *t* of Gad, Ramoth in	Josh 21:38	4294
and the half *t* of Manasseh,	Josh 22:1	4294
Now to the one half of the *t* of	Josh 22:7	7626
the half *t* of Manasseh returned,	Josh 22:9	7626
the half *t* of Manasseh built	Josh 22:10	7626
the half *t* of Manasseh have built	Josh 22:11	7626
Gad, and to the half *t* of Manasseh	Josh 22:13	7626
Gad, and to the half *t* of Manasseh	Josh 22:15	7626
the half *t* of Manasseh answered,	Josh 22:21	7626
in those days the *t* of the	Judg 18:1	7626
or that thou be a priest unto a *t*	Judg 18:19	7626
the *t* of Dan until the day of the	Judg 18:30	7626
men through all the *t* of Benjamin	Judg 20:12	7626
be to day one *t* lacking in Israel	Judg 21:3	7626
There is one *t* cut off from	Judg 21:6	7626
that a *t* be not destroyed out of	Judg 21:17	7626
at that time, every man to his *t*	Judg 21:24	7626
the families of the *t* of Benjamin	1Sa 9:21	7626
the *t* of Benjamin was taken	1Sa 10:20	7626
When he had caused the *t* of	1Sa 10:21	7626
widow's son of the *t* of Naphtali	1Kin 7:14	4294
but will give one *t* to thy son	1Kin 11:13	7626
(But he shall have one *t* for my	1Kin 11:32	7626
And unto his son will I give one *t*	1Kin 11:36	7626
of David, but the *t* of Judah only	1Kin 12:20	7626
with the *t* of Benjamin, an	1Kin 12:21	7626
none left but the *t* of Judah only	2Kin 17:18	7626
half the *t* of Manasseh, of,	1Chr 5:18	7626
the children of the half *t* of	1Chr 5:23	7626
the half *t* of Manasseh, and	1Chr 5:26	7626
And out of the *t* of Benjamin	1Chr 6:60	4294
were left of the family of that *t*	1Chr 6:61	4294
cities given out of the half *t*	1Chr 6:61	4294
out of the half *t* of Manasseh	1Chr 6:61	
families out of the *t* of Issachar	1Chr 6:62	4294
and out of the *t* of Asher	1Chr 6:62	4294
out of the *t* of Naphtali, and out	1Chr 6:62	4294
out of the *t* of Manasseh in	1Chr 6:62	4294
families, out of the *t* of Reuben	1Chr 6:63	4294
of Reuben, and out of the *t* of Gad	1Chr 6:63	4294
Gad, and out of the *t* of Zebulun	1Chr 6:63	4294
of the *t* of the children of Judah	1Chr 6:65	4294
out of the *t* of the children of	1Chr 6:65	4294
out of the *t* of the children of	1Chr 6:65	4294
coasts out of the *t* of Ephraim	1Chr 6:66	4294
And out of the half *t* of Manasseh	1Chr 6:70	4294
family of the half *t* of Manasseh	1Chr 6:71	4294
And out of the *t* of Issachar	1Chr 6:72	4294
And out of the *t* of Asher	1Chr 6:74	4294
And out of the *t* of Naphtali	1Chr 6:76	4294
given out of the *t* of Zebulun	1Chr 6:77	4294
given them out of the *t* of Reuben	1Chr 6:78	4294
And out of the *t* of Gad	1Chr 6:80	4294
of the half *t* of Manasseh	1Chr 12:31	4294
and of the half *t* of Manasseh	1Chr 12:37	7626
sons were named of the *t* of Levi	1Chr 23:14	7626
the half *t* of Manasseh, for every	1Chr 26:32	7626
of the half *t* of Manasseh	1Chr 27:20	7626
Of the half *t* of Manasseh in	1Chr 27:21	
and chose not the *t* of Ephraim	Ps 78:67	7626
But chose the *t* of Judah, the	Ps 78:68	7626
that in what *t* the stranger	Eze 47:23	7626
of Phanuel, of the *t* of Aser	Lk 2:36	5443
Cis, a man of the *t* of Benjamin	Acts 13:21	5443
of Abraham, of the *t* of Benjamin	Rom 11:1	5443
of the *t* of Benjamin, an Hebrew	Phil 3:5	5443
spoken pertaineth to another *t*	Heb 7:13	5443
of which *t* Moses spake nothing	Heb 7:14	5443
behold, the Lion of the *t* of Juda	Rev 5:5	5443
Of the *t* of Juda were sealed	Rev 7:5	5443
Of the *t* of Reuben were sealed	Rev 7:5	5443
Of the *t* of Gad were sealed	Rev 7:5	5443
Of the *t* of Aser were sealed	Rev 7:6	5443
Of the *t* of Nepthalim were sealed	Rev 7:6	5443
Of the *t* of Manasses were sealed	Rev 7:6	5443
Of the *t* of Simeon were sealed	Rev 7:7	5443
Of the *t* of Levi were sealed	Rev 7:7	5443
Of the *t* of Issachar were sealed	Rev 7:7	5443
Of the *t* of Zabulon were sealed	Rev 7:8	5443
Of the *t* of Joseph were sealed	Rev 7:8	5443
Of the *t* of Benjamin were sealed	Rev 7:8	5443

TRIBES

people, as one of the *t* of Israel	Gen 49:16	7626
these are the twelve *t* of Israel	Gen 49:28	7626
to the twelve *t* of Israel	Ex 24:4	7626
they be according to the twelve *t*	Ex 28:21	7626
name, according to the twelve *t*	Ex 39:14	7626
princes of the *t* of their fathers	Num 1:16	4294
who were the princes of the *t*	Num 7:2	4294
in his tents according to their *t*	Num 24:2	7626
the *t* of their fathers they shall	Num 26:55	7626
the *t* concerning the children of	Num 30:1	4294
throughout all the *t* of Israel	Num 31:4	4294
the chief fathers of the *t* of the	Num 32:28	4294
according to the *t* of your	Num 33:54	4294
commanded to give unto the nine *t*	Num 34:13	4294
The two *t* and the half tribe have	Num 34:15	4294
other *t* of the children of Israel	Num 36:3	4294
but every one of the *t* of the	Num 36:9	4294
and known among your *t*, and I will	Deut 1:13	7626
So I took the chief of your *t*	Deut 1:15	7626
tens, and officers among your *t*	Deut 1:15	7626
me, even all the heads of your *t*	Deut 5:23	7626
all your *t* to put his name there	Deut 12:5	7626
LORD shall choose in one of thy *t*	Deut 12:14	7626
God giveth thee, throughout thy *t*	Deut 16:18	7626
hath chosen him out of all thy *t*	Deut 18:5	7626
your captains of your *t*, your	Deut 29:10	7626
evil out of all the *t* of Israel	Deut 29:21	7626
unto me all the elders of your *t*	Deut 31:28	7626
the *t* of Israel were gathered	Deut 33:5	7626
twelve men out of the *t* of Israel	Josh 3:12	7626
unto the number of the *t* of the	Josh 4:5	7626
the *t* of the children of Israel	Josh 4:8	7626
be brought according to your *t*	Josh 7:14	7626
and brought Israel by their *t*	Josh 7:16	7626
to their divisions by their *t*	Josh 11:23	7626
the *t* of Israel for a possession	Josh 12:7	7626
an inheritance unto the nine *t*	Josh 13:7	7626
the *t* of the children of Israel	Josh 14:1	4294
the hand of Moses, for the nine *t*	Josh 14:2	4294
given the inheritance of two *t*	Josh 14:3	4294
the children of Joseph were two *t*	Josh 14:4	4294
the children of Israel seven *t*	Josh 18:2	7626
the *t* of the children of Israel	Josh 19:51	7626
the *t* of the children of Israel	Josh 21:1	4294
nine tribes out of those two *t*	Josh 21:16	7626
throughout all the *t* of Israel	Josh 22:14	4294
to be an inheritance for your *t*	Josh 23:4	7626
all the *t* of Israel to Shechem	Josh 24:1	7626
unto them among the *t* of Israel	Judg 18:1	7626
even of all the *t* of Israel	Judg 20:2	7626
throughout all the *t* of Israel	Judg 20:10	7626
the *t* of Israel sent men through	Judg 20:12	7626
Who is there among all the *t* of	Judg 21:5	7626
What one is there of the *t* of	Judg 21:8	7626
made a breach in the *t* of Israel	Judg 21:15	7626
the *t* of Israel to be my priest	1Sa 2:28	7626
the smallest of the *t* of Israel	1Sa 9:21	7626
before the LORD by your *t*	1Sa 10:19	7626
all the *t* of Israel to come near	1Sa 10:20	7626
made the head of the *t* of Israel	1Sa 15:17	7626
Then came all the *t* of Israel to	2Sa 5:1	7626
word with any of the *t* of Israel	2Sa 7:7	7626
is of one of the *t* of Israel	2Sa 15:2	7626
throughout all the *t* of Israel	2Sa 15:10	7626
throughout all the *t* of Israel	2Sa 19:9	7626
all the *t* of Israel unto Abel	2Sa 20:14	7626
now through all the *t* of Israel	2Sa 24:2	7626
Israel, and all the heads of the *t*	1Kin 8:1	4294
the *t* of Israel to build an house	1Kin 8:16	7626
and will give ten *t* to thee	1Kin 11:31	7626
chosen out of all the *t* of Israel	1Kin 11:32	7626
give it unto thee, even ten *t*	1Kin 11:35	7626
choose out of all the *t* of Israel	1Kin 14:21	7626
of the *t* of the sons of Jacob	1Kin 18:31	7626
chosen out of all *t* of Israel	2Kin 21:7	7626
Furthermore over the *t* of Israel	1Chr 27:16	7626
the princes of the *t* of Israel	1Chr 27:22	7626
of Israel, the princes of the *t*	1Chr 28:1	7626
and princes of the *t* of Israel	1Chr 29:6	7626
Israel, and all the heads of the *t*	2Chr 5:2	4294
I chose no city among all the *t*	2Chr 6:5	7626
after them out of all the *t* of	2Chr 11:16	7626
chosen out of all the *t* of Israel	2Chr 12:13	7626
chosen before all the *t* of Israel	2Chr 33:7	7626
to the number of the *t* of Israel	Ezr 6:17	7625
made the *t* of Israel to dwell in	Ps 78:55	7626
one feeble person among their *t*	Ps 105:37	7626

Whither the *t* go up, the *t* .... Ps 122:4 — 7626
the *t* of the LORD, unto the .... Ps 122:4 — 7626
are the stay of the *t* thereof .... Is 19:13 — 7626
to raise up the *t* of Jacob .... Is 49:6 — 7626
the *t* of thine inheritance .... Is 63:17 — 7626
the *t* of Israel his fellows, and .... Eze 37:19 — 7626
of Israel according to their *t* .... Eze 45:8 — 7626
to the twelve *t* of Israel .... Eze 47:13 — 7626
you according to the *t* of Israel .... Eze 47:21 — 7626
with you among the *t* of Israel .... Eze 47:22 — 7626
Now these are the names of the *t* .... Eze 48:1 — 7626
it out of all the *t* of Israel .... Eze 48:19 — 7626
As for the rest of the *t*, from .... Eze 48:23 — 7626
the *t* of Israel for inheritance .... Eze 48:29 — 7626
the names of the *t* of Israel .... Eze 48:31 — 7626
among the *t* of Israel have I made .... Hos 5:9 — 7626
according to the oaths of the *t* .... Hab 3:9 — 4294
of man, as of all the *t* of Israel .... Zec 9:1 — 7626
judging the twelve *t* of Israel .... Mt 19:28 — 5443
all the *t* of the earth mourn .... Mt 24:30 — 5443
judging the twelve *t* of Israel .... Lk 22:30 — 5443
Unto which promise our twelve *t* .... Acts 26:7 — 1429
to the twelve *t* which are .... Jas 1:1 — 5443
four thousand of all the *t* of the .... Rev 7:4 — 5443
t of the children of Israel .... Rev 21:12 — 5443

TRIBULATION
When thou art in *t*, and all these .... Deut 4:30 — 6862
deliver you in the time of your *t* .... Judg 10:14 — 6869
let him deliver me out of all *t* .... 1Sa 26:24 — 6869
for when *t* or persecution ariseth .... Mt 13:21 — 2347
For then shall be great *t* .... Mt 24:21 — 2347
Immediately after the *t* of those .... Mt 24:29 — 2347
But in those days, after that *t* .... Mk 13:24 — 2347
In the world ye shall have *t* .... Jn 16:33 — 2347
that we must through much *t* enter .... Acts 14:22 — 2347
T and anguish, upon every soul of .... Rom 2:9 — 2347
knowing that *t* worketh patience .... Rom 5:3 — 2347
shall *t*, or distress, or .... Rom 8:35 — 2347
patient in *t* .... Rom 12:12 — 2347
Who comforteth us in all our *t* .... 2Cor 1:4 — 2347
am exceeding joyful in all our *t* .... 2Cor 7:4 — 2347
before that we should suffer *t* .... 1Th 3:4 — 2346
t to them that trouble you .... 2Th 1:6 — 2347
your brother, and companion in *t* .... Rev 1:9 — 2347
I know thy works, and *t*, and .... Rev 2:9 — 2347
and ye shall have *t* ten days .... Rev 2:10 — 2347
adultery with her into great *t* .... Rev 2:22 — 2347
they which came out of great *t* .... Rev 7:14 — 2347

TRIBULATIONS
of all your adversities and your *t* .... 1Sa 10:19 — 6869
only so, but we glory in *t* also .... Rom 5:3 — 2347
that ye faint not at my *t* for you .... Eph 3:13 — 2347
persecutions and *t* that ye endure .... 2Th 1:4 — 2347

TRIBUTARIES
therein shall be *t* unto thee .... Deut 20:11 — 4522
dwelt among them, and became *t* .... Judg 1:30 — 4522
of Beth-anath became *t* unto them .... Judg 1:33 — 4522
prevailed, so that they became *t* .... Judg 1:35 — 4522

TRIBUTARY
provinces, how is she become *t* .... Lam 1:1 — 4522

TRIBUTE
bear, and became a servant unto *t* .... Gen 49:15 — 4522
levy a *t* unto the LORD of the men .... Num 31:28 — 4371
the LORD's *t* of the sheep was six .... Num 31:37 — 4371
which the LORD's *t* was threescore .... Num 31:38 — 4371
which the LORD's *t* was threescore .... Num 31:39 — 4371
of which the LORD's *t* was thirty .... Num 31:40 — 4371
And Moses gave the *t*, which was .... Num 31:41 — 4371
unto the LORD for God with a *t* of .... Deut 16:10 — 4530
unto this day, and serve under *t* .... Josh 16:10 — 4522
that they put the Canaanites to *t* .... Josh 17:13 — 4522
that they put the Canaanites to *t* .... Judg 1:28 — 4522
And Adoram was over the *t* .... 2Sa 20:24 — 4522
the son of Abda was over the *t* .... 1Kin 4:6 — 4522
a *t* of bondservice unto this day .... 1Kin 9:21 — 4522
sent Adoram, who was over the *t* .... 1Kin 12:18 — 4522
put the land to a *t* of an hundred .... 2Kin 23:33 — 6066
make to pay *t* until this day .... 2Chr 8:8 — 4522
sent Hadoram that was over the *t* .... 2Chr 10:18 — 4522
Jehoshaphat presents, and silver .... 2Chr 17:11 — 4853
then will they not pay toll, *t* .... Ezr 4:13 — 1093
and toll, *t*, and custom, was paid .... Ezr 4:20 — 1093
even of the priests, the river, ... Ezr 4:61 — 4061
not be lawful to impose toll, *t* .... Ezr 7:24 — 1093
borrowed money for the king's *t* .... Neh 5:4 — 4060
Ahasuerus laid a *t* upon the land .... Est 10:1 — 4522
but the slothful shall be under *t* .... Prov 12:24 — 4522
they that received *t* money came .... Mt 17:24 — 1323

said, Doth not your master pay *t* .... Mt 17:24 — 1323
of the earth take custom or *t* .... Mt 17:25 — 2778
it lawful to give *t* unto Caesar .... Mt 22:17 — 2778
Shew me the *t* money .... Mt 22:19 — 2778
Is it lawful to give *t* to Caesar .... Mk 12:14 — 2778
for us to give *t* unto Caesar .... Lk 20:22 — 5411
and forbidding to give *t* to Caesar .... Lk 23:2 — 5411
For for this cause pay ye *t* also .... Rom 13:6 — 5411
t to whom *t* is due .... Rom 13:7 — 5411

TRICKLETH
Mine eye *t* down, and ceaseth not, ... Lam 3:49 — 5064

TRIED
controversy and every stroke be *t* .... Deut 21:5
the word of the LORD is *t* .... 2Sa 22:31 — 6884
when he hath *t* me, I shall come .... Job 23:10 — 974
is that Job may be *t* unto the end .... Job 34:36 — 974
as silver *t* in a furnace of earth .... Ps 12:6 — 6884
thou hast *t* me, and shalt find .... Ps 17:3 — 6884
the word of the LORD is *t* .... Ps 18:30 — 6884
hast *t* us, as silver is *t* .... Ps 66:10 — 6884
the word of the LORD *t* him .... Ps 105:19 — 6884
a *t* stone, a precious corner .... Is 28:16 — 976
me, and *t* mine heart toward thee .... Jer 12:3 — 974
be purified, and made white, and *t* .... Dan 12:10 — 6884
and will try them as gold is *t* .... Zec 13:9 — 974
By faith Abraham, when he was *t* .... Heb 11:17 — 3985
for when he is *t*, he shall........................ Jas 1:12 — 1384
though it be *t* with fire .... 1Pet 1:7 — 1381
thou hast *t* them which say they .... Rev 2:2 — 3985
you into prison, that ye may be *t* .... Rev 2:10 — 3985
to buy of me gold *t* in the fire .... Rev 3:18 — 4448

TRIEST
my God, that thou *t* the heart .... 1Chr 29:17 — 974
that *t* the reins and the heart, ... Jer 11:20 — 974
that *t* the righteous, and seest .... Jer 20:12 — 974

TRIETH
For the ear *t* words, as the mouth .... Job 34:3 — 974
the righteous God *t* the hearts .... Ps 7:9 — 974
The LORD *t* the righteous .... Ps 11:5 — 974
but the LORD *t* the hearts .... Prov 17:3 — 974
men, but God, which *t* our hearts .... 1Th 2:4 — 1381

TRIMMED
nor *t* his beard, nor washed his .... 2Sa 19:24 — 6213
virgins arose, and *t* their lamps .... Mt 25:7 — 2885

TRIMMEST
Why *t* thou thy way to seek love .... Jer 2:33 — 3190

TRIUMPH
daughters of the uncircumcised *t* .... 2Sa 1:20 — 5937
let not mine enemies *t* over me .... Ps 25:2 — 5970
mine enemy doth not *t* over me .... Ps 41:11 — 7321
unto God with the voice of *t* .... Ps 47:1 — 7440
Philistia, *t* thou because of me .... Ps 60:8 — 7321
I will *t* in the works of thy .... Ps 92:4 — 7442
how long shall the wicked *t* .... Ps 94:3 — 5937
holy name, and to *t* in thy praise .... Ps 106:47 — 7623
over Philistia will I *t* .... Ps 108:9 — 7321
always causeth us to *t* in Christ .... 2Cor 2:14 — 2358

TRIUMPHED
LORD, for he hath *t* gloriously .... Ex 15:1 — 1342
LORD, for he hath *t* gloriously .... Ex 15:21 — 1342

TRIUMPHING
That the *t* of the wicked is short .... Job 20:5 — 7445
of them openly, *t* over them in it .... Col 2:15 — 2358

TROAS (tro'-as) A seaport of Phrygia in Asia Minor.
passing by Mysia came down to *T* .... Acts 16:8 — 5174
Therefore loosing from *T*, we came .... Acts 16:11 — 5174
going before tarried for us at *T* .... Acts 20:5 — 5174
came unto them to *T* in five days .... Acts 20:6 — 5174
when I came to *T* to preach .... 2Cor 2:12 — 5174
that I left at *T* with Carpus .... 2Ti 4:13 — 5174

TRODDEN
give the land that he hath *t* upon .... Deut 1:36 — 1869
have *t* shall be thine inheritance .... Josh 14:9 — 1869
thou hast *t* down strength .... Judg 5:21 — 1869
old way which wicked men have *t* .... Job 22:15 — 1869
The lion's whelps have not *t* it .... Job 28:8 — 1869
Thou hast *t* down all them that .... Ps 119:118 — 5541
thereof, and it shall be *t* down .... Is 5:5 — 4823
as a carcase *t* under feet .... Is 14:19 — 947
t down, whose land the rivers .... Is 18:2 — 4001
t under foot, whose land the .... Is 18:7 — 4001
Moab shall be *t* down under him, ... Is 25:10 — 1758
even as straw is *t* down for the .... Is 25:10 — 1758
of Ephraim, shall be *t* under feet .... Is 28:3 — 7429
then ye shall be *t* down by it .... Is 28:18 — 4823

I have *t* the winepress alone	Is 63:3	1869
have *t* down thy sanctuary	Is 63:18	947
they have *t* my portion under foot	Jer 12:10	947
The Lord hath *t* under foot all my	Lam 1:15	5541
the Lord hath *t* the virgin	Lam 1:15	1869
which ye have *t* with your feet	Eze 34:19	7429
and the host to be *t* under foot	Dan 8:13	4823
now shall she be *t* down as the	Mic 7:10	4823
to be *t* under foot of men	Mt 5:13	2662
and it was *t* down, and the fowls of	Lk 8:5	2662
Jerusalem shall be *t* down of the	Lk 21:24	3961
who hath *t* under foot the Son of	Heb 10:29	2662
winepress was *t* without the city	Rev 14:20	3961

TRODE

t the grapes, and made merry, and	Judg 9:27	1869
t them down with ease over	Judg 20:43	1869
the people *t* upon him in the gate	2Kin 7:17	7429
for the people *t* upon him in the	2Kin 7:20	7429
and he *t* her under foot	2Kin 9:33	7429
in Lebanon, and *t* down the thistle	2Kin 14:9	7429
in Lebanon, and *t* down the thistle	2Chr 25:18	7429
that they *t* one upon another	Lk 12:1	2662

TROGYLLIUM *(tro-jil'-le-um) A coastal town in Ionia in Asia Minor.*

arrived at Samos, and tarried at *T*	Acts 20:15	5175

TROOP

And Leah said, A *t* cometh	Gen 30:11	1409
Gad, a *t* shall overcome him	Gen 49:19	1416
Shall I pursue after this *t*	1Sa 30:8	1416
after Abner, and became one *t*	2Sa 2:25	92
and Joab came from pursuing a *t*	2Sa 3:22	1416
by thee I have run through a *t*	2Sa 22:30	1416
were gathered together into a *t*	2Sa 23:11	2416
the *t* of the Philistines pitched	2Sa 23:13	2416
by thee I have run through a *t*	Ps 18:29	1416
that prepare a table for that *t*	Is 65:11	1409
bring a *t* suddenly upon them	Jer 18:22	1416
the *t* of robbers spoileth without	Hos 7:1	1416
hath founded his *t* in the earth	Amos 9:6	92

TROOPS

The *t* of Tema looked, the	Job 6:19	734
His *t* come together, and raise up	Job 19:12	1416
by *t* in the harlots' houses	Jer 5:7	
as *t* of robbers wait for a man,	Hos 6:9	1416
in *t*, O daughter of *t*	Mic 5:1	1416
he will invade them with his *t*	Hab 3:16	

TROPHIMUS *(trof-im-us) A companion of Paul.*

and of Asia, Tychicus and *T*	Acts 20:4	5161
him in the city *T* an Ephesian	Acts 21:29	5161
but *T* have I left at Miletum sick	2Ti 4:20	5161

TROUBLE

camp of Israel a curse, and *t* it	Josh 6:18	5916
the Lord shall *t* thee this day	Josh 7:25	5916
and thou art one of them that *t* me	Judg 11:35	5916
Hezekiah, This day is a day of *t*	2Kin 19:3	6869
in my *t* I have prepared for the	1Chr 22:14	6040
But when they in their *t* did turn	2Chr 15:4	6862
and he hath delivered them to *t*	2Chr 29:8	2189
to affright them, and to *t* them	2Chr 32:18	926
and in the time of their *t*	Neh 9:27	6869
let not all the *t* seem little	Neh 9:32	8513
yet *t* came	Job 3:26	7267
neither doth *t* spring out of the	Job 5:6	5999
Yet man is born unto *t*, as the	Job 5:7	5999
is of few days, and full of *t*	Job 14:1	7267
T and anguish shall make him	Job 15:24	6862
his cry when *t* cometh upon him	Job 27:9	6869
not I weep for him that was in *t*	Job 30:25	7186,3117
quietness, who then can make *t*	Job 34:29	7561
reserved against the time of *t*	Job 38:23	6862
how are they increased that *t* me	Ps 3:1	6862
oppressed, a refuge in times of *t*	Ps 9:9	6869
consider my *t* which I suffer of	Ps 9:13	6040
hidest thou thyself in times of *t*	Ps 10:1	6869
those that *t* me rejoice when I am	Ps 13:4	6862
Lord hear thee in the day of *t*	Ps 20:1	6869
for *t* is near	Ps 22:11	6869
For in the time of *t* he shall	Ps 27:5	7451
for thou hast considered my *t*	Ps 31:7	6040
upon me, O Lord, for I am in *t*	Ps 31:9	6887
thou shalt preserve me from *t*	Ps 32:7	6862
their strength in the time of *t*	Ps 37:39	6869
will deliver him in time of *t*	Ps 41:1	7451
a very present help in *t*	Ps 46:1	6869
And call upon me in the day of *t*	Ps 50:15	6869
he hath delivered me out of all *t*	Ps 54:7	6869
and refuge in the day of my *t*	Ps 59:16	6862
Give us help from *t*	Ps 60:11	6862

hath spoken, when I was in *t*	Ps 66:14	6862
for I am in *t*	Ps 69:17	6887
They are not in *t* as other men	Ps 73:5	5999
In the day of my *t* I sought the	Ps 77:2	6869
in vanity, and their years in *t*	Ps 78:33	928
wrath, and indignation, and *t*	Ps 78:49	6869
Thou calledst in *t*, and I	Ps 81:7	6869
In the day of my *t* I will call	Ps 86:7	6869
I will be with him in *t*	Ps 91:15	6869
from me in the day when I am in *t*	Ps 102:2	6862
cried unto the Lord in their *t*	Ps 107:6	6862
cried unto the Lord in their *t*	Ps 107:13	6862
they cry unto the Lord in their *t*	Ps 107:19	6862
their soul is melted because of *t*	Ps 107:26	7451
they cry unto the Lord in their *t*	Ps 107:28	6862
Give us help from *t*	Ps 108:12	6862
I found *t* and sorrow	Ps 116:3	6869
T and anguish have taken hold on	Ps 119:143	6862
Though I walk in the midst of *t*	Ps 138:7	6869
I shewed before him my *t*	Ps 142:2	6869
sake bring my soul out of *t*	Ps 143:11	6869
righteous is delivered out of *t*	Prov 11:8	6869
but the just shall come out of *t*	Prov 12:13	6869
the revenues of the wicked is *t*	Prov 15:6	5916
great treasure and *t* therewith	Prov 15:16	4103
time of *t* is like a broken tooth	Prov 25:19	6869
they are a *t* unto me	Is 1:14	2960
and behold at darkness, dimness	Is 8:22	6869
And behold at eveningtide *t*	Is 17:14	1091
For it is a day of *t*, and of	Is 22:5	4103
in *t* have they visited thee	Is 26:16	6862
into the land of *t* and anguish,	Is 30:6	6869
salvation also in the time of *t*	Is 33:2	6869
Hezekiah, This day is a day of *t*	Is 37:3	6869
answer, nor save him out of his *t*	Is 46:7	6869
in vain, nor bring forth for *t*	Is 65:23	928
the time of their *t* they will say	Jer 2:27	7451
save thee in the time of thy *t*	Jer 2:28	7451
for a time of health, and behold *t*	Jer 8:15	1205
at all in the time of their *t*	Jer 11:12	7451
that they cry unto me for their *t*	Jer 11:14	7451
the saviour thereof in time of *t*	Jer 14:8	6869
the time of healing, and behold *t*	Jer 14:19	1205
it is even the time of Jacob's *t*	Jer 30:7	6869
for in the day of *t* they shall be	Jer 51:2	7451
mine enemies have heard of my *t*	Lam 1:21	7451
is come, the day of *t* is near	Eze 7:7	4103
the foot of man *t* them any more	Eze 32:13	4103
nor the hoofs of beasts *t* them	Eze 32:13	1804
interpretation thereof, *t* thee	Dan 4:19	927
let not thy thoughts *t* thee	Dan 5:10	927
and out of the north shall *t* him	Dan 11:44	926
and there shall be a time of *t*	Dan 12:1	6869
a strong hold in the day of *t*	Nah 1:7	6869
that I might rest in the day of *t*	Hab 3:16	6869
day is a day of wrath, a day of *t*	Zeph 1:15	6869
unto her, Why *t* ye the woman	Mt 26:10	2873,3930
why *t* ye her	Mk 14:6	3930
unto him, Lord, *t* not thyself	Lk 7:6	4660
t not the Master	Lk 8:49	4660
shall answer and say, *T* me not	Lk 11:7	2873
that we *t* not them, which from	Acts 15:19	3926
Jews, do exceedingly *t* our city	Acts 16:20	1613
him said, *T* not yourselves	Acts 20:10	2350
such shall have *t* in the flesh	1Cor 7:28	2347
comfort them which are in any *t*	2Cor 1:4	2347
of our *t* which came to us in Asia	2Cor 1:8	2347
but there be some that *t* you	Gal 1:7	5015
were even cut off which *t* you	Gal 5:12	387
From henceforth let no man *t* me	Gal 6:17	2873,3930
tribulation to them that *t* you	2Th 1:6	2346
Wherein I suffer *t*, as an evil	2Ti 2:9	2553
of bitterness springing up *t* you	Heb 12:15	1776

TROUBLED

Ye have *t* me to make me to stink	Gen 34:30	5916
the morning that his spirit was *t*	Gen 41:8	6470
for they were *t* at his presence	Gen 45:3	926
t the host of the Egyptians,	Ex 14:24	2000
Joshua said, Why hast thou *t* us	Josh 7:25	5916
My father hath *t* the land	1Sa 14:29	5916
evil spirit from the Lord *t* him	1Sa 16:14	1204
Saul, and saw that he was sore *t*	1Sa 28:21	926
and all the Israelites were *t*	2Sa 4:1	926
he answered, I have not *t* Israel	1Kin 18:18	5916
Syria was sore *t* for this thing	2Kin 6:11	5590
of Judah, and *t* them in building,	Ezr 4:4	1089
it toucheth thee, and thou art *t*	Job 4:5	926
so, why should not my spirit be *t*	Job 21:4	7114
Therefore am I *t* at his presence	Job 23:15	926
the people shall be *t* at midnight	Job 34:20	1607

didst hide thy face, and I was *t*	Ps 30:7	926
I am *t*.	Ps 38:6	5753
the waters thereof roar and be *t*	Ps 46:3	2560
they were *t*, and hasted away	Ps 48:5	926
I remembered God, and was *t*	Ps 77:3	1993
I am so *t* that I cannot speak	Ps 77:4	6470
the depths also were *t*	Ps 77:16	7264
them be confounded and *t* for ever	Ps 83:17	926
anger, and by thy wrath are we *t*	Ps 90:7	926
Thou hidest thy face, they are *t*	Ps 104:29	926
the wicked is as a *t* fountain	Prov 25:26	7515
Many days and years shall ye be *t*	Is 32:10	7264
be *t*, ye careless ones	Is 32:11	7264
But the wicked are like the the *t* sea	Is 57:20	1644
therefore my bowels are *t* for him	Jer 31:20	1993
my bowels are *t*	Lam 1:20	2560
fail with tears, my bowels are *t*	Lam 2:11	2560
the people of the land shall be *t*	Eze 7:27	926
sea shall be *t* at thy departure	Eze 26:18	926
afraid, they shall be *t* in their	Eze 27:35	7481
wherewith his spirit was *t*	Dan 2:1	6470
my spirit was *t* to know the dream	Dan 2:3	6470
and the visions of my head was *t* me	Dan 4:5	927
one hour, and his thoughts *t* him	Dan 4:19	927
changed, and his thoughts *t* him	Dan 5:6	927
was king Belshazzar greatly *t*	Dan 5:9	927
and the visions of my head *t* me	Dan 7:15	927
Daniel, my cogitations much *t* me	Dan 7:28	927
their way as a flock, they were *t*	Zec 10:2	6031
had heard these things, he was *t*	Mt 2:3	5015
walking on the sea, they were *t*	Mt 14:26	5015
see that ye be not *t*	Mt 24:6	2360
For they all saw him, and were *t*	Mk 6:50	5015
and rumours of wars, be ye not *t*	Mk 13:7	2360
when Zacharias saw him, he was *t*	Lk 1:12	5015
she was *t* at his saying, and cast	Lk 1:29	1298
careful and *t* about many things	Lk 10:41	5182
he said unto them, Why are ye *t*	Lk 24:38	5015
into the pool, and *t* the water	Jn 5:4	5015
have no man, when the water is *t*	Jn 5:7	5015
groaned in the spirit, and was *t*	Jn 11:33	5015,1438
Now is my soul *t*	Jn 12:27	5015
he was *t* in spirit, and testified,	Jn 13:21	5015
Let not your heart be *t*	Jn 14:1	5015
Let not your heart be *t*, neither	Jn 14:27	5015
out from us have *t* you with words	Acts 15:24	5015
they *t* the people and the rulers	Acts 17:8	5015
We are *t* on every side, yet not	2Cor 4:8	2346
but we were *t* on every side	2Cor 7:5	2346
And to you who are *t* rest with us	2Th 1:7	2346
not soon shaken in mind, or be *t*	2Th 2:2	2360
of their terror, neither be *t*	1Pet 3:14	5015

TROUBLEDST

t the waters with thy feet, and	Eze 32:2	1804

TROUBLER

the *t* of Israel, who transgressed	1Chr 2:7	5916

TROUBLES

many evils and *t* shall befall them	Deut 31:17	6869
t are befallen them, that this	Deut 31:21	6869
He shall deliver thee in six *t*	Job 5:19	6869
The *t* of my heart are enlarged	Ps 25:17	6869
Israel, O God, out of all his *t*	Ps 25:22	6869
and saved him out of all his *t*	Ps 34:6	6869
them out of all their *t*	Ps 34:17	6869
hast shewed me great and sore *t*	Ps 71:20	6869
For my soul is full of *t*	Ps 88:3	7451
tongue keepeth his soul from *t*	Prov 21:23	6869
the former *t* are forgotten	Is 65:16	6869
and there shall be famines and *t*	Mk 13:8	5016

TROUBLEST

why *t* thou the Master any further	Mk 5:35	4660

TROUBLETH

an evil spirit from God *t* thee	1Sa 16:15	1204
him, Art thou he that *t* Israel	1Kin 18:17	5916
about thee, and sudden fear *t* thee	Job 22:10	926
heart soft, and the Almighty *t* me	Job 23:16	926
he that is cruel *t* his own flesh	Prov 11:17	5916
He that *t* his own house shall	Prov 11:29	5916
is greedy of gain *t* his own house	Prov 15:27	5916
is in thee, and no secret *t* thee	Dan 4:9	598
Yet because this widow *t* me	Lk 18:5	3930,2873
but he that *t* you shall bear his	Gal 5:10	5015

TROUBLING

There the wicked cease from *t*	Job 3:17	7267
the *t* of the water stepped in was	Jn 5:4	5015

TROUBLOUS

and the wall, even in *t* times	Dan 9:25	5916

TROUGH

and emptied her pitcher into the *t*	Gen 24:20	8268

TROUGHS

t when the flocks came to drink	Gen 30:38	8268
filled the *t* to water their	Ex 2:16	7298

TROW

I *t* not	Lk 17:9	1380

TRUCEBREAKERS

Without natural affection, *t*	2Ti 3:3	786

TRUE

we are *t* men, thy servants are no	Gen 42:11	3651
If ye be *t* men, let one of your	Gen 42:19	3651
And we said unto him, We are *t* men	Gen 42:31	3651
shall I know that ye are *t* men	Gen 42:33	3651
no spies, but that ye are *t* men	Gen 42:34	3651
diligently, and, behold, it be *t*	Deut 17:4	571
But if this thing be *t*, and the	Deut 22:20	571
house, and give me a *t* token	Josh 2:12	571
now it is *t* that I am thy near	Ruth 3:12	551
art that God, and thy words be *t*	2Sa 7:28	571
It was a *t* report that I heard in	1Kin 10:6	571
is *t* in the name of the LORD	1Kin 22:16	571
It was a *t* report which I heard	2Chr 9:5	571
hath been without the *t* God	2Chr 15:3	571
and *t* laws, good statutes and	Neh 9:13	571
the judgments of the LORD are *t*	Ps 19:9	571
Thy word is *t* from the beginning	Ps 119:160	571
A *t* witness delivereth souls	Prov 14:25	571
But the LORD is the *t* God	Jer 10:10	571
said to Jeremiah, The LORD be a *t*	Jer 42:5	571
hath executed *t* judgment between	Eze 18:8	571
spake and said unto them, Is it *t*	Dan 3:14	6656
answered and said unto the king, T	Dan 3:24	3330
answered and said, The thing is *t*	Dan 6:12	3330
the morning which was told is *t*	Dan 8:26	571
and the thing was *t*, but the time	Dan 10:1	571
Execute *t* judgment, and shew mercy	Zec 7:9	571
Master, we know that thou art *t*	Mt 22:16	227
Master, we know that thou art *t*	Mk 12:14	227
commit to your trust the *t* riches	Lk 16:11	228
That was the *t* Light, which	Jn 1:9	228
set to his seal that God is *t*	Jn 3:33	227
when the *t* worshippers shall	Jn 4:23	228
And herein is that saying *t*	Jn 4:37	228
of myself, my witness is not *t*	Jn 5:31	227
which he witnesseth of me is *t*	Jn 5:32	227
you the *t* bread from heaven	Jn 6:32	228
that sent him, the same is *t*	Jn 7:18	227
myself, but he that sent me is *t*	Jn 7:28	228
thy record is not *t*	Jn 8:13	227
of myself, yet my record is *t*	Jn 8:14	227
yet if I judge, my judgment is *t*	Jn 8:16	227
the testimony of two men is *t*	Jn 8:17	227
but he that sent me is *t*	Jn 8:26	227
John spake of this man were *t*	Jn 10:41	227
I am the *t* vine, and my Father is	Jn 15:1	228
might know thee the only *t* God	Jn 17:3	228
bare record, and his record is *t*	Jn 19:35	228
and he knoweth that he saith *t*	Jn 19:35	2227
we know that his testimony is *t*	Jn 21:24	227
wist not that it was *t* which was	Acts 12:9	227
yea, let God be *t*, but every man	Rom 3:4	227
But as God is *t*, our word toward	2Cor 1:18	4103
as deceivers, and yet *t*	2Cor 6:8	227
in righteousness and *t* holiness	Eph 4:24	3588,225
t yokefellow, help those women	Phil 4:3	1103
brethren, whatsoever things are *t*	Phil 4:8	227
to serve the living and *t* God	1Th 1:9	228
This is a *t* saying, If a man	1Ti 3:1	4103
This witness is *t*	Titus 1:13	227
of the *t* tabernacle, which the	Heb 8:2	228
which are the figures of the *t*	Heb 9:24	228
Let us draw near with a *t* heart	Heb 10:22	228
testifying that this is the *t*	1Pet 5:12	227
them according to the *t* proverb	2Pet 2:22	227
unto you, which thing is *t* in him	1Jn 2:8	227
past, and the *t* light now shineth	1Jn 2:8	228
that we may know him that is *t*	1Jn 5:20	228
and we are in him that is *t*	1Jn 5:20	228
This is the *t* God, and eternal	1Jn 5:20	228
and ye know that our record is *t*	3Jn 12	227
he that is holy, he that is *t*	Rev 3:7	228
t witness, the beginning of the	Rev 3:14	228
How long, O Lord, holy and *t*	Rev 6:10	228
t are thy ways, thou King of	Rev 15:3	228
Even so, Lord God Almighty, *t*	Rev 16:7	228
For *t* and righteous are his	Rev 19:2	228
These are the *t* sayings of God	Rev 19:9	228
upon him was called Faithful and T	Rev 19:11	228

T

for these words are *t* and faithful .... Rev 21:5 — 228
These sayings are faithful and *t* .... Rev 22:6 — 228

TRULY

t Lamech seventy and sevenfold .... Gen 4:24 — 571
t with my master, tell me .... Gen 24:49 — 571
and deal kindly and *t* with me .... Gen 47:29 — 571
but *t* his younger brother shall .... Gen 48:19 — 199
But as *t* as I live, all the earth .... Num 14:21 — 199
As *t* as I live, saith the LORD, ... Num 14:28
Thou shalt *t* tithe all the .... Deut 14:22
will deal kindly and *t* with thee .... Josh 2:14 — 571
T the LORD hath delivered into............. Josh 2:24 — 3588
Now therefore, if ye have done *t* .... Judg 9:16 — 571
If ye then have dealt *t* and .... Judg 9:19 — 571
but *t* as the LORD liveth, and as .... 1Sa 20:3 — 199
For *t* my words shall not be false........... Job 36:4 — 551
T my soul waiteth upon God .... Ps 62:1 — 389
T God is good to Israel, even to .... Ps 73:1 — 389
O LORD, *t* I am thy servant..................... Ps 116:16 — 577
they that deal *t* are his delight .... Prov 12:22 — 530
T the light is sweet, and a .... Eccl 11:7
T in vain is salvation hoped for .... Jer 3:23 — 403
t in the LORD our God is the .... Jer 3:23 — 403
T this is a grief, and I must bear .... Jer 10:19 — 389
that the LORD hath *t* sent him .... Jer 28:9 — 571
hath kept my judgments, to deal *t* .... Eze 18:9 — 571
But *t* I am full of power by the .... Mic 3:8 — 199
The harvest *t* is plenteous, but .... Mt 9:37 — 3303
Elias *t* shall first come, and .... Mt 17:11 — 3303
T this was the Son of God .... Mt 27:54 — 230
The spirit *t* is ready, but the .... Mk 14:38 — 3303
T this man was the Son of God .... Mk 15:39 — 230
unto them, The harvest *t* is great .... Lk 10:2 — 3303
***T* ye bear witness that ye allow** .... Lk 11:48 — 686
but teachest the way of God *t* .... Lk 20:21 — 1909,225
***t* the Son of man goeth, as it was** .... Lk 22:22 — 3303
in that saidst thou *t* .... Jn 4:18 — 227
many other signs *t* did Jesus in .... Jn 20:30 — 3303
For John *t* baptized with water .... Acts 1:5 — 3303
For Moses *t* said unto the fathers .... Acts 3:22 — 3303
The prison *t* found we shut with .... Acts 5:23 — 3303
T the signs of an apostle were .... 2Cor 12:12 — 3303
they *t* were many priests, because .... Heb 7:23 — 3303
And *t*, if they had been mindful of......... Heb 11:15 — 3303
t our fellowship is with the .... 1Jn 1:3 — 1161

TRUMP

O my soul, the sound of the *t* .... Jer 4:19 — 7782
in Gibeah, and the *t* in Ramah .... Hos 5:8 — 2689
of an eye, at the last *t* .... 1Cor 15:52 — 4536
archangel, and with the *t* of God .... 1Th 4:16 — 4536

TRUMPET

when the *t* soundeth long, they .... Ex 19:13 — 3104
the voice of the *t* exceeding loud.......... Ex 19:16 — 7782
the voice of the *t* sounded long .... Ex 19:19 — 7782
lightnings, and the noise of the *t* .... Ex 20:18 — 7782
Then shalt thou cause the *t* of .... Lev 25:9 — 7782
t sound throughout all your land .... Lev 25:9 — 7782
And if they blow but with one *t* .... Num 10:4
when ye hear the sound of the *t*............. Josh 6:5 — 7782
people heard the sound of the *t* .... Josh 6:20 — 7782
that he blew a *t* in the mountain .... Judg 3:27 — 7782
came upon Gideon, and he blew a *t* ...... Judg 6:34 — 7782
he put a *t* in every man's hand, ... Judg 7:16 — 7782
When I blow with a *t*, I and all .... Judg 7:18 — 7782
Saul blew the *t* throughout all .... 1Sa 13:3 — 7782
So Joab blew a *t*, and all the .... 2Sa 2:28 — 7782
and with the sound of the *t* .... 2Sa 6:15 — 7782
as ye hear the sound of the *t*................. 2Sa 15:10 — 7782
And Joab blew the *t*, and the people .... 2Sa 18:16 — 7782
and he blew a *t*, and said, We have ...... 2Sa 20:1 — 7782
And he blew a *t*, and they retired .... 2Sa 20:22 — 7782
and blow ye with the *t*, and say,............ 1Kin 1:34 — 7782
And they blew the *t*............................... 1Kin 1:39 — 7782
Joab heard the sound of the *t* .... 1Kin 1:41 — 7782
he that sounded the *t* was by me .... Neh 4:18 — 7782
ye hear the sound of the *t*...................... Neh 4:20 — 7782
he that it is the sound of the *t* .... Job 39:24 — 7782
the LORD with the sound of a *t* .... Ps 47:5 — 7782
Blow up the *t* in the new moon, in .... Ps 81:3 — 7782
him with the sound of the *t* .... Ps 150:3 — 7782
and when he bloweth a *t*, hear ye .... Is 18:3 — 7782
that the great *t* shall be blown............... Is 27:13 — 7782
not, lift up thy voice like a *t* .... Is 58:1 — 7782
and say, Blow ye the *t* in the land .... Jer 4:5 — 7782
and hear the sound of the *t* .... Jer 4:21 — 7782
Jerusalem, and blow the *t* in Tekoa ...... Jer 6:1 — 7782
Hearken to the sound of the *t* .... Jer 6:17 — 7782
war, nor hear the sound of the *t* .... Jer 42:14 — 7782
blow the *t* among the nations, ... Jer 51:27 — 7782

They have blown the *t*, even to.............. Eze 7:14 — 8628
come upon the land, he blow the *t* .... Eze 33:3 — 7782
heareth the sound of the *t* .... Eze 33:4 — 7782
He heard the sound of the *t*................... Eze 33:5 — 7782
the sword come, and blow not the *t* ...... Eze 33:6 — 7782
Set the *t* to thy mouth .... Hos 8:1 — 7782
Blow ye the *t* in Zion, and sound........... Joel 2:1 — 7782
Blow the *t* in Zion, sanctify a .... Joel 2:15 — 7782
and with the sound of the *t* .... Amos 2:2 — 7782
Shall a *t* be blown in the city,................. Amos 3:6 — 7782
A day of the *t* and alarm against .... Zeph 1:16 — 7782
and the Lord GOD shall blow the *t*......... Zec 9:14 — 7782
do not sound a *t* before thee .... Mt 6:2 — 4537
angels with a great sound of a *t* .... Mt 24:31 — 4536
For if the *t* give an uncertain .... 1Cor 14:8 — 4536
for the *t* shall sound, and the .... 1Cor 15:52 — 4536
And the sound of a *t*, and the voice .... Heb 12:19 — 4536
me a great voice, as of a *t* .... Rev 1:10 — 4536
as it were of a *t* talking with me .... Rev 4:1 — 4536
of the *t* of the three angels .... Rev 8:13 — 4536
the sixth angel which had the *t* .... Rev 9:14 — 4536

TRUMPETERS

the *t* by the king, and all the .... 2Kin 11:14 — 2689
It came even to pass, as the *t* .... 2Chr 5:13 — 2689
singers sang, and the *t* sounded .... 2Chr 29:28 — 2690
and musicians, and of pipers, and *t*........ Rev 18:22 — 4538

TRUMPETS

a memorial of blowing of *t*...................... Lev 23:24
Make thee two *t* of silver .... Num 10:2 — 2689
priests, shall blow with the *t* .... Num 10:8 — 2689
ye shall blow an alarm with the *t* .... Num 10:9 — 2689
ye shall blow with the *t* over .... Num 10:10 — 2689
a day of blowing the *t* unto you............. Num 29:1
the *t* to blow in his hand .... Num 31:6 — 2689
the ark seven *t* of rams' horns .... Josh 6:4 — 7782
the priests shall blow with the *t* .... Josh 6:8 — 7782
let seven priests bear seven *t* of........... Josh 6:6 — 7782
t of rams' horns passed on before......... Josh 6:8 — 7782
the LORD, and blew with the *t* .... Josh 6:8 — 7782
the priests that blew with the *t* .... Josh 6:9 — 7782
going on, and blowing with the *t* .... Josh 6:9 — 7782
seven priests bearing seven *t* of........... Josh 6:13 — 7782
continually, and blew with the *t* .... Josh 6:13 — 7782
going on, and blowing with the *t* .... Josh 6:13 — 7782
when the priests blew with the *t*........... Josh 6:16 — 7782
when the priests blew with the *t*........... Josh 6:20 — 7782
in their hand, and their *t* .... Judg 7:8 — 7782
then blow ye the *t* also on every .... Judg 7:18 — 7782
and they blew the *t*, and brake the .... Judg 7:19 — 7782
And the three companies blew the *t*....... Judg 7:20 — 7782
the *t* in their right hands to .... Judg 7:20 — 7782
And the three hundred blew the *t*.......... Judg 7:22 — 7782
top of the stairs, and blew with *t* .... 2Kin 9:13 — 7782
the land rejoiced, and blew with *t* .... 2Kin 11:14 — 2689
of silver, snuffers, basons, *t*.................. 2Kin 12:13 — 2689
and with cymbals, and with *t*................. 1Chr 13:8 — 2689
did blow with the *t* before the .... 1Chr 15:24 — 2689
sound of the cornet, and with *t* .... 1Chr 15:28 — 2689
Jahaziel the priests with *t* .... 1Chr 16:6 — 2689
them Heman and Jeduthun with *t* .... 1Chr 16:42 — 2689
and twenty priests sounding with *t* .... 2Chr 5:12 — 2689
lifted up their voice with the *t*............... 2Chr 5:13 — 2689
the priests sounded *t* before them 2Chr 7:6
t to cry alarm against you .... 2Chr 13:12 — 2689
and the priests sounded with the *t* .... 2Chr 13:14 — 2689
and with shouting, and with *t* .... 2Chr 15:14 — 2689
t unto the house of the LORD .... 2Chr 20:28 — 2689
the princes and the *t* by the king .... 2Chr 23:13 — 2689
land rejoiced, and sounded with *t*.......... 2Chr 23:13 — 2689
David, and the priests with the *t* .... 2Chr 29:26 — 2689
of the LORD began also with the *t*.......... 2Chr 29:27 — 2689
priests in their apparel with *t* .... Ezr 3:10 — 2689
of the priests' sons with *t* .... Neh 12:35 — 2689
Zechariah, and Hananiah, with *t* .... Neh 12:41 — 2689
He saith among the *t*, Ha, ha .... Job 39:25 — 2689
With *t* and sound of cornet make a....... Ps 98:6 — 2689
and to them were given seven *t* .... Rev 8:2 — 4536
angels which had the seven *t* .... Rev 8:6 — 4536

TRUST

come and put your *t* in my shadow .... Judg 9:15 — 2620
whose wings thou art come to *t*............. Ruth 2:12 — 2620
in him will I *t* .... 2Sa 22:3 — 2620
buckler to all them that *t* in him............ 2Sa 22:31 — 2620
Now on whom dost thou *t*, that............. 2Kin 18:20 — 982
of Egypt unto all that *t* on him .... 2Kin 18:21 — 982
unto me, We *t* in the LORD our God .... 2Kin 18:22 — 982
put thy *t* on Egypt for chariots .... 2Kin 18:24 — 982
Hezekiah make you *t* in the LORD .... 2Kin 18:30 — 982
because they put their *t* in him.............. 1Chr 5:20 — 982

king of Assyria, Whereon do ye *t* 2Chr 32:10   982
he put no *t* in his servants..................Job 4:18   539
whose *t* shall be a spider's web.............Job 8:14   4009
he slay me, yet will I *t* in him.................Job 13:15   3176
he putteth no *t* in his saints...................Job 15:15   539
him that is deceived *t* in vanity ....Job 15:31   539
therefore *t* thou in him..........................Job 35:14   2342
Wilt thou *t* him, because his ....Job 39:11   982
all they that put their *t* in him ....Ps 2:12   2620
and put your *t* in the LORD ....Ps 4:5   982
that put their *t* in thee rejoice................Ps 5:11   2620
my God, in thee do I put my *t*.................Ps 7:1   2620
thy name will put their *t* in thee ....Ps 9:10   982
In the LORD put I my *t* ....Ps 11:1   2620
for in thee do I put my *t* ....Ps 16:1   2620
t in thee from those that rise up ....Ps 17:7   2620
my strength, in whom I will *t*..................Ps 18:2   2620
to all those that *t* in him ....Ps 18:30   2620
Some *t* in chariots, and some in.............Ps 20:7   2620
O my God, I *t* in thee ....Ps 25:2   982
for I put my *t* in thee ....Ps 25:20   2620
In thee, O LORD, do I put my *t* ....Ps 31:1   2620
but I *t* in the LORD ....Ps 31:6   982
t in thee before the sons of men ....Ps 31:19   2620
none of them that *t* in him shall ....Ps 34:22   2620
t under the shadow of thy wings...........Ps 36:7   2620
T in the LORD, and do good ....Ps 37:3   982
t also in him ....Ps 37:5   982
save them, because they *t* in him ....Ps 37:40   2620
and fear, and shall *t* in the LORD ....Ps 40:3   982
man that maketh the LORD his *t*.............Ps 40:4   4009
For I will not *t* in my bow ....Ps 44:6   982
They that *t* in their wealth, and ....Ps 49:6   982
I *t* in the mercy of God for ever..............Ps 52:8   982
but I will *t* in thee.................................Ps 55:23   982
I am afraid, I will *t* in thee ....Ps 56:3   982
his word, in God I have put my *t*............Ps 56:4   982
In God have I put my *t* ....Ps 56:11   982
I will *t* in the covert of thy ....Ps 61:4   2620
T in him at all times ....Ps 62:8   982
T not in oppression, and become ....Ps 62:10   982
in the LORD, and shall *t* in him...............Ps 64:10   2620
In thee, O LORD, do I put my *t* ....Ps 71:1   2620
thou art my *t* from my youth ....Ps 71:5   4004
I have put my *t* in the Lord GOD, ...Ps 73:28   4268
in him will I *t* ....Ps 91:2   982
and under his wings shalt thou *t*............Ps 91:4   2620
O Israel, *t* thou in the LORD ....Ps 115:9   982
O house of Aaron, *t* in the LORD ....Ps 115:10   982
that fear the LORD, *t* in the LORD ....Ps 115:11   982
It is better to *t* in the LORD ....Ps 118:8   2620
It is better to *t* in the LORD ....Ps 118:9   2620
for I *t* in thy word.................................Ps 119:42   982
They that *t* in the LORD shall be ....Ps 125:1   982
in thee is my *t*.......................................Ps 141:8   2620
for in thee do I *t* ....Ps 143:8   982
my shield, and he in whom I *t*................Ps 144:2   2620
Put not your *t* in princes........................Ps 146:3   982
T in the LORD with all thine....................Prov 3:5   982
That thy *t* may be in the LORD, I............Prov 22:19   4009
but he that putteth his *t* in the ....Prov 28:25   982
but whoso putteth his *t* in the................Prov 29:25   982
unto them that put their *t* in him ....Prov 30:5   2620
her husband doth safely *t* in her ....Prov 31:11   982
I will *t*, and not be afraid ....Is 12:2   982
poor of his people shall *t* in it ....Is 14:32   2620
T ye in the LORD for ever ....Is 26:4   982
to *t* in the shadow of Egypt....................Is 30:2   2620
the *t* in the shadow of Egypt your ....Is 30:3   2622
t in oppression and perverseness...........Is 30:12   982
t in chariots, because they are...............Is 31:1   982
now on whom dost thou *t*, that..............Is 36:5   982
of Egypt to all that *t* in him ....Is 36:6   982
to me, We *t* in the LORD our God ....Is 36:7   982
put thy *t* on Egypt for chariots ....Is 36:9   982
Hezekiah make you *t* in the LORD ....Is 36:15   982
that *t* in graven images, that say............Is 42:17   982
let him *t* in the name of the LORD ....Is 50:10   982
me, and on mine arm shall they *t*...........Is 51:5   3176
but he that putteth his *t* in me...............Is 57:13   2620
they *t* in vanity, and speak lies ....Is 59:4   982
T ye not in lying words, saying, ...Jer 7:4   982
ye *t* in lying words, that cannot ....Jer 7:8   982
called by my name, wherein ye *t*............Jer 7:14   982
and *t* ye not in any brother ....Jer 9:4   982
makest this people to *t* in a lie...............Jer 28:15   982
and he caused you to *t* in a lie ....Jer 29:31   982
because thou hast put thy *t* in me ....Jer 39:18   982
and all them that *t* in him ....Jer 46:25   982
and let thy widows *t* in me ....Jer 49:11   982
But thou didst *t* in thine own ....Eze 16:15   982

if he *t* to his own righteousness, ...Eze 33:13   982
because thou didst *t* in thy way...............Hos 10:13   982
t in the mountain of Samaria,.................Amos 6:1   982
T ye not in a friend, put ye not ....Mic 7:5   539
and he knoweth them that *t* in him ....Nah 1:7   2620
they shall *t* in the name of the ....Zeph 3:12   2620
in his name shall the Gentiles *t* ....Mt 12:21   1679
t in riches to enter into the ....Mk 10:24   *3982*
commit to your *t* the true riches............Lk 16:11   *4100*
you, even Moses, in whom ye *t* ....Jn 5:45   *1679*
in him shall the Gentiles *t*......................Rom 15:12   1679
for I *t* to see you in my journey, ...Rom 15:24   1679
but I *t* to tarry a while with you 1Cor 16:7   1679
that we should not *t* in ourselves 2Cor 1:9   3982
in whom we *t* that he will yet 2Cor 1:10   1679
I *t* ye shall acknowledge even to............2Cor 1:13   1679
such I *t* have we through Christ to 2Cor 3:4   4006
I *t* also are made manifest in..................2Cor 5:11   1679
If any man *t* to himself that he...............2Cor 10:7   3982
But I *t* that ye shall know that 2Cor 13:6   1679
But I *t* in the Lord Jesus to send.............Phil 2:19   1679
But I *t* in the Lord that I also..................Phil 2:24   3892
whereof he might *t* in the flesh ....Phil 3:4   3982
to be put in *t* with the gospel 1Th 2:4   4100
God, which was committed to my *t*.........1Ti 1:11   4100
because we *t* in the living God, ...1Ti 4:10   1679
nor *t* in uncertain riches, but in 1Ti 6:17   1679
that which is committed to thy *t*..............1Ti 6:20
for I *t* that through your prayers ....Philem 22   1679
And again, I will put my *t* in him ....Heb 2:13   3982
for we *t* we have a good ....Heb 13:18   3982
but I *t* to come unto you, and 2Jn 12   1679
But I *t* I shall shortly see thee,................3Jn 14   1679

TRUSTED
gods, their rock in whom they *t* ....Deut 32:37   2620
But Sihon *t* not Israel to pass ....Judg 11:20   539
because they *t* unto the liers in ....Judg 20:36   982
He *t* in the LORD God of Israel 2Kin 18:5   982
But I have *t* in thy mercy.......................Ps 13:5   982
Our fathers *t* in thee ....Ps 22:4   982
they *t*, and thou didst deliver ....Ps 22:4   982
they *t* in thee, and were not...................Ps 22:5   982
He *t* on the LORD that he would...............Ps 22:8   1556
I have *t* also in the LORD........................Ps 26:1   982
my heart *t* in him, and I am helped ....Ps 28:7   982
But I *t* in thee, O LORD...........................Ps 31:14   982
because we have *t* in his holy................Ps 33:21   982
own familiar friend, in whom I *t*............Ps 41:9   982
but *t* in the abundance of his ....Ps 52:7   982
in God, and *t* not in his salvation ....Ps 78:22   982
For thou hast *t* in thy wickedness..........Is 47:10   982
forgotten me, and *t* in falsehood ....Jer 13:25   982
because thou hast *t* in thy works............Jer 48:7   982
that *t* in her treasures, saying,...............Jer 49:4   982
his servants that *t* in him ....Dan 3:28   7365
she *t* not in the LORD ....Zeph 3:2   982
He *t* in God ....Mt 27:43   3982
him all his armour wherein he *t*............Lk 11:22   3982
t in themselves that they were ....Lk 18:9   3982
But we *t* that it had been he...................Lk 24:21   1679
his glory, who first *t* in Christ ....Eph 1:12   4276
In whom ye also *t*, after that ye ....Eph 1:13   1679
who *t* in God, adorned themselves, ...1Pet 3:5   1679

TRUSTEDST
walls come down, wherein thou *t*...........Deut 28:52   982
thy fenced cities, wherein thou *t* ....Jer 5:17   982
the land of peace, wherein thou *t* ....Jer 12:5   982

TRUSTEST
confidence is this wherein thou *t* 2Kin 18:19   982
thou *t* upon the staff of this...................2Kin 18:21   982
God in whom thou *t* deceive thee 2Kin 19:10   982
confidence is this wherein thou *t* ....Is 36:4   982
thou *t* in the staff of this ....Is 36:6   982
Let not thy God, in whom thou *t*............Is 37:10   982

TRUSTETH
he *t* that he can draw up Jordan ....Job 40:23   982
For the king *t* in the LORD.......................Ps 21:7   982
but he that *t* in the LORD ....Ps 32:10   982
blessed is the man that *t* in him............Ps 34:8   2620
for my soul *t* in thee ....Ps 57:1   2620
blessed is the man that *t* in thee ....Ps 84:12   982
save thy servant that *t* in thee ....Ps 86:2   982
so is every one that *t* in them.................Ps 115:8   982
so is every one that *t* in them.................Ps 135:18   982
He that *t* in his riches shall ....Prov 11:28   982
whoso *t* in the LORD, happy is he ....Prov 16:20   982
He that *t* in his own heart is a ....Prov 28:26   982
because he *t* in thee ....Is 26:3   982
Cursed be the man that *t* in man..........Jer 17:5   982

TRUSTING (continued)

is the man that *t* in the LORD .... Jer 17:7 · 982
the maker of his work *t* therein.............. Hab 2:18 · 982
t in God, and continueth in .... 1Ti 5:5 · *1679*

TRUSTING

his heart is fixed, *t* in the LORD.............. Ps 112:7 · 982

TRUSTY

removeth away the speech of the *t* .... Job 12:20 · 539

TRUTH

my master of his mercy and his *t* .... Gen 24:27 · 571
all the mercies, and of all the *t* .... Gen 32:10 · 571
whether there be any *t* in you .... Gen 42:16 · 571
men, such as fear God, men of *t* .... Ex 18:21 · 571
and abundant in goodness and *t* .... Ex 34:6 · 571
and, behold, if it be *t*, and the .... Deut 13:14 · 571
a God of *t* and without iniquity, ... Deut 32:4 · 530
and serve him in sincerity and in *t* .... Josh 24:14 · 571
If in *t* ye anoint me king over .... Judg 9:15 · 571
serve him in *t* with all your .... 1Sa 12:24 · 571
Of a *t* women have been kept from. 1Sa 21:5 · 3588,518
LORD shew kindness and *t* unto you ...... 2Sa 2:6 · 571
mercy and *t* be with thee........................ 2Sa 15:20 · 571
me in *t* with all their heart .... 1Kin 2:4 · 571
as he walked before thee in *t* .... 1Kin 3:6 · 571
of the LORD in thy mouth is *t*................ 1Kin 17:24 · 571
Of a *t*, LORD, the kings of...................... 2Kin 19:17 · 551
I have walked before thee in *t*................ 2Kin 20:3 · 571
good, if peace and *t* be in my days........ 2Kin 20:19 · 571
t to me in the name of the LORD............ 2Chr 18:15 · 571
t before the LORD his God...................... 2Chr 31:20 · 571
with words of peace and *t* .... Est 9:30 · 571
I know it is so of a *t* .... Job 9:2 · 551
and speaketh the *t* in his heart.............. Ps 15:2 · 571
Lead me in thy *t*, and teach me .... Ps 25:5 · 571
t unto such as keep his covenant .... Ps 25:10 · 571
and I have walked in thy *t* .... Ps 26:3 · 571
shall it declare thy *t* .... Ps 30:9 · 571
hast redeemed me, O LORD God of *t* ...... Ps 31:5 · 571
and all his works are done in *t* .... Ps 33:4 · 530
thy *t* from the great congregation .... Ps 40:10 · 571
thy *t* continually preserve me .... Ps 40:11 · 571
O send out thy light and thy *t*................ Ps 43:3 · 571
ride prosperously because of *t* .... Ps 45:4 · 571
thou desirest *t* in the inward .... Ps 51:6 · 571
cut them off in thy *t* .... Ps 54:5 · 571
send forth his mercy and his *t* .... Ps 57:3 · 571
heavens, and thy *t* unto the clouds .... Ps 57:10 · 571
may be displayed because of the .... Ps 60:4 · 7189
O prepare mercy and *t*, which may .... Ps 61:7 · 571
in the *t* of thy salvation.......................... Ps 69:13 · 571
with the psaltery, even thy *t* .... Ps 71:22 · 571
Mercy and *t* are met together .... Ps 85:10 · 571
T shall spring out of the earth .... Ps 85:11 · 571
I will walk in thy *t* .... Ps 86:11 · 571
and plenteous in mercy and *t*................ Ps 86:15 · 571
t shall go before thy face .... Ps 89:14 · 571
thou swarest unto David in thy *t* .... Ps 89:49 · 530
his *t* shall be thy shield and .... Ps 91:4 · 571
and the people with his *t* .... Ps 96:13 · 530
his *t* toward the house of Israel .... Ps 98:3 · 530
his *t* endureth to all generations............ Ps 100:5 · 530
thy *t* reacheth unto the clouds .... Ps 108:4 · 571
ever and ever, and are done in *t* .... Ps 111:8 · 571
the *t* of the LORD endureth for................ Ps 117:2 · 571
I have chosen the way of *t*...................... Ps 119:30 · 530
take not the word of *t* utterly .... Ps 119:43 · 571
and thy law is the *t* .... Ps 119:142 · 571
and all thy commandments are *t*............ Ps 119:151 · 571
LORD hath sworn in *t* unto David............ Ps 132:11 · 571
thy lovingkindness and for thy *t* .... Ps 138:2 · 571
to all that call upon him in *t*.................. Ps 145:18 · 571
which keepeth *t* for ever .... Ps 146:6 · 571
Let not mercy and *t* forsake thee............ Prov 3:3 · 571
For my mouth shall speak *t* .... Prov 8:7 · 571
He that speaketh *t* sheweth forth .... Prov 12:17 · 530
The lip of *t* shall be established.............. Prov 12:19 · 571
t shall be to them that devise .... Prov 14:22 · 571
By mercy and *t* iniquity is purged .... Prov 16:6 · 571
Mercy and *t* preserve the king .... Prov 20:28 · 571
the certainty of the words of *t* .... Prov 22:21 · 571
of *t* to them that send unto thee .... Prov 22:21 · 571
Buy the *t*, and sell it not .... Prov 23:23 · 571
was upright, even words of *t*.................. Eccl 12:10 · 571
Of a *t* many houses shall be .... Is 5:9 · 518,3808
the Holy One of Israel, in *t* .... Is 10:20 · 571
he shall sit upon it in *t* in the .... Is 16:5 · 571
of old are faithfulness and *t* .... Is 25:1 · 544
which keepeth the *t* may enter in .... Is 26:2 · 529
Of a *t*, LORD, the kings of...................... Is 37:18 · 551
I have walked before thee in *t*................ Is 38:3 · 571

the pit cannot hope for thy *t* .... Is 38:18 · 571
children shall make known thy *t*............ Is 38:19 · 571
shall be peace and *t* in my days............ Is 39:8 · 571
shall bring forth judgment unto *t* .... Is 42:3 · 571
or let them hear, and say, It is *t* .... Is 43:9 · 571
the God of Israel, but not in *t* .... Is 48:1 · 571
justice, nor any pleadeth for *t* .... Is 59:4 · 530
for *t* is fallen in the street, and.............. Is 59:14 · 571
Yea, *t* faileth.. Is 59:15 · 571
and I will direct their work in *t*.............. Is 61:8 · 571
bless himself in the God of *t* .... Is 65:16 · 548
earth shall swear by the God of *t* .... Is 65:16 · 548
swear, The LORD liveth, in *t* .... Jer 4:2 · 571
judgment, that seeketh the *t* .... Jer 5:1 · 530
are not thine eyes upon the *t* .... Jer 5:3 · 530
t is perished, and is cut off from .... Jer 7:28 · 530
valiant for the *t* upon the earth .... Jer 9:3 · 530
and will not speak the *t* .... Jer 9:5 · 571
for of a *t* the LORD hath sent me .... Jer 26:15 · 571
them the abundance of peace and *t* ...... Jer 33:6 · 571
Of a *t* it is, that your God is a................ Dan 2:47 · 7187
of heaven, all whose works are *t*............ Dan 4:37 · 7187
and asked him the *t* of all this .... Dan 7:16 · 3330
know the *t* of the fourth beast................ Dan 7:19 · 3321
it cast down the *t* to the ground............ Dan 8:12 · 571
iniquities, and understand thy *t*............ Dan 9:13 · 571
is noted in the scripture of *t*.................. Dan 10:21 · 571
And now will I shew thee the *t* .... Dan 11:2 · 571
the land, because there is no *t* .... Hos 4:1 · 571
Thou wilt perform the *t* to Jacob............ Mic 7:20 · 571
shall be called a city of *t* .... Zec 8:3 · 571
and I will be their God, in *t*.................... Zec 8:8 · 571
every man the *t* to his neighbour .... Zec 8:16 · 571
execute the judgment of *t* .... Zec 8:16 · 571
therefore love the *t* and peace................ Zec 8:19 · 571
The law of *t* was in his mouth, and........ Mal 2:6 · 571
Of a *t* thou art the Son of God .... Mt 14:33 · 230
And she said, *T*, Lord .... Mt 15:27 · 3483
and teachest the way of God in *t* .... Mt 22:16 · 225
before him, and told him all the *t* .... Mk 5:33 · 225
but teachest the way of God in *t*............ Mk 12:14 · 225
Master, thou hast said the *t*.................... Mk 12:32 · 225
But I tell you of a *t*, many...................... Lk 4:25 · 225
But I tell you of a *t*, there be................ Lk 9:27 · 230
Of a *t* I say unto you, that he .... Lk 12:44 · 230
Of a *t* I say unto you, that this .... Lk 21:3 · 230
Of a *t* this fellow also was with.............. Lk 22:59 · 225
the Father,) full of grace and *t* .... Jn 1:14 · 225
grace and *t* came by Jesus Christ .... Jn 1:17 · 225
But he that doeth *t* cometh to the........ Jn 3:21 · 225
the Father in spirit and in *t*................... Jn 4:23 · 225
worship him in spirit and in *t* .... Jn 4:24 · 225
and he bare witness unto the *t*.............. Jn 5:33 · 225
This is of a *t* that prophet that .... Jn 6:14 · 230
Of a *t* this is the Prophet .... Jn 7:40 · 230
And ye shall know the *t*, and the.......... Jn 8:32 · 225
the *t* shall make you free .... Jn 8:32 · 225
a man that hath told you the *t*.............. Jn 8:40 · 225
beginning, and abode not in the *t* .... Jn 8:44 · 225
because there is no *t* in him .... Jn 8:44 · 225
And because I tell you the *t* .... Jn 8:45 · 225
And if I say the *t*, why do ye not .... Jn 8:46 · 225
unto him, I am the way, the *t* .... Jn 14:6 · 225
Even the Spirit of *t*............................... Jn 14:17 · 225
the Father, even the Spirit of *t* .... Jn 15:26 · 225
Nevertheless I tell you the *t* .... Jn 16:7 · 225
Howbeit when he, the Spirit of *t* .... Jn 16:13 · 225
he will guide you into all *t* .... Jn 16:13 · 225
Sanctify them through thy *t* .... Jn 17:17 · 225
thy word is *t* .... Jn 17:17 · 225
might be sanctified through the *t* .... Jn 17:19 · 225
I should bear witness unto the *t* .... Jn 18:37 · 225
that is of the *t* heareth my voice .... Jn 18:37 · 225
Pilate saith unto him, What is *t*.............. Jn 18:38 · 225
For of a *t* against thy holy child .... Acts 4:27 · 225
Of a *t* I perceive that God is no .... Acts 10:34 · 225
but speak forth the words of *t*................ Acts 26:25 · 225
who hold the *t* in unrighteousness .... Rom 1:18 · 225
Who changed the *t* of God into a .... Rom 1:25 · 225
t against them which commit such .... Rom 2:2 · 225
contentious, and do not obey the *t*........ Rom 2:8 · 225
knowledge and of the *t* in the law.......... Rom 2:20 · 225
For if the *t* of God hath more .... Rom 3:7 · 225
I say the *t* in Christ, I lie not, ... Rom 9:1 · 225
the circumcision for the *t* of God .... Rom 15:8 · 225
bread of sincerity and *t* .... 1Cor 5:8 · 225
iniquity, but rejoiceth in the *t*................ 1Cor 13:6 · 225
report that God is in you of a *t*.............. 1Cor 14:25 · 3689
but by manifestation of the *t* .... 2Cor 4:2 · 225
By the word of *t*, by the power of .... 2Cor 6:7 · 225
we spake all things to you in *t* .... 2Cor 7:14 · 225

I made before Titus, is found a *t* 2Cor 7:14   225
As the *t* of Christ is in me, no 2Cor 11:10   225
for I will say the *t* 2Cor 12:6   225
against the *t*, but for the *t* 2Cor 13:8   225
that the *t* of the gospel might ....Gal 2:5   225
according to the *t* of the gospel ....Gal 2:14   225
that ye should not obey the *t* ....Gal 3:1   225
enemy, because I tell you the *t* ....Gal 4:16   226
you that ye should not obey the *t* ....Gal 5:7   225
after that ye heard the word of *t* ....Eph 1:13   225
But speaking the *t* in love ....Eph 4:15   226
by him, as the *t* is in Jesus ....Eph 4:21   225
speak every man *t* with his ....Eph 4:25   226
goodness and righteousness and *t* ....Eph 5:9   226
your loins girt about with *t* ....Eph 6:14   226
way, whether in pretence, or in *t* ....Phil 1:18   226
the word of the *t* of the gospel ....Col 1:5   226
it, and knew the grace of God in *t* ....Col 1:6   226
word of men, but as it is in *t* 1Th 2:13   230
received not the love of the *t* 2Th 2:10   225
be damned who believed not the *t* 2Th 2:12   225
of the Spirit and belief of the *t* 2Th 2:13   225
come unto the knowledge of the *t* 1Ti 2:4   225
apostle, (I speak the *t* in Christ 1Ti 2:7   225
the pillar and ground of the *t* 1Ti 3:15   225
them which believe and know the *t* 1Ti 4:3   225
minds, and destitute of the *t* 1Ti 6:5   225
rightly dividing the word of *t* 2Ti 2:15   225
Who concerning the *t* have erred 2Ti 2:18   225
to the acknowledging of the *t* 2Ti 2:25   225
to come to the knowledge of the *t* 2Ti 3:7   225
so do these also resist the *t* 2Ti 3:8   225
turn away their ears from the *t* 2Ti 4:4   225
of the *t* which is after godliness ....Titus 1:1   225
of men, that turn from the *t* ....Titus 1:14   225
received the knowledge of the *t* ....Heb 10:26   225
begat he us with the word of *t* ....Jas 1:18   225
not, and lie not against the *t* ....Jas 3:14   225
if any of you do err from the *t* ....Jas 5:19   225
the *t* through the Spirit unto 1Pet 1:22   225
be established in the present *t* 2Pet 1:12   225
way of *t* shall be evil spoken of 2Pet 2:2   225
darkness, we lie, and do not the *t* 1Jn 1:6   225
ourselves, and the *t* is not in us 1Jn 1:8   225
is a liar, and the *t* is not in him 1Jn 2:4   225
you because ye know not the *t* 1Jn 2:21   225
it, and that no lie is of the *t* 1Jn 2:21   225
you of all things, and is *t* 1Jn 2:27   227
but in deed and in *t* 1Jn 3:18   225
we know that we are of the *t* 1Jn 3:19   225
Hereby know we the spirit of *t* 1Jn 4:6   225
witness, because the Spirit is *t* 1Jn 5:6   225
children, whom I love in the *t* 2Jn 1   225
all they that have known the *t* 2Jn 1   225
the Son of the Father, in *t* 2Jn 3   225
of thy children walking in *t* 2Jn 4   225
Gaius, whom I love in the *t* 3Jn 1   225
of the *t* that is in thee, even as 3Jn 3   225
even as thou walkest in the *t* 3Jn 3   225
hear that my children walk in *t* 3Jn 4   225
might be fellowhelpers to the *t* 3Jn 8   225
of all men, and of the *t* itself 3Jn 12   225

TRUTH'S
for thy mercy, and for thy *t* sake ....Ps 115:1   571
For the *t* sake, which dwelleth in 2Jn 2   225

TRY
I will *t* them for thee there ....Judg 7:4   6884
to *t* him, that he might know all 2Chr 32:31   5254
morning, and *t* him every moment..........Job 7:18   974
Doth not the ear *t* words ....Job 12:11   974
his eyes behold, his eyelids *t* ....Ps 11:4   974
t my reins and my heart..........................Ps 26:2   6884
t me, and know my thoughts ....Ps 139:23   974
thou mayest know and *t* their way ....Jer 6:27   974
I will melt them, and *t* them ....Jer 9:7   974
I *t* the reins, even to give every ....Jer 17:10   974
t our ways, and turn again to the ....Lam 3:40   2713
to *t* them, and to purge, and to ....Dan 11:35   6884
will *t* them as gold is tried....................Zec 13:9   974
the fire shall *t* every man's work............1Cor 3:13   1381
the fiery trial which is to *t* you 1Pet 4:12   4314,3986
but *t* the spirits whether they................1Jn 4:1   1381
to *t* them that dwell upon the ....Rev 3:10   3985

TRYING
that the *t* of your faith worketh..............Jas 1:3   1383

TRYPHAENA See TRYPHENA.

TRYPHENA *(tri-fe'-nah) A Christian in Rome.*
Salute *T* and Tryphosa, who labour ....Rom 16:12   5170

TRYPHOSA *(tri-fo'-sah) A Christian in Rome.*
Salute Tryphena and *T*, who labour........Rom 16:12   5173

TUBAL *(tu'-bal)*
    1. A son of Japeth.
Magog, and Madai, and Javan, and *T*....Gen 10:2   8422
Magog, and Madai, and Javan, and *T*....1Chr 1:5   8422
    2. Migrants to Sicily and Spain.
and Lud, that draw the bow, to *T*...........Is 66:19   8422
Javan, *T*, and Meshech, they were ....Eze 27:13   8422
There is Meshech, *T*, and all her ....Eze 32:26   8422
the chief prince of Meshech and *T*.........Eze 38:2   8422
the chief prince of Meshech and *T*.........Eze 38:3   8422
the chief prince of Meshech and *T*.........Eze 39:1   8422

TUBAL-CAIN *(tu'-bal-cain) Son of Lamech.*
And Zillah, she also bare *T*....................Gen 4:22   8423
and the sister of *T* was Naamah............Gen 4:22   8423

TUMBLED
a cake of barley bread *t* into the ....Judg 7:13   2015

TUMULT
What meaneth the noise of this *t* 1Sa 4:14   1995
me thy servant, I saw a great *t*..............2Sa 18:29   1995
thy *t* is come up into mine ears,.............2Kin 19:28   7600
waves, and the *t* of the people ....Ps 65:7   1995
the *t* of those that rise up ....Ps 74:23   7588
For, lo, thine enemies make a *t*..............Ps 83:2   1993
noise of the *t* the people fled ....Is 33:3   1995
thy rage against me, and thy *t* ....Is 37:29   7600
with the noise of a great *t* he ....Jer 11:16   1999
Therefore shall a *t* arise among..............Hos 10:14   7588
and Moab shall die with *t*, with ....Amos 2:2   7588
that a great *t* from the LORD ....Zec 14:13   4103
but that rather a *t* was made ....Mt 27:24   2351
of the synagogue, and seeth the *t* ....Mk 5:38   2351
not know the certainty for the *t* ....Acts 21:34   2351
with multitude, nor with *t*......................Acts 24:18   2351

TUMULTS
behold the great *t* in the midst..............Amos 3:9   4103
stripes, in imprisonments, in *t* 2Cor 6:5   181
whisperings, swellings, *t*........................2Cor 12:20   181

TUMULTUOUS
a *t* noise of the kingdoms of ....Is 13:4   7588
of stirs, a *t* city, a joyous city..................Is 22:2   1993
crown of the head of the *t* ones ....Jer 48:45   1121,7588

TURN
t in, I pray you, into your ....Gen 19:2   5493
that I may *t* to the right hand, ...Gen 24:49   6437
until thy brother's fury *t* away ....Gen 27:44   7725
brother's anger *t* away from thee ....Gen 27:45   7725
And Moses said, I will now *t* aside ....Ex 3:3   5493
children of Israel, that they *t*................Ex 14:2   7725
enemies *t* their backs unto thee............Ex 23:27   2015
T from thy fierce wrath, and ....Ex 32:12   7725
Or if the raw flesh *t* again......................Lev 13:16   7725
T ye not unto idols, nor make to ....Lev 19:4   6437
To morrow *t* you, and get you into ....Num 14:25   6437
we will not *t* to the right hand..............Num 20:17   5186
we will not *t* into the fields, or..............Num 21:22   5186
the ass, to *t* her into the way ....Num 22:23   5186
where was no way to *t* either to ....Num 22:26   5186
For if ye *t* away from after him,..............Num 32:15   7725
your border shall *t* from the ....Num 34:4   5437
T you, and take your journey, and ....Deut 1:7   6437
t you, and take your journey into ....Deut 1:40   6437
t you northward..................................Deut 2:3   6437
I will neither *t* unto the right..................Deut 2:27   5493
if thou *t* to the LORD thy God, and ....Deut 4:30   7725
ye shall not *t* aside to the right ....Deut 5:32   5493
For they will *t* away thy son from ....Deut 7:4   5493
ye *t* aside, and serve other gods,...........Deut 11:16   5493
but *t* aside out of the way which ....Deut 11:28   5493
because he hath spoken to *t* you ....Deut 13:5   5627
that the LORD may *t* from the ....Deut 13:17   7725
Then shalt thou *t* it into money ....Deut 14:25   5414
thou shalt *t* in the morning, and ....Deut 16:7   6437
that his heart *t* not away ....Deut 17:17   5493
that he *t* not aside from the way ....Deut 17:20   5493
dig therewith, and shalt *t* back ....Deut 23:13   7725
in thee, and *t* away from thee................Deut 23:14   7725
LORD thy God will *t* thy captivity............Deut 30:3   7725
if thou *t* unto the LORD thy God ....Deut 30:10   7725
But if thine heart *t* away........................Deut 30:17   6437
then will they *t* unto other gods, ...Deut 31:20   6437
t aside from the way which I have ....Deut 31:29   5493
t not from it to the right hand ....Josh 1:7   5493
to *t* away this day from following ....Josh 22:16   7725
But that ye must *t* away this day ....Josh 22:18   7725
to *t* from following the LORD ....Josh 22:23   7725

T

t this day from following the	Josh 22:29	7725
that ye *t* not aside therefrom to	Josh 23:6	5493
strange gods, then he will *t*	Josh 24:20	7725
T in, my lord, *t* in to me	Judg 4:18	5493
Therefore we *t* again to thee now,	Judg 11:8	7725
let us *t* in into this city of the	Judg 19:11	5493
We will not *t* aside hither into	Judg 19:12	5493
we any of us *t* into his house	Judg 20:8	5493
Naomi said, *T* again, my daughters	Ruth 1:11	7725
T again, my daughters, go your	Ruth 1:12	7725
t aside, sit down here	Ruth 4:1	5493
yet *t* not aside from following	1Sa 12:20	5493
And *t* ye not aside	1Sa 12:21	5493
t thee; behold, I am	1Sa 14:7	5186
t again with me, that I may	1Sa 15:25	7725
t again with me, that I may	1Sa 15:30	7725
footmen that stood about him, *T*	1Sa 22:17	5437
T thou, and fall upon the priests	1Sa 22:18	5437
T thee aside to thy right hand or	2Sa 2:21	5186
But Asahel would not *t* aside from	2Sa 2:21	5493
T thee aside from following me	2Sa 2:22	5493
Howbeit he refused to *t* aside	2Sa 2:23	5493
none can *t* to the right hand or	2Sa 14:19	
Let him *t* to his own house, and	2Sa 14:24	5437
t the counsel of Ahithophel into	2Sa 15:31	
unto him, *T* aside, and stand here	2Sa 18:30	5437
t back again, that I may die in	2Sa 19:37	7725
shall *t* again to thee, and confess	1Kin 8:33	7725
t from their sin, when thou	1Kin 8:35	7725
shall at all *t* from following me	1Kin 9:6	7725
for surely thou will *t* away your	1Kin 11:2	5186
people *t* again unto their lord	1Kin 12:27	7725
nor *t* again by the same way that	1Kin 13:9	7725
nor *t* again to go by the way that	1Kin 13:17	7725
t thee eastward, and hide thyself	1Kin 17:3	6437
T thine hand, and carry me out of	1Kin 22:34	2015
t again unto the king that sent	2Kin 1:6	7725
to us, that he shall *t* in thither	2Kin 4:10	5493
t thee behind me	2Kin 9:18	5437
t thee behind me	2Kin 9:19	5437
T ye from your evil ways, and keep	2Kin 17:13	7725
How then wilt thou *t* away the	2Kin 18:24	7725
I will *t* thee back by the way by	2Kin 19:28	7725
T again, and tell Hezekiah the	2Kin 20:5	7725
to *t* the kingdom of Saul to him,	1Chr 12:23	5437
t away from them, and come upon	1Chr 14:14	5437
t from their sin, when thou dost	2Chr 6:26	7725
they are carried captive, and *t*	2Chr 6:37	7725
t not away the face of thine	2Chr 6:42	7725
face, and *t* from their wicked ways	2Chr 7:14	7725
But if ye *t* away, and forsake my	2Chr 7:19	7725
did *t* unto the Lord God of Israel	2Chr 15:4	7725
T thine hand, that thou mayest	2Chr 18:33	2015
t away from following the Lord	2Chr 25:27	5493
fierce wrath may *t* away from us	2Chr 29:10	7725
t again unto the Lord God of	2Chr 30:6	7725
of his wrath may *t* away from you	2Chr 30:8	7725
For if ye *t* again unto the Lord,	2Chr 30:9	7725
will not *t* away his face from you	2Chr 30:9	5493
would not *t* his face from him	2Chr 35:22	5437
But if ye *t* unto me, and keep my	Neh 1:9	7725
t their reproach upon their own	Neh 4:4	7725
against them to *t* them to thee	Neh 9:26	7725
Now when every maid's *t* was come	Est 2:12	8447
Now when the *t* of Esther, the	Est 2:15	8447
which of the saints wilt thou *t*	Job 5:1	6437
T from him, that he may rest,	Job 14:6	8159
is in one mind, and who can *t* him	Job 23:13	7725
They *t* the needy out of the way	Job 24:4	5186
man shall *t* again unto dust	Job 34:15	7725
how long will ye *t* my glory into	Ps 4:2	
If he *t* not, he will whet his	Ps 7:12	7725
neither did I *t* again till they	Ps 18:37	7725
shalt thou make them *t* their back	Ps 21:12	
shall remember and *t* unto the Lord	Ps 22:27	7725
T thee unto me, and have mercy	Ps 25:16	6437
nor such as *t* aside to lies	Ps 40:4	7750
Thou makest us to *t* back from the	Ps 44:10	7725
then shall mine enemies *t* back	Ps 56:9	7725
O *t* thyself to us again	Ps 60:1	7725
t unto me according to the	Ps 69:16	6437
T us again, O God, and cause thy	Ps 80:3	7725
T us again, O God of hosts, and	Ps 80:7	7725
T us again, O Lord God of hosts,	Ps 80:19	7725
T us, O God of our salvation, and	Ps 85:4	7725
but let them not *t* again to folly	Ps 85:8	7725
O *t* unto me, and have mercy upon	Ps 86:16	6437
the work of them that *t* aside	Ps 101:3	7750
that they *t* not again to cover	Ps 104:9	7725
to *t* away his wrath, lest he	Ps 106:23	7725
T away mine eyes from beholding	Ps 119:37	5674

T away my reproach which I fear	Ps 119:39	5674
those that fear thee *t* unto me	Ps 119:79	7725
As for such as *t* aside unto their	Ps 125:5	5186
T again our captivity, O Lord, as	Ps 126:4	7725
sake *t* not away the face of thine	Ps 132:10	7725
he will not *t* from it	Ps 132:11	7725
T you at my reproof	Prov 1:23	7725
by it, *t* from it, and pass away	Prov 4:15	7847
T not to the right hand nor to	Prov 4:27	5186
is simple, let him *t* in hither	Prov 9:4	5493
is simple, let him *t* in hither	Prov 9:16	5493
he *t* away his wrath from him	Prov 24:18	7725
shame, and thine infamy *t* not away	Prov 25:10	7725
but wise men *t* away wrath	Prov 29:8	7725
the dust, and all *t* to dust again	Eccl 3:20	7725
and the shadows flee away, *t*	Song 2:17	5437
T away thine eyes from me, for	Song 6:5	5437
I will *t* my hand upon thee, and	Is 1:25	7725
To *t* aside the needy from	Is 10:2	5186
every man *t* to his own people	Is 13:14	6437
out, and who shall *t* it back	Is 14:27	7725
they shall *t* the rivers far away	Is 19:6	2186
He will surely violently *t*	Is 22:18	6801
she shall *t* to her hire, and shall	Is 23:17	7725
that *t* the battle to the gate	Is 28:6	7725
t aside the just for a thing of	Is 29:21	5186
t aside out of the path, cause	Is 30:11	5186
when ye *t* to the right hand, and	Is 30:21	
hand, and when ye *t* to the left	Is 30:21	
T ye unto him from whom the	Is 31:6	7725
How then wilt thou *t* away the	Is 36:9	7725
I will *t* thee back by the way by	Is 37:29	7725
If thou *t* away thy foot from the	Is 58:13	7725
to Zion, and unto them that *t* from	Is 59:20	7725
her occasion who can *t* her away	Jer 2:24	7725
surely thy anger shall *t* from me	Jer 2:35	7725
all these things, *T* thou unto me	Jer 3:7	7725
T, O backsliding children, saith	Jer 3:14	7725
and shalt not *t* away from me	Jer 3:19	7725
neither will I *t* back from it	Jer 4:28	7725
t back thine hand as a	Jer 6:9	7725
shall he *t* away, and not return	Jer 8:4	7725
he *t* it into the shadow of death,	Jer 13:16	7760
t from their evil, I will repent	Jer 18:8	7725
to *t* away thy wrath from them	Jer 18:20	7725
I will *t* back the weapons of war	Jer 21:4	5437
T ye again now every one from his	Jer 25:5	7725
t every man from his evil way,	Jer 26:3	7725
I will *t* away your captivity, and	Jer 29:14	7725
for I will *t* their mourning into	Jer 31:13	2015
t thou me, and I shall be turned	Jer 31:18	7725
t again, O virgin of Israel	Jer 31:21	7725
t again to these thy cities	Jer 31:21	7725
that I will not *t* away from them	Jer 32:40	7725
ear to *t* from their wickedness	Jer 44:5	7725
t back, dwell deep, O inhabitants	Jer 49:8	6437
shall *t* every one to his people	Jer 50:16	6437
iniquity, to *t* away thy captivity	Lam 2:14	7725
To *t* aside the right of a man	Lam 3:35	5186
our ways, and *t* again to the Lord	Lam 3:40	7725
T thou us unto thee, O Lord, and	Lam 5:21	7725
he *t* not from his wickedness, nor	Eze 3:19	7725
man doth *t* from his righteousness	Eze 3:20	7725
thou shalt not *t* thee from one	Eze 4:8	2015
My face will *t* also from them	Eze 7:22	5437
but *t* thee yet again, and thou	Eze 8:6	7725
T thee yet again, and thou shalt	Eze 8:13	7725
t thee yet again, and thou shalt	Eze 8:15	7725
t yourselves from your idols	Eze 14:6	7725
t away your faces from all your	Eze 14:6	7725
But if the wicked will *t* from all	Eze 18:21	7725
t yourselves from all your	Eze 18:30	7725
wherefore *t* yourselves, and live	Eze 18:32	7725
wicked of his way to *t* from it	Eze 33:9	7725
if he do not *t* from his way	Eze 33:9	7725
that the wicked *t* from his way	Eze 33:11	7725
t ye, *t* ye from your evil ways	Eze 33:11	7725
if he *t* from his sin, and do that	Eze 33:14	7725
But if the wicked *t* from his	Eze 33:19	7725
I will *t* unto you, and ye shall be	Eze 36:9	6437
I will *t* thee back, and put hooks	Eze 38:4	7725
to *t* thine hand upon the desolate	Eze 38:12	7725
I will *t* thee back, and leave but	Eze 39:2	7725
our God, that we might *t* from our	Dan 9:13	7725
After this shall he *t* his face	Dan 11:18	7725
he shall cause it to *t* upon him	Dan 11:18	7725
Then he shall *t* his face toward	Dan 11:19	7725
they that *t* many to righteousness	Dan 12:3	7725
their doings to *t* unto their God	Hos 5:4	7725
Therefore *t* thou to thy God	Hos 12:6	7725
with you words, and *t* to the Lord	Hos 14:2	7725

t ye even to me with all your	Joel 2:12	7725
and *t* unto the LORD your God	Joel 2:13	7725
I will not *t* away the punishment	Amos 1:3	7725
I will not *t* away the punishment	Amos 1:6	7725
I will *t* mine hand against Ekron	Amos 1:8	7725
I will not *t* away the punishment	Amos 1:9	7725
I will not *t* away the punishment	Amos 1:11	7725
I will not *t* away the punishment	Amos 1:13	7725
I will not *t* away the punishment	Amos 2:1	7725
I will not *t* away the punishment	Amos 2:4	7725
I will not *t* away the punishment	Amos 2:6	7725
t aside the way of the meek	Amos 2:7	5186
Ye who *t* judgment to wormwood, and	Amos 5:7	2015
they *t* aside the poor in the gate	Amos 5:12	5186
I will *t* your feasts into	Amos 8:10	2015
let them *t* every one from his	Jonah 3:8	7725
Who can tell if God will *t*	Jonah 3:9	7725
t away from his fierce anger,	Jonah 3:9	7725
He will *t* again, he will have	Mic 7:19	7725
them, and *t* away their captivity	Zeph 2:7	7725
For then will I *t* to the people a	Zeph 3:9	2015
when I *t* back your captivity	Zeph 3:20	7725
T ye unto me, saith the LORD of	Zec 1:3	7725
I will *t* unto you, saith the LORD	Zec 1:3	7725
T ye now from your evil ways, and	Zec 1:4	7725
T you to the strong hold, ye	Zec 9:12	7725
with their children, and *t* again	Zec 10:9	7725
I will *t* mine hand upon the	Zec 13:7	7725
did *t* many away from iniquity	Mal 2:6	7725
that *t* aside the stranger from	Mal 3:5	5186
he shall *t* the heart of the	Mal 4:6	7725
cheek, *t* to him the other also	Mt 5:39	4762
borrow of thee *t* not thou away	Mt 5:42	654
feet, and *t* again and rend you	Mt 7:6	4762
him that is in the field not *t*	Mk 13:16	1994
shall he *t* to the Lord their God	Lk 1:16	1994
to *t* the hearts of the fathers to	Lk 1:17	1994
if not, it shall *t* to you again	Lk 10:6	344
times in a day *t* again to thee	Lk 17:4	1994
it shall *t* to you for a testimony	Lk 21:13	576
seeking to *t* away the deputy from	Acts 13:8	1294
life, lo, we *t* to the Gentiles	Acts 13:46	4762
t from these vanities unto the	Acts 14:15	1994
to *t* them from darkness to light,	Acts 26:18	1994
t to God, and do works meet for	Acts 26:20	1994
shall *t* away ungodliness from	Rom 11:26	654
when it shall *t* to the Lord	2Cor 3:16	1994
how *t* ye again to the weak and	Gal 4:9	1994
For I know that this shall *t* to	Phil 1:19	576
from such *t* away	2Ti 3:5	665
they shall *t* away their ears from	2Ti 4:4	654
of men, that *t* from the truth	Titus 1:14	654
if we *t* away from him that	Heb 12:25	654
we *t* about their whole body	Jas 3:3	3329
to *t* from the holy commandment	2Pet 2:21	1994
over waters to *t* them to blood	Rev 11:6	4762

TURNED

a flaming sword which *t* every way	Gen 3:24	2015
the men *t* their faces from thence	Gen 18:22	6437
they *t* in unto him, and entered	Gen 19:3	5493
t in to a certain Adullamite,	Gen 38:1	5186
he *t* unto her by the way, and said	Gen 38:16	5186
he *t* himself about from them, and	Gen 42:24	5437
LORD saw that he *t* aside to see	Ex 3:4	5493
it was *t* again as his other flesh	Ex 4:7	7725
the rod which *t* to a serpent	Ex 7:15	2015
and they shall be *t* to blood	Ex 7:17	2015
were in the river were *t* to blood	Ex 7:20	2015
And Pharaoh *t* and went into his	Ex 7:23	6437
he *t* himself, and went out from	Ex 10:6	6437
the LORD *t* a mighty strong west	Ex 10:19	2015
servants was *t* against the people	Ex 14:5	2015
They have *t* aside quickly out of	Ex 32:8	5493
And Moses *t*, and went down from the	Ex 32:15	6437
And he *t* again into the camp	Ex 33:11	7725
the hair in the plague is *t* white	Lev 13:3	2015
the hair thereof be not *t* white	Lev 13:4	2015
it have *t* the hair white, and	Lev 13:10	2015
it is all *t* white	Lev 13:13	2015
if the plague be *t* into white	Lev 13:17	2015
and the hair thereof be *t* white	Lev 13:20	2015
in the bright spot be *t* white	Lev 13:25	2015
because ye are *t* away from the	Num 14:43	7725
wherefore Israel *t* away from him	Num 20:21	5186
And they *t* and went up by the way	Num 21:33	6437
the ass *t* aside out of the way,	Num 22:23	5186
t from me these three times	Num 22:33	5186
unless she had *t* from me, surely	Num 22:33	5186
LORD may be *t* away from Israel	Num 25:4	7725
hath *t* my wrath away from the	Num 25:11	7725

t again unto Pi-hahiroth, which	Num 33:7	7725
And they *t* and went up into the	Deut 1:24	6437
Then we *t*, and took our journey	Deut 2:1	6437
Elath, and from Ezion-gaber, we *t*	Deut 2:8	6437
Then we *t*, and went up the way to	Deut 3:1	6437
they are quickly *t* aside out of	Deut 9:12	5493
So I *t* and came down from the	Deut 9:15	6437
ye had *t* aside quickly out of the	Deut 9:16	5493
I *t* myself and came down from the	Deut 10:5	6437
but the LORD thy God *t* the curse	Deut 23:5	2015
that they are *t* unto other gods	Deut 31:18	6437
but *t* their backs before their	Josh 7:8	6437
So the LORD *t* from the fierceness	Josh 7:26	7725
t back upon the pursuers	Josh 8:20	2015
city ascended, then they *t* again	Josh 8:21	7725
And Joshua at that time *t* back	Josh 11:10	7725
t from Sarid eastward toward the	Josh 19:12	7725
they *t* quickly out of the way	Judg 2:17	5493
But he himself *t* again from the	Judg 3:19	7725
when he had *t* in unto her into	Judg 4:18	5493
the children of Israel *t* again	Judg 8:33	7725
he *t* aside to see the carcase of	Judg 14:8	5493
and *t* tail to tail, and put a	Judg 15:4	6437
they *t* in thither, and said unto	Judg 18:3	5493
they *t* thitherward, and came to	Judg 18:15	5493
So they *t* and departed, and put the	Judg 18:21	6437
they *t* their faces, and said unto	Judg 18:23	5437
were too strong for him, he *t*	Judg 18:26	6437
they *t* aside thither, to go in and	Judg 19:15	5493
And when the men of Israel *t* again	Judg 20:41	2015
Therefore they *t* their backs	Judg 20:42	6437
And they *t* and fled toward the	Judg 20:45	6437
But six hundred men *t* and fled to	Judg 20:47	6437
the men of Israel *t* again upon	Judg 20:48	7725
the man was afraid, and *t* himself	Ruth 3:8	3943
And he *t* aside, and sat down	Ruth 4:1	5493
t not aside to the right hand or	1Sa 6:12	5493
but *t* aside after lucre, and took	1Sa 8:3	5186
shalt be *t* into another man	1Sa 10:6	2015
that when he had *t* his back to go	1Sa 10:9	6437
one company *t* unto the way that	1Sa 13:17	6437
another company *t* the way to	1Sa 13:18	6437
another company *t* to the way of	1Sa 13:18	6437
even they also *t* to be with the	1Sa 14:21	7725
and whithersoever he *t* himself	1Sa 14:47	6437
for he is *t* back from following	1Sa 15:11	7725
as Samuel *t* about to go away, he	1Sa 15:27	5437
So Samuel *t* again after Saul	1Sa 15:31	7725
he *t* from him toward another, and	1Sa 17:30	5437
And Doeg the Edomite *t*, and he fell	1Sa 22:18	5437
So David's young men *t* their way	1Sa 25:12	2015
the bow of Jonathan *t* not back	2Sa 1:22	7734
in going he *t* not to the right	2Sa 2:19	5186
he *t* aside, and stood still	2Sa 18:30	5437
the victory that day was *t* into	2Sa 19:2	2015
t not again until I had consumed	2Sa 22:38	7725
howbeit the kingdom is *t* about	1Kin 2:15	5437
for Joab had *t* after Adonijah,	1Kin 2:28	5186
though he *t* not after Absalom	1Kin 2:28	5186
the king *t* his face about, and	1Kin 8:14	5437
So she *t* and went to her own	1Kin 10:13	6437
his wives *t* away his heart	1Kin 11:3	5186
that his wives *t* away his heart	1Kin 11:4	5186
because his heart was *t* from the	1Kin 11:9	5186
t not aside from any thing that	1Kin 15:5	5493
that thou hast *t* their heart back	1Kin 18:37	5437
and, behold, a man *t* aside	1Kin 20:39	5493
t away his face, and would eat no	1Kin 21:4	5437
they *t* aside to fight against him	1Kin 22:32	5493
that they *t* back from pursuing	1Kin 22:33	7725
he *t* not aside from it, doing	1Kin 22:43	5493
the messengers *t* back unto him	2Kin 1:5	7725
unto them, Why are ye now *t* back	2Kin 1:5	7725
he *t* back, and looked on them, and	2Kin 2:24	6437
he *t* in thither to eat bread	2Kin 4:8	5493
he *t* into the chamber, and lay	2Kin 4:11	5493
So he *t* and went away in a rage	2Kin 5:12	6437
when the man *t* again from his	2Kin 5:26	2015
Joram *t* his hands, and fled, and	2Kin 9:23	2015
So the king of Assyria *t* back	2Kin 15:20	7725
t he from the house of the LORD	2Kin 16:18	5437
Then he *t* his face to the wall,	2Kin 20:2	5437
t not aside to the right hand or	2Kin 22:2	5493
And as Josiah *t* himself, he spied	2Kin 23:16	6437
that *t* to the LORD with all his	2Kin 23:25	7725
Notwithstanding the LORD *t* not	2Kin 23:26	7725
t his name to Jehoiakim, and took	2Kin 23:34	5437
then he *t* and rebelled against him	2Kin 24:1	7725
t the kingdom unto David the son	1Chr 10:14	5437
And Ornan *t* back, and saw the angel	1Chr 21:20	7725
And the king *t* his face, and	2Chr 6:3	5437

T

So she *t*, and went away to her own .... 2Chr 9:12 — 2015
the wrath of the LORD *t* from him .... 2Chr 12:12 — 7725
they *t* back again from pursuing .... 2Chr 18:32 — 7725
Egypt, but they *t* from them, and .... 2Chr 20:10 — 5493
have *t* away their faces from the .... 2Chr 29:6 — 5437
of the LORD, and *t* their backs .... 2Chr 29:6 — 5414
and *t* his name to Jehoiakim .... 2Chr 36:4 — 5437
t the heart of the king of .... Ezr 6:22 — 5437
God for this matter be *t* from us .... Ezr 10:14 — 7725
t back, and entered by the gate of .... Neh 2:15 — 7725
neither *t* they from their wicked .... Neh 9:35 — 7725
howbeit our God *t* the curse into .... Neh 13:2 — 2015
(though it was *t* to the contrary, ... Est 9:1 — 2015
the month which was *t* unto them .... Est 9:22 — 2015
paths of their way are *t* aside .... Job 6:18 — 3943
t me over into the hands of the .... Job 16:11 — 3399
whom I loved are *t* against me .... Job 19:19 — 2015
Yet his meat in his bowels is *t* .... Job 20:14 — 2015
under it is *t* up as it were fire .... Job 28:5 — 2015
Terrors are *t* upon me .... Job 30:15 — 2015
My harp also is *t* to mourning .... Job 30:31 —
If my step hath *t* out of the way .... Job 31:7 — 5186
Because they *t* back from him, and .... Job 34:27 — 5493
it is *t* round about by his .... Job 37:12 — 2015
It is *t* as clay to the seal .... Job 38:14 — 2015
sorrow is *t* into joy before him .... Job 41:22 — 1750
slingstones are *t* with him into .... Job 41:28 — 2015
the LORD *t* the captivity of Job, ... Job 42:10 — 7725
When mine enemies are *t* back .... Ps 9:3 — 7725
The wicked shall be *t* into hell .... Ps 9:17 — 7725
Thou hast *t* for me my mourning .... Ps 30:11 — 2015
my moisture is *t* into the drought .... Ps 32:4 — 2015
let them be *t* back and brought to .... Ps 35:4 — 5472
Our heart is not *t* back, neither .... Ps 44:18 — 5472
He *t* the sea into dry land .... Ps 66:6 — 2015
which hath not *t* away my prayer .... Ps 66:20 — 5493
let them be *t* backward, and put to .... Ps 70:2 — 5472
Let them be *t* back for a reward .... Ps 70:3 — 7725
t back in the day of battle .... Ps 78:9 — 2015
many a time *t* he his anger away, ... Ps 78:38 — 7725
Yea, they *t* back and tempted God, ... Ps 78:41 — 7725
had *t* their rivers into blood .... Ps 78:44 — 2015
But *t* back, and dealt unfaithfully .... Ps 78:57 — 5472
they were *t* aside like a .... Ps 78:57 — 2015
and *t* my hand against their .... Ps 81:14 — 7725
thou hast *t* thyself from the .... Ps 85:3 — 7725
Thou hast also *t* the edge of his .... Ps 89:43 — 7725
He *t* their heart to hate his .... Ps 105:25 — 2015
He *t* their waters into blood, and .... Ps 105:29 — 2015
Which *t* the rock into a standing .... Ps 114:8 — 2015
t my feet unto thy testimonies .... Ps 119:59 — 7725
When the LORD *t* the again .... Ps 126:1 — 7725
and *t* back that hate Zion .... Ps 129:5 — 5472
I *t* myself to behold wisdom, and .... Eccl 2:12 — 6437
whither is thy beloved *t* aside .... Song 6:1 — 6437
all this his anger is not *t* away .... Is 5:25 — 7725
all this his anger is not *t* away .... Is 9:12 — 7725
all this his anger is not *t* away .... Is 9:17 — 7725
all this his anger is not *t* away .... Is 9:21 — 7725
all this his anger is not *t* away .... Is 10:4 — 7725
with me, thine anger is *t* away .... Is 12:1 — 7725
hath he *t* into fear unto me .... Is 21:4 — 7760
wheel *t* about upon the cummin .... Is 28:27 — 5437
Lebanon shall be *t* into a .... Is 29:17 — 7725
thereof shall be *t* into pitch .... Is 34:9 — 2015
Then Hezekiah *t* his face toward .... Is 38:2 — 5437
They shall be *t* back, they shall .... Is 42:17 — 5472
a deceived heart hath *t* him aside .... Is 44:20 — 5186
rebellious, neither *t* away back .... Is 50:5 — 5472
we have *t* every one to his own .... Is 53:6 — 6437
judgment is *t* away backward, and .... Is 59:14 — 5253
therefore he was *t* to be their .... Is 63:10 — 2015
how then art thou *t* into the .... Jer 2:21 — 2015
for they have *t* their back unto .... Jer 2:27 — 6437
sister Judah hath not *t* unto me .... Jer 3:10 — 7725
of the LORD is not *t* back from us .... Jer 4:8 — 7725
have *t* away these things, and your .... Jer 5:25 — 5186
houses shall be *t* unto others .... Jer 6:12 — 5437
every one *t* to his own course, as the ... Jer 8:6 — 7725
they are *t* back to the iniquities .... Jer 11:10 — 7725
then they should have *t* them from .... Jer 23:22 — 7725
and all faces are *t* into paleness .... Jer 30:6 — 2015
turn thou me, and I shall be *t* .... Jer 31:18 — 7725
Surely after that I was *t* .... Jer 31:19 — 7725
they have *t* unto me the back, and .... Jer 32:33 — 6437
But afterward they *t*, and caused .... Jer 34:11 — 7725
And ye were now *t*, and had done .... Jer 34:15 — 7725
But ye *t* and polluted my name, and ..... Jer 34:16 — 7725
the mire, and they are *t* away back ...... Jer 38:22 — 5472
seen them dismayed and *t* away back ... Jer 46:5 — 5472
for they also are *t* back, and are .... Jer 46:21 — 6437

how hath Moab *t* the back with .... Jer 48:39 — 6437
they have *t* them away on the .... Jer 50:6 — 7725
for my feet, he hath *t* me back .... Lam 1:13 — 7725
mine heart is *t* within me .... Lam 1:20 — 2015
Surely against me is he *t* .... Lam 3:3 — 7725
He hath *t* aside my ways, and .... Lam 3:11 — 5493
Our inheritance is *t* to strangers .... Lam 5:2 — 2015
our dance is *t* into mourning .... Lam 5:15 — 2015
thee, O LORD, and we shall be *t* .... Lam 5:21 — 7725
they *t* not when they went .... Eze 1:9 — 5437
they *t* not when they went .... Eze 1:12 — 5437
they *t* not when they went .... Eze 1:17 — 5437
they *t* not as they went, but to .... Eze 10:11 — 5437
they *t* not as they went .... Eze 10:11 — 5437
also *t* not from beside them .... Eze 10:16 — 5437
whose branches *t* toward him .... Eze 17:6 — 6437
she is *t* unto me .... Eze 26:2 — 5437
He *t* about to the west side, and .... Eze 42:19 — 5437
thy fury be *t* away from thy city .... Dan 9:16 — 7725
was *t* in me into corruption .... Dan 10:8 — 2015
vision my sorrows are *t* upon me .... Dan 10:16 — 2015
Ephraim is a cake not *t* .... Hos 7:8 — 2015
mine heart is *t* within me .... Hos 11:8 — 2015
for mine anger is *t* away from him .... Hos 14:4 — 7725
The sun shall be *t* into darkness .... Joel 2:31 — 2015
for ye have *t* judgment into gall, ... Amos 6:12 — 2015
that they *t* from their evil way .... Jonah 3:10 — 7725
For the LORD hath *t* away the .... Nah 2:2 — 7725
right hand shall be *t* unto thee .... Hab 2:16 — 5437
them that are *t* back from the .... Zeph 1:6 — 5472
yet ye *t* not to me, saith the .... Hag 2:17 —
Then I *t*, and lifted up mine eyes, ... Zec 5:1 — 7725
And I *t*, and lifted up mine eyes, ... Zec 6:1 — 7725
All the land shall be *t* as a .... Zec 14:10 — 5437
he *t* aside into the parts of .... Mt 2:22 — 402
But Jesus *t* him about, and when he .... Mt 9:22 — 1994
But he *t*, and said unto Peter, Get .... Mt 16:23 — 4672
t him about in the press, and said .... Mk 5:30 — 1994
But when he had *t* about and looked ... Mk 8:33 — 1994
they *t* back again to Jerusalem, ... Lk 2:45 — 5290
t him about, and said unto the .... Lk 7:9 — 4762
he *t* to the woman, and said unto .... Lk 7:44 — 4762
But he *t*, and rebuked them, and .... Lk 9:55 — 4762
he *t* him unto his disciples, and .... Lk 10:23 — 4762
and he *t*, and said unto them, ... Lk 14:25 — 4762
t back, and with a loud voice .... Lk 17:15 — 5290
And the Lord *t*, and looked upon .... Lk 22:61 — 4762
Then Jesus *t*, and saw them .... Jn 1:38 — 4762
your sorrow shall be *t* into joy .... Jn 16:20 — 1096
she *t* herself back, and saw Jesus ...... Jn 20:14 — 4762
She *t* herself, and saith unto him, ... Jn 20:16 — 4762
The sun shall be *t* into darkness .... Acts 2:20 — 4762
in their hearts *t* back again into .... Acts 7:39 — 4762
Then God *t*, and gave them up to .... Acts 7:42 — 4762
Saron saw him, and *t* to the Lord .... Acts 9:35 — 1994
believed, and *t* unto the Lord .... Acts 11:21 — 1994
among the Gentiles are *t* to God .... Acts 15:19 — 1994
But Paul, being grieved, *t* .... Acts 16:18 — 1994
These that have *t* the world .... Acts 17:6 — 387
t away much people, saying that .... Acts 19:26 — 3179
how ye *t* to God from idols to .... 1Th 1:9 — 1994
have *t* aside unto vain jangling .... 1Ti 1:6 — 1824
are already *t* aside after Satan .... 1Ti 5:15 — 1824
are in Asia be *t* away from me .... 2Ti 1:15 — 654
truth, and shall be *t* unto fables .... 2Ti 4:4 — 654
t to flight the armies of the .... Heb 11:34 — 2827
which is lame be *t* out of the way .... Heb 12:13 — 1624
yet are they *t* about with a very .... Jas 3:4 — 3329
your laughter be *t* to mourning .... Jas 4:9 — 3344
The dog is *t* to his own vomit .... 2Pet 2:22 — 1994
I *t* to see the voice that spake .... Rev 1:12 — 1994
And being *t*, I saw seven golden .... Rev 1:12 — 1994

TURNEST

and whithersoever thou *t* thyself .... 1Kin 2:3 — 6437
That thou *t* thy spirit against .... Job 15:13 — 7725
Thou *t* man to destruction .... Ps 90:3 — 7725

TURNETH

the soul that *t* after such as .... Lev 20:6 — 6437
whose heart *t* away this day from ...... Deut 29:18 — 6437
when Israel *t* their backs before .... Josh 7:8 — 2015
t toward the sunrising to .... Josh 19:27 — 7725
And then the coast *t* to Ramah .... Josh 19:29 — 7725
and the coast *t* to Hosah .... Josh 19:29 — 7725
then the coast *t* westward to .... Josh 19:34 — 7725
neither *t* he back from the sword .... Job 39:22 — 7725
He *t* rivers into a wilderness, and ...... Ps 107:33 — 7760
He *t* the wilderness into a .... Ps 107:35 — 7760
of the wicked he *t* upside down .... Ps 146:9 — 5791
A soft answer *t* away wrath .... Prov 15:1 — 7725
whithersoever it *t*, it prospereth .... Prov 17:8 — 6437

he *t* it whithersoever he will .... Prov 21:1 — 5186
As the door *t* upon his hinges, so .... Prov 26:14 — 5437
He that *t* away his ear from .... Prov 28:9 — 5493
beasts, and *t* not away for any .... Prov 30:30 — 7725
south, and *t* about unto the north .... Eccl 1:6 — 5437
that *t* aside by the flocks of thy .... Song 1:7 — 5844
For the people *t* not unto him .... Is 9:13 — 7725
t it upside down, and scattereth............. Is 24:1 — 5753
that *t* wise men backward, and .... Is 44:25 — 7725
as a wayfaring man that *t* aside .... Jer 14:8 — 5186
t herself to flee, and fear hath.................. Jer 49:24 — 6437
yea, she sigheth, and *t* backward .... Lam 1:8 — 7725
he *t* his hand against me all the .... Lam 3:3 — 7725
But when the righteous *t* away .... Eze 18:24 — 7725
When a righteous man *t* away from ...... Eze 18:26 — 7725
when the wicked man *t* away from .... Eze 18:27 — 7725
and *t* away from all his .... Eze 18:28 — 7725
day that he *t* from his wickedness .... Eze 33:12 — 7725
When the righteous *t* from his .... Eze 33:18 — 7725
t the shadow of death into the .... Amos 5:8 — 2015

TURNING

wiping it, and *t* it upside down................ 2Kin 21:13 — 2015
gate, and at the *t* of the wall, and .... 2Chr 26:9 — 4740
hardened his heart from *t* unto........ 2Chr 36:13 — 7257
the armoury at the *t* of the wall .... Neh 3:19 — 4740
from the *t* of the wall unto the .... Neh 3:20 — 4740
of Azariah unto the *t* of the wall .... Neh 3:24 — 4740
over against the *t* of the wall .... Neh 3:25 — 4740
For the *t* away of the simple .... Prov 1:32 — 4878
Surely your *t* of things upside .... Is 29:16 — 2017
two leaves apiece, two *t* leaves .... Eze 41:24 — 4142
t away he hath divided our fields........... Mic 2:4 — 7725
But Jesus *t* unto them said, ... Lk 23:28 — 4762
t about, seeth the disciple whom .... Jn 21:20 — 1994
in *t* away every one of you from .... Acts 3:26 — 654
t him to the body said, Tabitha, ... Acts 9:40 — 1994
variableness, neither shadow of *t* .... Jas 1:17 — 5157
t the cities of Sodom and Gomorrah... 2Pet 2:6 — 5077
t the grace of our God into .... Jude 4 — 3346

TURTLE

the voice of the *t* is heard in................... Song 2:12 — 8449
and the *t* and the crane and the .... Jer 8:7 — 8449

TURTLEDOVE

a ram of three years old, and a *t* .... Gen 15:9 — 8449
and a young pigeon, or a *t* .... Lev 12:6 — 8449
thy *t* unto the multitude of the .... Ps 74:19 — 8449

TURTLEDOVES

he shall bring his offering of *t* .... Lev 1:14 — 8449
which he hath committed, two *t* .... Lev 5:7 — 8449
if he be not able to bring two *t* .... Lev 5:11 — 8449
And two *t*, or two young pigeons, ... Lev 14:22 — 8449
he shall offer the one of the *t*.............. Lev 14:30 — 8449
day he shall take to him two *t* .... Lev 15:14 — 8449
the law of the Lord, A pair of *t*.............. Lk 2:24 — 5167

TURTLES

lamb, then she shall bring two *t* .... Lev 12:8 — 8449
day she shall take unto her two *t*........... Lev 15:29 — 8449
eighth day he shall bring two *t* .... Num 6:10 — 8449

TUTORS

But is under *t* and governors until .... Gal 4:2 — 2012

TWAIN

my son in law in the one of the *t*........... 1Sa 18:21 — 8147
and shut the door upon them *t* .... 2Kin 4:33 — 8147
with *t* he covered his face, and .... Is 6:2 — 8147
with *t* he covered his feet, and .... Is 6:2 — 8147
his feet, and with *t* he did fly................. Is 6:2 — 8147
me, when they cut the calf in *t*............... Jer 34:18 — 8147
both *t* shall come forth out of .... Eze 21:19 — 8147
thee to go a mile, go with him *t* .... Mt 5:41 — 1417
they *t* shall be one flesh .... Mt 19:5 — 1417
Wherefore they are no more *t*................. Mt 19:6 — 1417
Whether of them *t* did the will of .... Mt 21:31 — 1417
Whether of the *t* will ye that I................. Mt 21:27 — 1417
in *t* from the top to the bottom............. Mt 27:51 — 1417
they *t* shall be one flesh .... Mk 10:8 — 1417
so then they are no more *t* .... Mk 10:8 — 1417
in *t* from the top to the bottom............. Mk 15:38 — 1417
make in himself of *t* one new man......... Eph 2:15 — 1417

TWELFTH

On the *t* day Ahira the son of .... Num 7:78 — 8147,6240
oxen before him, and he with the *t*. 1Kin 19:19 — 8147,6240
In the *t* year of Joram the son of.... 2Kin 8:25 — 8147,6240
In the *t* year of Ahaz king of........... 2Kin 17:1 — 8147,6240
king of Judah, in the *t* month .... 2Kin 25:27 — 8147,6240
to Eliashib, the *t* to Jakim, ... 1Chr 24:12 — 8147,6240
The *t* to Hashabiah, he, his sons,.... 1Chr 25:19 — 8147,6240
The *t* captain for the *t*...................... 1Chr 27:15 — 8147,6240

in the *t* year he began to purge ...... 2Chr 34:3 — 8147,6240
on the *t* day of the first month .... Ezr 8:31 — 8147,6240
in the *t* year of king Ahasuerus ...... Est 3:7 — 8147,6240
month to month, to the *t* month ...... Est 3:7 — 8147,6240
the thirteenth day of the *t* month.... Est 3:13 — 8147,6240
the thirteenth day of the *t* month.... Est 8:12 — 8147,6240
Now in the *t* month, that is, the ...... Est 9:1 — 8147,6240
king of Judah, in the *t* month .... Jer 52:31 — 8147,6240
in the *t* day of the month, the .... Eze 29:1 — 8147,6240
the *t* year, in the *t* month .... Eze 32:1 — 8147,6240
came to pass also in the *t* year ...... Eze 32:17 — 8147,6240
in the *t* year of our captivity .... Eze 33:21 — 8147,6240
the *t*, an amethyst .... Rev 21:20 — 1428

TWELVE

Seth were nine hundred and *t*........ Gen 5:8 — 8147,6240
T years they served Chedorlaomer.. Gen 14:4 — 8147,6240
t princes shall he beget, and I...... Gen 17:20 — 8147,6240
t princes according to their .... Gen 25:16 — 8147,6240
Now the sons of Jacob were *t* .... Gen 35:22 — 8147,6240
said, Thy servants are *t* brethren ... Gen 42:13 — 8147,6240
We be *t* brethren, sons of our........ Gen 42:32 — 8147,6240
these are the *t* tribes of Israel........ Gen 49:28 — 8147,6240
where were *t* wells of water, and ..... Ex 15:27 — 8147,6240
t pillars, according to the .... Ex 24:4 — 8147,6240
to the *t* tribes of Israel...................... Ex 24:4 — 8147,6240
of the children of Israel, *t* .... Ex 28:21 — 8147,6240
they be according to the *t* tribes.... Ex 28:21 — 8147,6240
of the children of Israel, *t*.............. Ex 39:14 — 8147,6240
name, according to the *t* tribes ...... Ex 39:14 — 8147,6240
flour, and bake *t* cakes thereof ...... Lev 24:5 — 8147,6240
princes of Israel, being *t* men.......... Num 1:44 — 8147,6240
six covered wagons, and *t* oxen...... Num 7:3 — 8147,6240
t chargers of silver .... Num 7:84 — 8147,6240
t silver bowls, *t* spoons of .... Num 7:84 — 8147,6240
The golden spoons were *t*, full of..... Num 7:86 — 8147,6240
were *t* bullocks, the rams *t* .... Num 7:87 — 8147,6240
the lambs of the first year *t*............. Num 7:87 — 8147,6240
of the goats for sin offering *t* .... Num 7:87 — 8147,6240
the house of their fathers *t* rods...... Num 17:2 — 8147,6240
fathers' houses, even *t* rods .... Num 17:6 — 8147,6240
ye shall offer *t* young bullocks .... Num 29:17 — 8147,6240
tribe, *t* thousand armed for war...... Num 31:5 — 8147,6240
threescore and *t* thousand beeves, ... Num 31:33 — 8147
tribute was threescore and *t*.................. Num 31:38 — 8147
in Elim were *t* fountains of water ... Num 33:9 — 8147,6240
I took *t* men of you, one of a........... Deut 1:23 — 8147,6240
Now therefore take you *t* men out .. Josh 3:12 — 8147,6240
Take you *t* men out of the people, ... Josh 4:2 — 8147,6240
t stones, and ye shall carry them.... Josh 4:3 — 8147,6240
Then Joshua called the *t* men .... Josh 4:4 — 8147,6240
took up *t* stones out of the midst ... Josh 4:8 — 8147,6240
Joshua set up *t* stones in the........... Josh 4:9 — 8147,6240
those *t* stones, which they took ...... Josh 4:20 — 8147,6240
were *t* thousand, even all the men... Josh 8:25 — 8147,6240
t cities with their villages .... Josh 18:24 — 8147,6240
t cities with their villages .... Josh 19:15 — 8147,6240
of the tribe of Zebulun, *t* cities .... Josh 21:7 — 8147,6240
were by their lot *t* cities .... Josh 21:40 — 8147,6240
into *t* pieces, and sent her into .... Judg 19:29 — 8147,6240
the congregation sent thither *t*........ Judg 21:10 — 8147,6240
over by number *t* of Benjamin........ 2Sa 2:15 — 8147,6240
t of the servants of David .... 2Sa 2:15 — 8147,6240
of Ish-tob *t* thousand men .... 2Sa 10:6 — 8147,6240
me now choose out *t* thousand........ 2Sa 17:1 — 8147,6240
Solomon had *t* officers over all........ 1Kin 4:7 — 8147,6240
chariots, and *t* thousand horsemen.. 1Kin 4:26 — 8147,6240
a line of *t* cubits did compass......... 1Kin 7:15 — 8147,6240
It stood upon *t* oxen, three .... 1Kin 7:25 — 8147,6240
one sea, and *t* oxen under the sea .. 1Kin 7:44 — 8147,6240
t lions stood there on the one .... 1Kin 10:20 — 8147,6240
t thousand horsemen, whom he ...... 1Kin 10:26 — 8147,6240
on him, and rent it in *t* pieces .... 1Kin 11:30 — 8147,6240
to reign over Israel, *t* years .... 1Kin 16:23 — 8147,6240
And Elijah took *t* stones................... 1Kin 18:31 — 8147,6240
who was plowing with *t* yoke of .... 1Kin 19:19 — 8147,6240
king of Judah, and reigned *t* years . 2Kin 3:1 — 8147,6240
Manasseh was *t* years old when ...... 2Kin 21:1 — 8147,6240
of the tribe of Zebulun, *t* cities .... 1Chr 6:63 — 8147,6240
the gates were two hundred and *t* .. 1Chr 9:22 — 8147,6240
and his brethren an hundred and *t* 1Chr 15:10 — 8147,6240
with his brethren and sons were *t*... 1Chr 25:9 — 8147,6240
his sons, and his brethren, were *t*... 1Chr 25:10 — 8147,6240
his sons, and his brethren, were *t*... 1Chr 25:11 — 8147,6240
his sons, and his brethren, were *t*... 1Chr 25:12 — 8147,6240
his sons, and his brethren, were *t*... 1Chr 25:13 — 8147,6240
his sons, and his brethren, were *t*... 1Chr 25:14 — 8147,6240
his sons, and his brethren, were *t*... 1Chr 25:15 — 8147,6240
his sons, and his brethren, were *t*... 1Chr 25:16 — 8147,6240
his sons, and his brethren, were *t*... 1Chr 25:17 — 8147,6240
his sons, and his brethren, were *t*... 1Chr 25:18 — 8147,6240

T

his sons, and his brethren, were *t* ...	1Chr 25:19	8147,6240
his sons, and his brethren, were *t* ...	1Chr 25:20	8147,6240
his sons, and his brethren, were *t* ...	1Chr 25:21	8147,6240
his sons, and his brethren, were *t* ...	1Chr 25:22	8147,6240
his sons, and his brethren, were *t* ...	1Chr 25:23	8147,6240
his sons, and his brethren, were *t* ...	1Chr 25:24	8147,6240
his sons, and his brethren, were *t* ...	1Chr 25:25	8147,6240
his sons, and his brethren, were *t* ...	1Chr 25:26	8147,6240
his sons, and his brethren, were *t* ...	1Chr 25:27	8147,6240
his sons, and his brethren, were *t* ...	1Chr 25:28	8147,6240
his sons, and his brethren, were *t* ...	1Chr 25:29	8147,6240
his sons, and his brethren, were *t* ...	1Chr 25:30	8147,6240
his sons, and his brethren, were *t* ...	1Chr 25:31	8147,6240
t thousand horsemen, which he	2Chr 1:14	8147,6240
It stood upon *t* oxen, three	2Chr 4:4	8147,6240
One sea, and *t* oxen under it	2Chr 4:15	8147,6240
t lions stood there on the one	2Chr 9:19	8147,6240
chariots, and *t* thousand horsemen	2Chr 9:25	8147,6240
With *t* hundred chariots, and	2Chr 12:3	505
Manasseh was *t* years old when	2Chr 33:1	8147,6240
two thousand eight hundred and *t* .	Ezr 2:6	8147,6240
of Jorah, an hundred and *t*	Ezr 2:18	8147,6240
t he goats, according to the	Ezr 6:17	8648,6236
Then I separated *t* of the chief	Ezr 8:24	8147,6240
t bullocks for all Israel, ninety	Ezr 8:35	8147,6240
t he goats for a sin offering	Ezr 8:35	8147,6240
t years, I and my brethren have	Neh 5:14	8147,6240
of Hariph, an hundred and *t*	Neh 7:24	8147,6240
after that she had been *t* months	Est 2:12	8147,6240
in the valley of salt *t* thousand	Ps 60:*t*	8147,6240
t brasen bulls that were under	Jer 52:20	8147,6240
a fillet of *t* cubits did compass	Jer 52:21	8147,6240
the altar shall be *t* cubits long	Eze 43:16	8147,6240
t broad, square in the four	Eze 43:16	8147,6240
to the *t* tribes of Israel	Eze 47:13	8147,6240
At the end of *t* months he walked	Dan 4:29	8648,6236
with an issue of blood *t* years	Mt 9:20	*1427*
called unto him his *t* disciples	Mt 10:1	*1427*
names of the *t* apostles are these	Mt 10:2	*1427*
These *t* Jesus sent forth, and	Mt 10:5	*1427*
end of commanding his *t* disciples	Mt 11:1	*1427*
that remained *t* baskets full	Mt 14:20	*1427*
ye also shall sit upon *t* thrones	Mt 19:28	*1427*
judging the *t* tribes of Israel	Mt 19:28	*1427*
the *t* disciples apart in the way	Mt 20:17	*1427*
Then one of the *t*, called Judas	Mt 26:14	*1427*
was come, he sat down with the *t*	Mt 26:20	*1427*
spake, lo, Judas, one of the *t*	Mt 26:47	*1427*
me more than *t* legions of angels	Mt 26:53	*1427*
And he ordained *t*, that they	Mk 3:14	*1427*
the *t* asked of him the parable	Mk 4:10	*1427*
had an issue of blood *t* years	Mk 5:25	*1427*
for she was of the age of *t* years	Mk 5:42	*1427*
And he called unto him the *t*	Mk 6:7	*1427*
they took up *t* baskets full of	Mk 6:43	*1427*
They say unto him, *T*	Mk 8:19	*1427*
And he sat down, and called the *t*	Mk 9:35	*1427*
And he took again the *t*, and began	Mk 10:32	*1427*
went out unto Bethany with the *t*	Mk 11:11	*1427*
And Judas Iscariot, one of the *t*	Mk 14:10	*1427*
the evening he cometh with the *t*	Mk 14:17	*1427*
unto them, It is one of the *t*	Mk 14:20	*1427*
spake, cometh Judas, one of the *t*	Mk 14:43	*1427*
And when he was *t* years old	Lk 2:42	*1427*
and of them he chose *t*, whom also	Lk 6:13	*1427*
and the *t* were with him,	Lk 8:1	*1427*
about *t* years of age, and she lay	Lk 8:42	*1427*
having an issue of blood *t* years	Lk 8:43	*1427*
called his *t* disciples together	Lk 9:1	*1427*
to wear away, then came the *t*	Lk 9:12	*1427*
that remained to them *t* baskets	Lk 9:17	*1427*
Then he took unto him the *t*	Lk 18:31	*1427*
being of the number of the *t*	Lk 22:3	*1427*
down, and the *t* apostles with him	Lk 22:14	*1427*
judging the *t* tribes of Israel	Lk 22:30	*1427*
was called Judas, one of the *t*	Lk 22:47	*1427*
filled *t* baskets with the	Jn 6:13	*1427*
Then said Jesus unto the *t*	Jn 6:67	*1427*
them, Have not I chosen you *t*	Jn 6:70	*1427*
betray him, being one of the *t*	Jn 6:71	*1427*
Are there not *t* hours in the day	Jn 11:9	*1427*
But Thomas, one of the *t*, called	Jn 20:24	*1427*
Then the *t* called the multitude	Acts 6:2	*1427*
and Jacob begat the *t* patriarchs	Acts 7:8	*1427*
And all the men were about *t*	Acts 19:7	*1177*
that there are yet but *t* days	Acts 24:11	*1177*
Unto which promise our *t* tribes	Acts 26:7	*1429*
was seen of Cephas, then of the *t*	1Cor 15:5	*1427*
to the *t* tribes which are	Jas 1:1	*1427*
of Juda were sealed *t* thousand	Rev 7:5	*1427*
of Reuben were sealed *t* thousand	Rev 7:5	*1427*
of Gad were sealed *t* thousand	Rev 7:5	*1427*
of Aser were sealed *t* thousand	Rev 7:6	*1427*
Nepthalim were sealed *t* thousand	Rev 7:6	*1427*
Manasses were sealed *t* thousand	Rev 7:6	*1427*
of Simeon were sealed *t* thousand	Rev 7:7	*1427*
of Levi were sealed *t* thousand	Rev 7:7	*1427*
Issachar were sealed *t* thousand	Rev 7:7	*1427*
of Zabulon were sealed *t* thousand	Rev 7:8	*1427*
of Joseph were sealed *t* thousand	Rev 7:8	*1427*
Benjamin were sealed *t* thousand	Rev 7:8	*1427*
upon her head a crown of *t* stars	Rev 12:1	*1427*
had *t* gates, and at the gates	Rev 21:12	*1427*
gates, and at the gates *t* angels	Rev 21:12	*1427*
the *t* tribes of the children of	Rev 21:12	*1427*
of the city had *t* foundations	Rev 21:14	*1427*
of the *t* apostles of the Lamb	Rev 21:14	*1427*
the reed, *t* thousand furlongs	Rev 21:16	*1427*
the *t* gates were *t* pearls	Rev 21:21	*1427*
which bare *t* manner of fruits, and	Rev 22:2	*1427*

TWENTIETH

t day of the month, was the earth	Gen 8:14	6242
t day of the month at even	Ex 12:18	6242
it came to pass on the *t* day of	Num 10:11	6242
in the *t* year of Jeroboam king of	1Kin 15:9	6242
t year of king Jehoash the	2Kin 12:6	6242
t year of Joash the son of	2Kin 13:1	6242
in the *t* year of Jotham the son	2Kin 15:30	6242
seven and *t* day of the month, that	2Kin 25:27	6242
to Pethahiah, the *t* to Jehezekel,	1Chr 24:16	6242
t to Jachin, the two and	1Chr 24:17	6242
to Jachin, the two and *t* to Gamul,	1Chr 24:17	6242
t to Delaiah, the four and	1Chr 24:18	6242
Delaiah, the four and *t* to Maaziah	1Chr 24:18	6242
The *t* to Eliathah, he, his sons,	1Chr 25:27	6242
t to Hothir, he, his sons, and his	1Chr 25:28	6242
t to Giddalti, he, his sons, and	1Chr 25:29	6242
t to Mahazioth, he, his sons, and	1Chr 25:30	6242
t to Romamti-ezer, he, his sons,	1Chr 25:31	6242
t day of the seventh month he	2Chr 7:10	6242
on the *t* day of the month	Ezr 10:9	6242
the month Chisleu, in the *t* year	Neh 1:1	6242
in the *t* year of Artaxerxes the	Neh 2:1	6242
from the *t* year even unto the two	Neh 5:14	6242
on the three and *t* day thereof	Est 8:9	6242
t year, the word of the LORD hath	Jer 25:3	6242
three and *t* year of Nebuchadrezzar	Jer 52:30	6242
five and *t* day of the month, that	Jer 52:31	6242
t year, in the first month, in	Eze 29:17	6242
t year of our captivity, in the	Eze 40:1	6242
t day of the first month, as I	Dan 10:4	6242
t day of the sixth month, in the	Hag 1:15	6242
t day of the month, came the word	Hag 2:1	6242
t day of the ninth month, in the	Hag 2:10	6242
t day of the ninth month, even	Hag 2:18	6242
t day of the month, saying,	Hag 2:20	6242
t day of the eleventh month,	Zec 1:7	6242

TWENTY

shall be an hundred and *t* years	Gen 6:3	6242
nine and *t* years, and begat Terah	Gen 11:24	6242
there shall be *t* found there	Gen 18:31	6242
hundred and seven and *t* years old	Gen 23:1	6242
This *t* years have I been with	Gen 31:38	6242
Thus have I been *t* years in thy	Gen 31:41	6242
t he goats, two hundred ewes, and	Gen 32:14	6242
two hundred ewes, and *t* rams,	Gen 32:14	6242
t she asses, and ten foals	Gen 32:15	6242
for *t* pieces of silver	Gen 37:28	6242
t cubits, and the breadth of one	Ex 26:2	6242
t boards on the south side	Ex 26:18	6242
of silver under the *t* boards	Ex 26:19	6242
side there shall be *t* boards	Ex 26:20	6242
the *t* pillars thereof and their	Ex 27:10	6242
their *t* sockets shall be of brass	Ex 27:10	6242
his *t* pillars and their *t*	Ex 27:11	6242
shall be an hanging of *t* cubits	Ex 27:16	6242
(a shekel is *t* gerahs	Ex 30:13	6242
from *t* years old and above, shall	Ex 30:14	6242
The length of one curtain was *t*	Ex 36:9	6242
t boards for the south side	Ex 36:23	6242
silver he made under the *t* boards	Ex 36:24	6242
north corner, he made *t* boards	Ex 36:25	6242
Their pillars were *t*, and their	Ex 38:10	6242
and their brasen sockets *t*	Ex 38:10	6242
cubits, their pillars were *t*	Ex 38:11	6242
and their sockets of brass *t*	Ex 38:11	6242
t cubits was the length, and the	Ex 38:18	6242
the gold of the offering, was *t*	Ex 38:24	6242
from *t* years old and upward, for	Ex 38:26	6242
shall be of the male from *t* years	Lev 27:3	6242
years old even unto *t* years old	Lev 27:5	6242

shall be of the male *t* shekels	Lev 27:5	6242
t gerahs shall be the shekel	Lev 27:25	6242
From *t* years old and upward, all	Num 1:3	6242
from *t* years old and upward, by	Num 1:18	6242
every male from *t* years old	Num 1:20	6242
every male from *t* years old	Num 1:22	6242
from *t* years old and upward, all	Num 1:24	6242
from *t* years old and upward, all	Num 1:26	6242
from *t* years old and upward, all	Num 1:28	6242
from *t* years old and upward, all	Num 1:30	6242
from *t* years old and upward, all	Num 1:32	6242
from *t* years old and upward, all	Num 1:34	6242
from *t* years old and upward, all	Num 1:36	6242
from *t* years old and upward, all	Num 1:38	6242
from *t* years old and upward, all	Num 1:40	6242
from *t* years old and upward, all	Num 1:42	6242
from *t* years old and upward, all	Num 1:45	6242
a month old and upward, were *t*	Num 3:39	6242
were numbered of them, were *t*	Num 3:43	6242
(the shekel is *t* gerahs	Num 3:47	6242
was an hundred and *t* shekels	Num 7:86	6242
of the peace offerings were *t*	Num 7:88	6242
from *t* and five years old and	Num 8:24	6242
neither ten days, nor *t* days	Num 11:19	6242
from *t* years old and upward, which	Num 14:29	6242
the sanctuary, which is *t* gerahs	Num 18:16	6242
that died in the plague were *t*	Num 25:9	6242
from *t* years old and upward,	Num 26:2	6242
from *t* years old and upward	Num 26:4	6242
the families of the Simeonites, *t*	Num 26:14	6242
that were numbered of them were *t*	Num 26:62	6242
from *t* years old and upward, shall	Num 32:11	6242
And Aaron was an hundred and *t*	Num 33:39	6242
hundred and *t* years old this day	Deut 31:2	6242
and *t* years old when he died	Deut 34:7	6242
all the cities are *t* and nine,	Josh 15:32	6242
t and two cities with their	Josh 19:30	6242
t years he mightily oppressed the	Judg 4:3	6242
And there returned of the people *t*	Judg 7:3	6242
t thousand men that drew sword	Judg 8:10	6242
And he judged Israel *t* and three	Judg 10:2	6242
a Gileadite, and judged Israel *t*	Judg 10:3	6242
even *t* cities, and unto the plain	Judg 11:33	6242
days of the Philistines *t* years	Judg 15:20	6242
And he judged Israel *t* years	Judg 16:31	6242
at that time out of the cities *t*	Judg 20:15	6242
of the Israelites that day *t*	Judg 20:21	6242
of the Benjamites that day *t*	Judg 20:35	6242
fell that day of Benjamin were *t*	Judg 20:46	6242
for it was *t* years	1Sa 7:2	6242
made, was about *t* men, within as	1Sa 14:14	6242
to Hebron, and *t* men with him	2Sa 3:20	6242
horsemen, and *t* thousand footmen	2Sa 8:4	6242
the Syrians two and *t* thousand men	2Sa 8:5	6242
had fifteen sons and *t* servants	2Sa 9:10	6242
t thousand footmen, and of king	2Sa 10:6	6242
that day of *t* thousand men	2Sa 18:7	6242
sons and his *t* servants with him	2Sa 19:17	6242
six toes, four and *t* in number	2Sa 21:20	6242
the end of nine months and *t* days	2Sa 24:8	6242
t oxen out of the pastures, and an	1Kin 4:23	6242
Solomon gave Hiram *t* thousand	1Kin 5:11	6242
and *t* measures of pure oil	1Kin 5:11	6242
and the breadth thereof *t* cubits	1Kin 6:2	6242
t cubits was the length thereof,	1Kin 6:3	6242
he built *t* cubits on the sides of	1Kin 6:16	6242
forepart was *t* cubits in length	1Kin 6:20	6242
t cubits in breadth	1Kin 6:20	6242
t cubits in the height thereof	1Kin 6:20	6242
t thousand oxen, and an hundred and	1Kin 8:63	6242
and an hundred and *t* thousand sheep	1Kin 8:63	6242
to pass at the end of *t* years	1Kin 9:10	6242
then king Solomon gave Hiram *t*	1Kin 9:11	6242
t talents, and brought it to king	1Kin 9:28	6242
t talents of gold, and of spices	1Kin 10:10	6242
reigned were two and *t* years	1Kin 14:20	6242
over all Israel in Tirzah, *t*	1Kin 15:33	6242
In the *t* and sixth year of Asa	1Kin 16:8	6242
him, and killed him, in the *t*	1Kin 16:10	6242
In the *t* and seventh year of Asa	1Kin 16:15	6242
reigned over Israel in Samaria *t*	1Kin 16:29	6242
and there a wall fell upon *t*	1Kin 20:30	6242
and he reigned *t* and five years in	1Kin 22:42	6242
t loaves of barley, and full ears	2Kin 4:42	6242
t years old was Ahaziah when he	2Kin 8:26	6242
over Israel in Samaria was *t*	2Kin 10:36	6242
He was *t* and five years old when	2Kin 14:2	6242
he began to reign, and reigned *t*	2Kin 14:2	6242
In the *t* and seventh year of	2Kin 15:1	6242
in Samaria, and reigned *t* years	2Kin 15:27	6242
t years old was he when he began	2Kin 15:33	6242

T years old was Ahaz when he	2Kin 16:2	6242
T and five years old was he when	2Kin 18:2	6242
and he reigned *t* and nine years in	2Kin 18:2	6242
Amon was *t* and two years old when	2Kin 21:19	6242
Jehoahaz was *t* and three years old	2Kin 23:31	6242
Jehoiakim was *t* and five years old	2Kin 23:36	6242
Zedekiah was *t* and one years old	2Kin 24:18	6242
t cities in the land of Gilead	1Chr 2:22	6242
t thousand and six hundred	1Chr 7:2	6242
reckoned by their genealogies *t*	1Chr 7:7	6242
was *t* thousand and two hundred	1Chr 7:9	6242
apt to the war and to battle was *t*	1Chr 7:40	6242
and of his father's house *t*	1Chr 12:28	6242
children of Ephraim *t* thousand	1Chr 12:30	6242
And of the Danites expert in war *t*	1Chr 12:35	6242
battle, an hundred and *t* thousand	1Chr 12:37	6242
and his brethren an hundred and *t*	1Chr 15:5	6242
and his brethren two hundred and *t*	1Chr 15:6	6242
horsemen, and *t* thousand footmen	1Chr 18:4	6242
the Syrians two and *t* thousand men	1Chr 18:5	6242
fingers and toes were four and *t*	1Chr 20:6	6242
Of which, *t* and four thousand were	1Chr 23:4	6242
the LORD, from the age of *t* years	1Chr 23:24	6242
were numbered from *t* years old	1Chr 23:27	6242
the year, of every course were *t*	1Chr 27:1	6242
and in his course were *t* and four	1Chr 27:2	6242
in his course likewise were *t*	1Chr 27:4	6242
and in his course were *t* and four	1Chr 27:5	6242
and in his course were *t* and four	1Chr 27:7	6242
and in his course were *t* and four	1Chr 27:8	6242
and in his course were *t* and four	1Chr 27:9	6242
and in his course were *t* and four	1Chr 27:10	6242
and in his course were *t* and four	1Chr 27:11	6242
and in his course were *t* and four	1Chr 27:12	6242
and in his course were *t* and four	1Chr 27:13	6242
and in his course were *t* and four	1Chr 27:14	6242
and in his course were *t* and four	1Chr 27:15	6242
number of them from *t* years old	1Chr 27:23	6242
t thousand measures of beaten	2Chr 2:10	6242
t thousand measures of barley, and	2Chr 2:10	6242
t thousand baths of wine, and	2Chr 2:10	6242
wine, and *t* thousand baths of oil	2Chr 2:10	6242
cubits, and the breadth *t* cubits	2Chr 3:3	6242
t cubits, and the height was an	2Chr 3:4	6242
and the height was an hundred and *t*	2Chr 3:4	6242
t cubits, and the breadth thereof	2Chr 3:8	6242
and the breadth thereof *t* cubits	2Chr 3:8	6242
the cherubims were *t* cubits long	2Chr 3:11	6242
spread themselves forth *t* cubits	2Chr 3:13	6242
t cubits the length thereof, and	2Chr 4:1	6242
t cubits the breadth thereof, and	2Chr 4:1	6242
t priests sounding with trumpets	2Chr 5:12	6242
Solomon offered a sacrifice of *t*	2Chr 7:5	6242
and an hundred and *t* thousand sheep	2Chr 7:5	6242
to pass at the end of *t* years	2Chr 8:1	6242
t talents of gold, and of spices	2Chr 9:9	6242
and begat *t* and eight sons, and	2Chr 11:21	6242
fourteen wives, and begat *t*	2Chr 13:21	6242
began to reign, and he reigned *t*	2Chr 20:31	6242
Amaziah was *t* and five years old	2Chr 25:1	6242
began to reign, and he reigned *t*	2Chr 25:1	6242
he numbered them from *t* years old	2Chr 25:5	6242
Jotham was *t* and five years old	2Chr 27:1	6242
t years old when he began to	2Chr 27:8	6242
Ahaz was *t* years old when he	2Chr 28:1	6242
t thousand in one day, which were	2Chr 28:6	6242
t years old, and he reigned nine	2Chr 29:1	6242
nine and *t* years in Jerusalem	2Chr 29:1	6242
and the Levites from *t* years old	2Chr 31:17	6242
t years old when he began to	2Chr 33:21	6242
Jehoahaz was *t* and three years old	2Chr 36:2	6242
Jehoiakim was *t* and five years old	2Chr 36:5	6242
t years old when he began to	2Chr 36:11	6242
of silver, nine and *t* knives,	Ezr 1:9	6242
children of Bebai, six hundred *t*	Ezr 2:11	6242
Azgad, a thousand two hundred *t*	Ezr 2:12	6242
of Bezai, three hundred *t*	Ezr 2:17	6242
children of Hashum, two hundred *t*	Ezr 2:19	6242
of Beth-lehem, an hundred *t*	Ezr 2:21	6242
The men of Anathoth, an hundred *t*	Ezr 2:23	6242
of Ramah and Gaba, six hundred *t*	Ezr 2:26	6242
The men of Michmas, an hundred *t*	Ezr 2:27	6242
of Beth-el and Ai, two hundred *t*	Ezr 2:28	6242
of Harim, three hundred and *t*	Ezr 2:32	6242
Hadid, and Ono, seven hundred *t*	Ezr 2:33	6242
children of Asaph, an hundred *t*	Ezr 2:41	6242
six thousand seven hundred and *t*	Ezr 2:67	6242
from *t* years old and upward, to	Ezr 3:8	6242
the son of Bebai, and with him *t*	Ezr 8:11	6242
his brethren and their sons, *t*	Ezr 8:19	6242
two hundred and *t* Nethinims	Ezr 8:20	6242

T

Also *t* basons of gold, of a	Ezr 8:27	6242
So the wall was finished in the *t*	Neh 6:15	6242
children of Bebai, six hundred *t*	Neh 7:16	6242
two thousand three hundred *t*	Neh 7:17	6242
of Hashum, three hundred *t*	Neh 7:22	6242
of Bezai, three hundred *t*	Neh 7:23	6242
The men of Anathoth, an hundred *t*	Neh 7:27	6242
of Ramah and Gaba, six hundred *t*	Neh 7:30	6242
men of Michmas, an hundred and *t*	Neh 7:31	6242
of Beth-el and Ai, an hundred *t*	Neh 7:32	6242
of Harim, three hundred and *t*	Neh 7:35	6242
Hadid, and Ono, seven hundred *t*	Neh 7:37	6242
thousand seven hundred and *t* asses	Neh 7:69	6242
the work *t* thousand drams of gold	Neh 7:71	7239
gave was *t* thousand drams of gold	Neh 7:72	7239
Now in the *t* and fourth day of	Neh 9:1	6242
Gabbai, Sallai, nine hundred *t*	Neh 11:8	6242
of the house were eight hundred *t*	Neh 11:12	6242
men of valour, an hundred *t*	Neh 11:14	6242
hundred and seven and *t* provinces	Est 1:1	6242
India unto Ethiopia, an hundred *t*	Est 8:9	6242
all the Jews, to the hundred *t*	Est 9:30	6242
chariots of God are *t* thousand	Ps 68:17	7239
t years old when he began to	Jer 52:1	6242
three thousand Jews and three and *t*	Jer 52:28	6242
be by weight, *t* shekels a day	Eze 4:10	6242
t men, with their backs toward	Eze 8:16	6242
door of the gate five and *t* men	Eze 11:1	6242
t cubits, door against door	Eze 40:13	6242
and the breadth five and *t* cubits	Eze 40:21	6242
and the breadth five and *t* cubits	Eze 40:25	6242
long, and five and *t* cubits broad	Eze 40:29	6242
t cubits long, and five cubits	Eze 40:30	6242
long, and five and *t* cubits broad	Eze 40:33	6242
and the breadth five and *t* cubits	Eze 40:36	6242
length of the porch was *t* cubits	Eze 40:49	6242
and the breadth, *t* cubits	Eze 41:2	6242
the length thereof, *t* cubits	Eze 41:4	6242
t cubits, before the temple	Eze 41:4	6242
chambers was the wideness of *t*	Eze 41:10	6242
Over against the *t* cubits which	Eze 42:3	6242
t thousand reeds, and the breadth	Eze 45:1	6242
t thousand, and the breadth of ten	Eze 45:3	6242
t thousand of length, and the ten	Eze 45:5	6242
for a possession for *t* chambers	Eze 45:5	6242
t thousand long, over against the	Eze 45:6	6242
And the shekel is *t* gerahs	Eze 45:12	6242
t shekels, five and *t* shekels	Eze 45:12	6242
t thousand reeds in breadth, and	Eze 48:8	6242
t thousand in length, and of ten	Eze 48:9	6242
t thousand in length, and toward	Eze 48:10	6242
five and *t* thousand in length	Eze 48:10	6242
t thousand in length, and ten	Eze 48:13	6242
t thousand, and the breadth ten	Eze 48:13	6242
t thousand, shall be a profane	Eze 48:15	6242
t thousand by five and	Eze 48:20	6242
thousand by five and *t* thousand	Eze 48:20	6242
t thousand of the oblation toward	Eze 48:21	6242
t thousand toward the west border	Eze 48:21	6242
t princes, which should be over	Dan 6:1	6243
Persia withstood me one and *t* days	Dan 10:13	6242
one came to an heap of *t* measures	Hag 2:16	6242
of the press, there were but *t*	Hag 2:16	6242
the length thereof is *t* cubits	Zec 5:2	6242
against him with *t* thousand	Lk 14:31	1501
t or thirty furlongs, they see	Jn 6:19	1501
were about an hundred and *t*	Acts 1:15	1501
And sounded, and found it *t* fathoms	Acts 27:28	1501
in one day three and *t* thousand	1Cor 10:8	1501
the throne were four and *t* seats	Rev 4:4	1501
t elders sitting, clothed in	Rev 4:4	1501
t elders fall down before him	Rev 4:10	1501
t elders fell down before the	Rev 5:8	1501
t elders fell down and worshipped	Rev 5:14	1501
t elders, which sat before God on	Rev 11:16	1501
t elders and the four beasts fell	Rev 19:4	1501

TWENTY'S

I will not destroy it for *t* sake	Gen 18:31	6242

TWICE

dream was doubled unto Pharaoh *t*	Gen 41:32	6471
it shall be *t* as much as they	Ex 16:5	4932
day they gathered *t* as much bread	Ex 16:22	4932
with his rod he smote the rock *t*	Num 20:11	6471
avoided out of his presence *t*	1Sa 18:11	6471
which had appeared unto him *t*	1Kin 11:9	6471
himself there, not once nor *t*	2Kin 6:10	8147
without Jerusalem once or *t*	Neh 13:20	8147
For God speaketh once, yea *t*	Job 33:14	8147
will not answer: yea, *t*	Job 40:5	8147
also the LORD gave Job *t* as much	Job 42:10	4932

t have I heard this	Ps 62:11	8147
he live a thousand years *t* told	Eccl 6:6	6471
night, before the cock crow *t*	Mk 14:30	1364
unto him, Before the cock crow *t*	Mk 14:72	1364
I fast *t* in the week, I give	Lk 18:12	1364
t dead, plucked up by the roots	Jude 12	1364

TWIGS

off the top of his young *t*	Eze 17:4	3242
top of his young *t* a tender one	Eze 17:22	3127

TWILIGHT

David smote them from the *t* even	1Sa 30:17	5399
And they rose up in the *t*, to go	2Kin 7:5	5399
they arose and fled in the *t*	2Kin 7:7	5399
stars of the *t* thereof be dark	Job 3:9	5399
the adulterer waiteth for the *t*	Job 24:15	5399
In the *t*, in the evening, in the	Prov 7:9	5399
and carry it forth in the *t*	Eze 12:6	5939
I brought it forth in the *t*	Eze 12:7	5939
bear upon his shoulder in the *t*	Eze 12:12	5939

TWINED

with ten curtains of fine *t* linen	Ex 26:1	7806
fine *t* linen of cunning work	Ex 26:31	7806
fine *t* linen, wrought with	Ex 26:36	7806
hangings for the court of fine *t*	Ex 27:9	7806
fine *t* linen, wrought with	Ex 27:16	7806
five cubits of fine *t* linen	Ex 27:18	7806
fine *t* linen, with cunning work	Ex 28:6	7806
and scarlet, and fine *t* linen	Ex 28:8	7806
and of scarlet, and of fine *t* linen	Ex 28:15	7806
made ten curtains of fine *t* linen	Ex 36:8	7806
and scarlet, and fine *t* linen	Ex 36:35	7806
fine *t* linen, of needlework	Ex 36:37	7806
of the court were of fine *t* linen	Ex 38:9	7806
round about were of fine *t* linen	Ex 38:16	7806
and scarlet, and fine *t* linen	Ex 38:18	7806
and scarlet, and fine *t* linen	Ex 39:2	7806
and scarlet, and fine *t* linen	Ex 39:5	7806
and scarlet, and fine *t* linen	Ex 39:8	7806
and purple, and scarlet, and *t* linen	Ex 39:24	7806
and linen breeches of fine *t* linen	Ex 39:28	7806
And a girdle of fine *t* linen	Ex 39:29	7806

TWINKLING

in the *t* of an eye, at the last	1Cor 15:52	4493

TWINS

behold, there were *t* in her womb	Gen 25:24	8380
that, behold, *t* were in her womb	Gen 38:27	8380
whereof every one bear *t*, and none	Song 4:2	8382
like two young roes that are *t*	Song 4:5	8380
whereof every one beareth *t*	Song 6:6	8382
like two young roes that are *t*	Song 7:3	8380

TWO See APPENDIX.

TWOEDGED

mouth, and a *t* sword in their hand	Ps 149:6	6374
as wormwood, sharp as a *t* sword	Prov 5:4	6310
and sharper than any *t* sword	Heb 4:12	1366
of his mouth went a sharp *t* sword	Rev 1:16	1366

TWOFOLD

ye make him *t* more the child of	Mt 23:15	1366

TYCHICUS (tik'-ik-us) *A co-worker with Paul.*

and of Asia, *T* and Trophimus	Acts 20:4	5190
know my affairs, and how I do, *T*	Eph 6:21	5190
from Rome unto the Ephesians by *T*	Eph *s*	5190
my state shall *T* declare unto you	Col 4:7	5190
from Rome to the Colossians by *T*	Col *s*	5190
And *T* have I sent to Ephesus	2Ti 4:12	5190
send Artemas unto thee, or *T*	Titus 3:12	5190

TYRANNUS (ti-ran'-nus) *An Ephesian schoolmaster.*

daily in the school of one *T*	Acts 19:9	5181

TYRE *(tire)* See TYRUS. *A coastal city of Phoenicia.*

to Ramah, and to the strong city *T*	Josh 19:29	6865
Hiram king of *T* sent messengers	2Sa 5:11	6865
And came to the strong hold of *T*	2Sa 24:7	6865
Hiram king of *T* sent his servants	1Kin 5:1	6865
sent and fetched Hiram out of *T*	1Kin 7:13	6865
and his father was a man of *T*	1Kin 7:14	6876
(Now Hiram the king of *T* had	1Kin 9:11	6865
Hiram came out from *T* to see the	1Kin 9:12	6865
Now Hiram king of *T* sent	1Chr 14:1	6865
they of *T* brought much cedar wood	1Chr 22:4	6876
sent to Huram the king of *T*	2Chr 2:3	6865
the king of *T* answered in writing	2Chr 2:11	6865
Dan, and his father was a man of *T*	2Chr 2:14	6876
them of Zidon, and to them of *T*	Ezr 3:7	6876
There dwelt men of *T* also therein	Neh 13:16	6876
the daughter of *T* shall be there	Ps 45:12	6865

with the inhabitants of *T*	Ps 83:7	6865
behold Philistia, and, *T*, with	Ps 87:4	6865
The burden of *T*	Is 23:1	6865
sorely pained at the report of *T*	Is 23:5	6865
hath taken this counsel against *T*	Is 23:8	6865
that *T* shall be forgotten seventy	Is 23:15	6865
years shall *T* sing as an harlot	Is 23:15	6865
years, that the Lord will visit *T*	Is 23:17	6865
what have ye to do with me, O *T*	Joel 3:4	6865
done in you, had been done in *T*	Mt 11:21	5184
It shall be more tolerable for *T*	Mt 11:22	5184
and departed into the coasts of *T*	Mt 15:21	5184
and they about *T* and Sidon, a great	Mk 3:8	5184
and went into the borders of *T*	Mk 7:24	5184
departing from the coasts of *T*	Mk 7:31	5184
and from the sea coast of *T*	Lk 6:17	5184
mighty works had been done in *T*	Lk 10:13	5184
it shall be more tolerable for *T*	Lk 10:14	5184
highly displeased with them of *T*	Acts 12:20	5185
sailed into Syria, and landed at *T*	Acts 21:3	5184
we had finished our course from *T*	Acts 21:7	5184

TYRIAN See Tyre.

TYRUS *(ti'-rus)* See Tyre. *Same as Tyre.*

And all the kings of *T*, and all the	Jer 25:22	6865
Ammonites, and to the king of *T*	Jer 27:3	6865
Philistines, and to cut off from *T*	Jer 47:4	6865
because that *T* hath said against	Eze 26:2	6865
Behold, I am against thee, O *T*	Eze 26:3	6865
they shall destroy the walls of *T*	Eze 26:4	6865
Behold, I will bring upon *T*	Eze 26:7	6865
Thus saith the Lord God to *T*	Eze 26:15	6865
man, take up a lamentation for *T*	Eze 27:2	6865
And say unto *T*, O thou that art	Eze 27:3	6865
O *T*, thou hast said, I am of	Eze 27:3	6865
thy wise men, O *T*, that were in	Eze 27:8	6865
thee, saying, What city is like *T*	Eze 27:32	6865
of man, say unto the prince of *T*	Eze 28:2	6865
a lamentation upon the king of *T*	Eze 28:12	6865
serve a great service against *T*	Eze 29:18	6865
he no wages, nor his army, for *T*	Eze 29:18	6865
Ephraim, as I saw *T*, is planted	Hos 9:13	6865
For three transgressions of *T*	Amos 1:9	6865
will send a fire on the wall of *T*	Amos 1:10	6865
T, and Zidon, though it be very	Zec 9:2	6865
T did build herself a strong hold	Zec 9:3	6865

U

UCAL *(u'-cal)* An obscure name.

Ithiel, even unto Ithiel and *U*	Prov 30:1	401

UEL *(u'-el)* Married a foreigner in exile.

Maadai, Amram, and, *U*,	Ezr 10:34	177

ULAI *(u'-lahee)* A river near Susa.

and I was by the river of *U*	Dan 8:2	195
voice between the banks of *U*	Dan 8:16	195

ULAM *(u'-lam)*
    1. A son of Sheresh.

and his sons were *U* and Rakem	1Chr 7:16	198
And the sons of *U*	1Chr 7:17	198

    2. A son of Eshek.

U his firstborn, Jehush the	1Chr 8:39	198
the sons of *U* were mighty men of	1Chr 8:40	198

ULLA *(ul'-la)* An Asherite chief.

And the sons of *U*	1Chr 7:39	5925

UMMAH *(um'-mah)* A city in Asher.

U also, and Aphek, and Rehob	Josh 19:30	5981

UNACCUSTOMED

as a bullock *u* to the yoke	Jer 31:18	3808,3925

UNADVISEDLY

so that he spake *u* with his lips	Ps 106:33	981

UNAWARES

Jacob stole away *u* to Laban the	Gen 31:20	3820,3824
thou hast stolen away *u* to me	Gen 31:26	3820,3824
which killeth any person at *u*	Num 35:11	7684
any person *u* may flee thither	Num 35:15	7684
which should kill his neighbour *u*	Deut 4:42	1097,1847
slayer that killeth any person *u*	Josh 20:3	7684
person at *u* might flee thither	Josh 20:9	7684
destruction come upon him at *u*	Ps 35:8	3045
and so that day come upon you *u*	Lk 21:34	160
of false brethren *u* brought in	Gal 2:4	3920
some have entertained angels *u*	Heb 13:2	2990
there are certain men crept in *u*	Jude 4	3921

UNBELIEF

works there because of their *u*	Mt 13:58	570
said unto them, Because of your *u*	Mt 17:20	570
he marvelled because of their *u*	Mk 6:6	570
help thou mine *u*	Mk 9:24	570
and upbraided them with their *u*	Mk 16:14	570
shall their *u* make the faith of	Rom 3:3	570
at the promise of God through *u*	Rom 4:20	570
because of *u* they were broken off	Rom 11:20	570
if they abide not still in *u*	Rom 11:23	543
obtained mercy through their *u*	Rom 11:30	543
God hath concluded them all in *u*	Rom 11:32	543
because I did it ignorantly in *u*	1Ti 1:13	570
in any of you an evil heart of *u*	Heb 3:12	570
could not enter in because of *u*	Heb 3:19	570
entered not in because of *u*	Heb 4:6	543
fall after the same example of *u*	Heb 4:11	543

UNBELIEVERS

him his portion with the *u*	Lk 12:46	571
brother, and that before the *u*	1Cor 6:6	571
in those that are unlearned, or *u*	1Cor 14:23	571
unequally yoked together with *u*	2Cor 6:14	571

UNBELIEVING

But the *u* Jews stirred up the	Acts 14:2	544
For the *u* husband is sanctified	1Cor 7:14	571
the *u* wife is sanctified by the	1Cor 7:14	571
But if the *u* depart, let him	1Cor 7:15	571
are defiled and *u* is nothing pure	Titus 1:15	571
But the fearful, and, *u*, and the	Rev 21:8	571

UNBLAMEABLE

death, to present you holy and *u*	Col 1:22	299
hearts *u* in holiness before God	1Th 3:13	299

UNBLAMEABLY

u we behaved ourselves among you	1Th 2:10	274

UNCERTAIN

if the trumpet give an *u* sound	1Cor 14:8	82
highminded, nor trust in *u* riches	1Ti 6:17	83

UNCERTAINLY

I therefore so run, not as *u*	1Cor 9:26	82

UNCHANGEABLE

ever, hath an *u* priesthood	Heb 7:24	531

UNCIRCUMCISED

the *u* man child whose flesh of	Gen 17:14	6189
give our sister to one that is *u*	Gen 34:14	6190
Pharaoh hear me, who am of *u* lips	Ex 6:12	6189
the Lord, Behold, I am of *u* lips	Ex 6:30	6189
for no *u* person shall eat thereof	Ex 12:48	6189
count the fruit thereof as *u*	Lev 19:23	6189
years shall it be as *u* unto you	Lev 19:23	6189
if then their *u* hearts be humbled	Lev 26:41	6189
for they were *u*, because they had	Josh 5:7	6189
take a wife of the *u* Philistines	Judg 14:3	6189
and fall into the hand of the *u*	Judg 15:18	6189
over unto the garrison of these *u*	1Sa 14:6	6189
for who is this *u* Philistine	1Sa 17:26	6189
this *u* Philistine shall be as one	1Sa 17:36	6189
lest these *u* come and thrust me	1Sa 31:4	6189
the daughters of the *u* triumph	2Sa 1:20	6189
lest these *u* come and abuse me	1Chr 10:4	6189
no more come into thee the *u*	Is 52:1	6189
behold, their ear is *u*, and they	Jer 6:10	6189
which are circumcised with the *u*	Jer 9:25	6190
for all these nations are *u*	Jer 9:26	6189
of Israel are *u* in the heart	Jer 9:26	6189
of the *u* by the hand of strangers	Eze 28:10	6189
shalt lie in the midst of the *u*	Eze 31:18	6189
down, and be thou laid with the *u*	Eze 32:19	6189
they are gone down, they lie *u*	Eze 32:21	6189
which are gone down *u* into the	Eze 32:24	6189
all of them *u*, slain by the sword	Eze 32:25	6189
all of them *u*, slain by the sword	Eze 32:26	6189
mighty that are fallen of the *u*	Eze 32:27	6189
be broken in the midst of the *u*	Eze 32:28	6189
they shall lie with the *u*	Eze 32:29	6189
they lie *u* with them that be	Eze 32:30	6189
be laid in the midst of the *u*	Eze 32:32	6189
u in heart, and *u* in flesh	Eze 44:7	6189
u in heart, nor *u* in flesh	Eze 44:9	6189
u in heart and ears, ye do always	Acts 7:51	564
Saying, Thou wentest in to men *u*	Acts 11:3	203,2192
faith which he had yet being *u*	Rom 4:11	1722,3588,203

which he had being yet *u*	Rom 4:12	*1722,3588,203*
let him not become *u*	1Cor 7:18	*1986*

UNCIRCUMCISION

law, thy circumcision is made *u*	Rom 2:25	*203*
Therefore if the *u* keep the	Rom 2:26	*203*
shall not his *u* be counted for	Rom 2:26	*203*
shall not *u* which is by nature,	Rom 2:27	*203*
by faith, and *u* through faith	Rom 3:30	*203*
only, or upon the *u* also	Rom 4:9	*203*
he was in circumcision, or in *u*	Rom 4:10	*203*
Not in circumcision, but in *u*	Rom 4:10	*203*
Is any called in *u*	1Cor 7:18	*203*
u is nothing, but the keeping of	1Cor 7:19	*203*
of the *u* was committed unto me	Gal 2:7	*203*
availeth any thing, nor *u*	Gal 5:6	*203*
availeth any thing, nor *u*	Gal 6:15	*203*
who are called *U* by that which is	Eph 2:11	*203*
the *u* of your flesh, hath he	Col 2:13	*203*
Greek nor Jew, circumcision nor *u*	Col 3:11	*203*

UNCLE

the sons of Uzziel the *u* of Aaron	Lev 10:4	*1730*
Either his *u*, or his uncle's son,	Lev 25:49	*1730*
Saul's *u* said unto him and to his	1Sa 10:14	*1730*
And Saul's *u* said, Tell me, I pray	1Sa 10:15	*1730*
And Saul said unto his *u*, He told	1Sa 10:16	*1730*
Abner, the son of Ner, Saul's *u*	1Sa 14:50	*1730*
David's *u* was a counsellor	1Chr 27:32	*1730*
of Abihail the *u* of Mordecai	Est 2:15	*1730*
thine *u* shall come unto thee	Jer 32:7	*1730*
a man's *u* shall take him up, and	Amos 6:10	*1730*

UNCLEAN

Or if a soul touch any *u* thing	Lev 5:2	*2931*
it be a carcase of an *u* beast	Lev 5:2	*2931*
or a carcase of *u* cattle.	Lev 5:2	*2931*
the carcase of *u* creeping things	Lev 5:2	*2931*
he also shall be *u*, and guilty	Lev 5:2	*2931*
any *u* thing shall not be eaten	Lev 7:19	*2931*
soul that shall touch any *u* thing	Lev 7:21	*2932*
of man, or any *u* beast, or any	Lev 7:21	*2931*
or any abominable *u* thing	Lev 7:21	*2931*
holy and unholy, and between *u*	Lev 10:10	*2931*
he is *u* unto you	Lev 11:4	*2931*
he is *u* unto you	Lev 11:5	*2931*
he is *u* unto you	Lev 11:6	*2931*
he is *u* to you	Lev 11:7	*2931*
they are *u* to you	Lev 11:8	*2931*
And for these ye shall be *u*	Lev 11:24	*2930*
of them shall be *u* until the even	Lev 11:24	*2930*
clothes, and be *u* until the even	Lev 11:25	*2930*
cheweth the cud, are *u* unto you	Lev 11:26	*2931*
one that toucheth them shall be *u*	Lev 11:26	*2930*
on all four, those are *u* unto you	Lev 11:27	*2931*
carcase shall be *u* until the even	Lev 11:27	*2930*
clothes, and be *u* until the even	Lev 11:28	*2930*
they are *u* unto you	Lev 11:28	*2931*
These also shall be *u* unto you	Lev 11:29	*2931*
These are *u* to you among all that	Lev 11:31	*2931*
shall be *u* until the even	Lev 11:31	*2930*
dead, doth fall, it shall be *u*	Lev 11:32	*2930*
it shall be *u* until the even	Lev 11:32	*2930*
whatsoever is in it shall be *u*	Lev 11:33	*2930*
such water cometh shall be *u*	Lev 11:34	*2930*
in every such vessel shall be *u*	Lev 11:34	*2930*
their carcase falleth shall be *u*	Lev 11:35	*2930*
for they are *u*, and shall be	Lev 11:35	*2931*
and shall be *u* unto you.	1Cor 11:35	*2931*
toucheth their carcase shall be *u*	Lev 11:36	*2930*
thereon, it shall be *u* unto you	Lev 11:38	*2931*
thereof shall be *u* until the even	Lev 11:39	*2930*
clothes, and be *u* until the even	Lev 11:40	*2930*
clothes, and be *u* until the even	Lev 11:40	*2930*
ye make yourselves *u* with them	Lev 11:43	*2930*
make a difference between the *u*	Lev 11:47	*2931*
then she shall be *u* seven days	Lev 12:2	*2930*
for her infirmity shall she be *u*	Lev 12:2	*2930*
then she shall be *u* two weeks	Lev 12:5	*2930*
look on him, and pronounce him *u*	Lev 13:3	*2930*
the priest shall pronounce him *u*	Lev 13:8	*2930*
the priest shall pronounce him *u*	Lev 13:11	*2930*
for he is *u*	Lev 13:11	*2931*
appeareth in him, he shall be *u*	Lev 13:14	*2930*
flesh, and pronounce him to be *u*	Lev 13:15	*2930*
for the raw flesh is *u*	Lev 13:15	*2931*
the priest shall pronounce him *u*	Lev 13:20	*2930*
the priest shall pronounce him *u*	Lev 13:22	*2930*
the priest shall pronounce him *u*	Lev 13:25	*2930*
the priest shall pronounce him *u*	Lev 13:27	*2930*
the priest shall pronounce him *u*	Lev 13:30	*2930*
he is *u*	Lev 13:36	*2931*

He is a leprous man, he is *u*	Lev 13:44	*2931*
shall pronounce him utterly *u*	Lev 13:44	*2930*
lip, and shall cry, *U*, *u*	Lev 13:45	*2931*
he is *u*	Lev 13:46	*2931*
it is *u*	Lev 13:51	*2931*
it is *u*	Lev 13:55	*2931*
it clean, or to pronounce it *u*	Lev 13:59	*2930*
is in the house be not made *u*	Lev 14:36	*2930*
into an *u* place without the city	Lev 14:40	*2931*
without the city into an *u* place	Lev 14:41	*2931*
it is *u*	Lev 14:44	*2931*
out of the city into an *u* place	Lev 14:45	*2931*
shut up shall be *u* until the even	Lev 14:46	*2930*
To teach when it is *u*, and when it	Lev 14:57	*2931*
because of his issue he is *u*	Lev 15:2	*2931*
lieth that hath the issue, is *u*	Lev 15:4	*2930*
whereon he sitteth, shall be *u*	Lev 15:4	*2930*
in water, and be *u* until the even	Lev 15:5	*2930*
in water, and be *u* until the even	Lev 15:6	*2930*
in water, and be *u* until the even	Lev 15:7	*2930*
in water, and be *u* until the even	Lev 15:8	*2930*
that hath the issue shall be *u*	Lev 15:9	*2930*
him shall be *u* until the even	Lev 15:10	*2930*
in water, and be *u* until the even	Lev 15:10	*2930*
in water, and be *u* until the even	Lev 15:11	*2930*
in water, and be *u* until the even	Lev 15:16	*2930*
water, and be *u* until the even	Lev 15:17	*2930*
in water, and be *u* until the even	Lev 15:18	*2930*
her shall be *u* until the even	Lev 15:19	*2930*
upon in her separation shall be *u*	Lev 15:20	*2930*
that she sitteth upon shall be *u*	Lev 15:20	*2930*
in water, and be *u* until the even	Lev 15:21	*2930*
in water, and be *u* until the even	Lev 15:22	*2930*
he shall be *u* until the even	Lev 15:23	
him, he shall be *u* seven days	Lev 15:24	*2930*
bed whereon he lieth shall be *u*	Lev 15:24	*2930*
she shall be *u*	Lev 15:25	*2931*
she sitteth upon shall be *u*	Lev 15:26	*2931*
toucheth those things shall be *u*	Lev 15:27	*2930*
in water, and be *u* until the even	Lev 15:27	*2930*
him that lieth with her that is *u*	Lev 15:33	*2931*
in water, and be *u* until the even	Lev 17:15	*2930*
brother's wife, it is an *u* thing	Lev 20:21	*5079*
between clean beasts and *u*	Lev 20:25	*2931*
and between *u* fowls	Lev 20:25	*2931*
I have separated from you as *u*	Lev 20:25	*2930*
any thing that is *u* by the dead	Lev 22:4	*2931*
thing, whereby he may be made *u*	Lev 22:5	*2930*
any such shall be *u* until even	Lev 22:6	*2930*
And if it be any *u* beast, of which	Lev 27:11	*2931*
And if it be of an *u* beast	Lev 27:27	*2931*
not make himself *u* for his father	Num 6:7	*2930*
be *u* by reason of a dead body	Num 9:10	*2931*
the firstling of *u* beasts shalt	Num 18:15	*2931*
priest shall be *u* until the even	Num 19:7	*2930*
shall be *u* until the even	Num 19:8	*2930*
clothes, and be *u* until the even	Num 19:10	*2930*
of any man shall be *u* seven days	Num 19:11	*2930*
sprinkled upon him, he shall be *u*	Num 19:13	*2931*
the tent, shall be a *u* seven days	Num 19:14	*2930*
no covering bound upon it, is *u*	Num 19:15	*2931*
or a grave, shall be *u* seven days	Num 19:16	*2930*
for an *u* person they shall take	Num 19:17	*2930*
upon the *u* on the third day	Num 19:19	*2931*
But the man that shall be *u*	Num 19:20	*2930*
he is *u*	Num 19:20	*2931*
separation shall be *u* until even	Num 19:21	*2930*
whatsoever the *u* person toucheth	Num 19:22	*2930*
person toucheth shall be *u*	Num 19:22	*2930*
toucheth it shall be *u* until even	Num 19:22	*2930*
the *u* and the clean may eat	Deut 12:15	*2931*
the *u* and the clean shall eat of	Deut 12:22	*2931*
therefore they are *u* unto you	Deut 14:7	*2931*
not the cud, it is *u* unto you	Deut 14:8	*2931*
it is *u* unto you	Deut 14:10	*2931*
thing that flieth is *u* unto you	Deut 14:19	*2931*
the *u* and the clean person shall	Deut 15:22	*2931*
that he see no *u* thing in thee	Deut 23:14	*6172*
away ought thereof for any *u* use	Deut 26:14	*2931*
the land of your possession be *u*	Josh 22:19	*2931*
drink, and eat not any *u* thing	Judg 13:4	*2931*
drink, neither eat any *u* thing	Judg 13:7	*2932*
strong drink, nor eat any *u* thing	Judg 13:14	*2932*
that none which was *u* in any	2Chr 23:19	*2931*
is an *u* land with the filthiness	Ezr 9:11	*5079*
bring a clean thing out of an *u*	Job 14:4	*2931*
and their life is among the *u*	Job 36:14	*6945*
good and to the clean, and to the *u*	Eccl 9:2	*2931*
because I am a man of *u* lips	Is 6:5	*2931*
the midst of a people of *u* lips	Is 6:5	*2931*
the *u* shall not pass over it	Is 35:8	*2931*

thee the uncircumcised and the *u* .... Is 52:1 | 2931
out from thence, touch no *u* thing .... Is 52:11 | 2931
But we are all as an *u* thing .... Is 64:6 | 2931
it is *u* .... Lam 4:15 | 2931
shewed difference between the *u* .... Eze 22:26 | 2931
them to discern between the *u* .... Eze 44:23 | 2931
they shall eat *u* things in .... Hos 9:3 | 2931
If one that is *u* by a dead body.............. Hag 2:13 | 2931
touch any of these, shall it be *u* .... Hag 2:13 | 2930
answered and said, It shall be *u* .... Hag 2:13 | 2930
that which they offer there is *u* .... Hag 2:14 | 2931
the *u* spirit to pass out of the................ Zec 13:2 | 2932
gave them power against *u* spirits .... Mt 10:1 | 169
When the *u* spirit is gone out of............ Mt 12:43 | 169
synagogue a man with an *u* spirit .... Mk 1:23 | 169
when the *u* spirit had torn him,.............. Mk 1:26 | 169
commandeth he even the *u* spirits .... Mk 1:27 | 169
u spirits, when they saw him,................. Mk 3:11 | 169
they said, He hath an *u* spirit .... Mk 3:30 | 169
the tombs a man with an *u* spirit .... Mk 5:2 | 169
out of the man, thou *u* spirit.................. Mk 5:8 | 169
the *u* spirits went out, and .... Mk 5:13 | 169
and gave them power over *u* spirits ...... Mk 6:7 | 169
young daughter had an *u* spirit .... Mk 7:25 | 169
which had a spirit of an *u* devil.............. Lk 4:33 | 169
power he commandeth the *u* spirits ...... Lk 4:36 | 169
that were vexed with *u* spirits .... Lk 6:18 | 169
(For he had commanded the *u* .... Lk 8:29 | 169
And Jesus rebuked the *u* .... Lk 9:42 | 169
When the *u* spirit is gone out of............ Lk 11:24 | 169
which were vexed with *u* spirits .... Acts 5:16 | 169
For *u* spirits, crying with loud .... Acts 8:7 | 169
any thing that is common or *u* .... Acts 10:14 | 169
not call any man common or *u* .... Acts 10:28 | 169
for nothing common or *u* hath at .... Acts 11:8 | 169
that there is nothing *u* of itself .... Rom 14:14 | 2839
that esteemeth any thing to be *u* .... Rom 14:14 | 2839
to him it is *u* .... Rom 14:14 | 2839
else were your children *u* .... 1Cor 7:14 | 169
Lord, and touch not the *u* thing .... 2Cor 6:17 | 169
nor *u* person, nor covetous man, ... Eph 5:5 | 169
of an heifer sprinkling the *u* .... Heb 9:13 | 2840
I saw three *u* spirits like frogs .... Rev 16:13 | 169
foul spirit, and a cage of every *u* .... Rev 18:2 | 169

UNCLEANNESS

Or if he touch the *u* of man .... Lev 5:3 | 2932
whatsoever *u* it be that a man................ Lev 5:3 | 2932
the LORD, having his *u* upon him .... Lev 7:20 | 2932
unclean thing, as the *u* of man .... Lev 7:21 | 2932
that is to be cleansed from his *u* .... Lev 14:19 | 2932
this shall be his *u* in his issue .... Lev 15:3 | 2932
from his issue, it is his *u* .... Lev 15:3 | 2932
her *u* shall be as the days of her............ Lev 15:25 | 2932
as the *u* of her separation .... Lev 15:26 | 2932
the LORD for the issue of her *u* .... Lev 15:30 | 2932
children of Israel from their *u* .... Lev 15:31 | 2932
that they die not in their *u* .... Lev 15:31 | 2932
because of the *u* of the children............ Lev 16:16 | 2932
them in the midst of their *u* .... Lev 16:16 | 2932
hallow it from the *u* of the .... Lev 16:19 | 2932
as she is put apart for her *u* .... Lev 18:19 | 2932
the LORD, having his *u* upon him .... Lev 22:3 | 2932
or a man of whom he may take *u*........... Lev 22:5 | 2930
whatsoever *u* he hath .... Lev 22:5 | 2932
to *u* with another instead of thy .... Num 5:19 | 2932
his *u* is yet upon him .... Num 19:13 | 2932
of *u* that chanceth him by night .... Deut 23:10 | 7137
he hath found some *u* in her .... Deut 24:1 | 6172
for she was purified from her *u* .... 2Sa 11:4 | 2932
brought out all the *u* that they .... 2Chr 29:16 | 2932
one end to another with their *u* .... Ezr 9:11 | 2932
me as the *u* of a removed woman .... Eze 36:17 | 2932
According to their *u* and according .... Eze 39:24 | 2932
of Jerusalem for sin and for *u* .... Zec 13:1 | 5079
of dead men's bones, and of all *u*.......... Mt 23:27 | 167
God also gave them up to *u*.................... Rom 1:24 | 167
your members servants to *u*................... Rom 6:19 | 167
and have not repented of the *u* .... 2Cor 12:21 | 167
Adultery, fornication, *u*, ... Gal 5:19 | 167
to work all *u* with greediness .... Eph 4:19 | 167
But fornication, and all *u* .... Eph 5:3 | 167
fornication, *u*, inordinate .... Col 3:5 | 167
was not of deceit, nor of *u* .... 1Th 2:3 | 167
For God hath not called us unto *u* .... 1Th 4:7 | 167
after the flesh in the lust of *u* .... 2Pet 2:10 | 3394

UNCLEANNESSES

also save you from all your *u* .... Eze 36:29 | 2932

UNCLE'S

a man shall lie with his *u* wife................ Lev 20:20 | 1733
he hath uncovered his *u* nakedness .... Lev 20:20 | 1730
Either his uncle, or his *u* son .... Lev 25:49 | 1733
that is, Esther, his *u* daughter .... Est 2:7 | 1733
So Hanameel mine *u* son came to me ..... Jer 32:8 | 1733
the field of Hanameel my *u* son............. Jer 32:9 | 1733
the sight of Hanameel mine *u* son .... Jer 32:12 | 1733

UNCLOTHED

not for that we would be *u* .... 2Cor 5:4 | 1562

UNCOMELY

himself *u* toward his virgin .... 1Cor 7:36 | 807
our *u* parts have more abundant .... 1Cor 12:23 | 809

UNCONDEMNED

They have beaten us openly *u* .... Acts 16:37 | 178
a man that is a Roman, and *u* .... Acts 22:25 | 178

UNCORRUPTIBLE

changed the glory of the *u* God .... Rom 1:23 | 862

UNCORRUPTNESS

in doctrine shewing *u*, gravity, ... Titus 2:7 | 90

UNCOVER

U not your heads, neither rend .... Lev 10:6 | 6544
kin to him, to *u* their nakedness............. Lev 18:6 | 1540
of thy mother, shalt thou not *u* .... Lev 18:7 | 1540
thou shalt not *u* her nakedness .... Lev 18:7 | 1540
father's wife shalt thou not *u* .... Lev 18:8 | 1540
their nakedness thou shalt not *u* .... Lev 18:9 | 1540
their nakedness thou shalt not *u* .... Lev 18:10 | 1540
thou shalt not *u* her nakedness .... Lev 18:11 | 1540
Thou shalt not *u* the nakedness of .... Lev 18:12 | 1540
Thou shalt not *u* the nakedness of .... Lev 18:13 | 1540
Thou shalt not *u* the nakedness of .... Lev 18:14 | 1540
Thou shalt not *u* the nakedness of .... Lev 18:15 | 1540
thou shalt not *u* her nakedness .... Lev 18:15 | 1540
Thou shalt not *u* the nakedness of .... Lev 18:16 | 1540
Thou shalt not *u* the nakedness of .... Lev 18:17 | 1540
daughter, to *u* her nakedness .... Lev 18:17 | 1540
to *u* her nakedness, beside the .... Lev 18:18 | 1540
unto a woman to *u* her nakedness .... Lev 18:19 | 1540
and shall *u* her nakedness .... Lev 20:18 | 1540
thou shalt not *u* the nakedness of .... Lev 20:19 | 1540
garments, shall not *u* his head .... Lev 21:10 | 6544
u the woman's head, and put the .... Num 5:18 | 6544
u his feet, and lay thee down .... Ruth 3:4 | 1540
u thy locks, make bare the leg,............. Is 47:2 | 1540
u the thigh, pass over the rivers .... Is 47:2 | 1540
for he shall *u* the cedar work .... Zeph 2:14 | 6168

UNCOVERED

and he was *u* within his tent.................. Gen 9:21 | 1540
hath *u* his father's nakedness .... Lev 20:11 | 1540
he hath *u* his sister's nakedness .... Lev 20:17 | 1540
she hath *u* the fountain of her .... Lev 20:18 | 1540
he hath *u* his uncle's nakedness .... Lev 20:20 | 1540
he hath *u* his brother's nakedness .... Lev 20:21 | 1540
u his feet, and laid her down .... Ruth 3:7 | 1540
of Israel today, who *u* himself................ 2Sa 6:20 | 1540
even with their buttocks *u* .... Is 20:4 | 2834
and horsemen, and Kir *u* the shield .... Is 22:6 | 6168
Thy nakedness shall be *u*, yea, ... Is 47:3 | 1540
I have *u* his secret places, and he .... Jer 49:10 | 1540
and thine arm shall be *u*, and thou .... Eze 4:7 | 2834
also, and let thy foreskin be *u* .... Hab 2:16 | 1540
they *u* the roof where he was .... Mk 2:4 | 648
her head *u* dishonoureth her head .... 1Cor 11:5 | 177
that a woman pray unto God *u* .... 1Cor 11:13 | 177

UNCOVERETH

for he *u* his near kin .... Lev 20:19 | 6168
because he *u* his father's skirt .... Deut 27:20 | 1540
fellows shamelessly *u* himself............... 2Sa 6:20 | 1540

UNCTION

But ye have an *u* from the Holy .... 1Jn 2:20 | 5545

UNDEFILED

Blessed are the *u* in the way................. Ps 119:1 | 8549
my sister, my love, my dove, my *u* .... Song 5:2 | 8535
My dove, my *u* is but one .... Song 6:9 | 8535
us, who is holy, harmless, *u* .... Heb 7:26 | 283
honourable in all, and the bed *u* .... Heb 13:4 | 283
u before God and the Father is.............. Jas 1:27 | 283
inheritance incorruptible, and *u* .... 1Pet 1:4 | 283

UNDER See APPENDIX.

UNDERGIRDING

up, they used helps, *u* the ship .... Acts 27:17 | 5269

UNDERNEATH See APPENDIX.

U

UNDERSETTERS

and the four corners thereof had *u*	1Kin 7:30	3802
under the laver were *u* molten	1Kin 7:30	3802
there were four *u* to the four	1Kin 7:34	3802
the *u* were of the very base	1Kin 7:34	3802

UNDERSTAND

that they may not *u* one another's	Gen 11:7	8085
that thou canst *u* a dream to	Gen 41:15	8085
then ye shall *u* that these men	Num 16:30	3045
U therefore this day, that the	Deut 9:3	3045
U therefore, that the LORD thy	Deut 9:6	3045
whose tongue thou shalt not *u*	Deut 28:49	8085
for we *u* it	2Kin 18:26	8085
the LORD made me *u* in writing by	1Chr 28:19	7919
the women, and those that could *u*	Neh 8:3	995
caused the people to *u* the law	Neh 8:7	995
and caused them to *u* the reading	Neh 8:8	995
even to *u* the words of the law	Neh 8:13	7919
cause me to *u* wherein I have	Job 6:24	995
u what he would say unto me	Job 23:5	995
thunder of his power who can *u*	Job 26:14	995
neither do the aged *u* judgment	Job 32:9	995
Also can any *u* the spreadings of	Job 36:29	995
see if there were any that did *u*	Ps 14:2	7919
Who can *u* his errors	Ps 19:12	995
see if there were any that did *u*	Ps 53:2	7919
know not, neither will they *u*	Ps 82:5	995
neither doth a fool *u* this	Ps 92:6	995
U, ye brutish among the people	Ps 94:8	995
things, even they shall *u* the	Ps 107:43	995
Make me to *u* the way of thy	Ps 119:27	995
I *u* more than the ancients,	Ps 119:100	995
To a *u* a proverb, and the	Prov 1:6	995
Then shalt thou *u* the fear of the	Prov 2:5	995
Then shalt thou *u* righteousness	Prov 2:9	995
O ye simple, *u* wisdom	Prov 8:5	995
of the prudent is to *u* his way	Prov 14:8	995
and he will *u* knowledge	Prov 19:25	995
how can a man then *u* his own way	Prov 20:24	995
Evil men *u* not judgment	Prov 28:5	995
that seek the LORD *u* all things	Prov 28:5	995
for though he *u* he will not	Prov 29:19	995
people, Hear ye indeed, but *u* not	Is 6:9	995
u with their heart, and convert,	Is 6:10	995
whom shall he make to *u* doctrine	Is 28:9	995
a vexation only to *u* the report	Is 28:19	995
of the rash shall *u* knowledge	Is 32:4	995
tongue, that thou canst not *u*	Is 33:19	998
for we *u* it	Is 36:11	8085
u together, that the hand of the	Is 41:20	7919
and believe me, and *u* that I am he	Is 43:10	995
their hearts, that they cannot *u*	Is 44:18	7919
they are shepherds that cannot *u*	Is 56:11	995
is the wise man, that may *u* this	Jer 9:12	995
whose words thou canst not *u*	Eze 3:6	8085
make this man to *u* the vision	Dan 8:16	995
but he said unto me, *U*, O son of	Dan 8:17	995
our iniquities, and *u* thy truth	Dan 9:13	7919
therefore the matter, and	Dan 9:23	995
Know therefore and *u*, that from	Dan 9:25	7919
u the words that I speak unto	Dan 10:11	995
thou didst set thine heart to *u*	Dan 10:12	995
Now I am come to make thee *u* what	Dan 10:14	995
they that *u* among the people	Dan 11:33	7919
and none of the wicked shall *u*	Dan 12:10	995
but the wise shall *u*	Dan 12:10	995
people that doth not *u* shall fall	Hos 4:14	995
wise, and he shall *u* these things	Hos 14:9	995
neither *u* they his counsel	Mic 4:12	995
they hear not, neither do they *u*	Mt 13:13	4920
ye shall hear, and shall not *u*	Mt 13:14	4920
should *u* with their heart, and	Mt 13:15	4920
and said unto them, Hear, and *u*	Mt 15:10	4920
Do not ye yet *u*, that whatsoever	Mt 15:17	3539
Do ye not yet *u*, neither remember	Mt 16:9	3539
How is it that ye do not *u* that I	Mt 16:11	3539
place, (whoso readeth, let him *u*	Mt 24:15	3539
hearing they may hear, and not *u*	Mk 4:12	4920
unto me every one of you, and *u*	Mk 7:14	4920
perceive ye not yet, neither *u*	Mk 8:17	4920
them, How is it that ye do not *u*	Mk 8:21	4920
not, (let him that readeth *u*	Mk 13:14	3539
neither *u* I what thou sayest	Mk 14:68	1987
see, and hearing they might not *u*	Lk 8:10	4920
that they might *u* the scriptures	Lk 24:45	4920
Why do ye not *u* my speech	Jn 8:43	1097
nor *u* with their heart, and be	Jn 12:40	3539
Because that thou mayest *u*	Acts 24:11	1097
ye shall hear, and shall not *u*	Acts 28:26	4920
u with their heart, and should be	Acts 28:27	4920

they that have not heard shall *u*	Rom 15:21	4920
Wherefore I give you to *u*	1Cor 12:3	1107
u all mysteries, and all knowledge	1Cor 13:2	1492
ye may *u* my knowledge in the	Eph 3:4	3539
But I would ye should *u*, brethren	Phil 1:12	1097
Through faith we *u* that the	Heb 11:3	3539
of the things that they *u* not	2Pet 2:12	50

UNDERSTANDEST

what *u* thou, which is not in us	Job 15:9	995
thou *u* my thought afar off	Ps 139:2	995
not, neither *u* what they say	Jer 5:15	8085
and said, *U* thou what thou readest	Acts 8:30	1097

UNDERSTANDETH

u all the imaginations of the	1Chr 28:9	995
God *u* the way thereof, and he	Job 28:23	995
u not, is like the beasts that	Ps 49:20	995
They are all plain to him that *u*	Prov 8:9	995
knowledge is easy unto him that *u*	Prov 14:6	995
glorieth glory in this, that he *u*	Jer 9:24	7919
u* it not, then cometh the wicked	Mt 13:19	4920
he that heareth the word, and *u* it	Mt 13:23	4920
There is none that *u*, there is	Rom 3:11	4920
for no man *u* him	1Cor 14:2	191
seeing he *u* not what thou sayest	1Cor 14:16	1492

UNDERSTANDING

spirit of God, in wisdom, and in *u*	Ex 31:3	8394
spirit of God, in wisdom, in *u*	Ex 35:31	8394
u to know how to work all manner	Ex 36:1	8394
Take you wise men, and *u*, and known	Deut 1:13	995
your *u* in the sight of the	Deut 4:6	998
nation is a wise and *u* people	Deut 4:6	995
neither is there any *u* in them	Deut 32:28	8394
and she was a woman of good *u*	1Sa 25:3	7922
an *u* heart to judge thy people	1Kin 3:9	8085
for thyself *u* to discern judgment	1Kin 3:11	995
given thee a wise and an *u* heart	1Kin 3:12	995
u exceeding much, and largeness of	1Kin 4:29	8394
he was filled with wisdom, and *u*	1Kin 7:14	8394
were men that had *u* of the times	1Chr 12:32	998
the LORD give thee wisdom and *u*	1Chr 22:12	998
son, endued with prudence and *u*	2Chr 2:12	998
sent a cunning man, endued with *u*	2Chr 2:13	998
who had *u* in the visions of God	2Chr 26:5	995
and for Elnathan, men of *u*	Ezr 8:16	995
us they brought us a man of *u*	Ezr 8:18	7922
and all that could hear with *u*	Neh 8:2	995
one having knowledge, and having *u*	Neh 10:28	995
But I have *u* as well as you	Job 12:3	3824
and in length of days *u*	Job 12:12	8394
and strength, he hath counsel and *u*	Job 12:13	8394
and taketh away the *u* of the aged	Job 12:20	2940
thou hast hid their heart from *u*	Job 17:4	7922
the spirit of my *u* causeth me to	Job 20:3	998
by his *u* he smiteth through the	Job 26:12	8394
and where is the place of *u*	Job 28:12	998
and where is the place of *u*	Job 28:20	998
and to depart from evil is *u*	Job 28:28	998
of the Almighty giveth them *u*	Job 32:8	995
hearken unto me, ye men of *u*	Job 34:10	3824
If now thou hast *u*, hear this	Job 34:16	998
Let men of *u* tell me, and let a	Job 34:34	3824
declare, if thou hast *u*	Job 38:4	998
or who hath given *u* to the heart	Job 38:36	998
neither hath he imparted to her *u*	Job 39:17	998
or as the mule, which have no *u*	Ps 32:9	995
sing My praises with *u*	Ps 47:7	7919
of my heart shall be of *u*	Ps 49:3	8394
a good *u* have all they that do	Ps 111:10	7922
Give me *u*, and I shall keep thy	Ps 119:34	995
give me *u*, that I may learn thy	Ps 119:73	995
I have more *u* than all my	Ps 119:99	7919
Through thy precepts I get *u*	Ps 119:104	995
give me *u*, that I may know thy	Ps 119:125	995
it giveth *u* unto the simple	Ps 119:130	995
give me *u*, and I shall live	Ps 119:144	995
give me *u* according to thy word	Ps 119:169	995
his *u* is infinite	Ps 147:5	8394
to perceive the words of *u*	Prov 1:2	998
a man of *u* shall attain unto wise	Prov 1:5	995
wisdom, and apply thine heart to *u*	Prov 2:2	8394
and liftest up thy voice for *u*	Prov 2:3	8394
his mouth cometh knowledge and *u*	Prov 2:6	8394
preserve thee, *u* shall keep thee	Prov 2:11	8394
good *u* in the sight of God and man	Prov 3:4	7922
and lean not unto thine own *u*	Prov 3:5	998
wisdom, and the man that getteth *u*	Prov 3:13	8394
by *u* hath he established the	Prov 3:19	8394
of a father, and attend to know *u*	Prov 4:1	998
Get wisdom, get *u*	Prov 4:5	998

and with all thy getting get *u*	Prov 4:7	998
wisdom, and bow thine ear to my *u*	Prov 5:1	8394
adultery with a woman lacketh *u*	Prov 6:32	3820
and call *u* thy kinswoman	Prov 7:4	998
the youths, a young man void of *u*	Prov 7:7	3820
and *u* put forth her voice	Prov 8:1	8394
and, ye fools, be ye of an *u* heart	Prov 8:5	995
I am *u*	Prov 8:14	998
as for him that wanteth *u*	Prov 9:4	3820
and go in the way of *u*	Prov 9:6	998
and the knowledge of the holy is *u*	Prov 9:10	998
and as for him that wanteth *u*	Prov 9:16	3820
him that hath *u* wisdom is found	Prov 10:13	995
the back of him that is void of *u*	Prov 10:13	3820
but a man of *u* hath wisdom	Prov 10:23	8394
but a man of *u* holdeth his peace	Prov 11:12	8394
vain persons is void of *u*	Prov 12:11	3820
Good *u* giveth favour	Prov 13:15	7922
is slow to wrath is of great *u*	Prov 14:29	8394
in the heart of him that hath *u*	Prov 14:33	995
him that hath *u* seeketh knowledge	Prov 15:14	995
but a man of *u* walketh uprightly	Prov 15:21	8394
he that heareth reproof getteth *u*	Prov 15:32	3820
to get *u* rather to be chosen than	Prov 16:16	998
U is a wellspring of life unto	Prov 16:22	7922
A man void of *u* striketh hands,	Prov 17:18	3820
Wisdom is before him that hath *u*	Prov 17:24	995
a man of *u* is of an excellent	Prov 17:27	8394
his lips is esteemed a man of *u*	Prov 17:28	995
A fool hath no delight in *u*	Prov 18:2	8394
he that keepeth *u* shall find good	Prov 19:8	8394
and reprove one that hath *u*	Prov 19:25	995
but a man of *u* will draw it out	Prov 20:5	8394
the way of *u* shall remain in the	Prov 21:16	7919
There is no wisdom nor *u* nor	Prov 21:30	8394
also wisdom, and instruction, and *u*	Prov 23:23	998
and by *u* it is established	Prov 24:3	8394
the vineyard of the man void of *u*	Prov 24:30	3820
but by a man of *u* and knowledge	Prov 28:2	995
that hath *u* searcheth him out	Prov 28:11	995
The prince that wanteth *u* is also	Prov 28:16	8394
man, and have not the *u* of a man	Prov 30:2	998
wise, nor yet riches to men of *u*	Eccl 9:11	995
him, the spirit of wisdom and *u*	Is 11:2	998
quick *u* in the fear of the LORD	Is 11:3	7306
for it is a people of no *u*	Is 27:11	998
the *u* of their prudent men shall	Is 29:14	998
him that framed it, He had no *u*	Is 29:16	995
erred in spirit shall come to *u*	Is 29:24	998
and shewed to him the way of *u*	Is 40:14	8394
there is no searching of his *u*	Is 40:28	8394
is there knowledge nor *u* to say	Is 44:19	8394
feed you with knowledge and *u*	Jer 3:15	7919
children, and they have none *u*	Jer 4:22	995
O foolish people, and without *u*	Jer 5:21	3820
stretched out the heaven by his *u*	Jer 51:15	8394
with thine *u* thou hast gotten	Eze 28:4	8394
u science, and such as had ability	Dan 1:4	995
Daniel had *u* in all visions and	Dan 1:17	995
And in all matters of wisdom and *u*	Dan 1:20	998
and knowledge to them that know *u*	Dan 2:21	999
mine *u* returned unto me, and I	Dan 4:34	4486
the days of thy father light and *u*	Dan 5:11	7924
spirit, and knowledge, and *u*	Dan 5:12	7924
is in thee, and that light and *u*	Dan 5:14	7924
u dark sentences, shall stand up	Dan 8:23	995
forth to give thee skill and *u*	Dan 9:22	998
the thing, and had *u* of the vision	Dan 10:1	998
And some of them of *u* shall fall	Dan 11:35	7919
and idols according to their own *u*	Hos 13:2	8394
there is none *u* in him	Obad 7	8394
u out of the mount of Esau	Obad 8	8394
said, Are ye also yet without *u*	Mt 15:16	801
them, Are ye so without *u* also	Mk 7:18	801
all the heart, and with all the *u*	Mk 12:33	4907
having had perfect *u* of all	Lk 1:3	3877
him were astonished at his *u*	Lk 2:47	4907
Then opened he their *u*, that they	Lk 24:45	3563
Without *u*, covenantbreakers,	Rom 1:31	801
to nothing the *u* of the prudent	1Cor 1:19	4907
prayeth, but my *u* is unfruitful	1Cor 14:14	3563
and I will pray with the *u* also	1Cor 14:15	3563
and I will sing with the *u* also	1Cor 14:15	3563
rather speak five words with my *u*	1Cor 14:19	3563
Brethren, be not children in *u*	1Cor 14:20	5424
be ye children, but in *u* be men	1Cor 14:20	5424
The eyes of your *u* being	Eph 1:18	1271
Having the *u* darkened, being,	Eph 4:18	1271
but *u* what the will of the Lord	Eph 5:17	4920
peace of God, which passeth all *u*	Phil 4:7	3563
will in all wisdom and spiritual *u*	Col 1:9	4907

riches of the full assurance of *u*	Col 2:2	4907
u neither what they say, nor	1Ti 1:7	4920
Lord give thee *u* in all things	2Ti 2:7	4907
is come, and hath given us an *u*	1Jn 5:20	1271
Let him that hath *u* count the	Rev 13:18	3563

UNDERSTOOD

they knew not that Joseph *u* them	Gen 42:23	8085
they were wise, that they *u* this	Deut 32:29	7919
they *u* that the ark of the LORD	1Sa 4:6	3045
u that Saul was come in very deed	1Sa 26:4	3045
all Israel *u* that day that it was	2Sa 3:37	3045
because they had *u* the words that	Neh 8:12	995
u of the evil that Eliashib did	Neh 13:7	995
this, mine ear hath heard and *u* it	Job 13:1	995
have I uttered that I *u* not	Job 42:3	995
then *u* I their end	Ps 73:17	995
I heard a language that I *u* not	Ps 81:5	3045
Our fathers *u* not thy wonders in	Ps 106:7	7919
have ye not *u* from the	Is 40:21	995
They have not known nor *u*	Is 44:18	995
at the vision, but none *u* it	Dan 8:27	995
u by books the number of the	Dan 9:2	995
and he *u* the thing, and had	Dan 10:1	995
And I heard, but I *u* not	Dan 12:8	995
Have ye *u* all these things	Mt 13:51	4920
Then *u* they how that he bade them	Mt 16:12	4920
Then the disciples *u* that he	Mt 17:13	4920
When Jesus *u* it, he said unto	Mt 26:10	1097
But they *u* not that saying, and	Mk 9:32	50
they *u* not the saying which he	Lk 2:50	4920
But they *u* not this saying, and it	Lk 9:45	50
they *u* none of these things	Lk 18:34	4920
They *u* not that he spake to them	Jn 8:27	1097
but they *u* not what things they	Jn 10:6	1097
These things *u* not his disciples	Jn 12:16	1097
his brethren would have *u* how	Acts 7:25	4920
but they *u* not	Acts 7:25	4920
having *u* that he was a Roman	Acts 23:27	3129
when he *u* that he was of Cilicia	Acts 23:34	4441
being *u* by the things that are	Rom 1:20	3539
I *u* as a child, I thought as a	1Cor 13:11	5426
by the tongue words easy to be *u*	1Cor 14:9	2154
are some things hard to be *u*	2Pet 3:16	1425

UNDERTAKE

oppressed; *u* for me	Is 38:14	6148

UNDERTOOK

the Jews *u* to do as they had	Est 9:23	6901

UNDO

to *u* the heavy burdens, and to let	Is 58:6	5425
at that time I will *u* all that	Zeph 3:19	6213

UNDONE

thou art *u*, O people of Chemosh	Num 21:29	6
he left nothing *u* of all that the	Josh 11:15	5493
for I am *u*	Is 6:5	1820
done, and not to leave the other *u*	Mt 23:23	
done, and not to leave the other *u*	Lk 11:42	

UNDRESSED

gather the grapes of thy vine *u*	Lev 25:5	5139
the grapes in it of thy vine *u*	Lev 25:11	5139

UNEQUAL

are not your ways *u*	Eze 18:25	3808,8505
are not your ways *u*	Eze 18:29	3808,8505

UNEQUALLY

Be ye not *u* yoked together with	2Cor 6:14	2086

UNFAITHFUL

Confidence in an *u* man in time of	Prov 25:19	898

UNFAITHFULLY

dealt *u* like their fathers	Ps 78:57	898

UNFEIGNED

by the Holy Ghost, by love *u*	2Cor 6:6	505
a good conscience, and of faith *u*	1Ti 1:5	505
the *u* faith that is in thee	2Ti 1:5	505
unto *u* love of the brethren	1Pet 1:22	505

UNFRUITFUL

choke the word, and he becometh *u*	Mt 13:22	175
choke the word, and it becometh *u*	Mk 4:19	175
but my understanding is *u*	1Cor 14:14	175
with the *u* works of darkness	Eph 5:11	175
uses, that they be not *u*	Titus 3:14	175
u in the knowledge of our Lord	2Pet 1:8	175

UNGIRDED

he *u* his camels, and gave straw and	Gen 24:32	6605

U

UNGODLINESS

from heaven against all *u*	Rom 1:18	763
and shall turn away *u* from Jacob	Rom 11:26	763
they will increase unto more *u*	2Ti 2:16	763
Teaching us that, denying *u*	Titus 2:12	763

UNGODLY

the floods of *u* men made me	2Sa 22:5	1100
Shouldest thou help the *u*	2Chr 19:2	7563
God hath delivered me to the *u*	Job 16:11	5760
and to princes, Ye are *u*	Job 34:18	7563
not in the counsel of the *u*	Ps 1:1	7563
The *u* are not so	Ps 1:4	7563
Therefore the *u* shall not stand	Ps 1:5	7563
but the way of the *u* shall perish	Ps 1:6	7563
hast broken the teeth of the *u*	Ps 3:7	7563
the floods of *u* men made me	Ps 18:4	1100
my cause against an *u* nation	Ps 43:1	3808,2623
Behold, these are the *u*, who	Ps 73:12	7563
An *u* man diggeth up evil	Prov 16:27	1100
An *u* witness scorneth judgment	Prov 19:28	1100
on him that justifieth the *u*	Rom 4:5	765
in due time Christ died for the *u*	Rom 5:6	765
lawless and disobedient, for the *u*	1Ti 1:9	765
be saved, where shall the *u*	1Pet 4:18	765
the flood upon the world of the *u*	2Pet 2:5	765
those that after should live *u*	2Pet 2:6	764
of judgment and perdition of *u* men	2Pet 3:7	765
u men, turning the grace of our	Jude 4	765
to convince all that are *u* among	Jude 15	763
u deeds which they have	Jude 15	763
deeds which they have *u* committed	Jude 15	764
all their hard speeches which *u*	Jude 15	765
walk after their own *u* lusts	Jude 18	763

UNHOLY

put difference between holy and *u*	Lev 10:10	2455
the ungodly and for sinners, for *u*	1Ti 1:9	462
to parents, unthankful, *u*	2Ti 3:2	462
an *u* thing, and hath done despite	Heb 10:29	2839

UNICORN

as it were the strength of a *u*	Num 23:22	7214
as it were the strength of a *u*	Num 24:8	7214
Will the *u* be willing to serve	Job 39:9	7214
Canst thou bind the *u* with his	Job 39:10	7214
Lebanon and Sirion like a young *u*	Ps 29:6	7214
thou exalt like the horn of an *u*	Ps 92:10	7214

UNICORNS

his horns are like the horns of *u*	Deut 33:17	7214
heard me from the horns of the *u*	Ps 22:21	7214
the *u* shall come down with them,	Is 34:7	7214

UNITE

u my heart to fear thy name	Ps 86:11	3161

UNITED

mine honour, be not thou *u*	Gen 49:6	3161

UNITY

brethren to dwell together in *u*	Ps 133:1	3162
Endeavouring to keep the *u* of the	Eph 4:3	1775
we all come in the *u* of the faith	Eph 4:13	1775

UNJUST

me from the deceitful and *u* man	Ps 43:1	5766
the hope of *u* men perisheth	Prov 11:7	205
u gain increaseth his substance,	Prov 28:8	8636
An *u* man is an abomination to the	Prov 29:27	5766
but the *u* knoweth no shame	Zeph 3:5	5767
rain on the just and on the *u*	Mt 5:45	94
the lord commended the *u* steward	Lk 16:8	93
he that is *u* in the least is	Lk 16:10	94
in the least is *u* also in much	Lk 16:10	94
said, Hear what the *u* judge saith	Lk 18:6	93
as other men are, extortioners, *u*	Lk 18:11	94
the dead, both of the just and *u*	Acts 24:15	94
another, go to law before the *u*	1Cor 6:1	94
for sins, the just for the *u*	1Pet 3:18	94
to reserve the *u* unto the day of	2Pet 2:9	94
He that is *u*, let him be *u*	Rev 22:11	91

UNJUSTLY

How long will ye judge *u*, and	Ps 82:2	5766
of uprightness will he deal *u*	Is 26:10	5765

UNKNOWN

this inscription, TO THE *U* GOD	Acts 17:23	57
For he that speaketh in an *u*	1Cor 14:2	
He that speaketh in an *u* tongue	1Cor 14:4	
in an *u* tongue pray that he may	1Cor 14:13	
For if I pray in an *u* tongue	1Cor 14:14	
ten thousand words in an *u* tongue	1Cor 14:19	
If any man speak in an *u* tongue	1Cor 14:27	

As *u*, and yet well known	2Cor 6:9	50
was *u* by face unto the churches	Gal 1:22	50

UNLADE

the ship was to *u* her burden	Acts 21:3	670

UNLAWFUL

Ye know how that it is an *u* thing	Acts 10:28	111
day to day with their *u* deeds	2Pet 2:8	459

UNLEARNED

and perceived that they were *u*	Acts 4:13	62
the *u* say Amen at thy giving of	1Cor 14:16	2399
and there come in those that are *u*	1Cor 14:23	2399
one that believeth not, or one *u*	1Cor 14:24	2399
u questions avoid, knowing that	2Ti 2:23	521
understood, which they that are *u*	2Pet 3:16	261

UNLEAVENED

them a feast, and did bake *u* bread	Gen 19:3	4682
roast with fire, and *u* bread	Ex 12:8	4682
Seven days shall ye eat *u* bread	Ex 12:15	4682
observe the feast of *u* bread	Ex 12:17	4682
at even, ye shall eat *u* bread	Ex 12:18	4682
habitations shall ye eat *u* bread	Ex 12:20	4682
they baked *u* cakes of the dough	Ex 12:39	4682
Seven days thou shalt eat *u* bread	Ex 13:6	4682
U bread shall be eaten seven days	Ex 13:7	4682
shalt keep the feast of *u* bread	Ex 23:15	4682
(thou shalt eat *u* bread seven	Ex 23:15	4682
u bread, and cakes as	Ex 29:2	4682
wafers *u* anointed with oil	Ex 29:2	4682
u bread that is before the LORD	Ex 29:23	4682
The feast of *u* bread shalt thou	Ex 34:18	4682
Seven days thou shalt eat *u* bread	Ex 34:18	4682
it shall be *u* cakes of fine flour	Lev 2:4	4682
or *u* wafers anointed with oil	Lev 2:4	4682
pan, it shall be of fine flour *u*	Lev 2:5	4682
with *u* bread shall it be eaten in	Lev 6:16	4682
u cakes mingled with oil, and	Lev 7:12	4682
u wafers anointed with oil, and	Lev 7:12	4682
two rams, and a basket of *u* bread	Lev 8:2	4682
And out of the basket of *u* bread	Lev 8:26	4682
the LORD, he took one *u* cake	Lev 8:26	4682
feast of *u* bread unto the LORD	Lev 23:6	4682
seven days ye must eat *u* bread	Lev 23:6	4682
And a basket of *u* bread, cakes of	Num 6:15	4682
wafers of *u* bread anointed with	Num 6:15	4682
LORD, with the basket of *u* bread	Num 6:17	4682
one *u* cake out of the basket, and	Num 6:19	4682
one *u* wafer, and shall put them	Num 6:19	4682
keep it, and eat it with *u* bread	Num 9:11	4682
seven days shall *u* bread be eaten	Num 28:17	4682
shalt thou eat *u* bread therewith	Deut 16:3	4682
Six days thou shalt eat *u* bread	Deut 16:8	4682
in the feast of *u* bread, and in	Deut 16:16	4682
u cakes, and parched corn in the	Josh 5:11	4682
u cakes of an ephah of flour	Judg 6:19	4682
the *u* cakes, and lay them upon	Judg 6:20	4682
touched the flesh and the *u* cakes	Judg 6:21	4682
consumed the flesh and the *u* cakes	Judg 6:21	4682
it, and bake *u* bread thereof	1Sa 28:24	4682
but they did eat of the *u* bread	2Kin 23:9	4682
meat offering, and for the *u* cakes	1Chr 23:29	4682
even in the feast of *u* bread	2Chr 8:13	4682
of *u* bread in the second month	2Chr 30:13	4682
of *u* bread seven days with great	2Chr 30:21	4682
the feast of *u* bread seven days	2Chr 35:17	4682
kept the feast of *u* bread seven	Ezr 6:22	4682
u bread shall be eaten	Eze 45:21	4682
of *u* bread the disciples came to	Mt 26:17	106
of the passover, and of *u* bread	Mk 14:1	106
And the first day of *u* bread	Mk 14:12	106
the feast of *u* bread drew nigh	Lk 22:1	106
Then came the day of *u* bread	Lk 22:7	106
(Then were the days of *u* bread	Acts 12:3	106
after the days of *u* bread	Acts 20:6	106
ye may be a new lump, as ye are *u*	1Cor 5:7	106
but with the *u* bread of sincerity	1Cor 5:8	106

UNLESS See APPENDIX.

UNLOOSE

am not worthy to stoop down and *u*	Mk 1:7	3089
whose shoes I am not worthy to *u*	Lk 3:16	3089
latchet I am not worthy to *u*	Jn 1:27	3089

UNMARRIED

I say therefore to the *u* and	1Cor 7:8	22
if she depart, let her remain *u*	1Cor 7:11	22
He that is *u* careth for the	1Cor 7:32	22
The *u* woman careth for the things	1Cor 7:34	22

UNMERCIFUL

natural affection, implacable, *u*	Rom 1:31	415

UNMINDFUL
Rock that begat thee thou art *u* .... Deut 32:18   7876

UNMOVABLE
brethren, be ye stedfast, *u* 1Cor 15:58   277

UNMOVEABLE
stuck fast, and remained *u* .... Acts 27:41   761

UNNI (*un'-nee*) A Levite.
and Shemiramoth, and Jehiel, and *U* 1Chr 15:18   6042
and Shemiramoth, and Jehiel, and *U* 1Chr 15:20   6042
Also Bakbukiah and *U*, their .... Neh 12:9   6042

UNOCCUPIED
days of Jael, the highways were *u* .... Judg 5:6   2308

UNPERFECT
did see my substance, yet being *u* .... Ps 139:16

UNPREPARED
come with me, and find you *u* 2Cor 9:4   532

UNPROFITABLE
Should he reason with *u* talk .... Job 15:3   5532
cast ye the *u* servant into outer .... Mt 25:30   888
you, say, We are *u* servants .... Lk 17:10   888
way, they are together become *u* .... Rom 3:12   889
for they are *u* and vain .... Titus 3:9   512
Which in time past was to thee *u* .... Philem 11   890
for that is *u* for you .... Heb 13:17   255

UNPROFITABLENESS
for the weakness and *u* thereof.............. Heb 7:18   512

UNPUNISHED
hand, the wicked shall not be *u* .... Prov 11:21   5352
join in hand, he shall not be *u* .... Prov 16:5   5352
glad at calamities shall not be *u* .... Prov 17:5   5352
A false witness shall not be *u* .... Prov 19:5   5352
A false witness shall not be *u* .... Prov 19:9   5352
name, and should ye be utterly *u* .... Jer 25:29   5352
Ye shall not be *u* .... Jer 25:29   5352
will not leave thee altogether *u* .... Jer 30:11   5352
will I not leave thee wholly *u* .... Jer 46:28   5352
he that shall altogether go *u* .... Jer 49:12   5352
thou shalt not go *u*, but thou................. Jer 49:12   5352

UNQUENCHABLE
burn up the chaff with *u* fire................. Mt 3:12   762
chaff he will burn with fire *u* .... Lk 3:17   762

UNREASONABLE
to me *u* to send a prisoner .... Acts 25:27   249
that we may be delivered from *u* 2Th 3:2   824

UNREBUKEABLE
this commandment without spot, *u* 1Ti 6:14   423

UNREPROVEABLE
and unblameable and *u* in his sight....... Col 1:22   410

UNRIGHTEOUS
the wicked to be an *u* witness .... Ex 23:1   2555
riseth up against me as the *u* .... Job 27:7   5767
wicked, out of the hand of the *u* .... Ps 71:4   5765
unto them that decree *u* decrees .... Is 10:1   205
way, and the *u* man his thoughts .... Is 55:7   205
not been faithful in the *u* mammon ...... Lk 16:11   94
Is God *u* who taketh vengeance .... Rom 3:5   94
Know ye not that the *u* shall not 1Cor 6:9   94
For God is not *u* to forget your .... Heb 6:10   94

UNRIGHTEOUSLY
do such things, and all that do *u* .... Deut 25:16   5766

UNRIGHTEOUSNESS
Ye shall do no *u* in judgment.................. Lev 19:15   5766
Ye shall do no *u* in judgment.................. Lev 19:35   5766
my rock, and there is no *u* in .... Ps 92:15   5766
him that buildeth his house by *u* .... Jer 22:13   3808,6664
friends of the mammon of *u* .... Lk 16:9   93
same is true, and no *u* is in him .... Jn 7:18   93
u of men, who hold the truth in .... Rom 1:18   93
of men, who hold the truth in *u* .... Rom 1:18   93
Being filled with all *u*, ... Rom 1:29   93
do not obey the truth, but obey *u* .... Rom 2:8   93
But if our *u* commend the .... Rom 3:5   93
as instruments of *u* unto sin .... Rom 6:13   93
Is there *u* with God .... Rom 9:14   93
hath righteousness with *u* 2Cor 6:14   458
of *u* in them that perish........................ 2Th 2:10   93
the truth, but had pleasure in *u* 2Th 2:12   93
For I will be merciful to their *u* .... Heb 8:12   93
And shall receive the reward of *u*.......... 2Pet 2:13   93
Bosor, who loved the wages of *u* 2Pet 2:15   93
sins, and to cleanse us from all *u* 1Jn 1:9   93
All *u* is sin.. 1Jn 5:17   93

UNRIPE
shake off his *u* grape as the vine .... Job 15:33   1154

UNRULY
brethren, warn them that are *u* 1Th 5:14   813
children not accused of riot or *u* .... Titus 1:6   506
For there are many *u* and vain .... Titus 1:10   506
it is an *u* evil, full of deadly .... Jas 3:8   183

UNSATIABLE
Assyrians, because thou wast *u* ..... Eze 16:28   1115,7654

UNSAVOURY
froward thou wilt shew thyself *u* 2Sa 22:27   6617
Can that which is *u* be eaten.................. Job 6:6   8602

UNSEARCHABLE
Which doeth great things and *u* .... Job 5:9   369,2714
and his greatness is *u* .... Ps 145:3   369,2714
depth, and the heart of kings is *u* ... Prov 25:3   369,2714
how *u* are his judgments, and his .... Rom 11:33   419
Gentiles the *u* riches of Christ .... Eph 3:8   421

UNSEEMLY
with men working that which is *u* .... Rom 1:27   808
Doth not behave itself *u*, seeketh 1Cor 13:5

UNSHOD
Withhold thy foot from being *u* .... Jer 2:25   3182

UNSKILFUL
is *u* in the word of righteousness .... Heb 5:13   552

UNSPEAKABLE
Thanks be unto God for his *u* gift 2Cor 9:15   411
into paradise, and heard *u* words.......... 2Cor 12:4   731
believing, ye rejoice with joy *u* 1Pet 1:8   412

UNSPOTTED
to keep himself *u* from the world .... Jas 1:27   784

UNSTABLE
U as water, thou shalt not excel .... Gen 49:4   6349
minded man is *u* in all his ways .... Jas 1:8   182
beguiling *u* souls................................... 2Pet 2:14   793
u wrest, as they do also the 2Pet 3:16   793

UNSTOPPED
the ears of the deaf shall be *u* .... Is 35:5   6605

UNTAKEN
day remaineth the same vail *u* 2Cor 3:14   3361,348

UNTEMPERED
others daubed it with *u* morter .... Eze 13:10   8602
them which daub it with *u* morter .... Eze 13:11   8602
that ye have daubed with *u* morter .... Eze 13:14   8602
that have daubed it with *u* morter .... Eze 13:15   8602
have daubed them with *u* morter .... Eze 22:28   8602

UNTHANKFUL
for he is kind unto the *u* .... Lk 6:35   884
disobedient to parents, *u*....................... 2Ti 3:2   884

UNTIL See APPENDIX.

UNTIMELY
Or as an hidden *u* birth I had not .... Job 3:16   5309
like the *u* birth of a woman, that .... Ps 58:8   5309
that an *u* birth is better than he............ Eccl 6:3   5309
as a fig tree casteth her *u* figs............... Rev 6:13   3653

UNTO See APPENDIX.

UNTOWARD
yourselves from this *u* generation .... Acts 2:40   4646

UNWALLED
beside *u* towns a great many................. Deut 3:5   6521
that dwelt in the *u* towns....................... Est 9:19   6519
go up to the land of *u* villages .... Eze 38:11

UNWASHEN
but to eat with *u* hands defileth............ Mt 15:20   449
defiled, that is to say, with *u* .... Mk 7:2   449
but eat bread with *u* hands.................... Mk 7:5   449

UNWEIGHED
And Solomon left all the vessels *u* 1Kin 7:47

UNWISE
the Lord, O foolish people and *u* .... Deut 32:6   3808,2450
he is an *u* son .... Hos 13:13   3808,2450
both to the wise, and to the *u* .... Rom 1:14   453
Wherefore be ye not *u*, but.................... Eph 5:17   878

UNWITTINGLY
if a man eat of the holy thing *u* .... Lev 22:14   7684
unawares and *u* may flee thither .... Josh 20:3   1097,1847
because he smote his neighbour *u* . Josh 20:5   1097,1847

U

UNWORTHILY
and drink this cup of the Lord, *u* 1Cor 11:27   *371*
For he that eateth and drinketh *u* 1Cor 11:29   *371*

UNWORTHY
judge yourselves *u* of everlasting ... Acts 13:46   *3756,514*
are ye *u* to judge the smallest 1Cor 6:2   *370*

UP See APPENDIX.

UPBRAID
Zalmunna, with whom ye did *u* me .... Judg 8:15   2778
Then began he to *u* the cities .... Mt 11:20   3679

UPBRAIDED
u them with their unbelief and .... Mk 16:14   3679

UPBRAIDETH
to all men liberally, and *u* not .... Jas 1:5   3679

UPHARSIN (u-far'-sin) See PERES. *Part of the "hand-writing on the wall."*
written, MENE, MENE, TEKEL, *U* .... Dan 5:25   6537

UPHAZ (u'-faz) *A place in southern Arabia.*
from Tarshish, and gold from *U* .... Jer 10:9   210
were girded with fine gold of *U* .... Dan 10:5   210

UPHELD
and my fury, it *u* me .... Is 63:5   5564

UPHOLD
u me with thy free spirit .... Ps 51:12   5564
Lord is with them that *u* my soul .... Ps 54:4   5564
U me according unto thy word, ... Ps 119:116   5564
but honour shall *u* the humble in .... Prov 29:23   8551
I will *u* thee with the right hand .... Is 41:10   8551
Behold my servant, whom I *u* .... Is 42:1   8551
wondered that there was none to *u* .... Is 63:5   5564
They also that *u* Egypt shall fall .... Eze 30:6   5564

UPHOLDEN
Thy words have *u* him that was .... Job 4:4   6965
and his throne is *u* by mercy .... Prov 20:28   5582

UPHOLDEST
thou *u* me in mine integrity, and .... Ps 41:12   8551

UPHOLDETH
but the LORD *u* the righteous .... Ps 37:17   5564
for the LORD *u* him with his hand .... Ps 37:24   5564
thy right hand *u* me .... Ps 63:8   8551
The LORD *u* all that fall, and .... Ps 145:14   5564

UPHOLDING
u all things by the word of his .... Heb 1:3   *5342*

UPON See APPENDIX.

UPPER
on the *u* door post of the houses, ... Ex 12:7   4947
put a covering upon his *u* lip .... Lev 13:45   8222
or the *u* millstone to pledge .... Deut 24:6   7393
And he gave her the *u* springs .... Josh 15:19   5942
unto Beth-horon the *u* springs .... Josh 16:5   5945
And Caleb gave her the *u* springs .... Judg 1:15   5942
his *u* chamber that was in Samaria 2Kin 1:2   5944
by the conduit of the *u* pool 2Kin 18:17   5945
the top of the *u* chamber of Ahaz 2Kin 23:12   5944
Beth-horon the nether, and the *u* 1Chr 7:24   5945
of the *u* chambers thereof, and of 1Chr 28:11   5944
he overlaid the *u* chambers with 2Chr 3:9   5944
Also he built Beth-horon the *u* 2Chr 8:5   5945
the *u* watercourse of Gihon 2Chr 32:30   5945
the *u* pool in the highway of the .... Is 7:3   5945
the *u* pool in the highway of the .... Is 36:2   5945
Now the *u* chambers were shorter .... Eze 42:5   5945
lodge in the *u* lintels of it .... Zeph 2:14   3730
shew you a large *u* room furnished ...... Mk 14:15   *508*
shew you a large *u* room furnished ...... Lk 22:12   *508*
in, they went up into an *u* room .... Acts 1:13   5253
they laid her in an *u* chamber .... Acts 9:37   5253
brought him into the *u* chamber .... Acts 9:39   5253
the *u* coasts came to Ephesus .... Acts 19:1   *510*
were many lights in the *u* chamber .... Acts 20:8   *5250*

UPPERMOST
in the *u* basket there was of all .... Gen 40:17   5945
berries in the top of the *u* bough .... Is 17:6
an *u* branch, which they left .... Is 17:9
love the *u* rooms at feasts, and .... Mt 23:6   *4411*
and the *u* rooms at feasts .... Mk 12:39   *4411*
for ye love the *u* seats in the .... Lk 11:43   *4410*

UPRIGHT
my sheaf arose, and also stood *u* .... Gen 37:7
the floods stood *u* as an heap .... Ex 15:8
of your yoke, and made you go *u* .... Lev 26:13   6968
the LORD liveth, thou hast been *u* 1Sa 29:6   3477
I was also *u* before him, and have 2Sa 22:24   8549

with the *u* man thou wilt shew 2Sa 22:26   8549
man thou wilt shew thyself *u* 2Sa 22:26   8552
for the Levites were more *u* in 2Chr 29:34   3477
and that man was perfect and *u* .... Job 1:1   3477
an *u* man, one that feareth God, ... Job 1:8   3477
an *u* man, one that feareth God, ... Job 2:3   3477
If thou wert pure and *u* .... Job 8:6   3477
the just *u* man is laughed to .... Job 12:4   8549
U men shall be astonied at this, ... Job 17:8   3477
God, which saveth the *u* in heart .... Ps 7:10   3477
privily shoot at the *u* in heart .... Ps 11:2   3477
his countenance doth behold the *u* .... Ps 11:7   3477
I was also *u* before him, and I .... Ps 18:23   8549
with an *u* man thou wilt shew .... Ps 18:25   8549
man thou wilt shew thyself *u* .... Ps 18:25   8549,8552
then shall I be *u*, and I shall be .... Ps 19:13   8552
but we are risen, and stand *u* .... Ps 20:8
Good and *u* is the LORD .... Ps 25:8   3477
joy, all ye that are *u* in heart .... Ps 32:11   3477
for praise is comely for the *u* .... Ps 33:1   3477
righteousness to the *u* in heart .... Ps 36:10   3477
slay such as be of *u* conversation .... Ps 37:14   3477
LORD knoweth the days of the *u* .... Ps 37:18   8549
the perfect man, and behold the *u* .... Ps 37:37   3477
the *u* shall have dominion over .... Ps 49:14   3477
all the *u* in heart shall glory .... Ps 64:10   3477
To shew that the LORD is *u* .... Ps 92:15   3477
all the *u* in heart shall follow .... Ps 94:15   3477
and gladness for the *u* in heart .... Ps 97:11   3477
heart, in the assembly of the *u* .... Ps 111:1   3477
of the *u* shall be blessed .... Ps 112:2   3477
Unto the *u* there ariseth light in .... Ps 112:4   3477
O LORD, and *u* are thy judgments .... Ps 119:137   3477
them that are *u* in their hearts .... Ps 125:4   3477
the *u* shall dwell in thy presence .... Ps 140:13   3477
For the *u* shall dwell in the land .... Prov 2:21   3477
of the LORD is strength to the *u* .... Prov 10:29   8537
of the *u* shall guide them .... Prov 11:3   3477
of the *u* shall deliver them .... Prov 11:6   3477
of the *u* the city is exalted .... Prov 11:11   3477
but such as are *u* in their way .... Prov 11:20   8549
mouth of the *u* shall deliver them .... Prov 12:6   3477
keepeth him that is *u* in the way .... Prov 13:6   8537
of the *u* shall flourish .... Prov 14:11   3477
prayer of the *u* is his delight .... Prov 15:8   3477
The highway of the *u* is to depart .... Prov 16:17   3477
and the transgressor for the *u* .... Prov 21:18   3477
but as for the *u*, he directeth .... Prov 21:29   3477
but the *u* shall have good things .... Prov 28:10   8549
The bloodthirsty hate the *u* .... Prov 29:10   8535
he that is *u* in the way is .... Prov 29:27   3477
I found, that God hath made man *u* ...... Eccl 7:29   3477
and that which was written was *u* .... Eccl 12:10   3476
the *u* love thee .... Song 1:4   4339
thou, most *u*, dost weigh the path .... Is 26:7   3477
They are as the palm tree, but .... Jer 10:5   4749
but he touched me, and set me *u* .... Dan 8:18   5977
I speak unto thee, and stand *u* .... Dan 10:11   5977
whole kingdom, and *u* ones with him ... Dan 11:17   3477
and there is none *u* among men .... Mic 7:2   3477
the most *u* is sharper than a .... Mic 7:4   3477
is lifted up is not *u* in him .... Hab 2:4   3474
a loud voice, Stand *u* on thy feet .... Acts 14:10   *3717*

UPRIGHTLY
He that walketh *u*, and worketh .... Ps 15:2   8549
do ye judge *u*, O ye sons of men .... Ps 58:1   4339
the congregation I will judge *u* .... Ps 75:2   4339
he withhold from them that walk *u* ...... Ps 84:11   8549
is a buckler to them that walk *u* .... Prov 2:7   8537
He that walketh *u* walketh surely .... Prov 10:9   8537
a man of understanding walketh *u* .... Prov 15:21   3474
Whoso walketh *u* shall be saved .... Prov 28:18   8549
righteously, and speaketh *u* .... Is 33:15   4339
and they abhor him that speaketh *u* ..... Amos 5:10   8549
do good to him that walketh *u* .... Mic 2:7   3477
u according to the truth of the .... Gal 2:14   *3716*

UPRIGHTNESS
or for the *u* of thine heart, dost .... Deut 9:5   3476
and in *u* of heart with thee 1Kin 3:6   3483
in integrity of heart, and in *u* 1Kin 9:4   3476
the heart, and hast pleasure in *u* 1Chr 29:17   3476
in the *u* of mine heart I have 1Chr 29:17   4339
thy hope, and the *u* of thy ways .... Job 4:6   8537
shall be of *u* of my heart .... Job 33:3   3476
thousand, to shew unto man his *u* .... Job 33:23   3476
judgment to the people in *u* .... Ps 9:8   4339
Let integrity and *u* preserve me .... Ps 25:21   3476
ever, and are done in truth and *u* .... Ps 111:8   3477
will praise thee with *u* of heart .... Ps 119:7   3476
lead me into the land of *u* .... Ps 143:10   4334

Who leave the paths of *u*, to walk	Prov 2:13	3476
walketh in his *u* feareth the LORD	Prov 14:2	3476
is the poor that walketh in his *u*	Prov 28:6	8537
The way of the just is *u*	Is 26:7	4339
in the land of *u* will he deal	Is 26:10	5229
beds, each one walking in his *u*	Is 57:2	5228

UPRISING

knowest my downsitting and mine *u*	Ps 139:2	6965

UPROAR

noise of the city being in an *u*	1Kin 1:41	1993
there be an *u* among the people	Mt 26:5	2351
lest there be an *u* of the people	Mk 14:2	2351
and set all the city on an *u*	Acts 17:5	2350
in question for this day's *u*	Acts 19:40	4714
after the *u* was ceased, Paul	Acts 20:1	2351
that all Jerusalem was in an *u*	Acts 21:31	4797
before these days madest an *u*	Acts 21:38	387

UPSIDE

wiping it, and turning it *u* down	2Kin 21:13	5921,6440
of the wicked he turneth *u* down	Ps 146:9	
it waste, and turneth it *u* down	Is 24:1	5921,6440
u down shall be esteemed as the	Is 29:16	
world *u* down are come hither also	Acts 17:6	389

UPWARD

Fifteen cubits *u* did the waters	Gen 7:20	4605
from twenty years old and *u*	Ex 38:26	4605
From twenty years old and *u*	Num 1:3	4605
names, from twenty years old and *u*	Num 1:18	4605
male from twenty years old and *u*	Num 1:20	4605
male from twenty years old and *u*	Num 1:22	4605
names, from twenty years old and *u*	Num 1:24	4605
names, from twenty years old and *u*	Num 1:26	4605
names, from twenty years old and *u*	Num 1:28	4605
names, from twenty years old and *u*	Num 1:30	4605
names, from twenty years old and *u*	Num 1:32	4605
names, from twenty years old and *u*	Num 1:34	4605
names, from twenty years old and *u*	Num 1:36	4605
names, from twenty years old and *u*	Num 1:38	4605
names, from twenty years old and *u*	Num 1:40	4605
names, from twenty years old and *u*	Num 1:42	4605
from twenty years old and *u*	Num 1:45	4605
old and *u* shalt thou number them	Num 3:15	4605
the males, from a month old and *u*	Num 3:22	4605
the males, from a month old and *u*	Num 3:28	4605
the males, from a month old and *u*	Num 3:34	4605
the males from a month old and *u*	Num 3:39	4605
of Israel from a month old and *u*	Num 3:40	4605
of names, from a month old and *u*	Num 3:43	4605
u even until fifty years old, all	Num 4:3	4605
u until fifty years old shalt	Num 4:23	4605
u even unto fifty years old shalt	Num 4:30	4605
u even unto fifty years old,	Num 4:35	4605
u even unto fifty years old,	Num 4:39	4605
u even unto fifty years old,	Num 4:43	4605
u even unto fifty years old,	Num 4:47	4605
u they shall go in to wait upon	Num 8:24	4605
from twenty years old and *u*	Num 14:29	4605
from twenty years old and *u*	Num 26:2	4605
from twenty years old and *u*	Num 26:4	4605
all males from a month old and *u*	Num 26:62	4605
Egypt, from twenty years old and *u*	Num 32:11	4605
to Akrabbim, from the rock, and *u*	Judg 1:36	4605
u he was higher than any of the	1Sa 9:2	4605
people from his shoulders and *u*	1Sa 10:23	4605
were able to put on armour, and *u*	2Kin 3:21	4605
root downward, and bear fruit *u*	2Kin 19:30	4605
from the age of thirty years and *u*	1Chr 23:3	4605
from the age of twenty years and *u*	1Chr 23:24	4605
males, from three years old and *u*	2Chr 31:16	4605
from twenty years old and *u*	2Chr 31:17	4605
from twenty years old and *u*	Ezr 3:8	4605
unto trouble, as the sparks fly *u*	Job 5:7	1361
the spirit of man that goeth *u*	Eccl 3:21	4605
king and their God, and look *u*	Is 8:21	4605
root downward, and bear fruit *u*	Is 37:31	4605
mine eyes fail with looking *u*	Is 38:14	4791
and their wings were stretched *u*	Eze 1:11	4605
appearance of his loins even *u*	Eze 1:27	4605
and from his loins even *u*, as the	Eze 8:2	4605
still *u* to the side chambers	Eze 41:7	4605
still *u* round about the house	Eze 41:7	4605
breadth of the house was still *u*	Eze 41:7	4605
altar and *u* shall be four horns	Eze 43:15	4605
you, consider from this day and *u*	Hag 2:15	4605
Consider now from this day and *u*	Hag 2:18	4605

UR *(ur)*

1. A district in Mesopotamia.

nativity, in *U* of the Chaldees	Gen 11:28	218
with them from *U* of the Chaldees	Gen 11:31	218
thee out of *U* of the Chaldees	Gen 15:7	218
forth out of *U* of the Chaldees	Neh 9:7	218

2. Father of Eliphal.

Hararite, Eliphal the son of *U*	1Chr 11:35	218

URBANE *(ur'-bane) A Christian in Rome.*

Salute *U*, our helper in Christ,	Rom 16:9	3779

URBANUS See URBANE.

URGE

began to *u* him vehemently	Lk 11:53	1758

URGED

And he *u* him, and he took it	Gen 33:11	6484
u him, so that his soul was vexed	Judg 16:16	509
depart, his father in law *u* him	Judg 19:7	6484
when they *u* him till he was	2Kin 2:17	6484
And he *u* him to take it	2Kin 5:16	6484
he *u* him, and bound two talents of	2Kin 5:23	6555

URGENT

Egyptians were *u* upon the people	Ex 12:33	2388
the king's commandment was *u*	Dan 3:22	2685

URI *(u'-ri)*

1. Father of Bezaleel.

by name Bezaleel the son of *U*	Ex 31:2	221
by name Bezaleel the son of *U*	Ex 35:30	221
And Bezaleel the son of *U*, the son	Ex 38:22	221
And Hur begat *U*	1Chr 2:20	221
and *U* begat Bezaleel	1Chr 2:20	221
altar, that Bezaleel the son of *U*	2Chr 1:5	221

2. Father of Geber.

Geber the son of *U* was in the	1Kin 4:19	221
Shallum, and Telem, and *U*	Ezr 10:24	221

URIAH *(u-ri'-ah)* See URIAH'S, URIAS, URIJAH.

1. Husband of Bathsheba.

Eliam, the wife of *U* the Hittite	2Sa 11:3	223
saying, Send me *U* the Hittite	2Sa 11:6	223
And Joab sent *U* to David	2Sa 11:6	223
when *U* was come unto him, David	2Sa 11:7	223
And David said to *U*, Go down to	2Sa 11:8	223
U departed out of the king's	2Sa 11:8	223
But *U* slept at the door of the	2Sa 11:9	223
U went not down unto his house,	2Sa 11:10	223
unto his house, David said unto *U*	2Sa 11:10	223
U said unto David, The ark, and	2Sa 11:11	223
And David said to *U*, Tarry here to	2Sa 11:12	223
So *U* abode in Jerusalem that day,	2Sa 11:12	223
Joab, and sent it by the hand of *U*	2Sa 11:14	223
Set ye *U* in the forefront of the	2Sa 11:15	223
that he assigned *U* unto a place	2Sa 11:16	223
and *U* the Hittite died also	2Sa 11:17	223
Thy servant *U* the Hittite is dead	2Sa 11:21	223
thy servant *U* the Hittite is dead	2Sa 11:24	223
when the wife of *U* heard that	2Sa 11:26	223
heard that *U* her husband was dead	2Sa 11:26	223
thou hast killed *U* the Hittite	2Sa 12:9	223
hast taken the wife of *U* the	2Sa 12:10	223
U the Hittite	2Sa 23:39	223
in the matter of *U* the Hittite	1Kin 15:5	223
U the Hittite, Zabad the son of	1Chr 11:41	223

2. A rebuilder of Jerusalem's wall.

Meremoth the son of *U* the priest	Ezr 8:33	223

3. A priest who aided Isaiah.

U the priest, and Zechariah the	Is 8:2	223

URIAH'S *(u-ri'-ahz) Refers to Uriah 1.*

child that *U* wife bare unto David	2Sa 12:15	223

URIAS *(u-ri'-as) Greek form of Uriah 1.*

her that had been the wife of *U*	Mt 1:6	3774

URIEL *(u'-re-el)*

1. Son of Tahath.

U his son, Uzziah his son, and	1Chr 6:24	222
U the chief, and his brethren an	1Chr 15:5	222
and for the Levites, for *U*	1Chr 15:11	222

2. Father of Micaiah.

the daughter of *U* of Gibeah	2Chr 13:2	222

URIJAH *(u-ri'-jah)* See URIAH.

1. A priest in Jerusalem.

king Ahaz sent to *U* the priest	2Kin 16:10	223
U the priest built an altar	2Kin 16:11	223
so *U* the priest made it against	2Kin 16:11	223
king Ahaz commanded *U* the priest	2Kin 16:15	223
Thus did *U* the priest, according	2Kin 16:16	223

2. A priest who rebuilt the wall.

repaired Meremoth the son of *U*	Neh 3:4	223
of *U* the son of Koz another piece	Neh 3:21	223

U

3. A priest who aided Ezra.
and Shema, and Anaiah, and *U* .... Neh 8:4   223
   4. A prophet killed by Jehoiakim.
LORD, *U* the son of Shemaiah of .... Jer 26:20   223
but when *U* heard it, he was .... Jer 26:21   223
they fetched forth *U* out of Egypt .... Jer 26:23   223

URIM *(u'-rim) A symbolic object in the High Priest's breastplate.*
the breastplate of judgment the *U* .... Ex 28:30   224
he put in the breastplate the *U* .... Lev 8:8   224
the judgment of *U* before the LORD .... Num 27:21   224
thy *U* be with thy holy one, whom .... Deut 33:8   224
not, neither by dreams, nor by *U* 1Sa 28:6   224
there stood up a priest with *U* .... Ezr 2:63   224
there stood up a priest with *U* .... Neh 7:65   224

US See APPENDIX.

USE See APPENDIX.

USED See APPENDIX.

USES See APPENDIX.

USEST
as thou *u* to do unto those that.............. Ps 119:132   4941

USETH
or that *u* divination, or an...................... Deut 18:10
brought which the king *u* to wear .... Est 6:8
of the wise *u* knowledge aright.............. Prov 15:2
The poor *u* intreaties .... Prov 18:23   1696
that *u* his neighbour's service................. Jer 22:13
every one that *u* proverbs shall .... Eze 16:44
For every one that *u* milk is .... Heb 5:13   3348

USING See APPENDIX.

USURER
thou shalt not be to him as a *u*.............. Ex 22:25   5383

USURP
nor to *u* authority over the man,............ 1Ti 2:12   831

USURY
neither shalt thou lay upon him *u* .... Ex 22:25   5392
Take thou no *u* of him, or .... Lev 25:36   5392
not give him thy money upon *u* .... Lev 25:37   5392
not lend upon *u* to thy brother .... Deut 23:19   5391
u of money, *u* of victuals,...................... Deut 23:19   5392
u of any thing that is lent upon .... Deut 23:19   5392
of any thing that is lent upon *u* .... Deut 23:19   5391
stranger thou mayest lend upon *u*........ Deut 23:20   5391
thou shalt not lend upon *u* .... Deut 23:20   5391
and said unto them, Ye exact *u* .... Neh 5:7   5383
pray you, let us leave off this *u* .... Neh 5:10   5383
putteth not out his money to *u* .... Ps 15:5   5392
He that by *u* and unjust gain................ Prov 28:8   5392
as with the taker of *u* .... Is 24:2   5383
so with the giver of *u* to him .... Is 24:2   5378
I have neither lent on *u* .... Jer 15:10   5383
nor men have lent to me on *u* .... Jer 15:10   5383
that hath not given forth upon *u* .... Eze 18:8   5392
Hath given forth upon *u*, and hath....... Eze 18:13   5392
hath not received *u* nor increase........... Eze 18:17   5392
thou hast taken *u* and increase, and..... Eze 22:12   5392
have received mine own with *u* .... Mt 25:27   5110
have required mine own with *u* .... Lk 19:23   5110

US-WARD
and thy thoughts which are to *u* .... Ps 40:5   413
of his power to *u* who believe.......... Eph 1:19   1519,2248
but is longsuffering to *u*................... 2Pet 3:9   1519,2248

UTHAI *(u'-thahee)*
   1. Son of Ammihud.
U the son of Ammihud, the son of 1Chr 9:4   5793
   2. A clan leader with Ezra.
U, and Zabbud, and with them .... Ezr 8:14   5793

UTMOST
of my progenitors unto the *u* .... Gen 49:26
of Arnon, which is in the *u* coast........... Num 22:36   7097
see the *u* part of the people .... Num 22:41   7097
shalt see but the *u* part of them .... Num 23:13   7097
the land of Judah, unto the *u* sea .... Deut 34:2   314
and all that are in the *u* corners............ Jer 9:26   7112
and all that are in the *u* corners............ Jer 25:23   7112
them that are in the *u* corners............... Jer 49:32   7112
against her from the *u* border................. Jer 50:26   7093
his hinder part toward the *u* sea .... Joel 2:20   314
for she came from the *u* parts of .... Lk 11:31   4009

UTTER
if he do not *u* it, then he shall .... Lev 5:1   5046
if ye *u* not this our business .... Josh 2:14   5046
if thou *u* this our business, then .... Josh 2:20   5046
awake, awake, *u* a song .... Judg 5:12   1696

whom I appointed to *u* destruction 1Kin 20:42
u words out of their heart .... Job 8:10   3318
a wise man *u* vain knowledge .... Job 15:2   6030
nor my tongue *u* deceit........................... Job 27:4   1897
my lips shall *u* knowledge clearly .... Job 33:3   4448
I will *u* dark sayings of old...................... Ps 78:2   5042
How long shall they *u* and speak .... Ps 94:4   5042
Who can *u* the mighty acts of the .... Ps 106:2   4448
My lips shall *u* praise, when thou .... Ps 119:171   5042
They shall abundantly *u* the .... Ps 145:7   5042
but a false witness will *u* lies .... Prov 14:5   6315
heart shall *u* perverse things .... Prov 23:33   1696
man cannot *u* it...................................... Eccl 1:8   1696
hasty to *u* any thing before God............ Eccl 5:2   3318
to *u* error against the LORD, to .... Is 32:6   1696
u it even to the end of the earth .... Is 48:20   3318
I will *u* my judgments against .... Jer 1:16   1696
u his voice from his holy........................ Jer 25:30   5414
u a parable unto the rebellious .... Eze 24:3   4911
thereof were toward the *u* court............. Eze 40:31   2435
thereof were toward the *u* court............. Eze 40:37   2435
brought me forth into the *u* court .... Eze 42:1   2435
which was for the *u* court .... Eze 42:3   2435
toward the *u* court on the .... Eze 42:7   2435
in the *u* court was fifty cubits .... Eze 42:8   2435
goeth into them from the *u* court .... Eze 42:9   2435
the holy place into the *u* court .... Eze 42:14   2435
they go forth into the *u* court .... Eze 44:19   2435
even into the *u* court to the .... Eze 44:19   2435
them not out into the *u* court .... Eze 46:20   2435
brought me forth into the *u* court .... Eze 46:21   2435
u gate by the way that looketh .... Eze 47:2   2531
the LORD shall *u* his voice before .... Joel 2:11   5414
u his voice from Jerusalem .... Joel 3:16   5414
u his voice from Jerusalem .... Amos 1:2   5414
flood he will make an *u* end of............... Nah 1:8   3617
he will make an *u* end .... Nah 1:9   3617
shall be no more *u* destruction .... Zec 14:11
I will *u* things which have been .... Mt 13:35   2044
except we by the tongue words 1Cor 14:9   1325
it is not lawful for a man to *u* 2Cor 12:4   2980

UTTERANCE
as the Spirit gave them *u*...................... Acts 2:4   669
ye are enriched by him, in all *u*............ 1Cor 1:5   3056
in every thing, in faith, and *u* 2Cor 8:7   3056
that *u* may be given unto me, that .... Eph 6:19   3056
would open unto us a door of *u* .... Col 4:3   3056

UTTERED
or *u* ought out of her lips,...................... Num 30:6   4008
and that which she *u* with her lips .... Num 30:8   4008
Jephthah *u* all his words before .... Judg 11:11   1696
and the most High *u* his voice 2Sa 22:14   5414
before me, and *u* my words to him .... Neh 6:19   3318
To whom hast thou *u* words .... Job 26:4   5046
therefore have I *u* that I .... Job 42:3   5046
he *u* his voice, the earth melted............. Ps 46:6   5414
Which my lips have *u*, and my mouth ... Ps 66:14   6475
have they *u* their voice, from .... Jer 48:34   5414
a noise of their voice is *u* .... Jer 51:55   5414
the deep *u* his voice, and lifted .... Hab 3:10   5414
with groanings which cannot be *u* .... Rom 8:26   215
things to say, and hard to be *u* .... Heb 5:11   3004
seven thunders *u* their voices .... Rev 10:3   2980
seven thunders had *u* their voices .... Rev 10:4   2980
things which the seven thunders *u* .... Rev 10:4   2980

UTTERETH
For thy mouth *u* thine iniquity, (*u*,...... Job 15:5   502
Day unto day *u* speech, and night......... Ps 19:2   5042
she *u* her voice in the streets .... Prov 1:20   5414
in the city she *u* her words .... Prov 1:21   559
he that *u* a slander, is a fool.................. Prov 10:18   3318
A fool *u* all his mind .... Prov 29:11   3318
When he *u* his voice, there is a.............. Jer 10:13   5414
When he *u* his voice, there is a.............. Jer 51:16   5414
he *u* his mischievous desire .... Mic 7:3   1696

UTTERING
u from the heart words of........................ Is 59:13   1897

UTTERLY
for I will *u* put out the .... Ex 17:14   502
If her father *u* refuse to give .... Ex 22:17   5042
only, he shall be *u* destroyed .... Ex 22:20   5414
but thou shalt *u* overthrow them .... Ex 23:24   559
shall pronounce him *u* unclean............. Lev 13:44   3318
I abhor them, to destroy them *u*............ Lev 26:44   3615
that soul shall *u* be cut off .... Num 15:31
then I will *u* destroy their...................... Num 21:2
they *u* destroyed them and their .... Num 21:3
But if her husband hath *u* made .... Num 30:12

u destroyed the men, and the women..... Deut 2:34
we *u* destroyed them, as we did............. Deut 3:6
u destroying the men, women, and........ Deut 3:6
that ye shall soon *u* perish from .... Deut 4:26
upon it, but shall *u* be destroyed .... Deut 4:26
smite them, and *u* destroy them .... Deut 7:2
but thou shalt *u* detest it .... Deut 7:26
and thou shalt *u* abhor it...................... Deut 7:26
Ye shall *u* destroy all the places .... Deut 12:2
of the sword, destroying it *u*................. Deut 13:15
But thou shalt *u* destroy them .... Deut 20:17
ye will *u* corrupt yourselves................... Deut 31:29
Sihon and Og, whom ye *u* destroyed..... Josh 2:10
they *u* destroyed all that was in .... Josh 6:21
until he had *u* destroyed all the............. Josh 8:26
taken Ai, and had *u* destroyed it .... Josh 10:1
the king thereof he *u* destroyed .... Josh 10:28
therein he *u* destroyed that day .... Josh 10:35
but destroyed it *u*, and all the .... Josh 10:37
u destroyed all the souls that .... Josh 10:39
but *u* destroyed all that breathed........... Josh 10:40
of the sword, *u* destroying them .... Josh 11:11
he *u* destroyed them, as Moses the .... Josh 11:12
that he might destroy them *u* .... Josh 11:20
them *u* with their cities .... Josh 11:21
but did not *u* drive them out .... Josh 17:13
Zephath, and *u* destroyed it .... Judg 1:17
and did not *u* drive them out .... Judg 1:28
that thou hadst *u* hated her .... Judg 15:2
Ye shall *u* destroy every male, and......... Judg 21:11
u destroy all that they have, and............ 1Sa 15:3
u destroyed all the people with............... 1Sa 15:8
good, and would not *u* destroy them 1Sa 15:9
and refuse, that they destroyed *u*........... 1Sa 15:9
and the rest we have *u* destroyed........... 1Sa 15:15
u destroy the sinners the 1Sa 15:18
have *u* destroyed the Amalekites 1Sa 15:20
should have been *u* destroyed................ 1Sa 15:21
his people Israel *u* to abhor him 1Sa 27:12
the heart of a lion, shall *u* melt............... 2Sa 17:10
they shall be *u* burned with fire 2Sa 23:7
also were not able *u* to destroy............... 1Kin 9:21
all lands, by destroying them *u* 2Kin 19:11
and destroyed them *u* unto this day 1Chr 4:41
u to slay and destroy them 2Chr 20:23
until they had *u* destroyed them............. 2Chr 31:1
that my fathers *u* destroyed................... 2Chr 32:14
thou didst not *u* consume them .... Neh 9:31
fall, he shall not be *u* cast down .... Ps 37:24
they are *u* consumed with terrors .... Ps 73:19
will I not *u* take from him .... Ps 89:33
O forsake not me *u* .... Ps 119:8   3966
word of truth *u* out of my mouth .... Ps 119:43   3966
for love, it would *u* be contemned .... Song 8:7
And the idols he shall *u* abolish............. Is 2:18   3632
man, and the land be *u* desolate .... Is 6:11
the LORD shall *u* destroy the .... Is 11:15
be *u* emptied, and *u* spoiled.................. Is 24:3
The earth is *u* broken down .... Is 24:19
he hath *u* destroyed them, he hath .... Is 34:2
to all lands by destroying them *u*........... Is 37:11
and the young men shall *u* fall .... Is 40:30
The LORD hath *u* separated me from..... Is 56:3
those nations shall be *u* wasted .... Is 60:12
for every brother will *u* supplant .... Jer 9:4
I will *u* pluck up and destroy that .... Jer 12:17
Hast thou *u* rejected Judah .... Jer 14:19
will *u* forget you, and I will .... Jer 23:39
will *u* destroy them, and make them...... Jer 25:9
and should ye be *u* unpunished.............. Jer 25:29
u destroy after them, saith the .... Jer 50:21
her up as heaps, and destroy her *u*........ Jer 50:26
destroy ye *u* all her host........................ Jer 51:3
of Babylon shall be *u* broken .... Jer 51:58
But thou hast *u* rejected us.................... Lam 5:22
Slay *u* old and young, both maids, ... Eze 9:6
shall it not *u* wither, when the................ Eze 17:10
make themselves *u* bald for thee............ Eze 27:31
make the land of Egypt *u* waste .... Eze 29:10
destroy, and *u* to make away many........ Dan 11:44
but I will *u* take them away .... Hos 1:6
the king of Israel *u* be cut off .... Hos 10:15
saving that I will not *u* destroy............... Amos 9:8
and say, We be *u* spoiled....................... Mic 2:4   7703
he is *u* cut off .... Nah 1:15   3605
I will *u* consume all things from .... Zeph 1:2
his right eye shall be *u* darkened .... Zec 11:17
there is *u* a fault among you 1Cor 6:7   3654
shall *u* perish in their own 2Pet 2:12   2704
she shall be *u* burned with fire.............. Rev 18:8   2618

UTTERMOST

in the *u* edge of another curtain .... Ex 26:4   7020
in the *u* side of another curtain .... Ex 36:11   7020
the *u* edge of the curtain in the .... Ex 36:17   7020
were in the *u* parts of the camp .... Num 11:1   7097
a city in the *u* of thy border .... Num 20:16   7097
even unto the *u* sea shall your .... Deut 11:24   314
was the *u* part of the south coast .... Josh 15:1   7097
the sea at the *u* part of Jordan .... Josh 15:5   7097
the *u* cities of the tribe of the .... Josh 15:21   7097
Saul tarried in the *u* part of................... 1Sa 14:2   7097
from the *u* part of the one wing............. 1Kin 6:24   7098
the *u* part of the other were ten 1Kin 6:24   7098
the *u* part of the camp of Syria 2Kin 7:5   7097
came to the *u* part of the camp 2Kin 7:8   7097
out unto the *u* part of the heaven .... Neh 1:9   7097
the *u* parts of the earth for thy .... Ps 2:8   657
They also that dwell in the *u* .... Ps 65:8   7098
dwell in the *u* parts of the sea .... Ps 139:9   319
the *u* part of the rivers of Egypt .... Is 7:18   7097
From the *u* part of the earth have .... Is 24:16   3671
thou hast paid the *u* farthing .... Mt 5:26   2078
for she came from the *u* parts of .... Mt 12:42   4009
from the *u* part of the earth to .... Mk 13:27   206
the earth to the *u* part of heaven .... Mk 13:27   206
unto the *u* part of the earth .... Acts 1:8   2078
I will know the *u* of your matter .... Acts 24:22   1231
wrath is come upon them to the *u* 1Th 2:16   5056
the *u* that come unto God by him .... Heb 7:25   3838

UZ (uz) A son of Aram.

U, and Hul, and Gether, and Mash .... Gen 10:23   5780
are these; *U*, and Aran .... Gen 36:28   5780
Arphaxad, and Lud, and Aram, and *U*... 1Chr 1:17   5780
of Dishan; *U*, and Aran 1Chr 1:42   5780
There was a man in the land of *U* .... Job 1:1   5780
and all the kings of the land of *U* .... Jer 25:20   5780
that dwellest in the land of *U*................ Lam 4:21   5780

UZAI (u'-zahee) Father of Palal.

Palal the son of *U*, over against .... Neh 3:25   186

UZAL (u'-zal) A son of Joktan.

And Hadoram, and *U*, and Diklah,........ Gen 10:27   187
Hadoram also, and *U*, and Diklah, ... 1Chr 1:21   187

UZZA (uz'-zah) See UZZAH.

1. Name of the burial ground of Manasseh and Amon.
his own house, in the garden of *U* 2Kin 21:18   5798
his sepulchre in the garden of *U* 2Kin 21:26   5798
2. Son of Shimei.
son, Shimei his son, *U* his son, ... 1Chr 6:29   5798
3. A brother of Ahihud.
Gera, he removed them, and begat *U* 1Chr 8:7   5798
4. Touched the Ark and died.
and *U* and Ahio drave the cart 1Chr 13:7   5798
U put forth his hand to hold the 1Chr 13:9   5798
of the LORD was kindled against *U*........ 1Chr 13:10   5798
the LORD had made a breach upon *U* 1Chr 13:11   5798
5. A family of Nethinims.
The children of *U*, the children .... Ezr 2:49   5798
of Gazzam, the children of *U* .... Neh 7:51   5798

UZZAH (uz'-zah) See UZZA. Same as Uzza 4.

and *U* and Ahio, the sons of 2Sa 6:3   5798
U put forth his hand to the ark 2Sa 6:6   5798
of the LORD was kindled against *U*......... 2Sa 6:7   5798
the LORD had made a breach upon *U* 2Sa 6:8   5798

UZZEN-SHEERAH See UZZEN-SHERAH.

UZZEN-SHERAH (uz'-zen-she'-rah) A city in Ephraim.

the nether, and the upper, and *U*............ 1Chr 7:24   242

UZZI (uz'-zi)

1. A son of Bukki.
begat Bukki, and Bukki begat *U*............ 1Chr 6:5   5813
U begat Zerahiah, and Zerahiah 1Chr 6:6   5813
U his son, Zerahiah his son, ... 1Chr 6:51   5813
The son of Zerahiah, the son of *U* .... Ezr 7:4   5813
2. Father of Izrahiah.
U, and Rephaiah, and Jeriel, and 1Chr 7:2   5813
And the sons of *U* 1Chr 7:3   5813
3. Son of Bela.
Ezbon, and *U*, and Uzziel, and.............. 1Chr 7:7   5813
4. A family of exiles.
of Jeroham, and Elah the son of *U* 1Chr 9:8   5813
5. An overseer of Levites.
Jerusalem was *U* the son of Bani .... Neh 11:22   5813
6. A priest descended from Jedaiah.
of Jedaiah, *U* .... Neh 12:19   5813
and Shemaiah, and Eleazar, and *U*....... Neh 12:42   5813

UZZIA (uz-zi'-ah) A "mighty man" of David.

U the Ashterathite, Shama and 1Chr 11:44   5814

U

UZZIAH (uz-zi'-ah)

1. A king of Judah.

thirtieth year of *U* king of Judah	2Kin 15:13	5818
year of Jotham the son of *U*	2Kin 15:30	5818
son of *U* king of Judah to reign	2Kin 15:32	5818
to all that his father *U* had done	2Kin 15:34	5818
all the people of Judah took *U*	2Chr 26:1	5818
Sixteen years old was *U* when he	2Chr 26:3	5818
And the Ammonites gave gifts to *U*	2Chr 26:8	5818
Moreover *U* built towers in	2Chr 26:9	5818
Moreover *U* had an host of	2Chr 26:11	5818
U prepared for them throughout	2Chr 26:14	5818
And they withstood *U* the king	2Chr 26:18	5818
It appertaineth not unto thee, *U*	2Chr 26:18	5818
Then *U* was wroth, and had a censer	2Chr 26:19	5818
U the king was a leper unto the	2Chr 26:21	5818
Now the rest of the acts of *U*	2Chr 26:22	5818
So *U* slept with his fathers, and	2Chr 26:23	5818
to all that his father *U* did	2Chr 27:2	5818
and Jerusalem in the days of *U*	Is 1:1	5818
In the year that king *U* died I	Is 6:1	5818
the son of Jotham, the son of *U*	Is 7:1	5818
son of Beeri, in the days of *U*	Hos 1:1	5818
in the days of *U* king of Judah	Amos 1:1	5818
in the days of *U* king of Judah	Zec 14:5	5818

2. Son of Uriel.

U his son, and Shaul his son	1Chr 6:24	5818

3. Father of Jehonathan.

was Jehonathan the son of *U*	1Chr 27:25	5818

4. Married a foreigner in exile.

and Shemaiah, and Jehiel, and *U*	Ezr 10:21	5818

5. A family of exiles.

Athaiah the son of *U*, the son of	Neh 11:4	5818

UZZIEL (uz-zi'-el)

1. A son of Kohath.

Amram, and Izhar, and Hebron, and *U*	Ex 6:18	5816
And the sons of *U*	Ex 6:22	5816
the sons of *U* the uncle of Aaron,	Lev 10:4	5816
Amram, and Izehar, Hebron, and *U*	Num 3:19	5816
shall be Elizaphan the son of *U*	Num 3:30	5816
Amram, Izhar, and Hebron, and *U*	1Chr 6:2	5816
Amram, and Izhar, and Hebron, and *U*	1Chr 6:18	5816
Of the sons of *U*	1Chr 15:10	5816
Amram, Izhar, Hebron, and *U*	1Chr 23:12	5816
Of the sons of *U*	1Chr 23:20	5816
Of the sons of *U*	1Chr 24:24	5816

2. A son of Ishi.

and Neariah, and Rephaiah, and *U*	1Chr 4:42	5816

3. A son of Bela.

Ezbon, and Uzzi, and *U*, and Jerimoth	1Chr 7:7	5816

4. A sanctuary servant.

Bukkiah, Mattaniah, *U*, Shebuel,	1Chr 25:4	5816

5. A Levite who cleansed the Temple.

Shemaiah, and *U*	2Chr 29:14	5816

6. A repairer of Jerusalem's wall.

repaired *U* the son of Harhaiah	Neh 3:8	5816

UZZIELITES (uz-zi'-el-ites) Descendants of Uzziel 1.

and the family of the *U*	Num 3:27	5817
the Hebronites, and the *U*	1Chr 26:23	5817

V

VAGABOND

a *v* shalt thou be in the earth	Gen 4:12	5110
be a fugitive and a *v* in the earth	Gen 4:14	5110
Then certain of the *v* Jews	Acts 19:13	4022

VAGABONDS

Let his children be continually *v*	Ps 109:10	5128

VAIL

therefore she took a *v*, and	Gen 24:65	6809
from her, and covered her with a *v*	Gen 38:14	6809
away, and laid by her *v* from her	Gen 38:19	6809
And thou shalt make a *v* of blue	Ex 26:31	6532
hang up the *v* under the taches	Ex 26:33	6532
the *v* the ark of the testimony	Ex 26:33	6532
the *v* shall divide unto you	Ex 26:33	6532
shalt set the table without the *v*	Ex 26:35	6532
of the congregation without the *v*	Ex 27:21	6532
the *v* that is by the ark of the	Ex 30:6	6532
with them, he put a *v* on his face	Ex 34:33	4533
speak with him, he took the *v* off	Ex 34:34	4533
Moses put the *v* upon his face	Ex 34:35	4533
seat, and the *v* of the covering,	Ex 35:12	6532
And he made a *v* of blue, and purple	Ex 36:35	6532
and the sockets of the *v*	Ex 38:27	6532
skins, and the *v* of the covering,	Ex 39:34	6532
and cover the ark with the *v*	Ex 40:3	6532
set up the *v* of the covering, and	Ex 40:21	6532
northward, without the *v*	Ex 40:22	6532
of the congregation before the *v*	Ex 40:26	6532
before the *v* of the sanctuary	Lev 4:6	6532
the LORD, even before the *v*	Lev 4:17	6532
the *v* before the mercy seat	Lev 16:2	6532
small, and bring it within the *v*	Lev 16:12	6532
and bring his blood within the *v*	Lev 16:15	6532
he shall not go in unto the *v*	Lev 21:23	6532
Without the *v* of the testimony,	Lev 24:3	6532
shall take down the covering *v*	Num 4:5	6532
of the altar, and within the *v*	Num 18:7	6532
Bring the *v* that thou hast upon	Ruth 3:15	4304
And he made the *v* of blue, and	2Chr 3:14	6532
the *v* that is spread over all	Is 25:7	4541
which put a *v* over his face, that	2Cor 3:13	2571
this day remaineth the same *v*	2Cor 3:14	2571
which *v* is done away in Christ	2Cor 3:14	
the *v* is upon their heart	2Cor 3:15	2571
the *v* shall be taken away	2Cor 3:16	2571

VAILS

linen, and the hoods, and the *v*	Is 3:23	7289

VAIN

and let them not regard *v* words	Ex 5:9	8267
the name of the LORD thy God in *v*	Ex 20:7	7723
that taketh his name in *v*	Ex 20:7	7723
and ye shall sow your seed in *v*	Lev 26:16	7385
your strength shall be spent in *v*	Lev 26:20	7385
the name of the LORD thy God in *v*	Deut 5:11	7723
that taketh his name in *v*	Deut 5:11	7723
For it is not a *v* thing for you	Deut 32:47	7386
wherewith Abimelech hired *v*	Judg 9:4	7386
were gathered *v* men to Jephthah	Judg 11:3	7386
then should ye go after *v* things	1Sa 12:21	8414
for they are *v*	1Sa 12:21	8414
Surely in *v* have I kept all that	1Sa 25:21	8267
servants, as one of the *v* fellows	2Sa 6:20	7386
they followed vanity, and became *v*	2Kin 17:15	1891
sayest, they are but *v* words	2Kin 18:20	8193
there are gathered unto him *v* men	2Chr 13:7	7386
be wicked, why then labour I in *v*	Job 9:29	1892
For he knoweth *v* men	Job 11:11	7723
For *v* man would be wise, though	Job 11:12	5014
a wise man utter *v* knowledge	Job 15:2	7307
Shall *v* words have an end	Job 16:3	7307
How then comfort ye me in *v*	Job 21:34	1892
why then are ye thus altogether *v*	Job 27:12	1891
doth Job open his mouth in *v*	Job 35:16	1892
her labour is in *v* without fear	Job 39:16	7385
Behold, the hope of him is in *v*	Job 41:9	3576
and the people imagine a *v* thing	Ps 2:1	7385
I have not sat with *v* persons	Ps 26:4	7723
An horse is a *v* thing for safety	Ps 33:17	8267
every man walketh in a *v* shew	Ps 39:6	
surely they are disquieted in *v*	Ps 39:6	1892
for *v* is the help of man	Ps 60:11	7723
and become not *v* in robbery	Ps 62:10	1891
I have cleansed my heart in *v*	Ps 73:13	7385
hast thou made all men in *v*	Ps 89:47	7723
for *v* is the help of man	Ps 108:12	7723
I hate *v* thoughts	Ps 119:113	
they labour in *v* that build it	Ps 127:1	7723
the watchman waketh but in *v*	Ps 127:1	7723
It is *v* for you to rise up early,	Ps 127:2	7723
thine enemies take thy name in *v*	Ps 139:20	7723
Surely in *v* the net is spread in	Prov 1:17	2600
followeth *v* persons is void of	Prov 12:11	7386
v persons shall have poverty	Prov 28:19	7386
and take the name of my God in *v*	Prov 30:9	
is deceitful, and beauty is *v*	Prov 31:30	1892
all the days of his *v* life which	Eccl 6:12	1892
Bring no more *v* oblations	Is 1:13	7723
For the Egyptians shall help in *v*	Is 30:7	1892
(but they are but *v* words) I have	Is 36:5	8193
it, he created it not in *v*	Is 45:18	8414
seed of Jacob, Seek ye me in *v*	Is 45:19	8414
Then I said, I have laboured in *v*	Is 49:4	7385
my strength for nought, and in *v*	Is 49:4	1892
They shall not labour in *v*	Is 65:23	7385
after vanity, and are become *v*	Jer 2:5	1891
In *v* have I smitten your children	Jer 2:30	7723

Truly in *v* is salvation hoped for	Jer 3:23	8267
How long shall thy *v* thoughts	Jer 4:14	205
in *v* shalt thou make thyself fair	Jer 4:30	7723
the founder melteth in *v*	Jer 6:29	7723
Lo, certainly in *v* made he it	Jer 8:8	8267
the pen of the scribes is in *v*	Jer 8:8	8267
the customs of the people are *v*	Jer 10:3	1892
they make you *v*	Jer 23:16	1891
in *v* shalt thou use many	Jer 46:11	7723
none shall return in *v*	Jer 50:9	7387
and the people shall labour in *v*	Jer 51:58	7385
Thy prophets have seen *v* and	Lam 2:14	7723
eyes as yet failed for our *v* help	Lam 4:17	1892
that I have not said in *v* that I	Eze 6:10	2600
more any *v* vision nor flattering	Eze 12:24	7723
Have ye not seen a *v* vision	Eze 13:7	7723
they comfort in *v*	Zec 10:2	1892
have said, It is *v* to serve God	Mal 3:14	7723
use not *v* repetitions, as the	Mt 6:7	
But in *v* they do worship me,	Mt 15:9	3155
Howbeit in *v* do they worship me,	Mk 7:7	3155
and the people imagine *v* things	Acts 4:25	2756
but became *v* in their	Rom 1:21	3154
for he beareth not the sword in *v*	Rom 13:4	1500
of the wise, that they are *v*	1Cor 3:20	3152
you, unless ye have believed in *v*	1Cor 15:2	1500
was bestowed upon me was not in *v*	1Cor 15:10	2756
risen, then is our preaching *v*	1Cor 15:14	2756
and your faith is also *v*	1Cor 15:14	2756
be not raised, your faith is *v*	1Cor 15:17	3152
labour is not in *v* in the Lord	1Cor 15:58	2756
receive not the grace of God in *v*	2Cor 6:1	2756
you should be in *v* in this behalf	2Cor 9:3	2761
I should run, or had run, in *v*	Gal 2:2	2756
the law, then Christ is dead in *v*	Gal 2:21	1432
ye suffered so many things in *v*	Gal 3:4	1500
if it be yet in *v*	Gal 3:4	1500
bestowed upon you labour in *v*	Gal 4:11	1500
Let us not be desirous of *v* glory	Gal 5:26	2755
no man deceive you with *v* words	Eph 5:6	2756
Christ, that I have not run in *v*	Phil 2:16	2756
neither laboured in *v*	Phil 2:16	2756
v deceit, after the tradition of	Col 2:8	2756
in unto you, that it was not in *v*	1Th 2:1	2756
you, and our labour be in *v*	1Th 3:5	2756
have turned aside unto *v* jangling	1Ti 1:6	3150
v babblings, and oppositions of	1Ti 6:20	2757
But shun profane and *v* babblings	2Ti 2:16	2757
v talkers and deceivers, specially	Titus 1:10	3151
for they are unprofitable and *v*	Titus 3:9	3152
heart, this man's religion is *v*	Jas 1:26	3152
O *v* man, that faith without works	Jas 2:20	2756
that the scripture saith in *v*	Jas 4:5	2761
from your *v* conversation received	1Pet 1:18	3152

VAINGLORY

be done through strife or *v*	Phil 2:3	2754

VAINLY

v puffed up by his fleshly mind,	Col 2:18	1500

VAIZATHA See VAJEZATHA.

VAJEZATHA (*va-jez'-a-thah*) *A son of Haman.*

and Arisai, and Aridai, and V	Est 9:9	2055

VALE

together in the *v* of Siddim	Gen 14:3	6010
with them in the *v* of Siddim	Gen 14:8	6010
the *v* of Siddim was full of	Gen 14:10	6010
sent him out of the *v* of Hebron	Gen 37:14	6010
plain, in the hills, and in the *v*	Deut 1:7	8219
and of the south, and of the *v*	Josh 10:40	8219
sycomore trees are in the *v*	1Kin 10:27	8219
that are in the *v* for abundance	2Chr 1:15	8219
mountains, in the cities of the *v*	Jer 33:13	8219

VALIANT

saw any strong man, or any *v* man	1Sa 14:52	2428
in playing, and a mighty *v* man	1Sa 16:18	2428
only be thou *v* for me, and fight	1Sa 18:17	1121,2428
to Abner, Art not thou a *v* man	1Sa 26:15	
All the *v* men arose, and went all	1Sa 31:12	2428
be strengthened, and be ye *v*	2Sa 2:7	1121,2428
where he knew that *v* men were	2Sa 11:16	2428
be courageous, and be *v*	2Sa 13:28	1121,2428
And he also that is *v*, whose heart	2Sa 17:10	1121,2428
they which be with him are *v* men	2Sa 17:10	2428
of Jehoiada, the son of a *v* man	2Sa 23:20	2428
v men that drew the sword	2Sa 24:9	2428
for thou art a *v* man, and bringest	1Kin 1:42	2428
of *v* men, men able to bear	1Chr 5:18	2428
they were *v* men of might in their	1Chr 7:2	1368
of Issachar were *v* men of might	1Chr 7:5	1368

They arose, all the *v* men	1Chr 10:12	2428
the son of a *v* man of Kabzeel,	1Chr 11:22	2428
Also the *v* men of the armies were	1Chr 11:26	1368
mighty men, and with all the *v* men	1Chr 28:1	2428
with an army of *v* men of war	2Chr 13:3	1368
of the LORD, that were *v* men	2Chr 26:17	2428
in one day, which were all *v* men	2Chr 28:6	2428
hundred threescore and eight *v* men	Neh 11:6	2428
threescore *v* men are about it, of	Song 3:7	1368
are about it, of the *v* of Israel	Song 3:7	1368
down the inhabitants like a *v* man	Is 10:13	3524
their *v* ones shall cry without	Is 33:7	691
but they are not *v* for the truth	Jer 9:3	1396
Why are thy *v* men swept away	Jer 46:15	47
red, the *v* men are in scarlet	Nah 2:3	2428
waxed *v* in fight, turned to	Heb 11:34	2478

VALIANTEST

twelve thousand men of the *v*	Judg 21:10	1121,2428

VALIANTLY

and Israel shall do *v*	Num 24:18	2428
behave ourselves *v* for our people	1Chr 19:13	2388
Through God we shall do *v*	Ps 60:12	2428
Through God we shall do *v*	Ps 108:13	2428
right hand of the LORD doeth *v*	Ps 118:15	2428
right hand of the LORD doeth *v*	Ps 118:16	2428

VALLEY

at the *v* of Shaveh, which is the	Gen 14:17	6010
his tent in the *v* of Gerar	Gen 26:17	5158
Isaac's servants digged in the *v*	Gen 26:19	5158
and the Canaanites dwelt in the *v*	Num 14:25	6010
and pitched in the *v* of Zared	Num 21:12	5158
And from Bamoth in the *v*, that is	Num 21:20	1516
they went up unto the *v* of Eshcol	Num 32:9	5158
and came unto the *v* of Eshcol	Deut 1:24	5158
unto the river Arnon half the *v*	Deut 3:16	5158
So we abode in the *v* over against	Deut 3:29	1516
in the *v* over against Beth-peor,	Deut 4:46	1516
down the heifer unto a rough *v*	Deut 21:4	5158
the heifer's neck there in the *v*	Deut 21:4	5158
heifer that is beheaded in the *v*	Deut 21:6	5158
and the plain of the *v* of Jericho	Deut 34:3	1237
he buried him in a *v* in the land	Deut 34:6	1516
brought them unto the *v* of Achor	Josh 7:24	6010
The *v* of Achor, unto this day	Josh 7:26	6010
now there was a *v* between them	Josh 8:11	1516
night into the midst of the *v*	Josh 8:13	6010
and thou, Moon, in the *v* of Ajalon	Josh 10:12	6010
south of Chinneroth, and in the *v*	Josh 11:2	8219
unto the *v* of Mizpeh eastward	Josh 11:8	1237
all the land of Goshen, and the *v*	Josh 11:16	8219
of Israel, and the *v* of the same	Josh 11:16	8219
even unto Baal-gad in the *v* of	Josh 11:17	1237
from Baal-gad in the *v* of Lebanon	Josh 12:7	1237
in the mount of the *v*,	Josh 13:19	6010
And in the *v*, Beth-aram, and	Josh 13:27	6010
toward Debir from the *v* of Achor	Josh 15:7	6010
the border went up by the *v* of	Josh 15:8	1516
before the *v* of Hinnom westward	Josh 15:8	1516
of the *v* of the giants northward	Josh 15:8	6010
And in the *v*, Eshtaol, and Zoreah,	Josh 15:33	8219
of the *v* have chariots of iron	Josh 17:16	6010
they who are of the *v* of Jezreel	Josh 17:16	6010
before the *v* of the son of Hinnom	Josh 18:16	1516
which is in the *v* of the giants	Josh 18:16	6010
and descended to the *v* of Hinnom	Josh 18:16	1516
Beth-hoglah, and the *v* of Keziz,	Josh 18:21	6010
are in the *v* of Jiphthah-el,	Josh 19:14	1516
to the *v* of Jiphthah-el toward	Josh 19:27	1516
and in the south, and in the *v*	Judg 1:9	8219
out the inhabitants of the *v*	Judg 1:19	6010
suffer them to come down to the *v*	Judg 1:34	6010
he was sent on foot into the *v*	Judg 5:15	6010
and pitched in the *v* of Jezreel	Judg 6:33	6010
by the hill of Moreh, in the *v*	Judg 7:1	6010
Midian was beneath him in the *v*	Judg 7:8	6010
of the east lay along in the *v*	Judg 7:12	6010
loved a woman in the *v* of Sorek	Judg 16:4	5158
it was in the *v* that lieth by	Judg 18:28	6010
their wheat harvest in the *v*	1Sa 6:13	6010
the border that looketh to the *v*	1Sa 13:18	1516
of Amalek, and laid wait in the *v*	1Sa 15:5	5158
and pitched by the *v* of Elah	1Sa 17:2	6010
there was a *v* between them	1Sa 17:3	1516
of Israel, were in the *v* of Elah	1Sa 17:19	6010
until thou come to the *v*	1Sa 17:52	1516
thou slewest in the *v* of Elah	1Sa 21:9	6010
were on the other side of the *v*	1Sa 31:7	6010
themselves in the *v* of Rephaim	2Sa 5:18	6010
themselves in the *v* of Rephaim	2Sa 5:22	6010

of the Syrians in the *v* of salt 2Sa 8:13   1516
pitched in the *v* of Rephaim 2Sa 23:13   6010
some mountain, or into some *v* 2Kin 2:16   1516
Make this *v* full of ditches 2Kin 3:16   5158
yet that *v* shall be filled with 2Kin 3:17   5158
in the *v* of salt ten thousand 2Kin 14:7   1516
which is in the *v* of the children............2Kin 23:10   1516
the father of the *v* of Charashim............1Chr 4:14   1516
even unto the east side of the *v* 1Chr 4:39   1516
were in the *v* saw that they fled............1Chr 10:7   6010
encamped in the *v* of Rephaim 1Chr 11:15   6010
themselves in the *v* of Rephaim 1Chr 14:9   6010
spread themselves abroad in the *v* 1Chr 14:13   6010
the *v* of salt eighteen thousand 1Chr 18:12   1516
in the *v* of Zephathah at Mareshah........2Chr 14:10   1516
themselves in the *v* of Berachah............2Chr 20:26   6010
The *v* of Berachah, unto this day............2Chr 20:26   6010
people, and went to the *v* of salt 2Chr 25:11   1516
the corner gate, and at the *v* gate 2Chr 26:9   1516
in the *v* of the son of Hinnom 2Chr 28:3   1516
in the *v* of the son of Hinnom 2Chr 33:6   1516
the west side of Gihon, in the *v* 2Chr 33:14   5158
came to fight in the *v* of Megiddo 2Chr 35:22   1237
out by night by the gate of the *v* ....Neh 2:13   1516
and entered by the gate of the *v* ....Neh 2:15   1516
The *v* gate repaired Hanun, and the ......Neh 3:13   1516
Beer-sheba unto the *v* of Hinnom ....Neh 11:30   1516
Lod, and Ono, the *v* of craftsmen ....Neh 11:35   1516
The clods of the *v* shall be sweet ....Job 21:33   5158
He paweth in the *v*, and rejoiceth ....Job 39:21   6010
the *v* of the shadow of death ....Ps 23:4   1516
smote of Edom in the *v* of salt ....Ps 60:*t*   1516
and mete out the *v* of Succoth ....Ps 60:6   6010
the *v* of Baca make it a well ....Ps 84:6   6010
and mete out the *v* of Succoth ....Ps 108:7   6010
ravens of the *v* shall pick it out..............Prov 30:17   5158
nuts to see the fruits of the *v* ....Song 6:11   5158
ears in the *v* of Rephaim ....Is 17:5   6010
The burden of the *v* of vision..................Is 22:1   1516
God of hosts in the *v* of vision ....Is 22:5   1516
which is on the head of the fat *v*............Is 28:4   1516
be wroth as in the *v* of Gibeon ....Is 28:21   6010
Every *v* shall be exalted, and ....Is 40:4   1516
As a beast goeth down into the *v* ....Is 63:14   1237
the *v* of Achor a place for the................Is 65:10   6010
see thy way in the *v*, know what ....Jer 2:23   1516
which is in the *v* of the son of ....Jer 7:31   1516
nor the *v* of the son of Hinnom,............Jer 7:32   1516
of Hinnom, but the *v* of slaughter ....Jer 7:32   1516
go forth unto the *v* of the son of ....Jer 19:2   1516
nor The *v* of the son of Hinnom,............Jer 19:6   1516
of Hinnom, but The *v* of slaughter ....Jer 19:6   1516
thee, O inhabitant of the *v* ....Jer 21:13   6010
the whole *v* of the dead bodies,..............Jer 31:40   6010
which are in the *v* of the son of ....Jer 32:35   1516
and in the cities of the *v* ....Jer 32:44   8219
off with the remnant of their *v* ....Jer 47:5   6010
the *v* also shall perish, and the..............Jer 48:8   6010
in the valleys, thy flowing *v*..................Jer 49:4   6010
of the *v* which was full of bones ....Eze 37:1   1237
were very many in the open *v* ....Eze 37:2   1237
the *v* of the passengers on the ....Eze 39:11   1516
shall call it The *v* of Hamon-gog ....Eze 39:11   1516
buried it in the *v* of Hamon-gog ....Eze 39:15   1516
bow of Israel in the *v* of Jezreel............Hos 1:5   6010
the *v* of Achor for a door of hope ....Hos 2:15   6010
down into the *v* of Jehoshaphat ....Joel 3:2   6010
come up to the *v* of Jehoshaphat ....Joel 3:12   6010
multitudes in the *v* of decision ....Joel 3:14   6010
Lord is near in the *v* of decision............Joel 3:14   6010
and shall water the *v* of Shittim ....Joel 3:18   5158
the stones thereof into the *v* ....Mic 1:6   1516
Hadadrimmon in the *v* of Megiddon........Zec 12:11   1237
and there shall be a very great *v*............Zec 14:4   1516
flee to the *v* of the mountains ....Zec 14:5   1516
for the *v* of the mountains shall ....Zec 14:5   1516
Every *v* shall be filled, and every............Lk 3:5   5327

VALLEYS

As the *v* are they spread forth, ...Num 24:6   5158
and depths that spring out of *v* ....Deut 8:7   1237
it, is a land of hills and *v* ....Deut 11:11   1237
Jordan, in the hills, and in the *v* ....Josh 9:1   8219
In the mountains, and in the *v*..............Josh 12:8   8219
hills, but he is not God of the *v* 1Kin 20:28   6010
put to flight all them of the *v* 1Chr 12:15   6010
v was Shaphat the son of Adlai 1Chr 27:29   6010
To dwell in the cliffs of the *v* ....Job 30:6   5158
will he harrow the *v* after thee..............Job 39:10   6010
the *v* also are covered over with............Ps 65:13   6010
they go down by the *v* unto the..............Ps 104:8   1237

He sendeth the springs into the *v* ....Ps 104:10   5158
of Sharon, and the lily of the *v*..............Song 2:1   6010
all of them in the desolate *v* ....Is 7:19   5158
that thy choicest *v* shall be full..............Is 22:7   6010
are on the head of the fat *v* of..............Is 28:1   1516
fountains in the midst of the *v* ....Is 41:18   1237
slaying the children in the *v* ....Is 57:5   5158
Wherefore gloriest thou in the *v* ....Jer 49:4   6010
hills, to the rivers, and to the *v* ....Eze 6:3   1516
the mountains like doves of the *v* ....Eze 7:16   1516
in all the *v* his branches are ....Eze 31:12   1516
fill the *v* with thy height ....Eze 32:5   1516
in thy hills, and in thy *v* ....Eze 35:8   1516
hills, to the rivers, and to the *v* ....Eze 36:4   1516
hills, to the rivers, and to the *v* ....Eze 36:6   1516
the *v* shall be cleft, as wax ....Mic 1:4   6010

VALOUR

armed, all the mighty men of *v*................Josh 1:14   2428
thereof, and the mighty men of *v* ....Josh 6:2   2428
thirty thousand mighty men of *v* ....Josh 8:3   2428
him, and all the mighty men of *v* ....Josh 10:7   2428
men, all lusty, and all men of *v* ....Judg 3:29   2428
with thee, thou mighty man of *v* ....Judg 6:12   2428
Gileadite was a mighty man of *v*............Judg 11:1   2428
men from their coasts, men of *v* ....Judg 18:2   2428
all these were men of *v* ....Judg 20:44   2428
all these were men of *v* ....Judg 20:46   2428
Jeroboam was a mighty man of *v*............1Kin 11:28   2428
he was also a mighty man in *v*................2Kin 5:1   2428
and all the mighty men of *v* 2Kin 24:14   2428
and Jahdiel, mighty men of *v* 1Chr 5:24   2428
of their fathers, mighty men of *v* 1Chr 7:7   2428
of their fathers, mighty men of *v* 1Chr 7:9   2428
of their fathers, mighty men of *v* 1Chr 7:11   2428
house, choice and mighty men of *v* 1Chr 7:40   2428
sons of Ulam were mighty men of *v* 1Chr 8:40   2428
for they were all mighty men of *v* 1Chr 12:21   2428
mighty men of *v* for the war 1Chr 12:25   2428
And Zadok, a young man mighty of *v*......1Chr 12:28   2428
and eight hundred, mighty men of *v* 1Chr 12:30   2428
for they were mighty men of *v* 1Chr 26:6   2428
and his brethren, men of *v* 1Chr 26:30   2428
men of *v* at Jazer of Gilead 1Chr 26:31   2428
And his brethren, men of *v* 1Chr 26:32   2428
chosen men, being mighty men of *v* 2Chr 13:3   2428
all these were mighty men of *v* 2Chr 14:8   2428
the men of war, mighty men of *v* 2Chr 17:13   2428
men of *v* three hundred thousand 2Chr 17:14   2428
hundred thousand mighty men of *v* 2Chr 17:16   2428
Eliada a mighty man of *v*, and with 2Chr 17:17   2428
of *v* out of Israel for an hundred............2Chr 25:6   2428
mighty men of *v* were two thousand 2Chr 26:12   2428
cut off all the mighty men of *v*................2Chr 32:21   2428
their brethren, mighty men of *v*..............Neh 11:14   2428

VALUE

priest, and the priest shall *v* him............Lev 27:8   6186
that vowed shall the priest *v* him ....Lev 27:8   6186
And the priest shall *v* it, whether ....Lev 27:12   6186
ye are all physicians of no *v*..................Job 13:4   457
ye are of more *v* than many ....Mt 10:31   *1308*
of the children of Israel did *v* ....Mt 27:9   *5091*
ye are of more *v* than many ....Lk 12:7   *1308*

VALUED

be *v* at fifty shekels of silver ....Lev 27:16   5541
It cannot be *v* with the gold of ....Job 28:16   5541
shall it be *v* with pure gold......................Job 28:19   5541
the price of him that was *v* ....Mt 27:9   *5091*

VALUEST

as thou *v* it, who art the priest,..............Lev 27:12   6187

VANIAH (*va-ni'-ah*) *Married a foreigner in exile.*
V, Meremoth, Eliashib,............................Ezr 10:36   2057

VANISH

What time they wax warm, they *v* ....Job 6:17   6789
heavens shall *v* away like smoke ....Is 51:6   4414
be knowledge, it shall *v* away 1Cor 13:8   2673
and waxeth old is ready to *v* away ....Heb 8:13   854

VANISHED

is their wisdom *v*....................................Jer 49:7   5628
and he *v* out of their sight ....Lk 24:31   *1096,855*

VANISHETH

the cloud is consumed and *v* away ....Job 7:9   3212
for a little time, and then *v* away ....Jas 4:14   *853*

VANITIES

provoked me to anger with their *v* ....Deut 32:21   1892
of Israel to anger with their *v* 1Kin 16:13   1892
of Israel to anger with their *v* 1Kin 16:26   1892

hated them that regard lying *v*	Ps 31:6	1892
Vanity of *v*, saith the Preacher,	Eccl 1:2	1892
saith the Preacher, vanity of *v*	Eccl 1:2	1892
words there are also divers *v*	Eccl 5:7	1892
Vanity of *v*, saith the Preacher	Eccl 12:8	1892
graven images, and with strange *v*	Jer 8:19	1892
the stock is a doctrine of *v*	Jer 10:8	1892
Are there any among the *v* of the	Jer 14:22	1892
lying *v* forsake their own mercy	Jonah 2:8	1892
from these *v* unto the living God	Acts 14:15	3152

VANITY

and they followed *v*, and became	2Kin 17:15	1892
am I made to possess months of *v*	Job 7:3	7723
for my days are *v*	Job 7:16	1892
him that is deceived trust in *v*	Job 15:31	7723
for *v* shall be his recompence	Job 15:31	7723
mischief, and bring forth *v*	Job 15:35	205
If I have walked with *v*, or if my	Job 31:5	7723
Surely God will not hear *v*	Job 35:13	7723
how long will ye love *v*, and seek	Ps 4:2	7385
under his tongue is mischief and *v*	Ps 10:7	205
They speak *v* every one with his	Ps 12:2	7723
not lifted up his soul unto *v*	Ps 24:4	7723
at his best state is altogether *v*	Ps 39:5	1892
surely every man is *v*	Ps 39:11	1892
he come to see me, he speaketh *v*	Ps 41:6	7723
Surely men of low degree are *v*	Ps 62:9	1892
are altogether lighter than *v*	Ps 62:9	1892
their days did he consume in *v*	Ps 78:33	1892
thoughts of man, that they are *v*	Ps 94:11	1892
away mine eyes from beholding *v*	Ps 119:37	7723
Man is like to *v*	Ps 144:4	1892
Whose mouth speaketh *v*, and their	Ps 144:8	7723
children, whose mouth speaketh *v*	Ps 144:11	7723
Wealth gotten by *v* shall be	Prov 13:11	1892
a lying tongue is a *v* tossed to	Prov 21:6	1892
that soweth iniquity shall reap *v*	Prov 22:8	205
Remove far from me *v* and lies	Prov 30:8	7723
V of vanities, saith the Preacher	Eccl 1:2	1892
saith the Preacher, *v* of vanities	Eccl 1:2	1892
all is *v*.	Eccl 1:2	1892
and, behold, all is *v* and vexation	Eccl 1:14	1892
and, behold, this also is *v*	Eccl 2:1	1892
and, behold, all was *v* and vexation	Eccl 2:11	1892
in my heart, that this also is *v*	Eccl 2:15	1892
for all is *v* and vexation of	Eccl 2:17	1892
This is also *v*	Eccl 2:19	1892
This also is *v* and a great evil	Eccl 2:21	1892
This is also *v*	Eccl 2:23	1892
This also is *v* and vexation of	Eccl 2:26	1892
for all is *v*.	Eccl 3:19	1892
This is also *v* and vexation of	Eccl 4:4	1892
and I saw *v* under the sun	Eccl 4:7	1892
This is also *v*, yea, it is a sore	Eccl 4:8	1892
Surely this also is *v* and vexation	Eccl 4:16	1892
this is also *v*	Eccl 5:10	1892
this is *v*, and it is an evil	Eccl 6:2	1892
For he cometh in with *v*, and	Eccl 6:4	1892
this is also *v* and vexation of	Eccl 6:9	1892
be many things that increase *v*	Eccl 6:11	1892
this also is *v*	Eccl 7:6	1892
have I seen in the days of my *v*	Eccl 7:15	1892
this is also *v*	Eccl 8:10	1892
There is a *v* which is done upon	Eccl 8:14	1892
I said that this also is *v*	Eccl 8:14	1892
all the days of the life of thy *v*	Eccl 9:9	1892
the sun, all the days of thy *v*	Eccl 9:9	1892
All that cometh is *v*.	Eccl 11:8	1892
for childhood and youth are *v*	Eccl 11:10	1892
V of vanities, saith the preacher	Eccl 12:8	1892
all is *v*.	Eccl 12:8	1892
draw iniquity with cords of *v*	Is 5:18	7723
the nations with the sieve of *v*	Is 30:28	7723
to him less than nothing, and *v*	Is 40:17	8414
the judges of the earth as *v*	Is 40:23	8414
Behold, they are all *v*	Is 41:29	205
a graven image are all of them *v*	Is 44:9	8414
v shall take them	Is 57:13	1892
of the finger, and speaking *v*	Is 58:9	205
they trust in *v*, and speak lies	Is 59:4	8414
from me, and have walked after *v*	Jer 2:5	1892
They are *v*, and the work of errors	Jer 10:15	1892
fathers have inherited lies, *v*	Jer 16:19	1892
me, they have burned incense to *v*	Jer 18:15	7723
They are *v*, the work of errors	Jer 51:18	1892
They have seen *v* and lying	Eze 13:6	7723
Because ye have spoken *v*, and seen	Eze 13:8	7723
be upon the prophets that see *v*	Eze 13:9	7723
Therefore ye shall see no more *v*	Eze 13:23	7723
Whiles they see *v* unto thee	Eze 21:29	7723

with untempered morter, seeing *v*	Eze 22:28	7723
surely they are *v*	Hos 12:11	7723
shall weary themselves for very *v*	Hab 2:13	7385
For the idols have spoken *v*	Zec 10:2	205
creature was made subject to *v*	Rom 8:20	3153
walk, in the *v* of their mind,	Eph 4:17	3153
speak great swelling words of *v*	2Pet 2:18	3153

VAPORS

he causeth the *v* to ascend from	Jer 10:13	5387
he causeth the *v* to ascend from	Jer 51:16	5387

VAPOUR

rain according to the *v* thereof	Job 36:27	108
the cattle also concerning the *v*	Job 36:33	5927
blood, and fire, and *v* of smoke	Acts 2:19	822
It is even a *v*, that appeareth	Jas 4:14	822

VAPOURS

He causeth the *v* to ascend from	Ps 135:7	5387
and hail; snow, and *v*	Ps 148:8	7008

VARIABLENESS

of lights, with whom is no *v*	Jas 1:17	3883

VARIANCE

set a man at *v* against his father	Mt 10:35	1369
Idolatry, witchcraft, hatred, *v*	Gal 5:20	2054

VASHNI (*vash'-ni*) *A son of Samuel.*

the firstborn *V*, and Abiah	1Chr 6:28	2059

VASHTI (*vash'-ti*) *A Persian queen, succeeded by Esther.*

Also *V* the queen made a feast for	Est 1:9	2060
To bring *V* the queen before the	Est 1:11	2060
But the queen *V* refused to come	Est 1:12	2060
unto the queen *V* according to law	Est 1:15	2060
V the queen hath not done wrong	Est 1:16	2060
V the queen to be brought in	Est 1:17	2060
That *V* come no more before king	Est 1:19	2060
was appeased, he remembered *V*	Est 2:1	2060
the king be queen instead of *V*	Est 2:4	2060
and made her queen instead of *V*	Est 2:17	2060

VAUNT

lest Israel *v* themselves against	Judg 7:2	6286

VAUNTETH

charity *v* not itself, is not	1Cor 13:4	4068

VEDAN See Dan.

VEHEMENT

fire, which hath a most *v* flame	Song 8:6	3050
that God prepared a *v* east wind	Jonah 4:8	2759
what *v* desire, yea, what zeal,	2Cor 7:11	1972

VEHEMENTLY

But he spake the more *v*, If I	Mk 14:31	1722,4053
the stream beat *v* upon that house	Lk 6:48	4366
which the stream did beat *v*	Lk 6:49	4366
the Pharisees began to urge him *v*	Lk 11:53	1171
and scribes stood and *v* accused him	Lk 23:10	2159

VEIL

the walls took away my *v* from me	Song 5:7	7289
the *v* of the temple was rent in	Mt 27:51	2665
the *v* of the temple was rent in	Mk 15:38	2665
the *v* of the temple was rent in	Lk 23:45	2665
entereth into that within the *v*	Heb 6:19	2665
And after the second *v*, the	Heb 9:3	2665
consecrated for us, through the *v*	Heb 10:20	2665

VEIN

there is a *v* for the silver	Job 28:1	4161

VENGEANCE

v shall be taken on him sevenfold	Gen 4:15	5358
To me belongeth *v*, and recompence	Deut 32:35	5359
I will render *v* to mine enemies	Deut 32:41	5359
will render *v* to his adversaries,	Deut 32:43	5359
as the Lord hath taken *v* for thee	Judg 11:36	5360
shall rejoice when he seeth the *v*	Ps 58:10	5359
O LORD God, to whom *v* belongeth	Ps 94:1	5360
to whom *v* belongeth, shew thyself	Ps 94:1	5360
tookest *v* of their inventions	Ps 99:8	5358
To execute *v* upon the heathen, and	Ps 149:7	5360
he will not spare in the day of *v*	Prov 6:34	5359
For it is the day of the LORD's *v*	Is 34:8	5359
behold, your God will come with *v*	Is 35:4	5359
I will take *v*, and I will not meet	Is 47:3	5359
on the garments of *v* for clothing	Is 59:17	5359
LORD, and the day of *v* of our God	Is 61:2	5359
For the day of *v* is in mine heart	Is 63:4	5359
heart, let me see thy *v* on them	Jer 11:20	5360
heart, let me see thy *v* on them	Jer 20:12	5360
the Lord God of hosts, a day of *v*	Jer 46:10	5360
for it is the *v* of the LORD	Jer 50:15	5360
take *v* upon her	Jer 50:15	5358

in Zion the *v* of the LORD our God	Jer 50:28	5360
LORD our God, the *v* of his temple	Jer 50:28	5360
this is the time of the LORD's *v*	Jer 51:6	5360
because it is the *v* of the LORD	Jer 51:11	5360
of the LORD, the *v* of his temple	Jer 51:11	5360
thy cause, and take *v* for thee	Jer 51:36	5360
Thou hast seen all their *v*	Lam 3:60	5360
cause fury to come up to take *v*	Eze 24:8	5359
the house of Judah by taking *v*	Eze 25:12	5359
I will lay my *v* upon Edom by the	Eze 25:14	5360
and they shall know my *v*, saith	Eze 25:14	5360
have taken *v* with a despiteful	Eze 25:15	5359
I will execute great *v* upon them	Eze 25:17	5360
when I shall lay my *v* upon them	Eze 25:17	5360
And I will execute *v* in anger	Mic 5:15	5359
will take *v* on his adversaries	Nah 1:2	5358
For these be the days of *v*	Lk 21:22	1557
yet *v* suffereth not to live	Acts 28:4	1349
Is God unrighteous who taketh *v*	Rom 3:5	3709
for it is written, *V* is mine	Rom 12:19	1557
In flaming fire taking *v* on them	2Th 1:8	1557
V belongeth unto me, I will	Heb 10:30	1557
suffering the *v* of eternal fire	Jude 7	1349

VENISON

Esau, because he did eat of his *v*	Gen 25:28	6718
to the field, and take me some *v*	Gen 27:3	6720
went to the field to hunt for *v*	Gen 27:5	6718
Bring me *v*, and make me savoury	Gen 27:7	6718
I pray thee, sit and eat of my *v*	Gen 27:19	6718
me, and I will eat of my son's *v*	Gen 27:25	6718
arise, and eat of his son's *v*	Gen 27:31	6718
where is he that hath taken *v*	Gen 27:33	6718

VENOM

dragons, and the cruel *v* of asps	Deut 32:33	7219

VENOMOUS

saw the *v* beast hang on his hand	Acts 28:4	

VENT

belly is as wine which hath no *v*	Job 32:19	6605

VENTURE

a certain man drew a bow at a *v*	1Kin 22:34	8537
a certain man drew a bow at a *v*	2Chr 18:33	8537

VERIFIED

so shall your words be *v*, and ye	Gen 42:20	539
let thy word, I pray thee, be *v*	1Kin 8:26	539
God of Israel, let thy word be *v*	2Chr 6:17	539

VERILY

We are *v* guilty concerning our	Gen 42:21	61
V my sabbaths ye shall keep	Ex 31:13	389
I *v* thought that thou hadst	Judg 15:2	559
V our lord king David hath made	1Kin 1:43	61
V she hath no child, and her	2Kin 4:14	61
but I will *v* buy it for the full	1Chr 21:24	7069
are *v* estranged from me	Job 19:13	389
the land, and thou shalt be fed	Ps 37:3	530
v every man at his best state is	Ps 39:5	389
V there is a reward for the	Ps 58:11	389
v he is a God that judgeth in the	Ps 58:11	389
But *v* God hath heard me	Ps 66:19	403
V I have cleansed my heart in	Ps 73:13	389
V thou art a God that hidest	Is 45:15	403
V it shall be well with thy	Jer 15:11	518,3808
v I will cause the enemy to	Jer 15:11	518
For *v* I say unto you, Till heaven	Mt 5:18	281
V I say unto thee, Thou shalt by	Mt 5:26	281
V I say unto you, They have their	Mt 6:2	281
V I say unto you, They have their	Mt 6:5	281
V I say unto you, They have their	Mt 6:16	281
V I say unto you, I have not	Mt 8:10	281
V I say unto you, It shall be	Mt 10:15	281
for *v* I say unto you, Ye shall	Mt 10:23	281
v I say unto you, he shall in no	Mt 10:42	281
V I say unto you, Among them that	Mt 11:11	281
For *v* I say unto you, That many	Mt 13:17	281
V I say unto you, There be some	Mt 16:28	281
for *v* I say unto you, If ye have	Mt 17:20	281
V I say unto you, Except ye be	Mt 18:3	281
v I say unto you, he rejoiceth	Mt 18:13	281
V I say unto you, Whatsoever ye	Mt 18:18	281
V I say unto you, That a rich man	Mt 19:23	281
V I say unto you, That ye which	Mt 19:28	281
V I say unto you, If ye have	Mt 21:21	281
V I say unto you, That the	Mt 21:31	281
V I say unto you, All these	Mt 23:36	281
v I say unto you, There shall not	Mt 24:2	281
V I say unto you, This generation	Mt 24:34	281
V I say unto you, That he shall	Mt 24:47	281
V I say unto you, I know you not	Mt 25:12	281

V I say unto you, Inasmuch as ye	Mt 25:40	281
V I say unto you, Inasmuch as ye	Mt 25:45	281
V I say unto you, Wheresoever	Mt 26:13	281
V I say unto you, that one of you	Mt 26:21	281
V I say unto thee, That this	Mt 26:34	281
V I say unto you, All sins shall	Mk 3:28	281
V I say unto you, It shall be	Mk 6:11	281
v I say unto you, There shall no	Mk 8:12	281
V I say unto you, That there be	Mk 9:1	281
them, Elias *v* cometh first, and	Mk 9:12	3303
v I say unto you, he shall not	Mk 9:41	281
V I say unto you, Whosoever shall	Mk 10:15	281
V I say unto you, There is no man	Mk 10:29	281
For *v* I say unto you, That	Mk 11:23	281
V I say unto you, That this poor	Mk 12:43	281
V I say unto you, that this	Mk 13:30	281
V I say unto you, Wheresoever	Mk 14:9	281
V I say unto you, One of you	Mk 14:18	281
V I say unto you, I will drink no	Mk 14:25	281
V I say unto thee, That this day,	Mk 14:30	281
V I say unto you, No prophet is	Lk 4:24	281
v I say unto you, It shall be	Lk 11:51	3483
v I say unto you, that he shall	Lk 12:37	281
v I say unto you, Ye shall not	Lk 13:35	281
V I say unto you, Whosoever shall	Lk 18:17	281
V I say unto you, There is no man	Lk 18:29	281
V I say unto you, This generation	Lk 21:32	281
V I say unto thee, To day shalt	Lk 23:43	281
And he saith unto him, *V*, *v*,	Jn 1:51	281
and said unto him, *V*, *v*	Jn 3:3	281
Jesus answered, *V*, *v*	Jn 3:5	281
V, *v*, I say unto thee, We	Jn 3:11	281
and said unto them, *V*, *v*	Jn 5:19	281
V, *v*, I say unto you, He	Jn 5:24	281
V, *v*, I say unto you, The	Jn 5:25	281
answered them and said, *V*, *v*	Jn 6:26	281
Jesus said unto them, *V*, *v*	Jn 6:32	281
V, *v*, I say unto you, He	Jn 6:47	281
Jesus said unto them, *V*, *v*	Jn 6:53	281
Jesus answered them, *V*, *v*	Jn 8:34	281
V, *v*, I say unto you, If a	Jn 8:51	281
Jesus said unto them, *V*, *v*	Jn 8:58	281
V, *v*, I say unto you, He	Jn 10:1	281
Jesus unto them again, *V*, *v*	Jn 10:7	281
V, *v*, I say unto you, Except	Jn 12:24	281
V, *v*, I say unto you, The	Jn 13:16	281
V, *v*, I say unto you, He	Jn 13:20	281
and testified, and said, *V*, *v*	Jn 13:21	281
V, *v*, I say unto thee, The	Jn 13:38	281
V, *v*, I say unto you, He	Jn 14:12	281
V, *v*, I say unto you, That	Jn 16:20	281
V, *v*, I say unto you,	Jn 16:23	281
V, *v*, I say unto you, When	Jn 21:18	281
nay *v*; but let them	Acts 16:37	1063
John *v* baptized with the baptism	Acts 19:4	3303
I am a man which am a Jew, born	Acts 22:3	3303
I *v* thought with myself, that I	Acts 26:9	3303,3767
For circumcision *v* profiteth	Rom 2:25	3303
Yes *v*, their sound went into all	Rom 10:18	3304
It hath pleased them *v*	Rom 15:27	1063
For I *v*, as absent in body, but	1Cor 5:3	3303
V that, when I preach the gospel,	1Cor 9:18	
For thou *v* givest thanks well,	1Cor 14:17	3303
v righteousness should have been	Gal 3:21	3689
For *v*, when we were with you, we	1Th 3:4	2532
For *v* he took not on him the	Heb 2:16	1222
Moses *v* was faithful in all his	Heb 3:5	3303
For men *v* swear by the greater	Heb 6:16	3303
v they that are of the sons of	Heb 7:5	3303
For there is *v* a disannulling of	Heb 7:18	3303
Then *v* the first covenant had	Heb 9:1	3303
For they *v* for a few days	Heb 12:10	3303
Who *v* was foreordained before the	1Pet 1:20	3303
in him *v* is the love of God	1Jn 2:5	230

VERITY

The works of his hands are *v*	Ps 111:7	571
of the Gentiles in faith and *v*	1Ti 2:7	225

VERMILION

with cedar, and painted with *v*	Jer 22:14	8350
the Chaldeans pourtrayed with *v*	Eze 23:14	8350

VERY See APPENDIX.

VESSEL

But the earthen *v* wherein it is	Lev 6:28	3627
whether it be any *v* of wood	Lev 11:32	3627
skin, or sack, whatsoever *v* it be	Lev 11:32	3627
And every earthen *v*, whereinto any	Lev 11:33	3627
in every such *v* shall be unclean	Lev 11:34	3627
an earthen *v* over running water	Lev 14:5	3627
an earthen *v* over running water	Lev 14:50	3627

the *v* of earth, that he toucheth	Lev 15:12	3627
every *v* of wood shall be rinsed	Lev 15:12	3627
take holy water in an earthen *v*	Num 5:17	3627
And every open *v*, which hath no	Num 19:15	3627
water shall be put thereto in a *v*	Num 19:17	3627
thou shalt not put any in thy *v*	Deut 23:24	3627
were sanctified this day in the *v*	1Sa 21:5	3627
pray thee, a little water in a *v*	1Kin 17:10	3627
unto her son, Bring me yet a *v*	2Kin 4:6	3627
unto her, There is not a *v* more	2Kin 4:6	3627
them in pieces like a potter's *v*	Ps 2:9	3627
I am like a broken *v*	Ps 31:12	3627
come forth a *v* for the finer	Prov 25:4	3627
v that is broken in pieces	Is 30:14	5035
v into the house of the LORD	Is 66:20	3627
the *v* that he made of clay was	Jer 18:4	3627
so he made it again another *v*	Jer 18:4	3627
as one breaketh a potter's *v*	Jer 19:11	3627
is he a *v* wherein is no pleasure	Jer 22:28	3627
ye shall fall like a pleasant *v*	Jer 25:34	3627
and put them in an earthen *v*	Jer 32:14	3627
not been emptied from *v* to *v*	Jer 48:11	3627
like a *v* wherein is no pleasure	Jer 48:38	3627
me, he hath made me an empty *v*	Jer 51:34	3627
and fitches, and put them in one *v*	Eze 4:9	3627
a pin of it to hang any *v* thereon	Eze 15:3	3627
as a *v* wherein is no pleasure	Hos 8:8	3627
carry any *v* through the temple	Mk 11:16	4632
a candle, covereth it with a *v*	Lk 8:16	4632
there was set a *v* full of vinegar	Jn 19:29	4632
for he is a chosen *v* unto me	Acts 9:15	4632
a certain *v* descending unto him,	Acts 10:11	4632
the *v* was received up again into	Acts 10:16	4632
saw a vision, A certain *v* descend	Acts 11:5	4632
lump to make one *v* unto honour	Rom 9:21	4632
possess his *v* in sanctification	1Th 4:4	4632
he shall be a *v* unto honour	2Ti 2:21	4632
the wife, as unto the weaker *v*	1Pet 3:7	4632

VESSELS

best fruits in the land in your *v*	Gen 43:11	3627
v of wood, and in *v* of stone	Ex 7:19	3627
he make it, with all these *v*	Ex 25:39	3627
all the *v* thereof thou shalt make	Ex 27:3	3627
All the *v* of the tabernacle in	Ex 27:19	3627
And the table and all his *v*	Ex 30:27	3627
and the candlestick and his *v*	Ex 30:27	3627
of burnt offering with all his *v*	Ex 30:28	3627
and his staves, and all his *v*	Ex 35:13	3627
grate, his staves, and all his *v*	Ex 35:16	3627
he made the *v* which were upon the	Ex 37:16	3627
made he it, and all the *v* thereof	Ex 37:24	3627
And he made all the *v* of the altar	Ex 38:3	3627
all the *v* thereof made he of	Ex 38:3	3627
it, and all the *v* of the altar,	Ex 38:30	3627
The table, and all the *v* thereof	Ex 39:36	3627
in order, and all the *v* thereof	Ex 39:37	3627
brass, his staves, and all his *v*	Ex 39:39	3627
all the *v* of the service of the	Ex 39:40	3627
hallow it, and all the *v* thereof	Ex 40:9	3627
the burnt offering, and all his *v*	Ex 40:10	3627
anointed the altar and all his *v*	Lev 8:11	3627
and over all the *v* thereof	Num 1:50	3627
tabernacle, and all the *v* thereof	Num 1:50	3627
the *v* of the sanctuary wherewith	Num 3:31	3627
thereof, and all the *v* thereof	Num 3:36	3627
and all the oil *v* thereof	Num 4:9	3627
all the *v* thereof within a	Num 4:10	3627
put upon it all the *v* thereof	Num 4:14	3627
basons, all the *v* of the altar	Num 4:14	3627
all the *v* of the sanctuary, as	Num 4:15	3627
sanctuary, and in the *v* thereof	Num 4:16	3627
the altar and all the *v* thereof	Num 7:1	3627
all the silver *v* weighed two	Num 7:85	3627
come nigh the *v* of the sanctuary	Num 18:3	3627
upon the tent, and upon all the *v*	Num 19:18	3627
gold, and *v* of brass and iron, are	Josh 6:19	3627
the *v* of brass and of iron, they	Josh 6:24	3627
thou art athirst, go unto the *v*	Ruth 2:9	3627
for the bread is spent in our *v*	1Sa 9:7	3627
the *v* of the young men are holy,	1Sa 21:5	3627
brought with him *v* of silver	2Sa 8:10	3627
and *v* of gold, and *v* of brass	2Sa 8:10	3627
beds, and basons, and earthen *v*	2Sa 17:28	3627
and all these *v*, which Hiram made	1Kin 7:45	3627
Solomon left all the *v* unweighed	1Kin 7:47	3627
Solomon made all the *v* that	1Kin 7:48	3627
the silver, and the gold, and the *v*	1Kin 7:51	3627
all the holy *v* that were in the	1Kin 8:4	3627
Solomon's drinking *v* were of gold	1Kin 10:21	3627
all the *v* of the house of the	1Kin 10:21	3627

v of silver, and *v* of gold,	1Kin 10:25	3627
the LORD, silver, and gold, and *v*	1Kin 15:15	3627
borrow thee *v* abroad of all thy	2Kin 4:3	3627
all thy neighbours, even empty *v*	2Kin 4:3	3627
shalt pour out into all those *v*	2Kin 4:4	3627
sons, who brought the *v* to her	2Kin 4:5	3627
when the *v* were full, that she	2Kin 4:6	3627
the way was full of garments and *v*	2Kin 7:15	3627
any *v* of gold	2Kin 12:13	3627
or *v* of silver, of the money that	2Kin 12:13	3627
all the *v* that were found in the	2Kin 14:14	3627
all the *v* that were made for Baal	2Kin 23:4	3627
cut in pieces all the *v* of gold	2Kin 24:13	3627
all the *v* of brass wherewith they	2Kin 25:14	3627
of all these *v* was without weight	2Kin 25:16	3627
the charge of the ministering *v*	1Chr 9:28	3627
were appointed to oversee the *v*	1Chr 9:29	3627
and the pillars, and the *v* of brass	1Chr 18:8	3627
with him all manner of *v* of gold	1Chr 18:10	3627
of the LORD, and the holy *v* of God	1Chr 22:19	3627
nor any *v* of it for the service	1Chr 23:26	3627
for all the *v* of service in the	1Chr 28:13	3627
all these *v* in great abundance	2Chr 4:18	3627
Solomon made all the *v* that were	2Chr 4:19	3627
all the holy *v* that were in the	2Chr 5:5	3627
all the drinking *v* of king	2Chr 9:20	3627
all the *v* of the house of the	2Chr 9:20	3627
v of silver, and *v* of gold,	2Chr 9:24	3627
dedicated, silver, and gold, and *v*	2Chr 15:18	3627
whereof were made *v* for the house	2Chr 24:14	3627
even *v* to minister, and to offer	2Chr 24:14	3627
and spoons, and *v* of gold and silver	2Chr 24:14	3627
all the *v* that were found in the	2Chr 25:24	3627
the *v* of the house of God	2Chr 28:24	3627
cut in pieces the *v* of the house	2Chr 28:24	3627
offering, with all the *v* thereof	2Chr 29:18	3627
table, with all the *v* thereof	2Chr 29:18	3627
Moreover all the *v*, which king	2Chr 29:19	3627
also carried of the *v* of the	2Chr 36:7	3627
with the goodly *v* of the house of	2Chr 36:10	3627
all the *v* of the house of God,	2Chr 36:18	3627
all the goodly *v* thereof	2Chr 36:19	3627
their hands with *v* of silver	Ezr 1:6	3627
the *v* of the house of the LORD	Ezr 1:7	3627
and ten, and other *v* a thousand	Ezr 1:10	3627
All the *v* of gold and of silver	Ezr 1:11	3627
the *v* also of gold and silver of	Ezr 5:14	3984
And said unto him, Take these *v*	Ezr 5:15	3984
silver *v* of the house of God,	Ezr 6:5	3984
The *v* also that are given thee	Ezr 7:19	3984
the silver, and the gold, and the *v*	Ezr 8:25	3627
silver *v* an hundred talents, and	Ezr 8:26	3627
two *v* of fine copper, precious as	Ezr 8:27	3627
the *v* are holy also	Ezr 8:28	3627
the silver, and the gold, and the *v*	Ezr 8:30	3627
the *v* weighed in the house of our	Ezr 8:33	3627
where are the *v* of the sanctuary,	Neh 10:39	3627
the frankincense, and the *v*	Neh 13:5	3627
I again the *v* of the house of God	Neh 13:9	3627
they gave them drink in *v* of gold	Est 1:7	3627
(the *v* being diverse one from	Est 1:7	3627
even in *v* of bulrushes upon the	Is 18:2	3627
all *v* of small quantity, from the	Is 22:24	3627
quantity, from the *v* of cups	Is 22:24	3627
even to all the *v* of flagons	Is 22:24	3627
that bear the *v* of the LORD	Is 52:11	3627
abominable things is in their *v*	Is 65:4	3627
they returned with their *v* empty	Jer 14:3	3627
the *v* of the LORD's house shall	Jer 27:16	3627
that the *v* which are left in the	Jer 27:18	3627
of the *v* that remain in this city	Jer 27:19	3627
concerning the *v* that remain in	Jer 27:21	3627
all the *v* of the LORD's house	Jer 28:3	3627
to bring again the *v* of the	Jer 28:6	3627
and oil, and put them in your *v*	Jer 40:10	3627
to wander, and shall empty his *v*	Jer 48:12	3627
their curtains, and all their *v*	Jer 49:29	3627
all the *v* of brass wherewith they	Jer 52:18	3627
of all these *v* was without weight	Jer 52:20	3627
men and *v* of brass in thy market	Eze 27:13	3627
with part of the *v* of the house	Dan 1:2	3627
he brought the *v* into the	Dan 1:2	3627
silver *v* which his father	Dan 5:2	3984
v that were taken out of the	Dan 5:3	3984
they have brought the *v* of his	Dan 5:23	3984
with their precious *v* of silver	Dan 11:8	3627
the treasure of all pleasant *v*	Hos 13:15	3627
draw out fifty *v* out of the press	Hag 2:16	
down, and gathered the good into *v*	Mt 13:48	30
oil in their *v* with their lamps	Mt 25:4	30
of cups, and pots, brasen *v*	Mk 7:4	

with much longsuffering the *v* of	Rom 9:22	4632
of his glory on the *v* of mercy	Rom 9:23	4632
have this treasure in earthen *v*	2Cor 4:7	4632
there are not only *v* of gold	2Ti 2:20	4632
all the *v* of the ministry	Heb 9:21	4632
as the *v* of a potter shall they	Rev 2:27	4632
wood, and all manner *v* of ivory	Rev 18:12	4632
all manner *v* of most precious	Rev 18:12	4632

VESTMENTS

Bring forth *v* for all the	2Kin 10:22	3830
And he brought them forth *v*	2Kin 10:22	4403

VESTRY

said unto him that was over the *v*	2Kin 10:22	4458

VESTURE

upon the four quarters of thy *v*	Deut 22:12	3682
them, and cast lots upon my *v*	Ps 22:18	3830
as a *v* shalt thou change them, and	Ps 102:26	3830
upon my *v* did they cast lots	Mt 27:35	2441
for my *v* they did cast lots	Jn 19:24	2441
as a *v* shalt thou fold them up,	Heb 1:12	4018
clothed with a *v* dipped in blood	Rev 19:13	2440
And he hath on his *v* and on his	Rev 19:16	2440

VESTURES

and arrayed him in *v* of fine linen	Gen 41:42	899

VEX

Thou shalt neither *v* a stranger	Ex 22:21	3238
sister, to *v* her, to uncover her	Lev 18:18	6887
in your land, ye shall not *v* him	Lev 19:33	3238
V the Midianites, and smite them	Num 25:17	6887
For they *v* you with their wiles	Num 25:18	6887
shall *v* you in the land wherein	Num 33:55	6887
how will he then *v* himself	2Sa 12:18	6213,7451
for God did *v* them with all	2Chr 15:6	2000
How long will ye *v* my soul	Job 19:2	3013
v them in his sore displeasure	Ps 2:5	926
v it, and let us make a breach	Is 7:6	6973
and Judah shall not *v* Ephraim	Is 11:13	6887
I will also *v* the hearts of many	Eze 32:9	3707
thee, and awake that shall *v* thee	Hab 2:7	2111
hands to *v* certain of the church	Acts 12:1	2559

VEXATION

shall send upon thee cursing, *v*	Deut 28:20	4103
all is vanity and *v* of spirit	Eccl 1:14	7469
that this also is *v* of spirit	Eccl 1:17	7475
v of spirit, and there was no	Eccl 2:11	7469
for all is vanity and *v* of spirit	Eccl 2:17	7469
of the *v* of his heart, wherein he	Eccl 2:22	7475
also is vanity and *v* of spirit	Eccl 2:26	7469
is also vanity and *v* of spirit	Eccl 4:4	7469
full with travail and *v* of spirit	Eccl 4:6	7469
also is vanity and *v* of spirit	Eccl 4:16	7475
is also vanity and *v* of spirit	Eccl 6:9	7469
shall not be such as was in her *v*	Is 9:1	4164
and it shall be a *v* only to	Is 28:19	2113
and shall howl for *v* of spirit	Is 65:14	7667

VEXATIONS

but great *v* were upon all the	2Chr 15:5	4103

VEXED

and the Egyptians *v* us, and our	Num 20:15	7489
that oppressed them and *v* them	Judg 2:18	1766
And that year they *v* and oppressed	Judg 10:8	7492
so that his soul was *v* unto death	Judg 16:16	7114
he turned himself, he *v* them	1Sa 14:47	7561
And Amnon was so *v*, that he fell	2Sa 13:2	3334
for her soul is *v* within her	2Kin 4:27	4843
hand of their enemies, who *v* them	Neh 9:27	6887
the Almighty, who hath *v* my soul	Job 27:2	4843
for my bones are *v*	Ps 6:2	926
My soul is also sore *v*	Ps 6:3	926
mine enemies be ashamed and sore *v*	Ps 6:10	926
rebelled, and *v* his holy Spirit	Is 63:10	6087
which art infamous and much *v*	Eze 22:5	4103
thee have they *v* the fatherless	Eze 22:7	3238
and have *v* the poor and needy	Eze 22:29	3238
is grievously *v* with a devil	Mt 15:22	1139
for he is lunatick, and sore *v*	Mt 17:15	3958
they that were *v* with unclean	Lk 6:18	3791
them which were *v* with unclean	Acts 5:16	3791
v with the filthy conversation of	2Pet 2:7	2669
v his righteous soul from day to	2Pet 2:8	928

VIAL

Then Samuel took a *v* of oil	1Sa 10:1	6378
poured out his *v* upon the earth	Rev 16:2	5357
poured out his *v* upon the sea	Rev 16:3	5357
poured out his *v* upon the rivers	Rev 16:4	5357
poured out his *v* upon the sun	Rev 16:8	5357

his *v* upon the seat of the beast	Rev 16:10	5357
v upon the great river Euphrates	Rev 16:12	5357
poured out his *v* into the air	Rev 16:17	5357

VIALS

golden *v* full of odours, which	Rev 5:8	5357
golden *v* full of the wrath of God	Rev 15:7	5357
pour out the *v* of the wrath of	Rev 16:1	5357
angels which had the seven *v*	Rev 17:1	5357
angels which had the seven *v* full	Rev 21:9	5357

VICTORY

the *v* that day was turned into	2Sa 19:2	8668
LORD wrought a great *v* that day	2Sa 23:10	8668
and the LORD wrought a great *v*	2Sa 23:12	8668
the power, and the glory, and the *v*	1Chr 29:11	5331
holy arm, hath gotten him the *v*	Ps 98:1	3467
He will swallow up death in *v*	Is 25:8	5331
he send forth judgment unto *v*	Mt 12:20	3534
Death is swallowed up in *v*	1Cor 15:54	3534
O grave, where is thy *v*	1Cor 15:55	3534
which giveth us the *v* through our	1Cor 15:57	3534
this is the *v* that overcometh the	1Jn 5:4	3529
had gotten the *v* over the beast	Rev 15:2	3528

VICTUAL

prepared for themselves any *v*	Ex 12:39	6720
to fetch *v* for the people, that	Judg 20:10	6720
provided *v* for king Solomon	1Kin 4:27	3557
captains in them, and store of *v*	2Chr 11:11	3978
and he gave them *v* in abundance	2Chr 11:23	4202

VICTUALS

Sodom and Gomorrah, and all their *v*	Gen 14:11	400
nor lend him thy *v* for increase	Lev 25:37	400
usury of money, usury of *v*	Deut 23:19	400
the people, saying, Prepare you *v*	Josh 1:11	6720
Take *v* with you for the journey,	Josh 9:11	6720
And the men took of their *v*	Josh 9:14	6718
the people took *v* in their hand	Judg 7:8	6720
and a suit of apparel, and thy *v*	Judg 17:10	4241
the LORD for him, and gave him *v*	1Sa 22:10	6720
which provided *v* for the king	1Kin 4:7	3557
him an house, and appointed him *v*	1Kin 11:18	3899
any *v* on the sabbath day to sell	Neh 10:31	7668
in the day wherein they sold *v*	Neh 13:15	6718
captain of the guard gave him *v*	Jer 40:5	737
for then had we plenty of *v*	Jer 44:17	3899
the villages, and buy themselves *v*	Mt 14:15	1033
round about, and lodge, and get *v*	Lk 9:12	1979

VIEW

Go *v* the land, even Jericho	Josh 2:1	7200
saying, Go up and *v* the country	Josh 7:2	7270
went, and stood to *v* afar off	2Kin 2:7	5048
were to *v* at Jericho saw him	2Kin 2:15	5048

VIEWED

And the men went up and *v* Ai	Josh 7:2	7370
I *v* the people, and the priests,	Ezr 8:15	995
v the walls of Jerusalem, which	Neh 2:13	7663
v the wall, and turned back, and	Neh 2:15	7663

VIGILANT

the husband of one wife, *v*	1Ti 3:2	3524
Be sober, be *v*	1Pet 5:8	1127

VILE

brother should seem *v* unto thee	Deut 25:3	7034
unto this man do not so *v* a thing	Judg 19:24	5039
his sons made themselves *v*	1Sa 3:13	7043
but every thing that was *v*	1Sa 15:9	5240
And I will yet be more *v* than thus	2Sa 6:22	7043
and reputed *v* in your sight	Job 18:3	2933
Behold, I am *v*	Job 40:4	7043
In whose eyes a *v* person is	Ps 15:4	959
The *v* person shall be no more	Is 32:5	5036
For the *v* person will speak	Is 32:6	5036
forth the precious from the *v*	Jer 15:19	2151
and will make them like *v* figs	Jer 29:17	8182
for I am become *v*	Lam 1:11	2151
estate shall stand up a *v* person	Dan 11:21	959
for thou art *v*	Nah 1:14	7043
filth upon thee, and make thee *v*	Nah 3:6	5034
gave them up unto *v* affections	Rom 1:26	819
Who shall change our *v* body	Phil 3:21	5014
in also a poor man in *v* raiment	Jas 2:2	4508

VILELY

of the mighty is *v* cast away	2Sa 1:21	1602

VILER

they were *v* than the earth	Job 30:8	5217

VILEST

when the *v* men are exalted	Ps 12:8	2149

VILLAGE

Go into the *v* over against you, ... Mt 21:2 — 2968
way into the *v* over against you .... Mk 11:2 — 2968
went throughout every city and *v* .... Lk 8:1 — 2968
went, and entered into a *v* of the .... Lk 9:52 — 2968
And they went to another *v* .... Lk 9:56 — 2968
that he entered into a certain *v* .... Lk 10:38 — 2968
And as he entered into a certain *v* .... Lk 17:12 — 2968
Go ye into the *v* over against you .... Lk 19:30 — 2968
same day to a *v* called Emmaus .... Lk 24:13 — 2968
And they drew nigh unto the *v* .... Lk 24:28 — 2968

VILLAGES

out of the houses, out of the *v* .... Ex 8:13 — 2691
But the houses of the *v* which .... Lev 25:31 — 2691
Heshbon, and in all the *v* thereof .... Num 21:25 — 1323
and they took the *v* thereof .... Num 21:32 — 1323
the *v* thereof, and called it Nobah .... Num 32:42 — 1323
the cities and the *v* thereof .... Josh 13:23 — 2691
families, the cities, and their *v* .... Josh 13:28 — 2691
are twenty and nine, with their *v* .... Josh 15:32 — 2691
fourteen cities with their *v* .... Josh 15:36 — 2691
sixteen cities with their *v* .... Josh 15:41 — 2691
nine cities with their *v* .... Josh 15:44 — 2691
Ekron, with her towns and her *v* .... Josh 15:45 — 2691
lay near Ashdod, with their *v* .... Josh 15:46 — 2691
Ashdod with her towns and her *v* .... Josh 15:47 — 2691
Gaza with her towns and her *v* .... Josh 15:47 — 2691
eleven cities with their *v* .... Josh 15:51 — 2691
nine cities with their *v* .... Josh 15:54 — 2691
ten cities with their *v* .... Josh 15:57 — 2691
six cities with their *v* .... Josh 15:59 — 2691
two cities with their *v* .... Josh 15:60 — 2691
six cities with their *v* .... Josh 15:62 — 2691
all the cities with their *v* .... Josh 16:9 — 2691
twelve cities with their *v* .... Josh 18:24 — 2691
fourteen cities with their *v* .... Josh 18:28 — 2691
thirteen cities and their *v* .... Josh 19:6 — 2691
four cities and their *v* .... Josh 19:7 — 2691
all the *v* that were round about .... Josh 19:8 — 2691
twelve cities with their *v* .... Josh 19:15 — 2691
these cities with their *v* .... Josh 19:16 — 2691
sixteen cities with their *v* .... Josh 19:22 — 2691
families, the cities and their *v* .... Josh 19:23 — 2691
twenty and two cities with their *v* .... Josh 19:30 — 2691
these cities with their *v* .... Josh 19:31 — 2691
nineteen cities with their *v* .... Josh 19:38 — 2691
families, the cities and their *v* .... Josh 19:39 — 2691
these cities with their *v* .... Josh 19:48 — 2691
the *v* thereof, gave they to Caleb .... Josh 21:12 — 2691
The inhabitants of the *v* ceased .... Judg 5:7 — 6520
inhabitants of his *v* in Israel .... Judg 5:11 — 6520
of fenced cities, and of country *v* .... 1Sa 6:18 — 3724
And their *v* were, Etam, and Ain, ... 1Chr 4:32 — 2691
all their *v* that were round about .... 1Chr 4:33 — 2691
the *v* thereof, they gave to Caleb .... 1Chr 6:56 — 2691
that dwelt in the *v* of the .... 1Chr 9:16 — 2691
by their genealogy in their *v* .... 1Chr 9:22 — 2691
brethren, which were in their *v* .... 1Chr 9:25 — 2691
in the cities, and in the *v* .... 1Chr 27:25 — 3723
and Shocho with the *v* thereof .... 2Chr 28:18 — 1323
and Timnah with the *v* thereof .... 2Chr 28:18 — 1323
Gimzo also and the *v* thereof .... 2Chr 28:18 — 1323
one of the *v* in the plain of Ono .... Neh 6:2 — 3715
And for the *v*, with their fields, ... Neh 11:25 — 2691
in the *v* thereof, and at Dibon, and ...... Neh 11:25 — 2691
in the *v* thereof, and at Jekabzeel, ... Neh 11:25 — 1323
Jekabzeel, and in the *v* thereof, ... Neh 11:25 — 1323
Beer-sheba, and in the *v* thereof, ... Neh 11:27 — 1323
at Mekonah, and in the *v* thereof, ... Neh 11:28 — 1323
Zanoah, Adullam, and in their *v* .... Neh 11:30 — 2691
at Azekah, and in the *v* thereof .... Neh 11:30 — 1323
Aija, and Beth-el, and in their *v* .... Neh 11:31 — 1323
and from the *v* of Netophathi .... Neh 12:28 — 2691
them *v* round about Jerusalem .... Neh 12:29 — 2691
Therefore the Jews of the *v* .... Est 9:19 — 6521
in the lurking places of the *v* .... Ps 10:8 — 2691
let us lodge in the *v* .... Song 7:11 — 3723
the *v* that Kedar doth inhabit .... Is 42:11 — 2691
go up to the land of unwalled *v* .... Eze 38:11 — 6519
with his staves the head of his *v* .... Hab 3:14 — 6518
went about all the cities and *v* .... Mt 9:35 — 2968
away, that they may go into the *v* .... Mt 14:15 — 2968
And he went round about the *v* .... Mk 6:6 — 2968
round about, and into the *v* .... Mk 6:36 — 2968
whithersoever he entered, into *v* .... Mk 6:56 — 2968
he went through the cities and *v* .... Lk 13:22 — 2968
in many *v* of the Samaritans .... Acts 8:25 — 2968

VILLANY

For the vile person will speak *v* .... Is 32:6 — 5039
they have committed *v* in Israel .... Jer 29:23 — 5039

VINE

dream, behold, a *v* was before me .... Gen 40:9 — 1612
in the *v* were three branches .... Gen 40:10 — 1612
Binding his foal unto the *v* .... Gen 49:11 — 1612
his ass's colt unto the choice *v* .... Gen 49:11 — 8321
the grapes of thy *v* undressed .... Lev 25:5 — 5139
grapes in it of thy *v* undressed .... Lev 25:11 — 5139
that is made of the *v* tree .... Num 6:4 — 3196
their *v* is of the *v* of Sodom .... Deut 32:32 — 1612
Then said the trees unto the *v* .... Judg 9:12 — 1612
the *v* said unto them, Should I .... Judg 9:13 — 1612
of any thing that cometh of the *v* .... Judg 13:14 — 1612
safely, every man under his *v* .... 1Kin 4:25 — 1612
gather herbs, and found a wild *v* .... 2Kin 4:39 — 1612
eat ye every man of his own *v* .... 2Kin 18:31 — 1612
v dressers in the mountains, and .... 2Chr 26:10 — 3755
off his unripe grape as the *v* .... Job 15:33 — 1612
hast brought a *v* out of Egypt .... Ps 80:8 — 1612
and behold, and visit this *v* .... Ps 80:14 — 1612
v by the sides of thine house .... Ps 128:3 — 1612
to see whether the *v* flourished .... Song 6:11 — 1612
shall be as clusters of the *v* .... Song 7:8 — 1612
let us see if the *v* flourish .... Song 7:12 — 1612
and planted it with the choicest *v* .... Is 5:2 — 8321
languish, and the *v* of Sibmah .... Is 16:8 — 1612
weeping of Jazer the *v* of Sibmah .... Is 16:9 — 1612
the *v* languisheth, all the .... Is 24:7 — 1612
fields, for the fruitful *v* .... Is 32:12 — 1612
the leaf falleth off from the *v* .... Is 34:4 — 1612
and eat ye every one of his *v* .... Is 36:16 — 1612
Yet I had planted thee a noble *v* .... Jer 2:21 — 8321
plant of a strange *v* unto me .... Jer 2:21 — 1612
the remnant of Israel as a *v* .... Jer 6:9 — 1612
there shall be no grapes on the *v* .... Jer 8:13 — 1612
O *v* of Sibmah, I will weep for .... Jer 48:32 — 1612
What is the *v* tree more than any .... Eze 15:2 — 1612
As the *v* tree among the trees of .... Eze 15:6 — 1612
a spreading *v* of low stature .... Eze 17:6 — 1612
so it became a *v*, and brought .... Eze 17:6 — 1612
this *v* did bend her roots toward .... Eze 17:7 — 1612
that it might be a goodly *v* .... Eze 17:8 — 1612
mother is like a *v* in thy blood .... Eze 19:10 — 1612
Israel is an empty *v*, he bringeth .... Hos 10:1 — 1612
as the corn, and grow as the *v* .... Hos 14:7 — 1612
He hath laid my *v* waste, and .... Joel 1:7 — 1612
The *v* is dried up, and the fig .... Joel 1:12 — 1612
the *v* do yield their strength .... Joel 2:22 — 1612
shall sit every man under his *v* .... Mic 4:4 — 1612
out, and marred their *v* branches .... Nah 2:2 — 2156
yea, as yet the *v*, and the fig .... Hag 2:19 — 1612
man his neighbour under the *v* .... Zec 3:10 — 1612
the *v* shall give her fruit, and .... Zec 8:12 — 1612
neither shall your *v* cast her .... Mal 3:11 — 1612
henceforth of this fruit of the *v* .... Mt 26:29 — 288
no more of the fruit of the *v* .... Mk 14:25 — 288
not drink of the fruit of the *v* .... Lk 22:18 — 288
I am the true *v*, and my Father is .... Jn 15:1 — 288
itself, except it abide in the *v* .... Jn 15:4 — 288
I am the *v*, ye are the branches .... Jn 15:5 — 288
either a *v*, figs? .... Jas 3:12 — 288
clusters of the *v* of the earth .... Rev 14:18 — 288
and gathered the *v* of the earth .... Rev 14:19 — 288

VINEDRESSERS

of the poor of the land to be *v* .... 2Kin 25:12 — 3755
shall be your plowmen and your *v* .... Is 61:5 — 3755
of the poor of the land for *v* .... Jer 52:16 — 3755
howl, O ye *v*, for the wheat and .... Joel 1:11 — 3755

VINEGAR

and shall drink no *v* of wine .... Num 6:3 — 2558
or *v* of strong drink, neither .... Num 6:3 — 2558
bread, and dip thy morsel in the *v* ...... Ruth 2:14 — 2558
my thirst they gave me *v* to drink .... Ps 69:21 — 2558
As *v* to the teeth, and as smoke to ...... Prov 10:26 — 2558
as *v* upon nitre, so is he that .... Prov 25:20 — 2558
They gave him *v* to drink mingled .... Mt 27:34 — 3690
a spunge, and filled it with *v* .... Mt 27:48 — 3690
ran and filled a spunge full of *v* .... Mk 15:36 — 3690
coming to him, and offering him *v* .... Lk 23:36 — 3690
there was set a vessel full of *v* .... Jn 19:29 — 3690
and they filled a spunge with *v* .... Jn 19:29 — 3690
therefore had received the *v* .... Jn 19:30 — 3690

VINES

of seed, or of figs, or of *v* .... Num 20:5 — 1612
A land of wheat, and barley, and *v* ...... Deut 8:8 — 1612
He destroyed their *v* with hail .... Ps 78:47 — 1612
He smote their *v* also and their .... Ps 105:33 — 1612
the *v* with the tender grape give .... Song 2:13 — 1612
little foxes, that spoil the *v* .... Song 2:15 — 3754
for our *v* have tender grapes .... Song 2:15 — 3754

v at a thousand silverlings	Is 7:23	1612
they shall eat up thy *v* and thy	Jer 5:17	1612
Thou shalt yet plant *v* upon the	Jer 31:5	3754
And I will destroy her *v* and her	Hos 2:12	1612
neither shall fruit be in the *v*	Hab 3:17	1612

VINEYARD

an husbandman, and he planted a *v*	Gen 9:20	3754
cause a field or *v* to be eaten	Ex 22:5	3754
and of the best of his own *v*	Ex 22:5	3754
manner thou shalt deal with thy *v*	Ex 23:11	3754
And thou shalt not glean thy *v*	Lev 19:10	3754
thou gather every grape of thy *v*	Lev 19:10	3754
six years thou shalt prune thy *v*	Lev 25:3	3754
sow thy field, nor prune thy *v*	Lev 25:4	3754
man is he that hath planted a *v*	Deut 20:6	3754
not sow thy *v* with divers seeds	Deut 22:9	3754
hast sown, and the fruit of thy *v*	Deut 22:9	3754
comest into thy neighbour's *v*	Deut 23:24	3754
gatherest the grapes of thy *v*	Deut 24:21	3754
thou shalt plant a *v*, and shalt	Deut 28:30	3754
Naboth the Jezreelite had a *v*	1Kin 21:1	3754
Naboth, saying, Give me thy *v*	1Kin 21:2	3754
thee for it a better *v* than it	1Kin 21:2	3754
unto him, Give me thy *v* for money	1Kin 21:6	3754
I will give thee another *v* for it	1Kin 21:6	3754
I will not give thee my *v*	1Kin 21:6	3754
I will give thee the *v* of Naboth	1Kin 21:7	3754
take possession of the *v* of	1Kin 21:15	3754
to the *v* of Naboth the Jezreelite	1Kin 21:16	3754
behold, he is in the *v* of Naboth	1Kin 21:18	3754
the *v* which thy right hand hath	Ps 80:15	3657
by the *v* of the man void of	Prov 24:30	3754
of her hands she planteth a *v*	Prov 31:16	3754
but mine own *v* have I not kept	Song 1:6	3754
Solomon had a *v* at Baal-hamon	Song 8:11	3754
he let out the *v* unto keepers	Song 8:11	3754
My *v*, which is mine, is before me	Song 8:12	3754
Zion is left as a cottage in a *v*	Is 1:8	3754
for ye have eaten up the *v*	Is 3:14	3754
song of my beloved touching his *v*	Is 5:1	3754
My wellbeloved hath a *v* in a very	Is 5:1	3754
I pray you, betwixt me and my *v*	Is 5:3	3754
could have been done more to my *v*	Is 5:4	3754
tell you what I will do to my *v*	Is 5:5	3754
For the *v* of the LORD of hosts is	Is 5:7	3754
ten acres of *v* shall yield one	Is 5:10	3754
sing ye unto her, A *v* of red wine	Is 27:2	3754
Many pastors have destroyed my *v*	Jer 12:10	3754
house, nor sow seed, nor plant *v*	Jer 35:7	3754
neither have we *v*, nor field, nor	Jer 35:9	3754
the field, and as plantings of a *v*	Mic 1:6	3754
to hire labourers into his *v*	Mt 20:1	290
a day, he sent them into his *v*	Mt 20:2	290
Go ye also into the *v*, and	Mt 20:4	290
unto them, Go ye also into the *v*	Mt 20:7	290
the lord of the *v* saith unto his	Mt 20:8	290
said, Son, go work to day in my *v*	Mt 21:28	290
householder, which planted a *v*	Mt 21:33	290
him, and cast him out of the *v*	Mt 21:39	290
lord therefore of the *v* cometh	Mt 21:40	290
will let out his *v* unto other	Mt 21:41	290
A certain man planted a *v*	Mk 12:1	290
husbandmen of the fruit of the *v*	Mk 12:2	290
him, and cast him out of the *v*	Mk 12:8	290
therefore the lord of the *v* do	Mk 12:9	290
and will give the *v* unto others	Mk 12:9	290
had a fig tree planted in his *v*	Lk 13:6	290
said he unto the dresser of his *v*	Lk 13:7	289
A certain man planted a *v*	Lk 20:9	290
give him of the fruit of the *v*	Lk 20:10	290
Then said the lord of the *v*	Lk 20:13	290
So they cast him out of the *v*	Lk 20:15	290
the lord of the *v* do unto them	Lk 20:15	290
and shall give the *v* to others	Lk 20:16	290
who planteth a *v*, and eateth not	1Cor 9:7	290

VINEYARDS

us inheritance of fields and *v*	Num 16:14	3754
the fields, or through the *v*	Num 20:17	3754
into the fields, or into the *v*	Num 21:22	3754
the LORD stood in a path of the *v*	Num 22:24	3754
which thou diggedst not, *v*	Deut 6:11	3754
Thou shalt plant *v*, and dress them	Deut 28:39	3754
of the *v* and oliveyards which ye	Josh 24:13	3754
the fields, and gathered their *v*	Judg 9:27	3754
and unto the plain of the *v*	Judg 11:33	3754
and came to the *v* of Timnath	Judg 14:5	3754
the standing corn, with the *v*	Judg 15:5	3754
Go and lie in wait in the *v*	Judg 21:20	3754
dances, then come ye out of the *v*	Judg 21:21	3754
will take your fields, and your *v*	1Sa 8:14	3754

tenth of your seed, and of your *v*	1Sa 8:15	3754
give every one of you fields and *v*	1Sa 22:7	3754
garments, and oliveyards, and *v*	2Kin 5:26	3754
and wine, a land of bread and *v*	2Kin 18:32	3754
year sow ye, and reap, and plant *v*	2Kin 19:29	3754
over the *v* was Shimei the	1Chr 27:27	3754
over the increase of the *v* for	1Chr 27:27	3754
We have mortgaged our lands, *v*	Neh 5:3	3754
and that upon our lands and *v*	Neh 5:4	3754
for other men have our lands and *v*	Neh 5:5	3754
this day, their lands, their *v*	Neh 5:11	3754
of all goods, wells digged, *v*	Neh 9:25	3754
he beholdeth not the way of the *v*	Job 24:18	3754
And sow the fields, and plant *v*	Ps 107:37	3754
I planted me *v*	Eccl 2:4	3754
they made me the keeper of the *v*	Song 1:6	3754
of camphire in the *v* of En-gedi	Song 1:14	3754
Let us get up early to the *v*	Song 7:12	3754
in the *v* there shall be no	Is 16:10	3754
and wine, a land of bread and *v*	Is 36:17	3754
year sow ye, and reap, and plant *v*	Is 37:30	3754
and they shall plant *v*, and eat the	Is 65:21	3754
v shall be possessed again in	Jer 32:15	3754
the land of Judah, and gave them *v*	Jer 39:10	3754
and shall build houses, and plant *v*	Eze 28:26	3754
I will give her her *v* from thence	Hos 2:15	3754
when your gardens and your *v*	Amos 4:9	3754
ye have planted pleasant *v*	Amos 5:11	3754
in all *v* shall be wailing	Amos 5:17	3754
and they shall plant *v*, and drink	Amos 9:14	3754
and they shall plant *v*, but not	Zeph 1:13	3754

VINTAGE

threshing shall reach unto the *v*	Lev 26:5	1210
the *v* shall reach unto the sowing	Lev 26:5	1210
better than the *v* of Abi-ezer	Judg 8:2	1210
they gather the *v* of the wicked	Job 24:6	3754
made their *v* shouting to cease	Is 16:10	1210
grapes when the *v* is done	Is 24:13	1210
for the *v* shall fail, the	Is 32:10	1210
thy summer fruits and upon thy *v*	Jer 48:32	1210
as the grapegleanings of the *v*	Mic 7:1	1210
the forest of the *v* is come down	Zec 11:2	1208

VIOL

And the harp, and the *v*, the tabret	Is 5:12	5035
That chant to the sound of the *v*	Amos 6:5	5035

VIOLATED

Her priests have *v* my law	Eze 22:26	2554

VIOLENCE

and the earth was filled with *v*	Gen 6:11	2555
is filled with *v* through them	Gen 6:13	2555
or in a thing taken away by *v*	Lev 6:2	1498
thou savest me from *v*	2Sa 22:3	2555
him that loveth *v* his soul hateth	Ps 11:5	2555
for I have seen *v* and strife in	Ps 55:9	2555
ye weigh the *v* of your hands in	Ps 58:2	2555
their soul from deceit and *v*	Ps 72:14	2555
v covereth them as a garment	Ps 73:6	2555
and drink the wine of *v*	Prov 4:17	2555
but *v* covereth the mouth of the	Prov 10:6	2555
but *v* covereth the mouth of the	Prov 10:11	2555
of the transgressors shall eat *v*	Prov 13:2	2555
A man that doeth *v* to the blood	Prov 28:17	6231
because he had done no *v*, neither	Is 53:9	2555
the act of *v* is in their hands	Is 59:6	2555
V shall no more be heard in thy	Is 60:18	2555
v and spoil is heard in her	Jer 6:7	2555
I spake, I cried out, I cried *v*	Jer 20:8	2555
do no *v* to the stranger, the	Jer 22:3	2554
and for oppression, and for *v*	Jer 22:17	4835
The *v* done to me and to my flesh	Jer 51:35	2555
v in the land, ruler against	Jer 51:46	2555
V is risen up into a rod of	Eze 7:11	2555
crimes, and the city is full of *v*	Eze 7:23	2555
they have filled the land with *v*	Eze 8:17	2555
because of the *v* of all them that	Eze 12:19	2555
pledge, hath spoiled none by *v*	Eze 18:7	1500
poor and needy, hath spoiled by *v*	Eze 18:12	1500
pledge, neither hath spoiled by *v*	Eze 18:16	1500
spoiled his brother by *v*	Eze 18:18	1499
filled the midst of thee with *v*	Eze 28:16	2555
remove and spoil, and execute	Eze 45:9	2555
for the *v* against the children of	Joel 3:19	2555
saith the LORD, who store up *v*	Amos 3:10	2555
cause the seat of *v* to come near	Amos 6:3	2555
For thy *v* against thy brother	Obad 10	2555
from the *v* that is in their hands	Jonah 3:8	2555
covet fields, and take them by *v*	Mic 2:2	1497
rich men thereof are full of *v*	Mic 6:12	2555
even cry out unto thee of *v*	Hab 1:2	2555

for spoiling and *v* are before me .... Hab 1:3   2555
They shall come all for *v* .... Hab 1:9   2555
for the *v* of the land, of the .... Hab 2:8   2555
For the *v* of Lebanon shall cover .... Hab 2:17   2555
for the *v* of the land, of the .... Hab 2:17   2555
fill their masters' houses with *v* .... Zeph 1:9   2555
they have done *v* to the law .... Zeph 3:4   2554
one covereth *v* with his garment .... Mal 2:16   2555
the kingdom of heaven suffereth *v* .... Mt 11:12   *971*
Do *v* to no man, neither accuse .... Lk 3:14   *1286*
and brought them without *v* .... Acts 5:26   *970*
soldiers for the *v* of the people .... Acts 21:35   *970*
with great *v* took him away out of .... Acts 24:7   *970*
broken with the *v* of the waves .... Acts 27:41   *970*
Quenched the *v* of fire, escaped .... Heb 11:34   *1411*
Thus with *v* shall that great city .... Rev 18:21   *3731*

VIOLENT
hast delivered me from the *v* man 2Sa 22:49   2555
his *v* dealing shall come down .... Ps 7:16   2555
hast delivered me from the *v* man .... Ps 18:48   2555
the assemblies of *v* men have .... Ps 86:14   6184
preserve me from the *v* man .... Ps 140:1   2555
preserve me from the *v* man .... Ps 140:4   2555
evil shall hunt the *v* man to .... Ps 140:11   2555
A *v* man enticeth his neighbour, ... Prov 16:29   2555
v perverting of judgment and .... Eccl 5:8   1499
and the *v* **take it by force** .... Mt 11:12   *973*

VIOLENTLY
servants had *v* taken away .... Gen 21:25   1497
restore that which he took *v* away .... Lev 6:4   1500
thine ass shall be *v* taken away .... Deut 28:31   1497
because he hath *v* taken away an .... Job 20:19   1497
they *v* take away flocks, and feed .... Job 24:2   1497
He will surely *v* turn and toss .... Is 22:18
And he hath *v* taken away his .... Lam 2:6   2554
the whole herd of swine ran *v* .... Mt 8:32
the herd ran *v* down a steep place .... Mk 5:13
the herd ran *v* down a steep place .... Lk 8:33

VIOLS
the grave, and the noise of thy *v* .... Is 14:11   5035
will not hear the melody of thy *v* .... Amos 5:23   5035

VIPER
come the young and old lion, the *v* .... Is 30:6   660
is crushed breaketh out into a *v* .... Is 59:5   660
there came a *v* out of the heat, ... Acts 28:3   *2191*

VIPER'S
the *v* tongue shall slay him .... Job 20:16   660

VIPERS
said unto them, O generation of *v* .... Mt 3:7   *2191*
O generation of *v*, **how can ye,** .... Mt 12:34   *2191*
Ye serpents, ye generation of *v* .... Mt 23:33   *2191*
of him, O generation of *v* .... Lk 3:7   *2191*

VIRGIN
was very fair to look upon, a *v* .... Gen 24:16   1330
that when the *v* cometh forth to .... Gen 24:43   5959
And for his sister a *v*, that is .... Lev 21:3   1330
but he shall take a *v* of his own .... Lev 21:14   1330
an evil name upon a *v* of Israel .... Deut 22:19   1330
If a damsel that is a *v* be .... Deut 22:23   1330
a man find a damsel that is a *v* .... Deut 22:28   1330
both the young man and the *v* .... Deut 32:25   1330
for she was a *v* 2Sa 13:2   1330
for my lord the king a young *v* 1Kin 1:2   1330
The *v* the daughter of Zion hath 2Kin 19:21   1330
a *v* shall conceive, and bear a son .... Is 7:14   5959
more rejoice, O thou oppressed *v* .... Is 23:12   1330
The *v*, the daughter of Zion, hath .... Is 37:22   1330
O *v* daughter of Babylon, sit on .... Is 47:1   1330
For as a young man marrieth a *v* .... Is 62:5   1330
for the *v* daughter of my people .... Jer 14:17   1330
the *v* of Israel hath done a very .... Jer 18:13   1330
shalt be built, O *v* of Israel .... Jer 31:4   1330
Then shall the *v* rejoice in the .... Jer 31:13   1330
O *v* of Israel, turn again to .... Jer 31:21   1330
up into Gilead, and take balm, O *v* .... Jer 46:11   1330
the Lord hath trodden the *v* .... Lam 1:15   1330
thee, O *v* daughter of Zion .... Lam 2:13   1330
Lament like a *v* girded with .... Joel 1:8   1330
The *v* of Israel is fallen .... Amos 5:2   1330
a *v* shall be with child, and shall .... Mt 1:23   *3933*
To a *v* espoused to a man whose .... Lk 1:27   *3933*
if a *v* marry, she hath not sinned 1Cor 7:28   *3933*
also between a wife and a *v* 1Cor 7:34   *3933*
himself uncomely toward his *v* 1Cor 7:36   *3933*
his heart that he will keep his *v* 1Cor 7:37   *3933*
you as a chaste *v* to Christ 2Cor 11:2   *3933*

VIRGINITY
And he shall take a wife in her *v* .... Lev 21:13   1331
the tokens of the damsel's *v* unto .... Deut 22:15   1331
are the tokens of my daughter's *v* .... Deut 22:17   1331
the tokens of *v* be not found for .... Deut 22:20   1331
the mountains, and bewail my *v* .... Judg 11:37   1331
bewailed her *v* upon the mountains .... Judg 11:38   1331
they bruised the teats of their *v* .... Eze 23:3   1331
they bruised the breasts of her *v* .... Eze 23:8   1331
an husband seven years from her *v* ...... Lk 2:36   *3932*

VIRGIN'S
and the *v* name was Mary .... Lk 1:27   *3933*

VIRGINS
money according to the dowry of *v* .... Ex 22:17   1330
four hundred young *v*, that had .... Judg 21:12   1330
daughters that were *v* apparelled 2Sa 13:18   1330
fair young *v* sought for the king .... Est 2:2   1330
young *v* unto Shushan the palace .... Est 2:3   1330
in his sight more than all the *v* .... Est 2:17   1330
when the *v* were gathered together .... Est 2:19   1330
the *v* her companions that follow .... Ps 45:14   1330
therefore do the *v* love thee .... Song 1:3   5959
concubines, and *v* without number .... Song 6:8   5959
up young men, nor bring up *v* .... Is 23:4   1330
her *v* are afflicted, and she is in .... Lam 1:4   1330
my *v* and my young men are gone .... Lam 1:18   1330
the *v* of Jerusalem hang down .... Lam 2:10   1330
my *v* and my young men are fallen .... Lam 2:21   1330
In that day shall the fair *v* .... Amos 8:13   1330
of heaven be likened unto ten *v* .... Mt 25:1   *3933*
Then all those *v* **arose, and** .... Mt 25:7   *3933*
Afterward came also the other *v* .... Mt 25:11   *3933*
same man had four daughters, *v* .... Acts 21:9   *3933*
Now concerning *v* I have no 1Cor 7:25   *3933*
for they are *v* .... Rev 14:4   *3933*

VIRTUE
that *v* had gone out of him .... Mk 5:30   *1411*
for there went *v* out of him .... Lk 6:19   *1411*
perceive that *v* **is gone out of me** .... Lk 8:46   *1411*
if there be any *v*, and if there be .... Phil 4:8   *703*
that hath called us to glory and *v* 2Pet 1:3   *703*
diligence, add to your faith *v* 2Pet 1:5   *703*
and to *v* knowledge 2Pet 1:5   *703*

VIRTUOUS
doth know that thou art a *v* woman .... Ruth 3:11   2428
A *v* woman is a crown to her .... Prov 12:4   2428
Who can find a *v* woman .... Prov 31:10   2428

VIRTUOUSLY
Many daughters have done *v* .... Prov 31:29   2428

VISAGE
his *v* was so marred more than any ...... Is 52:14   4758
Their *v* is blacker than a coal .... Lam 4:8   8389
the form of his *v* was changed .... Dan 3:19   600

VISIBLE
heaven, and that are in earth, *v* .... Col 1:16   *3707*

VISION
the LORD came unto Abram in a *v* .... Gen 15:1   4236
make myself known unto him in a *v* ...... Num 12:6   4758
which saw the *v* of the Almighty, ... Num 24:4   4236
which saw the *v* of the Almighty, ... Num 24:16   4236
there was no open *v* 1Sa 3:1   2377
Samuel feared to shew Eli the *v* 1Sa 3:15   4758
words, and according to all this *v* 2Sa 7:17   2384
words, and according to all this *v* 1Chr 17:15   2377
in the *v* of Isaiah the prophet 2Chr 32:32   2377
chased away as a *v* of the night .... Job 20:8   2384
in a *v* of the night, when deep .... Job 33:15   2384
thou spakest in *v* to thy holy one .... Ps 89:19   2377
Where there is no *v*, the people .... Prov 29:18   2377
The *v* of Isaiah the son of Amoz, ... Is 1:1   2377
A grievous *v* is declared unto me .... Is 21:2   2380
The burden of the valley of *v* .... Is 22:1   2384
GOD of hosts in the valley of *v* .... Is 22:5   2384
they err in *v*, they stumble in .... Is 28:7   7203
shall be as a dream of a night *v* .... Is 29:7   2377
the *v* of all is become unto you .... Is 29:11   2380
they prophesy unto you a false *v* .... Jer 14:14   2377
they speak a *v* of their own heart .... Jer 23:16   2377
also find no *v* from the LORD .... Lam 2:9   2377
for the *v* is touching the whole .... Eze 7:13   2377
they seek a *v* of the prophet .... Eze 7:26   2377
according to the *v* that I saw in .... Eze 8:4   4758
brought me in a *v* by the Spirit .... Eze 11:24   4758
So the *v* that I had seen went up .... Eze 11:24   4758
are prolonged, and every *v* faileth .... Eze 12:22   2377
at hand, and the effect of every *v* .... Eze 12:23   2377
vain *v* nor flattering divination .... Eze 12:24   2377

The ν that he seeth is for many	Eze 12:27	2377
Have ye not seen a vain ν	Eze 13:7	4236
appearance of the ν which I saw	Eze 43:3	4758
even according to the ν that I	Eze 43:3	4758
the visions were like the ν that	Eze 43:3	4758
revealed unto Daniel in a night ν	Dan 2:19	2376
and said, I saw in my ν by night	Dan 7:2	2376
Belshazzar a ν appeared unto me	Dan 8:1	2377
And I saw in a ν	Dan 8:2	2377
and I saw in a ν, and I was by the	Dan 8:2	2377
spake, How long shall be the ν	Dan 8:13	2377
I, even I Daniel, had seen the ν	Dan 8:15	2377
make this man to understand the ν	Dan 8:16	4758
time of the end shall be the ν	Dan 8:17	4758
the ν of the evening and the	Dan 8:26	4758
wherefore shut thou up the ν	Dan 8:26	2377
and I was astonished at the ν	Dan 8:27	4758
seen in the ν at the beginning	Dan 9:21	2377
the matter, and consider the ν	Dan 9:23	2377
and to seal up the ν and prophecy,	Dan 9:24	2377
and had understanding of the ν	Dan 10:1	4758
And I Daniel alone saw the ν	Dan 10:7	4759
that were with me saw not the ν	Dan 10:7	4759
left alone, and saw this great ν	Dan 10:8	4759
for yet the ν is for many days	Dan 10:14	2377
by the ν my sorrows are turned	Dan 10:16	4758
themselves to establish the ν	Dan 11:14	2377
The ν of Obadiah	Obad 1	2377
you, that ye shall not have a ν	Mic 3:6	2377
The book of the ν of Nahum the	Nah 1:1	2377
answered me, and said, Write the ν	Hab 2:2	2377
For the ν is yet for an appointed	Hab 2:3	2377
be ashamed every one of his ν	Zec 13:4	2384
Tell the ν to no man, until the	Mt 17:9	3705
he had seen a ν in the temple	Lk 1:22	3701
they had also seen a ν of angels	Lk 24:23	3701
and to him said the Lord in a ν	Acts 9:10	3705
hath seen in a ν a man named	Acts 9:12	3705
He saw in a ν evidently about the	Acts 10:3	3705
doubted in himself what this ν	Acts 10:17	3705
While Peter thought on the ν	Acts 10:19	3705
and in a trance I saw a ν, A	Acts 11:5	3705
but thought he saw a ν	Acts 12:9	3705
a ν appeared to Paul in the night	Acts 16:9	3705
And after he had seen the ν	Acts 16:10	3705
Lord to Paul in the night by a ν	Acts 18:9	3705
disobedient unto the heavenly ν	Acts 26:19	3705
And thus I saw the horses in the ν	Rev 9:17	3706

VISIONS

unto Israel in the ν of the night	Gen 46:2	4759
in the ν of Iddo the seer against	2Chr 9:29	2378
had understanding in the ν of God	2Chr 26:5	7200
thoughts from the ν of the night	Job 4:13	2384
and terrifiest me through ν	Job 7:14	2384
were opened, and I saw ν of God	Eze 1:1	4759
brought me in the ν of God to	Eze 8:3	4759
which see ν of peace for her, and	Eze 13:16	2377
In the ν of God brought he me	Eze 40:2	4759
the ν were like the vision that I	Eze 43:3	4759
Daniel had understanding in all ν	Dan 1:17	2377
the ν of thy head upon thy bed,	Dan 2:28	2376
the ν of my head troubled me	Dan 4:5	2376
tell me the ν of my dream that I	Dan 4:9	2376
Thus were the ν of mine head in	Dan 4:10	2376
I saw in the ν of my head upon my	Dan 4:13	2376
ν of his head upon his bed	Dan 7:1	2376
After this I saw in the night ν	Dan 7:7	2376
I saw in the night ν, and, behold,	Dan 7:13	2376
the ν of my head troubled me	Dan 7:15	2376
prophets, and I have multiplied ν	Hos 12:10	2377
your young men shall see ν	Joel 2:28	2384
and your young men shall see ν	Acts 2:17	3706
I will come to ν and revelations	2Cor 12:1	3701

VISIT

and God will surely ν you, and	Gen 50:24	6485
saying, God will surely ν you	Gen 50:25	6485
saying, God will surely ν you	Ex 13:19	6485
I ν I will ν their sin upon	Ex 32:34	6485
therefore I do ν the iniquity	Lev 18:25	6485
thou shalt ν thy habitation, and	Job 5:24	6485
shouldest ν him every morning	Job 7:18	6485
awake to ν all the heathen	Ps 59:5	6485
heaven, and behold, and ν this vine	Ps 80:14	6485
Then will I ν their transgression	Ps 89:32	6485
O ν me with thy salvation	Ps 106:4	6485
years, that the Lord will ν Tyre	Is 23:17	6485
neither shall they ν it	Jer 3:16	6485
Shall I not ν for these things	Jer 5:9	6485
Shall I not ν for these things	Jer 5:29	6485
at the time that I ν them they	Jer 6:15	6485

Shall I not ν them for these	Jer 9:9	6485
their iniquity, and ν their sins	Jer 14:10	6485
ν me, and revenge me of my	Jer 15:15	6485
I will ν upon you the evil of	Jer 23:2	6485
be until the day that I ν them	Jer 27:22	6485
at Babylon I will ν you, and	Jer 29:10	6485
there shall he be until I ν him	Jer 32:5	6485
him, the time that I will ν him	Jer 49:8	6485
come, the time that I will ν thee	Jer 50:31	6485
he will ν thine iniquity, O	Lam 4:22	6485
I will ν upon her the days of	Hos 2:13	6485
their iniquity, and ν their sins	Hos 8:13	6485
iniquity, he will ν their sins	Hos 9:9	6485
ν the transgressions of Israel	Amos 3:14	6485
will also ν the altars of Beth-el	Amos 3:14	6485
the Lord their God shall ν them	Zeph 2:7	6485
which shall not ν those that be	Zec 11:16	6485
it came into his heart to ν his	Acts 7:23	1980
at the first did ν the Gentiles	Acts 15:14	1980
ν our brethren in every city	Acts 15:36	1980
To ν the fatherless and widows in	Jas 1:27	1980

VISITATION

be visited after the ν of all men	Num 16:29	6486
thy ν hath preserved my spirit	Job 10:12	6486
what will ye do in the day of ν	Is 10:3	6486
in the time of their ν they shall	Jer 8:12	6486
time of their ν they shall perish	Jer 10:15	6486
even the year of their ν	Jer 11:23	6486
them, even the year of their ν	Jer 23:12	6486
upon them, and the time of their ν	Jer 46:21	6486
upon Moab, the year of their ν	Jer 48:44	6486
day is come, the time of their ν	Jer 50:27	6486
time of their ν they shall perish	Jer 51:18	6486
The days of ν are come, the days	Hos 9:7	6486
of thy watchmen and thy ν cometh	Mic 7:4	6486
knewest not the time of thy ν	Lk 19:44	1984
glorify God in the day of ν	1Pet 2:12	1984

VISITED

the Lord ν Sarah as he had said,	Gen 21:1	6485
me, saying, I have surely ν you	Ex 3:16	6485
Lord had ν the children of Israel	Ex 4:31	6485
or if they be ν after the	Num 16:29	6485
that Samson ν his wife with a kid	Judg 15:1	6485
of Moab how that the Lord had ν	Ruth 1:6	6485
And the Lord ν Hannah, so that she	1Sa 2:21	6485
is not so, he hath ν in his anger	Job 35:15	6485
thou hast ν me in the night	Ps 17:3	6485
he shall not be ν with evil	Prov 19:23	6485
after many days shall they be ν	Is 24:22	6485
therefore hast thou ν and	Is 26:14	6485
Lord, in trouble have they ν thee	Is 26:16	6485
Thou shalt be ν of the Lord of	Is 29:6	6485
this is the city to be ν	Jer 6:6	6485
them away, and have not ν them	Jer 23:2	6485
After many days thou shalt be ν	Eze 38:8	6485
for the Lord of hosts hath ν his	Zec 10:3	6485
I was sick, and ye ν me	Mt 25:36	1980
and in prison, and ye ν me not	Mt 25:43	1980
for he hath ν and redeemed his	Lk 1:68	1980
dayspring from on high hath ν us	Lk 1:78	1980
and, That God hath ν his people	Lk 7:16	1980

VISITEST

the son of man, that thou ν him	Ps 8:4	6485
Thou ν the earth, and waterest it	Ps 65:9	6485
the son of man, that thou ν him	Heb 2:6	1980

VISITETH

and when he ν, what shall I answer	Job 31:14	6485

VISITING

ν the iniquity of the fathers	Ex 20:5	6485
ν the iniquity of the fathers	Ex 34:7	6485
ν the iniquity of the fathers	Num 14:18	6485
ν the iniquity of the fathers	Deut 5:9	6485

VOCATION

of the ν wherewith ye are called	Eph 4:1	2821

VOICE

they heard the ν of the Lord God	Gen 3:8	6963
I heard thy ν in the garden, and I	Gen 3:10	6963
hearkened unto the ν of thy wife	Gen 3:17	6963
the ν of thy brother's blood	Gen 4:10	6963
wives, Adah and Zillah, Hear my ν	Gen 4:23	6963
Abram hearkened to the ν of Sarai	Gen 16:2	6963
unto thee, hearken unto her ν	Gen 21:12	6963
against him, and lift up her ν	Gen 21:16	6963
And God heard the ν of the lad	Gen 21:17	6963
the ν of the lad where he is	Gen 21:17	6963
because thou hast obeyed my ν	Gen 22:18	6963
Because that Abraham obeyed my ν	Gen 26:5	6963

obey my *v* according to that which .... Gen 27:8   6963
only obey my *v*, and go fetch me .... Gen 27:13   6963
and said, The *v* is Jacob's *v* .... Gen 27:22   6963
And Esau lifted up his *v*, and wept .... Gen 27:38   6963
Now therefore, my son, obey my *v* .... Gen 27:43   6963
kissed Rachel, and lifted up his *v* .... Gen 29:11   6963
me, and hath also heard my *v* .... Gen 30:6   6963
with me, and I cried with a loud *v* .... Gen 39:14   6963
he heard that I lifted up my *v* .... Gen 39:15   6963
came to pass, as I lifted up my *v* .... Gen 39:18   6963
And they shall hearken to thy *v* .... Ex 3:18   6963
believe me, nor hearken unto my *v* .... Ex 4:1   6963
to the *v* of the first sign .... Ex 4:8   6963
believe the *v* of the latter sign .... Ex 4:8   6963
signs, neither hearken unto thy *v* .... Ex 4:9   6963
obey his *v* to let Israel go .... Ex 5:2   6963
to the *v* of the LORD thy God .... Ex 15:26   6963
Hearken now unto my *v*, I will .... Ex 18:19   6963
to the *v* of his father in law .... Ex 18:24   6963
if ye will obey my *v* indeed .... Ex 19:5   6963
the *v* of the trumpet exceeding .... Ex 19:16   6963
when the *v* of the trumpet sounded .... Ex 19:19   6963
spake, and God answered him by a *v* .... Ex 19:19   6963
Beware of him, and obey his *v* .... Ex 23:21   6963
if thou shalt indeed obey his *v* .... Ex 23:22   6963
the people answered with one *v* .... Ex 24:3   6963
It is not the *v* of them that .... Ex 32:18   6963
neither is it the *v* of them that .... Ex 32:18   6963
hear the *v* of swearing, and is a .... Lev 5:1   6963
then he heard the *v* of one .... Num 7:89   6963
congregation lifted up their *v* .... Num 14:1   6963
and have not hearkened to my *v* .... Num 14:22   6963
unto the LORD, and hear our *v* .... Num 16:16   6963
LORD hearkened to the *v* of Israel .... Num 21:3   6963
LORD heard the *v* of your words .... Deut 1:34   6963
LORD would not hearken to your *v* .... Deut 1:45   6963
ye heard the *v* of the words .... Deut 4:12   6963
only ye heard a *v* .... Deut 4:12   6963
and shalt be obedient unto his *v* .... Deut 4:30   6963
Did ever people hear the *v* of God .... Deut 4:33   6963
heaven he made thee to hear his *v* .... Deut 4:36   6963
thick darkness, with a great *v* .... Deut 5:22   6963
when ye heard the *v* out of the .... Deut 5:23   6963
we have heard his *v* out of the .... Deut 5:24   6963
if we hear the *v* of the LORD our .... Deut 5:25   6963
that hath heard the *v* of the .... Deut 5:26   6963
LORD heard the *v* of your words .... Deut 5:28   6963
I have heard the *v* of the words .... Deut 5:28   6963
unto the *v* of the LORD your God .... Deut 8:20   6963
him not, nor hearkened to his *v* .... Deut 9:23   6963
his commandments, and obey his *v* .... Deut 13:4   6963
to the *v* of the LORD thy God .... Deut 13:18   6963
unto the *v* of the LORD thy God .... Deut 15:5   6963
again the *v* of the LORD my God .... Deut 18:16   6963
will not obey the *v* of his father .... Deut 21:18   6963
or the *v* of his mother, and that, ... Deut 21:18   6963
he will not obey our *v* .... Deut 21:20   6963
our fathers, the LORD heard our *v* .... Deut 26:7   6963
to the *v* of the LORD my God .... Deut 26:14   6963
and to hearken unto his *v* .... Deut 26:17   6963
obey the *v* of the LORD thy God .... Deut 27:10   6963
the men of Israel with a loud *v* .... Deut 27:14   6963
unto the *v* of the LORD thy God .... Deut 28:1   6963
unto the *v* of the LORD thy God .... Deut 28:2   6963
unto the *v* of the LORD thy God .... Deut 28:15   6963
unto the *v* of the LORD thy God .... Deut 28:45   6963
obey the *v* of the LORD thy God .... Deut 28:62   6963
shalt obey his *v* according to all .... Deut 30:2   6963
obey the *v* of the LORD, and do all .... Deut 30:8   6963
unto the *v* of the LORD thy God .... Deut 30:10   6963
and that thou mayest obey his *v* .... Deut 30:20   6963
the *v* of Judah, and bring him unto .... Deut 33:7   6963
they obeyed not the *v* of the LORD .... Josh 5:6   6963
nor make any noise with your *v* .... Josh 6:10   6963
hearkened unto the *v* of a man .... Josh 10:14   6963
have obeyed my *v* in all that I .... Josh 22:2   6963
we serve, and his *v* will we obey .... Josh 24:24   6963
but ye have not obeyed my *v* .... Judg 2:2   6963
that the people lifted up their *v* .... Judg 2:4   6963
and have not hearkened unto my *v* .... Judg 2:20   6963
but ye have not obeyed my *v* .... Judg 6:10   6963
mount Gerizim, and lifted up his *v* .... Judg 9:7   6963
God hearkened to the *v* of Manoah .... Judg 13:9   6963
they knew the *v* of the young man .... Judg 18:3   6963
Let not thy *v* be heard among us, ... Judg 18:25   6963
would not hearken to the *v* of .... Judg 20:13   6963
and they lifted up their *v* .... Ruth 1:9   6963
And they lifted up their *v* .... Ruth 1:14   6963
moved, but her *v* was not heard 1Sa 1:13   6963
not unto the *v* of their father 1Sa 2:25   6963

Hearken unto the *v* of the people 1Sa 8:7   6963
therefore hearken unto their *v* 1Sa 8:9   6963
refused to obey the *v* of Samuel 1Sa 8:19   6963
to Samuel, Hearken unto their *v* 1Sa 8:22   6963
I have hearkened unto your *v* in 1Sa 12:1   6963
LORD, and serve him, and obey his *v* 1Sa 12:14   6963
will not obey the *v* of the LORD, ... 1Sa 12:15   6963
the *v* of the words of the LORD 1Sa 15:1   6963
thou not obey the *v* of the LORD 1Sa 15:19   6963
I have obeyed the *v* of the LORD 1Sa 15:20   6963
as in obeying the *v* of the LORD? 1Sa 15:22   6963
the people, and obeyed their *v* 1Sa 15:24   6963
hearkened unto the *v* of Jonathan 1Sa 19:6   6963
that Saul said, Is this thy *v* 1Sa 24:16   6963
And Saul lifted up his *v*, and wept 1Sa 24:16   6963
see, I have hearkened to thy *v* 1Sa 25:35   6963
And Saul knew David's *v* 1Sa 26:17   6963
and said, Is this thy *v* 1Sa 26:17   6963
And David said, It is my *v* 1Sa 26:17   6963
Samuel, she cried with a loud *v* 1Sa 28:12   6963
obeyedst not the *v* of the LORD 1Sa 28:18   6963
thine handmaid hath obeyed thy *v* 1Sa 28:21   6963
also unto the *v* of thine handmaid 1Sa 28:22   6963
and he hearkened unto their *v* 1Sa 28:23   6963
were with him lifted up their *v* 1Sa 30:4   6963
and the king lifted up his *v* 2Sa 3:32   6963
he would not hearken unto our *v* 2Sa 12:18   6963
he would not hearken unto her *v* 2Sa 13:14   6963
sons came, and lifted up their *v* 2Sa 13:36   6963
the country wept with a loud *v* 2Sa 15:23   6963
and the king cried with a loud *v* 2Sa 19:4   6963
any more the *v* of singing men 2Sa 19:35   6963
he did hear my *v* out of his 2Sa 22:7   6963
and the most High uttered his *v* 2Sa 22:14   6963
of Israel with a loud *v*, saying, ... 1Kin 8:55   6963
And the LORD heard the *v* of Elijah 1Kin 17:22   6963
But there was no *v*, nor any that 1Kin 18:26   6963
that there was neither *v* 1Kin 18:29   6963
and after the fire a still small *v* 1Kin 19:12   6963
behold, there came a *v* unto him 1Kin 19:13   6963
And he hearkened unto their *v* 1Kin 20:25   6963
hast not obeyed the *v* of the LORD 1Kin 20:36   6963
but there was neither *v*, nor 2Kin 4:31   6963
no man there, neither *v* of man 2Kin 7:10   6963
and if ye will hearken unto my *v* 2Kin 10:6   6963
not the *v* of the LORD their God 2Kin 18:12   6963
cried with a loud *v* in the Jews' 2Kin 18:28   6963
whom hast thou exalted thy *v* 2Kin 19:22   6963
by lifting up the *v* with joy 1Chr 15:16   6963
up their *v* with the trumpets 2Chr 5:13   6963
sware unto the LORD with a loud *v* 2Chr 15:14   6963
of Israel with a loud *v* on high 2Chr 20:19   6963
their *v* was heard, and their 2Chr 30:27   6963
Then they cried with a loud *v* in 2Chr 32:18   6963
their eyes, wept with a loud *v* .... Ezr 3:12   6963
answered and said with a loud *v* .... Ezr 10:12   6963
cried with a loud *v* unto the LORD .... Neh 9:4   6963
him not, they lifted up their *v* .... Job 2:12   6963
let no joyful *v* come therein .... Job 3:7
hear not the *v* of the oppressor .... Job 3:18   6963
the *v* of the fierce lion, and the .... Job 4:10   6963
there was silence, and I heard a *v* .... Job 4:16   6963
that he had hearkened unto my *v* .... Job 9:16   6963
into the *v* of them that weep .... Job 30:31   6963
I have heard the *v* of thy words .... Job 33:8   6963
hearken to the *v* of my words .... Job 34:16   6963
attentively the noise of his *v* .... Job 37:2   6963
After it a *v* roareth .... Job 37:4   6963
with the *v* of his excellency .... Job 37:4   6963
not stay them when his *v* is heard .... Job 37:4   6963
marvellously with his *v* .... Job 37:5   6963
thou lift up thy *v* to the clouds .... Job 38:34   6963
thou thunder with a *v* like him .... Job 40:9   6963
I cried unto the LORD with my *v* .... Ps 3:4   6963
Hearken unto the *v* of my cry .... Ps 5:2   6963
My *v* shalt thou hear in the .... Ps 5:3   6963
hath heard the *v* of my weeping .... Ps 6:8   6963
he heard my *v* out of his temple, ... Ps 18:6   6963
and the Highest gave his *v* .... Ps 18:13   6963
where their *v* is not heard .... Ps 19:3   6963
with the *v* of thanksgiving .... Ps 26:7   6963
O LORD, when I cry with my *v* .... Ps 27:7   6963
Hear the *v* of my supplications, ... Ps 28:2   6963
heard the *v* of my supplications .... Ps 28:6   6963
The *v* of the LORD is upon the .... Ps 29:3   6963
The *v* of the LORD is powerful .... Ps 29:4   6963
the *v* of the LORD is full of .... Ps 29:4   6963
The *v* of the LORD breaketh the .... Ps 29:5   6963
The *v* of the LORD divideth the .... Ps 29:7   6963
The *v* of the LORD shaketh the .... Ps 29:8   6963

The *v* of the LORD maketh the	Ps 29:9	6963
the *v* of my supplications when I	Ps 31:22	6963
house of God, with the *v* of joy	Ps 42:4	6963
For the *v* of him that reproacheth	Ps 44:16	6963
he uttered his *v*, the earth	Ps 46:6	6963
unto God with the *v* of triumph	Ps 47:1	6963
Because of the *v* of the enemy	Ps 55:3	6963
and he shall hear my *v*	Ps 55:17	6963
not hearken to the *v* of charmers	Ps 58:5	6963
Hear my *v*, O God, in my prayer	Ps 64:1	6963
make the *v* of his praise to be	Ps 66:8	6963
attended to the *v* of my prayer	Ps 66:19	6963
out his *v*, and that a mighty *v*	Ps 68:33	6963
Forget not the *v* of thine enemies	Ps 74:23	6963
I cried unto God with my *v*	Ps 77:1	6963
even unto God with my *v*	Ps 77:1	6963
The *v* of thy thunder was in the	Ps 77:18	6963
people would not hearken to my *v*	Ps 81:11	6963
and attend to the *v* of my	Ps 86:6	6963
the floods have lifted up their *v*	Ps 93:3	6963
To day if ye will hear his *v*	Ps 95:7	6963
the harp, and the *v* of a psalm	Ps 98:5	6963
By reason of the *v* of my groaning	Ps 102:5	6963
hearkening unto the *v* of his word	Ps 103:20	6963
at the *v* of thy thunder they	Ps 104:7	6963
not unto the *v* of the LORD	Ps 106:25	6963
LORD, because he hath heard my *v*	Ps 116:1	6963
The *v* of rejoicing and salvation	Ps 118:15	6963
Hear my *v* according unto thy	Ps 119:149	6963
Lord, hear my *v*	Ps 130:2	6963
to the *v* of my supplications	Ps 130:2	6963
hear the *v* of my supplications, O	Ps 140:6	6963
give ear unto my *v*, when I cry	Ps 141:1	6963
I cried unto the LORD with my *v*	Ps 142:1	6963
with my *v* unto the LORD did I	Ps 142:1	6963
she uttereth her *v* in the streets	Prov 1:20	6963
and liftest up thy *v* for	Prov 2:3	6963
not obeyed the *v* of my teachers	Prov 5:13	6963
and understanding put forth her *v*	Prov 8:1	6963
my *v* is to the sons of man	Prov 8:4	6963
blesseth his friend with a loud *v*	Prov 27:14	6963
a fool's *v* is known by multitude	Eccl 5:3	6963
should God be angry at thy *v*	Eccl 5:6	6963
bird of the air shall carry the *v*	Eccl 10:20	6963
rise up at the *v* of the bird	Eccl 12:4	6963
The *v* of my beloved	Song 2:8	6963
the *v* of the turtle is heard in	Song 2:12	6963
countenance, let me hear thy *v*	Song 2:14	6963
for sweet is thy *v*, and thy	Song 2:14	6963
it is the *v* of my beloved that	Song 5:2	6963
the companions hearken to thy *v*	Song 8:13	6963
moved at the *v* of him that cried	Is 6:4	6963
Also I heard the *v* of the Lord	Is 6:8	6963
Lift up thy *v*, O daughter of	Is 10:30	6963
mountain, exalt the *v* unto them	Is 13:2	6963
their *v* shall be heard even unto	Is 15:4	6963
They shall lift up their *v*	Is 24:14	6963
Give ye ear, and hear my *v*	Is 28:23	6963
thy *v* shall be, as of one that	Is 29:4	6963
unto thee at the *v* of thy cry	Is 30:19	6963
cause his glorious *v* to be heard	Is 30:30	6963
For through the *v* of the LORD	Is 30:31	6963
he will not be afraid of their *v*	Is 31:4	6963
hear my *v*, ye careless daughters	Is 32:9	6963
cried with a loud *v* in the Jews'	Is 36:13	6963
whom hast thou exalted thy *v*	Is 37:23	6963
The *v* of him that crieth in the	Is 40:3	6963
The *v* said, Cry	Is 40:6	6963
lift up thy *v* with strength	Is 40:9	6963
nor cause his *v* to be heard in	Is 42:2	6963
cities thereof lift up their *v*	Is 42:11	6963
with a *v* of singing declare ye,	Is 48:20	6963
that obeyeth the *v* of his servant	Is 50:10	6963
thanksgiving, and the *v* of melody	Is 51:3	6963
Thy watchmen shall lift up the *v*	Is 52:8	6963
with the *v* together shall they	Is 52:8	6963
lift up thy *v* like a trumpet, and	Is 58:1	6963
to make your *v* to be heard on	Is 58:4	6963
the *v* of weeping shall be no more	Is 65:19	6963
heard in her, nor the *v* of crying	Is 65:19	6963
A *v* of noise from the city	Is 66:6	6963
a *v* from the temple	Is 66:6	6963
a *v* of the LORD that rendereth	Is 66:6	6963
tree, and ye have not obeyed my *v*	Jer 3:13	6963
A *v* was heard upon the high	Jer 3:21	6963
obeyed the *v* of the LORD our God	Jer 3:25	6963
For a *v* declareth from Dan, and	Jer 4:15	6963
give out their *v* against the	Jer 4:16	6963
For I have heard a *v* as of a	Jer 4:31	6963
the *v* of the daughter of Zion,	Jer 4:31	6963
their *v* roareth like the sea	Jer 6:23	6963

I them, saying, Obey my *v*	Jer 7:23	6963
not the *v* of the LORD their God	Jer 7:28	6963
the *v* of mirth	Jer 7:34	6963
the *v* of gladness	Jer 7:34	6963
the *v* of the bridegroom	Jer 7:34	6963
and the *v* of the bride	Jer 7:34	6963
Behold the *v* of the cry of the	Jer 8:19	6963
can men hear the *v* of the cattle	Jer 9:10	6963
them, and have not obeyed my *v*	Jer 9:13	6963
For a *v* of wailing is heard out	Jer 9:19	6963
When he uttereth his *v*, there is	Jer 10:13	6963
iron furnace, saying, Obey my *v*	Jer 11:4	6963
and protesting, saying, Obey my *v*	Jer 11:7	6963
the *v* of mirth	Jer 16:9	6963
the *v* of gladness	Jer 16:9	6963
the *v* of the bridegroom	Jer 16:9	6963
and the *v* of the bride	Jer 16:9	6963
my sight, that it obey not my *v*	Jer 18:10	6963
hearken to the *v* of them that	Jer 18:19	6963
and lift up thy *v* in Bashan	Jer 22:20	6963
that thou obeyedst not my *v*	Jer 22:21	6963
take from them the *v* of mirth	Jer 25:10	6963
the *v* of gladness	Jer 25:10	6963
the *v* of the bridegroom	Jer 25:10	6963
the *v* of the bride	Jer 25:10	6963
utter his *v* from his holy	Jer 25:30	6963
A *v* of the cry of the shepherds,	Jer 25:36	6963
obey the *v* of the LORD your God	Jer 26:13	6963
We have heard a *v* of trembling	Jer 30:5	6963
the *v* of them that make merry	Jer 30:19	6963
A *v* was heard in Ramah,	Jer 31:15	6963
Refrain thy *v* from weeping, and	Jer 31:16	6963
but they obeyed not thy *v*	Jer 32:23	6963
The *v* of joy	Jer 33:11	6963
the *v* of gladness	Jer 33:11	6963
the *v* of the bridegroom	Jer 33:11	6963
the *v* of the bride	Jer 33:11	6963
the *v* of them that shall say,	Jer 33:11	6963
Thus have we obeyed the *v* of	Jer 35:8	6963
the *v* of the LORD, which I speak	Jer 38:20	6963
LORD, and have not obeyed his *v*	Jer 40:3	6963
we will obey the *v* of the LORD	Jer 42:6	6963
when we obey the *v* of the LORD	Jer 42:6	6963
neither obey the *v* of the LORD	Jer 42:13	6963
obeyed the *v* of the LORD your God	Jer 42:21	6963
obeyed not the *v* of the LORD	Jer 43:4	6963
they obeyed not the *v* of the LORD	Jer 43:7	6963
have not obeyed the *v* of the LORD	Jer 44:23	6963
The *v* thereof shall go like a	Jer 46:22	6963
A *v* of crying shall be from	Jer 48:3	6963
Jahaz, have they uttered their *v*	Jer 48:34	6963
The *v* of them that flee and escape	Jer 50:28	6963
their *v* shall roar like the sea,	Jer 50:42	6963
When he uttereth his *v*, there is	Jer 51:16	6963
destroyed out of her the great *v*	Jer 51:55	6963
a noise of their *v* is uttered	Jer 51:55	6963
Thou hast heard my *v*	Lam 3:56	6963
as the *v* of the Almighty, the	Eze 1:24	6963
the *v* of speech, as the noise of	Eze 1:24	6963
there was a *v* from the firmament	Eze 1:25	6963
I heard a *v* of one that spake	Eze 1:28	6963
behind me a *v* of a great rushing	Eze 3:12	6963
cry in mine ears with a loud *v*	Eze 8:18	6963
also in mine ears with a loud *v*	Eze 9:1	6963
as the *v* of the Almighty God when	Eze 10:5	6963
my face, and cried with a loud *v*	Eze 11:13	6963
that his *v* should no more be	Eze 19:9	6963
to lift up the *v* with shouting	Eze 21:22	6963
a *v* of a multitude being at ease	Eze 23:42	6963
shall cause their *v* to be heard	Eze 27:30	6963
of one that hath a pleasant *v*	Eze 33:32	6963
his *v* was like a noise of many	Eze 43:2	6963
mouth, there fell a *v* from heaven	Dan 4:31	7032
with a lamentable *v* unto Daniel	Dan 6:20	7032
v of the great words which the	Dan 7:11	7032
I heard a man's *v* between the	Dan 8:16	6963
obeyed the *v* of the LORD our God	Dan 9:10	6963
that they might not obey thy *v*	Dan 9:11	6963
for we obeyed not his *v*	Dan 9:14	6963
the *v* of his words like the	Dan 10:6	6963
words like the *v* of a multitude	Dan 10:6	6963
Yet heard I the *v* of his words	Dan 10:9	6963
when I heard the *v* of his words	Dan 10:9	6963
shall utter his *v* before his army	Joel 2:11	6963
utter his *v* from Jerusalem	Joel 3:16	6963
utter his *v* from Jerusalem	Amos 1:2	6963
cried I, and thou heardest my *v*	Jonah 2:2	6963
thee with the *v* of thanksgiving	Jonah 2:9	6963
and let the hills hear thy *v*	Mic 6:1	6963
The LORD's *v* crieth unto the city	Mic 6:9	6963
lead her as with the *v* of doves	Nah 2:7	6963

the *v* of thy messengers shall no............ Nah 2:13   6963
the deep uttered his *v*, and lifted .... Hab 3:10   6963
my lips quivered at the *v*...................... Hab 3:16   6963
even the *v* of the day of the LORD........... Zeph 1:14   6963
their *v* shall sing in the windows .... Zeph 2:14   6963
She obeyed not the *v* .... Zeph 3:2   6963
obeyed the *v* of the LORD their .... Hag 1:12   6963
obey the *v* of the LORD your God .... Zec 6:15   6963
There is a *v* of the howling of .... Zec 11:3   6963
a *v* of the roaring of young lions .... Zec 11:3   6963
In Rama was there a *v* heard .... Mt 2:18   5456
The *v* of one crying in the..................... Mt 3:3   5456
lo a *v* from heaven, saying, This .... Mt 3:17   5456
any man hear his *v* in the streets........... Mt 12:19   5456
behold a *v* out of the cloud, ... Mt 17:5   5456
hour Jesus cried with a loud *v* .... Mt 27:46   5456
he had cried again with a loud *v* .... Mt 27:50   5456
The *v* of one crying in the..................... Mk 1:3   5456
And there came a *v* from heaven .... Mk 1:11   5456
torn him, and cried with a loud *v* .... Mk 1:26   5456
And cried with a loud *v*, and said, ... Mk 5:7   5456
a *v* came out of the cloud, saying .... Mk 9:7   5456
hour Jesus cried with a loud *v* .... Mk 15:34   5456
And Jesus cried with a loud *v* .... Mk 15:37   5456
And she spake out with a loud *v*........... Lk 1:42   5456
For, lo, as soon as the *v* of thy .... Lk 1:44   5456
The *v* of one crying in the..................... Lk 3:4   5456
a *v* came from heaven, which said,........ Lk 3:22   5456
devil, and cried out with a loud *v* .... Lk 4:33   5456
before him, and with a loud *v* said .... Lk 8:28   5456
there came a *v* out of the cloud,........... Lk 9:35   5456
And when the *v* was past, Jesus was ..... Lk 9:36   5456
of the company lifted up her *v* .... Lk 11:27   5456
with a loud *v* glorified God,................... Lk 17:15   5456
praise God with a loud *v* for all .... Lk 19:37   5456
Jesus had cried with a loud *v* .... Lk 23:46   5456
I am the *v* of one crying in the................ Jn 1:23   5456
because of the bridegroom's *v* .... Jn 3:29   5456
hear the *v* of the Son of God................ Jn 5:25   5456
in the graves shall hear his *v* .... Jn 5:28   5456
neither heard his *v* at any time .... Jn 5:37   5456
and the sheep hear his *v* .... Jn 10:3   5456
for they know his *v* .... Jn 10:4   5456
they know not the *v* of strangers .... Jn 10:5   5456
bring, and they shall hear my *v* .... Jn 10:16   5456
My sheep hear my *v*, and I know .... Jn 10:27   5456
spoken, he cried with a loud *v* .... Jn 11:43   5456
Then came there a *v* from heaven .... Jn 12:28   5456
This *v* came not because of me,........... Jn 12:30   5456
that is of the truth heareth my *v* .... Jn 18:37   5456
with the eleven, lifted up his *v*............... Acts 2:14   5456
they lifted up their *v* to God.................. Acts 4:24   5456
the *v* of the Lord came unto him,........... Acts 7:31   5456
Then they cried out with a loud *v* .... Acts 7:57   5456
down, and cried with a loud *v* .... Acts 7:60   5456
spirits, crying with loud *v*..................... Acts 8:7   5456
heard a *v* saying unto him, Saul, ... Acts 9:4   5456
him stood speechless, hearing a *v*......... Acts 9:7   5456
And there came a *v* to him, Rise, ... Acts 10:13   5456
the *v* spake unto him again the .... Acts 10:15   5456
I heard a *v* saying unto me, Arise .... Acts 11:7   5456
But the *v* answered me again from .... Acts 11:9   5456
And when they knew Peter's *v*............... Acts 12:14   5456
saying, It is the *v* of a god .... Acts 12:22   5456
Said with a loud *v*, Stand upright .... Acts 14:10   5456
But Paul cried with a loud *v*.................. Acts 16:28   5456
all with one *v* about the space of........... Acts 19:34   5456
heard a *v* saying unto me, Saul, ... Acts 22:7   5456
but they heard not the *v* of him .... Acts 22:9   5456
shouldest hear the *v* of his mouth .... Acts 22:14   5456
Except it be for this one *v*.................... Acts 24:21   5456
death, I gave my *v* against them .... Acts 26:10   5586
I heard a *v* speaking unto me, and........ Acts 26:14   5456
Festus said with a loud *v* .... Acts 26:24   5456
I know not the meaning of the *v* 1Cor 14:11   5456
that by my *v* I might teach others 1Cor 14:19   5456
with you now, and to change my *v* .... Gal 4:20   5456
with the *v* of the archangel, and............ 1Th 4:16   5456
To day if ye will hear his *v* .... Heb 3:7   5456
To day if ye will hear his *v* .... Heb 3:15   5456
To day if ye will hear his *v* .... Heb 4:7   5456
of a trumpet, and the *v* of words............ Heb 12:19   5456
which *v* they that heard intreated .... Heb 12:19
Whose *v* then shook the earth............... Heb 12:26   5456
when there came such a *v* to him 2Pet 1:17   5456
this *v* which came from heaven we......... 2Pet 1:18   5456
man's *v* forbad the madness of the........ 2Pet 2:16   5456
day, and heard behind me a great *v*....... Rev 1:10   5456
to see the *v* that spake with me .... Rev 1:12   5456
his *v* as the sound of many waters .... Rev 1:15   5456
if any man hear my *v*, and open the..... Rev 3:20   5456

the first *v* which I heard was as .... Rev 4:1   5456
angel proclaiming with a loud *v* .... Rev 5:2   5456
I heard the *v* of many angels .... Rev 5:11   5456
Saying with a loud *v*, Worthy is .... Rev 5:12   5456
I heard a *v* in the midst of the .... Rev 6:6   5456
I heard the *v* of the fourth beast............ Rev 6:7   5456
And they cried with a loud *v* .... Rev 6:10   5456
with a loud *v* to the four angels .... Rev 7:2   5456
And cried with a loud *v*, saying,............ Rev 7:10   5456
of heaven, saying with a loud *v* .... Rev 8:13   5456
I heard a *v* from the four horns .... Rev 9:13   5456
And cried with a loud *v*, as when a .... Rev 10:3   5456
I heard a *v* from heaven saying .... Rev 10:4   5456
of the *v* of the seventh angel .... Rev 10:7   5456
the *v* which I heard from heaven .... Rev 10:8   5456
they heard a great *v* from heaven .... Rev 11:12   5456
I heard a loud *v* saying in heaven.......... Rev 12:10   5456
I heard a *v* from heaven .... Rev 14:2   5456
as the *v* of many waters .... Rev 14:2   5456
as the *v* of a great thunder................... Rev 14:2   5456
I heard the *v* of harpers harping .... Rev 14:2   5456
Saying with a loud *v*, Fear God,............ Rev 14:7   5456
them, saying with a loud *v* .... Rev 14:9   5456
I heard a *v* from heaven saying .... Rev 14:13   5456
crying with a loud *v* to him that .... Rev 14:15   5456
I heard a great *v* out of the .... Rev 16:1   5456
there came a great *v* out of the .... Rev 16:17   5456
he cried mightily with a strong *v*............ Rev 18:2   5456
And I heard another *v* from heaven .... Rev 18:4   5456
the *v* of harpers, and musicians,........... Rev 18:22   5456
the *v* of the bridegroom and of the .... Rev 18:23   5456
great *v* of much people in heaven .... Rev 19:1   5456
a *v* came out of the throne, ... Rev 19:5   5456
were the *v* of a great multitude.............. Rev 19:6   5456
as the *v* of many waters .... Rev 19:6   5456
as the *v* of mighty thunderings.............. Rev 19:6   5456
and he cried with a loud *v*.................... Rev 19:17   5456
I heard a great *v* out of heaven .... Rev 21:3   5456

VOICES

before God, and lifted up their *v* .... Judg 21:2   6963
all the people lifted up their *v* 1Sa 11:4   6963
And they lifted up their *v* .... Lk 17:13   5456
And they were instant with loud *v*.......... Lk 23:23   5456
the *v* of them and of the chief .... Lk 23:23   5456
nor yet the *v* of the prophets .... Acts 13:27   5456
had done, they lifted up their *v*.............. Acts 14:11   5456
word, and then lifted up their *v* .... Acts 22:22   5456
so many kinds of *v* in the world............. 1Cor 14:10   5456
lightnings and thunderings and *v*.......... Rev 4:5   5456
and there were *v*, and thunderings,........ Rev 8:5   5456
v of the trumpet of the three .... Rev 8:13   5456
seven thunders uttered their *v* .... Rev 10:3   5456
thunders had uttered their *v* .... Rev 10:4   5456
and there were great *v* in heaven .... Rev 11:15   5456
and there were lightnings, and *v* .... Rev 11:19   5456
And there were *v*, and thunders, and...... Rev 16:18   5456

VOID

the earth was without form, and *v* .... Gen 1:2   922
them *v* on the day he heard them........... Num 30:12   6565
her husband hath made them *v*............. Num 30:12   6565
it, or her husband may make it *v*............ Num 30:13   6565
v after that he hath heard them .... Num 30:15   6565
they are a nation *v* of counsel .... Deut 32:28   6
in a *v* place in the entrance of 1Kin 22:10   1637
they sat in a *v* place at the.................... 2Chr 18:9   1637
Thou hast made *v* the covenant of .... Ps 89:39   5010
for they have made *v* thy law................. Ps 119:126   6565
a young man *v* of understanding, ... Prov 7:7   2638
of him that is *v* of understanding .... Prov 10:13   2638
He that is *v* of wisdom despiseth .... Prov 11:12   2638
persons is *v* of understanding .... Prov 12:11   2638
A man *v* of understanding striketh .... Prov 17:18   2638
of the man *v* of understanding .... Prov 24:30   2638
it shall not return unto me *v* .... Is 55:11   7387
and, lo, it was without form, and *v* .... Jer 4:23   922
I will make *v* the counsel of .... Jer 19:7   1238
She is empty, and *v*, and waste .... Nah 2:10   4003
v of offence toward God, and .... Acts 24:16   677
Do we then make *v* the law through....... Rom 3:31   2673
the law be heirs, faith is made *v*............ Rom 4:14   2758
any man should make my glorying *v*..... 1Cor 9:15   2758

VOLUME

in the *v* of the book it is....................... Ps 40:7   4039
I come (in the *v* of the book it .... Heb 10:7   2777

VOLUNTARILY

peace offerings *v* unto the LORD .... Eze 46:12   5071

VOLUNTARY

his own *v* will at the door of the	Lev 1:3	7522
or a *v* offering, it shall be	Lev 7:16	5071
a *v* burnt offering or peace	Eze 46:12	5071
of your reward in a *v* humility	Col 2:18	2309

VOMIT

and he shall *v* them up again	Job 20:15	6958
thou hast eaten shalt thou *v* up	Prov 23:8	6958
thou be filled therewith, and *v* it	Prov 25:16	6958
As a dog returneth to his *v*	Prov 26:11	6892
a drunken man staggereth in his *v*	Is 19:14	6892
For all tables are full of *v*	Is 28:8	6892
Moab also shall wallow in his *v*	Jer 48:26	6892
dog is turned to his own *v* again	2Pet 2:22	1829

VOMITED

it *v* out Jonah upon the dry land	Jonah 2:10	6958

VOMITETH

the land itself *v* out her	Lev 18:25	6958

VOPHSI (vof-si) A spy sent to the Promised Land.

of Naphtali, Nahbi the son of V	Num 13:14	2058

VOW

And Jacob vowed a *v*, saying, If	Gen 28:20	5088
and where thou vowedst a *v* unto me	Gen 31:13	5088
sacrifice of his offering be a *v*	Lev 7:16	5088
unto the Lord to accomplish his *v*	Lev 22:21	5088
but for a *v* it shall not be	Lev 22:23	5088
a man shall make a singular *v*	Lev 27:2	5088
separate themselves to *v*	Num 6:2	5087
a *v* of a Nazarite, to	Num 6:2	5088
All the days of the *v* of his	Num 6:5	5088
according to the *v* which he vowed	Num 6:21	5088
or a sacrifice in performing a *v*	Num 15:3	5088
for a sacrifice in performing a *v*	Num 15:8	5088
And Israel vowed a *v* unto the Lord	Num 21:2	5088
If a man *v*	Num 30:2	5087
a *v* unto the Lord	Num 30:2	5088
If a woman also *v* a	Num 30:3	5087
a *v* unto the Lord	Num 30:3	5088
And her father hear her *v*, and her	Num 30:4	5088
shall make her *v* which she vowed	Num 30:8	5088
But every *v* of a widow, and of her	Num 30:9	5088
Every *v*, and every binding oath to	Num 30:13	5088
vows which ye *v* unto the Lord	Deut 12:11	5087
of the Lord thy God for any *v*	Deut 23:18	5088
When thou shalt *v* a	Deut 23:21	5088
a *v* unto the Lord thy God	Deut 23:21	5088
But if thou shalt forbear to *v*	Deut 23:22	5088
Jephthah vowed a *v* unto the Lord	Judg 11:30	5088
to his *v* which he had vowed	Judg 11:39	5088
And she vowed a *v*, and said, O Lord	1Sa 1:11	5088
the yearly sacrifice, and his *v*	1Sa 1:21	5088
pray thee, let me go and pay my *v*	2Sa 15:7	5088
For thy servant vowed a *v* while I	2Sa 15:8	5088
thee shall the *v* be performed	Ps 65:1	5088
V, and pay unto the Lord your God	Ps 76:11	5087
When thou vowest a *v* unto God	Eccl 5:4	5088
is it that thou shouldest not *v*	Eccl 5:5	5087
than that thou shouldest *v*	Eccl 5:5	5087
oblation; yea, they shall *v*	Is 19:21	5087
a *v* unto the Lord	Is 19:21	5088
for he had a *v*	Acts 18:18	2171
four men which have a *v* on them	Acts 21:23	2171

VOWED

And Jacob *v* a vow, saying, If God	Gen 28:20	5087
that *v* shall the priest value him	Lev 27:8	5087

law of the Nazarite who hath *v*	Num 6:21	5087
according to the vow which he *v*	Num 6:21	5087
Israel *v* a vow unto the Lord, and	Num 21:2	5087
had at all an husband, when she *v*	Num 30:6	5088
he shall make her vow which she *v*	Num 30:8	5088
if she *v* in her husband's house,	Num 30:10	5087
thou hast *v* unto the Lord thy God	Deut 23:23	5087
Jephthah *v* a vow unto the Lord,	Judg 11:30	5087
to his vow which he had *v*	Judg 11:39	5087
she *v* a vow, and said, O Lord of	1Sa 1:11	5087
which I have *v* unto the Lord, in	2Sa 15:7	5087
For thy servant *v* a vow while I	2Sa 15:8	5087
v unto the mighty God of Jacob	Ps 132:2	5087
pay that which thou hast *v*	Eccl 5:4	5087
perform our vows that we have *v*	Jer 44:25	5087
I will pay that that I have *v*	Jonah 2:9	5087

VOWEDST

where thou *v* a vow unto me	Gen 31:13	5087

VOWEST

nor any of thy vows which thou *v*	Deut 12:17	5087
When thou *v* a vow unto God, defer	Eccl 5:4	5087

VOWETH

hath in his flock a male, and *v*	Mal 1:14	5087

VOWS

offer his oblation for all his *v*	Lev 22:18	5088
your gifts, and beside all your *v*	Lev 23:38	5088
in your set feasts, beside your *v*	Num 29:39	5088
then all her *v* shall stand	Num 30:4	5088
not any of her *v*, or of her bonds	Num 30:5	5088
then her *v* shall stand, and her	Num 30:7	5088
then all her *v* shall stand	Num 30:11	5088
out of her lips concerning her *v*	Num 30:12	5088
then he establisheth all her *v*	Num 30:14	5088
offerings of your hand, and your *v*	Deut 12:6	5088
all your choice *v* which ye vow	Deut 12:11	5088
nor any of thy *v* which thou	Deut 12:17	5088
things which thou hast, and thy *v*	Deut 12:26	5088
thee, and thou shalt pay thy *v*	Job 22:27	5088
I will pay my *v* before them that	Ps 22:25	5088
pay thy *v* unto the most High	Ps 50:14	5088
Thy *v* are upon me, O God	Ps 56:12	5088
For thou, O God, hast heard my *v*	Ps 61:5	5088
that I may daily perform my *v*	Ps 61:8	5088
I will pay thee my *v*,	Ps 66:13	5088
I will pay my *v* unto the Lord now	Ps 116:14	5088
I will pay my *v* unto the Lord now	Ps 116:18	5088
this day have I payed my *v*	Prov 7:14	5088
holy, and after *v* to make enquiry	Prov 20:25	5088
and what, the son of my *v*	Prov 31:2	5088
perform our *v* that we have vowed	Jer 44:25	5088
ye will surely accomplish your *v*	Jer 44:25	5088
and surely perform your *v*	Jer 44:25	5088
unto the Lord, and made *v*	Jonah 1:16	5088
thy solemn feasts, perform thy *v*	Nah 1:15	5088

VOYAGE

that this *v* will be with hurt	Acts 27:10	4144

VULTURE

And the *v*, and the kite after his	Lev 11:14	1676
kite, and the *v* after his kind,	Deut 14:13	1772

VULTURE'S

which the *v* eye hath not seen	Job 28:7	344

VULTURES

there shall the *v* also be	Is 34:15	1772

W

WADI ZERED See Zared.

WAFER

one *w* out of the basket of the	Ex 29:23	7550
a cake of oiled bread, and one *w*	Lev 8:26	7550
the basket, and one unleavened *w*	Num 6:19	7550

WAFERS

of it was like *w* made with honey	Ex 16:31	6838
w unleavened anointed with oil	Ex 29:2	7550
or unleavened *w* anointed with oil	Lev 2:4	7550
unleavened *w* anointed with oil,	Lev 7:12	7550
w of unleavened bread anointed	Num 6:15	7550

WAG

be astonished, and *w* his head	Jer 18:16	5110
w their head at the daughter of	Lam 2:15	5128
by her shall hiss, and *w* his hand	Zeph 2:15	5128

WAGES

tell me, what shall thy *w* be	Gen 29:15	4909
And he said, Appoint me thy *w*	Gen 30:28	7939
me, and changed my *w* ten times	Gen 31:7	4909
thus, The speckled shall be thy *w*	Gen 31:8	7939
thou hast changed my *w* ten times	Gen 31:41	4909
for me, and I will give thee thy *w*	Ex 2:9	7939
the *w* of him that is hired shall	Lev 19:13	6468
his neighbour's service without *w*	Jer 22:13	2600
yet had he no *w*, nor his army,	Eze 29:18	7939
and it shall be the *w* for his army	Eze 29:19	7939
he that earneth *w* earneth *w*	Hag 1:6	7936
oppress the hireling in his *w*	Mal 3:5	7939
and be content with your *w*	Lk 3:14	3800
And he that reapeth receiveth *w*	Jn 4:36	3408
For the *w* of sin is death	Rom 6:23	3800

taking *w* of them, to do you	2Cor 11:8	3800
son of Bosor, who loved the *w* of	2Pet 2:15	3408

WAGGING

by reviled him, *w* their heads,	Mt 27:39	2795
w their heads, and saying, Ah,	Mk 15:29	2795

WAGON

a *w* for two of the princes, and	Num 7:3	5699

WAGONS

take you *w* out of the land of	Gen 45:19	5699
and Joseph gave them *w*, according	Gen 45:21	5699
when he saw the *w* which Joseph	Gen 45:27	5699
in the *w* which Pharaoh had sent	Gen 46:5	5699
before the LORD, six covered *w*	Num 7:3	5699
And Moses took the *w* and the oxen,	Num 7:6	5699
Two *w* and four oxen he gave unto	Num 7:7	5699
And four *w* and eight oxen he gave	Num 7:8	5699
against them with chariots, *w*	Eze 23:24	7393

WAHEB See DID.

WAIL

w for the multitude of Egypt, and	Eze 32:18	5091
Therefore I will *w* and howl, I	Mic 1:8	5594
the earth shall *w* because of him	Rev 1:7	2875

WAILED

and them that wept and *w* greatly	Mk 5:38	214

WAILING

and fasting, and weeping, and *w*	Est 4:3	4553
will I take up a weeping and *w*	Jer 9:10	5092
make haste, and take up a *w* for us	Jer 9:18	5092
For a voice of *w* is heard out of	Jer 9:19	5092
mouth, and teach your daughters *w*	Jer 9:20	5092
neither shall there be *w* for them	Eze 7:11	5089
bitterness of heart and bitter *w*	Eze 27:31	4553
in their *w* they shall take up a	Eze 27:32	5204
W shall be in all streets	Amos 5:16	4553
are skilful of lamentation to *w*	Amos 5:16	4553
And in all vineyards shall be *w*	Amos 5:17	4553
I will make a *w* like the dragons,	Mic 1:8	4553
there shall be *w* and gnashing of	Mt 13:42	2805
there shall be *w* and gnashing of	Mt 13:50	2805
fear of her torment, weeping and *w*	Rev 18:15	3996
heads, and cried, weeping and *w*	Rev 18:19	3996

WAIT

And if a man lie not in *w*, but God	Ex 21:13	6658
they shall *w* on their priest's	Num 3:10	8104
in to *w* upon the service of the	Num 8:24	6633
or hurl at him by laying of *w*	Num 35:20	6660
him any thing without laying of *w*	Num 35:22	6660
lie in *w* for him, and rise up	Deut 19:11	693
ye shall lie in *w* against the	Josh 8:4	693
their liers in *w* on the west of	Josh 8:13	6119
in *w* for him in the top of the	Judg 9:25	693
thee, and lie in *w* in the field	Judg 9:32	693
they laid *w* against Shechem in	Judg 9:34	693
were with him, from lying in *w*	Judg 9:35	3993
laid *w* in the field, and looked,	Judg 9:43	693
laid *w* for him all night in the	Judg 16:2	693
Now there were men lying in *w*	Judg 16:9	693
there were liers in *w* abiding in	Judg 16:12	693
set liers in *w* round about Gibeah	Judg 20:29	693
the liers in *w* of Israel came	Judg 20:33	693
in *w* which they had set beside	Judg 20:36	693
And the liers in *w* hasted, and	Judg 20:37	693
the liers in *w* drew themselves	Judg 20:37	693
men of Israel and the liers in *w*	Judg 20:38	693
lie in *w* in the vineyards	Judg 21:20	693
how he laid *w* for him in the way,	1Sa 15:2	
Amalek, and laid *w* in the valley	1Sa 15:5	693
servant against me, to lie in *w*	1Sa 22:8	693
rise against me, to lie in *w*	1Sa 22:13	693
what should I *w* for the LORD any	2Kin 6:33	3176
Because their office was to *w* on	1Chr 23:28	3027
and did not then *w* by course	2Chr 5:11	8104
the Levites *w* upon their business	2Chr 13:10	
and of such as lay in *w* by the way	Ezr 8:31	693
of my appointed time will I *w*	Job 14:14	3176
If I *w*, the grave is mine house	Job 17:13	6960
or if I have laid *w* at my	Job 31:9	693
abide in the covert to lie in *w*	Job 38:40	695
He lieth in *w* secretly as a lion	Ps 10:9	693
he lieth in *w* to catch the poor	Ps 10:9	693
let none that *w* on thee be	Ps 25:3	6960
on thee do I *w* all the day	Ps 25:5	6960
for I *w* on thee	Ps 25:21	6960
W on the LORD	Ps 27:14	6960
w, I say, on the LORD	Ps 27:14	6960
the LORD, and *w* patiently for him	Ps 37:7	2342
but those that *w* upon the LORD	Ps 37:9	6960

W on the LORD, and keep his way,	Ps 37:34	6960
And now, Lord, what *w* I for	Ps 39:7	6960
and I will *w* on thy name	Ps 52:9	6960
my steps, when they *w* for my soul	Ps 56:6	6960
lo, they lie in *w* for my soul	Ps 59:3	693
his strength will I *w* upon thee	Ps 59:9	8104
My soul, *w* thou only upon God	Ps 62:5	1826
eyes fail while I *w* for my God	Ps 69:3	3176
Let not them that *w* on thee	Ps 69:6	6960
they that lay *w* for my soul take	Ps 71:10	8104
These *w* all upon thee	Ps 104:27	7663
so our eyes *w* upon the LORD our	Ps 123:2	
w for the LORD, my soul doth *w*	Ps 130:5	6960
The eyes of all *w* upon thee	Ps 145:15	7663
with us, let us lay *w* for blood	Prov 1:11	693
they lay *w* for their own blood	Prov 1:18	693
lieth in *w* at every corner	Prov 7:12	693
wicked are to lie in *w* for blood	Prov 12:6	693
but *w* on the LORD, and he shall	Prov 20:22	6960
She also lieth in *w* as for a prey	Prov 23:28	693
Lay not *w*, O wicked man, against	Prov 24:15	693
I will *w* upon the LORD, that	Is 8:17	2442
And therefore will the LORD *w*	Is 30:18	2442
are all they that *w* for him	Is 30:18	2442
But they that *w* upon the LORD	Is 40:31	6960
and the isles shall *w* for his law	Is 42:4	3176
not be ashamed that *w* for me	Is 49:23	6960
the isles shall *w* upon me	Is 51:5	6960
we *w* for light, but behold	Is 59:9	6960
Surely the isles shall *w* for me	Is 60:9	6960
they lay *w*, as he that setteth	Jer 5:26	7789
but in heart they layeth his *w*	Jer 9:8	696
therefore we will *w* upon thee	Jer 14:22	6960
was unto me as a bear lying in *w*	Lam 3:10	693
is good unto them that *w* for him	Lam 3:25	6960
quietly *w* for the salvation of	Lam 3:26	1748
they laid *w* for us in the	Lam 4:19	693
as troops of robbers *w* for a man	Hos 6:9	2442
an oven, whiles they lie in *w*	Hos 7:6	693
and *w* on thy God continually	Hos 12:6	6960
they all lie in *w* for blood	Mic 7:2	693
I will *w* for the God of my	Mic 7:7	3176
though it tarry, *w* for it	Hab 2:3	2442
Therefore *w* ye upon me, saith the	Zeph 3:8	2442
that a small ship should *w* on him	Mk 3:9	4342
Laying *w* for him, and seeking to	Lk 11:54	1748
unto men that *w* for their lord	Lk 12:36	4327
but *w* for the promise of the	Acts 1:4	4037
And when the Jews laid *w* for him	Acts 20:3	1096,1917
me by the lying in *w* of the Jews	Acts 20:19	1917
son heard of their lying in *w*	Acts 23:16	1747
for there lie in *w* for him of	Acts 23:21	1748
that the Jews laid *w* for the man	Acts 23:30	1917
laying *w* in the way to kill him	Acts 25:3	4160,1747
then do we with patience *w* for it	Rom 8:25	553
let us *w* on our ministering	Rom 12:7	
they which *w* at the altar are	1Cor 9:13	4332
For we through the Spirit *w* for	Gal 5:5	553
whereby they lie in *w* to deceive	Eph 4:14	3180
to *w* for his Son from heaven,	1Th 1:10	362

WAITED

I have *w* for thy salvation, O	Gen 49:18	6960
w for the king by the way, and	1Kin 20:38	5975
and she *w* on Naaman's wife	2Kin 5:2	1961,6440
then they *w* on their office	1Chr 6:32	5975
they that *w* with their children	1Chr 6:33	5975
Who hitherto *w* in the king's gate	1Chr 9:18	
the priests *w* on their offices	2Chr 7:6	5975
These *w* on the king, beside those	2Chr 17:19	8334
the porters *w* at every gate	2Chr 35:15	
priests and for the Levites that *w*	Neh 12:44	5975
the companies of Sheba *w* for them	Job 6:19	6960
and he is *w* for of the sword	Job 15:22	6822
Unto me men gave ear, and *w*	Job 29:21	3176
they *w* for me as for the rain	Job 29:23	3176
when I *w* for light, there came	Job 30:26	3176
Now Elihu had *w* till Job had	Job 32:4	2442
Behold, I *w* for your words	Job 32:11	3176
When I had *w*, (for they spake not	Job 32:16	3176
I *w* patiently for the LORD	Ps 40:1	6960
they *w* not for his counsel	Ps 106:13	2442
The wicked have *w* for me to	Ps 119:95	6960
we have *w* for him, and he will	Is 25:9	6960
we have *w* for him, we will be	Is 25:9	6960
O LORD, have we *w* for thee	Is 26:8	6960
we have *w* for thee	Is 33:2	6960
Now when she saw that she had *w*	Eze 19:5	3176
of Maroth *w* carefully for good	Mic 1:12	2342
w upon me knew that it was the	Zec 11:11	8104
which also *w* for the kingdom of	Mk 15:43	4327

the people w for Zacharias, and	Lk 1:21	4328
who also himself w for the	Lk 23:51	4327
of them that w on him continually	Acts 10:7	4342
And Cornelius w for them, and had	Acts 10:24	4328
Now while Paul w for them at	Acts 17:16	1551
of God w in the days of Noah	1Pet 3:20	1551

WAITETH

the adulterer w for the twilight	Job 24:15	8104
Our soul w for the LORD	Ps 33:20	2442
Truly my soul w upon God	Ps 62:1	1747
Praise w for thee, O God in Sion	Ps 65:1	1747
My soul w for the Lord more than	Ps 130:6	
so he that w on his master shall	Prov 27:18	8104
prepared for him that w for him	Is 64:4	2442
Blessed is he that w, and cometh	Dan 12:12	2442
nor w for the sons of men	Mic 5:7	3176
expectation of the creature w for	Rom 8:19	553
the husbandman w for the precious	Jas 5:7	1551

WAITING

cease w upon the service thereof	Num 8:25	6635
w at the posts of my doors	Prov 8:34	8104
w for the consolation of Israel	Lk 2:25	4327
for they were all w for him	Lk 8:40	4328
w for the moving of the water	Jn 5:3	1551
w for the adoption, to wit, the	Rom 8:23	553
w for the coming of our Lord	1Cor 1:7	553
and into the patient w for Christ	2Th 3:5	

WAKE

sleep a perpetual sleep, and not w	Jer 51:39	6974
sleep a perpetual sleep, and not w	Jer 51:57	6974
w up the mighty men, let all the	Joel 3:9	5782
us, that, whether we w or sleep	1Th 5:10	1127

WAKED

w me, as a man that is wakened	Zec 4:1	5782

WAKENED

Let the heathen be w, and come up	Joel 3:12	5782
a man that is w out of his sleep..,	Zec 4:1	5782

WAKENETH

he w morning by morning	Is 50:4	5782
he w mine ear to hear as the	Is 50:4	5782

WAKETH

city, the watchman w but in vain	Ps 127:1	8245
I sleep, but my heart w	Song 5:2	5782

WAKING

Thou holdest mine eyes w	Ps 77:4	8109

WALK

w through the land in the length	Gen 13:17	1980
w before me, and be thou perfect	Gen 17:1	1980
me, The LORD, before whom I w	Gen 24:40	1980
my fathers Abraham and Isaac did w	Gen 48:15	1980
whether they will w in my law	Ex 16:4	3212
them the way wherein they must w	Ex 18:20	3212
w abroad upon his staff, then	Ex 21:19	1980
neither shall ye w in their	Lev 18:3	3212
mine ordinances, to w therein	Lev 18:4	3212
ye shall not w in the manners of	Lev 20:23	3212
If ye w in my statutes, and keep	Lev 26:3	3212
I will w among you, and will be	Lev 26:12	1980
if ye w contrary unto me, and will	Lev 26:21	3212
but will w contrary unto me	Lev 26:23	1980
Then will I also w contrary unto	Lev 26:24	1980
unto me, but w contrary unto me	Lev 26:27	1980
Then I will w contrary unto you	Lev 26:28	1980
Ye shall w in all the ways which	Deut 5:33	3212
to w in his ways, and to fear him	Deut 8:6	3212
w after other gods, and serve them	Deut 8:19	1980
to w in all his ways, and to love	Deut 10:12	3212
to w in all his ways, and to	Deut 11:22	3212
Ye shall w after the LORD your	Deut 13:4	3212
thy God commanded thee to w in	Deut 13:5	3212
thy God, and to w ever in his ways	Deut 19:9	3212
to w in his ways, and to keep his	Deut 26:17	3212
LORD thy God, and w in his ways	Deut 28:9	1980
though I w in the imagination of	Deut 29:19	3212
to w in his ways, and to keep his	Deut 30:16	3212
w through the land, and describe	Josh 18:8	1980
to w in all his ways, and to keep	Josh 22:5	3212
the way of the LORD to w therein	Judg 2:22	3212
sit in judgment, and w by the way	Judg 5:10	1980
should w before me for ever	1Sa 2:30	1980
he shall w before mine anointed	1Sa 2:35	1980
thy sons w not in thy ways	1Sa 8:5	1980
to w in his ways, to keep his	1Kin 2:3	3212
to w before me in truth with all	1Kin 2:4	3212
And if thou wilt w in my ways	1Kin 3:14	3212
as thy father David did w	1Kin 3:14	1980

if thou wilt w in my statutes, and	1Kin 6:12	3212
all my commandments to w in them	1Kin 6:12	3212
that w before thee with all their	1Kin 8:23	1980
that they w before me as thou	1Kin 8:25	3212
good way wherein they should w	1Kin 8:36	3212
to w in all his ways, and to keep	1Kin 8:58	3212
to w in his statutes, and to keep	1Kin 8:61	3212
And if thou wilt w before me	1Kin 9:4	3212
wilt w in my ways, and do that is	1Kin 11:38	1980
been a light thing for him to w	1Kin 16:31	3212
But Jehu took no heed to w in the	2Kin 10:31	3212
to w after the LORD, and to keep	2Kin 23:3	3212
that w before thee with all their	2Chr 6:14	1980
heed to their way to w in my law	2Chr 6:16	3212
good way, wherein they should w	2Chr 6:27	3212
to w in thy ways, so long as they	2Chr 6:31	3212
thee, if thou wilt w before me	2Chr 7:17	3212
to w after the LORD, and to keep	2Chr 34:31	3212
ought ye not to w in the fear of	Neh 5:9	3212
to w in God's law, which was	Neh 10:29	3212
The wicked w on every side, when	Ps 12:8	1980
though I w through the valley of	Ps 23:4	3212
I will w in mine integrity	Ps 26:11	3212
W about Zion, and go round about	Ps 48:12	5437
that I may w before God in the	Ps 56:13	1980
God, and refused to w in his law	Ps 78:10	3212
they w on in darkness	Ps 82:5	1980
from them that w uprightly	Ps 84:11	1980
I will w in thy truth	Ps 86:11	1980
they shall w, O LORD, in the	Ps 89:15	1980
my law, and w not in my judgments	Ps 89:30	3212
I will w within my house with a	Ps 101:2	1980
feet have they, but they w not	Ps 115:7	1980
I will w before the LORD in the	Ps 116:9	1980
who w in the law of the LORD	Ps 119:1	1980
they w in his ways	Ps 119:3	1980
And I will w at liberty	Ps 119:45	1980
Though I w in the midst of	Ps 138:7	3212
know the way wherein I should w	Ps 143:8	3212
w not thou in the way with them	Prov 1:15	3212
buckler to them that w uprightly	Prov 2:7	1980
to w in the ways of darkness	Prov 2:13	3212
That thou mayest w in the way of	Prov 2:20	3212
Then shalt thou w in thy way	Prov 3:23	3212
the living which w under the sun	Eccl 4:15	1980
that knoweth to w before the	Eccl 6:8	1980
w in the ways of thine heart, and	Eccl 11:9	1980
ways, and we will w in his paths	Is 2:3	3212
let us w in the light of the LORD	Is 2:5	3212
w with stretched forth necks and	Is 3:16	1980
not w in the way of this people	Is 8:11	1980
That w to go down into Egypt, and	Is 30:2	1980
w ye in it, when ye turn to the	Is 30:21	3212
but the redeemed shall w there	Is 35:9	1980
and they shall w, and not faint	Is 40:31	3212
and spirit to them that w therein	Is 42:5	1980
for they would not w in his ways	Is 42:24	1980
w in the light of your fire, and	Is 50:11	3212
brightness, but we w in darkness	Is 59:9	1980
neither shall they w any more	Jer 3:17	3212
shall w with the house of Israel	Jer 3:18	3212
w therein, and ye shall find rest	Jer 6:16	3212
they said, We will not w therein	Jer 6:16	3212
into the field, nor w by the way	Jer 6:25	3212
neither w after other gods to	Jer 7:6	3212
w after other gods whom ye know	Jer 7:9	1980
w ye in all the ways that I have	Jer 7:23	1980
neighbour will w with slanders	Jer 9:4	1980
which w in the imagination of	Jer 13:10	1980
w after other gods, to serve them	Jer 13:10	1980
behold, ye w every one after the	Jer 16:12	1980
but we will w after our own	Jer 18:12	1980
to w in paths, in a way not cast	Jer 18:15	1980
commit adultery, and w in lies	Jer 23:14	1980
to w in my law, which I have set	Jer 26:4	1980
I will cause them to w by the	Jer 31:9	1980
shew us the way wherein we may w	Jer 42:3	1980
is desolate, the foxes w upon it	Lam 5:18	1980
That they may w in my statutes,	Eze 11:20	3212
W ye not in the statutes of your	Eze 20:18	3212
w in my statutes, and keep my	Eze 20:19	3212
w in the statutes of life,	Eze 33:15	1980
I will cause men to w upon you	Eze 36:12	3212
cause you to w in my statutes, and	Eze 36:27	3212
they shall also w in my judgments	Eze 37:24	3212
before the chambers was a w of	Eze 42:4	4109
those that w in pride he is able	Dan 4:37	1981
to w in his laws, which he set	Dan 9:10	3212
They shall w after the LORD	Hos 11:10	3212
and the just shall w in them	Hos 14:9	3212
they shall w every one in his	Joel 2:8	3212

W

Can two w together, except they	Amos 3:3	3212
ways, and we will w in his paths	Mic 4:2	3212
For all people will w every one	Mic 4:5	3212
we will w in the name of the LORD	Mic 4:5	3212
and to w humbly with thy God	Mic 6:8	3212
Ahab, and ye w in their counsels	Mic 6:16	3212
they shall stumble in their w	Nah 2:5	1979
Thou didst w through the sea with	Hab 3:15	1869
he will make me to w upon mine	Hab 3:19	1869
that they shall w like blind men	Zeph 1:17	1980
whom the LORD hath sent to w to	Zec 1:10	1980
If thou wilt w in my ways	Zec 3:7	3212
to w among these that stand by	Zec 3:7	4108
sought to go that they might w to	Zec 6:7	1980
w to and fro through the earth	Zec 6:7	1980
and they shall w up and down in his	Zec 10:12	1980
or to say, Arise, and w	Mt 9:5	4043
their sight, and the lame w	Mt 11:5	4043
maimed to be whole, the lame to w	Mt 15:31	4043
Arise, and take up thy bed, and w	Mk 2:9	4043
Why w not thy disciples according	Mk 7:5	4043
or to say, Rise up and w	Lk 5:23	4043
that the blind see, the lame w	Lk 7:22	4043
the men that w over them are not	Lk 11:44	4043
Nevertheless I must w to day	Lk 13:33	4198
which desire to w in long robes	Lk 20:46	4043
ye have one to another, as ye w	Lk 24:17	4043
him, Rise, take up thy bed, and w	Jn 5:8	4043
unto me, Take up thy bed, and w	Jn 5:11	4043
unto thee, Take up thy bed, and w	Jn 5:12	4043
for he would not w in Jewry	Jn 7:1	4043
me shall not w in darkness	Jn 8:12	4043
If any man w in the day, he	Jn 11:9	4043
But if a man w in the night	Jn 11:10	4043
W while ye have the light, lest	Jn 12:35	4043
Christ of Nazareth rise up and w	Acts 3:6	4043
we had made this man to w	Acts 3:12	4043
nations to w in their own ways	Acts 14:16	4198
neither to w after the customs	Acts 21:21	4043
but who also w in the steps of	Rom 4:12	4748
also should w in newness of life	Rom 6:4	4043
who w not after the flesh, but	Rom 8:1	4043
who w not after the flesh, but	Rom 8:4	4043
Let us w honestly, as in the day	Rom 13:13	4043
are ye not carnal, and w as men	1Cor 3:3	4043
called every one, so let him w	1Cor 7:17	4043
(For we w by faith, not by sight	2Cor 5:7	4043
will dwell in them, and w in them	2Cor 6:16	1704
For though we w in the flesh	2Cor 10:3	4043
W in the Spirit, and ye shall not	Gal 5:16	4043
let us also w in the Spirit	Gal 5:25	4748
as many as w according to this	Gal 6:16	4748
ordained that we should w in them	Eph 2:10	4043
beseech you that ye w worthy of	Eph 4:1	4043
w not as other Gentiles w	Eph 4:17	4043
w in love, as Christ also hath	Eph 5:2	4043
w as children of light	Eph 5:8	4043
See then that ye w circumspectly	Eph 5:15	4043
let us by the same rule, let us	Phil 3:16	4748
mark them which w so as ye have	Phil 3:17	4043
(For many w, of whom I have told	Phil 3:18	4043
That ye might w worthy of the	Col 1:10	4043
Jesus the Lord, so w ye in him	Col 2:6	4043
W in wisdom toward them that are	Col 4:5	4043
That ye would w worthy of God	1Th 2:12	4043
received of us how ye ought to w	1Th 4:1	4043
That ye may w honestly toward	1Th 4:12	4043
some which w among you disorderly	2Th 3:11	4043
But chiefly them that w after the	2Pet 2:10	4198
w in darkness, we lie, and do not	1Jn 1:6	4043
But if we w in the light, as he	1Jn 1:7	4043
in him ought himself also so to w	1Jn 2:6	4043
that we w after his commandments	2Jn 6	4043
the beginning, ye should w in it	2Jn 6	4043
hear that my children w in truth	3Jn 4	4043
who should w after their own	Jude 18	4198
they shall w with me in white	Rev 3:4	4043
neither can see, nor hear, nor w	Rev 9:20	4043
his garments, lest he w naked	Rev 16:15	4043
saved shall w in the light of it	Rev 21:24	4043

WALKED

Enoch w with God after he begat	Gen 5:22	1980
And Enoch w with God	Gen 5:24	1980
generations, and Noah w with God	Gen 6:9	1980
her maidens w along by the	Ex 2:5	1980
But the children of Israel w upon	Ex 14:29	1980
also have w contrary unto me	Lev 26:40	1980
that I also have w contrary unto	Lev 26:41	3212
For the children of Israel w	Josh 5:6	1980
the way which their fathers w in	Judg 2:17	1980

the travellers w through byways	Judg 5:6	3212
w through the wilderness unto the	Judg 11:16	3212
his sons w not in his ways, but	1Sa 8:3	1980
I have w before you from my	1Sa 12:2	1980
his men w all that night through	2Sa 2:29	1980
but have w in a tent and in a	2Sa 7:6	1980
all the places wherein I have w	2Sa 7:7	1980
w upon the roof of the king's	2Sa 11:2	1980
according as he w before thee in	1Kin 3:6	1980
me as thou hast w before me	1Kin 8:25	1980
before me, as David thy father w	1Kin 9:4	1980
have not w in my ways, to do that	1Kin 11:33	1980
he w in all the sins of his	1Kin 15:3	3212
w in the way of his father, and in	1Kin 15:26	3212
w in the way of Jeroboam, and in	1Kin 15:34	3212
thou hast w in the way of	1Kin 16:2	3212
For he w in all the way of	1Kin 16:26	3212
he w in all the ways of Asa his	1Kin 22:43	3212
w in the way of his father, and in	1Kin 22:52	3212
and w in the house to and fro	2Kin 4:35	3212
he w in the way of the kings of	2Kin 8:18	3212
he w in the way of the house of	2Kin 8:27	3212
made Israel sin, but w therein	2Kin 13:6	1980
but he w therein	2Kin 13:11	1980
But he w in the way of the kings	2Kin 16:3	3212
w in the statutes of the heathen,	2Kin 17:8	3212
but w in the statutes of Israel	2Kin 17:19	3212
For the children of Israel w in	2Kin 17:22	3212
how I have w before thee in truth	2Kin 20:3	1980
he w in all the way that his	2Kin 21:21	3212
all the way that his father w in	2Kin 21:21	1980
w not in the way of the LORD	2Kin 21:22	1980
w in all the way of David his	2Kin 22:2	3212
I have w with all Israel, spake I	1Chr 17:6	1980
thee whithersoever thou hast w	1Chr 17:8	1980
my law, as thou hast w before me	2Chr 6:16	3212
before me, as David thy father w	2Chr 7:17	1980
years they w in the way of David	2Chr 11:17	1980
because he w in the first ways of	2Chr 17:3	3212
w in his commandments, and not	2Chr 17:4	1980
he w in the way of Asa his father	2Chr 20:32	3212
he w in the way of the kings of	2Chr 21:6	3212
Because thou hast not w in the	2Chr 21:12	1980
But hast w in the way of the	2Chr 21:13	3212
He also w in the ways of the	2Chr 22:3	1980
He w also after their counsel, and	2Chr 22:5	1980
For he w in the ways of the kings	2Chr 28:2	3212
w in the ways of David his father	2Chr 34:2	3212
Mordecai w every day before the	Est 2:11	1980
by his light I w through darkness	Job 29:3	3212
If I have w with vanity, or if my	Job 31:5	1980
mine heart w after mine eyes, and	Job 31:7	1980
or hast thou w in the search of	Job 38:16	1980
for I have w in mine integrity	Ps 26:1	1980
and I have w in thy truth	Ps 26:3	1980
w unto the house of God in	Ps 55:14	1980
they w in their own counsels	Ps 81:12	3212
me, and Israel had w in my ways	Ps 81:13	1980
In the way wherein I w have they	Ps 142:3	1980
The people that w in darkness	Is 9:2	1980
as my servant Isaiah hath w naked	Is 20:3	1980
how I have w before thee in truth	Is 38:3	1980
have w after vanity, and are	Jer 2:5	3212
w after things that do not profit	Jer 2:8	1980
but w in the counsels and in the	Jer 7:24	3212
served, and after whom they have w	Jer 8:2	1980
my voice, neither w therein	Jer 9:13	1980
But have w after the imagination	Jer 9:14	3212
their ear, but w every one in the	Jer 11:8	3212
have w after other gods, and have	Jer 16:11	3212
thy voice, neither w in thy law	Jer 32:23	1980
nor w in my law, nor in my	Jer 44:10	1980
nor w in his law, nor in his	Jer 44:23	1980
statutes, they have not w in them	Eze 5:6	1980
have not w in my statutes,	Eze 5:7	1980
for ye have not w in my statutes	Eze 11:12	1980
hast thou not w after their ways	Eze 16:47	1980
Hath w in my statutes, and hath	Eze 18:9	1980
judgments, hath w in my statutes	Eze 18:17	1980
they w not in my statutes, and	Eze 20:13	1980
w not in my statutes, but	Eze 20:16	1980
they w not in my statutes,	Eze 20:21	1980
Thou hast w in the way of thy	Eze 23:31	1980
thou hast w up and down in the	Eze 28:14	1980
At the end of twelve months he w	Dan 4:29	1981
because he willingly w after the	Hos 5:11	1980
the which their fathers have w	Amos 2:4	1980
the lion, even the old lion, w	Nah 2:11	1980
trees, and said, We have w to	Zec 1:11	1980
So they w to and fro through the	Zec 6:7	1980
he w with me in peace and equity,	Mal 2:6	1980

that we have *w* mournfully before	Mal 3:14	1980
he *w* on the water, to go to Jesus	Mt 14:29	4043
Now as he *w* by the sea of Galilee	Mk 1:16	4043
the damsel arose, and *w*	Mk 5:42	4043
form unto two of them, as they *w*	Mk 16:12	4043
And looking upon Jesus as he *w*	Jn 1:36	4043
whole, and took up his bed, and *w*	Jn 5:9	4043
went back, and *w* no more with him	Jn 6:66	4043
these things Jesus *w* in Galilee	Jn 7:1	4043
And Jesus *w* in the temple in	Jn 10:23	4043
Jesus therefore *w* no more openly	Jn 11:54	4043
And he leaping up stood, and *w*	Acts 3:8	4043
mother's womb, who never had *w*	Acts 14:8	4043
And he leaped and *w*	Acts 14:10	4043
as if we *w* according to the flesh	2Cor 10:2	4043
w we not in the same spirit	2Cor 12:18	4043
w we not in the same steps	2Cor 12:18	4043
But when I saw that they *w* not	Gal 2:14	3716
Wherein in time past ye *w*	Eph 2:2	4043
In the which ye also *w* some time	Col 3:7	4043
when we *w* in lasciviousness	1Pet 4:3	4198
also so to walk, even as he *w*	1Jn 2:6	4043

WALKEDST

and *w* whither thou wouldest	Jn 21:18	4043

WALKEST

when thou *w* by the way, and when	Deut 6:7	3212
when thou *w* by the way, when thou	Deut 11:19	3212
w abroad any whither, that thou	1Kin 2:42	1980
when thou *w* through the fire,	Is 43:2	3212
that thou thyself also *w* orderly	Acts 21:24	4748
now *w* thou not charitably	Rom 14:15	4043
thee, even as thou *w* in the truth	3Jn 3	4043

WALKETH

What man is this that *w* in the	Gen 24:65	1980
For the LORD thy God *w* in the	Deut 23:14	1980
behold, the king *w* before you	1Sa 12:2	1980
own feet, and he *w* upon a snare	Job 18:8	1980
he *w* in the circuit of heaven	Job 22:14	1980
of iniquity, and *w* with wicked men	Job 34:8	3212
Blessed is the man that *w* not in	Ps 1:1	1980
He that *w* uprightly, and worketh	Ps 15:2	1980
Surely every man *w* in a vain shew	Ps 39:6	1980
their tongue *w* through the earth	Ps 73:9	1980
the pestilence that *w* in darkness	Ps 91:6	1980
he that *w* in a perfect way, he	Ps 101:6	1980
who *w* upon the wings of the wind	Ps 104:3	1980
that *w* in his ways	Ps 128:1	1980
man, *w* with a froward mouth	Prov 6:12	1980
that *w* uprightly surely	Prov 10:9	3212
He that *w* with wise men shall be	Prov 13:20	1980
He that *w* in his uprightness	Prov 14:2	1980
man of understanding *w* uprightly	Prov 15:21	1980
the poor that *w* in his integrity	Prov 19:1	1980
The just man *w* in his integrity	Prov 20:7	1980
poor that *w* in his uprightness	Prov 28:6	1980
Whoso *w* uprightly shall be saved	Prov 28:18	1980
but whoso *w* wisely, he shall be	Prov 28:26	1980
but the fool *w* in darkness	Eccl 2:14	1980
he that is a fool *w* by the way	Eccl 10:3	1980
He that *w* righteously, and	Is 33:15	1980
that *w* in darkness, and hath no	Is 50:10	1980
which *w* in a way that was not	Is 65:2	1980
in man that *w* to direct his steps	Jer 10:23	1980
w after the imagination of his	Jer 23:17	1980
heart *w* after the heart of their	Eze 11:21	1980
do good to him that *w* uprightly	Mic 2:7	1980
he *w* through dry places, seeking	Mt 12:43	1330
he *w* through dry places, seeking	Lk 11:24	1330
for he that *w* in darkness knoweth	Jn 12:35	4043
every brother that *w* disorderly	2Th 3:6	4043
w about, seeking whom he may	1Pet 5:8	4043
w in darkness, and knoweth not	1Jn 2:11	4043
who *w* in the midst of the seven	Rev 2:1	4043

WALKING

w in the garden in the cool of	Gen 3:8	1980
he knoweth thy *w* through this	Deut 2:7	3212
w in the statutes of David his	1Kin 3:3	3212
in *w* in the way of Jeroboam, and	1Kin 16:19	3212
and fro in the earth, and from *w* up	Job 1:7	1980
and fro in the earth, and from *w* up	Job 2:2	1980
or the moon *w* in brightness	Job 31:26	1980
princes *w* as servants upon the	Eccl 10:7	1980
forth necks and wanton eyes, *w*	Is 3:16	1980
And he did so, *w* naked and barefoot	Is 20:2	1980
each one *w* in his uprightness	Is 57:2	1980
revolters, *w* with slanders	Jer 6:28	1980
in the midst of the fire, and	Dan 3:25	1981
If a man *w* in the spirit and	Mic 2:11	1980
w by the sea of Galilee, saw two	Mt 4:18	4043

went unto them, *w* on the sea	Mt 14:25	4043
disciples saw him *w* on the sea	Mt 14:26	4043
w upon the sea, and would have	Mk 6:48	4043
when they saw him *w* upon the sea	Mk 6:49	4043
and said, I see men as trees, *w*	Mk 8:24	4043
as he was *w* in the temple, there	Mk 11:27	4043
w in all the commandments and	Lk 1:6	4198
they see Jesus *w* on the sea	Jn 6:19	4043
with them into the temple, *w*	Acts 3:8	4043
And all the people saw him *w*	Acts 3:9	4043
w in the fear of the Lord, and in	Acts 9:31	4198
not *w* in craftiness, nor handling	2Cor 4:2	4043
w after their own lusts,	2Pet 3:3	4198
found of thy children *w* in truth	2Jn 4	4043
w after their own lusts	Jude 16	4198

WALL

selfwill they digged down a *w*	Gen 49:6	7794
whose branches run over the *w*	Gen 49:22	7791
the waters were a *w* unto them on	Ex 14:22	2346
the waters were a *w* unto them on	Ex 14:29	2346
in sight are lower than the *w*	Lev 14:37	7023
no *w* round about them shall be	Lev 25:31	2346
a *w* being on this side, and a *w*	Num 22:24	1447
she thrust herself unto the *w*	Num 22:25	7023
Balaam's foot against the *w*	Num 22:25	7023
reach from the *w* of the city	Num 35:4	7023
for her house was upon the town *w*	Josh 2:15	2346
and she dwelt upon the *w*	Josh 2:15	2346
the *w* of the city shall fall down	Josh 6:5	2346
that the *w* fell down flat, so	Josh 6:20	2346
smite David even to the *w* with it	1Sa 18:11	7023
even to the *w* with the javelin	1Sa 19:10	7023
he smote the javelin into the *w*	1Sa 19:10	7023
times, even upon a seat by the *w*	1Sa 20:25	7023
They were a *w* unto us both by	1Sa 25:16	2346
any that pisseth against the *w*	1Sa 25:22	7023
any that pisseth against the *w*	1Sa 25:34	7023
his body to the *w* of Beth-shan	1Sa 31:10	7023
his sons from the *w* of Beth-shan	1Sa 31:12	7023
that they would shoot from the *w*	2Sa 11:20	2346
a millstone upon him from the *w*	2Sa 11:21	2346
why went ye nigh the *w*	2Sa 11:21	2346
from off the *w* upon thy servants	2Sa 11:24	2346
the roof over the gate unto the *w*	2Sa 18:24	2346
were with Joab battered the *w*	2Sa 20:15	2346
be thrown to thee over the *w*	2Sa 20:21	2346
by my God have I leaped over a *w*	2Sa 22:30	7791
the *w* of Jerusalem round about	1Kin 3:1	2346
that springeth out of the *w*	1Kin 4:33	7023
against the *w* of the house he	1Kin 6:5	7023
for without in the *w* of the house	1Kin 6:6	2346
wing of the one touched the one *w*	1Kin 6:27	7023
other cherub touched the other *w*	1Kin 6:27	7023
posts were a fifth part of the *w*	1Kin 6:31	2346
tree, a fourth part of the *w*	1Kin 6:33	2346
the *w* of Jerusalem, and Hazor, and	1Kin 9:15	2346
him that pisseth against the *w*	1Kin 14:10	7023
not one that pisseth against a *w*	1Kin 16:11	7023
there a *w* fell upon twenty and	1Kin 20:30	2346
him that pisseth against the *w*	1Kin 21:21	7023
eat Jezebel by the *w* of Jezreel	1Kin 21:23	2426
for a burnt offering upon the *w*	2Kin 3:27	2346
chamber, I pray thee, on the *w*	2Kin 4:10	7023
Israel was passing by upon the *w*	2Kin 6:26	2346
and he passed by upon the *w*	2Kin 6:30	2346
him that pisseth against the *w*	2Kin 9:8	7023
her blood was sprinkled on the *w*	2Kin 9:33	7023
brake down the *w* of Jerusalem	2Kin 14:13	2346
of the people that are on the *w*	2Kin 18:26	2346
me to the men which sit on the *w*	2Kin 18:27	2346
Then he turned his face to the *w*	2Kin 20:2	7023
reaching to the *w* of the house	2Chr 3:11	7023
reaching to the *w* of the house	2Chr 3:12	7023
brake down the *w* of Jerusalem	2Chr 25:23	2346
and brake down the *w* of Gath	2Chr 26:6	2346
the *w* of Jabneh, and the	2Chr 26:6	2346
the *w* of Ashdod, and built cities	2Chr 26:6	2346
gate, and at the turning of the *w*	2Chr 26:9	2346
on the *w* of Ophel he built much	2Chr 27:3	2346
up all the *w* that was broken	2Chr 32:5	2346
the towers, and another *w* without	2Chr 32:5	2346
of Jerusalem that were on the *w*	2Chr 32:18	2346
a *w* without the city of David	2Chr 33:14	2346
and brake down the *w* of Jerusalem	2Chr 36:19	2346
this house, and to make up this *w*	Ezr 5:3	846
and to give us a *w* in Judah	Ezr 9:9	1447
the *w* of Jerusalem also is broken	Neh 1:3	2346
for the *w* of the city, and for the	Neh 2:8	7023
by the brook, and viewed the *w*	Neh 2:15	2346
us build up the *w* of Jerusalem	Neh 2:17	2346

Jerusalem unto the broad *w*	Neh 3:8	2346
on the *w* unto the dung gate	Neh 3:13	2346
the *w* of the pool of Siloah by	Neh 3:15	2346
armoury at the turning of the *w*	Neh 3:19	
from the turning of the *w* unto	Neh 3:20	
Azariah unto the turning of the *w*	Neh 3:24	
over against the turning of the *w*	Neh 3:25	
out, even unto the *w* of Ophel	Neh 3:27	2346
heard that we builded the *w*	Neh 4:1	2346
even break down their stone *w*	Neh 4:3	2346
So built we the *w*	Neh 4:6	2346
all the *w* was joined together	Neh 4:6	2346
we are not able to build the *w*	Neh 4:10	2346
in the lower places behind the *w*	Neh 4:13	2346
we returned all of us to the *w*	Neh 4:15	2346
They which builded on the *w*	Neh 4:17	2346
and we are separated upon the *w*	Neh 4:19	2346
I continued in the work of this *w*	Neh 5:16	2346
heard that I had builded the *w*	Neh 6:1	2346
which cause thou buildest the *w*	Neh 6:6	2346
So the *w* was finished in the	Neh 6:15	2346
when the *w* was built, and I had	Neh 7:1	2346
at the dedication of the *w* of	Neh 12:27	2346
people, and the gates, and the *w*	Neh 12:30	2346
the princes of Judah upon the *w*	Neh 12:31	2346
upon the *w* toward the dung gate	Neh 12:31	2346
David, at the going up of the *w*	Neh 12:37	2346
the half of the people upon the *w*	Neh 12:38	2346
furnaces even unto the broad *w*	Neh 12:38	2346
them, Why lodge ye about the *w*	Neh 13:21	2346
by my God have I leaped over a *w*	Ps 18:29	7791
as a bowing *w* shall ye be	Ps 62:3	7023
as an high *w* in his own conceit	Prov 18:11	2346
the stone *w* thereof was broken	Prov 24:31	1444
behold, he standeth behind our *w*	Song 2:9	3796
If she be a *w*, we will build upon	Song 8:9	2346
I am a *w*, and my breasts like	Song 8:10	2346
tower, and upon every fenced *w*	Is 2:15	2346
and break down the *w* thereof	Is 5:5	1447
ye broken down to fortify the *w*	Is 22:10	2346
ones is as a storm against the *w*	Is 25:4	7023
to fall, swelling out in a high *w*	Is 30:13	2346
of the people that are on the *w*	Is 36:11	2346
me to the men that sit upon the *w*	Is 36:12	2346
turned his face toward the *w*	Is 38:2	7023
We grope for the *w* like the blind	Is 59:10	7023
this people a fenced brasen *w*	Jer 15:20	2346
a fire in the *w* of Damascus	Jer 49:27	2346
the *w* of Babylon shall fall	Jer 51:44	2346
the *w* of the daughter of Zion	Lam 2:8	2346
the rampart and the *w* to lament	Lam 2:8	2346
O *w* of the daughter of Zion, let	Lam 2:18	2346
set it for a *w* of iron between	Eze 4:3	7023
I looked, behold a hole in the *w*	Eze 8:7	7023
me, Son of man, dig now in the *w*	Eze 8:8	7023
and when I had digged in the *w*	Eze 8:8	7023
pourtrayed upon the *w* round about	Eze 8:10	7023
thou through the *w* in their sight	Eze 12:5	7023
through the *w* with mine hand	Eze 12:7	7023
the *w* to carry out thereby	Eze 12:12	7023
and one built up a *w*, and, lo,	Eze 13:10	2434
when the *w* is fallen, shall it	Eze 13:12	7023
the *w* that ye have daubed with	Eze 13:15	7023
I accomplish my wrath upon the *w*	Eze 13:15	7023
The *w* is no more, neither they	Eze 13:15	7023
she saw men pourtrayed upon the *w*	Eze 23:14	7023
every *w* shall fall to the ground	Eze 38:20	2346
behold a *w* on the outside of the	Eze 40:5	2346
he measured the *w* of the house	Eze 41:5	7023
they entered into the *w* which was	Eze 41:6	7023
not hold in the *w* of the house	Eze 41:6	7023
The thickness of the *w*, which was	Eze 41:9	7023
the *w* of the building was five	Eze 41:12	7023
by all the *w* round about within	Eze 41:17	7023
made, and on the *w* of the temple	Eze 41:20	7023
the *w* that was without over	Eze 42:7	1447
w of the court toward the east	Eze 42:10	1444
before the *w* toward the east	Eze 42:12	1448
it had a *w* round about, five	Eze 42:20	2346
the *w* between me and them, they	Eze 43:8	7023
of the *w* of the king's palace	Dan 5:5	3797
shall be built again, and the *w*	Dan 9:25	2742
thy way with thorns, and make a *w*	Hos 2:6	1447
shall climb the *w* like men of war	Joel 2:7	2346
they shall run upon the *w*	Joel 2:9	2346
will send a fire on the *w* of Gaza	Amos 1:7	2346
send a fire on the *w* of Tyrus	Amos 1:10	2346
kindle a fire in the *w* of Rabbah	Amos 1:14	2346
and leaned his hand on the *w*	Amos 5:19	7023
upon a *w* made by a plumbline	Amos 7:7	2346
shall make haste to the *w* thereof	Nah 2:5	2346

sea, and her *w* was from the sea	Nah 3:8	2346
the stone shall cry out of the *w*	Hab 2:11	7023
will be unto her a *w* of fire	Zec 2:5	2346
let him down by the *w* in a basket	Acts 9:25	5038
shall smite thee, thou whited *w*	Acts 23:3	5109
a basket was I let down by the *w*	2Cor 11:33	5038
middle *w* of partition between us	Eph 2:14	
And had a *w* great and high, and had	Rev 21:12	5038
the *w* of the city had twelve	Rev 21:14	5038
gates thereof, and the *w* thereof	Rev 21:15	5038
And he measured the *w* thereof	Rev 21:17	5038
of the *w* of it was of jasper	Rev 21:18	5038
the foundations of the *w* of the	Rev 21:19	5038

WALLED

sell a dwelling house in a *w* city	Lev 25:29	2346
w city shall be established for	Lev 25:30	2346
in the land, and the cities are *w*	Num 13:28	1219
are great and *w* up to heaven	Deut 1:28	1219

WALLOW

sackcloth, and *w* thyself in ashes	Jer 6:26	6428
w yourselves in the ashes, ye	Jer 25:34	6428
Moab also shall *w* in his vomit	Jer 48:26	5606
they shall *w* themselves in the	Eze 27:30	6428

WALLOWED

Amasa *w* in blood in the midst of	2Sa 20:12	1556
fell on the ground, and *w* foaming	Mk 9:20	2947

WALLOWING

was washed to her *w* in the mire	2Pet 2:22	2946

WALLS

if the plague be in the *w* of the	Lev 14:37	7023
be spread in the *w* of the house	Lev 14:39	7023
cities were fenced with high *w*	Deut 3:5	2346
fenced *w* come down, wherein thou	Deut 28:52	2346
threescore great cities with *w*	1Kin 4:13	2346
against the *w* of the house round	1Kin 6:5	7023
be fastened in the *w* of the house	1Kin 6:6	7023
he built the *w* of the house	1Kin 6:15	7023
house, and the *w* of the cieling	1Kin 6:15	7023
the *w* with boards of cedar	1Kin 6:16	7023
he carved all the *w* of the house	1Kin 6:29	7023
the way of the gate between two *w*	2Kin 25:4	2346
brake down the *w* of Jerusalem	2Kin 25:10	2346
to overlay the *w* of the houses	1Chr 29:4	7023
the *w* thereof, and the doors	2Chr 3:7	7023
and graved cherubims on the *w*	2Chr 3:7	7023
the nether, fenced cities, with *w*	2Chr 8:5	2346
cities, and make about them *w*	2Chr 14:7	2346
and have set up the *w* thereof	Ezr 4:12	7791
the *w* set up again, then will	Ezr 4:13	7791
the *w* thereof set up, by this	Ezr 4:16	7791
and timber is laid in the *w*	Ezr 5:8	3797
this house, and to make up these *w*	Ezr 5:9	846
viewed the *w* of Jerusalem, which	Neh 2:13	2346
heard that the *w* of Jerusalem	Neh 4:7	2346
Which make oil within their *w*	Job 24:11	7791
build thou the *w* of Jerusalem	Ps 51:18	2346
go about it upon the *w* thereof	Ps 55:10	2346
Peace be within thy *w*, and	Ps 122:7	2426
that is broken down, and without *w*	Prov 25:28	2346
the keepers of the *w* took away my	Song 5:7	2346
of vision, breaking down the *w*	Is 22:5	7023
also a ditch between the two *w*	Is 22:11	2346
fort of thy *w* shall he bring down	Is 25:12	2346
salvation will God appoint for *w*	Is 26:1	2346
thy *w* are continually before me	Is 49:16	2346
mine house and within my *w* a place	Is 56:5	2346
of strangers shall build up thy *w*	Is 60:10	2346
thou shalt call thy Salvation	Is 60:18	2346
I have set watchmen upon thy *w*	Is 62:6	2346
against all the *w* thereof round	Jer 1:15	2346
brasen *w* against the whole land,	Jer 1:18	2346
Go ye up upon her *w*, and destroy	Jer 5:10	8284
which besiege you without the *w*	Jer 21:4	2346
by the gate betwixt the two *w*	Jer 39:4	2346
and brake down the *w* of Jerusalem	Jer 39:8	2346
are fallen, her *w* are thrown down	Jer 50:15	2346
standard upon the *w* of Babylon	Jer 51:12	2346
The broad *w* of Babylon shall be	Jer 51:58	2346
way of the gate between the two *w*	Jer 52:7	2346
brake down all the *w* of Jerusalem	Jer 52:14	2346
of the enemy the *w* of her palaces	Lam 2:7	2346
they shall destroy the *w* of Tyrus	Eze 26:4	2346
set engines of war against thy *w*	Eze 26:9	2346
thy *w* shall shake at the noise of	Eze 26:10	2346
and they shall break down thy *w*	Eze 26:12	2346
army were upon thy *w* round about	Eze 27:11	2346
shields upon thy *w* round about	Eze 27:11	2346
are talking against thee by the *w*	Eze 33:30	7023

all of them dwelling without w .... Eze 38:11   2346
the building, with the w thereof .... Eze 41:13   7023
the w thereof, were of wood .... Eze 41:22   7023
like as were made upon the w .... Eze 41:25   7023
day that thy w are to be built .... Mic 7:11   1447
w for the multitude of men .... Zec 2:4
By faith the w of Jericho fell .... Heb 11:30   5038

WANDER
when God caused me to w from my ...... Gen 20:13   8582
your children shall w in the .... Num 14:33   7462
he made them w in the wilderness .... Num 32:13   5128
the blind to w out of the way .... Deut 27:18   7686
causeth them to w in a wilderness .... Job 12:24   8582
unto God, they w for lack of meat .... Job 38:41   8582
Lo, then would I w far off .... Ps 55:7   5074
Let them w up and down for meat, ... Ps 59:15   5128
and causeth them to w in the .... Ps 107:40   8582
O let me not w from thy .... Ps 119:10   7686
they shall w every one to his .... Is 47:15   8582
people, Thus have they loved to w .... Jer 14:10   5128
that shall cause him to w .... Jer 48:12   6808
they shall w from sea to sea, and .... Amos 8:12   5128

WANDERED
w in the wilderness of Beer-sheba .... Gen 21:14   8582
of Israel w in the wilderness .... Josh 14:10   1980
They w in the wilderness in a .... Ps 107:4   8582
they w through the wilderness .... Is 16:8   8582
They have w as blind men in the .... Lam 4:14   5128
when they fled away and w, they .... Lam 4:15   5128
My sheep w through all the .... Eze 34:6   7686
or three cities w unto one city .... Amos 4:8   5128
they w about in sheepskins and .... Heb 11:37   4022
they w in deserts, and in .... Heb 11:38   4105

WANDERERS
Lord, that I will send unto him w .... Jer 48:12   6808
they shall be w among the nations .... Hos 9:17   5074

WANDEREST
and under every green tree thou w .... Jer 2:20   6808

WANDERETH
He w abroad for bread, saying, ... Job 15:23   5074
The man that w out of the way of .... Prov 21:16   8582
As a bird that w from her nest .... Prov 27:8   5074
so is a man that w from his place .... Prov 27:8   5074
bewray not him that w .... Is 16:3   5074
none shall gather up him that w .... Jer 49:5   5074

WANDERING
and, behold, he was w in the field .... Gen 37:15   8582
As the bird by w, as the swallow .... Prov 26:2   5110
the eyes than the w of the desire .... Eccl 6:9   1981
as a w bird cast out of the nest, ... Is 16:2   5074
w about from house to house 1Ti 5:13   4022
w stars, to whom is reserved the .... Jude 13   4107

WANDERINGS
Thou tellest my w .... Ps 56:8   5112

WANT
nakedness, and in w of all things .... Deut 28:48   2640
for she shall eat them for w of .... Deut 28:57   2640
a place where there is no w of .... Judg 18:10   4270
there is no w of any thing .... Judg 19:19   4270
the rock for w of a shelter .... Job 24:8   1097
For w and famine they were .... Job 30:3   2639
seen any perish for w of clothing .... Job 31:19   1097
I shall not w .... Ps 23:1   2637
for there is no w to them that .... Ps 34:9   4270
Lord shall not w any good thing .... Ps 34:10   2637
and thy w as an armed man .... Prov 6:11   4270
but fools die for w of wisdom .... Prov 10:21   2638
is destroyed for w of judgment .... Prov 13:23   3808
the belly of the wicked shall w .... Prov 13:25   2637
but in the w of people is the .... Prov 14:28   657
every one that is hasty only to w .... Prov 21:5   4270
the rich, shall surely come to w .... Prov 22:16   4270
and thy w as an armed man .... Prov 24:34   4270
shall fail, none shall w her mate .... Is 34:16   6485
David shall never w a man to sit .... Jer 33:17   3772
shall the priests the Levites w a .... Jer 33:18   3772
the son of Rechab shall not w .... Jer 35:19   3772
stricken through for w of the .... Lam 4:9
That they may w bread and water, ... Eze 4:17   2637
w of bread in all your places .... Amos 4:6   2640
but she of her w did cast in all .... Mk 12:44   5304
and he began to be in w .... Lk 15:14   5302
may be a supply for their w 2Cor 8:14   5303
also may be a supply for your w 2Cor 8:14   5303
supplieth the w of the saints 2Cor 9:12   5303
Not that I speak in respect of w .... Phil 4:11   5304

WANTED
we have w all things, and have .... Jer 44:18   2637
And when they w wine, the mother .... Jn 2:3   5302
when I was present with you, and w 2Cor 11:9   5302

WANTETH
for his need, in that which he w .... Deut 15:8   2637
as for him that w understanding .... Prov 9:4   2638
as for him that w understanding .... Prov 9:16   2638
of words there w not sin .... Prov 10:19   2308
The prince that w understanding .... Prov 28:16   2638
so that he w nothing for his soul .... Eccl 6:2   2638
round goblet, which w not liquor .... Song 7:2   2637

WANTING
let none be w 2Kin 10:19   6485
whosoever shall be w, he shall 2Kin 10:19   6485
with words, yet they are w to him .... Prov 19:7   3808
that which is w cannot be .... Eccl 1:15   2642
in the balances, and art found w .... Dan 5:27   2627
in order the things that are w .... Titus 1:5   3007
that nothing be w unto them .... Titus 3:13   3007
be perfect and entire, w nothing .... Jas 1:4   3007

WANTON
w eyes, walking and mincing as .... Is 3:16   8265
begun to wax w against Christ 1Ti 5:11   2691
pleasure on the earth, and been w .... Jas 5:5   4684

WANTONNESS
not in chambering and w, not in .... Rom 13:13   766
of the flesh, through much w 2Pet 2:18   766

WANTS
let all thy w lie upon me .... Judg 19:20   4270
and he that ministered to my w .... Phil 2:25   5532

WAR
That these made w with Bera king .... Gen 14:2   4421
when there falleth out any w .... Ex 1:10   4421
the people repent when they see w .... Ex 13:17   4421
The Lord is a man of w .... Ex 15:3   4421
sworn that the Lord will have w .... Ex 17:16   4421
There is a noise of w in the camp .... Ex 32:17   4421
able to go forth to w in Israel .... Num 1:3   6635
that were able to go forth to w .... Num 1:20   6635
that were able to go forth to w .... Num 1:22   6635
that were able to go forth to w .... Num 1:24   6635
that were able to go forth to w .... Num 1:26   6635
that were able to go forth to w .... Num 1:28   6635
that were able to go forth to w .... Num 1:30   6635
that were able to go forth to w .... Num 1:32   6635
that were able to go forth to w .... Num 1:34   6635
that were able to go forth to w .... Num 1:36   6635
that were able to go forth to w .... Num 1:38   6635
that were able to go forth to w .... Num 1:40   6635
that were able to go forth to w .... Num 1:42   6635
able to go forth to w in Israel .... Num 1:45   6635
if ye go to w in your land .... Num 10:9   4421
are able to go to w in Israel .... Num 26:2   6635
Arm some of yourselves unto the w .... Num 31:3   6635
of Israel, shall ye send to the w .... Num 31:4   6635
twelve thousand armed for w .... Num 31:5   6635
And Moses sent them to the w .... Num 31:6   6635
of Eleazar the priest, to the w .... Num 31:6   6635
men of w which went to the battle .... Num 31:21   6635
them that took the w upon them .... Num 31:27   4421
men of w which went out to battle .... Num 31:28   4421
which the men of w had caught .... Num 31:32   6635
of them that went out to w .... Num 31:36   6635
of w which are under our charge .... Num 31:49   4421
(For the men of w had taken spoil .... Num 31:53   6635
Shall your brethren go to w .... Num 32:6   4421
go armed before the Lord to w .... Num 32:20   4421
pass over, every man armed for w .... Num 32:27   6635
on every man his weapons of w .... Deut 1:41   4421
the generation of the men of w .... Deut 2:14   4421
all the men of w were consumed .... Deut 2:16   4421
all that are meet for the w .... Deut 3:18   2438
by signs, and by wonders, and by w ..... Deut 4:34   4421
but will make w against thee .... Deut 20:12   4421
in making w against it to take it .... Deut 20:19   3898
the city that maketh w with thee .... Deut 20:20   4421
forth to w against thine enemies .... Deut 21:10   4421
wife, he shall not go out to w .... Deut 24:5   6635
for w passed over before the Lord .... Josh 4:13   6635
were males, even all the men of w .... Josh 5:4   4421
all the people that were men of w .... Josh 5:6   4421
compass the city, all ye men of w .... Josh 6:3   4421
all the people of w with thee .... Josh 8:1   4421
arose, and all the people of w .... Josh 8:3   4421
people of w that were with him .... Josh 8:11   4421
Gibeon, and made w against it .... Josh 10:5   3898
and all the people of w with him .... Josh 10:7   4421

the men of *w* which went with him	Josh 10:24	4421
and all the people of *w* with him	Josh 11:7	4421
Joshua made *w* a long time with	Josh 11:18	4421
And the land rested from *w*	Josh 11:23	4421
even so is my strength now, for *w*	Josh 14:11	4421
And the land had rest from *w*	Josh 14:15	4421
because he was a man of *w*	Josh 17:1	4421
to go up to *w* against them	Josh 22:12	6635
might know, to teach them *w*	Judg 3:2	4421
judged Israel, and went out to *w*	Judg 3:10	4421
then was *w* in the gates	Judg 5:8	3901
of Ammon made *w* against Israel	Judg 11:4	3898
of Ammon made *w* against Israel	Judg 11:5	3898
doest me wrong to *w* against me	Judg 11:27	3898
men appointed with weapons of *w*	Judg 18:11	4421
appointed with their weapons of *w*	Judg 18:16	4421
were appointed with weapons of *w*	Judg 18:17	4421
all these were men of *w*	Judg 20:17	4421
not to each man his wife in the *w*	Judg 21:22	4421
and to make his instruments of *w*	1Sa 8:12	4421
there was sore *w* against the	1Sa 14:52	4421
mighty valiant man, and a man of *w*	1Sa 16:18	4421
he a man of *w* from his youth	1Sa 17:33	4421
and Saul set him over the men of *w*	1Sa 18:5	4421
And there was *w* again	1Sa 19:8	4421
all the people together to *w*	1Sa 23:8	4421
the Philistines make *w* against me	1Sa 28:15	3898
and the weapons of *w* perished	2Sa 1:27	4421
Now there was long *w* between the	2Sa 3:1	4421
while there was *w* between the	2Sa 3:6	4421
did, and how the *w* prospered	2Sa 11:7	4421
all the things concerning the *w*	2Sa 11:18	4421
matters of the *w* unto the king	2Sa 11:19	4421
and thy father is a man of *w*	2Sa 17:8	4421
had yet *w* again with Israel	2Sa 21:15	4421
He teacheth my hands to *w*	2Sa 22:35	4421
and shed the blood of *w* in peace	1Kin 2:5	4421
put the blood of *w* upon his	1Kin 2:5	4421
but they were men of *w*, and his	1Kin 9:22	4421
there was *w* between Rehoboam and	1Kin 14:30	4421
there was *w* between Rehoboam and	1Kin 15:6	4421
there was *w* between Abijam and	1Kin 15:7	4421
there was *w* between Asa and Baasha	1Kin 15:16	4421
there was *w* between Asa and Baasha	1Kin 15:32	4421
or whether they be come out for *w*	1Kin 20:18	4421
years without *w* between Syria	1Kin 22:1	4421
Joram the son of Ahab to the *w*	2Kin 8:28	4421
hand of Jehoahaz his father by *w*	2Kin 13:25	4421
ten thousand, and took Selah by *w*	2Kin 14:7	4421
Israel came up to Jerusalem to *w*	2Kin 16:5	4421
counsel and strength for the *w*	2Kin 18:20	4421
all that were strong and apt for *w*	2Kin 24:16	4421
all the men of *w* fled by night by	2Kin 25:4	4421
that was set over the men of *w*	2Kin 25:19	4421
they made *w* with the Hagarites	1Chr 5:10	4421
shoot with bow, and skilful in *w*	1Chr 5:18	4421
that went out to the *w*	1Chr 5:18	6635
they made *w* with the Hagarites,	1Chr 5:19	4421
slain, because the *w* was of God	1Chr 5:22	4421
were bands of soldiers for *w*	1Chr 7:4	4421
soldiers, fit to go out for *w*	1Chr 7:11	6635
of them that were apt to the *w*	1Chr 7:40	6635
the mighty men, helpers of the *w*	1Chr 12:1	4421
men fit for the battle, that	1Chr 12:8	6635
that were ready armed to the *w*	1Chr 12:23	6635
hundred, ready armed to the *w*	1Chr 12:24	6635
mighty men of valour for the *w*	1Chr 12:25	6635
went forth to battle, expert in *w*	1Chr 12:33	4421
with all instruments of *w*	1Chr 12:33	4421
of the Danites expert in *w* twenty	1Chr 12:35	4421
went forth to battle, expert in *w*	1Chr 12:36	4421
instruments of *w* for the battle	1Chr 12:37	6635
All these men of *w*, that could	1Chr 12:38	4421
(for Hadarezer had *w* with Tou	1Chr 18:10	4421
that there arose *w* at Gezer with	1Chr 20:4	4421
there was *w* again with the	1Chr 20:5	4421
And yet again there was *w* at Gath	1Chr 20:6	4421
because thou hast been a man of *w*	1Chr 28:3	4421
If thy people go out to *w* against	2Chr 6:34	4421
but they were men of *w*, and chief	2Chr 8:9	4421
there was *w* between Abijah and	2Chr 13:2	4421
with an army of valiant men of *w*	2Chr 13:3	4421
he had no *w* in those years	2Chr 14:6	4421
there was no more *w* unto the five	2Chr 15:19	4421
made no *w* against Jehoshaphat	2Chr 17:10	3898
and the men of *w*, mighty men of	2Chr 17:13	4421
thousand ready prepared for the *w*	2Chr 17:18	6635
and we will be with thee in the *w*	2Chr 18:3	4421
son of Ahab king of Israel to *w*	2Chr 22:5	4421
choice men, able to go forth to *w*	2Chr 25:5	6635
men, that went out to *w* by bands	2Chr 26:11	6635
that made *w* with mighty power, to	2Chr 26:13	4421
against them that came from the *w*	2Chr 28:12	6635
set captains of *w* over the people	2Chr 32:6	4421
put captains of *w* in all the	2Chr 33:14	2428
the house wherewith I have	2Chr 35:21	4421
in *w* from the power of the sword	Job 5:20	4421
changes and *w* are against me	Job 10:17	6635
against the day of battle and *w*	Job 38:23	4421
He teacheth my hands to *w*	Ps 18:34	4421
though *w* should rise against me,	Ps 27:3	4421
butter, but *w* was in his heart	Ps 55:21	7128
thou the people that delight in *w*	Ps 68:30	7128
but when I speak, they are for *w*	Ps 120:7	4421
are they gathered together for *w*	Ps 140:2	4421
which teacheth my hands to *w*	Ps 144:1	4421,7128
and with good advice make *w*	Prov 20:18	4421
counsel thou shalt make thy *w*	Prov 24:6	4421
a time of *w*, and a time of peace	Eccl 3:8	4421
there is no discharge in that *w*	Eccl 8:8	4421
is better than weapons of *w*	Eccl 9:18	7128
hold swords, being expert in *w*	Song 3:8	4421
shall they learn *w* any more	Is 2:4	4421
The mighty man, and the man of *w*	Is 3:2	4421
the sword, and thy mighty in the *w*	Is 3:25	4421
toward Jerusalem to *w* against it	Is 7:1	4421
and from the grievousness of *w*	Is 21:15	4421
I have counsel and strength for *w*	Is 36:5	4421
is come forth to make *w* with thee	Is 37:9	3898
they that *w* against thee shall be	Is 41:12	4421
stir up jealousy like a man of *w*	Is 42:13	4421
of the trumpet, the alarm of *w*	Jer 4:19	4421
Prepare ye *w* against her	Jer 6:4	4421
array as men for *w* against thee	Jer 6:23	4421
of Babylon maketh *w* against us	Jer 21:2	3898
of *w* that are in your hands	Jer 21:4	4421
and against great kingdoms, of *w*	Jer 28:8	4421
the hands of the men of *w* that	Jer 38:4	4421
saw them, and all the men of *w*	Jer 39:4	4421
were found there, and the men of *w*	Jer 41:3	4421
of Ahikam, even mighty men of *w*	Jer 41:16	4421
of Egypt, where we shall see no *w*	Jer 42:14	4421
mighty and strong men for the *w*	Jer 48:14	4421
of *w* to be heard in Rabbah of the	Jer 49:2	4421
all the men of *w* shall be cut off	Jer 49:26	4421
all her men of *w* shall be cut off	Jer 50:30	4421
art my battle ax and weapons of *w*	Jer 51:20	4421
the men of *w* are affrighted	Jer 51:32	4421
up, and all the men of *w* fled	Jer 52:7	4421
had the charge of the men of *w*	Jer 52:25	4421
company make for him in the *w*	Eze 17:17	4421
engines of *w* against thy walls	Eze 26:9	6904
were in thine army, they men of *w*	Eze 27:10	4421
merchandise, and all thy men of *w*	Eze 27:27	4421
to hell with their weapons of *w*	Eze 32:27	4421
mighty men, and with all men of *w*	Eze 39:20	4421
same horn made *w* with the saints	Dan 7:21	7129
unto the end of the *w* desolations	Dan 9:26	4421
climb the wall like men of *w*	Joel 2:7	4421
Prepare *w*, wake up the mighty men	Joel 3:9	4421
let all the men of *w* draw near	Joel 3:9	4421
by securely as men averse from *w*	Mic 2:8	4421
they even prepare *w* against him	Mic 3:5	4421
shall they learn *w* any more	Mic 4:3	4421
going to make *w* against another	Lk 14:31	*4171*
his men of *w* set him at nought	Lk 23:11	*4753*
we do not *w* after the flesh	2Cor 10:3	*4754*
by them mightest *w* a good warfare	1Ti 1:18	*4754*
your lusts that *w* in your members	Jas 4:1	*4754*
ye fight and *w*, yet ye have not,	Jas 4:2	*4170*
lusts, which *w* against the soul	1Pet 2:11	*4754*
pit shall make *w* against them	Rev 11:7	*4171*
And there was *w* in heaven	Rev 12:7	*4171*
went to make *w* with the remnant	Rev 12:17	*4171*
who is able to make *w* with him	Rev 13:4	*4170*
him to make *w* with the saints	Rev 13:7	*4171*
These shall make *w* with the Lamb	Rev 17:14	*4170*
he doth judge and make *w*	Rev 19:11	*4170*
gathered together to make *w*	Rev 19:19	*4171*

WARD

he put them in *w* in the house of	Gen 40:3	4929
and they continued a season in *w*	Gen 40:4	4929
him in the of his lord's house	Gen 40:7	4929
put me in *w* in the captain of the	Gen 41:10	4929
all together into *w* three days	Gen 42:17	4929
And they put him in *w*, that he	Lev 24:12	4929
And they put him in *w*, because it	Num 15:34	4929
keep the house, and put them in *w*	2Sa 20:3	4931
kept the house of Saul	1Chr 12:29	4931
And they cast lots, *w* against	1Chr 25:8	4931
against *w*, as well	1Chr 25:8	4929

of the going up, *w* against *w*	1Chr 26:16	4929
man of God, *w* over against *w*	Neh 12:24	4929
were porters keeping the *w* at the	Neh 12:25	4929
porters kept the *w* of their God	Neh 12:45	4931
the *w* of the purification,	Neh 12:45	4931
and I am set in my *w* whole nights	Is 21:8	4931
a captain of the *w* was there	Jer 37:13	6488
And they put him in *w* in chains	Eze 19:9	5474
past the first and the second *w*	Acts 12:10	*5438*

WARDROBE

son of Harhas, keeper of the *w*	2Kin 22:14	899
son of Hasrah, keeper of the *w*	2Chr 34:22	899

WARDS

the house of the tabernacle, by *w*	1Chr 9:23	4931
having *w* one against another, to	1Chr 26:12	4931
appointed the *w* of the priests and	Neh 13:30	4931

WARE

w or any victuals on the sabbath	Neh 10:31	4728
brought fish, and all manner of *w*	Neh 13:16	4377
sellers of all kind of *w* lodged	Neh 13:20	4465
w no clothes, neither abode in	Lk 8:27	*1737*
They were *w* of it, and fled unto	Acts 14:6	*4894*
Of whom be thou *w* also	2Ti 4:15	*5442*

WARES

Gather up thy *w* out of the land,	Jer 10:17	3666
multitude of the *w* of thy making	Eze 27:16	4639
multitude of the *w* of thy making	Eze 27:18	4639
When thy *w* went forth out of the	Eze 27:33	5801
cast forth the *w* that were in the	Jonah 1:5	3627

WARFARE

their armies together for *w*	1Sa 28:1	6635
that her *w* is accomplished, that	Is 40:2	6635
Who goeth a *w* any time at his own	1Cor 9:7	*4754*
weapons of our *w* are not carnal	2Cor 10:4	*4752*
by them mightest war a good *w*	1Ti 1:18	*4752*

WARM

and the flesh of the child waxed *w*	2Kin 4:34	2552
What time they wax *w*, they vanish	Job 6:17	2215
How thy garments are *w*, when he	Job 37:17	2525
but how can one be *w* alone	Eccl 4:11	3179
will take thereof, and *w* himself	Is 44:15	2552
himself, and saith, Aha, I am *w*	Is 44:16	2552
there shall not be a coal to *w* at	Is 47:14	2552
clothe you, but there is none *w*	Hag 1:6	2527

WARMED

if he were not *w* with the fleece	Job 31:20	2552
and *w* himself at the fire	Mk 14:54	2328
and they *w* themselves	Jn 18:18	2328
stood with them, and *w* himself	Jn 18:18	2328
And Simon Peter stood and *w* himself	Jn 18:25	2328
them, Depart in peace, be ye *w*	Jas 2:16	2328

WARMETH

the earth, and *w* them in the dust,	Job 39:14	2552
he *w* himself, and saith, Aha, I am	Is 44:16	2552

WARMING

And when she saw Peter *w* himself	Mk 14:67	*2328*

WARN

ye shall even *w* them that they	2Chr 19:10	2094
nor speakest to *w* the wicked from	Eze 3:18	2094
Yet if thou *w* the wicked, and he	Eze 3:19	2094
if thou *w* the righteous man	Eze 3:21	2094
blow the trumpet, and *w* the people	Eze 33:3	2094
at my mouth, and *w* them from me	Eze 33:7	2094
to *w* the wicked from his way	Eze 33:8	2094
if thou *w* the wicked of his way	Eze 33:9	2094
I ceased not to *w* every one night	Acts 20:31	3560
but as my beloved sons I *w* you	1Cor 4:14	3560
w them that are unruly, comfort	1Th 5:14	3560

WARNED

w him of, and saved himself there,	2Kin 6:10	2094
Moreover by them is thy servant *w*	Ps 19:11	2094
surely live, because he is *w*	Eze 3:21	2094
trumpet, and the people be not *w*	Eze 33:6	2094
being *w* of God in a dream that	Mt 2:12	5537
being *w* of God in a dream, he	Mt 2:22	5537
who hath *w* you to flee from the	Mt 3:7	5263
who hath *w* you to flee from the	Lk 3:7	5263
was *w* from God by an holy angel	Acts 10:22	5537
being *w* of God of things not seen	Heb 11:7	5537

WARNING

To whom shall I speak, and give *w*	Jer 6:10	5749
my mouth, and give them *w* from me	Eze 3:17	2094
and thou givest him not *w*, nor	Eze 3:18	2094
because thou hast not given him *w*	Eze 3:20	2094
of the trumpet, and taketh not *w*	Eze 33:4	2094

of the trumpet, and took not *w*	Eze 33:5	2094
But he that taketh *w* shall	Eze 33:5	2094
w every man, and teaching every	Col 1:28	*3560*

WARP

Whether it be in the *w*, or woof	Lev 13:48	8359
or in the skin, either in the *w*	Lev 13:49	8359
in the garment, either in the *w*	Lev 13:51	8359
that garment, whether *w* or woof	Lev 13:52	8359
in the garment, either in the *w*	Lev 13:53	8359
out of the skin, or out of the *w*	Lev 13:56	8359
in the garment, either in the *w*	Lev 13:57	8359
And the garment, either *w*, or woof	Lev 13:58	8359
woollen or linen, either in the *w*	Lev 13:59	8359

WARRED

they *w* against the Midianites, as	Num 31:7	6633
Moses divided from the men that *w*	Num 31:42	6633
w against Israel, and sent and	Josh 24:9	3898
of the acts of Jeroboam, how he *w*	1Kin 14:19	3898
besieged Samaria, and *w* against it	1Kin 20:1	3898
might that he shewed, and how he *w*	1Kin 22:45	3898
king of Syria *w* against Israel	2Kin 6:8	3898
he did, and his might, how he *w*	2Kin 14:28	3898
w against the Philistines, and	2Chr 26:6	3898

WARRETH

No man that *w* entangleth himself	2Ti 2:4	*4754*

WARRING

king of Assyria *w* against Libnah	2Kin 19:8	3898
king of Assyria *w* against Libnah	Is 37:8	3898
w against the law of my mind, and	Rom 7:23	*497*

WARRIOR

of the *w* is with confused noise	Is 9:5	5431

WARRIORS

chosen men, which were *w*	1Kin 12:21	6213,4421
chosen men, which were *w*	2Chr 11:1	6213,4421

WARS

in the book of the *w* of the LORD	Num 21:14	4421
had not known all the *w* of Canaan	Judg 3:1	4421
for Hadadezer had *w* with Toi	2Sa 8:10	4421
of the LORD his God for the *w*	1Kin 5:3	4421
abundantly, and hast made great *w*	1Chr 22:8	4421
there were *w* between Rehoboam and	2Chr 12:15	4421
from henceforth thou shalt have *w*	2Chr 16:9	4421
the acts of Jotham, and all his *w*	2Chr 27:7	4421
He maketh *w* to cease unto the end	Ps 46:9	4421
hear of *w* and rumours of *w*	Mt 24:6	*4171*
hear of *w* and rumours of *w*	Mk 13:7	*4171*
But when ye shall hear of *w*	Lk 21:9	*4171*
From whence come *w* and fightings	Jas 4:1	*4171*

WAS See APPENDIX.

WASH

w your feet, and rest yourselves	Gen 18:4	7364
w your feet, and ye shall rise up	Gen 19:2	7364
camels, and water to *w* his feet	Gen 24:32	7364
down to *w* herself at the river	Ex 2:5	7364
let them *w* their clothes	Ex 19:10	3526
and shalt *w* them with water	Ex 29:4	7364
w the inwards of him, and his legs	Ex 29:17	7364
foot also of brass, to *w* withal	Ex 30:18	7364
and his sons shall *w* their hands	Ex 30:19	7364
they shall *w* with water, that	Ex 30:20	7364
So they shall *w* their hands	Ex 30:21	7364
and *w* them with water	Ex 40:12	7364
and put water there, to *w* withal	Ex 40:30	7364
and his legs shall he *w* in water	Lev 1:9	7364
But he shall *w* the inwards	Lev 1:13	7364
thou shalt *w* that whereon it was	Lev 6:27	3526
he did *w* the inwards and the legs,	Lev 9:14	7364
of them shall *w* their clothes	Lev 11:25	3526
of them shall *w* his clothes	Lev 11:28	3526
carcase of it shall *w* his clothes	Lev 11:40	3526
carcase of it shall *w* his clothes	Lev 11:40	3526
he shall *w* his clothes, and be	Lev 13:6	3526
he shall *w* his clothes, and be	Lev 13:34	3526
priest shall command that they *w*	Lev 13:54	3526
of skin it be, which thou shalt *w*	Lev 13:58	3526
be cleansed shall *w* his clothes	Lev 14:8	3526
w himself in water, that he may	Lev 14:8	7364
he shall *w* his clothes, also he	Lev 14:9	3526
also he shall *w* his flesh in	Lev 14:9	7364
in the house shall *w* his clothes	Lev 14:47	3526
in the house shall *w* his clothes	Lev 14:47	3526
his bed shall *w* his clothes	Lev 15:5	3526
the issue shall *w* his clothes	Lev 15:6	3526
the issue shall *w* his clothes	Lev 15:7	3526
then he shall *w* his clothes	Lev 15:8	3526
those things shall *w* his clothes	Lev 15:10	3526

he shall *w* his clothes, and bathe	Lev 15:11	3526
w his clothes, and bathe his flesh	Lev 15:13	3526
then he shall *w* all his flesh in	Lev 15:16	7364
her bed shall *w* his clothes	Lev 15:21	3526
she sat upon shall *w* his clothes	Lev 15:22	3526
shall *w* his clothes, and bathe	Lev 15:27	3526
shall he *w* his flesh in water	Lev 16:4	7364
he shall *w* his flesh with water	Lev 16:24	7364
the scapegoat shall *w* his clothes	Lev 16:26	3526
burneth them shall *w* his clothes	Lev 16:28	3526
he shall both *w* his clothes	Lev 17:15	3526
But if he *w* them not, nor bathe	Lev 17:16	3526
unless he *w* his flesh with water	Lev 22:6	7364
let them *w* their clothes, and so	Num 8:7	3526
the priest shall *w* his clothes	Num 19:7	3526
her shall *w* his clothes in water	Num 19:8	3526
of the heifer shall *w* his clothes	Num 19:10	3526
w his clothes, and bathe himself	Num 19:19	3526
of separation shall *w* his clothes	Num 19:21	3526
ye shall *w* your clothes on the	Num 31:24	3526
shall *w* their hands over the	Deut 21:6	7364
he shall *w* himself with water	Deut 23:11	7364
W thyself therefore, and anoint	Ruth 3:3	7364
w the feet of the servants of my	1Sa 25:41	7364
down to thy house, and *w* thy feet	2Sa 11:8	7364
w in Jordan seven times, and thy	2Kin 5:10	7364
may I not *w* in them, and be clean	2Kin 5:12	7364
then, when he saith to thee, *W*	2Kin 5:13	7364
and five on the left, to *w* in them	2Chr 4:6	7364
sea was for the priests to *w* in	2Chr 4:6	7364
If I *w* myself with snow water, and	Job 9:30	7364
I will *w* mine hands in innocency	Ps 26:6	7364
W me throughly from mine iniquity	Ps 51:2	3526
w me, and I shall be whiter than	Ps 51:7	3526
he shall *w* his feet in the blood	Ps 58:10	7364
W you, make you clean	Is 1:16	7364
For though thou *w* thee with nitre	Jer 2:22	3526
w thine heart from wickedness	Jer 4:14	3526
for whom thou didst *w* thyself	Eze 23:40	7364
anoint thine head, and *w* thy face	Mt 6:17	3538
for they *w* not their hands when	Mt 15:2	3538
except they *w* their hands oft	Mk 7:3	3538
from the market, except they *w*	Mk 7:4	907
began to *w* his feet with tears,	Lk 7:38	1026
w in the pool of Siloam, (which	Jn 9:7	3538
Go to the pool of Siloam, and *w*	Jn 9:11	3538
began to *w* the disciples' feet,	Jn 13:5	3538
him, Lord, dost thou *w* my feet	Jn 13:6	3538
him, Thou shalt never *w* my feet	Jn 13:8	3538
If I *w* thee not, thou hast no	Jn 13:8	3538
needeth not save to *w* his feet	Jn 13:10	3538
ye also ought to *w* one another's	Jn 13:14	3538
w away thy sins, calling on the	Acts 22:16	628

WASHED

them water, and they *w* their feet	Gen 43:24	7364
he *w* his face, and went out, and	Gen 43:31	7364
he *w* his garments in wine, and his	Gen 49:11	3526
and they *w* their clothes	Ex 19:14	3526
his sons *w* their hands and their	Ex 40:31	7364
came near unto the altar, they *w*	Ex 40:32	7364
and his sons, and *w* them with water	Lev 8:6	7364
he *w* the inwards and the legs in	Lev 8:21	7364
on the plague, after that it is *w*	Lev 13:55	3526
it shall be *w* the second time	Lev 13:58	3526
shall be *w* with water, and be	Lev 15:17	3526
purified, and they *w* their clothes	Num 8:21	3526
they *w* their feet, and did eat and	Judg 19:21	7364
David arose from the earth, and *w*	2Sa 12:20	7364
nor *w* his clothes, from the day	2Sa 19:24	3526
one *w* the chariot in the pool of	1Kin 22:38	7857
and they *w* his armour	1Kin 22:38	7364
the burnt offering they *w* in them	2Chr 4:6	1740
When I *w* my steps with butter, and	Job 29:6	7364
vain, and *w* my hands in innocency	Ps 73:13	7364
eyes, and yet is not *w* from their	Prov 30:12	7364
I have *w* my feet	Song 5:3	7364
w with milk, and fitly set	Song 5:12	7364
When the Lord shall have *w* away	Is 4:4	7364
neither wast thou *w* in water to	Eze 16:4	7364
Then *w* I thee with water	Eze 16:9	7364
I throughly *w* away thy blood from	Eze 16:9	7857
where they *w* the burnt offering	Eze 40:38	1740
w his hands before the multitude,	Mt 27:24	633
but she hath *w* my feet with tears	Lk 7:44	1026
he had not first *w* before dinner	Lk 11:38	907
He went his way therefore, and *w*	Jn 9:7	3538
and I went and *w*, and I received	Jn 9:11	3538
put clay upon mine eyes, and I *w*	Jn 9:15	3538
He that is *w* needeth not save to	Jn 13:10	3068
So after he had *w* their feet	Jn 13:12	3538

Lord and Master, have *w* your feet	Jn 13:14	3538
whom when they had *w*, they laid	Acts 9:37	3068
of the night, and *w* their stripes	Acts 16:33	3068
but ye are *w*, but ye are	1Cor 6:11	628
if she have *w* the saints' feet,	1Ti 5:10	3538
our bodies *w* with pure water	Heb 10:22	3068
the sow that was *w* to her	2Pet 2:22	3068
w us from our sins in his own	Rev 1:5	3068
have *w* their robes, and made them	Rev 7:14	4150

WASHEST

thou *w* away the things which grow	Job 14:19	7857

WASHING

somewhat dark after the *w* of it	Lev 13:56	3526
the roof he saw a woman *w* herself	2Sa 11:2	7364
that every one put them off for *w*	Neh 4:23	4325
shorn, which came up from the *w*	Song 4:2	7367
of sheep which go up from the *w*	Song 6:6	7367
as the *w* of cups, and pots, brasen	Mk 7:4	909
of men, as the *w* of pots and cups	Mk 7:8	909
out of them, and were *w* their nets	Lk 5:2	637
cleanse it with the *w* of water by	Eph 5:26	3067
by the *w* of regeneration, and	Titus 3:5	3067

WASHINGS

in meats and drinks, and divers *w*	Heb 9:10	909

WASHPOT

Moab is my *w*	Ps 60:8	5518,7366
Moab is my *w*	Ps 108:9	5518,7366

WAST

Who told thee that thou *w* naked	Gen 3:11	
for out of it *w* thou taken	Gen 3:19	
of God, and thou *w* pleased with me	Gen 33:10	
manner when thou *w* his butler	Gen 40:13	1961
remember that thou *w* a servant in	Deut 5:15	1961
thou shalt remember that thou *w* a	Deut 15:15	1961
that thou *w* a bondman in Egypt	Deut 16:12	1961
because thou *w* a stranger in his	Deut 23:7	1961
that thou *w* a bondman in Egypt	Deut 24:18	1961
thou shalt remember that thou *w* a	Deut 24:22	1961
behind thee, when thou *w* faint	Deut 25:18	
of Egypt, which thou *w* afraid of	Deut 28:60	
with whose maidens thou *w*	Ruth 3:2	
When thou *w* little in thine own	1Sa 15:17	
w thou not made the head of the	1Sa 15:17	
How *w* thou not afraid to stretch	2Sa 1:14	
thou *w* slain in thine high places	2Sa 1:25	
thou *w* he that leddest out and	2Sa 5:2	1961
thou *w* he that leddest out and	1Chr 11:2	1961
or *w* thou made before the hills	Job 15:7	
Where *w* thou when I laid the	Job 38:4	1961
thou it, because thou *w* then born	Job 38:21	
thou *w* a God that forgavest them,	Ps 99:8	1961
Jordan, that thou *w* driven back	Ps 114:5	
though thou *w* angry with me,	Is 12:1	
wherein thou *w* made to serve	Is 14:3	
spoiledst, and thou *w* not spoiled	Is 33:1	
Since thou *w* precious in my sight,	Is 43:4	
w called a transgressor from the	Is 48:8	
of youth, when thou *w* refused	Is 54:6	
therefore thou *w* not grieved	Is 57:10	
as thou *w* ashamed of Assyria	Jer 2:36	
O Babylon, and thou *w* not aware	Jer 50:24	
in the day thou *w* born thy navel	Eze 16:4	
neither *w* thou washed in water to	Eze 16:4	
thou *w* not salted at all, nor	Eze 16:4	
but thou *w* cast out in the open	Eze 16:5	
in the day that thou *w* born	Eze 16:5	
thee when thou *w* in thy blood	Eze 16:6	
thee when thou *w* in thy blood	Eze 16:6	
is grown, whereas thou *w* naked	Eze 16:7	
Thus *w* thou decked with gold and	Eze 16:13	
thou *w* exceeding beautiful, and	Eze 16:13	
of thy youth, when thou *w* naked	Eze 16:22	1961
bare, and *w* polluted in thy blood	Eze 16:22	1961
because thou *w* unsatiable	Eze 16:29	
yet thou *w* not satisfied herewith	Eze 16:29	
thou *w* corrupted more than they	Eze 16:47	
in the place where thou *w* created	Eze 21:30	
thou *w* not purged, thou shalt not	Eze 24:13	
that *w* inhabited of seafaring men	Eze 26:17	
which *w* strong in the sea, she and	Eze 26:17	
thou *w* replenished, and made very	Eze 27:25	
in the day that thou *w* created	Eze 28:13	
thou *w* upon the holy mountain of	Eze 28:14	1961
Thou *w* perfect in thy ways from	Eze 28:15	
from the day that thou *w* created	Eze 28:15	
even thou *w* as one of them	Obad 11	
Thou also *w* with Jesus of Galilee	Mt 26:69	2258
thou also *w* with Jesus of	Mk 14:67	2258

W

when thou *w* under the fig tree, I	Jn 1:48	5607
Thou *w* altogether born in sins,	Jn 9:34	
say unto thee, When thou *w* young	Jn 21:18	2258
for thou *w* slain, and hast	Rev 5:9	
God Almighty, which art, and *w*	Rev 11:17	2258
O Lord, which art, and *w*, and	Rev 16:5	2258

WASTE

And I will make your cities *w*	Lev 26:31	2723
be desolate, and your cities *w*	Lev 26:33	2723
have laid them *w* even unto Nophah	Num 21:30	8074
in the *w* howling wilderness	Deut 32:10	8414
The barrel of meal shall not *w*	1Kin 17:14	3615
lay *w* fenced cities into ruinous	2Kin 19:25	7582
of wickedness *w* them any more	1Chr 17:9	1086
my fathers' sepulchres, lieth *w*	Neh 2:3	2720
we are in, how Jerusalem lieth *w*	Neh 2:17	2720
in former time desolate and *w*	Job 30:3	4875
satisfy the desolate and *w* ground	Job 38:27	4875
laid *w* his dwelling place	Ps 79:7	8074
boar out of the wood doth *w* it	Ps 80:13	3765
And I will lay it *w*	Is 5:6	1326
the *w* places of the fat ones	Is 5:17	2723
in the night Ar of Moab is laid *w*	Is 15:1	7703
the night Kir of Moab is laid *w*	Is 15:1	7703
for it is laid *w*, so that there	Is 23:1	7703
for your strength is laid *w*	Is 23:14	7703
the earth empty, and maketh it *w*	Is 24:1	1110
The highways lie *w*, the wayfaring	Is 33:8	8074
to generation it shall lie *w*	Is 34:10	2717
have laid *w* all the nations	Is 37:18	2717
w defenced cities into ruinous	Is 37:26	7582
I will make *w* mountains and hills,	Is 42:15	2717
they that made thee *w* shall go	Is 49:17	2717
For thy *w* and thy desolate places,	Is 49:19	2723
he will comfort all her *w* places	Is 51:3	2723
ye *w* places of Jerusalem	Is 52:9	2723
thee shall build the old *w* places	Is 58:12	2723
and they shall repair the *w* cities	Is 61:4	2721
our pleasant things are laid *w*	Is 64:11	2723
yelled, and they made his land *w*	Jer 2:15	8047
and thy cities shall be laid *w*	Jer 4:7	5327
should this city be laid *w*	Jer 27:17	2723
for Noph shall be *w* and desolate	Jer 46:19	8047
a desolation, a reproach, a *w*	Jer 49:13	2721
w and utterly destroy after them,	Jer 50:21	2717
Moreover I will make thee *w*	Eze 5:14	2723
the cities shall be laid *w*	Eze 6:6	2717
that your altars may be laid *w*	Eze 6:6	2717
are inhabited shall be laid *w*	Eze 12:20	2717
and he laid *w* their cities	Eze 19:7	2717
be replenished, now she is laid *w*	Eze 26:2	2717
of Egypt shall be desolate and *w*	Eze 29:9	2723
make the land of Egypt utterly *w*	Eze 29:10	2723
w shall be desolate forty years	Eze 29:12	2717
and I will make the land *w*	Eze 30:12	8074
I will lay thy cities *w*, and thou	Eze 35:4	2723
and the *w* and desolate and ruined	Eze 36:35	2720
so shall the *w* cities be filled	Eze 36:38	2720
Israel, when they shall be always *w*	Eze 38:8	2723
He hath laid my vine *w*, and barked	Joel 1:7	8047
of Israel shall be laid *w*	Amos 7:9	2717
and they shall build the *w* cities	Amos 9:14	8074
they shall *w* the land of Assyria	Mic 5:6	7489
She is empty, and void, and *w*	Nah 2:10	1110
thee, and say, Nineveh is laid *w*	Nah 3:7	7703
I made their streets *w*, that none	Zeph 3:6	2717
houses, and this house lie *w*	Hag 1:4	2720
Because of mine house that is *w*	Hag 1:9	2720
his heritage *w* for the dragons of	Mal 1:3	8077
saying, To what purpose is this *w*	Mt 26:8	684
Why was this *w* of the ointment	Mk 14:4	684

WASTED

carcases be *w* in the wilderness	Num 14:33	8552
the Kenite shall be *w*, until	Num 24:22	1197
of the men of war were *w* out from	Deut 2:14	8552
And the barrel of meal shall not *w*	1Kin 17:16	3615
w the country of the children of	1Chr 20:1	7843
they that *w* us required of us	Ps 137:3	8437
cities be *w* without inhabitant	Is 6:11	7582
the sea, and the river shall be *w*	Is 19:5	2717
those nations shall be utterly *w*	Is 60:12	2717
and they are *w* and desolate, as at	Jer 44:6	2723
midst of the cities that are *w*	Eze 30:7	2717
The field is *w*, the land mourneth	Joel 1:10	7703
for the corn is *w*	Joel 1:10	7703
there *w* his substance with	Lk 15:13	1287
unto him that he had *w* his goods	Lk 16:1	1287
the church of God, and *w* it	Gal 1:13	4199

WASTENESS

trouble and distress, a day of *w*	Zeph 1:15	7722

WASTER

brother to him that is a great *w*	Prov 18:9	7843
I have created the *w* to destroy	Is 54:16	7843

WASTES

And they shall build the old *w*	Is 61:4	2723
thereof shall be perpetual *w*	Jer 49:13	2723
they that inhabit those *w* of the	Eze 33:24	2723
in the *w* shall by the sword	Eze 33:27	2723
to the valleys, to the desolate *w*	Eze 36:4	2723
and the *w* shall be builded	Eze 36:10	2723
cities, and the *w* shall be builded	Eze 36:33	2723

WASTETH

But man dieth, and *w* away	Job 14:10	2522
the destruction that *w* at noonday	Ps 91:6	7736
He that *w* his father, and chaseth	Prov 19:26	7703

WASTING

w and destruction are in their	Is 59:7	7701
w nor destruction within thy	Is 60:18	7701

WATCH

The LORD *w* between me and thee,	Gen 31:49	6822
that in the morning *w* the LORD	Ex 14:24	821
in the beginning of the middle *w*	Judg 7:19	821
and they had but newly set the *w*	Judg 7:19	8104
of the host in the morning *w*	1Sa 11:11	821
to *w* him, and to slay him in the	1Sa 19:11	8104
kept the *w* lifted up his eyes	2Sa 13:34	6822
of the *w* of the king's house	2Kin 11:5	4931
shall ye keep the *w* of the house	2Kin 11:6	4931
even they shall keep the *w* of the	2Kin 11:7	4931
the *w* tower in the wilderness	2Chr 20:24	4707
shall keep the *w* of the LORD	2Chr 23:6	4931
w ye, and keep them, until ye	Ezr 8:29	8245
set a *w* against them day and night	Neh 4:9	4929
of Jerusalem, every one in his *w*	Neh 7:3	4929
that thou settest a *w* over me	Job 7:12	4929
dost thou not *w* over my sin	Job 14:16	8104
is past, and as a *w* in the night	Ps 90:4	821
I *w*, and am as a sparrow alone	Ps 102:7	8245
than they that *w* for the morning	Ps 130:6	8104
than they that *w* for the morning	Ps 130:6	8104
Set a *w*, O LORD, before my mouth	Ps 141:3	8108
w in the watchtower, eat, drink	Is 21:5	6822
all that *w* for iniquity are cut	Is 29:20	8245
a leopard shall *w* over their	Jer 5:6	8245
so will I *w* over them, to build,	Jer 31:28	8245
I will *w* over them for evil, and	Jer 44:27	8245
of Babylon, make the *w* strong	Jer 51:12	4929
w the way, make thy loins strong,	Nah 2:1	6822
I will stand upon my *w*, and set me	Hab 2:1	4931
will *w* to see what he will say	Hab 2:1	6822
in the fourth *w* of the night	Mt 14:25	5438
W therefore	Mt 24:42	1127
in what *w* the thief would come	Mt 24:43	5438
W therefore, for ye know neither	Mt 25:13	1127
tarry ye here, and *w* with me	Mt 26:38	1127
could ye not *w* with me one hour	Mt 26:40	1127
W and pray, that ye enter not into	Mt 26:41	1127
said unto them, Ye have a *w*	Mt 27:65	2892
sealing the stone, and setting a *w*	Mt 27:66	2892
some of the *w* came into the city,	Mt 28:11	2892
about the fourth *w* of the night	Mk 6:48	5438
Take ye heed, *w* and pray	Mk 13:33	69
and commanded the porter to *w*	Mk 13:34	1127
W ye therefore	Mk 13:35	1127
I say unto you I say unto all, *W*	Mk 13:37	1127
tarry ye here, and *w*	Mk 14:34	1127
couldest not thou *w* one hour	Mk 14:37	1127
W ye and pray, lest ye enter into	Mk 14:38	1127
keeping *w* over their flock by	Lk 2:8	5438
if he shall come in the second *w*	Lk 12:38	5438
or come in the third *w*	Lk 12:38	5438
W ye therefore, and pray always,	Lk 21:36	69
Therefore *w*, and remember, that by	Acts 20:31	1127
W ye, stand fast in the faith,	1Cor 16:13	1127
w in the same with thanksgiving	Col 4:2	1127
but let us *w* and be sober	1Th 5:6	1127
But *w* thou in all things, endure	2Ti 4:5	3525
for they *w* for your souls, as	Heb 13:17	69
therefore sober, and *w* unto prayer	1Pet 4:7	3525
If therefore thou shalt not *w*	Rev 3:3	1127

WATCHED

they *w* the house to kill him	Ps 59:t	8104
All my familiars *w* for my halting	Jer 20:10	8104
that like as I have *w* over them	Jer 31:28	8245
in our watching we have *w* for a	Lam 4:17	6822
hath the LORD *w* upon the evil	Dan 9:14	8245

W

thief would come, he would have *w*	Mt 24:43	*1127*
And sitting down they *w* him there	Mt 27:36	*5083*
And they *w* him, whether he would	Mk 3:2	*3906*
And the scribes and Pharisees *w* him	Lk 6:7	*3906*
thief would come, he would have *w*	Lk 12:39	*1127*
the sabbath day, that they *w* him	Lk 14:1	*3906*
And they *w* him, and sent forth	Lk 20:20	*3906*
they *w* the gates day and night to	Acts 9:24	*3906*

WATCHER

head upon my bed, and, behold, a *w*	Dan 4:13	*5894*
And whereas the king saw a *w*	Dan 4:23	*5894*

WATCHERS

that *w* come from a far country,	Jer 4:16	*5341*
matter is by the decree of the *w*	Dan 4:17	*5894*

WATCHES

appoint *w* of the inhabitants of	Neh 7:3	*4931*
were over against them in the *w*	Neh 12:9	*4931*
meditate on thee in the night *w*	Ps 63:6	*821*
Mine eyes prevent the night *w*	Ps 119:148	*821*
in the beginning of the *w* pour	Lam 2:19	*821*

WATCHETH

The wicked *w* the righteous, and	Ps 37:32	*6822*
it *w* for thee	Eze 7:6	*6974*
Blessed is he that *w*, and keepeth	Rev 16:15	*1127*

WATCHFUL

Be *w*, and strengthen the things	Rev 3:2	*1127*

WATCHING

sat upon a seat by the wayside *w*	1Sa 4:13	*6822*
w daily at my gates, waiting at	Prov 8:34	*8245*
in our *w* we have watched for a	Lam 4:17	*6822*
w Jesus, saw the earthquake, and	Mt 27:54	*5083*
lord when he cometh shall find *w*	Lk 12:37	*1127*
w thereunto with all perseverance	Eph 6:18	*69*

WATCHINGS

in tumults, in labours, in *w*	2Cor 6:5	*70*
in *w* often, in hunger and thirst,	2Cor 11:27	*70*

WATCHMAN

the *w* went up to the roof over	2Sa 18:24	*6822*
the *w* cried, and told the king	2Sa 18:25	*6822*
the *w* saw another man running	2Sa 18:26	*6822*
the *w* called unto the porter, and	2Sa 18:26	*6822*
the *w* said, Me thinketh the	2Sa 18:27	*6822*
there stood a *w* on the tower in	2Kin 9:17	*6822*
the *w* told, saying, The messenger	2Kin 9:18	*6822*
the *w* told, saying, He came even	2Kin 9:20	*6822*
city, the *w* waketh but in vain	Ps 127:1	*8104*
Lord said unto me, Go, set a *w*	Is 21:6	*6822*
He calleth to me out of Seir, *W*	Is 21:11	*8104*
W, what of the night	Is 21:11	*8104*
The *w* said, The morning cometh,	Is 21:12	*8104*
I have made thee a *w* unto the	Eze 3:17	*6822*
coasts, and set him for their *w*	Eze 33:2	*6822*
But if the *w* see the sword come,	Eze 33:6	*6822*
I have set thee a *w* unto the	Eze 33:7	*6822*
The *w* of Ephraim was with my God	Hos 9:8	*6822*

WATCHMAN'S

will I require at the *w* hand	Eze 33:6	*6822*

WATCHMEN

the *w* of Saul in Gibeah of	1Sa 14:16	*6822*
tower of the *w* to the fenced city	2Kin 17:9	*5341*
tower of the *w* to the fenced city	2Kin 18:8	*5341*
The *w* that go about the city	Song 3:3	*8104*
The *w* that went about the city	Song 5:7	*8104*
Thy *w* shall lift up the voice	Is 52:8	*6822*
His *w* are blind	Is 56:10	*6822*
I have set *w* upon thy walls, O	Is 62:6	*8104*
Also I set *w* over you, saying,	Jer 6:17	*6822*
that the *w* upon the mount Ephraim	Jer 31:6	*5341*
the watch strong, set up the *w*	Jer 51:12	*8104*
the day of thy *w* and thy	Mic 7:4	*6822*

WATCHTOWER

Prepare the table, watch in the *w*	Is 21:5	*6844*
upon the *w* in the daytime	Is 21:8	*4707*

WATER

went out of Eden to *w* the garden	Gen 2:10	*8248*
a fountain of *w* in the wilderness	Gen 16:7	*4325*
Let a little *w*, I pray you, be	Gen 18:4	*4325*
and took bread, and a bottle of *w*	Gen 21:14	*4325*
the *w* was spent in the bottle, and	Gen 21:15	*4325*
her eyes, and she saw a well of *w*	Gen 21:19	*4325*
went, and filled the bottle with *w*	Gen 21:19	*4325*
Abimelech because of a well of *w*	Gen 21:25	*4325*
of *w* at the time of the evening	Gen 24:11	*4325*
time that women go out to draw *w*	Gen 24:11	*4325*
I stand here by the well of *w*	Gen 24:13	*4325*

of the city come out to draw *w*	Gen 24:13	*4325*
drink a little *w* of thy pitcher	Gen 24:17	*4325*
I will draw *w* for thy camels also	Gen 24:19	*4325*
ran again unto the well to draw *w*	Gen 24:20	*4325*
w to wash his feet, and the men's	Gen 24:32	*4325*
Behold, I stand by the well of *w*	Gen 24:43	*4325*
the virgin cometh forth to draw *w*	Gen 24:43	*4325*
a little *w* of thy pitcher to	Gen 24:43	*4325*
down unto the well, and drew *w*	Gen 24:45	*4325*
Isaac digged again the wells of *w*	Gen 26:18	*4325*
found there a well of springing *w*	Gen 26:19	*4325*
herdmen, saying, The *w* is ours	Gen 26:20	*4325*
and said unto him, We have found *w*	Gen 26:32	*4325*
w ye the sheep, and go and feed	Gen 29:7	*8248*
then we *w* the sheep	Gen 29:8	*8248*
was empty, there was no *w* in it	Gen 37:24	*4325*
Joseph's house, and gave them *w*	Gen 43:24	*4325*
Unstable as *w*, thou shalt not	Gen 49:4	*4325*
Because I drew him out of the *w*	Ex 2:10	*4325*
and they came and drew *w*, and filled	Ex 2:16	
troughs to *w* their father's flock	Ex 2:16	*8248*
also drew *w* enough for us, and	Ex 2:19	
shalt take of the *w* of the river	Ex 4:9	*4325*
the *w* which thou takest out of	Ex 4:9	*4325*
lo, he goeth out unto the *w*	Ex 7:15	*4325*
to drink of the *w* of the river	Ex 7:18	*4325*
and upon all their pools of *w*	Ex 7:19	*4325*
not drink of the *w* of the river	Ex 7:21	*4325*
about the river for *w* to drink	Ex 7:24	*4325*
not drink of the *w* of the river	Ex 7:24	*4325*
lo, he cometh forth to the *w*	Ex 8:20	*4325*
it raw, nor sodden at all with *w*	Ex 12:9	*4325*
in the wilderness, and found no *w*	Ex 15:22	*4325*
where were twelve wells of *w*	Ex 15:27	*4325*
there was no *w* for the people to	Ex 17:1	*4325*
Give us *w* that we may drink	Ex 17:2	*4325*
the people thirsted there for *w*	Ex 17:3	*4325*
and there shall come *w* out of it	Ex 17:6	*4325*
that is in the *w* under the earth	Ex 20:4	*4325*
shall bless thy bread, and thy *w*	Ex 23:25	*4325*
and shalt wash them with *w*	Ex 29:4	*4325*
and thou shalt put *w* therein	Ex 30:18	*4325*
they shall wash with *w*, that	Ex 30:20	*4325*
powder, and strawed it upon the *w*	Ex 32:20	*4325*
neither eat bread, nor drink *w*	Ex 34:28	*4325*
the altar, and shalt put *w* therein	Ex 40:7	*4325*
congregation, and wash them with *w*	Ex 40:12	*4325*
put *w* there, to wash withal	Ex 40:30	*4325*
and his legs shall he wash in *w*	Lev 1:9	*4325*
the inwards and the legs with *w*	Lev 1:13	*4325*
be both scoured, and rinsed in *w*	Lev 6:28	*4325*
his sons, and washed them with *w*	Lev 8:6	*4325*
the inwards and the legs in *w*	Lev 8:21	*4325*
is done, it must be put into *w*	Lev 11:32	*4325*
that on which such *w* cometh shall	Lev 11:34	*4325*
pit, wherein there is plenty of *w*	Lev 11:36	*4325*
But if any *w* be put upon the seed	Lev 11:38	*4325*
an earthen vessel over running *w*	Lev 14:5	*4325*
was killed over the running *w*	Lev 14:6	*4325*
his hair, and wash himself in *w*	Lev 14:8	*4325*
also he shall wash his flesh in *w*	Lev 14:9	*4325*
an earthen vessel over running *w*	Lev 14:50	*4325*
slain bird, and in the running *w*	Lev 14:51	*4325*
the bird, and with the running *w*	Lev 14:52	*4325*
clothes, and bathe himself in *w*	Lev 15:5	*4325*
clothes, and bathe himself in *w*	Lev 15:6	*4325*
clothes, and bathe himself in *w*	Lev 15:7	*4325*
clothes, and bathe himself in *w*	Lev 15:8	*4325*
clothes, and bathe himself in *w*	Lev 15:10	*4325*
and hath not rinsed his hands in *w*	Lev 15:11	*4325*
clothes, and bathe himself in *w*	Lev 15:11	*4325*
of wood shall be rinsed in *w*	Lev 15:12	*4325*
and bathe his flesh in running *w*	Lev 15:13	*4325*
he shall wash all his flesh in *w*	Lev 15:16	*4325*
shall be washed with *w*, and be	Lev 15:17	*4325*
shall both bathe themselves in *w*	Lev 15:18	*4325*
clothes, and bathe himself in *w*	Lev 15:21	*4325*
clothes, and bathe himself in *w*	Lev 15:22	*4325*
clothes, and bathe himself in *w*	Lev 15:27	*4325*
shall he wash his flesh in *w*	Lev 16:4	*4325*
flesh with *w* in the holy place	Lev 16:24	*4325*
clothes, and bathe his flesh in *w*	Lev 16:26	*4325*
clothes, and bathe his flesh in *w*	Lev 16:28	*4325*
clothes, and bathe himself in *w*	Lev 17:15	*4325*
unless he wash his flesh with *w*	Lev 22:6	*4325*
take holy *w* in an earthen vessel	Num 5:17	*4325*
shall take, and put it into the *w*	Num 5:17	*4325*
bitter *w* that causeth the curse	Num 5:18	*4325*
bitter *w* that causeth the curse	Num 5:19	*4325*
this *w* that causeth the curse	Num 5:22	*4325*
blot them out with the bitter *w*	Num 5:23	*4325*

bitter *w* that causeth the curse	Num 5:24	4325
the *w* that causeth the curse	Num 5:24	4325
cause the woman to drink the *w*	Num 5:26	4325
he hath made her to drink the *w*	Num 5:27	4325
that the *w* that causeth the curse	Num 5:27	4325
Sprinkle *w* of purifying upon them	Num 8:7	4325
and he shall bathe his flesh in *w*	Num 19:7	4325
her shall wash his clothes in *w*	Num 19:8	4325
and bathe his flesh in *w*	Num 19:8	4325
of Israel for a *w* of separation	Num 19:9	4325
because the *w* of separation was	Num 19:13	4325
running *w* shall be put thereto in	Num 19:17	4325
take hyssop, and dip it in the *w*	Num 19:18	4325
clothes, and bathe himself in *w*	Num 19:19	4325
the *w* of separation hath not been	Num 19:20	4325
that he that sprinkleth the *w* of	Num 19:21	4325
he that toucheth the *w* of	Num 19:21	4325
And there was no *w* for the	Num 20:2	4325
neither is there any *w* to drink	Num 20:5	4325
and it shall give forth his *w*	Num 20:8	4325
forth to them *w* out of the rock	Num 20:8	4325
we fetch you *w* out of this rock	Num 20:10	4325
the *w* came out abundantly, and the	Num 20:11	4325
This is the *w* of Meribah	Num 20:13	4325
we drink of the *w* of the wells	Num 20:17	4325
if I and my cattle drink of thy *w*	Num 20:19	4325
my word at the *w* of Meribah	Num 20:24	4325
no bread, neither is there any *w*	Num 21:5	4325
together, and I will give them *w*	Num 21:16	4325
He shall pour the *w* out of his	Num 24:7	4325
me at the *w* before their eyes	Num 27:14	4325
that is the *w* of Meribah in	Num 27:14	4325
purified with the *w* of separation	Num 31:23	4325
ye shall make go through the *w*	Num 31:23	4325
Elim were twelve fountains of *w*	Num 33:9	4325
where was no *w* for the people to	Num 33:14	4325
also buy *w* of them for money	Deut 2:6	4325
give me *w* for money, that I may	Deut 2:28	4325
good land, a land of brooks of *w*	Deut 8:7	4325
and drought, where there was no *w*	Deut 8:15	4325
who brought thee forth *w* out of	Deut 8:15	4325
neither did eat bread nor drink *w*	Deut 9:9	4325
neither eat bread, nor drink *w*	Deut 9:18	4325
how he made the *w* of the Red sea	Deut 11:4	4325
drinketh *w* of the rain of heaven	Deut 11:11	4325
shall pour it upon the earth as *w*	Deut 12:16	4325
shalt pour it upon the earth as *w*	Deut 12:24	4325
pour it upon the ground as *w*	Deut 15:23	4325
with *w* in the way, when ye came	Deut 23:4	4325
on, he shall wash himself with *w*	Deut 23:11	4325
thy wood unto the drawer of thy *w*	Deut 29:11	4325
up the *w* of the Red sea for you	Josh 2:10	4325
to the brink of the *w* of Jordan	Josh 3:8	4325
were dipped in the brim of the *w*	Josh 3:15	4325
the people melted, and became as *w*	Josh 7:5	4325
drawers of *w* unto all the	Josh 9:21	4325
drawers of *w* for the house of my	Josh 9:23	4325
drawers of *w* for the congregation	Josh 9:27	4325
the fountain of the *w* of Nephtoah	Josh 15:9	4325
give me also springs of *w*	Josh 15:19	4325
unto the *w* of Jericho on the east	Josh 16:1	4325
give me also springs of *w*	Judg 1:15	4325
I pray thee, a little *w* to drink	Judg 4:19	4325
the clouds also dropped *w*	Judg 5:4	4325
in the places of drawing *w*	Judg 5:11	4325
He asked *w*, and she gave him milk	Judg 5:25	4325
of the fleece, a bowl full of *w*	Judg 6:38	4325
bring them down unto the *w*	Judg 7:4	4325
down the people unto the *w*	Judg 7:5	4325
lappeth of the *w* with his tongue	Judg 7:5	4325
down upon their knees to drink *w*	Judg 7:6	4325
the jaw, and there came *w* thereout	Judg 15:19	4325
together to Mizpeh, and drew *w*	1Sa 7:6	4325
young maidens going out to draw *w*	1Sa 9:11	4325
I then take my bread, and my *w*	1Sa 25:11	4325
at his bolster, and the cruse of *w*	1Sa 26:11	4325
the cruse of *w* from Saul's	1Sa 26:12	4325
the cruse of *w* that was at his	1Sa 26:16	4325
and they made him drink *w*	1Sa 30:11	4325
eaten no bread, nor drunk any *w*	1Sa 30:12	4325
are as *w* spilt on the ground,	2Sa 14:14	4325
They be gone over the brook of *w*	2Sa 17:20	4325
Arise, and pass quickly over the *w*	2Sa 17:21	4325
the beginning of harvest until *w*	2Sa 21:10	4325
the *w* of the well of Beth-lehem	2Sa 23:15	4325
drew *w* out of the well of	2Sa 23:16	4325
bread nor drink *w* in this place	1Kin 13:8	4325
saying, Eat no bread, nor drink *w*	1Kin 13:9	4325
drink *w* with thee in this place	1Kin 13:16	4325
eat no bread nor drink *w* there	1Kin 13:17	4325
that he may eat bread and drink *w*	1Kin 13:18	4325

bread in his house, and drank *w*	1Kin 13:19	4325
drunk *w* in the place, of the	1Kin 13:22	4325
thee, Eat no bread, and drink no *w*	1Kin 13:22	4325
as a reed is shaken in the *w*	1Kin 14:15	4325
a little *w* in a vessel, that I	1Kin 17:10	4325
cave, and fed them with bread and *w*	1Kin 18:4	4325
the land, unto all fountains of *w*	1Kin 18:5	4325
cave, and fed them with bread and *w*	1Kin 18:13	4325
and said, Fill four barrels with *w*	1Kin 18:33	4325
the *w* ran round about the altar	1Kin 18:35	4325
he filled the trench also with *w*	1Kin 18:35	4325
licked up the *w* that was in the	1Kin 18:38	4325
and a cruse of *w* at his head	1Kin 19:6	4325
with *w* of affliction, until I	1Kin 22:27	4325
but the *w* is naught, and the	2Kin 2:19	4325
and there was no *w* for the host	2Kin 3:9	4325
which poured *w* on the hands of	2Kin 3:11	4325
valley shall be filled with *w*	2Kin 3:17	4325
good tree, and stop all wells of *w*	2Kin 3:19	4325
there came *w* by the way of Edom,	2Kin 3:20	4325
and the country was filled with *w*	2Kin 3:20	4325
and the sun shone upon the *w*	2Kin 3:22	4325
the Moabites saw the *w* on the	2Kin 3:22	4325
they stopped all the wells of *w*	2Kin 3:25	4325
beam, the ax head fell into the *w*	2Kin 6:5	4325
w before them, that they may eat	2Kin 6:22	4325
a thick cloth, and dipped it in *w*	2Kin 8:15	4325
brought *w* into the city, are they	2Kin 20:20	4325
the *w* of the well of Beth-lehem	1Chr 11:17	4325
drew *w* out of the well of	1Chr 11:18	4325
with *w* of affliction, until I	2Chr 18:26	4325
of Assyria come, and find much *w*	2Chr 32:4	4325
he did eat no bread, nor drink *w*	Ezr 10:6	4325
the *w* gate toward the east	Neh 3:26	4325
street that was before the *w* gate	Neh 8:1	4325
the *w* gate from the morning until	Neh 8:3	4325
and in the street of the *w* gate	Neh 8:16	4325
broughtest forth *w* for them out	Neh 9:15	4325
gavest them *w* for their thirst	Neh 9:20	4325
even unto the *w* gate eastward	Neh 12:37	4325
of Israel with bread and with *w*	Neh 13:2	4325
can the flag grow without *w*	Job 8:11	4325
If I wash myself with snow *w*	Job 9:30	1119
the scent of *w* it will bud	Job 14:9	4325
which drinketh iniquity like *w*	Job 15:16	4325
Thou hast not given *w* to the	Job 22:7	4325
who drinketh up scorning like *w*	Job 34:7	4325
he maketh small the drops of *w*	Job 36:27	4325
a tree planted by the rivers of *w*	Ps 1:3	4325
I *w* my couch with my tears	Ps 6:6	4529
I am poured out like *w*, and all my	Ps 22:14	4325
hart panteth after the *w* brooks	Ps 42:1	4325
and thirsty land, where no *w* is	Ps 63:1	4325
river of God, which is full of *w*	Ps 65:9	4325
we went through fire and through *w*	Ps 66:12	4325
as showers that *w* the earth	Ps 72:6	2222
The clouds poured out *w*	Ps 77:17	4325
shed like *w* round about Jerusalem	Ps 79:3	4325
came round about me daily like *w*	Ps 88:17	4325
the wilderness into a standing *w*	Ps 107:35	4325
it come into his bowels like *w*	Ps 109:18	4325
turned the rock into a standing *w*	Ps 114:8	4325
no fountains abounding with *w*	Prov 8:24	4325
is as when one letteth out *w*	Prov 17:14	4325
the heart of man is like deep *w*	Prov 20:5	4325
of the LORD, as the rivers of *w*	Prov 21:1	4325
be thirsty, give him *w* to drink	Prov 25:21	4325
As in *w* face answereth to face,	Prov 27:19	4325
earth that is not filled with *w*	Prov 30:16	4325
I made me pools of *w*	Eccl 2:6	4325
to *w* therewith the wood that	Eccl 2:6	8248
dross, thy wine mixed with *w*	Is 1:22	4325
and as a garden that hath no *w*	Is 1:30	4325
of bread, and the whole stay of *w*	Is 3:1	4325
with joy shall ye draw *w* out of	Is 12:3	4325
for the bittern, and pools of *w*	Is 14:23	4325
I will *w* thee with my tears, O	Is 16:9	7301
brought *w* to him that was thirsty	Is 21:14	4325
walls for the *w* of the old pool	Is 22:11	4325
I will *w* it every moment	Is 27:3	8248
or to take *w* withal out of the	Is 30:14	4325
the *w* of affliction, yet shall	Is 30:20	4325
as rivers of *w* in a dry place, as	Is 32:2	4325
and the thirsty land springs of *w*	Is 35:7	4325
I have digged, and drunk *w*	Is 37:25	4325
When the poor and needy seek *w*	Is 41:17	4325
make the wilderness a pool of *w*	Is 41:18	4325
and the dry land springs of *w*	Is 41:18	4325
For I will pour *w* upon him that	Is 44:3	4325
as willows by the *w* courses	Is 44:4	4325
he drinketh no *w*, and is faint	Is 44:12	4325

springs of w shall he guide them	Is 49:10	4325
stinketh, because there is no w	Is 50:2	4325
garden, and like a spring of w	Is 58:11	4325
arm, dividing the w before them	Is 63:12	4325
cisterns, that can hold no w	Jer 2:13	4325
given us w of gall to drink,	Jer 8:14	4325
give them w of gall to drink	Jer 9:15	4325
thy loins, and put it not in w	Jer 13:1	4325
came to the pits, and found no w	Jer 14:3	4325
and make them drink the w of gall	Jer 23:15	4325
And in the dungeon there was no w	Jer 38:6	4325
eye, mine eye runneth down with w	Lam 1:16	4325
pour out thine heart like w	Lam 2:19	4325
of w for the destruction of the	Lam 3:48	4325
We have drunken our w for money	Lam 5:4	4325
shalt drink also w by measure	Eze 4:11	4325
and they shall drink w by measure	Eze 4:16	4325
That they may want bread and w	Eze 4:17	4325
and all knees shall be weak as w	Eze 7:17	4325
drink thy w with trembling and	Eze 12:18	4325
drink their w with astonishment	Eze 12:19	4325
thou washed in w to supple thee	Eze 16:4	4325
Then washed I thee with w	Eze 16:9	4325
that he might w it by the furrows	Eze 17:7	8248
and all knees shall be weak as w	Eze 21:7	4325
set it on, and also pour w into it	Eze 24:3	4325
and thy dust in the midst of the w	Eze 26:12	4325
in their height, all that drink w	Eze 31:14	4325
best of Lebanon, all that drink w	Eze 31:16	4325
I will also w with thy blood the	Eze 32:6	8248
will I sprinkle clean w upon you	Eze 36:25	4325
us pulse to eat, and w to drink	Dan 1:12	4325
that give me my bread and my w	Hos 2:5	4325
out my wrath upon them like w	Hos 5:10	4325
is cut off as the foam upon the w	Hos 10:7	4325
shall w the valley of Shittim	Joel 3:18	8248
unto one city, to drink w	Amos 4:8	4325
of bread, nor a thirst for w	Amos 8:11	4325
let them not feed, nor drink w	Jonah 3:7	4325
is of old like a pool of w	Nah 2:8	4325
overflowing of the w passed by	Hab 3:10	4325
out of the pit wherein is no w	Zec 9:11	4325
you with w unto repentance	Mt 3:11	5204
went up straightway out of the w	Mt 3:16	5204
w only in the name of a disciple	Mt 10:42	5204
bid me come unto thee on the w	Mt 14:28	5204
of the ship, he walked on the w	Mt 14:29	5204
into the fire, and oft into the w	Mt 17:15	5204
a tumult was made, he took w	Mt 27:24	5204
I indeed have baptized you with w	Mk 1:8	5204
coming up out of the w, he saw	Mk 1:10	5204
a cup of w to drink in my name	Mk 9:41	5204
you a man bearing a pitcher of w	Mk 14:13	5204
all, I indeed baptize you with w	Lk 3:16	5204
thou gavest me no w for my feet	Lk 7:44	5204
and they were filled with w	Lk 8:23	5204
the wind and the raging of the w	Lk 8:24	5204
he commandeth even the winds and w	Lk 8:25	5204
dip the tip of his finger in w	Lk 16:24	5204
meet you, bearing a pitcher of w	Lk 22:10	5204
them, saying, I baptize with w	Jn 1:26	5204
am I come baptizing with w	Jn 1:31	5204
he that sent me to baptize with w	Jn 1:33	5204
them, Fill the waterpots with w	Jn 2:7	5204
tasted the w that was made wine	Jn 2:9	5204
servants which drew the w knew	Jn 2:9	5204
thee, Except a man be born of w	Jn 3:5	5204
because there was much w there	Jn 3:23	5204
a woman of Samaria to draw w	Jn 4:7	5204
he would have given thee living w	Jn 4:10	5204
then hast thou that living w	Jn 4:11	5204
of this w shall thirst again	Jn 4:13	5204
the w that I shall give him shall	Jn 4:14	5204
but the w that I shall give him	Jn 4:14	5204
w springing up into everlasting	Jn 4:14	5204
unto him, Sir, give me this w	Jn 4:15	5204
Galilee, where he made the w wine	Jn 4:46	5204
waiting for the moving of the w	Jn 5:3	5204
into the pool, and troubled the w	Jn 5:4	5204
after the troubling of the w	Jn 5:4	5204
when the w is troubled, to put me	Jn 5:7	5204
shall flow rivers of living w	Jn 7:38	5204
that he poureth w into a bason	Jn 13:5	5204
came there out blood and w	Jn 19:34	5204
For John truly baptized with w	Acts 1:5	5204
way, they came unto a certain w	Acts 8:36	5204
the eunuch said, See, here is w	Acts 8:36	5204
and they went down both into the w	Acts 8:38	5204
they were come up out of the w	Acts 8:39	5204
Can any man forbid w, that these	Acts 10:47	5204
said, John indeed baptized with w	Acts 11:16	5204

with the washing of w by the word	Eph 5:26	5204
Drink no longer w, but use a	1Ti 5:23	5202
of calves and of goats, with w	Heb 9:19	5204
and our bodies washed with pure w	Heb 10:22	5204
forth at the same place sweet w	Jas 3:11	
can no fountain both yield salt w	Jas 3:12	5204
is, eight souls were saved by w	1Pet 3:20	5204
These are wells without w	2Pet 2:17	504
out of the w and in the w	2Pet 3:5	5204
then was, being overflowed with w	2Pet 3:6	5204
This is he that came by w	1Jn 5:6	5204
not by w only, but by w	1Jn 5:6	5204
in earth, the spirit, and the w	1Jn 5:8	5204
clouds they are without w	Jude 12	504
w as a flood after the woman	Rev 12:15	5204
the w thereof was dried up, that	Rev 16:12	5204
fountain of the w of life freely	Rev 21:6	5204
me a pure river of w of life	Rev 22:1	5204
let him take the w of life freely	Rev 22:17	5204

WATERCOURSE

also stopped the upper w of Gihon	2Chr 32:30	4161,4325
Who hath divided a w for the	Job 38:25	8585

WATERED

w the whole face of the ground	Gen 2:6	8248
that it was well w every where	Gen 13:10	4945
of that well they w the flocks	Gen 29:2	8248
w the sheep, and put the stone	Gen 29:3	8248
w the flock of Laban his mother's	Gen 29:10	8248
and helped them, and w their flock	Ex 2:17	8248
enough for us, and w the flock	Ex 2:19	8248
watereth shall be w also himself	Prov 11:25	3384
and thou shalt be like a w garden	Is 58:11	7302
their soul shall be as a w garden	Jer 31:12	7302
I have planted, Apollos w	1Cor 3:6	4222

WATEREDST

w it with thy foot, as a garden	Deut 11:10	8248

WATEREST

Thou visitest the earth, and w it	Ps 65:9	7783
Thou w the ridges thereof	Ps 65:10	7301

WATERETH

He w the hills from his chambers	Ps 104:13	8248
he that w shall be watered also	Prov 11:25	7301
but w the earth, and maketh it	Is 55:10	7301
any thing, neither he that w	1Cor 3:7	4222
planteth and he that w are one	1Cor 3:8	4222

WATERFLOOD

Let not the w overflow me	Ps 69:15	7641,4325

WATERING

flocks in the gutters in the w	Gen 30:38	4325
Also by w he wearieth the thick	Job 37:11	7377
the stall, and lead him away to w	Lk 13:15	4222

WATERPOT

The woman then left her w	Jn 4:28	5201

WATERPOTS

were set there six w of stone	Jn 2:6	5201
unto them, Fill the w with water	Jn 2:7	5201

WATERS

God moved upon the face of the w	Gen 1:2	4325
a firmament in the midst of the w	Gen 1:6	4325
it divide the w from the w	Gen 1:6	4325
divided the w which were under	Gen 1:7	4325
under the firmament from the w	Gen 1:7	4325
Let the w under the heaven be	Gen 1:9	4325
together of the w called he Seas	Gen 1:10	4325
Let the w bring forth abundantly	Gen 1:20	4325
which the w brought forth	Gen 1:21	4325
fill the w in the seas, and let	Gen 1:22	4325
bring a flood of w upon the earth	Gen 6:17	4325
the flood of w was upon the earth	Gen 7:6	4325
because of the w of the flood	Gen 7:7	4325
that the w of the flood were upon	Gen 7:10	4325
the w increased, and bare up the	Gen 7:17	4325
And the w prevailed, and were	Gen 7:18	4325
ark went upon the face of the w	Gen 7:18	4325
the w prevailed exceedingly upon	Gen 7:19	4325
cubits upward did the w prevail	Gen 7:20	4325
the w prevailed upon the earth an	Gen 7:24	4325
over the earth, and the w assuaged	Gen 8:1	4325
the w returned from off the earth	Gen 8:3	4325
and fifty days the w were abated	Gen 8:3	4325
the w decreased continually until	Gen 8:5	4325
until the w were dried up from	Gen 8:7	4325
to see if the w were abated from	Gen 8:8	4325
for the w were on the face of the	Gen 8:9	4325
so Noah knew that the w were	Gen 8:11	4325
the w were dried up from off the	Gen 8:13	4325

W

off any more by the *w* of a flood	Gen 9:11	4325
the *w* shall no more become a	Gen 9:15	4325
upon the *w* which are in the river	Ex 7:17	4325
thine hand upon the *w* of Egypt	Ex 7:19	4325
smote the *w* that were in the	Ex 7:20	4325
all the *w* that were in the river	Ex 7:20	4325
out his hand over the *w* of Egypt	Ex 8:6	4325
dry land, and the *w* were divided	Ex 14:21	4325
the *w* were a wall unto them on	Ex 14:22	4325
that the *w* may come again upon	Ex 14:26	4325
the *w* returned, and covered the	Ex 14:28	4325
the *w* were a wall unto them on	Ex 14:29	4325
the *w* were gathered together	Ex 15:8	4325
they sank as lead in the mighty *w*	Ex 15:10	4325
again the *w* of the sea upon them	Ex 15:19	4325
could not drink of the *w* of Marah	Ex 15:23	4325
which when he had cast into the *w*	Ex 15:25	4325
the *w* were made sweet	Ex 15:25	4325
and they encamped there by the *w*	Ex 15:27	4325
ye eat of all that are in the *w*	Lev 11:9	4325
hath fins and scales in the *w*	Lev 11:9	4325
rivers, of all that move in the *w*	Lev 11:10	4325
living thing which is in the *w*	Lev 11:10	4325
hath no fins nor scales in the *w*	Lev 11:12	4325
creature that moveth in the *w*	Lev 11:46	4325
not drink of the *w* of the well	Num 21:22	4325
and as cedar trees beside the *w*	Num 24:6	4325
and his seed shall be in many *w*	Num 24:7	4325
is in the *w* beneath the earth	Deut 4:18	4325
is in the *w* beneath the earth	Deut 5:8	4325
to Jotbath, a land of rivers of *w*	Deut 10:7	4325
eat of all that are in the *w*	Deut 14:9	4325
Israel at the *w* of Meribah-kadesh	Deut 32:51	4325
didst strive at the *w* of Meribah	Deut 33:8	4325
shall rest in the *w* of Jordan	Josh 3:13	4325
that the *w* of Jordan shall be cut	Josh 3:13	4325
the *w* that come down from above	Josh 3:13	4325
That the *w* which came down from	Josh 3:16	4325
That the *w* of Jordan were cut off	Josh 4:7	4325
the *w* of Jordan were cut off	Josh 4:7	4325
that the *w* of Jordan returned	Josh 4:18	4325
the *w* of Jordan from before you	Josh 4:23	4325
the *w* of Jordan from before the	Josh 5:1	4325
together at the *w* of Merom	Josh 11:5	4325
them by the *w* of Merom suddenly	Josh 11:7	4325
passed toward the *w* of En-shemesh	Josh 15:7	4325
out to the well of *w* of Nephtoah	Josh 18:15	4325
in Taanach by the *w* of Megiddo	Judg 5:19	4325
before them the *w* unto Beth-barah	Judg 7:24	4325
took the *w* unto Beth-barah and	Judg 7:24	4325
before me, as the breach of *w*	2Sa 5:20	4325
and have taken the city of *w*	2Sa 12:27	4325
pavilions round about him, dark *w*	2Sa 22:12	4325
he drew me out of many *w*	2Sa 22:17	4325
it together, and smote the *w*	2Kin 2:8	4325
fell from him, and smote the *w*	2Kin 2:14	4325
and when he also had smitten the *w*	2Kin 2:14	4325
forth unto the spring of the *w*	2Kin 2:21	4325
the LORD, I have healed these *w*	2Kin 2:21	4325
So the *w* were healed unto this	2Kin 2:22	4325
better than all the *w* of Israel	2Kin 5:12	4325
ye every one the *w* of his cistern	2Kin 18:31	4325
I have digged and drunk strange *w*	2Kin 19:24	4325
hand like the breaking forth of *w*	1Chr 14:11	4325
his mighty men to stop the *w* of	2Chr 32:3	4325
as a stone into the mighty *w*	Neh 9:11	4325
are poured out like the *w*	Job 3:24	4325
sendeth *w* upon the fields	Job 5:10	4325
remember it as *w* that pass away	Job 11:16	4325
Behold, he withholdeth the *w*	Job 12:15	4325
As the *w* fail from the sea, and	Job 14:11	4325
The *w* wear the stones	Job 14:19	4325
and abundance of *w* cover thee	Job 22:11	4325
He is swift as the *w*	Job 24:18	4325
and heat consume the snow *w*	Job 24:19	4325
are formed from under the *w*	Job 26:5	4325
He bindeth up the *w* in his thick	Job 26:8	4325
hath compassed the *w* with bounds	Job 26:10	4325
Terrors take hold on him as *w*	Job 27:20	4325
even the *w* forgotten of the foot	Job 28:4	4325
and he weigheth the *w* by measure	Job 28:25	4325
My root was spread out by the *w*	Job 29:19	4325
me as a wide breaking in of *w*	Job 30:14	4325
breadth of the *w* is straitened	Job 37:10	4325
for the overflowing of *w*, or a	Job 38:25	4325
The *w* are hid as with a stone, and	Job 38:30	4325
abundance of *w* may cover thee	Job 38:34	4325
round about him were dark *w*	Ps 18:11	4325
Then the channels of *w* were seen	Ps 18:15	4325
took me, he drew me out of many *w*	Ps 18:16	4325
he leadeth me beside the still *w*	Ps 23:2	4325

voice of the LORD is upon the *w*	Ps 29:3	4325
the LORD is upon many *w*	Ps 29:3	4325
w they shall not come nigh unto	Ps 32:6	4325
He gathereth the *w* of the sea	Ps 33:7	4325
Though the *w* thereof roar and be	Ps 46:3	4325
away as *w* which run continually	Ps 58:7	4325
for the *w* are come in unto my	Ps 69:1	4325
I am come into deep *w*, where the	Ps 69:2	4325
hate me, and out of the deep *w*	Ps 69:14	4325
w of a full cup are wrung out to	Ps 73:10	4325
the heads of the dragons in the *w*	Ps 74:13	4325
The *w* saw thee, O God, the *w*	Ps 77:16	4325
sea, and thy path in the great *w*	Ps 77:19	4325
he made the *w* to stand as an heap	Ps 78:13	4325
caused *w* to run down like rivers	Ps 78:16	4325
that the *w* gushed out, and the	Ps 78:20	4325
I proved thee at the *w* of Meribah	Ps 81:7	4325
mightier than the noise of many *w*	Ps 93:4	4325
beams of his chambers in the *w*	Ps 104:3	4325
the *w* stood above the mountains	Ps 104:6	4325
He turned their *w* into blood	Ps 105:29	4325
the rock, and the *w* gushed out	Ps 105:41	4325
the *w* covered their enemies	Ps 106:11	4325
him also at the *w* of strife	Ps 106:32	4325
that do business in great *w*	Ps 107:23	4325
the flint into a fountain of *w*	Ps 114:8	4325
Rivers of *w* run down mine eyes,	Ps 119:136	4325
Then the had overwhelmed us,	Ps 124:4	4325
Then the proud *w* had gone over	Ps 124:5	4325
out the earth above the *w*	Ps 136:6	4325
me, and deliver me out of great *w*	Ps 144:7	4325
his wind to blow, and the *w* flow	Ps 147:18	4325
ye *w* that be above the heavens	Ps 148:4	4325
Drink *w* out of thine own cistern	Prov 5:15	4325
running *w* out of thine own well	Prov 5:15	
rivers of *w* in the streets	Prov 5:16	4325
that the *w* should not pass his	Prov 8:29	4325
Stolen *w* are sweet, and bread	Prov 9:17	4325
of a man's mouth are as deep *w*	Prov 18:4	4325
As cold *w* to a thirsty soul, so	Prov 25:25	4325
who hath bound the *w* in a garment	Prov 30:4	4325
Cast thy bread upon the *w*	Eccl 11:1	4325
of gardens, a well of living *w*	Song 4:15	4325
eyes of doves by the rivers of *w*	Song 5:12	4325
Many *w* cannot quench love,	Song 8:7	4325
the *w* of Shiloah that go softly	Is 8:6	4325
up upon them the *w* of the river	Is 8:7	4325
the LORD, as the *w* cover the sea	Is 11:9	4325
For the *w* of Nimrim shall be	Is 15:6	4325
For the *w* of Dimon shall be full	Is 15:9	4325
like the rushing of mighty *w*	Is 17:12	4325
rush like the rushing of many *w*	Is 17:13	4325
vessels of bulrushes upon the *w*	Is 18:2	4325
the *w* shall fail from the sea, and	Is 19:5	4325
nets upon the *w* shall languish	Is 19:8	4325
together the *w* of the lower pool	Is 22:9	4325
by great *w* the seed of Sihor, the	Is 23:3	4325
a flood of mighty *w* overflowing	Is 28:2	4325
the *w* shall overflow the hiding	Is 28:17	4325
streams of *w* in the day of the	Is 30:25	4325
are ye that sow beside all *w*	Is 32:20	4325
his *w* shall be sure	Is 33:16	4325
the wilderness shall *w* break out	Is 35:6	4325
one the *w* of his own cistern	Is 36:16	4325
Who hath measured the *w* in the	Is 40:12	4325
When thou passest through the *w*	Is 43:2	4325
sea, and a path in the mighty *w*	Is 43:16	4325
because I give *w* in the	Is 43:20	4325
come forth out of the *w* of Judah	Is 48:1	4325
he caused the *w* to flow out of	Is 48:21	4325
rock also, and the *w* gushed out	Is 48:21	4325
the sea, the *w* of the great deep	Is 51:10	4325
this is as the *w* of Noah unto me	Is 54:9	4325
for as I have sworn that the *w* of	Is 54:9	4325
that thirsteth, come ye to the *w*	Is 55:1	4325
whose *w* cast up mire and dirt	Is 57:20	4325
spring of water, whose *w* fail not	Is 58:11	4325
the fire causeth the *w* to boil	Is 64:2	4325
me the fountain of living *w*	Jer 2:13	4325
of Egypt, to drink the *w* of Sihor	Jer 2:18	4325
to drink the *w* of the river	Jer 2:18	4325
As a fountain casteth out her *w*	Jer 6:7	4325
Oh that my head were *w*, and mine	Jer 9:1	4325
and our eyelids gush out with *w*	Jer 9:18	4325
a multitude of *w* in the heavens	Jer 10:13	4325
sent their little ones to the *w*	Jer 14:3	4325
me as a liar, and as *w* that fail	Jer 15:18	4325
be as a tree planted by the *w*	Jer 17:8	4325
LORD, the fountain of living *w*	Jer 17:13	4325
or shall the cold flowing *w* that	Jer 18:14	4325
the rivers of *w* in a straight way	Jer 31:9	4325

W

by the great *w* that are in Gibeon	Jer 41:12	4325
whose *w* are moved as the rivers	Jer 46:7	4325
his *w* are moved like the rivers	Jer 46:8	4325
w rise up out of the north, and	Jer 47:2	4325
for the *w* also of Nimrim shall be	Jer 48:34	4325
A drought is upon her *w*	Jer 50:38	4325
O thou that dwellest upon many *w*	Jer 51:13	4325
a multitude of *w* in the heavens	Jer 51:16	4325
her waves do roar like great *w*	Jer 51:55	4325
W flowed over mine head	Lam 3:54	4325
wings, like the noise of great *w*	Eze 1:24	4325
he placed it by great *w*, and set	Eze 17:5	4325
planted in a good soil by great *w*	Eze 17:8	4325
in thy blood, planted by the *w*	Eze 19:10	4325
of branches by reason of many *w*	Eze 19:10	4325
thee, and great *w* shall cover thee	Eze 26:19	4325
have brought thee into great *w*	Eze 27:26	4325
depths of the *w* thy merchandise	Eze 27:34	4325
The *w* made him great, the deep	Eze 31:4	4325
because of the multitude of *w*	Eze 31:5	4325
for his root was by great *w*	Eze 31:7	4325
the *w* exalt themselves for their	Eze 31:14	4325
and the great *w* were stayed	Eze 31:15	4325
and troubledst the *w* with thy feet	Eze 32:2	4325
thereof from beside the great *w*	Eze 32:13	4325
Then will I make their *w* deep	Eze 32:14	4325
and to have drunk of the deep *w*	Eze 34:18	4325
voice was like a noise of many *w*	Eze 43:2	4325
w issued out from under the	Eze 47:1	4325
the *w* came down from under from	Eze 47:1	4325
there ran out *w* on the right side	Eze 47:2	4325
and he brought me through the *w*	Eze 47:3	4325
the *w* were to the ancles	Eze 47:3	4325
and brought me through the *w*	Eze 47:4	4325
the *w* were to the knees	Eze 47:4	4325
the *w* were to the loins	Eze 47:4	4325
for the *w* were risen	Eze 47:5	4325
w to swim in, a river that could	Eze 47:5	4325
These *w* issue out toward the east	Eze 47:8	4325
the sea, the *w* shall be healed	Eze 47:8	4325
because these *w* shall come	Eze 47:9	4325
because their *w* they issued	Eze 47:12	4325
even to the *w* of strife in Kadesh	Eze 47:19	4325
unto the *w* of strife in Kadesh	Eze 48:28	4325
which was upon the *w* of the river	Dan 12:6	4325
which was upon the *w* of the river	Dan 12:7	4325
for the rivers of *w* are dried up	Joel 1:20	4325
rivers of Judah shall flow with *w*	Joel 3:18	4325
that calleth for the *w* of the sea	Amos 5:8	4325
But let judgment run down as *w*	Amos 5:24	4325
that calleth for the *w* of the sea	Amos 9:6	4325
The *w* compassed me about, even to	Jonah 2:5	4325
as the *w* that are poured down a	Mic 1:4	4325
that had the *w* round about it,	Nah 3:8	4325
Draw thee *w* for the siege,	Nah 3:14	4325
the LORD, as the *w* cover the sea	Hab 2:14	4325
through the heap of great *w*	Hab 3:15	4325
that living *w* shall go out from	Zec 14:8	4325
the sea, and perished in the *w*	Mt 8:32	5204
him into the fire, and into the *w*	Mk 9:22	5204
journeyings often, in perils of *w*	2Cor 11:26	4215
his voice as the sound of many *w*	Rev 1:15	5204
them unto living fountains of *w*	Rev 7:17	5204
and upon the fountains of *w*	Rev 8:10	5204
part of the *w* became wormwood	Rev 8:11	5204
and many men died of the *w*	Rev 8:11	5204
have power over *w* to turn them to	Rev 11:6	5204
heaven, as the voice of many *w*	Rev 14:2	5204
and the sea, and the fountains of *w*	Rev 14:7	5204
upon the rivers and fountains of *w*	Rev 16:4	5204
And I heard the angel of the *w* say	Rev 16:5	5204
whore that sitteth upon many *w*	Rev 17:1	5204
The *w* which thou sawest, where	Rev 17:15	5204
and as the voice of many *w*	Rev 19:6	5204

WATERSPOUTS

unto deep at the noise of thy *w*	Ps 42:7	6794

WATERSPRINGS

and the *w* into dry ground	Ps 107:33	4161,4325
water, and dry ground into *w*	Ps 107:35	4161,4325

WAVE

shalt *w* them for a	Ex 29:24	5130
them for a *w* offering	Ex 29:24	8573
and *w* it for a	Ex 29:26	5130
it for a *w* offering before	Ex 29:26	8573
the breast of the *w* offering	Ex 29:27	8573
for a *w* offering before the LORD	Lev 7:30	8573
For the *w* breast and the heave	Lev 7:34	8573
waved them for a *w* offering	Lev 8:27	8573
waved it for a *w* offering before	Lev 8:29	8573

for a *w* offering before the LORD	Lev 9:21	8573
the *w* breast and heave shoulder	Lev 10:14	8573
the *w* breast shall they bring	Lev 10:15	8573
to *w* it for a *w* offering	Lev 10:15	5130
w them for a	Lev 14:12	5130
them for a *w* offering before	Lev 14:12	8573
the priest shall *w* them for a	Lev 14:24	5130
for a *w* offering before the LORD	Lev 14:24	8573
he shall *w* the sheaf before the	Lev 23:11	5130
the sabbath the priest shall *w* it	Lev 23:11	5130
ye *w* the sheaf an he lamb without	Lev 23:12	5130
the sheaf of the *w* offering	Lev 23:15	8573
two *w* loaves of two tenth deals	Lev 23:17	8573
the priest shall *w* them with the	Lev 23:20	5130
for a *w* offering before the LORD	Lev 23:20	8573
shall *w* the offering before the	Num 5:25	5130
the priest shall *w* them for a	Num 6:20	5130
for a *w* offering before the LORD	Num 6:20	8573
for the priest, with the *w* breast	Num 6:20	8573
with all the *w* offerings of the	Num 18:11	8573
shall be thine, as the *w* breast	Num 18:18	8573
For he that wavereth is like a *w*	Jas 1:6	2830

WAVED

of the heave offering, which is *w*	Ex 29:27	5130
that the breast may be *w* for a	Lev 7:30	5130
w them for a wave offering before	Lev 8:27	5130
w it for a wave offering before	Lev 8:29	5130
the right shoulder Aaron for a	Lev 9:21	5130
for a trespass offering to be *w*	Lev 14:21	8573

WAVERETH

For he that *w* is like a wave of	Jas 1:6	1252

WAVERING

profession of our faith without *w*	Heb 10:23	186
let him ask in faith, nothing *w*	Jas 1:6	1252

WAVES

When the *w* of death compassed me,	2Sa 22:5	4867
and treadeth upon the *w* of the sea	Job 9:8	1116
here shall thy proud *w* be stayed	Job 38:11	1530
all thy *w* and thy billows are gone	Ps 42:7	4867
of the seas, the noise of their *w*	Ps 65:7	1530
hast afflicted me with all thy *w*	Ps 88:7	4867
when the *w* thereof arise, thou	Ps 89:9	1530
the floods lift up their *w*	Ps 93:3	1796
yea, than the mighty *w* of the sea	Ps 93:4	4867
which lifteth up the *w* thereof	Ps 107:25	1530
so that the *w* thereof are still	Ps 107:29	1530
righteousness as the *w* of the sea	Is 48:18	1530
divided the sea, whose *w* roared	Is 51:15	1530
though the *w* thereof toss	Jer 5:22	1530
the sea when the *w* thereof roar	Jer 31:35	1530
the multitude of the *w* thereof	Jer 51:42	1530
when her *w* do roar like great	Jer 51:55	1530
the sea causeth his *w* to come up	Eze 26:3	1530
billows and thy *w* passed over me	Jonah 2:3	1530
and shall smite the *w* in the sea	Zec 10:11	1530
the ship was covered with the *w*	Mt 8:24	2949
midst of the sea, tossed with *w*	Mt 14:24	2949
the *w* beat into the ship, so that	Mk 4:37	2949
the sea and the *w* roaring	Lk 21:25	4535
broken with the violence of the *w*	Acts 27:41	2949
Raging *w* of the sea, foaming out	Jude 13	2949

WAX

And my wrath shall *w* hot, and I	Ex 22:24	
my wrath may *w* hot against them	Ex 32:10	
why doth thy wrath *w* hot against	Ex 32:11	
not the anger of my lord *w* hot	Ex 32:22	
or stranger *w* rich by thee	Lev 25:47	
that dwelleth by him *w* poor	Lev 25:47	
place, and his eyes began to *w* dim	1Sa 3:2	
What time they *w* warm, they	Job 6:17	
root thereof *w* old in the earth	Job 14:8	
my heart is like *w*	Ps 22:14	1749
as *w* melteth before the fire, so	Ps 68:2	1749
The hills melted like *w* at the	Ps 97:5	1749
all of them shall *w* old like a	Ps 102:26	
fatness of his flesh shall *w* lean	Is 17:4	
neither shall his face now *w* pale	Is 29:22	
they all shall *w* old as a garment	Is 50:9	
the earth shall *w* old like a	Is 51:6	
our hands *w* feeble	Jer 6:24	
as *w* before the fire, and as the	Mic 1:4	1749
the love of many shall *w* cold	Mt 24:12	5594
yourselves bags which *w* not old	Lk 12:33	3822
begun to *w* wanton against Christ	1Ti 5:11	2691
men and seducers shall *w* worse	2Ti 3:13	4298
they all shall *w* old as doth a	Heb 1:11	3822

WAXED

After I am *w* old shall I have	Gen 18:12	
And the man *w* great, and went	Gen 26:13	
the famine *w* sore in the land of	Gen 41:56	
multiplied, and *w* exceeding mighty	Ex 1:7	
multiplied, and *w* very mighty	Ex 1:20	
and when the sun *w* hot, it melted	Ex 16:21	
w louder and louder, Moses spake,	Ex 19:19	
and Moses' anger *w* hot, and he cast	Ex 32:19	
Moses, Is the LORD's hand *w* short	Num 11:23	
Thy raiment *w* not old upon thee,	Deut 8:4	
But Jeshurun *w* fat, and kicked	Deut 32:15	
round about, that Joshua *w* old	Josh 23:1	
hath many children is *w* feeble	1Sa 2:5	
but David *w* stronger and stronger,	2Sa 3:1	1980
and the house of Saul *w* weaker	2Sa 3:1	1980
and David *w* faint	2Sa 21:15	
and the flesh of the child *w* warm	2Kin 4:34	
So David *w* greater and greater	1Chr 11:9	1980
But Abijah *w* mighty, and married	2Chr 13:21	
Jehoshaphat *w* great exceedingly	2Chr 17:12	1980
But Jehoiada *w* old, and was full	2Chr 24:15	
their clothes *w* not old, and their	Neh 9:21	
for this man Mordecai *w* greater	Est 9:4	1980
my bones *w* old through my roaring	Ps 32:3	
Damascus is *w* feeble, and turneth	Jer 49:24	
of them, and his hands *w* feeble	Jer 50:43	
the he goat *w* very great	Dan 8:8	
which *w* exceeding great, toward	Dan 8:9	
it *w* great, even to the host of	Dan 8:10	
this people's heart is *w* gross	Mt 13:15	3975
w strong in spirit, and was in the	Lk 1:80	2901
w strong in spirit, filled with	Lk 2:40	2901
and it grew, and *w* a great tree	Lk 13:19	1096
Then Paul and Barnabas *w* bold	Acts 13:46	3955
heart of this people is *w* gross	Acts 28:27	3975
w valiant in fight, turned to	Heb 11:34	1096
w rich through the abundance of	Rev 18:3	4147

WAXEN

because the cry of them is *w*	Gen 19:13	
If thy brother be *w* poor, and hath	Lev 25:25	
And if thy brother be *w* poor	Lev 25:35	
that dwelleth by thee be *w* poor	Lev 25:39	
clothes are not *w* old upon you	Deut 29:5	
thy shoe is not *w* old upon thy	Deut 29:5	
and filled themselves, and *w* fat	Deut 31:20	
thou art *w* fat, thou art grown	Deut 32:15	
children of Israel were *w* strong,	Josh 17:13	
they are become great, and *w* rich	Jer 5:27	
They are *w* fat, they shine	Jer 5:28	
w great, and thou art come to	Eze 16:7	

WAXETH

it *w* old because of all mine	Ps 6:7	
w old is ready to vanish away	Heb 8:13	1095

WAXING

w confident by my bonds, are much	Phil 1:14	3982

WAY See APPENDIX.

WAYFARING

he saw a *w* man in the street of	Judg 19:17	732
to dress for the *w* man that was	2Sa 12:4	732
lie waste, the *w* man ceaseth	Is 33:8	5674,734
the *w* men, though fools, shall	Is 35:8	1980,1870
a lodging place of *w* men	Jer 9:2	732
as a *w* man that turneth aside to	Jer 14:8	732

WAYMARKS

Set thee up *w*, make thee high	Jer 31:21	6725

WAYS See APPENDIX.

WAYSIDE

sat upon a seat by the *w* watching.	1Sa 4:13	3197,1870
they have spread a net by the *w*	Ps 140:5	3027,4570

WE See APPENDIX.

WEAK

whether they be strong or *w*	Num 13:18	7504
never dried, then shall I be *w*	Judg 16:7	2470
were occupied, then shall I be *w*	Judg 16:11	2470
go from me, and I shall become *w*	Judg 16:17	2470
And I am this day *w*, though	2Sa 3:39	7390
w handed, and will make him afraid	2Sa 17:2	7504
and let not your hands be *w*	2Chr 15:7	7503
hast strengthened the *w* hands	Job 4:3	7504
for I am *w*	Ps 6:2	536
My knees are *w* through fasting	Ps 109:24	3782
Art thou also become *w* as we	Is 14:10	2470
Strengthen ye the *w* hands	Is 35:3	7504
and all knees shall be *w* as water	Eze 7:17	3212
How is thine heart, saith the	Eze 16:30	535

and all knees shall be *w* as water	Eze 21:7	3212
let the *w* say, I am strong	Joel 3:10	2523
is willing, but the flesh is *w*	Mt 26:41	772
is ready, but the flesh is *w*	Mk 14:38	772
ye ought to support the *w*	Acts 20:35	770
And being not *w* in faith, he	Rom 4:19	770
in that it was *w* through the	Rom 8:3	770
Him that is *w* in the faith	Rom 14:1	770
another, who is *w*, eateth herbs	Rom 14:2	770
or is offended, or is made *w*	Rom 14:21	770
to bear the infirmities of the *w*	Rom 15:1	102
God hath chosen the *w* things of	1Cor 1:27	772
we are *w*, but ye are strong	1Cor 4:10	772
conscience being *w* is defiled	1Cor 8:7	772
stumblingblock to them that are *w*	1Cor 8:9	770
is *w* be emboldened to eat those	1Cor 8:10	772
shall the *w* brother perish	1Cor 8:11	770
and wound their *w* conscience	1Cor 8:12	770
To the *w* became I as *w*	1Cor 9:22	770
as *w*, that I might gain the *w*	1Cor 9:22	770
For this cause many are *w*	1Cor 11:30	770
but his bodily presence is *w*,	2Cor 10:10	770
reproach, as though we had been *w*	2Cor 11:21	770
Who is *w*, and I am not *w*	2Cor 11:29	770
for when I am *w*, then am I strong	2Cor 12:10	770
in me, which to you-ward is not *w*	2Cor 13:3	770
For we also are *w* in him, but we	2Cor 13:4	770
For we are glad, when we are *w*	2Cor 13:9	770
God, how turn ye again to the *w*	Gal 4:9	772
the feebleminded, support the *w*	1Th 5:14	772

WEAKEN

ground, which didst *w* the nations	Is 14:12	2522

WEAKENED

land *w* the hands of the people of	Ezr 4:4	7503
hands shall be *w* from the work	Neh 6:9	7503
He *w* my strength in the way	Ps 102:23	6031

WEAKENETH

w the strength of the mighty	Job 12:21	7503
for thus he *w* the hands of the	Jer 38:4	7503

WEAKER

house of Saul waxed *w* and *w*	2Sa 3:1	1800
the wife, as unto the *w* vessel	1Pet 3:7	772

WEAKNESS

the *w* of God is stronger than men	1Cor 1:25	772
And I was with you in *w*, and in	1Cor 2:3	769
it is sown in *w*	1Cor 15:43	769
my strength is made perfect in *w*	2Cor 12:9	769
though he was crucified through *w*	2Cor 13:4	769
going before for the *w* and	Heb 7:18	772
out of *w* were made strong, waxed	Heb 11:34	769

WEALTH

And all their *w*, and all their	Gen 34:29	2428
mine hand hath gotten me this *w*	Deut 8:17	2428
that giveth thee power to get *w*	Deut 8:18	2428
her husband's, a mighty man of *w*	Ruth 2:1	2428
in all the *w* which God shall give	1Sa 2:32	
even of all the mighty men of *w*	2Kin 15:20	2428
and thou hast not asked riches, *w*	2Chr 1:11	5233
and I will give thee riches, and *w*	2Chr 1:12	5233
their peace or their *w* for ever	Ezr 9:12	2896
seeking the *w* of his people, and	Est 10:3	2896
They spend their days in *w*	Job 21:13	2896
I rejoiced because my *w* was great	Job 31:25	2428
not increase thy *w* by their price	Ps 44:12	
They that trust in their *w*	Ps 49:6	2428
and leave their *w* to others	Ps 49:10	2428
W and riches shall be in his house	Ps 112:3	1952
strangers be filled with thy *w*	Prov 5:10	3581
The rich man's *w* is his strong	Prov 10:15	1952
W gotten by vanity shall be	Prov 13:11	1952
the *w* of the sinner is laid up	Prov 13:22	2428
The rich man's *w* is his strong	Prov 18:11	1952
W maketh many friends	Prov 19:4	1952
whom God hath given riches and *w*	Eccl 5:19	5233
to whom God hath given riches, *w*	Eccl 6:2	5233
the *w* of all the heathen round	Zec 14:14	2428
that by this craft we have our *w*	Acts 19:25	2142
own, but every man another's *w*	1Cor 10:24	

WEALTHY

broughtest us out into a *w* place	Ps 66:12	7310
get you up unto the *w* nation	Jer 49:31	7961

WEANED

And the child grew, and was *w*	Gen 21:8	1580
the same day that Isaac was *w*	Gen 21:8	1580
not go up until the child be *w*	1Sa 1:22	1580
tarry until thou have *w* him	1Sa 1:23	1580
gave her son suck until she *w* him	1Sa 1:23	1580

And when she had *w* him, she took 1Sa 1:24   1580
whom Tahpenes *w* in Pharaoh's 1Kin 11:20   1580
a child that is *w* of his mother .... Ps 131:2   1580
my soul is even as a *w* child .... Ps 131:2   1580
the *w* child shall put his hand on .... Is 11:8   1580
them that are *w* from the milk................ Is 28:9   1580
Now when she had *w* Lo-ruhamah .... Hos 1:8   1580

WEAPON

smite him with an hand *w* of wood .... Num 35:18   3627
shalt have a paddle upon thy *w*............. Deut 23:13   240
man having his *w* in his hand.............. 2Chr 23:10   7973
and with the other hand held a *w*.......... Neh 4:17   7973
He shall flee from the iron *w*.............. Job 20:24   5402
No *w* that is formed against thee .... Is 54:17   3627
with his destroying *w* in his hand .... Eze 9:1   3627
man a slaughter *w* in his hand .... Eze 9:2   3627

WEAPONS

take, I pray thee, thy *w*, thy .... Gen 27:3   3627
girded on every man his *w* of war .... Deut 1:41   3627
men appointed with *w* of war .... Judg 18:11   3627
men appointed with their *w* of war .... Judg 18:16   3627
that were appointed with *w* of war.......... Judg 18:17   3627
brought my sword nor my *w* with me 1Sa 21:8   3627
fallen, and the *w* of war perished 2Sa 1:27   3627
every man with his *w* in his hand 2Kin 11:8   3627
every man with his *w* in his hand 2Kin 11:11   3627
every man with his *w* in his hand 2Chr 23:7   3627
Wisdom is better than *w* of war .... Eccl 9:18   3627
the *w* of his indignation, to.................... Is 13:5   3627
I will turn back the *w* of war .... Jer 21:4   3627
thee, every one with his *w* .... Jer 22:7   3627
forth the *w* of his indignation................ Jer 50:25   3627
Thou art my battle ax and *w* of war ..... Jer 51:20   3627
down to hell with their *w* of war .... Eze 32:27   3627
shall set on fire and burn the *w*.............. Eze 39:9   5402
they shall burn the *w* with fire............... Eze 39:10   5402
with lanterns and torches and *w* .... Jn 18:3   3696
(For the *w* of our warfare are not 2Cor 10:4   3696

WEAR

Thou wilt surely *w* away, both .... Ex 18:18   5034
The woman shall not *w* that which .... Deut 22:5   1961
Thou shalt not *w* a garment of .... Deut 22:11   3847
incense, to *w* an ephod before me.......... 1Sa 2:28   5375
persons that did *w* a linen ephod 1Sa 22:18   5375
brought which the king useth to *w*.......... Est 6:8   3847
The waters *w* the stones .... Job 14:19   7833
own bread, and *w* our own apparel....... Is 4:1   3847
shall *w* out the saints of the .... Dan 7:25   1080
neither shall they *w* a rough .... Zec 13:4   3847
they that *w* soft clothing are in .... Mt 11:8   *5409*
And when the day began to *w* away ...... Lk 9:12   *2827*

WEARETH

to him that *w* the gay clothing................ Jas 2:3   *5409*

WEARIED

so that they *w* themselves to find .... Gen 19:11   3811
offering, nor *w* thee with incense .... Is 43:23   3021
thou hast *w* me with thine..................... Is 43:24   3021
Thou art *w* in the multitude of .... Is 47:13   3811
Thou art *w* in the greatness of............... Is 57:10   3021
for my soul is *w* because of................... Jer 4:31   5888
the footmen, and they have *w* thee........ Jer 12:5   3811
thou trustedst, they *w* thee .... Jer 12:5
She hath *w* herself with lies, and........... Eze 24:12   3811
and wherein have I *w* thee .... Mic 6:3   3811
Ye have *w* the LORD with your............... Mal 2:17   3021
Yet ye say, Wherein have we *w* him ...... Mal 2:17   3021
being *w* with his journey, sat .... Jn 4:6   2872
against himself, lest ye be *w*.................. Heb 12:3   2577

WEARIETH

by watering he *w* the thick cloud .... Job 37:11   2959
the foolish *w* every one of them .... Eccl 10:15   3021

WEARINESS

and much study is a *w* of the flesh .... Eccl 12:12   3024
said also, Behold, what a *w* is it .... Mal 1:13   4972
In *w* and painfulness, in watchings......... 2Cor 11:27   2873

WEARING

priest in Shiloh, *w* an ephod................... 1Sa 14:3   5375
w the crown of thorns, and the .... Jn 19:5   *5409*
of *w* of gold, or of putting on of............. 1Pet 3:3   *4025*

WEARISOME

w nights are appointed to me .... Job 7:3   5999

WEARY

I am *w* of my life because of the............ Gen 27:46   6973
thee, when thou wast faint and *w*........... Deut 25:18   3023
for he was fast asleep and *w*................. Judg 4:21   5774
bread unto thy men that are *w*............... Judg 8:15   3286

people that were with him, came *w*....... 2Sa 16:14   5889
will come upon him while he is *w*........... 2Sa 17:2   3023
said, The people is hungry, and *w* 2Sa 17:29   5889
Philistines until his hand was *w* 2Sa 23:10   3021
and there the *w* be at rest .... Job 3:17   3019
My soul is *w* of my life........................... Job 10:1   5354
But now he hath made me *w* .... Job 16:7   3811
not given water to the *w* to drink .... Job 22:7   5889
I am *w* with my groaning........................ Ps 6:6   3021
thine inheritance, when it was *w* .... Ps 68:9   3811
I am *w* of my crying .... Ps 69:3   3021
neither be *w* of his correction .... Prov 3:11   6973
lest he be *w* of thee, and so hate .... Prov 25:17   7646
I am *w* to bear them .... Is 1:14   3811
None shall be *w* nor stumble among ...... Is 5:27   5889
it a small thing for you to *w* men .... Is 7:13   3811
but will ye *w* my God also....................... Is 7:13   3811
that Moab is *w* on the high place........... Is 16:12   3811
ye may cause the *w* to rest.................... Is 28:12   5889
of a great rock in a *w* land..................... Is 32:2   5889
earth, fainteth not, neither is *w* .... Is 40:28   3021
the youths shall faint and be *w* .... Is 40:30   3021
they shall run, and not be *w* .... Is 40:31   3021
but thou hast been *w* of me .... Is 43:22   3021
they are a burden to the *w* beast........... Is 46:1   5889
a word in season to him that is *w* .... Is 50:4   3287
seek her will not *w* themselves .... Jer 2:24   3286
I am *w* with holding in............................ Jer 6:11   3811
w themselves to commit iniquity .... Jer 9:5   3811
I am *w* with repenting .... Jer 15:6   3811
I was *w* with forbearing, and I............... Jer 20:9   3811
For I have satiated the *w* soul................ Jer 31:25   5889
in the fire, and they shall be *w* .... Jer 51:58   3286
and they shall be *w*............................... Jer 51:64   3286
the people shall *w* themselves for .... Hab 2:13   3286
by her continual coming she *w* me ...... Lk 18:5   *5299*
And let us not be *w* in well doing .... Gal 6:9   *1573*
brethren, be not *w* in well doing............ 2Th 3:13   *1573*

WEASEL

the *w*, and the mouse, and the .... Lev 11:29   2467

WEATHER

Fair *w* cometh out of the north .... Job 37:22   2091
taketh away a garment in cold *w* .... Prov 25:20   3117
ye say, It will be fair *w*.......................... Mt 16:2   *2105*
morning, It will be foul *w* to day .... Mt 16:3   *5494*

WEAVE

flax, and they that *w* networks.............. Is 19:9   707
eggs, and *w* the spider's web................. Is 59:5   707

WEAVER

and in fine linen, and of the *w* .... Ex 35:35   707
I have cut off like a *w* my life................. Is 38:12   707

WEAVER'S

of his spear was like a *w* beam 1Sa 17:7   707
of whose spear was like a *w* beam 2Sa 21:19   707
hand was a spear like a *w* beam 1Chr 11:23   707
spear staff was like a *w* beam 1Chr 20:5   707
days are swifter than a *w* shuttle .... Job 7:6

WEAVEST

If thou *w* the seven locks of my .... Judg 16:13   707

WEB

seven locks of my head with the *w*........ Judg 16:13   4545
pin of the beam, and with the *w* .... Judg 16:14   4545
whose trust shall be a spider's *w*........... Job 8:14   1004
eggs, and weave the spider's *w*............. Is 59:5   6980

WEBS

Their *w* shall not become garments .... Is 59:6   6980

WEDDING

them that were bidden to the *w* .... Mt 22:3   *1062*
The *w* is ready, but they which .... Mt 22:8   *1062*
the *w* was furnished with guests .... Mt 22:10   *1062*
man which had not on a *w* garment ...... Mt 22:11   *1062*
in hither not having a *w* garment .... Mt 22:12   *1062*
when he will return from the *w* .... Lk 12:36   *1062*
thou art bidden of any man to a *w* .... Lk 14:8   *1062*

WEDGE

a *w* of gold of fifty shekels..................... Josh 7:21   3956
the *w* of gold, and his sons, and............ Josh 7:24   3956
a man than the golden *w* of Ophir .... Is 13:12

WEDLOCK

judge thee, as women that break *w*....... Eze 16:38   5003

WEEDS

the *w* were wrapped about my head ...... Jonah 2:5   5488

WEEK

Fulfil her *w*, and we will give.................. Gen 29:27   7620
Jacob did so, and fulfilled her *w* .... Gen 29:28   7620

the covenant with many for one *w*	Dan 9:27	7620
in the midst of the *w* he shall	Dan 9:27	7620
toward the first day of the *w*	Mt 28:1	4521
morning the first day of the *w*	Mk 16:2	4521
early the first day of the *w*	Mk 16:9	4521
I fast twice in the *w*, I give	Lk 18:12	4521
Now upon the first day of the *w*	Lk 24:1	4521
The first day of the *w* cometh	Jn 20:1	4521
being the first day of the *w*	Jn 20:19	4521
And upon the first day of the *w*	Acts 20:7	4521
Upon the first day of the *w* let	1Cor 16:2	4521

WEEKS

thou shalt observe the feast of *w*	Ex 34:22	7620
then she shall be unclean two *w*	Lev 12:5	7620
the LORD, after your *w* be out	Num 28:26	7620
Seven *w* shalt thou number unto	Deut 16:9	7620
seven *w* from such time as thou	Deut 16:9	7620
of *w* unto the LORD thy God with a	Deut 16:10	7620
bread, and in the feast of *w*	Deut 16:16	7620
bread, and in the feast of *w*	2Chr 8:13	7620
us the appointed *w* of the harvest	Jer 5:24	7620
Seventy *w* are determined upon thy	Dan 9:24	7620
the Prince shall be seven *w*	Dan 9:25	7620
and threescore and two *w*	Dan 9:25	7620
two *w* shall Messiah be cut off	Dan 9:26	7620
Daniel was mourning three full *w*	Dan 10:2	7620
till three whole *w* were fulfilled	Dan 10:3	7620

WEEP

mourn for Sarah, and to *w* for her	Gen 23:2	1058
and he sought where to *w*	Gen 43:30	1058
w throughout their families	Num 11:10	1058
for they *w* unto me, saying, Give	Num 11:13	1058
aileth the people that they *w*	1Sa 11:5	1058
until they had no more power to *w*	1Sa 30:4	1058
w over Saul, who clothed you in	2Sa 1:24	1058
w for the child, while it was	2Sa 12:21	1058
rend thy clothes, and *w* before me	2Chr 34:27	1058
mourn not, nor *w*	Neh 8:9	1058
and his widows shall not *w*	Job 27:15	1058
Did not I *w* for him that was in	Job 30:25	1058
into the voice of them that *w*	Job 30:31	1058
A time to *w*, and a time to laugh	Eccl 3:4	1058
to Dibon, the high places, to *w*	Is 15:2	1065
I will *w* bitterly, labour not to	Is 22:4	1065
thou shalt *w* no more	Is 30:19	1058
of peace shall *w* bitterly	Is 33:7	1058
of tears, that I might *w* day	Jer 9:1	1058
my soul shall *w* in secret places	Jer 13:17	1058
and mine eye shall *w* sore, and run	Jer 13:17	1830
W ye not for the dead, neither	Jer 22:10	1058
but *w* sore for him that goeth	Jer 22:10	1058
I will *w* for thee with the	Jer 48:32	1058
For these things I *w*	Lam 1:16	1058
neither shalt thou mourn nor *w*	Eze 24:16	1058
ye shall not mourn nor *w*	Eze 24:23	1058
they shall *w* for thee with	Eze 27:31	1058
Awake, ye drunkards, and *w*	Joel 1:5	1058
w between the porch and the altar,	Joel 2:17	1058
it not at Gath, *w* ye not at all	Mic 1:10	1058
Should I *w* in the fifth month,	Zec 7:3	1058
them, Why make ye this ado, and *w*	Mk 5:39	2799
Blessed are ye that *w* now	Lk 6:21	2799
for ye shall mourn and *w*	Lk 6:25	2799
on her, and said unto her, *W* not	Lk 7:13	2799
but he said, *W* not	Lk 8:52	2799
w* not for me, but *w* for	Lk 23:28	2799
goeth unto the grave to *w* there	Jn 11:31	2799
I say unto you, That ye shall *w*	Jn 16:20	2799
Paul answered, What mean ye to *w*	Acts 21:13	2799
rejoice, and *w* with them that *w*	Rom 12:15	2799
And they that *w*, as though they	1Cor 7:30	2799
Be afflicted, and mourn, and *w*	Jas 4:9	2799
Go to now, ye rich men, *w*	Jas 5:1	2799
the elders saith unto me, *W* not	Rev 5:5	2799
merchants of the earth shall *w*	Rev 18:11	2799

WEEPEST

to her, Hannah, why *w* thou	1Sa 1:8	1058
say unto her, Woman, why *w* thou	Jn 20:13	2799
saith unto her, Woman, why *w* thou	Jn 20:15	2799

WEEPETH

was told Joab, Behold, the king *w*	2Sa 19:1	1058
And Hazael said, Why *w* my lord	2Kin 8:12	1058
He that goeth forth and *w*, bearing	Ps 126:6	1058
She *w* sore in the night, and her	Lam 1:2	1058

WEEPING

who were *w* before the door of the	Num 25:6	1058
so the days of *w* and mourning for	Deut 34:8	1065
her along *w* behind her to Bahurim	2Sa 3:16	1058

they went up, *w* as they went up	2Sa 15:30	1058
the noise of the *w* of the people	Ezr 3:13	1065
and when he had confessed, *w*	Ezr 10:1	1058
among the Jews, and fasting, and *w*	Est 4:3	1065
My face is foul with *w*, and on my	Job 16:16	1065
LORD hath heard the voice of my *w*	Ps 6:8	1065
w may endure for a night, but joy	Ps 30:5	1065
bread, and mingled my drink with *w*	Ps 102:9	1065
one shall howl, *w* abundantly	Is 15:3	1065
Luhith with *w* shall they go it up	Is 15:5	1065
I will bewail with the *w* of Jazer	Is 16:9	1065
the Lord GOD of hosts call to *w*	Is 22:12	1065
the voice of *w* shall be no more	Is 65:19	1065
was heard upon the high places, *w*	Jer 3:21	1065
the mountains will I take up a *w*	Jer 9:10	1065
They shall come with *w*, and with	Jer 31:9	1065
Ramah, lamentation, and bitter *w*	Jer 31:15	1065
Rahel *w* for her children refused	Jer 31:15	1058
Refrain thy voice from *w*, and	Jer 31:16	1065
meet them, *w* all along as he went	Jer 41:6	1058
of Luhith continual *w* shall go up	Jer 48:5	1065
weep for thee with the *w* of Jazer	Jer 48:32	1065
of Judah together, going and *w*	Jer 50:4	1058
there sat women *w* for Tammuz	Eze 8:14	1058
heart, and with fasting, and with *w*	Joel 2:12	1065
of the LORD with tears, with *w*	Mal 2:13	1065
a voice heard, lamentation, and *w*	Mt 2:18	2805
Rachel *w* for her children, and	Mt 2:18	2799
there shall be *w* and gnashing of	Mt 8:12	2805
there shall be *w* and gnashing of	Mt 22:13	2805
there shall be *w* and gnashing of	Mt 24:51	2805
there shall be *w* and gnashing of	Mt 25:30	2805
And stood at his feet behind him *w*	Lk 7:38	2799
There shall be *w* and gnashing of	Lk 13:28	2805
When Jesus therefore saw her *w*	Jn 11:33	2799
the Jews also *w* which came with	Jn 11:33	2799
stood without at the sepulchre *w*	Jn 20:11	2799
and all the widows stood by him *w*	Acts 9:39	2799
you often, and now tell you even *w*	Phil 3:18	2799
for the fear of her torment, *w*	Rev 18:15	2799
dust on their heads, and cried, *w*	Rev 18:19	2799

WEIGH

found it to *w* a talent of gold,	1Chr 20:2	4948
until ye *w* them before the chief	Ezr 8:29	8254
ye *w* the violence of your hands	Ps 58:2	6424
dost *w* the path of the just	Is 26:7	6424
w silver in the balance, and hire	Is 46:6	8254
then take thee balances to *w*	Eze 5:1	4948

WEIGHED

Abraham *w* to Ephron the silver,	Gen 23:16	8254
the silver vessels *w* two thousand	Num 7:85	
and by him actions are *w*	1Sa 2:3	8505
his spear's head *w* six hundred	1Sa 17:7	
he *w* the hair of his head at two	2Sa 14:26	8254
the weight of whose spear *w* three	2Sa 21:16	
w unto them the silver, and the	Ezr 8:25	8254
I even *w* unto their hand six	Ezr 8:26	8254
the vessels *w* in the house of our	Ezr 8:33	8254
O that my grief were throughly *w*	Job 6:2	8254
silver be *w* for the price thereof	Job 28:15	8254
Let me be *w* in an even balance,	Job 31:6	8254
w the mountains in scales, and the	Is 40:12	8254
w him the money, even seventeen	Jer 32:9	8254
w him the money in the balances	Jer 32:10	8254
Thou art *w* in the balances, and	Dan 5:27	8625
So they *w* for my price thirty	Zec 11:12	8254

WEIGHETH

he *w* the waters by measure	Job 28:25	8505
but the LORD *w* the spirits	Prov 16:2	8505

WEIGHING

charger of silver *w* an hundred	Num 7:85	
w ten shekels apiece, after the	Num 7:86	

WEIGHT

golden earring of half a shekel *w*	Gen 24:22	4948
hands of ten shekels *w* of gold	Gen 24:22	4948
of his sack, our money in full *w*	Gen 43:21	4948
of each shall there be a like *w*	Ex 30:34	
in judgment, in meteyard, in *w*	Lev 19:35	4948
deliver you your bread again by *w*	Lev 26:26	4948
the *w* thereof was an hundred and	Num 7:13	
the *w* whereof was an hundred and	Num 7:19	
the *w* whereof was an hundred and	Num 7:25	
charger of the *w* of an hundred	Num 7:31	4948
the *w* whereof was an hundred and	Num 7:37	4948
charger of the *w* of an hundred	Num 7:43	4948
the *w* whereof was an hundred and	Num 7:49	4948
charger of the *w* of an hundred	Num 7:55	4948
the *w* whereof was an hundred and	Num 7:61	4948

the *w* whereof was an hundred and	Num 7:67	4948
the *w* whereof was an hundred and	Num 7:73	4948
the *w* whereof was an hundred and	Num 7:79	4948
shalt have a perfect and just *w*	Deut 25:15	68
wedge of gold of fifty shekels *w*	Josh 7:21	4948
the *w* of the golden earrings that	Judg 8:26	4948
the *w* of the coat was five	1Sa 17:5	4948
the *w* whereof was a talent of	2Sa 12:30	4948
shekels after the king's *w*	2Sa 14:26	68
the *w* of whose spear weighed	2Sa 21:16	4948
hundred shekels of brass in *w*	2Sa 21:16	4948
neither was the *w* of the brass	1Kin 7:47	4948
Now the *w* of gold that came to	1Kin 10:14	4948
all these vessels was without *w*	2Kin 25:16	4948
six hundred shekels of gold by *w*	1Chr 21:25	4948
and brass in abundance without *w*	1Chr 22:3	4948
and of brass and iron without *w*	1Chr 22:14	4948
of gold by *w* for things of gold	1Chr 28:14	4948
all instruments of silver by *w*	1Chr 28:14	4948
Even the *w* for the candlesticks	1Chr 28:15	4948
by *w* for every candlestick, and	1Chr 28:15	4948
the candlesticks of silver by *w*	1Chr 28:15	4948
by *w* he gave gold for the tables	1Chr 28:16	4948
he gave gold by *w* for every bason	1Chr 28:17	4948
likewise silver by *w* for every	1Chr 28:17	4948
of incense refined gold by *w*	1Chr 28:18	4948
the *w* of the nails was fifty	2Chr 3:9	4948
for the *w* of the brass could not	2Chr 4:18	4948
Now the *w* of gold that came to	2Chr 9:13	4948
the Levites the *w* of the silver	Ezr 8:30	4948
By number and by *w* of every one	Ezr 8:34	4948
all the *w* was written at that	Ezr 8:34	4948
To make the *w* for the winds	Job 28:25	4948
but a just *w* is his delight	Prov 11:1	68
A just *w* and balance are the	Prov 16:11	6425
all these vessels was without *w*	Jer 52:20	4948
thou shalt eat shall be by *w*	Eze 4:10	4946
and they shall eat bread by *w*	Eze 4:16	4948
he cast the *w* of lead upon the	Zec 5:8	68
aloes, about an hundred pound *w*	Jn 19:39	
exceeding and eternal *w* of glory	2Cor 4:17	922
let us lay aside every *w*	Heb 12:1	3591
stone about the *w* of a talent	Rev 16:21	5006

WEIGHTIER

have omitted the *w* matters of the	Mt 23:23	926

WEIGHTS

Just balances, just *w*, a just	Lev 19:36	68
not have in thy bag divers *w*	Deut 25:13	68
all the *w* of the bag are his work	Prov 16:11	68
Divers *w*, and divers measures,	Prov 20:10	68
Divers *w* are an abomination unto	Prov 20:23	68
and with the bag of deceitful *w*	Mic 6:11	68

WEIGHTY

A stone is heavy, and the sand *w*	Prov 27:3	5192
For his letters, say they, are *w*	2Cor 10:10	926

WELFARE

And he asked them of their *w*	Gen 43:27	7965
they asked each other of their *w*	Ex 18:7	7965
king David, to enquire of his *w*	1Chr 18:10	7965
the *w* of the children of Israel	Neh 2:10	2896
my *w* passeth away as a cloud	Job 30:15	3444
should have been for their *w*	Ps 69:22	7965
seeketh not the *w* of this people	Jer 38:4	7965

WELL

If thou doest *w*, shalt thou not	Gen 4:7	3190
and if thou doest not *w*, sin lieth	Gen 4:7	3190
that it may be *w* with me for thy	Gen 12:13	3190
he entreated Abram *w* for her sake	Gen 12:16	3190
that it was *w* watered every where	Gen 13:10	
Wherefore the *w* was called	Gen 16:14	875
were old and *w* stricken in age	Gen 18:11	
her eyes, and she saw a *w* of water	Gen 21:19	875
Abimelech because of a *w* of water	Gen 21:25	875
me, that I have digged this *w*	Gen 21:30	875
was old, and *w* stricken in age	Gen 24:1	
down without the city by a *w* of	Gen 24:11	875
I stand here by the *w* of water	Gen 24:13	5869
and she went down to the *w*	Gen 24:16	5869
again unto the *w* to draw water	Gen 24:20	875
ran out unto the man, unto the *w*	Gen 24:29	5869
he stood by the camels at the *w*	Gen 24:30	5869
And I came this day unto the *w*	Gen 24:42	5869
Behold, I stand by the *w* of water	Gen 24:43	5869
and she went down unto the *w*	Gen 24:45	5869
from the way of the *w* Lahai-roi	Gen 24:62	
and Isaac dwelt by the *w* Lahai-roi	Gen 25:11	883
found there a *w* of springing	Gen 26:19	875
he called the name of the *w* Esek	Gen 26:20	875

And they digged another *w*, and	Gen 26:21	875
from thence, and digged another *w*	Gen 26:22	875
there Isaac's servants digged a *w*	Gen 26:25	875
the *w* which they had digged	Gen 26:32	875
behold a *w* in the field, and, lo,	Gen 29:2	875
for out of that *w* they watered	Gen 29:2	875
And he said unto them, Is he *w*	Gen 29:6	7965
And they said, He is *w*	Gen 29:6	7965
was beautiful and *w* favoured	Gen 29:17	3303
and I will deal *w* with thee	Gen 32:9	3190
whether it be *w* with thy brethren	Gen 37:14	7965
and *w* with the flocks	Gen 37:14	7965
a goodly person, and *w* favoured	Gen 39:6	3303
me when it shall be *w* with thee	Gen 40:14	3303
the river seven *w* favoured kine	Gen 41:2	3303
did eat up the seven *w* favoured	Gen 41:4	3303
kine, fatfleshed and *w* favoured	Gen 41:18	3303
and said, Is your father *w*	Gen 43:27	7965
and it pleased Pharaoh *w*, and his	Gen 45:16	
even a fruitful bough by a *w*	Gen 49:22	5869
God dealt *w* with the midwives	Ex 1:20	3190
and he sat down by a *w*	Ex 2:15	875
I know that he can speak *w*	Ex 4:14	
And Moses said, Thou hast spoken *w*	Ex 10:29	3651
as *w* the stranger, as he that is	Lev 24:16	
as *w* for the stranger, as for one	Lev 24:22	
for it was *w* with us in Egypt	Num 11:18	2895
for we are *w* able to overcome it	Num 13:30	
that is the *w* whereof the LORD	Num 21:16	875
sang this song, Spring up, O *w*	Num 21:17	875
The princes digged the *w*, the	Num 21:18	875
not drink of the waters of the *w*	Num 21:22	875
of the sons of Joseph hath said *w*	Num 36:5	3651
hear the small as *w* as the great	Deut 1:17	
And the saying pleased me *w*	Deut 1:23	
as *w* as unto you, and until they	Deut 3:20	
day, that it may go *w* with thee	Deut 4:40	3190
maidservant may rest as *w* as thou	Deut 5:14	
and that it may go *w* with thee	Deut 5:16	3190
they have *w* said all that they	Deut 5:28	3190
that it might be *w* with them	Deut 5:29	3190
and that it may be *w* with you	Deut 5:33	2895
that it may be *w* with thee	Deut 6:3	3190
that it may be *w* with thee	Deut 6:18	3190
but shalt *w* remember what the	Deut 7:18	
that it may go *w* with thee	Deut 12:25	3190
thee, that it may go *w* with thee	Deut 12:28	3190
house, because he is *w* with thee	Deut 15:16	2895
They have *w* spoken that which	Deut 18:17	3190
that it may go *w* with thee	Deut 19:13	2895
heart faint as *w* as his heart	Deut 20:8	
that it may be *w* with thee	Deut 22:7	3190
as *w* the stranger, as he that was	Josh 8:33	
went out to the *w* of waters of	Josh 18:15	4599
and pitched beside the *w* of Harod	Judg 7:1	5878
if ye have dealt *w* with Jerubbaal	Judg 9:16	2895
for she pleaseth me *w*	Judg 14:3	
and she pleased Samson *w*	Judg 14:7	
as *w* the men of every city, as	Judg 20:48	3190
thee, that it may be *w* with thee	Ruth 3:1	3190
thee the part of a kinsman, *w*	Ruth 3:13	2896
said Saul to his servant, *W* said	1Sa 9:10	2896
with his hand, and thou shalt be *w*	1Sa 16:16	2895
me now a man that can play *w*	1Sa 16:17	3190
so Saul was refreshed, and was *w*	1Sa 16:23	2895
it pleased David *w* to be the	1Sa 18:26	
came to a great *w* that is in	1Sa 19:22	953
If he say thus, It is *w*	1Sa 20:7	2896
that thou hast dealt *w* with me	1Sa 20:7	2896
enemy, will he let him go *w* away	1Sa 24:19	2896
I know *w* that thou shalt surely	1Sa 24:20	
shall have dealt *w* with my lord	1Sa 25:31	3190
And he said, *W*	2Sa 3:13	2896
him again from the *w* of Sirah	2Sa 3:26	953
as *w* to the women as men, to	2Sa 6:19	
devoureth one as *w* as another	2Sa 11:25	2090
And the saying pleased Absalom *w*	2Sa 17:4	
which had a *w* in his court	2Sa 17:18	375
that they came up out of the *w*	2Sa 17:21	375
and said unto the king, All is *w*	2Sa 18:28	7965
day, then it had pleased thee *w*	2Sa 19:6	
the water of the *w* of Beth-lehem	2Sa 23:15	953
water out of the *w* of Beth-lehem	2Sa 23:16	953
And Bath-sheba said, *W*	1Kin 2:18	2896
thou didst *w* that it was in thine	1Kin 8:18	3190
answered and said, It is *w* spoken	1Kin 18:24	2896
And she said, It shall be *w*	2Kin 4:23	7965
say unto her, Is it *w* with thee	2Kin 4:26	7965
is it *w* with thy husband	2Kin 4:26	7965
is it *w* with the child	2Kin 4:26	7965
And she answered, It is *w*	2Kin 4:26	7965

to meet him, and said, Is all w	2Kin 5:21	7965
And he said, All is w	2Kin 5:22	7965
said one to another, We do not w	2Kin 7:9	3651
and one said unto him, Is all w	2Kin 9:11	7965
Because thou hast done w in	2Kin 10:30	2895
and it shall be w with you	2Kin 25:24	3190
the water of the w of Beth-lehem	1Chr 11:17	953
water out of the w of Beth-lehem	1Chr 11:18	953
as w the small as the great, the	1Chr 25:8	
as w the small as the great,	1Chr 26:13	
thou didst w in that it was in	2Chr 6:8	2895
and also in Judah things went w	2Chr 12:12	2896
as w to the great as to the small	2Chr 31:15	
valley, even before the dragon w	Neh 2:13	5869
I have understanding as w as you	Job 12:3	71
Mark w, O Job, hearken unto me	Job 33:31	7181
Mark ye w her bulwarks, consider	Ps 48:13	
when thou doest w to thyself	Ps 49:18	3190
my steps had w nigh slipped	Ps 73:2	369
So they did eat, and were w filled	Ps 78:29	3966
the valley of Baca make it a w	Ps 84:6	4599
As w the singers as the players	Ps 87:7	
Thou hast dealt w with thy	Ps 119:65	2896
be, and it shall be w with thee	Ps 128:2	2896
and that my soul knoweth right w	Ps 139:14	
running waters out of thine own w	Prov 5:15	875
of a righteous man is a w of life	Prov 10:11	4726
When it goeth w with the	Prov 11:10	2898
but with the w advised is wisdom	Prov 13:10	
man looketh w to his going	Prov 14:15	995
Then I saw, and considered it w	Prov 24:32	3190
flocks, and look w to thy herds	Prov 27:23	
There be three things which go w	Prov 30:29	3190
She looketh w to the ways of her	Prov 31:27	6822
be w with them that fear God	Eccl 8:12	2896
it shall not be w with the wicked	Eccl 8:13	2896
a w of living waters, and streams	Song 4:15	875
Learn to do w	Is 1:17	3190
that it shall be w with him	Is 3:10	2896
instead of w set hair baldness	Is 3:24	4639
of wines on the lees w refined	Is 25:6	
they could not w strengthen their	Is 33:23	3651
The LORD is w pleased for his	Is 42:21	2654
LORD unto me, Thou hast w seen	Jer 1:12	3190
you, that it may be w unto you	Jer 7:23	3190
it shall be w with thy remnant	Jer 15:11	2896
thee w in the time of evil	Jer 15:11	
and then it was w with him	Jer 22:15	2896
then it was w with him	Jer 22:16	2896
so it shall be w unto thee	Jer 38:20	3190
look w to him, and do him no harm	Jer 39:12	
and I will look w unto thee	Jer 40:4	
and it shall be w with you	Jer 40:9	3190
that it may be w with us, when we	Jer 42:6	2896
we plenty of victuals, and were w	Jer 44:17	2896
bones under it, and make it boil w	Eze 24:5	7571
consume the flesh, and spice it w	Eze 24:10	
can play w on an instrument	Eze 33:32	
said unto me, Son of man, mark w	Eze 44:5	
mark w the entering in of the	Eze 44:5	
inherit it, one as w as another	Eze 47:14	
but w favoured, and skilful in all	Dan 1:4	2896
which I have made; w	Dan 3:15	
LORD, Doest thou w to be angry	Jonah 4:4	3190
Doest thou w to be angry for the	Jonah 4:9	3190
I do w to be angry, even unto	Jonah 4:9	3190
these days to do w unto Jerusalem	Zec 8:15	3190
Son, in whom I am w pleased	Mt 3:17	2106
to do w on the sabbath days	Mt 12:12	2573
in whom my soul is w pleased	Mt 12:18	2106
w did Esaias prophesy of you,	Mt 15:7	2573
Son, in whom I am w pleased	Mt 17:5	2106
W done, thou good and faithful	Mt 25:21	2095
W done, good and faithful servant	Mt 25:23	2095
Son, in whom I am w pleased	Mk 1:11	2106
W hath Esaias prophesied of you	Mk 7:6	2573
Full w ye reject the commandment	Mk 7:9	2573
saying, He hath done all things w	Mk 7:37	2573
that he had answered them w	Mk 12:28	2573
And the scribe said unto him, W	Mk 12:32	2573
both were now w stricken in years	Lk 1:7	4260
my wife w stricken in years	Lk 1:18	4260
in thee I am w pleased	Lk 3:22	2106
when all men shall speak w of you	Lk 6:26	2573
And if it bear fruit, w	Lk 13:9	2573
And he said unto him, W, thou good	Lk 19:17	2095
said, Master, thou hast w said	Lk 20:39	2573
and when men have w drunk, then	Jn 2:10	3184
Now Jacob's w was there	Jn 4:6	4077
his journey, sat thus on the w	Jn 4:6	4077
to draw with, and the w is deep	Jn 4:11	5421

father Jacob, which gave us the w	Jn 4:12	5421
a w of water springing up into	Jn 4:14	4077
said unto her, Thou hast w said	Jn 4:17	2573
Say we not w that thou art a	Jn 8:48	2573
Lord, if he sleep, he shall do w	Jn 11:12	4982
and ye say w	Jn 13:13	2573
but if w, why smitest thou me	Jn 18:23	2573
thou hast w done that thou art	Acts 10:33	2573
the Holy Ghost as w as we	Acts 10:47	2532
ye keep yourselves, ye shall do w	Acts 15:29	2095
Fare ye w	Acts 15:29	2095
Which was w reported of by the	Acts 16:2	3140
no wrong, as thou very w knowest	Acts 25:10	2573
W spake the Holy Ghost by Esaias	Acts 28:25	2573
in w doing seek for glory	Rom 2:7	18
W; because of unbelief	Rom 11:20	2573
he will keep his virgin, doeth w	1Cor 7:37	2573
giveth her in marriage doeth w	1Cor 7:38	2573
as w as other apostles, and as the	1Cor 9:5	2532
of them God was not w pleased	1Cor 10:5	2106
For thou verily givest thanks w	1Cor 14:17	2573
As unknown, and yet w known	2Cor 6:9	1921
ye might w bear with him	2Cor 11:4	2573
zealously affect you, but not w	Gal 4:17	2573
Ye did run w	Gal 5:7	2573
And let us not be weary in w doing	Gal 6:9	2570
That it may be w with thee	Eph 6:3	2095
Notwithstanding ye have w done	Phil 4:14	2573
for this is w pleasing unto the	Col 3:20	2101
brethren, be not weary in w doing	2Th 3:13	2569
One that ruleth w his own house	1Ti 3:4	2573
children and their own houses w	1Ti 3:12	2573
used the office of a deacon w	1Ti 3:13	2573
W reported of for good works	1Ti 5:10	3140
Let the elders that rule w be	1Ti 5:17	2573
at Ephesus, thou knowest very w	2Ti 1:18	957
and to please them w in all things	Titus 2:9	1510,2101
preached, as w as unto them	Heb 4:2	2509
such sacrifices God is w pleased	Heb 13:16	2100
thy neighbour as thyself, ye do w	Jas 2:8	2573
thou doest w	Jas 2:19	2573
for the praise of them that do w	1Pet 2:14	17
that with w doing ye may put to	1Pet 2:15	15
but if, when ye do w, and suffer	1Pet 2:20	15
ye are, as long as ye do w	1Pet 3:6	15
be so, that ye suffer for w doing	1Pet 3:17	15
of their souls to him in w doing	1Pet 4:19	16
Son, in whom I am w pleased	2Pet 1:17	2106
whereunto ye do w that ye take	2Pet 1:19	2573
a godly sort, thou shalt do w	3Jn 6	2573

WELLBELOVED

A bundle of myrrh is my w unto me	Song 1:13	1730
Now will I sing to my w a song of	Is 5:1	3039
My w hath a vineyard in a very	Is 5:1	3039
yet therefore one son, his w	Mk 12:6	27
Salute my w Epaenetus, who is the	Rom 16:5	27
The elder unto the w Gaius	3Jn 1	27

WELLFAVOURED

of the whoredoms of the w harlot	Nah 3:4	

WELLPLEASING

a sacrifice acceptable, w to God	Phil 4:18	2101
you that which is w in his sight	Heb 13:21	2101

WELL'S

great stone was upon the w mouth	Gen 29:2	875
rolled the stone from the w mouth	Gen 29:3	875
upon the w mouth in his place	Gen 29:3	875
roll the stone from the w mouth	Gen 29:8	875
rolled the stone from the w mouth	Gen 29:10	875
a covering over the w mouth	2Sa 17:19	875

WELLS

For all the w which his father's	Gen 26:15	875
Isaac digged again the w of water	Gen 26:18	875
where were twelve w of water	Ex 15:27	5869
we drink of the water of the w	Num 20:17	875
w digged, which thou diggedst not	Deut 6:11	953
good tree, and stop all w of water	2Kin 3:19	4599
they stopped all the w of water	2Kin 3:25	4599
in the desert, and digged many w	2Chr 26:10	953
goods, w digged, vineyards, and	Neh 9:25	953
water out of the w of salvation	Is 12:3	4599
These are w without water, clouds	2Pet 2:17	4077

WELLSPRING

Understanding is a w of life unto	Prov 16:22	4726
the w of wisdom as a flowing	Prov 18:4	4726

WEN

broken, or maimed, or having a w	Lev 22:22	2990

WENCH
and a *w* went and told them 2Sa 17:17   8198

WENT See APPENDIX.

WENTEST
because thou *w* up to thy father's .... Gen 49:4   5927
when thou *w* out of Seir, when .... Judg 5:4   3318
when thou *w* to fight with the .... Judg 8:1   1980
which thou *w* to seek are found 1Sa 10:2   1980
with thee whithersoever thou *w* 2Sa 7:9   1980
why *w* thou not with my friend 2Sa 16:17   1980
Wherefore *w* not thou with me, ... 2Sa 19:25   1980
when thou *w* forth before thy .... Ps 68:7   3318
even thither *w* thou up to offer .... Is 57:7   5927
thou *w* to the king with ointment, ... Is 57:9   7788
when thou *w* after me in the .... Jer 2:2   3212
even the way which thou *w* .... Jer 31:21   1980
Thou *w* forth for the salvation of .... Hab 3:13   3318
Thou *w* in to men uncircumcised, ... Acts 11:3   1525

WEPT
him, and lift up her voice, and *w* .... Gen 21:16   1058
And Esau lifted up his voice, and *w* .... Gen 27:38   1058
and lifted up his voice, and *w* .... Gen 29:11   1058
and they *w* .... Gen 33:4   1058
Thus his father *w* for him .... Gen 37:35   1058
himself about from them, and *w* .... Gen 42:24   1058
into his chamber, and *w* there .... Gen 43:30   1058
And he *w* aloud .... Gen 45:2
his brother Benjamin's neck, and *w* ...... Gen 45:14   1058
and Benjamin *w* upon his neck .... Gen 45:14   1058
all his brethren, and *w* upon them .... Gen 45:15   1058
w on his neck a good while .... Gen 46:29   1058
w upon him, and kissed him .... Gen 50:1   1058
Joseph *w* when they spake unto him ...... Gen 50:17   1058
and, behold, the babe *w* .... Ex 2:6   1058
children of Israel also *w* again .... Num 11:4   1058
for ye have *w* in the ears of the .... Num 11:18   1058
have *w* before him, saying, Why .... Num 11:20   1058
and the people *w* that night .... Num 14:1   1058
ye returned and *w* before the LORD .... Deut 1:45   1058
the children of Israel *w* for .... Deut 34:8   1058
lifted up their voice, and *w* .... Judg 2:4   1058
And Samson's wife *w* before him .... Judg 14:16   1058
she *w* before him the seven days, ... Judg 14:17   1058
w before the LORD until even, and .... Judg 20:23   1058
came unto the house of God, and *w* ...... Judg 20:26   1058
lifted up their voices, and *w* sore .... Judg 21:2   1058
they lifted up their voice, and *w* .... Ruth 1:9   1058
lifted up their voice, and *w* again .... Ruth 1:14   1058
therefore she *w*, and did not eat 1Sa 1:7   1058
prayed unto the LORD, and *w* sore 1Sa 1:10   1058
lifted up their voices, and *w* 1Sa 11:4   1058
w one with another, until David 1Sa 20:41   1058
And Saul lifted up his voice, and *w* 1Sa 24:16   1058
him lifted up their voice and *w* 1Sa 30:4   1058
And they mourned, and *w*, and fasted ... 2Sa 1:12   1058
voice, and *w* at the grave of Abner 2Sa 3:32   1058
and all the people *w* 2Sa 3:32   1058
all the people *w* again over him 2Sa 3:34   1058
was yet alive, I fasted and *w* 2Sa 12:22   1058
and lifted up their voice and *w* 2Sa 13:36   1058
and all his servants *w* very sore 2Sa 13:36   1058
all the country *w* with a loud 2Sa 15:23   1058
w as he went up, and had his head 2Sa 15:30   1058
the chamber over the gate, and *w* 2Sa 18:33   1058
and the man of God *w* 2Kin 8:11   1058
w over his face, and said, O my 2Kin 13:14   1058
And Hezekiah *w* sore 2Kin 20:3   1058
rent thy clothes, and *w* before me 2Kin 22:19   1058
their eyes, *w* with a loud voice .... Ezr 3:12   1058
for the people *w* very sore .... Ezr 10:1   1058
these words, that I sat down and *w* ...... Neh 1:4   1058
For all the people *w*, when they .... Neh 8:9   1058
they lifted up their voice, and *w* .... Job 2:12   1058
When I *w*, and chastened my soul .... Ps 69:10   1058
there we sat down, yea, we *w* .... Ps 137:1   1058
And Hezekiah *w* sore .... Is 38:3   1058
he *w*, and made supplication unto .... Hos 12:4   1058
And he went out, and *w* bitterly .... Mt 26:75   2799
seeth the tumult, and them that *w* .... Mk 5:38   2799
And when he thought thereon, he *w* ..... Mk 14:72   2799
with him, as they mourned and *w* .... Mk 16:10   2799
mourned to you, and ye have not *w* ... Lk 7:32   2799
And all *w*, and bewailed her .... Lk 8:52   2799
he beheld the city, and *w* over it, ... Lk 19:41   2799
And Peter went out, and *w* bitterly .... Lk 22:62   2799
Jesus *w* .... Jn 11:35   1145
and as she *w*, she stooped down, and ... Jn 20:11   2799
And they all *w* sore, and fell on .... Acts 20:37

that weep, as though they *w* not 1Cor 7:30   2799
I *w* much, because no man was .... Rev 5:4   2799

WERE See APPENDIX.

WERT
If thou *w* pure and upright .... Job 8:6
O that thou *w* as my brother, that .... Song 8:1
w graffed in among them, and with .... Rom 11:17
For if thou *w* cut out of the .... Rom 11:24
w graffed contrary to nature into .... Rom 11:24
I would thou *w* **cold or hot** .... Rev 3:15   1498

WEST
his tent, having Beth-el on the *w* .... Gen 12:8   3220
thou shalt spread abroad to the *w* .... Gen 28:14   3220
turned a mighty strong *w* wind .... Ex 10:19   3220
w side shall be hangings of fifty .... Ex 27:12   3220
for the *w* side were hangings of .... Ex 38:12   3220
On the *w* side shall be the .... Num 2:18   3220
this shall be your *w* border .... Num 34:6   3220
on the *w* side two thousand cubits .... Num 35:5   3220
of the LORD, possess thou the *w* .... Deut 33:23   3220
and Ai, on the *w* side of Ai .... Josh 8:9   3220
on the *w* side of the city .... Josh 8:12   3220
in wait on the *w* of the city .... Josh 8:13   3220
and in the borders of Dor on the *w* .... Josh 11:2   3220
Canaanite on the east and on the *w* ...... Josh 11:3   3220
on this side Jordan on the *w* .... Josh 12:7   3220
the *w* border was to the great sea .... Josh 15:12   3220
this was the *w* quarter .... Josh 18:14   3220
and the border went out on the *w* .... Josh 18:15   3220
reacheth to Asher on the *w* side .... Josh 19:34   3220
and three looking toward the *w* 1Kin 7:25   3220
the porters, toward the east, *w* 1Chr 9:24   3220
toward the east, and toward the *w* 1Chr 12:15   4628
and three looking toward the *w* 2Chr 4:4   3220
the *w* side of the city of David 2Chr 32:30   4628
on the *w* side of Gihon, in the 2Chr 33:14   4628
from the east, nor from the *w* .... Ps 75:6   4628
As far as the east is from the *w* .... Ps 103:12   4628
from the east, and from the *w* .... Ps 107:3   4628
of the Philistines toward the *w* .... Is 11:14   3220
east, and gather thee from the *w* .... Is 43:5   4628
rising of the sun, and from the *w* .... Is 45:6   4628
from the north and from the *w* .... Is 49:12   3220
the name of the LORD from the *w* .... Is 59:19   4628
the *w* was seventy cubits broad .... Eze 41:12   3220
He turned about to the *w* side .... Eze 42:19   3220
from the *w* side westward, and from ..... Eze 45:7   3220
from the *w* border unto the east .... Eze 45:7   3220
The *w* side also shall be .... Eze 47:20   3220
This is the *w* side .... Eze 47:20   3220
for these are his sides east and *w* .... Eze 48:1   3220
the east side unto the *w* side .... Eze 48:2   3220
east side even unto the *w* side .... Eze 48:3   3220
the east side unto the *w* side .... Eze 48:4   3220
the east side unto the *w* side .... Eze 48:5   3220
east side even unto the *w* side .... Eze 48:6   3220
the east side unto the *w* side .... Eze 48:7   3220
the east side unto the *w* side .... Eze 48:8   3220
the east side unto the *w* side .... Eze 48:8   3220
toward the *w* ten thousand in .... Eze 48:10   3220
the *w* side four thousand and five .... Eze 48:16   3220
toward the *w* two hundred and fifty ...... Eze 48:17   3220
thousand toward the *w* border .... Eze 48:21   3220
the east side unto the *w* side .... Eze 48:23   3220
the east side unto the *w* side .... Eze 48:24   3220
the east side unto the *w* side .... Eze 48:25   3220
the east side unto the *w* side .... Eze 48:26   3220
the east side unto the *w* side .... Eze 48:27   3220
At the *w* side four thousand and .... Eze 48:34   3220
an he goat came from the *w* on the ...... Dan 8:5   4628
children shall tremble from the *w* .... Hos 11:10   3220
country, and from the *w* country .... Zec 8:7   3996,8121
toward the east and toward the *w* .... Zec 14:4   3220
shall come from the east and *w* .... Mt 8:11   1424
east, and shineth even unto the *w* ...... Mt 24:27   1424
ye see a cloud rise out of the *w* .... Lk 12:54   1424
come from the east, and from the *w* .... Lk 13:29   1424
and lieth toward the south *w* .... Acts 27:12   3047
and north *w* .... Acts 27:12   5566
and on the *w* three gates .... Rev 21:13   1424

WESTERN
And as for the *w* border, ye shall .... Num 34:6   3220

WESTWARD
and southward, and eastward, and *w* .... Gen 13:14   3220
w thou shalt make six boards .... Ex 26:22   3220
tabernacle, for the two sides *w* .... Ex 26:27   3220
tabernacle *w* he made six boards .... Ex 36:27   3220
of the tabernacle for the sides *w* .... Ex 36:32   3220

pitch behind the tabernacle *w* .... Num 3:23   3220
Pisgah, and lift up thine eyes *w* .... Deut 3:27   3220
were on the side of Jordan *w* .... Josh 5:1   3220
before the valley of Hinnom *w* .... Josh 15:8   3220
from Baalah *w* unto mount Seir .... Josh 15:10   3220
goeth down *w* to the coast of .... Josh 16:3   3220
Tappuah *w* unto the river Kanah .... Josh 16:8   3220
went up through the mountains *w* .... Josh 18:12   3220
and reacheth to Carmel *w*, and to .... Josh 19:26   3220
coast turneth *w* to Aznoth-tabor .... Josh 19:34   3220
brethren on this side Jordan *w* .... Josh 22:7   3220
off, even unto the great sea *w* .... Josh 23:4   3996,8121
w Gezer, with the towns thereof 1Chr 7:28   4628
and Hosah the lot came forth *w* 1Chr 26:16   4628
At Parbar *w*, four at the causeway 1Chr 26:18   4628
of Israel on this side Jordan *w* 1Chr 26:30   4628
of the city, from the west side *w* .... Eze 45:7   3220
was a place on the two sides *w* .... Eze 46:19   3220
eastward, and ten thousand *w* .... Eze 48:18   3220
w over against the five and twenty .... Eze 48:21   3220
I saw the ram pushing *w*, and .... Dan 8:4   3220

WET

They are *w* with the showers of .... Job 24:8   7372
let it be *w* with the dew of .... Dan 4:15   6647
let it be *w* with the dew of .... Dan 4:23   6647
they shall *w* thee with the dew of .... Dan 4:25   6647
his body was *w* with the dew of .... Dan 4:33   6647
his body was *w* with the dew of .... Dan 5:21   6647

WHALE

Am I a sea, or a *w*, that thou .... Job 7:12   8577
and thou art as a *w* in the seas .... Eze 32:2   8565

WHALE'S

and three nights in the *w* belly .... Mt 12:40   *2785*

WHALES

And God created great *w*, and every ...... Gen 1:21   8577

WHAT See APPENDIX.

WHATSOEVER See APPENDIX.

WHEAT

went in the days of *w* harvest .... Gen 30:14   2406
But the *w* and the rie were not .... Ex 9:32   2406
of the firstfruits of *w* harvest .... Ex 34:22   2406
the best of the wine, and of the *w* .... Num 18:12   1715
A land of *w*, and barley, and vines, ... Deut 8:8   2406
with the fat of kidneys of *w* .... Deut 32:14   2406
threshed *w* by the winepress .... Judg 6:11   2406
after, in the time of *w* harvest .... Judg 15:1   2406
of barley harvest and of *w* harvest........ Ruth 2:23   2406
their *w* harvest in the valley 1Sa 6:13   2406
Is it not *w* harvest to day 1Sa 12:17   2406
though they would have fetched *w* 2Sa 4:6   2406
basons, and earthen vessels, and *w* 2Sa 17:28   2406
of *w* for food to his household 1Kin 5:11   2406
Now Ornan was threshing *w* 1Chr 21:20   2406
the *w* for the meat offering 1Chr 21:23   2406
thousand measures of beaten *w* 2Chr 2:10   2406
Now therefore the *w*, and the 2Chr 2:15   2406
and ten thousand measures of *w* 2Chr 27:5   2406
offerings of the God of heaven, *w* .... Ezr 6:9   2591
and to an hundred measures of *w* .... Ezr 7:22   2591
Let thistles grow instead of *w* .... Job 31:40   2406
also with the finest of the *w* .... Ps 81:16   2406
thee with the finest of the *w* .... Ps 147:14   2406
in a mortar among *w* with a pestle .... Prov 27:22   7383
heap of *w* set about with lilies .... Song 7:2   2406
and cast in the principal *w* .... Is 28:25   2406
They have sown *w*, but shall reap.......... Jer 12:13   2406
What is the chaff to the *w*? .... Jer 23:28   1250
the goodness of the Lord, for *w* .... Jer 31:12   1715
have treasures in the field, of *w* .... Jer 41:8   2406
Take thou also unto thee *w* .... Eze 4:9   2406
traded in thy market *w* of Minnith .... Eze 27:17   2406
part of an ephah of an homer of *w* .... Eze 45:13   2406
O ye vinedressers, for the *w* .... Joel 1:11   2406
And the floors shall be full of *w* .... Joel 2:24   1250
and ye take from him burdens of *w*....... Amos 5:11   1250
sabbath, that we may set forth *w* .... Amos 8:5   1250
yea, and sell the refuse of the *w* .... Amos 8:6   1250
gather his *w* into the garner .... Mt 3:12   4621
came and sowed tares among the *w* ..... Mt 13:25   4621
ye root up also the *w* with them .... Mt 13:29   4621
but gather the *w* into my barn .... Mt 13:30   4621
will gather the *w* into his garner .... Lk 3:17   4621
he said, An hundred measures of *w* ..... Lk 16:7   4621
you, that he may sift you as *w* .... Lk 22:31   4621
Except a corn of *w* fall into the .... Jn 12:24   4621
and cast out the *w* into the sea............ Acts 27:38   4621
bare grain, it may chance of *w* 1Cor 15:37   4621

say, A measure of *w* for a penny............ Rev 6:6   *4621*
wine, and oil, and fine flour, and *w* ...... Rev 18:13   *4621*

WHEATEN

of *w* flour shalt thou make them .... Ex 29:2   2406

WHEEL

and the height of a *w* was a cubit........... 1Kin 7:32   212
was like the work of a chariot *w* 1Kin 7:33   212
O my God, make them like a *w* .... Ps 83:13   1534
and bringeth the *w* over them .... Prov 20:26   212
or the *w* broken at the cistern .... Eccl 12:6   1534
neither is a cart *w* turned about............. Is 28:27   212
break it with the *w* of his cart .... Is 28:28   1536
behold one *w* upon the earth by .... Eze 1:15   212
were a *w* in the middle of a *w* .... Eze 1:16   212
one *w* by one cherub, and another .... Eze 10:9   212
another *w* by another cherub .... Eze 10:9   212
as if a *w* had been in the midst .... Eze 10:10   212
had been in the midst of a *w* .... Eze 10:10   212
unto them in my hearing, O *w* .... Eze 10:13   1534

WHEELS

And took off their chariot *w* .... Ex 14:25   212
Why tarry the *w* of his chariots .... Judg 5:28   6471
And every base had four brasen *w* 1Kin 7:30   212
And under the borders were four *w* 1Kin 7:32   212
the axletrees of the *w* were 1Kin 7:32   212
the work of the *w* was like the 1Kin 7:33   212
and their *w* like a whirlwind .... Is 5:28   1534
he wrought a work on the *w* .... Jer 18:3   70
and at the rumbling of his *w* .... Jer 47:3   1534
The appearance of the *w* and their .... Eze 1:16   212
went, the *w* went by them..................... Eze 1:19   212
the earth, the *w* were lifted up .... Eze 1:19   212
the *w* were lifted up over against .... Eze 1:20   212
the living creature was in the *w* .... Eze 1:20   212
the *w* were lifted up over against .... Eze 1:21   212
the living creature was in the *w* .... Eze 1:21   212
the noise of the *w* over against .... Eze 3:13   212
and said, Go in between the *w* .... Eze 10:2   1534
Take fire from between the *w* .... Eze 10:6   1534
he went in, and stood beside the *w* .... Eze 10:6   212
looked, behold the four *w* by the .... Eze 10:9   212
the appearance of the *w* was as .... Eze 10:9   212
hands, and their wings, and the *w* .... Eze 10:12   212
even the *w* that they four had .... Eze 10:12   212
As for the *w*, it was cried unto .... Eze 10:13   212
went, the *w* went by them..................... Eze 10:16   212
the same *w* also turned not from .... Eze 10:16   212
the *w* also were beside them, and......... Eze 10:19   212
their wings, and the *w* beside them....... Eze 11:22   212
thee with chariots, wagons, and *w* .... Eze 23:24   1534
of the horsemen, and of the *w*.............. Eze 26:10   1534
flame, and his *w* as burning fire............ Dan 7:9   1535
noise of the rattling of the *w* .... Nah 3:2   212

WHELP

Judah is a lion's *w*................................ Gen 49:9   1482
of Dan he said, Dan is a lion's *w* .... Deut 33:22   1482
old lion, walked, and the lion's *w* .... Nah 2:11   1482

WHELPS

bear robbed of her *w* in the field 2Sa 17:8   1121
the stout lion's *w* are scattered .... Job 4:11   1121
The lion's *w* have not trodden it, ... Job 28:8   1121
a bear robbed of her *w* meet a man .... Prov 17:12
they shall yell as lions' *w* .... Jer 51:38   1484
nourished her *w* among young lions...... Eze 19:2   1482
And she brought up one of her *w* .... Eze 19:3   1482
then she took another of her *w* .... Eze 19:5   1482
a bear that is bereaved of her *w* .... Hos 13:8
tear in pieces enough for his *w* .... Nah 2:12   1484

WHEN See APPENDIX.

WHENCE See APPENDIX.

WHENSOEVER

w the stronger cattle did .... Gen 30:41   3605
w ye will ye may do them good .... Mk 14:7   *3752*
W I take my journey into Spain, ... Rom 15:24   *5613,1437*

WHERE See APPENDIX.

WHEREABOUT

of the business *w* I send thee 1Sa 21:2   834

WHEREAS See APPENDIX.

WHEREBY See APPENDIX.

WHEREFORE See APPENDIX.

WHEREIN See APPENDIX.

WHEREINSOEVER

Howbeit *w* any is bold 2Cor 11:21   *1722,3739,302*

WHEREINTO
w any of them falleth,................ Lev 11:33   834,413,8432
I bring into the land w he went....... Num 14:24   824,8432
save that one w his disciples.......... Jn 6:22   *1519,3739*

WHEREOF See APPENDIX.

WHEREON
the land w thou liest, to thee.......... Gen 28:13   834,5921
for the place w thou standest is..... Ex 3:5   834,5921
and also the ground w they are..... Ex 8:21   834,5921
thou shalt wash that w it was........ Lev 6:27   834,5921
w he lieth that hath the issue,........ Lev 15:4
w he sitteth, shall be unclean....... Lev 15:4
w he sat that hath the issue.......... Lev 15:6   834,5921
w is the seed of copulation,........ Lev 15:17   834,5921
or on any thing w she sitteth......... Lev 15:23   834,5921
all the bed w he lieth shall be...... Lev 15:24   834,5921
Every bed w she lieth all the........ Lev 15:26   834,5921
Every place w the soles of your........... Deut 11:24   834
for the place w thou standest is........ Josh 5:15   834,5921
Surely the land w thy feet have........... Josh 14:9   834
w they set down the ark of the....... 1Sa 6:18   834,5921
the tables w the shewbread was............ 2Chr 4:19   5921
W do ye trust, that ye abide in....... 2Chr 32:10   5921,4100
fallen upon the bed w Esther was.......... Est 7:8
him to be in safety, w he resteth........ Job 24:23
w there hang a thousand bucklers,........ Song 4:4   5921
w if a man lean, it will go into........ Is 36:6   834,5921
the sticks w thou writest shall........ Eze 37:20   834,5921
find a colt tied, w never man sat..... Mk 11:2   *1909,3739*
the hill w their city was built...... Lk 4:29   *1909,3739*
them, and took up that w he lay..... Lk 5:25   *1909,3739*
a colt tied, w yet never man sat..... Lk 19:30   *1909,3739*
reap that w ye bestowed no labour........ Jn 4:38   *3739*

WHERESOEVER See APPENDIX.

WHERETO
w might the strength of their.................. Job 30:2   4100
prosper in the thing w I sent it....... Is 55:11   834
w we have already attained, let...... Phil 3:16   *1519,3739*

WHEREUNTO See APPENDIX.

WHEREUPON See APPENDIX.

WHEREWITH
blessing w his father blessed him.......... Gen 27:41   834
w the Egyptians oppress them.............. Ex 3:9   834
thine hand, w thou shalt do signs.......... Ex 4:17   834
the bread w I have fed you in the....... Ex 16:32   834
w thou smotest the river, take in........... Ex 17:5   834
things w the atonement was made......... Ex 29:33   834
of the sanctuary w they minister......... Num 3:31   834
w the odd number of them is to be........ Num 3:48
thereof, w they minister unto it.............. Num 4:9   834
w they minister in the sanctuary........ Num 4:12   834
w they minister about it, even........ Num 4:14   834
w they that were burnt had............ Num 16:39   834
w they have beguiled you in the............ Num 25:18   834
her bond w she hath bound her........... Num 30:4   834
every bond w she hath bound her......... Num 30:4   834
or of her bonds w she hath bound......... Num 30:5   834
of her lips, w she bound her soul........ Num 30:6   834
her bonds w she bound her soul.......... Num 30:7   834
w she bound her soul, of none................ Num 30:8   834
w they have bound their souls,........ Num 30:9   834
every bond w she bound her soul.......... Num 30:11   834
w he may die, and he die, he is a..... Num 35:17   834
w he may die, and he die, he is a.......... Num 35:18   834
w a man may die, seeing him not,........ Num 35:23   834
w the LORD was wroth against you........ Deut 9:19   834
of that w the LORD thy God hath............ Deut 15:14   834
vesture, w thou coverest thyself............ Deut 22:12   834
w thine enemies shall distress......... Deut 28:53   834
w thine enemies shall distress................ Deut 28:55   834
w thine enemy shall distress thee......... Deut 28:57   834
of thine heart w thou shalt fear............ Deut 28:67   834
w Moses the man of God blessed........ Deut 33:1   834
w he stretched out the spear,................ Josh 8:26   834
Oh my Lord, w shall I save Israel.......... Judg 6:15   4100
w Abimelech hired vain and light.......... Judg 9:4
w by me they honour God and man,........ Judg 9:9   834
w thou saidst, Who is Abimelech,........... Judg 9:38   834
w thou mightest be bound to................ Judg 16:6   4100
thee, w thou mightest be bound............ Judg 16:10   4100
tell me w thou mightest be bound......... Judg 16:13   834
tell us w we shall send it to his........... 1Sa 6:2   4100
w they have forsaken me, and.............. 1Sa 8:8
for w should he reconcile himself......... 1Sa 29:4   4100
so that the hatred w he hated her.......... 2Sa 13:15   834
than the love w he had loved her........... 2Sa 13:15   834
w shall I make the atonement,................ 2Sa 21:3   4100

w I have made supplication before......... 1Kin 8:59   834
thereof, w Baasha had builded........... 1Kin 15:22   834
in his sin w he made Israel to................ 1Kin 15:26   834
by his provocation w he provoked........... 1Kin 15:30   834
in his sin w he made Israel to................ 1Kin 15:34   834
in his sin w he made Israel to................ 1Kin 16:26   834
for the provocation w thou hast........... 1Kin 21:22   834
And the LORD said unto him, W........... 1Kin 22:22   4100
his might w he fought against............... 2Kin 13:12   834
beside his sin w he made Judah to........ 2Kin 21:16   834
w his anger was kindled against........... 2Kin 23:26   834
of brass w they ministered.................... 2Kin 25:14   834
w Solomon made the brasen sea, and.... 1Chr 18:8
after the numbering w David his......... 1Chr 2:17   834
thereof, w Baasha was building........... 2Chr 16:6   834
And the LORD said unto him, W........... 2Chr 18:20   4100
against the house w I have war............. 2Chr 35:21
w thou didst testify against them........ Neh 9:34   834
or with speeches w he can do no......... Job 15:3
w they have reproached thee, O............ Ps 79:12   834
W thine enemies have reproached,........ Ps 89:51   834
w they have reproached the................... Ps 89:51   834
w he hath girded himself...................... Ps 93:1
for a girdle w he is girded..................... Ps 109:19
So shall I have w to answer him............ Ps 119:42   1697
W the mower filleth not his hand......... Ps 129:7
king Solomon with the crown w his...... Song 3:11
This is the rest w ye may cause............. Is 28:12   834
w the servants of the king of................. Is 37:6   834
w I said I would benefit them................. Jer 18:10   834
w their enemies, and they that.............. Jer 19:9   834
w ye fight against the king of................ Jer 21:4   834
this is the name w she shall be.............. Jer 33:16   834
of brass w they ministered.................... Jer 52:18   834
w the LORD hath afflicted me in............ Lam 1:12   834
the daubing w ye have daubed it........... Eze 13:12   834
w ye there hunt the souls to make......... Eze 13:20   834
w I fed thee, thou hast even set............ Eze 16:19   834
his labour w he served against it.......... Eze 29:20   834
w they shall lament her .... Eze 32:16
for their idols w they had...................... Eze 36:18
w they slew the burnt offering............... Eze 40:42   834
w his spirit was troubled, and his......... Dan 2:1
W shall I come before the LORD, ... Mic 6:6   4100
this shall be the plague w the................ Zec 14:12   834
w the LORD will smite the heathen......... Zec 14:18   834
him for the fear w he feared me .... Mal 2:5
his savour, w shall it be salted .... Mt 5:13   *1722,5101*
blasphemies w soever they shall .... Mk 3:28   *3745*
his saltness, w will ye season it ..... Mk 9:50   *1722,5101*
savour, w shall it be seasoned ...... Lk 14:34   *1722,5101*
unto him, Make ready w I may sup ...... Lk 17:8   *5101*
with the towel w he was girded............. Jn 13:5   *3739*
that the love w thou hast loved .... Jn 17:26   *3739*
things w one may edify another .... Rom 14:19
by the comfort w we ourselves are......... 2Cor 1:4   *3739*
but by the consolation w he was............ 2Cor 7:7   *3739*
w I think to be bold against some.......... 2Cor 10:2   *3739*
w Christ hath made us free................... Gal 5:1   *3739*
for his great love w he loved us .... Eph 2:4   *3739*
of the vocation w ye are called .... Eph 4:1   *3739*
w ye shall be able to quench all ..... Eph 6:16   *1722,3739*
for all the joy w we joy for your 1Th 3:9   *3739*
w he was sanctified, an unholy .... Heb 10:29   *1722,3739*

WHEREWITHAL
W shall a young man cleanse his.......... Ps 119:9
or, W shall we be clothed .... Mt 6:31   *5101*

WHET
If I w my glittering sword, and .... Deut 32:41   8150
he turn not, he will w his sword............. Ps 7:12   3913
Who w their tongue like a sword,.......... Ps 64:3   8150
be blunt, and he do not w the edge........ Eccl 10:10   7043

WHETHER See APPENDIX.

WHICH See APPENDIX.

WHILE See APPENDIX.

WHILES
W they see vanity unto thee, ... Eze 21:29
w they divine a lie unto thee, to............. Eze 21:29
w they minister in the gates of .... Eze 44:17
w he tasted the wine, commanded .... Dan 5:2
w I was speaking, and praying, and....... Dan 9:20   5750
w I was speaking in prayer, even............ Dan 9:21
like an oven, w ye lie in wait .... Hos 7:6
w thou art in the way with him...... Mt 5:25   *2193,3755*
W it remained, was it not thine .... Acts 5:4
W by the experiment of this 2Cor 9:13

W

WHILST

put to death w it is yet morning	Judg 6:31	5704
w I leave it, and come down to you	Neh 6:3	834
W it is yet in his greenness, and	Job 8:12	5704
w ye searched out what to say	Job 32:11	5704
own nets, w that I withal escape	Ps 141:10	5704
W their children remember their	Jer 17:2	
w we are at home in the body, we	2Cor 5:6	
w he remembereth the obedience of	2Cor 7:15	
w ye were made a gazingstock both	Heb 10:33	
w ye became companions of them	Heb 10:33	

WHIP

A w for the horse, a bridle for	Prov 26:3	7752
The noise of a w, and the noise of	Nah 3:2	7752

WHIPS

father hath chastised you with w	1Kin 12:11	7752
father also chastised you with w	1Kin 12:14	7752
my father chastised you with w	2Chr 10:11	7752
my father chastised you with w	2Chr 10:14	7752

WHIRLETH

it w about continually, and the	Eccl 1:6	1980

WHIRLWIND

take up Elijah into heaven by a w	2Kin 2:1	5591
Elijah went up by a w into heaven	2Kin 2:11	5591
Out of the south cometh the w	Job 37:9	5492
LORD answered Job out of the w	Job 38:1	5591
the LORD unto Job out of the w	Job 40:6	5591
shall take them away as with a w	Ps 58:9	8175
and your destruction cometh as a w	Prov 1:27	5492
As the w passeth, so is the	Prov 10:25	5492
flint, and their wheels like a w	Is 5:28	5492
like a rolling thing before the w	Is 17:13	5492
the w shall take them away as	Is 40:24	5591
away, and the w shall scatter them	Is 41:16	5591
and with his chariots like a w	Is 66:15	5492
and his chariots shall be as a w	Jer 4:13	5492
a w of the LORD is gone forth in	Jer 23:19	5591
forth in fury, even a grievous w	Jer 23:19	5591
a great w shall be raised up from	Jer 25:32	5591
the w of the LORD goeth forth	Jer 30:23	5591
forth with fury, a continuing w	Jer 30:23	5591
a w came out of the north, a	Eze 1:4	7307,5591
shall come against him like a w	Dan 11:40	8175
wind, and they shall reap the w	Hos 8:7	5492
with the w out of the floor	Hos 13:3	5590
a tempest in the day of the w	Amos 1:14	5492
the LORD hath his way in the w	Nah 1:3	5492
came out as a w to scatter me	Hab 3:14	5590
But I scattered them with a w	Zec 7:14	5590

WHIRLWINDS

As w in the south pass through	Is 21:1	5492
and shall go with w of the south	Zec 9:14	5591

WHISPER

All that hate me w together	Ps 41:7	3907
speech shall w out of the dust	Is 29:4	6850

WHISPERED

David saw that his servants w	2Sa 12:19	3907

WHISPERER

a w separateth chief friends	Prov 16:28	5372

WHISPERERS

deceit, malignity; w,	Rom 1:29	5588

WHISPERINGS

wraths, strifes, backbitings, w	2Cor 12:20	5587

WHIT

and all the spoil thereof every w	Deut 13:16	3632
And Samuel told him every w	1Sa 3:18	1697
every w whole on the sabbath day	Jn 7:23	3650
his feet, but is clean every w	Jn 13:10	3650
not a w behind the very chiefest	2Cor 11:5	3367

WHITE

every one that had some w in it	Gen 30:35	3836
pilled w strakes in them	Gen 30:37	3836
made the w appear which was in	Gen 30:37	3836
I had three w baskets on my head	Gen 40:16	2751
wine, and his teeth w with milk	Gen 49:12	3836
and it was like coriander seed, w	Ex 16:31	3836
hair in the plague is turned w	Lev 13:3	3836
If the bright spot be w in the	Lev 13:4	3836
the hair thereof be not turned w	Lev 13:4	3836
if the rising be w in the skin	Lev 13:10	3836
and it have turned the hair w	Lev 13:10	3836
it is all turned w	Lev 13:13	3836
turn again, and be changed unto w	Lev 13:16	3836
if the plague be turned into w	Lev 13:17	3836
of the boil there be a w rising	Lev 13:19	3836

or a bright spot, w	Lev 13:19	3836
and the hair thereof be turned w	Lev 13:20	3836
there be no w hairs therein, and	Lev 13:21	3836
that burneth have a w bright spot	Lev 13:24	3836
somewhat reddish, or w	Lev 13:24	3836
in the bright spot be turned w	Lev 13:25	3836
there be no w hair in the bright	Lev 13:26	3836
bright spots, even w bright spots	Lev 13:38	3836
skin of their flesh be darkish w	Lev 13:39	3836
bald forehead, a w reddish sore	Lev 13:42	3836
be w reddish in his bald head	Lev 13:43	3836
Miriam became leprous, w as snow	Num 12:10	
Speak, ye that ride on w asses	Judg 5:10	6715
his presence a leper w as snow	2Kin 5:27	
being arrayed in w linen	2Chr 5:12	
Where were w, green, and blue,	Est 1:6	2353
a pavement of red, and blue, and w	Est 1:6	1858
in royal apparel of blue and w	Est 8:15	2353
any taste in the w of an egg	Job 6:6	7388
it was w as snow in Salmon	Ps 68:14	
Let thy garments be always w	Eccl 9:8	3836
My beloved is w and ruddy, the	Song 5:10	6703
they shall be as w as snow	Is 1:18	3835
in the wine of Helbon, and w wool	Eze 27:18	6713
sit, whose garment was w as snow	Dan 7:9	
and to purge, and to make them w	Dan 11:35	3835
Many shall be purified, and made w	Dan 12:10	3835
the branches thereof are made w	Joel 1:7	3835
there red horses, speckled, and w	Zec 1:8	3836
And in the third chariot w horses	Zec 6:3	3836
the w go forth after them	Zec 6:6	3836
not make one hair w or black	Mt 5:36	3022
and his raiment was w as the light	Mt 17:2	3022
and his raiment w as snow	Mt 28:3	3022
shining, exceeding w as snow	Mk 9:3	3022
as no fuller on earth can w them	Mk 9:3	3021
side, clothed in a long w garment	Mk 16:5	3022
was altered, and his raiment was w	Lk 9:29	3022
for they are w already to harvest	Jn 4:35	3022
And seeth two angels in w sitting	Jn 20:12	3022
men stood by them in w apparel	Acts 1:10	3022
w like wool, as w as snow	Rev 1:14	3022
manna, and will give him a w stone	Rev 2:17	3022
and they shall walk with me in w	Rev 3:4	3022
shall be clothed in w raiment	Rev 3:5	3022
w raiment, that thou mayest be	Rev 3:18	3022
sitting, clothed in w raiment	Rev 4:4	3022
And I saw, and behold a w horse	Rev 6:2	3022
w robes were given unto every one	Rev 6:11	3022
the Lamb, clothed with w robes	Rev 7:9	3022
which are arrayed in w robes	Rev 7:13	3022
made them w in the blood of the	Rev 7:14	3021
And I looked, and behold a w cloud	Rev 14:14	3022
w linen, and having their breasts	Rev 15:6	2986
arrayed in fine linen, clean and w	Rev 19:8	2986
opened, and behold a w horse	Rev 19:11	3022
heaven followed him upon w horses	Rev 19:14	3022
clothed in fine linen, w	Rev 19:14	3022
And I saw a great w throne	Rev 20:11	3022

WHITED

for ye are like unto w sepulchres	Mt 23:27	2867
God shall smite thee, thou w wall	Acts 23:3	2867

WHITER

me, and I shall be w than snow	Ps 51:7	3835
than snow, they were w than milk	Lam 4:7	6705

WHITHER See APPENDIX.

WHITHERSOEVER

thou mayest prosper w thou goest	Josh 1:7	3605,834
thy God is with thee w thou goest	Josh 1:9	3605,834
w thou sendest us, we will go	Josh 1:16	3605,834
W they went out, the hand of the	Judg 2:15	3605,834
w he turned himself, he vexed	1Sa 14:47	3605,834
David went out w Saul sent him	1Sa 18:5	3605,834
Keilah, and went w they could go	1Sa 23:13	834
I was with thee w thou wentest	2Sa 7:9	3605,834
LORD preserved David w he went	2Sa 8:6	3605,834
LORD preserved David w he went	2Sa 8:14	3605,834
and w thou turnest thyself	1Kin 2:3	3605,834,8033
w thou shalt send them, and shall	1Kin 8:44	1870,834
he prospered w he went forth	2Kin 18:7	3605,834
with thee w thou hast walked	1Chr 17:8	3605,834
LORD preserved David w he went	1Chr 18:6	3605,834
LORD preserved David w he went	1Chr 18:13	3605,834
w the king's commandment	Est 4:3	4725,834
w the king's commandment and his	Est 8:17	834
w it turneth, it prospereth	Prov 17:8	413,3605,834
he turneth it w he will	Prov 21:1	5921,3605,834
W the spirit was to go, they	Eze 1:20	5921,834,8033
or on the left, w thy face is set	Eze 21:16	575

w the rivers shall come,	Eze 47:9	413,3605,834,8033
I will follow thee *w* thou goest	Mt 8:19	*3699,1437*
w he entered, into villages, or	Mk 6:56	*3699,302*
I will follow thee *w* thou goest	Lk 9:57	*3699,302*
bring me on my journey *w* I go	1Cor 16:6	*3757,1437*
helm, *w* the governor listeth	Jas 3:4	*3699,302*
which follow the Lamb *w* he goeth	Rev 14:4	*3699,302*

WHO See APPENDIX.

WHOLE

watered the *w* face of the ground	Gen 2:6	854,3605
compasseth the *w* land of Havilah	Gen 2:11	854,3605
compasseth the *w* land of Ethiopia	Gen 2:13	854,3605
that were under the *w* heaven	Gen 7:19	3605
were on the face of the *w* earth	Gen 8:9	3605
and of them was the *w* earth	Gen 9:19	3605
the *w* earth was of one language,	Gen 11:1	3605
upon the face of the *w* earth	Gen 11:4	3605
Is not the *w* land before thee	Gen 13:9	3605
so the *w* age of Jacob was an	Gen 47:28	
covered the face of the *w* earth	Ex 10:15	3605
and the *w* assembly of the	Ex 12:6	3605
the *w* congregation of the	Ex 16:2	3605
to kill this *w* assembly with	Ex 16:3	854,3605
as Aaron spake unto the *w*	Ex 16:10	3605
the *w* mount quaked greatly	Ex 19:18	3605
burn the *w* ram upon the altar	Ex 29:18	854,3605
the *w* rump, it shall he take off	Lev 3:9	8549
Even the *w* bullock shall he carry	Lev 4:12	854,3605
if the *w* congregation of Israel	Lev 4:13	3605
he shall offer one out of the *w*	Lev 7:14	3605
Moses burnt the *w* ram upon the	Lev 8:21	854,3605
the *w* house of Israel, bewail the	Lev 10:6	3605
within a *w* year after it is sold	Lev 25:29	8552
the charge of the *w* congregation	Num 3:7	3605
thou shalt gather the *w* assembly	Num 8:9	854,3605
of a *w* piece shalt thou make them	Num 10:2	4749
But even a *w* month, until it come	Num 11:20	3117
that they may eat a *w* month	Num 11:21	3117
the *w* congregation said unto them	Num 14:2	3605
you, according to your *w* number	Num 14:29	3605
even the *w* congregation, into the	Num 20:1	3605
Israel, even the *w* congregation,	Num 20:22	3605
that are under the *w* heaven	Deut 2:25	3605
all nations under the *w* heaven	Deut 4:19	3605
of the LORD thy God of *w* stones	Deut 27:6	8003
that the *w* land thereof is	Deut 29:23	3605
w burnt sacrifice upon thine	Deut 33:10	3632
in the camp, till they were *w*	Josh 5:8	2421
of Moses, an altar of *w* stones	Josh 8:31	8003
not to go down about a *w* day	Josh 10:13	8549
So Joshua took the *w* land	Josh 11:23	854,3605
the *w* congregation of the	Josh 18:1	3605
the *w* congregation of the	Josh 22:12	3605
Thus saith the *w* congregation of	Josh 22:16	3605
with the *w* congregation of Israel	Josh 22:18	3605
and was there four *w* months	Judg 19:2	3117
the *w* congregation sent some to	Judg 21:13	3605
because my life is yet *w* in me	2Sa 1:9	3605
good to the *w* house of Benjamin	2Sa 3:19	3605
even among the *w* multitude of	2Sa 6:19	3605
the *w* family is risen against	2Sa 14:7	3605
the *w* house he overlaid with gold	1Kin 6:22	3605
also the *w* altar that was by the	1Kin 6:22	3605
the *w* kingdom out of his hand	1Kin 11:34	854,3605
For the *w* house of Ahab shall	2Kin 9:8	3605
blessed the *w* congregation of	2Chr 6:3	854,3605
and sought him with their *w* desire	2Chr 15:15	3605
to and fro throughout the *w* earth	2Chr 16:9	3605
The *w* number of the chief of the	2Chr 26:12	3605
the *w* assembly took counsel to	2Chr 30:23	3605
them, according to the *w* law	2Chr 33:8	3605
The *w* congregation together was	Ezr 2:64	3605
The *w* congregation together was	Neh 7:66	3605
the *w* kingdom of Ahasuerus	Est 3:6	3605
he woundeth, and his hands make *w*	Job 5:18	7495
and seeth under the *w* heaven	Job 28:24	3605
Or who hath disposed the *w* world	Job 34:13	3605
directeth it under the *w* heaven	Job 37:3	3605
is under the *w* heaven is mine	Job 41:11	3605
thee, O LORD, with my *w* heart	Ps 9:1	3605
situation, the joy of the *w* earth	Ps 48:2	3605
offering and *w* burnt offering	Ps 51:19	3632
let the *w* earth be filled with	Ps 72:19	854,3605
of the LORD of the *w* earth	Ps 97:5	3605
he brake the *w* staff of bread	Ps 105:16	3605
praise the LORD with my *w* heart	Ps 111:1	3605
and that seek him with the *w* heart	Ps 119:2	3605
With my *w* heart have I sought	Ps 119:10	3605
shall observe it with my *w* heart	Ps 119:34	3605
thy favour with my *w* heart	Ps 119:58	3605
keep thy precepts with my *w* heart	Ps 119:69	3605
I cried with my *w* heart	Ps 119:145	
will praise thee with my *w* heart	Ps 138:1	3605
and *w*, as those that go down into	Prov 1:12	8549
but the *w* disposing thereof is of	Prov 16:33	3605
shewed before the *w* congregation	Prov 26:26	
the conclusion of the *w* matter	Eccl 12:13	3605
for this is the *w* duty of man	Eccl 12:13	3605
the *w* head is sick	Is 1:5	3605
and the *w* heart faint	Is 1:5	3605
the *w* stay of bread	Is 3:1	3605
and the *w* stay of water	Is 3:1	3605
the *w* earth is full of his glory	Is 6:3	3605
his *w* work upon mount Zion	Is 10:12	854,3605
to destroy the *w* land	Is 13:5	3605
The *w* earth is at rest, and is	Is 14:7	3605
that is purposed upon the *w* earth	Is 14:26	3605
w Palestina, because the rod of	Is 14:29	3605
w Palestina, art dissolved	Is 14:31	3605
and I am set in my ward *w* nights	Is 21:8	3605
even determined upon the *w* earth	Is 28:22	3605
The God of the *w* earth shall he	Is 54:5	3605
brasen walls against the *w* land	Jer 1:18	3605
turned unto me with her *w* heart	Jer 3:10	3605
for the *w* land is spoiled	Jer 4:20	3605
The *w* land shall be desolate	Jer 4:27	3605
The *w* city shall flee for the	Jer 4:29	3605
even the *w* seed of Ephraim	Jer 7:15	3605
the *w* land trembled at the sound	Jer 8:16	3605
the *w* land is made desolate,	Jer 12:11	3605
unto me the *w* house of Israel	Jer 13:11	3605
the *w* house of Judah, saith the	Jer 13:11	3605
man of contention to the *w* earth	Jer 15:10	3605
that cannot be made *w* again	Jer 19:11	7495
return unto me with their *w* heart	Jer 24:7	3605
this *w* land shall be a desolation	Jer 25:11	3605
the *w* valley of the dead bodies,	Jer 31:40	3605
my *w* heart and with my *w* soul	Jer 32:41	3605
the *w* house of the Rechabites	Jer 35:3	3605
the *w* army of the Chaldeans that	Jer 37:10	3605
I will pluck up, even this *w* land	Jer 45:4	3605
of the *w* earth cut in asunder	Jer 50:23	3605
praise of the *w* earth surprised	Jer 51:41	3605
her *w* land shall be confounded,	Jer 51:47	3605
of beauty, The joy of the *w* earth	Lam 2:15	3605
the *w* remnant of thee will I	Eze 5:10	3605
touching the *w* multitude thereof	Eze 7:13	3605
And their *w* body, and their backs,	Eze 10:12	3605
Behold, when it was *w*, it was	Eze 15:5	8549
beasts of the *w* earth with thee	Eze 32:4	3605
When the *w* earth rejoiceth, I	Eze 35:14	3605
bones are the *w* house of Israel	Eze 37:11	3605
mercy upon the *w* house of Israel	Eze 39:25	3605
they may keep the *w* form thereof	Eze 43:11	3605
the top of the mountain the *w*	Eze 43:12	3605
be for the *w* house of Israel	Eze 45:6	3605
mountain, and filled the *w* earth	Dan 2:35	3606
over the *w* province of Babylon	Dan 2:48	3606
should be over the *w* kingdom	Dan 6:1	3606
to set him over the *w* realm	Dan 6:3	3606
and shall devour the *w* earth	Dan 7:23	3606
of the kingdom under the *w* heaven	Dan 7:27	3606
west on the face of the *w* earth	Dan 8:5	3605
for under the *w* heaven hath not	Dan 9:12	3605
till three *w* weeks were fulfilled	Dan 10:3	3117
the strength of his *w* kingdom	Dan 11:17	3605
away captive the *w* captivity	Amos 1:6	8003
up the *w* captivity to Edom	Amos 1:9	8003
against the *w* family which I	Amos 3:1	3605
unto the Lord of the *w* earth	Mic 4:13	3605
but the *w* land shall be devoured	Zeph 1:18	3605
run to and fro through the *w* earth	Zec 4:10	3605
stand by the Lord of the *w* earth	Zec 4:14	3605
over the face of the *w* earth	Zec 5:3	3605
robbed me, even this *w* nation	Mal 3:9	3605
not that thy *w* body should be	Mt 5:29	*3650*
not that thy *w* body should be	Mt 5:30	*3650*
thy *w* body shall be full of light	Mt 6:22	*3650*
thy *w* body shall be full of	Mt 6:23	*3650*
the *w* herd of swine ran violently	Mt 8:32	*3956*
the *w* city came out to meet Jesus	Mt 8:34	*3956*
They that be *w* need not a	Mt 9:12	*2480*
touch his garment, I shall be *w*	Mt 9:21	*4982*
thy faith hath made thee *w*	Mt 9:22	*4982*
woman was made *w* from that hour	Mt 9:22	*4982*
and it was restored *w*, like as the	Mt 12:13	*5199*
the *w* multitude stood on the	Mt 13:2	*3956*
of meal, till the *w* was leavened	Mt 13:33	*3650*
as touched were made perfectly *w*	Mt 14:36	*1295*
was made *w* from that very hour	Mt 15:28	*3390*
dumb to speak, the maimed to be *w*	Mt 15:31	*5199*

if he shall gain the *w* world	Mt 16:26	3650
shall be preached in the *w* world	Mt 26:13	3650
unto him the *w* band of soldiers	Mt 27:27	3650
They that are *w* have no need of	Mk 2:17	2480
hand was restored *w* as the other	Mk 3:5	5199
the *w* multitude was by the sea on	Mk 4:1	3956
but his clothes, I shall be *w*	Mk 5:28	4982
thy faith hath made thee *w*	Mk 5:34	4982
in peace, and be *w* of thy plague	Mk 5:34	5199
ran through that *w* region round	Mk 6:55	3650
many as touched him were made *w*	Mk 6:56	4982
man, if he shall gain the *w* world	Mk 8:36	3650
thy faith hath made thee *w*	Mk 10:52	4982
more than all *w* burnt offerings	Mk 12:33	3646
preached throughout the *w*	Mk 14:9	3650
the *w* council, and bound Jesus, and	Mk 15:1	3650
and they call together the *w* band	Mk 15:16	3650
the *w* land until the ninth hour	Mk 15:33	3650
the *w* multitude of the people	Lk 1:10	3956
They that are *w* need not a	Lk 5:31	5198
hand was restored *w* as the other	Lk 6:10	5199
the *w* multitude sought to touch	Lk 6:19	3956
found the servant *w* that had been	Lk 7:10	5198
Then the *w* multitude of the	Lk 8:37	537
published throughout the *w* city	Lk 8:39	3650
thy faith hath made thee *w*	Lk 8:48	4982
only, and she shall be made *w*	Lk 8:50	4982
if he gain the *w* world, and lose	Lk 9:25	3650
thy *w* body also is full of light	Lk 11:34	3650
If thy *w* body therefore be full	Lk 11:36	3650
the *w* shall be full of light, as	Lk 11:36	3650
of meal, till the *w* was leavened	Lk 13:21	3650
thy faith hath made thee *w*	Lk 17:19	4982
the *w* multitude of the disciples	Lk 19:37	3956
dwell on the face of the *w* earth	Lk 21:35	3956
the *w* multitude of them arose, and	Lk 23:1	537
himself believed, and his *w* house	Jn 4:53	3650
w of whatsoever disease he had	Jn 5:4	5199
unto him, Wilt thou be made *w*	Jn 5:6	5199
immediately the man was made *w*	Jn 5:9	5199
answered them, He that made me *w*	Jn 5:11	5199
unto him, Behold, thou art made *w*	Jn 5:14	5199
was Jesus, which had made him *w*	Jn 5:15	5199
every whit *w* on the sabbath day	Jn 7:23	5199
that the *w* nation perish not	Jn 11:50	3650
man, by what means he is made *w*	Acts 4:9	4982
this man stand here before you *w*	Acts 4:10	5199
saying pleased the *w* multitude	Acts 6:5	3956
Jesus Christ maketh thee *w*	Acts 9:34	2390
that a *w* year they assembled	Acts 11:26	3650
sabbath day came almost the *w*	Acts 13:44	3956
and elders, with the *w* church	Acts 15:22	3650
the *w* city was filled with	Acts 19:29	3650
Paul dwelt two *w* years in his own	Acts 28:30	3650
spoken of throughout the *w* world	Rom 1:8	3650
know that the *w* creation groaneth	Rom 8:22	3956
mine host, and of the *w* church	Rom 16:23	3650
leaven leaveneth the *w* lump	1Cor 5:6	3650
If the *w* body were an eye, where	1Cor 12:17	3650
If the *w* were hearing, where	1Cor 12:17	3650
If therefore the *w* church be come	1Cor 14:23	3650
he is a debtor to do the *w* law	Gal 5:3	3650
leaven leaveneth the *w* lump	Gal 5:9	3650
Of whom the *w* family in heaven and	Eph 3:15	3958
From whom the *w* body fitly joined	Eph 4:16	3958
Put on the *w* armour of God, that	Eph 6:11	3650
take unto you the *w* armour of God	Eph 6:13	3650
and I pray God your *w* spirit	1Th 5:23	3648
be stopped, who subvert *w* houses	Titus 1:11	3650
whosoever shall keep the *w* law	Jas 2:10	3650
and able also to bridle the *w* body	Jas 3:2	3650
and we turn about their *w* body	Jas 3:3	3650
that it defileth the *w* body	Jas 3:6	3650
also for the sins of the *w* world	1Jn 2:2	3650
the *w* world lieth in wickedness	1Jn 5:19	3650
which deceiveth the *w* world	Rev 12:9	3650
of the earth and of the *w* world	Rev 16:14	3650

WHOLESOME

A *w* tongue is a tree of life	Prov 15:4	4832
and consent not to *w* words	1Ti 6:3	5198

WHOLLY

it shall be *w* burnt	Lev 6:22	3632
for the priest shall be *w* burnt	Lev 6:23	3632
thou shalt not *w* reap the corners	Lev 19:9	3615
they are *w* given unto him out of	Num 3:9	
spread over it a cloth *w* of blue	Num 4:6	3632
For they are *w* given unto me from	Num 8:16	
they have not *w* followed me	Num 32:11	4390
for they have *w* followed the LORD	Num 32:12	4390
because he hath *w* followed the	Deut 1:36	4390

but I *w* followed the LORD my God	Josh 14:8	4390
because thou hast *w* followed the	Josh 14:9	4390
because that he *w* followed the	Josh 14:14	4390
I had *w* dedicated the silver unto	Judg 17:3	6942
a burnt offering *w* unto the LORD	1Sa 7:9	3632
will be *w* at thy commandment	1Chr 28:21	3605
being *w* at ease and quiet	Job 21:23	3605
that thou art *w* gone up to the	Is 22:1	3605
thee a noble vine, *w* a right seed	Jer 2:21	3605
she is *w* oppression in the midst	Jer 6:6	3605
it shall be *w* carried away	Jer 13:19	7965
If ye *w* set your faces to enter	Jer 42:15	7760
I not leave thee *w* unpunished	Jer 46:28	5352
but it shall be *w* desolate	Jer 50:13	3605
and all the house of Israel *w*	Eze 11:15	3605
and it shall rise up *w* as a flood	Amos 8:8	3605
it shall rise up *w* like a flood	Amos 9:5	3605
saw the city *w* given to idolatry	Acts 17:16	
very God of peace sanctify you *w*	1Th 5:23	3651
give thyself *w* to them	1Ti 4:15	1510,1722

WHOM See APPENDIX.

WHOMSOEVER

With *w* thou findest thy gods, let	Gen 31:32	834
With *w* of thy servants it be	Gen 44:9	834
w he toucheth that hath the issue	Lev 15:11	3605,834
of *w* I say unto thee, This shall	Judg 7:4	834
So whom the LORD our God shall drive	Judg 11:24	3605,834
of men, and giveth it to *w* he will	Dan 4:17	4479
of men, and giveth it to *w* he will	Dan 4:25	4479
of men, and giveth it to *w* he will	Dan 4:32	4479
he appointeth over it *w* he will	Dan 5:21	4479,1768
he to *w* the Son will reveal him	Mt 11:27	3739,1437
but on *w* it shall fall, it will	Mt 21:44	3739,302
W I shall kiss, that same is he	Mt 26:48	3739,302
W I shall kiss, that same is he	Mk 14:44	3739,302
them one prisoner, *w* they desired	Mk 15:6	3746
and to *w* I will I give it	Lk 4:6	3739,1437
For unto *w* much is given, of him	Lk 12:48	3956,3739
but on *w* it shall fall, it will	Lk 20:18	3739,302
He that receiveth *w* I send	Jn 13:20	1437,1500
that on *w* I lay hands, he may	Acts 8:19	3739,302
w ye shall approve by your	1Cor 16:3	3739,1437

WHORE

daughter, to cause her to be a *w*	Lev 19:29	2181
shall not take a wife that is a *w*	Lev 21:7	2181
profane herself by playing the *w*	Lev 21:9	2181
to play the *w* in her father's	Deut 22:21	2181
There shall be no *w* of the	Deut 23:17	6948
shalt not bring the hire of a *w*	Deut 23:18	2181
played the *w* against him, and went	Judg 19:2	2181
For a *w* is a deep ditch	Prov 23:27	2181
seed of the adulterer and the *w*	Is 57:3	2181
Thou hast played the *w* also with	Eze 16:28	2181
w that sitteth upon many waters	Rev 17:1	4204
thou sawest, where the *w* sitteth	Rev 17:15	4204
the beast, these shall hate the *w*	Rev 17:16	4204
for he hath judged the great *w*	Rev 19:2	4204

WHOREDOM

behold, she is with child by *w*	Gen 38:24	2183
lest the land fall to *w*, and the	Lev 19:29	2181
to commit *w* with Molech, from	Lev 20:5	2181
w with the daughters of Moab	Num 25:1	2181
through the lightness of her *w*	Jer 3:9	2184
neighings, the lewdness of thy *w*	Jer 13:27	2184
men, and didst commit *w* with them	Eze 16:17	2181
unto thee on every side for thy *w*	Eze 16:33	8457
and commit ye *w* after their	Eze 20:30	2181
and poured their *w* upon her	Eze 23:8	8457
and they defiled her with their *w*	Eze 23:17	8457
thy *w* brought from the land of	Eze 23:27	2184
they, nor their kings, by their *w*	Eze 43:7	2184
Now let them put away their *w*	Eze 43:9	2184
the land hath committed great *w*	Hos 1:2	2181
they shall commit *w*, and shall not	Hos 4:10	2181
W and wine and new wine take away	Hos 4:11	2184
your daughters shall commit *w*	Hos 4:13	2181
your daughters when they commit *w*	Hos 4:14	2181
they have committed *w* continually	Hos 4:18	2181
now, O Ephraim, thou committest *w*	Hos 5:3	2181
there is the *w* of Ephraim	Hos 6:10	2184

WHOREDOMS

forty years, and bear your *w*	Num 14:33	2184
so long as the *w* of thy mother	2Kin 9:22	2183
like to the *w* of the house of	2Chr 21:13	2181
hast polluted the land with thy *w*	Jer 3:2	2184
Is this of thy *w* a small matter	Eze 16:20	8457
thy *w* thou hast not remembered	Eze 16:22	8457
passed by, and multiplied thy *w*	Eze 16:25	8457

and hast increased thy *w*, to	Eze 16:26	8457
in thee from other women in thy *w*	Eze 16:34	8457
none followeth thee to commit *w*	Eze 16:34	2181
through thy *w* with thy lovers	Eze 16:36	8457
And they committed *w* in Egypt	Eze 23:3	
they committed *w* in their youth	Eze 23:3	
she committed her *w* with them	Eze 23:7	8457
left she her *w* brought from Egypt	Eze 23:8	8457
in her *w* more than her sister in	Eze 23:11	8457
more than her sister in her *w*	Eze 23:11	8457
And that she increased her *w*	Eze 23:11	2183
So she discovered her *w*, and	Eze 23:14	8457
Yet she multiplied her *w*, in	Eze 23:18	8457
of thy *w* shall be discovered	Eze 23:19	8457
both thy lewdness and thy *w*	Eze 23:29	2183
thou also thy lewdness and thy *w*	Eze 23:29	8457
Will they now commit *w* with her	Eze 23:35	8457
Go, take unto thee a wife of *w*	Eze 23:43	8457
and children of *w*	Hos 1:2	2183
put away her *w* out of her sight	Hos 1:2	2183
for they be the children of *w*	Hos 2:2	2183
for the spirit of *w* hath caused	Hos 2:4	2183
for the spirit of *w* is in the	Hos 4:12	2183
the *w* of the wellfavoured harlot	Hos 5:4	2183
selleth nations through her *w*	Nah 3:4	2183
	Nah 3:4	2183

WHOREMONGER

For this ye know, that no *w*	Eph 5:5	4205

WHOREMONGERS

For *w*, for them that defile	1Ti 1:10	4205
but *w* and adulterers God will	Heb 13:4	4205
abominable, and murderers, and *w*	Rev 21:8	4205
are dogs, and sorcerers, and *w*	Rev 22:15	4205

WHORE'S

and thou hadst a *w* forehead	Jer 3:3	2181

WHORES

They give gifts to all *w*	Eze 16:33	2181
themselves are separated with *w*	Hos 4:14	2181

WHORING

they go a *w* after their gods, and	Ex 34:15	2181
daughters go a *w* after their gods	Ex 34:16	2181
thy sons go a *w* after their gods	Ex 34:16	2181
after whom they have gone a *w*	Lev 17:7	2181
off, and all that go a *w* after him	Lev 20:5	2181
to go a *w* after them, I will even	Lev 20:6	2181
after which ye use to go a *w*	Num 15:39	2181
go a *w* after the gods of the	Deut 31:16	2181
but they went a *w* after other	Judg 2:17	2181
Israel went thither a *w* after it	Judg 8:27	2181
went a *w* after Baalim, and made	Judg 8:33	2181
went a *w* after the gods of the	1Chr 5:25	2181
of Jerusalem to go a *w*, like to	2Chr 21:13	2181
all them that go a *w* from thee	Ps 73:27	2181
works, and went a *w* with their own	Ps 106:39	2181
which go a *w* after their idols	Eze 6:9	2181
hast gone a *w* after the heathen	Eze 23:30	2181
they have gone a *w* from under	Hos 4:12	2181
thou hast gone a *w* from thy God	Hos 9:1	2181

WHORISH

For by means of a *w* woman a man	Prov 6:26	2181
I am broken with their *w* heart	Eze 6:9	2181
the work of an imperious *w* woman	Eze 16:30	2181

WHOSE See APPENDIX.

WHOSO See APPENDIX.

WHOSOEVER See APPENDIX.

WHY See APPENDIX.

WICKED

But the men of Sodom were *w*	Gen 13:13	7451
destroy the righteous with the *w*	Gen 18:23	7563
to slay the righteous with the *w*	Gen 18:25	7563
the righteous should be as the *w*	Gen 18:25	7563
was *w* in the sight of the LORD	Gen 38:7	7451
and I and my people are *w*	Ex 9:27	7563
put not thine hand with the *w* to	Ex 23:1	7563
for I will not justify the *w*	Ex 23:7	7563
it is a *w* thing	Lev 20:17	2617
from the tents of these *w* men	Num 16:26	7563
be not a thought in thy *w* heart	Deut 15:9	1100
which have committed that *w* thing	Deut 17:5	7451
then keep thee from every *w* thing	Deut 23:9	7451
the righteous, and condemn the *w*	Deut 25:1	7563
if the *w* man be worthy to be	Deut 25:2	7563
the *w* shall be silent in darkness	1Sa 2:9	7563
Wickedness proceedeth from the *w*	1Sa 24:13	7563
Then answered all the *w* men	1Sa 30:22	7451
as a man falleth before *w* men	2Sa 3:34	5766

when *w* men have slain a righteous	2Sa 4:11	7563
thy servants, condemning the *w*	1Kin 8:32	7563
wrought *w* things to provoke the	2Kin 17:11	7451
thy servants, by requiting the *w*	2Chr 6:23	7563
face, and turn from their *w* ways	2Chr 7:14	7451
that *w* woman, had broken up the	2Chr 24:7	4849
turned they from their *w* works	Neh 9:35	7451
and enemy is this *w* Haman	Est 7:6	7451
by letters that his *w* device	Est 9:25	7451
There the *w* cease from troubling	Job 3:17	7563
of the *w* shall come to nought	Job 8:22	7563
destroyeth the perfect and the *w*	Job 9:22	7563
is given into the hand of the *w*	Job 9:24	7563
If I be *w*, why then labour I in	Job 9:29	7561
shine upon the counsel of the *w*	Job 10:3	7563
Thou knowest that I am not *w*	Job 10:7	7561
If I be *w*, woe unto me	Job 10:15	7561
But the eyes of the *w* shall fail	Job 11:20	7563
The *w* man travaileth with pain	Job 15:20	7563
me over into the hands of the *w*	Job 16:11	7563
light of the *w* shall be put out	Job 18:5	7563
such are the dwellings of the *w*	Job 18:21	5767
the triumphing of the *w* is short	Job 20:5	7563
every hand of the *w* shall come	Job 20:22	6001
the portion of a *w* man from God	Job 20:29	7563
Wherefore do the *w* live, become	Job 21:7	7563
counsel of the *w* is far from me	Job 21:16	7563
is the candle of the *w* put out	Job 21:17	7563
are the dwelling places of the *w*	Job 21:28	7563
That the *w* is reserved to the day	Job 21:30	7451
old way which *w* men have trodden	Job 22:15	205
counsel of the *w* is far from me	Job 22:18	7563
they gather the vintage of the *w*	Job 24:6	7563
Let mine enemy be as the *w*	Job 27:7	7563
the portion of a *w* man with God	Job 27:13	7563
And I brake the jaws of the *w*	Job 29:17	5767
Is not destruction to the *w*	Job 31:3	5767
iniquity, and walketh with *w* men	Job 34:8	7562
fit to say to a king, Thou art *w*	Job 34:18	1100
He striketh them as *w* men in the	Job 34:26	7563
because of his answers for *w* men	Job 34:36	205
preserveth not the life of the *w*	Job 36:6	7563
fulfilled the judgment of the *w*	Job 36:17	7563
that he might be shaken out of	Job 38:13	7563
from the *w* their light is	Job 38:15	7563
tread down the *w* in their place	Job 40:12	7563
of the *w* come to an end	Ps 7:9	7563
God is angry with the *w* every day	Ps 7:11	
thou hast destroyed the *w*	Ps 9:5	7563
the *w* is snared in the work of	Ps 9:16	7563
The *w* shall be turned into hell,	Ps 9:17	7563
The *w* in his pride doth persecute	Ps 10:2	7563
For the *w* boasteth of his heart's	Ps 10:3	7563
The *w*, through the pride of his	Ps 10:4	7563
Wherefore doth the *w* contemn God	Ps 10:13	7563
Break thou the arm of the *w*	Ps 10:15	7563
the *w* bend their bow, they make	Ps 11:2	7563
but the *w* and him that loveth	Ps 11:5	7563
Upon the *w* he shall rain snares,	Ps 11:6	7563
The *w* walk on every side, when	Ps 12:8	7563
From the *w* that oppress me, from	Ps 17:9	7563
deliver my soul from the *w*	Ps 17:13	7563
of the *w* have inclosed me	Ps 22:16	7489
and will not sit with the *w*	Ps 26:5	7563
When the *w*, even mine enemies and	Ps 27:2	7489
Draw me not away with the *w*	Ps 28:3	7563
let the *w* be ashamed, and let them	Ps 31:17	7563
Many sorrows shall be to the *w*	Ps 32:10	7563
Evil shall slay the *w*	Ps 34:21	7563
of the *w* saith within my heart	Ps 36:1	7563
not the hand of the *w* remove me	Ps 36:11	7563
who bringeth *w* devices to pass	Ps 37:7	4209
while, and the *w* shall not be	Ps 37:10	7563
The *w* plotteth against the just,	Ps 37:12	7563
The *w* have drawn out the sword,	Ps 37:14	7563
better than the riches of many *w*	Ps 37:16	7563
the arms of the *w* shall be broken	Ps 37:17	7563
But the *w* shall perish, and the	Ps 37:20	7563
The *w* borroweth, and payeth not	Ps 37:21	7563
seed of the *w* shall be cut off	Ps 37:28	7563
The *w* watcheth the righteous, and	Ps 37:32	7563
when the *w* are cut off, thou	Ps 37:34	7563
I have seen the *w* in great power	Ps 37:35	7563
the end of the *w* shall be cut off	Ps 37:38	7563
he shall deliver them from the *w*	Ps 37:40	7563
bridle, while the *w* is before me	Ps 39:1	7563
But unto the *w* God saith, What	Ps 50:16	7563
of the oppression of the *w*	Ps 55:3	7563
The *w* are estranged from the womb	Ps 58:3	7563
his feet in the blood of the *w*	Ps 58:10	7563
merciful to any *w* transgressors	Ps 59:5	205

profane *w* prince of Israel, whose	Eze 21:25	7563
of them that are slain, of the *w*	Eze 21:29	7563
the land into the hand of the *w*	Eze 30:12	7451
When I say unto the *w*	Eze 33:8	7563
O *w* man, thou shalt surely die	Eze 33:8	7563
speak to warn the *w* from his way	Eze 33:8	7563
that *w* man shall die in his	Eze 33:8	7563
if thou warn the *w* of his way to	Eze 33:9	7563
no pleasure in the death of the *w*	Eze 33:11	7563
but that the *w* turn from his way	Eze 33:11	7563
as for the wickedness of the *w*	Eze 33:12	7563
Again, when I say unto the *w*	Eze 33:14	7563
If the *w* restore the pledge, give	Eze 33:15	7563
But if the *w* turn from his	Eze 33:19	7563
but the *w* shall do wickedly	Dan 12:10	7563
none of the *w* shall understand	Dan 12:10	7563
wickedness in the house of the *w*	Mic 6:10	7563
them pure with the *w* balances	Mic 6:11	7562
and will not at all acquit the *w*	Nah 1:3	7563
against the LORD, a *w* counsellor	Nah 1:11	1100
for the *w* shall no more pass	Nah 1:15	1100
for the *w* doth compass about the	Hab 1:4	7563
holdest thy tongue when the *w*	Hab 1:13	7563
head out of the house of the *w*	Hab 3:13	7563
and the stumblingblocks with the *w*	Zeph 1:3	7563
between the righteous and the *w*	Mal 3:18	7563
And ye shall tread down the *w*	Mal 4:3	7563
other spirits more *w* than himself	Mt 12:45	4191
it be also unto this *w* generation	Mt 12:45	4190
it not, then cometh the *w* one	Mt 13:19	4190
are the children of the *w* one.	Mt 13:38	4190
sever the *w* from among the just,	Mt 13:49	4190
A *w* and adulterous generation	Mt 16:4	4190
O thou *w* servant, I forgave thee	Mt 18:32	4190
miserably destroy those *w* men	Mt 21:41	2556
answered and said unto him, Thou *w*	Mt 25:26	4190
other spirits more *w* than himself	Lk 11:26	4191
will I judge thee, thou *w* servant	Lk 19:22	4190
by *w* hands have crucified and	Acts 2:23	459
a matter of wrong or *w* lewdness	Acts 18:14	4190
among yourselves that *w* person	1Cor 5:13	4190
all the fiery darts of the *w*	Eph 6:16	4190
enemies in your mind by *w* works	Col 1:21	4190
And then shall that *W* be revealed	2Th 2:8	459
from unreasonable and *w* men	2Th 3:2	4190
the filthy conversation of the *w*	2Pet 2:7	113
led away with the error of the *w*	2Pet 3:17	113
ye have overcome the *w* one	1Jn 2:13	4190
and ye have overcome the *w* one	1Jn 2:14	4190
as Cain, who was of that *w* one	1Jn 3:12	4190
that *w* one toucheth him not	1Jn 5:18	4190

WICKEDLY

I pray you, brethren, do not so *w*	Gen 19:7	7489
in doing *w* in the sight of the	Deut 9:18	7561
nay, I pray you, do not so *w*	Judg 19:23	7489
But if ye shall still do *w*	1Sa 12:25	7489
have not *w* departed from my God	2Sa 22:22	7561
I have sinned, and I have done *w*	2Sa 24:17	5753
hath done *w* above all that the	2Kin 21:11	7489
have done amiss, and have dealt *w*	2Chr 6:37	7561
king of Israel, who did very *w*	2Chr 20:35	7561
mother was his counsellor to do *w*	2Chr 22:3	7561
done right, but we have done *w*	Neh 9:33	7561
Will ye speak *w* for God	Job 13:7	5766
Yea, surely God will not do *w*	Job 34:12	7561
have not *w* departed from my God	Ps 18:21	7561
speak *w* concerning oppression	Ps 73:8	7451
hath done *w* in the sanctuary	Ps 74:3	7489
iniquity, we have done *w*	Ps 106:6	7561
For they speak against thee *w*	Ps 139:20	4209
iniquity, and have done *w*, and have	Dan 9:5	7561
we have sinned, we have done *w*	Dan 9:15	7561
such as do *w* against the covenant	Dan 11:32	7561
but the wicked shall do *w*	Dan 12:10	7561
the proud, yea, and all that do *w*	Mal 4:1	7564

WICKEDNESS

God saw that the *w* of man was	Gen 6:5	7451
how then can I do this great *w*	Gen 39:9	7451
it is *w*	Lev 18:17	2154
and the land become full of *w*	Lev 19:29	2154
a wife and her mother, it is *w*	Lev 20:14	2154
that there be no *w* among you	Lev 20:14	2154
but for the *w* of these nations	Deut 9:4	7564
but for the *w* of these nations	Deut 9:5	7564
of this people, nor to their *w*	Deut 9:27	7562
any such *w* as this is among you	Deut 13:11	7451
that hath wrought *w* in the sight	Deut 17:2	7451
because of the *w* of thy doings	Deut 28:20	7455
God rendered the *w* of Abimelech	Judg 9:56	7451
Israel, Tell us, how was this *w*	Judg 20:3	7451

What *w* is this that is done among	Judg 20:12	7451
and see that your *w* is great	1Sa 12:17	7451
ye have done all this *w*	1Sa 12:20	7451
W proceedeth from the wicked	1Sa 24:13	7562
the *w* of Nabal upon his own head	1Sa 25:39	7451
doer of evil according to his *w*	2Sa 3:39	7451
of *w* afflict them any more	2Sa 7:10	5766
but if *w* shall be found in him,	1Kin 1:52	7451
Thou knowest all the *w* which	1Kin 2:44	7451
return thy *w* upon thine own head	1Kin 2:44	7451
perversely, we have committed *w*	1Kin 8:47	7561
work *w* in the sight of the LORD	1Kin 21:25	7451
he wrought much *w* in the sight of	2Kin 21:6	7451
children of *w* waste them any more	1Chr 17:9	5766
they that plow iniquity, and sow *w*	Job 4:8	5999
he seeth *w* also	Job 11:11	205
away, and let not *w* dwell in thy	Job 11:14	5766
Though *w* be sweet in his mouth,	Job 20:12	7451
Is not thy *w* great	Job 22:5	7451
w shall be broken as a tree	Job 24:20	5766
My lips shall not speak *w*	Job 27:4	5766
it from God, that he should do *w*	Job 34:10	7562
Thy *w* may hurt a man as thou art	Job 35:8	7562
not a God that hath pleasure in *w*	Ps 5:4	7562
their inward part is very *w*	Ps 5:9	1942
Oh let the *w* of the wicked come	Ps 7:9	7451
seek out his *w* till thou find	Ps 10:15	7562
according to the *w* of their	Ps 28:4	7455
lovest righteousness, and hatest *w*	Ps 45:7	7562
and strengthened himself in his *w*	Ps 52:7	1942
W is in the midst thereof	Ps 55:11	1942
for *w* is in their dwellings, and	Ps 55:15	7451
Yea, in heart ye work *w*	Ps 58:2	5766
than to dwell in the tents of *w*	Ps 84:10	7562
nor the son of *w* afflict him	Ps 89:22	5766
shall cut them off in their own *w*	Ps 94:23	7451
for the *w* of them that dwell	Ps 107:34	7451
For they eat the bread of *w*	Prov 4:17	7562
w is an abomination to my lips	Prov 8:7	7562
Treasures of *w* profit nothing	Prov 10:2	7562
wicked shall fall by his own *w*	Prov 11:5	7564
man shall not be established by *w*	Prov 12:3	7562
but *w* overthroweth the sinner	Prov 13:6	7564
wicked is driven away in his *w*	Prov 14:32	7451
abomination to kings to commit *w*	Prov 16:12	7562
the wicked for their *w*	Prov 21:12	7451
his *w* shall be shewed before the	Prov 26:26	7451
mouth, and saith, I have done no *w*	Prov 30:20	205
of judgment, that *w* was there	Eccl 3:16	7562
that prolongeth his life in his *w*	Eccl 7:15	7451
things, and to know the *w* of folly	Eccl 7:25	7562
neither shall *w* deliver those	Eccl 8:8	7562
For *w* burneth as the fire	Is 9:18	7564
For thou hast trusted in thy *w*	Is 47:10	7451
and to smite with the fist of *w*	Is 58:4	7562
to loose the bands of *w*, to undo	Is 58:6	7562
against them touching all their *w*	Jer 1:16	7451
Thine own *w* shall correct thee,	Jer 2:19	7451
with thy whoredoms and with thy *w*	Jer 3:2	7451
wash thine heart from *w*, that	Jer 4:14	7451
this is thy *w*, because it is	Jer 4:18	7451
waters, so she casteth out her *w*	Jer 6:7	7451
it for the *w* of my people Israel	Jer 7:12	7451
no man repented him of his *w*	Jer 8:6	7451
for the *w* of them that dwell	Jer 12:4	7451
for I will pour their *w* upon them	Jer 14:16	7451
We acknowledge, O LORD, our *w*	Jer 14:20	7562
and confounded for all thy *w*	Jer 22:22	7451
in my house have I found their *w*	Jer 23:11	7451
that none doth return from his *w*	Jer 23:14	7451
for all whose *w* I have hid my	Jer 33:5	7451
Because of their *w* which they	Jer 44:3	7451
their ear to turn from their *w*	Jer 44:5	7451
forgotten the *w* of your fathers	Jer 44:9	7451
the *w* of the kings of Judah, and	Jer 44:9	7451
the *w* of their wives, and your own	Jer 44:9	7451
of their wives, and your own *w*	Jer 44:9	7451
the *w* of your wives, which they	Jer 44:9	7451
Let all their *w* come before thee	Lam 1:22	7451
wicked, and he turn not from his *w*	Eze 3:19	7562
into *w* more than the nations	Eze 5:6	7564
is risen up into a rod of *w*	Eze 7:11	7562
it came to pass after all thy *w*	Eze 16:23	7451
Before thy *w* was discovered, as	Eze 16:57	7451
the *w* of the wicked shall be upon	Eze 18:20	7564
from his *w* that he hath committed	Eze 18:27	7564
I have driven him out for his *w*	Eze 31:11	7562
as for the *w* of the wicked, he	Eze 33:12	7564
day that he turneth from his *w*	Eze 33:12	7562
But if the wicked turn from his *w*	Eze 33:19	7564
discovered, and the *w* of Samaria	Hos 7:1	7451

that I remember all their *w* .... Hos 7:2 — 7451
make the king glad with their *w* .... Hos 7:3 — 7451
All their *w* is in Gilgal .... Hos 9:15 — 7451
for the *w* of their doings I will .... Hos 9:15 — 7455
Ye have plowed *w*, ye have reaped .... Hos 10:13 — 7562
unto you because of your great *w* .... Hos 10:15 — 7451
for their *w* is great .... Joel 3:13 — 7451
for their *w* is come up before me .... Jonah 1:2 — 7451
of *w* in the house of the wicked .... Mic 6:10 — 7562
hath not thy *w* passed continually .... Nah 3:19 — 7451
And he said, This is *w* .... Zec 5:8 — 7564
shall call them, The border of *w* .... Mal 1:4 — 7564
yea, they that work *w* are set up .... Mal 3:15 — 7564
But Jesus perceived their *w* .... Mt 22:18 — 4189
Thefts, covetousness, *w*, deceit, ... Mk 7:22 — 4189
part is full of ravening and *w* .... Lk 11:39 — 4189
Repent therefore of this thy *w* .... Acts 8:22 — 2549
man, if there be any *w* in him .... Acts 25:5 — 5129,824
unrighteousness, fornication, *w* .... Rom 1:29 — 4189
with the leaven of malice and *w* .... 1Cor 5:8 — 4189
spiritual *w* in high places .... Eph 6:12 — 4189
and the whole world lieth in *w* .... 1Jn 5:19 — 4190

WIDE
shalt open thine hand *w* unto him .... Deut 15:8 — 6605
thine hand *w* unto thy brother .... Deut 15:11 — 6605
and good, and the land was *w* .... 1Chr 4:40 — 7342,3027
mouth *w* as for the latter rain .... Job 29:23
me as a *w* breaking in of waters .... Job 30:14 — 7342
opened their mouth *w* against me .... Ps 35:21 — 7337
open thy mouth *w*, and I will fill .... Ps 81:10 — 7337
w sea, wherein are things .... Ps 104:25 — 7342,3027
but he that openeth *w* his lips .... Prov 13:3
a brawling woman and in a *w* house ...... Prov 21:9 — 2267
a brawling woman and in a *w* house ...... Prov 25:24 — 2267
against whom make ye a *w* mouth .... Is 57:4 — 7337
saith, I will build me a *w* house .... Jer 22:14 — 4060
be set *w* open unto thine enemies .... Nah 3:13 — 6605
for *w* is the gate, and broad is .... Mt 7:13 — 4116

WIDENESS
w of twenty cubits round about .... Eze 41:10 — 7341

WIDOW
Remain a *w* at thy father's house, ... Gen 38:11 — 490
Ye shall not afflict any *w* .... Ex 22:22 — 490
A *w*, or a divorced woman, or .... Lev 21:14 — 490
if the priest's daughter be a *w* .... Lev 22:13 — 490
But every vow of a *w*, and of her .... Num 30:9 — 490
judgment of the fatherless and *w* .... Deut 10:18 — 490
and the fatherless, and the *w* .... Deut 14:29 — 490
and the fatherless, and the *w* .... Deut 16:11 — 490
and the fatherless, and the *w* .... Deut 16:14 — 490
for the fatherless, and for the *w* .... Deut 24:19 — 490
for the fatherless, and for the *w* .... Deut 24:20 — 490
for the fatherless, and for the *w* .... Deut 24:21 — 490
the fatherless, and the *w* .... Deut 26:12 — 490
to the fatherless, and to the *w* .... Deut 26:13 — 490
of the stranger, fatherless, and *w* .... Deut 27:19 — 490
answered, I am indeed a *w* woman .... 2Sa 14:5 — 490
a *w* woman, even he lifted up his .... 1Kin 11:26 — 490
I have commanded a *w* woman there .... 1Kin 17:9 — 490
the *w* woman was there gathering .... 1Kin 17:10 — 490
upon the *w* with whom I sojourn .... 1Kin 17:20 — 490
and doeth not good to the *w* .... Job 24:21 — 490
caused the eyes of the *w* to fail .... Job 31:16 — 490
They slay the *w* and the stranger, ... Ps 94:6 — 490
be fatherless, and his wife a *w* .... Ps 109:9 — 490
he relieveth the fatherless and *w* .... Ps 146:9 — 490
establish the border of the *w* .... Prov 15:25 — 490
the fatherless, plead for the *w* .... Is 1:17 — 490
the cause of the *w* come unto them .... Is 1:23 — 490
I shall not sit as a *w*, neither .... Is 47:8 — 490
the fatherless, and the *w* .... Jer 7:6 — 490
the fatherless, nor the *w* .... Jer 22:3 — 490
how is she become as a *w* .... Lam 1:1 — 490
vexed the fatherless and the *w* .... Eze 22:7 — 490
they take for their wives a *w* .... Eze 44:22 — 490
or a *w* that had a priest before .... Eze 44:22 — 490
And oppress not the *w*, nor the .... Zec 7:10 — 490
the hireling in his wages, the *w* .... Mal 3:5 — 490
And there came a certain poor *w* .... Mk 12:42 — 5503
That this poor *w* hath cast more .... Mk 12:43 — 5503
she was a *w* of about fourscore and .... Lk 2:37 — 5503
Sidon, unto a woman that was a *w* .... Lk 4:26 — 5503
son of his mother, and she was a *w* .... Lk 7:12 — 5503
there was a *w* in that city .... Lk 18:3 — 5503
Yet because this *w* troubleth me .... Lk 18:5 — 5503
he saw also a certain poor *w* .... Lk 21:2 — 5503
that this poor *w* hath cast in .... Lk 21:3 — 5503
But if any *w* have children or .... 1Ti 5:4 — 5503
Now she that is a *w* indeed .... 1Ti 5:5 — 5503

Let not a *w* be taken into the .... 1Ti 5:9 — 5503
heart, I sit a queen, and am no *w* .... Rev 18:7 — 5503

WIDOWHOOD
and put on the garments of her *w* .... Gen 38:19 — 491
day of their death, living in *w* .... 2Sa 20:3 — 491
day, the loss of children, and *w* .... Is 47:9 — 489
the reproach of thy *w* any more .... Is 54:4 — 491

WIDOW'S
she put her *w* garments off from .... Gen 38:14 — 491
nor take a *w* raiment to pledge .... Deut 24:17 — 490
He was a *w* son of the tribe of .... 1Kin 7:14 — 490
they take the *w* ox for a pledge .... Job 24:3 — 490
I caused the *w* heart to sing for .... Job 29:13 — 490

WIDOWS
and your wives shall be *w*, and your ...... Ex 22:24 — 490
Thou hast sent *w* away empty .... Job 22:9 — 490
and his *w* shall not weep .... Job 27:15 — 490
fatherless, and a judge of the *w* .... Ps 68:5 — 490
their *w* made no lamentation .... Ps 78:64 — 490
mercy on their fatherless and *w* .... Is 9:17 — 490
that *w* may be their prey, and that .... Is 10:2 — 490
Their *w* are increased to me above .... Jer 15:8 — 490
of their children, and be *w* .... Jer 18:21 — 490
and let thy *w* trust in me .... Jer 49:11 — 490
fatherless, our mothers are as *w* .... Lam 5:3 — 490
her many *w* in the midst thereof .... Eze 22:25 — 490
many *w* were in Israel in the days .... Lk 4:25 — 5503
because their *w* were neglected in .... Acts 6:1 — 5503
all the *w* stood by him weeping, ... Acts 9:39 — 5503
he had called the saints and *w* .... Acts 9:41 — 5503
therefore to the unmarried and *w* .... 1Cor 7:8 — 5503
Honour *w* that are *w* indeed .... 1Ti 5:3 — 5503
But the younger *w* refuse .... 1Ti 5:11 — 5503
or woman that believeth have *w* .... 1Ti 5:16 — 5503
relieve them that are *w* indeed .... 1Ti 5:16 — 5503
w in their affliction, and to keep .... Jas 1:27 — 5503

WIDOWS'
for ye devour *w* houses, and for a .... Mt 23:14 — 5503
Which devour *w* houses, and for a .... Mk 12:40 — 5503
Which devour *w* houses, and for a .... Lk 20:47 — 5503

WIFE
and shall cleave unto his *w* .... Gen 2:24 — 802
were both naked, the man and his *w* ..... Gen 2:25 — 802
his *w* hid themselves from the .... Gen 3:8 — 802
hearkened unto the voice of thy *w* .... Gen 3:17 — 802
to his *w* did the LORD God make .... Gen 3:21 — 802
And Adam knew Eve his *w* .... Gen 4:1 — 802
And Cain knew his *w* .... Gen 4:17 — 802
And Adam knew his *w* again .... Gen 4:25 — 802
ark, thou, and thy sons, and thy *w* .... Gen 6:18 — 802
went in, and his sons, and his *w* .... Gen 7:7 — 802
the sons of Noah, and Noah's *w* .... Gen 7:13 — 802
forth of the ark, thou, and thy *w* .... Gen 8:16 — 802
went forth, and his sons, and his *w* .... Gen 8:18 — 802
the name of Abram's *w* was Sarai .... Gen 11:29 — 802
and the name of Nahor's *w*, Milcah, ... Gen 11:29 — 802
in law, his son Abram's *w* .... Gen 11:31 — 802
And Abram took Sarai his *w* .... Gen 12:5 — 802
that he said unto Sarai his *w* .... Gen 12:11 — 802
they shall say, This is his *w* .... Gen 12:12 — 802
because of Sarai Abram's *w* .... Gen 12:17 — 802
not tell me that she was thy *w* .... Gen 12:18 — 802
I might have taken her to me to *w* .... Gen 12:19 — 802
now therefore behold thy *w* .... Gen 12:19 — 802
and they sent him away, and his *w* .... Gen 12:20 — 802
up out of Egypt, he, and his *w* .... Gen 13:1 — 802
Now Sarai Abram's *w* bare him no .... Gen 16:1 — 802
Sarai Abram's *w* took Hagar her .... Gen 16:3 — 802
to her husband Abram to be his *w* .... Gen 16:3 — 802
unto Abraham, As for Sarai thy *w* .... Gen 17:15 — 802
Sarah thy *w* shall bear thee a son .... Gen 17:19 — 802
unto him, Where is Sarah thy *w* .... Gen 18:9 — 802
Sarah thy *w* shall have a son .... Gen 18:10 — 802
Lot, saying, Arise, take thy *w* .... Gen 19:15 — 802
hand, and upon the hand of his *w* .... Gen 19:16 — 802
But his *w* looked back from behind .... Gen 19:26 — 802
And Abraham said of Sarah his *w* .... Gen 20:2 — 802
for she is a man's *w* .... Gen 20:3 — 1166
therefore restore the man his *w* .... Gen 20:7 — 802
and she became my *w* .... Gen 20:12 — 802
and restored him Sarah his *w* .... Gen 20:14 — 802
and God healed Abimelech, and his *w* .. Gen 20:17 — 802
because of Sarah Abraham's *w* .... Gen 20:18 — 802
his mother took him a *w* out of .... Gen 21:21 — 802
Abraham buried Sarah his *w* in the ...... Gen 23:19 — 802
that thou shalt not take a *w* unto .... Gen 24:3 — 802
take a *w* unto my son Isaac .... Gen 24:4 — 802
thou shalt take a *w* unto my son .... Gen 24:7 — 802

the *w* of Nahor, Abraham's brother	Gen 24:15	802
Sarah my master's *w* bare a son to	Gen 24:36	802
Thou shalt not take a *w* to my son	Gen 24:37	802
kindred, and take a *w* unto my son	Gen 24:38	802
thou shalt take a *w* for my son of	Gen 24:40	802
let her be thy master's son's *w*	Gen 24:51	802
took Rebekah, and she became his *w*	Gen 24:67	802
Then again Abraham took a *w*	Gen 25:1	802
Abraham buried, and Sarah his *w*	Gen 25:10	802
old when he took Rebekah to *w*	Gen 25:20	802
intreated the LORD for his *w*	Gen 25:21	802
him, and Rebekah his *w* conceived	Gen 25:21	802
of the place asked him of his *w*	Gen 26:7	802
for he feared to say, She is my *w*	Gen 26:7	802
was sporting with Rebekah his *w*	Gen 26:8	802
Behold, of a surety she is thy *w*	Gen 26:9	802
lightly have lien with thy *w*	Gen 26:10	802
w shall surely be put to death	Gen 26:11	802
to *w* Judith the daughter of Beeri	Gen 26:34	802
if Jacob take a *w* of the	Gen 27:46	802
Thou shalt not take a *w* of the	Gen 28:1	802
take thee a *w* from thence of the	Gen 28:2	802
to take him a *w* from thence	Gen 28:6	802
Thou shalt not take a *w* of the	Gen 28:6	802
sister of Nebajoth, to be his *w*	Gen 28:9	802
said unto Laban, Give me my *w*	Gen 29:21	802
him Rachel his daughter to *w* also	Gen 29:28	802
gave him Bilhah her handmaid to *w*	Gen 30:4	802
her maid, and gave her Jacob to *w*	Gen 30:9	802
saying, Get me this damsel to *w*	Gen 34:4	802
I pray you give her him to *w*	Gen 34:8	802
but give me the damsel to *w*	Gen 34:12	802
the son of Adah the *w* of Esau	Gen 36:10	802
son of Bashemath the *w* of Esau	Gen 36:10	802
were the sons of Adah Esau's *w*	Gen 36:12	802
the sons of Bashemath Esau's *w*	Gen 36:13	802
the daughter of Zibeon, Esau's *w*	Gen 36:14	802
the sons of Aholibamah Esau's *w*	Gen 36:17	802
the sons of Aholibamah Esau's *w*	Gen 36:18	802
the daughter of Anah, Esau's *w*	Gen 36:18	802
Judah took a *w* for Er his	Gen 38:6	802
Onan, Go in unto thy brother's *w*	Gen 38:8	802
he went in unto his brother's *w*	Gen 38:9	802
daughter of Shuah Judah's *w* died	Gen 38:12	802
she was not given unto him to *w*	Gen 38:14	802
that his master's *w* cast her eyes	Gen 39:7	802
and said unto his master's *w*	Gen 39:8	802
but thee, because thou art his *w*	Gen 39:9	802
master heard the words of his *w*	Gen 39:19	802
he gave him to *w* Asenath the	Gen 41:45	802
Ye know that my *w* bare me two	Gen 44:27	802
The sons of Rachel Jacob's *w*	Gen 46:19	802
buried Abraham and Sarah his *w*	Gen 49:31	802
buried Isaac and Rebekah his *w*	Gen 49:31	802
took to *w* a daughter of Levi	Ex 2:1	
And Moses took his *w* and his sons	Ex 4:20	802
Jochebed his father's sister to *w*	Ex 6:20	802
sister of Naashon, to *w*	Ex 6:23	802
of the daughters of Putiel to *w*	Ex 6:25	802
in law, took Zipporah, Moses' *w*	Ex 18:2	802
his *w* unto Moses into the	Ex 18:5	802
am come unto thee, and thy *w*	Ex 18:6	802
shalt not covet thy neighbour's *w*	Ex 20:17	802
then his *w* shall go out with him	Ex 21:3	802
If his master have given him a *w*	Ex 21:4	802
the *w* and her children shall be	Ex 21:4	802
say, I love my master, my *w*	Ex 21:5	802
If he take him another *w*	Ex 21:10	
surely endow her to be his *w*	Ex 22:16	802
father's *w* shalt thou not uncover	Lev 18:8	802
thou shalt not approach to his *w*	Lev 18:14	802
she is thy son's *w*	Lev 18:15	802
the nakedness of thy brother's *w*	Lev 18:16	802
shalt thou take a *w* to her sister	Lev 18:18	802
carnally with thy neighbour's *w*	Lev 18:20	802
adultery with another man's *w*	Lev 20:10	802
adultery with his neighbour's *w*	Lev 20:10	802
w hath uncovered his father's	Lev 20:11	802
And if a man take a *w* and her	Lev 20:14	802
man shall lie with his uncle's *w*	Lev 20:20	1753
a man shall take his brother's *w*	Lev 20:21	802
not take a *w* that is a whore	Lev 21:7	802
And he shall take a *w* in her	Lev 21:13	802
a virgin of his own people to *w*	Lev 21:14	802
them, If any man's *w* go aside	Num 5:12	802
him, and he be jealous of his *w*	Num 5:14	802
him, and he be jealous of his *w*	Num 5:14	802
man bring his *w* unto the priest	Num 5:15	802
when a *w* goeth aside to another	Num 5:29	802
him, and he be jealous over his *w*	Num 5:30	802
name of Amram's *w* was Jochebed	Num 26:59	802
Moses, between a man and his *w*	Num 30:16	802
shall be *w* unto one of the family	Num 36:8	802
thou desire thy neighbour's *w*	Deut 5:21	802
or the *w* of thy bosom, or thy	Deut 13:6	802
is there that hath betrothed a *w*	Deut 20:7	802
thou wouldest have her to thy *w*	Deut 21:11	802
husband, and she shall be thy *w*	Deut 21:13	802
If any man take a *w*, and go in	Deut 22:13	802
my daughter unto this man to *w*	Deut 22:16	802
and she shall be his *w*	Deut 22:19	802
he hath humbled his neighbour's *w*	Deut 22:24	802
of silver, and she shall be his *w*	Deut 22:29	802
man shall not take his father's *w*	Deut 22:30	802
When a man hath taken a *w*	Deut 24:1	802
she may go and be another man's *w*	Deut 24:2	
die, which took her to be his *w*	Deut 24:3	802
not take her again to be his *w*	Deut 24:4	802
When a man hath taken a new *w*	Deut 24:5	802
shall cheer up his *w* which he	Deut 24:5	802
the *w* of the dead shall not marry	Deut 25:5	802
unto her, and take her to him to *w*	Deut 25:5	802
like not to take his brother's *w*	Deut 25:7	2994
then let his brother's *w* go up to	Deut 25:7	2994
Then shall his brother's *w* come	Deut 25:9	2994
the *w* of the one draweth near for	Deut 25:11	802
he that lieth with his father's *w*	Deut 27:20	802
Thou shalt betroth a *w*, and	Deut 28:30	802
toward the *w* of his bosom, and	Deut 28:54	802
I give Achsah my daughter to *w*	Josh 15:16	802
gave him Achsah his daughter to *w*	Josh 15:17	802
I give Achsah my daughter to *w*	Judg 1:12	802
gave him Achsah his daughter to *w*	Judg 1:13	802
the *w* of Lapidoth, she judged	Judg 4:4	802
of Jael the *w* of Heber the Kenite	Judg 4:17	802
Then Jael Heber's *w* took a nail	Judg 4:21	802
Jael the *w* of Heber the Kenite be	Judg 5:24	802
And Gilead's *w* bare him sons	Judg 11:2	802
his *w* was barren, and bare not	Judg 13:2	802
Manoah arose, and went after his *w*	Judg 13:11	802
and Manoah and his *w* looked on	Judg 13:19	802
his *w* looked on it, and fell on	Judg 13:20	802
more appear to Manoah and to his *w*	Judg 13:21	802
And Manoah said unto his *w*	Judg 13:22	802
But his *w* said unto him, If the	Judg 13:23	802
now therefore get her for me to *w*	Judg 14:2	802
to take a *w* of the uncircumcised	Judg 14:3	802
that they said unto Samson's *w*	Judg 14:15	802
Samson's *w* wept before him, and	Judg 14:16	802
But Samson's *w* was given to his	Judg 14:20	802
Samson visited his *w* with a kid	Judg 15:1	802
go in to my *w* into the chamber	Judg 15:1	802
because he had taken his *w*	Judg 15:6	802
his daughter unto Benjamin to *w*	Judg 21:1	802
be he that giveth a *w* to Benjamin	Judg 21:18	802
catch you every man his *w* of the	Judg 21:21	802
not to each man his *w* in the war	Judg 21:22	802
the country of Moab, he, and his *w*	Ruth 1:1	802
and the name of his *w* Naomi	Ruth 1:2	802
the *w* of the dead, to raise up	Ruth 4:5	802
the *w* of Mahlon, have I purchased	Ruth 4:10	802
have I purchased to be my *w*	Ruth 4:10	802
Boaz took Ruth, and she was his *w*	Ruth 4:13	802
he gave to Peninnah his *w*	1Sa 1:4	802
and Elkanah knew Hannah his *w*	1Sa 1:19	802
And Eli blessed Elkanah and his *w*	1Sa 2:20	802
his daughter in law, Phinehas' *w*	1Sa 4:19	802
the name of Saul's *w* was Ahinoam	1Sa 14:50	802
Merab, her will I give thee to *w*	1Sa 18:17	802
unto Adriel the Meholathite to *w*	1Sa 18:19	802
gave him Michal his daughter to *w*	1Sa 18:27	802
and Michal David's *w* told him	1Sa 19:11	802
and the name of his *w* Abigail	1Sa 25:3	802
young men told Abigail, Nabal's *w*	1Sa 25:14	802
his *w* had told him these things,	1Sa 25:37	802
Abigail, to take her to him to *w*	1Sa 25:39	802
thee, to take thee to him to *w*	1Sa 25:40	802
of David, and became his *w*	1Sa 25:42	802
Michal his daughter, David's *w*	1Sa 25:44	802
the Carmelitess, Nabal's *w*	1Sa 27:3	802
Abigail the *w* of Nabal the	1Sa 30:5	802
save to every man his *w* and his	1Sa 30:22	802
Abigail Nabal's *w* the Carmelite	2Sa 2:2	802
of Abigail the *w* of Nabal the	2Sa 3:3	802
Ithream, by Eglah David's *w*	2Sa 3:5	802
saying, Deliver me my *w* Michal	2Sa 3:14	802
the *w* of Uriah the Hittite	2Sa 11:3	802
and to drink, and to lie with my *w*	2Sa 11:11	802
when the *w* of Uriah heard that	2Sa 11:26	802
to his house, and she became his *w*	2Sa 11:27	802
hast taken his *w* to be thy *w*	2Sa 12:9	802
hast taken the *w* of Uriah the	2Sa 12:10	802

of Uriah the Hittite to be thy *w*	2Sa 12:10	802
that Uriah's *w* bare unto David	2Sa 12:15	802
David comforted Bath-sheba his *w*	2Sa 12:24	802
me Abishag the Shunammite to *w*	1Kin 2:17	802
to Adonijah thy brother to *w*	1Kin 2:21	802
the daughter of Solomon to *w*	1Kin 4:11	802
the daughter of Solomon to *w*	1Kin 4:15	802
daughter, whom he had taken to *w*	1Kin 7:8	
unto his daughter, Solomon's *w*	1Kin 9:16	802
so that he gave him to *w* the	1Kin 11:19	802
the sister of his own *w*	1Kin 11:19	802
And Jeroboam said to his *w*	1Kin 14:2	802
not known to be the *w* of Jeroboam	1Kin 14:2	802
And Jeroboam's *w* did so, and arose,	1Kin 14:4	802
the *w* of Jeroboam cometh to ask a	1Kin 14:5	802
said, Come in, thou *w* of Jeroboam	1Kin 14:6	802
And Jeroboam's *w* arose, and	1Kin 14:17	802
that he took to *w* Jezebel the	1Kin 16:31	802
But Jezebel his *w* came to him	1Kin 21:5	802
Jezebel his *w* said unto him, Dost	1Kin 21:7	802
whom Jezebel his *w* stirred up	1Kin 21:25	802
and she waited on Naaman's *w*	2Kin 5:2	802
the daughter of Ahab was his *w*	2Kin 8:18	802
Give thy daughter to my son to *w*	2Kin 14:9	802
the *w* of Shallum the son of	2Kin 22:14	802
begat children of Azubah his *w*	1Chr 2:18	802
then Abiah Hezron's *w* bare him	1Chr 2:24	802
Jerahmeel had also another *w*	1Chr 2:26	802
the name of the *w* of Abishur was	1Chr 2:29	802
to Jarha his servant to *w*	1Chr 2:35	802
the sixth, Ithream by Eglah his *w*	1Chr 3:3	802
his *w* Jehudijah bare Jered the	1Chr 4:18	802
the sons of his *w* Hodiah the	1Chr 4:19	802
Machir took to *w* the sister of	1Chr 7:15	802
Maachah the *w* of Machir bare a	1Chr 7:16	802
And when he went in to his *w*	1Chr 7:23	802
And he begat of Hodesh his *w*	1Chr 8:9	802
My *w* shall not dwell in the house	2Chr 8:11	802
of Jerimoth the son of David to *w*	2Chr 11:18	802
he had the daughter of Ahab to *w*	2Chr 21:6	802
the *w* of Jehoiada the priest	2Chr 22:11	802
Give thy daughter to my son to *w*	2Chr 25:18	802
the *w* of Shallum the son of	2Chr 34:22	802
which took a *w* of the daughters	Ezr 2:61	802
of Barzillai the Gileadite to *w*	Neh 7:63	802
for his friends, and Zeresh his *w*	Est 5:10	802
Then said Zeresh his *w* and all his	Est 5:14	802
And Haman told Zeresh his *w*	Est 6:13	802
wise men and Zeresh his *w* unto him	Est 6:13	802
Then said his *w* unto him, Dost	Job 2:9	802
My breath is strange to my *w*	Job 19:17	802
Then let my *w* grind unto another,	Job 31:10	802
be fatherless, and his *w* a widow	Ps 109:9	802
Thy *w* shall be as a fruitful vine	Ps 128:3	802
rejoice with the *w* of thy youth	Prov 5:18	802
goeth in to his neighbour's *w*	Prov 6:29	802
Whoso findeth a *w* findeth a good	Prov 18:22	802
the contentions of a *w* are a	Prov 19:13	802
a prudent *w* is from the Lord	Prov 19:14	802
Live joyfully with the *w* whom	Eccl 9:9	802
the children of the married *w*	Is 54:1	
a *w* of youth, when thou wast	Is 54:6	802
They say, If a man put away his *w*	Jer 3:1	802
Surely as a *w* treacherously	Jer 3:20	802
neighed after his neighbour's *w*	Jer 5:8	802
husband with the *w* shall be taken	Jer 6:11	802
Thou shalt not take thee a *w*	Jer 16:2	802
But as a *w* that committeth	Eze 16:32	802
hath defiled his neighbour's *w*	Eze 18:6	802
and defiled his neighbour's *w*	Eze 18:11	802
not defiled his neighbour's *w*	Eze 18:15	802
with his neighbour's *w*	Eze 22:11	802
and at even my *w* died	Eze 24:18	802
every one his neighbour's *w*	Eze 33:26	802
take unto thee a *w* of whoredoms	Hos 1:6	802
for she is not my *w*, neither am I	Hos 2:2	802
Syria, and Israel served for a *w*	Hos 12:12	802
and for a *w* he kept sheep	Hos 12:12	802
Thy *w* shall be an harlot in the	Amos 7:17	802
the *w* of thy youth, against whom	Mal 2:14	802
and the *w* of thy covenant	Mal 2:14	802
against the *w* of his youth	Mal 2:15	802
her that had been the *w* of Urias	Mt 1:6	
not to take unto thee Mary thy *w*	Mt 1:20	1135
him, and took unto him his *w*	Mt 1:24	1135
Whosoever shall put away his *w*	Mt 5:31	1135
whosoever shall put away his *w*	Mt 5:32	1135
sake, his brother Philip's *w*	Mt 14:3	1135
him to be sold, and his *w*, and	Mt 18:25	1135
to put away his *w* for every cause	Mt 19:3	1135
mother, and shall cleave to his *w*	Mt 19:5	1135

Whosoever shall put away his *w*	Mt 19:9	1135
case of the man be so with his *w*	Mt 19:10	1135
or father, or mother, or *w*	Mt 19:29	1135
his brother shall marry his *w*	Mt 22:24	1135
first, when he had married a *w*	Mt 22:25	
left his *w* unto his brother	Mt 22:25	1135
whose *w* shall she be of the seven	Mt 22:28	1135
his *w* sent unto him, saying, Have	Mt 27:19	1135
sake, his brother Philip's *w*	Mk 6:17	1135
for thee to have thy brother's *w*	Mk 6:18	1135
for a man to put away his *w*	Mk 10:2	1135
and mother, and cleave to his *w*	Mk 10:7	1135
Whosoever shall put away his *w*	Mk 10:11	1135
or father, or mother, or *w*	Mk 10:29	1135
leave his *w* behind him, and leave	Mk 12:19	1135
his brother should take his *w*	Mk 12:19	1135
and the first took a *w*, and dying	Mk 12:20	1135
whose *w* shall she be of them	Mk 12:23	1135
for the seven had her to *w*	Mk 12:23	1135
his *w* was of the daughters of	Lk 1:5	1135
thy *w* Elisabeth shall bear thee a	Lk 1:13	1135
my *w* well stricken in years	Lk 1:18	1135
days his *w* Elisabeth conceived	Lk 1:24	1135
be taxed with Mary his espoused *w*	Lk 2:5	1135
Herodias his brother Philip's *w*	Lk 3:19	1135
Joanna the *w* of Chuza Herod's	Lk 8:3	1135
another said, I have married a *w*	Lk 14:20	1135
not his father, and mother, and *w*	Lk 14:26	1135
Whosoever putteth away his *w*	Lk 16:18	1135
Remember Lot's *w*	Lk 17:32	1135
or parents, or brethren, or *w*	Lk 18:29	1135
any man's brother die, having a *w*	Lk 20:28	1135
his brother should take his *w*	Lk 20:28	1135
and the first took a *w*, and died	Lk 20:29	1135
And the second took her to *w*	Lk 20:30	1135
whose *w* of them is she	Lk 20:33	1135
for seven had her to *w*	Lk 20:33	1135
Mary the *w* of Cleophas, and Mary	Jn 19:25	
Ananias, with Sapphira his *w*	Acts 5:1	1135
his *w* also being privy to it, and	Acts 5:2	1135
of three hours after, when his *w*	Acts 5:7	1135
from Italy, with his *w* Priscilla	Acts 18:2	1135
Felix came with his *w* Drusilla	Acts 24:24	1135
one should have his father's *w*	1Cor 5:1	1135
let every man have his own *w*	1Cor 7:2	1135
render unto the *w* due benevolence	1Cor 7:3	1135
also the *w* unto the husband	1Cor 7:3	1135
The *w* hath not power of her own	1Cor 7:4	1135
power of his own body, but the *w*	1Cor 7:4	1135
Let not the *w* depart from her	1Cor 7:10	1135
not the husband put away his *w*	1Cor 7:11	1135
hath a *w* that believeth not	1Cor 7:12	1135
husband is sanctified by the *w*	1Cor 7:14	1135
the unbelieving *w* is sanctified	1Cor 7:14	1135
For what knowest thou, O *w*	1Cor 7:16	1135
whether thou shalt save thy *w*	1Cor 7:16	1135
Art thou bound unto a *w*	1Cor 7:27	1135
Art thou loosed from a *w*	1Cor 7:27	1135
seek not a *w*	1Cor 7:27	1135
world, how he may please his *w*	1Cor 7:33	1135
is difference also between a *w*	1Cor 7:34	1135
The *w* is bound by the law as long	1Cor 7:39	1135
power to lead about a sister, a *w*	1Cor 9:5	1135
the husband is the head of the *w*	Eph 5:23	1135
that loveth his *w* loveth himself	Eph 5:28	1135
and shall be joined unto his *w*	Eph 5:31	1135
so love his *w* even as himself	Eph 5:33	1135
the *w* see that she reverence her	Eph 5:33	1135
blameless, the husband of one *w*	1Ti 3:2	1135
deacons be the husbands of one *w*	1Ti 3:12	1135
old, having been the *w* of one man	1Ti 5:9	1135
blameless, the husband of one *w*	Titus 1:6	1135
giving honour unto the *w*	1Pet 3:7	1134
his *w* hath made herself ready	Rev 19:7	1135
shew thee the bride, the Lamb's *w*	Rev 21:9	1135

WIFE'S

And Adam called his *w* name Eve	Gen 3:20	802
they will slay me for my *w* sake	Gen 20:11	802
his *w* name was Mehetabel, the	Gen 36:39	802
of thy father's *w* daughter	Lev 18:11	802
his *w* sons grew up, and they	Judg 11:2	802
his *w* name was Mehetabel, the	1Chr 1:50	802
whose *w* name was Maachah	1Chr 8:29	802
Jehiel, whose *w* name was Maachah	1Chr 9:35	802
he saw his *w* mother laid, and sick	Mt 8:14	3994
But Simon's *w* mother lay sick of	Mk 1:30	3994
Simon's *w* mother was taken with a	Lk 4:38	3994

W

WILD

And he will be a *w* man	Gen 16:12	6501
will also send *w* beasts among you	Lev 26:22	7704
the *w* goat, and the pygarg	Deut 14:5	689
the pygarg, and the *w* ox	Deut 14:5	8377
to the *w* beasts of the earth	1Sa 17:46	2416
men upon the rocks of the *w* goats	1Sa 24:2	3277
was as light of foot as a *w* roe	2Sa 2:18	7704
gather herbs, and found a *w* vine	2Kin 4:39	7704
gathered thereof *w* gourds his lap	2Kin 4:39	7704
there passed by a *w* beast that	2Kin 14:9	7704
there passed by a *w* beast that	2Chr 25:18	7704
Doth the *w* ass bray when he hath	Job 6:5	6501
man be born like a *w* ass's colt	Job 11:12	6501
as *w* asses in the desert, go they	Job 24:5	6501
w goats of the rock bring forth	Job 39:1	3277
Who hath set out the *w* ass free	Job 39:5	6501
loosed the bands of the *w* ass	Job 39:5	6171
or that the *w* beast may break	Job 39:15	7704
the *w* beasts of the field are	Ps 50:11	2123
the *w* beast of the field doth	Ps 80:13	2123
the *w* asses quench their thirst	Ps 104:11	6501
are a refuge for the *w* goats	Ps 104:18	3277
and it brought forth *w* grapes	Is 5:2	891
grapes, brought it forth *w* grapes	Is 5:4	891
But *w* beasts of the desert shall	Is 13:21	6728
the *w* beasts of the islands shall	Is 13:22	338
dens for ever, a joy of *w* asses	Is 32:14	6501
The *w* beasts of the desert shall	Is 34:14	6728
with the *w* beasts of the island	Is 34:14	338
the streets, as a *w* bull in a net	Is 51:20	8377
A *w* ass used to the wilderness,	Jer 2:24	6501
the *w* asses did stand in the high	Jer 14:6	6501
Therefore the *w* beasts of the	Jer 50:39	6728
the *w* beasts of the islands shall	Jer 50:39	338
his dwelling was with the *w* asses	Dan 5:21	6167
Assyria, a *w* ass alone by himself	Hos 8:9	6501
the *w* beast shall tear them	Hos 13:8	7704
his meat was locusts and *w* honey	Mt 3:4	66
and he did eat locusts and *w* honey	Mk 1:6	66
and was with the *w* beasts	Mk 1:13	2342
w beasts, and creeping things, and	Acts 10:12	2342
w beasts, and creeping things, and	Acts 11:6	2342
being a *w* olive tree, wert	Rom 11:17	65
olive tree which is *w* by nature	Rom 11:24	65

WILDERNESS

unto El-paran, which is by the *w*	Gen 14:6	4057
by a fountain of water in the *w*	Gen 16:7	4057
wandered in the *w* of Beer-sheba	Gen 21:14	4057
and he grew, and dwelt in the *w*	Gen 21:20	4057
And he dwelt in the *w* of Paran	Gen 21:21	4057
that found the mules in the *w*	Gen 36:24	4057
into this pit that is in the *w*	Gen 37:22	4057
three days' journey into the *w*	Ex 3:18	4057
Go into the *w* to meet Moses	Ex 4:27	4057
may hold a feast unto me in the *w*	Ex 5:1	4057
that they may serve me in the *w*	Ex 7:16	4057
go three days' journey into the *w*	Ex 8:27	4057
to the Lord your God in the *w*	Ex 8:28	4057
the way of the *w* of the Red sea	Ex 13:18	4057
in Etham, in the edge of the *w*	Ex 13:20	4057
the land, the *w* hath shut them in	Ex 14:3	4057
taken us away to die in the *w*	Ex 14:11	4057
than that we should die in the *w*	Ex 14:12	4057
they went out into the *w* of Shur	Ex 15:22	4057
and they went three days in the *w*	Ex 15:22	4057
of Israel came unto the *w* of Sin	Ex 16:1	4057
against Moses and Aaron in the *w*	Ex 16:2	4057
have brought us forth into this *w*	Ex 16:3	4057
that they looked toward the *w*	Ex 16:10	4057
upon the face of the *w* there lay	Ex 16:14	4057
wherewith I have fed you in the *w*	Ex 16:32	4057
journeyed from the *w* of Sin	Ex 17:1	4057
and his wife unto Moses into the *w*	Ex 18:5	4057
day came they into the *w* of Sinai	Ex 19:1	4057
of Sinai, and had pitched in the *w*	Ex 19:2	4057
unto the Lord, in the *w* of Sinai	Lev 7:38	4057
him go for a scapegoat into the *w*	Lev 16:10	4057
the hand of a fit man into the *w*	Lev 16:21	4057
he shall let go the goat in the *w*	Lev 16:22	4057
unto Moses in the *w* of Sinai	Num 1:1	4057
numbered them in the *w* of Sinai	Num 1:19	4057
in the *w* of Sinai, and they had no	Num 3:4	4057
unto Moses in the *w* of Sinai	Num 3:14	4057
unto Moses in the *w* of Sinai	Num 9:1	4057
month at even in the *w* of Sinai	Num 9:5	4057
journeys out of the *w* of Sinai	Num 10:12	4057
cloud rested in the *w* of Paran	Num 10:12	4057

how we are to encamp in the *w*	Num 10:31	4057
and pitched in the *w* of Paran	Num 12:16	4057
sent them from the *w* of Paran	Num 13:3	4057
land from the *w* of Zin unto Rehob	Num 13:21	4057
of Israel, unto the *w* of Paran	Num 13:26	4057
would God we had died in this *w*	Num 14:2	4057
he hath slain them in the *w*	Num 14:16	4057
which I did in Egypt and in the *w*	Num 14:22	4057
get you into the *w* by the way of	Num 14:25	4057
carcases shall fall in this *w*	Num 14:29	4057
they shall fall in this *w*	Num 14:32	4057
shall wander in the *w* forty years	Num 14:33	4057
your carcases be wasted in the *w*	Num 14:33	4057
in this *w* they shall be consumed,	Num 14:35	4057
children of Israel were in the *w*,	Num 15:32	4057
and honey, to kill us in the *w*	Num 16:13	4057
of the Lord into this *w*, that we	Num 20:4	4057
up out of Egypt to die in the *w*	Num 21:5	4057
in the *w* which is before Moab,	Num 21:11	4057
which is in the *w* that cometh out	Num 21:13	4057
from the *w* they went to Mattanah	Num 21:18	4057
out against Israel into the *w*	Num 21:23	4057
but he set his face toward the *w*	Num 24:1	4057
of Israel in the *w* of Sinai	Num 26:64	4057
They shall surely die in the *w*	Num 26:65	4057
Our father died in the *w*, and he	Num 27:3	4057
Meribah in Kadesh in the *w* of Zin	Num 27:14	4057
them wander in the *w* forty years	Num 32:13	4057
yet again leave them in the *w*	Num 32:15	4057
which is in the edge of the *w*	Num 33:6	4057
the midst of the sea into the *w*	Num 33:8	4057
days' journey in the *w* of Etham	Num 33:8	4057
sea, and encamped in the *w* of Sin	Num 33:11	4057
their journey out of the *w* of Sin	Num 33:12	4057
and pitched in the *w* of Sinai	Num 33:15	4057
and pitched in the *w* of Zin	Num 33:36	4057
w of Zin along by the coast of	Num 34:3	4057
on this side Jordan in the *w*	Deut 1:1	4057
all that great and terrible *w*	Deut 1:19	4057
And in the *w*, where thou hast seen	Deut 1:31	4057
the *w* by the way of the Red sea	Deut 1:40	4057
the *w* by the way of the Red sea	Deut 2:1	4057
thy walking through this great *w*	Deut 2:7	4057
by the way of the *w* of Moab	Deut 2:8	4057
I sent messengers out of the *w* of	Deut 2:26	4057
Namely, Bezer in the *w*, in the	Deut 4:43	4057
thee these forty years in the *w*	Deut 8:2	4057
through that great and terrible *w*	Deut 8:15	4057
Who fed thee in the *w* with manna	Deut 8:16	4057
Lord thy God to wrath in the *w*	Deut 9:7	4057
them out to slay them in the *w*	Deut 9:28	4057
And what he did unto you in the *w*	Deut 11:5	4057
from the *w* and Lebanon, from the	Deut 11:24	4057
have led you forty years in the *w*	Deut 29:5	4057
land, and in the waste howling *w*	Deut 32:10	3452
Meribah-kadesh, in the *w* of Zin	Deut 32:51	4057
From the *w* and this Lebanon even	Josh 1:4	4057
of war, died in the *w* by the way	Josh 5:4	4057
people that were born in the *w* by	Josh 5:5	4057
walked forty years in the *w*	Josh 5:6	4057
them, and fled by the way of the *w*	Josh 8:15	4057
the people that fled to the *w*	Josh 8:20	4057
in the *w* wherein they chased them	Josh 8:24	4057
and in the springs, and in the *w*	Josh 12:8	4057
of Israel wandered in the *w*	Josh 14:10	4057
the *w* of Zin southward was the	Josh 15:1	4057
In the *w*, Beth-arabah, Middin, and	Josh 15:61	4057
to the *w* that goeth up from	Josh 16:1	4057
were at the *w* of Beth-aven	Josh 18:12	4057
they assigned Bezer in the *w* upon	Josh 20:8	4057
ye dwelt in the *w* a long season	Josh 24:7	4057
of Judah into the *w* of Judah	Judg 1:16	4057
flesh with the thorns of the *w*	Judg 8:7	4057
of the city, and thorns of the *w*	Judg 8:16	4057
through the *w* unto the Red sea	Judg 11:16	4057
they went along through the *w*	Judg 11:18	4057
from the *w* even unto Jordan	Judg 11:22	4057
of Israel unto the way of the *w*	Judg 20:42	4057
fled toward the *w* unto the rock	Judg 20:45	4057
fled to the *w* unto the rock	Judg 20:47	4057
with all the plagues in the *w*	1Sa 4:8	4057
the valley of Zeboim toward the *w*	1Sa 13:18	4057
left those few sheep in the *w*	1Sa 17:28	4057
abode in the *w* in strong holds	1Sa 23:14	4057
in a mountain in the *w* of Ziph	1Sa 23:14	4057

David was in the w of Ziph in a	1Sa 23:15	4057
and his men were in the w of Maon	1Sa 23:24	4057
a rock, and abode in the w of Maon	1Sa 23:25	4057
after David in the w of Maon	1Sa 23:25	4057
David is in the w of En-gedi	1Sa 24:1	4057
and went down to the w of Paran	1Sa 25:1	4057
David heard in the w that Nabal	1Sa 25:4	4057
out of the w to salute our master	1Sa 25:14	4057
that this fellow hath in the w	1Sa 25:21	4057
and went down to the w of Ziph	1Sa 26:2	4057
to seek David in the w of Ziph	1Sa 26:2	4057
But David abode in the w, and he	1Sa 26:3	4057
Saul came after him into the w	1Sa 26:3	4057
by the way of the w of Gibeon	2Sa 2:24	4057
over, toward the way of the w	2Sa 15:23	4057
will tarry in the plain of the w	2Sa 15:28	4057
as be faint in the w may drink	2Sa 16:2	4057
this night in the plains of the w	2Sa 17:16	4057
and weary, and thirsty, in the w	2Sa 17:29	4057
buried in his own house in the w	1Kin 2:34	4057
And Baalath, and Tadmor in the w	1Kin 9:18	4057
went a day's journey into the w	1Kin 19:4	4057
on thy way to the w of Damascus	1Kin 19:15	4057
The way through the w of Edom	2Kin 3:8	4057
of the w from the river Euphrates	1Chr 5:9	4057
Bezer in the w with her suburbs,	1Chr 6:78	4057
the hold to the w men of might	1Chr 12:8	4057
LORD, which Moses made in the w	1Chr 21:29	4057
of the LORD had made in the w	2Chr 1:3	4057
And he built Tadmor in the w	2Chr 8:4	4057
the brook, before the w of Jeruel	2Chr 20:16	4057
and went forth into the w of Tekoa	2Chr 20:20	4057
toward the watch tower in the w	2Chr 20:24	4057
of God laid upon Israel in the w	2Chr 24:9	4057
forsookest them not in the w	Neh 9:19	4057
didst thou sustain them in the w	Neh 9:21	4057
came a great wind from the w	Job 1:19	4057
in a w where there is no way	Job 12:24	8414
the w yieldeth food for them and	Job 24:5	6160
fleeing into the w in former time	Job 30:3	6723
on the w, wherein there is no man	Job 38:26	4057
Whose house I have made the w	Job 39:6	6160
voice of the LORD shaketh the w	Ps 29:8	4057
the LORD shaketh the w of Kadesh	Ps 29:8	4057
far off, and remain in the w	Ps 55:7	4057
when he was in the w of Judah	Ps 63:t	4057
drop upon the pastures of the w	Ps 65:12	4057
thou didst march through the w	Ps 68:7	3452
in the w shall bow before him	Ps 72:9	6728
to the people inhabiting the w	Ps 74:14	6728
He clave the rocks in the w	Ps 78:15	4057
provoking the most High in the w	Ps 78:17	6723
Can God furnish a table in the w	Ps 78:19	4057
oft did they provoke him in the w	Ps 78:40	4057
guided them in the w like a flock	Ps 78:52	4057
in the day of temptation in the w	Ps 95:8	4057
I am like a pelican of the w	Ps 102:6	4057
the depths, as through the w	Ps 106:9	4057
But lusted exceedingly in the w	Ps 106:14	4057
them, to overthrow them in the w	Ps 106:26	4057
in the w in a solitary way	Ps 107:4	4057
He turneth rivers into the w	Ps 107:33	4057
He turneth the w into a standing	Ps 107:35	4057
causeth them to wander in the w	Ps 107:40	8414
led his people through the w	Ps 136:16	4057
It is better to dwell in the w	Prov 21:19	4057
of the w like pillars of smoke	Song 3:6	4057
is this that cometh up from the w	Song 8:5	4057
That made the world as a w	Is 14:17	4057
of the land from Sela to the w	Is 16:1	4057
they wandered through the w	Is 16:8	4057
it for them that dwell in the w	Is 23:13	6728
forsaken, and left like a w	Is 27:10	4057
the w be a fruitful field, and the	Is 32:15	4057
judgment shall dwell in the w	Is 32:16	4057
Sharon is like a w	Is 33:9	6160
The w and the solitary place shall	Is 35:1	4057
for in the w shall waters break	Is 35:6	4057
voice of him that crieth in the w	Is 40:3	4057
I will make the w a pool of water	Is 41:18	4057
I will plant in the w the cedar	Is 41:19	4057
Let the w and the cities thereof	Is 42:11	4057
I will even make a way in the w	Is 43:19	4057
because I give waters in the w	Is 43:20	4057
up the sea, I make the rivers a w	Is 50:2	4057
and he will make her w like Eden	Is 51:3	4057
the deep, as an horse in the w	Is 63:13	4057
are a w, Zion is a w	Is 64:10	4057
thou wentest after me in the w	Jer 2:2	4057
Egypt, that led us through the w	Jer 2:6	4057
A wild ass used to the w, that	Jer 2:24	4057

Have I been a w unto Israel	Jer 2:31	4057
for them, as the Arabian in the w	Jer 3:2	4057
the w toward the daughter of my	Jer 4:11	4057
lo, the fruitful place was a w	Jer 4:26	4057
Oh that I had in the w a lodging	Jer 9:2	4057
of the w a lamentation, because	Jer 9:10	4057
and is burned up like a w, that	Jer 9:12	4057
corners, that dwell in the w	Jer 9:26	4057
my pleasant portion a desolate w	Jer 12:10	4057
all high places through the w	Jer 12:12	4057
passeth away by the wind of the w	Jer 13:24	4057
the parched places in the w	Jer 17:6	4057
yet surely I will make thee a w	Jer 22:6	4057
places of the w are dried up	Jer 23:10	4057
of the sword found grace in the w	Jer 31:2	4057
and be like the heath in the w	Jer 48:6	4057
of the nations shall be a w	Jer 50:12	4057
a desolation, a dry land, and a w	Jer 51:43	6160
like the ostriches in the w	Lam 4:3	4057
they laid wait for us in the w	Lam 4:19	4057
because of the sword of the w	Lam 5:9	4057
than the w toward Diblath	Eze 6:14	4057
And now she is planted in the w	Eze 19:13	4057
Egypt, and brought them into the w	Eze 20:10	4057
rebelled against me in the w	Eze 20:13	4057
out my fury upon them in the w	Eze 20:13	4057
up my hand unto them in the w	Eze 20:15	4057
I make an end of them in the w	Eze 20:17	4057
said unto their children in the w	Eze 20:18	4057
my anger against them in the w	Eze 20:21	4057
mine hand unto them also in the w	Eze 20:23	4057
you into the w of the people	Eze 20:35	4057
in the w of the land of Egypt	Eze 20:36	4057
were brought Sabeans from the w	Eze 23:42	4057
will leave thee thrown into the w	Eze 29:5	4057
they shall dwell safely in the w	Eze 34:25	4057
she was born, and make her as a w	Hos 2:3	4057
her, and bring her into the w	Hos 2:14	4057
found Israel like grapes in the w	Hos 9:10	4057
I did know thee in the w, in the	Hos 13:5	4057
the LORD shall come up from the w	Hos 13:15	4057
devoured the pastures of the w	Joel 1:19	4057
devoured the pastures of the w	Joel 1:20	4057
them, and behind them a desolate w	Joel 2:3	4057
the pastures of the w do spring	Joel 2:22	4057
and Edom shall be a desolate w	Joel 3:19	4057
led you forty years through the w	Amos 2:10	4057
and offerings in the w forty years	Amos 5:25	4057
of Hemath unto the river of the w	Amos 6:14	6166
a desolation, and dry like a w	Zeph 2:13	4057
waste for the dragons of the w	Mal 1:3	4057
preaching in the w of Judaea	Mt 3:1	2048
The voice of one crying in the w	Mt 3:3	2048
the w to be tempted of the devil	Mt 4:1	2048
went ye out into the w to see	Mt 11:7	2048
we have so much bread in the w	Mt 15:33	2047
The voice of one crying in the w	Mk 1:3	2048
John did baptize in the w	Mk 1:4	2048
the spirit driveth him into the w	Mk 1:12	2048
he was there in the w forty days	Mk 1:13	2048
men with bread here in the w	Mk 8:4	2047
the son of Zacharias in the w	Lk 3:2	2048
The voice of one crying in the w	Lk 3:4	2048
was led by the Spirit into the w	Lk 4:1	2048
And he withdrew himself into the w	Lk 5:16	2048
went ye out into the w for to see	Lk 7:24	2048
driven of the devil into the w	Lk 8:29	2048
leave the ninety and nine in the w	Lk 15:4	2048
the voice of one crying in the w	Jn 1:23	2048
lifted up the serpent in the w	Jn 3:14	2048
fathers did eat manna in the w	Jn 6:49	2048
unto a country near to the w	Jn 11:54	2048
there appeared to him in the w of	Acts 7:30	2048
Red sea, and in the w forty years	Acts 7:36	2048
w with the angel which spake to	Acts 7:38	2048
the space of forty years in the w	Acts 7:42	2048
tabernacle of witness in the w	Acts 7:44	2048
he their manners in the w	Acts 13:18	2048
leddest out into the w four	Acts 21:38	2048
for they were overthrown in the w	1Cor 10:5	2048
in the city, in perils in the w	2Cor 11:26	2047
in the day of temptation in the w	Heb 3:8	2048
whose carcases fell in the w	Heb 3:17	2048
And the woman fled into the w	Rev 12:6	2048
that she might fly into the w	Rev 12:14	2048
me away in the spirit into the w	Rev 17:3	2048

WILES

For they vex you with their w	Num 25:18	5231
stand against the w of the devil	Eph 6:11	3180

W

WILFULLY
For if we sin *w* after that we .... Heb 10:26   *1596*

WILILY
They did work *w*, and went and made .... Josh 9:4   *6195*

WILL See APPENDIX.

WILLETH
So then it is not of him that *w* .... Rom 9:16   *2309*

WILLING See APPENDIX.

WILLINGLY See APPENDIX.

WILLOW
waters, and set it as a *w* tree .... Eze 17:5   *6851*

WILLOWS
of thick trees, and *w* of the brook .... Lev 23:40   *6155*
the *w* of the brook compass him .... Job 40:22   *6155*
upon the *w* in the midst thereof .... Ps 137:2   *6155*
carry away to the brook of the *w* .... Is 15:7   *6155*
as *w* by the water courses .... Is 44:4   *6155*

WILT
if thou *w* take the left hand, ... Gen 13:9
what *w* thou give me, seeing I go .... Gen 15:2
and whither *w* thou go .... Gen 16:8
W thou also destroy the righteous .... Gen 18:23
w thou also destroy and not spare .... Gen 18:24
w thou destroy all the city for .... Gen 18:28
w thou slay also a righteous .... Gen 20:4
thou *w* not deal falsely with me .... Gen 21:23
saying, But if thou *w* give it .... Gen 23:13
unto her, *W* thou go with this man .... Gen 24:58
That thou *w* do us no hurt, as we .... Gen 26:29
if thou *w* do this thing for me, I .... Gen 30:31
What *w* thou give me, that thou .... Gen 38:16
W thou give me a pledge, till .... Gen 38:17
If thou *w* send our brother with .... Gen 43:4
But if thou *w* not send him, we .... Gen 43:5
the hand of him whom thou *w* send ...... Ex 4:13
if thou *w* not let my people go, ... Ex 8:21
them go, and *w* hold them still, ... Ex 9:2
that thou *w* not let them go .... Ex 9:17
How long *w* thou refuse to humble .... Ex 10:3
if thou *w* not redeem it, then .... Ex 13:13
If thou *w* diligently hearken to .... Ex 15:26
w do that which is right in his .... Ex 15:26
w give ear to his commandments, ... Ex 15:26
Thou *w* surely wear away, both .... Ex 18:18
if thou *w* make me an altar of .... Ex 20:25
if thou *w* forgive their sin .... Ex 32:32
me know whom thou *w* send with me .... Ex 33:12
w thou put out the eyes of these .... Num 16:14
w thou be wroth with all the .... Num 16:22
If thou *w* indeed deliver this .... Num 21:2
when thou *w* ease thyself abroad, ... Deut 23:13
if thou *w* not hearken unto the .... Deut 28:15
If thou *w* not observe to do all .... Deut 28:58
away, so that thou *w* not hear .... Deut 30:17
what *w* thou do unto thy great .... Josh 7:9
Caleb said unto her, What *w* thou .... Judg 1:14
If thou *w* go with me, then I will .... Judg 4:8
but if thou *w* not go with me, ... Judg 4:8
If thou *w* save Israel by mine .... Judg 6:36
thou *w* save Israel by mine hand .... Judg 6:37
W not thou possess that which .... Judg 11:24
if thou *w* offer a burnt offering, ... Judg 13:16
If thou *w* redeem it, redeem it .... Ruth 4:4
but if thou *w* not redeem it, then .... Ruth 4:4
if thou *w* indeed look on the 1Sa 1:11
but *w* give unto thine handmaid a 1Sa 1:11
How long *w* thou be drunken 1Sa 1:14
w thou deliver them into the hand 1Sa 14:37
How long *w* thou mourn for Saul, ... 1Sa 16:1
wherefore then *w* thou sin against 1Sa 19:5
if thou *w* take that, take it 1Sa 21:9
that thou *w* not cut off my seed 1Sa 24:21
that thou *w* not destroy my name 1Sa 24:21
know and consider what thou *w* do 1Sa 25:17
that thou *w* neither kill me, nor 1Sa 30:15
w thou deliver them into mine 2Sa 5:19
w thou not tell me 2Sa 13:4
Joab said, Wherefore *w* thou run 2Sa 18:22
why *w* thou swallow up the 2Sa 20:19
thou *w* shew thyself merciful 2Sa 22:26
man thou *w* shew thyself upright 2Sa 22:26
the pure thou *w* shew thyself pure 2Sa 22:27
with the froward thou *w* shew 2Sa 22:27
the afflicted people thou *w* save 2Sa 22:28
or *w* thou flee three months 2Sa 24:13
if thou *w* walk in my ways, to 1Kin 3:14
if thou *w* walk in my statutes, and 1Kin 6:12

if thou *w* walk before me, as 1Kin 9:4
thee, and *w* keep my statutes and my ... 1Kin 9:4
if thou *w* hearken unto all that I............ 1Kin 11:38
w walk in my ways, and do that is 1Kin 11:38
If thou *w* be a servant unto this 1Kin 12:7
w serve them, and answer them, and 1Kin 12:7
If thou *w* give me half thine 1Kin 13:8
W thou go with me to battle to 1Kin 22:4
w thou go with me against Moab to 2Kin 3:7
Wherefore *w* thou go to him to day 2Kin 4:23
I know the evil that thou *w* do 2Kin 8:12
strong holds *w* thou set on fire.............. 2Kin 8:12
their young men *w* thou slay with 2Kin 8:12
w dash their children, and rip up 2Kin 8:12
How then *w* thou turn away the............ 2Kin 18:24
w thou deliver them into mine 1Chr 14:10
that thou *w* build him an house 1Chr 17:25
if thou *w* walk before me, as 2Chr 7:17
of Judah, *W* thou go with me to............ 2Chr 18:3
our affliction, then thou *w* hear 2Chr 20:9
O our God, *w* thou not judge them 2Chr 20:12
But if thou *w* go, do it, be 2Chr 25:8
and when *w* thou return .... Neh 2:6
the king unto her, What *w* thou .... Est 5:3
with thee, *w* thou be grieved .... Job 4:2
which of the saints *w* thou turn .... Job 5:1
How long *w* thou not depart from .... Job 7:19
How long *w* thou speak these .... Job 8:2
I know that thou *w* not hold me .... Job 9:28
w thou bring me into dust again .... Job 10:9
thou *w* not acquit me from mine .... Job 10:14
W thou break a leaf driven to and .... Job 13:25
w thou pursue the dry stubble .... Job 13:25
thou *w* have a desire to the work .... Job 14:15
that thou *w* bring me to death .... Job 30:23
w thou condemn him that is most .... Job 34:17
W thou hunt the prey for the lion .... Job 38:39
W thou trust him, because his.............. Job 39:11
or *w* thou leave thy labour to him .... Job 39:11
W thou believe him, that he will............ Job 39:12
W thou also disannul my judgment ...... Job 40:8
w thou condemn me, that thou .... Job 40:8
w thou take him for a servant for .... Job 41:4
W thou play with him as with a .... Job 41:5
or *w* thou bind him for thy .... Job 41:5
thou, LORD, *w* bless the righteous .... Ps 5:12
with favour *w* thou compass him as ...... Ps 5:12
his heart, Thou *w* not require it .... Ps 10:13
thou *w* prepare their heart .... Ps 10:17
thou *w* cause thine ear to hear .... Ps 10:17
How long *w* thou forget me, O LORD ...... Ps 13:1
how long *w* thou hide thy face .... Ps 13:1
For thou *w* not leave my soul in .... Ps 16:10
neither *w* thou suffer thine Holy .... Ps 16:10
Thou *w* shew me the path of life .... Ps 16:11
upon thee, for thou *w* hear me .... Ps 17:6
thou *w* shew thyself merciful .... Ps 18:25
man thou *w* shew thyself upright .... Ps 18:25
the pure thou *w* shew thyself pure .... Ps 18:26
thou *w* shew thyself froward .... Ps 18:26
For thou *w* save the afflicted .... Ps 18:27
but *w* bring down high looks................ Ps 18:27
For thou *w* light my candle .... Ps 18:28
LORD, how long *w* thou look on .... Ps 35:17
thou *w* hear, O Lord my God................ Ps 38:15
thou *w* not deliver him unto the............ Ps 41:2
thou *w* make all his bed in his.............. Ps 41:3
heart, O God, thou *w* not despise .... Ps 51:17
w not thou deliver my feet from............ Ps 56:13
W not thou, O God, which hadst .... Ps 60:10
Thou *w* prolong the king's life .... Ps 61:6
in righteousness *w* thou answer us .... Ps 65:5
w thou be angry for ever .... Ps 79:5
how long *w* thou be angry against .... Ps 80:4
if thou *w* hearken unto me .... Ps 81:8
W thou be angry with us for ever .... Ps 85:5
w thou draw out thine anger to .... Ps 85:5
W thou not revive us again.................... Ps 85:6
for thou *w* answer me .... Ps 86:7
W thou shew wonders to the dead .... Ps 88:10
w thou hide thyself for ever .... Ps 89:46
O when *w* thou come unto me .... Ps 101:2
W not thou, O God, who hast cast .... Ps 108:11
w not thou, O God, go forth with .... Ps 108:11
saying, When *w* thou comfort me .... Ps 119:82
when *w* thou execute judgment on .... Ps 119:84
of trouble, thou *w* revive me .... Ps 138:7
Surely thou *w* slay the wicked, O .... Ps 139:19
if thou *w* receive my words, and .... Prov 2:1
why *w* thou, my son, be ravished .... Prov 5:20
How long *w* thou sleep, O sluggard .... Prov 6:9

when *w* thou arise out of thy .... Prov 6:9
W thou set thine eyes upon that............ Prov 23:5
Thou *w* keep him in perfect peace,......... Is 26:3
thou *w* ordain peace for us .... Is 26:12
forth, thou *w* debate with it .... Is 27:8
How then *w* thou turn away the............. Is 36:9
to night *w* thou make an end of me........ Is 38:12
to night *w* thou make an end of me........ Is 38:13
so *w* thou recover me, and make me ...... Is 38:16
w thou call this a fast, and an .... Is 58:5
W thou refrain thyself for these.............. Is 64:12
w thou hold thy peace, and afflict .... Is 64:12
W thou not from this time cry .... Jer 3:4
If thou *w* return, O Israel, saith............. Jer 4:1
and if thou *w* put away thine .... Jer 4:1
thou art spoiled, what *w* thou do .... Jer 4:30
then how *w* thou do in the .... Jer 12:5
What *w* thou say when he shall .... Jer 13:21
w thou not be made clean .... Jer 13:27
w thou be altogether unto me as a .... Jer 15:18
How long *w* thou go about, O thou .... Jer 31:22
w thou not surely put me to death .... Jer 38:15
w thou not hearken unto me .... Jer 38:15
If thou *w* assuredly go forth unto .... Jer 38:17
But if thou *w* not go forth to the .... Jer 38:18
how long *w* thou cut thyself .... Jer 47:5
thou *w* bring the day that thou .... Lam 1:21
w thou destroy all the residue of .... Eze 9:8
w thou make a full end of the .... Eze 11:13
W thou judge them, son of man,........... Eze 20:4
son of man, *w* thou judge them .... Eze 20:4
w thou judge, *w* thou judge the .... Eze 22:2
w thou judge Aholah and Aholibah ...... Eze 23:36
W thou yet say before him that .... Eze 28:9
W thou not shew us what thou .... Eze 37:18
what *w* thou give .... Hos 9:14
thou *w* cast all their sins into .... Mic 7:19
Thou *w* perform the truth to Jacob .... Mic 7:20
shall I cry, and thou *w* not hear............. Hab 1:2
of violence, and thou *w* not save .... Hab 1:2
I said, Surely thou *w* fear me .... Zeph 3:7
thou *w* receive instruction..................... Zeph 3:7
how long *w* thou not have mercy on ...... Zec 1:12
If thou *w* walk in my ways .... Zec 3:7
if thou *w* keep my charge, then .... Zec 3:7
if thou *w* fall down and worship me ...... Mt 4:9
Or how *w* thou say to thy brother,......... Mt 7:4
him, saying, Lord, if thou *w* .... Mt 8:2   2309
W thou then that we go and gather ..... Mt 13:28   2309
be it unto thee even as thou *w* .... Mt 15:28   2309
if thou *w*, let us make here three .... Mt 17:4   2309
but if thou *w* enter into life, ... Mt 19:17   2309
If thou *w* be perfect, go and sell .... Mt 19:21   2309
And he said unto her, What *w* thou ...... Mt 20:21   2309
Where *w* thou that we prepare for .... Mt 26:17   2309
not as I will, but as thou *w* .... Mt 26:39
and saying unto him, If thou *w*............... Mk 1:40   2309
Ask of me whatsoever thou *w* .... Mk 6:22   2309
What *w* thou that I should do unto .... Mk 10:51   2309
Where *w* thou that we go and .... Mk 14:12   2309
not what I will, but what thou *w*........... Mk 14:36   2309
If thou therefore *w* worship me .... Lk 4:7
him, saying, Lord, if thou *w*................... Lk 5:12   2309
w thou that we command fire to............ Lk 9:54   2309
What *w* thou that I shall do unto .... Lk 18:41   2309
Where *w* thou that we prepare .... Lk 22:9   2309
w thou rear it up in three days .... Jn 2:20
unto him, *W* thou be made whole .... Jn 5:6   2309
now, whatsoever thou *w* ask of God ...... Jn 11:22
W thou lay down thy life for my .... Jn 13:38
how is it that thou *w* manifest .... Jn 14:22
w thou at this time restore again .... Acts 1:6
Because thou *w* not leave my soul.......... Acts 2:27
neither *w* thou suffer thine Holy .... Acts 2:27
W thou kill me, as thou diddest .... Acts 7:28   2309
what *w* thou have me to do .... Acts 9:6   2309
w thou not cease to pervert the .... Acts 13:10
W thou go up to Jerusalem, and .... Acts 25:9
Thou *w* say then unto me, Why doth ...... Rom 9:19
Thou *w* say then, The branches .... Rom 11:19
W thou then not be afraid of the .... Rom 13:3   2309
knowing that thou *w* also do more .... Philem 21
But *w* thou know, O vain man, that ...... Jas 2:20   2309

WIMPLES

apparel, and the mantles, and the *w*...... Is 3:22   4304

WIN

thought to *w* them for himself 2Chr 32:1   1234
but dung, that I may *w* Christ .... Phil 3:8   2770

WIND

God made a *w* to pass over the .... Gen 8:1   7307
the east *w* sprung up after them .... Gen 41:6
thin, and blasted with the east *w* .... Gen 41:23
ears blasted with the east *w* .... Gen 41:27
the LORD brought an east *w* upon .... Ex 10:13   7307
the east *w* brought the locusts .... Ex 10:13   7307
turned a mighty strong west *w*............... Ex 10:19   7307
by a strong east *w* all that night .... Ex 14:21   7307
Thou didst blow with thy *w*..................... Ex 15:10   7307
went forth a *w* from the LORD .... Num 11:31   7307
was seen upon the wings of the *w* 2Sa 22:11   7307
heaven was black with clouds and *w* 1Kin 18:45   7307
strong *w* rent the mountains, and......... 1Kin 19:11   7307
but the LORD was not in the *w* 1Kin 19:11   7307
after the *w* an earthquake 1Kin 19:11   7307
the LORD, Ye shall not see *w* 2Kin 3:17   7307
there came a great *w* from the .... Job 1:19   7307
that is desperate, which are as *w*........... Job 6:26   7307
O remember that my life is *w* .... Job 7:7   7307
of thy mouth be like a strong *w* .... Job 8:2   7307
and fill his belly with the east *w* .... Job 15:2   7307
They are as stubble before the *w* .... Job 21:18   7307
The east *w* carrieth him away, and ...... Job 27:21
they pursue my soul as the *w* .... Job 30:15   7307
Thou liftest me up to the *w* .... Job 30:22   7307
quieteth the earth by the south *w* .... Job 37:17
but the *w* passeth, and cleanseth .... Job 37:21   7307
the east *w* upon the earth .... Job 38:24
chaff which the *w* driveth away .... Ps 1:4   7307
did fly upon the wings of the *w*............... Ps 18:10   7307
small as the dust before the *w* .... Ps 18:42   7307
Let them be as chaff before the *w* .... Ps 35:5   7307
ships of Tarshish with an east *w* .... Ps 48:7   7307
He caused an east *w* to blow in .... Ps 78:26
power he brought in the south *w* .... Ps 78:26
a *w* that passeth away, and cometh ...... Ps 78:39   7307
as the stubble before the *w* .... Ps 83:13   7307
For the *w* passeth over it, and it .... Ps 103:16   7307
walketh upon the wings of the *w* .... Ps 104:3   7307
and raiseth the stormy *w*, which .... Ps 107:25   7307
he bringeth the *w* out of his .... Ps 135:7   7307
he causeth his *w* to blow, and the......... Ps 147:18   7307
stormy *w* fulfilling his word .... Ps 148:8   7307
his own house shall inherit the *w* .... Prov 11:29   7307
is like clouds and *w* without rain........... Prov 25:14   7307
The north *w* driveth away rain............... Prov 25:23   7307
Whosoever hideth her hideth the *w* ...... Prov 27:16   7307
hath gathered the *w* in his fists .... Prov 30:4   7307
The *w* goeth toward the south, and ...... Eccl 1:6   7307
the *w* returneth again according............ Eccl 1:6   7307
he that hath laboured for the *w*............. Eccl 5:16   7307
observeth the *w* shall not sow................. Eccl 11:4   7307
Awake, O north *w* .... Song 4:16
of the wood are moved with the *w*.......... Is 7:2   7307
with his mighty *w* shall he shake .... Is 11:15   7307
of the mountains before the *w*............... Is 17:13   7307
have as it were brought forth *w* .... Is 26:18   7307
he stayeth his rough *w* in the day .... Is 27:8   7307
the day of the east *w* .... Is 27:8
be as an hiding place from the *w* .... Is 32:2   7307
the *w* shall carry them away, and........... Is 41:16   7307
their molten images are *w*....................... Is 41:29   7307
but the *w* shall carry them all .... Is 57:13   7307
and our iniquities, like the *w*................. Is 64:6   7307
snuffeth up the *w* at her pleasure.......... Jer 2:24   7307
A dry *w* of the high places in the .... Jer 4:11   7307
Even a full *w* from those places............. Jer 4:12   7307
And the prophets shall become *w*........... Jer 5:13   7307
bringeth forth the *w* out of his .... Jer 10:13   7307
away by the *w* of the wilderness .... Jer 13:24   7307
snuffed up the *w* like dragons .... Jer 14:6   7307
with an east *w* before the enemy .... Jer 18:17   7307
The *w* shall eat up all thy .... Jer 22:22   7307
up against me, a destroying *w* .... Jer 51:1   7307
bringeth forth the *w* out of his .... Jer 51:16   7307
part thou shalt scatter in the *w* .... Eze 5:2   7307
I will scatter toward every *w* all .... Eze 12:14   7307
and a stormy *w* shall rend it .... Eze 13:11   7307
it with a stormy *w* in my fury .... Eze 13:13   7307
when the east *w* toucheth it .... Eze 17:10   7307
the east *w* dried up her fruit .... Eze 19:12   7307
the east *w* hath broken thee in .... Eze 27:26   7307
he unto me, Prophesy unto the *w* .... Eze 37:9   7307
son of man, and say to the *w* .... Eze 37:9   7307
the *w* carried them away, that no .... Dan 2:35   7308
The *w* hath bound her up in her .... Hos 4:19   7307
For they have sown the *w*, and they ...... Hos 8:7   7307
Ephraim feedeth on *w* .... Hos 12:1   7307
and followeth after the east *w*............... Hos 12:1
an east *w* shall come .... Hos 13:15

the *w* of the LORD shall come up	Hos 13:15	7307
the mountains, and createth the *w*	Amos 4:13	7307
sent out a great *w* into the sea	Jonah 1:4	7307
God prepared a vehement east *w*	Jonah 4:8	7307
faces shall sup up as the east *w*	Hab 1:9	
and the *w* was in their wings	Zec 5:9	7307
A reed shaken with the *w*	Mt 11:7	417
for the *w* was contrary	Mt 14:24	417
But when he saw the *w* boisterous	Mt 14:30	417
come into the ship, the *w* ceased	Mt 14:32	417
And there arose a great storm of *w*	Mk 4:37	417
And he arose, and rebuked the *w*	Mk 4:39	417
the *w* ceased, and there was a	Mk 4:39	417
of man is this, that even the *w*	Mk 4:41	417
for the *w* was contrary unto them	Mk 6:48	417
and the *w* ceased	Mk 6:51	417
A reed shaken with the *w*	Lk 7:24	417
down a storm of *w* on the lake	Lk 8:23	417
Then he arose, and rebuked the *w*	Lk 8:24	417
And when ye see the south *w* blow	Lk 12:55	
The *w* bloweth where it listeth,	Jn 3:8	4151
by reason of a great *w* that blew	Jn 6:18	417
heaven as of a rushing mighty *w*	Acts 2:2	4157
the *w* not suffering us, we sailed	Acts 27:7	417
And when the south *w* blew softly	Acts 27:13	
arose against it a tempestuous *w*	Acts 27:14	417
and could not bear up into the *w*	Acts 27:15	417
hoised up the mainsail to the *w*	Acts 27:40	4154
and after one day the south *w* blew	Acts 28:13	
about with every *w* of doctrine	Eph 4:14	417
wave of the sea driven with the *w*	Jas 1:6	416
when she is shaken of a mighty *w*	Rev 6:13	417
that the *w* should not blow on the	Rev 7:1	417

WINDING

they went up with *w* stairs into	1Kin 6:8	3583
a *w* about still upward to the	Eze 41:7	5437
for the *w* about of the house went	Eze 41:7	4141

WINDOW

A *w* shalt thou make to the ark,	Gen 6:16	6672
that Noah opened the *w* of the ark	Gen 8:6	2474
the Philistines looked out at a *w*	Gen 26:8	2474
them down by a cord through the *w*	Josh 2:15	2474
line of scarlet thread in the *w*	Josh 2:18	2474
bound the scarlet line in the *w*	Josh 2:21	2474
of Sisera looked out at a *w*	Judg 5:28	2474
Michal let David down through a *w*	1Sa 19:12	2474
daughter looked through a *w*	2Sa 6:16	2474
her head, and looked out at a *w*	2Kin 9:30	2474
And he lifted up his face to the *w*	2Kin 9:32	2474
And he said, Open the *w* eastward	2Kin 13:17	2474
out at a *w* saw king David dancing	1Chr 15:29	2474
For at the *w* of my house I looked	Prov 7:6	2474
there sat in a *w* a certain young	Acts 20:9	2376
through a *w* in a basket was I let	2Cor 11:33	2376

WINDOWS

the *w* of heaven were opened	Gen 7:11	699
the *w* of heaven were stopped, and	Gen 8:2	699
house he made *w* of narrow lights	1Kin 6:4	2474
there were *w* in three rows, and	1Kin 7:4	8261
and posts were square, with the *w*	1Kin 7:5	8260
the LORD would make *w* in heaven	2Kin 7:2	699
the LORD should make *w* in heaven	2Kin 7:19	699
look out of the *w* be darkened	Eccl 12:3	699
wall, he looketh forth at the *w*	Song 2:9	2474
for the *w* from on high are open,	Is 24:18	699
And I will make thy *w* of agates	Is 54:12	8121
cloud, and as the doves to their *w*	Is 60:8	699
For death is come up into our *w*	Jer 9:21	2474
chambers, and cutteth him out *w*	Jer 22:14	2474
there were narrow *w* to the little	Eze 40:16	2474
w were round about inward	Eze 40:16	2474
And their *w*, and their arches, and	Eze 40:22	2474
And there were *w* in it and in the	Eze 40:25	2474
thereof round about, like those *w*	Eze 40:25	2474
and there were *w* in it and in the	Eze 40:29	2474
and there were *w* therein and in the	Eze 40:33	2474
and the *w* to it round about	Eze 40:36	2474
The door posts, and the narrow *w*	Eze 41:16	2474
and from the ground up to the *w*	Eze 41:16	2474
and the *w* were covered	Eze 41:16	2474
And there were narrow *w* and palm	Eze 41:26	2474
his *w* being open in his chamber	Dan 6:10	3551
enter in at the *w* like a thief	Joel 2:9	2474
their voice shall sing in the *w*	Zeph 2:14	2474
will not open you the *w* of heaven	Mal 3:10	699

WINDS

To make the weight for the *w*	Job 28:25	7307
I will scatter into all *w* them	Jer 49:32	7307
four *w* from the four quarters of	Jer 49:36	7307

scatter them toward all those *w*	Jer 49:36	7307
will I scatter into all the *w*	Eze 5:10	7307
a third part into all the *w*	Eze 5:12	7307
shall be scattered toward all *w*	Eze 17:21	7307
Come from the four *w*, O breath,	Eze 37:9	7307
the four *w* of the heaven strove	Dan 7:2	7308
ones toward the four *w* of heaven	Dan 8:8	7307
toward the four *w* of heaven	Dan 11:4	7307
as the four *w* of the heaven	Zec 2:6	7307
the *w* blew, and beat upon that	Mt 7:25	417
the *w* blew, and beat upon that	Mt 7:27	417
Then he arose, and rebuked the *w*	Mt 8:26	417
of man is this, that even the *w*	Mt 8:27	417
his elect from the four *w*	Mt 24:31	417
his elect from the four *w*	Mk 13:27	417
for he commandeth even the *w*	Lk 8:25	417
because the *w* were contrary	Acts 27:4	417
great, and are driven of fierce *w*	Jas 3:4	417
without water, carried about of *w*	Jude 12	417
holding the four *w* of the earth	Rev 7:1	417

WINDY

hasten my escape from the *w* storm	Ps 55:8	7307

WINE

And he drank of the *w*, and was	Gen 9:21	3196
Noah awoke from his *w*, and knew	Gen 9:24	3196
of Salem brought forth bread and *w*	Gen 14:18	3196
let us make our father drink *w*	Gen 19:32	3196
their father drink *w* that night	Gen 19:33	3196
make him drink *w* this night also	Gen 19:34	3196
father drink *w* that night also	Gen 19:35	3196
and he brought him *w*, and he drank	Gen 27:25	3196
the earth, and plenty of corn and *w*	Gen 27:28	8492
corn and *w* have I sustained him	Gen 27:37	8492
he washed his garments in *w*	Gen 49:11	3196
His eyes shall be red with *w*	Gen 49:12	3196
an hin of *w* for a drink offering	Ex 29:40	3196
Do not drink *w* nor strong drink,	Lev 10:9	3196
offering thereof shall be of *w*	Lev 23:13	3196
He shall separate himself from *w*	Num 6:3	3196
and shall drink no vinegar of *w*	Num 6:3	3196
that the Nazarite may drink *w*	Num 6:20	3196
the fourth part of an hin of *w*	Num 15:5	3196
the third part of an hin of *w*	Num 15:7	3196
a drink offering half an hin of *w*	Num 15:10	3196
the oil, and all the best of the *w*	Num 18:12	8492
shalt thou cause the strong *w* to	Num 28:7	7491
half an hin of *w* unto a bullock	Num 28:14	3196
of thy land, thy corn, and thy *w*	Deut 7:13	8492
gather in thy corn, and thy *w*	Deut 11:14	8492
tithe of thy corn, or of thy *w*	Deut 12:17	8492
the tithe of thy corn, of thy *w*	Deut 14:23	8492
for oxen, or for sheep, or for *w*	Deut 14:26	3196
gathered in thy corn and thy *w*	Deut 16:13	3342
also of thy corn, of thy *w*	Deut 18:4	8492
but shalt neither drink of the *w*	Deut 28:39	3196
not leave thee either corn, *w*	Deut 28:51	8492
have ye drunk *w* or strong drink	Deut 29:6	3196
Their *w* is the poison of dragons,	Deut 32:33	3196
drank the *w* of their drink	Deut 32:38	3196
shall be upon a land of corn and *w*	Deut 33:28	8492
w bottles, old, and rent, and bound	Josh 9:4	3196
And these bottles of *w*, which we	Josh 9:13	3196
unto them, Should I leave my *w*	Judg 9:13	8492
drink not *w* nor strong drink, and	Judg 13:4	3196
now drink no *w* nor strong drink,	Judg 13:7	3196
let her drink *w* or strong drink	Judg 13:14	3196
w also for me, and for thy	Judg 19:19	3196
put away thy *w* from thee	1Sa 1:14	3196
neither *w* nor strong drink	1Sa 1:15	3196
ephah of flour, and a bottle of *w*	1Sa 1:24	3196
and another carrying a bottle of *w*	1Sa 10:3	3196
with bread, and a bottle of *w*	1Sa 16:20	3196
loaves, and two bottles of *w*	1Sa 25:18	3196
when the *w* was gone out of Nabal,	1Sa 25:37	3196
piece of flesh, and a flagon of *w*	2Sa 6:19	
Amnon's heart is merry with *w*	2Sa 13:28	3196
summer fruits, and a bottle of *w*	2Sa 16:1	3196
and the *w*, that such as be faint	2Sa 16:2	3196
own land, a land of corn and *w*	2Kin 18:32	8492
and the fine flour, and the *w*	1Chr 9:29	3196
figs, and bunches of raisins, and *w*	1Chr 12:40	3196
piece of flesh, and a flagon of *w*	1Chr 16:3	
of the vineyards for the *w*	1Chr 27:27	3196
and twenty thousand baths of *w*	2Chr 2:10	3196
and the barley, the oil, and the *w*	2Chr 2:15	3196
store of victual, and of oil and *w*	2Chr 11:11	3196
the firstfruits of corn, *w*	2Chr 31:5	8492
for the increase of corn, and *w*	2Chr 32:28	8492
the God of heaven, wheat, salt, *w*	Ezr 6:9	2562
and to an hundred baths of *w*	Ezr 7:22	2562

the king, that *w* was before him	Neh 2:1	3196
and I took up the *w*, and gave it	Neh 2:1	3196
the money, and of the corn, the *w*	Neh 5:11	8492
and had taken of them bread and *w*	Neh 5:15	3196
ten days store of all sorts of *w*	Neh 5:18	3196
of all manner of trees, of *w*	Neh 10:37	8492
of the corn, of the new *w*	Neh 10:39	8492
the tithes of the corn, the new *w*	Neh 13:5	8492
tithe of the corn and the new *w*	Neh 13:12	8492
as also *w*, grapes, and figs, and	Neh 13:15	3196
royal *w* in abundance, according	Est 1:7	3196
of the king was merry with *w*	Est 1:10	3196
unto Esther at the banquet of *w*	Est 5:6	3196
second day at the banquet of *w*	Est 7:2	3196
of *w* in his wrath went into the	Est 7:7	3196
the place of the banquet of *w*	Est 7:8	3196
drinking *w* in their eldest	Job 1:13	3196
drinking *w* in their eldest	Job 1:18	3196
my belly is as *w* which hath no	Job 32:19	3196
their corn and their *w* increased	Ps 4:7	8492
us to drink the *w* of astonishment	Ps 60:3	3196
there is a cup, and the *w* is red	Ps 75:8	3196
man that shouteth by reason of *w*	Ps 78:65	3196
w that maketh glad the heart of	Ps 104:15	3196
shall burst out with new *w*	Prov 3:10	8492
and drink the *w* of violence	Prov 4:17	3196
she hath mingled her *w*	Prov 9:2	3196
drink of the *w* which I have	Prov 9:5	3196
W is a mocker, strong drink is	Prov 20:1	3196
he that loveth *w* and oil shall not	Prov 21:17	3196
They that tarry long at the *w*	Prov 23:30	3196
they that go to seek mixed *w*	Prov 23:30	4469
thou upon the *w* when it is red	Prov 23:31	3196
it is not for kings to drink *w*	Prov 31:4	3196
w unto those that be of heavy	Prov 31:6	3196
mine heart to give myself unto *w*	Eccl 2:3	3196
drink thy *w* with a merry heart	Eccl 9:7	3196
for laughter, and *w* maketh merry	Eccl 10:19	3196
for thy love is better than *w*	Song 1:2	3196
remember thy love more than *w*	Song 1:4	3196
much better is thy love than *w*	Song 4:10	3196
I have drunk my *w* with my milk	Song 5:1	3196
like the best *w* for my beloved	Song 7:9	3196
cause thee to drink of spiced *w*	Song 8:2	3196
dross, like *w* mixed with water	Is 1:22	5435
until night, till *w* inflame them	Is 5:11	3196
viol, the tabret, and pipe, and *w*	Is 5:12	3196
them that are mighty to drink *w*	Is 5:22	3196
tread out no *w* in their presses	Is 16:10	3196
eating flesh, and drinking *w*	Is 22:13	3196
The new *w* mourneth, the vine	Is 24:7	8492
shall not drink *w* with a song	Is 24:9	3196
is a crying for *w* in the streets	Is 24:11	3196
ye unto her, A vineyard of red *w*	Is 27:2	2561
of them that are overcome with *w*	Is 28:1	3196
they also have erred through *w*	Is 28:7	3196
drink, they are swallowed up of *w*	Is 28:7	3196
they are drunken, but not with *w*	Is 29:9	3196
own land, a land of corn and *w*	Is 36:17	8492
their own blood, as with sweet *w*	Is 49:26	6071
and drunken, but not with *w*	Is 51:21	3196
yea, come, buy *w* and milk without	Is 55:1	3196
Come ye, say they, I will fetch *w*	Is 56:12	3196
stranger shall not drink thy *w*	Is 62:8	8492
As the new *w* is found in the	Is 65:8	8492
bottle shall be filled with *w*	Jer 13:12	3196
bottle shall be filled with *w*	Jer 13:12	3196
like a man whom *w* hath overcome	Jer 23:9	3196
Take the *w* cup of this fury at my	Jer 25:15	3196
of the LORD, for wheat, and for *w*	Jer 31:12	8492
chambers, and give them *w* to drink	Jer 35:2	3196
of the Rechabites pots full of *w*	Jer 35:5	3196
and I said unto them, Drink ye *w*	Jer 35:5	3196
But they said, We will drink no *w*	Jer 35:6	3196
us, saying, Ye shall drink no *w*	Jer 35:6	3196
to drink no *w* all our days, we,	Jer 35:8	3196
commanded his sons not to drink *w*	Jer 35:14	3196
but ye, gather ye *w*, and summer	Jer 40:10	3196
unto Mizpah, and gathered *w*	Jer 40:12	3196
I have caused *w* to fail from the	Jer 48:33	3196
the nations have drunken of her *w*	Jer 51:7	3196
their mothers, Where is corn and *w*	Lam 2:12	3196
in the *w* of Helbon, and white wool	Eze 27:18	3196
Neither shall any priest drink *w*	Eze 44:21	3196
meat, and of the *w* which he drank	Dan 1:5	3196
nor with the *w* which he drank	Dan 1:8	3196
the *w* that they should drink	Dan 1:16	3196
drank *w* before the thousand	Dan 5:1	2562
whiles he tasted the *w*,	Dan 5:2	2562
They drank *w*, and praised the gods	Dan 5:4	2562
concubines, have drunk *w* in them	Dan 5:23	2562

came flesh nor *w* in my mouth	Dan 10:3	3196
know that I gave her corn, and *w*	Hos 2:8	8492
my *w* in the season thereof, and	Hos 2:9	8492
shall hear the corn, and the *w*	Hos 2:22	8492
other gods, and love flagons of *w*	Hos 3:1	6025
Whoredom and *w* and new	Hos 4:11	3196
new *w* take away the heart	Hos 4:11	8492
made him sick with bottles of *w*	Hos 7:5	3196
assemble themselves for corn and *w*	Hos 7:14	8492
the new *w* shall fail in her	Hos 9:2	8492
They shall not offer *w* offerings	Hos 9:4	8492
shall be as the *w* of Lebanon	Hos 14:7	8492
and howl, all ye drinkers of *w*	Joel 1:5	3196
because of the new *w*	Joel 1:5	6071
the new *w* is dried up, the oil	Joel 1:10	8492
I will send you corn, and *w*	Joel 2:19	8492
and the fats shall overflow with *w*	Joel 2:24	8492
an harlot, and sold a girl for *w*	Joel 3:3	3196
mountains shall drop down new *w*	Joel 3:18	6071
they drink the *w* of the condemned	Amos 2:8	3196
ye gave the Nazarites *w* to drink	Amos 2:12	3196
but ye shall not drink *w* of them	Amos 5:11	3196
That drink *w* in bowls, and anoint	Amos 6:6	3196
the mountains shall drop sweet *w*	Amos 9:13	6071
vineyards, and drink the *w* thereof	Amos 9:14	3196
I will prophesy unto thee of *w*	Mic 2:11	3196
with oil; and sweet *w*	Mic 6:15	8492
but shalt not drink *w*	Mic 6:15	3196
because he transgresseth by *w*	Hab 2:5	3196
but not drink the *w* thereof	Zeph 1:13	3196
upon the corn, and upon the new *w*	Hag 1:11	8492
do touch bread, or pottage, or *w*	Hag 2:12	3196
and make a noise as through *w*	Zec 9:15	3196
men cheerful, and new *w* the maids	Zec 9:17	8492
heart shall rejoice as through *w*	Zec 10:7	3196
do men put new *w* into old bottles	Mt 9:17	*3631*
the *w* runneth out, and the bottles	Mt 9:17	*3631*
they put new *w* into new bottles	Mt 9:17	*3631*
putteth new *w* into old bottles	Mk 2:22	*3631*
else the new *w* doth burst the	Mk 2:22	*3631*
the *w* is spilled, and the bottles	Mk 2:22	*3631*
but new *w* must be put into new	Mk 2:22	*3631*
him to drink *w* mingled with myrrh	Mk 15:23	*3631*
drink neither *w* nor strong drink	Lk 1:15	*3631*
putteth new *w* into old bottles	Lk 5:37	*3631*
else the new *w* will burst the	Lk 5:37	*3631*
But new *w* must be put into new	Lk 5:38	*3631*
old *w* straightway desireth new	Lk 5:39	*3631*
eating bread nor drinking *w*	Lk 7:33	*3631*
his wounds, pouring in oil and *w*	Lk 10:34	*3631*
And when they wanted *w*, the mother	Jn 2:3	*3631*
saith unto him, They have no *w*	Jn 2:3	*3631*
tasted the water that was made *w*	Jn 2:9	*3631*
beginning doth set forth good *w*	Jn 2:10	*3631*
hast kept the good *w* until now	Jn 2:10	*3631*
where he made the water *w*	Jn 4:46	*3631*
said, These men are full of new *w*	Acts 2:13	*1098*
to eat flesh, nor to drink *w*	Rom 14:21	*3631*
And be not drunk with *w*, wherein	Eph 5:18	*3631*
Not given to *w*, no striker, not	1Ti 3:3	*3943*
not given to much *w*, not greedy	1Ti 3:8	*3631*
but use a little *w* for thy	1Ti 5:23	*3631*
not soon angry, not given to *w*	Titus 1:7	*3943*
accusers, not given to much *w*	Titus 2:3	*3631*
lusts, excess of *w*, revellings,	1Pet 4:3	*3632*
thou hurt not the oil and the *w*	Rev 6:6	*3631*
made all nations drink of the *w*	Rev 14:8	*3631*
of the *w* of the wrath of God	Rev 14:10	*3631*
w of the fierceness of his wrath	Rev 16:19	*3631*
with the *w* of her fornication	Rev 17:2	*3631*
all nations have drunk of the *w*	Rev 18:3	*3631*
ointments, and frankincense, and *w*	Rev 18:13	*3631*

WINEBIBBER

Behold a man gluttonous, and a *w*	Mt 11:19	*3630*
Behold a gluttonous man, and a *w*	Lk 7:34	

WINEBIBBERS

Be not among *w*	Prov 23:20	5433,3196

WINEFAT

like him that treadeth in the *w*	Is 63:2	1660
it, and digged a place for the *w*	Mk 12:1	*5276*

WINEPRESS

and as the fulness of the *w*	Num 18:27	3342
and as the increase of the *w*	Num 18:30	3342
out of thy floor, and out of thy *w*	Deut 15:14	3342
Gideon threshed wheat by the *w*	Judg 6:11	1660
Zeeb they slew at the *w* of Zeeb	Judg 7:25	3342
of the barnfloor, or out of the *w*	2Kin 6:27	3342
of it, and also made a *w* therein	Is 5:2	3342
I have trodden the *w* alone	Is 63:3	6333

the daughter of Judah, as in a *w*	Lam 1:15	1660
the *w* shall not feed them, and the	Hos 9:2	3342
round about, and digged a *w* in it	Mt 21:33	3025
the great *w* of the wrath of God	Rev 14:19	3025
the *w* was trodden without the	Rev 14:20	3025
city, and blood came out of the *w*	Rev 14:20	3025
and he treadeth the *w* of the	Rev 19:15	3025,3631

WINEPRESSES

some treading *w* on the sabbath	Neh 13:15	1660
their walls, and tread their *w*	Job 24:11	3342
caused wine to fail from the *w*	Jer 48:33	3342
of Hananeel unto the king's *w*	Zec 14:10	3342

WINES

a feast of *w* on the lees, of fat	Is 25:6	8105
of *w* on the lees well refined	Is 25:6	8105

WING

was the one *w* of the cherub	1Kin 6:24	3671
cubits the other *w* of the cherub	1Kin 6:24	3671
the uttermost part of the one *w*	1Kin 6:24	3671
so that the *w* of the one touched	1Kin 6:27	3671
the *w* of the other cherub touched	1Kin 6:27	3671
one *w* of the one cherub was five	2Chr 3:11	3671
the other *w* was likewise five	2Chr 3:11	3671
reaching to the *w* of the other	2Chr 3:11	3671
one *w* of the other cherub was	2Chr 3:12	3671
the other *w* was five cubits also,	2Chr 3:12	3671
joining to the *w* of the other	2Chr 3:12	3671
there was none that moved the *w*	Is 10:14	3671
shall dwell all fowl of every *w*	Eze 17:23	3671

WINGED

every *w* fowl after his kind	Gen 1:21	3671
the likeness of any *w* fowl that	Deut 4:17	3671

WINGS

and how I bare you on eagles' *w*	Ex 19:4	3671
stretch forth their *w* on high	Ex 25:20	3671
the mercy seat with their *w*	Ex 25:20	3671
spread out their *w* on high	Ex 37:9	3671
covered with their *w* over the	Ex 37:9	3671
cleave it with the *w* thereof	Lev 1:17	3671
her young, spreadeth abroad her *w*	Deut 32:11	3671
them, beareth them on her *w*	Deut 32:11	84
under whose *w* thou art come to	Ruth 2:12	3671
was seen upon the *w* of the wind	2Sa 22:11	3671
forth the *w* of the cherubims	1Kin 6:27	3671
their *w* touched one another in	1Kin 6:27	3671
even under the *w* of the cherubims	1Kin 8:6	3671
spread forth their two *w* over the	1Kin 8:7	3671
that spread out their *w*, and	1Chr 28:18	
the *w* of the cherubims were	2Chr 3:11	3671
The *w* of these cherubims spread	2Chr 3:13	3671
even under the *w* of the cherubims	2Chr 5:7	3671
their *w* over the place of the ark	2Chr 5:8	3671
the goodly *w* unto the peacocks	Job 39:13	3671
or *w* and feathers unto the ostrich	Job 39:13	34
stretch her *w* toward the south	Job 39:26	3671
hide me under the shadow of thy *w*	Ps 17:8	3671
he did fly upon the *w* of the wind	Ps 18:10	3671
trust under the shadow of thy *w*	Ps 36:7	3671
said, Oh that I had *w* like a dove	Ps 55:6	83
in the shadow of thy *w* will I	Ps 57:1	3671
will trust in the covert of thy *w*	Ps 61:4	3671
shadow of thy *w* will I rejoice	Ps 63:7	3671
yet shall ye be as the *w* of a	Ps 68:13	3671
under his *w* shalt thou trust	Ps 91:4	3671
walketh upon the *w* of the wind	Ps 104:3	3671
If I take the *w* of the morning,	Ps 139:9	3671
certainly make themselves *w*	Prov 23:5	3671
that which hath *w* shall tell the	Eccl 10:20	3671
each one had six *w*	Is 6:2	3671
the stretching out of his *w* shall	Is 8:8	3671
Woe to the land shadowing with *w*	Is 18:1	3671
shall mount up with *w* as eagles	Is 40:31	83
Give *w* unto Moab, that it may	Jer 48:9	6731
and shall spread his *w* over Moab	Jer 48:40	3671
and spread his *w* over Bozrah	Jer 49:22	3671
faces, and every one had four *w*	Eze 1:6	3671
under their *w* on their four sides	Eze 1:8	3671
four had their faces and their *w*	Eze 1:8	3671
Their *w* were joined one to	Eze 1:9	3671
their *w* were stretched upward	Eze 1:11	3671
two *w* of every one were joined	Eze 1:11	3671
firmament were their *w* straight	Eze 1:23	3671
I heard the noise of their *w*	Eze 1:24	3671
they stood, they let down their *w*	Eze 1:24	3671
stood, and had let down their *w*	Eze 1:25	3671
w of the living creatures that	Eze 3:13	3671
w was heard even to the outer	Eze 10:5	3671
of a man's hand under their *w*	Eze 10:8	3671

backs, and their hands, and their *w*	Eze 10:12	3671
w to mount up from the earth	Eze 10:16	3671
the cherubims lifted up their *w*	Eze 10:19	3671
faces apiece, and every one four *w*	Eze 10:21	3671
hands of a man was under their *w*	Eze 10:21	3671
did the cherubims lift up their *w*	Eze 11:22	3671
A great eagle with great *w*	Eze 17:3	3671
another great eagle with great *w*	Eze 17:7	3671
was like a lion, and had eagle's *w*	Dan 7:4	1611
I beheld till the *w* thereof were	Dan 7:4	1611
the back of it four *w* of a fowl	Dan 7:6	1611
wind hath bound her up in her *w*	Hos 4:19	3671
women, and the wind was in their *w*	Zec 5:9	3671
had *w* like the *w* of a stork	Zec 5:9	3671
arise with healing in his *w*	Mal 4:2	3671
her chickens under her *w*, and ye	Mt 23:37	4420
doth gather her brood under her *w*	Lk 13:34	4420
had each of them six *w* about him	Rev 4:8	4420
the sound of their *w* was as the	Rev 9:9	4420
were given two *w* of a great eagle	Rev 12:14	4420

WINK

and what do thy eyes *w* at,	Job 15:12	7335
neither let them *w* with the eye	Ps 35:19	7169

WINKED

times of this ignorance God *w* at	Acts 17:30	5237

WINKETH

He *w* with his eyes, he speaketh	Prov 6:13	7169
He that *w* with the eye causeth	Prov 10:10	7169

WINNETH

and he that *w* souls is wise	Prov 11:30	3947

WINNOWED

which hath been *w* with the shovel	Is 30:24	2219

WINNOWETH

he *w* barley to night in the	Ruth 3:2	2219

WINTER

and cold and heat, and summer and *w*	Gen 8:22	2779
thou hast made summer and *w*	Ps 74:17	2779
the *w* is past, the rain is over	Song 2:11	5638
of the earth shall *w* upon them	Is 18:6	2778
I will smite the *w* house with the	Amos 3:15	2779
in summer and in *w* shall it be	Zec 14:8	2778
that your flight be not in the *w*	Mt 24:20	5494
that your flight be not in the *w*	Mk 13:18	5494
of the dedication, and it was *w*	Jn 10:22	5494
haven was not commodious to *w* in	Acts 27:12	3915
attain to Phenice, and there to *w*	Acts 27:12	3914
w with you, that ye may bring me	1Cor 16:6	3914
Do thy diligence to come before *w*	2Ti 4:21	5494
for I have determined there to *w*	Titus 3:12	3914

WINTERED

which had *w* in the isle, whose	Acts 28:11	3916

WINTERHOUSE

sat in the *w* in the ninth month	Jer 36:22	2779

WIPE

I will *w* Jerusalem as a man	2Kin 21:13	4229
w not out my good deeds that I	Neh 13:14	4229
the Lord GOD will *w* away tears	Is 25:8	4229
did *w* them with the hairs of her	Lk 7:38	1591
on us, we do *w* off against you	Lk 10:11	631
feet, and to *w* them with the towel	Jn 13:5	1591
God shall *w* away all tears from	Rev 7:17	1813
God shall *w* away all tears from	Rev 21:4	1813

WIPED

his reproach shall not be *w* away	Prov 6:33	4229
w* them with the hairs of her head	Lk 7:44	1591
w his feet with her hair, whose	Jn 11:2	1591
and *w* his feet with her hair	Jn 12:3	1591

WIPETH

wipe Jerusalem as a man *w* a dish	2Kin 21:13	4229
w her mouth, and saith, I have	Prov 30:20	4229

WIPING

w it, and turning it upside down	2Kin 21:13	4229

WIRES

thin plates, and cut it into *w*	Ex 39:3	6616

WISDOM

have filled with the spirit of *w*	Ex 28:3	2451
him with the spirit of God, in *w*	Ex 31:3	2451
are wise hearted I have put in *w*	Ex 31:6	2451
them up in *w* spun goats' hair	Ex 35:26	2451
him with the spirit of God, in *w*	Ex 35:31	2451
hath he filled with *w* of heart	Ex 35:35	2451
man, in whom the LORD put *w*	Ex 36:1	2451
in whose heart the LORD had put *w*	Ex 36:2	2451
for this is your *w* and your	Deut 4:6	2451

Nun was full of the spirit of *w*	Deut 34:9	2451
according to the *w* of an angel of	2Sa 14:20	2451
went unto all the people in her *w*	2Sa 20:22	2451
Do therefore according to thy *w*	1Kin 2:6	2451
saw that the *w* of God was in him	1Kin 3:28	2451
And God gave Solomon *w* and	1Kin 4:29	2451
Solomon's *w* excelled the	1Kin 4:30	2451
country, and all the *w* of Egypt	1Kin 4:30	2451
people to hear the *w* of Solomon	1Kin 4:34	2451
earth, which had heard of his *w*	1Kin 4:34	2451
And the LORD gave Solomon *w*	1Kin 5:12	2451
and he was filled with *w*, and	1Kin 7:14	2451
of Sheba had seen all Solomon's *w*	1Kin 10:4	2451
own land of thy acts and of thy *w*	1Kin 10:6	2451
thy *w* and prosperity exceedeth the	1Kin 10:7	2451
before thee, and that hear thy *w*	1Kin 10:8	2451
of the earth for riches and for *w*	1Kin 10:23	2451
sought to Solomon, to hear his *w*	1Kin 10:24	2451
and all that he did, and his *w*	1Kin 11:41	2451
Only the LORD give thee *w*	1Chr 22:12	7922
Give me now *w* and knowledge, that	2Chr 1:10	2451
but hast asked *w* and knowledge for	2Chr 1:11	2451
W and knowledge is granted unto	2Chr 1:12	2451
Sheba had seen the *w* of Solomon	2Chr 9:3	2451
land of thine acts, and of thy *w*	2Chr 9:5	2451
of thy *w* was not told me	2Chr 9:6	2451
before thee, and hear thy *w*	2Chr 9:7	2451
kings of the earth in riches and *w*	2Chr 9:22	2451
of Solomon, to hear his *w*	2Chr 9:23	2451
after the *w* of thy God, that is	Ezr 7:25	2452
they die, even without *w*	Job 4:21	2451
is *w* driven quite from me	Job 6:13	8454
would shew thee the secrets of *w*	Job 11:6	2451
people, and *w* shall die with you	Job 12:2	2451
With the ancient is *w*	Job 12:12	2451
With him is *w* and strength, he	Job 12:13	2451
With him is strength and *w*	Job 12:16	8454
and it should be your *w*	Job 13:5	2451
dost thou restrain *w* to thyself	Job 15:8	2451
thou counseled him that hath no *w*	Job 26:3	2451
But where shall *w* be found	Job 28:12	2451
the price of *w* is above rubies	Job 28:18	2451
Whence then cometh *w*	Job 28:20	2451
the fear of the LORD, that is *w*	Job 28:28	2451
multitude of years should teach *w*	Job 32:7	2451
should say, We have found out *w*	Job 32:13	2451
peace, and I shall teach thee *w*	Job 33:33	2451
and his words were without *w*	Job 34:35	7919
he is mighty in strength and *w*	Job 36:5	3820
Who hath put *w* in the inward	Job 38:36	2451
Who can number the clouds in *w*	Job 38:37	2451
God hath deprived her of *w*	Job 39:17	2451
Doth the hawk fly by thy *w*	Job 39:26	998
mouth of the righteous speaketh *w*	Ps 37:30	2451
My mouth shall speak of *w*	Ps 49:3	2454
part thou shalt make me to know *w*	Ps 51:6	2451
we may apply our hearts unto *w*	Ps 90:12	2451
In *w* hast thou made them all	Ps 104:24	2451
and teach his senators *w*	Ps 105:22	2449
of the LORD is the beginning of *w*	Ps 111:10	2451
To him that by *w* made the heavens	Ps 136:5	8394
To know *w* and instruction	Prov 1:2	2451
To receive the instruction of *w*	Prov 1:3	7919
but fools despise *w* and	Prov 1:7	2451
W crieth without	Prov 1:20	2454
thou incline thine ear unto *w*	Prov 2:2	2451
For the LORD giveth *w*	Prov 2:6	2451
up sound *w* for the righteous	Prov 2:7	8454
When *w* entereth into thine heart,	Prov 2:10	2451
Happy is the man that findeth *w*	Prov 3:13	2451
The LORD by *w* hath founded the	Prov 3:19	2451
keep sound *w* and discretion	Prov 3:21	8454
Get *w*, get understanding	Prov 4:5	2451
W is the principal thing	Prov 4:7	2451
therefore get *w*	Prov 4:7	2451
have taught thee in the way of *w*	Prov 4:11	2451
My son, attend unto my *w*, and bow	Prov 5:1	2451
Say unto *w*, Thou art my sister	Prov 7:4	2451
Doth not *w* cry	Prov 8:1	2451
O ye simple, understand *w*	Prov 8:5	6195
For *w* is better than rubies	Prov 8:11	2451
I *w* dwell with prudence, and find	Prov 8:12	2451
Counsel is mine, and sound *w*	Prov 8:14	8454
W hath builded her house, she	Prov 9:1	2454
of the LORD is the beginning of *w*	Prov 9:10	2451
hath understanding *w* is found	Prov 10:13	2451
but fools die for want of *w*	Prov 10:21	3820
but a man of understanding hath *w*	Prov 10:23	2451
of the just bringeth forth *w*	Prov 10:31	2451
but with the lowly is *w*	Prov 11:2	2451
He that is void of *w* despiseth	Prov 11:12	3820

be commended according to his *w*	Prov 12:8	7922
but with the well advised is *w*	Prov 13:10	2451
A scorner seeketh *w*, and findeth	Prov 14:6	2451
The *w* of the prudent is to	Prov 14:8	2451
W resteth in the heart of him	Prov 14:33	2451
joy to him that is destitute of *w*	Prov 15:21	3820
the LORD is the instruction of *w*	Prov 15:33	2451
better is it to get *w* than gold	Prov 16:16	2451
in the hand of a fool to get *w*	Prov 17:16	2451
W is before him that hath	Prov 17:24	2451
and intermeddleth with all *w*	Prov 18:1	8454
the wellspring of *w* as a flowing	Prov 18:4	2451
He that getteth *w* loveth his own	Prov 19:8	3820
There is no *w* nor understanding	Prov 21:30	2451
cease from thine own *w*	Prov 23:4	998
will despise the *w* of thy words	Prov 23:9	7922
also *w*, and instruction, and	Prov 23:23	2451
Through *w* is an house builded	Prov 24:3	2451
W is too high for a fool	Prov 24:7	2454
knowledge of *w* be unto thy soul	Prov 24:14	2451
Whoso loveth *w* rejoiceth his	Prov 29:3	2451
The rod and reproof give *w*	Prov 29:15	2451
I neither learned *w*, nor have the	Prov 30:3	2451
She openeth her mouth with *w*	Prov 31:26	2451
search out by *w* concerning all	Eccl 1:13	2451
have gotten more *w* than all they	Eccl 1:16	2451
heart had great experience of *w*	Eccl 1:16	2451
And I gave my heart to know *w*	Eccl 1:17	2451
For in much *w* is much grief	Eccl 1:18	2451
yet acquainting mine heart with *w*	Eccl 2:3	2451
also my *w* remained with me	Eccl 2:9	2451
And I turned myself to behold *w*	Eccl 2:12	2451
Then I saw that *w* excelleth folly	Eccl 2:13	2451
is a man whose labour is in *w*	Eccl 2:21	2451
a man that is good in his sight *w*	Eccl 2:26	2451
W is good with an inheritance	Eccl 7:11	2451
For *w* is a defence, and money is a	Eccl 7:12	2451
that *w* giveth life to them that	Eccl 7:12	2451
W strengtheneth the wise more	Eccl 7:19	2451
All this have I proved by *w*	Eccl 7:23	2451
and to search, and to seek out *w*	Eccl 7:25	2451
a man's *w* maketh his face to	Eccl 8:1	2451
I applied mine heart to know *w*	Eccl 8:16	2451
nor device, nor knowledge, nor *w*	Eccl 9:10	2451
This *w* have I seen also under the	Eccl 9:13	2451
he by his *w* delivered the city	Eccl 9:15	2451
W is better than strength	Eccl 9:16	2451
the poor man's *w* is despised	Eccl 9:16	2451
W is better than weapons of war	Eccl 9:18	2451
him that is in reputation for *w*	Eccl 10:1	2451
his *w* faileth him, and he saith to	Eccl 10:3	3820
but *w* is profitable to direct	Eccl 10:10	2451
hand I have done it, and by my *w*	Is 10:13	2451
rest upon him, the spirit of *w*	Is 11:2	2451
for the *w* of their wise men shall	Is 29:14	2451
And *w* and knowledge shall be the	Is 33:6	2451
Thy *w* and thy knowledge, it hath	Is 47:10	2451
and what *w* is in them	Jer 8:9	2451
not the wise man glory in his *w*	Jer 9:23	2451
established the world by his *w*	Jer 10:12	2451
Is *w* no more in Teman	Jer 49:7	2451
is their *w* vanished	Jer 49:7	2451
established the world by his *w*	Jer 51:15	2451
With thy *w* and with thine	Eze 28:4	2451
By thy great *w* and by thy traffick	Eze 28:5	2451
against the beauty of thy *w*	Eze 28:7	2451
sealest up the sum, full of *w*	Eze 28:12	2451
thou hast corrupted thy *w* by	Eze 28:17	2451
favoured, and skilful in all *w*	Dan 1:4	2451
and skill in all learning and *w*	Dan 1:17	2451
And in all matters of *w* and	Dan 1:20	2451
w to Arioch the captain of the	Dan 2:14	2942
for *w* and might are his	Dan 2:20	2452
he giveth *w* unto the wise, and	Dan 2:21	2452
my fathers, who hast given me *w*	Dan 2:23	2452
any *w* that I have more than any	Dan 2:30	2452
light and understanding and *w*	Dan 5:11	2452
like the *w* of the gods, was found	Dan 5:11	2452
excellent *w* is found in thee	Dan 5:14	2452
the man of *w* shall see thy name	Mic 6:9	8454
But *w* is justified of her	Mt 11:19	4678
earth to hear the *w* of Solomon	Mt 12:42	4678
said, Whence hath this man this *w*	Mt 13:54	4678
what *w* is this which is given	Mk 6:2	4678
disobedient to the *w* of the just	Lk 1:17	5428
strong in spirit, filled with *w*	Lk 2:40	4678
And Jesus increased in *w* and	Lk 2:52	4678
But *w* is justified of all her	Lk 7:35	4678
earth to hear the *w* of Solomon	Lk 11:31	4678
Therefore also said the *w* of God	Lk 11:49	4678
For I will give you a mouth and *w*	Lk 21:15	4678

full of the Holy Ghost and *w*	Acts 6:3	4678
were not able to resist the *w*	Acts 6:10	4678
w in the sight of Pharaoh king of	Acts 7:10	4678
in all the *w* of the Egyptians	Acts 7:22	4678
depth of the riches both of the *w*	Rom 11:33	4678
not with *w* of words, lest the	1Cor 1:17	4678
I will destroy the *w* of the wise	1Cor 1:19	4678
made foolish the *w* of this world	1Cor 1:20	4678
For after that in the *w* of God	1Cor 1:21	4678
God the world by *w* knew not God	1Cor 1:21	4678
sign, and the Greeks seek after *w*	1Cor 1:22	4678
the power of God, and the *w* of God	1Cor 1:24	4678
who of God is made unto us *w*	1Cor 1:30	4678
with excellency of speech or of *w*	1Cor 2:1	4678
with enticing words of man's *w*	1Cor 2:4	4678
should not stand in the *w* of men	1Cor 2:5	4678
Howbeit we speak *w* among them	1Cor 2:6	4678
yet not the *w* of this world, nor	1Cor 2:6	4678
But we speak the *w* of God in a	1Cor 2:7	4678
in a mystery, even the hidden *w*	1Cor 2:7	4678
the words which man's *w* teacheth	1Cor 2:13	4678
For the *w* of this world is	1Cor 3:19	4678
given by the Spirit the word of *w*	1Cor 12:8	4678
sincerity, not with fleshly *w*	2Cor 1:12	4678
hath abounded toward us in all *w*	Eph 1:8	4678
may give unto you the spirit of *w*	Eph 1:17	4678
the church the manifold *w* of God	Eph 3:10	4678
knowledge of his will in all *w*	Col 1:9	4678
and teaching every man in all *w*	Col 1:28	4678
are hid all the treasures of *w*	Col 2:3	4678
a shew of *w* in will worship	Col 2:23	4678
dwell in you richly in all *w*	Col 3:16	4678
Walk in *w* toward them that are	Col 4:5	4678
If any of you lack *w*, let him ask	Jas 1:5	4678
his works with meekness of *w*	Jas 3:13	4678
This *w* descendeth not from above,	Jas 3:15	4678
But the *w* that is from above is	Jas 3:17	4678
Paul also according to the *w*	2Pet 3:15	4678
to receive power, and riches, and *w*	Rev 5:12	4678
Blessing, and glory, and *w*, and	Rev 7:12	4678
Here is *w*	Rev 13:18	4678
And here is the mind which hath *w*	Rev 17:9	4678

WISE

tree to be desired to make one *w*	Gen 3:6	7919
Egypt, and all the *w* men thereof	Gen 41:8	2450
look out a man discreet and *w*	Gen 41:33	2450
none so discreet and *w* as thou art	Gen 41:39	2450
Pharaoh also called the *w* men	Ex 7:11	2450
If thou afflict them in any *w*	Ex 22:23	6031
for the gift blindeth the *w*	Ex 23:8	6493
speak unto all that are *w* hearted	Ex 28:3	2450
are *w* hearted I have put wisdom	Ex 31:6	2450
every *w* hearted among you shall	Ex 35:10	2450
all the women that were *w* hearted	Ex 35:25	2450
every *w* hearted man, in whom the	Ex 36:1	2450
every *w* hearted man, in whose	Ex 36:2	2450
And all the *w* men, that wrought	Ex 36:4	2450
every *w* hearted man among them	Ex 36:8	2450
but ye shall in no *w* eat of it	Lev 7:24	
thou shalt in any *w* rebuke thy	Lev 19:17	3198
the field will in any *w* redeem it	Lev 27:19	
On this *w* ye shall bless	Num 6:23	
Take you *w* men, and understanding,	Deut 1:13	2450
w men, and known, and made them	Deut 1:15	2450
Surely this great nation is a *w*	Deut 4:6	2450
gift doth blind the eyes of the *w*	Deut 16:19	2450
Thou shalt in any *w* set him king	Deut 17:15	
shalt in any *w* bury him that day	Deut 21:23	
shalt in any *w* let the dam go	Deut 22:7	
O that they were *w*, that they	Deut 32:29	2449
in any *w* keep yourselves from the	Josh 6:18	
Else if ye do in any *w* go back	Josh 23:12	
Her *w* ladies answered her, yea,	Judg 5:29	2450
but in any *w* return him a	1Sa 6:3	
and fetched thence a *w* woman	2Sa 14:2	2450
and my lord is *w*, according to the	2Sa 14:20	2450
Then cried a *w* woman out of the	2Sa 20:16	2450
for thou art a *w* man, and knowest	1Kin 2:9	2450
lo, I have given thee a *w*	1Kin 3:12	2450
living child, and in no *w* slay it	1Kin 3:26	
living child, and in no *w* slay it	1Kin 3:27	
a *w* son over this great people	1Kin 5:7	2450
howbeit let me go in any *w*	1Kin 11:22	
a *w* counsellor, they cast lots	1Chr 26:14	7922
counsellor, a *w* man, and a scribe	1Chr 27:32	995
given to David the king a *w* son	2Chr 2:12	2450
Then the king said to the *w* men	Est 1:13	2450
Then said his *w* men and Zeresh his	Est 6:13	2450
He taketh the *w* in their own	Job 5:13	2450
He is *w* in heart, and mighty in	Job 9:4	2450

For vain man would be *w*, though	Job 11:12	3823
Should a *w* man utter vain	Job 15:2	2450
Which *w* men have told from their	Job 15:18	2450
I cannot find one *w* man among you	Job 17:10	2450
as he that is *w* may be profitable	Job 22:2	7919
Great men are not always *w*	Job 32:9	2449
Hear my words, O ye *w* men	Job 34:2	2450
let a *w* man hearken unto me	Job 34:34	2450
not any that are *w* of heart	Job 37:24	2450
Be *w* now therefore, O ye kings	Ps 2:10	7919
LORD is sure, making *w* the simple	Ps 19:7	2449
he hath left off to be *w*, and to	Ps 36:3	7919
not thyself in any *w* to do evil	Ps 37:8	
For he seeth that *w* men die	Ps 49:10	2450
and ye fools, when will ye be *w*	Ps 94:8	7919
Whoso is *w*, and will observe these	Ps 107:43	2450
A *w* man will hear, and will	Prov 1:5	2450
shall attain unto *w* counsels	Prov 1:5	
the words of the *w*, and their dark	Prov 1:6	2450
Be not *w* in thine own eyes	Prov 3:7	2450
The *w* shall inherit glory	Prov 3:35	2450
consider her ways, and be *w*	Prov 6:6	2449
Hear instruction, and be *w*	Prov 8:33	2449
rebuke a *w* man, and he will love	Prov 9:8	2450
Give instruction to a *w* man	Prov 9:9	2450
If thou be *w*, thou shalt	Prov 9:12	2449
thou shalt be *w* for thyself	Prov 9:12	2449
A *w* son maketh a glad father	Prov 10:1	2450
gathereth in summer is a *w* son	Prov 10:5	7919
The *w* in heart will receive	Prov 10:8	2450
W men lay up knowledge	Prov 10:14	2450
he that refraineth his lips is *w*	Prov 10:19	7919
be servant to the *w* of heart	Prov 11:29	2450
and he that winneth souls is *w*	Prov 11:30	2450
that hearkeneth unto counsel is *w*	Prov 12:15	2450
but the tongue of the *w* is health	Prov 12:18	2450
A *w* son heareth his father's	Prov 13:1	2450
The law of the *w* is a fountain of	Prov 13:14	2450
walketh with *w* men shall	Prov 13:20	2450
men shall be *w*	Prov 13:20	2449
Every *w* woman buildeth her house	Prov 14:1	2454
lips of the *w* shall preserve them	Prov 14:3	2450
A *w* man feareth, and departeth	Prov 14:16	2450
crown of the *w* is their riches	Prov 14:24	2450
favour is toward a *w* servant	Prov 14:35	7919
The tongue of the *w* useth	Prov 15:2	2450
The lips of the *w* disperse	Prov 15:7	2450
neither will he go unto the *w*	Prov 15:12	2450
A *w* son maketh a glad father	Prov 15:20	2450
The way of life is above to the *w*	Prov 15:24	7919
of life abideth among the *w*	Prov 15:31	2450
but a *w* man will pacify it	Prov 16:14	2450
The *w* in heart shall be called	Prov 16:21	2450
The heart of the *w* teacheth his	Prov 16:23	2450
A *w* servant shall have rule over	Prov 17:2	7919
a *w* man than an hundred stripes	Prov 17:10	995
holdeth his peace, is counted *w*	Prov 17:28	2450
and the ear of the *w* seeketh	Prov 18:15	2450
mayest be *w* in thy latter end	Prov 19:20	2449
is deceived thereby is not *w*	Prov 20:1	2449
A *w* king scattereth the wicked,	Prov 20:26	2450
is punished, the simple is made *w*	Prov 21:11	2449
when the *w* is instructed, he	Prov 21:11	2450
and oil in the dwelling of the *w*	Prov 21:20	2450
A *w* man scaleth the city of the	Prov 21:22	2450
ear, and hear the words of the *w*	Prov 22:17	2450
My son, if thine heart be *w*	Prov 23:15	2449
Hear thou, my son, and be *w*	Prov 23:19	2449
he that begetteth a *w* child shall	Prov 23:24	2450
A *w* man is strong	Prov 24:5	2450
For by *w* counsel thou shalt make	Prov 24:6	
These things also belong to the *w*	Prov 24:23	2450
so is a *w* reprover upon an	Prov 25:12	2450
lest he be *w* in his own conceit	Prov 26:5	2450
Seest thou a man *w* in his own	Prov 26:12	2450
My son, be *w*, and make my heart	Prov 27:11	2449
Whoso keepeth the law is a *w* son	Prov 28:7	995
The rich man is *w* in his own	Prov 28:11	2450
but *w* men turn away wrath	Prov 29:8	2450
If a *w* man contendeth with a	Prov 29:9	2450
but a *w* man keepeth it in till	Prov 29:11	2450
earth, but they are exceeding *w*	Prov 30:24	2450
The *w* man's eyes are in his head	Eccl 2:14	2450
and why was I then more *w*	Eccl 2:15	2449
w more than of the fool for ever	Eccl 2:16	2450
And how dieth the *w* man	Eccl 2:16	2450
he shall be a *w* man or a fool	Eccl 2:19	2450
shewed myself *w* under the sun	Eccl 2:19	2449
a *w* child than an old and foolish	Eccl 4:13	2450
For what hath the *w* more than the	Eccl 6:8	2450
The heart of the *w* is in the	Eccl 7:4	2450

to hear the rebuke of the *w* .... Eccl 7:5   2450
oppression maketh a *w* man mad .... Eccl 7:7   2450
neither make thyself over *w* .... Eccl 7:16   2449
Wisdom strengtheneth the *w* more .... Eccl 7:19   2450
I said, I will be *w* .... Eccl 7:23   2449
Who is as the *w* man .... Eccl 8:1   2450
a *w* man's heart discerneth both .... Eccl 8:5   2450
though a *w* man think to know it, ... Eccl 8:17   2450
that the righteous, and the *w* .... Eccl 9:1   2450
neither yet bread to the *w* .... Eccl 9:11   2450
was found in it a poor *w* man .... Eccl 9:15   2450
The words of *w* men are heard in .... Eccl 9:17   2450
A *w* man's heart is at his right .... Eccl 10:2   2450
The words of a *w* man's mouth are .... Eccl 10:12   2450
because the preacher was *w* .... Eccl 12:9   2450
The words of the *w* are as goads .... Eccl 12:11   2450
them that are *w* in their own eyes .... Is 5:21   2450
the counsel of the *w* counsellors .... Is 19:11   2450
Pharaoh, I am the son of the *w* .... Is 19:11   2450
where are thy *w* men .... Is 19:12   2450
of their *w* men shall perish .... Is 29:14   2450
Yet he also is *w*, and will bring .... Is 31:2   2450
that turneth *w* men backward .... Is 44:25   2450
they are *w* to do evil, but to do .... Jer 4:22   2450
How do ye say, We are *w*, and the .... Jer 8:8   2450
The *w* men are ashamed, they are .... Jer 8:9   2450
Who is the *w* man, that may .... Jer 9:12   2450
Let not the *w* man glory in his .... Jer 9:23   2450
all the *w* men of the nations .... Jer 10:7   2450
priest, nor counsel from the *w* .... Jer 18:18   2450
her princes, and upon her *w* men .... Jer 50:35   2450
drunk her princes, and her *w* men .... Jer 51:57   2450
thy *w* men, O Tyrus, that were in .... Eze 27:8   2450
the *w* men thereof were in thee .... Eze 27:9   2450
destroy all the *w* men of Babylon .... Dan 2:12   2445
that the *w* men should be slain .... Dan 2:13   2445
to slay the *w* men of Babylon .... Dan 2:14   2445
the rest of the *w* men of Babylon .... Dan 2:18   2445
he giveth wisdom unto the *w* .... Dan 2:21   2445
to destroy the *w* men of Babylon .... Dan 2:24   2445
Destroy not the *w* men of Babylon .... Dan 2:24   2445
hath demanded cannot the *w* men .... Dan 2:27   2445
over all the *w* men of Babylon .... Dan 2:48   2445
the *w* men of Babylon before me .... Dan 4:6   2445
forasmuch as all the *w* men of my .... Dan 4:18   2445
said to the *w* men of Babylon, ... Dan 5:7   2445
Then came in all the king's *w* men .... Dan 5:8   2445
And now the *w* men, the astrologers ..... Dan 5:15   2445
they that be *w* shall shine as the .... Dan 12:3   7919
but the *w* shall understand .... Dan 12:10   7919
Who is *w*, and he shall understand .... Hos 14:9   2450
destroy the *w* men out of Edom .... Obad 8   2450
and Zidon, though it be very *w* .... Zec 9:2   2449
of Jesus Christ was on this *w* .... Mt 1:18   3779
there came *w* men from the east to .... Mt 2:1   3097
he had privily called the *w* men .... Mt 2:7   3097
that he was mocked of the *w* men .... Mt 2:16   3097
diligently enquired of the *w* men .... Mt 2:16   3097
shall in no *w* pass from the law .... Mt 5:18   3364
I will liken him unto a *w* man .... Mt 7:24   5429
be ye therefore *w* as serpents .... Mt 10:16   5429
he shall in no *w* lose his reward .... Mt 10:42
hast hid these things from the *w* .... Mt 11:25   4680
I in like *w* will tell you by what .... Mt 21:24
prophets, and *w* men, and scribes .... Mt 23:34   4680
w servant, whom his lord hath .... Mt 24:45   5429
And five of them were *w*, and five ...... Mt 25:2   5429
But the *w* took oil in their .... Mt 25:4   5429
And the foolish said unto the *w* .... Mt 25:8   5429
But the *w* answered, saying, Not .... Mt 25:9   5429
I will not deny thee in any *w* .... Mk 14:31
hast hid these things from the *w* .... Lk 10:21   4680
w steward, whom his lord shall .... Lk 12:42   5429
could in no *w* lift up herself .... Lk 13:11   3588,3838
child shall in no *w* enter therein .... Lk 18:17
to me I will in no *w* cast out .... Jn 6:37
on this *w* shewed he himself .... Jn 21:1   3779
And God spake on this *w*, That his .... Acts 7:6   3779
to corruption, he said on this *w* .... Acts 13:34   3779
which ye shall in no *w* believe .... Acts 13:41
both to the *w*, and to the unwise .... Rom 1:14   4680
Professing themselves to be *w* .... Rom 1:22   4680
No, in no *w*: .... Rom 3:9   3843
is of faith speaketh on this *w* .... Rom 10:6   3779
lest ye should be *w* in your own .... Rom 11:25   5429
Be not *w* in your own conceits .... Rom 12:16   5429
you *w* unto that which is good .... Rom 16:19   4680
To God only *w*, be glory through .... Rom 16:27   4680
will destroy the wisdom of the *w* 1Cor 1:19   4680
Where is the *w* 1Cor 1:20   4680
how that not many *w* men after the 1Cor 1:26   4680

of the world to confound the *w* 1Cor 1:27   4680
as a *w* masterbuilder, I have laid 1Cor 3:10   4680
you seemeth to be *w* in this world 1Cor 3:18   4680
become a fool, that he may be *w* 1Cor 3:18   4680
He taketh the *w* in their own 1Cor 3:19   4680
knoweth the thoughts of the *w* 1Cor 3:20   4680
sake, but ye are *w* in Christ 1Cor 4:10   5429
there is not a *w* man among you 1Cor 6:5   4680
I speak as to *w* men 1Cor 10:15   5429
among themselves, are not *w* 2Cor 10:12   4920
seeing ye yourselves are *w* 2Cor 11:19   5429
not as fools, but as *w*, ... Eph 5:15   4680
invisible, the only *w* God 1Ti 1:17   4680
which are able to make thee *w* 2Ti 3:15   4679
of the seventh day on this *w* .... Heb 4:4   3779
Who is a *w* man and endued with .... Jas 3:13   4680
To the only *w* God our Saviour, be .... Jude 25   4680
there shall in no *w* enter into it .... Rev 21:27   4680

WISELY

Come on, let us deal *w* with them .... Ex 1:10   2449
sent him, and behaved himself *w* 1Sa 18:5   7919
behaved himself *w* in all his ways 1Sa 18:14   7919
that he behaved himself very *w* 1Sa 18:15   7919
w than all the servants of Saul 1Sa 18:30   7919
And he dealt *w*, and dispersed of 2Chr 11:23   995
of charmers, charming never so *w* .... Ps 58:5   2449
for they shall *w* consider of his .... Ps 64:9   7919
behave myself *w* in a perfect way .... Ps 101:2   7919
a matter *w* shall find good .... Prov 16:20   7919
The righteous man *w* considereth .... Prov 21:12   7919
but whoso walketh *w*, he shall be .... Prov 28:26   2451
not enquire *w* concerning this .... Eccl 7:10   2451
steward, because he had done *w* .... Lk 16:8   5430

WISER

For he was *w* than all men 1Kin 4:31   2449
maketh us *w* than the fowls of .... Job 35:11   2449
hast made me *w* than mine enemies ...... Ps 119:98   2449
a wise man, and he will be yet *w* .... Prov 9:9   2449
The sluggard is *w* in his own .... Prov 26:16   2450
Behold, thou art *w* than Daniel .... Eze 28:3   2450
w* than the children of light .... Lk 16:8   5429
foolishness of God is *w* than men 1Cor 1:25   4680

WISH

according to thy *w* in God's stead .... Job 33:6   6310
and put to shame that *w* me evil .... Ps 40:14   2655
they have more than heart could *w* .... Ps 73:7   4906
For I could *w* that myself were .... Rom 9:3   2172
and this also we *w*, even your 2Cor 13:9   2172
I *w* above all things that thou 3Jn 2   2172

WISHED

w in himself to die, and said, It .... Jonah 4:8   7592
of the stern, and *w* for the day .... Acts 27:29   2172

WISHING

to sin by *w* a curse to his soul .... Job 31:30   7592

WIST

for they *w* not what it was .... Ex 16:15   3045
that Moses *w* not that the skin of .... Ex 34:29   3045
though he *w* it not, yet is he .... Lev 5:17   3045
w it not, and it shall be forgiven .... Lev 5:18   3045
but I *w* not whence they were .... Josh 2:4   3045
but he *w* not that there were .... Josh 8:14   3045
he *w* not that the LORD was .... Judg 16:20   3045
For he *w* not what to say .... Mk 9:6   1492
neither *w* they what to answer .... Mk 14:40   1492
w ye not that I must be about my .... Lk 2:49   1492
that was healed *w* not who it was .... Jn 5:13   1492
w not that it was true which was .... Acts 12:9   1492
I *w* not, brethren, that he was .... Acts 23:5   1492

WIT

to *w* whether the LORD had made .... Gen 24:21   3045
to *w* what would be done to him .... Ex 2:4   3045
to *w*, for Machir the firstborn of .... Josh 17:1
David not knowing thereof, to *w* 1Kin 2:32
for the doors of the house, to *w* 1Kin 7:50
he saddled for him the ass, to *w* 1Kin 13:23
not from after them, to *w* 2Kin 10:29
of their father's house, to *w* 1Chr 7:2
Israel after their number, to *w* 1Chr 27:1
To *w*, the two pillars, and the 2Chr 4:12
the LORD is not with Israel, to *w* 2Chr 25:7
Then Amaziah separated them, to *w* 2Chr 25:10
for the burnt offerings, to *w* 2Chr 31:3
possession in their cities, to *w* .... Neh 11:3
purifications accomplished, to *w* .... Est 2:12
To *w*, Jerusalem, and the cities of .... Jer 25:18
serve himself of them, to *w* .... Jer 34:9
To *w*, the prophets of Israel .... Eze 13:16

waiting for the adoption, to *w* .... Rom 8:23
To *w*, that God was in Christ, ... 2Cor 5:19 5613
we do you to *w* of the grace of 2Cor 8:1 1107

WITCH
Thou shalt not suffer a *w* to live .... Ex 22:18 3784
of times, or an enchanter, or a *w* .... Deut 18:10 3784

WITCHCRAFT
For rebellion is as the sin of *w* 1Sa 15:23 7081
and used enchantments, and used *w* 2Chr 33:6 3784
Idolatry, *w*, hatred, variance, ... Gal 5:20 5331

WITCHCRAFTS
Jezebel and her *w* are so many 2Kin 9:22 3785
I will cut off *w* out of thine .... Mic 5:12 3785
harlot, the mistress of *w* .... Nah 3:4 3785
and families through her *w* .... Nah 3:4 3785

WITH See APPENDIX.

WITHAL
and bowls thereof, to cover *w* .... Ex 25:29 2004
for the staves to bear it *w* .... Ex 30:4 1992
his foot of brass, to wash *w* .... Ex 30:18
of the sanctuary, to make it *w* .... Ex 36:3
bowls, and his covers to cover *w* .... Ex 37:16 2004
for the staves to bear it *w* .... Ex 37:27
sides of the altar, to bear it *w* .... Ex 38:7
and put water there, to wash *w* .... Ex 40:30
be that a man shall be defiled *w* .... Lev 5:3
to reconcile *w* in the holy place .... Lev 6:30
feet, to leap *w* upon the earth .... Lev 11:21 2004
be holy to praise the LORD *w* .... Lev 19:24
the bowls, and covers to cover *w* .... Num 4:7
in their right hands to blow *w* .... Judg 7:20
w of a beautiful countenance, and 1Sa 16:12 5973
w how he had slain all the 1Kin 19:1 834,3605
that Manasseh had provoked him *w* 2Kin 23:26
overlay the walls of the houses *w* 1Chr 29:4
to minister, and to offer *w* 2Chr 24:14
to shoot arrows and great stones *w* 2Chr 26:15
man *w* whom the king delighteth to .... Est 6:9
a potsherd to scrape himself *w* .... Job 2:8
own nets, whilst that I *w* escape .... Ps 141:10 3162
they shall *w* be fitted in thy .... Prov 22:18 3162
or to take water *w* out of the pit .... Is 30:14
that thou shalt sow the ground *w* .... Is 30:23
baptized *w* shall ye be baptized ...... Mk 10:39
_w_ it shall be measured to you .... Lk 6:38
not *w* to signify the crimes laid .... Acts 25:27
is given to every man to profit *w* 1Cor 12:7
W praying also for us, that God .... Col 4:3 260
And *w* they learn to be idle, ... 1Ti 5:13 260
But *w* prepare me also a lodging .... Philem 22 260

WITHDRAW
unto the priest, *W* thine hand 1Sa 14:19 622
If God will not *w* his anger .... Job 9:13 7725
W thine hand far from me .... Job 13:21 7368
That he may *w* man from his .... Job 33:17 5493
W thy foot from thy neighbour's .... Prov 25:17 3365
also from this *w* not thine hand .... Eccl 7:18 3240
neither shall thy moon *w* itself .... Is 60:20 622
the stars shall *w* their shining .... Joel 2:10 622
the stars shall *w* their shining .... Joel 3:15 622
that ye *w* yourselves from every 2Th 3:6 4724
from such *w* thyself 1Ti 6:5 868

WITHDRAWEST
Why *w* thou thy hand, even thy .... Ps 74:11 7725

WITHDRAWETH
He *w* not his eyes from the .... Job 36:7 1639

WITHDRAWN
have *w* the inhabitants of their .... Deut 13:13 5080
but my beloved had *w* himself .... Song 5:6 2559
he hath not *w* his hand from .... Lam 2:8 7725
that hath *w* his hand from .... Eze 18:8 7725
he hath *w* himself from them .... Hos 5:6 2502
he was *w* from them about a .... Lk 22:41 645

WITHDREW
w the shoulder, and hardened their Neh 9:29 5414,5437
Nevertheless I *w* mine hand .... Eze 20:22 7725
knew it, he *w* himself from thence .... Mt 12:15 402
But Jesus *w* himself with his .... Mk 3:7 402
he *w* himself into the wilderness, ... Lk 5:16 5298
but when they were come, he *w* .... Gal 2:12 5288

WITHER
his leaf also shall not *w* .... Ps 1:3 5034
the grass, and *w* as the green herb ...... Ps 37:2 5034
the reeds and flags shall *w* .... Is 19:6 7060
thing sown by the brooks, shall *w* .... Is 19:7 3001

blow upon them, and they shall *w* .... Is 40:24 3001
and the herbs of every field *w* .... Jer 12:4 3001
off the fruit thereof, that it *w* .... Eze 17:9 3001
it shall *w* in all the leaves of .... Eze 17:9 3001
shall it not utterly *w*, when the .... Eze 17:10 3001
it shall *w* in the furrows where .... Eze 17:10 3001
and the top of Carmel shall *w* .... Amos 1:2 3001

WITHERED
And, behold, seven ears, *w* .... Gen 41:23 6798
heart is smitten, and *w* like grass .... Ps 102:4 3001
and I am *w* like grass .... Ps 102:11 3001
for the hay is *w* away, the grass .... Is 15:6 3001
When the boughs thereof are *w* .... Is 27:11 3001
it is *w*, it is become like a .... Lam 4:8 3001
her strong rods were broken and *w* ...... Eze 19:12 3001
all the trees of the field, are *w* .... Joel 1:12 3001
because joy is *w* away from the .... Joel 1:12 3001
for the corn is *w* .... Joel 1:17 3001
piece whereupon it rained not *w* .... Amos 4:7 3001
and it smote the gourd that it *w* .... Jonah 4:7 3001
was a man which had his hand *w* .... Mt 12:10 3584
they had no root, they *w* away .... Mt 13:6 3583
And presently the fig tree *w* away .... Mt 21:19 3583
How soon is the fig tree *w* away .... Mt 21:20 3583
a man there which had a *w* hand .... Mk 3:1 3584
unto the man which had the *w* hand ..... Mk 3:3 3583
because it had no root, it *w* away ..... Mk 4:6 3583
which thou cursedst is *w* away .... Mk 11:21 3583
was a man whose right hand was *w* ...... Lk 6:6 3584
to the man which had the *w* hand .... Lk 6:8 3584
it *w* away, because it lacked .... Lk 8:6 3583
impotent folk, of blind, halt, *w*, ... Jn 5:3 3584
cast forth as a branch, and is *w* ...... Jn 15:6 3583

WITHERETH
it *w* before any other herb .... Job 8:12 3001
the evening it is cut down, and *w* .... Ps 90:6 3001
which *w* afore it groweth up .... Ps 129:6 3001
The grass *w*, the flower fadeth .... Is 40:7 3001
The grass *w*, the flower fadeth .... Is 40:8 3001
but it *w* the grass, and the flower .... Jas 1:11 3583
The grass *w*, and the flower 1Pet 1:24 3583
trees whose fruit *w*, without .... Jude 12 5352

WITHHELD
for I also *w* thee from sinning .... Gen 20:6 2820
seeing thou hast not *w* thy son .... Gen 22:12 2820
this thing, and hast not *w* thy son .... Gen 22:16 2820
who hath *w* from thee the fruit of .... Gen 30:2 4513
If I have *w* the poor from their .... Job 31:16 4513
I *w* not my heart from any joy .... Eccl 2:10 4513

WITHHELDEST
w not thy manna from their mouth, ... Neh 9:20 4513

WITHHOLD
none of us shall *w* from thee his .... Gen 23:6 3607
for he will not *w* me from thee 2Sa 13:13 4513
but who can *w* himself from .... Job 4:2 6113
W not thou thy tender mercies .... Ps 40:11 3607
no good thing will he *w* from them, ... Ps 84:11 4513
W not good from them to whom it .... Prov 3:27 4513
W not correction from the child .... Prov 23:13 4513
in the evening *w* not thine hand .... Eccl 11:6 3240
W thy foot from being unshod, and ...... Jer 2:25 4513

WITHHOLDEN
seeing the LORD hath *w* thee from 1Sa 25:26 4513
thou hast *w* bread from the hungry ...... Job 22:7 4513
from the wicked their light is *w* .... Job 38:15 4513
no thought can be *w* from thee, ... Job 42:2 1219
hast not *w* the request of his .... Ps 21:2 4513
Therefore the showers have been *w* ..... Jer 3:3 4513
your sins have *w* good things from .... Jer 5:25 4513
hath not *w* the pledge, neither .... Eze 18:16 2254
the drink offering is *w* from the .... Joel 1:13 4513
also I have *w* the rain from you, ... Amos 4:7 4513

WITHHOLDETH
he *w* the waters, and they dry up .... Job 12:15 6113
there is that *w* more than is meet .... Prov 11:24 4513
He that *w* corn, the people shall .... Prov 11:26 4513
now ye know what *w* that he might 2Th 2:6 2722

WITHIN See APPENDIX.

WITHOUT See APPENDIX.

WITHS
green *w* that were never dried .... Judg 16:7 3499
green *w* which had not been dried .... Judg 16:8 3499
And he brake the *w*, as a thread of .... Judg 16:9 3499

WITHSTAND
behold, I went out to *w* thee .... Num 22:32 7854
and could not *w* them 2Chr 13:7 2388

now ye think to *w* the kingdom of ....2Chr 13:8 — 2388
so that none is able to *w* thee ....2Chr 20:6 — 3320
and no man could *w* them......................Est 9:2 — 5975
against him, two shall *w* him..................Eccl 4:12 — 5975
the arms of the south shall not *w* ....Dan 11:15 — 5975
shall there be any strength to *w* ....Dan 11:15 — 5975
what was I, that I could *w* God...............Acts 11:17 — 2967
may be able to *w* in the evil day...........Eph 6:13 — 436

WITHSTOOD
they *w* Uzziah the king, and said ....2Chr 26:18 — 5975
of the kingdom of Persia *w* me one ....Dan 10:13 — 5975
name by interpretation) *w* them ....Acts 13:8 — 436
I *w* him to the face, because he ....Gal 2:11 — 436
Now as Jannes and Jambres *w* Moses...2Ti 3:8 — 436
for he hath greatly *w* our words ....2Ti 4:15 — 436

WITNESS
that they may be a *w* unto me ....Gen 21:30 — 5713
and let it be for a *w* between me ....Gen 31:44 — 5707
said, This heap is a *w* between me ....Gen 31:48 — 5707
God is *w* betwixt me and thee ....Gen 31:50 — 5707
This heap be *w*.......................................Gen 31:52 — 5707
and this pillar be *w*.................................Gen 31:52 — 5711
false *w* against thy neighbour ....Ex 20:16 — 5707
then let him bring it for *w* ....Ex 22:13 — 5707
the wicked to be an unrighteous *w* ......Ex 23:1 — 5707
the voice of swearing, and is a *w*...........Lev 5:1 — 5707
and there be no *w* against her ....Num 5:13 — 5707
the LORD in the tabernacle of *w*............Num 17:7 — 5715
went into the tabernacle of *w*................Num 17:8 — 5715
before the tabernacle of *w*.....................Num 18:2 — 5715
but one *w* shall not testify ....Num 35:30 — 5707
earth to *w* against you this day, ...Deut 4:26 — 5749
false *w* against thy neighbour ....Deut 5:20 — 5707
but at the mouth of one *w* he ....Deut 17:6 — 5707
One *w* shall not rise up against a ....Deut 19:15 — 5707
If a false *w* rise up against any ....Deut 19:16 — 5707
if the *w* be a false *w*...........................Deut 19:18 — 5707
that this song may be a *w* for me ....Deut 31:19 — 5707
shall testify against them as a *w* ....Deut 31:21 — 5707
may be there for a *w* against thee.........Deut 31:26 — 5707
But that it may be a *w* between us ......Josh 22:27 — 5707
but it is a *w* between us and you ....Josh 22:28 — 5707
for it shall be a *w* between us ....Josh 22:34 — 5707
this stone shall be a *w* unto us ....Josh 24:27 — 5713
shall be therefore a *w* unto you ....Josh 24:27 — 5713
The LORD be *w* between us.......................Judg 11:10 — 8085
w against me before the LORD, and ....1Sa 12:3 — 6030
them, The LORD is *w* against you ....1Sa 12:5 — 5707
and his anointed is *w* this day ....1Sa 12:5 — 5707
And they answered, He is *w*...................1Sa 12:5 — 5707
to bear *w* against him, saying, ...1Kin 21:10 — 5749
Israel, for the tabernacle of *w*...............2Chr 24:6 — 5715
wrinkles, which is a *w* against me ....Job 16:8 — 5707
up in me beareth *w* to my face ....Job 16:8 — 6030
my *w* is in heaven, and my record........Job 16:19 — 5707
the eye saw me, it gave *w* to me ....Job 29:11 — 5749
and as a faithful *w* in heaven................Ps 89:37 — 5707
A false *w* that speaketh lies, and ....Prov 6:19 — 5707
but a false *w* deceit ....Prov 12:17 — 5707
A faithful *w* will not lie ....Prov 14:5 — 5707
but a false *w* will utter lies ....Prov 14:5 — 5707
A true *w* delivereth souls ....Prov 14:25 — 5707
but a deceitful *w* speaketh lies ....Prov 14:25
A false *w* shall not be unpunished ....Prov 19:5 — 5707
A false *w* shall not be unpunished ....Prov 19:9 — 5707
An ungodly *w* scorneth judgment ....Prov 19:28 — 5707
A false *w* shall perish ....Prov 21:28 — 5707
Be not a *w* against thy neighbour ....Prov 24:28 — 5707
A man that beareth false *w* ....Prov 25:18 — 5707
countenance doth *w* against them ....Is 3:9 — 5707
for a *w* unto the LORD of hosts in..........Is 19:20 — 5707
given him for a *w* to the people ....Is 55:4 — 5707
even I know, and am a *w*, saith the ....Jer 29:23 — 5707
faithful between us, if we do ....Jer 42:5 — 5707
thing shall I take to *w* for thee ....Lam 2:13 — 5749
let the Lord GOD be *w* against you........Mic 1:2 — 5707
the LORD hath been *w* between thee ......Mal 2:14 — 5749
I will be a swift *w* against the ....Mal 3:5 — 5707
fornications, thefts, false *w*................Mt 15:19 — 5577
Thou shalt not bear false *w* ....Mt 19:18 — 5576
world for a *w* unto all nations ....Mt 24:14 — 3142
sought false *w* against Jesus, to............Mt 26:59 — 5577
is it which these *w* against thee ....Mt 26:62 — 2649
many things they *w* against thee ....Mt 27:13 — 2649
Do not steal, Do not bear false *w*........Mk 10:19 — 5576
all the council sought for *w*...................Mk 14:55 — 3141
For many bare false *w* against him.......Mk 14:56 — 5576
but their *w* agreed not together ....Mk 14:56 — 3141
bare false *w* against him, saying, ...Mk 14:57 — 5576
so did their *w* agree together ....Mk 14:59 — 3141

is it which these *w* against thee ....Mk 14:60 — 2649
many things they *w* against thee ....Mk 15:4 — 2649
And all bare him *w*, and wondered at ...Lk 4:22 — 3140
Truly ye bear *w* that ye allow the ......Lk 11:48 — 3140
Do not steal, Do not bear false *w*.......Lk 18:20 — 5576
said, What need we any further *w* ....Lk 22:71 — 3141
The same came for a *w* ....Jn 1:7 — 3141
to bear *w* of the Light, that all ....Jn 1:7 — 3140
was sent to bear *w* of that Light.............Jn 1:8 — 3140
John bare *w* of him, and cried, ...Jn 1:15 — 3140
and ye receive not our *w*....................Jn 3:11 — 3141
Jordan, to whom thou barest *w* ....Jn 3:26 — 3140
Ye yourselves bear me *w*, that I ....Jn 3:28 — 3140
If I bear *w* of myself..........................Jn 5:31 — 3140
of myself, my *w* is not true ....Jn 5:31 — 3141
is another that beareth *w* of me ....Jn 5:32 — 3140
I know that the *w* which he ....Jn 5:32 — 3141
John, and he bare *w* unto the truth ......Jn 5:33 — 3140
have greater *w* than that of John ......Jn 5:36 — 3141
bear *w* of me, that the Father ....Jn 5:36 — 3140
hath sent me, hath borne *w* of me........Jn 5:37 — 3140
I am one that bear *w* of myself ....Jn 8:18 — 3140
that sent me beareth *w* of me ....Jn 8:18 — 3140
Father's name, they bear *w* of me .....Jn 10:25 — 3140
And ye also shall bear *w*, because .....Jn 15:27 — 3140
spoken evil, bear *w* of the evil ....Jn 18:23 — 3140
I should bear *w* unto the truth ....Jn 18:37 — 3140
a *w* with us of his resurrection.............Acts 1:22 — 3144
great power gave the apostles *w* ....Acts 4:33 — 3142
tabernacle of *w* in the wilderness ....Acts 7:44 — 3142
To him give all the prophets *w*.............Acts 10:43 — 3140
he left not himself without *w*...............Acts 14:17 — 267
knoweth the hearts, bare them *w*.........Acts 15:8 — 3140
the high priest doth bear me *w* ....Acts 22:5 — 3140
For thou shalt be his *w* unto all............Acts 22:15 — 3144
so must thou bear *w* also at Rome........Acts 23:11 — 3140
a *w* both of these things which ....Acts 26:16 — 3144
For God is my *w*, whom I serve ....Rom 1:9 — 3144
their conscience also bearing *w* ....Rom 2:15 — 4828
itself beareth *w* with our spirit ....Rom 8:16 — 4828
bearing me *w* in the Holy Ghost ....Rom 9:1 — 4828
Thou shalt not bear false *w* ....Rom 13:9 — 5576
God is *w*...1Th 2:5 — 3144
This *w* is true ....Titus 1:13 — 3141
God also bearing them *w*, both ....Heb 2:4 — 4901
the Holy Ghost also is a *w* to us...........Heb 10:15 — 3140
by which he obtained *w* that he............Heb 11:4 — 3140
of them shall be a *w* against you ....Jas 5:3 — 3142
a *w* of the sufferings of Christ,.............1Pet 5:1 — 3144
and we have seen it, and bear *w* ....1Jn 1:2 — 3140
it is the Spirit that beareth *w* ....1Jn 5:6 — 3140
are three that bear *w* in earth..............1Jn 5:8 — 3140
If we receive the *w* of men ....1Jn 5:9 — 3141
the *w* of God is greater..........................1Jn 5:9 — 3141
for this is the *w* of God which he ....1Jn 5:9 — 3141
Son of God hath the *w* in himself..........1Jn 5:10 — 3141
Which have borne *w* of thy charity.......3Jn 6 — 3140
Christ, who is the faithful *w*..................Rev 1:5 — 3144
the Amen, the faithful and true *w* .....Rev 3:14 — 3144
were beheaded for the *w* of Jesus.........Rev 20:4 — 3141

WITNESSED
the men of Belial *w* against him...........1Kin 21:13 — 5749
being *w* by the law and the ....Rom 3:21 — 3140
Pilate *w* a good confession ....1Ti 6:13 — 3140
of whom it is *w* that he liveth...............Heb 7:8 — 3140

WITNESSES
be put to death by the mouth of *w* ....Num 35:30 — 5707
of two *w*, or three *w* ....Deut 17:6 — 5707
The hands of the *w* shall be first ....Deut 17:7 — 5707
at the mouth of two *w*............................Deut 19:15 — 5707
or at the mouth of three *w* ....Deut 19:15 — 5707
Ye are *w* against yourselves that ....Josh 24:22 — 5707
And they said, We are *w* ....Josh 24:22 — 5707
Ye are *w* this day, that I have................Ruth 4:9 — 5707
ye are *w* this day................................Ruth 4:10 — 5707
and the elders, said, We are *w* ....Ruth 4:11 — 5707
Thou renewest thy *w* against me ....Job 10:17 — 5707
for false *w* are risen up against.............Ps 27:12 — 5707
False *w* did rise up ....Ps 35:11 — 5707
took unto me faithful *w* to record ....Is 8:2 — 5707
let them bring forth their *w* ....Is 43:9 — 5707
Ye are my *w*, saith the LORD, and ....Is 43:10 — 5707
therefore ye are my *w*, saith the ....Is 43:12 — 5707
ye are even my *w* ....Is 44:8 — 5707
and they are their own *w* ....Is 44:9 — 5707
evidence, and sealed it, and took *w*.....Jer 32:10 — 5707
in the presence of the *w* that ....Jer 32:12 — 5707
the field for money, and take *w* ....Jer 32:25 — 5707
take *w* in the land of Benjamin,............Jer 32:44 — 5707
in the mouth of two or three *w* ....Mt 18:16 — 3144

Wherefore ye be *w* unto yourselves	Mt 23:31	*3140*
yea, though many false *w* came	Mt 26:60	*5575*
At the last came two false *w*	Mt 26:60	*5575*
what further need have we of *w*	Mt 26:65	*3144*
saith, What need we any further *w*	Mk 14:63	*3144*
And ye are *w* of these things	Lk 24:48	*3144*
ye shall be *w* unto me both in	Acts 1:8	*3144*
raised up, whereof we all are *w*	Acts 2:32	*3144*
whereof we are *w*	Acts 3:15	*3144*
we are his *w* of these things	Acts 5:32	*3144*
And set up false *w*, which said,	Acts 6:13	*3144*
the *w* laid down their clothes at	Acts 7:58	*3144*
we are *w* of all things which he	Acts 10:39	*3144*
but unto *w* chosen before of God,	Acts 10:41	*3144*
who are his *w* unto the people	Acts 13:31	*3144*
and we are found false *w* of God	1Cor 15:15	*5575*
In the mouth of two or three *w*	2Cor 13:1	*3144*
Ye are *w*, and God also, how holily	1Th 2:10	*3144*
but before two or three *w*	1Ti 5:19	*3144*
a good profession before many *w*	1Ti 6:12	*3144*
hast heard of me among many *w*	2Ti 2:2	*3144*
mercy under two or three *w*	Heb 10:28	*3144*
about with so great a cloud of *w*	Heb 12:1	*3144*
I will give power unto my two *w*	Rev 11:3	*3144*

WITNESSETH

witness which he *w* of me is true	Jn 5:32	*3140*
the Holy Ghost *w* in every city	Acts 20:23	*1263*

WITNESSING

w both to small and great, saying	Acts 26:22	*3140*

WIT'S

man, and are at their *w* end	Ps 107:27	*2451*

WITTINGLY

head, guiding his hands *w*	Gen 48:14	*7919*

WITTY

out knowledge of *w* inventions	Prov 8:12	

WIVES

And Lamech took unto him two *w*	Gen 4:19	*802*
And Lamech said unto his *w*	Gen 4:23	*802*
ye *w* of Lamech, hearken unto my	Gen 4:23	*802*
they took them *w* of all which	Gen 6:2	*802*
wife, and thy sons' *w* with thee	Gen 6:18	*802*
his wife, and his sons' *w* with him	Gen 7:7	*802*
the three *w* of his sons with them	Gen 7:13	*802*
sons, and thy sons' *w* with thee	Gen 8:16	*802*
his wife, and his sons' *w* with him	Gen 8:18	*802*
And Abram and Nahor took them *w*	Gen 11:29	*802*
took unto the *w* which he had	Gen 28:9	*802*
Give me my *w* and my children, for	Gen 30:26	*802*
set his sons and his *w* upon camels	Gen 31:17	*802*
take other *w* beside my daughters	Gen 31:50	*802*
up that night, and took his two *w*	Gen 32:22	*802*
take their daughters to us for *w*	Gen 34:21	*802*
their *w* took they captive, and	Gen 34:29	*802*
Esau took his *w* of the daughters	Gen 36:2	*802*
And Esau took his *w*, and his sons,	Gen 36:6	*802*
sons of Zilpah, his father's *w*	Gen 37:2	*802*
your little ones, and for your *w*	Gen 45:19	*802*
and their little ones, and their *w*	Gen 46:5	*802*
loins, besides Jacob's sons' *w*	Gen 46:26	*802*
come not at your *w*	Ex 19:15	*802*
your *w* shall be widows, and your	Ex 22:24	*802*
which are in the ears of your *w*	Ex 32:2	*802*
to fall by the sword, that our *w*	Num 14:3	*802*
door of their tents, and their *w*	Num 16:27	*802*
Our little ones, our *w*, our	Num 32:26	*802*
But your *w*, and your little ones,	Deut 3:19	*802*
shall he multiply *w* to himself	Deut 17:17	*802*
If a man have two *w*, one beloved,	Deut 21:15	*802*
Your little ones, your *w*, and thy	Deut 29:11	*802*
Your *w*, your little ones, and your	Josh 1:14	*802*
their daughters to be their *w*	Judg 3:6	*802*
for he had many *w*	Judg 8:30	*802*
How shall we do for *w* for them	Judg 21:7	*802*
give them of our daughters to *w*	Judg 21:7	*802*
they gave them *w* which they had	Judg 21:14	*802*
How shall we do for *w* for them	Judg 21:16	*802*
not give them *w* of our daughters	Judg 21:18	*802*
Benjamin did so, and took them *w*	Judg 21:23	*802*
they took them *w* of the women of	Ruth 1:4	*802*
And he had two *w*	1Sa 1:2	*802*
they were also both of them his *w*	1Sa 25:43	*802*
even David with his two *w*	1Sa 27:3	*802*
and their *w*, and their sons, and	1Sa 30:3	*802*
David's two *w* were taken captives,	1Sa 30:5	*802*
and David rescued his two *w*	1Sa 30:18	*802*
up thither, and his two *w* also	2Sa 2:2	*802*
w out of Jerusalem, after he was	2Sa 5:13	*802*
thy master's *w* into thy bosom, and	2Sa 12:8	*802*

I will take thy *w* before thine	2Sa 12:11	*802*
he shall lie with thy *w* in the	2Sa 12:11	*802*
daughters, and the lives of thy *w*	2Sa 19:5	*802*
And he had seven hundred *w*	1Kin 11:3	*802*
his *w* turned away his heart	1Kin 11:3	*802*
that his *w* turned away his heart	1Kin 11:4	*802*
did he for all his strange *w*	1Kin 11:8	*802*
thy *w* also and thy children, even	1Kin 20:3	*802*
thy silver, and thy gold, and thy *w*	1Kin 20:5	*802*
for he sent unto me for my *w*	1Kin 20:7	*802*
the *w* of the sons of the prophets	2Kin 4:1	*802*
king's mother, and the king's *w*	2Kin 24:15	*802*
the father of Tekoa had two *w*	1Chr 4:5	*802*
for they had many *w* and sons	1Chr 7:4	*802*
Hushim and Baara were his *w*	1Chr 8:8	*802*
And David took more *w* at Jerusalem	1Chr 14:3	*802*
of Absalom above all his *w*	2Chr 11:21	*802*
(for he took eighteen *w*, and	2Chr 11:21	*802*
And he desired many *w*	2Chr 11:23	*802*
mighty, and married fourteen *w*	2Chr 13:21	*802*
with their little ones, their *w*	2Chr 20:13	*802*
people, and thy children, and thy *w*	2Chr 21:14	*802*
house, and his sons also, and his *w*	2Chr 21:17	*802*
And Jehoiada took for him two *w*	2Chr 24:3	*802*
our *w* are in captivity for this	2Chr 29:9	*802*
of all their little ones, their *w*	2Chr 31:18	*802*
have taken strange *w* of the	Ezr 10:2	*802*
our God to put away all the *w*	Ezr 10:3	*802*
and have taken strange *w*, to	Ezr 10:10	*802*
the land, and from the strange *w*	Ezr 10:11	*802*
them which have taken strange *w*	Ezr 10:14	*802*
w by the first day of the first	Ezr 10:17	*802*
found that had taken strange *w*	Ezr 10:18	*802*
that they would put away their *w*	Ezr 10:19	*802*
All these had taken strange *w*	Ezr 10:44	*802*
some of them had *w* by whom they	Ezr 10:44	*802*
sons, and your daughters, your *w*	Neh 4:14	*802*
of their *w* against their brethren	Neh 5:1	*802*
unto the law of God, their *w*	Neh 10:28	*802*
the *w* also and the children	Neh 12:43	*802*
Jews that had married *w* of Ashdod	Neh 13:23	*802*
our God in marrying strange *w*	Neh 13:27	*802*
all the *w* shall give to their	Est 1:20	*802*
be spoiled, and their *w* ravished	Is 13:16	*802*
with their fields and *w* together	Jer 6:12	*802*
will I give their *w* unto others	Jer 8:10	*802*
none to bury them, them, their *w*	Jer 14:16	*802*
let their *w* be bereaved of their	Jer 18:21	*802*
Take ye *w*, and beget sons and	Jer 29:6	*802*
take *w* for your sons, and give	Jer 29:6	*802*
adultery with their neighbours' *w*	Jer 29:23	*802*
no wine all our days, we, our *w*	Jer 35:8	*802*
So they shall bring out all thy *w*	Jer 38:23	*802*
and the wickedness of their *w*	Jer 44:9	*802*
and the wickedness of your *w*	Jer 44:9	*802*
w had burned incense unto other	Jer 44:15	*802*
your *w* have both spoken with your	Jer 44:25	*802*
they take for their *w* a widow	Eze 44:22	*802*
the king, and his princes, his *w*	Dan 5:2	*7695*
the king, and his princes, his *w*	Dan 5:3	*7695*
and thou, and thy lords, thy *w*	Dan 5:23	*7695*
them, their children, and their *w*	Dan 6:24	*5389*
of David apart, and their *w* apart	Zec 12:12	*802*
of Nathan apart, and their *w* apart	Zec 12:12	*802*
of Levi apart, and their *w* apart	Zec 12:13	*802*
of Shimei apart, and their *w* apart	Zec 12:13	*802*
family apart, and their *w* apart	Zec 12:14	*802*
suffered not to put away your *w*	Mt 19:8	*1135*
eat, they drank, they married *w*	Lk 17:27	*1135*
all brought us on our way, with *w*	Acts 21:5	*1135*
that both they that have *w* be as	1Cor 7:29	*1135*
W, submit yourselves unto your	Eph 5:22	*1135*
so let the *w* be to their own	Eph 5:24	*1135*
Husbands, love your *w*, even as	Eph 5:25	*1135*
love their *w* as their own bodies	Eph 5:28	*1135*
W, submit yourselves unto your	Col 3:18	*1135*
Husbands, love your *w*, and be not	Col 3:19	*1135*
Even so must their *w* be grave	1Ti 3:11	*1135*
Likewise, ye *w*, be in subjection	1Pet 3:1	*1135*
won by the conversation of the *w*	1Pet 3:1	*1135*

WIVES'

old *w* fables, and exercise thyself	1Ti 4:7	*1126*

WIZARD

a familiar spirit, or that is a *w*	Lev 20:27	*3049*
with familiar spirits, or a *w*	Deut 18:11	*3049*

WIZARDS

spirits, neither seek after *w*	Lev 19:31	*3049*
have familiar spirits, and after *w*	Lev 20:6	*3049*
had familiar spirits, and the *w*	1Sa 28:3	*3049*

have familiar spirits, and the *w* 1Sa 28:9   3049
dealt with familiar spirits and *w* 2Kin 21:6   3049
with familiar spirits, and the *w* 2Kin 23:24   3049
with a familiar spirit, and with *w* 2Chr 33:6   3049
unto *w* that peep, and that mutter .... Is 8:19   3049
familiar spirits, and to the *w*. .... Is 19:3   3049

WOE

W to thee, Moab.................................. Num 21:29   188
And they said, *W* unto us 1Sa 4:7   188
W unto us 1Sa 4:8   188
If I be wicked, *w* unto me .... Job 10:15   480
W is me, that I sojourn in Mesech .... Ps 120:5   190
Who hath *w* .... Prov 23:29   188
but *w* to him that is alone when .... Eccl 4:10   337
W to thee, O land, when thy king .... Eccl 10:16   337
W unto their soul .... Is 3:9   188
W unto the wicked .... Is 3:11   188
W unto them that join house to .... Is 5:8   1945
W unto them that rise up early in .... Is 5:11   1945
W unto them that draw iniquity .... Is 5:18   1945
W unto them that call evil good, ... Is 5:20   1945
W unto them that are wise in .... Is 5:21   1945
W unto them that are mighty to.............. Is 5:22   1945
Then said I, *W* is me.............................. Is 6:5   188
W unto them that decree .... Is 10:1   1945
W to the multitude of many people .... Is 17:12   1945
W to the land shadowing with .... Is 18:1   1945
leanness, my leanness, *w* unto me .... Is 24:16   188
W to the crown of pride, to the .... Is 28:1   1945
W to Ariel, to Ariel, the city .... Is 29:1   1945
W unto them that seek deep to .... Is 29:15   1945
W to the rebellious children, ... Is 30:1   1945
W to them that go down to Egypt .... Is 31:1   1945
W to thee that spoilest, and thou .... Is 33:1   1945
W unto him that striveth with his .... Is 45:9   1945
W unto him that saith unto his .... Is 45:10   1945
W unto us .... Jer 4:13   188
her hands, saying, *W* is me now .... Jer 4:31   188
W unto us .... Jer 6:4   188
W is me for my hurt............................ Jer 10:19   188
W unto thee, O Jerusalem, ... Jer 13:27   188
W is me, my mother, that thou .... Jer 15:10   188
W unto him that buildeth his .... Jer 22:13   1945
W be unto the pastors that .... Jer 23:1   1945
Thou didst say, *W* is me now .... Jer 45:3   188
W unto Nebo .... Jer 48:1   1945
W be unto thee, O Moab .... Jer 48:46   188
w unto them .... Jer 50:27   1945
w unto us, that we have sinned .... Lam 5:16   188
lamentations, and mourning, and *w* ...... Eze 2:10   1958
W unto the foolish prophets, that .... Eze 13:3   1945
W to the women that sew pillows .... Eze 13:18   1945
w, w unto thee .... Eze 16:23   188
W to the bloody city, to the pot .... Eze 24:6   188
W to the bloody city .... Eze 24:9   188
Howl ye, *W* worth the day .... Eze 30:2   1929
W be to the shepherds of Israel .... Eze 34:2   1945
W unto them. .... Hos 7:13   188
w also to them when I depart from .... Hos 9:12   188
W unto you that desire the day of .... Amos 5:18   1945
W to them that are at ease in .... Amos 6:1   1945
W to them that devise iniquity,.............. Mic 2:1   1945
W is me .... Mic 7:1   480
W to the bloody city .... Nah 3:1   1945
W to him that increaseth that .... Hab 2:6   1945
W to him that coveteth an evil .... Hab 2:9   1945
W to him that buildeth a town .... Hab 2:12   1945
W unto him that giveth his .... Hab 2:15   1945
W unto him that saith to the wood .... Hab 2:19   1945
W unto the inhabitants of the sea .... Zeph 2:5   1945
W to her that is filthy and .... Zeph 3:1   1945
W to the idol shepherd that .... Zec 11:17   1945
W unto thee, Chorazin, ... Mt 11:21   3759
w unto thee, Bethsaida .... Mt 11:21   3759
W unto the world because of .... Mt 18:7   3759
but w to that man by whom the .... Mt 18:7   3759
But w unto you, scribes and .... Mt 23:13   3759
W unto you, scribes and Pharisees,...... Mt 23:14   3759
W unto you, scribes and Pharisees,...... Mt 23:15   3759
W unto you, ye blind guides, ... Mt 23:16   3759
W unto you, scribes and Pharisees,...... Mt 23:23   3759
W unto you, scribes and Pharisees,...... Mt 23:25   3759
W unto you, scribes and Pharisees,...... Mt 23:27   3759
W unto you, scribes and Pharisees,...... Mt 23:29   3759
w unto them that are with child, ... Mt 24:19   3759
but w unto that man by whom the .... Mt 26:24   3759
But w to them that are with child.......... Mk 13:17   3759
but w to that man by whom the Son ...... Mk 14:21   3759
But w unto you that are rich .... Lk 6:24   3759
W unto you that are full .... Lk 6:25   3759

W unto you that laugh now .... Lk 6:25   3759
W unto you, when all men shall .... Lk 6:26   3759
W unto thee, Chorazin, ... Lk 10:13   3759
w unto thee, Bethsaida .... Lk 10:13   3759
But w unto you, Pharisees .... Lk 11:42   3759
W unto you, Pharisees .... Lk 11:43   3759
W unto you, scribes and Pharisees, ... Lk 11:44   3759
W unto you also, ye lawyers .... Lk 11:46   3759
W unto you! for ye build the .... Lk 11:47   3759
W unto you, lawyers .... Lk 11:52   3759
but w unto him, through whom they ...... Lk 17:1   3759
But w unto them that are with .... Lk 21:23   3759
but w unto that man by whom he is ...... Lk 22:22   3759
w is unto me, if I preach not the............ 1Cor 9:16   3759
W unto them. .... Jude 11   3759
saying with a loud voice, *W, w* .... Rev 8:13   3759
with a loud voice, *W, w, w*.................... Rev 8:13   3759
One *w* is past .... Rev 9:12   3759
The second *w* is past .... Rev 11:14   3759
the third *w* cometh quickly .... Rev 11:14   3759
W to the inhabiters of the earth .... Rev 12:12   3759

WOEFUL

neither have I desired the *w* day .... Jer 17:16   605

WOES

there come two *w* more hereafter .... Rev 9:12   3759

WOLF

Benjamin shall ravin as a *w* .... Gen 49:27   2061
The *w* also shall dwell with the .... Is 11:6   2061
The *w* and the lamb shall feed................ Is 65:25   2061
a *w* of the evenings shall spoil................ Jer 5:6   2061
sheep are not, seeth the *w* coming........ Jn 10:12   3074
and the *w* catcheth them, and .... Jn 10:12   3074

WOLVES

are like *w* ravening the prey .... Eze 22:27   2061
more fierce than the evening *w* .... Hab 1:8   2061
her judges are evening *w*...................... Zeph 3:3   2061
but inwardly they are ravening *w*. ...... Mt 7:15   3074
forth as sheep in the midst of *w* .... Mt 10:16   3074
I send you forth as lambs among *w* ...... Lk 10:3   3074
grievous *w* enter in among you .... Acts 20:29   3074

WOMAN

had taken from man, made he a *w* .... Gen 2:22   802
she shall be called *W*, because .... Gen 2:23   802
And he said unto the *w*, Yea, hath .... Gen 3:1   802
the *w* said unto the serpent, We .... Gen 3:2   802
And the serpent said unto the *w* .... Gen 3:4   802
when the *w* saw that the tree was .... Gen 3:6   802
The *w* whom thou gavest to be with ...... Gen 3:12   802
And the Lord God said unto the *w* .... Gen 3:13   802
the *w* said, The serpent beguiled .... Gen 3:13   802
put enmity between thee and the *w* .... Gen 3:15   802
Unto the *w* he said, I will...................... Gen 3:16   802
thou art a fair *w* to look upon .... Gen 12:11   802
the *w* that she was very fair.................... Gen 12:14   802
the *w* was taken into Pharaoh's .... Gen 12:15   802
for the *w* which thou hast taken .... Gen 20:3   802
Peradventure the *w* will not be .... Gen 24:5   802
if the *w* will not be willing to .... Gen 24:8   802
Peradventure the *w* will not .... Gen 24:39   802
let the same be the *w* whom the .... Gen 24:44   802
Shaul the son of a Canaanitish *w* .... Gen 46:10
the *w* conceived, and bare a son .... Ex 2:2   802
the *w* took the child, and nursed .... Ex 2:9   802
But every *w* shall borrow of her.............. Ex 3:22   802
Shaul the son of a Canaanitish *w* .... Ex 6:15
every *w* of her neighbour, jewels .... Ex 11:2   802
hurt a *w* with child, so that her .... Ex 21:22   802
If an ox gore a man or a *w* .... Ex 21:28   802
that he hath killed a man or a *w*............ Ex 21:29   802
unto the Lord, every man and *w* .... Ex 35:29   802
Let neither man nor *w* make any .... Ex 36:6   802
If a *w* have conceived seed, and .... Lev 12:2   802
If a man or *w* have a plague upon .... Lev 13:29   802
If a man also or a *w* have in............ Lev 13:38   802
The *w* also with whom man shall .... Lev 15:18   802
if a *w* have an issue, and her .... Lev 15:19   802
if a *w* have an issue of her blood .... Lev 15:25   802
an issue, of the man, and of the *w*.......... Lev 15:33   5347
not uncover the nakedness of a *w* .... Lev 18:17   802
unto a *w* to uncover her nakedness .... Lev 18:19   802
neither shalt any *w* stand before............ Lev 18:23   802
whosoever lieth carnally with a *w*.......... Lev 19:20   802
mankind, as he lieth with a *w* .... Lev 20:13   802
if a *w* approach unto any beast, ... Lev 20:16   802
thereto, thou shalt kill the *w* .... Lev 20:16   802
lie with a *w* having her sickness .... Lev 20:18   802
A man also or *w* that hath a.................. Lev 20:27   802
a *w* put away from her husband .... Lev 21:7   802

A widow, or a divorced *w*, or	Lev 21:14	
And the son of an Israelitish *w*	Lev 24:10	802
and this son of the Israelitish *w*	Lev 24:10	
When a man or *w* shall commit any	Num 5:6	802
shall set the *w* before the LORD	Num 5:18	802
her by an oath, and say unto the *w*	Num 5:19	802
the *w* with an oath of cursing	Num 5:21	802
the priest shall say unto the *w*	Num 5:21	802
the *w* shall say, Amen, amen	Num 5:22	802
he shall cause the *w* to drink the	Num 5:24	802
cause the *w* to drink the water	Num 5:26	802
the *w* shall be a curse among her	Num 5:27	802
if the *w* be not defiled, but be	Num 5:28	802
shall set the *w* before the LORD,	Num 5:30	802
this *w* shall bear her iniquity	Num 5:31	802
When either man or *w* shall	Num 6:2	802
Ethiopian *w* whom he had married	Num 12:1	802
for he had married an Ethiopian *w*	Num 12:1	802
w in the sight of Moses, and in	Num 25:6	
and the *w* through her belly	Num 25:8	802
was slain with the Midianitish *w*	Num 25:14	
w that was slain was Cozbi	Num 25:15	802
If a *w* also vow a vow unto the	Num 30:3	802
kill every *w* that hath known man	Num 31:17	802
an Hebrew man, or an Hebrew *w*	Deut 15:12	
thy God giveth, the man or *w*	Deut 17:2	802
bring forth that man or that *w*	Deut 17:5	802
gates, even that man or that *w*	Deut 17:5	802
among the captives a beautiful *w*	Deut 21:11	802
The *w* shall not wear that which	Deut 22:5	802
upon her, and say, I took this *w*	Deut 22:14	802
with a *w* married to an husband	Deut 22:22	802
that lay with the *w*, and the *w*	Deut 22:22	802
delicate *w* among you, which would	Deut 28:56	
should be among you man, or *w*	Deut 29:18	802
the *w* took the two men, and hid	Josh 2:4	802
was in the city, both man and *w*	Josh 6:21	802
house, and bring out thence the *w*	Josh 6:22	802
sell Sisera into the hand of a *w*	Judg 4:9	802
a certain *w* cast a piece of a	Judg 9:53	802
men say not of me, A *w* slew him	Judg 9:54	802
thou art the son of a strange *w*	Judg 11:2	802
of the LORD appeared unto the *w*	Judg 13:3	802
Then the *w* came and told her	Judg 13:6	802
the *w* as she sat in the field	Judg 13:9	802
the *w* made haste, and ran, and	Judg 13:10	802
the man that spakest unto the *w*	Judg 13:11	802
I said unto the *w* let her beware	Judg 13:13	802
the *w* bare a son, and called his	Judg 13:24	802
saw a *w* in Timnath of the	Judg 14:1	802
I have seen a *w* in Timnath of the	Judg 14:2	802
Is there never a *w* among the	Judg 14:3	802
went down, and talked with the *w*	Judg 14:7	802
his father went down unto the *w*	Judg 14:10	802
that he loved a *w* in the valley	Judg 16:4	802
Then came the *w* in the dawning of	Judg 19:26	802
the *w* his concubine was fallen	Judg 19:27	802
husband of the *w* that was slain	Judg 20:4	802
every *w* that hath lain by man	Judg 21:11	802
the *w* was left of her two sons and	Ruth 1:5	802
and, behold, a *w* lay at his feet	Ruth 3:8	802
know that thou art a virtuous *w*	Ruth 3:11	802
that a *w* came into the floor	Ruth 3:14	802
The LORD make the *w* that is come	Ruth 4:11	802
shall give thee of this young *w*	Ruth 4:12	5291
I am a *w* of a sorrowful spirit	1Sa 1:15	802
So the *w* went her way, and did eat	1Sa 1:18	802
So the *w* abode, and gave her son	1Sa 1:23	802
I am the *w* that stood by thee	1Sa 1:26	802
w for the loan which is lent to	1Sa 2:20	802
but slay both man and *w*, infant and	1Sa 15:3	802
son of the perverse rebellious *w*	1Sa 20:30	
she was a *w* of good understanding	1Sa 25:3	802
and left neither man nor *w* alive	1Sa 27:9	802
saved neither man nor *w* alive	1Sa 27:11	802
Seek me a *w* that hath a familiar	1Sa 28:7	802
there is a *w* that hath a familiar	1Sa 28:7	802
and they came to her by night	1Sa 28:8	802
the *w* said unto him, Behold, thou	1Sa 28:9	802
Then said the *w*, Whom shall I	1Sa 28:11	802
when the *w* saw Samuel, she cried	1Sa 28:12	802
the *w* spake to Saul, saying, Why	1Sa 28:12	802
the *w* said unto Saul, I saw gods	1Sa 28:13	802
the *w* came unto Saul, and saw that	1Sa 28:21	802
his servants, together with the *w*	1Sa 28:23	802
the *w* had a fat calf in the house	1Sa 28:24	802
with a fault concerning this *w*	2Sa 3:8	802
roof he saw a *w* washing herself	2Sa 11:2	802
the *w* was very beautiful to look	2Sa 11:2	802
sent and enquired after the *w*	2Sa 11:3	802
the *w* conceived, and sent and told	2Sa 11:5	802

did not a *w* cast a piece of a	2Sa 11:21	802
said, Put now this *w* out from me	2Sa 13:17	
and fetched thence a wise *w*	2Sa 14:2	802
but be as a *w* that had a long	2Sa 14:2	802
when the *w* of Tekoah spake to the	2Sa 14:4	802
answered, I am indeed a widow *w*	2Sa 14:5	802
And the king said unto the *w*	2Sa 14:8	802
the *w* of Tekoah said unto the	2Sa 14:9	802
Then the *w* said, Let thine	2Sa 14:12	802
the *w* said, Wherefore then hast	2Sa 14:13	802
king answered and said unto the *w*	2Sa 14:18	802
the *w* said, Let my lord the king	2Sa 14:18	802
the *w* answered and said, As thy	2Sa 14:19	802
she was a *w* of a fair countenance	2Sa 14:27	802
the *w* took and spread a covering	2Sa 17:19	802
came to the *w* to the house	2Sa 17:20	802
the *w* said unto them, They be	2Sa 17:20	802
cried a wise *w* out of the city	2Sa 20:16	802
the *w* said, Art thou Joab	2Sa 20:17	802
the *w* said unto Joab, Behold, his	2Sa 20:21	802
Then the *w* went unto all the	2Sa 20:22	802
And the one *w* said, O my lord, I	1Kin 3:17	802
this *w* dwell in one house	1Kin 3:17	802
that this *w* was delivered also	1Kin 3:18	802
And the other *w* said, Nay	1Kin 3:22	802
Then spake the *w* whose the living	1Kin 3:26	802
name was Zeruah, a widow *w*	1Kin 11:26	802
feign herself to be another *w*	1Kin 14:5	
a widow *w* there to sustain thee	1Kin 17:9	802
the widow *w* was there gathering	1Kin 17:10	802
things, that the son of the *w*	1Kin 17:17	802
the *w* said to Elijah, Now by this	1Kin 17:24	802
Now there cried a certain *w* of	2Kin 4:1	802
to Shunem, where was a great *w*	2Kin 4:8	802
the *w* conceived, and bare a son at	2Kin 4:17	802
wall, there cried a *w* unto him	2Kin 6:26	802
This *w* said unto me, Give my son	2Kin 6:28	802
the king heard the words of the *w*	2Kin 6:30	802
Then spake Elisha unto the *w*	2Kin 8:1	802
the *w* arose, and did after the	2Kin 8:2	802
that the *w* returned out of the	2Kin 8:3	802
body to life, that, behold, the *w*	2Kin 8:5	802
My lord, O king, this is the *w*	2Kin 8:5	802
And when the king asked the *w*	2Kin 8:6	802
said, Go, see now this cursed *w*	2Kin 9:34	
one of Israel, both man and *w*	1Chr 16:3	802
The son of a *w* of the daughters	2Chr 2:14	802
small or great, whether man or *w*	2Chr 15:13	802
sons of Athaliah, that wicked *w*	2Chr 24:7	
that whosoever, whether man or *w*	Est 4:11	802
is born of a *w* is of few days	Job 14:1	802
and he which is born of a *w*	Job 15:14	802
he be clean that is born of a *w*	Job 25:4	802
heart have been deceived by a *w*	Job 31:9	802
and pain, as of a *w* in travail	Ps 48:6	
like the untimely birth of a *w*	Ps 58:8	802
maketh the barren *w* to keep house	Ps 113:9	
deliver thee from the strange *w*	Prov 2:16	802
a strange *w* drop as an honeycomb	Prov 5:3	
son, be ravished with a strange *w*	Prov 5:20	
To keep thee from the evil *w*	Prov 6:24	802
of the tongue of a strange *w*	Prov 6:24	
For by means of a whorish *w* man	Prov 6:26	802
with a *w* lacketh understanding	Prov 6:32	802
may keep thee from the strange *w*	Prov 7:5	802
there met him a *w* with the attire	Prov 7:10	802
A foolish *w* is clamorous	Prov 9:13	802
A gracious *w* retaineth honour	Prov 11:16	802
so is a fair *w* which is without	Prov 11:22	802
A virtuous *w* is a crown to her	Prov 12:4	802
Every wise *w* buildeth her house	Prov 14:1	802
a pledge of him for a strange *w*	Prov 20:16	
housetop, than with a brawling *w*	Prov 21:9	802
with a contentious and an angry *w*	Prov 21:19	802
a strange *w* is a narrow pit	Prov 23:27	
housetop, than with a brawling *w*	Prov 25:24	
a pledge of him for a strange *w*	Prov 27:13	
day and a contentious *w* are alike	Prov 27:15	802
is the way of an adulterous *w*	Prov 30:20	802
For an odious *w* when she is	Prov 30:23	
Who can find a virtuous *w*	Prov 31:10	802
but a *w* that feareth the LORD,	Prov 31:30	802
find more bitter than death the *w*	Eccl 7:26	802
but a *w* among all those have I	Eccl 7:28	802
be in pain as a *w* that travaileth	Is 13:8	
the pangs of a *w* that travaileth	Is 21:3	
Like as a *w* with child, that	Is 26:17	
will I cry like a travailing *w*	Is 42:14	
or to the *w*, What hast thou	Is 45:10	802
Can a *w* forget her sucking child,	Is 49:15	802
hath called thee as a *w* forsaken	Is 54:6	802

a voice as of a *w* in travail	Jer 4:31	
of Zion to a comely and delicate *w*	Jer 6:2	
us, and pain, as of a *w* in travail	Jer 6:24	
take thee, as a *w* in travail	Jer 13:21	802
the pain as of a *w* in travail	Jer 22:23	
as a *w* in travail, and all faces	Jer 30:6	
the *w* with child and her that	Jer 31:8	
earth, A *w* shall compass a man	Jer 31:22	5347
to cut off from you man and *w*	Jer 44:7	802
as the heart of a *w* in her pangs	Jer 48:41	802
as the heart of a *w* in her pangs	Jer 49:22	802
have taken her, as a *w* in travail	Jer 49:24	
and pangs as of a *w* in travail	Jer 50:43	
will I break in pieces man and *w*	Jer 51:22	802
is as a menstruous *w* among them	Lam 1:17	
work of an imperious whorish *w*	Eze 16:30	802
hath come near to a menstruous *w*	Eze 18:6	802
as they go in unto a *w* that	Eze 23:44	802
as the uncleanness of a removed *w*	Eze 36:17	
love a *w* beloved of her friend,	Hos 3:1	802
travailing *w* shall come upon him	Hos 13:13	
have taken thee as a *w* in travail	Mic 4:9	
of Zion, like a *w* in travail	Mic 4:10	
this is a *w* that sitteth in the	Zec 5:7	802
on a *w* to lust after her hath	Mt 5:28	*1135*
And, behold, a *w*, which was	Mt 9:20	*1135*
the *w* was made whole from that	Mt 9:22	*1135*
like unto leaven, which a *w* took	Mt 13:33	*1135*
a *w* of Canaan came out of the	Mt 15:22	*1135*
answered and said unto her, O *w*	Mt 15:28	*1135*
And last of all the *w* died also	Mt 22:27	*1135*
There came unto him a *w* having an	Mt 26:7	*1135*
unto them, Why trouble ye the *w*	Mt 26:10	*1135*
also this, that this *w* hath done	Mt 26:13	
And a certain *w*, which had an	Mk 5:25	*1135*
But the *w* fearing and trembling,	Mk 5:33	*1135*
For a certain *w*, whose young	Mk 7:25	*1135*
The *w* was a Greek, a	Mk 7:26	*1135*
if a *w* shall put away her husband	Mk 10:12	*1135*
last of all the *w* died also	Mk 12:22	*1135*
at meat, there came a *w* having an	Mk 14:3	*1135*
unto a *w* that was a widow	Lk 4:26	*1135*
a *w* in the city, which was a	Lk 7:37	*1135*
what manner of *w* this is that	Lk 7:39	*1135*
And he turned to the *w*, and said	Lk 7:44	*1135*
unto Simon, Seest thou this *w*	Lk 7:44	
but this *w* since the time I came	Lk 7:45	
but this *w* hath anointed my feet	Lk 7:46	
And he said to the *w*, Thy faith	Lk 7:50	*1135*
a *w* having an issue of blood	Lk 8:43	*1135*
when the *w* saw that she was not	Lk 8:47	*1135*
a certain *w* named Martha received	Lk 10:38	*1135*
a certain *w* of the company lifted	Lk 11:27	*1135*
there was a *w* which had a spirit	Lk 13:11	*1135*
her to him, and said unto her, *W*	Lk 13:12	*1135*
And ought not this *w*, being a	Lk 13:16	
It is like leaven, which a *w* took	Lk 13:21	*1135*
Either what *w* having ten pieces	Lk 15:8	*1135*
Last of all the *w* died also	Lk 20:32	*1135*
And he denied him, saying, *W*	Lk 22:57	*1135*
Jesus saith unto her, *W*, what	Jn 2:4	*1135*
There cometh a *w* of Samaria to	Jn 4:7	*1135*
Then saith the *w* of Samaria unto	Jn 4:9	*1135*
of me, which am a *w* of Samaria	Jn 4:9	*1135*
The *w* saith unto him, Sir, thou	Jn 4:11	*1135*
The *w* saith unto him, Sir, give	Jn 4:15	*1135*
The *w* answered and said, I have no	Jn 4:17	*1135*
The *w* saith unto him, Sir, I	Jn 4:19	*1135*
Jesus saith unto her, *W*, believe	Jn 4:21	*1135*
The *w* saith unto him, I know that	Jn 4:25	*1135*
that he talked with the *w*	Jn 4:27	*1135*
The *w* then left her waterpot, and	Jn 4:28	*1135*
on him for the saying of the *w*	Jn 4:39	*1135*
And said unto the *w*, Now we	Jn 4:42	*1135*
unto him a *w* taken in adultery	Jn 8:3	*1135*
this *w* was taken in adultery, in	Jn 8:4	*1135*
the *w* standing in the midst	Jn 8:9	*1135*
up himself, and saw none but the *w*	Jn 8:10	*1135*
he said unto her, *W*	Jn 8:10	*1135*
A *w* when she is in travail hath	Jn 16:21	*1135*
he saith unto his mother, *W*	Jn 19:26	*1135*
And they say unto her, *W*, why	Jn 20:13	*1135*
Jesus saith unto her, *W*, why	Jn 20:15	*1135*
this *w* was full of good works and	Acts 9:36	
Timotheus, the son of a certain *w*	Acts 16:1	*1135*
a certain *w* named Lydia, a seller	Acts 16:14	*1135*
a *w* named Damaris, and others with	Acts 17:34	*1135*
leaving the natural use of the *w*	Rom 1:27	*2338*
For the *w* which hath an husband	Rom 7:2	*1135*
good for a man not to touch a *w*	1Cor 7:1	*1135*
let every *w* have her own husband	1Cor 7:2	
the *w* which hath an husband that	1Cor 7:13	*1135*
The unmarried *w* careth for the	1Cor 7:34	*1135*
and the head of the *w* is the man	1Cor 11:3	*1135*
But every *w* that prayeth or	1Cor 11:5	*1135*
For if the *w* be not covered, let	1Cor 11:6	*1135*
for a *w* to be shorn or shaven	1Cor 11:6	*1135*
but the *w* is the glory of the man	1Cor 11:7	*1135*
For the man is not of the *w*	1Cor 11:8	*1135*
but the *w* of the man	1Cor 11:8	*1135*
was the man created for the *w*	1Cor 11:9	*1135*
but the *w* for the man	1Cor 11:9	*1135*
For this cause ought the *w* to	1Cor 11:10	*1135*
neither is the man without the *w*	1Cor 11:11	*1135*
neither the *w* without the man, in	1Cor 11:11	*1135*
For as the *w* is of the man	1Cor 11:12	*1135*
even so is the man also by the *w*	1Cor 11:12	*1135*
is it comely that a *w* pray unto	1Cor 11:13	*1135*
But if a *w* have long hair, it is	1Cor 11:15	*1135*
sent forth his Son, made of a *w*	Gal 4:4	*1135*
heir with the son of the free *w*	Gal 4:30	*1658*
as travail upon a *w* with child	1Th 5:3	
Let the *w* learn in silence with	1Ti 2:11	*1135*
But I suffer not a *w* to teach	1Ti 2:12	*1135*
but the *w* being deceived was in	1Ti 2:14	*1135*
If any man or *w* that believeth	1Ti 5:16	
thou sufferest that *w* Jezebel	Rev 2:20	*1135*
a *w* clothed with the sun, and the	Rev 12:1	*1135*
the dragon stood before the *w*	Rev 12:4	*1135*
the *w* fled into the wilderness,	Rev 12:6	*1135*
he persecuted the *w* which brought	Rev 12:13	*1135*
to the *w* were given two wings of	Rev 12:14	*1135*
water as a flood after the *w*	Rev 12:15	*1135*
And the earth helped the *w*	Rev 12:16	*1135*
the dragon was wroth with the *w*	Rev 12:17	*1135*
I saw a *w* sit upon a scarlet	Rev 17:3	*1135*
the *w* was arrayed in purple and	Rev 17:4	*1135*
I saw the *w* drunken with the	Rev 17:6	*1135*
tell thee the mystery of the *w*	Rev 17:7	*1135*
mountains, on which the *w* sitteth	Rev 17:9	*1135*
the *w* which thou sawest is that	Rev 17:18	*1135*

WOMANKIND

not lie with mankind, as with *w*	Lev 18:22	802

WOMAN'S

his pledge from the *w* hand	Gen 38:20	802
according as the *w* husband will	Ex 21:22	802
the Israelitish *w* son blasphemed	Lev 24:11	802
the LORD, and uncover the *w* head	Num 5:18	802
offering out of the *w* hand	Num 5:25	802
shall a man put on a *w* garment	Deut 22:5	802
this *w* child died in the night	1Kin 3:19	802

WOMB

her, Two nations are in thy *w*	Gen 25:23	990
behold, there were twins in her *w*	Gen 25:24	990
Leah was hated, he opened her *w*	Gen 29:31	7358
from thee the fruit of the *w*	Gen 30:2	990
hearkened to her, and opened her *w*	Gen 30:22	7358
that, behold, twins were in her *w*	Gen 38:27	990
of the breasts, and of the *w*	Gen 49:25	7356
whatsoever openeth the *w* among	Ex 13:2	7358
instead of such as open every *w*	Num 8:16	7358
he cometh out of his mother's *w*	Num 12:12	7358
also bless the fruit of thy *w*	Deut 7:13	990
be a Nazarite unto God from the *w*	Judg 13:5	990
the *w* to the day of his death	Judg 13:7	990
unto God from my mother's *w*	Judg 16:17	990
there yet any more sons in my *w*	Ruth 1:11	4578
but the LORD had shut up her *w*	1Sa 1:5	7358
the LORD had shut up her *w*	1Sa 1:6	7358
Naked came I out of my mother's *w*	Job 1:21	990
not up the doors of my mother's *w*	Job 3:10	990
Why died I not from the *w*	Job 3:11	7358
brought me forth out of the *w*	Job 10:18	7358
carried from the *w* to the grave	Job 10:19	990
The *w* shall forget him	Job 24:20	7358
he that made me in the *w* make him	Job 31:15	990
did not one fashion us in the *w*	Job 31:15	7358
guided her from my mother's *w*	Job 31:18	990
as if it had issued out of the *w*	Job 38:8	7358
Out of whose *w* came the ice	Job 38:29	990
art he that took me out of the *w*	Ps 22:9	990
I was cast upon thee from the *w*	Ps 22:10	7358
wicked are estranged from the *w*	Ps 58:3	7358
have I been holden up from the *w*	Ps 71:6	990
from the *w* of the morning	Ps 110:3	7358
the fruit of the *w* is his reward	Ps 127:3	990
hast covered me in my mother's *w*	Ps 139:13	990
and the barren *w*	Prov 30:16	7356
and what, the son of my *w*	Prov 31:2	990
he came forth of his mother's *w*	Eccl 5:15	990

W

the *w* of her that is with child	Eccl 11:5	990
no pity on the fruit of the *w*	Is 13:18	990
thee, and formed thee from the *w*	Is 44:2	990
and he that formed thee from the *w*	Is 44:24	990
which are carried from the *w*	Is 46:3	7356
called a transgressor from the *w*	Is 48:8	990
LORD hath called me from the *w*	Is 49:1	990
me from the *w* to be his servant	Is 49:5	990
compassion on the son of her *w*	Is 49:15	990
to bring forth, and shut the *w*	Is 66:9	990
out of the *w* I sanctified thee	Jer 1:5	7358
Because he slew me not from the *w*	Jer 20:17	7358
her *w* to be always great with me	Jer 20:17	7358
forth out of the *w* to see labour	Jer 20:18	7358
the fire all that openeth the *w*	Eze 20:26	7356
from the birth, and from the *w*	Hos 9:11	990
give them a miscarrying *w*	Hos 9:14	7358
even the beloved fruit of their *w*	Hos 9:16	990
his brother by the heel in the *w*	Hos 12:3	990
so born from their mother's *w*	Mt 19:12	2836
Ghost, even from his mother's *w*	Lk 1:15	2836
thou shalt conceive in thy *w*	Lk 1:31	1064
of Mary, the babe leaped in her *w*	Lk 1:41	2836
and blessed is the fruit of thy *w*	Lk 1:42	2836
the babe leaped in my *w* for joy	Lk 1:44	2836
before he was conceived in the *w*	Lk 2:21	2836
the *w* shall be called holy to the	Lk 2:23	3388
Blessed is the *w* that bare thee	Lk 11:27	2836
second time into his mother's *w*	Jn 3:4	2836
from his mother's *w* was carried	Acts 3:2	2836
a cripple from his mother's *w*	Acts 14:8	2836
yet the deadness of Sarah's *w*	Rom 4:19	3388
separated me from my mother's *w*	Gal 1:15	2836

WOMBS

the *w* of the house of Abimelech	Gen 20:18	7358
the *w* that never bare, and the	Lk 23:29	2836

WOMEN

the *w* also, and the people	Gen 14:16	802
with Sarah after the manner of *w*	Gen 18:11	802
even the time that *w* go out to	Gen 24:11	
for the custom of *w* is upon me	Gen 31:35	802
lifted up his eyes, and saw the *w*	Gen 33:5	802
of a midwife to the Hebrew *w*	Ex 1:16	
Because the Hebrew *w* are not as	Ex 1:19	802
not as the Egyptian *w*	Ex 1:19	802
to thee a nurse of the Hebrew *w*	Ex 2:7	
all the *w* went out after her with	Ex 15:20	802
And they came, both men and *w*	Ex 35:22	802
all the *w* that were wise hearted	Ex 35:25	802
all the *w* whose heart stirred	Ex 35:26	802
of the *w* assembling, which	Ex 38:8	
ten *w* shall bake your bread in	Lev 26:26	802
took all the *w* of Midian captives	Num 31:9	802
Have ye saved all the *w* alive	Num 31:15	5347
But all the *w* children, that have	Num 31:18	802
of *w* that had not known man by	Num 31:35	802
destroyed the men, and the *w*	Deut 2:34	802
utterly destroying the men, *w*	Deut 3:6	802
But the *w*, and the little ones, and	Deut 20:14	802
the people together, men, and *w*	Deut 31:12	802
fell that day, both of men and *w*	Josh 8:25	802
of Israel, with the *w*, and the	Josh 8:35	802
Blessed above *w* shall Jael the	Judg 5:24	802
shall she be above *w* in the tent	Judg 5:24	802
also, about a thousand men and *w*	Judg 9:49	802
and thither fled all the men and *w*	Judg 9:51	802
the house was full of men and *w*	Judg 16:27	802
about three thousand men and *w*	Judg 16:27	802
the edge of the sword, with *w*	Judg 21:10	802
alive of the *w* of Jabesh-gilead	Judg 21:14	802
seeing the *w* are destroyed out of	Judg 21:16	802
took them wives of the *w* of Moab	Ruth 1:4	802
the *w* said unto Naomi, Blessed be	Ruth 4:14	802
the *w* her neighbours gave it a	Ruth 4:17	
how they lay with the *w* that	1Sa 2:22	802
w that stood by her said unto her	1Sa 4:20	
thy sword hath made *w* childless	1Sa 15:33	802
thy mother be childless among *w*	1Sa 15:33	802
that the *w* came out of all cities	1Sa 18:6	802
the *w* answered one another as	1Sa 18:7	802
kept themselves at least from *w*	1Sa 21:4	802
Of a truth *w* have been kept from	1Sa 21:5	802
edge of the sword, both men and *w*	1Sa 22:19	802
And had taken the *w* captives	1Sa 30:2	802
wonderful, passing the love of *w*	2Sa 1:26	802
Israel, as well to the *w* as men	2Sa 6:19	802
And the king left ten *w*, which	2Sa 15:16	802
voice of singing men and singing *w*	2Sa 19:35	
took the ten *w* his concubines	2Sa 20:3	802
Then came there two *w*, that were	1Kin 3:16	802

king Solomon loved many strange *w*	1Kin 11:1	802
w of the Moabites, Ammonites,	1Kin 11:1	
and rip up their *w* with child	2Kin 8:12	
all the *w* therein that were with	2Kin 15:16	
where the *w* wove hangings for the	2Kin 23:7	802
brethren two hundred thousand, *w*	2Chr 28:8	802
the singing *w* spake of Josiah in	2Chr 35:25	
hundred singing men and singing *w*	Ezr 2:65	
great congregation of men and *w*	Ezr 10:1	802
and five singing men and singing *w*	Neh 7:67	
the congregation both of men and *w*	Neh 8:2	802
midday, before the men and the *w*	Neh 8:3	802
him did outlandish *w* cause to sin	Neh 13:26	802
the *w* in the royal house which	Est 1:9	802
shall come abroad unto all *w*	Est 1:17	802
the palace, to the house of the *w*	Est 2:3	802
chamberlain, keeper of the *w*	Est 2:3	802
custody of Hegai, keeper of the *w*	Est 2:8	802
best place of the house of the *w*	Est 2:9	802
according to the manner of *w*	Est 2:12	802
things for the purifying of the *w*	Est 2:12	802
of the *w* unto the king's house	Est 2:13	802
into the second house of the *w*	Est 2:14	802
chamberlain, the keeper of the *w*	Est 2:15	802
king loved Esther above all the *w*	Est 2:17	802
and old, little children and *w*	Est 3:13	802
them, both little ones and *w*	Est 8:11	802
as one of the foolish *w* speaketh	Job 2:10	
in all the land were no *w* found	Job 42:15	802
were among thy honourable *w*	Ps 45:9	
mouth of strange *w* is a deep pit	Prov 22:14	
Thine eyes shall behold strange *w*	Prov 23:33	
Give not thy strength unto *w*	Prov 31:3	802
w singers, and the delights of the	Eccl 2:8	
know not, O thou fairest among *w*	Song 1:8	802
beloved, O thou fairest among *w*	Song 5:9	802
gone, O thou fairest among *w*	Song 6:1	802
oppressors, and *w* rule over them	Is 3:12	802
in that day seven *w* shall take	Is 4:1	802
day shall Egypt be like unto *w*	Is 19:16	802
the *w* come, and set them on fire	Is 27:11	802
Rise up, ye *w* that are at ease	Is 32:9	802
ye be troubled, ye careless *w*	Is 32:10	
Tremble, ye *w* that are at ease	Is 32:11	
the *w* knead their dough, to make	Jer 7:18	802
ye, and call for the mourning *w*	Jer 9:17	
and send for cunning *w*, that they	Jer 9:17	
hear the word of the LORD, O ye *w*	Jer 9:20	
all the *w* that are left in the	Jer 38:22	802
those *w* shall say, Thy friends	Jer 38:22	
had committed unto him men, and *w*	Jer 40:7	802
even mighty men of war, and the *w*	Jer 41:16	802
Even men, and *w*, and children, and	Jer 43:6	802
all the *w* that stood by, a great	Jer 44:15	802
people, to the men, and to the *w*	Jer 44:20	802
all the people, and to all the *w*	Jer 44:24	802
and they shall become as *w*	Jer 50:37	802
they became as *w*	Jer 51:30	802
Shall the *w* eat their fruit, and	Lam 2:20	802
The hands of the pitiful *w* have	Lam 4:10	802
They ravished the *w* in Zion	Lam 5:11	802
there sat *w* weeping for Tammuz	Eze 8:14	802
maids, and little children, and *w*	Eze 9:6	802
Woe to the *w* that sew pillows to	Eze 13:18	802
from other *w* in thy whoredoms	Eze 16:34	
as *w* that break wedlock and shed	Eze 16:38	802
upon thee in the sight of many *w*	Eze 16:41	802
Son of man, there were two *w*	Eze 23:2	802
and she became famous among *w*	Eze 23:10	802
and unto Aholibah, the lewd *w*	Eze 23:44	802
the manner of *w* that shed blood	Eze 23:45	
that all *w* may be taught not to	Eze 23:48	802
shall give him the daughter of *w*	Dan 11:17	802
his fathers, nor the desire of *w*	Dan 11:37	802
their *w* with child shall be	Hos 13:16	
up the *w* with child of Gilead	Amos 1:13	
The *w* of my people have ye cast	Mic 2:9	802
people in the midst of thee are *w*	Nah 3:13	802
and, behold, there came out two *w*	Zec 5:9	802
old *w* dwell in the streets of	Zec 8:4	
houses rifled, and the *w* ravished	Zec 14:2	802
Among them that are born of *w*	Mt 11:11	1135
about five thousand men, beside *w*	Mt 14:21	1135
were four thousand men, beside *w*	Mt 15:38	1135
Two *w* shall be grinding at the	Mt 24:41	1135
many *w* were there beholding afar	Mt 27:55	1135
angel answered and said unto the *w*	Mt 28:5	1135
There were also *w* looking on afar	Mk 15:40	1135
many other *w* which came up with	Mk 15:41	
blessed art thou among *w*	Lk 1:28	1135
and said, Blessed art thou among *w*	Lk 1:42	1135

Among those that are born of w	Lk 7:28	1135
And certain w, which had been	Lk 8:2	1135
Two w shall be grinding together	Lk 17:35	
great company of people, and of w	Lk 23:27	1135
the w that followed him from	Lk 23:49	1135
the w also, which came with him	Lk 23:55	1135
other w that were with them,	Lk 24:10	
certain w also of our company	Lk 24:22	1135
it even so as the w had said	Lk 24:24	1135
and supplication, with the w	Acts 1:14	1135
Lord, multitudes both of men and w	Acts 5:14	1135
w committed them to prison	Acts 8:3	1135
they were baptized, both men and w	Acts 8:12	1135
way, whether they were men or w	Acts 9:2	1135
up the devout and honourable w	Acts 13:50	1135
spake unto the w which resorted	Acts 16:13	1135
and of the chief w not a few	Acts 17:4	1135
of honourable w which were Greeks	Acts 17:12	1135
into prisons both men and w	Acts 22:4	1135
for even their w did change the	Rom 1:26	2338
Let your w keep silence in the	1Cor 14:34	1135
for it is a shame for w to speak	1Cor 14:35	1135
help those w which laboured with	Phil 4:3	
that w adorn themselves in modest	1Ti 2:9	1135
But (which becometh w professing	1Ti 2:10	1135
The elder as mothers	1Ti 5:2	
that the younger w marry, bear	1Ti 5:14	
captive silly w laden with sins	2Ti 3:6	1133
The aged w likewise, that they be	Titus 2:3	4247
may teach the young w to be sober	Titus 2:4	
W received their dead raised to	Heb 11:35	1135
in the old time the holy w also	1Pet 3:5	1135
And they had hair as the hair of w	Rev 9:8	1135
which were not defiled with w	Rev 14:4	1135

WOMEN'S
before the court of the w house	Est 2:11	802

WOMENSERVANTS
and oxen, and menservants, and w	Gen 20:14	8198
flocks, and menservants, and w	Gen 32:5	8198
took his two wives, and his two w	Gen 32:22	8198

WON
Out of the spoils w in battles	1Chr 26:27	
harder to be w than a strong city	Prov 18:19	
be w by the conversation of the	1Pet 3:1	2770

WONDER
and giveth thee a sign or a w	Deut 13:1	4159
And the sign or the w come to pass	Deut 13:2	4159
upon thee for a sign and for a w	Deut 28:46	4159
the w that was done in the land	2Chr 32:31	4159
I am as a w unto many	Ps 71:7	4159
w upon Egypt and upon Ethiopia	Is 20:3	4159
Stay yourselves, and w	Is 29:9	8539
even a marvellous work and a w	Is 29:14	6382
and the prophets shall w	Jer 4:9	8539
and regard, and w marvellously	Hab 1:5	8539
and they were filled with w	Acts 3:10	2285
Behold, ye despisers, and w	Acts 13:41	2296
appeared a great w in heaven	Rev 12:1	4592
appeared another w in heaven	Rev 12:3	4592
that dwell on the earth shall w	Rev 17:8	2296

WONDERED
w that there was no intercessor	Is 59:16	8074
I w that there was none to uphold	Is 63:5	8074
for they are men w at	Zec 3:8	4159
Insomuch that the multitude w	Mt 15:31	2296
themselves beyond measure, and w	Mk 6:51	2296
all they that heard it w at those	Lk 2:18	2296
w at the gracious words which	Lk 4:22	2296
And they being afraid w, saying	Lk 8:25	2296
But while they w every one at all	Lk 9:43	2296
and the people w	Lk 11:14	2296
yet believed not for joy, and w	Lk 24:41	2296
Moses saw it, he w at the sight	Acts 7:31	2296
he continued with Philip, and w	Acts 8:13	1839
all the world w after the beast	Rev 13:3	2296
I w with great admiration	Rev 17:6	2296

WONDERFUL
the LORD will make thy plagues w	Deut 28:59	6381
thy love to me was w, passing the	2Sa 1:26	6381
about to build shall be w great	2Chr 2:9	6381
things too w for me, which I knew	Job 42:3	6381
are thy w works which thou hast	Ps 40:5	6381
his w works that he hath done	Ps 78:4	6381
for his w works to the children	Ps 107:8	6381
for his w works to the children	Ps 107:15	6381
for his w works to the children	Ps 107:21	6381
for his w works to the children	Ps 107:31	6381
He hath made his w works to be	Ps 111:4	6381

Thy testimonies are w	Ps 119:129	6382
Such knowledge is too w for me	Ps 139:6	6383
things which are too w for me	Prov 30:18	6381
and his name shall be called W	Is 9:6	6382
for thou hast done w things	Is 25:1	6382
which is w in counsel, and	Is 28:29	6381
A w and horrible thing is	Jer 5:30	8047
and in thy name done many w works	Mt 7:22	*1411*
scribes saw the w things that he	Mt 21:15	2297
in our tongues the w works of God	Acts 2:11	3167

WONDERFULLY
when he had wrought w among them	1Sa 6:6	5953
for I am fearfully and w made	Ps 139:14	6395
therefore she came down w	Lam 1:9	6382
and he shall destroy w, and shall	Dan 8:24	6381

WONDERING
the man w at her held his peace,	Gen 24:21	7583
w in himself at that which was	Lk 24:12	2296
is called Solomon's, greatly w	Acts 3:11	1569

WONDEROUSLY
and the angel did w	Judg 13:19	6381

WONDERS
smite Egypt with all my w which I	Ex 3:20	6381
do all those w before Pharaoh	Ex 4:21	4159
my w in the land of Egypt	Ex 7:3	4159
that my w may be multiplied in	Ex 11:9	4159
did all these w before Pharaoh	Ex 11:10	4159
fearful in praises, doing w	Ex 15:11	6382
by temptations, by signs, and by w	Deut 4:34	4159
And the LORD shewed signs and w	Deut 6:22	4159
eyes saw, and the signs, and the w	Deut 7:19	4159
and with signs, and with w	Deut 26:8	4159
In all the signs and the w	Deut 34:11	4159
the LORD will do w among you	Josh 3:5	6381
works that he hath done, his w	1Chr 16:12	4159
w upon Pharaoh, and on all his	Neh 9:10	4159
thy w that thou didst among them	Neh 9:17	6381
yea, and w without number	Job 9:10	6381
I will remember thy w of old	Ps 77:11	6382
Thou art the God that doest w	Ps 77:14	6382
his w that he had shewed them	Ps 78:11	6381
his w in the field of Zoan	Ps 78:43	4159
Wilt thou shew w to the dead	Ps 88:10	6382
Shall thy w be known in the dark	Ps 88:12	6382
And the heavens shall praise thy w	Ps 89:5	6382
heathen, his w among all people	Ps 96:3	6381
his w, and the judgments of his	Ps 105:5	4159
them, and w in the land of Ham	Ps 105:27	4159
understood not thy w in Egypt	Ps 106:7	6381
of the LORD, and his w in the deep	Ps 107:24	6381
w into the midst of thee, O Egypt	Ps 135:9	4159
To him who alone doeth great w	Ps 136:4	6381
for w in Israel from the LORD of	Is 8:18	4159
w in the land of Egypt, even unto	Jer 32:20	4159
of Egypt with signs, and with w	Jer 32:21	4159
w that the high God hath wrought	Dan 4:2	8540
and how mighty are his w	Dan 4:3	8540
w in heaven and in earth, who hath	Dan 6:27	8540
shall it be to the end of these w	Dan 12:6	6382
I will shew w in the heavens and	Joel 2:30	4159
and shall shew great signs and w	Mt 24:24	*5059*
rise, and shall shew signs and w	Mk 13:22	*5059*
him, Except ye see signs and w	Jn 4:48	*5059*
I will shew w in heaven above, and	Acts 2:19	*5059*
of God among you by miracles and w	Acts 2:22	*5059*
and many w and signs were done by	Acts 2:43	*5059*
w may be done by the name of holy	Acts 4:30	*5059*
w wrought among the people	Acts 5:12	*5059*
of faith and power, did great w	Acts 6:8	*5059*
out, after that he had shewed w	Acts 7:36	*5059*
w to be done by their hands	Acts 14:3	*5059*
w God had wrought among the	Acts 15:12	*5059*
Through mighty signs and w	Rom 15:19	*5059*
in all patience, in signs, and w	2Cor 12:12	*5059*
all power and signs and lying w	2Th 2:9	*5059*
witness, both with signs and w	Heb 2:4	*5059*
And he doeth great w, so that he	Rev 13:13	*4592*

WONDROUS
him, talk ye of all his w works	1Chr 16:9	6381
and consider the w works of God	Job 37:14	6381
the w works of him which is	Job 37:16	4652
and tell of all thy w works	Ps 26:7	6381
have I declared thy w works	Ps 71:17	6381
Israel, who only doeth w things	Ps 72:18	6381
name is near thy w works declare	Ps 75:1	6381
and believed not for his w works	Ps 78:32	6381
thou art great, and doest w things	Ps 86:10	6381
talk ye of all his w works	Ps 105:2	6381

W works in the land of Ham, and...........Ps 106:22   6381
that I may behold w things out of ....Ps 119:18   6381
so shall I talk of thy w works................Ps 119:27   6381
of thy majesty, and of thy w works.........Ps 145:5   6381
us according to all his w works ....Jer 21:2   6381

WONDROUSLY
God, that hath dealt w with you ....Joel 2:26   6381

WONT
But if the ox were w to push with ....Ex 21:29   5056
was I ever w to do so unto thee ....Num 22:30   5532
and his men were w to haunt 1Sa 30:31   1980
They were w to speak in old time, ...2Sa 20:18   1696
more than it was w to be heated ....Dan 3:19   2370
w to release unto the people a ....Mt 27:15   1486
and, as he was w, he taught them ......Mk 10:1   1486
came out, and went, as he was w ...Lk 22:39   2596,1485
where prayer was w to be made ....Acts 16:13   3543

WOOD
Make thee an ark of gopher w ....Gen 6:14   6086
clave the w for the burnt ....Gen 22:3   6086
Abraham took the w of the burnt ....Gen 22:6   6086
he said, Behold the fire and the w ....Gen 22:7   6086
there, and laid the w in order ....Gen 22:9   6086
laid him on the altar upon the w ....Gen 22:9   6086
of Egypt, both in vessels of w ....Ex 7:19   6086
and badgers' skins, and shittim w.........Ex 25:5   6086
shall make an ark of shittim w.............Ex 25:10   6086
shalt make staves of shittim w ....Ex 25:13   6086
also make a table of shittim w ....Ex 25:23   6086
make the staves of shittim w ....Ex 25:28   6086
of shittim w standing up ....Ex 26:15   6086
thou shalt make bars of shittim w........Ex 26:26   6086
of shittim w overlaid with gold..............Ex 26:32
hanging five pillars of shittim w ....Ex 26:37
shalt make an altar of shittim w ....Ex 27:1   6086
the altar, staves of shittim w ....Ex 27:6   6086
of shittim w shalt thou make it ....Ex 30:1   6086
make the staves of shittim w ....Ex 30:5   6086
and badgers' skins, and shittim w.........Ex 35:7   6086
w for any work of the service.................Ex 35:24   6086
to set them, and in carving of w ....Ex 35:33   6086
for the tabernacle of shittim w ....Ex 36:20   6086
And he made bars of shittim w.............Ex 36:31   6086
four pillars of shittim w ....Ex 36:36   6086
made the ark of shittim w.......................Ex 37:1   6086
And he made staves of shittim w ....Ex 37:4   6086
And he made the table of shittim w ......Ex 37:10   6086
he made the staves of shittim w ....Ex 37:15   6086
the incense altar of shittim w ....Ex 37:25   6086
he made the staves of shittim w ....Ex 37:28   6086
of burnt offering of shittim w ....Ex 38:1   6086
he made the staves of shittim w ....Ex 38:6   6086
lay the w in order upon the fire ....Lev 1:7   6086
in order upon the w that is on ....Lev 1:8   6086
w that is on the fire which is..................Lev 1:12   6086
upon the w that is upon the fire ....Lev 1:17   6086
which is upon the w that is on................Lev 3:5   6086
and burn him on the w with fire.............Lev 4:12   6086
shall burn w on it every morning ....Lev 6:12   6086
whether it be any vessel of w................Lev 11:32   6086
birds alive and clean, and cedar w ....Lev 14:4   6086
he shall take it, and the cedar w ....Lev 14:6   6086
the house two birds, and cedar w.........Lev 14:49   6086
And he shall take the cedar w ....Lev 14:51   6086
living bird, and with the cedar w ....Lev 14:52   6086
every vessel of w shall be rinsed ....Lev 15:12   6086
lean, whether there be w therein ....Num 13:20   6086
hair, and all things made of w ....Num 31:20   6086
him with an hand weapon of w ....Num 35:18   6086
gods, the work of men's hands, w ....Deut 4:28   6086
mount, and make thee an ark of w ....Deut 10:1   6086
And I made an ark of shittim w ....Deut 10:3   6086
As when a man goeth into the w...........Deut 19:5   3293
his neighbour to hew w ....Deut 19:5   6086
shalt thou serve other gods, w..............Deut 28:36   6086
thy fathers have known, even w.............Deut 28:64   6086
from the hewer of thy w unto the..........Deut 29:11   6086
abominations, and their idols, w............Deut 29:17   6086
but let them be hewers of w ....Josh 9:21   6086
being bondmen, and hewers of w..........Josh 9:23   6086
made them that day hewers of w...........Josh 9:27   6086
then get thee up to the w country ....Josh 17:15   3293
for it is a w, and thou shalt cut ....Josh 17:18   3293
a burnt sacrifice with the w of..............Judg 6:26   6086
and they clave the w of the cart 1Sa 6:14   6086
all they of the land came to a w 1Sa 14:25   3293
the people were come into the w...........1Sa 14:26   3293
in the wilderness of Ziph in a w............1Sa 23:15   2793

and went to David into the w.................1Sa 23:16   2793
and David abode in the w, and 1Sa 23:18   2793
with us in strong holds in the w............1Sa 23:19   2793
of instruments made of fir w 2Sa 6:5   6086
battle was in the w of Ephraim..............2Sa 18:6   3293
the w devoured more people that 2Sa 18:8   3293
him into a great pit in the w 2Sa 18:17   3293
instruments of the oxen for w 2Sa 24:22   6086
covered them on the inside with w 1Kin 6:15   6086
cut it in pieces, and lay it on w 1Kin 18:23   6086
the other bullock, and lay it on w 1Kin 18:23   6086
And he put the w in order, and cut 1Kin 18:33   6086
in pieces, and laid him on the w 1Kin 18:33   6086
the burnt sacrifice, and on the w 1Kin 18:33   6086
the burnt sacrifice, and the w 1Kin 18:38   6086
forth two she bears out of the w 2Kin 2:24   3293
came to Jordan, they cut down w..........2Kin 6:4   6086
but the work of men's hands, w 2Kin 19:18   6086
Then shall the trees of the w.................1Chr 16:33   3293
the threshing instruments for w 1Chr 21:23   6086
brought much cedar w to David 1Chr 22:4   6086
of iron, and w for things of w 1Chr 29:2   6086
we will cut w out of Lebanon, as 2Chr 2:16   6086
scribe stood upon a pulpit of w ....Neh 8:4   6086
for the w offering, to bring it ....Neh 10:34   6086
for the w offering, at times ....Neh 13:31   6086
as straw, and brass as rotten w............Job 41:27   6086
boar out of the w doth waste it ....Ps 80:13   3293
As the fire burneth a w, and as ....Ps 83:14   3293
all the trees of the w rejoice..................Ps 96:12   3293
found it in the fields of the w.................Ps 132:6   3293
cleaveth w upon the earth ....Ps 141:7
Where no w is, there the fire.................Prov 26:20   6086
to burning coals, and w to fire...............Prov 26:21   6086
to water therewith the w that................Eccl 2:6   3293
he that cleaveth w shall be ....Eccl 10:9   6086
tree among the trees of the w ....Song 2:3   3293
a chariot of the w of Lebanon ....Song 3:9   6086
as the trees of the w are moved............Is 7:2   3293
up itself, as if it were no w ....Is 10:15   6086
pile thereof is fire and much w ....Is 30:33   6086
but the work of men's hands, w ....Is 37:19   6086
up the w of their graven image..............Is 45:20   6086
for w brass, and for stones iron ....Is 60:17   6086
thy mouth fire, and this people w...........Jer 5:14   6086
The children gather w, and the ....Jer 7:18   6086
Thou hast broken the yokes of w ....Jer 28:13   6086
her with axes, as hewers of w ....Jer 46:22   6086
our w is sold unto us.............................Lam 5:4   6086
and the children fell under the w ....Lam 5:13   6086
Shall w be taken thereof to do ....Eze 15:3   6086
of the countries, to serve w ....Eze 20:32   6086
Heap on w, kindle the fire,.....................Eze 24:10   6086
shall take no w out of the field..............Eze 39:10   6086
door, cieled with w round about.............Eze 41:16   6086
The altar of w was three cubits ....Eze 41:22   6086
and the walls thereof, were of w ....Eze 41:22   6086
silver, of brass, of iron, of w ....Dan 5:4   636
and gold, of brass, iron, w ....Dan 5:23   636
which dwell solitarily in the w ....Mic 7:14   3293
Woe unto him that saith to the w...........Hab 2:19   6086
Go up to the mountain, and bring w ......Hag 1:8   6086
an hearth of fire among the w ....Zec 12:6   6086
gold, silver, precious stones, w 1Cor 3:12   3586
gold and of silver, but also of w.............2Ti 2:20   3585
and brass, and stone, and of w ....Rev 9:20   3585
silk, and scarlet, and all thyine w..........Rev 18:12   3586
manner vessels of most precious w ....Rev 18:12   3586

WOODS
the wilderness, and sleep in the w ....Eze 34:25   3264

WOOF
Whether it be in the warp, or w ....Lev 13:48   6154
either in the warp, or in the w ....Lev 13:49   6154
either in the warp, or in the w ....Lev 13:51   6154
that garment, whether warp or w...........Lev 13:52   6154
either in the warp, or in the w ....Lev 13:53   6154
out of the warp, or out of the w ....Lev 13:56   6154
either in the warp, or in the w ....Lev 13:57   6154
And the garment, either warp, or w ....Lev 13:58   6154
linen, either in the warp, or w................Lev 13:59   6154

WOOL
put a fleece of w in the floor ....Judg 6:37   6785
hundred thousand rams, with the w 2Kin 3:4   6785
He giveth snow like w............................Ps 147:16   6785
She seeketh w, and flax, and ....Prov 31:13   6785
like crimson, they shall be as w............Is 1:18   6785
and the worm shall eat them like w ....Is 51:8   6785
in the wine of Helbon, and white w........Eze 27:18   6785
fat, and ye clothe you with the w ....Eze 34:3   6785

no *w* shall come upon them, whiles	Eze 44:17	6785
hair of his head like the pure *w*	Dan 7:9	6015
me my bread and my water, my *w*	Hos 2:5	6785
thereof, and will recover my *w*	Hos 2:9	6785
goats, with water, and scarlet *w*	Heb 9:19	2053
and his hairs were white like *w*	Rev 1:14	2053

WOOLLEN

is in, whether it be a *w* garment	Lev 13:47	6785
of linen, or of *w*	Lev 13:48	6785
in *w* or in linen, or any thing of	Lev 13:52	6785
in a garment of *w* or linen	Lev 13:59	6785
of linen and *w* come upon thee	Lev 19:19	8162
garment of divers sorts, as of *w*	Deut 22:11	6785

WORD

After these things the *w* of the	Gen 15:1	1697
the *w* of the LORD came unto him,	Gen 15:4	1697
it might be according to thy *w*	Gen 30:34	1697
and bring me *w* again	Gen 37:14	1697
according unto thy *w* shall all my	Gen 41:40	6310
to the *w* that Joseph had spoken	Gen 44:2	1697
speak a *w* in my lord's ears, and	Gen 44:18	1697
he said, Be it according to thy *w*	Ex 8:10	1697
did according to the *w* of Moses	Ex 8:13	1697
did according to the *w* of Moses	Ex 8:31	1697
He that feared the *w* of the LORD	Ex 9:20	1697
he that regarded not the *w* of the	Ex 9:21	1697
did according to the *w* of Moses	Ex 12:35	1697
Is not this the *w* that we did	Ex 14:12	1697
did according to the *w* of Moses	Ex 32:28	1697
did according to the *w* of the	Lev 10:7	1697
according to the *w* of the LORD	Num 3:16	6310
according to the *w* of the LORD	Num 3:51	6310
the *w* of the LORD by the hand of	Num 4:45	6310
thou shalt see now whether my *w*	Num 11:23	1697
and brought back *w* unto them	Num 13:26	1697
have pardoned according to thy *w*	Num 14:20	1697
hath despised the *w* of the LORD	Num 15:31	1697
my *w* at the water of Meribah	Num 20:24	6310
and I will bring you *w* again	Num 22:8	1697
beyond the *w* of the LORD my God	Num 22:18	6310
but yet the *w* which I shall say	Num 22:20	1697
but only the *w* that I shalt speak	Num 22:35	1697
the *w* that God putteth in my	Num 22:38	1697
the LORD put a *w* in Balaam's	Num 23:5	1697
put a *w* in his mouth, and said, Go	Num 23:16	1697
at his *w* shall they go out	Num 27:21	6310
at his *w* they shall come in, both	Num 27:21	6310
he shall not break his *w*, he	Num 30:2	1697
according to the *w* of the LORD	Num 36:5	6310
bring us *w* again by what way we	Deut 1:22	1697
unto us, and brought us *w* again	Deut 1:25	1697
unto the *w* which I command you	Deut 4:2	1697
to shew you the *w* of the LORD	Deut 5:5	1697
but by every *w* that proceedeth	Deut 8:3	
that he may perform the *w* which	Deut 9:5	1697
presume to speak a *w* in my name	Deut 18:20	1697
How shall we know the *w* which the	Deut 18:21	1697
and by their *w* shall every	Deut 21:5	6310
But the *w* is very nigh unto thee,	Deut 30:14	1697
for they have observed thy *w*	Deut 33:9	565
according to the *w* of the LORD	Deut 34:5	6310
Remember the *w* which Moses the	Josh 1:13	1697
neither shall any *w* proceed out	Josh 6:10	1697
according unto the *w* of the LORD	Josh 8:27	1697
There was not a *w* of all that	Josh 8:35	1697
I brought him *w* again as it was	Josh 14:7	1697
the LORD spake this *w* unto Moses	Josh 14:10	1697
According to the *w* of the LORD,	Josh 19:50	6310
according to the *w* of the LORD by	Josh 22:9	6310
Israel, and brought them *w* again	Josh 22:32	1697
only the LORD establish his *w*	1Sa 1:23	1697
the *w* of the LORD was precious in	1Sa 3:1	1697
neither was the *w* of the LORD yet	1Sa 3:7	1697
in Shiloh by the *w* of the LORD	1Sa 3:21	1697
the *w* of Samuel came to all	1Sa 4:1	1697
that I may shew thee the *w* of God	1Sa 9:27	1697
Then came the *w* of the LORD unto	1Sa 15:10	1697
hast rejected the *w* of the LORD	1Sa 15:23	1697
hast rejected the *w* of the LORD	1Sa 15:26	1697
could not answer Abner a *w* again	2Sa 3:11	1697
that the *w* of the LORD came unto	2Sa 7:4	1697
I a *w* with any of the tribes of	2Sa 7:7	1697
the *w* that thou hast spoken	2Sa 7:25	1697
speak one *w* unto my lord the king	2Sa 14:12	1697
The *w* of my lord the king shall	2Sa 14:17	1697
until there come *w* from you to	2Sa 15:28	1697
not a *w* of bringing the king back	2Sa 19:10	
they sent this *w* unto the king	2Sa 19:14	
the *w* of the LORD is tried	2Sa 22:31	565
by me, and his *w* was in my tongue	2Sa 23:2	4405

king's *w* prevailed against Joab	2Sa 24:4	1697
the *w* of the LORD came unto the	2Sa 24:11	1697
w which he spake concerning me	1Kin 2:4	1697
this *w* against his own life	1Kin 2:23	1697
he might fulfil the *w* of the LORD	1Kin 2:27	1697
Benaiah brought the king *w* again	1Kin 2:30	1697
The *w* that I have heard is good	1Kin 2:42	1697
the *w* of the LORD came to Solomon	1Kin 6:11	1697
will I perform my *w* with thee	1Kin 6:12	1697
performed his *w* that he spake	1Kin 8:20	1697
now, O God of Israel, let thy *w*	1Kin 8:26	1697
one *w* of all his good promise	1Kin 8:56	1697
But the *w* of God came unto	1Kin 12:22	1697
therefore to the *w* of the LORD	1Kin 12:24	1697
according to the *w* of the LORD	1Kin 12:24	1697
by the *w* of the LORD unto Beth-el	1Kin 13:1	1697
the altar in the *w* of the LORD	1Kin 13:2	1697
had given by the *w* of the LORD	1Kin 13:5	1697
charged me by the *w* of the LORD	1Kin 13:9	1697
said to me by the *w* of the LORD	1Kin 13:17	1697
unto me by the *w* of the LORD	1Kin 13:18	1697
that the *w* of the LORD came unto	1Kin 13:20	1697
unto the *w* of the LORD	1Kin 13:26	6310
according to the *w* of the LORD	1Kin 13:26	1697
saying which he cried by the *w* of	1Kin 13:32	1697
according to the *w* of the LORD	1Kin 14:18	1697
Then the *w* of the LORD came to	1Kin 16:1	1697
the *w* of the LORD against Baasha	1Kin 16:7	1697
according to the *w* of the LORD	1Kin 16:12	1697
according to the *w* of the LORD	1Kin 16:34	1697
years, but according to my *w*	1Kin 17:1	1697
the *w* of the LORD came unto him,	1Kin 17:2	1697
according unto the *w* of the LORD	1Kin 17:5	1697
the *w* of the LORD came unto him,	1Kin 17:8	1697
according to the *w* of the LORD	1Kin 17:16	1697
that the *w* of the LORD in thy	1Kin 17:24	1697
that the *w* of the LORD came to	1Kin 18:1	1697
the people answered him not a *w*	1Kin 18:21	1697
unto whom the *w* of the LORD came,	1Kin 18:31	1697
done all these things at thy *w*	1Kin 18:36	1697
the *w* of the LORD came to him, and	1Kin 19:9	1697
departed, and brought him *w* again	1Kin 20:9	1697
neighbour in the *w* of the LORD	1Kin 20:35	1697
displeased because of the *w* which	1Kin 21:4	1697
the *w* of the LORD came to Elijah	1Kin 21:17	1697
the *w* of the LORD came to Elijah	1Kin 21:28	1697
at the *w* of the LORD to day	1Kin 22:5	1697
let thy *w*, I pray thee	1Kin 22:13	1697
be like the *w* of one of them, and	1Kin 22:13	1697
thou therefore the *w* of the LORD	1Kin 22:19	1697
according unto the *w* of the LORD	1Kin 22:38	1697
God in Israel to enquire of his *w*	2Kin 1:16	1697
So he died according to the *w* of	2Kin 1:17	1697
The *w* of the LORD is with him	2Kin 3:12	1697
according to the *w* of the LORD	2Kin 4:44	1697
according to the *w* of Elisha	2Kin 6:18	1697
said, Hear ye the *w* of the LORD	2Kin 7:1	1697
according to the *w* of the LORD	2Kin 7:16	1697
according to the *w* of the LORD	2Kin 9:26	1697
said, This is the *w* of the LORD	2Kin 9:36	1697
nothing of the *w* of the LORD	2Kin 10:10	1697
according to the *w* of the LORD	2Kin 14:25	1697
This was the *w* of the LORD which	2Kin 15:12	1697
Hear the *w* of the great king, the	2Kin 18:28	1697
peace, and answered him not a *w*	2Kin 18:36	1697
This is the *w* that the LORD hath	2Kin 19:21	1697
that the *w* of the LORD came to	2Kin 20:4	1697
Hezekiah, Hear the *w* of the LORD	2Kin 20:16	1697
Good is the *w* of the LORD which	2Kin 20:19	1697
king, and brought the king *w* again	2Kin 22:9	1697
And they brought the king *w* again	2Kin 22:20	1697
according to the *w* of the LORD	2Kin 23:16	1697
according to the *w* of the LORD	2Kin 24:2	1697
even against the *w* of the LORD	1Chr 10:13	1697
according to the *w* of the LORD by	1Chr 11:3	1697
according to the *w* of the LORD	1Chr 11:10	1697
according to the *w* of the LORD	1Chr 12:23	6310
according to the *w* of the LORD	1Chr 15:15	1697
the *w* which he commanded to a	1Chr 16:15	1697
that the *w* of God came to Nathan,	1Chr 17:3	1697
spake I a *w* to any of the judges	1Chr 17:6	1697
king's *w* prevailed against Joab	1Chr 21:4	1697
for the king's *w* was abominable	1Chr 21:6	1697
therefore advise thyself what *w* I	1Chr 21:12	1697
But the *w* of the LORD came to me,	1Chr 22:8	1697
his *w* that he hath spoken	2Chr 6:10	1697
let thy *w* be verified, which thou	2Chr 6:17	1697
that the LORD might perform his *w*	2Chr 10:15	1697
But the *w* of the LORD came to	2Chr 11:2	1697
the *w* of the LORD came to	2Chr 12:7	1697
at the *w* of the LORD to day	2Chr 18:4	1697

let thy *w* therefore, I pray thee,	2Chr 18:12	1697
Therefore hear the *w* of the LORD	2Chr 18:18	1697
the princes, by the *w* of the LORD	2Chr 30:12	1697
and brought the king *w* back again	2Chr 34:16	1697
have not kept the *w* of the LORD	2Chr 34:21	1697
So they brought the king *w* again	2Chr 34:28	1697
the *w* of the LORD by the hand of	2Chr 35:6	1697
To fulfil the *w* of the LORD by	2Chr 36:21	1697
that the *w* of the LORD spoken by	2Chr 36:22	1697
that the *w* of the LORD by the	Ezr 1:1	1697
that whosoever shall alter this *w*	Ezr 6:11	6600
should do according to this *w*	Ezr 10:5	1697
the *w* that thou commandedst thy	Neh 1:8	1697
did according to the *w* of Memucan	Est 1:21	1697
As the *w* went out of the king's	Est 7:8	1697
and none spake a *w* unto him	Job 2:13	1697
by the *w* of thy lips I have kept	Ps 17:4	1697
the *w* of the LORD is tried	Ps 18:30	565
For the *w* of the LORD is right	Ps 33:4	1697
By the *w* of the LORD were the	Ps 33:6	1697
In God I will praise his *w*	Ps 56:4	1697
In God will I praise his *w*	Ps 56:10	1697
in the LORD will I praise his *w*	Ps 56:10	1697
The Lord gave the *w*	Ps 68:11	562
unto the voice of his *w*	Ps 103:20	1697
the *w* which he commanded to a	Ps 105:8	1697
Until the time that his *w* came	Ps 105:19	1697
the *w* of the LORD tried him	Ps 105:19	565
they rebelled not against his *w*	Ps 105:28	1697
land, they believed not his *w*	Ps 106:24	1697
He sent his *w*, and healed them, and	Ps 107:20	1697
heed thereto according to thy *w*	Ps 119:9	1697
Thy *w* have I hid in mine heart,	Ps 119:11	565
I will not forget thy *w*	Ps 119:16	1697
that I may live, and keep thy *w*	Ps 119:17	1697
thou me according to thy *w*	Ps 119:25	1697
thou me according unto thy *w*	Ps 119:28	1697
Stablish thy *w* unto thy servant,	Ps 119:38	565
thy salvation, according to thy *w*	Ps 119:41	565
for I trust in thy *w*	Ps 119:42	1697
take not the *w* of truth utterly	Ps 119:43	1697
Remember the *w* unto thy servant,	Ps 119:49	1697
for thy *w* hath quickened me	Ps 119:50	565
unto me according to thy *w*	Ps 119:58	565
O LORD, according unto thy *w*	Ps 119:65	1697
but now have I kept thy *w*	Ps 119:67	565
because I have hoped in thy *w*	Ps 119:74	1697
to thy *w* unto thy servant	Ps 119:76	565
but I hope in thy *w*	Ps 119:81	1697
Mine eyes fail for thy *w*, saying,	Ps 119:82	565
thy *w* is settled in heaven	Ps 119:89	1697
evil way, that I might keep thy *w*	Ps 119:101	1697
Thy *w* is a lamp unto my feet, and	Ps 119:105	1697
me, O LORD, according unto thy *w*	Ps 119:107	1697
I hope in thy *w*	Ps 119:114	1697
Uphold me according unto thy *w*	Ps 119:116	565
for the *w* of thy righteousness	Ps 119:123	565
Order my steps in thy *w*	Ps 119:133	565
Thy *w* is very pure	Ps 119:140	565
I hoped in thy *w*	Ps 119:147	1697
that I might meditate in thy *w*	Ps 119:148	565
quicken me according to thy *w*	Ps 119:154	565
because they kept not thy *w*	Ps 119:158	565
Thy *w* is true from the beginning	Ps 119:160	1697
my heart standeth in awe of thy *w*	Ps 119:161	1697
I rejoice at thy *w*, as one that	Ps 119:162	565
understanding according to thy *w*	Ps 119:169	1697
deliver me according to thy *w*	Ps 119:170	565
My tongue shall speak of thy *w*	Ps 119:172	565
doth wait, and in his *w* do I hope	Ps 130:5	1697
thy *w* above all thy name	Ps 138:2	565
For there is not a *w* in my tongue	Ps 139:4	4405
his *w* runneth very swiftly	Ps 147:15	1697
He sendeth out his *w*, and melteth	Ps 147:18	1697
He sheweth his *w* unto Jacob	Ps 147:19	1697
stormy wind fulfilling his *w*	Ps 148:8	1697
but a good *w* maketh it glad	Prov 12:25	1697
the *w* shall be destroyed	Prov 13:13	1697
The simple believeth every *w*	Prov 14:15	1697
a *w* spoken in due season, how	Prov 15:23	1697
A *w* fitly spoken is like apples	Prov 25:11	1697
Every *w* of God is pure	Prov 30:5	565
Where the *w* of a king is, there	Eccl 8:4	1697
Hear the *w* of the LORD, ye rulers	Is 1:10	1697
The *w* that Isaiah the son of Amoz	Is 2:1	1697
the *w* of the LORD from Jerusalem	Is 2:3	1697
despised the *w* of the Holy One of	Is 5:24	565
speak the *w*, and it shall not	Is 8:10	1697
speak not according to this *w*	Is 8:20	1697
The Lord sent a *w* into Jacob	Is 9:8	1697
This is the *w* that the LORD hath	Is 16:13	1697
for the LORD hath spoken this *w*	Is 24:3	1697
But the *w* of the LORD was unto	Is 28:13	1697
Wherefore hear the *w* of the LORD	Is 28:14	1697
make a man an offender for a *w*	Is 29:21	1697
Israel, Because ye despise this *w*	Is 30:12	1697
ears shall hear a *w* behind thee	Is 30:21	1697
peace, and answered him not a *w*	Is 36:21	1697
This is the *w* which the LORD hath	Is 37:22	1697
Then came the *w* of the LORD to	Is 38:4	1697
Hear the *w* of the LORD of hosts	Is 39:5	1697
Good is the *w* of the LORD which	Is 39:8	1697
but the *w* of our God shall stand	Is 40:8	1697
I asked of them, could answer a *w*	Is 41:28	1697
confirmeth the *w* of his servant	Is 44:26	1697
the *w* is gone out of my mouth in	Is 45:23	1697
I should know how to speak a *w* in	Is 50:4	1697
So shall my *w* be that goeth forth	Is 55:11	1697
spirit, and trembleth at my *w*	Is 66:2	1697
Hear the *w* of the LORD	Is 66:5	1697
ye that tremble at his *w*	Is 66:5	1697
To whom the *w* of the LORD came in	Jer 1:2	1697
Then the *w* of the LORD came unto	Jer 1:4	1697
Moreover the *w* of the LORD came	Jer 1:11	1697
I will hasten my *w* to perform it	Jer 1:12	1697
the *w* of the LORD came unto me	Jer 1:13	1697
Moreover the *w* of the LORD came	Jer 2:1	1697
Hear ye the *w* of the LORD	Jer 2:4	1697
see ye the *w* of the LORD	Jer 2:31	1697
wind, and the *w* is not in them	Jer 5:13	1699
of hosts, Because ye speak this *w*	Jer 5:14	1697
the *w* of the LORD is unto them a	Jer 6:10	1697
The *w* that came to Jeremiah from	Jer 7:1	1697
house, and proclaim there this *w*	Jer 7:2	1697
Hear the *w* of the LORD, all ye of	Jer 7:2	1697
have rejected the *w* of the LORD	Jer 8:9	1697
Yet hear the *w* of the LORD	Jer 9:20	1697
ear receive the *w* of his mouth	Jer 9:20	1697
Hear ye the *w* which the LORD	Jer 10:1	1697
The *w* that came to Jeremiah from	Jer 11:1	1697
according to the *w* of the LORD	Jer 13:2	1697
the *w* of the LORD came unto me	Jer 13:3	1697
Then the *w* of the LORD came unto	Jer 13:8	1697
thou shalt speak unto them this *w*	Jer 13:12	1697
The *w* of the LORD that came to	Jer 14:1	1697
thou shalt say this *w* unto them	Jer 14:17	1697
thy *w* was unto me the joy and	Jer 15:16	1697
The *w* of the LORD came also unto	Jer 16:1	1697
me, Where is the *w* of the LORD	Jer 17:15	1697
them, Hear ye the *w* of the LORD	Jer 17:20	1697
The *w* which came to Jeremiah from	Jer 18:1	1697
Then the *w* of the LORD came to me	Jer 18:5	1697
nor the *w* from the prophet	Jer 18:18	1697
And say, Hear ye the *w* of the LORD	Jer 19:3	1697
because the *w* of the LORD was	Jer 20:8	1697
But his *w* was in mine heart as a	Jer 20:9	
The *w* which came unto Jeremiah	Jer 21:1	1697
say, Hear ye the *w* of the LORD	Jer 21:11	1697
of Judah, and speak there this *w*	Jer 22:1	1697
Hear the *w* of the LORD, O king of	Jer 22:2	1697
earth, hear the *w* of the LORD	Jer 22:29	1697
and hath perceived and heard his *w*	Jer 23:18	1697
who hath marked his *w*, and heard	Jer 23:18	1697
and he that hath my *w*	Jer 23:28	1697
let him speak my *w* faithfully	Jer 23:28	1697
Is not my *w* like as a fire	Jer 23:29	1697
for every man's *w* shall be his	Jer 23:36	1697
Because ye say this *w*, The burden	Jer 23:38	1697
Again the *w* of the LORD came unto	Jer 24:4	1697
The *w* that came to Jeremiah	Jer 25:1	1697
the *w* of the LORD hath come unto	Jer 25:3	1697
Judah came this *w* from the LORD	Jer 26:1	1697
diminish not a *w*	Jer 26:2	1697
w unto Jeremiah from the LORD	Jer 27:1	1697
if the *w* of the LORD be with them	Jer 27:18	1697
this *w* that I speak in thine ears	Jer 28:7	1697
when the *w* of the prophet shall	Jer 28:9	1697
Then the *w* of the LORD came unto	Jer 28:12	1697
and perform my good *w* toward you	Jer 29:10	1697
ye therefore the *w* of the LORD	Jer 29:20	1697
Then came the *w* of the LORD unto	Jer 29:30	1697
The *w* that came to Jeremiah from	Jer 30:1	1697
Hear the *w* of the LORD, O ye	Jer 31:10	1697
The *w* that came to Jeremiah from	Jer 32:1	1697
The *w* of the LORD came unto me,	Jer 32:6	1697
according to the *w* of the LORD	Jer 32:8	1697
that this was the *w* of the LORD	Jer 32:8	1697
Then came the *w* of the LORD unto	Jer 32:26	1697
Moreover the *w* of the LORD came	Jer 33:1	1697
the *w* of the LORD came unto	Jer 33:19	1697
Moreover the *w* of the LORD came	Jer 33:23	1697
The *w* which came unto Jeremiah	Jer 34:1	1697

Yet hear the *w* of the LORD	Jer 34:4	1697
for I have pronounced the *w*	Jer 34:5	1697
This is the *w* that came unto	Jer 34:8	1697
Therefore the *w* of the LORD came	Jer 34:12	1697
The *w* which came unto Jeremiah	Jer 35:1	1697
Then came the *w* of the LORD unto	Jer 35:12	1697
that this *w* came unto Jeremiah	Jer 36:1	1697
Then the *w* of the LORD came to	Jer 36:27	1697
Then came the *w* of the LORD unto	Jer 37:6	1697
Is there any *w* from the LORD	Jer 37:17	1697
this is the *w* that the LORD hath	Jer 38:21	1697
Now the *w* of the LORD came unto	Jer 39:15	1697
The *w* that came to Jeremiah from	Jer 40:1	1697
that the *w* of the LORD came unto	Jer 42:7	1697
therefore hear the *w* of the LORD	Jer 42:15	1697
Then came the *w* of the LORD unto	Jer 43:8	1697
The *w* that came to Jeremiah	Jer 44:1	1697
As for the *w* that thou hast	Jer 44:16	1697
Hear the *w* of the LORD, all Judah	Jer 44:24	1697
hear ye the *w* of the LORD	Jer 44:26	1697
The *w* that Jeremiah the prophet	Jer 45:1	1697
The *w* of the LORD which came to	Jer 46:1	1697
The *w* that the LORD spake to	Jer 46:13	1697
The *w* of the LORD that came to	Jer 47:1	1697
The *w* of the LORD that came to	Jer 49:34	1697
The *w* that the LORD spake against	Jer 50:1	1697
The *w* which Jeremiah the prophet	Jer 51:59	1697
he hath fulfilled his *w* that he	Lam 2:17	565
The *w* of the LORD came expressly	Eze 1:3	1697
that the *w* of the LORD came unto	Eze 3:16	1697
therefore hear the *w* at my mouth	Eze 3:17	1697
the *w* of the LORD came unto me,	Eze 6:1	1697
hear the *w* of the Lord GOD	Eze 6:3	1697
Moreover the *w* of the LORD came	Eze 7:1	1697
Again the *w* of the LORD came unto	Eze 11:14	1697
The *w* of the LORD also came unto	Eze 12:1	1697
came the *w* of the LORD unto me	Eze 12:8	1697
Moreover the *w* of the LORD came	Eze 12:17	1697
the *w* of the LORD came unto me,	Eze 12:21	1697
the *w* that I shall speak shall	Eze 12:25	1697
house, will I say the *w*, and will	Eze 12:25	1697
Again the *w* of the LORD came to	Eze 12:26	1697
but the *w* which I have spoken	Eze 12:28	1697
the *w* of the LORD came unto me,	Eze 13:1	1697
hearts, Hear ye the *w* of the LORD	Eze 13:2	1697
that they would confirm the *w*	Eze 13:6	1697
the *w* of the LORD came unto me,	Eze 14:2	1697
The *w* of the LORD came again to	Eze 14:12	1697
the *w* of the LORD came unto me,	Eze 15:1	1697
Again the *w* of the LORD came unto	Eze 16:1	1697
O harlot, hear the *w* of the LORD	Eze 16:35	1697
the *w* of the LORD came unto me,	Eze 17:1	1697
Moreover the *w* of the LORD came	Eze 17:11	1697
The *w* of the LORD came unto me	Eze 18:1	1697
Then came the *w* of the LORD unto	Eze 20:2	1697
Moreover the *w* of the LORD came	Eze 20:45	1697
drop thy *w* toward the south, and	Eze 20:46	
the south, Hear the *w* of the LORD	Eze 20:47	1697
the *w* of the LORD came unto me,	Eze 21:1	1697
drop thy *w* toward the holy places	Eze 21:2	
Again the *w* of the LORD came unto	Eze 21:8	1697
The *w* of the LORD came unto me	Eze 21:18	1697
Moreover the *w* of the LORD came	Eze 22:1	1697
the *w* of the LORD came unto me,	Eze 22:17	1697
the *w* of the LORD came unto me,	Eze 22:23	1697
The *w* of the LORD came again unto	Eze 23:1	1697
the *w* of the LORD came unto me,	Eze 24:1	1697
Also the *w* of the LORD came unto	Eze 24:15	1697
The *w* of the LORD came unto me,	Eze 24:20	1697
The *w* of the LORD came again unto	Eze 25:1	1697
Hear the *w* of the Lord GOD	Eze 25:3	1697
that the *w* of the LORD came unto	Eze 26:1	1697
The *w* of the LORD came again unto	Eze 27:1	1697
The *w* of the LORD came again unto	Eze 28:1	1697
Moreover the *w* of the LORD came	Eze 28:11	1697
Again the *w* of the LORD came unto	Eze 28:20	1697
the *w* of the LORD came unto me,	Eze 29:1	1697
the *w* of the LORD came unto me,	Eze 29:17	1697
The *w* of the LORD came again unto	Eze 30:1	1697
that the *w* of the LORD came unto	Eze 30:20	1697
that the *w* of the LORD came unto	Eze 31:1	1697
that the *w* of the LORD came unto	Eze 32:1	1697
that the *w* of the LORD came unto	Eze 32:17	1697
Again the *w* of the LORD came unto	Eze 33:1	1697
thou shalt hear the *w* at my mouth	Eze 33:7	1697
Then the *w* of the LORD came unto	Eze 33:23	1697
hear what is the *w* that cometh	Eze 33:30	1697
the *w* of the Lord came unto me,	Eze 34:1	1697
shepherds, hear the *w* of the LORD	Eze 34:7	1697
shepherds, hear the *w* of the LORD	Eze 34:9	1697
Moreover the *w* of the LORD came	Eze 35:1	1697

of Israel, hear the *w* of the LORD	Eze 36:1	1697
hear the *w* of the Lord GOD	Eze 36:4	1697
Moreover the *w* of the LORD came	Eze 36:16	1697
dry bones, hear the *w* of the LORD	Eze 37:4	1697
The *w* of the LORD came again unto	Eze 37:15	1697
the *w* of the LORD came unto me,	Eze 38:1	1697
him, and have changed the king's *w*	Dan 3:28	4406
demand by the *w* of the holy ones	Dan 4:17	3983
While the *w* was in the king's	Dan 4:31	4406
whereof the *w* of the LORD came to	Dan 9:2	1697
when he had spoken this *w* unto me	Dan 10:11	1697
The *w* of the LORD that came unto	Hos 1:1	1697
The *w* of the LORD by Hosea	Hos 1:2	1699
of the *w* of the LORD by Hosea	Hos 1:2	1699
Hear the *w* of the LORD, ye	Hos 4:1	1697
The *w* of the LORD that came to	Joel 1:1	1697
he is strong that executeth his *w*	Joel 2:11	1697
Hear this *w* that the LORD hath	Amos 3:1	1697
Hear this *w*, ye kine of Bashan,	Amos 4:1	1697
Hear ye this *w* which I take up	Amos 5:1	1697
hear thou the *w* of the LORD	Amos 7:16	1697
drop not thy *w* against the house	Amos 7:16	
and fro to seek the *w* of the LORD	Amos 8:12	1697
Now the *w* of the LORD came unto	Jonah 1:1	1697
the *w* of the LORD came unto Jonah	Jonah 3:1	1697
according to the *w* of the LORD	Jonah 3:3	1697
For *w* came unto the king of	Jonah 3:6	1697
The *w* of the LORD that came to	Mic 1:1	1697
the *w* of the LORD from Jerusalem	Mic 4:2	1697
oaths of the tribes, even thy *w*	Hab 3:9	562
The *w* of the LORD which came unto	Zeph 1:1	1697
the *w* of the LORD is against you	Zeph 2:5	1697
came the *w* of the LORD by Haggai	Hag 1:1	1697
Then came the *w* of the LORD by	Hag 1:3	1697
came the *w* of the LORD by the	Hag 2:1	1697
According to the *w* that I	Hag 2:5	1697
came the *w* of the LORD by Haggai	Hag 2:10	1697
again the *w* of the LORD came unto	Hag 2:20	1697
came the *w* of the LORD unto	Zec 1:1	1697
came the *w* of the LORD unto	Zec 1:7	1697
This is the *w* of the LORD unto	Zec 4:6	1697
Moreover the *w* of the LORD came	Zec 4:8	1697
the *w* of the LORD came unto me,	Zec 6:9	1697
that the *w* of the LORD came unto	Zec 7:1	1697
Then came the *w* of the LORD of	Zec 7:4	1697
the *w* of the LORD came unto	Zec 7:8	1697
Again the *w* of the LORD of hosts	Zec 8:1	1697
the *w* of the LORD of hosts came	Zec 8:18	1697
The burden of the *w* of the LORD	Zec 9:1	1697
that it was the *w* of the LORD	Zec 11:11	1697
The burden of the *w* of the LORD	Zec 12:1	1697
The burden of the *w* of the LORD	Mal 1:1	1697
have found him, bring me *w* again	Mt 2:8	518
thou there until I bring thee *w*	Mt 2:13	2036
but by every *w* that proceedeth	Mt 4:4	4487
but speak the *w* only, and my	Mt 8:8	3056
cast out the spirits with his *w*	Mt 8:16	3056
whosoever speaketh a *w* against	Mt 12:32	3056
That every idle *w* that men shall	Mt 12:36	4487
one heareth the *w* of the kingdom	Mt 13:19	3056
the same is he that heareth the *w*	Mt 13:20	3056
ariseth because of the *w*, by and	Mt 13:21	3056
thorns is he that heareth the *w*	Mt 13:22	3056
of riches, choke the *w*, and he	Mt 13:22	3056
ground is he that heareth the *w*	Mt 13:23	3056
But he answered her not a *w*	Mt 15:23	3056
every *w* may be established	Mt 18:16	4487
no man was able to answer him a *w*	Mt 22:46	3056
Peter remembered the *w* of Jesus	Mt 26:75	4487
And he answered him to never a *w*	Mt 27:14	4487
did run to bring his disciples *w*	Mt 28:8	518
and he preached the *w* unto them	Mk 2:2	3056
The sower soweth the *w*	Mk 4:14	3056
the way side, where the *w* is sown	Mk 4:15	3056
taketh away the *w* that was sown	Mk 4:15	3056
who, when they have heard the *w*	Mk 4:16	3056
such as hear the *w*,	Mk 4:18	3056
things entering in, choke the *w*	Mk 4:19	3056
such as hear the *w*, and receive it	Mk 4:20	3056
parables spake he the *w* unto them	Mk 4:33	3056
Jesus heard the *w* that was spoken	Mk 5:36	3056
Making the *w* of God of none	Mk 7:13	3056
the *w* that Jesus said unto him	Mk 14:72	4487
confirming the *w* with signs	Mk 16:20	3056
and ministers of the *w*	Lk 1:2	3056
be it unto me according to thy *w*	Lk 1:38	4487
in peace, according to thy *w*	Lk 2:29	4487
the *w* of God came unto John the	Lk 3:2	4487
alone, but by every *w* of God	Lk 4:4	4487
for his *w* was with power	Lk 4:32	3056
saying, What a *w* is this	Lk 4:36	3056
upon him to hear the *w* of God	Lk 5:1	3056

nevertheless at thy *w* I will let	Lk 5:5	4487
but say in a *w*, and my servant	Lk 7:7	3056
The seed is the *w* of God	Lk 8:11	3056
taketh away the *w* out of their	Lk 8:12	3056
they hear, receive the *w* with joy	Lk 8:13	3056
and good heart, having heard the *w*	Lk 8:15	3056
are these which hear the *w* of God	Lk 8:21	3056
at Jesus' feet, and heard his *w*	Lk 10:39	3056
are they that hear the *w* of God	Lk 11:28	3056
speak a *w* against the Son of man	Lk 12:10	3056
remembered the *w* of the Lord	Lk 22:61	3056
w before God and all the people	Lk 24:19	3056
In the beginning was the *W*	Jn 1:1	3056
the *W* was with God	Jn 1:1	3056
and the *W* was God	Jn 1:1	3056
the *W* was made flesh, and dwelt	Jn 1:14	3056
the *w* which Jesus had said	Jn 2:22	3056
believed because of his own *w*	Jn 4:41	3056
the man believed the *w* that Jesus	Jn 4:50	3056
unto you, He that heareth my *w*	Jn 5:24	3056
ye have not his *w* abiding in you	Jn 5:38	3056
on him, If ye continue in my *w*	Jn 8:31	3056
because my *w* hath no place in you	Jn 8:37	3056
even because ye cannot hear my *w*	Jn 8:43	3056
gods, unto whom the *w* of God came	Jn 10:35	3056
the *w* that I have spoken, the	Jn 12:48	3056
the *w* which ye hear is not mine,	Jn 14:24	3056
w which I have spoken unto you	Jn 15:3	3056
Remember the *w* that I said unto	Jn 15:20	3056
that the *w* might be fulfilled	Jn 15:25	3056
and they have kept thy *w*	Jn 17:6	3056
I have given them thy *w*	Jn 17:14	3056
thy *w* is truth	Jn 17:17	3056
believe on me through their *w*	Jn 17:20	3056
received his *w* were baptized	Acts 2:41	3056
them which heard the *w* believed	Acts 4:4	3056
all boldness they may speak thy *w*	Acts 4:29	3056
they spake the *w* of God with	Acts 4:31	3056
that we should leave the *w* of God	Acts 6:2	3056
and to the ministry of the *w*	Acts 6:4	3056
And the *w* of God increased	Acts 6:7	3056
went every where preaching the *w*	Acts 8:4	3056
Samaria had received the *w* of God	Acts 8:14	3056
and preached the *w* of the Lord	Acts 8:25	3056
The *w* which God sent unto the	Acts 10:36	3056
That *w*, I say, ye know, which was	Acts 10:37	4487
on all them which heard the *w*	Acts 10:44	3056
had also received the *w* of God	Acts 11:1	3056
remembered I the *w* of the Lord	Acts 11:16	4487
preaching the *w* to none but unto	Acts 11:19	3056
But the *w* of God grew and	Acts 12:24	3056
they preached the *w* of God in the	Acts 13:5	3056
and desired to hear the *w* of God	Acts 13:7	3056
if ye have any *w* of exhortation	Acts 13:15	3056
to you is the *w* of this salvation	Acts 13:26	3056
together to hear the *w* of God	Acts 13:44	3056
It was necessary that the *w* of	Acts 13:46	3056
and glorified the *w* of the Lord	Acts 13:48	3056
the *w* of the Lord was published	Acts 13:49	3056
testimony unto the *w* of his grace	Acts 14:3	3056
they had preached the *w* in Perga	Acts 14:25	3056
should hear the *w* of the gospel	Acts 15:7	3056
and preaching the *w* of the Lord	Acts 15:35	3056
have preached the *w* of the Lord	Acts 15:36	3056
Ghost to preach the *w* in Asia	Acts 16:6	3056
spake unto him the *w* of the Lord	Acts 16:32	3056
in that they received the *w* with	Acts 17:11	3056
had knowledge that the *w* of God	Acts 17:13	3056
teaching the *w* of God among them	Acts 18:11	3056
heard the *w* of the Lord Jesus	Acts 19:10	3056
So mightily grew the *w* of God	Acts 19:20	3056
to the *w* of his grace, which is	Acts 20:32	3056
gave him audience unto this *w*	Acts 22:22	3056
after that Paul had spoken one *w*	Acts 28:25	4487
Not as though the *w* of God hath	Rom 9:6	3056
For this is the *w* of promise	Rom 9:9	3056
The *w* is nigh thee, even in thy	Rom 10:8	4487
the *w* of faith, which we preach	Rom 10:8	4487
and hearing by the *w* of God	Rom 10:17	4487
make the Gentiles obedient, by *w*	Rom 15:18	3056
the kingdom of God is not in *w*	1Cor 4:20	3056
by the Spirit the *w* of wisdom	1Cor 12:8	3056
to another the *w* of knowledge by	1Cor 12:8	3056
came the *w* of God out from you	1Cor 14:36	3056
our *w* toward you was not yea and	2Cor 1:18	3056
many, which corrupt the *w* of God	2Cor 2:17	3056
nor handling the *w* of God	2Cor 4:2	3056
unto us the *w* of reconciliation	2Cor 5:19	3056
By the *w* of truth, by the power	2Cor 6:7	3056
such as we are in *w* by letters	2Cor 10:11	3056
shall every *w* be established	2Cor 13:1	4487
all the law is fulfilled in one *w*	Gal 5:14	4487
the *w* communicate unto him that	Gal 6:6	4487
that ye heard the *w* of truth	Eph 1:13	4487
the washing of water by the *w*	Eph 5:26	4487
the Spirit, which is the *w* of God	Eph 6:17	4487
bold to speak the *w* without fear	Phil 1:14	3056
Holding forth the *w* of life	Phil 2:16	3056
the *w* of the truth of the gospel	Col 1:5	3056
for you, to fulfil the *w* of God	Col 1:25	3056
Let the *w* of Christ dwell in you	Col 3:16	3056
And whatsoever ye do in *w* or deed	Col 3:17	3056
came not unto you in *w* only	1Th 1:5	3056
received the *w* in much affliction	1Th 1:6	3056
out the *w* of the Lord not only in	1Th 1:8	3056
when ye received the *w* of God	1Th 2:13	3056
received it not as the *w* of men	1Th 2:13	3056
the *w* of God, which effectually	1Th 2:13	3056
say unto you by the *w* of the Lord	1Th 4:15	3056
neither by spirit, nor by *w*	2Th 2:2	3056
ye have been taught, whether by *w*	2Th 2:15	3056
and stablish you in every good *w*	2Th 2:17	3056
that the *w* of the Lord may have	2Th 3:1	3056
obey not our *w* by this epistle	2Th 3:14	3056
it is sanctified by the *w* of God	1Ti 4:5	3056
an example of the believers, in *w*	1Ti 4:12	3056
they who labour in the *w* and	1Ti 5:17	3056
but the *w* of God is not bound	2Ti 2:9	3056
rightly dividing the *w* of truth	2Ti 2:15	3056
their *w* will eat as doth a canker	2Ti 2:17	3056
Preach the *w*	2Ti 4:2	3056
his *w* through preaching, which is	Titus 1:3	3056
faithful *w* as he hath been taught	Titus 1:9	3056
that the *w* of God be not	Titus 2:5	3056
all things by the *w* of his power	Heb 1:3	4487
For if the *w* spoken by angels was	Heb 2:2	3056
but the *w* preached did not profit	Heb 4:2	3056
For the *w* of God is quick, and	Heb 4:12	3056
in the *w* of righteousness	Heb 5:13	3056
And have tasted the good *w* of God	Heb 6:5	4487
but the *w* of the oath, which was	Heb 7:28	3056
were framed by the *w* of God	Heb 11:3	4487
w should not be spoken to them	Heb 12:19	3056
And this *w*, Yet once more,	Heb 12:27	
have spoken unto you the *w* of God	Heb 13:7	3056
suffer the *w* of exhortation	Heb 13:22	3056
begat he us with the *w* of truth	Jas 1:18	3056
with meekness the engrafted *w*	Jas 1:21	3056
But be ye doers of the *w*, and not	Jas 1:22	3056
For if any be a hearer of the *w*	Jas 1:23	3056
If any man offend not in *w*	Jas 3:2	3056
of incorruptible, by the *w* of God	1Pet 1:23	3056
But the *w* of the Lord endureth	1Pet 1:25	4487
this is the *w* which by the gospel	1Pet 1:25	4487
desire the sincere milk of the *w*	1Pet 2:2	3050
to them which stumble at the *w*	1Pet 2:8	3056
that, if any obey not the *w*	1Pet 3:1	3056
they also may without the *w* be	1Pet 3:1	3056
also a more sure *w* of prophecy	2Pet 1:19	3056
that by the *w* of God the heavens	2Pet 3:5	3056
by the same *w* are kept in store,	2Pet 3:7	3056
have handled, of the *W* of life	1Jn 1:1	3056
him a liar, and his *w* is not in us	1Jn 1:10	3056
But whoso keepeth his *w*, in him	1Jn 2:5	3056
The old commandment is the *w*	1Jn 2:7	3056
the *w* of God abideth in you, and	1Jn 2:14	3056
children, let us not love in *w*	1Jn 3:18	3056
in heaven, the Father, the *W*	1Jn 5:7	3056
Who bare record of the *w* of God	Rev 1:2	3056
called Patmos, for the *w* of God	Rev 1:9	3056
strength, and hast kept my *w*	Rev 3:8	3056
hast kept the *w* of my patience	Rev 3:10	3056
that were slain for the *w* of God	Rev 6:9	3056
by the *w* of their testimony	Rev 12:11	3056
his name is called The *W* of God	Rev 19:13	3056
of Jesus, and for the *w* of God	Rev 20:4	3056

WORD'S

For thy *w* sake, and according to	2Sa 7:21	1697
ariseth for the *w* sake,	Mk 4:17	3056

WORDS

when he heard the *w* of Rebekah	Gen 24:30	1697
Abraham's servant heard their *w*	Gen 24:52	1697
Esau heard the *w* of his father	Gen 27:34	1697
these *w* of Esau her elder son	Gen 27:42	1697
he heard the *w* of Laban's sons,	Gen 31:1	1697
their *w* pleased Hamor, and Shechem	Gen 34:18	1697
more for his dreams, and for his *w*	Gen 37:8	1697
unto him according to these *w*	Gen 39:17	1697
master heard the *w* of his wife	Gen 39:19	1697
that your *w* may be proved,	Gen 42:16	1697
so shall your *w* be verified	Gen 42:20	1697

according to the tenor of these *w*	Gen 43:7	1697
he spake unto them these same *w*	Gen 44:6	1697
Wherefore saith my lord these *w*	Gen 44:7	1697
let it be according unto your *w*	Gen 44:10	1697
we told him the *w* of my lord	Gen 44:24	1697
they told him all the *w* of Joseph	Gen 45:27	1697
he giveth goodly *w*	Gen 49:21	561
unto him, and put *w* in his mouth	Ex 4:15	1697
Moses told Aaron all the *w* of the	Ex 4:28	1697
Aaron spake all the *w* which the	Ex 4:30	1697
and let them not regard vain *w*	Ex 5:9	1697
These are the *w* which thou shalt	Ex 19:6	1697
w which the LORD commanded him	Ex 19:7	1697
Moses returned the *w* of the	Ex 19:8	1697
Moses told the *w* of the people	Ex 19:9	1697
And God spake all these *w*, saying,	Ex 20:1	1697
perverteth the *w* of the righteous	Ex 23:8	1697
the people all the *w* of the LORD	Ex 24:3	1697
All the *w* which the LORD hath	Ex 24:3	1697
Moses wrote all the *w* of the LORD	Ex 24:4	1697
with you concerning all these *w*	Ex 24:8	1697
write upon these tables the *w*	Ex 34:1	1697
w I have made a covenant with	Ex 34:27	1697
the tables the *w* of the covenant	Ex 34:28	1697
These are the *w* which the LORD	Ex 35:1	1697
told the people the *w* of the LORD	Num 11:24	1697
And he said, Hear now my *w*	Num 12:6	1697
an end of speaking all these *w*	Num 16:31	1697
and spake unto him the *w* of Balak	Num 22:7	1697
said, which heard the *w* of God	Num 24:4	561
said, which heard the *w* of God	Num 24:16	561
These be the *w* which Moses spake	Deut 1:1	1697
LORD heard the voice of your *w*	Deut 1:34	1697
king of Heshbon with *w* of peace	Deut 2:26	1697
and I will make them hear my *w*	Deut 4:10	1697
ye heard the voice of the *w*	Deut 4:12	1697
thou heardest his *w* out of the	Deut 4:36	1697
These *w* the LORD spake unto all	Deut 5:22	1697
LORD heard the voice of your *w*	Deut 5:28	1697
the voice of the *w* of this people	Deut 5:28	1697
And these *w*, which I command thee	Deut 6:6	1697
written according to all the *w*	Deut 9:10	1697
w that were in the first tables	Deut 10:2	1697
lay up these my *w* in your heart	Deut 11:18	1697
hear all these *w* which I command	Deut 12:28	1697
unto the *w* of that prophet	Deut 13:3	1697
pervert the *w* of the righteous	Deut 16:19	1697
to keep all the *w* of this law	Deut 17:19	1697
will put my *w* in his mouth	Deut 18:18	1697
will not hearken unto my *w* which	Deut 18:19	1697
upon them all the *w* of this law	Deut 27:3	1697
the *w* of this law very plainly	Deut 27:8	1697
all the *w* of this law to do them	Deut 27:26	1697
not go aside from any of the *w*	Deut 28:14	1697
wilt not observe to do all the *w*	Deut 28:58	1697
These are the *w* of the covenant	Deut 29:1	1697
therefore the *w* of this covenant	Deut 29:9	1697
he heareth the *w* of this curse	Deut 29:19	1697
we may do all the *w* of this law	Deut 29:29	1697
spake unto all Israel	Deut 31:1	1697
to do all the *w* of this law	Deut 31:12	1697
the *w* of this law in a book	Deut 31:24	1697
I may speak these *w* in their ears	Deut 31:28	1697
of Israel the *w* of this song	Deut 31:30	1697
hear, O earth, the *w* of my mouth	Deut 32:1	561
spake all the *w* of this song in	Deut 32:44	1697
all these *w* to all Israel	Deut 32:45	1697
Set your hearts unto all the *w*	Deut 32:46	1697
to do, all the *w* of this law	Deut 32:46	1697
every one shall receive of thy *w*	Deut 33:3	1703
will not hearken unto thy *w* in	Josh 1:18	1697
she said, According unto your *w*	Josh 2:21	1697
hear the *w* of the LORD your God	Josh 3:9	1697
he read all the *w* of the law	Josh 8:34	1697
heard the *w* that the children of	Josh 22:30	1697
Joshua wrote these *w* in the book	Josh 24:26	1697
for it hath heard all the *w* of	Josh 24:27	561
angel of the LORD spake these *w*	Judg 2:4	1697
the men of Shechem all these *w*	Judg 9:3	1697
the *w* of Gaal the son of Ebed	Judg 9:30	1697
we do not so according to thy *w*	Judg 11:10	1697
Jephthah uttered all his *w* before	Judg 11:11	1697
w of Jephthah which he sent him	Judg 11:28	1697
Now let thy *w* come to pass	Judg 13:12	1697
she pressed him daily with her *w*	Judg 16:16	1697
none of his *w* fall to the ground	1Sa 3:19	1697
Samuel told all the *w* of the LORD	1Sa 8:10	1697
heard all the *w* of the people	1Sa 8:21	1697
the voice of the *w* of the LORD	1Sa 15:1	1697
commandment of the LORD, and thy *w*	1Sa 15:24	1697
heard those *w* of the Philistine	1Sa 17:11	1697
and spake according to the same *w*	1Sa 17:23	1697
when the *w* were heard which David	1Sa 17:31	1697
those *w* in the ears of David	1Sa 18:23	1697
his servants told David these *w*	1Sa 18:26	1697
laid up these *w* in his heart	1Sa 21:12	1697
stayed his servants with these *w*	1Sa 24:7	1697
Wherefore hearest thou men's *w*	1Sa 24:9	1697
end of speaking these *w* unto Saul	1Sa 24:16	1697
all those *w* in the name of David	1Sa 25:9	1697
hear the *w* of thine handmaid	1Sa 25:24	1697
king hear the *w* of his servant	1Sa 26:19	1697
because of the *w* of Samuel	1Sa 28:20	1697
have hearkened unto thy *w* which	1Sa 28:21	1697
wroth for the *w* of Ish-bosheth	2Sa 3:8	1697
According to all these *w*, and	2Sa 7:17	1697
thy *w* be true, and thou hast	2Sa 7:28	1697
So Joab put the *w* in her mouth	2Sa 14:3	1697
he put all these *w* in the mouth	2Sa 14:19	1697
the *w* of the men of Judah were	2Sa 19:43	1697
than the *w* of the men of Israel	2Sa 19:43	1697
Hear the *w* of thine handmaid	2Sa 20:17	1697
unto the LORD the *w* of this song	2Sa 22:1	1697
Now these be the last *w* of David	2Sa 23:1	1697
in after thee, and confirm thy *w*	1Kin 1:14	1697
I have done according to thy *w*	1Kin 3:12	1697
when Hiram heard the *w* of Solomon	1Kin 5:7	1697
And let these my *w*, wherewith I	1Kin 8:59	1697
Howbeit I believed not the *w*	1Kin 10:7	1697
them, and speak good *w* to them	1Kin 12:7	1697
the *w* which he had spoken unto	1Kin 13:11	1697
to pass, when Ahab heard those *w*	1Kin 21:27	1697
the *w* of the prophets declare	1Kin 22:13	1697
to meet you, and told you these *w*	2Kin 1:7	1697
the *w* that thou speakest in thy	2Kin 6:12	1697
the king heard the *w* of the woman	2Kin 6:30	1697
sayest, (but they are but vain *w*	2Kin 18:20	1697
and to thee, to speak these *w*	2Kin 18:27	1697
told him the *w* of Rab-shakeh	2Kin 18:37	1697
will heard all the *w* of Rab-shakeh	2Kin 19:4	1697
will reprove the *w* which the LORD	2Kin 19:4	1697
Be not afraid of the *w* which thou	2Kin 19:6	1697
hear the *w* of Sennacherib, which	2Kin 19:16	1697
the *w* of the book of the law	2Kin 22:11	1697
concerning the *w* of this book	2Kin 22:13	1697
hearkened unto the *w* of this book	2Kin 22:13	1697
even all the *w* of the book which	2Kin 22:16	1697
As touching the *w* which thou hast	2Kin 22:18	1697
the *w* of the book of the covenant	2Kin 23:2	1697
to perform the *w* of this covenant	2Kin 23:3	1697
who proclaimed these *w*	2Kin 23:16	1697
that he might perform the *w* of	2Kin 23:24	1697
According to all these *w*, and	1Chr 17:15	1697
For by the last *w* of David the	1Chr 23:27	1697
the king's seer in the *w* of God	1Chr 25:5	1697
Howbeit I believed not their *w*	2Chr 9:6	1697
them, and speak good *w* to them	2Chr 10:7	1697
And they obeyed the *w* of the LORD	2Chr 11:4	1697
And when Asa heard these *w*	2Chr 15:8	1697
the *w* of the prophets declare	2Chr 18:12	1697
by the *w* of the LORD, to cleanse	2Chr 29:15	1697
unto the LORD with the *w* of David	2Chr 29:30	1697
the *w* of Hezekiah king of Judah	2Chr 32:8	1697
the *w* of the seers that spake to	2Chr 33:18	1697
king had heard the *w* of the law	2Chr 34:19	1697
concerning the *w* of the book that	2Chr 34:21	1697
the *w* which thou hast heard	2Chr 34:26	1697
heardest his *w* against this place	2Chr 34:27	1697
the *w* of the book of the covenant	2Chr 34:30	1697
to perform the *w* of the covenant	2Chr 34:31	1697
hearkened not unto the *w* of Necho	2Chr 35:22	1697
of God, and despised his *w*	2Chr 36:16	1697
even a scribe of the *w* of the	Ezr 7:11	1697
at the *w* of the God of Israel	Ezr 9:4	1697
The *w* of Nehemiah the son of	Neh 1:1	1697
to pass, when I heard these *w*	Neh 1:4	1697
as also the king's *w* that he had	Neh 2:18	1697
when I heard their cry and these *w*	Neh 5:6	1697
their king, according to these *w*	Neh 6:6	1697
to the king according to these *w*	Neh 6:7	1697
before me, and uttered my *w* to him	Neh 6:19	1697
when they heard the *w* of the law	Neh 8:9	1697
w that were declared unto them	Neh 8:12	1697
to understand the *w* of the law	Neh 8:13	1697
his seed, and hast performed thy *w*	Neh 9:8	1697
and told Esther the *w* of Mordecai	Est 4:9	1697
they told to Mordecai Esther's *w*	Est 4:12	1697
for all the *w* of this letter	Est 9:26	1697
with *w* of peace and truth,	Est 9:30	1697
Thy *w* have upholden him that was	Job 4:4	4405
therefore my *w* are swallowed up	Job 6:3	1697

the prophet spake all these *w* .... Jer 34:6	1697
which have not performed the *w* of .... Jer 34:18	1697
instruction to hearken to my *w* .... Jer 35:13	1697
The *w* of Jonadab the son of .... Jer 35:14	1697
write therein all the *w* that I .... Jer 36:2	1697
of Jeremiah all the *w* of the LORD .... Jer 36:4	1697
the *w* of the LORD in the ears of .... Jer 36:6	1697
reading in the book the *w* of the .... Jer 36:8	1697
read Baruch in the book the *w* of .... Jer 36:10	1697
of the book all the *w* of the LORD .... Jer 36:11	1697
them all the *w* that he had heard .... Jer 36:13	1697
when they had heard all the *w* .... Jer 36:16	1697
tell the king of all these *w* .... Jer 36:16	1697
write all these *w* at his mouth .... Jer 36:17	1697
these *w* unto me with his mouth .... Jer 36:18	1697
told all the *w* in the ears of the .... Jer 36:20	1697
servants that heard all these *w* .... Jer 36:24	1697
the *w* which Baruch wrote at the .... Jer 36:27	1697
write in it all the former *w* that .... Jer 36:28	1697
the *w* of the book which Jehoiakim .... Jer 36:32	1697
besides unto them many like *w* .... Jer 36:32	1697
hearken unto the *w* of the LORD .... Jer 37:2	1697
heard the *w* that Jeremiah had .... Jer 38:1	1697
in speaking such *w* unto them .... Jer 38:4	1697
Let no man know of these *w* .... Jer 38:24	1697
w that the king had commanded .... Jer 38:27	1697
I will bring my *w* upon this city............ Jer 39:16	1697
LORD your God according to your *w* ...... Jer 42:4	1697
all the *w* of the LORD their God............ Jer 43:1	1697
him to them, even all these *w* .... Jer 43:1	1697
shall know whose *w* shall stand .... Jer 44:28	1697
that ye may know that my *w* shall .... Jer 44:29	1697
these *w* in a book at the mouth of .... Jer 45:1	1697
even all these *w* that are written .... Jer 51:60	1697
see, and shalt read all these *w* .... Jer 51:61	1697
Thus far are the *w* of Jeremiah.............. Jer 51:64	1697
neither be afraid of their *w* .... Eze 2:6	1697
be not afraid of their *w*, nor be .... Eze 2:6	1697
thou shalt speak my *w* unto them .... Eze 2:7	1697
and speak with my *w* unto them .... Eze 3:4	1697
whose *w* thou canst not understand...... Eze 3:6	1697
all my *w* that I shall speak unto .... Eze 3:10	1697
of my *w* be prolonged any more .... Eze 12:28	1697
as my people, and they hear thy *w*........ Eze 33:31	1697
for they hear thy *w*, but they do .... Eze 33:32	1697
have multiplied your *w* against me ...... Eze 35:13	1697
corrupt *w* to speak before me, ... Dan 2:9	4406
by reason of the *w* of the king .... Dan 5:10	4406
the king, when he heard these *w* .... Dan 6:14	4406
the great *w* which the horn spake .... Dan 7:11	4406
he shall speak great *w* against............ Dan 7:25	4406
And he hath confirmed his *w*................ Dan 9:12	1697
the voice of his *w* like the voice .... Dan 10:6	1697
Yet heard I the voice of his *w* .... Dan 10:9	1697
when I heard the voice of his *w* .... Dan 10:9	1697
understand the *w* that I speak .... Dan 10:11	1697
thy *w* were heard .... Dan 10:12	1697
and I am come for thy *w* .... Dan 10:12	1697
when he had spoken such *w* unto me...... Dan 10:15	1697
But thou, O Daniel, shut up the *w*........ Dan 12:4	1697
for the *w* are closed up and sealed ...... Dan 12:9	1697
slain them by the *w* of my mouth .... Hos 6:5	561
They have spoken *w*, swearing.............. Hos 10:4	1697
Take with you *w*, and turn to the .... Hos 14:2	1697
The *w* of Amos, who was among the ...... Amos 1:1	1697
is not able to bear all his *w* .... Amos 7:10	1697
but of hearing the *w* of the LORD .... Amos 8:11	1697
do not my *w* do good to him that .... Mic 2:7	1697
the *w* of Haggai the prophet, as............ Hag 1:12	1697
But my *w* and my statutes, which I ...... Zec 1:6	1697
that talked with me with good *w* .... Zec 1:13	1697
and comfortable *w* .... Zec 1:13	1697
Should ye not hear the *w* which .... Zec 7:7	1697
the *w* which the LORD of hosts .... Zec 7:12	1697
w by the mouth of the prophets .... Zec 8:9	1697
have wearied the LORD with your *w* ...... Mal 2:17	1697
Your *w* have been stout against me ...... Mal 3:13	1697
not receive, nor hear your *w* .... Mt 10:14	3056
For by thy *w* thou shalt be .... Mt 12:37	3056
by thy *w* thou shalt be condemned ...... Mt 12:37	3056
When they had heard these *w* .... Mt 22:22	
but my *w* shall not pass away.............. Mt 24:35	3056
the third time, saying the same *w* .... Mt 26:44	3056
of my *w* in this adulterous and............ Mk 8:38	3056
were astonished at his *w*.................... Mk 10:24	3056
Herodians, to catch him in his *w*.......... Mk 12:13	3056
but my *w* shall not pass away.......... Mk 13:31	3056
and prayed, and spake the same *w*........ Mk 14:39	3056
because thou believest not my *w* .... Lk 1:20	3056
of the *w* of Esaias the prophet .... Lk 3:4	3056
wondered at the gracious *w* which .... Lk 4:22	3056

shall be ashamed of me and of my *w* .... Lk 9:26	3056
they might take hold of his *w* .... Lk 20:20	3056
hold of his *w* before the people.............. Lk 20:26	4487
but my *w* shall not pass away .... Lk 21:33	3056
he questioned with him in many *w* .... Lk 23:9	3056
And they remembered his *w*, ... Lk 24:8	4487
their *w* seemed to them as idle.............. Lk 24:11	4487
These are the *w* which I spake .... Lk 24:44	3056
hath sent speaketh the *w* of God............ Jn 3:34	4487
how shall ye believe my *w* .... Jn 5:47	4487
the *w* that I speak unto you, they .... Jn 6:63	4487
thou hast the *w* of eternal life .... Jn 6:68	4487
he had said these *w* unto them .... Jn 7:9	
These *w* spake Jesus in the.................... Jn 8:20	4487
As he spake these *w*, many .... Jn 8:30	
He that is of God heareth God's *w* ...... Jn 8:47	4487
These *w* spake his parents, ... Jn 9:22	
which were with him heard these *w*........ Jn 9:40	
These are not the *w* of him that .... Jn 10:21	4487
And if any man hear my *w*, and .... Jn 12:47	4487
me, and receiveth not my *w* .... Jn 12:48	4487
the *w* that I speak unto you I .... Jn 14:10	4487
a man love me, he will keep my *w* ...... Jn 14:23	3056
my *w* abide in you, ye shall ask........ Jn 15:7	4487
These *w* spake Jesus, and lifted up .... Jn 17:1	
them the *w* which thou gavest me .... Jn 17:8	4487
When Jesus had spoken these *w* .... Jn 18:1	
unto you, and hearken to my *w*.............. Acts 2:14	4487
Ye men of Israel, hear these *w* .... Acts 2:22	3056
with many other *w* did he testify .... Acts 2:40	3056
Ananias hearing these *w* fell down .... Acts 5:5	3056
the people all the *w* of this life .... Acts 5:20	4487
speak blasphemous *w* against Moses .... Acts 6:11	4487
w against this holy place .... Acts 6:13	4487
the Egyptians, and was mighty in *w*...... Acts 7:22	3056
his house, and to hear *w* of thee............ Acts 10:22	4487
While Peter yet spake these *w*................ Acts 10:44	4487
Who shall tell thee *w*, whereby.............. Acts 11:14	4487
Gentiles besought that these *w*.............. Acts 13:42	4487
this agree the *w* of the prophets .... Acts 15:15	3056
from us have troubled you with *w* .... Acts 15:24	3056
exhorted the brethren with many *w*........ Acts 15:32	3056
told these *w* unto the magistrates .... Acts 16:38	4487
But if it be a question of *w* .... Acts 18:15	3056
to remember the *w* of the Lord .... Acts 20:35	3056
of all for the *w* which he spake .... Acts 20:38	3056
hear us of thy clemency a few *w* .... Acts 24:4	
but speak forth the *w* of truth .... Acts 26:25	4487
And when he had said these *w* .... Acts 28:29	
their *w* unto the ends of the .... Rom 10:18	4487
and by good *w* and fair speeches .... Rom 16:18	5542
not with wisdom of *w*, lest the................ 1Cor 1:17	3056
with enticing *w* of man's wisdom............ 1Cor 2:4	3056
not in the *w* which man's wisdom 1Cor 2:13	3056
tongue *w* easy to be understood............ 1Cor 14:9	3056
five *w* with my understanding 1Cor 14:19	3056
than ten thousand *w* in an unknown 1Cor 14:19	3056
paradise, and heard unspeakable *w* 2Cor 12:4	4487
(as I wrote afore in few *w* .... Eph 3:3	
no man deceive you with vain *w* .... Eph 5:6	3056
beguile you with enticing *w* .... Col 2:4	4086
at any time used we flattering *w* 1Th 2:5	3056
comfort one another with these *w* 1Th 4:18	3056
nourished up in the *w* of faith 1Ti 4:6	3056
and consent not to wholesome *w* 1Ti 6:3	3056
even the *w* of our Lord Jesus 1Ti 6:3	
about questions and strifes of *w*............ 1Ti 6:4	3055
Hold fast the form of sound *w* 2Ti 1:13	3056
strive not about *w* to no profit 2Ti 2:14	3054
he hath greatly withstood our *w* 2Ti 4:15	3056
of a trumpet, and the voice of *w*............ Heb 12:19	4487
a letter unto you in few *w*...................... Heb 13:22	
feigned *w* make merchandise of you 2Pet 2:3	3056
speak great swelling *w* of vanity 2Pet 2:18	
That ye may be mindful of the *w* 2Pet 3:2	4487
against us with malicious *w* 3Jn 10	3056
mouth speaketh great swelling *w*............ Jude 16	
remember ye the *w* which were .... Jude 17	4487
that hear the *w* of this prophecy............ Rev 1:3	3056
until the *w* of God shall be .... Rev 17:17	3056
for these *w* are true and faithful............ Rev 21:5	3056
w of the prophecy of this book .... Rev 22:18	3056
w of the book of this prophecy .... Rev 22:19	3056

WORK

God ended his *w* which he had made .... Gen 2:2	4399
from all his *w* which he had made .... Gen 2:2	4399
from all his *w* which God created .... Gen 2:3	4399
shall comfort us concerning our *w* .... Gen 5:29	4639
Let there more *w* be laid upon the.......... Ex 5:9	5656
of your *w* shall be diminished .... Ex 5:11	5656

W

Go therefore now, and *w*	Ex 5:18	5647
no manner of *w* shall be done in	Ex 12:16	4399
Israel saw that great *w* which the	Ex 14:31	3027
walk, and the *w* that they must do	Ex 18:20	4640
thou labour, and do all thy *w*	Ex 20:9	4399
in it thou shalt not do any *w*	Ex 20:10	4399
Six days thou shalt do thy *w*	Ex 23:12	4639
a paved *w* of a sapphire stone	Ex 24:10	4639
of beaten *w* shalt thou make them,	Ex 25:18	4749
of beaten *w* shall the candlestick	Ex 25:31	4749
be one beaten *w* of pure gold	Ex 25:36	4749
of cunning *w* shalt thou make them	Ex 26:1	4639
and fine twined linen of cunning *w*	Ex 26:31	4639
fine twined linen, with cunning *w*	Ex 28:6	4639
same, according to the *w* thereof	Ex 28:8	4639
With the *w* of an engraver in	Ex 28:11	4639
of wreathen *w* shalt thou make	Ex 28:14	4639
of judgment with cunning *w*	Ex 28:15	4639
after the *w* of the ephod thou	Ex 28:15	4639
ends of wreathen *w* of pure gold	Ex 28:22	4639
w round about the hole of it	Ex 28:32	4639
to *w* in gold, and in silver, and in	Ex 31:4	6213
to *w* in all manner of workmanship	Ex 31:5	6213
for whosoever doeth any *w* therein	Ex 31:14	4399
Six days may *w* be done	Ex 31:15	4399
doeth any *w* in the sabbath day	Ex 31:15	4399
And the tables were the *w* of God	Ex 32:16	4639
art shall see the *w* of the LORD	Ex 34:10	4639
Six days thou shalt *w*, but on the	Ex 34:21	5627
Six days shall *w* be done, but on	Ex 35:2	4399
whosoever doeth *w* therein shall	Ex 35:2	4399
to the *w* of the tabernacle of the	Ex 35:21	4399
wood for any *w* of the service	Ex 35:24	4399
to bring for all manner of *w*	Ex 35:29	4399
to *w* in gold, and in silver, and in	Ex 35:32	6213
to make any manner of cunning *w*	Ex 35:33	4399
to *w* all manner of	Ex 35:35	6213
all manner of *w*	Ex 35:35	4399
even of them that do any *w*	Ex 35:35	4399
and of those that devise cunning *w*	Ex 35:35	
to *w* all manner of	Ex 36:1	6213
of *w* for the service of the	Ex 36:1	4399
up to come unto the *w* to do it	Ex 36:2	4399
of Israel had brought for the *w*	Ex 36:3	4399
all the *w* of the sanctuary	Ex 36:4	4399
man from his *w* which they made	Ex 36:4	4399
enough for the service of the *w*	Ex 36:5	4399
more *w* for the offering of the	Ex 36:6	4399
for all the *w* to make it, and too	Ex 36:7	4399
the *w* of the tabernacle made ten	Ex 36:8	4399
of cunning *w* made he them	Ex 36:8	4639
cherubims made he it of cunning *w*	Ex 36:35	4639
of beaten *w* made he the	Ex 37:17	4749
it was one beaten *w* of pure gold	Ex 37:22	4749
according to the *w* of the	Ex 37:29	4639
the *w* in all the *w* of the holy	Ex 38:24	4399
to *w* it in the blue, and in the	Ex 39:3	6213
in the fine linen, with cunning *w*	Ex 39:3	4639
same, according to the *w* thereof	Ex 39:5	4639
made the breastplate of cunning *w*	Ex 39:8	4639
like the *w* of the ephod	Ex 39:8	4639
of wreathen *w* of pure gold	Ex 39:15	4639
the robe of the ephod of woven *w*	Ex 39:22	4639
fine linen of woven *w* for Aaron	Ex 39:27	4639
Thus was all the *w* of the	Ex 39:32	5656
children of Israel made all the *w*	Ex 39:42	5656
And Moses did look upon all the *w*	Ex 39:43	4399
So Moses finished the *w*	Ex 40:33	4399
it be, wherein it is done	Lev 11:32	4399
or in any *w* that is made of skin	Lev 13:51	4399
do no *w* at all, whether it be one	Lev 16:29	4399
Six days shall *w* be done	Lev 23:3	4399
ye shall do no *w* therein	Lev 23:3	4399
ye shall do no servile *w* therein	Lev 23:7	4399
ye shall do no servile *w* therein	Lev 23:8	4399
ye shall do no servile *w* therein	Lev 23:21	4399
Ye shall do no servile *w* therein	Lev 23:25	4399
ye shall do no *w* in that same day	Lev 23:28	4399
that doeth any *w* in that same day	Lev 23:30	4399
Ye shall do no manner of *w*	Lev 23:31	4399
ye shall do no servile *w* therein	Lev 23:35	4399
ye shall do no servile *w* therein	Lev 23:36	4399
to do the *w* in the tabernacle of	Num 4:3	
to do the *w* of the tabernacle of	Num 4:23	5656
to do the *w* of the tabernacle of	Num 4:30	5656
for the *w* in the tabernacle of	Num 4:35	5656
for the *w* in the tabernacle of	Num 4:39	5656
for the *w* in the tabernacle of	Num 4:43	5656
this *w* of the candlestick was of	Num 8:4	4639
the flowers thereof, was beaten *w*	Num 8:4	
do no manner of servile *w* therein	Num 28:18	4399

ye shall do no servile *w*	Num 28:25	4399
ye shall do no servile *w*	Num 28:26	4399
ye shall do no servile *w*	Num 29:1	4399
ye shall not do any *w* therein	Num 29:7	4399
ye shall do no servile *w*, and ye	Num 29:12	4399
ye shall do no servile *w* therein	Num 29:35	4399
all *w* of goats' hair, and all	Num 31:20	4639
the *w* of men's hands, wood and	Deut 4:28	4639
shalt labour, and do all thy *w*	Deut 5:13	4399
in it thou shalt not do any *w*	Deut 5:14	4399
God may bless thee in all the *w*	Deut 14:29	4639
thou shalt do no *w* with the	Deut 15:19	5647
thou shalt do no *w* therein	Deut 16:8	4399
thee in all the *w* of thine hands	Deut 24:19	4639
the *w* of the hands of the	Deut 27:15	4639
to bless all the *w* of thine hand	Deut 28:12	4639
in every *w* of thine hand, in the	Deut 30:9	4639
anger through the *w* of your hands	Deut 31:29	4639
He is the Rock, his *w* is perfect	Deut 32:4	6467
accept the *w* of his hands	Deut 33:11	6467
They did *w* wilily, and went and	Josh 9:4	6213
his *w* out of the field at even	Judg 19:16	4639
The LORD recompense thy *w*	Ruth 2:12	6467
your asses, and put them to his *w*	1Sa 8:16	4399
be that the LORD will *w* for us	1Sa 8:16	6213
officers which were over the *w*	1Kin 5:16	4399
the people that wrought in the *w*	1Kin 5:16	4399
gold fitted upon the carved *w*	1Kin 6:35	
porch, which was of the like *w*	1Kin 7:8	4649
cunning to *w* all works in brass	1Kin 7:14	6213
Solomon, and wrought all his *w*	1Kin 7:14	4399
And nets of checker *w*	1Kin 7:17	4639
and wreaths of chain *w*	1Kin 7:17	4639
were of lily *w* in the porch	1Kin 7:19	4639
the top of the pillars was lily *w*	1Kin 7:22	4639
so was the *w* of the pillars	1Kin 7:22	4399
the *w* of the bases was on this	1Kin 7:28	4639
certain additions made of thin *w*	1Kin 7:29	4639
was round after the *w* of the base	1Kin 7:31	4639
the *w* of the wheels was like the	1Kin 7:33	4639
was like the *w* of a chariot wheel	1Kin 7:33	4639
made an end of doing all the *w*	1Kin 7:40	4399
So was ended all the *w* that king	1Kin 7:51	4399
that were over Solomon's *w*	1Kin 9:23	4399
the people that wrought in the *w*	1Kin 9:23	4399
to anger with the *w* of his hands	1Kin 16:7	4639
thou hast sold thyself to *w* evil	1Kin 21:20	6213
which did sell himself to *w*	1Kin 21:25	6213
the hands of them that did the *w*	2Kin 12:11	4399
but the *w* of men's hands, wood and	2Kin 19:18	4639
the hand of the doers of the *w*	2Kin 22:5	4399
give it to the doers of the *w*	2Kin 22:5	4399
the hand of them that do the *w*	2Kin 22:9	4399
and the wreathen *w*, and	2Kin 25:17	7639
the second pillar with wreathen *w*	2Kin 25:17	7639
dwelt with the king for his *w*	1Chr 4:23	4399
all the *w* of the place most holy	1Chr 6:49	4399
very able men for the *w* of the	1Chr 9:13	4399
were over the *w* of the service,	1Chr 9:19	4399
they were employed in that *w* day	1Chr 9:33	4399
as every day's *w* required	1Chr 16:37	1697
cunning men for every manner of *w*	1Chr 22:15	4399
were to set forward the *w* of the	1Chr 23:4	4399
that did the *w* for the service of	1Chr 23:24	4399
the *w* of the service of the house	1Chr 23:28	4639
over them that did the *w* of the	1Chr 27:26	4399
for all the *w* of the service of	1Chr 28:13	4399
thou hast finished all the *w* for	1Chr 28:20	4399
and tender, and the *w* is great	1Chr 29:1	4399
for all manner of *w* to be made by	1Chr 29:5	4399
with the rulers of the king's *w*	1Chr 29:6	4399
a man cunning to *w* in gold	2Chr 2:7	6213
man of Tyre, skilful to *w* in gold	2Chr 2:14	6213
overseers to set the people a *w*	2Chr 2:18	5647
he made two cherubims of image *w*	2Chr 3:10	4639
like the *w* of the brim of a cup	2Chr 4:5	4639
Huram finished the *w* that he was	2Chr 4:11	4399
Thus all the *w* that Solomon made	2Chr 5:1	4399
make no servants for his *w*	2Chr 8:9	4399
Now all the *w* of Solomon was	2Chr 8:16	4399
for your *w* shall be rewarded	2Chr 15:7	6468
of Ramah, and let his *w* cease	2Chr 16:5	4399
gave it to such as did the *w* of	2Chr 24:12	4399
the *w* was perfected by them, and	2Chr 24:13	4399
till the *w* was ended, and until	2Chr 29:34	4399
in every *w* that he began in the	2Chr 31:21	4399
which were the *w* of the hands of	2Chr 32:19	4639
And the men did the *w* faithfully	2Chr 34:12	4399
of all that wrought the *w* in any	2Chr 34:13	4399
the treasure of the *w* threescore	Ezr 2:69	4399
to set forward the *w* of the house	Ezr 3:8	4399

Then ceased the *w* of the house of	Ezr 4:24	5673
and this *w* goeth fast on, and	Ezr 5:8	5673
Let the *w* of this house of God	Ezr 6:7	5673
in the *w* of the house of God	Ezr 6:22	4399
is this a *w* of one day or two	Ezr 10:13	4399
nor to the rest that did the *w*	Neh 2:16	4399
their hands for this good *w*	Neh 2:18	4399
necks to the *w* of their Lord	Neh 3:5	5656
for the people had a mind to *w*	Neh 4:6	6213
them, and cause the *w* to cease	Neh 4:11	4399
to the wall, every one unto his *w*	Neh 4:15	4399
of my servants wrought in the *w*	Neh 4:16	4399
one of his hands wrought in the *w*	Neh 4:17	4399
The *w* is great and large, and we	Neh 4:19	4399
So we laboured in the *w*	Neh 4:21	4399
I continued in the *w* of this wall	Neh 5:16	4399
were gathered thither unto the *w*	Neh 5:16	4399
saying, I am doing a great *w*	Neh 6:3	4399
why should the *w* cease, whilst I	Neh 6:3	4399
shall be weakened from the *w*	Neh 6:9	4399
this *w* was wrought of our God	Neh 6:16	4399
of the fathers gave unto the *w*	Neh 7:70	4399
gave to the treasure of the *w*	Neh 7:71	4399
for all the *w* of the house of our	Neh 10:33	4399
their brethren that did the *w* of	Neh 11:12	4399
and the singers, that did the *w*	Neh 13:10	4399
hast blessed the *w* of his hands	Job 1:10	4639
looketh for the reward of his *w*	Job 7:2	6467
despise the *w* of thine hands	Job 10:3	3018
a desire to the *w* of thine hands	Job 14:15	4639
On the left hand, where he doth *w*	Job 23:9	6213
desert, go they forth to their *w*	Job 24:5	6467
For the *w* of a man shall he	Job 34:11	6467
they all are the *w* of his hands	Job 34:19	4639
Then he sheweth them their *w*	Job 36:9	6467
Remember thou that magnify his *w*	Job 36:24	6467
that all men may know his *w*	Job 37:7	4639
the *w* of thy fingers, the moon and	Ps 8:3	4639
snared in the *w* of his own hands	Ps 9:16	6467
them after the *w* of their hands	Ps 28:4	4639
what *w* thou didst in their days,	Ps 44:1	6467
Yea, in heart ye *w* wickedness	Ps 58:2	6466
to every man according to his *w*	Ps 62:12	4639
and shall declare the *w* of God	Ps 64:9	6467
w thereof at once with axes	Ps 74:6	6603
I will meditate also of all thy *w*	Ps 77:12	6467
Let thy *w* appear unto thy	Ps 90:16	6467
establish thou the *w* of our hands	Ps 90:17	4639
the *w* of our hands establish thou	Ps 90:17	4639
hast made me glad through thy *w*	Ps 92:4	6467
me, proved me, and saw my *w*	Ps 95:9	6467
I hate the *w* of them that turn	Ps 101:3	6213
heavens are the *w* of thy hands	Ps 102:25	4639
Man goeth forth unto his *w*	Ps 104:23	6467
His *w* is honourable and glorious	Ps 111:3	6467
and gold, the *w* of men's hands	Ps 115:4	4639
It is time for thee, Lord, to *w*	Ps 119:126	6213
and gold, the *w* of men's hands	Ps 135:15	4639
works with men that *w* iniquity	Ps 141:4	5950
I muse on the *w* of thy hands	Ps 143:5	4639
The wicked worketh a deceitful *w*	Prov 11:18	6468
the weights of the bag are his *w*	Prov 16:11	4639
his *w* is brother to him that is a	Prov 18:9	4399
his doings, whether his *w* be pure	Prov 20:11	6467
as for the pure, his *w* is right	Prov 21:8	6467
Prepare thy *w* without, and make it	Prov 24:27	4399
to the man according to his *w*	Prov 24:29	6467
because the *w* that is wrought	Eccl 2:17	4639
the *w* that God maketh from the	Eccl 3:11	4639
for every purpose and for every *w*	Eccl 3:17	4639
evil *w* that is done under the sun	Eccl 4:3	4639
all travail, and every right *w*	Eccl 4:4	4639
destroy the *w* of thine hands	Eccl 5:6	4639
Consider the *w* of God	Eccl 7:13	4639
w that is done under the sun	Eccl 8:9	4639
evil *w* is not executed speedily	Eccl 8:11	4639
according to the *w* of the wicked	Eccl 8:14	4639
to the *w* of the righteous	Eccl 8:14	4639
Then I beheld all the *w* of God	Eccl 8:17	4639
the *w* that is done under the sun	Eccl 8:17	4639
for there is no *w*, nor device,	Eccl 9:10	4639
shall bring every *w* into judgment	Eccl 12:14	4639
the *w* of the hands of a cunning	Song 7:1	4639
they worship the *w* of their own	Is 2:8	4639
they regard not the *w* of the Lord	Is 5:12	6467
him make speed, and hasten his *w*	Is 5:19	4639
his whole *w* upon mount Zion	Is 10:12	4639
the *w* of his hands, neither shall	Is 17:8	4639
Moreover they that *w* in fine flax	Is 19:9	5647
Egypt to err in every *w* thereof	Is 19:14	4639
shall there be any *w* for Egypt	Is 19:15	4639
and Assyria the *w* of my hands	Is 19:25	4639
he may do his *w*, his strange *w*	Is 28:21	4639
a marvellous *w* among this people	Is 29:14	6381
this people, even a marvellous *w*	Is 29:14	6381
for shall the *w* say of him that	Is 29:16	4639
the *w* of mine hands, in the midst	Is 29:23	4639
the help of them that *w* iniquity	Is 31:2	6213
and his heart will *w* iniquity	Is 32:6	6213
the *w* of righteousness shall be	Is 32:17	4639
but the *w* of men's hands, wood and	Is 37:19	4639
is with him, and his *w* before him	Is 40:10	6468
of nothing, and your *w* of nought	Is 41:24	6467
I will *w*, and who shall let it	Is 43:13	6466
or thy *w*, He hath no hands	Is 45:9	6467
concerning the *w* of my hands	Is 45:11	6467
the Lord, and my *w* with my God	Is 49:4	6468
forth an instrument for his *w*	Is 54:16	4639
the *w* of my hands, that I may be	Is 60:21	4639
and I will direct their *w* in truth	Is 61:8	6468
is with him, and his *w* before him	Is 62:11	6468
and we all are the *w* of thy hand	Is 64:8	4639
their former *w* into their bosom	Is 65:7	6468
long enjoy the *w* of their hands	Is 65:22	4639
the *w* of the hands of the workman	Jer 10:3	4639
the *w* of the workman, and of the	Jer 10:9	4639
they are all the *w* of cunning men	Jer 10:9	4639
are vanity, and the *w* of errors	Jer 10:15	4639
sabbath day, neither do ye any *w*	Jer 17:22	4399
sabbath day, to do no *w* therein	Jer 17:24	4399
he wrought a *w* on the wheels	Jer 18:3	4399
and giveth him not for his *w*	Jer 22:13	6467
for thy *w* shall be rewarded,	Jer 31:16	6468
Great in counsel, and mighty in *w*	Jer 32:19	5950
anger with the *w* of their hands	Jer 32:30	4639
the *w* of the Lord deceitfully	Jer 48:10	4399
for this is the *w* of the Lord God	Jer 50:25	4399
recompense her according to her *w*	Jer 50:29	6467
in Zion the *w* of the Lord our God	Jer 51:10	4639
They are vanity, the *w* of errors	Jer 51:18	4639
according to the *w* of their hands	Lam 3:64	4639
the *w* of the hands of the potter	Lam 4:2	4639
their *w* was like unto the colour	Eze 1:16	4639
their *w* was as it were a wheel in	Eze 1:16	4639
wood be taken thereof to do any *w*	Eze 15:3	4399
Is it meet for any *w*	Eze 15:4	4399
was whole, it was meet for no *w*	Eze 15:5	4399
shall it be meet yet for any *w*	Eze 15:5	4399
thee also with broidered *w*	Eze 16:10	7553
linen, and silk, and broidered *w*	Eze 16:13	7553
the *w* of an imperious whorish	Eze 16:30	4639
Fine linen with broidered *w* from	Eze 27:7	7553
emeralds, purple, and broidered *w*	Eze 27:16	7553
in blue clothes, and broidered *w*	Eze 27:24	7553
ye *w* abomination, and ye defile	Eze 33:26	6213
with him he shall *w* deceitfully	Dan 11:23	6213
is a city of them that *w* iniquity	Hos 6:8	6466
all of it the *w* of the craftsmen	Hos 13:2	4639
any more to the *w* of our hands	Hos 14:3	4639
and *w* evil upon their beds	Mic 2:1	6466
more worship the *w* of thine hands	Mic 5:13	4639
for I will *w* a	Hab 1:5	6466
a *w* in your days	Hab 1:5	6467
maker of his *w* trusteth therein	Hab 2:18	3336
revive thy *w* in the midst of the	Hab 3:2	6467
for he shall uncover the cedar *w*	Zeph 2:14	731
did *w* in the house of the Lord of	Hag 1:14	4399
of the land, saith the Lord, and *w*	Hag 2:4	6213
so is every *w* of their hands	Hag 2:14	4639
they that *w* wickedness are set up	Mal 3:15	6213
from me, ye that *w* iniquity	Mt 7:23	2038
go *w* to day in my vineyard	Mt 21:28	2038
she hath wrought a good *w* upon me	Mt 26:10	2041
And he could there do no mighty *w*	Mk 6:5	1411
servants, and to every man his *w*	Mk 13:34	2041
she hath wrought a good *w* on me	Mk 14:6	2041
six days in which men ought to *w*	Lk 13:14	2038
that sent me, and to finish his *w*	Jn 4:34	2041
Father worketh hitherto, and I *w*	Jn 5:17	2038
that we might *w* the works of God	Jn 6:28	2038
unto them, This is the *w* of God	Jn 6:29	2041
what dost thou *w*	Jn 6:30	2038
said unto them, I have done one *w*	Jn 7:21	2041
I must *w* the works of him that	Jn 9:4	2038
night cometh, when no man can *w*	Jn 9:4	2038
For a good *w* we stone thee not	Jn 10:33	2041
I have finished the *w* which thou	Jn 17:4	2041
this counsel or this *w* be of men	Acts 5:38	2041
Saul for the *w* whereunto I have	Acts 13:2	2041
for I *w* a	Acts 13:41	2038
a *w* in your days	Acts 13:41	2040
a *w* which ye shall in no wise	Acts 13:41	2041

for the *w* which they fulfilled	Acts 14:26	2041
and went not with them to the *w*	Acts 15:38	2041
had much *w* to come by the boat	Acts 27:16	3433,2480
Which shew the *w* of the law	Rom 2:15	2041
did *w* in our members to bring	Rom 7:5	1754
we know that all things *w*	Rom 8:28	4903
For he will finish the *w*, and cut	Rom 9:28	3056
because a short *w* will the Lord	Rom 9:28	3056
otherwise *w* is no more *w*	Rom 11:6	2041
For meat destroy not the *w* of God	Rom 14:20	2041
Every man's *w* shall be made	1Cor 3:13	2041
every man's *w* of what sort it is	1Cor 3:13	2041
If any man's *w* abide which he	1Cor 3:14	2041
If any man's *w* shall be burned,	1Cor 3:15	2041
are not ye my *w* in the Lord	1Cor 9:1	2041
abounding in the *w* of the Lord	1Cor 15:58	2041
for he worketh the *w* of the Lord	1Cor 16:10	2041
may abound to every good *w*	2Cor 9:8	2041
But let every man prove his own *w*	Gal 6:4	2041
for the *w* of the ministry, for	Eph 4:12	2041
to *w* all uncleanness with	Eph 4:19	2039
w in you will perform it until	Phil 1:6	2041
w out your own salvation with	Phil 2:12	2716
Because for the *w* of Christ he	Phil 2:30	2041
being fruitful in every good *w*	Col 1:10	2041
without ceasing your *w* of faith	1Th 1:3	2041
to *w* with your own hands, as we	1Th 4:11	2038
the *w* of faith with power	2Th 1:11	2041
of iniquity doth already *w*	2Th 2:7	1754
you in every good word and *w*	2Th 2:17	2041
you, that if any would not *w*	2Th 3:10	2038
that with quietness they *w*	2Th 3:12	2038
of a bishop, he desireth a good *w*	1Ti 3:1	2041
diligently followed every good *w*	1Ti 5:10	2041
and prepared unto every good *w*	2Ti 2:21	2041
do the *w* of an evangelist, make	2Ti 4:5	2041
deliver me from every evil *w*	2Ti 4:18	2041
and unto every good *w* reprobate	Titus 1:16	2041
to be ready to every good *w*	Titus 3:1	2041
not unrighteous to forget your *w*	Heb 6:10	2041
in every good *w* to do his will	Heb 13:21	2041
let patience have her perfect *w*	Jas 1:4	2041
hearer, but a doer of the *w*	Jas 1:25	2041
is confusion and every evil *w*	Jas 3:16	4229
according to every man's *w*	1Pet 1:17	2041
man according as his *w* shall be	Rev 22:12	2041

WORKER
was a man of Tyre, a *w* in brass	1Kin 7:14	2790

WORKERS
Moreover the *w* with familiar	2Kin 23:24	
w of stone and timber, and all	1Chr 22:15	2796
punishment to the *w* of iniquity	Job 31:3	6466
in company with the *w* of iniquity	Job 34:8	6466
where the *w* of iniquity may hide	Job 34:22	6466
thou hatest all *w* of iniquity	Ps 5:5	6466
from me, all ye *w* of iniquity	Ps 6:8	6466
Have all the *w* of iniquity no	Ps 14:4	6466
with the *w* of iniquity, which	Ps 28:3	6466
There are the *w* of iniquity	Ps 36:12	6466
envious against the *w* of iniquity	Ps 37:1	6213
Have the *w* of iniquity no	Ps 53:4	6466
Deliver me from the *w* of iniquity	Ps 59:2	6466
insurrection of the *w* of iniquity	Ps 64:2	6466
when all the *w* of iniquity do	Ps 92:7	6466
all the *w* of iniquity shall be	Ps 92:9	6466
all the *w* of iniquity boast	Ps 94:4	6466
for me against the *w* of iniquity	Ps 94:16	6466
them forth with the *w* of iniquity	Ps 125:5	6466
and the gins of the *w* of iniquity	Ps 141:9	6466
shall be to the *w* of iniquity	Prov 10:29	6466
shall be to the *w* of iniquity	Prov 21:15	6466
from me, all ye *w* of iniquity	Lk 13:27	2040
are all *w* of miracles	1Cor 12:29	1411
as *w* together with him, beseech	2Cor 6:1	4903
are false apostles, deceitful *w*	2Cor 11:13	2040
Beware of dogs, beware of evil *w*	Phil 3:2	2040
fellow *w* unto the kingdom of God	Col 4:11	

WORKETH
all these things *w* God oftentimes	Job 33:29	6466
w righteousness, and speaketh the	Ps 15:2	6466
He that *w* deceit shall not dwell	Ps 101:7	6213
The wicked *w* a deceitful work	Prov 11:18	6213
and a flattering mouth *w* ruin	Prov 26:28	6213
w willingly with her hands	Prov 31:13	6213
What profit hath he that *w* in	Eccl 3:9	6213
the tongs both *w* in the coals	Is 44:12	6466
w it with the strength of his	Is 44:12	6466
w righteousness, those that	Is 64:5	6213
he *w* signs and wonders in heaven	Dan 6:27	5648

them, My Father *w* hitherto	Jn 5:17	2038
w righteousness, is accepted with	Acts 10:35	2038
peace, to every man that *w* good	Rom 2:10	2038
Now to him that *w* is the reward	Rom 4:4	2038
But to him that *w* not, but	Rom 4:5	2038
Because the law *w* wrath	Rom 4:15	2716
that tribulation *w* patience	Rom 5:3	2716
Love *w* no ill to his neighbour	Rom 13:10	2038
the same God which *w* all in all	1Cor 12:6	1754
But all these *w* that one and the	1Cor 12:11	1754
for he *w* the work of the Lord, as	1Cor 16:10	2038
So then death *w* in us, but life	2Cor 4:12	1754
w for us a far more exceeding and	2Cor 4:17	2716
For godly sorrow *w* repentance to	2Cor 7:10	2716
the sorrow of the world *w* death	2Cor 7:10	2716
w miracles among you, doeth he it	Gal 3:5	1754
but faith which *w* by love	Gal 5:6	1754
to the purpose of him who *w* all	Eph 1:11	1754
the spirit that now *w* in the	Eph 2:2	1754
to the power that *w* in us	Eph 3:20	1754
God which *w* in you both to will	Phil 2:13	1754
working, which *w* in me mightily	Col 1:29	1754
which effectually *w* also in you	1Th 2:13	1754
trying of your faith *w* patience	Jas 1:3	2716
For the wrath of man *w* not the	Jas 1:20	2716
neither whatsoever *w* abomination	Rev 21:27	4160

WORKFELLOW
Timotheus my *w*, and Lucius, and	Rom 16:21	4904

WORKING
like a sharp rasor, *w* deceitfully	Ps 52:2	6213
w salvation in the midst of the	Ps 74:12	6466
in counsel, and excellent in *w*	Is 28:29	8454
east shall be shut the six *w* days	Eze 46:1	4639
where, the Lord *w* with them, and	Mk 16:20	4903
men with men *w* that which is	Rom 1:27	2716
w death in me by that which is	Rom 7:13	2716
And labour, *w* with our own hands	1Cor 4:12	2038
have not we power to forbear *w*	1Cor 9:6	2038
To another the *w* of miracles	1Cor 12:10	1755
according to the *w* of his mighty	Eph 1:19	1753
by the effectual *w* of his power	Eph 3:7	1753
according to the effectual *w* in	Eph 4:16	1753
w with his hands the thing which	Eph 4:28	2038
according to the *w* whereby he is	Phil 3:21	1753
striving according to his *w*	Col 1:29	1753
the *w* of Satan with all power	2Th 2:9	1753
w not at all, but are busybodies	2Th 3:11	2038
his will, *w* in you that which is	Heb 13:21	4160
w miracles, which go forth unto	Rev 16:14	4160

WORKMAN
the engraver, and of the cunning *w*	Ex 35:35	2803
Dan, an engraver, and a cunning *w*	Ex 38:23	2803
work of the hands of a cunning *w*	Song 7:1	542
The *w* melteth a graven image, and	Is 40:19	2796
w to prepare a graven image	Is 40:20	2796
the work of the hands of the *w*	Jer 10:3	2796
from Uphaz, the work of the *w*	Jer 10:9	2796
the *w* made it.	Hos 8:6	2796
for the *w* is worthy of his meat	Mt 10:10	2040
a *w* that needeth not to be	2Ti 2:15	2040

WORKMANSHIP
knowledge, and in all manner of *w*	Ex 31:3	4399
to work in all manner of *w*	Ex 31:5	4399
knowledge, and in all manner of *w*	Ex 35:31	4399
according to all the *w* thereof	2Kin 16:10	4639
of *w* every willing skilful man	1Chr 28:21	4399
the *w* of thy tabrets and of thy	Eze 28:13	4399
For we are his *w*, created in	Eph 2:10	4161

WORKMEN
But they gave that to the *w*	2Kin 12:14	6213,4399
the money to be bestowed on *w*	2Kin 12:15	6213,4399
Moreover there are *w* with thee in	1Chr 22:15	6213,4399
the number of the *w* according to	1Chr 25:1	582,4399
So the *w* wrought, and the work	2Chr 24:13	6213,4399
w that had the oversight of the	2Chr 34:10	6213,4399
they gave it to the *w* that	2Chr 34:10	6213,4399
and to the hand of the *w*	2Chr 34:17	6213,4399
to set forward the *w* in the house	Ezr 3:9	
and the *w*, they are of men	Is 44:11	2796
with the *w* of like occupation	Acts 19:25	2040

WORKMEN'S
and her right hand to the *w* hammer	Judg 5:26	6001

WORK'S
highly in love for their *w* sake	1Th 5:13	2041

WORKS
let the people from their *w*	Ex 5:4	4639
them, saying, Fulfil your *w*	Ex 5:13	4639

serve them, nor do after their *w* .... Ex 23:24   4639
To devise cunning *w*, to work in.............. Ex 31:4
And to devise curious *w*, to work .... Ex 35:32
hath sent me to do all these *w* .... Num 16:28   4639
thee in all the *w* of thy hand .... Deut 2:7   4639
that can do according to thy *w*............... Deut 3:24   4639
God shall bless thee in all thy *w* .... Deut 15:10   4639
in all the *w* of thine hands.................. Deut 16:15   4639
had known all the *w* of the LORD .... Josh 24:31   4639
seen all the great *w* of the LORD .... Judg 2:7   4639
nor yet the *w* which he had done .... Judg 2:10   4639
According to all the *w* which they 1Sa 8:8   4639
because his *w* have been to 1Sa 19:4   4639
and cunning to work all *w* in brass....... 1Kin 7:14   4399
told him all the *w* that the man 1Kin 13:11   4639
with all the *w* of their hands 2Kin 22:17   4639
talk ye of all his wondrous *w* 1Chr 16:9
marvellous *w* that he hath done 1Chr 16:12
his marvellous *w* among all 1Chr 16:24
even all the *w* of this pattern 1Chr 28:19   4399
the LORD hath broken thy *w*............... 2Chr 20:37   4639
Hezekiah prospered in all his *w* 2Chr 32:30   4639
with all the *w* of their hands 2Chr 34:25   4639
according to these their *w*.................... Neh 6:14   4639
turned they from their wicked *w* .... Neh 9:35   4611
Therefore he knoweth their *w*............... Job 34:25   4566
and consider the wondrous *w* of God ..... Job 37:14
the wondrous *w* of him which is .... Job 37:16
dominion over the *w* of thy hands.......... Ps 8:6   4639
shew forth all thy marvellous *w* .... Ps 9:1
they have done abominable *w*.............. Ps 14:1   5949
and tell of all thy wondrous *w*............... Ps 26:7
they regard not the *w* of the LORD .... Ps 28:5   6468
all his *w* are done in truth..................... Ps 33:4   4640
he considereth all their *w*..................... Ps 33:15   4640
are thy wonderful *w* which thou .... Ps 40:5
behold the *w* of the LORD, what............. Ps 46:8   4659
How terrible art thou in thy *w* .... Ps 66:3   4639
Come and see the *w* of God .... Ps 66:5   4659
have I declared thy wondrous *w* .... Ps 71:17
GOD, that I may declare all thy *w* .... Ps 73:28   4399
is near thy wondrous *w* declare .... Ps 75:1
I will remember the *w* of the LORD .... Ps 77:11   4611
his wonderful *w* that he hath done .... Ps 78:4
God, and not forget the *w* of God .... Ps 78:7   4611
And forgat his *w*, and his wonders......... Ps 78:11   5949
believed not for his wondrous *w* .... Ps 78:32
there any *w* like unto thy *w* .... Ps 86:8   4639
triumph in the *w* of thy hands.............. Ps 92:4   4639
O LORD, how great are thy *w* .... Ps 92:5   4639
all his *w* in all places of his................. Ps 103:22   4639
satisfied with the fruit of thy *w* .... Ps 104:13   4639
O LORD, how manifold are thy *w* .... Ps 104:24   4639
the LORD shall rejoice in his *w*............. Ps 104:31   4639
talk ye of all his wondrous *w* .... Ps 105:2
marvellous *w* that he hath done .... Ps 105:5
They soon forgat his *w* .... Ps 106:13   4639
Wondrous *w* in the land of Ham, and.... Ps 106:22
the heathen, and learned their *w* .... Ps 106:35   4639
they defiled with their own *w*.............. Ps 106:39   4639
for his wonderful *w* to the.................... Ps 107:8
for his wonderful *w* to the.................... Ps 107:15
for his wonderful *w* to the.................... Ps 107:21
declare his *w* with rejoicing .... Ps 107:22   4639
These see the *w* of the LORD................. Ps 107:24   4639
for his wonderful *w* to the.................... Ps 107:31
The *w* of the LORD are great,................ Ps 111:2   4639
his wonderful *w* to be remembered .... Ps 111:4
his people the power of his *w* .... Ps 111:6   4639
The *w* of his hands are verity and .... Ps 111:7   4639
and declare the *w* of the LORD .... Ps 118:17   4639
so shall I talk of thy wondrous *w*........... Ps 119:27
forsake not the *w* of thine own .... Ps 138:8   4639
marvellous are thy *w*........................... Ps 139:14   4639
to practise wicked *w* with men .... Ps 141:4   5949
I meditate on all thy *w* .... Ps 143:5   6467
shall praise thy *w* to another .... Ps 145:4   4639
thy majesty, and of thy wondrous *w* ...... Ps 145:5   1697
tender mercies are over all his *w* .... Ps 145:9   4639
All thy *w* shall praise thee, O .... Ps 145:10   4639
his ways, and holy in all his *w* .... Ps 145:17   4639
of tapestry, with carved *w*.................... Prov 7:16
of his way, before his *w* of old .... Prov 8:22   4659
Commit thy *w* unto the LORD, and......... Prov 16:3   4639
to every man according to his *w* .... Prov 24:12   6467
let her own *w* praise her in the .... Prov 31:31   4639
I have seen all the *w* that are .... Eccl 1:14   4639
I made me great *w*.............................. Eccl 2:4   4639
Then I looked on all the *w* that............. Eccl 2:11   4639
a man should rejoice in his own *w* .... Eccl 3:22   4639
and the wise, and their *w*, are in .... Eccl 9:1   5652

for God now accepteth thy *w* .... Eccl 9:7   4639
not the *w* of God who maketh all .... Eccl 11:5   4639
also hast wrought all our *w* in us........... Is 26:12   4639
their *w* are in the dark, and they.......... Is 29:15   4639
their *w* are nothing .... Is 41:29   4639
thy righteousness, and thy *w* .... Is 57:12   4639
cover themselves with their *w* .... Is 59:6   4639
their *w* are *w* of iniquity .... Is 59:6   4639
For I know their *w* and their .... Is 66:18   4639
worshipped the *w* of their own .... Jer 1:16   4639
because ye have done all these *w*........... Jer 7:13   4639
according to all his wondrous *w*............. Jer 21:2
to anger with the *w* of your hands......... Jer 25:6   4639
provoke me to anger with the *w* of .... Jer 25:7   4639
according to the *w* of their own .... Jer 25:14   4639
wrath with the *w* of your hands .... Jer 44:8   4639
thou hast trusted in thy *w*.................... Jer 48:7   4639
down, and your *w* may be abolished ...... Eze 6:6   4639
of heaven, all whose *w* are truth .... Dan 4:37   4567
in all his *w* which he doeth .... Dan 9:14   4639
will never forget any of their *w*............. Amos 8:7   4639
And God saw their *w*, that they .... Jonah 3:10   4639
all the *w* of the house of Ahab.............. Mic 6:16   4639
that they may see your good *w* .... Mt 5:16   *2041*
in thy name done many wonderful *w* ... Mt 7:22
in the prison the *w* of Christ .... Mt 11:2   *2041*
most of his mighty *w* were done .... Mt 11:20
for if the mighty *w*, which were .... Mt 11:21
for if the mighty *w*, which have .... Mt 11:23
this wisdom, and these mighty *w* .... Mt 13:54
he did not many mighty *w* there............ Mt 13:58
therefore mighty *w* do shew forth .... Mt 14:2
every man according to his *w* .... Mt 16:27   *4234*
but do not ye after their *w* .... Mt 23:3   *2041*
But all their *w* they do for to be .... Mt 23:5   *2041*
that even such mighty *w* are.................. Mk 6:2
therefore mighty *w* do shew forth .... Mk 6:14
for if the mighty *w* had been done......... Lk 10:13
the mighty *w* that they had seen .... Lk 19:37
shew him greater *w* than these .... Jn 5:20   *2041*
for the *w* which the Father hath .... Jn 5:36   *2041*
the same *w* that I do, bear .... Jn 5:36   *2041*
that we might work the *w* of God .... Jn 6:28   *2041*
may see the *w* that thou doest .... Jn 7:3   *2041*
that the *w* thereof are evil .... Jn 7:7   *2041*
ye would do the *w* of Abraham.............. Jn 8:39   *2041*
but that the *w* of God should be .... Jn 9:3   *2041*
I must work the *w* of him that .... Jn 9:4   *2041*
the *w* that I do in my Father's .... Jn 10:25   *2041*
Many good *w* have I shewed you .... Jn 10:32   *2041*
which of those *w* do ye stone me........... Jn 10:32   *2041*
If I do not the *w* of my Father .... Jn 10:37   *2041*
ye believe not me, believe the *w*............ Jn 10:38   *2041*
dwelleth in me, he doeth the *w* .... Jn 14:10   *2041*
the *w* that I do shall he do also .... Jn 14:12   *2041*
greater *w* than these shall he do........... Jn 14:12   *2041*
the *w* which none other man did .... Jn 15:24   *2041*
tongues the wonderful *w* of God .... Acts 2:11
rejoiced in the *w* of their own .... Acts 7:41   *2041*
this woman was full of good *w*............... Acts 9:36   *2041*
Known unto God are all his *w* from .... Acts 15:18   *2041*
God, and do *w* meet for repentance ...... Acts 26:20   *2041*
what law? of *w*?................................... Rom 3:27   *2041*
if Abraham were justified by *w*.............. Rom 4:2   *2041*
imputeth righteousness without *w* .... Rom 4:6   *2041*
to election might stand, not of *w* .... Rom 9:11   *2041*
as it were by the *w* of the law .... Rom 9:32   *2041*
by grace, then is it no more of *w* .... Rom 11:6   *2041*
But if it be of *w*, then is it no .... Rom 11:6   *2041*
rulers are not a terror to good *w*............ Rom 13:3   *2041*
cast off the *w* of darkness .... Rom 13:12   *2041*
end shall be according to their *w*........... 2Cor 11:15   *2041*
not justified by the *w* of the law .... Gal 2:16   *2041*
and not by the *w* of the law.................. Gal 2:16   *2041*
for by the *w* of the law shall no............. Gal 2:16   *2041*
ye the Spirit by the *w* of the law .... Gal 3:2   *2041*
doeth he it by the *w* of the law .... Gal 3:5   *2041*
For as many as are of the *w* of .... Gal 3:10   *2041*
Now the *w* of the flesh are .... Gal 5:19   *2041*
Not of *w*, lest any man should................ Eph 2:9   *2041*
in Christ Jesus unto good *w*.................. Eph 2:10   *2041*
with the unfruitful *w* of darkness .... Eph 5:11   *2041*
enemies in your mind by wicked *w* .... Col 1:21   *2041*
professing godliness) with good *w* 1Ti 2:10   *2041*
Well reported of for good *w* 1Ti 5:10   *2041*
Likewise also the good *w* of some 1Ti 5:25   *2041*
good, that they be rich in good *w*........... 1Ti 6:18   *2041*
calling, not according to our *w*.............. 2Ti 1:9   *2041*
furnished unto all good *w* 2Ti 3:17   *2041*
reward him according to his *w* 2Ti 4:14   *2041*
but in *w* they deny him, being .... Titus 1:16   *2041*

thyself a pattern of good *w* ... Titus 2:7 *2041*
people, zealous of good *w* ... Titus 2:14 *2041*
Not by *w* of righteousness which ... Titus 3:5 *2041*
be careful to maintain good *w* ... Titus 3:8 *2041*
good *w* for necessary uses ... Titus 3:14 *2041*
heavens are the *w* of thine hands ... Heb 1:10 *2041*
set him over the *w* of thy hands ... Heb 2:7 *2041*
me, and saw my *w* forty years ... Heb 3:9 *2041*
although the *w* were finished from ... Heb 4:3 *2041*
the seventh day from all his *w* ... Heb 4:4 *2041*
also hath ceased from his own *w* ... Heb 4:10 *2041*
of repentance from dead *w* ... Heb 6:1 *2041*
dead *w* to serve the living God ... Heb 9:14 *2041*
to provoke unto love and to good *w* ... Heb 10:24 *2041*
say he hath faith, and have not *w* ... Jas 2:14 *2041*
Even so faith, if it hath not *w* ... Jas 2:17 *2041*
say, Thou hast faith, and I have *w* ... Jas 2:18 *2041*
shew me thy faith without thy *w* ... Jas 2:18 *2041*
I will shew thee my faith by my *w* ... Jas 2:18 *2041*
man, that faith without *w* is dead ... Jas 2:20 *2041*
Abraham our father justified by *w* ... Jas 2:21 *2041*
thou how faith wrought with his *w* ... Jas 2:22 *2041*
by *w* was faith made perfect ... Jas 2:22 *2041*
how that by *w* a man is justified ... Jas 2:24 *2041*
Rahab the harlot justified by *w* ... Jas 2:25 *2041*
so faith without *w* is dead also ... Jas 2:26 *2041*
his *w* with meekness of wisdom ... Jas 3:13 *2041*
they may by your good *w*, which ... 1Pet 2:12 *2041*
the *w* that are therein shall be ... 2Pet 3:10 *2041*
might destroy the *w* of the devil ... 1Jn 3:8 *2041*
Because his own *w* were evil ... 1Jn 3:12 *2041*
I know thy *w*, and thy labour, and ... Rev 2:2 *2041*
and repent, and do the first *w* ... Rev 2:5 *2041*
I know thy *w*, and tribulation, and ... Rev 2:9 *2041*
I know thy *w*, and where thou ... Rev 2:13 *2041*
I know thy *w*, and charity, and ... Rev 2:19 *2041*
faith, and thy patience, and thy *w* ... Rev 2:19 *2041*
one of you according to your *w* ... Rev 2:23 *2041*
keepeth my *w* unto the end, to him ... Rev 2:26 *2041*
I know thy *w*, that thou hast a ... Rev 3:1 *2041*
found thy *w* perfect before God ... Rev 3:2 *2041*
I know thy *w* ... Rev 3:8 *2041*
I know thy *w*, that thou art ... Rev 3:15 *2041*
not of the *w* of their hands ... Rev 9:20 *2041*
and their *w* do follow them ... Rev 14:13 *2041*
Great and marvellous are thy *w* ... Rev 15:3 *2041*
her double according to her *w* ... Rev 18:6 *2041*
the books, according to their *w* ... Rev 20:12 *2041*
every man according to their *w* ... Rev 20:13 *2041*

WORKS'

believe me for the very *w* sake ... Jn 14:11 *2041*

WORLD

and he hath set the *w* upon them ... 1Sa 2:8 8398
of the *w* were discovered, at the ... 2Sa 22:16 8398
the *w* also shall be stable, that ... 1Chr 16:30 8398
darkness, and chased out of the *w* ... Job 18:18 8398
Or who hath disposed the whole *w* ... Job 34:13 8398
the face of the *w* in the earth ... Job 37:12 8398
judge the *w* in righteousness ... Ps 9:8 8398
hand, O LORD, from men of the *w* ... Ps 17:14 2465
the foundations of the *w* were ... Ps 18:15 8398
their words to the end of the *w* ... Ps 19:4 8398
the ends of the *w* shall remember ... Ps 22:27 776
the *w*, and they that dwell therein ... Ps 24:1 8398
of the *w* stand in awe of him ... Ps 33:8 8398
ear, all ye inhabitants of the *w* ... Ps 49:1 2465
for the *w* is mine, and the fulness ... Ps 50:12 8398
the ungodly, who prosper in the *w* ... Ps 73:12 5769
the lightnings lightened the *w* ... Ps 77:18 8398
as for the *w* and the fulness ... Ps 89:11 8398
hadst formed the earth and the *w* ... Ps 90:2 8398
the *w* also is stablished, that it ... Ps 93:1 8398
the *w* also shall be established ... Ps 96:10 8398
judge the *w* with righteousness ... Ps 96:13 8398
His lightnings enlightened the *w* ... Ps 97:4 8398
the *w*, and they that dwell therein ... Ps 98:7 8398
shall he judge the *w*, and the ... Ps 98:9 8398
highest part of the dust of the *w* ... Prov 8:26 8398
he hath set the *w* in their heart ... Eccl 3:11 5769
will punish the *w* for their evil ... Is 13:11 8398
That made the *w* as a wilderness, ... Is 14:17 8398
the face of the *w* with cities ... Is 14:21 8398
All ye inhabitants of the *w* ... Is 18:3 8398
the *w* upon the face of the earth ... Is 23:17 776
the *w* languisheth and fadeth away, ... Is 24:4 8398
the inhabitants of the *w* will ... Is 26:9 8398
the inhabitants of the *w* fallen ... Is 26:18 8398
fill the face of the *w* with fruit ... Is 27:6 8398
the *w*, and all things that come ... Is 34:1 8398
with the inhabitants of the *w* ... Is 38:11 2309
nor confounded *w* without end ... Is 45:17 5769
proclaimed unto the end of the *w* ... Is 62:11 776
of the *w* men have not heard ... Is 64:4 5769
established the *w* by his wisdom ... Jer 10:12 8398
and all the kingdoms of the *w* ... Jer 25:26 776
established the *w* by his wisdom ... Jer 51:15 8398
and all the inhabitants of the *w* ... Lam 4:12 8398
at his presence, yea, the *w* ... Nah 1:5 8398
him all the kingdoms of the *w* ... Mt 4:8 *2889*
Ye are the light of the *w* ... Mt 5:14 *2889*
forgiven him, neither in this *w* ... Mt 12:32 *165*
neither in the *w* to come ... Mt 12:32
and the care of this *w*, and the ... Mt 13:22 *165*
from the foundation of the *w* ... Mt 13:35 *2889*
The field is the *w* ... Mt 13:38 *2889*
the harvest is the end of the *w* ... Mt 13:39 *165*
shall it be in the end of this *w* ... Mt 13:40 *165*
shall it be at the end of the *w* ... Mt 13:49 *165*
if he shall gain the whole *w* ... Mt 16:26 *2889*
Woe unto the *w* because of ... Mt 18:7 *2889*
coming, and of the end of the *w* ... Mt 24:3 *165*
shall be preached in all the *w* ... Mt 24:14 *3625*
beginning of the *w* to this time ... Mt 24:21 *2889*
you from the foundation of the *w* ... Mt 25:34 *2889*
shall be preached in the whole *w* ... Mt 26:13 *2889*
alway, even unto the end of the *w* ... Mt 28:20 *165*
And the cares of this *w*, and the ... Mk 4:19 *165*
man, if he shall gain the whole *w* ... Mk 8:36 *2889*
in the *w* to come eternal life ... Mk 10:30 *165*
preached throughout the whole *w* ... Mk 14:9 *2889*
unto them, Go ye into all the *w* ... Mk 16:15 *2889*
which have been since the *w* began ... Lk 1:70 *165*
that all the *w* should be taxed ... Lk 2:1 *3625*
of the *w* in a moment of time ... Lk 4:5 *3625*
if he gain the whole *w*, and lose ... Lk 9:25 *2889*
shed from the foundation of the *w* ... Lk 11:50 *2889*
the nations of the *w* seek after ... Lk 12:30 *2889*
for the children of this *w* are in ... Lk 16:8 *165*
in the *w* to come life everlasting ... Lk 18:30 *165*
The children of this *w* marry ... Lk 20:34 *165*
accounted worthy to obtain that *w* ... Lk 20:35 *165*
every man that cometh into the *w* ... Jn 1:9 *2889*
He was in the *w* ... Jn 1:10 *2889*
the *w* was made by him, and the ... Jn 1:10 *2889*
by him, and the *w* knew him not ... Jn 1:10 *2889*
taketh away the sin of the *w* ... Jn 1:29 *2889*
For God so loved the *w*, that he ... Jn 3:16 *2889*
into the *w* to condemn the *w* ... Jn 3:17 *2889*
but that the *w* through him might ... Jn 3:17 *2889*
that light is come into the *w* ... Jn 3:19 *2889*
the Christ, the Saviour of the *w* ... Jn 4:42 *2889*
that should come into the *w* ... Jn 6:14 *2889*
heaven, and giveth life unto the *w* ... Jn 6:33 *2889*
I will give for the life of the *w* ... Jn 6:51 *2889*
things, shew thyself to the *w* ... Jn 7:4 *2889*
The *w* cannot hate you ... Jn 7:7 *2889*
saying, I am the light of the *w* ... Jn 8:12 *2889*
ye are of this *w* ... Jn 8:23 *2889*
I am not of this *w* ... Jn 8:23 *2889*
I speak to the *w* those things ... Jn 8:26 *2889*
As long as I am in the *w* ... Jn 9:5 *2889*
I am the light of the *w* ... Jn 9:5 *2889*
Since the *w* began was it not ... Jn 9:32 *165*
judgment I am come into this *w* ... Jn 9:39 *2889*
sanctified, and sent into the *w* ... Jn 10:36 *2889*
he seeth the light of this *w* ... Jn 11:9 *2889*
God, which should come into the *w* ... Jn 11:27 *2889*
behold, the *w* is gone after him ... Jn 12:19 *2889*
***w* shall keep it unto life eternal** ... Jn 12:25 *2889*
Now is the judgment of this *w* ... Jn 12:31 *2889*
the prince of this *w* be cast out ... Jn 12:31 *2889*
I am come a light into the *w* ... Jn 12:46 *2889*
for I came not to judge the *w* ... Jn 12:47 *2889*
but to save the *w* ... Jn 12:47 *2889*
out of this *w* unto the Father ... Jn 13:1 *2889*
loved his own which were in the *w* ... Jn 13:1 *2889*
whom the *w* cannot receive, ... Jn 14:17 *2889*
while, and the *w* seeth me no more ... Jn 14:19
unto us, and not unto the *w* ... Jn 14:22 *2889*
not as the *w* giveth, give I unto ... Jn 14:27 *2889*
for the prince of this *w* cometh ... Jn 14:30 *2889*
But that the *w* may know that I ... Jn 14:31 *2889*
If the *w* hate you, ye know that ... Jn 15:18 *2889*
If ye were of the *w* ... Jn 15:19 *2889*
the *w* would love his own ... Jn 15:19 *2889*
but because ye are not of the *w* ... Jn 15:19 *2889*
I have chosen you out of the *w* ... Jn 15:19 *2889*
therefore the *w* hateth you ... Jn 15:19 *2889*
he will reprove the *w* of sin ... Jn 16:8 *2889*
the prince of this *w* is judged ... Jn 16:11 *2889*
lament, but the *w* shall rejoice ... Jn 16:20 *2889*

WORLDLY

WORLD'S

WORLDS

WORM

WORMS

until the morning, and it bred *w*	Ex 16:20	8438
for the *w* shall eat them	Deut 28:39	8438
My flesh is clothed with *w*	Job 7:5	7415
after my skin *w* destroy this body	Job 19:26	
dust, and the *w* shall cover them	Job 21:26	7415
under thee, and the *w* cover thee	Is 14:11	8438
their holes like *w* of the earth	Mic 7:17	2119
and he was eaten of *w*, and gave up	Acts 12:23	4662

WORMWOOD

you a root that beareth gall and *w*	Deut 29:18	3939
But her end is bitter as *w*	Prov 5:4	3939
them, even this people, with *w*	Jer 9:15	3939
Behold, I will feed them with *w*	Jer 23:15	3939
he hath made me drunken with *w*	Lam 3:15	3939
affliction and my misery, the *w*	Lam 3:19	3939
Ye who turn judgment to *w*	Amos 5:7	3939
the name of the star is called *W*	Rev 8:11	894
third part of the waters became *w*	Rev 8:11	894

WORSE See APPENDIX.

WORSHIP

I and the lad will go yonder and *w*	Gen 22:5	7812
and *w* ye afar off	Ex 24:1	7812
For thou shalt *w* no other god	Ex 34:14	7812
shouldest be driven to *w* them	Deut 4:19	7812
w them, I testify against you	Deut 8:19	7812
and serve other gods, and *w* them	Deut 11:16	7812
w before the LORD thy God	Deut 26:10	7812
w other gods, and serve them	Deut 30:17	7812
his face to the earth, and did *w*	Josh 5:14	7812
up out of his city yearly to *w*	1Sa 1:3	7812
with me, that I may *w* the LORD	1Sa 15:25	7812
that I may *w* the LORD thy God	1Sa 15:30	7812
go and serve other gods, and *w* them	1Kin 9:6	7812
people went to *w* before the one	1Kin 12:30	
the house of Rimmon to *w* there	2Kin 5:18	7812
shall ye fear, and him shall ye *w*	2Kin 17:36	7812
Ye shall *w* before this altar in	2Kin 18:22	7812
w the LORD in the beauty of	1Chr 16:29	7812
go and serve other gods, and *w* them	2Chr 7:19	7812
Ye shall *w* before one altar, and	2Chr 32:12	7812
in thy fear will I *w* toward thy	Ps 5:7	7812
the nations shall *w* before thee	Ps 22:27	7812
be fat upon earth shall eat and *w*	Ps 22:29	7812
w the LORD in the beauty of	Ps 29:2	7812
and *w* thou him	Ps 45:11	7812
All the earth shall *w* thee	Ps 66:4	7812
shalt thou *w* any strange god	Ps 81:9	7812
come and *w* before thee, O Lord	Ps 86:9	7812
O come, let us *w* and bow down	Ps 95:6	7812
O *w* the LORD in the beauty of	Ps 96:9	7812
w him, all ye gods	Ps 97:7	7812
our God, and *w* at his footstool	Ps 99:5	7812
our God, and *w* at his holy hill	Ps 99:9	7812
we will *w* at his footstool	Ps 132:7	7812
I will *w* toward thy holy temple,	Ps 138:2	7812
they *w* the work of their own	Is 2:8	7812
made each one for himself to *w*	Is 2:20	7812
shall *w* the LORD in the holy	Is 27:13	7812
Ye shall *w* before this altar	Is 36:7	7812
they fall down, yea, they *w*	Is 46:6	7812
and arise, princes also shall *w*	Is 49:7	7812
all flesh come to *w* before me	Is 66:23	7812
in at these gates to *w* the LORD	Jer 7:2	7812
to *w* them, shall even be as this	Jer 13:10	7812
to *w* them, and provoke me not to	Jer 25:6	7812
which come to *w* in the LORD's	Jer 26:2	7812
did we make her cakes to *w* her	Jer 44:19	6087
he shall *w* at the threshold of	Eze 46:2	7812
the people of the land shall *w* at	Eze 46:3	7812
w shall go out by the way of the	Eze 46:9	7812
down and *w* the golden image that	Dan 3:5	5457
fall down and *w* the golden image	Dan 3:10	5457
nor *w* the golden image which thou	Dan 3:12	5457
nor *w* the golden image which I	Dan 3:14	5457
w the image which I have made	Dan 3:15	5457
but if ye *w* not, ye shall be cast	Dan 3:15	5457
nor *w* the golden image which thou	Dan 3:18	5457
might not serve nor *w* any god	Dan 3:28	5457
thou shalt no more *w* the work of	Mic 5:13	7812
them that *w* the host of heaven	Zeph 1:5	7812
and them that *w* and that swear by	Zeph 1:5	7812
and men shall *w* him, every one	Zeph 2:11	7812
from year to year to *w* the King	Zec 14:16	7812
unto Jerusalem to *w* the King	Zec 14:17	7812
in the east, and are come to *w* him	Mt 2:2	4352
that I may come and *w* him also	Mt 2:8	4352
if thou wilt fall down and *w* me	Mt 4:9	4352
Thou shalt *w* the Lord thy God, and	Mt 4:10	4352

But in vain they do *w* me,	Mt 15:9	4576
Howbeit in vain do they *w* me	Mk 7:7	4576
If thou therefore wilt *w* me	Lk 4:7	4352,1799
Thou shalt *w* the Lord thy God, and	Lk 4:8	4352
then shalt thou have *w* in the	Lk 14:10	1391
is the place where men ought to *w*	Jn 4:20	4352
yet at Jerusalem, *w* the Father	Jn 4:21	4352
Ye *w* ye know not what	Jn 4:22	4352
we know what we *w*	Jn 4:22	4352
shall *w* the Father in spirit	Jn 4:23	4352
the Father seeketh such to *w* him	Jn 4:23	4352
they that *w* him must	Jn 4:24	4352
must *w* him in spirit	Jn 4:24	4352
that came up to *w* at the feast	Jn 12:20	4352
gave them up to *w* the host of	Acts 7:42	3000
figures which ye made to *w* them	Acts 7:43	4352
and had come to Jerusalem for to *w*	Acts 8:27	4352
Whom therefore ye ignorantly *w*	Acts 17:23	2151
men to *w* God contrary to the law	Acts 18:13	4576
I went up to Jerusalem for to *w*	Acts 24:11	3000
so *w* I the God of my fathers,	Acts 24:14	3000
down on his face he will *w* God	1Cor 14:25	4352
which *w* God in the spirit, and	Phil 3:3	3000
indeed a shew of wisdom in will *w*	Col 2:23	1479
let all the angels of God *w* him	Heb 1:6	4352
***w* before thy feet, and to know**	Rev 3:9	4352
w him that liveth for ever and	Rev 4:10	4352
that they should not *w* devils	Rev 9:20	4352
the altar, and them that *w* therein	Rev 11:1	4352
dwell upon the earth shall *w* him	Rev 13:8	4352
therein to *w* the first beast	Rev 13:12	4352
w the image of the beast should	Rev 13:15	4352
w him that made heaven, and earth,	Rev 14:7	4352
voice, If any man *w* the beast	Rev 14:9	4352
who *w* the beast and his image, and	Rev 14:11	4352
shall come and *w* before thee	Rev 15:4	4352
And I fell at his feet to *w* him	Rev 19:10	4352
w God	Rev 19:10	4352
I fell down to *w* before the feet	Rev 22:8	4352
w God	Rev 22:9	4352

WORSHIPPED

down his head, and *w* the LORD	Gen 24:26	7812
w the LORD, and blessed the LORD	Gen 24:48	7812
he *w* the LORD, bowing himself to	Gen 24:52	7812
then they bowed their heads and *w*	Ex 4:31	7812
And the people bowed the head and *w*	Ex 12:27	7812
them a molten calf, and have *w* it	Ex 32:8	7812
and all the people rose up and *w*	Ex 33:10	7812
his head toward the earth, and *w*	Ex 34:8	7812
w them, either the sun, or moon,	Deut 17:3	7812
w them, gods whom they knew not,	Deut 29:26	7812
interpretation thereof, that he *w*	Judg 7:15	7812
w before the LORD, and returned,	1Sa 1:19	7812
And he *w* the LORD there	1Sa 1:28	7812
and Saul *w* the LORD	1Sa 15:31	7812
into the house of the LORD, and *w*	2Sa 12:20	7812
top of the mount, where he *w* God	2Sa 15:32	7812
upon other gods, and have *w* them	1Kin 9:9	7812
have *w* Ashtoreth the goddess of	1Kin 11:33	7812
and went and served Baal, and *w* him	1Kin 16:31	7812
w him, and provoked to anger the	1Kin 22:53	7812
w all the host of heaven, and	2Kin 17:16	7812
w all the host of heaven, and	2Kin 21:3	7812
that his father served, and *w* them	2Kin 21:21	7812
heads, and *w* the LORD, and the king	1Chr 29:20	7812
ground upon the pavement, and *w*	2Chr 7:3	7812
gods, and *w* them, and served them	2Chr 7:22	7812
And all the congregation *w*	2Chr 29:28	7812
with him bowed themselves, and *w*	2Chr 29:29	7812
and they bowed their heads and *w*	2Chr 29:30	7812
w all the host of heaven, and	2Chr 33:3	7812
w the LORD with their faces to	Neh 8:6	7812
and *w* the LORD their God	Neh 9:3	7812
fell down upon the ground, and *w*	Job 1:20	7812
in Horeb, and *w* the molten image	Ps 106:19	7812
w the works of their own hands	Jer 1:16	7812
have sought, and whom they have *w*	Jer 8:2	7812
have served them, and have *w* them	Jer 16:11	7812
w other gods, and served them	Jer 22:9	7812
they *w* the sun toward the east	Eze 8:16	7812
w Daniel, and commanded that they	Dan 2:46	5457
down and *w* the golden image that	Dan 3:7	5457
mother, and fell down, and *w* him	Mt 2:11	4352
w him, saying, Lord, if thou wilt	Mt 8:2	4352
w him, saying, My daughter is	Mt 9:18	4352
w him, saying, Of a truth thou	Mt 14:33	4352
w him, saying, Lord, help me	Mt 15:25	4352
***w* him, saying, Lord, have**	Mt 18:26	4352
and held him by the feet, and *w* him	Mt 28:9	4352
And when they saw him, they *w* him	Mt 28:17	4352

Jesus afar off, he ran and *w* him, ... Mk 5:6   4352
him, and bowing their knees *w* him .... Mk 15:19   4352
And they *w* him, and returned to .... Lk 24:52   4352
Our fathers *w* in this mountain .... Jn 4:20   4352
And he *w* him .... Jn 9:38   4352
fell down at his feet, and *w* him............. Acts 10:25   4352
the city of Thyatira, which *w* God .... Acts 16:14   4576
Neither is *w* with men's hands, as .... Acts 17:25   2323
named Justus, one that *w* God .... Acts 18:7   4576
the truth of God into a lie, and *w* .... Rom 1:25   4573
that is called God, or that is *w* 2Th 2:4   4574
and *w*, leaning upon the top of his.......... Heb 11:21   4352
w him that liveth for ever and .... Rev 5:14   4352
throne on their faces, and *w* God, ... Rev 7:11   4352
fell upon their faces, and *w* God, ... Rev 11:16   4352
they *w* the dragon which gave .... Rev 13:4   4352
they *w* the beast, saying, Who is .... Rev 13:4   4352
and upon them which *w* his image .... Rev 16:2   4352
w God that sat on the throne, ... Rev 19:4   4352
beast, and them that *w* his image .... Rev 19:20   4352
God, and which had not *w* the beast ..... Rev 20:4   4352

WORSHIPPER
but if any man be a *w* of God .... Jn 9:31   2318
is a *w* of the great goddess Diana .... Acts 19:35   3511

WORSHIPPERS
he might destroy the *w* of Baal............. 2Kin 10:19   5647
all the *w* of Baal came, so that 2Kin 10:21   5647
vestments for all the *w* of Baal 2Kin 10:22   5647
Baal, and said unto the *w* of Baal 2Kin 10:23   5647
the Lord, but the *w* of Baal only 2Kin 10:23   5647
when the true *w* shall worship the .... Jn 4:23   4353
because that the *w* once purged .... Heb 10:2   3000

WORSHIPPETH
and the host of heaven *w* thee .... Neh 9:6   7812
yea, he maketh a god, and *w* it............. Is 44:15   7812
w it, and prayeth unto it, and............... Is 44:17   7812
w shall the same hour be cast .... Dan 3:6   5457
And whoso falleth not down and *w* .... Dan 3:11   5457
whom all Asia and the world *w* .... Acts 19:27   4576

WORSHIPPING
as he was *w* in the house of 2Kin 19:37   7812
fell before the Lord, *w* the Lord 2Chr 20:18   7812
as he was *w* in the house of .... Is 37:38   7812
w him, and desiring a certain .... Mt 20:20   4352
w of angels, intruding into those .... Col 2:18   2356

WORST See APPENDIX.

WORTH
it is *w* he shall give it me for a .... Gen 23:9   4392
the land is *w* four hundred .... Gen 23:15
unto him the *w* of thy estimation.......... Lev 27:23   4373
for he hath been *w* a double hired........ Deut 15:18   7939
but now thou art *w* ten thousand 2Sa 18:3   3644
give thee the *w* of it in money 1Kin 21:2   4242
liar, and make my speech nothing *w* ..... Job 24:25
heart of the wicked is little *w*................ Prov 10:20
Howl ye, Woe *w* the day .... Eze 30:2

WORTHIES
He shall recount his *w*.......................... Nah 2:5   117

WORTHILY
do thou *w* in Ephratah, and be .... Ruth 4:11   2428

WORTHY
I am not *w* of the least of all .... Gen 32:10   6994
shall he that is *w* of death be................ Deut 17:6
whereas he was not *w* of death .... Deut 19:6
have committed a sin *w* of death.......... Deut 21:22
in the damsel no sin *w* of death .... Deut 22:26
the wicked man be *w* to be beaten........ Deut 25:2   1121
unto Hannah he gave a *w* portion 1Sa 1:5   639
the Lord liveth, ye are *w* to die 1Sa 26:16   1121
the Lord, who is *w* to be praised.......... 2Sa 22:4
If he will shew himself a *w* man 1Kin 1:52   2428
for thou art *w* of death 1Kin 2:26   376
the Lord, who is *w* to be praised.......... Ps 18:3
saying, This man is *w* to die .... Jer 26:11
This man is not *w* to die .... Jer 26:16
I, whose shoes I am not *w* to bear .... Mt 3:11   2425
I am not *w* that thou shouldest .... Mt 8:8   2425
for the workman is *w* of his meat .... Mt 10:10   514
enter, enquire who in it is *w* .... Mt 10:11   514
And if the house be *w*, let your........... Mt 10:13   514
but if it be not *w*, let your................ Mt 10:13   514
more than me is not *w* of me .... Mt 10:37   514
more than me is not *w* of me .... Mt 10:37   514
after me, is not *w* of me................... Mt 10:38   514
they which were bidden were not *w*..... Mt 22:8   514
shoes I am not *w* to stoop down .... Mk 1:7   2425

therefore fruits *w* of repentance............. Lk 3:8   514
whose shoes I am not *w* to unloose........ Lk 3:16   2425
That he was *w* for whom he should .... Lk 7:4   514
for I am not *w* that thou .... Lk 7:6   2425
I myself *w* to come unto thee .... Lk 7:7   515
for the labourer is *w* of his hire .... Lk 10:7   514
and did commit things *w* of stripes ..... Lk 12:48   514
am no more *w* to be called thy son ...... Lk 15:19   514
am no more *w* to be called thy son ...... Lk 15:21   514
accounted *w* to obtain that world .... Lk 20:35   2661
that ye may be accounted *w* to........... Lk 21:36   2661
nothing *w* of death is done unto .... Lk 23:15   514
latchet I am not *w* to unloose .... Jn 1:27   514
that they were counted *w* to.................. Acts 5:41   2661
of his feet I am not *w* to loose .... Acts 13:25   514
his charge *w* of death or of bonds .... Acts 23:29   514
that very *w* deeds are done unto .... Acts 24:2   2735
committed any thing *w* of death............ Acts 25:11   514
had committed nothing *w* of death .... Acts 25:25   514
nothing *w* of death or of bonds .... Acts 26:31   514
commit such things are *w* of death .... Rom 1:32   514
of this present time are not *w* to .... Rom 8:18   514
beseech you that ye walk *w* of the......... Eph 4:1   516
That ye might walk *w* of the Lord .... Col 1:10   516
That ye would walk *w* of God................ 1Th 2:12   516
counted *w* of the kingdom of God 2Th 1:5   2661
would count you *w* of this calling 2Th 1:11   515
w of all acceptation, that Christ 1Ti 1:15   514
saying and *w* of all acceptation 1Ti 4:9   514
be counted *w* of double honour 1Ti 5:17   515
The labourer is *w* of his reward 1Ti 5:18   514
their own masters *w* of all honour 1Ti 6:1   514
w of more glory than Moses.................. Heb 3:3   515
suppose ye, shall he be thought *w*......... Heb 10:29   515
(Of whom the world was not *w*.............. Heb 11:38   514
Do not they blaspheme that *w* name ..... Jas 2:7   2570
for they are *w* .... Rev 3:4   514
Thou art *w*, O Lord, to receive .... Rev 4:11   514
Who is *w* to open the book, and to........ Rev 5:2   514
no man was found *w* to open .... Rev 5:4   514
Thou art *w* to take the book, and .... Rev 5:9   514
W is the Lamb that was slain to............. Rev 5:12   514
for they are *w* .... Rev 16:6   514

WOT
I *w* not who hath done this thing .... Gen 21:26   3045
w ye not that such a man as I can .... Gen 44:15   3045
we *w* not what is become of him............ Ex 32:1   3045
we *w* not what is become of him............ Ex 32:23   3045
for I *w* that he whom thou .... Num 22:6   3045
whither the men went I *w* not .... Josh 2:5   3045
I *w* that through ignorance ye did.......... Acts 3:17   1492
we *w* not what is become of him............ Acts 7:40   1492
W ye not what the scripture saith........... Rom 11:2   1492
yet what I shall choose I *w* not............... Phil 1:22   1107

WOTTETH
my master *w* not what is with me .... Gen 39:8   3045

WOULD See APPENDIX.

WOULDEST See APPENDIX.

WOUND
w for *w*, stripe for stripe .... Ex 21:25   6482
I *w*, and I heal.................................... Deut 32:39   4272
the blood ran out of the *w* into 1Kin 22:35   4347
my *w* is incurable without..................... Job 34:6   2671
But God shall *w* the head of his .... Ps 68:21   4272
he shall *w* the heads over many .... Ps 110:6   4272
A *w* and dishonour shall he get .... Prov 6:33   5061
The blueness of a *w* cleanseth .... Prov 20:30   6482
and healeth the stroke of their *w*........... Is 30:26   4347
my *w* is grievous .... Jer 10:19   4347
my *w* incurable, which refuseth to .... Jer 15:18   4347
incurable, and thy *w* is grievous .... Jer 30:12   4347
thee with the *w* of an enemy .... Jer 30:14   4347
his sickness, and Judah saw his *w* .... Hos 5:13   4205
heal you, nor cure you of your *w* .... Hos 5:13   4205
bread have laid a *w* under thee .... Obad 7   4204
For her *w* is incurable .... Mic 1:9   4347
thy *w* is grievous .... Nah 3:19   4347
w it in linen clothes with the .... Jn 19:40   1210
w him up, and carried him out, and...... Acts 5:6   4958
w their weak conscience, ye sin............. 1Cor 8:12   5180
and his deadly *w* was healed .... Rev 13:3   4127
beast, whose deadly *w* was healed........ Rev 13:12   4127
beast, which had the *w* by a sword .... Rev 13:14   4127

WOUNDED
He that is *w* in the stones, or .... Deut 23:1   1795
many were overthrown and *w*............... Judg 9:40   2491
the *w* of the Philistines fell 1Sa 17:52   2491
he was sore *w* of the archers 1Sa 31:3   2342

w them, that they could not arise	2Sa 22:39	4272
him, so that in smiting he *w* him	1Kin 20:37	6481
for I am *w*	1Kin 22:34	2470
and the Syrians *w* Joram	2Kin 8:28	5221
him, and he was *w* of the archers	1Chr 10:3	2342
for I am *w*	2Chr 18:33	2470
for I am sore *w*	2Chr 35:23	2470
and the soul of the *w* crieth out	Job 24:12	2491
I have *w* them that they were not	Ps 18:38	4272
suddenly shall they be *w*	Ps 64:7	4347
grief of those whom thou hast *w*	Ps 69:26	2491
needy, and my heart is *w* within me	Ps 109:22	2490
For she hath cast down many *w*	Prov 7:26	2491
but a *w* spirit who can bear	Prov 18:14	5218
me, they smote me, they *w* me	Song 5:7	6481
hath cut Rahab, and *w* the dragon	Is 51:9	2490
But he was *w* for our	Is 53:5	2490
for I have *w* thee with the wound	Jer 30:14	5221
remained but *w* men among them	Jer 37:10	1856
all her land the *w* shall groan	Jer 51:52	2491
when they swooned as the *w* in the	Lam 2:12	2491
sound of they fall, when the *w* cry	Eze 26:15	2491
the *w* shall be judged in the	Eze 28:23	2491
the groanings of a deadly *w* man	Eze 30:24	2491
the sword, they shall not be *w*	Joel 2:8	1214
Those with which I was *w* in the	Zec 13:6	5221
w him in the head, and sent him	Mk 12:4	
w him, and departed, leaving him	Lk 10:30	4127,2007
they *w* him also, and cast him out	Lk 20:12	*5135*
fled out of that house naked and *w*	Acts 19:16	*5135*
his heads as it were *w* to death	Rev 13:3	*4969*

WOUNDEDST

thou *w* the head out of the house	Hab 3:13	4272

WOUNDETH

he *w*, and his hands make whole	Job 5:18	4272

WOUNDING

for I have slain a man to my *w*	Gen 4:23	6482

WOUNDS

to be healed in Jezreel of the *w*	2Kin 8:29	4347
to be healed in Jezreel of the *w*	2Kin 9:15	4347
in Jezreel because of the *w* which	2Chr 22:6	4347
and multiplieth my *w* without cause	Job 9:17	6482
My *w* stink and are corrupt because	Ps 38:5	2250
in heart, and bindeth up their *w*	Ps 147:3	6094
words of a talebearer are as *w*	Prov 18:8	3859
who hath *w* without cause	Prov 23:29	6482
words of a talebearer are as *w*	Prov 26:22	3859
Faithful are the *w* of a friend	Prov 27:6	6482
but *w*, and bruises, and putrifying	Is 1:6	6482
me continually is grief and *w*	Jer 6:7	4347
and I will heal thee of thy *w*	Jer 30:17	4347
What are these *w* in thine hands	Zec 13:6	4347
And went to him, and bound up his *w*	Lk 10:34	*5134*

WOVE

where the women *w* hangings for	2Kin 23:7	707

WOVEN

it shall have a binding of *w* work	Ex 28:32	707
the robe of the ephod of *w* work	Ex 39:22	707
of fine linen of *w* work for Aaron	Ex 39:27	707
w from the top throughout	Jn 19:23	5307

WRAP

than that he can *w* himself in it	Is 28:20	3664
so they *w* it up	Mic 7:3	5686

WRAPPED

w herself, and sat in an open	Gen 38:14	5968
it is here *w* in a cloth behind	1Sa 21:9	3874
that he *w* his face in his mantle	1Kin 19:13	3874
w it together, and smote the	2Kin 2:8	1563
His roots are *w* about the heap	Job 8:17	5440
of his stones are *w* together	Job 40:17	8276
it is *w* up for the slaughter	Eze 21:15	4593
the weeds were *w* about my head	Jonah 2:5	2280
he *w* it in a clean linen cloth	Mt 27:59	*1794*
w him in the linen, and laid him	Mk 15:46	*1750*
w him in swaddling clothes, and	Lk 2:7	*4683*
the babe *w* in swaddling clothes	Lk 2:12	*4683*
w it in linen, and laid it in a	Lk 23:53	*1794*
but *w* together in a place by	Jn 20:7	*1794*

WRATH

that his *w* was kindled	Gen 39:19	639
and their *w*, for it was cruel	Gen 49:7	5678
thou sentest forth thy *w*, which	Ex 15:7	2740
my *w* shall wax hot, and I will	Ex 22:24	639
that my *w* may wax hot against	Ex 32:10	639
why doth thy *w* wax hot against	Ex 32:11	639
Turn from thy fierce *w*, and repent	Ex 32:12	639

lest *w* come upon all the people	Lev 10:6	7107
that there be no *w* upon the	Num 1:53	7110
the *w* of the LORD was kindled	Num 11:33	639
for there is *w* gone out from the	Num 16:46	7110
that there be no *w* any more upon	Num 18:5	7110
hath turned my *w* away from the	Num 25:11	2534
thy God to *w* in the wilderness	Deut 9:7	7107
Horeb ye provoked the LORD to *w*	Deut 9:8	7107
ye provoked the LORD to *w*	Deut 9:22	7107
then the LORD's *w* be kindled	Deut 11:17	639
in his anger, and in his *w*	Deut 29:23	2534
of their land in anger, and in *w*	Deut 29:28	2534
that I feared the *w* of the enemy	Deut 32:27	3708
lest *w* be upon us, because of the	Josh 9:20	7110
w fell on all the congregation of	Josh 22:20	7110
his fierce *w* upon Amalek,	1Sa 28:18	639
if so be that the king's *w* arise	2Sa 11:20	2534
for great is the *w* of the LORD	2Kin 22:13	2534
therefore my *w* shall be kindled	2Kin 22:17	2534
the fierceness of his great *w*	2Kin 23:26	639
because there fell *w* for it	1Chr 27:24	7110
my *w* shall not be poured out upon	2Chr 12:7	2534
the *w* of the LORD turned from him	2Chr 12:12	639
therefore is *w* upon thee from	2Chr 19:2	7110
so *w* come upon you, and upon your	2Chr 19:10	7110
w came upon Judah and Jerusalem	2Chr 24:18	7110
for the fierce *w* of the LORD is	2Chr 28:11	639
there is fierce *w* against Israel	2Chr 28:13	639
Wherefore the *w* of the LORD was	2Chr 29:8	7110
that his fierce *w* may turn away	2Chr 29:10	639
of his *w* may turn away from you	2Chr 30:8	639
therefore there was *w* upon him	2Chr 32:25	7110
so that the *w* of the LORD came	2Chr 32:26	7110
for great is the *w* of the LORD	2Chr 34:21	2534
therefore my *w* shall be poured	2Chr 34:25	2534
until the *w* of the LORD arose	2Chr 36:16	639
provoked the God of heaven unto *w*	Ezr 5:12	7265
for why should there be *w* against	Ezr 7:23	7109
his *w* is against all them that	Ezr 8:22	639
until the fierce *w* of our God for	Ezr 10:14	639
yet ye bring more *w* upon Israel	Neh 13:18	2740
arise too much contempt and *w*	Est 1:18	7110
when the *w* of king Ahasuerus was	Est 2:1	2534
then was Haman full of *w*	Est 3:5	2534
his *w* went into the palace garden	Est 7:7	2534
Then was the king's *w* pacified	Est 7:10	2534
For *w* killeth the foolish man, and	Job 5:2	3708
me secret, until thy *w* be past	Job 14:13	639
He teareth me in his *w*, who	Job 16:9	639
also kindled his *w* against me	Job 19:11	639
for *w* bringeth the punishments of	Job 19:29	2534
cast the fury of his *w* upon him	Job 20:23	639
flow away in the day of his *w*	Job 20:28	639
drink of the *w* of the Almighty	Job 21:20	2534
be brought forth to the day of *w*	Job 21:30	5678
Then was kindled the *w* of Elihu	Job 32:2	639
against Job was his *w* kindled	Job 32:2	639
three friends was his *w* kindled	Job 32:3	639
three men, then his *w* was kindled	Job 32:5	639
the hypocrites in heart heap up *w*	Job 36:13	639
Because there is *w*, beware lest	Job 36:18	2534
Cast abroad the rage of thy *w*	Job 40:11	639
My *w* is kindled against thee, and	Job 42:7	639
shall he speak unto them in his *w*	Ps 2:5	639
when his *w* is kindled but a	Ps 2:12	639
shall swallow them up in his *w*	Ps 21:9	639
Cease from anger, and forsake *w*	Ps 37:8	2534
O LORD, rebuke me not in thy *w*	Ps 38:1	7110
upon me, and in *w* they hate me	Ps 55:3	639
both living, and in his *w*	Ps 58:9	2740
Consume them in *w*, consume them	Ps 59:13	2534
Surely the *w* of man shall praise	Ps 76:10	2534
the remainder of *w* shalt thou	Ps 76:10	2534
The *w* of God came upon them, and	Ps 78:31	639
and did not stir up all his *w*	Ps 78:38	2534
the fierceness of his anger, *w*	Ps 78:49	5678
Pour out thy *w* upon the heathen	Ps 79:6	2534
Thou hast taken away all thy *w*	Ps 85:3	5678
Thy *w* lieth hard upon me, and thou	Ps 88:7	2534
Thy fierce *w* goeth over me	Ps 88:16	2740
shall thy *w* burn like fire	Ps 89:46	2534
and by thy *w* are we troubled	Ps 90:7	2534
our days are passed away in thy *w*	Ps 90:9	5678
to thy fear, so is thy *w*	Ps 90:11	5678
Unto whom I sware in my *w* that	Ps 95:11	639
of thine indignation and thy *w*	Ps 102:10	7110
in the breach, to turn away his *w*	Ps 106:23	2534
Therefore was the *w* of the LORD	Ps 106:40	639
through kings in the day of his *w*	Ps 110:5	639
when their *w* was kindled against	Ps 124:3	639
against the *w* of mine enemies	Ps 138:7	639

Riches profit not in the day of *w* .... Prov 11:4   5678
expectation of the wicked is *w* .... Prov 11:23   5678
A fool's *w* is presently known .... Prov 12:16   3708
He that is slow to *w* is of great .... Prov 14:29   639
but his *w* is against him that .... Prov 14:35   5678
A soft answer turneth away *w* .... Prov 15:1   2534
The *w* of a king is as messengers .... Prov 16:14   2534
The king's *w* is as the roaring of .... Prov 19:12   2197
A man of great *w* shall suffer .... Prov 19:19   2534
and a reward in the bosom strong *w* ...... Prov 21:14   2534
his name, who dealeth in proud *w* .... Prov 21:24   5678
and he turn away his *w* from him .... Prov 24:18   639
but a fool's *w* is heavier than .... Prov 27:3   3708
W is cruel, and anger is .... Prov 27:4   2534
but wise men turn away *w* .... Prov 29:8   639
so the forcing of *w* bringeth .... Prov 30:33   639
sorrow and *w* with his sickness .... Eccl 5:17   7110
Through the *w* of the LORD of .... Is 9:19   5678
of my *w* will I give him a charge .... Is 10:6   5678
LORD cometh, cruel both with *w* .... Is 13:9   5678
in the of the LORD of hosts, and .... Is 13:13   5678
in *w* with a continual stroke .... Is 14:6   5678
and his pride, and his *w* .... Is 16:6   5678
In a little *w* I hid my face from .... Is 54:8   7110
for in my *w* I smote thee, but in .... Is 60:10   7110
forsaken the generation of his *w* .... Jer 7:29   5678
at his *w* the earth shall tremble, ... Jer 10:10   7110
and to turn away thy *w* from them ...... Jer 18:20   2534
anger, and in fury, and in great *w* ...... Jer 21:5   7110
and in my fury, and in great *w* .... Jer 32:37   7110
In that ye provoke me unto *w* with ...... Jer 44:8   3707
I know his *w*, saith the LORD .... Jer 48:30   5678
Because of the *w* of the LORD it .... Jer 50:13   7110
in his *w* the strong holds of the .... Lam 2:2   5678
affliction by the rod of his *w* .... Lam 3:1   5678
for *w* is upon all the multitude .... Eze 7:12   2740
for my *w* is upon all the .... Eze 7:14   2740
in the day of the *w* of the LORD .... Eze 7:19   5678
I accomplish my *w* upon the wall .... Eze 13:15   2534
against thee in the fire of my *w* .... Eze 21:31   5678
blow upon you in the fire of my *w* .... Eze 22:21   5678
them with the fire of my *w* .... Eze 22:31   5678
in the fire of my *w* have I spoken .... Eze 38:19   5678
out my *w* upon them like water .... Hos 5:10   5678
anger, and took him away in my *w* .... Hos 13:11   5678
and he kept his *w* for ever .... Amos 1:11   5678
he reserveth *w* for his enemies .... Nah 1:2
in *w* remember mercy .... Hab 3:2   7267
was thy *w* against the sea, that .... Hab 3:8   5678
That day is a day of *w*, a day of .... Zeph 1:15   5678
them in the day of the LORD's *w* .... Zeph 1:18   5678
a great *w* from the LORD of hosts .... Zec 7:12   7110
your fathers provoked me to *w* .... Zec 8:14   7107
you to flee from the *w* to come .... Mt 3:7   3709
you to flee from the *w* to come .... Lk 3:7   3709
these things, were filled with *w* .... Lk 4:28   2372
the land, and *w* upon this people .... Lk 21:23   3709
but the *w* of God abideth on him .... Jn 3:36   3709
sayings, they were full of *w* .... Acts 19:28   2372
For the *w* of God is revealed from .... Rom 1:18   3709
w against the day of *w* .... Rom 2:5   3709
w against the day of *w* .... Rom 2:5   3709
unrighteousness, indignation and *w* ...... Rom 2:8   3709
Because the law worketh *w* .... Rom 4:15   3709
shall be saved from *w* through him .... Rom 5:9   3709
if God, willing to shew his *w* .... Rom 9:22   3709
of *w* fitted to destruction .... Rom 9:22   3709
but rather give place unto *w* .... Rom 12:19   3709
a revenger to execute *w* upon him .... Rom 13:4   3709
needs be subject, not only for *w* .... Rom 13:5   3709
hatred, variance, emulations, *w* .... Gal 5:20   2372
were by nature the children of *w* .... Eph 2:3   3709
not the sun go down upon your *w* .... Eph 4:26   3950
Let all bitterness, and *w*, and .... Eph 4:31   2372
of these things cometh the *w* of .... Eph 5:6   3709
provoke not your children to *w* .... Eph 6:4   3949
For which things' sake the *w* of .... Col 3:6   3709
anger, *w*, malice, blasphemy, ... Col 3:8   2372
delivered us from the *w* to come 1Th 1:10   3709
for the *w* is come upon them to 1Th 2:16   3709
God hath not appointed us to *w* 1Th 5:9   3709
lifting up holy hands, without *w* 1Ti 2:8   3709
So I sware in my *w*, They shall .... Heb 3:11   3709
he said, As I have sworn in my *w* .... Heb 4:3   3709
not fearing the *w* of the king .... Heb 11:27   2372
to hear, slow to speak, slow to *w* .... Jas 1:19   3709
For the *w* of man worketh not the .... Jas 1:20   3709
throne, and from the *w* of the Lamb ...... Rev 6:16   3709
the great day of his *w* is come .... Rev 6:17   3709
thy *w* is come, and the time of the .... Rev 11:18   3709
down unto you, having great *w* .... Rev 12:12   2372

wine of the *w* of her fornication .... Rev 14:8   2372
drink of the wine of the *w* of God .... Rev 14:10   2372
great winepress of the *w* of God .... Rev 14:19   2372
in them is filled up the *w* of God .... Rev 15:1   2372
golden vials full of the *w* of God .... Rev 15:7   2372
of the *w* of God upon the earth .... Rev 16:1   2372
wine of the fierceness of his *w* .... Rev 16:19   3709
wine of the *w* of her fornication .... Rev 18:3   2372
fierceness and *w* of Almighty God .... Rev 19:15   3709

WRATHFUL
let thy *w* anger take hold of them .... Ps 69:24   2740
A *w* man stirreth up strife .... Prov 15:18   2534

WRATHS
there be debates, envyings, *w* 2Cor 12:20   2372

WREATH
rows of pomegranates on each *w* 2Chr 4:13   7639

WREATHED
they are *w*, and come up upon my .... Lam 1:14   8276

WREATHEN
of *w* work shalt thou make them, ... Ex 28:14   5688
fasten the *w* chains to the ouches .... Ex 28:14   5688
the ends of *w* work of pure gold .... Ex 28:22   5688
thou shalt put the two *w* chains .... Ex 28:24   5688
the other two ends of the two *w* .... Ex 28:25   5688
the ends, of *w* work of pure gold .... Ex 39:15   5688
they put the two *w* chains of gold .... Ex 39:17   5688
the two ends of the two *w* chains .... Ex 39:18   5688
the *w* work, and pomegranates upon 2Kin 25:17   7639
had the second pillar with *w* work 2Kin 25:17   7639

WREATHS
work, and *w* of chain work, for the 1Kin 7:17   1434
the two *w* to cover the two 2Chr 4:12   7639
hundred pomegranates on the two *w* 2Chr 4:13   7639

WREST
decline after many to *w* judgment .... Ex 23:2   5186
Thou shalt not *w* the judgment of .... Ex 23:6   5186
Thou shalt not *w* judgment .... Deut 16:19   5186
Every day they *w* my words .... Ps 56:5   6087
that are unlearned and unstable *w* 2Pet 3:16   4761

WRESTLE
For we *w* not against flesh and .... Eph 6:12   2076,3823

WRESTLED
have I *w* with my sister, and I .... Gen 30:8   6617
there *w* a man with him until the .... Gen 32:24   79
out of joint, as he *w* with him .... Gen 32:25   79

WRESTLINGS
With great *w* have I wrestled with .... Gen 30:8   5319

WRETCHED
O *w* man that I am .... Rom 7:24   5005
and knowest not that thou art *w* .... Rev 3:17   5005

WRETCHEDNESS
and let me not see my *w* .... Num 11:15   7451

WRING
w off his head, and burn it on the .... Lev 1:15   4454
w off his head from his neck, but .... Lev 5:8   4454
of the earth shall *w* them out .... Ps 75:8   4680

WRINGED
w the dew out of the fleece, a .... Judg 6:38   4680

WRINGING
the *w* of the nose bringeth forth .... Prov 30:33   4330

WRINKLE
church, not having spot, or *w* .... Eph 5:27   4512

WRINKLES
And thou hast filled me with *w* .... Job 16:8   7059

WRITE
W this for a memorial in a book, ... Ex 17:14   3789
I will *w* upon these tables the .... Ex 34:1   3789
unto Moses, *W* thou these words .... Ex 34:27   3789
the priest shall *w* these curses .... Num 5:23   3789
w thou every man's name upon his .... Num 17:2   3789
thou shalt *w* Aaron's name upon .... Num 17:3   3789
thou shalt *w* them upon the posts .... Deut 6:9   3789
I will *w* on the tables the words .... Deut 10:2   3789
thou shalt *w* them upon the door .... Deut 11:20   3789
that he shall *w* him a copy of .... Deut 17:18   3789
then let him *w* her a bill of .... Deut 24:1   3789
w her a bill of divorcement, and .... Deut 24:3   3789
thou shalt *w* upon them all the .... Deut 27:3   3789
thou shalt *w* upon the stones all .... Deut 27:8   3789
Now therefore *w* ye this song for .... Deut 31:19   3789
the prophet, the son of Amoz, *w* 2Chr 26:22   3789
that we might *w* the names of the .... Ezr 5:10   3790

we make a sure covenant, and *w* it	Neh 9:38	3789
W ye also for the Jews, as it	Est 8:8	3789
w them upon the table of thine	Prov 3:3	3789
w them upon the table of thine	Prov 7:3	3789
roll, and *w* in it with a man's pen	Is 8:1	3789
that *w* grievousness which they	Is 10:1	3789
be few, that a child may *w* them	Is 10:19	3789
w it before them in a table, and	Is 30:8	3789
W ye this man childless, a man	Jer 22:30	3789
W thee all the words that I have	Jer 30:2	3789
parts, and *w* it in their hearts	Jer 31:33	3789
w therein all the words that I	Jer 36:2	3789
How didst thou *w* all these words	Jer 36:17	3789
w in it all the former words that	Jer 36:28	3789
w thee the name of the day, even	Eze 24:2	3789
w upon it, For Judah, and for the	Eze 37:16	3789
w upon it, For Joseph, the stick	Eze 37:16	3789
w it in their sight, that they	Eze 43:11	3789
W the vision, and make it plain	Hab 2:2	3789
Moses suffered to *w* a bill of	Mk 10:4	1125
to *w* unto thee in order, most	Lk 1:3	1125
and sit down quickly, and *w* fifty	Lk 16:6	1125
Take thy bill, and *w* fourscore	Lk 16:7	1125
the law, and the prophets, did *w*	Jn 1:45	1125
W not, The King of the Jews	Jn 19:21	1125
But that we *w* unto them, that	Acts 15:20	1989
certain thing to *w* unto my lord	Acts 25:26	1125
had, I might have somewhat to *w*	Acts 25:26	1125
I *w* not these things to shame you	1Cor 4:14	1125
that the things that I *w* unto you	1Cor 14:37	1125
For we *w* none other things unto	2Cor 1:13	1125
For to this end also did I *w*	2Cor 2:9	1125
is superfluous for me to *w* to you	2Cor 9:1	1125
being absent now I *w* to them	2Cor 13:2	1125
Therefore I *w* these things being	2Cor 13:10	1125
Now the things which I *w* unto you	Gal 1:20	1125
To *w* the same things to you, to	Phil 3:1	1125
ye need not that I *w* unto you	1Th 4:9	1125
ye have no need that I *w* unto you	1Th 5:1	1125
so I *w*	2Th 3:17	1125
These things *w* I unto thee	1Ti 3:14	1125
mind, and *w* them in their hearts	Heb 8:10	1924
and in their minds will I *w* them	Heb 10:16	1924
beloved, I now *w* unto you	2Pet 3:1	1125
And these things *w* we unto you	1Jn 1:4	1125
these things I *w* unto you	1Jn 2:1	1125
I *w* no new commandment unto you,	1Jn 2:7	1125
a new commandment I *w* unto you,	1Jn 2:8	1125
I *w* unto you, little children,	1Jn 2:12	1125
I *w* unto you, fathers, because ye	1Jn 2:13	1125
I *w* unto you, young men, because	1Jn 2:13	1125
I *w* unto you, little children,	1Jn 2:13	1125
Having many things to *w* unto you	2Jn 12	1125
I would not *w* with paper	2Jn 12	
I had many things to *w*, but I	3Jn 13	1125
not with ink and pen *w* unto thee	3Jn 13	
to *w* unto you of the common	Jude 3	1125
was needful for me to *w* unto you	Jude 3	1125
w in a book, and send it unto the	Rev 1:11	1125
W the things which thou hast seen	Rev 1:19	1125
angel of the church of Ephesus *w*	Rev 2:1	1125
angel of the church in Smyrna *w*	Rev 2:8	1125
angel of the church in Pergamos *w*	Rev 2:12	1125
angel of the church in Thyatira *w*	Rev 2:18	1125
angel of the church in Sardis *w*	Rev 3:1	1125
of the church in Philadelphia *w*	Rev 3:7	1125
I will *w* upon him the name of my	Rev 3:12	1125
I will *w* upon him my new name	Rev 3:12	
of the church of the Laodiceans *w*	Rev 3:14	1125
their voices, I was about to *w*	Rev 10:4	1125
thunders uttered, and *w* them not	Rev 10:4	1125
from heaven saying unto me, *W*	Rev 14:13	1125
And he saith unto me, *W*, Blessed	Rev 19:9	1125
And he said unto me, *W*	Rev 21:5	1125

WRITER

they that handle the pen of the *w*	Judg 5:14	5608
my tongue is the pen of a ready *w*	Ps 45:1	5608

WRITER'S

with a *w* inkhorn by his side	Eze 9:2	5608
which had the *w* inkhorn by his	Eze 9:3	5608

WRITEST

For thou *w* bitter things against	Job 13:26	3789
the sticks whereon thou *w* shall	Eze 37:20	3789

WRITETH

when he *w* up the people, that	Ps 87:6	3789

WRITING

the *w* was the *w* of God,	Ex 32:16	4385
pure gold, and wrote upon it a *w*	Ex 39:30	4385

tables, according to the first *w*	Deut 10:4	4385
when Moses had made an end of *w*	Deut 31:24	3789
in *w* by his hand upon me, even	1Chr 28:19	3789
the king of Tyre answered in *w*	2Chr 2:11	3791
there came a *w* to him from Elijah	2Chr 21:12	4385
according to the *w* of David king	2Chr 35:4	3791
according to the *w* of Solomon his	2Chr 35:4	4385
his kingdom, and put it also in *w*	2Chr 36:22	4385
his kingdom, and put it also in *w*	Ezr 1:1	4385
the *w* of the letter was written	Ezr 4:7	3791
according to the *w* thereof	Est 1:22	3791
according to the *w* thereof	Est 3:12	3791
The copy of the *w* for a	Est 3:14	3791
he gave him the copy of the *w* of	Est 4:8	3791
for the *w* which is written in the	Est 8:8	3791
according to the *w* thereof	Est 8:9	3791
to the Jews according to their *w*	Est 8:9	3791
The copy of the *w* for a	Est 8:13	3791
two days according to their *w*	Est 9:27	3791
The *w* of Hezekiah king of Judah,	Is 38:9	4385
in the *w* of the house of Israel,	Eze 13:9	3791
Whosoever shall read this *w*	Dan 5:7	3792
but they could not read the *w*	Dan 5:8	3792
me, that they should read this *w*	Dan 5:15	3792
now if thou canst read the *w*	Dan 5:16	3792
I will read the *w* unto the king	Dan 5:17	3792
and this *w* was written	Dan 5:24	3792
this is the *w* that was written,	Dan 5:25	3792
the decree, and sign the *w*	Dan 6:8	3792
king Darius signed the *w* and the	Dan 6:9	3792
Daniel knew that the *w* was signed	Dan 6:10	3792
him give her a *w* of divorcement	Mt 5:31	
to give a *w* of divorcement	Mt 19:7	975
And he asked for a *w* table	Lk 1:63	4093
the *w* was, JESUS OF NAZARETH	Jn 19:19	1125

WRITINGS

But if ye believe not his *w*	Jn 5:47	1121

WRITTEN

and commandments which I have *w*	Ex 24:12	3789
stone, *w* with the finger of God	Ex 31:18	3789
the tables were *w* on both their	Ex 32:15	3789
side and on the other were they *w*	Ex 32:15	3789
out of thy book which thou hast *w*	Ex 32:32	3789
and they were of them that were *w*	Num 11:26	3789
of stone *w* with the finger of God	Deut 9:10	3789
on them was *w* according to all	Deut 9:10	
this law that are *w* in this book	Deut 28:58	3789
which is not *w* in the book of	Deut 28:61	3789
all the curses that are *w* in this	Deut 29:20	3789
are *w* in this book of the law	Deut 29:21	3789
curses that are *w* in this book	Deut 29:27	3789
his statutes which are *w* in this	Deut 30:10	3789
to all that is *w* therein	Josh 1:8	3789
as it is *w* in the book of the law	Josh 8:31	3789
that is *w* in the book of the law	Josh 8:34	3789
Is not this *w* in the book of	Josh 10:13	3789
to do all that is *w* in the book	Josh 23:6	3789
it is *w* in the book of Jasher	2Sa 1:18	3789
as it is *w* in the law of Moses,	1Kin 2:3	3789
they are *w* in the book of the	1Kin 11:41	3789
are they not *w* in the book of the	1Kin 14:19	3789
are they not *w* in the book of the	1Kin 14:29	3789
are they not *w* in the book of the	1Kin 15:7	3789
are they not *w* in the book of the	1Kin 15:23	3789
are they not *w* in the book of the	1Kin 15:31	3789
are they not *w* in the book of the	1Kin 16:5	3789
are they not *w* in the book of the	1Kin 16:14	3789
are they not *w* in the book of the	1Kin 16:20	3789
are they not *w* in the book of the	1Kin 16:27	3789
as it was *w* in the letters which	1Kin 21:11	3789
are they not *w* in the book of the	1Kin 22:39	3789
are they not *w* in the book of the	1Kin 22:45	3789
are they not *w* in the book of the	2Kin 1:18	3789
are they not *w* in the book of the	2Kin 8:23	3789
are they not *w* in the book of the	2Kin 10:34	3789
are they not *w* in the book of the	2Kin 12:19	3789
are they not *w* in the book of the	2Kin 13:8	3789
are they not *w* in the book of the	2Kin 13:12	3789
according unto that which is *w* in	2Kin 14:6	3789
are they not *w* in the book of the	2Kin 14:15	3789
are they not *w* in the book of the	2Kin 14:18	3789
are they not *w* in the book of the	2Kin 14:28	3789
are they not *w* in the book of the	2Kin 15:6	3789
they are *w* in the book of the	2Kin 15:11	3789
they are *w* in the book of the	2Kin 15:15	3789
are they not *w* in the book of the	2Kin 15:21	3789
they are *w* in the book of the	2Kin 15:26	3789
they are *w* in the book of the	2Kin 15:31	3789
are they not *w* in the book of the	2Kin 15:36	3789
are they not *w* in the book of the	2Kin 16:19	3789

are they not *w* in the book of the	2Kin 20:20	3789
are they not *w* in the book of the	2Kin 21:17	3789
are they are not *w* in the book of	2Kin 21:25	3789
all that which is *w* concerning us	2Kin 22:13	3789
covenant that were *w* in this book	2Kin 23:3	3789
as it is *w* in the book of this	2Kin 23:21	3789
w in the book that Hilkiah the	2Kin 23:24	3789
are they not *w* in the book of the	2Kin 23:28	3789
are they not *w* in the book of the	2Kin 24:5	3789
these *w* by name came in the days	1Chr 4:41	3789
they were *w* in the book of the	1Chr 9:1	3789
that is *w* in the law of the LORD	1Chr 16:40	3789
they are *w* in the book of Samuel	1Chr 29:29	3789
are they not *w* in the book of	2Chr 9:29	3789
are they not *w* in the book of	2Chr 12:15	3789
are in the story of the prophet	2Chr 13:22	3789
they are *w* in the book of the	2Chr 16:11	3789
they are *w* in the book of Jehu	2Chr 20:34	3789
as it is *w* in the law of Moses,	2Chr 23:18	3789
they are *w* in the story of the	2Chr 24:27	3789
but did as it is *w* in the law in	2Chr 25:4	3789
are they not *w* in the book of the	2Chr 25:26	3789
they are *w* in the book of the	2Chr 27:7	3789
they are *w* in the book of the	2Chr 28:26	3789
time in such sort as it was *w*	2Chr 30:5	3789
passover otherwise than it was *w*	2Chr 30:18	3789
as it is *w* in the law of the LORD	2Chr 31:3	3789
they are *w* in the vision of	2Chr 32:32	3789
they are *w* in the book of	2Chr 33:18	3789
they are *w* among the sayings of	2Chr 33:19	3789
after all that is *w* in this book	2Chr 34:21	3789
are *w* in the book which they have	2Chr 34:24	3789
covenant which are *w* in this book	2Chr 34:31	3789
as it is *w* in the book of Moses	2Chr 35:12	3789
they are *w* in the lamentations	2Chr 35:25	3789
was *w* in the law of the LORD	2Chr 35:26	3789
they are *w* in the book of the	2Chr 35:27	3789
they are *w* in the book of the	2Chr 36:8	3789
as it is *w* in the law of Moses	Ezr 3:2	3789
feast of tabernacles, as it is *w*	Ezr 3:4	3789
letter was *w* in the Syrian tongue	Ezr 4:7	3789
unto him, wherein was *w* thus	Ezr 5:7	3790
and therein was a record thus *w*	Ezr 6:2	3790
as it is *w* in the book of Moses	Ezr 6:18	3792
all the weight was *w* at that time	Ezr 8:34	3789
Wherein was *w*, It is reported	Neh 6:6	3789
at the first, and found *w* therein,	Neh 7:5	3789
they found *w* in the law which the	Neh 8:14	3789
trees, to make booths, as it is *w*	Neh 8:15	3789
our God, as it is *w* in the law	Neh 10:34	3789
as it is *w* in the law, and the	Neh 10:36	3789
were *w* in the book of the	Neh 12:23	3789
and therein was found *w*, that the	Neh 13:1	3789
let it be *w* among the laws of the	Est 1:19	3789
it was *w* in the book of the	Est 2:23	3789
let it be *w* that they may be	Est 3:9	3789
there was *w* according to all that	Est 3:12	3789
name of king Ahasuerus was it *w*	Est 3:12	3789
And it was found *w*, that Mordecai	Est 6:2	3789
let it be *w* to reverse the	Est 8:5	3789
which is in the king's name	Est 8:8	3789
it was *w* according to all that	Est 8:9	3789
and as Mordecai had *w* unto them	Est 9:23	3789
and it was *w* in the book	Est 9:32	3789
are they not *w* in the book of the	Est 10:2	3789
Oh that my words were now *w*	Job 19:23	3789
that mine adversary had *w* a book	Job 31:35	3789
volume of the book it is *w* of me	Ps 40:7	3789
not be *w* with the righteous	Ps 69:28	3789
This shall be *w* for the	Ps 102:18	3789
in thy book all my members were *w*	Ps 139:16	3789
execute upon them the judgment *w*	Ps 149:9	3789
Have not I *w* to thee excellent	Prov 22:20	3789
and that which was *w* was upright	Eccl 12:10	3789
even every one that is *w* among	Is 4:3	3789
Behold, it is *w* before me	Is 65:6	3789
of Judah is *w* with a pen of iron	Jer 17:1	3789
from me shall be *w* in the earth	Jer 17:13	3789
even all that is *w* in this book	Jer 25:13	3789
which thou hast *w* from my mouth	Jer 36:6	3789
saying, Why hast thou *w* therein	Jer 36:29	3789
when he had *w* these words in a	Jer 45:1	3789
words that are *w* against Babylon	Jer 51:60	3789
and it was *w* within and without	Eze 2:10	3789
there was *w* therein lamentations,	Eze 2:10	3789
neither shall they be *w* in the	Eze 13:9	3789
and this writing was *w*	Dan 5:24	7560
And this is the writing that was *w*	Dan 5:25	7560
the oath that is *w* in the law of	Dan 9:11	3789
As it is *w* in the law of Moses,	Dan 9:13	3789
that shall be found *w* in the book	Dan 12:1	3789

I have *w* to him the great things	Hos 8:12	3789
a book of remembrance was *w*	Mal 3:16	3789
for thus it is *w* by the prophet	Mt 2:5	1125
But he answered and said, It is *w*	Mt 4:4	1125
for it is *w*, He shall give his	Mt 4:6	1125
said unto him, It is *w* again	Mt 4:7	1125
for it is *w*, Thou shalt worship	Mt 4:10	1125
For this is he, of whom it is *w*	Mt 11:10	1125
And said unto them, It is *w*	Mt 21:13	1125
of man goeth as it is *w* of him	Mt 26:24	1125
for it is *w*, I will smite the	Mt 26:31	1125
up over his head his accusation *w*	Mt 27:37	1125
As it is *w* in the prophets,	Mk 1:2	1125
of you hypocrites, as it is *w*	Mk 7:6	1125
how it is *w* of the Son of man,	Mk 9:12	1125
they listed, as it is *w* of him.	Mk 9:13	1125
saying unto them, Is it not *w*	Mk 11:17	1125
indeed goeth, as it is *w* of him	Mk 14:21	1125
for it is *w*, I will smite the	Mk 14:27	1125
of his accusation was *w* over	Mk 15:26	1924
(As it is *w* in the law of the	Lk 2:23	1125
As it is *w* in the book of the	Lk 3:4	1125
answered him, saying, It is *w*,	Lk 4:4	1125
for it is *w*, Thou shalt worship	Lk 4:8	1125
For it is *w*, He shall give his	Lk 4:10	1125
he found the place where it was *w*	Lk 4:17	1125
This is he, of whom it is *w*	Lk 7:27	1125
your names are *w* in heaven	Lk 10:20	1125
unto him, What is *w* in the law	Lk 10:26	1125
all things that are *w* by the	Lk 18:31	1125
Saying unto them, It is *w*	Lk 19:46	1125
said, What is this then that is *w*	Lk 20:17	1125
which are *w* may be fulfilled	Lk 21:22	1125
that this that is *w* must yet be	Lk 22:37	1125
a superscription also was *w* over	Lk 23:38	1125
which were *w* in the law of Moses,	Lk 24:44	1125
And said unto them, Thus it is *w*	Lk 24:46	1125
remembered that it was *w*, The	Jn 2:17	1125
as it is *w*, He gave them bread	Jn 6:31	1125
It is *w* in the prophets, And they	Jn 6:45	1125
It is also *w* in your law, that	Jn 8:17	1125
Is it not *w* in your law, I said,	Jn 10:34	1125
as it is *w*,	Jn 12:14	1125
that these things were *w* of him	Jn 12:16	1125
fulfilled that is *w* in their law	Jn 15:25	1125
it was *w* in Hebrew, and Greek, and	Jn 19:20	1125
What I have *w* I have *w*	Jn 19:22	1125
which are not *w* in this book	Jn 20:30	1125
But these are *w*, that ye might	Jn 20:31	1125
if they should be *w* every one	Jn 21:25	1125
the books that should be *w*	Jn 21:25	1125
For it is *w* in the book of Psalms	Acts 1:20	1125
as it is *w* in the book of the	Acts 7:42	1125
fulfilled all that was *w* of him	Acts 13:29	1125
as it is also *w* in the second	Acts 13:33	1125
as it is *w*,	Acts 15:15	1125
Gentiles which believe, we have *w*	Acts 21:25	1989
for it is *w*, Thou shalt not speak	Acts 23:5	1125
all things which are *w* in the law	Acts 24:14	1125
as it is *w*, The just shall live	Rom 1:17	1125
work of the law *w* in their hearts	Rom 2:15	1123
Gentiles through you, as it is *w*	Rom 2:24	1125
as it is *w*, That thou mightest be	Rom 3:4	1125
As it is *w*, There is none	Rom 3:10	1125
(As it is *w*, I have made thee a	Rom 4:17	1125
Now it was not *w* for his sake	Rom 4:23	1125
As it is *w*, For thy sake we are	Rom 8:36	1125
As it is *w*, Jacob have I loved,	Rom 9:13	1125
As it is *w*, Behold, I lay in Sion	Rom 9:33	1125
as it is *w*, How beautiful are the	Rom 10:15	1125
(According as it is *w*, God hath	Rom 11:8	1125
as it is *w*, There shall come out	Rom 11:26	1125
for it is *w*, Vengeance is mine	Rom 12:19	1125
For it is *w*, As I live, saith the	Rom 14:11	1125
but, as it is *w*, The reproaches	Rom 15:3	1125
For whatsoever things were *w*	Rom 15:4	4270
aforetime were *w* for our learning	Rom 15:4	4270
as it is *w*, For this cause I will	Rom 15:9	1125
I have *w* the more boldly unto you	Rom 15:15	1125
But as it is *w*, To whom he was	Rom 15:21	1125
W to the Romans from Corinthus,	Rom *s*	1125
For it is *w*, I will destroy the	1Cor 1:19	1125
That, according as it is *w*	1Cor 1:31	1125
But as it is *w*, Eye hath not seen	1Cor 2:9	1125
For it is *w*, He taketh the wise	1Cor 3:19	1125
of men above that which is *w*	1Cor 4:6	1125
But now I have *w* unto you not to	1Cor 5:11	1125
For it is *w* in the law of Moses,	1Cor 9:9	1125
our sakes, no doubt, this is *w*	1Cor 9:10	1125
neither have I *w* these things	1Cor 9:15	1125
as it is *w*, The people sat down	1Cor 10:7	1125

WRONG

WRONGED

WRONGETH

WRONGFULLY

WROTE

WROTH

all these things, he was very *w*	2Sa 13:21	2734
moved and shook, because he was *w*	2Sa 22:8	2734
But Naaman was *w*, and went away,	2Kin 5:11	7107
And the man of God was *w* with him	2Kin 13:19	7107
Then Asa was *w* with the seer, and	2Chr 16:10	3707
Then Uzziah was *w*, and had a	2Chr 26:19	2196
while he was *w* with the priests,	2Chr 26:19	2196
of your fathers was *w* with Judah	2Chr 28:9	2534
we builded the wall, he was *w*	Neh 4:1	2734
be stopped, then they were very *w*	Neh 4:7	2734
therefore was the king very *w*	Est 1:12	7107
those which kept the door, were *w*	Est 2:21	7107
and were shaken, because he was *w*	Ps 18:7	2734
the LORD heard this, and was *w*	Ps 78:21	5674
When God heard this, he was *w*	Ps 78:59	5674
was *w* with his inheritance	Ps 78:62	5674
thou hast been *w* with thine	Ps 89:38	5674
he shall be *w* as in the valley of	Is 28:21	7264
I was *w* with my people, I have	Is 47:6	7107
that I would not be *w* with thee	Is 54:9	7107
ever, neither will I be always *w*	Is 57:16	7107
of his covetousness was I *w*	Is 57:17	7107
I hid me, and was *w*, and he went on	Is 57:17	7107
behold, thou art *w*	Is 64:5	7107
Be not *w* very sore, O LORD,	Is 64:9	7107
the princes were *w* with Jeremiah	Jer 37:15	7107
thou art very *w* against us	Lam 5:22	7107
of the wise men, was exceeding *w*	Mt 2:16	2373
And his lord was *w*, and delivered	Mt 18:34	3710
the king heard thereof, he was *w*	Mt 22:7	3710
the dragon was *w* with the woman	Rev 12:17	3710

WROUGHT

because he had *w* folly in Israel	Gen 34:7	6213
what things I have *w* in Egypt	Ex 10:2	5953
twined linen, *w* with needlework	Ex 26:36	4639
twined linen, *w* with needlework	Ex 27:16	
Then *w* Bezaleel and Aholiab, and	Ex 36:1	6213
that *w* all the work of the	Ex 36:4	6213
hearted man among them that *w* the	Ex 36:8	6213
they *w* onyx stones inclosed in	Ex 39:6	6213
they have *w* confusion	Lev 20:12	6213
and of Israel, What hath God *w*	Num 23:23	6466
gold of them, even all *w* jewels	Num 31:51	4639
such abomination is *w* among you	Deut 13:14	6213
that hath *w* wickedness in the	Deut 17:2	6213
such abomination is *w* in Israel	Deut 17:4	6213
which hath not been *w* with	Deut 21:3	5647
she hath *w* folly in Israel	Deut 22:21	6213
the evils which they shall have *w*	Deut 31:18	6213
because he hath *w* folly in Israel	Josh 7:15	6213
folly that they have *w* in Israel	Judg 20:10	6213
mother in law with whom she had *w*	Ruth 2:19	6213
name with whom I *w* to day is Boaz	Ruth 2:19	6213
when he had *w* wonderfully among	1Sa 6:6	5953
LORD hath *w* salvation in Israel	1Sa 11:13	6213
who hath *w* this great salvation	1Sa 14:45	6213
for he hath *w* with God this day	1Sa 14:45	6213
the LORD *w* a great salvation for	1Sa 19:5	6213
Otherwise I should have *w*	2Sa 18:13	6213
the LORD *w* a great victory that	2Sa 23:10	6213
the LORD *w* a great victory	2Sa 23:12	6213
the people that *w* in the work	1Kin 5:16	6213
king Solomon, and *w* all his work	1Kin 7:14	6213
the brim thereof was *w* like the	1Kin 7:26	4639
the people that *w* in the work	1Kin 9:23	6213
Zimri, and his treason that he *w*	1Kin 16:20	7194
But Omri *w* evil in the eyes of	1Kin 16:25	6213
he *w* evil in the sight of the	2Kin 3:2	6213
that *w* upon the house of the LORD	2Kin 12:11	6213
w wicked things to provoke the	2Kin 17:11	6213

he *w* much wickedness in the sight	2Kin 21:6	6213
house of them that *w* fine linen	1Chr 4:21	5656
he set masons to hew *w* stones to	1Chr 22:2	1496
linen, and *w* cherubims thereon	2Chr 3:14	5927
he *w* that which was evil in the	2Chr 21:6	6213
the LORD, and also such as *w* iron	2Chr 24:12	2790
So the workmen *w*, and the work was	2Chr 24:13	6213
w that which was good and right and	2Chr 31:20	6213
he *w* much evil in the sight of	2Chr 33:6	6213
that *w* in the house of the LORD	2Chr 34:10	6213
that *w* the work in any manner of	2Chr 34:13	6213
half of my servants *w* in the work	Neh 4:16	6213
one of his hands *w* in the work	Neh 4:17	6213
that this work was *w* of our God	Neh 6:16	6213
and had *w* great provocations	Neh 9:18	6213
they *w* great provocations	Neh 9:26	6213
the hand of the LORD hath *w* this	Job 12:9	6213
who can say, Thou hast *w* iniquity	Job 36:23	6466
which thou hast *w* for them that	Ps 31:19	6466
her clothing is of *w* gold	Ps 45:13	4865
that which thou hast *w* for us	Ps 68:28	6466
How he had *w* his signs in Egypt,	Ps 78:43	7760
curiously *w* in the lowest parts	Ps 139:15	7551
all the works that my hands had *w*	Eccl 2:11	6213
because the work that is *w* under	Eccl 2:17	6213
for thou also hast *w* all our	Is 26:12	6466
we have not *w* any deliverance in	Is 26:18	6213
Who hath *w* and done it, calling	Is 41:4	6466
seeing thou hast *w* lewdness with	Jer 11:15	6213
he *w* a work on the wheels	Jer 18:3	6213
But I *w* for my name's sake, that	Eze 20:9	6213
But I *w* for my name's sake, that	Eze 20:14	6213
w for my name's sake, that it	Eze 20:22	6213
when I have *w* with you for my	Eze 20:44	6213
against it, because they *w* for me	Eze 29:20	6213
the high God hath *w* toward me	Dan 4:2	5648
for the sea *w*, and was tempestuous	Jonah 1:11	1980
for the sea *w*, and was tempestuous	Jonah 1:13	1980
which have *w* his judgment	Zeph 2:3	6466
These last have *w* but one hour	Mt 20:12	4160
for she hath *w* a good work upon	Mt 26:10	2038
mighty works are *w* by his hands,	Mk 6:2	1096
she hath *w* a good work on me	Mk 14:6	2038
manifest, that they are *w* in God	Jn 3:21	2038
wonders *w* among the people	Acts 5:12	1096
wonders God had *w* among the	Acts 15:12	4160
craft, he abode with them, and *w*	Acts 18:3	2038
God *w* special miracles by the	Acts 19:11	4160
what things God had *w* among the	Acts 21:19	4160
w in me all manner of	Rom 7:8	2716
which Christ hath not *w* by me	Rom 15:18	2716
Now he that hath *w* us for the	2Cor 5:5	2716
what carefulness it *w* in you	2Cor 7:11	2716
were *w* among you in all patience	2Cor 12:12	2716
(For he that *w* effectually in	Gal 2:8	1754
Which he *w* in Christ, when he	Eph 1:20	1754
but *w* with labour and travail	2Th 3:8	2038
w righteousness, obtained	Heb 11:33	2038
thou how faith *w* with his works	Jas 2:22	4903
have *w* the will of the Gentiles	1Pet 4:3	2716
not those things which we have *w*	2Jn 8	2038
that *w* miracles before him	Rev 19:20	4160

WROUGHTEST

and where *w* thou	Ruth 2:19	6213

WRUNG

the blood thereof shall be *w* out	Lev 1:15	4680
w out at the bottom of the altar	Lev 5:9	4680
of a full cup are *w* out to them	Ps 73:10	4680
cup of trembling, and *w* them out	Is 51:17	4680

X

XERXES See AHASUERUS.

XERXES' See AHASUERUS'.

Y

YAH See JAH.

YARN

brought out of Egypt, and linen *y*	1Kin 10:28	4723
received the linen *y* at a price	1Kin 10:28	4723
brought out of Egypt, and linen *y*	2Chr 1:16	4723
received the linen *y* at a price	2Chr 1:16	4723

YE See APPENDIX.

YEA See APPENDIX.

YEAR

six hundredth *y* of Noah's life	Gen 7:11	8141
in the six hundredth and first *y*	Gen 8:13	8141
in the thirteenth *y* they rebelled	Gen 14:4	8141
fourteenth *y* came Chedorlaomer	Gen 14:5	8141
at this set time in the next *y*	Gen 17:21	8141
in the same *y* an hundredfold	Gen 26:12	8141

Y

for all their cattle for that *y*	Gen 47:17	8141
When that *y* was ended, they came	Gen 47:18	8141
they came unto him the second *y*	Gen 47:18	8141
the first month of the *y* to you	Ex 12:2	8141
blemish, a male of the first *y*	Ex 12:5	8141
in his season from *y* to *y*	Ex 13:10	3117
in his season from *y* to *y*	Ex 13:10	3117
But the seventh *y* thou shalt let	Ex 23:11	8141
keep a feast unto me in the *y*	Ex 23:14	8141
which is in the end of the *y*	Ex 23:16	8141
Three times in the *y* all thy	Ex 23:17	8141
out from before thee in one *y*	Ex 23:29	8141
first *y* day by day continually	Ex 29:38	8141
in a *y* with the blood of the sin	Ex 30:10	8141
once in the *y* shall he make	Ex 30:10	8141
Thrice in the *y* shall all your	Ex 34:23	8141
the LORD thy God thrice in the *y*	Ex 34:24	8141
the first month in the second *y*	Ex 40:17	8141
and a lamb, both of the first *y*	Lev 9:3	8141
the first *y* for a burnt offering	Lev 12:6	8141
of the first *y* without blemish	Lev 14:10	8141
for all their sins once a *y*	Lev 16:34	8141
But in the fourth *y* all the fruit	Lev 19:24	8141
in the fifth *y* shall ye eat of	Lev 19:25	8141
without blemish of the first *y*	Lev 23:12	8141
without blemish of the first *y*	Lev 23:18	8141
two lambs of the first *y* for a	Lev 23:19	8141
unto the LORD seven days in the *y*	Lev 23:41	8141
But in the seventh *y* shall be a	Lev 25:4	8141
for it is a *y* of rest unto the	Lev 25:5	8141
And ye shall hallow the fiftieth *y*	Lev 25:10	8141
shall that fiftieth *y* be unto you	Lev 25:11	8141
In the *y* of this jubile ye shall	Lev 25:13	8141
What shall we eat the seventh *y*	Lev 25:20	8141
blessing upon you in the sixth *y*	Lev 25:21	8141
And ye shall sow the eighth *y*	Lev 25:22	8141
of old fruit until the ninth *y*	Lev 25:22	8141
bought it until the *y* of jubile	Lev 25:28	8141
within a whole *y* after it is sold	Lev 25:29	8141
within a full *y* may he redeem it	Lev 25:29	3117
within the space of a full *y*	Lev 25:30	8141
shall go out in the *y* of jubile	Lev 25:33	
serve thee unto the *y* of jubile	Lev 25:40	8141
y that he was sold to him unto	Lev 25:50	8141
sold to him unto the *y* of jubile	Lev 25:50	8141
few years unto the *y* of jubile	Lev 25:52	8141
shall go out in the *y* of jubile	Lev 25:54	8141
his field from the *y* of jubile	Lev 27:17	8141
even unto the *y* of the jubile	Lev 27:18	8141
even unto the *y* of the jubile	Lev 27:23	8141
In the *y* of the jubile the field	Lev 27:24	8141
in the second *y* after they were	Num 1:1	8141
first *y* for a trespass offering	Num 6:12	8141
one he lamb of the first *y*	Num 6:14	8141
first *y* without blemish for a sin	Num 6:14	8141
one ram, one lamb of the first *y*	Num 7:15	8141
goats, five lambs of the first *y*	Num 7:17	8141
one ram, one lamb of the first *y*	Num 7:21	8141
goats, five lambs of the first *y*	Num 7:23	8141
one ram, one lamb of the first *y*	Num 7:27	8141
goats, five lambs of the first *y*	Num 7:29	8141
one ram, one lamb of the first *y*	Num 7:33	8141
goats, five lambs of the first *y*	Num 7:35	8141
one ram, one lamb of the first *y*	Num 7:39	8141
goats, five lambs of the first *y*	Num 7:41	8141
one ram, one lamb of the first *y*	Num 7:45	8141
goats, five lambs of the first *y*	Num 7:47	8141
one ram, one lamb of the first *y*	Num 7:51	8141
goats, five lambs of the first *y*	Num 7:53	8141
one ram, one lamb of the first *y*	Num 7:57	8141
goats, five lambs of the first *y*	Num 7:59	8141
one ram, one lamb of the first *y*	Num 7:63	8141
goats, five lambs of the first *y*	Num 7:65	8141
one ram, one lamb of the first *y*	Num 7:69	8141
goats, five lambs of the first *y*	Num 7:71	8141
one ram, one lamb of the first *y*	Num 7:75	8141
goats, five lambs of the first *y*	Num 7:77	8141
one ram, one lamb of the first *y*	Num 7:81	8141
goats, five lambs of the first *y*	Num 7:83	8141
the lambs of the first *y* twelve	Num 7:87	8141
the lambs of the first *y* sixty	Num 7:88	8141
the first month of the second *y*	Num 9:1	8141
were two days, or a month, or a *y*	Num 9:22	3117
the second month, in the second *y*	Num 10:11	8141
even forty days, each day for a *y*	Num 14:34	8141
of the first *y* for a sin offering	Num 15:27	8141
two lambs of the first *y* without	Num 28:3	8141
lambs of the first *y* without spot	Num 28:9	8141
lambs of the first *y* without spot	Num 28:11	8141
throughout the months of the *y*	Num 28:14	8141
and seven lambs of the first *y*	Num 28:19	8141
ram, seven lambs of the first *y*	Num 28:27	8141
of the first *y* without blemish	Num 29:2	8141
and seven lambs of the first *y*	Num 29:8	8141
and fourteen lambs of the first *y*	Num 29:13	8141
lambs of the first *y* without spot	Num 29:17	8141
of the first *y* without blemish	Num 29:20	8141
of the first *y* without blemish	Num 29:23	8141
lambs of the first *y* without spot	Num 29:26	8141
of the first *y* without blemish	Num 29:29	8141
of the first *y* without blemish	Num 29:32	8141
of the first *y* without blemish	Num 29:36	8141
in the fortieth *y* after the	Num 33:38	8141
it came to pass in the fortieth *y*	Deut 1:3	8141
from the beginning of the *y* even	Deut 11:12	8141
y even unto the end of the *y*	Deut 11:12	8141
field bringeth forth *y* by *y*	Deut 14:22	8141
field bringeth forth *y* by *y*	Deut 14:22	8141
of thine increase the same *y*	Deut 14:28	8141
heart, saying, The seventh *y*	Deut 15:9	8141
the *y* of release, is at hand	Deut 15:9	8141
then in the seventh *y* thou shalt	Deut 15:12	8141
y by *y* in the place which the	Deut 15:20	8141
by *y* in the place which the LORD	Deut 15:20	8141
Three times in a *y* shall all thy	Deut 16:16	8141
he shall be free at home one *y*	Deut 24:5	8141
of thine increase the third *y*	Deut 26:12	8141
which is the *y* of tithing	Deut 26:12	8141
the solemnity of the *y* of release	Deut 31:10	8141
of the land of Canaan that *y*	Josh 5:12	8141
that *y* they vexed and oppressed	Judg 10:8	8141
the Gileadite four days in a *y*	Judg 11:40	8141
ten shekels of silver by the *y*	Judg 17:10	3117
And as he did so *y* by *y*	1Sa 1:7	8141
brought it to him from *y* to *y*	1Sa 2:19	3117
he went from *y* to *y* in circuit	1Sa 7:16	8141
Saul reigned one *y*	1Sa 13:1	8141
of the Philistines was a full *y*	1Sa 27:7	
after the *y* was expired, at the	2Sa 11:1	8141
David three years, after *y*	2Sa 21:1	8141
his month in a *y* made provision	1Kin 4:7	8141
gave Solomon to Hiram *y* by *y*	1Kin 5:11	8141
eightieth *y* after the children of	1Kin 6:1	8141
in the fourth *y* of Solomon's	1Kin 6:1	8141
In the fourth *y* was the	1Kin 6:37	8141
And in the eleventh *y*, in the	1Kin 6:38	8141
three times in a *y* did Solomon	1Kin 9:25	8141
one *y* was six hundred threescore	1Kin 10:14	8141
and mules, a rate *y* by *y*	1Kin 10:25	8141
in the fifth *y* of king Rehoboam	1Kin 14:25	8141
Now in the eighteenth *y* of king	1Kin 15:1	8141
in the twentieth *y* of Jeroboam	1Kin 15:9	8141
the second *y* of Asa king of Judah	1Kin 15:25	8141
Even in the third *y* of Asa king	1Kin 15:28	8141
In the third *y* of Asa king of	1Kin 15:33	8141
sixth *y* of Asa king of Judah	1Kin 16:8	8141
seventh *y* of Asa king of Judah,	1Kin 16:10	8141
seventh *y* of Asa king of Judah,	1Kin 16:15	8141
first *y* of Asa king of Judah	1Kin 16:23	8141
eighth *y* of Asa king of Judah	1Kin 16:29	8141
came to Elijah in the third *y*	1Kin 18:1	8141
for at the return of the *y* the	1Kin 20:22	8141
to pass at the return of the *y*	1Kin 20:26	8141
And it came to pass in the third *y*	1Kin 22:2	8141
fourth *y* of Ahab king of Israel	1Kin 22:41	8141
in Samaria the seventeenth *y* of	1Kin 22:51	8141
second *y* of Jehoram the son of	2Kin 1:17	8141
in Samaria the eighteenth *y* of	2Kin 3:1	8141
in the fifth *y* of Joram the son	2Kin 8:16	8141
In the twelfth *y* of Joram the son	2Kin 8:25	8141
and he reigned one *y* in Jerusalem	2Kin 8:26	8141
in the eleventh *y* of Joram the	2Kin 9:29	8141
the seventh *y* Jehoiada sent and	2Kin 11:4	8141
In the seventh *y* of Jehu Jehoash	2Kin 12:1	8141
twentieth *y* of king Jehoash the	2Kin 12:6	8141
twentieth *y* of Joash the son of	2Kin 13:1	8141
seventh *y* of Joash king of Judah	2Kin 13:10	8141
land at the coming in of the *y*	2Kin 13:20	8141
In the second *y* of Joash son of	2Kin 14:1	8141
In the fifteenth *y* of Amaziah the	2Kin 14:23	8141
seventh *y* of Jeroboam king of	2Kin 15:1	8141
eighth *y* of Azariah king of Judah	2Kin 15:8	8141
thirtieth *y* of Uzziah king of	2Kin 15:13	8141
thirtieth *y* of Azariah king of	2Kin 15:17	8141
In the fiftieth *y* of Azariah king	2Kin 15:23	8141
fiftieth *y* of Azariah king of	2Kin 15:27	8141
in the twentieth *y* of Jotham the	2Kin 15:30	8141
In the second *y* of Pekah the son	2Kin 15:32	8141
In the seventeenth *y* of Pekah the	2Kin 16:1	8141
In the twelfth *y* of Ahaz king of	2Kin 17:1	8141
Assyria, as he had done *y* by *y*	2Kin 17:4	8141
In the ninth *y* of Hoshea the king	2Kin 17:6	8141

it came to pass in the third y of	2Kin 18:1	8141
in the fourth y of king Hezekiah	2Kin 18:9	8141
which was the seventh y of Hoshea	2Kin 18:9	8141
even in the sixth y of Hezekiah	2Kin 18:10	8141
that is the ninth y of Hoshea	2Kin 18:10	8141
fourteenth y of king Hezekiah did	2Kin 18:13	8141
Ye shall eat this y such things	2Kin 19:29	8141
in the second y that which	2Kin 19:29	8141
and in the third y sow ye, and reap	2Kin 19:29	8141
the eighteenth y of king Josiah	2Kin 22:3	8141
the eighteenth y of king Josiah	2Kin 23:23	8141
him in the eighth y of his reign	2Kin 24:12	8141
pass in the ninth y of his reign	2Kin 25:1	8141
the eleventh y of king Zedekiah	2Kin 25:2	8141
which is the nineteenth y of king	2Kin 25:8	8141
thirtieth y of the captivity of	2Kin 25:27	8141
king of Babylon in the y that he	2Kin 25:27	8141
that after the y was expired	1Chr 20:1	8141
In the fortieth y of the reign of	1Chr 26:31	8141
all the months of the y, of every	1Chr 27:1	8141
in the fourth y of his reign	2Chr 3:2	8141
feasts, three times in the y	2Chr 8:13	8141
Solomon in one y was six hundred	2Chr 9:13	8141
and mules, a rate y by y	2Chr 9:24	8141
that in the fifth y of king	2Chr 12:2	8141
Now in the eighteenth y of king	2Chr 13:1	8141
in the fifteenth y of the reign	2Chr 15:10	8141
thirtieth y of the reign of Asa	2Chr 15:19	8141
thirtieth y of the reign of Asa	2Chr 16:1	8141
ninth y of his reign was diseased	2Chr 16:12	8141
one and fortieth y of his reign	2Chr 16:13	8141
Also in the third y of his reign	2Chr 17:7	8141
and he reigned one y in Jerusalem	2Chr 22:2	8141
in the seventh y Jehoiada	2Chr 23:1	8141
house of your God from y to y	2Chr 24:5	8141
came to pass at the end of the y	2Chr 24:23	8141
of Ammon gave him the same y an	2Chr 27:5	8141
pay unto him, both the second y	2Chr 27:5	8141
He in the first y of his reign	2Chr 29:3	8141
For in the eighth y of his reign	2Chr 34:3	8141
in the twelfth y he began to	2Chr 34:3	8141
in the eighteenth y of his reign	2Chr 34:8	8141
In the eighteenth y of the reign	2Chr 35:19	8141
when the y was expired, king	2Chr 36:10	8141
Now in the first y of Cyrus king	2Chr 36:22	8141
Now in the first y of Cyrus king	Ezr 1:1	8141
Now in the second y of their	Ezr 3:8	8141
So it ceased unto the second y of	Ezr 4:24	8140
But in the first y of Cyrus the	Ezr 5:13	8140
In the first y of Cyrus the king	Ezr 6:3	8140
which was in the sixth y of the	Ezr 6:15	8140
in the seventh y of Artaxerxes	Ezr 7:7	8141
was in the seventh y of the king	Ezr 7:8	8141
month Chisleu, in the twentieth y	Neh 1:1	8141
in the twentieth y of Artaxerxes	Neh 2:1	8141
the twentieth y even unto the two	Neh 5:14	8141
thirtieth y of Artaxerxes the	Neh 5:14	8141
that we would leave the seventh y	Neh 10:31	8141
at times appointed y by y	Neh 10:34	8141
at times appointed y by y	Neh 10:34	8141
all fruit of all trees, y by y	Neh 10:35	8141
thirtieth y of Artaxerxes king of	Neh 13:6	8141
In the third y of his reign	Est 1:3	8141
in the seventh y of his reign	Est 2:16	8141
Nisan, in the twelfth y of king	Est 3:7	8141
to their appointed time every y	Est 9:27	8141
be joined unto the days of the y	Job 3:6	8141
crownest the y with thy goodness	Ps 65:11	8141
In the y that king Uzziah died I	Is 6:1	8141
In the y that king Ahaz died was	Is 14:28	8141
In the y that Tartan came unto	Is 20:1	8141
the Lord said unto me, Within a y	Is 21:16	8141
add ye y to y	Is 29:1	8141
the y of recompences for the	Is 34:8	8141
the fourteenth y of king Hezekiah	Is 36:1	8141
Ye shall eat this y such as	Is 37:30	8141
the second y that which springeth	Is 37:30	8141
and in the third y sow ye, and reap	Is 37:30	8141
the acceptable y of the LORD	Is 61:2	8141
the y of my redeemed is come	Is 63:4	8141
in the thirteenth y of his reign	Jer 1:2	8141
unto the end of the eleventh y of	Jer 1:3	8141
even the y of their visitation	Jer 11:23	8141
be careful in the y of drought	Jer 17:8	8141
even the y of their visitation,	Jer 23:12	8141
people of Judah in the fourth y	Jer 25:1	8141
of Judah, that was the first y of	Jer 25:1	8141
From the thirteenth y of Josiah	Jer 25:3	8141
that is the three and twentieth y	Jer 25:3	8141
And it came to pass the same y	Jer 28:1	8141
king of Judah, in the fourth y	Jer 28:1	8141

this y thou shalt die, because	Jer 28:16	8141
the same y in the seventh month	Jer 28:17	8141
tenth y of Zedekiah king of Judah	Jer 32:1	8141
eighteenth y of Nebuchadrezzar	Jer 32:1	8141
it came to pass in the fourth y	Jer 36:1	8141
it came to pass in the fifth y of	Jer 36:9	8141
In the ninth y of Zedekiah king	Jer 39:1	8141
And in the eleventh y of Zedekiah	Jer 39:2	8141
in the fourth y of Jehoiakim the	Jer 45:1	8141
y of Jehoiakim the son of Josiah	Jer 46:2	8141
the y of their visitation, saith	Jer 48:44	8141
a rumour shall both come one y	Jer 51:46	8141
in another y shall come a rumour	Jer 51:46	8141
in the fourth y of his reign	Jer 51:59	8141
pass in the ninth y of his reign	Jer 52:4	8141
the eleventh y of king Zedekiah	Jer 52:5	8141
which was the nineteenth y of	Jer 52:12	8141
in the seventh y three thousand	Jer 52:28	8141
In the eighteenth y of	Jer 52:29	8141
twentieth y of Nebuchadrezzar	Jer 52:30	8141
thirtieth y of the captivity of	Jer 52:31	8141
king of Babylon in the first y of	Jer 52:31	8141
came to pass in the thirtieth y	Eze 1:1	8141
which was the fifth y of king	Eze 1:2	8141
appointed thee each day for a y	Eze 4:6	8141
And it came to pass in the sixth y	Eze 8:1	8141
it came to pass in the seventh y	Eze 20:1	8141
Again in the ninth y, in the	Eze 24:1	8141
it came to pass in the eleventh y	Eze 26:1	8141
In the tenth y, in the tenth	Eze 29:1	8141
pass in the seven and twentieth y	Eze 29:17	8141
it came to pass in the eleventh y	Eze 30:20	8141
it came to pass in the eleventh y	Eze 31:1	8141
it came to pass in the twelfth y	Eze 32:1	8141
to pass also in the twelfth y	Eze 32:17	8141
in the twelfth y of our captivity	Eze 33:21	8141
twentieth y of our captivity, in	Eze 40:1	8141
in the beginning of the y	Eze 40:1	8141
in the fourteenth y after that	Eze 40:1	8141
of the first y without blemish	Eze 46:13	8141
shall be his to the y of liberty	Eze 46:17	8141
In the third y of the reign of	Dan 1:1	8141
unto the first y of king Cyrus	Dan 1:21	8141
in the second y of the reign of	Dan 2:1	8141
In the first y of Belshazzar king	Dan 7:1	8140
In the third y of the reign of	Dan 8:1	8141
In the first y of Darius the son	Dan 9:1	8141
In the first y of his reign I	Dan 9:2	8141
In the third y of Cyrus king of	Dan 10:1	8141
in the first y of Darius the Mede	Dan 11:1	8141
offerings, with calves of a y old	Mic 6:6	8141
In the second y of Darius the	Hag 1:1	8141
in the second y of Darius the	Hag 1:15	8141
month, in the second y of Darius	Hag 2:10	8141
month, in the second y of Darius	Zec 1:1	8141
Sebat, in the second y of Darius	Zec 1:7	8141
in the fourth y of king Darius	Zec 7:1	8141
y to y to worship the King	Zec 14:16	8141
y at the feast of the passover	Lk 2:41	2094
Now in the fifteenth y of the	Lk 3:1	2094
the acceptable y of the Lord	Lk 4:19	1763
Lord, let it alone this y also	Lk 13:8	2094
being the high priest that same y	Jn 11:49	1763
but being high priest that y	Jn 11:51	1763
was the high priest that same y	Jn 18:13	1763
that a whole y they assembled	Acts 11:26	1763
And he continued there a y	Acts 18:11	1763
but also to be forward a y ago	2Cor 8:10	4070
that Achaia was ready a y ago	2Cor 9:2	4070
high priest alone once every y	Heb 9:7	1763
every y with blood of others	Heb 9:25	1763
y by y continually make the	Heb 10:1	1763
which they offered y by y	Heb 10:1	1763
again made of sins every y	Heb 10:3	1763
a city, and continue there a y	Jas 4:13	1763
and a day, and a month, and a y	Rev 9:15	1763

YEARLY

as a y hired servant shall he be	Lev 25:53	8141
went y to lament the daughter of	Judg 11:40	3117
y in a place which is on the	Judg 21:19	3117
up out of his city y to worship	1Sa 1:3	3117
unto the LORD the y sacrifice	1Sa 1:21	3117
husband to offer the y sacrifice	1Sa 2:19	3117
for there is a y sacrifice there	1Sa 20:6	3117
to charge ourselves y with the	Neh 10:32	8141
the fifteenth day of the same, y	Est 9:21	8141

YEARN

his bowels did y upon his brother	Gen 43:30	3648

YEARNED

for her bowels *y* upon her son	1Kin 3:26	3648

YEAR'S

feast of ingathering at the *y* end	Ex 34:22	8141
(for it was at every *y* end that	2Sa 14:26	3117

YEARS

and for seasons, and for days, and *y*	Gen 1:14	8141
Adam lived an hundred and thirty *y*	Gen 5:3	8141
Seth were eight hundred *y*	Gen 5:4	8141
were nine hundred and thirty *y*	Gen 5:5	8141
Seth lived an hundred and five *y*	Gen 5:6	8141
Enos eight hundred and seven *y*	Gen 5:7	8141
were nine hundred and twelve *y*	Gen 5:8	8141
And Enos lived ninety *y*, and begat	Gen 5:9	8141
Cainan eight hundred and fifteen *y*	Gen 5:10	8141
Enos were nine hundred and five *y*	Gen 5:11	8141
And Cainan lived seventy *y*	Gen 5:12	8141
eight hundred and forty *y*, and	Gen 5:13	8141
Cainan were nine hundred and ten *y*	Gen 5:14	8141
Mahalaleel lived sixty and five *y*	Gen 5:15	8141
Jared eight hundred and thirty *y*	Gen 5:16	8141
eight hundred ninety and five *y*	Gen 5:17	8141
lived an hundred sixty and two *y*	Gen 5:18	8141
he begat Enoch eight hundred *y*	Gen 5:19	8141
were nine hundred sixty and two *y*	Gen 5:20	8141
And Enoch lived sixty and five *y*	Gen 5:21	8141
begat Methuselah three hundred *y*	Gen 5:22	8141
three hundred sixty and five *y*	Gen 5:23	8141
an hundred eighty and seven *y*	Gen 5:25	8141
seven hundred eighty and two *y*	Gen 5:26	8141
were nine hundred sixty and nine *y*	Gen 5:27	8141
lived an hundred eighty and two *y*	Gen 5:28	8141
five hundred ninety and five *y*	Gen 5:30	8141
seven hundred seventy and seven *y*	Gen 5:31	8141
And Noah was five hundred *y* old	Gen 5:32	8141
shall be an hundred and twenty *y*	Gen 6:3	8141
Noah was six hundred *y* old when	Gen 7:6	8141
flood three hundred and fifty *y*	Gen 9:28	8141
Noah were nine hundred and fifty *y*	Gen 9:29	8141
Shem was an hundred *y* old	Gen 11:10	8141
Arphaxad two *y* after the flood	Gen 11:10	8141
he begat Arphaxad five hundred *y*	Gen 11:11	8141
Arphaxad lived five and thirty *y*	Gen 11:12	8141
Salah four hundred and three *y*	Gen 11:13	8141
And Salah lived thirty *y*, and begat	Gen 11:14	8141
Eber four hundred and three *y*	Gen 11:15	8141
And Eber lived four and thirty *y*	Gen 11:16	8141
Peleg four hundred and thirty *y*	Gen 11:17	8141
And Peleg lived thirty *y*, and begat	Gen 11:18	8141
begat Reu two hundred and nine *y*	Gen 11:19	8141
And Reu lived two and thirty *y*	Gen 11:20	8141
Serug two hundred and seven *y*	Gen 11:21	8141
And Serug lived thirty *y*, and begat	Gen 11:22	8141
he begat Nahor two hundred *y*	Gen 11:23	8141
And Nahor lived nine and twenty *y*	Gen 11:24	8141
Terah an hundred and nineteen *y*	Gen 11:25	8141
And Terah lived seventy *y*, and	Gen 11:26	8141
Terah were two hundred and five *y*	Gen 11:32	8141
five *y* old when he departed out	Gen 12:4	8141
Twelve *y* they served Chedorlaomer	Gen 14:4	8141
Take me an heifer of three *y* old	Gen 15:9	8027
old, and a she goat of three *y* old	Gen 15:9	8027
old, and a ram of three *y* old	Gen 15:9	3027
shall afflict them four hundred *y*	Gen 15:13	8141
dwelt ten *y* in the land of Canaan	Gen 16:3	8141
Abram was fourscore and six *y* old	Gen 16:16	8141
And when Abram was ninety *y* old	Gen 17:1	8141
unto him that is an hundred *y* old	Gen 17:17	8141
shall Sarah, that is ninety *y* old	Gen 17:17	8141
And Abraham was ninety *y* old	Gen 17:24	8141
his son was thirteen *y* old	Gen 17:25	8141
And Abraham was an hundred *y*	Gen 21:5	8141
hundred and seven and twenty *y* old	Gen 23:1	8141
these were the *y* of the life of	Gen 23:1	8141
these are the days of the *y* of	Gen 25:7	8141
hundred threescore and fifteen *y*	Gen 25:7	8141
old age, an old man, and full of *y*	Gen 25:8	8141
these are the *y* of the life of	Gen 25:17	
an hundred and seven and thirty *y*	Gen 25:17	8141
Isaac was forty *y* old when he	Gen 25:20	8141
Isaac was threescore *y* old when	Gen 25:26	8141
Esau was forty *y* old when he took	Gen 26:34	8141
I will serve thee seven *y* for	Gen 29:18	8141
Jacob served seven *y* for Rachel	Gen 29:20	8141
serve with me yet seven other *y*	Gen 29:27	8141
served with him yet seven other *y*	Gen 29:30	8141
This twenty *y* have I been with	Gen 31:38	8141
have I been twenty *y* in thy house	Gen 31:41	8141
fourteen *y* for thy two daughters	Gen 31:41	8141
and six *y* for thy cattle	Gen 31:41	8141

were an hundred and fourscore *y*	Gen 35:28	8141
Joseph, being seventeen *y* old	Gen 37:2	8141
to pass at the end of two full *y*	Gen 41:1	8141
The seven good kine are seven *y*	Gen 41:26	8141
the seven good ears are seven *y*	Gen 41:26	8141
came up after them are seven *y*	Gen 41:27	8141
wind shall be seven *y* of famine	Gen 41:27	8141
there come seven *y* of great	Gen 41:29	8141
after them seven *y* of famine	Gen 41:30	8141
of Egypt in the seven plenteous *y*	Gen 41:34	8141
food of those good *y* that come	Gen 41:35	8141
against the seven *y* of famine	Gen 41:36	8141
Joseph was thirty *y* old when he	Gen 41:46	8141
in the seven plenteous *y* the	Gen 41:47	8141
up all the food of the seven *y*	Gen 41:48	8141
sons before the *y* of famine came	Gen 41:50	8141
the seven *y* of plenteousness,	Gen 41:53	8141
the seven *y* of dearth began to	Gen 41:54	8141
For these two *y* hath the famine	Gen 45:6	8141
and yet there are five *y*, in the	Gen 45:6	8141
yet there are five *y* of famine	Gen 45:11	8141
Pharaoh, The days of the *y* of my	Gen 47:9	8141
are an hundred and thirty *y*	Gen 47:9	8141
the days of the *y* of my life been	Gen 47:9	8141
y of the life of my fathers in	Gen 47:9	8141
in the land of Egypt seventeen *y*	Gen 47:28	8141
was an hundred forty and seven *y*	Gen 47:28	8141
Joseph lived an hundred and ten *y*	Gen 50:22	8141
being an hundred and ten *y* old	Gen 50:26	8141
the *y* of the life of Levi were an	Ex 6:16	8141
were an hundred thirty and seven *y*	Ex 6:16	8141
the *y* of the life of Kohath were	Ex 6:18	8141
were an hundred thirty and three *y*	Ex 6:18	8141
the *y* of the life of Amram were	Ex 6:20	8141
an hundred and thirty and seven *y*	Ex 6:20	8141
And Moses was fourscore *y* old	Ex 7:7	8141
and Aaron fourscore and three *y*	Ex 7:7	8141
was four hundred and thirty *y*	Ex 12:40	8141
of the four hundred and thirty *y*	Ex 12:41	8141
of Israel did eat manna forty *y*	Ex 16:35	8141
servant, six *y* he shall serve	Ex 21:2	8141
six *y* thou shalt sow thy land, and	Ex 23:10	8141
are numbered, from twenty *y* old	Ex 30:14	8141
to be numbered, from twenty *y* old	Ex 38:26	8141
three *y* shall it be as	Lev 19:23	8141
Six *y* thou shalt sow thy field,	Lev 25:3	8141
six *y* thou shalt prune thy	Lev 25:3	8141
seven sabbaths of *y* unto thee	Lev 25:8	8141
unto thee, seven times seven *y*	Lev 25:8	8141
of *y* shall be unto thee forty	Lev 25:8	8141
be unto thee forty and nine *y*	Lev 25:8	8141
According to the number of *y*	Lev 25:15	8141
of *y* of the fruits he shall sell	Lev 25:15	8141
y thou shalt increase the price	Lev 25:16	8141
according to the fewness of *y*	Lev 25:16	8141
according to the number of the *y*	Lev 25:16	8141
bring forth fruit for three *y*	Lev 25:21	8141
count the *y* of the sale thereof	Lev 25:27	8141
be according unto the number of *y*	Lev 25:50	8141
If there be yet many *y* behind	Lev 25:51	8141
but few *y* unto the year of jubile	Lev 25:52	8141
according unto his *y* shall he	Lev 25:52	8141
if he be not redeemed in these *y*	Lev 25:54	8141
be of the male from twenty *y* old	Lev 27:3	8141
even unto sixty *y* old	Lev 27:3	8141
if it be from five *y* old even	Lev 27:5	8141
y old even unto twenty *y* old	Lev 27:5	8141
a month old even unto five *y* old	Lev 27:6	8141
And if it be from sixty *y* old	Lev 27:7	8141
according to the *y* that remain	Lev 27:18	8141
From twenty *y* old and upward, all	Num 1:3	8141
of the names, from twenty *y* old	Num 1:18	8141
every male from twenty *y* old	Num 1:20	8141
every male from twenty *y* old	Num 1:22	8141
of the names, from twenty *y* old	Num 1:24	8141
of the names, from twenty *y* old	Num 1:26	8141
of the names, from twenty *y* old	Num 1:28	8141
of the names, from twenty *y* old	Num 1:30	8141
of the names, from twenty *y* old	Num 1:32	8141
of the names, from twenty *y* old	Num 1:34	8141
of the names, from twenty *y* old	Num 1:36	8141
of the names, from twenty *y* old	Num 1:38	8141
of the names, from twenty *y* old	Num 1:40	8141
of the names, from twenty *y* old	Num 1:42	8141
their fathers, from twenty *y* old	Num 1:45	8141
From thirty *y* old and upward even	Num 4:3	8141
and upward even until fifty *y* old	Num 4:3	8141
From thirty *y* old and upward until	Num 4:23	8141
upward until fifty *y* old shalt	Num 4:23	8141
From thirty *y* old and upward even	Num 4:30	8141
upward even unto fifty *y* old	Num 4:30	8141

From thirty y old and upward even	Num 4:35	8141
and upward even unto fifty y old	Num 4:35	8141
From thirty y old and upward even	Num 4:39	8141
and upward even unto fifty y old	Num 4:39	8141
From thirty y old and upward even	Num 4:43	8141
and upward even unto fifty y old	Num 4:43	8141
From thirty y old and upward even	Num 4:47	8141
and upward even unto fifty y old	Num 4:47	8141
from twenty and five y old	Num 8:24	8141
from the age of fifty y they	Num 8:25	8141
seven y before Zoan in Egypt	Num 13:22	8141
whole number, from twenty y old	Num 14:29	8141
wander in the wilderness forty y	Num 14:33	8141
your iniquities, even forty y	Num 14:34	8141
of Israel, from twenty y old	Num 26:2	8141
of the people, from twenty y old	Num 26:4	8141
out of Egypt, from twenty y old	Num 32:11	8141
wander in the wilderness forty y	Num 32:13	8141
three y old when he died in mount	Num 33:39	8141
these forty y the LORD thy God	Deut 2:7	8141
Zered, was thirty and eight y	Deut 2:14	8141
these forty y in the wilderness	Deut 8:2	8141
did thy foot swell, these forty y	Deut 8:4	8141
At the end of three y thou shalt	Deut 14:28	8141
seven y thou shalt make a release	Deut 15:1	8141
unto thee, and serve thee six y	Deut 15:12	8141
to thee, in serving thee six y	Deut 15:18	8141
led you forty y in the wilderness	Deut 29:5	8141
hundred and twenty y old this day	Deut 31:2	8141
At the end of every seven y	Deut 31:10	8141
of old, consider the y of many	Deut 32:7	8141
twenty y old when he died	Deut 34:7	8141
walked forty y in the wilderness	Josh 5:6	8141
Joshua was old and stricken in y	Josh 13:1	8141
Thou art old and stricken in y	Josh 13:1	8141
Forty y old was I when Moses the	Josh 14:7	8141
as he said, these forty and five y	Josh 14:10	8141
this day fourscore and five y old	Josh 14:10	8141
being an hundred and ten y old	Josh 24:29	8141
being an hundred and ten y old	Judg 2:8	8141
served Chushan-rishathaim eight y	Judg 3:8	8141
And the land had rest forty y	Judg 3:11	8141
Eglon the king of Moab eighteen y	Judg 3:14	8141
And the land had rest fourscore y	Judg 3:30	8141
twenty y he mightily oppressed	Judg 4:3	8141
And the land had rest forty y	Judg 5:31	8141
into the hand of Midian seven y	Judg 6:1	8141
the second bullock of seven y old	Judg 6:25	8141
forty y in the days of Gideon	Judg 8:28	8141
had reigned three y over Israel	Judg 9:22	8141
judged Israel twenty and three y	Judg 10:2	8141
and judged Israel twenty and two y	Judg 10:3	8141
eighteen y, all the children of	Judg 10:8	8141
coasts of Arnon, three hundred y	Judg 11:26	8141
And Jephthah judged Israel six y	Judg 12:7	8141
And he judged Israel seven y	Judg 12:9	8141
and he judged Israel ten y	Judg 12:11	8141
and he judged Israel eight y	Judg 12:14	8141
hand of the Philistines forty y	Judg 13:1	8141
days of the Philistines twenty y	Judg 15:20	8141
And he judged Israel twenty y	Judg 16:31	8141
and they dwelled there about ten y	Ruth 1:4	8141
Now Eli was ninety and eight y old	1Sa 4:15	8141
And he had judged Israel forty y	1Sa 4:18	8141
for it was twenty y	1Sa 7:2	8141
he had reigned two y over Israel	1Sa 13:1	8141
with me these days, or these y	1Sa 29:3	8141
Saul's son was forty y old when	2Sa 2:10	8141
over Israel, and reigned two y	2Sa 2:10	8141
the house of Judah was seven y	2Sa 2:11	8141
He was five y old when the	2Sa 4:4	8141
David was thirty y old when he	2Sa 5:4	8141
to reign, and he reigned forty y	2Sa 5:4	8141
he reigned over Judah seven y	2Sa 5:5	8141
three y over all Israel and Judah	2Sa 5:5	8141
it came to pass after two full y	2Sa 13:23	8141
to Geshur, and was there three y	2Sa 13:38	8141
dwelt two full y in Jerusalem	2Sa 14:28	8141
And it came to pass after forty y	2Sa 15:7	8141
aged man, even fourscore y old	2Sa 19:32	8141
I am this day fourscore y old	2Sa 19:35	8141
in the days of David three y	2Sa 21:1	8141
Shall seven y of famine come unto	2Sa 24:13	8141
David was old and stricken in y	1Kin 1:1	3117
reigned over Israel were forty y	1Kin 2:11	8141
seven y reigned he in Hebron, and	1Kin 2:11	8141
three y reigned he in Jerusalem	1Kin 2:11	8141
to pass at the end of three y	1Kin 2:39	8141
So was he seven y in building it	1Kin 6:38	8141
building his own house thirteen y	1Kin 7:1	8141
to pass at the end of twenty y	1Kin 9:10	8141
once in three y came the navy of	1Kin 10:22	8141
over all Israel was forty y	1Kin 11:42	8141
reigned were two and twenty y	1Kin 14:20	8141
one y old when he began to reign,	1Kin 14:21	8141
reigned seventeen y in Jerusalem	1Kin 14:21	8141
Three y reigned he in Jerusalem	1Kin 15:2	8141
one y reigned he in Jerusalem	1Kin 15:10	8141
and reigned over Israel two y	1Kin 15:25	8141
in Tirzah, twenty and four y	1Kin 15:33	8141
over Israel in Tirzah, two y	1Kin 16:8	8141
to reign over Israel, twelve y	1Kin 16:23	8141
six y reigned he in Tirzah	1Kin 16:23	8141
Israel in Samaria twenty and two y	1Kin 16:29	8141
shall not be dew nor rain these y	1Kin 17:1	8141
they continued three y without	1Kin 22:1	8141
five y old when he began to reign	1Kin 22:42	8141
twenty and five y in Jerusalem	1Kin 22:42	8141
and reigned two y over Israel	1Kin 22:51	8141
of Judah, and reigned twelve y	2Kin 3:1	8141
also come upon the land seven y	2Kin 8:1	8141
land of the Philistines seven y	2Kin 8:2	8141
two y old was he when he began to	2Kin 8:17	8141
he reigned eight y in Jerusalem	2Kin 8:17	8141
twenty y old was Ahaziah when he	2Kin 8:26	8141
in Samaria was twenty and eight y	2Kin 10:36	8141
in the house of the LORD six y	2Kin 11:3	8141
Seven y old was Jehoash when he	2Kin 11:21	8141
forty y reigned he in Jerusalem	2Kin 12:1	8141
Samaria, and reigned seventeen y	2Kin 13:1	8141
in Samaria, and reigned sixteen y	2Kin 13:10	8141
five y old when he began to reign	2Kin 14:2	8141
twenty and nine y in Jerusalem	2Kin 14:2	8141
Jehoahaz king of Israel fifteen y	2Kin 14:17	8141
Azariah, which was sixteen y old	2Kin 14:21	8141
and reigned forty and one y	2Kin 14:23	8141
Sixteen y old was he when he	2Kin 15:2	8141
two and fifty y in Jerusalem	2Kin 15:2	8141
and reigned ten y in Samaria	2Kin 15:17	8141
in Samaria, and reigned two y	2Kin 15:23	8141
in Samaria, and reigned twenty y	2Kin 15:27	8141
twenty y old was he when he began	2Kin 15:33	8141
he reigned sixteen y in Jerusalem	2Kin 15:33	8141
Twenty y old was Ahaz when he	2Kin 16:2	8141
and reigned sixteen y in Jerusalem	2Kin 16:2	8141
in Samaria over Israel nine y	2Kin 17:1	8141
Samaria, and besieged it three y	2Kin 17:5	8141
five y old was he when he began	2Kin 18:2	8141
twenty and nine y in Jerusalem	2Kin 18:2	8141
the end of three y they took it	2Kin 18:10	8141
will add unto thy days fifteen y	2Kin 20:6	8141
Manasseh was twelve y old when he	2Kin 21:1	8141
fifty and five y in Jerusalem	2Kin 21:1	8141
two y old when he began to reign,	2Kin 21:19	8141
and he reigned two y in Jerusalem	2Kin 21:19	8141
Josiah was eight y old when he	2Kin 22:1	8141
thirty and one y in Jerusalem	2Kin 22:1	8141
three y old when he began to	2Kin 23:31	8141
five y old when he began to reign	2Kin 23:36	8141
he reigned eleven y in Jerusalem	2Kin 23:36	8141
became his servant three y	2Kin 24:1	8141
Jehoiachin was eighteen y old	2Kin 24:8	8141
one y old when he began to reign,	2Kin 24:18	8141
he reigned eleven y in Jerusalem	2Kin 24:18	8141
when he was threescore y old	1Chr 2:21	8141
and there he reigned seven y	1Chr 3:4	8141
he reigned thirty and three y	1Chr 3:4	8141
numbered from the age of thirty y	1Chr 23:3	8141
LORD, from the age of twenty y	1Chr 23:24	8141
were numbered from twenty y old	1Chr 23:27	8141
number of them from twenty y old	1Chr 27:23	8141
reigned over Israel was forty y	1Chr 29:27	8141
seven y reigned he in Hebron, and	1Chr 29:27	8141
three y reigned he in Jerusalem	1Chr 29:27	8141
to pass at the end of twenty y	2Chr 8:1	8141
every three y once came the ships	2Chr 9:21	8141
Jerusalem over all Israel forty y	2Chr 9:30	8141
son of Solomon strong, three y	2Chr 11:17	8141
for three y they walked in the	2Chr 11:17	8141
forty y old when he began to	2Chr 12:13	8141
reigned seventeen y in Jerusalem	2Chr 12:13	8141
He reigned three y in Jerusalem	2Chr 13:2	8141
his days the land was quiet ten y	2Chr 14:1	8141
rest, and he had no war in those y	2Chr 14:6	8141
after certain y he went down to	2Chr 18:2	8141
five y old when he began to reign	2Chr 20:31	8141
twenty and five y in Jerusalem	2Chr 20:31	8141
two y old when he began to reign,	2Chr 21:5	8141
he reigned eight y in Jerusalem	2Chr 21:5	8141
of time, after the end of two y	2Chr 21:19	3117
two y old was he when he began to	2Chr 21:20	8141
he reigned in Jerusalem eight y	2Chr 21:20	8141

two y old was Ahaziah when he	2Chr 22:2	8141
hid in the house of God six y	2Chr 22:12	8141
Joash was seven y old when he	2Chr 24:1	8141
he reigned forty y in Jerusalem	2Chr 24:1	8141
thirty y old was he when he died	2Chr 24:15	8141
five y old when he began to reign	2Chr 25:1	8141
twenty and nine y in Jerusalem	2Chr 25:1	8141
numbered them from twenty y old	2Chr 25:5	8141
Jehoahaz king of Israel fifteen y	2Chr 25:25	8141
Uzziah, who was sixteen y old	2Chr 26:1	8141
Sixteen y old was Uzziah when he	2Chr 26:3	8141
fifty and two y in Jerusalem	2Chr 26:3	8141
five y old when he began to reign	2Chr 27:1	8141
he reigned sixteen y in Jerusalem	2Chr 27:1	8141
twenty y old when he began to	2Chr 27:8	8141
and reigned sixteen y in Jerusalem	2Chr 27:8	8141
Ahaz was twenty y old when he	2Chr 28:1	8141
he reigned sixteen y in Jerusalem	2Chr 28:1	8141
when he was five and twenty y old	2Chr 29:1	8141
nine and twenty y in Jerusalem	2Chr 29:1	8141
of males, from three y old	2Chr 31:16	8141
and the Levites from twenty y old	2Chr 31:17	8141
Manasseh was twelve y old when he	2Chr 33:1	8141
fifty and five y in Jerusalem	2Chr 33:1	8141
twenty y old when he began to	2Chr 33:21	8141
reigned two y in Jerusalem	2Chr 33:21	8141
Josiah was eight y old when he	2Chr 34:1	8141
in Jerusalem one and thirty y	2Chr 34:1	8141
three y old when he began to	2Chr 36:2	8141
five y old when he began to reign	2Chr 36:5	8141
he reigned eleven y in Jerusalem	2Chr 36:5	8141
Jehoiachin was eight y old when	2Chr 36:9	8141
twenty y old when he began to	2Chr 36:11	8141
and reigned eleven y in Jerusalem	2Chr 36:11	8141
to fulfil threescore and ten y	2Chr 36:21	8141
the Levites, from twenty y old	Ezr 3:8	8141
that was builded these many y ago	Ezr 5:11	8140
the king, that is, twelve y	Neh 5:14	8141
forty y didst thou sustain them	Neh 9:21	8141
Yet many y didst thou forbear	Neh 9:30	8141
are thy y as man's days,	Job 10:5	8141
the number of y is hidden to the	Job 15:20	8141
When a few y are come, then I	Job 16:22	8141
multitude of y should teach	Job 32:7	8141
and their y in pleasures	Job 36:11	8141
number of his y be searched out	Job 36:26	8141
lived Job an hundred and forty y	Job 42:16	8141
with grief, and my y with sighing	Ps 31:10	8141
his y as many generations	Ps 61:6	8141
of old, the y of ancient times	Ps 77:5	8141
but I will remember the y of the	Ps 77:10	8141
in vanity, and their y in trouble	Ps 78:33	8141
For a thousand y in thy sight are	Ps 90:4	8141
we spend our y as a tale that is	Ps 90:9	8141
of our y are threescore y	Ps 90:10	8141
of strength they be fourscore y	Ps 90:10	8141
the y wherein we have seen evil	Ps 90:15	8141
Forty y long was I grieved with	Ps 95:10	8141
thy y are throughout all	Ps 102:24	8141
same, and thy y shall have no end	Ps 102:27	8141
the y of thy life shall be many	Prov 4:10	8141
others, and thy y unto the cruel	Prov 5:9	8141
the y of thy life shall be	Prov 9:11	8141
but the y of the wicked shall be	Prov 10:27	8141
hundred children, and live many y	Eccl 6:3	8141
so that the days of his y be many	Eccl 6:3	8141
he live a thousand y twice told	Eccl 6:6	8141
But if a man live many y, and	Eccl 11:8	8141
nor the y draw nigh, when thou	Eccl 12:1	8141
five y shall Ephraim be broken,	Is 7:8	8141
Zoar, an heifer of three y old	Is 15:5	
spoken, saying, Within three y	Is 16:14	8141
as the y of an hireling, and the	Is 16:14	8141
and barefoot three y for a sign	Is 20:3	8141
according to the y of an hireling	Is 21:16	8141
Tyre shall be forgotten seventy y	Is 23:15	8141
after the end of seventy y shall	Is 23:15	8141
pass after the end of seventy y	Is 23:17	8141
y shall ye be troubled, ye	Is 32:10	8141
will add unto thy days fifteen y	Is 38:5	8141
deprived of the residue of my y	Is 38:10	8141
I shall go softly all my y in the	Is 38:15	8141
child shall die an hundred y old	Is 65:20	8141
hundred y old shall be accursed	Is 65:20	8141
the king of Babylon seventy y	Jer 25:11	8141
when seventy y are accomplished,	Jer 25:12	8141
Within two full y will I bring	Jer 28:3	8141
within the space of two full y	Jer 28:11	8141
the Lord, That after seventy y be	Jer 29:10	8141
At the end of seven y let ye go	Jer 34:14	8141
and when he hath served thee six y	Jer 34:14	8141

as an heifer of three y old	Jer 48:34	
twenty y old when he began to	Jer 52:1	8141
he reigned eleven y in Jerusalem	Jer 52:1	8141
upon thee the y of their iniquity	Eze 4:5	8141
near, and art come even unto thy y	Eze 22:4	8141
shall it be inhabited forty y	Eze 29:11	8141
waste shall be desolate forty y	Eze 29:12	8141
At the end of forty y will I	Eze 29:13	8141
in the latter y thou shalt come	Eze 38:8	8141
prophesied in those days many y	Eze 38:17	8141
shall burn them with fire seven y	Eze 39:9	8141
so nourishing them three y	Dan 1:5	8141
about threescore and two y old	Dan 5:31	8140
by books the number of the y	Dan 9:2	8141
he would accomplish seventy y in	Dan 9:2	8141
in the end of y they shall join	Dan 11:6	8141
he shall continue more y than the	Dan 11:8	8141
after certain y with a great army	Dan 11:13	8141
even to the y of many generations	Joel 2:2	8141
I will restore to you the y that	Joel 2:25	8141
two y before the earthquake	Amos 1:1	8141
led you forty y through the	Amos 2:10	8141
and your tithes after three y	Amos 4:4	3117
in the wilderness forty y	Amos 5:25	8141
thy work in the midst of the y	Hab 3:2	8141
in the midst of the y make known	Hab 3:2	8141
these threescore and ten y	Zec 1:12	8141
as I have done these so many y	Zec 7:3	8141
month, even those seventy y	Zec 7:5	8141
days of old, and as in former y	Mal 3:4	8141
coasts thereof, from two y old	Mt 2:16	1332
with an issue of blood twelve y	Mt 9:20	2094
had an issue of blood twelve y	Mk 5:25	2094
she was of the age of twelve y	Mk 5:42	2094
both were now well stricken in y	Lk 1:7	2250
and my wife well stricken in y	Lk 1:18	2250
seven y from her virginity	Lk 2:36	2094
of about fourscore and four y	Lk 2:37	2094
And when he was twelve y old	Lk 2:42	2094
began to be about thirty y of age	Lk 3:23	2094
the heaven was shut up three y	Lk 4:25	2094
daughter, about twelve y of age	Lk 8:42	2094
having an issue of blood twelve y	Lk 8:43	2094
much goods laid up for many y	Lk 12:19	2094
these three y I come seeking	Lk 13:7	2094
a spirit of infirmity eighteen y	Lk 13:11	2094
hath bound, lo, these eighteen y	Lk 13:16	2094
these many y do I serve thee,	Lk 15:29	2094
six y was this temple in building	Jn 2:20	2094
an infirmity thirty and eight y	Jn 5:5	2094
him, Thou art not yet fifty y old	Jn 8:57	2094
For the man was above forty y old	Acts 4:22	2094
entreat them evil four hundred y	Acts 7:6	2094
And when he was full forty y old	Acts 7:23	5063
when forty y were expired, there	Acts 7:30	2094
sea, and in the wilderness forty y	Acts 7:36	2094
of forty y in the wilderness	Acts 7:42	2094
which had kept his bed eight y	Acts 9:33	2094
about the time of forty y	Acts 13:18	5063
space of four hundred and fifty y	Acts 13:20	2094
Benjamin, by the space of forty y	Acts 13:21	2094
continued by the space of two y	Acts 19:10	2094
that by the space of three y I	Acts 20:31	5148
many y a judge unto this nation	Acts 24:10	2094
Now after many y I came to bring	Acts 24:17	2094
But after two y Porcius Festus	Acts 24:27	1333
Paul dwelt two whole y in his own	Acts 28:30	1333
he was about an hundred y old	Rom 4:19	1541
these many y to come unto you	Rom 15:23	2094
in Christ above fourteen y ago	2Cor 12:2	2094
Then after three y I went up to	Gal 1:18	2094
Then fourteen y after I went up	Gal 2:1	2094
four hundred and thirty y after	Gal 3:17	2094
days, and months, and times, and y	Gal 4:10	1763
the number under threescore y old	1Ti 5:9	2094
the same, and thy y shall not fail	Heb 1:12	2094
me, and saw my works forty y	Heb 3:9	2094
with whom was he grieved forty y	Heb 3:17	2094
Moses, when he was come to y	Heb 11:24	1096,3173
the earth by the space of three y	Jas 5:17	1763
is with the Lord as a thousand y	2Pet 3:8	2094
and a thousand y as one day	2Pet 3:8	2094
Satan, and bound him a thousand y	Rev 20:2	2094
till the thousand y should be	Rev 20:3	2094
reigned with Christ a thousand y	Rev 20:4	2094
the thousand y were finished	Rev 20:5	2094
shall reign with him a thousand y	Rev 20:6	2094
when the thousand y are expired	Rev 20:7	2094

Y

YEARS'

came to pass at the seven y end 2Kin 8:3   8141
Either three y famine 1Chr 21:12   8141

YELL

they shall y as lions' whelps ....Jer 51:38   5286

YELLED

lions roared upon him, and y ....Jer 2:15   5414,6963

YELLOW

and there be in it a y thin hair ....Lev 13:30   6669
not, and there be in it no y hair ....Lev 13:32   6669
priest shall not seek for y hair ....Lev 13:36   6669
and her feathers with y gold ....Ps 68:13   3422

YES See APPENDIX.

YESTERDAY

your task in making brick both y ....Ex 5:14   8543
son of Jesse to meat, neither y 1Sa 20:27   8543
Whereas thou camest but y 2Sa 15:20   8543
Surely I have seen y the blood of 2Kin 9:26   570
(For we are but of y, and know ....Job 8:9   8543
are but as y when it is past ....Ps 90:4   865
Y at the seventh hour the fever ....Jn 4:52   5504
as thou diddest the Egyptian y ....Acts 7:28   5504
Jesus Christ the same y, and to ....Heb 13:8   5504

YESTERNIGHT

Behold, I lay y with my father ....Gen 19:34   570
of your father spake unto me y ....Gen 31:29   570
of my hands, and rebuked thee y ....Gen 31:42   570

YET See APPENDIX.

YIELD

y unto thee her strength ....Gen 4:12   5414
he shall y royal dainties ....Gen 49:20   5414
that it may y unto you the ....Lev 19:25   3254
And the land shall y her fruit ....Lev 25:19   5414
and the land shall y her increase ....Lev 26:4   5414
of the field shall y their fruit ....Lev 26:4   5414
land shall not y her increase ....Lev 26:20   5414
trees of the land y their fruits ....Lev 26:20   5414
and that the land y not her fruit ....Deut 11:17   5414
but y yourselves unto the LORD, ...2Chr 30:8   5414,3027
shall the earth y her increase ....Ps 67:6   5414
and our land shall y her increase ....Ps 85:12   5414
which may y fruits of increase ....Ps 107:37   6213
fair speech she caused him to y ....Prov 7:21   5186
of vineyard shall y one bath ....Is 5:10   6213
seed an homer shall y an ephah ....Is 5:10   6213
of the field shall y her fruit ....Eze 34:27   5414
and the earth shall y her increase ....Eze 34:27   5414
y your fruit to my people of ....Eze 36:8   5375
the bud shall y no meal ....Hos 8:7   6213
if so be it y, the strangers ....Hos 8:7   6213
the vine do y their strength ....Joel 2:22   5414
and the fields shall y no meat ....Hab 3:17   6213
did y fruit that sprang up and ....Mk 4:8   1325
But do not thou y unto them ....Acts 23:21   3982
Neither y ye your members as ....Rom 6:13   3936
but y yourselves unto God, as ....Rom 6:13   3936
that to whom ye y yourselves ....Rom 6:16   3936
even so now y your members ....Rom 6:19   3936
can no fountain both y salt water ....Jas 3:12   4160

YIELDED

y up the ghost, and was gathered ....Gen 49:33   1478
and bloomed blossoms, and y almonds ..Num 17:8   1580
y their bodies, that they might ....Dan 3:28   3052
with a loud voice, y up the ghost ....Mt 27:50   863
and choked it, and it y no fruit ....Mk 4:7   1325
at his feet, and y up the ghost ....Acts 5:10   1634
for as ye have y your members ....Rom 6:19   3936
and y her fruit every month ....Rev 22:2   591

YIELDETH

it y much increase unto the kings ....Neh 9:37   7235
the wilderness y food for them ....Job 24:5
the root of the righteous y fruit ....Prov 12:12   5414
it y the peaceable fruit of ....Heb 12:11   591

YIELDING

forth grass, the herb y seed ....Gen 1:11   2232
the fruit tree y fruit after his ....Gen 1:11   6213
herb y seed after his kind, and ....Gen 1:12   2232
his kind, and the tree y fruit ....Gen 1:12   6213
is the fruit of a tree y seed ....Gen 1:29   2232
for y pacifieth great offences ....Eccl 10:4   4832
neither shall cease from y fruit ....Jer 17:8   6213

YIRON See IRON.

YOKE

break his y from off thy neck ....Gen 27:40   5923
I have broken the bands of your y ....Lev 26:13   5923

and upon which never came y ....Num 19:2   5923
and which hath not drawn in the y ....Deut 21:3   5923
he shall put a y of iron upon thy ....Deut 28:48   5923
on which there hath come no y 1Sa 6:7   5923
And he took a y of oxen, and hewed 1Sa 11:7   6776
which a y of oxen might plow 1Sa 14:14   6776
Thy father made our y grievous 1Kin 12:4   5923
his heavy y which he put upon us, ...1Kin 12:4   5923
Make the y which thy father did 1Kin 12:9   5923
Thy father made our y heavy 1Kin 12:10   5923
heavy y, I will add to your y 1Kin 12:11   5923
My father made your y heavy 1Kin 12:14   5923
and I will add to your y 1Kin 12:14   5923
with twelve y of oxen before him 1Kin 19:19   6776
took a y of oxen, and slew them, ...1Kin 19:21   6776
Thy father made our y grievous 2Chr 10:4   5923
his heavy y that he put upon us, ...2Chr 10:9   5923
Ease somewhat the y that thy 2Chr 10:9   5923
Thy father made our y heavy 2Chr 10:10   5923
my father put a heavy y upon you 2Chr 10:11   5923
you, I will put more to your y 2Chr 10:11   5923
My father made your y heavy 2Chr 10:14   5923
camels, and five hundred y of oxen ....Job 1:3   6776
camels, and a thousand y of oxen ....Job 42:12   6776
hast broken the y of his burden ....Is 9:4   5923
his y from off thy neck, and the ....Is 10:27   5923
the y shall be destroyed because ....Is 10:27   5923
then shall his y depart from off ....Is 14:25   5923
hast thou very heavily laid thy y ....Is 47:6   5923
go free, and that ye break every y ....Is 58:6   4133
away from the midst of thee the y ....Is 58:9   4133
of old time I have broken thy y ....Jer 2:20   5923
have altogether broken the y ....Jer 5:5   5923
the y of the king of Babylon ....Jer 27:8   5923
the y of the king of Babylon ....Jer 27:11   5923
the y of the king of Babylon ....Jer 27:12   5923
I have broken the y of the king ....Jer 28:2   5923
for I will break the y of the ....Jer 28:4   5923
Hananiah the prophet took the y ....Jer 28:10   4133
Even so will I break the y of ....Jer 28:11   5923
the y from off the neck of the ....Jer 28:12   4133
I have put a y of iron upon the ....Jer 28:14   5923
break his y from off thy neck ....Jer 30:8   5923
a bullock unaccustomed to the y ....Jer 31:18   5923
the husbandman and his y of oxen ....Jer 51:23   6776
The y of my transgressions is ....Lam 1:14   5923
that he bear the y in his youth ....Lam 3:27   5923
have broken the bands of their y ....Eze 34:27   5923
that take off the y on their jaws ....Hos 11:4   5923
will I break his y from off thee ....Nah 1:13   4132
Take my y upon you, and learn of ......Mt 11:29   2218
For my y is easy, and my burden is .....Mt 11:30   2218
I have bought five y of oxen ....Lk 14:19   2201
to put a y upon the neck of the ....Acts 15:10   2218
again with the y of bondage ....Gal 5:1   2218
y count their own masters worthy 1Ti 6:1   2218

YOKED

Be ye not unequally y together 2Cor 6:14   2086

YOKEFELLOW

And I intreat thee also, true y ....Phil 4:3   4805

YOKES

Make thee bonds and y, and put them ...Jer 27:2   4133
Thou hast broken the y of wood ....Jer 28:13   4133
shalt make for them y of iron ....Jer 28:13   4133
shall break there the y of Egypt ....Eze 30:18   4133

YONDER

and I and the lad will go y ....Gen 22:5   3541
and scatter thou the fire y ....Num 16:37   1973
offering, while I meet the LORD y ....Num 23:15   3541
with them on y side Jordan ....Num 32:19   5676
Behold, y is that Shunammite 2Kin 4:25   5704,3541
mountain, Remove hence to y place .....Mt 17:20   1563
Sit ye here, while I go and pray y ....Mt 26:36   1563

YOU See APPENDIX.

YOUNG

wounding, and a y man to my hurt ....Gen 4:23   3206
that which thy y men have eaten ....Gen 14:24   5288
and a turtledove, and a y pigeon ....Gen 15:9   1469
and good, and gave it unto a y man ......Gen 18:7   5288
the house round, both old and y ....Gen 19:4   5288
and took two of his y men with him ......Gen 22:3   5288
And Abraham said unto his y men ....Gen 22:5   5288
Abraham returned unto his y men ....Gen 22:19   5288
she goats have not cast their y ....Gen 31:38   5288
and herds with y are with me ....Gen 33:13   5763
the y man deferred not to do the ....Gen 34:19   5288
there was there with us a y man ....Gen 41:12   5288
Moses said, We will go with our y ....Ex 10:9   5288

There shall nothing cast their *y*	Ex 23:26	
he sent *y* men of the children of	Ex 24:5	5288
Take one *y* bullock, and two rams	Ex 29:1	1121,1241
a *y* man, departed not out of the	Ex 33:11	5288
of turtledoves, or of *y* pigeons	Lev 1:14	1121
a *y* bullock without blemish unto	Lev 4:3	1121,1241
offer a *y* bullock for the sin	Lev 4:14	1121,1241
or two *y* pigeons, unto the LORD	Lev 5:7	1121
or two *y* pigeons, then he that	Lev 5:11	1121
Take thee a *y* calf for a sin	Lev 9:2	1121,1241
a *y* pigeon, or a turtledove, for	Lev 12:6	1121
two turtles, or two *y* pigeons	Lev 12:8	1121
or two *y* pigeons, such as he is	Lev 14:22	1121
turtledoves, or of the *y* pigeons	Lev 14:30	1121
or two *y* pigeons, and come before	Lev 15:14	1121
or two *y* pigeons, and bring them	Lev 15:29	1121
with a *y* bullock for a sin	Lev 16:3	1121,1241
kill it and her *y* both in one day	Lev 22:28	1121
one *y* bullock, and two rams	Lev 23:18	1121,1241
or two *y* pigeons, to the priest,	Num 6:10	1121
One *y* bullock, one ram, one lamb	Num 7:15	1121,1241
One *y* bullock, one ram, one lamb	Num 7:21	1121,1241
One *y* bullock, one ram, one lamb	Num 7:27	1121,1241
One *y* bullock, one ram, one lamb	Num 7:33	1121,1241
One *y* bullock, one ram, one lamb	Num 7:39	1121,1241
One *y* bullock, one ram, one lamb	Num 7:45	1121,1241
One *y* bullock, one ram, one lamb	Num 7:51	1121,1241
One *y* bullock, one ram, one lamb	Num 7:57	1121,1241
One *y* bullock, one ram, one lamb	Num 7:63	1121,1241
One *y* bullock, one ram, one lamb	Num 7:69	1121,1241
One *y* bullock, one ram, one lamb	Num 7:75	1121,1241
One *y* bullock, one ram, one lamb	Num 7:81	1121,1241
Then let them take a *y* bullock	Num 8:8	1121,1241
another *y* bullock shalt thou take	Num 8:8	1121,1241
And there ran a *y* man, and told	Num 11:27	5288
of Moses, one of his *y* men	Num 11:28	979
y bullock for a burnt offering	Num 15:24	1121,1241
and lift up himself as a *y* lion	Num 23:24	
y bullocks, and one ram, seven	Num 28:11	1121,1241
two *y* bullocks, and one ram, and	Num 28:19	1121,1241
two *y* bullocks, one ram, seven	Num 28:27	1121,1241
one *y* bullock, one ram, and seven	Num 29:2	1121,1241
one *y* bullock, one ram, and seven	Num 29:8	1121,1241
thirteen *y* bullocks, two rams, and	Num 29:13	1121,1241
ye shall offer twelve *y* bullocks	Num 29:17	1121,1241
ground, whether they be *y* ones	Deut 22:6	667
and the dam sitting upon the *y*	Deut 22:6	667
shalt not take the dam with the *y*	Deut 22:6	1121
the dam go, and take the *y* to thee	Deut 22:7	1121
the old, nor shew favour to the *y*	Deut 28:50	5288
toward her *y* one that cometh out	Deut 28:57	7988
her nest, fluttereth over her *y*	Deut 32:11	1469
shall destroy both the *y* man	Deut 32:25	970
in the city, both man and woman, *y*	Josh 6:21	5288
the *y* men that were spies went in	Josh 6:23	5288
him, Take thy father's bullock	Judg 6:25	6499
caught a *y* man of the men of	Judg 8:14	5288
unto his *y* man his armourbearer	Judg 9:54	5288
his *y* man thrust him through, and	Judg 9:54	5288
a *y* lion roared against him	Judg 14:5	3715
for so used the *y* men to do	Judg 14:10	970
And there was a *y* man out of	Judg 17:7	5288
the *y* man was unto him as one of	Judg 17:11	5288
the *y* man became his priest, and	Judg 17:12	5288
the voice of the *y* man the Levite	Judg 18:3	5288
the house of the *y* man the Levite	Judg 18:15	5288
for the *y* man which is with thy	Judg 19:19	5288
four hundred *y* virgins, that had	Judg 21:12	5291
have I not charged the *y* men that	Ruth 2:9	5288
that which the *y* men have drawn	Ruth 2:9	5288
glean, Boaz commanded his *y* men	Ruth 2:15	5288
Thou shalt keep fast by my *y* men	Ruth 2:21	5288
as thou followedst not *y* men	Ruth 3:10	970
shall give thee of this *y* woman	Ruth 4:12	5291
and the child was *y*	1Sa 1:24	
Wherefore the sin of the *y* men	1Sa 2:17	5288
and your goodliest *y* men, and your	1Sa 8:16	970
name was Saul, a choice *y* man	1Sa 9:2	970
they found *y* maidens going out to	1Sa 9:11	5291
the *y* man that bare his armour	1Sa 14:1	5288
Jonathan said to the *y* man that	1Sa 14:6	5288
Whose son art thou, thou *y* man	1Sa 17:58	5288
But if I say thus unto the *y* man	1Sa 20:22	5958
if the *y* men have kept themselves	1Sa 21:4	5288
the vessels of the *y* men are holy	1Sa 21:5	5288
And David sent out ten *y* men	1Sa 25:5	5288
men, and David said unto the *y* men	1Sa 25:5	5288
Ask thy *y* men, and they will shew	1Sa 25:8	5288
Wherefore let the *y* men find	1Sa 25:8	5288
And when David's *y* men came	1Sa 25:9	5288
So David's *y* men turned their way	1Sa 25:12	5288
But one of the *y* men told Abigail	1Sa 25:14	5288
saw not the *y* men of my lord	1Sa 25:25	5288
the *y* men that follow my lord	1Sa 25:27	5288
and let one of the *y* men come over	1Sa 26:22	5288
I am a *y* man of Egypt, servant to	1Sa 30:13	5288
of them, save four hundred *y* men	1Sa 30:17	5288
said unto the *y* man that told him	2Sa 1:5	5288
the *y* man that told him said, As	2Sa 1:6	5288
said unto the *y* man that told him	2Sa 1:13	5288
And David called one of the *y* men	2Sa 1:15	5288
Let the *y* men now arise, and play	2Sa 2:14	5288
lay thee hold on one of the *y* men	2Sa 2:21	5288
And David commanded his *y* men	2Sa 4:12	5288
And Mephibosheth had a *y* son	2Sa 9:12	6996
all the *y* men the king's sons	2Sa 13:32	5288
the *y* man that kept the watch	2Sa 13:34	5288
bring the *y* man Absalom again	2Sa 14:21	5288
summer fruit for the *y* men to eat	2Sa 16:2	5288
gently for my sake with the *y* man	2Sa 18:5	5288
that none touch the *y* man Absalom	2Sa 18:12	5288
ten *y* men that bare Joab's armour	2Sa 18:15	5288
Is the *y* man Absalom safe	2Sa 18:29	5288
Is the *y* man Absalom safe	2Sa 18:32	5288
do thee hurt, be as that *y* man is	2Sa 18:32	5288
for my lord the king a *y* virgin	1Kin 1:2	5291
Solomon seeing the *y* man that he	1Kin 11:28	5288
consulted with the *y* men that	1Kin 12:8	3206
the *y* men that were grown up with	1Kin 12:10	3206
after the counsel of the *y* men	1Kin 12:14	3206
Even by the *y* men of the princes	1Kin 20:14	5288
Then he numbered the *y* men of the	1Kin 20:15	5288
the *y* men of the princes of the	1Kin 20:17	5288
So these *y* men of the princes of	1Kin 20:19	5288
me, I pray thee, one of the *y* men	2Kin 4:22	5288
to me from mount Ephraim two *y*	2Kin 5:22	5288
LORD opened the eyes of the *y* man	2Kin 6:17	5288
their *y* men wilt thou slay with	2Kin 8:12	970
So the *y* man, even the *y* man	2Kin 9:4	5288
even the *y* man the prophet, went	2Kin 9:4	5288
a *y* man mighty of valour, and of	1Chr 12:28	5288
David said, Solomon my son is *y*	1Chr 22:5	5288
alone God hath chosen, is yet *y*	1Chr 29:1	5288
took counsel with the *y* men that	2Chr 10:8	3206
the *y* men that were brought up	2Chr 10:10	3206
after the advice of the *y* men	2Chr 10:14	3206
of Solomon, when Rehoboam was *y*	2Chr 13:7	5288
himself with a *y* bullock and seven	2Chr 13:9	1121,1241
of his reign, while he was yet *y*	2Chr 34:3	5288
who slew their *y* men with the	2Chr 36:17	970
compassion upon *y* man or maiden	2Chr 36:17	970
both *y* bullocks, and rams, and	Ezr 6:9	1123
Let there be fair *y* virgins	Est 2:2	5291
gather together all the fair *y*	Est 2:3	5291
cause to perish, all Jews, both *y*	Est 3:13	5288
mules, camels, and *y* dromedaries	Est 8:10	1121
house, and it fell upon the *y* men	Job 1:19	5288
lion, and the teeth of the *y* lions	Job 4:10	3715
Yea, *y* children despised me	Job 19:18	
The *y* men saw me, and hid	Job 29:8	5288
Buzite answered and said, I am *y*	Job 32:6	6810,3117
fill the appetite of the *y* lions	Job 38:39	3715
when thy *y* ones cry unto God,	Job 38:41	3206
they bring forth their *y* ones	Job 39:3	3206
Their *y* ones are in good liking,	Job 39:4	1121
is hardened against her *y* ones	Job 39:16	1121
Her *y* ones also suck up blood	Job 39:30	667
as it were a *y* lion lurking in	Ps 17:12	3715
and Sirion like a *y* unicorn	Ps 29:6	1121
The *y* lions do lack, and suffer	Ps 34:10	3715
I have been *y*, and now am old	Ps 37:25	5288
the great teeth of the *y* lions	Ps 58:6	3715
The fire consumed their *y* men	Ps 78:63	970
y he brought him to feed Jacob	Ps 78:71	5763
herself, where she may lay her *y*	Ps 84:3	667
the *y* lion and the dragon shalt	Ps 91:13	3715
The *y* lions roar after their prey	Ps 104:21	3715
shall a *y* man cleanse his way	Ps 119:9	5288
to the *y* ravens which cry	Ps 147:9	1121
Both *y* men, and maidens	Ps 148:12	970
to the *y* man knowledge and	Prov 1:4	5288
a *y* man void of understanding,	Prov 7:7	5288
The glory of *y* men is their	Prov 20:29	970
the *y* eagles shall eat it	Prov 30:17	1121
Rejoice, O *y* man, in thy youth	Eccl 11:9	970
beloved is like a roe or a *y* hart	Song 2:9	6082
be thou like a roe or a *y* hart	Song 2:17	6082
like two *y* roes that are twins	Song 4:5	6082
like two *y* roes that are twins	Song 7:3	6082
to a *y* hart upon the mountains of	Song 8:14	6082
they shall roar like *y* lions	Is 5:29	3715
that a man shall nourish a *y* cow	Is 7:21	1241

shall have no joy in their y men	Is 9:17	970
the y lion and the fatling	Is 11:6	3715
their y ones shall lie down	Is 11:7	3206
shall dash the y men to pieces	Is 13:18	5288
and the Ethiopians captives, y	Is 20:4	5288
neither do I nourish up y men	Is 23:4	970
anguish, from whence come the y	Is 30:6	3833
upon the shoulders of y asses	Is 30:6	
the y asses that ear the ground	Is 30:24	
the y lion roaring on his prey,	Is 31:4	3715
his y men shall be discomfited	Is 31:8	970
gently lead those that are with y	Is 40:11	5763
the y men shall utterly fall	Is 40:30	5288,970
For as a y man marrieth a virgin,	Is 62:5	970
The y lions roared upon him, and	Jer 2:15	3715
the assembly of y men together	Jer 6:11	970
the y men from the streets	Jer 9:21	970
the y men shall die by the sword	Jer 11:22	970
of the y men a spoiler at noonday	Jer 15:8	970
let their y men be slain by the	Jer 18:21	970
for the y of the flock and of the	Jer 31:12	1121
rejoice in the dance, both y men	Jer 31:13	970
his chosen y men are gone down to	Jer 48:15	970
Therefore her y men shall fall in	Jer 49:26	970
Therefore shall her y men fall in	Jer 50:30	970
and spare ye not her y men	Jer 51:3	970
will I break in pieces old and y	Jer 51:22	5288
will I break in pieces the y man	Jer 51:22	970
against me to crush my y men	Lam 1:15	970
my y men are gone into captivity	Lam 1:18	970
for the life of thy y children	Lam 2:19	
The y and the old lie on the	Lam 2:21	5288
my y men are fallen by the sword	Lam 2:21	970
they give suck to their y ones	Lam 4:3	1482
the y children ask bread, and no	Lam 4:4	
They took the y men to grind	Lam 5:13	970
the y men from their musick	Lam 5:14	970
Slay utterly old and y, both maids	Eze 9:6	970
off the top of his y twigs	Eze 17:4	3242
top of his y twigs a tender one	Eze 17:22	3127
her whelps among y lions	Eze 19:2	3715
it became a y lion, and it learned	Eze 19:3	3715
her whelps, and made him a y lion	Eze 19:5	3715
the lions, he became a y lion	Eze 19:6	3715
all of them desirable y men	Eze 23:6	970
all of them desirable y men	Eze 23:12	970
all of them desirable y men	Eze 23:23	970
The y men of Aven and of Pi-beseth	Eze 30:17	970
of the field bring forth their y	Eze 31:6	
Thou art like a y lion of the	Eze 32:2	3715
with all the y lions thereof,	Eze 38:13	3715
the face of a y lion toward the	Eze 41:19	3715
a y bullock for a sin offering	Eze 43:19	1121,1241
thou shalt offer a y bullock	Eze 43:23	1121,1241
shall also prepare a y bullock	Eze 43:25	1121,1241
thou shalt take a y bullock	Eze 45:18	1121,1241
be a y bullock without blemish	Eze 46:6	1121,1241
as a y lion to the house of Judah	Hos 5:14	3715
your y men shall see visions	Joel 2:28	970
of your y men for Nazarites	Amos 2:11	970
will a y lion cry out of his den,	Amos 3:4	3715
your y men have I slain with the	Amos 4:10	970
virgins and y men faint for thirst	Amos 8:13	970
as a y lion among the flocks of	Mic 5:8	3715
the feeding place of the y lions	Nah 2:11	3715
sword shall devour thy y lions	Nah 2:13	3715
her y children also were dashed	Nah 3:10	
him, Run, speak to this y man	Zec 2:4	5288
shall make the y men cheerful	Zec 9:17	970
a voice of the roaring of y lions	Zec 11:3	3715
off, neither shall seek the y one	Zec 11:16	5288
search diligently for the y child	Mt 2:8	3813
stood over where the y child was	Mt 2:9	3813
they saw the y child with Mary	Mt 2:11	3813
Arise, and take the y child	Mt 2:13	3813
seek the y child to destroy him	Mt 2:13	3813
he arose, he took the y child	Mt 2:14	3813
Arise, and take the y child	Mt 2:20	3813
which sought the y child's life	Mt 2:20	3813
And he arose, and took the y child	Mt 2:21	3813
The y man saith unto him, All	Mt 19:20	3495
But when the y man heard that	Mt 19:22	3495
whose y daughter had an unclean	Mk 7:25	2365
they brought y children to him,	Mk 10:13	3813
followed him a certain y man.	Mk 14:51	3495
the y men laid hold on him,	Mk 14:51	3495
they saw a y man sitting on the	Mk 16:5	3495
of turtledoves, or two y pigeons	Lk 2:24	3502
Y man, I say unto thee, Arise	Lk 7:14	3495
Jesus, when he had found a y ass	Jn 12:14	3678
I say unto thee, When thou wast y	Jn 21:18	3501

your y men shall see visions, and	Acts 2:17	3495
the y men arose, wound him up, and	Acts 5:6	3501
the y men came in, and found her	Acts 5:10	3495
they cast out their y children	Acts 7:19	1025
their clothes at a y man's feet	Acts 7:58	3494
a certain y man named Eutychus	Acts 20:9	3494
And they brought the y man alive	Acts 20:12	3816
Bring this y man unto the chief	Acts 23:17	3494
me to bring this y man unto thee	Acts 23:18	3494
captain then let the y man depart	Acts 23:22	3494
may teach the y women to be sober	Titus 2:4	3501
Y men likewise exhort to be sober	Titus 2:6	3501
y men, because ye have overcome	1Jn 2:13	3495
y men, because ye are strong, and	1Jn 2:14	3495

YOUNGER

knew what his y son had done unto	Gen 9:24	6996
And the firstborn said unto the y	Gen 19:31	6810
the firstborn said unto the y	Gen 19:34	6810
the y arose, and lay with him	Gen 19:35	6810
And the y, she also bare a son, and	Gen 19:38	6810
and the elder shall serve the y	Gen 25:23	6810
and put them upon Jacob her y son	Gen 27:15	6996
sent and called Jacob her y son	Gen 27:42	6996
and the name of the y was Rachel	Gen 29:16	6996
years for Rachel thy y daughter	Gen 29:18	6996
country, to give the y before the	Gen 29:26	6810
and said, Is this your y brother	Gen 43:29	6996
Ephraim's head, who was the y	Gen 48:14	6810
but truly his y brother shall be	Gen 48:19	6996
son of Kenaz, Caleb's y brother	Judg 1:13	6996
son of Kenaz, Caleb's y brother	Judg 3:9	6996
is not her y sister fairer than	Judg 15:2	6996
and the name of the y Michal	1Sa 14:49	6996
over against their y brethren	1Chr 24:31	6996
But now they that are y than I	Job 30:1	6810,3117
thy y sister, that dwelleth at	Eze 16:46	6996
thy sisters, thine elder and thy y	Eze 16:61	6996
the y of them said to his father,	Lk 15:12	3501
not many days after the y son	Lk 15:13	3501
among you, let him be as the y	Lk 22:26	3501
her, The elder shall serve the y	Rom 9:12	1640
and the y men as brethren	1Ti 5:1	3501
the y as sisters, with all purity	1Ti 5:2	3501
But the y widows refuse	1Ti 5:11	3501
therefore that the y women marry	1Ti 5:14	3501
Likewise, ye y, submit yourselves	1Pet 5:5	3501

YOUNGEST

the y is this day with our father	Gen 42:13	6996
except your y brother come hither	Gen 42:15	6996
But bring your y brother unto me	Gen 42:20	6996
the y is this day with our father	Gen 42:32	6996
bring your y brother unto me	Gen 42:34	6996
the y according to his youth	Gen 43:33	6810
cup, in the sack's mouth of the y	Gen 44:2	6996
at the eldest, and left at the y	Gen 44:12	6996
Except your y brother come down	Gen 44:23	6996
if our y brother be with us, then	Gen 44:26	6996
except our y brother be with us	Gen 44:26	6996
in his y son shall he set up the	Josh 6:26	6810
the y son of Jerubbaal was left	Judg 9:5	6996
said, There remaineth yet the y	1Sa 16:11	6996
And David was the y	1Sa 17:14	6996
gates thereof in his y son Segub	1Kin 16:34	6810
save Jehoahaz, the y of his sons	2Chr 21:17	6996
his y son king in his stead	2Chr 22:1	6996

YOUR See APPENDIX.

YOURS See APPENDIX.

YOURSELVES See APPENDIX.

YOUTH

of man's heart is evil from his y	Gen 8:21	5271
the youngest according to his y	Gen 43:33	6812
cattle from our y even until now	Gen 46:34	5271
her father's house, as in her y	Lev 22:13	5271
in her father's house in her y	Num 30:3	5271
being yet in her y in her	Num 30:16	5271
But the y drew not his sword	Judg 8:20	5288
he feared, because he was yet a y	Judg 8:20	5288
for thou art but a y, and he a man	1Sa 17:33	5288
and he a man of war from his y	1Sa 17:33	5271
for he was but a y, and ruddy, and	1Sa 17:42	5288
host, Abner, whose son is this y	1Sa 17:55	5288
befell me from thy y until now	2Sa 19:7	5271
servant fear the LORD from my y	1Kin 18:12	5271
to possess the iniquities of my y	Job 13:26	5271
are full of the sin of his y	Job 20:11	5934
As I was in the days of my y	Job 29:4	2779
Upon my right hand rise the y	Job 30:12	6526
(For from my y he was brought up	Job 31:18	5271

shall return to the days of his *y*	Job 33:25	5934
They die in *y*, and their life is	Job 36:14	5290
Remember not the sins of my *y*	Ps 25:7	5271
thou art my trust from my *y*	Ps 71:5	5271
thou hast taught me from my *y*	Ps 71:17	5271
and ready to die from my *y* up	Ps 88:15	5290
The days of his *y* hast thou	Ps 89:45	5934
so that thy *y* is renewed like the	Ps 103:5	5271
thou hast the dew of thy *y*	Ps 110:3	3208
so are children of the *y*	Ps 127:4	5271
have they afflicted me from my *y*	Ps 129:1	5271
have they afflicted me from my *y*	Ps 129:2	5271
be as plants grown up in their *y*	Ps 144:12	5271
forsaketh the guide of her *y*	Prov 2:17	5271
and rejoice with the wife of thy *y*	Prov 5:18	5271
Rejoice, O young man, in thy *y*	Eccl 11:9	3208
cheer thee in the days of thy *y*	Eccl 11:9	979
for childhood and *y* are vanity	Eccl 11:10	7839
thy Creator in the days of thy *y*	Eccl 12:1	979
thou hast laboured from thy *y*	Is 47:12	5271
even thy merchants, from thy *y*	Is 47:15	5271
shalt forget the shame of thy *y*	Is 54:4	5934
grieved in spirit, and a wife of *y*	Is 54:6	5271
thee, the kindness of thy *y*	Jer 2:2	5271
thou art the guide of my *y*	Jer 3:4	5271
labour of our fathers from our *y*	Jer 3:24	5271
from our *y* even unto this day, and	Jer 3:25	5271
hath been thy manner from thy *y*	Jer 22:21	5271
I did bear the reproach of my *y*	Jer 31:19	5271
done evil before me from their *y*	Jer 32:30	5271
Moab hath been at ease from his *y*	Jer 48:11	5271
that he bear the yoke in his *y*	Lam 3:27	5271
for from my *y* up even till now	Eze 4:14	5271
not remembered the days of thy *y*	Eze 16:22	5271
not remembered the days of thy *y*	Eze 16:43	5271
with thee in the days of thy *y*	Eze 16:60	5271
committed whoredoms in their *y*	Eze 23:3	5271
for in her *y* they lay with her,	Eze 23:8	5271
to remembrance the days of her *y*	Eze 23:19	5271
remembrance the lewdness of thy *y*	Eze 23:21	5271
Egyptians for the paps of thy *y*	Eze 23:21	5271
there, as in the days of her *y*	Hos 2:15	5271
for the husband of her *y*	Joel 1:8	5271
me to keep cattle from my *y*	Zec 13:5	5271
between thee and the wife of thy *y*	Mal 2:14	5271
against the wife of his *y*	Mal 2:15	5271
things have I kept from my *y* up	Mt 19:20	3503
these have I observed from my *y*	Mk 10:20	3503
these have I kept from my *y* up	Lk 18:21	3503
My manner of life from my *y*	Acts 26:4	3503
Let no man despise thy *y*	1Ti 4:12	3503

YOUTHFUL

Flee also *y* lusts	2Ti 2:22	3512

YOUTHS

ones, I discerned among the *y*	Prov 7:7	1121
Even the *y* shall faint and be	Is 40:30	5288

YOU-WARD

world, and more abundantly to *y*	2Cor 1:12	4314,5209
which to *y* is not weak, but is	2Cor 13:3	1519,5209
of God which is given me to *y*	Eph 3:2	1519,5209

Z

ZAANAIM (za-an-a'-im) See ZAANANNIM. *A plain in Naphtali.*

his tent unto the plain of Z	Judg 4:11	6815

ZAANAN (za'-an-an) See ZENAN. *A city of Judah.*

the inhabitant of Z came not	Mic 1:11	6630

ZA-ANANNIM See ZAANAIM.

ZAANANNIM (za-an-an'-nim) *Same as Zaanaim.*

was from Heleph, from Allon to Z	Josh 19:33	6815

ZAAVAN (za'-av-an) See ZAVAN. *A son of Ezer.*

Bilhan, and Z, and Akan	Gen 36:27	2190

ZABAD (za'-bad) See JOSABAD, JOZACHAR.
   1. A son of Nathan.

begat Nathan, and Nathan begat Z	1Chr 2:36	2066
Z begat Ephlal, and Ephlal begat	1Chr 2:37	2066
   2. Son of Tahath.
| Z his son, and Shuthelah his son, | 1Chr 7:21 | 2066 |
   3. A "mighty man" of David.
| the Hittite, Z the son of Ahlai, | 1Chr 11:41 | 2066 |
   4. A son of Shimeath.
| Z the son of Shimeath an | 2Chr 24:26 | 2066 |
   5. A son of Zatta.
| Mattaniah, and Jeremoth, and Z | Ezr 10:27 | 2066 |
   6. A son of Hasham.
| Mattenai, Mattathah, Z, Eliphelet | Ezr 10:33 | 2066 |
   7. A son of Nebo.
| Jeiel, Mattithiah, Z, Zebina, | Ezr 10:43 | 2066 |

ZABBAI (zab'-bahee) See ZACCAI.
   1. Married a foreigner in exile.

Jehohanan, Hananiah, Z, and Athlai	Ezr 10:28	2079
   2. Father of Baruch.
| After him Baruch the son of Z | Neh 3:20 | 2079 |

ZABBUD (zab'-bud) See ZACCUR. *An exile with Ezra.*

Uthai, and Z, and with them seventy	Ezr 8:14	2072

ZABDI (zab'-di) See ZACCHUR, ZICHRI.
   1. Father of Carmi.

the son of Carmi, the son of Z	Josh 7:1	2067
and Z was taken	Josh 7:17	2067
the son of Carmi, the son of Z	Josh 7:18	2067
   2. Son of Shimhi.
| And Jakim, and Zichri, and Z | 1Chr 8:19 | 2067 |
   3. A storekeeper in David's court.
| wine cellars was Z the Shiphmite | 1Chr 27:27 | 2067 |
   4. A Levite.
| the son of Micha, the son of Z | Neh 11:17 | 2067 |

ZABDIEL (zab'-de-el)
   1. Father of Jashobeam.

month was Jashobeam the son of Z	1Chr 27:2	2068
   2. An overseer of priests.
| and their overseer was Z, the son | Neh 11:14 | 2068 |

ZABUD (za'-bud) *A family of exiles.*

Z the son of Nathan was principal	1Kin 4:5	2071

ZABULON (zab'-u-lon) See ZEBULUN. *Greek form of Zebulon.*

sea coast, in the borders of Z	Mt 4:13	2194
The land of Z, and the land of	Mt 4:15	2194
Of the tribe of Z were sealed	Rev 7:8	2194

ZACCAI (zac'-cahee) See ZABBAI. *A family of exiles.*

The children of Z, seven hundred	Ezr 2:9	2140
The children of Z, seven hundred	Neh 7:14	2140

ZACCHAEUS (zak-ke'-us) *A tax collector visited by Jesus.*

behold, there was a man named Z	Lk 19:2	2195
and saw him, and said unto him, Z	Lk 19:5	2195
Z stood, and said unto the Lord	Lk 19:8	2195

ZACCHUR (zac'-cur) See ZACCUR. *Father of Shimei.*

Z his son, Shimei his son	1Chr 4:26	2139

ZACCUR (zac'-cur) See ZABBUD, ZABDI, ZACCHUR, ZICHRI.
   1. Father of Shammua.

of Reuben, Shammua the son of Z	Num 13:4	2139
   2. A sanctuary servant.
| Beno, and Shoham, and Z, and Ibri | 1Chr 24:27 | 2139 |
   3. A son of Asaph.
Z, and Joseph, and Nethaniah, and	1Chr 25:2	2139
The third to Z, he, his sons, and	1Chr 25:10	2139
the son of Michaiah, the son of Z	Neh 12:35	2139
   4. A rebuilder of Jerusalem's wall.
| to them builded Z the son of Imri | Neh 3:2 | 2139 |
   5. A Levite who renewed the covenant.
| Z, Sherebiah, Shebaniah, | Neh 10:12 | 2139 |
   6. Father of Hanan.
| to them was Hanan the son of Z | Neh 13:13 | 2139 |

ZACHARIAH (zak-a-ri'-ah) See ZECHARIAH.
   1. A king of Israel.

Z his son reigned in his stead	2Kin 14:29	2148
of Azariah king of Judah did Z	2Kin 15:8	2148
And the rest of the acts of Z	2Kin 15:11	2148
   2. Father of Abi.
| also was Abi, the daughter of Z | 2Kin 18:2 | 2148 |

ZACHARIAS (zak'-a-ri-as) See ZECHARIAH.
   1. Son of Barachias.

the blood of Z son of Barachias	Mt 23:35	2197
blood of Abel unto the blood of Z	Lk 11:51	2197
   2. Father of John the Baptist.
Judaea, a certain priest named Z	Lk 1:5	2197
when Z saw him, he was troubled,	Lk 1:12	2197
angel said unto him, Fear not, Z	Lk 1:13	2197
Z said unto the angel, Whereby	Lk 1:18	2197
And the people waited for Z	Lk 1:21	2197

And entered into the house of Z............Lk 1:40	2197	
and they called him Z, after the ....Lk 1:59	2197	
his father Z was filled with the ....Lk 1:67	2197	
the son of Z in the wilderness ....Lk 3:2	2197	

ZACHER (za'-kur) See ZECHARIAH. *Father of Gibeon.*
And Gedor, and Ahio, and Z ....1Chr 8:31 — 2144

ZADOK (za'-dok) See ZADOK'S.
1. A priest in David's time.

Z the son of Ahitub, and Ahimelech.......2Sa 8:17	6659
lo Z also, and all the Levites...............2Sa 15:24	6659
And the king said unto Z, Carry...........2Sa 15:25	6659
king said also unto Z the priest...............2Sa 15:27	6659
Z therefore and Abiathar carried 2Sa 15:29	6659
hast thou not there with thee Z 2Sa 15:35	6659
house, thou shalt tell it to Z 2Sa 15:35	6659
Then said Hushai unto Z and to 2Sa 17:15	6659
Then said Ahimaaz the son of Z...........2Sa 18:19	6659
the son of Z yet again to Joab 2Sa 18:22	6659
running of Ahimaaz the son of Z 2Sa 18:27	6659
And king David sent to Z and to 2Sa 19:11	6659
and Z and Abiathar were the priests 2Sa 20:25	6659
But Z the priest, and Benaiah the 1Kin 1:8	6659
Z the priest, and Benaiah the son 1Kin 1:26	6659
Call me Z the priest, and Nathan 1Kin 1:32	6659
let Z the priest and Nathan the 1Kin 1:34	6659
So Z the priest, and Nathan the 1Kin 1:38	6659
Z the priest took an horn of oil 1Kin 1:39	6659
hath sent with him Z the priest 1Kin 1:44	6659
Z the priest and Nathan the 1Kin 1:45	6659
Z the priest did the king put in.............1Kin 2:35	6659
Azariah the son of Z the priest................1Kin 4:2	6659
and Z and Abiathar were the priests 1Kin 4:4	6659
And Ahitub begat Z 1Chr 6:8	6659
and Z begat Ahimaaz.............................1Chr 6:8	6659
Z his son, Ahimaaz his son 1Chr 6:53	6659
And David called for Z and Abiathar 1Chr 15:11	6659
Z the priest, and his brethren the 1Chr 16:39	6659
Z the son of Ahitub, and Abimelech.......1Chr 18:16	6659
both Z of the sons of Eleazar, and,.........1Chr 24:3	6659
Z the priest, and Ahimelech the 1Chr 24:6	6659
presence of David the king, and Z.........1Chr 24:31	6659
of the Aaronites, Z 1Chr 27:17	6659
chief governor, and Z to be priest 1Chr 29:22	6659
of the house of Z answered him 2Chr 31:10	6659
The son of Shallum, the son of Z ....Ezr 7:2	6659
these are the sons of Z among the ....Eze 40:46	6659
Levites that be of the seed of Z ....Eze 43:19	6659
the Levites, the sons of Z ....Eze 44:15	6659
are sanctified the sons of Z...................Eze 48:11	6659
2. Father of Jerusha.	
was Jerusha, the daughter of Z 2Kin 15:33	6659
was Jerushah, the daughter of Z............2Chr 27:1	6659
3. Son of Ahitub.	
And Ahitub begat Z, and Zadok begat .. 1Chr 6:12	6659
begat Zadok, and Z begat Shallum,.......1Chr 6:12	6659
son of Meshullam, the son of Z 1Chr 9:11	6659
4. A warrior in David's army.	
And Z, a young man mighty of 1Chr 12:28	6659
5. The son of Baana.	
them repaired Z the son of Baana..........Neh 3:4	6659
6. A priest who rebuilt the wall.	
After them repaired Z the son of ....Neh 3:29	6659
7. A renewer of the covenant.	
Meshezabeel, Z, Jaddua, ...Neh 10:21	6659
8. A son of Meraioth.	
son of Meshullam, the son of Z ....Neh 11:11	6659
9. A Temple servant.	
Z the scribe, and of the Levites,.............Neh 13:13	6659

ZADOKITES See ZADOK'S.

ZADOK'S (za'-doks) Refers to Zadok 1.
their two sons, Ahimaaz Z son ....2Sa 15:36 — 6659

ZAHAM (za'-ham) *A son of Rehoboam.*
Jeush, and Shamariah, and Z ....2Chr 11:19 — 2093

ZAIR (za'-ur) *A city in Edom.*
So Joram went over to Z, and all ....2Kin 8:21 — 6811

ZALAPH (za'-laf) *Father of Hanun.*
and Hanun the sixth son of Z ....Neh 3:30 — 6764

ZALMON (zal'-mon) See ILAI, SALMON.
1. A hill in Ephraim.
Abimelech gat him up to mount Z ....Judg 9:48 — 6756
2. A "mighty man" of David.
Z the Ahohite, Maharai the....................2Sa 23:28 — 6756

ZALMONAH (zal'-mo-nah) *An Israelite encampment in the wilderness.*
from mount Hor, and pitched in Z...........Num 33:41 — 6758
And they departed from Z, and ....Num 33:42 — 6758

ZALMUNNA (zal-mun'-nah) *A Midianite king.*

and I am pursuing after Zebah and Z ...Judg 8:5	6759
Z now in thine hand, that we ....Judg 8:6	6759
Z into mine hand, then I will...................Judg 8:7	6759
Z were in Karkor, and their hosts ....Judg 8:10	6759
Z fled, he pursued after them, and.........Judg 8:12	6759
two kings of Midian, Zebah and Z ....Judg 8:12	6759
and said, Behold Zebah and Z ....Judg 8:15	6759
Z now in thine hand, that we ....Judg 8:15	6759
Then said he unto Zebah and Z.............Judg 8:18	6759
Z said, Rise thou, and fall upon ....Judg 8:21	6759
Gideon arose, and slew Zebah and Z ....Judg 8:21	6759
their princes as Zebah, and as Z ....Ps 83:11	6759

ZAMZUMMIMS (zam-zum'-mims) See ZUZIMS. *A tribe in Canaan.*
and the Ammonites call them Z ....Deut 2:20 — 2157

ZAMZUMMITES See ZAMZUMMIMS.

ZANOAH (za-no'-ah)
1. A city on the plain of Judah.
And Z, and En-gannim, Tappuah, and ...Josh 15:34 — 2182
Hanun, and the inhabitants of Z............Neh 3:13 — 2182
Z, Adullam, and in their villages, ...Neh 11:30 — 2182
2. A city in the hills of Judah.
And Jezreel, and Jokdeam, and Z ....Josh 15:56 — 2182
3. A descendant of Caleb.
and Jekuthiel the father of Z..................1Chr 4:18 — 2182

ZAPHENATH-PANEAH See ZAPHNATH-PAANEAH.

ZAPHNATH-PAANEAH (zaf-nath-pa-a-ne'-ah) *Name given to Joseph by Pharaoh.*
And Pharaoh called Joseph's name Z ....Gen 41:45 — 6847

ZAPHON (za'-fon) *A city in Gad.*
and Beth-nimrah, and Succoth, and Z ...Josh 13:27 — 6829

ZARA (za'-rah) See ZARAH, ZERAH. *Greek form of Zarah; an ancestor of Jesus.*
Judas begat Phares and Z of Thamar....Mt 1:3 — 2196

ZARAH (za'-rah) See ZARA, ZERAH. *A son of Judah.*
and his name was called Z ....Gen 38:30 — 2226
Onan, and Shelah, and Pharez, and Z...Gen 46:12 — 2226

ZAREAH (za'-re-ah) See ZAREATHITES, ZORAH. *A city in Judah.*
And at En-rimmon, and at Z, and at ......Neh 11:29 — 6881

ZAREATHITES (za'-re-ath-ites) See ZORATHITES. *Descendants of Shobal.*
of them came the Z, and the ....1Chr 2:53 — 6882

ZARED (za'-red) See ZERED. *A brook near the Dead Sea.*
and pitched in the valley of Z ....Num 21:12 — 2218

ZAREPHATH (zar'-e-fath) See SAREPTA. *A city in Phoenicia.*
Arise, get thee to Z, which ....1Kin 17:9 — 6886
So he arose and went to Z ....1Kin 17:10 — 6886
of the Canaanites, even unto Z...............Obad 20 — 6886

ZARETAN (zar'-e-tan) See ZARTANAH, ZEREDATHAH. *A city in Ephraim.*
the city Adam, that is beside Z ....Josh 3:16 — 6891

ZARETHAN See ZARTHAN.

ZARETH-SHAHAR (za'-reth-sha-har) *A city in Reuben.*
Z in the mount of the valley,...................Josh 13:19 — 6890

ZARHITES (zar'-hites)
1. Descendants of Zerah, the Simeonite.
Of Zerah, the family of the Z ....Num 26:13 — 2227
and he took the family of the Z ....Josh 7:17 — 2227
the family of the Z man by man ....Josh 7:17 — 2227
Sibbecai the Hushathite, of the Z..........1Chr 27:11 — 2227
the Netophathite, of the Z ....1Chr 27:13 — 2227
2. Descendants of Zerah, son of Judah.
of Zerah, the family of the Z...................Num 26:20 — 2227

ZARTANAH (zar'-ta-nah) See ZARETAN, ZARTHAN. *Same as Zaretan.*
which is by Z beneath Jezreel,................1Kin 4:12 — 6891

ZARTHAN (zar'-than) See ZARETAN, ZARTANAH. *Same as Zaretan.*
clay ground between Succoth and Z ......1Kin 7:46 — 6891

ZATTHU (zath'-u) See ZATTU. *A renewer of the covenant.*
Parosh, Pahath-moab, Elam, Z ....Neh 10:14 — 2240

ZATTU (zat'-tu) See ZATTHU. *A family of exiles.*
The children of Z, nine hundred ....Ezr 2:8 — 2240
And of the sons of Z ....Ezr 10:27 — 2240
The children of Z, eight hundred ....Neh 7:13 — 2240

ZAVAN (za'-van) See ZAAVAN. *Son of Ezer.*
Bilhan, and Z, and Jakan 1Chr 1:42   2190

ZAZA (za'-zah) *A son of Jonathan.*
Peleth, and Z 1Chr 2:33   2117

ZEAL
his z to the children of Israel 2Sa 21:2   7065
with me, and see my z for the LORD 2Kin 10:16   7068
the z of the LORD of hosts shall 2Kin 19:31   7068
For the z of thine house hath ....Ps 69:9   7068
My z hath consumed me, because ....Ps 119:139   7068
The z of the LORD of hosts will ....Is 9:7   7068
the z of the LORD of hosts shall ....Is 37:32   7068
and was clad with z as a cloke ....Is 59:17   7068
where is thy z and thy strength, ...Is 63:15   7068
I the LORD have spoken it in my z ....Eze 5:13   7068
The z of thine house hath eaten ....Jn 2:17   2205
record that they have a z of God ....Rom 10:2   2205
what vehement desire, yea, what z........2Cor 7:11   2205
your z hath provoked very many 2Cor 9:2   2205
Concerning z, persecuting the ....Phil 3:6   2205
that he hath a great z for you ....Col 4:13   2205

ZEALOT See ZELOTES.

ZEALOUS
while he was z for my sake among........Num 25:11   7065
because he was z for his God................Num 25:13   7065
and they are all z of the law.................Acts 21:20   2207
was z toward God, as ye all are............Acts 22:3   2207
as ye are z of spiritual gifts.................1Cor 14:12   2207
being more exceedingly z of the ....Gal 1:14   2207
peculiar people, z of good works ....Titus 2:14   2207
be z therefore, and repent ....Rev 3:19   2206

ZEALOUSLY
They z affect you, but not well ....Gal 4:17   2206
But it is good to be z affected ....Gal 4:18   2206

ZEBADIAH (zeb-ad-i'-ah)
   1. Grandson of Elpael.
And Z, and Arad, and Ader, ...1Chr 8:15   2069
   2. A son of Elpael.
And Z, and Meshullam, and Hezeki 1Chr 8:17   2069
   3. A warrior in David's army.
And Joelah, and Z, the sons of...............1Chr 12:7   2069
   4. A Levite gatekeeper.
Z the third, Jathniel the fourth, ...1Chr 26:2   2069
   5. A son of Asahel.
of Joab, and Z his son after him 1Chr 27:7   2069
   6. A messenger for King Jehoshaphat.
even Shemaiah, and Nethaniah, and Z .2Chr 17:8   2069
   7. Son of Ishmael.
Z the son of Ishmael, the ruler 2Chr 19:11   2069
   8. A family of exiles.
Z the son of Michael, and with him.......Ezr 8:8   2069
   9. Married a foreigner in exile.
Hanani, and Z ....Ezr 10:20   2069

ZEBAH (ze'-bah) *A king of Midian.*
faint, and I am pursuing after Z ....Judg 8:5   2078
Succoth said, Are the hands of Z ....Judg 8:6   2078
when the LORD hath delivered Z ....Judg 8:7   2078
Now Z and Zalmunna were in Karkor, ...Judg 8:10   2078
And when Z and Zalmunna fled, he ......Judg 8:12   2078
took the two kings of Midian, Z...............Judg 8:12   2078
men of Succoth, and said, Behold Z ......Judg 8:15   2078
me, saying, Are the hands of Z ....Judg 8:15   2078
Then said he unto Z and Zalmunna, ...Judg 8:18   2078
Then Z and Zalmunna said, Rise ....Judg 8:21   2078
And Gideon arose, and slew Z ....Judg 8:21   2078
yea, all their princes as Z.......................Ps 83:11   2078

ZEBAIM (ze-ba'-im) *Residence of some exiles in Babylonia.*
the children of Pochereth of Z ....Ezr 2:57   6380
the children of Pochereth of Z ....Neh 7:59   6380

ZEBEDEE (zeb'-e-dee) See ZEBEDEE'S. *Father of James and John.*
two brethren, James the son of Z ....Mt 4:21   2199
in a ship with Z their father ....Mt 4:21   2199
James the son of Z, and John his ....Mt 10:2   2199
him Peter and the two sons of Z ....Mt 26:37   2199
thence, he saw James the son of Z ....Mk 1:19   2199
they left their father Z in the..................Mk 1:20   2199
And James the son of Z, and John ....Mk 3:17   2199
And James and John, the sons of Z ....Mk 10:35   2199
James, and John, the sons of Z ....Lk 5:10   2199
Cana in Galilee, and the sons of Z ....Jn 21:2   2199

ZEBEDEE'S (zeb'-e-dees)
of Z children with her sons....................Mt 20:20   2199
and the mother of Z children ....Mt 27:56   2199

ZEBIDAH See ZEBUDAH.

ZEBINA (ze-bi'-nah) *Married a foreigner in exile.*
Jeiel, Mattithiah, Zabad, Z.....................Ezr 10:43   2081

ZEBOIIM (ze-boy'-im) See ZEBOIM. *City destroyed with Sodom and Gomorrah.*
of Admah, and Shemeber king of Z........Gen 14:2   6636
king of Admah, and the king of Z...........Gen 14:8   6636

ZEBOIM (ze-bo'-im) See ZEBOIIM.
   1. Same as Zeboiim.
and Gomorrah, and Admah, and Z ....Gen 10:19   6636
Sodom, and Gomorrah, Admah, and Z ..Deut 29:23   6636
how shall I set thee as Z ....Hos 11:8   6636
   2. A city in Benjamin.
valley of Z toward the wilderness 1Sa 13:18   6650
Hadid, Z, Neballat,.................................Neh 11:34   6650

ZEBUDAH (ze-bu'-dah) *Mother of King Jehoshaphat.*
And his mother's name was Z.................2Kin 23:36   2081

ZEBUL (ze'-bul) *A ruler of Shechem.*
and Z his officer ....Judg 9:28   2083
when Z the ruler of the city....................Judg 9:30   2083
Gaal saw the people, he said to Z...........Judg 9:36   2083
Z said unto him, Thou seest the ....Judg 9:36   2083
Then said Z unto him, Where is ....Judg 9:38   2083
Z thrust out Gaal and his brethren.........Judg 9:41   2083

ZEBULONITE (zeb'-u-lon-ite) See ZEBULONITES. *A descendant of Zebulun 1.*
And after him Elon, a Z, judged ....Judg 12:11   2075
And Elon the Z died, and was buried ......Judg 12:12   2075

ZEBULUN (zeb'-u-lun) See ZABULON, ZEBULONITE, ZEBULONITES.
   1. A son of Jacob.
and she called his name Z ....Gen 30:20   2074
Levi, and Judah, and Issachar, and Z....Gen 35:23   2074
And the sons of Z ....Gen 46:14   2074
Z shall dwell at the haven of the............Gen 49:13   2074
Issachar, Z, and Benjamin,....................Ex 1:3   2074
Levi, and Judah, Issachar, and Z 1Chr 2:1   2074
   2. Descendants of Zebulun.
Of Z; Eliab the...................................... Num 1:9   2074
Of the children of Z, by their..................Num 1:30   2074
of them, even of the tribe of Z...............Num 1:31   2074
Then the tribe of Z ....Num 2:7   2074
be captain of the children of Z...............Num 2:7   2074
prince of the children of Z ....Num 7:24   2074
of Z was Eliab the son of Helon ....Num 10:16   2074
Of the tribe of Z, Gaddiel the ....Num 13:10   2074
Of the sons of Z after their ....Num 26:26   2074
of the tribe of the children of Z ....Num 34:25   2074
Reuben, Gad, and Asher, and Z,............Deut 27:13   2074
And of Zebulun he said, Rejoice, Z ....Deut 33:18   2074
of Z according to their families...............Josh 19:10   2074
of Z according to their families...............Josh 19:16   2074
to Beth-dagon, and reacheth to Z ....Josh 19:27   2074
reacheth to Z on the south side, ...Josh 19:34   2074
of Gad, and out of the tribe of Z ....Josh 21:7   2074
Levites, out of the tribe of Z ....Josh 21:34   2074
Neither did Z drive out the ....Judg 1:30   2074
Naphtali and of the children of Z............Judg 4:6   2074
And Barak called Z and Naphtali to ......Judg 4:10   2074
out of Z they that handle the pen ....Judg 5:14   2074
Z and Naphtali were a people that.........Judg 5:18   2074
messengers unto Asher, and unto Z ......Judg 6:35   2074
in Aijalon in the country of Z ....Judg 12:12   2074
of Gad, and out of the tribe of Z 1Chr 6:63   2074
were given out of the tribe of Z 1Chr 6:77   2074
Of Z, such as went forth to.....................1Chr 12:33   2074
them, even unto Issachar and Z 1Chr 12:40   2074
Of Z, Ishmaiah the son of Obadiah........1Chr 27:19   2074
Ephraim and Manasseh even unto Z 2Chr 30:10   2074
of Z humbled themselves, and came 2Chr 30:11   2074
and Manasseh, Issachar, and Z 2Chr 30:18   2074
their council, the princes of Z ....Ps 68:27   2074
lightly afflicted the land of Z...................Is 9:1   2074
unto the west side, Z a portion ....Eze 48:26   2074
And by the border of Z, from the ....Eze 48:27   2074
gate of Issachar, one gate of Z...............Eze 48:33   2074

ZEBULUNITES (zeb'-u-lun-ites) *Descendants of Zebulun.*
Z according to those that were ....Num 26:27   2075

ZECHARIAH (zek-a-ri'-ah) See ZACCUR, ZACHARIAH, ZACHARIAS, ZACHER.
   1. A chief Reubenite.
were the chief, Jeiel, and Z 1Chr 5:7   2148
   2. A Levite gatekeeper.
Z the son of Meshelemiah was................1Chr 9:21   2148
Z the firstborn, Jediael the 1Chr 26:2   2148

Z

Then for Z his son, a wise 1Chr 26:14 2148
was Abijah, the daughter of Z 2Chr 29:1 2148
   3. A Benjamite.
And Gedor, and Ahio, and Z, and 1Chr 9:37 2148
   4. A Levite musician.
brethren of the second degree, Z 1Chr 15:18 2148
And Z, and Aziel, and Shemiramoth, ... 1Chr 15:20 2148
Asaph the chief, and next to him Z 1Chr 16:5 2148
   5. A Tabernacle priest.
and Nethaneel, and Amasai, and Z 1Chr 15:24 2148
   6. A son of Isshiah.
sons of Isshiah; Z 1Chr 24:25 2148
   7. Son of Hosah.
Tebaliah the third, Z the fourth 1Chr 26:11 2148
   8. A chief of Manasseh.
in Gilead, Iddo the son of Z 1Chr 27:21 2148
   9. A messenger of King Jehoshaphat.
Ben-hail, and to Obadiah, and to Z 2Chr 17:7 2148
   10. Father of Jehaziel.
Then upon Jahaziel the son of Z 2Chr 20:14 2148
   11. A son of Jehoshaphat.
Azariah, and Jehiel, and Z 2Chr 21:2 2148
   12. Son of Jehoida.
the Spirit of God came upon Z the 2Chr 24:20 2148
   13. A prophet in King Uzziah's time.
And he sought God in the days of Z 2Chr 26:5 2148
   14. A Levite who cleansed the Temple.
Z, and Mattaniah 2Chr 29:13 2148
   15. An overseer of the Temple repairs.
and Z and Meshullam, of the sons of 2Chr 34:12 2148
   16. A prince of Judah.
Hilkiah and Z and Jehiel, rulers of 2Chr 35:8 2148
   17. A prophet in Judah.
Z the son of Iddo, prophesied .... Ezr 5:1 2148
the prophet and Z the son of Iddo .... Ezr 6:14 2148
came the word of the LORD unto Z .... Zec 1:1 2148
came the word of the LORD unto Z .... Zec 1:7 2148
Z in the fourth day of the ninth .... Zec 7:1 2148
the word of the LORD came unto Z .... Zec 7:8 2148
   18. A son of Pharosh.
sons of Pharosh; Z .... Ezr 8:3 2148
   19. A son of Bebai.
Z the son of Bebai, and with him .... Ezr 8:11 2148
Elnathan, and for Nathan, and for Z...... Ezr 8:16 2148
   20. Married a foreigner in exile.
Mattaniah, Z, and Jehiel, and Abdi, ... Ezr 10:26 2148
   21. A prince who aided Ezra.
and Hashum, and Hashbadana, Z .... Neh 8:4 2148
   22. A descendant of Pharez.
the son of Uzziah, the son of Z .... Neh 11:4 2148
   23. A son of Shiloni.
the son of Joiarib, the son of Z .... Neh 11:5 2148
   24. Father of a resettler in Jerusalem.
the son of Amzi, the son of Z .... Neh 11:12 2148
   25. A priest in Joiakim's time.
Of Iddo, Z .... Neh 12:16 2148
   26. A priest who dedicated the wall.
Z the son of Jonathan, the son of .... Neh 12:35 2148
Miniamin, Michaiah, Elioenai, Z .... Neh 12:41 2148
   27. Son of Jeber.
and Z the son of Jeberechiah .... Is 8:2 2148

ZECHER See ZACHER.

ZEDAD *(ze'-dad) A place near Hamath.*
forth of the border shall be to Z .... Num 34:8 6657
way of Hethlon, as men go to Z .... Eze 47:15 6657

ZEDEKIAH *(zed-e-ki'-ah)* See MATTANIAH, ZEDEKIAH'S, ZIDKIJAH.
   1. A false prophet.
Z the son of Chenaanah made him 1Kin 22:11 6667
But Z the son of Chenaanah went 1Kin 22:24 6667
Z the son of Chenaanah had made 2Chr 18:10 6667
Then Z the son of Chenaanah came 2Chr 18:23 6667
   2. Name given to Mattaniah by Nebuchadnezzar.
stead, and changed his name to Z 2Kin 24:17 6667
Z was twenty and one years old 2Kin 24:18 6667
that Z rebelled against the king 2Kin 24:20 6667
unto the eleventh year of king Z 2Kin 25:2 6667
the sons of Z before his eyes 2Kin 25:7 6667
eyes, and put out the eyes of Z 2Kin 25:7 6667
the second Jehoiakim, the third Z 1Chr 3:15 6667
made Z his brother king over 2Chr 36:10 6667
Z was one and twenty years old 2Chr 36:11 6667
Z the son of Josiah king of Judah .... Jer 1:3 6667
when king Z sent unto him Pashur .... Jer 21:1 6667
unto them, Thus shall ye say to Z .... Jer 21:3 6667
I will deliver Z king of Judah .... Jer 21:7 6667
So will I give Z the king of .... Jer 24:8 6667
to Jerusalem unto Z king of Judah .... Jer 27:3 6667
I spake also to Z king of Judah .... Jer 27:12 6667

of the reign of Z king of Judah .... Jer 28:1 6667
(whom Z king of Judah sent unto .... Jer 29:3 6667
the tenth year of Z king of Judah .... Jer 32:1 6667
For Z king of Judah had shut him .... Jer 32:3 6667
Z king of Judah shall not escape .... Jer 32:4 6667
And he shall lead Z to Babylon .... Jer 32:5 6667
speak to Z king of Judah, and tell .... Jer 34:2 6667
of the LORD, O Z king of Judah .... Jer 34:4 6667
unto Z king of Judah in Jerusalem .... Jer 34:6 6667
after that the king Z had made a .... Jer 34:8 6667
Z king of Judah and his princes .... Jer 34:21 6667
king Z the son of Josiah reigned .... Jer 37:1 6667
Z the king sent Jehucal the son .... Jer 37:3 6667
Then Z the king sent, and took him .... Jer 37:17 6667
Jeremiah said unto king Z .... Jer 37:18 6667
Then Z the king commanded that .... Jer 37:21 6667
Then Z the king said, Behold, he .... Jer 38:5 6667
Then Z the king sent, and took .... Jer 38:14 6667
Then Jeremiah said unto Z .... Jer 38:15 6667
So Z the king sware secretly unto .... Jer 38:16 6667
Then said Jeremiah unto Z .... Jer 38:17 6667
Z the king said unto Jeremiah, I .... Jer 38:19 6667
Then said Z unto Jeremiah, Let no .... Jer 38:24 6667
the ninth year of Z king of Judah .... Jer 39:1 6667
And in the eleventh year of Z .... Jer 39:2 6667
that when Z the king of Judah saw .... Jer 39:4 6667
overtook Z in the plains of .... Jer 39:5 6667
of Z in Riblah before his eyes .... Jer 39:6 6667
as I gave Z king of Judah into .... Jer 44:30 6667
of the reign of Z king of Judah .... Jer 49:34 6667
when he went with Z the king of .... Jer 51:59 6667
Z was one and twenty years old .... Jer 52:1 6667
that Z rebelled against the king .... Jer 52:3 6667
unto the eleventh year of king Z .... Jer 52:5 6667
overtook Z in the plains of .... Jer 52:8 6667
the sons of Z before his eyes .... Jer 52:10 6667
Then he put out the eyes of Z .... Jer 52:11 6667
   3. Grandson of Jehoiakim.
Jeconiah his son, Z his son 1Chr 3:16 6667
   4. A false prophet denounced by Jeremiah.
of Z the son of Maaseiah, which .... Jer 29:21 6667
saying, The LORD make thee like Z .... Jer 29:22 6667
   5. A prince of Judah.
Z the son of Hananiah, and all the......... Jer 36:12 6667

ZEDEKIAH'S *(zed-e-ki'-ahs) Refers to Zedekiah 2.*
Moreover he put out Z eyes .... Jer 39:7 6667

ZEEB *(ze'-eb) A Midianite prince.*
of the Midianites, Oreb and Z .... Judg 7:25 2062
Z they slew at the winepress of.............. Judg 7:25 2062
they slew at the winepress of Z .... Judg 7:25 2062
Z to Gideon on the other side .... Judg 7:25 2062
the princes of Midian, Oreb and Z .... Judg 8:3 2062
their nobles like Oreb, and like Z .... Ps 83:11 2062

ZELA See ZELAH.

ZELAH *(ze'-lah) A city in Benjamin.*
And Z, Eleph, and Jebusi, which is .... Josh 18:28 6762
in the country of Benjamin in Z 2Sa 21:14 6762

ZELEK *(ze'-lek) A "mighty man" of David.*
Z the Ammonite, Nahari the 2Sa 23:37 6768
Z the Ammonite, Naharai the 1Chr 11:39 6768

ZELOPHEHAD *(ze-lo'-fe-had) Son of Hepher.*
Z the son of Hepher had no sons, ... Num 26:33 6765
of the daughters of Z were Mahlah .... Num 26:33 6765
Then came the daughters of Z .... Num 27:1 6765
The daughters of Z speak right .... Num 27:7 6765
Z our brother unto his daughters .... Num 36:2 6765
concerning the daughters of Z .... Num 36:6 6765
Moses, so did the daughters of Z .... Num 36:10 6765
and Noah, the daughters of Z .... Num 36:11 6765
But Z, the son of Hepher, the son .... Josh 17:3 6765
and the name of the second was Z 1Chr 7:15 6765
and Z had daughters 1Chr 7:15 6765

ZELOTES *(ze-lo-teze)* See CANAANITE, SIMON. *Surname of Simon, disciple of Jesus.*
of Alphaeus, and Simon called Z .... Lk 6:15 2208
the son of Alphaeus, and Simon Z .... Acts 1:13 2208

ZELZAH *(zel'-zah) A city in Benjamin.*
in the border of Benjamin at Z 1Sa 10:2 6766

ZEMARAIM *(zem-a-ra'-im)* See ZEMARITE.
   1. A city in Benjamin.
And Beth-arabah, and Z, and Beth-el,.... Josh 18:22 6787
   2. A mountain in Ephraim.
And Abijah stood up upon mount Z 2Chr 13:4 6787

ZEMARITE *A descendant of Canaan.*
And the Arvadite, and the Z .... Gen 10:18 6786
And the Arvadite, and the Z 1Chr 1:16 6786

ZEMIRA (ze-mi'-rah) *A son of Becher.*
Z, and Joash, and Eliezer, and 1Chr 7:8   2160

ZEMIRAH See ZEMIRA.

ZENAN (ze'-nan) See ZAANAN. *A city in Judah.*
Z, and Hadashah, and Migdal-gad, ... Josh 15:37   6799

ZENAS (ze'-nas) *A Christian lawyer.*
Bring Z the lawyer and Apollos on .... Titus 3:13   2211

ZEPHANIAH (zef-a-ni'-ah)
   1. A priest in exile.
Z the second priest, and the three 2Kin 25:18   6846
Z the son of Maaseiah the priest, ... Jer 21:1   6846
to Z the son of Maaseiah the .... Jer 29:25   6846
Z the priest read this letter in .... Jer 29:29   6846
Z the son of Maaseiah the priest .... Jer 37:3   6846
Z the second priest, and the three .... Jer 52:24   6846
   2. An ancestor of Samuel.
the son of Azariah, the son of Z 1Chr 6:36   6846
   3. A prophet.
came unto Z the son of Cushi .... Zeph 1:1   6846
   4. Son of Josiah the priest.
the house of Josiah the son of Z .... Zec 6:10   6846
Jedaiah, and to Hen the son of Z........... Zec 6:14   6846

ZEPHATH (ze'-fath) See HORMAH. *A city in Simeon.*
the Canaanites that inhabited Z .... Judg 1:17   6857

ZEPHATHAH (zef-a-thah) *A valley in Judah.*
in the valley of Z at Mareshah............ 2Chr 14:10   6859

ZEPHI (ze'-fi) See ZEPHO. *Son of Eliphaz.*
Teman, and Omar, Z, and Gatam, ... 1Chr 1:36   6825

ZEPHO (ze'-fo) See ZEPHI. *Same as Zephi.*
of Eliphaz were Teman, Omar, Z .... Gen 36:11   6825
duke Teman, duke Omar, duke Z .... Gen 36:15   6825

ZEPHON (ze'-fon) See ZEPHONITES, ZIPHION. *A son of Gad.*
of Z, the family of the................................ Num 26:15   6827

ZEPHONITES (zef-on-ites) *Descendants of Zephon.*
of Zephon, the family of the Z .... Num 26:15   6831

ZER (zur) *A city in Naphtali.*
the fenced cities are Ziddim, Z .... Josh 19:35   6863

ZERAH (ze'-rah) See EZRAHITE, ZARAH, ZARHITES, ZOHAR.
   1. A son of Reuel.
and Z, Shammah, and Mizzah .... Gen 36:13   2226
duke Nahath, duke Z, duke Shammah .. Gen 36:17   2226
Nahath, Z, Shammah, and Mizzah........ 1Chr 1:37   2226
   2. Father of Jobab.
Jobab the son of Z of Bozrah .... Gen 36:33   2226
Jobab the son of Z of Bozrah 1Chr 1:44   2226
   3. Son of Judah.
of Z, the family of the Zarhites .... Num 26:20   2226
the son of Zabdi, the son of Z .... Josh 7:1   2226
the son of Zabdi, the son of Z .... Josh 7:18   2226
with him, took Achan the son of Z .... Josh 7:24   2226
son of Z commit a trespass in the .... Josh 22:20   2226
in law bare him Pharez and Z 1Chr 2:4   2226
And the sons of Z 1Chr 2:6   2226
And of the sons of Z 1Chr 9:6   2226
children of Z the son of Judah .... Neh 11:24   2226
   4. A son of Simeon.
Of Z, the family of the Zarhites .... Num 26:13   2226
were, Nemuel, and Jamin, Jarib, Z 1Chr 4:24   2226
   5. Son of Iddo.
Z his son, Jeaterai his son 1Chr 6:21   2226
   6. Father of Ethni.
The son of Ethni, the son of Z 1Chr 6:41   2226
   7. An Ethiopian king.
there came out against them Z the 2Chr 14:9   2226

ZERAHIAH (zer-a-hi'-ah)
   1. An ancestor of Ezra.
And Uzzi begat Z, and Z....................... 1Chr 6:6   2228
Z, and Z begat Meraioth, ... 1Chr 6:6   2228
his son, Uzzi his son, Z his son,........... 1Chr 6:51   2228
The son of Z, the son of Uzzi,................ Ezr 7:4   2228
   2. Father of Elihoenai.
Elihoenai the son of Z, and with .... Ezr 8:4   2228

ZERAHITE See ZARHITES.

ZERED (ze'-red) See ZARED. *Same as Zared.*
I, and get you over the brook Z.............. Deut 2:13   2218
And we went over the brook Z .... Deut 2:13   2218
we were come over the brook Z .... Deut 2:14   2218

ZEREDA (zer'-e-dah) *A city north of Mt. Ephraim.*
son of Nebat, an Ephrathite of Z 1Kin 11:26   6868

ZEREDAH See ZEREDATHAH.

ZEREDATHAH (ze-red'-a-thah) See ZARTHAN, ZERERATH. *A city in Manasseh.*
clay ground between Succoth and Z 2Chr 4:17   6868

ZERERAH See ZERERATH.

ZERERATH (zer'-e-rath) See ZARTHAN, ZEREDATHAH. *A district in Manasseh.*
host fled to Beth-shittah in Z .... Judg 7:22   6888

ZERESH (ze'-resh) *Wife of Haman.*
for his friends, and Z his wife .... Est 5:10   2238
Then said Z his wife and all his.............. Est 5:14   2238
And Haman told Z his wife and all .... Est 6:13   2238
Z his wife unto him, If Mordecai .... Est 6:13   2238

ZERETH (ze'-reth) *A descendant of Judah.*
And the sons of Helah were, Z 1Chr 4:7   6889

ZERETH-SHAHAR See ZERETH.

ZERI (ze'-ri) See IZRI. *Son of Jeduthun.*
Gedaliah, and Z, and Jeshaiah, ... 1Chr 25:3   6874

ZEROR (ze'-ror) *Ancestor of King Saul.*
the son of Abiel, the son of Z................. 1Sa 9:1   6872

ZERUAH (ze-ru'-ah) *Mother of Jeroboam 1.*
whose mother's name was Z 1Kin 11:26   6871

ZERUBBABEL (ze-rub'-ba-bel) See SHESHBAZZAR, ZOROBABEL. *A leader of a group of exiles.*
And the sons of Pedaiah were, Z 1Chr 3:19   2216
and the sons of Z.................................... 1Chr 3:19   2216
Which came with Z .... Ezr 2:2   2216
Z the son of Shealtiel, and his............... Ezr 3:2   2216
began Z the son of Shealtiel, and .... Ezr 3:8   2216
Then they came to Z, and to the .... Ezr 4:2   2216
But Z, and Jeshua, and the rest of........ Ezr 4:3   2216
Then rose up Z the son of .... Ezr 5:2   2217
Who came with Z, Jeshua, Nehemiah.... Neh 7:7   2216
up with Z the son of Shealtiel .... Neh 12:1   2216
And all Israel in the days of Z .... Neh 12:47   2216
unto Z the son of Shealtiel .... Hag 1:1   2216
Then Z the son of Shealtiel, and .... Hag 1:12   2216
spirit of Z the son of Shealtiel .... Hag 1:14   2216
Speak now to Z the son of .... Hag 2:2   2216
Yet now be strong, O Z, saith the .... Hag 2:4   2216
Speak to Z, governor of Judah,.............. Hag 2:21   2216
of hosts, will I take thee, O Z .... Hag 2:23   2216
is the word of the LORD unto Z............... Zec 4:6   2216
before Z thou shalt become a................ Zec 4:7   2216
The hands of Z have laid the.................. Zec 4:9   2216
in the hand of Z with those seven.......... Zec 4:10   2216

ZERUIAH (ze-ru-i'-ah) *Sister of David.*
and to Abishai the son of Z.................... 1Sa 26:6   6870
And Joab the son of Z, and the 2Sa 2:13   6870
there were three sons of Z there 2Sa 2:18   6870
the sons of Z be too hard for me............ 2Sa 3:39   6870
Joab the son of Z was over the 2Sa 8:16   6870
Now Joab the son of Z perceived........... 2Sa 14:1   6870
the son of Z unto the king 2Sa 16:9   6870
I to do with you, ye sons of Z 2Sa 16:10   6870
sister to Z Joab's mother........................ 2Sa 17:25   6870
the hand of Abishai the son of Z............ 2Sa 18:2   6870
But Abishai the son of Z answered........ 2Sa 19:21   6870
I to do with you, ye sons of Z 2Sa 19:22   6870
the son of Z succoured him 2Sa 21:17   6870
the brother of Joab, the son of Z............ 2Sa 23:18   6870
armourbearer to Joab the son of Z........ 2Sa 23:37   6870
conferred with Joab the son of Z 1Kin 2:5   6870
what Joab the son of Z did to me 1Kin 2:5   6870
priest, and for Joab the son of Z 1Kin 2:22   6870
Whose sisters were Z, and Abigail 1Chr 2:16   6870
And the sons of Z 1Chr 2:16   6870
Joab the son of Z went first up 1Chr 11:6   6870
armourbearer of Joab the son of Z 1Chr 11:39   6870
Abishai the son Z slew the 1Chr 18:12   6870
Joab the son of Z was over the 1Chr 18:15   6870
son of Ner, and Joab the son of Z 1Chr 26:28   6870
Joab the son of Z began to number........ 1Chr 27:24   6870

ZETHAM (ze'-tham) *A descendant of Laadan.*
the chief was Jehiel, and Z 1Chr 23:8   2241
Z, and Joel his brother, which 1Chr 26:22   2241

ZETHAN (ze'-than) *A son of Bilhan.*
and Ehud, and Chenaanah, and Z........ 1Chr 7:10   2133

ZETHAR (ze'-thar) *A servant of King Ahasuerus.*
Harbona, Bigtha, and Abagtha, Z .... Est 1:10   2242

ZEUS See MERCURIUS.

ZIA (zi'-ah) *A Gadite in Bashan.*
Sheba, and Jorai, and Jachan, and Z 1Chr 5:13   2127

Z

ZIBA (zi'-bah) *A servant of King Saul.*

Saul a servant whose name was Z	2Sa 9:2	6717
king said unto him, Art thou Z	2Sa 9:2	6717
Z said unto the king, Jonathan	2Sa 9:3	6717
Z said unto the king, Behold, he	2Sa 9:4	6717
Then the king called to Z	2Sa 9:9	6717
Now Z had fifteen sons and twenty	2Sa 9:10	6717
Then said Z unto the king,	2Sa 9:11	6717
all that dwelt in the house of Z	2Sa 9:12	6717
Z the servant of Mephibosheth met	2Sa 16:1	6717
And the king said unto Z, What	2Sa 16:2	6717
Z said, The asses be for the	2Sa 16:2	6717
Z said unto the king, Behold, he	2Sa 16:3	6717
Then said the king to Z, Behold,	2Sa 16:4	6717
Z said, I humbly beseech thee	2Sa 16:4	6717
Z the servant of the house of	2Sa 19:17	6717
said, Thou and Z divide the land	2Sa 19:29	6717

ZIBEON (zib'-e-un)
1. Grandfather of Adah.

Anah the daughter of Z the Hivite	Gen 36:2	6649
of Anah the daughter of Z	Gen 36:14	6649

2. A son of Seir.

Lotan, and Shobal, and Z, and Anah,	Gen 36:20	6649
And these are the children of Z	Gen 36:24	6649
he fed the asses of Z his father	Gen 36:24	6649
duke Lotan, duke Shobal, duke Z	Gen 36:29	6649
Lotan, and Shobal, and Z, and Anah,	1Chr 1:38	6649
And the sons of Z	1Chr 1:40	6649

ZIBIA (zib'-e-ah) *Son of Hodesh.*

of Hodesh his wife, Jobab, and Z	1Chr 8:9	6644

ZIBIAH (zib'-e-ah) *Mother of King Jehoash.*

mother's name was Z of Beer-sheba	2Kin 12:1	6645
name also was Z of Beer-sheba	2Chr 24:1	6645

ZICHRI (zik'-ri) See ZITHRI.
1. A son of Izhar.

Korah, and Nepheg, and Z	Ex 6:21	2147

2. A Benjamite.

And Jakim, and Z, and Zabdi,	1Chr 8:19	2147

3. Son of Shishak.

And Abdon, and Z, and Hanan,	1Chr 8:23	2147

4. Son of Jeroham.

And Jaresiah, and Eliah, and Z	1Chr 8:27	2147

5. Son of Asaph.

the son of Micah, the son of Z	1Chr 9:15	2147

6. Descendant of Eliezer.

Z his son, and Shelomith his son	1Chr 26:25	2147

7. Father of Eliezer.

was Eliezer the son of Z	1Chr 27:16	2147

8. Father of Amasiah.

next him was Amasiah the son of Z	2Chr 17:16	2147

9. Father of Elishaphat.

and Elishaphat the son of Z	2Chr 23:1	2147

10. A "mighty man" of Ephraim.

And Z, a mighty man of Ephraim,	2Chr 28:7	2147

11. Father of Joel.

Joel the son of Z was their	Neh 11:9	2147

12. A priest with Zerubbabel.

Of Abijah, Z	Neh 12:17	2147

ZICRI See ZICHRI.

ZIDDIM (zid'-dim) *A city in Naphtali.*

And the fenced cities are Z	Josh 19:35	6661

ZIDKIJAH (zid-ki'-jah) See ZEDEKIAH. *A clan leader who renewed the covenant.*

the son of Hachaliah, and Z	Neh 10:1	6667

ZIDON (zi'-don)
1. A city in Asher.

and his border shall be unto Z	Gen 49:13	6721
them, and chased them unto great Z	Josh 11:8	6721
and Kanah, even unto great Z	Josh 19:28	6721
Accho, nor the inhabitants of Z	Judg 1:31	6721
gods of Syria, and the gods of Z	Judg 10:6	6721
because it was far from Z	Judg 18:28	6721
came to Dan-jaan, and about to Z	2Sa 24:6	6721
Zarephath, which belongeth to Z	1Kin 17:9	6721
and drink, and oil, unto them of Z	Ezr 3:7	6722
thou whom the merchants of Z	Is 23:2	6721
Be thou ashamed, O Z	Is 23:4	6721
oppressed virgin, daughter of Z	Is 23:12	6721
of Tyrus, and all the kings of Z	Jer 25:22	6721
of Tyrus, and to the king of Z	Jer 27:3	6721
Z every helper that remaineth	Jer 47:4	6721
The inhabitants of Z and Arvad	Eze 27:8	6721
of man, set thy face against Z	Eze 28:21	6721
Behold, I am against thee, O Z	Eze 28:22	6721
ye to do with me, O Tyre, and Z	Joel 3:4	6721
Tyrus, and Z, though it be very	Zec 9:2	6721

2. A son of Canaan.

Canaan begat Z his firstborn, and	1Chr 1:13	6721

ZIDONIANS (zi-do'-ne-uns) See SIDONIANS.
Inhabitants of Zidon.

The Z also, and the Amalekites, and	Judg 10:12	6722
after the manner of the Z	Judg 18:7	6722
and they were far from the Z	Judg 18:7	6722
Moabites, Ammonites, Edomites, Z	1Kin 11:1	6722
Ashtoreth the goddess of the Z	1Kin 11:5	6722
Ashtoreth the goddess of the Z	1Kin 11:33	6722
daughter of Ethbaal king of the Z	1Kin 16:31	6722
the abomination of the Z, and for	2Kin 23:13	6722
for the Z and they of Tyre brought	1Chr 22:4	6722
north, all of them, and all the Z	Eze 32:30	6722

ZIF (zif) *Second month of the Hebrew year.*

reign over Israel, in the month Z	1Kin 6:1	2099
of the LORD laid, in the month Z	1Kin 6:37	2099

ZIHA (zi'-hah)
1. A family of exiles.

the children of Z, the children	Ezr 2:43	6727
the children of Z, the children	Neh 7:46	6727

2. An overseer of Temple servants.

and Z and Gispa were over the	Neh 11:21	6727

ZIKLAG (zik'-lag) *A city in Judah.*

And Z, and Madmannah, and	Josh 15:31	6860
And Z, and Beth-marcaboth, and	Josh 19:5	6860
Then Achish gave him Z that day	1Sa 27:6	6860
wherefore Z pertaineth unto the	1Sa 27:6	6860
were come to Z on the third day	1Sa 30:1	6860
south, and Z, and smitten Z	1Sa 30:1	6860
and we burned Z with fire	1Sa 30:14	6860
And when David came to Z, he sent	1Sa 30:26	6860
and David had abode two days in Z	2Sa 1:1	6860
hold of him, and slew him in Z	2Sa 4:10	6860
at Bethuel, and at Hormah, and at Z	1Chr 4:30	6860
are they that came to David to Z	1Chr 12:1	6860
As he went to Z, there fell to	1Chr 12:20	6860
And at Z, and at Mekonah, and in the	Neh 11:28	6860

ZILLAH (zil'-lah) *A wife of Lamech.*

Adah, and the name of the other Z	Gen 4:19	6741
And Z, she also bare Tubal-cain,	Gen 4:22	6741
said unto his wives, Adah and Z	Gen 4:23	6741

ZILLETHAI See ZILTHAI.

ZILPAH (zil'-pah) *Handmaid of Leah.*

Leah Z his maid for an handmaid	Gen 29:24	2153
left bearing, she took Z her maid	Gen 30:9	2153
Z Leah's maid bare Jacob a son	Gen 30:10	2153
Z Leah's maid bare Jacob a second	Gen 30:12	2153
And the sons of Z, Leah's handmaid	Gen 35:26	2153
of Bilhah, and with the sons of Z	Gen 37:2	2153
These are the sons of Z, whom	Gen 46:18	2153

ZILTHAI (zil'-thahee)
1. Son of Shimhi.

And Elienai, and Z, and Eliel,	1Chr 8:20	6769

2. A warrior in David's army.

and Jozabad, and Elihu, and Z	1Chr 12:20	6769

ZIMMAH (zim'-mah)
1. A son of Jahath.

son, Jahath his son, Z his son,	1Chr 6:20	2155

2. A Gershonite.

The son of Ethan, the son of Z	1Chr 6:42	2155

3. Father of Joah.

Joah the son of Z, and Eden the	2Chr 29:12	2155

ZIMRAN (zim'-ran) *A son of Abraham.*

And she bare him Z, and Jokshan, and	Gen 25:2	2175
she bare Z, and Jokshan, and Medan,	1Chr 1:32	2175

ZIMRI (zim'-ri)
1. A Simeonite.

with the Midianitish woman, was Z	Num 25:14	2174

2. A king of Israel.

And his servant Z, captain of half	1Kin 16:9	2174
Z went in and smote him, and killed	1Kin 16:10	2174
Thus did Z destroy all the house	1Kin 16:12	2174
did Z reign seven days in Tirzah	1Kin 16:15	2174
Z hath conspired, and hath also	1Kin 16:16	2174
when Z saw that the city was	1Kin 16:18	2174
Now the rest of the acts of Z	1Kin 16:20	2174
Had Z peace, who slew his master	2Kin 9:31	2174

3. A son of Zerah.

Z, and Ethan, and Heman, and Calcol,	1Chr 2:6	2174

4. Son of Jehoadah.

begat Alemeth, and Azmaveth, and Z	1Chr 8:36	2174
and Z begat Moza,	1Chr 8:36	2174
begat Alemeth, and Azmaveth, and Z	1Chr 9:42	2174
and Z begat Moza	1Chr 9:42	2174

5. *An unspecified place.*
And all the kings of Z, and all the .... Jer 25:25 — 2174

ZIN (zin) *A wilderness south of Judah.*
the wilderness of Z unto Rehob .... Num 13:21 — 6790
desert of Z in the first month .... Num 20:1 — 6790
my commandment in the desert of Z .... Num 27:14 — 6790
in Kadesh in the wilderness of Z .... Num 27:14 — 6790
and pitched in the wilderness of Z........ Num 33:36 — 6790
of Z along by the coast of Edom .... Num 34:3 — 6790
of Akrabbim, and pass on to Z .... Num 34:4 — 6790
in the wilderness of Z.......................... Deut 32:51 — 6790
of Edom the wilderness of Z .... Josh 15:1 — 6790
and passed along to Z, and.................. Josh 15:3 — 6790

ZINA (zi'-nah) *A son of Shimei.*
sons of Shimei were, Jahath, Z............. 1Chr 23:10 — 2126

ZION (zi'-un) *See SION, ZION'S. A term for Jerusalem.*
David took the strong hold of Z .... 2Sa 5:7 — 6726
of the city of David, which is Z .... 1Kin 8:1 — 6726
daughter of Z hath despised thee .... 2Kin 19:21 — 6726
they that escape out of mount Z........... 2Kin 19:31 — 6726
David took the castle of Z .... 1Chr 11:5 — 6726
of the city of David, which is Z .... 2Chr 5:2 — 6726
my king upon my holy hill of Z .... Ps 2:6 — 6726
to the LORD, which dwelleth in Z .... Ps 9:11 — 6726
in the gates of the daughter of Z .... Ps 9:14 — 6726
of Israel were come out of Z................. Ps 14:7 — 6726
and strengthen thee out of Z................. Ps 20:2 — 6726
of the whole earth, is mount Z .... Ps 48:2 — 6726
Let mount Z rejoice, let the .... Ps 48:11 — 6726
Walk about Z, and go round about .... Ps 48:12 — 6726
Out of Z, the perfection of .... Ps 50:2 — 6726
good in thy good pleasure unto Z .... Ps 51:18 — 6726
of Israel were come out of Z................. Ps 53:6 — 6726
For God will save Z, and will .... Ps 69:35 — 6726
this mount Z, wherein thou hast............ Ps 74:2 — 6726
and his dwelling place in Z .... Ps 76:2 — 6726
the mount which he loved .... Ps 78:68 — 6726
of them in Z appeareth before God .... Ps 84:7 — 6726
The LORD loveth the gates of Z .... Ps 87:2 — 6726
of Z it shall be said, This and .... Ps 87:5 — 6726
Z heard, and was glad .... Ps 97:8 — 6726
The LORD is great in Z .... Ps 99:2 — 6726
shalt arise, and have mercy upon Z ...... Ps 102:13 — 6726
When the LORD shall build up Z .... Ps 102:16 — 6726
declare the name of the LORD in Z .... Ps 102:21 — 6726
the rod of thy strength out of Z .... Ps 110:2 — 6726
in the LORD shall be as mount Z .... Ps 125:1 — 6726
turned again the captivity of Z.............. Ps 126:1 — 6726
LORD shall bless thee out of Z .... Ps 128:5 — 6726
and turned back that hate Z .... Ps 129:5 — 6726
For the LORD hath chosen Z .... Ps 132:13 — 6726
descended upon the mountains of Z....... Ps 133:3 — 6726
and earth bless thee out of Z .... Ps 134:3 — 6726
Blessed be the LORD out of Z .... Ps 135:21 — 6726
we wept, when we remembered Z.......... Ps 137:1 — 6726
Sing us one of the songs of Z .... Ps 137:3 — 6726
reign for ever, even thy God, O Z .... Ps 146:10 — 6726
praise thy God, O Z .... Ps 147:12 — 6726
let the children of Z be joyful................ Ps 149:2 — 6726
Go forth, O ye daughters of Z .... Song 3:11 — 6726
the daughter of Z is left as a .... Is 1:8 — 6726
Z shall be redeemed with judgment .... Is 1:27 — 6726
for out of Z shall go forth the .... Is 2:3 — 6726
the daughters of Z are haughty .... Is 3:16 — 6726
of the head of the daughters of Z .... Is 3:17 — 6726
pass, that he that is left in Z................ Is 4:3 — 6726
the filth of the daughters of Z .... Is 4:4 — 6726
every dwelling place of mount Z .... Is 4:5 — 6726
hosts, which dwelleth in mount Z .... Is 8:18 — 6726
his whole work upon mount Z .... Is 10:12 — 6726
O my people that dwellest in Z.............. Is 10:24 — 6726
the mount of the daughter of Z .... Is 10:32 — 6726
and shout, thou inhabitant of Z .... Is 12:6 — 6726
That the LORD hath founded Z .... Is 14:32 — 6726
the mount of the daughter of Z .... Is 16:1 — 6726
of the LORD of hosts, the mount Z .... Is 18:7 — 6726
of hosts shall reign in mount Z .... Is 24:23 — 6726
I lay in Z for a foundation a .... Is 28:16 — 6726
be, that fight against mount Z .... Is 29:8 — 6726
shall dwell in Z at Jerusalem .... Is 30:19 — 6726
come down to fight for mount Z............. Is 31:4 — 6726
the LORD, whose fire is in Z .... Is 31:9 — 6726
he hath filled Z with judgment.............. Is 33:5 — 6726
The sinners in Z are afraid .... Is 33:14 — 6726
Look upon Z, the city of our .... Is 33:20 — 6726
for the controversy of Z .... Is 34:8 — 6726
and come to Z with songs and .... Is 35:10 — 6726
The virgin, the daughter of Z .... Is 37:22 — 6726
they that escape out of mount Z .... Is 37:32 — 6726

O Z, that bringest good tidings,............ Is 40:9 — 6726
The first shall say to Z, Behold, ... Is 41:27 — 6726
in Z for Israel my glory .... Is 46:13 — 6726
But Z said, The LORD hath .... Is 49:14 — 6726
For the LORD shall comfort Z .... Is 51:3 — 6726
and come with singing unto Z............... Is 51:11 — 6726
of the earth, and say unto Z................. Is 51:16 — 6726
put on thy strength, O Z .... Is 52:1 — 6726
thy neck, O captive daughter of Z .... Is 52:2 — 6726
that saith unto Z, Thy God.................... Is 52:7 — 6726
when the LORD shall bring again Z .... Is 52:8 — 6726
And the Redeemer shall come to Z .... Is 59:20 — 6726
The Z of the Holy One of Israel .... Is 60:14 — 6726
appoint unto them that mourn in Z .... Is 61:3 — 6726
Say ye to the daughter of Z .... Is 62:11 — 6726
Z is a wilderness, Jerusalem a .... Is 64:10 — 6726
for as soon as Z travailed .... Is 66:8 — 6726
family, and I will bring you to Z............ Jer 3:14 — 6726
Set up the standard toward Z................ Jer 4:6 — 6726
the voice of the daughter of Z .... Jer 4:31 — 6726
the daughter of Z to a comely .... Jer 6:2 — 6726
war against thee, O daughter of Z .... Jer 6:23 — 6726
Is not the LORD in Z .... Jer 8:19 — 6726
of wailing is heard out of Z .... Jer 9:19 — 6726
hath thy soul lothed Z .... Jer 14:19 — 6726
Z shall be plowed like a field,............... Jer 26:18 — 6726
an Outcast, saying, This is Z .... Jer 30:17 — 6726
let us go up to Z unto the LORD .... Jer 31:6 — 6726
come and sing in the height of Z .... Jer 31:12 — 6726
They shall ask the way to Z with........... Jer 50:5 — 6726
to declare in Z the vengeance of........... Jer 50:28 — 6726
let us declare in Z the work of .... Jer 51:10 — 6726
they have done in Z in your sight .... Jer 51:24 — 6726
shall the inhabitant of Z say.................. Jer 51:35 — 6726
The ways of Z do mourn, because .... Lam 1:4 — 6726
from the daughter of Z all her............... Lam 1:6 — 6726
Z spreadeth forth her hands, and.......... Lam 1:17 — 6726
of Z with a cloud in his anger .... Lam 2:1 — 6726
tabernacle of the daughter of Z .... Lam 2:4 — 6726
and sabbaths to be forgotten in Z .... Lam 2:6 — 6726
the wall of the daughter of Z .... Lam 2:8 — 6726
daughter of Z sit upon the ground .... Lam 2:10 — 6726
thee, O virgin daughter of Z .... Lam 2:13 — 6726
Lord, O wall of the daughter of Z .... Lam 2:18 — 6726
The precious sons of Z,........................ Lam 4:2 — 6726
and hath kindled a fire in Z .... Lam 4:11 — 6726
is accomplished, O daughter of Z .... Lam 4:22 — 6726
They ravished the women in Z............... Lam 5:11 — 6726
Because of the mountain of Z .... Lam 5:18 — 6726
Blow the trumpet in Z, and .... Joel 2:1 — 6726
Blow the trumpet in Z, sanctify a .... Joel 2:15 — 6726
Be glad then, ye children of Z .... Joel 2:23 — 6726
for in mount Z and in Jerusalem .... Joel 2:32 — 6726
The LORD also shall roar out of Z .... Joel 3:16 — 6726
the LORD your God dwelling in Z .... Joel 3:17 — 6726
for the LORD dwelleth in Z .... Joel 3:21 — 6726
said, The LORD will roar from Z............. Amos 1:2 — 6726
Woe to them that are at ease in Z .... Amos 6:1 — 6726
But upon mount Z shall be.................... Obad 17 — 6726
Z to judge the mount of Esau .... Obad 21 — 6726
of the sin to the daughter of Z .... Mic 1:13 — 6726
They build up Z with blood .... Mic 3:10 — 6726
Therefore shall Z for your sake .... Mic 3:12 — 6726
for the law shall go forth of Z .... Mic 4:2 — 6726
them in mount Z from henceforth .... Mic 4:7 — 6726
strong hold of the daughter of Z .... Mic 4:8 — 6726
to bring forth, O daughter of Z .... Mic 4:10 — 6726
and let our eye look upon Z .... Mic 4:11 — 6726
Arise and thresh, O daughter of Z .... Mic 4:13 — 6726
Sing, O daughter of Z .... Zeph 3:14 — 6726
and to Z, Let not thine hands be .... Zeph 3:16 — 6726
for Z with a great jealousy .... Zec 1:14 — 6726
and the LORD shall yet comfort Z .... Zec 1:17 — 6726
Deliver thyself, O Z, that...................... Zec 2:7 — 6726
Sing and rejoice, O daughter of Z......... Zec 2:10 — 6726
I was jealous for Z with great .... Zec 8:2 — 6726
I am returned unto Z, and will .... Zec 8:3 — 6726
Rejoice greatly, O daughter of Z .... Zec 9:9 — 6726
and raised up thy sons, O Z .... Zec 9:13 — 6726

ZION'S (zi'-uns)
For Z sake will I not hold my .... Is 62:1 — 6726

ZIOR (zi'-or) *A city in Judah.*
which is Hebron, and Z........................ Josh 15:54 — 6730

ZIPH (zif) *See ZIPHITES.*
1. A city in southeast Judah.
Z, and Telem, and Bealoth,.................. Josh 15:24 — 2128
a mountain in the wilderness of Z .... 1Sa 23:14 — 2128
in the wilderness of Z in a wood .... 1Sa 23:15 — 2128
arose, and went to Z before Saul .... 1Sa 23:24 — 2128

went down to the wilderness of Z 1Sa 26:2   2128
seek David in the wilderness of Z 1Sa 26:2   2128
And Gath, and Mareshah, and Z 2Chr 11:8   2128
  2. A city in Judah near Carmel.
Maon, Carmel, and Z, and Juttah, ... Josh 15:55   2128
  3. A descendant of Caleb.
which was the father of Z 1Chr 2:42   2128
  4. A son of Jehalaleel.
Z, and Ziphah, Tiria, and Asareel 1Chr 4:16   2128

ZIPHAH *(zi'-fah) A son of Jehalaleel.*
Ziph, and Z, Tiria, and Asareel 1Chr 4:16   2129

ZIPHIMS *(zif'-ims) See* ZIPHITES. *Same as Ziphites.*
A Psalm of David, when the Z came ... Ps 54:t   2130

ZIPHION *(zif'-e-on) See* ZEPHON. *A son of Gad.*
Z, and Haggi, Shuni, and Ezbon, Eri ...... Gen 46:16   6837

ZIPHITES *(zif'-ites) See* ZIPHIMS. *Inhabitants of Ziph.*
Then came up the Z to Saul to 1Sa 23:19   2130
the Z came unto Saul to Gibeah, ... 1Sa 26:1   2130

ZIPHRON *(zif'-ron) A place in northern Palestine.*
And the border shall go on to Z .... Num 34:9   2202

ZIPPOR *(zip'-por) Father of Balak.*
Balak the son of Z saw all that .... Num 22:2   6834
Balak the son of Z was king of .... Num 22:4   6834
said unto God, Balak the son of Z .... Num 22:10   6834
Thus saith Balak the son of Z .... Num 22:16   6834
hearken unto me, thou son of Z .... Num 23:18   6834
Then Balak the son of Z, king of .... Josh 24:9   6834
better than Balak the son of Z .... Judg 11:25   6834

ZIPPORAH *(zip-po-'rah) Wife of Moses.*
and he gave Moses Z his daughter .... Ex 2:21   6855
Then Z took a sharp stone, and cut .... Ex 4:25   6855
Moses' father in law, took Z .... Ex 18:2   6855

ZITHRI *(zith'-ri) See* ZICHRI. *A son of Uzziel.*
Mishael, and Elzaphan, and Z .... Ex 6:22   5644

ZIV See ZIF.

ZIZ *(ziz) A place in Judah.*
they come up by the cliff of Z 2Chr 20:16   6732

ZIZA *(zi'-zah) See* ZIZAH.
  1. Son of Ziphi.
Z the son of Shiphi, the son of 1Chr 4:37   2124
  2. A son of Rehoboam.
bare him Abijah, and Attai, and Z 2Chr 11:20   2124

ZIZAH *(zi'-zah) See* ZINA, ZIZA. *Son of Shimei.*
was the chief, and Z the second 1Chr 23:11   2125

ZOAN *(zo'-an) An Egyptian city.*
seven years before Z in Egypt .... Num 13:22   6814
land of Egypt, in the field of Z .... Ps 78:12   6814
and his wonders in the field of Z .... Ps 78:43   6814
Surely the princes of Z are fools............. Is 19:11   6814
The princes of Z are become fools.......... Is 19:13   6814
For his princes were at Z........................ Is 30:4   6814
desolate, and will set fire in Z................. Eze 30:14   6814

ZOAR *(zo'-ar) A Canaanite city.*
of Egypt, as thou comest unto Z .... Gen 13:10   6820
and the king of Bela, which is Z .... Gen 14:2   6820
the king of Bela (the same is Z .... Gen 14:8   6820
the name of the city was called Z.......... Gen 19:22   6820
the earth when Lot entered into Z .... Gen 19:23   6820
And Lot went up out of Z, and dwelt ..... Gen 19:30   6820
for he feared to dwell in Z .... Gen 19:30   6820
the city of palm trees, unto Z................ Deut 34:3   6820
his fugitives shall flee unto Z................. Is 15:5   6820
from Z even unto Horonaim, as an........ Jer 48:34   6820

ZOBA *(zo'-bah) See* ZOBAH. *A district in northern Syria.*
Beth-rehob, and the Syrians of Z.......... 2Sa 10:6   6678
and the Syrians of Z, and of Rehob, ... 2Sa 10:8   6678

ZOBAH *(zo'-bah) See* ZOBA. *Same as Zoba.*
Edom, and against the kings of Z........... 1Sa 14:47   6678
the son of Rehob, king of Z 2Sa 8:3   6678
to succour Hadadezer king of Z 2Sa 8:5   6678
son of Rehob, king of Z 2Sa 8:12   6678
Igal the son of Nathan of Z 2Sa 23:36   6678
from his lord Hadadezer king of Z 1Kin 11:23   6678
a band, when David slew them of Z 1Kin 11:24   6678
Hadarezer king of Z unto Hamath 1Chr 18:3   6678
came to help Hadarezer king of Z 1Chr 18:5   6678
the host of Hadarezer king of Z 1Chr 18:9   6678
out of Syria-maachah, and out of Z....... 1Chr 19:6   6678

ZOBEBAH *(zo-be'-bah) A daughter of Coz.*
And Coz begat Anub, and Z, and the..... 1Chr 4:8   6637

ZOHAR *(zo'-har) See* ZERAH, ZEROR.
  1. Father of Ephron.
for me to Ephron the son of Z .... Gen 23:8   6714
Ephron the son of Z the Hittite .... Gen 25:9   6714
  2. Son of Simeon.
Jamin, and Ohad, and Jachin, and Z ..... Gen 46:10   6714
Jamin, and Ohad, and Jachin, and Z ..... Ex 6:15   6714

ZOHELETH *(zo'-he-leth) A stone near En-rogel.*
and fat cattle by the stone of Z 1Kin 1:9   2120

ZOHETH *(zo'heth) Son of Ishi.*
And the sons of Ishi were, Z.................... 1Chr 4:20   2105

ZOPHAH *(zo'-fah) Son of Helem.*
Z, and Imna, and Shelesh, and Amal..... 1Chr 7:35   6690
The sons of Z 1Chr 7:36   6690

ZOPHAI *(zo'-fahee) See* ZUPH. *Brother of Samuel.*
Z his son, and Nahath his son, ... 1Chr 6:26   6689

ZOPHAR *(zo'-far)*
the Shuhite, and Z the Naamathite........ Job 2:11   6691
Then answered Z the Naamathite, ... Job 11:1   6691
Then answered Z the Naamathite, ... Job 20:1   6691
Z the Naamathite went, and did .... Job 42:9   6691

ZOPHIM *(zo'-fim) A peak on Mt. Pisgah.*
brought him into the field of Z .... Num 23:14   6839

ZORAH *(zo'-rah) See* ZAREAH, ZORATHITES, ZOREAH,
ZORITES. *A city in Judah.*
coast of their inheritance was Z .... Josh 19:41   6681
And there was a certain man of Z.......... Judg 13:2   6681
in the camp of Dan between Z................ Judg 13:25   6681
him up, and buried him between Z .... Judg 16:31   6681
coasts, men of valour, from Z .... Judg 18:2   6681
came unto their brethren to Z .... Judg 18:8   6681
family of the Danites, out of Z .... Judg 18:11   6681
And Z, and Aijalon, and Hebron, ... 2Chr 11:10   6681

ZORATHITES *(zo'-rath-ites) Descendants of Shobal.*
These are the families of the Z 1Chr 4:2   6882

ZOREAH *(zo'-re-ah) Same as Zorah.*
And in the valley, Eshtaol, and Z .... Josh 15:33   6881

ZORITES *(zo'-rites) See* ZAREATHITES, ZORATHITES.
Descendants of Salma.
half of the Manahethites, the Z 1Chr 2:54   6882

ZOROBABEL *(zo-rob'-a-bel) See* ZERUBBABEL. *Father of
Abiud; ancestor of Jesus.*
and Salathiel begat Z............................. Mt 1:12   2216
And Z begat Abiud................................ Mt 1:13   2216
of Rhesa, which was the son of Z .... Lk 3:27   2216

ZUAR *(zu'-ar) Father of Nethaneel.*
Nethaneel the son of Z .... Num 1:8   6686
Nethaneel the son of Z shall be .... Num 2:5   6686
second day Nethaneel the son of Z......... Num 7:18   6686
of Nethaneel the son of Z .... Num 7:23   6686
was Nethaneel the son of Z.................... Num 10:15   6686

ZUPH *(zuf)*
  1. An ancestor of Samuel.
the son of Tohu, the son of Z 1Sa 1:1   6689
The son of Z, the son of Elkanah, ... 1Chr 6:35   6689
  2. A district in Jerusalem.
they were come to the land of Z............. 1Sa 9:5   6689

ZUPHITE See ZUPH.

ZUR *(zur)*
  1. Father of Cozbi.
was Cozbi, the daughter of Z .... Num 25:15   6698
namely, Evi, and Rekem, and Z .... Num 31:8   6698
of Midian, Evi, and Rekem, and Z .... Josh 13:21   6698
  2. Son of Jeiel.
And his firstborn son Abdon, and Z 1Chr 8:30   6698
his firstborn son Abdon, then Z 1Chr 9:36   6698

ZURIEL *(zu'-re-el) Son of Abihail.*
Merari was Z the son of Abihail .... Num 3:35   6700

ZURISHADDAI *(zu-re-shad'-da-i) Father of Shelumiel.*
Shelumiel the son of Z .... Num 1:6   6701
shall be Shelumiel the son of Z.............. Num 2:12   6701
fifth day Shelumiel the son of Z .... Num 7:36   6701
of Shelumiel the son of Z .... Num 7:41   6701
Simeon was Shelumiel the son of Z........ Num 10:19   6701

ZUZIMS *(zu'-zims) See* ZAMZUMMIMS. *A tribe in the
land of Ham.*
the Z in Ham, and the Emims in .... Gen 14:5   2104

APPENDIX OF ARTICLES, CONJUNCTIONS, PREPOSITIONS, ETC.

A

Gen 1:6; 29; 2:5; 6; 7; 8; 10; 21; 22; 24; 3:6; 24; 4:1; 2(2); 12(2); 14(2); 15; 17; 23(2); 25; 26; 5:3; 28; 6:9; 16(2); 17; 8:1; 7; 8; 21; 9:11(2); 13(2); 14; 15; 20; 23; 25; 10:8; 9; 12; 30; 11:2; 4(3); 12:1; 2(2); 8; 10; 11; 13:7; 16; 14:23(2); 15:1; 9(4); 12; 13(3); 15; 17(2); 18; 16:7; 11; 12; 15; 17:4; 5; 7; 8; 11; 16(2); 17; 19; 20; 18:4; 5; 7(2); 10; 13(2); 14; 18; 19:3; 9; 20(2); 26; 28; 30; 31; 37; 38; 20:3(3); 4; 6; 7; 9; 16(2); 21:2; 7; 8; 13; 14; 16(2); 18; 19; 21; 25; 27; 30; 32; 33; 22:2; 6; 7; 8(2); 13(3); 23(4); 6; 9(2); 18; 20(2); 24:3; 4; 7; 11; 16; 17; 22(2); 29; 36; 37; 38; 40; 43; 55; 65; 25:1; 8; 27(3); 26:1; 8(2); 9; 19; 25; 28; 30; 35; 27:11(2); 12(3); 27; 34; 36; 44; 46; 28:1; 2; 3; 4; 6(3); 11; 12; 18; 20; 22; 29:2(2); 14; 20; 22; 32; 33; 34; 35; 30:5; 6; 7; 10; 11; 12; 15; 20; 21; 23; 30; 31:10; 11; 13; 24; 44(2); 45(2); 48; 32:13; 16; 18; 24; 28; 33:18; 19(2); 34:14; 35:11(2); 14(3); 16; 20; 37:1; 3; 5; 9; 15; 24; 25; 31; 38:1; 2(2); 3; 4; 5; 6; 11; 14; 17(2); 28; 39:2; 6; 14; 20; 40:4; 5; 8; 9; 19; 20; 41:2; 7; 11; 12; 15(2); 18; 33; 38(2); 42; 43:2; 6; 11(3); 44:15; 18; 19(2); 20(3); 25; 33; 45:7(2); 8(2); 46:3; 10; 29; 47:11; 22; 26; 48:4; 7; 16; 19(2); 49:6(2); 9(2); 10; 14; 15; 17; 19; 21; 22(3); 27; 30(2); 50:9; 10(2); 11; 13(2); 16; 26 **Ex** 1:8; 16(3); 2:1(2); 2(2); 7; 14(2); 15; 22(3); 3:2(2); 8(3); 12; 17; 19; 4:2; 3; 4; 10; 16; 26(2); 26; 5:1; 11; 6:12(2); 6; 7(2); 10; 7; 9; 19; 22; 11:6; 7(2); 8; 12:3(2); 5; 13; 14(3); 19; 21; 22; 30(2); 38; 42; 45; 46; 48; 13:5; 6; 9(3); 12; 13; 16; 21(3); 14:20; 21; 22; 23(2); 24; 28(2); 31; 32(3); 33; 15:2; 3; 16; 20; 25(2); 16:4; 14; 25; 33; 35; 17:12; 14(2); 18:3; 12; 16; 19:5; 6; 9; 16; 18(2); 19; 20:5; 21:4; 7(2); 8; 12; 13(2); 14; 16; 18; 20(2); 21; 22; 28(2); 29(2); 30; 31; 32(2); 33(4); 22:1(3); 2; 5(2); 7; 9(2); 10(2); 14; 15; 3:1(2); 5; 6; 7; 12; 16; 17; 4:22; 12; 14; 20; 21; 22; 23(2); 24; 28(2); 31; 32(3); 33; 5:1(2); 2(3); 3; 4(2); 6(4); 7(3); 9; 10; 11(2); 12(2); 13; 15(4); 17; 18(2); 19; 6:2(3); 3; 6(2); 7(2); 10(3); 11; 12(2); 19(4); 21(3); 24; 25(2); 26; 38:4; 23; 25; 26(2); 27(2); 39:7; 9(2); 10(3); 11(2); 12; 13(2); 14; 21; 23; 26(4); 28; 29; 30(2); 31; 40:34(; 35(; 39; 26:7; 13(2); 14(2); 16(3); 31; 27:4; 21; 28:45(3); 11; 12; 16(2); 17(3); 18(2); 19; 20(2); 21; 28; 29; 32; 33; 34; 35; 30:5; 6; 7; 10; 11; 12; 15; 20; 21; 23; 30; 31:10; 11; 13; 24 **Lev** 1:3(2); 9(2); 10(2); 13(2); 12; 1; 3:1(2); 5; 6; 7; 12; 16; 17; 4:2; 3(2); 12; 14; 20; 21; 22; 23(2); 24; 28(2); 31; 32(3); 33; 5:1(2); 2(3); 3; 4(2); 6(4); 7(3); 9; 10; 11(2); 12(2); 13; 15(4); 17; 18(2); 19; 6:2(3); 3; 6(2); 7(2); 10(3); 11; 12(2); 19(4); 21(3); 24; 25(2); 26; 26(2); 27(2); 39:7; 9(2); 10(3)

Num 1:4; 3:15; 22; 28; 34; 39; 40; 43; 50; 4:6; 7; 8(2); 9; 10(2); 11(2); 12(3); 13; 14; 5:6(2); 12; 13; 21; 23; 27; 29; 6:2(2); 11(2); 12(2); 14(2); 15; 17; 20; 7:3; 13; 15; 16; 17; 19; 21; 22; 23; 25; 27; 28; 29; 31; 33; 34; 35; 37; 39; 40; 41; 43(2); 45; 46; 47; 49; 51; 8:4; 7; 11; 12(2); 13(2); 19; 21; 8:25(2); 9:3; 10; 11; 13; 14; 20(2); 21(2); 22(2); 10:7; 11; 21; 22; 22:23(2); 8; 12; 22:7; 10; 17; 21; 22; 23(2); 24; 30; 34:16; 17; 18; 20; 21; 22; 23; 24:16; 25:8; 23; 30(2); 1Chr 2:34; 5:25; 6:33; 7:16; 23; 9:13; 10:4; 13; 11:3; 11; 13; 14; 20; 22(4); 23(4); 42; 12:2; 4; 14; 22; 28; 34; 38; 13:7; 11; 14:12; 15:15(2); 13; 27; 28; 29; 16:3(3); 5; 15; 17; 19; 42; 17:6; 8; 9; 17(3); 21; 24; 18:4; 19:6; 20:2; 5; 6; 21:3; 5; 13; 16; 22:9(2); 14; 25:3; 26:14; 17(2); 30; 27:5; 32(3); 28:3; 9(2); 29:15; 19; 21(3); 28; **2Chr** 1:4; 6; 9; 14; 16; 17; 2:7; 12; 13; 14(2); 18;

Deut 1:11; 23; 25; 31; 33(2); 39; 2:5(2); 9(2); 10; 19; 20; 21; 35; 3:4; 5; 7; 11(2); 4:6; 12; 16; 20; 23; 24(2); 25; 31; 34(3); 5:2; 9; 15(3); 22; 6:8; 15; 21; 7:6; 8; 9; 16; 21; 23; 26(2); 8:5; 7(2); 8(2); 9(2); 9:2; 3; 6; 12; 13; 14; 16; 26; 10:7; 15; 17(3); 11:9; 10; 11; 12; 18; 26(2); 27; 28; 12:11; 13:1(4); 14:2; 21; 15:1; 3; 7; 9; 15; 18; 16:8; 10(2); 12; 15; 16; 19(2); 21; 17:8; 14; 15; 18(2); 18:3; 6; 10; 11(4); 15; 18; 20; 22; 19:3; 5(2); 15; 16; 18; 20:1; 5; 6; 7; 10; 19(2); 21:4; 11(2); 13; 15; 17; 18(2); 20(2); 22:5(3); 6; 8(2); 11; 13; 14; 17; 19; 22(2); 23; 24(1); 3; 5(2); 6; 7; 17; 18; 19; 22; 25:1; 2; 5; 7; 13(2); 14(2); 15(2); 26:2; 5(3); 8; 9; 15; 27:3; 14; 15; 28:22(2); 30(2); 33; 35; 36; 37(2); 46(2); 48; 49(2); 50; 65; 29:13(2); 18; 22; 31:6; 7; 14; 15(2); 16; 19; 21; 23(2); 24; 26; 32:4; 20; 21; 22; 28; 34:6; 10; **Josh** 1:6; 9; 18; 2:12; 15; 3:4; 12; 4:2; 4; 5; 6; 7; 5:6; 13; 6:5(2); 18; 20; 7:1; 21(2); 26; 8:2; 11; 14; 17; 27; 28; 29(2); 32; 35; 9:6(2); 7; 9; 11; 15; 16; 10:2; 8; 10; 13; 14; 16; 17; 20; 11:14; 18; 19; 12:6; 7; 14:15; 15:3; 13; 18; 19(2); 17:1(2); 2; 14; 15; 17; 18; 18:9; 14; 20:4; 21:13; 21; 27; 32; 38; 44; 22:10; 14; 17; 20; 25; 27; 28; 34; 23:1; 10; 13; 24:7; 13; 19; 25(2); 26; 27(2); 32; 33; **Judg** 1:14; 15(2); 24; 26; 2:3; 17; 3:9; 15(4); 16(2); 17; 19; 20(2); 25; 27; 28; 29; 4:4; 9; 16; 18; 19(2); 21; 5:7; 8; 12; 14; 18; 25; 28; 30(3); 6:8; 17; 19(3); 26; 31; 34; 37; 38; 7:5; 13(5); 14; 16; 18; 8:14; 18; 20; 24; 25; 26; 27(2); 31; 32; 33; 9:8(2); 48; 49; 51; 53(3); 54; 10:1; 3; 11:1; 2; 30; 31; 33; 39; 40; 12:11; 13; 13:2; 5(2); 6; 7(2); 15; 16; 19(3); 23(2); 24; 14:1; 2; 3(2); 5; 6; 8(2); 15; 16; 19(3); 20; 12; 16(3); 15:1(2); 3; 4; 15(2); 16:4; 9; 12; 17(2); 19; 23; 17:1; 3(2); 4(2); 7(2); 8; 9(2); 10(3); 3; 18:10(3); 14(2); 19(6); 22; 23; 27; 28; 19:1(2); 3; 5; 12; 15; 17; 24(2); 29; 20:10(2); 38; 40; 21:5; 15; 17; 18; 19(2); **Ruth** 1:1(2); 2:1(2); 3; 7; 10; 11; 12; 3:8; 9; 11; 12(3); 13; 14; 4:1; 3; 7(2); 13; 14; 15(2); 17(2); **1Sa** 1:1; 5; 9(2); 11(2); 15(2); 16; 20; 24; 25; 2:3; 13; 18(2); 19; 25; 27; 34; 35(2); 36(3); 3:11; 20; 4:5; 7; 10; 12; 13; 17; 20; 5:9; 11; 6:3; 7; 8(2); 9; 14(3); 17; 19; 7:9(2); 10; 12; 8:5; 6; 10; 19; 22; 9:1(3); 2(4); 6; 7; 8; 9(3); 12; 15; 16; 21; 27; 10:1; 3; 5(5); 10; 12; 19; 25; 26; 11:1; 2(2); 7; 13; 12:1; 12; 13; 17; 19; 13:4; 6; 9; 12; 14; 21; 14:1; 2; 4(2); 10; 12; 14; 15; 20; 25; 29; 30; 33; 36; 39; 41; 43; 15:5; 12; 18; 28; 29; 16:1; 12; 16(2); 17; 18(4); 20(2); 17:3(2); 4(2); 5; 6; 7(2); 8(2); 20; 21; 22; 23; 25; 29; 33; 34; 38(2); 40(2); 41; 45(2); 49; 51; 55; 18:6; 8; 12; 16; 20; 21; 25; 29; 30; 19:2; 3(2); 6; 9; 13; 15; 20(3); 21; 24(2); 20:2; 12; 13; 25; 27; 28; 29; 30; 31; 34; 16(2); 17; 18(4); 20(2); 21(2); 22; 25:2; 6; 8; 12; 13(2); 16; 22; 20:3; 6; 8; 16; 20; 21; 25; 29; 35; 41; 21:2(2); 5(2); 7; 9; 22:2; 6; 8; 13; 18; 23:5; 7; 14; 15; 18; 25; 27; 24:3; 14(2); 19; 25:2(2); 3(2); 8; 10; 16; 17(2); 28; 29(2); 36(2); 37; 41; 26:12; 13; 15; 20(2); 27:5; 7; 10; 28:7(4); 9; 12; 14; 22; 24; 29:1; 30:12(2); 13; 17; 25; 26; 31:4; 13; **2Sa** 1:2; 13; 2:17; 18; 28; 3:7; 8(2); 11; 13; 20; 21; 22(2); 29(2); 33; 34; 38(2); 4:2; 4; 5; 10; 11; 5:2; 3; 23; 24; 6:3; 8; 14; 16; 19(3); 7:6(2); 7; 9; 10(2); 19(2); 23(2); 24; 8:2; 4; 13; 9:2; 3; 8; 12; 10:6; 11:2; 8; 14; 16; 21(3); 27; 12:3; 4; 24; 30; 13:1; 2; 3(2); 6; 9; 18; 14:2(4); 5; 11; 17; 18(3); 19; 25; 18:23(2); 6; 7; 8(2); 9; 19; 42; 3; 4; 5; 10; 11; 12; 13; 14; 19(5); 22(2); 25; 26; 30; 31(2); 31:10; 15; 16(2); 30; **Eccl** 1:3; 2:19(2);

2Chr 1:4; 6; 9; 14; 16; 17; 2:7; 12; 13; 14(2); 18;

Est 1:3; 5; 6; 9; 19; 2:5(2); 18(2); 23; 3:4; 8; 13; 14; 4:1(2); 5; 14; 5:9; 14; 8:11; 13; 15(2); 17(2); 9:17; 18; 19(2); 22; 10:1; **Job** 1:1; 3; 6; 8; 13; 14; 19; 2:1; 3; 4; 8; 13; 3:3; 5; 23; 4:12(2); 15; 16; 17; 5:26(2); 6:15; 22; 27; 7:1; 2(2); 6; 12(3); 20(2); 8:2; 9; 14; 20; 9:2; 3; 17; 19; 25; 32; 10:16; 20; 21; 22; 12:5; 14; 18; 24; 25; 13:25; 27; 28(2); 14:1; 2(2); 4; 7; 9; 13; 14; 15; 17; 15:2; 14; 21; 24; 16:8; 14; 21(2); 22; 17:3; 6(2); 7; 18:8(2); 10; 19:10; 15; 23; 29; 20:5; 8(2); 26; 29; 21:11; 13; 22(2); 6; 14; 16; 28; 24:3; 5; 8; 9; 14; 20; 24; 25; 25:4; 26:14; 27:13; 18(2); 20; 21; 28:11(2); 12(2); 26; 29:14(2); 16; 25; 30:5; 14; 15; 29(2); 31:1(2); 3; 9; 12; 18; 23; 30; 34; 35; 36; 37; 32:8; 33:15(2); 23(2); 24; 25; 34:9; 11; 13; 18; 20; 29(2); 34; 35:8; 36:2; 16; 18; 37:4; 18; 20; 38:3; 9; 14; 25(2); 28; 30; 39:20; 40:7; 9; 17; 23; 41:1; 2; 4(2); 5; 6; 15; 18; 20; 21; 24(2); 29; 31(2); 32; 34; 42:8; 11; 12(2); **Ps** 1:3; 2:1; 9(2); 12; 3:t; 3; 4:t; 5:t; 4; 12; 6:t; 7:2; 15; 8:t; 5; 9:t; 9; 6; 9(2); 10:9; 11:t; 1; 12:t; 2; 6; 13:t; 14:t; 15:t; 3; 4; 16:6; 17:t; 12(2); 18:t; 8; 10; 19; 29(2); 30; 31; 34; 43; 19:t; 4; 5(3); 20:t; 21:t; 3; 9; 11; 22:t; 6; 12(2); 13; 15; 20; 31; 23:t; 5; 24:t; 4; 25:t; 26:t; 27:t; 5; 28:t; 2; 6; 13; 56:t; 57:4; 6(2); 58:4; 8(2); 9; 11(3); 59:6(2); 14(2); 60:4; 61:t; 3(2); 62:t; 3(3); 8; 9; 63:t; 1; 10; 64:t; 3; 6; 65:t; 66:t; 1; 12; 67:t; 68:t; 5(2); 6; 9; 13; 33; 69:t; 4; 8; 11; 22(2); 30; 70:t; 3; 71:7; 72:t; 73:t; 1; 6(2); 19; 20; 22; 27; 74:5; 75:t; 5; 8; 76:t; 6; 77:t; 13; 17; 20; 78:2; 5(2); 8(2); 14(2); 19; 21; 38; 39; 50; 52; 57; 65; 66; 79:t; 4(2); 80:t; 1; 6; 8; 81:t; 1; 2; 82:t; 82:t; 83:t; 2; 4; 13; 14; 84:t; 3; 6; 10(3); 11; 85:t; 86:t; 15; 17; 87:t; 88:t; 4; 89:3; 8; 13; 37; 41; 90:t; 4(2); 5(2); 9; 91:7; 12; 92:t; 1; 3; 6(2); 12; 94:2; 20; 95:1; 2; 3(2); 10; 96:1; 97:3; 98:t; 1; 4(2); 5; 6; 99:8; 100:t; 1; 101:t; 2(2); 4(2); 5; 6; 102:t; 6; 7; 11; 26(2); 103:t; 13; 15; 104:2(2); 4; 6; 9; 18; 105:8; 10; 12; 16; 17(2); 39(2); 41; 106:18; 19; 36; 39; 107:4; 7; 27; 29; 33; 34; 35; 36; 41; 108:t; 109:t; 2; 3; 6; 9; 19; 25; 29; 110:t; 4; 111:10; 112:5; 113:9; 114:1; 8(2); 118:5; 119:9; 19; 63; 69; 78; 83; 105(2); 110; 161; 164; 176; 120:t; 2; 121:t; 122:t; 3; 123:t; 2; 124:t; 6; 7; 125:t; 126:t; 127:t; 4; 128:t; 3; 129:t; 1; 2; 130:t; 131:t; 2(2); 132:t; 5; 17; 133:t; 134:t; 136:12(2); 137:3; 4; 138:t; 139:t; 4; 140:t; 3; 5(2); 141:t; 3; 5; 142:t; 3; 143:t; 6; 144:t; 4; 8; 9(2); 11; 12; 15; 147:10; 148:6; 14; 149:1; 6; **Prov** 1:5(2); 6; 27; 2:7; 3:12; 18; 30; 4:1; 9; 24; 5:3; 4; 10; 20(2); 6:1; 5(2); 12(3); 17(2); 19; 23; 24; 26(3); 27; 30; 32; 33; 34; 7:7; 10; 19; 20; 22; 23(2); 8:27; 9:7(3); 8(2); 9(2); 13; 14; 10:1(3); 4; 5(2); 8; 10; 11(2); 13; 18(2); 23(2); 11:2; 7; 12; 15; 16; 18; 20; 22; 25(2); 26; 27; 30; 34(2); 35; 15:1; 4(3); 5; 12; 13(2); 15(2); 17(2); 18; 20(3); 21; 23(2); 30; 16:2; 7; 8; 9; 10; 11; 14(2); 15; 18; 20; 22; 25(2); 27; 28(2); 31; 32; 17:1; 7; 8; 9; 11; 14(2); 15; 18; 20; 22; 23(2); 25; 26; 2:1; 2; 3; 4(2); 8(2); 9; 10; 14(2); 15; 16(2); 17; 18; 19; 23; 24; 25; 26; 20:1; 2(2); 3; 5; 6; 8; 11; 15(2); 16(3); 17; 19; 23; 24; 25; 26; 30; 21:2; 4; 6(2); 9(3); 14(2); 15(3); 17; 20; 21; 23; 24; 25; 26; 29:5(2); 6; 8(2); 9(2); 9; 21; 24; 27(4); 28; 32; 34; 24:5(2); 7; 8; 14; 16; 25; 26; 28; 33(3); 25:2(2); 4; 9; 11; 12; 13; 14; 15(2); 18(4); 19(2); 20; 23; 24(2); 25(2); 26(3); 28; 26:1; 3(3); 4; 5; 6(2); 7; 8(3); 9(1); 12(2); 13(2); 16; 17; 18; 21; 22; 23(2); 27(2); 28(2); 27:1; 2; 3(2); 6; 8(2); 9; 10(2); 12; 13(3); 14(2); 15(3); 17; 20; 21; 23; 24; 25; 26; 29:5(2); 6; 8(2); 9(2); 11(2); 12; 15; 19; 20(2); 21; 22; 23; 24; 25; 30:2; 4; 5; 6; 10; 11; 12; 13; 14; 19(5); 22(2); 25; 26; 30; 31(2); 31:10; 15; 16(2); 30; **Eccl** 1:3; 2:19(2);

21(3); 24; 26; 3:1(2); 2(4); 3(4); 4(4); 5(4); 6(4); 7(4); 8(4); 12; 17; 19(2); 22; 4:4; 8(2); 9; 12; 13(2); 5:3(2); 4; 8; 12; 13; 14; 16; 6:2(2); 3; 6; 12(2); 7:1; 5; 6; 7(2); 8; 12(2); 15(2); 20; 28(2); 8:1(2); 4; 5; 9; 12; 13; 14; 15; 17(3); 9:4(2); 5; 6; 7; 14(2); 15; 10:1(2); 2(2); 3(2); 8(2); 11; 12(2); 14(2); 16; 19; 20; 11:2; 7; 8; 12:5; 12; **Song** 1:9; 13; 14; 2:9(2); 13; 17(2); 3:4; 9; 4:1; 2; 3(3); 4; 12(3); 15(2); 5:11; 13; 6:5; 6; 7(2); 7:1; 2; 4; 7; 13; 8:6(3); 7; 8; 9(3); 10; 11(2); 12; 14(2); **Is** 1:4(2); 8(5); 9; 14; 30; 31; 2:20; 3:6; 7; 16; 17; 24(4); 4:5(3); 6(4); 5:1(3); 2(2); 7; 9; 18; 28; 29; 6:1; 5(2); 6; 12; 13(2); 7:6(2); 8; 11; 13; 14(3); 20; 21(2); 23(2); 8:1(2); 3; 11; 12(2); 14(5); 19; 9:2; 6(2); 8; 10:6; 7; 13; 14; 16(2); 17(2); 18; 19; 22; 23; 24; 25; 26; 34; 11:1(2); 6; 10; 13:2; 4(3); 5; 6; 8; 12(2); 14; 14:6; 17; 19(2); 23; 29(2); 31; 15:5; 16:2; 4; 17:1(2); 7; 9; 11; 12(2); 13; 18:2(3); 3; 4(2); 7(3); 19:1; 4(2); 14(2); 17; 19; 20(4); 21; 23; 24; 20:3; 21:1; 2; 3; 6; 7(4); 8; 9(2); 16; 22(2); 5; 11; 16(2); 17; 18(2); 21; 23(3); 23:3; 10; 11; 24:9; 11; 20(2); 25:2(4); 4(5); 5(2); 26:1; 16; 17; 20; 27:2; 10; 11; 28:1; 2(4); 4; 5(2); 6; 10(2); 13(2); 15; 16(5); 19; 20; 22; 27(4); 29:3; 6; 10(2); 12(3); 15; 16(5); 19; 20; 22; 27; 28; 29(3); 30; 31; 33; 31:4; 7; 8(2); 32:1; 2(5); 14(2); 15(2); 18; 19; 33:9; 19(4); 20(2); 21; 23; 34:4(2); 6(2); 13; 14; 35:4(2); 7; 8; 36:2; 6; 13; 16; 17(3); 21; 37:3; 7(2); 18; 30; 32; 33; 38:3; 7; 12(2); 13; 14(3); 21(2); 39:1; 3; 40:3; 11; 12(2); 15(3); 16; 19; 20(3); 22(2); 41:12; 15; 18; 28; 42:3; 6(2); 10; 13(2); 14; 16; 22(3); 24; 43:16(2); 19(4); 44:8; 9; 10(2); 13(3); 15(3); 17; 19; 20(2); 22(2); 45:15; 19; 20; 21(2); 46:1; 6(2); 11(2); 47:3; 7; 8; 9; 14; 48:8; 18; 20; 49:2(2); 6(2); 7; 8(2); 11; 15; 18; 21; 50:2; 4; 7; 9; 11; 51:4(2); 6; 8; 10; 12; 20(2); 53:2(3); 3; 7(2); 12; 54:6(2); 7; 8(2); 55:4(2); 5; 13; 56:3; 5(2); 57:4(2); 6(2); 7; 8; 15; 58:1; 2; 5(5); 11(2); 13; 59:5; 15; 17(2); 19(2); 60:6; 15; 22(4); 61:10(2); 62:1; 2; 3(2); 5(2); 7; 10; 12; 63:14(2); 16; 64:6; 10(3); 65:1; 2(2); 3; 5(2); 8; 9; 10(2); 11; 15; 17; 18(2); 22; 66:2; 3(3); 5; 8; 9; 10(2); 11; 15; 17; 18; 20; **Jer** 1:5; 6; 7; 11; 13; 18; 2(2); 5(2); 7; 10; 11; 14(2); 21(3); 23; 24; 27(2); 30; 31(2); 32(2); 3:1; 3; 8; 14(2); 19(2); 20; 21; 4:6; 11; 12; 13; 15; 16; 17; 19; 20; 26; 27; 29; 31(2); 5:1; 3; 6(3); 9; 10; 15(3); 18; 19; 22; 23(2); 26; 27; 29; 30; 6:1; 2; 6; 7; 8; 9(2); 10; 20; 22(2); 24; 27(2); 7:5; 11; 28; 21; 29; 31(2); 32(2); 3:1; 3; 8; 14(2); 19(2); 20; 27; 29; 33(2); 34; 37; 39; 43(4); 46(2); 54(2); 55; 57; 59; 60; 63; 52:21; 22; 23; 34(2); **Lam** 1:1; 13; 15; 17; 2:1; 3; 6; 7(2); 8; 18; 20; 22; 3:10(2); 12; 14; 26; 27; 35; 36; 39(2); 44; 47; 52; 53; 64; 4:6; 8(2); 11; 17; **Eze** 1:4(4); 5; 7; 8; 10(2); 14; 16(3); 25; 26(3); 28; 2:3; 5(2); 6; 9(2); 3:5(2); 6; 9; 12(2); 13(2); 17; 20(2); 26(2); 27; 4:1; 2(2); 3(2); 6; 10; 5:1(2); 2(5); 3; 4; 12(4); 14; 15(2); 16; 17; 8; 9; 7:11; 21(2); 23; 26; 8:2; 3; 7; 8; 11; 17; 9:1; 2(2); 4; 10:1(2); 8; 9; 10; 13(2); 14(3); 21; 11:8; 13(2); 16; 19; 22; 23; 24; 34:8; 9; 13; 15; 17; 22; 24; 12:2(2); 3; 6; 13(2); 17(2); 22; 18:5(3); 6; 7; 20; 22(2); 23; 23(2); 25; 26; 34:8; 9; 13; 15; 17; 22; 24; 12:2(2); 3; 6; 13(2); 17(2); 22; 18:5(3); 6; 7; 20; 22(2); 23; 19:1; 2; 3; 5; 6; 10; 13; 16; 26; **Rom** 1:1; 10; 25; 28; 2:14;

6; 7; 9; 11; 18; 11:3; 5; 7; 10; 11; 13(2); 15; 18; 20; 21; 22; 23; 24; 25(2); 34; 35; 38; 39; 40; 12:1(2); 7; 11; **Hos** 1:2; 3; 4; 6; 8; 2:3(2); 6; 12; 15; 18; 3:1; 4(3); 4:1; 12; 16(3); 5:1(2); 2; 7; 12; 14(2); 6:4; 8; 9; 7:6; 8; 11; 16; 8:8; 9; 10; 12; 14; 9:1(2); 7; 8(2); 11; 12; 13; 14; 10:3; 4; 6; 14; 15; 11:1; 4; 10; 11(2); 12:1; 2; 7; 12(2); 13(2); 13:7(2); 8(2); 10; 11; 13; 14:8; **Joel** 1:6(3); 8; 14(2); 15; 2:2(4); 3(3); 5(2); 9; 14(3); 15(2); 19; 20; 3:3(2); 4; 8; 18; 19(2); 5(2); 9; 14(3); 15(2); 19; 20; 3:3(2); 4; 8; 18; 19(2); **Amos** 1:4; 7; 10; 12; 14(2); 2:2; 5; 6; 7; 13; 3:4(2); 5(3); 6(2); 12(3); 4:5; 11; 5:1; 3; 12; 19(4); 24; 6:10; 13; 14; 7:4; 7(3); 8(2); 14; 17; 8:1; 2; 6; 8; 10; 11(3); 9:5; 9; **Obad** 1; 7; 12; 18(2); **Jonah** 1:3; 4(2); 16; 17; 3:4; 5; 4:2; 5; 6(2); 7; 8; 10(2); **Mic** 1:4; 6; 8; 14; 2:2(2); 4(2); 5; 10; 11; 3:6; 12; 4:3; 7(2); 9; 10; 5:1; 7; 8(2); 6:2; 6; 16; 7:2; 3; 4(2); 5(2); 6; 8; 17; 18; **Nah** 1:7; 11; 14; 2:8; 3:2; 3(2); 6; 8; 17; 18; **Hab** 1:5; 10; 2:5; 6(2); 12(2); 18; 3:1; 14; **Zeph** 1:7; 10(2); 13(2); 15(5); 16; 18; 2:4; 9; 13(2); 15(2); 3:9; 13; 18; 20(2); **Hag** 1:6; 11; 2:6; 13; 15(2); 23; **Zec** 1:8(2); 14; 15; 16; 2:1(2); 5; 9; 3:2; 5(2); 4:1; 2(2); 7; 5:1; 2; 7(2); 9; 6:13; 14; 7:12; 14; 8:3; 13(2); 23; 9:3; 6; 7(2); 9; 13; 15; 16; 10:2(2); 7; 11:3(2); 13; 15; 16; 12:2; 3; 6(2); 11; 13:1; 4; 14:4; 10; 13; **Mal** 1:6(4); 11; 13; 14(3); 2:2; 11; 15; 3:2; 3; 5; 8; 9; 10; 12; 16; 17; 4:6; **Mt** 1:19(2); 20; 21; 23(2); 2:6; 12; 13; 18; 19; 22; 23(2); 3:4; 16; 17; 4:5; 6; 18; 21; 5:1; 14; 15(3); 22; 28; 31; 38(2); 41; 6:2; 16; 7:4; 9; 10(2); 17; 18(2); 24(2); 25; 26; 8:2; 4; 16; 17; 18; 20; 21; 24; 26; 30; 32; 9:1; 2(2); 9; 12; 16; 18; 20; 33(2); 10:18; 29; 34; 35; 36; 41(6); 42(2); 11:7; 8; 9(2); 11; 18; 19(2); 12:10; 11; 12(2); 14; 20; 22; 29; 32; 35; 38; 39; 41; 42; 43; 13:2; 3; 21; 24; 31(2); 32; 33; 34; 42; 44(2); 45; 47; 52; 57; 14:5; 8; 11; 13; 14; 15; 22; 23; 26; 33; 15:5; 11(2); 20(2); 22(2); 23; 29; 33; 34; 16:1; 4(2); 26(2); 17:5(2); 14; 20; 27; 18:2; 6; 12; 17; 23; 19:3; 5; 7; 23; 24(3); 20:1; 2(2); 9; 10; 13; 20; 28; 29; 21:2; 9; 19(2); 21; 22; 25(2); 33(3); 43; 46; 22:2(2); 11; 12; 15; 16; 17(2); 23; 24:7; 10; 11; 14; 16(2); 17; 19; 32; 40; 42; 45(2); 46; 50; 54(2); 57; 59; 60; 63; 52:21; 22; 23; 34(2); **Mk** 1:6(2); 10; 11; 16; 19; 20; 30; 35(2); 40; 44; 2:2(2); 3:1(2); 7; 8; 9; 13; 24; 27; 4:1(2); 3; 17; 21(4); 26; 31; 34; 37; 38; 39; 5:2; 7; 11; 13; 25; 42; 6:4; 5; 8; 10; 11; 15; 19; 20; 21(2); 25; 28; 29; 31(2); 32; 34; 35; 46; 49; 7:11(2); 15; 26(2); 29; 31(2); 32; 34; 35; 46; 49; 7:11(2); 15; 26(2); 8:4; 7; 10; 11; 12; 22; 36; 37; 9:7(2); 14; 17; 21; 36; 39; 41; 42; 10:2; 4; 7; 12; 15; 16; 17; 18; 21(2); 17:3(2); 4; 5; 10; 18:2(2); 7; 21(3); 22; 23; 19:1; 5; 6; 11; 12(2); 13; 15(2); 16; 17; 20; 20:1; 2; 3(2); 4; 6; 11; 21:1(2); 2; 3; 10; 11(2); 12; 15; 17; 19; 20(3); 27; 22:1; 15

17; 19(2); 20; 21; 22; 25; 28; 29; 3:4; 5; 7; 25; 28; 4:11; 17; 5:7(2); 7:1; 21; 8:24; 9:9; 27; 28; 29; 33; 10:2; 14; 19; 21; 11:5; 9(4); 17; 24; 12:1; 13:3; 4; 14:13; 15:8; 12; 23; 26; 16:1; 2; 23; **1Cor** 1:22; 23; 2:7; 11; 3:10; 14; 18; 4:1; 2; 3; 6; 9; 21; 5:5; 6; 7; 11(4); 6:1; 5; 7; 18; 20; 7:12(2); 5; 12; 15(2); 21; 22; 23; 26; 27(3); 28; 34(2); 35; 8:7; 9; 9:5(2); 7(3); 8; 11; 17(2); 20; 24; 25; 27; 10:13; 27; 30; 11:6(2); 7; 13; 14(2); 15(3); 28; 12:31; 13:1; 11(5); 14(2); 17; 11(2); 22; 25; 26(4); 35; 37; 15:38; 44(4); 45(2); 51; 52; 16:7; 9; **2Cor** 1:10; 15; 23; 2:6; 7; 12; 15; 3:13; 18; 4:17(2); 5:1; 17; 6:2; 13; 18; 7:8(2); 9; 11; 14; 8:2; 10; 11(2); 12(2); 14(2); 9:2; 5; 7; 10:6; 13; 11:1; 2; 5; 16(3); 20(5); 23; 25(2); 32; 33(2); 12:2; 3; 4; 6; 7; 11; 17; 18(2); 13:3; S:1; 32; 33(2); 12:2; 3; 4; 6; 7; 11; 17; 18(2); 13:3; S:1; **Gal** 2:3; 14; 16; 18; 3:13(2); 15; 19; 20(2); 21; 25; 4:1(2); 4; 7(3); 18; 22(2); 27; 5:3; 9; 6:1(2); 3; 7; **Eph** 3:7; 4:13; 5:2(2); 12; 27; 31; 32; 6:21; **Phil** 1:6; 23(2); 2:7; 8; 9; 15; 22; 3:5; 4:17; 18(2); **Col** 1:7; 23; 2:15; 17; 18; 23; 3:13; 4:1; 3; 7(2); 9; 11; 12; 13; **1Th** 2:5; 7; 11; 17; 4:16; 5:2; 3; 4; **2Th** 1:5; 6; 2:3; 11; 3:15; **1Ti** 1:5(2); 8; 9; 13(2); 15; 16; 18; 19; 2:2; 6; 7(2); 12; 3:14(2); 3; 5; 6; 7; 9; 10; 13(2); 4:2; 6; 9; 5:1; 5; 9; 23; 6:9; 12; 13; 19; **2Ti** 1:7; 11(2); 2:3; 4; 5; 11; 15; 17; 20; 21(2); 22; 3:5; 15; 4:7; 8; **Titus** 1:1; 7; 8(2); 12; 2:7; 14; 3:8; 10; **Philem** 1:1; 9; 15; 16(3); 17; 22; S:1; **Heb** 1:4; 5(2); 7; 8; 11; 12; 2:2; 6; 7; 9; 17; 3:5(2); 6; 4:1; 4; 7(2); 9; 12; 14; 5:6; 8; 13; 6:18; 7:2; 3; 12; 16; 17; 18; 19; 21; 22(2); 8:2; 4; 6(2); 8; 10(2); 13; 9:1; 2; 9; 11; 16; 17; 10:1; 3; 5; 15; 20; 22; 27; 31; 32; 33; 34; 37; 11:2; 4; 6; 8; 9; 10; 11; 14; 16(2); 19; 21; 23; 25; 35; 39; 12:1; 10; 19; 20(2); 28; 29; 13:9; 18; 22; **Jas** 1:1; 6; 8; 11; 18; 23(4); 25(2); 2:2(3); 3; 11; 14; 15; 18; 24; 3:2; 4; 5(3); 5; 16; 17; 20(2); **1Pet** 1:3; 6; 19; 22; 2:4; 5; 6; 8(2); 9(3); 10; 16; 19; 3:4; 9; 15; 16; 20; 21; 4:15(3); 16; 19; 5:1(2); 2; 4; 8; 10; 12; 14; **2Pet** 1:1; 17; 19(3); 2:3; 5; 17; 19; 3:8(2); 10(2); 13; **1Jn** 1:10; 2:4; 8; 22; 3:15; 4:20(2); 5:10; 16(2); 17; **2Jn** 4; 5; 7; 8; **3Jn** 6; 22; **Rev** 1:10(2); 11; 13(2); 14; 15; 16; 2:10; 14(2); 17(2); 18; 20(2); 22; 27(2); 3:1; 3; 4; 8; 12; 4:1(2); 2; 3(3); 6; 7(5); 5:1; 2(2); 6; 9; 12; 6:2(3); 4; 5(2); 6(4); 8; 10; 11; 12; 13(2); 14; 7:2; 9; 10; 8:3; 8; 10(2); 12; 13; 9:1; 2(2); 5(2); 11; 13; 15(3); 10:1(2); 2; 3(2); 4; 11:1(2); 3; 12(2); 13; 12:1(3); 3(2); 5(2); 6(2); 10; 12; 14(3); 15; 13:1; 2(3); 5; 11(2); 14; 16; 18; 14:1; 2(2); 3; 7; 9; 13; 14(3); 15; 17; 18; 21(2); 17:3(2); 4; 5; 10; 18:2(2); 7; 21(3); 22; 23; 19:1; 5; 6; 11; 12(2); 13; 15(2); 16; 17; 20; 20:1; 2; 3(2); 4; 6; 11; 21:1(2); 2; 3; 10; 11(2); 12; 15; 17; 19; 20(3); 27; 22:1; 15

ABOUT

235, 247, 413, 854, 1157, 1980, 2559, 3803, 4524, 5027, 5048, 5362, 5437, 5439, 5440, 5473, 5489, 5503, 5921, 5922, 6213, 7751, 1330, 1722, 1909, 1994, 2021, 2212, 2596, 2943, 2944, 2945, 3163, 3195, 3329, 3840, 3936, 3985, 4012, 4013, 4015, 4016, 4017, 4019, 4022, 4024, 4029, 4037, 4038, 4043, 4060, 4064, 4066, 4084, 4225, 4762, 4814, 5418, 5613, 5616, 5618

Gen 23:17; 35:5; 37:7; 38:24; 39:11; 41:25; 28; 42; 48; 42:24; 46:34; **Ex** 7:24; 9:18; 11:4; 12:37; 13:18; 16:13; 19:12; 23; 25:11; 24; 25:27; 27:17; 28:32; 33(2); 34; 29:16; 20; 30:3(2); 32:28; 37:2; 11; 12(2); 26(2); 38:16; 20; 31(2); 39:23; 25; 26; 40:8; 33; **Lev** 1:5; 11; 3:2; 8; 13; 6:5; 7:2; 8:15; 19; 24; 9:12; 18; 14:41; 16:18; 25:31; 44; **Num** 1:50; 53; 2:2; 3:26; 37; 4:4; 14; 26; 32; 11:8; 24; 31; 32; 16:24; 34; 49; 22:4; 32:33; 34:12; 35:2; 4; **Deut** 6:14; 12:10; 13:7; 17:14; 21:2; 25:19; 31:21; 32:10; **Josh** 2:5; 3:4; 4:13; 6:3; 11; 15; 7:3; 4; 5; 8:12; 10:13; 11:6; 15:12; 16:6; 18:20; 19:8; 21:11; 42; 44; 23:1; **Judg** 2:12; 14; 3:29; 7:21; 8:10; 26; 9:49; 16:27; 17:2; 19:22; 20:5; 29; 31; 39; 43; **Ruth** 1:4; 19; 2:17; **1Sa** 1:20; 4:2; 20; 5:8(2); 9; 10; 9:13; 16; 22; 26; 13:15; 14:2; 14; 21; 15:12; 27; 17:42; 20:12; 21:5; 22:2; 6; 7; 17; 24; 26; 25:13; 38; 26:5; 7; 31:9; **2Sa** 3:12; 4:5; 5:9; 7:1; 14:20; 18:15; 20:26; 22:6; 12; 24:6; **1Kin** 2:5; 15; 3:1; 4:24; 31; 5:3; 6:5(3); 6; 29; 7:12; 15; 18; 20; 23(2); 24(2); 36; 8:14; 18:32; 35; 19:2; 20:6; 22:6; 36; **2Kin** 3:25; 4:16; 6:14; 17; 7:1; 18; 8:21; 11:7; 8; 11; 17:15; 23:5; 25:1; 4; 10; 17; **1Chr** 4:33; 6:55; 9:27; 10:9; 11:8(2); 15:22; 18:17; 22:9; 28:12; **2Chr** 2:9; 4:2; 3(2); 13:13; 14:7; 14; 15:15; 17:9; 10; 18:31; 34; 20:30; 23:2; 7; 16; 33:14; 34:6; **Ezr** 1:6; 10:15; **Neh** 5:17; 6:16; 12:28; 29; 13:21; **Job** 1:5; 10(3); 8:17; 10:8; 11:18; 16:13; 19:12; 20:23; 22:10; 29:5; 30:18; 37:12; 40:22; 41:14; **Ps** 3:6; 7:7; 17:9; 18:5; 11; 27:6; 32:7; 10; 34:7; 40:12; 44:13; 48:12(2); 49:5; 50:3; 55:10; 59:6; 14; 73:6; 76:11; 78:28; 79:3; 4; 88:17(2); 89:7; 8; 97:2; 3; 109:3; 118:10; 11(2); 12; 125:2(2); 128:3; 139:11; 140:9; 142:7; **Prov** 1:9; 3:3; 6:22; 21; 20:19; **Eccl** 1:6(2); 2:20; 12:5; **Song** 3:2; 3; 7; 5:7; 7:2; **Is** 3:18; 15:8; 23:16; **Jer** 26:20; 28:27; 29:3; 42:25; 49:18; 50:11; 60:4; **Jer** 1:15; 2:36; 4:17; 6:3; 12:9; 14:18; 17:26; 21:14; 25:9; 31:22; 39; 32:44; 33:13; 41:14; 46:5; 14; 48:17; 39; 49:5; 50:14; 15; 29; 32; 51:2; 52:4; 7; 14; 22; 23; **Lam** 1:17; 2:3; 22; 3:7; **Eze** 1:4; 18; 27(2); 28; 4:2; 5:2; 5; 6; 7(2); 12; 14; 15; 6:5; 13; 8:10; 16; 10:12; 11:12; 12:14; 16:10; 37; 57(2); 23:24; 27:11(2); 28:24; 26; 31:4; 32:22; 23; 24;

25; 26; 34:26; 36:4; 7; 36; 37:2; 40:5; 14; 16(2); 17; 25; 29; 30; 33; 36; 43; 41:5; 6; 7(3); 8; 10; 11; 12; 16(2); 17; 19; 42:15; 16; 17; 19; 20; 43:12; 13; 17(2); 20; 45:1; 2(2); 46:23(3); 47:2; 48:35; **Dan** 5:7; 16; 29; 31; 9:16; 21; **Hos** 7:2; 11:12; **Joel** 3:11; 12; **Amos** 3:11; **Jonah** 2:3; 5(3); 6; **Nah** 3:8; **Hab** 1:4; **Zec** 2:5; 7:7; 9:8; 12:2; 6; 14:14; **Mt** 1:11; 3:4; 5; 4:23; 8:18; 9:22; 35; 14:21; 35; 18:6; 20:3; 5; 6; 9; 21:33; 27:46; **Mk** 1:6; 28; 2:2; 3:5; 8; 32; 34(2); 4:10; 5:13; 30; 32; 6:6; 36; 44; 48; 55(2); 8:9; 33; 9:8; 14; 42; 10:23; 11:11; 12:1; 14:51; 15:17; **Lk** 1:56; 65; 2:9; 37; 49; 3:3; 23; 4:14; 37; 6:10; 7:9; 17; 8:37; 42; 9:12; 14; 28; 10:40; 41; 12:35; 13:8; 17:2; 19:43; 22:41; 49; 59; 23:44; 24:13; **Jn** 1:39; 3:25; 4:6; 6:10; 19; 7:14; 19; 20; 10:24; 11:18; 44; 19:14; 39; 20:7; 21:20; **Acts** 1:15; 2:10; 41; 3:3; 4:4; 5:7; 16; 36; 9:3; 29; 10:3; 9; 38; 11:19; 12:1; 8; 13:11; 18; 20; 14:6; 20; 15:2; 18:14; 19:7; 23; 34; 20:3; 21:31; 22:6(2); 24:6; 25:7; 15; 24; 26:13; 21; 27:27; 30; **Rom** 4:19; 10:3; 15:19; **1Cor** 9:5; 13; **2Cor** 4:10; **Eph** 4:14; 6:14; **1Ti** 5:13; 6:4; **2Ti** 2:14; **Titus** 3:9; **Heb** 8:5; 9:4; 11:30; 37; 12:1; 13:9; **Jas** 3:3; 4; **1Pet** 5:8; **Jude** 7; 9; 12; **Rev** 1:13; 4:3; 4; 6; 8; 5:11; 7:11(2); 8:1; 10:4; 16:21; 20:9

ABOVE

4480, 4605, 4791, 5291, 5921, 5922, *507, 509, 511, 1883, 1909, 3844, 4012, 4117, 4253, 5228, 5231*

Gen 1:7; 20; 3:14(2); 6:16; 7:17; 27:39; 28:13; 48:22; 49:25; 26; **Ex** 18:11; 19:5; 20:4; 25:21; 22; 26:14; 24; 28:27; 28; 29:13; 22; 30:14; 36:19; 39:20; 21; 40:19; 20; **Lev** 3:4; 10; 15; 4:9; 7:4; 8:16; 25; 9:10; 19; 11:21; 27:7; **Num** 3:49; 4:25; 12:3; 16:3; **Deut** 4:39; 5:8; 7:6; 14; 10:15; 14:2; 17:20; 25:3; 26:19; 28:1; 13; 43; 30:5; **Josh** 2:11; 3:13; 16; **Judg** 5:24(2); **1Sa** 2:29; **2Sa** 22:17; 49; **1Kin** 7:3; 11; 20; 25; 29; 31; 8:7; 23; 14:9; 22; 16:30; **2Kin** 21:11; 25:28; **1Chr** 5:2; 16:25; 23:27; 27:6; 29:3; 11; **2Chr** 2:5; 4:4; 5:8; 11:21; 24:20; 25:5; 34:4; **Neh** 3:28; 7:2; 8:5; 9:5; 12:37; 39(3); **Est** 2:17; 3:1; 5:11; **Job** 3:4; 18:16; 28:18; 31:2; 28; **Ps** 8:1; 10:5; 18:16; 48; 27:6; 45:7; 50:4; 57:5(2); 11(2); 78:23; 95:3; 96:4; 97:9(2); 99:2; 103:11; 104:6; 108:4; 5(2); 113:4(2); 119:127(2); 135:5; 136:6; 137:6; 138:2; 144:7; 148:4; 13; **Prov** 8:28; 15:24; 31:10; **Eccl** 2:7; 3:19; **Is** 2:2; 6:2; 7:11; 14:13; 14; 45:8; **Jer** 4:28; 15:8; 17:9; 31:37; 35:4; 52:32; **Lam** 1:13; **Eze** 1:22; 26(2); 10:1; 19; 11:22; 16:43; 29:15; 31:5; 37:8; 41:17; 20; **Dan** 6:3; 11:5; 36; 37; **Amos** 2:9; **Mic** 4:1; **Nah** 3:16; **Mt** 10:24(2); **Lk** 3:20; 6:40; 13:2; 4; **Jn** 3:31(3); 6:13; 8:23; 19:11; **Acts** 2:19; 4:22; 26:13; **Rom** 10:6; 14:5; **1Cor** 4:6; 10:13; 15:6; **2Cor** 1:8; 11:23; 12:2; 6; 7(2); **Gal** 1:14; 4:26; **Eph** 1:21; 3:20; 4:6; 10; 6:16; **Phil** 2:9; **Col** 3:1; 2; 14; **2Th** 2:4; **Philem** 1:16; **Heb** 1:9; 10:8; **Jas** 1:17; 3:15; 17; 5:12; **1Pet** 4:8; **3Jn** 2

ACCORDING

413, 834, 1767, 3605, 3644, 3651, 4481, 5921, 6310, 6440, 6903, 7272, *2526, 2530, 2531, 2596, 4314, 5613*

Gen 6:22; 7:5; 18:10; 14; 21; 21:23; 25:13; 16; 27:8; 19; 30:34; 33:14; 34:12; 36:40; 43; 39:17; 40:5; 41:11; 12; 40; 54; 43:7; 33(2); 44:2; 7; 10; 45:21; 47:12; 49:28; 50:6; 12; **Ex** 6:16; 17; 19; 25; 26; 8:10; 13; 31; 12:3; 4(2); 21; 25; 35; 16:16(2); 18; 21; 17:1; 21:22; 31; 22:17; 24:4; 25:9; 35; 26:30; 28:8; 10; 21(2); 29:35; 41(2); 30:37; 31:11; 32:28; 36:1; 37:21; 29; 38:21; 39:5; 14(3); 32; 42; 40:16; **Lev** 4:3; 35; 5:10; 12; 9:16; 10:7; 12:2; 25:15(2); 16(3); 50(2); 51; 52; 26:21; 27:8; 16; 17; 18; 25; 27(2); **Num** 1:18; 20; 22; 24; 26; 28; 30; 32; 34; 36; 38; 40; 42; 54; 2:10; 18; 34(2); 3:16; 20; 22; 34; 51; 4:31; 33; 37; 41; 45; 49(3); 6:21; 7:5; 7; 8; 8:4; 20; 9:3(2); 5; 12; 14(2); 20(2); 10:13; 14; 18; 22; 28; 14:17; 19; 20; 29; 15:12(2); 24; 17:2(2); 6; 18:16; 23:23; 24:2; 26:18; 22; 25; 27; 37; 43; 47; 50; 53; 54; 55; 56; 29:6; 18; 21; 24; 27; 30; 33; 37; 40; 30:2; 33:2(2); 54; 34:14(2); 35:8; 24; 36:5; **Deut** 1:3; 30; 41; 46; 3:24(2); 4:34; 9:10; 10:4; 9; 10; 12:15; 16:10; 17; 17:10(2); 11(2); 18:16; 23:23; 24:8; 25:2; 26:13; 14; 29:21; 30:2; 31:5; 32:8; 34:5; **Josh** 1:7; 8; 17; 2:21; 4:5; 8; 10; 7:14(2); 8:8; 27; 34; 10:32; 35; 37; 11:23(2); 12:7; 13:15; 24; 15:12; 13; 20; 16:5; 17:4; 18:4; 10; 11; 20; 21; 28; 19:1; 8; 10; 16; 17; 23; 24; 31; 32; 39; 40; 48; 50; 21:33; 44; 22:9; 24:5; **Judg** 8:35; 9:16; 11:10; 36; 39; 20:10; 21:23; **Ruth** 3:6; **1Sa** 2:35; 6:4; 18; 8:8; 13:8; 14:7; 17:23; 23:20; 25:9; 30; **2Sa** 3:39; 7:17(2); 21; 22; 9:11; 14:20; 22:21(2); 25(2); 24:19; **1Kin** 2:6; 3:6; 12; 4:28; 5:6; 10; 6:3; 38; 7:9; 36; 8:32; 39; 43; 56; 9:4; 11; 11:37; 12:24; 13:5; 26; 14:18; 24; 15:29; 16:12; 34; 17:1; 5; 15; 16; 18:31; 20:4; 21:26; 22:38; 53; **2Kin** 1:17; 2:22; 4:16; 17; 44; 5:14; 6:18; 7:16; 9:26; 10:17; 30; 11:9; 14:3; 6; 25; 15:3; 34; 16:3; 10; 11; 16; 17:13; 18:3; 21:8(2); 22:13; 23:16; 19; 25; 32; 35(2); 37; 24:2; 3; 9; 19; **1Chr** 6:19; 32; 49; 9:9; 11:3; 10; 12:23; 15:15; 16:40; 17:15(2); 17; 19; 20; 23:11; 31; 24:3; 4; 19; 25:1; 2; 6; 26:13; 31; 28:15; **2Chr** 3:4; 8; 4:7; 6:23; 30; 33; 7:17; 18; 8:13; 14; 17:14; 23:8; 24:6; 25:5; 26:4; 11; 27:2; 29:2; 15; 25; 30:6; 16; 19; 31:2; 16; 32:25; 33:8; 34:32; 35:4(2); 5; 6; 10; 12; 13; 15; 16; 26; **Ezr** 3:4; 7; 6:9; 13; 14(2); 17; 7:6; 9; 14; 9:1; 10:3(2); 5; 8; **Neh** 2:8; 5:12; 13; 19; 6:6; 7; 14; 8:18; 9:27; 28; 12:24; 45; 13:22; 24; **Est** 1:7; 8(2); 15; 21; 22(2); 2:12; 18; 3:12(2); 4:16; 17; 8:9(4); 9:13; 27(2); 31; **Job** 1:5; 20:18; 33:6; 34:11; 33; 36:27; 42:9; **Ps** 7:8(2); 17; 18:20(2); 24(2); 20:4; 25:7; 28:4(2); 33:22; 35:24; 48:10; 51:1(2); 62:12; 69:16; 74:5; 78:72; 79:11; 90:11; 15; 103:10; 106:45; 109:26; 119:9; 25; 28; 41; 58; 65; 76; 91; 107; 116; 124; 149(2); 154; 156; 159; 169; 170; 150:2; **Prov** 12:8; 24:12; 29; 26:4; 5; **Eccl** 1:6; 8:14(2); **Is** 8:20; 9:3; 10:26; 21:16; 23:15; 27:7; 44:13; 59:18; 63:7(3); **Jer** 2:28; 3:15; 11:4; 13(2); 13:2; 17:10(2); 21:2; 14; 25:14(2); 26:20; 27:12; 31:32; 32:8; 11; 19(2); 35:10; 18; 36:8; 38:27; 40:3; 42:4; 5; 20; 50:21; 29(2); 52:2; **Lam** 3:32; 64; **Eze** 4:4; 5; 9; 5:7; 7:3; 8; 9; 27; 8:4; 14:4; 18:24; 30; 20:44(2); 23:24; 24:14(2); 24; 25:14(2); 35:11(2); 36:19(2); 39:24(2); 40:24; 28; 29; 32; 33; 35; 42:11(2); 12; 43:3(2); 44:24; 45:8; 25(4); 46:7; 47:10; 12; 13; 21; **Dan** 4:8; 35; 6:8; 12; 8:4; 9:16; 11:3; 4; 16; 36; **Hos** 3:1; 9:10; 10:1(2); 12:2(2); 13:2; 6; **Jonah** 3:3; **Mic** 7:15; **Hab** 3:9; **Hag** 2:5; **Zec** 1:6(2); 5:3(2); **Mal** 2:9; **Mt** 2:16; 9:29; 16:27; 25:15; **Mk** 7:5; **Lk** 1:9; 38; 2:22; 24; 29; 39; 5:14; 12:47; 23:56; **Jn** 7:24; 18:31; **Acts** 2:30; 4:35; 7:44; 11:29; 13:23; 22:3; 12; 24:6; **Rom** 1:3; 4; 2:2; 6; 16; 4:18; 8:27; 28; 9:3; 11; 10:2; 11:5; 8; 12:3; 6(2); 15:5; 16:25(2); 26; **1Cor** 1:31; 3:8; 10; 15:3; 4; **2Cor** 1:17; 4:13; 5:10; 8:12(2); 9:7; 10:2; 13; 15; 11:15; 13:10; **Gal** 1:4; 2:14; 3:29; 6:16; **Eph** 1:4; 5; 7; 9; 11; 19; 2:2(2); 3:7; 11; 16; 20; 4:7; 16; 22; 6:5; **Phil** 1:20; 3:21; 4:19; **Col** 1:11; 25; 29; 3:22; **2Th** 1:12; **1Ti** 1:11; 18; 6:3; **2Ti** 1:1; 8; 9(2); 2:8; 4:14; **Titus** 1:1; 3; 3:5; 7; **Heb** 2:4; 7:5; 8:4; 5; 9; 9:19; **Jas** 2:8; **1Pet** 1:2; 3; 14; 17; 3:7; 4:6(2); 19; **2Pet** 1:3; 2:22; 3:13; 15; **1Jn** 5:14; **Rev** 2:23; 18:6; 20:12; 13; 21:17; 22:12

AFAR

4801, 7350, 7368, *3112, 3113, 3467, 4207*

Gen 22:4; 37:18; **Ex** 2:4; 20:18; 21; 24:1; 33:7; **Num** 9:10; **1Sa** 26:13; **2Kin** 2:7; 4:25; **Ezr** 3:13; **Neh** 12:43; **Job** 2:12; 36:3; 25; 39:25; 29; **Ps** 10:1; 38:11; 65:5; 138:6; 139:2; **Prov** 31:14; **Is** 23:7; 59:14; 66:19; **Jer** 23:23; 30:10; 31:10; 46:27; 51:50; **Mic** 4:3; **Mt** 26:58; 27:55; **Mk** 5:6; 11:13; 14:54; 15:40; **Lk** 16:23; 17:12; 18:13; 22:54; 23:49; **Acts** 2:39; **Eph** 2:17; **Heb** 11:13; **2Pet** 1:9; **Rev** 18:10; 15; 17

AFTER

167, 310, 311, 314, 413, 834, 870, 1767, 1836, 3602, 4480, 4481, 5921, 6256, 6310, 7093, 7097, 7272, *516, 1207, 1223, 1230, 1377, 1534, 1567, 1722, 1836, 1872, 1887, 1894, 1899, 1905, 1909, 1934, 1938, 1971, 1984, 2089, 2517, 2596, 2614, 2628, 3195, 3326, 3693, 3694, 3753, 3765, 3779, 4023, 4137, 4329, 4459, 5225, 5613, 5615*

Gen 1:11; 12(2); 21(2); 24(2); 25(3); 26; 4:17; 5:3; 4; 7; 10; 13; 16; 19; 22; 26; 30; 6:4; 20(3); 7:10; 14(4); 8:3; 19; 9:9; 28; 10:1; 5(2); 20(2); 31(3); 32(2); 11:10; 11; 13; 15; 17; 19; 21; 23; 25; 13:14; 14:17; 15:1; 16:3; 13; 17:7(2); 8; 9; 10; 19; 18:5; 11; 12; 19; 25; 19:6; 31; 22:1; 20; 23:19; 24:55; 67; 25:11; 26; 26:18(2); 31:23; 30; 36; 32:29; 33:2; 7; 35:5; 12; 36:40; 37:17; 38:24; 39:7; 19; 40:1; 13; 41:3; 6; 19; 23; 27; 30; 44:4; 45:15; 23; 48:1; 4; 6(2); 50:14; **Ex** 3:20; 5:19; 7:25; 10:14; 11:8; 14:4; 8; 9; 10; 23; 28; 15:20; 16:1; 17:1; 18:2; 21:9; 23:2; 24; 25:9; 40; 28:15; 43; 29:29; 30:12; 13; 24; 25; 32; 35; 32:4; 33:8; 34:15; 16(2); 27; 37:19; 38:24; 25; 26; **Lev** 5:15; 11:14; 15; 16; 19; 22(4); 29; 13:7; 35; 55; 56; 14:8; 43(3); 48; 15:28; 16:1; 17:7; 18:3(2); 19:31; 20:5; 6(3); 23:11; 15; 16; 25:15; 29; 46; 48; 26:33; 27:3; 18; **Num** 1:1; 2; 18; 20; 22; 24; 26; 28; 30; 32; 34; 36; 38; 40; 42; 47; 2:34; 3:15; 47; 50; 4:2; 15; 29; 34(2); 44; 46(2); 6:19; 20; 21; 7:13; 19; 25; 31; 37; 43; 49; 55; 61; 67; 73; 79; 85; 86; 88; 8:15; 22; 9:1; 17; 12:14; 13:25; 14:34; 15:13; 39(2); 16:29; 18:16; 25:8; 13; 26:1; 12; 15; 20; 23; 26; 28; 35; 37; 38; 41; 42(2); 44; 48; 57; 27:21; 28:24; 26; 29:18; 21; 24; 27; 30; 33; 37; 30:15; 32:15; 42; 33:3; 38; 35:28; **Deut** 1:4; 8; 3:11; 14; 4:37; 40; 45; 46; 6:14; 8:19; 9:4; 10:15; 11:4; 28; 12:8; 15; 20; 21; 25; 28; 30(2); 13:2; 4; 14:13; 14; 15; 18; 26; 16:13; 18:9; 20:18; 21:13; 22:2; 24:4; 9; 28:14; 29:22; 31:16; 27; 29; **Josh** 1:1; 2:5; 7(2); 3:2; 3; 5:4; 11; 12; 6:9; 13; 15; 7:25; 8:6; 16(2); 17(2); 9:16; 10:14; 19; 13:23; 28; 19:47; 20:5; 22:27; 23:1; 24:6; 20; 29; **Judg** 1:1; 6; 2:10; 17; 3:22; 28(2); 31; 4:14; 16(2); 5:14; 6:34; 35; 7:23; 8:5; 12; 27; 33; 10:1; 3; 12:8; 11; 13; 13:11; 18; 14:8; 15:1; 7; 16:22; 18:7; 29; 19:3; 20:45; **Ruth** 1:15; 16; 2:2; 3; 7; 9; 18; 4:4; **1Sa** 1:9(2); 20; 5:9; 6:12; 7:2; 8:3; 10:5; 11:5; 7(2); 12:21; 13:4; 14; 14:12; 13(2); 22; 36; 37; 15:31; 17:27; 30(2); 35; 53; 18:30; 20:37; 38; 22:20; 23:25; 28; 24:8; 14(4); 21; 25:13; 19; 38; 42(2); 26:3; 18; 30:8; **2Sa** 1:1; 6; 10; 2:1; 19; 24; 25; 28; 3:26; 5:13; 7:12; 8:1; 10:1; 11:1; 3; 12:28; 13:1; 17; 18; 23; 14:26; 15:1; 7; 13; 16; 17; 18; 17:1; 6(2); 21; 18:16; 18; 22; 20:2; 6; 7(2); 10; 11; 13(2); 14; 21:1; 14; 18; 23:4; 9; 10; 11; 24:10; **1Kin** 1:6; 13; 14; 17; 20; 24; 27; 30; 35; 40; 2:28(2); 3:12; 18; 6:1; 7:11; 31; 37; 9:21; 11:2; 4; 5(2); 6; 10; 15; 12:14; 13:14; 23(2); 31; 33; 15:4; 16:24; 17:7; 13; 17; 18:1; 28; 19:11; 12(2); 20; 21; 20:15; 21:1; **2Kin** 1:1; 5:20; 21(2); 6:24; 7:14; 15; 8:2; 9:25; 27; 10:29; 14:17; 19; 22; 17:15; 33; 34(4); 40; 18:5; 21:2; 23:3; 25; 25:5; **1Chr** 2:24; 5:1; 25; 6:31; 7:4; 9; 8:8; 9:25; 10:2(2); 11:12; 14:14; 15:13; 17:11; 18:1; 19:1; 20:1; 4; 23:24; 24:30; 27:1; 7; 34; 28:8; 29:14; 21; **2Chr** 1:12; 2:17; 3:3; 4:20; 8:8; 13; 10:5; 14; 11:16; 20; 13:9; 19; 17:4; 18:2; 19(2); 20:1; 35; 21:18; 19; 22:4; 5; 23:21; 24:4; 17; 25:14; 15; 20; 25; 27(2); 26:2; 17; 28:3; 30:16; 31:2; 32:1; 9; 33:14; 34:3; 21; 31; 35:4; 5; 20; 36:14; **Ezr** 2:61; 69; 3:10; 5:4; 12; 7:1; 18; 25; 9:10; 13; 10:16; **Neh** 3:16; 17; 18; 20; 21; 22; 23(2); 24; 25; 27; 29(2); 30(2); 31; 4:13; 5:8; 6:4(2); 7:63; 9:28; 10:34; 11:8; 12:32; 38; 13:6; 19; **Est** 1:22; 2:1; 12; 3:1; 12; 8:9; 9:26; **Job** 3:1; 10:6(2); 18:20; 19:26; 21:3; 21; 33; 29:22; 30:5(2); 31:7; 37:4; 39:8; 10; 41:32; 42:7; 8; 16; **Ps** 4:2; 10:4; 16:4; 27:4; 28:4; 35:4; 38:12; 40:14; 42:1(2); 49:11; 17; 51:t, 54:3; 63:8; 68:25; 70:2; 78:34; 86:14; 103:10; 104:21; 110:4; 119:40; 85; 88; 150; 143:6; 144:12; **Prov** 2:3; 6:25; 7:22; 15:9; 20:7; 25; 21:21; 28:19; **Eccl** 1:11; 2:12; 18; 3:22; 4:16; 6:12; 7:14; 9:3; 10:14; 11:1; 12:2; **Song** 1:4; **Is** 1:23; 5:17; 10:24; 26; 11:3(2); 23:15; 17; 24:22; 43:10; 44:13; 45:14; 49:20; 51:1; 65:2; **Jer** 2:2; 5; 8; 23; 25; 3:7; 17; 5:8; 7:6; 9; 8:2; 9:14(2); 16; 22; 11:10; 12:6; 15; 13:6; 9; 10; 16:11; 12; 16; 18:12; 23:17; 24:1; 25:6; 26; 28:12; 29:2; 10; 30:17; 18; 31:19(2); 33; 32:18; 39; 34:8; 35:15; 36:27; 39:5; 40:1; 41:4; 16; 42:7; 16; 49:37; 50:21; 51:46; 52:8; **Eze** 5:2; 12; 6:9; 7:27; 9:5; 11:12; 21; 12:14; 16:23; 47(2); 20:16; 24; 30(2); 23:15; 30; 45(2); 48; 29:16; 33:20; 31; 34:6; 36:11; 38:8; 39:14; 26; 40:1; 21; 22; 24; 41:5; 43:13; 44:10; 26; 45:11; 46:12; 17; 19; 48:31; **Dan** 2:39; 3:29; 4:26; 7:6; 7; 24; 8:1; 9:26; 11:13; 18; 23; **Hos** 2:5; 7; 13; 5:8; 11; 6:2; 7:4; 11:10; 12:1; **Joel** 2:2; **Amos** 2:4; 7; 4:4; 10; 7:1; **Zec** 2:8; 6:6; 7:14; **Mt** 1:12; 3:11; 5:6; 28; 6:9; 32; 10:38; 12:39; 15:12; 23; 16:4; 24; 17:1; 18:32; 23:3; 24:29; 25:19; 26:2; 32; 73; 27:31; 53; 63; **Mk** 1:7; 14; 17; 20; 36; 2:1; 4:28; 8:12; 25; 31; 34; 9:2; 31; 12:34; 13:24; 14:1; 28; 70; 16:12; 14; 19; **Lk** 1:24; 59; 2:27; 42; 46; 5:27; 6:1; 7:11; 9:23; 28; 10:1; 12:4; 5; 30; 13:9; 14:27; 29; 15:4; 13; 17:23; 19:14; 20:40; 21:8; 26; 22:20; 58; 59; 23:26; 55; **Jn** 1:15; 27; 30; 35; 2:6; 12; 3:22; 4:43; 5:1; 4; 6:1; 23; 7:1; 8:15; 11:7; 11; 12:19; 13:5; 12; 27; 19:28; 38; 20:26; 21:1; 14; **Acts** 1:2; 3; 8; 3:24; 5:4; 7; 37(2); 7:5; 7; 36; 45; 9:23; 10:24; 37; 41; 12:4; 13:15; 20; 22; 25; 36; 14:24; 15:1; 13; 16; 17; 23; 33; 36; 16:7; 10; 17:27; 18:1; 18; 23; 19:4; 21(2); 20:1; 6; 18; 29; 30; 21:1; 15; 21; 36; 22:29; 23:3; 25; 24:1; 10; 14; 17; 24; 27; 25:1; 13; 26; 26:5; 27:14; 21; 28:6; 11; 13; 17; 25; **Rom** 2:5; 3:11; 5:14; 6:19; 7:22; 8:1(2); 4(2); 5(2); 12; 13; 9:30; 31; 10:20; 14:19; **1Cor** 1:21; 22; 26; 7:7(2); 40; 10:6; 18; 11:25; 12:28; 14:1; 15:6; 7; 32; **2Cor** 5:16(2); 7:9; 11; 9:14; 10:3; 7; 11:17; 18; **Gal** 1:11; 18; 2:1; 14; 3:15; 17; 25; 4:9; 23; 29(2); **Eph** 1:11; 13(2); 15; 4:24; **Phil** 1:8; 2:26; 3:12; **Col** 2:8(3); 22; 3:10; **1Th** 2:2; **2Th** 2:9; 3:6; **1Ti** 5:15; 24; 6:10; 11; **2Ti** 4:3; **Titus** 1:1; 4; 3:4; 10; **Heb** 3:5; 4:7; 11; 5:6; 10; 6:15; 20; 7:2; 11(2); 15; 16(2); 17; 21; 8:10; 9:3; 17; 27; 10:12; 15; 16; 26; 32; 36; 11:8; 30; 12:10; **Jas** 3:9; **1Pet** 3:5; 5:10; **2Pet** 1:15; 2:6; 10; 20; 21; 3:3; **2Jn** 6; **3Jn** 6; **Jude** 7; 11; 16; 18; **Rev** 4:1; 7:1; 9; 11:11; 12:15; 13:3; 15:5; 18:1; 14; 19:1; 20:3

AFTERWARD

310, 314, 3651, *1208, 1534, 1899, 2517, 2547, 3347, 5023, 5305*

Gen 10:18; 15:14; 32:20; 38:30; **Ex** 5:1; 34:32; **Lev** 14:19; 36; 16:26; 28; 22:7; **Num** 5:26; 12:16; 19:7; 31:2; 24; 32:22; **Deut** 17:7; 24:21; **Josh** 2:16; 8:34; 10:26; 24:5; **Judg** 1:9; 7:11; 16:4; 19:5; **1Sa** 24:5; 8; **2Sa** 3:28; **1Chr** 2:21; **2Chr** 35:14; **Ezr** 3:5; **Neh** 6:10; **Ps** 73:24; **Is** 1:26; 9:1; **Jer** 21:7; 34:11; 46:26; 49:6; **Eze** 41:1; 43:1; 47:1; 5; **Dan** 8:27; **Hos** 3:5; **Joel** 2:28; **Mt** 4:2; 21:29; 32; 25:11; **Mk** 4:17; 16:14; **Lk** 4:2; 8:1; 17:8; 18:4; **Jn** 5:14; **Acts** 13:21; **1Cor** 15:23; 46; **Heb** 4:8; 12:11; 17; **Jude** 5

AGAIN

310, 322, 1571, 1906, 1946, 3138, 3254, 5437, 5750, 7725, 7999, 8138, 8145, 8579, *313, 321, 326, 330, 344, 364, 375, 450, 456, 467, 470, 479, 483, 486, 488, 509, 518, 523, 560, 591, 600, 618, 654, 1208, 1364, 1453, 1515, 1519, 1880, 1994, 3326, 3588, 3825, 4388, 4762, 5290*

Gen 4:2; 25; 8:10; 12; 21(2); 14:16; 15:16; 18:29; 19:9; 22:5; 24:5; 6; 8; 20; 25:1; 26:18; 28:15; 21; 29:3; 33; 34; 35; 30:7; 19; 31; 35:9; 37:14; 22; 38:4; 5; 26; 40:21; 42:24; 37; 43:2; 12(2); 13; 21; 44:8; 25; 46:4; 48:21; 50:5; **Ex** 4:7(3); 10:8; 29; 14:13; 26; 15:19; 21:19; 23:4; 24:14; 33:11; 34:35; **Lev** 13:6; 7; 16; 14:39; 43; 20:2; 24:20; 25:48; 51; 52; 26:26; **Num** 11:4; 12:14; 15; 17:10; 22:8; 15; 25; 34; 23:16; 32:15; 33:7; 35:32; **Deut** 1:22; 25; 5:30; 13:16; 15:3; 18:16; 22:1; 2; 4; 23:11; 24:4; 13; 19; 20; 28:68(2); 30:9; 33:11; **Josh** 5:2; 8:21;

14:7; 18:4; 8; 9; 22:28; 32; **Judg** 3:12; 19; 4:1; 20; 6:18; 8:9; 33; 9:37; 10:6; 11:8; 9; 13; 14; 13:1; 8; 9; 15:19; 16:22; 19:3; 7; 20:22; 23; 25; 28; 41; 48; 21:14; **Ruth** 1:11; 12; 14; 21; 4:3; **1Sa** 3:5; 6(2); 8; 21; 4:5; 5:3; 11; 6:21; 9:8; 15:25; 30; 31; 16:10; 17:30; 19:8; 15; 21; 20:17; 23:4; 23; 25:12; 27:4; 29:4; 30:12; **2Sa** 1:9; 2:22; 3:11; 26; 34; 5:22; 6:1; 12:23; 14:13; 14; 21; 29; 15:8; 25; 29; 16:19; 18:22; 19:24; 30; 37; 20:10; 21:15; 18; 19; 22:38; 24:1; **1Kin** 1:45; 2:30; 41; 8:33; 34; 12:5; 12; 20; 21; 27(2); 13:4; 6(2); 9; 17; 33; 17:21; 22; 18:37; 43; 19:6; 7; 20; 20:5; 9; **2Kin** 1:6; 11; 13; 2:18; 4:22; 29; 31; 38; 43; 5:10; 14; 26; 7:8; 9:18; 20; 36; 13:25; 19:9; 30; 20:5; 21:3; 22:9; 20; 24:7; **1Chr** 13:3; 14:13; 14; 20:5; 6; 21:12; 27; **2Chr** 6:25; 10:5; 12; 11:1; 12:11; 13:20; 18:18; 32; 19:4; 20:27; 24:11; 19; 25:10; 28:11; 17; 30:6; 9(2); 32:25; 33:3; 13; 34:16; 28; **Ezr** 2:1; 4:13; 16; 6:5; 21; 9:14; **Neh** 7:6; 8:17; 9:28; 29; 13:9; 21; **Est** 4:10; 6:12; 7:2; 8:3; **Job** 2:1; 6:29; 10:9; 16; 12:14; 23; 14:7; 14; 20:15; 29:22; 34:15; **Ps** 18:37; 37:21; 60:1; 68:22(2); 71:20(2); 78:39; 80:3; 7; 19; 85:6; 8; 104:9; 107:26; 39; 126:1; 4; 6; 140:10; **Prov** 2:19; 3:28; 19:17; 19; 24; 23:35; 24:16; 26:15; **Eccl** 1:6; 7; 3:20; 4:4; 11; 8:14; **Is** 7:10; 8:5; 10:20; 11:11; 24:20; 37:31; 38:8; 46:8; 49:5; 20; 51:22; 52:8; **Jer** 3:1(2); 12:15; 15:19; 16:15; 18:4; 19:11; 23:3; 24:4; 6; 25:5; 27:16; 28:3; 4; 6; 29:14; 30:3; 18; 31:4(2); 16; 17; 21(2); 23; 32:15; 37; 33:10; 12; 13; 36:28; 37:8; 41:16; 46:16; 48:47; 49:6; 39; 50:19; **Lam** 3:40; **Eze** 3:20; 4:6; 5:4; 7:7; 8:6; 13; 15; 11:14; 12:26; 14:12; 16:1; 53(2); 18:1; 27; 21:8; 18; 23:1; 24:1; 25:1; 26:21; 27:1; 28:1; 20; 29:14; 30:1; 33:1; 14; 15; 34:4; 16; 37:4; 15; 39:25; 27; 47:1; 4(2); **Dan** 2:7; 9:25; 10:18; **Hos** 1:6; **Joel** 3:1; **Amos** 7:8; 13; 8:2; 14; 9:14; **Jonah** 2:4; **Mic** 7:19; **Zeph** 3:20; **Hag** 2:20; **Zec** 2:1; 12; 4:1; 12; 8:15; 30; 10:6; 9; 10; 12:6; **Mal** 2:13; **Mt** 2:8; 4:7; 8; 5:33; 7:2; 6; 11:4; 13:44; 45; 47; 16:21; 17:9; 23; 18:19; 19:24; 20:5; 19; 21:36; 22:1; 4; 26:32; 42; 43; 44; 52; 72; 27:3; 50; 63; **Mk** 2:1; 13; 3:1; 20; 4:1; 5:21; 7:31; 8:13; 25; 31; 10:1(2); 10; 24; 32; 34; 11:27; 12:4; 5; 13:16; 14:39; 40; 61; 69; 70(2); 15:4; 12; 13; **Lk** 2:34; 45; 4:20; 6:30; 34; 35; 38; 8:37; 55; 9:8; 19; 39; 42; 10:6; 17; 35; 13:20; 14:6; 12; 15:24; 32; 17:4; 18:33; 20:11; 12; 23:11; 20; 24:7; **Jn** 1:35; 3:3; 7; 4:3; 13; 46; 54; 6:15; 39; 8:2; 8; 12; 21; 9:15; 17; 24; 26; 27; 10:7; 17; 18; 19; 31; 39; 40; 11:7; 8; 23; 24; 38; 12:22; 28; 39; 13:12; 14:3; 28; 16:16; 17; 19; 22; 28; 18:7; 27; 33; 38; 40; 19:4; 9; 37; 20:9; 10; 21; 26; 21:1; 16; **Acts** 1:6; 7:26; 39; 10:15; 16; 11:9; 10; 13:33; 37; 14:21; 15:16(2); 16; 17:3; 32; 18:21; 20:11; 21:6; 22:17; 27:28; **Rom** 4:25; 8:15; 34; 10:7; 11:23; 35; 15:10; 11; 12; **1Cor** 3:20; 7:5; 12:21; 15:4; **2Cor** 1:16; 2:1; 3:1; 5:12; 15; 10:7; 11:16; 12:19; 21; 13:2; **Gal** 1:9; 17; 2:1; 18; 4:9(2); 19; 5:1; 3; **Phil** 1:26; 2:28; 4:4; 10; 16; **1Th** 2:18; 3:9; 4:14; **Titus** 2:9; **Philem** 1:12; **Heb** 1:5; 6; 2:13(2); 4:5; 7; 5:12; 6:1; 6; 10:30; 11:35; 13:20; **Jas** 5:18; **1Pet** 1:3; 23; 2:23; **2Pet** 2:20; 22; **1Jn** 2:8; **Rev** 10:8; 11; 19:3; 20:5

AGAINST

413, 834, 4136, 4775, 5048, 5227, 5704, 5921, 5922, 5973, 5978, 5980, 6440, 6640, 6655, 6903, 6965, 7125, 210, 368, 470, 471, 481, 483, 495, 497, 561, 596, 1519, 1537, 1690, 1693, 1715, 1722, 1727, 1909, 2018, 2019, 2596, 2620, 2649, 2691, 2702, 2713, 2729, 3326, 3844, 4012, 4314, 4366, 5396

Gen 4:8; 14:15; 15:10; 16:12(2); 20:6; 21:16(2); 30:2; 32:25; 34:30; 37:18; 39:9; 40:2(3); 41:36; 42:22; 36; 43:18; 25; 44:18; 50:20; **Ex** 1:10; 4:14; 7:15; 8:12; 9:17; 10:16(2); 11:7(2); 12:12; 14:2; 5; 25; 27; 15:7; 24; 16:2; 7(2); 8(3); 17:3; 19:11; 15; 20:16; 23:29; 33; 25:27; 37; 26:17; 35; 28:27; 32:10; 11; 12; 33; 37:14; 39:20; 40:24; **Lev** 4:2(2); 13; 14; 22; 27; 5:19; 6:2; 17:10; 19:16; 18; 20:3; 5(2); 6; 26:17; 40; **Num** 5:6; 7; 12; 13; 27; 8:2; 3; 10:9; 21; 11:18; 33; 12:1; 8; 9; 13:31; 14:2(2); 9; 27(2); 29; 35; 36; 16:3(2); 11(2); 19; 38; 41(2); 42(2); 17:5; 10; 20:2(2); 18; 20; 24; 21:1; 5(2); 7(2); 23(2); 26; 33; 22:5; 34; 23:23(2); 24:10; 25:3; 4; 26:9(3); 27:3; 14; 30:9; 31:3; 7; 16; 32:13; 23; 35:30; **Deut** 1:1; 26; 41; 43; 44; 2:15; 19; 32; 3:1; 29; 4:26; 46; 5:20; 6:15; 7:4; 8:19; 9:7; 16; 19; 23; 24; 11:17; 30; 15:9(2); 19:11; 15; 16(2); 18; 20:1; 3; 4; 10; 12; 18; 19(2); 20; 21:10; 22:14; 17; 26; 23:4; 9; 24:15; 28:7(2); 25; 48; 49; 29:7; 20; 27; 30:19; 31:17; 19; 21; 26; 27; 28; 32:49; 51; 33:11; 34:1; 6; **Josh** 1:18; 3:16; 5:13; 7:1; 13; 20; 8:3; 4; 5; 14(2); 22; 33(2); 9:1; 18; 10:5; 6; 21; 25; 29; 31(2); 34(2); 36; 38; 11:5; 7; 20; 18:17; 18; 19:47; 22:11; 12; 16(2); 18; 19(2); 22; 29; 31; 33; 23:16; 24:9; 11; 22; **Judg** 1:1(2); 3; 5; 8; 9; 10; 11; 2:14; 15; 20; 3:8; 10; 12; 4:24; 5:14; 20; 23; 6:2; 3; 31; 32; 39; 7:2; 22; 24; 9:18; 31; 33; 34; 43; 45; 50; 52; 10:7; 9(3); 10; 18; 11:4; 5; 8; 9; 12; 20; 25(2); 27(2); 32; 12:1; 3; 20:1; 4; 5; 15:10; 14; 16:5; 18:9; 19:2; 10; 20:5; 9; 11; 14; 18; 19; 20(2); 23(2); 24; 25; 28; 30(2); 31; 34; 43; **Ruth** 1:13; 21; **1Sa** 2:25(2); 3:12; 4:1; 2; 5:9; 7:6; 7; 10; 13; 9:14; 11:1; 12:3; 5; 9; 12; 14; 15:3(3); 23; 14:5(2); 30; 33; 34; 47(6); 52; 15:7; 18; 17:2; 9; 21; 28; 33; 35; 55; 18:21; 19:4(3); 5; 20:30; 22:8(2); 13(2); 23:1; 3; 9; 28; 24:6; 7; 10; 11;

AGO

1Sa 9:20; **2Kin** 19:25; **Ezr** 5:11; **Is** 22:11; 37:26; **Mt** 11:21; **Mk** 9:21; **Lk** 10:13; **Acts** 10:30; 15:7; **2Cor** 8:10; 9:2; 12:2

AH

162, 253, 1945, 3758

Ps 35:25; **Is** 1:4; 24; **Jer** 1:6; 4:10; 14:13; 22:18(4); 32:17; 34:5; **Eze** 4:14; 9:8; 11:13; 20:49; 21:15; **Mk** 15:29

AHA

253

Ps 35:21(2); 40:15(2); 70:3(2); **Is** 44:16; **Eze** 25:3; 26:2; 36:2

ALAS

160, 162, 188, 253, 994, 1930, 1945, 3759

Num 12:11; 24:23; **Josh** 7:7; **Judg** 6:22; 11:35; **1Kin** 13:30; **2Kin** 3:10; 6:5; 15; **Jer** 30:7; **Eze** 6:11; **Joel** 1:15; **Amos** 5:16(2); **Rev** 18:10(2); 16(2); 19(2)

ALIKE

259, 834, 1571, 3162, 7737

Deut 12:22; 15:22; **1Sa** 30:24; **Job** 21:26; **Ps** 33:15; 139:12; **Prov** 20:10; 27:15; **Eccl** 9:2; 11:6; **Rom** 14:5

ALL

622, 1571, 3162, 3605, 3606, 3632, 3650, 3885, 4393, 4557, 5973, 7230, 8552, 537, 1273, 2527, 3122, 3364, 3367, 3650, 3654, 3745, 3762, 3779, 3829, 3832, 3833, 3837, 3843, 3956, 4219, 4561, 5033

Gen 1:26; 29; 2:1; 2; 3; 20; 3:14(2); 17; 20; 4:21; 5:5; 8; 11; 14; 17; 20; 23; 27; 31; 6:2; 12; 13; 17; 19; 21; 22; 7:1; 3; 5; 11; 14; 15; 16; 19; 21; 22(2); 8:1; 17; 9:2(2); 3; 10; 11; 15(2); 16; 17; 29; 10:21; 29; 11:6; 8; 9(2); 12:3; 5; 20; 13:1; 10; 11; 14:3; 7; 11(2); 16; 20; 15:10; 16:12; 17:8; 23(2); 27; 18:18; 25; 26; 28; 19:2(4); 4; 17; 25(2); 28; 31; 20:7; 8(2); 16(2); 18; 21:6; 12; 22; 22:18; 23:10; 17(2); 18; 24:1; 2; 10; 20; 36; 54; 66; 25:4; 5; 18; 25; 26:3; 4(2); 11; 15; 27:33; 37; 28:11; 14; 15; 22; 29:3; 8; 13; 22; 30:32(3); 35(2); 40; 31:1(2); 6; 8(2); 12(2); 16; 18(2); 21; 34; 37(2); 43; 54; 32:5; 4(2); 6; 36:6(3); 37:3; 4; 35(2); 39:3; 4; 5(2); 6; 8; 22; 40:17; 20; 41:8(2); 19; 29; 30; 35; 37; 39; 40; 41; 43; 44; 45; 46; 48; 51(2); 54(2); 55(2); 56(2); 57(2); 42:6; 11; 17; 29; 36; 45:1; 8(2); 9; 10; 11; 13(2); 15; 22(2); 24; 26(2); 27; 32; 47:1; 12; 13(2); 14; 15; 17; 20; 48:15; 16; 49:28; 50:7(2); 8; 14; 15; **Ex** 1:5; 6(2); 14(2); 22; 3:15; 20; 4:19; 21; 28(2); 29; 5:12; 23; 6:29; 7:2; 19(2); 20; 24; 8:2; 4; 16; 17(2); 24; 9:4; 6; 9(2); 11; 14(2); 16; 19; 22; 24; 25(2); 10:6(2); 12; 13(2); 14(2); 15(2); 19; 22; 23; 11:5(3); 8; 12:6(2); 15; 16; 17; 20; 26(2); 27; 32; 47:1; 12; 13(2); 14; 15; 17; 20; 48:15; 16; 49:28; 50:7(2); 8; 14; 15; 13:2; 7; 9(2); 11; 18; 24; 29; 15:1; 6(2); 14(2); 16; 19:5; 7; 8(2); 11; 16; 20:1; 9; 11; 18; 24; 22:9; 23; 26; 23:13; 17; 22; 27(2); 24:3(4); 4; 7; 8; 25:9(2); 36; 39; 26:8; 27:3; 17; 19(4); 28:3; 31; 38; 29:12; 13; 24; 35; 30:27; 28; 31:3; 5; 6(2); 7; 8; 9; 11; 32:3; 13; 26; 29(3); 30; 31; 32(2); 35:1; 4; 10; 13; 16; 20; 21; 22; 25; 26; 29; 31; 35; 36:1(2); 8; 38:3(2); 4; 7; 9; 22; 37:22; 24:2; 1; 10; 20; 36; 40:9; 10; 16; 36; 38(2); **Lev** 1:9; 13; 2:2; 13; 16; 3:3; 9; 14; 16; 17; 4:7; 8(2); 11; 18; 19; 26; 30; 31; 34; 35; 6:3; 5; 7; 9; 15; 18; 29; 7:3; 9(2); 10; 18; 8:3; 10; 11; 16; 25; 27; 36; 9:5; 23; 24; 10:3; 6; 11; 11:2; 9; 10(2); 20(2); 21; 23; 27(2); 31; 34(2); 42(2); 13:12; 13(2); 14:8(2); 9(2); 36; 45; 46; 54; 15:16; 24(2); 25; 26; 16:2; 16; 17; 21(3); 22; 29; 30; 33; 34; 17:4; 13; 18:24; 27; 19:2; 7; 13; 20; 23; 24; 37(2); 20:5; 22(2); 23; 21:24; 22(2); 18(3); 23:3; 14; 21; 31; 38(2); 42; 24:14(2); 16; 25:7; 9; 10(2); 24; 26:14; 15; 18; 27; 44; 27:9; 10; 13; 25; 28; 30; 31; 33; **Num** 1:2; 3; 18; 20; 22; 24; 26; 28; 30; 32; 34; 36; 40; 42; 45(2); 46; 50(3); 54; 2:9; 16; 24; 31; 32; 34; 3:8; 12; 13(3); 22; 26; 28; 31; 34; 36(2); 39(2); 40; 41(2); 42; 43; 45; 4:3; 9; 10; 12; 14(2); 15; 16(2); 23; 26(2); 27(4); 31; 32(2); 33; 37; 41; 46; 5:9; 30; 6:4; 5; 6; 8; 7:1(2); 85; 86; 87; 88; 8:7; 16; 17; 18; 20(2); 9:3(2); 5; 12; 10:3; 25; 11:6; 11; 12; 13; 14; 22; 29; 33(4); 12:3; 7; 13:3; 26(2); 32; 14:1; 2; 5; 7; 10(2); 11;

15; 21; 22; 29; 35; 36; 39; 15:13; 22; 23; 24; 25; 26(2); 33; 35; 36; 39; 40; 16:3; 5; 6; 10; 11; 16; 19(2); 22(2); 26; 28; 29(2); 30; 31; 32(2); 33; 34; 41; 17:2; 9(2); 12; 18:3; 4; 8; 11; 12(2); 15; 19; 21; 28; 29(2); 19:14(2); 18; 20:14; 27; 29(2); 21:23; 25(3); 26; 33; 34; 35; 22:2; 4; 38; 23:6; 13; 25(2); 26; 24:17; 25:4; 6; 26:2(2); 43; 62; 27:2; 16; 19; 20; 21(2); 22; 29:40; 30:2; 4; 6; 11; 14(2); 31:4; 7; 9(4); 10(2); 11(2); 13; 15; 18; 20(4); 23; 27; 30; 35; 51; 52; 32:13; 15; 21; 26; 33:3; 4; 52(4); 35:3; 7; 29; **Deut** 1:1; 3; 7; 18; 19; 30; 31; 41; 2:7; 14; 16; 32; 33; 34; 36; 3:1; 2; 3; 4(2); 5; 7; 10(3); 13(3); 14; 18; 21(2); 4:3; 6; 7; 8; 9; 10; 19(2); 29(2); 30; 34; 49; 5:1; 3; 13; 22; 23; 26; 27(2); 28; 29; 31; 33; 6:2(2); 5(3); 11; 19; 22; 24; 25; 7:6; 7; 14; 15(2); 16; 18; 19; 8:1; 2; 13; 19; 9:10; 18; 10:12(3); 14; 15; 11:3; 6(2); 7; 8; 13(2); 22(2); 23; 25; 32; 12:1; 2; 5; 7; 8; 10; 11(2); 14; 15; 18; 28; 13:3(2); 9; 11; 15; 16(2); 18; 14:2; 9(2); 11; 20; 22; 28; 29; 15:5; 10(2); 18; 19; 16:3; 4(2); 15(2); 16; 18; 17:7; 10; 13; 14; 19(2); 18:1; 5; 6(2); 7; 12; 16; 18; 19:8; 9; 20:11; 14(2); 15; 18; 21:6; 14; 17; 21(2); 23; 22:3; 5; 19; 29; 23:6; 20; 24:8; 19; 25:16(2); 18; 19; 26:2; 12; 13; 14; 16(2); 18; 19; 27:1; 3; 8; 9; 14; 15; 16; 17; 18; 19; 20; 21; 22; 23; 24; 25; 26(2); 28:1(2); 2; 8; 10; 12; 15(2); 20; 25; 26; 32; 33; 37; 40; 42; 45; 47; 48; 52(4); 55; 57; 58; 60; 64; 29:2(4); 9; 10(2); 20; 21(2); 24; 27; 29; 30:1(2); 2(3); 3; 6(2); 7; 8; 10(2); 31:1; 5; 7; 9; 11(2); 12; 18; 28; 30; 32:4; 27; 44; 46(2); 6(2); 33:3; 12; 34:1; 2(2); 11(3); 12(3) **Josh** 1:2; 4; 5; 7; 8; 14; 16; 17; 18; 2:3; 9; 13; 18; 22; 23; 24(2); 3:1; 7; 11; 13; 15(2); 17(2); 4:1; 10; 11; 14(2); 18; 24; 5:1(2); 4(2); 5(2); 6; 8; 6:3; 5; 17(2); 19; 21; 22; 23(2); 24; 25; 27; 7:3(2); 7; 9; 15; 23; 24(2); 25; 8:1; 3; 4; 5; 11; 13; 14; 15; 16; 21; 24(3); 25(2); 26; 33; 34(2); 35(2); 9:1(2); 5; 9; 10; 11; 18; 19(2); 21; 24(2); 10:2; 5; 6; 7(2); 9; 15; 21; 24; 25; 28; 29; 30; 31; 32(2); 34; 35(2); 36; 37(4); 38; 39(2); 40(3); 41; 42; 43; 11:4; 5; 6; 7; 10; 11; 12(2); 14; 15; 16(3); 17; 18; 19; 21(2); 23; 12:1; 5; 24; 13:2(2); 4; 5; 14(5); 15(2); 24; 1; 2; 17(2); 18; 27(2); 31(3); 33; 12(2); 18; 28; 30; 32:4; 27; 44; 46(2); 6(2); 33:3; 12; 34:1; 2(2); 11(3); 12(3) **Judg** 1:25; 2:4; 7(3); 10; 18; 3:1; 3; 19; 29(2); 4:13(2); 15(2); 16; 5:31; 6:9; 13(2); 31; 33; 35; 37; 39; 40; 7:1; 6; 7; 8; 12; 14; 18(2); 21; 22; 23; 24(2); 8:10(2); 12; 27; 34; 35; 9:1; 2(2); 3(2); 6(2); 14; 25; 34; 44; 45; 46; 47; 48; 49(2); 51(2); 53; 57; 10:8; 18; 11:8; 11; 20; 21(2); 22; 26; 12:4; 13:13; 14; 23; 14:3; 16:2(2); 3; 17; 18(2); 27; 30(2); 31; 18:1; 31; 19:6; 9; 13; 20; 25; 29; 30; 20:1; 2(2); 6; 7; 8; 10(2); 11; 12; 16; 17; 25; 26(2); 33; 34; 35; 37; 44; 46(2); 48(2); 21:5; **Ruth** 1:19; 2:11; 21; 3:5; 6; 11(2); 16; 4:7; 9(3); 11; **1Sa** 1:4; 11; 21; 2:14(2); 22(2); 23; 28(2); 29; 32; 33; 3:12; 17; 20; 4:1; 5; 8; 13; 5:8; 11(2); 6:4; 18; 7:2; 3(2); 5; 13; 15; 16; 8:4; 5; 7; 8; 10; 20; 21; 9:6; 19; 20(2); 21; 10:9; 11; 18; 19; 20; 24(3); 25; 11:1; 2(2); 3; 4; 7; 10; 15(2); 12:1(2); 7; 18; 19(2); 20(2); 24; 13:3; 4; 7; 10; 14:7; 15; 20; 24(3); 25; 11:1; 2(2); 3; 4; 7; 10; 15(2); 12:1(2); 7; 18; 19(2); 20(2); 24; 13:3; 4; 7; 10; 14:7; 15; 20; 24; 38; 39; 40; 47; 52; 15:3; 6; 8; 9; 11; 16:11; 17:11; 19; 24; 46; 47; 18:5; 6; 14; 16; 22; 30; 19:1; 5; 7; 18; 24(2); 20:6(2); 22:1; 4; 6; 7; 8; 11(2); 14; 15(2); 16; 22; 23:8; 20; 23(2); 24:2; 25:1; 6; 7; 9; 12; 16; 17; 21(2); 22; 28; 30; 26:12; 24; 27:11; 28:3; 4; 20(3); 29:1; 30:6; 8; 16(2); 18; 19; 20; 22; 31; 31:6; 12(2); **2Sa** 1:11; 2:9; 28; 29(2); 30; 32; 3:12; 18; 19; 21(2); 23; 25; 29; 31; 32; 34; 35; 36(2); 37(2); 4:1; 7; 9; 5:1; 3; 5; 17; 6:1; 2; 5(2); 11; 12; 14; 15; 19(2); 21; 7:1; 3; 7(2); 9; 11; 17(2); 21; 22; 8:4; 9; 11; 14(2); 15(2); 9:7; 9(2); 11; 12; 10:7; 9; 17; 19; 11:1; 9; 18; 22; 12:12; 16; 29; 31(2); 13:9; 21; 23; 25; 27; 29; 30; 31; 32; 33; 34; 14:19(2); 20; 25; 15:6; 10; 14; 16; 17; 18(4); 22(2); 23(3); 24(2); 30; 16:4; 6(3); 8; 11; 14; 15; 18; 21(2); 22; 23; 17:2; 3(3); 4; 10; 11; 12; 13; 14; 16; 22; 24; 18:4; 5(2); 8; 17; 28; 31; 32; 19:2; 5; 6; 7; 8(2); 9(2); 11; 14(2); 15; 20; 20; 30; 31; 40; 41(2); 42(2); 20:7; 12; 13; 14(2); 15; 22; 23; 21:9; 14; 22; 23; 31; 23:5(3); 6; 39; 24:2; 7; 8; 23; **1Kin** 1:3; 9(2); 19; 20; 25; 29; 39; 40; 41; 49; 2:2; 3; 4(2); 15; 26; 44; 3:13; 15; 28; 4:1; 7; 10; 11; 12; 21(2); 24(3); 25; 27; 30(2); 31(2); 34(2); 5:6; 8; 10; 13; 6:10; 12; 18; 22; 29; 38(2); 7:1; 5; 9; 14(2); 23; 25; 33; 37; 40; 45; 47; 48; 51; 8:1; 2; 3; 4; 5; 14(2); 16; 22(2); 23; 38; 39; 40; 43(2); 48; 50; 52; 53; 54; 55; 56(2); 58; 59; 60; 62; 63; 65; 66; 9:1; 4; 6; 7; 9; 11; 19(2); 20; 10(2); 3; 4; 13; 15; 21(2); 23; 24; 29; 11:8; 13; 16; 25; 28; 32; 34; 37; 38; 41; 42; 12:1; 3; 12; 13; 14; 16; 20(2); 21; 23; 31; 25:3(3); 6; 39; 24:2; 7; 8; 23; **2Kin** 3:6; 19; 21(2); 25(2); 4:3; 4; 13; 5:12; 15(2); 21; 22; 6:24; 7:13(2); 15; 8:4; 6(2); 21; 23; 9:5; 7; 11; 14; 10:5; 9(2); 11(2); 17; 18; 19(3); 21(2); 20; 12:2; 4(2); 9; 12; 18(2); 19; 13:18; 21; 22; 28; 15:3; 6; 16(2); 18; 20; 21; 26; 29; 31; 34; 36; 16:10; 11; 15(3); 16; 17:5; 9; 11; 13(3); 16(2); 20; 22; 23; 29; 18:3; 5; 12; 13; 19(3); 21(2); 23(2); 24; 28; 28(2); 7:2; 10; 13; 15; 23; 25; 27; 8:2; 3(2); 12; 16;

19(2); 20; 21; 22; 24; 25(4); 26; 28; 32; 37; 24:3; 5; 7; 9; 13(2); 14(4); 16(2); 19; 25:1; 4; 5; 9; 10; 14; 16; 17; 23; 26; 29; 30; **1Chr** 1:23; 33; 2:4; 6; 23; 3:9; 4:27; 33; 5:10; 16; 17; 20; 6:48; 49(2); 60; 7:3; 5(2); 8; 11; 40; 8:38; 40; 9:1; 9; 22; 29; 10:6; 7; 11(2); 12; 11:1; 3; 4; 10; 12:15(2); 21; 32; 33; 37; 38(3); 13:2(2); 4(2); 5; 6; 8(2); 14; 14:8(2); 17(2); 15:3; 27; 28; 16:9; 14; 23; 24; 25; 26; 30; 32; 36; 40; 43; 17:2; 6; 8; 10; 15(2); 19(2); 20; 18:4; 9; 10; 11; 13; 14(2); 19:8; 10; 17; 20:3(2); 21:3; 4; 5; 12; 22; 22:5; 9; 15; 17; 23:2; 28; 29; 31; 28:1(3); 4(2); 5; 8(2); 9(2); 12(2); 13(2); 14(4); 19(2); 20; 21(3); 29:1; 2(2); 3; 5; 10; 11(2); 12(2); 14; 15; 16(2); 17; 18(2); 19(2); 20; 21; 23; 24(2); 25; 26; 30(2); **2Chr** 1:2(2); 3; 17; 2:5; 17; 4:4; 16; 18; 19; 5:1(3); 2; 3; 4; 5; 6; 8; 11; 17; 20; 22; 8:4; 6(4); 7; 16; 9:1; 2; 12; 14; 20(2); 22; 23; 26; 28; 30; 10:1; 3; 12; 16(2); 11:3; 13(2); 16; 21; 23(2); 12:1; 9; 13; 13:4; 15; 14:5; 8; 14(2); 15:2; 5; 6; 8; 9; 12(2); 15(2); 17; 16:4; 6; 17:2; 5; 9; 10; 18:9; 19; 20:3; 5; 6; 8(2); 10; 13; 16; 17; 20; 21; 24:2; 5; 7; 10(2); 14; 23(2); 25:5; 7; 12; 24(2); 26:1; 4; 14; 20; 27:2; 7; 28:6; 14; 15(2); 23; 26; 29:2; 16; 18(3); 19; 24(2); 28(2); 29; 32; 34; 36; 30:1; 2; 4; 5; 6; 14; 22; 25(2); 31:1(5); 5(2); 18(2); 19(2); 20; 21; 32:4; 5; 7; 9(2); 13; 14; 21; 22; 23; 27; 28; 30; 31; 33; 33:3; 5; 7; 8; 14; 15; 19; 22; 25; 34:7(2); 9(2); 12; 13; 16; 21; 24; 25; 28; 29; 30(3); 31(2); 32; 33(4); 35:3; 7(2); 13; 16; 18(2); 20; 24; 25; 36:14(2); 17; 18(2); 19(2); 22; 23(2); **Ezr** 1:1; 2; 3; 5; 6(2); 11(2); 2:42; 58; 70; 3:5; 8; 11; 4:5; 20; 5:7; 6:12; 17; 20(2); 21; 7:6; 13; 16(2); 21; 25(2); 28; 8:20; 21; 22(2); 25; 34; 35(2); 9:13; 10:3; 5; 7; 8; 9(2); 12; 14(2); 16; 17; 44; **Neh** 4:6; 8; 12; 15; 16; 5:13; 16; 18(2); 19; 6:9; 16(2); 7:60; 73; 8:1; 2; 3; 5(3); 6; 9(2); 11; 12; 13; 15; 17; 9:2; 5; 6(4); 10(2); 25; 32(2); 33; 38; 10:28; 29; 33; 35(2); 37(2); 11:2; 6; 18; 20; 24; 12:27; 47; 13:3; 6; 8; 12; 15; 16; 18; 20; 26; 27; 30; **Est** 1:3; 5; 8; 13; 16(3); 17; 18; 20(2); 22; 2:3(2); 15; 17(2); 18; 3:1; 2; 6; 8(2); 12; 13(2); 14; 4:1; 7; 11; 13; 16; 17; 5:11; 13; 14; 6:10; 13; 8:5; 9; 11; 12; 13; 9:2(2); 3; 4; 5; 20(2); 24; 26; 27; 29; 30; 10:2; 3; **Job** 1:3; 5; 10; 11; 12; 22; 2:4; 10; 11; 4:14; 8:13; 9:28; 12:9; 10; 13:1; 4; 27; 14:14; 15:20; 16:2; 7; 17:7; 10; 19:19; 20:26; 24:24; 27:3; 12; 28:3; 21; 29:19; 30:23; 31:4; 12; 33:1; 11; 29; 34:15; 19; 21; 36:19; 37:7; 38:7; 18; 40:20; 41:34(2); 42:11(4); 15; **Ps** 2:12; 3:7; 5(5); 11; 6:6; 7; 8; 10; 7:1; 8:1; 6; 7; 9; 9:1; 14; 17; 10:4; 5; 12:3; 14:3(2); 4; 16:3; 18:4; 22; 30; 19:4; 20:3; 4; 5; 21:8; 22:7; 14; 17; 23(2); 27(2); 29(2); 23:6; 25:5; 10; 18; 22; 26:7; 27:4; 31:11; 23; 24; 32:3; 11; 33:4; 6; 8(2); 11; 13; 14; 34:1; 4; 6; 17; 35:10; 28; 38:6; 9; 12; 39:8; 12; 40:16; 41:3; 7; 42:7; 44:8; 17; 22; 45:8; 13; 16; 17; 47:1; 2; 7; 49:1(2); 11; 50:11; 51:9; 52:4; 54:7; 56:5; 57:2; 5; 11; 59:5; 8; 62:3; 8; 64:8; 9; 10; 65:2; 5; 66:1; 4; 16; 67:2; 3; 5; 7; 69:19; 70:4; 71:8; 15; 24; 72:5; 11(2); 17; 73:14; 27; 28; 74:3; 8; 17; 75:3; 8; 10; 76:9; 11; 77:12; 78:14; 32; 38; 51; 79:13; 80:12; 82:5; 6; 8; 83:11; 18; 85:2; 3; 5; 86:5; 9; 12; 87:2; 7; 88:7; 89:1; 4; 7; 16; 40; 41; 42; 47; 50; 90:1; 9; 14; 91:11; 92:7; 9; 94:4; 15; 95:3; 96:1; 3; 4; 5; 9; 12(2); 97:6; 7(2); 9(2); 98:3; 4; 99:2; 100:1; 5; 101:8(2); 102:8; 12; 15; 24; 26; 103:1; 2; 3(2); 6; 19; 21; 22(2); 104:20; 24; 27; 105:2; 7; 21; 31; 35; 36(2); 106:2; 3; 31; 46; 48; 107:18; 42; 108:5; 109:11; 111:2; 7; 10; 113:4; 116:11; 12; 14; 18; 117:1(2); 118:10; 119:6; 13; 14; 20; 63; 86; 90; 91; 96; 97; 99; 118; 119; 128(2); 151; 168; 172; 121:7; 128:5; 129:5; 130:8; 132:1; 134:1; 135:5; 6; 9; 11; 13; 136:25; 138:2; 4; 139:3; 16; 143:5; 12; 144:13; 145:9(2); 10; 13; 14(2); 15; 17(2); 9(2); 10; 11(2); 14; 146:6; 10; 147:4; 148:2(2); 3; 7; 9(2); 10; 11(2); 14; 149:9; **Prov** 1:13; 14; 25; 30; 3:5; 6; 9; 15; 17; 4:22; 26; 5:14; 19; 21; 6:31; 8:8; 9; 11; 16; 36; 10:12; 14:23; 15:15; 16:2; 4; 11; 17:17; 18:1; 19:7; 20:8; 27; 21:26; 22:2; 23:17; 24:4; 31; 26:10; 28:5; 29:11; 12; 30:4; 27; 31:8; 12; 21; 29; **Eccl** 1:2; 3; 7; 8; 13; 14(2); 16; 2:3; 5; 7; 8; 9; 10(2); 11(2); 14; 16; 17; 18; 19; 20; 22; 23; 3:13; 19(2); 20(3); 4:1; 4; 8; 15; 16(2); 5:9; 16; 17; 18(2); 6:2; 6; 7; 12; 7:2; 15; 18; 21; 23; 28; 8:9; 17; 9:1(3); 2(2); 3; 4(2); 9; 11; 10:19; 11:5; 8(2); 9; 12:4; 8; **Song** 1:13; 3:6; 8; 4:4; 7; 10; 14(2); 7:13; 8:7; **Is** 1:5; 2(2); 13(2); 14(2); 16(2); 4:5; 5:25; 28; 7:19(3); 24; 25; 8:7(3); 9; 12; 9:9; 12; 17; 21; 10:4; 14; 23; 11:9; 12:5; 13:7; 14:9(2); 10; 18(2); 26; 15:2; 16:14; 18:3; 6; 19:8; 10; 21:2; 9; 16; 22:3(2); 24(3); 23:9(2); 17; 24:7; 11; 25:6; 7(2); 8(2); 26:12; 14; 15; 27:9(2); 28:8; 24; 29:7(2); 8; 11; 20; 30:5; 18; 31:3; 32:13; 32:13; 15; 19; 21; 31; 34(2); 35:1; 13; 14; 16:14; 26; 17:10; 27; 29; 18:12; 21; 22; 28; 31; 43; 19:7; 37; 48; 20:6; 32; 35; 36; 38; 22(2); 23; 24; 25; 27(2); 44; 47; **Jn** 1:3; 7; 16; 2:15; 24; 3:26; 31(2); 35; 4:25; 29; 45; 5:20; 22; 23; 28; 6:37; 39; 45; 7:21; 8:2; 10:8; 29; 41; 11:48; 49; 12:32; 13:3; 10; 11; 18; 35; 14:26(2); 15:15; 21; 16:13; 15; 30; 17:2; 7; 10; 21; 18:4; 38; 40; 19:11; 28; 21:11; 17; **Acts** 1:1; 8; 14; 18; 19; 21; 24; 2:1; 2; 4; 7(2); 12; 14; 17; 32; 36; 39; 44(2); 45; 47; 3:9; 11; 16; 18; 21(2); 24; 29; 31; 32; 33; 5:5; 11; 12; 17; 20; 21; 23; 34; 36; 37; 6:15; 7:10(2); 11; 14; 22; 50; 8:1; 10; 27; 37; 40; 9:14; 21; 26; 31; 32; 35; 39; 40; 42; 10:2; 8; 12; 22; 33(2); 36; 37; 38; 39; 41; 43; 44; 11:10; 14; 23; 28; 12:11; 13:10(3); 22; 24; 29; 39(2); 49; 14:15; 16; 27; 15:3; 4; 12; 17(2);

18; 16:3; 26; 28; 32; 33; 34; 17:5; 7; 11; 15; 21; 22; 24; 25(2); 26(2); 30; 31; 18:2; 8; 17; 21; 23(2); 19:7; 10; 17(2); 19; 26; 27; 34; 20:18; 19; 25; 26; 27; 28; 32; 35; 36; 37; 38; 21:5; 18; 20; 21; 24; 27; 28; 30; 31; 22:3; 5; 10; 12; 15; 30; 23:1; 24:3(2); 5; 8; 14; 25:8; 24(2); 26:2; 3; 4; 14; 20; 29; 27:20; 24; 33; 35; 36; 37; 44; 28:30; 31; **Rom** 1:5; 7; 8; 18; 29; 3:9; 12; 19; 22(2); 23; 4:11; 16(2); 5:12(2); 18(2); 7:8; 8:28; 32(2); 36; 37; 9:5; 6; 7; 17; 10:12(2); 16; 18; 21; 11:26; 32(2); 36; 12:4; 17; 18; 13:7; 14:2; 10; 20; 15:11(2); 13; 14; 33; 16:4; 15; 19; 24; 26; **1Cor** 1:2; 5(2); 10; 2:10; 15; 3:21; 22; 4:13; 6:12(3); 7:7; 17; 8:1; 6(2); 9:12; 19(2); 22(3); 24; 25; 10:1(2); 2; 3; 4; 11; 17; 23(4); 31; 33(2); 11:2; 5; 12; 18; 12:6(2); 11; 12; 13(2); 19; 26(2); 29(4); 30(3); 13:2(3); 3; 7(4); 14:5; 18; 21; 23; 24(3); 26; 31(3); 33; 40; 15:3; 7; 8; 10; 19; 22(2); 24(2); 25; 27(3); 28(4); 29; 39; 51(2); 16:12; 14; 20; 24; **2Cor** 1:1(2); 3; 4; 20; 2:3(2); 5; 9; 3:2; 18; 4:15; 5:10; 14(2); 15; 17; 18; 6:4; 10; 7:1; 4; 11; 13; 14; 15; 16; 8:7; 18; 9:8(3); 11; 13; 10:6; 11:6; 9; 28; 12:12; 19; 13:2; 13; 14; **Gal** 1:2; 2:14; 3:8; 10; 22; 26; 28; 4:1; 12; 26; 5:14; 6:6; 10; **Eph** 1:3; 8; 10; 11; 15; 21; 22(2); 23(2); 2:3; 21; 3:8; 9(2); 18; 19; 20; 21; 4:2; 6(4); 10(2); 13; 15; 19; 31(2); 5:3; 9; 13; 20; 6:13; 16(2); 18(3); 21; 24; **Phil** 1:1; 4; 7(2); 8; 9; 13(2); 20; 25; 2:14; 17; 21; 26; 29; 3:8(2); 21; 4:5; 7; 12; 13; 18; 19; 22; 23; **Col** 1:4; 6; 9; 10; 11(2); 16(2); 17(2); 18; 19; 20; 28; 2:2; 3; 9; 10; 13; 19; 22; 3:8; 11(2); 14; 16; 17; 20; 22; 4:7; 9; 12; **1Th** 1:2; 7; 2:15; 3:7; 9; 12; 13; 4:6; 10(2); 5:5; 14; 15; 21; 22; 26; 27; **2Th** 1:3; 4; 10; 11; 2:4; 9; 10; 12; 3:2; 11; 16(2); 18; **1Ti** 1:15; 16; 2:1(2); 2(2); 4; 6; 11; 3:4; 11; 4:8; 9; 10; 15; 5:2; 20; 6:1; 10; 13; 17; **2Ti** 1:15; 2:7; 10; 24; 3:9; 11; 12; 16; 17; 4:2; 5; 8; 16; 17; 21; **Titus** 1:15; 2:7; 9; 10(2); 11; 14; 15; 3:2(2); 15(2); **Philem** 1:5; **Heb** 1:2; 3; 6; 11; 14; 2:8(3); 10(2); 11; 15; 17; 3:2; 4; 5; 16; 4:4; 13; 15; 5:9; 6:16; 7:2; 7; 8:5; 11; 9:3; 8; 17; 19(2); 21; 22; 10:10; 11:13; 39; 12:8; 14; 23; 13:4; 18; 24(2); 25; **Jas** 1:2; 5; 8; 21; 2:10; 3:2; 4:16; 5:12; **1Pet** 1:15; 24(2); 2:1(3); 17; 18; 3:8; 4:7; 8; 11; 5:5; 7; 10; 14; **2Pet** 1:3; 5; 3:4; 9; 11(2); 16; **1Jn** 1:5; 7; 9; 2:16; 19; 20; 27; 3:20; 5:17; **2Jn** 1; **3Jn** 2; 12; **Jude** 3; 15(4); **Rev** 1:2; 7; 2:23; 3:10; 4:11; 5:6; 13; 7:4; 9; 11; 17; 8:3; 7; 11:6; 12:5; 13:3; 7; 8; 12; 16; 14:8; 15:4; 18:3; 12(3); 14(2); 17; 19; 21; 22(2); 23(3); 24; 19:5; 17; 18; 21; 21:4; 5; 7; 8; 19; 25; 22:21

ALMOST

4592, *3195, 3641, 4975*

Ex 17:4; **Ps** 73:2; 94:17; 119:87; **Prov** 5:14; **Acts** 13:44; 19:26; 21:27; 26:28; 29; **Heb** 9:22

ALONE

259, 905, 909, 2308, 4422, 7503, 7662, 7896, *863, 1438, 1439, 2398, 2596, 2651, 3440, 3441*

Gen 2:18; 32:24; 42:38; 44:20; **Ex** 14:12; 18:14; 18; 24:2; 32:10; **Lev** 13:46; **Num** 11:14; 17; 23:9; **Deut** 1:9; 12; 9:14; 32:12; 33:28; **Josh** 22:20; **Judg** 3:20; 11:37; **1Sa** 21:1; **2Sa** 16:11; 18:24; 25; 26; **1Kin** 11:29; **2Kin** 4:27; 19:15; 23:18(2); **1Chr** 29:1; **Ezr** 6:7; **Neh** 9:6; **Est** 3:6; **Job** 1:15; 16; 17; 19; 7:16; 19; 9:8; 10:20; 13:13; 15:19; 31:17; **Ps** 83:18; 86:10; 102:7; 136:4; 148:13; **Prov** 9:12; **Eccl** 4:8; 10; 11; **Is** 2:11; 17; 5:8; 14:31; 37:16; 44:24; 49:21; 51:2; 63:3; **Jer** 15:17; 49:31; **Lam** 3:28; **Dan** 10:7; 8; **Hos** 4:17; 8:9; **Mt** 4:4; 14:23; 15:14; 18:15; **Mk** 1:24; 4:10; 34; 6:47; 14:6; 15:36; **Lk** 4:4; 34; 5:21; 6:4; 9:18; 36; 10:40; 13:8; **Jn** 6:15; 22; 8:9; 16; 29; 11:48; 12:7; 24; 16:32(2); 17:20; **Acts** 5:38; 19:26; **Rom** 4:23; 11:3; **Gal** 6:4; **1Th** 3:1; **Heb** 9:7; **Jas** 2:17

ALONG

1980, 6967

Ex 2:5; 9:23; **Num** 21:22; 34:3; **Deut** 2:27; **Josh** 10:10; 15:3(2); 6; 10; 11; 16:2; 17:7; 18:18; 19; 19:13; **Judg** 7:12; 13; 9:25; 37; 11:18; 26; 20:37; **1Sa** 6:12; 28:20; **2Sa** 3:16; 16:13; **2Kin** 11:11; **2Chr** 23:10; **Jer** 41:6

ALREADY

3528, *2235, 4258, 5348*

Ex 1:5; **2Chr** 28:13; **Neh** 5:5; **Eccl** 1:10; 2:12; 3:15; 4:2; 6:10; **Mal** 2:2; **Mt** 5:28; 17:12; **Mk** 15:44; **Lk** 12:49; **Jn** 3:18; 4:35; 9:22; 27; 11:17; 19:33; **Acts** 11:11; 27:9; **1Cor** 5:3; **2Cor** 12:21; **Phil** 3:12(2); 16; **2Th** 2:7; **1Ti** 5:15; **2Ti** 2:18; **1Jn** 4:3; **Rev** 2:25

ALSO

176, 389, 637, 638, 1571, 3541, 3651, 5704, 7683, *260, 1161, 1211, 2504, 2528, 2532, 2546, 2548, 2579, 3761, 4828, 4879, 4901, 5037*

Gen 1:16; 2:9; 3:6; 18; 21; 22; 4:4; 22; 26; 6:3; 4; 11; 7:3; 8:2; 8; 10:21; 12:15; 13:5; 16; 14:7; 16(2); 15:14; 16:13; 17:16; 18:12; 23; 24; 19:21; 34; 35; 38; 20:4; 6; 21:13; 22:20; 24; 24:14; 19; 44; 46(2); 53; 26:21; 27:31; 34; 38; 45; 29:27; 28; 30(2); 33; 30:3; 6; 15; 30; 31:15; 32:6; 18; 33:7; 35:17; 37:7; 38:10; 11; 22; 24; 40:15; 16; 42:22; 43:8; 13; 44:9; 10; 16; 29; 45:20; 46:4; 34; 47:3; 18; 48:11; 19(2); 50:18; 23; **Ex** 1:10; 2:19; 3:9; 4:9; 14; 6:4; 5; 7:11(2); 23; 8:21; 32; 10:24; 25; 26; 12:32(2); 38; 15:4; 18:23; 19:22; 21:6; 29; 35; 23:9; 24:11; 25:23; 29:15; 22; 44; 30:18(2); 23; 31:13; 33:12; 17; 35:14; 37:12; 26; **Lev** 5:2; 7:16; 8:8; 9; 9:4; 18; 11:29; 40; 13:18; 38; 47; 14:9; 15:18; 20; 18:19; 28; 20:13; 27; 22:12; 23:27; 39; 26:16; 22; 24; 28; 39; 40; 41; 42(2); 43; **Num** 3:1; 4:22; 6:17; 9:2; 10:10; 11:4; 10; 12:2; 15:15; 16:10; 17; 34; 18:2; 3; 8; 28; 20:11; 22:19; 33; 24:12; 18; 24; 25; 27:13; 28:26; 30:3; 31:8; 33:4; 35:2; **Deut** 1:37(2); 2:6; 11; 12; 20; 3:3; 17; 20; 7:13; 8:5; 9:8; 19; 20; 10:10; 14; 15:17; 18:4; 20:6; 23:12; 26:13; 28:51; 61; 29:15; 31:2; 32:24; 25; 33:28; **Josh** 1:15; 2:12; 7:11(3); 10:30; 39; 13:3; 22; 15:19; 17:1; 2; 9; 19:30; 20:1; 22:7; 24:5; 18; **Judg** 1:15; 18; 22; 2:3; 10; 21; 3:22; 31; 5:4; 15; 6:35; 7:18; 8:9; 22; 31; 9:2; 19; 49; 10:9; 10; 12; 15:5; 17:2; 19:10; 16; 19; 20:48; **Ruth** 1:5; 12(2); 17; 2:16; 21; 3:15; 4:5; **1Sa** 1:6; 28; 2:15; 26; 3:12; 17; 4:17(2); 8:8; 20; 10:11; 12; 26; 12:14; 13:4; 14:15; 21; 22; 44; 15:1; 23; 29; 17:38; 18:5; 19:11; 20; 21; 22; 23; 24(2); 20:15; 22:17; 23:17; 25; 24:8; 25:13; 22; 43(2); 26:25; 28:19(2); 22; 30:21; **2Sa** 1:4(2); 18; 2:2; 6; 7; 24; 3:9; 12; 19(2); 35; 4:2; 5:2; 15; 18; 7:11; 19; 8:3; 11; 10:14; 11:12; 17; 21; 24; 12:13; 14; 13:36; 14:7; 15:19(2); 21; 23; 24; 27; 34; 17:5; 10; 18:2; 22; 26; 19:13; 40; 43; 20:14; 26; 21:20; 22:10; 20; 24; 36; 41; 44; 49; 23:20; **1Kin** 1:6; 14; 22; 33; 46; 48; 2:5; 22; 23; 3:13; 18; 4:13; 15; 28; 33; 6:22; 32; 33; 7:2; 8; 20; 31; 8:24; 9:21; 10:11; 12; 12:14; 13:5; 11; 18; 24; 14:23; 24; 15:13; 16:7; 16; 17:20; 18:35; 19:2; 20:3; 10; 21:19; 23; 22:22; **2Kin** 1:11; 2:13; 14; 3:18; 5:1; 6:31; 7:4; 8; 8:1; 9:27; 10:2; 5; 11:17; 13:6; 16:14; 17:19; 18:2; 21:11; 22:19; 23:5; 19; 27; 24:4; **1Chr** 1:14; 21; 51; 2:9; 26; 49; 3:6; 18; 6:3; 48; 67; 79; 7:10; 12; 25; 28; 8:13; 18; 32; 9:29; 38; 10:13; 11:10; 22; 26; 12:38; 13:2; 15:27; 16:6; 25; 30; 38; 17:9; 17; 18:4; 11; 20:2; 6; 21:23; 22:4; 14; 17; 23:26; 24:30; 26:6; 10; 27:4; 30; 32; 28:13; 14; 15; 17; 21; 29:9; 17; **2Chr** 2:8; 14; 3:7; 12; 15; 4:2; 6; 8; 14; 16; 19; 5:6; 12; 7:6; 8; 8:5; 14; 9:4; 10; 12:5; 9; 12; 13:2; 3; 11; 14:5; 15; 15:16; 17:7; 11; 18:21; 19:11; 20:1; 21:4; 10; 13; 17; 22:2; 3; 5; 23:13; 18; 24:1; 7; 12; 20; 25:6; 24; 26:3; 10(2); 20; 27:1; 5; 28:2; 4; 5; 8; 18(2); 29:7; 22; 27; 35; 30:1; 12; 31:1; 3; 6; 19; 32:5; 17; 28; 30; 33:4; 6; 19; 34:13; 27; 35:9; 36:7; 13; 22; **Ezr** 1:1; 7; 3:4; 7; 4:20; 5:10; 14; 6:5; 11; 7:19; 24; 8:6; 14; 16; 20; 27; 28; 35; 10:4; 23; 24; 28; **Neh** 1:3; 2:6; 18; 3:3; 8; 29; 5:3; 4; 9; 11; 13; 16; 18; 6:7; 19; 7:61; 8:7; 18; 9:13; 20; 23; 37; 10:32; 36; 11:1; 15; 22; 31; 12:9; 10; 22; 29; 43(2); 13:15; 16; 22; 23; **Est** 1:9; 16; 2:8; 3:11; 4:8; 16; 5:12; 7:8; 9; 8:8; 9:13; 15; **Job** 1:3; 6; 16; 17; 18; 2:1; 5:25; 7:1; 9:11; 20; 11:11; 19; 12:15; 13:2; 16; 27; 14:2; 16:4; 12; 17; 19; 17:6; 7; 9; 19:11; 20:9; 22:28; 24:15; 22; 30:11; 31; 31:28; 32:3; 10; 17(2); 33:6; 19; 36:1; 10; 29; 33; 37:1; 11; 39:30; 40:8; 14; 42:9; 10; 11; 13; **Ps** 1:3; 5:11; 6:3; 7:13; 9:9; 16:7; 9; 18:7; 9; 13; 19; 23; 35; 40; 19:10; 13; 26:1; 27:7; 28:9; 29:6; 35:3; 37:4; 5; 38:10; 12; 20; 40:2; 45:10; 52:6; 55:10; 60:7; 62:12; 65:8; 13(2); 68:1; 8; 18; 69:11; 21; 31; 36; 71:18; 19; 22; 24; 72:8; 12; 15; 74:16; 75:10; 76:2; 77:12; 16; 17; 78:14; 16; 20; 21; 27; 46; 48; 55; 62; 70; 81:16; 83:8; 84:6; 89:5; 11; 21; 25; 27; 29; 43; 92:11; 93:1; 95:4; 96:10; 99:4; 105:23; 33; 36; 37; 106:9; 16; 27; 28; 32; 42; 46; 107:32; 38; 108:8; 109:3; 10; 25; 119:3; 23; 24; 41; 46; 48; 132:12; 16; 139:17; 141:5; 145:19; 148:6; 14; **Prov** 1:26; 4:4; 9:2; 11:25; 17:26; 18:3; 9; 19:2; 21:13; 23:23; 28; 24:23; 25:1; 26:4; 28:16; 30:31; 31:15; 28; **Eccl** 1:5; 17; 2:1; 7; 8; 9; 14; 15; 19; 21; 23; 24; 26; 3:11; 13; 4:4; 8; 14; 16(2); 5:7; 10; 16; 17; 19; 6:3; 9; 7:6; 14; 18; 21; 22; 8:10; 14; 16; 9:3; 6; 12; 13; 10:3; 14; 11:2; 12:5; **Song** 1:16; 7:8; **Is** 2:7(2); 8; 5:2; 6; 6:1; 8; 7:13; 20; 8:5; 11:6; 13; 12:2; 13:3; 16; 18; 14:10; 13; 23; 17:3; 19:8; 13; 21:12; 22:9; 11; 23:12; 24:5; 26:12; 21; 28:7; 17; 29; 29:19; 24; 30:5; 22; 31:2; 5; 32:4; 7; 33:2; 34:3; 11; 14(2); 15; 38:22; 40:24; 44:19; 45:16; 46:11(2); 48:12; 13; 19; 21; 49:6; 7; 56:6; 57:8; 15; 18; 60:14; 16; 17; 21; 62:3; 66:4; 21; **Jer** 1:3; 2:8; 16; 33; 34; 36; 3:6; 8; 4:12; 6:14; 17; 7:27; 9:16; 10:5; 13:23; 14:5; 16:1; 8; 19:5; 20:1; 23:14(2); 25:14; 26:20; 27:6; 12; 16; 28:14; 29:24; 30:19; 20; 31:36; 37; 33:21; 35:15; 36:6; 38:25; 39:6; 40:5; 41:3; 43:13; 46:21(2); 48:2; 7; 8; 26(2); 34; 49:17; 50:24(2); 51:22; 23; 52:10; 17; 18; 22; 25; **Lam** 2:9; 3:8; 16; 4:21; **Eze** 1:5; 10; 3:13; 21; 4:1; 2; 4; 9; 11; 5:3; 11; 7:2; 18; 22; 24; 8:13; 18; 9:1; 10; 10:16; 17; 19; 12:1; 13; 13:21; 16:10; 11; 17; 19; 24; 26; 28; 39(2); 40; 41; 43; 52(2); 17:5; 7; 13; 22; 18:4; 19:4; 20:12; 15; 23; 25; 28; 39; 21:9; 17; 19; 23:26; 35; 37; 24:3; 5; 15; 25; 25:13; 26:4; 27:19; 30:6; 10; 13; 18; 31:17; 32:6; 9; 13; 17; 33:30; 36:1; 26; 29; 33; 37:24; 27; 38:10; 39:16; 40:8; 12; 14; 42; 41:8; 14; 43:21; 25; 44:30; 45:5; 47:20; **Dan** 6:22; 7:6; 8:25(2); 10:6; 11:1; 8; 14; 17; 22; 41; 42; **Hos** 2:11; 3:3; 4:3; 5; 6(2); 5:5; 6:11; 7:11; 8:6; 9:12; 10:6; 8; 11:3; 12:2; 10; **Joel** 1:12; 20; 2:12; 29; 3:2; 6; 16; **Amos** 1:5; 2:10; 3:14; 4:6; 7; 7:6; 12; 9:14; **Jonah** 4:11; **Mic** 3:3; 4:11; 5:13; 6:13; 7:12; **Nah** 3:10; 11(2); **Hab** 1:8; 2:5; 15; 16; **Zeph** 1:4; 9; 13; 2:12; 3:12; **Zec** 3:7(2); 4:9; 8:6; 21; 9:2; 5; 11; 10:10; 11:8(2); 12:7; 13:2; 14:14; **Mal** 1:13; 2:9; **Mt** 2:8; 3:10; 5:39; 40; 6:14; 21; 10:4; 32; 33; 12:45; 13:22; 23; 26; 29; 15:3; 16; 16:1; 18; 17:12; 18:33; 35; 19:3; 28; 20:4; 7; 21:21; 24; 22:26; 27; 23:26; 28; 24:27; 37; 39; 44; 25:11; 17; 22; 41; 44; 26:13; 35; 69; 71; 73; 27:41; 44; 57; **Mk** 1:19; 38; 2:15; 21; 26; 28; 3:19; 4:36; 5:16; 7:18; 8:7; 34; 38; 11:25; 29; 12:6; 22; 14:9; 31; 67; 15:31; 40; 41; 43; **Lk** 1:3; 35; 36; 2:4; 35; 3:9; 12; 21; 4:23; 41; 43; 5:10; 36; 39; 6:4; 5; 6; 13; 14; 16; 29(2); 31; 32; 33; 34; 36; 7:8; 49; 8:36; 9:61; 10:1; 39; 11:1; 4; 18; 30; 34(2); 40; 45; 46; 49; 12:8(2); 34; 40; 54; 13:6; 8; 14:12(2); 26; 16:1; 10(2); 14; 22; 28; 17:24; 26; 28; 18:15; 19:9; 19; 20:3; 11; 12; 31; 32; 21:2; 22:20; 24; 39; 56; 58; 59; 68; 23:7; 27; 32; 35; 36; 38; 51; 55; 24:22; 23; **Jn** 3:23; 4:45; 5:18; 19; 27; 6:24; 36; 67; 7:3; 10; 47; 52; 8:17; 19; 9:15; 27; 40; 10:16; 11:16; 33; 52; 12:9; 10; 18; 26; 42; 13:9; 14; 32; 34; 14:1; 3; 7; 12; 19; 15:20(2); 23; 27; 17:1; 18; 19; 20; 21; 24; 18:2; 5; 17; 25; 19:23; 39; 20:8; 21:3; 20; 25; **Acts** 1:3; 11; 2:22; 26; 3:17; 5:2; 16; 32; 37; 7:45; 8:13; 19; 9:32; 10:26; 45; 11:1; 18; 30; 12:3; 13:5; 9; 22; 33; 35; 14:1; 5; 15; 15:27; 32; 35(2); 17:6; 12; 13; 28(2); 19:17; 19; 21; 27; 20:21; 30; 21:13; 16; 24; 28; 22:5(2); 20; 29; 23:11; 30; 33; 35; 24:6; 9; 15; 26; 25:22; 24; 26:10; 26; 29; 27:10; 12; 36; 28:9; 10; **Rom** 1:6; 13; 15; 16; 24; 27; 2:9; 10; 12; 15; 3:7; 29(2); 4:6; 9; 11; 12; 16; 21; 24; 5:2; 3; 11; 15; 6:4; 5; 8; 11; 7:4; 8:11; 17; 21; 23; 26; 29; 30(3); 32; 34; 9:1; 10; 24; 25; 27; 11:1; 5; 16; 21; 22; 23; 31(2); 13:5; 6; 15:7; 14(3); 22; 27; 16:2; 4; 7; **1Cor** 1:8; 16; 2:13; 4:8; 5:12; 6:14; 7:3; 4; 22; 34; 40; 9:8; 10:6; 9; 10; 13; 11:1; 6; 12; 19; 23; 25; 12:12; 13:12; 14:15(2); 19; 34; 15:1; 2; 3; 8; 14; 18; 21; 28; 40; 42; 48(2); 49; 16:4; 10; **2Cor** 1:5; 6; 7; 11; 14(2); 22; 2:9; 10; 3:6; 4:10; 11; 13; 14; 5:5; 11; 6:1; 13; 8:6(2); 7; 10; 11; 14; 19; 21; 9:6(2); 12; 10:11; 14; 11:15; 18; 21; 13:4; 9; **Gal** 2:1; 10; 13; 17; 5:21; 25; 6:1; 7; **Eph** 1:11; 13(2); 15; 21; 2:3; 22; 4:9; 10; 5:2; 25; 6:9; 21; **Phil** 1:15; 20; 29; 2:4; 5; 9; 18; 19; 24; 27; 3:4; 12; 20; 4:3(2); 10; 15; **Col** 1:6; 7; 8; 9; 29; 2:11; 12; 3:4; 7; 8; 13; 15; 4:1; 3(2); 16; **1Th** 1:5; 8; 2:8; 10; 13(2); 14; 3:6; 4:6; 8; 14; 5:11; 24; **2Th** 1:5; 11; **1Ti** 2:9; 3:10; 5:13; 20; 25; 6:12; **2Ti** 1:5; 12; 2:2; 5; 10; 11; 12(2); 20; 22; 3:1; 8; 9; 4:8; 15; **Titus** 3:3; 14; **Philem** 1:9; 21; 22; **Heb** 1:2; 2:4; 14; 3:2; 4:10; 5:2; 3; 5; 6; 7:2(2); 9; 12; 25; 8:3; 6; 9:1; 16; 10:15; 11:11; 19; 32; 12:1; 26; 13:3; 12; **Jas** 1:11; 2:2; 11; 19; 25; 26; 3:2; 4; 5:8; **1Pet** 2:5; 6; 8; 18; 21; 3:1; 5; 18; 19; 21; 4:6; 13; 5:1(2); **2Pet** 1:19; 2:1; 3:10; 15; 16(2); 17; **1Jn** 1:3; 2:2; 6; 23; 24; 3:4; 4:11; 21; 5:1; **2Jn** 1; **3Jn** 12; **Jude** 8; 14; **Rev** 1:7; 9; 2:6; 15; 3:10; 21; 6:11; 11:8; 14:17

ALTHOUGH

272, 3588, *1487, 2532, 2543*

Ex 13:17; **Josh** 22:17; **2Sa** 23:5(2); **1Kin** 20:5; **Est** 7:4; **Job** 2:3; 5:6; 35:14; **Jer** 31:32; **Eze** 7:13; 11:16(2); **Hab** 3:17; **Mk** 14:29; **Heb** 4:3

ALTOGETHER

259, 1571, 3162, 3605, 3617, *1722, 3650, 3843, 4183*

Gen 18:21; **Ex** 11:1; 19:18; **Num** 16:13; 23:11; 24:10; 30:14; **Deut** 16:20; **2Chr** 12:12; **Est** 4:14; **Job** 13:5; 27:12; **Ps** 19:9; 39:5; 50:21; 53:3; 62:9; 139:4; **Song** 5:16; **Is** 10:8; **Jer** 5:5; 10:8; 15:18; 30:11; 49:12; **Jn** 9:34; **Acts** 26:29; **1Cor** 5:10; 9:10

AM

1961, *1510, 1511, 5607*

Gen 4:9; 15:1; 7; 17:1; 18:12; 13; 27; 22:1; 7; 11; 23:4; 24:24; 34; 25:22; 30; 32; 26:24(2); 27:1; 2; 11; 18; 19; 24; 32; 46; 28:13; 15; 30:2; 13; 31:11; 13; 32:10(2); 35:11; 37:13; 38:25; 41:44; 43:14; 45:3; 4; 46:2; 3; 49:29; 50:19; **Ex** 3:4; 6; 8; 11; 14(3); 19; 4:10(2); 6:2; 6; 7; 8; 12; 29; 30; 7:5; 17; 8:22; 9:29; 10:2; 12:12; 14:4; 18; 15:26; 16:12; 18:6; 20:2; 5; 22:27; 29:46(2); 31:13; **Lev** 8:35; 10:13; 11:44(2); 45(2); 18:2; 4; 5; 6; 21; 30; 19:2; 3; 4; 10; 12; 14; 16; 18; 25; 28; 30; 31; 32; 34; 36; 37; 20:7; 8; 24; 26; 21:8; 12; 22:2; 3; 8; 30; 31; 32; 33; 23:22; 43; 24:22; 25:17; 38; 55; 26:1; 2; 13; 44; 45; **Num** 3:13; 41; 45; 10:10; 11:14; 21; 15:41(2); 18:20; 22:30; 37; 38; **Deut** 1:9; 42; 5:6; 9; 26:3; 29:6; 31:2; 27; 32:39; **Josh** 5:14; 14:10; 11; 17:14; 23:2; 14; **Judg** 4:19; 6:10; 15; 8:5; 9:2;

13:11; 17:9; 18:4; 19:18(2); **Ruth** 1:12; 2:10; 3:9; 12; 4:4; **1Sa** 1:8; 15; 26; 3:4; 5; 6; 8; 16; 4:16; 9:19; 21; 12:2; 3; 14:7; 16:2; 5; 17:8; 43; 58; 18:18; 23; 22:12; 28:15; 30:13; **2Sa** 1:3; 7; 8; 13; 26; 2:20; 3:8; 39; 7:18; 9:8; 11:5; 14:5; 15; 32; 15:26; 19:20; 22; 35; 20:17; 19; 24:14; **1Kin** 3:7; 8:20; 13:14; 18; 31; 14:6; 17:12; 18:8; 12; 36; 19:4; 10; 14; 20:4; 13; 28; 22:4; 34; **2Kin** 2:10; 3:7; 5:7; 16:7; 18:25; 19:23; 21:12; **1Chr** 17:16; 21:13; 29:14; **2Chr** 2:6; 9; 6:10(2); 18:3; 33; 35:23; **Ezr** 9:6; **Neh** 6:3; 11; **Est** 5:12; **Job** 1:15; 16; 17; 19; 7:3; 4; 8; 12; 20; 9:20; 28; 32; 10:7; 15; 11:4; 12:3; 4; 13:2; 16:6; 19:7; 10; 15; 20; 21:6; 23:15(2); 30:9(2); 19; 29; 32:6; 18; 33:6(2); 9(2); 34:5; 40:4; **Ps** 6:2; 6; 13:4; 17:3; 22:2; 6; 14; 25:16; 28:7; 31:9; 12(2); 22; 35:3; 37:25; 38:6(2); 8; 17; 39:4; 10; 12; 40:12; 17; 46:10; 50:7; 52:8; 56:3; 69:2; 3; 8; 17; 20; 29; 70:5; 71:7; 18; 73:23; 77:4; 81:10; 86:1; 2; 88:4(2); 8; 15(2); 102:2; 6(2); 7; 11; 109:22; 23(2); 116:16(2); 119:19; 63; 83; 94; 107; 120; 125; 141; 120:7; 139:14; 18; 21; 142:6; 143:12; **Prov** 8:14; 20:9; 26:19; 30:2; **Eccl** 1:16; **Song** 1:5; 6; 2:1; 5; 5:1; 8; 6:3; 7:10; 8:10; **Is** 1:11; 14; 6:5(2); 8; 10:13; 19:11; 21:8; 29:12; 33:24; 36:10; 37:24; 38:10; 14; 41:4; 10(2); 42:8; 43:3; 5; 10; 11; 12; 13; 15; 25; 44:5; 6(2); 16; 24; 45:3; 5; 6; 18; 22; 46:4; 9(2); 47:8; 10; 48:12(3); 16; 17; 49:21; 23; 26; 51:12; 15; 52:6; 56:3; 58:9; 60:16; 65:1(2); 5; **Jer** 1:6; 7; 8; 19; 2:23; 35; 3:12; 14; 4:19; 6:11(2); 8:21(2); 9:24; 15:6; 16; 20; 20:7; 21:13; 23:9; 23; 30; 31; 32; 24:7; 26:14; 29:23; 30:11; 31:9; 32:27; 36:5; 38:19; 42:11; 46:28; 50:31; 51:25; **Lam** 1:11; 14; 20; 3:1; 54; 63; **Eze** 5:8; 6:7; 9; 10; 13; 14; 7:4; 9; 27; 11:10; 12; 12:11; 15; 16; 20; 25; 13:8; 9; 14; 20; 21; 23; 14:8; 15:7; 16:62; 63; 20:5; 7; 12; 19; 20; 26; 38; 42; 44; 21:3; 22:16; 26; 23:49; 24:24; 27; 25:5; 7; 11; 17; 26:3; 6; 27:3; 28:2; 9; 22(2); 23; 24; 26; 29:3; 6; 9; 10; 16; 21; 30:8; 19; 22; 25; 26; 32:15; 33:29; 34:10; 27; 30; 31; 35:3; 4; 9; 12; 15; 36:9; 11; 23; 38; 37:6; 13; 38:3; 23; 39:1; 6; 7; 22; 27; 28; 44:28(2); **Dan** 9:22; 23; 10:11; 12; 14; 20; **Hos** 2:2; 11:9; 12:8; 9; 13:4; 14:8; **Joel** 2:27(2); 3:10; 17; **Amos** 2:13; **Jonah** 1:9; 2:4; **Mic** 3:8; 7:1; **Nah** 2:13; 3:5; **Hab** 2:1; **Zeph** 2:15; **Hag** 1:13; 2:4; **Zec** 1:14; 15; 16; 8:3; 10:6; 11:5; 13:5(2); **Mal** 1:14; 3:6; **Mt** 3:11; 17; 5:17(2); 8:8; 9; 9:13; 28; 10:34; 35; 11:29; 15:24; 16:13; 15; 17:5; 18:20; 20:15; 22; 23; 22:32; 24:5; 26:32; 61; 27:24; 43; 28:20; **Mk** 1:7; 11; 8:27; 29; 10:38; 39; 12:26; 13:6; 14:28; 62; **Lk** 1:18; 19(2); 3:16; 22; 4:43; 5:8; 7:6; 8; 9:18; 20; 12:49; 50; 51; 15:19; 21; 16:3; 4(2); 24; 18:11; 21:8; 22:27; 33; 58; 70; **Jn** 1:20; 21; 23; 27; 31; 3:28(2); 4:9; 26; 5:7; 43; 6:35; 41; 48; 51; 7:28(2); 29; 33; 34; 36; 8:12; 16; 18; 23(2); 24; 28; 58; 9:5(2); 9; 39; 10:7; 9; 10; 11; 14(2); 36; 11:15; 25; 12:26; 46; 13:13; 19; 33; 14:3; 6; 10; 11; 20; 15:1; 5; 16:28; 32; 17:10; 11; 14; 16; 24; 18:5; 6; 8; 17; 25; 35; 37; 19:21; 20:17; **Acts** 7:32; 34; 9:5; 10; 10:21; 26; 13:25(3); 18:6; 10; 20:26; 21:13; 39(2); 22:3(2); 8; 23:6(2); 24:21; 26:2; 6; 7; 15; 25; 26; 29; 27:23; 28:20; **Rom** 1:14; 15; 16; 3:7; 7:14; 24; 8:38; 11:1; 3; 13; 14:14; 15:14; 29; 16:19; **1Cor** 1:12; 3:4(2); 4:4; 9:1(2); 2; 22; 10:30; 11:1; 12:15(2); 16(2); 13:1; 2; 12; 15:9(2); 10(2); 16:17; **2Cor** 7:4(2); 14; 10:1(2); 2; 11:2; 21; 22(3); 23; 29; 12:10(2); 11(2); 14; 13:1; **Gal** 2:19; 20; 4:11; 12(2); 16; 18; **Eph** 3:8; 6:20; **Phil** 1:17; 23; 3:12; 4:11; 12; 18; **Col** 1:23; 25; 2:5; 4:3; **1Ti** 1:15; 2:7; **2Ti** 1:5; 11; 12(2); 4:6; **Jas** 1:13; **1Pet** 1:16; 5:1; **2Pet** 1:13; 17; **Rev** 1:8; 9; 11; 17; 18(2); 2:23; 3:17; 21; 18:7; 19:10; 21:6; 22:9; 13; 16

AMONG

413, 854, 996, 997, 1460, 1767, 4480, 5921, 5973, 7130, 8432, *303, 575, 1223, 1519, 1537, 1722, 1909, 2596, 3319, 3326, 3844, 4045, 4314, 4315, 4814, 5216, 5259*

Gen 17:10; 12; 23; 23:6; 10; 24:3; 30:32(2); 33(2); 35; 41; 34:22; 30(2); 35:2; 36:30; 40:20; 42:5; 47:6; **Ex** 2:5; 7:5; 9:20; 10:2; 12:31; 49; 13:2; 13; 15:11; 17:7; 25:8; 28:1; 29:45; 46; 30:12; 13; 14; 31:14; 32:25; 34:9; 10; 19; 35:5; 10; 36:8; **Lev** 6:18; 29; 7:6; 33; 34; 11:2; 3; 13; 27; 29; 31; 42; 15:31; 16:16; 29; 17:4; 8; 9; 10(2); 12; 13; 18:26; 29; 19:8; 16; 34; 20:3; 5; 6; 14; 18; 21:1; 4; 10; 15; 22:3; 32; 23:29; 30; 24:10; 25:33; 45; 26:11; 12; 22; 25; 33; 38; **Num** 1:47; 49; 2:33; 3:12(2); 41(2); 42; 45; 4:2; 18; 5:21; 27; 8:6; 14; 16; 19(2); 9:7; 13; 14; 11:1; 3; 4; 20; 21; 12:6; 13:2; 14:11; 13; 14; 42; 15:14; 23; 26; 29(2); 30; 16:3; 21; 33; 45; 47; 17:6; 18:6; 20(2); 23; 24; 19:10; 20; 21:6; 23:9; 21; 25:7; 11; 14; 26:62(2); 64; 27:4(2); 7; 31:16; 17; 32:30; 33:4; 54; 35:6; 15; 34; **Deut** 1:13; 15; 42; 2:14; 15; 16; 4:3; 27(2); 6:15; 7:14(2); 20; 21; 13:1; 11; 13; 14; 14:6; 15:4; 7; 16:11; 17:2; 7; 15; 18:2; 10; 18; 19:19; 20; 21:9; 11; 21; 22:21; 24; 23:10; 16; 24:7; 26:11; 28:37; 54; 56; 64; 65; 29:17; 18(2); 30:1; 31:16; 17; 32:26; 34; 46; 51; **Josh** 3:5; 10; 4:6; 7:11; 12; 13; 21; 8:9; 33; 35; 9:7; 16; 22; 10:1; 13:13; 22; 14:3; 15; 15:13; 16:9; 10; 17:4(2); 6; 9; 18:2; 4; 7; 19:49; 20:4; 9; 22:7; 14; 19; 31; 23:7(2); 12; 24:5; 17; 23; **Judg** 1:16; 29; 30; 32; 33; 3:5; 5:8; 9; 13; 14; 16; 10:16; 12:4(2); 14:3(2); 18:1; 25; 20:12; 16; 21:5; 12; **Ruth** 2:7; 15; 4:10; **1Sa** 2:8; 4:3; 17; 6:6; 7:3; 9:2; 22; 10:10; 11(2); 12; 22; 23; 24; 14:15; 30; 34; 39; 15:6(2); 33; 16:1; 17:12; 19:24; 22:14; 31:9; **2Sa** 6:19(2); 15:31; 16:20; 17:9; 19:28; 22:50; 23:8; 18(2); 22; **1Kin** 3:13; 5:6; 6:13; 7:51; 8:53; 9:7; 11:20; 14:7; 21:9; 12; **2Kin** 4:13; 9:2; 11:2; 17:25; 26; 18:5; 35; 20:15; 23:9; **1Chr** 4:23; 7:5; 11:20; 24; 25; 12:1; 4; 16:8; 24(2); 31; 18:14; 21:6; 23:6; 24:4(2); 26:12(2); 19(2); 30; 31(3); 27:6; 28:4; **2Chr** 5:1; 6:5; 7:13; 20; 11:22; 20:25; 22:11; 24:16; 23; 26:6; 28:15; 31:19(2); 32:14; 33:11; 19; 35:13; 36:23; **Ezr** 1:3; 2:62; 65; 10:18; **Neh** 1:8; 4:11; 5:17; 6:6; 7:64; 9:17; 10:34; 11:17; 13:26; **Est** 1:19; 3:8; 4:3; 9:21; 28; 10:3; **Job** 1:6; 2:1; 8; 15:19; 17:10; 18:19; 28:10; 30:5; 7; 33:23; 34:4; 37; 36:14; 39:25; 41:6; 42:15; **Ps** 9:11; 12:1; 18:49; 21:10; 22:18; 28; 31:11(2); 35:18; 44:11; 14(2); 45:9; 12; 46:10; 55:15; 57:4(2); 9(2); 67:2; 68:13; 17; 18; 25; 74:9; 77:14; 78:45; 49; 60; 79:10; 80:6; 82:1; 86:8; 88:5; 89:6; 94:8; 96:3(2); 10; 99:6(2); 104:10; 12; 105:1; 27; 37; 106:27; 35; 47; 108:3(2); 109:30; 110:6; 126:2; 136:11; **Prov** 1:14; 6:19; 7:7(2); 14:9; 15:31; 17:2; 23:20(2); 28; 27:22; 30:14; 30; 31:23; **Eccl** 6:1; 7:28(2); 9:3; 17; **Song** 1:8; 2:2(2); 3(2); 16; 4:2; 5; 5:9; 10; 6:1; 3; 6; **Is** 2:4; 4:3; 5:27; 8:15; 16; 10:16; 12:4; 24:13; 29:14; 19; 33:14(2); 36:20; 39:4; 41:28; 42:23; 43:9; 12; 44:4; 14; 48:14; 50:10; 51:18; 57:6; 61:9(2); 65:4; 66:19(2); **Jer** 3:19; 4:3; 5:26; 6:15; 18; 27; 8:12; 17; 9:16; 10:7; 11:9(2); 12:14; 14:22; 18:13; 24:10; 25:16; 27; 29:18; 32; 31:7; 32:20; 37:4; 10; 39:14; 40:1; 5; 6; 11; 41:8(2); 44:8; 46:18; 48:27; 49:15(2); 50:2; 23; 46; 51:27; 41; **Lam** 1:1(2); 2; 3; 17; 2:9; 4:15; 20; **Eze** 1:1; 13; 2:5; 6; 3:15; 25; 4:13; 5:14; 6:8; 9; 13; 9:2; 11:1; 9; 16(2); 12:10; 12; 15; 16; 13:19; 15:2; 6; 16:14; 18:18; 19:2(2); 6; 11; 20:9; 23; 38; 22:15; 26; 30; 23:10; 25:10; 27:24; 36; 28:19; 25; 29:12(2); 30:23; 26(2); 31:3; 10; 14; 18; 32:9; 21; 33:6; 33; 34:12; 24; 35:11; 36:19; 21; 22; 23; 24; 30; 37:21; 39:6; 21; 28; 40:46; 44:9; 47:22(4); **Dan** 1:6; 19; 4:35; 7:8; 11:24; 33; **Hos** 5:9; 7:7; 8; 8:8; 10; 9:17; 10:14; 13:15; **Joel** 2:17; 19; 25; 3:2; 9; **Amos** 1:1; 2:16; 4:10; 9:9; **Obad** 1; 2; 4; **Mic** 3:11; 4:3; 5:2; 8(3); 7:2; **Nah** 3:8; **Hab** 1:5; **Zeph** 3:20; **Hag** 2:3; 5; **Zec** 1:8; 10; 11; 3:7; 7:14; 8:13; 10:9; 12:6; 8; 14:13; **Mal** 1:10; 11(2); 14; **Mt** 2:6; 4:23; 9:35; 11:11; 12:11; 13:7; 22; 25; 32; 49; 16:7; 8; 20:26(2); 27; 21:38; 23:11; 26:5; 27:35; 56; 28:15; **Mk** 1:27; 4:7; 18; 5:3; 6:4; 41; 8:16; 19; 20; 9:33; 34; 10:26; 43(2); 12:7; 13:10; 15:31; 40; 16:3; **Lk** 1:1; 25; 28; 42; 2:44; 4:36; 7:16; 28; 8:7; 14; 9:46; 48; 10:3; 30; 36; 16:15; 19:2; 39; 20:14; 22:17; 23; 24; 26; 27; 37; 55; 24:5; 47; **Jn** 1:14; 26; 6:9; 43; 52; 7:12; 35(2); 43; 8:7; 9:16; 10:19; 11:54; 56; 12:19; 20; 42; 15:24; 16:17; 19; 19:24(2); 21:23; **Acts** 1:21; 2:22; 3:23; 4:12; 15; 17; 34; 5:12; 34; 6:3; 8; 10:22; 12:18; 13:26; 14:14; 15:7; 12; 19; 22; 17:33; 34; 18:11; 20:25; 29; 32; 21:19; 21; 34; 23:10; 24:5; 21; 25:5; 6; 26:3; 4; 18; 27:22; 28:4; 25; 29; **Rom** 1:5; 6; 13(2); 2:24; 8:29; 11:17; 12:3; 15:9; 16:7; **1Cor** 1:10; 11; 2:2; 6; 3:3; 18; 5:1(2); 2; 13; 6:5; 7; 11:18; 19(2); 30; 15:12; **2Cor** 1:19; 6:17; 10:1; 12; 11:6; 26; 12:12; 21; **Gal** 1:16; 2:2; 3:1; 5; **Eph** 2:3; 3:8; 5:3; **Phil** 2:15; **Col** 1:27; 4:16; **1Th** 1:5; 2:7; 10; 5:12; 13; 15; **2Th** 1:10; 3:7; 11; **2Ti** 2:2; **Heb** 5:1; **Jas** 1:26; 3:6; 13; 4:1; 5:13; 14; **1Pet** 2:12; 4:8; 5:1; 2; **2Pet** 2:1(2); 8; **3Jn** 9; **Jude** 15; **Rev** 2:13; 7:15; 14:4

AN

Gen 2:18; 20; 4:3; 22; 5:3; 6; 18; 25; 28; 6:3; 14; 7:24; 8:11; 20; 9:20; 11:10; 25; 12:7; 8; 13:18; 15:9; 12; 16:1(2); 17:7; 8; 13; 17; 19; 21:5; 20; 22:9; 23:1; 25:7; 8; 17; 25; 26:12; 25; 28; 27:30; 29:24; 31:46; 33:17; 19; 20; 34:31; 35:1; 3; 7; 8; 28; 37:33; 36; 38:14; 15; 39:1(2); 14; 41:12; 16; 42:23; 43:12; 32; 44:20; 46:34; 47:9; 28; 48:4; 49:9; 13; 17; 33; 50:22; 25; 26; **Ex** 2:3; 11(2); 19; 4:20; 6:8; 16; 18; 20; 10:13; 26; 12:3; 14; 16(2); 17; 24; 45; 13:13; 14:8; 15:2; 8; 25; 16:16; 18; 32; 33; 36(2); 17:15; 18:3; 19:6; 13; 20:24; 25; 21:2; 6; 28; 33(2); 22:1(2); 10(2); 11; 15; 23:1; 20; 22(2); 24:4; 25:2; 10; 25; 26:36; 27:1; 9; 11; 16; 18; 28:4; 11; 18; 19(2); 20; 32(2); 29:18; 25; 28(2); 36; 37(2); 40(2); 41; 30:1; 10; 13; 14; 15(2); 16; 24; 25(3); 31; 31:18; 32:5; 30; 33:2; 34:20; 35:2; 5(2); 22; 24; 36:37; 37:12; 38:9; 11; 23(2); 25; 27; 39:11; 12(2); 13; 23(2); 40:10; 15; **Lev** 1:2; 9; 13; 17; 2:2; 4; 9; 16; 3:3; 5; 9; 14; 4:20; 26; 31; 35; 5:2; 4; 6; 10; 11; 13; 16; 18; 6:7; 20; 7:5; 14; 18; 25; 32; 8:21; 28; 33; 34; 9:7(2); 17; 11:10; 11; 12; 13; 20; 23; 41; 42; 12:7; 8; 13:11; 28; 14:5; 18; 19; 20; 21; 29; 31; 40; 41; 45; 50; 53; 15:13; 15; 19; 25; 30; 32; 33; 16:6; 10; 11; 16; 17(2); 18; 20; 24; 30; 33(3); 34(2); 17:3; 4; 11(2); 19:20; 22; 20:13; 21; 21:14; 22:10; 12; 22; 27; 23:3; 7; 8(2); 12; 13; 14; 18; 21; 24; 25; 27(2); 28; 35; 36(3); 37; 24:7; 8; 10(2); 25:40; 46; 50; 26:8(2); 27:9; 27; **Num** 2:9; 16; 24(2); 31; 4:15; 5:2; 8; 15(3); 17; 19; 21(2); 26; 6:11; 7:3; 13; 19; 25; 31; 37; 43; 49; 55; 61; 67; 73; 79; 85; 86; 8:11; 12; 13; 15; 19; 21(2); 9:7; 10:5; 6(2); 7; 8; 9; 12:1; 13:32; 14:7; 15:3; 4; 5; 6; 7; 9; 10(2); 13; 14; 15; 19; 20; 21; 25; 28(2); 16:31; 46; 47; 18:8; 17; 21; 24; 26; 28; 19:17; 20:16; 22:22; 23:3; 25:13(2); 26:53; 27:7; 28:5(2); 7; 14(3); 18; 22; 25; 26; 30; 29:1; 5; 7; 12; 30:2; 6; 10; 31:29; 50(2); 32:14; 33:3; 39; 54; 34:2; 35:16; 18; 36:2; 8; **Deut** 4:21; 38; 5:29; 7:6; 25; 26; 10:1; 3; 13:16; 14:2; 21(2); 15:4; 12(2); 17; 17:1; 18:10(2); 12; 19:10; 20:9; 16; 19; 21:3; 23; 22:10(2); 14; 19(2); 22; 23; 23:3; 7(2); 24:4; 14; 25:5; 16; 19; 26:1; 8; 12; 19; 27:5(2); 15; 25; 28:9; 22(2); 30; 37; 29:4; 8; 31:2; 24; 32:11; 45; 33:7; 34:7; **Josh** 1:6; 2:1; 3:13; 16; 7:13; 8:2; 24; 28; 30; 31; 10:20; 11:23; 13:6; 7; 14:3; 13; 17:4(2); 6; 19:49(2); 51(2); 22:10; 11; 14; 16; 19; 23; 26; 29; 23:4; 24:19; 25; 26; 29; 32; **Judg** 2:1; 8; 3:18; 31; 4:21; 6:11(2); 19; 22(2); 24; 26; 8:10; 27; 9:23; 46; 48; 11:1; 12:5; 13:6; 16; 21; 14:4; 15:15; 16(2); 17; 19; 16:1; 3; 17:5(2); 18:1; 14; 19:9; 16; 28; 20:10(2); 16; 35; 38; 21:4; 17; **Ruth** 1:12(2); 2:17; **1Sa** 1:1; 2:28; 31; 32(2); 3:12; 4:18; 7:17; 9:6; 10:13; 13:10; 14:3; 14; 27; 28; 35; 48; 16:2; 14; 15; 16; 20; 23; 17:5; 12; 17; 38; 18:1; 25; 19:13; 16; 20:36; 21:7; 23:6; 24:16; 25:18; 42; 26:13; 19; 28:14; 29:4; 9; 30:11; 13; 14; 25; **2Sa** 1:8; 13; 2:25; 3:14; 29; 5:11; 6:18; 7:2; 5; 7; 11; 13; 27; 8:4; 11:2; 19; 13:36; 14:17; 20; 15:19; 16:1(2); 17:25; 18:10; 19:26; 27; 23:5; 14; 21; 38(2); 24:3; 18; 21; 25; **1Kin** 1:39; 41(2); 52; 2:24; 36; 3:1; 9; 12; 4:23; 5:3; 5(2); 7:2; 8; 26; 31; 40; 8:13; 16; 17; 18; 20; 31; 36; 54; 63; 10:10; 29(2); 11:7; 14; 18; 25; 26; 12:21; 31; 13:11; 14; 18; 14:21; 31; 15:13; 16:32; 17:12; 18:4; 10; 13; 32; 19:5; 11; 20:20; 25; 29; 30; 22:9; 25; **2Kin** 1:8; 9; 3:4(2); 4:9; 24; 43; 6:15; 25; 9:2; 5; 17; 10:25; 11:4; 16:10; 11; 18:31; 19:32; 35; 23:33; 25:19; **1Chr** 2:34; 5:21; 6:49; 8:40; 11:23; 12:14; 37; 14:1; 15:5; 7; 10; 27; 16:2; 17; 29; 17:1; 4; 5; 6; 10; 12; 25; 18:4; 21:3; 5; 15; 18; 22; 26; 22:6; 7; 8; 10; 14; 27:4; 28:2; 3; 8; 10; 29:16; **2Chr** 1:17(2); 2:1(2); 3; 4(2); 6(2); 12(2); 17; 3:4; 16; 4:1; 5; 8; 5:12; 6:2; 5; 7; 8; 22; 27; 7:1; 5; 12; 21; 9:9; 11:1; 12:13; 13:3; 13; 14:8; 9; 15:16; 17:18; 18:24; 20:23; 21:18; 24:10; 15; 26; 25:6(2); 26:11; 13; 27:5; 28:6; 29:17; 24; 29; 32; 32:8; 21; 35:25; 36:3; 23; **Ezr** 1:2; 2:3; 18; 21; 23; 27; 30; 41; 42; 4:3; 6; 17; 6:17; 7:22(4); 8:3; 10; 12; 26(2); 9:11; 12; 10:17; **Neh** 4:2; 5:12; 17; 6:5; 13; 7:8; 24; 26; 27; 31; 32; 44; 45; 10:29; 33; 11:14; 19; **Est** 1:1; 4; 8:9; **Job** 1:8; 10; 2:3; 11; 3:16; 4:16; 6:6; 7:1; 13:16; 14:3; 4; 6; 16:3; 18:2; 19:15; 24; 20:19; 26:10; 28:3; 31:6; 11(2); 28; 33:23; 40:9; 15; 41:1; 2; 42:11; 16; **Ps** 5:9; 7:9; 11:6; 18:25; 26:12; 27:3; 31:2; 33:2; 7; 16; 17; 38:4; 39:5; 40:2; 41:8; 43:1; 48:7; 50:21; 55:12; 64:5; 7; 68:15; 21; 69:8; 13; 31; 72:16; 78:13; 26; 55; 84:3; 88:8; 92:3; 10; 96:8; 101:5; 102:3; 6; 105:10; 106:20; 119:96; 111; 142; 127:3; 132:5; 135:12(2); 136:21; 22; 140:11; 141:5; 144:9; 145:13; **Prov** 1:9; 4:9; 5:3; 6:11; 16; 18; 7:10; 13; 22; 8:5; 7; 10:25; 11:9; 13:22; 15:8; 9; 19; 26; 16:5; 12; 18; 19; 24; 27; 17:1; 10; 11; 27; 18:11; 19:15; 28; 20:3; 21; 23; 21:4; 19; 22:24; 23:5; 6; 18; 32; 24:3; 9; 34; 25:12(3); 19; 20; 23; 27:6; 7; 28:10; 22; 29:6; 22; 27(2); 30:19; 20; 23(2); 31; **Eccl** 4:6; 13; 5:6; 6:1; 2; 3(2); 7:11; 8:3; 11; 12; 9:2; 3; 12(2); 10:5(2); 8; **Song** 4:4; 13; 6:4; 10; 7:2; **Is** 1:13; 21; 30; 3:7; 5:10(2); 26; 6:13; 9:17(2); 10:6; 11:10; 12; 16; 14:19; 15:5; 16:4; 11; 14; 17:6; 9; 18:3; 19:19; 21:16; 22:16(2); 23:15; 16; 24:13; 25:2; 29:5; 8; 21; 30:5; 13; 17(2); 28; 32:2; 33:1; 34:13; 35:6; 8; 36:16; 37:33; 36; 38:12; 13; 41:24; 43:23; 44:14; 19; 45:17; 48:4; 49:8; 18; 53:10; 54:16; 55:3; 13; 56:5; 7; 58:5; 59:17; 60:15; 19; 61:8; 63:12; 13; 64:6; 65:9; 20(4); 66:3(3); 14; 20(2); 24; **Jer** 1:11; 14; 18; 2:7; 19; 3:18; 4:7; 5:15; 16; 6:26; 9:2; 8; 11; 10:10; 11:19; 14:12; 18:17; 19:8; 21:5; 22:19; 23:14; 40; 24:7; 25:9(2); 11; 18(2); 36; 26:8; 9; 29:11; 18(2); 30:14; 17; 31:3; 32; 32:14; 40; 33:9; 12; 34:9(2); 14; 22; 42:18(2); 43:1; 44:12(2); 22(2); 27; 46:19; 22; 47:2; 48:34; 40; 49:2; 14; 50:9; 51:29; 34; 37(3); 41; 63; 52:23; 25; **Lam** 1:15; 2:4(2); 5; 5:10; **Eze** 1:10(2); 24; 2:9; 3:5; 6; 9; 4:3; 11; 5:15(2); 7:2; 5(2); 6; 8:3; 10:14; 11:19; 13:11; 13; 16:3(2); 24(2); 30; 31; 45(2); 60; 17:13; 22; 20:17; 21:25; 29; 23:24; 31:3; 33:32; 35:5; 36:3; 26; 37:10; 26; 38:10; 40:5; 19; 23; 27; 42(2); 43; 47(2); 41:7; 13(2); 14; 15; 42:2; 8; 15; 43:13; 23; 44:28; 45:1(2); 4; 11(2); 13(4); 14(2); 24(4); 46:5(3); 7(4); 11(4); 14(2); 47:22; **Dan** 2:46; 3:1; 4; 27; 4:3; 13; 23; 34; 5:12; 6:1; 3; 7:14; 27; 8:5; 12; 9:24; 10:10; 11:6; 7; 12:7; **Hos** 3:1; 2(2); 4(2); 6:10; 11; 7:4; 6; 7; 8:1; 10:1; 11; 13:13; 15; **Joel** 2:1; 3:3; **Amos** 3:11; 12; 15; 5:3(2); 13; 7:2; 14(2); 17; 8:10; **Obad** 1; **Jonah** 1:9; 3:3; **Mic** 1:6; 7(2); 15; 2:3; 8; 6:16; **Nah** 1:8; 9; **Hab** 2:3; 9; **Zeph** 1:10; 3:12; **Hag** 2:16; **Zec** 5:6; 11; 7:12; 9:9(2); 16; 12:6; 13:5; **Mal** 1:10; 13; 2:11; 12; 3:3; 4:1; **Mt** 2:19; 4:2; 8; 5:14; 38(2); 8:30; 9:16; 20; 10:12; 11:1; 12:1; 3; 35; 39; 13:8; 23; 28; 52; 14:7; 16:23; 17:1; 27; 18:12; 17; 28; 19:29; 20:1; 21:2; 5(2); 24:44; 50; 25:24; 35; 37; 42; 44; 26:5; 7; 30; 72; **Mk** 1:23; 2:21; 25; 3:19; 26; 30; 4:8; 20; 5:2; 25; 6:20; 27; 7:22; 24; 25; 32; 9:2; 10:30; 12:1; 14:2; 3; 26; 15:43; **Lk** 1:11; 18; 69; 2:36; 4:5; 33; 5:36; 6:3; 7; 45; 48; 49; 7:37; 8:8; 15; 32; 43; 9:28; 10:34; 11:12; 29; 12:1; 40; 46; 14:5(2); 32; 15:4; 16:2; 6; 7; 19:21; 22; 21:18; 22:37; 43; 44; 24:42; **Jn** 1:22; 47; 2:16; 5:4; 5; 6:60; 10:12; 13; 12:15; 29; 13:15; 19:31; 39; 21:11; **Acts** 1:13; 15; 2:30; 3:3; 6:15; 7:30; 47; 8:27; 9:37; 10:3; 22; 28; 11:13; 12:21; 13:17; 14:5; 17:5; 23; 18:24; 19:40; 20:32; 21:16; 26; 29; 31; 38; 23:9; 21; 27; 25:11; 27:12; 34; **Rom** 1:1; 23; 2:20; 3:13; 4:19; 7:2; 3; 11:1; 14:13; 16:16; **1Cor** 1:1; 5:9; 11(3); 6:15; 16; 7:13;

8:4; 7; 9:1; 2; 25; 12:17; 14:2; 4; 8; 13; 14; 19; 26; 27; 15:9; 52; 16:20; **2Cor** 1:1; 2:11; 5:1; 6:15; 8:14; 10:11; 11:7; 14; 12:2; 5; 12; 13:12; **Gal** 1:1; 8; 2:5; 4:7; 14; 24; 5:13; 6:1; **Eph** 1:1; 11; 2:21; 22; 5:2; 5; 6:20; **Phil** 1:28; 3:5; 17; 4:18; **Col** 1:1; 2:16; **1Th** 5:8; 26; **2Th** 3:9; 15; **1Ti** 1:1; 2:7; 4:12; 5:1; 8; 19(2); **2Ti** 1:1; 9; 11; 2:9; 4:5; **Titus** 1:1; 3:10; **Philem** 1:9; **Heb** 3:12; 4:15; 5:5; 10; 6:6; 16(2); 17; 19; 20; 7:16; 20; 21(2); 24; 26; 8:1; 9:11; 13; 10:21; 22; 29; 34; 11:7; 8; 16; 12:22; 13:10; **Jas** 3:8; 5:10; **1Pet** 1:1; 4; 2:5; 9; 21; 3:15; 4:15; 5:1; **2Pet** 1:1; 11; 2:6(2); 14; **1Jn** 2:1; 7; 20; 5:20; **2Jn** 7; **Jude** 7; **Rev** 2:7; 11; 17; 29; 3:6; 8; 13; 22; 4:3; 7:4; 8:1; 5; 13; 9:15; 11:9; 11; 19; 13:9; 14; 14:1; 16:18; 19:17; 20:1; 21:17; 19; 20

AND

Gen 1:1; 2(4); 3(2); 4(2); 5(4); 6(2); 7(3); 8(3); 9(3); 10(3); 11(3); 12(4); 13(2); 14(5); 15(2); 16(2); 17; 18(4); 19(2); 20(2); 21(4); 22(4); 23(2); 24(4); 25(4); 26(6); 27; 28(8); 29(2); 30(4); 31(4); 2:1(2; 2(2); 3(3); 4(2); 5(3); 6; 7(3); 8(2); 9(4); 10(3); 12(2); 13; 14(3); 15; 16; 17; 18; 19(4); 20(3); 21(4); 22(2); 23(2); 24(3); 25(3); 3:1; 2; 4; 5(2); 6(6); 7(4); 8(3); 9(2); 10; 11; 12(2); 13(3); 14(3); 15(5); 16(3); 17(2); 18(2); 19; 20; 21(2); 22(6); 24(2); 4:1(4); 2(2); 3; 4(4); 5(3); 6(2); 7(3); 8(3); 9(2); 10; 11; 12(2); 13(4); 14(4); 15(2); 16(2); 17(5); 18(4); 19(2); 20(2); 21(2); 22(3); 24; 25(3); 26(2); 5:2(3); 3(4); 4(3); 5(3); 6(3); 7(4); 8(3); 9(2); 10(4); 11(3); 12(2); 13(4); 14(3); 15(3); 16(4); 17(3); 18(3); 19(3); 20(3); 21(3); 22(3); 23(2); 24; 25(3); 26(2); 5:2:3(3); 4(3); 5(3); 6(3); 7(4); 8(2); 9(2); 10(4); 11(3); 12(4); 13(4); 1:1; 2:6(2); 3; 4(2); 5(2); 6(2); 7(4); 9(2); 10(4); 11; 12(2); 13; 14; 15(2); 16(8); 17(2); 18(2); 19; 20(2); 21(3); 22(2); 23(7); 24(2); 25; 26(2); 27(2); 28(2); 29(3); 10:1(2); 2(6); 3(3); 4(3); 6(6); 7(7); 8; 10(4); 11(3); 12(2); 13(4); 14(3); 15(2); 16(3); 17(3); 18(4); 19(4); 20; 22(4); 23(4); 24(2); 25(2); 26(4); 27(3); 28(3); 29(3); 30; 32; 11:1(2); 2(2); 3(4); 4(3); 5(2); 6(4); 7; 8; 9; 10; 11(3); 12(3); 13(4); 14(2); 15(4); 16(3); 17(4); 18(2); 19(4); 20(3); 21(4); 22(2); 23(3); 24(3); 25(4); 26(3); 27(2); 28; 29(4); 31(6); 32(3); 12(12(2); 2(4); 3(3); 4(3); 5(2); 6(4); 7(3); 8(5); 9; 10(2); 11; 12; 13; 14; 15(2); 16(8); 17(2); 18(2); 19; 20(4); 13(14(2); 2(2); 3; 4; 5(2); 6(6); 7(4); 8(4); 10(3); 11(2); 12(2); 13; 14(5); 15; 16; 17; 18(3); 14(12; 2(3); 4; 5(5); 6; 7(4); 8(6); 9(3); 10(5); 11(4); 12(3); 13(4); 14(3); 15(4); 16(5); 17(2); 18(3); 19(3); 20(2); 21(10); 22(6); 23(3); 24(2); 15:1; 2(2); 3(2); 4; 5(4); 6(2); 7; 8; 9(5; 10(3); 11; 12(2); 13(3); 14(2); 15; 17(3); 19(2); 20(3); 21(4); 16:1; 2(2); 3(2); 4(3); 5(3); 6; 7; 8(3); 9(5); 10(2); 11(3); 12(3); 13; 14; 15(2); 16(2); 17:14(2); 15:7(2); 18(3); 19(3); 20(2); 21(4); 16:1; 7(2); 9; 10; 11(2); 12; 13(2); 15(4); 20; 23(2); 24; 25(2); 26; 27(4); 28(5); 29(2); 30(5); 31(2); 32; 33(4); 34(3); 35(4); 37(2); 38(2); 20:14(3); 2(3); 3; 4; 5(2); 6; 7(4); 8(3); 9(3); 10; 11(2); 12(2); 13; 14(6); 15; 16(2); 17(4); 21:1(2; 2; 3; 4; 5; 6; 7; 8; 9; 10; 11; 12(2); 13(4); 14(8); 15(2); 16(5); 17(3); 18; 19(3); 20(4); 21; 24(2); 25(2); 26(5); 31(2); 32; 33(4); 34(3); 35(4); 37(2); 38(2); 20:14(2); 2(3); 3; 4; 5(2); 6; 7(4); 8(3); 9; 10; 11(2); 12(2); 13; 14(3); 15(2); 16; 17(3); 18(3); 19; 21(3); 22(4); 23; 24(4); 25(2); 26(3); 27(2); **Ex** 1:3; 4; 2:3; 4(2); 5; 6(3); 7(5); 9(2); 10(3); 11(2); 12(2); 13; 14(3); 15(2); 16(2); 17; 18(3); 19(2); 20(2); 21(2); 2:1(2); 2(3); 3(4); 4(3); 5(6); 6(2); 7(2); 8(2); 9(6); 3:1; 2; 3; 4; 5; 6(2); 7(3); 8(6); 9; 11(5; 12(2); 13; 14(6); 15(6); 16(2); 17(2); 18(5); 19(2); 20; 21(3); 22; 23(3); 24(4); 25; 26(2); 27(2); 29(5; 29(4); 30(4); 31(4); 32(3); 33(3); 34(4); 44:1(2); 2(3); 3; 4(3); 5; 6(2); 7; 9; 10(2); 11; 12(4); 14(3); 15; 16(2); 17(2); 18; 21(3); **Lev** 1:1(2); 2(2); 4(2); 5(3); 6(2); 7(2); 8(2); 9(2); 10; 11(2); 12(3); 13(3); 14; 15(4); 16(2); 17(2); 2:1(3); 2(4); 3(2); 4; 5; 6; 7; 8(2); 9(2); 10(3); 12(2); 13(4); 14; 15; 16(5); 17(3); 18(4); 6:1; 2(2); 3(2); 4; 5; 6; 7; 8(2); 9(2); 10(2); 11; 12(2); 13(3); 14(2); 15(3); 16; 4:1; 2; 4(3); 5(2); 6(2); 7; 8(2); 9(2); 10(3); 9:3; 10; 11(5); 12; 13(4); 14; 15(2); 16; 17(2); 18(2); 19(2); 20(3); 21(2); 22(2); 24(2); 25(3); 26(3); 27(2); 29(2); 30(3); 31(4); 32; 33(4); 34(3); 35(4); 5:1(3); 2(2); 3; 4; 5; 6(2); 7(2); 8(2); 9(2); 10(3); 12(2); 13(4; 14; 15; 16(3); 17(3); 18(4); 6:1; 2(2); 3(2); 4; 5(2); 6; 7; 8(2); 9(2); 10; 11(2); 12(2); 13(3); 14(2); 15(4); 16(2); 17(4); 19; 20; 21(2); 22; 23; 24(2); 25(2); 28(2); 30; 7:2; 3(2); 4(3); 5; 8; 9(3); 10(2); 11; 12(2); 14(2); 15(3); 16; 4:1; 2; 4(3); 5(2); 6(2); 7(2); 8(2); 9(2); 10; 12(4); 14; 16(5); 17(2); 18(2); 19(2); 20(4); 21(4); 22(3); 23(5); 24(5); 25(7); 26(5); 27(3); 28(2); 29(2); 30(10); 31(4); 32(2); 35(2); 36; 9:1(3); 2(3); 3(4); 4(2); 5; 6(4); 7(2); 8; 10(4); 11; 12(4); 13(2); 14(5); 15(3); 16(4); 17; 19(4); 20; 21; 10:11(2); 3(2); 5(2); 6(2); 7; 8(2); 9(2); 10(4); 13(3); 14(2); 16(4); 17(3); 18(3); 19(3); 22(3); 24; 25(2); 26; 27; 28(2); 29(2); 30(5); 32(2); 33(2); 34;

6(3); 7(2); 8(3); 9; 10; 11(2); 12; 13(2); 14(3); 15(3); 16(4); 17(3); 18(2); 19(2); 20(2); 21(2); 22(3); 23(3); 24(2); 25(2); 26(2); 27; 28(2); 29(2); 30(3); 31(3); 32(5); 33(2); 34; 35(7); 36(3); 37(5); 38; 39(3); 40(5); 41; 42; 43(6); 31:1(2); 2(2); 3(3); 4(3); 5(4); 6; 7(2); 8; 9; 10(4); 11(2); 12(3); 13(2); 14(3); 15; 16; 17(2); 18(2); 19(2); 20; 21(3); 22; 23(2); 24(2); 25; 26(2); 27(4); 28(2); 30; 31(2); 32; 33(4); 34(3); 35(2); 36(4); 37; 38(2); 39(4); 40; 37:1; 2; 3(2); 4(3); 3:4; 5(3); 6; 7(2); 8(2); 9(2); 10(2); 11(4); 12(3); 13(3); 14(3); 15; 16; 17(2); 18(2); 19(2); 20; 21(3); 22; 23(3); 24(2); 25; 26(2); 27(2); 28(2); 29(3); 10:1(2; 2(6); 3(3); 4(3); 7(7); 8; 10(4); 11(3); 13(4); 14(2); 15(2); 16(8); 17(2); 18(2); 19; 20; 21(2); 22(6); 24(2); 4:1(4); 2; 3(4); 5(3); 6(6); 7(4); 8(3); 9(2); 10; 11; 12(2); 13(3); 14(4); 15(2); 16(3); 17(4); 18(4); 19(2); 20(2); 21(2); 22(3); 24; 25(3); 26(2); 5:2(3); 3; 3:1; 2; 4; 5(2); 6(6); 7(4); 8(3); 9(2); 10; 11; 12; 13; 14(4); 15(2); 16(2); 17(5); 18(4); 19(2); 20(2); 21(2); 22(3); 24(3); 25(3); 26(2); 5:2; 3(4); 4(3); 4:3(2); 3(4); 5(2); 6(4); 7; 8; 9(5; 10(3); 11; 5:1; 2(2); 3(2); 4; 5(4); 6(2); 7; 8; 9(5); 10(2); 11; 13(3); 14(2); 15; 17(3); 19(2); 20(3); 21(4); 6:1; 2(2); 3(4); 4(3); 5(2); 6(4); 7; 8; 9(5); 10(2); 11; 12(2); 13; 14; 15(2); 16(2); 17(4); 18(2); 19(2); 20(2); 21(7); 23; 24(4); 25; 26; 27(2); 28(2); 29(5); 30; 31(5); 32(4); 33(2); 34; 47:1(7); 2(2); 3(3); 5(2); 6(2); 7(3); 8; 9(4); 10(3); 11; 12; 13(4); 14; 15(2); 16(2); 17(4); 18; 19; 20(2); 21(7); 23; 24(4); 25; 26; 27(2); 28(2); 29(5); 30; 31(5); 32(4); 34; 47:1(7); 2(2); 3(3); 4(3); 5(2); 6(2); 7(3); 8(2); 9(3); 10(3); 11(2); 12(3); 13(4); 14(3); 15(3); 16(2); 17(3); 18(5); 19(3); 21(3); 22; 24(2); 25(2); 26(3); 27(2); 28(2); 46:1(3); 2(3); 4(3); 5(4); 6(4); 7(3); 8(2); 9(4); 10(2); 11(5); 13; 15(4); 16(3); 19; 20(2); 21; 22(2); 24; 27(4); 28(3); 29(3); 30(3); 31(4); 32; 33(2); 34(2); 35(2); 36:1(3); 2(3); 3; 4(2); 5; 6(2); 7; 8(4); 9(2); 10(2); 11; 12(2); 13; 14; 15(3); 17(4); 18(6); 19(4); 20(2); 22; 24(3); 25(4); 26(4); 27(2); 28(2); 29(3); 30(4); 31(4); 39:1(4); 2(4); 3(5); 5(4); 6; 7; 8(4); 9; 10(2); 12(2); 13(4); 14; 16; 15(3); 17(4); 18(6); 19(4); 18(2); 19(2); 20(2); 21(2); 22; 23; 24(4); 25(2); 26(2); 27(2); 28(3); 29(4); 30(2); 31; 32; 33(4); 34(3); 35(2); 36(2); 37(2); 38(4); 39(3); 40(4); 41(2); 43(3); 40:1; 3(2); 4(4); 5(2); 6; 7(3); 8(2); 9(6); 10(4); 11(3); 12(3); 13(4); 14(2); 15; 17; 18(5); 19(2); 20(4); 21(3); 22; 23; 24; 25(2); 26(2); 27(2); 28(3); 29(4); 30(3); 31; 32; 33(4); 34(3); 35(2); 36; 38; **Lev** 1:1(2); 2(2); 4(2); 5(2); 6(2); 7(2); 8(2); 9(2); 10; 11(2); 12(3); 13(3); 14; 15(4); 16(2); 17(2); 2:1(3); 2(4); 3; 4; 5; 6(2); 7(2); 8(2); 9(2); 10(3); 12(2); 13(3); 14(2); 15(3); 16(2); 17(2); 18(2); 19(2); 20; 21(2); 22(2); 23; 24(2); 25(3); 26; 27; 28(2); 29(2); 30(5); 32(2); 33(2); 34;

18; 19(2); 20(2); 21(3); 14:1; 2(2); 4(4); 5(4); 6(2); 7(3); 8(3); 9(4); 10(4); 11; 13(2); 14; 15; 16(3); 17(5); 18(2); 19(4); 20(4); 21(4); 22(3); 23(3); 24(3); 25; 26(2); 27(4); 28(4); 29(2); 30; 31(4); 15:1(3); 2(4); 4; 7; 8(2); 14; 16; 17; 18; 19(2); 20(3); 21(2); 22(3); 23; 24; 25(4); 26(4); 27(4); 16:1(3); 2(2); 3(2); 4(2); 5(2); 6(2); 7(2); 8(3); 9(4); 10(2); 11; 12(3); 13(3); 14; 16; 17(4); 18; 19(2); 20(3); 21(2); 22(3); 23(2); 24; 25(3); 26; 27(4); 28(4); 29(2); 30; 31(4); 15:1(3); 2(4); 4(4); 5(2); 6(2); 7(3); 8(2); 9(3); 10(3); 11(3); 12(5); 13(3); 14(3); 15(2); 16(3); 17; 18(5); 25:1; 3(3); 4(5); 5(3); 6; 7(2); 8(2); 9(2); 10(6); 11(3); 12(4); 13(2); 14; 16; 17(4); 18; 19(2); 20(2); 21(2); 22(3); 23(2); 24; 25(3); 26; 27(2); 28; 29(3); 30; 31(4); 32; 33(3); 34; 35(3); 36(4); 37(4); 27:1(3); 2(3); 3(3); 4(2); 5; 6(2); 7(2); 9(3); 10(3); 11(2); 13; 14; 17(4); 18(6); 19(4); 20(2); 22; 24(2); 25(4); 26(4); 27(6); 28(2); 29(3); 30(4); 31(6); 32(3); 33; 34(3); 35; 37(4); 8:1; 2(6); 3; 6(3); 7(6); 9; 11(4); 14(2); 15(6); 16(5); 17(2); 18(3); 19(2); 20(4); 21(4); 22(3); 23(5); 24(5); 25(7); 26(5); 27(3); 28(2); 29(2); 30(10); 31(4); 32(2); 35(2); 36; 9:1(3); 2(3); 3(4); 4(2); 5; 6(4); 7(2); 8; 10(4); 11; 12(4); 13(2); 14(5); 15(3); 16(4); 17; 19(4); 20; 21; 10:11(2); 3(2); 5(2); 6(2); 7; 8(2); 9(2); 10(4); 13(3); 14(2); 16(4); 17(3); 18(3); 19(3); 22(3); 24; 25(2); 26; 27; 28(2); 29(2); 30(5); 32(2); 33(2); 34;

35(2); 37; 38; 39; 40(3); 41; 42; 44; 46(3); 47(3); 12:1; 2; 3; 4(2); 5(2); 6(2); 7(2); 8(4); 13:1(2); 2; 3(5); 4(2); 5(3); 6(5); 8; 10(4); 11(2); 12(2); 13; 15(2); 16; 17(2); 18; 19(3); 20(2); 21(2); 22; 23(2); 24; 25(2); 26(2); 27(2); 28(3); 30(2); 31(3); 32(4); 33; 34(4); 36; 37(2); 39; 40; 41; 42; 43; 45(4); 49(2); 50(2); 51; 53(2); 54; 55(3); 56(2); 57; 58(2); 14:1; 3(3); 4(4); 5; 6(5); 7(3); 8(5); 9(4); 10(4); 11(2); 12(4); 13(2); 14(4); 15(2); 16(2); 17(3); 18(2); 19(3); 20(4); 21(4); 22(3); 23; 24(3); 25(5); 26; 27; 28(3); 29; 30; 31(2); 33(2); 34; 35(2); 36; 37(2); 38; 39(3); 40; 41(2); 42(4); 43(4); 44(2); 45(4); 47(2); 48(3); 49(4); 50; 51(7); 52(6); 53(2); 54; 55(2); 56(3); 57; 15:1(2); 2; 3; 4; 5(3); 6(3); 7(3); 8(3); 9; 10(4); 11(4); 12(2); 13(4); 14(3); 15(3); 16(2); 17(3); 18; 19(3); 20; 21(3); 22(3); 23; 24(3); 25; 26; 27(4); 28; 29(2); 30(3); 32(2); 33(4); 16:1(2); 2; 3; 4(4); 5(2); 6(3); 7(2); 8(2); 9(2); 10; 11(4); 12(3); 13; 14(3); 15(4); 16(3); 17(4); 18(5); 19(3); 20(3); 21(4); 22(2); 23(3); 24(7); 25; 26(3); 27(5); 28(3); 29(2); 31; 32(3); 33(5); 34(2); 17:1; 2(3); 4(2); 5; 6(2); 7; 8; 9; 10(2); 11; 13(3); 15(3); 18:1; 2; 3; 4; 5; 17; 21; 25(2); 26(2); 27; 30; 19:1; 2; 3(2); 5; 6(2); 7; 8; 9; 10(2); 12; 16; 17; 19; 20(2); 21; 22(2); 23(2); 25; 29; 30; 32(2); 33; 34; 36; 37(2); 20:1; 3(3); 4(2); 5(3); 6(3); 7; 8(2); 10(2); 11; 12; 14(3); 15(2); 16(3); 17(4); 18(4); 19; 20; 21; 22(2); 23(2); 24(2); 25(4); 26(2); 21:1(2); 2(4); 3; 6(2); 9; 10(2); 13; 16; 22(2); 24(4); 22:1; 2(2); 4; 6; 7(2); 9; 11; 13(2); 14(2); 15; 17; 18(4); 21; 25; 26; 27(2); 28(2); 29; 31; 23:1; 2; 6; 9; 10(2); 11; 12; 13(2); 14; 15; 16; 18(4); 19; 20; 21; 22(2); 23(2); 24(2); 25(4); 26(2); 27; 28(2); 29; 30; 31; 32; 33(2); 35(2); 36; 37(2); 38(3); 39; 40(4); 41; 44; 24:1; 5(2); 6; 7; 9(3); 10(3); 11(4); 12; 13; 14(3); 15; 16(2); 17(3); 18(2); 19(3); 20(2); 21; 22(2); 23(3); 25:1; 2; 3(2); 6(5); 7(2); 8(3); 10(4); 14; 15; 16; 18(3); 19(3); 20; 21; 22(2); 23; 24; 25(2); 26(2); 27; 28(2); 29; 30; 31; 32; 33; 34; 35(2); 36; 37(2); 38; 39(2); 40; 41(2); 42; 43(2); 44(2); 45; 46(3); 50(5); 51(3); 52(2); 53; 54; 2:1(2); 3(2); 4(4); 5(2); 6(4); 7; 8(4); 9(3); 10; 11(4); 12(2); 13(4); 14; 15(5); 16(5); 18; 19(3); 20(2); 21(4); 22; 23(4); 24(3); 25; 26(4); 27(2); 28(4); 29; 30(4); 31(3); 32(3); 34(2); 3:1; 2(3); 4(5); 5; 6; 7(2); 8(2); 9(2); 10(4); 11; 12; 13; 14; 15; 16; 17(3); 18(2); 19(3); 20(2); 21; 22(2); 24; 25(3); 26(4); 27; 28(2); 30; 31; 32; 33(2); 34(3); 35; 36(7); 37(4); 38(3); 39(4); 40(3); 41(2); 42; 43(5); 44; 45(2); 46(3); 47(2); 48(2); 49; 5:1; 2(2); 3; 4(2); 5; 6; 7(3); 9; 10; 11; 12; 13(5); 14(5); 15; 16(2); 17(3); 18(4); 19(3); 20(2); 21(3); 22; 23(2); 24(3); 25; 26; 27(4); 28(2); 29; 30; 31; 32; 32(3); 33; 34; 35(2); 36; 37(2); 38; 39(2); 40; 41(2); 42; 43(2); 44(2); 45; 46(3); 50(5); 51(3); 52(2); 53; 54; 2:1(2); 3(2); 4(4); 5(2); 6(4); 7; 8(4); 9(3); 10; 11(4); 12(2); 13(4); 14; 15; 16(3); 17(3); 18(2); 19(3); 20(2); 21(2); 22(2); 23(4); 24(3); 25(2); 26(4); 27(2); 28(4); 29; 30(4); 31(3); 32(3); 34(2); 3:1; 2(3); 4(5); 5; 6; 7(2); 8(2); 9(2); 49; 53; 55; 59; 61; 65; 67; 71; 73; 77; 79; 83; 85(2); 86; 87; 88(2); 89(2); 8:1; 2; 3; 4; 5; 6; 7(4); 8; 9(2); 10(2); 11; 12(3); 13(3); 14; 15(3); 17; 18; 19(3); 20(3); 21(4); 22(2); 23; 24(2); 25(2); 26; 9:1; 3; 4; 5; 6(3); 7; 8(2); 9; 11(2); 13(2); 14(4); 15; 16; 17(2); 18; 19(2); 20(2); 21; 22; 23; 10:1; 2; 3; 4; 8(2); 9(3); 10(3); 11; 12(2); 13; 14; 15; 16; 17(3); 18(2); 19; 20; 21(2); 22(2); 23; 24; 25(2); 26; 27; 30(2); 31(2); 32; 33; 34; 35(2); 36; 11:1(5); 2(2); 3; 4(3); 5(4); 7(2); 8(6); 9; 10; 11(2); 15(2); 16(3); 17(5); 18(3); 20(2); 21(2); 22; 23; 24(4); 25(6); 26(4); 27(4); 28(2); 29(2); 30(2); 31(5); 32(5); 33(2); 34; 35(2); 12(2); 14; 15(2); 16(2); 18; 19(2); 20; 21; 23(4); 24(2); 25(3); 26; 27; 28; 29; 30; 32(3); 33(4); 34(4); 35(3); 22:1(2); 2; 3(2); 4(2); 5; 6(2); 7(4); 8(3); 9(2); 10; 11; 12; 13(2); 14(3); 15(2); 16; 17; 18(3); 20(3); 21(3); 23(5); 24; 25(3); 26(2); 27(3); 28(2); 29; 30(2); 31(4); 32; 33(3); 34(4); 35(3); 36(2); 37(2); 38; 39; 40(4); 41(2); 42(3); 43(3); 44(3); 45; 46; 47; 48; 49; 50(3); 53:1; 2(3); 3; 5(2); 6(2); 7(4); 8(3); 9(2); 10(2); 11(2); 12(3); 13(2); 14(2); 15(2); 16(4); 17(3); 18(2); 19; 20(2); 21(3); 22; 23(3); 24(2); 25(2); 26; 27(3); 28; 29(3); 34:1(2); 2(4); 3(2); 4(2); 6; 7(2); 8(2); 9; 11; 12(3); 13; 14(2); 15(2); 16(2); 18(2); 19; 20; 21(4); 22(4); 23(4); 24; 3:1(5); 2; 3(2); 4; 6; 7; 8; 9; 10; 11; 12(2); 13(4); 14; 15; 16; 17(4); 18(2); 19; 20(3); 21; 22(2); 23(6); 26(3); 27; 28(4); 29; 30:10(3); 2(4); 3(3); 4; 5(4); 6(3); 7(2); 8(3); 9(3); 10(3); 12(2); 13(2); 14; 15; 16(5); 17(2); 18; 19(4); 20(4); 31:1(2); 2(3); 3(3); 4(3); 5; 6; 7(4); 8; 9(3); 10; 12(6); 13(2); 14(5); 15(2); 16(5); 17(5); 18; 19(7); 21(2); 22; 23(4); 24; 26; 27(2); 28(3); 29(2); 30; 32:1(2); 4(2); 5; 6(2); 7(2); 10; 12; 13(2); 14(4); 15(2); 18; 19(2); 20; 21; 22(2); 23; 24(2); 25(2); 27(2); 30(2); 32; 33; 34; 35(2); 36(2); 37; 38(3); 39(4); 40(4); 41(2); 42(3); 43(3); 44(3); 45; 46; 47; 48; 49; 50(3); 33:1; 2(3); 3; 5(2); 6(2); 7(4); 8(3); 9(2);

2(2); 3(2); 4(3); 5(3); 6(4); 7(5); 8; 9(2); 10(2); 11(2); 12; 13(3); 14; 15(4); 16(4); 17(2); 18(4); 19(3); 20(5); 21(4); 23(2); 24(3); 25(3); 26(3); 27(8); 28(3); 29(3); 30; 31(3); 32(2); 33(4); 34(3); 35(4); 36(2); 37(3); 38; 39(2); 40(4); 41(3); 42(2); 43(7); 44(5); 45(5); 46; 47; 48(8); 49(5); 50(2); 51(5); 52(3); 53(2); 54(4); 55; 57(2); 10:1(2); 2(4); 3(3); 4(2); 5(2); 6(10); 7(3); 8(2); 9(2); 10(2); 11(3); 12(4); 13; 14; 15; 16(3); 17(3); 18(2); 11:1(2); 2(4); 3(4); 4; 5; 6(2); 7(3); 8(3); 9(2); 10; 11(3); 12; 13(2); 14; 15; 16(2); 17(2); 18(4); 19(2); 20(2); 21(3); 22(2); 23; 25; 26(4); 27; 29(4); 30(2); 31; 32; 33(2); 34(4); 35(4); 36; 37(4); 38(4); 39(3); 12:14(2); 2(3); 3(3); 4(3); 5(2); 6(4); 7(2); 8; 9(4); 10; 11(2); 12(2); 13; 14(4); 15(2); 13:1(2); 2(3); 3(4); 4(2); 5(3); 6(2); 7(2); 8(2); 9(2); 10(4); 11(5); 12(2); 13; 15; 16(2); 17; 18; 19(4); 20(3); 21; 22; 23; 24(4); 25(2); 14:1(2); 2(4); 3(2); 4; 5(4); 6(3); 7(3); 8(4); 9(6); 10; 11; 12(3); 13(2); 14(3); 15(2); 16(6); 17(3); 18(3); 19(7); 15:1; 2; 3; 4(5); 5(4); 6(5); 7(2); 8(4); 9(2); 10; 11(2); 12(2); 13(4); 14(4); 15(4); 16; 17(2); 18(5); 19(3); 20; 16:1(2); 2(4); 3(8); 4; 5(5); 6(2); 7(2); 8(2); 9(2); 10(2); 11(2); 12(4); 13(3); 14(5); 15(2); 16(7); 17(3); 18(5); 19(5); 20(5); 21(4); 23; 24(2); 25(4); 26; 27(4); 28(3); 29(3); 30(4); 30(4); 31(6); 17:1; 2(3); 3(2); 4(4); 5(4); 6(2); 7(2); 8(2); 9(3); 10(6); 11(2); 12(3); 18:1; 2(3); 3(4); 4(4); 5; 6; 7(6); 8(3); 9(4); 10; 11(2); 12(2); 13(2); 14(4); 15(2); 13:1(2); 3(4); 4(2); 5(2); 6(2); 7(2); 8(3); 9; 10(2); 11(3); 12(4); 13; 14; 15(3); 16(2); 17(2); 18(3); 19(3); 20; 21; 4:1(3); 2(3); 3; 4(2); 5; 6(2); 7(2); 9(2); 10(4); 11(3); 12(3); 13(3); 14(3); 15(2); 16(3); 17(6); 18(5); 19(5); 20; 21(3); 22; 5:1(2); 2; 3(3); 4(3); 6(3); 7(2); 8(4); 9(4); 10(2); 11(4); 12(2); 6:1; 2(2); 3(2); 4(2); 5(4); 6(2); 7(3); 8(3); 9; 10(2); 11(3); 12(4); 13(4); 14(4); 15(5); 16; 17; 18(2); 19(4); 20(2); 21(2); 7:1(4); 2(5); 3; 4(3); 5; 6(2); 7(2); 8(3); 9(2); 10(4); 11(2); 12(2); 13; 14(4); 15(2); 16(2); 17(2); 18(4); 19; 20(4); 21; 22(3); 23; 25; 26(4); 27; 29(4); 30(2); 31; 32(2); 33(3); 34(2); 35(4); 36(4); 3:1(2); 2(2); 4; 5(5); 6(5); 8(2); 9(2); 10(3); 11; 13; 14; 15(3); 16(2); 17(2); 18(3); 19(3); 20; 21; 4:1(3); 2(3); 3; 4(2); 5; 6(2); 7(2); 9(2); 10(4); 11(3); 12(3); 13(3); 14(3); 15(2); 16(3); 17(6); 18(5); 19(5); 20; 21(3); 22; 5:1(2)(2); 3; 4; 14:1; 2(2); 13:1(4); 14(2); 15; 16(2); 17(2); 18(4); 19(2); 20; 21(2); 22; 23; 24(3); 25; 26(5); 27(7); 28(2); 29; 30(2); 31; 32(2); 33(2); 34; 35(2); 16:1(2); 2(3); 3(3); 4(4); 5(5); 6(2); 8(2); 9; 10; 11(5); 12(5); 13; 14(4); 15; 16; 17; 18(4); 19(4); 20; 21(2); 22; 23(4); 24(3); 25(3); 26(2); 27(1); 1:3(2); 2(3); 3(4); 5(3); 6(3); 7; 8; 9(4); 9(4); 5(3); 6(5); 7; 8; 9(4); 10; 11(4); 12; 13; 14(2); 15(5); 12:1(2); 2(5); 3(2); 4; 6(3); 7; 8; 9(4); 10; 11(3); 12(2); 13; 14(4); 15; 16; 17; 18(4); 19(4); 20; 21(2); 22; 23(4); 24(3); 25(3); 26(2); 27(1); 1:3(2); 2(3); 3(4); 5(3); 6(3); 7; 8; 9(4); 10(2); 11; 12(2); 13(4); 22:1(3); 2(5); 3(4); 4(2); 5(3); 6(2); 7(3); 8(2); 9(3); 10; 11(2); 12(4); 13(4); 14(4);

16(2); 17(4); 18(6); 19(6); 20(2); 21; 22; 23:1; 2(4); 3; 4(2); 5(4); 6; 7(3); 8(2); 9(2); 11; 12(2); 13(5); 14(3); 15(2); 16(3); 17(4); 18(3); 20; 21; 22(3); 23(4); 24(3); 25(4); 26(6); 27; 28; 29(2); 24:1; 2(2); 3(4); 4(2); 5; 6; 7(2); 8(4); 9; 10(2); 11(3); 12(2); 15(5); 16(3); 17; 18; 20(2); 21; 22(3); 23(5); 25:1(6); 2(5); 3(5); 4; 5(4); 6(3); 7; 8(2); 9(2); 10(3); 11(3); 12(5); 13(5); 14; 15; 16; 17(2); 18(7); 19; 20(4); 21; 22; 23:4(4); 24(4); 25; 26(3); 27; 28; 29(2); 30(2); 32; 33(3); 34; 35(2); 36(2); 37(2); 38; 39(4); 40; 41(3); 42(5); 43; 26:1; 2(3); 3; 4; 5(6); 6(3); 7(4); 8; 9(2); 10; 11; 12(3); 13; 14(3); 15(2); 16(2); 17(4); 18(3); 20; 21; 22(3); 23(4); 24(3); 25(2); 27:1(2); 2(3); 3(3); 4(2); 5; 7(2); 9(2); 10(4); 11(3); 12(3); 13(3); 14; 15(2); 23; 26; 27; 28(4); 10:1; 2(4); 3; 4(2); 5(6); 6(2); 7(3); 8; 9(2); 10(2); 11(2); 12(3); 13(3); 2Sa 1:1; 2(3); 3(2); 4(6); 5(2); 6(3); 7(3); 8(2); 9; 10(4); 11(2); 12(6); 13(2); 14; 15(4); 16; 17(2); 22; 19; 20; 21:4(2); 22(4); 23; 25(2); 26; 27(2); 28(3); 29(3); 30(3); 31:1(2); 2(5); 3(3); 4(4); 5(7); 6(3); 7(7); 8(2); 9(4); 10(2); 11; 12(5); 13(3); 2Sa 1:1; 2(3); 3(2); 4(6); 5(2); 6(3); 13(2); 14; 15(4); 16; 17(2); 22; 2:1(4); 2(2); 3(2); 4(3); 5(3); 6(3); 7(2); 8(2); 9(2); 10:1; 2(4); 3; 4(2); 5(6); 19(2); 20(2); 21(3); 22; 23(4); 24(2); 25(3); 26; 27; 28(2); 29(5); 30(3); 31(2); 32(3); 32(5); 3(4); 9(2); 10(2); 11; 12(2); 13; 14; 15(2); 16(2); 17; 18; 19; 20; 21(4); 22; 23:1; 24(2); 25(3); 26; 27(2); 28(2); 29(2); 30; 31(5); 32(4); 33(2); 34; 35(2); 36(2); 37; 38(2); 39(2); 4:1(2); 2(2); 3(2); 4(7); 5(4); 6(4); 7(3); 8; 9(3); 10; 11; 12(6); 5:1(2); 2(3); 3(5); 4; 5(4); 6(2); 7(3); 8:2; 9:1(2); 2(2); 3(4); 4; 5; 6(2); 7(3); 8:2; 9:1(2); 2(2); 3(4); 22; 23; 26(3); 27(2); 28(2); 29(2); 30(2); 31; 32(2); 33(3); 34(2); 35(4); 36(4); 3:1(2); 2(2); 4; 5(5); 6(5); 7(2); 8(3); 9(2); 11(2); 12(5); 13(3); 14(2); 15(3); 16(2); 17(2); 18(3); 19(3); 20; 21; 4:1(3); 2(3); 3; 4(2); 5; 6(2); 7(2); 9(2); 10(4); 11(3); 12(3); 13(3); 14(3); 15(2); 16(3); 17(6); 18(5); 19(5); 20; 21(3); 22; 5:1(2); 2; 3(3); 4(3); 6(3); 7(2); 8(4); 9(4); 10(2); 11(4); 12(2); 6:1; 2(2); 3(2); 4(2); 5(4); 6(2); 7(3); 8(3); 9; 10(2); 11(3); 12(4); 13(4); 14(4); 15(5); 16; 17; 18(2); 19(4); 20(2); 21(2); 22; 23; 24(3); 25; 26(5); 27(7); 28(2); 29; 30(2); 31; 32(2); 33(2); 34; 35(2); 16:1(2); 2(3); 3(3); 4(4); 5(5); 6(2); 8(2); 9; 10; 11(5); 12(5); 13; 14(4); 15; 16; 17; 18(4); 19(4); 20; 21(2); 22; 23(4); 24(3); 25(3); 26(2); 27(1); 1Kin 1:1(2); 2(2); 3(2); 4(3); 5(3); 6(3); 7(3); 8(5); 9(3); 10; 11; 12; 13(3); 14; 15(3); 16(3); 17(2); 18; 19(2); 20(2); 21(3); 22; 23(2); 24(6); 25(2); 3:1; 2(2); 4(3); 6(2); 7(4); 8(2); 9(5); 10; 11(2); 12(3); 13(3); 14; 15; 16(2); 17(3); 18(3); 19; 20(2); 21(5); 22; 23(2); 24(2); 25(6); 26(2); 27(3); 28(2); 29(5); 30(3); 31; 32; 33; 34(7); 35(6); 36(3); 37(4); 38(5); 39(5); 40(3); 41(3); 42(4); 43(2); 44(2); 5:1; 2(3); 3; 4(3); 5(6); 6; 7(4); 8(2); 9(2); 10(4); 11(6); 12(3); 13(5); 14(5); 16; 17; 18(2); 19; 20; 21(2); 22(2); 23(5); 24(4); 25(3); 26(8); 27(2); 6:1; 2(3); 3(3); 4; 5(2); 6(5); 7(2); 8(2); 9(3); 10(3); 12; 13; 14; 15(4); 16(2); 17(6); 17(6); 18(2); 19; 20; 21(2); 22(2); 23(5); 24(4); 25(3); 26(8); 27(2); 6:1; 2(3); 3(3); 4; 5(2); 6(5); 7(2); 8(2); 9(3); 10(3); 12; 13; 14; 15(4); 16(2); 17(6); 18(2); 19; 20; 21(2); 22(2); 23(4); 24(3); 31; 32(3); 33(4); 34; 5:1; 2; 5; 6(2); 7(2); 8(3); 9(4); 10;

11(2); 12(4); 13(2); 14(3); 15(3); 16; 17(3); 18(4); 6:1(2); 2(3); 3(2); 4; 5(3); 6(2); 7; 8(2); 9(3); 10(2); 11; 12(2); 13(2); 14; 15(4); 16(2); 17; 18(2); 19; 20(5); 21(2); 22; 23; 24(2); 25(2); 26; 27(4); 28; 29(4); 30(2); 31(2); 32(6); 34(2); 35(4); 36(2); 38(2); 7:1; 2(2); 3; 4(2); 5(3); 6(5); 7; 8; 9(10); 12(3); 13(2); 14; 15; 16(2); 17(3); 18(3); 19; 20(2); 21(5); 22; 23(3); 24; 25(5); 26(2); 27(3); 28(2); 29(5); 30(3); 31(4); 32(4); 33(4); 34(2); 35(3); 36(3); 37; 38(2); 39; 40(3); 41(2); 43(2); 44(2); 45(4); 46; 47; 48(2); 49(4); 50(7); 51(3); 8:1; 2; 3(2); 4(4); 5(3); 6(2); 7; 8(2); 9(3); 10(2); 11; 12(2); 13(2); 14; 15(4); 16; 17; 18(2); 19; 20(4); 21; 22(2); 23(2); 24; 26; 27; 28(2); 29(2); 30(4); 31(2); 33(3); 34(2); 35(3); 36(3); 37; 38(2); 39(2); 42(3); 43(2); 44(2); 45(2); 46(2); 47(3); 48(4); 49(2); 50(3); 51; 52; 54(2); 55(2); 58(3); 59(3); 60; 61; 62(2); 63(5); 64(4); 65(3); 66(4); 9:1(3); 3(4); 4(4); 6(4); 7(3); 8(4); 9(4); 10(2); 11(2); 12(2); 13(2); 14; 15(7); 16(4); 17(2); 18(2); 19(6); 20(2); 22(5); 23; 25(3); 26; 27; 28(4); 10:1; 2(4); 3; 4(2); 5(6); 6(2); 7(3); 8; 9(4); 10; 11; 12(3); 13(3); 14; 15; 16; 17(2); 18; 19(3); 20(2); 21(2); 22(3); 23; 24; 25(6); 26(6); 27(2); 28(2); 29(6); 11:1; 3(3); 4; 5; 6(2); 7; 8(2); 9; 10; 11(3); 13; 14; 15; 16; 17; 18(6); 19; 20(2); 21(2); 22; 23; 24; 25(5); 26; 27(3); 28(2); 29(3); 30(2); 31(2); 32; 33(5); 34; 35; 36; 37(3); 38(6); 39; 40(3); 41(3); 42; 43(3); 12:1; 2(4); 3; 4(2); 5(2); 6(2); 7; 8(2); 9(2); 10; 11; 12(3); 13(2); 14(2); 15(3); 16; 17(2); 18(2); 19; 20(5); 21; 22(2); 23(2); 24; 26; 27; 28(2); 29; 30(4); 31(2); 32(3); 33(4); 34(3); 36(3); 37; 38(2); 39(4); 40(2); 41(2); 42(4); 45(2); 46(2); 47(3); 48(4); 49(2); 50(3); 51; 52; 54(2); 55(2); 58(3); 59(3); 60; 61; 62(2); 63(5); 64(4); 65(3); 66(4); 9:1(3); 3(4); 4(4); 6(4); 7(3); 8(4); 9(4); 10(2); 11(2); 12(2); 13(2); 14; 15(7); 16(4); 17(2); 18(2); 19(6); 20(2); 21(2); 22(3); 23; 24; 25(6); 26(6); 27(2); 28(2); 29(6); 11:1; 3(3); 4; 5; 6(2); 7; 8(2); 9; 10; 11(3); 13; 14; 15; 16; 17; 18(4); 19(5); 20(5); 21(2); 22(4); 23(3); 24(3); 25(2); 26(3); 27(3); 28; 29; 30; 31; 32(3); 33; 34(3); 16:2(3); 3(2); 4; 5(2); 6(2); 7(4); 8; 9; 10(5); 11; 13(2); 14; 15(2); 16(4); 17(3); 18(3); 19; 20; 21; 22(3); 23; 24; 25(2); 26; 27(2); 28(2); 29; 30; 31; 32(2); 33(2); 34(3); 16:2(3); 3(2); 4; 5(2); 6(2); 7(4); 8; 9; 10(4); 11(7); 12(3); 13(5); 14(4); 15(2); 16(2); 17(2); 18(4); 19(4); 20(5); 21(2); 22(3); 23(3); 24(3); 25(2); 26(3); 27(3); 28; 29; 30; 31; 32(3); 33; 34(3); 16:2(3); 3(2); 4; 5(2); 6(2); 7(4); 8; 9; 10(4); 11; 12(4); 13(5); 14(4); 15(2); 16(2); 17(2); 18(4); 19(4); 20(5); 21(2); 22(3); 23(3); 24(3); 25(2); 26(3); 27(3); 28; 29; 30; 31; 3; 4; 5; 7(2); 9(3); 10(3); 11(2); 12(2); 13(3); 14(6);

15(2); 16(3); 17; 18; 19(2); 20(2); 21(2); 22; 23(2); 24; 27; 28(4); 29(2); 15:1; 2(3); 3; 4; 5(3); 6(2); 7(2); 8; 9; 10(4); 11; 12; 13(2); 14(4); 15(2); 16(3); 17(2); 18; 19(2); 20(2); 21(2); 22(2); 23; 24; 25(5); 26(2); 27(2); 28; 29(8); 30(4); 31(2); 33(3); 34; 35; 36; 37; 38(3); 16:2(2); 3; 4(4); 5(2); 6(3); 7(3); 8(4); 9(4); 10(4); 11; 12(3); 13(4); 14(3); 15(9); 17(4); 18(2); 20(3); 17:2; 3(2); 4(3); 5(2); 6(4); 7; 8(2); 9(2); 10(3); 11(2); 13(5); 15(6); 16(5); 17(5); 18; 20(3); 21(3); 24(8); 25; 26(2); 27(3); 28(2); 29; 30(3); 31(4); 32; 33; 34; 35; 36(3); 37(5); 38; 39; 41(2); 18:2(3); 3; 4(4); 6; 7(4); 8; 9(2); 10; 11(4); 12(2); 13; 14(3); 15(2); 16(2); 17(7); 18(3); 19; 20; 21; 22(3); 23; 24(2); 25; 26(3); 27(2); 28(2); 30; 31(4); 32(6); 34(2); 36; 37(3); 19:1(3); 2(3); 3(4); 4; 6; 7(3); 8; 9; 11; 12(3); 13(3); 14(4); 15(3); 16(3); 17; 18(2); 21; 22(3); 23(5); 24(2); 25; 26(3); 27(3); 28(3); 29(6); 30(2); 31; 32; 33; 34; 35(4); 36(3); 37(4); 20:1(3); 2; 3(3); 4; 5; 6(5); 7(4); 8(2); 9; 10; 11(2); 12; 13(7); 14(3); 15; 16; 17(2); 18; 19(2); 20(5); 21(2); 21:1(3); 2; 3(4); 4; 5; 6(5); 7(3); 8; 9; 10; 11(2); 12; 13(4); 14(4); 15; 17(2); 18(3); 19; 20; 21; 22(3); 23; 24(2); 25; 26(3); 27(2); 28(2); 30; 31(4); 32(4); 34(2); 36; 37(3); 19:1(3); 2(3); 3(4); 4; 6; 7(3); 8; 9; 11; 12(3); 13(3); 14(4); 15(3); 16(3); 17; 18(2); 21; 22(3); 23(5); 24(2); 25; 26(3); 27(3); 28(3); 29(6); 30(2); 31; 32; 33; 34; 35(4); 36(3); 37(4); 20:1(3); 2; 3(3); 4; 5; 6(5); 7(4); 8(2); 9; 10; 11(2); 12; 13(7); 14(3); 15; 16; 17(2); 18; 19(2); 20(5); 21(4); 22(2); 23(3); 24(3); 25(3); 28(7; 29(5); 30(4); 31(2); 32(4); 33(3); 34(3); 35(4); 36(4); 37(5); 38(3); 39(3); 40(4); 8:1; 2; 3(4); 3(3); 5(2); 6(2); 7(5); 8(2); 9(4); 10(2); 11(2); 12(3); 13; 14(2); 15(3); 16(3); 17(4); 18(2); 19(3); 20(2); 21(3); 22(3); 23(3); 23(3); 24(3); 25(2); 26(3); 27(3); 28; 29; 31(5); 32(2); 34; 35; 36(2); 37; 21:1(2); 2; 3(4); 4; 5(2); 6(7; 7(3); 8(3); 9; 10(4); 11(2); 12; 13(8); 14(6); 15; 16; 17(2); 18(2); 19; 20(5); 21(4); 22(2); 23(5); 24; 25; 27(3); 26:1; 2; 3(4); 5(2); 6(7; 7(3); 8(3); 9; 10(4); 11(2); 12; 13(8); 14(6); 15; 16; 17(2); 18(2); 19; 20(5); 21(4); 22(2); 23(5); 24; 25; 27(3); 26:1; 2; 3(4); 5(2); 6(7; 7(3); 8(3); 9; 10(4); 11(2); 12; 13(8); 14(6); 15; 16; 17(2); 18(2); 19; 20(5); 21(4); 22(2); 23(5); 24; 25; 27(3); 27; 34; 35; 36; 40; 32:3; 6(4); 7; 8; 12; 16; 20;

33:1; 3; 4; 8; 16; 17; 18; 19; 20; 21; 22; 24; 26(2); 27(3); 28; 31; 33; 34:1; 2; 5; 8; 10; 11; 14; 15; 17; 18; 20(3); 21; 24; 25; 27; 28; 29; 33; 34; 35; 37; 35:1; 3; 4; 5(2); 8; 11; 36:1; 2; 3; 5(2); 7; 8(2); 9; 10; 11(2); 12; 14; 15; 16; 17; 26; 28; 30; 32; 37:1; 2; 3; 4; 6; 8; 9; 10; 12; 14; 15(2); 13; 20; 23; 27(2); 29; 30; 35; 38; 40; 39:4; 6; 8; 12; 13; 14; 15; 18; 21; 22; 23; 24; 25(2); 26; 27; 28(2); 29; 30; 40:1; 3; 6; 7; 10(3); 11(2); 12(2); 13; 16; 21; 23; 41:18; 19; 21; 22; 27; 42:1; 2; 4(2); 6(2); 7(2); 8(4); 9(3); 10; 11(6); 12(3); 13; 14(3); 15(2); 16(3); 17; **Ps** 1:2(2); 3(2); 2:1; 2(2); 3; 5; 8(2); 11; 12; 3:3; 4; 5; 4:1; 2; 4(2); 5; 7; 8; 5:2; 3; 6; 7; 6:10(2); 7:1; 5(2); 6; 8; 9; 11; 12; 14(2); 15; 16; 17; 8:2(2); 3; 4; 5; 6; 8; 10; 17; 10:3; 7(3); 10; 14; 15; 16; 18; 11:5; 6(2); 12:2; 3; 13:3; 4; 14:2; 4; 7; 15:2(2); 4; 16:3; 5; 9; 17:3; 6; 12; 14(2); 18(2); 2(4); 4; 6(2); 7(2); 8; 9; 10(2); 11; 12; 13(2); 14(3); 15; 17; 21; 22; 23; 26; 27(2); 28; 29(2); 31; 23(4); 6(2); 24(1); 3; 5; 7(2); 8(2); 25:5; 6; 8; 9; 10(2); 13; 14; 16(2); 18(2); 19; 20; 21; 26:2(2); 3; 5; 7; 8; 10; 11; 12; 14; 28:3; 4; 5; 7(3); 8; 9(2); 29:1; 6; 9(2); 30:t; 1; 2; 4; 6; 7; 8; 10; 11; 12; 31:3(2); 7; 8; 9; 10(2); 11; 15; 17; 18; 23(4); 24; 32:2; 4; 6; 7; 8; 10; 11; 13; 33:2; 4; 5; 6; 9(2); 12; 19; 20; 34:t; 2; 3; 4; 6; 7; 8; 10; 11; 12; 14; 28:3; 4; 5; 7; 3; 4; 5(2); 6(2); 7; 8; 9(2); 10(2); 11; 12(2); 13(2); 14(2); 15(2); 16(2); 17; 18; 19(2); 20(3); 21; 22; 23; 24; 25(2); 26; 27; 28; 29:1; 2; 4; 5; 6; 9; 10; 11; 12; 14; 15; 16; 17; 18(2); 19; 20; 21; 22; 23; 24; 25(2); 26; 27; 28:2; 8; 13; 15; 22; 24; 29:1; 6; 10; 11; 12(2); 13; 15; 16; 20; 21; 22; 23; 28; 30; 31; 32; 31:2(2); 5(2); 6; 7(2); 9(2); 12; 13(2); 15(2); 16; 17; 28(2); 30; 31; **Eccl** 1:4; 5(2); 6(2); 13(2); 14(2); 15; 16(2); 17(3); 18; 2:1; 2; 3; 5(2); 7(3); 8(6); 9; 10(2); 11(4); 12(3); 14; 15; 16; 17; 19(2); 21(3); 22; 23; 24(2); 26(4); 3:1; 2(2); 3(2); 4(2); 5(2); 6(2); 7(2); 8(2); 12; 14; 15(2); 16(2); 17(2); 18; 20; 21; 4:1(4); 4(2); 5; 6; 7; 8(2); 12(2); 13(2); 16; 5:1; 2(2); 3; 5; 7; 8(3); 11; 14(2); 15; 16; 17(2); 18; 6:2; 5(2); 6; 7; 8(3); 10(2); 11(2); 12; 16; 17(2); 20; 23; 24; 25; 23:2; 7; 8; 10; 12; 14; 18; 19(2); 21(2); 22(2); 23(3); 24; 25(2); 26; 27(2); 28; 32; 33; 35(2); 24:2; 3; 4(2); 6; 9; 11; 12(2); 13; 14; 15; 16; 17(3); 19; 20; 21(2); 22; 23; 4; 9; 10; 11; 12(2); 13; 15; 16; 20; 21; 22; 23; 24; 27; 28; 27:2; 4; 5; 6; 7; 8(2); 9(4); 10; 11; 12; 13; 14; 48:1(2); 3; 3(3); 4(2); 5(2); 6(2); 7; 8; 9; 11; 12; 13; 14(2); 15; 16(2); 18; 19; 21(2); 49:1; 2(3); 3; 4(2); 5(2); 6(4); 7(4); 8(3); 9; 11(2); 13(3); 14; 17; 18(3); 19(3); 21(4); 22(3); 23(4); 25(2); 26(4); 50:1; 2; 3; 5; 6(2); 7; 10(2); 11; 51:1; 2(3); 3(4); 4(2); 5(2); 6(4); 8(2); 9(3); 10; 14; 16(4); 17; 19(3); 21(2); 22; 23(2); 24; 25(3); 26(3); 28(4); 29:1; 3; 4; 5; 6; 7(2); 8(2); 9(2); 10; 11; 12(4); 54:1; 2(2); 3(3); 4; 5; 6(2); 7(2); 8(2); 9(2); 10; 11; 12(4); 54:1; 2; 3(3); 4; 5; 6; 7(2); 8(2); 10; 11; 12(3); 13; 14; 15; 16; 55:1(4); 2(3); 3(3); 4; 5(2); 7(4); 9; 10(5); 11; 12(3); 13(2); 56:1(2); 2(2); 4(2); 5(3); 6(2); 7(2); 11; 12(3); 57:1(2); 3; 4; 7; 8(3); 9(4); 11(3); 12; 13; 14; 15(4); 16; 17(3); 18(3); 19(2); 20; 58:1(2); 2; 3(3); 4(2); 5(3); 6(2); 7(2); 8(2); 9(3); 10(3); 11(5); 12(2); 13(3); 14(2); 15:9; 59:2(3); 3; 4(2); 5(2); 6; 7; 8; 10; 11; 12(2); 13(4); 14(3); 60:1; 2(2); 3(2); 4(2); 5(3); 6(3); 7; 8; 9(3); 10(2); 11; 12; 13(2); 14(2); 15; 16(3); 17(4); 18; 19; 20; 22; 61:1; 2; 4(2); 5(4); 6; 7; 8(2); 9(2); 10; 11(2); 62:1(2); 2(3); 3; 4(2); 5; 7(2); 8(2); 9(2); 11; 12(2); 63:2; 3(4); 4; 5(4); 6(3); 7(3); 9(4); 10(2); 11; 15(4); 16; 17; 64:5(2); 6(3); 7(2); 8(2); 11(2); 12; 65:3; 4(2); 7(2); 8; 9(4); 10(2); 11; 12(2); 14; 15(2); 16(2); 17(2); 18(2); 19(3); 21(4); 22(3); 23; 24(2); 25(3); **Jer** 1:5(2); 7; 9(2); 10(5); 11; 13(3); 15(4); 16(3); 17(2); 18(3); 19; 2(2); 3; 4; 5(2); 6(3); 7(3); 8(3); 9; 10(4); 12; 13; 15(2); 16; 18; 19(4); 20(3); 22; 25(2); 26(2); 27(3); 37(2); 3:1(2); 2(3); 3(2); 5; 6(2); 7(2); 8(3); 9(3); 10; 11; 12(4); 13(4); 15(2); 16(2); 17; 18; 19(3); 21(2); 22; 23; 24(2); 25(3); 4:1; 2; 4(2); 5(3); 6(2); 7; 8; 9(4); 10; 11; 13; 15; 16; 18; 20; 21; 22; 23(4); 24(2); 25(2); 26(3); 28(3); 29(3); 30; 31; 5:1(5); 2; 5(3); 6(2); 7(2); 9; 10; 11; 12; 13(2); 14(2); 15(7); 16; 18; 20(3); 24(3); 25; 28; 29(3); 31(2); 33(3); 34(3); 8:1(4); 2(7); 3; 4; 5(2); 6; 7; 9; 11(4); 12; 13(2); 14; 15; 16; 17(2); 18(5); 19(2); 20; 21(3); 22(3); 24; 25(2); 23:3(2); 9; 12; 14(4); 15(4); 16; 17(4); 19; 20(3); 22(2); 25(3);

26(3); 28(2); 30; 23:1; 2(2); 3(4); 4(2); 5(4); 6(2); 8(3); 9(2); 10(2); 11; 12; 13(2); 14(2); 15; 16; 17; 18(3); 20; 22(2); 23; 24; 28; 29; 31; 32(3); 33; 34(4); 35(2); 36; 37; 38; 39(4); 40(2); 24:1(4); 2; 3(2); 6(5); 7(3); 8(4); 9(3); 10(3); 25:2; 3(3); 4(2); 5(4); 6(4); 9(9); 10(3); 11(3); 12(4); 13; 14(3); 15; 16(3); 17; 18(4); 19(3); 20(7); 21(2); 22(3); 23(3); 24(2); 25(3); 26(4); 27(4); 28; 29; 30(2); 32; 33; 34(4); 35; 36; 37; 38; 26:2; 3; 4; 5; 6; 7(2); 8(2); 9(2); 10; 11(2); 12(2); 13(3); 14; 15(2); 16(2); 17; 18(3); 19(3); 20(2); 21(4); 22(2); 23(3); 27:2(2); 3(5); 4; 5(3); 6(2); 7(5); 8(5); 10(2); 11(3); 12(3); 13(2); 15(2); 16; 17; 18(3); 19(3); 20(2); 21(2); 22(2); 28:1(3); 3; 4; 5; 6; 7; 8(4); 10; 11(2); 13; 14(2); 29:1(3); 2(5); 3; 5(3); 6(6); 7(2); 8; 10; 11; 12(3); 13(2); 14(5); 16(2); 17(2); 18(6); 19; 21(2); 22(2); 23(3); 25(2); 26(2); 28(3); 29; 31(2); 32; 30:3(3); 4(2); 5; 6(2); 8(2); 9; 10(5); 11; 12; 16(3); 17; 18(3); 19(5); 20(2); 21(4); 22(2); 24; 31:1; 4(2); 5; 6; 7(2); 8(4); 9(2); 10(3); 11; 12(8); 13(3); 14(2); 15; 16(2); 17; 18(2); 19; 23(2); 24(3); 25; 26(2); 27(2); 28(6); 29; 31; 33(3); 34(3); 35(2); 37; 39(2); 40(3); 32:2; 3(2); 4(3); 5(2); 6; 8(2); 9(2); 10(4); 11(2); 12(2); 13; 14(2); 15(2); 17(3); 18; 19(2); 20(4); 21(5); 22(2); 23(2); 24(5); 25(2); 28(2); 29(4); 30; 31; 32(4); 33(3); 35(2); 36(3); 37(4); 38(2); 39(3); 40; 41(2); 43; 44(8); 33:3(3); 4(2); 5(2); 6(4); 7(3); 8(3); 9(5); 10(4); 11(3); 12(2); 13(4); 14; 15(3); 16(2); 18(2); 19; 20(3); 21; 22; 25(3); 26(3); 34:1(4); 2(3); 3(5); 5(2); 7(2); 9; 10(3); 11(4); 14; 15(3); 16(5); 17(3); 18(2); 19(3); 20(3); 21(4); 22(6); 35:2(3); 3(3); 4; 5(3); 10(2); 11(2); 13(2); 14; 15(2); 17(2); 18(3); 36:1; 2(3); 3; 4; 5; 6(2); 7(2); 8; 9(2); 12(6); 14(2); 15(2); 16; 17; 18; 19(4); 20(4); 21(3); 22; 23(2); 25(2); 26(3); 27; 28; 29(4); 30(2); 31(6); 32(2); 37:1; 3(2); 4; 5; 8(4); 10(2); 11; 13(2); 14; 17(4); 18:1(3); 2(2); 4; 6(3); 8; 9; 10; 11(4); 12(3); 13(2); 14(2); 15; 17(3); 18(2); 19(2); 20; 22(4); 23(3); 24; 25(3); 27(2); 28; 39:1(2); 2; 3(2); 4(4); 5(2); 6; 7; 48:1(2); 2; 3; 6; 7(3); 8(3); 9; 10; 11(3); 12(2); 13; 14; 15(2); 16; 17(2); 18(2); 19(3); 20; 21(3); 22(3); 23(3); 24(3); 25; 26; 28(2); 29(3); 31; 32; 33(4); 34; 35; 36; 37(2); 38; 39; 40; 41(2); 42; 43(2); 44; 45(3); 46; 49:1; 2(2); 3(4); 5(2); 6; 10(4); 11; 12; 13(2); 14(3); 15; 16; 17; 18(2); 19(2); 20; 22(3); 23(3); 24(3); 26; 27(2); 28(2); 29(4); 30; 32(4); 33(2); 36(3); 37(3); 38(3); 50:1; 2(3); 3(2); 4(4); 5; 7; 8(2); 9(2); 10; 11; 12; 16(2); 17; 18; 19(5); 20(4); 21(3); 22; 23; 24; 25; 26; 26:2; 3; 4(3); 5; 6; 26:2; 3; 4; 5(2); 6; 7(2); 8(2); 9(2); 10; 11(2); 12(2); 13(3); 14; 15(2); 16(2); 17; 18(3); 19(3); 20(2); 21(4); 22(2); Lam 1:1; 2; 3; 4; 6(2); 7(3); 8; 11; 12; 13(2); 14; 17; 18(2); 19; 21; 22(2); 2:1(2); 2(2); 3; 4; 5(2); 6(4); 8; 9(2); 10; 11; 12; 14(3); 15; 16; 17(2); 18; 20(3); 21(3); 22; 3:2; 4; 5(2); 8; 10; 11; 12; 14; 17; 18(2); 19(2); 20; 26; 28; 37; 38; 48(2); 49; 42; 43; 45; 47(2); 49; 50; 53; 60; 61; 62; 63; 66; 4:4; 6; 11(2); 12(2); 13; 15; 21(2); 5:1; 3; 5; 6; 7(2); 11; 13; 20; 21; Eze 1:1; 3; 4(5); 5; 6(2); 7(3); 8(3); 10(2); 11(2); 12(2); 13(4); 14(4); 16(4); 17; 18; 19(2); 20; 21(2); 22; 3(2); 4; 5(2); 6; 3(2); 4(5); 6; 3(5); 7; 8; 9(2); 10(3); 11; 12(4); 13; 14(3); 14; 15(4); 16(8); 17(8); 18(4); 19; 20(2); 21(8); 22(2); 24; 25; 26; 27; 28(2); 29; 30(2); 31; 32(4); 33(3); 34; 35; Dan 1:3; 3(3); 4(6); 5(2); 6; 7(3); 9; 10(2); 11; 12(2); 13(2); 14; 15(2); 16(2); 17(4); 19(3); 20(3); 21; 2:1(2); 2(4); 5(2); 6(4); 7(2); 8; 9(2); 9:8(2); 10; 12(3); 15; 16(4); 17(3); 5:1(4); 2(4); 3; 4; 6:7(3); 8(2); 9; 10(3); 11(2); 12(3); 14(5); 15; 16(2); 17(2); 18; 9:2(5); 3(4); 5(2); 6(4); 7(4); 8(4); 9:4(3); 6; 7(2); 5(3); 7; 8; 9(2); 10(3); 11; 12(4); 13(3); 14; 15(4); 16; 20(3); 21; 22(2); 23(3); 24:2; 5; 26; 27; 28(2); 29; 30(2); 31; 32(4); 33(3); 34; 35; Dan 1:3; 3(3); 4(6); 5(2); 6; 7(3); 9; 10(2); 11; 12(2); 13(2); 14; 15(2); 16(2); 17(4); 19(3); 20(3); 21; 2:1; 2; 4; 5(2); 7(2); 8(3); 9(2); 10(2); 12(2); 13(3); 14(2); 15(2); 19; 20; 21(2); 22; 23(2); 47:1(2); 2(2); 3(2); 4(2); 5; 6(2); 7; 8(2); 9(3); 10; 11; 12(4); 14(2); 15; 16; 17(4); 18(5); 19(2); 22(3); 23; 48:1; 2; 3; 4; 5; 6; 7; 8(4); 9(2); 10(7); 12; 13(5); 14(4); 15(4); 7:1; 2(2); 3(2); 5(3); 6(3); 7(3); 8; 9(2); 10(2); 11(3); 12(2); 13; 14; 15(2); 16; 17(2); 20(2); 21; 22(6); 23; 7:5(3); 6(3); 7(2); 8; 9; 10; 11(3); 2:1; 2; 3(4); 5(3); 6; 7(3); 8(4); 9(4); 10(2); 11(2); 12(4); 13(5); 14(2); 15(4); 16(2); 17; 18(7); 19(4); 20; 21(2); 22(4); 23(4); 3:1; 2(2); 3(2); 4(5); 5(4); 4:2(5); 3(2); 5(2); 8; 9(3); 10(2); 11(3); 12(3); 13(4); 14; 15; 19; 5:1(3); 2; 3(2); 4; 5(2); 6; 8; 11; 12; 13(2); 14(3); 15(2); 6:13(3); 2; 3(2); 4; 5; 6(2); 8; 9; 7:1(3); 2; 3; 7; 9(2); 10(2); 14(3); 15; 8:1; 4(2); 7; 10; 13(2); 14(3); 9:2(2); 3; 5; 7; 8; 10(2); 11(2); 14; 17; 10:5; 6; 8(3); 10; 11(3); 12; 14; 11:1; 2; 4(2); 6(3); 7; 9(2); 11(2); 12(2); 12:1(4); 2; 3; 4(3); 6(2); 8; 9; 10(2); 12(3); 13(2); 14; 13:24(3); 3(2); 4; 6(2); 8; 9; 10(2); 15(2); 16; 14:2(2); 5; 6(2); 7; 8; 9(3); Joel 1:2; 3(2); 4(2); 5(2); 6(2); 7(2); 9; 11; 12(2); 14(2); 15; 16; 19; 20; 2:1; 2(3); 3(3); 4; 7(2); 8; 9; 10(2); 11(3); 12(3); 13(6); 14(3); 16(2); 17(3); 18; 19(5); 20(5); 21; 22; 23(3); 24(3); 25(3); 26(4); 27(4); 28(3); 29(2); 30(4); 31(2); 32(3); 3:1(2); 2(4); 4(5); 5(2); 6; 7; 8(3); 10; 11(2); 12; 15(2); 16(4); 17; 18(5); 19; 20; Amos 1:1; 2(4); 3; 5(3); 6; 8(4); 9(2); 11(4); 13; 14; 15(2); 2:3; 3(2); 4(5); 5; 6(2); 7(3); 8(2); 9(2); 10; 11(2); 12; 14; 15; 16; 3:5; 6(2); 9(4); 4:1; 2; 3(2); 4(5); 5(3); 6(2); 7(4); 9(4); 10(2); 11(2); 12; 13(3); 5:3; 4; 5(2); 6(3); 7; 8(4); 10; 11; 12(2); 14(2); 15(2); 16(3); 17; 18; 19(3); 20(2); 21; 22; 24; 25; 26; 6:1; 2(2); 3; 4(3); 5; 6; 7; 8; 9; 10(4); 11(2); 12; 14; 7:1(2); 2; 4(3); 7; 8(2); 9(3); 11; 12(2); 13; 14(2); 15(2); 16; 17(5); 8:1; 2(2); 3; 5(2); 6(2); 8(4); 9(2); 10(6); 12(4); 13; 14(3); 9:1(4); 3(4); 4(4); 5(5); 6(2); 7(2); 8; 9; 11(3); 12; 13(3); 14(6); 15(2); Obad 1(2); 4; 7; 8; 9; 10; 11(2); 16(2); 17(2); 18(6); 19(5); 20(2); 21(2); Jonah 1:2; 3(3); 4; 5(4); 6; 7(3); 8(2); 9(3); 10; 11; 12(2); 13; 14(2); 15(2); 16(2); 17(2); 2:2(3); 3(2); 7; 10(2); 3:1; 2; 3; 4(4); 5(2); 6(4); 7(3); 8(3); 9(2); 10(3); 4:1; 2(5); 5(3); 6(2); 7; 8(4); 9(2); 10; 11(3); Mic 1:1(2); 2(2); 3(2); 4(3); 5(2); 6(3); 7(4); 8(3); 16; 2:1; 2(6); 4(2); 10; 11(2); 13(4); 3:1(2); 2(2); 3(4); 5(2); 6(5); 7; 8(3); 9(2); 10; 11(3); 12(2); 4:1(2); 2(7); 3(4); 4(2); 5(2); 6(2); 7(3); 8; 10(3); 11; 13(5); 5:3(4); 5(3); 6(3); 7; 8(3); 9; 10(2); 11(2); 12(2); 6:1; 3(3); 4(3); 14; 15(3); 16(2); 7:2; 3(2); 4; 9(2); 10; 12(4); 14; 16; 17; 18; 19; 20; Nah 1:2(3); 3(4); 4(4); 5(3); 6(2); 7; 8; 10; 12; 13; 14(2); 2:2; 3; 5; 6; 7(2); 9; 10(6); 11(3); 12(3); 13(4); 3:1; 2(3); 3(4); 4; 5(3); 6(3); 7(2); 8; 9(3); 10(2); 11; 14; 16; 17; 18; Hab 1:2(2); 3(4); 4; 5(2); 6; 7(2); 8(3); 9; 10(3); 11(2); 12; 13(2); 14; 15(2); 16(2); 17; 2:1(3); 2(3); 3; 5(3); 6(3); 7(2); 8(2); 10; 11; 12; 13; 15; 16(2); 17(3); 18; 19(2); 3:2(3); 4(2); 5; 6(3); 7; 8; 10(2); 11(2); 16; 17(2); 19(2); Zeph 1:3(4); 4(3); 5(4); 6(2); 8(3); 9; 10(3); 12(2); 13(4); 14; 15(4); 16(2); 17(3); 2:4(2); 6(3); 7(2); 8(2); 9(4); 10; 11; 13(4); 14(2); 15(2); 3:1; 4; 7; 11; 12(2); 13(2); 14; 16; 19(4); 20; Hag 1:1; 4; 6(2); 8(4); 9(3); 10; 11(9); 12(3); 14(5); 15; 2:1; 2(2); 3; 4(3); 6(4); 7(3); 8; 9; 10; 12(3); 14(4); 15(2); 17(2); 18(2); 19; 20(2); 21; 22(6); 23; Zec 1:3; 4; 5; 6(4); 7; 8(4); 9; 10(3); 11(5); 12(3); 13(2); 14; 15(2); 16; 17(3); 18(2); 19(3); 20; 21; 2:1(2); 2(2); 3(2); 4(2); 5; 6; 9(2); 10(2); 11(4); 12(2); 3:1(2); 2; 3; 4(4); 5(3); 6; 7(3); 8; 9; 10; 4:1(2); 2(5); 3(2); 4; 5(2); 6; 7; 9(2); 10(2); 11(3); 12(3); 13; 14(4); 5:1(3); 3(4); 5(3); 6(2); 7(3); 8(2); 9(5); 11(3); 6:1(5); 2; 3(3); 4; 5(2); 6(2); 7(6); 8; 9; 10(3); 11(3); 12(3); 13(5); 14(4); 15(4); 7:1; 2(2); 3(2); 5(3); 6(3); 7(3); 8; 9; 12; 8:2; 3(3); 8; 2; 3(4); 4; 6; 7(3); 8(2); 9(5); 14:1; 2(5); 3; 4(6); 5(3); 6; 8(3); 9(3); 10(6); 11(2); 12(3); 13(3); 14(4); 15(4); 7:1; 2(2); 3(2); 5(3); 6(3); 7(3); 8; 9; 12; 8:2; 3(3); 4; 6; 7; 9(2); 10(4); 11(5); 12(2); 13(3); 14; 15; 16; 17(2); 18; 19(6); 20; 21(2); 22(2); 9:1; 2(2); 3(3); 4(2); 5(5); 6(2); 7(4); 8(3); 9(3); 10(6); 13(2); 14(4); 15(6); 16; 17(2); 10:1; 2(2); 3(2); 5(3); 6(5); 7(3); 8(2); 9(4); 10(4); 11(5); 12(3); 11:5(3); 6(4); 7(4); 8(2); 9(2); 10(2); 11(2); 12(2); 13(3); 14; 15; 16; 17(2); 12:1(2); 2; 3; 4(3); 5; 6(4); 7; 8(2); 9(2); 10(6); 13:1; 3(2); 4(4); 6; 7(3); 8(2); 9(5); 14:1(3); 3; 4(6); 5(3); 6; 8(3); 9(3); 10(6); 11(2); 12(3); 13(3); 14(4); 15(3); 16(2); 17; 18(2); 19; 20; 21(5); Mal 1:3(3); 4(3); 5(2); 6(3); 7; 8(3); 9; 11(2); 12; 13(4); 14(3); 2:1; 2(2); 3(2); 4; 5(3); 6(3); 7; 9; 11(3); 12(2); 13(2); 14(2); 15(3); 17; 3:1(2); 2(3); 3(5); 4(2); 5(8); 7(2); 8; 10(2); 11(2); 12; 14(2); 15; 16(4); 17(2); 18(3); 4:1(3); 2(2); 3; 4; 5; 6(3); Mt 1:2(3); 3(4); 4(3); 5(3); 6(2); 7(3); 8(3); 9(3); 10(3); 11(2); 12(2); 13(3); 14(3); 15(3); 16; 17(2); 19; 21(2); 23(2); 24; 25(2); 2:2; 3; 4(2); 5; 6; 8(5); 9(2); 11(6); 12; 13(3); 14(2); 15; 16(4); 18(3); 20(3); 21(4); 22(3); 3:2; 4(4); 5(2); 6; 7; 8(2); 9(2); 10; 11(2); 13(3); 15; 16(2); 17; 18(2); 19(2); 20(2); 21(3); 22(3); 23(4); 24(7); 25(5); 5:1(2); 2(2); 6; 11(2); 12; 13; 15(2); 16; 18; 19(2); 20; 21; 22; 23; 24; 25(2); 29(3); 30(3); 32; 38; 40(2); 41; 42; 43; 44(2); 45(3); 47; 6:2; 4; 5(2); 6(2); 12; 13(3); 17; 18; 19(3); 20; 24(3); 25; 28; 29; 30; 33(2); 7:2; 3; 4; 5; 6(2); 7(3); 8(2); 12; 13(2); 14(2); 19; 22(2); 23; 24; 25(5); 26(2);

27(6); 28; 29; 8:2(2); 3(3); 4(2); 5; 6; 7(2); 8(2); 9(6); 10; 11(5); 12; 13(3); 14(2); 15(4); 16(2); 17; 19(2); 20(2); 21(2); 22; 23; 24; 25(2); 26(4); 27; 28; 29; 30; 32(4); 33(4); 34(2); 9:1(3); 2(2); 3; 4; 5; 6; 7(2); 8; 9(4); 10(4); 11(2); 13(2); 14; 15(2); 16; 17(3); 18(3); 19(3); 20(2); 22(2); 23(3); 24; 25(2); 26; 27(2); 28(2); 30(2); 33(3); 35(5); 36; 10:1(3); 2(2); 3(3); 4; 5(2); 7; 11(2); 12; 13; 14; 15; 16; 17; 18(3); 21(4); 22; 25; 26; 27; 28(2); 29; 35(2); 36; 37; 38(2); 39; 40; 41; 42; 11:1(2); 3; 4(3); 5(3); 6; 7; 9; 12(2); 13; 14; 16; 17(3); 18; 19(4); 21(2); 22; 23(4); 27(2); 28(2); 29(3); 30; 12:1(3); 3; 4; 5; 7; 9; 10(2); 11(3; 13(2); 14; 15(2); 16; 18; 20; 21; 22(4); 23(2); 25(3); 26; 27; 29(2); 30; 31; 32; 33(2); 35; 37; 38; 39(3); 40(2); 41(2); 42(2); 43; 44(2); 45(4); 46; 47; 48(2); 49(3); 50(2); 13:1; 2(3); 3; 4(3); 5; 6(2); 7(3); 8; 10(2); 11; 12; 13; 14(4); 15(6); 16; 17(4); 19(2); 20; 21; 22(3); 23(2); 25(2); 26; 27; 28; 30(2); 31; 32(2); 33; 34; 36(2); 37; 39; 40; 41(2); 42(2); 44(3); 46(2); 47; 48(2); 49; 50(2); 52; 53; 54(3); 55(4); 56; 57(2); 58; 14:2(2); 3(2); 5; 6; 8; 9(2); 10(2); 11(3); 12(5); 13; 14(4); 15(3); 17(2); 19(7); 20(3); 21(2); 22(2); 23(2); 25; 26(2); 28(2); 29(2); 30; 31(3); 32; 33; 34; 35(2); 36(2); 15:1; 3; 4(2); 6; 8; 10(3); 12; 13; 14; 15; 16; 17; 18; 21(2); 22(2); 23(2); 24; 25; 26(2); 27; 28(2); 29(4); 30(4); 31(2); 32(3); 33; 34(3); 35; 36(6); 37(3); 38(2); 39(3); 16:1; 2; 3(2); 4(4); 5; 6(2); 7; 9; 10; 11; 12; 14(2); 16(2); 17(3); 18; 19(3); 21(5); 22; 24; 25; 26; 27(2); 28; 29(2); 30; 20:2(2); 3(2); 4(3); 5; 6(2); 7(3); 8; 9; 10; 11; 12(2); 13; 14; 16; 17(2); 18(3); 19(4); 20; 21(2); 22(2); 23(3); 24; 25(2); 27; 28; 29; 32(2); 33; 34; 35(5); 36(2); 37; 38(2); 39(3); 41; 43; 45; 48; 49(3); 50; 51(3); 25:1; 2(2); 3; 5; 6; 7; 8; 9(2); 10(3); 12; 14; 15(3); 16(2); 17; 18(2); 19; 20(2); 21; 22; 23; 24; 25(2); 26(3); 27; 28; 29; 30(2); 31; 32; 33; 35(3); 36; 37(2); 38(2); 39; 40(2); 41; 42(2); 43(4); 44; 46; 26:1; 2; 3(2); 7; 9; 15(3); 16; 18(2); 19(2); 21; 22(2); 23(2); 24; 25(3); 26; 27(2); 28; 29(2); 30(2); 31; 32; 33; 33(3); 34(3); 35(3); 36(2); 37(2); 38(2); 39; 40(2); 41; 42(2); 43(4); 44; 46; 26:1; 2(4); 3; 4(2); 5(2); 6(2); 7(3); 8(3); 9(4); 10; 11; 12(2); 13; 14(2); 15(2); 16; 17(3); 18(8); 19(2); 20; 21; 22(2); 23(2); 24; 25(3); 26(2); 27(2); 28(2); 29(2); 30; 31(5); 32(2); 33; 34(3); 35(3); 36(2); 37; 38; 39(2); 40(3); 41(3); 42(2); 43(2); 44(2); 46; 48(5); 51(3); 52(2); 53(3); 54(2); 55; 56; 57; 58; 59; 60(3); 61(2); 62; 64(2); 66(2); 28:1; 2(4); 3; 4(2); 5(2); 7(3); 8(3); 9(4); 10; 11; 12(2); 13; 14(2); 15(2); 16; 17; 18(3); 19(3); 20; **Mk** 1:4; 5(3); 6(4); 7(2); 9(2); 10(2); 11; 12; 13(3); 15(3); 16; 17(2); 18(2); 19(2); 20(3); 21(3); 22(2); 23(2); 26(2); 27(2); 28; 29(2); 30; 31(5); 32(2); 33; 34(3); 35(3); 36(2); 37; 38; 39(2); 40(3); 41(3); 42(2); 43(2); 44(2); 45(3) 2:1(2); 2(2); 3; 4(2); 6; 8; 9(2); 11(2); 12(2); 13(3); 14(4); 15(4); 18(5); 19; 20; 21; 22(3); 23(2); 24; 25(3); 26(2); 27(2); 27(5); 30; 32(2); 33; 34; 35; 36(2); 37(2); 38(3) 39(5); 40; 41(3); 5:1; 2; 3; 4(3); 5(4); 6; 7(2); 9(2); 10; 12; 13(5); 14(4); 15(6); 16(2); 17; 18; 19(2); 20(3); 21(2); 22(2); 23(3); 24(3); 25; 26(3); 27; 29(2); 30(2); 31(2); 32; 33(3); 34(2); 37(3); 38(4); 39(2); 40; 4(2); 5(2); 6(2); 7(4); 8; 9; 10; 11(2); 12(2); 13(3); 14(3); 15(2); 16; 17; 18(2); 20(2); 21; 22(2); 23(3); 24(2); 25; 26; 27(5); 30; 32(2); 33; 34; 35; 36(2); 37(2); 38(3); 39(5); 40; 41(3); 5:1; 2; 3; 4(3); 5(4); 6; 7(2); 9(2); 10; 12; 13(5); 14(4); 15(6); 16(2); 17; 18; 19(2); 20(3); 21(2); 22(2); 23(3); 24(3); 25; 26(3); 27; 29(2); 30(2); 31(2); 32; 33(3); 34(2); 35; 36; 38(2); 39; 40; 41; 42(2); 43(2); 44; 45(2); 46; 47; 48(3); 49; 50(3); 51(4); 53(2); 54; 55(2); 56(3); 7:1; 2; 3; 4; 5; 6; 8(2); 9; 10(2); 12; 13; 14(4); 15(6); 16; 17(4); 19(2); 20; 21; 22(3); 23(2); 25(2); 26; 27; 28; 30(2); 31; 32(2); 33; 34; 36(2); 37; 39; 40; 41(2); 42(2); 44(3); 46(2); 47; 48(2); 49; 50(2); 52; 53; 54(3); 55(4); 56; 57(2); 58; 14:2(2); 3(2); 5; 6; 8; 9(2); 10(2); 11(3); 12(5); 13; 14(4); 15(3); 17(2); 19(7); 20(3); 21(2); 22(2); 23(2); 24; 25; 26; 27(5); 18:2(2); 3(2); 5; 6; 8; 9(2); 12(4); 13(2); 15(2); 17(2); 18(3); 19; 20(3); 21; 22; 24; 25(4); 26; 27(2); 28(2); 29(3); 30(2); 31(2); 34(2); 36(2); 37(4); 38(2); 39; 40(3); 42; 43(3); 44(2); 45; 46(2); 47(2); 48(3); 49; 50; 51(3); 52(4); 3:1(4); 2; 3; 5(3); 6; 8; 9(2); 10; 11(2); 12; 13; 14(2); 15(2); 16; 17(2); 22(2); 23; 4:1(2); 4:1(2); 3; 4; 5(2); 6(2); 7(4); 9; 10(3); 11; 12(2); 13(2); 14(2); 15(2); 16(2); 17(3); 18; 19(3); 20(2); 21(2); 22(3); 23; 24(2); 26; 27(2); 28(2); 29(3); 30; 31; 32(3); 33; 34; 35; 36(2); 37(3); 38; 6:1(3); 2; 3(2); 4(3); 5; 6(3); 7(2); 8(4); 10(3); 11(2); 12(2); 13(2); 14(3); 15(2); 16(2); 17(8); 18(2); 19(2); 20(2); 22(3); 23; 25; 28; 29(2); 30; 31; 32(3); 33(3); 34(3); 35(4); 37(2); 38; 39; 41; 42; 43; 44(2); 45; 46(2); 47(2); 48(3); 49; 50; 51(3); 5:1(2); 2(3); 3(2); 4(2); 5; 6; 7; 8(2); 9(2); 10; 12(2); 13; 14(3); 15; 16; 17; 18(5); 19; 20(2); 22(3); 23; 24; 25(7); 27; 28; 29; 30; 31; 32(3); 35; 37; 38(2); 39; 40(2); 41; 42; 46; 48(5); 51(3); 52(2); 53(3); 54(2); 55; 56; 57; 58; 59; 60(3); 61(2); 62; 64(2); 66(2); 28:1; 2(4); 3; 4(2); 5(2); 7(3); 8(3); 9(4); 10; 11; 12(2); 13; 14(2); 15(2); 16; 17; 18(3); 19(3); 20;

20(2); 21(3); 22; 23(2); 24(3); 26(4); 27; 28(2); 30(2); 12:2; 3; 4(2); 6(2); 7(5); 8(5); 9(3); 10(4); 11(3); 12; 13; 14(2); 15; 16(2); 17(4); 19(5); 20(3); 21(2); 22(2); 23(3); 24; 25(3); 13:1(5); 2(2); 3(3); 4; 5(2); 6; 7(2); 10(2); 11(5); 13(2); 14(2); 15(3); 16(2); 17(2); 18; 19; 20(2); 21(2); 22(2); 25; 26(2); 27; 28; 29(2); 31; 32; 34; 36(2); 38; 39; 41(2); 42; 43(2); 44; 45(2); 46(3); 48(3); 49; 50(5); 51; 52(2); 14:1(3); 2; 3(2); 4(2); 5(3); 6(3); 7; 8; 9; 10(2); 11; 12(2); 13(2); 14(2); 15(5); 17(3); 18; 19(3); 20(2); 21(4); 22(2); 23(2); 24; 25; 26; 27(3); 28; 15:1(2); 2(5); 3(3); 4(4); 5; 6(2); 7(4); 8; 9(2); 12(3); 13(2); 15; 16(3); 17; 20(3); 22(3); 23(5); 24; 25; 27; 28; 29(3); 30; 32(3); 33; 35(2); 36(3); 37; 38; 39(3); 40(2); 41(2); 16:1(3); 2; 3(2); 4(2); 5(2); 6(2); 8; 9(3); 10; 11; 12(3); 13(3); 14; 15(4); 16; 17(2); 18(3); 19(3); 20; 21; 22(3); 23; 24; 25(4); 26(3); 27(3); 29(4); 30(2); 31(3); 32(3); 33(4); 34(2); 35; 36(2); 37(3); 38(2); 39(4); 40(4); 17:1; 2(2); 3(3); 4(5); 5(4); 6(2); 7; 8(2); 9(2); 10(2); 11; 12; 13; 14(2); 15(3); 17(2); 18(3); 19; 21; 22; 23; 24(2); 25(2); 26(3); 27; 28(2); 29; 30; 32(2); 34(3); 18:1; 2(2); 3(2); 4(3); 5(3); 6(3); 7(2); 8(3); 9; 10; 11(2); 13(2); 14(2); 15(2); 16; 17(2); 18(5); 19(3); 21; 22; 23; 24(2); 25(2); 26(3); 27; 28(2); 29(2); 30(4); 23:1(2); 2; 3; 4; 5(3); 7(3); 9(3); 10(3); 11(2); 12(2); 14(3); 15; 16(3); 17; 18(3); 19(2); 20; 21; 22; 23(4); 24(2); 25(4); 26(3); 27; 28(4); 30(5); 31; 32(4); 33(4); 34(2); 35; 37; 38; 39; 40(3); 22:1; 2(2); 3(2); 4; 5(2); 6(2); 7(2); 8(2); 9(2); 10(4); 11; 12(3); 14(3); 13; 14; 15; 16(2); 16(2); 17; 18(3); 19(3); 20(2); 21; 24; 25; 26; 27; 25:2(3); 3; 4; 5; 6(2); 7(3); 8; 9; 9:10(3); 11; 12(4); 13; 14(2); 15(2); 16(2); 16:3; 6; 7(2); 10(2); 11(5); 13(2); 14(2); 15(3); 16(2); 17(2); 18; 19; 20(2); 21(2); 22(2); 25; 26(2); 27; 28; 29(2); 31; 32; 34; 36(2); 38; 39; 41(2); 42; 43(2); 44; 45(2); 46(3); 48(3); 49; 50(5); 51; 52(2); 14:1(3); 2; 3(2); 4(2); 6(2); 7(5); 8(5); 9(3); 10(4);

21; 23; 24(2); 26; 30; 31(4); 32; 5:2(3); 3; 5; 9(2); 11; 14(2); 18; 19(3); 20; 23; 25; 26; 27; 29; 30; 31(3); 32; 33; 6:2; 3; 4(2); 5; 7; 9; 10; 12; 13; 14; 15; 17(2); 18(3); 19; 21(2); 22; 23(2); **Phil** 1:1(2); 2(2); 7(2); 9(3); 10; 11; 13; 14; 15(2); 18(2); 19; 20; 21; 23; 25(3); 27; 28(2); 30; 2:1; 7(2); 8(2); 9; 10(2); 11; 12; 13; 14; 15(2); 17(3); 18; 25(3); 26; 27; 28; 29; 3:3(2); 8(2); 9; 10(2); 13; 15; 17; 18; 19; 4:1(2); 2; 3(2); 4; 6; 7(2); 8; 9(4); 12(4); 15; 16; 18; 20(2); **Col** 1:1; 2(3); 3; 4; 6(2); 9(2); 10; 11; 13; 16(3); 17(2); 18; 20; 21(2); 22(2); 23(3); 24; 26; 28; 2:1(2); 2(3); 3; 4; 5(2); 7(2); 8(2); 10(2); 13(2); 14; 18(3); 19(2); 20; 21(2); 22; 23(4); 24; 26; 28; 2:1(2); 2(3); 3; 3:3; 5; 10; 11; 12; 13; 14; 15(2); 16(3); 17(2); 19; 23(2); 25; 4:1; 2; 7(2); 8; 9; 10; 11; 12; 13; 14; 15(2); 16(2); 17; **S:1**; **1Th** 1:1(5); 3(3); 5(2); 6(2); 7; 8; 9(2); 10; 2:2; 9(2); 10(3); 11(2); 12; 15(4); 18; 20; 3:2(4); 4; 5; 6(3); 7; 10(2); 11(3); 12; 14; 15; 16(2); 17(2); 5:1; 3(2); 5; 6; 7; 8(2); 11; 12(3); 13(2); 15; 23(4); 2Th 1:1(3); 2(2); 3; 4(2); 7; 8; 9; 10; 11(2); 12(2); 2:1; 3; 4; 6; 8(2); 9(2); 10; 11; 13(2); 15; 16(3); 17(2); 2(3); 4; 5(2); 6; 7(2); 8; 9; 13; 15; 16(3); 17(2); 19; 2; 2(3); 4; 6(2); 5(2); 6; 7; 8(2); 11; 12(3); 13(2); 15; 23(4); **1Ti** 1:1; 2(2); 4; 5(2); 9(4); 10; 12; 13(2); 14(2); 15; 17(2); 19; 20; 2:1; 2(3); 3; 4; 5(2); 7(3); 8; 9; 14; 15(2); 3:7; 10; 12; 13; 15; 16; 4:1; 3(2); 4; 5; 6; 7(2); 8; 9; 10; 11; 16(2); 5:1; 4(2); 5(4); 7; 8(2); 13(3); 16; 17; 18; 21(2); 23; 24; 25; 6:1; 2(3); 3; 4; 5; 6(2); 7(2); 8(2); 9(4); 10; 11; 13; 14; **2Ti** 1:2(2); 3; 5(2); 7(2); 9(2); 10(2); 11(2); 12; 13; 15; 16; 17; 18; 2:2; 5; 7; 16; 17(2); 18; 19; 20(4); 21(2); 23; 24; 26; 3:6; 7; 8; 12; 13(3); 14; 15; 16; 4:1(3); 2; 4(2); 6; 8; 10; 11; 12; 13; 17(3); 18(3); 19(2); 21(4); **Titus** 1:1(2); 4(2); 5; 9; 10(2); 14; 15(2); 16(2); 2:9; 12(2); 13(2); 14; 15(2); 3:1; 3(3); 4; 5; 8(2); 9(4); 10; 11; 13; 14; **Philem** 1:1(2); 2(3); 3(2); 5(2); 7; 9; 11; 16; **Heb** 1:1; 3(2); 5(2); 6(2); 7(2); 8; 9; 10(2); 11; 12(3); 2:2(2); 3; 4(3); 7(2); 9; 10; 11; 13(3); 14; 15; 17; 3:1; 5; 6; 9; 10(2); 18; 4:4; 5; 6; 12(7); 13; 16; 5:1; 2; 3; 4; 7(3); 9; 11; 12(2); 14; 6:1; 2(3); 3; 4(2); 5(2); 6; 7; 8(2); 9; 10(2); 11; 12; 14; 15; 16; 19(2); 7:1; 2; 5; 6; 7; 8; 9; 11; 15; 18; 20; 21; 23; 26; 27; 8:2(2); 3; 5; 8; 9; 10(3); 11(2); 12(2); 13; 15; 19(5); 21; 22(2); 27; 28; 10:1; 4; 5; 6; 8(3); 11(2); 16; 17; 20; 21; 22; 24(2); 25; 27; 29(2); 30; 33(2); 34(2); 37(2); 11:4; 5; 6; 7; 8; 9; 10; 11; 12(2); 13(4); 15; 17; 20; 21; 22; 23; 28; 32(6); 36(3); 37; 38(3); 39; 12:1(2); 2(2); 3; 5; 6; 8(2); 9; 11; 12(3); 13; 14; 15; 18(3); 19(2); 20; 21(2); 22(2); 23(3); 24(2); 27; 28; 13:1; 2; 3(2); 4; 5; 6(2); 7; 8(2); 9; 11; 12; 13; 14; 15(2); 16(2); 18; 19; 20; 21; 22(2); 24; 25; **Jas** 1:1; 4; 5(2); 6; 11(2); 14; 15; 17(2); 21(2); 22; 23; 24(2); 25; 26; 27(4); 2:2; 3(3); 4; 5; 6; 9; 10; 12; 13; 14; 15; 16(2); 18(2); 19; 22; 23(3); 24; 25; 2:3; 4; 5; 6; 9; 10; 12; 13; 14; 15; 16(2); 8(2); 9; 10; 11(2); 12(3); 13(4); 14; 15; 17; 5:1; 2; 3(3); 4; 5; 6(2); 7; 8; 9; 10; 11; 12(2); 13(4); 16; 17; 18(2); 5:1(2); 4; 5(2); 11(2); **1Pet** 1:1; 2(2); 3; 4(2); 7(2); 8; 10; 11; 13; 17; 18; 19; 21(2); 23; 24(2); 25; 2:1(4); 4; 6; 8(2); 11; 14; 16; 18; 20; 25; 3:3; 4; 6; 7; 10(2); 11(2); 12; 13; 14(2); 15(2); 19; 22(3); 4:3; 4(2); 5; 7; 8; 10; 11; 13; 17(4); 18; 19; 21(2); 22(2); 23(3); 24(3); 4:3(3); 4; 5; 6; 8(2); 9; 11; 13; 14; 15; 16; 17; 18; **1Jn** 1:1; 2(4); 3(3); 4; 5(2); 6(2); 7; 8; 9(2); 10; 2:1; 2(2); 3; 4(2); 8(2); 9; 10; 11(2); 14(2); 16(2); 17(2); 18; 20; 21; 22; 24; 25; 27(4); 28(2); 3:2; 3; 5(2); 9; 10; 12(3); 15; 16; 17(2); 18; 19(2); 20; 22(2); 23(2); 24(3); 4:3(3); 4; 5; 6(2); 7; 9; 10; 12; 13; 14(2); 15; 16(4); 20; 21; 5:1; 2; 3; 4; 6(3); 7(2); 8(4); 11(2); 12; 13; 14; 15; 16; 17; 18; 19(2); 20(4); **2Jn** 1(2); 2; 3(3); 5; 6; 7; 9(2); 10; 12(2); **3Jn** 2; 3; 5; 10(3); 12(3); 13; 14; **Jude** 1(3); 2(2); 3; 4(2); 6; 7(3); 8; 11(2); 14; 15(2); 16; 22; 23; 24; 25(3); **Rev** 1:1(2); 2(2); 3(2); 4(4); 5(4); 6(5); 7(3); 8(4); 9(4); 10; 11(10); 12(2); 13(2); 14(2); 15(2); 16(3); 17(3); 18(4); 19(2); 20(2); 2:2(6); 3(4); 5(3); 8(3); 9(4); 10(2); 11(3); 12(4); 13; 14; 15; 16(3); 17(3); 18(4); 19(2); 20(2); 22(6); 3(4); 27; 28; 3:1(3); 2; 3(4); 4; 5(2); 7(4); 8(3); 9(3); 12(4); 14(2); 16; 17; 18(2); 19(6); 20(2); 21(2); 22; 23; 24; 25(3); 26; 27; 28; 4(2); 5; 6; 7(4); 8(3); 9(3); 11(2); 12(13); 13(14);

14(4); 15; 16(6); 17(4); 18; 19(3); 20(2); 21(3); 22(6); 23(3); 24(3); 19:1(4); 2(2); 3(3); 4(4); 5(3); 6(3); 7(3); 8(2); 9(2); 10(3); 11(6); 12(2); 13(2); 14(2); 15(4); 16(3); 17(3); 18(7); 19(4); 20(3); 21(2); 20:1(2); 2(3); 3(4); 4(8); 6(3); 7; 8(2); 9(5); 10(6); 11(4); 12(5); 13(4); 14(2); 15; 21:1(4); 2; 3(3); 4(2); 5(3); 6(3); 7(2); 8(8); 9(2); 10(3); 11; 12(5); 13; 14(2); 15(3); 16(5); 17(3); 18(2); 19; 21(2); 22(2); 23(2); 24(3); 25; 26(2); 27; 22:1(2); 2(3); 3(3); 4(2); 5(4); 6(3); 8(4); 9(2); 10; 11(3); 12(2); 13(3); 14; 15(6); 16(3); 17(5); 19(3)

ANOTHER

250, 251, 259, 269, 312, 317, 321, 376, 1668, 1836, 2088, 2090, 2114, 3671, 5234, 5997, 7453, 7468, 8145, 8264, 240, 243, 245, 246, 1438, 1520, 2087, 3588, 3739, 4299, 4835

Gen 4:25; 11:3; 15:10; 26:21; 22; 31; 29:19; 30:24; 31:49; 37:9; 19; 42:1; 21; 28; 43:7; 33; **Ex** 10:23; 16:15; 18:16; 21:10; 18; 22:5; 9; 25:20; 26:3(2); 4; 5; 17; 19; 21; 25; 36:10(2); 11; 12; 13; 22; 24; 26; 37:8; 9; 19; **Lev** 7:10; 19:11; 20:10; 25:14; 17; 46; 26:37; 27:20; **Num** 5:19; 20; 29; 8:8; 14:4; 24; 23:13; 27; 36:9; **Deut** 4:34; 20:5; 6; 7; 21:15; 24:2; 25:11; 28:30; 32; 29:28; **Judg** 2:10; 6:29; 9:37; 10:18; 16:7; 11; **Ruth** 2:8; 3:14; **1Sa** 2:25; 10:3(2); 6; 9; 11; 13:18(2); 14:16; 17:30; 18:7; 20:41(2); 21:11; 29:5; **2Sa** 15:25; 18:20; 26(2); **1Kin** 6:27; 7:8; 11:23; 13:10; 14:5; 6; 18:6; 20:37; 21:6; 22:20; **2Kin** 1:1; 3:23; 7:3; 6; 8; 9; 10:21; 14:8; 11; 21:16; **1Chr** 2:26; 16:20; 17:5; 24:5; 26:12; **2Chr** 18:19; 20:23; 25:17; 21; 32:5; **Ezr** 4:21; 9:11; **Neh** 3:19; 21; 24; 27; 30; 4:19; 9:3; **Est** 1:7; 19; 4:14; 9:19; 22; **Job** 1:16; 17; 18; 13:9; 19:27; 21:25; 31:8; 10; 41:16; 17; **Ps** 16:4; 75:7; 105:13(2); 109:8; 145:4; **Prov** 25:9; 27:2; **Eccl** 1:4; 4:10; 8:9; **Song** 5:9(2); **Is** 3:5; 6:3; 13:8; 28:11; 42:8; 44:5(2); 48:11; 57:8; 65:15; 22(2); 66:23(2); **Jer** 3:1; 13:14; 18:4; 14; 22:26; 25:26; 36:28; 32; 46:16; 51:31(2); 46; **Eze** 1:9; 11; 3:13; 4:8; 17; 10:9(2); 12:3; 15:7; 17:7; 19:5; 22(2); 24:23; 33:30; 37:16; 17; 40:13; 26; 49; 41:6; 11; 47:14; **Dan** 2:39(2); 43; 5:6; 17; 7:3; 5; 6; 8; 24; 8:13; **Hos** 3:3; 4:4; **Joel** 1:3; 2:8; **Amos** 4:7; **Nah** 2:4; **Zec** 2:3; 8:21; 11:9; **Mal** 3:16; **Mt** 2:12; 8:9; 21; 10:23; 11:3; 13:24; 31; 33; 19:9; 21:33; 35(2); 22:5; 24:2; 10(2); 25:15(2); 32; 26:71; 27:38; **Mk** 4:41; 9:10; 50; 10:11; 12; 12:4; 5; 13:2; 14:19; 58; 16:12; **Lk** 2:15; 6:6; 11; 7:8; 19; 20; 32; 8:25; 9:56; 59; 61; 12:1; 14:19; 20; 31; 16:7; 12; 18; 19:20; 44; 20:11; 21:6; 22:58; 59; 24:17; 32; **Jn** 4:33; 37; 5:7; 32; 43; 44; 13:22; 34(2); 35; 14:16; 15:12; 17; 18:15; 19:37; 21:18; **Acts** 1:20; 2:7; 12; 7:18; 26; 10:28; 12:17; 13:35; 17:7; 19:32; 38; 21:6; 34; **Rom** 1:27; 2:1; 15; 21; 7:3(2); 4; 23; 9:21; 12:5; 10(2); 16; 13:8(2); 14:2; 4; 5(2); 13; 19; 15:5; 7; 14; 20; 16:16; **1Cor** 3:4; 10; 4:6; 7; 6:1; 7; 7:7; 10:29; 11:21; 33; 12:8; 9(2); 10(5); 25; 14:30; 15:39(3); 40; 41(3); 16:20; **2Cor** 10:16; 11:4(3); 13:12; **Gal** 1:6; 7; 5:13; 15(2); 26(2); 6:4; **Eph** 4:2; 25; 32(2); 5:21; **Col** 3:9; 13(2); 16; **1Th** 3:12; 4:9; 18; 5:11; **1Ti** 5:21; **Titus** 3:3; **Heb** 3:13; 4:8; 5:6; 7:11; 13; 15; 10:24; 25; **Jas** 2:25; 4:11; 12; 5:9; 16(2); **1Pet** 1:22; 3:8; 4:10; 5:5; 14; **1Jn** 1:7; 3:11; 23; 4:7; 11; 12; **2Jn** 5; **Rev** 6:4(2); 7:2; 8:3; 10:1; 11:10; 12:3; 13:11; 14:6; 8; 15; 17; 18; 15:1; 16:7; 18:1; 4; 20:12

ANOTHER'S

7453, 240, 2087

Gen 11:7; **Ex** 21:35; **Jn** 13:14; **1Cor** 10:24; **Gal** 6:2

ANSWER

559, 1696, 1697, 3045, 4405, 4617, 5421, 6030, 6600, 7725, 8421, 470, 611, 612, 625, 626, 1906, 2036, 5538

Gen 30:33; 41:16; 45:3; **Deut** 20:11; 21:7; 25:9; 27:15; **Josh** 4:7; **Judg** 5:29; **1Sa** 2:16; 20:10; **2Sa** 3:11; 24:13; **1Kin** 9:9; 12:6; 7; 9; 18:29; **2Kin** 4:29; 18:36; **2Chr** 10:6; 9; 10; **Ezr** 4:17; 5:5; 11; **Neh** 5:8; **Est** 4:13; 15; **Job** 5:1; 9:3; 14; 15; 32; 13:22(2); 14:15; 19:16; 20:2; 3; 23:5; 31:14; 35; 32:1; 3; 5; 14; 17; 20; 33:5; 12; 32; 35:4; 12; 38:3; 40:2; 4; 5; **Ps** 27:7; 65:5; 86:7; 91:15; 102:2; 108:6; 119:42; 143:1; **Prov** 1:28; 15:1; 23; 28; 16:1; 22:21; 24:26; 26:4; 5; 27:11; 29:19; **Song** 5:6; **Is** 14:32; 30:19; 36:21; 41:28; 46:7; 50:2; 58:9; 65:12; 24; 66:4; **Jer** 5:19; 7:27; 23:9; 33:3; 42:4; 44:20; **Eze** 14:4; 7; 21:7; **Dan** 3:16; **Joel** 2:19; **Mic** 3:7; **Hab** 2:1; 11; **Zec** 13:6; **Mt** 22:46; 25:37; 40; 44; 45; **Mk** 11:29; 30; 14:40; **Lk** 11:7; 12:11; 13:25; 14:6; 20:3; 26; 21:14; 22:68; **Jn** 1:22; 19:9; **Acts** 24:10; 25:16; 26:2; **Rom** 11:4; **1Cor** 9:3; **2Cor** 5:12; **Col** 4:6; **2Ti** 4:16; **1Pet** 3:15; 21

ANSWERED

559, 1697, 6030, 7725, 8421, *611, 626*

Gen 18:27; 23:5; 10; 14; 24:50; 27:37; 39; 31:14; 31; 36; 43; 34:13; 35:3; 40:18; 41:16; 42:22; 43:28; **Ex** 4:1; 15:21; 19:8; 19; 24:3; **Num** 11:28; 22:18; 23:12; 26; 32:31; **Deut** 1:14; 41; **Josh** 1:16; 2:14; 7:20; 9:24; 15:19; 17:15; 22:21; 24:16; **Judg** 5:29; 7:14; 8:8(2); 18; 25; 11:13; 15:6; 10; 18:14; 19:28; 20:4; **Ruth** 2:4; 6; 11; 3:9; **1Sa** 1:15; 17; 3:4; 6; 10; 16; 4:17; 20; 5:8; 6:4; 9:8; 12; 19; 21; 10:12; 22; 11:2; 12:5; 14:12; 28; 37; 39; 44; 16:18; 17:27; 30; 58; 18:7; 19:17; 20:28; 32; 21:4; 5; 22:9; 12; 14; 23:4; 25:10; 26:6; 14; 22; 28:6; 15; 29:9; 30:8; 22; **2Sa** 1:4; 7; 8; 13; 2:20; 4:9; 9:6; 13:12; 32; 14:5; 18; 19; 32; 15:21; 18:3; 29; 32; 19:21; 26; 38; 42; 43; 20:17(2); 20; 21:1; 5; 22:42; **1Kin** 1:28; 36; 43; 2:22; 30; 3:27; 11:22; 12:13; 16; 13:6; 18:8; 18; 21; 24; 26; 20:4; 11; 14; 21:6; 20; 22:15; **2Kin** 1:8; 10; 11; 12; 2:5; 3:8; 11; 4:13; 14; 26; 6:2; 3; 16; 22; 28; 7:2; 13; 19; 8:12; 13; 14; 9:19; 22; 10:13; 15; 18:36; 20:10; 15; **1Chr** 12:17; 21:3; 26; 28; **2Chr** 2:11; 7:22; 10:13; 14; 16; 18:3; 25:9; 29:31; 31:10; 34:15; 23; **Ezr** 10:2; 12; **Neh** 2:20; 6:4; 8:6; **Est** 1:16; 5:4; 7; 6:7; 7:3; 5; **Job** 1:7; 9; 2:2; 4; 4:1; 6:1; 8:1; 9:1; 16; 11:1; 2; 12:1; 15:1; 16:1; 18:1; 19:1; 20:1; 21:1; 22:1; 23:1; 25:1; 26:1; 32:6; 12; 15; 16; 34:1; 38:1; 40:1; 3; 6; 42:1; **Ps** 18:41; 81:7; 99:6; 118:5; **Is** 6:11; 21:9; 36:21; 39:4; **Jer** 7:13; 11:5; 23:35; 37; 35:17; 36:18; 44:15; **Eze** 24:20; 37:3; **Dan** 2:5; 7; 8; 10; 14; 15; 20; 26; 27; 47; 3:16; 24; 25; 4:19; 5:17; 6:12; 13; **Amos** 7:14; **Mic** 6:5; **Hab** 2:2; **Hag** 2:12; 13; 14; **Zec** 1:10; 11; 12; 13; 19; 3:4; 4:4; 5; 6; 11; 12; 13; 5:2; 6:4; 5; **Mt** 4:4; 8:8; 11:4; 25; 12:38; 39; 48; 13:11; 37; 14:28; 15:3; 13; 15; 23; 24; 26; 28; 16:2; 16; 17; 17:4; 11; 17; 19:4; 27; 20:13; 22; 21:21; 24; 27; 29; 30; 22:1; 29; 24:4; 25:9; 12; 26; 26:23; 25; 33; 63; 66; 27:12; 14; 21; 25; 28:5; **Mk** 3:33; 5:9; 6:37; 7:6; 28; 8:4; 28; 9:5; 12; 17; 38; 10:3; 5; 20; 29; 51; 11:14; 29; 33; 12:28; 29; 34; 35; 14:20; 48; 61; 15:3; 5; 9; 12; **Lk** 1:35; 60; 3:16; 4:4; 8; 7:43; 8:21; 50; 9:49; 10:28; 41; 11:45; 13:14; 15; 14:5; 17:20; 37; 19:40; 20:3; 7; 24; 22:51; 23:3; 9; **Jn** 1:21; 26; 48; 49; 50; 2:18; 19; 3:3; 5; 9; 10; 27; 4:10; 13; 17; 5:7; 11; 17; 19; 6:7; 26; 29; 43; 68; 70; 7:16; 20; 21; 46; 47; 52; 8:14; 19; 33; 34; 39; 48; 49; 54; 9:3; 11; 20; 25; 27; 30; 34; 36; 10:25; 32; 33; 34; 11:9; 12:23; 30; 34; 13:7; 8; 26; 36; 38; 14:23; 16:31; 18:5; 8; 20; 23; 30; 34; 35; 36; 37; 19:7; 11; 15; 22; 20:28; 21:5; **Acts** 3:12; 4:19; 5:8; 29; 8:24; 34; 37; 9:13; 10:46; 11:9; 15:13; 19:15; 21:13; 22:8; 28; 24:10; 25; 25:4; 8; 9; 12; 16; 26:1; **Rev** 7:13

ANSWERING

488, 611, 5274

Mt 3:15; **Mk** 11:22; 33; 12:17; 24; 13:2; 5; 15:2; **Lk** 1:19; 4:12; 5:5; 22; 31; 6:3; 7:22; 40; 9:19; 20; 41; 10:27; 30; 13:2; 8; 14:3; 15:29; 17:17; 20:34; 39; 23:40; 24:18; **Titus** 2:9

ANSWERS

8666, *612*

Job 21:34; 34:36; **Lk** 2:47

ANY

259, 376, 1697, 1991, 3254, 3605, 3606, 3972, 4310, 5315, 5750, 5769, *1520, 1530, 1536, 1538, 2089, 3361, 3362, 3364, 3367, 3370, 3379, 3381, 3387, 3588, 3762, 3763, 3765, 3956, 4218, 4455, 4458, 5100, 5150*

Gen 3:1; 4:15; 8:12; 21(2); 9:11(2); 14:23; 17:5; 12; 18:14; 19:12; 22; 22:12; 24:16; 30:31; 31:14; 35:10; 36:31; 39:9; 23; 42:16; 43:34; 47:6; **Ex** 1:10; 8:29; 9:29; 10:15; 23; 11:6; 7; 12:39; 16:24; 20:4(3); 10; 17; 21:23; 22:9; 10; 20; 22; 23; 25; 31; 24:14(2); 30:32; 33(2); 31:14; 15; 32:24; 34:3; 10; 24; 35:24; 33; 35; 36:6; **Lev** 1:2; 2:1; 11(2); 4:2(2); 13; 22; 27(2); 5:2; 11; 17; 6:3; 7; 27; 30; 7:8; 15; 18; 19; 21(3); 24; 26; 27; 11:10; 32(3); 33; 35; 37(2); 38(2); 39; 43; 44; 13:24; 48; 49; 51; 52; 53; 57; 59; 15:2; 6; 10(2); 16; 22; 23; 24; 17:10; 12; 13; 18:6; 21; 23(2); 24; 26(3); 29; 30; 19:17; 18; 26; 28(2); 20:2; 4; 16; 25; 21:5; 9; 11; 17; 18; 22:4; 5; 6; 11; 23; 24; 25; 23:22; 30; 24:17; 25:25; 32; 49; 26:1; 27:9; 11; 19; 20; **Num** 4:15; 5:6; 10; 12; 6:3; 9; 9:10; 12; 14:23; 15:27; 17:13; 18:5; 20; 19:11; 13; 20:5; 19; 21:5; 9; 22:38(2); 23:23; 29:7; 30:5; 15; 31:19(2); 35:11; 15; 22; 23; 26; 30(2); 36:3; 8; **Deut** 2:19; 37; 4:16; 17(2); 18(2); 23; 25; 32; 5:8(3); 14(2); 21; 25; 7:7; 8:9; 12:17; 13:11; 14:1; 3; 21; 15:7; 21(2); 16:4; 5; 21; 22; 17:1(2); 2; 3; 15; 18:6; 10; 16; 19:11; 15(3); 16; 20; 21:23; 22:1; 6; 7; 8; 13; 23:10; 18; 19; 24; 24:5; 7; 10; 13; 26:14; 27:5; 15; 21; 28:14; 55; 29:23; 30:4; 31:13; 32:28; 39; **Josh** 1:5; 2:11(2); 19; 5:1; 12; 6:10(2); 18; 7:12; 8:31; 10:21; 11:11; 14; 13:33; 20:3; 9; 21:45; 23:12; 13; **Judg** 2:14; 21; 4:20(2); 11:25; 13:4; 7; 14(2); 16:17; 18:7(2); 10; 28; 19:19; 20:8(2); 21:1; 12; **Ruth** 1:11; 2:22; **1Sa** 2:2; 13; 16; 3:17; 5:5; 6:3; 9:2; 10:23; 12:3; 4; 13:22; 14:24(2); 28; 52(2); 18:25; 20:12; 26; 39; 21:2; 22:15; 25:15; 22; 34; 27:1(2); 30:2; 12; 19; **2Sa** 2:1; 28; 7:6; 7; 10; 22; 9:1; 3; 10:19; 13:2; 14:10; 11; 14; 32; 15:2; 4; 5; 11; 19:22; 28; 29; 35; 42; 21:4; 5; **1Kin** 1:6; 2:36; 42; 3:12; 13; 5:6; 6:7; 8:31; 38; 10:3; 20; 11:22; 15:5; 17; 29; 18:26; 29(2); 20:33; 39; **2Kin** 2:21; 4:2; 29(2); 6:33; 10:5; 14; 24; 12:4; 5; 13; 14:26(3); 18:5; 33; 21:8; 23:25; 24:7; **1Chr** 1:43; 17:6; 9; 20; 19:19; 23:26; 26:28; 27:1; 28:21; 29:25; **2Chr** 1:12; 2:14; 6:5; 29; 8:15; 9:9; 19; 20; 23:19; 32:13; 15; 33:8; 34:13; **Ezr** 1:4; 7:24; **Neh** 2:12(2); 5:16; 10:31; **Job** 4:20; 5:1; 4; 6:6; 7:10; 8:12; 9:33; 10:22; 15:11; 16:17; 18:19; 20:9; 21:22; 22:3; 25:3; 31:7; 19(2); 32:21; 33:13; 27; 32; 34:27; 31; 36:5; 29; 37:24; **Ps** 4:6; 14:2; 33:17; 34:10; 37:8; 38:3; 49:7; 53:2; 59:5; 74:9(2); 81:9; 86:8; 91:10; 109:12; 115:17; 119:133; 135:17; 139:24; 141:4; 146:2; 147:20; **Prov** 1:17; 6:35; 14:34; 28:17; 30:2; 30; 31:5; **Eccl** 1:10; 11; 2:10; 3:14; 5:2; 6:5; 9:5(2); 6(2); **Is** 1:5; 2:4; 7(2); 19:15; 26:18; 27:3; 30:20; 33:20; 35:9; 36:18; 44:8; 51:18; 52:14; 53:9; 54:4; 56:2; 59:4; 62:4; **Jer** 3:16; 17; 5:1; 9:4; 10:20; 14:22; 17:22; 18:18; 20:9; 22:11; 30; 23:24; 31:12; 40; 32:27; 33:26; 34:10; 35:7; 36:24; 37:17; 38:5; 42:21; 44:26; 48:9; 49:33; 50:40; 51:43; 44; **Lam** 1:12; 3:49; **Eze** 5:9; 11; 7:11; 13; 9:6; 12:24; 28; 14:11; 15:2; 3(2); 4; 5; 16:5; 41; 63; 18:3; 7; 8; 10; 11; 16; 23; 21:5; 23:27; 24:13; 27:36; 28:19; 24; 29:15; 31:8; 32:13; 33:6; 34:10; 29; 36:14; 15(3); 37:22; 23(2); 39:7; 10; 15; 28; 29; 44:9; 13; 18; 21; 31; 46:16; **Dan** 2:10; 30(2); 3:28; 29; 6:4; 5; 7; 12; 8:4; 11:15; 37; **Hos** 13:10; 14:3; 8; **Joel** 2:2; 3:17; **Amos** 6:10; 7:8; 13; 8:2; 7; **Obad** 18; **Jonah** 3:7; **Mic** 4:3; **Zeph** 3:15; **Hag** 2:12; 13; **Zec** 8:10(2); 9:8; 13:3; **Mal** 2:13; **Mt** 4:6; 5:25; 40; 10:5; 11:27; 12:19; 13:15; 19; 16:24; 18:19; 21:3; 22:16; 46(2); 24:17; 23; **Mk** 1:44; 4:12; 22; 23; 5:4; 35; 7:16; 8:26; 9:8; 22; 30; 35; 11:3; 13; 16(2); 25; 12:21; 34; 13:5; 15; 21; 14:31; 63; 15:44; 16:8(2); 18; **Lk** 3:14; 4:11; 40; 8:17; 27; 43; 9:23; 36; 10:19; 11:11; 14:8; 26; 15:29; 19:8(2); 31; 20:21; 27; 28; 36; 40; 21:34; 22:16; 35; 71; 24:41; **Jn** 1:3; 18; 46; 2:25; 4:33; 5:37; 6:46; 51; 7:4; 17; 37; 48; 51; 8:33; 9:22; 31; 32; 10:9; 28; 11:9; 57; 12:26(2); 47; 14:14; 16:30; 18:31; 21:5; **Acts** 4:12; 32; 34; 9:2; 10:14; 28; 47; 11:8; 13:15; 17:25; 19:2; 38; 39; 24:12; 20; 25:5; 8; 11; 16; 17; 24; 27:12; 22; 34; 42; 28:21(2); **Rom** 1:10; 6:2; 8:9; 33; 39; 9:11; 11:14; 13:8; 9; 14:13; 14; 21; 15:18; **1Cor** 1:15; 16; 2:2; 3:7; 12; 14; 15; 17; 18; 5:11; 6:1; 12; 7:12; 18(2); 36; 8:2(2); 3; 9; 10; 9:7; 15; 27; 10:19(2); 27; 28; 11:16; 34; 14:27; 30; 35; 37; 38; 16:22; **2Cor** 1:4; 2:5; 10(2); 3:5; 5:17; 6:3; 7:14; 8:23; 10:7; 11:3; 21; 12:6; 17; **Gal** 1:8; 9(2); 2:2; 5:6; 6:15; **Eph** 2:9; 5:5; 27; 6:8; **Phil** 2:1(4); 3:4; 11; 15; 4:8(2); **Col** 2:4; 8; 23; 3:13(2); **1Th** 1:8; 2:5; 9; 4:6; 5:15; **2Th** 2:3; 3:8(2); 10; 14; **1Ti** 1:10; 5:4; 8; 16; 6:3; **Titus** 1:6; **Heb** 1:5; 13; 2:1; 3:12; 13; 4:1; 11; 12; 13; 10:38; 12:15(2); 16; 19; **Jas** 1:5; 7; 13; 23; 26; 3:2; 5:12; 13(2); 14; 19; **1Pet** 3:1; 6; 4:11(2); 16; **2Pet** 1:20; 3:9; **1Jn** 2:1; 15; 27; 4:12; 5:14; 16; **2Jn** 10; **Rev** 3:20; 7:1; 16(2); 9:4(2); 11:5(2); 12:8; 13:9; 14:9; 18:11; 22; 21:4; 27; 22:18; 19

APART

905, 5079, 5674, 6395, *659, 2398, 2596*

Ex 13:12; **Lev** 15:19; 18:19; **Ps** 4:3; **Eze** 22:10; **Zec** 12:12(5); 13(4); 14(2); **Mt** 14:13; 23; 17:1; 19; 20:17; **Mk** 6:31; 9:2; **Jas** 1:21

ARE

1526

Gen 2:4; 6:9; 7:2; 8; 9:2; 19; 10:1; 20; 31; 32; 11:10; 27; 18:5; 24; 19:5; 15; 20:7; 16; 25:7; 12; 13; 16(2); 17; 19; 23; 27:22; 41; 46; 29:4; 21; 31:12; 15; 43(3); 49; 32:17; 33:5; 8; 13(2); 15; 34:21; 22; 35:2; 26; 36:1; 5; 9; 10; 13; 16; 17(3); 18; 19(2); 20; 21; 24; 26; 27; 28; 29; 30; 31; 40; 37:2; 17; 38:25(2); 40:12; 18; 41:26(2); 27; 42:9(2); 10; 11(3); 12; 13; 14; 16; 21; 31(2); 33; 34(2); 36; 43:18; 44:16; 45:6; 11; 16; 46:8; 18; 22; 25; 31; 32; 47:1(2); 3; 4; 5; 9; 48:5; 8; 9; 49:5(2); 28; 50:3(2); **Ex** 1:1; 9; 19(3); 2:18; 3:7; 4:18; 19; 5:5; 16; 17(2); 6:15; 16; 19; 24; 25; 26; 27(2); 7:17; 8:21; 9:27; 10:8; 11; 12:13; 14:3; 15:4; 16:7; 8(2); 16; 19:6; 21:1; 24:14; 25:22; 26; 28:3; 4; 24; 29:33; 30:13; 14; 31:6; 32:2; 22; 33:5; 16; 35:1; 39:6; 40:4; **Lev** 4:12(2); 13; 5:17; 10:14; 11:2(2); 8; 9; 13(2); 26; 27; 28; 31; 32; 35; 42; 12:6; 14:37; 16:4; 18:17; 24; 23:2; 4; 17; 37; 42; 25:7; 23; 33; 42; 44; 45; 55(2); 26:25; 36; 39; 46; 27:34; **Num** 1:3; 5; 17; 44; 2:32; 3:1; 2; 3; 9; 13; 18; 20; 21; 27; 33; 46(2); 4:15; 20; 41; 6:13; 8:16; 17; 9:7(2); 10:4; 29; 31; 11:21; 13:16; 28; 30; 31; 32; 14:9; 35; 43(2); 15:13; 15; 16:3; 5; 11; 37; 38; 18:6; 16; 17; 18; 20:16; 22:4; 6; 9; 12; 24:3; 5; 6; 15; 26:2; 7; 14; 18; 22; 25; 27; 30; 34; 35; 36; 37(2); 41; 42(2); 47; 50; 57; 58; 63; 27:1; 30:14; 16; 31:12; 49; 32:14; 33:1; 2; 51; 34:17; 19; 29; 35:33; 36:3; 4; 13; **Deut** 1:2; 10; 11; 20; 28; 2:4; 25; 3:18; 4:4; 20; 30; 32; 45; 5:3; 6:1; 14; 7:6; 17; 20; 8:9; 9:12; 29; 11:12; 30; 12:1; 9; 13:7; 13; 14:1; 2; 4; 7; 9; 12; 29; 16:11; 14; 17:14; 18:12; 20:2; 15(2); 21:2; 6; 22:5; 17; 23:8; 18; 24:14; 25:16; 27:12; 28:58; 29:1; 5; 20; 21; 27; 29; 30:1; 10; 31:17; 18; 21; 32:4; 5; 20; 21; 28; 32(2); 37; 33:3; 17(3); 27; **Josh** 2:3(2); 3:8; 4:9; 6:17(2); 19; 7:3; 21; 8:5; 9:8(2); 9; 11; 13; 22; 23; 25; 10:6; 17; 12:1; 7; 13:14; 17; 30; 32; 14:1; 15:32; 16:3; 17:3; 9; 16(2); 18:3; 19:14; 29; 35; 51; 21:9; 22:10; 17; 23:14; 15; 24:22(2); 23; **Judg** 3:1; 5:11; 6:2; 7:2(2); 4; 18; 8:6; 15(2); 9:2; 18; 10:4(2); 11:7(2); 12:3; 4; 15:10(2); 11; 12; 18:9; 24; 19:18; 20:7; 13; 32; 39; 21:16; **Ruth** 1:11; 4:9; 10; 11; 18; **1Sa** 2:3; 4(2); 8; 4:8; 17; 6:17; 9:20; 10:2; 7; 12:2; 21; 16:11; 16; 17:8; 19:22; 20:21; 22; 21:5; 26:16; 29:10; **2Sa** 1:4(3); 19; 25; 27; 3:28; 5:1; 8; 7:9; 11:11; 13:33; 14:14; 20; 15:3; 13; 15; 16:4; 21; 17:2; 10; 12; 16; 19:11; 12(3); 20:19; 22:28; 39; 24:14; **1Kin** 1:20; 45; 4:8; 13; 8:8; 9:13; 10:8(2); 27; 11:41; 13:3; 32; 14:19; 29; 15:7; 23; 31; 16:5; 14; 20; 27; 18:22; 25; 20:3; 17; 23; 31; 22:39; 45; **2Kin** 1:5; 18; 3:23; 5:12; 6:9; 16; 7:12; 13(5); 8:23; 9:22; 10:2(2); 5; 13(2); 34; 12:19; 13:8; 12; 14:15; 18; 28; 15:6; 11; 15; 21; 26; 31; 36; 16:19; 18:20; 26; 34(2); 35; 19:3; 4; 20:14; 15; 20; 21:17; 25(2); 23:28; 24:5; **1Chr** 1:29; 31; 33; 43; 54; 2:1; 18; 55; 4:2; 4; 12; 18; 22; 5:14; 6:19; 31; 33; 50; 54; 65; 7:8; 33; 8:6(2); 38; 40; 9:33; 44; 11:1; 10; 12:1; 15; 18; 23; 13:2(2); 14:4; 15:12; 16:14; 26; 27(2); 17:8; 19:3; 21:3; 13; 22:15; 24:1; 26:19; 29:15(2); 17; 29; **2Chr** 1:15; 2:7; 3:3; 6:37; 7:14; 8:11; 9:7(2); 27; 29; 11:10; 12:15; 13:7; 8; 9; 10; 22; 16:11; 17:14; 19:3; 20:12; 34; 23:6; 24:26; 27; 25:26; 26:18; 27:7; 28:10; 26; 29:9; 19; 30:6; 32:32; 33:18; 19; 34:21; 24; 31; 35:25; 27; 36:8; **Ezr** 2:1; 4:10; 12; 5:4; 11; 6:6; 9; 7:13; 19; 21; 25; 8:1; 13; 28(3); 9:6; 15; 10:3; 13(3); **Neh** 1:3(3); 10; 2:3; 17(2); 4:2; 4; 10; 19; 5:2; 5; 17; 6:8; 7:6; 9:6; 36(2); 37; 10:39; 11:3; 7; 12:1; **Est** 1:16; 3:8; 4:16; 7:4; 8:5; 9; 9:13; 10:2; **Job** 1:19; 3:8; 19; 22; 24; 4:9; 10; 11; 19; 20; 5:4(2); 6:3; 4; 7; 16; 17; 18; 21(2); 25; 26; 7:1; 3; 6(2); 8; 16; 8:9(2); 13; 17; 9:25; 26; 10:5(2); 17; 20; 11:6; 12:2; 6; 16; 13:4(2); 12; 23; 14:5(2); 21; 15:10; 11; 15; 28; 16:2; 22; 17:1(2); 2; 7; 11(2); 18:3; 21; 19:3; 13; 19; 22; 20:11; 25; 21:7; 9; 18; 22; 24(2); 28; 33; 22:10; 12; 14; 19; 29; 23:14; 24:1; 8; 13; 17; 23; 24(3); 25:2; 5; 26:5; 11; 14; 27:12; 28:4(2); 6; 30:1; 15; 17; 30; 31:40; 32:6; 9; 34:18; 19; 21; 25; 35:5; 36:7(2); 20; 37:17; 24; 38:6; 30; 35; 39:4; 30; 40:17; 18(2); 41:14; 15; 17; 18; 23(2); 25; 28; 29; 30; **Ps** 1:4(2); 2:12; 3:1(2); 6:2; 9:3; 6; 15; 10:5(2); 8; 16; 12:4; 6; 8; 14:1; 3(2); 16:3; 6; 11; 17:2; 10; 14(2); 18:38; 19:8; 9; 10; 20:8(2); 21:11; 22:14; 25:10; 15; 17; 19; 27:12; 31:10; 15; 32:11; 33:4; 34:15(2); 18; 19; 35:19; 20; 36:3; 6; 12(2); 37:23; 28; 34; 38:4(2); 5; 7; 14; 19(3); 20; 39:6; 40:5(3); 12; 42:7; 44:13; 22(2); 45:5; 47:9; 49:14; 50:11; 51:17; 53:1; 3; 54:3; 55:4; 5; 10; 56:5; 8; 12; 57:4(2); 6; 58:3; 4; 59:3; 7; 62:9(3); 65:5; 8; 13(2); 68:6; 17; 69:1; 4(2); 5; 9; 19; 71:13; 24(2); 72:20; 73:1; 4; 5(2); 8; 10; 12; 19(2); 27; 74:20; 75:3; 76:5; 6; 77:19; 79:1; 4(2); 8; 11; 82:5; 6(2); 83:5; 84:1; 4; 5; 85:10; 86:8; 14; 87:3; 7; 88:5; 89:7; 11; 14; 49; 90:4; 5(2); 7(2); 9; 10; 92:5(2); 93:5; 94:11; 95:4; 7; 96:5; 6(2); 97:2(2); 100:3; 102:3(2); 8(2); 11; 20; 22; 24; 25; 103:6; 14; 15; 104:16; 17; 18; 24; 25; 28; 29; 30; 105:7; 106:3; 107:17; 27; 29; 30; 38; 39; 109:2; 4; 24; 111:2; 7(2); 8; 113:6; 115:4; 8; 15; 16; 116:11; 118:12; 119:1; 2; 21; 24; 39; 75; 84; 85; 86; 91; 98; 99; 103; 111; 129; 137; 138; 143; 150; 151; 156; 157; 168; 172; 120:7; 122:5; 123:3; 4; 124:7; 125:2; 4; 126:3; 127:3; 4(2); 135:15; 18; 139:12; 14; 17; 18; 140:2; 141:6(2); 7; 8; 142:6; 144:4; 145:9; 146:8; **Prov** 1:19; 2:15; 3:15; 17(2); 20; 4:22; 23; 5:6; 11; 21; 6:16; 23; 8:8; 9; 11; 18; 32; 9:17; 18(2); 10:6; 11:20(4); 12:5(2); 6; 7(2); 10; 22(2); 13:8; 14:4; 12; 18; 15:3; 11; 15; 22(2); 26(2); 16:2; 11(2); 13; 24; 25; 17:6(2); 15; 24; 18:4; 7; 8; 19; 21; 19:7; 13; 14; 21; 29; 20:7; 10; 15; 23; 24; 22:3; 4; 5; 26; 23:3; 24:11(2); 21; 25:1; 26:7; 21; 22; 23; 25; 28; 27:6(2); 12; 15; 20(2); 24; 25; 26(2); 28:1; 2; 29:2; 12; 16; 30:12; 13(2); 14; 15(2); 18; 24(2); 25; 26; 29; 31:8; 21; 25; **Eccl** 1:8; 11; 13; 14; 2:14; 23; 3:18; 20; 4:1; 2(2); 9; 5:7; 11; 7:19; 21; 8:8; 13; 9:1; 3; 12(3); 16; 17; 10:12; 11:10; 12:3; 11(2); **Song** 1:10; 17; 3:7; 4:2(2); 3(2); 5(2); 11; 13; 5:11; 12; 13; 14; 15; 6:6; 7; 8; 7:1(2); 3(2); 9; 13; 8:6; **Is** 1:4(2); 7; 14; 15; 23; 2:6; 13; 14; 3:8; 12; 16; 4:2; 5:12; 13(2); 21; 22; 28; 7:2; 8:18; 9:10(2); 16(2); 10:8; 14; 20; 29; 14:19; 16:4; 7; 8(3); 17:2; 19:11; 12(2); 13(3); 21:3; 22:2; 3(4); 9; 23:8(2); 24:6(2); 17; 18; 21; 22; 25:1; 26:9; 14(2); 27:7; 9; 11; 28:1(2); 7(3); 8; 9; 15; 27(2); 29:9; 15; 20; 30:18; 27; 31:1(2); 3; 32:7; 9; 11; 20; 33:13(2); 14; 23; 35:4; 36:5; 11; 19(2); 20; 37:3; 39:3; 40:11; 15(2); 17(2); 22; 41:23(2); 24; 29(3); 42:9; 17; 22(3); 43:10; 12; 17(2); 44:7; 8; 9(2); 11; 45:16; 19; 20; 24; 46:1; 2; 3(2); 10; 12; 48:1(2); 7; 49:9; 16; 51:1(2); 19; 20; 52:7; 53:5; 54:1; 55:8(2); 9(2); 56:8; 10(3); 11(2); 57:1; 4; 6; 20; 58:7; 59:3; 6; 7(2); 10; 12(2); 60:8; 61:1; 9; 11; 63:8; 15; 19; 64:6(2); 8(2); 9; 10; 11; 65:5; 11; 16(2); 22; 23; 24; **Jer** 2:5(2); 11; 15; 28(2); 31; 4:13(2); 17; 20; 22(2); 5:3; 4(2); 6(2); 7; 10; 16; 23; 26; 27(2); 28; 6:4; 20; 23; 28(3); 29(2); 7:4; 10; 8:8; 9(2); 16; 20; 9:3; 10(3); 19(2); 25; 26(3); 10:2; 3; 5; 8; 9; 15; 20(3); 21; 11:10; 16; 12:1; 4; 9; 12; 13:22; 23; 14:2; 7;

9; 18; 22; 15:2(4); 8; 16:3; 17(2); 20; 18:6; 21:4; 7; 22:6; 17; 20; 28(2); 23:10; 11; 14; 26; 24:2; 3; 5; 8; 25:12; 22; 23; 26; 31; 34; 37; 27:5; 18; 29:1; 4; 16; 17; 22; 25; 30:4; 6; 31:20; 29; 32:19; 24; 35; 33:4; 10; 34:21; 35:14; 37:19; 38:19; 22(3); 40:15; 41:12; 42:2; 11; 43:11(3); 44:2; 6; 10; 14; 24; 27; 28; 46:5(2); 7; 8; 12; 15; 21(3); 23(2); 48:14; 15; 17; 32; 36; 41; 46; 49:23; 32; 50:2(2); 11; 15(2); 37; 38; 42; 51:4; 7; 18; 30; 32(2); 43; 51(2); 56; 60; 64; **Lam** 1:2(2); 4(2); 5(2); 6(2); 14; 16; 18; 20; 21; 22; 2:9(2); 11; 21; 3:22; 23; 4:1; 2; 5; 8; 9; 18; 19; 5:3(2); 5; 7; 12; 17; **Eze** 2:4; 5; 7; 3:7; 26; 27; 5:2; 5; 6; 7(2); 14; 15; 7:9; 11:2; 7; 12; 15; 12:2; 10; 14; 20; 22; 23; 27; 13:4; 14:5; 16:7; 27; 38; 52; 57; 18:2; 4; 25; 29(2); 20:3; 30; 34; 21:14; 24(2); 29; 22:9; 18(2); 19; 27; 23:45; 24:19; 25:9; 26:6; 18; 19; 27:4; 27; 28:8; 24; 25; 29:12(2); 30:7(2); 31:12(3); 14; 32:20; 21; 22; 23; 24; 25; 26; 27(2); 28; 29; 30(2); 32; 33:24; 27; 30; 34:3; 12; 30; 31; 35:8; 12(2); 36:2; 3(2); 4(2); 7; 8; 20(2); 35(2); 36; 37:11(3); 38:7; 11; 12(2); 20; 22; 40:46; 42:13; 14(2); 43:13; 18; 27; 44:10; 45:14; 46:24; 48:1(2); 11; 15; 29; 30; **Dan** 1:10; 2:20; 28; 3:12; 16; 4:3(2); 18; 35; 37; 5:23; 7:17(2); 24; 8:20; 23; 9:7(2); 16(2); 19; 24; 26; 10:16; 12:9; **Hos** 1:9; 10(2); 2:12; 4:4; 6; 14; 5:2; 6:5; 7:2; 4; 7(2); 9; 16; 8:9; 9:6; 7(2); 15; 11:7; 8; 12:7; 11(2); 14:3; 9; **Joel** 1:6; 7; 12; 17(2); 18(2); 20; **Amos** 4:1; 5:16; 6:1(2); 6; 9:7; 8; 12; **Obad** 6(2); **Jonah** 4:11; **Mic** 1:4; 5(2); 16; 2:7; 13; 4:11; 6:10; 12; 16; 7:6; 11; **Nah** 1:3; 6; 10; 2:3; 3:13; 17(2); **Hab** 1:3(2); 6; 7; 8(2); 15; 3:6; **Zeph** 1:6; 8; 11(2); 12; 3:3(2); 4; 6(2); 18(2); **Hag** 1:6; **Zec** 1:5; 9; 10; 15; 19; 21(2); 3:8; 4:2; 4; 10; 11; 14; 6:4; 5; 6; 10; 15; 8:16; 17; 11:2; 13:6; **Mal** 1:4; 2:8; 3:6; 7; 9; 15(2); **Mt** 1:17(3); 2:2; 18; 20; 5:3; 4; 5; 6; 7; 8; 9; 10(2); 11; 13; 14; 15; 6:5; 26; 7:15; 8:26; 9:12; 17; 37; 10:2; 28; 29; 30; 31; 11:5(2); 8; 11; 27; 28; 12:5; 48; 13:15; 16; 38(2); 39; 40; 56; 15:16; 20; 17:26; 18:20; 19:6; 12(2); 26; 30; 20:22(2); 25; 22:4(3); 14(2); 21(2); 30(2); 23:8; 13; 25; 27(2); 28; 31; 37; 24:8; 19; 25:8; 26:55; **Mk** 2:17(2); 4:11(2); 15; 16(2); 17; 18(2); 20(2); 40; 5:9; 6:2; 3; 7:15; 18; 9:23; 10:8; 27; 31; 42; 12:17(2); 25(3); 13:1; 8; 17; 25; 32; 14:36; 48; **Lk** 1:1; 4:18; 5:20; 31(2); 38; 6:21(2); 22; 24; 25; 7:22(2); 25(2); 28; 31; 32; 47(2); 48; 8:12; 13; 14(2); 15; 21; 9:12; 55; 61; 10:2; 8; 9; 17; 20(2); 22; 23; 11:7; 21; 28; 41; 44(2); 12:6; 7(2); 24; 37; 38; 13:14; 23; 25; 27; 30(2); 34; 14:17; 16:8; 15; 17:10(2); 17; 18; 18:11; 27(2); 31; 19:42; 20:34; 35; 36(2); 37; 21:21(3); 22; 23; 26; 22:10; 25; 28; 38; 23:29(2); 24:17(2); 18; 38; 44; 48; **Jn** 3:21; 4:35(2); 38; 5:28; 39; 6:9; 49; 58; 63(2); 64; 69; 7:7; 23; 47; 49; 8:10; 23(2); 31; 37; 44; 47; 53; 9:28; 40; 10:8; 12; 16; 21; 26; 30; 34; 11:9; 13:10; 11; 17; 35; 14:2; 15:3; 5; 6; 14; 19; 16:15; 30; 17:7; 9; 10(2); 11(2); 14; 16; 22; 20:23(2); 29; 30; 31; 21:25; **Acts** 2:7; 13; 15; 32; 39; 3:15; 25; 5:9; 25; 32; 7:1; 26; 10:4; 21; 31; 33(2); 39; 13:27; 31; 39; 14:11; 15(2); 15:18; 19; 23; 16:17; 21; 28; 17:6; 22; 28; 29; 19:15; 26; 37; 38(2); 40; 20:32; 21:20(2); 21(2); 24; 22:3; 10; 23:15; 21; 35; 24:2; 11; 14; 25:5; 24; 26:3; 18; 26; 28:27; **Rom** 1:6; 15; 20(3); 28; 32; 2:2; 8; 13; 14; 18; 19; 3:9(2); 12(2); 15; 16; 19; 25; 4:7(3); 12; 14; 6:2; 4; 13; 14; 15; 16; 21; 7:4; 6; 8:1; 5(2); 8; 9; 12; 14(2); 16; 18; 24; 28; 36(2); 37; 9:4; 5; 6(2); 7(2); 8(3); 26; 10:15; 19; 11:14; 16; 28(2); 29; 33; 36; 12:5; 13:1; 3; 6; 14:8; 20; 15:1; 14; 26; 27; 16:7; 10; 11; 14; 15; 18; **1Cor** 1:2; 5; 11(2); 18; 24; 26; 27; 28(3); 30; 2:6; 12; 14(2); 3:2; 3(2); 4; 8; 9(3); 16; 17; 20; 21; 22; 23; 4:8(2); 9; 10(6); 11(2); 13(2); 18; 19; 5:2; 4; 7; 12(2); 13; 6:2; 4; 11(3); 12(3); 15; 19; 20(2); 7:14; 23; 33; 8:4; 5; 6(2); 8(2); 9; 10; 9:1; 2; 12; 13; 20(2); 21(2); 10:11(2); 13; 17(2); 18; 22; 23(3); 11:19; 30; 32(2); 12:4; 5; 6; 12; 13; 20; 22; 27; 29(4); 14:10; 12; 22; 23(2); 25; 32; 34; 37; 15:2; 6; 15; 17; 18(2); 19; 23; 27; 29(2); 35; 40; 48(4); 16:9; 18; **2Cor** 1:1; 4(2); 7; 14(2); 20; 24; 2:11; 15(2); 16; 17; 3:2; 3; 5; 18; 4:3; 8(2); 11; 15; 18(6); 5:4; 6(3); 8; 11(2); 17(2); 18; 20; 6:12(2); 16; 7:3; 6; 8:23; 10:4; 7; 10; 11(3); 12; 14; 11:13; 19; 22(3); 23; 28; 13:4; 6; 9(3); **Gal** 1:2; 6; 2:15; 17; 3:3(2); 7(2); 9; 10(3); 25; 26; 28; 29; 4:6; 8; 9; 12; 24(2); 28; 31; 5:4(2); 17; 18; 19(2); 24; 6:1; 10; 13; **Eph** 1:1; 10(2); 2:5; 8; 10; 11; 13; 19; 20; 22; 4:1; 4; 25; 30; 5:4; 8; 12; 13(2); 16; 30; 6:5; **Phil** 1:1; 7; 10; 11; 13; 14; 2:21; 3:3; 13(2); 18; 4:3; 8(6); 21; 22; **Col** 1:2; 16(2); 2:3; 10; 11; 12; 17; 20; 22; 3:1; 3; 5; 15; 4:5; 9; 11(2); 13; 15; **1Th** 2:10; 14; 15; 19; 20; 3:3; 4:9; 10; 12; 13; 15(2); 17; 5:4; 5(2); 7; 8; 12; 14; **2Th** 1:3; 7; 2:13; 3:11(2); 12; **1Ti** 2:2; 3:7; 5:3; 15; 16; 24; 25(2); 6:1; 2(2); 17; **2Ti** 1:15(2); 2:19; 20; 26; 3:3; 6; 15; **Titus** 1:5; 10; 12; 15(2); 3:8; 9; 15; **Philem** 1:7; **Heb** 1:10; 14; 2:10(2); 11(2); 14; 18; 3:6; 14; 4:13; 15; 5:2; 11; 12; 14; 6:9; 7:5; 13; 8:4; 9:15; 17; 22; 24; 10:8; 10; 14; 39; 11:3; 12:1; 8(2); 11; 18; 22; 23; 27(2); 13:3; 11; **Jas** 1:1; 2:4(2); 7; 9; 16; 3:4(2); 9; 5:2(2); 4; 17; **1Pet** 1:5; 6; 12; 2:5; 9; 10; 14; 25; 3:6(2); 9; 12(2); 14; 4:6; 13; 14; 5:1; 9(2); 14; **2Pet** 1:4; 2:10(2); 11; 13; 15; 17(2); 19; 20; 3:5; 7(2); 10; 16(2); **1Jn** 2:5; 12; 14; 15; 18; 3:2; 10; 19; 22; 4:1(2); 4; 5; 6; 17; 5:3; 7(2); 8; 19; 20; **2Jn** 7; **Jude** 1; 4; 7; 12(2); 15; 16; **Rev** 1:3; 4(2); 11; 19; 20(2); 2:2(3); 9(3); 18; 3:2; 4; 9(2); 4:5; 11; 5:6; 8; 13(2); 7:13(2); 14; 15; 8:13; 9:14; 10:6(3); 11:4; 15; 13:8; 14:4(3); 5; 12; 13; 18; 15:3(2); 4; 16:6; 7; 14; 17:9; 10(2); 12; 14(2); 15; 18:3; 14(2); 19:2; 9(3); 20:7; 8; 10; 21:4; 5; 12; 16; 22; 24; 27; 22:6; 14; 15; 18; 19

ART

383, 4640, *1488, 2192, 5078, 5607*

Gen 3:9; 14; 19; 4:6; 11; 12:11; 13; 13:14; 16:11; 17:8; 20:3; 23:6; 24:23; 47; 60; 26:16; 29; 27:18; 24; 32; 28:4; 29:14; 15; 32:17; 39:9; 41:39; 44:18; 45:19; 46:30; 47:8; 49:3; 8; 9; **Ex** 4:25; 26; 18:18; 30:25; 35; 33:3; 34:10; **Lev** 27:12; **Num** 14:14(2); 21:29; **Deut** 2:18; 4:30; 38; 7:6; 19; 8:10; 12; 9:1; 6; 14:2; 21; 24; 17:14; 18:9; 26:1; 27:3; 9; 28:10; 32:15(3); 18; 33:29; **Josh** 5:13; 13:1; 17:17; **Judg** 8:18; 11:2; 12; 25; 35; 12:5; 13:3; 11; **Ruth** 2:9; 11; 12; 3:9(2); 11; 16; **1Sa** 8:5; 10:2; 5; 17:28; 33(2); 58; 19:3; 21:1; 24:17; 26:14; 15; 28:12; 29:9; 30:13; **2Sa** 1:8; 13; 2:20; 7:22; 24; 28; 9:2; 12:7; 13:4; 15:2; 19; 27; 16:8(2); 21; 18:3; 19:13; 20:9; 17; 22:29; **1Kin** 1:42; 2:9; 26; 6:12; 13:14; 18; 17:18; 24; 18:7; 17; 36; 37; 20:36; 22:4; **2Kin** 1:4; 6; 16; 3:7; 4:4; 19:15; 19; **1Chr** 17:26; 29:11; **2Chr** 14:11; 16:14; 18:3; 20:6; 7; 25:16; **Ezr** 7:14; 9:15; **Neh** 2:2; 9:6; 7; 8; 17; 31; 33; **Est** 4:14; **Job** 4:5; 15:7; 17:14(2); 22:3; 30:21; 31:24; 33:12; 34:18; 35:8; **Ps** 2:7; 3:3; 5:4; 8:4; 10:14; 16:2; 22:1; 3; 9; 10; 23:4; 25:5; 31:3; 4; 14; 32:7; 40:17; 42:5(2); 11(2); 43:2; 5(2); 44:4; 45:2; 63:1; 65:5; 66:3; 68:35; 70:5; 71:3; 5(2); 6; 7; 76:4; 7(2); 77:14; 83:18; 86:5; 10(2); 15; 89:17; 26; 90:2; 92:8; 93:2; 97:9(2); 102:27; 104:1(2); 110:4; 118:21; 28(2); 119:12; 57; 68; 114; 137; 151; 137:8; 139:3; 8(2); 140:6; 142:5; 143:10; **Prov** 6:2(2); 3; 7:4; 24:24; **Eccl** 10:17; **Song** 1:15(2); 16; 2:14; 4:1(2); 7; 6:4; 7:6; **Is** 14:8; 10(2); 12(2); 19; 31; 22:1; 2; 25:1; 26:15; 37:16; 20; 41:8; 9; 43:1; 44:17; 21(2); 45:15; 47:8; 13; 48:4; 49:3; 51:9; 10; 12; 16; 57:8; 10; 63:2; 16(2); 64:5; 8; **Jer** 2:21; 23; 27; 3:4; 22; 4:30; 10:6; 12:1; 2; 14:9; 22; 15:6; 17:14; 17; 20:7; 22:6; 31:18; 39:17; 49:12; 50:24(2); 51:20; **Lam** 5:22; **Eze** 3:5; 16:7; 34; 45(2); 54; 22:4(2); 5; 24; 23:30; 26:17; 27:3(2); 28:2; 3; 14; 31:2; 18; 32:2(2); 33:32; 38:13; 17; 40:4; **Dan** 2:26; 37; 38; 4:18; 22; 5:13(2); 27(2); 9:23; **Hos** 2:23(2); **Obad** 2; 5; **Jonah** 1:8; 4:2; **Mic** 2:7; **Nah** 1:14; 3:8; **Hab** 1:12; 13; 2:16; **Zec** 4:7; **Mt** 2:6; 5:25; 6:9; 8:29; 11:3; 23; 14:33; 16:14; 16; 17; 18; 23; 22:16; 25:24; 26:50; 73; 27:11; **Mk** 1:11; 24(2); 3:11; 8:29; 12:14; 34; 14:61; 70(2); 15:2; **Lk** 1:28(2); 42; 3:22; 4:34(2); 41; 7:19; 20; 10:15; 41; 11:2; 12:58; 13:12; 14:8; 10; 15:31; 16:25; 19:21; 22:32; 58; 67; 70; 23:3; 40; 24:18; **Jn** 1:19; 21(2); 22; 42; 49(2); 3:2; 10; 4:12; 19; 5:14; 6:69; 7:52; 8:25; 48; 53; 57; 9:28; 11:27; 17:21; 18:17; 25; 33; 37; 19:9; 12; 21:12; **Acts** 4:24; 8:23; 9:5; 10:33; 12:15; 13:33; 17:29; 21:22; 38; 22:8; 27; 26:1; 15; 24; **Rom** 2:1(2); 17; 19(2); 3:4; 9:20; 14:4; **1Cor** 7:21; 27(2); **Gal** 4:7; **1Ti** 6:12; **Heb** 1:5; 12; 2:6; 5:5; 6; 7:17; 21; 12:5; **Jas** 2:11; 4:11; 12; **Rev** 2:5; 9; 3:1; 15; 16; 17; 4:11; 5:9; 11:17(2); 15:4; 16:5(2)

AS

5613

Gen 3:5; 22; 4:20(2); 21; 7:9; 16; 8:21; 9:3; 10:9; 19(2); 30; 11:2; 12:4; 13:10(2); 16; 16:6; 17:4; 15; 20; 23; 18:5; 25; 33(2); 19:8; 14; 28; 21:1(2); 4; 16; 22:14; 17(2); 23:9(2); 24:22; 51; 25:18; 26:4; 29(2); 27:4; 9; 12; 14; 19; 23; 27; 30(2); 42; 46; 28:6; 14; 31:2; 5; 26; 32:12; 25; 28; 31; 33:10; 14; 34:12; 15; 22; 31; 35:18; 36:24; 38:11; 29; 39:10; 18; 40:10; 22; 41:13; 19; 21; 38; 39(2); 49; 54; 42:27; 35; 43:6; 17; 34; 44:1(2); 3(2); 15; 17; 18; 47:11; 21; 30; 48:5; 7; 20(2); 49:4; 9(2); 16; 27; 50:6; 12; 20(2); **Ex** 1:17; 19; 2:14; 4:6; 7; 5:7; 13; 14; 20; 7:6; 10; 13; 20; 22; 8:15; 19; 27; 9:12; 17; 18; 24; 29(2); 30; 35; 10:10; 14; 11:6; 12:25; 28; 31; 32; 36; 48; 50; 13:11; 14:28; 15:5; 7; 8; 10; 16(2); 16:5(2); 10; 14(2); 22; 24; 34; 17:10; 18:21; 19:18; 21:7; 22(2); 22:25; 23:15; 24:10(2); 27:8; 28:32; 30:37; 32:1; 13; 17; 19(2); 23; 33:9; 11; 34:4; 10; 18; 35:22(2); 38:21; 39:1; 5; 6; 7; 21; 23; 26; 29; 31; 43; 40:15; 19; 21; 23; 25; 27; 29; 32; **Lev** 2:12; 4:10; 20; 21; 26(2); 31; 35; 5:13(2); 6:17(2); 7:7; 10(2); 19; 21; 8:4; 9; 13; 17; 21; 29; 31; 34; 9:7; 10; 15; 21; 10:5; 15; 18; 11:4; 12:5; 13:43; 14:6; 13; 22; 30; 31; 35; 15:25; 26(2); 16:15; 34; 18:19(2); 22; 28; 19:16; 18; 23(2); 34(2); 20:6; 13; 25; 22:13; 24:16(2); 19; 20; 22(2); 23; 25:31; 39; 40(2); 42; 46; 53; 26:19(2); 34(2); 35(2); 36; 37; 27:12; 14; 21; 23; **Num** 1:19; 2:17; 33; 3:16; 42; 51; 4:15; 29; 49; 5:4; 8:3; 16; 19; 21; 22; 9:15; 18(2); 10:31; 11:7(2); 8; 12; 31(3); 12:10; 12; 13:21; 33; 14:15; 17; 19; 21(2); 28(3); 32; 15:14; 15; 20; 36; 16:31; 40(3); 45; 47; 17:11; 18:6; 7; 18(2); 24; 27(2); 30(2); 20:9; 27; 21:34; 22:4; 8; 23:2; 22; 24(2); 30; 24:1; 6(4); 8; 9(2); 26:4; 27:11; 13; 17; 22; 23; 28:8(2); 31:7; 31; 41; 47; 32:25; 27; 31; 33:56; 34:6; 36:10; **Deut** 1:10; 11(2); 17(2); 19; 21; 31; 40; 44; 2:1; 5; 10; 11; 12; 14; 21; 22; 29; 30; 3:2; 6; 20(2); 4:5; 7; 8; 20; 32; 33; 38; 5:12; 14(2); 16; 26; 31; 32; 6:3; 8; 16; 19; 24; 25; 8:5; 18; 20; 9:3(2); 18; 21(2); 25; 10:5; 9; 15; 22; 11:4; 10(2); 18; 21; 25; 12:9; 12; 15(2); 16; 19(2); 20; 21; 22; 24; 13:6; 11; 17; 14:7; 15:6; 21; 22(2); 23; 16:9; 10; 17; 17:14; 16; 18:2; 7; 14; 19:5; 6; 8; 19; 20:8(2); 17; 22:11; 26; 23:23; 24:8; 26:15; 18; 19; 27:3; 28:9; 29; 49(2); 62; 63; 29:13(2); 28; 30:9; 31:3; 4; 13(2); 21; 32:2(4); 10; 11; 31; 50; 33:20; 25; 34:9; **Josh** 1:3; 5; 15; 17(2); 2:7(2); 11(2); 3:7; 13(2); 15; 4:8(2); 12; 14; 18; 23; 5:5; 14; 6:22; 7:5; 8:2; 5; 6; 15; 19(2); 29(2); 31(2); 33(3); 9:4; 21; 25; 10:1; 2; 11; 28; 30; 39(2); 40; 11:4; 9; 12; 13; 15; 20; 13:6; 8; 14; 33; 14:2; 5; 7; 10; 11(4); 12; 15:18; 63; 17:14; 21:8; 22:4; 23:5; 8; 9; 10; 15; 24:15; **Judg** 1:7; 20; 2:3; 15(2); 22; 3:1(2); 2; 4:22; 5:31; 6:5; 16; 27; 36; 37; 7:5; 12; 17; 8:8; 18; 19; 21; 33(2); 9:33(3); 36; 48; 11:36; 13:9; 23(2); 14:6; 20; 15:10; 11; 14; 16:7; 9; 11; 20; 17:8; 11; 19:22; 20:1; 8; 11; 30; 31; 32; 39; 48(2); **Ruth** 1:8; 3:10; 13; **1Sa** 1:7; 12; 26; 28(2); 2:2; 16(2); 3:10; 4:9; 5:10; 6:6; 12; 7:10; 9:11; 13(2); 20; 27; 10:7; 12:15; 23; 13:5; 7; 10(2); 14:14; 39; 45; 15:22(2); 23(2); 27; 33; 16:7; 17:20(2); 23; 36; 55; 57; 18:1; 3; 6; 7; 10; 19:6; 7; 9; 20; 20:3(2); 13; 17; 20; 21; 23; 25; 31(2); 36; 41(2); 42; 22:8; 13; 14; 23:11; 24:4; 13; 18; 25:15(2); 20; 25; 26(3); 29; 34; 37; 26:10; 16; 20; 24; 27:8; 28:10; 17; 29:6; 8; 9; 10(2); 30:24; **2Sa** 1:6; 21; 2:18(2); 23(2); 27; 3:9; 33; 34; 36; 4:4; 6; 9; 5:20; 25; 6:16; 18(2); 19(2); 20; 7:10; 11; 15; 25; 8:3; 9:8; 11(2); 10:2; 11:11(2); 25(2); 12:3; 5; 13:13(2); 29; 35; 36(2); 14:2; 11; 13; 14; 17; 19; 25; 15:10(2); 21(2); 26; 30(2); 34; 16:2; 5; 13(2); 19; 23; 17:3; 8; 10; 11; 12(2); 18:32; 33; 19:3; 14; 18; 27; 30; 20:8; 22:23; 31; 43(3); 45(2); 23:4(2); 6; 24:19; 23; **1Kin** 1:29; 30; 37; 41; 2:3; 24(2); 31; 38; 3:6(2); 14; 4:20; 29; 5:5; 12; 8:20; 24; 25; 43; 53; 57; 59; 61; 9:2; 4; 5; 10:10; 27(2); 11:4; 6; 11; 33; 38(2); 12:12; 17; 13:6; 18; 20; 21; 14:6; 7; 8; 10; 15; 15:3; 11; 16:2; 9; 11(2); 31; 17:1; 11; 12; 13; 18:7; 10; 12(2); 15; 32(2); 19:2; 5; 20:11; 12; 34; 36(4); 39; 40; 21:11(2); 26; 22:4(3); 14; 17; **2Kin** 1:16; 2:2(2); 4(2); 6(2); 11; 19; 23; 3:7(3); 14; 22(2); 4:8(2); 30(2); 40; 5:16; 20; 27(2); 6:5; 26; 7:7; 10; 13(2); 17; 18; 8:5; 18; 19; 27; 9:17; 22; 31; 37; 10:2(2); 12; 15; 25(2); 11:8(2); 14; 12:9; 13:5; 21; 23; 14:3; 4; 5(2); 15:9; 17:2; 4; 11; 23; 41; 19:12; 26(4); 29; 37; 21:3; 13; 20; 22:18; 23:16; 21; 27; 24:13; 25:15; 22; **1Chr** 5:1; 6:26; 12:8(2); 20; 33; 36; 14:16; 15:15; 29; 16:37; 17:1; 9; 13; 23; 18:3; 21:3; 15; 17; 21; 22:7; 11; 23:24; 24:19; 25:8(3); 26:13(2); 21; 28:2; 7; 29:11; 15(2); 17; 23; 25; **2Chr** 1:12; 15(3); 2:3; 16(2); 3:16; 4:6; 5:13(2); 6:8; 10; 15; 16; 31; 33; 7:17(2); 18; 8:7; 14; 9:9; 27(2); 10:12; 17; 11:16; 13:10; 15; 16:3; 18:3(2); 13; 16; 20:9; 20; 21; 33; 21:6; 7; 23:3; 13; 18(2); 24:12(2); 25:4; 16; 26:5(2); 29:8; 31(2); 30:5; 7; 8; 31:3; 5(2); 15(2); 32:17; 19; 33:22; 23; 34:26; 35:12; 18; 36:21(2); **Ezr** 2:62; 3:1; 2; 4(2); 4:2; 3; 6:18; 21; 7:14; 25; 27; 28; 8:27; 31; 9:7; 13; 15; 10:3; 12; **Neh** 1:1; 2:16; 18; 5:5(2); 12; 6:8; 11(2); 7:64; 8:1; 15; 9:10; 11; 23; 24; 10:34; 36; 13:15; **Est** 2:9; 20(2); 3:11; 4:14; 5:5; 8; 13; 6:10; 7:8; 8:8; 9:2; 22; 23(2); 27(2); 31(2); **Job** 2:10; 3:6; 16(2); 4:8; 5:7; 14; 25; 26; 6:7; 15(2); 26; 7:2(2); 9; 20; 9:26(2); 32; 10:4; 5(2); 9; 10; 16; 19; 22(2); 11:8(2); 16; 17; 20; 12:3(3); 4; 5; 13:9; 28(2); 14:2; 6; 11; 15:24; 33(2); 16:4; 21; 17:6; 7; 10; 15; 18:3; 20; 19:11; 22; 20:8(2); 21:4; 18(2); 33; 22:2; 8; 24(2); 23:10; 24:5; 14; 17; 18; 20; 24(2); 26:3; 27:2; 6; 7(2); 16(2); 18(2); 20; 21; 28:5(2); 29:2(2); 4; 14; 18; 23(2); 25(2); 30:5; 14; 15(2); 18; 31:18; 33; 36; 37; 32:19; 34:3; 26; 35:8; 37:18; 38:8; 14(2); 19; 30; 39:16; 20; 40:15; 18; 41:5; 15; 20; 24(4); 27(2); 29; 42:7; 9; 10(2); 15; **Ps** 5:7; 12; 10:5; 9; 11:1; 12:6; 14:4; 17:8; 12(2); 15; 18:30; 42(2); 44(2); 19:5(2); 21:9; 22:13; 25:10; 26:11; 27:12; 31:12; 32:9(2); 33:7; 22; 34:18; 35:5; 13; 14(2); 37:2; 6(2); 14; 20; 22; 38:4; 10; 13(2); 14; 39:5(2); 12; 40:4; 16; 41:12; 42:1; 10; 44:22; 48:6; 8; 50:21; 53:4; 55:16; 20; 58:3(2); 7(2); 8; 9; 61:6; 62:3(2); 63:2; 5; 65:3; 66:10; 68:2(2); 13; 14; 15(2); 17; 21; 69:13; 70:4; 71:7; 72:5(2); 6; 7; 17(2); 73:1; 2; 5; 6(2); 19; 20; 22; 74:5; 77:13; 78:8; 13; 15; 27(2); 65; 83:9(3); 10; 11(2); 13; 14(2); 87:7(2); 88:4; 89:10; 11; 29; 36; 37(2); 90:4(2); 5(2); 9; 92:7; 95:8(2); 102:3; 7; 26; 103:11; 12(2); 13; 15(3); 18; 104:2; 6; 17; 33(2); 106:9; 107:10; 109:17(2); 18(2); 19; 23; 29; 116:2(2); 118:12; 119:14(2); 70(2); 111; 132; 162; 122:3; 123:2(2); 124:6; 7; 125:1; 2; 5(2); 126:4; 127:4; 128:3; 129:6; 131:2(2); 133:3(2); 137:8; 139:12; 16; 140:9; 141:2(2); 7; 143:3; 6; 144:4; 12(2); 147:20; **Prov** 1:12(2); 27(2); 2:4(2); 3:12; 4:18; 19; 5:3; 4(2); 19; 6:5(2); 11(2); 7:2; 22(2); 23; 8:26; 30; 9:4; 16; 10:20; 23; 25; 26(2); 11:19; 20; 22; 28; 12:4; 15:19; 16:14; 15; 24; 27; 17:8; 14; 18:4(2); 8; 11; 19:12(2); 24; 20:2; 19; 21:1; 8; 29; 23:5; 7; 28; 34(2); 24:29; 34(2); 25:12; 13; 16; 20(2); 25; 26; 26:1(2); 2(2); 8; 9; 11; 14; 18; 21; 22; 27:8; 19; 21; 28:1; 4; 15; 30:14(2); 31:8; **Eccl** 2:8; 13(2); 15; 16; 3:19; 4:1; 5:15(2); 16; 6:12; 7:6; 26; 8:1; 13; 9:2(2); 12(2); 10:5; 7; 11:5; 12:7; 11(2); **Song** 1:3; 5(2); 7; 14; 2:2; 3; 4:1; 11; 5:11(2); 12; 13(2); 14(2); 15(3); 6:4(3); 5; 6; 7; 10(4); 13; 7:4(2); 8; 8:1; 6(4); 10; **Is** 1:7; 8(3); 9; 18(4); 26(2); 30(2); 31(2); 3:9; 12; 16; 5:18; 24(3); 6:13(2); 7:2; 8:6; 9:1; 3; 4; 18; 19; 10:9(3); 10; 11; 14(2); 15(3); 18; 20; 22; 26; 32; 11:9; 16; 13:4; 6; 8(2); 14(2); 17; 19; 14:10;

17; 19(2); 24(2); 16:2; 3; 14; 17:3; 5(2); 6; 9; 13; 19:14; 20:3; 21:1; 3; 22:16; 23; 23:5; 10; 15; 24:2(6); 13(2); 22; 25:4; 5; 10; 11; 26:17; 18; 19; 20; 27:7; 9; 28:2(2); 4; 21(2); 29:2; 4; 5; 7; 8(2); 11; 13; 16; 17; 30:13; 14; 17(2); 22; 26(2); 27; 28; 29(2); 31:4; 5; 32:2(3); 33:4; 11; 12(2); 34:4(3); 35:1; 6; 37:12; 27(4); 30; 38; 38:12; 13; 14; 19; 40:6; 15(3); 17; 22(3); 23; 24; 31; 41:2(2); 11; 12(2); 15; 25(2); 42:13; 19(3); 43:17; 44:4(2); 7; 22(2); 47:3; 4; 8; 14; 48:18(2); 19; 49:18(3); 26; 50:4; 9; 51:9; 12; 13; 20; 23(2); 52:14; 53:2(2); 3; 7(2); 54:6; 9(2); 55:9; 10; 56:12; 58:2; 4; 5; 8; 10; 59:10(3); 12; 17(2); 21; 60:8(2); 61:10(2); 11(2); 62:1(2); 5(2); 63:13; 14; 64:2; 6(3); 65:8; 22; 66:3(4); 8(2); 13; 20; 22; **Jer** 2:26; 36; 3:2; 5; 20; 4:13(2); 17; 31(2); 5:8; 9; 16; 19; 26; 27; 29; 6:7; 9(2); 23; 24; 26; 7:14; 15; 8:6; 9:8; 9; 22(2); 10:5; 6; 7; 11:5; 12:8; 9; 16; 13:5; 10; 11; 21(2); 24; 14:8(2); 9(2); 15:2(4); 18(2); 19; 16:4; 17:8; 11; 16; 22; 18:4; 6(2); 17; 19:11; 12; 13; 20:9; 11; 16; 21:7; 22:23; 24; 23:12; 14(2); 27; 29; 34; 24:8; 25:18; 30; 38; 26:11; 14(2); 18; 27:13; 30:6; 20; 31:5; 10; 12; 18; 23; 28; 32:20; 31; 42; 33:7; 11; 22; 38:16; 39:12; 40:3; 10; 41:6(2); 42:2; 18; 43:11(3); 12; 44:6; 13; 14; 16; 17; 22; 23; 30; 46:7(2); 18(3); 22; 26; 48:8; 13; 34; 40; 41; 49:16(2); 18; 22(2); 24; 50:8; 9; 11(2); 15; 18; 26; 37; 40; 43; 51:14; 27; 30; 38; 49; **Lam** 1:1; 15; 17; 20; 22; 2:4; 5; 6; 7; 12; 22; 3:6; 10(2); 12; 45; 4:2; 6; 14; 17(2); 5:3; 21; **Eze** 1:1; 4; 10; 13; 14; 15; 16; 18; 22; 24(2); 26(2); 27(3); 28; 3:3; 9; 23; 4:12; 5:11; 7:17; 20; 8:1; 2(3); 9:10; 11; 10:1(2); 5; 9; 10(2); 11(2); 13; 11:16; 21; 12:4(2); 7(2); 11; 23; 14:10; 16; 18; 20; 15:6; 16:4; 7; 31; 32; 38; 44; 47; 48(2); 50; 57; 59; 17:5; 16; 19; 18:3; 4; 18; 20:3; 31; 32(2); 33; 36; 39; 21:7; 10; 23; 22:20; 22; 23:16(2); 18; 20; 44; 24:18; 22; 26:3; 10; 28:2; 6; 16; 30:9; 18; 32:2; 33:11; 12; 17; 27; 31(2); 32; 34:8; 12; 17; 19; 35:6; 11; 15; 36:17; 38(2); 37:7(2); 10; 38:16; 40:2; 40; 41:21; 25; 42:6; 9; 11(4); 12; 43:22; 46:5; 7; 11; 12; 47:10; 14(2); 15; 22; 48:1; 8; 11; 23; **Dan** 1:4; 13; 17; 2:29; 30; 40(3); 41; 42; 43; 45; 4:18; 25; 32; 33; 35; 5:12; 6:4; 10; 22; 7:4; 9(2); 12; 28; 8:5; 15; 18; 9:7; 12; 13; 15; 10:4; 6(2); 17; 11:29(2); 32; 12:1; 3(2); **Hos** 1:10; 2:3(2); 15(2); 4:4; 7; 16(2); 5:12(2); 14(2); 6:3(3); 4(2); 5; 9; 7:4; 6; 7; 12(2); 8:1; 8; 12; 9:1; 4; 9; 10(2); 11; 13; 10:4; 7(2); 11; 14; 11:2; 4; 8(2); 11(2); 12:9; 11; 13:3(4); 7(2); 8; 14:5(3); 6(2); 7(3); **Joel** 1:15; 2:2; 3; 4(2); 5; 32; **Amos** 2:9; 13; 3:12; 4:11(2); 5:11; 14; 16; 19; 24(2); 7:15; 8:8(2); 10(2); 9:5; 7; 9; 11; **Obad** 4; 11; 15; 16(2); **Jonah** 1:14; **Mic** 1:4(2); 6(2); 8; 16; 2:8(2); 12(2); 3:3(2); 4; 12(2); 4:9; 12; 5:7(2); 8(2); 15; 7:1(2); 4; 10; 14; **Nah** 1:10(3); 2:2; 7; 3:6; 15(2); 17(2); **Hab** 1:8; 9(2); 14(2); 2:5(2); 14; 3:4; 14(2); **Zeph** 1:8; 17(2); 2:2; 9(3); **Hag** 1:12; 2:3; 19; 23; **Zec** 1:4; 6; 2:4; 6; 4:1; 5:3(2); 7:3; 12; 13; 8:11; 13; 14; 9:1; 3(2); 7(2); 11; 13; 14; 15(2); 16(3); 10:2; 3; 5; 6; 7; 8; 12:8(3); 10(2); 11; 13:9(2); 14:3; 5; 10; 15; **Mal** 2:9; 3:3(2); 4(2); 17; 4:1; 2; **Mt** 1:18; 24; 5:48; 6:2; 5; 7; 10; 12; 16; 7:29(2); 8:13; 9:9; 10; 15(2); 32; 36; 10:7; 16(3); 25(2); 11:7; 12:13; 40; 13:40; 43; 14:5; 36(2); 15:28; 33; 17:2(2); 9; 20; 18:3; 4; 17; 19; 25; 33; 19:19; 20:14; 28; 29; 21:6; 18; 23; 26; 22:9(2); 10(2); 30; 31; 39; 23:37; 24:3; 21; 27; 37; 38; 44; 25:14; 32; 40; 45; 26:7; 19; 21; 24; 26; 39(2); 55; 27:10; 32; 65(2); 28:1; 3; 4; 6; 9; 15; **Mk** 1:2; 16; 22(2); 42(2); 2:2; 14; 15; 19(2); 23; 3:5; 10(2); 20; 4:4; 18; 20; 26; 33; 36; 5:36(2); 6:15; 31; 34; 56(2); 7:4; 6; 8; 8:24; 9:3(2); 9; 13; 26; 10:1; 15; 32; 46; 11:2(2); 6; 20; 27; 12:25; 26; 31; 33; 13:1; 3; 19; 34; 14:3; 16; 18; 21; 22; 45(2); 48; 66; 15:8; 16:7; 10; 12; 14; **Lk** 1:1; 2; 23(2); 44(2); 55; 70; 2:15; 20; 23; 43; 3:4; 15; 23; 4:16; 5:1; 14; 17; 6:3; 10; 22; 31; 34; 36; 40; 8:5; 6(2); 23; 42; 9:18; 29; 33; 34; 42; 53; 54; 57; 10:3; 7; 8; 18; 27; 33; 38; 11:1(2); 2; 8(2); 27; 30; 36; 37; 41; 44; 53; 12:58; 13:34; 14:1; 22; 15:19; 25; 30(2); 17:6; 11; 12; 14; 24; 26; 28; 18:11(2); 13; 17; 35; 19:9; 11; 32; 33; 36; 20:1; 21:5; 6; 35; 22:13; 22; 26(2); 27; 29; 31; 39; 44; 52; 56; 66(2); 23:7(2); 14; 24; 26; 24:4; 5; 11; 17; 24; 28; 30; 36; 39; 50(2); **Jn** 1:12(2); 14; 23; 36; 3:14; 4:51; 5:21; 23; 26; 30; 6:11(2); 31; 57; 58; 59; 7:10; 28; 38; 8:6; 20; 28; 30; 9:1; 5(2); 29; 10:15; 26; 11:20(2); 29(2); 56; 12:14; 50; 13:15; 33; 34; 14:27; 31; 15:4; 6; 9; 10; 12; 16:21(2); 17:2(3); 11; 14; 16; 18; 21; 22; 23; 18:6(2); 19:40; 20:9; 11; 21; 21:8; 9(2); **Acts** 1:10; 11; 19; 2:2; 3; 4; 15; 22; 39(2); 45; 47; 3:6; 11; 12; 17; 24(2); 4:1; 6(2); 34(2); 35; 5:11(2); 15; 35; 36(2); 37(2); 6:15; 7:5(2); 26; 28; 31; 40; 42; 44; 48; 51; 8:3; 16; 32; 36; 9:3; 17; 18; 32; 38; 10:9; 11; 25; 27; 29(2); 45(2); 47(2); 11:5; 15(2); 17(2); 19(2); 22(2); 12:13; 18(2); 13:1; 2; 17; 25; 33; 34; 48(2); 14:20; 15:8; 11; 15; 24; 16:4; 16; 17:2; 14; 23; 25; 28; 29; 19:2; 20:3; 9; 21:10; 25; 31; 37; 22:3; 5; 6; 23; 25; 23:11; 15; 20; 31; 24:10; 25; 25:10; 18; 26:12; 24; 29; 27:25; 27; 30(2); 28:10; 15(2); 22; **Rom** 1:13; 15(2); 17; 21; 28; 2:12(4); 24; 3:4; 5; 7; 8(2); 10; 4:1; 6; 17(2); 5:12; 15; 16; 18; 19; 21; 6:3; 4; 13(3); 19; 7:1(2); 2; 8:14(2); 26; 36(2); 9:5; 6; 13; 25; 27; 29(2); 32; 33; 10:15; 11:8; 13; 26; 28(2); 30; 12:3; 4; 18(2); 13:9; 13; 14:11; 15:3; 7; 9; 15; 21; 16:2; **1Cor** 1:6; 31; 2:9; 3:1(3); 3; 5; 10; 15; 4:1; 7; 8; 9; 13; 14; 17; 18; 5:1(2); 3(2); 7; 7:7; 8; 17(2); 25; 29; 30(3); 31; 39(2); 8:1; 2; 4; 5; 7; 9:5(3); 8; 20(2); 21; 22; 26(2); 10:6; 7(2); 8; 9; 10; 13; 15; 33; 11:1; 2; 5; 7; 12; 25(2); 26(2); 12:2; 11; 12; 18; 13:1; 11(3); 12; 14:12; 33; 34; 15:8; 22; 38; 48(2); 49; 58; 16:1; 2; 10; 12; **2Cor** 1:5; 7; 14(2); 18; 23; 2:17(3); 3:1; 3; 5; 13; 18(2); 4:1; 13; 5:20; 6:1; 4; 8; 9(3); 10(3); 13; 16; 7:14; 8:5; 6; 7; 11; 15; 9:1; 3; 5(2); 7; 9; 10:2; 7; 9; 11; 14(3); 11:2; 3; 10; 12; 15; 16; 17; 21(2); 23; 12:20(2); 13:2; 7; **Gal** 1:9; 2:7; 14(2); 3:6; 10(2); 16(2); 27(2); 4:1(2); 12(2); 14(2); 28; 29; 5:14; 21; 6:10; 12(2); 16(2); **Eph** 1:4; 2:3; 3:3; 5; 4:4; 17; 21; 32; 5:1; 2; 3; 8; 15(2); 22; 23; 24; 25; 28; 29; 33; 6:5; 6(2); 7; 20; **Phil** 1:7(2); 20; 27; 2:8; 12(2); 15; 22; 23; 3:5; 12; 15(2); 17; 4:15; **Col** 1:6(2); 7; 2:1(2); 6; 7; 20; 3:12; 13; 18; 22; 23; 4:4; **1Th** 1:5; 2:2; 4(2); 5; 6; 7; 11(2); 13(2); 14; 3:4; 6; 12; 4:1; 5; 6; 9; 11; 13; 5:2; 3; 4; 6; 11; **2Th** 1:3; 2:2(2); 4; 3:1; 15(2); **1Ti** 1:3; 5:1(2); 2(2); 6:1(2); **2Ti** 2:3; 9; 17; 3:8; 9; **Titus** 1:5; 7; 9; 2:3; **Philem** 1:9; 14; 16; 17; **Heb** 1:4; 11; 12; 2:14; 3:2; 3; 5; 6; 7; 8; 15; 4:2(2); 3(2); 7; 10; 15; 5:3; 4; 6; 12; 6:19; 7:9; 20; 27; 8:5; 9:8; 9; 25; 27; 10:25(2); 11:7; 9; 12(4); 27; 29; 12:5; 7; 16; 20; 27; 13:3(2); 5; 17; **Jas** 1:10; 2:8; 9; 12; 26; 5:3; 5; 17; **1Pet** 1:14; 15; 18(2); 19; 24(2); 2:2; 4; 5; 11; 12; 13; 14; 16(2); 25; 3:6(3); 7(2); 8; 16; 4:1; 10(2); 11(2); 12; 13; 15(4); 16; 19; 5:3; 8; 12; **2Pet** 1:3; 13(2); 14; 19; 21; 2:1; 12; 13; 3:4; 8(2); 9; 10; 15; 16(2); **1Jn** 1:7; 2:6; 18; 27(2); 3:2; 3; 7; 12; 23; 4:17; **2Jn** 4; 5; 6; **3Jn** 2; 3; **Jude** 7; 10; **Rev** 1:10; 14(3); 15(2); 16; 17; 2:24(3); 27(2); 3:3; 19(2); 21; 4:1; 7; 5:6; 13; 6:1; 11; 12(2); 13; 14; 8:8; 10; 12; 9:2; 3; 5; 7(2); 8(2); 9(2); 17; 10:1(2); 3; 7; 9; 10(3); 11:6(2); 12:4(2); 15; 13:2(2); 3; 11; 15(2); 14:2(2); 3; 15:2; 16:3; 15; 18; 17:12(2); 18:6; 17(2); 19:6(3); 12; 20:8; 21:2; 11; 16(2); 21; 22:1; 12

ASIDE

2015, 3943, 5186, 5265, 5437, 5493, 5844, 6437, 7750, 7847, *402, 565, 659, 863, 1824, 2398, 2596, 5087, 5298*

Ex 3:3; 4; 32:8; **Num** 5:12; 19; 20; 29; 22:23; **Deut** 5:32; 9:12; 16; 11:16; 28; 17:20; 28:14; 31:29; **Josh** 23:6; **Judg** 14:8; 19:12; 15; **Ruth** 4:1(2); **1Sa** 6:12; 8:3; 12:20; 21; **2Sa** 2:21(2); 22; 23; 3:27; 6:10; 18:30(2); **1Kin** 15:5; 20:39; 22:32; 43; **2Kin** 4:4; 22:2; **1Chr** 13:13; **Job** 6:18; **Ps** 14:3; 40:4; 78:57; 101:3; 125:5; **Song** 1:7; 6:1; **Is** 10:2; 29:21; 30:11; 44:20; **Jer** 14:8; 15:5; **Lam** 3:11; 35; **Amos** 2:7; 5:12; **Mal** 3:5; **Mt** 2:22; **Mk** 7:8; 33; **Lk** 9:10; **Jn** 13:4; **Acts** 4:15; 23:19; 26:31; **1Ti** 1:6; 5:15; **Heb** 12:1; **1Pet** 2:1

ASK

1156, 1245, 1875, 7592, *154, 523, 1833, 1905, 2065, 4441*

Gen 32:29; 34:12; **Num** 27:21; **Deut** 4:32(2); 13:14; 32:7; **Josh** 4:6; 21; 15:18; **Judg** 1:14; 18:5; **1Sa** 12:19; 25:8; 28:16; **2Sa** 14:18; 20:18; **1Kin** 2:16; 20; 22(2); 3:5; 14:5; **2Kin** 2:9; **2Chr** 1:7; 20:4; **Job** 12:7; **Ps** 2:8; **Is** 7:11(2); 12; 45:11; 58:2; **Jer** 6:16; 15:5; 18:13; 23:33; 30:6; 38:14; 48:19; 50:5; **Lam** 4:4; **Dan** 6:7; 12; **Hos** 4:12; **Hag** 2:11; **Zec** 10:1; **Mt** 6:8; 7:7; 9; 10; 11; 14:7; 18:19; 20:22; 21:22; 24; 22:46; 27:20; **Mk** 6:22; 23; 24; 9:32; 10:38; 11:29; 12:34; **Lk** 6:9; 30; 9:45; 11:9; 11(2); 12; 13; 12:48; 19:31; 20:3; 40; 22:68; **Jn** 1:19; 9:21; 23; 11:22; 13:24; 14:13; 14; 15:7; 16; 16:19; 23(2); 24; 26; 30; 18:21; 21:12; **Acts** 3:2; 10:29; **1Cor** 14:35; **Eph** 3:20; **Jas** 1:5; 6; 4:2; 3(2); **1Jn** 3:22; 5:14; 15; 16

ASKED

1156, 1245, 7592, 7593, *154, 1905, 2065, 3004, 4441*

Gen 24:47; 26:7; 32:29; 37:15; 38:21; 40:7; 43:7; 27; 44:19; **Ex** 18:7; **Josh** 9:14; 19:50; **Judg** 1:1; 5:25; 6:29; 13:6; 20:18; 23; **1Sa** 1:17; 20; 27; 8:10; 14:37; 19:22; 20:6; 28; **1Kin** 3:10; 11(5); 13; 10:13; **2Kin** 2:10; 8:6; **2Chr** 1:11(3); 9:12; **Ezr** 5:9; 10; **Neh** 1:2; **Job** 21:29; **Ps** 21:4; 105:40; **Is** 30:2; 41:28; 65:1; **Jer** 36:17; 37:17; 38:27; **Dan** 2:10; 7:16; **Mt** 12:10; 16:13; 17:10; 22:23; 35; 41; 27:11; **Mk** 4:10; 5:9; 6:25; 7:5; 17; 8:5; 23; 27; 9:11; 16; 21; 28; 33; 10:2; 10; 17; 12:18; 28; 13:3; 14:60; 61; 15:2; 4; 44; **Lk** 1:63; 3:10; 8:9; 30; 9:18; 15:26; 18:18; 36; 40; 20:21; 27; 21:7; 22:64; 23:3; 6; **Jn** 1:21; 25; 4:10; 5:12; 9:2; 15; 19; 16:24; 18:7; 19; **Acts** 1:6; 3:3; 4:7; 5:27; 10:18; 23:19; 34; 25:20; **Rom** 10:20

ASKING

7592, 154, 1905, 2065

1Sa 12:17; **1Chr** 10:13; **Ps** 78:18; **Lk** 2:46; **Jn** 8:7; **1Cor** 10:25; 27

AT

176, 389, 413, 681, 996, 1157, 3027, 3117, 3162, 3926, 4118, 4480, 5704, 5705, 5921, 5973, 5980, 6440, 6544, 7126, 7138, 7535, *345, 575, 630, 1065, 1159, 1223, 1368, 1369, 1448, 1451, 1519, 1531, 1537, 1657, 1715, 1722, 1764, 1847, 1848, 1909, 2178, 2186, 2527, 2579, 2596, 2621, 2625, 2919, 3195, 3317, 3367, 3379, 3568, 3571, 3654, 3762, 3763, 3826, 3843, 3844, 4012, 4218, 4314, 4363, 4412, 4455, 4648, 4814, 4873*

Gen 3:24; 4:7; 6:6; 8:6; 9:5(3); 13:3; 4; 14:17; 17:21; 18:14; 19:1; 6; 11; 20:13; 21:2; 22; 32; 22:19; 23:10; 18; 24:11; 21; 30; 55; 57; 63; 25:32; 26:8; 27:41; 28:19; 31:10; 33:10; 19; 38:1; 5; 11; 41:1; 21; 43:16; 18; 19; 20; 25; 33; 44:12(2); 45:3; 48:3; 49:13; 19; 23; 27; **Ex** 2:5; 4:25; 5:23; 8:32; 9:14; 12:9; 18(2); 22; 29; 41; 16:6; 12; 13; 18:5; 22; 26; 19:15; 17; 22:23; 26; 28:7; 14; 22; 29:39; 41; 42; 30:8; 32:4; 33:8; 9; 10; 34:22; 35:15; 36:29; 38:8; 39:15; 40:8; 28; **Lev** 1:3; 15; 3:2; 4:7(2); 18(2); 25; 30; 34; 5:9; 6:20; 7:18; 8:15; 31; 33; 35; 9:9; 13:5; 37; 14:11; 15:24; 16:2; 7; 29; 17:6; 18:9; 19:5; 7; 20; 22:19; 29; 23:5; 32; 25:32; 26:32; 27:10; 13; 16; 31; 33; **Num** 3:39; 4:27; 6:6; 18; 9:2; 3; 5; 11; 15; 18(2); 23(3); 10:3; 11:6; 20; 35; 13:30; 16:34; 19:19; 20:24; 21:11; 15; 30; 33; 34; 22:4; 20; 38; 23:25(2); 24:1; 27:14; 21(2); 28:4; 8; 30:4; 6; 7; 11; 14(2); 31:12; 33:14; 16; 17; 19; 21; 26; 27; 30; 32; 34; 35; 38; 34:5; 9; 12; 35:11; 20; 26; **Deut** 1:4; 9; 16; 18; 2:32; 34; 3:1; 2; 4; 8; 12; 18; 21; 23; 4:14; 46; 5:5; 6:24; 7:21; 22; 8:16; 19; 9:11; 18; 19; 22(3); 25; 10:1; 8; 10; 14:28; 15:1; 9; 16:4; 6(4); 17:6(2); 19:15(2); 21:14; 23:24; 24:5; 15; 28:29; 67; 31:10; 32:35; 51; 33:3; 8(2); **Josh** 5:2; 3; 10; 6:16; 26; 7:7; 8:5; 6; 14; 29; 9:6; 10; 14; 16; 10:10; 16; 17; 21; 27; 42; 11:5; 10; 21; 12:4(2); 15:4; 5; 7; 8; 11; 63; 16:3; 7; 8; 17:9; 18:1; 9; 12; 14; 19(2); 19:22; 29; 33; 51; 20:4; 9; 21:2; 3; 22:11; 12; **Judg** 3:2; 29; 4:4; 10; 5:27(2); 28; 7:25; 8:18; 9:5; 41; 11:39; 12:2; 6(2); 10; 13:23(2); 25; 14:4; 16:3; 20; 28; 30; 18:27; 29; 19:16; 22; 26; 27; 20:15; 16; 20; 30; 31; 32; 33; 21:14; 22; 24; **Ruth** 2:14; 3:7; 8(2); 10; 14; **1Sa** 2:22; 29(2); 3:2; 10; 11; 6:10; 9:8; 10:2; 13:11; 14:18; 16:4; 17:1; 15; 18:10; 19; 19:19; 22; 20:5(2); 6; 16; 20; 25; 33; 35; 21:1; 4; 22:8; 13; 14; 23:29; 25:1; 24; 26:7; 8; 11; 16; 27:3; 28:7; 30:8; 21; 31:13; **2Sa** 2:32; 3:30; 32; 4:5; 6:4; 8:3; 9:7; 10; 11; 13; 10:5; 8; 11:1(2); 9; 13; 13:5; 6; 14:26(2); 15:8; 14; 16:3; 6(2); 13; 23; 17:7; 9; 19:9; 28; 32; 42; 20:3; 8; 18; 21:18; 22:16(2); 23:8; 24:8; 24; **1Kin** 1:6; 2:7; 8; 26; 39; 3:20; 5:14; 7:30; 8:2; 9; 59; 61; 65; 9:2; 6; 8; 10; 10:22; 26; 28; 11:29; 12:27; 13:20; 14:1; 6; 15:18; 27; 18:19; 27; 36(2); 44; 19:6; 20:9; 16; 22; 26; 22:5; 20; 28; 34; 35; 48; **2Kin** 2:3; 5; 15; 18; 4:17; 37; 5:9; 20; 6:32; 7:3; 8:3; 22; 29; 9:7; 24; 27; 30; 31; 10:8; 12; 14; 11:6(2); 12:4; 13:20; 14:10; 11; 13; 20; 16:6; 10; 17:25; 18:10; 16; 33; 19:21; 36; 20:12; 23:6; 8; 11; 15; 29; 33; 24:3; 10; 25:21; 25; **1Chr** 2:55; 4:28; 29(3); 30(3); 31(3); 8:29; 9:34; 38; 11:11; 13; 16; 17; 12:22; 32; 13:3; 14:3; 15:13; 29; 16:33; 39; 17:9; 19:5; 20:1(2); 4(2); 6; 21:19; 28; 29(2); 23:30; 26:18(3); 31; 28:7; 21; **2Chr** 1:3; 4; 6; 13; 14; 15; 16; 3:1; 5:10; 12; 7:8; 8:1; 14; 17; 9:1; 25; 13:18; 14:10; 15:10; 15; 16; 16:2; 7; 18:4; 9; 19; 33; 19:4; 20:16; 22:5; 6(2); 23:5(2); 13(2); 19; 24:8(2); 11; 21; 23; 25:19; 21; 23; 26:9(3); 28:16; 30:1; 3; 5; 13; 21; 31:13; 32:9; 33; 33:14; 35:15; 17; 23; 36:3; 7; **Ezr** 1:2; 2:68; 3:8; 4:10; 11; 17; 24; 5:2; 3; 17(2); 6:2; 3; 5(2); 9; 12; 17; 18; 7:12; 8:17(2); 21; 29; 34; 9:4; 5; 10:3; 14; **Neh** 2:12; 3:19; 4:22; 5:17; 6:1; 7; 7:5; 9:37; 10:34; 11:1; 2; 4; 6; 22; 24; 25(3); 26(3); 27(2); 28(2); 29(3); 30(2); 31; 32; 12:25; 27; 37(2); 44; 13:6; 19; 31; **Est** 1:12; 4:8; 14; 5:6; 13; 6:10; 7:2; 3(2); 8:3; 9; 14; 9:14; 15; 18; **Job** 2:10; 3:13; 17; 5:22; 23; 9:23; 12:5; 15:12; 23; 16:4; 12; 17:8; 18:12; 20; 19:25; 21:12; 23; 22:21; 23:15; 26:11; 27:23; 29:21; 31:9; 29; 34:20; 37:1; 39:22; 27; 41:9; 26; 29; **Ps** 7:4; 9:3; 10:5; 11:2; 12:5; 16:8; 11; 18:12; 15(2); 25:13; 30:t, 4; 34:1; 35:8; 26; 37:13; 39:5; 12; 42:7; 52:6; 55:6; 17; 20; 59:6; 8; 14; 62:8; 64:4(2); 7; 65:8; 68:2; 8(2); 12; 29; 73:3; 74:6; 76:6; 80:16; 81:7; 83:9; 10; 91:6; 7(2); 97:5(2); 12; 99:5; 9; 104:7(2); 105:22; 106:3; 7(2); 32; 107:27; 109:6; 31; 110:1; 5; 114:7(2); 118:13; 119:20; 45; 62; 162; 123:4; 132:6; 7; 135:21; 141:7; **Prov** 1:23; 25; 26; 4:19; 5:11; 19; 7:6; 12; 19; 20; 8:3(4); 34(2); 9:14; 14:9; 19; 16:7; 17:5; 17; 20:21; 21:13; 23:30; 32; 24:19; 28:18; 29:21; 30:17; **Eccl** 5:6; 8; 10:2(2); 12:4; 6(2); **Song** 1:7; 12; 2:9; 7:13; 8:11; **Is** 1:12; 26(2); 6:4; 7:3; 23; 9:1; 10:26; 28; 29; 32; 13:6; 8; 14:7; 8; 9; 16:2; 4; 17:7; 14; 19:1; 19; 20:2; 21:3(2); 22:7; 23:5(2); 26:11; 27:13; 28:15; 29:5; 30:2; 4; 13; 17(2); 19(2); 32:9; 11; 33:3(2); 37:22; 37; 39:1; 42:14; 47:14; 50:2(2); 51:17; 20; 52:14; 15; 59:10; 60:4; 14; 64:1; 2; 3; 66:2; 5; 8; **Jer** 1:15; 17; 2:12; 24; 3:17; 4:9; 11; 19; 26; 5:22; 6:4; 15(2); 7:2; 12; 8:1; 12; 16; 10:2(2); 10; 18; 11:12; 15:8; 17:11; 27; 18:7; 9; 20:16; 23:23; 32; 25:15; 17; 28; 33; 26:19; 27:18; 29:10; 25; 31:1; 12; 32:20; 33:7; 11; 15; 34:8; 14; 16(2); 35:11; 36:10; 17; 27; 39:10; 40:10; 41:3; 43:9; 44:1(3); 6; 22; 23; 45:1; 46:27; 47:3(3); 48:11; 41; 49:17; 21(2); 22; 50:11; 13; 14; 46; 51:31; 49; **Lam** 1:7; 20; 2:15(2); 3:56(2); **Eze** 2:6; 3:9; 15; 16; 17; 18; 20; 8:5; 16; 9:6(2); 10:19; 11:1; 12:4; 23; 14:3; 16:4(2); 25; 46(2); 57; 18:23; 20:32; 21:19; 21(2); 22; 22:13(2); 23:42; 24:18; 26:10; 15;

16(2); 18; 27:3; 28; 35; 36; 28:19; 29:7; 13; 30:18; 31:16; 32:10(2); 33:6; 7; 8; 34:10; 35:15; 36:8; 11; 37:22; 38:10; 11; 18; 20; 39:20; 40:40(2); 44(2); 41:12; 44:11; 17; 25; 46:2; 3; 19; 47:1; 7; 48:28; 32; 33; 34; **Dan** 1:5; 15; 18; 2:10; 3:5; 7; 8; 15; 4:4; 8; 29; 34; 36; 5:3; 6:24; 8:1; 2; 17; 19; 27; 9:7; 15; 21; 23; 10:3; 11:27(2); 29; 40(2); 43; 12:1(2); 13; **Hos** 1:5; 2:16; 4:12; 5:8; 9:10; 11:7; **Joel** 1:15; 2:1; 9; **Amos** 3:5; 9; 4:3(2); 4; 6:1; 7:13; 8:9; **Obad** 7; **Mic** 1:10(2); 3:4; 7:16; **Nah** 1:3; 5(2); 3:10; **Hab** 1:10; 2:3; 5; 19; 3:5; 11(2); 16; **Zeph** 1:7(2); 12; 2:4; 3:19; 20; **Zec** 1:11; 15; 3:1; 8; 7:5; 11:13; 12:8; 14:7; 14; **Mal** 1:10; 13; 2:7; 8; 13; **Mt** 3:2; 4:6; 17; 5:25; 34; 40; 7:13; 28; 8:6; 9:9; 10; 10:7; 35; 11:22; 25; 12:1; 41; 13:15; 49; 14:1; 9; 15:17; 30; 18:1; 29; 19:4; 22:33; 23:6; 24; 24:33; 41; 25:6; 27; 26:7; 18(2); 45; 46; 60; 27:15; **Mk** 1:15; 22; 32; 33; 2:14; 15; 4:12; 5:22; 23; 6:3; 7:25; 9:12; 10:22; 24; 11:1; 18; 12:2; 4; 17; 39; 13:29; 35(3); 14:3; 42; 54; 15:6; 34; 16:2; 14; **Lk** 1:10; 14; 29; 2:18; 33; 41; 47; 4:11; 18; 22; 32; 5:5; 8; 9; 27; 7:9; 37; 38; 49; 8:19; 26; 35; 41; 9:31; 43(2); 61(2); 10:14; 32; 39; 11:5; 32; 12:40; 46; 13:1; 24; 25; 14:10; 14; 15; 17; 15:29; 16:20; 17:16; 19:5; 23; 29; 30; 37; 42; 20:10; 26; 37; 40; 46; 21:30; 31; 34; 37; 22:27(2); 30; 40; 23:7(2); 11; 12; 17; 18; 24:12; 22; 27; 30; 47; **Jn** 1:18; 2:10; 13; 23; 4:21; 45(2); 46; 47; 52; 53; 5:2; 4; 28; 37; 6:21; 39; 40; 41; 44; 54; 61; 7:2; 11; 23; 8:7; 9; 59; 10:22; 40; 11:24; 32; 49; 55; 12:2; 16; 20; 13:28; 14:20; 16:4; 26; 18:16; 38; 39; 19:11; 39; 42; 20:11; 12(2); 19; 21:1; 20; **Acts** 1:6; 19; 2:5; 14; 3:1; 2; 10(2); 12; 4:6; 11; 18; 35; 37; 5:2; 9; 10; 15; 7:13; 26; 29; 31; 58; 8:1(2); 14; 35; 40; 9:10; 13; 19; 22; 27; 28; 32; 35; 36; 10:11; 25; 30; 11:8; 15; 12:13; 13:1; 5; 12; 27; 14:8; 15:14; 16:2; 4; 25; 17:13; 16; 30; 18:22; 24; 19:1; 17; 26; 27; 20:5; 14; 15(2); 16; 18; 21:3; 11; 13; 24; 22:3; 23:11; 23; 25:4; 8; 10; 15; 23; 24; 26:4(2); 13; 20; 32; 27:3; 28:12; **Rom** 1:10; 15; 3:26; 4:20; 8:34; 9:9; 32; 11:5; 13:12; 14:10; 15:26; 16:1; S:1; **1Cor** 1:2; 7:39; 8:10; 9:7; 13; 11:34; 14:16; 27; 35; 15:6; 23; 29; 32; 52; 16:8; 12(2); **2Cor** 1:1; 4:18(2); 5:6; 8:14; **Gal** 4:12; 13; **Eph** 1:1; 20; 2:12; 3:13; **Phil** 1:1; 2:10; 4:5; 10; **Col** 1:2; 2:1; **1Th** 2:2; 5; 19; 3:1; 13; 5:13; **2Th** 2:2; 3:11; **1Ti** 1:3; 5:4; **2Ti** 1:18; 2:26; 3:11(3); 4:1; 6; 8; 13; 16; 20(2); **Titus** 2:5; **Heb** 1:1; 5; 13; 2:1; 3; 7:13; 9:17; 12:2; 13:23; **Jas** 3:11; **1Pet** 1:7; 13; 2:8; 4:7; 17(2); 5:13; **1Jn** 1:5; 2:28; 4:12; **Rev** 1:3; 17; 3:20; 8:3; 18:14; 21; 22(2); 23(2); 19:2; 10; 21:12; 25; 22:10

AWAY

310, 1197, 1272, 1473, 1497, 1540, 1541, 1546, 1589, 1639, 1870, 1898, 1920, 2219, 2763, 2846, 2862, 3212, 3318, 3988, 4422, 5074, 5077, 5111, 5186, 5265, 5493, 5496, 5674, 5709, 5710, 6378, 7311, 7368, 7617, 7628, 7673, 7726, 7953, *115, 142, 337, 343, 520, 522, 565, 577, 580, 595, 617, 628, 630, 645, 646, 649, 654, 657, 665, 667, 683, 726, 851, 863, 868, 1294, 1544, 1593, 1599, 1601, 1602, 1808, 1813, 1821, 1854, 2210, 2673, 3179, 3334, 3350, 3351, 3895, 3911, 3928, 4014, 4879, 5217*

Gen 12:20; 15:11; 18:3; 21:14; 25; 24:54; 56; 59; 25:6; 26:27; 29; 31; 27:35; 36(2); 44; 45; 28:5; 6; 30:15; 23; 25; 31:1; 9; 18; 20; 26(2); 27(3); 42; 35:2; 38:19; 40:15; 42:36; 43:14; 44:3; 45:24; **Ex** 2:9; 17; 8:8; 28; 10:17; 19; 12:15; 28; 13:19; 22; 14:11; 15:15; 18:18; 19:24; 22:10; 23:25; 33:23; **Lev** 1:16; 3:4; 10; 15; 4:9; 31(2); 35(2); 6:2; 4; 7:4; 14:40; 43; 16:21; 21:7; 25:25; 26:39(2); 44; **Num** 4:13; 11:6; 14:43; 17:10; 20:21; 21:7; 24:22; 25:4; 11; 27:4; 32:15; 36:4; **Deut** 7:4; 15; 13:5(2); 10; 15:13; 16; 18; 17:7; 12; 17; 19:13; 19; 21:9; 21; 22:19; 21; 22; 24; 29; 23:14; 24:4; 7; 26:13; 14; 28:26; 31; 29:18; 30:17(2); **Josh** 2:21; 5:9; 7:13; 8:3; 16; 18:8; 22:6; 7; 16; 18; 24:14; 23; **Judg** 3:18; 4:15; 17; 5:21; 8:21; 9:21; 10:16; 11:13; 15; 38; 15:17; 16:3; 14; 18:24(2); 19:2; 20:13; 31; **1Sa** 1:14; 5:11; 6:3; 8; 7:3; 4; 9:26; 10:25; 14:16; 15:27; 17:26; 19:10; 17; 20:13; 22; 29; 21:6; 23:5; 26; 24:19; 25:10; 26:12; 27:9; 28:3; 25; 30:2; 18; 22; **2Sa** 1:21; 3:21; 22; 23; 24; 4:7; 11; 5:6; 7:15(2); 10:4; 12:13; 13:16; 17:18; 18:3; 9; 19:3; 41; 22:46; 23:6; 9; 24:10; **1Kin** 2:31; 39; 8:46; 48; 66; 11:2; 3; 4; 13; 14:8; 10(2); 26(3); 15:12; 22; 16:3; 19:4; 10; 14; 20:6; 24; 34(2); 41; 21:4; 21; 22:43; **2Kin** 2:3; 5; 9; 3:2; 4:27; 5:2; 11; 12; 6:23; 32; 7:15; 12:3; 18; 14:4; 17:6; 11; 23; 28; 33; 18:11; 22; 24; 32; 20:18; 23:11; 19; 24; 34; 24:14; 15; 25:11(2); 14; 15; 21; **1Chr** 5:6; 21; 26; 6:15; 7:21; 8:8; 13; 9:1; 10:12; 12:19; 14:14; 17:13; 19:4; 21:8; **2Chr** 6:36; 42; 7:10; 19; 9:12; 12:9(2); 14:3; 5; 13; 15; 15:8; 17; 16:6; 17:6; 19:3; 20:25(2); 33; 21:17; 25:12; 27; 28:5; 8(2); 17; 21; 29:6; 10; 19; 30:8; 9; 14(2); 32:12; 33:15; 34:33; 35:23; 36:20; **Ezr** 2:1(2); 5:12; 8:35; 9:4; 10:3; 6; 8; 19; **Neh** 7:6(2); **Est** 2:6(3); 4:4; 8:3; **Job** 1:15; 17; 21; 4:21; 6:15; 7:9; 21; 8:4; 20; 9:12; 25; 26; 34; 11:14; 16; 12:17; 19; 20(2); 24; 14:10; 19; 20; 15:12; 30; 20:8(2); 19; 28; 21:18; 22:9; 23; 24:2; 3; 10; 27:2; 8; 20; 21; 28:4; 30:12; 15; 32:22; 33:21; 34:5; 20(2); 36:18; **Ps** 1:4; 2:3; 18:22; 45; 27:9; 28:3; 31:13; 34:t, 37:20; 36; 39:10; 11; 48:5; 49:17; 51:11; 52:5; 55:6; 58:7; 8; 9; 64:8; 65:3; 66:20; 68:2(2); 69:4; 78:38; 39; 79:9; 85:3; 88:8; 90:5; 9; 10; 102:24; 104:7; 29; 106:23; 112:10; 119:37; 39; 119; 132:10; 137:3; 144:4; **Prov** 1:19; 32; 4:15; 16; 24; 6:33; 10:3; 14:32; 15:1; 19:26; 20:8; 30; 22:27; 23:5; 24:18; 25:4; 5; 10; 20; 23; 28:9; 29:8; 30:30; **Eccl** 1:4; 3:5; 6; 5:15; 11:10; **Song** 2:10; 13; 17; 4:6; 5:7; 6:5; **Is** 1:4; 13; 16; 25(2); 3:1; 18; 4:1; 4; 5:5; 23; 24; 25; 29; 6:7; 12; 8:4; 9:12; 17; 21; 10:2; 4; 27; 12:1; 15:6; 7; 16:10; 17:1; 18:5; 19:6; 7; 20:4; 22:4; 17; 24:4(2); 25:8(2); 27:9; 28:17; 29:5; 30:22; 31:7; 35:10; 36:7; 9; 17; 39:7; 40:24; 41:9; 16; 49:19; 25; 50:1(2); 5; 51:6; 11; 52:5; 57:1(2); 13; 58:9; 13; 59:13; 14; 64:6; **Jer** 1:3; 2:24; 3:1; 8; 19; 4:1; 4; 5:10; 25; 6:4; 29; 7:29; 33; 8:4; 13; 13:17; 19(2); 24; 15:15; 16:5; 18:20; 22:10; 23:2; 24:1; 5; 27:20; 28:3; 6; 29:1(2); 4(2); 7; 14(2); 32:40; 33:26; 37:13; 14; 38:22; 39:9(2); 40:1(2); 7; 41:10(2); 14; 43:3; 12; 46:5; 6; 15; 21; 48:9; 49:19; 29; 50:6; 17; 44; 51:50; 52:15(2); 18; 19; 27; 28; 29; 30; **Lam** 2:6; 14; 4:9; 15; 22; **Eze** 3:14; 4:17; 11:18; 14:6; 16:9; 50; 18:24; 26; 27; 28; 31; 20:7; 8; 23:25; 26; 29; 24:16; 23; 26:16; 30:4; 33:4; 6; 10; 34:4; 16; 36:26; 38:13(2); 43:9; 44:10(2); 22; 45:9; **Dan** 1:16; 2:35; 4:14; 7:12; 14; 26; 8:11; 9:16; 11:12; 31; 44; 12:11; **Hos** 1:6; 2:2; 9; 17; 4:3; 11; 5:14(2); 6:4; 9:11; 17; 13:3; 11; 14:2; 4; **Joel** 1:7; 12; **Amos** 1:3; 6(2); 9; 11; 13; 2:1; 4; 6; 16; 4:2; 10; 5:23; 6:3; 7:11; 12; 9:1; **Obad** 11; **Jonah** 3:9; **Mic** 1:11; 2:2; 4; 9; **Nah** 2:2; 7; 8; 3:10; 16; 17; **Zeph** 2:7; 3:11; 15; **Zec** 3:4; 7:11; 9:7; 10:11; 14:12(3); **Mal** 2:3; 6; 16; 3:7; **Mt** 1:11; 17(2); 19; 5:31; 32; 40; 42; 8:31; 13:6; 12; 19; 36; 48; 14:15; 22; 23; 15:23; 32; 39; 19:3; 7; 8; 9(2); 22; 21:19; 20; 22:13; 24:35(2); 39; 25:29; 46; 26:42(2); 44; 57; 27:2; 31; 64; 28:13; 16; **Mk** 1:43; 2:20; 21; 4:6; 15; 36; 5:10; 6:36; 45; 46; 8:3; 9; 26; 9:18; 10:2; 4; 11; 12; 22; 50; 11:21; 12:3; 4; 13:31(2); 14:36; 39; 44; 53; 15:1; 16; 16:3; 4; **Lk** 1:25; 53; 2:15; 5:35; 6:29; 30; 8:6; 12; 13; 38; 9:12(2); 25; 10:42; 11:52; 13:15; 16:3; 18(2); 17:31; 19:26; 20:10; 11; 21:24; 32; 33(2); 23:18; 26; 24:2; **Jn** 1:29; 4:8; 5:13; 6:22; 67; 10:40; 11:39; 41; 48; 12:11; 14:28; 15:2; 16:7(2); 18:13; 19:15(2); 16; 31; 38; 20:1; 2; 10; 13; 15; **Acts** 3:26; 5:37; 7:27; 43; 8:33; 39; 10:23; 13:3; 8; 17:10; 14; 19:26; 20:6; 30; 21:36; 22:16; 22; 24:7; 27:20; **Rom** 11:1; 2; 15; 26; 27; **1Cor** 5:2; 13; 7:11; 12; 31; 12:2; 13:8; 10; 11; **2Cor** 3:7; 11; 14(2); 16; 5:17; **Gal** 2:13; **Eph** 4:25; 31; **Col** 1:23; **2Th** 2:3; **1Ti** 1:19; **2Ti** 1:15; 3:5; 6; 4:4; **Heb** 6:6; 8:13; 9:26; 10:4; 9; 11; 35; 12:25; **Jas** 1:10; 11; 14; 4:14; **1Pet** 1:4; 24; 3:21; 5:4; **2Pet** 3:10; 17; **1Jn** 2:17; 3:5; **Rev** 7:17; 12:15; 16:20; 17:3; 20:11; 21:1; 4(2); 10; 22:19(2)

BACK

268, 310, 322, 1354, 1355, 1458, 1639, 1973, 2015, 2820, 3607, 4185, 4513, 5253, 5437, 5472, 5493, 5637, 6203, 6437, 6544, 7725, 7926, *617, 650, 3557, 3577, 3694, 4762, 5288, 5289, 5290*

Gen 14:16; 19:9; 26; 38:29; 39:9; **Ex** 14:21; 18:2; 23:4; 33:23; **Num** 9:7; 13:26; 22:34; 24:11; **Deut** 23:13; **Josh** 8:20; 26; 11:10; 23:12; **Judg** 11:35; 18:26; **Ruth** 1:15; 2:6; **1Sa** 10:9; 15:11; 25:34; **2Sa** 1:22; 12:23; 15:20; 25; 17:3; 18:16; 19:10; 11; 12; 37; 43; **1Kin** 13:18; 19; 20; 22; 23; 26; 29; 14:9; 28; 18:37; 19:20; 21; 22:26; 33; **2Kin** 1:5(2); 2:13; 24; 8:29; 15:20; 19:28; 20:9; **1Chr** 21:20; **2Chr** 13:14; 18:25; 32; 19:4; 25:13; 34:16; **Neh** 2:15; **Job** 23:12; 26:9; 33:18; 30; 34:27; 39:22; **Ps** 9:3; 14:7; 19:13; 21:12; 35:4; 44:10; 18; 53:6; 56:9; 70:3; 78:9; 41; 57; 80:18; 85:1; 114:3; 5; 129:3; 5; **Prov** 10:13; 19:29; 26:3; **Is** 14:27; 31:2; 37:29; 38:17; 42:17; 43:6; 50:5; 6; **Jer** 2:27; 4:8; 28; 6:9; 8:5; 11:10; 18:17; 21:4; 32:33; 38:22; 40:5(2); 42:4; 46:5(2); 21; 47:3; 48:10; 39; 49:8; **Lam** 1:13; 2:3; **Eze** 23:35; 24:14; 38:4; 8; 39:2; 44:1; **Dan** 7:6; **Hos** 4:16; **Nah** 2:8; **Zeph** 1:6; 3:20; **Mt** 24:18; 28:2; **Mk** 13:16; **Lk** 2:45; 8:37; 9:62; 17:15; 31; **Jn** 6:66; 20:14; **Acts** 5:2; 3; 7:39; 20:20; **Rom** 11:10; **Heb** 10:38; 39; **Jas** 5:4

BE

1510, 1961

Gen 1:3; 6; 9; 14(2); 15; 22; 28; 29; 2:18; 23; 24; 3:5(2); 6; 12; 16; 4:7(2); 12; 14(2); 15; 24; 6:3; 15; 19; 21; 8:17; 9:1; 2; 3; 6; 7; 11(2); 13; 14; 16; 20; 25(2); 26(2); 27; 10:8; 11:4; 6; 12:2; 3; 13; 13:8(2); 16; 14:19; 20; 15:4(2); 5(2); 13; 15; 16:2; 3; 5; 10; 12(2); 17:1; 4; 5(2); 7; 8; 10; 11; 12; 13(2); 14; 15; 16(2); 17; 18:4; 11; 18; 24; 25(3); 29; 30(2); 31; 32(2); 19:9; 15; 17; 22; 20:9; 21:10; 12(2); 30; 22:14; 18; 23:8; 24:5; 8(2); 14; 27; 41(2); 44; 51; 60; 25:22; 23(2); 24; 26:3; 4; 11; 22; 28; 27:13; 21; 29(3); 33; 39; 45; 28:3; 9; 14(2); 20; 21; 22; 29:4; 7; 8; 15; 26; 29; 34; 30:32; 33; 34; 31:3; 8(2); 30; 44; 52(2); 32:12; 18; 28; 33:14; 34:7; 10; 15(3); 17(2); 22(2); 23; 30; 35:2; 10(2); 11(2); 36:43; 37:14; 27; 32; 35; 38:9; 11; 15; 23; 24; 29; 39:10; 40:14; 41:21; 27; 30; 31(2); 36(2); 40(3); 52; 42:15; 16(3); 19(2); 20; 32; 33; 43:3; 5; 9; 11; 14; 23; 29; 44:9(2); 10(3); 17; 26(2); 30; 34; 45:5; 6; 10; 46:15; 47:19(2); 24; 25; 48:5; 6(2); 16; 19(2); 21; 49:6; 7; 8; 10; 12; 13(2); 17; 20; 26; 29; 50:18; **Ex** 1:16(2); 2:4; 3:12(2); 4:12; 14; 15; 16(4); 18; 5:8; 9; 11; 18; 21; 6:7; 14(2); 7:1; 17; 19; 8:10; 21; 22; 23; 9:3; 9; 15; 16; 19(2); 22; 28; 29; 10:5; 7; 10; 14; 21(2); 24; 26; 11:6(2); 9; 12:2(2); 4; 5; 13(2); 14; 15; 16(4); 19(3); 25; 32; 33; 42(2); 46; 48(2); 49; 13:3; 5; 6; 7(3); 9(2); 11; 12; 14; 16; 14:4; 15:9; 14; 15; 16; 16:5; 8; 12; 23; 26; 32; 33; 34; 17:4; 18:10; 19(2); 21; 22(2); 23; 19:5; 6; 11; 12; 13(2); 15; 20:12; 20; 26; 21:4; 7; 8; 12; 15; 16(2); 17; 19(2); 20; 21; 22; 28(3); 29(2); 30; 31; 32; 34; 36(2); 22:2(3); 3(3); 4(2); 5; 6; 7(2); 8(2); 9(2); 10; 11; 12; 13; 14; 15(2); 16; 19; 20; 24; 25; 30; 31; 23:1; 12; 13(2); 22; 26; 30; 33; 24:7; 12; 25:7; 10; 12; 14; 15(2); 17; 20; 23; 27; 28; 31(2); 34; 35; 36(2); 38; 26:2; 3(2); 6; 7; 8(2); 11; 16(2); 17; 20; 24(4); 25; 31; 32; 37; 27:1(2); 2; 5; 7(2); 9; 10(2); 11; 12; 13; 14; 15; 16(2); 17(2); 18; 19; 21; 28:7; 8; 11; 16(3); 17(2); 18; 20; 21(2); 28(2); 30; 32(2); 35(2); 37(2); 38(3); 43(2); 29:9; 10; 21; 26; 28(2); 29(3); 34; 37(2); 42; 43; 45; 30:2(4); 4; 12; 13; 16; 21; 25; 29(2); 31; 32(2); 33; 34; 36; 37; 38; 31:14(2); 15(2); 32:4; 8; 33:16(2); 19(2); 23; 34:2; 3; 12; 25; 35:2(3); 9; 27; 29; 36:6; 18; 34; 37:3; 27; 38:5; 26; 39:7; 21(2); 37; 40:4; 9; 10; 15; **Lev** 1:3; 4; 9; 10; 14; 15; 2:1; 2; 3; 4; 5(2); 7(2); 10; 11; 12; 13; 3:1(2); 6; 12; 17; 4:2; 12; 13(2); 15; 20; 22; 26; 27(2); 31; 35; 5:2(3); 3(4); 4(3); 5(2); 7; 9; 10; 11; 13(2); 16; 17; 18; 6:4; 7; 9; 12(2); 13; 16; 17; 18(2); 21; 22; 23(2); 25; 26; 27; 28(3); 30(2); 7:6; 9; 14; 15; 16(3); 17; 18(4); 19(3); 20; 21; 24; 25; 26; 27(2); 30; 31; 36; 8:5; 33; 10:3(2); 9; 14; 15; 11:7; 10; 11; 12; 13; 20; 23; 24(2); 25; 26; 27; 28; 29; 31(2); 32(6); 33; 34(4); 35(4); 36(2); 37(2); 38(2); 39; 40(2); 41(2); 43; 44; 45(2); 47(2); 12:2(2); 3; 4; 5; 7; 8(2); 13:2(2); 3; 4(3); 5; 6(2); 7; 9; 10(2); 14; 15; 16; 17; 19(2); 20(2); 21(3); 24; 25(2); 26(3); 27; 28; 30(2); 31; 32(2); 33; 34(3); 36; 37; 39; 42; 43; 45; 46(3); 47; 48; 49(2); 51; 52; 53; 55(2); 56; 58(4); 14:2(2); 3; 4; 5; 7; 8(2); 9(2); 11; 14; 17; 18; 19; 20; 21(2); 22; 25; 28; 29; 31; 34; 36; 37; 39; 41; 44; 46; 53; 15:3(2); 4; 5; 6; 7; 8; 9; 10(2); 11; 12(2); 13; 16; 17(2); 18; 19(3); 20(2); 21; 22; 23(2); 24(3); 25(2); 26(2); 27(2); 28(2); 16:4(2); 10(2); 17; 29(2); 30; 31; 34; 17:3; 4(2); 7; 8; 9; 10; 13(2); 14; 15(3); 18:9; 29; 19:2; 6(2); 7(2); 8; 20(2); 22; 23(2); 24; 29; 31; 34; 20:2(2); 7; 9(2); 10; 11(2); 12(2); 13(2); 14(2); 15; 16(2); 17; 18; 21; 26(2); 27(2); 21:1; 3; 6(2); 8; 9; 17; 18; 20; 22:3(2); 4; 5; 6; 7; 12; 13; 18; 20; 21(3); 23; 25(2); 27(2); 28; 30; 32; 33; 23:2; 3; 10; 11; 13(2); 14; 15; 17(2); 18; 20; 21(2); 27(2); 29(3); 30; 31; 32; 34; 35; 36; 37; 39(2); 41; 24:3; 5; 7; 9; 12; 16(2); 17; 19; 20; 21; 25:4; 6; 7; 8; 10; 11; 12; 23; 25; 26; 28; 30(2); 31(2); 34; 35(2); 38; 39(2); 40; 42; 44; 45; 46; 48; 49; 50(2); 51; 53; 54; 26:12(2); 13; 17; 20; 22; 23; 25; 26; 32; 33; 34; 41; 43; 44; 45; 27:2; 3(2); 4(2); 5(2); 6(3); 7(3); 8; 9(2); 10; 11; 12(2); 14(2); 15; 16(2); 18; 19; 20; 21(2); 25(2); 26(2); 27(3); 28; 29(3); 32; 33(3); **Num** 1:4; 51(2); 53; 2:3; 5(2); 7; 10(2); 12(2); 14; 18(2); 20(2); 22; 25(2); 27(2); 29; 3:10; 12; 13; 24; 25; 30; 31; 32; 36; 38(2); 45; 46; 48; 4:4; 7; 27; 28; 45; 5:6; 8(2); 9; 10(2); 13(5); 14(4); 19; 20; 27(2); 28(3); 30; 31; 6:5(2); 12; 13; 25; 7:5; 8:14; 19; 9:10(2); 13; 10:7; 8; 9(2); 10; 31; 32(2); 35; 11:16; 20; 22(2); 12:6; 12; 14(3); 13:18; 19(2); 20(3); 28; 31; 14:3; 11; 17; 21; 31; 33; 35; 40; 42; 43; 15:2; 11; 14; 15(2); 16; 19; 24(2); 25; 26; 28; 30(2); 31(2); 34; 35; 39; 40; 41; 16:7(2); 16; 22; 26; 29; 38; 40(2); 17:3; 10; 13; 18:2; 4; 5; 7; 9(2); 10; 13; 14; 15(2); 16; 18; 23; 27; 30; 19:7; 8; 9; 10(2); 11; 12(3); 13(2); 14; 16; 17; 19; 20(2); 21(2); 22(2); 20:24; 26; 21:22; 27; 22:11; 23:9; 10; 23; 24:7(3); 18(2); 20; 22; 25:4; 26:53; 54; 55; 56; 27:4; 11; 13; 17; 20; 28:7(2); 14; 15; 17; 18; 19; 20; 24; 26; 31; 29:3; 8; 9; 13; 14; 18; 21; 24; 27; 30; 33; 37; 31:2; 23(2); 24; 32:5; 22(3); 23; 26; 29; 32; 33:54; 55; 34:3(2); 4; 5; 6; 7; 8; 9(2); 12(2); 35:3; 5(2); 6; 7; 8; 10; 11; 12; 14; 15; 16; 17; 18; 21; 27; 29; 30; 31; 33; 36:3(4); 4(3); 8; **Deut** 1:1; 17; 21; 29; 39; 42; 2:4; 25; 4:19; 20; 26; 27; 30; 5:16; 29; 33; 6:2; 3; 6; 8; 10; 11; 15; 18; 25; 7:4; 6; 10; 14(2); 16; 18; 20; 21; 23; 24; 25; 26; 8:14; 19; 20; 10:5; 16; 11:8; 15; 16; 17(2); 18; 21; 24(2); 25; 12:11; 21; 23; 27; 30(2); 13:5; 9; 14; 16(2); 14:2; 19; 24(2); 29; 15:4; 7; 9(3); 10; 12; 16; 17; 21(2); 16:4; 8; 17:2; 4(2); 6(2); 7; 9; 18; 19; 20; 18:3(2); 10; 13; 22; 19:10(2); 15; 17; 18; 20:1; 2; 3; 9; 11(3); 20(2); 21:1(2); 3; 5; 8(2); 13(2); 14; 15; 16; 22(2); 23; 22:2(2); 6(2); 7; 9; 19; 20(2); 22; 23; 28; 29; 23:10; 11; 13; 14; 17; 21; 22; 24:2; 3; 4; 5(2); 7; 12; 13; 14; 15; 16(3); 19; 20; 21; 25:1; 2(4); 6(2); 9; 10; 15; 19; 26:1; 3; 12; 17; 18; 19; 27:2; 4(2); 15; 16; 17; 18; 19; 20; 21; 22; 23; 24; 25; 26; 28:3(2); 4; 5; 6(2); 7; 10; 13(2); 16(2); 17; 18; 19(2); 20; 23(2); 24; 25(2); 26; 27; 29; 31(4); 32(2); 33; 34; 35; 44(2); 45; 46; 51; 54; 56; 61; 62; 63; 68; 29:13; 18(2); 30:4; 17; 31:6(2); 7; 8(2); 16; 17(2); 19; 21; 23(2); 26; 32:20; 24; 38; 43; 50; 33:6; 7(2); 8; 13; 20; 24(2); 25(2); 28; 29; **Josh** 1:4; 5(2); 6; 7; 9(3); 17; 18(3); 2:3; 14; 16; 17; 19(6); 20; 21; 3:4; 7; 13; 4:6; 7; 6:17; 26; 7:12; 14(2); 15(2); 8:1; 4; 8; 9:6; 13; 20; 21; 23; 10:25(2); 11:6; 13:1; 14:9; 12(3); 15:4; 17:15(2); 18(3); 20:3; 6; 21:13; 21; 27; 32; 38; 22:18(2); 19; 22; 27; 28; 34; 23:4; 6; 13; 16; 24:27(2); **Judg** 2:3(2); 3:6; 4:9; 20; 5:24(2); 31; 6:13(2); 16; 23; 31(2); 37(2); 39(3); 7:4; 11; 17; 8:5; 9:9; 11; 13; 24; 31; 33; 10:18; 11:6; 8; 9; 10; 26; 27; 31(2); 37; 13:5; 7; 8; 14:11; 15:3; 7; 16:6; 7(2); 9; 10; 11(2); 12; 13; 14; 17(2); 20; 28; 17:2; 10; 18:5; 9; 19(3); 25; 19:6(2); 9; 20; 28; 20:9; 21:3; 5; 17(3); 18; 22(3); **Ruth** 1:11; 16; 17; 2:4; 9; 12; 13; 19; 20; 3:1; 4; 10; 13; 14; 18; 4:10(2); 11; 12;

14(2); 15; **1Sa** 1:14; 22; 28; 2:9; 10; 28; 30(2); 31; 32; 33; 34; 3:9; 14; 20; 4:9(2); 19; 5:8; 6:3(2); 4; 8:11(2); 13(3); 17; 20; 9:13(2); 16; 10:1; 6; 7; 21; 11:3; 7; 9; 13; 12:15; 25; 13:14; 14:6; 10; 21; 24(2); 28; 39; 40(2); 15:1; 11; 13; 18; 33; 16:16; 17:9(3); 25; 26; 27; 36; 37; 18:17(3); 18; 21(3); 22; 23; 25; 26; 27; 19:6; 11; 22; 20:3; 7(2); 8; 9; 12; 13; 18(2); 23; 29; 31; 32; 42; 22:3; 15; 23; 23:3; 17(2); 20; 21; 23; 24:12; 13; 15; 20(2); 25:6(3); 10; 11; 24; 26; 27; 29; 31; 32; 33(2); 39; 41; 26:9; 19(2); 24; 25; 27:11; 12; 28:13; 19; 29:4(2); 10; 30:24; **2Sa** 1:5; 16; 21(2); 2:5; 7(2); 26(2); 3:12; 17; 35; 39; 5:2; 8; 14; 24; 6:22(3); 7:8; 11; 12; 14(2); 16(2); 24; 26(2); 28; 29; 10:5; 11(2); 12; 11:15; 20; 24; 12:9; 10; 22; 28; 13:12; 13; 15; 25; 28(2); 14:2(2); 9(2); 14(2); 15; 17(2); 25; 32; 15:20; 21(2); 33; 34(2); 35; 16:2(2); 12; 18; 19; 21; 17:3; 8(2); 9; 10; 11; 12(2); 13(2); 16; 17; 20; 18:25; 28; 32; 19:7; 13; 21; 22(2); 35; 37; 42; 43; 20:1; 4; 20(2); 21; 21:5; 6; 22:4(2); 44; 45; 46; 47(2); 23:1; 3; 4; 5; 6(2); 7(2); 8; 17; 24:3; 13; 17; 21; 22; **1Kin** 1:2; 5; 21; 35(2); 37; 48; 52; 2:2; 7; 19; 21; 24; 33; 37(2); 39; 45(2); 3:8; 13; 26; 5:6; 7; 9; 6:6; 8:5; 15; 16(2); 26; 29(2); 31; 33; 37(4); 38; 46; 51; 52; 53; 56; 57; 59; 61; 9:3; 7; 8; 10:9; 27(2); 11:37; 38(2); 12:7(2); 10; 13:2(2); 3(2); 6; 14:2(3); 5(2); 6; 10; 17:1; 4; 18:21; 24; 27; 31; 36; 19:15; 16(2); 20:6; 18(2); 23; 25; 39(2); 40; 21:7; 22:3; 13; 22; **2Kin** 1:10; 12; 13; 14; 15; 2:9(2); 10(2); 16; 21; 3:17; 4:1; 10; 13(2); 14; 23; 5:10; 12; 13; 17; 22; 23; 6:3; 8; 16(2); 7:1; 2; 12; 18; 19; 8:13; 29; 9:10; 15(2); 37; 10:6; 9; 15; 19(2); 23; 24; 11:5; 6(2); 8(2); 15; 17; 12:5; 15; 14:6(3); 15:19; 16:15; 18:23; 29; 30; 19:4; 6; 10; 11; 25; 26; 29; 20:8; 17(2); 18; 19; 22:17(2); 20; 23:27; 25:12; 24(2); **1Chr** 1:10; 4:10; 5:1; 6:17; 9:22; 11:2; 6; 12:17(3); 18(2); 13:2; 14:15; 15:16; 16:15; 25(2); 30(2); 31; 36; 38; 17:7; 9; 10; 11(3); 13(2); 14; 21; 23; 24(3); 27(2); 19:5; 12(2); 13; 21:3(2); 12; 17(3); 22; 22:5(2); 9(3); 10(2); 11; 13(2); 16(2); 19; 28:4(2); 6(2); 7; 9; 10; 20(3); 21(3); 29:2(2); 5; 10; 14; 22(2); **2Chr** 1:9; 2:8; 9; 12; 14; 18(2); 4:18; 5:6; 13; 6:4; 5(2); 6(2); 17; 20; 22; 24; 28(4); 29; 36; 40(2); 41; 7:13; 15; 16(2); 18; 20; 21; 22; 9:8(2); 10:7(2); 10; 11:22; 12:7; 8; 13:8; 9; 15:2(2); 7(3); 13; 18:3; 10; 12; 14; 21; 19:7; 11(2); 20:2; 15; 17(2); 20; 22:6; 23:4; 5(2); 7(2); 14; 16; 25:8; 14; 16; 26:15; 18; 29:11; 24; 30:7; 8; 19; 31:4; 32:7(3); 14; 33:4; 34:25(2); 28; 35:3; 36:22; 23; **Ezr** 1:1; 3; 4:12; 13(2); 15; 16; 21(2); 5:8; 15; 17(2); 6:3(2); 4; 5; 6; 8(2); 9; 11(3); 12; 7:20; 21; 23(2); 24; 26(2); 27; 9:12; 14(2); 10:3; 4(2); 8; 14; **Neh** 1:6; 11; 2:3; 6; 7; 17; 4:5; 7; 12; 14; 22; 5:5; 8; 13; 14; 6:6; 7; 9(2); 13; 7:3(3); 5; 8:10; 11; 9:5; 10:38; 11:23; 13:5; 19(4); **Est** 1:17(2); 19(2); 20; 22; 2:2; 3; 4; 9; 3:9(2); 14(2); 4:14; 5:3; 6(2); 14(3); 6:6; 8; 9(2); 11; 13; 7:2(2); 3; 4(2); 8:5(2); 13(2); 9:1; 12(2); 13(2); 14; 25; 28; **Job** 1:5; 21; 3:4; 6; 7; 9; 17; 4:2; 17(2); 5:1; 11(2); 21(2); 22; 23(2); 24; 25; 6:3; 6; 14; 28; 29; 7:4; 21; 8:2; 14(2); 22; 9:2; 29; 10:15(2); 11:2(2); 12(2); 14; 15; 17(2); 18; 20; 12:14(2); 13:5; 16; 18; 14:7; 12(2); 13; 15:14(2); 29; 31; 32(2); 34; 17:8; 9; 18:2; 4(2); 5; 6(2); 7; 12(2); 14; 15; 16(2); 18; 20; 19:4; 27; 29; 20:8(2); 12; 18; 21; 22; 26; 21:2; 4; 5; 30; 32; 33; 22:2(2); 21; 23; 25; 28; 23:7; 24:20(2); 23(2); 25; 25:4(2); 27:7; 14(2); 15; 19; 28:12; 15(2); 16; 17; 18; 19; 31:6; 8; 11; 22; 28; 31; 32:20; 33:3; 7; 21; 23; 25; 26; 30; 34:10; 20(2); 29; 30; 31; 33; 36; 35:2; 3(2); 6; 7; 36:4; 8(2); 16(2); 26; 37:6; 20(2); 38:11; 13; 15; 39:9; 40:8; 41:9; 17; 23; 32; 42:2; **Ps** 1:3; 2:10(2); 12; 3:2; 6; 4:4; 6; 5:11; 6:10(2); 7:3; 9:2; 9; 17; 18; 19; 20; 10:2; 6(2); 11:3; 6; 13:2; 14:7; 15:5; 16:4; 8; 17:15; 18:3(2); 45; 46(2); 19:10; 13(2); 14; 21:7; 13; 22:11; 19; 25; 26; 29; 30; 31; 24:7; 25:2; 3(2); 20; 26:11; 27:1; 3; 6; 14; 28:1(2); 6; 30:6; 10; 12; 31:1; 2; 7; 17(3); 18; 21; 24; 32:6; 9(2); 10; 11; 33:22; 34:1; 2; 18; 21; 22; 35:4(2); 5; 6; 9; 22; 26(2); 27(2); 36:2(2); 3; 8; 12; 37:1; 2; 3; 9; 10(2); 14; 15; 17; 18; 19(2); 20; 22(3); 24; 28; 36; 38(2); 38:18; 21; 39:13; 40:5(2); 13; 14(2); 15; 16(2); 41:2; 4; 10; 13; 42:8; 45:12; 14(2); 15; 16; 17; 46:2(2); 3; 5; 10(3); 48:1; 11; 14; 49:3; 16; 50:3; 22; 51:4(2); 7(2); 13; 19; 53:6; 55:6; 20; 22; 56:1; 2; 11; 57:1(3); 5(2); 11(2); 58:3; 7; 59:5; 12; 13; 15; 60:4; 5; 62:2; 3(2); 6; 9; 63:5; 10; 11; 64:7; 10; 65:1; 4; 66:8; 9; 20; 67:1; 2; 4; 68:1; 3; 13; 19; 23; 35; 69:6(2); 14; 23; 25; 28(2); 32; 70:2(2); 3; 4(2); 71:1; 3; 6; 8; 12; 13(2); 72:14; 15(3); 16; 17(2); 18; 19(2); 74:14; 75:10; 76:7; 8; 11(2); 77:2; 7; 9; 78:6; 8; 79:2; 5; 10; 80:3; 4; 7; 17; 19; 81:9; 83:1; 4; 17(2); 84:4; 10; 85:5; 86:3; 17; 87:5; 7; 88:11; 12; 89:2; 6(2); 7(2); 16; 17; 21; 24(2); 37; 52; 90:10; 14; 17; 91:4; 5; 15; 92:7; 9; 10; 13; 14; 93:1; 94:8; 13; 96:4(2); 10(2); 11; 12; 97:1; 7; 98:8; 99:1; 100:4; 101:6; 102:18(2); 26; 28; 104:5; 34(2); 35(2); 106:8; 46; 48; 107:30; 108:5; 6; 109:7(2); 8; 9; 10; 12(2); 13(2); 14(2); 15; 17; 19; 20; 28; 29; 110:3; 111:4; 5; 112:2(2); 3; 6(2); 7; 8; 9; 10; 113:2; 3; 9; 118:24; 26; 119:6; 46; 58; 74; 76; 78; 80(2); 116; 117; 122; 128; 132; 120:3(2); 121:3; 122:7; 8; 124:6; 125:1(2); 4; 5; 127:5; 128:2(2); 3; 4; 129:5; 6; 8; 130:2; 4; 132:9; 135:21; 137:8(2); 9; 138:6; 139:11; 24; 140:10; 11; 141:2; 5(3); 143:2; 7; 144:1; 12(2); 13; 14(3); 145:3; 14; 148:4; 149:2; 5; 6; **Prov** 1:9; 31; 33; 2:22(2); 3:7; 8; 10; 11; 15; 22; 24(2); 25; 26; 35; 4:10; 12; 26; 5:10(2); 16; 17; 18; 19(2); 20; 22; 6:1; 6; 15; 18; 27; 28; 29; 31; 33; 8:5; 6; 11(2); 33; 9:9; 11(2); 12(2); 10:9; 24; 27; 28; 29; 30; 31; 11:6; 9; 18; 21(2); 25(2); 26; 29; 31; 12:3(2); 8(2); 11; 14(2); 19; 21; 24; 13:4; 9; 11; 13(2); 18(2); 20(2); 21; 14:11; 14(2); 22; 16:3; 5; 7; 16; 19; 21; 31; 17:5; 11; 14; 18:19; 20(2); 19:2; 5; 9; 20; 23; 20:3; 11(2); 13; 17; 20; 21(2); 21:13; 15; 17(2); 18; 20; 22:1; 5; 9; 11; 13; 18; 19; 26; 23:2; 3; 4; 15; 17; 18; 19; 20; 25; 34; 24:1(2); 4; 8; 11; 14(3); 17; 19; 20(2); 25; 28; 25:5; 7(2); 16; 17; 21(2); 26:4; 5; 26; 27:11; 14; 18; 23; 28:2; 6; 9; 18; 20(2); 22; 25; 26; 29:1; 14; 19; 25; 30:6; 9(2); 10; 18; 24; 29; 31:6; 30; **Eccl** 1:9(2); 10; 11; 13; 15(2); 2:16; 18; 19; 3:2; 10; 14(2); 15; 22; 4:11; 13; 5:1; 2(3); 6; 8; 10; 6:3(2); 4; 11; 12; 7:9(2); 14; 16; 17(2); 23; 26; 8:1; 3; 7(2); 12(2); 13; 14(2); 15; 17; 9:8; 10:9(2); 10; 14(2); 11:2; 3(2); 6; 8; 12:2; 3; 4(2); 5(3); 6(3); 12; 14(2); **Song** 1:4; 7; 2:17; 7:8; 8:1; 3; 7; 8; 9(2); 14; **Is** 1:5; 18(4); 19; 20; 26; 27; 28(2); 29(2); 30; 31; 2:2(2); 6; 11(3); 12(2); 17(3); 22; 3:4; 5; 6(2); 7; 10; 11(2); 24; 4:1; 2(2); 3; 5; 6; 5:5(2); 6; 8(2); 9; 15(3); 16(2); 24; 27(3); 28; 29; 6:10; 11(2); 12; 13(3); 7:4(2); 8(2); 9; 16; 23(2); 25(2); 8:4; 9(3); 12; 13(2); 14; 15(3); 21; 22; 9:1; 5; 6(2); 7; 19; 20(2); 21; 10:2; 17; 18; 19; 22; 24; 27(2); 30; 33(2); 11:5; 9; 10(2); 11; 13; 16(2); 12:2; 13:7; 8(4); 10; 14; 15; 16(2); 19; 20(2); 21; 22; 14:1; 14; 15; 20(2); 29; 31; 15:2; 4(2); 6; 9; 16:2(2); 4; 5; 6; 10(2); 14(2); 17:1; 2; 3; 4; 5(2); 6; 9(2); 11; 13; 18:6; 7; 19:1; 5; 6; 7(2); 9; 10; 15; 16(2); 17(2); 18; 19; 20; 21; 22; 23; 24; 25; 20:5; 6; 21:17; 22:7; 14; 18; 21; 23; 25(3); 23:2; 4; 5; 15; 16; 18(3); 24:2; 3; 9; 13(2); 18; 20(2); 22(3); 23; 25:2(2); 5; 9(2); 10; 26:1; 10; 11; 20; 27:9; 10; 11; 12; 13; 28:3; 4; 5; 10; 13; 18(2); 19; 21; 22(2); 28; 29:2(2); 4(3); 5(3); 6; 7; 8(2); 14; 16; 17(2); 22; 30:3; 5; 8; 13; 14; 15(2); 16; 17; 18(2); 19; 20; 23; 25; 26(2); 28; 30; 31; 32; 31:4; 8; 9; 32:2; 3; 4; 5(2); 10; 11; 14(3); 15(3); 17; 19; 33:1; 2(2); 4; 6; 10; 12(2); 16(3); 20(3); 21; 24; 34:3(2); 4(2); 5; 7; 9; 10; 12(2); 13; 15; 35:1; 2; 4; 5(2); 7; 8(3); 9(2); 36:8; 14; 15; 37:4; 6; 10; 11; 26; 27; 30; 38:7; 39:6(2); 7; 8; 40:4(3); 5; 9; 20; 24(2); 25; 30; 31; 41:6; 7; 10; 11(2); 12; 22; 23; 42:2; 4; 17(2); 43:2(2); 9(3); 10; 26; 44:8; 9; 11(3); 15; 21; 26(2); 27; 28(2); 45:1; 14; 16; 17(2); 18; 22; 24; 25; 46:5; 13; 47:1; 3(2); 5; 7; 11; 12(3); 14(2); 15; 48:11; 14; 49:3; 5(4); 6(2); 9; 11; 13; 19(2); 22; 23(2); 24; 25(2); 26; 50:7(2); 51:3; 6(2); 7; 8; 11; 12(2); 14; 19; 52:3; 11; 12; 13(2); 53:11; 54:3; 4(3); 5; 9; 10(2); 13(2); 14(2); 55:6; 11; 12; 13(2); 56:1; 5; 6; 7(2); 12; 57:16; 58:4; 8; 10; 11; 12(2); 60:2; 4; 5(2); 7; 11(3); 12; 18; 19(2); 20(2); 21(2); 61:3(2); 5; 6; 7; 9; 10; 62:2; 3; 4(4); 8; 12; 63:3; 10; 16; 64:5; 9; 65:10; 13(3); 17; 18; 19; 20(2); 25; 66:5(2); 8(2); 10; 11(2); 12(2); 13; 14; 16; 17; 24(2); **Jer** 1:8; 17; 2:10; 12(3); 36; 3:1; 3; 16(2); 17; 4:7; 9; 11; 13; 14; 27; 28; 29; 5:1; 6; 9; 13; 29; 6:6; 8; 11; 12; 15; 22; 7:20(2); 23(3); 32(2); 33; 34; 8:2(3); 3; 12; 13; 14; 17; 9:2; 9; 10:2; 5(2); 10; 21; 11:3; 4(2); 5; 11; 19; 23; 12:13; 16; 13:10; 11; 12(2); 15; 19(3); 21; 27(2); 14:8; 9; 15(2); 16; 15:1; 4; 11; 18(2); 19; 16:4(5); 6; 14; 17:5; 6; 8(3); 11; 13(2); 14(2); 17; 18(4); 27; 18:14; 16; 20; 21(4); 22; 23; 19:6; 7; 8; 11(2); 13; 20:6; 10; 11(2); 14(2); 15; 16; 17; 18; 21:2; 9; 10; 22:19; 22; 23; 23:1; 3; 4(2); 6(2); 12(2); 26; 36; 40; 24:2; 3; 7(2); 8; 9(2); 10; 25:11; 16(2); 27; 28; 29(2); 32; 33(3); 36; 26:3; 9(2); 18; 27:16; 17; 18(2); 22(2); 28:9; 29:4; 6; 7; 8(2); 10; 14(2); 17; 18(2); 22; 26; 30:7; 10(3); 13; 16(2); 18; 19(2); 20(2); 21; 22(2); 31:1(2); 4(2); 6; 12; 14; 15; 16; 18; 30; 33(3); 37; 38; 40(2); 32:4; 5; 15; 36; 38(2); 43; 33:9; 10(2); 12; 16(2); 20; 21; 22; 24; 25; 26; 34:3; 16; 17; 20; 35:7; 36:3; 7; 19; 30; 37:17; 20; 38:3; 4; 17; 18; 20; 22; 23(2); 39:16; 17; 18; 40:9; 15; 42:2; 5; 6(3); 11(2); 17; 18(2); 44:8(2); 12(3); 26; 27(2); 29; 46:10; 11; 19; 23; 24(2); 26; 27(2); 47:2; 6(3); 7; 48:2(2); 3; 4; 6; 7; 8; 9; 10(2); 13; 26; 28; 30; 33; 34; 37(2); 38; 39; 41; 42; 43; 44; 46; 49:2(4); 5(2); 10; 13; 17(2); 22; 23; 26; 32; 33; 36; 37; 50:5; 8; 9(2); 10(2); 12(3); 13(3); 19; 20(3); 26; 30; 36; 37; 38; 39(2); 41; 51:2; 6; 8(2); 26; 29; 35; 46; 47; 58(3); 62; 63; 64; **Lam** 1:12; 17; 21; 2:6; 20; 3:6; 29(2); 4:9(2); 21(2); 5:6; 21; **Eze** 2:6(6); 8; 3:9(2); 12; 20; 26(2); 4:3(2); 7; 10; 17; 5:12; 13(2); 15; 16; 6:4(2); 6(6); 8; 9; 13; 7:4; 11; 16; 17(2); 18; 19(2); 24; 25; 26; 27(2); 9:4; 11:3; 11(2); 16; 20(2); 12:3(2); 11; 13; 19; 20(2); 24; 25; 28(2); 13:9(3); 11; 12; 13; 14(2); 21(2); 14:3; 9; 10; 11(3); 15; 16(2); 18; 22(3); 15:3; 5; 16:16; 20; 25; 28; 42(2); 52; 54; 61; 63; 17:8; 14; 15; 20; 21; 23; 18:5; 13; 20(2); 22; 24; 30; 19:9; 14(2); 20:3; 9; 12; 14; 20; 22; 31(2); 32(2); 41; 47(2); 48; 21:7(4); 11(2); 12(3); 13; 14; 15; 23(2); 24(2); 26; 27; 32(3); 22:5(2); 14; 21; 22; 23:25; 29; 32; 33; 46; 48; 24:8; 10; 11(3); 12; 13; 23; 25; 27(3); 25:10; 26:2; 5; 6; 13; 14(2); 16; 17; 18; 20; 21(3); 27:7; 30; 34; 35(3); 36(2); 28:9; 19(3); 22(2); 23; 24; 25; 29:5; 7; 9; 11; 12; 14; 15; 16; 19; 30:3; 4(2); 7(2); 8; 11; 13; 16; 18; 21(2); 31:13; 16; 17; 18(2); 32:6; 10; 12; 15; 19; 25; 27; 28; 30(2); 31; 32; 33:4; 5; 6; 10; 12; 13; 16; 27(2); 28; 34:2; 10; 14; 22; 23; 24; 26; 27; 28; 29; 35:4; 10; 15; 36:3; 9; 10(2); 12; 23; 25; 28(2); 32(2); 33; 34; 37; 38; 37:19; 20; 21; 22(3); 23(2); 24; 25; 26; 27(3); 28; 38:7(2); 8; 9; 16(2); 19; 20; 21; 23; 39:4; 12; 13(2); 16; 19(2); 20; 25; 28; 42:13; 43:10; 11; 12; 13(3); 14(2); 15(2); 16; 17(3); 19; 27; 44:2(3); 7; 11; 14; 17; 28; 29; 30; 31; 45:1(3); 2; 3; 4(2); 6; 7(2); 8; 11(2); 12(2); 17; 21; 46:1(3); 2; 4; 5(2); 6(2); 11; 16(2); 17(2); 18; 47:5; 8; 9(2); 10(2); 11(2); 12(2); 13; 15; 17; 20; 22; 48:8(2); 9; 10(2); 11; 12; 13; 15(2); 16; 17; 18(3); 20; 21(3); 22; 28; 31; 35; **Dan** 1:13; 2:5(2); 9; 13(2); 20; 28; 40; 41(2); 42; 44(2); 3:6; 11; 15(2); 17; 18; 19; 28; 29(2); 4:1; 15(2); 16(2); 19; 23(2); 25; 26; 27(2); 32; 5:7(2); 10; 12; 16(2); 17; 29; 6:1; 7; 8; 12; 15; 17; 25; 26(2); 7:14; 23(2); 24; 25; 27; 8:13(2); 14; 17; 19(2); 24; 25; 26; 9:16; 25(2); 26(2); 27; 10:19(3); 11:2; 4(3); 5(3); 6; 10(2); 11(2); 12(2); 15; 16; 17; 19; 20; 22(2); 25; 27(2); 28; 29; 30; 32; 34; 36(2); 41; 43; 12:1(3); 3; 4; 6; 7(2); 8; 10; 11(2); 13; **Hos** 1:9; 10(3); 11(2); 2:4; 16; 17; 3:3(2); 4:3; 6; 9; 19; 5:9(2); 12; 14; 7:4; 16; 8:4; 5; 6; 7; 8; 11; 9:4(3); 6; 12; 17; 10:2; 6(2); 8; 10; 14; 15; 11:5; 13:3; 7; 10; 14(3); 15(2); 16(2); 14:5; 6; 7; **Joel** 1:11; 2:2; 6; 8; 10; 18; 19; 21; 22; 23; 24; 26(2); 27; 31; 32(2); 3:12; 15; 16; 17; 19(2); **Amos** 3:3; 6(3); 11(2); 12; 14; 5:6; 14; 15(2); 16; 17; 20; 6:2; 7; 7:3; 6; 9(2); 11; 17(2); 8:3(2); 5; 8; 9:1; 3; 5; 15; **Obad** 9(2); 10; 15; 16; 17(2); 18(2); 21; **Jonah** 1:4; 6; 11; 12; 3:4; 7; 8; 4:4; 6; 9(2); **Mic** 1:2; 4(2); 7(2); 14; 2:4; 11; 3:6(3); 7; 12; 4:1(2); 10(2); 11; 5:2(2); 4; 5; 7; 8; 9(2); 6:7; 14(2); 7:4; 8; 10; 11(2); 13; 16(2); 17; **Nah** 1:10(2); 12(2); 14; 2:3(2); 5; 6(2); 7(2); 13; 3:11(2); 12(2); 13; **Hab** 1:5; 10; 2:5; 7; 9; 14; 16(3); 3:17(3); **Zeph** 1:10; 17; 18(2); 2:3(2); 4(2); 5; 6; 7; 9; 11; 12; 14; 3:7; 8; 11(2); 13; 14; 16(2); **Hag** 1:2; 8; 2:4(3); 9; 12; 13(2); **Zec** 1:4; 9; 16(2); 17; 19; 2:4; 5(2); 9; 11(2); 13; 3:9; 4:5; 12; 13; 5:3(2); 11; 6:13(2); 14; 8:3; 5; 6(2); 8(2); 9(2); 11; 12; 13(2); 19; 9:1(2); 2; 4; 5(3); 7(2); 10(2); 14; 15; 16; 10:5(2); 6; 7(2); 10; 11; 11:5; 9(2); 16; 17(3); 12:2; 3(2); 5; 6; 8(2); 10; 11; 13:1; 2; 4; 7; 8(2); 14:1; 2(2); 4; 6; 7(3); 8(2); 9(2); 10(2); 11(2); 12; 13; 14; 15(2); 17(2); 18; 19; 20(2); 21(2); **Mal** 1:5; 6(2); 8; 9; 11(3); 14; 2:4; 3:4; 5; 10(2); 12; 17; 4:1; 3; **Mt** 1:22; 23; 2:4; 13; 15; 18; 23(2); 3:13; 14; 15; 4:1; 3(2); 6; 14; 5:4; 6; 9; 12; 13(3); 14; 18; 19(2); 21; 22(3); 24; 25; 29; 30; 37; 45; 48; 6:1; 4; 5(2); 7; 8; 9; 10; 16; 21; 22(2); 23(3); 31; 33; 7:1; 2(2); 7(2); 8; 13; 14; 26; 8:3; 8; 12(2); 13; 17; 9:2(2); 5; 12; 15; 21; 22; 29; 10:13(2); 15; 16; 18; 19; 21; 22(2); 23; 25; 26(2); 36; 11:6; 22; 23; 24; 12:11; 17; 27; 31(2); 32(2); 37(2); 39; 40; 45; 13:12(2); 15; 35; 40; 42; 49; 50; 14:9; 27(2); 28; 15:5; 6; 13; 14; 28; 31; 16:2; 3; 4; 19(2); 21(2); 22(2); 23(2); 28; 17:4; 7; 9; 17; 20; 22; 23; 18:3; 7; 8; 9; 12; 13; 16; 17; 18(2); 19; 25(2); 19:5; 9; 10; 12; 21; 25; 30(2); 20:16(2); 18; 22; 23(2); 26(3); 27(2); 28; 33; 21:4; 13; 21(3); 43; 44; 22:13; 28; 23:4; 5; 7; 8; 10; 11; 12(2); 26; 31; 24:2(2); 3(2); 6; 7; 9(2); 10; 13; 14; 16; 20; 21(2); 22(3); 27; 28; 29(2); 34; 37; 39; 40(2); 41(2); 43; 44; 51; 25:1; 9; 29(2); 30; 32; 26:2; 5; 13(2); 31(2); 33(2); 37; 39; 42; 46; 54(2); 56; 63; 27:22; 23; 25; 26; 35; 40; 42; 49; 58; 64(2); 28:10; **Mk** 1:41; 2:5; 9; 20; 22(2); 3:14; 24; 25; 26; 28; 4:12(2); 21(2); 22; 24(2); 25(2); 31; 39; 5:18; 23; 28; 34; 36; 43; 6:9; 11; 27; 50(2); 7:4; 11(2); 24; 27; 34; 8:12; 31(2); 33(2); 38(2); 9:1; 5; 12; 19; 34; 35(2); 43; 45(2); 47; 49(2); 10:8; 12; 26; 31; 33; 38; 39; 40; 41; 43(3); 44(2); 45; 49(2); 11:2; 10; 17; 23(2); 12:7; 23; 13:2(2); 4(3); 7(3); 8(2); 9(2); 10; 11; 12; 13(2); 14; 18; 19(2); 20; 24; 25; 30; 14:2; 9(2); 19; 27(2); 29; 33(2); 49; 64; 15:15; 16:6; 16(2); **Lk** 1:15(2); 20(3); 29; 32(2); 33; 34; 35(2); 37; 38; 45; 57; 60; 66; 68; 71; 76; 2:1; 3; 5; 6; 10; 12; 23; 34; 35; 49; 3:5(4); 7; 12; 14; 23; 4:3(2); 7; 9; 5:13; 15; 23; 35; 37; 38; 6:17; 20; 21; 35(2); 36; 37(3); 38(2); 40; 7:7; 23; 8:9; 12; 17(2); 18(2); 38; 43; 48; 50; 9:22(3); 25; 26(2); 27; 33; 41; 44; 46; 48; 51; 10:5; 6; 11; 12; 14; 15; 42; 11:2(2); 9(2); 10; 18; 19; 29; 30; 35; 36(2); 46; 50; 51; 12:2(2); 3(2); 4; 9; 10(2); 19; 20(2); 26; 29; 31; 34; 35; 39; 40; 45; 47; 48(2); 49; 50(2); 52; 53; 55; 58; 13:14; 16; 23; 24; 28; 30(2); 32; 33; 14:8; 11(2); 12; 14(2); 23; 26; 27; 31; 33(2); 34; 15:7; 14; 19; 21; 23; 24; 32; 16:2; 21; 31; 17:6(2); 24; 25; 26; 30; 31; 34(3); 35(2); 36(2); 37; 18:13; 14(2); 26; 31; 32(2); 40; 19:7; 15; 19; 26(2); 38; 20:6; 13; 14; 18; 25(2); 35; 21:6(2); 7(2); 8; 9; 11(2); 15; 16(2); 17; 22(2); 23; 24(3); 25; 26; 32; 34; 36; 22:7; 16; 24; 26(2); 37; 42(2); 52; 23:23; 24; 31; 32; 35; 37; 39; 43; 24:7(2); 20; 36; 44; 47; 49; **Jn** 1:25; 31; 42; 3:2; 3; 4(2); 5; 7; 9; 14; 17; 20; 21; 27; 4:14; 5:6; 34; 6:12; 20; 45; 7:4; 17; 23; 8:5; 33(2); 36; 41; 55; 9:3; 22; 25; 27; 31; 39; 10:9; 16; 24; 35; 11:4; 12:23; 26; 31; 32; 34; 36; 38; 40; 42; 13:18; 24; 32; 14:1; 3; 13; 17; 21; 27(2); 15:7; 8; 11; 25; 16:1; 20(2); 24; 32; 33; 17:11; 12; 19; 21(2); 22; 23; 24; 26; 18:9; 28; 32; 36; 19:16; 24(2); 28; 31(2); 36(2); 20:15; 19; 21; 26; 27; 21:18; 25(2); **Acts** 1:5; 8; 20; 22(2); 2:14; 20; 21; 24; 25; 38; 47; 3:14; 19(2); 23; 25; 4:9; 10; 12; 19; 28; 30; 5:31; 36; 38; 39(2); 7:7; 35; 8:20; 22; 36; 9:6; 17; 10:42; 47; 48; 11:14; 16; 28; 12:19; 13:11; 22; 28; 38; 39; 42; 47(2); 14:3; 9; 15:1(2); 11; 24; 16:13; 15; 30; 31; 17:18; 27; 18:6; 9; 15(2); 19:2; 26; 27(3); 36(2); 39; 40; 20:16; 21:13; 14(2); 24; 26; 33; 34; 37; 22:5; 10; 15; 16; 24(2); 23:3; 11; 29; 35; 24:4; 15; 21; 25:4; 5; 6; 9; 10; 11(2); 17; 19; 20; 21(2); 26:3; 8; 23; 28; 27:10; 20; 22(2); 24; 25(2); 26; 31; 28:27; 28; **Rom** 1:1; 4; 7(2); 11; 12; 19; 22; 2:12; 13; 25; 26; 3:4(2); 8; 19; 20; 25; 26; 4:11(3); 13; 14; 16(2); 17; 18; 24; 5:9; 10; 15; 19; 6:5; 6; 8; 11; 17; 7:2; 3(4); 4; 10; 8:4; 6(2); 7; 9; 10; 17(2); 18(2); 21; 26; 29(2); 31(2); 39; 9:7; 17; 26; 27(2); 33; 10:1; 9; 11; 13; 15; 11:6; 9; 10; 12; 15(2); 16(2); 17; 19; 20; 22; 23; 24(2); 25(3); 26; 35; 36; 12:2(2); 9; 10;

16(2); 18; 21; 13:1(2); 3; 4; 5; 9; 14:4; 5; 9; 14; 15; 16; 15:5; 12; 16(2); 24(2); 31(2); 32; 33; 16:11; 20; 24; 27; **1Cor** 1:1; 2; 3; 8; 10(2); 17; 3:13(2); 15(2); 18(2); 4:2; 3; 6; 16; 17; 5:2; 5; 7; 11; 6:2; 5; 7; 9; 12; 16; 7:5; 11; 12; 13; 18; 21; 23; 25; 26; 27; 29; 34; 39(2); 8:5(2); 10; 9:2; 10; 12; 15; 19; 23; 27; 10:1; 7; 13(2); 21; 27; 30; 33; 11:1; 6(5); 16; 18; 19(2); 27; 31; 32; 12:13(2); 22; 23; 25; 26; 13:3; 8(3); 10; 14:7; 9(2); 10; 11(2); 20(3); 23; 26; 27; 28; 30; 31; 34; 37; 38(2); 40; 15:9; 12; 13; 14; 15; 17; 22; 26; 28(3); 33; 37; 51; 52(2); 54; 57; 58; 16:2; 4; 6; 10; 13; 14; 22; 23; 24; **2Cor** 1:2; 3; 4; 6(2); 7; 11; 16; 17; 2:4; 7; 9; 14; 3:3; 7; 8; 9; 16; 4:3; 7; 10; 11; 5:2; 3(2); 4(2); 8(2); 9; 10; 13(2); 17; 20; 21(2); 6:3; 13; 14; 16(2); 17; 18(2); 7:10; 11; 8:9; 10; 11; 12; 13; 14(3); 16; 23; 9:3(2); 4; 5; 15; 10:2(2); 8; 11; 15; 11:3; 6; 7; 12; 15(2); 12:6(2); 7(2); 11; 13; 14; 15(2); 16; 20(2); 13:1; 5(2); 7; 11(4); 14; **Gal** 1:3; 5; 7; 8; 9; 10; 2:3; 6(2); 9; 11; 16(2); 17; 3:4; 8; 9; 15(2); 18; 22; 23; 24; 29; 4:1; 9; 12; 18; 19; 20; 21; 30; 5:1; 2; 10(2); 15; 18; 26; 6:1(2); 3; 7; 9; 12; 16; 18; **Eph** 1:2; 3; 4; 12; 22; 3:6; 10; 16; 18; 19; 21; 4:14; 21; 23; 26; 31; 32; 5:1; 3; 7; 17; 18(2); 24; 27; 31(2); 6:3; 5; 8; 10; 11; 13; 16; 19; 23; 24; **Phil** 1:2; 10; 20(3); 23; 26; 27(2); 30; 2:1; 2; 3; 5; 6; 15; 17; 19; 28; 3:9; 15(3); 17; 21; 4:2; 5; 6(2); 8(2); 9; 11; 12(3); 20; 23; **Col** 1:2; 9; 12; 16; 20; 23; 2:2; 5; 20; 3:1; 15; 19; 21; 4:6; 16; 18; **1Th** 1:1; 2:4; 9; 16; 3:1; 3; 5; 4:11; 13; 17(2); 5:6; 7; 8; 13; 14; 23; 27; 28; **2Th** 1:5; 7; 9; 10(2); 12; 2:2(2); 3; 6; 7; 8; 10; 12; 3:1; 2; 8; 13; 14; 16; 18; **1Ti** 1:7; 10; 17; 2:1; 4; 6; 12; 15; 3:2; 8; 10; 11; 12; 4:3; 4(2); 6; 12; 5:7; 9; 13; 16; 17; 22; 25; 6:1; 8; 9; 16; 17; 18; 21; **2Ti** 1:4; 8(2); 15; 2:1; 2; 4; 6; 11; 15; 21; 24; 3:2; 9; 17; 4:2; 4; 6; 15; 16; 17; 18; 22(2); **Titus** 1:6; 7; 9; 11; 13; 2:2; 3; 4; 5(2); 6; 8(2); 9; 3:1(2); 2; 7; 8; 12; 13; 14; 15; **Philem** 1:8; 14; 22; 25; **Heb** 1:5(2); 12; 14; 2:3; 17(2); 3:5; 12; 13; 4:15; 5:5; 11; 12(2); 6:8; 12; 7:11; 8:4; 10(2); 12; 9:16; 23; 10:2; 13; 29; 11:16; 18; 24; 40; 12:3; 8; 9; 10; 11; 13(2); 15; 16; 18; 19; 20; 27; 28; 13:2; 5(2); 9(2); 19; 21; 25; **Jas** 1:4; 5; 13; 18; 19; 22; 23; 25; 26; 2:12; 15; 16; 3:1; 4; 10; 17; 4:4; 9(2); 14; 5:3; 7; 8; 9; 12; 15; 16; **1Pet** 1:2; 3; 5; 6; 7(2); 13(2); 15; 16; 21; 2:3; 6; 7; 13; 18; 20; 3:1(2); 3; 4; 7; 8(3); 13; 14(2); 15; 16; 17; 4:6; 7; 11(2); 13(2); 14; 16; 17; 18; 5:1; 5(2); 8(2); 11; 14; **2Pet** 1:2; 4; 8(2); 11; 12(2); 15; 2:1; 2; 4; 9; 12; 3:2; 8; 10; 11(2); 12; 14(2); 16; 18; **1Jn** 1:4; 2:19; 28; 3:1; 2(2); 4:10; 14; **2Jn** 2; 3; 12; **3Jn** 2; 8; 14; **Jude** 2; 18; 19; 25; **Rev** 1:4; 6; 19; 2:10(2); 11; 19; 27; 3:2; 5; 18(2); 19; 4:1; 5:13; 6:11(2); 17; 7:12; 9:5; 10:6; 7; 9; 11:5; 9; 18; 12:2; 4; 15; 13:10; 15; 14:10; 16:5; 12; 17:17; 18:4; 8; 21(2); 22(4); 23; 19:7; 8; 20:3(2); 6; 7; 10; 21:3(3); 4(2); 7(2); 25(2); 22:3(2); 4; 5; 6; 11(4); 12; 21

BECAME

481, 748, 1431, 1891, 1934, 1961, 2388, 3054, 5235, 5647, 6148, 6452, 8082, *1096, 1402, 1519, 3154, 3471, 4241, 4433*

Gen 2:7; 10; 6:4; 19:26; 20:12; 21:20; 24:67; 26:13; 44:32; 47:20; 26; 49:15; **Ex** 2:10; 4:3; 4; 7:10; 12; 8:17(2); 9:10; 24; 36:13; **Num** 12:10; 26:10; **Deut** 26:5; **Josh** 7:5; 14:14; 24:32; **Judg** 1:30; 33; 35; 8:27; 15:14; 17:5; 12; **Ruth** 4:16; **1Sa** 10:12; 16:21; 18:29; 22:2; 25:37; 42; **2Sa** 2:25; 4:4; 8:2; 6; 14; 11:27; **1Kin** 11:24; 12:30; 13:6; 33; 34; **2Kin** 17:3; 15; 24:1; **1Chr** 18:2; 6; 13; 19:19; **2Chr** 27:6; **Neh** 9:25; **Est** 8:17; **Ps** 69:11; 83:10; 109:25; **Jer** 51:30; **Eze** 17:6(2); 19:3; 6; 23:10; 31:5; 34:5; 8(2); 36:4; **Dan** 2:35(2); 8:4; 10:15; **Obad** 12; **Mt** 28:4; **Mk** 9:3; **Acts** 10:10; **Rom** 1:21; 22; 6:18; **1Cor** 9:20; 22; 13:11; **2Cor** 8:9; **Phil** 2:8; **1Th** 1:6; 2:14; **Heb** 2:10; 5:9; 7:26; 10:33; 11:7; **Rev** 6:12(2); 8:8; 11; 16:3; 4

BECAUSE

182, 413, 834, 843, 854, 1115, 1558, 1697, 1768, 1870, 3027, 3282, 3588, 3605, 3606, 3651, 4480, 4481, 4616, 5668, 5750, 5921, 6118, 6119, 6440, 6448, 6903, 8471, 8478, *473, 575, 1063, 1223, 1360, 1537, 1722, 1752, 1893, 1894, 1909, 2443, 2530, 3704, 3739, 3754, 3759, 4314, 5484*

Gen 2:3; 23; 3:10; 14; 17; 20; 5:29; 7:7; 11:9; 12:13; 17; 16:11; 18:20(2); 19:13; 20:11; 18; 21:11; 12(2); 13; 25; 31; 22:16; 18; 25:21; 28; 26:5; 7; 9; 20; 27:20; 23; 41; 46; 28:11; 29:15; 33; 34; 30:18; 20; 31:30; 31; 32:32; 33:11(2); 34:7; 13; 19; 27; 35:7; 36:7; 37:3; 38:15; 26; 39:9; 23; 41:32; 57; 43:18(2); 32; 46:30; 47:20; 49:4; **Ex** 1:12; 19; 21; 2:10; 4:26; 5:21; 8:12; 9:11; 12:39; 13:8; 14:11; 17:7(2); 16; 18:15; 19:18; 29:33; 34; 32:35; 40:35; **Lev** 6:4; 9; 10:13; 11:4; 5; 6; 14:48; 15:2; 16:16(2); 19:8; 20; 20:3; 21:23; 22:7; 25; 26:10; 35; 43(3); **Num** 3:13; 6:7; 12; 7:9; 9:13; 11:3; 14; 20; 34; 12:1; 13:24; 14:16; 22; 24; 43; 15:31; 34; 19:13; 20; 20:12; 13; 24; 21:4; 22:3(2); 22; 29; 32; 25:13; 26:62; 27:4; 30:5; 14; 32:11; 17; 19; 35:28; **Deut** 1:27; 36; 2:5; 9; 19; 25; 4:3; 37; 7:7; 8(2); 8:20; 9:18; 25; 28(2); 12:20; 13:5; 10; 14:8; 29; 15:2; 10; 16(2); 16:15; 18:12; 19:6; 20:3; 21:14; 22:19; 21; 24(2); 29; 23:4(2); 5; 7; 24:1; 27:20; 28:20; 45; 47; 55; 62; 29:25; 31:17; 29; 32:3; 19; 47; 51(2); 33:21; **Josh** 2:9; 11; 24; 5:1; 6; 7; 6:1; 17; 25; 7:12; 15(2); 9:9; 18; 20; 24(2); 10:2(2); 42; 11:6; 14:9; 14; 17:1; 6; 20:5; 22:31; 23:3; **Judg** 1:19; 2:18; 20; 3:12; 5:23; 6:2; 6; 7; 22; 27; 30(2); 31; 32; 8:20; 24; 9:18; 10:10; 11:13; 12:4; 13:22; 14:17; 15:6; 18:28; 20:36; 21:15; 22; **1Sa** 1:6; 20; 2:1; 25; 3:13; 4:21(2); 6:19(2); 8:18; 9:13; 16; 10:1; 12:10; 22; 13:11; 14; 14:29; 15:23; 24; 16:7; 17:32; 18:3; 12; 16; 19:4(2); 20:17; 18; 34; 21:8; 22:17(2); 24:5; 25:28; 26:12; 16; 21; 28:18; 20; 30:6; 13; 16; 22; **2Sa** 1:9; 10; 12; 2:6; 3:11; 30; 6:8; 12; 8:10; 10:5; 12:6(2); 10; 14; 25; 13:22; 14:15; 26; 16:8; 10; 18:20; 19:21; 26; 42; 21:1; 7; 22:8; 20; 23:6; **1Kin** 1:50; 2:7; 26(2); 3:2; 11; 19; 7:47; 8:11; 33; 35; 64; 9:9; 10:9; 11:9; 33; 34; 14:13; 15; 16; 15:5; 13; 30; 16:7; 17:7; 19:7; 14; 20:28; 36; 42; 21:2; 4; 6; 20; 29; **2Kin** 1:3; 6; 16; 17; 5:1; 8:12; 29; 9:14; 10:30; 13:4; 23; 15:16; 17:26; 18:12; 19:28; 21:11; 15; 22:7; 13; 17; 19; 23:26; **1Chr** 1:19; 4:9; 41; 5:9; 20; 22; 7:21; 23; 9:27; 12:1; 13:10; 11; 14:2; 15:13; 22; 16:33; 41; 18:10; 19:2; 21:8; 30; 22:8; 23:28; 27:23; 24; 28:3; 29:3; 9; **2Chr** 1:11; 2:11; 6:24; 26; 7:2; 6; 7; 22; 8:11; 9:8; 12:2; 5; 14; 13:18; 14:6; 7; 15:16; 16:7; 8; 10; 17:3; 20:37; 21:3; 7; 10; 12; 22:6(2); 9; 24:16; 20; 24; 25:16; 20; 26:20; 27:6; 28:6; 9; 19; 23; 30:3; 34:21; 25; 27; 35:14; 36:15; **Ezr** 3:3; 11(2); 4:14; 8:22; 9:4; 15; 10:6; 9; **Neh** 4:9; 5:3; 9; 15; 18; 6:18; 8:12; 9:37; 38; 13:2; 29; **Est** 1:15; 8:7; 9:3; 24; **Job** 3:10; 6:20; 8:9; 11:16; 18; 15:27; 17:12; 18:15; 20:19(2); 23:17; 29:12; 30:11; 31:25(2); 32:1; 2; 3; 4; 34:27; 36; 35:12; 15; 36:18; 38:21(2); 39:11; 17; **Ps** 5:8; 11; 6:7(2); 7:6; 8:2; 13:6; 14:6; 16:8; 18:7; 19; 27:11; 28:5; 6; 31:10; 33:21; 37:1; 7(2); 40; 38:3(2); 5; 20; 39:9; 41:11; 42:9; 43:2; 44:3; 45:4; 48:11; 52:9; 53:5; 55:3(2); 19; 59:9; 60:4; 8; 63:3; 7; 68:29; 69:7; 18; 78:22; 86:17; 91:9; 14(2); 97:8; 102:10; 106:33; 107:11; 17(2); 26; 30; 109:16; 21; 116:1; 2; 118:1; 119:53; 56; 62; 74; 100; 136; 139; 158; 164; 122:9; **Prov** 1:24; 21:7; 22:22; 24:13; 19; **Eccl** 2:17; 18; 4:9; 5:20; 8:6; 11; 13; 15; 17; 10:15; 12:3; 5; 9; **Song** 1:3; 6(2); 3:8; **Is** 2:6; 3:8; 16; 5:13; 24; 6:5; 7:5; 24; 8:20; 10:27; 14:20; 29; 15:1(2); 17:9; 10; 19:16; 17; 20; 22:4; 24:5; 26:3; 28:15; 28; 30:12; 31:1(2); 32:14; 37:29; 40:7; 43:20; 48:4; 49:7; 50:2; 51:13; 53:9; 12; 55:5; 60:5; 9; 61:1; 64:7; 65:12; 16(2); 66:4; **Jer** 2:35(2); 4:4; 17; 18(2); 19; 28; 31; 5:6; 14; 6:19; 30; 7:13; 8:14; 19; 9:10; 13; 19(2); 10:5; 12:4; 11; 13; 13:17; 25; 14:4; 5; 6; 16; 15:4; 17; 16:11; 18; 17:13; 18:15; 19:4; 8; 13; 15; 20:8; 17; 21:12; 22:9; 15; 23:9(3); 10; 38; 25:8; 16; 27; 37; 38(2); 26:3; 28:16; 29:15; 19; 23; 25; 31; 32; 30:14; 15; 17; 31:15; 19; 32:24; 32; 35:16; 17; 18; 39:18; 40:3; 41:9; 18(2); 44:3; 22(2); 23(2); 46:15; 21; 23; 47:4; 48:7; 36; 42; 45; 50:7; 11(3); 13; 24; 51:11; 51; 55; 56; **Lam** 1:3(2); 4; 8; 16(2); 2:11; 3:22; 28; 51; 5:9; 10; 18; **Eze** 3:20; 21; 5:7; 9; 11; 6:9; 7:19; 12:19; 13:8; 10(2); 22; 14:5; 15; 15:8; 16:15; 28; 36; 43; 63; 18:18; 28; 20:16; 24; 21:7; 13; 24(2); 28; 22:19; 23:30(2); 35; 45; 24:13; 25:3; 6; 8; 12; 15; 26:2; 28:2; 5; 6; 17; 29:6; 9; 20; 31:5; 10; 33:29; 34:5; 8(2); 21; 35:5; 10; 15; 36:2; 3; 6; 13; 39:23; 44:2; 7; 12; 47:9; 12; **Dan** 2:8; 3:22; 29; 4:9; 6:3; 23; 7:11; 9:7; 8; 11; 16; 11:35; **Hos** 4:1; 6; 10; 13; 19; 5:1; 11; 7:13; 8:1; 11; 9:6; 17; 10:3; 5(2); 13; 15; 11:5; 6; **Joel** 1:5; 11; 12; 18; 2:20; 3:5; 19; **Amos** 1:3; 6; 9; 11; 13; 2:1; 4; 6; 4:12; **Jonah** 1:10; **Mic** 2:1; 10; 6:13; 7:9; 13; 17; 18; **Nah** 3:4; 11; **Hab** 1:16; 2:3; 5; 8(2); 17; **Zeph** 1:17; 2:10; 3:11; **Hag** 1:9; **Zec** 8:10; 9:8(3); 10:2; 5; 11:2; **Mal** 2:2; 14; **Mt** 2:18; 5:36; 7:14; 9:36; 11:20; 25; 12:41; 13:5; 6; 11; 13; 21; 58; 14:5; 15:32; 16:7; 8; 17:20; 18:7; 32; 19:8; 20:7; 15; 31; 21:46; 23:29; 24:12; 26:31; 33; 27:6; 19; **Mk** 1:34; 3:9; 30; 4:5; 6; 29; 5:4; 6:6; 34; 7:19; 8:2; 16; 17; 9:38; 41; 11:18; 12:24; 14:27; 15:42; 16:14; **Lk** 1:7; 20; 2:4; 7; 4:18; 5:19; 8:6; 30; 9:7; 49; 53; 10:20; 11:8(2); 18; 12:17; 13:2; 14; 15:27; 16:8; 17:9; 18:5; 19:3; 11(2); 17; 21; 31; 44; 23:8; **Jn** 1:50; 2:24; 3:18; 19; 23; 29; 4:41; 42; 5:16; 18; 27; 30; 6:2; 26(2); 41; 7:1; 7; 22; 23; 30; 39; 43; 8:22; 37; 43; 44; 45; 47; 9:16; 22; 10:13; 17; 26; 33; 36; 11:9; 10; 42; 12:6; 11; 30; 39; 42; 13:29; 14:12; 17; 19; 28; 15:19; 21; 27; 16:3; 4; 6; 9; 10; 11; 16; 17; 21; 27; 32; 17:14; 19:7; 31; 42; 20:13; 29; 21:17; **Acts** 2:6; 24; 27; 4:21; 6:1; 8:11; 20; 10:45; 12:3; 20; 23; 13:27; 14:12; 16:3; 17:18; 31; 18:2; 3; 20:16; 22:29; 30; 24:11; 25:20; 26:2; 3; 27:4; 9; 12; 28:2(2); 18; 20; **Rom** 1:19; 21; 3:2; 4:15; 5:5; 6:15; 19; 8:7; 10(2); 21; 27; 9:7; 28; 32; 11:20; 14:23; 15:15; **1Cor** 1:25; 2:14; 3:13; 6:7; 11:10; 12:15; 16; 15:9; 15; **2Cor** 2:13; 5:14; 7:13; 11:7; 11; **Gal** 2:4; 11; 3:19; 4:6; 16; **Eph** 4:18; 5:6; 16; **Phil** 1:7; 2:26; 30; 4:17; **1Th** 2:8; 9; 13; 4:6; **2Th** 1:3; 10; 2:10; 13; 3:9; **1Ti** 1:13; 4:10; 5:12; 6:2(2); **Philem** 1:7; **Heb** 3:19; 4:6; 6:13; 7:23; 24; 8:9; 10:2; 11:5; 11; 23; **Jas** 1:10; 4:2; 3; **1Pet** 1:16; 2:21; 5:8; **1Jn** 2:8; 11; 12; 13(3); 14(2); 21(2); 3:1; 9; 12; 14; 16; 22; 4:1; 4; 9; 13; 17; 18; 19; 5:6; 10; **3Jn** 7; **Jude** 16; **Rev** 1:7; 2:4; 14; 20; 3:10; 16; 17; 5:4; 8:11; 11:10; 17; 12:12; 14:8; 16:5; 11; 21

BECOME

142, 444, 816, 1086, 1197, 1431, 1891, 1961, 2015, 2470, 2973, 3988, 4390, 4911, 6004, 6105, 6213, 6238, 6275, 8631, *889, 1096, 1402, 1519, 1986, 2289, 2673, 4241*

Gen 3:22; 9:15; 18:18; 24:35; 32:10; 34:16; 37:20; 48:19(2); **Ex** 4:9; 7:9; 19; 8:16; 9:9; 15:2; 6; 23:29; 32:1; 23; **Lev** 19:29; **Num** 5:24; 27; **Deut** 27:9; 28:37; **Josh** 9:13; **Judg** 16:17; **1Sa** 28:16; **2Sa** 7:24; **1Kin** 2:15; 14:3; **2Kin** 21:14; 22:19; **Est** 2:11; **Job** 7:5; 15:28; 21:7; 30:19; 21; **Ps** 14:3; 28:1; 53:3; 62:10; 69:8; 22(2); 79:4; 109:7; 118:14; 21; 22; 119:83; **Prov** 29:21; **Is** 1:21; 22; 7:24; 12:2; 14:10(2); 19:11; 13; 29:11; 34:9; 35:7; 59:6; 60:22; **Jer** 2:5; 3:1; 5:13; 27; 7:11; 10:21; 22:5; 26:18; 49:13; 50:23; 37; 51:37; 41; **Lam** 1:1(2); 2; 6; 11; 4:1; 3; 8; **Eze** 22:4; 18; 19; 26:5; 36:35(2); 37:17; **Dan** 4:22; 9:16; 11:23; **Hos** 12:8; 13:15; 16; **Jonah** 4:5; **Mic** 3:12; **Zeph** 1:13; 2:15; **Zec** 4:7; **Mt** 18:3; 21:42; **Mk** 1:17; 12:10; **Lk** 20:17; **Jn** 1:12; **Acts** 4:11; 7:40; 12:18; **Rom** 3:12; 19; 4:18; 6:22; 7:4; 13; **1Cor** 3:18; 7:18; 8:9; 13:1; 15:20; **2Cor** 5:17; 12:11; **Gal** 4:16; 5:4; **Titus** 2:1; **Philem** 1:6; **Heb** 5:12; **Jas** 2:4; 11; **Rev** 11:15; 18:2

BEEN

1934, 1961, *1096, 1304, 1511, 2075, 2076, 2192, 2258, 3918, 4160, 4357, 5607*

Gen 13:3; 26:8; 31:5; 38; 41; 42; 38:26; 45:6; 46:32; 34; 47:9; **Ex** 2:22; 9:18; 14:12; 18:3; 21:29; 34:10; **Lev** 10:19; 13:7; **Num** 19:20; **Deut** 2:7; 4:32(2); 9:7; 24; 15:18; 21:3; 31:27; **Josh** 7:7; 9:4; 10:27; 23:9; **Judg** 16:8; 17; **Ruth** 2:11; **1Sa** 1:13; 4:7; 9; 17; 9:24; 14:29; 30; 38; 15:21; 18:19; 19:4; 20:13; 21:5; 25:28; 34; 29:3; 6; 8; **2Sa** 1:21; 26; 12:8; 13:20; 32; 14:32(2); 15:34; **1Kin** 1:37; 2:26; 14:8; 16:31; 17:7; 19:10; 14; **2Kin** 4:13; 20:12; **1Chr** 17:8; 28:3; 29:25; **2Chr** 1:12; 15:3; 23:9; **Ezr** 2:1; 4:18; 19(2); 20; 5:16; 8:35; 9:2; 4; 7(2); 8; 10:6; 8; **Neh** 2:1; 5:15; 7:6; 13:10; **Est** 2:6(2); 12; 4:11; 6:3; 7:4; **Job** 3:13(2); 16; 10:19(3); 22:9; 31:9; 27; 38:17; 42:11; **Ps** 25:6; 27:9; 35:14; 37:25; 42:3; 50:8; 18; 59:16; 60:1; 61:3; 63:7; 69:22; 71:6; 73:14; 85:1; 89:38; 90:1; 94:17; 115:12; 119:54; 71; 92; 124:1; 2; 143:3; **Prov** 7:26; **Eccl** 1:9; 10; 16; 2:12; 3:15(2); 4:3; 16; 6:10; **Is** 1:6; 9(2); 5:4; 17:10; 23:16; 25:4; 26:17; 18(2); 30:24; 38:9; 39:1; 40:21; 42:14; 43:4; 22; 48:18; 19(2); 49:21; 52:15; 57:11; 60:15; 66:2; **Jer** 2:31; 3:2; 3(2); 4:17; 15:9; 20:17; 22:21; 28:8; 32:31; 34:14; 42:18; 43:5; 44:18; 48:11(2); 50:6; 29; 51:5; 7; **Eze** 2:5; 4:14; 10:10; 11:17; 16:31; 20:41; 43; 22:13; 28:13; 29:6; 33:33; 34:12; 38:8; **Dan** 5:15; 9:12(2); **Hos** 5:1; 2; **Joel** 1:2; 2:2; **Obad** 16; **Mic** 5:2; **Zeph** 3:19; **Zec** 1:2; **Mal** 1:9; 2:9; 14; 3:13; **Mt** 1:6; 5:31; 33; 38; 43; 11:21; 23(2); 13:35; 23:30(2); 25:21; 23; 26:9; 24(2); **Mk** 5:4(2); 18; 6:49; 8:2; 14:5(2); 21; 15:44; 16:10; 11; **Lk** 1:4; 70; 2:44; 4:16; 7:10; 8:2; 10:13(2); 16:11; 12; 19:17; 24:21; **Jn** 5:6; 9:18; 11:21; 32; 39; 12:1; 38; 14:9; 15:27; **Acts** 1:16; 4:13; 16; 5:26; 6:15; 7:52; 9:18; 10:11; 11:5; 13:1; 46; 14:19; 26; 15:7; 16:27; 19:21; 20:18; 23:10; 27; 24:10; 19; 26; 25:14; 26:32; **Rom** 6:5; 9:29(2); 11:34; 15:22; 27; 16:2; **1Cor** 1:11; 12:13; **2Cor** 11:6; 21; 25; 12:11; **Gal** 3:1; 21(2); 27; 4:15; 5:13; **Eph** 3:9; 4:21; **Phil** 2:26; **Col** 1:26; 2:7; 4:11; **1Th** 2:6; **2Th** 2:15; **1Ti** 5:9; **2Ti** 3:14; **Titus** 1:9; **Heb** 8:7(2); 11:15; 13:9; **Jas** 3:7; 5:5; **2Pet** 2:21; **1Jn** 2:19; **Rev** 5:6; 17:2

BEFORE

413, 639, 854, 2958, 2962, 3808, 3942, 4136, 4551, 4608, 5021, 5048, 5084, 5226, 5227, 5703, 5704, 5869, 5921, 5973, 6440, 6471, 6903, 6905, 6924, 6925, 6931, 7130, 7223, 7228, 8032, 8543, *561, 575, 1715, 1725, 1726, 1773, 1799, 1909, 2228, 2596, 2713, 2714, 3319, 3362, 3764, 3844, 3908, 3936, 4250, 4253, 4254, 4256, 4257, 4264, 4267, 4270, 4275, 4277, 4278, 4280, 4281, 4282, 4293, 4295, 4296, 4299, 4300, 4301, 4302, 4304, 4308, 4309, 4310, 4314, 4315, 4363, 4383, 4384, 4386, 4391, 4401, 4412, 4413*

Gen 2:5(2); 6:11; 13; 7:1; 10:9(2); 11:28; 12:15; 13:9; 10; 13; 17:1; 18; 18:8; 22; 19:4; 13; 27; 20:15; 23:3; 12; 17; 18; 19; 24:7; 15; 33; 40; 45; 51; 25:9; 18; 27:4; 7(2); 10; 33; 29:26; 30:30; 33; 38; 39; 41; 31:2; 5; 32; 35; 37; 32:3; 16; 17; 20; 21; 33:3; 12; 14(2); 18; 34:10; 36:31; 37:18; 40:9; 41:43; 46; 50; 42:6; 24; 43:9; 14; 15; 33; 34; 44:14; 45:1; 5; 7; 28; 46:28; 47:6; 7; 10; 19; 48:5; 15; 20; 49:8; 30; 50:13; 16; 18; **Ex** 4:3; 21; 6:12; 30; 7:9; 10(2); 8:20; 26; 9:10; 11; 13; 10:1; 3; 10; 14; 11:10; 12:34; 13:21; 22; 14:2(2); 9; 19(2); 16:9; 33; 34; 17:5; 6; 18:12; 19:2; 7; 20:3; 20; 21:1; 22:9; 23:15; 17; 20; 23; 27; 28(2); 29; 30; 31; 25:30; 27:21(2); 28:12; 25; 29; 30(2); 35; 38; 29:10; 11; 23; 24; 25; 26; 42; 30:6(2); 8; 16; 36; 32:1; 5; 23; 34; 33:2; 19(2); 34:3; 6; 10; 11; 20; 23; 24(2); 34; 39:18; 40:5; 6; 23; 25; 26; **Lev** 1:3; 5; 11; 3:1; 7; 8; 12; 13; 4:4(2); 6(2); 7; 14; 15(2); 17(2); 18; 24; 6:7; 14(2); 25; 7:30; 8:26; 27; 29; 9:2; 4; 5(2); 21; 24; 10:1; 2; 3; 4; 15; 17; 19; 12:7; 14:11; 12; 16; 18; 23; 24; 27; 29; 31; 36; 15:14; 15; 30; 16:1; 2; 7; 10; 12; 13; 14; 15; 18; 30; 17:4; 18:23; 24; 27; 28; 30; 19:14; 22; 32; 20:23; 23:11; 20; 28; 40; 24:3; 4; 6; 8; 26:7; 8; 17; 37(2); 27:8; 11; **Num** 3:4(2);

6; 7; 38(2); 5:16; 18; 25; 30; 6:12; 16; 20; 7:3(2); 10; 8:9; 10; 11; 13(2); 21; 22(2); 9:6(2); 10:9; 10; 33; 35; 11:6; 20; 13:22; 30; 14:5; 10; 14; 37; 42; 43; 15:15; 25; 28; 16:2; 7; 9; 16; 17; 38; 40; 43; 17:4; 7; 9; 10; 18:2; 19; 19:3; 4; 20:3; 8; 9; 10; 21:11; 22:32; 25:4; 6; 26:61; 27:2(3); 5; 14; 17(2); 19(2); 21(2); 22(2); 31:50; 54; 32:4; 17; 20; 21(2); 22(4); 27; 29(2); 32; 33:7(2); 8; 47; 52; 55; 35:12; 36:1(2); **Deut** 1:8; 21; 22; 30(2); 33; 38; 42; 45; 2:12; 21; 22; 31; 33; 3:18; 28; 4:8; 10; 32; 34; 38; 44; 5:7; 6:19; 22; 25; 7:1; 2; 22; 24; 8:20; 9:2; 3(2); 4(2); 5; 17; 18; 25; 10:8; 11; 11:23; 25; 26; 32; 12:7; 12; 18(2); 29; 30; 14:23; 26; 15:20; 16:11; 16(2); 17:12; 18; 18:7; 12; 19:17(2); 21:16; 22:6; 17; 23:14; 24:4; 13; 25:2; 26:4; 5; 10(2); 13; 27:7; 28:7(2); 25(2); 31(2); 66; 29:2; 10; 15; 30:1; 15; 19; 31:3(3); 5; 8; 11(2); 21; 32:52; 33:1; 10; 27; **Josh** 1:5; 14; 2:8; 3:1; 6(2); 10; 11; 14; 4:5; 7; 12; 13; 18; 23(2); 5:1; 6:4; 5; 6; 7; 8; 9; 13(2); 20; 26; 7:4; 5; 6; 8; 12(2); 13; 23; 8:5; 6(2); 10; 11; 14; 15; 33(2); 35; 9:24; 10:5; 8; 10; 11; 12; 14; 11:6; 13:3; 6; 25; 14:15; 15:7; 8; 15; 17:4(3); 7; 18:1; 6; 8; 10; 14; 16; 19:11; 46; 51; 20:6; 9; 21:44; 22:27; 29; 23:5; 9(2); 13; 24:1; 8; 12(2); 18; **Judg** 1:10; 11; 23; 2:3; 14; 21; 3:2; 27; 4:14; 15; 23; 5:5(2); 6:9; 18; 7:24; 8:13; 28; 9:39; 40; 11:9; 11; 23; 24; 33; 12:5; 14:16; 17; 18; 16:3; 20; 18:6; 21; 20:23; 26(2); 28; 32; 35; 39; 42; 21:2; **Ruth** 3:14; 4:4(2); **1Sa** 1:12; 15; 19; 22; 2:11; 15; 17; 18; 21; 28; 30; 35; 3:1; 4:2; 3; 17; 5:3; 4; 6:20; 7:6; 10; 8:11; 20; 9:12; 13; 15; 19; 24(2); 27; 10:5; 8; 19; 25; 11:15(2); 12:2(2); 3(2); 7; 16; 14:13; 21; 15:30(2); 33; 16:6; 8; 10; 16; 21; 22; 17:7; 31; 41; 57; 18:13; 16; 19:24; 20:1(2); 21:6; 7; 13; 22:4; 23:18; 24; 25:19; 23; 26:1; 3; 19; 20; 28:22; 25(2); 30:20; 31:1; **2Sa** 2:14; 17; 24; 3:28; 31; 34; 5:3; 20; 24; 6:4; 5; 14; 16; 17; 21(4); 7:15; 16; 18; 23; 26; 29; 10:6; 9; 13; 14; 15; 16; 18; 19; 11:13; 12:11; 12(2); 20; 13:9; 14:33; 15:1; 18; 18:7; 28; 19:8; 13; 17; 18; 28; 20:8; 21:9; 22:13; 23; 24; 24:13; 20; **1Kin** 1:2; 5; 23(2); 25; 28; 32; 2:4; 26; 45; 3:6; 12; 15; 16; 22; 24; 6:3(2); 7; 17; 21; 7:6(2); 49; 8:5; 8; 22; 23; 25(2); 28; 31; 33; 50; 54; 59; 62; 64(2); 65; 9:3; 4; 6; 25; 10:8; 11:7; 36; 12:6; 8; 30; 13:6; 14:9; 24; 15:3; 16:25; 30; 33; 17:1; 3; 5; 18:15; 46; 19:11(2); 19; 20:27; 21:10; 13; 26; 29(2); 22:10; 21; **2Kin** 1:13; 2:9; 15; 3:14; 24; 4:12; 31; 38; 43; 44; 5:15; 16; 23; 25; 6:22; 32; 8:9; 10:4; 11:18; 14:12; 15:10; 16:3; 14; 17:2; 8; 11; 18:5; 22; 19:14; 15; 26; 32; 20:3; 21:2; 9; 11; 22:10; 19(2); 23:3; 13; 25; 25:7; 29; **1Chr** 1:43; 5:25; 6:32; 10:1; 11:3; 13; 13:8; 10; 14:15; 15:24; 16:1; 4; 6; 29; 30; 37(2); 39; 17:8; 13; 16; 21; 24; 25; 27; 19:7; 9; 10; 14(2); 15; 16(2); 18; 19; 21:12; 30; 22:5; 18(2); 23:13; 31; 24:2; 6(2); 28:4; 29:10; 15; 22; 25; **2Chr** 1:5; 6; 10; 12; 13; 2:4; 6; 3:15; 17; 4:20; 5:6; 9; 6:12; 13; 14; 16; 19; 22; 24(2); 36; 7:4; 6; 7; 17; 19; 8:12; 14; 9:7; 11; 10:6; 8; 13:13; 14; 15; 16; 14:5; 7; 12(2); 13(2); 15:8; 18:9; 20; 19:2; 11; 20:5; 7; 9; 13; 16; 18; 21; 23:17; 24:14; 25:8; 14; 22; 26:19; 27:6; 28:3; 9; 14; 29:11; 19; 23; 30:9; 31:20; 32:12; 33:2; 7; 9; 12; 19; 23; 34:18; 24; 27(3); 31; 36:12; **Ezr** 3:12; 4:18; 23; 7:19; 28(2); 8:21; 29; 9:15(2); 10:1; 6; **Neh** 1:4; 6; 2:1; 13; 4:2; 5(2); 5:15; 6:19; 8:1; 2; 3(3); 9:8; 11; 24; 28; 32; 35; 12:36; 13:4; 19; **Est** 1:3; 11; 16; 17; 19; 2:11; 23; 3:7; 4:2; 6; 8; 6:1; 9; 11; 13(2); 7:6; 8; 9; 8:1; 3; 4; 5; 9:11; 25; **Job** 1:6; 2:1(2); 3:24; 4:15; 16; 19; 8:12; 16; 10:21; 13:15; 16; 15:4; 7; 32; 18:20; 21:8; 18; 33; 23:4; 17; 26:6; 30:11; 33:5; 35:14; 41:10; 22; 42:10; 11; **Ps** 5:8; 16:8; 18:6; 12; 22; 23; 42; 22:25; 27; 29; 23:5; 26:3; 31:19; 22; 34:t; 35:5; 36:1; 38:9; 17; 39:1; 5; 13; 41:12; 42:2; 44:15; 50:3; 8; 21; 51:3; 52:9; 54:3; 56:13; 57:6; 58:9; 61:7; 62:8; 68:1; 2; 3; 4; 7; 25; 69:19; 22; 72:9; 11; 73:22; 78:55; 79:11; 80:2; 9; 83:13; 84:7; 85:13; 86:9; 14; 88:1; 2; 89:14; 23; 36; 90:2; 8; 95:2; 6; 96:6; 9; 13; 97:3; 98:6; 9; 100:2; 101:3; 102:t, 28; 105:17; 106:23; 109:15; 116:9; 119:30; 46; 67; 168; 169; 170; 138:1; 139:5; 141:2; 3; 142:2(2); 147:17; **Prov** 4:25; 5:21; 8:22; 25(2); 30; 14:19; 15:11; 33; 16:18(2); 17:14; 24; 18:12(2); 13; 16; 22:29(2); 23:1; 25:5; 26; 26:26; 27:4; 30:7; **Eccl** 1:10; 16; 2:7; 9; 26; 3:14; 4:16; 5:2; 6; 6:8; 7:17; 8:12; 13; 9:1; **Song** 8:12; **Is** 1:12; 16; 7:16; 8:4(2); 9:3; 12; 13:16; 17:13(2); 14; 23:18; 24:23; 28:4; 30:8; 11; 36:7; 37:14; 27; 33; 38:3; 40:10; 17; 41:1; 2; 42:9; 16; 43:10; 13; 45:1(2); 2; 47:14; 48:5; 7; 19; 49:16; 52:12; 53:2; 7; 55:12; 57:16; 58:8; 59:12; 61:11; 62:11; 63:12; 65:6; 12; 24; 66:4; 7(2); 22; 23; **Jer** 1:5(2); 17; 2:22; 6:7; 21; 7:10; 8:2; 9:13; 13:16(2); 15:1; 9; 19; 17:16; 18:17; 20; 23; 19:7; 21:8; 24:1; 26:4; 28:8(2); 29:21; 30:20; 31:36(2); 32:12; 13; 30; 31; 33:9; 18; 24; 34:5; 15; 18; 35:5; 19; 36:7; 9; 22; 37:20; 38:10; 26; 39:6; 16; 40:4; 42:2; 9; 44:10(2); 47:1; 49:19; 37(2); 50:8; 44; 52:10; 33; **Lam** 1:5; 6; 22; 2:3; 19; 3:35; **Eze** 2:10; 3:20; 4:1; 6:4; 5; 8:1; 11; 9:6; 14:1; 3; 4; 7; 16:18; 19; 50; 57; 20:1; 9; 14; 41; 21:6; 22:30; 23:24; 41; 28:9; 17; 30:24; 32:10; 33:31; 36:17; 23; 37:20; 38:16; 40:12; 22; 26; 47; 41:4; 12; 22; 42:1; 2; 4; 8; 11; 12; 13; 43:24; 44:3; 4; 11; 12; 15; 22; 45:7(2); 46:3; 9; **Dan** 1:5; 13; 18; 19; 2:2; 9; 10; 11; 24; 25; 31; 36; 3:3; 13; 4:6; 7; 8(2); 5:1; 13; 15; 17; 19; 23; 6:10; 11; 12; 13; 18; 22(2); 26; 7:7; 8; 10(2); 13; 20; 8:3; 4; 6; 7; 15; 9:10; 13; 18; 20; 10:12; 16; 11:16; 22; **Hos** 7:2; **Joel** 1:16; 2:3(2); 6; 10; 11; 31; **Amos** 1:1; 2:9; 4:3; 9:4; **Jonah** 1:2; 4:2; **Mic** 1:4; 2:13(2); 6:1; 4; 6(3); **Nah** 1:6; 2:1; **Hab** 1:3; 2:20; 3:5; **Zeph** 2:2(4); 3:20; **Hag** 1:12; 2:14; 15; **Zec** 2:13; 3:1; 3; 4; 8; 9; 4:7; 6:5; 7:2; 8:10; 21; 22; 12:8; 14:4; 5; 20; **Mal** 2:5; 9; 3:1; 11; 14; 16; 4:5; **Mt** 1:18; 2:9; 5:12; 16; 24; 6:1; 2; 8; 7:6; 8:29; 10:18; 32(2); 33(2); 11:10(2); 14:6; 8; 22; 17:2; 21:9; 31; 24:25; 38; 25:32; 26:32; 34; 70; 75; 27:11; 24; 29; 28:7; **Mk** 1:2(2); 35; 2:12; 3:11; 5:33; 6:41; 45; 8:6(2); 7; 9:2; 10:32; 11:9; 13:9; 14:28; 30; 72; 15:42; 16:7; **Lk** 1:6; 8; 17; 75; 76; 2:21; 26; 31; 5:18; 19; 25; 7:27(2); 8:28; 47(2); 9:16; 52; 10:1; 8; 11:6; 38; 12:6; 8(2); 9(2); 14:2; 15:18; 16:15; 18:39; 19:4; 27; 28; 20:26; 21:12(2); 14; 36; 22:15; 34; 47; 61; 23:12; 14; 53; 24:19; 43; **Jn** 1:15(2); 27; 30(2); 48; 3:28; 5:7; 6:62; 7:51; 8:58; 9:8; 10:4; 8; 11:55; 12:1; 37; 13:1; 19; 14:29; 15:18; 17:5; 24; **Acts** 1:16; 2:20; 25; 31; 3:18; 20; 4:10; 28; 5:23; 27; 36; 6:6; 7:2; 40; 45; 46; 52; 8:32; 9:15; 10:4; 17; 30; 33; 41; 12:6; 14; 13:24; 14:13; 16:29; 34; 17:26; 18:17; 19:9; 19; 20:5; 13; 21:29; 38; 22:30; 23:1; 30; 33; 24:19; 20; 25:9; 16; 26(2); 26:2; 26; 27:24; **Rom** 2:13; 3:9; 18; 19; 4:2; 17; 9:29; 14:10; 22; 16:7; **1Cor** 2:7; 4:5; 6:1(2); 6; 10:27; 11:21; **2Cor** 1:15; 5:10; 7:3; 14; 8:10; 24; 9:5(2); 12:19; 13:2; **Gal** 1:9; 17; 20; 2:12; 14; 3:1; 8; 17; 23; 5:21; **Eph** 1:4(2); 2:10; **Phil** 3:13; **Col** 1:5; 17; **1Th** 2:2; 3:4; 9; 13; **1Ti** 1:13; 18; 5:4; 19; 20; 21(2); 24; 6:12; 13(2); **2Ti** 1:9; 2:14; 4:1; 21; S:1; **Titus** 1:2; **Heb** 6:18; 7:18; 10:15; 11:5; 12:1; 2; **Jas** 1:27; 2:6; 5:9; **1Pet** 1:20; **2Pet** 2:11; 3:2; 17; **1Jn** 2:28; 3:19; **3Jn** 6; **Jude** 4; 17; 24; **Rev** 1:4; 2:14; 3:2; 5(2); 8; 9; 4:5; 6(2); 10(2); 5:8; 7:9(2); 11; 15; 8:2; 3; 4; 9:13; 10:11; 11:4; 16; 12:4; 10; 13:12; 14:3(2); 5; 15:4; 16:19; 19:20; 20:12; 22:8

BEFOREHAND

4271, 4294, 4303, 4305

Mk 13:11; **2Cor** 9:5; **1Ti** 5:24; 25; **1Pet** 1:11

BEGAN

2490, 2974, 3246, 5927, 6751, 8271, *746, 756, 2020, 2192, 2983*

Gen 4:26; 6:1; 9:20; 10:8; 41:54; 44:12; **Num** 25:1; **Deut** 1:5; **Judg** 13:25; 16:19; 22; 19:25; 20:31; 39; 40; **1Sa** 3:2; **2Sa** 2:10; 5:4; **1Kin** 6:1; 14:21; 15:25; 33; 16:8; 11; 23; 29; 22:41; 42; 51; **2Kin** 3:1; 8:16; 17; 26; 9:29; 10:32; 11:21; 12:1; 13:1; 10; 14:2; 23; 15:1; 2; 13; 17; 23; 27; 32; 33; 37; 16:1; 2; 17:1; 18:1; 2; 21:1; 19; 22:1; 23:31; 36; 24:8; 18; 25:27; **1Chr** 1:10; 27:24; **2Chr** 3:1; 2; 12:13; 13:1; 20:22; 31; 21:5; 20; 22:2; 24:1; 25:1; 26:3; 27:1; 8; 28:1; 29:1; 17; 27(2); 31:7; 10; 21; 33:1; 21; 34:1; 3(2); 36:2; 5; 9; 11; **Ezr** 3:6; 8; 5:2; 7:9; **Neh** 4:7; 13:19; **Jer** 52:1; **Eze** 9:6; **Jonah** 3:4; **Mt** 4:17; 11:7; 20; 12:1; 16:21; 22; 26:22; 37; 74; 28:1; **Mk** 1:45; 2:23; 4:1; 5:17; 20; 6:2; 7; 34; 55; 8:11; 31; 32; 10:28; 32; 41; 47; 11:15; 12:1; 13:5; 14:19; 33; 65; 69; 71; 15:8; 18; **Lk** 1:70; 3:23; 4:21; 5:7; 21; 7:15; 24; 38; 49; 9:12; 11:29; 53; 12:1; 14:18; 30; 15:14; 24; 19:37; 45; 20:9; 22:23; 23:2; **Jn** 4:52; 9:32; 13:5; **Acts** 1:1; 2:4; 3:21; 8:35; 10:37; 11:15; 18:26; 24:2; 27:35; **Rom** 16:25; **2Ti** 1:9, **Titus** 1:2; **Heb** 2:3

BEGIN

2490, 8462, *756, 3195*

Gen 11:6; **Deut** 2:24; 25; 31; 16:9; **Josh** 3:7; **Judg** 10:18; 13:5; **1Sa** 3:12; 22:15; **2Kin** 8:25; **Neh** 11:17; **Jer** 25:29; **Eze** 9:6; **Mt** 24:49; **Lk** 3:8; 12:45; 13:25; 26; 14:9; 29; 21:28; 23:30; **2Cor** 3:1; **1Pet** 4:17(2); **Rev** 10:7

BEGINNING

227, 1931, 5769, 7218, 7223, 7225, 8462, *509, 746, 756, 4412, 4413*

Gen 1:1; 10:10; 13:3; 41:21; 49:3; **Ex** 12:2; **Deut** 11:12; 21:17; 32:42; **Judg** 7:19; **Ruth** 1:22; 3:10; **2Sa** 21:9; 10; **2Kin** 17:25; **1Chr** 17:9; **Ezr** 4:6; **Job** 8:7; 42:12; **Ps** 111:10; 119:160; **Prov** 1:7; 8:22; 23; 9:10; 17:14; 20:21; **Eccl** 3:11; 7:8; 10:13; **Is** 1:26; 18:2; 7; 40:21; 41:4; 26; 46:10; 48:3; 5; 7; 16; 64:4; **Jer** 17:12; 26:1; 27:1; 28:1; 49:34; **Lam** 2:19; **Eze** 40:1; **Dan** 9:21; 23; **Hos** 1:2; **Amos** 7:1; **Mic** 1:13; **Mt** 14:30; 19:4; 8; 20:8; 24:8; 21; **Mk** 1:1; 10:6; 13:19; **Lk** 1:2; 23:5; 24:27; 47; **Jn** 1:1; 2; 2:10; 11; 6:64; 8:9; 25; 44; 15:27; 16:4; **Acts** 1:22; 11:4; 15; 15:18; 26:5; **Eph** 3:9; **Phil** 4:15; **Col** 1:18; **2Th** 2:13; **Heb** 1:10; 3:14; 7:3; **2Pet** 2:20; 3:4; **1Jn** 1:1; 2:7(2); 13; 14; 24(2); 3:8; 11; **2Jn** 5; 6; **Rev** 1:8; 3:14; 21:6; 22:13

BEGUN

2490, *756, 1728, 2691, 4278*

Num 16:46; 47; **Deut** 2:31; 3:24; **Est** 6:13; 9:23; **Mt** 18:24; **2Cor** 8:6; 10; **Gal** 3:3; **Phil** 1:6; **1Ti** 5:11

BEHIND

268, 310, 3498, 5975, *2641, 3693, 3694, 5278, 5302, 5303*

Gen 18:10; 19:17; 26; 22:13; 32:18; 20; **Ex** 10:26; 11:5; 14:19(2); **Lev** 25:51; **Num** 3:23; **Deut** 25:18; **Josh** 8:2; 4; 14; 20; **Judg** 18:12; 20:40; **1Sa** 21:9; 24:8; 30:9; 10; **2Sa** 1:7; 2:20; 23; 3:16; 5:23; 10:9; 13:34; **1Kin** 10:19; 14:9; **2Kin** 6:32; 9:18; 19; 11:6; **1Chr** 19:10; **2Chr** 13:13(2); 14; **Neh** 4:13; 16; 9:26; **Ps** 50:17; 139:5; **Song** 2:9; **Is** 9:12; 30:21; 38:17; 57:8; 66:17; **Eze** 3:12; 23:35; 41:15; **Joel** 2:3(2); 14; **Zec** 1:8; **Mt** 9:20; 16:23; **Mk** 5:27; 8:33; 12:19; **Lk** 2:43; 4:8; 7:38; 8:44; **1Cor** 1:7; **2Cor** 11:5; 12:11; **Phil** 3:13; **Col** 1:24; **Rev** 1:10; 4:6

BEING

1961, 5750, *1096, 1909, 2070, 5225, 5605, 5607*

Gen 18:12; 19:16; 21:4; 24:27; 34:30; 35:29; 37:2; 50:26; **Ex** 12:34; 13:15; 22:14; 28:16; 32:18; 39:9; **Lev** 21:4; 24:8; **Num** 1:44; 22:24; 30:3; 16; 31:32; 32:38; **Deut** 3:13; 17:8; 22:24; 32:31; **Josh** 9:23; 21:10; 24:29; **Judg** 2:8; 9:5; **1Sa** 2:18; 15:23; 26; 26:13; **2Sa** 8:13; 13:4; 14; 19:3; 21:16; **1Kin** 1:41; 2:27; 11:17; 15:13; 16:7; 20:15; **2Kin** 8:16; 10:6; 12:11; **1Chr** 9:19; 24:6; **2Chr** 5:12; 13:3; 15:16; 21:20; 26:21; **Ezr** 6:11; 10:19; **Neh** 6:11; **Est** 1:3; 7; 3:15; 8:14; **Job** 4:7; 21:23; 42:17; **Ps** 49:12; 65:6; 69:4; 78:9; 38; 83:4; 104:33; 107:10; 139:16; 146:2; **Prov** 3:26; 29:1; **Song** 3:8; 10; **Is** 3:26; 17:1; 40:13; 65:20; **Jer** 2:25; 12:11; 17:16; 31:36; 34:9; 40:1; 48:2; 42; **Eze** 17:10; 23:42; 47:8; 48:22; **Dan** 3:27; 5:31; 6:10; 8:22; 9:21; **Mt** 1:19; 23; 24; 2:12; 22; 7:11; 12:34; 14:8; **Mk** 3:5; 5:41; 8:1; 9:33; 14:3; 15:22; 34; **Lk** 1:74; 2:5; 3:1(2); 2; 19; 21; 23; 4:1; 2; 15; 7:29; 30; 8:25; 11:13; 13:16; 14:21; 16:23; 20:36; 21:12; 22:3; 44; **Jn** 1:38; 41; 4:6; 9; 5:13; 6:71; 7:50; 8:9; 10:33; 11:49; 51; 13:2; 14:25; 18:26; 19:38; 20:19; 26; **Acts** 1:3; 4; 2:23; 30; 33; 3:1; 4:2; 23; 36; 5:2; 7:55; 13:4; 12; 14:8; 15:3; 21; 25; 32; 40; 16:18; 20; 21; 37; 17:28; 18:25; 19:40; 20:9; 22:11; 26:11; 27:2; 18; **Rom** 1:20; 29; 2:18; 3:21; 24; 4:11; 12; 19; 21; 5:1; 9; 10; 6:9; 18; 22; 7:6; 9:11; 10:3; 11:17; 12:5; 15:16; **1Cor** 4:12(2); 13; 7:18; 21; 22(2); 8:7; 9:21; 10:17; 12:12; **2Cor** 5:3; 4; 8:17; 9:11; 10:1; 11:9; 12:16; 13:2; 10(2); **Gal** 1:14; 2:3; 14; 3:13; **Eph** 1:11; 18; 2:11; 12; 20; 3:17; 4:18; 19; **Phil** 1:6; 11; 2:2; 6; 8; 3:10; **Col** 1:10; 2:2; 13; **1Th** 2:8; 17; **1Ti** 2:14; 3:6; 10; **2Ti** 1:4; 3:13; **Titus** 1:16; 3:7; 11; **Philem** 1:9; **Heb** 1:3; 4; 2:18; 4:1; 2; 5:9; 7:2; 12; 9:11; 11:4; 7; 37; 13:3; **Jas** 1:25; 2:17; **1Pet** 1:7; 23; 2:8; 24; 3:5; 7; 18; 22; 5:3(2); **2Pet** 3:6; 12; 17; **Rev** 1:12; 12:2; 14:4

BENEATH

4295, 8478, *2736*

Gen 35:8; **Ex** 20:4; 26:24; 27:5; 28:33; 32:19; 36:29; 38:4; **Deut** 4:18; 39; 5:8(2); 28:13; 33:13; **Josh** 2:11; **Judg** 7:8; **1Kin** 4:12; 7:29; 8:23; **Job** 18:16; **Prov** 15:24; **Is** 14:9; 51:6; **Jer** 31:37; **Amos** 2:9; **Mk** 14:66; **Jn** 8:23; **Acts** 2:19

BESIDE

310, 413, 657, 681, 854, 905, 1107, 1115, 2108, 3027, 5921, 5973, 5980, 6654, *846, 1839, 1909, 3105, 4862, 5565*

Gen 26:1; 31:50; **Ex** 12:37; 14:9; 29:12; **Lev** 1:16; 6:10; 9:17; 10:12; 18:18; 23:38(4); **Num** 5:8; 20; 6:21; 11:6; 16:49; 24:6; 28:10; 15; 23; 24; 31; 29:6; 11; 16; 19; 22; 25; 28; 31; 34; 38; 39; 31:8; **Deut** 3:5; 4:35; 11:30; 18:8; 19:9; 29:1; **Josh** 3:16; 7:2; 12:9; 13:4; 17:5; 22:19; 29; **Judg** 6:37; 7:1; 8:26(2); 11:34; 20:15; 17; 36; **Ruth** 2:14; 4:4; **1Sa** 2:2; 4:1; 19:3; **2Sa** 7:22; 13:23; 15:2; 18; **1Kin** 3:20; 4:23; 5:16; 9:26; 10:13; 15; 19; 11:25; 13:31; **2Kin** 11:20; 12:9; 21:16; **1Chr** 3:9; 17:20; **2Chr** 9:12; 14; 17:19; 20:1; 26:19; 31:16; **Ezr** 1:4; 6; 2:65; **Neh** 5:15; 17; 7:67; 8:4; **Job** 1:14; **Ps** 23:2; 73:25; **Song** 1:8; **Is** 32:20; 43:11; 44:6; 8; 45:5; 6; 21(2); 47:8; 10; 56:8; 64:4; **Jer** 36:21; **Eze** 9:2; 10:6; 16; 19; 11:22; 32:13; **Dan** 11:4; **Hos** 13:4; **Zeph** 2:15; **Mt** 14:21; 15:38; 25:20; 22; **Mk** 3:21; **Lk** 16:26; 24:21; **Acts** 26:24; **2Cor** 5:13; 11:28; **2Pet** 1:5

BESIDES

905, 5750, 5921, *3063, 4359*

Gen 19:12; 46:26; **Lev** 7:13; **1Kin** 22:7; **2Chr** 18:6; **Is** 26:13; **Jer** 36:32; **1Cor** 1:16; **Philem** 1:19

BETTER

2896, 3027, 3148, 3190, 3504, *1308, 2570, 2573, 2909, 3081, 3123, 4052, 4284, 4851, 5242, 5543*

Gen 29:19; **Ex** 14:12; **Num** 14:3; **Judg** 8:2; 9:2; 11:25; 18:19; **Ruth** 4:15; **1Sa** 1:8; 15:22; 28; 27:1; **2Sa** 17:14; 18:3; **1Kin** 1:47; 2:32; 19:4; 21:2; **2Kin** 5:12; **2Chr** 21:13; **Est** 1:19; **Ps** 37:16; 63:3; 69:31; 84:10; 118:8; 9; 119:72; **Prov** 3:14; 8:11; 19; 12:9; 15:16; 17; 16:8; 16; 19; 32; 17:1; 19:1; 22; 21:9; 19; 25:7; 24; 27:5; 10; 28:6; **Eccl** 2:24; 3:22; 4:3; 6; 9; 13; 5:5; 6:3; 9; 11; 7:1; 2; 3(2); 5; 8(2); 10; 8:15; 9:4; 16; 18; 10:11; **Song** 1:2; 4:10; **Is** 56:5; **Lam** 4:9; **Eze** 36:11; **Dan** 1:20; **Hos** 2:7; **Amos** 6:2; **Jonah** 4:3; 8; **Nah** 3:8; **Mt** 6:26; 12:12; 18:6; 8; 9; **Mk** 9:42; 43; 45; 47; **Lk** 5:39; 12:24; 17:2; **Rom** 3:9; **1Cor** 7:9; 38; 8:8; 9:15; 11:17; **Phil** 1:23; 2:3; **Heb** 1:4; 6:9; 7:7; 19; 22; 8:6(2); 9:23; 10:34; 11:16; 35; 40; 12:24; **1Pet** 3:17; **2Pet** 2:21

BETWEEN

996, 997, 5921, 5973, 8432, *1722, 3307, 3319, 3326, 3342, 4314*

Gen 3:15(2); 9:12; 13; 15; 16; 17; 10:12; 13:3; 7; 8(2); 15:17; 16:5; 14; 17:2; 7; 10; 20:1; 31:44; 48; 49; 48:12; 49:10; 14; **Ex** 8:23; 9:4; 11:7; 13:9; 16; 14:2; 20; 16:1; 18:16; 22:11; 25:22; 26:33; 28:33; 30:18; 31:13; 17; 39:25(2); 40:7; 30; **Lev** 10:10(2); 11:47(2); 20:25(2); 26:46; **Num** 7:89; 11:33; 13:23; 16:48; 21:13; 26:56; 30:16(2); 31:27(2); 35:24; **Deut** 1:1; 16(2); 39; 5:5; 6:8; 11:18; 14:1; 17:8(3); 19:17; 25:1; 28:57; 33:12; **Josh** 3:4; 8:9; 11; 12; 18:11; 22:25; 27; 28; 34; 24:7; **Judg** 4:5; 17; 9:23; 11:10; 27; 13:25; 15:4; 16:25; 31; 20:38; **1Sa** 4:4; 7:12; 14; 14:4; 42; 17:1; 3; 6; 20:3; 23; 42(2); 24:12; 15; 26:13; **2Sa** 3:1; 6; 6:2; 18:9; 24; 19:35; 21:7(2); **1Kin** 3:9; 5:12; 7:28; 29; 46; 14:30; 15:6; 7; 16; 19(2); 32; 18:6; 21; 42; 22:1; 34; **2Kin** 9:24; 11:17(2); 16:14; 19:15; 25:4; **1Chr** 13:6; 21:16; **2Chr** 4:17; 12:15; 13:2; 16:3(2); 18:33; 19:10(2); 23:16(3); **Neh** 3:32; **Job** 41:16; **Ps** 80:1; 99:1; **Prov** 18:18; **Is** 22:11; 37:16; 59:2; **Jer** 7:5; 34:18; 19; 42:5; 52:7; **Lam** 1:3; **Eze** 4:3; 8:3; 16; 10:2(2); 6(2); 7(2); 18:8; 20:12; 20; 22:26(2); 34:17(2); 20(2); 22; 40:7; 41:10; 18; 42:20; 43:8; 44:23(2); 47:16; 48:22; **Dan** 7:5; 8:5; 16; 21; 11:45; **Hos** 2:2; **Joel** 2:17; **Jonah** 4:11; **Zec** 5:9; 6:1; 13; 9:7; 11:14; **Mal** 2:14; 3:18(2); **Mt** 18:15; 23:35; **Lk** 11:51; 16:26; 23:12; **Jn** 3:25; **Acts** 12:6; 15:9; 39; 23:7; 26:31; **Rom** 1:24; 10:12; **1Cor** 6:5; 7:34; **Eph** 2:14; **1Ti** 2:5

BEYOND

1973, 5674, 5675, 5676, 5921, *1537, 1900, 2596, 4008, 4053, 5228, 5233, 5236, 5238, 5239, 5249*

Gen 35:21; 50:10; 11; **Lev** 15:25; **Num** 22:18; 24:13; **Deut** 3:20; 25; 30:13; **Josh** 9:10; 13:8; 18:7; **Judg** 3:26; 5:17; **1Sa** 20:22; 36; 37; **2Sa** 10:16; **1Kin** 4:12; 14:15; **1Chr** 19:16; **2Chr** 20:2; **Ezr** 4:17; 20; 6:6(2); 8; 7:21; 25; **Neh** 2:7; 9; 12:38; **Is** 7:20; 9:1; 18:1; **Jer** 22:19; 25:22; **Amos** 5:27; **Zeph** 3:10; **Mt** 4:15; 25; 19:1; **Mk** 3:8; 6:51; 7:37; **Jn** 1:28; 3:26; 10:40; **Acts** 7:43; **2Cor** 8:3; 10:14; 16; **Gal** 1:13; **1Th** 4:6

BOTH

413, 1571, 3162, 8147, *297, 1417, 2532, 5037*

Gen 2:25; 3:7; 6:7; 7:21; 23; 8:17; 9:23; 19:4; 11; 36; 21:27; 31; 22:6; 8; 24:25; 44; 27:45; 31:37; 36:24; 40:5; 41:10; 42:35; 43:8; 44:9; 16; 46:34; 47:3; 19; 48:13; 50:9; **Ex** 5:14; 7:19; 8:4; 9:25; 12:12; 31; 13:2; 15; 18:18; 22:9; 11; 26:24; 29:44; 32:15; 35:22; 25; 34; 36:29(2); 37:26; **Lev** 6:28; 8:11; 9:3; 15:18; 16:21; 17:15; 20:11; 12; 13; 14; 18; 21:22; 22:28; 25:41; 44; 54; 27:28; 33; **Num** 3:13; 5:3; 7:1; 13; 19; 25; 31; 37; 43; 49; 55; 61; 67; 73; 79; 8:17; 9:14; 12:5; 15:15; 29; 16:11; 25:8; 27:21; 31:11; 19; 26; 28; 47; 35:15; **Deut** 19:17; 21:15; 22:22(2); 24; 23:18; 30:19; 32:25; **Josh** 6:21; 8:25; 14:11; 17:16; **Judg** 5:30; 6:5; 8:22; 10:10; 15:5; 19:6; 8; 19; **Ruth** 1:5; **1Sa** 2:26; 34; 3:11; 5:4; 9; 6:18; 9:26; 12:14; 25; 14:11; 15:3; 17:36; 20:11; 42; 22:19; 25:6; 16; 43; 26:25; **2Sa** 8:18; 9:13; 15:25; 16:23; 17:18; **1Kin** 3:13; 6:5; 15; 16; 25; 7:12; 50; **2Kin** 2:11; 3:17; 6:15; 17:41; 21:12; 23:2; 15; 25:26; **1Chr** 12:2; 15; 15:12; 16:3; 23:29; 24:3; 28:15; 29:12; **2Chr** 20:25; 24:16; 25:21; 26:10; 27:5; 31:17; 32:26; **Ezr** 3:5; 6:9; **Neh** 1:6; 4:16; 8:2; 10:9; 12:27; 28; 45; **Est** 1:5; 20; 2:23; 3:13; 8:11; 9:20; **Job** 9:33; 15:10; **Ps** 4:8; 49:2; 58:9; 64:6; 76:6; 104:25; 115:13; 135:8; 139:12; 148:12; **Prov** 17:15; 20:10; 12; 24:22; 26:10; 27:3; 29:13; **Eccl** 4:3; 6; 8:5; 11:6; **Is** 1:31; 7:16; 8:14; 10:18; 13:9; 18:5; 31:3; 38:15; 44:12; **Jer** 5:24; 9:10; 14:18; 16:6; 21:6; 23:11; 26:5; 28:8; 31:13; 32:11; 14; 36:16; 44:25; 46:12; 50:3; 51:12; 46; **Lam** 3:26; **Eze** 9:6; 14:22; 15:4; 21:19; 23:13; 29; 34:11; 39:9; 42:11; **Dan** 8:13; 11:27; **Mic** 5:8; 7:3; **Nah** 3:3; **Zeph** 2:14; **Zec** 6:13; 12:2; **Mt** 9:17; 10:28; 12:22; 13:30; 15:14; 22:10; **Mk** 6:30; 7:37; **Lk** 1:6; 7; 2:46; 5:7; 36; 38; 6:39; 7:42; 21:16; 22:33; **Jn** 2:2; 4:36; 7:28; 9:37; 11:48; 57; 12:28; 15:24(2); 20:4; **Acts** 1:1; 8; 13; 2:29; 36; 4:27; 5:14; 8:12; 38(2); 10:39; 14:1(2); 5; 19:10; 20:21; 21:12; 22:4; 23:8; 24:15; 25:24; 26:16; 22; 29; 28:23; **Rom** 1:12; 14(2); 3:9; 11:33; 14:9(2); **1Cor** 1:2; 24; 4:5; 11; 6:13; 14; 7:29; 34; **2Cor** 9:10; **Eph** 1:10; 2:14; 16; 18; **Phil** 1:7; 2:13; 4:9; 12(3); **1Th** 2:15; 5:15; **2Th** 3:4; **1Ti** 4:10; 16; **Titus** 1:9; **Philem** 1:16; **Heb** 2:4; 11; 5:1; 14; 6:19; 9:9; 19; 21; 10:33; 11:21; **Jas** 3:12; **2Pet** 3:1; 18; **2Jn** 9; **Jude** 25; **Rev** 13:15; 16; 19:5; 18(2); 20

BRING

338, 503, 622, 858, 935, 1069, 1431, 1876, 1980, 2142, 2342, 2381, 2986, 3051, 3205, 3212, 3254, 3318, 3381, 3513, 3533, 3665, 3947, 4608, 4672, 5060, 5066, 5080, 5107, 5375, 5381, 5414, 5437, 5647, 5674, 5924, 5927, 6049, 6213, 6315, 6398, 6509, 6779, 6805, 7034, 7126, 7311, 7392, 7665, 7725, 7760, 7817, 7896, 7971, 8045, 8074, 8213, 8317, *71, 114, 321, 363, 518, 520, 667, 1295, 1396, 1402, 1521, 1533, 1625, 1627, 1863, 2018, 2036, 2097, 2592, 2609, 2615, 2673, 3919, 4160, 4311, 4317, 4374, 5062, 5088, 5179, 5342, 5461*

Gen 1:11; 20; 24; 3:16; 18; 6:17; 19; 8:17; 9:7; 14; 18:16; 19; 19:5; 8; 12; 24:5; 6; 8; 27:4; 5; 7; 10; 12; 25; 28:15; 37:14; 38:24; 40:14; 41:32; 42:20; 34; 37(2); 38; 43:7; 9; 16; 44:21; 29; 31; 32; 45:13; 19; 46:4; 48:9; 21; 50:20; 24; **Ex** 3:8; 10; 11; 17; 6:6; 8; 13; 26; 27; 7:4; 5; 8:3; 18; 10:4; 11:1; 12:51; 13:5; 11; 15:17; 16:5; 18:19; 22; 21:6(2); 22:13; 23:4; 19; 20; 23; 25:2; 26:33; 27:20; 29:3; 4; 8; 32:2; 12; 33:12; 34:26; 35:5; 29; 36:5; 40:4(2); 12; 14; **Lev** 1:2(2); 5; 10; 13; 14; 15; 2:2; 4; 8(2); 11; 4:3; 4; 5; 14; 16; 23; 28; 32(2); 5:6; 7(2); 8; 11(2); 12; 15; 18; 6:6; 21; 7:29; 30(2); 10:15; 12:6; 8(2); 14:23; 15:29; 16:9; 11; 12; 15; 20; 17:5(2); 18:3; 19:21; 20:22; 23:10; 17; 24:2; 14; 23; 25:21; 26:10; 21; 25; 31; 32; 27:9; **Num** 3:6; 5:9; 15(2); 16; 6:10; 12; 16; 8:9; 10; 11:16; 13:20; 14:8; 16; 24; 31; 37; 15:4; 9; 10; 18; 25; 27; 16:9; 17; 17:10; 18:2; 13; 15; 19:2; 3; 20:5; 8; 12; 25; 22:8; 23:27; 27:17; 28:26; 32:5; **Deut** 1:17; 22; 4:38; 6:23; 7:1; 26; 9:3; 28; 12:6; 11; 14:28; 17:5; 21:4; 12; 19; 22:1; 2; 8; 14; 15; 21; 24; 23:18; 24:11; 26:2; 28:36; 49; 60; 61; 63; 68; 29:27; 30:5; 12; 13; 31:23; 33:7; **Josh** 2:3; 18; 6:22; 10:22; 18:6; 23:15; **Judg** 6:13; 18; 30; 7:4; 11:9; 19:3; 22; 24; **Ruth** 3:15; **1Sa** 1:22; 4:4; 6:7; 9:7(2); 23; 11:12; 13:9; 14:18; 34; 15:32; 16:17; 19:15; 20:8; 23:9; 27:11; 28:8; 11(2); 15; 30:7; 15(2); **2Sa** 2:3; 3:12; 13; 6:2; 9:10; 12:23; 13:10; 14:10; 21; 15:8; 14; 25; 17:3; 13; 14; 19:11; 12; 22:28; **1Kin** 1:33; 2:9; 3:24; 5:9; 8:1; 4; 32; 34; 10:29; 12:21; 13:18; 14:10; 17:11; 13; 20:33; 21:21; 29(2); **2Kin** 2:20(2); 3:15; 4:6; 41; 6:19; 10:22; 12:4; 19:3; 22:16; 20; 23:4; **1Chr** 9:28; 13:3; 5; 6; 12; 15:3; 12; 14; 25; 16:29; 21:2; 12; 22:19; **2Chr** 2:16; 5:2; 5; 6:25; 11:1; 24:6; 9; 19; 28:13; 29:31; 31:10; 34:24; 28; **Ezr** 1:8; 11; 3:7; 8:17; 30; **Neh** 1:9; 5:5; 8:1; 9:29; 10:31; 34; 35; 36; 37; 38; 39; 11:1; 12:27; 13:18(2); **Est** 1:11; 3:9; 6:1; 9; 14; **Job** 6:22; 10:9; 14:4; 9; 15:35; 18:14; 30:23; 33:30; 38:32; 39:1; 2; 3; 12; 40:12; 20; **Ps** 18:27; 25:17; 37:5; 6; 38:t, 43:3; 55:23; 59:11; 60:9; 68:22(2); 29; 70:t, 71:20; 72:3; 10; 76:11; 81:2; 92:14; 94:23; 96:8; 104:14; 108:10; 142:7; 143:11; 144:13; **Prov** 4:8; 19:24; 26:15; 27:1; 29:8; 23; **Eccl** 3:22; 11:9; 12:14; **Song** 8:2; 11; **Is** 1:13; 5:2; 4; 7:17; 14:2; 15:9; 23:4(2); 9; 25:5; 11; 12(2); 28:21; 31:2; 33:11; 37:3; 38:8; 41:21; 22; 42:1; 3; 7; 16; 43:5; 6; 8; 9; 45:8; 21; 46:8; 11; 13; 49:5; 22; 52:8; 55:10; 56:7; 58:7; 59:4; 60:6; 9; 11; 17(2); 63:6; 65:9; 23; 66:4; 8; 9(3); 20(2); **Jer** 3:14; 4:6; 5:15; 6:19; 8:1; 10:24; 11:8; 11; 23; 12:2; 15; 15:19; 16:15; 17:18; 21; 24; 18:22; 19:3; 15; 23:3; 12; 40; 24:6; 25:9; 13; 29; 26:15; 27:11; 12; 22; 28:3; 4; 6; 29:14; 30:3; 18; 31:8; 23; 32; 32:37; 42; 33:6; 11; 35:2; 17; 36:31; 38:23; 39:16; 41:5; 42:17; 45:5; 48:44; 47; 49:5; 6; 8; 16; 32; 36; 37; 39; 50:19; 51:40; 44; 64; **Lam** 1:21; **Eze** 5:17; 6:3; 7:24; 11:7; 8; 9; 12:4; 13; 13:14; 14:17; 16:40; 53(2); 17:8; 20; 23; 20:6; 15; 34; 35; 37; 38; 41; 42; 21:29; 23:22; 46; 24:6; 26:7; 19; 20; 28:7; 8; 18(2); 29:4; 8; 14; 31:6; 32:3; 9; 33:2; 34:13(2); 16; 36:11; 24; 37:6; 12; 21; 38:4; 16; 17; 39:2; 25; 47:12; **Dan** 1:3; 18; 2:24; 3:13; 4:6; 5:2; 7; 9:24; **Hos** 2:14; 7:12; 9:12; 13; 16; **Joel** 3:1; 2; **Amos** 3:11; 4:1; 4; 6:10; 8:10; 9:2; 14; **Obad** 3; 4; **Jonah** 1:13; **Mic** 1:15; 4:10; 7:9; **Zeph** 1:17; 2:2; 3:5; 10; 20; **Hag** 1:6; 8; **Zec** 3:8; 4:7; 5:4; 8:8; 10:6; 10(2); 13:9; **Mal** 3:10; **Mt** 1:21; 23; 2:8; 13; 3:8; 5:23; 7:18(2); 14:18; 17:17; 21:2; 28:8; **Mk** 4:20; 7:32; 8:22; 9:19; 11:2; 12:15; 15:22; **Lk** 1:31; 2:10; 3:8; 5:18; 19; 6:43; 8:14; 15; 9:41; 12:11; 14:21; 15:22; 23; 19:27; 30; **Jn** 10:16; 14:26; 15:2; 16; 18:29; 19:4; 21:10; **Acts** 5:28; 7:6; 9:2; 21; 12:4; 17:5; 22:5; 23:10; 15; 17; 18; 20; 24; 24:17; **Rom** 7:4; 5; 10:6; 7; 15; **1Cor** 1:19; 28; 4:5; 17; 9:27; 16:3; 6; **2Cor** 11:20; **Gal** 2:4; 3:24; **Eph** 6:4; **1Th** 4:14; **2Ti** 4:11; 13; **Titus** 3:13; **1Pet** 3:18; **2Pet** 2:1(2); 11; **2Jn** 10; **3Jn** 6; **Jude** 9; **Rev** 21:24; 26

BRINGETH

935, 1069, 1319, 2142, 2659, 3318, 3381, 3615, 5060, 5107, 5148, 5414, 5927, 6213, 6331, 6445, 6779, 7725, 7737, 7817, 8213, *399, 616, 1521, 1544, 2592, 4160, 4393, 4992, 5088, 5342*

Ex 6:7; **Lev** 11:45; 17:4; 9; **Deut** 8:7; 14:22; **1Sa** 2:6(2); 7; **2Sa** 18:26; 22:48; 49; **Job** 12:6; 22; 19:29; 28:11; **Ps** 1:3; 14:7; 33:10; 37:7; 53:6; 68:6; 107:28; 30; 135:7; **Prov** 10:31; 16:30; 18:16; 19:26; 20:26; 21:27; 29:15; 21; 25; 30:33(3); 31:14; **Eccl** 2:6; **Is** 8:7; 26:5(2); 40:23; 26; 41:27; 43:17; 52:7(2); 54:16; 61:11; **Jer** 4:31; 10:13; 51:16; **Eze** 29:16; **Hos** 10:1; **Nah** 1:15; **Hag** 1:11; **Mt** 3:10; 7:17(2); 19; 12:35(2); 13:23; 52; 17:1; **Mk** 4:28; **Lk** 3:9; 6:43; 45(2); **Jn** 12:24; 15:5; **Col** 1:6; **Titus** 2:11; **Heb** 1:6; 6:7; **Jas** 1:15(2)

BRINGING

935, 2142, 3318, 5375, 7725, *71, 163, 1863, 1898, 4160, 5342*

Ex 12:42; 36:6; **Num** 5:15; 14:36; **2Sa** 19:10; 43; **1Kin** 10:22; **2Kin** 21:12; **2Chr** 9:21; **Neh** 13:15; **Ps** 126:6; **Jer** 17:26(2); **Eze** 20:9; **Dan** 9:12; **Mt** 21:43; **Mk** 2:3; **Lk** 24:1; **Acts** 5:16; **Rom** 7:23; **2Cor** 10:5; **Heb** 2:10; 7:19; **2Pet** 2:5

BROUGHT

539, 622, 656, 857, 858, 935, 1197, 1310, 1319, 1431, 1468, 1540, 1541, 1589, 1809, 1820, 1946, 1961, 2254, 2342, 2659, 2986, 2987, 3205, 3212, 3218, 3318, 3381, 3467, 3474, 3533, 3665, 3766, 3947, 4161, 4355, 4551, 5060, 5066, 5090, 5148, 5265, 5375, 5414, 5437, 5493, 5674, 5927, 5954, 6030, 6213, 6565, 6819, 7126, 7127, 7136, 7235, 7311, 7323, 7392, 7617, 7725, 7730, 7760, 7817, 7971, 8213, 8239, 8317, *71, 321, 397, 654, 985, 1080, 1096, 1325, 1402, 1521, 1533, 1627, 1806, 1850, 2018, 2049, 2064, 2097, 2164, 2476, 2601, 2609, 2865, 2989, 3350, 3860, 3920, 3930, 3936, 4160, 4254, 4311, 4317, 4374, 4851, 4939, 5013, 5044, 5088, 5142, 5342, 5461, 5842*

Gen 1:12; 21; 2:19; 22; 4:3; 4; 14:16(2); 18; 15:5; 7; 19:16; 17; 20:9; 24:53; 67; 26:10; 27:14; 20; 25(2); 31; 33; 29:13; 23; 30:14; 39; 31:39; 33:11; 37:2; 28; 32; 38:25; 39:1(2); 14; 17; 40:10; 41:14; 47; 43:2; 12; 17; 18(2); 21; 22; 23; 24; 26; 44:8; 46:7; 32; 47:7; 14; 17; 48:10; 12; 13; 50:23; **Ex** 2:10; 3:12; 8:7; 12; 9:19; 10:8; 13(2); 12:17; 39; 13:3; 9; 14; 16; 15:19; 22; 26; 16:3; 6; 32; 17:3; 18:1; 26; 19:4; 17; 20:2; 22:8; 29:10; 46; 32:1; 3; 4; 6; 8; 11; 21; 23; 33:1; 35:21; 22; 23; 24(2); 25; 27; 29; 36:3(2); 39:33; 40:21; **Lev** 6:30; 8:6; 13; 14; 18; 22; 24; 9:5; 9; 15; 16; 17; 10:18; 13:2; 9; 14:2; 16:27; 19:36; 22:27; 33; 23:14; 15; 43; 24:11; 25:38; 42; 55; 26:13; 41; 45; **Num** 6:13; 7:3(2); 9:13; 11:31; 12:15; 13:23; 26; 32; 14:3; 15:33; 36; 41; 16:10; 13; 14; 17:8; 9; 20:4; 16; 21:5; 22:41; 23:7; 14; 22; 28; 24:8; 25:6; 27:5; 31:12; 50; 54; 32:17; **Deut** 1:25(2); 27; 4:20; 37; 5:6; 15; 6:10; 12; 21; 23; 7:8; 19; 8:14; 15; 9:4; 12; 26; 28; 11:29; 13:5; 10; 16:1; 20:1; 22:19; 26:8; 9; 10; 13; 29:25; 31:20; 21; 33:14; **Josh** 2:6; 6:23(2); 7:7; 14; 16; 17(2); 18; 23; 24; 8:23; 10:23; 24; 14:7; 22:32; 24:5; 6; 7; 8; 17; 32; **Judg** 1:7; 2:1; 12; 3:17; 5:25; 6:8(2); 19; 7:5; 25; 11:35; 14:11; 15:13; 16:8; 18; 21; 31; 18:3; 19:3; 21; 25; 21:12; **Ruth** 1:21; 2:18; **1Sa** 1:24; 25; 2:14; 19; 5:1; 2; 10; 6:21; 7:1(2); 8:8; 9:22; 10:18; 27; 12:6; 8; 14:34; 15:15; 20; 16:12; 17:54; 57; 18:27; 19:7; 20:8; 21:8; 14; 15; 22:4; 23:5; 25:27; 35; 28:25; 30:7; 11; 16; **2Sa** 1:10; 2:8; 3:22; 26; 4:8; 10; 6:3; 4; 12; 15; 17; 7:6; 18; 8:2; 6; 7; 10; 10:16; 12:30; 31; 13:10; 11; 18; 14:23; 17:28; 19:41; 21:8; 13; 22:20; 23:16; **1Kin** 1:3; 38; 53; 2:30; 40; 3:1; 24; 4:21; 28; 5:17; 6:7; 7:51; 8:4; 6; 16; 21; 9:9(2); 28; 10:11(2); 25; 28; 12:28; 13:20; 23; 26; 29; 14:28; 15:15; 17:6; 20; 23; 18:40; 20:9; 39; 22:37; **2Kin** 4:5; 20; 42; 5:2; 6; 20; 10:1; 6; 8; 22; 24; 26; 11:4; 12; 19; 12:4; 9; 13; 16; 14:20; 16:14; 17:4; 7; 24; 27; 36; 19:25; 20:11; 20; 22:4; 9; 20; 23:6; 8; 30; 24:16; 25:6; 20; **1Chr** 5:26; 10:12; 11:18; 19; 12:40; 13:13; 14:17; 15:28; 16:1; 17:5; 16; 18:2; 6; 7; 8; 11; 20:2; 3; 22:4; **2Chr** 1:4; 16; 17(2); 5:1; 5; 7; 6:5; 7:22(2); 8:11; 18; 9:10(2); 12; 14(2); 24; 28; 10:8; 10; 12:11; 13:18; 15:11; 18; 16:2; 17:5; 11(2); 19:4; 22:9; 23:11; 14; 20; 24:10; 11; 14; 25:12; 14; 23; 28; 28:5; 8; 15; 19; 27; 29:4; 16; 21; 23; 31; 32; 30:15; 31:5(2); 6; 12; 32:23; 30; 33:11; 13; 34:9; 14(2); 16; 28; 35:24; 36:10; 17; 18; **Ezr** 1:7(2); 11; 4:2; 10; 5:14; 6:5(2); 8:18; **Neh** 4:15; 5:5; 8:2; 16; 9:18; 33; 12:31; 13:9; 12; 15; 16; 19; **Est** 1:17; 2:7; 8; 20; 6:8; 11; 9:11; **Job** 4:12; 10:18; 14:21; 21:30; 32; 24:24; 31:18; 42:11; **Ps** 7:14; 18:19; 20:8; 22:15; 30:3; 35:4; 26; 40:2; 45:14(2); 15; 71:24; 73:19; 78:16; 26; 54; 71; 79:8; 80:8; 81:10; 85:1; 89:40; 90:2; 105:30; 37; 40; 43; 106:42; 43; 107:12; 14; 39; 116:6; 136:11; 142:6; **Prov** 6:26; 8:24; 25; 30; **Eccl** 12:4; **Song** 1:4; 2:4; 3:4; 8:5(2); **Is** 1:2; 2:12; 5:2; 4; 15; 14:11; 15; 15:1(2); 18:7; 21:14; 23:13; 25:5; 26:18; 29:4; 20; 37:26; 43:14; 23; 45:10; 48:15; 49:21; 51:18(2); 53:7; 59:16; 60:11; 62:9; 63:5; 11; 66:7; 8; **Jer** 2:6; 7; 27; 7:22; 10:9; 11:4; 7; 19; 15:8; 16:14; 15; 20:3; 15; 23:7; 8; 24:1; 26:23; 27:16; 32:21; 42; 34:11; 13; 16; 35:4; 37:14; 38:22; 39:5; 40:3; 41:16; 44:2; 50:25; 51:10; 52:26; 31; **Lam** 2:2; 22; 3:2; 4:5; **Eze** 8:3; 7; 14; 16; 11:1; 24; 12:7(2); 14:22(3); 17:6; 24; 19:3; 4; 9(2); 20:10; 14; 22; 28; 21:7; 23:8; 27; 42; 27:6; 15; 26; 29:5; 30:11;

31:18; 34:4; 37:13; 38:8(2); 39:27; 40:1; 2; 3; 4;
17; 24; 28; 32; 35; 48; 49; 41:1; 42:1(2); 15; 43:1;
5; 44:1; 4; 7; 46:19; 21; 47:1; 2; 3; 4(2); 6; 8; **Dan**
1:2; 9; 18; 2:25; 3:13; 5:3; 13(2); 15; 23; 6:16; 17;
18; 24; 7:13; 9:14; 15; 11:6; **Hos** 12:13; **Amos**
2:10; 3:1; 9:7; **Obad** 7; **Jonah** 2:6; **Mic** 5:3; 6:4;
Nah 2:7; **Hag** 1:9; 2:19; **Zec** 10:11; **Mal** 1:13(2);
Mt 1:12; 25; 4:24; 8:16; 9:2; 32; 10:18; 11:23;
12:22; 25; 13:8; 26; 14:11(2); 35; 16:8; 17:16;
18:24; 19:13; 21:7; 22:19; 25:20; 27:3; **Mk** 1:32;
4:8; 21; 29; 6:27; 28; 9:17; 20; 10:13(2); 11:7;
12:16; 13:9; **Lk** 1:57; 2:7; 22; 27; 3:5; 4:9; 16; 40;
5:11; 18; 7:37; 10:34; 11:17; 12:16; 18:15; 40;
19:35; 21:12; 22:54; 23:14; **Jn** 1:42; 4:33; 7:45;
8:3; 9:13; 18:16; 19:13; 39; **Acts** 4:34; 37; 5:2;
15; 19; 21; 26; 27; 36; 6:12; 7:36; 40; 45; 9:8;
27; 30; 39; 11:26; 12:6; 17; 13:1; 17; 14:13; 15:3;
16:16; 20; 30; 34; 39; 17:15; 19; 18:12; 19:12; 19;
24; 37; 20:12; 21:5; 16; 28; 29; 22:3; 24; 30; 23:18;
28; 31; 25:6; 17; 18; 23; 26; 27:24; **Rom** 15:24;
1Cor 6:12; 15:54; **2Cor** 1:16; **Gal** 2:4; **1Th** 3:6;
1Ti 5:10; 6:7; **2Ti** 1:10; S:1; **Heb** 13:11; 20; **Jas**
5:18; **1Pet** 1:13; **2Pet** 2:19; **Rev** 12:5; 13

BROUGHTEST

935, 3318, 5927

Ex 32:7; **Num** 14:13; **Deut** 9:28; 29; **2Sa** 5:2;
1Kin 8:51; 53; **1Chr** 11:2; **Neh** 9:7; 15; 23; **Ps**
66:11; 12

BUT

235

Gen 2:6; 17; 20; 3:3; 4:2; 5; 6:8; 18; 8:9; 9:4;
11:30; 12:12; 13:13; 15:4; 10; 16; 16:6; 17:5; 15;
21; 18:15; 22; 27; 32; 19:2; 4; 10; 14; 26; 20:3(2);
4; 12; 21:23; 26; 22:7; 23:6; 13; 24:4; 33; 38; 25:6;
28; 26:29; 27:22; 38; 28:17; 19; 29:17; 20; 31;
30:42; 31:5; 7; 29; 33; 34; 35; 47; 32:28; 34:12;
15; 17; 35:8; 10; 16; 18; 37:11; 22; 35; 38:20;
39:8; 9; 21; 40:14; 22; 23; 41:8; 21; 24; 54; 42:4;
7; 8; 10; 12; 20; 34; 43:5; 34; 44:17; 45:8; 22;
46:12; 47:18; 30; 48:7; 19; 21; 49:19; 24; 50:20(2);
Ex 1:12; 16; 17(2); 2:15; 17; 3:22; 4:1; 10; 21;
5:16; 17; 6:3; 9; 7:4; 12; 8:15; 18; 29; 9:6; 30; 32;
10:8; 20; 29; 15:19; 16:8; 20; 26; 17:12; 18:22; 26;
19:13; 24; 20:10; 19; 21:13; 14; 18; 28; 29(2);
22:15; 23:11; 22; 24; 24:2; 29:14; 33; 31:15;
32:18; 33:11; 23; 34:13; 20; 21; 34; 35:2; 36:38;
40:37; **Lev** 1:9; 13; 17; 2:12; 5:8; 11; 6:28; 7:16;
17; 20; 24; 31; 8:17; 9:10; 10:6; 11:4; 5; 6; 11; 23;
36; 38; 12:5; 13:6; 7; 14; 21(2); 23; 26(2); 28; 33;
35; 37; 14:9; 53; 15:28; 16:10; 17:16; 19:14; 15;
18; 24; 34; 20:24; 21:2; 4; 14; 22:11; 13(2); 20;
23; 32; 23:3; 8; 25; 25:4; 17; 28; 31; 34; 36; 40;
43; 46; 52; 26:14; 15; 23; 27; 45; 27:8; 13; 18; 21;
29; **Num** 1:47; 50; 53; 2:33; 3:38; 4:15; 19; 20;
5:8; 20; 28; 6:12; 7:9; 8:26; 9:13; 22; 10:4; 7(2);
30; 11:6; 20; 26(2); 12:14; 13:31; 14:10; 21; 24;
31; 32; 38; 41; 44; 15:30; 16:9; 30; 41; 18:2; 17;
23; 24; 19:12; 20; 21:22; 23; 22:20; 24; 35; 23:13;
26; 24:1; 4; 11; 13; 16; 17(2); 20; 26:33; 64; 27:3;
28:19; 27; 29:8; 36; 30:5; 8; 9; 31:18; 32:17; 31:18;
32:17; 23; 27; 30; 33:55; 35:8; 20; 22; 26; 28; 30;
31; 33; 36:9; **Deut** 1:17; 26; 38; 40; 43; 45; 2:11;
12; 21; 30; 3:7; 19; 26; 28; 4:4; 9; 12; 20; 22(2);
26; 29; 5:3; 14; 31; 7:5; 8; 15; 18; 23; 26; 8:3; 18;
9:4; 5; 19; 10:12; 11:7; 11; 28; 12:5; 10; 14; 18;
13:9; 14:7; 12; 20; 15:3; 6(2); 8; 16:6; 17:6; 16;
18:14; 20; 22; 19:11; 13; 21; 20:12; 14; 16; 17;
21:14; 17; 23; 22:7; 20; 25; 26; 23:5; 11; 20; 22;
24; 25; 24:5; 18; 25:15; 26:14; 28:15; 38; 39; 40;
41; 65; 29:15; 20; 30:14; 17(2); 32:15; 52;
34:4; 6; **Josh** 1:8; 14; 2:4; 6; 22; 5:5; 12; 14; 6:13;
19; 22; 7:1; 3(2); 12; 8:4; 9; 14; 9:12; 19; 21; 10:16;
19; 30; 37; 40; 11:13; 14; 20; 13:13; 33; 14:3; 8;
15:63; 16:10; 17:3(2); 8; 12; 13; 14; 18; 18:7;
21:12; 22:3; 5; 7; 18; 19; 27; 28; 23:8; 9; 13; 24:4;
10; 12; 15; 21; **Judg** 1:19; 21; 25; 27; 29; 30;
32; 33; 35; 2:2; 3; 17(2); 3:15; 16; 19; 4:8; 16;
5:31; 6:10; 13; 34; 39(2); 7:6; 10; 19; 8:20; 9:9;
11; 20; 51; 11:16; 17(2); 18; 20(2); 27; 13:3; 6; 7;
9; 21; 23; 14:4; 6; 9; 13; 16; 20; 15:1(2); 13(2); 19;
16:21; 17:6; 19:10(2); 16; 18; 24; 25; 28; 20:9; 13;
14; 32; 34; 40; 42; 47; **Ruth** 1:14; 17; 2:8; 3:3;
13; 4:4; **1Sa** 1; 2; 5(2); 11; 13; 15; 22; 2:15; 16;
18; 25; 30; 4:20; 5:6; 6:3; 9; 7:10; 8:3; 6; 7; 19;
9:4(2); 7; 27; 10:12; 16; 19; 27(2); 12:10; 12; 15(2);
20; 23; 25; 13:8; 14; 16; 20; 22; 14:1; 10; 26; 27;
37; 39; 41; 45; 50; 54; 18:8(2); 16; 17; 19; 25(2);
19:2; 10; 20:2; 3(2); 5; 7; 13; 15; 22; 39; 21:4; 6;
22:17; 23; 23:14; 24; 27; 24:7; 10; 12; 13; 22;
25:3; 14; 15; 19; 25; 29; 31; 37; 44; 26:3; 7; 11;
19; 23; 28:23(2); 29:2; 8; 30:2; 6; 10; 24; 31:4;
2Sa 2:8; 10; 21; 31; 3:1; 13; 22; 26; 4:12; 5:17;
23; 6:10; 7:2; 6; 15; 19; 8:4; 9:10; 10:11; 11:1; 9;
13; 27; 12:3; 4; 12; 17; 19; 21; 23(2); 13:3; 9; 14;
16; 20; 21; 25; 27; 34; 37; 14:2; 6; 25; 29; 15:3;
10; 20; 26; 34; 16:18; 17:16; 18; 18:3(2); 20(2);
22; 23; 29; 19:4; 21; 27; 28; 37; 20:2; 3; 5; 10; 21;
21:2; 7; 8; 17; 22:19; 28; 42(2); 23:6; 7; 12; 16;
21; 23; 24:3; 17; 24; **1Kin** 1:1; 4; 8; 10; 19; 26;
52; 2:7; 8; 9; 26; 30; 33; 3:7; 11; 21; 22(2); 23;

26(2); 5:4; 7:1; 31; 8:16; 19; 27; 41; 9:6(2); 22(2);
24; 11:1; 10; 12; 13; 22; 32; 34; 35; 39; 12:8; 10;
11; 14; 17; 20; 22; 13:18; 22; 33; 14:4; 9; 14;
15:14; 16:22; 25; 17:1; 12; 13; 18:12; 18; 21; 22;
25; 26; 19:4; 11(2); 12; 20:9; 16; 23; 27; 28; 30;
21:5; 15; 25; 29; 22:8(2); 16; 18; 24; 30; 31; 48;
49; **2Kin** 1:3; 4; 6; 12; 2:10; 17; 19; 3:2; 5; 11;
15; 18; 24; 26; 4:27; 31; 41; 5:1; 11; 15; 16(2); 17;
20(2); 25; 6:5; 12; 19; 32(2); 7:2; 4; 10; 19; 8:13;
9:15; 18; 27; 35; 10:4; 9; 18; 19; 23; 31; 11:2; 15;
12:3; 6; 7; 9; 14; 13:6; 7; 11; 19; 22; 14:6(2); 11;
17; 27; 15:25; 16:3; 5; 17:2; 14; 18; 19; 36; 39;
40; 18:6; 12; 20(2); 22; 27; 36; 19:18; 27; 20:10;
21:9; 22:18; 23:9; 23; 35; 25:12; 25; **1Chr** 2:30;
34; 4:27; 5:1; 2; 6:49; 56; 7:14; 10:4; 11:18(2); 25;
12:17; 19; 13:13; 15:2; 16:5; 19; 26; 17:1; 5; 14;
18:4; 19:3; 12; 18; 20:1; 7; 21:3; 6; 8; 13; 17(2);
24; 30; 22:8; 23:11; 17; 22; 24:2; 27:23; 24; 28:3;
9; 29:1; 14; **2Chr** 1:4; 11; 2:6; 4:6; 5:9; 6:2; 6; 8;
9; 18; 32; 7:19; 8:8; 9(2); 10:8; 11; 14(2); 17;
18; 11:2; 12:7; 13:10; 11; 13; 21; 15:2; 4; 5; 17;
16:12; 17:4; 18:6; 7(2); 15; 17; 29; 31; 19:6; 20:10;
12; 15; 21:3; 13; 20; 22:10; 11; 23:6(2); 7; 24:15;
19; 22; 25; 25:2; 4(3); 7; 8; 9; 12; 20; 27; 26:16;
18; 28:1; 9; 10; 20; 21; 23; 27; 29:34; 30:8; 10;
18; 32:8; 9; 25; 33:12; 10; 22; 23; 35:13; 21(2);
22; 36:13; 16; **Ezr** 2:59; 62; 3:6; 12; 4:3(2); 5:5;
12; 13; 8:22; 9:9; 10:13; **Neh** 1:9; 2:12; 3; 10; 20;
3:3; 5; 14; 15; 4:1; 7; 5:15(2); 6:2; 8; 12; 7:4; 61;
64; 9:16; 17(2); 28; 29; 33; 11:3; 21; 13:2; 6; 24;
Est 1:12; 16; 17; 2:15; 3:2; 15; 4:4; 11; 14; 5:9;
12; 6:12; 13; 7:4; 9:10; 15; 16(2); 18; 25; **Job** 1:11;
2:5; 6; 10; 3:9; 21; 4:2; 5; 16; 5:3; 15; 6:1; 14; 25;
7:21; 8:9; 15(2); 9:2; 11; 15; 18; 35; 11:5; 20; 12:7;
3; 7; 13:4; 15; 14:10; 21; 22; 16:5; 7; 12; 20; 17:10;
19:7(2); 28; 20:5; 13; 21:1; 22:8; 18; 20; 23:6; 8(2);
9; 10; 13; 24:24; 26:1; 14(2); 27:17; 19; 28:12;
30:1; 31:32; 32:8; 16; 35:10; 12; 15; 36:6; 7; 12;
13; 17; 37:21; 38:11; 40:5(2); 42:5; **Ps** 1:2; 4; 6;
2:12; 3:3; 4:3; 5:7; 11; 6:3; 7:9; 9:7; 20; 11:5; 13:5;
15:4; 16:3; 18:17; 27; 41(2); 20:7; 8; 22:2; 3; 6; 9;
19; 24; 26:11; 28:3; 30:5(2); 31:6; 11; 14; 32:10;
34:10; 19; 35:13; 15; 20; 37:9; 11; 17; 20; 21; 28;
36; 38; 39; 38:13; 19; 40:17; 41:10; 44:3; 7; 9;
49:15; 50:16; 21; 52:7; 8; 55:13; 21; 23(2); 59:8;
16; 62:4; 63:9; 11(2); 64:7; 66:12; 19; 68:3; 6; 21;
69:13; 20(2); 29; 70:5; 71:7; 14; 73:2; 4; 25; 26;
28; 74:6; 75:7; 8; 9; 10; 77:10; 78:7; 30; 38; 39;
50; 52; 53; 57; 68; 81:11; 15; 82:7; 85:8; 86:15;
88:13; 89:24; 38; 90:4; 91:7; 92:8; 10; 94:15; 22;
96:5; 102:12; 26; 27; 103:17; 105:12; 106:7; 14;
15; 25; 35; 43; 109:4; 16; 21; 28(2); 115:1; 3; 5(2);
6(2); 7(2); 16; 18; 118:10; 11; 13; 17; 18; 119:23;
61; 67; 69; 70; 78; 81; 87; 95; 96; 113; 161; 163;
120:7; 125:1; 5; 127:1; 5; 130:4; 132:11;
135:16(2); 17; 136:15; 138:6; 139:4; 12; 141:8;
142:4; 145:20; 146:9; **Prov** 1:7; 25; 28(2); 33;
2:22; 3:1; 32; 33; 34; 35; 4:18; 5:4; 6:31; 32; 8:36;
9:12; 18; 10:1; 2; 3; 4; 5; 6; 7; 8; 9; 10; 11; 12; 13;
14; 17; 19; 21; 23; 24; 25; 27; 28; 29; 30; 31; 32;
11:1; 2; 3; 4; 5; 6; 9; 11; 12; 13; 14; 17; 18; 20;
21; 23; 24; 26; 27; 28; 12:1; 2; 3; 4; 5; 6; 7; 8; 10;
11; 12; 13; 15; 16; 17; 18; 19(2); 20; 21; 22; 23;
24; 25; 26; 27; 13:1; 2; 3; 4; 5; 6; 8; 9; 10; 11; 12;
13; 15; 16; 17; 18; 19; 20; 21; 24; 25; 14:1; 2;
3; 4; 5; 6; 8; 9; 11; 12; 15; 16; 18; 20; 21; 22; 23;
24; 25; 28; 29; 30; 31; 32; 33; 34; 35; 15:1; 2; 4;
5; 6; 7; 8; 9; 13; 14; 15; 18; 19; 20; 21; 22; 25; 26;
27; 28; 29; 32; 16:2; 9; 14; 22; 25; 33; 17:3; 9; 22;
24; 18:2; 14; 17; 23; 19:4; 12; 16; 20:3; 5; 6; 14;
15; 17; 21; 22; 21:2; 5; 8; 12; 13; 15; 20; 26; 28;
29; 31; 22:3; 3; 23:7; 17; 24:16; 25; 25:2; 27:3;
4; 6; 7; 12; 28:1; 8; 11; 14; 16; 18; 19; 20; 25; 26;
27; 28; 29:2; 6; 14; 18; 19; 20; 21; 22; 25; 26;
28(2); 40; 41; 24:6; 16; 21; 24; 29; 37; 49; **Jn** 1:8;
12; 13; 17; 20; 26; 31; 33; 2:9; 10; 21; 24; 3:8; 13;
15; 16; 17; 18; 21; 28; 29; 30; 36; 4:2; 14(2); 23;
32; 5:7; 17; 18; 19; 22; 24; 30; 34(2); 36; 42; 47;
6:9; 20; 22; 26; 27; 32; 36; 38; 39; 64; 7:6; 7;
10(2); 12; 16; 18; 22; 24; 26; 27; 28; 29; 30; 39;
41; 44; 49; 8:5; 6; 10; 12; 14; 16; 26; 28; 35; 37;
40; 42; 49; 55(2); 59; 9:3; 9; 18; 21; 28; 31; 41;
10:1; 2; 5; 6; 8; 10; 26; 33; 38; 39; 41;
11:4; 10; 11; 13; 20; 22; 30; 42; 46; 51; 52; 54;
12:2; 6; 8; 9; 10; 16; 24; 27; 30; 43; 46; 48;
49; 13:7; 9; 10(2); 18; 36; 14:6; 10; 17; 19; 21; 23;
24:7; 14; 27; 25:4; 9; 11; 19; 21; 25; 26:16;
20; 25(2); 29; 27:10; 14; 21; 22; 27; 39; 41; 43;
28:6; 16; 19; 22; **Rom** 1:13; 21; 32; 2:2; 5; 8(2);
10; 13; 25; 29(2); 3:4; 5; 21; 27; 4:2; 4; 5(2); 10;
12; 13; 16; 20; 24; 5:3; 8; 11; 13; 15; 16; 20; 6:10;
11; 13; 14; 15; 17(2); 22; 23; 7:2; 3; 6; 7; 8; 9; 13;
14; 15; 17; 18; 19; 20; 23; 24; 25; 32; 9:7; 8; 10;
10; 11; 13; 16; 20; 24; 31; 32; 10:2; 6; 8; 16; 18; 19;
20; 21; 11:4; 6; 7; 11; 15; 18(2); 20; 22; 28; 12(2);
3; 16; 19; 21; 13:1; 3; 4; 5; 8; 14; 14:1; 10; 13; 14;
15; 17; 20; 15:3; 21; 23; 25; 16:4; 18; 19; 26; **1Cor**
1:10; 14; 17; 18; 23; 24; 27; 30; 2:4; 5; 7; 9; 10; 4;
11; 12; 13; 14; 15; 16; 3:1; 5; 6; 7; 10; 11; 12; 14;
15; 17; 20; 15:3; 21; 23; 25; 16:4; 18; 19; 26; **1Cor**
13(2); 17; 18; 7:4(2); 6; 7; 9; 10; 11; 12; 14; 15(2);

17; 19; 21; 28(2); 29; 32; 33; 34; 35; 36; 37; 38; 39; 40; 8:1; 3; 4; 6(2); 8; 9; 12; 9:12; 15; 17; 21; 24; 25; 27; 10:5; 13(3); 20; 23(2); 24; 28; 29; 33; 11:3; 5; 6; 7; 8; 9; 12; 15; 16; 17; 28; 32; 12:3; 4; 5; 6; 7; 11; 14; 18; 20(2); 24; 25; 31; 13:6; 8; 10; 11; 12(2); 13; 14:1; 2; 3; 4; 5; 14; 17; 20; 22(3); 24; 28; 33; 34; 38; 15:6; 10(3); 13; 20; 23; 27; 35; 37; 38; 39; 40; 46; 51; 57; 16:7; 8; 11; 12(2); **2Cor** 1:9(2); 12; 18; 19; 24; 2:1; 2; 4; 5(2); 13; 17(2); 3:3(2); 5; 6(2); 7; 14; 15; 18; 4:2(2); 3; 5; 7; 8; 9(2); 12; 16; 17; 18(2); 5:4; 11; 12; 15; 6:4; 12; 7:5; 7; 8; 9; 10; 12; 14; 8:5; 8; 10; 14; 16; 17; 19; 21; 22; 9:6; 12; 10:1; 2; 4; 10; 12; 13(2); 15; 17; 18; 11:3; 6(2); 12; 17; 12:5; 6; 14(2); 16; 19; 13:3; 4; 6; 7; 8; **Gal** 1:1; 7; 8; 11; 12; 15; 17; 19; 23; 2:2; 3; 6; 7; 11; 12; 14; 16; 17; 20; 3:11; 12; 15; 16; 18; 20; 22; 23; 25; 4:2; 4; 7; 9; 14; 17; 18; 23(2); 26; 29; 31; 5:6; 10; 13; 15; 18; 22; 6:4; 8; 13; 14; 15; **Eph** 1:21; 2:4; 13; 19; 4:7; 9; 15; 20; 28; 29; 5:3; 4; 8; 11; 13; 15; 17; 18; 27; 29; 32; 6:4; 6; 12; 21; **Phil** 1:12; 17; 20; 22; 28; 29; 2:3; 4; 7; 12; 19; 22; 24; 25; 27(2); 3:1; 7; 8(2); 9; 12; 13; 4:6; 10(2); 15; 17; 18; 19; **Col** 1:26; 2:17; 3:8; 11; 22; 25; **1Th** 1:5; 8; 2:2; 4(2); 7; 8; 13; 17; 18; 3:6; 4:7; 8; 9; 10; 13; 5:1; 4; 6; 8; 9; 15; **2Th** 2:12; 13; 3:3; 8; 9; 11; 13; 15; **1Ti** 1:8; 9; 13; 2:10; 12(2); 14; 3:3; 15; 4:7; 8; 12; 5:1; 4; 6; 8; 11; 13; 19; 23; 6:2; 4; 6; 9; 11; 17; **2Ti** 1:7; 8; 9; 10; 17; 2:9; 14; 16; 20(2); 22; 23; 24; 3:5; 9; 10; 11; 13; 14; 4:3; 5; 8; 13; 16; 20; **Titus** 1:3; 8; 15(2); 16; 2:1; 10; 3:2; 4; 5; 9; **Philem** 1:11; 14(2); 16(2); 22; **Heb** 1:8; 11; 12; 13; 2:6; 8; 9; 16; 3:4; 6; 13; 17; 18; 4:2; 13; 15; 5:4; 5; 14; 6:8; 9; 12; 7:3; 6; 8; 16; 19; 21; 24; 28; 8:6; 9:7; 11; 12; 23; 24; 26; 27; 10:3; 5; 12; 25; 27; 32; 38; 39(2); 11:6; 13; 16; 12:8; 10; 11; 13; 22; 26(2); 13:4; 14; 16; 19; **Jas** 1:4; 6; 10; 11; 14; 22; 25(2); 26; 2:6; 9; 20; 3:8; 14; 15; 17; 4:6(2); 11(2); 16; 5:12(2); **1Pet** 1:12; 15; 19; 20; 23; 25; 2:4; 7; 9; 10(2); 16; 18; 20; 23; 25; 3:4; 9; 12; 14; 15; 18; 21; 4:2; 6; 7; 13; 14; 15; 16; 5:2(2); 3; 10; **2Pet** 1:9; 16; 21; 2:1; 4; 5; 10; 12; 16; 22; 3:7; 8; 9(2); 10; 18; **1Jn** 1:7; 2:2; 5; 7; 11; 16; 17; 19(2); 20; 21; 22; 23; 27(2); 3:2; 17; 18; 4:1; 10; 18; 5:5; 6; 18; **2Jn** 1; 5; 8; 12; **3Jn** 9; 11(2); 13; 14; **Jude** 6; 9; 10(2); 17; 20; **Rev** 2:6; 9(2); 14; 24; 25; 3:5; 9; 9:4; 5; 11; 10:7; 9; 11:2; 12:12; 14:3; 17:12; 19:12; 20:5; 6; 21:8; 27; 22:3

BY

Gen 7:2(2); 3; 9:6; 11; 10:5; 32; 14:6; 15; 16:2; 7(2); 18:2; 8; 19:36; 20:3; 21:23; 28; 29; 22:13; 16; 23:20; 24:3; 11; 13; 30; 43; 25:11; 13; 16(2); 26:18; 27:40; 29:2; 30:3; 27; 40; 31:24; 31; 39(2); 40; 53; 32:16; 33:8; 35:4; 36:37; 40; 37:28; 38:14; 16; 18; 19; 20; 21; 24; 25; 39:10(2); 12; 16; 41:1; 3; 31; 32; 47; 42:15; 16; 23; 38; 43:32(3); 45:1; 7; 23; 24; 47:13; 48:7; 49:17; 22; 24; 25(2); **Ex** 2:3; 5; 15; 23(2); 3:7; 19; 4:4; 13; 24; 6:3(2); 7:4; 15; 8:24; 9:35; 12:14; 17; 26; 31; 51; 13:3; 14; 16; 21(3); 22(2); 14:2; 9; 20; 21; 15:16; 27; 16:3(2); 18:8; 13; 14; 19:19; 20:26; 21:3(2); 4; 22:25; 26; 23:30; 25:14; 26:9(2); 28:28; 29:11; 18; 25; 28; 32; 38; 41; 43; 30:4; 6; 20; 31:2; 32:13; 27; 33:6; 12; 17; 21; 22(2); 34:6; 7; 35:29; 30; 36:16(2); 37:3; 5; 27; 38:21; 39:4; 21; 40:29; 38(2); **Lev** 1:5; 9; 13; 16; 17; 2:2; 3; 9; 10; 11; 14; 16; 3:3; 4; 5; 9(2); 10; 11; 14; 15; 16; 4:9; 35; 5:12; 15; 17; 6:2; 17; 18; 7:4; 5; 25; 30; 34; 35; 36; 8:21; 28; 36; 10:11; 12; 13; 15(2); 16:21; 31; 19:12; 31; 20:25(3); 21:6; 9; 21; 22:4; 22; 27; 23:8; 13; 18; 25; 27; 36(2); 37; 24:7; 8; 9(2); 25:39; 47(3); 26:7; 8; 23(2); 26; 46; 27:2; **Num** 1:2(2); 3; 17; 18(2); 20(3); 22(3); 24(2); 26(2); 28(2); 30(2); 32(2); 34(2); 36(2); 38(2); 40(2); 42; 45; 52(2); 2:2; 12; 17; 20; 25; 27; 32; 34; 3:15; 17; 18; 19; 20; 26(2); 43; 47; 49; 4:2; 22; 26(2); 29; 32; 36; 37; 38; 40; 42; 45; 49; 5:2; 19; 6:9; 11; 7:84; 9:6; 7; 10; 16(2); 21(2); 23; 10:13; 34; 11:31; 12:2(2); 13:3; 22; 29(2); 14:3; 14(2); 18; 25; 36; 37; 43; 15:3; 10; 13; 14; 23; 24; 25; 28; 16:40; 18:8(2); 11; 17; 19; 32; 20:17; 18; 19; 23; 21:1; 4; 18; 22; 33; 22:1; 5; 23:3; 6; 15; 17; 24:6; 26:3; 55; 63(2); 27:2; 23; 28:2; 3(2); 6; 8; 13; 19; 24; 29:6; 13; 36; 30:3; 10; 31:12; 17; 18; 35; 33:2; 10; 48; 49; 50; 54; 34:3; 13; 18; 35:1; 20; 30; 33; 36:2(2); 13(2); **Deut** 1:2; 7; 19; 22; 33(3); 40; 2:1; 8(2); 27; 30; 36(2); 3:12; 4:34(7); 48; 5:5; 15; 31; 6:7; 13; 7:22; 8:3(2); 9:29(2); 10:20; 11:19; 30; 12:30; 14:22; 15:20; 16:1; 18:1; 20:19; 21:5; 17; 22:4; 23:10(2); 24:9; 25:2; 11; 17; 18; 27:16; 28:10; 68; 29:16; 33:12; 14(2); 29; **Josh** 2:12; 15; 18; 3:4(2); 4:6; 5:1; 4; 5; 7; 13; 7:14(2); 16; 17; 18; 8:3; 15; 9:13; 18; 19; 10:18; 11:7; 23; 13:6; 14; 16; 22; 29; 31; 32; 14:2(2); 15:1; 6; 8; 16:1; 6; 8; 17:2(2); 18:9; 20; 19:51; 20:2; 8; 9; 21:2; 4; 5; 6; 7; 8(2); 9; 40(2); 22:9; 10; 23:4; 7; 24:26; **Judg** 2:18; 3:1; 4(2); 15; 19(2); 4:11; 5:10; 19; 22; 6:11; 25; 27(2); 28; 30; 36; 37; 7:1; 5; 7; 12; 8:11; 9:6; 9; 25; 32; 34; 37(2); 11:18; 26; 16:5; 26; 17:10; 18:3; 16; 28; 19:11; 14; 20:5; 9; 21:7; 11; 12; **Ruth** 2:8; 21; 23; 4:1; **1Sa** 1:7; 9; 26; 2:3; 9; 16; 23; 28; 3:21; 4:13; 18; 20; 5:2; 6:8; 9; 9:23; 10:2; 19(2); 21; 11:7; 9; 14:4; 6(2); 36; 16:9; 20; 17:2; 23; 26; 35; 43; 52; 18:25; 30; 20:7; 9; 19; 25(2); 23:7; 24:3; 21; 25:13; 16; 20; 22; 34; 26:3; 7; 24(2); 27:1; 28:6(3); 8(2); 10; 15(2); 17; 29:1; 2(2); 30:15; 24; **2Sa** 1:6; 12; 2:13; 15; 16; 24; 3:5; 18; 6:2; 7; 10:2; 8; 11:14; 12:14; 25; 13:31; 32; 34; 15:30; 36; 16:2; 13; 17:11; 17; 22; 18:4(3); 23; 19:3; 7; 37; 20:9; 11; 12; 21; 21:10(2); 22(2); 22:9; 30(2); 35; 23:2; 4; 15; 16; 24:16; **1Kin** 1:9(2); 17; 27; 30; 2:8; 23; 25; 29; 42; 3:5; 4:12; 20; 5:9; 11; 14; 6:21; 22; 7:20; 8:38(2); 43; 53; 56; 9:8; 10:5; 25; 29; 12:15; 13:1(2); 2; 5; 9(2); 10; 17(2); 18; 24(3); 25(2); 28; 32; 14:4; 18; 15:13; 29; 30; 16:7; 12; 13(2); 34; 17:3; 5; 16; 20; 24; 18:4; 6(2); 13; 24; 19:2; 11; 19; 20:14(2); 38; 39(2); 21:1; 23; 22:8; 19; 28; **2Kin** 2:1; 7; 11; 13; 23; 3:11; 20; 4:8; 9; 27; 5:1; 2; 6:14; 26; 30; 8:8; 21; 9:27(2); 36; 10:6; 10; 33; 11:11; 14(2); 16(2); 19; 13:7; 25; 14:7; 9; 25; 27; 16:15; 17:4; 6; 13(3); 23; 18:11; 17; 31; 19:7; 11; 23; 28(2); 33(2); 20:11; 21:10; 23:3; 7; 11; 24:2; 25:4(3); **1Chr** 1:48; 3:3; 4:38; 41; 5:7; 10; 17; 6:15; 61; 63; 65(2); 78; 7:4; 5; 7; 9; 11; 29; 8:28; 9:1; 22; 23; 28; 11:3; 11; 14; 18; 12:22; 31; 14:11; 15:16; 16:41; 17:21; 18:3; 19:4; 9; 20:8(2); 21:15; 25; 26; 23:3(2); 24(2); 27; 31; 24:5; 27; 26:16; 25; 27:1; 28:1; 12; 14(2); 15(2); 16; 17(2); 18; 19; 29:5; 8; **2Chr** 1:17; 2:16; 3:3; 5:11; 14; 6:23(4); 33; 34; 7:6; 12; 14; 20; 21; 8:14; 18; 9:4; 18; 24; 10:15; 12:7; 13:5; 16:14; 18:7; 27; 19:5; 20:15; 16; 21:9; 15(3); 19; 22:7; 23:10(2); 13; 15; 18(2); 24:11(2); 13; 25:18; 26:11(2); 15; 28:15; 29:9; 15; 25; 27; 30:12; 21; 31:6; 15; 17(2); 19(2); 32:11(2); 33:8; 34:14; 35:4; 6; 20; 36:13; 15; 21; 22; **Ezr** 1:1; 8; 2:62; 3:4; 11; 4:16; 23; 5:5; 6:9; 7:23; 8:3; 18; 20; 31; 33; 34(2); 9:11; 10:16; 17; 44; **Neh** 1:10(2); 2:6; 13(2); 15(2); 3:15; 23; 25; 4:3; 12; 18(2); 7:3; 5; 64; 8:14; 18; 9:9; 12(2); 14; 19(2); 30; 10:29; 34; 35; 12:37; 13:18; 25; 26; **Est** 1:12; 15; 2:14; 3:13; 15; 7:7; 8:5; 10; 14; 9:25; **Job** 4:9(2); 6:16; 9:11; 11:7; 15:30; 16:12; 17:7; 18:8; 9; 20:29; 21:29; 22:30; 26:12; 13; 27:11; 28:8; 9; 25; 29:3; 19; 30:4; 18; 31:9; 11; 23; 28; 30; 33; 33:18; 35:9(2); 36:12; 22; 31; 32; 37:10; 11; 12; 17; 19; 38:2; 24; 39:9; 26; 41:18; 25; 42:5; **Ps** 1:3; 5:10; 9:16; 10:10; 17:4; 7; 18:8; 29(2); 34; 19:11; 30:7; 33:6(2); 16(2); 17; 37:23; 38:8; 39:10; 41:11; 44:3; 12; 16; 48:4; 49:7; 50:5; 54:1(2); 56:7; 59:11; 63:10; 11; 65:5; 6; 66:7; 68:4; 71:6; 72:3; 73:23; 74:7; 13; 77:20; 78:17; 18; 26; 49; 55; 64; 65; 72; 79:10; 80:12; 88:9; 89:35; 39; 41; 90:7(2); 10; 91:5(2); 94:20; 102:5; 104:8(2); 12; 106:22; 107:7; 119:9; 121:6(2); 128:3; 129:8; 134:1; 136:5; 8; 9; 137:1; 140:5; 147:4; **Prov** 3:19(2); 20; 28; 29; 4:15; 6:26; 7:26; 8:2; 15; 16; 30; 9:11; 11:5; 11(2); 12:3; 13; 14; 13:2; 10; 11(2); 14:4; 15:13; 23; 16:6(2); 12; 20:4; 11; 18; 28; 21:6; 22:4; 24:3; 4; 6; 30(2); 25:15; 26:2(2); 6; 17(2); 26; 28; 27:9; 28:2; 8; 29:4; 19; 30:27; 31:18; **Eccl** 1:13; 5:3; 9; 14; 7:3; 11; 23; 26; 27; 9:1; 15; 10:3; 18; 12:11; 12; **Song** 1:7; 8; 2:7(2); 3:1; 5(2); 5:4; 12; 7:4; **Is** 1:7; 3:5(2); 25; 4:1; 4(2); 5(2); 7:20(2); 9:1; 10:13(2); 34; 13:15; 15:5; 18:2; 19:7(3); 20:2; 22:3; 5; 14; 23:3; 26:13; 27:7; 9; 12; 28:18; 19(3); 29:13; 32:8; 34:17; 36:2; 16; 37:7; 11; 24(2); 29(2); 34(2); 38:8; 16; 40:26(3); 41:3; 42:16; 43:1; 7; 44:4; 5(2); 24; 45:3; 4; 23; 46:3; 48:1(2); 17; 49:10; 19; 50:4; 51:18; 19; 52:12; 53:11; 54:15; 60:19; 62:2; 8(2); 63:12; 19; 64:4; 65:1; 5; 15; 16; 66:16(2); **Jer** 2:8; 17; 34; 4:26; 5:7(2); 22; 31; 6:5; 25; 7:10; 11; 14; 30; 8:3; 5; 10:12(3); 14; 11:21; 22(2); 12:16(2); 13:5; 24; 14:9; 12(3); 15; 15:16; 16:4(2); 17:2; 8(2); 11; 19; 20; 21; 18:21(2); 19:2; 7(2); 20:2; 4; 21:9(3); 22:2; 4; 5; 8; 13(2); 23:27; 32(2); 25:29; 27:3; 5(2); 8; 13(3); 29:3; 19; 22; 31:9; 32; 35(2); 32:17; 34; 36(3); 33:4(2); 34:4; 15; 35:4; 37:2; 38:2(3); 11; 23; 39:4(3); 18; 41:12; 17; 42:17(3); 22(3); 44:12(4); 13(3); 15; 18(2); 26; 27(2); 46:2; 6; 10; 18; 48:19; 49:3; 9; 13; 17; 50:1; 13; 51:14; 15(3); 17(2); 52:7(5); **Lam** 1:12; 14; 2:15; 21; 3:1; 5:12; **Eze** 1:3; 5; 15; 19; 3:15; 23; 4:10; 11; 16(2); 5:12; 14; 6:11(3); 12(2); 8:3; 9:2; 3; 11; 10:9(3); 15; 16; 20; 22; 11:10; 24; 12:3; 4; 7; 13:19; 22; 14:3; 7; 13; 14; 20; 16:6; 8; 15; 25; 36; 56; 61; 17:5; 7; 8; 9; 14; 17; 18; 21; 18:7; 12; 16; 18; 19:7; 10(2); 20:3; 31(2); 21:12; 22:7(2); 12; 23:21; 25(2); 24:6; 21; 25:12; 13; 14; 15; 26:6; 10; 11; 27:12; 16; 34; 28:5(2); 10; 16; 17; 18(2); 23; 29:7; 30:5; 6; 10; 12; 17; 31:7; 9; 12; 14; 18; 32:12; 20; 21; 22; 23; 24; 25; 26; 29(2); 30; 31; 33:27; 30; 34:13; 35:5; 36:17(2); 34; 37; 37:2; 18; 38:17; 39:15; 23; 40:2; 5; 7; 18; 22; 28; 38; 41; 49(2); 41:7; 17(2); 42:20; 43:3; 4; 6; 7(2); 8(3); 13; 44:2(2); 3(2); 45:1; 46:2(2); 8(2); 9(5); 14; 16; 18; 21; 47:2; 12; 16; 18; 22; 48:2; 3; 4; 5; 6; 7; 8; 12; 20; 24; 25; 26; 27; 28; 29; **Dan** 4:17(2); 27(2); 30; 5:10; 7:2; 8; 16; 8:2; 11; 12; 24; 25; 9:2; 3; 5; 10; 11; 12; 18; 19; 10:4; 16; 11:2; 12; 16; 18; 21; 32; 33(4); 12:7; **Hos** 1:2; 7(6); 2:17; 4:2; 6:5(2); 9; 7:4; 16; 8:4; 9; 11:3; 12:3(2); 10(2); 13(2); 13:7; 16; 14:1; **Amos** 2:8; 4:2; 5:3(2); 6:8; 10; 13; 7:2; 4; 5; 7; 8; 11; 17(2); 8:2; 5; 7; 8; 14; 9:5; 10; 12; **Obad** 5; 9; **Jonah** 2:2; 3:7; **Mic** 2:2; 5; 8; 12; 13; 3:8; 7:18; **Nah** 1:6; **Hab** 1:16; 2:4; 5; 10; 12; 3:10; 13; **Zeph** 1:5(2); 18; 2:12; 15; 3:6; **Hag** 1:1; 3; 2:1; 10; 13; 22; **Zec** 1:8; 3:5; 7; 4:3; 6(3); 14; 5:4; 7:7; 12; 8:9; 9:8; 11; **Mal** 1:1; 9; 2:10; **Mt** 1:22; 2:5; 14; 15; 17; 23; 3:3; 4:4(2); 14; 15; 18; 5:21; 26; 27; 33; 34; 35(2); 36; 6:27; 7:16; 20; 8:17; 28; 9:25; 11:12; 12:17; 24; 27(2); 28; 33; 37(2); 13:1; 4; 14; 19; 21(2); 35; 14:13; 15:3; 5(2); 6; 17:21; 18:7; 28; 20:30(2); 21:4; 23; 24; 27; 22:1; 31; 23:16(2); 18(2); 20(3); 21(3); 22(3); 24:15; 26:4; 24; 63; 73; 27:9; 32; 35; 39; 64; 28:9; 13; **Mk** 1:16; 31; 2:13; 14; 3:22; 4:1(2); 2; 4; 15; 5:4; 7; 21; 22; 41; 6:2; 7; 25(2); 32; 39; 40(2); 48; 7:11(2); 26; 8:3; 23; 27; 9:2; 27; 29(2); 33; 34; 10:1; 46; 11:4; 20; 28; 29; 33; 12:1; 36; 13:14; 14:1; 19; 21; 47; 69; 70; 15:21; 29; 35; **Lk** 1:61; 70; 77; 2:8; 18; 26; 27; 3:19; 4:1; 4(2); 5:1; 2; 15; 17; 19; 6:44; 8:4; 5; 12; 20; 36; 54; 9:7; 14; 47; 10:4; 19; 31(2); 32; 11:3; 19(2); 13:17; 16:22; 17:6; 7(2); 18:5; 31; 35; 36; 37; 19:8; 15; 24; 20:2; 8; 21:9(2); 16; 24; 22:22; 56; 23:8; 24:4; 12; 32; **Jn** 1:3; 10; 17(2); 42; 3:2; 34; 5:2; 6:15; 18; 57(2); 7:50; 8:9(2); 59; 9:1; 7; 21; 10:1; 2; 3; 9; 11:39; 42; 12:11; 29; 13:35; 14:6; 16:30; 18:22; 19:7; 25; 26; 39; 20:7; 21:19; **Acts** 1:3; 10; 16; 25; 2:16; 22(2); 23(2); 33; 43; 3:7; 12; 16; 18; 21; 4:7(2); 9; 10(2); 16; 25; 30(2); 36; 5:10; 12; 15; 19; 6:10; 7:25; 35; 42; 53; 9:8; 13; 25(2); 36; 39; 10:6; 22; 32; 36; 11:4; 5; 28; 30; 12:9; 20; 13:4; 8; 11; 19; 21; 36; 39(2); 45; 14:3; 15:3; 7; 9; 12; 23; 27; 40; 16:2; 8; 13; 16; 17:10; 23; 29; 31; 18:3; 9; 21; 28; 19:10; 11; 13; 25; 20:16; 19; 31; 21:19; 22:11; 20; 24; 25; 23:2; 4; 10; 11; 19; 31; 24:2(2); 8; 21; 25:14; 26:18; 27:2; 11; 12; 13; 16; 23; 28:16; 25; **Rom** 1:2; 4; 5; 10(2); 12; 17; 20; 2:7; 12; 14; 16; 27(2); 3:20(2); 21; 22; 24; 27(2); 28; 30; 4:2; 16; 5:1; 2(2); 5; 9; 10(2); 11; 12(2); 15(2); 16(2); 17(3); 18(2); 19(2); 21; 6:4(2); 7:2; 4; 5; 7; 8; 11(2); 13(2); 8:11; 14; 20; 24; 9:10(2); 32(2); 10:5; 17(2); 19(2); 11:6; 14; 20; 24; 12:1; 2; 14:14; 15:16; 18(2); 19; 24; 28; 32; 16:18; 26; S:1; **1Cor** 1:4; 5; 9; 10; 11; 21(2); 2:10; 3:5; 13; 15; 4:4; 6:2; 11; 14; 7:6; 14(2); 39; 8:6(2); 9; 9:22; 27; 10:30; 11:12; 12:3(2); 8(2); 9(2); 13; 14:6(4); 9; 19; 27(3); 30; 31; 15:2; 10; 21(2); 31; 16:2; 3; 7; S:1; **2Cor** 1:1; 4; 5; 11(3); 12; 16; 19(2); 20; 24; 2:2; 14; 3:3; 10; 18; 4:2; 14; 16; 5:7(2); 18; 20; 6:6(6); 7(3); 8(2); 7:6; 7(2); 9; 13; 8:5; 8(2); 14; 19; 20; 9:12; 13; 14; 10:1; 9; 11; 12; 15; 11:3; 26(2); 33; 12:17; 13:4(2); S:1; **Gal** 1:1(2); 12; 15; 22; 2:2(2); 5; 15; 16(5); 17; 20; 21; 3:2(2); 3; 5(2); 11(2); 18; 19; 21; 22; 24; 26; 4:8; 22(2); 23; 5:4; 5; 6; 13; 6:14; **Eph** 1:1; 5; 2:3; 5; 8; 11(2); 13; 16; 18; 3:3; 5; 6; 7; 9; 10; 12; 16; 17; 21; 4:14; 16; 21; 5:13; 26; S:1; **Phil** 1:11; 14; 20(2); 26; 28; 3:9; 11; 16; 4:6; 19; S:1; **Col** 1:1; 16(2); 17; 20(2); 21; 2:11; 18; 19; 3:17; 4:18; S:1; **1Th** 3:3; 5; 7; 4:1; 2; 15; 5:9; 27; **2Th** 2:1(2); 2(3); 3; 14; 15; 3:12; 14; 16; **1Ti** 1:1; 18; 4:5; 14; 5:21; **2Ti** 1:1; 6; 10; 14; 2:26; 3:16; 4:17; **Titus** 1:9; 3:5(2); 7; **Philem** 1:6; 7; S:1; **Heb** 1:1; 2(2); 3(2); 4; 2:2; 3(2); 9; 10; 3:4; 16; 5:3; 8; 14; 6:7; 13(2); 16; 17; 18; 7:2; 11; 19; 21; 22; 23; 25; 8:6; 9; 9:11; 12(2); 15; 22; 26; 10:1; 8; 10; 14; 19; 20; 33; 38; 11:2; 3; 4(3); 5; 7(3); 8; 9; 12; 17; 20; 21; 22; 23; 24; 27; 29(2); 30; 31; 13:11; 15; S:1; **Jas** 2:7; 12; 18; 21; 22; 24(2); 25; 5:4; 12(3); 17; **1Pet** 1:3; 5; 12; 18; 21; 23; 25; 2:5; 12; 14; 24; 3:1; 18; 19; 20; 21; 5:2; 10; 12; **2Pet** 1:4; 13; 21(2); 2:2; 3:1; 2; 5; 7; **1Jn** 3:24; 5:2; 6(3); **3Jn** 14; **Jude** 1; 12; 23; **Rev** 1:1; 5:9; 8:13; 9:2; 18(4); 20; 10:6; 12:11(2); 13:14(2); 14:20; 18:15; 17; 19; 23; 21:25

CAME

857, 858, 935, 1691, 1916, 1934, 1946, 1961, 1980, 2015, 3212, 3318, 3329, 3381, 3847, 3996, 4161, 4291, 4672, 5060, 5066, 5182, 5312, 5437, 5559, 5674, 5927, 5954, 6293, 6473, 6555, 6743, 7126, 7127, 7725, *191, 305, 565, 1096, 1237, 1240, 1448, 1525, 1531, 1607, 1831, 1904, 1910, 1994, 1998, 2064, 2113, 2186, 2240, 2597, 2658, 2718, 2944, 2983, 3415, 3719, 3854, 3918, 3922, 3928, 4130, 4334, 4370, 4863, 4869, 4872, 4884, 4905, 5342*

Gen 4:3; 8; 6:1; 4; 7:10; 8:6; 11; 13; 10:14; 11:2; 5; 31; 12:5; 11; 14; 13:18; 14:1; 5; 7; 13; 15:1; 4; 11; 17; 19:1; 5; 8; 9(2); 17; 29; 34; 20:3; 13; 21:22; 22:1; 9; 20; 23:2; 24:15(2); 16; 22; 30(2); 32; 42; 45; 52; 62; 25:11; 25; 26; 29; 26:8; 32(2); 27:1; 18; 27; 30(2); 35; 29:1; 9; 10; 13; 23; 25; 30:16; 25; 30; 38(2); 41; 31:10; 24; 32:6; 13; 33:1; 3; 6; 7(2); 18(2); 34:7; 20; 25(2); 27; 35:6; 9; 17; 18; 22; 27; 36:16; 17; 18; 29; 30; 40; 37:14; 18; 23; 25; 38:1; 9; 18; 24; 27; 28(2); 29(2); 30; 39:5; 7; 10; 11; 13; 14; 15; 16; 17; 18; 19; 40:1; 6; 20; 41:1; 2; 3; 5; 8; 13; 14; 18; 19; 22; 27; 50; 57; 42:5(2); 6; 29; 35; 43:2; 19; 20; 21(2); 25; 26; 44:14; 18; 24(2); 45:4; 25; 46:1; 6; 8; 26(2); 27; 28; 47:1; 15; 18; 48:1; 5; 7; 50:10; **Ex** 1:1(2); 5; 21; 2:5; 11; 16; 17; 18; 23(2); 3:1; 4:24; 5:15; 20; 23; 6:28; 8:6; 24; 10:3; 12:29; 41(2); 51; 13:3; 4; 8; 15; 17; 14:20(2); 24; 28; 15:23; 27; 16:1; 10; 13(2); 22(2); 27; 35(2); 17:8; 11; 18:5; 7; 12; 13; 19:1; 7; 16; 20; 21:3; 22:15; 24:3; 32:19(2); 24; 30; 33:7; 8; 9; 34:29(3); 32; 34(2); 35:21; 22; 36:4; 40:17; 32; **Lev** 9:1; 22; 23; 24; **Num** 4:47; 7:1; 9:6; 10:11; 21; 35; 11:20; 25(2); 12:4; 5(2); 13:22; 23; 26; 27; 14:45; 16:27; 31; 35; 42; 43; 17:8; 19:2; 20:1; 11; 20; 22; 28; 21:1; 7; 9; 23; 22:7; 9; 16; 20; 39; 41; 23:17; 24:2; 25:6; 26:1; 27:1; 31:14; 48; 32:2; 11; 16; 33:9; 36:1; **Deut** 1:3; 19; 22; 24; 31; 44; 2:14; 16; 23; 32; 3:1; 4:11; 45; 5:23(2); 9:7; 11; 15; 10:5; 11:5; 10; 22:14; 23:4; 29:7(2); 16; 31:24; 32:17; 44; 33:2(2); 21; **Josh** 1:1; 2:1; 2; 4; 5; 8; 10; 22; 23; 3:1; 2; 14; 16(2); 4:1; 11; 18; 19; 22; 5:1; 4(2); 5(2); 6; 8; 13; 6:1; 8; 9; 11; 13; 15; 16; 20; 8:11; 14; 24; 9:1; 12; 16; 17; 10:1; 9; 11; 20; 24(2); 27; 33; 11:1; 5; 7; 21; 14:6; 15:18(2); 16:7; 17:4; 13; 18:9; 11; 19:1; 10; 17; 24; 32; 40; 21:1; 4; 45; 22:10; 15; 23:1; 24:6; 11; 29; **Judg** 1:1; 14(2); 28; 2:1; 4; 19; 3:10; 20; 22; 24; 27; 4:5; 22(2); 5:14; 19; 23; 6:3(2); 5(2); 7; 11; 25; 34; 35; 7:9; 13; 19; 8:4; 15; 33; 9:25; 26; 42; 52; 57; 11:4; 13;

16(2); 18(2); 29; 34(2); 35; 39; 13:6(2); 9; 10; 11; 20; 14:2; 5; 6; 9; 11; 14(2); 15; 17; 19; 15:1; 6; 14(2); 17; 19(2); 16:4; 5; 16; 18; 25; 31; 17:8; 18:2; 7; 8; 13; 15; 17; 27; 19:1; 5; 10; 16; 22; 26; 30; 20:4; 21; 24; 26; 33; 34; 42; 48(2); 21:2; 4; 5(2); 8(2); 14; **Ruth** 1:1; 2; 19(2); 22; 2:3; 4; 6; 7; 3:7; 8; 14; 16; 4:1; **1Sa** 1:12; 19; 20; 2:13; 14; 15; 19; 27; 3:2; 10; 4:1; 5; 12; 13(2); 14; 16; 18; 19; 5:10(2); 6:14; 7:1; 2; 11; 13; 8:1; 4; 9:12; 14; 15; 26; 10:9; 10(2); 11; 13; 14; 11:1; 4; 5; 6; 7; 9(2); 11(2); 12:12; 13:5; 8; 10(2); 17; 22; 14:1; 19; 20; 25; 15:2; 5; 6; 10; 12; 13; 32; 35; 16:4; 6; 13; 21; 23; 17:20; 22; 23; 34; 41; 48(2); 18:1; 6(3); 10(2); 13; 16; 19; 30; 19:18; 22; 23; 20:1; 27; 35; 38; 21:1; 5; 22:5; 11; 23:6(2); 19; 25; 27; 24:1; 3; 5; 16; 25:9; 12; 20(2); 36; 37; 38; 26:1; 3; 5; 7; 15; 27:9; 28:1; 4; 8; 21; 30:1; 3; 9; 12; 21(2); 23; 26; 31:7; 8(2); 12; **2Sa** 1:1; 2(3); 2:1; 4; 23(3); 29; 32; 3:6; 20; 22; 23; 24(2); 25; 35; 4:4(2); 5; 6; 7; 5:1; 3; 17; 18; 20; 22; 6:6; 16; 20; 7:1; 4(2); 8:1; 5; 10:1; 2; 8; 14; 16; 17; 11:1; 2; 4; 14; 16; 22; 23; 12:1; 4; 18; 20(2); 13:1; 23; 24; 30(2); 34; 36(2); 14:31; 33(2); 15:1; 2; 5; 6; 7; 13; 18; 32(2); 37(2); 16:5(4); 11; 14; 15; 16; 17:18; 20; 21(2); 24; 27; 18:4; 25; 31; 19:5; 8; 15(2); 16; 24(2); 25; 31; 41; 20:3; 12; 15; 21:18; 22:10; 23:13; 24:6(2); 7; 8; 11; 13; 18; **1Kin** 1:22; 28; 32; 40; 42; 47; 53; 2:7; 8; 13; 28; 30; 39; 3:15; 16; 18; 4:27; 34; 5:7; 6:1; 11; 7:14; 8:3; 9; 10; 9:1; 10; 12; 24; 28; 10:1; 2; 7; 10; 12; 14; 22; 29; 11:4; 15; 18(2); 29; 12:2; 3; 12; 20; 22; 13:1; 4; 10; 11; 12; 20(2); 21; 23; 25; 29; 31; 14:4; 6; 17(2); 25(2); 15:21; 29; 16:1; 7; 11; 18; 31; 17:2; 7; 8; 10; 17; 22; 18:1(2); 17; 21; 27; 29; 30; 31; 36(2); 44; 45; 19:3; 4; 7; 9(2); 13; 20:5; 12; 13; 19; 22; 26; 28; 30; 32; 33; 43; 21:1; 4; 5; 13; 15; 16; 17; 27; 28; 22:2(2); 15; 21; 32; 33; **2Kin** 1:6; 7; 10; 12; 13; 14; 2:1; 3; 4; 5; 9; 11; 15; 18; 23; 24; 3:5; 15(2); 20(2); 24; 4:6; 7; 11; 25(2); 27(2); 38; 39; 40; 42; 5:7; 9; 13; 14; 15; 24; 6:4; 14; 18; 20; 23; 24; 30; 32; 33; 7:8(2); 10(2); 17; 18; 8:3; 5; 7; 9; 14; 15; 9:5; 11(2); 17; 18; 19; 20; 22; 36; 10:7(2); 8; 9; 12; 17; 21(3); 25; 11:9; 13; 16; 19; 12:10; 13:14; 21; 14:5; 13; 15:12; 14; 19; 29; 16:5; 6; 11; 17:3; 5; 28; 18:1; 9(2); 17(2); 18; 37; 19:1; 5; 33; 35; 37; 20:1; 4(2); 14(2); 21:15; 22:3; 9; 11; 23:9; 17; 18; 34; 24:1; 3; 7; 10; 11; 20; 25:1(2); 8; 23; 25(2); 26; 27; **1Chr** 1:12; 2:53; 55; 4:41; 5:2; 7:21; 22; 10:7; 8(2); 11:3; 12:1; 16; 18; 19; 22; 23; 38; 13:9; 14:9; 11; 15:26; 29(2); 17:1; 3(2); 16; 18:1; 5; 19:1; 2; 7(2); 9; 15; 17; 20:1(2); 4; 21:4; 11; 21; 22:8; 24:7; 28; 25:9; 26:14; 16; 27:1; **2Chr** 1:13; 5:4; 10; 11; 13; 7:1; 3; 11; 8:1; 9:1; 6; 13; 21; 10:2; 3; 12; 11:2; 14; 16; 12:1; 2(2); 3; 4; 5; 7; 9; 11; 13:15; 14:9(2); 14; 15:1; 5; 16:1; 5; 7; 18:20; 23; 31; 32; 20:1(2); 2; 4; 10; 14; 24; 25; 28; 21:12; 17; 19; 22:1; 8; 23:2; 12; 20; 24:4; 11(2); 17; 18; 20; 23(3); 24; 25:3; 7; 14; 16; 20; 28:9; 12; 20; 29:15; 17; 30:11; 25(2); 27; 31:5; 8; 32:1; 21; 26; 34:9; 19; 35:20; 22; 36:6; **Ezr** 2:1; 2; 68; 4:2; 12; 5:3; 5; 16; 7:8; 9; 8:32; 9:1; 10:6; **Neh** 1:1; 2; 4; 2:1; 9; 11; 4:1; 7; 12(2); 15; 16; 5:17; 6:1; 10; 16; 17; 7:1; 5; 6; 7; 73; 13:3; 6; 7; 19; 21; **Est** 1:1; 17; 2:8; 13; 14; 3:4; 4:2; 3; 4; 9; 5:1; 5; 10; 6:6; 12; 14; 7:1; 8:1; 17; 9:25; **Job** 1:6(2); 14; 16; 17; 18; 19; 21; 2:1(2); 11; 3:11; 26; 4:14; 6:20; 26:4; 29:13; 30:14; 26(2); 38:29; 42:11; **Ps** 18:6; 9; 27:2; 51:t; 52:t; 54:t, 78:21; 31; 88:17; 105:19; 23; 31; 34; **Prov** 7:15; **Eccl** 5:15(2); 16; 9:14; **Song** 4:2; **Is** 7:1; 11:16; 20:1; 30:4; 36:1(2); 3; 22; 37:1; 5; 34; 38; 38:1; 4; 39:3(2); 41:5; 48:3; 5; 50:2; 66:7; **Jer** 1:2; 3; 4; 11; 13; 2:1; 3:9; 7:1; 25; 31; 8:15; 11:1; 13:3; 6; 8; 14:1; 3; 16:1; 17:16; 18:1; 5; 19:5; 14; 20:3; 18; 21:1; 24:4; 25:1; 26:1; 8; 10; 27:1; 28:1; 12; 29:30; 30:1; 32:1; 6; 8; 23; 26; 35; 33:1; 19; 23; 34:1; 8; 12; 35:1; 11(2); 12; 36:1(2); 9(2); 14; 16; 23; 27; 37:4; 6; 11; 38:27; 39:1; 3; 4; 15; 40:1; 8; 12; 13; 41:1(2); 4; 5; 6; 7; 13; 42:1; 7(2); 43:1; 7(2); 8; 44:1; 21; 46:1; 47:1; 49:34; 52:3; 4(2); 12; 31; **Lam** 1:9; **Eze** 1:1; 3; 4; 5; 3:15; 16(2); 4:14; 6:1; 7:1; 8:1; 9:2; 8; 10:6; 11:13; 14; 12:1; 8; 17; 21; 26; 13:1; 14:1; 2; 12; 15:1; 16:1; 23; 17:1; 3; 11; 18:1; 20:1(2); 2; 45; 21:1; 8; 18; 22:1; 17; 23; 23:1; 17; 39; 40; 24:1; 15; 20; 25:1; 26:1(2); 27:1; 28:1; 11; 20; 29:1; 17(2); 30:1; 20(2); 31:1(2); 32:1(2); 17(2); 33:1; 21(2); 22(2); 23; 34:1; 35:1; 36:16; 37:7; 8; 10; 15; 38:1; 40:6; 43:2; 3; 4; 46:9; 47:1; **Dan** 1:1; 2:2; 29; 3:8; 26(2); 4:7; 8; 13; 28; 5:5; 8; 10; 6:12; 20; 24; 7:3; 8; 10; 13(2); 16; 20; 22(2); 8:2; 3; 5; 6; 8; 9; 15; 17(2); 9:2; 23; 10:3; 13; 18; **Hos** 1:1; 2:15; **Joel** 1:1; **Amos** 6:1; 7:2; **Obad** 5(2); **Jonah** 1:1; 6; 2:7; 3:1; 6; 4:8; 10; **Mic** 1:1; 11; 12; **Hab** 3:3; 14; **Zeph** 1:1; **Hag** 1:1; 3; 9; 14; 2:1; 5; 10; 16(2); 20; **Zec** 1:1; 7; 4:1; 8; 5:9; 6:1; 9; 7:1(2); 4; 8; 12; 8:1; 10; 18; 10:4; 14:16; **Mt** 1:18; 2:1; 9; 21; 23; 3:1; 4:3; 11; 13; 5:1; 7:25; 27; 28; 8:2; 5; 19; 25; 34; 9:1; 10(2); 14; 18; 20; 23; 28; 10:34; 11:1; 18; 19; 12:42; 44; 13:4; 10; 25; 27; 36; 53; 14:12; 15; 33; 34; 15:1; 12; 22; 23; 25; 29; 30; 39; 16:1; 13; 17:7; 9; 14; 19; 24; 18:1; 21; 31; 19:1(2); 3; 16; 20:9; 10; 20; 28; 21:14; 19; 23; 28; 30; 32; 22:11; 23; 24:1; 3; 39; 25:10; 11; 20; 22; 24; 36; 39; 26:1; 7; 17; 43; 47; 49; 50; 60(2); 69; 73; 27:32; 53; 57; 62; 28:1; 2; 9; 11; 13; 18; **Mk** 1:9(2); 11; 14; 26; 31; 38; 40; 45; 2:15; 17; 23; 3:8; 13; 22; 31; 4:4(2); 5:1; 27; 33; 35; 6:1; 22; 25; 29; 33; 34; 35; 53; 7:1(2); 25; 31; 8:3; 10; 11; 9:7; 9; 14; 21; 25; 26; 33; 10:2; 17; 45; 46; 50; 11:1; 13(2); 12:28; 42; 14:3; 16; 32; 15:41; 43; 16:2; **Lk** 1:8; 22; 23; 28; 41; 57; 59(2); 65; 2:1; 9; 15; 16; 27; 46; 51; 3:2; 3; 7; 12; 21; 22; 4:16; 31; 35; 41; 42; 5:1; 7; 12; 15; 17; 32; 6:1; 6; 12; 17(2); 7:4; 11; 12; 14; 16; 33; 45; 8:1; 19; 22; 23; 24; 35; 40; 41; 44; 47; 51; 55; 9:12; 18; 28; 33; 34; 35; 37; 51; 57; 10:31; 32; 33; 38; 40; 11:1; 14; 24; 27; 31; 13:6; 31; 14:1; 21; 15:17; 20; 25; 28; 16:21; 22; 17:11; 14; 27; 18:3; 35; 19:5; 6; 15; 16; 18; 20; 29; 20:1(2); 27; 21:38; 22:7; 39; 66; 23:48; 55; 24:1; 4; 15; 23; 30; 51; **Jn** 1:7; 11; 17; 39; 3:2; 13; 22; 23; 26; 4:27; 30; 46; 6:23; 24; 38; 41; 42; 51; 58; 7:45; 50; 8:1; 2(2); 14; 42(2); 9:7; 10:8; 24; 35; 11:17; 19; 29; 33; 44; 45; 12:1; 9; 20; 21; 27; 28; 30; 47; 16:27; 28; 17:8; 18:37; 19:5; 32; 33; 34; 38; 39(2); 20:3; 4; 8; 18; 19; 24; 26; 21:8; **Acts** 2:2; 6; 43; 4:1; 5; 5:5; 7; 10; 11; 16; 21; 22; 25; 6:12; 7:4; 11; 23; 31; 45; 8:7; 36; 40; 9:3; 21; 32(2); 37; 43; 10:13; 29; 45; 11:5; 22; 23; 26; 27; 28; 12:7; 10; 12; 13; 20; 13:13; 14; 31; 44; 51; 14:1; 19; 20; 24; 15:1; 6; 30; 16:1; 8; 11; 16; 18; 29; 39; 17:1; 13; 18:1; 2; 19; 24; 19:1(2); 6; 18; 20:2; 6; 7; 14; 15(2); 18; 21:1(2); 7; 8; 10; 31; 33; 35; 22:6; 11; 13; 17; 27; 23:14; 27; 33; 24:7; 17; 24; 27; 25:7; 13; 27:5; 8; 44; 28:3; 8; 9; 13(2); 15; 16; 17; 21; 23; 30; **Rom** 5:18(2); 7:9; 9:5; **1Cor** 2:1(2); 14:36(2); 15:21(2); **2Cor** 1:8; 23; 2:3; 12; 11:9; **Gal** 1:21; 2:4; 12; 3:23; **Eph** 2:17; **1Th** 1:5; 3:4; 6; **1Ti** 1:15; **2Ti** 3:11; **Heb** 3:16; 11:15; **2Pet** 1:17; 18; 21; **1Jn** 5:6; **3Jn** 3; **Rev** 5:7; 7:13; 14; 8:3; 4; 9:3; 14:15; 17; 18; 20; 15:6; 16:17; 19; 17:1; 19:5; 20:9; 21:9

CAMEST

935, 1518, 1980, 3318, 3381, 7126, 7725, *1096, 1525, 1831, 2064*

Gen 16:8; 24:5; 27:33; **Ex** 23:15; 34:18; **Num** 22:37; **Deut** 2:37; 16:3(2); 6; **1Sa** 13:11; 17:28; **2Sa** 11:10; 15:20; **1Kin** 13:9; 14; 17; 22; **2Kin** 19:28; **Neh** 9:13; **Is** 37:29; 64:3; **Jer** 1:5; **Eze** 32:2; **Mt** 22:12; **Jn** 6:25; 16:30; **Acts** 9:17

CAN

3045, 3201, 3202, *1097, 1410, 1492, 2480*

Gen 4:13; 13:16; 31:43; 39:9; 41:15; 38; 44:1; 15; **Ex** 4:14; 5:11; **Lev** 14:30; **Num** 23:10; **Deut** 1:12; 3:24; 7:17; 9:2; 31:2; 32:39; **Judg** 14:12; **1Sa** 9:6; 16:2; 17; 18:8; 26:9; 28:2; **2Sa** 7:20; 12:22; 23; 14:19; 15:36; 19:35(3); **1Kin** 5:6; **1Chr** 17:18; **2Chr** 1:10; 2:7; 8; **Est** 8:6(2); **Job** 3:22; 4:2; 6:6; 8:11(2); 9:12; 10:7; 11:10; 12:14; 14:4; 15:3; 22:2; 13; 17; 23:13; 25:4(2); 26:14; 34:29(2); 36:23; 26; 29; 38:37(2); 40:14; 19; 23; 41:13(2); 14; 16; 42:2; **Ps** 11:3; 19:12; 22:29; 40:5; 49:7; 56:4; 11; 58:9; 78:19; 20(2); 89:6(2); 106:2(2); 118:6; 147:17; **Prov** 6:27; 28; 18:14; 20:6; 9; 24; 26:16; 31:10; **Eccl** 2:12; 25(2); 3:11; 14; 4:11; 6:12; 7:13; 24; 8:7; 10:14; **Song** 8:7; **Is** 28:20(2); 38:18; 43:9; 13; 46:7; 49:15; 56:11; **Jer** 2:13; 24; 28; 32; 4:4; 5:1; 22(2); 9:10(2); 13:23; 14:22(2); 17:9; 21:12; 23:24; 31:37; 33:20; 38:5; 47:7; **Lam** 2:13; **Eze** 22:14(2); 28:3; 33:32; 37:3; **Dan** 2:9; 10; 11; 3:29; 4:35; 10:17; **Joel** 2:11; **Amos** 3:3; 5; 8; **Jonah** 3:9; **Mic** 3:11; 5:8; **Nah** 1:6(2); **Mt** 6:24; 27; 7:18; 9:15; 12:29; 34; 16:3(2); 19:25; 23:33; 27:65; **Mk** 2:7; 19; 3:23; 27; 7:15; 8:4; 9:3; 29; 39; 10:26; 38; 39; **Lk** 5:21; 34; 6:39; 12:4; 25; 56; 16:13; 26; 18:26; 20:36; **Jn** 1:46; 3:2; 4(2); 9; 27; 5:19; 30; 44; 6:44; 52; 60; 65; 9:4; 16; 10:21; 14:5; 15:4; 5; **Acts** 8:31; 10:47; 24:13; **Rom** 8:7; 31; **1Cor** 2:14; 3:11; 12:3; **2Cor** 13:8; **Phil** 4:13; **1Th** 3:9; **1Ti** 6:7; 16(2); **Heb** 5:2; 10:1; 11; **Jas** 2:14; 3:8; 12(2); **1Jn** 4:20; **Rev** 3:8; 9:20

CANNOT

369, 408, 518, 1077, 1097, 1115, 3045, 3201, 3202, 3308, 3808, *176, 180, 215, 368, 551, 761, 893, 1410, 1492, 1735, 2192, 2480, 3361, 3467, 3756*

Gen 19:19; 22; 24:50; 29:8; 31:35; 32:12; 34:14; 38:22; 43:22; 44:22; 26; **Ex** 10:5; 19:23; **Lev** 14:21; **Num** 22:18; 23:20; 24:13; 35:33; **Deut** 28:35; **Josh** 24:19; **Judg** 11:35; 14:13; **Ruth** 4:6(2); **1Sa** 12:21; 17:39; 55; 25:17; **2Sa** 5:6; 14:14; 23:6; **1Kin** 3:8; 8:27; 18:12; **2Chr** 2:6; 6:18; 24:20; **Ezr** 9:15; **Neh** 6:3; **Job** 5:12; 6:30; 9:3; 12:14; 14:5; 17:10; 19:8; 23:8; 9(2); 28:15; 16; 17; 31:31; 33:21; 36:18; 37:5; 19; 23; 41:17; 23; 26; 28; **Ps** 40:5; 77:4; 88:8; 93:1; 125:1; 139:6; **Prov** 30:21; **Eccl** 1:8; 15(2); 8:17; 10:14; **Song** 8:7; **Is** 1:13; 29:11; 38:18(2); 44:18(2); 20; 45:20; 50:2; 56:10; 11; 57:20; 59:1(2); 14; **Jer** 1:6; 4:19; 5:22; 6:10; 7:8; 10:5(2); 14:9; 18:6; 19:11; 24:3; 8; 29:17; 33:22; 36:5; 46:23; 49:23; **Lam** 3:7; 4:18; **Dan** 2:27; **Hos** 1:10; **Jonah** 4:11; **Hab** 2:5; **Mt** 5:14; 6:24; 7:18; 19:11; 21:27; 26:53; 27:42; **Mk** 2:19; 3:24; 25; 26; 7:18; 11:33; 15:31; **Lk** 11:7; 13:33; 14:14; 20; 26; 27; 33; 16:3; 13; 26; **Jn** 3:3; 5; 7:7; 34; 36; 8:14; 21; 22; 43; 10:35; 13:33; 37; 14:17; 15:4; 16:12; 18; **Acts** 4:16; 20; 5:39; 15:1; 19:36; 27:31; **Rom** 8:8; 26; **1Cor** 7:9; 10:21(2); 12:21; 15:50; **2Cor** 12:2(2); 3; **Gal** 3:17; 5:17; **1Ti** 5:25; **2Ti** 2:13; **Titus** 1:2; 2:8; **Heb** 4:15; 9:5; 12:27; 28; **Jas** 1:13; 4:2; **2Pet** 1:9; 2:14; **1Jn** 3:9

CANST

3201, 3202, *1097, 1410, 1492*

Gen 41:15; **Ex** 33:20; **Deut** 28:27; **Josh** 7:13; **Judg** 16:15; **1Sa** 30:15; **2Kin** 8:1; **Ezr** 7:16; **Job** 11:7(2); 8(2); 22:11; 33:5; 38:31; 32(2); 33; 34; 35; 39:1; 2; 10; 20; 40:9; 41:1; 2; 7; 42:2; **Prov** 3:15; 5:6; 30:4; **Is** 33:19(2); **Jer** 2:23; 12:5; **Eze** 3:6; **Dan** 5:16(2); **Hab** 1:13; **Mt** 5:36; 8:2; **Mk** 1:40; 9:22; 23; **Lk** 5:12; 6:42; **Jn** 3:8; 13:36; **Acts** 21:37; **Rev** 2:2

CAST

1299, 1457, 1602, 1644, 1740, 1760, 1920, 1972, 2186, 2219, 2490, 2904, 3032, 3034, 3240, 3332, 3333, 3381, 3384, 3423, 3766, 3782, 3874, 3988, 4048, 4054, 4131, 4166, 4788, 5060, 5077, 5080, 5203, 5221, 5307, 5375, 5394, 5414, 5422, 5437, 5499, 5549, 5619, 5927, 6080, 6327, 6437, 6696, 7290, 7324, 7368, 7412, 7760, 7817, 7843, 7921, 7971, 7993, 7995, 8210, 8213, 8216, 8628, *114, 577, 641, 656, 683, 906, 1000, 1260, 1544, 1570, 1601, 1614, 1620, 1685, 1911, 1977, 2210, 2598, 2630, 2975, 3036, 3679, 3860, 4016, 4160, 4496, 5011, 5020*

Gen 21:10; 15; 31:38; 51; 37:20; 22; 24; 39:7; **Ex** 1:22; 4:3(2); 25; 7:9; 10; 12; 10:19; 15:4; 25; 22:31; 23:26; 25:12; 26:37; 32:19; 24; 34:24; 36:36; 37:3; 13; 38:5; 27; **Lev** 1:16; 14:40; 16:8; 18:24; 20:23; 26:30; 44; **Num** 19:6; 35:22; 23; **Deut** 6:19; 7:1; 9:4; 17; 21; 28:40; 29:28; **Josh** 8:29; 10:11; 27; 13:12; 18:6; 8; 10; **Judg** 6:28; 30; 31; 8:25; 9:53; 15:17; **1Sa** 14:42; 18:11; 20:33; **2Sa** 1:21; 11:21; 16:6; 13; 18:17; 20:12; 15; 22; **1Kin** 7:15; 24(2); 46; 9:7; 13:24; 25; 28; 14:9; 24; 18:42; 19:19; 21:26; **2Kin** 2:16; 21; 3:25; 4:41; 6:6; 7:15; 9:25; 26; 10:25; 13:21; 23; 16:3; 17:8; 20; 19:18; 32; 21:2; 23:6; 12; 27; 24:20; **1Chr** 24:31; 25:8; 26:13; 14; 28:9; **2Chr** 4:3(2); 17; 7:20; 11:14; 13:9; 20:11; 24:10; 25:8; 12; 26:14; 28:3; 29:19; 30:14; 33:2; 15; **Neh** 1:9; 6:16; 9:26; 10:34; 11:1; 13:8; **Est** 3:7; 9:24; **Job** 8:4; 20; 15:33; 18:7; 8; 20:15; 23; 22:29; 27:22; 29:24; 30:19; 39:3; 40:11; 41:9; **Ps** 2:3; 5:10; 17:13; 18:42; 22:10; 18; 36:12; 37:14; 24; 42:5; 6; 11; 43:2; 5; 44:2; 9; 23; 51:11; 55:3; 22; 56:7; 60:1; 8; 10; 62:4; 71:9; 74:1; 7; 76:6; 77:7; 78:49; 55; 80:8; 89:38; 44; 94:14; 102:10; 108:9; 11; 140:10; 144:6; **Prov** 1:14; 7:26; 16:33; 22:10; **Eccl** 3:5; 6; 11:1; **Is** 2:20; 5:24; 6:13; 14:19; 16:2; 19:8; 25:7; 26:19; 28:2; 25(2); 30:22; 31:7; 34:3; 17; 37:19; 33; 38:17; 41:9; 57:14(2); 20; 58:7; 62:10(2); 66:5; **Jer** 6:6; 15; 7:15(2); 29; 8:12; 9:19; 14:16; 15:1; 16:13; 18:15; 22:7; 19; 26; 28(2); 23:39; 26:23; 28:16; 31:37; 33:24; 26; 36:23; 30; 38:6; 9; 11; 12; 41:7; 9; 14; 50:26; 51:34; 63; 52:3; **Lam** 2:1; 7; 10; 3:31; 53; **Eze** 4:2; 5:4; 6:4; 7:19; 11:16; 15:4; 16:5; 18:31; 19:12; 20:7; 8; 21:22; 23:35; 26:8; 27:30; 28:16; 17; 31:16; 32:4; 18; 36:5; 43:24; **Dan** 3:6; 11; 15; 20; 21; 24; 6:7; 12; 16; 24; 7:9; 8:7; 10; 11; 12; 11:12; 15; **Hos** 8:3; 5; 9:17; 14:5; **Joel** 1:7; 3:3; **Amos** 1:11; 4:3; 8:3; 8; **Obad** 11; **Jonah** 1:5; 7(2); 12; 15; 2:3; 4; **Mic** 2:5; 9; 4:7; 7:19; **Nah** 3:6; 10; **Zeph** 3:15; **Zec** 1:21; 5:8(2); 9:4; 10:6; 11:13(2); **Mal** 3:11; **Mt** 3:10; 4:6; 12; 5:13; 25; 29(2); 30(2); 6:30; 7:5(2); 6; 19; 22; 8:12; 16; 31; 9:33; 10:1; 8; 12:24; 26; 27(2); 28; 13:42; 47; 48; 50; 15:17; 26; 30; 17:19; 27; 18:8(2); 9(2); 30; 21:12; 21; 39; 22:13; 25:30; 27:5; 35; 44; **Mk** 1:34; 39; 3:15; 23; 4:26; 6:13; 7:26; 27; 9:18; 22; 28; 42; 45; 47; 11:7; 15; 23; 12:4; 8; 41(2); 43(2); 44(2); 14:51; 16:9; 17; **Lk** 1:29; 3:9; 4:9; 29; 6:22; 42; 9:25; 40; 11:18; 19(2); 20; 12:5; 28; 58; 13:19; 32; 14:35; 17:2; 19:35; 43; 45; 20:12; 15; 21:3; 4(2); 22:41; 23:19; 25; 34; **Jn** 3:24; 6:37; 8:7; 59; 9:34; 35; 12:31; 15:6(2); 19:24(2); 21:6(2); 7; **Acts** 7:19; 21; 58; 12:8; 16:23; 37; 22:23; 27:19; 26; 29; 30; 38; 43; **Rom** 11:1; 2; 13:12; **1Cor** 7:35; **2Cor** 4:9; 7:6; **Gal** 4:30; **1Ti** 5:12; **Heb** 10:35; **2Pet** 2:4; **Rev** 2:10; 14; 22; 4:10; 8:5; 7; 8; 12:4; 9(3); 10; 13; 15; 16; 14:19; 18:19; 21; 19:20; 20:3; 10; 14; 15

CAUSE

657, 834, 1697, 1700, 1779, 1961, 2600, 3651, 4616, 4941, 5252, 5414, 5438, 5668, 7379, 7387, 7945, 8267, *156, 158, 846, 873, 1223, 1352, 1432, 1500, 1752, 2289, 2596, 3056, 3588, 4160, 5124, 5484*

Gen 7:4; 45:1; **Ex** 8:5; 9:16; 18; 21:19; 22:5; 9; 23:2; 3; 6; 27:20; 29:10; **Lev** 14:41; 19:29; 24:2; 19; 25:9; 26:16; **Num** 5:24; 26; 16:5(2); 11; 27:5; 7; 8; 28:7; 35:30; **Deut** 1:17; 38; 3:28; 12:11; 17:16; 24:4; 25:2; 28:7; 25; 31:7; **Josh** 5:4; 20:4; 23:7; **1Sa** 17:29; 19:5; 24:15; 25:39; 28:9; **2Sa** 3:35; 13:13; 16; 15:4; **1Kin** 1:33; 5:9; 8:31; 45; 49; 59(2); 11:27; 12:15; **2Kin** 19:7; **1Chr** 21:3; **2Chr** 6:35; 39; 10:15; 19:10; 32:20; **Ezr** 4:15; 21; 5:5; **Neh** 4:11; 6:6; 13:26; **Est** 3:13; 5:5; 8:11; **Job** 2:3; 5:8; 6:24; 9:17; 13:18; 20:2; 23:4; 24:7; 10; 29:16; 31:13; 34:11; 28; 38:26; 27; **Ps** 7:4; 9:4; 10:17; 25:3; 35:1; 7(2); 19; 23; 27; 43:1; 67:1; 69:4; 71:2; 74:22; 76:8; 80:3; 7; 9; 19; 85:4; 109:3; 119:78; 154; 161; 140:12; 143:8(2); **Prov** 1:11; 3:30; 4:16; 8:21; 18:17; 22:23; 23:11; 29; 24:28; 25:9; 29:7; 31:8; 9; **Eccl** 2:20; 5:6; 7:10; 10:1; **Song** 8:2; 13; **Is** 1:23; 3:12; 9:16; 10:30; 13:10; 11; 27:6; 28:12; 30:11; 30; 32:6; 37:7; 41:21; 42:2; 49:8; 51:22; 52:4; 58:14; 61:11; 66:9(2); **Jer** 3:12;

5:28(2); 7:3; 7; 34; 11:20; 13:16; 14:22; 15:4; 11; 16:9; 21(2); 17:4; 18:2; 19:7; 9; 20:12; 22:16; 23:27; 32; 25:15; 29:8; 30:3; 13; 21; 31:2; 9; 32:35(2); 37; 44; 33:7; 11; 15; 26; 34:22; 36:29; 37:20; 38:23; 26; 42:12; 48:12; 35; 49:2; 37; 50:9; 34; 51:27; 36; **Lam** 3:32; 36; 52; 59; **Eze** 3:3; 5:1; 13; 9:1; 14:15; 23; 16:2; 21; 41; 20:4; 37; 21:17; 30; 23:48; 24:8; 26; 25:7; 26:3; 13; 17; 27:30; 29:4; 14; 21; 30:13; 22; 32:4; 12; 14; 34:10; 15; 25; 26; 36:12; 15(2); 27; 33; 37:5; 12; 39:2; 3; 44:23; 30; **Dan** 2:12; 8:25; 9:17; 27; 11:18(2); 39; **Hos** 1:4; 2:11; **Joel** 2:23; 3:11; **Amos** 5:27; 6:3; 8:9; **Jonah** 1:7; 8; **Mic** 7:9; **Hab** 1:3; **Zec** 8:12; 13:2; **Mt** 5:22; 32; 10:21; 19:3; 5; **Mk** 10:7; 13:12; **Lk** 8:47; 21:16; 23:22; **Jn** 12:18; 27; 15:25; 18:37; **Acts** 10:21; 13:28; 19:40; 23:28; 25:14; 28:18; 20; **Rom** 1:26; 13:6; 15:9; 22; 16:17; **1Cor** 4:17; 11:10; 30; **2Cor** 4:16; 5:13; 7:12(2); **Eph** 3:1; 14; 5:31; **Phil** 2:18; **Col** 1:9; 4:16; **1Th** 2:13; 3:5; **2Th** 2:11; **1Ti** 1:16; **2Ti** 1:12; **Titus** 1:5; **Heb** 2:11; 9:15; **1Pet** 4:6; **Rev** 12:15; 13:15

CAUSED

1961, 5414, *3076, 4160*

Gen 2:5; 21; 20:13; 41:52; **Ex** 14:21; 36:6; **Lev** 24:20; **Num** 31:16; **Deut** 34:4; **Judg** 16:19; **1Sa** 10:20; 21; 20:17; **2Sa** 7:11; **1Kin** 1:38; 44; 2:19; 20:33; **2Kin** 17:17; **2Chr** 8:2; 13:13; 21:11; 33:6; 34:32; **Ezr** 6:12; **Neh** 8:7; 8; **Est** 5:14; **Job** 29:13; 31:16; 39; 37:15; 38:12; **Ps** 66:12; 78:13; 16; 26; 119:49; **Prov** 7:21; **Is** 19:14; 43:23; 48:21; 63:14; **Jer** 12:14; 13:11; 15:8; 18:15; 23:13; 22; 29:4; 7; 14; 31; 32:23; 34:11; 16; 48:4; 33; 50:6; 51:49; **Lam** 2:6; 17; 3:13; **Eze** 3:2; 16:7; 20:10; 26; 22:4; 23:37; 24:13; 29:18; 31:15(2); 32:23; 24; 25; 26; 32; 37:2; 39:28; 44:12; 46:21; 47:6; **Dan** 9:21; **Hos** 4:12; **Amos** 2:4; 4:7(2); **Jonah** 3:7; **Zec** 3:4; **Mal** 2:8; **Jn** 11:37; **Acts** 15:3; **2Cor** 2:5

CAUSETH

5414, *2358, 2716, 4160*

Num 5:18; 19; 22; 24(2); 27; **Job** 12:24; 20:3; 37:13; **Ps** 104:14; 107:40; 135:7; 147:18; **Prov** 10:5; 10; 14:35; 17:2; 18:18; 19:26; 27; 28:10; **Is** 61:11; 64:2; **Jer** 10:13; 51:16; **Eze** 26:3; 44:18; **Mt** 5:32; **2Cor** 2:14; 9:11; **Rev** 13:12; 16

CHILDREN'S

1121, *3813, 5043*

Gen 31:16; 45:10; **Ex** 9:4; 34:7; **Deut** 4:25; **Josh** 14:9; **2Kin** 17:41; **Job** 19:17; **Ps** 103:17; 128:6; **Prov** 13:22; 17:6; **Jer** 2:9; 31:29; **Eze** 18:2; 37:25; **Mt** 15:26; **Mk** 7:27; 28

CITIES

5892, 7141, 8179, *4172*

Gen 13:12; 19:25(2); 29(2); 35:5; 41:35; 48; 47:21; **Ex** 1:11; **Lev** 25:32(2); 33; 34; 26:25; 31; 33; **Num** 13:19; 28; 21:2; 3; 25(2); 31:10; 32:16; 17; 24; 26; 33(2); 36; 38; 35:2(2); 3; 4; 5; 6(3); 7(2); 8(2); 11(2); 12; 13(2); 14(3); 15; **Deut** 1:22; 28; 2:34; 35; 37; 3:4(2); 5; 7; 10(2); 12; 19; 4:41; 42; 6:10; 9:1; 13:12; 19:1; 2; 5; 7; 9; 11; 20:15(2); 16; 21:2; **Josh** 9:17(2); 10:2; 19; 20; 37; 39; 11:12; 13; 14; 21; 13:10; 17; 21; 23; 25; 28; 30; 31; 14:4; 12; 15:9; 21; 32; 36; 41; 44; 51; 54; 57; 59; 60; 62; 16:9(2); 17:9(2); 12; 18:9; 21; 24; 28; 19:6; 7; 8; 15; 16; 22; 23; 30; 31; 35; 38; 39; 48; 20:2; 4; 9; 21:2; 3; 4; 5; 6; 7; 8; 9; 16; 18; 19(2); 20; 22; 24; 25; 26; 27; 29; 31; 32; 33(2); 35; 37; 39; 40(2); 41(2); 42(2); 24:13; **Judg** 10:4; 11:26; 33; 12:7; 20:14; 15; 42; 48; 21:23; **1Sa** 6:18(2); 7:14; 18:6; 30:29(2); 31:7; **2Sa** 2:1; 3; 8:8; 10:12; 12:31; 20:6; 24:7; **1Kin** 4:13; 8:37; 9:11; 12; 13; 19(3); 10:26; 12:17; 13:32; 15:20; 23; 20:34; 22:39; **2Kin** 3:25; 13:25(2); 17:6; 9; 24(2); 26; 29; 18:11; 13; 19:25; 23:5; 8; 19; **1Chr** 2:22; 23; 4:31; 32; 33; 6:57; 60(2); 61(2); 62; 63; 64; 65; 66; 67; 9:2; 10:7; 13:2; 18:8; 19:7; 13; 20:3; 27:25; **2Chr** 1:14; 6:28; 8:2; 4; 5; 6(3); 9:25; 10:17; 11:5; 10; 12:4; 13:19; 14:5; 6; 7; 14(2); 15:8; 16:4(2); 17:2(2); 7; 9; 12; 13; 19; 19:5; 10; 20:4; 21:3; 23:2; 24:5; 25:13; 26:6; 27:4; 28:18; 31:1(2); 6; 15; 19; 32:1; 29; 33:14; 34:6; **Ezr** 2:70(2); 3:1; 4:10; 10:14; **Neh** 7:73(2); 8:15; 9:25; 10:37; 11:1; 3(2); 20; 12:44; **Est** 9:2; **Job** 15:28; **Ps** 9:6; 69:35; **Is** 1:7; 6:11; 14:17; 21; 17:2; 9; 19:18; 33:8; 36:1; 37:26; 40:9; 42:11; 44:26; 54:3; 61:4; 64:10; **Jer** 1:15; 2:15; 28; 4:5; 7; 16; 26; 5:6; 17; 7:17; 34; 8:14; 9:11; 10:22; 11:6; 12; 13; 13:19; 17:26; 20:16; 22:6; 25:18; 26:2; 31:21; 23; 24; 32:44(4); 33:10; 12; 13(4); 34:1; 7(3); 22; 36:6; 9; 40:5; 10; 44:2; 6; 17; 21; 48:9; 15; 24; 28; 49:1; 13; 18; 50:32; 40; 51:43; **Lam** 5:11; **Eze** 6:6; 12:20; 19:7; 25:9(2); 26:19; 29:12(2); 30:7(2); 17; 35:4; 9; 36:4; 10; 33; 35; 38; 39:9; **Dan** 11:15; **Hos** 8:14(2); 11:6; 13:10; **Amos** 4:6; 8; 9:14; **Obad** 20; **Mic** 5:11; 14; 7:12; **Zeph** 1:16; 3:6; **Zec** 1:12; 17; 7:7; 8:20; **Mt** 9:35; 10:23; 11:1; 20; 14:13; **Mk** 6:33; 56; **Lk** 4:43; 13:22; 19:17; 19; **Acts** 5:16; 8:40; 14:6; 16:4; 26:11; **2Pet** 2:6; **Jude** 7; **Rev** 16:19

COME

Gen 4:14; 6:13; 18; 20; 7:1; 9:14; 12:11; 12; 14; 15:4; 14; 16; 17:6; 18:5; 21; 19:22; 31; 32; 20:4; 13; 22:5; 24:13; 14; 31; 43; 26:27; 27:21; 26; 40; 28:21; 30:16; 33(2); 31:44; 32:8; 11; 33:14; 34:5; 35:11; 16; 37:10; 13; 20; 23; 27; 38:16(2); 41:29; 35; 54; 42:7; 9; 10; 12; 15; 21; 44:23; 30; 31; 34; 45:4; 9; 11; 16; 18; 19; 46:31; 33; 47:1; 4; 5; 24; 48:7; 49:6; 10; 50:5; **Ex** 1:10(2); 19; 2:18; 3:8; 9; 10; 13; 18; 21; 4:8; 9; 7:15; 8:3; 4; 5; 9:19; 10:12; 26; 11:8; 12:23; 25(2); 26; 48; 13:14; 14:26; 16:5; 9; 17:6; 18:6; 8; 15; 16; 19:2; 9; 11; 13; 15; 22; 23; 24(2); 20:20; 24; 21:14; 22:9; 27; 23:27; 24:1; 2(2); 12; 14(2); 25:32; 33; 28:43(2); 30:20; 32:1; 26; 33:5; 22; 34:2; 3; 30; 35:10; 36:2; **Lev** 4:23; 28; 10:3; 4; 6; 12:4; 13:16; 14:8; 34; 35; 39; 43; 44; 48; 15:14; 16:2; 3; 17; 23; 24; 26; 28; 19:19; 23; 21:21(2); 23; 23:10; 25:2; 22; 25; **Num** 1:1; 4:5; 15; 5:14(2); 27; 6:5; 6; 8:19; 9:1; 10:29; 11:17; 20; 23; 12:4; 13:21; 33; 14:30; 15:2; 18; 16:5(2); 12; 14; 40; 17:5; 18:3; 4; 22; 19:7; 14; 20:5; 18; 21:8; 27; 22:5; 6; 11(2); 14; 17; 20; 36; 38; 23:3; 7(2); 13; 27; 24:14; 17; 19; 24(2); 26:29; 27:21; 31:24; 33:38; 55; 56; 34:2; 35:10; 26; 32; **Deut** 1:20; 22; 2:14; 4:30; 46; 6:20; 7:12; 10:1; 11:13; 29; 12:5; 9; 13:2; 14:29; 15:19; 17:9; 14; 18:6(2); 9; 19; 22; 20:2; 21:2; 5; 23:10; 11; 24:1; 9; 25:1; 9; 17; 26:1; 3; 27:12; 28:1; 2; 7; 15(2); 24; 43; 45; 52; 63; 29:19; 22(2); 30:1(2); 31:2; 11; 17; 21; 32:35; 33:16; **Josh** 2:3(2); 18; 3:4; 8; 9; 13(2); 15; 4:6; 16; 17; 18; 21; 5:14; 6:5; 19; 7:14(3); 8:5(2); 6; 9:6; 8; 9; 10:4; 6; 24; 11:20; 14:11; 18:4; 8; 20:6; 22:24; 27; 28; 23:7; 14; 15(2); **Judg** 1:3; 24; 34; 3:27; 4:20; 22; 6:4; 18(2); 7:13; 17; 24; 8:9; 9:10; 12; 14; 15(2); 20(2); 24; 29; 31; 33; 36; 37(2); 43; 11:6; 7; 12; 33; 12:3; 13:5; 8; 12; 17; 15:10(2); 12; 16:2; 17; 18; 18:10; 19:11; 13; 23; 29; 20:10; 41; 21:3; 21(2); 22; **Ruth** 1:19; 2:11; 12; 14; 4:3; 11; **1Sa** 1:11; 20; 2:3; 31; 34; 36(2); 4:3; 6; 7; 5:5; 6:7; 21; 9:5(2); 9; 10; 13(2); 14; 16; 25; 10:3; 5(3); 6; 7; 8(2); 11; 20; 21; 22; 11:3; 10; 14; 12:8; 13:12; 14:1; 6; 9; 10; 11; 12(2); 26; 16:2; 5(2); 6; 11; 16; 17:8(2); 25(2); 28; 44; 45; 52; 19:16; 20:9; 11; 19; 21; 24; 37; 21:15; 22:3; 23:3; 7; 10; 11(2); 15; 20(2); 23(2); 27; 24:14; 25:8; 19; 30; 34; 40; 26:4; 10; 20; 22; 29:10; 30:1; 31:4; **2Sa** 1:9; 2:24; 3:23; 26; 5:6(2); 8; 13; 23; 25; 6:9; 7:19; 9:6; 10:11; 11:7; 12:4(2); 13:5; 6(2); 11; 35; 14:3; 15; 29(2); 32(2); 15:4; 28; 32; 16:7(2); 16; 17:2; 6; 9; 12; 17; 27; 19:11; 18; 20; 25; 30; 33; 39; 20:16; 17; 24:13; 21; **1Kin** 1:12; 14; 21; 23; 35(2); 42; 45; 2:30; 41; 3:7; 6:1; 8:10; 19; 31; 42; 10:2; 11:2; 12:1; 5; 12; 20; 21; 13:7; 15; 22; 32; 14:6; 13; 15:17; 19; 17:18; 21; 18:12(2); 30; 19:17; 20:17; 18(2); 22; 33(2); 22:27; **2Kin** 1:4; 6; 9; 10; 11; 12; 16; 3:21; 4:1; 4; 22; 32; 36; 5:6; 8; 10; 11; 22; 6:9; 20; 7:4; 5; 6; 9(2); 12; 8:1; 7; 9:16; 30; 34; 10:6; 16; 25; 11:9; 14:8; 16:7; 12; 18:13; 17; 25; 31; 32; 19:3; 9; 23; 28; 32(2); 33; 20:14; 17; **1Chr** 9:25; 10:4; 11:5; 12:17(2); 31; 14:14; 16:29; 17:11; 17; 19:3; 9; 24:19; 29:12; 14; **2Chr** 1:10; 5:11; 6:9; 22; 32(2); 8:11; 9:1; 10:1; 5; 12; 11:1; 13:13; 16:1; 18:14; 19:10(2); 20:11; 16; 22; 22:7; 23:6; 8; 15; 25:10; 14; 17; 28:17; 29:31; 30:1; 5; 9; 32:2; 4; 21; 35:21; **Ezr** 3:1; 8; 4:12; 6:21; 8:35; 9:13; 10:8; 14; **Neh** 2:7; 10; 17; 4:8; 11; 6:2; 3(2); 7; 10(2); 8:17; 9:32; 13:1; 22; **Est** 1:12; 17; 19; 2:12; 15; 4:11(2); 14; 5:4; 8; 12; 6:4; 5; 8:6; 9:26; **Job** 2:11(2); 3:6; 7; 25(2); 4:5; 5:26; 7:9; 8:22; 9:32; 13:13; 16; 14:14; 21; 15:21; 16:22; 17:10; 18:20; 19:12; 20:22; 22:21; 23:3; 10; 26:10; 34:28; 37:13; 38:11; 41:13; 16; **Ps** 5:7; 7:9; 16; 9:6; 14:7; 17:2; 22:31; 24:7; 9; 32:6; 9; 34:11; 35:8; 36:11; 40:7; 41:6; 42:2; 44:17; 46:8; 50:3; 52:t, 53:6; 55:5; 65:2; 66:5; 16; 68:31; 69:1; 2; 27; 71:18; 72:6; 78:4; 6; 79:1; 11; 80:2; 83:4; 86:9; 88:2; 8; 91:7; 10; 95:1; 2; 6; 96:8; 100:2; 101:2; 102:1; 13; 18; 109:17; 18; 119:41; 77; 169; 170; 126:6; 132:3; 144:5; **Prov** 1:11; 3:28; 5:8; 6:3; 11; 15; 7:18; 20; 9:5; 10:24; 11:27; 12:13; 20:13; 22:16; 23:21; 24:25; 34; 25:4; 7; 26:2; 28:22; 31:25; **Eccl** 1:7; 11(2); 16; 2:16; 4:16; 7:18; 8:10; 9:2; 12:1; **Song** 2:10; 12; 13; 4:8; 16(2); 5:1; 7:11; **Is** 1:12; 18; 23; 2:2; 3; 5; 3:24; 4:3; 5:6; 19; 26; 7:7; 17; 18; 19; 21; 22; 23; 24; 25; 8:7; 10; 21; 10:3; 12; 20; 27; 28; 11:1; 11; 13:5; 6; 22; 14:3; 8; 24; 29; 31; 16:8; 12(2); 17:4; 19:1; 23; 21:12; 22:7; 20; 23:15; 17; 24:10; 18; 21; 26:20; 27:6; 11; 12; 13(2); 28:15; 29:24; 30:6; 8; 29; 31:4; 32:10; 13; 34:1(2); 3; 5; 7; 13; 35:4(2); 10; 36:10; 16; 17; 37:3; 9; 24; 29; 33(2); 34; 39:3; 6; 40:10; 41:1(2); 22; 23; 25(2); 42:9; 23; 44:7; 45:11; 14(3); 20; 24; 47:1; 9(2); 11(2); 13; 48:1; 16; 49:12; 18; 50:8; 51:11; 19; 52:1; 54:14; 55:1(3); 3; 13(2); 56:1; 9; 12; 57:1; 59:19; 20; 60:1; 3; 4(2); 5; 6; 7; 13; 14; 63:4; 64:1; 65:5; 17; 24; 66:15; 18(2); 23(2); **Jer** 1:15; 2:3; 31; 3:16(2); 18; 22; 4:4; 7; 9; 12; 13; 16; 5:12; 19; 6:3; 26; 7:10; 32; 8:16; 9:17(2); 21; 25; 10:22; 12:9(2); 12; 15; 16; 13:18; 20; 22; 15:2; 16:10; 14; 19; 17:15; 19; 24; 26; 18:14; 18(2); 19:6; 20:6; 21:13; 22:23; 23:5; 7; 17; 25:3; 12; 31; 26:2; 27:3; 7; 8; 28:9; 30:3; 8; 31:9; 12; 16; 17; 27; 28; 31; 38; 32:7; 23; 24(2); 29; 33:5; 14; 35:11; 36:6; 14; 29; 37:5; 7; 8; 19; 38:25; 40:3; 4(3); 10; 41:6; 42:4; 16; 46:9(2); 13; 18; 21; 22; 47:5; 48:2; 8; 12; 16; 18(2); 21; 45; 49:2; 4; 9; 14; 19; 22; 36; 39; 50:4; 5; 9; 26; 27; 31; 41; 44; 51:10; 13; 27; 33; 42; 46(2); 47; 48; 50; 51; 52; 53; 56; 60; **Lam** 1:4; 14; 22; 3:47; 4:18; 5:1; **Eze** 5:4; 7:2; 3; 5; 6(3); 7(2); 10; 12; 26; 9:6; 11:5; 16; 18; 12:16; 25; 27; 13:18; 14:22; 16:7; 16; 33; 17:12; 18:6; 20:3; 21:19(2); 20; 24; 25; 27; 29; 22:3; 4; 23:24; 40; 24:8; 14; 26; 26:3(2); 16; 27:29; 30:4; 6; 9; 32:11; 33:3; 4; 6(2); 30; 31; 33; 34:26; 36:8; 37:9; 12; 38:8; 9; 10(2); 13; 15; 16; 18(3); 39:2; 8; 11; 17; 40:46; 44:13(2); 15; 16; 17(2); 25; 45:4; 46:9; 47:9(3); 10; 20; 22; 23; **Dan** 2:29(2); 45; 3:2; 26(2); 4:24; 8:7; 23; 9:13; 22; 23; 26; 10:12; 14; 20(2); 11:6; 7; 9; 10; 11; 13; 15; 21; 23; 29; 30; 40; 45; **Hos** 1:5; 10; 11; 2:21; 4:15; 6:1; 3; 8:1; 9:4; 7(2); 10:8; 12; 13:13; 15(2); **Joel** 1:6; 13; 15; 2:20(2); 23; 28; 31; 32; 3:9; 11(2); 12; 13; 18(2); **Amos** 4:2; 4; 10; 5:5; 9; 6:3; 9; 8:2; 9; 11; 9:13; **Obad** 21; **Jonah** 1:2; 7; 4:6; **Mic** 1:3; 9(2); 15; 2:13; 3:11; 4:1; 2(2); 8(2); 5:2; 5; 10; 6:6(2); 7:12; **Nah** 1:11; 2:1; 3:7; **Hab** 1:8; 9; 2:3; **Zeph** 1:8; 10; 12; 2:2(2); **Hag** 1:2; 2:7; 22; **Zec** 1:21(2); 2:6; 10; 6:10(2); 15(2); 7:13; 8:13; 20(2); 22; 23; 11:2; 12:9(2); 13:2; 3; 4; 8; 14:5; 6; 7; 13; 16; 17; 18(2); 19; 21; **Mal** 3:1(2); 5; 4:6; **Mt** 2:2; 6; 8; 11; 3:7(2); 5:17(2); 24; 26; 6:10; 7:15; 8:1; 7; 8; 9; 11; 14; 16; 28; 29; 32; 9:13; 15; 18; 28; 10:12; 13; 23; 34; 35; 11:3; 14; 28; 12:28; 32; 44; 13:32; 49; 54; 14:23; 28; 29(2); 32; 15:18; 16:5; 24; 27; 17:10; 11; 12; 14; 24; 25; 18:7; 11; 19:14; 21; 20:8; 21:1; 10; 23; 38; 22:3; 4; 23:35; 36; 24:5; 6; 14; 17; 42; 43; 50; 25:31; 34; 26:20; 50; 55; 27:1; 33; 40; 42; 49; 57; 64; 28:6; 14; **Mk** 1:17; 24; 25; 29; 2:3; 4; 18; 20; 4:22; 29; 35; 5:2; 8; 15; 18; 23; 39; 6:2; 21; 31; 47; 54; 7:4; 15; 23; 30; 8:34; 9:1; 11; 13; 25; 28; 29; 10:14; 21; 30; 35; 11:11; 12; 15; 19; 23; 27(2); 12:7; 9; 14; 18; 13:6; 29; 14:8; 41; 45; 48; 15:30; 33; 36; 42; 16:1; **Lk** 1:35; 43; 2:15; 3:7; 4:34; 35; 36; 5:7; 17; 35; 7:3; 7; 8; 19; 20(2); 34; 8:4; 17; 19; 29; 41; 9:23; 26; 37; 51; 54; 56; 10:1; 9; 11; 35; 11:2; 6; 20; 22; 33; 12:37; 38(2); 39; 46; 49; 51; 13:7; 14; 29; 35; 14:9; 17; 20; 23; 26; 27; 15:27; 30; 16:26; 28; 17:1(2); 7; 20; 22; 31; 18:16; 22; 30; 35; 40; 19:5; 9; 10; 13; 29; 37; 41; 43; 20:14; 16; 21:6; 7; 8; 9; 28; 31; 34; 35; 36; 22:14; 18; 45; 52(2); 23:33; 24:12; 18; **Jn** 1:31; 39; 46(2); 2:4; 3:2; 19; 26; 4:15; 16; 25; 29; 40; 45; 47(2); 49; 54; 5:14; 24; 29; 40; 43(2); 6:5; 14; 15; 16; 17; 37; 44; 65; 7:6; 8; 28; 30; 34; 36; 37; 41; 8:14; 20; 21; 22; 9:39; 10:10; 11:27; 28; 30; 32; 34; 43; 48; 56; 12:12; 23; 35; 46; 13:1; 3; 19(2); 33; 14:3; 18; 23; 28; 29(2); 15:22; 26; 16:4; 7; 8; 13(2); 21; 28; 32; 17:1; 11; 13; 18:4; 21:4; 9; 12; 22; 23; **Acts** 1:6; 8; 11; 13; 2:1; 17; 20; 21; 3:19; 23; 5:38; 7:3; 7; 34(2); 8:15; 24; 27; 31; 39; 9:26; 38; 39; 10:4; 21; 27; 28; 33; 11:2; 11; 20; 12:11; 13:40; 14:11; 27; 15:4; 16:7; 9; 15; 18; 37; 17:6; 15; 18:2; 5; 27; 19:4; 32; 20:11; 18; 21:11; 17; 22(2); 22:6; 17; 23:15; 35; 24:8; 22; 23; 25; 25:1; 7; 17; 23; 26:7; 22; 27:7; 16; 27; 28:6; 17; **Rom** 1:10; 13; 3:8; 23; 5:14; 8:38; 9:9; 26; 11:11; 25; 26; 15:23; 24; 28; 29(2); 32; 16:19; **1Cor** 1:7; 2:6; 3:22; 4:5; 18; 19; 21; 7:5; 10:11; 11:17; 18; 20; 26; 33; 34(2); 13:10; 14:6; 23(2); 24; 26; 15:35; 16:2; 3; 5; 10; 11; 12(3); **2Cor** 1:15; 16; 2:1; 6:17; 7:5; 9:4; 10:14; 12:1; 14; 20; 21; 13:2; **Gal** 2:11; 12; 21; 3:14; 19; 25; 4:4; **Eph** 1:21; 2:7; 4:13; **Phil** 1:27; 2:24; **Col** 1:6; 2:17; 4:10; **1Th** 1:10; 2:16; 18; **2Th** 1:10; 2:3(2); **1Ti** 2:4; 3:14; 4:8; 13; 6:19; **2Ti** 3:1; 7; 4:3; 9; 21; **Titus** 3:12; **Heb** 2:5; 4:1; 16; 6:5; 7:5; 25; 8:8; 9:11(2); 10:1; 7; 9; 37(2); 11:20; 24; 12:18; 22; 13:14; 23; **Jas** 2:2(2); 4:1(2); 5:1; **1Pet** 1:10; 4:17; **2Pet** 3:3; 9; 10; **1Jn** 2:18; 4:2; 3(2); 5:20; **2Jn** 7; 10; 12; **3Jn** 10; **Rev** 1:1; 4; 8; 2:5; 16; 25; 3:3(2); 9; 10; 11; 20; 4:1; 8; 6:1; 3; 5; 7; 17; 9:12; 10:1; 11:12; 17; 18; 12:10; 12; 13:13; 14:7; 15; 15:4; 16:13; 15; 17:1; 10; 18:1; 4; 8; 10; 17; 19:7; 17; 20:1; 21:9; 22:7; 12; 17(3); 20(2)

COMEST

935, 2199, 7126, *2064*

Gen 10:19; 13:10; 24:41; **Deut** 2:19; 20:10; 23:24; 25; 28:6; 19; **Judg** 17:9; 18:23; 19:17; **1Sa** 15:7; 16:4; 17:43; 45; **2Sa** 1:3; 3:13; **1Kin** 2:13; 19:15; **2Kin** 5:25; 9:2; **Job** 1:7; 2:2; **Jer** 51:61; **Jonah** 1:8; **Mt** 3:14; **Lk** 23:42; **2Ti** 4:13

COMETH

857, 935, 1961, 1980, 3318, 3381, 4672, 5034, 5060, 5414, 5674, 5927, 6293, 6437, 6627, 6631, 7131, 7698, 7725, *305, 1096, 1511, 1607, 1831, 1999, 2064, 2186, 2591, 2597, 3854, 4334, 4905*

Gen 24:43; 29:6; 30:11; 32:6; 37:19; 48:2; **Ex** 4:14; 8:20; 13:12; 28:35; 29:30; **Lev** 11:34; **Num** 1:51; 3:10; 38; 5:30; 12:12; 17:13; 18:7; 21:13; 26:5; **Deut** 18:8; 23:11; 13; 28:57; **Judg** 11:31; 13:14; **1Sa** 4:3; 9:6; 11:7; 20:27; 29; 25:8; 28:14; **2Sa** 13:5; 18:27; **1Kin** 8:41; 14:5(2); **2Kin** 4:10; 6:32; 9:18; 20; 10:2; 11:8(2); 12:4; 9; **1Chr** 16:33; 29:16; **2Chr** 13:9; 20:2; 9; 12; 23:7(2); **Job** 3:21; 24; 5:6; 21; 26; 14:2; 18; 20:25(2); 21:17; 27:9;

28:5; 20; 36:32; 37:9; 22; **Ps** 30:5; 62:1; 75:6; 78:39; 96:13(2); 98:9; 118:26; 121:1; 2; **Prov** 1:26; 27(3); 2:6; 3:25; 11:2(2); 8; 13:5; 10; 12; 18:3(2); 17; 29:26; **Eccl** 1:4; 2:12; 4:14; 5:3; 6:4; 11:8; **Song** 2:8; 3:6; 8:5; **Is** 13:9; 21:1; 9; 12; 24:18; 26:21; 28:29; 30:13; 27; 42:5; 55:10; 62:11; 63:1; **Jer** 6:20; 22; 17:6; 8; 18:14; 43:11; 46:7; 20(2); 47:4; 50:3; 51:54; **Lam** 3:37; **Eze** 4:12; 7:25; 14:4(2); 7; 20:32; 21:7(2); 24:24; 30:9; 33:30; 31; 33; 47:9; **Dan** 11:16; 12:12; **Hos** 7:1; **Joel** 2:1; **Mic** 1:3; 5:6; 7:4; **Hab** 3:16; **Zec** 9:9; 14:1; **Mal** 4:1(2); **Mt** 3:11; 13; 5:37; 8:9; 13:19; 15:11; 17:27; 18:7; 21:5; 9; 40; 23:39; 24:27; 44; 46; 25:6; 13; 19; 26:36; 40; 45; **Mk** 1:7; 3:20; 4:15; 5:22; 38; 6:48; 7:20; 8:22; 38; 9:12; 10:1; 11:9; 10; 13:35; 14:17; 37; 41; 43; 66; **Lk** 3:16; 6:47; 7:8; 8:12; 49; 11:25; 12:36; 37; 40; 43; 54; 55; 13:35; 14:10; 31; 15:6; 17:20; 18:8; 19:38; **Jn** 1:9; 15; 30; 3:8; 20; 21; 31(2); 4:5; 7; 21; 23; 25; 35; 5:44; 6:33; 35; 37; 45; 50; 7:27; 31; 42; 9:4; 10:10; 11:38; 12:13; 15; 22; 13:6; 14:6; 30; 15:25; 16:2; 25; 32; 18:3; 20:1; 2; 6; 21:13; **Acts** 10:32; 13:25; 18:21; **Rom** 4:9; 10:17; **1Cor** 15:24; **2Cor** 11:4; 28; **Gal** 5:8; **Eph** 5:6; **Col** 3:6; **1Th** 5:2; 3; **1Ti** 6:4; **Heb** 6:7; 10:5; 11:6; **Jas** 1:17; **Jude** 14; **Rev** 1:7; 3:12; 11:14; 17:10

COMING

857, 935, 1980, 3318, 3381, 3996, 4126, 5182, 5674, 7122, 7272, *305, 602, 1096, 1525, 1529, 1531, 1660, 1904, 2064, 2186, 2597, 3854, 3952, 4334*

Gen 24:63; 30:30; **Num** 22:16; 33:40; **Judg** 5:28; **1Sa** 10:5; 16:4; 22:9; 25:26; 33; 29:6(2); **2Sa** 3:25; 24:20; **2Kin** 10:15; 13:20; 19:27; **2Chr** 22:7; **Ezr** 3:8; **Ps** 19:5; 37:13; 121:8; **Prov** 8:3; **Is** 14:9; 32:19; 37:28; 44:7; **Jer** 8:7; **Dan** 4:23; **Mic** 7:15; **Hab** 3:4; **Mal** 3:2; 4:5; **Mt** 8:28; 16:28; 24:3; 27; 30; 37; 39; 48; 25:27; 26:64; **Mk** 1:10; 6:31; 13:26; 36; 14:62; 15:21; **Lk** 2:38; 9:42; 12:45; 18:5; 19:23; 21:26; 27; 23:26; 29; 36; **Jn** 1:27; 29; 47; 5:7; 25; 28; 10:12; 11:20; 12:12; **Acts** 7:52; 9:12; 28; 10:3; 25; 13:24; 17:10; 27:33; **Rom** 15:22; **1Cor** 1:7; 15:23; 16:17; **2Cor** 7:6; 7; 13:1; **Phil** 1:26; **1Th** 2:19; 3:13; 4:15; 5:23; **2Th** 2:1; 8; 9; **Jas** 5:7; 8; **1Pet** 2:4; **2Pet** 1:16; 3:4; 12; **1Jn** 2:28; **Rev** 13:11; 21:2

CONCERNING

182, 413, 854, 1697, 5921, 5922, 6655, *1519, 2596, 3056, 3754, 4012, 4314, 5228*

Gen 5:29; 12:20; 19:21; 24:9; 26:32; 42:21; **Ex** 6:8; 24:8; **Lev** 4:2; 13; 22; 26; 27; 5:6; 18; 6:3; 18; 23:2; 27:32; **Num** 8:20; 22; 9:8; 10:29; 14:30; 30:1; 12(2); 32:28; 36:6; **Josh** 14:6; 23:14; **Judg** 15:3; 21:5; **Ruth** 4:7(2); **1Sa** 3:12; 25:30; **2Sa** 3:8; 7:25(2); 11:18; 13:39; 14:8; 18:5; **1Kin** 2:4; 27; 5:8(2); 6:12; 8:41; 10:1; 11:2; 10; 22:8; 18; 23; **2Kin** 10:10; 17:15; 19:21; 32; 22:13(2); **1Chr** 11:10; 17:23(2); 19:2; 22:12; 13; 23:14; 24:21; 29; 26:1; 21; **2Chr** 6:32; 8:15(2); 12:15; 15:16; 24:27; 31:6; 9; 34:21; 26; **Ezr** 5:5; 17; 6:3; 7:14; 10:2; **Neh** 1:2(2); 9:23; 11:23; 24; 13:14; 22; **Est** 3:2; 9:26; **Job** 36:33(2); **Ps** 7:t, 17:4; 73:8; 90:13; 106:34; 119:128; 152; 135:14; **Eccl** 1:13; 3:18; 7:10; **Is** 1:1; 2:1; 8:1; 16:13; 23:5; 29:22; 30:7; 37:9; 22; 33; 45:11(2); **Jer** 7:22; 14:1; 15; 16:3(4); 18:7(2); 9(2); 22:18; 23:15; 25:1; 27:19(4); 21; 29:31; 30:4(2); 32:36; 33:4(2); 39:11; 42:19; 44:1; 49:1; 7; 23; 28(2); 52:21; **Lam** 1:17; **Eze** 13:16; 14:7; 22(2); 18:2; 21:28(2); 36:6; 44:5; 45:14; 47:14; **Dan** 2:18; 5:29; 6:4; 5; 12; 17; 7:12; 8:13; **Amos** 1:1; **Obad** 1; **Mic** 1:1; 3:5; **Nah** 1:14; **Hag** 2:11; **Mt** 4:6; 11:7; 16:11; **Mk** 5:16; 7:17; **Lk** 2:17; 7:24; 18:31; 22:37; 24:19; 27; 44; **Jn** 7:12; 32; 9:18; 11:19; **Acts** 1:16; 2:25; 8:12; 13:34; 19:8; 39; 21:24; 22:18; 23:15; 24:24; 25:16; 28:21; 22; 23; **Rom** 1:3; 9:5; 27; 11:28; 16:19; **1Cor** 5:3; 7:1; 25; 8:4; 12:1; 16:1; **2Cor** 8:23; 11:21; **Eph** 4:22; 5:32; **Phil** 3:6; 4:15; **1Th** 3:2; 4:13; 5:18; **1Ti** 1:19; 6:21; **2Ti** 2:18; 3:8; **Heb** 7:14; 11:20; 22; **1Pet** 4:12; **2Pet** 3:9; **1Jn** 2:26

COULD

3045, 3201, 3202, 3546, 5074, 5234, *102, 1410, 1415, 2192, 2480, 2489, 5342*

Gen 13:6; 27:1; 36:7; 37:4; 41:8; 21; 24; 43:7; 45:1; 3; 48:10; **Ex** 2:3; 7:21; 24; 8:18; 9:11; 12:39; 15:23; **Num** 9:6; **Josh** 7:12; 15:63; 17:12; **Judg** 1:19; 2:14; 3:22; 6:27; 12:6; 14:14; 17:8; 20:16; **Ruth** 3:14; **1Sa** 3:2; 4:15; 10:21; 23:13; 30:10; 21; **2Sa** 1:10; 3:11; 17:20; 22:39; **1Kin** 5:3; 8:5; 11; 13:4; 14:4; **2Kin** 3:26; 4:40; 16:5; **1Chr** 12:2; 8; 33; 38; 21:30; **2Chr** 4:18; 5:6; 14; 7:2; 13:7; 14:13; 20:25; 25:5; 15; 29:34; 30:3; 32:14; 34:12; **Ezr** 2:59; 3:13; 5:5; **Neh** 7:61; 8:2; 3; 13:24; **Est** 6:1; 7:4; 9:2; **Job** 4:16; 16:4(2); 31:23; **Ps** 37:36; 55:12; 73:7; 78:44; **Song** 5:6; **Is** 5:4; 7:1; 30:5; 33:23(2); 41:28; 46:2; **Jer** 6:15; 8:12; 15:1; 20:9; 24:2; 44:22; **Lam** 4:14; 17; **Eze** 31:8; 47:5(2); **Dan** 5:8; 15; 6:4; 8:4; 7; **Hos** 5:13; **Jonah** 1:13; **Mt** 17:16; 19; 26:40; 27:24; **Mk** 1:45; 2:4; 3:20; 5:3; 4; 6:5; 19; 7:24; 9:18; 28; 14:8; **Lk** 1:22; 5:19; 6:48; 8:19; 43; 9:40; 13:11; 14:6; 19:3; 48; 20:7; 26; **Jn** 9:33; 11:37; 12:39; 21:25; **Acts** 4:14; 11:17; 13:39; 21:34; 22:11; 25:7; 27:15; 43; **Rom** 8:3; 9:3; **1Cor** 3:1; 13:2; **2Cor** 3:7; 13; 11:1; **Gal** 3:21; **1Th** 3:1; 5; **Heb** 3:19; 6:13; 9:9; 12:20; **Rev** 7:9; 14:3

DAY'S

3117, *2250, 4594*

Num 11:31(2); **1Kin** 19:4; **1Chr** 16:37; **Est** 9:13; **Jonah** 3:4; **Lk** 2:44; **Acts** 1:12; 19:40

DAYS

1242, 3117, 3118, 6153, 8543, *1909, 2250, 5066*

Gen 1:14; 3:14; 17; 5:4; 5; 8; 11; 14; 17; 20; 23; 27; 31; 6:3; 4; 7:4(2); 10; 12; 17; 24; 8:3; 6; 10; 12; 9:29; 10:25; 11:32; 14:1; 17:12; 21:4; 34; 24:55; 25:7; 24; 26:1; 15; 18; 27:41; 44; 29:20; 21; 30:14; 35:28; 29; 37:34; 40:12; 13; 18; 19; 42:17; 47:9(4); 49:1; 50:3(3); 4; 10; **Ex** 2:11; 7:25; 10:22; 23; 12:15; 19; 13:6; 7; 15:22; 16:26; 29; 20:9; 11; 12; 22:30; 23:12; 15; 26; 24:16; 18; 29:30; 35; 37; 31:15; 17; 34:18; 21; 28; 35:2; **Lev** 8:33(3); 35; 12:2(2); 4(2); 5; 6; 13:4; 5; 21; 26; 31; 33; 46; 50; 54; 14:8; 38; 15:13; 19; 24; 25(3); 26; 28; 22:27; 23:3; 6; 8; 16; 34; 36; 39; 40; 41; 42; **Num** 6:4; 5(2); 6; 8; 12(2); 13; 9:19; 20; 22; 10:10; 11:19(4); 12:14(2); 15; 13:25; 14:34(2); 19:11; 14; 16; 20:29; 24:14; 28:17; 24; 29:12; 31:19; **Deut** 1:46(2); 2:1; 4:9; 10; 26; 30; 32; 40; 5:13; 16; 33; 6:2(2); 9:9; 11; 18; 25; 10:10; 11:9; 21(3); 12:1; 16:3(2); 4; 8; 13; 15; 17:9; 19; 20; 19:17; 22:7; 19; 29; 23:6; 25:15; 26:3; 30:18; 20; 31:14; 29; 32:7; 47; 33:25; 34:8(2); **Josh** 1:5; 11; 2:16; 22; 3:2; 4:14; 6:3; 14; 9:16; 20:6; 22:3; 24:31(2); **Judg** 2:7(2); 18; 5:6(2); 8:28; 11:40; 14:12; 14; 17; 15:20; 17:6; 18:1(2); 19:1; 4; 20:27; 28; 21:25; **Ruth** 1:1; **1Sa** 1:11; 2:31; 3:1; 7:13; 15; 9:20; 10:8; 13:8; 11; 14:52; 17:12; 16; 18:26; 20:19; 21:5; 25:10; 28; 38; 28:1; 29:3; 30:12; 13; 31:13; **2Sa** 1:1; 7:12; 16:23; 20:4; 21:1; 9(2); 24:8; **1Kin** 2:1; 11; 38; 3:2; 13; 14; 4:21; 25; 8:40; 65(3); 10:21; 11:12; 25; 34; 12:5; 14:20; 30; 15:5; 6; 14; 16; 32; 16:15; 34; 17:15; 18:1; 19:8; 20:29; 21:29(2); 22:46; **2Kin** 2:17; 8:20; 10:32; 12:2; 13:3; 22; 15:18; 29; 37; 18:4; 20:1; 6; 17; 19; 23:22(2); 29; 24:1; 25:29; 30; **1Chr** 1:19; 4:41; 5:10; 17(2); 7:2; 22; 9:25; 10:12; 12:39; 13:3; 17:11; 21:12; 22:9; 23:1; 29:15; 28; **2Chr** 7:8; 9(2); 9:20; 10:5; 13:20; 14:1; 15:17; 20:25; 21:8; 24:2; 14; 15; 26:5; 29:17; 30:21; 22; 23(2); 32:24; 26; 34:33; 35:17; 18; 36:9; **Ezr** 4:2; 5; 7; 6:22; 8:15; 32; 9:7; 10:8; 9; **Neh** 1:4; 2:11; 5:18; 6:15; 17; 8:17; 18; 12:7; 12; 22; 23; 26(2); 46; 47(2); 13:6; 15; 23; **Est** 1:1; 2; 4(2); 5(2); 2:12; 21; 4:11; 16; 9:22(2); 26; 27; 28(2); 31; **Job** 1:5; 2:13; 3:6; 7:1(2); 6; 16; 8:9; 9:25; 10:5(3); 20; 12:12; 14:1; 5; 14; 15:20; 17:1; 11; 21:13; 24:1; 29:2; 4; 18; 30:16; 27; 32:7; 33:25; 36:11; 38:12; 21; 42:17; **Ps** 21:4; 23:6; 27:4; 34:12; 37:18; 19; 39:4; 5; 44:1; 49:5; 55:23; 72:7; 77:5; 78:33; 89:29; 45; 90:9; 10; 12; 14; 15; 94:13; 102:3; 11; 23; 24; 103:15; 109:8; 119:84; 128:5; 143:5; 144:4; **Prov** 3:2; 16; 9:11; 10:27; 15:15; 28:16; 31:12; **Eccl** 2:3; 16; 23; 5:17; 18; 20; 6:3; 12; 7:10; 15; 8:12; 13; 15; 9:9(2); 11:1; 8; 9; 12:1(2); **Is** 1:1; 2:2; 7:1; 17; 13:22; 23:7; 15; 24:22; 30:26; 32:10; 38:1; 5; 10; 20; 39:6; 8; 51:9; 53:10; 60:20; 63:9; 11; 65:20(2); 22(2); **Jer** 1:2; 3; 2:32; 3:6; 16; 18; 5:18; 6:11; 7:32; 9:25; 13:6; 16:9; 14; 17:11; 19:6; 20:18; 22:30; 23:5; 6; 7; 20; 25:34; 26:18; 30:3; 24; 31:27; 29; 31; 33; 38; 32:14; 33:14; 15; 16; 35:1; 7(2); 8; 36:2; 37:16; 42:7; 46:26; 48:12; 47; 49:2; 39; 50:4; 20; 51:47; 52; 52:33; 34; **Lam** 1:7(2); 2:17; 4:18; 5:21; **Eze** 3:15; 16; 4:4; 5(2); 6; 8; 9(2); 5:2; 12:22; 23; 25; 27; 16:22; 43; 60; 22:4; 14; 23:19; 38:8; 16; 17; 43:25; 26; 27; 44:26; 45:21; 23(2); 25; 46:1; **Dan** 1:12; 14; 15; 18; 2:28; 44; 4:34; 5:11; 6:7; 12; 7:9; 13; 22; 8:14; 26; 27; 10:2; 13; 14(2); 11:20; 33; 12:11; 12; 13; **Hos** 1:1(2); 2:11; 13; 15; 3:3; 4; 5; 6:2; 9:7(2); 9; 10:9; 12:9; **Joel** 1:2(2); 2:29; 3:1; **Amos** 1:1(2); 4:2; 5:21; 8:11; 9:11; 13; **Jonah** 1:17; 3:4; **Mic** 1:1; 4:1; 7:14; 15; 20; **Hab** 1:5; **Zeph** 1:1; **Hag** 2:16; **Zec** 8:6; 9; 10; 11; 15; 23; 14:5; **Mal** 3:4; 7; **Mt** 2:1; 3:1; 4:2; 9:15; 11:12; 12:5; 10; 12; 40(2); 15:32; 17:1; 23:30; 24:19; 22(2); 29; 37; 38; 26:2; 61; 27:40; 63; **Mk** 1:9; 13; 2:1; 20(2); 26; 3:4; 8:1; 2; 31; 9:2; 13:17; 19; 20(2); 24; 14:1; 58; 15:29; **Lk** 1:5; 23; 24; 25; 39; 75; 2:1; 6; 21; 22; 43; 46; 4:2(2); 25; 31; 5:35(2); 6:2; 9; 12; 9:28; 36; 13:14; 15:13; 17:22(2); 26(2); 28; 19:43; 20:1; 21:6; 22; 23; 23:29; 24:18; **Jn** 2:12; 19; 20; 4:40; 43; 11:6; 17; 39; 12:1; 20:26; **Acts** 1:3; 5; 15; 2:17; 18; 3:24; 5:36; 37; 6:1; 7:41; 45; 9:9; 19; 23; 37; 43; 10:30; 48; 11:27; 28; 12:3; 13:31; 41; 15:36; 16:12; 18; 17:2; 20:6(3); 21:4; 5; 10; 15; 26; 27; 38; 24:1; 11; 24; 25:1; 6; 13; 14; 27:7; 20; 28:7; 12; 14; 17; **Gal** 1:18; 4:10; **Eph** 5:16; **Col** 2:16; **2Ti** 3:1; **Heb** 1:2; 5:7; 7:3; 8:8; 10; 10:16; 32; 11:30; 12:10; **Jas** 5:3; **1Pet** 3:10; 20; **2Pet** 3:3; **Rev** 2:10; 13; 9:6; 10:7; 11:3; 6; 9; 11; 12:6

DAYS'

3117

Gen 30:36; 31:23; **Ex** 3:18; 5:3; 8:27; **Num** 10:33(2); 33:8; **Deut** 1:2; **1Sa** 11:3; **2Sa** 24:13; **2Kin** 3:9; **Jonah** 3:3

DID

1580, 1961, 2052, 5648, 6213, 7965, *15, 91, 1731, 3000, 4160, 4238*

Gen 3:6(2); 12; 13; 21; 6:22(2); 7:5; 20; 11:9(2); 18:8; 13; 19:3(2); 21:1; 22:1; 23; 24:54; 25:28; 34; 26:20; 30; 27:25; 29:25; 28; 30:40; 41; 31:46; 54; 35:5; 38:10; 11; 39:3; 6; 19; 22; 23; 40:17; 23; 41:4; 12; 20; 42:20; 25; 43:3; 17; 30; 32; 44:2; 45:5; 21; 47:22; 48:15; 50:12; 15; 16; 17; **Ex** 1:11; 17; 2:13; 4:30; 5:8; 19; 6:8; 7:6(2); 10; 11; 20; 22(2); 23; 8:7; 13; 17; 18; 24; 31; 9:6; 7; 10:11; 15; 11:10; 12:28(2); 35; 50(2); 51; 13:8; 14:4; 12; 31; 16:3; 17; 18; 24; 35(2); 17:2; 6; 10; 18:7; 14; 24; 19:4; 24:11; 32:12; 21; 28; 33:4; 34:28; 35:24; 25; 36:22; 29; 39:3; 21; 32(2); 43; 40:16(2); **Lev** 4:20; 8:4; 9; 36; 9:14; 10:7; 16:15; 34; 24:23; 26:35; 27:24; **Num** 1:54(2); 2:34; 4:37; 41; 5:4(2); 7:18; 24; 30; 36; 8:3; 20(2); 22; 9:5; 10:21; 11:5; 25; 14:22; 37; 17:11(2); 20:27; 21:14; 22:37; 23:2; 30; 25:2; 27:22; 31:31; 32:8; 36:10; **Deut** 1:30; 32; 2:12; 22; 29; 3:6; 4:3; 4; 33; 34; 5:23; 7:7; 18; 8:3; 4; 9:9; 18; 11:3; 4; 5; 6; 7; 12:30; 24:9; 25:17; 29:2; 31:4; 32:12; 38; 33:9; 34:9; **Josh** 2:10; 11(2); 4:8; 18; 20; 23; 5:4; 11; 12; 14; 15; 6:14; 9:4; 9; 10; 26; 10:23; 28(2); 30(2); 39; 42; 11:9; 12; 13; 15(2); 12:6; 13:12; 22; 32; 14:5; 17:13; 22:20; 33; 24:5; 13; 17; **Judg** 1:21; 27; 28; 29; 30; 31; 32; 33; 2:7; 11; 17; 22; 3:7; 12; 16; 4:1; 5:17; 6:1; 13; 20; 27(2); 40; 8:1; 15; 25; 9:27; 56; 57; 10:6; 11; 12; 11:7; 25(2); 26; 39; 13:1; 19; 21; 14:9; 15:11; 16:21; 17:6; 19:4; 6; 8; 21; 21:22; 23; 25; **Ruth** 2:14; 19; 3:6; 4:11; **1Sa** 1:7(2); 18; 2:11; 14; 22; 27; 28(2); 3:7; 19; 4:20; 6:6; 10; 7:4; 14; 9:24; 12:7; 13:6; 14:32; 43; 15:2; 16:4; 19:5; 20:34; 21:11; 22:15; 17; 18; 25:4; 27:11; 28:24; 25; 30:11; **2Sa** 1:2; 2:3; 3:36; 5:25; 7:17; 8:11; 9:6; 13; 11:7(2); 13; 20; 21; 12:3; 6; 17; 20; 31; 13:8; 29; 14:4; 15:6; 17:15; 19:19; 28; 43; 20:6; 21:6; 22:7(2); 11; 23; 37; 43(3); 23:17; 22; 24:23; **1Kin** 1:16; 31; 2:5(2); 35; 42; 3:4; 14; 21; 5:18; 7:15; 18; 23; 46; 51; 8:4; 64; 9:21; 22; 24; 25; 10:29; 11:6(2); 7; 8; 16; 25; 33; 38; 41; 12:9; 11; 32; 13:19; 22; 14:4; 16; 21; 22; 24; 29; 15:4; 5; 7; 11(2); 23; 26; 28; 31; 34; 16:5; 7; 12; 14; 15; 19; 25; 27; 30; 33; 34; 17:5; 15(2); 16; 18:13; 34(2); 19:6; 8; 21; 20:25; 33(2); 21:11; 13; 25; 26(2); 22:18; 39; 52; **2Kin** 1:18; 2:18; 4:1; 28(2); 44; 6:6; 29; 7:8; 8:2; 18(2); 23; 25; 27(2); 9:27; 34; 10:19; 34; 11:3; 9; 10; 12:2; 11; 19; 13:2; 7; 8; 11; 12; 25; 14:3(3); 4; 15; 24; 28; 15:3; 6; 8; 9; 18; 21; 24; 26; 28; 31; 34(2); 36; 16:2; 16; 19; 17:2; 9; 11; 14; 22; 40(2); 41; 18:3(2); 4; 11; 13; 16; 21:2; 3; 9; 11; 17; 20(2); 25; 22:2; 23:9; 12; 13; 19; 24; 28; 32; 37; 24:3; 5; 9; 11; 19; 25:11; 13; 27; 29; **1Chr** 4:27; 9:22; 11:19; 24; 14:16; 15:13; 24; 17:15; 23:24; 26:27; 27:26; 29:22; **2Chr** 1:7; 2:7; 4:2; 3; 16; 17; 5:5; 11; 8:8; 9; 10:9; 12:14; 13:20; 14:2; 15:4; 6; 18:16; 17; 19:8; 20:35(2); 21:6; 10; 22:4; 23:8; 24:2; 7; 11; 12; 25:2; 4; 12; 27; 26:4(2); 22; 27:2(3); 5; 28:1; 16; 22; 29:2; 19; 34; 30:18; 22; 24; 31:20; 21; 32:3; 9; 33; 33:2; 17; 22(2); 34:2; 6; 12; 32; 35:3; 12; 18; 36:5; 8; 9; 12; **Ezr** 1:8; 11; 5:14; 6:13; 21; 10:6; 16; **Neh** 2:16(2); 3:3; 5:13; 15; 9:25; 28; 11:12; 13:7; 10; 18(2); 26(2); **Est** 1:8; 21; 2:4; 11; 20; 3:1; 2; 5; 4:17; 5:12; 8:1; 9:5; **Job** 1:5; 2:10; 3:11; 12; 6:22; 28:27; 30:25; 31:13; 15(2); 32; 34(2); 42:9; 11; **Ps** 14:2; 18:10(2); 22; 36; 37; 42(2); 31:11; 35:11; 15; 41:9; 44:3; 45:9; 51:5; 53:2(2); 55:12; 66:6; 68:12; 78:12; 25; 29; 33; 36; 38; 40; 102:19; 105:35; 106:34; 43; 119:23(2); 135:6; 139:16; 142:1; **Prov** 1:29; **Is** 5:25; 6:2; 9:1; 10:10; 13:1; 14:16; 20:2; 22:12; 38:14(2); 42:24; 48:3; 53:4; 58:2; 65:12(4); 66:4(3); **Jer** 7:12; 26; 11:8; 14:6(2); 15:4; 16; 22:15; 26:19(2); 31:19; 36:8; 37:2; 38:12; 41:1; 44:19; 21; 46:15; 17; 21; 52:2; 21; 33; **Lam** 1:7(2); 4:5; **Eze** 3:3; 6:13; 11:22; 12:7; 16:49; 17:7; 18:18; 20:8(2); 17; 24:18; 27:25; 31:6; 34:6; 8; 43:22; 46:12; **Dan** 1:15; 3:24; 4:7; 33; 6:10; 7:9; 8:4; 27; 10:3; **Hos** 2:8; 9:17; 10:9; 13:5; **Amos** 1:11(3); 5:19; 7:4; **Obad** 14(2); **Jonah** 3:10; 4:8; **Nah** 2:12; **Hab** 1:1; 3:6; 7; **Hag** 1:9; 12; 14; **Zec** 1:4; 6; 21; 7:5; 6(3); 9:3; **Mal** 2:6; 15; **Mt** 1:24; 2:22; 9:19; 12:3; 4; 13:58; 14:20; 15:7; 37; 38; 17:2; 19:7; 20:5; 21:6; 15; 25; 31; 36; 42; 25:44; 45(2); 26:12; 19; 21; 67; 27:9; 35; 51; 28:4; 8; 15; **Mk** 1:4; 6; 32; 2:25; 26; 3:8; 4:8; 5:20; 6:20; 42; 44; 8:6; 8; 10:3; 11:31; 12:44(2); 14:18; 22; 59; 65; 15:19; **Lk** 4:2; 6:1; 3; 4; 10; 23; 26; 49; 7:38; 9:15; 17; 43; 53; 54; 11:40; 12:47; 48; 15:16; 17:9; 27; 28; 19:22; 24:32; 43; **Jn** 1:45; 2:11; 23; 24; 4:29; 39; 45; 54; 5:16; 6:2; 14; 23; 26; 31; 49; 58; 7:5; 19; 8:40; 9:2; 18; 22; 26; 27; 10:8; 41; 11:45; 12:36; 42; 15:24; 18:15; 26; 34; 19:24(2); 20:4; 30; 21:7; 25; **Acts** 2:22; 26; 31; 40; 46; 3:17(2); 4:25; 5:28; 6:8; 7:27; 35; 51; 8:6; 9:9; 36; 10:39; 41; 11:17; 30; 12:8; 14:17; 15:8; 14; 16:18; 19:14; 21:9; 26:10(2); 22; **Rom** 1:26; 28; 3:3; 5:20; 7:5; 8:29(2); 30;

10:19; **1Cor** 4:8; 10:3; 4; 15:27; **2Cor** 1:17; 2:9; 5:20; 7:8; 12; 8:5; 12:16; 17; 18; **Gal** 2:12; 4:8; 5:7(2); **Phil** 4:14; **2Th** 3:8; **1Ti** 1:13; **2Ti** 4:14; **Heb** 3:16; 4:2; 4; 10; 7:19; 27; 9:9; **1Pet** 1:11; 12; 2:22; **Rev** 12:4; 13:14; 19:2; 21:23

DIDST

6213

Gen 12:18; 18:15; 20:6; 21:26; 31:27(2); 39; **Ex** 15:10; 40:15; **Num** 21:34; **Deut** 3:2; 9:7; 32:14; 33:8(2); **Josh** 2:18; 8:2; **Judg** 12:1; 13:8; **1Sa** 3:6; 8; 15:19(3); 19:5; 20:19; 25:25; **2Sa** 11:10; 12:12; 21(2); 13:16; 18:11; 19:28; **1Kin** 1:13; 2:44; 8:18; 53; 20:9; 21:10; **1Chr** 17:22; **2Chr** 2:3(2); 6:8; 16:8; 20:7; 34:27(2); **Neh** 9:7; 9; 10; 11; 17; 21; 22; 28; 30; 31; 34; **Ps** 22:4; 9; 30:7; 39:9; 40:6; 44:1; 2(2); 60:10; 68:7; 9(2); 73:18; 74:13; 15; 76:8; 80:9; **Is** 14:12; 22:8; 47:6; 7(2); 48:6; 54:1(2); 57:9(3); 63:14; 64:3; **Jer** 32:22; 36:17; 45:3; **Lam** 1:10; **Eze** 16:13(2); 15; 16; 17; 36; 23:40; 27:33; 29:7; 35:15; **Dan** 10:12; **Hos** 10:13; **Hab** 3:8; 9; 12(2); 14; 15; **Mt** 13:27; 14:31; 20:13; **Lk** 7:46; 19:21; **Jn** 17:8; **Acts** 11:3; **1Cor** 4:7(2); **Heb** 2:7; **Rev** 17:7

DO

1167, 1580, 3190, 3318, 4640, 5647, 5648, 5674, 5933, 6213, 6466, 6467, *14, 15, 17, 1107, 1398, 1754, 2005, 2038, 2140, 2192, 2480, 2554, 2698, 2716, 3056, 3930, 4160, 4238, 4704, 4982*

Gen 6:17; 9:13; 11:6(2); 16:6; 18:5; 17; 19; 25(2); 29; 30; 19:7; 8(2); 22; 21:23; 22:12; 24:42; 25:32; 26:29; 27:37; 46; 30:31; 31:16; 29; 43; 32:12; 34:14; 19; 37:13; 39:9; 11; 40:8; 41:9; 25; 28; 34; 55; 42:1; 18; 22; 43:11; 44:7; 17; 45:17; 19; 47:30; **Ex** 1:16; 3:20; 4:15; 17; 21; 5:4; 17; 6:1; 8:8; 26; 9:5; 15:26; 17:2; 4; 18:16; 20; 23; 19:8; 20:9; 10; 21:7; 11; 22:30; 23:2; 12; 22; 24; 24:3; 7; 14; 29:1; 35; 41; 31:11; 32:14; 18; 33:5; 17; 34:10(2); 15; 35:1; 9; 35; 36:2; 39:1; 41; **Lev** 4:2; 3; 20(2); 5:1; 4(2); 8:34; 9:6; 10:9; 16:15; 16; 29; 18:3(2); 4; 5; 25; 19:15; 29; 35; 37; 20:4; 8; 22; 21:6; 15; 23; 22:9; 16; 31; 23:3; 7; 8; 21; 25; 28; 31; 35; 36; 25:18(2); 45; 26:3; 14; 15; 16; 27:11; **Num** 2:5; 3:7; 8; 4:3; 19; 23; 30; 37; 41; 47; 5:6; 6:21; 7:5; 8:7; 15; 19; 22; 26(2); 9:14; 10:29; 32(2); 11:27; 14:28; 35; 41; 15:12; 13; 14(2); 20; 39; 40; 16:6; 9; 28; 18:6; 23; 21:34; 22:17; 18; 20; 30; 23:19; 26; 24:13; 14; 18; 28:18; 25; 26; 29:1; 7; 12; 35; 39; 30:2; 31:19; 32:20; 23; 24; 25; 31; 33:56(2); **Deut** 1:14; 18; 44; 3:2; 21; 24; 4:1; 5; 6; 14; 25; 5:1; 13; 14; 27; 31; 32; 6:1; 3; 18; 24; 25; 7:11; 12; 19; 8:1; 16; 19; 11:22; 32; 12:1; 4; 8(2); 14; 25; 30; 31; 32; 13:11; 18; 15:5; 17; 19; 16:8; 12; 17:10(2); 11; 12; 13; 19; 18:7; 9; 12; 14; 19:9; 19; 20:3; 15; 18; 21:9; 22:3(3); 5; 26; 24:8(2); 18; 22; 25:16(2); 26:16(2); 27:10; 26; 28:1; 13; 15; 20; 58; 63; 29:9(2); 14; 29; 30:5; 8; 12; 13; 14; 31:4; 5; 12; 29; 32:6; 46; 34:11; **Josh** 1:2; 7; 8; 16; 2:24; 3:5; 6:3; 7:9; 8:2; 8; 9:20; 25(2); 10:25; 22:5; 24; 27; 23:6; 12; 24:13; 20; **Judg** 6:27; 7:17(3); 8:3; 9:33; 48(2); 10:15; 11:10; 12; 36; 13:8; 12; 17; 14:10; 15:3; 10; 17:13; 18:14(2); 18; 19:23(2); 24(2); 20:9; 10; 21:7; 11; 16; **Ruth** 1:17; 2:9; 3:4; 5; 11; 13(3); 4:11; **1Sa** 1:23; 2:23; 35; 3:11; 17; 18; 5:8; 6:2; 6; 7:3; 8:8; 10:2; 7; 8; 11:10; 12:16; 25; 14:7; 36; 40; 44; 16:3; 20:2; 4; 13(2); 30; 22:3; 24:4; 6; 25:17; 22; 26:21; 25; 28:2; 15; 29:3; 30:23; **2Sa** 3:8; 9(2); 18; 35; 7:3; 23; 25; 9:11; 10:12; 11:11; 12:9; 12; 13:2; 12(2); 15:4; 5; 15; 26; 16:10; 11; 20; 17:6; 18:4; 32; 19:13; 18; 19; 22(2); 27; 37; 38(2); 20:6; 17; 21:3; 4; 23:17; 24:12; **1Kin** 1:30; 2:6; 9; 23; 31; 38; 3:28; 5:8; 8:32; 39; 43(2); 9:1; 4; 10:9; 11:12; 33; 38; 12:6; 27; 14:8; 17:13; 18; 18:34(2); 19:2; 20:9(2); 10; 24; 22:22; **2Kin** 2:9; 3:13; 4:2; 16; 28; 5:13; 6:15; 27; 31; 7:9; 8:12; 13; 9:18; 19; 10:5(2); 19; 11:5; 17:12; 15; 17; 34(2); 36; 37; 41; 18:12; 19:31; 20:9; 21:8; 9; 22:9; 13; **1Chr** 11:19; 12:32; 13:4; 16:21; 22; 40; 17:2; 23; 19:13; 21:8; 10; 23; 28:7; 10; 20; 29:19; **2Chr** 6:23; 33; 7:17; 9:8; 14:4; 18:21; 19:6; 7; 9; 10; 20:12; 22:3; 23:4; 25:8; 9; 30:12; 32:10; 33:8; 9; 34:16; 21; 35:6; 21; **Ezr** 4:2(2); 3; 22; 6:8; 7:10; 18(2); 21; 26; 10:4; 5; 11; 12; **Neh** 1:9; 2:12; 19; 4:2; 5:9; 12(2); 6:2; 13; 9:24; 29; 10:29; 13:17; 21; 27; **Est** 1:8; 15; 3:11; 4:11; 5:5; 8; 6:6; 10; 7:5; 9:13; 23; **Job** 6:4; 26; 7:20; 9:13; 10:2; 11:8; 13:2; 9; 10; 14; 20; 15:3; 12; 16:4; 17:10; 19:22; 20:2; 21:7; 29; 22:17; 24:1; 31:14; 32:9; 34:10; 12; 32; 36:28; 37:12; 24; 39:1; 41:8; 42:2; **Ps** 2:1; 7:1; 11:3; 12:2; 16:1; 25:1; 5; 31:1; 34:10; 14; 16; 36:3; 37:3; 8; 27; 38:15; 40:8; 41:7; 50:16; 51:18; 56:4; 11; 58:1(2); 60:12; 64:4; 71:1; 75:1(2); 80:12; 82:3; 83:9; 86:4; 89:50; 92:7; 95:10; 103:18; 20; 21; 104:20; 105:14; 15; 107:23; 108:13; 109:21; 111:10; 118:6; 119:3; 21; 35; 83; 109; 113; 132; 141; 153; 157; 163; 164; 176; 125:4; 129:8; 130:5; 131:1; 137:6; 139:21; 143:8; 10; **Prov** 2:14; 3:27; 6:3; 30; 8:13; 10:23; 14:22; 17:7; 19:7(2); 19; 20:30; 21:3; 7; 15; 24:8; 29; 25:8; 28:12; 31:12; **Eccl** 2:3; 11; 12; 3:12; 4:8; 5:1; 6:6; 8:11; 12; 9:10(2); 10:10; 11:5; **Song** 1:3; 8:8; **Is** 1:16; 17; 5:5; 9:13; 10:3; 11; 14:21; 19:15; 21; 23:4; 24:4; 7; 18; 27:3; 28:21; 29:13; 14; 37:32; 38:7; 19; 41:23(2); 42:9; 16; 43:19; 45:7; 46:10; 11; 48:11; 14; 55:2; 56:1; 57:4; 58:4; 64:6; 65:8; **Jer** 2:8; 18(2); 4:22(2); 30; 5:28; 31; 7:10; 14; 17; 19(2); 8:8; 14; 9:7; 10:5(2); 11:4; 6; 8; 15; 12:5; 13:12; 23(2); 14:7; 21(2); 17:22; 24; 18:6; 8; 10; 12; 19:12; 22:3(2); 4; 15; 17; 23:24; 32; 25:6; 26:3; 14; 28:6; 29:32; 30:6; 31:20; 32:23; 35; 40; 41; 33:9; 18; 36:3; 38:5; 39:12(2); 40:16; 42:2; 3; 5; 20; 44:4; 17; 50:15; 21; 29; 51:47; 52; 55; **Lam** 1:4; 22; 2:11; **Eze** 2:4; 5:9(2); 6:10; 7:27; 8:6; 9; 12; 13; 11:20; 15:3; 16:5; 18:5; 21; 20:11; 13; 19; 21(2); 21:24; 22:14; 23:30; 48; 24:14; 22; 24; 25:8; 14; 33:9; 14; 19; 31; 32; 34:2; 35:11; 15; 36:11; 22; 27; 32; 36; 37; 37:24; 28; 39:17; 43:11; 44:13; 45:20; 25; **Dan** 3:14; 4:26; 9:18; 19; 11:3; 16; 17; 24; 27; 28; 30; 32(3); 36; 39; 12:10; **Hos** 4:18; 6:4(2); 7:10; 15; 9:5; 10:3; 15; 12:1; 14:8; **Joel** 1:18; 2:21; 22(2); 3:4; **Amos** 3:7; 10; 4:12(2); **Jonah** 1:11; 3:10; 4:9; **Mic** 2:3; 7(2); 11; 6:8; 7:3; **Nah** 1:9; **Zeph** 1:12(2); 3:5; 13; **Hag** 2:3; 12; **Zec** 1:5; 6; 21; 5:10; 8:15; 16; 9:12; 12:7; **Mal** 1:10; 2:2; 10; 4:1; 3; **Mt** 5:6; 15; 19; 44; 46; 47(2); 6:1; 2(2); 7; 20; 26; 28; 32; 7:12(2); 16; 8:9; 29; 9:14; 17; 28; 11:3; 4; 12:2(2); 12; 27; 50; 13:13; 41; 14:2; 15:2; 3; 9; 17; 16:9; 11; 13; 17:25; 18:10; 35; 19:16; 18; 20:13; 15; 32; 21:21; 24; 27; 40; 22:29; 23:3(3); 5; 26:72; 27:19; 22; **Mk** 1:24; 27; 2:18; 24; 3:4(2); 35; 5:7; 6:5; 14; 7:7; 8; 12; 13; 18; 8:18; 21; 27; 9:22; 39; 10:17; 19(4); 35; 36; 51; 11:3; 5; 26; 28; 29; 33(2); 12:9; 24; 27; 13:11; 14:7; 15:8; 12; **Lk** 2:27; 3:10; 11; 12; 14(2); 4:23; 34; 5:30; 33; 6:2(2); 9(2); 11; 27; 31(2); 33(3); 35; 44; 46; 7:4; 8; 8:21; 28; 10:11; 25; 28; 37; 11:19; 39; 12:4; 17; 18; 26; 30; 56; 13:32; 15:29; 16:3; 4; 17:10; 18:18; 20(4); 41; 19:31; 48; 20:8; 13; 15; 22:19; 23; 23:31; 34; 24:38; **Jn** 2:4; 5; 3:2; 11; 4:34; 5:19(2); 30; 36; 45; 6:6; 28; 38; 7:4; 17; 26; 31; 8:11; 28; 29; 38; 39; 41; 43; 44; 46; 49; 9:15; 16; 33; 10:25; 32; 37; 38; 11:12; 47; 13:7; 15; 17; 27; 14:12(3); 13; 14; 31; 15:5; 14; 21; 16:3; 19; 31; 17:4; 21:21; **Acts** 1:1; 2:11; 37; 4:16; 28; 5:35; 7:26; 51(2); 9:6(2); 10:6; 14:15; 15:29; 36; 16:20; 28; 30; 37; 17:7; 19:36; 21:23; 22:10(2); 23:21; 24:10; 16; 25:9; 26:9; 20; **Rom** 1:28; 32(2); 2:3; 8; 14; 3:8; 31; 7:15(3); 16; 17; 19(2); 20(2); 21; 8:3; 5; 13; 25; 12:8; 15; 13:3; 4; 15:31; **1Cor** 5:12(2); 6:2; 7(2); 8; 7:36; 9:3; 13; 17; 23; 25; 10:22; 31(2); 11:24; 25; 26; 12:30(2); 15:29; 35; 16:1; 5; 10; **2Cor** 1:17; 3:1; 5:4; 7:8; 8:1; 10; 23; 10:3; 7; 11:8; 12(2); 12:19; 13:7(2); 8; **Gal** 1:10(2); 2:10; 14(2); 21; 3:10; 4:21; 5:3; 11; 17; 21; 6:10; **Eph** 3:20; 6:9; 21; **Phil** 1:18; 2:13; 14; 18; 3:8; 13; 4:9; 13; **Col** 1:9; 3:13; 17(2); 23(2); **1Th** 3:12; 4:10; 11; 5:6; 11; 24; **2Th** 3:4(2); **1Ti** 1:4; 6:2; 18; **2Ti** 2:23; 3:8; 4:5; 9; 21; **Philem** 1:14; 19; 21; **Heb** 3:10; 4:3; 13; 6:3; 10; 11; 10:7; 9; 11:3; 29; 13:6; 16; 17; 19; 21; **Jas** 1:16; 2:6; 7; 8; 11(2); 12; 4:5; 15; 17; 5:19; **1Pet** 1:21; 2:14; 20; 3:6; 11; 12; 4:11; **2Pet** 1:10; 19; 3:16; **1Jn** 1:6; 2:3; 3:22; 4:14; 5:16; **3Jn** 6; **Rev** 2:5; 3:9; 18; 9:19; 13:14; 14:13; 19:10; 21:24; 22:9; 14

DOEST

5648, 6213, 6466, *4160, 4238*

Gen 4:7(2); 21:22; **Ex** 18:14; 17; **Deut** 12:28; 14:29; 15:18; **Judg** 11:27; **2Sa** 3:25; **1Kin** 2:3; 19:9; 13; 20:22; **Job** 9:12; 35:6(2); **Ps** 49:18; 77:14; 86:10; 119:68; **Eccl** 8:4; **Jer** 11:15; 15:5; **Eze** 12:9; 16:30; 24:19; **Dan** 4:35; **Jonah** 4:4; 9; **Mt** 6:2; 3; 21:23; **Mk** 11:28; **Lk** 20:2; **Jn** 2:18; 3:2; 7:3; 13:27; **Acts** 22:26; **Rom** 2:1; 3; **Jas** 2:19; **3Jn** 5(2)

DOETH

1580, 5648, 6213, 7760, *15, 91, 2554, 4160, 4238, 4374*

Gen 31:12; **Ex** 31:14; 15; 35:2; **Lev** 4:27; 6:3; 23:30; **Num** 15:30; 24:23; **Job** 5:9; 9:10; 23:13; 24:21; 37:5; **Ps** 1:3; 14:1; 3; 15:3; 5; 53:1; 3; 72:18; 106:3; 118:15; 16; 136:4; **Prov** 6:32; 11:17; 15:7; 17:21; 22; 28:17; **Eccl** 2:2; 3:14(2); 7:20; 8:3; **Is** 49:18; 56:2; **Jer** 5:19; 48:10; **Eze** 17:15; 18:10; 11; 14; 24(2); 27; **Dan** 4:35; 9:14; **Amos** 9:12; **Mal** 2:12; 17; **Mt** 6:3; 7:21; 24; 26; 8:9; **Lk** 6:47; 49; 7:8; **Jn** 3:20; 21; 5:19(2); 20; 7:4; 51; 9:31; 11:47; 14:10; 15:15; 16:2; **Acts** 15:17; 26:31; **Rom** 2:9; 3:12; 10:5; 13:4; **1Cor** 6:18; 7:37; 38(2); **Gal** 3:5; 12; **Eph** 6:8; **Col** 3:25; **Jas** 4:17; **1Jn** 2:17; 29; 3:7; 10; **3Jn** 10; 11(2); **Rev** 13:13

DOING

854, 4640, 5949, 6213, *15, 16, 92, 1096, 1398, 2041, 2109, 2554, 2569, 4160*

Gen 31:28; 44:5; **Ex** 15:11; **Num** 20:19; **Deut** 9:18; **1Kin** 7:40; 16:19; 22:43; **2Kin** 21:16; **1Chr** 22:16; **2Chr** 20:32; **Ezr** 9:1; **Neh** 6:3; **Job** 32:22; **Ps** 64:9; 66:5; 118:23; **Is** 56:2; 58:13(2); **Mt** 21:42; 24:46; **Mk** 12:11; **Lk** 12:43; **Acts** 10:38; 24:20; **Rom** 2:7; 12:20; **2Cor** 8:11; **Gal** 6:9; **Eph** 6:6; 7; **2Th** 3:13; **1Ti** 4:16; 5:21; **1Pet** 2:15; 3:17(2); 4:19

DOINGS

4611, 4640, 5949

Lev 18:3(2); **Deut** 28:20; **Judg** 2:19; **1Sa** 25:3; **2Chr** 17:4; **Ps** 9:11; 77:12; **Prov** 20:11; **Is** 1:16; 3:8; 10; 12:4; **Jer** 4:4; 18; 7:3; 5; 11:18; 17:10; 18:11; 21:12; 14; 23:2; 22; 25:5; 26:3; 13; 32:19; 35:15; 44:22; **Eze** 14:22; 23; 20:43; 44; 21:24; 24:14; 36:17; 19; 31; **Hos** 4:9; 5:4; 7:2; 9:15; 12:2; **Mic** 2:7; 3:4; 7:13; **Zeph** 3:7; 11; **Zec** 1:4; 6

DONE

466, 1254, 1580, 1639, 1697, 1961, 3254, 3615, 5414, 5647, 5648, 5953, 6213, 6466, 7760, 8552, *91, 1096, 1796, 2673, 2716, 4160, 4238*

Gen 3:13; 14; 4:10; 8:21; 9:24; 12:18; 18:21; 20:5; 9(3); 10; 21:23; 26; 22:16; 24:15; 19(2); 22; 45; 66; 26:10; 29; 27:19; 45; 28:15; 29:25; 26; 30:26; 31:26; 28; 34:7; 40:15; 42:28; 44:5; 15; **Ex** 1:18; 2:4; 3:16; 5:23; 10:2; 12:16(2); 13:8; 14:5; 18:1; 8; 9; 21:31; 31:15; 34:10; 33; 35:2; 39:43(2); **Lev** 4:2; 13(2); 22(2); 27; 5:16; 17; 6:7; 8:5; 34; 11:32; 18:27; 19:22(2); 23:3; 24:19(2); 20; **Num** 5:7; 27; 12:11; 15:11; 34; 16:28; 22:2; 28; 23:11; 27:4; 32:13; **Deut** 3:21; 10:21; 12:31; 19:19; 20:18; 25:9; 26:14; 29:24; 32:27; **Josh** 5:8; 7:19; 20; 9:3; 24; 10:1(2); 32; 35; 37; 39(2); 22:24; 23:3; 8; 24:7; 20; 31; **Judg** 1:7; 2:2; 10; 3:12; 6:29(2); 8:2; 9:16(2); 24; 48; 11:37; 14:6; 15:6; 7; 10; 11(2); 19:30; 20:12; **Ruth** 2:11; 3:3; 16; **1Sa** 4:16; 6:9; 8:8; 11:7; 12:17; 20; 24; 13:11; 13; 14:43; 17:26; 27; 29; 19:18; 20:1; 32; 34; 24:19; 25:30; 26:16; 18; 28:9; 17; 18; 29:8; 31:11; **2Sa** 2:6; 3:24; 7:21; 11:27; 12:5; 21; 13:12; 14:20; 21; 15:24; 16:10; 21:11; 23:20; 24:10(2); 17(2); **1Kin** 1:6; 27; 3:12; 8:47; 66; 9:8; 11:11; 13:11; 14:9; 22; 15:3; 18:36; 19:1; 20; 22:53; **2Kin** 4:13; 14; 5:13; 7:12; 8:4; 10:10; 30(2); 15:3; 9; 34; 17:4; 19:11; 25; 20:3; 21:11(2); 15; 23:17; 19; 32; 37; 24:9; 19; **1Chr** 10:11; 11:22; 16:12; 17:19; 21:8(2); 17(2); **2Chr** 6:37; 7:21; 11:4; 16:9; 24:16; 22; 25:16; 29:2; 6; 36; 30:5; 32:13; 25; 31; **Ezr** 6:12; 7:21; 23; 9:1; 10:3; **Neh** 5:19; 6:8; 9; 8:17; 9:33(2); 13:14; **Est** 1:16; 2:1; 4:1; 6:3(2); 6; 9; 11; 9:12(2); 14; **Job** 21:31; 34:29; 32; **Ps** 7:3; 14:1; 22:31; 33:4; 9; 40:5; 50:21; 51:4; 52:9; 53:1; 66:16; 71:19; 74:3; 78:4; 98:1; 105:5; 106:6; 21; 109:27; 111:8; 115:3; 119:121; 166; 120:3; 126:2; 3; **Prov** 3:30; 4:16; 24:29; 30:20; 32; 31:29; **Eccl** 1:9(2); 13; 14; 2:12; 4:1; 3; 8:9; 10; 14; 16; 17; 9:3; 6; **Is** 5:4(2); 10:11; 13; 12:5; 24:13; 25:1; 33:13; 37:11; 26; 38:3; 15; 41:4; 20; 44:23; 46:10; 48:5; 53:9; **Jer** 2:23; 3:5; 6; 7; 16; 5:13; 7:13; 14; 30; 8:6; 11:17; 16:12; 18:13; 22:8; 30:15; 24; 31:37; 32:23; 30; 32; 34:15; 35:10; 18; 38:9(2); 40:3; 41:11; 42:10; 44:17; 48:19; 50:15; 29; 51:12; 24; 35; 52:2; **Lam** 1:12; 21; 22; 2:17; 20; **Eze** 3:20; 5:7; 9; 9:4; 11; 11:12; 12:11(2); 28; 14:23(2); 16:47; 48(2); 51; 54; 59; 63; 17:18; 24; 18:13; 14; 19(2); 22; 24; 26; 23:38; 39; 24:22; 24; 33:16; 39:8; 24; 43:11; 44:14; **Dan** 6:22; 9:5; 12(2); 15; 11:24; 36; **Hos** 2:5; **Joel** 2:20; **Amos** 3:6; **Obad** 15(2); **Jonah** 1:10; 14; **Mic** 6:3; **Zeph** 3:4; **Zec** 7:3; **Mal** 2:13; **Mt** 1:22; 6:10; 7:22; 8:13; 11:20; 21(2); 23(2); 13:28; 17:12; 18:19; 31(2); 21:4; 21(2); 23:23; 25:21; 23; 40(2); 26:13; 42; 56; 27:23; 54; 28:11; **Mk** 4:11; 5:14; 19; 20; 32; 33; 6:30; 7:37; 9:13; 13:30; 14:8; 9; 15:8; 14; **Lk** 1:49; 3:19; 4:23; 5:6; 8:34; 35; 39(2); 56; 9:7; 10; 10:13(2); 11:2; 42; 13:17; 14:22; 16:8; 17:10(2); 22:42; 23:8; 15; 22; 31; 41; 47; 48; 24:21; 35; **Jn** 1:28; 5:16; 29(2); 7:21; 31; 11:46; 12:16; 18; 37; 13:12; 15; 15:7; 24; 18:35; 19:36; **Acts** 2:43; 4:7; 9; 16; 21; 28; 30; 5:7; 8:13; 9:13; 10:16; 33; 11:10; 12:9; 13:12; 14:3; 11; 13; 18; 27; 15:4; 21:14; 33; 24:2; 25:10; 26:26; 28:9; **Rom** 9:11; **1Cor** 5:2; 3; 9:15; 13:10; 14:26; 40; 16:14; **2Cor** 3:7; 11; 14; 5:10(2); 7:12; **Eph** 5:12; 6:13; **Phil** 2:3; 4:14; **Col** 3:25; 4:9; **Titus** 3:5; **Heb** 10:29; 36; **Rev** 16:17; 21:6; 22:6

DOWN

935, 1288, 1438, 1457, 1760, 2040, 2904, 3212, 3332, 3381, 3665, 3766, 3782, 3996, 4174, 4295, 4535, 4606, 4769, 5117, 5128, 5181, 5183, 5186, 5242, 5243, 5307, 5422, 5456, 5493, 6131, 6201, 6915, 7250, 7252, 7257, 7323, 7491, 7503, 7665, 7673, 7743, 7812, 7817, 7901, 7971, 8045, 8058, 8213, 8214, 8257, *345, 347, 377, 387, 597, 1308, 1581, 1931, 2504, 2506, 2507, 2521, 2523, 2524, 2596, 2597, 2598, 2601, 2609, 2621, 2625, 2630, 2647, 2662, 2667, 2673, 2679, 2701, 2718, 2736, 2778, 2875, 3879, 3935, 4098, 4496, 4776, 4781, 4782, 5011, 5294, 5465*

Gen 11:5; 7; 12:10; 15:11; 12; 17; 18:21; 19:4; 33; 35; 21:16; 23:12; 24:11; 14; 16; 18; 26; 45; 46; 48; 26:2; 27:29(2); 28:11; 37:10; 25(2); 35; 38:1; 39:1(2); 42:2; 3; 6; 38(2); 43:4; 5; 7; 11; 15; 20; 22; 28; 44:11; 21; 23; 26(2); 29; 31; 45:9; 13; 46:3; 4; 49:6; 8; 9; 14; 50:18; **Ex** 2:5; 15; 3:8; 7:10; 12; 9:19; 11:8(2); 17:11; 12; 19:11; 14; 20; 21; 24; 25; 20:5; 22:26; 23:24(2); 32:1; 6; 7; 15; 34:13; 29(2); **Lev** 9:22; 11:35; 14:45; 18:23; 19:16; 20:16; 22:7; 26:1; 6; 30; **Num** 1:51; 4:5; 10:17; 11:17; 25; 12:5; 13:23; 24; 14:45; 16:30; 33; 20:15; 28; 21:15; 22:27; 31; 23:24; 24:9; 25:2; 33:52; 34:11; 12; **Deut** 1:25; 5:9; 6:7; 7:5(2); 9:3; 12; 15; 18; 25(2); 10:5; 22; 11:19; 30; 12:3; 16:6;

19:5; 20:19; 20; 21:4; 22:4; 23:11; 24:13; 15; 19; 25:2; 26:4; 5; 15; 28:24; 43; 52; 33:3; 28; **Josh** 1:4; 2:8; 15; 18; 3:13; 16(2); 4:8; 6:5; 20; 7:5; 8:29(2); 10:11(2); 13; 27(2); 15:10; 16:3; 7; 17:15; 18; 18:16; 18; 24:4; **Judg** 1:9; 34; 2:2; 19; 3:25; 27; 28; 4:14; 15; 5:11; 14; 21; 27(2); 6:25(2); 26; 28(2); 30(2); 31; 32; 7:4; 5(2); 6; 9; 10(2); 11(2); 24; 8:9; 17; 9:36; 37; 45; 48; 49; 11:37; 14:1; 5; 7; 10; 18; 19; 15:8; 12; 16:21; 31; 19:6; 14; 15; 26; 27; 20:21; 25; 32; 39; 43; **Ruth** 3:3; 4(2); 6; 7(2); 13; 4:1(3); 2(2); **1Sa** 2:6; 3:2; 3; 5(2); 6; 9(2); 6:15; 18; 21; 9:25; 27; 10:5; 8(2); 13:12; 20; 14:16; 36; 37; 15:6; 12; 16:11; 17:8; 28(2); 52; 19:12; 24; 20:19; 24; 21:13; 22:1; 23:4; 6; 8; 11(2); 20(2); 25; 25:1; 20(2); 26:2; 6(2); 29:4; 30:15(2); 16; 24; 31:1; **2Sa** 2:13; 16; 23(2); 24; 3:35; 5:17; 8:2; 11:8; 9; 10(2); 13; 13:5; 6; 8; 15:20; 24; 17:18; 18:28; 19:16; 18; 20; 24; 31; 20:15; 21:15; 22:10; 28; 48; 23:13; 20; 21; **1Kin** 1:25; 33; 38; 53; 2:6; 8; 9; 19; 5:9; 8:33; 17:23; 18:30; 40; 42; 44; 19:4; 6; 10; 14; 21:4; 16; 18(2); 22:2; 36; **2Kin** 1:2; 4; 6; 9; 10(2); 11; 12(2); 14; 15(2); 16; 2:2; 3:12; 25; 5:14; 18; 21; 6:4; 6; 9; 18; 33; 7:17; 8:29; 9:16; 24; 33(2); 10:13; 27(2); 11:6; 18; 19; 12:20; 13:14; 21; 14:9; 13; 16:17; 18:4; 19:16; 23; 20:10; 11; 21:13; 23:5; 7; 8; 12(2); 14; 15; 25:10; **1Chr** 5:22; 7:21; 10:1; 11:15; 22; 23; 29:20; **2Chr** 6:13; 7:1; 3; 13:17; 14:3(2); 15:16; 18:2; 34; 20:16; 22:6; 23:17; 20; 25:8; 12; 14; 18; 23; 26:6; 31:1(2); 32:30; 33:3; 34:4(2); 7(2); 36:3; 19; **Ezr** 6:11; 9:3; 10:1; 16; **Neh** 1:3; 4; 2:13; 3:15; 4:3; 6:3(2); 16; 9:13; **Est** 3:15; 8:3; **Job** 1:7; 20; 2:2; 8; 13; 6:21; 7:4; 9; 19; 8:12; 11:19; 12:14; 14:2; 7; 12; 17:3; 16; 18:7; 20:11; 15; 18; 21:13; 26; 22:16; 20; 29; 27:19; 29:24; 31:10; 32:13; 33:24; 36:27; 40:12; 41:1; 9; **Ps** 3:5; 4:8; 7:5; 16; 9:15; 14:2; 17:11; 13; 18:9; 27; 20:8; 22:29; 23:2; 28:1; 30:3; 9; 31:2; 35:14; 36:12; 37:2; 14; 24; 38:6; 42:5; 6; 11; 43:5; 44:5; 25; 50:1; 53:2; 55:15; 23; 56:7; 57:6; 59:11; 15; 60:12; 62:4; 72:6; 11; 73:18; 74:6; 7; 75:7; 78:16; 24; 31; 80:12; 14; 16; 85:11; 86:1; 88:4; 89:23; 40; 44; 90:6; 95:6; 102:10; 19; 104:8; 19; 22; 107:12(2); 23; 26; 108:13; 109:23; 113:3; 115:17; 119:118; 136; 133:2(2); 137:1; 139:3; 143:3; 7; 144:5; 145:14; 146:8; 9; 147:6; **Prov** 1:12; 3:20; 24(2); 5:5; 7:26; 27; 14:1; 18:8; 21:22; 22:17; 23:34; 24:31; 25:26; 28; 26:22; **Eccl** 1:5; 3:3; **Song** 2:3; 6:2; 11; 7:9; **Is** 2:9; 11; 17; 5:5(2); 15; 9:10(2); 10:4; 6; 13; 33; 34; 11:6; 7; 14:8; 11; 12; 15; 19; 30; 16:8; 17:2; 18:2; 5; 21:3; 22:5(2); 10; 19; 25; 24:1; 10; 19; 25:5; 10(2); 11; 12; 26:5; 6; 27:10; 28:2; 18; 29:4; 16; 30:2; 30; 31; 31:1; 3; 4; 32:19; 33:9; 20; 34:4; 5; 7; 37:24; 38:8(2); 18; 42:10; 43:14; 17; 44:14; 15; 17; 19; 45:8(2); 14; 46:1; 2; 6; 47:1; 49:23; 50:11; 51:23; 52:2; 4; 55:10; 56:10; 58:5; 60:14; 20; 63:6(2); 14; 15; 18; 64:1(2); 3(2); 65:10; 12; **Jer** 1:10(2); 3:25; 4:26; 6:6; 15; 8:12; 9:18; 13:17; 18(2); 14:17; 15:9; 18:2; 3; 7; 21:13; 22:1; 7; 24:6; 25:37; 26:10; 31:28(2); 40; 33:4; 12; 36:12; 15; 38:6; 11; 39:8; 42:10; 45:4; 46:5; 23; 48:2; 5; 15; 18; 20; 39; 49:16; 50:15; 27; 51:25; 40; 52:14; **Lam** 1:9; 16; 2:1; 2(2); 10; 17; 18; 3:48; 49; 50; 63; **Eze** 1:13; 24; 25; 6:4; 6; 11:13; 13:14(2); 16:39(2); 17:24; 19:2; 6; 12; 24:16; 26:4; 9; 11(2); 12; 16; 20(2); 27:29; 28:8; 14; 30:4; 6; 25; 31:12; 14; 15; 16; 17; 18; 32:18(2); 19; 21; 24(2); 25; 27; 29; 30(2); 34:15; 18; 26; 37:1; 38:20; 39:10; 47:1; 8; **Dan** 3:5; 6; 7; 10; 11; 15; 23; 4:13; 14; 23(2); 5:19; 6:14; 7:9; 23; 8:7; 10; 11; 12; 11:12; 26; **Hos** 2:18; 7:12; 10:2; **Joel** 1:17; 2:23; 3:2; 11; 13; 18; **Amos** 2:8; 3:11; 5:24; 6:2; 8:9; 9:2; **Obad** 3; 4; 16; **Jonah** 1:3(2); 5; 2:6; **Mic** 1:3; 4; 6; 12; 3:6; 5:8; 11; 6:14; 7:10; **Nah** 1:6; 12; **Zeph** 1:11; 2:7; 14; 15; 3:13; **Hag** 2:22; **Zec** 10:5; 11; 12; 11:2; **Mal** 1:4; 11; 4:3; **Mt** 2:11; 3:10; 4:6; 9; 7:19; 8:1; 11; 32; 9:10; 11:23; 13:48; 14:19; 29; 15:29; 30; 35; 17:9; 14; 18:26; 29; 21:8; 24:2; 17; 26:20; 27:5; 19; 36; 40; 42; **Mk** 1:7; 40; 2:4; 3:11; 22; 5:13; 33; 6:39; 40; 8:6; 9:9; 35; 11:8; 13:2; 15; 15:30; 36; 46; **Lk** 1:52; 2:51; 3:9; 4:9; 20; 29; 31; 5:3; 4; 5; 8; 19; 29; 6:17; 38; 7:36; 8:5; 23; 28; 33; 41; 47; 9:14; 15; 37; 42; 44; 54; 10:15; 30; 31; 11:37; 12:18; 37; 13:7; 9; 29; 14:8; 10; 28; 31; 16:6; 17:7; 16; 31; 18:14; 19:5; 6; 21; 22; 21:6; 24; 22:14; 41; 44; 55(2); 23:53; 24:5; 12; **Jn** 2:12; 3:13; 4:47; 49; 51; 5:4; 7; 6:10(2); 11; 16; 33; 38; 41; 42; 50; 51; 58; 8:2; 6; 8; 10:15; 17; 18(2); 11:32; 13:12; 37; 38; 15:13; 19:13; 20:5; 11; **Acts** 4:35; 5:5; 10; 7:15; 34; 58; 60; 8:5; 15; 26; 38; 9:25; 30; 32; 40; 10:11; 20; 21; 25; 11:5; 12:19; 13:14; 29; 14:11; 25; 15:1; 16; 16:8; 13; 29; 17:6; 18:22; 19:35; 20:9(2); 10; 36; 21:5; 10; 32; 22:30; 23:10; 15; 20; 24:22; 25:5; 6; 7; 27:27; 30; 28:6; **Rom** 10:6; 11:3; 10; 16:4; **1Cor** 10:7; 14:25; 15:24; **2Cor** 4:9; 7:6; 10:4; 5; 11:33; **Eph** 2:14; 4:26; **Heb** 1:3; 10:12; 11:30; 12:2; 12; **Jas** 1:17; 5:4; **1Pet** 1:12; **2Pet** 2:4; **1Jn** 3:16(2); **Rev** 1:13; 3:12; 21; 4:10; 5:8; 14; 10:1; 12:10; 12; 13:13; 18:1; 21; 19:4; 20:1; 9; 21:2; 22:8

EACH

259, 376, 802, 905, *240, 303, 1538*

Gen 15:10; 34:25; 40:5(2); 41:11; 12; 45:22; **Ex** 18:7; 30:34; **Lev** 24:7; **Num** 1:44; 7:3; 11; 85(2); 14:34; 16:17; 17:6; 29:14; 15; **Josh** 18:4; 22:14(2); **Judg** 8:18; 21:22; **Ruth** 1:8; 9; **1Kin** 4:7; 6:23; 22:10; **2Kin** 9:21; 15:20; **1Chr** 20:6(2); **2Chr** 3:15; 4:13; 9:18; **Neh** 13:24; **Ps** 85:10; **Is** 2:20; 6:2; 35:7; 57:2; **Eze** 4:6; 40:16; 48; **Lk** 13:15; **Acts** 2:3; **Phil** 2:3; **2Th** 1:3; **Rev** 4:8

EITHER

176, 376, 518, 1571, 3588, 8145, *1782, 2228, 2532*

Gen 31:24; 29; **Lev** 10:1; 13:49; 51; 53; 57; 58; 59; 22:23; 25:49; **Num** 6:2; 22:26; 24:13; **Deut** 17:3; 28:51; **Judg** 9:2; **1Sa** 20:2; 25:31; 30:2; **1Kin** 7:15; 10:19; 18:27; **1Chr** 21:12; **2Chr** 18:9; **Eccl** 9:1; 11:6; **Is** 7:11; 17:8; **Eze** 21:16; **Mt** 6:24; 12:33; **Lk** 6:42; 15:8; 16:13; **Jn** 19:18; **Acts** 17:21; **1Cor** 14:6; **Phil** 3:12; **Jas** 3:12; **Rev** 22:2

ELSE

369, 518, 3588, 3808, 5750, *686, 1490, 1893, 2087, 2532*

Gen 30:1; 42:16; **Ex** 8:21; 10:4; **Num** 20:19; **Deut** 4:35; 39; **Josh** 23:12; **Judg** 7:14; **2Sa** 3:35; 15:14; **1Kin** 8:60; 20:39; 21:6; **1Chr** 21:12; **2Chr** 23:7; **Neh** 2:2; **Ps** 51:16; **Eccl** 2:25; **Is** 45:5; 6; 14; 18; 21; 22; 46:9; 47:8; 10; **Joel** 2:27; **Mt** 6:24; 9:17; 12:29; 33; **Mk** 2:21; 22; **Lk** 5:37; 14:32; 16:13; **Jn** 14:11; **Acts** 17:21; 24:20; **Rom** 2:15; **1Cor** 7:14; 14:16; 15:29; **Phil** 1:27; **Rev** 2:5; 16

ENOUGH

1767, 1952, 3027, 3605, 4672, 7227, 7644, 7654, *566, 713, 714, 2425, 2880, 4052*

Gen 24:25; 33:9; 11; 34:21; 45:28; **Ex** 2:19; 9:28; 36:5; **Deut** 1:6; 2:3; **Josh** 17:16; **2Sa** 24:16; **1Kin** 19:4; **1Chr** 21:15; **2Chr** 31:10; **Prov** 27:27; 28:19; 30:15; 16; **Is** 56:11; **Jer** 49:9; **Hos** 4:10; **Obad** 5; **Nah** 2:12; **Hag** 1:6; **Mal** 3:10; **Mt** 10:25; 25:9; **Mk** 14:41; **Lk** 15:17; 22:38; **Acts** 27:38

EVEN

227, 389, 637, 853, 1571, 1887, 3588, 3602, 3651, 4334, 5704, 5705, 6153, 6664, 7535, *737, 891, 1063, 1096, 1161, 2089, 2193, 2504, 2531, 2532, 2536, 2548, 3303, 3483, 3676, 3739, 3761, 3779, 3796, 3798, 5037, 5158, 5613, 5615, 5618*

Gen 6:17; 9:3; 10:9; 19; 21; 13:3; 10; 14:23; 19:1; 4; 9; 20:5; 21:10; 23:7; 10; 24:11; 26:28; 27:34; 38; 34:29; 35:14; 37:18; 42:28; 44:18; 46:18; 34; 47:2; 21; 49:22; 25; **Ex** 3:1; 4:16; 22; 23; 9:18; 10:12; 21; 11:5; 12:15; 18(2); 19; 38; 41; 14:23; 16:6; 12; 13; 18:14; 23:31; 25:9; 19; 27:5; 28:1; 8; 17; 42; 29:27; 28; 39; 41; 30:8; 21; 23; 33; 38; 32:29; 35:35; 36:2; 37:3; 9; 38:21; 24; 39:37; 43; **Lev** 1:2; 2:14; 3:14; 4:12; 17; 5:12; 6:5; 15; 7:8; 20; 21; 25; 27; 8:9; 11:11; 22; 24; 25; 27; 28; 31; 32; 39; 40(2); 13:12; 18; 30; 38; 14:9; 31; 46; 15:5; 6; 7; 8; 10(2); 11; 16; 17; 18; 19; 21; 22; 23; 27; 16:32; 17:5; 9; 10; 13; 15; 18:9; 10; 29; 19:21; 20:6; 10; 22:6; 23:2; 4; 5; 16; 18; 32(3); 24:7; 26:16; 28; 34; 43; 27:3(2); 5; 6; 18; 23; 24; 32; **Num** 1:21; 23; 25; 27; 29; 31; 33; 35; 37; 39; 41; 43; 46; 3:22; 38; 47; 4:3; 14; 30; 35; 39; 40; 43; 44; 47; 48; 5:8; 26; 6:4; 7:10; 8:8; 16; 9:3; 5; 11; 13; 15; 21; 11:20; 12:8; 14:19; 34(2); 37; 45; 15:23; 16:5(2); 17:6; 18:21; 26; 29; 19:7; 8; 10; 19; 21; 22; 20:1; 22; 29; 21:24; 26; 30(2); 25:13; 14; 27:21; 28:4; 8; 31:47; 51; 32:4; 33(2); 33:49; 34:2; 6; 36:10; **Deut** 1:44; 2:22; 23; 36; 3:16(2); 17(2); 4:5; 13; 19; 20; 24; 30; 48; 49; 5:3; 23; 9:9; 11; 21; 10:15; 11:12; 24; 12:5; 22; 30; 31; 13:7; 16:3; 4; 6; 17:5; 12; 18:20; 20:14; 21:3; 22:26; 23:2; 3; 16; 18; 23; 25:18; 26:9; 28:59; 64(2); 67(2); 29:24; 31:21; 32:31; 39; 33:4; **Josh** 1:2; 4; 2:1; 24; 3:16; 5:4; 10; 6:17; 25; 7:5; 11(2); 8:4; 11; 13; 25; 28; 9:20; 27; 10:41(2); 11:4; 17(2); 12:2; 3; 7; 13:3; 8; 24; 27; 31; 14:10; 11; 15:1; 5; 13; 46; 16:5; 17:11; 17; 19:1; 28; 32; 50; 21:20; 23:4; 12; 24:2; 12; 18; **Judg** 3:1; 9; 4:13; 5:3; 5; 11; 15; 6:3; 25; 7:22; 8:14; 19; 27; 9:40; 11:13; 22(2); 33(2); 36; 18:15; 19:16; 20:1; 2; 23; 26; 33; 21:2; **Ruth** 2:7; 15; 17; **1Sa** 3:20; 5:6; 6:18; 19; 7:14; 8:8; 14; 14:21; 22; 17:40; 52; 18:4; 11; 19:10; 20:4; 5; 16; 25; 25:25; 27; 26:8; 27:3; 8; 28:3; 17; 30:17; 26; **2Sa** 1:2; 12; 2:5; 3:9; 10; 15; 6:5; 19; 7:6; 23; 8:2; 10:4; 11:13; 23; 14:25; 15:12; 21; 17:11; 18:5; 19:11; 14; 32; 20:2; 21; 22:42; 23:4; 24:2; 7; 15(2); **1Kin** 1:26; 30(2); 37; 48; 2:22; 4:12; 24; 25; 29; 33; 6:16(3); 7:7; 9; 10; 42; 51; 8:4; 6; 29; 39; 65; 11:26; 35; 12:27; 30; 33; 13:34; 14:14; 26; 15:13; 28; 16:7; 18:22; 26; 19:10; 14; 20:3; 14; 15; 21:11; 13; 19; 22:35; **2Kin** 3:24; 26; 4:3; 5:22; 7:6; 7; 13; 8:6; 9; 9:4; 6; 20; 10:3; 14; 33; 11:2; 5; 7; 12:4; 14:10; 29; 15:20; 17:16; 18:8; 10; 21; 19:15; 19; 22; 20:14; 21:15; 22:16; 24:14; 16(2); 25:22; 23; **1Chr** 2:23; 4:15; 39; 42; 5:8; 24; 26; 6:39; 10:13; 11:2; 8; 12:2; 40; 13:5; 14:16; 16:16; 19; 17:7; 24(2); 20:3; 21:2; 12; 17; 23:24; 30; 24:31; 25:7; 26:12; 21; 31; 28:15; 19; 20; 21; 29:4; 21; **2Chr** 2:3; 9; 5:7; 13(2); 6:21; 33; 39; 8:10; 13(2); 9:26; 11:6; 13:3; 5; 17:7; 8; 18:13; 21; 34; 19:10; 20:4; 24:14; 25:13; 19; 26:8; 19; 28:10; 27; 30:5; 10; 18; 27; 31:16; 33:14; 34:6; 11; 24; 27; 33; **Ezr** 1:8; 3:3; 4:5; 11; 5:1; 16; 6:8; 7:11; 21; 8:25; 26; 9:1; **Neh** 2:13; 3:1; 10; 21; 24; 27; 4:3(2); 13; 5:8; 11; 13; 14; 15; 8:13; 9:6; 12:23; 37; 38; 39; 43; 13:26; **Est** 1:1; 4; 2:18; 3:6; 13; 4:2; 5:3; 6; 6:10; 7:2; **Job** 4:8; 21; 5:5; 6:9; 10:21; 15:26; 17:5; 11; 18:13; 21:6; 23:2; 3; 13; 24:17; 25:5; 28:4; 31:6; 34:17; 36:16; 41:9; 42:16; **Ps** 18:6; 41; 21:4; 24:9; 26:12; 27:2; 35:23; 39:t, 2; 40:3; 45:12; 47:9; 48:14; 50:1; 7; 55:19; 57:4(2); 59:12; 64:3; 65:4; 67:6; 68:8; 17; 19; 24; 26; 71:16; 22; 73:1; 74:3; 11; 76:7; 77:1; 78:6; 54; 84:2; 3; 90:2; 11; 91:9; 105:17; 20; 106:7; 38; 107:43; 108:1; 109:16; 113:8; 115:16; 118:27; 119:41; 112; 121:8; 125:2; 131:2; 133:2; 3; 136:22; 137:7; 139:10; 11; 146:10; 148:14; **Prov** 2:16; 3:12; 8:16; 14:13; 20; 16:4; 7; 17:15; 28; 20:11; 12; 22:19; 23:15; 28:9; 30:1(2); **Eccl** 2:12; 15; 3:19; 4:16; 7:25; 9:1; 11:5; 12:10; **Song** 4:2; **Is** 1:6; 13; 4:3; 5:9; 7:6; 17; 23; 8:7; 8; 9:7; 9; 10:21; 23; 13:3; 5; 12; 14:9; 18; 15:4; 16:6; 8; 18:2; 19:13; 22; 24; 20:4; 22:15; 24; 23:4; 24:15; 16; 25:5; 10; 12; 26:5(2); 6; 27:1; 28:22; 29:7; 8; 14; 32:7; 35:2; 4; 37:16; 20; 23; 38:11; 12; 13; 39:3; 40:30; 41:3; 12; 28; 43:7; 11; 19; 25; 44:8; 17; 28; 45:4; 12; 24; 46:4(3); 47:15; 48:5; 6; 7; 11; 15; 20; 49:10; 19; 25; 51:12; 22; 55:3; 56:5; 7; 57:6; 7; 9; 11; 65:6; 66:2; **Jer** 3:25; 4:12; 6:11; 13(2); 19; 7:11; 15; 25; 8:10(2); 9:15; 22; 10:11; 11:7; 13; 23; 12:6(2); 12; 13:10; 13; 14; 18; 15:13; 16:5; 17:4; 10; 27; 19:11; 12; 21:5; 22:25; 23:12; 19; 33; 34; 39; 24:2; 25:3; 13; 31; 33; 28:6; 11; 29:23; 30:7; 31:2; 19; 21; 32:9; 20; 31; 33:10; 24; 34:20; 36:2; 12; 39:3; 12; 14; 40:7; 8; 12; 41:1; 3; 5; 10; 16; 42:1; 2; 5; 8; 43:1; 6; 7; 44:10; 12(2); 15; 45:4; 46:25; 48:32; 34(3); 44; 49:37; 50:7; 21; 51:9; 56; 60; **Lam** 4:3; **Eze** 1:27(2); 2:3; 4:1; 13; 14; 5:8; 6:3; 7:14; 8:2(2); 6; 9:1; 10:2; 5; 12; 11:15; 17; 12:4; 7; 13:10; 13; 20; 14:10; 22; 16:19; 37; 59; 17:9; 16; 19; 18:11; 18; 20:11; 13; 21; 31; 21:13; 28; 22:4; 18; 23:34; 24:2; 4; 9; 18; 29:10; 30:3; 32:6; 16; 18; 31; 32; 33:18; 34:11; 20; 23; 30; 35:6; 11; 15; 36:2; 10; 12; 37:19; 25; 38:4; 39:17; 40:14; 41:17; 42:12; 43:1; 3; 8; 13; 14(2); 44:6; 7; 10; 19; 47:10; 19; 48:3; 6; 10; 28; **Dan** 1:21; 2:43; 4:15; 23; 5:14; 6:26; 7:11; 18; 20; 8:1; 10; 11; 15; 9:5; 11; 21; 25; 27; 11:1; 4; 10; 11; 24(2); 30; 35; 41; 12:1; 4; **Hos** 2:20; 5:14; 9:16; 12:5; **Joel** 1:2; 12; 2:2; 12; 14; **Amos** 2:11; 3:11; 5:1; 20; 8:4; 12; 14; **Obad** 7; 8; 11; 20; **Jonah** 2:5; 3:5; 4:9; **Mic** 1:9; 2:2; 8; 10; 11; 3:4; 5; 4:7; 8; 10; 7:12(2); **Nah** 2:11; 3:12; **Hab** 1:2; 3:9; 13; **Zeph** 1:14; 18; 2:5; 9; 11; 3:8; 10; 15; 20; **Hag** 2:18; **Zec** 3:2; 6:10; 13; 7:1; 5(2); 8:23; 9:7; 10(2); 12; 11:7; 10; 14; 12:6; 14:16; 17; **Mal** 1:10; 11; 12; 2:2; 3; 3:1; 7; 9; 15; **Mt** 5:46; 47; 48; 6:29; 7:12; 17; 8:16; 27; 9:18; 11:26; 12:8; 45; 13:12; 15:28; 18:14; 33; 20:8; 14; 28; 23:8; 10; 28; 37; 24:27; 33; 25:29; 26:20; 38; 27:57; 28:20; **Mk** 1:27; 32; 4:25; 35; 36; 41; 6:2; 47; 10:45; 11:6; 19; 12:44; 13:22; 29; 35; 14:30; 54; 15:42; **Lk** 1:2; 15; 2:15; 6:33; 8:18; 25; 9:54; 10:11; 17; 21; 12:7; 41; 57; 17:30; 18:11; 19:26; 32; 37; 42; 44; 20:37; 24:24; **Jn** 1:12; 3:13; 14; 5:21; 23; 45; 6:16; 57; 8:9; 25; 41; 43; 10:15; 11:22; 37; 12:50; 14:17; 31; 15:10; 26; 17:14; 16; 18; 22; 20:21; 21:25; **Acts** 2:39; 4:10; 5:37; 39; 9:17; 10:41; 11:5; 12:15; 15:8; 11; 20:11; 22:17; 26:11; 27:25; **Rom** 1:13; 20; 26; 28; 3:22; 4:6; 17; 5:7; 14; 18; 21; 6:4; 19; 7:4; 8:23; 34; 9:10; 17; 24; 30; 10:8; 11:5; 31; 15:3; 6; **1Cor** 1:6; 2:7; 11; 3:1; 5; 4:11; 5:7; 7:7; 8; 9:14; 10:33; 11:1; 5; 12; 14; 12:2; 13:12; 14:7; 12; 15:22; 24; 16:1; **2Cor** 1:3; 8; 13; 14; 19; 3:10; 15; 18; 7:14; 10:7; 13; 11:12; 13:9; **Gal** 2:16; 3:6; 4:3; 14; 29; 5:12; 14; **Eph** 1:10; 2:3; 5; 15; 4:4; 15; 32; 5:12; 23; 25; 29; 33; **Phil** 1:7; 15; 2:8; 3:15; 18; 21; 4:16; **Col** 1:14; 26; 3:13; **1Th** 1:10; 2:2; 4; 7; 14; 18; 19; 3:4; 12; 13; 4:3; 5; 13; 14; 5:11; **2Th** 2:9; 16; 3:1; 10; **1Ti** 3:11; 6:3; **2Ti** 2:9; **Titus** 1:12; 15; **Philem** 1:19; **Heb** 1:9; 4:12; 5:14; 6:20; 7:4; 11:12; 19; **Jas** 2:17; 3:5; 9; 4:1; 14; **1Pet** 1:9; 2:8; 21; 3:4; 6; 21; 4:10; **2Pet** 1:14; 2:1(2); 3:15; **1Jn** 2:6; 9; 18; 25; 27; 3:3; 7; 4:3; 5:4; 6; 20; **3Jn** 2; 3; **Jude** 7; 23; **Rev** 1:7; 2:13(2); 27; 3:4; 21; 6:13; 14:20; 16:7; 17:11; 18:6; 21:11; 22:20

EVERY

259, 376, 802, 1397, 3605, 3632, 5437, 7218, *303, 537, 1330, 1519, 1520, 1538, 2596, 3650, 3836, 3837, 3840, 3956, 5100, 5101, 5956*

Gen 1:21(2); 25; 26; 28; 29(2); 30(4); 31; 2:5(2); 9; 16; 19(3); 20; 3:1; 14; 24; 4:14; 22; 6:5; 17; 19(2); 20(2); 7:2; 4; 8; 14(5); 21(2); 23; 8:1; 17(2); 19(3); 20(2); 21; 9:2(2); 3; 5(2); 10(3); 12; 15; 16; 10:5; 13:10; 16:12(2); 17:10; 12; 23; 19:4; 20:13; 27:29; 30:33; 35; 32:16; 34:15; 22; 23; 24; 41:48; 42:25; 35; 43:21; 44:1; 11(2); 13; 45:1; 46:34; 47:20; 49:28; **Ex** 1:1; 22(2); 3:22; 7:12; 9:19; 22; 25(2); 10:5; 12; 15; 11:2(2); 12:3; 4; 16; 44; 13:12;

13; 14:7; 16:4; 16(3); 18; 21(2); 29; 18:22(2); 26; 25:2; 26:2; 27:18; 28:21; 29:36; 30:7; 12; 13; 14; 31:14; 32:27(4); 29; 33:7; 8; 10; 34:19; 35:10; 21(2); 22; 23; 24(2); 29; 36:1; 2(2); 3; 4; 8; 30; 38:26(2); 39:14; **Lev** 2:13; 6:12; 18; 23; 7:6; 10; 11:15; 21; 26(2); 33; 34; 35; 41; 46(2); 15:4(2); 12; 17(2); 20(2); 26; 17:15; 19:3; 8; 10; 20:9; 23:37; 24:8; 25:10(2); 13; 27:28; **Num** 1:2; 4(2); 20; 22; 52(2); 2:2; 17; 34; 3:15; 4:19; 30; 35; 39; 43; 47; 49; 5:2(2); 9; 10; 7:5; 8:16; 17; 11:10; 13:2(2); 15:12; 16:3; 17(2); 18; 27; 17:2(2); 6; 9; 18:7; 9(4); 10; 11; 13; 14; 15; 29; 31; 19:15; 21:8; 23:2; 4; 14; 30; 25:5; 26:54; 28:10; 14; 21; 29:14; 30:4; 9; 11; 13(2); 31:4; 5; 6; 17(2); 23; 50; 53; 32:18; 27; 29; 33:54; 34:18; 35:8; 15; 36:7; 8(2); 9; **Deut** 1:16; 22; 41; 2:34; 3:6; 20; 4:4; 8:3; 11:24; 12:2; 8; 13; 31; 13:16; 14:6; 14; 19; 15:1; 2; 16:17; 19:3; 20:13; 21:5(2); 23:9; 24:16; 26:11; 28:61(2); 30:9; 31:10; 33:3; **Josh** 1:3; 3:12; 4:2; 4; 5; 10; 6:5; 20; 11:14; 21:42; 24:28; **Judg** 2:6; 5:30; 7:5(2); 7; 8; 16; 18; 21; 22; 8:24; 25; 34; 9:49; 55; 16:5; 17:6; 20:16; 48; 21:11(2); 21; 24(2); 25; **1Sa** 2:36; 3:11; 18; 4:10; 8:22; 10:25; 12:11; 13:2; 20; 14:20; 34(3); 47; 15:9; 20:15; 22:2(3); 7; 23:14; 25:10; 13(2); 26:23; 27:3; 30:6; 22; **2Sa** 2:3; 16; 27; 6:19(2); 13:9; 29; 37; 14:26; 15:4; 30; 36; 18:17; 19:8; 20:1; 2; 12; 22; 21:20(2); **1Kin** 1:49; 4:25; 27; 28; 5:3; 4; 7:30(2); 36; 38(2); 8:38; 39; 9:8; 10:25; 11:15; 16; 12:24; 14:23(2); 19:18; 20:20; 24; 22:17; 28; 36(2); **2Kin** 3:19(4); 25(2); 6:2; 8:9; 9:13; 11:8; 9; 11; 12:4(2); 5; 14:6; 12; 16:4; 17:10(2); 29(2); 18:31(3); 23:35; 25:9; 30; **1Chr** 9:27; 32; 13:1; 2; 16:3(2); 37; 43; 22:15; 18; 23:30; 26:13; 32; 27:1; 28:14; 15(2); 16; 17(2); 21; **2Chr** 1:2; 2:14; 6:29; 30; 7:21; 8:13; 14(2); 9:21; 24; 10:16; 11:4; 12; 23; 13:11(3); 14:7; 18:16; 20:23; 27; 23:7; 8; 10; 25:4; 22; 28:4; 24; 25; 29:35; 30:17; 18; 31:1; 2; 16; 19; 21; 32:22; 35:15; **Ezr** 2:1; 3:4; 5; 6:5; 8:34; 9:4; 10:14; **Neh** 3:28; 4:15; 17; 18; 22; 23; 5:7; 13; 7:3(2); 6; 8:16; 10:28; 31; 11:3; 20; 23; 12:47; 13:10; 30; **Est** 1:8; 22(4); 2:11; 12; 13; 3:12(4); 14; 4:3; 6:13; 8:9(2); 11; 13; 17(2); 9:27; 28(4); **Job** 1:4; 10; 2:11; 12; 7:18(2); 12:10; 18:11; 19:10; 20:22; 21:33; 24:6; 28:10; 34:11; 36:25; 37:7; 39:8; 40:11; 12; 42:2; 11(2); **Ps** 7:11; 12:2; 8; 29:9; 31:13; 32:6; 39:5; 6; 11; 50:10; 53:3; 56:5; 58:8; 62:12; 63:11; 64:6; 65:12; 68:30; 69:34; 71:18; 21; 73:14; 84:7; 92:2; 104:11; 115:8; 119:101; 104; 128; 160; 128:1; 135:18; 145:2; 16; 150:6; **Prov** 1:19; 2:9; 3:18; 7:12; 13:16; 14:1; 15; 15:3; 16:5; 19:6; 20:3; 6; 18; 21:2; 5; 24:12; 26; 27:7; 24; 29:26; 30:5; **Eccl** 3:1(2); 11; 13; 17(2); 4:4; 5:19; 8:6; 9; 10:3; 15; 12:14(2); **Song** 3:8; 4:2; 6:6; 8:11; **Is** 1:23; 2:12(2); 15(2); 3:5(2); 4:3; 5; 7:22; 23; 9:5; 17(2); 20; 13:7; 14(2); 15(2); 14:18; 15:2; 3; 16:7; 19:2(2); 7; 14; 17; 24:10; 27:3; 30:25(2); 32; 31:7; 33:2; 34:15; 36:16(3); 40:4(2); 41:6(2); 43:7; 44:23; 45:23(2); 47:15; 51:13; 52:5; 53:6; 54:17; 55:1; 56:6; 11; 57:5; 58:6; **Jer** 1:15; 2:20(2); 3:6(2); 13; 4:29; 5:6; 8; 6:3; 13(2); 25; 8:6; 10(2); 9:4(3); 5; 20; 10:14(2); 11:8; 12:4; 15(2); 13:12(2); 15:10; 16:12; 16(2); 17:10; 18:11; 12; 16; 19:8; 9; 20:7; 10; 22:7; 8; 23:17; 27; 30; 35(2); 36; 25:5; 26:3; 29:26; 30:6; 16; 31:25; 30(2); 34(2); 32:19; 34:9(2); 10(2); 14; 15; 16(2); 17(2); 35:15; 36:3; 7; 37:10; 43:6; 47:4; 48:8; 37(2); 49:5; 17; 29; 50:13; 16(2); 42; 51:6; 9; 17(2); 29; 45; 56; 52:34; **Lam** 2:19; 3:23; 4:1; **Eze** 1:6(2); 9; 11; 12; 23(2); 6:13(3); 7:16; 8:10; 11; 12; 9:1; 2; 10:14; 19; 21(2); 22; 11:5; 12:14; 22; 23; 13:18; 14:4; 7; 16:15; 24; 25(2); 31(2); 33; 44; 17:23; 18:30; 19:8; 20:7; 8; 28; 39; 47(2); 21:7(2); 10; 22:6; 23:22; 24:4; 26:16; 28:13; 23; 29:18(2); 32:10(2); 33:20; 26; 30; 34:6; 8; 36:3; 37:21; 38:20; 21; 39:4; 17(3); 40:7; 41:5(2); 10; 18; 43:25; 44:5; 29; 30(2); 45:20; 46:13; 14; 15; 18; 21; 47:9(2); **Dan** 3:10; 29; 6:12; 26; 11:36; 12:1; **Hos** 4:3; 9:1; **Joel** 2:7; 8; **Amos** 2:8; 4:3; 4; 8:3; 8; 10; **Obad** 9; **Jonah** 1:5; 7; 3:8; **Mic** 4:4; 5; 7:2; **Hab** 1:10; **Zeph** 2:11; 15; 3:5; 19; **Hag** 1:9; 2:14; 22; **Zec** 3:10; 5:3(2); 7:9; 8:4; 10; 16; 10:1; 4; 11:6; 9; 12:4(2); 12; 14; 13:4; 14:13; 16; 21; **Mal** 1:11; 2:10; 17; **Mt** 3:10; 4:4; 7:8; 17; 19; 21; 26; 8:33; 9:35(2); 12:25(2); 36; 13:47; 52; 15:13; 16:27; 18:16; 35; 19:3; 29; 20:9; 10; 25:15; 29; 26:22; **Mk** 1:45; 7:14; 8:25; 9:49(2); 13:34; 15:24; 16:15; 20; **Lk** 2:3; 23; 41; 3:5(2); 9; 4:4; 37; 40; 5:17; 6:30; 40; 44; 8:1; 4; 9:6; 43; 10:1; 11:4; 10; 17; 16:5; 16; 19; 18:14; 19:15; 26; 43; **Jn** 1:9; 2:10; 3:8; 20; 6:7; 40; 45; 7:23; 53; 13:10; 15:2(2); 16:32; 18:37; 19:23; 21:25; **Acts** 2:5; 6; 8; 38; 43; 45; 3:23; 26; 4:35; 5:16; 42; 8:3; 4; 10:35; 11:29; 13:27; 14:23; 15:21(2); 36; 16:26; 17:27; 30; 18:4; 20:23; 31; 21:26; 28; 22:19; 26:11; 28:2; 22; **Rom** 1:16; 2:6; 9; 10; 3:2; 4; 19; 10:4; 12:3(2); 5; 13:1; 14:5(2); 11(2); 12; 15:2; **1Cor** 1:2; 5; 12; 3:5; 8; 10; 13(2); 4:5; 17(2); 6:18; 7:2(2); 7; 17(2); 20; 24; 8:7; 9:25; 10:24; 11:3; 4; 5; 21; 12:7; 11; 18; 14:26; 15:23; 30; 38; 16:2; 16; **2Cor** 2:14; 4:2; 8; 5:10; 7:5; 8:7; 9:7; 8; 11; 10:5(2); 13:1; **Gal** 3:10; 13; 5:3; 6:4; 5; **Eph** 1:21; 4:7; 14; 16(2); 25; 5:24; 33; **Phil** 1:3; 4; 18; 2:4(2); 9; 10; 11; 4:6; 12; 21; **Col** 1:10; 15; 23; 28(3); 4:6; **1Th** 1:8; 2:11; 4:4; 5:18; **2Th** 1:3; 2:17; 3:6; 17; **1Ti** 2:8; 4:4; 5:10; **2Ti** 2:19; 21; 4:18; **Titus** 1:5; 16; 3:1; **Philem** 1:6; **Heb** 2:2; 9; 3:4; 5:1; 13; 6:11; 8:3; 11(2); 9:7; 19; 25; 10:3; 11; 12:1; 6; 13:21; **Jas** 1:14; 17(2); 19; 3:7; 16; **1Pet** 1:17; 2:13; 3:15; 4:10; **1Jn** 2:29; 3:3; 4:1; 2; 3; 7; 5:1; **Rev** 1:7; 2:23; 5:8; 9; 13; 6:11; 14; 15(2); 14:6; 16:3; 20; 21; 18:2(2); 17; 20:13; 21:21; 22:2; 12; 18

EXCEPT

369, 518, 905, 1115, 3588, 3808, 3861, 3884, 7535, *1508, 1509, 2228, 3362, 3923, 4133*

Gen 31:42; 32:26; 42:15; 43:3; 5; 10; 44:23; 26; 47:26; **Num** 16:13; **Deut** 32:30; **Josh** 7:12; **1Sa** 25:34; **2Sa** 3:9; 13; 5:6; **2Kin** 4:24; **Est** 2:14; 4:11; **Ps** 127:1(2); **Prov** 4:16; **Is** 1:9; **Dan** 2:11; 3:28; 6:5; **Amos** 3:3; **Mt** 5:20; 12:29; 18:3; 19:9; 24:22; 26:42; **Mk** 3:27; 7:3; 4; 13:20; **Lk** 9:13; 13:3; 5; **Jn** 3:2; 3; 5; 27; 4:48; 6:44; 53; 65; 12:24; 15:4(2); 19:11; 20:25; **Acts** 8:1; 31; 15:1; 24:21; 26:29; 27:31; **Rom** 7:7; 9:29; 10:15; **1Cor** 7:5; 14:5; 6; 7; 9; 15:36; **2Cor** 12:13; 13:5; **2Th** 2:3; **2Ti** 2:5; **Rev** 2:5; 22

EXCEPTED

1622

1Cor 15:27

FAR

1419, 2008, 2186, 2486, 3966, 4801, 5048, 5079, 7350, 7352, 7368, 7369, *891, 2193, 2436, 3112, 3113, 3117, 3123, 4054, 4183, 4206, 5231, 5236*

Gen 18:25(2); 44:4; **Ex** 8:28; 23:7; **Num** 2:2; **Deut** 12:21; 13:7; 14:24; 20:15; 28:49; 29:22; 30:11; **Josh** 3:16; 8:4; 9:6; 9; 22; **Judg** 9:17; 18:7; 28; 19:11; **1Sa** 2:30; 20:9; 22:15; **2Sa** 15:17; 20:20(2); 23:17; **1Kin** 8:41; 46; **2Kin** 20:14; **2Chr** 6:32; 36; 26:15; **Ezr** 6:6; **Neh** 4:19; **Est** 9:20; **Job** 5:4; 11:14; 13:21; 19:13; 21:16; 22:18; 23; 30:10; 34:10; **Ps** 10:5; 22:1; 11; 19; 27:9; 35:22; 38:21; 55:7; 71:12; 73:27; 88:8; 18; 97:9; 103:12(2); 109:17; 119:150; 155; **Prov** 4:24; 5:8; 15:29; 19:7; 22:5; 15; 25:25; 27:10; 30:8; 31:10; **Eccl** 2:13; 7:23; 24; **Is** 5:26; 6:12; 8:9; 10:3; 13:5; 17:13; 19:6; 22:3; 26:15; 29:13; 30:27; 33:13; 17; 39:3; 43:6; 46:11; 12; 13; 49:1; 12; 19; 54:14; 57:9; 19; 59:9; 11; 60:4; 9; **Jer** 2:5; 4:16; 5:15; 6:20; 8:19; 12:2; 25:26; 27:10; 48:24; 47; 49:30; 51:64; **Lam** 1:16; 3:17; **Eze** 6:12; 7:20; 8:6; 11:15; 16; 12:27; 22:5; 23:40; 43:9; 44:10; **Dan** 9:7; 11:2; **Joel** 2:20; 3:6; 8; **Amos** 6:3; **Mic** 4:7; 7:11; **Hab** 1:8; **Zec** 6:15; 10:9; **Mt** 15:8; 16:22; 21:33; 25:14; **Mk** 6:35(2); 7:6; 8:3; 12:1; 34; 13:34; **Lk** 7:6; 15:13; 19:12; 20:9; 22:51; 24:29; 50; **Jn** 21:8; **Acts** 11:19; 22; 17:27; 22:21; 28:15; **Rom** 13:12; **2Cor** 4:17; 10:14; **Eph** 1:21; 2:13; 4:10; **Phil** 1:23; **Heb** 7:15

FARTHER

4008, 4260, 4281

Mt 26:39; **Mk** 1:19; 10:1

FATHER'S

1, 1730

Gen 9:23; 12:1; 20:13; 24:7; 23; 38; 40; 26:15; 28:21; 29:9; 12; 31:1(2); 5; 14; 19; 30; 35:22; 37:2; 12; 38:11(2); 41:51; 46:31(2); 47:12; 48:17; 49:4; 8; 50:1; 8; 22; **Ex** 2:16; 6:20; 15:2; **Lev** 16:32; 18:8(2); 11; 12(2); 14; 20:11(2); 17; 19; 22:13(2); **Num** 2:2; 18:1; 27:7; 10; 30:3; 16; 36:11; **Deut** 22:21(2); 30(2); 27:20(2); **Josh** 2:12; 18; 6:25; **Judg** 6:15; 25; 27; 9:5; 18; 11:2; 7; 14:15; 19; 19:2; 3; **1Sa** 2:31; 9:20; 17:15; 25; 34; 18:2; 18; 22:1; 11; 16; 22; 24:21; **2Sa** 3:7; 29; 9:7; 14:9; 15:34; 16:19; 21; 22; 19:28; 24:17; **1Kin** 11:12; 17; 12:10; 18:18; **2Kin** 10:3; 23:30; 24:17; **1Chr** 5:1; 7:2; 40; 12:28; 21:17; 23:11; **2Chr** 2:13; 10:10; 21:13; 36:1; **Ezr** 2:59; **Neh** 1:6; 7:61; **Est** 4:14; **Ps** 45:10; **Prov** 4:3; 6:20; 13:1; 15:5; 27:10; **Is** 7:17; 22:23; 24; **Jer** 35:14; **Eze** 18:14; 22:11; **Mt** 26:29; **Lk** 2:49; 9:26; 12:32; 15:17; 16:27; **Jn** 2:16; 5:43; 6:39; 10:25; 29; 14:2; 24; 15:10; **Acts** 7:20; **1Cor** 5:1; **Rev** 14:1

FATHERS

1, 2, *3962, 3964, 3967, 3970, 3971*

Gen 15:15; 31:3; 46:34; 47:3; 9; 30; 48:15; 16; 21; 49:29; **Ex** 3:13; 15; 16; 4:5; 6:25; 10:6(2); 12:3; 13:5; 11; 20:5; 34:7; **Lev** 25:41; 26:39; 40; **Num** 1:2; 4; 16; 18; 20; 22; 24; 26; 28; 30; 32; 34; 36; 38; 40; 42; 44; 45; 47; 2:32; 34; 3:15; 20; 4:2; 22; 29; 34; 38; 40; 42; 46; 7:2; 11:12; 13:2; 14:18; 23; 17:2(2); 3; 20:15(2); 26:55; 31:26; 32:8; 28; 33:54; 34:14(2); 36:1(2); 3; 4; 7; 8; **Deut** 1:8; 11; 21; 35; 4:1; 31; 37; 5:3; 9; 6:3; 10; 18; 23; 7:8; 12; 13; 8:1; 3; 16; 18; 9:5; 10:11; 15; 22; 11:9; 21; 12:1; 13:6; 17; 19:8(2); 24:16(2); 26:3; 7; 15; 27:3; 28:11; 36; 64; 29:13; 25; 30:5(2); 9; 20; 31:7; 16; 20; 32:17; **Josh** 1:6; 4:6; 21; 5:6; 14:1; 18:3; 19:51; 21:1(2); 43; 44; 22:14; 28; 24:2; 6(2); 14; 15; 17; **Judg** 2:1; 10; 12; 17; 19; 20; 22; 3:4; 6:13; 21:22; **1Sa** 12:6; 7; 8(2); 15; **2Sa** 7:12; **1Kin** 1:21; 2:10; 8:1; 21; 34; 40; 48; 53; 57; 58; 9:9; 11:21; 43; 13:22; 14:15; 20; 22; 31(2); 15:8; 12; 24(2); 16:6; 28; 19:4; 21:3; 4; 22:40; 50(2); **2Kin** 8:24(2); 9:28; 10:35; 12:18; 21; 13:9; 13; 14:6(2); 16; 20; 22; 29; 15:7(2); 9; 22; 38(2); 16:20(2); 17:13; 14; 15; 41; 19:12; 20:17; 21; 21:8; 15; 18; 22; 22:13; 20; 23:32; 37; 24:6; **1Chr** 4:38; 5:13; 15; 24(2); 25; 6:19; 7:4; 7; 9; 11; 8:6; 10; 13; 28; 9:9(2); 13; 19; 33; 34; 12:17; 30; 15:12; 17:11; 23:9; 24(2); 24:4(2); 6; 30; 31(2); 26:13; 21; 26; 31; 32; 27:1; 29:6; 15; 18; 20; **2Chr** 1:2; 5:2; 6:25; 31; 38; 7:22; 9:31; 11:16; 12:16; 13:12; 18; 14:1; 4; 15:12; 16:13; 17:14; 19:4; 8; 20:6; 33; 21:1(2); 10; 19; 23:2; 24:18; 24; 25:4(2); 5; 28; 26:2; 12; 23(2); 27:9; 28:6; 9; 25; 27; 29:5; 6; 9; 30:7(2); 8; 19; 22; 31:17; 32:13; 14; 15; 33; 33:8; 12; 20; 34:21; 28; 32; 33; 35:4; 5; 24; 36:15; **Ezr** 1:5; 2:68; 3:12; 4:2; 3; 15; 5:12; 7:27; 8:1; 28; 29; 9:7; 10:11; 16(2); **Neh** 7:70; 71; 8:13; 9:2; 9; 16; 23; 32; 34; 36; 10:34; 11:13; 12:12; 22; 23; 13:18; **Job** 8:8; 15:18; 30:1; **Ps** 22:4; 39:12; 44:1; 45:16; 49:19; 78:3; 5; 8; 12; 57; 95:9; 106:6; 7; 109:14; **Prov** 17:6; 19:14; 22:28; **Is** 14:21; 37:12; 39:6; 49:23; 64:11; 65:7; **Jer** 2:5; 3:18; 24; 25; 6:21; 7:7; 14; 18; 22; 25; 26; 9:14; 16; 11:4; 5; 7; 10; 13:14; 14:20; 16:3; 11; 12; 13; 15; 19; 17:22; 19:4; 23:27; 39; 24:10; 25:5; 30:3; 31:29; 32; 32:18; 22; 34:5; 13; 14; 35:15; 44:3; 9; 10; 17; 21; 47:3; 50:7; **Lam** 5:7; **Eze** 2:3; 5:10(2); 18:2; 20:4; 18; 27; 30; 36; 42; 36:28; 37:25; 47:14; **Dan** 2:23; 9:6; 8; 16; 11:24(2); 37; 38; **Hos** 9:10; **Joel** 1:2; **Amos** 2:4; **Mic** 7:20; **Zec** 1:2; 4; 5; 6; 8:14; **Mal** 2:10; 3:7; 4:6(2); **Mt** 23:30; 32; **Lk** 1:17; 55; 72; 6:23; 26; 11:47; 48; **Jn** 4:20; 6:31; 49; 58; 7:22; **Acts** 3:13; 22; 25; 5:30; 7:2; 11; 12; 15; 19; 32; 38; 39; 44; 45(2); 51; 52; 13:17; 32; 36; 15:10; 22:1; 3; 14; 24:14; 26:6; 28:17; 25; **Rom** 9:5; 15:8; **1Cor** 4:15; 10:1; **Gal** 1:14; **Eph** 6:4; **Col** 3:21; **1Ti** 1:9; **Heb** 1:1; 3:9; 8:9; 12:9; **1Pet** 1:18; **2Pet** 3:4; **1Jn** 2:13; 14

FATHERS'

1, *3962*

Ex 6:14; 10:6; **Num** 17:6; 26:2; 32:14; **Neh** 2:3; 5; **Eze** 20:24; 22:10; **Dan** 11:24; **Rom** 11:28

FEW

259, 4213, 4557, 4591, 4592, 4962, 7116, *1024, 3641, 4935*

Gen 24:55; 27:44; 29:20; 34:30; 47:9; **Lev** 25:52; 26:22; **Num** 9:20; 13:18; 26:54; 56; 35:8(2); **Deut** 4:27; 26:5; 28:62; 33:6; **Josh** 7:3; **1Sa** 14:6; 17:28; **2Kin** 4:3; **1Chr** 16:19(2); **2Chr** 29:34; **Neh** 2:12; 7:4; **Job** 10:20; 14:1; 16:22; **Ps** 105:12(2); 109:8; **Eccl** 5:2; 9:14; 12:3; **Is** 10:7; 19; 24:6; **Jer** 30:19; 42:2; **Eze** 5:3; 12:16; **Dan** 11:20; **Mt** 7:14; 9:37; 15:34; 20:16; 22:14; 25:21; 23; **Mk** 6:5; 8:7; **Lk** 10:2; 12:48; 13:23; **Acts** 17:4; 12; 24:4; **Eph** 3:3; **Heb** 12:10; 13:22; **1Pet** 3:20; **Rev** 2:14; 20; 3:4

FEWER

4592

Num 33:54

FOR

3588, *1063*

Gen 1:14(3); 15; 29; 30; 2:5; 9; 17; 18; 20(2); 3:5; 6; 17; 19(2); 22; 4:23; 25; 5:24; 6:3; 7; 12; 13; 21(3); 7:1; 4; 8:9(2); 21(2); 9:3; 6; 12; 13; 10:25; 11:3(2); 12:10; 13; 16; 13:6; 8; 15(2); 17; 14:13; 15:6; 16; 16:10; 13; 17:4; 5; 7; 8; 13; 15; 19; 20; 18:5; 14; 15; 19; 24; 26; 28; 29; 31; 32; 19:8; 13; 14; 17; 21; 22; 30; 20:3(2); 6; 7(2); 11; 18; 21:2; 7; 10; 12; 16; 17; 18; 30; 22:2; 3; 7; 8; 12; 13; 16; 23:2(2); 8; 9(2); 13; 18; 20; 24:10; 14; 19; 20; 22; 23; 31(2); 32; 40; 44(2); 62; 65; 25:21; 30; 26:3; 7(2); 9; 14; 15; 16; 18; 21; 22(3); 24(2); 27:5; 9; 36(2); 37; 41; 28:11; 15; 18(2); 22; 29:2; 9; 15; 18; 20(2); 21; 24; 25; 27; 32; 30:13; 15; 16; 26(2); 27(2); 30(2); 31; 33(2); 31:12; 14; 15; 16; 18; 31; 32; 35; 41(2); 44; 45; 49; 52; 32:10; 11; 12; 13; 20; 26; 28; 30; 33:10; 17; 19; 34:8; 14; 21(3); 22; 35:18; 36:7; 37:7; 8(2); 17; 27; 28; 34; 35(2); 38:6; 11; 14; 16; 39:5; 40:15; 17; 41:8; 19; 31; 32; 36; 49; 51; 52; 55; 57; 42:2; 4; 5; 18; 19; 23; 25; 27; 30; 33; 38; 43:5; 9(2); 10; 16; 18; 25; 30; 32(4); 44:4; 14; 17; 18; 22; 26; 32(3); 34; 45:3; 5; 6; 11; 19(2); 20; 21; 23; 26; 46:3; 32; 34; 47:4(4); 13; 14; 15(2); 16; 17(6); 19; 20(2); 21; 22; 23(2); 24(5); 48:4; 7; 10; 14; 18; 49:6; 7(2); 13; 18; 30; 50:3(3); 5; 10; 13(2); 17; 19; 20; **Ex** 1:5; 11; 18; 19; 2:3; 7; 9; 19; 22; 3:5; 6; 7; 15; 4:1; 19; 5:7; 8; 18; 23; 6:1; 7; 8; 9(2); 7:9; 12; 24(2); 8:8; 9(3); 17; 25(2); 26; 28; 9:2; 11; 14; 15; 16(2); 19; 27; 28; 30; 31; 32; 10:1; 5; 9; 10; 11; 12; 15; 16; 23; 26; 28; 12:3; 4(2); 12; 13; 14(2); 15; 17(2); 19; 21; 23; 24(2); 30; 31; 33; 39(2); 42; 44; 48; 13:3; 9(3); 16(3); 17; 19;

14:3; 12(2); 13(2); 14; 25(2); 15:1; 17; 18; 19; 21; 23; 25; 26; 16:3; 4; 7; 8; 9; 15; 16(2); 22; 23; 25; 27; 29; 32; 33; 17:1; 3; 14(2); 16; 18:1(2); 3; 4; 8; 9; 11; 12; 18(2); 19; 22; 19:2; 5; 7; 9; 11; 23; 20:5; 7; 11; 20; 25; 21:2; 6; 19; 21; 23; 24(4); 25(3); 26; 27; 30; 36; 22:1(2); 2; 3(3); 9(6); 13; 15; 21; 27(3); 23:7; 8; 9; 15; 21(2); 23; 31; 33; 24:14; 25:6(3); 12; 26; 27; 26:14; 15; 17; 18; 19(2); 20; 22; 23; 24(2); 26; 27(3); 29(2); 36; 37(2); 27:4; 6; 9(3); 11; 12; 16; 20; 21; 28:2(3); 4; 12(2); 29; 40(5); 43; 29:9; 22; 24; 25(2); 26; 27(2); 28(2); 36(3); 37; 40; 41; 30:4(2); 12; 15; 16(2); 17(2); 12; 13; 14(2); 16; 17(2); 32:1(2); 7; 12; 13; 18(2); 23(3); 25; 29; 30; 33:3(2); 5; 16; 17; 20; 34:7; 9(2); 10; 12; 14(2); 18; 24; 27(2); 35:8(3); 9(2); 14(2); 15; 17; 19; 21(2); 24; 27(2); 28(3); 36:1; 3; 5; 6; 14; 19; 20; 22; 23(2); 24(2); 26(3); 28; 29(3); 39; 16:11; 28; 34; 37; 38(2); 39; 46(2); 47; 17:3(2); 6; 8; 10; 18:4; 6; 7; 8; 9(2); 11; 16; 17(2); 19(2); 21(2); 23; 26(2); 31(2); 19:9(3); 10(2); 17(2); 19(2); 21(2); 2(6); 3; 5; 6; 7; 8(2); 9; 10; 14(2); 17(3); 21; 24(2); 5; 6; 7; 8(4); 9; 10(2); 13(3); 14(4); 15(7); 16(3); 17(4); 3(2); 4:13(2); 19(2); 24(2); 25(2); 26(2); 45:t; 2; 3; 4; 8; 14(2); 49:t; 7; 46:t; 47:t; 2; 4; 7; 9; 48:t; 2; 3; 4; 8; 14(2); 49:t; 7; 46:t; 47:t; 2; 4; 7; 9; 48:t; 50:6; 8; 10; 12; 51:3; 16; 52:5; 8; 9(2); 53:5; 54:3; 6; 7; 55:3; 6; 9; 12; 15; 16; 18; 56:1; 2; 5; 6; 9(2); 13; 57:1; 2; 6; 10; 58:11; 59:3(4); 7; 9; 12(2); 15; 60:2; 11; 12; 61:3(2); 4; 5; 7; 8; 62:5; 8; 16; 17; 60:2; 11; 12; 63:1(2); 10; 64:9; 65:1; 3; 9; 13; 66:7; 10; 16; 67:4(2); 68:10; 16; 18(2); 28; 69:1; 3; 6(2); 7; 9; 13; 16; 17; 20(2); 21; 22; 26; 35; 33; 70:3; 71:3; 5; 10(2); 11; 12; 15; 24(2); 72:t; 12; 15; 17; 19; 73:2; 3; 4; 14; 16; 26; 27; 28; 74:1; 4; 10; 12; 19; 20; 75:1; 6; 8; 9; 77:7; 8(2); 78:5; 18; 20; 29; 32(2); 37; 39; 58; 69; 79:5; 7; 8; 9(2); 13; 80:15; 17; 81:4(2); 5; 15; 82:8; 83:2; 5; 10; 17; 84:t; 2(2); 3; 10; 11; 85:t; 5; 8; 86:1; 2; 3; 4; 5; 7; 10; 12; 13; 17; 87:t; 88:t; 1; 8; 9; 12(2); 89:1; 2(2); 4; 6; 11; 17; 18; 28(2); 29; 36; 37; 46; 52; 90:4; 7; 9; 10; 91:5(2); 6(2); 11; 92:t; 4; 7; 8; 9(2); 93:5; 94:13; 14; 16(2); 95:3; 7; 96:4; 5; 13(2); 97:9; 11(2); 98:1; 9; 99:3; 5; 9; 100:5; 102:3; 9; 10; 12; 13; 14; 18; 19; 103:6; 9; 11; 14; 15; 16; 104:5; 8; 24(2); 105:8; 10(2); 14; 16; 17; 32; 38; 39; 42; 106:1(3); 8; 13; 31(2); 32; 43; 45; 107:1(3); 8(2); 9; 15(2); 16; 21(2); 25; 31(2); 34; 36; 108:4; 12; 13; 109:2; 4; 5(2); 9; 21(2); 22; 31; 110:4; 111:3; 8; 9; 112:3; 6; 9; 113:2; 115:1(2); 18; 116:7; 8; 12; 117:2(2); 118:1(2); 2; 3; 4; 12; 21; 29(3); 119:20; 22; 28; 35; 39; 42; 43; 44; 45; 50; 66; 71; 76; 77; 78; 81; 82; 83; 85; 89; 91; 93; 94; 95; 98; 99; 102; 110; 111(2); 115; 118; 120; 122(2); 123(2); 126(2); 131(2); 152; 153; 155; 160; 166; 168; 172; 173; 174; 176; 120:7(2); 121:8; 122:5; 6; 8; 123:3; 125:1; 2; 3; 5; 126:2; 3; 127:1; 2(2); 128:2; 130:5; 6(3); 7; 131:1; 3; 132:5(2); 9; 10; 12; 13; 14(2); 16; 17; 133:1; 3(2); 135:3(2); 4(2); 5; 7; 12; 13; 14; 136:1(3); 2(2); 3(2); 4(2); 5(2); 6(2); 7(2); 8(2); 9(2); 10(2); 11(2); 12(2); 13(2); 14(2); 15(2); 16(2); 17(2); 18(2); 19(2); 20(2); 21(3); 22(2); 23(2); 24(2); 25(2); 26(2); 137:3; 138:2(3); 5; 8; 139:4; 6; 13; 14; 20; 140:2; 5(2); 9; 141:5; 6; 9; 142:3; 4; 6(2); 7; 143:2; 3; 8(2); 10; 11(2); 12; 145:1; 2; 11; 146:5; 6; 7; 10; 147:1(2); 8; 13; 20; 148:5; 6; 13; 149:4; 150:2; **Prov** 1:9; 11(2); 16; 18(2); 29; 32; 2:3; 4(2); 6; 7; 18; 21; 3:2; 12; 14; 26; 32; 4:2; 3; 13; 16; 17; 23; 5:3; 21; 6:1; 23; 26(2); 34; 7:6; 19; 23; 26; 8:6; 7; 11; 32; 35; 9:4; 11; 12; 16; 10:13; 21; 11:15:12:6; 12; 6; 19(2); 26; 32; 4:2; 3; 6; 11; 33:1(2); 4; 9; 11; 12; 17; 20; 21; 34:9; 35:2; 27:5; 6; 7; 18; 21; 21:4; 14; 19; 21; 28:2(2); 4; 6(2); 8; 17; 26; 23:7; 14(2); 16; 24:3; 5(3); 8; 15; 16; 17; 24; 27:8; 15; 12(2); 13; 18; 20(2); 24(2); 25; 14(2); 15(7); 16; 17(2); 18(2); 20; 6:2; 4; 7; 8; 12(3); 7:2; 5; 6; 9; 10; 13; 18; 20; 22; 8:3; 7(2); 15; 16; 9:1; 4(2); 5(2); 6; 7; 8; 9; 10; 12(2); 15; 16; 10:1(4); 17; 19; 20; 11:1; 2; 6; 7; 8; 9; 10; 12:13; 14; **Song** 1:2; 7; 2:5; 11; 14; 15; 3:10; 4:4; 5:2; 4; 6:5; 7:6; 9; 13; 8:6; 7; 8(2); 11; **Is** 1:2; 17; 20; 29(2); 30; 2:3; 10(2); 12; 19(2); 20; 21(2); 22; 3:1; 7; 8; 9; 10; 11; 12; 14; 4:2; 5; 6(3); 5:7(3); 10; 18(2); 22(2); 23; 25(2); 8:4; 10; 11; 14(5); 17; 18(2); 19; 9:4; 5; 6; 7; 12; 13; 16; 17(2); 18; 19; 21; 20(3); 10:4; 7; 8(2); 15; 16; 18(2); 19; 31; 33(2); 22; 4:11; 20; 5:2; 18; 23; 27; 6:3; 4; 8; 9; 9:17; 32; 10:16; 27; 28; 7:2; 16; 21; 8:4; 6; 8; 9; 9:17; 32; 10:16; 19; 32; 35(3); 38:1; 14; 17(2); 18(2); 21(2); 39:1;

2Sa 1:9; 12(4); 16; 21; 26; 2:7; 26; 3:6; 8; 14; 17; 18; 22; 27; 37; 39; 4:2; 7; 5:12(2); 6:6; 7; 17; 7:3; 5; 10; 13(2); 16(2); 17; 20; 21; 24(2); 13:6; 7; 8; 11; 15; 23; 24; 26; 29; 35; 16:1(2); 7(2); 11; 12; 17:8; 12; 17; 20; 21; 26; 28:1; 33; 39(2); 42; 47; 18:11; 17(2); 19:5(2); 13; 20:4; 6(2); 8(2); 9; 15; 17; 21; 22; 23; 26; 29; 31(2); 34(2); 2:2(2); 3(2); 7(2); 12:13(2); 24:4(2); 7; 16; 20; 25:3; 16; 22; 26; 30; **1Chr** 4:14; 13; 39; 40; 41; 42; 5:1; 2; 20; 22; 6:26; 49(2); 54; 70; 7:4(2); 11; 9:1; 13; 26; 33; 10:4; 13(2); 11:9; 19; 20; 21; 12:8; 18; 19; 21; 22; 25; 29; 37; 39(2); 40; 13:3; 4; 9; 14:2; 10; 15; 15:1(2); 2(2); 3; 11(3); 12; 13(2); 22; 23; 24; 16:1; 17(2); 21; 25; 26; 34(3); 36; 41; 42; 17:2; 5; 9; 12; 14(2); 17(2); 18(2); 19; 22(2); 25; 29; 37; 39(2); 40; 13:3; 4; 9; 14:2; 21; 32(2); 34; 38; 39; 40; 41; 46(3); 47; 56; 57(2); 62; 67(2); 68; 69:8; 13; 16; 26; 29; 30:9(3); 11; 12; 13; 20; 31:6; 7; 18; 19(2); 20; 22; 23; 31; 10; 14; 20; 140:2; 5(2); 9; 141:5(2); 2; 21; 146:5; 6; 7; 10; 147:1(2); 8; 13; 20; 148:5; 6; 13; 149:4; 150:2;

11:4; 11; 12; 15; 13:7(2); 8; 16; 19; 24; 26; 14:7; 16; 20; 15:5; 22; 23; 25; 31; 34; 16:12; 17; 21(2); 17:1; 4; 10(2); 15; 18:4; 8; 10(2); 19:15; 17; 21; 24; 25; 27; 29; 20:2; 5; 7; 18; 21; 21:4; 14; 19; 21; 28; 22:4; 6(2); 8; 17; 26; 23:7; 14(2); 16; 24:3; 5(3); 8; 15; 16; 17; 24; 27:8; 14; 22; 28:1(2); 5; 15(2); 17; 18; 24; 25; 26(2); 29:13; 23(3); 30:3; 4; 23(2); 25(2); 26(2); 31:2; 11; 12; 18; 19; 24; 32:4; 6(2); 8; 17; 26; 23:7; 14(2); 16; 24:3; 5(3); 8; 15; 16; 17; 24; 27:8; 14; 22; 28:1(2); 5; 15(2); 16; 17; 18; 24; 32:1; 11(2); 13; 15; 16(2); 18(2); 19(2); 20; 21(3); 22(2); 23(2); 24(2); 25(2); 26(2); 137:3; 138:2(3); 5; 8; 139:4; 6; 13; 14; 20; 140:2(2); 5(2); 9; 141:5; 6; 9; 142:3; 4; 6(2); 7; 143:2; 3; 8(2); 10; 11(2); 12; 145:1; 2; 11; 146:5; 6; 7; 10; 147:1(2); 8; 13; 20; 148:5; 6; 13; 149:4; 150:2; **Prov** 1:9; 11(2); 16; 18(2); 29; 32; 2:3; 4(2); 6; 7; 18; 21; 3:2; 12; 14; 26; 32; 4:2; 3; 13; 16; 17; 23; 5:3; 21; 6:1; 23; 26(2); 34; 7:6; 19; 23; 26; 8:6; 7; 11; 32; 35; 9:4; 11; 12; 16; 10:13; 21; 11:15(2); 12:6; 18:6; 16; 19:10(2); 18; 19; 29(2); 20:3; 16(2); 21:8; 12; 18(2); 25; 29; 22:9; 11; 18; 23; 26; 23:3; 5; 7; 9; 11; 13; 18; 21; 27; 28; 24:2; 6; 7; 16; 20; 22; 27; 25:3(2); 4; 7; 13; 16; 22; 27; 26:1; 3(3); 25; 27:1; 10; 13(2); 21(2); 24(2); 26; 27(4); 28:2; 8; 21(2); 29:5; 14; 19; 30:8; 18; 21(2); 22; 23; 30; 31:4(3); 8; 10; 21(2); 29; **Eccl** 1:4; 18; 2:3; 10; 12; 16(2); 17; 21(2); 22; 23; 26; 3:12; 14; 17(3); 19(2); 22(2); 4:4; 8; 9; 10(2); 14; 5:1; 2; 3; 4; 7; 8; 9; 13; 16; 18(2); 20; 6:2; 4; 7; 8; 12(3); 7:2; 3; 5; 6; 9; 10; 12; 13; 18; 20; 22; 8:3; 7(2); 15; 16; 9:1; 4(2); 5(2); 6; 7; 8; 9; 10; 12(2); 15; 16; 10:1(4); 17; 19; 20; 11:1; 2; 6; 7; 8; 9; 10; 12:13; 14; **Song** 1:2; 7; 2:5; 11; 14; 15; 3:10; 4:4; 5:2; 4; 6:5; 7:6; 9; 13; 8:6; 7; 8(2); 11; **Is** 1:2; 17; 20; 29(2); 30; 2:3; 10(2); 12; 19(2); 20; 21(2); 22; 3:1; 7; 8; 9; 10; 11; 12; 14; 4:2; 5; 6(3); 5:7(3); 10; 18(2); 22(2); 23; 25(2); 6:5; 7; 14; 7:9; 10; 13; 14; 4:2; 5; 7; 8; 14(2); 16; 5:4; 8; 9; 10; 20; 21; 27; 11; 28:5(2); 6(2); 8; 10; 11; 15; 16; 19; 20; 21(2); 27:11; 28:5(2); 6(2); 8; 10; 11; 15; 16; 19; 20; 21(3); 30:4; 7; 8(2); 15; 16; 18(2); 19; 31; 33(2); 4(4); 7(2); 9; 32:6; 10; 13(3); 14(2); 15; 17; 33:2; 5; 22; 34:2; 5; 6; 8(2); 13; 16; 17(2); 35:1; 6; 8; 36:5; 9(2); 11; 14; 16; 21; 37:3; 4; 8; 19; 32; 35(3); 38:1; 14; 17(2); 18(2); 21(2); 39:1;

8; 40:2(2); 3; 5; 8; 10; 16; 26; 41:7; 10(2); 13; 17; 22; 28; 42:4; 6(2); 21; 22(2); 23; 24(2); 43:1; 3(3); 4(2); 5; 7(2); 14; 21; 25; 44:3; 7; 10; 14; 15(2); 17; 18; 21; 22; 23(2); 45:4; 13; 18; 22; 46:9; 13; 47:1; 4; 5; 7; 9(2); 10; 48:2; 8; 9(3); 11(3); 21; 49:4; 6; 8; 10; 13; 19; 20; 23(2); 25; 50:1(2); 2; 7; 51:2; 3; 4(2); 6(2); 8(2); 10; 11; 12; 54:1; 3; 4(3); 5; 7; 9(2); 10; 14(2); 15(2); 16; 55:2(2); 4; 5; 7; 8; 9(2); 13; 47:1; 49:4; 5; 7; 9(2); 10; 14(2); 15(2); 16; 17; 20; 22; 23(2); 66:2; 5; 10(2); 12; 15; 16; 18; 20; 21(2); 22; 24; Jer 1:6; 7; 8; 12; 15; 16; 18; 20; 2:10; 11; 13; 20; 22; 25; 27; 28; 37; 3:2; 5; 8; 10; 12; 14; 18; 21; 22; 23; 24(2); 4:3; 6; 8(2); 13; 15; 20; 22; 27; 28; 29; 31(2); 5:4; 5; 7; 9; 10; 11; 22; 26; 29; 6:1; 4(2); 6; 11; 12; 13; 16(3); 22; 27; 29; 7:5; 7; 12; 16(3); 22; 29; 30; 32; 33(2); 34; 8:2; 10; 11; 14; 15(2); 16; 17; 21; 9:1; 2; 3(3); 4; 7(2); 10(2); 12; 17(2); 18; 19; 21; 24; 26; 10:2; 3(2); 5; 7; 14; 16(2); 17; 20; 35:6(2); 9; 11(2); 14; 19; 36:7; 31; 37:3; 4; 9; 10; 11; 15; 17; 38:2(2); 4(2); 5; 9(2); 27; 39:16(2); 18(2); 40:4; 10; 16; 41:8; 9; 18; 42:2(3); 5; 10; 11; 12; 22; 28(2); 47:3; 4; 48:1; 5(2); 7; 9; 14; 18; 20; 26; 27(3); 31; 32; 34; 36(2); 37; 38; 44; 46; 49:3(2); 8; 12; 13; 15; 16; 23; 30; 33(2); 37; 50:3; 9; 14; 15; 16; 20(2); 24; 25; 27; 29; 31; 38; 39; 44; 46; 24:7; 9; 10; 16; 17; 23; 25(2); 27; 13:5; 16; 19(2); 20; 27; 29; 31; 2Pet 1:8; 10; 11; 16; 17; 21; 2:4; 8; 16; 17; 18; 19; 20; 21(2); 3:4; 5; 12; 13; 14; 18; 1Jn 1:2; 2:2(3); 12; 16; 17; 19; 3:2; 4; 8(2); 9; 11; 16(2); 20; 4:7; 8; 10; 20; 5:1; 9; 16(2); 2Jn 2(2); 7; 11; 3Jn 3; 7; Jude 3(2); 4; 7; 11(2); 13; 21; Rev 1:3; 6; 9(2); 18; 2:3; 3:2; 4; 8; 4:9; 10; 11(2); 5:9; 13; 14; 6:6(2); 9(2); 11; 17; 7:12; 17; 8:12; 9:15(2); 19(2); 10:6; 11:2; 15; 12:4; 10; 12; 14; 13:18; 14:4; 5; 7; 11; 17:14; 17; 18:3; 5; 7; 8; 9(2); 11; 15; 17; 19; 20; 23(2); 19:2(2); 3; 6; 7; 8; 10; 20:4(2); 10; 11; 21:1; 2; 4; 5; 22; 23; 25; 22:2; 5(2); 9; 10; 15; 18

FOREMOST
7223

Gen 32:17; 33:2; 2Sa 18:27

FORTH
935, 1310, 1319, 1518, 1645, 1876, 1921, 2254, 2330, 2342, 2351, 2590, 2904, 2986, 3205, 3209, 3318, 3329, 4161, 4163, 4866, 5066, 5107, 5132, 5265, 5312, 5375, 5414, 5608, 5674, 5975, 6213, 6398, 6440, 6509, 6556, 6566, 6605, 6631, 6779, 7126, 7737, 7971, 8317, 8444, 321, 392, 584, 616, 649, 669, 985, 1032, 1080, 1519, 1544, 1554, 1584, 1599, 1600, 1607, 1614, 1631, 1632, 1731, 1754, 1804, 1806, 1821, 1831, 1854, 1901, 1907, 1911, 2164, 2564, 2592, 2604, 2609, 3004, 3318, 3319, 3860, 3855, 3860, 3928, 4160, 4193, 4254, 4261, 4270, 4295, 4311, 4388, 4393, 4486, 5087, 5088, 5319, 5348

Gen 1:11; 12; 20; 21; 24; 3:16; 18; 22; 23; 8:7(2); 8; 9; 10; 12; 16; 17; 18; 19; 9:7; 18; 10:11; 11:31; 12:5; 14:18; 15:4; 5; 19:10; 16; 17; 22:10; 24:43; 45; 53; 30:39; 38:24; 25; 29; 39:13; 40:10(2); 41:47; 42:15; Ex 3:10; 11; 12; 4:4(2); 14; 5:20; 7:4; 5; 8:3; 5; 18; 20; 9:9; 10; 22; 23; 10:13; 22; 12:31; 39; 46; 13:8; 16; 14:11; 27; 15:7; 13; 16:3; 32; 19:1; 17; 22; 24; 25:20; 29:46; 32:11; Lev 4:12; 21; 6:11; 14:3; 45; 16:24; 27; 22:27; 24:14; 23; 25:21; 38; 42; 55; 26:10; 13; 45; Num 1:3; 20; 22; 24; 26; 28; 30; 32; 34; 36; 48; 40; 42; 2:9; 16; 11:20; 31; 12:15; 17:8; 19:3; 20:8(2); 16; 24:6; 8; 26:4; 31:13; 33:1; 34:4; 8; Deut 1:27; 2:23; 4:20; 45; 46; 6:12; 8:14; 15; 9:12; 26; 14:22; 28; 16:1; 3(2); 6; 17:5; 21:2; 10; 22:15; 23:4; 9; 12; 24:9; 25:11; 17; 26:8; 29:25; 33:2; 14(2); Josh 2:3; 5:5; 8:9; 10:23; 18:11; 17(2); 19:1; Judg 1:24; 3:21; 23; 5:25; 31; 6:8; 18; 21; 9:8; 43; 11:31; 14:12; 13; 14(2); 16; 15:15; 19:22; 25; 20:21; 25; 33; Ruth 1:7; 2:18; 1Sa 11:7; 12:8; 14:11; 27; 17:20; 55; 18:30(2); 22:3; 17; 23:13; 24:6; 10; 26:9; 11; 23; 30:21; 2Sa 1:14; 5:20; 6:6; 11:1; 12:30; 31; 13:39; 15:5; 16; 17; 16:5; 11; 18:2(2); 3; 12; 19:7(2); 20:8; 22:20; 49; 1Kin 2:30; 36; 6:27; 8:7; 16; 19; 22; 38; 51; 9:9; 13:4(2); 19:11; 20:33; 21:13; 22:21; 22(2); 2Kin 2:3; 21; 23; 24;

6:15; 8:3; 9:11; 15; 10:22(2); 25; 26; 11:7; 12; 15; 18:7; 19:3; 31; 21:15; 23:4; **1Chr** 12:33; 36; 13:9; 14:11; 15; 16:23; 19:16; 20:1; 24:7; 25:9; 26:16; **2Chr** 1:17; 3:13; 5:8; 6:5; 9; 12; 13; 29; 7:22; 20:20(2); 21:9; 23:14; 25:5; 11; 26:6; 29:5; 23; 32:21; **Ezr** 1:7(2); 8; 6:5; **Neh** 4:16; 8:15; 16; 9:7; 15; 13:8; 21; **Est** 4:6; 5:9; **Job** 1:11; 12(2); 2:5; 7; 5:6; 8:16; 10:18; 11:17; 14:2; 9; 15:35; 21:11; 30; 23:10; 24:5; 28:9; 11; 30:5; 38:8; 27; 32; 39:1; 2; 3; 4; 40:20; **Ps** 1:3; 7:14; 9:1; 14; 17:2; 18:19; 19:6; 37:6; 44:9; 51:15; 55:20; 57:3; 66:2; 68:7; 71:15; 78:52; 79:13; 80:1; 88:8; 90:2; 92:2; 14; 96:2; 104:14; 20; 23; 30; 105:30; 37; 43; 106:2; 107:7; 108:11; 113:2; 115:18; 121:8; 125:3; 5; 126:6; 138:7; 141:2; 143:6; 144:6; 13; 146:4; 147:15; 17; **Prov** 7:15; 8:1; 24; 25; 9:3; 10:31; 12:17; 25:4; 6; 8; 27:1; 30:27; 33(3); 31:20; **Eccl** 2:6; 5:15; 7:18; 10:1; **Song** 1:3; 8; 12; 2:9; 13; 3:11; 6:10; 7:11; 12; 8:5(2); **Is** 1:15; 2:3; 3:16; 5:2(2); 4(2); 25; 7:3; 25; 11:1; 13:10; 14:7; 29; 23:4; 25:11(2); 26:18; 27:8; 28:19; 29; 31:4; 32:20; 33:11; 34:1; 36:3; 37:3; 9; 32; 36; 41:21; 22; 42:1; 3; 5; 9; 13; 43:8; 9; 13; 43:8; 9; 17; 19; 21; 44:23; 24; 45:8; 10; 48:1; 3; 20; 49:9; 13; 17; 51:5; 13; 18; 52:9; 54:1; 2; 3; 16; 55:10; 11; 12(2); 58:8(2); 9; 59:4; 60:6; 61:11(3); 62:1; 65:9; 23; 66:7; 8(2); 9(2); 24; **Jer** 1:5; 9; 14; 2:27; 37; 4:4; 7; 31; 6:25; 7:25; 10:13; 20(2); 11:4; 12:2; 14:18; 15:1; 2; 19; 17:22; 19:2; 20:3; 18; 22:11; 19; 23:15; 19; 25:32; 26:23; 29:16; 30:23; 31:4; 24; 39; 32:21; 34:13; 37:5; 7; 12; 38:2; 8; 17; 18; 21; 22; 39:4; 41:6; 42:18(2); 43:12; 44:6; 17; 46:4; 9; 48:7; 45; 49:5; 50:8; 25; 51:10; 16; 44; 52:7; 31; **Lam** 1:17; **Eze** 1:13; 22; 3:22; 23; 5:4; 7:10; 8:3; 9:7(2); 10:7; 11:7; 12:4(3); 6; 7(2); 12; 14:22(2); 16:14; 17:2; 6(2); 7; 8; 23; 18:8; 13; 20:6; 9; 10; 22; 38; 21:3; 4; 5; 19; 24:12; 27:7; 10; 33; 28:18; 29:21; 30:9; 31:5; 6; 32:2; 4; 33:30; 36:8; 20; 38:4; 8; 39:9; 42:1; 15; 44:5; 19; 46:2; 8; 9(2); 10(2); 12(2); 21; 47:3; 8; 10; 12; **Dan** 2:13; 14; 3:26(2); 5:5; 7:10; 8:9; 9:15; 22; 23; 25; 10:20; 11:11(2); 13; 42; 44; **Hos** 6:3; 5; 9:13; 16; 10:1; 13:13; 14:5; **Joel** 2:16; 3:18; **Amos** 5:3; 7:17; 8:3; 5; **Jonah** 1:5; 12; 15; **Mic** 1:9; 4:2; 10(2); 5:2(2); 3; 7:9; **Hab** 1:4; 3:5; 13; **Zeph** 2:2; **Hag** 1:11; 2:19; **Zec** 1:16; 2:3; 6; 3:8; 4:7; 5:3; 4; 5(2); 6; 6:5; 6(3); 7; 9:11; 14; 10:4; 12:1; 14:2; 3; **Mal** 4:2; **Mt** 1:21; 23; 25; 2:16; 3:8; 10; 7:17(2); 18(2); 19; 8:3; 9:9; 25; 38; 10:5; 16; 12:13(2); 20; 35(2); 49; 13:3; 8; 9; 25; 38; 10:5; 16; 12:13(2); 20; 35(2); 49; 13:3; 8; 23; 24; 26; 31; 41; 43; 49; 52; 14:2; 14; 31; 15:18; 16:21; 21:43; 22:3; 4; 7; 46; 24:26; 32; 25:1; **Mk** 1:38; 41; 2:12; 13; 3:3; 5; 6; 14; 4:8; 20; 28; 29; 6:7; 14; 17; 24; 7:26; 8:11; 9:29; 10:17; 11:1; 13:28; 14:13; 16; 16:20; **Lk** 1:1; 31; 57; 2:7; 3:7; 8; 9; 5:13; 27; 6:8(2); 10; 43(2); 45(2); 7:17; 8:14; 15; 22; 27; 10:2; 3; 12:16; 37; 14:7; 15:22; 20:9; 20; 21:30; 22:53; **Jn** 1:43; 2:10; 11; 5:29; 8:42; 10:4; 11:43; 44; 53; 12:13; 24; 15:2; 5; 6; 16:28; 30; 18:1; 4; 19:4(2); 5; 13; 17; 20:3; 21:3; 18; **Acts** 1:26; 2:33; 4:30; 5:10; 15; 19; 34; 7:7; 9:30; 40; 11:22; 12:1; 4; 6; 13:4; 16:3; 17:18; 21:2; 23:28; 24:2; 25:17; 23; 26; 26:1; 25; 27:21; **Rom** 3:25; 7:4; 5; 10:21; **1Cor** 4:9; 6:11; **Gal** 3:1; 4:4; 6; 27; **Phil** 2:16; 3:13; **Col** 1:6; **1Ti** 1:16; **Heb** 1:14; 7; 13:13; **Jas** 1:15(2); 3:11; 5:18; **1Pet** 2:9; **3Jn** 7; **Jude** 7; **Rev** 5:6; 6:2; 12:5; 13; 16:14

FRO

Gen 8:7; **2Kin** 4:35; **2Chr** 16:9; **Job** 1:7; 2:2; 7:4; 13:25; **Ps** 107:27; **Prov** 21:6; **Is** 24:20; 33:4; 49:21; **Jer** 5:1; 49:3; **Eze** 27:19; **Dan** 12:4; **Joel** 2:9; **Amos** 8:12; **Zec** 1:10; 11; 4:10; 6:7(3); **Eph** 4:14

FROM

575

Gen 1:4; 6; 7; 14; 18; 2:2; 3; 6; 10; 22; 3:8; 23(2); 4:1; 10; 11(2); 14(2); 16; 6:7; 17; 7:4; 23; 8:2; 3; 7; 8(2); 11; 13; 9:10; 24; 10:19; 30; 11:2; 6; 8; 9; 31; 12:1(2); 8; 13:3; 9; 11; 14(2); 17; 14:23; 15:18; 16(2); 8; 17:14; 22; 18:2; 3; 16; 17; 22; 25(2); 19:4; 24; 26; 20:1; 6; 13; 22:12; 23:3; 6; 24:5; 7(3); 8; 41(2); 46; 50; 62; 25:6; 18; 23(2); 26:16; 22; 23; 26; 27; 31; 27:9; 30(2); 39; 40; 45(2); 28:2; 6; 10; 29:3; 8; 10; 30:2; 32; 31:13; 16; 27; 31; 40; 49; 32:11(2); 33:18; 35:1; 7; 13; 16; 36:6; 37:25; 38:1; 14; 17; 19; 20; 39:5; 9; 40:19(2); 41:42; 46; 42:2; 7; 24(2); 43:34; 44:28; 29; 45:1; 46:5; 34; 47:10; 18; 21; 48:7; 12; 16; 17; 49:9; 10(2); 24; 26; 32; 50:25; 26; **Ex** 2:15; 3:5; 4:3; 5:4; 5; 19; 20; 6:6; 7; 26; 27; 7:5; 8:8(2); 9; 11(4); 12; 29(4); 30; 31(3); 9:15; 33; 10:5; 6; 11; 17; 18; 23; 28; 11:5; 8; 12:5(2); 15(2); 19; 29; 31; 37; 41; 42; 13:3(2); 10; 14(2); 20; 22; 14:5; 19; 25; 15:22; 16:1; 4; 6; 32; 17:1; 14; 16; 18:4; 10; 13; 19; 2:9; 3:2(3); 10; 14(2); 20; 22; 14:5; 15; 22; 16:1; 4; 6; 18; 24; 25; 26; 29(4); 30; 31(3); 9:15; 10:5; 11; 17; 18; 23; 11:5; 12:5; 15; 19; 29; 31; 37; 41; 13:3; 10; 14; 16:1; 4; 6; 18; 24; 25; 26; **Ex** 2:15; 3:5; 4:3; 5:4; 5; 19; 20; 6:6; 7; 9:1; 9; 10; 18:29; 19:8; 20:3; 4; 5; 6; 18; 24; 25; 26;

21:7; 22:2; 3; 4; 25; 27; 23:15(2); 29; 30; 32; 24:3; 8; 25:41; 50; 26:36; 27:3; 5; 6; 7; 17; 18; **Num** 1:3; 18; 20; 22; 24; 26; 28; 30; 32; 34; 36; 38; 40; 42; 45; 3:12; 15; 22; 28; 34; 39; 40; 43; 4:2; 3; 13; 18; 23; 30; 35; 39; 43; 47; 5:13; 19; 31; 6:3; 4; 7:89(2); 8:6; 14; 16; 19; 24; 25; 9:13; 17; 21; 10:9; 11; 11:31(2); 35; 12:10; 14; 15; 16; 13:3; 21; 14:9; 13; 19; 29; 43; 15:23; 30; 16:9; 15; 21; 24; 26; 27; 33; 35; 45; 46(2); 17:5; 9; 10; 18:6; 9; 16; 26; 30; 32; 19:13; 20; 20:6; 9; 14; 21; 22:5; 16; 33(2); 23:7; 9(2); 13(2); 24:11; 24; 25:4; 7; 8; 11; 26:2; 4; 62; 27:4; 30:14; 31:14; 42; 32:7; 8; 11; 15; 21; 33:3; 5; 6; 7; 8; 9; 10; 11; 34:3; 4(2); 5; 7; 8; 10; 35:4(2); 5; 10; 36:2(4); 7; 9; **Deut** 1:2; 19; 2:8(3); 12; 14(2); 15; 16; 22; 36(2); 3:4; 8; 12; 16; 17; 4:2; 3; 9; 26; 29; 32; 34; 38; 48; 5:6; 6:12; 15; 19; 23; 7:4; 8; 15; 20; 24; 8:14; 9:4(2); 5; 7; 12; 14; 15; 23; 24; 10:5; 6; 7(2); 11:10; 12; 17; 23; 24(2); 12:10; 21; 29; 30; 32; 13:5(2); 7(2); 10(2); 13; 17; 14:24; 15:7; 12; 13; 16; 18; 16:9; 17:7; 11; 12; 15; 20; 18:3(2); 6; 12; 15; 18; 19; 19:5; 13; 19; 20:15; 21:9; 13; 21; 22:1; 4; 8; 21; 22:1; 4; 8; 21; 22; 24; 23:1; 4; 5(2); 8(2); 9; 23:1; 14; 14; 16; 18(2); 25:4(2); 8(2); 9; 2; 23:1; 14; 14; 16; 18(2); 25:4(2); 8(2); 27:12; 28:9(2); 19; 22; 29; 29:13; 15; 30:6; 11; 14; 27; 31:6; 8; 32:2(2); 15; 33:15(3); 34:4(2); 10; 17; 36:2; 37:8; 14; 20; 38:7; 12(2); 13; 17; 39:3(3); 7; 40:21(2); 27(2); 41:2; 4; 9(2); 25(2); 26; 42:7; 10; 11; 43:5(2); 6(2); 44:2; 8; 24; 45:6(2); 8; 21(2); 46:3(2); 7; 10(2); 11(2); 12; 47:11; 12; 13; 14; 15; 48:3; 5; 6; 7; 8(2); 16(2); 19; 20; 49:1(3); 5; 12; 4; 24; 50:6; 51:4; 8; 52:2(2); 11; 53:3; 8(2); 54:8; 10; 14(2); 55:10; 56:2(2); 3; 6; 11; 57:1; 58:7; 9; 13(2); 59:2; 9; 11; 13(2); 15; 19(2); 20; 21; 60:4; 6; 9; 63:1(2); 16(2); 17(2); 64:7; 65:16; 66:6(2); 23(2); **Jer** 2:5; 25(2); 35; 37; 3:1; 4; 19; 20; 23(2); 24; 25; 4:6; 7(2); 8; 12; 14; 15(2); 16; 28; 5:15; 25; 6:8; 13(2); 20(2); 22(2); 7:1; 28; 34(2); 8:10(2); 13; 16; 9:2; 3; 21(2); 10:9(2); 11(2); 13; 11:1; 4; 15; 19; 12:2; 12; 14; 13:6; 7; 20; 25; 15:7; 19; 16:5(2); 16(2); 17(2); 19; 17:4; 5; 8; 12; 13; 16; 26(6); 18:1; 8; 11; 14(2); 15; 18(3); 20; 22; 23; 19:14; 20:13; 17; 21:1; 2; 7(3); 22:20; 21; 23:8; 14; 15; 22(2); 30; 24:1; 10; 25:3; 5(2); 10; 30(2); 32(2); 33; 26:1; 3; 10; 27:1; 10; 16; 20; 28:3; 6; 10; 11; 12; 29:1(2); 2; 4; 14(2); 20; 30:1; 8; 10(2); 21; 31:8(2); 11; 13; 16(3); 34; 36(2); 38; 32:1; 30; 31(2); 40(2); 33:5; 8; 34:1; 8; 12; 14; 21; 35:1; 15; 36:1; 2(2); 4; 6; 7; 9; 29; 28:3; 38:10; 14; 25; 40:1(2); 4; 41:5(3); 6; 14; 15; 16(3); 42:1; 4; 8; 21; 43:5; 12; 44:5; 12; 46:16; 27(2); 47:4; 48:2; 3; 10; 11(2); 18; 33(3); 34(2); 42; 44; 49:5; 7; 14; 16; 19(2); 32; 36; 38; 50:6; 9(2); 16; 26; 39; 41(2); 44(2); 51:16; 25; 45; 48; 53; 54(2); 64; 52:3; 8; 29; **Lam** 1:6; 13; 14; 16; 2:1; 3; 8; 9; 3:17; 18; 50; 66; 5:14(2); 16; 19; **Eze** 1:19; 21; 25; 27(2); 3:12; 17; 18; 19(2); 20; 4:8; 10; 11; 14; 6:9; 7:20; 22; 26(2); 8:2(2); 6; 9:2; 3; 10:2; 4; 6(2); 7; 16(2); 18; 19; 11:15; 17; 18; 23; 24; 12:3; 16; 19; 13:20; 22; 14:5; 6(2); 7; 8; 9; 11; 13; 17; 19; 21; 15:7; 16:9; 34; 41; 42; 17:22; 18:8; 17; 21; 23; 20:17; 34; 38; 41; 47; 21:3; 4(2); 22:5; 26; 23:8; 17; 18(2); 22; 27(2); 28; 40; 42; 24:13; 16; 25; 25:7; 9; 16; 18; 25; 29:10; 13; 30:6; 9; 31:12; 32:13; 33:6; 7; 8; 9(2); 11(2); 12; 14; 18; 19; 30; 34:10(2); 13(2); 35:7; 36:24; 25(2); 29; 33; 37:9; 21; 38:8; 15; 39:2; 22; 23; 24; 27; 29; 40:13; 15; 19; 23; 27; 41:7; 16; 20; 42:6; 7; 16(2); 18; 19; 43:8; 17; 18(2); 44:7; 10; 13; 44:10(2); 15; 45:1; 3; 4; 5; 6; 7(3); 9; 46:18; 47:1(2); 2; 3(2); 12; 48:1; 8; 15; 16; 28; **Dan** 2:1; 5; 8; 15; 3:17; 4:3; 13; 14(2); 16; 23; 31(2); 32; 33; 34; 5:20(2); 21; 24; 6:18; 20; 27; 7:3(2); 4; 7; 10; 19; 23; 24; 8:5; 9:5(2); 13; 16; 25; 10:12; 11:22; 12:11; **Hos** 1:2; 2:2; 15; 4:12; 5:3; 6; 7:4; 13; 8:6; 9:1; 11(3); 12; 10:5; 9; 11:2; 7; 10; 12; 9; 13:4; 14(3); 15; 14:4; **Joel** 1:5; 9; 12; 13; 15; 16; 2:20; 3:6; 16; 20; **Amos** 1:2(2); 5(2); 8(2); 2:3; 9(2); 10; 14; 3:1; 5; 11; 4:7; 5:11; 12; 19; 23; 6:2; 14; 8:12(2); 9:3; 7(2); 8; **Obad** 1; **Jonah** 1:3(2); 10; 15; 2:6; 3:6; 6(2); 8(2); 9; 10; 4:3; 6; **Mic** 1:2; 12; 16; 2:3; 4; 8(2); 9(2); 3:2(2); 3; 4; 4:2; 7; 10; 5:2(2); 6; 7; 6:5; 7:5; 12(5); 20; **Nah** 1:12; 13; 3:7; 8; **Hab** 1:8; 12; 2:9; 3:3(2); 17; **Zeph** 1:2; 3; 4; 6; 10(3); 2:11; 3:10; **Hag** 1:10(2); 2:15(2); 18(3); 19; **Zec** 1:4(2); 2:6; 3:4(2); 6:1; 5; 10; 7:12; 8:7(2); 9:5; 7; 10(4); 13:5; 14:2; 5; 8; 10(3); 13; 16; **Mal** 1:5; 11; 2:6; 3:5; 7(2); **Mt** 1:17(3); 21; 24; 2:1; 16; 3:7; 13; 17; 4:17; 21; 25(5); 5:18; 29; 30; 42; 6:13; 7:23; 8:1; 11; 30; 9:9; 15; 16; 22; 11:12; 25; 12:15; 38; 42; 44; 13:12; 27; 35; 49; 14:2; 15:8; 18; 27; 28; 29; 16:1; 21; 22; 17:9(2); 18; 18:8; 9; 35; 19:1; 8; 12; 20; 20:8; 29; 21:8; 25(2); 43; 22:46; 23:34; 35; 24:1; 29;

31(2); 25:28; 29; 32(2); 34; 41; 26:16; 39; 42; 47; 27:31; 40; 42; 45; 51; 55; 64; 28:2(2); 7; 8; **Mk** 1:9; 11; 42; 45; 2:20; 21; 3:7(2); 8(3); 22; 4:25; 5:35; 6:1; 2; 10; 14; 16; 7:1; 4; 6; 15; 17; 18; 21; 23; 24; 31; 33; 8:3; 4; 11; 9:9(2); 10; 10:1; 6; 20; 11:12; 20; 30; 31; 12:2; 25; 34; 13:19; 27(2); 14:35; 36; 43; 52; 15:20; 30; 32; 38; 16:3; 8; **Lk** 1:2; 3; 15; 26; 38; 45; 48; 50; 52; 71(2); 78; 2:1; 4; 15; 36; 37; 3:7; 22; 4:1; 9; 13; 42; 5:3; 8; 10; 13; 35; 6:17; 22; 7:6; 8:18; 37; 49; 9:5; 7; 33; 37; 39; 45; 54; 10:7; 18; 21; 30; 42; 11:4; 7; 16; 22; 31; 50; 51; 12:36; 52; 58; 13:12; 15; 16; 27; 29(4); 16:3; 18; 21; 26(2); 30; 31; 17:7; 29; 18:21; 34; 19:8; 24; 26(2); 39; 42; 20:4; 5; 35; 21:11; 22:41; 42; 43; 45; 23:5; 49; 55; 24:2; 9; 13; 46; 49; 51; **Jn** 1:6; 19; 32; 2:22; 3:2; 13; 27; 31(2); 4:11; 5:24; 34; 41; 44; 6:23; 31; 32(2); 33; 38; 41; 42; 50; 51; 58; 64; 66; 7:29; 8:23(2); 25; 42; 44; 9:1; 29; 30; 10:5; 18; 32; 11:41; 53; 12:1; 9; 17; 27; 28; 32; 36; 13:3; 4; 14:7; 15:26(2); 27; 16:22; 27; 28; 30; 17:8; 15; 18:3; 28; 36; 19:11; 12; 23; 27; 20:1; 9; 21:8; 14; **Acts** 1:4; 11; 12(2); 22(2); 25; 2:2; 40; 46; 3:2; 15; 19; 23; 24; 26; 4:2; 10; 5:38; 41; 7:3; 4; 33; 39; 8:10; 26; 33; 9:3; 8; 14; 18; 10:17; 21; 22; 23; 37; 41; 11:4; 5; 9; 11; 27; 12:7; 10; 11; 19; 25; 13:4; 8; 13(2); 14; 29; 30; 31; 34; 39(2); 46; 14:8; 15; 17; 19; 26; 15:1; 18; 19; 20(4); 24; 29(5); 33; 38(2); 39; 16:11; 12; 17:3; 27; 31; 33; 18:1; 2(2); 5; 6; 16; 21; 19:9; 12(2); 35; 20:6; 9; 17; 18; 20; 26; 21:1(2); 7; 10; 25(4); 22:5; 6; 22; 29; 30; 23:10; 21; 24:18; 25:1; 7; 26:4; 5; 10; 12; 13; 17(2); 18(2); 23; 26; 27:4; 21; 34; 43; 28:13; 15; 17; 23; **Rom** 1:4; 7; 17; 18; 20; 4:24; 5:9; 14; 6:4; 7; 9; 13; 17; 18; 20; 22; 7:2; 3; 4; 6; 24; 8:2; 11(2); 21; 35; 39; 9:3; 10:6; 7; 9; 11:15; 26; 15:19; 22; 31; S:1; **1Cor** 1:3(2); 4:7; 5:2; 13; 7:10; 27; 9:19; 10:14; 14:36; 15:12; 20; 41; 47; S:1; **2Cor** 1:2(2); 10; 2:3; 13; 3:1; 18; 5:2; 6; 8; 6:17; 7:1; 11:3; 9(2); 12; 12:8; S:1; **Gal** 1:1; 3(2); 4; 6; 8; 15; 2:12; 3:13; 4:1; 24; 5:4; 6:17; S:1; **Eph** 1:2(2); 20; 2:12(2); 3:9; 4:16; 18; 31; 5:14; 6:6; 23; S:1; **Phil** 1:2(2); 5; 3:20; 4:15; 18; S:1; **Col** 1:2; 13; 18; 23; 26(2); 2:12; 19; 20; 4:16; S:1; **1Th** 1:1; 8; 9; 10(3); 2:17; 3:6; 4:3; 16; 5:22; S:1; **2Th** 1:2; 7; 9(2); 2:2; 13; 3:2; 3; 6; S:1; **1Ti** 1:2; 6; 4:1; 3; 5:13; 6:5; 10; S:1; **2Ti** 1:2; 3; 15; 2:8; 19; 21; 3:5; 15; 4:4; 18; S:1; **Titus** 1:4; 14; 2:14; S:1; **Philem** 1:3; S:1; **Heb** 3:12; 4:3; 4; 10(2); 5:1; 7; 6:1; 7; 7:1; 6; 26; 8:11; 9:14; 10:13; 22; 11:15; 19(2); 12:25(2); 13:20; S:1; **Jas** 1:17(2); 27; 3:15; 17; 4:1; 7; 5:19; 20(2); **1Pet** 1:3; 12; 18(2); 21; 2:11; 3:10; 4:1; **2Pet** 1:9; 17(2); 18; 2:8; 14; 18; 21; 3:4; 17; **1Jn** 1:1; 7; 9; 2:7(2); 13; 14; 19; 20; 24(2); 3:8; 11; 14; 17; 4:21; 5:21; **2Jn** 3(2); 4; 5; 6; **Jude** 14; 24; **Rev** 1:4(2); 5(2); 2:5; 3:10; 12; 6:4; 16(2); 7:2; 17; 8:10; 9:1; 6; 13; 10:1; 4; 8; 11:11; 12; 12:14; 13:8; 13; 14:2; 3; 4; 13(3); 18; 15:8(2); 16:17; 17:8; 18:1; 4; 14(2); 20:1; 9; 11; 21:2; 4; 10; 22:19(2)

FRONT

6440

2Sa 10:9; **2Chr** 3:4

FURTHER

3148, 3254, 5750, 6329, *1339, 2089, 4118, 4206*

Num 22:26; **Deut** 20:8; **1Sa** 10:22; **Est** 9:12; **Job** 38:11; 40:5; **Ps** 140:8; **Eccl** 8:17; 12:12; **Mt** 26:65; **Mk** 5:35; 14:63; **Lk** 22:71; 24:28; **Acts** 4:17; 21; 12:3; 21:28; 24:4; 27:28; **2Ti** 3:9; **Heb** 7:11

FURTHERMORE

637, 5750, *1161, 1534, 3063*

Ex 4:6; **Deut** 4:21; 9:13; **1Sa** 26:10; **1Chr** 17:10; 27:16; 29:1; **2Chr** 4:9; **Job** 34:1; **Eze** 8:6; 23:40; **2Cor** 2:12; **1Th** 4:1; **Heb** 12:9

GIVEN

1167, 1478, 1576, 2505, 2603, 3052, 3254, 3289, 5221, 5375, 5414, 5462, 6213, 7760, 7761, *1325, 1377, 1402, 1433, 1547, 2227, 3860, 3930, 3943, 4272, 4337, 4369, 5483*

Gen 1:29; 30; 9:3; 15:3; 18; 16:5; 20:16; 21:7; 24:35; 36; 27:37; 29:33; 30:6; 18(2); 31:9; 33:5; 38:14; 43:23; 48:9; 22; **Ex** 5:16; 18; 16:15; 29; 21:4; 31:6; **Lev** 6:17; 7:34; 36; 10:14; 17; 17:11; 19:20; 20:3; **Num** 3:9; 8:16; 19; 16:14; 18:6; 7; 8(2); 11; 12; 19; 21; 24; 26; 20:12; 24; 21:29; 26:54; 62; 27:12; 32:5; 7; 9; 33:53; **Deut** 1:3; 2:5; 9; 19; 24; 3:18; 19; 20(3); 8:10; 9:23; 12:15; 21; 13:12; 16:17; 20:14; 22:17; 25:19; 26:9; 10; 11; 12; 13; 14; 15; 28:31; 32; 52; 53; 29:4; 26; **Josh** 1:3; 13(2); 15(2); 2:9; 14; 6:2; 16; 8:1; 14:3; 15:19; 17:14; 18:3; 22:4; 7; 23:1; 13; 15; 16; 24:13; 33; **Judg** 1:15; 14:20; 15:6; 18; 18:10; **Ruth** 2:12; **1Sa** 1:27; 15:28; 18:19(2); 22:13; 25:27; 44; 28:17; 30:23; **2Sa** 4:10; 7:1; 9:9; 12:8; 14; 17:7; 18:11; 19:42; 22:36; 41; **1Kin** 1:48; 2:21; 3:6; 12; 13; 5:4; 7; 8:36; 56; 9:7; 12; 13; 16; 12:8; 13:5; 18:26; **2Kin** 5:1; 17; 8:29; 9:15; 23:11; 25:30; **1Chr** 5:1; 6:61; 63; 71; 77; 78; 22:18(2); 23:25; 28:5; 29:3; 14; **2Chr** 2:12; 6:27; 7:20; 14:6; 7; 20:11; 22:6; 25:9; 32:29; 34:14; 18; 36:23; **Ezr** 1:2; 4:21; 6:4; 8; 9; 7:6; 19; 9:13; **Neh** 2:7; 10:29; 13:5; 10; **Est** 2:3; 9; 13; 3:11; 14; 15; 4:8; 5:3; 7:3; 8:7; 13; 14; 9:14; **Job** 3:20; 23; 9:24; 10:18; 15:19; 22:7; 24:23; 33:4; 34:13; 37:10; 38:36; 39:19; **Ps** 16:7; 18:35; 40; 21:2; 44:11; 60:4; 61:5; 71:3; 72:15; 78:24; 63; 79:2; 111:5; 112:9; 115:16; 118:18; 120:3; 124:6; **Prov** 19:17; 23:2; 24:21; **Eccl** 1:13; 3:10; 5:19(2); 6:2; 8:8; 9:9; 12:11; **Is** 3:11; 8:18; 9:6; 23:11; 33:16; 35:2; 37:10; 43:28; 47:6; 8; 50:4; 55:4; **Jer** 3:8; 18; 6:13; 8:10; 13; 14; 11:18; 12:7; 13:20; 15:9; 21:10; 25:5; 27:5; 6(2); 28:14; 32:22; 24; 25; 43; 35:15; 38:3; 18; 39:17; 44:20; 47:7; 50:15; 52:34; **Lam** 1:11; 2:7; 5:6; **Eze** 3:20; 4:15; 11:15; 15:6; 16:17; 34; 17:18; 18:7; 8; 13; 16; 20:15; 21:11; 28:25; 29:5; 20; 33:24; 35:12; 37:25; 47:11; **Dan** 2:23; 37; 38; 4:16; 5:28; 7:4; 6; 11; 14; 22; 25; 27; 8:12; 11:6; 11; **Hos** 2:9; 12; **Joel** 2:23; 3:3; **Amos** 4:6; 9:15; **Nah** 1:14; **Mt** 7:7; 9:8; 10:19; 12:39; 13:11(2); 12; 14:9; 11; 16:4; 19:11; 20:23; 21:43; 22:30; 25:29; 26:9; 28:18; **Mk** 4:11; 24; 25; 5:43; 6:2; 8:12; 10:40; 12:25; 13:11; 14:5; 23; 44; **Lk** 6:38; 8:10; 18; 11:9; 29; 12:48; 17:27; 19:15; 26; 20:34; 35; 22:19; **Jn** 1:17; 3:27; 35; 4:10; 5:26; 27; 36; 6:11; 23; 39; 65; 7:39; 11:57; 12:5; 13:3; 15; 17:2(2); 7; 8; 9; 11; 14; 22; 24(2); 18:11; 19:11; **Acts** 1:2; 3:16; 4:12; 5:32; 8:18; 17:16; 31; 20:2; 21:40; 24:26; 27:24; **Rom** 5:5; 11:8; 35; 12:3; 6; 13; 15:15; **1Cor** 1:4; 2:12; 3:10; 11:15; 24; 12:7; 8; 24; 16:1; **2Cor** 1:11; 22; 5:5; 18; 9:9; 10:8; 12:7; 13:10; **Gal** 2:9; 3:21(2); 22; 4:15; **Eph** 3:2; 7; 8; 4:7; 19; 5:2; 6:19; **Phil** 1:29; 2:9; **Col** 1:25; **1Th** 4:8; **2Th** 2:16; **1Ti** 3:2; 3; 8; 4:14; **2Ti** 1:7; 9; 3:16; **Titus** 1:7(2); 2:3; **Philem** 1:22; **Heb** 2:13; 4:8; **Jas** 1:5; **2Pet** 1:3; 4; 3:15; **1Jn** 3:24; 4:13; 5:11; 20; **Rev** 6:2; 4(2); 8; 11; 7:2; 8:2; 3; 9:1; 3; 5; 11:1; 2; 12:14; 13:5(2); 7(2); 16:6; 8; 20:4

GIVETH

1478, 3052, 5414, 5415, *1325, 3330, 3930, 5087, 5524*

Gen 49:21; **Ex** 16:29; 20:12; 25:2; **Lev** 20:2; 4; 27:9; **Num** 5:10; **Deut** 2:29; 4:1; 21; 40; 5:16; 8:18; 9:6; 11:17; 31; 12:1; 9; 10(2); 13:1; 15:4; 7; 16:5; 18; 20; 17:2; 14; 18:9; 19:1; 2; 3; 10; 14; 21:1; 23; 24:3; 4; 25:15; 19; 26:1; 2; 27:2; 3; 28:8; **Josh** 1:11; 15; **Judg** 11:24; 21:18; **Job** 5:10; 14:10; 32:8; 33:13; 34:29; 35:10; 12; 36:6; 31; **Ps** 18:50; 37:21; 68:35; 119:130(2); 127:2; 136:25; 144:10; 146:7; 147:9; 16; **Prov** 2:6; 3:34; 13:15; 17:4(2); 19:6; 21:26; 22:9; 16; 23:31; 24:26; 26:8; 28:27; 31:15; **Eccl** 2:26(2); 5:18; 6:2; 7:12; 8:15; **Is** 40:29; 42:5; **Jer** 5:24; 22:13; 31:35; **Lam** 3:30; **Dan** 2:21; 4:17; 25; 32; **Hab** 2:15; **Mt** 5:15; **Jn** 3:34; 6:32; 33; 37; 10:11; 14:27; 21:13; **Acts** 17:25; **Rom** 12:8; 14:6(2); **1Cor** 3:7; 7:38(2); 15:38; 57; **2Cor** 3:6; **1Ti** 6:17; **Jas** 1:5; 4:6(2); **1Pet** 4:11; 5:5; **Rev** 22:5

GO

236, 258, 833, 935, 980, 1718, 1869, 1946, 1961, 1980, 2498, 2559, 3051, 3212, 3318, 3381, 3518, 4609, 4994, 5066, 5181, 5186, 5265, 5362, 5437, 5472, 5493, 5674, 5927, 5930, 6213, 6310, 6485, 6544, 6585, 6805, 6806, 6923, 7126, 7368, 7503, 7686, 7725, 7751, 7847, 7971, 8582, 8637, *33, 71, 305, 565, 630, 863, 1330, 1525, 1607, 1831, 1994, 2064, 2212, 2597, 3327, 3928, 4043, 4198, 4254, 4281, 4313, 4320, 4334, 4782, 4905, 5217, 5233, 5342*

Gen 3:14; 8:16; 9:10; 11:3; 4; 7(2); 31; 12:5; 19; 13:9(2); 15:2; 15; 16:2; 8; 18:21; 19:2; 34; 22:5; 24:4; 11; 38; 42; 51; 55; 56; 58(2); 26:2; 16; 27:3; 9; 13; 28:2; 20; 29:7; 21; 30:3; 25; 26; 31:18; 32:26(2); 33:12(2); 35:1; 3; 37:14; 17; 30; 35; 38:8; 16; 41:55; 42:15; 19; 38(2); 43:2; 4; 5; 8; 13; 44:25; 26(2); 33; 34; 45:1; 9; 17; 28; 46:3; 4; 31; 50:5; 6; **Ex** 2:7; 8; 3:11; 16; 18; 19; 20; 21(2); 4:12; 18(2); 19; 21; 23(2); 26; 27; 5:1; 2(2); 3; 7; 8; 11; 17; 18; 6:1; 11(2); 7:14; 16; 8:1(2); 2; 3; 8; 20; 21; 25; 27; 28(2); 29(2); 32; 9:1(2); 2; 7; 13; 17; 28; 35; 10:1; 3; 4; 7; 8(2); 9(2); 10; 11; 20; 24(2); 26; 27; 11:1(2); 4; 8; 10; 12:22; 31; 13:15; 17; 21; 14:5; 15; 16; 21; 16:4; 29; 17:5(2); 9; 18:23; 19:10; 12; 21; 20:26; 21:2; 3(2); 4; 5; 7; 11; 26; 27; 23:23; 24:2; 30:20; 32:1; 7; 23; 27; 30; 34(2); 33:1; 3; 14; 15; 34:9; 15; 16(2); 24; **Lev** 6:13; 8:33; 9:7; 10:7; 9; 11:27; 14:3; 36(2); 38; 53; 15:16; 16:10; 18; 22; 26; 19:16; 20:5; 6; 21:11; 12; 23; 25:28; 30; 31; 33; 54; 26:6; 13; **Num** 1:3; 20; 22; 24; 26; 28; 30; 32; 34; 36; 38; 40; 42; 45; 2:24; 31; 4:19; 20; 5:12; 22; 8:15; 24; 10:5; 9; 30; 32; 13:17; 30; 31; 14:40; 42; 44; 15:39; 16:30; 46; 20:17; 19(2); 20; 21:22; 22:12; 13; 18; 20; 35; 23:3; 16; 24:13; 14; 26:2; 27:17(2); 21; 31:3; 23(2); 32:6; 9; 17; 20; 21; 34:4; 9; 11; 12; **Deut** 1:7; 8; 21; 22; 26; 28; 33; 37; 38; 39; 41(2); 42; 2:27; 3:25; 27; 28; 4:1; 5; 14; 21(2); 22(2); 26; 34; 40; 5:16; 27; 30; 6:1; 14; 18; 8:1; 9:1; 5; 23; 10:11; 11:8(2); 11; 28; 31; 12:10; 25; 26; 28; 13:2; 6; 13; 14:25; 15:12; 13; 16; 16:7; 19:13; 21; 20:5; 6; 7; 8; 21:13; 14; 22:1; 7; 13; 23:10; 12; 24:2; 5; 10; 15; 19; 20; 25:5; 7; 26:2; 3; 27:3; 28:14(2); 25; 41; 29:18; 30:12; 13; 18; 31:2(2); 3(2); 6; 7; 8; 13; 16(2); 21; 32:47; 52; 34:4; **Josh** 1:2; 11; 16; 2:1; 16; 19; 3:3; 4; 6:3; 22; 7:2; 3(2); 8:1; 3; 4; 9:11; 12; 10:13; 14:11; 18:3; 4; 8; 22:9; 12; 33; 23:12(2); **Judg** 1:1; 2; 3; 25; 2:1; 6; 4:6; 8(4); 9; 5:11; 6:14; 7:3; 4(4); 7; 10(2); 11; 9:9; 11; 13; 38; 10:14; 11:8; 35; 37; 38; 12:1; 5; 15:1(2); 5; 16:17; 20; 17:9; 18:2; 5; 6(2); 9(2); 10; 19; 19:5; 9; 15; 25; 27; 20:8; 9; 14; 18(2); 23(2); 28(2); 21:10; 20; 21; **Ruth** 1:8; 11; 12; 16; 18; 2:2(2); 8(2); 9(2); 22; 3:4; 17; **1Sa** 1:17; 22; 3:9; 5:11; 6:6; 8; 20; 8:20; 22; 9:3; 6(2); 7; 9; 10; 13; 14; 19(2); 10:3; 8; 9; 11:14; 12:21; 14:1; 4; 6; 9; 10; 36; 37; 15:3; 6; 18; 27; 16:1; 2; 17:32; 33; 37; 39(2); 55; 18:2; 19:3; 17; 20:5; 11; 13; 19; 21; 22; 28; 29; 40; 42; 23:2(2); 4; 8; 13(2); 22; 23; 24:19; 25:5; 19; 35; 26:6(2); 11; 19; 28:1; 7; 29:4(2); 7; 8; 9; 30:10; **2Sa** 1:15; 2:1(3); 3:16; 21; 5:19(2); 23; 24; 7:3; 5; 11:1; 8; 10; 11; 12:23; 13:7; 13; 24; 25(2); 26(2); 27; 39; 14:8; 21; 30; 15:7; 9; 20(2); 22; 16:9; 21; 17:11; 18:2; 3; 21; 19:7(2); 15; 20; 26; 34; 36; 37; 38; 20:11; 21:17; 24:1; 2; 12; 18; **1Kin** 1:13; 53; 2:2; 6; 29; 36; 3:7; 8:44; 9:6; 11:2; 10; 17; 21; 22(2); 12:24; 27(2); 28; 13:8; 16; 17; 14:3; 7; 15:17; 17:12; 13; 18:1; 5; 8; 11; 14; 43(2); 44; 19:11; 15; 20; 20:22; 31; 33; 42(2); 21:16; 18; 22:4; 6(2); 12; 15(2); 20; 22(2); 25; 48; 49; **2Kin** 1:2; 3(2); 6; 15; 2:16; 18; 23(2); 3:7(2); 8; 4:3; 7; 23; 24; 29; 5:5(2); 10; 19; 24; 6:2(2); 3(2); 13; 22; 7:5; 9; 14; 8:1; 8; 10; 9:1; 2; 15(2); 34; 10:13; 24; 25; 11:7; 9; 12:17; 17:27; 18:21; 25; 19:31; 20:5; 8; 9(2); 10; 22:4; 13; **1Chr** 7:11; 14:10(2); 14; 15; 17:4; 11; 20:1; 21:2; 10; 18; 30; **2Chr** 1:10; 6:34; 7:19; 11:4; 14:11; 16:1; 3; 18:2; 3; 5(2); 11; 14(2); 19; 21(2); 24; 29; 20:16; 17; 27; 36; 37; 21:13; 23:6; 8; 24:5; 25:5; 7; 8; 10; 13; 26:18; 20; 34:21; 36:23; **Ezr** 1:3; 5; 5:15; 7:9; 13(2); 28; 8:31; 9:11; **Neh** 3:15; 4:3; 6:11(2); 8:10; 15; 9:12; 15; 19; 23; **Est** 1:19; 2:12; 13; 15; 4:8; 16(2); 5:14; **Job** 4:21; 6:18; 10:21; 15:13; 30; 16:22; 17:16; 20:26; 21:13; 29; 23:8; 24:5; 10; 27:6; 31:37; 37:8; 38:35; 39:4; 41:19; 42:8; **Ps** 22:29; 26:4; 28:1; 30:3; 9; 32:8; 38:6; 39:13; 42:9; 43:2; 4; 48:12; 49:19; 55:10; 15; 58:3; 59:6; 14; 60:10; 63:9; 66:13; 71:16; 73:27; 78:52; 80:18; 84:7; 85:13; 88:4; 89:14; 104:8(2); 26; 105:20; 107:7; 23; 26; 108:11; 115:17; 118:19; 119:35; 122:1; 4; 129:8; 132:3; 7; 139:7; 143:7; **Prov** 1:12; 2:19; 3:28; 4:13; 14; 5:5; 23; 6:3; 6; 28; 7:25; 9:6; 15; 14:7; 15:12; 18:8; 19:7; 22:6; 10; 24; 23:30; 25:8; 26:22; 27:10; 28:10; 30:27; 29; **Eccl** 2:1; 3:20; 5:15; 16; 6:6; 7:2(2); 8:3; 9:3; 7; 10:15; 12:5; **Song** 1:8; 3:2; 3; 4; 11; 6:6; 7:8; 11; **Is** 2:3(3); 19; 21; 3:16; 5:5; 24; 6:8; 9; 7:3; 6; 8:6; 7; 8; 11:15; 13:2; 14:19; 15:5; 18:2; 20:2; 21:2; 6; 22:15; 23:16; 27:4; 28:13; 30:2; 8; 31:1; 33:21; 34:10; 35:9; 36:6; 10; 37:32; 38:5; 10; 15; 18; 22; 42:10; 13; 45:2; 13; 16; 48:17; 20; 49:9; 17; 51:23; 52:11(2); 12(3); 54:9; 55:12; 58:6; 8; 60:20; 62:1; 10(2); 66:24; **Jer** 1:7; 2:2; 25; 37; 3:1; 12; 4:5; 29; 5:10; 6:4; 5; 25; 7:12; 9:2; 10:5; 11:12; 13:1; 4; 6; 14:18(2); 15:1; 2; 5; 16:5; 8; 17:19(2); 18:2; 11; 19:1; 2; 10; 20:6; 21:2; 12; 22:1; 20; 22; 25:6; 32; 27:18; 28:13; 29:12; 30:16; 31:4; 6; 22; 24; 39; 34:2; 3; 9; 10(2); 11; 14(2); 35:2; 11; 13; 15; 36:5; 6; 19; 37:12; 38:17; 18; 21; 39:16; 40:1; 4(2); 5(4); 15; 41:10; 17; 42:14; 15; 17; 19; 22; 43:2; 12; 44:12; 46:8; 11; 16; 19; 22; 48:5; 7; 49:3; 12(2); 28; 50:4; 6; 8; 21; 27; 33; 51:9; 45; 50; **Lam** 4:18; **Eze** 1:12; 20(2); 3:1; 4; 11; 22; 24; 25; 6:9; 8:6; 9; 9:4; 5; 7; 10:2; 12:4(2); 11; 12; 13:20; 14:11; 17; 15:7; 20:10; 29; 39; 21:4; 16; 23:44; 24:14; 26:11; 20; 30:9; 17; 18; 31:14; 32:18; 19; 24; 25; 29; 30; 38:11(2); 39:9; 40:26; 42:14; 44:3; 19; 46:2; 8(2); 9(3); 10(4); 12; 47:8(2); 15; **Dan** 11:44; 12:9; 13; **Hos** 1:2; 2:5; 7; 3:1; 4:15; 5:6; 14; 15; 7:11; 12; 11:3; **Joel** 2:16; **Amos** 1:5; 15; 2:7; 4:3; 5:5; 27; 6:2(2); 7(2); 7:12; 15; 17; 8:9; 9:4; **Jonah** 1:2; 3; 3:2; **Mic** 1:8; 2:3; 3:6; 4:2(2); 10(2); 5:8; **Nah** 3:14; **Hab** 1:4; **Hag** 1:8; **Zec** 6:5; 6(3); 7; 8; 10; 8:21(3); 23; 9:14(2); 14:2; 3; 8; 16; 18; **Mal** 4:2; **Mt** 2:8; 20; 22; 5:24; 41(2); 7:13; 8:4; 9; 13; 21; 31; 32; 9:6; 13; 10:5; 6; 7; 11; 11:4; 13:28; 14:15; 22; 29; 16:21; 17:27; 18:15; 19:21; 24; 20:4; 7; 14; 18; 21:2; 28; 30; 31; 22:9; 23:13(2); 24:26; 25:6; 9; 46; 26:18; 32; 36; 27:65; 28:7; 10(2); 19; **Mk** 1:38; 44; 2:11; 5:19; 34; 6:36; 37; 38; 45; 7:29; 8:26; 9:43; 10:21; 25; 33; 52; 11:2; 6; 12:38; 13:15; 14:12; 13; 14; 28; 42; 16:7; 15; **Lk** 1:17; 76; 2:15; 5:14; 24; 7:8; 22; 50; 8:14; 22; 31; 48; 51; 9:5; 12; 13; 51; 53; 59; 60; 61; 10:3; 7; 10; 37; 11:5; 13:32; 14:4; 10(2); 18; 19; 21; 23; 15:4; 18; 28; 17:7; 14; 19; 23; 18:25; 31; 19:30; 21:8; 22:8; 33; 68; 23:22; **Jn** 1:43; 4:4; 16; 50; 6:67; 68; 7:3; 8(2); 19; 33; 35(2); 8:11; 14(2); 21(2); 22; 9:7; 11; 10:9; 11:7; 11; 15; 16; 44; 13:33; 36; 14:2; 3; 4; 12; 28(2); 31; 15:16; 16:5; 7(2); 10; 16; 17; 28; 18:8; 19:12; 20:17; 21:3(2); **Acts** 1:11; 25; 3:3; 13; 4:15; 21; 23; 5:20; 40; 7:40; 8:26; 29; 9:6; 11; 15; 10:20; 11:12; 22; 12:17; 15:2; 33; 36; 16:3; 7; 10; 35; 36(2); 17:9; 14; 18:6; 19:21; 20:1; 13; 22; 21:4; 12; 22:10; 23:10; 23; 32; 24:25; 25:5; 9; 12; 20; 27:3; 28:18; 26; **Rom** 15:25; **1Cor** 5:10; 6:1; 7; 10:27; 16:4(2); 6; **2Cor** 9:5; **Gal** 2:9; **Eph** 4:26; **Phil** 2:23; **1Th** 4:6; **Heb** 6:1; 11:8; 13:13; **Jas** 4:13(2); 5:1; **Rev** 3:12; 10:8; 13:10; 16:1; 14; 17:8; 20:8

GOEST

935, 1980, 3213, 3318, 5927, *565, 5217*

Gen 10:19; 30; 25:18; 28:15; 32:17; **Ex** 4:21; 33:16; 34:12; **Num** 14:14; **Deut** 7:1; 11:10; 29; 12:29; 20:1; 21:10; 23:20; 28:6; 19; 21; 63; 30:16; 32:50; **Josh** 1:7; 9; **Judg** 14:3; 19:17; **Ruth** 1:16; **1Sa** 27:8; 28:22; **2Sa** 15:19; **1Kin** 2:37; 42; **Ps** 44:9; **Prov** 4:12; 6:22; **Eccl** 5:1; 9:10; **Jer** 45:5; **Zec** 2:2; **Mt** 8:19; **Lk** 9:57; 12:58; **Jn** 11:8; 13:36; 14:5; 16:5

GOETH

732, 925, 935, 1869, 1980, 3212, 3318, 3381, 3518, 3996, 4609, 5186, 5493, 5648, 5674, 5927, 6437, 7126, 7847, *305, 565, 1525, 1607, 2212, 2597, 4198, 4254, 4334, 5217, 5562*

Gen 2:14; 32:20; 33:14; 38:13; **Ex** 7:15; 22:26; 28:29; 30; 35; **Lev** 11:21; 27; 42(2); 14:46; 15:32; 16:17; 22:3; 4; 27:21; **Num** 5:29; 21:15; **Deut** 1:30; 9:3; 11:30; 19:5; 20:4; 23:9; 24:13; **Josh** 10:10; 11:17; 12:7; 16:1; 2; 3; 19:12(2); 13; 27; 34; **Judg** 5:31; 20:31; 21:19; **1Sa** 6:9; 22:14; 30:24; **2Kin** 5:18; 11:8; 12:20; **2Chr** 23:7; **Ezr** 5:8; **Job** 7:9; 9:11; 34:8; 37:2; 39:21; 41:20; 21; **Ps** 17:1; 41:6; 68:21; 88:16; 97:3; 104:23; 126:6; 146:4; **Prov** 6:29; 7:22(2); 11:10; 16:18; 20:19; 26:9; 20; 31:18; **Eccl** 1:5; 6; 3:21(2); 12:5; **Song** 7:9; **Is** 28:19; 30:29; 55:11; 59:8; 63:14; **Jer** 5:6; 6:4; 21:9; 22:10; 30:23; 38:2; 44:17; 49:17; 50:13; **Eze** 7:14; 33:31; 40:40; 42:9; 44:27; 48:1; **Hos** 6:4; 5; **Zec** 5:3; 5; 6; **Mt** 8:9; 12:45; 13:44; 15:11; 17; 17:21; 18:12; 26:24; 28:7; **Mk** 3:13; 7:19; 14:21; 45; 16:7; **Lk** 7:8; 11:26; 22:22; **Jn** 3:8; 7:20; 10:4; 11:31; 12:35; **Acts** 8:26; **1Cor** 6:6; 9:7; **Jas** 1:24; **1Jn** 2:11; **Rev** 14:4; 17:11; 19:15

GOING

235, 838, 935, 1980, 3212, 3318, 3381, 3996, 4161, 4174, 4608, 5362, 5674, 5927, 5944, 6807, 7751, 8444, 8582, *71, 305, 565, 1330, 1607, 2212, 2597, 4105, 4108, 4198, 4254, 4260, 4281*

Gen 12:9; 15:12; 37:25; **Ex** 17:12; 23:4; 37:18; 19; 21; **Lev** 11:20; **Num** 32:7; 34:4; **Deut** 16:6; 33:18; **Josh** 1:4; 6:9; 11; 13; 7:5; 10:11; 27; 15:7; 18:17; 23:14; **Judg** 1:36; 19:18; 28; **1Sa** 9:11; 27; 10:3; 17:20; 29:6; **2Sa** 2:19; 3:25; 5:24; **1Kin** 17:11; 22:36; **2Kin** 2:23; 9:27; 19:27; **1Chr** 14:15; 26:16; **2Chr** 11:4; 18:34; **Neh** 3:19; 31; 32; 12:37; **Job** 1:7; 2:2; 33:24; 28; **Ps** 19:6; 50:1; 104:19; 113:3; 121:8; 144:14; **Prov** 7:27; 14:15; 30:29; **Is** 13:10; 37:28; **Jer** 48:5(2); 50:4; **Eze** 27:19; 40:31; 34; 37; 44:5; 46:12; **Dan** 6:14; 9:25; **Hos** 6:3; **Jonah** 1:3; **Mal** 1:11; **Mt** 4:21; 20:17; 26:46; 28:11; **Mk** 6:31; 10:32; **Lk** 14:31; **Jn** 4:51; 8:59; **Acts** 9:28; 20:5; **Rom** 10:3; **1Ti** 5:24; **Heb** 7:18; **1Pet** 2:25; **Jude** 7

GOINGS

838, 1979, 4161, 4163, 4570, 4703, 6471, 6806, 8444

Num 33:2(2); 34:5; 8; 9; 12; **Josh** 15:4; 7; 11; 16:3; 8; 18:12; 14; **Job** 34:21; **Ps** 17:5; 40:2; 68:24(2); 140:4; **Prov** 5:21; 20:24; **Is** 59:8; **Eze** 42:11; 43:11; 48:30; **Mic** 5:2

GONE

230, 235, 369, 656, 935, 1540, 1961, 1980, 2114, 3212, 3318, 3381, 4059, 4161, 4185, 5128, 5186, 5362, 5437, 5472, 5493, 5674, 5927, 6805, 7725, 7751, 7847, 8582, *305, 402, 565, 576, 1276, 1330, 1339, 1525, 1578, 1607, 1826, 1831, 3985, 4105, 4198, 4260, 4570, 5055*

Gen 27:30; 28:7; 31:30; 34:17; 42:33; 44:4; 49:9; **Ex** 9:29; 12:32; 16:14; 19:1; 33:8; **Lev** 17:7; **Num** 5:19; 20; 7:89; 13:32; 16:46; 21:28; **Deut** 9:9; 13:13; 17:3; 23:23; 27:4; 32:36; **Josh** 2:7; 4:23; 23:16; **Judg** 3:24; 4:12; 14; 18:24; 20:3; **Ruth** 1:13; 15; **1Sa** 14:3; 17; 15:12(2); 20; 20:41; 25:37; **2Sa** 2:27; 3:7; 22; 23; 24; 6:13; 13:15; 17:20; 22; 23:9; 24:8; **1Kin** 1:25; 2:41; 9:16; 11:15; 13:24; 14:9; 10; 18:12; 20:40; 21:18; 22:13; **2Kin** 1:4; 6; 16; 2:9; 5:2; 6:15; 7:12; 20:4; 11; **1Chr** 14:15; 17:5; **Job** 1:5; 7:4; 19:10; 23:12; 24:24; 28:4; **Ps** 14:3; 19:4; 38:4; 10; 42:4; 7; 47:5; 51:t, 53:3; 73:2; 77:8; 89:34; 103:16; 109:23; 119:176; 124:4; 5; **Prov** 7:19; 20:14; **Eccl** 8:10; **Song** 2:11; 5:6; 6:1; 2; **Is** 1:4; 5:13; 10:29; 15:2; 8; 16:8; 22:1; 24:11; 38:8(2); 41:3; 45:23; 46:2; 51:5; 53:6; 57:8; **Jer** 2:5; 23; 3:6; 4:7; 5:23; 9:10; 10:20; 14:2; 15:6; 9; 23:15; 19; 29:16; 34:21; 40:5; 44:8; 14; 28; 48:11; 15(2); 32; 50:6; **Lam** 1:3; 5; 6; 18; **Eze** 7:10; 9:3; 13:5; 19:14; 23:30; 24:6; 31:12; 32:21; 24; 27; 30; 36:20; 37:21; 44:10; **Dan** 2:5; 8; 14; 10:20; **Hos** 4:12; 8:9; 9:1; 6; **Amos** 8:5; **Jonah** 1:5; **Mic** 1:16; 2:13; **Mal** 3:7; **Mt** 10:23; 12:43; 14:34; 18:12(2); 25:8; 26:71; **Mk** 1:19; 5:30; 7:29; 30; 10:17; **Lk** 2:15; 5:2; 8:46; 11:14; 24; 19:7; 24:28; **Jn** 4:8; 6:22; 7:10; 12:19; 13:31; **Acts** 13:6; 42; 16:6; 19; 18:22; 20:2; 25; 24:6; 26:31; 27:28; **Rom** 3:12; **1Pet** 3:22; **2Pet** 2:15; **1Jn** 4:1; **Jude** 11

GOOD

1319, 1580, 2492, 2617, 2623, 2869, 2895, 2896, 2898, 3190, 3191, 3276, 3474, 3788, 3966, 5750, 6743, 6965, 7368, 7522, 7965, 7999, 8232, *14, 15, 18, 515, 865, 979, 2095, 2097, 2106, 2107, 2108, 2109, 2133, 2162, 2140, 2163, 2425, 2480, 2565, 2567, 2570, 2573, 3112, 4851, 5358, 5542, 5543, 5544*

Gen 1:4; 10; 12; 18; 21; 25; 31; 2:9(2); 12; 17; 18; 3:5; 6; 22; 15:15; 18:7; 19:8; 21:16; 24:12; 50; 25:8; 26:29; 27:9; 46; 30:20; 31:24; 29; 32:12; 40:16; 41:5; 22; 24; 26(2); 35; 37; 43:28; 44:4; 45:18; 20; 23; 46:29; 49:15; 50:20; **Ex** 3:8; 18:17; 21:34; 22:11; 13; 14; 15; **Lev** 5:4; 24:18; 27:10(2); 12; 14; 33; **Num** 10:29(2); 13:19; 20; 14:7; 23:19; 24:13; **Deut** 1:14; 25; 35; 39; 2:4; 3:25; 4:15; 21; 22; 6:11; 18(2); 24; 8:7; 10; 16; 9:6; 10:13; 11:17; 12:28; 26:11; 28:12; 63; 30:5; 9(2); 15; 31:6; 7; 23; 33:16; **Josh** 1:6; 8; 9; 18; 9:25; 10:25; 21:45; 23:11; 13; 14; 15(2); 16; 24:20; **Judg** 8:32; 9:11; 10:15; 17:13; 18:9; 22; 19:24; **Ruth** 2:22; **1Sa** 1:23; 2:24; 3:18; 11:10; 12:23; 14:36; 40; 15:9; 19:4(2); 20:12; 24:4; 17; 19; 25:3; 8; 15; 21; 30; 26:16; 29:6; 9; **2Sa** 3:19(2); 4:10; 6:19; 10:12(2); 13:22; 14:17; 32; 15:3; 26; 16:12; 17:7; 14; 18:27(2); 19:18; 27; 35; 37; 38; 24:22; **1Kin** 1:42; 2:38; 42; 3:9; 8:36; 56; 12:7; 14:13; 15; 21:2; 22:8; 13(2); 18; **2Kin** 3:19(2); 25(2); 7:9; 8:9; 10:5; 20:3; 19(2); **1Chr** 4:40; 13:2; 16:3; 34; 19:13(2); 21:23; 22:13; 28:8; 20; 29:3; 28; **2Chr** 5:13; 6:27; 7:3; 10:7; 14:2; 18:7; 12(2); 17; 19:3; 11; 24:16; 30:18; 22; 31:20; **Ezr** 3:11; 5:17; 7:9; 18; 8:18; 22; 9:12; 10:4; **Neh** 2:8; 18(2); 5:9; 19; 6:19; 9:13; 20; 36; 13:14; 31; **Est** 3:11; 5:4; 7:9; 8:17; 9:19; 22; **Job** 2:10; 5:27; 7:7; 9:25; 10:3; 13:9; 15:3; 21:16; 22:18; 21; 24:21; 30:26; 34:4; 39:4; **Ps** 4:6; 14:1; 3; 25:8; 27:14; 31:24; 34:8; 10; 12; 14; 35:12; 36:3; 4; 37:3; 23; 27; 38:20(2); 39:2; 45:1; 51:18(2); 52:3; 9; 53:1; 3; 54:6; 69:16; 73:1; 28; 84:11; 85:12; 86:5; 17; 92:1; 100:5; 103:5; 104:28; 106:1; 5; 107:1; 109:5; 21; 111:10; 112:5; 118:1; 29; 119:39; 66; 68(2); 71; 122; 122:9; 125:4(2); 128:5; 133:1; 135:3; 136:1; 143:10; 145:9; 147:1; **Prov** 2:9; 20; 3:4; 27; 4:2; 11:17; 23; 27; 12:2; 14; 25; 13:2; 15; 21; 22; 14:14; 19; 22; 15:3; 23; 30; 16:20; 29; 17:13; 20; 22; 26; 18:5; 22; 19:2; 8; 20:18; 23; 22:1; 24:13; 23; 25; 25:25; 27; 28:10; 21; 31:12; 18; **Eccl** 2:3; 24; 26(2); 3:12(2); 13; 4:8; 9; 5:11; 18(2); 6:3; 6; 12; 7:1; 11; 18; 20; 9:2(2); 18; 11:6; 12:9; 14; **Song** 1:3; 2:13; **Is** 1:19; 5:20(2); 7:15; 16; 38:3; 39:8; 40:9(2); 41:6; 23; 27; 52:7(3); 55:2; 61:1; 65:2; **Jer** 4:22; 5:25; 6:16; 8:15; 10:5; 13:10; 23; 14:11; 19; 17:6; 18:4; 10; 11; 20(2); 21:10; 24:2; 3(2); 5(2); 6; 26:14; 29:10; 32; 32:39; 40; 41; 42; 33:9; 11; 14; 39:16; 40:4(2); 42:6; 44:27; **Lam** 3:25; 26; 27; 38; **Eze** 16:50; 17:8; 18:18; 20:25; 24:4; 34:14(2); 18; 36:31; **Dan** 4:2; **Hos** 4:13; 8:3; **Amos** 5:14; 15; 9:4; **Mic** 1:12; 2:7; 3:2; 6:8; 7:2; **Nah** 1:7; 15; **Zeph** 1:12; **Zec** 1:13; 11:12; **Mal** 2:13; 17; **Mt** 3:10; 5:13; 16; 44; 45; 7:11(2); 17(2); 18(2); 19; 8:30; 9:2; 22; 11:26; 12:33(2); 34; 35(3); 13:8; 23; 24; 27; 37; 38; 48; 14:27; 17:4; 19:10; 16(2); 17(2); 20:15; 22:10; 25:21; 23; 26:10; 24; **Mk** 3:4; 4:8; 20; 6:50; 9:5; 50; 10:17; 18(2); 49; 14:6; 7; 21; **Lk** 1:3; 53; 2:10; 14; 3:9; 6:9; 27; 33(2); 35; 38; 43(2); 45(3); 8:8; 15(2); 48; 9:33; 10:21; 42; 11:13; 12:32; 14:34; 16:25; 18:18; 19(2); 19:17; 23:50; **Jn** 1:46; 2:10(2); 5:29; 7:12; 10:11(2); 14; 32; 33; 16:33; **Acts** 4:9; 9:36; 10:22; 38; 11:24; 14:17; 15:7; 25; 28; 38; 18:18; 22:12; 23:1; 11; 27:22; 25; 36; **Rom** 2:10; 3:8; 12; 5:7; 7:12; 13(2); 16; 18(2); 19; 21; 8:28; 9:11; 10:15; 11:24; 12:2; 9; 21; 13:3(2); 4; 14:16; 21; 15:2; 16:18; 19; **1Cor** 5:6; 7:1; 8; 26(2); 15:33; **2Cor** 5:10; 6:8; 9:8; 13:11; **Gal** 4:18(2); 6:6; 10; **Eph** 1:5; 9; 2:10; 4:28; 29; 6:7; 8; **Phil** 1:6; 15; 2:13; 19; 4:8; **Col** 1:10; **1Th** 3:1; 6(2); 5:15; 21; **2Th** 1:11; 2:16; 17; **1Ti** 1:5; 8; 18; 19; 2:3; 10; 3:1; 2; 7; 13; 4:4; 6(2); 5:4; 10(2); 25; 6:12(2); 13; 18(2); 19; **2Ti** 1:14; 2:3; 21; 3:3; 17; 4:7; **Titus** 1:8; 16; 2:3; 5; 7; 10; 14; 3:1; 8(2); 14; **Philem** 1:6; **Heb** 5:14; 6:5; 9:11; 10:1; 24; 11:2; 12; 39; 13:9; 16; 18; 21; **Jas** 1:17; 2:3; 3:13; 17; 4:17; **1Pet** 2:12; 18; 3:10; 11; 13; 16(2); 21; 4:10; **1Jn** 3:17; **3Jn** 11(2); 12

GOODLY

117, 145, 155, 410, 1926, 1935, 2530, 2532, 2896, 3303, 4261, 4758, 6287, 6643, 7443, 8231, 8233, 8389, *2573, 2986*

Gen 27:15; 39:6; 49:21; **Ex** 2:2; 39:28; **Lev** 23:40; **Num** 24:5; 31:10; **Deut** 3:25; 6:10; 8:12; **Josh** 7:21; **1Sa** 9:2; 16:12; **2Sa** 23:21; **1Kin** 1:6; **2Chr** 36:10; 19; **Job** 39:13; **Ps** 16:6; 80:10; **Jer** 3:19; 11:16; **Eze** 17:8; 23; **Hos** 10:1; **Joel** 3:5; **Zec** 10:3; 11:13; **Mt** 13:45; **Lk** 21:5; **Jas** 2:2; **Rev** 18:14

GOODNESS

2617, 2896, 2898, *19, 5543, 5544*

Ex 18:9; 33:19; 34:6; **Num** 10:32; **Judg** 8:35; **2Sa** 7:28; **1Kin** 8:66; **1Chr** 17:26; **2Chr** 6:41; 7:10; 32:32; 35:26; **Neh** 9:25; 35; **Ps** 16:2; 21:3; 23:6; 27:13; 31:19; 33:5; 52:1; 65:4; 11; 68:10; 107:8; 9; 15; 21; 31; 144:2; 145:7; **Prov** 20:6; **Is** 63:7; **Jer** 2:7; 31:12; 14; 33:9; **Hos** 3:5; 6:4; 10:1; **Zec** 9:17; **Rom** 2:4(2); 11:22(3); 15:14; **Gal** 5:22; **Eph** 5:9; **2Th** 1:11

GOTTEN

622, 3254, 4672, 5414, 6213, 7069, 7408, *645*

Gen 4:1; 12:5; 31:1; 18(2); 46:6; **Ex** 14:18; **Lev** 6:4; **Num** 31:50; **Deut** 8:17; **2Sa** 17:13; **Job** 28:15; 31:25; **Ps** 98:1; **Prov** 13:11; 20:21; **Eccl** 1:16; **Is** 15:7; **Jer** 48:36; **Eze** 28:4(2); 38:12; **Dan** 9:15; **Acts** 21:1; **Rev** 15:2

GREATER

1419, 1431, 1980, 7227, 7235, *3187, 3286, 4055, 4119*

Gen 1:16; 4:13; 39:9; 41:40; 48:19; **Ex** 18:11; **Num** 14:12; **Deut** 1:28; 4:38; 7:1; 9:1; 14; 11:23; **Josh** 10:2; **1Sa** 14:30; **2Sa** 13:15; 16; **1Kin** 1:37; 47; **1Chr** 11:9(2); **2Chr** 3:5; **Est** 9:4(2); **Job** 33:12; **Lam** 4:6; **Eze** 8:6; 13; 15; 43:14; **Dan** 11:13; **Amos** 6:2; **Hag** 2:9; **Mt** 11:11(2); 12:6; 41; 42; 23:14; 17; 19; **Mk** 4:32; 12:31; 40; **Lk** 7:28(2); 11:31; 32; 12:18; 20:47; 22:27; **Jn** 1:50; 4:12; 5:20; 36; 8:53; 10:29; 13:16(2); 14:12; 28; 15:13; 20; 19:11; **Acts** 15:28; **1Cor** 14:5; 15:6; **Heb** 6:13; 16; 9:11; 11:26; **Jas** 3:1; **2Pet** 2:11; **1Jn** 3:20; 4:4; 5:9; **3Jn** 4

GREATEST

1419, 4768, *3173, 3187*

1Chr 12:14; 29; **Job** 1:3; **Jer** 6:13; 8:10; 31:34; 42:1; 8; 44:12; **Jonah** 3:5; **Mt** 13:32; 18:1; 4; 23:11; **Mk** 9:34; **Lk** 9:46; 22:24; 26; **Acts** 8:10; **1Cor** 13:13; **Heb** 8:11

GREATLY

3966, 7227, 7230, 7690, *1568, 1569, 1971, 3029, 3171, 4183, 4970, 5479*

Gen 3:16; 7:18; 24:35; 31:30; 32:7; **Ex** 19:18; **Num** 11:10; 14:39; 22:17; 24:11; **Deut** 6:3; 15:4; 17:17; **Josh** 10:2; **Judg** 2:15; 6:6; **1Sa** 11:6; 15; 12:18; 15:11; 16:21; 17:11; 28:5; 30:6; 31:4; **2Sa** 10:5; 12:5; 24:10; **1Kin** 5:7; 18:3; **2Kin** 6:11; **1Chr** 4:38; 10:4; 16:25; 19:5; 21:8; 29:9; **2Chr** 25:10; 33:12; **Neh** 8:12; **Job** 3:25; **Ps** 6:3; 10; 21:1; 28:7; 38:6; 45:11; 47:9; 48:1; 62:2; 65:9; 71:23; 78:59; 89:7; 96:4; 105:24; 107:38; 109:30; 112:1; 116:10; 145:3; **Prov** 23:24; **Eccl** 8:6; **Is** 42:17; 61:10; **Jer** 3:1; 4:10; 9:19; 20:11; **Eze** 20:13; 25:12; 27:35; **Dan** 5:9; 6:14; 7:28; 9:23; 10:11; 19; **Obad** 2; **Zec** 9:9; **Mt** 17:6; 27:14; 54; **Mk** 6:51; 9:6; 15; 26; 10:14; 41; 12:27; **Lk** 2:9; 24:4; **Jn** 3:29; **Acts** 3:11; 4:2; 6:7; 16:18; 18:27; **2Cor** 10:15; **Phil** 1:8; 4:10; **1Th** 3:6; **2Ti** 1:4; 4:15; **1Pet** 1:6; **2Jn** 4; **3Jn** 3

GREATNESS

1419, 1420, 1433, 4768, 7230, 7238, *3174*

Ex 15:7; 16; **Num** 14:19; **Deut** 3:24; 5:24; 9:26; 11:2; 32:3; **1Chr** 17:19; 21; 29:11; **2Chr** 9:6; 24:27; **Neh** 13:22; **Est** 10:2; **Ps** 66:3; 71:21; 79:11; 145:3; 6; 150:2; **Prov** 5:23; **Is** 40:26; 57:10; 63:1; **Jer** 13:22; **Eze** 31:2; 7; 18; **Dan** 4:22; 7:27; **Eph** 1:19

HAD

935, 1961, 3426, 3884, 7760, *1096, 1510, 1746, 2192, 2258, 2722, 2983, 3844, 5607*

Gen 1:31; 2:2(2); 3; 5; 8; 22; 3:1; 4:4; 5; 5:4; 6:6; 12; 7:9; 16; 8:6; 9:24; 11:3(2); 30; 12:1; 4; 5(2); 16; 20; 13:1; 3; 4; 5; 14:13; 16:1; 3; 4; 5; 17:23; 18:8; 33; 19:17; 20:4; 18; 21:1(2); 2; 4; 9; 25; 22:3; 9; 23:16; 24:1; 2; 15; 16; 19; 21; 22; 29; 45; 48; 65(2); 66; 25:5; 6; 26:8; 14; 15(2); 18(3); 32; 27:17; 30; 31; 28:6; 9; 18; 29:16; 20; 30:9; 25; 35; 38; 43; 31:18(2); 19; 21; 25; 32; 34; 42; 32:23; 33:10; 19; 34:5; 7; 13; 19; 27; 35:16; 36:6; 38:15; 30; 39:1; 4; 5(3); 6(2); 13; 40:1; 16; 22; 41:21(2); 43; 54; 43:2(2); 6; 10(2); 23; 44:2; 45:27(2); 46:1; 5; 6; 47:11; 22; 27; 48:11; 49:33; 50:14; **Ex** 2:6(2); 16; 25; 4:28(2); 30; 31(2); 5:14; 7:10; 13; 22; 25; 8:12; 15; 19; 9:12; 35; 10:15; 23; 12:28; 39; 13:17; 19; 14:12; 15:25; 16:3; 18(2); 17:10; 18:1(2); 2; 8(2); 9(2); 24; 19:2; 31:18; 32:4; 20; 25; 29; 33:5; 34:4; 32; 33; 35:25; 29; 36:1; 2; 3; 7; 22; 39:43(3); 40:23; **Lev** 10:5; 19; 21:3; 24:23; **Num** 1:48; 3:4; 7:1(3); 8:4; 22; 12:1(2); 14; 13:32; 14:2(2); 24; 16:31; 39; 20:3; 21:9; 26; 22:2; 33(2); 23:2; 30;

26:33; 65; 27:3; 30:6; 31:32; 35; 53; 32:1; 9; 13; 33:4; **Deut** 1:3; 4; 39; 41; 2:12; 7:8; 9:16(4); 21; 25; 10:5; 15; 19:19; 29:26; 31:24; 32:30(2); 34:9; **Josh** 2:6(2); 11; 4:4; 5:1; 5; 7; 8; 12(2); 6:8; 10; 22(2); 23; 25; 7:7; 24; 25; 8:13; 18; 19; 20; 21; 24; 26; 33; 9:3; 4; 16; 18; 21; 10:1(6); 13; 20; 27; 32; 33; 35; 37; 39(2); 11:1; 14; 14:3; 15; 17:1; 3; 6(2); 8; 11; 18:2; 19:2; 9; 49; 21:4; 5; 6; 7; 10; 20; 45; 22:7; 23:1; 24:31(2); **Judg** 1:8(2); 19; 2:6; 7; 10; 15(2); 3:1; 11; 12; 16; 18; 20; 30; 4:3; 11; 18; 24; 5:26; 31; 6:3; 27; 7:19; 8:3; 8; 19; 24; 30(2); 34; 35; 9:22; 10:4(2); 11:34; 39; 12:9; 14; 14:4; 6(2); 9; 18(2); 20; 15:5; 6; 17; 19; 16:8; 18; 17:3(2); 5; 18:1; 7; 27(2); 28; 19:6; 17; 20:36; 21:1; 5; 12; 14; 15; **Ruth** 1:6(2); 2:1; 17; 18(2); 19; 3:7; 16; **1Sa** 1:2(3); 5; 6; 9(2); 13; 20; 24; 3:8; 4:18; 5:9(2); 6:6; 16; 19(2); 7:14; 9:2; 15; 10:9; 13; 20; 21; 26; 13:1; 4(2); 8; 10; 21; 14:11; 17; 22; 24; 30(2); 15:35; 17:5; 6; 12; 20; 21; 39; 40; 18:1; 19:18; 20:34; 37; 22:21; 24:5; 10; 16; 18; 25:2; 21; 34; 35; 37; 44; 26:5; 28:3(3); 20; 24; 30:1; 2; 4; 12(2); 16(2); 18; 19; 21; 31:11; **2Sa** 1:1; 21; 2:27; 30; 31; 3:7; 17; 22; 30; 4:2; 4; 5:12(2); 17; 25; 6:8; 13; 17; 18; 22; 23; 7:1; 8:9; 10(2); 11; 9:2; 10; 12; 11:10; 13; 22; 27; 12:2; 3(2); 6; 8; 13:1; 3; 10; 11; 15; 18; 22; 23; 28; 29; 36; 14:2; 6; 32; 33; 15:2; 24; 30; 16:23; 17:14; 18; 20; 18:18; 33; 19:6(3); 8; 24; 32; 43; 20:3; 5; 8; 21:2; 11; 12(3); 15; 20; 22:1; 38; 23:8; 18; 20; 21; 22; 24:8; 10; **1Kin** 1:6; 41; 2:28; 41; 3:1; 10; 21; 28; 4:2; 7; 11; 14; 24(2); 26; 34; 5:1(2); 15; 6:22; 7:8(2); 20; 28; 30(2); 37; 51; 8:11; 54; 66; 9:1; 2; 10; 11; 12; 16; 19; 24; 27; 10:4(2); 7; 15; 19; 22; 24; 26; 28; 11:3; 9; 10; 15; 16; 29; 12:8; 12; 32(2); 33(2); 13:4; 5; 11(2); 12; 23(3); 28; 31; 14:22(2); 26; 15:3; 12; 13; 15(2); 20; 22; 29; 16:31; 32; 17:7; 19:1(2); 21:1; 4(2); 11(2); 22:31; 53; **2Kin** 1:17(2); 2:14; 3:2; 4:12; 15; 17; 20; 5:1; 2(2); 7; 8(2); 13; 6:23; 30; 7:6; 15; 17; 18; 8:1; 5(2); 29; 9:14; 15; 31; 10:1; 17; 25; 11:15; 12:6; 11; 18; 13:7(2); 23(2); 25; 14:5; 15:3; 9; 34; 16:11; 18; 17:4(2); 7(3); 8; 12; 15; 20; 23; 28; 29; 35; 18:4; 16; 18; 19:8; 20:11; 12(2); 21:3; 7; 16; 24; 22:11; 23:5; 8; 11; 12(2); 13; 15; 19(2); 26; 29; 32; 37; 24:7; 9; 13(2); 19; 20; 25:16; 17; 22; 23; **1Chr** 2:22; 26; 34(2); 52; 4:5; 22; 27(2); 40; 6:31; 32; 49; 66; 7:4; 15; 8:8; 38; 40; 9:23; 28; 31; 44; 10:9; 11; 13; 11:10; 11; 20; 22; 24; 12:15; 29; 32; 39; 13:11; 14; 14:2; 4; 12; 15:3; 27; 16:1; 2; 18:9; 10(2); 19:6; 17; 21:28; 23:11; 17; 22; 24:2; 19; 28; 26:9; 10; 26; 28(2); 27:23; 28:2(2); 12; 29:25; **2Chr** 1:3; 4(3); 5; 12; 14; 16; 2:17; 3:1; 5:1; 14; 6:13(2); 7:1; 2; 6; 7; 10; 8:1; 2; 6; 11; 12; 14; 18; 9:3(2); 6; 12; 23; 25; 10:2; 6; 11:14; 15; 12:1(2); 2; 9; 13; 14:6(3); 8; 15:8; 11; 15; 16; 18(2); 16:14; 17:2; 5; 9; 13; 18:1; 2; 10; 30; 20:21; 23; 27; 29; 33; 21:2; 6; 7; 10; 22:1; 7; 9(2); 23:8; 9; 18; 21; 24:7; 10; 14; 16; 22; 24; 25:3; 26:5; 10; 11; 19; 20; 28:3; 6; 17; 18(2); 29:2; 22; 29; 34; 36; 30:2; 3(2); 5; 17; 18; 31:1; 10; 32:27; 29; 33:2; 3; 4; 7(2); 9; 15; 22; 23; 25; 34:4; 7(2); 8; 9; 10; 11; 19; 22; 35:20; 24; 36:13; 14; 15; 17; 20; 21; **Ezr** 1:5; 7(2); 2:1(2); 3:7; 12; 5:12; 14; 6:13; 21; 22; 7:6; 10; 8:20; 22; 25; 35; 9:4; 10:1(2); 6; 8; 17; 18; 44(3); **Neh** 1:2; 2:1; 9; 12; 16; 18; 4:6; 15; 18; 5:15(2); 6:1(2); 12(2); 18; 7:1; 6(2); 67; 8:1; 4; 12; 14; 17; 9:18(2); 28(2); 10:28; 11:16; 12:29; 43; 13:3; 5; 10; 23; **Est** 1:8; 2:1; 6(3); 7; 10(2); 12; 15; 20(2); 3:2; 4; 6; 12; 4:5; 7(2); 17; 5:5; 11(2); 12; 6:2; 4; 13; 14; 7:4(2); 9(2); 10; 8:1; 2; 3; 16; 17; 9:1; 16; 23(2); 24(2); 26(2); 31(2); **Job** 2:11; 3:13; 15; 16; 26; 6:20; 9:16(3); 10:18(2); 19; 22:8; 24:16; 29:12; 31:25; 31; 35; 32:3(2); 4(2); 16; 38:8; 42:7; 10; 11(2); 12; 13; **Ps** 27:13(2); 35:14; 42:4; 51:t, 55:6; 73:2; 74:5; 78:11; 23; 24(2); 43; 44; 54; 81:13(2); 84:10; 89:7; 94:17(2); 105:26; 106:21; 23; 119:51; 56; 87; 92; 124:1; 2; 3; 4(2); 5; **Prov** 8:26; 24:31; **Eccl** 1:16; 2:7(2); 11(2); 18; 4:1(2); 8:10(2); **Song** 3:4; 5:6; 8:11; **Is** 1:9; 6:2; 6; 22:11; 26:13; 29:16; 37:8; 38:9; 17; 21; 22; 39:1(2); 41:3; 48:18; 19; 49:21; 52:15(2); 53:9; 59:10; 60:10; **Jer** 2:21; 3:7; 8; 4:23; 5:7; 6:15; 8:12; 9:2; 11:19; 13:7; 16:15; 19:14; 23:8; 22(2); 24:1(2); 2(2); 25:17; 26:8(2); 19; 28:12; 29:1; 32:3; 16; 34:8; 10; 11; 15(2); 16; 18; 36:4; 11; 13; 16; 23; 25; 27; 32; 37:4; 10; 15; 16; 38:1; 7; 27; 39:5; 10; 40:1(2); 7(2); 11(2); 41:2; 4; 9(3); 10; 11; 14; 16(3); 18; 43:1(2); 5; 6; 44:15; 17; 20; 45:1; 52:2; 3; 20; 25; **Lam** 1:7; 9; 2:17(2); **Eze** 1:5; 6(2); 8(2); 10(3); 16; 23(2); 25; 27; 3:6; 8:8; 9:3; 11; 10:6; 10(2); 12; 14; 21; 11:24; 25; 16:14; 17; 17:3; 18; 19:5; 11; 20:6; 15; 24(3); 28; 23:10; 19; 32; 39; 29:18(2); 33:15; 21; 22; 35:5(2); 36:18(2); 21(2); 40:10; 26; 31; 34; 37; 41:6; 18; 23; 24; 42:6; 15; 20; 44:22; 25; 47:3; 7; **Dan** 1:4; 9; 11; 17; 18; 2:24; 3:2; 3(2); 7; 27(2); 4:12; 21; 5:2; 6:24(2); 7:1; 4; 5; 6(2); 7(2); 12; 20; 8:3; 5; 6(2); 15; 9:21; 10:1; 11; 15; 19; **Hos** 1:8; 2:23; 12:3; 4; **Amos** 7:2; **Obad** 5; 16; **Jonah** 1:10; 17; 3:10; 4:10; **Nah** 3:8; **Hab** 3:4; **Hag** 1:12; **Zec** 1:12; 5:9; 7:2; 10:6; 11:10; **Mal** 2:15; **Mt** 1:6; 24; 25; 2:3; 4; 7; 9; 11; 16; 3:4; 4:2; 12; 24; 7:28; 9:8; 10:1; 11:1; 2; 21; 23; 12:7; 10; 13:5(2); 6; 46(2); 53; 14:3; 13; 21; 23; 35; 16:5; 17:8; 18:24; 25(2); 32; 33(2); 19:1; 22; 20:2; 11; 34; 21:28; 32; 45; 22:11; 22; 25; 28; 34(2); 23:30; 24:43; 25:16; 17; 18; 20; 22; 24; 26:1; 8; 19; 24(2); 30; 57; 27:2; 3; 16; 18; 26; 29; 31; 34; 50; 59; 60; 28:12; 16; **Mk** 1:19; 22; 26; 37; 42; 2:4; 25; 3:1; 3; 5; 8; 10(2); 4:5(2); 6; 36; 5:3; 4(2); 15; 18; 19; 20; 25; 26(3); 27; 30; 32; 40; 6:17(2); 18; 19; 30(2); 31; 41; 46; 49; 53; 7:14; 25; 32; 8:7; 9; 14(2); 23; 33; 34; 9:8; 9; 34; 36; 10:22; 11:6; 11; 12:12; 22; 23; 28; 44; 13:20; 14:4; 16; 21; 23; 26; 44; 15:7(2); 8; 10; 15; 20; 24; 44; 16:1; 9; 10; 11(2); 14; 19; **Lk** 1:3; 7; 22; 58; 2:17; 20; 26; 36; 39; 43; 3:19; 4:13; 16; 17; 33; 35; 40; 5:4; 6; 9; 11; 6:8; 7:1; 10; 13; 39; 41; 42; 8:2; 8; 27; 29(2); 39; 42; 43; 47; 9:8; 10; 11; 36; 10:13(2); 33; 39; 11:38; 12:39; 13:1; 6; 11; 14; 17; 14:2; 15:9; 11; 14; 20; 16:1(2); 8; 17:6; 19:15(2); 28; 32; 37; 20:19; 33; 21:4; 22:13; 55; 61; 64; 23:8; 13; 25; 46; 51; 24:1; 14; 21; 23; 24; 37; 40; **Jn** 2:9; 15; 22(2); 4:1; 18; 50; 5:4; 5; 6; 13; 15; 16; 18; 46; 6:11; 13; 14; 19; 23; 25; 60; 7:9; 8:3; 10; 19; 9:6; 8; 15; 18(2); 22; 35(2); 11:6; 13; 17; 21; 28; 32; 43; 45; 46; 57; 12:1; 6; 9; 14; 16; 18; 37; 13:3; 12(2); 21; 26; 29(2); 14:7; 15:22(3); 24(3); 17:5; 18:1; 6; 18; 22; 24; 38; 19:23; 30; 20:12; 14; 18(2); 20; 22; 21:15; 19; **Acts** 1:2(2); 9; 17; 2:30; 44; 45; 3:10; 12; 18; 4:7; 13; 15; 21; 23; 31; 32; 35; 5:23; 27; 34; 40; 6:6; 15; 7:5; 17; 36; 44(3); 60; 8:11(2); 14; 25; 27(2); 9:18; 19; 27(3); 31; 33; 37; 38; 41; 10:8; 11; 17(2); 24; 31; 11:1; 5; 6; 13; 23; 26; 12:4; 12; 16; 17; 19; 25; 13:1; 3; 5; 6; 19; 22; 24; 29; 36; 14:8; 9; 11; 18; 19; 21(2); 23(2); 24; 25; 26; 27(3); 15:2; 4; 7; 12; 13; 30; 31; 33; 16:6; 10(2); 23; 27; 34; 40; 17:1; 9; 13; 18:2; 18; 22; 23; 26; 27; 19:6; 13; 21; 35; 41; 20:2(2); 11; 13; 16; 36; 21:1; 3; 5; 6; 7; 9; 19(2); 29(2); 33; 40; 22:29; 23:7; 12; 13; 30; 34; 24:10; 19; 25:6; 12; 14; 19; 21; 25; 26; 26:30; 32; 27:4; 5; 7; 13; 16; 17; 28; 30; 35(2); 38; 40; 28:3; 6; 9; 11; 18; 19; 23; 25; 29(2); **Rom** 1:2; 4:11; 12; 21; 5:14; 6:21; 7:7(3); 9:10; 23; 29(2); **1Cor** 1:15; 2:8; 7:29; 11:24; 25; 14:19; **2Cor** 1:9; 12; 2:13; 3:10; 7:5; 12; 8:6; 15(4); 9:5; 11:21; **Gal** 1:23; 2:2; 3:21; 4:15; 22; **Eph** 2:3; **Phil** 2:26(2); 27; 3:12; **1Th** 1:9; 2:2; **2Th** 2:12; **Titus** 1:5; **Heb** 1:3; 2:14; 3:16; 17; 4:8; 5:7; 6:15; 7:6; 8:7; 9:1; 4(2); 19; 10:2; 6; 12; 15; 34; 11:5(2); 11; 15(2); 17; 26; 31; 36; 12:9; **Jas** 2:21; 25(2); **1Pet** 2:10; **2Pet** 2:21; **1Jn** 2:7; 19; **2Jn** 5; **3Jn** 13; **Rev** 1:16; 4:4; 7; 8; 5:6; 8; 6:2; 3; 5(2); 7; 9; 12; 8:1; 6; 9; 9:8; 9; 10; 11; 14; 19; 10:2; 3; 4; 10; 13:11; 14(2); 15; 17; 14:18(2); 15:2; 16:2; 17:1; 18:19; 19:12; 20; 20:4(2); 21:9; 12(2); 14; 15; 23; 22:8

HAND

405, 854, 2026, 2225, 2947, 2948, 3027, 3028, 3079, 3221, 3225, 3231, 3325, 3709, 4672, 7126, 7138, 8040, 8041, 8042, *1448, 1451, 1764, 2021, 2186, 5495, 5496, 5497*

Gen 3:22; 4:11; 8:9; 9:2; 5(3); 13:9(2); 14:15; 20; 22; 16:6; 12(2); 19:10; 16(3); 21:18; 30; 22:6; 10; 12; 24:2; 9; 10; 18; 49; 25:26; 27:17; 41; 30:35; 31:29; 39; 32:11(2); 13; 16; 33:10; 19; 35:4; 37:22; 27; 38:18; 20(2); 28(2); 29; 30; 39:3; 4; 6; 8; 12; 13; 22; 23; 40:11(2); 13; 21; 41:35; 42(2); 44; 42:37; 43:9; 12(2); 15; 21; 26; 44:17; 46:4; 47:29; 48:13(4); 14(2); 17(2); 18; 22; 49:8; **Ex** 2:19; 3:8; 19; 20; 4:2; 4(3); 6(3); 7(2); 13; 17; 20; 21; 5:21; 6:1(2); 7:4; 5; 15; 17; 19; 8:5; 6; 17; 9:3; 15; 22; 10:12; 21; 22; 12:11; 13:3; 9(2); 14; 16(2); 14:8; 16; 21; 22; 26; 27; 29; 30; 15:6(2); 9; 12; 20; 16:3; 17:5; 9; 11(2); 18:9; 10(3); 19:13; 21:13; 16; 20; 24(2); 22:4; 8; 11; 23:1; 31; 24:11; 25:25; 29:20; 32:4; 11; 15; 33:22; 23; 34:4; 29; 35:29; 38:15(2); 21; **Lev** 1:4; 3:2; 8; 13; 4:4; 24; 29; 33; 8:23; 36; 9:22; 10:11; 14:14; 15; 16; 17(2); 18; 25; 26; 27; 28(2); 29; 32; 16:21; 22:25; 25:14; 28; 26:25; 46; **Num** 4:28; 33; 37; 45; 49; 5:18; 25; 6:21; 7:8; 9:23; 10:13; 11:15; 23; 15:23; 16:40; 20:11; 17; 20; 21:2; 26; 34; 22:7; 23; 26; 29; 31; 25:7; 27:18; 23; 31:6; 33:1; 3; 35:18; 21; 25; 36:13; **Deut** 1:27; 2:7; 15; 24; 27; 30; 3:2; 8; 24; 4:34; 5:15; 32; 6:8; 21; 7:8(2); 19; 24; 8:17; 9:26; 10:3; 11:2; 18; 12:6; 7; 11; 17; 13:9(2); 17; 14:25; 29; 15:3; 7; 8; 9; 10; 11; 16:10; 17:11; 20; 19:5; 12; 21(2); 23:20; 25; 24:1; 3; 25:11(2); 12; 26:4; 8; 28:8; 12; 14; 20; 32; 30:9; 32:27; 35; 39; 40; 41; 33:2; 3; 34:12; **Josh** 1:7; 2:19; 4:24; 5:13; 6:2; 7:7; 8:1; 7; 18(3); 19; 26; 9:25; 26; 10:6; 8; 19; 30; 32; 11:8; 14:2; 17:7; 19:27; 20:2; 5; 9; 21:2; 8; 44; 22:9; 31; 23:6; 24:8; 10; 11; **Judg** 1:2; 4; 35; 2:15; 16; 18; 23; 3:4; 8; 10(2); 21; 28; 30; 4:2; 7; 9; 14; 21; 24; 5:26(2); 6:1; 2; 9(2); 14; 21; 36; 37; 7:2; 6; 7; 8; 9; 14; 15; 16; 8:6; 7; 15; 22; 9:17; 29; 48; 10:12; 11:21; 12:3; 13:1; 5; 14:6; 15:12; 13; 15; 17; 18(2); 16:18; 23; 26; 29; 17:3; 18:19; 20:28; 48; **Ruth** 1:13; 4:5; 9; **1Sa** 2:13; 4:3; 8; 5:6; 7; 9; 11; 6:3; 5; 9; 12; 7:3; 8; 13; 9:8; 16; 10:18(2); 12:3; 4; 5; 9(3); 10; 11; 15; 13:22; 14:10; 12; 19; 26; 27(2); 37; 43; 16:16; 23; 17:22; 37; 40(2); 46; 49; 50; 57; 18:10(2); 17(2); 21; 25; 19:5; 9(2); 20:16; 19; 21:3(2); 4; 8; 22:6; 17(2); 23:4; 6; 7; 11; 12; 14; 16; 17; 20; 24:4; 6; 10(2); 11(2); 12; 13; 15; 18; 20; 25:8; 26; 33; 35; 39; 26:8; 9; 11; 18; 23(2); 27:1(2); 28:17; 19(2); 21; 30:23; **2Sa** 1:14; 2:19; 21; 3:8; 12; 18(3); 4:11; 5:19(2); 6:6; 8:1; 10:2; 10; 11:14; 12:7; 25; 13:5; 6; 10; 19; 14:16; 19(2); 15:5; 16:6; 8; 18:2(3); 12(2); 14; 28; 19:9(2); 20:9; 10; 21; 21:20; 22(2); 22:1(2); 23:10(2); 21(2); 24:14(2); 16(2); 17; **1Kin** 2:19; 25; 46; 7:26; 8:15; 24; 42; 53; 56; 11:12; 26; 27; 31; 34; 35; 13:4(2); 6(2); 14:18; 15:18; 16:7; 17:11; 18:9; 44; 46; 20:6; 13; 28; 42; 22:3; 6; 12; 15; 19; 34; **2Kin** 3:10; 13; 15; 18; 4:29; 5:11; 18; 24; 6:7; 7:2; 17; 8:8; 20; 22; 9:1; 7; 10:15(2); 11:8; 11; 12:15; 13:3(2); 5; 16(2); 25(2); 14:5; 25; 27; 15:19(2); 16:7(2); 17:7; 20; 39; 18:21; 29; 30; 33; 34; 35(2); 19:10; 14; 19; 20:6; 21:14; 22:2; 5; 7; 9; 23:8; 13; **1Chr** 4:10; 5:10; 20; 6:15; 39; 44; 11:23(2); 12:2; 13:9; 10; 14:10(2); 11; 16:7; 18:1; 19:11; 20:6; 8(2); 21:13(2); 15; 16; 17; 22:18; 26:28; 28:19; 29:8; 12(2); 16; **2Chr** 3:17(2); 4:6; 7; 6:15; 32; 10:15; 12:5; 7; 13:8; 16; 16:7; 8; 17:5; 18:5; 11; 14; 18; 33; 20:6; 21:10(2); 23:7; 10; 18; 24:11; 24; 25:15; 20; 26:11(2); 13; 19; 28:5(2); 9; 30:6; 12; 16; 31:13; 32:11; 13; 14(2); 15(3); 17(2); 22(2); 33:8; 34:2; 9; 10; 17(2); 35:6; 36:17; **Ezr** 1:8; 5:12; 6:12; 7:6; 9; 14; 25; 28; 8:18; 22; 26; 31(2); 33; 9:2; 7; **Neh** 1:10; 2:8; 18; 4:17; 6:5; 8:4(2); 9:14; 27(2); 28; 30; 11:24; 12:31; **Est** 2:21; 3:10; 5:2; 6:2; 9; 8:7; 9:2; 10; 15; **Job** 1:11; 12; 2:5; 6; 10; 5:15; 6:9; 23(2); 9:24; 33; 10:7; 11:14; 12:6; 9; 10; 13:14; 21; 15:23; 25; 19:21; 20:22; 21:5; 16; 23:9(2); 26:13; 27:11; 22; 28:9; 29:9; 20; 30:12; 21; 24; 31:21; 25; 27; 33:7; 34:20; 35:7; 37:7; 40:4; 14; 41:8; **Ps** 10:12; 14; 16:8; 11; 17:7; 14; 18:(2); 35; 20:6; 21:8(2); 26:10; 31:5; 8; 15(2); 32:4; 36:11; 37:24; 33; 38:2; 39:10; 44:2; 3; 45:4; 9; 48:10; 60:5; 63:8; 71:4(2); 73:23; 74:11(2); 75:8; 77:10; 20; 78:42; 54; 61; 80:15; 17(2); 81:14; 82:4; 88:5; 89:13(2); 21; 25(2); 42; 48; 91:7; 95:4; 7; 97:10; 98:1; 104:28; 106:10(2); 26; 41; 42; 107:2; 108:6; 109:6; 27; 31; 110:1; 5; 118:15; 16(2); 119:109; 173; 121:5; 123:2(2); 127:4; 129:7; 136:12; 137:5; 138:7(2); 139:5; 10(2); 142:4; 144:7(2); 8(2); 11(3); 145:16; 149:6; **Prov** 1:24; 3:16(2); 27; 4:27; 6:1; 3; 5(2); 10:4(2); 11:21(2); 12:24; 16:5(2); 17:16; 19:24; 21:1; 26:6; 9; 15; 27:16; 30:32; 31:20; **Eccl** 2:24; 5:14; 15; 7:18; 9:1; 10; 10:2; 11:6; **Song** 2:6(2); 5:4; 8:3(2); **Is** 1:12; 25; 3:6; 5:25(2); 6:6; 8:11; 9:12; 17; 20(2); 21; 10:4; 5; 10; 13; 14; 32; 11:8; 11; 14; 15; 13:2; 6; 14:26; 27; 19:4; 16; 22:21; 23:11; 25:10; 26:11; 28:2; 4; 30:21; 31:3; 34:17; 36:6; 15; 18; 19; 20(2); 37:10; 14; 20; 38:6; 40:2; 10; 12; 41:10; 13; 20; 42:6; 43:13; 44:5; 20; 45:1; 47:6; 48:13(2); 49:2; 22; 50:2; 11; 51:16; 17; 18; 22; 23; 53:10; 54:3; 56:2; 57:10; 59:1; 62:3(2); 8; 63:12; 64:8; 66:2; 14; **Jer** 1:9; 6:9; 12; 11:21; 12:7; 15:6; 17; 21(2); 16:21; 18:4; 6(2); 20:4; 5; 13; 21:5; 7(3); 10; 12; 22:3; 24; 25(4); 23:23; 25:15; 17; 28; 26:14; 24(2); 27:3; 6; 8; 29:3; 21; 31:11; 32; 32:3; 4(2); 21; 24; 25; 28(2); 36; 43; 34:2; 3(2); 20(2); 21(3); 36:14(2); 37:17; 38:3; 5; 16; 18(2); 19; 23(2); 39:17; 40:4; 41:5; 42:11; 43:3; 9; 44:25; 30(3); 46:24; 26(3); 50:15; 51:7; 25; **Lam** 1:7; 10; 14; 2:3; 4; 7; 8; 3:3; 5:6; 8; 12; **Eze** 1:3; 2:9; 3:14; 18; 20; 22; 6:11; 14; 8:1; 3; 11; 9:1; 2; 10:2; 7; 8; 12:7; 23; 13:9; 21(2); 23; 14:9; 13; 16:27; 39; 46(2); 49; 17:18; 18:8; 17; 20:5(2); 6; 15; 22; 23; 28; 33; 34; 42; 21:11; 16; 22; 24; 31; 22:13; 23:9(2); 28(2); 31; 25:7; 13; 14; 16; 27:15; 28:9; 10; 29:7; 30:10; 12(2); 22; 24; 25; 31:11; 33:6; 8; 22; 34:10; 27; 35:3; 36:7; 8; 37:1; 17; 19(2); 20; 38:12; 39:3(2); 21; 23; 40:1; 3; 5(2); 43; 43:13; 44:12; 46:7; 47:3; 14; **Dan** 1:2; 2:38; 3:17; 4:35; 5:5(2); 23; 24; 7:25; 8:4; 7; 25(2); 9:15; 10:10; 11:11; 16; 41; 42; 12:7(2); **Hos** 2:10; 7:5; 12:7; **Joel** 1:15; 2:1; 3:8; **Amos** 1:8; 5:19; 7:7; 9:2; **Jonah** 4:11(2); **Mic** 2:1; 4:10; 5:9; 12; 7:16; **Hab** 2:16; 3:4; **Zeph** 1:4; 7; 2:13; 15; **Zec** 2:1; 9; 3:1; 4:10; 8:4; 11:6(3); 12:6; 13:7; 14:13(3); **Mal** 1:10; 13; 2:13; **Mt** 3:2; 12; 4:17; 5:30; 6:3(2); 8:3; 15; 9:18; 25; 10:7; 12:10; 13; 49; 14:31; 18:8; 20:21; 23; 22:13; 44; 25:33; 34; 41; 26:18; 23; 45; 46; 51; 64; 27:29; 38; **Mk** 1:15; 31; 41; 3:1; 3; 5(2); 5:41; 7:32; 8:23; 9:27; 43; 10:37(2); 40(2); 12:36; 14:42; 62; 15:27; 16:19; **Lk** 1:1; 66; 71; 74; 3:17; 5:13; 6:6; 8; 10(2); 8:54; 9:62; 15:22; 20:42; 21:30; 31; 22:21; 69; 23:33; **Jn** 2:13; 3:35; 7:2; 10:28; 29; 39; 11:44; 55; 18:22; 19:42; 20:25; 27; **Acts** 2:25; 33; 34; 3:7; 4:28; 30; 5:31; 7:25; 35; 50; 55; 56; 9:8; 12; 41; 11:21; 12:11; 17; 13:11(2); 16; 19:33; 21:3; 40; 22:11; 23:19; 26:1; 28:3; 4; **Rom** 8:34; 13:12; **1Cor** 12:15; 21; 16:21; **2Cor** 6:7; 10:16; **Gal** 3:19; 6:11; **Eph** 1:20; **Phil** 4:5; **Col** 3:1; 4:18; **2Th** 2:2; 3:17; **2Ti** 4:6; **Philem** 1:19; **Heb** 1:3; 13; 8:1; 9; 10:12; 12:2; **1Pet** 3:22; 4:7; 5:6; **Rev** 1:3; 16; 17; 20; 2:1; 5:1; 7; 6:5; 8:4; 10:2; 5; 8; 10; 13:16; 14:9; 14; 17:4; 19:2; 20:1; 22:10

HANDS

2651, 3027, 3028, 3709, *849, 886, 2902, 4084, 4475, 5495, 5499*

Gen 5:29; 16:9; 20:5; 24:22; 30; 47; 27:16; 22(2); 23(2); 31:42; 37:21; 22; 39:1; 43:22; 48:14; 49:24(2); **Ex** 9:29; 33; 15:17; 17:12(3); 29:10; 15; 19; 24(2); 25; 30:19; 21; 32:19; 35:25; 40:31; **Lev** 4:15; 7:30; 8:14; 18; 22; 24; 27(2); 28; 15:11; 16:12; 21; 24:14; **Num** 5:18; 6:19; 8:10; 12; 24:10; 27:23; **Deut** 1:25; 3:3; 4:28; 9:15; 17; 12:18; 16:15; 17:7(2); 20:13; 21:6; 7; 10; 24:19; 27:15; 31:29; 33:7; 11; 34:9; **Josh** 2:24; **Judg** 2:14(2); 6:13; 7:2; 11; 19; 20(2); 8:3; 6; 15; 34; 9:16; 10:7(2); 11:30; 32; 12:2; 3; 13:23; 14:9; 15:14; 16:24; 18:10; 19:27; **1Sa** 5:4; 7:14; 10:4; 11:7; 14:13; 48; 17:47; 21:13; 30:15; **2Sa** 2:7; 3:34; 4:1; 12; 16:21; 21:9; 22:21; 35; 23:6; **1Kin** 8:22; 38; 54; 14:27; 16:7; **2Kin** 3:11; 4:34(2); 5:20; 9:23; 35; 10:24; 11:12; 16; 12:11; 13:16(2); 19:18; 22:17; **1Chr** 12:17; 25:2; 3; 6; 29:5; **2Chr** 6:4; 12; 13; 29; 8:18; 12:10; 15:7; 23:15; 29:23; 32:19;

34:25; 35:11; **Ezr** 1:6; 4:4; 5:8; 6:22; 9:5; 10:19; **Neh** 2:18; 4:17; 6:9(2); 8:6; 9:24; 13:21; **Est** 3:6; 9; 9:16; **Job** 1:10; 4:3; 5:12; 18; 9:30; 10:3; 8; 11:13; 14:15; 16:11; 17; 17:3; 9; 20:10; 22:30; 27:23; 30:2; 31:7; 34:19; 37; **Ps** 7:3; 8:6; 9:16; 18:20; 24; 34; 22:16; 24:4; 26:6; 10; 28:2; 4; 5; 44:20; 47:1; 55:20; 58:2; 63:4; 68:31; 73:13; 76:5; 78:72; 81:6; 88:9; 90:17(2); 91:12; 92:4; 95:5; 98:8; 102:25; 111:7; 115:4; 7; 119:48; 73; 125:3; 128:2; 134:2; 135:15; 138:8; 140:4; 141:2; 143:5; 6; 144:1; **Prov** 6:10; 17; 12:14; 14:1; 17:18; 21:25; 22:26; 24:33; 30:28; 31:13; 16; 19(2); 20; 31; **Eccl** 2:11; 4:5; 6; 5:6; 7:26; 10:18; **Song** 5:5; 14; 7:1; **Is** 1:15(2); 2:8; 3:11; 5:12; 13:7; 17:8; 19:25; 25:11(3); 29:23; 31:7; 33:15; 35:3; 37:19; 45:9; 11; 12; 49:16; 55:12; 59:3; 6; 60:21; 65:2; 22; **Jer** 1:16; 2:37; 4:31; 6:24; 10:3; 9; 19:7; 21:4; 23:14; 25:6; 7; 14; 30:6; 32:30; 33:13; 38:4(2); 44:8; 47:3; 48:37; 50:43; **Lam** 1:14; 17; 2:15; 19; 3:41; 64; 4:2; 6; 10; **Eze** 1:8; 7:17; 21; 27; 10:7; 12; 21; 11:9; 13:22; 16:11; 21:7; 14; 17; 22:14; 23:37; 42; 45; 25:6; **Dan** 2:34; 45; 3:15; 10:10; **Hos** 14:3; **Obad** 13; **Jonah** 3:8; **Mic** 5:13; 7:3; **Nah** 3:19; **Hab** 3:10; **Zeph** 3:16; **Hag** 1:11; 2:14; 17; **Zec** 4:9(2); 8:9; 13; 13:6; **Mt** 4:6; 15:2; 20; 17:22; 18:8; 28; 19:13; 15; 21:46; 26:45; 50; 67; 27:24; **Mk** 5:23; 6:2; 5; 7:2; 3; 5; 8:23; 25; 9:31; 43; 10:16; 14:41; 46; 58(2); 65; 16:18; **Lk** 4:11; 40; 6:1; 9:44; 13:13; 20:19; 21:12; 22:53; 23:46; 24:7; 39; 40; 50; **Jn** 7:30; 44; 8:20; 13:3; 9; 19:3; 20:20; 25; 27; 21:18; **Acts** 2:23; 4:3; 5:12; 18; 6:6; 7:41; 48; 8:17; 18; 19; 9:17; 11:30; 12:1; 7; 13:3; 14:3; 17:24; 25; 19:6; 11; 26; 20:34; 21:11(2); 27; 24:7; 27:19; 28:8; 17; **Rom** 10:21; **1Cor** 4:12; **2Cor** 5:1; 11:33; **Gal** 2:9; **Eph** 2:11; 4:28; **Col** 2:11; **1Th** 4:11; **1Ti** 2:8; 4:14; 5:22; **2Ti** 1:6; **Heb** 1:10; 2:7; 6:2; 9:11; 24; 10:31; 12:12; **Jas** 4:8; **1Jn** 1:1; **Rev** 7:9; 9:20; 20:4

HAPPEN

579, 7136, *4819*

1Sa 28:10; **Prov** 12:21; **Is** 41:22; **Mk** 10:32

HAPPENED

1961, 7122, 7136, *1096, 4819*

1Sa 6:9; **2Sa** 1:6; 20:1; **Est** 4:7; **Jer** 44:23; **Lk** 24:14; **Acts** 3:10; **Rom** 11:25; **1Cor** 10:11; **Phil** 1:12; **1Pet** 4:12; **2Pet** 2:22

HAST

1961, 3426, *2192, 5224*

Gen 3:11; 13; 14; 17(2); 4:10; 14; 12:18; 15:3; 18:5; 19:12(2); 19(2); 21; 20:3; 9(3); 10; 21:23; 29; 22:12; 16(2); 18; 24:14(2); 26:10; 27:20; 36; 38; 45; 29:25(2); 30:15; 31:26(2); 28(2); 30; 36; 37(2); 41; 32:10; 28(2); 33:9; 37:10; 38:23; 29; 39:17; 45:10; 11; 47:25; 30; **Ex** 3:12; 4:10; 5:22(2); 23; 9:19; 10:29; 12:44; 13:12; 14:11(2); 15:7; 13(3); 16; 17; 17:3; 20:25; 23:16(2); 29:36; 32:11; 21; 32; 33:1; 12(3); 17(2); **Num** 5:19; 20; 11:11; 21; 14:17; 19; 16:13; 14; 22:28; 29; 30; 32; 23:11(2); 24:10; 27:13; **Deut** 1:14; 31; 2:7; 3:24; 4:33; 8:10; 12(2); 13; 9:2; 12; 26(2); 12:26; 13:2; 6; 16:13; 17:4; 21:8; 10; 11; 14; 22:3; 9; 23:23(2); 24:19; 26:10; 12(2); 13; 14; 15; 17; 28:20; 32:18; **Josh** 2:17; 20; 7:7; 19; 25; 14:9; 15:19; 17:14; 17; **Judg** 1:15; 5:21; 6:36; 37; 8:1; 22; 9:38; 11:12; 35; 36; 14:16(2); 15:11; 18; 16:10; 13; 15(2); 18:3; **Ruth** 2:11(2); 13(2); 19; 3:10; 15; **1Sa** 1:17; 4:20; 12:4(2); 13:11; 13(2); 14; 14:43; 15:23; 26; 17:28; 45; 19:17; 20:8; 19; 30; 22:13(2); 24:17; 18(2); 19; 25:6; 7; 31; 33; 26:15; 16; 28:12; 15; 29:4; 6; 8; **2Sa** 1:26; 3:7; 24(2); 6:22; 7:18; 19; 21; 24; 25(2); 27; 28; 29; 11:19; 12:9(4); 10(2); 14; 21; 14:13; 15:35; 16:8; 10; 18:21; 22; 19:5; 6; 22:36; 37; 40(2); 41; 44(2); 49(2); **1Kin** 1:6; 11; 24; 27; 2:8; 26; 43; 3:6(3); 7; 8; 11(5); 13; 8:24(2); 25; 29; 36; 44; 48; 9:3(2); 13; 11:11; 22; 13:21(2); 22; 14:8; 9(3); 16:2(2); 17:13; 20; 18:18; 37; 20:13; 25; 36; 40; 42; 21:19; 20(2); 22; **2Kin** 1:16; 2:10; 4:2; 13; 5:8; 6:22; 9:18; 19; 10:30(2); 14:10; 17:26; 19:6; 11; 15; 20; 22(2); 23(2); 25; 20:19; 22:18; 19(2); 23:17; **1Chr** 17:8; 16; 17(2); 19; 21; 23(2); 25; 26; 22:8(3); 28:3(2); 20; 29:17; **2Chr** 1:8(2); 9; 11(3); 6:15(3); 16(2); 17; 20; 27(2); 34; 38; 16:7; 9; 19:3(2); 20:11; 37; 21:12; 13(3); 24:6; 25:15; 16(2); 19; 26:18; 34:26; **Ezr** 9:11; 13(2); 10:12; **Neh** 1:10; 6:7; 9:6; 8; 33; 37; **Est** 6:10(2); 13; **Job** 1:8; 10(2); 2:3; 4:3(2); 4; 7:20; 10:4; 9; 10; 11(2); 12; 13; 18; 11:4; 14:5; 15:8; 16:7; 8; 17:4; 22:6; 7(2); 9; 15; 26:2; 3(2); 4; 33:8; 32; 34:16; 36:17; 21; 23; 37:18; 38:4; 12; 16(2); 17; 18; 22(2); 39:19; 40:9; **Ps** 3:7(2); 4:1; 7; 7:6; 8:1; 2; 3; 5(2); 6; 9:4; 5(3); 6; 10; 10:14; 17; 16:2; 17:3(3); 18:35; 36; 39(2); 40; 43(2); 48; 21:2(2); 5; 6(2); 22:1; 15; 21; 27:9; 30:1(2); 2; 3(2); 7; 11(2); 31:5; 7(2); 8(2); 19(2); 35:22; 39:5; 40:5; 6(2); 42:9; 44:7(2); 9; 11(2); 19; 50:16; 18; 21; 51:8; 52:9; 53:5; 56:13; 59:16; 60:1(3); 2(2); 3(2); 4; 61:3; 5(2); 63:7; 65:9; 66:10(2); 12; 68:10; 18(3); 28; 69:19; 26(2); 71:3; 17; 19; 20; 23; 73:23; 27; 74:1; 2(3); 16; 17(2); 77:14; 15; 80:8(2); 12; 85:1(2); 2(2); 3(2); 86:9; 13; 17; 88:6; 7; 8(2); 18; 89:10(2); 11; 12; 13; 38(2); 39(2); 40(2); 42(2); 43(2); 44; 45(2); 47; 90:1; 8; 15; 91:9; 92:4; 102:10; 25; 104:8; 9; 24; 26; 108:11; 109:27; 110:3; 116:8; 16; 118:13; 21; 119:4; 21; 49; 65; 75; 90; 93; 98; 102; 118; 138; 152; 171; 137:8; 138:2; 139:1; 5; 13(2); 140:7; **Prov** 3:28; 6:1; 22:27; 23:8; 24:14; 25:16; 30:32(2); **Eccl** 5:4; 7:22; **Song** 1:15; 4:1; 9(2); **Is** 2:6; 3:6; 9:3; 4; 14:13; 20; 17:10(2); 22:16(3); 23:16; 25:1; 2; 4; 26:12; 14; 15(2); 37:6; 11; 16; 21; 23(2); 24(2); 26; 38:17(2); 39:8; 40:28(2); 43:4; 22(2); 23(2); 24(4); 45:4; 5; 10; 47:6; 10(3); 12; 15; 48:6; 49:20; 51:13; 17(2); 23; 57:6(2); 7; 8(3); 10; 11(3); 60:15; 62:8; 63:17; 64:7(2); **Jer** 1:12; 2:17(2); 18(2); 19; 23; 27; 28; 33; 3:1; 2(3); 5; 6; 13(2); 4:10; 19; 5:3(2); 12:2; 3; 5; 13:4; 21; 25; 14:19(2); 22; 15:6; 10; 17; 20:6; 7(2); 26:9; 28:6; 13; 16; 29:25; 27; 30:13; 31:18; 32:17; 20(2); 21; 22; 23; 24; 25; 36:6; 14; 29(2); 38:25; 39:18; 44:16; 48:7; 50:24; 51:62; 63; **Lam** 1:21(2); 22; 2:20; 21(2); 22; 3:17; 42; 43(3); 44; 45; 56; 58(2); 59; 60; 61; 5:22; **Eze** 3:19; 20; 21; 4:6; 8; 5:11; 8:12; 15; 17; 9:11; 16:7; 17; 18; 19; 20(3); 21; 22; 24(2); 25(3); 26(2); 28(2); 29; 31; 37(3); 43(2); 47; 48; 51(3); 52(3); 54; 58; 59(2); 63; 22:4(4); 8(2); 12(3); 13; 23:30; 31; 35; 41; 25:6; 27:3; 28:2; 4(2); 5; 6; 13; 14; 16; 17; 18; 31:10; 32:9; 33:9; 35:5(2); 6; 10; 11; 12; 36:13; 38:13; 43:23; 47:6; **Dan** 2:23(3); 3:10; 12(2); 18; 5:22; 23(3); 6:12; 13; 9:7; 15(2); 10:19; **Hos** 4:6(2); 9:1(2); 10:9; 13:9; 14:1; **Obad** 15; **Jonah** 1:10; 14; 2:6; 4:10(2); **Mic** 7:20; **Nah** 3:16; **Hab** 1:12(2); 2:8; 10(2); **Zeph** 3:11; **Zec** 1:12; **Mal** 1:2; 2:14; **Mt** 5:26; 6:6; 8:13; 11:25(2); 17:27; 18:15; 19:21; 20:12; 21:16; 25:21; 23; 24(2); 25; 26:25; 64; 27:46; **Mk** 10:21; 12:32; 15:34; **Lk** 1:4; 30; 2:31; 48; 7:43; 10:21(2); 28; 11:27; 12:19; 20; 59; 13:26; 14:22; 15:30; 18:22; 19:17; 20:39; 24:18; **Jn** 2:10; 4:11(2); 17; 18(2); 6:68; 7:20; 8:48; 52; 57; 9:37; 11:41; 42; 13:8; 38; 14:9; 17:2(2); 3; 7; 9; 11; 18; 21; 23(3); 24(2); 25; 26; 18:35; 20:15; 29(2); **Acts** 1:24; 2:28; 4:24; 25; 27; 5:4(2); 8:20; 21; 10:33; 22:15; 23:11; 19; 22; 24:10; 25:12; 26:16; **Rom** 2:20; 9:20; 14:22; **1Cor** 4:7; 7:28; 8:10; **Col** 4:17; **1Ti** 4:6; 6:12; **2Ti** 1:13; 2:2; 3:10; 14(3); 15; **Philem** 1:5; **Heb** 1:9; 10; 2:8; 10:5; 6; **Jas** 2:18; **Rev** 1:19; 2:2(2); 3(4); 4; 6; 13; 14; 15; 3:1; 3; 4; 8(3); 10; 11; 4:11; 5:9; 10; 11:17(2); 16:5; 6

HATH

413, 1172, 1961, 3426, 4672, *2192, 5220, 5224*

Gen 1:20; 3:1; 3; 4:11; 25; 5:29; 14:20; 16:2; 11; 17:14; 18:19; 19:13; 19; 21:6; 12; 17; 26; 22:20; 23:9; 24:27; 35(2); 36(2); 44; 51; 56; 26:22; 27:27; 33; 35; 36(2); 29:32; 33(2); 30:2; 6(3); 18; 20; 23; 27; 30; 31:1(2); 5; 7; 9; 15(2); 16(2); 42; 33:5; 11; 37:20; 33; 38:24; 26; 39:8(2); 9; 14; 41:25; 39; 51; 52; 42:28; 43:23; 44:16; 45:6; 8; 9; 46:32; 34; 47:18; 48:9; 11; **Ex** 3:13; 14; 15; 18; 4:1; 5; 11; 5:3; 23; 7:16; 9:18; 10:12; 12:25; 13:9; 14:3; 15:1(2); 4; 6; 21(2); 16:6; 9; 15; 16; 23; 29; 17:16; 18:10(2); 19:8; 21:8(2); 29(3); 36(2); 22:11; 24:3; 7; 8; 32:24; 33; 35:1; 10; 30; 31; 34; 35; **Lev** 4:3; 22; 23; 28(2); 35; 5:1; 5; 6; 7; 10; 13; 16; 19; 6:2; 4(2); 5; 7; 10; 7:8; 8:34(2); 10:6; 11; 15; 17; 11:9; 12; 42; 12:7; 13:4; 7; 12; 13; 17; 31; 33; 41; 50; 14:43(2); 48; 15:2; 4; 6; 7; 8; 9; 11(2); 12; 13; 32; 33; 16:20; 17:2; 4; 19:8; 22(2); 20:3; 9; 11; 17; 18(2); 20; 21; 27; 21:3; 17; 18(2); 20(2); 21(2); 23; 22:4; 5; 6; 20; 23; 24:14; 19; 20; 25:25; 28; 27:22; 28; **Num** 5:2; 7; 27; 6:9; 21; 10:29; 12:2(2); 14:3; 16; 24; 40; 15:22; 23; 31(2); 16:5; 9; 10; 28; 29; 19:2; 15; 20(2); 20:14; 16; 21:28; 29; 22:10; 23:7; 8(2); 12; 17; 19(2); 20; 21(2); 22; 23; 24:3(2); 4; 6; 8; 11; 15(2); 16; 25:11; 27:4; 30:1; 4(2); 5; 12(2); 15; 31:17; 19(2); 50; 32:7; 21; 24; 31; 36:5; **Deut** 1:10; 11; 21(2); 27; 36(2); 2:7(2); 3:18; 20; 21; 4:3; 7; 8; 19; 20; 23; 32(2); 34; 5:12; 16; 24; 26; 32; 33; 6:3; 17; 19; 20; 25; 7:1; 6; 8; 8:10; 17; 9:3; 4(2); 28; 10:9; 21; 22; 11:4; 25; 29; 12:7; 12; 15; 20; 21(2); 13:5; 10; 12; 17; 14:2; 10; 24; 27; 29; 15:14; 18; 16:10; 11; 17; 17:2; 3; 16; 18:2; 5; 14; 21; 22(2); 19:1; 8; 18; 20:5(2); 6(2); 7(2); 13; 14; 17; 21:1; 3(2); 5; 10; 16; 17; 22:3; 17; 19; 21; 24; 29; 23:1; 24:1(2); 5(2); 25:10; 19; 26:9(2); 11; 16; 18(2); 19(2); 27:3; 28:9; 52; 53; 55; 29:4; 13(2); 22; 24; 30:1; 3; 31:2; 3; 7; 32:6(2); 27; **Josh** 1:13(2); 15; 2:9; 14; 24; 6:16; 22; 7:11; 15(3); 8:31; 10:4; 19; 14:10; 17:14; 18:3; 22:4; 25; 23:3(2); 5; 9(2); 10; 13; 14(2); 15; 16; 24:20; 27; **Judg** 1:7; 2:20; 3:28; 4:6; 14; 6:13; 25; 29(2); 30(2); 31; 32; 7:2; 14; 15; 8:3; 7; 11:23; 36(2); 13:10; 15:6; 10; 16:17; 18; 23; 24; 18:4; 10; 21:11; **Ruth** 1:20; 21(3); 2:7; 11; 20; 4:14; 15; **1Sa** 1:27; 2:5(2); 8; 3:17; 4:3; 7; 17; 6:7; 9; 7:12; 9:24; 10:1; 2; 22; 24; 11:13; 12:13; 22; 24; 13:14(2); 14:10; 12; 29; 38; 45(2); 15:11; 16; 22; 23; 26; 28(2); 33; 16:8; 9; 10; 22; 17:36; 18:7; 22; 19:4; 20:13; 15; 22; 26; 29(2); 32; 21:2(2); 11; 22:8(2); 23:7(2); 10; 11; 22; 25:21(2); 26; 27; 28; 30; 31; 34; 39(3); 26:8; 27:12; 28:7(2); 9(2); 17(2); 18; 21; 29:3; 30:23(2); **2Sa** 1:16; 3:9; 18; 23; 29; 4:8; 9; 5:20; 6:12; 7:27; 9:3; 11; 10:3(2); 12:5; 13; 13:20; 24; 30; 32; 14:19; 20; 22; 30; 15:4; 16:8(2); 10; 11; 21; 17:6; 7; 21; 18:19; 28; 31; 19:27; 42; 20:21; 22:21; 25; 36; 23:5; **1Kin** 1:19(3); 25(2); 26; 29; 37; 43; 44; 48; 51; 2:24(2); 31; 38; 5:4; 7; 8:15; 20; 56(2); 9:8; 9; 12:11; 13:3; 26(2); 14:11; 16:16(2); 18:10; 19:18; 22:23(2); 28; **2Kin** 1:9; 11; 2:2; 4; 6; 16; 3:7; 10; 13; 4:2; 14; 27(2); 5:20; 22; 6:29; 32; 7:6; 8:1; 4; 9; 10; 13; 10:10; 14:10; 17:26; 18:22(2); 27(2); 33; 19:4(2); 16; 21(3); 20:9; 21:11(3); 22:10; 16; **1Chr** 14:11; 15:2; 16:12; 17; 17:25; 19:3; 22:11; 18(2); 23:25; 28:4; 5(2); 10; 29:1; **2Chr** 2:11(2); 12; 15; 6:1; 4; 10(2); 7:21; 22; 8:11; 13:6; 14:7; 15:3; 18:22(2); 27; 20:37; 23:3; 24:20; 25:8; 16; 28:9; 29:8; 11; 30:8; 31:10; 32:12; 34:18; 36:23(2); **Ezr** 1:2(2); 4:3; 18; 19(2); 5:3; 16; 6:12; 7:27; 28; 9:2; 8; 9(2); **Neh** 9:32; **Est** 1:15; 16; 5:5; 8; 6:3; **Job** 1:10; 11; 12; 16; 21; 2:4; 3:23; 5:16; 6:5; 7:8; 9:4(2); 10:12; 12:9; 13; 13:1(2); 16:7; 11; 12(2); 17:6; 9; 19:6(2); 8(2); 9; 10(2); 11; 13; 21; 20:15; 19(3); 21:21; 31; 23:10; 11; 17; 26:2; 3; 6; 10; 13(2); 27:2(2); 8; 28:6; 7; 30:11; 19; 31:5; 7(2); 17; 27(2); 32:14; 19; 33:2; 4(2); 34:5(2); 9; 13(2); 35; 35:15; 36:23; 38:5(2); 25; 28(2); 29; 36(2); 39:5(2); 17(2); 19; 41:11; 42:7; **Ps** 2:7; 4:3; 5:4; 6:8; 9; 7:12; 13; 14; 9:7; 10:6; 11(2); 13; 13:6; 14:1; 16:7; 18:20; 24; 35(2); 19:4; 22:24(2); 31; 24:2; 4(2); 28:6; 31:21; 33:12; 35:8; 21; 27; 36:3; 37:16; 40:3; 41:9; 44:15; 45:2; 7; 46:8; 50:1; 2; 53:1; 5(2); 54:7(2); 55:5; 18; 20(2); 60:6; 62:11; 66:14; 16; 19(2); 20; 68:10; 28; 69:7; 9; 20; 31; 71:11; 72:12; 74:3; 18; 77:9(2); 78:4; 69; 80:15; 84:3; 88:4; 91:14(2); 93:1; 98:1(2); 2(2); 3; 100:3; 101:5; 102:19; 103:10; 12; 19; 104:16; 105:5; 8; 107:2; 16; 108:7; 109:11; 110:4; 111:4; 5; 6; 9; 112:9(2); 115:3(2); 12; 16; 116:1; 2; 7; 118:18(2); 24; 27; 119:20; 50; 53; 139; 167; 120:6; 124:6; 126:2; 3; 127:5; 129:4; 132:11; 13(2); 135:4; 136:24; 138:6; 143:3(3); 146:5; 147:13(2); 20; 148:6(2); 150:6; **Prov** 3:19(2); 7:20; 26; 9:1(2); 2(3); 3; 10:13; 23; 12:9; 13:4; 7(2); 14:20; 21; 31; 32; 33; 15:14; 15; 23; 16:4; 22; 17:8; 16; 20(2); 21; 24; 27; 18:2; 24; 19:17(2); 23; 25; 20:12; 22:9; 23:6; 29(6); 24:29; 25:8; 28; 28:11; 22; 30:4(4); 15; **Eccl** 1:3; 9; 10; 13; 2:12; 21; 22(2); 3:9; 10; 11(2); 15(2); 19; 4:3(2); 8; 10; 5:4; 16(2); 17; 19(2); 6:2; 5(2); 6; 8(2); 10; 7:13; 14; 29; 8:8(2); 15; 9:9; 10:20; **Song** 1:4; 6; 3:8; 8:6; 8; **Is** 1:2; 12; 20; 30; 5:1; 14; 25(2); 6:7; 8:18; 9:2; 8; 10:10; 12; 14; 28; 12:5; 14:4; 5; 9; 24; 27; 32; 16:13; 14; 19:12; 14; 17; 20:3; 21:4; 6; 9; 16; 17; 22:25; 23:4; 8; 9; 11; 24:3; 6; 25:8; 27:7; 28:2; 25; 29:4; 8; 10(3); 30:24; 33; 31:4; 33:5; 8(2); 14; 34:2(2); 6; 16(2); 17(2); 36:7; 12(2); 18; 37:4(2); 17; 22(3); 38:7; 15(2); 40:2; 5; 12; 13(2); 20; 21; 26; 41:4; 20(2); 26; 42:25(2); 43:27; 44:10; 18; 20; 23(2); 45:9; 18; 21(2); 47:10; 48:5(2); 13(2); 14(2); 16; 20; 49:1(2); 2(3); 10; 13; 14(2); 21(2); 50:4; 5; 10; 51:9; 10(2); 13; 18(2); 52:9(2); 10; 53:1; 2; 4; 6; 10; 12; 54:6; 10; 55:1; 5; 56:3(2); 58:14; 59:3; 60:9; 61:1(2); 9; 10(2); 62:8; 11; 63:7(2); 64:4(2); 65:20; 66:2; 8(2); **Jer** 2:11; 30; 37; 3:3; 6(2); 10; 11; 24; 4:17; 27; 5:23; 6:6; 24; 30; 7:29; 8:14; 21; 9:12; 10:12(3); 11:15(2); 16; 17; 18; 13:15; 14:19; 15:9(3); 16:10; 18:13(2); 15; 20:3; 13; 22:8; 21; 23:9; 17; 18(3); 28(2); 35(2); 37(2); 25:3; 4; 5; 13; 31; 36; 38; 26:11; 13; 15; 16; 27:13; 28:9; 15; 29:15; 26; 31; 32; 31:3; 11; 22; 32:31; 33:24(2); 34:14(2); 35:8; 16; 18; 36:7; 28; 38:21; 40:2; 3(2); 5; 14; 42:18; 19; 21; 43:2; 45:3; 46:10; 12(2); 17; 47:7(2); 48:8; 11(4); 36; 39; 42; 49:1(2); 16; 20(2); 24; 30(2); 50:6; 14; 15(2); 17(2); 25(2); 29(2); 43; 45(2); 51:5; 7; 10; 11; 12; 14; 15(3); 30; 34(6); 44; 49; 51; 55; **Lam** 1:2; 5; 8; 9; 10(2); 12; 13(4); 14(2); 15(3); 17; 2:1; 2(5); 3(2); 4; 5(4); 6(4); 7(3); 8(3); 9; 17(6); 22; 3:1; 2; 4(2); 5; 6; 7(2); 9(2); 11(2); 12; 13; 15(2); 16(2); 20; 28; 4:11(4); 16; **Eze** 2:3; 5; 3:20; 4:14; 5:6; 6:9; 7:10(2); 8:12; 9:9; 12:9; 13:6; 14:9; 15:5; 16:48; 51; 17:12; 13(3); 18; 19(2); 20; 18:6(4); 7(5); 8(4); 9(2); 11; 12(5); 13(3); 14; 15(3); 16(5); 17(4); 19(3); 21; 22(2); 24(3); 26; 27; 28; 19:14(2); 21:11; 22:11(3); 13; 28; 24:12; 24; 25:12(2); 26:2; 27:26; 29:3; 9; 31:10; 33:13; 16(2); 32; 33; 36:2; 44:2; 25; **Dan** 1:10; 2:27; 37; 38(2); 45; 3:5; 28; 4:2; 5:26; 6:22(2); 27; 9:12(3); 14; 11:12; **Hos** 1:2; 2:5(2); 12; 4:1; 12; 19; 5:6; 6:1(2); 11; 7:4; 8; 12; 8:3; 5; 7; 9; 11; 14(2); 10:1; 12:2; 13:16; **Joel** 1:2; 4(6); 6; 7(2); 19(2); 20; 2:2; 20; 23; 25; 26; 32; 3:8; **Amos** 3:1; 4; 6; 8(2); 4:2; 6:8; 7:1; 4; 10; 8:1; 7; 9:6; **Obad** 3; 18; **Jonah** 1:9; **Mic** 2:4(3); 4:4; 5:1; 3; 6:2; 8; 9; **Nah** 1:3; 14; 2:2; 3:19; **Hab** 2:18; **Zeph** 1:7(2); 3:15(2); **Hag** 2:19; **Zec** 1:2; 6; 10; 2:8; 9; 11; 3:2; 4:9; 10; 6:15; 7:7; 12; 10:3(2); 13:4; **Mal** 1:4; 9; 14; 2:10; 11(3); 14; **Mt** 3:7; 5:23; 28; 31; 33; 38; 43; 8:20; 9:6; 22; 11:11; 15; 18; 13:9; 12(3); 21; 27; 28; 43; 44(2); 54; 56; 15:13; 16:17; 19:6; 29; 20:7; 21:3; 24:45; 25:28; 29(3); 26:10; 12; 13; 65; 27:23; **Mk** 2:10; 3:22; 26; 29; 30; 4:9; 25(3); 5:19(2); 34; 6:2; 7:6; 37; 9:17; 22; 10:9; 29; 52; 11:3; 12:43; 13:20(2); 14:6; 8; 9; 15:14; **Lk** 1:25; 36; 47; 48; 49; 51(2); 52; 53(2); 54; 68; 69; 78; 2:15; 3:7; 11(3); 4:18(2); 5:24; 7:5; 16; 20; 33; 44; 45; 46; 50; 8:8; 16; 18(2); 39; 46; 48; 9:58; 10:40; 42; 11:33; 12:5(2); 44; 13:16; 25; 14:29; 33; 35; 15:5; 9; 27(2); 30; 17:19; 18:29; 42; 19:16; 18; 24; 25; 26(3); 31; 34; 20:24; 21:3; 4; 22:29; 31; 36(2); 23:22; 41; 24:34; 39; **Jn** 1:18(2); 2:17; 3:13; 18; 29; 32; 33(2); 34; 35; 36; 4:33; 44; 5:22; 23; 24; 26(2); 27; 30; 36(2); 37(2); 38; 6:9; 27; 29; 39(2); 44; 45(2); 46(2); 47; 54; 57; 7:29; 31; 38; 42; 8:10; 28; 29; 37; 40; 9:3; 17; 21; 30; 10:20; 21; 36; 11:39; 12:7; 38(2); 40; 48; 13:18; 14:9(2); 21; 30; 15:9; 13; 16:6; 15; 21;

17:14; 25; 18:11; 19:11; 20:21; **Acts** 1:7; 2:24; 32; 33; 36; 3:13; 15; 16(2); 18; 21; 4:16; 5:3; 31; 32; 7:50; 9:12; 13; 14; 17; 10:15; 28; 11:8; 9; 18; 12:11(2); 13:23; 33(2); 47; 15:14; 21; 17:7; 26(2); 31(4); 19:26; 20:28(2); 21:28; 22:14; 23:9; 17; 18; 24:6; 25:25; 27:24; 28:4; **Rom** 1:19; 3:1; 7; 25; 4:1; 2; 5:15; 21; 6:9; 7:1; 2; 8:2; 20; 9:6; 18; 19; 21; 24; 31; 10:9; 16; 11:1; 2; 7(2); 8; 32; 34(2); 35; 12:3; 13:8; 14:3; 15:18; 26; 27; 16:2(2); **1Cor** 1:11; 20; 27(2); 28; 2:9(2); 10; 16; 3:14; 4:9; 5:2; 3; 6:14; 7:4(2); 7; 12; 13; 15; 17(2); 25; 28; 37(2); 9:14; 10:13; 12:12; 18(2); 24; 28; 14:26(5); 15:25; 27; 38; 16:2; **2Cor** 1:21; 22; 2:5; 3:6; 4:4; 6; 5:5(2); 10; 18(2); 19; 21; 6:14(2); 15(2); 16(2); 7:8; 8:12(2); 9:2; 9(2); 10:8; 13; 13:10; **Gal** 3:1(2); 13; 22; 4:6; 27(2); 5:1; **Eph** 1:3; 4; 6; 8; 9; 22; 2:1; 5; 6; 10; 14(2); 3:9; 4:32; 5:2(2); 5; **Phil** 1:6; 2:9; 22; 3:4; 4:10; **Col** 1:12; 13(2); 21; 26; 2:12; 13; 18; 3:25; 4:13; **1Th** 2:12; 4:7; 8; 5:9; **2Th** 2:13; 16(2); **1Ti** 1:12; 4:3; 5:8; 6:16(2); **2Ti** 1:7; 9; 10(2); 2:4; 4:10; 15; **Titus** 1:3; 9; 2:11; **Philem** 1:18; **Heb** 1:2(2); 4; 9; 2:5; 13; 18; 3:3(2); 4:10; 7:24; 8:6; 13; 9:20; 26; 10:14; 20; 29(3); 30; 35; 11:10; 16; 12:26; 13:5; **Jas** 1:12; 15; 2:5(2); 13; 14; 17; 3:7; 5:7; **1Pet** 1:3; 15; 2:9; 3:18; 4:1(3); 10; 5:10; **2Pet** 1:3(2); 9; 14; 3:15; **1Jn** 2:11; 23(2); 25; 27; 3:1; 3; 6; 15; 17; 24; 4:12; 13; 16; 18; 20(2); 5:9; 10(2); 11; 12(4); 20; **2Jn** 9(2); **3Jn** 11; 12; **Jude** 6; **Rev** 1:6; 2:7; 11; 12; 17; 18; 29; 3:1; 6; 7; 13; 22; 5:5; 9:11; 10:7; 12:6; 12; 13:18; 16:9; 17:7; 9; 17; 18:5; 6; 7; 20; 19:2(2); 7; 16; 20:6(2)

HAVE

383, 935, 1167, 1934, 1961, 3045, 3318, 3426, 3947, 4672, 5375, 5674, 5921, 474, 568, 1099, 1526, 1699, 1751, 2070, 2071, 2076, 2192, 2701, 2983, 3335, 3918, 5224, 5225

Gen 1:26; 28; 29; 30; 4:1; 20; 23; 6:7(2); 7:1; 4; 8:21; 9:3; 17; 11:6(2); 12:19; 14:22; 23; 24; 15:18; 16:5; 13; 17:5; 20(2); 18:3; 10; 12; 14; 21; 27; 31; 19:8(2); 21; 20:5; 9; 16; 21:7(3); 23; 30; 22:16; 24:19; 25; 31; 33; 26:10(2); 27; 29(3); 32; 27:19; 33(2); 37(3); 40; 28:15(2); 22; 29:34; 30:3; 8(2); 16; 18; 20; 26(2); 27(2); 29; 31:6; 12; 27; 38(3); 41; 43; 51; 32:4; 5(2); 30; 33:9; 10(2); 11; 34:30; 35:17; 37:6; 8; 9; 32; 40:8; 15; 41:15(2); 28; 41; 42:2; 36; 43:7; 21; 22; 44:4; 5; 15; 19; 20; 45:13; 46:30; 32(2); 47:1; 4; 9(2); 23; 26; 29; 48:22; 49:18; 23; 26; 50:4; 5; **Ex** 1:18(2); 2:20; 22; 3:7(2); 9; 12; 16; 17; 4:11; 21; 5:14; 21; 6:4; 5(2); 12; 7:1; 9:16; 27; 10:1; 2(2); 6; 16; 12:17; 31; 32; 14:5(2); 13; 18; 15:5; 17; 26; 16:3; 12; 32; 17:16; 18:3; 16; 19:4; 20:2; 3; 22(2); 21:4(2); 8; 9; 31(2); 22:3; 8; 23:13; 20; 24:12; 14; 26:2; 28:3; 7; 32; 29:35; 31:2; 3; 6(3); 11; 32:7; 8(5); 9; 13; 30; 31(2); 34; 33:13; 16; 34:9; 10; 27; **Lev** 4:13; 14; 6:3; 17; 7:7; 8; 10; 33; 34(2); 10:17; 18; 19(3); 11:10; 11; 13; 21; 23; 12:2; 13:2; 10; 13; 24; 29; 38; 55; 15:19; 25; 16:4; 17:7; 11; 18:27; 19:23; 31; 36; 20:6; 12; 13; 24(2); 25; 26; 22:13; 23:7; 14; 24; 39; 24:22; 25:26; 31; 44; 26:9; 13; 26; 37; 40; 41(2); 27:20; **Num** 3:12; 32; 4:15; 5:7; 8; 18; 19; 20; 27; 8:16; 18; 19; 9:14; 11:11; 12(2); 13; 15; 18; 20(2); 12:11(2); 13:32; 14:11; 14; 15; 20; 22(3); 27; 28; 29; 31; 35; 40; 15:22; 29; 16:15(2); 28; 30; 41; 18:6; 7; 8(2); 11; 12; 19; 20(2); 21; 23; 24(3); 26; 30; 32; 20:4; 5; 12; 15; 17; 24; 21:5; 7(2); 30(2); 34; 22:28; 34; 38; 23:4(2); 20; 24:19; 25:13; 18; 27:8; 9; 10; 11; 12; 17; 28:25; 26; 29:1; 7; 12; 35; 30:9; 31:15; 18; 49; 50; 32:4; 5; 11; 12; 17; 18; 23; 30; 33:53; 34:6; 14(2); 15; 35:3; 8(2); 13; 22; 28; **Deut** 1:6; 8; 28(2); 41; 2:3; 5; 9; 19; 24; 31; 3:19(2); 20(2); 21; 4:3; 5; 9; 25; 5:7; 24(2); 26; 28(4); 6:10; 11; 7:16; 24; 9:7; 8; 12(2); 13; 20; 23; 24; 10:21; 11:2(2); 7; 28; 12:21; 31(2); 13:13(2); 17; 14:9; 15:21; 17:3; 5; 18:1; 2; 8; 17(2); 20; 19:14; 19; 20:9; 18; 21:7(2); 11; 14; 15(2); 18(2); 22; 23:12; 13; 25:5; 13; 14; 15(2); 26:10; 13(4); 14(4); 28:21; 31; 36; 40; 48; 51; 64; 65; 66; 29:2; 3; 5; 6(2); 16; 17; 19; 25; 30:1; 3; 15; 19; 31:5; 13; 16; 18; 20(2); 21; 27; 29; 32:5; 21(2); 33:9(2); 34:4; **Josh** 1:3; 8; 9; 15(2); 2:10; 12; 13; 3:4; 5:9; 6:2; 7:11(4); 20(2); 8:1; 6; 8(2); 9:9; 19; 22; 24; 10:8; 11:20; 13:6; 8; 14:9; 17:16; 17; 18; 18:7(2); 22:2(2); 3(2); 11; 16(2); 23; 24(2); 25; 27; 31(2); 23:3; 4(2); 8; 15; 16(2); 24:7(2); 13; 22; **Judg** 1:2; 7; 2:1; 2(2); 20; 3:19; 20; 5:13(2); 30(2); 6:10; 14; 17; 22; 7:9; 8:2; 9:16(4); 18(2); 19; 48(2); 10:10(2); 13; 14; 15; 11:27; 35; 13:15; 22; 23(3); 14:2; 6; 15(2); 16; 15:7; 11; 16; 16:17; 17:13; 18:9; 14; 24(2); 20:5(2); 6; 10; 21:7; 18; **Ruth** 1:8; 12(3); 2:9(2); 10; 21; 3:3; 18; 4:9; 10; **1Sa** 1:15(2); 16; 20; 23; 28; 2:5; 15; 29; 3:12; 13; 14; 4:9; 5:10; 6:21; 7:6; 8:7(2); 8(2); 18; 19; 9:7; 8; 16; 24; 10:19(2); 11:9; 12:1(2); 2; 3(5); 5; 10(3); 13(2); 17; 19; 20; 13:12; 13; 14:29; 33; 15:3; 11; 13; 15(2); 20(4); 21; 24(2); 30; 16:1(2); 7; 18; 17:25; 29; 39; 18:8(3); 19; 19:4; 20:1; 3; 7; 12; 23; 29; 42; 21:2(2); 4; 5; 8; 14; 15(2); 22:8; 13; 22; 23:21; 27; 24:10; 11; 17; 25:7; 11; 21; 30(2); 31; 35(2); 26:16; 18; 19(2); 21(3); 27:5; 10; 28:9; 15; 21(2); 22; 29:3; 6; 8(2); 9; 10; 30:22; **2Sa** 1:10; 16; 2:5(2); 6; 7; 3:8; 4:6; 10(2); 11; 7:6(2); 7; 9(2); 11; 22; 9:9; 10; 12:8; 13; 27(2); 13:9; 28; 32; 14:15; 21; 22; 29; 31; 32; 15:7; 26; 34; 36; 16:10; 19; 17:15; 18:11; 13(2); 18; 19:5; 20; 22; 28; 29; 34; 41(2); 42; 43(2); 20:1(2); 21:4; 16; 22:22(2); 24; 30(2); 38; 39; 24:10(3); 17(3); **1Kin** 1:35; 44; 45(2); 2:14; 23; 42; 43; 3:12(2); 13; 5:8; 8:13; 20; 21; 27; 28; 33; 35; 43; 44; 47(3); 48; 50(3); 59; 9:3(2); 4; 6; 7(2); 9(2); 11:11; 13; 32(2); 33(3); 36(2); 12:9; 16(2); 14:15; 15:19; 17:4; 9; 12; 18; 18:9; 18(2); 36; 19:10(2); 14(2); 18(2); 20; 20:4; 5; 28; 31; 21:2; 20; 22:11; 17(2); **2Kin** 2:21; 3:13; 23; 27; 5:6; 13; 7:12; 17; 9:3; 5; 6; 12; 26; 10:8; 19; 24; 11:15; 13:17; 19; 17:38; 18:14; 20; 34; 35; 19:6; 11; 12(2); 17; 18(2); 20; 24(2); 25(3); 20:3(2); 5(2); 9; 15(3); 17; 21:7; 8; 15(2); 22:4; 5; 8; 9(3); 13; 17(2); 19; 23:27(2); **1Chr** 11:19; 15:12; 17:5(2); 6(2); 8(3); 20; 21:8(3); 17(2); 22:14(2); 28:6; 29:2; 3(4); 14; 16; 17(2); 19; **2Chr** 1:11; 12(3); 2:13; 6:2; 6(2); 10; 11; 18; 19; 24; 26; 33; 34; 37(3); 38(2); 39; 7:12(2); 16; 17; 18; 19; 20(2); 10:9; 16(2); 12:5(2); 7; 13:7; 9(2); 10; 11; 14:7(2); 11; 16:3; 9; 18:16(2); 20:8; 12; 21:15; 23:14; 24:20; 25:9; 28:9; 11; 13; 29:6(3); 7(2); 9; 18; 19; 31; 31:10(2); 32:13; 17; 33:7; 8(2); 34:15; 17(2); 21; 24; 25(2); 27; 35:21(2); 23; **Ezr** 4:3; 12; 14(2); 15; 16; 19; 20(2); 6:9; 11; 12; 7:15; 20; 9:1; 2(2); 7(2); 10; 11; 10:2(2); 10(2); 13; 14; **Neh** 1:6(2); 7(2); 9; 2:5; 20; 4:5; 5:3; 4; 5; 8; 14; 19; 6:13; 14; 9:33; 34; 35; 37; 10:37; 13:14; 29; **Est** 1:18; 3:9; 4:11; 5:4; 8; 7:3; 8:5; 7(2); 9:1; 12(2); **Job** 1:5; 15; 17; 3:9; 13(2); 4:4; 8; 5:3; 27; 6:8; 10(2); 15; 24; 7:20; 8:4(2); 18; 10:8; 19(2); 12:3; 13:18; 14:15; 22; 15:17; 18(2); 16:2; 3; 10(3); 15; 18; 17:13; 14; 18:17; 19; 19:3; 4; 14(2); 21(2); 20:3; 7; 21:3; 15; 29; 22:9; 15; 25; 26; 23:11; 12(2); 24:7; 19; 27:12; 28:8; 22; 30:1(3); 11; 13; 16; 31:5; 9(2); 16(2); 17; 18; 19; 20; 21; 24(2); 28; 30; 39(2); 32:13; 33:2; 8; 24; 27; 34:2; 31; 32; 35:3; 36:2; 9; 16; 38:17; 23; 39:6; 40:5; 42:3; 5; 7; 8; **Ps** 2:4; 6; 7; 3:6; 4:1; 5:10; 6:2; 7:3; 4(2); 8:6; 9:13; 10:2; 12:4; 13:4; 5; 14:1; 4; 6; 16:6; 8; 17:4; 6; 11(2); 14; 18:21(2); 29(2); 37; 38; 43; 19:13; 22:12(2); 16(2); 25:6; 16; 26:1(2); 3; 4; 5; 8; 27:4; 7; 30:10; 31:4; 6; 9; 13; 17; 32:5; 9; 33:21; 35:7(2); 25(2); 37:14(2); 25(2); 35; 38:8; 40:9(2); 10(3); 12(2); 41:4; 42:3; 44:1(2); 17(2); 18; 20; 45:1; 8; 48:8(2); 9; 49:14; 50:5; 8; 51:1; 4; 53:1; 4(2); 54:3; 55:9; 12(2); 19; 56:4; 11; 57:6(2); 59:8; 62:11; 63:2; 66:14; 68:13; 24; 69:7; 22; 35; 71:6; 17; 18; 72:8; 73:7; 13; 14; 25; 28; 74:7(2); 8; 18; 20; 76:5(2); 77:5; 78:3(2); 79:1(2); 2; 3; 6(2); 7; 12; 81:14; 15(2); 16(2); 82:6; 83:2; 3; 4; 5; 8; 85:10; 86:14(2); 16; 88:1; 9(2); 13; 16; 89:2; 3(2); 19(2); 20(2); 35; 51(2); 90:15; 93:3(2); 94:20; 95:10; 98:3; 102:9; 13; 27; 104:12; 33; 106:6(3); 109:2; 5; 111:2; 10; 115:5(2); 6(2); 7(2); 116:10; 118:26; 119:6; 7; 10; 11; 13; 14; 15; 22; 26; 30(2); 31; 40; 42; 43; 47; 48; 51(2); 52; 54; 55(2); 57; 61(2); 66; 67; 69; 71; 73; 74; 79; 85; 92; 94; 95; 96; 99; 101; 102; 106; 110; 111; 112; 117; 121; 126; 133; 139; 143; 152; 161; 165; 166; 168; 173; 174; 176; 123:2; 3(2); 129:1; 2(2); 130:1; 131:2; 132:14; 17; 135:16(2); 17; 140:3; 4; 5(3); 141:9; 142:3; 143:3; 146:2; 147:20; 149:9; **Prov** 1:14; 24(2); 25; 3:30; 4:11(2); 6; 5:12; 13; 7:14(2); 15; 16; 17; 26; 8:14; 9:5; 13:3; 14:26; 17:2(2); 19:10; 20:4; 9; 22:19; 20; 28; 23:24; 35(2); 24:23; 25:7; 27:27; 28:10; 13; 19(2); 21; 27; 29:21; 30:2; 3; 7; 20; 27; 31:11; 29; **Eccl** 1:14; 16(2); 2:19(3); 3:10; 19; 4:9; 11; 16; 5:13; 18; 6:1; 3; 7:12; 15; 23; 27; 28(2); 29(2); 8:9; 9:5; 6; 13; 10:5; 7; 12:1; **Song** 1:6; 9; 2:15; 5:1(3); 3(2); 6:5; 7:13; 8:8; 12; **Is** 1:2(2); 4(2); 6; 9(2); 29(2); 2:8; 3:9; 14; 4:4(2); 5:4(2); 13; 24; 6:5; 12; 7:5; 17; 8:4; 19; 9:2; 17(2); 10:1; 11; 13(4); 14; 29; 13:3(2); 18; 14:1; 24(2); 15:7(2); 16:6; 8; 10; 17:7; 8; 18:2; 7; 19:3; 13; 14; 21:2; 3; 10(2); 22:3; 9; 10(2); 11; 23:2; 12; 24:5; 16(3); 25:9(2); 26:1; 8; 9; 13; 16; 17; 18(5); 27:11; 28:7(2); 15(4); 22; 29:13; 30:2; 7; 18; 29; 31:6; 7; 33:2; 13; 36:5; 19; 20; 37:6; 11; 12(2); 18; 19(2); 25(2); 26(3); 38:3(2); 5(2); 12; 39:4(3); 6; 40:21(3); 29; 41:8; 9(2); 25; 42:1; 4; 6; 14(2); 16; 24; 43:1(2); 4; 7(3); 8(2); 10; 12(3); 14(2); 21; 23; 27; 28(2); 44:1; 2; 8(2); 16; 18; 19(3); 21; 22(2); 45:1; 4(2); 8; 12(3); 13; 19; 20; 21; 23; 24; 46:4; 11(2); 47:6; 48:3; 5; 6; 10(2); 15(3); 16; 19; 49:4(2); 8(2); 13; 15; 16; 20; 21; 50:1(3); 2; 7; 11(2); 51:16(2); 20; 22; 23; 52:3; 5; 53:6(2); 54:7; 8; 9(2); 16(2); 55:4; 7; 56:11; 57:11; 16; 18; 58:3(2); 5; 6; 59:2(2); 3; 8; 21; 60:10; 61:7; 62:6; 9(2); 63:3; 18(2); 64:4; 5; 6; 65:2; 7; 10; 66:2; 3; 19(2); 24; **Jer** 1:9; 10; 16(2); 18; 2:5(2); 11; 13(2); 16; 20; 23; 25; 27; 29; 30; 31; 32; 34; 35; 3:3; 13; 18; 20; 21(2); 25(2); 4:10; 18; 22(3); 28(2); 31; 5:3(4); 5(2); 7; 11; 12; 19; 21(2); 22; 25(2); 31; 6:2; 10; 14; 19; 23; 24; 27; 7:11; 13; 14; 15; 23; 25; 30(2); 31; 8:2(5); 3; 6; 9; 11; 13; 14; 16; 19; 9:5; 13(2); 14; 16(2); 19(2); 10:11; 21; 25(2); 11:5; 10; 13; 17; 20; 12:2; 5; 6(2); 7(3); 8; 10(3); 11; 12; 13(2); 14; 15(2); 13:11; 14; 27; 14:3; 7; 10(2); 13; 14; 16; 20; 15:5; 8(2); 10(2); 15; 16:2; 5; 10; 11(6); 12; 18(2); 19; 17:4; 13; 16(2); 18:8; 15(2); 20; 22; 19:4(5); 5; 13(2); 15(2); 20:12; 17; 21:7(2); 10; 22:9; 12; 23:2(2); 3; 11; 13; 14; 17; 20(2); 21(2); 22; 25(3); 27; 36; 38; 24:5; 25:3(2); 4; 7; 8; 13; 35; 26:4; 5; 11; 12; 27:5(2); 6(2); 8; 15; 28:2; 8; 14(2); 29:4; 7(2); 9; 14; 15; 18; 19; 20; 23(4); 32; 30:2; 5; 11; 14(2); 15; 18; 24(2); 31:3(2); 18; 20; 25(2); 28; 29; 37; 32:23; 29; 30(2); 32; 33(2); 37; 42(2); 33:5(2); 8(3); 14; 21; 24(2); 25; 26; 34:5; 17; 18(2); 35:7; 8; 9; 10(2); 14; 15(3); 16; 17(5); 18; 36:2; 30; 31; 37:18(2); 38:2; 9(3); 22(2); 25; 40:3(2); 10; 41:8; 42:4; 10; 12; 14; 19; 21(2); 43:10; 44:2(2); 3; 9(2); 10; 12; 13; 14; 17; 18(2); 22; 23(3); 25(2); 26; 45:4(2); 46:5; 12; 28; 48:2; 4; 5; 29; 33; 34; 38; 49:9; 10(2); 12; 13; 14; 23; 24; 31; 37; 50:6(4); 7(2); 17; 18; 21; 24; 51:7; 9; 24; 30(3); 32; 50; 51; **Lam** 1:2; 8; 11; 18; 20; 21(2); 2:7; 10(2); 14(3); 16(4); 22; 3:21; 32; 42(2); 46; 53; 4:10; 12(2); 13; 14(2); 17; 5:4; 5; 6; 7(2); 8; 14; 16; **Eze** 2:3; 3:6; 8; 9; 17; 4:5; 6; 14; 15; 5:5; 6(2); 7(3); 9; 11; 13(2); 15; 17; 6:8; 9; 10; 7:4; 9; 14; 20; 8:17(2); 18; 9:1; 5; 10; 11; 11:5; 6(2); 7; 8; 12(2); 15; 16(2); 17; 12:2(2); 6; 11; 22; 28; 13:3; 5; 6(2); 7(3); 8; 10; 12; 14; 15; 22(2); 14:3; 9; 22(2); 23(2); 15:6; 8; 16:5; 7; 27(2); 17:21; 24(6); 18:2; 3; 23; 31; 32; 20:27(2); 41; 43(2); 44; 48; 21:5; 15; 17; 23; 24; 25; 29; 32; 22:4; 7(3); 10(2); 12; 13; 14; 22; 25(3); 26(5); 28; 29(3); 31(3); 23:9; 34; 37(3); 38(3); 39; 40; 24:8; 13(2); 14; 21; 22; 25:15(2); 26:5; 14; 27:4; 5(2); 6(2); 11; 26; 28:10; 14; 16; 22; 25(2); 26; 29:3; 5; 6; 9; 20; 30:8; 12; 16(2); 21; 31:9; 11(2); 12(3); 32:24; 25(2); 27; 32; 33:7; 11; 29(2); 34:4(6); 12; 18(2); 19(2); 21(2); 24; 27; 35:11; 12; 13(3); 36:3; 5(2); 6(2); 7; 22; 23; 33; 36; 37:13; 14; 23; 24; 25(2); 38:8; 12; 17; 19; 39:5; 8; 15; 19; 21(2); 24; 25; 26(2); 27; 28(2); 29; 41:6; 43:8(3); 11; 44:7(2); 8(2); 12; 13; 18(2); 45:5; 10; 21; 47:13; 22; 48:11; 13; 23; 24; **Dan** 2:3; 9; 25; 26; 30; 3:12; 14; 15; 25; 28; 4:9; 18; 26; 30; 5:7; 14; 15; 16(2); 23(2); 6:2; 7; 22(2); 9:5(4); 6; 7; 8; 9; 10; 11(2); 15(2); 10:16; 11:5; 24; 30(2); 43; 12:7; **Hos** 1:6; 7; 2:4; 12; 23; 4:10(2); 12; 18; 5:1; 2; 4; 7(2); 9; 6:5(2); 7(2); 10; 7:1; 2; 5; 6; 7; 9; 13(4); 14; 15; 8:1; 4(3); 7; 10; 12; 9:9; 10:1; 3; 4; 13(3); 12:8; 10(2); 13:2; 6; 14:8(2); **Joel** 1:18; 3:2; 3(2); 4; 5(2); 6; 7; 19; 21; **Amos** 1:3; 13; 2:4(3); 3:2; 4; 5; 15; 4:6(2); 7; 8; 9(2); 10(5); 11(2); 5:11(2); 14; 25; 26; 6:12; 13; 9:7; 15; **Obad** 1; 2; 5; 7(3); 12(3); 13(3); 14(2); 16; **Jonah** 2:9; **Mic** 2:5; 9(2); 13(2); 3:4; 6; 4:6; 9; 5:2; 12; 15; 6:3(2); 12; 7:1; 9; 19; **Nah** 1:12; 2:2; **Hab** 1:14; 3:2; **Zeph** 1:6; 17; 2:3; 8(2); 10(2); 3:4(2); 6; 19; **Hag** 1:6(2); 2:23; **Zec** 1:4; 11; 12; 19; 21; 2:6; 3:4; 9; 4:2; 9; 6:8; 7:3; 8:15; 23; 9:8; 11; 13; 10:2(3); 6; 8(2); 12:10; 14:12; 18; **Mal** 1:2; 6; 7; 10; 12; 13; 2:2; 4; 8(2); 9(3); 10; 13; 17(2); 3:7; 8(2); 9; 13(2); 14(3); **Mt** 2:2; 8; 15; 3:9; 14; 5:13; 21; 27; 33; 38; 40; 43; 46; 6:1; 2(2); 5; 8; 16; 32; 7:22(2); 8:10; 20(2); 29; 9:13; 27; 10:8; 23; 25; 11:5; 17(4); 21; 23(2); 12:3; 5; 7(2); 11; 18; 13:12; 15; 17(3); 35; 51; 14:4; 5; 17; 15:6; 22; 32(2); 33; 34; 16:7; 8; 17:12; 15; 20; 18:12; 26; 29; 33; 19:4; 12; 16; 20; 21; 27(2); 28; 20:10; 12(2); 30; 31; 21:13; 16; 21; 22:4; 31; 23:23(2); 30; 37; 24:25; 43(2); 25:20; 22; 26; 27(2); 29; 40(2); 26:9; 11(2); 65(2); 27:4(2); 19(2); 43; 65; 28:7; 20; **Mk** 1:8; 24; 2:17; 19; 25; 3:15; 4:15; 16; 17; 23; 40; 5:7; 6:18; 19; 36; 38; 48; 7:4; 13; 16; 24; 8:2(3); 5; 16; 17(2); 9:1; 13; 17; 22; 50(3); 10:20; 21; 23; 28(2); 47; 48; 11:17; 22; 23; 24; 25; 12:10; 26; 43; 13:23; 14:5(2); 7(2); 64; **Lk** 1:1; 14; 62; 70; 2:30; 44; 48; 3:8; 4:23; 34; 5:5(2); 26; 6:3; 24; 32; 33; 34; 7:9; 22; 32(4); 39; 40; 8:13; 14; 18; 28; 9:3; 9; 13; 58(2); 10:13; 24(3); 11:5; 6; 41; 42; 52; 12:3(2); 4; 17; 24; 30; 33; 39(2); 48; 50; 13:26; 34; 14:5; 10; 18(2); 19(2); 20; 28; 34; 15:6; 9; 16; 17; 18; 21; 31; 16:11; 12; 24; 28; 29; 17:8; 10(2); 13; 18:21; 22; 24; 28; 38; 39; 19:8; 14; 17; 20; 23; 46; 21:4; 22:15; 28; 31; 32; 37; 71; 23:8; 14(2); 22; 24:17; 20; 21; 25; 26; 28; 39; 41; **Jn** 1:16; 41; 45; 2:3; 4; 10; 3:11; 12; 15; 16; 4:9; 10(2); 17(2); 32; 42; 5:7; 26; 29(2); 36; 37; 38; 39; 40; 42; 46; 6:36; 40; 53; 70; 7:21; 23; 44; 45; 48; 8:6; 12; 19; 26(2); 28; 38(2); 40; 41; 49; 55; 9:27; 41; 10:10(2); 16; 18(3); 32; 11:34; 37(2); 12:8(2); 28; 34; 35; 36; 48; 49; 13:12; 14; 15(2); 18; 26; 29; 34; 35; 14:2; 7(2); 9; 25; 26; 28; 29; 15:3; 9; 10; 11; 12; 15(3); 16(2); 19; 20(2); 22; 24; 27; 16:1; 3; 4; 6; 12; 22; 24; 25; 27(2); 33(4); 17:4(2); 6(2); 7; 8(4); 12; 13; 14; 18; 22; 25(2); 26; 18:8; 9; 20; 21; 23; 30; 35; 39; 19:7; 10(2); 11; 15; 22(2); 20:2(2); 13(2); 15; 25; 29(2); 31; 21:5; 10; **Acts** 1:1; 4; 11; 16; 21; 2:23(2); 36; 3:6(2); 24(2); 4:7; 20; 5:9(2); 21; 26; 28; 6:11; 14; 7:25; 26; 34(3); 42; 52(3); 53(2); 8:24; 9:6; 13; 10:10; 14; 20; 29; 47; 12:6; 13:2; 15; 22; 27; 33; 46; 47; 14:13; 15:24(2); 26; 27; 36; 16:3; 15; 27; 36; 37(2); 17:3; 6; 28(2); 18:10; 19:2(2); 21; 25; 30; 33; 37; 38; 20:18; 20(2); 24; 25; 27; 33; 34; 35; 21:23(2); 25; 22:29; 30; 23:1; 10; 14(2); 20; 21(2); 27; 28; 29; 24:5; 6; 15; 16; 19; 20; 23; 25; 26; 25:8; 10; 11; 15; 16(2); 24; 25; 26(3); 26:16; 32; 27:21(3); 29; 30; 33; 28:6; 17; 18; 20; 27; **Rom** 1:5; 10; 13(2); 32; 2:12(2); 14; 3:9; 13; 17; 23; 4:17; 5:1; 2; 11; 12; 6:5; 14; 17; 19; 22; 8:9; 15(2); 23; 9:2; 9; 13(2); 15(4); 17; 18; 30; 10:2; 3; 14(2); 16; 18; 21; 11:3; 4(2); 11; 30(2); 31; 32; 12:4(2); 13:3; 14:22; 15:4; 15; 17; 19; 20; 21; 22; 27; 28(2); 31; 16:4; 17; 19; **1Cor** 2:8; 9; 12; 16; 3:2; 6; 10; 4:5; 6; 8; 11; 15(3); 17; 5:1; 2; 3; 11; 12; 6:4; 19; 7:2(2); 25; 28; 29; 32; 40; 8:1; 9:1; 4; 5; 6; 11; 12; 15(2); 16; 17; 19; 27; 10:20; 11:3; 10; 14; 15; 16; 22(2); 23; 12:1; 13; 21(2); 23; 24; 25; 30; 13:1; 2(3); 3; 15:1; 2; 15; 19; 24(2); 31; 32; 34; 49; 54(2); 16:1; 12; 15; 17; 18; **2Cor** 1:8; 12; 14; 15; 24; 2:3; 4; 5; 3:4; 12; 4:1(2); 2; 7; 13; 5:1; 12; 16; 6:2(2); 7:2(3); 3; 11; 14; 16; 8:10; 11; 18; 22(3); 9:3; 11:2; 4(3); 6; 7(2); 9; 25; 12:11(2); 21(3); 13:2; **Gal** 1:8; 9; 13; 2:4; 16; 3:4; 21(2); 27(2); 4:9; 11; 12; 15(2); 5:10; 13; 21; 24; 6:10; 11; 13; **Eph** 1:7; 11; 2:18; 3:2; 12; 4:19; 20; 21(2); 28; 5:11; 6:22; **Phil** 1:7; 12; 2:12; 16; 20; 27; 3:3; 4; 8; 13; 16; 17; 18; 4:9; 11; 14; 18; **Col** 1:4; 14; 18; 23; 2:1(2); 6; 7; 23; 3:9;

10; 13; 4:1; 8; 11; **1Th** 2:6; 8; 14(2); 15; 18; 3:5; 6; 4:1; 6; 12; 13(2); 5:1; **2Th** 2:15; 3:1; 2; 4; 9; 14; **1Ti** 1:6; 19; 20; 2:4; 3:7; 13; 5:4; 10(5); 11; 12; 16; 6:2; 10; 21; **2Ti** 1:3; 12(2); 2:18; 4:7(3); 12; 20; **Titus** 3:5; 8; 12; **Philem** 1:7; 10; 12; 13(2); 19; 20; **Heb** 1:5; 2:1; 3:10; 4:3(2); 8; 13; 14; 15; 5:2; 5; 11; 12(2); 14; 6:4; 5; 10(2); 18(2); 19; 7:5; 28; 8:1(2); 3; 7; 9:26; 10:2(2); 26; 34; 36(2); 38; 11:15(2); 12:4; 5; 9; 17; 28; 13:2; 5; 7(2); 9(2); 10(2); 14; 17; 18; 22; 24; **Jas** 1:4; 2:1; 3; 6; 9; 13; 14; 18; 3:14; 4:2(3); 5:3; 4(2); 5(2); 6; 10; 11(2); 15; **1Pet** 1:10; 12; 2:2; 3; 10; 4:3; 8; 5:10; 12; **2Pet** 1:1; 15; 16; 19; 2:14; 15; 20; 21(2); **1Jn** 1:1(4); 2; 3(2); 5; 6; 7; 8; 10; 2:1; 7; 13(3); 14(4); 18; 19; 20; 21; 24(2); 26; 27; 28; 3:14; 17; 21; 4:3; 4; 14; 16; 17; 21; 5:13(2); 14; 15; **2Jn** 1; 4; 6; 8; **3Jn** 4; 6; 9; **Jude** 11; 15(2); 22; **Rev** 1:18; 2:4; 10; 14; 20; 24(2); 25; 3:2; 4; 8; 9; 17; 7:3; 14; 9:3; 4; 11:6(2); 7; 12:17; 13:9; 14:11; 16:6; 17:2(2); 12; 13; 18:3(2); 5; 9; 19:10; 21:8; 22:14; 16

HAVING

1167, 5414, 846, 1722, 1746, 2192, 5225, 5607

Gen 12:8; **Lev** 7:20; 20:18; 22:3; 22; **Num** 24:4; 16; **Deut** 10:3; **Judg** 1:7; 19:3; **Ruth** 1:13; **1Sa** 22:6; 26:2; **1Kin** 22:10; **1Chr** 4:42; 21:16; 26:12; **2Chr** 5:12; 11:12; 23:10; **Ezr** 9:5; **Neh** 10:28(2); 13:4; **Est** 6:12; **Ps** 13:2; **Prov** 6:7; 18:1; **Is** 6:6; 41:15; **Jer** 41:5(2); **Eze** 38:11; 40:44; 44:11; **Dan** 8:20; **Mic** 1:11; **Zec** 9:9; **Mt** 7:29; 8:9; 9:36; 15:30; 18:8; 9; 22:12; 24; 25; 26:7; **Mk** 6:34; 8:1; 18(2); 9:43; 45; 47; 11:13; 12:6; 28; 14:3; 51; **Lk** 1:3; 5:39; 7:8; 8:15; 43; 9:62; 11:36; 15:4; 8; 17:7; 19:15; 20:28; 23:14; 46; **Jn** 4:45; 5:2; 7:15; 13:1; 2; 30; 18:3; 10; **Acts** 2:24; 33; 47; 3:26; 4:37; 12:20; 14:19; 16:24; 18:18; 19:1; 29; 22:12; 23:27; 24:22; 26:10; 22; 27:33; **Rom** 2:14; 9:11; 12:6; 15:23(2); **1Cor** 6:1; 7:37; 11:4; 12:24; **2Cor** 2:3; 4:13; 6:10; 7:1; 9:8; 10:6; 15; **Gal** 3:3; **Eph** 1:5; 9; 2:12; 15; 16; 4:18; 5:27; 6:13; 14(2); **Phil** 1:23; 25; 30; 2:2; 3:9; 4:18; **Col** 1:20; 2:13; 15; 19; **1Th** 1:6; **1Ti** 1:6; 19; 3:4; 4:2; 8; 5:9; 12; 6:8; **2Ti** 2:19; 3:5; 4:3; 10; **Titus** 1:6; 2:8; **Philem** 1:21; **Heb** 7:3; 9:12; 10:1; 19; 21; 22; 11:13(2); 39; 40; **1Pet** 1:8; 2:12; 3:8; 16; **2Pet** 1:4; 2:14; **2Jn** 12; **Jude** 5; 16; 19; **Rev** 5:6; 8; 7:2; 8:3; 9:17; 12:3; 12; 13:1; 14:1; 6; 14; 17; 15:1; 2; 6(2); 17:3; 4; 18:1; 20:1; 21:11

HE

1931, 846

Gen 1:5; 10; 16; 27(2); 31; 2:2(3); 3; 8(2); 19; 21(2); 3; 3:1; 6; 10; 11; 16(2); 17; 22; 23; 24(2); 4:4; 5; 9; 10; 17; 20; 21; 26; 5:1; 2; 4(2); 5; 7; 8; 10; 11; 13; 14; 16; 17; 18; 19; 20; 22; 24; 26; 27; 29; 30; 31; 6:3; 6; 22; 8:6; 7; 8; 9; 10(2); 12; 9:6; 20; 21(2); 25(2); 26; 27; 29; 10:8; 9; 11:11; 13; 15; 17; 19; 21; 23; 25; 12:4; 7; 8(2); 11(2); 16(3); 20; 13:1(2); 3; 4; 14:13; 14; 15(2); 16; 18; 19; 20; 15:4; 5(2); 6(2); 7; 8; 9; 10(2); 13; 16:4; 8; 12(2); 17:1(2); 18(2); 14; 20; 22; 24; 25; 18:1; 2(3); 7; 8(3); 9; 10; 19(2); 33; 19:1; 2; 3(2); 9; 14; 16; 17; 21; 25; 27; 28; 29; 30(3); 33; 35; 20:4; 5(2); 7(2); 13; 16(2); 21:1; 2; 6; 7(2); 11; 12(2); 13; 14; 15(2); 16; 20; 21; 22; 25; 41:1; 5; 8; 11; 12(2); 13; 14; 28; 43(3); 45; 46; 48; 49; 51; 52; 55; 42:2; 4; 6; 7(2); 9; 12; 17; 21(2); 24; 27(2); 28; 29(2); 30(2); 31; 34; 44:1; 2; 5; 6(2); 10(2); 12; 14; 16; 17; 18(2); 31(2); 45:1; 2; 4; 8; 14; 15; 22(2); 23; 24(2); 26(2); 46:1; 2; 3; 7; 28; 29; 47:2; 17; 21; 22; 29; 30; 31; 48:1; 9; 10(3); 12; 15; 17; 19(3); 20(2); 49:4; 8; 9(2); 11; 13; 15; 19; 20; 21; 27(2); 28; 31; 33; 50:6; 10; 12; 14(2); 16; 21; 22; 24; 26; **Ex** 1:9; 16; 21; 2:2; 2; 10; 11(2); 12(3); 13(2); 14; 15(2); 18; 20(3); 21; 22(2); 3:1; 2; 6(2); 7; 13; 16; 4:11; 14; 16(3); 20(3); 21; 22; 26(2); 30(2); 5:21; 6:26; 27; 30; 7:11; 22; 14:4; 6; 7(2); 8(3); 9; 18:4(4); 21; 24; 25; 14:2(2); 5(2); 6; 7; 11; 15; 16(2); 17(4); 18(4); 21; 23; 25; 14:2(2); 5(2); 6; 7; 11; 15; 16(2); 17(4); 18(4); 21; 23; 25; 22(2); 24(2); 25(2); 27(2); 28(3); 15:23(3); 3; 5; 6; 9(2); 12; 13; 15; 16; 18(2); 25; 26; 28(2); 31; 33(3); 34(2); 35; 36; 16:2; 3; 4; 13; 14; 18; 19; 17:2; 4(2); 7; 8(3); 9; 18:4; 20; 24; 26; 27; 30; 31; 19:3; 4; 5; 7; 8; 9; 10; 13; 15(2); 16

Josh 1:15; 17; 18(2); 2:11; 3:1; 10; 4:4; 21; 23; 5:6(2); 7; 13; 14; 6:7; 26(2); 7:6; 15(5); 17(3); 18; 24; 8:4; 10; 12; 14(2); 18; 19; 26(2); 27; 29; 32(2); 33; 34; 9:9; 10; 22; 26; 27; 10:1(2); 7; 12; 28(4); 30(3); 32; 33; 35(2); 37(2); 39(5); 40; 11:1; 9; 11; 12; 14; 21; 23; 26(2); 27(2); 30(3); 31; 17:2; 3; 4; 7; 8(3); 9; 18(4); 20; 24; 26; 29; 27; 30; 31; 32; 34; 17:5(2); 6; 35; **Judg** 1:7; 11; 12; 13; 19; 20; 25; 2:3; 7; 2:10(2); 14(2); 15; 16(2); 17(4); 18(4); 21; 23; 25; 14:2(2); 5(2); 6; 7; 11; 15; 16(2); 17(4); 18(4); 21; 23; 25; 27(2); 28; 31; 3:1; 5; 6; 9; 6:19; 20; 22; 24(2); 25(2); 26; 28(2); 31; 33; 34(2); 35; 36; 16:2; 3; 4; 13; 14; 11:2; 3; 5; 8; 13; 14; 15; 16; 17(4); 19(2); 20; 25:1; 9(2); 19; 22; 25; 27; 28; 29; **1Chr** 1:10; 2:3; 21(2); 23; 3:4(2); 4:10; 5:1(2); 6; 9; 20; 26; 6:10; 7:23(2); 8:7; 8; 9; 11; 10:3; 4; 5;

13(2); 14; 11:2; 8; 11; 13; 19; 20(2); 21(3); 22(2); 23(2); 25; 12:1; 18; 19(2); 20; 13:10(3); 14; 14:4; 15:3; 22(2); 16:2; 3; 4; 12; 14; 15; 16; 21(2); 25; 33; 34; 37; 40; 17:12; 13; 18:2; 3; 6; 10(2); 11; 13(2); 19:3; 5; 8; 10; 11; 12; 17; 20:2; 3; 6; 7; 21:3; 6; 7; 15(2); 19; 26; 27; 28; 30; 22:2; 6; 10(2); 11; 18(2); 23:1; 2; 13(2); 25:10; 11; 12; 13; 14; 15; 16; 17; 18; 19; 20; 21; 22; 23; 24; 25; 26; 27; 28; 29; 30; 31; 26:10; 27:23; 24; 28:4(2); 5; 6(2); 7; 9(2); 12; 14; 16; 17; 20; 29:27(3); 28; **2Chr** 1:4; 5; 14(2); 15; 2:11(2); 18; 3:2; 4; 5(2); 6; 7; 8(2); 9; 10; 14; 15; 16; 17; 4:1; 2; 6; 7; 8(2); 9; 10; 11; 14(2); 21; 5:1; 13; 6:1; 4(2); 9; 10; 11; 12; 13; 7:3; 7; 10; 11; 21; 22; 8:4(2); 5; 11(2); 12; 14; 9:2; 3; 4; 8; 16; 25; 26; 27; 31; 10:2; 4; 5; 6; 8; 9; 15; 18; 11:1(2); 6; 11; 12; 15(2); 20; 21; 22; 23(3); 12:1; 4; 9(2); 12(2); 13(2); 14(2); 13(2); 20; 14:3; 5; 6(2); 7(2); 15:2(3); 4; 8(2); 9; 15; 16; 18(2); 16:1; 3; 5; 6; 8; 10; 12; 14; 17:2; 3; 5; 6; 7; 8; 11; 12; 13; 18:2(3); 3; 7; 14(2); 16; 17; 18; 19; 21; 27; 33; 34; 19:4; 5; 9; 20:15; 21(2); 31(3); 32; 36; 21:2; 3(2); 4; 5(2); 6(3); 7(2); 9; 10; 11; 19; 20(3); 22:2(2); 3; 4; 5; 6(3); 7(2); 8; 9(3); 12; 23:3; 7(3); 10; 19; 20; 24:1(2); 3; 5; 15(3); 16; 19; 20; 22(2); 25; 25:1(2); 2; 3; 4; 5; 6; 14; 15; 16; 20; 21; 24; 27; 26:2; 3(2); 4; 5(2); 6; 8; 10(3); 15(3); 16(2); 19; 20; 21; 23; 27:1(2); 2(2); 3(2); 4(2); 5; 6; 8(2); 28:1(3); 2; 3; 4; 5; 9(2); 19; 21; 22(2); 23(2); 24; 25; 29:1(2); 3; 4; 8; 21(2); 23; 25; 30:6; 8; 19; 31:3; 4; 21(2); 32:2; 3; 5; 6; 9; 17; 21(2); 23; 24(2); 26; 27; 29; 31; 33:1(2); 3(2); 4; 5; 6(3); 7(2); 12(2); 13(2); 14; 15(2); 16; 19(2); 21; 22; 34:1(2); 2; 3(3); 4(2); 5; 6; 7(2); 15:2(3); 16; 18:2(3); 19; 30; 32; 35:2; 21(2); 22; 24(2); 36:2(2); 5(3); 8; 9(3); 12; 13(2); 14; 15; 17(2); 18; 20; 22; 23; **Ezr** 1:1; 2; 3; 4; 3:11; 5:12; 14; 6:17; 7:6; 8; 9(2); 8:23; 31; 35; 10:1; 6(3); **Neh** 1:2; 2:8; 18; 20; 3:12; 14; 15; 4:1; 2; 3(2); 18; 5:13; 6:10; 12; 13; 18; 7:2; 8:3; 5(2); 10; 18; 9:29; 12:8; 13:2; 5; **Est** 1:3; 4; 10; 20; 22; 2:1; 4; 7; 9(2); 17; 18; 3:4(3); 6; 4:4; 5; 8; 11; 5:5; 9(2); 10(2); 11; 14; 6:1; 4; 7:5(2); 7; 8; 10; 8:1; 2; 3; 5; 7; 10; 9:25(3); 30; **Job** 1:10; 11(2); 12; 16; 17; 18; 2:3; 4; 5; 6; 8(2); 10; 4:18(2); 5:12; 13; 15; 18(2); 19; 20; 6:5; 9; 14; 7:9; 10; 8:4; 6; 15(2); 16; 18; 20; 21; 9:3(2); 4; 11(2); 12; 16(2); 17; 18; 19; 22; 23; 24(2); 32; 11:6; 10; 11(3); 12:4; 5; 13; 14(2); 13(3); 14(3); 15(4); 16(4); 17(2); 18; 20(2); 24; 28; 45:9; 13(2); 18(3); 46:4; 6; 7(3); 48:12; 14; 15; 21(3); 49:1; 2(3); 6; 7; 10(2); 50:4(2); 8; 9; 51:3(2); 12; 13; 14(2); 52:6; 9; 13; 15; 53:2(2); 3(2); 4; 5(2); 7(5); 8(3); 9(2); 10(3); 11(2); 12(4); 54:5; 55:1; 5; 6(2); 7(2); 57:2; 13; 17; 58:9; 59:2; 5; 15; 16; 17(2); 18(2); 60:9; 61:1; 3; 10(2); 62:7(2); 63:7; 8(2); 9(3); 10(2); 11(3); 64:4; 65:16(2); 66:6(3); 8; 9; **Jer** 2:14(2); 17; 26; 3:1; 5(2); 4:7; 13; 5:12; 24; 26; 8:4; 8; 9:8; 12(2); 24; 10:10; 12(2); 13(3); 16; 11:16; 12:4; 13:16(2); 21; 14:10; 22; 15:4; 16:15; 17:6; 8; 11; 18:3; 4(2); 19:14; 20:4; 10; 13; 17; 21:2; 7(2); 9(3); 10; 22:4; 10; 11; 12; 16; 19; 28(2); 23:6; 20(2); 28; 31; 25:30(2); 31(2); 38; 26:11; 13; 16; 19(2); 21; 27:20; 29:21; 28; 31; 32(3); 30:7; 21; 24; 31:10; 11; 20; 32:3; 5(2); 28; 33:1; 15; 21; 24; 34:2; 3; 14; 16; 35:8; 14; 16; 18; 36:4; 12; 13; 18; 21; 23; 25(2); 30; 37:2(2); 13(2); 14; 17; 38:6(2); 7; 9; 10; 12; 19; 20(3); 22; 50:8; 19; 34(2); 44; 45(3); 51:6; 12; 15(2); 16(3); 19; 25; 29; 33; 34(2); 44; 16; 17; 25(3); 26; 27; 31; 3:1; 2; 3; 4; 5(3); 8; 9; 10; 12; 13(2); 14(2); 16; 17; 21; 22(2); 23; 26; 27(2); 29; 30; 33; 34; 4:1(2); 2; 4; 9(2); 10; 11; 13; 21; 24; 25(3); 26; 27; 29; 30; 31; 32; 33(2); 34(2); 36; 38; 39; 40; 5:2; 4; 5; 6(2); 8; 9(2); 10(2); 18(3); 20; 21; 22(2); 32; 34; 35; 36; 37; 38; 39(2); 40(2); 41; 43; 6:1; 2; 5(2); 6(2); 7; 10; 14; 16(2); 17; 19; 20(3); 23; 26; 27; 31; 34(2); 37; 38; 39; 40; 41(2); 42; 43; 44; 45; 46; 47; 48(2); 49; 53; 55; 66; 68; 70; 71; 72; 74; 75; 27:3(2); 5; 12(2); 14; 18; 19; 23; 24(2); 26(3); 34(2); 42(3); 43(3); 50; 58; 59; 60(2); 63; 64; 28:6(3); 7(2); **Mk** 1:6; 8; 10; 13; 16(2); 19(2); 20; 21; 22; 23; 26; 27; 31; 34; 35; 38; 39; 42(2); 43; 45; 2:1(2); 2; 4; 5; 8; 10; 12; 13(2); 14(3); 16; 17; 23; 25(3); 26; 27; 3:1; 2; 3; 4; 5(3); 8; 9; 10; 12; 13(2); 14(2); 16; 17; 21; 22(2); 23; 26; 27(2); 29; 30; 33; 34; 4:1(2); 2; 4; 9(2); 10; 11; 13; 21; 24; 25(3); 26; 27; 29; 30; 33; 34(2); 35; 36; 38; 39; 40; 5:2; 4; 5; 6(2); 8; 9(2); 10(2); 18(3); 20; 21; 22(2); 32; 34; 35; 36; 37; 38; 39(2); 40(2); 41; 43; 6:1; 2; 5(2); 6(2); 7; 10; 14; 16(2); 17; 20; 23; 27; 31; 34(2); 37; 38; 39(2); 42(3); 43; 45; 2:1(2); 4; 9(2); 10; 11; 12(2); 14(2); 16; 18(3); 19; 20(2); 21(2); 22(2); 24(2); 25(2); 27; 28; 29; 31; 32; 33(2); 34(2); 36; 38(2); 40; 41; 42; 10:1(3); 3; 5; 11; 13; 14; 15; 16; 17; 20; 22(2); 30; 32; 34; 36; 46; 47(2); 48(2); 49; 50; 52; 11:1; 3; 7; 9; 11(2); 12; 13(4); 17; 19; 23(3); 27; 31; 32; 12(2); 13(3); 3; 13; 20(2); 21; 27; 36; 14:3; 11(2); 13; 14; 15; 16; 17; 20(2); 21; 23(3); 24; 31; 32; 33(2); 34(2); 36; 38; 9:1; 2; 6; 9; 12(2); 14(2); 16; 18(3); 19; 20(2); 21(2); 25; 26(2); 27; 28; 29; 30; 31(3); 33(2); 35; 36(3); 38(2); 40; 41; 42; 10:1(3); 3; 5; 11; 13; 14; 15; 16; 17; 20; 22(2); 30; 32; 34; 36; 46; 47(2); 48(2); 49; 50; 52; 11:1; 3; 7; 9; 11(2); 12; 13(4); 15; 16; 21; 27; 28; 32; 34(2); 35; 37; 38; 43; 13:1; 3; 13; 20(2); 21; 27; 36; 14:3; 11(2); 13; 14; 15; 16; 17; 20; 23(3); 26; 27; 29; 30; 31(3); 32; 33(3); 34(2); 35; 36; 37; 38; 39; 40(2); 41; 42; 43; 44(2); 45(2); 52; 54; 61; 68(2); 70; 71; 72(2); 15:2; 3; 6; 8; 10; 11; 14; 15; 23; 28; 31(2); 35; 39(2); 41; 44(3); 45(2); 46; 47; 16:6(3); 7(2); 9(2); 11; 12; 14(2); 15; 16(2); 19; **Lk** 1:8; 9; 12; 15(2); 16; 17; 21; 22(4); 23; 25; 32; 33; 48; 49; 51(2); 52; 53(2); 54; 55; 60; 62; 63; 64; 68; 70; 73; 74; 2:4; 21; 26(2); 27; 28; 42; 49; 50; 51; 3:3; 7; 11; 13; 15; 16; 17(2); 18; 20; 4:2(2); 9; 10; 13; 15; 16(3); 17(2); 18(2); 20(2); 21; 23; 24; 30; 35; 36; 38; 39; 40; 41(2); 42(2); 43; 44; 5:1; 3(3); 4(2); 5(2); 6; 8(3); 9; 11; 12; 13; 14(2); 15(2); 16; 17(2); 18(2); 19; 20; 21(2); 23; 24; 27; 28(2); 33; 36(2); 39(2); 40; 42; 43; 44; 48; 49; 50; 51(2); 53; 55; 59(2); 10:1; 2(2); 16(3); 18; 22; 23; 26; 27; 28; 29; 31(2); 32; 33(4); 35(2); 37(2); 38; 11:1(2); 12(2); 14; 15; 17; 22(3); 23(2); 24(2); 25(2); 26; 27; 28; 29; 33; 37(2); 38(2); 40; 46; 53; 12:1; 5; 9; 13; 14; 15(2); 16; 17; 18; 21; 22; 28; 36(2); 37(2); 38; 39; 43; 44(2); 46(2); 48; 54; 58; 13:6(2); 7; 8; 10; 12; 13; 17; 18; 20; 22; 23; 25; 27; 32; 35; 14:1; 4; 7(2); 9; 10(2); 11; 12; 15(2); 16; 25; 26; 28; 29; 31(3); 35; 15:3; 4(2); 5(2); 6(2); 11; 12; 14(2); 15(2); 16; 17(2); 20(2); 24; 25(2); 26; 27(2); 28; 29; 31; 16:1(2); 2; 5; 6(2); 7(3); 8; 10(2); 13(2); 15; 22(2); 24(2); 26; 27; 28; 30; 31; 17:1; 2(2); 4; 7; 9(2); 11(2); 12; 14(2); 15(2); 16; 19; 20(2); 24(2); 33; 37; 18:1; 4(2); 7; 8(2); 9; 14; 15; 21; 22; 23(3); 24(2); 27; 29; 31; 32; 33; 35; 36; 38; 39(2); 40(2); 41; 43; 19:2; 3(2); 4(2); 5; 6; 7; 9; 11(2); 12; 13(4); 14(2); 15(2); 16; 17; 20; 22; 25; 29; 33; 37(2); 38(2); 40; 44(2); 46(2); 47; 48; 20:1; 2; 3; 5; 9; 10; 11; 12; 16; 17; 19; 23; 25; 28; 30; 37; 38; 41; 44; 45; 21:1; 2; 3; 5; 8; 10; 29; 37(2); 22:4(2); 5; 8; 10(2); 12; 13; 14; 15; 17; 19;

Prov 2:7(2); 8; 3:6; 12(2); 19; 29; 30; 33; 34(2); 4:4; 5:21; 22; 23(2); 6:13(3); 14(2); 15; 19; 29; 30(2); 31(3); 32; 33; 34; 35(2); 7:8; 19; 20; 22; 8:26; 27(2); 28(2); 29(2); 36; 9:7(2); 8(2); 9(2); 18; 10:3; 4; 5(2); 9(2); 10; 17(2); 18(2); 19; 22; 11:12; 13; 15(2); 17; 19; 25; 26; 27(2); 28; 29; 30; 12:1; 2; 8; 9(2); 11(2); 15; 17; 27; 13:3(2); 11; 13; 18; 20; 24(2); 14:2(2); 17; 21(3); 29(2); 31(2); 15:5; 9; 10; 12; 15; 18; 24; 25; 27(2); 29; 32(2); 16:5; 7; 17; 20(2); 26; 30(2); 32(3); 17:5; 9(2); 20; 19:1; 2; 5; 7; 8(2); 9; 16(2); 17(3); 23(2); 25; 26; 20:4; 14(2); 19; 22; 21:1(2); 13; 17(2); 21; 26; 27; 29; 22:5; 6(3); 8; 9(2); 11; 12; 14; 16(2); 22; 27; 29(2); 23:7(3); 9; 11; 13; 24; 34(2); 24:7; 8; 12(4); 17; 18; 24; 29; 25:10; 13; 17; 20(2); 21; 28; 26:5; 6; 8(2); 17; 24; 25; 27; 27:14; 18; 28:6(2); 7; 8(2); 9; 10; 13; 14; 16; 18; 19(2); 20; 22; 23(2); 25(2); 26(2); 27(2); 29:1; 3; 4; 9; 17(2); 18(2); 19(2); 21; 24; 27; 30:5; 6; 10; 22(2); 31; 31:11; 23; 28; **Eccl** 1:3; 5; 18; 2:19(2); 21; 22; 24(2); 26(2); 3:9(2); 11(2); 4:3; 8(2); 10(2); 14(2); 5:4; 8; 10(2); 12; 14; 15(4); 16(3); 17(2); 18; 20; 6:2(2); 3(2); 4; 5; 6(2); 10(2); 12; 7:13; 18; 8:3; 7; 8; 13(2); 17(2); 9:2(2); 9; 15; 10:3(3); 8; 9; 10(2); 15; 11:4(2); 12:4; 9(2); **Song** 1:13; 2:4; 7; 8; 9(2); 16; 3:5; 10; 5:6(2); 16; 6:3; 8:4; 11; **Is** 1:1; 11; 2:3; 4; 12; 18; 19; 21; 22; 3:7; 4:3(2); 5:2(2); 7; 14; 25; 26; 6:2(3); 6; 7; 9; 11; 7:13; 15(2); 22; 8:7; 8(3); 14; 9:1; 15(2); 20(2); 10:7; 8; 13; 16; 24; 26; 28(3); 32(2); 34; 11:3; 4(3); 12; 15; 16; 12:2; 5; 13:9; 14:6(2); 30; 15:2; 16:5; 6; 12(2); 17:5; 8; 14; 18:3(2); 5; 19:16; 20(2); 22(2); 20:2; 21:4; 6; 7(2); 8; 9(2); 11; 22:8; 16; 18; 19; 21; 22(2); 23; 23:11(2); 12; 13; 24:18(2); 25:7; 8(2); 9; 11(3); 12; 26:3; 5(4); 10(2); 27:1; 5(2); 6; 7(3); 8; 9; 10; 11(2); 28:4(2); 9(2); 11; 12; 16; 20; 21(2); 24; 25(2); 28; 29:8(5; 10; 11; 12; 16(2); 30:14(2); 18(3); 19(3); 23; 32; 31:2; 3(2); 4; 5(2); 8; 9; 32:6; 7; 8; 33:4(2); 5(2); 8(3); 15:2(3); 12; 14; 37:1; 2; 7; 8(2); 9(4); 33; 34(2); 38; 38:7; 9; 12; 13; 15; 19; 21; 39:1(2); 4; 8; 40:6; 11(2); 19; 24(2); 26; 42:1; 3; 4; 5; 13(3); 43:1; 10; 13; 25; 44:12(2); 13(3); 14(3); 15(4); 16(4); 17(2); 18; 20(2); 24; 28; 45:9; 13(2); 18(3); 46:4; 6; 7(3); 48:12; 14; 15; 21(3); 49:1; 2(3); 6; 7; 10(2); 50:4(2); 8; 9; 51:3(2); 12; 13; 14(2); 52:6; 9; 13; 15; 53:2(2); 3(2); 4; 5(2); 7(5); 8(3); 9(2); 10(3); 11(2); 12(4); 54:5; 55:1; 5; 6(2); 7(2); 57:2; 13; 17; 58:9; 59:2; 5; 15; 16; 17(2); 18(2); 60:9; 61:1; 3; 10(2); 62:7(2); 63:7; 8(2); 9(3); 10(2); 11(3); 64:4; 65:16(2); 66:6(3); 8; 9; **Jer** 2:14(2); 17; 26; 3:1; 5(2); 4:7; 13; 5:12; 24; 26; 8:4; 8; 9:8; 12(2); 24; 10:10; 12(2); 13(3); 16; 11:16; 12:4; 13:16(2); 21; 14:10; 22; 15:4; 16:15; 17:6; 8; 11; 18:3; 4(2); 19:14; 20:4; 10; 13; 17; 21:2; 7(2); 9(3); 10; 22:4; 10; 11; 12; 16; 19; 28(2); 23:6; 20(2); 28; 31; 25:30(2); 31(2); 38; 26:11; 13; 16; 19(2); 21; 27:20; 29:21; 28; 31; 32(3); 30:7; 21; 24; 31:10; 11; 20; 32:3; 5(2); 28; 33:1; 15; 21; 24; 34:2; 3; 14; 16; 35:8; 14; 16; 18; 36:4; 12; 13; 18; 21; 23; 25(2); 30; 37:2(2); 13(2); 14; 17; 38:6(2); 7; 9; 10; 12; 19; 20(3); 22; 50:8; 19; 34(2); 44; 45(3); 51:6; 12; 15(2); 16(3); 19; 25; 29; 33; 34(2); 44; **Lam** 1:13(4); 14; 15; 2:2(3); 3(3); 4(3); 5(3); 6(2); 7(2); 8(3); 9; 17(6); 3:2; 3(4); 4(2); 7(2); 8; 9(2); 10; 11(2); 12; 13(4); **Eze** 2:1; 2; 3; 10; 3:1; 2; 3; 4; 10; 19(2); 20(3); 21(3); 22; 27(2); 4:15; 16; 6:12(3); 7:15(2); 20; 8:3; 5; 6; 7; 8; 9; 12; 13; 14; 15; 16; 17; 9:1; 3(2); 5; 7; 9; 10:2(2); 5; 6(2); 11:2; 12:12(2); 13(3); 27(2); 13:22; 14:9; 17:4(2); 5(2); 7; 9; 13; 15(4); 16(3); 18(3); 19(2); 20(2); 21; 23(2); 24(5); 26(2); 27(2); 28:4; 19:4; 6(2); 7(2); 8; 20:11; 13; 21; 49; 21:11; 21(3); 23; 27; 24:24; 26; 26:8(2); 9(2); 10; 11(2); 29:9; 18(2); 19; 20; 30:11; 24; 25; 31:5; 7; 10; 11; 15; 32:25; 32; 33:3(2); 5(2); 6; 9(2); 12(3); 13(4); 14; 15(3); 16(3); 18; 19; 22(2); 24; 34:12; 17; 23(3); 37:3; 4; 9; 10; 11; 38:17; 39:15; 40:2; 3(2); 5; 6; 43:7(3); 8; 10(2); 13(2); 5; 22(4); 23(2); 24(2); 25(2); 27; 28(2); 29(3); 30; 31; 32(2); 36; 37; 38(2); 39(3); 40(2); 41; 43; 19:2; 3(3); 4(2); 5; 6; 7; 9; 11(2); 13(4); 14(3); 15(3); 17(2); 18; 21; 23; 24; 25; 26; 28(2); 29(2); 30; 31; 32(2); 33; 34; 35; 36; 37; 38; 43; 54; 58; 13:6(2); 7; 8; 10; 12; 13; 17; 18; 20; 22; 23; 25; 27; 28; 29; 33; 35; 14:1; 4; 7(2); 9(2); 10; 15; 16; 17(2); 15:2(2); 4(2); 5(2); 6(2); 11; 12; 14(2); 15(2); 16; 17(2); 20(2); 24; 25(2); 26; 27(2); 28; 29; 31; **Dan** 1:2(2); 3; 5; 7; 8(4); 10; 14; 18; 20; 2:15; 16(2); 21(3); 22(2); 24; 29; 38; 49; 3:1; 11; 17; 19; 20; 25; 4:14; 17; 25; 29; 32; 33; 35; 37; 5:2; 12; 19(9); 20; 21(4); 29; 6:4; 7; 10(3); 14(2); 16; 20(2); 23; 26; 27; 7:1; 6; 23; 24(2); 25; 8:4; 5; 6; 7(2); 12(2); 14; 22; 27(3); 10:1; 11(2); 12; 15; 21; 19; 20; 11:2(2); 4(2); 5; 6(3); 8; 10; 11; 12(3); 16(2); 17(3); 18(2); 19(2); 20; 21; 23(2); 24(4); 25(2); 27; 28(2); 29(3); 30; 31(2); 32; 38; 39(3); 40(2); 41; 43; 49; 2:3; 4(2); 5; 6; 7; 9; 11(2); 12; 15(4); 17; 19; 22; 24; 25; 26; 28(2); 29(2); 32; 36; 37; 40; 41(2); 45; 47; 20:1; 2; 3; 5; 9; 10; 11; 12; 16; 17; 19; 23; 25; 28; 30; 37; 38; 41; 44; 45; 21:1; 2; 3; 5; 8; 10; 29; 37(2); 22:4(2); 5; 8; 10(2); 12; 13; 14; 15; 17; 19; **Hos** 1:3; 5:6; 11; 13; 6:1(4); 2(2); 3; 11; 7:4; 5; 8; 9(2); 8:1; 13; 9:9(2); 10:1(2); 2(2); 12; 11:5; 10(2); 12:1; 2; 3(2); 4(4); 7(2); 12; 13; 14; 13:1(3); 13(2); 15(2); 14:5; 9(2); **Joel** 1:6; 7(2); 2:11; 13; 14; 20; 23(2); **Amos** 1:1;

2; 11(2); 15; 2:1; 9; 15(3); 16; 3:4(2); 7; 11; 4:2; 13; 5:6; 6:10(3); 11; 7:1; 2; 5; 7; 8(2); 9:1(3); 3; 5; 6(2); **Obad** 12; **Jonah** 1:3(2); 5; 9; 10(2); 12; 2:2; 3:4; 6(2); 7; 10(3); 4:1; 2; 5; 8; 9; **Mic** 1:1; 9; 11; 15; 2:4(3); 11; 3:4(2); 5; 4:2; 3; 12; 5:1; 2; 3; 4(2); 5; 6(3); 8; 6:2; 8; 7:3; 9(2); 12; 18(2); 19(3); **Nah** 1:2; 4; 7; 8; 9; 12; 15; 2:1; 5; **Hab** 1:11; 13; 2:1; 2; 5(2); 9(2); 3:4; 6(2); 16(2); 19(2); **Zeph** 1:7; 12; 18; 2:11; 13; 14; 3:5(3); 15; 17(4); **Hag** 1:6; **Zec** 1:6; 8; 19; 21; 2:2; 8(2); 13; 3:1; 4(2); 4:6; 7; 13; 14; 5:2; 3; 6(2); 8(3); 11; 6:7; 8; 12(2); 13(3); 7:13; 9:4; 7(3); 9; 10; 10:11; 11:16; 12:8; 13:3; 4; 5; 14:3; **Mal** 1:8; 9(2); 2:5; 6; 7; 11; 13; 15(3); 16; 17; 3:1(2); 2(2); 3(2); 11; 4:6; **Mt** 1:20; 21; 25; 2:2; 3; 4(2); 7; 8; 14(2); 16(3); 21; 22(3); 23(2); 3:3; 7(2); 11(2); 12(2); 15; 16(2); 4:2(2); 3; 4; 6; 12; 13; 19; 21(2); 24; 5:1(2); 2; 19; 45; 6:24(2); 30; 7:8; 9; 10(2); 21; 29; 8:1; 9(3); 10; 14; 15; 16; 18; 23; 24; 26(2); 28; 32; 34; 9:1; 6; 7; 9(3); 12; 18; 22(2); 24; 25; 28; 29; 34; 36(2); 37; 38; 10:1(2); 2(2); 11:1; 2; 3; 6; 10; 11(2); 15; 18; 19; 21(2); 24; 5:1(2); 2; 19; 45; 6:24(2); 30; 7:8; 9; 10(2); 21; 29; 8:1; 9(3); 10; 14; 15; 16; 18; 23; 24; 26(2); 28; 32; 34; 9:1; 6; 7; 9(3); 12; 18; 22(2); 24; 25; 28; 29; 34; 36(2); 37; 38; 10:1(2); 2; 3; 6; 10; 11(2); 15:2(3); 18; 19; 20; 27; 12:3(2); 4; 9(2); 11(2); 13(2); 15(2); 18; 19; 20(3); 22; 26; 29(2); 30(2); 39; 43; 44(3); 45; 46; 48; 49; 13:2; 3; 4; 11; 12(2); 19; 20(2); 21(2); 22(2); 23(2); 24; 28; 29; 31; 33; 34; 37(2); 44(2); 46(2); 52; 53; 54(2); 58; 14:2; 5(2); 7; 9; 10; 13; 14; 18; 19(2); 22; 23(3); 29(2); 30(3); 33(2); 34; 36; 4; 6; 10; 13; 23; 24; 26; 30; 35; 36; 39; 16:1; 2; 4; 8; 12; 13; 15; 20(2); 21; 23; 26; 27; 17:5; 13; 15(2); 18; 23; 25(2); 28; 30(2); 32; 34; 19:1; 2; 4(2); 8; 11; 12; 13; 15; 17; 18; 22(2); 20:2(2); 3; 5; 6; 7; 13; 19; 21; 23; 21:3; 9; 10; 14; 15; 17(2); 18(2); 19(2); 23(2); 25; 27; 28; 29(2); 30(2); 31; 32; 33; 41; 45; 26:1; 7; 10; 16; 18; 20; 21; 23(2); 24; 25; 27; 37; 38; 39; 40; 42; 43; 44; 45; 46; 47; 48(2); 49; 53; 65; 66; 68; 70; 71; 72; 74; 75; 27:3(2); 5; 12(2); 14; 18; 19; 23; 24(2); 26(3); 34(2); 42(3); 43(3); 50; 58; 59; 60(2); 63; 64; 28:6(3); 7(2); **Mk** 1:6; 8; 10; 13; 16(2); 19(2); 20; 21; 22; 23; 26; 27; 31; 34; 35; 38; 39; 42(2); 43; 45; 2:1(2); 2; 4; 5; 8; 10; 12; 13(2); 14(3); 16; 17; 23; 25(3); 26; 27; 3:1; 2; 3; 4; 5(3); 8; 9; 10; 12; 13(2); 14(2); 16; 17; 21; 22(2); 23; 26; 27(2); 29; 30; 33; 34; 4:1(2); 2; 4; 9(2); 10; 11; 13; 21; 24; 25(3); 26; 27; 29; 30; 33; 34(2); 35; 36; 38; 39; 40; 5:2; 4; 5; 6(2); 8; 9(2); 10(2); 18(3); 20; 21; 22(2); 32; 34; 35; 36; 37; 38; 39(2); 40(2); 41; 43; 6:1; 2; 5(2); 6(2); 7; 10; 14; 16(2); 17; 20(3); 21; 22(3; 4); 24; 25(2); 26; 27; 29; 30; 31; 33(2); 34; 36(2); 37(2); 38; 9:1; 2; 6; 9; 12(2); 14(2); 16; 18(3); 19; 20(2); 21(2); 25; 26(2); 27; 28; 29; 30; 31(3); 33(2); 35; 36(3); 38(2); 40; 41; 42; 10:1(3); 3; 5; 11; 13; 14; 15; 16; 17; 20; 22(2); 30; 32; 34; 36; 46; 47(2); 48(2); 49; 50; 52; 11:1; 3; 7; 9; 11(2); 12; 13(4); 15; 16; 17; 20; 21; 23(3); 27; 28; 32; 34(2); 35; 37; 39; 40(2); 41; 42; 43; 44(2); 45(2); 52; 54; 61; 68(2); 70; 71; 72(2); 15:2; 3; 6; 8; 10; 11; 14; 15; 23; 28; 31(2); 35; 39(2); 41; 44(3); 45(2); 46; 47; 16:6(3); 7(2); 9(2); 11; 12; 14(2); 15; 16(2); 19; **Lk** 1:8; 9; 12; 15(2); 16; 17; 21; 22(4); 23; 25; 32; 33; 48; 49; 51(2); 52; 53(2); 54; 55; 60; 62; 63; 64; 68; 70; 73; 74; 2:4; 21; 26(2); 27; 28; 42; 49; 50; 51; 3:3; 7; 11; 13; 15; 16; 17(2); 18; 20; 4:2(2); 9; 10; 13; 15; 16(3); 17(2); 18(2); 20(2); 22; 24; 25(2); 27(2); 28; 34; 36; 39; 6:1; 4; 5; 6; 7; 8; 20(2); 12; 13(3); 14; 17; 20; 35; 39; 47; 48; 49; 7:1(2); 3(3); 4(2); 5(2); 6; 8(3); 9; 11; 12; 13; 14(2); 15(2); 19; 20; 21(2); 23; 24; 27; 28(2); 33; 36(2); 39(2); 40; 42; 43(3); 44; 48; 50; 50; 8:1; 4; 5; 6; 7; 8(3); 9; 11; 12; 14; 15; 16; 17(2); 18; 20(2); 21; 23; 24; 30; 35; 36; 38; 39; 40; 41(2); 42(2); 43; 44; 5:1; 3(3); 4(2); 5(2); 6; 8(3); 9; 11; 12; 13; 14(2); 15(2); 16; 17(2); 18(2); 19; 20; 21(2); 23; 24; 27; 28(2); 33; 36(2); 39(2); 40; 42; 43; 44; 48; 49; 50; 51(2); 53; 55; 59(2); 10:1; 2(2); 16(3); 18; 22; 23; 26; 27; 28; 29; 31(2); 32; 33(4); 35(2); 37(2); 38; 11:1(2); 12(2); 14; 15(2); 16; 17; 22(3); 23(2); 24(2); 25(2); 26; 27; 28; 29; 33; 37(2); 38(2); 40; 46; 53; 12:1; 5; 9; 13; 14; 15(2); 16; 17; 18; 21; 22; 28; 36(2); 37(2); 38; 39; 43; 44(2); 46(2); 48; 54; 58; 13:6(2); 7; 8; 10; 12; 13; 17; 18; 20; 22; 23; 25; 27; 32; 35; 14:1; 4; 7(2); 9; 10(2); 11; 12; 15(2); 16; 25; 26; 28; 29; 31(3); 35; 15:3; 4(2); 5(2); 6(2); 11; 12; 14(2); 15(2); 16; 17(2); 20(2); 24; 25(2); 26; 27(2); 28; 29; 31; 16:1(2); 2; 5; 6(2); 7(3); 8; 10(2); 13(2); 15; 22(2); 24(2); 26; 27; 28; 30; 31; 17:1; 2(2); 4; 7; 9(2); 11(2); 12; 14(2); 15(2); 16; 19; 20(2); 24(2); 33; 37; 18:1; 4(2); 7; 8(2); 9; 14; 15; 21; 22; 23(3); 24(2); 27; 29; 31; 32; 33; 35; 36; 38; 39(2); 40(2); 41; 43; 19:2; 3(2); 4(2); 5; 6; 7; 9; 11(2); 12; 13(4); 14(2); 15(2); 16; 17; 20; 22; 25; 26; 28; 29; 33; 37(2);

Ps 1:1(2); 3(2); 2:4; 5; 12; 3:4; 4; 7:1; 2; 12(3); 13(2); 14; 15(2); 9:7; 8(2); 12; 18; 12; 10:5; 6; 8(2); 9(4); 10; 11(3); 13; 11:6; 13:6; 15:2; 3; 4(2); 16:8; 18:t; 6; 7; 9; 10(2); 11; 14(2); 16(3); 17; 19(3); 20; 30; 33; 34; 41; 48; 50; 19:4; 20:6; 21:1; 4; 7; 22:8(3); 9; 24(4); 28; 31; 23:2(2); 3(2); 24:2; 4; 5; 10; 25:8(2); 12(3); 14; 15; 27:5(3); 14; 28:5; 6; 8; 29:6; 31:21; 24; 32:1; 2; 4; 10; 33:5; 7(2); 9(2); 10; 36:4; 7(2); 9(2); 10(2); 12; 13; 14; 36:2; 3; 4(3); 37:4; 5; 6; 13; 23; 24(2); 26; 33; 34; 36(3); 39; 40; 39:6; 40:1; 2; 3; 41:1; 2; 5; 6(4); 8(2); 44:21; 45:11; 46:6; 8; 9(3); 47:2; 3; 4(2); 9; 48:14; 49:9; 10; 12; 15; 17(2); 18(2); 19; 50:4(2); 9; 51:t; 52:5; 54:5; 7; 55:12; 17; 18; 19; 20(2); 22(2); 56:1; 57:t; 3; 58:7; 9; 10(2); 11; 60:t; 12; 61:7; 62:2(2); 6(2); 63:t; 65:4; 66:5; 6; 7; 16; 17; 19; 68:6; 20; 33; 35; 71:6; 72:2; 4(2); 6; 8; 12(2); 13; 14; 15(2); 74:5; 75:7; 8; 76:3; 12(2); 77:1; 7; 9; 78:4; 5(2); 11; 12; 13(2); 14; 15; 16; 20(3); 23; 25; 26(2); 27; 28; 29; 33; 34; 38; 39(2); 42; 43; 45; 46; 47; 48; 49; 50(2); 53; 54; 55; 59; 60(2); 62; 66(2); 67; 68; 69(2); 70; 71; 72; 81:5(3); 16; 82:1; 84:11; 85:8; 87:6; 89:26; 41; 48(2); 91:1; 2; 3; 4; 11; 14(2); 15; 92:12; 15; 93:1(2); 94:9(4); 10(4); 14; 23; 95:5; 7; 96:4; 10; 13(3); 97:10(2); 98:1; 2; 3; 9(2); 99:1; 2; 5; 6; 7(2); 100:3(2); 101:6(2); 7(2); 102:t; 12; 17; 19; 23(2); 103:7; 9(2); 10; 12; 14(2); 15; 104:10; 13; 14(2); 16; 19; 32(2); 105:5; 7; 8(2); 9; 14(2); 16(2); 17; 18; 21; 24; 25; 26(2); 28; 29; 31; 32; 33; 34; 36; 37; 39; 40; 41; 43; 106:1; 2; 3(2); 9(2); 10; 15; 23(3); 26; 33; 40; 41; 43; 44(2); 45; 46; 107:1; 2; 6; 7; 9; 12; 14; 16; 19; 20; 25; 28; 29; 30; 33; 35; 36; 38; 40; 41; 108:13; 109:7; 11; 15; 16(2); 17(2); 18; 19; 31; 110:6(3); 7(2); 111:4; 5(2); 6(2); 9(2); 112:4; 5; 6; 7; 9(2); 10; 113:7; 8; 9; 115:3(2); 9; 10; 11; 12(3); 13; 16; 116:1; 2; 6; 118:1; 18; 26; 29; 120:1; 121:3(2); 4; 7; 123:2; 126:6; 127:2; 129:4; 7; 130:8; 132:2; 11; 13; 135:6; 7(3); 14; 136:1; 137:8; 9; 138:6(2); 142:t; 143:3(2); 144:2; 10; 145:19(2); 20; 146:4; 5; 9(2); 147:2; 3; 4(2); 6; 9; 10(2); 12; 13(2); 14; 15; 16(2); 17; 18(2); 19; 20; 148:5; 6(2); 14; 149:4;

22; 25; 26(3); 27(4); 31; 33; 34; 35; 36(3); 37; 38; 39(2); 40(2); 41; 44; 45(2); 47(2); 51; 56; 57; 59; 60; 61; 67; 70; 23:2; 3; 5; 6; 7(3); 8(4); 9(2); 13; 17; 22(2); 23; 25(2); 26; 35(2); 42; 46(2); 47; 50; 51; 53; 24:6(3); 12; 17; 19; 21; 23; 25; 27; 28(2); 29; 30(2); 31; 32(2); 35; 38; 40(2); 41; 43; 44; 45; 50(2); 51(2); **Jn** 1:8; 10; 11; 12; 15(3); 18; 20; 21(2); 23; 27; 30(2); 31; 33(2); 36(2); 39(2); 41; 42(2); 51; 2:5; 8; 12(2); 15(2); 21; 22(2); 23(2); 24; 25; 3:3; 4(2); 5; 13; 16; 18(3); 21; 22; 26; 29; 30; 31(3); 32(2); 33; 34; 36(2); 4:3; 4; 5; 10; 18; 25(2); 26; 27; 32; 36(3); 39; 40(2); 43; 45(2); 46; 47(4); 50; 51; 52(2); 54; 5:4; 6(2); 11(2); 13; 16; 18; 19(2); 20; 21; 23; 24; 26; 27; 32; 33; 35; 38; 46; 6:2; 3; 5; 6(3); 11(2); 12; 15; 20; 29; 31; 33; 35(2); 39; 41; 42; 46(2); 47; 51; 56; 57(2); 58; 59(2); 61; 62; 65; 71(2); 7:1; 4; 9(2); 10; 11; 12(2); 17; 18(2); 25; 26; 27(2); 28(2); 29; 31; 35(2); 36; 38; 39; 50; 51; 8:1; 2(2); 6; 7(2); 8; 10; 12; 20; 22(2); 23; 24; 26; 27; 28; 29; 30; 42; 44(4); 47; 51; 52; 54; 56; 9:1; 2; 6(3); 7; 8(2); 9(4); 11; 12(2); 15(3); 16; 17(3); 18; 19; 20; 21(3); 22(2); 23; 25(2); 26(2); 27; 29; 30(2); 31; 33; 35(2); 36(2); 37; 38(2); 10:1; 2; 3; 4(2); 6; 9; 12; 13; 20; 35; 39; 40; 11:3; 4; 6(4); 7; 9(2); 10; 11(2); 12(2); 13; 17(2); 24; 25(3); 33; 36; 39(2); 43(2); 44; 51(2); 52; 56; 57(2); 12:1; 6(3); 9(2); 14; 17; 18; 25(2); 33(2); 35(2); 37; 38; 40; 41; 44; 45; 48; 49; 13:1(2); 3; 4; 5(2); 6; 10; 11(2); 12(2); 16(2); 18; 19; 20(2); 21; 22; 24(2); 25; 26(3); 28; 29; 30; 31; 14:9; 10; 12(3); 16(2); 17; 21(3); 23; 24; 26; 15:2(2); 5; 6; 16; 23; 26; 16:2; 8(2); 13(6); 14(2); 15; 17; 18(2); 23; 17:2; 18:1(2); 5; 6(2); 7; 8; 9; 13; 14; 17; 22; 25; 30; 32(2); 38(2); 19:7(2); 8; 11; 13; 14; 16; 17; 21; 26(2); 27; 30(2); 33; 35(3); 38(2); 41; 20:5(2); 8; 9; 18; 20(2); 22(2); 25; 27; 21:1; 6; 7(2); 14; 15(2); 16(3); 17(3); 19(4); 20; 22; 23(2); **Acts** 1:2(3); 3; 4; 7; 9(2); 10; 17; 18; 22; 25(2); 26; 2:24; 25; 29; 30; 31; 33; 34; 40; 3:5; 7; 8; 10; 12; 13; 18; 20; 22; 4:9; 32; 35; 5:37; 6:10; 7:2(3); 4(2); 5(4); 8; 10; 12; 15; 21; 23; 24; 25; 26; 27; 29; 31(2); 36(2); 38; 44(3); 55; 60(3); 8:3; 6; 11; 13(2); 16; 18; 19; 27; 31(3); 32(3); 37; 38(2); 39; 40(2); 9:2(2); 3(2); 4; 5; 6; 8; 9; 10; 11; 12; 13; 14; 15; 16; 18; 19(2); 20(2); 21(2); 26(2); 27(3); 28; 29; 32; 33; 34; 38; 39; 41(2); 43; 10:3; 4(3); 6(2); 7; 8(2); 10(2); 17; 21; 23; 27(2); 28; 32(2); 35; 36; 39; 41; 42(2); 48; 11:13(2); 16; 17; 22; 23; 24; 26(2); 12:2; 3(2); 4(2); 7; 8(2); 9(2); 11; 12(2); 17(3); 19(2); 23(2); 13:11; 12; 17; 18; 19(2); 20; 22(3); 25(2); 28; 31; 33; 34(2); 35; 36; 37; 14:9; 10; 12; 17(2); 19; 20(2); 27; 15:8; 41; 16:1; 10; 18; 27; 29; 33(2); 34(2); 17:16; 17; 18(2); 24; 25(2); 27; 31(5); 18:3(2); 4; 6; 7; 11; 16; 18; 19(2); 20; 21; 22(2); 23(2); 25; 26; 27(2); 28; 19:2; 3; 8; 9; 21; 22(2); 25; 31; 34; 35; 41(2); 20:2(2); 3(2); 9; 11(2); 13; 14; 16(2); 17; 18; 28; 35; 36(2); 38; 21:4; 11(2); 14; 19(2); 33(2); 34(2); 35(2); 37; 40(2); 22:2(2); 8; 14; 21; 22; 24(2); 26; 27; 29(3); 30(3); 23:5; 6; 7; 15(2); 16; 17; 18; 20; 23; 25; 27; 34(4); 35(2); 24:2; 22; 23(2); 24; 25; 26(3); 25:1; 3; 4; 5; 6(2); 7; 8; 12; 16; 20; 22; 24; 25(2); 26:15; 23; 24; 25; 30; 32; 27:6; 35(4); 28:4; 5; 6(2); 15; 17; 23; 29; **Rom** 1:2; 2:28; 29; 3:26; 29(2); 4:2; 10; 11(3); 12; 13; 17; 18; 19(2); 20; 21(2); 6:7; 10(4); 7:1; 2; 8:9; 11; 24; 27(2); 29(3); 30(6); 32(2); 34; 9:15; 18(4); 19; 23(2); 24; 25; 28; 10:21; 11:2(2); 7; 21; 32; 12:3; 7; 8(4); 20; 13:4(3); 8; 14:2; 4(2); 6(7); 9; 18; 22(2); 23(3); 15:10; 12; 21; **1Cor** 1:31; 2:14; 15(2); 16; 3:7(2); 8(2); 10; 14(2); 15(2); 18; 19; 4:4; 5:2; 6:16(2); 17; 18; 7:13; 20; 22(2); 24; 32(2); 33(2); 36(3); 37(2); 38(2); 8:2(3); 9:10(3); 10:12(2); 22; 11:7; 23; 24(2); 25(2); 26; 29; 12:11; 14:2(2); 3; 4(2); 5(3); 11; 13; 16(2); 24(2); 25; 15:4(2); 5; 6; 7; 8; 12; 15(2); 24(2); 25(2); 27(3); 16:10(2); 11; 12(2); **2Cor** 1:10; 21; 2:2; 5; 4:14; 5:5; 10; 15; 17; 21; 6:2; 15; 7:7(2); 15; 8:6(2); 9(2); 12; 15(2); 17(2); 23; 9:6(2); 7; 9(2); 10; 10:7(2); 17; 18; 11:4; 12:4; 6(2); 9; 13:4(2); **Gal** 1:4; 23(2); 2:8; 11; 12(2); 3:5(2); 16; 4:1(2); 23(2); 29; 5:3; 10(2); 6:3(2); 4; 7; 8(2); **Eph** 1:4; 6; 8; 9; 10; 20(2); 2:1; 4; 7; 14; 16; 3:3; 11; 16; 4:8(3); 9(2); 10(2); 11; 28; 5:14; 23; 26; 27; 28; 6:8(2); 22; **Phil** 1:6; 2:8; 22; 25; 26(2); 27; 30; 3:4(2); 21; **Col** 1:17; 18(2); 21; 2:13; 15; 18; 3:25(2); 4:8; 10; 13; **1Th** 1:10; 3:13; 4:8; 5:24; **2Th** 1:10; 2:4(2); 6; 7(2); 14; 3:6; 10; 14; **1Ti** 1:12; 3:1; 5; 6; 7(2); 5:8; 6:4; 15; **2Ti** 1:12; 16; 17(2); 18(2); 2:4; 5(2); 12; 13(2); 21; 4:11; 15; **Titus** 1:9(2); 2:8; 14; 3:5; 6; 11; **Philem** 1:13; 15; 18; **Heb** 1:2(2); 3; 4; 5(2); 6(2); 7; 8; 13; 2:5; 8(2); 9; 11(2); 14(2); 16(2); 17; 18(2); 3:3; 4; 17; 18; 4:3; 4; 7; 8; 10(2); 5:1; 2; 3; 4; 5; 6; 7(2); 8(3); 9; 13; 6:13(2); 15(2); 7:6; 8(2); 10; 13; 17; 20; 24; 25(2); 27(2); 8:4(2); 5(2); 6(2); 8; 13(2); 9:7; 12; 15; 19; 21; 25; 26(2); 28; 10:5(2); 8; 9(3); 12; 14; 15; 20; 23; 28; 29(2); 37; 11:4(3); 5(3); 6(3); 7; 8(4); 9; 10; 16; 17(2); 19; 21; 22; 23(2); 24; 26; 27(2); 28(2); 12:6(2); 7; 10; 17(4); 26; 13:5; 12; 23; **Jas** 1:6; 7; 9; 10(2); 12(2); 13(2); 14; 18; 23; 24(2); 25; 2:5; 10; 11; 13; 14; 21; 23; 4:6(2); 7; 8; 10; 11; 5:6; 7; 15; 17; 18; 20; **1Pet** 1:15; 2:6; 7; 23(3); 3:10; 13; 18; 19; 4:1; 2; 14(2); 5:6; 7; 8; **2Pet** 1:9(2); 17; 2:19; **1Jn** 1:7; 9; 2:2; 4; 6(3); 9(2); 10; 11(2); 17; 22(2); 23; 25; 28; 29; 3:2(2); 3; 5; 7(2); 8(2); 9(2); 10; 12; 14; 16; 23; 24(4); 4:4(2); 6(2); 8; 10; 13(2); 15; 16; 17; 18; 19; 20(5); 21; 5:5(2); 6; 9; 10(3); 12(2); 14; 15; 16(3); 18; **2Jn** 9(2); 11; **3Jn** 10(2); 11(2); **Jude** 6; 9; **Rev** 1:1; 2; 3; 7; 16; 17; 18; 2:1; 7; 11(2); 12; 17(2); 23; 26; 27; 29; 3:1; 5; 6; 7(4); 12; 13; 20; 22; 4:3; 5:7; 8; 6:2(2); 3; 5(2); 7; 9; 12; 7:2; 14; 15; 8:1; 3; 9:2; 5; 10:2(2); 3; 7(2); 9; 11; 11:5; 15; 12:9; 12(2); 13(2); 15; 13:6; 10(2); 11(2); 12; 13(2); 14; 15; 16; 17; 14:4; 10; 16; 17; 16:15(2); 16; 17:3; 10(2); 11; 14; 15; 18:2; 22; 19:2; 9(2); 10; 11(2); 12(2); 13; 15(3); 16; 17; 20; 20:2; 3(2); 6; 21:3; 5(2); 6; 7(2); 10; 15; 16; 17; 22:1; 6; 7; 9; 10; 11(4); 20

HER

846

Gen 2:22; 3:6(2); 15; 4:11; 12; 8:9(3); 11; 12:15(2); 16; 19(2); 16:2; 3(3); 4(2); 5; 6(3); 7; 9(2); 10; 11; 13; 17:15(2); 16(4); 19:33; 20:4; 6; 7; 13; 21:10; 12; 14(2); 16(2); 17; 19; 23:2; 24:15(2); 16(2); 17; 18(2); 20; 21; 22; 28; 43; 45(3); 46(2); 47(3); 51(2); 53(2); 55(2); 57; 58; 59; 60; 61; 64; 67(2); 25:1; 22; 23; 24(2); 26:9; 27:6; 15(3); 17; 42(2); 29:9; 12(2); 19(2); 20; 21; 23(2); 27; 28; 29; 31; 30:1; 3(2); 4(2); 9(2); 15; 16; 21; 22(2); 31:19; 35; 33:2; 7; 34:2(4); 8; 11(2); 35:17; 18; 20; 38:2(2); 8; 11; 14(3); 15(3); 16; 18(2); 19(3); 20; 22; 23(3); 24(2); 25; 26(2); 27(2); 39:7; 10(3); 12; 13; 14; 16; 40:10; 48:7; **Ex** 2:5(2); 8; 9; 10; 3:22(3); 4:25; 11:2; 15:20(2); 18:2; 3; 6(2); 21:4(2); 8(5); 9(2); 10(3); 11; 22(2); 22:16(2); 17(2); **Lev** 11:19; 12:2; 4(2); 5(2); 6; 7(3); 8; 15:19(3); 20; 21; 23; 24(2); 25(5); 26(4); 28; 29; 30(2); 33(3); 18:7; 11; 15; 17(5); 18(4); 19(2); 20; 25; 19:20; 29; 20:14; 17; 18(4); 21:3; 7; 9; 13; 22:13(3); 28; 25:19; 22; 26:4; 20; 34(2); 43; **Num** 5:13(3); 15(2); 16(2); 18; 19; 24; 27(6); 29; 30; 31; 12:12; 13; 14(4); 16:30; 32; 19:3(3); 4(2); 5(4); 8; 22:23; 25; 33; 25:8; 26:10; 59; 30:3(2); 4(8); 5(8); 6(2); 7(5); 8(6); 9(2); 10(2); 11(5); 12(6); 13(2); 14(6); 15; 16(2); 36:8; **Deut** 11:6; 17; 14:18; 20:7(2); 21:11(2); 12(3); 13(6); 14(5); 22:13(2); 14(4); 15; 16; 17; 19; 21(4); 23(2); 25(3); 27(2); 28(2); 29(3); 24:1(5); 3(5); 4(3); 25:5(4); 8; 11(2); 12(2); 28:30; 56(5); 57(3); 32:11(4); 22; **Josh** 2:14; 15; 17; 6:17; 22; 23(4); 25; 8:2(2); 10:1(2); 39; 13:17; 15:18(3); 19; 45(2); 47(4); 17:11(6); 16; 21:13(2); 14(2); 15(2); 16(3); 17(2); 18(2); 21(2); 22(2); 23(2); 24(2); 25(2); 27(2); 28(2); 29(2); 30(2); 31(2); 32(3); 34(2); 35(2); 36(2); 37(2); 38(2); 39(2); **Judg** 1:14(3); 15; 27(5); 4:5; 8; 18; 19; 20; 21; 22; 5:26(2); 27(2); 29(2); 11:26(2); 34; 35; 37; 38(3); 39(2); 13:3; 6; 9(2); 10; 13; 14(3); 14:2; 3; 8; 16; 17(2); 15:1; 2(6); 6(3); 16:1; 5(2); 7; 8; 9; 11; 13; 16; 17(2); 18(2); 19; 19:2; 3(5); 25(4); 26; 27(2); 28(2); 29(3); 20:6(2); **Ruth** 1:3; 5(2); 6; 7(2); 8(2); 9; 10; 14(2); 15(2); 18(2); 22(2); 2:1; 2; 3; 10; 11; 14(2); 15(2); 16(2); 18(2); 19(3); 20(2); 22; 23; 3:1(2); 5; 6(2); 7; 15; 16(3); 4:13(2); 16; 17; **1Sa** 1:4(2); 5; 6(4); 7; 8(2); 12; 13(3); 14; 18(2); 19; 22; 23(3); 24; 2:19; 4:19(4); 20(3); 21(2); 18:17; 21; 25:19(2); 20; 23; 35(2); 39; 40; 41; 42; 28:7(2); 10; 13; 14; **2Sa** 3:15(2); 16(3); 6:16; 23; 11:4(4); 26(2); 27; 12:24(2); 13:1; 2; 5; 6; 8; 10; 11(2); 14(3); 15(4); 16; 17; 18(3); 19(5); 20(3); 14:2; 3; 4; 5; 17:8; 20:17; 22; 21:10; **1Kin** 1:2(3); 3; 4; 31; 2:19(2); 20; 3:1; 17; 20(2); 26(3); 27; 9:24(2); 10:2; 3(3); 5; 13(4); 14:5(2); 6; 15:13(2); 17:10; 11; 13; 15; 19(2); 20; 21:6; **2Kin** 4:2; 5(3); 6(2); 9; 12; 13; 14(2); 15(2); 17; 20; 22; 24; 25; 26(2); 27(4); 30; 36; 37; 5:3; 6:28; 29(2); 8:2; 3(2); 5(3); 6; 9:10; 22; 30(2); 33(4); 34; 35(3); 11:1; 3; 14; 15(3); 16; 19:21; 22:14; **1Chr** 2:18; 5:16; 6:57; 58(2); 59(2); 60(3); 67(2); 68(2); 69(2); 70(2); 71(2); 72(2); 73(2); 74(2); 75(2); 76(3); 77(2); 78(2); 79(2); 80(2); 81(2); 7:29(4); 15:29; 18:1; **2Chr** 8:11; 9:1; 2(3); 4; 12(3); 11:20; 15:16(2); 22:10; 23:13; 14(3); 15(2); 34:22; 36:21; **Est** 1:11; 19; 2:1; 7; 9(6); 10(3); 11; 13(2); 14; 15(2); 17(2); 20(3); 4:4(2); 5; 8(3); 5:1; 3; 12; 8:1; **Job** 2:10; 5:16; 9:6; 21:10; 31:10; 18; 39:14; 16(2); 17(2); 26; 27; 29; 30; **Ps** 34:2; 45:13; 14(2); 46:5(2); 48:3; 12; 13(2); 55:11; 58:4; 67:6; 68:13; 31; 69:15; 80:11(2); 12(2); 84:3; 85:12; 87:5(2); 102:13; 14; 104:17; 107:42; 123:2; 132:15(2); 16(2); 137:5; **Prov** 1:20; 21; 2:4(2); 16; 17(2); 18(2); 19; 3:15; 16(2); 17(2); 18(2); 4:6(2); 8(2); 13(2); 5:3; 4; 5(2); 6; 8(2); 19(3); 6:6; 8(2); 25(3); 29; 7:5; 8(2); 11(2); 21(2); 22; 25(2); 26; 27; 8:1; 9:1(2); 2(3); 3; 14; 18; 12:4; 14:1(2); 17:12; 25; 27:8; 16; 30:20; 23; 28; 31:10; 11(2); 12; 13; 14; 15(2); 16; 17(2); 18(2); 19(2); 20(2); 21(2); 22; 23; 25; 26(2); 27; 28(4); 31(4); **Eccl** 7:26(3); 11:5; **Song** 2:13; 3:4; 6:9(6); 8:5; 9(2); **Is** 1:27; 3:26; 4:5; 5:14; 7:16; 9:1(2); 10:11(2); 13:10; 13; 22(2); 16:8; 21:9; 23:3; 7(2); 17; 18(3); 24:2; 26:17(2); 21(2); 27:2; 29:7(3); 34:12; 13; 15(3); 16; 37:22; 40:2(4); 49:15(2); 51:3(3); 18(2); 52:11; 53:7; 61:10; 11; 65:18; 19; 66:7; 8; 10(4); 11(2); 12(3); **Jer** 2:23; 24(6); 32(2); 3:1; 7; 8(3); 9; 10(2); 20; 4:17; 31(3); 5:10(2); 6:3(2); 4; 5; 6; 7(3); 8:7; 19(2); 9:20; 12:7; 9; 15:9; 17:8(2); 19:15; 20:17; 30:18; 31:8; 15(2); 44:17; 18; 19(4); 25; 46:21(2); 22; 23; 48:4; 15; 19; 28; 41; 49:2; 4; 14; 19(2); 22; 24(2); 26(2); 50:2(2); 3(2); 9; 10; 13; 14; 15(6); 26(5); 27; 29(3); 30(2); 35(2); 36; 37(2); 38; 44(2); 51:2(3); 3(2); 4; 6(2); 7; 8(2); 9(2); 27(3); 28; 30(2); 33(2); 36(2); 43; 45; 47(3); 48; 52(2); 53(2); 55(2); 56(2); 57(5); 58; 64; **Lam** 1:2(7); 3(2); 4(3); 5(5); 6(2); 7(7); 8(3); 9(3); 10(2); 11; 17(2); 2:5; 7; 9(5); 16; 4:6; 7; 13(3); **Eze** 5:5; 6; 12:19; 13:16; 16:2; 32; 44; 45(2); 46(2); 48; 49(2); 53(2); 55(2); 57; 17:7(3); 9; 19:2; 3; 5(2); 11(3); 12(2); 14(2); 22:2(2); 3; 10; 24; 25(2); 26; 27; 28; 23:4; 5(2); 7; 8(5); 9(2); 10(5); 11(5); 12; 14; 16; 17(3); 18(4); 19(2); 31; 42; 43(2); 44; 24:7(2); 8; 12(3); 26:4(4); 6; 17; 28:22(2); 23(4); 29:12; 19(3); 30:4(2); 6; 7; 8; 18(5); 31:4(2); 32:7; 16(4); 18; 20(2); 22; 23(2); 24(2); 25(3); 26(2); 29(2); 33:28; 34:27(2); 36:38; 44:22; **Dan** 11:6(3); 7; 17; **Hos** 1:6; 2:2(6); 3(5); 4; 6; 7; 8(2); 9; 10(3); 11(5); 12(2); 13(4); 14(3); 15(3); 17; 23(2); 3:1; 2; 3; 4:18; 19(2); 9:2; 10; 10:7; 11; 14; 13:8; 16; **Joel** 1:8; 2:16; 22; 3:17; **Amos** 4:3; 5:2(2); **Obad** 1; **Jonah** 1:15; 2:6; **Mic** 1:9; 4:6(3); 7(2); 11; 7:5; 6(2); 10(2); **Nah** 2:7(2); 13; 3:4(2); 7; 8; 9; 10(3); **Zeph** 2:14; 15(2); 3:1; 2; 3(3); 4(2); 19(2); **Hag** 1:10; 2:3; **Zec** 2:5(2); 5:11; 7:7; 8:2; 12(2); 9:4(2); 5; 12:6; 14:10; **Mal** 3:11; **Mt** 1:6; 19(3); 20; 25(2); 2:18; 5:28(2); 31; 32(2); 8:15(2); 9:18; 22; 25; 10:35(2); 11:19; 14:4; 7; 8; 9; 11; 15:23(2); 28(2); 19:7; 9; 20:20; 21; 21:2; 22:28; 23:37(2); 24:29; 26:13; **Mk** 1:30; 31(3); 5:23; 29(2); 32; 33; 34; 41; 43; 6:17; 23; 24; 26; 28; 7:26; 27; 29; 30(2); 10:4; 11; 12; 12:21; 22; 23; 44(2); 13:24; 28; 14:5; 6(2); 9; 16:11; **Lk** 1:5; 28; 29; 30; 35; 36(2); 38; 41; 45; 56(2); 58(4); 61; 2:7; 19; 22; 36; 51; 4:38; 39(2); 7:12; 13(3); 35; 38; 44; 47; 48; 8:43; 44; 48; 52; 54; 55(2); 56; 10:38; 40; 41; 42; 11:27; 12:53(2); 13:12(3); 13; 34(2); 15:9(2); 16:18(2); 18:5(2); 20:30; 31; 33; 21:4; **Jn** 2:4; 4:7; 10; 13; 16; 17; 21; 26; 27; 28(2); 8:3; 7; 10; 11; 11:1; 2; 5; 23; 25; 28(2); 31(3); 33(2); 40; 12:3; 7; 16:21; 18:16; 19:27; 20:13; 15; 16; 17; 18; **Acts** 5:8; 9; 10(4); 7:21; 8:27; 9:37; 40; 41(3); 12:15; 16:15; 16; 18; 19; 19:27; 21:3; 27:15; 32; **Rom** 7:2(2); 3(2); 9:12; 25; 16:2(2); **1Cor** 7:2; 4; 10; 11(2); 12; 13(2); 34; 36; 38(2); 39(2); 11:5(2); 6(2); 10; 15(3); 13:5; **Gal** 4:25; 30; **Eph** 5:33; **1Th** 2:7; **Jas** 1:4; 5:18; **2Pet** 2:22; **2Jn** 1; **Rev** 2:21(2); 22(2); 23; 6:13; 12:1(2); 4; 5; 6; 14; 15; 16; 17; 14:8; 18; 16:19; 17:2; 4(2); 5; 6; 7; 16(3); 18:3(3); 4(3); 5(2); 6(4); 7(2); 8(2); 9(4); 10; 11; 15(2); 18; 19; 20(2); 24; 19:2(2); 3; 8; 21:2; 11; 22:2

HERE

645, 1988, 2005, 2008, 2009, 2088, 2236, 3541, 4672, 6311, 8033, 8552, *848, 1759, 3918, 3936, 4840, 5602*

Gen 16:13; 19:12; 15; 21:23; 22:1; 5; 7; 11; 24:13; 27:1; 18; 31:11; 37; 37:13; 40:15; 42:33; 46:2; 47:23; **Ex** 3:4; 24:14; 33:16; **Num** 14:40; 22:8; 19; 23:1(2); 15; 29(2); 32:6; 16; **Deut** 5:3; 31; 12:8; 29:15(2); **Josh** 18:6; 8; 21:9; **Judg** 4:20; 18:3; 19:9; 24; 20:7; **Ruth** 2:8; 4:1; 2; **1Sa** 1:26; 3:4; 5; 6; 8; 16; 9:8; 11; 12:3; 14:34; 16:11; 21:8; 9(2); 22:12; 23:3; 29:3; **2Sa** 1:7; 11:12; 15:26; 18:30; 20:4; 24:22; **1Kin** 2:30; 18:8; 11; 14; 19:9; 13; 20:40; 22:7; **2Kin** 2:2; 4; 6; 3:11(2); 7:3; 4; 10:23; **1Chr** 29:17; **2Chr** 18:6; **Job** 38:11; 35; **Ps** 132:14; **Is** 6:8; 21:9; 22:16(3); 28:10; 13; 52:5; 58:9; **Eze** 8:6; 9; 17; **Hos** 7:9; **Mt** 12:41; 42; 14:8; 17; 16:28; 17:4(2); 20:6; 24:2; 23; 26:36; 38; 28:6; **Mk** 6:3; 8:4; 9:1; 5; 13:1; 21; 14:32; 34; 16:6; **Lk** 4:23; 9:12; 27; 33; 11:31; 32; 17:21; 23; 19:20; 22:38; 24:6; 41; **Jn** 6:9; 11:21; 32; **Acts** 4:10; 8:36; 9:10; 14; 10:33; 16:28; 24:19; 20; 25:24(2); **Col** 4:9; **Heb** 7:8; 13:14; **Jas** 2:3(2); **1Pet** 1:17; **Rev** 13:10; 18; 14:12(2); 17:9

HEREAFTER

268, 310, 311, 1836, *575, 737, 2089, 3195, 3326, 3370, 3568, 5028*

Is 41:23; **Eze** 20:39; **Dan** 2:29; 45; **Mt** 26:64; **Mk** 11:14; **Lk** 22:69; **Jn** 1:51; 13:7; 14:30; **1Ti** 1:16; **Rev** 1:19; 4:1; 9:12

HERS

Deut 21:15; **1Sa** 25:42; **2Kin** 8:6; **Job** 39:16

HERSELF

5315, *844, 846, 1438*

Gen 18:12; 20:5; 24:65; 38:14; **Ex** 2:5; **Lev** 15:28; 21:9; **Num** 22:25; 30:3; **Judg** 5:29; **Ruth** 2:10; **1Sa** 4:19; 25:23; 41; **2Sa** 11:2; **1Kin** 14:5; **2Kin** 4:37; **Job** 39:18; **Ps** 84:3; **Prov** 31:22; **Is** 5:14; 34:14; 61:10; **Jer** 3:11; 4:31; 49:24; **Eze** 22:3(2); 23:7; 24:12; **Hos** 2:13; **Zec** 9:3; **Mt** 9:21; **Mk** 4:28; **Lk** 1:24; 13:11; **Jn** 20:14; 16; **Heb** 11:11; **Rev** 2:20; 18:7; 19:7

HIGH

376, 753, 1111, 1116, 1361, 1362, 1363, 1364, 1386, 1419, 1870, 4546, 4605, 4608, 4791, 4796, 4869, 5375, 5920, 5943, 5945, 5946, 6381, 6877, 6967, 7218, 7311, 7312, 7315, 7319, 7413, 7682, 8203, 8205, 8564, 8643, *507, 749, 2032, 2409, 3173, 5308, 5310, 5311, 5313*

Gen 7:19; 14:18; 19; 20; 22; 29:7; **Ex** 14:8; 25:20; 37:9; 39:31; **Lev** 21:10; 26:22; 30; **Num** 11:31; 20:17; 19; 21:22; 28; 22:41; 23:3; 24:16; 33:3; 52; 35:25; 28(2); **Deut** 2:27; 3:5; 12:2; 26:19; 28:1; 43; 52; 32:8; 13; 27; 33:29; **Josh** 20:6; **Judg** 5:18; **1Sa** 9:12; 13; 14; 19; 25; 10:5; 13; 13:6; **2Sa** 1:19; 25; 22:3; 14; 34; 49; 23:1; **1Kin** 3:2; 3; 4;

6:10; 23; 7:15; 35; 9:8; 11:7; 12:31; 32; 13:2; 32; 33(2); 14:23(2); 15:14; 21:9; 12; 22:43(2); **2Kin** 12:3(2); 10; 14:4(2); 15:4(2); 35(2); 16:4; 17:9; 10; 11; 29; 32(2); 18:4; 22; 19:22; 21:3; 22:4; 8; 23:4; 5; 8(2); 9; 13; 15(3); 19; 20; **1Chr** 11:23; 14:2; 16:39; 17:17; 21:29; **2Chr** 1:3; 13; 3:15; 6:13; 7:21; 11:15; 14:3; 5; 15:17; 17:6; 20:19; 33; 21:11; 23:20; 24:11; 27:3; 28:4; 25; 31:1; 32:12; 33:3; 17; 19; 34:3; 4; 9; **Neh** 3:1; 20; 25; 13:28; **Est** 5:14; 7:9; **Job** 5:11; 11:8; 16:19; 21:22; 22:12; 25:2; 31:2; 38:15; 39:18; 27; 41:34; **Ps** 7:7; 17; 9:2; 18:2; 27; 33; 21:7; 46:4; 47:2; 49:2; 50:14; 56:2; 57:2; 62:9; 68:15; 16; 18; 69:29; 71:19; 73:11; 75:5; 77:10; 78:17; 35; 56; 58; 69; 82:6; 83:18; 89:13; 91:1; 9; 14; 92:1; 8; 93:4; 97:9; 99:2; 101:5; 103:11; 104:18; 107:11; 41; 113:4; 5; 131:1; 138:6; 139:6; 144:2; 149:6; 150:5; **Prov** 8:2; 9:14; 18:11; 21:4; 24:7; **Eccl** 12:5; **Is** 2:13; 14; 15; 6:1; 10:12; 33; 13:2; 14:14; 15:2; 16:12; 22:16; 24:18; 21(2); 25:12; 26:5; 30:13; 25(2); 32:15; 33:5; 16; 36:7; 37:23; 40:9; 26; 41:18; 49:9; 52:13; 57:7; 15(2); 58:4; 14; **Jer** 2:20; 3:2; 6; 21; 4:11; 7:29; 31; 12:12; 14:6; 17:2; 3; 12; 19:5; 20:2; 25:30; 26:18; 31:21; 32:35; 48:35; 49:16; 51:58; **Lam** 3:35; 38; **Eze** 1:18; 6:3; 6; 13; 16:16; 24; 25; 31; 39; 17:22(2); 24; 20:28; 29; 21:26; 31:3; 4; 34:6; 14; 36:2; 40:2; 42; 41:22; 43:7; **Dan** 3:6; 4:2; 17; 24; 25; 32; 34; 5:18; 21; 7:18; 22; 25(2); 27; 8:3; **Hos** 7:16; 10:8; 11:7; **Amos** 4:13; 7:9; **Obad** 3; **Mic** 1:3; 5; 3:12; 6:6; **Hab** 2:9; 3:10; 19; **Zeph** 1:16; **Hag** 1:1; 12; 14; 2:2; 4; **Zec** 3:1; 8; 6:11; **Mt** 4:8; 17:1; 26:3; 51; 57; 58; 62; 63; 65; **Mk** 2:26; 5:7; 6:21; 9:2; 14:47; 53; 54; 60; 61; 63; 66; **Lk** 1:78; 3:2; 4:5; 8:28; 22:50; 54; 24:49; **Jn** 11:49; 51; 18:10; 13; 15(2); 16; 19:2; 24; 26; 19:31; **Acts** 4:6(2); 5:17; 21; 24; 27; 7:1; 48; 9:1; 13:17; 16:17; 22:5; 23:2; 4; 5; 24:1; 25:2; **Rom** 12:16; 13:11; **2Cor** 10:5; **Eph** 4:8; 6:12; **Phil** 3:14; **Heb** 1:3; 2:17; 3:1; 4:14; 15; 5:1; 5; 10; 6:20; 7:1; 26; 27; 28; 8:1; 3; 9:7; 11; 25; 10:21; 13:11; **Rev** 21:10; 12

HIM

846

Gen 1:27; 2:15; 18(2); 20; 3:9; 23; 4:7; 8; 15(4); 19; 26; 5:1; 24; 6:6; 22; 7:5; 7; 16(2); 23; 8:1; 8; 9(2); 11; 12; 18; 9:8; 24; 10:21; 12(3); 4(2); 7; 20(2); 13:1; 11; 14; 14:5; 17(2); 19; 20; 15:4; 5(2); 6; 7; 9; 10; 12; 16:1; 12; 13; 17:1; 3; 17; 19(2); 20(4); 22; 23; 27; 18:1; 2; 9; 10; 18; 19(3); 29; 30; 19:3; 5; 6; 16(3); 21; 26; 30; 32; 34(2); 35; 20:3; 6; 9; 14; 21:2; 3(2); 4; 5; 7; 16(2); 18(2); 21; 22:1; 2; 3(2); 9(2); 11; 12; 13(2); 23:5; 14; 24:5; 6; 9; 18; 19; 24; 25; 32; 33; 35; 36; 47; 54; 25:2; 9; 21; 33; 26:2; 7; 9; 12; 14; 20; 24; 26; 31; 32(2); 27:1(2); 12; 13; 22; 23(2); 25(2); 26; 27(2); 32; 33; 37(3); 39; 41; 42; 44; 45; 28:1(3); 6(4); 29:5; 13(4); 14(2); 25; 30; 33; 30; 34; 30:4; 16; 20; 27; 29; 37; 31:2; 7; 14; 15; 20; 23(3); 24; 32; 32:1; 3; 6; 7; 11; 19; 17; 34:6; 8; 35:2; 6; 7; 9; 10; 11; 13; 14; 15; 18; 26; 29; 36:5; 37:3; 4(3); 5; 8(2); 10(2); 11; 13; 14(2); 15(2); 18(3); 20(3); 21(2); 22(4); 23; 24(2); 27(2); 33(2); 36; 38:5; 7; 10; 14; 18; 39:1(2); 3; 4(2); 5; 12(2); 15; 17; 19; 20(2); 21(2); 23; 40:7; 8; 9; 21; 41:12; 13; 14; 33; 34; 42; 43(3); 45; 50; 42:4; 6; 8; 10; 16; 24; 29; 31; 37(3); 38; 43:3; 5; 7; 9(4); 19; 26(2); 32(2); 33; 34(2); 44:7; 9; 14; 18; 20; 21(2); 24; 28; 29; 32; 45:1(2); 3; 9; 15; 26; 27(2); 28; 46:5; 6; 7(2); 20; 27; 28; 29; 31; 47:7; 18(2); 29; 31; 48:1; 10; 13; 17; 49:9; 11; 23(3); 26; 50:1(2); 9; 12; 13(2); 14; 15; 17; 26; **Ex** 1:16; 2:2(2); 3(2); 4; 6; 10(2); 12; 13; 20; 22; 3:2; 4; 18; 4:2; 6; 11; 13; 15; 16; 18; 23; 24(2); 26; 27(2); 28(2); 6:2; 20(2); 23(2); 25(2); 7:16; 8:1; 20; 9:1; 13; 29; 10:1; 3; 7; 28; 12:4; 44; 48; 49; 13:14; 19; 14:6; 15:2(2); 25; 16:8; 17:10; 12; 18:7; 17; 19:3; 7; 19; 24; 20:7; 21:3; 4(2); 6(3); 10; 13; 14(2); 16; 19(2); 22; 26; 27; 29; 30(2); 31; 36; 22:2; 3(2); 7; 12; 13; 17; 21; 25(2); 26; 23:4; 5(3); 21(3) 24:2; 14; 18; 28:1; 3; 41; 43(2); 29:5; 7; 17; 21(2); 29; 30:21; 31:3; 6; 18; 32:1(2); 23; 26(2); 33; 33:4; 15; 34:4; 5; 6; 20; 29; 30; 31; 32; 34; 35; 35:5; 21; 31; 36:2; 3; 38:23; 40:13(2); 16; **Lev** 1:3; 4(2); 4:3; 12; 14; 19; 21; 26(2); 31(2); 35; 5:2; 3; 4; 6; 10(2); 13(2); 16(2); 18(2); 6:2; 4; 5; 7(2); 7:18; 20; 8:2; 4; 7(6); 8; 12(2); 30(2); 9:9; 12; 13; 18; 13:3(2); 4; 5(2); 6(2); 8; 10; 11(2); 12; 13; 14; 15; 16; 17(2); 22:3; 23; 24:12; 10; 13(3); 16; 18; 24; 25; 26; 27; 31; 32; 33; 34; 36; 37; 39; 41; 43; 46; 47; 48; 49(3); 50(4); 52(2); 53(2); 54; 26:46; 27:8(2); 18; 19; 23; 24(2); **Num** 2:5; 12; 7:89(3); 8:2; 9:7; 14; 10:30; 11:20; 25(2); 29; 30; 12:6(2); 8; 13:27; 31; 14:24(2); 36; 15:28(2); 29(2); 31; 33(2); 34(2); 35; 36(2); 16:5(4); 10; 11; 25; 40; 17:6; 19:13(2); 17; 22(2); 33; 34; 20:2; 3; 4; 5(2); 6; 9; 21:2; 3; 8; 12; 15; 17; 22:3; 4; 24:9; 11; 12; 14(3); 16; 19; 20; 23(2); 25; 27; 28(2); 30; 35; 36; 37(2); 39; 41; 43; 47; 48; 49(3); 50(4); 52(2); 54; 26:46; 27:8(2); 18; 19; 23; 24(2); **Num** 2:5; 12; 7:89(3); 8:2; 9:7; 14; 10:30; 11:20; 25(2); 29; 30; 12:6(2); 8; 13:27; 31; 14:24(2); 36; 15:28(2); 29(2); 31; 33(2); 34(2); 35; 36(2); 16:5(4); 10; 11; 25; 40; 17:6; 19:13(2); 18; 20:9; 18; 19; 20; 21; 21:24; 34(3); 35(2); 22:5; 7; 16; 20; 22(2); 32; 36; 40; 41; 23:4; 6; 9(2); 13; 14; 17(3); 21; 24:2; 8; 9; 17(2); 19; 25:12; 13; 26:54; 27:11; 18; 19(2); 20; 21(2); 22(2); 23(2); 31:17; 18; 35; 32:15;

16; 21; 35:16; 17; 18; 19(2); 20(2); 21(3); 22(2); 23(2); 25; 27; 30; 32; 33; **Deut** 1:3; 16; 36; 38; 2:24; 30(2); 33(2); 3:2(3); 3(2); 28(2); 4:7; 20; 25; 29(2); 34; 35; 42; 5:11; 6:13; 16; 7:9; 10(4); 8:6; 9:18; 20; 23; 10:8; 9; 12; 18; 20(2); 11:13; 22; 13:4(3); 8(4); 9(3); 10; 14:27; 15:8(2); 9; 10(2); 12; 13(2); 14(2); 18; 17:7(2); 15; 18; 19; 18:4; 5(2); 15; 18; 19; 20; 22; 19:6(3); 11(3); 12(2); 13; 16; 19; 20:5; 6; 7; 8; 21:1; 2; 5; 15; 17; 18; 19(2); 21; 22; 23; 22:2(2); 4; 18; 19; 26; 23:10; 16(2); 24:1; 7(2); 13; 15; 25:2; 3(2); 5; 8(2); 9; 10; 11(3); 26:3; 28:44; 55; 29:15(2); 20(2); 21; 30:20; 31:7; 14; 29; 32:10(4); 12(2); 13(2); 15; 16(2); 33:7(3); 9; 11(2); 12(2); 16(2); 24(2); 34:1; 4; 6; 9(2); 11; **Josh** 1:18; 2:19; 23; 4:14; 5:3; 13(3); 14; 6:5; 7; 20; 7:3; 19; 24; 25; 26; 8:11; 14; 23; 9:6; 9(2); 10:7; 15; 23; 24; 29; 31; 33(2); 34; 36; 38; 43; 11:7; 9; 13:1; 14:6; 7; 13; 15:16; 17; 18(2); 19:50; 20:4(2); 5(2); 22:5(2); 14; 27; 30; 24:3(2); 14; 22; 30; 33(2); **Judg** 1:3; 5; 6(2); 7; 12; 13; 14(2); 15; 24; 2:9; 3:10; 13; 15; 16; 19(2); 20; 23; 27; 28; 31; 4:6; 7; 10; 13; 14; 18(2); 19(2); 21; 22(2); 5:13; 25; 31; 6:12(2); 13; 14; 15; 16; 17; 19; 20; 23; 25; 27; 31(5); 32(2); 34; 35; 7:1; 3; 5; 8; 9; 19; 8:1(2); 3; 4; 8(2); 14(2); 31; 9:3; 4(2); 16; 19; 21; 23; 24(2); 26; 28(2); 33; 34; 35; 36; 38(2); 40(2); 44; 48(3); 54(3); 10:3; 6; 11:2(2); 3; 11; 15; 19; 28; 34; 36; 12:5; 6(3); 8; 11; 13; 13:6; 10; 11; 12; 18; 23; 24; 25; 14:3; 5; 6(2); 11(2); 13; 16; 17; 18(2); 19; 15:1; 10; 12; 13(3); 14(2); 16:2(3); 5(4); 8; 9; 12(2); 14; 15; 16(2); 19(4); 20; 21(3); 24; 25; 26; 31(3); 17:9(2); 10; 11(3); 18:3; 5; 19; 25; 26; 19:1; 2(2); 3(4); 8; 11; 18:3; 5; 22(3); 5; 8; 9; 19; 8:10; 11; 12; 13; 3(2); 7; 10:2; 22; 26; 9(4); 11(4); 23:1; 11(4); 14; 24:3; 6; 16; 21(2); 22; 23; 25:6(3); 7; 10; 13; 15(2)4; 16; 24:3; 6; 16; 21(2); 22; 23; 25:6(3); 7; 10; 13; 15(2)4; 16; 24:3; 6; 16; 21(2); 22; 23; 25:6(3); 7; 10; 13; 15(2)4; 16; 14:6; 7; 13; 15:16; 17; 18(2); 19:50; 20:4(2); 5(2); **Ruth** 2:2; 4; 10; 3:13; 4:1; 15; **1Sa** 1:11; 17; 20; 22; 23(2); 24(3); 27; 28; 2:3; 16(2); 19(2); 25(2); 27; 28; 35; 36; 3:7; 13; 18(4); 19; 5:3; 4; 6:3; 4; 8; 7:3; 9; 8:5; 10; 9; 6; 13(2); 16; 17; 10:1; 9; 10(2); 11; 14; 16; 19; 21; 23; 24(2); 26; 27(2); 11:3; 5; 12:14; 24; 13:2; 7; 8; 10(2); 14(2); 15(2); 14:2; 7; 13(2); 17; 20; 24(3); 25; 33; 34; 36; 37; 39; 43; 52(2); 15:2; 12; 16; 18; 28; 32; 16:1; 3; 6; 7; 8; 11; 13; 14; 15; 17; 18; 21(2); 17:7; 7; 9(2); 15(2); 16; 14:6; 20(2); 22(2); 15:21; 24(2); 26; 31; 18:6; 7; 9(2); 10(2); 11(2); 14; 20; 21; 19:11; 16; 28; 20:7; 9(3); 11; 14; 16; 22; 23(2); 24; 25; 26(2); 27; 29; 21:15(2); 19; 21; 31; 33(3); 22:3; 14; 21; 27; 23:3; 4; 7; 8; 9(2); 13; 14; 15; 24:1; 10; 20(2); 23; 25:2; 26:2; 3; 6; 14; 27:9; 15; 20(2); 21(2); 22; 23(2); 29:12(2); 13; 30:25; 31:14; 15; 29(2); 37(2); 32:13; 14; 33:13; 23; 24(2); 26; 34:11; 13; 17; 19; 27; 28; 29; 35:6(2); 7; 14(3); 36:11; 22; 23; 28; 37:16; 18; 19; 20; 23; 24; 39:11(2); 12; 20; 23; 40:2(2); 9; 11; 12; 19(2); 20; 22(2); 41:4; 5(2); 6(2); 8; 9(2); 10; 11; 13; 22; **Ps** 2:12; 3:2; 4:3(2); 5:12; 7:4(2); 5; 13; 8:4(2); 5(2); 6; 10:9; 11:5; 12:5(3); 13:4; 17:13(2); 18:1; 6; 11; 12; 23; 30; 20:6; 21:2; 3; 4; 5; 6(2); 22:8(4); 23(3); 24(2); 25; 26; 29; 30; 24:6; 25:12; 14; 28:7(2); 32:6; 10; 33:2; 3; 8; 18; 21; 34:5; 6(2); 7; 8; 9; 19; 22; 35:8(2); 10(4); 25; 37:5; 7(2); 12; 13; 22(2); 24; 32; 33(2); 34; 40; 41:1; 2(3); 3; 8; 42:5; 11; 43:5; 44:16; 45:11; 49:7; 17; 50:3(2); 18; 23; 51:t; 52:t; 6; 53:5; 55:12; 20; 56:t; 57:3; 59:t; 61:7; 62:1; 4; 5; 8(2) 63:1; 64:4; 10; 66:6; 17; 67:7; 68:1(2); 4(2); 33; 69:26; 30; 34; 71:11(3); 72:9; 11(2); 12; 15(2); 17(2); 74:14; 76:11(2); 78:17; 34; 36(2); 37; 40(2); 58(2); 70; 71; 79:10; 81:15; 85:9; 13; 89:7; 20; 21; 22(2); 23; 24; 27; 28(2); 33; 41; 43; 45; 91:2; 14(2); 15(4); 16(2); 92:15; 94:12; 13; 95:2; 96:6; 9; 97:2; 3; 7; 98:1; 100:4; 101:5(2); 103:11; 13; 17; 104:34; 105:2(2); 21; 106:7; 10; 23; 29; 31; 32; 43; 107:32(2); 41; 109:6; 7; 12; 17(2); 19(2); 30; 31; 111:5; 113:8; 116:2; 117:1; 119:2; 42; 120:6; 126:6; 130:7; 135:1; 136:4; 5; 6; 7; 10; 13; 16; 17; 140:11; 141:5; 142:2(2); 144:3(2); 145:18(2); 19; 20; 147:11; 148:1; 2(2); 3(2); 4; 14; 149:2(2); 3; 150:1; 2(2); 3(2); 4(2); 5(2); **Prov** 3:6; 6:16; 7:10; 13(3); 20; 21(2); 8:9; 30(3); 9:4(3); 16(3); 10:13(2); 24; 26; 11:18; 26(2); 27; 12:14; 13:6; 18; 24(2); 14:2; 6; 7; 31; 33; 35; 15:9; 10; 12; 14; 21; 16:7; 13; 22; 26; 29; 17:8; 11; 24; 25; 18:9; 13; 16(2); 17; 19:7(3); 17; 19; 21:25; 22:15; 23:6; 13; 14; 24; 24:18(2); 24(2); 25; 29; 25:13; 21(2); 26:4; 12; 15; 17; 24; 25; 27; 27:11; 13; 14; 22; 28:8; 11; 17; 22; 29:20; 21; 23; 30:5; 31:1; 6; 7; 12; **Eccl** 2:26; 3:14; 22(2); 4:10(2); 12(2); 16; 5:12; 18; 19; 20; 6:2; 10; 12; 7:14; 8:3; 4; 6; 7; 12; 15(2); 9:2(2); 4; 17; 10:1; 3; 8; 14(2); 11:8; **Song** 1:2; 3:1(3); 2(3); 3; 4(4); 11; 5:4; 6(3); 8; 12; 19; 24(2); 46:7(5); 48:14; 14; 13(2); 15; 19(2); 21; 22; 23(2); 24(2); 27:6; 7(2); 11; 12; 28:9; 14(2); 29:26; 31; 30:8; 10; 21; 31:2; 10(2); 11(2); 20(4); 32:3; 4; 5; 9; 10; 33:13; 34:2; 14; 36:4; 8; 15; 22; 31; 37:4; 14(2); 15(2); 17(2); 21; 38:6; 11; 13; 14; 27(2); 39:5(3); 7(2); 9; 12(4); 14(2); 40:1(2); 2; 5(3); 6; 7; 14; 41:1; 2(2); 3; 7; 11; 12; 13; 16; 42:8; 9; 11; 43:1; 44:20; 45:4; 46:10; 25; 27; 48:11; 12(2); 17(2); 19; 26; 27; 35(2); 39; 49:5; 8(2); 19; 50:16; 17(2); 32(2); 43; 51:3(2); 44; 52:8;

9(2); 11(3); 31; 32(2); 33; 34; **Lam** 1:17; 2:19; 3:24; 25(2); 28; 30(2); **Eze** 1:3; 2:2; 3:18; 20(2); 27(2); 7:15; 9:4; 5; 10:7; 12:13(2); 14(2); 13:22; 14:4; 7(2); 8(2); 9(2); 10(2); 17:6(2); 7(2); 12; 13(2); 15(2); 16(2); 17; 20(3); 18:13; 20(2); 22; 32; 19:4(2); 5; 8(2); 9(3); 21:26(2); 27; 24:27; 28:9(2); 29:2(2); 20; 30:11; 24; 31:4(2); 8(2); 9(2); 11(3); 12(3); 15(3); 16; 17; 32:2; 21(2); 22; 25; 26; 33:2; 4; 5; 12; 16; 27; 35:7(2); 37:19; 38:2; 21; 22(3); 40:46; 43:6; 44:26; 45:20; 46:12; 47:23; **Dan** 2:1; 16; 22; 24; 25; 46; 48(2); 3:28; 4:8; 16(2); 19; 23; 34; 35; 5:6; 9; 11; 17; 19(2); 20; 21; 24; 29; 6:3(2); 4; 5; 6; 14(2); 16; 18(2); 22; 23(2); 7:10(3); 13(2); 14(2); 16; 27; 8:4; 6; 7(5); 11; 12; 9:4; 9; 11; 10:16; 11:1; 5; 11; 16(2); 17(3); 18(2); 22; 23; 25; 26; 30; 40(2); 44; 45; 12:7; **Hos** 1:3; 4; 6; 4:17; 5:6; 14; 7:5; 9; 10; 8:3; 11; 12; 9:4; 17; 11:1; 7; 12:2; 4(2); 14(3); 13:11; 13; 14:2; 4; 8(2); **Joel** 2:13; 14; 20; **Amos** 1:5; 8; 2(3); 3:5; 14; 5:8; 10(2); 11; 19(2); 6:10(3); 9:13; **Obad** 7; **Jonah** 1:6(2); 8; 10; 11; 15; 3:6(2); 4:5; 6; **Mic** 1:4; 2:7; 3(3); 5:5; 6:5; 6; 7:9; 15; **Nah** 1:5; 6; 7; 15; **Hab** 2:4; 5(2); 6(4); 9; 12; 15(3); 19; 20; 3:5; **Zeph** 1:6; 2:11; 3:9; **Hag** 1:12; **Zec** 1:8; 2:3; 4; 3:1; 4(3); 5; 4:11; 12; 5:4; 6:12; 8:10; 23; 9:8(2); 10:4(4); 12(1); 10(2); 13:3(4); 6; **Mal** 2:5(2); 12; 17; 3:16; 17; 18(3); 4:4; **Mt** 1:20; 24(2); 2:2; 3; 5; 8(2); 11(2); 13; 3:5; 6; 13; 14; 15(2); 16(2); 4:3; 5(2); 6; 7; 8(2); 9; 10(2); 11(2); 20; 22; 24; 25; 5:1; 25; 31; 39; 40; 41; 42(2); 6:8; 7:8; 9; 10; 11; 24; 8:1; 2; 3; 4; 5(2); 7(2); 16; 18; 19; 20; 21; 22; 23; 25(2); 27; 28; 31; 34(2); 9:2; 9(2); 10; 14; 18; 19; 20; 24; 27; 28(2); 32; 10:1; 4; 28; 32; 33; 40; 11:3; 15; 27; 12:2; 3; 4(2); 10(2); 14(2); 15; 16; 18; 22(2); 32(2); 46; 47; 48(3); 12; 9; 10; 12(2); 27; 28; 36; 43; 51; 57; 14:2; 3(2); 4; 5(2); 9; 13; 15; 17; 22; 26; 28; 31(2); 33; 35(2); 36; 15:4; 12; 15; 22; 23; 25; 30; 32; 33; 16:1; 17; 22(2); 24; 17:3; 5; 10; 12(2); 14(2); 16(2); 17; 18; 19; 23; 25; 26(2); 18(2); 6; 15(2); 17; 21(2); 22; 24(2); 25; 26; 27(2); 28(3); 29; 30; 32(2); 34(2); 19:2; 3(3); 7; 10; 11; 13; 16; 17; 18; 20; 21; 27; 20:7; 18; 19(2); 20(3); 21; 22; 25; 26; 27; 29; 33; 34; 21:7; 14; 16; 19; 21; 22; 23(2); 35(2); 37; 42; 43; 45; 46(2); 23:15; 21; 22; 24:1(2); 3; 15; 17; 18; 47; 50; 51(2); 25:6; 10; 21; 23; 26; 28(2); 29; 31; 32; 37; 44; 26:4; 7; 15(2); 16; 17; 18; 28; 29; 24; 25(2); 33; 34; 35; 37; 47; 48(2); 49; 54; 56(2); 7:1; 5; 10; 12; 14; 15(3); 16; 17(3); 18(2); 22; 23; 25; 26; 30; 35; 37; 39; 43; 44(3); 45; 48; 51; 52; 8:2; 3; 4; 6(2); 7(2); 13; 19; 20; 25; 26; 29; 30; 31(2); 33; 35(2); 36; 38; 39; 41; 44; 48; 52; 55(4); 57; 59; 9:2; 3; 4; 7; 8; 9; 10; 12; 13; 15; 17; 18(2); 21; 23; 24; 26; 28; 31; 34(2); 35; 36; 37; 39; 40; 41; 44; 48; 52; 55(4); 57; 59; 9:2; 3; 4; 7; 8; 9; 10; 12; 13; 17; 18(2); 21; 23; 24; 31; 34(2); 31; 35(2); 36; 37; 38; 39; 40; 47; 54; 57; 58(2); 8:2; 11; 20; 30(2); 31; 35; 38; 39; 41; 44; 48; 52; 55(4); 57; 59; 9:2; 3; 4; 7; 8; 9; 10; 12; 13; 17; 18(2); 21; 23; 24; 25(2); 30; 31; 35; 38; 39; 40; 47; 54; 57; 58; 8:2; 11; 20; 30(2); 31; 35; 38; 39; 40; 10:3(2); 4(2); 7; 11; 13; 15; 19; 21; 23; 25(2); 26; 27; 35(2); 38; 40(2); 41; 43(2); 48; 11:2; 13; 26(2); 12:4(5); 5; 6; 7(2); 8(2); 9; 10; 16; 17; 19(2); 20; 23; 13:9; 11(2); 22; 27(2); 28; 29(3); 30; 31; 34; 39; 14:9; 19; 20; 15:21; 38; 16:3(3); 9; 32; 17:15(2); 16; 17; 18; 19(2); 23; 27(2); 28; 31; 34; 18:12; 17; 18; 20; 26(2); 27; 19:2; 4(2); 22; 30; 31(2); 33; 38; 20:1; 3; 4; 10(3); 14; 16; 18; 37; 38; 21:8; 11; 12; 17(2); 21; 27; 29; 30; 31; 32; 33; 34; 36; 40; 22:9; 13; 18; 19; 22; 24(2); 25; 27; 29(3); 30(2); 23:2(2); 3; 9; 10(2); 11; 15(3); 17(2); 18(3); 19(3); 20; 21(2); 22; 23; 24; 27; 28(2); 30; 31; 32; 33; 35; 24:2; 7; 8; 10; 23(2); 24; 26(4); 25:2(2); 3(3); 5; 15; 16; 19; 21(2); 22; 25; 26; 27; 26:26; 27:3; 28:6; 8(2); 16; 21(2); 23; 30; 31; **Rom** 1:20; 21; 3:26; 4:3; 4; 5(2); 17; 22; 23; 24; 5:9; 14; 6:4; 6; 8; 9; 7:4; 8:11; 17; 20; 32(2); 37; 9:11; 16(2); 20; 33; 10:9; 11; 12; 14(2); 11:4; 35(2); 36(3); 12:8; 20(2); 13:4; 14:1; 3(5); 4; 14(2); 15; 15:11; 12; 16:25; **1Cor** 1:5; 30; 31; 2:2; 9; 11; 14; 16; 3:17; 18; 5:3; 7:12(2); 13; 15; 17; 18(2); 36; 8:3; 6(2); 10; 10:12; 11:14; 28; 34; 12:18; 14:2; 11; 13; 28(2); 37; 38; 15:27(2); 28(3); 38; 16:2(2); 11:3; 12; 22; **2Cor** 1:19; 20(2); 2:7(2); 8; 5:9; 15; 16; 21(2); 6:1; 7:14; 15; 8:18; 9:7; 10:7; 17; 11:4; 12:18; 13:4(2); **Gal** 1:1; 6; 8; 9; 16; 18; 2:11; 13; 3:6; 4:29; 5:8; 6:6(2); **Eph** 1:4(2); 10; 11; 17; 20(2); 22; 23; 2:18; 3:12; 20; 21; 4:15; 21(2); 28(3); 6:9; **Phil** 1:29; 2:7; 9(2); 22; 23; 27(2); 28(2); 29; 3:9; 10; **Col** 1:16(3); 17; 19; 20(2); 2:6; 7; 9; 10; 12(3); 13; 3:4; 10(2); 17; 4:10; 13; **1Th** 4:14; 5:10; **2Th** 1:12; 2:1; 9; 3:14; 15(2); **1Ti** 1:16; 5:1; **2Ti** 1:12; 18; 2:4(2); 11(2); 12(2); 26; 4:11; 14; **Titus** 1:16; **Philem** 1:12; 15; 17; **Heb** 1:5; 6; 2:3; 6(2); 7(3); 8(3); 10; 13; 14; 16(2); 17; 3:2(2); 4:13; 5:5; 7(2); 9; 6:6; 7:1; 6; 10; 21(2); 25; 9:9; 28; 10:30; 38; 11:5; 6(2); 9; 11; 12; 19(2); 27; 12:2; 3; 5; 25(3); 13:13; 15; **Jas** 1:5(2); 6; 12; 2:3(2); 5; 14; 23; 3:13; 4:17(2); 5:13(2); 14(3); 15(2); 19; 20; **1Pet** 1:8; 21(3); 2:6; 9; 14; 23; 3:6; 10; 11(2); 22; 4:5; 11(2); 16(2); 19; 5:7; 11; **2Pet** 1:3; 17; 18; 3:14; 15; 18; **1Jn** 1:5(2); 6; 2:9; 3:1; 2(2); 3; 5; 6(3); 9; 12; 15; 17(2); 28(2); 29; 3:1; 2(2); 3; 5; 6(3); 9; 12; 15; 17(2); 28(2); 4:9; 13; 15; 16; 19; 21; 5:1(3); 10; 14; 15; 16; 20(2); **2Jn** 10(2); 11; **Jude** 9; 15; 24; **Rev** 1:1; 4; 5; 6; 7(3); 17; 2:7(2); 11; 17(3); 26; 28; 29; 3:6; 12(3); 13; 20(2); 21; 22; 4:8; 9; 10(2); 5:1; 7; 13; 14; 6:2(2); 4; 8(2); 5; 8(2); 16; 7:14; 15; 8:3; 9:1; 10:6; 9; 12:9; 11; 13:2; 4; 5(2); 7(2); 8; 9; 12; 18; 14:1; 7(2); 15; 18; 16:8; 9; 17:14; 19:5; 7; 10; 11; 14; 19; 20(2); 21; 20:2; 3(3); 6; 11; 21:6; 22:3; 11(4); 17(3); 18

HIMSELF

Gen 14:15; 18:2; 19:1; 22:8; 23:7; 12; 24:52; 27:42; 30:36; 32:21; 33:3; 41:14; 42:7; 24; 43:31; 32; 45:1(2); 46:29; 47:31; 48:2; 12; **Ex** 10:6; 21:3(2); 4; **Lev** 7:8; 9:8; 14:8; 15:5; 6; 7; 8; 10; 11; 13; 21; 22; 27; 16:6(2); 11(3); 17; 24; 17:15; 21:4(2); 11; 22:8; 25:26; 47; 49; 27:8; **Num** 6:3; 5; 6; 7; 16:9; 19:12(2); 13; 23:24; 25:3; 31:53; 35:19; 36:7; 9; **Deut** 7:6; 14:2; 17:16; 17(2); 23:11; 28:9; 29:13; 19; 32:36; 33:21; **Josh** 22:23; **Judg** 3:19; 20; 4:11; 6:31; 7:5; 9:5; 16:30; **Ruth** 3:8; **1Sa** 2:14; 3:21; 8:11; 10:19; 22; 14:47; 17:16; 18:4; 14; 15; 30; 20:24; 41; 21:13; 23:19; 23; 24:8; 25:31; 26:1; 28:8; 14; 29:4; 30:6; 31; **2Sa** 3:6; 31; 6:20(2); 7:23; 9:8; 12:18; 20; 13:6;

14:22; 33; 15:23; 17:23; 18:18; 21; 24:20; **1Kin** 1:5; 23; 47; 5:2; 5:3; 2:19; 11:29; 15:15; 16:9; 17:21; 18:2; 6(2); 42; 19:4(2); 20:11; 16; 38; 21:25; 29(2); 22:30; **2Kin** 4:34; 35; 5:14; 6:10; 19:1; 23:16; **1Chr** 12:1; 13:13; 21:21; **2Chr** 12:1; 12; 13; 13:9; 12; 15:18; 16:9; 14; 17:1; 16; 18:29; 34; 20:3; 35; 36; 21:4; 23:1; 25:11; 14; 26:8; 20; 32:1; 5; 9; 26; 27; 33:12; 23(2); 35:22; 36:12; **Ezr** 10:1; 8; **Est** 5:10; **Job** 1:12; 2:1; 8; 4:2; 9:4; 15:25; 17:8; 18:4; 22:2; 23:9; 27:10; 32:2; 34:9; 14; 41:25; **Ps** 4:3; 10:10; 14; 35:8; 36:2; 4; 37:35; 50:6; 52:7; 54:t; 55:12; 68:30; 87:5; 93:1; 109:18; 113:6; 132:18; 135:4; 14; **Prov** 5:22; 9:7(2); 11:25; 12:9; 13:7(2); 14:14; 16:4; 26; 18:1; 24; 21:13; 22:3; 25:9; 14; 27:12; 28:10; 29:15; **Eccl** 5:9; 10:12; **Song** 2:9; 3:9; 5:6; **Is** 2:9; 20; 3:5; 7:14; 8:13; 19:17; 22:16; 28:20(2); 31:4; 37; 38:15; 44:5(2); 14; 15; 16; 23; 45:18; 56:3; 59:15; 61:10; 63:12; 64:7; 65:16(2); **Jer** 10:23; 16:20; 23:24; 29:26; 27; 31:18; 34:9; 37:12; 43:12; 48:26; 42; 49:10; 51:3; 14; **Lam** 1:9; **Eze** 7:13; 14:7; 24:22; 25:12; 45:22; **Dan** 1:8(2); 6:14; 8:11; 25; 9:26; 11:36(2); 37; **Hos** 5:6; 7:8; 8:9; 10:1; 13:1; **Amos** 2:14; 15(2); 6:8; **Jonah** 4:8; **Hab** 2:6; **Mt** 6:4; 8:17; 12:15; 26; 45(2); 13:21; 16:24; 18:4; 23:12(2); 27:3; 5; 42; 57; **Mk** 3:7; 21; 26; 5:5; 30; 6:17; 8:34; 12:33; 36; 37; 14:54; 67; 15:31; **Lk** 3:23; 5:16; 6:3; 7:39; 9:23; 25; 10:1; 29; 11:18; 26; 12:17; 21; 37; 47; 14:11(2); 15:15; 17; 16:3; 18:4; 11; 14(2); 19:12; 20:42; 23:2; 7; 35; 51; 24:12; 15; 27; 36; **Jn** 2:24; 4:2; 12; 44; 53; 5:13; 18; 19; 20; 26(2); 37; 6:6; 15; 61; 7:4; 18; 8:7; 10; 22; 59; 9:21; 11:38; 51; 12:36; 13:4; 32; 16:13; 27; 18:18; 19; 7; 12; 21:1(2); 7; 14; **Acts** 1:3; 2:34; 5:13; 36; 7:26; 8:9; 13; 34; 9:26; 10:17; 12:11; 14:17; 16:27; 18:19; 19:22; 31; 20:13; 21:26; 25:4; 8; 16; 25; 26:1; 24; 27:3; 28:16; **Rom** 12:3; 14:7(2); 12; 22; 15:3; **1Cor** 2:15; 3:15; 18; 7:36; 11:28; 29; 14:4; 8; 28; 37; 15:28; **2Cor** 5:18; 19; 10:7(2); 18; 11:14; 20; **Gal** 1:4; 2:12; 20; 6:3(2); 4; **Eph** 1:5; 9; 2:15; 20; 5:2; 25; 27; 28; 33; **Phil** 2:7; 8; 3:21; **Col** 1:20; **1Th** 3:11; 4:16; **2Th** 2:4(2); 16; 3:16; **1Ti** 2:6; **2Ti** 2:4; 13; 21; **Titus** 2:14(2); 3:11; **Heb** 1:3; 2:14; 6:13; 7; 7; 14; 9:7; 14; 25; 26; 12:3; **Jas** 1:24; 27; **1Pet** 2:23; **1Jn** 2:6; 3:3; 5:10; 18; **3Jn** 10; **Rev** 19:12; 21:3

HIS

Gen 1:11; 12(2); 21; 24(2); 25(2); 27; 2:2(2); 3; 7; 21; 24(3); 25; 3:8; 15; 20; 21; 22; 4:1; 2; 4(2); 5(2); 7; 8(2); 17(2); 21; 23; 25(2); 26; 5:3(3); 29; 6:3; 5; 6; 9; 12; 20; 7:2(2); 7(3); 13; 14(3); 8:9; 18(3); 21(2); 9:1; 6; 8; 21; 22(2); 24(2); 25; 26; 27; 10:5; 10; 15; 25(2); 11:28(2); 31(4); 12:5(2); 8; 11; 12; 17; 20(2); 13:1; 3(2); 10; 12; 18; 14:12; 14(2); 15; 16(2); 17; 16:3; 11; 12(2); 15; 17:3; 14(2); 17(2); 19(2); 23(3); 24; 25(2); 26; 27; 18:2; 19(2); 33; 19:1; 3; 14(3); 16(3); 26; 30(2); 37; 38; 20:2; 7; 8; 14; 17(2); 21:2; 3; 4; 5; 7; 11; 21; 22; 23:3; 6; 9; 10; 18; 19; 24:2(2); 7; 9(2); 10(3); 15; 19; 24; 26; 27(2); 29(3); 32(2); 40; 48; 59; 61; 63; 67(3); 25:6; 8; 9; 10; 11; 17; 18; 21(2); 25; 26(3); 28; 30; 34(2); 26:7; 8; 11(2); 15(2); 17; 18(2); 25; 26(2); 27:12(2); 5; 10; 11; 13; 14(3); 16(2); 19; 20; 22; 23(2); 26; 27; 28; 29; 30(2); 32(2); 40; 48; 59; 61; 63; 67(3); 27:2(2); 3; 4(2); 5; 8; 9; 10(3); 11; 13; 14; 15; 16; 27(3); 30; 33; 34; 35(2); 36; 37; 38; 39(3); 37:1; 2(3); 3(2); 4(2); 5; 8(3); 9; 10(3); 11; 12(2); 13; 23(3); 30(2); 31; 32(2); 34; 35(2); 36; 37; 38; 39(3); 37:1; 2(3); 3(2); 4(2); 5; 8(3); 9; 10(3); 11; 12(2); 13; 23(3); 30(2); 31; 32(2); 34; 35(2); 36; 37; 38; 39(3); 38:1; 3; 4; 5; 6; 7; 9; 11(2); 12(2); 13; 16; 20(2); 28(2); 29(3); 30(3); 39:2; 3(2); 5; 7; 8; 9; 11; 12(2); 13; 15; 16(2); 18; 19(3); 49:1; 10; 11(4); 12(2); 13; 15; 16; 17; 20; 24(2); 26; 28; 31(2); 33(3); 50:1; 2(2); 4; 7(2); 8(2); 10; 12; 13; 14(3); 18(2); 20; 21; 22; 24; 3:1; 6; 14; 16; 17; 18; 19; 34:3; 4; 5(4); 13; 19; 20; 24(3); 26(2); 30(2); 32; 33; 34; 35(2); 36; 37; 38; 39(3); 37:1; 2(3); 4(2); 5(2); 6; 7(5); 8; 15(3); 18; 25; 26; 28; 29(4); 31(2); 47:2; 3; 5; 7; 11(2); 22; 23; 24; 46:1(2); 4; 6; 7(5); 8; 15(3); 18; 25; 26; 28; 29(4); 31(2); 47:2; 3; 5; 7; 11(2); 22; 23; 24; 48:1; 9; 12(2); 13(2); 14(3); 17(3); 18(2); 19(3); 49:1; 10; 11(4); 12(2); 13; 15; 16; 17; 20; 24(2); 26; 28; 31(2); 33(3); 50:1; 2(2); 4; 7(2); 8(2); 10; 12; 13; 14(3); 18(2); 20; 24; **Ex** 1:1; 6; 9; 22; 2:4; 7; 10; 11(2); 12; 21; 22; 24; 3:1; 6; 13; 4:4(2); 6(3); 7(4); 14; 15(2); 18; 20; 23(3); 25(2); 26; 27; 32:2; 21; 25; 5:2; 21; 21; 6:7; 10; 12:4(3); 6(3); 7(4); 9(2); 17(3); 22; 29(3); 30(3); 39:2; 3(2); 5; 7; 8; 9; 11; 12(2); 13; 15; 16(2); 18; 19(3); 28:1; 4; 12; 21; 29; 30; 35; 38; 41; 43(2); 29:4; 6; 7; 8(3); 10; 14(2); 15; 16; 17(3); 19; 20(2); 21(6);

24; 27; 28; 29; 30; 31; 32; 35; 44; 30:12; 18; 19; 21; 27(2); 28(2); 30; 33; 38; 31:8(2); 9(2); 10; 14; 32:11; 14; 15; 19; 27(5); 29(2); 33:4; 8; 10; 11(2); 34:4; 8; 15; 20; 26; 29; 30; 33; 35; 35:11(7); 13(2); 14(2); 15; 16(4); 17; 19; 21(2); 34; 36:4; 24(2); 37:16(4); 17(5); 20(2); 23(3); 39:5; 14; 21; 27; 33(6); 39(4); 40(4); 41; 40:10; 11; 12; 14; 18(2); 31; **Lev** 1:3(2); 4; 6; 9(2); 10; 11; 12(3); 14(2); 15; 16(2); 2:1; 2; 3; 10; 3:1; 2(2); 6; 7; 8(2); 12; 13; 14; 4:3; 4; 6; 11(5); 17; 19; 22; 23(3); 24; 25(2); 26(2); 28(4); 29; 30; 33; 34; 35; 5:1; 4; 6(3); 7; 8(2); 10; 11; 12; 13; 15; 17; 18; 6:2(2); 5; 6; 9; 10(3); 11; 15; 16; 20; 22(2); 25; 7:13(2); 15; 16(2); 18(2); 20(2); 21; 25; 27; 29(3); 30; 31; 33; 34; 35; 8:2; 6; 9(2); 11(2); 14; 15; 17(3); 18; 22; 23(2); 27; 30(6); 31(2); 36; 9:1; 9; 22; 10:1; 3; 6; 12; 11:14; 15; 16; 22(4); 25; 27; 28; 29; 40(2); 12:3; 13:2(3); 3; 4; 5; 6; 7; 11; 12(2); 13; 23; 28; 34; 35; 37; 40; 41(3); 42(2); 43(2); 44(2); 45(3); 46; 55; 14:2; 8(3); 9(7); 14(2); 15; 16(3); 17(3); 19; 23; 25(2); 26; 27(2); 28(3); 32; 47(2); 15:2(2); 3(7); 5(2); 6; 7; 8; 10; 11(2); 13(4); 15; 16; 21; 22; 27; 16:4(2); 6(2); 11; 12; 14(2); 15; 17; 19; 21; 24(3); 26(2); 28(2); 32; 17:2; 4; 9; 10; 15; 16(2); 18:14; 19:3(2); 8(2); 21; 22; 20:2; 3(2); 4; 5; 6; 9(5); 10; 11(2); 12; 17(6); 19; 20(2); 21(2); 21:1; 2(6); 3; 4; 7; 10(3); 11(2); 12(2); 14; 15(2); 17; 20(2); 21; 22; 24; 22:2; 3; 6; 7; 11(3); 18(4); 21; 23; 23:29; 30; 37; 24:9; 11; 14; 15(2); 19; 25:10(2); 13; 25(3); 27; 28; 30; 33; 41(3); 48; 49(3); 50; 51; 52(2); 54; 27:8; 14; 15(2); 16; 17; 18; 22; 28; 31; **Num** 1:4; 44; 52(2); 2:2; 4; 6; 8; 11; 13; 15; 17; 19; 21; 23; 26; 28; 30; 3:7; 9; 10; 38; 48; 51; 4:5; 9(3); 15; 19(3); 25; 27; 49(2); 5:7; 9; 10(2); 14(2); 15; 18; 30; 6:4; 5(3); 7(6); 8; 9(3); 11; 12(2); 13; 14; 16(2); 17(2); 18(2); 19; 21(4); 23; 25; 26; 7:5; 11; 12; 13; 19; 25; 31; 37; 43; 49; 55; 61; 67; 73; 79; 8:8; 13; 19; 22; 9:2; 3; 7; 13(3); 10:14; 18; 22; 25; 11:1; 10; 28; 29; 12:12; 14:24; 15:4; 24(2); 30; 31(2); 16:4; 5(2); 6; 17(3); 18; 40; 17:2; 9; 19:3; 4; 5; 7(2); 8(2); 10; 13; 19; 21; 20:8; 11(2); 21; 24; 25; 26(3); 28(2); 21:23(2); 24; 26(2); 29(2); 33; 34(2); 35(3); 22:5; 18; 21; 22(2); 23(2); 31(4); 23:6; 7; 10; 16; 17; 18; 21; 24:1; 2(2); 3; 4; 7(4); 8(2); 10; 13; 15; 16; 18; 20(2); 21; 23; 25(2); 25:5; 6; 7; 13(2); 26:54; 27:1; 3; 4; 8(2); 9(2); 10(2); 11(4); 21(2); 23; 28:10; 15; 24; 31; 29:6(2); 16(2); 22(2); 25(2); 28(2); 31(2); 34(2); 38(2); 30:2(3); 4; 7; 11; 14(2); 16(2); 31:6; 32:18; 21; 42; 33:54; 35:8(2); 21; 23(2); 25; 26; 27; 28(2); 32; 36:2; 7; 8; 9; **Deut** 1:16; 31; 36; 41; 2:12; 24; 30(2); 31(2); 32; 33(2); 34; 3:1; 2(2); 3; 4; 11; 14; 20; 4:13; 30; 36(3); 37(2); 40(2); 42; 47; 5:11; 21(5); 24(3); 6:2(2); 13; 17(2); 22; 7:3(2); 7; 9; 10; 8:2; 5; 6; 11(3); 18; 9:23; 10:6(2); 8; 9(2); 12; 13; 20; 11:1(4); 2(3); 3(3); 14; 22; 12:5(2); 8; 11; 21; 13:4(2); 17; 18; 14:13; 14; 15; 21; 23; 24; 15:2(3); 8; 17; 16:2; 6; 11; 17:2; 17; 18; 19(2); 20(5); 18:1; 5; 6; 7(2); 8; 10(2); 18; 19:4; 5(3); 6; 9; 11; 12; 18; 19; 20:5; 6; 7; 8(3); 21:16; 17(2); 18(2); 19(4); 20; 21; 23; 22:1; 3(2); 4; 19(2); 24; 26; 29(2); 30(2); 23:1; 2; 7; 15(2); 24:1(2); 2; 3(2); 4; 5; 7; 10(2); 12; 13; 15(3); 16; 25:2(2); 6(2); 7(3); 8; 9(5); 10(2); 26:2; 17(5); 18(2); 27:10(2); 16(2); 17; 20(2); 22(3); 23; 24; 28:1; 9; 12(2); 15(2); 40; 45(2); 54(4); 55; 29:2(2); 12; 19; 20(2); 23(2); 30:2; 8; 10(2); 16(4); 20; 32:4(2); 5; 9(2); 10; 15; 19(2); 36(2); 43(5); 50; 33:1; 2; 3; 6; 7(3); 9(4); 11(2); 12; 13; 16; 17(3); 21; 24(2); 26; 28; 34:6; 7(2); 9; 11(2); **Josh** 2:19(3); 3:15; 4:5; 14; 18; 5:13(3); 14(2); 6:26(2); 27; 7:6(2); 18; 22; 24(6); 26; 8:1(3); 14; 18; 19; 26; 29; 9:24; 10:21; 33; 11:15; 13:27; 15:17; 17:3; 6; 10; 20:4; 5(2); 6(2); 21:12; 22:5(2); 20; 29; 24:3; 4; 10; 24; 28; 30; 33; **Judg** 1:2; 3; 6(2); 13; 17; 25; 2:6; 9; 3:10(2); 16(2); 20; 21(3); 22; 24(3); 4:7(2); 10; 11; 13; 15(4); 17; 21; 22; 5:11; 17; 26(2); 28(2); 31; 6:11; 13; 21(2); 27(2); 31; 32; 7:5(2); 7; 8; 11; 13; 14(2); 21; 22; 8:20(2); 21; 24; 25; 27(2); 29; 30; 31; 32; 9:1(2); 3; 5(2); 7; 16(2); 17; 18(2); 19; 21; 24; 26; 28; 30; 31; 41; 48(2); 49; 53; 54(2); 55; 56(2); 10:16; 11:2; 3; 11; 20(2); 21; 23; 32; 34(3); 35; 39; 12:9; 13:2; 5; 6(2); 7; 11; 19; 20; 21; 22; 23; 24; 14:2(2); 3(3); 4(2); 5(2); 6(3); 9(2); 10; 19(2); 20(2); 15:1; 6(2); 14(3); 15; 17; 19; 16:3; 5; 9; 12; 14; 16; 17; 18(2); 19(2); 20; 21; 22; 29(2); 30(3); 31(3); 17:2(2); 3(2); 4(2); 5(2); 6; 11; 12; 18:4; 26; 30; 19:2; 3; 4; 5; 7; 9(3); 10; 11; 12; 13; 15; 16; 17; 21; 24; 25; 27(2); 28; 29(2); 20:8(2); 21:1; 21; 22; 24(3); 25; **Ruth** 1:1(2); 2(2); 6; 2:1; 5; 15; 20; 22; 3:4; 7(2); 8; 14; 4:5; 7(2); 8; 10(3); 13; 14; 17; **1Sa** 1:1; 3; 4; 11(2); 19; 20; 21(2); 23; 2:9; 10(2); 11; 13; 19; 20; 22; 3:2(2); 9; 12; 13(2); 19; 4:10; 12(2); 13; 15; 18; 19; 5:3(2); 4(2); 7; 11; 6:2; 3; 5; 9(2); 7:1; 15; 17(2); 8:1; 2(2); 3(2); 11(3); 12(4); 14; 15(2); 16; 17; 22; 9:2; 3; 5; 7; 10; 15; 22; 10:1(2); 9; 14; 16; 23; 25; 27; 11:6; 7; 12:3; 5; 14; 22(3); 13:2; 14(2); 16; 20(4); 22; 14:1(2); 6; 7; 12(2); 13(4); 14; 17; 20; 26(2); 27(5); 34(3); 45; 47; 49; 50; 15:1; 27; 34; 35; 16:1; 4; 5; 7(2); 10; 13; 16; 17; 20; 21; 23; 17:5; 6(2); 7(2); 13; 15; 17; 22(2); 25(2); 28; 33; 34; 35(2); 38(2); 39(2); 40(4); 43; 49(5); 51(2); 54(2); 57; 18:1; 2; 3; 4(4); 7(2); 10; 11; 13; 14; 22(2); 26; 27(2); 30; 19:1(2); 4(3); 5(2); 7; 9(4); 13; 16; 24; 20:6; 17; 25; 27; 32; 33; 34; 36; 38; 40(2); 41; 21:7; 11(2); 12; 13(3); 14; 22:1(2); 6(3); 7; 11; 15; 23:5; 6; 8; 11; 13; 14; 15; 16; 18; 22(2); 24; 25; 26(3); 24:2; 3(2); 6; 7(2); 8; 16; 19; 22; 25:1; 2; 3(2); 4; 10; 13(4); 17; 20; 24; 25(2); 36; 37(2); 39(2); 42; 43; 44; 26:5; 7(2); 9; 10; 11; 16; 18; 19; 23(2); 25(2); 27:1(2); 3(3); 8; 11; 12; 28:3; 5; 7(2); 14; 18; 23; 25; 29:2; 4(2); 5(2); 11; 30:1; 3; 6(3); 12; 18; 22(2); 24(2); 26; 31; 31:2; 4(2); 5(2); 6(3); 7; 8; 9(2); 10(2); 12; **2Sa** 1:2(2); 4; 5; 6; 10(2); 11; 12; 17; 2:2; 3(2); 16(3); 21; 27; 29; 32(2); 3:2; 3; 8(2); 12; 27; 29; 30; 32; 38; 39; 4:1; 4(3); 6; 7(3); 8; 9; 10; 11(3); 12; 5:6; 12(2); 21; 6:6; 7; 11; 14; 17; 19; 20(2); 21; 7:1(2); 12; 13; 14; 25; 27; 8:3; 10; 15; 9:3; 6; 9; 11; 13; 10:1(2); 2(3); 3; 10; 11:1; 2; 9(2); 10; 13(3); 27(2); 12:3(4); 4(2); 9(2); 15; 17; 19(2); 20(2); 21; 24(2); 25; 30; 13:2; 8; 17; 18; 22(2); 24; 28; 29; 31(2); 32; 33; 34; 36; 37; 14:7(2); 9; 13; 14; 15; 16; 22(2); 24(2); 25(3); 26(2); 30; 31; 33; 15:5; 12; 14; 16; 18; 22; 25; 30(2); 32(2); 16:6(2); 9; 11; 12; 13; 18; 19; 22; 17:6; 8; 18; 23(6); 18:9; 14; 17; 18(2); 19; 24; 25; 28; 19:2; 4; 8; 11(2); 17(2); 19; 24(3); 30; 39; 41; 20:1; 3(2); 8; 10(2); 21(2); 22; 21:1; 2; 4; 6; 12; 13; 14(2); 15; 22; 22:1; 7(2); 9(2); 10; 14; 16; 23(2); 25; 31; 51(3); 23:2; 8; 10(2); 18; 21(2); 23; 24:14; 16; 20(2); 21; **1Kin** 1:2; 6(2); 9; 10; 21; 23; 37; 47; 49; 51; 2:1; 3(5); 4; 5(4); 6; 9; 10; 12(2); 15; 19(2); 22; 23; 32(2); 33(4); 34; 35; 40(3); 3:1; 3; 6; 15; 4:7(2); 21; 25(2); 26; 27; 28; 31; 32; 34; 5:1(2); 3(2); 10; 11; 7:1(2); 8; 14(2); 23; 51; 8:6; 14; 15(2); 20; 22; 28; 31; 32(3); 38(2); 39; 54(2); 56(3); 58(4); 59(2); 61(2); 66(2); 9:11; 15; 16; 19(3); 22(5); 27; 10:5(5); 13; 24(2); 25; 11:3(2); 4(5); 6; 8; 9; 17; 19; 20; 21; 23; 26; 27(2); 33; 34(2); 35; 36; 41; 43(4); 12:4; 6; 15; 18; 24; 26; 33; 13:4(2); 11; 12; 13; 19; 24; 27; 28; 30(2); 31(2); 33; 14:2; 4(2); 8; 18; 20(3); 21(2); 31(5); 15:2; 3(4); 4(2); 5; 6; 8(3); 10; 11; 12; 13; 14; 15; 18; 23(3); 24(5); 26(2); 28; 29; 30; 34; 16:3; 4; 5; 6(3); 7(2); 9(3); 10; 11(3); 13; 19(2); 20; 26; 27; 28(3); 34(3); 17:17; 19; 23; 18:3; 7; 42(2); 43; 46; 19:3(2); 6; 13(2); 19; 20:1; 11; 12; 20; 24; 31; 35; 38; 39; 41; 42(2); 43; 21:4(3); 5; 7; 8(2); 11(2); 25; 27(2); 29(3); 22:3; 10; 17; 19(3); 22; 31(2); 34; 35; 36(2); 38(2); 40(3); 42; 43; 45; 46; 50(5); 52(2); 53; **2Kin** 1:2; 8; 9; 10; 11; 12; 13(2); 16; 17; 2:8; 12; 3:2(3); 25; 27(2); 4:12; 18; 19(2); 20; 25; 32; 34(6); 35; 37; 38; 39; 43; 5:1; 3; 4; 6; 7(2); 8; 9(2); 11(2); 13; 14; 15; 20; 23; 25; 26; 27; 6:7; 8; 11; 12; 15; 17; 24; 30(2); 32(2); 7:12; 13; 8:11; 14; 15(2); 18; 19(2); 20; 24(4); 26; 9:2; 3; 6; 11(2); 13; 21(2); 23; 24(4); 25(2); 26; 28(3); 31; 32; 36; 10:3; 10; 11(3); 15; 16; 19(2); 24; 31; 34; 35(3); 11:2; 8(2); 9; 11(2); 18(2); 12:1; 2; 5; 17; 18(2); 20; 21(4); 13:8; 9(3); 12; 13(2); 14(2); 16(2); 21; 23(2); 24(2); 25; 14:2; 3(2); 5(3); 6; 15; 16(3); 20; 21; 22; 25; 28; 29(3); 15:2; 3; 5; 7(4); 9; 10; 14; 15; 18; 19(2); 22(3); 25(2); 30; 33; 34; 38(5); 16:2(2); 3; 13(4); 15; 20(4); 17:3; 15(3); 18; 20; 23(2); 18:2; 3; 6; 12; 21; 29; 31(3); 33; 19:1; 4; 7(2); 19; 23(2); 37(4); 20:2; 13(5); 20; 21(3); 21:1; 3; 6; 7; 10; 11; 12; 16; 17; 18(4); 19; 20; 21(2); 22; 23; 24(2); 26(3); 22:1; 2; 11; 23:3(3); 10(2); 18(2); 25(3); 26(2); 29; 30(3); 31; 32; 34(2); 35; 36; 37; 24:1(2); 2; 3; 6(3); 7; 8; 9; 11; 12(5); 15; 17(3); 18; 20; 25:1(2); 5; 7; 28; 29(2); 30(2); **1Chr** 1:13; 19(2); 43; 44; 45; 46(2); 47; 48; 49; 50(3); 2:4; 13; 18; 35(2); 42; 3:3; 10(3); 11(3); 12(3); 13(3); 14(2); 16(2); 17; 4:9(3); 18; 19; 23; 25(3); 26(3); 27; 5:1(2); 2; 4(3); 5(3); 6; 7; 6:20(3); 21(4); 22(3); 23(3); 24(4); 26(2); 27(3); 29(3); 30(3); 39(2); 49; 50(3); 51(3); 52(3); 53(2); 7:14; 16(3); 18; 20(4); 21(2); 22; 23(3); 24; 25(3); 26(3); 27(2); 35; 8:1; 8; 9; 10; 30; 37(3); 39(2); 9:5; 19(2); 36; 43(3); 10:2; 4(2); 5; 6(2); 7; 8; 9(2); 10(2); 12; 13; 11:10; 11; 20; 23; 25; 45; 12:15; 19; 28; 13:9; 10; 14; 14:2(2); 4; 15:3; 5; 6; 7; 8; 9; 10; 17; 16:7; 8(2); 9; 10; 11(2); 12(3); 13(2); 14; 15; 16; 23; 24(2); 27(2); 29; 34; 37; 39; 41; 43(2); 17:1; 11; 12; 13; 14; 21; 23; 25; 18:3; 10(2); 14; 19:1(2); 2(2); 3; 7; 11; 13; 15; 19; 20:2; 8; 21:3; 13; 16(2); 20; 21; 23; 27; 22:5; 6; 9(3); 10(2); 17; 18; 23:1; 13(2); 14; 25; 25:9; 10(2); 11(2); 12(2); 13(2); 14(2); 15(2); 16(2); 17(2); 18(2); 19(2); 20(2); 21(2); 22(2); 23(2); 24(2); 25(2); 26(2); 27(2); 28(2); 29(2); 30(2); 31(2); 26:6; 10; 14(2); 15; 22; 25(6); 26; 28; 29; 30; 31; 32; 27:2; 4(2); 5; 6(2); 7(2); 8; 9; 10; 11; 12; 13; 14; 15; 28:1; 2; 6; 7; 11; 19; 20; 29:5; 23; 28(2); 30(2); **2Chr** 1:1(2); 8; 13; 2:1; 11; 12; 14; 15; 17; 3:1; 2; 4:16; 5:1; 7; 13; 6:3; 4(2); 10; 12; 13(2); 19; 22; 23(3); 29(3); 30; 7:3; 6; 10; 11; 8:1; 6; 9(3); 14; 18; 9:4(5); 8; 23(2); 24; 31(4); 10:4; 6; 15; 18; 11:4; 12; 14; 21(2); 22; 23; 12:8; 13(2); 14; 16(3); 13:2; 5; 6; 12; 17; 22(2); 14:1(4); 2; 11; 13; 15:9; 17; 18; 16:4; 5; 12(4); 13(2); 14; 17:1(2); 2; 3; 4(2); 5; 6; 7(2); 18:8; 9; 16; 18(3); 21; 33; 34; 19:1; 20:18(2); 20; 21; 25; 30; 31; 32; 21:1(4); 4(2); 7; 8; 9(2); 10(2); 17(3); 18; 19(4); 22:1(2); 2; 3(2); 4(3); 9; 11; 23:7(2); 8; 10(2); 11; 13; 17(2); 24:1; 11; 13; 16; 22(2); 25(2); 27(3); 25:1; 3(2); 4; 11; 14; 22; 28; 26:1; 2; 3; 4; 8; 15; 16(3); 19(2); 20; 21(2); 23(4); 27:1; 2; 6(2); 7(2); 9(3); 28:1; 3; 5; 22; 25; 26(2); 27(3); 29:1; 2; 3; 10; 19(2); 25; 30:2; 6; 8(2); 9; 19(2); 27; 31:1; 2; 3; 8; 10; 12; 13; 16; 20; 21(2); 32:3(2); 8; 9(2); 12(2); 14; 15; 16(2); 17; 21(3); 25; 26; 30; 31; 32; 33(4); 33:3; 6; 7; 10; 12(2); 13(2); 18(2); 19(3); 20(4); 22(2); 23; 24(2); 25(2); 34:2; 3(2); 4; 8(2); 19; 27; 31(6); 33; 35:3; 4; 8; 9; 22; 23; 24(2); 26; 27; 36:1; 4(3); 5; 7; 8(3); 10; 12; 13(2); 15(3); 16(3); 17; 18; 20; 22; 23(2); **Ezr** 1:1; 3(2); 4; 7; 2:1; 68; 3:2(2); 3; 9(3); 11; 4:6; 5:6; 15; 17; 6:5; 7; 10; 11(2); 12; 7:6(2); 9; 10; 11; 13; 14; 15; 23; 28; 8:17; 18(2); 19; 22(2); 25(2); 9:8; 10:8; 11; 18; **Neh** 1:5; 2:1; 20; 3:1; 10; 12; 17; 23; 28; 29; 30; 4:2; 15; 17; 18(2); 22; 5:7; 13(2); 6:5(2); 11; 18; 19; 7:3(2); 6; 8:4(2); 16; 9:8(2); 10(2); 10:29(2); 11:3; 13; 17; 20; 12:8; 36; 45; 47; 13:10; 26; 30; **Est** 1:2; 3(3); 4(2); 8; 12(2); 20; 22; 2:3; 7(2); 8; 15; 16(2); 17; 18(2); 3:1; 10(2); 4:1; 3; 4; 11; 17; 5:1; 2(2); 10(2); 11(2); 14(2); 6:6; 8; 12(2); 13(4); 7:5; 7(2); 8:2; 3(2); 5(2); 7; 17; 9:1; 4; 25(3); 10:2(2); 3(3); **Job** 1:3; 4(2); 10(3); 13(2); 20(2); 2:3; 4; 5(2); 6; 7(2); 9; 10; 11; 12; 13; 3:1(2); 19; 4:9; 17; 18(2); 5:3; 4; 18; 26; 6:5; 9; 14; 7:1; 2; 10(2); 8:12; 15; 16(2); 17; 18; 19; 9:5; 13; 33; 34(2); 11:5; 12:4; 5; 11; 16; 13:8; 11(2); 14:5(3); 6; 18; 20; 21; 22(2); 15:2; 15(2); 20; 21; 23; 25; 26(2); 27(3); 29; 30(2); 31; 32(2); 33(2); 16:9(3); 12; 13; 21; 17:5(2); 9; 18:4(2); 5; 6(2); 7(2); 8; 11; 12(2); 13(2); 14(2); 15(3); 16(2); 17; 19(2); 20; 19:6; 11(2); 12; 20:6(2); 7; 9; 10(2); 11(2); 12(2); 13; 14(2); 15; 18; 20; 21(2); 22; 23(2); 25; 26(2); 27; 28(3); 21:17; 19(2); 20(2); 21(2); 23; 24(2); 25; 31(2); 22:22(2); 23:3; 6; 11(2); 12(2); 13; 15; 24:1; 6; 15; 22; 23; 25:2; 3(2); 5; 26:8; 9(2); 11; 12(2); 13(2); 14(2); 27:1; 8; 9; 14(2); 15; 18; 19; 21; 22; 23; 28:9; 10; 29:1; 3(2); 17; 30:24(2); 31:20; 23; 30; 31; 32:1; 2; 3(2); 5; 12; 14; 33:10; 13; 17; 18(2); 19(2); 20(2); 21(2); 22(2); 23; 25(2); 26(2); 28(2); 30; 34:11; 14(3); 19; 21(2); 27; 29; 35; 36; 37(3); 35:15; 16; 36:7; 15; 18; 22; 23; 24; 26; 29; 30; 37:1; 2(2); 3; 4(2); 5; 6; 7; 11; 12; 13; 15; 38:12; 32(2); 41(2); 39:6; 8; 10; 11; 18; 19; 20; 21; 40:16(4); 17(2); 18(2); 19; 23; 24(2); 41:1; 2(2); 7(2); 12(3); 13(2); 14(2); 15(2); 18(2); 19; 20; 21(2); 22; 23; 24; 33; 42:10; 11(4); 12; 16(2); **Ps** 1:2(2); 3(3); 2:2; 5(2); 12; 3:t, 4; 7:12(2); 13; 16(4); 17; 8:6; 9:7; 11; 16; 10:2; 3; 4(2); 5(3); 6; 7(2); 8; 9(2); 10; 11(2); 13; 15; 16; 11:4(3); 5; 7; 12:2; 14:1; 6; 7; 15:2; 3(3); 4; 5; 17:12; 18:t, 6(2); 8(2); 9; 11(2); 12; 13; 14; 22(2); 24; 30; 50(3); 19:1; 5; 6(2); 12; 20:6(3); 21:2(2); 3; 5; 9; 22:24; 29; 31; 23:3; 24:3; 4; 5; 25:9; 10(2); 13(2); 14; 22; 27:4; 5(2); 6; 28:5; 8; 29:2; 9(2); 11(2); 30:4(2); 5(2); 31:21; 23; 33:4; 6; 11; 12; 14; 17; 18; 21; 34:t, 1; 3; 6; 9; 15; 20; 22; 35:8; 9; 14; 27; 36:1; 2(2); 3; 4; 37:7; 10; 12; 13; 23; 24; 25; 26; 28; 30; 31(3); 33; 34; 38:13; 39:5; 11; 40:4; 41:2; 3(2); 5; 6; 9; 42:5; 8(2); 46:6; 47:8; 48:1; 49:7; 16; 17; 18; 19; 50:4; 6; 23; 52:7(3); 53:1; 6; 54:7; 55:20(2); 21(3); 56:4; 10(2); 57:3(2); 58:7(2); 9; 10; 59:9; 60:6; 61:6; 62:4; 12; 64:9; 65:6; 66:2(2); 5; 7(2); 8; 20; 67:1; 68:1; 4(2); 5; 21(2); 33; 34(2); 35; 69:33; 36(2); 72:7; 9; 14; 17(2); 19(2); 73:10; 76:1; 2(2); 77:8(2); 9; 78:4(2); 7; 10; 11(2); 20; 22; 26; 32; 37; 38(2); 42; 43(2); 49; 50; 52; 54(2); 56; 61(2); 62(2); 66; 69; 70; 71(2); 72(2); 79:7; 81:6(2); 85:8(2); 9; 13; 87:1; 89:23(2); 24; 25(2); 29(2); 30; 36(2); 39; 40(2); 41; 42(2); 43; 44(2); 45; 48; 91:4(3); 11; 14; 94:14(2); 95:2; 4(2); 5(2); 7(3); 96:2(2); 3(2); 6; 8(2); 13; 97:2; 3; 4; 6(2); 10; 12; 98:1(2); 2(2); 3(2); 99:5; 6(2); 7; 9; 100:2; 3(2); 4(3); 5(2); 101:5; 102:t, 16; 19; 21; 103:1; 2; 7(2); 9; 11; 13; 15; 17; 18(2); 19(2); 20(3); 21(3); 22(2); 104:3(2); 4(2); 13; 15; 19; 23(2); 31; 105:1(2); 2; 3; 4(2); 5(3); 6(2); 7; 8; 9; 19; 21(2); 22(3); 24; 25(2); 26; 27; 28; 42(2); 43(2); 45(2); 106:1; 2; 8(2); 12(2); 13(2); 23(2); 24; 26; 33(2); 40(2); 45(2); 107:1; 8(2); 15(2); 20; 21(2); 22; 24; 31(2); 108:7; 109:6; 7; 8(2); 9(2); 10; 11; 12; 13; 14(2); 18(3); 31; 110:5; 111:3(2); 4; 5; 6(2); 7(2); 9(3); 10(2); 112:1; 2; 3(2); 5; 7; 8(3); 9(2); 10; 113:4; 8; 114:2(2); 116:2; 12; 14; 15; 18; 117:2; 118:1; 2; 3; 4; 29; 119:2; 3; 9; 125:2; 126:6; 127:2; 3; 5; 128:1; 129:7(2); 130:5; 8; 131:2; 132:1; 7(2); 13; 18(2); 133:2; 135:3; 4; 7; 9; 12; 14(2); 136:1; 2; 3; 4; 5; 6; 7; 8; 9; 10; 11; 12; 13; 14; 15(2); 16(2); 17; 18; 19; 20; 21; 22(2); 23; 24; 25; 26; 140:8; 144:4; 10; 145:3; 9(2); 12(2); 17(2); 21; 146:4(3); 5(2); 147:5; 9; 11; 15(2); 17(2); 18(2); 19(3); 20; 148:2(2); 8; 13(2); 14(2); 149:1; 3; 4; 9; 150:1(2); 2(2); **Prov** 2:6; 8; 3:11; 20; 31; 32; 5:21; 22(2); 23; 6:13(3); 14; 15; 27(2); 28; 29; 30; 31; 32; 33; 7:23(2); 8:22(2); 29(2); 30; 31; 36; 10:1; 9; 15; 19; 11:1; 5(2); 7; 8; 9(2); 12(2); 17(2); 19; 20; 28; 29; 12:4; 8; 10; 11; 13; 14; 15; 22; 26; 13:1; 2; 3(3); 8; 16; 22; 24(2); 25; 14:2(2); 8; 10(2); 14; 15; 20; 21; 26; 31; 32(2); 35; 15:5; 8; 20; 23; 27; 32; 16:2; 7; 9(2); 10; 11; 15; 17(2); 23(2); 26; 27; 29; 30(2); 32; 17:5; 12; 13; 18; 19; 21; 25; 27; 28(2); 18:2; 6; 7(3); 9; 11(2); 14; 17(2); 20(2); 19:1(2); 2; 3(2); 4; 7; 8; 11(2); 12; 13; 16(2); 18; 22; 24(3); 26(2); 20:2; 6; 7(2); 8; 11(2); 14; 16; 17; 19; 20(3); 24; 28; 21:2; 8; 10(2); 13; 23(3); 24; 25; 29(2); 22:5; 8; 9; 11(2); 16; 25; 29; 23:3; 6; 7(2); 14; 31; 24:7; 12; 15; 18; 26; 29; 25:5; 13; 18; 22; 28; 26:4; 5(2); 11(2); 12; 14(2); 15(3); 16; 19; 24; 25; 26; 27:8; 13; 14; 16; 17; 18; 21; 22; 28:6(2); 7; 8; 9(2); 10; 11; 13; 14; 16; 18; 19; 24(2); 25; 26; 27; 29:1; 3(2); 5(2); 10; 11; 12; 14; 15; 20; 21(2); 24; 25; 30:4(3); 6; 10; 17(2); 31:1; 7(2); **Eccl** 1:3; 5; 6; 2:14; 21; 22(2); 23(3); 24(2); 26; 3:11; 12; 13; 22(2); 4:4; 5(2); 8(2); 10; 14; 15; 5:14; 15(3); 17(2); 18(3); 19(2); 20(2); 6:2; 3(2); 4; 7; 12; 7:2; 15(3); 8:1(2); 3; 9; 12; 13; 15(2); 16; 9:12; 15; 16; 10:2(2); 3; 13(2); 12:5; 13; **Song** 1:2; 4; 12; 2:3(2); 4; 6(2); 16; 3:7; 8(2); 11(3); 4:16(2); 5:4; 11(2); 12; 13(2); 14(2); 15(2); 16; 6:2; 7:10; 8:3(2); 7; 10; **Is** 1:3(2); 2:3(2); 10; 19; 20(2); 21; 22; 3:5; 6(2); 8; 11; 14; 5:1; 7; 12; 19; 25(4); 6:1; 2(2); 3; 6; 7:2(2); 14; 8:3; 7(3); 8; 17; 9:4(3); 6(2); 7(2); 11; 12(2); 17(2); 19; 20; 21(2); 10:4(2); 7(2); 12(2); 16(2); 17(3); 18(2); 19; 24; 26; 27(2); 28; 32; 11:1; 3(2); 4(2); 5(2); 8; 10; 11(2); 15(2); 16; 12:4(3); 13:5; 10; 13; 14(2);

14:17; 18; 21; 25(2); 27; 29; 31; 32; 15:4; 5; 16:6(4); 12; 17:4; 5; 7(2); 8(2); 9; 19:1; 2(2); 14; 22:21; 22; 23; 24; 23:11; 24:2; 23; 25:4; 8; 9; 11(2); 26:21; 27:1; 8; 9; 28:4; 5; 21(4); 24; 26; 28(2); 29:8(2); 22; 23; 30:4(2); 26; 27(3); 28; 30(3); 31:2; 3; 4; 7(2); 8; 9(3); 32:6; 33:6; 15(3); 16(2); 17; 34:2; 14; 16; 17; 36:6; 16(3); 18; 37:1; 4; 7(2); 20; 24(2) 38(4); 38:2; 9; 39:2(5); 40:10(3); 11(3); 12; 13; 26; 28; 41:2(3); 3; 6(2); 42:2; 4; 10; 12; 13; 21; 24(2); 25; 44:5; 6; 11; 12(2); 13; 17; 19; 20; 26(2); 45:1; 9; 10; 11; 13; 46:7(3); 47:4; 15; 48:2; 14(2); 15; 16; 19; 20; 49:2(2); 5; 7; 13(2); 50:10(2); 51:14; 15; 17; 22; 52(2); 9; 10; 14(2); 53:5; 6; 7(2); 8; 9(3); 10(4); 11(2); 12; 54:5; 16; 55:7(2); 56:2; 3; 6; 10; 11(2); 57:2; 13; 17(2); 18(2); 58:5(2); 59:1; 2; 16(2); 17; 18(2); 19; 60:2; 22; 62:8(2); 11(2); 63:1(2); 7(2); 9(3); 10; 11(3); 12; 65:15; 20; 66:5; 6; 13; 14(3); 15(3); 16; **Jer** 1:2; 9; 15; 2:3; 15(2); 35; 3:1; 5; 4:7(3); 13(2); 26; 5:8; 24; 6:3; 21; 7:5; 29; 8:1; 6(2); 16(2); 9:4; 5; 8(3); 20; 23(3); 10:10(2); 12(3); 13(2); 14(2); 16(2); 23; 25; 11:19; 12:15(2); 13:23(2); 16:12; 17:5; 10(2); 11(2); 18:11; 12; 16; 18; 19:3; 9; 20:9(2); 21:2; 7; 9; 22:4(2); 7; 8; 10; 11; 13(4); 18; 28; 30(2) 23:6(2); 9; 14; 17; 18(2); 20; 27; 30; 34; 35(2); 36; 24:8; 25:4; 5; 19(3); 30(3); 38(2) 26:3; 21(2); 23; 27:7(3); 8; 12; 28:11; 29:32; 30:6(2); 8; 18; 21; 24; 31:10; 30(2); 34(2); 35; 32:4(2); 18; 19(2); 33:2; 11; 21; 26; 34:1(2); 3(2); 9(3); 10(2); 14; 15; 16(2); 17(2); 21; 35:3(2); 14; 15; 18; 36:3; 7; 14; 17; 18; 24; 30; 31(2) 37:2; 10; 17; 38:2; 39:1; 6; 40:3; 42:11; 43:10(2); 12; 44:21; 23(3); 30(4); 46:15; 17; 26; 47:3(3); 48:7(2); 10 11(4); 12; 15; 16; 17; 25; 26; 29(4); 30(2); 35; 40; 49:1(2); 2; 3(2); 10(4); 20; 22; 50:16(2); 17; 18; 19(2); 25(2); 28(2); 32; 34; 43; 45; 51:3(2); 5; 6; 9; 11(2); 15(3); 16(2); 17(2); 19(2); 21(2); 23(2); 28; 31; 34; 44; 45; 59; 52:1; 3; 4(2); 8; 10; 11; 27; 31; 32(2); 33(4); 34(3); **Lam** 1:10; 12; 14; 17; 18; 2:1(3); 2; 3(2); 4(3); 5; 6(3); 7(3); 11; 3; 12; 13; 22; 27; 29; 30; 32; 34; 36; 39; 4:4; 11(2); 20; **Eze** 1:15; 27(2); 3:12; 18(4); 19(3); 20(4); 7:13; 16; 20; 8:2(2); 11(2); 12; 9:1(2); 2(3); 3; 11; 10:7; 12:12(3); 14; 13:22; 14:4(5); 7(4); 16:15; 17:4; 14; 15; 17; 18; 19; 20; 21(2); 22; 18:6(2); 7(2); 8; 11; 12; 13; 14 15(2); 16; 17(2); 18(4); 21; 22(2); 23; 24(4); 26(2); 27(2); 28; 30; 19:7; 9; 20:7; 39; 21:3; 4; 5; 21; 22; 30; 22:11(4); 25:9(2); 26:3; 9; 10; 11; 29:3; 18(2); 8; 30:10:11; 22(2); 24; 31:2; 3; 4; 5(3); 6(3); 7(3); 8(3); 9; 10(3); 12; 13(2); 13; 13(2); 14; 16; 17; 25; 26; 29(4); 30(2); 35; 40; 49:1(2); 31; 34; 44; 45; 59; 52:1; 3; 4(2); 8; 10; 11; 27; 31; 32(2); 33(4); 34(3); **Lam** 1:10; 12; 14; 17; 18; 2:1(3); 2; 3(2); 4(3); 8; 10; 11; 27; 31; 2; 3(2); 4(3); 5; 6(2); 7(3); 8; 12; 3; 12; 13; 22; 27; 29; 30; 32; 34; 36; 39; 4:4; 11(2); 20; **Eze** 1:15; 27(2); 3:12; 18(4); 19(3); 20(4); 7:13; 16; 20; 8:2(2); 11(2); 9; 12; 9:1(2); 3; 11; 10:7; 12:12(3); 14; 13:22; 14:4(5); 16:15; 17:4; 14; 15; 17; 18; 19; 20; 21(2); 22; 18:6(2); 8; 8; 14; 18(2); 19:6; 12; 31; 33; 20:7; 10; 28; 32; 38; 21:11; 19; 22:14(2); 15; 20; 30; 23:29; 30; 24:8; 23; 24; 27:3; 28:3; 4; 8; 23; 30; **Rom** 1:2; 3; 5; 9; 20; 2:4; 6; 18; 26; 3:7; 20; 24; 25(2); 26; 4:5; 13; 19; 23; 5:8; 9; 10(2); 6:3; 5(2); 16; 8:3; 9; 11; 28; 29; 32; 9:19; 22(2); 23; 11:1; 2; 22; 33(2); 34; 12; 13:10; 14:4; 5; 13; 15:2(2); 9; 10; 16:13; 15; **1Cor** 1:9; 29; 2:10; 3:8(2); 5:1; 6:5; 14; 18; 7:2; 4; 7; 11; 33; 36; 37(4); 9:7; 10; 10:24; 28; 11:4(2); 7; 21; 14:25(2); 30; 15:10; 23(2); 25; 27; 38; 16:12; **2Cor** 2:11; 14; 3:7; 13; 5:10; 7:7; 12(2); 13; 15; 8:9; 17; 9:7; 9; 15; 10:10(3); 11:3; 15; 33; **Gal** 1:15; 16; 3:16; 4:4; 6; 5:10; 6:4; 5; 8; **Eph** 1:5; 6; 7(2); 9(2); 11; 12; 14; 18(2); 19(2); 20; 22; 23; 2:4; 7(2); 10; 15; 3:5; 6; 7; 16(2); 4:25; 28; 5:28; 29; 30(3); 31(2); 33; 6:10; 7; 16(2); 4:25; 28; 5:28; 29; 30(3); 31(2); 33; 6:10 **Phil** 1:29; 2:4; 13; 30; 3:10(3); 21; 4:19; **Col** 1:9; 11; 13; 14; 20; 22(2); 24; 26; 29; 2:14; 18; 3:9; 4:15; **1Th** 1:10; 2:11; 12; 19; 3:13; 4:4; 6; 8; **2Th** 1:7; 9; 10; 11; 2:6; 8(2); **1Ti** 3:4(2); 5; 5:8(2); 18; 6:1; 15; **2Ti** 1:8; 9; 2:19; 26; 4:1(2); 8; 14; 18; **Titus** 1:3; 3:5; 7; **Heb** 1:2; 3(3); 7(2); 2:4; 8; 17; 3:2; 5; 6; 7; 15; 18; 4:1; 4; 7; 10(3); 13; 5:7; 6:10; 17; 7:10; 27; 8:11(2); 9:12; 10:13(2); 20; 30; 11:4; 5; 7; 17; 21; 22; 23; 12:10; 16; 13:12; 13; 15; 21(2); **Jas** 1:8; 11; 14; 18(2); 23; 24; 25; 26(2); 2:21; 22; 3:13; 4:11(2); 5:20; **1Pet** 1:8; 2:9; 21; 22; 24(2); 3:10(2); 12; 4:2; 13; 5:10; **2Pet** 1:3; 9; 16; 2:8; 16; 22; 3:4; 9; 13; 16; **1Jn** 1:3; 7; 10; 2:3; 4; 5; 9; 10; 11(2); 12; 28; 3:9; 10; 12(3); 14; 15; 16; 17(2); 22(2); 23(2); 24; 4:9; 10; 12; 3; 20(3); 21; 5:2; 3(2); 9; 10; 11; 16; 20; **2Jn** 6; 11; **3Jn** 7; 10; **Jude** 14; 24; **Rev** 1:1(3); 4; 5; 6; 14(3); 15(2); 16(4); 17(2); 2:1; 5; 18(2); 3:5(3); 21; 6:5; 8; 17; 7:15; 9:11; 10:1(3); 2(3); 5; 7; 11:15; 19(2); 12:3; 4; 5; 7(2); 9; 10; 15; 16; 13:1(2); 2(4); 3(2); 6(3); 17; 18:14:1; 7; 9(4); 10; 11(2); 14(2); 16; 19; 15:2(3); 8; 16:2(2); 3; 4; 8; 10(2); 12; 15(2); 17; 19; 17:17; 18:1; 19:2(2); 5; 7; 10; 12(2); 13; 15; 16(2); 19; 20; 21; 20:1; 4(2); 7; 21:3; 7; 22:3; 4(2); 6(2); 12; 14; 19

HOW

Gen 26:9; 27:20; 28:17; 30:29(2); 38:29; 39:9; 44:8; 16; 34; 47:8; 18; **Ex** 2:18; 6:12; 30; 9:29; 10:2; 3; 7; 11:7; 16:28; 18:8; 19:4; 36:1; **Num** 10:31; 14:11(2); 27; 20:15; 23:8(2); 24:5; **Deut** 1:12; 31; 7:17; 9:7; 11:4(2); 6; 12:30; 18:21; 25:18; 29:16(2); 31:27; 32:30; **Josh** 2:10; 9:7; 24; 10:1(2); 14:12; 18:3; **Judg** 13:12(2); 16:15; 18:7; 20:3; 21:7; 16; **Ruth** 1:6; 2:11; 3:18; **1Sa** 1:14; 2:22; 10:27; 12:24; 14:29; 30; 15:2; 16:1; 2; 17:18; 23:3; 24:10; 18; 28:9; **2Sa** 1:4; 5; 14; 19; 25; 27; 2:22; 26; 4:11; 6:9; 20; 11:7(3); 12:18; 16:11; 18:19; 19:2; 34; 24:3; **1Kin** 3:7; 5:3; 8:27; 12:6; 14:19(2); 18:13; 21; 19:1; 20:7; 21:29; 22:16; 45; **2Kin** 5:7; 13; 6:15; 32; 8:5; 9:25; 10:4; 14:15; 28(2); 17:28; 18:24; 19:25; 20:3; 20; **1Chr** 13:12; 18:9; 19:5; **2Chr** 6:18; 7:3; 18:15; 20:11; 32:15; 33:19; **Ezr** 7:22; **Neh** 2:6; 17; **Est** 2:11; 5:11; 8:6(2); **Job** 4:19; 6:25; 7:19; 8:2(2); 9:2; 14; 13:23; 15:16; 18:2; 19:2; 21:17(2); 34; 22:12; 13; 25:4(2); 6; 26:2(2); 3(2); 14; 34:19; 37:17; **Ps** 3:1; 4:2(2); 6:3; 8:1; 9; 11:1; 13:1(2); 2(2); 21:1; 31:19; 35:17; 36:7; 39:4; 44:2(2); 62:3; 66:3; 73:11; 19; 74:9; 10; 22; 78:40; 43; 79:5; 80:4; 82:2; 84:1; 89:46; 47; 50; 90:13; 92:5; 94:3(2); 4; 104:24; 119:84; 97; 103; 159; 132:2; 133:1(2); 137:4; 139:17(2); **Prov** 1:22; 5:12; 6:9; 15:11; 23; 16:16; 19:7; 20:24; 21:27; 30:13; **Eccl** 2:16; 4:11; 10:15; 11:5; **Song** 4:10(2); 5:3(2); 7:1; 6:2; **Is** 1:21; 6:11; 14:4; 12(2); 19:11; 20:6; 36:9; 37:26; 38:3; 48:11; 50:4; 52:7; **Jer** 2:21; 23; 3:19; 4:14; 21; 5:7; 8:8; 9:7; 19; 12:4; 5(2); 15:5; 22:23; 23:26; 31:22; 36:17; 46:13; 47:5; 6; 7; 48:14; 17; 39(2); 49:25; 50:23(2); 51:41(3); **Lam** 1:1(3); 2:1; 4:1(2); 2; **Eze** 14:21; 15:5; 16:30; 26:17; 33:10; **Dan** 4:3(2); 8:13; 10:17; 12:6; **Hos** 8:5; 11:8(4); **Joel** 1:18; **Obad** 5; 6(2); **Mic** 2:4; **Hab** 1:2; 2:6; **Zeph** 2:15; **Hag** 2:3; **Zec** 1:12; 9:17(2); **Mt** 6:23; 28; 7:4; 11(2); 10:19; 25; 12:4; 5; 12; 14; 26; 29; 34; 15:34; 16:9; 10; 11; 12; 21; 17:17(2); 18:12; 21; 21:20; 22:12; 15; 43; 45; 23:33; 37; 26:54; 27:13; **Mk** 2:16; 26; 3:6; 23; 4:13; 27; 40; 5:16; 19; 20; 6:38; 8:5; 19; 20; 21; 9:12; 19(2); 21; 10:23; 24; 11:18; 12:26; 35; 41; 14:1; 11; 15:4; 34; 58; 62; 2:49; 6:4; 42; 7:22; 8:18; 39(2); 47; 9:41; 10:26; 11:13(2); 18; 12:11; 24; 27; 28; 50; 56; 13:34; 14:7; 15:17; 16:2; 5; 7; 18:24; 19:15; 20:41; 44; 21:5; 22:2; 4; 61; 23:55; 24:6; 20; 35; **Jn** 3:4; 9; 12; 4:1; 9; 5:44; 47; 6:42; 52; 7:15; 8:33; 9:10; 15; 16; 19; 26; 10:24; 11:36; 12:19; 34; 14:5; 9; 22; 28; **Acts** 2:8; 4:21; 5:9; 7:25; 8:31; 9:13; 16; 27(2); 10:28; 38; 11:13; 16; 12:14; 17; 13:32; 14:27; 15:7; 14; 36; 19:35; 20:20; 35(2); 21:20; 23:30; **Rom** 3:6; 4:10; 6:2; 7:1; 18; 8:32; 10:14(3); 15(2); 11:2; 12; 24; 33; **1Cor** 1:26; 3:10; 6:3; 7:16; 32; 33; 34; 10:1; 14:7; 9; 16; 26; 15:3; 12; 35; **2Cor** 3:8; 7:15; 8:2; 12:4; 13:5; **Gal** 1:13; 4:9; 13; 6:11; **Eph** 3:3; 6:21; **Phil** 1:8; 2:23; 4:12(2); **Col** 4:6; **1Th** 1:9; 2:10; 11; 4:1; 4; **2Th** 3:7; **1Ti** 3:5(2); 15; **2Ti** 1:18; **Philem** 1:16; 19; **Heb** 2:3; 7:4; 8:6; 9:14; 10:29; 12:17; **Jas** 2:22; 24; 3:5; **2Pet** 2:9; **1Jn** 3:17; 4:20; **Jude** 5; 18; **Rev** 2:2; 3:3; 6:10; 18:7

HUNDRED

Gen 5:3; 4; 5; 6; 7; 8; 10; 11; 13; 14; 16; 17; 18; 19; 20; 22; 23; 25; 26; 27; 28; 30; 31; 32; 6:3; 15; 7:6; 24; 8:3; 9:28; 29; 11:10; 11; 13; 15; 17; 19; 21; 23; 25; 32; 14:14; 15:13; 17:17; 21:5; 23:1; 15; 16; 25:7; 17; 32:6; 14(2); 33:1; 19; 35:28; 45:22; 47:9; 28; 50:22; 26; **Ex** 6:16; 18; 20; 12:37; 40; 41; 14:7; 27:9; 11; 18; 30:23(3); 24; 38:9; 11; 24; 25(2); 26(2); 27(3); 28; 29; **Lev** 26:8(2); **Num** 1:21; 23; 25; 27; 29; 31; 33; 35; 37; 39; 41; 43; 46(2); 2:4; 6; 8; 9(2); 11; 13; 15; 16(2); 19; 21; 23; 24(2); 26; 28; 30; 31(2); 32(2); 3:22; 28; 34; 43; 46; 50; 4:36; 40; 44; 48; 7:13; 19; 25; 31; 37; 43; 45; 49; 55; 61; 67; 73; 79; 85(2); 86; 11:21; 16:2; 17; 35; 49; 26:7; 10; 14; 18; 22; 25; 27; 34; 37; 41; 43; 47; 50; 51(2); 31:28; 32; 36(2); 37; 39; 43(2); 45; 52; 33:39; **Deut** 22:19; 31:2; 34:7; **Josh** 7:21; 24:29; 32; **Judg** 3:31; 4:3; 13; 7:6; 7; 8; 16; 19; 22; 8:4; 10; 26; 11:26; 15:4; 16:5; 17:2; 3; 4; 18:11; 16; 17; 20:2; 10(2); 15; 16; 17; 35; 47; 21:12; **1Sa** 11:8; 13:15; 14:2; 15:4; 17:7; 18:25; 27; 22:2; 23:13; 25:13(2); 18(3); 27:2; 30:9; 10(2); 17; 21; **2Sa** 2:31; 3:14; 8:4(2); 10:18; 14:26; 15:11; 18; 16:1(3); 21:16; 23:8; 18; 24:9(2); **1Kin** 4:23; 5:16; 6:1; 7:2; 20; 42; 8:63; 9:23; 28; 10:10; 14; 16(2); 17; 26; 29(2); 11:3(2); 12:21; 18; 20; 22; 20:15; 29; 22:6; **2Kin** 3:4(2); 26; 4:43; 14:13; 18:14; 19:35; 23:33; **1Chr** 4:42; 5:18; 21(2); 7:2; 9; 11; 8:40; 9:6; 9; 11; 11; 20; 12:14; 24; 25; 26; 27; 30; 32; 35; 37; 15:5; 6; 7; 8; 10; 18:4; 21:3; 5(2); 25; 22:14; 25:7; 26:30; 32; 29:7; **2Chr** 1:14; 17(2); 2:2; 17(2); 18; 3:4; 8; 16; 4:8; 13; 5:12; 7:5; 8:10; 18; 9:9; 13; 15(2); 16(2); 11:1; 12:3; 13:3(2); 17; 14:8(2); 9; 15:11; 17:11(2); 14; 15; 16; 17; 18; 18:5; 24:15; 25:5; 6(2); 9; 23; 26:12; 13(2); 27:5; 28:6; 8; 29:32(2); 33; 35:8(2); 9; 36:3; **Ezr** 1:10; 11; 2:3; 4; 5; 6; 7; 8; 9; 10; 11; 12; 13; 15; 17; 18; 19; 21; 23; 25; 26; 27; 28; 30; 31; 32; 33; 34; 35; 36; 38; 41; 42; 58; 60; 64; 65(2); 66(2); 67(2); 69; 6:17(3); 7:22(4); 8:3; 4; 5; 9; 10; 12; 20; 26(3); **Neh** 5:17; 7:8; 9; 10; 11; 12; 13; 14; 15; 16; 17; 18; 20; 22; 23; 24; 26; 27; 28; 30; 31; 32; 33; 34; 35; 36; 37; 38; 39; 41; 44; 45; 60; 62; 66; 67(2); 68(2); 69(2); 70; 71; 11:6; 8; 12; 13; 14; 18; 19; **Est** 1:1; 4; 8:9; 9:6; 12; 15; 30; **Job** 1:3(2); 42:16; **Prov** 17:10; **Eccl** 6:3; 8:12; **Song** 8:12; **Is** 37:36; 65:20(2); **Jer** 52:23; 29; 30(2); **Eze** 4:5; 9; 40:19; 23; 27; 47:2; 41:13(2); 14; 15; 42:2; 8; 16; 17; 18; 19; 20(2); 45:2(2); 15; 48:16(4); 17(4); 30; 32; 33; 34; **Dan** 6:1; 8:14; 12:11; 12; **Amos** 5:3(2); **Mt** 18:12; 28; **Mk** 4:8; 20; 6:37; 14:5; **Lk** 7:41; 15:4; 16:6; 7; **Jn** 6:7; 12:5; 19:39; 21:8; 11; **Acts** 1:15; 5:36; 7:6; 13:20; 23:23(2); 27:37; **Rom** 4:19; **1Cor** 15:6; **Gal** 3:17; **Rev** 7:4; 9:16; 11:3; 12:6; 13:18; 14:1; 3; 20; 21:17

I

589, 1473

Gen 1:29; 30; 2:18; 3:10(4); 11; 12; 13; 15; 16; 17; 4:1; 9(2); 13; 14(2); 23; 6:7(3); 13; 17(2); 18; 7:1; 4(3); 8:21(3); 9:3; 5(3); 9(2); 11; 12; 13; 14; 15; 16(2); 17; 12:1; 2(2); 3; 7; 11; 13; 19; 13:8; 9(3); 15; 16; 17; 14:22; 23(3); 15:1; 2; 7; 8(2); 14; 18; 16:2(2); 5(2); 8; 10; 13; 17:1; 2; 5; 6(2); 7; 8(2); 16(2); 19; 20(3); 21; 18:3(2); 4; 5; 10; 12(2); 13; 14; 15; 17(2); 19; 21(2); 26(2); 27; 28(2); 29; 30(3); 31(2); 32(2); 19:2; 7; 8(2); 19(2); 21(2); 22; 34; 20:5; 6(3); 9; 11; 13; 16; 21:7; 13; 18; 23; 24; 26(2); 30; 22:1; 2; 5; 7; 11; 12; 16; 17(2); 23:4(2); 8; 11(3); 13(3); 24:2; 3(2); 5; 7; 12; 13; 14(5); 17; 19; 23; 24; 27; 31; 33(2); 34; 37; 39; 40; 42(2); 43(3); 44; 45(3); 46(2); 47(2); 48; 49; 56; 58; 25:22; 30(2); 32; 26:2; 3(4); 4; 9(2); 24(2); 27:1; 2(2); 3; 4(3); 6; 7; 8; 9; 11; 12(2); 18; 19(3); 21(2); 24; 25; 32; 33; 37(4); 41; 45(2); 46; 28:13(2); 15(4); 16; 20; 21; 22(2); 29:18; 19(2); 21; 25; 33; 34; 35; 30:1; 2; 3; 8(2); 13; 14; 16; 18; 20; 25; 26(2); 27(3); 28; 29; 30(2); 31(2); 32; 34; 31:3; 5; 6; 10; 11(2); 12; 13; 27; 31(2); 35; 38(2); 39(2); 40; 41(2); 43; 44; 51; 52; 32:4; 5(3); 9; 10(3); 11(2); 12; 20(2); 26; 29; 30; 33:8; 9; 10(4); 11(2); 12; 14(3); 34:8; 11; 12; 30(3); 35:3(2); 11; 12(3); 37:6(2); 9; 10; 13(2); 14; 16(2); 17; 30(2); 35; 38:16; 17; 18; 22; 23; 25(2); 26(2); 39:9(2); 14; 15; 18; 40:8; 11(2); 14; 15(2); 16(2); 41:9; 11; 15(2); 17; 19; 21; 22; 24; 28; 40; 41; 44; 42:2(2); 14; 18; 22; 33; 34(2); 37(2); 43:9(2); 14(2); 23; 44:15; 17; 18; 28(2); 30; 32(2); 33; 34(2); 45:3; 4(2); 11; 18; 28(2); 46:2; 3(2); 4(2); 30; 31; 47:16; 23; 29(3); 30(2); 48:4(2); 5; 7; 9(2); 11; 19(2); 21; 22(2); 49:1; 7; 18; 29; 31; 50:4(2); 5(4); 17; 19; 21; 24; **Ex** 2:7; 9; 10; 22; 3:3; 4; 6; 7(2); 8; 9; 10; 11(3); 12(2); 13; 14(3); 16; 17(2); 19; 20(2); 21; 4:10(2); 11; 12; 13; 14; 15; 18; 21(2); 23(2); 5:2(3); 10; 23; 6:1; 2; 3(2); 4; 5(2); 6(4); 7(3); 8(4); 29; 30; 7:1; 2; 3; 4; 5(2); 17(3); 16; 17(2); 19; 20(2); 21; 4:10(2); 11; 12; 13; 14; 15; 18; 21(2); 23(2); 5:2(3); 10; 23; 6:1; 2; 3(2); 4; 5(2); 6(4); 7(3); 8(4); 29(2); 30; 7:1; 2; 3; 4; 5(2); 16; 17(2); 29; 8:1; 2; 4; 8(2); 12:12(3); 13(3); 17; 13:8; 15(2); 14:4(3); 17(3); 18(2); 15:1; 2(2); 9(4); 26(3); 16:4(2); 12(2); 32(2); 17:4; 6; 9; 14; 18:3; 6; 11; 16(2); 19; 19:4(2); 9(2); 20:2; 5; 22; 24(3); 21:5(2); 13; 22:23; 24; 27(2); 23:7; 13; 15; 20(2); 21(2); 25; 26; 27(2); 28; 29; 30; 31(2); 24:12(2); 25:8; 9; 16; 21; 22(3); 28:3; 29:35; 42; 43; 44(2); 45; 46(3); 30:6; 36; 31:2; 3; 6(4); 11; 13; 32:8; 9; 10(2); 13(3); 14; 16(2); 17(2); 18; 19(4); 22(2); 23; 34:1; 9; 10(3); 11(2); 12; 10(3); 11(2); 18; 24; 27; **Lev** 6:17; 7:34; 8:31; 35; 10:3(2); 13; 18; 19; 11:44(2); 45(2); 14:34(2); 16:2; 17:10; 11; 12; 14; 18:2; 3; 4; 5; 6; 21; 24; 25; 30; 19:2; 3; 4; 10; 12; 14; 16; 18; 25; 28; 30; 31; 32; 34; 36; 37; 20:3; 5; 6; 7; 8; 22; 23(2); 24(3); 26; 21:8; 12; 15; 22; 3; 8; 9; 16; 30; 31; 32(2); 33; 23:10; 22; 30; 40(3); 24:22; 25:2; 5(2); 21; 23; 24; 27(2); 21; 48; 42; 6(2); 9; 11; 12; 13(2); 16(2); 17(2); 18; 19(4); 22(2); 23; 34:1; 9(2); 10(3); **Num** 3:12(2); 13(3); 41; 45; 5:3; 6:27; 8:16; 17(2); 18; 19; 9:8; 10:10; 29; 30(2); 31; 11:11; 12(2); 13; 14; 15(2); 17(2); 21(2); 12:6; 8; 11; 13; 13:2; 14:11; 12; 17; 19; 20; 21; 22; 23; 24; 27(2); 28(2); 30; 31; 35(2); 15:2; 18; 41(2); 16:8; 15(2); 21; 26; 28; 45; 17:4; 5(2); 18:6(2); 7; 8(2); 12; 19; 20; 21; 24(2); 26; 20:12; 17; 18; 19(3); 24; 21:2; 16; 34; 22:6(4); 8; 11; 16; 17(3); 18; 19(2); 20; 28; 29(2); 30(3); 32; 33; 34; 35; 37(2); 38(3); 23(3); 4; 8(2); 9(2); 11; 12; 13; 15; 22; 24:10; 11; 12; 13(2); 14(2); 17(2); 25:11; 12; 27:12; 32:8; 11; 33:53; 56(2); 35:34(2); **Deut** 1:8; 9(2); 12; 13; 15; 16; 17; 18; 20; 23; 29; 35; 36; 39; 42; 43; 2:5(2); 9(2); 13; 19(2); 24; 25; 26; 27(2); 28(3); 29; 31; 3:2; 12; 13; 15; 16; 18; 19(2); 20; 21; 23; 25; 4:1; 2(2); 5; 8; 10; 21(2); 22(2); 26; 40; 5:1; 5; 6; 9; 28; 31(2); 6:2; 6; 7:11; 17(2); 8:1; 11; 19; 9:9(3); 12; 13; 14(2); 15; 16; 17; 18(2); 19; 20; 21(2); 24; 25(2); 26; 10:2; 3; 5; 10; 11; 11:2; 8; 13; 14; 15; 22; 26; 27; 28; 32; 12:11; 14; 20; 21; 28; 30; 32; 13:18; 15:5; 11; 16; 17:3; 14; 18:16; 18(2); 19; 20; 19:7; 9; 22:14(3); 16; 17; 24:8; 18; 22; 25:8; 26:3(2); 10; 13(3); 14(3); 27:1; 4; 10; 28:1; 13; 14; 15; 68; 29:5; 6; 14; 19(2); 30:1; 2; 8; 11; 15; 16; 31:2(2); 5; 14; 16; 17(2); 18; 20(2); 21(3); 23(2); 27(2); 28; 29(2); 32:1; 3; 20(2); 21(2); 23(2); 24; 26(3); 27; 39(6); 40(2); 41(2); 42; 46; 49; 52; 33:9; 34:4(3); **Josh** 1:2; 3(2); 5(3); 6; 9; 2:4; 5; 9; 12(2); 3:7(3); 5:9; 14; 6(2); 10; 7:8; 11; 12; 19; 20(2); 21(2); 8:1; 5; 8; 18; 10:8; 11:6; 13:6(2); 14:7(2); 8; 10; 11(2); 12; 15:16; 17:14; 18:4; 6; 8; 20:2; 22:2; 23:2; 4(2); 14; 24:3; 4(2); 5(4); 6; 7; 8(3); 10(2); 11; 12; 13; **Judg** 1:2; 3; 7; 12; 2:1(4); 3(2); 20; 21; 22; 3:19; 20; 4:7(2); 8(2); 9; 19(2); 22; 5:3(3); 7(2); 6:8; 9; 10(2); 14; 15(2); 16; 17; 18(3); 22; 37(2); 39(2); 7:4(3); 7; 9; 13; 17(2); 18(2); 8:2; 3; 5(2); 7; 9(2); 19; 23; 24; 9:2(2); 9; 11; 13; 29; 38; 48; 10:11; 12; 11:9; 11; 27; 31(2); 35(2); 37(2); 12:2(2); 3(2); 13:4; 6; 7; 11; 16; 18; 16:6; 7; 9; 10; 11; 15; 17(3); 20; 26(2); 28(3); 17:2; 3(2); 9(3); 10; 13(2); 18:4; 24(2); 19:6; 8; 9; 11; 18(3); 23; 24; 20:4(2); 6; 23; 28(3); **Ruth** 1:12(4); 16(2); 17(2); 21; 2:2; 7; 9; 10(2); 13; 19; 5; 9; 11; 12(2); 13; 4:4(4); 6(3); 9; 10; **1Sa** 1:8; 11; 15(2); 16; 20; 22(2); 26;

27(2); 28; 2:1; 16; 23; 24; 27; 28(2); 29; 30(2); 31; 33; 35(2); 36(2); 3:4; 5(2); 6(2); 8; 11; 12(4); 13(2); 14; 16; 17; 4:16(2); 7:5; 8:7; 8; 9:8(2); 16(2); 17; 18; 19(2); 21; 23(2); 24(2); 26; 27; 10:2; 8(2); 15; 18; 11:2(2); 12:1; 2(2); 3(7); 7; 17; 23(2); 13:11; 12(3); 14:7; 24; 29(2); 37; 40; 43(2); 15:2; 6; 11; 13; 14; 16; 20; 24(3); 25(2); 26; 30; 16:1(3); 2(2); 3(2); 5; 7; 18; 22; 17:8; 9; 28; 29; 35(2); 39(2); 43; 44; 45; 46(2); 55; 58; 18:11; 17; 18(2); 21; 23; 19:2; 3(4); 15; 17; 20:1; 3; 4; 5(2); 9(2); 12(3); 13; 14(2); 20(2); 21(2); 22; 23; 29(3); 30; 36; 21:2(3); 5; 8; 15; 22:3(2); 23:2; 4; 11(2); 12; 17(2); 20; 25:7; 8; 11(3); 19; 21; 22; 24; 25(2); 28; 35; 26:6; 8(2); 11(2); 18; 19; 21(3); 23; 27:1(3); 5(2); 8; 29:8; 8:2; 7; 8(2); 11; 13(5); 15(2); 16(2); 22; 9; 3(2); 30:7; 8(2); 13(2); 15; **2Sa** 1:3; 4; 6; 7(2); 8(2); 9; 10(3); 13; 16; 26; 2:1(2); 6; 20; 22(2); 3:8; 9; 13(2); 14; 18; 21; 28; 35; 39; 4:10(2); 5:19(2); 6:21; 22(2); 7:2(2); 3(7); 7; 17; 23(2); 13:11; 12(3); 14; 16; 17(2); 18; 19(2); 21(3); 23; 27(3); 5(2); 8(2); 7; 9(2); 10(2); 11; 11(2); 12; 78:2(2); 81:5(2); 6; 7(3); 8; 10(2); 12; 14; 16; 82:6; 84:10; 85:8; 86:1; 2; 3; 4; 7; 11; 12(2); 87:4; 88:1; 4(2); 8(2); 9(2); 13; 15(3); 89:1(2); 2; 3(4); 19; 14(2); 20(2); 23; 25; 27; 28; 29; 32; 33; 34; 35(2); 50; 91:2(2); 14(2); 15(3); 16; 92:4; 10; 94:18; 95:10; 11; 101:1(2); 2(2); 3(2); 4; 5(2); 8(2); 102:2(2); 4; 6; 9; 10(3); 11; 12; 13; 14; 104:33(4); 34; 105:11; 106:5(3); 108:1; 2; 3(2); 7(2); 9(2); 109:4; 22; 23(2); 25; 30(2); 110:1; 111:1; 116:1; 2(2); 3; 4(2); 6; 9; 10(3); 11; 12; 13; 14; 16(2); 17; 18; 118:5; 6; 7; 10; 11; 12; 13; 17; 19(2); 21; 25(2); 28(2); 119:6(2); 7(2); 8; 10; 11(2); 13; 14; 15; 16(2); 17; 18; 19; 22; 26; 27; 30(3); 31; 32; 33; 34(2); 35; 39; 40; 42(2); 43; 44; 46(2); 47; 48(3); 51; 52; 55; 56(2); 57(2); 58; 59; 60; 61; 62; 63(3); 69; 70; 71(2); 73; 74; 75; 76; 77; 78; 80; 81; 83(2); 87; 88; 92; 93; 94(2); 95; 96; 97; 99; 100(2); 101(2); 102; 104(2); 106(3); 107; 108; 109; 110; 111; 112; 113(2); 114; 115; 116; 117(2); 119; 120; 121; 125(2); 127; 128(2); 131(2); 134; 141(2); 144; 145(2); 146(2); 147(2); 148; 152; 157; 158; 159; 162; 163(2); 164; 166; 167; 168; 173; 174; 176(2); 120:1; 5(2); 121:1; 122:1; 8; 9; 123:1; 130:1; 5(2); 6; 131:1; 2; 132:3; 4; 5; 11; 12; 14(2); 15(2); 16; 17(2); 18; 135:5; 137:5; 6(2); 138:1(2); 2; 3; 7; 139:6; 7(2); 8(2); 9; 11; 14(2); 15; 18(3); 21(2); 22(2); 140:6; 12; 141:1(2); 10; 142:1(2); 2(2); 3; 4; 5(2); 6(2); 7; 143:5(3); 6; 7; 8(3); 9; 12; 144:2; 9(2); 145:1(2); 2(2); 5; 6; 146:2(4); **Prov** 1:23(2); 24(2); 26(2); 28; 3:28; 4:2; 3; 11(2); 5:12; 14; 7:6; 7; 14(2); 15(2); 16; 17; 8:4; 6; 12; 13; 14(2); 17; 20; 21(2); 23; 24; 25; 27; 30(2); 9:5; 20:9(2); 22; 22:13; 19; 20; 21; 23:35(4); 24:29(2); 30; 32; 26:19; 27:11; 30:2; 3; 7(2); 9(2); 18; 20; **Eccl** 1:12; 13; 14; 16(2); 17(2); 2:1(2); 2; 3(2); 4(3); 5; 6; 7(2); 8(2); 9; 10(2); 11(2); 12; 13; 14; 15(3); 17; 18(3); 19(2); 20(2); 24; 25; 3:10; 12; 14; 16; 17; 18; 22; 4:1; 2; 4; 7(2); 8; 15; 5:13; 18; 6:1; 3; 7:15; 23(3); 25; 26; 27; 28(3); 29; 8:2; 9; 10; 12; 14; 15; 16; 17; 9:1; 11; 13; 16; 10:5; 7; 12:1; **Song** 1:5; 6(2); 7; 9; 2:1; 3; 5; 7; 16; 3:1(3); 2(4); 3; 4(4); 5; 4:6; 5:1(4); 2; 3(4); 5; 6(4); 8(2); 6:3; 11; 12; 7:8(3); 10; 12; 13; 8:1(3); 2(2); 4; 5; 10(2); 11(2); 12; 13; 14(2); **Is** 1:2; 11(2); 13; 14; 15(2); 24; 25; 26; 3:4; 7; 5:1; 3; 4(2); 5(3); 6(2); 6:1; 5(4); 8(4); 11; 7:12(2); 8:2; 3; 11; 17(2); 18; 10:6(2); 11(2); 12; 13(4); 14; 12:1; 2; 13:3(2); 11(2); 12; 13; 17; 14:13(3); 14(2); 22; 23(2); 24(2); 25; 30; 15:9; 16:9(2); 10; 18:4(2); 19:2; 3; 4; 11; 21:2; 3(2); 10(2); 17; 22:4(2); 19; 20; 21(2); 23(2); 24(2); 16; 25:1(2); 26:9(2); 27:3(3); 4(2); 28:16; 17; 22; 29:2; 3(2); 11(2); 12(2); 14; 30:7; 33:10(3); 13; 24; 36:5(2); 8(2); 10; 11; 17; 37:7(2); 24(3); 25(2); 26(3); 28; 29(2); 35; 38:3(2); 5(3); 6(2); 8; 10(3); 11(3); 12; 13; 14(3); 15(2); 17; 19; 22(2); 39:4; 40:6; 25; 41:4(2); 8; 9(2); 10(5); 13(2); 14; 15; 17(2); 18(2); 19(2); 25; 27; 28(2); 42:1(2); 6; 7(3); 10(2); 11(2); 43:1(2); 2; 3(2); 4(2); 5(2); 6(3); 7(2); 10(2); 11(2); 12(3); 14; 15; 19(2); 20; 21; 25(2); 28; 44:1; 2; 6; 7(2); 8(2); 16(2); 19(5); 21; 45:2(2); 3(4); 4; 5(3); 6; 7; 8(2); 12; 13(2); 14(3); 15; 16(4); 19; 43:1(2); 2; 3(2); 4(2); 5; 6; 7(3); 10(2); 11(2); 12(3); 14; 15; 19(2); 20; 21; 23; 25(2); 28; 44:1; 2; 6; 7(2); 8(2); 16(2); 19(5); 21; 45:2(2); 3(4); 4; 5(3); 6; 7; 8(2); 12; 13(2); 14(3); 15; 16(4); 19; **Jer** 1:5(4); 6(3); 7(3); 8; 9; 10; 11(2); 12; 13(2); 15; 16; 17(2); 18; 19; 2:2; 7; 9(2); 20(2); 21; 23(2); 25(2); 30; 31; 34; 35(3); 3:7; 8(2); 12(3); 14(3); 15; 18; 19(3); 22; 4:6; 10; 12; 19(2); 21; 23; 24; 25; 26; 27; 28(3); 31; 5:1; 4; 5; 7(2); 9; 14; 15; 18; 29; 6:2; 8; 10; 11(2); 12; 15; 17; 19; 21; 27; 7:3; 7(2); 11; 12(3); 13; 14(3); 15(2); 16; 22(2); 23(3); 25; 31; 34; 8:3; 6(2); 10; 13(2); 15; 16; 18(3); 19(2); 23; 9:1(2); 2(2); 6; 7; 8; 9; 11; 12; 15(2); 20:4(2); 5(2); 7(3); 8(3); 9(4); 10; 12; 14; 18; 21:2; 4(2); 5; 6; 7; 8; 10; 13; 14(2);

22:5; 6; 7; 14; 21(2); 24(2); 25; 26; 23:2; 3(2); 4; 5; 8; 9; 11; 12; 13; 14; 15; 21(2); 23; 24(2); 25(3); 30; 31; 32(2); 33; 34; 38; 39(4); 40; 24:3; 5(2); 6(4); 7(3); 8; 9(2); 10(2); 25:3; 6; 9; 10; 12; 13(2); 14; 15; 16; 17; 27; 29(2); 26:2; 3(2); 4; 5; 6; 14; 27:5; 6(2); 8(2); 10; 11; 12; 15(2); 16; 22(2); 28:2; 3; 4(2); 7; 11; 14(2); 16; 29:4; 7; 9; 10; 11(2); 12; 14(6); 17; 18(2); 19; 20; 21; 23(2); 31; 32(2); 30:2; 3(3); 6; 8; 9; 10; 11(5); 14; 15; 16; 17(2); 18; 19(2); 20; 21; 22; 31:1; 2; 3(2); 4; 8; 9(3); 13; 14; 18(3); 19(6); 20(3); 23; 25(2); 26; 27; 28(2); 31; 32(3); 33(2); 34(2); 37; 32:3; 5; 8(2); 9; 10; 11; 12; 13; 16(2); 27; 28; 31; 33; 35; 37(4); 38; 39; 40(3); 41(2); 42(3); 44; 33:3; 5(2); 6(2); 7; 8(2); 9(2); 11; 14(2); 15; 22; 25; 26(3); 34:2; 5; 13(2); 17(2); 18; 20; 21; 22(2); 35:3; 4; 5(2); 14; 15(2); 17(4); 36:2(2); 3(2); 5(2); 18; 31(3); 37:14; 18; 20(3); 38:14; 15(2); 16(2); 19; 20(2); 25; 26; 39:16; 17; 18; 40:4(2); 10; 15(2); 42:4(4); 10(4); 11; 12; 17; 19; 21; 43:10(2); 12; 44:2; 4(2); 10; 11; 12; 13(2); 26; 27; 29; 30(2); 45:3(2); 4(4); 5(2); 46:5; 8(2); 18; 25; 26; 27; 28(5); 48:12; 30; 31(2); 32; 33; 35; 38; 44; 47; 49:2; 5; 6; 8(2); 10(2); 11; 13; 14; 15; 16; 19(2); 27; 32(2); 35; 36; 37(4); 38; 39; 50:9; 18(2); 19; 20(2); 21; 24; 31(2); 32; 44(2); 51:1; 14; 20(2); 21(2); 22(3); 23(3); 24; 25(2); 36(2); 39(2); 40; 44(2); 47; 52; 57; 64; **Lam** 1:11; 14; 16; 18(2); 19; 20(2); 21; 2:13(4); 22; 3:1; 7; 8; 14; 17; 18; 21(2); 24; 54(2); 55; 57; 63; **Eze** 1:1(2); 4; 15; 24; 27(2); 28(3); 2:1; 2; 3; 4; 8(2); 9; 3:2; 3(2); 6; 8; 9; 10; 12; 13; 14; 15(2); 17; 18(2); 20(2); 22; 23(3); 26; 27(2); 4:5; 6; 8; 13; 14(2); 15; 16; 5:2; 5; 8(2); 9(3); 10(2); 11(3); 12(2); 13(4); 14; 15(2); 16(3); 17(3); 6:3(3); 4; 5(2); 7; 8; 9; 10(3); 12; 13; 14(2); 7:3; 4(3); 8(2); 9(3); 20; 21; 22; 24(2); 27(3); 8:1; 2; 4; 5; 6; 7; 8; 10; 18(3); 9:8(2); 10(2); 11; 10:1; 9; 15; 20(2); 22; 11:1; 5; 7; 8; 9; 10(2); 11; 12; 13(2); 16(3); 17(2); 19(3); 20; 21; 24; 25; 12:6; 7(6); 11(2); 13(2); 14(2); 15(2); 16(2); 20; 23; 25(4); 28; 13:7; 8; 9; 13; 14(2); 15; 20(2); 21(2); 22; 23(2); 14:3; 4; 5; 7; 8(3); 9(2); 11; 13; 15; 16; 17(2); 18; 19; 20; 21; 22(2); 23(2); 15:6(2); 7(3); 8; 16:6(3); 7; 8(3); 9(3); 10(3); 11(2); 12; 14; 17; 19(2); 27; 37(2); 38(2); 39; 41; 42(2); 43; 48; 50(2); 53(2); 59; 60(2); 61; 62(2); 63; 17:16; 19(2); 20(2); 21; 22(2); 23; 24(2); 18:3; 23; 30; 32; 20:3(2); 5(3); 6(2); 7(2); 8(2); 9(2); 10; 11; 12(2); 13(2); 14(2); 15(3); 17; 18; 19; 20; 21(2); 22(2); 23(2); 25; 26(3); 28(2); 29; 31(3); 33(2); 34; 35(2); 36(2); 37(2); 38(3); 40(2); 41(3); 42(3); 44(2); 47; 48; 49; 21:3; 4; 5; 15; 17(3); 24; 27(2); 30(2); 31(2); 32; 22:4; 13; 14(2); 15; 16; 19; 20(2); 21; 22; 26; 30(3); 31(3); 23:9; 13; 22(2); 24; 25; 27; 28; 30; 31; 34; 43; 46; 48; 49; 24:8; 9; 13(2); 14(5); 16; 18(3); 20; 21; 22; 24; 25; 27; 25:4; 5(2); 7(5); 9; 11(2); 13(2); 14; 16(2); 17(3); 26:2; 3; 4; 5; 6; 7; 13; 14(2); 19(2); 20(2); 21; 27:3; 28:2(2); 7; 9; 10; 14; 16(2); 17(2); 18(2); 22(4); 23(2); 24; 25(2); 26(2); 29:3(2); 4(3); 5(2); 6; 8; 9(2); 10(2); 12(2); 13; 14; 15; 16; 19; 20; 21(3); 30:8(2); 10; 12(3); 13(3); 14; 15(2); 16; 18; 19(2); 21; 22(2); 23; 24(2); 25(3); 26(2); 31:9; 11(2); 15(4); 16(2); 32:3; 4(3); 5; 6; 7(3); 8; 9(2); 10(2); 12; 13; 14; 15(3); 32; 33:2; 6; 7; 8(2); 11(2); 13; 14; 20; 22; 27(2); 28; 29(2); 30; 34:8; 10(3); 11(2); 12; 13; 14; 15(2); 16(3); 17; 20(2); 22(2); 23; 24(2); 25; 26(2); 27(2); 29; 30; 31; 35:3(3); 4(2); 6(2); 7; 8; 9(2); 11(4); 12(2); 13; 14; 15(2); 36:5; 6; 7; 9(2); 10; 11(3); 12; 15; 18; 19(2); 21; 22; 23(3); 24; 25(2); 26(4); 27; 28(2); 29(2); 30; 32; 33(2); 36(3); 37(2); 38; 37:3; 5; 6(2); 7(3); 8; 10; 12; 13(2); 14(2); 19; 21; 22; 23(2); 25; 26(2); 27; 28; 38:3; 4(2); 11(2); 16(2); 17(2); 19; 21; 22(2); 23(3); 39:1; 2; 3; 4; 5; 6(2); 7(3); 8; 11; 13; 17; 19; 21(3); 22; 23; 24; 25; 27; 28(2); 29(2); 40:4(2); 41:8; 43:3(5); 6; 7; 8; 9; 27; 44:4(2); 5; 12; 14; 28(2); 47:5; 7; 14; **Dan** 1:10; 12; 2:3; 8; 9; 23; 24; 25; 26; 30; 3:14; 15; 25; 29; 4:2; 4; 5; 6; 7; 8; 9(2); 10; 13; 18; 30; 34(3); 36; 37; 5:11; 14; 16; 17; 6:22; 26; 7:2; 4; 6; 7; 8; 9; 11(2); 13; 15; 16; 19; 21; 28; 8:2(5); 3; 4; 5; 6; 7; 13; 15(2); 16; 17(2); 18; 19; 27(3); 9:2; 3; 4; 16; 20; 21(2); 22; 23; 10:2; 3(2); 4; 5; 7; 8(2); 9(3); 11(3); 12; 13; 14; 15(2); 16(2); 19; 20(3); 21; 11:1(2); 2; 12:5; 7; 8(3); **Hos** 1:4; 5; 6(2); 7; 9; 2:2; 3; 4; 5; 6; 7; 8; 9; 10; 11; 12(2); 13; 14; 15; 17; 18(2); 19(2); 20; 21(2); 23(3); 3:2; 3(2); 4:5; 6(2); 7; 9; 14; 5:2; 3; 9; 10; 12; 14(4); 15; 6:4(2); 5(2); 6; 10; 11; 7:1; 2; 12(3); 13; 15; 8:4; 10; 12; 14; 9:10(2); 12(2); 13; 15(3); 16; 10:10; 11(2); 11:1; 3(2); 4(3); 8(4); 9(4); 11; 12:8(2); 9; 10(2); 13:4; 5; 7(2); 8(2); 10; 11; 14(4); 14:4(2); 5; 8(3); **Joel** 1:19; 2:19(2); 20; 25(2); 27(2); 28; 29; 30; 3:1; 2; 4; 7; 8; 10; 12; 17; 21(2); **Amos** 1:3; 4; 5; 6; 7; 8(2); 9; 10; 11; 12; 13; 14; 2:1; 2; 3; 4; 5; 6; 9(2); 10; 11; 13; 3:1; 2(2); 14(2); 15; 4:6; 7(2); 9; 10(3); 11; 12(2); 5:1; 12; 17; 21(3); 22(2); 23; 27; 6:8(2); 14; 7:2(2); 5(2); 8(3); 9; 14(3); 15; 8:2(2); 7; 9(2); 10(3); 11; 9:1(2); 2; 3(2); 4(2); 7; 8(2); 9(2); 11(3); 14; 15(2); **Obad** 2; 4; 8; **Jonah** 1:9(2); 12; 2:2(2); 4(3); 6; 7; 9(3); 3:2; 4:2(4); 3; 9; 11; **Mic** 1:6(3); 7; 8(3); 15; 2:3; 11; 12(3); 3:1(2); 8; 9; 4:6(3); 7; 13(3); 5:10(2); 11; 12; 13; 14(2); 15; 6:3(2); 4(2); 6(2); 7; 11; 13; 14; 16; 7:1; 7(2); 8(3); 9(3); 15; **Nah** 1:12(2); 13; 14(2); 2:13(3); 3:5(3); 6; 7; **Hab** 1:2; 5; 6; 2:1(3); 3:2; 7; 16(3); 18(2); **Zeph** 1:2; 3(3); 4(2); 8; 9; 12; 17; 2:5; 8; 9; 15; 3:6(2); 7(2); 8(2); 9; 11; 12; 18; 19(3); 20(4); **Hag** 1:8(2); 9; 11; 13; 2:4; 5; 6; 7(2); 9; 15; 17; 19; 21; 22(3); 23(2); **Zec** 1:3; 6; 8; 9(2); 14; 15(2); 16; 18; 19; 21; 2:1; 2; 5; 6; 9; 10(2); 11; 3:4(2); 5; 7; 8; 9(3); 4:2(2); 4; 5; 11; 12; 13; 5:1; 2(2); 4; 6; 9; 10; 6:1; 4; 7:3(2); 13; 14; 8:2(2); 3; 7; 8(2); 10; 11; 12; 13; 14(2); 15; 17; 21; 9:6; 7; 8(2); 10; 11; 12(2); 13; 10:3; 6(6); 8(2); 9; 10(2); 12; 11:5; 6(3); 7(5); 8; 9(2); 10(3); 12; 13(2); 14(2); 16; 12:2; 3; 4(2); 6; 9; 10; 13:2(2); 5(2); 6; 7; 9(3); 14:2; **Mal** 1:2(2); 3; 4; 6(2); 9; 10(2); 13; 14; 2:2(3); 3; 4; 5; 9; 3:1; 5(2); 6(2); 7; 10; 11; 17(2); 4:3; 4; 5; 6; **Mt** 2:8; 13; 15; 3:9; 11(3); 14; 17; 4:9; 19; 5:17(2); 18; 20; 22; 26; 28; 32; 34; 39; 44; 6:2; 5; 16; 25; 29; 7:23(2); 24; 8:3; 7; 8; 9(2); 10(2); 11; 19; 9:13(2); 21(2); 28; 10:15; 16; 23; 27; 32; 33; 34(2); 35; 42; 11:9; 10; 11; 16; 22; 24; 25; 28; 29; 12:6; 7; 18(2); 27; 28; 31; 36; 44(2); 13:13; 15; 17; 30; 35(2); 14:27; 15:24; 32(2); 16:11; 13; 15; 18(2); 19; 28; 17:5; 12; 16; 17(2); 20; 18:3; 10; 13; 18; 19; 20; 21; 22; 26; 29; 32; 33; 19:9; 16(2); 20(2); 23; 24; 28; 20:4; 13; 14; 15(2); 22(2); 23; 32; 21:21; 24(3); 27(2); 29; 30; 31; 43; 22:4; 32; 44; 23:34; 36; 37; 39; 24:2; 5; 25; 34; 47; 25:12(2); 20; 21; 22; 23; 24; 25; 26(3); 27; 35(3); 36(2); 40; 42(2); 43; 45; 26:13; 15; 18; 21; 22; 25; 29(3); 31; 32(2); 33; 34; 35(2); 36; 39; 42; 48; 53; 55; 61; 63; 64; 70; 72; 74; 27:4(2); 17; 19; 21; 22; 24; 43; 63; 28:5; 7; 20(2); **Mk** 1:2; 7(2); 8; 11; 17; 24; 38(2); 41; 2:11; 17; 3:28; 5:7(2); 23; 28(2); 41; 6:11; 16; 22; 23; 24; 25; 50; 8:2; 3; 12; 19; 24; 27; 29; 9:1; 13; 17; 18; 19(2); 24; 25; 41; 10:15; 17(2); 20; 29; 36; 38(2); 39(2); 51(2); 11:23; 24; 29(3); 33(2); 12:15; 26; 36; 43; 13:6; 23; 30; 37(2); 14:9; 14; 18; 19(2); 25(3); 27; 28(2); 29; 30; 31(2); 32; 36; 44; 49; 58(2); 62; 68(2); 71; 15:9; 12; **Lk** 1:18(2); 19; 34; 2:10; 48; 49; 3:8; 16(3); 22; 4:6(3); 24; 25; 34; 43(2); 5:5; 8; 13; 24; 32; 6:9; 27; 46; 47; 7:6; 7; 8(2); 9(2); 14; 26; 27; 28; 31; 40; 43; 44; 45; 47; 8:28(2); 46; 9:9(2); 18; 20; 27; 38; 40; 41; 57; 61; 10:3; 12; 18; 19; 21; 24; 25; 35(2); 11:6; 7; 8; 9; 18; 19; 20; 24(2); 49; 51; 12:4; 5(2); 8; 17(2); 18(3); 19; 22; 27; 37; 44; 49(2); 50(2); 51(2); 59; 13:3; 5; 7; 8; 18; 20; 24; 25; 27(2); 32(3); 33; 34; 35; 14:18(3); 19(3); 20(2); 24; 15:6; 7; 9(2); 10; 17; 18(2); 21; 29(3); 31; 16:2; 3(3); 4(2); 9; 24; 27; 28; 17:4; 8(2); 9; 34; 18:4; 5; 8; 11(2); 12(3); 14; 17; 18; 21; 29; 41(2); 19:5; 8(3); 13; 20; 21; 22(4); 23; 26; 27; 40; 20:3; 8(2); 13(2); 43; 21:3; 8; 15; 32; 22:11; 15(2); 16(2); 18(2); 27; 29; 32; 33; 34; 35; 37; 53; 57; 58; 60; 67; 68; 70; 23:4; 14; 15; 16; 22(2); 43; 46; 24:39; 44(2); 49; **Jn** 1:15; 20; 21; 23; 26; 27; 30; 31(2); 32; 33; 34; 48; 50(2); 51; 2:4; 19; 3:3; 5; 7; 11; 12(2); 28(3); 30; 4:14(2); 15; 17(2); 19; 25; 26; 29; 32; 35; 38; 39; 5:7(2); 17; 19; 24; 25; 30(4); 31; 32; 34(2); 36(2); 41; 42; 43; 45; 6:20; 26; 32; 35; 36; 37; 38; 39; 40; 41; 42; 44; 47; 48; 51(3); 53; 54; 56; 57; 63; 65; 70; 7:7; 8; 17; 21; 23; 28(2); 29(2); 33(2); 34; 36; 8:11; 12; 14(6); 15; 16(3); 18; 21(2); 22; 23(2); 24(2); 25; 26(3); 28(3); 29; 34; 37; 38(2); 40; 42(2); 45; 46; 49(2); 50; 51; 54; 55(5); 58(2); 9:4; 5(2); 9; 11(2); 12; 15; 25(4); 27; 36; 38; 39; 10:1; 7(2); 9; 10; 11; 14; 15(2); 16(2); 17(2); 18(4); 25(2); 26; 27; 28; 30; 32; 34; 36(2); 37; 38(2); 11:11(2); 15(2); 22; 24; 25; 27; 40; 41; 42(2); 12:24; 26; 27(2); 28; 32(2); 40; 46; 47(2); 48; 49(3); 50(3); 13:7; 8; 12; 13; 14; 15(2); 16; 18(3); 19(2); 20(2); 21; 26(2); 33(4); 34(2); 36; 37(2); 38; 14:2(2); 3(3); 4; 6; 9; 10(3); 11; 12(3); 13; 14; 16; 18(2); 19; 20(2); 21; 25; 26; 27(3); 28(5); 29; 30; 31(2); 15:1; 3; 4; 5(2); 9; 10; 11; 12; 14; 15(4); 16; 17; 19; 20; 22; 24; 26; 16:1; 4(4); 5; 6; 7(5); 10; 12; 15; 16; 17; 19; 20; 22; 23; 25(3); 26(2); 27; 28(2); 32; 33(2); 17:4(2); 5; 6; 8(2); 9(2); 10; 11(2); 12(3); 13(2); 14(2); 15; 16; 18; 19; 20; 21; 22; 23; 24(2); 25; 26(2); 18:5; 6; 8(2); 9; 11; 17; 20(3); 21(2); 23; 25; 26; 35; 36; 37(4); 38; 39(2); 19:4(2); 6; 10; 15; 21; 22(2); 28; 20:13; 15; 17(2); 21; 25(2); 21:3; 15; 16; 17; 18; 22(2); 23(2); 25; **Acts** 1:1; 2:17; 18; 19; 25(2); 35; 3:6(3); 17; 5:38; 7:3; 7; 32; 34(4); 43; 56; 8:19; 23; 31; 34; 37; 9:5; 10; 13; 16; 10:14; 20; 21; 26; 28; 29(3); 30(2); 33; 34; 37; 11:5(2); 6(2); 7; 8; 11; 15; 16; 17(2); 12:11; 13:2; 22; 25(3); 33; 34; 41; 47; 15:16(3); 16:18; 30; 17:3; 22; 23(3); 18:6(2); 10(2); 14; 15; 21(2); 19:15(2); 21(2); 20:18(2); 20; 22; 24(3); 25(2); 26(2); 27; 29; 31; 32; 33; 35; 21:13; 37; 39(2); 22:1; 3; 4; 5; 6; 7; 8(2); 10(2); 11(2); 13; 17(3); 19(2); 20; 21; 28(2); 23:1; 5; 6(2); 27; 28(2); 29; 30; 35; 24:4(2); 10(2); 11; 14(2); 16; 17; 20; 21(2); 22; 25(2); 25:8; 10(3); 11(3); 15; 16; 17; 18; 20(2); 21(2); 22; 25(2); 26(3); 26:2(3); 3(2); 5; 6; 7; 9(2); 10(3); 11(2); 12; 13; 14; 15(2); 16(2); 17; 19; 22; 25; 26(2); 27; 29(2); 27:10; 22; 23(2); 25; 34; 28:17(2); 19(2); 20(2); 27; **Rom** 1:8; 9(2); 10; 11(2); 12; 13(3); 14; 15; 16; 3:5; 7; 26; 4:17; 6:19; 7:1; 7(2); 9(2); 10; 14; 15(6); 16(3); 17; 18(2); 19(4); 20(3); 21(2); 22; 23; 24; 25(2); 8:18; 38; 9:1(2); 2; 3; 9; 13(2); 15(4); 17(2); 25; 33; 10:2; 18; 19(3); 20(2); 21; 11:1(2); 3; 4; 11; 13(3); 14; 19; 25; 27; 12:1; 3; 19; 14:11; 14; 15:8; 9; 14; 15; 16; 17(2); 18; 19; 20(2); 22; 24(4); 25; 28(2); 29(3); 30; 31(2); 32; 16:1; 4; 17; 19(2); 22; **1Cor** 1:4; 10; 12(5); 14(2); 15; 16(3); 19; 2:1(2); 2; 3; 3:1; 2; 4(2); 6; 10; 4:3(2); 4(2); 6; 8; 9; 14(2); 15; 16; 17(2); 18; 19; 21; 5:3(2); 9; 11; 12; 6:5; 12; 15; 7:6; 7(2); 8(2); 10(2); 12; 17; 25(2); 26(2); 28; 29; 32; 35(2); 40(2); 8:13(2); 9:1(3); 2(2); 6; 8; 15(2); 16(3); 17(2); 18(3); 19(3); 20(3); 21; 22(4); 23(2); 26(2); 27(3); 10:1; 15(2); 19; 20(2); 29; 30(3); 33; 11:1; 2(2); 3; 17(2); 18(2); 22(3); 23(2); 34(2); 12:1; 3; 15(2); 16(2); 21(2); 31; 13:1(2); 2(4); 3(2); 11(6); 12(3); 14:5; 6(3); 11(2); 14; 15(4); 18(2); 19(2); 21; 37; 15:1(2); 2; 3(2); 9(2); 10(4); 11; 31(3); 32; 34; 50; 51; 16:1; 2; 3(2); 4; 5(3); 6(2); 7(2); 8; 10; 11; 12; 15; 17; **2Cor** 1:13; 15; 17(4); 23(2); 2:1(2); 2; 3(4); 4(2); 5; 8; 9(2); 10(4); 12; 13(3); 4:13(2); 5:8; 11; 6:2(2); 13; 16(2); 17; 7:3(2); 4(2); 7; 8(4); 9; 12(2); 14(3); 16(2); 8:3; 8; 10; 13; 22; 9:2(2); 3(2); 5; 6; 10:1; 2(4); 8(2); 9(2); 11:2(3); 3; 5(2); 6; 7(2); 8; 9(4); 11; 12(3); 16(2); 17(2); 18; 21(3); 22(3); 23(2); 24; 25(4); 29(2); 30(2); 31; 33; 12:1; 2(3); 3(2); 5(2); 6(4); 7(2); 8; 9; 10(3); 11(4); 13; 14(3); 15(3); 16(2); 17(2); 18(2); 20(5); 21(2); 13:1; 2(5); 6; 7; 10(2); **Gal** 1:6; 9; 10(4); 11; 12(2); 13; 16(2); 17(2); 18; 19; 20(2); 21; 2:1; 2(3); 10; 11; 14(2); 18(3); 19(2); 20(5); 21; 3:2; 15; 17; 4:1; 11(2); 12(3); 13; 15; 16(2); 18; 19; 20(2); 5:2; 3; 10; 11(3); 12; 16; 21(2); 6:11; 14(2); 17; **Eph** 1:15(2); 3:1; 3; 7; 8; 13; 14; 4:1; 17; 5:32; 6:19; 20(3); 21; 22; **Phil** 1:3; 7; 8; 9; 12; 17; 18; 19; 20; 22(3); 23; 25(2); 27(2); 2:16(2); 17(2); 19(3); 20; 23(2); 24(2); 25; 27; 28(2); 3:4(2); 7; 8(3); 10; 11; 12(4); 13(2); 14; 18; 4:2; 3; 4; 10; 11(3); 12(3); 13; 15; 17(2); 18(2); **Col** 1:20; 23; 25; 29; 2:1(2); 4; 5(2); 4:3; 4(2); 8; 13; **1Th** 2:18; 3:5(2); 4:9; 13; 5:1; 23; 27; **2Th** 2:5(2); 3:17; **1Ti** 1:3(2); 12; 13(2); 15; 16; 18; 20; 2:1; 7(2); 8; 12; 3:14; 15; 4:13; 5:14; 21; 6:13; **2Ti** 1:3(3); 4; 5(2); 6; 11; 12(5); 2:7; 9; 10; 3:11; 4:1; 6; 7(3); 12; 13; 16; 17; 20; **Titus** 1:5(2); 3:8; 12(2); **Philem** 1:4; 8; 9; 10(2); 12; 13; 14; 19(3); 21(2); 22(2); **Heb** 1:5(2); 13; 2:12(2); 13(2); 3:10; 11; 4:3; 5:5; 6:14(2); 7:9; 8:8; 9(3); 10(3); 12(2); 10:7(2); 9; 16(3); 17; 30; 11:32; 12:21; 26; 13:5; 6; 19(2); 22(2); 23; **Jas** 1:13; 2:18(2); **1Pet** 1:16; 2:6; 11; 5:1; 12(2); **2Pet** 1:12; 13(2); 14; 15; 17; 3:1(2); **1Jn** 2:1; 4; 7; 8; 12; 13(3); 14(2); 21; 26; 4:20; 5:13; 16; **2Jn** 1(2); 4(2); 5(2); 12(2); **3Jn** 1; 2; 3; 4; 9; 10(2); 13(2); 14(2); **Jude** 3; 5; **Rev** 1:8; 9; 10; 11; 12(2); 17(3); 18(2); 2:2; 4; 5; 6; 7; 9(2); 10; 13; 14; 15; 16; 17; 19; 20; 21; 22; 23(3); 24(2); 25; 26; 27; 28; 3:1; 2; 3(2); 5(2); 8(2); 9(3); 10; 11; 12(3); 15(2); 16; 17; 18; 19(2); 20(2); 21(2); 4:1(3); 2; 4; 5:1; 2; 4; 6; 11(2); 13; 6:1(2); 2; 3; 5(2); 6; 7; 8; 9; 12; 7:1; 2; 4; 9; 14; 8:2; 13; 9:1; 13; 16; 17; 10:1; 4(2); 5; 8; 9; 10(2); 11:3; 12:10; 13:1; 2; 3; 11; 14:1; 2(2); 6; 13; 14; 15:1; 2; 5; 16:1; 5; 7; 13; 15; 17:1; 3; 6(3); 7; 18:1; 4; 7; 19:1; 6; 10(2); 11; 17; 19; 20:1; 4(2); 11; 12; 21:1; 2; 3; 5; 6(2); 7; 9; 22; 22:7; 8(3); 9; 12; 13; 16(2); 18; 20

IF

176, 194, 432, 518, 834, 2005, 2006, 3588, 3808, 3863, 3884, 6112, *148, 1437, 1477, 1487, 1489, 1490, 1499, 1512, 1513, 1535, 2579, 3379*

Gen 4:7(2); 24; 8:8; 13:9(2); 16; 15:5; 18:3; 21; 26; 28; 30; 20:7; 23:8; 13; 24:8; 41; 42; 49(2); 25:22; 27:46; 28:20; 30:27; 31; 31:8(2); 50(2); 32:8; 33:10; 13; 34:15; 17; 22; 37:26; 42:19; 37; 38; 43:4; 5; 9; 11; 14; 44:22; 26; 29; 32; 47:6; 16; 29; 50:4; **Ex** 1:16(2); 4:8; 9; 23; 8:2; 21; 9:2; 10:4; 12:4; 13:13; 15:26; 18:23; 19:5; 20:25(2); 21:2; 3(2); 4; 5; 7; 8; 9; 10; 11; 13; 14; 16; 18; 19; 20; 21; 22; 23; 26; 27; 28; 29; 30; 32; 33(2); 35; 36; 22:1; 2; 3(2); 4; 5; 6; 7(2); 8; 10; 12; 13; 14; 15(2); 16; 17; 23; 25; 26; 23:4; 5; 22; 33; 24:14; 29:34; 32:32(2); 33:13; 15; 34:9; 20; 40:37; **Lev** 1:2; 3; 10; 14; 2:4; 5; 7; 14; 3:1(2); 6; 7; 12; 4:2; 3; 13; 23; 27; 28; 32; 5:1(2); 2(2); 3; 4; 7; 11; 15; 17; 6:2; 28; 7:12; 16; 18; 10:19; 11:37; 38; 39; 12:2; 5; 8; 13:4; 5; 6; 7; 8; 10; 12; 13; 16; 17; 20; 21(2); 22; 23; 24; 25; 26; 27; 28; 29; 30; 31; 32; 34; 35; 36; 37; 38; 39; 42; 43; 49; 51; 53; 55; 56; 57; 58; 14:3; 21; 37; 39; 43; 44; 48; 15:8; 16; 19; 23; 24; 25(2); 28; 17:16; 18:5; 19:5; 6; 7; 33; 20:4; 12; 13; 14; 15; 16; 17; 18; 20; 21; 21:9; 22:9; 11; 12; 13; 14; 24:19; 25:14; 20; 25(2); 26; 28; 29; 30; 33; 35; 39; 47; 49; 51; 52; 54; 26:3; 14; 15(2); 18; 21; 23; 27; 40; 41; 27:4; 5; 6; 7(2); 8; 9; 10; 11; 13; 15; 16; 17; 18; 19; 20(2); 22; 27(2); 31; 33; **Num** 5:8; 12; 14; 19(2); 20(2); 27; 28; 6:9; 9:10; 14; 10:4; 9; 32; 11:15(2); 12:6; 14; 14:8; 15; 15:14; 22; 24; 27; 16:29(2); 30; 19:12; 20:19; 21:2; 9; 22:18; 20; 34; 24:13; 27:8; 9; 10; 11; 30:2; 3; 5; 6; 8; 10; 12; 14; 15; 32:5; 15; 20(2); 23; 29; 30; 33:55; 35:16; 17; 18; 20; 22; 26; 36:3; **Deut** 4:29(2); 30; 5:25; 6:25; 7:12; 17; 8:19; 11:13; 22; 27; 28; 12:21; 13:1; 6; 12; 14; 14:24(2); 15:5; 7; 12; 16; 21(2); 17:2; 8; 18:6; 21; 22; 19:8; 9; 11; 16; 18; 20:11; 12; 21:1; 14; 15(2); 18; 22; 22:2(2); 6; 8; 13; 20; 22; 23; 25; 28; 23:10; 22; 24:3(2); 7; 12; 25:1; 2; 3; 5; 7; 8; 28:1; 2; 9; 13; 15; 58; 30:4; 10(2); 17; 32:41; **Josh** 2:14; 19; 20; 8:15; 9:4; 14:12; 17:15(2); 20:5; 22:19; 22(2); 23(2); 24; 23:12; 24:15; 20; **Judg** 4:8(2); 6:13; 17; 31; 36; 37; 7:10; 8:19; 9:15(2); 16(2); 19; 20; 36; 11:9; 10; 30; 36; 12:5; 13:16; 23; 14:12; 13; 18; 16:7; 11; 13; 17; 21:21; **Ruth** 1:12(2); 17; 3:13(2); 4:4(2); **1Sa** 1:11; 2:16(2); 25(2); 3:9; 17; 6:3; 9(2); 7:3; 9:7; 10:22; 11:3; 12:14; 15; 25; 14:9; 10; 30; 16:2; 17:9(2); 19:11; 20:6; 7(2); 8; 9; 10; 12; 13; 21; 22; 29; 21:4; 9; 23:3; 23; 24:19; 25:22; 26:19(2); 27:5; **2Sa** 3:35; 7:14; 10:11(2); 11:20; 12:8; 18; 13:26; 14:32; 15:8; 25; 26; 33; 34; 16:23; 17:3; 6; 13; 18:3(2); 25; 19:6; 7; 13; **1Kin** 1:52(2); 2:4; 23; 3:14; 6:12; 8:31; 35; 37(4); 44; 46; 47; 9:4; 6; 11:38; 12:7; 27; 13:8; 16:31; 18:21(2); 19:2; 20:10; 39; 21:2; 6; 22:28; **2Kin** 1:10; 12; 2:10(2); 4:29(2); 5:13; 6:27; 31; 7:2; 4(4); 9; 19; 9:15; 10:6(2); 15; 24; 18:21; 22;

23; 20:19; 21:8; **1Chr** 12:17(2); 13:2; 19:12(2); 22:13; 28:7; 9(2); **2Chr** 6:22; 24; 26; 28(4); 32; 34; 36; 37; 38; 7:13(3); 14; 17; 19; 10:7; 15:2(2); 18:27; 20:9; 25:8; 30:9(2); **Ezr** 4:13; 16; 5:17; **Neh** 1:8; 9; 2:5(2); 7; 4:3; 9:29; 10:31; 13:21; **Est** 1:19; 3:9; 4:14; 16; 5:4; 8(2); 6:13; 7:3(2); 4; 8:5(2); 9:13; **Job** 4:2; 5:1; 6:28; 8:4; 5; 6; 18; 9:3; 13; 16; 19(2); 20(2); 23; 24; 27; 29; 30; 10:14; 15(2); 11:10; 13; 14; 13:10; 19; 14:7; 14; 16:4; 17:13; 19:5; 21:4; 15; 22:23; 24:17; 25; 27:14; 29:24; 31:5(2); 7(2); 9(2); 13; 16; 19; 20(2); 21; 24; 25; 26; 29; 31; 33; 38; 39; 33:5; 23; 27; 32; 33; 34:14(2); 16; 32; 35:3; 6(2); 7; 36:8; 11; 12; 37:20; 38:4; 5; 8; 18; **Ps** 7:3(2); 4; 12; 11:3; 14:2; 28:1; 40:5; 41:6; 44:20; 50:12; 53:2; 59:15; 62:10; 66:18; 73:15; 81:8; 89:30; 31; 90:10; 95:7; 124:1; 2; 130:3; 132:12; 137:5; 6(2); 139:8(2); 9; 11; 18; 24; **Prov** 1:10; 11; 2:1; 3; 4; 3:30; 6:1(2); 30; 31; 9:12(2); 16:31; 19:19; 22:18; 27; 23:2(2); 13; 15; 24:10; 11; 12; 5:8; 6:3; 10:4; 10; 11:3(2); 8; **Song** 1:8; 5:8; 7:12; 8:7; 9(2); **Is** 1:19; 20; 5:30; 7:9; 8:20; 10:15(3); 21:12; 36:6; 7; 8; 47:11; 12(2); 51:13; 58:9; 10; 13; 59:10; 66:3(4); **Jer** 2:10; 28; 3:1; 4:1(2); 5:1(2); 7:5(2); 6; 12:5(2); 16; 17; 13:17; 22; 14:18(2); 15:2; 19(2); 17:24; 27; 18:8; 10; 21:2; 22:4; 5; 23:22; 25:28; 26:3; 4; 15; 27:18(2); 31:36; 37; 33:20; 25(2); 38:15(2); 17; 18; 21; 25; 40:4(2); 42:5; 10; 13; 15; 49:9(2); 51:8; **Lam** 1:12; 2:6; 3:29; **Eze** 3:19; 21; 10:10; 14:9; 15; 17; 19; 16:47; 18:5; 10; 14; 21; 20:11; 13; 21; 39; 21:13; 33:2; 3; 4; 6(2); 8; 9(2); 10; 13; 14; 15; 19; 43:11; 46:16; 17; **Dan** 5:6; 9; 3:15(2); 17; 18; 4:27; 5:16; **Hos** 6:3; 8:7; **Joel** 2:14; 3:4; **Amos** 3:4; 5:19; 6:9; **Obad** 5(3); **Jonah** 1:6; 3:9; **Mic** 2:11; 5:8; **Nah** 3:12; **Hag** 2:12; 13; **Zec** 3:7(2); 6:15; 8:6; 11:12(2); 14:18; **Mal** 1:6(2); 8(2); 2:2(2); 3:10; **Mt** 4:3; 6; 9; 5:13; 23; 29; 30; 40; 46; 47; 6:14; 15; 22; 23(2); 30; 7:9; 10; 11; 8:2; 31; 9:21; 10:13(2); 25; 11:14; 21; 23; 12:7; 11; 26; 27; 28; 14:28; 15:14; 16:24; 26; 17:4; 20; 18:8; 9; 12; 15(2); 16; 17(2); 19; 35; 19:10; 17; 21; 21:3; 21(2); 24; 25; 26; 22:24; 45; 23:30; 24:23; 24; 26; 43; 48; 26:24; 39; 42; 27:40; 42; 43; 28:14; **Mk** 1:40; 3:24; 25; 26; 4:23; 26; 5:28; 6:56; 7:11; 16; 8:3; 23; 36; 9:22; 23; 35; 43; 45; 47; 50; 10:12; 11:3; 13; 25; 26; 31; 32; 12:19; 13:21; 22; 14:21; 31; 35; 15:44; 16:18; **Lk** 4:3; 7; 9; 5:12; 36; 6:32; 33; 34; 7:39; 9:23; 25; 10:6(2); 13; 11:11(2); 12; 13; 18; 19; 20; 36; 12:26; 28; 38; 39; 45; 49; 13:9(2); 14:26; 34; 15:4; 8; 16:11; 12; 30; 31; 17:3(2); 4; 6; 19:8; 31; 40; 42; 20:5; 6; 28; 22:42; 67; 68; 23:31; 35; 37; 39; **Jn** 1:25; 3:12(2); 4:10; 5:31; 43; 47; 6:51; 62; 7:4; 17; 23; 37; 8:16; 19; 24; 31; 36; 39; 42; 46; 51; 52; 54; 55; 9:22; 31; 33; 41; 10:9; 24; 35; 37; 38; 11:9; 10; 12; 21; 32; 40; 48; 57; 12:24; 26(2); 32; 47; 13:8; 14; 17(2); 32; 35; 14:2; 3; 7; 14; 15; 23; 28; 15:6; 7; 10; 14; 18; 19; 20(2); 22; 24; 16:7(2); 18; 23(2); 30; 36; 19:12; 20:15; 21:22; 23; 25; **Acts** 4:9; 5:38; 39; 8:22; 37; 9:2; 13:15; 15:29; 16:15; 17:27; 18:14; 15; 21; 19:38; 39; 20:16; 23:9; 24:19; 20; 25:5; 11(2); 26:5; 32; 27:12; 39; **Rom** 1:10; 2:25(2); 26; 27; 3:3; 5; 7; 4:2; 14; 24; 5:10; 15; 6:5; 8; 7:2(2); 16; 20; 8:9(2); 10; 11; 13(2); 17(2); 25; 31; 9:22; 10:9; 11:6(2); 12; 14; 15; 16(2); 17; 18; 21; 22; 23; 24; 12:18; 20(2); 13:4; 9; 14:15; 23; 15:24; 27; **1Cor** 3:12; 14; 15; 17; 18; 4:7(2); 19; 5:11; 6:2; 4; 7; 8; 9; 11; 12; 13; 15; 21; 28(2); 36(2); 39; 40; 8:2; 3; 8(2); 10; 13; 9:2; 11(2); 12; 16; 17(2); 10:27; 28; 30; 11:5; 6(2); 14; 15; 16; 31; 34; 12:15; 16; 17(2); 19; 14:6; 8; 11; 14; 23; 24; 27; 28; 30; 35; 37; 38; 15:2; 12; 13; 14; 16; 17; 19; 29; 32(2); 16:4; 7; 10; 22; **2Cor** 2:2; 5; 10; 3:7; 9; 11; 4:3; 5:1; 3; 14; 17; 7:14; 8:12; 9:4; 10:2; 7; 9; 11:4(2); 15; 16; 20(5); 30; 13:2(2); **Gal** 1:9; 10; 2:14; 17; 18; 21; 3:4; 15; 18; 21; 29; 4:7; 15; 5:2(2); 15; 6:1; 3; 9; **Eph** 3:2; 4:21; **Phil** 1:22; 2:1(4); 17; 3:4; 11; 12; 15; 4:8(2); **Col** 1:23; 2:20; 3:1; 13; 4:10; **1Th** 3:8; 4:14; **2Th** 3:10; 14; **1Ti** 1:8; 10; 2:15; 3:1; 5; 15; 4:4; 6; 5:4; 8; 10(5); 16; 6:3; **2Ti** 2:5; 11; 12(2); 13; 21; 25; **Titus** 1:6; **Philem** 1:17; 18; **Heb** 2:2; 3; 3:6; 7; 14; 15; 4:3; 5; 6; 6:3; 7:11; 8:4; 7; 9:13; 10:26; 38; 11:15; 12:7; 8; 20; 25(2); 13:23; **Jas** 1:5; 23; 26; 2:2; 8; 9; 11(2); 15; 17; 3:2; 14; 4:11; 15; 5:15; 19; **1Pet** 1:6; 17; 2:3; 19; 20(2); 3:1; 13; 14; 17; 4:11(2); 14; 16; 17; 18; **2Pet** 1:8; 10; 2:4; 20; **1Jn** 1:6; 7; 8; 9; 10; 2:1; 3; 15; 19; 24; 29; 3:13; 20; 21; 4:11; 12; 20; 5:9; 14; 15; 16; **2Jn** 10; **3Jn** 6; 10; **Rev** 1:15; 3:3; 20; 11:5(2); 13:9; 14:9; 22:18; 19

1722

Gen 1:1; 6; 11; 12; 14; 15; 17; 20; 22(2); 26; 27(2); 29; 2:3; 4; 5; 8; 9; 17; 3:3; 5; 8(2); 10; 16; 17; 19; 4:3; 8; 12; 14; 16; 20; 22; 5:1(2); 2; 3; 6:4(3); 5; 8; 9; 14; 16(2); 17; 7:1; 7; 9; 11(2); 13; 15; 16(3); 22(2); 23; 8:1; 4; 5; 9; 11(3); 13(2); 14; 17; 21; 9:6; 7; 13; 14; 16; 27; 10:5(2); 8; 10; 20(2); 25; 31; 32(2); 11:2; 28(2); 31; 32; 12:3; 5; 6; 10(2); 13(3); 7; 12(2); 17(2); 18(2); 14:1; 3; 4; 5(4); 6; 7; 12; 15:1; 3; 6; 10; 13; 15(2); 16; 18; 16:2; 3; 4(2); 5; 6; 7(2); 12; 17:7; 9; 12; 13(2); 17; 21; 18:1; 6; 9; 11; 12; 18; 19(2); 24; 26; 27(2); 29; 2:3; 4; 5; 6(4); 8; 10; 12; 15; 16(3); 17; 21; 9:6; 7; 13; 14; 16; 27; 10:5(2); 8; 10; 20(2); 25; 31; 32(2); 11:2; 28(2); 30; 32; 34; 38; 16:2; 7; 13; 17; 18(2); 21; 26; 27; 45; 49; 17:4; 7; 18:10; 11; 13(2); 14; 15; 20; 21; 31(1); 19:5; 7; 8(2); 9; 14(2); 16; 17; 18; 19; 20:1(2); 5; 12; 13; 15; 16(2); 23; 27; 28; 21:1; 5; 10; 11; 12; 13; 14(3); 20(2); 25(3); 27; 31; 22:1; 7; 13; 18; 21; 23(2); 24; 26; 29; 31(2); 34; 36(2); 38; 23:5; 11; 16; 21(2); 24:2; 7; 14; 21; 25:1; 7; 13; 21; 22; 23(2); 24; 26; 29; 31(2); 34; 36(2); 38; 39; 41; 43; 47; 5:3; 17(2); 18(2); 23; 6:5; 9; 18; 7:10; 84; 8:15; 17; 19; 22(2); 24; 26; 9:1(2); 3(2); 5; 7; 10; 13(2); 14; 17; 18; 20; 21; 22; 23; 10:9; 10(3); 11; 12; 14; 29; 31; 33; 11:1; 5; 8(3); 9; 10; 11; 12; 15; 18(2); 25; 26(2); 27; 12:5(2); 6(3); 7; 8; 14:2; 15; 16; 13:19(4); 22; 28; 29(2); 32; 33(2); 14:2(2); 8; 10; 13; 14(2); 16; 22(2); 25; 28; 29; 31; 32; 33(2); 34; 35; 40; 45; 15:3(3); 8; 13; 14; 15; 21; 26; 30; 32; 34; 38; 16:2; 7; 13; 17; 18(2); 21; 26; 27; 45; 49; 17:4; 7; 18:10; 11; 13(2); 14; 15; 19; 20:1(2); 5; 12; 13; 15; 16(2); 23; 27; 28; 21:1; 5; 10; 11; 12; 13; 14(3); 20(2); 25(3); 27; 31; 22:1; 5; 6(6); 7; 16(2); 17; 22(2); 14:2(2); 3; 7; 9; 15(2); 16; 19; 22(2); 27(2); 33; 34; 39; 43; 45; 15:2; 4; 5; 12; 14; 17; 19; 21; 22(2); 33(2); 16:12; 13; 18(2); 22; 17:1; 2; 8; 12; 19; 20; 21; 22; 25; 28; 40(4); 45; 46; 49(2); 50; 54; 57; 18:5(2); 10(2); 13; 14; 16; 18(2); 24; 27(2); 19:2(2); 3; 5; 7(2); 9(2); 11; 13; 15; 16(2); 18; 19; 22(2); 23(2); 24; 20:1; 3; 5; 8; 13; 19; 24; 29(2); 34; 35; 42(2); 21:3; 5(2); 6; 9(2); 11; 12; 13; 15; 22:2(2); 4; 5; 8(3); 11(2); 14(2); 23; 23:3; 6; 7; 14(4); 15(2); 16; 18; 19(3); 23; 24(2); 25(2); 29; 24:1; 3(2); 10; 11(3); 20; 25:1; 2(3); 3; 4; 5; 6; 7; 8(2); 9; 15; 21; 24(2); 28; 29; 34; 35; 36; 37; 26:1; 2; 3(2); 4; 5; 7; 15(2); 18; 19; 20; 21; 24(2); 27:1(2); 5(4); 7; 11; 28:1; 3(2); 4(2); 20; 21; 24; 29:1; 2; 3; 4; 5; 6(4); 7; 8; 9; 10:2; 11; 10:6; 11; 28(3); 29(3); 30(3); 31; 31:1; 7; 8; 9; 10; **2Sa** 1:1; 9; 18; 20(2); 23(2); 24; 25(2); 2:3; 11; 16(2); 19; 23; 26; 27; 32(2); 3:2; 5; 7; 17; 19(3); 21; 22(3); 23; 25; 27; 30; 32; 38; 4:1; 7; 10; 11; 12(3); 5:2(3); 3; 5(2); 6(2); 9; 14; 18; 22; 24; 6:3; 11; 16; 17(3); 18; 20; 22(2); 7:1; 2; 8:3(3); 6; 3; 7; 14; 9(2); 10; 18; 19; 23; 27; 8:6; 13; 14; 9:4(2); 10; 12; 13; 10:1; 4; 8(3); 9; 10; 17; 11(2); 4; 12; 14; 30; 13:5; 6; 8; 12; 13; 16; 20; 23; 30; 14:3; 6; 13; 19(2); 20; 22(2); 25(2); 28; 32; 15:4; 7; 8; 9; 10; 11; 17; 21(2); 25; 26; 27; 27(2);

28; 16:2; 4; 8(2); 19(3); 21; 22(2); 23; 17:3; 8(2); 9(2); 11; 12; 16; 18(2); 23(2); 25; 26; 29; 18:6; 10; 12(2); 14(2); 17; 18(3); 25; 19:3; 6; 8(2); 10; 13; 22; 24; 27; 30; 33; 37; 43(3); 20:1(2); 3(3); 8(2); 9; 10(2); 12(2); 15(2); 18; 19(2); 22; 21:1; 2; 4; 5; 6; 9(4); 12; 14(3); 16; 19; 20(2); 22; 22:1; 3; 7; 19; 20; 25; 31; 23:2; 3; 5; 7; 8; 12; 13(2); 14(2); 17; 20(2); 21; 39; 24:3; 5(2); 9; 10; 11; 13(2); 14; 18; **1Kin** 1:1; 2; 6; 13; 14; 15; 19; 22; 23; 25; 30; 35; 41; 42; 45; 52; 2:3(3); 4; 5(2); 6; 8; 10; 11(2); 26; 27; 34(2); 35(2); 36; 38; 39; 46; 3:2; 3(2); 5(2); 6(3); 7; 8; 14; 17(2); 18(2); 19; 20(2); 21(2); 25; 26; 27; 28; 4:7; 8; 9(2); 10; 11; 13(3); 15; 16(2); 17; 18; 19(3); 20; 27; 31; 33; 5:1; 5; 9(2); 14; 15; 16; 6:1(3); 6(2); 7(3); 8; 12(3); 19; 20(4); 27; 37(2); 38(3); 7:3; 4(2); 5; 14(2); 19; 20; 21; 24(2); 35; 46(2); 51; 8:1; 2; 4; 6; 8; 9; 12; 13(2); 17; 18(2); 20; 22; 23; 25; 30; 31; 32; 33; 34; 36; 37(2); 39; 40; 43; 45; 47(2); 48; 49; 52; 58; 61; 65; 9:4(2); 11; 16; 18(2); 19(3); 21; 23; 25; 26(2); 27; 10:2; 5; 6; 9; 11; 14; 17; 20; 21; 22; 24; 26; 27(2); 11:2(3); 6; 7; 12; 14; 15(2); 16; 19; 20(2); 21; 22; 24; 29(2); 30; 33(2); 36; 38(2); 40; 41; 42; 43(2); 12:2(2); 16(2); 17; 25; 26; 27; 29(2); 32(4); 33(2); 13:2; 4(2); 8(2); 11(2); 16(2); 19; 22; 24; 25(2); 28; 30; 31; 32(2); 14:5; 6(2); 8; 10; 11(2); 13(2); 15; 19; 20; 21(2); 22; 24; 25; 27; 29; 31(2); 15:1; 2; 3; 4; 5(2); 7; 8(2); 9; 10; 11; 13; 15; 17; 18; 21; 23(3); 24(2); 25; 26(3); 28(2); 31; 33(2); 34(3); 16:2; 4(2); 5; 6(2); 7(3); 8(2); 9(3); 10(3); 13; 14; 15(2); 16; 19(5); 20; 23(2); 25; 26(2); 27; 28(2); 29(2); 30; 31; 32(2); 34(3); 17:6(2); 7; 10; 11; 12(3); 17; 24; 18:1; 2; 4; 7; 13; 18; 23; 27; 32; 33(2); 36; 38; 45; 19:8; 11(3); 12; 13(3); 16; 18; 20:6(2); 12(3); 16; 23; 24; 25; 29(2); 34(2); 35; 37; 21:1; 2; 8(2); 9; 11(2); 13(2); 18(2); 19; 20; 21; 24(2); 25; 26; 27; 29(2); 22:2; 3; 10(2); 16; 17; 22; 23; 25; 27(2); 28; 35; 37; 38; 39; 40; 41; 42; 43(3); 45; 46; 47; 49; 50(2); 51; 52(4); **2Kin** 1:2(2); 3; 6; 13; 14; 16; 17(2); 18; 2:12; 21; 24; 3:1; 2; 18; 20; 21; 22; 24; 25; 27; 4:2(2); 4; 8; 10; 15; 29; 33; 35; 36; 37; 38; 40; 41; 42; 5:1; 3; 4; 8; 10; 12(2); 14; 15(2); 18(4); 19; 20; 23; 24; 25; 6:6; 8; 12(2); 13; 20; 25; 32; 7:1; 2; 3; 4; 5; 7; 12(2); 13(2); 15; 17; 18; 19; 20; 8:2; 8; 15(2); 16; 17; 18(2); 20; 23; 24(2); 25; 26; 27(3); 28; 29(2); 9:1; 2; 8; 10; 15(2); 16; 17; 21(2); 24; 25; 26; 27; 28(3); 29; 31; 34; 36; 37; 10:1; 5; 7; 8(2); 9; 11; 12; 16; 17; 19; 24; 25; 29(2); 30(3); 31; 32(2); 34; 35(2); 36; 11:2; 3; 4; 5; 8(2); 9; 10; 11; 15; 18; 20; 12:1(2); 2; 3; 6; 9; 10(3); 18(2); 19; 20; 21(2); 13:1(2); 2; 5; 6; 8; 9(2); 10(2); 11; 12; 13; 17; 20; 24; 14:1; 2; 3; 5; 6; 7; 8; 9(3); 11; 14(2); 15; 16(2); 18; 19; 20; 23(2); 24; 28; 29; 15:1; 2; 3; 5; 6; 7(2); 8(2); 9; 10; 11; 13(2); 14(2); 15; 17(2); 18; 19; 20; 21; 22; 23(2); 24; 25(3); 26; 27(2); 28; 29; 30(2); 31; 32; 33; 34; 35; 36; 37; 38(2); 16:1; 2(2); 3; 4; 8(2); 18; 19; 20(2); 17:1(2); 2; 4(2); 6(4); 8; 9; 10; 11; 14; 17; 19; 22; 24(2); 26; 28; 29(2); 31; 32; 18:1; 2; 3; 4; 5; 9; 10; 11(3); 13; 15(2); 17; 22(2); 26(3); 28; 30; 19:7; 10; 12; 27; 28(2); 29(2); 35(2); 37(2); 20:1(2); 3(2); 11; 13(3); 15(2); 17(2); 18; 19; 20; 21; 21:1; 2; 4(2); 5; 6; 7(3); 15; 16(2); 17; 18(3); 19; 20; 21(2); 22; 23; 24; 25; 26(3); 22:1; 2(2); 3; 5; 8; 9; 14(2); 20; 23:2(2); 3; 4; 5(3); 8(2); 9; 10; 11(2); 12; 14; 16; 19(2); 21; 22; 23(2); 24(4); 28; 29; 30(3); 31; 32; 33(3); 34; 36; 37; 24:1; 5; 6; 8; 9; 12; 13(2); 17; 18; 19; 20; 25:1(3); 3; 5; 8; 11; 13(3); 15(2); 19(3); 21; 22; 24; 25; 27(3); 28; **1Chr** 1:19; 43; 44; 45; 46(2); 47; 48; 49; 50; 2:3; 4; 6; 7; 21; 22; 24; 3:1; 4(2); 5; 4:22; 38; 41(2); 5:8; 9(2); 10(2); 11; 12; 16(4); 17(2); 18; 20(2); 22; 23; 6:10(2); 31; 32; 54; 55; 62; 67; 71; 76; 78; 80; 7:2(2); 5; 21; 23; 29; 8:8; 28; 32; 9:1; 2(2); 3; 9; 16; 18(2); 20; 22(3); 24; 25; 26; 28; 31; 33(2); 35; 10:1; 7(2); 8; 10(2); 12; 11:2(2); 3; 7; 10; 14; 15; 16; 19; 22(2); 23; 12:2; 15; 17; 21; 33; 35; 36; 40; 13:2(2); 3; 4; 7; 14; 14:4; 9; 11; 13; 15; 15:1; 29; 16:1; 2; 10; 14; 19; 27(2); 29; 35; 39; 40; 17:1(2); 2; 4; 5; 8; 9; 14(2); 17; 19; 21; 25; 18:6; 12; 13; 19:1; 4; 9(2); 10; 11; 13; 17(2); 18; 20:2; 3; 8; 21:12; 13; 16(2); 18; 19; 23; 28; 29(2); 22:2; 3(2); 4; 7; 8; 9; 14(2); 15; 23:11; 13; 25; 28(3); 29; 31(2); 32; 24:3; 19; 31; 25:5; 6; 7; 26:12; 27; 30(2); 31; 27:1(2); 2; 4; 5; 6; 7; 8; 9; 10; 11; 12; 13; 14; 15; 21; 24; 25(4); 28; 29(2); 28:2; 8(2); 13; 19; 29:2; 11(2); 12(2); 17(2); 18; 21; 25(2); 27(2); 28(2); 29(3); **2Chr** 1:1; 2; 3; 7; 8; 9; 10; 11; 14; 15; 2:2; 7(7); 8; 9; 11; 14(10); 16; 17; 18; 3:1(3); 2(2); 4; 10; 16; 4:2; 3; 6(3); 7; 8; 17(2); 18; 5:1; 3(2); 5; 7; 10; 12; 13; 6:1; 5; 7; 8(3); 10; 11; 12; 13; 14(2); 16(2); 18; 22; 24; 28(2); 29; 31(2); 32; 37(2); 38; 40; 41; 7:8; 9; 10; 11(2); 15; 18; 8:4(2); 6(2); 8; 11; 13(4); 17; 9:1(2); 4; 5; 8; 11; 13; 16; 19; 20; 22; 23; 25; 27(3); 29(3); 30; 31(2); 10:2; 16(2); 17; 11:3; 5(2); 10(2); 11; 12; 13; 17; 23; 12:2; 5; 12; 13(2); 15; 16(2); 13:1; 2; 3(2); 4; 8; 11; 20; 22; 14:1(3); 2; 6(2); 10(2); 11; 14; 15; 15:4; 5(2); 9; 10(2); 16; 16:1(2); 9; 10(2); 11; 12(3); 13; 14(3); 17:1; 2(3); 3; 4; 5(2); 6; 7(2); 9; 12; 13(2); 19; 18:1; 2; 3; 9(3); 15; 16; 21; 22; 26(2); 27; 34; 19:1; 3(2); 5; 6; 8; 9; 10; 11; 20:2; 5(2); 6(2); 9(3); 14; 17; 20(2); 24; 25(2); 26; 27; 31; 32(2); 34(2); 36; 21:1(2); 3; 5; 6(2); 8; 9; 11; 12(2); 13; 17; 18; 19; 20(3); 22:1; 2; 3; 4; 6; 9; 11; 12; 23:1; 2; 3; 5; 6; 7(2); 8; 9; 10; 13; 14; 17; 18(2); 19(2); 24:1; 2; 6; 9(2); 10; 11; 13; 14; 16(2); 21; 25(3); 27(2); 25:1; 2; 4(2); 10; 12; 17; 18(3); 21; 24; 26; 27; 28; 26:1; 3; 4; 5(2); 7; 8; 9; 10(5); 15; 17; 19(3); 20; 21; 23(2); 27:1; 2; 4(2); 7; 8; 9(2); 28:1(2); 2; 3(2); 4; 6(2); 9; 13; 22; 24(2); 25; 26; 27(3); 29:1; 2; 3(2); 4; 6; 7; 9; 10; 16; 17(2); 18; 19(2); 25; 31; 34; 35(2); 30:2(2); 5; 12; 13; 14; 15; 16; 17; 25; 26(2); 31:1(2); 2; 3; 4(2); 5(2); 6(2); 7(2); 11; 12; 15(2); 16; 17; 18(2); 19(2); 21(4); 32:5(2); 6; 10(2); 18; 21; 23; 24; 26; 29; 30; 31(3); 32(2); 33(2); 33:1; 2; 4(2); 5; 6(2); 7(3); 12; 14(3); 15(2); 17; 18(2); 20(2); 21; 22; 24; 25; 34:1; 2(2); 3(2); 4(2); 6; 8; 10(2); 13; 15; 17; 21(3); 22(2); 24; 28; 30(2); 31(2); 32; 33; 35:1; 2; 3; 5; 10(2); 12; 13(3); 14; 15; 18; 19; 22; 24(2); 25(3); 26; 27; 36:1(2); 2; 3; 5(2); 6; 7; 8(3); 9(2); 11; 12; 14; 17; 22(2); 23(2); **Ezr** 1:1(2); 2; 3(2); 4(2); 5; 7; 2:42; 68; 70(2); 3:1; 2; 8(2); 9; 10; 11; 4:4; 6(2); 7(3); 8; 10; 15(2); 17; 23; 5:1(2); 8(2); 13; 14; 15(2); 16(2); 17; 6:1(2); 2(2); 3; 5; 7; 15; 18(3); 22; 7:1; 6; 7; 8(2); 10; 13; 14; 15; 16(2); 17; 25; 27(2); 8:1; 15; 22; 29; 31; 33; 9:2; 7; 8(2); 9(4); 14; 15; 10:2; 9; 13; 14; 16; **Neh** 1:1(3); 3(2); 11; 2:1(3); 5; 12(2); 15; 17; 20; 3:17; 26; 4:2; 4; 11; 13; 16; 17; 20; 21; 22; 5:5; 9; 14; 16; 18; 6:2(2); 5(2); 7; 10(2); 11; 14; 15(2); 16; 17; 18(2); 19; 7:3; 73(2); 8:5; 7; 8(2); 14(3); 15(2); 16(4); 18; 9:1; 3(2); 9; 12(3); 15; 17; 19(3); 21; 23; 24; 25(2); 27; 28; 29; 30; 33; 35(3); 36; 37; 10:29; 34; 36(2); 37; 11:1(2); 3(4); 17; 18; 20(2); 21; 24; 25(3); 27; 28; 30(2); 31; 36(2); 12:7; 9; 12; 22; 23; 26(2); 39; 40; 46; 47(2); 13:1(2); 6(2); 7(2); 11; 15(4); 16; 19; 23; 24(2); 27; 28; 30; **Est** 1:1; 2(2); 3; 5(2); 7(2); 9; 10; 12; 14; 16; 17(2); 22; 2:3; 5; 12; 14(3); 15(2); 16(2); 17; 19; 21(2); 22; 23; 3:2; 3; 7(2); 8; 12; 13; 14; 15; 4:3(2); 8; 11; 13; 16(2); 5:1(2); 2(3); 8; 9; 12; 14; 6:4; 5(2); 6(2); 7:3; 5; 7; 8; 9; 8:5(3); 8(2); 9; 10; 11; 12; 13; 15; 17(2); 9:1(3); 2; 4; 6; 11; 12(2); 13; 15; 16; 19; 20; 31; 32; 10:2; **Job** 1:1; 4; 5(2); 7(2); 8; 10; 12; 13; 18; 22; 2:2(2); 3; 6; 10; 3:3; 20(2); 23; 26; 4:13; 18; 19(3); 21; 5:4; 13; 14(3); 19(2); 20(2); 23; 24; 26(3); 6:2; 4; 6; 10; 13; 29; 30; 7:11(2); 21(2); 8:12; 16; 9:4(2); 5; 29; 31; 32; 10:1; 13; 11:4; 14(2); 18; 12:5; 9; 10; 12; 24; 25; 13:14(2); 15; 27; 14:8(2); 13; 17; 15:9; 15(2); 21(2); 28(2); 31; 16:4; 8; 9; 15; 17; 19; 17:2; 3; 13; 16; 18:3; 4; 6; 10(2); 15; 17; 19; 19:2; 8; 15(2); 23; 24; 26; 28; 20:11; 12; 14; 20; 22(2); 26(2); 28; 21:7; 8; 13(2); 16; 17; 21(2); 23; 25; 26; 32; 34(2); 22:8; 12; 14; 22; 26; 23:6; 13; 24:5; 6; 7; 13; 14; 16(2); 17; 18; 23; 25:2; 5; 26:8; 27:3(2); 10; 15; 20; 28:13; 14; 29:2(2); 4; 7; 18; 20(2); 25; 30:1; 2; 3; 6(3); 10; 14(2); 17(2); 24; 25; 28; 31:6; 15(2); 21; 26; 32; 33; 32:1; 5; 8; 22; 33:2; 5; 6; 8; 9; 11; 12; 15(3); 34:8; 20; 24(2); 25; 26; 35:10; 14; 15(2); 16; 36:4; 5; 8(2); 11(2); 13; 14; 15(2); 20; 31; 37:8; 12; 16; 21; 23(3); 38:16; 32; 33; 36; 37; 40(3); 39:4; 10; 14(2); 16; 21(2); 40:12; 13(2); 16(2); 21; 41:9; 22; 23; 42:6; 8; 11; 15; **Ps** 1:1(3); 2(2); 3; 5(2); 2:4(2); 5(2); 9; 12; 3:2; 4:1; 4; 5; 7(2); 8(2); 5:3(2); 4; 5; 7(2); 8; 9; 10; 11(2); 6:1(2); 5(2); 7:1; 2; 3; 5; 6; 8; 10; 8:1; 9; 9:2; 4; 8(2); 9; 10; 11; 14(2); 15(2); 16; 19; 20; 10:1; 2(2); 4; 6(2); 8(2); 9(3); 11; 13; 11:1; 2; 4(2); 12:5; 6; 13:2(2); 5(2); 14:1; 5(2); 15:1(2); 2; 4; 16:1; 3(2); 6; 7; 9; 10; 11; 17:3; 5; 7; 10; 11; 12; 14; 15; 18:t, 2; 6; 13; 18; 19; 24; 30; 42; 19:4; 11; 14; 20:1; 5(2); 7(2); 21:1(2); 5; 7; 9(2); 13; 22:2(2); 4; 5; 8; 14; 22; 25; 23:2; 3; 5; 6; 24:3; 7; 8; 9; 25:2; 5; 8; 9; 12; 20; 26:1(2); 3; 4; 6; 10; 11; 12(2); 27:3; 4(2); 5(3); 6; 9; 11; 13; 28:3; 7; 29:2; 9; 30:5(2); 6; 9; 31:1(2); 6; 7(2); 8; 9; 14; 15; 17; 19; 20(2); 21; 22; 24; 32:2; 6(2); 8; 9; 10; 11(2); 33:1; 4; 7; 8; 18; 19; 21(2); 22; 34:1; 2; 8; 22; 35:7; 9(2); 15; 16; 18; 20; 25; 27; 36:2; 4; 5; 9; 10; 37:3(2); 4; 5; 7(2); 8; 11; 19(2); 23; 31; 33; 35; 39; 40; 38:1(2); 2; 3(2); 7; 14; 15; 39:6(2); 7; 40:3(2); 5; 7; 9; 16; 41:1; 3; 9; 12; 42:4; 5(2); 8(2); 10; 11; 43:5; 44:1(2); 3; 6; 8; 17; 19; 45:4; 5; 9; 14; 16; 17; 46:1; 5; 8; 9(2); 10; 48:1(2); 3; 6; 8(2); 9; 49:5; 6(2); 12; 14(3); 20; 50:15; 16; 21; 22; 51:t, 4; 5(2); 6(2); 10; 16; 18; 52:1; 7(2); 8(2); 53:1; 5; 54:5; 55:2; 3; 7; 9; 10; 11; 14; 15; 18; 21; 23; 56:t, 3; 4(2); 7; 8; 10(2); 11; 13; 57:t, 1(2); 58:2(2); 6; 7; 9; 10; 11; 59:3; 7; 8; 12; 13(2); 16(2); 60:t, 6; 61:4(2); 62:4; 7(2); 8; 9; 10(2); 63:t, 1; 2; 4; 6; 7; 11; 64:1; 4; 5; 10(3); 65:1; 4; 5; 8; 66:3; 5; 6; 9; 14; 18; 68:5; 6(2); 14(2); 16(2); 17(2); 21; 23(2); 24; 26; 30; 34; 69:1; 2; 12; 13(3); 17; 21; 25; 35; 70:4; 71:1; 2; 9; 16; 72:4; 7; 9; 14; 16; 17; 73:4; 5; 11; 12(2); 13(2); 18; 19; 21; 25; 28; 74:3; 4; 8(2); 12; 13; 14; 75:8; 76:1(2); 2(2); 7; 77:2(2); 6; 9; 13; 18; 19(2); 78:2; 5(2); 7; 9; 10; 12(3); 14; 15; 17; 18; 19; 22(2); 26(2); 28; 30; 33(2); 37; 40(2); 43(2); 51(2); 52; 55; 66; 79:10; 80:5; 81:3(2); 5; 7(2); 9; 12; 13; 82:1; 5; 83:4; 12; 84:4; 5(2); 7; 10(3); 12; 85:6; 9; 13; 86:2; 5; 7; 11; 15; 87:1; 5; 7; 88:5; 6(3); 11(2); 12(2); 13; 89:2; 5; 6; 7(2); 10; 12; 15; 16(2); 17; 19; 24; 25(2); 30; 37; 43; 47; 49; 50; 90:1; 4(2); 5; 6(2); 8; 9; 91:1; 2; 6; 11; 12; 15; 92:2; 4; 12; 13(2); 14; 15; 94:5; 15; 17; 19; 23; 95:4; 8(3); 10; 11; 96:6; 9; 97:11; 12; 98:2; 99:2; 4; 7; 101:2; 6; 7; 102:2(3); 14; 16; 21(2); 23; 24; 103:8; 19; 20; 22; 104:3; 22; 24; 27; 31; 34; 105:3; 7; 12(2); 18; 23; 27; 30(2); 31; 32; 35; 36; 39; 41; 106:5; 7; 14(2); 16; 18; 19; 21; 22; 23; 25; 26; 27; 29; 47; 107:4(3); 5; 6; 10(3); 13; 14; 16; 19; 23(2); 24; 28; 32(2); 40; 108:7; 109:13; 16; 17; 110:2; 3(2); 5; 7; 111:1(2); 8; 112:1; 3; 4; 6; 7; 113:6(2); 115:3; 8; 9; 10; 11; 116:9; 11; 14; 15; 18; 19(2); 118:5(2); 8(2); 9(2); 10; 11; 12; 15; 23; 24; 26; 119:1(2); 3; 11; 14(2); 15; 16; 19; 23; 35; 37; 40; 42; 43; 47; 48; 50; 51; 54; 55; 70; 74; 75; 78; 80; 81; 83; 89; 92; 109; 114; 133; 147; 148; 161; 120:1; 5(2); 121:8; 123:1; 124:8; 125:1; 4; 126:4; 5(2); 127:1(2); 4; 5; 128:1; 129:8; 130:5; 7; 131:1(2); 3; 132:6; 11; 133:1; 134:1; 2; 135:2(2); 6(3); 17; 18; 136:10; 15; 23; 137:2; 4; 7; 138:3(2); 5; 7; 139:4; 8; 9; 13; 15(2); 16(2); 18; 20; 24(2); 140:2; 7; 11; 13; 141:5; 6; 8; 142:t, 3; 5; 143:1(2); 2; 3; 8(2); 144:2; 12; 13; 14(2); 15; 145:15; 17(2); 18; 146:3(3); 4; 5; 147:3; 10(2); 11(3); 14; 148:1; 149:1; 2(2); 3; 4; 5; 6(2); 150:1(2); **Prov** 1:14; 15; 17(2); 20; 21(3); 22; 2:13; 14; 15; 20; 21(2); 3:4; 5; 6; 7; 12; 16(2); 23; 27; 33; 4:3; 11(2); 14; 21; 5:10; 14(2); 16; 23; 6:8(2); 14; 18; 25; 27; 29; 34; 7:9(3); 11; 12(2); 25; 8:2(2); 3; 8(2); 20(2); 22; 31; 9:4; 6; 9; 14; 16; 17; 18; 10:5(2); 8; 13; 17; 19; 11:4; 6; 8; 14; 20; 21; 22; 28; 31; 12:4; 6; 15; 20; 25; 27; 28(2); 13:6; 23; 14:2(2); 3; 7; 13; 14; 23; 26; 28(2); 32(2); 33(2); 15:3; 4; 6(2); 22; 23; 16:1; 2; 5(2); 10(2); 15; 20; 21; 27; 31; 17:8; 12; 16; 18; 24; 18:2; 5; 9; 11; 17; 21; 19:1(2); 20; 21; 24; 20:4; 5; 7; 8; 20; 21:1; 2; 9(2); 10; 14(2); 16; 19; 20; 24; 22:5; 6; 13; 15; 18; 19; 20; 22; 29; 23:7; 9; 17; 19; 28; 31; 34; 24:6; 7; 10; 23; 27; 25:5; 6(2); 7; 8; 11; 13; 19(2); 20; 24(2); 26:1(2); 5; 7; 8; 9; 12; 13(2); 15; 16; 19; 25; 27:10; 14; 15; 19; 22; 28:6(2); 10(2); 11; 18; 25; 26; 29:2; 6; 11; 20; 22; 23; 25; 27; 30:4(2); 5; 9; 12; 19(2); 25; 26; 28; 29; 32; 31:8; 11; 23; 25; 26; 31; **Eccl** 1:1; 12; 16; 18; 2:1; 3; 5; 7(2); 9; 10; 14(2); 15(2); 16; 21(3); 23; 24; 26; 3:9; 10; 11(2); 12(2); 17; 18; 22; 4:14; 15; 16; 5:2; 4; 7; 8; 14; 15; 16; 17; 19; 20; 6:4(2); 12; 7:4(2); 8(2); 9(2); 14(2); 15(3); 19; 8:2; 3; 8(2); 10; 11; 9:1(2); 3; 6; 9(2); 10; 12(3); 15; 17; 10:1; 6(2); 16; 17; 20(2); 11:3; 5; 6(2); 8; 9(4); 12:1(2); 3; 4; 5; 9; **Song** 1:4; 9; 14; 2:12; 14(2); 3:2(2); 8(2); 11(2); 4:7; 5:4; 6:2; 13; 7:4; 5; 11; 8:8; 10; 13; **Is** 1:1; 6; 7; 8(2); 11; 21; 2:2(2); 3; 5; 6; 10; 11; 17; 20; 22; 3:7(2); 14; 18; 25; 4:1; 2; 3(3); 6; 5:1; 2; 4; 8; 9; 11; 12; 16(2); 21(2); 25; 30(2); 6:1; 5; 6; 12; 13(2); 7:1; 3; 6; 11(2); 18(3); 19(2); 20; 21; 22; 23; 8:1; 6; 9(3); 11; 18(2); 20; 9:1(2); 2(2); 3; 4; 5; 9; 14; 17; 18; 10:3(2); 5; 7; 17; 20(2); 23; 24; 25; 27; 11:3; 9; 10; 11; 15; 16; 12:1; 4; 5; 6; 13:3; 4; 8; 10; 13(2); 17; 20; 22(2); 14:1; 2; 3; 6(2); 13(2); 18(2); 20; 25; 28; 30; 31; 32; 15:1(2); 3(2); 5; 16:3; 5(3); 10(2); 17:4; 5; 6(3); 9; 11(3); 18:2; 4(2); 5; 7; 19:1; 3; 9; 10; 14(3); 16; 17; 18(2); 19(2); 20; 21; 23; 24(2); 20:1; 6; 21:1; 5; 8(2); 13(2); 22:2; 3; 5; 7; 8; 12; 14; 16; 20; 23; 25(2); 23:1; 13; 15; 24:10; 11; 12; 13; 15(2); 18; 21; 22(2); 23(2); 25:4; 5; 6; 7; 8; 9(2); 10; 11; 26:1(2); 2; 3(2); 4(2); 8; 9(2); 10; 12; 16; 17(3); 18(2); 19; 27:1(2); 2; 4(2); 8(2); 9; 12; 13(4); 28:4; 5; 6; 7(2); 14; 16; 20; 21(2); 25(2); 29(2); 29:15; 18; 19(2); 21; 23; 24; 30:2(2); 3; 7; 8(2); 12; 13; 14(2); 15(3); 19; 21; 23(2); 25; 26; 28; 29; 32(2); 31:1(2); 7; 9(2); 32:1(2); 2(2); 13; 16(2); 18(3); 19; 33:2; 12; 14; 17; 34:5; 6(2); 11; 13(2); 35:6(2); 7; 36:1; 2; 6(2); 7; 11(3); 13; 15; 37:7; 10; 12; 28; 29(2); 30; 36(2); 38(2); 38:1(2); 3(2); 8; 10; 11; 15; 16; 17; 20; 39:2(3); 4(2); 6(2); 7; 8; 40:3(2); 11; 12(4); 14; 22; 24; 26; 41:16(2); 18(2); 19(2); 42:1; 2; 4; 6; 7; 12; 16; 17; 22(2); 24; 43:4; 14; 16(2); 19(2); 20(2); 26; 44:7; 12; 13; 16; 19(2); 20; 23; 45:2(2); 13; 14(2); 17; 18; 19(3); 23; 24; 25; 46:6; 7; 13; 47:1; 8; 9(3); 10(2); 13; 48:1(2); 10; 16; 49:2(2); 3; 4(2); 5; 8(2); 9(3); 20; 21; 22; 50:4; 10(2); 11(3); 51:6; 7; 9(2); 14; 16(2); 20; 52:6; 10; 53:9(2); 10; 54:6; 8; 14; 16; 17; 55:2; 11; 56:5; 7; 9; 57:2(2); 5; 6; 10; 13; 15; 17; 58:2; 3; 10; 11; 12; 14; 59:4; 6; 7; 8; 9; 10(2); 13; 14; 19; 20; 21; 60:10(2); 18; 22; 61:3; 6; 7(2); 8; 10(2); 11; 62:3(2); 4; 7; 9; 63:1(3); 2(2); 3(2); 4; 6(2); 9(3); 13; 64:5(2); 65:2; 3; 4(2); 5; 8(2); 10; 16(3); 18; 19(3); 23; 25; 66:3; 4; 8; 13; 17(2); 20(3); **Jer** 1:1(2); 2(2); 3(2); 5; 9; 2:2(3); 5; 17; 18(2); 19; 23; 24(2); 27; 28; 30; 34; 37; 3:2(2); 6; 16(2); 18; 23(2); 25; 4:2(5); 5(3); 11; 19; 20; 30; 31; 5:1; 6; 7; 8; 13; 14; 18; 19(2); 20(2); 24(2); 30; 31; 6:1(2); 3; 6; 7; 10; 11; 16; 23; 24; 26; 29; 7:2(2); 3; 4; 6; 7(2); 8; 10; 11; 12; 17(2); 22; 23; 24(2); 30(2); 31(2); 32; 8:3; 7; 8(2); 9; 12; 16; 18; 19(3); 22; 9:2; 4; 6; 8; 23(3); 24(3); 26(3); 10:5; 6; 7; 13; 14(2); 15; 23(2); 24; 11:4; 6(2); 7; 8; 12; 14; 15; 17; 21; 12:2; 5(2); 8; 16; 13:1; 4; 10; 17; 21; 22; 25; 27; 14:4; 5; 6; 8(2); 9; 13; 14; 15(2); 16; 15:4; 7; 11(2); 13; 14; 15; 17; 16:2; 3(2); 6; 7; 9(2); 19; 17:3; 4(2); 5; 6(3); 7; 8; 11; 13; 17; 19(3); 20; 21; 24; 25; 27(2); 18:4; 6(2); 10; 15(3); 17; 21; 23; 19:4; 7; 9; 10; 11; 14; 20:1; 2(2); 6; 7; 9(3); 16; 21:4; 5(3); 7; 9; 12; 14; 22:2; 3; 4(2); 12; 15; 20; 21; 23(2); 30(2); 23:5; 6; 8; 11; 12; 13(2); 14(2); 18; 19; 20; 22; 24; 25; 26; 29; 24:8(2); 9; 25:1; 5; 13; 23; 24; 34; 26:1; 2(2); 4; 7; 9(2); 10; 14; 15; 16; 18; 20; 27:1; 11; 15; 18(2); 19; 21(2); 28:1(5); 5(3); 7(2); 11; 15; 17; 29:5; 7; 8; 9; 10; 15; 16; 21; 22(2); 23(2); 25; 26(4); 28(2); 29; 31; 30:2; 6; 8; 10; 11; 24; 31:2; 4; 9; 10; 12; 13; 15; 17; 22; 23(2); 24(2); 29; 32; 33(2); 32:1; 2(2); 7; 8(3); 9; 10; 12(3); 14; 15; 19(2); 20(2); 23(2); 34; 35; 37(3); 40; 41; 43; 44(6); 33:1; 5(2); 10(3); 12(2); 13(6); 15(2); 16; 20; 34:5; 6; 13; 15(3); 17; 18; 35:1; 7(2); 8; 9; 10; 15; 36:1; 6(4); 8(2); 9(3); 10(5); 13; 14(3); 15(2); 18; 20(3); 21(2); 22(2); 23; 28(2); 30(2); 32; 37:1; 4; 10; 12; 13; 15(2); 17; 18; 21(2); 38:2; 4(2); 5; 6(3); 7(3); 9(3); 13; 14; 22(2); 28; 39:1(2); 2(2); 3(2); 5(2); 6; 9; 10; 15; 16; 17; 18; 40:1; 6; 7(2); 9; 10(2); 11(3); 13; 15(2); 41:1(2); 5; 8; 10(2); 12; 17; 18; 42:10; 13; 16(2); 20; 22; 43:4; 5; 8; 9(5); 12(2); 13; 44:1(2); 3; 6(2); 8(2); 9(2); 10(2); 12; 13; 15(2); 16; 17(2); 21(2); 23(3); 24; 26(3); 27; 29; 45:1(2); 3; 5;

46:2(2); 10; 11; 14(4); 19; 21; 25; 26; 27; 28; 48:2; 5(2); 6; 7(2); 11; 18; 20; 26(2); 28(3); 35(2); 38; 41(2); 44; 47; 49:1; 2; 4(2); 7; 11; 16; 18(2); 21; 22; 24; 26(2); 27; 32; 33; 34; 38; 39; 50:2(2); 4(2); 5; 9(2); 14; 16; 20(2); 22; 23; 25; 28; 30(2); 32; 37; 39; 42; 43; 51:1; 2; 3; 4(2); 6; 7; 10; 13; 16; 17; 18; 20; 21(2); 22(3); 23(3); 24(2); 27; 30; 39; 44; 46(3); 47; 58(2); 59; 60; 62; 52:1; 2; 3; 4(3); 6(3); 8; 9; 10; 11(2); 12(2); 15; 17(2); 19(2); 20; 25(2); 27(2); 28; 29; 30; 31(4); 32; **Lam** 1:2; 4; 7(2); 9; 12; 15(2); 19; 20; 2:1(2); 2; 3; 4; 5; 6(2); 7(2); 11; 12; 17; 19(3); 20; 21(2); 22(2); 3:6; 10(2); 11; 20(2); 24; 27; 29; 36; 41; 45; 53; 57; 66; 4:1; 3; 5(2); 6; 7; 8; 10; 11; 13; 14; 17; 18; 19; 20; 21; 5:11(2); **Eze** 1:1(3); 2; 3; 16; 20; 21; 28(2); 3:3; 10; 14(2); 18; 19; 20; 4:9; 12; 14; 16; 5:2(2); 3(2); 4; 5; 6; 7; 8(2); 9; 10(2); 12; 13(2); 14; 15(4); 6:6; 7; 9; 10; 13; 14; 7:4; 7; 9; 13; 15(2); 19(2); 20; 8:1(4); 3; 4; 5; 7; 8(2); 9; 10; 11(2); 12(2); 18(2); 9:1(2); 2(2); 4; 5; 7; 8; 10:1; 2(3); 3; 6; 8; 10; 13; 17; 19; 11:2; 6; 7; 10; 11(2); 12; 15; 16; 20; 24; 12:2; 3(2); 4(2); 5; 6(2); 7(3); 8; 10; 12; 13; 15; 22; 23; 25; 13:4; 5(2); 9(2); 13(3); 14; 21; 14:3; 4; 5; 7(2); 14; 16; 18; 19; 20; 23; 16:4(2); 5(2); 6(3); 12; 15; 22(2); 24; 29; 31(4); 34(3); 38; 41; 43; 47; 49(2); 51; 52; 53; 54(2); 56; 59; 60; 17:4; 5; 8(2); 9; 10; 15; 16(2); 17; 20; 23(2); 18:3; 9; 17; 18; 22; 24(3); 26; 32; 19:4; 8; 9(2); 10; 11; 12; 13(2); 20:1(2); 5(2); 6; 8; 9(2); 11; 13(4); 14; 15; 16; 17; 18(2); 19; 21(3); 22(2); 23; 26(2); 27(2); 36; 40(3); 41; 43; 47(2); 21:20; 21; 22; 23; 24(2); 30(2); 31; 32; 22:3; 4(2); 6; 7(3); 9(3); 10(2); 11(2); 12; 13; 14; 15; 16(2); 18; 20(2); 21(2); 22(2); 24; 25(2); 27; 30; 23:3(2); 8; 11(3); 15; 19(2); 21; 31; 32; 37; 38; 39; 43; 44(3); 45; 24:1(3); 7; 11; 12; 13; 18(2); 25; 26; 27; 25:4(2); 6; 10; 14; 26:1(2); 5; 6; 8; 12; 15; 17; 18(2); 20(3); 27:4; 8; 9(2); 10(2); 11; 12; 13; 14; 16; 17; 18(2); 19(2); 20; 21(2); 22; 24(3); 25(2); 26; 27(4); 30; 32(2); 34(3); 35; 28:2(2); 8; 9; 12; 13(3); 14; 15(2); 18; 22(3); 23; 25(3); 29:1(3); 3; 4; 12; 17(3); 21(2); 30:4(2); 5; 6; 7(2); 8; 9(3); 13; 14(2); 16; 18; 19; 20(3); 24; 31:1(3); 2; 3; 6; 7(2); 8(3); 9; 10(2); 12; 14(2); 15; 16; 17; 18(3); 32:1(3); 2; 3; 10; 17(2); 19; 20; 23(2); 24; 25(3); 26; 27; 28; 32(2); 33:6; 8; 9; 10; 11; 12(3); 15; 21(3); 22(2); 27(4); 30; 34:12(2); 13; 14(3); 25(2); 26; 27; 29; 35:5(2); 8(3); 36:2; 3; 5; 6(2); 15; 17; 23(2); 27; 28; 31; 33(2); 34; 38; 37:1(2); 2; 6; 8; 14(2); 17; 19(2); 20; 22; 24; 25; 26; 28; 38:8; 12; 14; 16(2); 17(2); 18; 19(4); 23; 39:6; 7(2); 9; 11(2); 15; 26; 27(2); 40:1(5); 2; 3(2); 5; 25(2); 27; 29(2); 33; 39; 44; 41:6(2); 42:3; 6; 8; 10; 12; 43:7(2); 8(2); 9; 11(2); 16; 17; 18; 21; 44:2(2); 3; 5; 7(4); 8; 9(2); 11; 13; 17(2); 19; 24(3); 27(2); 28; 29; 30; 45:1; 2(2); 3; 8(2); 16; 17(4); 18(2); 21(2); 25(3); 46:1; 3(2); 4; 6; 8; 9(3); 10(3); 11(2); 21; 22; 23; 47:3; 5; 19; 22; 23; 48:8(3); 9(2); 10(5); 13(2); 15(2); 18; 21; 22; 28; **Dan** 1:1; 4(5); 8; 14; 15; 17(2); 18(2); 20(2); 2:1; 4; 5; 16; 19; 22; 24(2); 25(2); 27; 28(2); 40(2); 41; 44(2); 45; 49; 3:1(2); 13; 16; 20; 21; 24; 25; 28; 29; 30; 4:1; 4(2); 6; 7; 8(2); 9; 10(2); 12(2); 13; 15(3); 17; 18; 21; 23(2); 25; 29; 31; 32; 35; 36; 37; 5:2; 3; 5; 7(2); 8; 9; 11(4); 12; 13; 14(2); 15; 16; 20; 21; 23(2); 27; 29; 30; 6:3; 4; 10; 19(2); 22; 23; 24; 25; 26; 27(2); 28(2); 7:1; 2; 5; 7(2); 8; 13; 15(2); 19; 20; 23; 28(2); 8:1; 2(4); 6; 7; 18; 19; 22; 23; 25(2); 9:1; 2(2); 6; 10; 11; 13; 14; 21(2); 24; 25; 27; 10:1; 2; 3; 4; 5; 6; 8(2); 9; 14; 17(2); 21(2); 11:1; 2; 6(2); 7; 14; 16; 20(4); 21(2); 38; 39; 45; 12:1; 2; 6; 7; 13; **Hos** 1:1(2); 5; 10; 2:3; 9(2); 10; 15(2); 18; 19(4); 20; 21; 23; 3:5; 4:1; 5(2); 16; 19; 5:4; 5; 8(2); 9; 11; 15; 6:2(2); 9; 10; 7:1; 2; 5; 6(2); 16; 8:6; 9:2; 3(2); 5(2); 6; 8(2); 9; 10(2); 13; 15; 10:4(2); 9; 10(2); 12(2); 13(2); 14(2); 15; 11:9; 11; 12:3; 4; 7; 8(2); 9(2); 11(3); 13:1(2); 5(2); 9; 10; 11(2); 13; 16; 14:3; 9; **Joel** 1:2(2); 13; 2:1(2); 5; 8; 9(2); 15; 23(2); 26; 27; 29; 30(2); 32(3); 3:1(2); 13; 14(2); 17; 18; 19; 21; **Amos** 1:1(2); 14(3); 2:7; 8; 16; 3:4; 5; 6(2); 9(5); 10; 12(4); 13; 14; 4:1; 6(2); 5:6(2); 7; 10; 11; 12; 13; 15; 16(2); 17; 20; 21; 25; 6:1(2); 6; 9; 13; 14; 7:1; 7; 8; 10; 17(2); 8:3(2); 9(2); 11; 13; 9:1; 3(2); 6(2); 9; 11(2); **Obad** 1; 3(2); 7; 8; 11(2); 12(3); 13(3); 14(2); 18; 20; **Jonah** 1:4; 5; 17; 2:3; 7; 3:6; 8; 4:2; 5; 8; 10(2); **Mic** 1:1; 10(2); 11; 13; 2:1; 4; 5; 11; 12; 3:3; 4; 4:1(2); 2; 5(2); 6; 7; 9(2); 10(3); 13; 5:1; 2; 4(2); 5; 6; 7; 8(2); 10; 15; 6:10; 12; 13(2); 14; 16; 7:2; 5(3); 6(2); 8; 11(2); 12; 14(4); 18; **Nah** 1:3(3); 6; 7(2); 13; 2:1; 3(2); 4(2); 5; 10; 12; 13; 3:10(2); 13; 17(2); 18; **Hab** 1:5; 15(2); 2:4; 13; 19; 20; 3:2(3); 7; 11; 12(2); 16(2); 17(2); 18(2); **Zeph** 1:1; 8; 9; 10; 12; 18(2); 2:3; 7(2); 14(4); 15(2); 3:2; 5; 11(2); 12(2); 13; 15; 16; 17(2); 19; 20; **Hag** 1:1(3); 4; 6; 8; 13; 14; 15(2); 2:1(2); 3(3); 9; 10(2); 12; 15; 17; 19; 20; 22; 23; **Zec** 1:1(2); 7; 8; 16; 2:1; 5; 10; 11(2); 12; 3:7; 9; 10; 4:10; 5:4; 7; 9; 11; 6:2(2); 3(2); 8; 14; 15; 7:1(3); 3(2); 5; 7; 10; 12; 8:3; 4(2); 5; 6(3); 8(3); 9(2); 10; 11; 15; 16; 17; 22; 23; 9:1; 4; 6; 7; 16; 10:1(2); 2; 3; 5(2); 7; 9; 11; 12(2); 11:8; 11; 13; 16(2); 12:2; 3(2); 4; 5(2); 6(4); 8; 9; 10(2); 11(3); 13:1; 2; 3; 4; 6(2); 8; 14:1; 3; 4(2); 5; 6; 8(3); 9; 10; 11; 12(2); 13; 14; 15; 20(2); 21(4); **Mal** 1:7; 10; 11; 12; 14; 2:6(3); 9; 11(2); 17(2); 3:1; 3; 4(2); 5; 8; 10; 11; 17; 4:2; 3; 4; **Mt** 1:20(2); 2:1(2); 2; 5; 6; 9; 12; 13; 16(2); 18; 19(2); 22(3); 23; 3:1(2); 3; 6; 12; 17; 4:6; 13(2); 16(2); 21; 23; 5:3; 8; 12; 15; 16; 18; 19(2); 20; 21; 22(3); 25; 28; 45; 48; 6:1; 2(2); 4(2); 5(2); 6(2); 9; 10(2); 18(2); 20; 23; 29; 7:3(2); 4; 11; 13(2); 15; 21; 22(4); 8:10; 11; 13; 24; 32; 9:4; 10; 16; 25; 31; 33; 35; 10:9; 11; 15; 16; 17; 19; 20; 23; 27(3); 28; 32; 33; 35(2); 41(2); 42(2); 11:1; 2; 6; 8(2); 11; 16; 21(3); 23(2); 24; 26; 29; 12:5(2); 6; 18; 19; 21; 32(2); 36; 40(2); 41; 42; 45; 50; 13:3; 10; 13; 14; 19; 21; 24; 27; 30(2); 31; 32; 33; 34; 35; 40(2); 43; 44; 54; 57(3); 14:2; 3; 8; 10; 11; 24; 25; 33; 15:9; 17; 32; 33; 16:3; 17; 19(2); 26; 27; 28; 17:5; 22; 18:1; 2; 4; 5; 6(2); 10(2); 14; 16; 18(2); 19; 20(2); 19:21; 28(2); 20:1; 3; 17; 21; 21:8(2); 9(2); 12; 14; 15; 18; 19; 22; 24; 28; 32; 33; 41; 42(2); 22:11; 12; 15; 16; 28; 30(3); 36; 43; 23:2; 6; 7; 9; 13(2); 30(2); 34; 39; 24:5; 7; 14; 15; 16; 18; 19; 20; 26(2); 30(2); 38(2); 40; 43; 44; 45; 48; 50(2); 25:4; 10; 18; 25; 31; 35; 36; 38; 39; 43(2); 44; 26:6(2); 12; 13; 23; 29; 55(2); 58; 61; 64; 67; 69; 27:4; 5; 7; 19; 29; 40; 43; 44; 51; 59; 60(2); 28:1; 18(2); 19; **Mk** 1:2; 3; 4; 5; 9(2); 11; 13; 14; 19; 20; 23; 35; 39; 45; 2:1; 6; 8(2); 15; 20; 26; 3:23; 29; 4:1; 2; 11; 15; 17; 19; 28; 29; 31(2); 36; 38; 5:4; 5(2); 13; 14(2); 15; 20; 27; 29; 30(2); 33; 34; 39; 40; 6:2; 4(2); 8; 10; 11; 14; 17; 22; 25(2); 27; 28; 29; 40; 47; 48; 51; 55; 56; 7:7; 32; 8:1; 4; 12; 14; 26; 37; 38(2); 9:33; 36(2); 37; 38; 39; 41; 42; 50; 10:10; 16; 21; 24; 30(2); 32; 37; 52; 11:4; 8(2); 9; 10(2); 15; 20; 22; 23; 25; 26; 27; 12:4; 11; 13; 14; 23; 25(2); 26(2); 35; 38(3); 39; 41; 42; 43; 44(2); 13:6; 8; 9; 11; 14; 16; 17; 18; 19; 24; 25; 26; 29; 32; 35; 14:3(2); 14; 17; 20; 25; 30; 31; 49; 60; 62; 66; 15:1; 7; 29; 38; 41; 43; 46(2); 16:2; 5; 12; 17; **Lk** 1:1(2); 3; 5; 6; 7; 8; 15; 17; 18; 19; 20; 21; 22; 25; 26; 28; 29; 31; 36; 39; 41; 44(2); 47; 51; 54; 66; 69; 75; 79(2); 80(2); 2:1; 7(3); 8(2); 11; 12(2); 14; 16; 19; 21; 23; 24; 25; 27; 28; 29; 34; 38(2); 40; 43; 44; 46(2); 51; 52(2); 3:1(2); 2; 4(2); 15(2); 17; 18; 20; 22(2); 4:2; 5; 11; 14; 15; 20; 21; 23(2); 24; 25(2); 27(2); 28; 33; 35; 44; 5:7; 12; 18(2); 19; 22; 29; 35; 6:1; 8; 12(2); 17; 23(3); 41(2); 42(3); 7:1; 7; 9; 21; 23; 25(2); 28; 32; 37(2); 45; 50; 8:10; 13; 15; 16; 23; 27(2); 29; 34(2); 35; 48; 51; 9:12; 14; 26(2); 31; 36; 48; 49; 57; 10:7; 12; 13(3); 20(2); 21(3); 26; 34; 11:1; 2(3); 6; 7; 21; 26; 31; 32; 33(2); 35; 37; 43(2); 52(2); 12:1; 3(4); 12; 15; 27; 28; 33; 38(2); 42; 45; 46(2); 52; 53(4); 58; 13:4(2); 6; 10; 11; 14(2); 19; 21; 24(2); 26(2); 28; 29; 35; 14:8; 10(2); 15; 21; 23; 15:4; 7; 10; 14(2); 21; 25; 28; 16:8; 10(4); 11; 12; 15; 19; 23(3); 24(2); 25; 17:4(2); 6; 24; 26(2); 27; 28; 30; 31(3); 34(2); 36; 18:2; 3; 9; 12; 17; 22; 30(2); 19:17; 20; 30; 36; 38(3); 42; 43; 44; 47; 20:1; 31; 33; 34; 35; 42; 45; 46(3); 21:2; 3; 4(2); 6; 8; 11; 14; 19; 21(3); 23(2); 25(3); 27; 37(3); 38(2); 22:6; 10; 16; 19; 20; 28; 30; 37; 44; 53; 55; 23:4; 9; 11; 14; 19; 22; 29; 31(2); 38; 40; 43; 45; 53(3); 24:1; 3; 4; 6; 12; 18(2); 19; 27; 29; 35(2); 36; 38; 44(3); 47; 49; 53; **Jn** 1:1; 2; 4; 5; 10; 18; 23; 28; 45; 47; 2:1; 11; 14; 19; 20(2); 23(3); 25; 3:13; 14; 15; 16; 18; 21; 23; 4:14; 18; 20(2); 21; 23(2); 24(2); 31; 44; 53; 5:2; 3; 4; 6; 13; 14; 26(2); 28(2); 35; 38; 39; 42; 43(2); 45; 6:10(2); 31; 37; 45; 49; 53; 56(2); 59(2); 61; 7:1(2); 4; 5; 9; 10; 18; 28; 37; 8:1; 2; 3(2); 4(2); 5; 9; 12; 17; 20(2); 21; 24(2); 31; 33; 35; 37; 44(2); 9:3; 5; 7; 34; 10:2; 9(2); 23(2); 25; 34; 38(2); 11:6; 9(2); 10(2); 13; 17; 20; 24; 25; 26; 30; 31; 33; 38; 52; 56; 12:13; 25; 35; 36; 46; 48; 13:1; 21; 31; 32(2); 14:1(2); 2; 10(3); 11(2); 13(2); 14; 17; 20(3); 26; 30; 15:2; 4(4); 5(2); 6; 7(2); 9; 10(2); 11; 16; 25; 16:21; 23(2); 24; 25(2); 26; 33(2); 17:10; 11(2); 12(2); 13(2); 21(3); 23(3); 26(2); 18:13; 15; 16; 20(3); 26; 38; 19:4; 6; 13(3); 17; 18; 20; 40; 41(2); 20:5(2); 7; 8; 12; 19; 25; 26; 30(2); 21:2; 8; **Acts** 1:2; 7; 8(3); 10; 11; 13; 14; 15(2); 18; 19; 20; 21; 2:1; 6; 8; 9(3); 10(2); 11; 12; 17; 18; 19(2); 22; 26; 27; 31; 37; 38; 42(3); 46; 3:6; 11; 13; 16(2); 22; 25; 26; 4:3; 7; 12; 16; 17; 18; 19; 24; 5:4(2); 7; 10; 12; 18; 20; 21; 22; 25(2); 28; 34(2); 37; 40; 42(2); 6:1(2); 7; 15; 7:2(2); 4; 5; 6; 7(2); 10; 12; 16; 17; 20(2); 22(3); 29; 30(3); 34; 35; 36(3); 38(3); 39; 41(2); 42(2); 44; 45; 48; 51; 8:8; 9; 16; 21(2); 23(2); 25; 28; 33; 40; 9:10; 11; 12(2); 17; 20; 21; 22; 25; 27(2); 28; 29; 31(2); 37(2); 42; 43; 10:1; 3(2); 17; 23; 25; 27; 30(2); 31(2); 32; 35; 39(2); 43; 48; 11:1; 3; 5(2); 13; 22; 26; 27; 28; 29; 12:4; 5; 7; 14; 21; 13:1; 5; 13; 14; 17; 18; 19; 27; 28; 29; 33(2); 35; 40; 41(2); 43; 14:1; 3; 8; 11(2); 14; 16(2); 17; 22; 23; 25; 15:21(2); 23; 33; 35; 36; 39; 16:3; 5(2); 6; 9; 12; 18; 24; 29; 32; 34; 36; 17:2; 11(2); 16; 17(2); 21; 22(2); 24; 28; 31(3); 18:2; 4; 5; 9; 10; 18; 21; 23; 24; 25(2); 26; 19:5; 9; 10; 16; 21; 22; 27; 29; 30; 39; 40(2); 20:6; 8; 9; 10; 13; 14; 16; 19; 22; 23; 29; 21:18; 27; 29; 31; 39; 40; 22:2; 3(3); 17(2); 19; 23:1; 6(2); 9; 10; 11; 16; 21; 35; 24:3; 12(3); 14(2); 18; 20; 21; 24; 25:3; 5; 14; 26:3; 10(2); 11; 13; 14; 16; 18; 21; 26; 27:12; 20; 21; 27; 31; 35; 37(2); 39; 28:7; 8; 9; 11(2); 18; 30(2); **Rom** 1:2; 7; 9(2); 15; 18; 19; 21; 27(2); 28; 32; 2:7; 12; 14; 15; 16; 17; 19; 20; 28; 29(2); 3:4; 9; 16; 20; 24; 25; 26; 4:10(4); 12; 18; 19; 20; 5:2; 3; 5; 6; 8; 11; 13; 17; 6:1; 4; 5(2); 10(2); 12(2); 21; 7:5(2); 6(2); 8; 13; 17; 18(2); 20; 22; 23(2); 8:1; 2; 3(3); 4; 8; 9(3); 10; 11(2); 18; 20; 22; 37; 39; 9:1(2); 2; 7; 17; 25; 26; 28; 33; 10:6; 8(2); 9; 14(2); 11:17; 19; 22; 23(3); 25(3); 30; 32; 12:4; 5; 10; 11(2); 12(3); 16; 17; 18; 20; 13:4; 9; 13(4); 14:1; 5; 13; 17; 18; 22; 15:12; 13(2); 15(2); 17; 23; 24; 27; 29; 30; 31; 16:2(2); 3; 5; 7; 8; 9; 10; 11; 12(2); 13; 22; **1Cor** 1:2(2); 5(3); 6; 7; 8; 10(2); 13; 15; 21; 29; 30; 31; 2:3(3); 4; 5(2); 7; 11; 13; 3:1; 16; 18; 19; 21; 4:2; 6(2); 10; 15(2); 17(3); 20(2); 21(2); 5:3(2); 4; 5; 9; 6:4; 11; 19; 20(2); 7:15; 17; 18; 20; 22; 28; 34(2); 37(2); 38(2); 39; 8:4(2); 5(2); 6; 7; 10; 9:1; 2; 9; 10(2); 18; 24; 25; 10:2(2); 5; 8; 19; 25; 28; 33; 11:2; 11; 13; 17; 18; 21; 22(2); 23; 24; 25(2); 34; 12:6; 18; 25; 27; 28; 13:6(2); 9(2); 10; 12; 14:2(2); 4; 7; 10; 13; 14; 19(2); 20(3); 21; 23; 24; 25; 27; 28; 33; 34; 35; 40; 15:2(2); 10; 17; 18; 19(2); 22(2); 23; 28; 30; 31; 41; 42(2); 43(4); 52(2); 54; 58(3); 16:2; 11; 13; 19(2); 24; **2Cor** 1:1; 4(2); 5; 6; 8; 9(3); 10; 12(2); 14(2); 15; 19; 20(2); 21; 22; 2:1; 3; 5; 9; 10; 13; 14(2); 15(2); 17(2); 3:2; 3(2); 7; 9; 10; 14(2); 18; 4:2(2); 4; 6(2); 7; 8; 10(2); 11; 12(2); 5:1; 2; 4; 6; 10; 11; 12(2); 17; 19; 20; 21; 6:1; 2(3); 3; 4(5); 5(6); 12(2); 13; 16(2); 7:1; 3; 4; 7; 9; 11(3); 12; 13; 14; 16(2); 8:2; 6; 7(5); 18; 20; 21(2); 22(2); 9:3(2); 4; 7; 8; 11; 14; 10:1; 3; 6; 11(2); 14; 16(2); 17; 11:1; 3; 6(3); 7; 9; 10(2); 17; 23(4); 25; 26(12); 27(5); 32; 33; 12:2(2); 3; 5; 7; 9(2); 10(5); 11(2); 12(2); 18(2); 19; 13:1; 3(2); 4; 5(2); 11; **Gal** 1:13(2); 14(2); 16; 22; 23; 24; 2:2; 4(3); 6; 8(2); 16; 20(2); 21; 3:3; 4(2); 8; 10(2); 11; 12; 17; 19; 26; 28; 4:3; 9; 11; 14; 18; 19(2); 20; 25(2); 5:1; 6; 10; 14(2); 16; 21; 25(2); 6:1(2); 4(2); 6(2); 9(2); 12; 13; 14; 15; 17; **Eph** 1:1; 3(2); 4(2); 6; 7; 8; 9; 10(5); 11; 12; 13(2); 15; 16; 17; 18; 20(2); 21(2); 23; 2:1; 2(2); 3(2); 4; 5; 6(2); 7(2); 10(2); 11(3); 12; 13; 15(3); 16; 21(2); 22; 3:3; 4; 5; 6; 9; 10; 11; 12; 15; 16; 17(2); 20; 21; 4:2; 3; 4; 6; 13; 14; 15(2); 16(2); 17(2); 18; 21; 23; 24; 5:2; 5; 8; 9; 12; 19(2); 20; 21; 24; 33; 6:1; 4; 5; 9; 10(2); 12; 13; 18; 20; 21; 24; **Phil** 1:4; 5; 6; 7(3); 8; 9(2); 13(3); 14; 18(2); 20(2); 22; 23; 24; 26; 27; 28; 29; 30(2); 2:1; 3; 5(2); 6; 7; 8; 10(2); 12(2); 13; 15(2); 16(3); 19; 22; 24; 25; 29(2); 3:1; 3(3); 4(2); 6; 9; 14; 15; 19; 20; 4:1; 2; 3(2); 4; 6; 9; 10; 11(2); 12; 15; 16; 19; 21; **Col** 1:2; 4; 5(2); 6(3); 8; 9; 10(2); 12; 14; 16(2); 18; 19; 20(2); 21; 22(2); 23; 24(2); 27; 28(2); 29; 2:1; 2; 3; 5(3); 6; 7(2); 9; 10; 11(2); 12; 13; 15; 16(3); 18; 20; 23(2); 3:3; 4; 7(2); 10; 11; 15(2); 16(4); 17(2); 18; 20; 22(2); 4:1; 2(2); 3; 5; 7; 12(2); 13(2); 15(2); 16; 17; **1Th** 1:1(2); 2; 3(2); 5(4); 6; 7; 8(2); 9; 2:1(2); 2; 3; 4; 13(2); 14(2); 17(2); 19; 3:2; 5; 7; 8; 10; 12; 13; 4:4; 5; 6; 10; 14; 16; 17(2); 5:2; 4; 7(2); 12; 13; 18(2); **2Th** 1:1; 4(3); 8; 10(3); 12(2); 2:2; 4; 6; 10; 12; 17; 3:4; 6; 13; 17; **1Ti** 1:2; 4; 13; 14; 16; 2:2(2); 3; 6; 7(2); 9(2); 11; 12; 14; 15(2); 3:4; 9; 11; 13(2); 15; 16(3); 4:1; 2; 6(2); 10; 12(6); 14; 16(2); 5:5(2); 6; 7; 17; 6:9; 13; 15; 16; 17(3); 18; 19; **2Ti** 1:1; 3; 5(3); 6(2); 9; 13(2); 14; 15; 17; 18(2); 2:1(2); 7; 10; 14; 20; 25; 3:1; 12; 14; 15; 16; 4:2; 5; **Titus** 1:2; 3; 5(3); 13; 16; 2:2(3); 3; 7(2); 9; 10; 12; 3:1; 3; 8; 15; **Philem** 1:2; 4; 6(2); 7; 8; 10; 11; 13(2); 16(2); 20(2); 21; 23; **Heb** 1:1(2); 2; 6; 10; 2:5; 6; 8(3); 10; 12; 13; 17(2); 18; 3:2; 5; 8(3); 10; 11; 12(2); 15; 17; 19; 4:2; 3; 4; 5; 6; 7; 13; 15; 16; 5:1; 6; 7(2); 13; 6:7; 10; 18; 7:9; 10; 19; 8:1; 5; 9(2); 10; 13; 9:9; 10; 12; 23; 24; 26; 10:3; 6; 7; 16; 22; 32; 34(3); 38; 11:9(3); 12; 13; 18; 19; 26; 34; 37; 38(3); 12:3; 9; 23; 13:3(2); 4; 18; 21(3); 22; **Jas** 1:6; 8; 9; 10; 11; 23; 25; 27; 2:2(3); 3; 4; 5; 10; 16; 3:2(2); 3; 7; 14; 18; 4:1; 5(2); 10; 16; 5:5(2); 10; 14; **1Pet** 1:4; 5; 6; 8; 11; 14; 15; 17; 20; 21(2); 22; 2:6(2); 10; 12; 22; 24; 3:1; 4(2); 5(3); 15(2); 16; 18; 19; 20; 4:1(2); 2; 3; 6(2); 11; 15; 19; 5:6; 9(3); 14; **2Pet** 1:4; 8(2); 12(2); 13(2); 15; 17; 18; 19(2); 21; 2:1; 5; 8; 10; 11; 12; 13; 18; 19; 22; 3:1; 3; 5; 7; 10(2); 11; 14; 16(3); 18(2); **1Jn** 1:5; 6; 7(2); 8; 10; 2:4; 5(2); 6; 8(2); 9(2); 10(2); 11(2); 14; 15(2); 16; 24(4); 27(2); 28; 3:3; 5; 6; 9; 10; 14; 15; 17; 18(4); 22; 24(3); 4:2; 3(2); 4(2); 9; 12(2); 13(2); 15(2); 16(3); 17(2); 18(2); 5:7; 8(2); 10; 11; 14; 19; 20(2); **2Jn** 1; 2; 3; 4; 6; 7; 9(2); **3Jn** 1; 2; 3(2); 4; **Jude** 1; 4; 5; 6; 7; 10; 11(2); 12; 16; 18; 20; 21; **Rev** 1:4; 5; 9(3); 10; 11(2); 13; 15; 16(2); 20; 2:1(2); 7; 8; 12; 13; 17; 18; 24; 3:1; 4(2); 5; 7; 12; 18; 20; 21(2); 4:1; 2(3); 3; 4; 6; 5:1; 3(2); 6(2); 13(3); 6:5; 6; 15(2); 7:3; 9; 13; 14; 15; 17; 8:1; 9; 9:4; 6; 10; 11(2); 14; 17; 19(2); 10:2; 7; 8; 9; 10; 11:3; 5; 6; 8; 9; 12; 13; 15; 19(2); 12:1; 2; 3; 7; 8; 10; 12; 13:6(2); 8; 13; 14; 16(2); 14:1; 5; 6; 9(2); 10(2); 13; 14; 15; 16; 17; 18; 19; 15:1(2); 5; 6; 16:3; 16; 19; 17:3; 4(2); 8; 17; 18:6; 7; 8; 10; 16; 17(2); 19(2); 22(3); 23(2); 24; 19:1; 8; 11; 13; 14(2); 17(2); 20:1; 4; 6; 8; 12; 13(2); 15; 21:8; 10; 14; 23; 24; 27(2); 22:2; 3; 4; 14; 16; 18; 19

INASMUCH

1115, 3588, *1909, 2526, 2596, 3745*

Deut 19:6; **Ruth** 3:10; **Mt** 25:40; 45; **Rom** 11:13; **Phil** 1:7; **Heb** 3:3; 7:20; **1Pet** 4:13

INDEED

61, 389, 546, 551, 552, 1571, *230, 235, 1063, 2532, 3303, 3689*

Gen 17:19; 20:12; 37:8(2); 10; 40:15; 43:20; 44:5; **Ex** 19:5; 23:22; **Lev** 10:18; **Num** 12:2; 21:2; 22:37; **Deut** 2:15; 21:16; **Josh** 7:20; **1Sa** 1:11; 2:30; **2Sa** 14:5; 15:8; **1Kin** 8:27; **2Kin** 14:10; **1Chr** 4:10; 21:17; **Job** 19:4; 5; **Ps** 58:1; **Is** 6:9(2); **Jer** 22:4; **Mt** 3:11; 13:32; 20:23; 23:27; 26:41; **Mk** 1:8; 9:13; 10:39; 11:32; 14:21; **Lk** 3:16;

11:48; 23:41; 24:34; **Jn** 1:47; 4:42; 6:55(2); 7:26; 8:31; 36; **Acts** 4:16; 11:16; 22:9; **Rom** 6:11; 8:7; 14:20; **1Cor** 11:7; **2Cor** 8:17; 11:1; **Phil** 1:15; 2:27; 3:1; **Col** 2:23; **1Th** 4:10; **1Ti** 5:3; 5; 16; **1Pet** 2:4

INSIDE

1004

1Kin 6:15

INSOMUCH

1519, 5620

Ps 106:40; **Mal** 2:13; **Mt** 8:24; 12:22; 13:54; 15:31; 24:24; 27:14; **Mk** 1:27; 45; 2:2; 12; 3:10; 9:26; **Lk** 12:1; **Acts** 1:19; 5:15; **2Cor** 1:8; 8:6; **Gal** 2:13

INSTEAD

8478

Gen 2:21; 4:25; 44:33; **Ex** 4:16(2); 5:12; **Num** 3:12; 41(2); 45(2); 5:19; 20; 29; 8:16(2); 10:31; **Judg** 15:2; **2Sa** 17:25; **1Kin** 3:7; **2Kin** 14:21; 17:24; **1Chr** 29:23; **2Chr** 12:10; **Est** 2:4; 17; **Job** 31:40(2); **Ps** 45:16; **Is** 3:24(5); 55:13(2); **Jer** 22:11; 37:1; **Eze** 16:32

INTO

413, 5704, 5921, 8432, 891, 1519, 1531, 1722, 1909, 2080, 2596, 3350, 5259

Gen 2:7; 10; 15; 6:18; 19; 7:1; 7; 9; 13; 15; 8:9(2); 9:2; 11:31; 12:5(2); 10; 11; 14; 15; 13:1; 14:20; 16:5; 18:6; 19:2; 3; 10; 23; 21:32; 22:2; 24:20; 32; 67; 26:2; 27:17; 28:15; 29:1; 30:35; 31:33(4); 32:7; 16; 36:6; 37:20; 22; 24; 28; 35; 36; 39:4; 11; 20; 40:3; 11(2); 13; 15; 21; 41:57; 42:17; 25; 37; 43:17; 18; 24; 26; 30; 45:4; 25; 46:3; 4; 6; 7; 8; 26; 27; 28; 47:14; 48:5; 16; 49:6; 33; 50:13; 14; **Ex** 1:1; 22; 3:18; 4:6(2); 7(2); 19; 21; 27; 5:3; 7:23; 8:3(5); 21; 24(3); 27; 9:20; 10:4; 19; 11:4; 13:5; 11; 14:22; 28; 15:1; 4; 5; 19; 21; 22; 25; 16:3; 18:5; 7; 27; 19:1; 12; 21:13; 23:19; 20; 31; 24:12; 13; 15; 18(2); 25:14; 16; 26:11; 27:7; 29:3; 30; 30:20; 32:24; 33:5; 8; 9; 11; 37:5; 38:7; 39:3(2); 40:20; 21; 32; 35; **Lev** 1:6; 12; 6:30; 8:20; 9:23; 10:9; 11:32; 12:4; 13:17; 14:7; 8; 15; 26; 34; 36; 40; 41; 45; 46; 53; 16:2; 3; 10; 21; 23(2); 26; 28; 19:23; 23:10; 25:2; 26:25; 32; 36; 41; **Num** 4:3; 30; 35; 39; 43; 5:17; 22; 24; 27; 7:89; 11:30; 13:17; 14:3; 4; 8; 16; 24; 25; 30; 40; 15:2; 18; 16:14; 30; 33; 47; 17:8; 19:6; 7; 14; 20:1; 4; 12; 15; 24; 27; 21:2; 22(2); 23; 27; 29; 34; 22:13; 23(2); 41; 23:14; 24:4; 16; 25:8; 27:12; 31:24; 27; 54; 32:7; 9; 32; 33:8; 38; 51; 34:2; 35:10; 28; 36:12; **Deut** 1:22; 24; 27; 31; 40; 41; 43; 2:1; 24; 29; 30; 3:2; 3; 27; 5:5; 30; 6:10; 7:1; 24; 26; 8:7; 9:9; 21; 28; 10:1; 3; 22; 11:5; 13:16; 14:6; 25; 17:8; 18:9; 19:3; 5; 11; 12; 20:13; 21:10; 23:1; 2(2); 3(2); 5; 8; 11; 18; 24; 25; 24:10; 26:5; 9; 28:25; 38; 41; 68; 29:12(2); 28; 30:5; 31:20; 21; 23; 32:26; 49; **Josh** 2:1; 3; 18; 19; 24; 3:11; 4:5; 6:2; 11; 14; 19; 20; 22; 24; 7:7; 8:1; 7; 13; 18; 19; 10:8; 19(2); 20; 27; 30; 32; 11:8; 13:5; 18:5; 6; 9; 20:4; 5; 21:44; 22:13; 24:4; 8(2); 11; **Judg** 1:2; 3(2); 4; 16; 24; 25; 26; 34; 2:14(2); 23; 3:8; 10; 21; 28; 4:2; 7; 9; 14; 18; 21(2); 22; 5:15; 6:1; 5; 13; 7:2; 7; 9; 13; 14; 15(2); 16; 8:3; 7; 9:27(2); 42; 43; 46; 10:7(2); 11:19; 21; 30; 32; 12:3; 13:1; 15:1; 5; 12; 13; 18(2); 16:23; 24; 18:10; 18; 19:3; 11; 12; 15; 21; 22; 23; 29(3); 20:4; 8; 28; **Ruth** 1:2; 2:18; 3:14; 15; 4:11; **1Sa** 2:14; 36; 4:3; 5; 6; 7; 10; 13; 5:2; 5; 6:14; 19; 7:1; 13; 9:13; 14(2); 22; 25; 10:6; 11:11; 12:8; 9(3); 14:10; 12; 21; 26; 37; 17:22; 46; 47; 49; 19:10; 20:8; 11(2); 35; 42; 21:15; 22:5(2); 23:4; 7(2); 11; 12; 14; 16; 20; 25; 24:4; 10; 18; 26:3; 8; 10; 23; 27:1; 28:19(2); 29:11; 30:15; 23; 31:9; **2Sa** 2:1; 3:8; 34; 4:6; 7; 5:8; 19(2); 6:10(2); 12; 16; 10:2; 10; 14; 11:11; 23; 12:8; 20; 13:10(2); 15:25; 27; 31; 37(2); 16:8; 17:13(2); 17; 18:6; 17; 19:2; 3; 5; 20:12; 21:9; 22:7; 20; 23:11; 24:14(2); **1Kin** 1:15; 28; 3:1; 6:8(2); 8:6; 11:17; 40; 13:18; 14:12; 28(2); 15:15; 18; 16:18; 21; 17:19; 21; 22; 23; 18:5; 9; 19:4; 20:2; 13; 28; 30(3); 33; 39; 21:4; 22:6; 12; 15; 25; 30(2); 35; **2Kin** 2:1; 11; 16; 3:10; 13; 18; 4:4; 11; 32; 39(2); 41; 5:18; 6:5; 20; 23; 7:4; 8(2); 12; 8(2); 9:6; 26; 10:15; 21; 23; 24; 11:4; 13; 16; 18; 12:4(3); 9(2); 11; 13; 15; 16; 13:3(2); 21; 17:6; 20; 18:21; 30; 19:1; 10; 14; 18; 19(2); 25; 28; 32; 33; 37; 20:4; 18; 17; 20; 21:14; 22:4; 5; 7; 9; 20; 23:2; 12; 24:15; **1Chr** 5:20; 6:15; 10:9; 11:15; 12:8; 13:13; 14:10(2); 17; 16:7; 19:2; 15; 21:13(2); 27; 22:18; 19; 23:6; 24:19; **2Chr** 5:7; 6:41; 7:2; 10; 11; 9:4; 12:11(2); 13:16; 15:12; 18; 16:8; 18:5; 11; 14; 24; 20:20; 21:17(2); 23:1; 6; 7; 12; 20; 24:10; 24; 25:20; 26:16; 27:2; 28:5(2); 9; 27; 29:4; 16(3); 31; 30:8; 9; 14; 15; 31:1; 10; 16; 32:1; 21; 33:13; 34:7; 9; 14; 17; 30; 36:17; **Ezr** 5:8; 12(2); 14; 15; 9:7; 10:6; **Neh** 2:7; 8; 5:5; 6:11; 7:5; 8:1; 9:11(2); 22; 23; 24; 27; 30; 10:29(2); 34; 38; 12:44; 13:1; 2; 15; **Est** 1:22(2); 2:14; 16; 3:9; 13; 4:1; 2; 11; 6:4; 7:7; 8; 9:22; **Job** 3:6; 9:24; 10:9; 12:6; 16; 19; 31; 11:8; 13:11; **Jas** 1:2; 25; 4:13; 5:4; 12;

1961, 2076

Gen 1:11; 29(2); 30; 2:9; 11(3); 12(2); 13(2); 14(3); 18; 23; 3:3; 13; 17; 22; 4:6; 9; 13; 5:1; 6:3; 13(2); 15; 17(2); 21; 7:15; 8:17; 21; 9:4; 10; 12(2); 15; 16; 17(2); 18; 10:9; 12; 11:6; 9; 12:12; 18; 19; 13:9; 18; 14:2; 3; 6; 7; 8; 15; 17; 23; 15:2; 3; 13; 16; 16:6; 14; 17:4; 10; 12(3); 13(2); 14; 17(2); 18:9; 14; 20(2); 21; 19:8; 13; 20(3); 31(2); 37; 38; 20:2; 3; 5(2); 7; 11; 12(2); 13(2); 15; 16; 21:13; 17; 22; 22:7; 14; 17; 23:2; 9(2); 11; 15(2); 19; 20; 24:23; 35; 51; 65(2); 25:9; 18; 26:7(2); 9(2); 10; 20; 33; 27:11; 20; 22; 27; 33; 36; 28:16; 17(3); 29:6(2); 7(2); 19; 25; 30:15; 30; 33; 31:5; 14; 16; 29; 32; 35; 36(2); 43; 48; 50(2); 32:2; 8; 18(2); 20; 27; 29; 30; 32; 33:11; 17; 18; 34:14; 21; 35:6(2); 10; 19; 20; 27; 36:1; 8; 19; 43; 37:10; 22; 26; 27; 30; 33(2); 38:14; 18; 21; 24; 39:8; 9; 40:8; 12; 18; 41:15; 16; 25(2); 26; 28(2); 32(2); 38(2); 39; 42:2; 13(2); 14; 21; 22; 28(3); 30; 32(2); 36(2); 38(2); 43:7; 27(2); 28(2); 29; 32; 44:5; 10; 15; 16; 17; 20(2); 28; 30; 31; 45:12; 20; 26(2); 28(2); 46:33; 34; 47:3; 4; 6; 18(2); 23; 48:1; 7; 18; 49:9; 14; 21; 22; 24; 28; 29; 30(2); 32; 5:10; 11(2); 20; **Ex** 1:22; 2:6; 14; 18; 20(2); 3:3; 5; 9; 11; 13; 15(2); 16; 4:2; 14; 22; 5:2; 16(2); 22; 7:14; 17; 18; 8:10; 19; 26; 9:3(2); 4; 14; 27; 28; 29; 10:5; 7; 9; 10; 12:11; 19; 22(2); 27; 42(2); 43; 44; 48; 49; 13:2; 8; 14; 14:12; 15:2(3); 3(2); 6; 11(2); 26; 16:1; 15(2); 16; 23(2); 25; 26; 32; 36; 17:3; 7; 18:11; 14; 17; 18(2); 19; 5; 20:4(3); 10(2); 11; 17; 20; 21; 30; 22:16; 25; 27(2); 31; 23:16; 21; 25:3; 26:5; 10; 27:21; 28:8; 26; 29:1; 13(2); 14; 18(2); 21; 22(2); 23; 25; 27(4); 28; 30; 32; 34; 38; 30:6(2); 10; 13; 32; 31:7; 13; 14; 15; 17; 32:1; 5; 9; 17; 18(2); 23; 26; 33:13; 16; 21; 34:9; 10; 14(2); 19(2); 35:4; 5; 36:25; 38:21; 26; 40:9; **Lev** 1:5; 8(2); 12(2); 13; 17(2); 2:3; 6; 8(2); 9; 10(2); 15; 16; 3:3; 4(2); 5(3); 9; 10(2); 11; 14; 15(2); 16(2); 4:3; 5; 7(2); 8; 9(2); 14; 16; 18(3); 21; 22; 24; 31; 35; 5; 8; 9; 11; 13(2); 14; 17; 19; 6:4; 9(2); 14; 15; 17(2); 20(2); 25(3); 27; 28; 29; 30; 7:1(2); 4(3); 5; 6; 7(3); 9(2); 11; 15; 24; 35; 37; 8:5; 28; 31; 9:6; 10:3; 7; 12; 13; 17; 11:3; 4; 5; 6; 7; 10; 26; 32; 33; 36; 37; 46; 12:7; 13:2(2); 15; 16; 9:3(2); 4; 14; 27; 28; 29; 10:5; 7; 8; 10; 12; 11:8; 13:11; **Num** 1:51; 3:26; 47; 48; 4:15; 16; 24; 25; 26(2); 28; 31; 33; 5:2; 15; 17; 18; 29(2); 6:4; 7; 8; 13; 18; 19; 20; 21; 8:24; 9:13(2); 10:7; 11:6(2); 14; 17; 20; 23; 12:7(2); 12; 13:18; 19; 20; 27; 32; 14:7; 9(2); 18; 42; 15:25; 29; 16:3; 5; 11; 13; 40; 46(2); 18:11(2); 13(2); 16; 19; 31; 19:2(2); 9(2); 14(2); 15; 16; 20; 20:5(2); 13; 21:5(2); 8; 11; 13(2); 14; 16; 20; 28; 30; 22:5(2); 7; 31; 20; 30; 1; 9; 31:20; 21; 32:4; 19; 33:6; 7; 36; 34:2; 13; 35:16; 17; 18; 21; 31; 32; 33; 36:6; **Deut** 1:14; 16; 17(2); 25; 28; 2:36(2); 3:11; 12; 16; 24; 25; 4:6(2); 7(2); 8; 17; 18; 24; 31; 32; 35(2); 38; 39(2); 44; 48(2); 5:8(3); 14(2); 21; 26; 6:4; 15; 18; 24; 7:9; 21; 25(2); 26; 8:13(2); 18(2); 9:3; 13; 10:9; 14(2); 15; 17; 21(2); 11:10; 11; 12; 8; 12; 18; 22(2); 28; 13:6; 11; 14; 15; 18; 14:8; 10; 19; 21; 15:2(2); 3; 9; 16; 16:11; 17; 20; 17:12(2); 4; 6; 15; 18; 18:2; 22; 19:4; 6(2); 16; 17; 20:1; 4; 5; 6; 7; 8(2); 11; 14; 19; 21:2; 3; 4; 6; 9; 16; 17(2); 20(2); 23; 22:5; 29; 23:13; 14; 20; 31:6; 8; 11; 12; 17; 32:4(3); 5; 6; 9(2); 20; 21; 22; 27; 28; 31; 32; 33; 34; 35; 36(3)? 47(2); 49(4); 33:1; 7; 17; 22; 26; 27; 29(2); 34:1; 4; **Josh** 1:2; 8; 9; 2:9; 11; 3:10; 16; 4:24; 5:4; 9; 15; 6:7; 7:2; 13; 15; 8:18; 31; 34; 9:12(2); 10:13; 11:4; 12:2(2); 9; 13:2; 3(2); 4; 9(2); 16(2); 25; 28; 14:11; 15:7(2); 8(2); 9; 10; 12; 13; 20; 25; 49; 54; 60; 16:8; 17:10; 16; 18; 18:7; 13; 14; 16; 17; 28(2); 19:8; 11; 16; 23; 31; 39; 48; 20:7; 21:11; 22:9; 16; 22; 23; 33; 34; 23:3; 6; 10; 24:17; 18; 19(2); 30; **Judg** 1:26; 4:11; 14(2); 20; 5:9; 28; 6:12; 13; 15; 24; 25; 31; 7:1; 3; 14; 8:2; 21(2); 9:2; 3; 18; 28(3); 32; 33(2); 38(3); 10:8; 18; 13:17; 18; 14:3; 15; 18(2); 15:2; 11; 19; 16:2(2); 9; 15; 17:2; 18:6; 9; 10(2); 12; 14; 19; 24; 19:10; 12; 18; 19; 24(2); 30; 20:1; 23; 31; **Ruth** 1:13; 15; 19; 2:5; 6; 19; 20; 22; 3:2; 12(2); 4:3; 4; 11; 15; 17(2); **1Sa** 1:8; 2:1(2); 2(3); 3; 5; 20; 24; 35; 36; 3:17; 18; 4:7; 16; 17(2); 21; 22(2); 5:7; 6:3; 9; 20; 9:6(2); 7(2); 9; 11; 12(3); 16; 18; 19; 20(2); 24; 10:1; 5; 7; 11(3);

12(2); 24; 11:12; 12:5(3); 6; 17(2); 13:5; 14:1; 2; 6; 7; 17; 15:7; 11; 12; 22; 23(2); 28; 29; 32; 16:6; 12; 16(2); 18(2); 19; 17:25(2); 26; 29; 46; 47; 55; 56; 18:18; 19:14; 17; 19; 22; 24; 20:1(2); 2; 3; 5; 6; 7(2); 18; 21; 26(2); 37; 21:3(2); 4(2); 5; 8; 9(3); 11; 14; 22:8(3); 14(3); 17; 23:7; 19; 22(2); 24:1; 6; 10; 11; 14; 16; 25:10(2); 17(2); 25(4); 29; 26:1; 3; 11; 15; 16(2); 17(2); 18; 20; 27:1; 28:7; 14(2); 15; 16(2); 29:1; 3; 5; 6; 30:20; 24; **2Sa** 1:9(2); 18; 19; 21; 2:7; 16; 3:12; 13; 23; 24(2); 29; 38; 4:10; 5:7; 6:2; 7:3(2); 18; 19; 22(2); 23; 26; 9:1(2); 2; 3(2); 4(2); 8; 11:3; 21; 24; 12:14; 18; 19(2); 21; 23; 13:16(2); 20; 23; 28; 30; 32; 33; 35; 14:5; 7(2); 13; 15; 17; 19; 20; 30; 15:2; 3; 31; 16:3; 17; 17:2; 3; 7; 8; 9(2); 10(3); 11; 14; 20; 29; 18:3; 13; 18(2); 20; 25; 27(2); 28; 29; 32(2); 19:9; 10; 11; 26; 27(2); 30; 42; 20:8; 11; 21; 21:1; 22:2; 3; 4; 31(3); 32(2); 33; 35; 48; 51; 23:5; 15; 17; 24:16; 21; **1Kin** 1:9; 25; 27; 41; 45; 2:3; 15(2); 22; 29; 38; 42; 44; 3:6; 8; 9; 22(4); 23(4); 27; 4:12(2); 13; 20; 29; 33; 5:4; 6; 6:1; 17; 38; 8:1; 2; 21; 23; 24; 35(2); 41; 43; 46; 60(2); 9:8; 15; 26; 11:7; 11; 33; 38; 12:24; 28; 32; 13:3; 26; 31; 14:2; 5; 10; 13; 15; 15:19; 17:3; 5; 24; 18:8; 10(2); 11; 14; 24; 27(4); 39(2); 41; 43; 19:4; 7; 20:3; 6; 28(2); 32(2); 21:2; 5; 14(2); 15; 18(3); 21; 22:3; 7; 8; 13; 16; 32; **2Kin** 1:3(2); 6(2); 8; 16(2); 2:14; 19(2); 3:11(2); 12; 18; 23; 4:1(2); 4; 6; 9; 13; 14(2); 23; 25; 26(4); 27; 31; 40; 5:3; 4; 6; 8; 15; 21; 22; 26; 6:1; 11; 12; 13(2); 19(2); 32; 33; 7:4; 9; 8:5(2); 7; 13; 9:8; 11; 12; 13; 17; 18; 19; 20; 22; 23; 27; 32; 34; 36; 37; 10:5; 15(3); 30; 33; 11:5; 12:4(2); 14:6; 18:10; 17; 19; 21; 22; 19:3(2); 9; 13; 21; 28; 30; 20:3; 10; 15; 17; 19(2); 22:4; 5; 13(4); 23:10; 17(2); 21; 25:4; 8; **1Chr** 1:27; 5:1; 6:10; 7:31; 11:4; 5; 11; 17; 12:17; 13:6(2); 11; 14:15; 16:14; 25(2); 32; 34; 40; 17:2(2); 16; 20(2); 21; 24; 19:13; 21:15; 17(2); 23; 24; 22:1(2); 5(2); 14; 16; 18(2); 19; 23:29(2); 27:6; 29:1(3); 5; 11(4); 12(2); 14; 15; 16; **2Chr** 1:10; 12; 2:4; 5(2); 6; 5:2; 9; 13; 6:11; 14; 15; 26(2); 32(2); 33; 36; 40; 7:3; 15; 21; 11:4; 12:6; 13:4; 6; 10; 12; 14:7; 11; 15:2; 16:3; 7; 9; 18:6; 7(2); 31; 19:2; 6; 7; 11; 20:2; 6(2); 9; 15; 34; 22:9; 23:4; 18; 25:4; 7; 9; 26:23; 28:11; 13(2); 22; 29:10; 30:9; 31:3; 10(2); 32:7; 8(2); 34:21(4); 35:12; 21; 36:23(2); **Ezr** 1:2; 3(4); 4; 5; 9; 2:68; 3:2; 4; 11; 4:11; 15; 19; 24; 5:2; 8(2); 15; 16(2); 17; 6:2; 5(2); 12; 18(2); 7:11; 14; 15; 16; 17; 23; 25; 27; 8:1; 22(2); 9:6; 7; 11; 13; 15; 10:2; 13(2); 23; **Neh** 1:3; 2:2(2); 19; 4:10(2); 14; 19; 5:5(2); 9; 14; 6:6; 7; 11; 8:9(2); 10(3); 11; 15; 9:5; 6; 10; 18; 33; 10:34; 36; 13:11; 17; **Est** 1:1; 19; 20; 2:7; 16; 3:7(3); 8(2); 11; 13; 4:11(2); 16; 5:3; 6(2); 7; 6:3; 4; 8; 7:2(2); 5(2); 6; 8:8; 9; 12; 9:1; 12(2); 24; **Job** 1:8; 10; 12; 16; 2:3; 6; 3:3; 19; 20(2); 23(2); 25(2); 4:5; 6; 19; 21; 5:4; 7; 13; 17; 27; 6:6(2); 11(2); 12(2); 13(2); 14; 16; 17; 26; 28; 29; 30; 7:1; 5(2); 7; 9; 17; 8:12; 16; 19; 9:2; 4; 19; 22; 24(2); 32; 33; 35; 10:1; 3; 7; 13; 22; 11:4; 6; 8; 9; 18; 12:4; 5(3); 10; 12; 13; 16; 24; 13:9; 19; 28; 14:1(2); 2; 7; 10; 17; 18; 15:9; 11; 14(2); 16; 20; 21; 22; 23(2); 31; 16:6; 8; 16(2); 17; 19(2); 17:1; 3; 7; 12; 13; 15; 16; 18:8; 10; 15; 21; 19:7; 17; 28; 29; 20:5; 7; 14(2); 23(2); 25; 26; 29; 21:4; 8; 9; 15; 16(2); 17; 21; 28; 30; 22:2; 3(2); 5; 12; 18; 20; 29; 30; 23:2(2); 8; 13; 14; 24:14; 17; 18(2); 22; 25:3; 4; 6(2); 26:2; 3; 6; 8; 14; 27:3(2); 8; 11; 13; 14; 19; 28:1; 2(2); 5; 7; 11; 12; 13; 14(2); 18; 20; 21; 28(2); 30:16; 18; 30; 31; 31:2; 3; 11(2); 12; 28; 35; 32:8; 19(2); 33:9; 12; 19; 21; 24; 34:4; 6; 7; 17; 18; 22; 31; 36; 35:2; 10; 14; 15; 36:4(2); 5(2); 14; 16; 18; 26; 37:1; 4; 10(2); 12; 16; 18; 21; 22; 23; 38:2; 14; 15; 19(2); 21; 24; 26(2); 30; 39:8; 11; 16(2); 20; 22; 24; 30; 40:11; 12; 16(2); 19; 41:9; 10(2); 11(2); 16; 22; 24; 33(2); 34; 42:3; 7(2); 8; **Ps** 1:1; 2; 2:12; 3:2; 8; 4:3; 5:9(3); 6:3; 5; 7; 7:2; 4; 8; 10; 11; 15; 8:1; 4; 9; 9:6; 15; 16(2); 10:4; 7(2); 16; 11:4(2); 12:4; 14:1(2); 3; 5; 6; 15:4; 16:3; 5; 8; 9; 11; 17:12; 13; 18:2; 3; 30(3); 31(2); 32; 34; 47; 19:3(2); 4; 5; 6(2); 7(2); 8; 9; 11(2); 21:5; 22:11(2); 14(2); 15; 28(2); 23:1; 24:1; 6; 8; 10(2); 25:8; 11; 12; 14; 26:3; 10(2); 27:1(2); 28:3; 7; 8(2); 29:3(2); 4(2); 30:5; 9; 31:9; 10; 19; 32:1(3); 2(2); 4; 6; 33:1; 4; 5; 12(2); 16(2); 17; 18; 20; 34:8(2); 9; 12; 16; 18; 20; 35:10(2); 36:1; 4; 5; 6; 7; 9; 37:13; 16; 26(2); 31; 33; 37; 39(2); 38:3(2); 7; 9(2); 10; 17; 20; 39:1; 4; 5(2); 7; 11; 40:4; 7; 8; 41:1; 42:3; 6; 10; 11; 43:5; 44:15; 17; 18; 25; 45:1(2); 2; 6(2); 11; 13(2); 46:1; 4; 5; 7(2); 11(2); 47:2(2); 5; 7; 9; 48:1; 2; 3; 10(2); 14; 49:8; 11; 12; 13; 16(2); 20(2); 50:6; 10; 12; 51:3; 52:t, 7; 9; 53:1(2); 3(2); 54:4(2); 6; 55:4; 11; 15; 56:9; 57:4; 6; 7(2); 10; 58:4; 11(2); 59:9; 17; 60:7(4); 8; 11; 12; 61:2(2); 62:2(2); 5; 6(2); 7(2); 8; 63:1; 3; 64:6; 65:4; 9; 66:5; 10; 68:2; 5; 15; 16; 17; 20(2); 27; 34(2); 35; 69:2; 3; 13; 16; 71:11; 18; 19(2); 73:1; 4; 11; 25; 26; 28; 74:9(2); 12; 16(2); 75:1; 7; 8(3); 76:1(2); 2; 12; 77:8; 10; 13(2); 19; 79:10(2); 80:16(2); 83:8; 18; 84:5(2); 10; 11; 12; 85:9; 12; 86:8; 13; 87:1; 88:3; 89:7; 8; 10; 11; 13(2); 15; 18(2); 19; 34; 41; 47; 48; 90:4; 6; 9; 10(2); 11; 91:2; 9; 92:1; 7; 15(3); 93:1(3); 2; 4; 94:12; 22(2); 95:3; 4; 5; 7; 10; 96:4(2); 12; 97:11; 99:2(2); 3; 5; 9; 100:3(2); 5(2); 102:t, 4; 13; 103:1; 5; 8; 11(2); 12; 16; 17; 104:13; 20; 24; 25; 26; 105:7; 106:1; 107:1; 26; 40; 43; 108:1; 4; 8(4); 9; 12; 13; 109:19; 21; 22; 27; 111:3; 4; 9; 10; 112:1; 4; 7; 8; 113:3; 4; 5; 115:2; 3; 8; 9; 10; 11; 116:5(2); 15; 117:2; 118:1; 6; 8; 9; 14(2); 15; 16; 22; 23(2); 24; 27; 29; 119:38; 50; 64; 70; 71; 72; 77; 89; 90; 96; 97; 105; 109; 118; 126; 140; 142(2); 144; 155; 160; 174; 120:5; 121:5(2); 122:3(2); 123:4; 124:7(2); 8; 125:2; 127:2; 3; 5; 128:1; 129:4; 130:4; 7(2); 131:1; 2(2); 132:14; 133:1; 2; 135:3(2); 5(2); 17; 18; 136:1; 138:5; 139:4; 6(2); 17; 140:3; 141:8; 143:4(2); 10; 144:3; 4; 8; 10; 11; 15(4); 145:3(2); 8; 9; 13; 17; 18; 146:3; 5(2); 6; 147:1(3); 5(2); 148:13(2); **Prov** 1:7; 17; 19; 2:7; 10; 3:13; 14; 15; 16; 18(2); 27(2); 32(2); 33; 4:7; 13; 16; 18; 19; 5:3; 4; 6:14; 23(2); 26; 30; 34; 7:11; 12; 19(2); 23; 27; 8:4; 7; 8; 11; 13; 14; 19; 34; 9:4; 10(2); 13(2); 16; 17; 10:1; 5(2); 7; 11; 13(3); 14; 15(2); 17; 18; 19; 20(2); 23; 25(2); 26; 29; 32; 11:1(2); 2; 8; 10; 11(2); 12; 13; 14(2); 15(2); 17; 22(2); 23(2); 24(3); 30(2); 12:1; 4(2); 8; 9(2); 11; 13; 15(2); 16; 18(2); 19; 20(2); 26; 27; 28(2); 13:5; 6; 7(2); 10; 12; 14; 15; 17; 19(2); 22; 23(3); 14:2; 3; 4(2); 6; 8(2); 9; 12; 13(2); 16; 17(2); 20; 21; 23; 24(2); 26; 27; 28(2); 29(3); 30; 32; 33(2); 34; 35(2); 15:4(2); 5; 6(2); 8(2); 9; 10; 13; 15; 16; 17(2); 18; 19(2); 21(2); 23; 24; 27; 29; 33(2); 16:1; 5(2); 6; 8; 10; 12(2); 14; 15(2); 16; 17; 19; 20; 22(2); 25; 27; 29; 31; 32(2); 33(2); 17:1; 3; 5; 8; 14; 16; 17; 24; 25; 26; 27; 28(2); 18:5; 7; 9(3); 10; 11; 12(2); 13; 17; 19; 24; 19:1(3); 2; 4; 6; 10; 11; 12(2); 13; 14; 18; 22(2); 26; 20:1(4); 2; 3; 5; 11; 14(3); 15; 16; 17; 18; 23; 25(2); 27; 28; 29(2); 21:1; 2; 3; 4; 5; 6; 8(2); 9; 11(3); 15; 19; 20; 24; 27; 30; 31(2); 22:1; 2; 6; 7; 13; 14(2); 15; 18; 22; 23:1; 5; 7(2); 11; 18; 22; 27(2); 31; 24:3(2); 5; 6; 7; 9(2); 10; 13(2); 23; 25:2(2); 3; 7; 11; 12; 13; 14; 15; 16; 18; 19; 20; 24; 25; 26; 27(2); 28(2); 26:1; 7; 8; 9; 12; 13(2); 16; 17; 19; 20(2); 21; 26; 27:3(2); 4(3); 5; 7; 8; 10(2); 13; 21; 28:3; 6(2); 7(2); 11; 12(2); 14; 15; 16; 18; 21; 24(2); 25; 26; 29:6; 9; 18(2); 20(2); 24; 27(3); 30:4(2); 5(2); 9; 11; 12(2); 13; 14; 15; 16(2); 20; 21; 22; 23(2); 28; 30; 31; 31:4(2); 6; 10; 14; 15; 18; 21; 22; 23; 26; 30(2); **Eccl** 1:2; 7; 8; 9(4); 10(2); 11; 14; 15(2); 17; 18; 2:1; 2; 15; 16(2); 17(3); 19; 21(3); 23; 24; 26(3); 3:1; 2; 12; 13; 15(3); 17; 19; 22(2); 4:3(2); 4(2); 6; 8(6); 10; 12; 13; 14; 16(2); 5:2; 3; 5; 8; 9(2); 10; 11; 12; 13; 14; 16; 18(2); 19; 6:1(2); 2(2); 3; 7(2); 9(2); 10(4); 11; 12; 7:1; 2(2); 3(2); 4(2); 5; 6(2); 8(2); 10; 11(2); 12(3); 15(2); 18; 20; 24; 26; 8:1; 4(2); 6(2); 8(2); 9(2); 10; 11(2); 14(3); 16(2); 17; 9:1; 2(3); 3(4); 4(3); 5; 6(2); 9; 10; 11; 16(2); 18; 10:1; 2; 3(2); 5; 6; 10; 11; 13(2); 14; 16; 17; 19; 11:5(2); 7(2); 8; 12:4; 5; 8; 12(2); 13; **Song** 1:1; 2; 3; 13; 14; 16; 2:2; 3; 6; 9; 11(2); 12(2); 14(2); 16; 3:6; 7; 4:1; 2; 3; 4; 7; 10(2); 11; 12; 5:2(2); 9(2); 10; 11; 14; 15; 16(4); 6:1(2); 2; 3; 5; 6; 9(3); 10; 7:2(2); 4(2); 5(2); 7; 10; 8:5; 6(2); 12(2); **Is** 1:5; 6; 7(2); 8; 11; 13(2); 21; 22; 2:7(4); 8; 12(2); 22(2); 3:7; 8(2); 14; 4:3(2); 5:7; 16; 25(3); 30; 6:3(2); 5; 7; 13; 7:2; 8(2); 9(2); 13; 18(2); 20; 22; 8:10; 20(2); 9:5; 6(2); 12(2); 15(2); 17(3); 19; 21(2); 10:4(2); 5; 7; 9(3); 28(2); 29(2); 31; 12:1; 2(3); 4; 5; 6; 13:6; 15(2); 22; 14:6; 7(2); 8; 9; 11(2); 16; 26(4); 27; 29; 15:1(2); 2; 6(2); 8; 16:4; 6; 9; 10; 12(2); 13; 17:1; 14(2); 18:1; 5(2); 19:11; 20:6; 21:2; 9(2); 22:5; 15; 25; 23:1(3); 3(2); 7(2); 10; 14; 24:5; 10(2); 11(3); 12(2); 13; 19(3); 25:4; 7; 9(2); 10; 26:3; 4; 7; 8; 11; 17; 19; 27:1; 4; 7; 9; 11; 28:1; 4(2); 8; 12(2); 14; 20; 27; 28; 29; 29:8(2); 11(4); 12(2); 13; 17; 20(2); 30:7; 9; 14; 18; 21; 27; 29; 33(3); 31:2; 3; 4; 9; 33:5; 6; 9(2); 17; 18(3); 22(3); 23; 34:1; 2; 6(2); 8; 36:4; 6; 7; 37:3(2); 4; 9; 13; 22; 29; 31; 38:3; 8; 12(2); 16; 22; 39:4(2); 6; 8; 40:2(2); 6(2); 7; 10; 16; 20; 22; 26; 27(2); 28(2); 41:7; 17; 24; 26(4); 42:8; 10; 19(3); 21; 22; 43:7; 9; 11; 13; 14; 44:3; 6; 8(2); 10; 12(2); 16; 19; 20; 28; 45:5(2); 6(2); 14(3); 18; 21(2); 22; 23; 46:9(2); 47:1; 4; 48:2; 4; 22; 49:4; 6; 7; 20; 50:1(3); 2(2); 4; 8(2); 9; 10; 51:5(2); 7; 13; 15; 18(2); 52:5(2); 6; 53:1; 2; 3; 7(2); 54:5(2); 9; 17(3); 55:2(2); 6; 56:1; 2; 57:1; 6; 10; 15(2); 19(2); 21; 58:5(2); 6; 7; 59:1; 5; 6; 8; 9; 11(2); 14(2); 21(2); 60:1(2); 61:1; 62:11; 63:1(2); 4(2); 11(2); 15; 16; 64:5; 7; 10; 11; 65:4; 6; 8(2); 66:1(4); 2; 3; **Jer** 1:13; 2:6; 8; 14(3); 19(2); 22; 25; 26(3); 34; 3:6; 23(2); 4:7(3); 8; 18(2); 20(2); 22; 31(2); 5:12; 13; 15(2); 16; 19; 27; 30; 6:6(2); 7(2); 10(2); 11; 13; 14; 16; 18; 25; 29; 7:10; 11(2); 14; 28(3); 30; 31; 8:5; 8(2); 9; 10; 11; 16; 18; 19(2); 20(2); 22(3); 9:6; 8; 12(3); 19; 21(2); 10:5; 6(2); 7; 8; 9(2); 10(2); 13; 14(4); 16(4); 19(3); 20(2); 22; 23(2); 11:5; 9; 15; 19; 12:8; 9; 11; 13:4; 10; 17; 20; 25; 14:2; 4; 17; 19(2); 15:9; 10; 14; 18; 16:10(2); 17; 19; 21; 17:1(2); 7(2); 9; 12; 15; 18:6; 12; 19:2; 20:11; 15; 21:12; 22:14; 28(3); 23:6; 9; 10(3); 15; 19; 28; 29; 33; 25:3; 13; 18; 29; 38; 26:11; 16; 28:6; 29:26; 28; 30:7(3); 12(2); 13; 15; 17; 21; 31:9; 17; 20(2); 35; 32:7(2); 8(4); 14(2); 17; 18; 24(2); 25; 27; 34; 43(2); 33:2; 5; 11; 12; 16; 34:8; 15; 36:7; 37:7; 14; 17(2); 38:5(2); 9(3); 14; 21; 40:3; 4; 41:17; 43:9; 13; 44:22; 23; 45:3; 46:7; 10; 17; 18(2); 20; 47:2; 5(2); 48:1(3); 4; 11; 15(2); 16; 17; 19; 20(3); 21; 25(2); 29; 32; 33; 38; 39; 41; 47; 49:3; 7(3); 10(2); 14; 19(3); 21; 23(2); 24; 25; 29; 50:2(3); 15; 17; 22; 23(2); 25; 27; 31; 34(2); 35; 36(2); 37(2); 38(2); 44(3); 46(2); 51:6; 8; 9(2); 11(2); 13; 16; 17(4); 19(4); 31; 33(2); 41(3); 42(2); 48; 55; 56(2); 57; 52:28; **Lam** 1:1(2); 3; 4; 6; 8; 9; 12(2); 14; 16; 17(2); 18; 20(2); 21; 22; 2:9; 11; 12; 13; 15; 16; 3:3; 18; 20; 22; 23; 24; 25; 26; 27; 30; 37; 47; 4:1(2); 3; 6; 8(3); 15; 18(2); 22; 5:1; 2; 4; 8; 15(2); 16; 17; 18; **Eze** 1:28; 3:21; 4:14; 5:5; 6:12(3); 7:2; 3; 5; 6(3); 7(3); 10(2); 11; 12(2); 13(2); 14; 15(3); 19; 23(2); 8:17; 9:6; 9(2); 10:15; 20; 11:3(2); 7; 15; 23; 12:12; 19; 22; 27; 13:12(2); 15; 16; 15:2(2); 4(3); 5; 16:3; 7; 20; 30; 34(2); 44(2); 46(2); 17:12; 18:4; 5; 9; 10; 18; 19; 21; 25(2); 27; 29; 19:2; 10; 13; 14(2); 20:6; 15; 29(2); 21:9; 10(2); 11(2); 13; 14; 15(2); 16; 25; 26(2); 27; 28(2); 29; 22:18; 22; 24; 25; 23:4; 20(2); 22; 28; 37; 45; 24:6(2); 7; 13; 24; 27; 25:8; 26:2(3); 10; 15; 27:27; 32; 28:2; 3; 5; 29:3; 9; 30:3(2); 5; 12; 31:10; 18; 32:16; 20; 22; 23; 24; 25; 26; 29; 33:6; 14; 16; 17(2); 19; 20; 21; 24; 27; 30; 34:5; 12; 36:35; 37:11; 19; 38:8(3); 39:4; 8(3); 40:45(2); 46(2); 41:4; 22(2); 42:13; 15; 43:4; 12(2); 13; 44:3; 9; 22; 26; 31; 45:13; 14; 20; 46:11; 20; 47:16(2); 17; 18; 19; 20; 48:12; 14; 22; 29; 35; **Dan** 2:5; 8; 9; 10(2); 11(3); 15; 22; 28; 30; 36; 43; 45; 47(2); 3:4; 14; 15; 17; 25; 29; 4:3(2); 8; 9; 17; 18; 22(2); 24(3); 30; 31(2); 34(2); 37; 5:11(2); 14(2); 23; 25; 26; 28; 6:12; 13; 15; 20; 26; 7:14; 27; 28; 8:2; 21(3); 26; 9:11(2); 13(2); 14; 17; 18; 10:4; 14; 17; 21(2); 11:35; 36; 12:12; **Hos** 2:2; 4:1; 13; 17; 18; 5:1; 3(2); 4; 11; 6:3; 4; 8(2); 10(2); 7:7; 8; 11; 8:3; 5; 6; 8(2); 9:7(2); 8; 13; 15; 16(2); 10:1; 2; 5; 7; 10; 11(2); 12; 11:8; 12; 12:1; 5; 7; 11; 13:3; 4; 8; 9; 10; 12(2); 13; 14:4; 8; 9; **Joel** 1:5; 6; 9; 10(3); 11; 12(2); 13; 15; 16; 17(2); 2:1; 3; 4; 11(3); 13; 17; 3:13(3); 14; **Amos** 2:11; 13(2); 15; 16; 3:5; 4:3; 13(2); 5:2(3); 8; 11; 13; 18(2); 27; 6:8; 10(2); 7:2; 5; 10; 13(2); 8:2; 9:5; 6(2); 9; 11; **Obad** 1; 3; 7; 15; 20; **Jonah** 1:2; 7; 8(3); 12; 2:9; 3:8; 4:3; 8; **Mic** 1:2; 5(3); 9(3); 13; 2:1(2); 3; 7; 8; 10(2); 13; 3:1; 7; 11; 4:6; 9(2); 5:2; 6:8; 10; 12; 7:1(2); 2(2); 4(2); 10(2); 18; **Nah** 1:2(2); 3; 5; 6; 7; 11; 15; 2:1; 3; 8; 9; 10(2); 11; 3:1; 3(2); 7; 17; 18; 19(2); **Hab** 1:4; 13; 16; 2:3; 4(2); 5(2); 6; 13; 19(2); 20; 3:19; **Zeph** 1:7; 14(2); 15; 2:5; 15(3); 3:1; 5; 6(2); 8; 15; 17; **Hag** 1:2; 4; 6; 9; 10(2); 2:3(2); 6; 8(2); 13; 14(4); 19; **Zec** 1:7; 11; 2:2(2); 13; 3:2; 4:1; 6; 5:2; 3; 5; 6(3); 7; 8; 6:12; 7:13; 8:23(2); 9:9; 11; 17(2); 10:5; 11:2(2); 3(3); 9; 16; 12:8; 10; 13:7; 9(4); 14:4; 16; **Mal** 1:6(2); 7; 8(2); 10; 12(2); 13; 14; 2:1; 7; 11; 14; 17(2); 3:2; 14(2); **Mt** 1:16; 20(2); 23; 2:2(2); 5; 3:2; 3; 9; 10(2); 11; 12; 17; 4:4; 6; 7; 10; 13; 16; 17; 5:3; 10; 12; 13; 14; 16; 22; 29; 30; 32; 34; 35(2); 37; 45; 48(2); 6:1; 6; 10; 13; 18; 21; 22; 23(2); 25; 30(2); 34; 7:3(2); 4; 6; 9; 11; 12; 13(2); 14(2); 19; 21; 8:27; 9:5; 15; 16(2); 18; 24; 37; 10:2; 7; 10; 11; 20; 24; 25; 26; 28; 32; 33; 37(2); 38; 11:6; 10(2); 11(2); 14; 16; 19; 30(2); 12:2; 6; 8; 10; 12(2); 18; 23; 25; 26; 28; 30(2); 33; 41; 42; 43; 44; 45; 48; 50(2); 13:11(2); 14; 15; 19; 20; 21; 22; 23; 24; 31; 32(3); 33; 37; 38; 39(2); 44; 45; 47; 52(3); 55(2); 57; 14:2(2); 4; 15(2); 26; 27; 15:5; 8; 17; 22; 26; 28; 16:2(2); 3; 7; 11; 17; 26; 17:4; 5; 12; 15; 18:1; 4; 8; 9; 10; 11; 12; 14(2); 19; 23; 19:3; 9; 10; 11; 12; 14; 17(2); 24; 26; 20:1(2); 4; 7; 14; 15(2); 23(2); 21:9; 10; 11; 13; 20; 21; 38; 42(3); 22:2; 8; 17; 20; 23; 32; 36; 38; 39; 42; 45; 23:8; 9(2); 10; 11; 15; 16(2); 17; 18(3); 19; 26; 38; 39; 24:6; 17; 18; 23; 26(2); 28; 32(2); 33; 45; 46; 50; 25:14; 25; 26:2(2); 8; 18; 22; 24(2); 25; 26; 28(2); 31; 38; 41(2); 45(2); 46; 48; 62; 66; 68; 27:4; 6(2); 17; 22; 33; 37; 46; 64; 28:6(2); 7; 15; 18; **Mk** 1:2; 15(2); 27(2); 2:9; 16; 19; 21; 22; 24; 26; 28; 3:4; 17; 21; 29; 33; 35; 4:11; 15; 21; 22; 26; 29(2); 31(3); 32; 40; 41; 5:9(2); 35; 39; 41; 6:2(2); 3; 4; 15(2); 16(2); 18; 35(2); 50; 7:2; 6(2); 11(2); 15; 27; 29; 34; 8:16; 21; 9:5; 7; 12; 13(2); 21; 26; 31(2); 39; 40(2); 42; 43; 44; 45; 46; 47; 48; 50; 10:2; 14; 18(2); 24; 25; 27; 29; 40(2); 11:9; 17; 21; 25; 26; 12:7; 10; 11; 14; 16; 18; 27; 28; 29(2); 30; 31(2); 32(2); 33; 35; 37; 13:11; 15; 16; 21(2); 28(2); 29; 33; 34; 14:8; 14; 19(2); 20; 21(2); 22; 24(2); 27; 34; 38(2); 41(3); 42; 44; 58; 60; 69; 15:22; 34; 42; 16:6(2); 16; **Lk** 1:13; 28; 36; 42; 43; 45; 49(2); 50; 61(2); 63; 2:4; 11(2); 15; 23; 24; 34; 49; 3:4; 8; 9(2); 13; 17; 4:4; 6; 8; 10; 12; 18; 21; 22; 24; 36; 5:21; 23; 34; 39; 6:2; 4; 5; 9; 20; 23; 35; 36; 40(2); 41(2); 42(3); 44; 45(2); 47; 48; 49; 7:16; 22; 23; 27(2); 28(3); 34; 35; 39(2); 47; 49; 8:10; 11(2); 17; 25(2); 26; 30; 46; 49; 52; 9:9; 19; 25; 33; 35; 38; 48; 50(2); 56; 62; 10:2; 7; 9; 11; 22(2); 26; 29; 42; 11:4; 6; 7; 8; 11; 17; 20; 23(2); 24; 26; 27; 29; 31; 32; 34(5); 35; 39; 40(2); 12:1; 2; 6; 21(2); 23(2); 26; 28(2); 32; 34; 42; 43; 46; 48; 54; 56; 57; 13:18; 19; 21; 25; 35(2); 14:3; 15; 22(2); 29; 32; 34; 35; 15:4; 10; 24(2); 27; 31; 32(2); 16:2; 10(5); 12(2); 15(2); 16; 17; 18; 25; 26; 17:1; 7; 21; 30; 31; 37; 18:16; 19(2); 25; 29; 19:7; 9(2); 10; 20; 46(2); 20:2; 14; 17(3); 22; 27; 33; 38; 41; 44; 21:9; 20; 30; 31; 37; 22:1; 11; 19(2); 20(2); 21; 22; 26(2); 27(2); 37; 38; 53; 59; 64; 23:2; 15; 33; 38; 24:6(2); 21; 29(2); 34; 39; 46; **Jn** 1:15; 18; 19; 27(2); 30(2); 33; 34; 38; 41; 42; 47; 2:4; 10; 3:4; 6(4); 8(2); 13; 18(2); 19(2); 29(2); 31(4); 33; 4:5; 9; 10; 11; 18; 20; 22; 23; 24; 25(2); 29; 34; 37; 42; 54; 5:2(2); 7; 10(2); 12; 24; 25(2); 27; 28; 30; 31; 32(2); 45; 6:1; 7; 9; 14; 20; 29; 31; 33; 39; 40; 42(2); 45; 46; 50; 51; 55(2); 58; 60; 63; 70; 7:4; 6(2); 8; 11; 12; 16; 18(2); 22; 25; 26; 27(2); 28; 36; 40; 41; 8:7; 13; 14; 16; 17(2); 19; 26; 29; 34; 39; 44(2); 47; 50; 52; 53; 54(3); 9:4; 7; 8; 9(2); 11; 12; 16(2); 17; 19; 20; 21; 23; 24; 29; 30(2); 36; 37; 10:1; 2; 12; 13; 20; 29(2); 34; 38; 11:3; 4; 10; 14; 16; 28; 50; 12:13; 14; 19; 23; 27; 31; 34; 35; 50; 13:10(2); 16(2); 19; 25; 26; 31(2); 14:21; 22; 24; 26; 28; 29; 15:1; 6(2); 8; 12; 20; 25; 26; 16:7; 8; 11; 13; 17; 18; 21(4); 32(2); 17:1; 3; 12; 17; 18:31; 36(2); 37; 38; 19:13; 17; 30; 35; 40; 20:16; 31; 21:7; 14; 20; 22; 23; 24(2); **Acts** 1:7; 8; 11;

12; 19(2); 20; 2:15; 16; 25; 29(2); 34; 39; 3:2; 11; 16; 4:9; 11(2); 12(2); 16; 24; 36; 5:9; 17; 32; 6:2; 9; 7:33; 34; 37; 38; 40; 42; 49(3); 8:10; 21; 26; 33; 36; 37; 9:5; 11; 15; 20; 21; 22; 36; 10:4; 5; 6; 14; 21; 28(2); 31; 32(2); 34; 35; 36; 42; 11:13; 12:15; 22; 13:8; 9; 11; 26; 33; 38; 40; 15:15; 16; 17; 19; 16:12; 17:3; 7; 19; 24; 25; 29; 19:4; 27; 28; 34; 35(2); 38; 20:10; 32; 35; 21:22; 28; 22:22; 25(2); 26; 23:5; 8; 19; 25:14; 16(2); 26:14; 18; 27:8; 12; 16; 33; 34; 28:4; 22; 27; 28; **Rom** 1:8; 9; 12; 15; 16; 17(2); 18; 19; 25; 26; 27; 2:2; 11; 24(2); 25; 27; 28(4); 29(4); 3:1; 4; 5; 8; 10(2); 11(2); 12; 13(2); 14; 18; 20; 21; 22(2); 24; 27(2); 28; 29(2); 30; 4:4; 5; 8; 14; 15(2); 16(4); 17; 5:5(2); 13(2); 14; 15(2); 16(2); 6:6; 7(2); 21; 23(2); 7:2(2); 3(2); 4; 7; 12; 13(2); 14; 16; 17; 18(3); 20; 21; 23; 8:1; 6(2); 7(2); 9; 10(2); 24(2); 27; 33; 34(4); 36; 39; 9:5; 8; 9; 13; 14; 16; 30; 33; 10:1; 4; 5; 6(2); 7; 8(2); 10; 12(2); 15; 20; 11:5; 6(4); 8; 11; 16; 23; 24; 25; 26; 27; 12:1; 2; 3; 6; 9(2); 19(2); 13:1; 3; 4(3); 7; 9; 10; 11(2); 12(2); 14:1; 2; 4; 11; 14(2); 17; 18; 20; 21(3); 22; 23(3); 15:3; 9; 15; 21; 27; 16:1(2); 5(2); 19(2); 25; 26; **1Cor** 1:2; 4; 9; 13; 18(2); 19; 20(3); 25(2); 30; 31; 2:9; 12; 15(2); 3:3; 5(2); 7; 10; 11(2); 13; 17; 19(2); 23; 4:2; 3; 4; 6; 17; 20; 5:1(3); 6; 7; 11; 6:5(2); 7; 13; 16(2); 17(2); 18; 19(2); 7:1; 8; 9; 14(2); 15; 18(2); 19(2); 22(4); 24; 26(2); 29; 32; 33; 34(2); 35; 39(2); 40; 8:3; 4(2); 6; 7(2); 10; 9:3; 9; 10; 11; 16(2); 17; 18; 25; 10:7; 13(2); 16(2); 19(3); 25; 26; 27; 28(2); 29; 11:3(3); 5; 7(2); 8; 11; 12(2); 13; 14; 15(2); 20; 21(2); 24(2); 25; 12:3; 6; 7; 8; 12(2); 14; 15; 16; 13:4(2); 5; 10(3); 13; 14:5; 7; 9; 10; 14; 15; 17; 21; 24(2); 25; 26; 33; 15:12; 13; 14(2); 16; 17; 20; 26; 27(2); 36; 39(2); 40(2); 41; 42(3); 43(4); 44(4); 45; 46(3); 47(2); 48(2); 54(2); 55(2); 56(2); 58; 16:9; 15; 19; **2Cor** 1:1; 6(3); 7; 12; 18; 21; 2:2(2); 3; 6; 16; 3:5; 11(2); 13; 14; 15(2); 17(3); 4:3; 4; 13; 16; 17; 5:2; 5; 13(2); 17; 6:2(2); 11(2); 7:4(2); 14; 15; 8:10; 12; 15; 18; 19; 20; 23; 9:1; 8; 9; 12; 10:6; 7(2); 10; 15(2); 18; 11:3; 10; 14; 15; 21; 29(2); 31; 12:1; 4; 9(2); 13; 13:1; 3(2); 5; 7; **Gal** 1:7; 11; 2:16; 17; 21; 3:10(2); 11(2); 12; 13(2); 16; 18; 20(2); 21; 25; 28(3); 4:1; 2; 15; 18; 22; 24; 25(3); 26(3); 27; 29; 5:3(2); 4; 11; 14; 22; 23; 6:3; 6; 7; 14; **Eph** 1:14; 18; 19; 21(2); 23; 2:4; 8; 11; 14; 3:2; 5; 8; 9; 13; 15; 18; 20; 4:4; 6; 7; 9; 10; 15; 18; 21; 22; 24; 28; 29; 5:5; 9; 10; 12; 13; 17; 18; 23(3); 24; 32; 6:1; 2; 9(2); 17; **Phil** 1:7; 8; 18; 21(2); 22; 23; 24; 28; 29; 2:9; 11; 13; 3:1(2); 6; 9(3); 19(3); 20; 21; 4:5; **Col** 1:5; 6(2); 7; 15; 17; 18(2); 23; 24(2); 25; 26; 27(2); 2:10; 17; 3:3; 4; 5; 10; 11(2); 14; 18; 20; 25; 4:1; 7; 9; 11; 12; 15; 16; **1Th** 1; 8; 2:5; 13; 16; 19; 3:10; 4:3; 6; 5:15; 18; 21; 24; **2Th** 1:3; 5; 6; 2:2; 4(3); 9; 3:1; 3; 17; **1Ti** 1:1; 4; 5; 8; 9; 10; 14; 15; 20; 2:3; 5; 3:1; 13; 15; 16; 4:4; 5; 8(3); 9; 10; 14; 5:4; 6; 8; 8; 18; 6:3; 4; 5; 6; 7; 10; 15; 20; S:1; **2Ti** 1:1; 5; 6; 10; 12; 13; 2:1; 5; 9; 10; 11; 17; 18; 3:15; 16(2); 4:6; 8; 10; 11(2); **Titus** 1:1; 3; 13; 15(2); 2:8; 3:8; 10; 11(2); **Philem** 1:6; 8; 12; **Heb** 1:8(2); 2; 8; 11; 14; 18; 3:4(2); 13; 15; 4:7; 10; 12(2); 13(2); 14; 5:1; 2; 4; 13(2); 6:4; 7; 8(3); 10; 16; 20; 7:2; 5; 6; 7; 8; 12; 14; 15; 16; 17; 21; 22; 36; 10:4; 5; 6; 14; 3(2); 6; 10; 14; 18; 3:4(2); 13; 15; 4:7; 10; 16; 20; 22; 24; 27; 10:3; 4; 7; 15; 16; 18(2); 20; 23; 25; 31; 11:1; 6(3); 7; 10; 12; 16(2); 27; 12:1; 2; 7; 13; 29; 13:4; 6; 9; 11; 15; 16; 17; 21; 23; **Jas** 1:6; 8; 9; 10; 11; 12(2); 13; 14(2); 15; 17(2); 21; 23; 26; 27; 2:10; 17; 19; 20; 24; 26(2); 3:2; 5; 6(3); 7; 8; 13; 15; 16(2); 17(2); 18; 4:4(2); 12(2); 14(2); 16; 17; 5:3; 4; 11; 13(2); 14; **1Pet** 1:13; 15; 16; 24; 25(2); 2:3; 6; 7(2); 15; 19; 20(2); 3:4(2); 12; 13(2); 15; 17; 20; 22(2); 4:5; 7; 12; 14(2); 17; 5:2; 12; 13; **2Pet** 1:4; 9; 17; 20; 2:17; 19(2); 20; 22(2); 3:4; 8; 9(2); 15; **1Jn** 1:3; 5(3); 7; 8; 9; 10; 2:2; 4(2); 5; 7; 8(2); 9(2); 10; 12; 15; 16(3); 18(2); 21; 22(3); 25; 27(2); 29(2); 3:2; 3; 4; 5; 7(2); 8; 9(2); 10; 11; 15; 20; 23; 4:2(2); 3(4); 4(3); 6; 7(2); 8; 10; 12; 15; 16; 17(2); 18(2); 20; 5:1(3); 3; 4(2); 5(2); 6(3); 9; 11(2); 14; 16(2); 17; 18(2); 20(4); **2Jn** 6(2); 7(2); 11; **3Jn** 3; 11(3); 12; **Jude** 13; 24; **Rev** 1:3(2); 4(2); 5; 8(2); 9; 2:7; 8; 13; 3:7(2); 12; 4:8(2); 5:2; 12; 13; 6:13; 14; 17; 7:17; 8:11; 9:11(2); 12; 13; 19; 10:8; 11:2(2); 8; 14; 18; 12:10(2); 12; 14; 13:4(2); 10; 18(3); 14:7; 8(2); 10; 12; 15(2); 17; 15:1; 16:15; 17; 17:8(3); 9; 10(2); 11(3); 14; 18; 18:2(3); 8; 10; 17; 18; 19; 19:7; 8; 10; 13; 20:2; 5; 6; 8; 12; 14; 21:3; 6(2); 8; 16; 17; 23; 22:7; 10; 11(4); 12; 17

846

Gen 1:4; 6; 7; 9; 10; 11; 12; 15; 18; 21; 24; 25; 28; 29; 30; 31; 2:3(2); 5(3); 10; 11; 13; 14; 15(2); 17; 18; 3:3(2); 6; 15; 17(2); 18; 19; 4:3; 8; 12; 14; 6:1; 6(2); 7; 12; 14; 15(3); 16(2); 21(2); 7:4; 10; 17; 8:6; 13; 9:5; 13; 14; 16; 23; 10:9; 11:2; 9; 12:11; 12; 13; 14; 13:10; 15; 17(3); 14:1; 15:6; 7; 8; 17(2); 16:2; 6; 10; 14; 17:11; 18:6; 7(2); 8; 10; 11; 21; 28; 29; 30; 31; 32; 19:13; 17; 20(2); 29; 34; 20:13; 15; 21:12; 14(2); 16; 22; 26; 22:1; 6; 14(2); 20(2); 23:8; 9(2); 11(2); 13(2); 24:14; 15; 22; 30; 43; 52; 65; 25:11; 22; 26:8; 21; 22; 36; 27:1; 4; 5; 10; 20(3); 25(2); 30; 31; 33; 40; 28:12(2); 13(2); 16; 18(2); 29:2; 7(2); 10; 13; 19; 23; 25(2); 26; 30:15; 25; 28; 30(2); 33; 34; 35; 41; 31:2; 5; 10; 22; 29;

32; 35; 37; 39(2); 44; 45; 47(2); 48; 32:8; 18; 29; 33:11; 15; 20; 34:7; 21; 25; 35:8; 12; 17; 18; 22(2); 37:5; 9; 10; 14; 21; 23; 24; 25; 26; 32(2); 33(2); 38:1; 9(2); 13; 17; 18; 23; 24(2); 27; 28; 29; 39:5; 7; 10; 11; 13; 15; 18; 19; 22; 23; 40:1; 8; 10(2); 12; 14; 20; 41:1; 7; 8; 13(2); 15(2); 16; 21; 24; 31; 32(2); 42; 43; 49; 42:6; 14; 27; 28; 35; 43:2; 11; 12(2); 21(2); 44:5; 9; 10(2); 24; 31; 45:8; 12; 16; 28; 46:33; 47:18; 24; 26; 48:1; 14; 17(2); 19(2); 49:4; 7(2); 15; 28; 50:9; 11; 20(2); **Ex** 1:10; 16(2); 21; 2:3(2); 5; 6; 9(2); 11; 18; 20; 3:21; 4:3(4); 4(3); 6; 7(2); 8; 9(2); 24; 25; 5:11; 19; 22; 6:8(2); 28; 7:9(2); 10; 8:10; 16; 17; 26; 9:8; 9; 10(2); 18; 24(2); 28; 10:10; 13; 11:6(2); 12:2; 4; 5; 6(2); 7(2); 8; 9; 10(2); 11(3); 14(2); 22; 25; 26; 27; 29; 34; 39; 41(2); 42; 46; 47; 48; 51; 13:2; 5; 9; 11(2); 13; 14; 15; 16; 17; 14:2; 5; 12; 16; 20(3); 24; 27; 15:23; 16:5(2); 10; 13; 15(3); 16; 18; 19; 20(2); 21(2); 22; 24(2); 25; 26(2); 27; 31(2); 32; 33; 34; 17:6; 11; 12; 14; 15; 18:13; 18; 22(2); 19:12; 23(3); 16; 18; 23; 20:8; 10; 11; 18; 25(3); 21:26; 29; 31; 33; 34; 35; 36; 22:1(2); 4; 7; 9; 10(2); 11(2); 12; 13(2); 14(3); 15(4); 26; 27; 30(2); 30(2); 23:4; 11; 13; 21; 24; 25(4); 26(4); 27(3); 38:1; 2(2); 4; 7; 8; 21; 30; 39:3(2); 4(3); 5; 9; 10; 18; 19; 20; 21; 23; 30; 31(2); 43(2); 40:4; **Lev** 1:3; 4; 6; 9; 10; 11; 12; 13(3); 15(2); 16; 17(4); 2:1; 2(3); 4; 5; 6(2); 7; 8(2); 9(2); 10; 15(2); 16(2); 3:1(3); 2; 4; 5(2); 6; 7; 8; 9; 10; 11(2); 12; 13(2); 15; 16; 17; 4:5; 8; 9; 10; 14; 17; 19; 20; 21; 24(2); 25; 26; 30; 31(2); 32; 33; 34; 35; 5:1(2); 2(2); 3(3); 4(3); 5; 8; 9; 10; 11(2); 12(4); 13; 16(2); 17; 18(2); 19; 6:3; 4; 5(3); 7; 9(2); 12(4); 13; 14; 18(3); 20; 21(3); 22; 23; 24(3); 25; 26(2); 27; 28(3); 30(3); 31(2); 32; 39; 42; 43; 47; 48; 49; 50; 51; 52(2); 54; 55(5); 56(2); 57(2); 58(2); 59(2); 14:6; 9; 13; 14; 15; 25; 35(2); 36; 43; 44(2); 45; 46; 48; 53; 57(2); 15:3; 23(2); 25; 16:12; 14; 15; 18(2); 19(3); 29; 31; 17:3; 4; 9(2); 11(2); 13; 14(3); 15; 18:8; 16; 17; 22; 25; 28(2); 19:5; 6(3); 7(3); 8; 23(2); 25; 20:14; 17; 21; 24(2); 21:24; 22:7; 9(2); 11; 14(2); 20; 21; 23; 27(2); 28(2); 29; 30(2); 32(2); 14:3; 7; 8; 11; 13; 14; 23; 24; 35; 41; 15:11; 19; 20; 24; 25(2); 26; 28; 34; 39(2); 16:4; 7; 9; 31; 42(2); 17:5; 8; 18:10(3); 11; 13; 15; 19; 23; 26; 27; 29; 30(2); 31(2); 32(3); 19:6; 9(2); 10; 12; 15; 18(2); 21; 22; 20:5; 8; 19; 21:8(3); 9(2); 14; 17; 18; 28; 22:34; 41; 23:19(2); 20; 22; 23; 27; 24:1; 8; 25:7; 13; 26; 1; 6; 12; 32; 34; 35(4); 37; 27:4; 5; 6; 7(2); 9; 10(3); 11; 12(4); 13; 14(4); 14(4); 17; 18; 19(3); 20; 21; 24; 26(3); 27(5); 30; 33(5); **Num** 1:50(2); 51(2); 3:26; 4:5; 6; 9; 10(2); 11; 14(4); 15; 25; 5:7(2); 10; 13; 15(2); 17; 25; 26; 27; 6:9; 18; 7:1(3); 5; 10; 84; 88; 8:24; 9:3(3); 11(2); 12(3); 15; 16(2); 20; 21(2); 22(2); 10:11; 29; 32(2); 35; 36; 11:1(2); 8(6); 9; 14; 17(2); 18; 20(2); 25(2); 31(3); 33; 12(2); 13:18; 19; 20; 23; 27(2); 30(2); 32(2); 14:3; 7; 8; 11; 13; 14; 23; 24; 35; 41; 15:11; 19; 20; 24; 25(2); 26; 28; 34; 39(2); 16:4; 7; 9; 31; 42(2); 17:5; 8; 18:10(3); 11; 13; 15; 19; 23; 26; 27; 29; 30(2); 31(2); 32(3); 19:6; 9(2); 10; 12; 15; 18(2); 21; 22; 20:5; 8; 19; 21:8(3); 9(2); 14; 17; 18; 28; 22:34; 41; 23:19(2); 20; 22; 23; 27; 24:1; 8; 25:7; 13; **Deut** 1:3; 17(2); 21; 24; 25(2); 36; 38; 39(2); 2:16; 19; 24; 3:9; 11(2); 18; 26; 27; 4:2; 5; 14; 26(2); 32; 35; 38; 39; 40; 5:12; 14; 16; 23; 27(2); 29; 31; 33; 6:1; 3(2); 10; 18; 24; 25; 7:1; 12; 25(2); 26(4); 8:9; 18(2); 19; 9:6; 11; 13; 21(4); 10:15; 11:8; 10(2); 11; 12; 13; 29(2); 31; 12:1; 16; 24(2); 25(2); 28; 32(2); 13:14; 15; 16(3); 14:8(2); 9; 11; 24; 25; 28; 15:2(3); 3; 4; 9; 16; 14:8(2); 10; 21(3); 24; 25; 28; 15:2(3); 3; 4; 9; 16; 17; 18; 20; 21(2); 22(2); 23; 16:3; 7; 17:4(3); 14; 18; 19; 18:3; 19(2); 22; 19:2; 13; 14; 20:2; 5(2); 3; 7; 14; 16; 22:2(4); 7; 23:11; 13; 16; 20; 21(3); 3; 7; 14; 16; 22:2(4); 7; 23:11; 13; 16; 20; 21(3); 22; 24:1(2); 3; 13; 15(3); 19(2); 20; 21(2); 25:2; 6; 8; 9; 19(3); 26:1(2); 2; 4; 10; 27:2; 4; 15; 28:1; 15; 21; 24; 38; 63(2); 67(2); 68; 29:8; 19; 22; 23; 27; 28; 30:1; 5; 11(2); 12(4); 13(4); 14; 16; 18; 31:6; 7; 8; 9; 13; 19(2); 21(2); 22; 24; 26(2); 32:19; 27; 47(3); 34:4(2); **Josh** 1:1; 7; 11; 15; 2:2; 5(2); 14; 19; 21; 3:2; 3(2); 4(2); 13; 14; 4:1; 7; 11; 18; 24; 5:1; 8; 13; 6:5; 8; 11; 15; 16; 17; 18; 20; 26; 7:9; 11; 14; 15; 19; 21; 22(2); 8:2; 5; 7; 8; 14(2); 18; 19; 24(2); 25; 28; 29; 31; 9:1; 12(2); 16; 24; 25; 10:1(2); 2; 4; 5; 11; 14; 20; 24; 27; 28(3); 31(2); 32(2); 34(2); 35(2); 36; 37:3; 4; 12; 13; 20; 38:5; 8(2); 9; 10; 13(2); 14; 16; 20; 21; 26; 29; 39:12; 24; 40:2; 24; 42:7; **Ps** 6:7; 7:2; 5; 12; 15; 10:11; 13; 14(2); 17:12; 18:8; 32; 47; 19:6; 21:4; 22:14; 30; 24:2(2); 25:11; 30:9; 33:9(2); 34:14; 35:9; 15; 21; 25; 37:5; 10; 34; 38:10; 39:4; 9; 40:3; 7; 14; 41:6; 48:5; 8; 13; 49:8; 50:3; 51:16; 52:9(2); 54:6; 55:10(2); 12(3); 13; 60:2(2); 4; 12; 63:9; 65:9(3); 10; 68:9; 11; 14(2); 16; 69:18; 22; 35; 36; 73:16; 28; 74:11; 75:3; 8; 78:28; 80:8; 9(3); 10; 13(2);

16(2); 81:10; 84:6; 86:17; 87:5; 89:37; 39; 90:4; 6(2); 10; 13; 17; 91:7; 92:1; 7; 93:1; 94:7; 15; 95:5; 10; 96:10; 99:3; 100:3; 101:3; 103:16(3); 104:5; 6; 20; 32; 105:12; 28; 106:9; 32; 107:42; 108:13; 109:17(2); 18; 19; 23; 27; 112:10; 114:3; 118:8; 9; 23; 24; 119:20; 33; 34; 71; 90; 97; 106; 126; 130; 140; 175; 124:1; 2; 127:1; 2; 128:2; 129:6; 132:6(2); 11; 13; 14; 133:1; 2; 135:3; 136:14; 137:7(2); 139:4; 6(2); 141:5(2); 144:10; 147:1(2); **Prov** 2:21; 22; 3:8; 14; 25; 27(3); 28; 4:5; 15(3); 23; 6:22(3); 32; 7:23; 8:11; 33; 9:12; 10:22(2); 23; 24; 11:10; 11; 15; 19; 24; 26; 27; 12:25(2); 13:12; 19; 14:1; 6; 15:23; 16:12; 14; 16; 19; 22; 26; 31; 17:8(3); 14; 16; 21; 18:5; 10; 13(2); 21; 19:2; 11; 19; 23; 24; 20:3; 5; 11; 14(2); 25; 21:1; 9; 15; 19; 20; 27; 22:6; 15; 18; 23:23; 31(3); 32; 35(2); 24:3; 12(3); 13; 14; 18(2); 23; 27; 31; 32(2); 25:2; 7(2); 10; 16; 24; 27; 26:15(2); 27; 28; 27:14; 28:8; 24; 29:4; 7; 11; 24; 30:15; 16; 17(2); 21; 31:4(2); 15; 16; 24; **Eccl** 1:6; 8; 9; 10(2); 2:2(2); 15(2); 18; 21; 24; 3:10; 13; 14(4); 4:8; 5:4; 5; 6; 18(2); 6:1; 2(2); 10(2); 7:2(2); 5; 11; 12; 18; 23; 24; 8:7; 8; 12; 13; 14(2); 17(4); 9:10; 12; 13; 14(4); 15; 10:8; 11:1; 3; 7; 12:7(2); 14(2); **Song** 3:4; 7; 10; 5:2; 3; 6:13; 8:7(2); 13; **Is** 1:6; 7(2); 13; 20; 21(2); 31; 2:2(2); 3:9; 10; 11; 24; 4:3; 5:2(5); 4(3); 5(2); 6(3); 14; 18; 19(2); 29(2); 6:2; 7; 13(2); 7:1(3); 2; 6(2); 7(2); 8; 11; 13; 18; 20; 21; 22; 23(2); 25; 8:1; 10(2); 20; 21(2); 9:7(2); 8; 18; 10:7; 12; 13; 15(3); 17; 20; 26; 27; 30; 11:10; 11; 15; 16; 13:6; 9; 14; 17; 20(2); 14:3; 9(2); 23(2); 24(2); 27(2); 32; 15:5; 16:2; 5; 12(2); 17:1; 4; 5(2); 6; 10; 19:1; 16(2); 17; 20; 21; 22; 20:1; 21:1; 3(2); 17; 22:5; 7; 11; 14; 20; 25(2); 23:1(2); 9; 13(2); 15; 17; 18; 24:1(2); 2; 9; 13; 18; 20(2); 21; 25:2; 8; 9; 26:5(3); 6; 15; 18; 20; 27:3(4); 8(2); 11; 12; 13; 28:4(3); 15; 18; 19(4); 20(2); 28(3); 29:2; 5; 8; 11; 16(2); 17; 30:8(3); 14(2); 19; 21; 22; 23; 32(2); 33(3); 31:5(2); 32:19; 34:1; 5; 6; 8; 10(3); 11(3); 13; 16(2); 17(2); 35:2(2); 8(3); 9; 36:1; 6(2); 7; 10(2); 11; 37:1(2); 4; 9; 14(2); 26(3); 27; 33(2); 35; 38; 38:8; 15; 17; 21; 40:5(2); 7; 9; 19; 21; 22; 41:4; 5; 7(3); 20; 23; 42:5(2); 21; 25(3); 43:9; 13; 19(2); 44:7(2); 8; 12(2); 13(5); 14; 15(4); 17(3); 19(2); 23; 45:8; 9; 12; 18(4); 21; 46:6; 8; 11(4); 13; 47:7; 10; 11; 14; 48:5(3); 6; 11; 16; 20; 49:6; 50:1; 2; 51:9; 10; 22; 23; 52:6; 53:3; 10; 54:14; 55:10(2); 11(4); 13; 56:2(2); 6; 57:1; 8; 11; 20; 58:5(2); 7; 14; 59:1(2); 11; 15(2); 16; 60:22; 61:11; 62:9(4); 63:5; 18; 65:6; 8(2); 9; 24; 66:18; 23; **Jer** 1:3; 12; 2:19; 34; 3:5; 7; 9; 16(4); 17; 4:4; 9; 11; 18(2); 23; 28(3); 5:1; 12; 13; 14; 15(2); 19; 20; 22(3); 31; 6:10; 11; 19; 7:11; 12; 20; 23; 29; 30; 31; 32; 8:8; 16; 9:8; 12; 10:4(3); 5; 7; 18; 19; 23; 11:5(2); 16(2); 18(2); 12:8(2); 11(3); 15; 16; 13:1(2); 2; 4; 5; 6; 7(2); 16(2); 17; 19(2); 27; 14:5; 7; 15:2; 8; 9; 11; 16:10; 14; 17:1; 9; 15; 21; 24; 27(2); 18:4(2); 7; 9; 10(2); 19:4; 5(2); 15; 20:3; 4; 10; 21:10(2); 12; 14(2); 22:14; 15; 16; 17; 23:18; 19; 20; 25:12(2); 13; 15; 18; 28; 26:8; 21; 27:5(2); 8; 11; 28:1; 10; 29:7; 30:3; 7(3); 8; 23; 24(2); 31:10; 28; 33; 39; 40; 32:3; 7; 8; 10; 23; 24(3); 28; 29; 31(2); 34; 35; 36; 43(2); 33:2(2); 5; 6; 9(2); 34:2; 22(3); 35:11; 36:1; 3; 7; 9; 15(2); 16; 21(2); 23(3); 28; 32; 37:8(2); 11; 14; 38:3; 15; 18; 20; 25; 39:1; 4; 40:3; 4(3); 5; 9; 15; 41:1; 4(2); 6; 7; 9(2); 13; 42:4(2); 6(3); 7; 16; 17; 20; 21; 43:1; 44:21; 46:10; 20; 23; 26; 47:6; 7(3); 48:1; 2(2); 9; 20(2); 30(2); 39; 44; 49:2; 12; 17; 18; 23; 27; 33; 39; 50:13(2); 15; 21; 29; 32; 38; 39(2); 51:11(2); 33; 62(3); 63(3); 52:3; 4(3); 21(2); 22; 31; **Lam** 1:12; 13; 21; 2:6; 16; 3:22; 26; 27; 28; 37(2); 4:4; 8(2); 11; 15; 5:18; **Eze** 1:1; 4; 13; 16; 26; 27(3); 28; 2:10(2); 3:3(2); 16; 4:1(2); 2(5); 3(4); 4(2); 7; 10; 12(2); 5:1; 2; 5; 13; 15(2); 17; 7:6(2); 10; 19; 20(2); 21(2); 22(2); 8:1; 17; 9:8; 10:1; 6; 7(2); 11; 13; 11:3; 7(2); 13; 12:3; 6(2); 7(2); 11; 13; 23; 25(2); 13:7; 10; 11(3); 12(2); 13(2); 14(2); 15(2); 14:13(3); 14; 15(2); 16; 17; 18; 19(2); 20; 21; 22; 23; 15:3; 4(4); 5(5); 16:14; 15; 16; 19(2); 23; 17:4(2); 5(3); 6(2); 7; 8(4); 9(4); 10(5); 14(2); 19; 21; 22(2); 23(3); 24; 18:4; 20; 19:3(3); 20:1; 9; 14; 22; 28; 42; 47; 48(2); 21:5; 7(3); 10(4); 11(4); 12(2); 13(2); 14; 15(2); 17; 19; 23; 27(4); 28; 30; 32; 22:3; 14(2); 20(2); 30; 23:32; 34(3); 39; 41; 24:3(2); 4(2); 5(3); 6(3); 7(3); 8(2); 10; 11(5); 14(3); 25; 26; 25:3(2); 13(2); 15; 26:1; 5(3); 14; 17; 28:10; 18; 21; 29:3; 9; 11(3); 15(2); 16; 17; 18; 19; 20; 30:3; 6; 9; 12; 20; 21(3); 25; 31:1; 32:1; 15; 17; 33:9; 13; 21; 33; 34:18; 24; 35:2; 3; 7; 10; 15(2); 36:5; 10; 17; 18; 29; 32; 34; 36(2); 37; 37:14(2); 16(2); 26; 38:8; 10; 14; 16; 18; 39:5; 8(2); 11(3); 13; 14; 15(2); 40:22; 25; 26(2); 29(2); 31; 33; 34; 35; 36; 37; 49; 41:15; 18; 19; 42:15; 20(2); 43:3; 11; 17; 18; 20(3); 21; 22; 23; 26; 27; 44:1; 2(4); 3(2); 6; 7; 17; 24; 28; 31; 45:3; 4; 6; 9; 17; 19; 46:1(2); 6; 9; 13; 14; 16; 17(2); 23; 47:5; 9; 10(2); 12; 14(2); 22(2); 23; 48:8; 11; 14(2); 18; 19; 21; 35; **Dan** 1:1; 2:7; 11(2); 40; 41; 44(2); 45; 47; 3:1; 4; 14; 17; 18; 19; 4:2; 12(3); 14; 15; 17(2); 21; 22; 23(2); 25; 27; 31; 32; 5:21; 26; 6:1; 5; 8; 17; 7:4(2); 5(5); 6(2); 7(6); 23(2); 26; 8:2; 8; 10(2); 12(2); 15; 22; 26; 27; 9:13; 14; 27; 11:12; 18; 27; 29; 35; 12:6; 7; **Hos** 1:5; 10(3); 2:7; 16; 21; 6:4; 7:4; 6; 9; 8:4; 5; 6(3); 7(3); 13; 14; 9:7; 10:5(4); 6; 10; 12; 13:2; **Joel** 1:3; 5; 7(2); 15; 2:1; 2; 11; 28; 32; 3:8; 18; **Amos** 1:14; 2:2; 5; 11; 3:6; 4:7(3); 5:6(2); 13; 15; 18; 20; 6:9; 7:1; 2; 3; 4; 13(2); 8:8(2); 9; 10; 12; 9:4; 5(2); 6; 8; 11; **Obad** 15; 18; **Jonah** 1:2; 3; 5; 13; 14; 2:10; 3:2; 7; 10; 4:1; 3; 5; 6(2); 7(2); 8(2); 10; **Mic** 1:5; 7; 9; 10; 2:1(2); 4; 10(2); 13; 3:1; 6; 4:1(3); 4; 8; 5:10; 6:9; 7:3; 10; **Nah** 1:4; 3:1; 7; 8; 9; 15; **Hab** 1:5; 10; 2:2(2); 3(5); 11; 13; 18; 19(3); **Zeph** 1:8; 10; 12; 14; 2:3; 14; 3:16; 18; **Hag** 1:4; 6; 8; 9(3); 2:3(3); 6; 12; 13(2); 18; **Zec** 1:16; 21; 4:2; 3; 7; 9; 5:3(2); 4(4); 6; 8; 11(2); 7:1; 13; 8:6(2); 13; 20; 23; 9:2; 5(2); 10:7; 11:9(2); 10; 11(2); 13; 12:3(2); 9; 13:2; 3; 4; 8; 9; 14:4; 6; 7(3); 8(2); 10; 11; 13; 16; 17; **Mal** 1:8(3); 12; 13(2); 2:2(2); 3; 13; 3:10; 14(2); 16; 4:1; **Mt** 1:22; 2:5; 9; 15; 23; 3:15(2); 4:4; 6; 7; 10; 14; 5:13(2); 15(2); 21; 27; 29(3); 30(3); 31; 33; 34; 35(2); 38; 43; 6:10; 7:2; 7(2); 8; 14; 25(2); 27(2); 28; 8:9; 10; 13; 17; 9:8; 10; 11; 16; 29; 30; 33; 10:11; 12; 13(2); 15; 19; 20; 25; 39(2); 11:1; 10; 12; 14; 16; 22; 23; 24; 26; 12:2; 10; 11(3); 12; 13(2); 15; 17; 24; 32(2); 39; 41; 42; 44; 45; 13:11(2); 19; 20; 23; 27; 32(2); 35; 40; 46; 48; 49; 53; 14:4; 9; 11; 12; 13; 15; 26; 27; 28; 15:5; 26(2); 28; 16:2(2); 3; 4; 7; 11(2); 17; 18; 22; 25(2); 17:4; 6; 20; 18:6; 7; 8; 9(3); 13; 14; 17; 19; 19:1; 3; 8; 9; 10; 11; 12(2); 24; 25; 20:11; 15; 23(2); 24; 26; 21:4; 13(2); 19(2); 20; 21; 25; 32; 33(3); 34; 42; 44(2); 22:5; 17; 39; 23:16; 18(2); 20; 21; 24:23; 24; 26; 33; 25:28; 40(2); 45(2); 26:1; 7; 8; 10; 12; 22; 24(2); 25; 26(3); 27(2); 29; 31; 39; 42; 54; 61; 62; 27:6(2); 24; 29; 35; 40; 48(2); 59; 60; 65; 28:1; 2; **Mk** 1:2; 9; 45; 2:1; 4; 9; 12; 15; 16; 17; 21; 23; 3:4; 5; 21; 4:4(2); 5(3); 6(3); 7(2); 11; 16; 19; 20; 22; 24; 30; 31(2); 32(3); 33; 37; 40; 5:14(2); 16(2); 43; 6:11; 15(2); 16; 18; 22; 23; 28(2); 29(2); 49; 50; 56; 7:6; 11; 18; 19; 24; 27(2); 36; 8:16; 17; 21; 26; 35(2); 36; 9:5; 12; 13; 21; 22; 30; 33; 42; 43(2); 45(2); 47(2); 50; 10:2; 14; 24; 25; 27; 40(2); 41; 43; 47; 11:2; 13; 14(2); 17(2); 18; 30; 12:1(2); 11; 14; 15; 16; 13:11; 14; 22; 29; 14:3; 5; 11; 19(2); 20; 21(2); 22; 23(2); 25; 27; 35; 41; 60; 70; 15:2; 17; 23; 25; 29; 35; 36; 42; 45; 16:4; 13; 18; **Lk** 1:3; 8; 23; 38; 41; 59; 2:1; 6; 15; 17; 18; 20; 23; 26; 43; 46; 49; 3:4; 21; 4:3; 4; 6; 8; 10; 12; 17; 20; 39; 42; 5:1; 8; 12; 17; 6:1; 4; 6; 9(2); 12; 13; 38(2); 48(2); 49; 7:8; 11; 27; 39; 8:1; 5(2); 6(3); 7(2); 10; 15; 16(3); 20; 21; 22; 29; 34; 36; 40; 50; 9:7; 11; 18; 24(2); 28; 33(2); 36; 37; 39; 45(2); 51; 57; 10:6(2); 12; 14; 21; 38; 11:1; 9(2); 10; 14(2); 25; 27; 28; 29; 32; 33; 38; 51; 12:10(2); 32; 49; 50; 54; 55; 56; 13:7(2); 8(3); 9(2); 18; 19(3); 21; 33; 14:1; 3; 18; 22; 28; 29(2); 34; 35(2); 15:4; 5(2); 8; 9; 22; 23; 32; 16:2; 16; 17; 22; 17:1; 2; 6; 11; 14; 22; 26(2); 28; 29; 30; 31; 33(2); 18:15; 25; 26; 35; 36; 43; 19:7; 15; 24; 29; 41; 46(2); 20:1; 4; 7; 9; 13; 16; 18(2); 22; 24; 21:5; 13; 14; 21; 35; 22:16; 17; 19; 22; 23; 36; 38; 44; 64; 66; 23:3; 24; 26; 44; 53(3); 24:4; 10; 15; 21; 24; 29; 30(2); 39; 43; 46(2); 51; **Jn** 1:5; 27; 32; 39; 2:5; 8; 9; 17; 19; 20; 3:8(3); 27; 4:6; 9; 10; 53; 5:10(2); 13; 15; 6:17; 20; 31; 39; 42; 45; 60; 61; 63; 65; 71; 7:7(2); 10; 17; 22; 51; 8:9; 17; 44; 54; 56; 9:4; 14; 27; 32; 37; 10:10; 17; 18(4); 22(2); 34; 11:2; 22; 38(2); 42; 50; 57; 12:14; 24(3); 25(2); 28(2); 29(2); 13:19(2); 24; 25; 26(3); 30; 14:2; 8; 14; 17; 21; 22; 27; 29(2); 15:2(2); 4; 7; 16; 18(2); 16:7; 14; 15; 23; 17:26; 18:10; 11; 14; 18; 25; 28; 31; 34; 19:2; 11; 14; 19; 20; 24(3); 29(2); 30; 31; 35; 40; 20:1; 14; 27; 21:4; 6; 7(2); 8; 12; **Acts** 1:7; 19; 20; 2:2; 3; 15; 17; 21; 24(2); 3:10; 12; 17; 23; 4:3; 5; 10; 14; 16; 17; 19; 37(2); 5:2(2); 4(4); 7; 9; 38; 39(2); 6:2; 15; 7:5(2); 23; 31(2); 42; 44; 53; 9:5; 6; 18; 32; 37; 42; 43; 10:4; 11; 28; 42; 11:4; 5(2); 26; 30; 12:3; 9; 15(2); 18; 22; 13:17; 33; 38; 41; 46(2); 14:1; 6; 15:5; 15; 16; 22; 25; 28; 34; 16:16; 35; 17:14; 18:14; 15(2); 19:1; 19; 39; 20:16; 35; 21:1; 3; 20; 22; 35; 22:6; 10; 17; 22; 25; 23:5; 12; 30; 31; 24:3; 21; 25:16; 27; 26:8; 14; 27:1; 8; 14; 25(2); 28(2); 35; 39(2); 44; 28:8; 17; 19; 22; 28(2); **Rom** 1:16; 17; 19; 2:24; 27; 3:4; 10; 19; 27; 30; 4:3; 10; 16(2); 17; 22; 23(2); 24; 5:16; 6:12; 7:11; 13; 16; 17(2); 20(2); 8:3; 7; 25; 33; 34; 36; 9:12; 13; 16; 20; 26(2); 28; 32(2); 33; 10:8; 15; 11:6(3); 7; 8; 26; 35; 12:8; 18; 19; 13:9; 11; 14:6(2); 11; 14; 20; 21; 22; 15:3; 9; 21; 26; 27; **1Cor** 1:11; 18; 19; 21; 31; 2:8; 9; 3:2; 13(3); 19; 4:2; 3; 7(2); 9; 12; 5:1; 6:5; 13; 7:1; 5; 8; 9; 21(2); 26; 29; 31; 8:7; 9:9; 10; 11; 15(2); 25; 27; 10:7; 13; 16(2); 28; 11:6; 13; 14; 15; 18; 24; 25; 12:6; 15; 16; 18; 26(2); 13:3; 8; 14:7; 9; 10; 15; 21; 26; 27; 34; 35; 36; 15:11; 27; 32; 36; 37; 38(2); 42(2); 43(4); 44(2); 45; 16:4; 6; 15; **2Cor** 1:6(2); 2:10(2); 3:16; 4:3; 13; 5:10; 13(2); 7:8; 11; 12; 8:11; 12; 15; 9:1; 5; 9; 11:15; 17(2); 12:1; 4; 8; 13(2); 16; **Gal** 1:12(2); 13; 15; 2:6; 3:4; 5; 6; 10; 11; 13; 15(2); 17; 18(2); 19(2); 4:15; 18; 22; 27; 29; **Eph** 2:8; 3:5; 4:9; 29; 5:3; 12; 25; 26; 27(2); 29; 6:3; **Phil** 1:6; 7; 20; 27; 29; 2:6; 13; 23; 25; 3:1; 21; S:1; **Col** 1:6(3); 9; 19; 2:14(2); 15; 3:18; 23; 4:4; 16; 17; **1Th** 2:1; 13(2); 3:1; 4; 4:10; 5:24; **2Th** 1:3; 6; 3:1; **1Ti** 1:8; 13; 4:4; 5; 5:16; 6:7; **2Ti** 2:11; 4:16; **Titus** 1; **Philem** 1:14; 19(2); **Heb** 2:10; 17; 3:13; 15; 17; 4:1; 2; 6(2); 7; 6:4; 7(2); 17; 18; 7:8; 11; 14; 15; 8:3; 9:5; 17; 23; 27; 10:4; 7; 31; 11:2; 4; 6; 18; 12:11; 13; 17; 20; 13:9; 17; **Jas** 1:2; 5; 11(2); 15(2); 2:14; 16; 17; 23; 3:6(2); 8; 4:3; 14; 17(2); 5:3; 7; 17(2); **1Pet** 1:7; 11; 12; 16; 2:6; 13; 20(4); 3:3; 4; 11; 17; 4:4; 11; 12; 17; **2Pet** 1:13; 2:13; 21(2); 22; **1Jn** 1:2; 2:18(2); 21; 27; 3:1; 2; 4:3(2); 5:6; 16; **2Jn** 6; **Jude** 3; **Rev** 1:1; 11; 2:17; 3:8; 4:1; 5:6; 6:1; 11; 14; 7:2; 8:3; 5(2); 8; 10(2); 12; 9:4; 5; 6; 7; 9; 10:1; 9(4); 10(3); 11:2(2); 6; 12:4; 13:3; 7; 18; 14:3; 19; 15:2; 16:3; 17; 18:21; 19:6; 10; 15; 20:11; 13; 21:6; 16; 18; 21; 22; 23(2); 24(2); 25; 26; 27; 22:2; 3; 9

ITS

Lev 25:5

ITSELF

2088, 846, 1438, 5565

Gen 1:11; 12; **Lev** 7:24; 17:15; 18:25; 22:8; 25:11; **Deut** 14:21; **1Kin** 7:34; **Job** 10:22; **Ps** 41:6; 68:8; **Prov** 18:2; 23:31; 27:16; 25; **Is** 10:15(4); 37:30; 55:2; 60:20; **Jer** 31:24; **Eze** 1:4; 4:14; 17:14; 29:15; 44:31; **Dan** 7:5; **Mt** 6:34; 12:25(2); **Mk** 3:24; 25; **Lk** 11:17; **Jn** 15:4; 20:7; 21:25; **Rom** 8:16; 21; 26; 14:14; **1Cor** 11:14; 13:4; 5; **2Cor** 10:5; **Eph** 4:16; **Heb** 9:24; **3Jn** 12

LARGE

3027, 4800, 7304, 7337, 7342, *2425, 3173, 4080, 5118*

Gen 34:21; **Ex** 3:8; **Judg** 18:10; **2Sa** 22:20; **Neh** 4:19; 7:4; 9:35; **Ps** 18:19; 31:8; 118:5; **Is** 22:18; 30:23; 33; **Jer** 22:14; **Eze** 23:32; **Hos** 4:16; **Mt** 28:12; **Mk** 14:15; **Lk** 22:12; **Gal** 6:11; **Rev** 21:16

LARGENESS

7341

1Kin 4:29

LEAST

176, 389, 4591, 6810, 6994, 6996, 7535, *1646, 1647, 1848, 2534, 2579, 3398*

Gen 24:55; 32:10; **Num** 11:32; **Judg** 3:2; 6:15; **1Sa** 9:21; 21:4; **2Kin** 18:24; **1Chr** 12:14; **Is** 36:9; **Jer** 6:13; 8:10; 31:34; 42:1; 8; 44:12; 49:20; 50:45; **Amos** 9:9; **Jonah** 3:5; **Mt** 2:6; 5:19(2); 11:11; 13:32; 25:40; 45; **Lk** 7:28; 9:48; 12:26; 16:10(2); 19:42; **Acts** 5:15; 8:10; **1Cor** 6:4; 15:9; **Eph** 3:8; **Heb** 8:11

LEAVE

2308, 3241, 3322, 3498, 3499, 5157, 5203, 5414, 5800, 6168, 7503, 7592, 7604, 7662, 8338, *447, 657, 782, 863, 1459, 1544, 2010, 2641*

Gen 2:24; 28:15; 33:15; 42:33; 44:22(2); **Ex** 16:19; 23:11; **Lev** 7:15; 16:23; 19:10; 22:30; 23:22; **Num** 9:12; 10:31; 22:13; 32:15; **Deut** 28:51; 54; **Josh** 4:3; **Judg** 9:9; 13; **Ruth** 1:16; 2:16; **1Sa** 9:5; 14:36; 20:6; 28; 25:22; **2Sa** 14:7; **1Kin** 8:57; **2Kin** 2:2; 4; 6; 4:30; 43; 13:7; **1Chr** 28:8; **Ezr** 9:8; 12; **Neh** 5:10; 6:3; 10:31; 13:6; **Job** 9:27; 10:1; 39:11; **Ps** 16:10; 17:14; 27:9; 37:33; 49:10; 119:121; 141:8; **Prov** 2:13; 17:14; **Eccl** 2:18; 21; 10:4; **Is** 10:3; 65:15; **Jer** 9:2; 14:9; 17:11; 18:14; 30:11; 44:7; 46:28; 48:28; 49:9; 11; **Eze** 6:8; 12:16; 16:39; 22:20; 23:29; 29:5; 32:4; 39:2; **Dan** 4:15; 23; 26; **Hos** 12:14; **Joel** 2:14; **Amos** 5:3(2); 7; **Obad** 5; **Zeph** 3:12; **Mal** 4:1; **Mt** 5:24; 18:12; 19:5; 23:23; **Mk** 5:13; 10:7; 12:19(2); **Lk** 11:42; 15:4; 19:44; **Jn** 14:18; 27; 16:28; 32; 19:38; **Acts** 2:27; 6:2; 18:18; 21:6; **1Cor** 7:13; **2Cor** 2:13; **Eph** 5:31; **Heb** 13:5; **Rev** 11:2

LEAVING

863, 2641, 5277

Mt 4:13; **Lk** 10:30; **Rom** 1:27; **Heb** 6:1; **1Pet** 2:21

LESS

657, 4295, 4591, 6996, *253, 820, 1640, 1647, 2276, 3398*

Ex 16:17; 30:15; **Num** 22:18; 26:54; 33:54; **1Sa** 22:15; 25:36; **1Kin** 8:27; **2Chr** 6:18; 32:15; **Ezr** 9:13; **Job** 4:19; 9:14; 11:6; 25:6; 34:19; **Prov** 17:7; 19:10; **Is** 40:17; **Eze** 15:5; **Mk** 4:31; 15:40; **1Cor** 12:23; **2Cor** 12:15; **Eph** 3:8; **Phil** 2:28; **Heb** 7:7

LESSER

6996, 7716

Gen 1:16; **Is** 7:25; **Eze** 43:14

LEST

634, 1077, 1115, 3808, 6435, *1519, 2443, 3361, 3379, 3381, 3588*

Gen 3:3; 22; 4:15; 11:4; 14:23; 19:15; 17; 19; 26:7; 9; 32:11; 38:9; 11; 23; 42:4; 44:34; 45:11; **Ex** 1:10; 5:3; 13:17; 19:21; 22; 24; 20:19; 23:29; 33; 33:3; 34:12(2); 15; **Lev** 10:6(2); 7; 9; 19:29; 22:9; **Num** 4:15; 20; 16:26; 34; 18:22; 32; 20:18; **Deut** 1:42; 4:9(2); 16; 19; 23; 6:12; 15; 7:22; 25; 26; 8:12; 9:28; 11:17; 19:6; 20:5; 6; 7; 8; 22:9; 24:15; 25:3; 29:18(2); 32:27(2); **Josh** 2:16; 6:18; 9:20; 24:27; **Judg** 7:2; 14:15; 18:25; **Ruth** 4:6; **1Sa** 9:5; 13:19; 15:6; 20:3; 27:11; 29:4; 31:4; **2Sa** 1:20(2); 12:28; 13:25; 14:11; 15:14; 17:16; 20:6; **2Kin** 2:16; **1Chr** 10:4; **Job** 32:13; 34:30; 36:18; 42:8; **Ps** 2:12; 7:2; 13:3; 4; 28:1; 32:9; 38:16; 50:22; 59:11; 91:12; 106:23; 125:3; 140:8; 143:7; **Prov** 5:6; 9; 10; 9:8; 20:13; 22:25; 24:18; 25:8; 10; 16; 17; 26:4; 5; 30:6; 9(2); 10; 31:5; **Eccl** 7:21; **Is** 6:10; 27:3; 28:22; 36:18; 48:5; 7; **Jer** 1:17; 4:4; 6:8(2); 10:24; 21:12; 37:20; 38:19; 51:46; **Hos** 2:3; **Amos** 5:6; **Zec** 7:12; **Mal** 4:6; **Mt** 4:6; 5:25; 7:6; 13:15; 29; 15:32; 17:27; 25:9; 26:5; 27:64; **Mk** 3:9; 4:12; 13:5; 36; 14:2; 38; **Lk** 4:11; 8:12; 12:58; 14:8; 12; 29; 16:28; 18:5; 21:34; 22:46; **Jn** 3:20; 5:14; 12:35; 42; 18:28; **Acts** 5:26; 39; 13:40; 23:10; 27:17; 29; 42; 28:27; **Rom** 11:21; 25; 15:20; **1Cor** 1:15; 17; 8:9; 13; 9:12; 27; 10:12; **2Cor** 2:3; 7; 11; 4:4; 9:3; 4; 11:3; 12:6; 7(2); 20(2); 21; 13:10; **Gal** 2:2; 4:11; 6:1; 12; **Eph** 2:9; **Phil** 2:27; **Col** 2:4; 8; 3:21; **1Th** 3:5; **1Ti** 3:6; 7; **Heb** 2:1; 3:12; 13; 4:1; 11; 11:28; 12:3; 13; 15(2); 16; **Jas** 5:9; 12; **2Pet** 3:17; **Rev** 16:15

LET

3240, 3381, 5117, 5186, 5414, 6544, 7503, 7725, 7971, *630, 863, 1439, 1554, 1832, 1929, 2010, 2524, 2722, 2967, 5465*

Gen 1:3; 6(2); 9(2); 11; 14(2); 15; 20; 22; 24; 26(2); 11:3; 4(2); 7; 13:8; 14:24; 18:4; 30; 32; 19:8; 20; 32; 34; 21:12; 16; 24:14(3); 17; 18; 44; 45; 46; 51; 55; 60; 26:28(2); 27:29(2); 31; 30:26; 31:32; 35; 44(2); 32:26(2); 33:12(2); 14; 15(2); 34:11; 21(3); 23; 35:3; 37:17; 20; 21; 27(2); 38:16; 23; 24; 41:33; 34(2); 35(2); 42:16; 19; 43:9; 44:9; 10; 18(2); 33(2); 46:30; 47:4; 6; 25; 48:16(2); 49:21; 50:5; **Ex** 1:10; 3:18; 19; 20; 4:18; 21; 23(2); 26; 5:1; 2(2); 3; 4; 7; 8; 9(2); 17; 6:1; 11; 7:14; 16; 8:1; 2; 8; 20; 21; 28; 29; 32; 9:1; 2; 7; 8; 13; 17; 28; 35; 10:3; 4; 7; 10(2); 20; 24(2); 27; 11:1(2); 2; 10; 12:4; 10; 48(2); 13:15; 17; 14:5; 12; 25; 16:19; 29; 17:11; 18:22; 27; 19:10; 22; 24; 20:19; 21:8; 26; 27; 22:7; 13; 23:11; 13; 24:14; 25:8; 32:10; 22; 24; 26; 33:12; 34:3(2); 9; 35:5; 36:6; **Lev** 1:3; 4:3; 10:6; 14:7; 53; 16:10; 22; 26; 18:21; 19:19; 21:17; 24:14(2); 25:27; **Num** 5:8; 6:5; 8:7(2); 8; 9:2; 10:35(2); 11:15; 31; 12:12; 14(2); 13:30; 14:4(2); 17; 16:38; 20:17; 21:22; 27; 22:16; 23:10(2); 27:16; 31:3; 32:5; 33:55; 36:6; **Deut** 2:27; 30; 3:25; 26; 9:14; 13:2(2); 6; 13; 15:12; 13; 18:16(2); 20:3; 5; 6; 7; 8; 21:14; 22:7; 24:1; 25:7; 32:38; 33:6(2); 7; 8; 16; 24(3); **Josh** 2:15; 18; 4:22; 6:6; 7; 7:3(2); 8:22; 9:15; 20; 21(2); 10:28; 30; 22:23; 26; 24:28; **Judg** 1:25; 2:6; 5:31(2); 6:31(2); 32; 39(4); 7:3; 7; 9:15; 19; 20(2); 10:14; 11:17; 19; 37(2); 12:5; 13:8; 12; 13; 14(2); 15; 15:5; 16:30; 18:25; 19:6; 11; 13; 20; 25; 28; 20:32; **Ruth** 2:2; 7; 9; 13; 15; 16; 3:13; 14; 4:12; **1Sa** 1:18; 2:3; 16; 3:18; 19; 4:3; 5:8; 11; 6:6; 9:5; 6; 9; 10; 19; 10:7; 11:14; 13:3; 14:1; 6; 36(3); 16:16; 22; 17:8; 32; 18:2; 17(2); 19:4; 12; 17; 20:3; 5; 11; 16; 29(2); 21:2; 13; 22:3; 15; 24:19; 25:8; 24(2); 25; 26; 27; 41; 26:8; 11; 19(2); 20; 22; 24(2); 27:5; 28:22; 29:4; **2Sa** 1:21(2); 2:7; 14(2); 3:29(2); 5:24; 7:26(2); 29(2); 10:12; 11:12; 25; 13:5; 6; 24; 25; 26; 27; 32; 33; 14:11; 12; 18; 24(2); 32(2); 15:7; 14; 26; 16:9; 10; 11(2); 17:1; 5; 18:19; 22; 23; 19:19; 30; 37(2); 20:11; 21:6; 24:14(2); 17; 22; **1Kin** 1:2(4); 12; 31; 34; 51; 2:6; 7; 21; 3:26; 8:26; 57; 59; 61; 11:21; 22; 17:21; 18:23(2); 24; 36; 40; 19:2; 20; 20:11; 23; 31; 32; 42; 21:7; 22:8; 13; 17; 49; **2Kin** 1:10; 12; 13; 14; 2:9; 16; 4:10(2); 27; 5:8; 24; 6:2(2); 7:4; 13(2); 9:15; 17; 10:19; 25; 11:8; 15; 12:5(2); 13:21; 14:8; 17:27(2); 18:29; 30; 19:10; 20:10; 22:5(2); 23:18(3); **1Chr** 13:2; 3; 16:10; 31(3); 32(2); 17:23; 24(2); 27; 19:13(2); 21:13(2); 17; 23; **2Chr** 1:9; 2:15; 6:17; 40(2); 41(2); 14:7; 11; 15:7; 16:1; 5; 18:7; 12; 16; 19:7; 20:10; 23:6; 14; 25:7; 17; 32:15; 36:23; **Ezr** 1:3; 4; 4:2; 5:15; 17(2); 6:3(2); 4; 5; 7(2); 9; 11(3); 12; 7:23; 26; 10:3(2); 14(2); **Neh** 1:6; 11; 2:3; 7; 17; 18; 4:5; 22; 5:10; 6:2; 7; 10(2); 7:3(2); 9:32; **Est** 1:19(3); 2:2; 3(2); 4; 3:9; 5:4; 8; 12; 14; 6:5; 8; 9; 10; 7:3; 8:5; 9:13(2); **Job** 3:3; 4(3); 5(3); 6(3); 7(2); 8; 9(3); 6:9; 10; 29; 7:16; 19; 9:34(2); 10:20; 11:14; 13:13(2); 21; 22; 15:31; 16:18; 21:2; 27:6; 7; 30:11; 31:6; 8(3); 10(2); 22; 40; 32:21(2); 34:4(2); 34(2); 40:2; **Ps** 2:3; 5:10; 11(3); 6:10(2); 7:5(2); 9; 9:19(2); 10:2; 17:2(2); 18:46; 19:13; 14; 20:9; 22:8; 25:2(2); 3(2); 20; 21; 31:1; 17(3); 18; 33:8(2); 22; 34:3; 35:4(2); 5(2); 6(2); 8(3); 19(2); 24; 25(2); 26(2); 27(3); 36:11(2); 40:11; 14(2); 15; 16(2); 43:3(2); 48:11(2); 55:15(2); 57:5; 11; 58:7(2); 8; 59:10; 12; 13; 14(2); 15; 66:7; 67:3(2); 4; 5(2); 68:1(3); 2; 3(3); 69:6(2); 14(2); 15(3); 22(2); 23; 24; 25(2); 27; 28; 29; 34; 70:2(2); 3; 4(3); 71:1; 8; 13(2); 72:19; 74:8; 21(2); 76:11; 78:28; 79:8; 10; 11; 80:17; 83:4; 12; 17(2); 85:8; 88:2; 90:13; 16; 17; 95:1(2); 2; 6(2); 96:11(3); 12; 97:1(2); 98:7; 8(2); 99:1(2); 3; 102:1; 104:35(2); 105:3; 20; 106:48; 107:2; 22; 32; 109:6; 7(2); 8(2); 9; 10(2); 11(2); 12(2); 13(2); 14(2); 15; 17(2); 18; 19; 20; 28(3); 29(2); 118:2; 3; 4; 119:10; 41; 76; 77; 78; 79; 80; 116; 122; 133; 169; 170; 173; 175(2); 122:1; 129:5; 6; 130:2; 7; 131:3; 132:9(2); 137:5; 6; 140:9; 10(2); 11; 141:2; 4; 5(2); 10; 145:21; 148:5; 13; 149:2(2); 3(2); 5(2); 6; 150:6; **Prov** 1:11(2); 12; 14; 3:1; 3; 21; 4:4; 13; 21; 25(2); 26; 5:16; 17; 18; 19(2); 6:25; 7:18(2); 25; 9:4; 16; 17:12; 19:18; 23:17; 26; 24:17; 27:2; 28:17; 31:7; 31; **Eccl** 5:2(2); 9:8(2); 11:8; 9; 12:13; **Song** 1:2; 2:14(2); 3:4; 4:16; 7:11(2); 12(2); 8:11; **Is** 1:18; 2:3; 5; 3:6; 4:1; 5:19(2); 7:6(2); 8:13(2); 16:4; 19:12(2); 21:6; 22:13; 26:10; 27:5; 29:1; 34:1; 36:14; 15; 37:10; 38:21; 41:1(4); 22(2); 42:11(3); 12; 43:9(4); 13; 26; 44:7; 11(2); 45:8(4); 9; 13; 21; 47:13; 50:8(2); 10; 54:2; 55:2; 7(2); 56:3(2); 57:13; 58:6; 66:5; **Jer** 2:28; 4:5; 5:24; 6:4; 5(2); 8:14(2); 9:18; 20; 23(3); 24; 11:19(2); 20; 12:1; 14:17(2); 15:1; 19; 17:15; 18(4); 18:18(3); 21(3); 22; 23; 20:12; 14; 16(2); 23:28(2); 27:11; 18; 29:8; 31:6; 34:9; 10(2); 11; 14(2); 35:11; 36:19; 37:20; 38:4; 6; 11; 24; 40:1; 5; 15; 42:2; 46:6; 9; 16; 48:2; 49:11; 50:5; 26; 27; 29; 33; 51:3; 9; 10; 50; **Lam** 1:22; 2:18(2); 3:40; 41; **Eze** 1:24; 25; 3:27(2); 7:12; 9:5; 11:3; 13:20; 21:14; 24:5; 6; 10; 39:7; 43:9; 10; 44:6; 45:9; **Dan** 1:12; 13; 2:7; 4:14; 15(2); 16(3); 19; 23(2); 27; 5:10(2); 12; 17; 9:16; 10:19; **Hos** 2:2; 4:4; 15; 17; 6:1; 13:2; **Joel** 1:3; 2:1; 16; 17(2); 3:9(2); 10; 12; **Amos** 4:1; 5:24; **Obad** 1; **Jonah** 1:7; 14; 3:7(2); 8(2); **Mic** 1:2; 4:2; 11(2); 6:1; 7:14; **Hab** 2:16; 20; **Zeph** 3:16; **Zec** 3:5; 7:10; 8:9; 13; 17; 21; 11:9(3); **Mal** 2:15; **Mt** 5:16; 31; 37; 40; 6:3; 7:4; 8:22; 10:13(2); 11:15; 13:9; 30; 43; 15:4; 14; 16:24; 17:4; 18:17; 19:6; 12; 20:26; 27; 21:19; 33; 38(2); 41; 24:15; 16; 17; 18; 26:39; 46; 27:22; 23; 42; 43; 49(2); **Mk** 1:24; 38; 2:4; 4:9; 23; 35; 7:10; 16; 27; 8:34; 9:5; 10:9; 11:6; 12:1; 7; 13:14(2); 15; 16; 14:6; 42; 15:32; 36(2); **Lk** 2:15; 3:11(2); 4:34; 5:4; 5; 19; 6:42; 8:8; 22; 9:23; 33; 44; 60; 61; 12:35; 13:8; 14:4; 35; 15:23; 16:29; 17:31(2); 20:9; 14; 21:21(3); 22:26; 36(2); 68; 23:22; 35; **Jn** 7:37; 8:7; 11:7; 15; 16; 44; 48; 12:7; 26; 14:1; 27(2); 31; 18:8; 19:12; 24; **Acts** 1:20(3); 2:29; 36; 3:13; 4:17; 21; 23; 5:38; 40; 9:25; 10:11; 11:5; 15:33; 36; 16:35; 36; 37; 17:9; 19:38; 23:9; 22; 24:20; 23; 25:5; 27:15; 30; 32; 28:18; **Rom** 1:13; 3:4; 8; 6:12; 11:9; 10; 12:6; 7; 8; 9; 13:1; 12(2); 13; 14:3(2); 5; 13; 16; 19; 15:2; **1Cor** 1:31; 3:10; 18(2); 21; 4:1; 5:8; 7:2(2); 3; 9; 10; 11(2); 12; 13; 15; 17; 18(2); 20; 24; 36(2); 10:8; 9; 12; 24; 11:6(2); 28(2); 34; 14:13; 26; 27(2); 28(2); 29(2); 30; 34; 35; 37; 38; 40; 15:32; 16:2; 11; 14; 22; **2Cor** 7:1; 9:7; 10:7; 11; 17; 11:16; 33; **Gal** 1:8; 9; 5:25; 26; 6:4; 6; 9; 10; 17; **Eph** 4:26; 28(2); 29; 31; 5:3; 6; 24; 33; **Phil** 1:27; 2:3(2); 5; 3:15; 16(2); 4:5; 6; **Col** 2:16; 18; 3:15; 16; 4:6; **1Th** 5:6(2); 8; **2Th** 2:3; 7; **1Ti** 2:11; 3:10(2); 12; 4:12; 5:4; 9; 16(2); 17; 6:1; 2; 8; **2Ti** 2:19; **Titus** 2:15; 3:14; **Philem** 1:20; **Heb** 1:6; 2:1; 4:1; 11; 14; 16; 6:1; 10:22; 23; 24; 12:1(2); 13; 28; 13:1; 5; 13; 15; **Jas** 1:4; 5; 6; 7; 9; 13; 19; 3:13; 4:9; 5:12; 13(2); 14(2); 20; **1Pet** 3:3; 4; 10; 11(2); 4:11(2); 15; 16(2); 19; **1Jn** 2:24; 3:7; 18; 4:7; **Rev** 2:7; 11; 17; 29; 3:6; 13; 22; 13:9; 18; 19:7; 22:11(4); 17(3)

LETTING

Ex 8:29

LIKE

251, 1571, 1819, 1821, 1823, 1825, 1922, 2088, 2421, 2654, 2803, 3541, 3644, 3651, 4711, 4911, 4915, 5973, 5974, 7737, *407, 499, 871, 1381, 1503, 2470, 2472, 2504, 2532, 3663, 3664, 3665, 3666, 3667, 3779, 3945, 3946, 4832, 5024, 5108, 5613, 5615, 5616, 5618*

Gen 13:10; 25:25; **Ex** 7:11; 8:10; 9:14; 24; 11:6(2); 15:11(2); 16:31(2); 23:11; 24:17; 25:33(2); 34; 28:11; 21; 36; 30:32; 33; 34; 38; 34:1; 4; 37:19; 20; 39:8; 14; 30; **Lev** 13:2; **Num** 23:10; **Deut** 4:32; 7:26; 10:1; 3; 17:14; 18:8; 15; 18; 22:3; 25:7; 8; 29:23; 33:17(2); 26; 29; 34:10; **Josh** 10:14; **Judg** 7:12; 11:17; 13:6; 16:12; 17; **Ruth** 2:13; 4:11(2); 12; **1Sa** 2:2; 4:9(2); 8:5; 20; 10:24; 17:7; 19:24; 21:9; 25:36; 26:15; **2Sa** 7:9; 22; 23(2); 18:27; 21:19; 22:34; **1Kin** 3:12(2); 13; 5:6; 7:8(2); 26; 33; 8:23; 10:20; 12:32; 16:3; 7; 18:44; 20:25; 27; 21:22(2); 25; 22:13; **2Kin** 3:2(2); 5:14; 9:9(2); 20; 13:7; 14:3; 16:2; 17:14; 15; 18:5; 32; 23:25(2); 25:17; **1Chr** 4:27; 11:23; 12:8; 22; 14:11; 17:8; 20; 21; 20:5; 27:23; **2Chr** 1:9; 12; 4:5; 6:14; 9:19; 18:12; 21:6; 13; 19; 22:4; 28:1; 30:7(2); 26; 33:2; 35:18; **Neh** 6:5; 13:26; **Est** 2:20; **Job** 1:8; 2:3; 3:24; 5:26; 7:1; 8:2; 10:10; 11:12; 12:25; 13:12; 14:2; 9; 15:16; 16:14; 19:10; 20:7; 21:11; 30:19; 32:19; 34:7(2); 36:22; 38:3; 40:7; 9(2); 17; 18; 41:18; 31(2); 33; 42:8; **Ps** 1:3; 4; 2:9; 7:2; 17:12; 18:33; 22:14(2); 15; 28:1; 29:6(2); 31:12; 35:10; 36:6; 37:2; 35; 39:11; 44:11; 49:12; 14; 20; 52:2; 8; 55:6; 58:4(2); 8; 59:6; 14; 64:3; 71:19; 72:6; 16(2); 73:5; 77:20; 78:16; 27; 52(2); 57(2); 65; 69(2); 79:3; 5; 80:1; 10; 82:7(2); 83:11(2); 13; 86:8(2); 88:5; 17; 89:8; 46; 90:5; 92:10; 12(2); 97:5; 102:3; 4; 6(2); 9; 11(2); 26; 103:5; 13; 104:2; 105:41; 107:27; 41; 109:18(3); 23; 113:5; 114:4(2); 6(2); 115:8; 118:12; 119:83; 119; 176; 126:1; 128:3; 133:2; 135:18; 140:3; 143:7; 144:4; 147:16(2); 17; **Prov** 12:18; 17:22; 18:19; 20:5; 23:32(2); 25:11; 14; 19; 28; 26:4; 17; 23; 28:3; 31:14; **Song** 2:9; 17; 3:6; 4:2; 3(2); 4; 5; 11; 5:13; 6:12; 7:1; 2(2); 3; 4; 5(2); 7; 8; 9; 8:10; 14; **Is** 1:9; 18; 2:6; 3:18; 5:28(2); 29(2); 30; 9:18; 10:6; 13; 16; 11:7; 16; 13:4; 14:10; 14; 19; 16:11; 17:12(2); 13(2); 18:4(2); 19:16; 20:3; 22:18; 24:20(2); 26:17; 27:10; 29:5; 30:33; 31:4; 33:4; 9; 36:17; 38:12; 14; 40:11; 42:13; 14; 46:5; 9; 48:19; 49:2; 50:7; 51:3(2); 6(3); 8(2); 53:6; 57:20; 58:1; 11(2); 59:10; 11(2); 19; 63:2; 64:6; 65:25; 66:12(2); 14; 15; **Jer** 2:30; 4:4; 5:19; 6:23; 9:3; 12; 10:6; 7; 16; 11:19; 12:3; 14:6; 17:6; 21:12; 23:9(2); 29(2); 24:2; 5; 25:34; 26:6; 9; 18; 29:17; 22(2); 30:7; 31:28; 32:42; 36:32; 38:9; 46:8(2); 20; 21; 22; 48:6; 28; 36(2); 38; 49:19(2); 50:42(2); 44(2); 51:19; 33; 34; 38; 40(2); 55; 52:22; **Lam** 1:6; 12; 21; 2:3; 4(2); 13; 18; 19; 3:52; 4:3; 8; 5:10; **Eze** 1:7(2); 13(2); 16; 24; 2:8; 5:9; 7:16; 12:11; 13:4; 16:16; 18:10; 14; 19:10; 20:36; 22:25; 27; 23:18; 20; 25:8; 26:4; 14; 19; 27:32(2); 31:2; 8(3); 18; 32:2; 14; 36:35; 37; 38:9(2); 40:3; 25; 41:25; 42:11; 43:2; 3; 45:25; **Dan** 1:19; 2:35; 3:25; 4:33(2); 5:11; 21(2); 7:4; 5; 6; 8; 9(2); 13; 10:6(3); 16; 18; 11:40; **Hos** 2:3; 4:9(2); 5:10(2); 6:7; 7:6; 11; 16; 9:10; 11; 11:10; 13:8; 14:8; **Joel** 1:8; 2:2; 5(2); 7(2); 9; **Amos** 2:9; 5:6; 6:5; 9:5; 9; **Jonah** 1:4; **Mic** 1:8; 4:10; 7:17(2); 18; **Nah** 1:6; 2:4(2); 8; 3:12; 15; **Hab** 3:19; **Zeph** 1:17; 2:13; **Zec** 1:6; 5:9; 9:15; 10:7; 12:6(2); 14:5; 20; **Mal** 3:2(2); **Mt** 3:16; 6:8; 29; 11:16; 12:13; 13:31; 33; 44; 45; 47; 52; 20:1; 21:24; 22:2; 39; 23:27; 28:3; **Mk** 1:10; 4:31; 7:8; 13; 12:31; 13:29; **Lk** 3:22; 6:23; 47; 48; 49; 7:31; 32; 12:27; 36; 13:18; 19; 21; 20:31; **Jn** 1:32; 7:46; 8:55; 9:9; **Acts** 1:11; 2:3; 3:22; 7:37; 8:32; 11:17; 14:15; 17:29; 19:25; **Rom** 1:23; 28; 6:4; 9:29; **1Cor** 16:13; **Gal** 5:21; **Phil** 3:21; **1Th** 2:14; **1Ti** 2:9; **Heb** 2:17; 4:15; 7:3; **Jas** 1:6; 23; 5:17; **1Pet** 3:21; **2Pet** 1:1; **1Jn** 3:2; **Jude** 7; **Rev** 1:13; 14; 15; 2:18(2); 4:3(2); 6; 7(3); 9:7(2); 10; 19; 11:1; 13:2; 4; 11; 14:14; 16:13; 18:18; 21; 21:11(2); 18

LIKEWISE

1571, 2063, 3162, 3651, *36, 437, 2532, 3668, 3779, 3898, 5615*

Ex 22:30; 26:4; 27:11; 36:11; **Lev** 7:1; **Deut** 9:23; 12:30; 15:17; 22:3; **Judg** 1:3; 7:5; 17; 8:8; 9:49; **1Sa** 14:22; 19:21; 31:5; **2Sa** 1:11; 17:5; **1Kin** 11:8; **1Chr** 10:5; 18:8; 19:15; 23:30; 24:31; 27:4; 28:16; 17; 29:24; **2Chr** 3:11; 29:22; **Neh** 4:22; 5:10; **Est** 1:18; 4:16; **Job** 31:38; 37:6; **Ps** 49:10; 52:5; **Eccl** 7:22; **Is** 30:24; **Jer** 40:11; **Eze** 13:17; 40:16; 46:3; **Nah** 1:12; **Mt** 17:12; 18:35; 20:5; 10; 21:30; 36; 22:26; 24:33; 25:17; 26:35; 27:41; **Mk** 4:16; 12:21; 14:31; 15:31; **Lk** 2:38; 3:11; 14; 5:33; 6:31; 10:32; 37; 13:3; 5; 14:33; 15:7; 10; 16:25; 17:10; 28; 31; 19:19; 21:31; 22:20; 36; **Jn** 5:19; 6:11; 21:13; **Acts** 3:24; **Rom** 1:27; 6:11; 8:26; 16:5; **1Cor** 7:3; 4; 22; 14:9; **Gal** 2:13; **Col** 4:16; **1Ti** 3:8; 5:25; **Titus** 2:3; 6; **Heb** 2:14; **Jas** 2:25; **1Pet** 3:1; 7; 4:1; 5:5; **Jude** 8; **Rev** 8:12

LOW

120, 1809, 3665, 3766, 4295, 4355, 6030, 6819, 7817, 8213, 8216, 8217, 8219, 8482, *5011, 5013, 5014*

Deut 28:43; **Judg** 11:35; **1Sa** 2:7; **1Chr** 27:28; **2Chr** 9:27; 26:10; 28:18; 19; **Job** 5:11; 14:21; 24:24; 40:12; **Ps** 49:2; 62:9; 79:8; 106:43; 107:39; 116:6; 136:23; 142:6; **Prov** 29:23; **Eccl** 10:6; 12:4(2); **Is** 2:12; 17; 13:11; 25:5; 12; 26:5(2); 29:4; 32:19(2); 40:4; **Lam** 3:55; **Eze** 17:6; 24; 21:26; 26:20; **Lk** 1:48; 52; 3:5; **Rom** 12:16; **Jas** 1:9; 10

LOWER

2637, 8217, 8481, 8482, *1642, 2737*

Gen 6:16; **Lev** 13:20; 21; 26; 14:37; **Neh** 4:13; **Ps** 8:5; 63:9; **Prov** 25:7; **Is** 22:9; 44:23; **Eze** 40:18; 19; 42:5; 43:14; **Eph** 4:9; **Heb** 2:7; 9

LOWEST

7048, 8481, 8482, *2078*

Deut 32:22; **1Kin** 12:31; 13:33; **2Kin** 17:32; **Ps** 86:13; 88:6; 139:15; **Eze** 41:7; 42:6; **Lk** 14:9; 10

MADE

752, 1129, 1443, 2342, 2672, 3322, 3335, 3627, 3738, 3772, 3835, 4639, 5221, 5414, 5648, 5927, 5975, 6087, 6213, 6235, 6466, 6555, 6743, 7194, 7236, 7495, 7502, 7543, 7737, 7739, 7760, 7761, 7896, *208, 272, 319, 347, 461, 591, 626, 770, 805, 871, 886, 1080, 1096, 1107, 1165, 1215, 1232, 1239, 1295, 1303, 1392, 1402, 1511, 1517, 1519, 1586, 1642, 1659, 1743, 1770, 1839, 1861, 2005, 2049, 2090, 2092, 2134, 2227, 2301, 2390, 2427, 2525, 2559, 2673, 2680, 2721, 2722, 2749, 2758, 2841, 3021, 3076, 3182, 3421, 3447, 3471, 3489,*

3666, 3670, 3822, 3903, 3982, 4087, 4147, 4160, 4161, 4198, 4222, 4364, 4483, 4692, 4732, 4776, 4832, 4955, 4982, 5014, 5048, 5055, 5087, 5293, 5319, 5487, 5499

Gen 1:7; 16(2); 25; 31; 2:2(2); 3; 4; 9; 22; 3:1; 7; 5:1; 6:6; 7; 7:4; 8:1; 6; 9:6; 13:4; 14:2; 23; 15:18; 17:5; 19:3; 33; 35; 21:6; 8; 27; 32; 23:17; 20; 24:11; 21; 37; 46(2); 26:22; 30; 27:14; 30; 31; 37; 29:22; 30:37; 31:46; 33:17; 37:3; 7; 9; 39:3; 4; 5; 23; 40:20; 41:43(2); 51; 42:7; 43:25; 28; 30; 45:1; 8; 9; 46:29; 47:26; 49:24; 33; 50:5; 6; 10; **Ex** 1:13; 14(2); 21; 2:14; 4:11; 5:21; 7:1; 9:20; 14:6; 21; 15:17; 25(2); 16:31; 18:25; 20:11; 24:8; 25:31; 33(2); 34; 26:31; 29:18; 25; 33; 36; 41; 30:20; 31:17; 18; 32:4; 5; 8; 20(2); 25; 31; 35(2); 34:8; 27; 35:21; 29(2); 36:4; 8(2); 11(2); 12(2); 13; 14(2); 17(2); 18; 19; 20; 23; 24; 25; 27; 28; 31; 33; 34; 35(2); 36; 37; 37:1; 2; 4; 6; 7(2); 8; 10; 11; 12(2); 15; 16; 17(2); 19(2); 20; 23; 24; 25; 26; 27; 28; 29; 38:1; 2; 3(2); 4; 6; 7; 8; 9; 22; 28; 30; 39:1(2); 2; 4; 8; 9; 15; 16; 19; 20; 22; 24; 25; 27; 30; 42; **Lev** 1:9; 13; 17; 2:2; 3; 7; 8; 9; 10; 11(2); 16; 3:3; 5; 9; 11; 14; 16; 4:35; 5:12; 6:17; 18; 21; 7:5; 25; 30; 35; 8:21; 28; 10:12; 13; 15; 13:48; 51; 14:11; 36; 16:17; 20; 21:6; 21; 22:5; 27; 23:8; 13; 18; 25; 27; 36(2); 37; 43; 24:7; 9; 26:13; 46; **Num** 4:15; 26; 5:8; 27; 6:4; 8:4; 21; 11:8; 14:36; 15:10; 13; 14; 25; 16:31; 39; 47; 18:17; 20:5; 21:9; 25:13; 28:2; 3; 6; 8; 13; 19; 24; 29:6; 13; 36; 30:12(2); 31:20(2); 32:13; **Deut** 1:15; 2:30; 4:23; 36; 5:2; 3; 9:9; 12; 16; 21; 10:3; 5; 22; 11:4; 18:1; 20:9; 26:12; 19; 29:1; 25; 31:16; 24; 32:6; 13(2); 15; 45; **Josh** 2:17; 20; 5:3; 8:15; 24; 28; 9:4; 15(2); 16; 27; 10:1; 4; 5; 20; 11:18; 19; 13:14; 14:8; 19:49; 51; 22:25; 28; 24:25; **Judg** 2:1; 3:16; 18; 5:13(2); 6:2; 19; 8:27; 33; 9:6; 16; 18; 27; 11:4; 5; 11; 13:10; 15; 14:10; 15:17; 16:19; 25; 27; 17:4; 5; 18:24; 27; 31; 21:5; 15; **1Sa** 2:19; 28; 3:13; 4:18; 8:1; 9:22; 10:13; 11:15; 12:1; 8; 13:10; 12; 14:14; 15:17; 33; 35; 16:8; 9; 10; 18:1; 3; 13; 20:16; 22:8; 23:18; 26; 24:16; 25:18; 27:10; 12; 30:11; 14; 21; 25; **2Sa** 2:9; 3:6; 20; 4:4; 5:3; 6:5; 8; 18; 7:9; 10:19; 11:13; 19; 12:31; 13:6; 8; 10; 36; 14:15; 15:4; 17:25; 22:5; 12; 36; 23:5; **1Kin** 1:41; 43; 2:24; 3:1(2); 7; 15; 4:7; 5:12; 6:4; 5; 6; 7; 21; 23; 31; 33; 7:6; 7; 8; 16; 18; 23; 27; 29; 37; 38; 40(3); 45; 48; 51; 8:9; 21; 38; 54; 59; 9:3; 26; 10:9; 12; 16; 17; 18; 20; 27(2); 11:28; 12:4; 10; 14; 18; 20; 28; 31(2); 32(2); 33; 13:33; 14:7; 9; 15; 16; 26; 27; 15:12; 13; 22; 26; 30; 34; 16:2(2); 13; 16; 26; 33; 18:26; 32; 20:34(2); 21:22; 22:11; 39; 44; 48; 52; **2Kin** 3:2; 3; 7:6; 8:20; 9:21; 10:16; 25; 27; 29; 31; 11:4; 12; 17; 12:13; 20; 13:2; 6; 7; 11; 14:19; 21; 24; 15:9; 15; 18; 24; 28; 30; 16:3; 11; 17:8; 15; 16(2); 19; 21(2); 29(2); 30(3); 31; 32; 35; 38; 18:4; 19:15; 20:20; 21:3; 6; 7; 11; 16; 24; 22:7; 23:3; 4; 12(2); 15(2); 19; 30; 34; 24:13; 17; 25:16; 22; 23; **1Chr** 5:10; 19; 9:30; 31; 11:3; 12:18; 13:11; 15:1; 13; 16:2; 5; 16; 26; 17:8; 18:8; 19:6; 19; 21:29; 22:8; 23:1; 5; 26:10; 32; 28:2; 19; 29:2; 5; 19; 22; **2Chr** 1:3; 5; 8; 9; 11; 15(2); 2:11; 12; 3:8; 10; 14; 15; 16(2); 4:1; 2; 6; 7; 8(2); 9; 11; 14(2); 18; 19; 21; 5:1; 10; 6:11; 13; 29; 40; 7:1; 6; 7; 9; 15; 9:8; 11; 15; 16; 17; 19; 27(2); 10:4; 10; 14; 18; 11:12; 15; 17; 22; 12:9; 10; 13:8; 9; 15:16; 16:14(2); 17:10; 18:10; 20:23; 27; 36; 21:7; 8; 11; 13; 19; 22:1; 23:3; 11; 16; 24:8; 9; 10; 14; 17; 25:5; 16; 27; 26:1; 5; 13; 15; 28:2; 19; 24; 25; 29:17; 24(2); 29; 32:5; 27; 33:3; 7; 9; 22; 25; 34:4; 31; 33; 35:14; 25; 36:1; 4; 10; 13; 22; **Ezr** 1:1; 4:15; 19(3); 23; 5:13; 14; 17(2); 6:1(2); 3; 11(2); 12; 22; 10:5; 7; 17; **Neh** 3:16; 4:7; 9; 6:9; 8:4; 16; 17; 9:6; 18; 10:32; 12:43; 13:13; 25; 26; **Est** 1:3; 5; 9; 2:17; 18(2); 23; 5:14(2); 7:9; 9:17; 18; 19; **Job** 1:10; 17; 2:11; 4:14; 7:3; 10:8; 9; 15:7; 16:7(2); 17:6; 13; 28:18; 26; 31:1; 15; 24; 33:4; 38:9; 39:6; 40:15; 19; 41:33; **Ps** 7:12; 15(2); 8:5; 9:15; 18:4; 11; 35; 43; 21:6(2); 30:1; 7; 8; 33:6; 39:5; 45:1; 8; 46:8; 49:16; 50:5; 52:7; 60:2; 3; 69:11; 72:15; 74:17; 77:6; 78:13; 50; 52; 55; 64; 86:9; 88:8; 89:3; 39; 42; 43; 44; 47; 91:9; 92:4; 95:5; 96:5; 98:2; 100:3; 103:7; 104:24; 26; 105:9; 21; 24; 28; 106:19; 46; 111:4; 115:15; 118:24; 119:60; 73; 98; 126; 121:2; 124:8; 129:3; 134:3; 136:5; 7; 14; 139:14; 15; 143:3; 146:6; 148:6; 149:2; **Prov** 8:26; 11:25; 13:4; 14:33; 15:19; 16:4; 20:9; 12; 21:11; 22:19; 28:25; **Eccl** 1:15; 2:4; 5; 6; 3:11; 7:3; 13; 29; 10:19; **Song** 1:6; 3:9; 10; 6:12; **Is** 2:8; 17; 20; 5:2; 14:3; 16; 17; 16:10; 17:4; 8; 21:2; 22:11; 25:2; 26:14; 27:11; 28:15(2); 22; 25; 29:16(2); 30:33; 31:7; 34:6; 7; 37:16; 40:4(2); 41:2; 43:7; 24; 44:2; 45:12; 18; 46:4; 49:1; 2(2); 17; 51:10; 12; 52:10; 53:9; 12; 57:8; 16; 59:8; 63:17; 66:2; 8; **Jer** 1:18; 2:7; 15; 28; 5:3; 8:8; 10:11; 12; 25; 11:10; 12:10; 11(2); 13:22; 27; 14:22; 17:23; 18:4(2); 19:11; 20:8; 25:17; 26:8; 27:5; 29:26; 31:32; 32:17; 20; 34:8; 13; 15; 18; 36:25; 37:1; 15; 38:16; 40:5; 7; 41:2; 9; 18; 43:1; 46:10; 16; 49:10; 51:7; 15; 34; 63; 52:20; **Lam** 1:13; 14; 2:7; 8; 3:4; 7; 9; 11; 15; 45; **Eze** 3:8; 9; 17; 6:6; 7:20; 13:5; 6; 22(2); 16:24; 25; 17:13; 16; 24; 19:5; 20:5; 9; 28; 21:15; 21; 24; 22:4(2); 13; 25; 26:10; 15; 27:5; 6(2); 11; 24; 25; 29:3; 9; 18; 31:4; 6; 9; 16; 36:3; 39:26; 40:14; 17; 41:18; 19; 20; 25(2); 42:15; 43:23; 46:23; **Dan** 2:5; 15; 17; 23(2); 38; 45; 48(2); 3:1; 10; 15; 29; 4:5; 6; 5:1; 11; 21; 29; 7:4; 16; 21; 9:1; 4; 13; 11:23; 12:10; **Hos** 5:9; 7:5; 6; 8:4(2); 6; 11; 10:1; 12:4; 13:2; **Joel** 1:7(2); 18; **Amos** 4:10; 5:26; 7:2; 7; **Obad** 2; **Jonah** 1:9; 16; 4:5; 6; **Nah** 2:3; 11; **Hab** 2:17; 3:9; **Zeph** 3:6; **Zec** 7:12; 9:13; 10:3; 11:10; **Mal** 2:9; **Mt** 4:3; 9:16; 22(2); 11:1; 14:36; 15:6; 28; 18:25; 19:4(2); 12(2); 20:12; 21:13; 22:2; 5; 23:15; 24:45; 25:6; 16; 26:19; 27:24; 64; 66; **Mk** 2:21; 27; 5:34; 6:21; 56; 8:25; 10:6; 52; 11:17; 14:4; 16; 58(2); 15:7; **Lk** 1:62; 2:2; 15; 17; 3:5(2); 4:3; 5:29; 8:17; 48; 50; 9:15; 11:40; 12:14; 13:13; 14:12; 16; 17:19; 19:6; 46; 22:13; 23:12; 19; 24:22; 28; **Jn** 1:3(3); 10; 14; 31; 2:9; 15; 3:21; 4:1; 46; 5:4; 6; 9; 11; 14; 15; 7:23; 8:33; 9:3; 6; 11; 14; 39; 12:2; 15:15; 17:23; 18:18; 19:7; 23; **Acts** 1:1; 2:28; 36; 3:12; 16; 25; 4:9; 24; 35; 7:10; 13(2); 27; 35; 41; 43; 48; 50; 8:2; 3; 9:39; 10:10; 17; 12:5; 20; 21; 13:32; 14:2; 5; 15; 15:7; 16:13; 24; 17:24(2); 26; 18:12; 19:24; 26; 33; 20:28; 21:40; 22:6; 23:13; 26:6; 27:40; **Rom** 1:3; 20; 23; 2:25; 4:14(2); 17; 5:19(2); 6:18; 22; 7:13; 8:2; 20; 9:20; 29; 10:10; 20; 11:9; 14:21; 15:8; 27; 16:26(2); **1Cor** 1:17; 20; 30; 3:13; 4:9; 13; 7:21; 9:19; 22; 11:19; 12:13; 14:25; 15:22; 45(2); **2Cor** 2:2; 3:6; 10; 4:10; 11; 5:1; 11(2); 21(2); 7:8(2); 9(2); 14; 10:16; 11:6; 12:9; **Gal** 3:3; 13; 16; 19; 4:4(2); 5:1; **Eph** 1:6; 9; 2:6; 11; 13; 14; 3:3; 5; 7; 5:13; **Phil** 2:7(2); 3:10; 4:6; **Col** 1:12; 20; 23; 25; 26; 2:11; 15; **1Ti** 1:9; 19; 2:1; **2Ti** 1:10; **Titus** 3:7; **Heb** 1:2; 4; 2:9; 17; 3:14; 5:5; 9; 6:4; 13; 20; 7:3; 12; 16; 19; 20; 21; 22; 26; 8:9; 13; 9:2; 8; 11; 24; 10:3; 13; 33; 11:3; 22; 34; 40; 12:23; 27; **Jas** 1:10; 2:22; 3:9; **1Pet** 2:7; 3:22; **2Pet** 1:16; 2:12; **1Jn** 2:19; 4:17; 18; 5:10; **Rev** 1:6; 5:10; 7:14; 8:11; 14:7; 8; 15:4; 17:2; 18:15; 19(2); 19:7

MADEST

3045, 3772, 6213, 387, 1642

Neh 9:8; 14; **Ps** 8:6; 80:15; 17; **Eze** 16:17; 29:7; **Jonah** 4:10; **Acts** 21:38; **Heb** 2:7

MAKE

1124, 1254, 1443, 2015, 3331, 3335, 3635, 3772, 3823, 5414, 5674, 6014, 6213, 6381, 7760, 7761, 7896, 8074, *142, 347, 805, 1107, 1303, 1325, 1510, 1519, 1659, 1710, 1793, 2005, 2090, 2116, 2146, 2165, 2350, 2433, 2476, 2511, 2525, 2625, 2673, 2675, 2758, 2936, 2973, 3076, 3753, 3856, 3868, 4052, 4062, 4087, 4115, 4121, 4122, 4135, 4137, 4160, 4170, 4294, 4336, 4400, 4621, 4679, 4692, 4766, 4820, 4921, 4931, 5037, 5055, 5087, 5319, 5461*

Gen 1:26; 2:18; 3:6; 21; 6:14(2); 15; 16(2); 9:12; 11:3; 4; 12:2(2); 13:16; 17:2; 6(2); 20(2); 18:6(2); 19:32; 34; 21:13; 18; 24:3; 26:4; 28; 27:4; 7; 9; 28:3; 31:44; 32:12; 34:9; 30; 35:1; 3; 40:14; 43:16; 46:3; 47:6(2); 48:4(2); 20; **Ex** 5:5; 7; 8; 16; 12:4; 18:16; 20:4; 23(2); 24; 25; 21:34; 22:3; 5; 6; 11; 12; 13; 14; 15; 23:13; 27; 32; 33; 25:8; 9; 10; 11; 13; 17; 18(2); 19(2); 23; 24; 25(2); 26; 28; 29(2); 31; 37; 39; 40; 26:1(2); 4(2); 5(2); 6; 7(2); 10; 11; 14; 15; 17; 18; 19; 22; 23; 26; 29; 31; 36; 37; 27:1; 2; 3(2); 4(2); 6; 8(2); 9; 28:2; 3; 4(2); 6; 11; 13; 14; 15(3); 22; 23; 26; 27; 31; 33; 36; 39(2); 40(3); 42; 29:2; 37; 30:1(2); 3; 4(2); 5; 10(2); 15; 16; 18; 25; 32; 35; 37(2); 38; 31:6; 32:1; 10; 23; 30; 33:19; 34:10; 12; 15; 16; 17; 35:10; 33; 36:3; 5; 6; 7; 22; **Lev** 1:4; 4:20; 26; 31; 35; 5:6; 10; 13; 16(2); 18; 6:7; 8:15; 34; 9:7(2); 10:17; 11:43(2); 47; 12:7; 8; 14:18; 19; 20; 21; 29; 31; 53; 15:15; 30; 16:6; 10; 11; 16; 17; 18; 24; 27; 30; 32; 33(3); 34; 17:11; 19:4; 22; 28; 20:25; 21:5(2); 22:22; 24; 23:22; 28; 24:18; 25:9; 26:1; 6; 9; 19; 22; 31; 27:2; **Num** 5:21(2); 22; 6:7; 11; 25; 8:7; 12; 19; 10:2(2); 12:6; 14:4; 12; 30; 15:3(2); 25; 28(2); 38; 16:13; 30; 38; 46; 17:5; 21:8; 23:19; 28:22; 30; 29:5; 30:8; 13; 15; 31:23(2); 50; **Deut** 1:11; 13; 4:10; 16; 23; 25; 5:8; 7:2; 3; 8:3; 9:14; 10:1; 13:14; 14:1; 15:1; 16:18; 21; 19:18; 20:9; 11; 12(2); 21:14; 16; 22:8; 12; 26:19; 28:11; 13; 21; 24; 59; 29:1; 14; 30:9; 32:26; 35; 39; 42; **Josh** 1:8; 5:2; 6:5; 10; 18(2); 7:3; 19; 9:6; 7; 11; 22:25; 23:7; 12; **Judg** 2:2; 9:48; 16:25; 17:3; 20:38; **Ruth** 3:3; 4:11; **1Sa** 1:6; 2:8; 24; 29; 3:12; 6:5; 7; 8:5; 12; 22; 9:12; 11:1; 2; 12:22; 13:19; 17:25; 18:25; 20:38; 22:7; 25:28; 28:2; 15(2); 29:4; **2Sa** 3:12; 13; 21; 7:11; 21; 23; 11:25; 13:5; 6; 15:14; 20; 17:2; 21:3; 23:5; **1Kin** 1:37; 47(2); 2:42; 8:29; 33; 47; 9:22; 11:34; 12:1; 4; 9; 10; 16:3; 19; 21; 17:13(2); 19:2; 20:34; 21:22; **2Kin** 3:16; 4:10; 5:7; 6:2; 7:2; 19; 9:2; 9; 21; 10:5; 18:30; 31; 21:8; 23:10; **1Chr** 6:49; 11:10; 12:31; 38(2); 16:8; 42; 17:21; 22; 21:3; 22:5; 28:4; 29:12; **2Chr** 4:11; 16; 5:13; 6:21; 22; 24; 7:11; 20; 8:8; 9; 10:1; 10; 11:22; 14:7; 20:36; 25:8; 29:10; 24; 30:5; 35:21; **Ezr** 5:3; 4; 9; 6:8; 7:13; 21; 10:3; 11; **Neh** 2:4; 8; 4:2; 8:12; 15; 9:38; 10:33; **Est** 1:20; 4:8(2); 5:5; 6:10; 7:7; 9:22; **Job** 5:18; 8:5; 6; 9:15; 30; 11:3(2); 19(2); 13:11; 21; 23; 15:24; 18:2; 11; 19:3; 20:2; 22:27; 24:11; 25(2); 28:25; 31:15; 33:7; 34:29; 35:9; 39:20; 27; 40:19; 41:3; 4; 6; 28; **Ps** 5:8; 6:6; 11:2; 21:9; 12(2); 22:9; 31:16; 34:2; 36:8; 38:22; 39:4; 8; 40:13; 17; 41:3; 45:16; 17; 46:4; 51:6; 8; 55:2; 57:1; 59:6; 14; 64:8; 66:1; 2; 8; 69:23; 70:1(2); 5(2); 71:12; 16; 78:5; 81:1; 83:2; 11; 13; 15; 84:6; 87:4; 89:1; 27; 29; 90:15; 95:1; 2; 98:4(2); 6; 100:1; 104:15; 17; 105:1; 106:8; 110:1; 115:8; 119:27; 35; 135; 132:17; 135:18; 139:8; 141:1; 142:1; 145:12; **Prov** 1:16; 23; 6:3; 14:9; 20:18; 25; 22:21; 24; 23:5; 24:6; 27; 27:11; 30:26; **Eccl** 2:24; 7:13; 16; **Song** 1:11; 8:14; **Is** 1:15; 16; 3:7; 5:19; 6:10(2); 7:6; 10:23; 11:3; 15; 12:4; 13:12; 20; 14:23; 16:3; 17:2; 11(2); 12(2); 19:10; 23:16; 25:6; 26:13; 27:5(2); 28:9; 16; 29:21; 32:6; 11; 33:1; 34:15; 36:15; 16; 37:9; 38:12; 13; 16; 19; 40:3; 41:15(2); 18; 42:15(2); 16; 21; 43:19; 44:9; 19; 45:2; 7; 14; 46:5; 47:2; 48:1; 15; 49:11; 17; 50:2; 3; 51:3; 4; 52:5; 53:10; 54:3; 12; 55:3; 56:7; 57:4; 58:4; 11; 59:7; 60:13; 15; 17; 61:8; 62:6; 7; 63:6; 12; 14; 64:2; 66:22; **Jer** 4:7; 16; 27; 30; 5:10; 14; 18; 6:8; 26; 7:16; 18; 9:11(2); 18; 10:22; 13:16; 15:14; 20; 16:6; 20; 18:4; 11; 16; 19:7; 8; 12; 20:4; 9; 22:6; 23:15; 16; 25:9; 12; 18; 26:6(2); 27:2; 18; 28:13; 29:17; 22; 30:10; 11(2); 19; 31:4; 13; 21; 31; 33; 32:40; 34:17; 22; 44:19; 46:27; 28(2); 48:26; 49:15; 16; 19; 20; 50:3; 44; 45; 51:11; 12; 25; 29; 36; 39(2); 57; **Lam** 4:21; **Eze** 3:26; 4:9; 5:14; 6:14; 7:14; 23; 24; 11:13; 12:23; 13:18; 20(2); 14:8; 15:8; 16:42; 17:17; 18:31; 20:17; 26; 31; 21:10(2); 22:30; 23:27; 24:5; 9; 17; 25:4; 5; 13; 26:4; 8; 12(2); 14; 19; 21; 27:5; 31; 29:10; 12; 30:9; 10; 12(2); 14; 21; 32:7; 8; 10; 14; 15; 34:25; 26; 28; 35:3; 7; 9; 11; 14; 37:19; 22; 26; 39:7; 42:20; 43:18; 27; 44:14; 45:15; 17; **Dan** 1:10; 2:5; 9; 25; 26; 30; 3:29; 4:6; 7; 18; 25; 32; 5:8; 15; 16(2); 17; 6:7; 26; 8:16; 19; 9:24(2); 27; 10:14; 11:6; 35; 44; **Hos** 2:3; 6; 12; 18(2); 5:2; 7:3; 10:11; 11:8; 12:1; 9; **Joel** 2:19; **Amos** 6:10; 8:4; 10; 9:14; **Mic** 1:6; 8; 16; 2:12; 3:5; 4:4; 7; 13(2); 6:13; 16; **Nah** 1:8; 9; 14; 2:1; 5; 3:6; 14; 15(2); **Hab** 2:2; 18; 3:2; 19(2); **Zeph** 1:18; 2:13; 3:13; 20; **Hag** 2:23; **Zec** 6:11; 9:15; 17; 10:1; 12:2; 3; 6; **Mal** 2:15; 3:17; **Mt** 1:19; 3:3; 4:19; 5:36; 8:2; 12:16; 33(2); 17:4; 22:44; 23:5; 14; 15(2); 25; 24:47; 25:21; 23; 27:65; **Mk** 1:3; 17; 40; 3:12; 5:39; 6:39; 9:5; 12:36; 40; 42; 14:15; **Lk** 1:17; 3:4; 5:12; 33; 34; 9:14; 33; 52; 11:39; 40; 12:37; 42; 44; 14:18; 31; 15:19; 29; 32; 16:9; 17:8; 19:5; 20:43; 47; 22:12; **Jn** 1:23; 2:16; 6:10; 15; 8:32; 36; 10:24; 14:23; **Acts** 2:28; 35; 7:40; 44; 9:34; 22:1; 18; 23:23; 26:16; 24; **Rom** 1:9; 3:3; 31; 9:21; 22; 23; 28; 13:14; 14:4; 19; 15:18; 26; **1Cor** 4:5; 6:15; 8:13(2); 9:15; 18; 10:13; **2Cor** 2:2; 9:5; 8; 10:12; 12:17; 18; **Gal** 2:18; 3:17; 6:12; **Eph** 2:15; 3:9; 5:13; 6:19; 21; **Col** 1:27; 4:4; 9; **1Th** 3:12; **2Th** 3:9; **2Ti** 3:15; 4:5; **Heb** 1:13; 2:10; 17; 7:25; 8:5(2); 8; 10; 9:9; 10:1; 16; 12:13; 13:21; **Jas** 3:18; **1Pet** 5:10; **2Pet** 1:8; 10; 2:3; **1Jn** 1:10; **Rev** 3:9(2); 12; 10:9; 11:7; 10; 12:17; 13:4; 7; 14; 17:14; 16; 19:11; 19; 21:5

MAKER

3335, 6213, 6466, 6467, *1217*

Job 4:17; 32:22; 35:10; 36:3; **Ps** 95:6; **Prov** 14:31; 17:5; 22:2; **Is** 1:31; 17:7; 22:11; 45:9; 11; 51:13; 54:5; **Jer** 33:2; **Hos** 8:14; **Hab** 2:18(2); **Heb** 11:10

MAKEST

6213, 7760, 7896, *2744, 4160*

Judg 18:3; **Job** 13:26; 22:3; **Ps** 4:8; 39:11; 44:10; 13; 14; 65:8; 10; 80:6; 104:20; 144:3; **Song** 1:7; **Is** 45:9; **Jer** 22:23; 28:15; **Eze** 16:31; **Hab** 1:14; 2:15; **Lk** 14:12; 13; **Jn** 8:53; 10:33; **Rom** 2:17; 23

MAKETH

3772, 5414, 6213, 6466, 7737, 7760, *393, 1252, 1308, 1793, 2165, 2390, 2525, 2617, 4160, 4977, 5241, 5319*

Ex 4:11; **Lev** 7:7; 14:11; 17:11; **Deut** 18:10; 20:20; 21:16; 24:7; 27:15; 18; 29:12; **1Sa** 2:6; 7(2); **2Sa** 22:33; 34; **Job** 5:18; 9:9; 12:17; 25; 15:27; 23:16; 25:2; 27:18; 35:11; 36:27; 41:31(2); 32; **Ps** 9:12; 18:32; 33; 23:2; 29:6; 9; 33:10; 40:4; 46:9; 104:3; 4; 15; 107:29; 36; 41; 113:9; 135:7; 147:8; 14; **Prov** 10:1; 4; 22; 12:4; 25(2); 13:7(2); 12; 15:13; 20; 30; 16:7; 18:16; 19:4; 28:20; 31:22; 24; **Eccl** 3:11; 7:7; 8:1; 10:19; 11:5; **Is** 19:17; 24:1(2); 27:9; 40:23; 43:16; 44:13; 15(2); 17; 24; 25(2); 46:6; 55:10; 59:15; **Jer** 4:19; 10:13; 17:5; 21:2; 29:26; 27; 48:28; 51:16; **Eze** 22:3; **Dan** 2:28; 29; 6:13; 11:31; 12:11; **Amos** 4:13; 5:8(2); **Nah** 1:4; **Mt** 5:45; **Mk** 7:37; **Lk** 5:36; **Jn** 19:12; **Acts** 9:34; **Rom** 5:5; 8:26; 27; 34; 11:2; **1Cor** 4:7; **2Cor** 2:2; 14; **Gal** 2:6; **Eph** 4:16; **Heb** 1:7; 7:28(2); **Rev** 13:13; 21:27; 22:15

MAN'S

120, 312, 376, 582, 606, 1167, 1397, *245, 435, 442, 444, 3494, 3762, 5100*

Gen 8:21(2); 9:5; 6; 16:12; 20:3; 42:11; 25; 35; 43:21; 44:1; 26; **Ex** 4:11; 12:44; 21:35; 22:5; 7; 30:32; **Lev** 7:8; 15:16; 20:10; **Num** 5:10; 12; 17:2; 5; 33:54; **Deut** 20:19; 24:2; 6; **Judg** 7:16; 22; 19:26; **Ruth** 2:19; **1Sa** 12:4; 14:20; 17:32; **2Sa** 12:4; 17:18; 25; **1Kin** 18:44; **2Kin** 12:4; 23:8; 25:9; **Est** 1:8; **Job** 10:5; 32:21; **Ps** 104:15; **Prov** 10:15; 12:14; 13:8; 16:7; 9; 18:4; 11; 16; 20; 19:21; 20:24; 27:9; 29:23; 26; **Eccl** 2:14; 8:1; 5;

9:16; 10:2; 12; **Is** 8:1; 13:7; **Jer** 3:1; 23:36; **Eze** 4:15; 10:8; 38:21; 39:15; 40:5; **Dan** 4:16; 5:5; 7:4; 8:16; **Amos** 6:10; **Jonah** 1:14; **Mic** 7:6; **Mt** 10:36; 41; 12:29; **Mk** 3:27; 12:19; **Lk** 6:22; 12:15; 16:12; 21; 20:28; **Jn** 18:17; **Acts** 5:28; 7:58; 11:12; 13:23; 17:29; 18:7; 20:33; 27:22; **Rom** 5:17; 19; 14:4; 15:20; **1Cor** 2:4; 13; 3:13(2); 14; 15; 4:3; 10:29; **2Cor** 4:2; 10:16; **Gal** 2:6; 3:15; **2Th** 3:8; **Jas** 1:26; **1Pet** 1:17; **2Pet** 2:16

MANY

1995, 3513, 3605, 7227, 7230, 7231, 7233, 7235, 7690, *2425, 3745, 4119, 4183, 4214, 5118*

Gen 17:4; 5; 21:34; 37:3; 23; 32; 34; **Ex** 5:5; 19:21; 23:2; 35:22; **Lev** 15:25; 25:51; **Num** 9:19; 10:36; 13:18; 22:3; 24:7; 26:54; 56; 35:8(2); **Deut** 1:11; 46; 2:1; 10; 21; 3:5; 7:1; 15:6(2); 25:3; 28:12; 31:17; 21; 32:7; **Josh** 11:4; 22:3; **Judg** 3:1; 7:2; 4; 8:30; 9:40; 16:24; **1Sa** 2:5; 6:19; 14:6; 25:10; **2Sa** 1:4; 2:23; 12:2; 22:17; 23:20; 24:3; **1Kin** 2:38; 4:20; 7:47; 11:1; 17:15; 18:1; 25; 22:16; **2Kin** 9:22; **1Chr** 4:27; 5:22; 7:4; 22; 8:40; 11:22; 21:3; 23:11; 17; 28:5; **2Chr** 11:23; 14:11; 16:8; 18:15; 26:10; 29:31; 30:17; 18; 32:23; **Ezr** 3:12(2); 5:11; 10:13(2); **Neh** 5:2; 6:17; 18; 7:2; 9:28; 30; 13:26; **Est** 1:4; 2:8; 4:3; 8:17; **Job** 4:3; 11:19; 13:23; 16:2; 23:14; 41:3; **Ps** 3:1; 2; 4:6; 18:16; 22:12; 25:19; 29:3; 31:13; 32:10; 34:12; 19; 37:16; 40:3; 5; 55:18; 56:2; 61:6; 71:7; 78:38; 93:4; 106:43; 110:6; 119:84; 157; 129:1; 2; **Prov** 4:10; 6:35; 7:26(2); 10:21; 14:20; 19:4; 6; 21; 28:2; 27; 29:26; 31:29; **Eccl** 5:7; 6:3(2); 11; 7:29; 11:1; 8(2); 12:9; 12; **Song** 8:7; **Is** 1:15; 2:3; 4; 5:9; 8:7; 15; 17:12; 13; 22:9; 23:16; 24:22; 31:1; 32:10; 42:20; 52:14; 15; 53:11; 12; 58:12; 60:15; 61:4; 66:16; **Jer** 3:1; 5:6; 11:15; 12:10; 13:6; 14:7; 16:16(2); 20:10; 22:8; 25:14; 27:7; 28:8; 32:14; 35:7; 36:32; 37:16; 42:2; 46:11; 16; 50:41; 51:13; **Lam** 1:22; **Eze** 3:6; 12:27; 16:41; 17:7; 9; 17; 19:10; 22:25; 26:3; 27:3; 15; 33; 32:3; 9; 10; 33:24; 37:2; 38:6; 8(2); 9; 15; 17; 22; 23; 39:27; 43:2; 47:7; 10; **Dan** 2:48; 8:25; 26; 9:27; 10:14; 11:12; 14; 18; 26; 33(2); 34; 39; 40; 41; 44; 12:2; 3; 4; 10; **Hos** 3:3; 4; 8:11; **Joel** 2:2; **Amos** 8:3; **Mic** 4:2; 3; 11; 13; 5:7; 8; **Nah** 1:12; 3:15(2); **Hab** 2:8; 10; **Zec** 2:11; 7:3; 8:20; 22; **Mal** 2:6; 8; **Mt** 3:7; 7:13; 22(2); 8:11; 16; 30; 9:10; 10:31; 13:3; 17; 58; 14:36; 15:30; 34; 16:9; 10; 21; 19:30; 20:16; 28; 22:9; 10; 14; 24:5(2); 10; 11(2); 12; 25:21; 23; 26:28; 60; 27:13; 19; 52; 53; 55; **Mk** 1:34(2); 2:2; 15(2); 3:10(2); 4:2; 33; 5:9; 26(2); 6:2; 13(2); 20; 31; 33; 34; 38; 56; 7:4; 8; 13; 8:5; 19; 20; 31; 9:12; 26; 10:31; 45; 48; 11:8; 12:5; 41; 13:6(2); 14:24; 56; 15:3; 4; 41; **Lk** 1:1; 14; 16; 2:34; 35; 3:18; 4:25; 27; 41; 7:11; 21(2); 47; 8:3; 30; 32; 9:22; 10:24; 41; 11:8; 53; 12:7; 19; 47; 13:24; 14:16; 15:13; 17; 29; 17:25; 21:8; 22:65; 23:8; 9; **Jn** 1:12; 2:12; 23; 4:39; 41; 6:9; 60; 66; 7:31; 40; 8:26; 30; 10:20; 32; 41; 42; 11:19; 45; 47; 55; 12:11; 37; 42; 14:2; 16:12; 17:2; 19:20; 20:30; 21:11; 25; **Acts** 1:3; 5; 2:39; 40; 43; 3:24; 4:4; 6; 34; 5:11; 12; 36; 37; 8:7(2); 25; 9:13; 23; 42; 43; 10:27; 45; 12:12; 13:31; 43; 48; 14:21; 15:32; 35; 16:18; 23; 17:12; 18:8; 19:18; 19; 20:8; 19; 21:10; 20; 24:10; 17; 25:7; 14; 26:9; 10; 27:7; 20; 28:10; 23; **Rom** 2:12(2); 4:17; 18; 5:15(2); 16; 19(2); 6:3; 8:14; 29; 12:4; 5; 15:23; 16:2; **1Cor** 1:26(3); 4:15; 8:5(2); 10:5; 17; 33; 11:30(2); 12:12(2); 14; 20; 14:10; 16:9; **2Cor** 1:11(2); 2:4; 6; 17; 4:15; 6:10; 8:22; 9:2; 12; 11:18; 12:21; **Gal** 1:14; 3:4; 10; 16; 27; 4:27; 6:12; 16; **Phil** 1:14; 3:15; 18; **Col** 2:1; **1Ti** 6:1; 9; 10; 12; **2Ti** 1:18; 2:2; **Titus** 1:10; **Heb** 2:10; 5:11; 7:23; 9:28; 11:12; 12:15; **Jas** 3:1; 2; **2Pet** 2:2; **1Jn** 2:18; 4:1; **2Jn** 7; 12; **3Jn** 13; **Rev** 1:15; 2:24; 3:19; 5:11; 8:11; 9:9; 10:11; 13:15; 14:2; 17:1; 18:17; 19:6; 12

MATTER

1419, 1697, 4406

Gen 24:9; 30:15; **Ex** 18:16; 22(2); 26; 23:7; **Num** 16:49; 25:18(2); 31:16; **Deut** 3:26; 17:8; 19:15; 22:26; **Ruth** 3:18; **1Sa** 10:16; 20:23; 39; 30:24; **2Sa** 1:4; 18:13; 19:42; 20:18; 21; **1Kin** 8:59; 15:5; **1Chr** 26:32; 27:1; **2Chr** 8:15; 24:5; **Ezr** 5:5(2); 17; 10:4; 9; 14; 15; 16; **Neh** 6:13; **Est** 2:23; 9:26; **Job** 19:28; 32:18; **Ps** 45:1; 64:5; **Prov** 11:13; 16:20; 17:9; 18:13; 25:2; **Eccl** 5:8; 10:20; 12:13; **Jer** 38:27; **Eze** 9:11; 16:20; **Dan** 1:14; 2:10; 23; 3:16; 4:17; 7:28(2); 9:23; **Mk** 1:45; 10:10; **Acts** 8:21; 11:4; 15:6; 17:32; 18:14; 19:38; 24:22; **1Cor** 6:1; **2Cor** 7:11; 9:5; **Gal** 2:6; **1Th** 4:6; **Jas** 3:5

MATTERS

1419, 1697, 4406

Ex 24:14; **Deut** 17:8; **1Sa** 16:18; **2Sa** 11:19; 15:3; 19:29; **2Chr** 19:11(2); **Neh** 11:24; **Est** 3:4; 9:31; 32; **Job** 33:13; **Ps** 35:20; 131:1; **Dan** 1:20; 7:1; **Mt** 23:23; **Acts** 18:15; 19:39; 25:20; **1Cor** 6:2; **1Pet** 4:15

MAY

194, 3201, *1410, 1832, 2481*

Gen 1:20; 3:2; 8:17; 9:16; 11:4; 7; 12:13; 16:2(2); 18:19; 19:5; 32; 34; 21:30; 23:4; 9; 24:14; 49; 56; 27:4(2); 7; 10(2); 19; 21; 25; 31; 29:21; 30:3; 25; 31:37; 32:5; 42:2; 16; 43:8; 14; 18; 44:21; 26; 46:34; 47:19; 49:1; **Ex** 2:7; 20; 3:18; 4:5; 23; 5:1; 9; 7:4; 16; 19(2); 8:1; 8(2); 9; 16; 20; 28; 29; 9:1; 13; 15; 16; 22; 10:2; 3; 7; 12; 17; 21(2); 25; 11:7; 9; 12:16; 13:9; 14:4; 12; 26; 16:4; 32; 17:2; 6; 19:9; 20:12; 20; 21:14; 23:11; 12(2); 25:8; 14; 28; 37; 26:5; 11; 27:5; 28:1; 3(2); 4; 28; 37; 38(2); 41; 29:46; 30:16; 29; 30; 31:6; 13; 15; 32:10(2); 29; 33:5; 13(2); 35:34; 40:13; 15; **Lev** 7:24; 30; 10:10; 11; 11:21; 22; 34(2); 39; 47(2); 14:8; 16:13; 30; 17:5(2); 13; 19:25; 21:3; 22:5(2); 12; 23:21; 43; 24:7; 25:27; 29(2); 31; 32; 34; 35; 36; 48(2); 49(3); **Num** 3:6; 4:19; 6:20; 7:5; 8:11; 9:7; 10:10; 11:13; 16; 21; 13:2; 15:39; 40; 16:21; 45; 18:2; 19:3; 22:6(2); 19; 25:4; 27:17(4); 20; 30:13(2); 31:23; 32:32; 35:6; 11; 15; 17; 18; 23; 36:8; **Deut** 2:6(2); 28(2); 4:1; 2; 10(2); 40; 5:1; 14; 16(2); 31; 33(3); 6:2; 3(2); 18; 7:4; 8:1; 18; 9:5; 14; 10:11; 11:8; 9; 18; 21; 12:15; 25; 28; 13:17; 14:10; 20; 21; 29; 17:19; 20; 19:3; 4; 12; 13; 21:16; 22:7; 19; 29; 23:20; 24:2; 4; 13; 19; 25:1; 3; 15; 26:12; 29:9; 13(2); 29; 30:12; 13; 19; 31:5; 12(2); 13; 14; 19; 26; 28; **Josh** 2:16; 3:4; 7; 4:6; 9:19; 10:4; 18:6; 8; 20:3; 4; 22:27(2); 28; **Judg** 1:3; 2:22; 6:30; 9:7; 11:6; 37; 13:14; 17; 14:13; 15; 15:12; 16:5(2); 25; 26(2); 28; 17:9; 18:5; 9; 19:9; 22; 20:10; 13; 21:18; **Ruth** 1:9; 11; 2:16; 3:1; 4:4; 14; **1Sa** 1:22; 2:36; 4:3; 6:8; 8:20(2); 9:16; 26; 27; 11:2; 3; 12; 12:7; 17; 14:6; 24; 15:25; 30; 17:10; 46; 18:21(2); 19:15; 20:5; 27:5; 28:7; 29:4; 8; 30:22; **2Sa** 3:21; 7:10; 29; 9:1; 3; 10; 11:15; 12:22; 13:5; 6; 10; 14:7; 15; 32; 15:20; 16:2; 4; 11; 12; 18:14; 19:26; 37; 20:16; 21:3; 24:2; 3; 12; 21; **1Kin** 1:2; 35; 2:4; 3:9; 8:29; 40; 43(2); 50; 52; 58; 60; 11:21; 36; 12:6; 9; 13:6; 16; 18; 15:19; 17:10; 12(2); 18:5; 37; 20:9; 21:2; 10; 22:8; 20; **2Kin** 3:11; 17; 4:22; 41; 42; 43; 5:12; 6:2; 13; 17; 20; 22; 28; 29; 7:9; 9:7; 18:27; 32; 19:4; 19; 22:4; **1Chr** 4:10; 13:2; 15:12; 16:35; 17:24; 27; 21:2; 10; 22(2); 23:25; 28:8; **2Chr** 1:10; 6:20; 31; 33(2); 7:16; 10:9; 12:8; 13:9; 16:3; 18:7; 19; 28:23; 29:10; 30:8; 35:6; **Ezr** 4:15; 6:10; 7:25; 9:8; 12; **Neh** 2:5; 7; 8; 4:22; 5:2; **Est** 2:3; 3:9; 4:11; 5:5; 14; 6:9; 8:8; **Job** 1:5; 5:11; 10:20; 13:13; 14:6; 19:29; 21:3; 22:2; 27:17; 31:6; 32:20; 33:17; 34:22; 36; 35:8(2); 36:25(2); 37:7; 12; 38:34; 35; 39:15(2); **Ps** 9:14; 20; 10:10; 18; 11:2; 22:17; 26:7; 27:4; 30:5; 12; 34:12; 39:4; 13; 41:10; 48:13; 50:4; 51:8; 56:13; 58:8; 59:13; 60:4; 5; 61:7; 8; 64:4; 65:4; 67:2; 68:23; 69:35; 71:3; 73:28; 76:7; 83:4; 16; 18; 84:3; 85:6; 9; 86:17; 90:12; 14; 101:6; 8; 104:9; 14; 106:5(3); 107:36; 37; 108:6; 109:15; 27; 111:6; 113:8; 119:17; 18; 73; 77; 116; 125; 124:1; 129:1; 142:7; 144:12(2); 13(2); 14; **Prov** 5:2; 7:5; 8:11; 21; 15:24; 18:2; 20:21; 22:19; 27:1; 11; **Eccl** 1:10; 2:26; 5:15; 6:10; 8:4; **Song** 4:16; 6:1; 13; **Is** 5:8; 11; 19(2); 7:15; 10:2(2); 19; 13:2; 19:15; 24:10; 26:2; 27:5; 28:12; 21; 30:1; 8; 18(2); 36:12; 37:4; 20; 41:20; 22; 23(2); 26(2); 42:18; 43:9; 10; 44:9; 13; 45:6; 46:5; 49:15; 20; 51:14; 16; 23; 55:6; 10; 60:11(2); 21; 64:2; 65:8; 66:11(2); **Jer** 6:10; 7:18; 23; 9:12(2); 17(2); 18; 10:18; 11:5; 19; 13:23; 26; 16:12; 21:2; 26:3; 28:14; 29:6(2); 32:14; 39; 33:21; 35:7; 36:3(3); 7; 42:3(3); 6; 12; 44:29; 46:10; 48:9; 49:19; 50:34; 44; 51:8; 39; **Lam** 2:13; 3:29; **Eze** 4:17; 6:6(4); 8; 11:20; 12:3; 16; 19; 14:5; 11(3); 15; 16:33; 37; 20:20; 21:5; 10; 11; 15; 19; 20; 23; 22:3; 23:48; 24:11(4); 25:10; 28:17; 34:10; 37:9; 38:16; 39:12; 17; 43:10; 11; 44:25; 30; 45:11; **Dan** 4:17; 27; 6:15; **Hos** 8:4; 13:10; **Amos** 5:14; 15; 6:10; 8:5(2); 6; 9:1; 12; **Obad** 9; **Jonah** 1:7; 11; **Mic** 6:5; 7:3; **Hab** 2:2; 9(2); **Zeph** 2:3; 3:8; 9; **Zec** 11:1; **Mal** 3:2; 3; 10; **Mt** 2:8; 5:16; 45; 6:2; 4; 5; 16; 9:6; 21; 14:15; 18:16; 19:16; 20:21; 33; 23:26; 35; 26:42; **Mk** 1:38; 2:10; 4:12(2); 32; 5:12; 23; 28; 6:36; 7:9; 10:17; 37; 11:25; 12:15; 14:7; 15:32; **Lk** 2:35; 5:24; 8:16; 9:12; 11:33; 50; 12:36; 14:10; 23; 16:4; 9; 24; 28; 17:8; 18:41; 20:13; 14; 21:22; 36; 22:8; 30; 31; **Jn** 1:22; 3:21; 4:36; 5:20; 6:5; 7; 30; 40; 50; 7:3; 10:38; 11:11; 15; 16; 42; 12:36; 13:18; 19; 14:3; 13; 16; 31; 15:2; 16; 16:4; 24; 17:1; 11; 21(3); 22; 23(2); 24; 26; 19:4; **Acts** 1:25; 3:19; 4:29; 30; 6:3; 8:19; 20; 22; 17:19; 19:40; 21:24(2); 37; 23:24; 25:11; 26:18; **Rom** 1:11(2); 12; 19; 3:8; 19(2); 6:1; 8:17; 11:10; 14; 31; 12:2; 14:2; 19; 15:6; 13; 17; 31(2); 32(2); **1Cor** 1:8; 2:16; 3:18; 5:5; 7; 7:5; 32; 33; 34(2); 35(2); 9:18; 24; 10:13; 33; 11:19; 14:1; 5; 10; 12; 13; 31(3); 15:28; 37; 16:6(2); 10; 11; **2Cor** 1:4; 11; 2:5; 4:7; 5:9; 10; 12; 8:11; 14(3); 9:3; 8; 10:2; 9; 11:2; 12(2); 16; 12:9; **Gal** 6:13; **Eph** 1:17; 18; 3:4; 17; 18; 4:15; 28; 29; 6:3; 11; 13; 19(2); 20; 21; **Phil** 1:9; 10(2); 26; 27; 2:15; 16; 19; 28(2); 3:8; 10; 12; 21; 4:17; **Col** 1:28; 4:4; 6; 12; **1Th** 3:13; 4:12(2); **2Th** 1:5; 12; 3:1; 2; 14; **1Ti** 1:20; 2:2; 4:15; 5:7; 16; 20; 6:19; **2Ti** 1:4; 18; 2:4; 10; 26; 3:17; 4:16; **Titus** 1:9; 13; 2:4; 8; 10; **Philem** 1:6; **Heb** 4:16; 5:1; 7:9; 10:9; 12:27; 28; 13:6; 17; 19; **Jas** 1:4; 2:18; 3:3; 4:3; 5:16; **1Pet** 2:2; 12; 15; 3:1; 16; 4:3; 11; 13; 5:6; 8; **2Pet** 1:15; 3:2; 14; **1Jn** 1:3; 4; 2:28; 4:17; 5:13(2); 20; **2Jn** 12; **Rev** 2:10; 14:13; 19:18; 22:14(2)

MAYEST

3201, *1410, 1832*

Gen 2:16; 23:6; 28:3; 4; 38:16; **Ex** 3:10; 8:10; 22; 9:14; 29; 10:2; 18:19; 24:12; 26:33; **Lev** 22:23; **Num** 10:2; 31; 23:13; 27; **Deut** 2:31; 4:40; 6:18; 7:22; 8:9; 11:14; 15; 12:15; 17; 20; 23; 14:21; 23; 15:3; 16:3; 5; 20; 17:15; 20:19; 22:3; 7; 23:20; 24; 25; 26:19; 27:3; 28:58; 30:6; 14; 16; 20(4); **Josh** 1:7(2); 8; **Judg** 9:33; 11:8; 19:9; **1Sa** 20:13; 24:4; 28:15; 22; **2Sa** 3:21; 15:34; 22:28; **1Kin** 1:12; 2:3; 31; 8:29; **2Kin** 5:6; 8:10; **1Chr** 22:12; 14; **2Chr** 1:11; 18:33; **Ezr** 7:17; **Neh** 1:6; 6:6; **Job** 40:8; **Ps** 32:6; 45:16; 94:13; 104:27; 130:4; **Prov** 2:20; 5:2; 19:20; **Is** 23:16; 43:26; 45:3; 47:12; 49:6; 9; **Jer** 4:14; 6:27; 30:13; **Eze** 16:54(2); 63; **Hab** 2:15; **Mk** 14:12; **Lk** 12:58; 16:2; **Acts** 8:37; 24:8; 11; **1Cor** 7:21; **Eph** 6:3; **1Ti** 3:15; **3Jn** 2; **Rev** 3:18(3)

ME

1691, 3165

Gen 3:12(2); 13; 4:10; 14(3); 25; 6:7; 13; 7:1; 9:12; 13; 15; 17; 12:12; 13; 18(2); 19; 13:8; 9; 14:21; 24; 15:2; 3; 9; 16:2; 5; 13(2); 17:1; 2; 4; 7; 10; 11; 18:21; 27; 31; 19:8; 19(2); 20; 20:5; 6; 9(2); 11; 13(3); 21:6(2); 16; 23(3); 26; 30; 22:12; 23:4; 8(2); 9(2); 11; 13(2); 15(2); 24:5; 7(3); 12; 17; 23; 27; 30; 37; 39; 40; 43; 44; 45; 48; 49(2); 54; 56(2); 25:30; 31; 32; 33; 26:7; 27(3); 27:3; 4(2); 7(2); 9; 12(2); 13(2); 19(2); 20; 25; 26; 31; 33; 34(2); 36(2); 38(2); 46; 28:20(3); 22; 29:15(2); 19; 21; 25(2); 27; 32; 33; 34; 30:1; 6(2); 13; 14; 16; 18; 20(2); 24; 25; 26(2); 27; 28; 29; 31(2); 33(2); 31:5(2); 7(2); 9; 11; 13; 26; 27(2); 28; 29; 31; 32; 35; 36; 40; 42(2); 44; 48; 49; 50; 51; 52; 32:9; 11(2); 16; 20(2); 26(2); 29; 33:10; 11; 13; 14; 15(3); 34:4; 11(2); 12(3); 30(4); 35:3(2); 37:9; 14; 16; 38:16(3); 17; 39:7; 8; 9; 12; 14(2); 15; 17(2); 18; 19; 40:8; 9; 14(4); 15; 41:10(2); 13; 16; 24; 51; 52; 42:20; 33; 34; 36(2); 43:6; 8; 9; 16; 29; 44:21; 27; 28; 29; 34; 45:1; 4; 5(2); 7; 8(2); 9(2); 10; 18; 46:30; 31; 47:29(2); 30(2); 31; 48:3(2); 4; 7(2); 9(2); 11; 15; 16; 49:29; 50:5(4); 20; **Ex** 2:9; 14; 3:9; 13(2); 14; 15; 16; 4:1; 18; 23; 25; 5:1; 22; 6:7; 12(2); 30; 7:16(2); 8:1; 8; 9; 20; 28; 9:1; 13; 14; 10:3(2); 17; 28; 11:8(2); 12:32; 13:2; 8; 14:15; 17; 18; 17:2; 4; 18:4; 15; 16; 19:5; 6; 20:3; 5; 6; 23; 24; 25; 22:23; 27; 29; 30; 31; 23:14; 15; 33; 24:12; 25:2; 8; 30; 28:1; 3; 4; 41; 29:1; 44; 30:30; 31; 31:13; 17; 32:2; 10; 23; 24; 26; 32; 33; 33:12(3); 13; 15; 18; 20; 21; 34:2; 20; 40:13; 15; **Lev** 10:3; 19; 14:35; 20:26; 22:2; 25:23; 55; 26:14; 18; 21(2); 23(2); 27(2); 40(2); **Num** 3:13; 41; 8:16(2); 11:11; 12; 13; 14; 15(3); 16; 14:11(2); 22; 23; 24; 27(2); 29; 35; 16:28; 29; 17:5; 10; 18:9; 20:12(2); 18; 21:22; 22:5; 6(2); 8; 10; 11; 13; 16; 17(2); 18; 19; 28; 29; 32; 33(3); 34(2); 37; 23:1(2); 3(2); 7(2); 10; 11; 13(2); 18; 27; 29(2); 24:12; 13; 27:14; 28:2(2); 32:11; **Deut** 1:14; 17; 22; 23; 37; 41; 42; 2:1; 2; 9; 17; 27; 28(2); 29; 31; 3:2; 25; 26(4); 4:5; 10(3); 14; 21; 5:7; 9; 10; 22; 23; 28(2); 29; 31; 7:4; 8:17; 9:4; 10; 11; 12; 13; 14; 19; 10:1(2); 4; 5; 10; 11; 17:14(2); 18:15; 16(2); 17; 26:10; 13; 14; 28:20; 31:2; 16; 19; 20; 28; 32:21(2); 34; 35; 39; 41; 51(2); **Josh** 2:4; 12(2); 7:19(2); 8:5; 10:4(2); 22; 14:6; 7; 8; 10; 11; 12(2); 15:19(3); 17:14(2); 18:4; 6; 8; 24:15; **Judg** 1:3; 7; 15(3); 3:28; 4:8(2); 18; 19; 5:13; 6:17(2); 39(2); 7:2(3); 17; 18; 8:5; 15; 24; 9:7; 9; 15; 48; 54(2); 10:12; 13; 11:7(3); 9(2); 12(2); 17; 27(2); 31; 35(2); 36; 37(2); 12:2; 3(3); 5; 13:6(2); 7; 10(2); 16; 14:2; 3(2); 12; 13(2); 16(3); 15:11; 12(2); 16:6; 7; 10(3); 11; 13(3); 15(3); 17; 18; 26; 28(2); 30; 17:2; 10(2); 13; 18:4(2); 24; 19:18; 19; 20; 20:5(3); **Ruth** 1:8; 11; 13(2); 16; 17(2); 20(3); 21(4); 2:2; 7; 10; 11; 13(2); 21; 3:5; 17(2); 4:4; **1Sa** 1:11; 27; 2:16; 28; 29; 30(4); 35; 36; 3:5; 6; 8; 17(2); 8:7; 8; 9:16; 18; 19(2); 21; 10:2; 8; 15; 12:1; 3; 12; 23; 13:9; 11; 12; 14:12; 33; 34; 42; 43; 15:1; 11(2); 16; 20; 25; 30(2); 32; 16:1; 2; 3; 5; 17(2); 19; 22; 17:8; 9(2); 10; 35; 37(2); 43; 44; 45; 18:8; 17; 19:15; 17(3); 20:2(2); 3; 5; 6(2); 8(3); 10; 14; 23; 28; 29(3); 31; 42; 21:2(2); 3; 8; 9; 14; 22:3; 8(5); 13(2); 15; 17; 23(2); 23:11; 12; 21; 22; 23; 24:10; 12(2); 15(2); 17; 18(3); 19; 21(2); 25:19; 21; 24(2); 32; 33; 34(2); 26:6; 8; 19(2); 24; 27:1(3); 5; 28:1; 7; 8(2); 9; 11; 12; 15(6); 16; 17; 19; 21; 22; 29:3(2); 6(2); 30:7; 13; 15(4); 31:4(3); **2Sa** 1:4; 7(2); 8; 9(5); 26(2); 2:7; 22; 3:8; 12; 14(2); 35; 39; 4:10; 5:20; 6:9; 21(2); 7:5(2); 7; 18; 10:2; 11(2); 11:6; 12:10; 22; 23; 13:4; 5; 6; 9; 11; 12; 13; 16(2); 17; 14:9; 10; 15; 16; 18; 19; 32(4); 15:4; 7; 8; 25(2); 26; 28; 33(2); 34; 36; 16:3; 9; 12; 17:1; 18:13; 19; 22; 23; 27; 29; 19:13(2); 19; 22; 25; 26(2); 33(2); 36; 38(2); 20:4; 20; 22:3; 5(2); 6(2); 17(2); 18(3); 19; 20(3); 21(2); 23; 25; 34; 36(2); 37; 40(3); 41(2); 44(3); 45(2); 48(2); 49(4); 23:2; 3; 5; 15; 17; 24:13; 14; 17; 24; **1Kin** 1:12; 13; 17; 24; 26(2); 28; 30; 32; 51; 2:4(2); 5; 7; 8(2); 15; 16; 17; 20; 23; 24(3); 30; 31; 42; 3:20; 24; 5:4; 6; 8; 9; 8:25(2); 9:3; 4; 6; 13; 10:7; 11:21; 22(2); 33; 36(2); 12:5; 9; 12; 24; 27; 13:6(2); 7; 8; 9; 13; 15; 17; 18; 27; 31; 14:2; 8; 9(2); 15:19(2); 16:2; 17:10; 11; 12; 13(2); 18; 19; 18:9; 12; 14; 19; 30; 37(2); 19:2; 18; 20; 20:5; 7; 10(2); 32; 35; 36; 37; 39; 21:2; 3; 6; 20; 22; 29(2); 22:4;

8; 14; 16; 18; 24; 28; 34; **2Kin** 2:2; 4; 6; 9; 10; 20; 3:7(2); 15; 4:2; 6; 22; 24; 27(2); 28; 5:7(2); 8; 11; 22(2); 6:11; 19; 28; 31; 8:4; 9; 10; 13; 14; 9:12; 18; 19; 10:6; 15; 16; 19; 16:7(2); 15; 18:14(2); 20; 22; 25; 27(2); 31(2); 19:6; 20; 27; 28; 20:8; 21:15; 22:10; 13; 15; 17(2); 19; **1Chr** 4:10(4); 10:4(2); 11:17; 19; 12:17(3); 13:12; 17:4; 6; 12; 16; 17; 19:2; 12(2); 21:2; 12; 13(2); 17; 22(2); 22:7; 8; 28:2(2); 3; 4(3); 5; 6; 19(2); 29:17; **2Chr** 1:8; 9; 10; 2:3; 7(2); 8; 9; 6:16; 7:17; 9:6; 10:5; 6; 9; 12; 11:4; 12:5; 13:4; 15:2; 16:3(2); 18:3; 7; 15; 17; 23; 27; 33; 20:20; 28:11; 23; 29:5; 34:18; 21; 23; 25(2); 27(2); 35:21(2); 23; 36:23(2); **Ezr** 1:2(2); 4:18; 21; 7:28(3); 8:1; 9:1; 4; **Neh** 1:3; 9; 2:2; 4; 5; 6(2); 7(2); 8(3); 9; 12(2); 14; 18(2); 4:18; 23; 5:15; 18(2); 19; 6:2(2); 4; 5; 12; 13; 14; 19(2); 12:40; 13:8; 14; 22(2); 28; 31; **Est** 4:16; 5:13; 7:3; 8; **Job** 2:3; 3:12; 25(2); 4:12; 14; 6:4(2); 8; 9(2); 13(2); 22(2); 23(2); 24(2); 28; 7:3; 8(3); 12; 13; 14(2); 16; 19(2); 20; 21; 9:11; 16; 17; 18(2); 19; 20(2); 28; 31(2); 34(2); 35; 10:2(3); 8(3); 9(2); 10(2); 11(2); 12; 14(2); 15; 16(2); 17(3); 18(2); 20; 13:13(2); 15; 19; 20; 21(2); 22(2); 23; 24; 26(2); 14:3; 13(4); 15:17; 16:7; 8(3); 9(4); 10(3); 11(2); 12(4); 13; 14(2); 20; 17:1; 2; 3(2); 6; 19:2; 3(2); 5(2); 6(2); 9; 10; 11(2); 12; 13(2); 14; 15; 16; 18(2); 19(2); 21(3); 22; 27; 28; 20:2; 3; 21:3; 4; 5; 16; 27; 34; 22:18; 23:5(2); 6(2); 10; 14; 16; 24:15; 25; 27:3; 5; 6; 7; 28:14(2); 29:2; 5(2); 6; 8; 11(4); 13; 14; 20; 21; 23; 30:1; 2; 10(2); 11(2); 12; 14(2); 15; 16(2); 17; 18; 19; 20(2); 21(2); 22(2); 23; 26; 27; 30; 31:6; 8; 13; 15; 18; 20; 23; 29; 34; 35(2); 36; 38; 32:10; 14; 18(2); 21(2); 22; 33:4(2); 5(2); 9; 10(2); 27; 31; 32; 33; 34:2; 10; 32; 34(2); 36:2; 38:3; 40:7; 8; 41:10; 11; 42:3; 4; 7; 8; **Ps** 2:7; 8; 3:1(2); 3; 4; 5(2); 6; 7; 4:1(3); 8(2); 5:7; 8; 6:1(2); 2(2); 4; 8; 7:1(3); 4; 6; 8(2); 9:13(3); 13:1(2); 2; 3; 4; 6; 16:1; 6; 7(2); 8; 11; 17:3(2); 4; 6(2); 8(2); 9(2); 15; 18:4(2); 5(2); 16(2); 17(3); 18; 19(3); 20(2); 22(2); 24; 32; 33; 35(3); 36; 39(3); 40(2); 43(3); 44(3); 47(2); 48(4); 19:12; 13; 22:1(2); 7(2); 9(2); 11; 12(2); 13; 15; 16(2); 17; 19(2); 21(2); 23:2(2); 3; 4(2); 5; 6; 25:2(2); 4(2); 5(2); 7; 16(2); 17; 19; 20(2); 21; 26:1; 2(2); 11(3); 27:2; 3(2); 5(3); 6; 7(2); 9(3); 10(2); 11(2); 12(2); 28:1(2); 3; 30:1(2); 2; 3; 10; 11(2); 31:1(2); 2(3); 3(2); 4(2); 5; 8; 9; 11(2); 13; 15(2); 16; 17; 21; 32:4; 7(2); 34:3; 4(2); 11; 35:1(2); 3; 7; 12; 13; 15(2); 16; 19(2); 21; 22; 24(2); 26; 36:11(2); 38:1(2); 2(2); 4; 10(2); 12; 16(3); 17; 19; 21(2); 22; 39:1; 3; 4; 8(2); 10; 13; 40:1; 2; 7; 11(2); 12(3); 13(2); 14; 15; 17; 41:4; 5; 6; 7(3); 9; 10(2); 11(2); 12(3); 42:3; 4; 5; 6; 7; 8; 9; 10(2); 11; 43:1(2); 2; 3(2); 5; 44:6; 15(2); 49:5; 15; 50:5(2); 8; 15(2); 23; 51:1; 2(2); 3; 5; 6; 7(2); 8; 10(2); 11(2); 12(2); 14; 54:1(2); 3; 7; 55:2(2); 3(2); 4(2); 5(2); 12(3); 16(2); 18(2); 56:1(3); 2(2); 4; 5; 9; 11; 12; 57:1(2); 2; 3(2); 6; 59:1(3); 2(2); 3; 4; 10(2); 60:5; 8; 9(2); 61:2; 3; 5; 63:8; 64:2; 65:3; 66:18; 19; 20; 69:1; 2; 4(2); 9(2); 12; 13(2); 14(4); 15(3); 16(2); 17; 18; 21(2); 29; 70:1(2); 5; 71:1; 2(4); 3; 4; 6; 9(2); 10; 12; 17; 18; 20(3); 21; 73:2; 16; 23; 24(2); 28; 77:1; 81:8; 11; 13; 86:1; 3; 7; 11; 13; 14; 16(2); 17(4); 87:4; 88:6; 7(2); 8(2); 14; 16(2); 17(2); 18; 89:26; 36; 91:14; 15; 92:4; 11; 94:16(2); 18; 19; 95:9(2); 101:2; 3; 4; 6(2); 102:2(3); 8(3); 10(2); 24; 103:1; 106:4(2); 108:6; 10(2); 109:2(2); 3(2); 5; 21(2); 22; 25; 26(2); 116:2; 3(2); 6; 12; 118:5(2); 6; 7(2); 10; 11(2); 12; 13(2); 18(2); 19; 21; 119:8; 10; 12; 19; 22; 23; 25; 26(2); 27; 28; 29(2); 30; 31; 33; 34; 35; 37; 40; 41; 42; 49; 50; 51; 53; 58; 61; 64; 66; 68; 69; 71; 72; 73(3); 74; 75; 77; 78; 79; 82; 84; 85; 86(2); 87; 88; 93; 94; 95(2); 98(2); 102; 107; 108; 110; 115; 116(2); 117; 121; 122; 124; 125; 132(2); 133; 134; 135; 139; 143; 144; 145; 146; 149; 153; 154(2); 156; 159; 161; 169; 170; 171; 173; 175; 120:1; 5; 122:1; 129:1; 2(2); 131:1; 138:3(2); 7(2); 8; 139:1(2); 5(2); 6; 10(2); 11(2); 13; 17; 19; 23(2); 24(2); 140:1(2); 4(2); 5(2); 9; 141:1; 4; 5(2); 9(2); 142:3(2); 4(2); 6; 7(2); 143:1; 3; 4(2); 7(2); 8(2); 9(2); 10(2); 11; 144:2; 7(2); 11(2); **Prov** 1:28(3); 33; 4:4(2); 5:7; 13; 7:14; 24; 8:15; 16; 17(3); 18; 21; 22; 32; 34; 35; 36(2); 9:11; 23:26; 35(2); 24:29; 27:11; 30:7; 8(4); 18; **Eccl** 1:16; 2:4(3); 5; 6; 7(2); 8(2); 9(2); 15; 17; 18; 7:23; 9:13; **Song** 1:2; 4(2); 6(4); 7; 13; 14; 2:4(2); 5(2); 6; 10; 14(2); 3:3; 4; 4:6; 8(2); 5:2; 6; 7(4); 6:5(2); 12; 7:10; 8:2; 3; 6; 12; 13; **Is** 1:2; 11; 12; 13; 14; 24(2); 3:7; 5:3; 6:5; 6; 8; 8:1; 2; 3; 5; 11(2); 18; 10:4; 12:1(2); 18:4; 21:3; 3; 4(2); 6; 11; 16; 22:4(2); 24:16; 26:9; 27:4(2); 5(2); 29:2; 13(4); 16; 30:1; 31:4; 36:5; 7; 10; 12(2); 16(2); 37:6; 21; 28; 29; 38:12(3); 13; 14; 15; 16(2); 20; 39:3; 40:25; 41:1; 43:10(3); 11; 20; 22(2); 23(2); 24(4); 26; 27; 44:6; 7; 8; 17; 21; 22; 45:4; 5(2); 6; 11(2); 19; 21(2); 22; 23; 46:3(2); 5(3); 9; 12; 47:8; 10(2); 48:12; 16(2); 19; 49:1(2); 2(3); 3; 5; 14(2); 16; 20(2); 21; 23; 50:4; 7; 8(3); 9(2); 51:1; 4(3); 5; 7; 54:9; 15; 17; 55:2; 3; 11; 56:3; 4; 57:8; 11(2); 13; 16; 17; 58:2(2); 59:21; 60:9; 61:1(3); 10(2); 63:3; 5(2); 15; 65:1(4); 3; 5; 6; 7; 10; 66:1; 22; 23; 24; **Jer** 1:4; 7; 9; 11; 12; 13; 14; 16; 2:1; 2; 5(2); 8(2); 13; 21; 22; 27(2); 29(2); 32; 35; 3:1; 4; 6; 7; 10; 11; 19(2); 20; 4:1; 12; 17; 19; 22; 31; 5:5; 7; 11; 19; 22; 6:7; 20(2); 7:10; 16; 18; 19; 26; 8:18; 19; 21; 9:3; 6; 24; 10:19; 20; 24(2); 11:6; 9; 11; 14; 17; 18(2); 19; 20; 12:1; 3(2); 8(2); 9; 11; 13:1; 3; 5; 6; 8; 11(2); 22; 25(2); 14:11; 14; 15:1(2); 6; 8; 10(4); 15(4); 16; 17; 18; 19; 16:1; 11(2); 12; 17:13; 14(2); 15; 16; 17; 18(3); 19; 24; 27; 18:5; 15; 19(2); 22; 23(2); 19:4; 20:7(2); 8; 11; 12; 14; 17(2); 22:6; 14; 16; 23:9; 14; 17; 24:1; 3; 4; 7(2); 25:3; 6; 7(2); 15; 17; 26:3; 4; 12; 14(2); 15(2); 27:2; 5; 28:1; 8; 29:12(2); 13(3); 30:20; 21(2); 31:3; 18(2); 26; 34; 36(2); 32:6; 8(2); 25; 27; 29; 30(2); 31; 32; 33; 39; 40; 33:3; 8(2); 9; 18; 22; 34:14; 15; 17; 18; 35:14; 15; 16; 19; 36:18; 37:7(2); 18; 20; 38:14; 15(2); 19(2); 21; 26; 39:18; 40:4(2); 10; 15; 42:9; 10; 20; 21; 44:3; 8; 45:3; 49:4; 11; 19(3); 50:44(3); 51:1; 34(5); 35; 53; **Lam** 1:12(2); 13(2); 14; 15(2); 16; 19; 20; 21(2); 22; 3:2(2); 3(2); 5(2); 6; 7; 10; 11(2); 12; 15(2); 16; 20; 52; 53; 60; 61; 62(2); **Eze** 2:1; 2(4); 3(3); 9; 10; 3:1; 2; 3; 4; 7; 10; 12(2); 14(3); 16; 17; 22(2); 24(4); 4:15; 16; 6:1; 9(2); 7:1; 8:1(2); 3(3); 5; 6; 7; 8; 9; 12; 13; 14; 15; 16; 17(2); 9:9; 10; 11; 11:1(2); 2; 5(2); 14; 24(3); 25; 12:1; 8; 17; 21; 26; 13:1; 19; 14:1(2); 2; 5; 7(2); 11; 12; 13; 15:1; 16:1; 20; 26; 43; 50; 17:1; 11; 20; 18:1; 20:1; 2; 3; 8(2); 12; 13; 20; 21; 27(2); 38; 39; 40; 45; 49; 21:1; 8; 18; 22:1; 12; 17; 18; 23; 30; 23:1; 35(2); 36; 37; 38; 24:1; 15; 19; 20; 25:1; 26:1; 2; 27:1; 28:1; 11; 20; 29:1; 17; 20; 30:1; 9; 20; 31:1; 32:1; 17; 33:1; 7; 21; 22(2); 23; 34:1; 35:1; 13(2); 36:16; 17; 37:1(3); 2; 3; 4; 9; 10; 11; 15; 38:1; 16; 39:23; 26; 40:1(2); 2(2); 3; 4; 17; 24; 28; 32; 35; 45; 48; 49; 41:1; 4; 22; 42:1(2); 13; 15; 43:1; 5(2); 6(2); 7; 8; 9; 18; 19(2); 44:1; 2; 4; 5; 10(2); 13(2); 15(5); 16; 46:19; 20; 21(2); 24; 47:1; 2(2); 3; 4(2); 6(3); 8; **Dan** 1:10; 2:5(2); 6(2); 8; 9(4); 23(2); 24; 26; 30(2); 4:2; 5(2); 6(2); 7; 8; 9; 18; 34; 36(4); 5:7; 15(2); 16; 6:22(2); 7:15; 16(2); 28(3); 8:1(3); 14; 15; 17; 18(3); 9:21; 22(2); 10:7; 8(2); 10(2); 11(2); 12; 13(2); 15; 16(2); 17(3); 18(2); 19(2); 21; **Hos** 2:5; 7; 12; 13; 16(2); 19(2); 20; 23; 3:1; 2; 3; 4:6; 7; 5:3; 15; 6:7; 7:7; 13(3); 14(2); 15; 8:2; 4; 11:7; 8; 12; 12:8(2); 13:4(2); 6; 9; 10; 14:8; **Joel** 2:12; 3:4(3); **Amos** 4:6; 8; 9; 10; 11; 5:4; 22; 23; 25; 7:1; 4; 7; 8; 15(2); 8:1; 2; 9:7; **Obad** 3; **Jonah** 1:2; 12(2); 2:2; 3(3); 5(2); 6; 7; 4:3(2); 8; **Mic** 2:4; 5:2; 6:3; 7:1; 7; 8(2); 9(2); 10; **Hab** 1:3(3); 2:1(2); 2; 3:14; 19; **Zeph** 2:15; 3:7; 8; 11; **Hag** 2:14; 17; **Zec** 1:3; 4; 9(2); 13; 14(2); 19(2); 20; 2:2; 3; 8; 9; 11; 3:1; 4:1(2); 2; 4; 5(2); 6; 8; 9; 13; 5:2; 3; 5(2); 10; 11; 6:4; 5; 8(2); 9; 15; 7:4; 5(2); 8:1; 14; 18; 9:13; 10:9; 11:7; 8; 11; 12; 13; 15; 12:10; 13:5; **Mal** 2:5; 6; 3:1; 5; 7; 8; 9; 10; 13; **Mt** 2:8; 3:11; 14; 4:9; 19; 7:4; 21; 22; 23; 8:2; 9; 21; 22; 9:9; 10:32; 33; 37(4); 38(2); 40(3); 11:6; 27; 28; 29; 12:30(3); 14:8; 18; 28; 30; 15:5; 8(3); 9; 22; 25; 32; 16:23(2); 24(2); 17:17; 27; 18:5; 6; 21; 26; 28; 29; 32; 19:14; 17; 21; 28; 20:13; 15; 21:2; 24; 22:18; 19; 23:39; 25:20; 22; 35(3); 36(3); 40; 41; 42(2); 43(3); 45; 26:10; 11; 15; 21; 23(2); 31; 34; 38; 39; 40; 42; 46; 53; 55(2); 75; 27:10; 46; 28:10; 18; **Mk** 1:7; 17; 40; 2:14; 5:7; 31; 6:22; 23; 25; 7:6(2); 7; 11; 14; 8:2; 33; 34(2); 38; 9:19; 37(4); 39; 42; 10:14; 18; 21; 47; 48; 11:29; 30; 12:15(2); 14:6; 7; 18(2); 20; 27; 30; 36; 42; 48; 49; 72; 15:34; **Lk** 1:3; 25(2); 38; 43(2); 48; 49; 2:49; 4:6; 7; 8; 18(3); 23; 5:8; 12; 27; 6:42; 46; 47; 7:8; 23; 42; 44; 45; 8:28; 45(2); 46(2); 9:23(2); 26; 48(3); 59(2); 61; 10:16(4); 22; 40(2); 11:5; 6; 7(2); 23(3); 12:8; 9; 13; 14; 13:27; 35; 14:18; 19; 26; 27; 15:6; 9; 12(2); 19; 29; 31; 16:3; 4; 24; 17:8; 18:3; 5(2); 13; 16; 19; 22; 38; 39; 19:27; 20:3; 23; 24; 22:19; 21(2); 28; 29; 34; 37(2); 42; 53; 61; 68(2); 23:14; 28; 42; 43; 24:39(2); 44; **Jn** 1:15(3); 27(2); 30(3); 33(2); 43; 48; 2:17; 3:28; 4:7; 9; 10; 15; 21; 29; 34; 39; 5:7(2); 11(2); 24; 30; 32(2); 36(3); 37(2); 39; 40; 43; 46(2); 6:26; 35(2); 36; 37(3); 38; 39(2); 40; 44(2); 45; 47; 56; 57(3); 65; 7:7; 16; 19; 23; 28(2); 29; 33; 34(2); 36(2); 37; 38; 8:12; 16; 18(2); 19(2); 21; 26; 28; 29(3); 37; 40; 42(2); 45; 46(2); 49; 54; 9:4; 11; 10:8; 9; 15; 17; 18; 25; 27; 29; 32; 37; 38(2); 11:25; 26; 41; 42(2); 12:8; 26(3); 27; 30; 32; 44(3); 45(2); 46; 48; 49(2); 50; 13:8; 13; 18(2); 20(3); 21; 33; 36(2); 38; 14:1; 6; 7; 9(2); 10(2); 11(3); 12; 15; 19(2); 20; 21(2); 23; 24(2); 28; 30; 31; 15:2; 4(2); 5(2); 6; 7; 9; 16; 18; 20; 21; 23; 24; 25; 26; 27; 16:3; 5(2); 9; 10; 14; 16(2); 17(2); 19(2); 23; 27; 32(2); 33; 17:4; 5; 6(2); 7; 8(2); 9; 11; 12; 18; 20; 21(2); 22; 23(3); 24(4); 25; 26; 18:8; 9; 11; 21(2); 23; 34; 35; 19:10; 11(2); 20:15; 17; 21; 29; 21:15; 16; 17(2); 19; 22; **Acts** 1:4; 8; 2:28(2); 29; 3:22; 5:8; 7:7; 28; 37; 42; 49; 8:19; 24(2); 31; 36; 9:4; 6; 15; 17; 10:28; 29; 30; 11:5; 7; 9; 11; 12(2); 12:8; 11; 13:2; 25; 15:13; 16:15; 20:19; 22; 23; 24; 34; 21:39; 22:5; 6; 7(2); 8; 9(2); 10; 11; 13(2); 18(2); 21; 27; 23:3(2); 11; 18(2); 19; 22; 30; 24:12; 13; 18; 19; 20; 25:5; 9; 11(2); 15; 24; 27; 26:3; 5; 13(2); 14(2); 18; 21(2); 28; 29; 27:21; 23; 25; 28:18(3); **Rom** 1:12; 15; 7:8; 11(2); 13(2); 17; 18(2); 20; 21; 23; 24; 8:2; 9:1; 19; 20; 10:20(2); 12:3; 14:11; 15:3; 15; 18; 30(2); 16:7; **1Cor** 1:11; 17; 3:10; 4:3; 4; 16; 6:12(2); 7:1; 9:3; 15(2); 16(2); 17; 10:23(2); 11:1; 2; 24; 25; 13:3; 14:11; 21; 15:8; 10(2); 32; 16:4; 6; 9; 11; 21; **2Cor** 1:17; 19; 2:2(2); 5; 12; 7:7; 9:1; 4; 11:1(2); 9; 10(2); 16(2); 28; 32; 12:1; 6(3); 7(2); 8; 9(2); 11; 13; 21; 13:3; 10; **Gal** 1:2; 11; 15(2); 16; 17; 24; 2:1; 3; 6(2); 7; 8; 9(2); 20(3); 4:12; 14; 15; 21; 6:14; 17; **Eph** 3:2; 3; 7; 8; 6:19(2); **Phil** 1:7; 12; 21; 26; 30(2); 2:18; 22; 23; 27; 30; 3:1; 7; 17; 4:3; 9; 10; 13; 15; 21; **Col** 1:25; 29; 4:11; 18; **1Ti** 1:12(3); 16; **2Ti** 1:8; 13; 15; 16; 17(2); 18; 2:2; 3:11(2); 4:8(3); 9; 10; 11(2); 14; 16(2); 17(3); 18(2); **Titus** 1:3; 3:12; 15; **Philem** 1:11; 13(2); 16; 17; 19; 20; 22; **Heb** 1:5; 2:13; 3:9(2); 8:10; 11; 10:5; 7; 30; 34; 11:32; 13:6; **Jas** 2:18; **2Pet** 1:14; **Jude** 3; **Rev** 1:10; 12; 17(2); 3:4; 18; 20; 21; 4:1; 5:5; 7:13; 14; 10:4; 8; 9(2); 11; 11:1; 14:13; 17:1(2); 3; 7; 15; 19:9(2); 10; 21:5; 6; 9(2); 10(2); 15; 22:1; 6; 8; 9; 10; 12

MEN

120, 376, 582, 606, 1121, 1167, 1397, 1400, 2145, 2388, 4962, 4974, 5315, *407, 435, 442, 444, 730, 3495, 4753, 5046*

Gen 4:26; 6:1; 2; 4(3); 11:5; 12:20; 13:13; 14:24(2); 17:23; 27; 18:2; 16; 22; 19:4(2); 5; 8; 10; 11; 12; 16; 20:8; 22:3; 5; 19; 24:13; 54; 59; 26:7(2); 29:22; 32:6; 28; 33:1; 13; 34:7; 20; 21; 22; 38:21; 22; 39:11; 14; 41:8; 42:11; 19; 31; 33; 34; 43:15; 16(2); 17; 18; 24; 33; 44:3; 4; 46:32; 47:2; 6; **Ex** 1:17; 18; 2:13; 4:19; 5:9; 7:11; 10:7; 11; 12:33; 37; 15:15; 17:9; 18:21(2); 25; 21:18; 22; 22:31; 24:5; 32:28; 34:23; 35:22; 36:4; 38:26; **Lev** 7:25; 18:27; 27:9; 29; **Num** 1:5; 17; 44; 5:6; 9:6; 7; 11:16; 24; 26; 28; 12:3; 13:2; 3; 16; 21; 31; 32; 14:22; 36; 37; 38; 16:2; 14; 26; 29(3); 30; 32; 35; 18:15; 22:9; 20; 35; 25:5; 26:10; 31:11; 21; 28; 32; 42; 49; 53; 32:11; 14; 34:17; 19; **Deut** 1:13; 15; 22; 23; 35; 2:14; 16; 34; 3:6; 4:3; 13:13; 19:17; 21:21; 22:21; 25:1; 11; 27:14; 29:10; 25; 31:12; 32:26; 33:6; **Josh** 1:14; 2:1; 2; 3; 4(2); 5(2); 7; 9; 14; 17; 23; 3:12; 4:2; 4; 5:4; 6; 6:2; 3; 9; 13; 22; 23; 7:2(2); 3; 4(2); 5(2); 8:3; 12; 14; 20; 21; 25(2); 9:6; 7; 14; 10:2; 6; 7; 18; 24(2); 18:4; 8; 9; 24:11; **Judg** 1:4; 3:29(2); 31; 4:6; 10; 14; 6:27(2); 28; 30; 7:6; 7; 8; 11; 16; 19; 23; 24; 8:1; 4; 5; 8(2); 9; 10(2); 14(2); 15(2); 16; 17; 18; 22; 9:2; 3; 6; 7; 18; 20(2); 23(2); 24; 25; 26; 28; 36; 39; 46; 47; 49(2); 51; 54; 55; 57; 11:3; 12:1; 4(2); 5; 14:10; 18; 19; 15:10; 11; 15; 16:9; 27(2); 18:2(2); 7; 11; 14; 16; 17(2); 22; 19:16; 22; 25; 20:5; 10; 11; 12; 13; 15(2); 16; 17(3); 20(2); 21; 22; 25; 31; 33; 34; 35; 36; 38; 39(2); 41(2); 42; 44(2); 45(2); 46(2); 47; 48(2); 21:1; 10; **Ruth** 2:9(2); 15; 21; 3:10; 4:2; **1Sa** 2:4; 17(2); 26; 4:2; 9(2); 5:7; 9; 12; 6:10; 15; 19(2); 20; 7:1; 11; 8:16; 22; 10:2; 3; 26; 11:1; 5; 8; 9(2); 10; 12; 15; 13:2; 6; 15; 14:2; 8; 12; 14; 22; 24; 15:4; 17:2; 12; 19; 24; 25; 26; 28; 52; 18:5; 27(2); 21:4; 5; 15; 22:2; 6; 19; 23:3; 5; 8; 11; 12(2); 13; 24; 25; 26(3); 24:2(2); 3; 4; 6; 22; 25:5(2); 8(2); 9; 11; 12; 13(2); 14; 15; 20; 25; 27; 26:2; 19; 22; 27:2; 3; 8; 28:1; 8; 29:2; 4; 11; 30:1; 3; 9; 10; 17; 21; 22(2); 31; 31:1; 6; 7(2); 12; **2Sa** 1:11; 15; 2:3; 4(2); 5; 14; 17; 21; 29; 30; 31(2); 32; 3:20(2); 34; 39; 4:2; 11; 12; 5:6; 21; 6:1; 19; 7:9; 14(2); 8:5; 13; 10:5; 6(2); 7; 9; 12; 18; 11:16; 17; 23; 12:1; 13:9; 32; 15:1; 6; 11; 13; 18; 22; 16:2; 6; 13; 15; 18; 17:1; 8(2); 10; 12; 14; 24; 18:7; 15; 28; 19:14; 16; 17; 28; 35; 41(3); 42(2); 43(4); 20:2; 4; 5; 7(2); 11; 21:6; 12; 17; 22:5; 23:3; 8; 9(2); 16; 17(2); 20; 22; 24:9(3); 15; **1Kin** 1:5; 8; 9; 10; 2:32; 4:31; 5:13; 8:2; 39; 9:22; 10:8; 11:18; 24; 12:6; 8(2); 10; 14; 21; 13:25; 18:13; 22; 20:14; 15; 17(2); 19; 30; 33; 21:10; 11; 13(2); 22:6; **2Kin** 2:7; 16; 17; 19; 3:26; 4:22; 40; 43; 5:22; 24; 6:20; 7:3; 8:12; 10:6(2); 11; 14; 24(2); 11:9; 12:15; 13:21; 15:20; 25; 17:24; 30(3); 18:27; 20:14; 23:2; 14; 17; 24:14; 16; 25:4; 19(3); 23(2); 24; 25; **1Chr** 4:12; 22; 42; 5:18(2); 21; 24(2); 7:2; 3; 4; 5; 7; 9; 11; 21; 40(2); 8:28; 40; 9:9; 13; 10:1; 7; 12; 11:10; 11; 19; 22; 26; 12:1; 8(2); 21; 25; 30; 32; 38; 16:31; 17:8; 18:5; 19:5(2); 8; 18; 21:5(2); 14; 22:15; 24:4(2); 26:6; 7; 8; 9; 12; 30; 31; 32; 28:1(2); 29:24; **2Chr** 2:2; 7; 14(2); 5:3; 6:18; 30; 8:9; 9:7; 10:6; 8(2); 10; 13; 14; 11:1; 13:3(4); 7; 15(2); 17; 14:8(2); 17:13(2); 14; 16; 17; 18:5; 22:1; 23:8; 24:24; 25:5; 6; 26:11; 12; 15; 17; 28:6; 14; 15; 31:19; 32:3; 21; 34:12; 30; 35:25; 36:17; **Ezr** 1:4; 2:2; 22; 23; 27; 28; 65; 3:12; 4:11; 21; 5:4; 10; 6:8; 7:28; 8:16(2); 10:1; 9; 17; **Neh** 1:2; 2:12; 3:2; 7; 22; 4:23; 5:5; 7:7; 26; 27; 28; 29; 30; 31; 32; 33; 67; 8:2; 3; 11:2; 6; 14(2); 13:16; **Est** 1:13; 6:13; 9:6; 12; 15; **Job** 1:3; 19; 4:13; 7:20; 11:3; 11; 15:10; 18; 17:8; 22:15; 29; 24:12; 27:23; 28:4; 29:8; 21; 30:5; 8; 31:31; 32:1; 5; 9; 33:15; 16; 27; 34:2; 8; 10; 24; 26; 34; 36; 35:12; 36:24; 37:7; 21; 24; 39:21; **Ps** 4:2; 9:20; 11:4; 12:1; 8; 14:2; 17:4; 14(2); 18:4; 21:10; 22:6; 26:9; 31:19; 33:13; 36:7; 45:2; 49:10; 18; 53:2; 55:23; 57:4; 58:1; 59:2; 62:9(2); 64:9; 66:5; 12; 68:18; 72:17; 73:5(2); 76:5; 78:31; 60; 63; 82:7; 83:18; 86:14; 89:47; 90:3; 105:12; 107:8(2); 15(2); 21(2); 31(2); 115:16; 116:11; 124:2; 139:19; 141:4; 145:6; 12; 148:12(2); **Prov** 2:20; 4:14; 6:30; 7:26; 8:4; 31; 10:14; 11:7; 16; 12:12; 13:20; 15:11; 16:6; 17:6; 18:16; 20:6; 29(2); 22:29; 23:28; 24:1; 9; 19; 25:1; 6; 27; 26:16; 28:5; 7; 12; 28; 29:8(2); 30:14; **Eccl** 2:3; 8(2); 3:10; 14; 18; 19; 6:1; 7:2; 19; 8:11; 14(2); 9:3; 11(2); 12; 14; 17; 12:3; **Song** 3:7; 4:4; **Is** 2:11; 17; 3:25; 5:3; 7; 13; 22; 6:12; 7:13; 24; 9:3; 17; 11:15; 13:18; 19:12; 21:9; 17; 22:2; 6; 23:4; 24:6; 26:19; 28:14; 29:11; 13; 14(2); 19; 31:3; 8; 35:8; 36:12; 38:16; 39:3; 40:30; 41:9; 14; 43:4; 44:11; 25; 45:14; 24; 46:8; 51:7; 52:14; 53:3; 57:1; 59:10; 60:11; 61:6; 64:4; 66:24; **Jer** 4:3; 4; 5:5; 16; 26(2); 6:11; 23; 30; 8:9; 9:2(2); 10; 21; 22; 10:7; 9; 11:2; 9; 21; 22; 23; 15:8; 10; 16:6; 7(2); 17:25; 18:11; 21(2); 19:10; 26:21; 22(2); 31:13; 32:19; 20; 32; 44; 33:5; 34:18; 35:13; 36:31; 37:10; 38:4; 9; 10; 11; 16; 39:4; 17; 40:7(2); 8; 9; 41:1; 2; 3; 5; 7; 8; 9; 12; 15; 16; 42:17; 43:2; 6; 9; 44:15; 19; 20; 27; 46:9; 15; 21;

47:2; 48:14; 15; 31; 36; 49:15; 22; 26(2); 28; 50:30(2); 35; 36; 51:3; 14; 30; 32; 56; 57(2); 52:7; 13; 25(3); **Lam** 1:15(2); 18; 2:15; 21; 3:33; 4:14(2); 5:13; 14; **Eze** 6:4; 13; 8:11; 16; 9:2; 4; 6; 11:1; 2; 15; 12:16; 14:3; 14; 16; 18; 15:3; 16:17; 19:3; 6; 21:14; 31; 22:9; 23:6; 7; 12; 14; 23; 40; 42; 45; 24:17; 22; 25:4; 10; 26:10; 17; 27:8; 9; 10; 11; 13; 15; 27; 30:5; 17; 31:14; 34:31; 35:8; 36:10; 12(2); 13; 14; 15; 37; 38; 38:20; 39:14; 20(2); 47:15; **Dan** 2:12; 13; 14; 18; 24(2); 27; 38; 43; 48; 3:12; 13; 20; 21; 22; 23; 24; 25; 27; 4:6; 17(2); 18; 25(2); 32(2); 33; 5:7; 8; 15; 21(2); 6:5; 11; 15; 24; 26; 9:7; 10:7; 16; **Hos** 6:7; 10:13; 13:2; **Joel** 1:2; 12; 2:7(2); 28(2); 3:9(2); **Amos** 2:11; 4:10; 6:9; 8:13; **Obad** 7(2); 8; 9; **Jonah** 1:10(2); 13; 16; **Mic** 2:8; 12; 5:5; 7; 6:12; 7:2; 6; **Nah** 2:3(2); 3:10(2); **Hab** 1:14; **Zeph** 1:12; 17(2); 2:11; **Hag** 1:11; **Zec** 2:4; 3:8; 7:2; 7; 8:4; 10; 23; 9:17; 10:5; 11:6; 14:11; **Mt** 2:1; 7; 16(2); 4:19; 5:11; 13; 15; 16; 19; 6:1; 2; 5; 14; 15; 16; 18; 7:12; 16; 8:27; 9:8; 17; 27; 28; 10:17; 22; 32; 33; 12:31(2); 36; 41; 13:17; 25; 14:21; 35; 15:9; 38; 16:13; 23; 17:22; 19:11; 12; 26; 20:30; 21:25; 26; 41; 22:16; 23:5; 7; 13; 28; 34; 26:33; 28:4; **Mk** 1:17; 37; 3:28; 5:20; 6:12; 44; 7:7; 8; 21; 8:4; 24; 27; 33; 9:31; 10:27; 11:30; 32(2); 12:14; 13:13; 14:51; **Lk** 1:25; 2:14; 3:15; 5:10; 18; 6:22; 26; 31; 38; 44; 7:20; 31; 9:14; 30; 32; 44; 11:31; 32; 44; 46; 12:8; 9; 36; 48; 13:4; 14; 14:24; 35; 16:15(2); 17:12; 34; 36; 18:1; 10; 11; 27; 20:4; 6; 20; 21:1; 17; 22:63; 23:11; 24:4; 7; **Jn** 1:4; 7; 2:10; 24; 3:19; 26; 4:20; 28; 38; 5:23; 41; 6:10(2); 14; 8:17; 11:48; 12:32; 43; 13:35; 15:6; 17:6; 18:3; **Acts** 1:10; 11; 16; 21; 24; 2:5; 13; 14; 17(2); 22; 29; 37; 45; 3:12; 4:4; 12; 13; 16; 21; 5:4; 6; 10; 14; 25; 29; 35(2); 36; 38(2); 6:3; 11; 7:2; 8:2; 3; 12; 9:2; 7; 38; 10:5; 17; 19; 21; 11:3; 11; 13; 20; 13:15; 16; 26; 38; 50; 14:11; 15; 15:1; 7; 13; 17; 22(2); 25; 26; 16:17; 20; 35; 17:12; 22; 26; 30; 31; 34; 18:13; 19:7; 19; 29; 35; 37; 20:26; 30; 21:23; 26; 28(2); 38; 22:1; 4; 15; 23:1; 6; 21; 24:16; 25:23; 24; 28:17; **Rom** 1:18; 27(3); 2:16; 29; 5:12; 18(2); 6:19; 11:4; 12:16; 17; 18; 14:18; 16:19; **1Cor** 1:25(2); 26; 2:5; 3:3; 21; 4:6; 9; 7:7; 23; 9:19; 22; 10:15; 33; 13:1; 14:2; 3; 20; 21; 15:19; 32; 39; 16:13; **2Cor** 3:2; 5:11; 8:13; 21; 9:13; **Gal** 1:1; 10(3); 3:15; 6:10; **Eph** 3:5; 9; 4:8; 14; 5:28; 6:7; **Phil** 2:7; 4:5; **Col** 2:8; 22; 3:23; **1Th** 1:5; 2:4; 6; 13; 15; 3:12; 5:14; 15; **2Th** 3:2(2); **1Ti** 2:1; 4; 5; 8; 4:10; 5:1; 24; 6:5; 9; **2Ti** 2:2; 24; 3:2; 8; 9; 13; 4:16; **Titus** 1:8; 14; 2:2; 6; 11; 3:2; 8; **Heb** 5:1(2); 6:16; 7:8; 28; 9:17; 27; 12:14; 23; **Jas** 1:5; 2:6; 3:9; 5:1; **1Pet** 2:4; 15; 17; 4:2; 6; **2Pet** 1:21; 3:7; 9; **1Jn** 2:13; 14; 5:9; **3Jn** 12; **Jude** 4(2); **Rev** 6:15(3); 8:11; 9:4; 6; 7; 10; 15; 18; 20; 11:13; 13:13; 14:4; 16:2; 8; 9; 18; 21(2); 18:13; 23; 19:18(2); 21:3

MEN'S

120, 582, *444, 4283*

Gen 24:32; 44:1; **Deut** 4:28; **1Sa** 24:9; **1Kin** 12:13; 13:2; **2Kin** 19:18; 23:20; **Ps** 115:4; 135:15; **Is** 37:19; **Jer** 48:41; **Hab** 2:8; 17; **Mt** 23:4; 27; **Lk** 9:56; 21:26; **Acts** 17:25; **2Cor** 10:15; **1Ti** 5:22; 24; **1Pet** 4:15; **Jude** 16

MIDST

1459, 2436, 2872, 2677, 2686, 3820, 3824, 7130, 8432, 8484, *3319, 3321, 3322*

Gen 1:6; 2:9; 3:3; 15:10; 19:29; 48:16; **Ex** 3:2; 4; 20; 8:22; 11:4; 14:16; 22; 23; 27; 29; 15:19; 23:25; 24:16; 18; 26:28; 27:5; 28:32; 33:3; 5; 34:12; 38:4; 39:23; **Lev** 16:16; **Num** 2:17; 5:3; 16:47; 19:6; 33:8; 35:5; **Deut** 4:11; 12; 15; 33; 34; 36; 5:4; 22; 23; 24; 26; 9:10; 10:4; 11:3; 6; 13:5; 16; 17:20; 18:15; 19:2; 23:14; 32:51; **Josh** 3:17; 4:3; 5; 8; 9; 10; 18; 7:13; 21; 23; 8:13; 22; 10:13; 13:9; 16; **Judg** 15:4; 18:20; 20:42; **1Sa** 11:11; 16:13; 18:10; **2Sa** 1:25; 4:6; 6:17; 18:14; 20:12; 23:12; 20; 24:5; **1Kin** 3:8; 6:27; 8:51; 20:39; 22:35; **2Kin** 6:20; **1Chr** 11:14; 16:1; 19:4; **2Chr** 6:13; 20:14; 32:4; **Neh** 4:11; 9:11; **Est** 4:1; **Job** 21:21; **Ps** 22:14; 22; 46:2; 5; 48:9; 55:10; 11; 57:6; 74:4; 12; 78:28; 102:24; 110:2; 116:19; 135:9; 136:14; 137:2; 138:7; **Prov** 4:21; 5:14; 8:20; 14:33; 23:34; 30:19; **Song** 3:10; **Is** 4:4; 5:2; 8; 25; 6:5; 12; 7:6; 10:23; 12:6; 16:3; 19:1; 3; 14; 19; 24; 24:13; 18; 25:11; 29:23; 30:28; 41:18; 52:11; 58:9; 66:17; **Jer** 6:1; 6; 9:6; 12:16; 14:9; 17:11; 21:4; 29:8; 30:21; 37:12; 41:7(2); 46:21; 48:45; 50:8; 37; 51:1; 6; 45; 47; 63; 52:25; **Lam** 1:15; 3:45; 4:13; **Eze** 1:4(2); 5; 5:2; 4; 5; 8; 10; 12; 6:7; 7:4; 9; 8:11; 9:4(3); 10:10; 11:7(2); 9; 11; 23; 12:2; 13:14; 14:8; 9; 15:4; 16:53; 17:16; 20:8; 21:32; 22:3; 7; 9; 13; 18; 19; 20; 21; 22(2); 25(2); 27; 23:39; 24:7; 26:5; 12; 15; 27:4; 25; 26; 27(2); 32; 34; 28:2; 8; 14; 16(2); 18; 22; 23; 29:3; 4; 12; 21; 30:7(2); 31:14; 17; 18; 32:20; 21; 25(2); 28; 32; 36:23; 37:1; 26; 28; 38:12; 39:7; 41:7; 43:7; 9; 46:10; 48:8; 10; 15; 21; 22; **Dan** 3:6; 11; 15; 21; 23; 24; 25; 26; 4:10; 7:15; 9:27; **Hos** 5:4; 11:9; **Joel** 2:27; **Amos** 2:3; 3:9(2); 6:4; 7:8; 10; **Jonah** 2:3; **Mic** 2:12; 5:7; 8; 10; 13; 14; 6:14; 7:14; **Nah** 3:13; **Hab** 2:19; 3:2(2); **Zeph** 2:14; 3:5; 11; 12; 15; 17; **Zec** 2:5; 10; 11; 5:4; 7; 8; 8:3; 8; 14:1; 4; **Mt** 10:16; 14:24; 18:2; 20; **Mk** 6:47; 7:31; 9:36; 14:60; **Lk** 2:46; 4:30; 35; 5:19; 6:8; 17:11; 21:21; 22:55; 23:45; 24:36; **Jn** 7:14; 8:3; 9; 59; 19:18; 20:19; 26; **Acts** 1:15; 18; 2:22; 4:7; 17:22; 27:21; **Phil** 2:15; **Heb** 2:12; **Rev** 1:13; 2:1; 7; 4:6; 5:6(2); 6:6; 7:17; 8:13; 14:6; 19:17; 22:2

MIGHT

202, 410, 1369, 1370, 2428, 3201, 3581, 3966, 5797, 5807, 6108, 8632, *1410, 1411, 2479, 2480*

Gen 12:19; 13:6; 17:18; 26:10; 30:34; 41; 31:27; 36:7; 37:22; 43:32; 49:3; **Ex** 10:1; 12:33; 36:18; 39:21(2); **Lev** 24:12; 26:45; **Num** 4:37; 41; 14:13; 22:41; **Deut** 2:30; 3:24; 4:14; 36; 42(2); 5:29; 6:1; 5; 23; 24; 8:3; 16(2); 17; 28:32; 29:6; 32:13; **Josh** 4:24(2); 11:20(3); 20:9; 22:16; 24; 27; 24:8; **Judg** 3:2; 5:31; 6:14; 9:24; 16:30; 18:7; **Ruth** 1:6; **1Sa** 4:4; 13:10; 14:14; 18:27; 20:6; **2Sa** 6:14; 10:10; 15:4; 17:14; 17; 22:41; **1Kin** 2:27; 7:7; 8:1; 16; 12:15; 15:17; 23; 16:5; 27; 19:4; 22:7; 45; **2Kin** 7:2; 19; 10:19; 34; 13:8; 12; 14:15; 28; 15:19; 20:20; 22:17; 23:10; 24; 25; 33; 24:16; **1Chr** 4:10; 7:2; 5; 12:8; 13:8; 29:2; 12; 30; **2Chr** 2:12; 6:5; 6; 10:15; 11:1; 16:1; 18:6; 20:6; 12; 25:20; 31:4; 32:18; 31; 34:25; 35:12; 15; 22; 36:22; **Ezr** 1:1; 5:10; 8:21; **Neh** 5:3; 10; 6:13(2); 7:5; 9:24; 10:37; **Est** 4:2; 10:2; **Job** 6:8; 9:33; 16:21; 23:3(2); 7; 30:2; 38:13(2); **Ps** 18:40; 68:18; 76:5; 78:6; 7; 8; 105:45; 106:8; 107:7; 109:16; 118:13; 119:11; 71; 101; 148; 145:6; **Prov** 22:21; **Eccl** 2:3; 3:18(2); 9:10; **Is** 11:2; 28:13; 33:13; 40:26; 29; 61:3(2); 64:1; **Jer** 9:1; 2; 23; 10:6; 13:11; 16:21; 17:23; 19:15; 20:17; 25:7; 26:19; 27:15(2); 43:3; 44:8(2); 49:35; 51:30; **Eze** 17:7; 8(3); 14(3); 15; 20:12; 26(2); 24:8; 32:29; 30; 36:3; 40:4; 41:6; **Dan** 1:4; 5; 8; 2:20; 23; 3:28; 4:6; 30; 5:2; 6:2; 17; 8:4; 9:11; 13; **Joel** 3:3; 6; **Amos** 1:13; **Jonah** 4:5; 6; **Mic** 3:8; 7:16; **Hab** 3:16; **Zec** 4:6; 6:7; 8:9; 11:10; 14; **Mal** 2:4; 15; **Mt** 1:22; 2:15; 23; 4:14; 8:17; 28; 12:10; 14; 17; 13:35; 14:36; 21:4; 32; 34; 22:15; 26:4; 9; 56; 27:35; **Mk** 3:2; 6; 14; 5:18; 6:56; 10:51; 11:13; 18; 12:2; 14:1; 5; 11; 35; 16:1; **Lk** 1:74; 4:29; 5:19; 6:7; 11; 8:9; 10(2); 38; 11:54; 15:29; 17:6; 19:15; 23; 48; 20:20(2); 22:2; 4; 23:23; 26; 24:45; **Jn** 1:7; 3:17; 5:34; 40; 6:28; 8:6; 9:36; 39(2); 10:10(2); 17; 11:4; 57; 12:9; 10; 38; 14:29; 15:11(2); 25; 16:33; 17:3; 12; 13; 19; 18:9; 28; 32; 19:24; 28; 31(2); 35; 38; 20:31(2); **Acts** 1:25; 4:21; 5:15; 7:19; 8:15; 9:2; 12; 21; 13:42; 15:17; 17:27; 20:24; 22:24; 24:26; 25:21; 26; 26:32; 27:12; **Rom** 1:10; 13; 3:26; 4:11(2); 16(2); 18; 5:20; 21; 6:6; 7:13(2); 8:4; 29; 9:11; 17(2); 23; 10:1; 11:14; 19; 32; 14:9; 15:4; 9; 16; **1Cor** 2:12; 4:6; 8; 5:2; 9:19; 20(2); 21; 22(2); 23; 14:19; **2Cor** 1:15; 2:4; 9; 4:10; 11; 15; 5:4; 21; 7:9; 12; 8:9; 9:5; 11:4; 7; 12:8; **Gal** 1:4; 16; 2:4; 5; 16; 19; 3:14(2); 22; 24; 4:5; 17; **Eph** 1:10; 21; 2:7; 16; 3:10; 16; 19; 4:10; 5:26; 27; 6:10; 22(2); **Phil** 3:4(2); 11; **Col** 1:9; 10; 11; 18; 2:2; 4:8; **1Th** 2:6; 16; 3:10(2); **2Th** 2:6; 10; 12; 3:8; **1Ti** 1:16; **2Ti** 4:17(2); **Titus** 2:14; 3:8; **Philem** 1:8; 13; **Heb** 2:14; 17; 6:18; 9:15; 10:36; 11:15; 35; 12:10; 18; 13:12; **Jas** 5:17; **1Pet** 1:7; 21; 3:18; 4:6; **2Pet** 1:4; 2:11; **1Jn** 2:19; 3:8; 4:9; **3Jn** 8; **Rev** 7:12; 12:14; 15; 13:17; 16:12

MINE

589, 3027, 5978, *846, 1683, 1698, 1699, 1700, 3427, 3450*

Gen 14:22; 15:3; 24:33; 45; 30:25; 30; 31:10; 40; 42; 43; 41:13; 44:21; 48:5(2); 49:6; **Ex** 7:4; 5; 17; 13:2; 17:9; 18:4; 19:5; 20:26; 21:14; 23:23; 32:34; 33:23; 34:19; **Lev** 18:4; 30; 20:26; 22:9; 25:23; **Num** 3:12; 13(2); 45; 8:14; 17; 10:30; 12:7; 14:28; 16:28; 18:8; 22:29; 23:11; 24:10; 13; **Deut** 8:17; 10:3; 26:13; 29:19; 32:22; 23; 41(2); 42; **Josh** 14:7; **Judg** 6:36; 37; 7:2; 8:7; 11:30; 16:17; 17:2; 19:23; **Ruth** 4:6; **1Sa** 2:1(2); 28; 29; 33; 35(2); 12:3; 14:24; 29; 43; 15:14; 17:46; 18:17; 19:17; 20:1; 21:3; 4; 23:7; 24:6; 10(3); 11; 12; 13; 25:33; 26:11; 18; 23; 24; 28:2; **2Sa** 5:19; 20; 6:22; 11:11; 14:5; 30; 16:12; 18:12(2); 13; 19:37; 22:4; 24; 35; 38; 41; 49; **1Kin** 1:33; 48; 2:15; 22; 3:26; 9:3(2); 10:6; 7; 11:21; 33; 14:8; 20:3(2); 21:20; **2Kin** 4:13; 5:26; 6:32; 10:6; 30(2); 18:34; 35(2); 19:28; 34; 20:6; 15; 21:14; **1Chr** 12:17(3); 14:10; 11(2); 16:22; 17:14; 16; 22:18; 28:2; 29:3; 17; **2Chr** 7:15(2); 16(2); 9:5; 6; 29:10; 32:13; 14(2); 15(2); 17(2); **Neh** 7:5; **Job** 3:10; 4:12; 16; 6:11; 7:7; 21; 9:20; 31; 10:6; 14; 15; 13:1(2); 14; 15; 23; 14:17; 16:4; 9; 17; 20; 17:2; 7; 13; 19:4; 10; 13; 15; 17; 27; 27:5; 7; 31:1; 6; 7(3); 9; 12; 22(2); 25; 33; 35; 32:6; 10; 17; 33:8; 40:4; 41:11; 42:5; **Ps** 3:3; 7; 5:8; 6:7(2); 10; 7:4; 5; 6; 8; 9:3; 13:2; 3; 4; 16:5; 17:3; 18:3; 23; 34; 37; 40; 48; 23:5; 25:2; 11; 15; 18; 19; 26:1; 3; 6; 11; 27:2; 6(2); 11; 12; 31:9; 10; 11(2); 15; 32:5; 8; 35:2; 13; 15; 19; 26; 38:4(2); 10; 18; 19; 20; 39:4; 5; 40:6; 12(2); 41:5; 9; 11; 12; 42:10; 49:4; 50:10; 11; 12; 51:2; 9; 54:4; 5; 7(2); 55:13(2); 56:2; 9; 59:1; 10; 60:7(3); 69:3; 4(2); 18; 19; 71:10; 77:4; 6; 88:8; 9; 18; 89:21; 92:11(3); 101:3; 6; 102:8; 105:15; 108:8(3); 109:20; 29; 116:8; 119:11; 18; 37; 82; 92; 98; 112; 121; 123; 136; 139; 148; 153; 157; 121:1; 123:1; 131:1; 132:4(2); 17; 138:7; 139:2; 22; 141:8; 143:9; 12; **Prov** 5:13; 8:14; 23:15; **Eccl** 1:16; 2:1; 3(2); 10; 3:17; 18; 7:25; 8:16; **Song** 1:6; 2:16; 6:3; 8:12; **Is** 1:15; 16; 24(2); 5:9; 6:5; 10:5(2); 25; 13:3; 16:4; 11; 19:25; 22:14; 29:23; 37:29; 35; 38:12; 14; 39:4; 42:1; 43:1; 25; 45:4; 47:6; 48:5; 9; 11(2); 13; 49:22; 50:4; 5; 8; 11; 51:5(2); 16; 56:5; 7(2); 60:7; 63:3; 4; 5; 6; 65:9; 12; 16; 22; 66:2; 4; **Jer** 2:7; 3:12; 15; 7:20; 9:1; 11:15; 12:3; 7(2); 8; 9; 14; 13:17; 14:17; 15:14; 16; 16:17(2); 18; 21; 17:4; 18:6; 20:9; 23:9; 24:6; 32:8; 12; 31; 37; 33:5; 42:18; 44:6; 28; 48:31; 36(2); 50:11; 51:25; **Lam** 1:16(2); 19; 20; 21; 2:11; 22; 3:19; 48; 49; 51(2); 52; 54; **Eze** 5:11; 13; 7:3; 4; 8; 9; 8:1; 3; 5; 18(2); 9:1; 5; 10; 11:20; 12:7; 13:9; 13; 14:13; 16:8; 18(2); 17:19; 18:4(2); 20:5(2); 6; 17; 22; 23; 28; 40; 42; 21:17; 31; 22:8; 13; 20; 26; 31; 23:4; 5; 39; 41(2); 25:7; 13; 14; 16; 29:3; 9; 35:3; 10; 36:7; 21; 22; 37:19; 43:8; 44:8; 12; 24; 47:14; **Dan** 4:4; 10; 34(2); 36; 8:3; 10:5; **Hos** 2:5; 10; 8:5; 13; 9:15; 11:8; 9; 13:11; 14; 14:4; **Amos** 1:8; 9:2; 4; **Jonah** 2:2; **Mic** 7:8; 10(2); **Hab** 1:12; 3:19; **Zeph** 1:4; 3:8; 10; **Hag** 1:9; 2:8(2); **Zec** 1:18; 2:1; 9; 5:1; 9; 6:1; 8:6; 9:8(2); 10:3; 11:14; 12:4; 13:7; **Mal** 1:6; 7; 10; 3:7; 10; 17; **Mt** 7:24; 26; 20:15; 23; 25:27; **Mk** 9:24; 10:40; **Lk** 1:44; 2:30; 9:38; 11:6; 18:3; 19:23; 27; **Jn** 2:4; 5:30(2); 6:38; 7:16; 8:50; 9:11; 15; 30; 10:14; 14:24; 16:14; 15(2); 17:10(2); **Acts** 11:6; 13:22; 21:13; 26:4; **Rom** 11:13; 12:19; 16:13; 23; **1Cor** 1:15; 4:3; 9:2; 3; 10:33; 16:21; **2Cor** 11:26; 30; 12:5; **Gal** 1:14; 6:11; **Phil** 1:4; 3:9; **2Th** 3:17; **Titus** 1:4; **Philem** 1:12; 18; 19; **Rev** 22:16

MORE

518, 637, 1058, 1490, 1980, 2351, 3148, 3254, 3499, 3513, 3588, 3651, 4480, 4481, 5674, 5736, 5750, 5922, 5973, 6105, 6440, 7138, 7227, 7231, 7235, 7608, 7725, 8145, *197, 243, 316, 414, 1065, 1308, 1508, 1617, 1833, 2001, 2089, 2115, 3122, 3123, 3185, 3187, 3370, 3745, 3761, 3765, 3844, 4053, 4055, 4056, 4057, 4119, 4179, 4325, 4369, 4707, 5112, 5228, 5236, 5245*

Gen 3:1; 8:12; 21(2); 9:11(2); 15; 17:5; 29:30; 32:28; 34:19; 35:10; 36:7; 37:3; 4; 5; 8; 9; 38:26(2); 44:23; **Ex** 1:9; 12(2); 5:7; 9; 8:29; 9:28; 29; 34; 10:28; 29; 11:1; 6; 14:13; 16:17; 30:15; 36:5; 6; **Lev** 6:5; 11:42; 13:5; 33; 54; 17:7; 26:18; 21; 27:20; **Num** 3:46; 8:25; 18:5; 22:15(2); 18; 19; 26:54; 33:54(2); **Deut** 1:11; 3:26; 5:22; 25; 7:7; 17; 10:16; 13:11; 17:13; 16; 18:16; 19:9; 20; 20:1; 28:68; 31:2; 27; **Josh** 2:11; 5:1; 12; 7:12; 10:11; 23:13; **Judg** 2:19; 8:28; 10:13; 13:21; 15:3; 16:30; 18:24; **Ruth** 1:11; 17; 3:10; **1Sa** 1:18; 2:3; 3:17; 7:13; 14:30; 44; 15:35; 18:2; 8; 29; 30; 20:13; 22:15; 23:3; 24:17; 25:22; 36; 26:21; 27:1; 4; 28:15; 30:4; **2Sa** 2:28(2); 3:9; 35; 4:11; 5:13; 6:22; 7:10(2); 20; 10:19; 11:25; 14:10; 11; 16:11; 18:8; 19:13; 28; 29; 35; 43; 20:6; 21:17; 23:23; **1Kin** 2:23; 32; 10:5; 10; 16:33; 19:2; 20:10; **2Kin** 2:12; 21; 4:6; 6:16; 23; 31; 9:35; 12:7; 8; 21:8; 9; 24:7; **1Chr** 4:9; 11:21; 14:3(2); 17:9(2); 18; 19:19; 21:3; 23:26; 24:4; **2Chr** 9:4; 10:11; 15:19; 20:25; 25:9; 28:13; 22; 29:34; 32:7; 16; 33:8; 23(2); **Ezr** 7:20; **Neh** 2:17; 13:18; 21; **Est** 1:19; 2:14; 17; 4:13; 6:6; **Job** 3:21; 4:17(2); 7:7; 8; 9; 10(2); 14:12; 15:16; 20:9(2); 23:12; 24:20; 32:15; 16; 34:19; 23; 31; 32; 35:2; 11; 41:8; 42:12; **Ps** 4:7; 10:18; 19:10; 39:13; 40:5; 12; 41:8; 52:3; 69:4; 71:14(2); 73:7; 74:9; 76:4; 77:7; 78:17; 83:4; 87:2; 88:5; 103:16; 104:35; 115:14(2); 119:99; 100; 130:6(2); 139:18; **Prov** 3:15; 4:18(2); 10:25; 11:24; 31; 12:26; 15:11; 17:10; 19:7; 21:3; 27; 26:12; 28:23; 29:20; 30:2; 31:7; **Eccl** 1:16; 2:9; 15; 16; 25; 4:2; 13; 5:1; 6:5; 8; 7:19; 26; 9:5; 6; 17; 10:10; **Song** 1:4; 5:9(2); **Is** 1:5(3); 13; 2:4; 5:4; 9:1; 10:20; 13:12; 15:9; 19:7; 23:10; 12; 26:21; 30:19; 20; 32:5; 38:11; 47:1; 5; 51:22; 52:1; 14(2); 54:1; 4; 9; 56:12; 60:18; 19; 20; 62:4(2); 8; 65:19; 20; **Jer** 2:31; 3:11; 16(2); 17; 7:32; 10:20; 11:19; 16:14; 19:6; 20:9; 22:10; 11; 12; 30; 23:4; 7; 36; 25:27; 30:8; 31:12; 29; 34(2); 40; 33:24; 34:10; 38:9; 42:18; 44:26; 46:23; 48:2; 49:7; 50:39; 51:44; **Lam** 2:9; 4:7; 15; 16; 22; **Eze** 5:6(2); 7; 9; 6:14; 12:23; 24; 25; 28; 13:15; 21; 23; 14:11(2); 21; 15:2; 16:41; 42; 47; 51; 52(2); 63; 18:3; 19:9; 20:39; 21:5; 13; 27; 32; 23:11(2); 27; 24:13; 27; 26:13; 14; 21; 27:36; 28:19; 24; 29:15(2); 16; 30:13; 32:13; 33:22; 34:10; 22; 28; 29(2); 36:12; 14(2); 15(3); 30; 37:22(2); 23; 39:7; 28; 29; 42:6; 43:7; 45:8; **Dan** 2:30; 3:19; 7:20; 11:8; **Hos** 1:6; 2:16; 17; 6:6; 9:15; 13:2(2); 14:3; 8; **Joel** 2:2; 19; 3:17; **Amos** 5:2; 7:8; 13; 8:2; 9:15; **Jonah** 4:11; **Mic** 4:3; 5:12; 13; **Nah** 1:12; 14; 15; 2:13; **Hab** 1:8; 13; **Zeph** 3:11; 15; **Zec** 9:8; 11:6; 13:2; 14:11; 21; **Mal** 2:13; **Mt** 5:37; 47; 6:25; 30; 7:11; 10:15; 25; 31; 37(2); 11:9; 22; 24; 12:45; 13:12; 18:13; 16; 19:6; 20:10; 31; 21:36; 22:46; 23:15; 25:20; 26:53; 27:23; **Mk** 1:45; 4:24; 6:11; 7:12; 36(2); 8:14; 9:8; 25; 10:8; 48; 12:33; 43; 14:5; 25; 31; 15:14; **Lk** 3:13; 5:15; 7:26; 9:13; 10:12; 14; 35; 11:13; 26; 12:4; 7; 23(2); 24; 28; 48; 14:8; 15:7; 19; 21; 18:30; 39; 20:36; 21:3; 22:16; 44; 23:5; **Jn** 4:1; 41; 5:14; 18; 6:66; 7:31; 8:11; 10:10; 11:54; 12:43; 14:19; 15:2; 4; 16:10; 21; 25; 17:11; 19:8; 21:15; **Acts** 4:19; 5:14; 8:39; 9:22; 13:34; 17:11; 18:26; 19:32; 20:25; 35; 38; 22:2; 23:13; 15; 20; 21; 24:10; 22; 25:6; 27:11; 12; **Rom** 1:25; 2:18; 3:7; 5:9; 10; 15; 17; 20; 6:9(2); 7:17; 20; 8:37; 11:6(4); 12; 24; 12:3;

14:13; 15:15; 23; **1Cor** 6:3; 9:19; 12:22(2); 23(2); 24; 31; 14:18; 15:10; **2Cor** 1:12; 2:4; 3:9; 11; 4:17; 5:16; 7:7; 13; 15; 8:17; 22; 10:8; 11:23(3); 12:15; **Gal** 1:14; 3:18; 4:7; 27; **Eph** 2:19; 4:14; 28; **Phil** 1:9(2); 14; 24; 26; 2:12; 28; 3:4; **1Th** 2:17; 4:1(2); 10(2); **2Ti** 2:16; 3:4; **Philem** 1:16; 21; **Heb** 1:4; 2:1; 3:3(2); 6:17; 7:15; 8:6; 12; 9:11; 14; 10:2; 17; 18; 25; 26; 11:4; 32; 12:19; 25; 26; 27; **Jas** 4:6; **1Pet** 1:7; **2Pet** 1:19; **Rev** 2:19; 3:12; 7:16(2); 9:12; 12:8; 18:11; 14; 21; 22(3); 23(2); 20:3; 21:1; 4(2); 22:3

MOREOVER

518, 637, 1571, 3148, 3254, 5750, *235, 1161, 2089, 2532, 3063, 3739*

Gen 24:25; 32:20; 45:15; 47:4; 48:22; **Ex** 3:6; 15; 11:3; 18:21; 26:1; 30:22; **Lev** 7:21; 26; 14:46; 18:20; 25:45; **Num** 13:28; 16:14; 33:56; 35:31; **Deut** 1:28; 39; 7:20; 28:45; 60; **Judg** 10:9; **Ruth** 4:10; **1Sa** 2:19; 12:23; 14:21; 17:37; 20:3; 24:11; 28:19; **2Sa** 7:10; 12:8; 15:4; 17:1; 13; 21:15; **1Kin** 1:47; 2:5; 14; 44; 8:41; 10:18; 14:14; **2Kin** 12:15; 21:16; 23:15; 24; **1Chr** 11:2; 12:40; 17:10; 18:12; 22:15; 23:5; 25:1; 26:4; 28:7; 29:3; **2Chr** 1:5; 2:12; 4:1; 20; 6:32; 7:7; 9:17; 17:6; 19:8; 21:11; 16; 23:9; 25:5; 26:9; 11; 27:4; 28:3; 29:19; 30; 31:4; 32:29; 35:1; 36:14; **Ezr** 6:8; 10:25; **Neh** 2:7; 3:6; 26; 5:14; 17; 6:17; 9:12; 22; 11:19; 12:8; **Est** 5:12; **Job** 27:1; 29:1; 35:1; 40:1; **Ps** 19:11; 78:67; 105:16; **Eccl** 3:16; 5:9; 6:5; 12:9; **Is** 3:16; 7:10; 8:1; 19:9; 29:5; 30:26; 39:8; **Jer** 1:11; 2:1; 8:4; 20:5; 25:10; 33:1; 23; 37:18; 39:7; 40:13; 44:24; 48:35; **Eze** 3:1; 10; 4:3; 16; 5:14; 7:1; 11:1; 12:17; 16:20; 29; 17:11; 19:1; 20:12; 45; 22:1; 23:36; 38; 28:11; 35:1; 36:16; 37:16; 26; 45:1; 46:18; 48:22; **Zec** 4:8; 5:6; **Mt** 6:16; 18:15; **Lk** 16:21; **Acts** 2:26; 11:12; 19:26; **Rom** 5:20; 8:30; **1Cor** 4:2; 10:1; 15:1; **2Cor** 1:23; 8:1; **1Ti** 3:7; **Heb** 9:21; 11:36; **2Pet** 1:15

MOST

2429, 2896, 3524, 3800, 4581, 4791, 5920, 5943, 5945, 5946, 6579, 6944, 7230, 8077, 8563, *40, 2236, 2903, 3122, 4118, 4119, 5310*

Gen 14:18; 19; 20; 22; **Ex** 26:33; 34; 29:37; 30:10; 29; 36; 40:10; **Lev** 2:3; 10; 6:17; 25; 29; 7:1; 6; 10:12; 17; 14:13; 21:22; 24:9; 27:28; **Num** 4:4; 19; 18:9(2); 10; 24:16; **Deut** 32:8; **2Sa** 22:14; 23:19; **1Kin** 6:16; 7:50; 8:6; **1Chr** 6:49; 23:13; **2Chr** 3:8; 10; 4:22; 5:7; 31:14; **Ezr** 2:63; **Neh** 7:65; **Est** 6:9; **Job** 34:17; **Ps** 7:17; 9:2; 21:6; 7; 45:3; 46:4; 47:2; 50:14; 56:2; 57:2; 73:11; 77:10; 78:17; 56; 82:6; 83:18; 91:1; 9; 92:1; 8; 107:11; **Prov** 20:6; **Song** 5:11; 16; 8:6; **Is** 14:14; 26:7; **Jer** 6:26; 50:31; 32; **Lam** 3:35; 38; 4:1; **Eze** 2:7; 23:12; 33:28; 29; 35:3; 7; 41:4; 42:13(2); 43:12; 44:13; 45:3; 48:12; **Dan** 3:20; 26; 4:17; 24; 25; 32; 34; 5:18; 21; 7:18; 22; 25(2); 27; 9:24; 11:15; 39; **Hos** 7:16; 11:7; 12:14; **Mic** 7:4; **Mt** 11:20; **Mk** 5:7; **Lk** 1:1; 3; 7:42; 43; 8:28; **Acts** 7:48; 16:17; 20:38; 23:26; 24:3; 26:5; 25; **1Cor** 14:27; 15:19; **2Cor** 12:9; **Heb** 7:1; **Jude** 20; **Rev** 18:12; 21:11

MUCH

634, 637, 834, 1431, 1571, 1767, 1931, 2479, 3254, 3498, 3515, 3588, 3605, 3966, 4180, 4276, 4767, 5704, 6079, 6581, 7114, 7225, 7227, 7230, 7235, 7690, *23, 1280, 2425, 2470, 2579, 3123, 3366, 3383, 3386, 3433, 3588, 3745, 3761, 4055, 4056, 4124, 4183, 4214, 5118, 5248*

Gen 23:9; 26:16; 30:43; 34:12; 41:49; 43:34; 44:1; 50:20; **Ex** 12:38; 42; 14:28; 16:5; 18; 22; 30:23; 36:5; 7; **Lev** 7:10; 13:7; 22; 27; 35; 14:21; **Num** 16:3; 7; 20:20; 21:4; 6; **Deut** 2:5; 3:19; 28:38; 31:27; **Josh** 11:4; 13:1; 19:9; 22:8(3); **Ruth** 1:13; **1Sa** 2:16; 14:30(2); 18:30; 19:2; 20:13; 23:3; 26:24(2); **2Sa** 4:11; 8:8; 13:34; 14:25; 16:11; 17:12; 18:33; **1Kin** 4:29; 8:27; 10:2; 12:28; **2Kin** 5:13; 10:18; 12:10; 21:6; 16; **1Chr** 18:8; 20:2; 22:4; 8; **2Chr** 2:16; 6:18; 14:13; 14; 17:13; 20:25; 24:11; 25:9; 13; 26:10; 27:3; 5; 28:8; 30:13; 32:4(2); 15; 27; 29; 33:6; 36:14; **Ezr** 7:22; 10:13; **Neh** 4:10; 6:16; 9:37; **Est** 1:18; **Job** 4:19; 9:14; 15:10; 16; 25:6; 31:25; 34:19; 42:10; **Ps** 19:10; 33:16; 35:18; 119:14; 107; **Prov** 7:21; 11:31; 13:23; 14:4; 15:6; 11; 16:16; 17:7; 19:7; 10; 24; 21:27; 25:16; 27; **Eccl** 1:18(2); 5:12; 17; 20; 7:16; 17; 9:18; 10:18; 12:12; **Song** 4:10; **Is** 21:7; 30:33; 56:12; **Jer** 2:22; 36; 40:12; **Eze** 14:21; 15:5; 17:15; 22:5; 23:32; 26:7; 33:31; **Dan** 4:12; 21; 7:5; 28; 11:13; **Joel** 2:6; **Jonah** 4:11; **Nah** 2:10; **Hag** 1:6; 9; **Mal** 3:13; **Mt** 6:7; 26; 30; 7:11; 10:25; 12:12; 13:5; 15:33; 26:9; **Mk** 1:45; 2:2; 3:20; 4:5; 5:10; 21; 24; 6:31; 34; 7:36; 10:14; 41; 12:41; **Lk** 5:15; 6:3; 34; 7:11; 12; 26; 47; 8:4; 9:37; 10:40; 11:13; 12:19; 24; 28; 48(3); 16:5; 7; 10(2); 18:13; 39; 19:15; 24:4; **Jn** 3:23; 6:10; 11; 7:12; 12:9; 12; 24; 14:30; 15:5; 8; **Acts** 5:8(2); 37; 7:5; 9:13; 10:2; 11:24; 26; 14:22; 15:7; 16:16; 18:10; 27; 19:2; 26; 20:2; 26:24; 27:9; 10; 16; **Rom** 1:15; 3:2; 5:9; 10; 15; 17; 20; 9:22; 11:12; 24; 12:18; 15:22; 16:6; 12; **1Cor** 2:3; 5:1; 6:3; 12:22; 16:19; **2Cor** 2:4; 3:9; 11; 6:4; 8:4; 15; 22; **Phil** 1:14; 2:12; **1Th** 1:5; 6; 2:2; **1Ti** 3:8; **2Ti** 4:14; **Titus** 2:3; **Philem** 1:8; 16; **Heb** 1:4; 7:22; 8:6; 9:14; 10:25; 29; 12:9; 20; 25; **Jas** 5:16; **1Pet** 1:7; **2Pet** 2:18; **Rev** 5:4; 8:3; 18:7(2); 19:1

MY

1700, 3450

Gen 2:23(2); 4:9; 13; 23(4); 6:3; 18; 9:9; 11; 13; 15; 12:13(2); 19; 13:8; 15:2; 3; 16:2; 5(2); 8; 17:2; 4; 7; 9; 10; 13; 14; 19; 21; 18:3; 12; 19:2; 8; 18; 19; 20; 34; 20:2; 5(4); 9; 11; 12(4); 13(2); 15; 21:10; 23(2); 30; 22:7(2); 8; 18; 23:4(2); 6; 8(2); 11(2); 13; 15; 24:2; 3; 4(3); 6; 7(3); 8(2); 12(2); 14; 18; 27(3); 35; 36(2); 37(2); 38(3); 39; 40(3); 41(3); 42(2); 44; 48(3); 49; 54; 56(2); 65; 26:5(5); 7(2); 9; 24; 27:1; 2; 4; 7; 8(2); 11; 12; 13(2); 18(2); 19; 20; 21(2); 24; 25(2); 26; 27; 31; 34; 36(2); 37; 38(2); 41(2); 43(3); 46(2); 28:21(2); 29:4; 14(2); 15; 21(2); 32(2); 34; 30:3(2); 6; 8; 15(2); 16; 18(3); 20; 23; 25; 26(3); 30; 32; 33(2); 31:5; 6; 7; 26; 28(2); 29; 30; 35; 36(2); 37(2); 39; 40; 41; 42(2); 43(4); 50(2); 32:4; 5; 9(2); 10; 11; 17; 18; 29; 30; 33:8; 9; 10(2); 11; 13; 14(2); 15; 34:8; 30; 35:3; 37:7(2); 16; 33; 35; 38:11; 26; 39:8(2); 15; 18; 40:9; 11; 16(2); 17; 41:9; 17; 22; 40(2); 51(2); 52; 42:10; 28(2); 36; 37(2); 38(2); 43:3; 5; 9; 14; 29; 44:2; 5; 7; 9; 10; 16(2); 17; 18(2); 19; 20; 22; 23; 24(2); 27(2); 29; 30; 32(2); 33; 34(2); 45:3; 9; 12(2); 13(3); 28; 46:31(2); 47:1(2); 6; 9(3); 18(3); 25; 29; 30; 48:9; 15(2); 16(2); 18; 19; 22(2); 49:3(3); 4; 6; 9; 26; 29(2); 50:5(3); 25; **Ex** 3:7; 10; 15(2); 20(2); 4:1; 10; 13; 18; 22(2); 23; 5:1; 6:3; 4; 5; 7:3(2); 4(2); 16; 8:1; 8; 20; 21; 22; 23; 9:1; 13; 14; 15; 16(2); 17; 27; 29; 10:1; 2; 3; 4; 17; 28(2); 11:9; 12:31; 13:15; 19; 15:2(4); 9(3); 16:4; 28(2); 18:4; 19; 19:5(2); 20:6; 24; 21:5(3); 22:24; 25; 23:18(2); 21; 27; 25:2; 29:43; 31:13; 32:10; 22; 33; 33:12; 14; 17; 19; 20; 22(2); 23(2); 34:9; 25; **Lev** 6:17; 15:31; 17:10; 18:4; 5(2); 26(2); 19:3; 12; 19; 30(2); 37(2); 20:3(3); 5; 6; 8; 22(2); 21:23; 22:2; 3; 31; 32; 23:2; 25:18(2); 21; 42; 55; 26:2(2); 3(2); 9; 11(2); 12; 15(4); 17; 25; 30; 42(3); 43(2); 44; **Num** 6:27; 10:30; 11:15; 23; 28; 29; 12:6; 7; 8; 11; 14:17; 22(3); 24; 34; 15:40; 20:19(2); 24; 21:2; 22:18; 38; 23:10; 12; 24:14; 25:11(3); 12; 27:14; 28:2(3); 32:25; 27; 36:2(2); **Deut** 2:28; 4:5; 10; 5:10; 29; 8:17; 9:4; 15; 17; 11:13; 18; 18:16; 18; 19(2); 20; 22:16; 17; 25:7(2); 26:5; 14(2); 31:16; 17(2); 18; 20; 27; 29; 32:1; 2(2); 20; 34; 39; 40; 41; 42; **Josh** 1:2; 7; 2:12; 13(4); 5:14; 7:11; 19; 21; 9:23; 14:8(2); 9; 11(2); 15:16; 22:2; 24:15; **Judg** 1:3; 7; 12; 2:1; 2; 20(2); 4:18; 5:9; 21; 6:10; 13; 15(3); 18; 8:19(2); 23; 9:9; 11(2); 13; 15; 17; 18; 29; 11:7; 12; 13; 19; 31; 35(2); 36; 37(2); 12:2; 3(3); 13:8; 18; 14:3; 16(3); 18(2); 15:1; 16:13; 17(2); 28; 17:2; 3(2); 13; 18:24; 19:23; 24; 20:4; 5; 6; 23; 28; **Ruth** 1:11(2); 12; 13; 16(2); 2:2; 8(2); 13; 21(2); 22; 3:1; 10; 11(2); 16; 18; 4:4; 6; 10; **1Sa** 1:15(2); 16; 26(2); 27; 2:1(2); 24; 28; 29(3); 32; 35; 3:6; 16; 4:16; 9:5; 16(3); 17; 21; 10:2; 12:2(2); 5; 14:29; 39; 40; 42; 15:11; 25; 30; 16:22; 18:17; 18(2); 21; 19:2; 3(2); 20:1(2); 2(2); 9; 12; 13(2); 15; 29(2); 42; 21:2; 8(2); 15(2); 22:3(2); 8(3); 12; 15; 23; 23:10; 12; 17(2); 24:6; 8; 10; 11(3); 15; 16; 21(3); 25:5; 11(4); 24; 25(2); 26(2); 27(2); 28(2); 29; 30; 31(3); 39; 41; 26:17(3); 18; 19; 20; 21(2); 23; 24; 25; 27:12; 28:9; 21(2); 29:6; 8; 9; 30:13; 15; 23; **2Sa** 1:9; 10; 26; 2:22; 3:7; 12; 13(2); 14; 18(2); 21; 28; 4:8; 9; 5:2; 7:5; 7; 8(2); 10; 11; 13; 14; 15; 18; 9:7; 10; 11(2); 11:11(3); 12:28; 13:4; 5(2); 6(2); 11; 12; 13; 20; 25; 26; 32; 33; 14:7(2); 9(2); 11; 12; 15; 16; 17(2); 18; 19(2); 20; 22; 24; 31; 15:7; 15; 21(2); 16:3; 4; 9; 11(3); 18:5; 18; 22; 28; 31; 32; 33(5); 19:4(3); 12(3); 13(2); 19(2); 20; 26(2); 27(2); 28(2); 30; 35; 37(3); 20:9; 22:2(3); 3(6); 7(4); 18; 19(2); 21(2); 22; 25(2); 29(2); 30; 33(2); 34(2); 35; 37(2); 39; 44; 47(2); 23:2; 5(3); 24:3(2); 17; 21; 22; 24; **1Kin** 1:2(2); 13(2); 17(2); 18; 20(2); 21(2); 24(2); 27(2); 29; 30(2); 31; 33; 35(2); 36; 37(2); 48; 2:15; 20; 24; 26(2); 31; 32; 38; 44; 3:6; 7(2); 14(3); 17; 20(2); 21(2); 22(2); 23(2); 26; 5:3; 4; 5(3); 6; 9(3); 6:12(4); 13; 8:15; 16(3); 17; 18(2); 19; 20; 24; 25(2); 26; 28; 29; 59; 9:3; 4(2); 6(2); 7(2); 13; 11:11(2); 13; 32; 33(3); 34(3); 36(2); 38(5); 12:10(2); 11(2); 14(2); 13:6; 30; 31; 14:7; 8(2); 15:19; 16:2(2); 17:1; 12; 18(2); 20; 21; 18:7; 10; 12; 13; 19:4(2); 10; 14; 20(2); 20:4; 6; 7(4); 9; 32; 34(2); 21:2; 3; 4; 6; 22:4(2); 49; **2Kin** 1:13; 14; 2:12(2); 19; 3:7(2); 4:1(2); 16; 19(2); 28; 29(2); 5:3; 6; 13; 18(2); 20; 22; 6:8; 12; 15; 21; 26; 28; 29; 8:5; 12; 9:7; 32; 10:6; 9; 15; 16; 13:14(2); 14:9; 17:13(3); 18:23; 24; 27; 19:12; 23; 24; 28(2); 34; 20:5; 6; 15; 19; 21:4; 7; 8; 15; 22:17; 23:27(2); **1Chr** 4:10; 11:2(2); 19; 16:22; 17:4; 6; 7(2); 9; 10; 13(2); 14; 25; 21:3(3); 17(2); 23; 22:5; 7(3); 8(2); 10(2); 11; 14; 28:2(2); 3; 4(3); 5(2); 6(3); 7(2); 9; 20; 29:1; 2(2); 3(3); 14; 17; 19; **2Chr** 1:8; 9; 11; 2:3; 4; 7; 8; 13; 14; 15; 6:4; 5(3); 6(2); 7; 8(2); 9; 10; 15; 16(3); 19; 40; 7:13; 14(3); 16; 17(2); 19(2); 20(3); 8:11; 10:10(2); 11(2); 14(2); 12:7; 8; 16:3; 18:3; 13; 25:16; 18; 29:11; 32:13; 14; 15; 33:4; 7; 34:25; **Ezr** 7:13; 28; 9:3(4); 5(6); 6(3); 10:3; **Neh** 1:2; 6; 9(2); 2:3(2); 5; 8; 12(2); 18; 4:16; 23(2); 5:10(2); 13; 14; 16; 17; 19; 6:9; 14; 19; 7:2; 5; 13:14(3); 19; 22; 29; 31; **Est** 4:16; 5:7(2); 8(2); 7:3(4); 4(2); 8:6(2); **Job** 1:5; 8; 21; 2:3; 3:10; 24(2); 4:14; 15(2); 5:8; 6:2(2); 3; 4; 7(2); 8; 11(2); 12(2); 13; 15; 21; 24; 29; 30(2); 7:5(2); 6; 7; 11(3); 13(3); 15(2); 16; 19; 21; 9:14; 15; 16; 17; 18; 21(2); 25; 27(2); 28; 30; 10:1(4); 6; 12; 15; 20; 11:4; 13:6(2); 14(3); 16; 17(2); 18; 19; 23(2); 26; 27(3); 14:14(2); 16(2); 17; 16:4; 5(2); 6; 7; 8(2); 12; 13(2); 15(2); 16(2); 17; 18(2); 19(2); 20; 17:1(2); 7; 11(3); 13; 14(3); 15(2); 19:2; 5; 8(2); 9(2); 12; 13; 14(2); 15; 16(2); 17(2); 19; 20(4); 21; 22; 23; 25; 26(2); 27; 20:2; 3(2); 21:2; 4(2); 6; 23:2(3); 4(2); 7; 11; 12; 16; 17; 24:25; 27:2(2); 3(2); 4(2); 6(2); 29:3; 4(2); 5; 6; 7; 14; 18(2); 19(2); 20(3); 21; 22(2); 24; 30:1; 10; 11; 12(2); 13(2); 15(2); 16; 17(2); 18(3); 22; 25; 27; 30(2); 31(2); 31:4(2); 5; 7; 8; 9; 10; 13(2); 17; 18(2); 20; 21(2); 22; 24(2); 25; 27(3); 30; 31; 32; 33(2); 35; 36; 37; 38; 32:17; 19; 20; 22; 33:1(2); 2(3); 3(3); 7(2); 11(2); 34:2; 5; 6(2); 16; 36; 35:2; 3; 10; 36:3(2); 4; 37:1; 38:10; 40:4; 8; 42:7(2); 8(3); **Ps** 2:6(2); 7; 3:2; 3; 4; 7; 4:1(2); 2; 7; 5:1(2); 2(3); 3(2); 8; 6:2; 3; 4; 6(4); 8; 9(2); 7:1(2); 2; 3(2); 5(2); 8; 10; 9:1; 4(2); 13; 11:1(2); 13:2(2); 3; 5; 14:4; 16:1; 2(3); 3; 4; 5(2); 7; 8; 9(3); 10; 17:1(2); 2; 3; 5(2); 6; 9; 13; 18:1; 2(8); 6(4); 17; 18(2); 20(2); 21; 24(2); 28(3); 29; 32; 33(2); 34; 36(2); 38; 46(2); 19:14(4); 22:1(3); 2; 9; 10(2); 14(3); 15(3); 16(2); 17; 18(2); 19; 20(2); 22; 25(2); 23:1; 3; 5(2); 6; 25:1; 2; 5; 7(2); 15; 17(2); 18(2); 20(2); 26:2(2); 9(2); 12; 27:1(3); 2(2); 3; 4; 7; 8(2); 9(2); 10(2); 28:1; 2(2); 6; 7(5); 30:1; 2; 3; 6; 7; 9; 10; 11(2); 12(2); 31:1; 2; 3(2); 4; 5; 7(2); 8; 9(2); 10(4); 11; 13; 14; 15; 22(2); 32:3(2); 4; 5(3); 7; 34:1; 2; 4; 35:1; 3; 4(2); 7; 9; 10; 11; 12; 13(3); 14; 17(2); 23(4); 24; 27; 28; 36:1; 38:3(3); 5(2); 7(2); 8; 9(2); 10(2); 11(4); 12(2); 15; 16; 17; 18; 21; 22; 39:1(3); 2(2); 3(2); 4; 5; 7; 8; 9; 12(4); 40:1; 2(2); 3; 5; 8(2); 9; 10; 12; 14; 17(3); 41:4; 7; 9; 42:1; 2; 3(2); 4; 5; 6(2); 8(2); 9; 10; 11(3); 43:1; 2; 4(2); 5(3); 44:4; 6(2); 15(2); 45:1(2); 49:3(2); 4; 5; 15; 50:5; 7; 16(2); 17; 51:1; 2; 3(2); 5; 9; 14(2); 15(2); 53:4; 54:2(2); 3; 4; 55:1(2); 2; 4; 8; 13; 17; 18; 56:4; 5; 6(2); 8(2); 11; 13(2); 57:1(2); 4; 6(2); 7(2); 8; 59:1; 3(3); 4; 9; 10(2); 11; 16(2); 17(3); 60:7; 8(2); 61:1(2); 2; 5; 8; 62:1(2); 2(3); 5(2); 6(3); 7(4); 63:1(3); 3; 4; 5(2); 6; 7; 8; 9; 64:1(3); 66:13; 14(2); 16; 17(2); 18; 19; 20; 68:22; 24(2); 69:1; 3(3); 5(2); 6(2); 7; 8(2); 10(2); 11; 13; 18; 19(3); 20; 21(2); 70:2(2); 5(2); 71:1; 3(3); 4; 5(3); 6(2); 7; 8; 9; 10; 12(2); 13(2); 15; 17; 21; 22; 23(2); 24(2); 73:2(2); 13(2); 21(2); 23; 26(4); 28; 74:12; 77:1(2); 2(3); 3; 6(2); 10; 78:1(3); 2; 81:8; 11(2); 13(2); 14; 83:13; 84:2(3); 3(2); 8; 10; 86:2(2); 4; 6(2); 7; 11; 12(2); 13; 14; 87:7; 88:1; 2(2); 3(2); 9; 13; 14; 15; 89:1; 3(2); 20(2); 21; 24(3); 26(3); 27; 28(2); 30(2); 31(2); 33(2); 34(2); 35; 47; 50; 91:2(3); 9; 14; 16; 92:10; 11(2); 15; 94:17(2); 18; 19(2); 22(3); 95:9; 10; 11(2); 101:2; 7(2); 102:1(2); 3(2); 4(2); 5(3); 9; 11; 23(2); 24(2); 103:1; 2; 22; 104:1(2); 33(2); 34; 35; 105:15; 108:1(2); 8; 9(2); 109:1; 4(2); 5; 20; 22; 24(2); 26; 30; 110:1(2); 111:1; 116:1(2); 4; 7; 8(2); 11; 14; 16; 18; 118:6; 7(2); 14(2); 21; 28(2); 119:5; 10; 13; 20; 24(2); 25; 26; 28; 32; 34; 36; 39; 43; 48; 50(2); 54(2); 57; 58; 59(2); 69; 76; 77; 80; 81; 92; 97; 99(2); 101; 103(2); 105(2); 108; 109(2); 111; 114(2); 115; 116; 120; 129; 131; 133; 139; 143; 145; 149; 154; 157; 161; 167; 168; 169; 170; 171; 172; 174; 175; 120:1; 2; 6; 121:1; 2; 122:8; 129:1; 2; 3; 130:2(2); 5; 6; 131:1; 2; 132:3(2); 12(2); 14; 137:5; 6(3); 138:1; 3; 139:2(2); 3(3); 4; 8; 13(2); 14; 15; 16(2); 23(2); 140:4; 6(2); 7(2); 141:1; 2(2); 3(2); 4; 5(2); 6; 8(2); 142:1(3); 2(2); 3(2); 4(2); 5(2); 6(2); 7; 143:1(2); 3(2); 4(2); 6(2); 7; 8; 10; 11; 12; 144:1(3); 2(6); 145:1; 21; 146:1; 2; **Prov** 1:8; 10; 15; 23(3); 24; 25(2); 30(2); 2:1(3); 3:1(3); 11; 21; 4:2; 3(2); 4(2); 5; 10(2); 20(3); 5:1(3); 7; 12; 13; 20; 6:1; 3; 20; 7:1(3); 2(2); 4; 6(2); 14; 16; 17; 24; 8:4; 6; 7(2); 8; 10; 19(2); 31; 32; 34(2); 9:5; 19:27; 20:9(2); 22:17; 23:15(2); 16; 19; 26(2); 24:13; 21; 27:11(2); 30:9; 31:2(3); **Eccl** 1:13; 16; 17; 2:7; 9; 10(5); 11; 15(2); 18; 19; 20; 4:8; 7:15; 28; 8:9; 9:1; 12:12; **Song** 1:6; 7; 9; 12; 13(2); 14; 15; 16; 2:2; 3(2); 6; 7; 8; 9; 10(3); 13(2); 14; 16; 17; 3:1(2); 2; 3; 4(2); 5; 4:1; 7; 8; 9(4); 10(2); 11; 12(2); 16(2); 5:1(9); 2(8); 3(2); 4(2); 5(3); 6(3); 7; 8; 10; 16(2); 6:2; 3(2); 4; 9(2); 12; 7:9; 10; 11; 12; 13; 8:1(2); 2(2); 3; 4; 10; 12; 14; **Is** 1:3; 12; 14; 25; 3:7; 12(2); 15; 5:1(3); 3; 4; 5; 13; 6:7; 7:13; 8:4(2); 16; 10:2; 6; 8; 10; 13(2); 14; 24; 11:9; 12:2(4); 13:3(3); 14:13; 25(2); 15:5; 16:9; 11; 18:4(2); 19:25(2); 20:3; 21:3; 4(2); 8(2); 10(2); 22:4; 20; 24:16(2); 25:1; 26:9(2); 19; 20; 27:5; 28:23(2); 29:23; 30:1; 2; 32:9(2); 13; 18; 33:13; 34:5(2); 16; 36:8; 9; 12; 19; 20(2); 37:12; 24; 25; 29(2); 35; 38:10(2); 12; 13; 15(2); 16; 17(2); 20; 39:4; 8; 40:1; 27(3); 41:8(2); 9; 10; 25; 42:1(3); 8(3); 14; 19(2); 43:4; 6(2); 7(2); 10(2); 12; 13; 20(2); 21; 44:1; 2; 3(2); 8; 17; 20; 21(2); 28(2); 45:4; 11(2); 12; 13(2); 23; 46:10(2); 11; 13(3); 47:6; 48:3; 5(2); 9(2); 11(2); 12; 13; 18; 49:1(2); 2; 3; 4(4); 5(2); 6(2); 11(2); 14; 16; 21; 22; 50:1; 2(2); 6(3); 7; 51:4(3); 5(2); 6(2); 7; 8(2); 16(2); 22; 52:4; 5(2); 6(2); 13; 53:8; 11; 54:8; 10(2); 55:8(2); 9(2); 11(2); 56:1(2); 4(2); 5; 6; 7(2); 57:11; 13; 14; 21; 58:1; 2; 13; 59:21(3); 60:7; 10(2); 13(2); 21(2); 61:10(2); 62:1; 9; 63:3(3); 4; 5; 6; 8; 65:1; 2; 3; 5; 8; 9(2); 10; 11; 13(3); 14; 15; 19; 22; 25; 66:1(3); 2; 5; 18; 19(3); 20; **Jer** 1:9(2); 12; 16; 2:7; 11; 13; 19; 27; 31; 32; 3:4(2); 13; 19; 4:1; 4; 11; 19(6); 20(2); 22; 31; 5:9; 14; 22; 26; 29; 31; 6:8; 12; 14; 19(2); 26; 27; 7:10;

11; 12(3); 14; 15; 20; 23(2); 25; 30(2); 31; 8:7; 11; 18; 19; 21; 22; 9:1(2); 2; 7; 9; 13(2); 10:19(2); 20(5); 11:4(2); 7; 10(2); 15; 20; 12:7; 10(3); 14; 16(4); 13:2; 10; 17; 14:14; 15; 17; 15:1(2); 6; 7; 10; 15; 18(2); 19; 16:5; 11; 17; 18; 19(3); 21(2); 17:3; 14; 16; 17; 18:2; 10(2); 15; 20; 22; 19:5; 15; 20:9; 10(2); 11; 12; 14; 15; 17(2); 18; 21:10; 12; 22:18; 21; 24; 23:1; 2(2); 3; 9; 11; 13; 22(3); 25; 27(3); 28(2); 29; 30; 32; 39; 24:7; 25:8; 9; 13; 15; 29; 26:4; 5; 27:5(2); 6; 15; 29:9; 10; 19(2); 21; 23; 32; 30:3; 10; 22; 31:1; 9; 14(2); 18; 19(2); 20(2); 26; 32; 33(2); 32:7; 8; 9; 31(2); 34; 35; 37; 38; 40; 41(2); 33:5(2); 20(2); 21(3); 22; 24; 25; 26; 34:15(2); 16; 18; 35:13; 15; 36:6; 37:20(2); 38:9; 26; 39:16; 42:18(2); 43:10; 44:4; 6; 10(2); 11; 26(2); 29; 45:3(2); 46:27; 28; 49:25; 37; 38; 50:6; 51:20; 34; 35(2); 45; **Lam** 1:9; 12; 13(2); 14(3); 15(2); 16(2); 18(3); 19(2); 20; 21; 22(3); 2:11(3); 21(2); 22; 3:4(3); 7; 8; 9(2); 11; 13; 14; 16; 17; 18(2); 19; 20; 21; 24(2); 48; 51; 53; 56(3); 58(2); 59(2); 4:3; 6; 10; **Eze** 1:28; 2:2; 7; 3:2; 3; 4; 10; 14; 17; 23; 24; 4:14(3); 5:6(4); 7(2); 11; 13(3); 6:12; 14; 7:8; 14; 22(2); 8:6; 9:6; 8; 10:2; 13; 19; 11:12(2); 13; 20(2); 12:7(2); 13(2); 28; 13:9; 10; 13(2); 15; 18; 19(2); 21; 23; 14:8(2); 9(2); 11; 19; 21; 15:7(2); 16:8; 14; 17(2); 19; 21; 27; 42(2); 60; 62; 17:19; 20(2); 18:9(2); 17(2); 19; 21; 25; 29; 20:8(2); 9; 11(2); 12; 13(4); 14; 15; 16(3); 19(2); 20; 21(5); 22; 24(3); 39; 44; 21:3; 4; 5; 10; 12(2); 17; 31; 22:8; 20; 21; 22; 26(2); 31; 23:18(2); 25; 38(2); 39; 24:13; 18; 21; 25:3; 14(4); 17; 28:25; 29:3; 30:15; 24; 25; 32:3(2); 10; 32; 33:7; 22(2); 31; 34:6(2); 8(5); 10(2); 11; 12; 15; 17; 19; 22; 23; 24; 26; 30; 31(2); 36:5(2); 6(2); 8; 12; 18; 20; 23; 27(3); 28; 37:12; 13; 14; 23; 24(3); 25(2); 26; 27(2); 28; 38:14; 16(2); 17; 18(2); 19(2); 20; 21; 39:7(3); 17; 19; 20; 21(3); 23; 24; 25; 29(2); 43:3; 7(3); 8(3); 44:4; 7(5); 8(2); 9; 11; 13; 15; 16(3); 23; 24(4); 45:8(2); 9; 46:18; 48:11; **Dan** 1:10(2); 2:3; 23; 3:14; 15; 4:4; 5(2); 8; 9; 10; 13(2); 18; 19; 24; 27; 30(2); 36(5); 5:13; 6:22; 26; 7:2; 15(3); 28(3); 8:17; 18; 9:3; 4(2); 18; 19; 20(5); 10:3; 8; 9(2); 10(2); 15; 16(4); 17(2); 19; 12:8; **Hos** 1:9; 10; 2:2; 5(6); 7; 9(4); 12(2); 23(3); 4:6; 8; 12; 5:10; 15(2); 6:5; 11; 7:2; 12; 8:1(2); 2; 12; 9:8; 17; 10:10; 11:1; 7; 8; 12:8; 13:11; **Joel** 1:6; 7(2); 13; 2:1; 25; 26; 27; 28; 29; 3:2(3); 3; 5(3); 17; **Amos** 2:7; 7:8; 15; 8:2; 9:3; 10; 12; 14; **Obad** 13; 16; **Jonah** 1:12; 2:2; 5; 6(2); 7(2); 4:2(2); 3; **Mic** 1:9; 2:4; 7; 8; 9(2); 3:3; 5; 6:3; 5; 7(4); 16; 7:1; 7(2); 9; **Hab** 1:12; 2:1; 3:16(3); 18; 19(3); **Zeph** 2:8; 9(2); 12; 3:8(3); 10(2); 11; **Hag** 2:5; 23; **Zec** 1:6(3); 9; 16; 17; 2:11; 3:7(4); 8; 4:4; 5; 6; 13; 5:4; 6:4; 8; 8:7; 8; 11:4; 8; 10(2); 12(2); 12:5; 13:5; 6; 7(2); 9(3); 14:5; **Mal** 1:6(2); 11(3); 14; 2:2; 4; 5(2); 9; 3:1; 17; 4:2; 4; **Mt** 2:6; 15; 3:17; 5:11; 7:21; 8:6; 8(2); 9; 21; 9:18; 10:18; 22; 32; 33; 39; 11:10; 27; 29; 30(2); 12:18(4); 44; 48(2); 49(2); 50(2); 13:30; 35; 15:13; 22; 16:17; 18; 25; 17:5; 15; 18:5; 10; 19; 20; 21; 35; 19:20; 29; 20:21; 23(4); 21:13; 28; 37; 22:4(3); 44(2); 24:5; 9; 35; 36; 48; 25:27(2); 34; 40; 26:12(2); 18(2); 26; 28; 29; 38; 39; 42; 53; 27:35(2); 46(2); 28:10; **Mk** 1:2; 11; 3:33(2); 34(2); 35(2); 5:9; 23; 30; 6:23; 8:35; 38; 9:7; 17; 37; 39; 41; 10:20; 29; 40(2); 51; 11:17; 12:6; 36(2); 13:6; 9; 13; 31; 14:8; 14; 22; 24; 34; 15:34(2); 16:17; **Lk** 1:18; 20; 25; 43; 44; 46; 47(2); 2:49; 3:22; 6:47; 7:6; 7; 8; 27; 44(2); 45; 46(2); 8:21(2); 9:24; 26; 35; 38; 48; 59; 61; 10:22; 29; 40; 11:7; 24; 12:4; 13; 17; 18(3); 19; 45; 14:23; 24; 26; 27; 33; 15:6; 17; 18; 24; 29; 16:3; 5; 24; 27; 18:21; 41; 19:8; 23(2); 46; 20:13; 42(2); 21:8; 12; 17; 33; 22:11; 19; 20; 28; 29; 30(2); 42; 23:46; 24:39(2); 49; **Jn** 2:16; 3:29; 4:34; 49; 5:17; 24; 30; 31; 43; 47; 6:32; 51; 54(2); 55(2); 56(2); 65; 7:6; 8; 16; 8:14; 16; 19(2); 21; 28; 31(2); 37; 38; 43(2); 49; 51; 52; 54(2); 56; 10:14; 15; 16; 17(2); 18; 25; 26; 27(2); 28; 29(2); 30; 32; 37; 11:21; 32; 12:7; 26(2); 27; 47; 48; 13:6; 8; 9(3); 35; 37; 38; 14:2; 7; 12; 13; 14; 15; 20; 21(2); 23(2); 24; 26; 27; 28; 15:1; 7; 8(2); 9; 10(3); 11; 12; 14; 15; 16; 20; 21; 23; 24; 16:5; 10; 23; 24; 26; 17:13; 24; 18:11; 36(4); 37; 19:24(2); 20:13; 17(4); 21; 25(2); 27(2); 28(2); 21:15; 16; 17; **Acts** 2:14; 17; 18(3); 25(2); 26(3); 27; 34(2); 7:34; 49(3); 50; 59; 9:15; 16; 10:30; 11:8; 13:22; 33; 15:7; 17; 19; 16:15; 20:24(2); 25; 29; 34; 22:1; 6; 24:14; 17; 25:26; 26:4(2); 10; 28:19; **Rom** 1:8; 9(3); 2:16; 3:7; 7:4; 18; 23(3); 9:1; 2; 3(2); 17(2); 25(2); 26; 10:1; 21; 11:3; 14; 27; 15:14; 24(3); 31; 16:3; 4; 5; 7(2); 8; 9; 11; 21(2); 25; **1Cor** 1:4; 11; 2:4(2); 4:14; 17(2); 5:4; 7:25; 40; 8:13(2); 9:1; 15; 17; 18(2); 27; 10:14; 29; 11:24; 25; 33; 13:3(2); 14:14(2); 18; 19(2); 15:58; 16:6; 18; 24; **2Cor** 1:16; 23; 2:3; 13(3); 6:13; 16; 18; 7:4(2); 8:10; 23; 11:1; 12:9(3); 21; **Gal** 1:13; 14(2); 15; 4:14(2); 19; 20; 6:17; **Eph** 1:16; 3:4; 13; 14; 6:10; 19; 21; **Phil** 1:3; 7(3); 8; 13; 14; 16; 19; 20(3); 22; 26; 2:2; 12(3); 25(2); 3:1; 8; 4:1(3); 3; 14; 16; 19; **Col** 1:24(2); 2:1; 4:7; 10; 11; 18; **1Ti** 1:2; 11; **2Ti** 1:2; 3(2); 6; 16; 2:1; 8; 3:10; 4:6; 7; 16; **Philem** 1:4(2); 10(2); 20; 23; 24; **Heb** 1:5; 13; 2:12; 13; 3:9; 10; 11(2); 4:3(2); 5; 5:5; 8:9; 10; 10:16; 34; 38; 12:5; 13:6; **Jas** 1:2; 16; 19; 2:1; 3; 5; 14; 18(2); 3:1; 10; 12; 5:10; 12; **1Pet** 5:13; **2Pet** 1:14; 15; 17; **1Jn** 2:1; 3:13; 18; **3Jn** 4; **Rev** 1:20; 2:3; 13(3); 16; 20; 26; 27; 3:5; 8(2); 10; 12(5); 16; 20; 21(2); 10:10(2); 11:3; 18:4; 21:7; 22:12

MYSELF

589, 5315, 846, 1683, 1691

Gen 3:10; 22:16; **Ex** 19:4; **Num** 8:17; 12:6; **Deut** 1:9; 12; 10:5; **Judg** 16:20; **Ruth** 4:6; **1Sa** 13:12; 20:5; 25:33; **2Sa** 18:2; 22:24; **1Kin** 18:15; 22:30; **2Kin** 5:18(2); **2Chr** 7:12; 18:29; **Neh** 5:7; **Est** 5:12; 6:6; **Job** 6:10; 7:20; 9:20; 27; 30; 10:1; 13:20; 19:4; 27; 31:17; 29; 42:6; **Ps** 18:23; 35:14; 55:12; 57:8; 101:2; 108:2; 109:4; 119:16; 47; 52; 131:1; 2; **Eccl** 2:3; 12; 14; 19; **Is** 33:10; 42:14; 43:21; 44:24; 45:23; **Jer** 8:18; 21:5; 22:5; 49:13; **Eze** 14:7; 20:5; 9; 29:3; 35:11; 38:23(2); **Dan** 10:3; **Mic** 6:6; **Hab** 3:16; **Zec** 7:3; **Lk** 7:7; 24:39; **Jn** 5:31; 7:17; 28; 8:14; 18; 28; 42; 54; 10:18; 12:49; 14:3; 10; 21; 17:19; **Acts** 10:26; 20:24; 24:10; 16; 25:22; 26:2(2); 9; **Rom** 7:25; 9:3; 11:4; 15:14; 16:2; **1Cor** 4:4; 6; 7:7; 9:19; 27; **2Cor** 2:1; 10:1; 11:7; 9(2); 16; 12:5; 13; **Gal** 2:18; **Phil** 2:24; 3:13; **Philem** 1:17

NAMELY

1722

Lev 1:10; **Num** 1:32; 9:15; 13:11; 31:8; **Deut** 4:43; 13:7; 20:17; **Judg** 3:3; 8:35; **1Chr** 6:57; 61; 9:23; 23:6; **Ezr** 10:18; **Neh** 12:35; **Est** 8:12; **Eccl** 5:13; **Is** 7:20; **Jer** 26:22; **Mk** 12:31; **Acts** 15:22; **Rom** 13:9

NEAR

413, 681, 3027, 5060, 5066, 5921, 5973, 7126, 7131, 7132, 7138, 7200, 7607, 7608, 316, 1448, 1451, 4139, 4317, 4334

Gen 12:11; 18:23; 19:9; 20; 20:4; 27:21; 22; 25(2); 26; 27; 29:10; 33:3; 6; 7(2); 37:18; 43:19; 44:18; 45:4(2); 10; 48:10; 13; **Ex** 12:48; 13:17; 14:20; 16:9; 19:22; 20:21; 24:2; 28:43; 30:20; 40:32; **Lev** 9:5; 10:4; 5; 18:6; 12; 13; 17; 20:19; 21:2; **Num** 3:6; 5:16; 16:5(2); 9; 10; 40; 17:13; 26:3; 63; 31:12; 48; 32:16; 33:48; 50; 34:15; 35:1; 36:1; 13; **Deut** 1:22; 4:11; 5:23; 27; 16:21; 21:5; 25:11; **Josh** 3:4; 10:24(2); 15:46; 17:4; 18:13; 21:1; **Judg** 18:22; 19:13; 20:24; 34; **Ruth** 2:20; 3:9; 12; **1Sa** 4:19; 7:10; 9:18; 10:20; 21; 14:36; 38; 17:16; 40; 41; 30:21; **2Sa** 1:15; 14:30; 18:25; 19:42; 20:16; 17; **1Kin** 8:46; 18:30(2); 36; 21:2; 22:24; **2Kin** 4:27; 5:13; **2Chr** 6:36; 18:23; 21:16; 29:31; **Est** 5:2; 9:1; **Job** 31:37; 33:22; 41:16; **Ps** 22:11; 32:9; 73:28; 75:1; 107:18; 119:151; 169; 148:14; **Prov** 7:8; 10:14; 27:10; **Is** 13:22; 26:17; 29:13; 33:13; 34:1; 41:1(2); 5; 45:20; 21; 46:13; 48:16; 50:8(2); 51:5; 54:14; 55:6; 56:1; 57:3; 19; 65:5; **Jer** 12:2; 25:26; 30:21; 42:1; 46:3; 48:16; 24; 52:25; **Lam** 3:57; 4:18; **Eze** 6:12; 7:7; 12; 9:1; 6; 11:3; 18:6; 22:4; 5; 30:3(2); 40:46; 44:13(2); 15; 16; 45:4; **Dan** 3:8; 26; 6:12; 7:13; 16; 8:17; 9:7; **Joel** 3:9; 14; **Amos** 6:3; **Obad** 15; **Zeph** 1:14(2); 3:2; **Mal** 3:5; **Mt** 21:34; 24:33; **Mk** 13:28; **Lk** 15:1; 18:40; 19:41; 21:8; 22:47; 24:15; **Jn** 3:23; 4:5; 11:54; **Acts** 7:31; 8:29; 9:3; 10:24; 21:33; 23:15; 27:27; **Heb** 10:22

NEARER

7138, 1452

Ruth 3:12; **Rom** 13:11

NEITHER

369, 408, 518, 1077, 1115, 1571, 3808, 3809, 4480, 235, 2228, 2532, 2542, 3361, 3366, 3383, 3756, 3761, 3762, 3777

Gen 3:3; 8:21; 9:11(2); 17:5; 19:17; 21:26(2); 22:12; 24:16; 29:7; 39:9; 45:6; **Ex** 4:8; 9; 10; 5:2; 23; 7:22; 23; 8:32; 9:29; 35; 10:6; 14; 23; 12:39; 46; 13:7; 16:24; 20:23; 26; 22:21; 25; 31; 23:2; 3; 13; 18; 24:2; 30:9; 32; 32:18; 34:3(2); 24; 25; 28; 36:6; **Lev** 2:13; 3:17; 5:11; 7:18; 10:6; 11:43; 44; 17:12; 18:3; 17; 18; 21; 23(2); 26; 19:9; 10; 11(2); 12; 13; 16; 19; 26; 27; 31; 21:5; 7; 11; 12; 15; 22:24; 25; 32; 23:14; 22; 25:4; 5; 11; 26:1(2); 6; 20; 44; 27:33; **Num** 1:49; 5:13; 6:3; 11:19; 14:9; 23; 16:15; 18:3; 20; 22; 32; 20:5; 17; 21:5; 23:19; 21; 23; 25; 35:23; 36:9; **Deut** 1:21; 29; 42; 2:9; 27; 4:2; 28; 31; 5:18; 19; 20; 21(2); 7:3; 16; 26; 8:3; 4; 9:9; 18; 13:8(3); 16:4; 19; 22; 17:17(2); 18:16; 20:3; 21:4; 7; 22:5; 24:5; 15; 16; 26:13; 14; 28:36; 39; 64; 65; 29:6; 14; 30:11; 13; 31:8(2); 32:28; 39; 33:9; **Josh** 1:9; 2:11; 5:1; 12; 6:10; 7:12; 8:1; 11:14; 23:7(2); **Judg** 1:27; 29; 30; 31; 33; 2:23; 6:4; 8:23; 35; 11:34; 13:6; 7; 14; 23; 20:8; **Ruth** 2:8; **1Sa** 1:15; 2:2; 3:7; 4:20; 5:5; 12:4; 13:22; 16:8; 9; 20:27; 21:8; 24:11; 25:7; 15; 26:12; 27:9; 11; 28:6; 15; 30:15; 19(3); **2Sa** 1:21; 2:28; 7:10; 22; 12:17; 13:22; 14:7; 14; 18:3; 19:6; 19; 24; 20:1; 21:4; 10; 24:24; **1Kin** 3:11; 12; 26; 5:4; 6:7; 7:47; 11:2; 12:16; 13:8; 16; 16:11; 17:14; 16; 18:29; 22:31; **2Kin** 3:17; 4:23; 31; 5:17; 6:19; 7:10; 10:14; 12:8; 13:7; 23; 17:34; 38; 18:30; 21:8; 23:25; **1Chr** 4:27; 17:9; 20; 19:19; 27:24; **2Chr** 1:11; 12; 6:5; 9:9; 13:20; 20:12; 25:4; 26:18; 30:3; 32:15; 33:8; 34:2; 28; 35:18; **Ezr** 9:12; 10:13; **Neh** 2:12(2); 16; 4:11; 23; 5:5; 16; 8:10; 11; 9:17; 19; 34; 35; **Est** 2:7; 3:8; 4:16; **Job** 3:4; 9; 26(2); 5:4; 6; 21; 22; 7:10; 8:20; 9:33; 15:29(2); 18:19; 20:9; 21:9; 23:12; 17; 28:13; 15; 19; 31:30; 32:9; 14; 21; 33:7; 9; 34:12; 35:13; 36:26; 39:7; 17; 22; 24; **Ps** 5:4; 6:1; 16:10; 18:37; 22:24; 26:4; 27:9; 33:17; 35:19; 37:1; 38:1; 3; 44:3; 6; 17; 18; 55:12; 69:15; 73:5; 74:9; 75:6; 78:37; 81:9; 82:5; 86:8; 91:10; 92:6; 94:7; 14; 103:9; 109:12; 115:7; 17; 121:4; 129:8; 131:1; 135:17; **Prov** 2:19; 3:11; 25; 4:5; 6:25; 35; 15:12; 22:22; 23:6; 24:1; 19; 27:10; 30:3; 8; **Eccl** 1:11; 4:8(3); 5:6; 6:10; 7:16; 17; 8:8(2); 13; 16; 9:5; 6; 11; **Song** 8:7; **Is** 1:6(2); 23; 2:4; 7(2); 3:7; 5:12; 27; 7:4; 7; 12; 8:12; 9:13; 17; 10:7; 11:3; 13:20(3); 16:10; 17:8; 19:15; 22:11; 23:4; 26:18; 28:27; 29:22; 31:1; 33:20; 21; 36:15; 40:28; 42:8; 24; 43:2; 10; 18; 23; 24; 44:8; 19; 47:7; 8; 49:10; 50:5; 51:7; 18; 53:9; 54:4; 10; 55:8; 56:3(2); 57:16; 59:1; 6; 9; 60:19; 20; 62:4; 64:4; 9; 66:19; 24; **Jer** 2:6; 3:16(4); 17; 4:28; 5:12(2); 15; 24; 6:15; 7:6; 16(2); 31; 8:12; 9:10; 13; 16; 23; 10:5; 11:14; 14:13; 14(2); 15:10; 16:2; 4; 5; 6; 7(2); 13; 17; 17:8; 16; 22(2); 23; 18:23; 19:4; 5; 21:7; 22:3; 10; 23:4; 25:33; 29:8; 32; 30:10; 32:23; 35; 33:18; 22; 34:14; 35:6; 7; 9; 36:24; 37:2; 38:16; 42:13; 44:3; 10; 48:11; 49:18; 31; 50:39; 40; 51:43; 62; **Eze** 2:6; 3:9; 4:14; 5:7(2); 11(2); 7:4; 9; 11; 13; 19; 8:18; 9:5; 10; 11:11; 12; 13:5; 9(2); 15; 14:11; 16; 18; 20; 16:4; 16; 49; 51; 17:17; 18:6(3); 8; 15; 16(2); 20; 20:8; 17; 18; 21; 22:26; 23:8; 24:14(2); 16(2); 29:11; 15; 31:14(2); 32:13; 33:12; 34:4(4); 8; 10; 28; 29; 36:14; 15(3); 37:22; 23; 38:11; 39:10; 29; 43:7; 44:20; 21; 22; 47:12; 48:14; **Dan** 3:27; 6:4; 18; 8:4; 9:6; 10; 10:3(2); 17; 11:6; 15(2); 17; 20; 37; **Hos** 2:2; 4:15; 9:4; 14:3; **Joel** 2:2; 8; **Amos** 2:14; 15(2); 5:22; 7:14; **Obad** 12(2); 14(2); **Jonah** 3:7; 4:10; **Mic** 2:3; 4:3; 12; **Hab** 2:5; 3:17; **Zeph** 1:12; 18; 3:13; **Zec** 8:10; 11:16; 13:4; **Mal** 1:10(2); 3:11; 4:1; **Mt** 5:15; 34; 35; 36; 6:15; 20; 26; 28; 7:6; 18; 9:17; 10:9; 10(2); 11:18; 27; 12:4; 19; 32(2); 13:13; 16:9; 10; 21:27; 22:16; 30; 46; 23:10; 13(2); 24:18; 20; 25:13; **Mk** 4:22; 5:4; 8:14; 17; 26; 11:26; 33; 12:21; 24; 25; 13:11; 15; 19; 32; 14:40; 59; 68; 16:8; 13; **Lk** 1:15; 3:14; 6:43; 7:7; 33; 8:17; 27; 43; 9:3(4); 10:4; 11:33; 12:2; 22; 24(2); 29; 33; 47; 14:12; 35; 15:29; 16:26; 31; 17:21; 18:2; 34; 20:8; 21; 35; 36; **Jn** 1:25; 3:20; 4:15; 21; 5:37; 6:24; 7:5; 8:11; 19; 42; 9:3; 10:28; 13:16; 14:17; 27; 17:20; **Acts** 2:27; 31; 4:12; 32; 34; 8:21; 9:9; 15:10; 16:21; 17:25; 19:37; 20:24; 21:21; 23:8; 12; 21; 24:12(3); 13; 18; 25:8(2); 27:20; 28:21(2); **Rom** 1:21; 2:28; 4:19; 6:13; 8:7; 38; 9:7; 11; 14:21; **1Cor** 2:9; 14; 3:2; 7(2); 5:8; 6:9; 8:8(2); 9:15; 10:7; 8; 9; 10; 32; 11:9; 11(2); 16; 15:50; **Gal** 1:1; 12(2); 17; 2:3; 3:28(3); 5:6; 6:13; 15; **Eph** 4:27; 5:4; 6:9; **Phil** 2:16; **Col** 3:11; **1Th** 2:5; 6; **2Th** 2:2; 3:8; 10; **1Ti** 1:4; 7; 5:22; **Heb** 4:13; 7:3; 9:12; 18; 10:8; **Jas** 1:13; 17; 5:12(3); **1Pet** 2:22; 3:14; 5:3; **2Pet** 1:8; **1Jn** 2:15; 3:6; 10; 18; **2Jn** 10; **3Jn** 10; **Rev** 3:15; 16; 5:3(2); 4; 7:3; 16(2); 9:4(2); 20; 21; 12:8; 20:4(2); 21:4(2); 23; 27; 22:5

NEVER

369, 408, 518, 1074, 1077, 1256, 1755, 3808, 3809, 5331, 5704, 5769, 5957, 165, 1519, 1520, 3364, 3368, 3588, 3761, 3762, 3763, 4219, 4455

Gen 34:12; 41:19; **Lev** 6:13; **Num** 19:2; **Deut** 15:11; **Judg** 2:1; 14:3; 16:7; 11; **2Sa** 12:10; **2Chr** 18:7; 21:17; **Job** 3:16; 9:30; 21:25; **Ps** 10:6; 11; 15:5; 30:6; 31:1; 49:19; 55:22; 58:5; 71:1; 119:93; **Prov** 10:30; 27:20(2); 30:15; **Is** 13:20; 14:20; 25:2; 56:11; 62:6; 63:19; **Jer** 20:11; 33:17; **Eze** 16:63; 26:21; 27:36; 28:19; **Dan** 2:44; 12:1; **Joel** 2:26; 27; **Amos** 8:7; 14; **Hab** 1:4; **Mt** 7:23; 9:33; 21:16; 42; 26:33; 27:14; **Mk** 2:12; 25; 3:29; 9:43; 45; 11:2; 14:21; **Lk** 15:29; 19:30; 23:29(2); 53; **Jn** 4:14; 6:35(2); 7:15; 46; 8:33; 51; 52; 10:28; 11:26; 13:8; 19:41; **Acts** 10:14; 14:8; **1Cor** 13:8; **2Ti** 3:7; **Heb** 10:1; 11; 13:5; **2Pet** 1:10

NEVERTHELESS

61, 389, 403, 518, 657, 1297, 1571, 3588, 7535, 235, 1161, 2544, 3305, 3676, 4133

Ex 32:34; **Lev** 11:4; 36; **Num** 13:28; 14:44; 18:15; 24:22; 31:23; **Deut** 14:7; 23:5; **Josh** 13:13; 14:8; **Judg** 1:33; 2:16; **1Sa** 8:19; 15:35; 20:26; 29:6; **2Sa** 5:7; 17:78; 23:16; **1Kin** 8:19; 15:4; 14; 23; 22:43; **2Kin** 2:10; 3:3; 13:6; 23:9; **1Chr** 11:5; 21:4; **2Chr** 12:8; 15:17; 19:3; 30:11; 33:17; 35:22; **Neh** 4:9; 9:26; 31; 13:26; **Est** 5:10; **Ps** 31:22; 49:12; 73:23; 78:36; 89:33; 106:8; 44; **Prov** 19:21; **Eccl** 9:16; **Is** 9:1; **Jer** 5:18; 26:24; 28:7; 36:25; **Eze** 3:21; 16:60; 20:17; 22; 33:9; **Dan** 4:15; **Jonah** 1:13; **Mt** 14:9; 26:39; 64; **Mk** 14:36; **Lk** 5:5; 13:33; 18:8; 22:42; **Jn** 11:15; 12:42; 16:7; **Acts** 14:17; 27:11; **Rom** 5:14; 15:15;

1Cor 7:2; 28; 37; 9:12; 11:11; **2Cor** 3:16; 7:6; 12:16; **Gal** 2:20; 4:30; **Eph** 5:33; **Phil** 1:24; 3:16; **2Ti** 1:12; 2:19; **Heb** 12:11; **2Pet** 3:13; **Rev** 2:4

NEXT

312, 3027, 4283, 4932, 5921, 7138, *839, 1206, 1836, 1887, 1966, 2064, 2087, 2192, 3342*

Gen 17:21; **Ex** 12:4; **Num** 2:5; 11:32; 27:11; **Deut** 21:3; 6; **Ruth** 2:20; **1Sa** 17:13; 23:17; 30:17; **2Kin** 6:29; **1Chr** 5:12; 16:5; **2Chr** 17:15; 16; 18; 28:7; 31:12; 15; **Neh** 3:2(2); 4(3); 5; 7; 8(2); 9; 10(2); 12; 17; 19; 13:13; **Est** 1:14; 10:3; **Jonah** 4:7; **Mt** 27:62; **Mk** 1:38; **Lk** 9:37; **Jn** 1:29; 35; 12:12; **Acts** 4:3; 7:26; 13:42; 44; 14:20; 16:11; 20:15(3); 21:8; 26; 25:6; 27:3; 18; 28:13

NO

Gen 8:9; 9:15; 11:30; 13:8; 15:3; 16:1; 26:29; 30:1; 31:50; 32:28; 37:22(2); 24; 32; 38:21; 22; 26; 40:8; 41:44; 42:11; 31; 34; 44:23; 45:1; 47:4; 13; **Ex** 2:12; 3:19; 5:7; 16; 18; 8:22; 9:26; 28(2); 10:14; 28; 29; 12:16; 19; 43; 48; 13:3; 7; 14:11; 13; 15:22; 16:4; 18; 19; 29; 17:1; 20:3; 21:8; 22; 22:2; 10; 23:8; 13; 32; 30:9; 12; 33:4; 20; 34:3; 7; 14; 17; 35:3; **Lev** 2:11(2); 5:11; 6:30; 7:23; 24; 26; 11:12; 12:4; 13:21; 26(2); 31; 32; 16:17; 29; 17:7; 12; 14; 19:15; 35; 20:14; 21:3; 21; 22:10; 13(2); 21; 23:3; 7; 8; 21; 25; 28; 31; 35; 36; 25:31; 36; 26:1; 37; 27:26; 28; **Num** 1:53; 3:4; 5:8; 13; 15; 19; 6:3; 5; 6; 8:19; 25; 26; 14:18; 16:40; 18:5; 20; 23; 24; 32; 19:2; 15; 20:2; 5; 21:5; 22:26; 23:23; 26:33; 62; 27:3; 4; 8; 9; 10; 11; 17; 28:18; 25; 26; 29:1; 12; 35; 33:14; 35:31; 32; **Deut** 1:39; 2:5; 3:26; 4:12; 15; 5:22; 7:2; 16; 24; 8:2; 15; 10:9; 16; 11:17; 25; 12:12; 13:11; 14:27; 29; 15:4; 19; 16:3; 4; 8; 17:13; 16; 18:1; 2; 19:20; 20:12; 21:14; 22:26; 23:14; 17; 22; 24:1; 6; 25:5; 28:26; 29; 32; 65; 68(2); 31:2; 32:12; 20; 39; 34:6; **Josh** 8:20; 31; 10:14; 11:20; 14:4; 17:3; 18:7; 22:25; 27; 23:9; 13; **Judg** 2:2; 4:20; 5:19; 6:4; 8:28; 10:13; 11:39; 13:5; 7; 21; 15:13; 17:6; 18:1; 7(2); 10; 28(2); 19:1; 15; 18; 19; 30; 21:12; 25; **1Sa** 1:2; 11; 15; 18; 2:3; 9; 24; 3:1; 6:7; 7:13; 10:14; 27; 11:3; 13:19; 14:6; 26; 15:35; 17:32; 50; 18:2; 20:15; 21; 34; 21:1; 2; 4; 6; 9; 25:31; 26:12; 21; 27:4; 28:10; 15; 20(2); 29:3; 30:4; 12; **2Sa** 1:21; 2:28; 6:23; 7:10; 12:6; 13:12; 16; 14:25; 15:3; 26; 18:13; 18; 20; 22; 20:1; 10; 21:4; 17; **1Kin** 1:1; 3:2; 18; 22; 26; 27; 6:18; 8:16; 23; 35; 46; 9:22; 10:5; 10; 12; 13:9; 17; 22(2); 17:7; 17; 18:10; 23(2); 25; 26; 21:4; 5; 22:17; 18; 47; **2Kin** 1:16; 17; 2:12; 3:9; 4:14; 41; 5:15; 25; 6:23; 7:5; 10; 9:35; 10:31; 12:7; 8; 17:4; 19:18; 22:7; 23:10; 18; 25; 25:3; **1Chr** 2:34; 12:17; 16:21; 22; 17:9; 22:16; 23:22; 26; 24:2; 28; **2Chr** 6:5; 14; 26; 36; 7:13; 8:9; 9:4; 13:9; 14:6; 11; 15:5; 19; 17:10; 18:16(2); 19:7; 20:12; 21:19; 22:9; 32:15; 35:18; 36:16; 17; **Ezr** 4:16; 9:14; 10:6; **Neh** 2:14; 17; 20; 6:1; 8; 13:19; 21; 26; **Est** 1:19; 2:14; 5:12; 8:8; 9:2; **Job** 3:7; 4:18; 5:19; 6:21; 7:7; 8; 9; 10; 9:25; 10:18; 11:3; 12:2; 14; 24; 13:4; 14:12; 15:3; 15; 19; 28; 16:18; 18:17; 19:7; 16; 20:9; 21; 23:6; 24:7; 15; 20; 22; 26:2; 3; 6; 28:7; 18; 30:13; 17; 32:3; 5; 15; 16; 19; 34:22; 32; 36:16; 19; 38:11; 26(2); 40:5; 41:8; 16; 42:2; 15; **Ps** 3:2; 5:9; 6:5; 10:18; 14:1; 3; 4; 19:3; 22:6; 23:4; 32:2; 9; 33:16; 34:9; 36:1; 38:3; 7; 14; 39:13; 40:17; 41:8; 50:9; 53:1; 3; 4; 5; 55:19; 63:1; 69:2; 70:5; 72:12; 73:4; 74:9; 77:7; 78:64; 81:9; 83:4; 84:11; 88:4; 5; 91:10; 92:15; 101:3; 102:27; 103:16; 104:35; 105:14; 15; 107:4; 40; 119:3; 142:4(2); 143:2; 144:14(2); 146:3; **Prov** 1:24; 3:30; 6:7; 8:24(2); 10:22; 25; 11:14; 12:21; 28; 14:4; 17:16; 20; 21; 18:2; 21:10; 30; 22:24; 24:20; 25:28; 26:20(2); 28:1; 3; 17; 24; 29:9; 18; 30:20; 27; 31; 31:7; 11; **Eccl** 1:9; 11; 2:11; 16; 3:11; 12; 19; 4:1(2); 8; 13; 16; 5:4; 6:3; 6; 7:21; 8:5; 8(2); 15; 9:1; 8; 10; 15; 10:11; 20; 12:1; 12; **Song** 4:7; 5:6; 8:8; **Is** 1:6; 13; 30; 5:6; 8; 13; 8:20; 9:7; 17; 19; 10:15; 20; 13:14; 18; 14:8; 15:6; 16:10(2); 19:7; 23:1(2); 10; 12(2); 24:10; 25:2; 26:21; 27:11(2); 28:8; 29:16; 30:7; 16; 19; 32:5; 33:8; 21; 34:16; 35:9; 37:19; 38:11; 40:20; 28; 29; 41:28(2); 43:10; 11; 12; 24; 44:6; 8; 12; 45:5; 9; 14; 20; 21; 47:1(2); 5; 6; 48:22; 50:2(3); 10; 51:22; 52:1; 11; 53:2(2); 9; 54:9; 17; 55:1; 57:1; 10; 21; 58:3; 59:8; 10; 15; 16(2); 60:15; 18; 19; 20; 62:4; 7; 8; 65:19; 20; **Jer** 2:6(2); 11; 13; 25(2); 30; 31; 3:3; 16; 4:22; 23; 25; 5:7; 6:10; 14; 23; 7:32(2); 8:6; 11; 13; 15; 22(2); 10:14; 11:19; 23; 12:11; 12; 14:3; 4; 5; 6; 19(2); 16:14; 19; 20; 17:21; 24(2); 18:12; 19:6; 11; 22:3(2); 10; 12; 28; 30; 23:4; 7; 17; 36; 25:6; 27; 35; 30:8; 13; 17; 31:29; 34(2); 33:24; 35:6(2); 8; 36:19; 38:6; 9; 24; 39:12; 40:15; 41:4; 42:14(2); 18; 44:2; 5; 17; 22; 26; 45:3; 46:25; 48:2; 8; 33; 38; 49:1(2); 7; 18; 33; 36; 50:14; 39; 40; 51:17; 43; 52:6; **Lam** 1:3; 6; 9; 2:9(2); 18; 4:4; 6; 15; 16; 22; 5:5; **Eze** 12:23; 24; 25; 13:10; 15; 16; 21; 23; 14:11; 15; 15:5; 16:34; 41; 42; 18:32; 19:9; 14; 20:39; 21:13; 27; 32; 22:26; 24:6; 17; 27; 26:13; 14; 21; 28:3; 9; 24; 29:11; 15; 16; 18; 30:13; 14; 15; 16; 33:11; 22; 34:5; 8; 22; 28; 29; 36:12; 14; 29; 30; 37:8; 22; 39:10; 43:7; 44:2; 9; 17; 25(2); 28; 45:8; **Dan** 1:4; 2:10; 35; 3:25; 27; 29; 4:9; 6:2; 15; 22; 23; 8:4; 7; 10:3; 8(2); 16; 17; **Hos** 1:6; 2:16; 17; 4:1; 4; 6; 8:7(2); 8; 9:15; 16; 10:3; 13:4(2); **Joel** 1:18; 2:19; 3:17; **Amos** 3:4; 5; 5:2; 20; 6:10; 7:14; 9:15; **Mic** 3:7; 4:9; 5:12; 13; 7:1; **Nah** 1:12; 14; 15; 2:13; 3:8; 18; 19; **Hab** 1:14; 2:19; 3:17(2); **Zeph** 2:5; 3:5; 6; 11; **Hag** 2:12; **Zec** 1:21; 4:5; 13; 7:14; 8:10; 17; 9:8; 11; 10:2; 11:6; 13:2; 5; 14:11; 17; 18; 21; **Mal** 1:10; **Mt** 5:18; 20; 26; 6:1; 24; 25; 31; 34; 8:4; 10; 28; 9:16; 30; 36; 10:19; 42; 11:27; 12:39; 13:5; 6; 16:4; 7; 8; 20; 17:8; 9; 19:6; 18; 20:7; 13; 21:19; 22:23; 24; 25; 46; 23:9; 24:4; 21; 22; 36(2); 25:3; 42(2); 26:55; **Mk** 1:45; 2:2(2); 17; 21; 22; 3:27; 4:5; 6; 7; 17; 40; 5:3(2); 37; 43; 6:5; 8(3); 31; 7:12; 24; 36; 8:12; 16; 17; 30; 9:3; 8; 9; 25; 39; 10:8; 29; 11:14; 12:14; 18; 19; 20; 22; 34; 13:11; 20; 32(2); 14:25; **Lk** 1:7; 33; 2:7; 3:13; 14; 4:24; 5:14; 36; 37; 39; 7:9; 44; 45; 8:13; 14; 16; 27; 51; 56; 9:13; 21; 36; 62; 10:4; 22; 11:20; 29; 33; 36; 12:4; 11; 17; 22; 33; 13:11; 15:7; 16; 19; 21; 16:2; 13; 18:17; 29; 20:22; 31; 22:36; 53; 23:4; 14; 15; 22; **Jn** 1:18; 21; 47; 2:3; 3:2; 13; 32; 4:9; 17(2); 27; 38; 44; 5:7; 14; 22; 6:37; 44; 53; 65; 66; 7:4; 13; 18; 27; 30; 44; 52; 8:10; 11(2); 15; 20; 37; 44; 9:4; 25; 41; 10:18; 29; 41; 11:10; 54; 13:8; 28; 14:6; 19; 15:4; 13; 22; 16:10; 21; 22; 25; 29; 17:11; 18:38; 19:4; 6; 9; 11; 15; 21:5; **Acts** 1:20; 4:17(2); 5:13; 23; 7:5(2); 11; 8:39; 9:7; 8; 10:34; 12:18; 13:28; 34; 37; 41; 15:2; 9; 24; 28; 16:28; 18:10; 15; 19:23; 24; 26; 40; 20:25; 33; 38; 21:25; 39; 23:8; 9; 22; 25:10; 11; 26; 27:20; 22; 28:2; 4; 5; 6; 18; 31; **Rom** 2:11; 3:9(2); 10; 12; 18; 20; 22; 4:15(2); 5:13; 6:9(2); 7:3; 17; 18; 20; 8:1; 10:12; 19; 11:6(4); 12:17; 13:1; 8; 10; 14:7; 13; 15:23; **1Cor** 1:7; 10; 29; 2:11; 15; 3:11; 18; 21; 4:6; 11; 5:11; 6:5; 7:25; 37; 8:13; 9:10; 10:13; 24; 25; 27; 11:16; 12:3(2); 21(2); 24; 25; 13:5; 14:2; 28; 15:12; 13; 16:2; 11; **2Cor** 2:13; 3:10; 5:16(2); 21; 6:3; 7:2(3); 5; 8:15; 20; 11:9; 10; 14; 15; 16; 13:7; **Gal** 2:5; 6(2); 16; 3:11; 15; 18; 25; 4:7; 8; 5:4; 23; 6:17; **Eph** 2:12; 19; 4:14; 28; 29; 5:5; 6; 11; 29; **Phil** 2:7; 20; 3:3; 4:15; **Col** 2:16; 18; 3:25; **1Th** 3:1; 3; 5; 4:6; 13; 5:1; **2Th** 2:3; 3:14; **1Ti** 1:3; 3:3; 4:12; 5:22; 23; 6:16(2); **2Ti** 2:4; 14; 3:9; 4:16; **Titus** 1:7; 2:8; 15; 3:2(2); **Heb** 5:4; 6:13; 7:13; 8:7; 12; 9:17; 22; 10:2; 6; 17; 18; 26; 38; 12:11; 14; 17; 13:10; 14; **Jas** 1:11; 13; 17; 2:11; 13; 3:8; 12; **1Pet** 2:22; 3:10; 4:2; **2Pet** 1:20; **1Jn** 1:5; 8; 2:7; 19; 21; 27; 3:5; 7; 15; 4:12; 18; **3Jn** 4; **Rev** 2:17; 3:7(2); 8; 11; 12; 5:3; 4; 7:9; 16; 10:6; 13:17; 14:3; 5; 11; 15:8; 17:12; 18:7(2); 11; 14; 21; 22(3); 23(2); 19:12; 20:3; 6; 11; 21:1; 4; 22; 23; 25; 27; 22:3; 5(2)

NONE

369, 376, 408, 657, 802, 1077, 1097, 1115, 1997, 3606, 3808, 5106, 6565, *208, 677, 1601, 2673, 2758, 3361, 3367, 3387, 3756, 3762, 3777, 5100*

Gen 23:6; 28:17; 39:9; 11; 41:8; 15; 24; 39; **Ex** 8:10; 9:14; 24; 11:6; 12:22; 15:26; 16:26; 27; 23:15; 34:20; **Lev** 18:6; 21:1; 22:30; 25:26; 26:6; 17; 36; 37; 27:29; **Num** 7:9; 9:12; 21:35; 30:8; 32:11; **Deut** 2:34; 3:3; 4:35; 39; 5:7; 7:15; 22:27; 28:31; 66; 32:36; 33:26; **Josh** 6:1(2); 8:22; 9:23; 10:21; 28; 30; 33; 37; 39; 40; 11:8; 13; 22; 13:14; 14:3; **Judg** 19:28; 21:8; 9; **Ruth** 4:4; **1Sa** 2:2(2); 3:19; 10:24; 14:24; 21:9; 22:8(2); **2Sa** 7:22; 14:6; 19; 25; 18:12; 22:42; **1Kin** 3:12; 8:60; 10:21; 12:20; 15:22; 21:25; **2Kin** 5:16; 6:12; 9:10; 15; 10:11; 19; 23; 25; 17:18; 18:5; 24:14; **1Chr** 15:2; 17:20; 23:17; 29:15; **2Chr** 1:12; 9:11; 20; 10:16; 16:1; 20:6; 24; 23:6; 19; **Ezr** 8:15; **Neh** 4:23; **Est** 1:8; 4:2; **Job** 1:8; 2:3; 13; 3:9; 10:7; 11:19; 18:15; 20:21; 29:12; 32:12; 35:10; 12; 41:10; **Ps** 7:2; 10:15; 14:1; 3; 18:41; 22:11; 29; 25:3; 33:10; 34:22; 37:31; 49:7; 50:22; 53:1; 3; 69:20(2); 25; 71:11; 73:25; 76:5; 79:3; 81:11; 86:8; 107:12; 109:12; 139:16; **Prov** 1:25; 30; 2:19; 3:31; **Song** 4:2; **Is** 1:31; 5:27(2); 29; 10:14; 14:6; 31; 17:2; 22:22(2); 34:10; 12; 16; 41:17; 26(3); 42:22(2); 43:13; 44:19; 45:5; 6(2); 14; 18; 21; 22; 46:9(2); 47:8; 10(2); 15; 50:2; 51:18; 57:1; 59:4; 11; 63:3; 5(2); 64:7; 66:4; **Jer** 4:4; 22; 7:33; 9:10; 12; 22; 10:6; 7; 20; 13:19; 14:16; 21:12; 23:14; 30:7; 10; 13; 34:9; 10; 35:14; 36:30; 42:17; 44:7; 14(2); 46:27; 48:33; 49:5; 50:3; 9; 20; 29; 32; 51:62; **Lam** 1:2; 4; 7; 17; 21; 2:22; 5:8; **Eze** 7:11; 14; 25; 12:28; 16:5; 34; 18:7; 22:30; 31:14; 33:16; 28; 34:6; 28; 39:26; 28; **Dan** 1:19; 2:11; 4:35; 6:4; 8:7; 27; 10:21; 11:16; 45; 12:10; **Hos** 2:10; 5:14; 7:7; 11:7; 12:8; **Joel** 2:27; **Amos** 5:2; 6; **Obad** 7; **Mic** 2:5; 3:11; 4:4; 5:8; 7:2; **Nah** 2:8; 9; 11; 3:3; **Zeph** 2:15; 3:6(2); 13; **Hag** 1:6; **Zec** 7:10; 8:17; **Mal** 2:15; **Mt** 12:43; 15:6; 19:17; 26:60(2); **Mk** 7:13; 10:18; 12:31; 32; 14:55; **Lk** 1:61; 3:11; 4:26; 27; 11:24; 13:6; 7; 14:24; 18:19; 34; **Jn** 6:22; 7:19; 8:10; 15:24; 16:5; 17:12; 18:9; 21:12; **Acts** 3:6; 4:12; 7:5; 8:16; 24; 11:19; 18:17; 20:24; 24:23; 25:11; 18; 26:22; 26; **Rom** 3:10; 11(2); 12; 4:14; 8:9; 9:6; 14:7; **1Cor** 1:14; 17; 2:8; 7:29; 8:4; 9:15; 10:32; 14:10; **2Cor** 1:13; **Gal** 1:19; 3:17; 5:10; **1Th** 5:15; **1Ti** 5:14; **1Pet** 4:15; **1Jn** 2:10; **Rev** 2:10; 24

NOR

176, 369, 408, 508, 518, 1077, 1115, 1571, 3808, 3809, 3908, 5703, *2228, 2532, 3361, 3364, 3366, 3383, 3756, 3761, 3777*

Gen 19:33; 35; 21:23(2); 45:5; 6; 49:10; **Ex** 4:1; 10; 10:6; 11:6; 12:9; 13:22; 20:5; 10(5); 17(5); 22:21; 28; 23:24(2); 26; 32; 30:9(2); 34:3; 10; 28; 36:6; **Lev** 2:11; 3:17; 10:9(2); 11:12; 26; 12:4; 13:34; 17:16; 18:26; 19:4; 14; 15; 18; 20; 26; 28; 20:19; 21:5; 10; 11; 12; 23; 22:22; 23:14(2); 25:4; 11; 20; 37; 26:1; 27:10; **Num** 5:15; 6:3; 9:12; 11:19(3); 18:3; 20:17; 23:25; **Deut** 1:45; 2:19; 27; 37(3); 4:28(3); 31; 5:9; 14(8); 7:2; 3; 7; 25; 9:9; 18; 23; 27(2); 10:9; 17; 12:12; 17(2); 32; 13:6; 8; 14:1; 8; 27; 29; 15:7; 19; 17:11; 16; 18:1; 22; 21:4; 22:30; 23:6; 17; 24:17(2); 26:14; 28:36; 39; 50; 64; 29:23(2); 31:6(2); 33:9; 34:7; **Josh** 1:5; 6:10; 10:25; 13:13; 22:19; 26; 28; 23:7(2); 24:12; 19; **Judg** 1:27(4); 30; 31(6); 33; 2:10; 19; 6:4(2); 11:15; 34; 13:4; 7; 14; 23; 14:16; 19:30; **1Sa** 1:15; 3:14; 5:5; 12:4; 21; 13:22; 15:29; 20:27; 31; 21:8; 22:15; 24:11; 25:31; 26:12; 27:9; 11; 28:6(2); 15; 18; 20; 30:12; 15; 19(3); **2Sa** 1:21; 2:19; 3:34; 13:22; 14:7; 19:6; 24(2); 21:4(2); 10; **1Kin** 3:8; 11; 26; 5:4; 6:7(2); 8:5; 57; 10:12; 12:24; 13:8; 9(2); 16(2); 17(2); 28; 16:11; 17:1; 18:26; 29(2); 20:8; 22:31; **2Kin** 3:14; 4:23; 31; 5:17; 6:10; 9:15; 14:6; 26(2); 17:35(3); 18:5; 12; 19:32(3); 20:13; 23:22(2); **1Chr** 21:24; 22:13; 23:26; 28:20(2); **2Chr** 1:11; 5:6; 6:14; 11:4; 15:5; 19:7(2); 20:15; 17; 21:12; 29:7; 32:7(2); 15; 34:2; **Ezr** 9:12; 14; 10:6; **Neh** 1:7(2); 2:16(4); 20(2); 4:23(3); 7:61; 8:9; 9:31; 34(2); 10:30; 13:25; **Est** 2:7; 10; 20; 3:2; 5; 4:16; 5:9; 9:28; **Job** 1:22; 3:10; 7:19; 14:12; 18:19(2); 24:13; 27:4; 28:8; 34:19; 22; 36:19; 41:12(2); 26; **Ps** 1:1(2); 5; 15:3(2); 5; 16:4; 19:3; 22:24; 24:4; 25:7; 26:9; 28:5; 37:25; 33; 40:4; 49:7; 50:9; 59:3; 66:20; 75:6(2); 78:42; 89:22; 33; 34; 91:5; 6(2); 103:10; 121:4; 6; 129:7; 131:1; 132:3; 144:14; 146:3; **Prov** 4:27; 5:13; 6:4; 8:26(2); 17:26; 21:30(2); 30:3; 8; 31:3; 4; **Eccl** 1:8; 3:14; 4:8; 5:10; 6:5; 8:16; 9:10(3); 11(3); 11:5; 12:1; 2; **Song** 2:7; 3:5; 8:4; **Is** 3:7; 5:6; 27(3); 8:12; 11:9; 14:21(2); 22:2; 23:4(2); 18; 28:28(2); 30:5(2); 31:4; 32:5; 34:10; 35:9; 37:33(3); 39:2; 40:16; 42:2(2); 4; 43:23; 44:9; 18; 19; 20; 45:13; 17; 46:7; 47:14; 48:1; 19; 49:10(2); 51:14; 52:12; 53:2; 54:9; 57:11; 58:13(2); 59:4; 21(2); 60:11; 18; 62:6; 64:4; 65:17; 19; 20; 23; 25; **Jer** 4:11; 5:4; 12; 6:19; 20; 25; 7:16; 22; 24; 26; 28; 32; 8:2; 13; 9:16; 11:8; 13:14(2); 14:16(2); 15:10; 17; 16:5; 6(2); 13; 17:21; 23; 18:18(2); 19:4(2); 5; 6; 20:9; 21:7; 22:3; 10; 23:4; 32; 25:4; 33; 35; 27:9(4); 31:40; 35:6; 7(3); 8; 9(3); 15; 36:24(2); 37:2(2); 19; 42:14(2); 21; 44:3; 5; 10(2); 23(3); 46:6; 49:31; 33; 51:5; 26; 62; **Lam** 2:22; 3:33; **Eze** 2:6; 3:18; 19; 7:11(2); 12; 12:24; 13:23; 14:16; 18; 20; 16:4; 47; 48; 18:17; 20:18; 44; 22:24; 23:27; 24:16; 22; 23; 28:24; 29:5; 11; 18; 31:8; 32:13; 37:23(2); 38:11; 43:7(2); 44:9; 13; 20; 22; 48:14; **Dan** 1:8; 2:10; 3:12; 14; 18; 27(2); 28; 5:8; 10; 23(2); 6:4; 13; 15; 10:3; 11:4; 6; 20; 24; 37(2); **Hos** 1:7(3); 10; 4:1(2); 4; 14; 15; 5:13; 7:10; **Amos** 5:5; 8:11; 9:10; **Obad** 13; **Jonah** 3:7(3); **Mic** 5:7; **Zeph** 1:6; 18; 3:13; **Zec** 1:4; 4:6; 7:10(2); 14; 8:10; 11:16(2); 14:6; 7; **Mal** 4:1; **Mt** 5:35; 6:20(2); 25; 26; 10:9(2); 10(2); 14; 24; 11:18; 12:19; 22:29; 30; 24:21; 25:13; **Mk** 6:11; 8:26; 12:25; **Lk** 1:15; 6:44; 7:33; 9:3; 10:4(2); 12:24(2); 14:12(2); 35; 17:23; 18:4; 20:35; 21:15; 22:68; 23:15; **Jn** 1:13(2); 25; 4:21; 5:37; 8:19; 9:3; 11:50; 12:40; 16:3; **Acts** 4:18; 8:21; 9:9; 13:27; 15:10; 19:37; 23:8; 12; 21; 24:12; 18; 25:8; 27:20; **Rom** 8:38(6); 39(3); 9:16; 14:21(2); **1Cor** 2:6; 9; 6:9(4); 10(5); 10:32(2); 12:21; **2Cor** 4:2; 7:12; **Gal** 3:28(3); 4:14; 5:6; 6:15; **Eph** 5:4(2); 5(2); **Col** 3:11(3); **1Th** 2:3(2); 5; 6(2); 5:5; **2Th** 2:2(2); **1Ti** 1:7; 2:12; 6:16; 17; **2Ti** 1:8; **Heb** 7:3; 9:25; 12:5; 18; 13:5; **2Pet** 1:8; **Rev** 3:15; 16; 5:3; 7:1(2); 3; 16; 9:20(2); 21(3); 14:11; 21:4

NOT

3808, *3756*

Gen 2:5(2); 17; 18; 20; 25; 3:1; 3; 4; 11; 17; 4:5; 7(2); 9; 12; 5:24; 6:3; 7:2; 8; 8:12; 21; 22; 9:4; 23; 11:7; 12:18; 13:6(2); 9; 14:23(2); 15:1; 4; 10; 13; 16; 16:10; 17:12; 14; 15; 18:3; 15; 21; 24; 25; 28; 29; 30(2); 31; 32(2); 19:7; 8; 17; 18; 20; 21; 31; 33; 35; 20:4; 5; 6; 7; 9; 11; 12; 21:10; 12; 16; 17; 23; 26; 22:12(2); 16; 24:3; 5; 6; 8(2); 21; 27; 33; 37; 39; 41; 49; 56; 26:2; 22; 24; 29; 27:1; 2; 12; 21; 23; 36(2); 28:1; 6; 8; 15; 16; 29:25; 26; 30:31; 33; 40; 42; 31:2; 5; 7; 15; 20; 24; 27; 28; 29; 32(2); 33; 34; 35(2); 38(2); 39; 52(2); 32:10; 25; 26; 32; 34:7; 17; 19; 23; 35:5; 10; 17; 36:7; 37:4; 13; 21; 27; 29; 30; 38:9; 14; 16; 20; 23; 26; 39:6; 8; 10; 23; 40:8; 23; 41:16; 21; 31; 36; 42:2; 4; 8; 13; 15; 20; 21; 22(3); 23; 32; 36(2); 37; 38; 43:3; 5(3); 8; 9; 23; 32; 44:4; 5; 15; 18; 26; 28; 30; 31; 32; 34; 45:1; 3; 5; 8; 9; 20; 24; 26; 46:3; 47:9; 18(2); 19(2); 22(2); 26; 29; 48:10; 11; 18; 49:4; 6(2); 10; 50:19; 21; **Ex** 1:8; 17; 19; 2:3; 3:2; 3; 5; 19(2); 21; 4:1(2); 8; 9; 10; 11; 14; 21; 5:2; 8; 9; 10; 11; 14; 19; 6:3; 9; 12; 7:4; 13; 16; 21; 24; 8:15; 18; 19; 21; 26(2); 28; 29(2); 31; 9:6; 7(2); 11; 12; 17; 18; 19; 21; 30; 32(2); 33; 10:7; 11; 15; 19; 20; 23; 26(2); 27; 11:7;

9; 10; 12:9; 13; 23; 30(2); 39(2); 45; 46; 13:13; 17; 22; 14:12; 13; 20; 28; 15:23; 16:8; 15; 20; 24; 25; 17:7; 18:17; 18; 19:12; 13(2); 15; 24; 20:4; 5; 7(2); 10; 13; 14; 15; 16; 17(2); 19; 20(2); 23; 25; 26; 21:5; 7; 8; 10; 11; 13; 18; 21; 28; 29; 33; 36; 22:8; 11(2); 13; 14; 15; 16; 18; 22; 25; 28; 29; 23:1(2); 2; 6; 7(2); 9; 18; 19; 21(2); 24; 29; 33; 24:2; 11; 25:15; 28:28; 32; 35; 43; 29:33; 34; 30:15(2); 20; 21; 32; 37; 32:1; 18; 22; 23; 32; 33:3; 11; 12; 15(2); 16; 20; 23; 34:10; 20; 25; 26; 29; 39:21; 23; 40:35; 37(2); **Lev** 1:17; 2:12; 4:2; 13; 22; 27; 5:1; 7; 8; 11; 17; 18; 6:12; 17; 23; 7:15; 18; 19; 8:33; 35; 10:1; 6; 7; 9; 17; 18; 11:4(2); 5; 6; 7; 8(2); 10; 11; 13; 26; 41; 42; 43; 47; 12:8; 13:4(2); 5; 6; 11; 21; 23; 28; 31; 32(2); 33; 34; 36; 53; 55(2); 14:32; 36; 48; 15:11; 31; 16:2(2); 13; 22; 17:4; 9; 16; 18:3(2); 7(2); 8; 9; 10; 11; 12; 13; 14(2); 15(2); 16; 17; 19; 20; 21; 22; 24; 26; 28; 30(2); 19:4; 7; 9; 10; 11; 12; 13(2); 14; 15; 16; 17(2); 18; 19(2); 20(3); 23; 26; 27; 28; 29; 31; 33; 20:4; 19; 22; 23; 25; 21:4; 5; 6; 7; 10; 14; 17; 18; 21; 23(2); 22:2; 4; 6; 8; 10; 12; 15; 20(2); 22; 23; 24; 25; 28; 23:22; 29; 25:5; 11; 14; 17; 20; 23; 28; 30(2); 34; 37; 39; 42; 43; 46; 53; 54; 26:11; 13; 14(2); 15; 18; 20; 21; 23; 26; 27; 31; 35; 44; 27:10; 11; 20(2); 22; 27; 33(2); **Num** 1:47; 49; 2:33; 4:15; 18; 19; 20; 5:3; 14; 19; 28; 6:7; 9:6; 7; 13(2); 19; 22; 10:7; 30; 31; 11:11; 14; 15; 17; 19; 23; 25; 26; 12:2; 7; 8(2); 11; 12; 14; 15; 13:20; 31; 14:3; 9(2); 16; 22; 23; 30; 41; 42(3); 43; 44; 15:22; 34; 39; 16:12; 14(2); 15(2); 28; 29; 40(2); 17:10; 18:3; 4; 17; 19:12(2); 13(2); 20(2); 20:12(2); 17(2); 18; 20; 24; 21:22(2); 23; 34; 22:12(2); 30; 34; 37(3); 23:8(2); 9; 12; 13; 19(3); 21; 24; 26; 24:1; 12; 17(2); 25:11; 26:11; 62; 64; 65; 27:3; 17; 29:7; 30:2; 5; 11; 12; 31:18; 23; 35; 49; 32:5; 9; 11; 18; 19; 23; 30; 33:55; 35:12; 23(2); 27; 30; 33; 34; 36:7; **Deut** 1:9; 17(2); 21; 26; 29; 32; 35; 37; 42(2); 43; 45; 2:5(3); 9(2); 19(2); 30; 36; 37; 3:2; 4(2); 11; 22; 26; 27; 4:2; 21(2); 22; 26; 31; 42; 5:3; 5; 8; 9; 11(2); 14; 17; 32; 6:10; 11(3); 14; 16; 7:3; 7; 10; 14; 18; 21; 22; 25; 8:3(2); 4; 9; 11(2); 16; 20; 9:4; 5; 6; 7; 23; 26; 27; 28; 10:10; 17; 11:2(3); 10; 16; 17; 28(2); 30; 12:4; 8; 9; 13; 16; 17; 19; 23(2); 24; 25; 30(2); 31; 32; 13:2; 3; 6; 8; 13; 16; 14:1; 3; 7(2); 8(2); 10(2); 12; 19; 21(2); 24; 27; 15:2; 6(2); 7; 9; 10; 13; 16; 18; 21; 23; 16:5; 16; 19(2); 21; 17:1; 3; 6; 11; 12; 15(2); 16; 17; 20(2); 18:9; 10; 14; 16(2); 19; 20; 21; 22(3); 19:4; 6(2); 10; 13; 14; 15; 21; 20:1; 3(3); 5; 6; 7; 15; 18; 19(2); 20; 21:1; 3(2); 7; 8; 14(2); 16; 18(2); 20; 23(2); 22:1; 2(2); 3; 4; 5; 6; 8; 9; 10; 11; 14; 17; 19; 20; 24; 28; 29; 30; 23:1; 2(2); 3(2); 4; 5; 6; 7(2); 10(2); 15; 16; 18; 19; 20; 21; 24; 25; 24:4(2); 5; 10; 12; 14; 16; 17; 19; 20; 21; 25:3; 4; 5; 6; 7(2); 8; 9; 12; 13; 14; 18; 19; 26:13; 14; 27:5; 26; 28:12; 13(2); 14; 15; 27; 29; 30(2); 31(2); 33; 40; 41; 44; 45; 47; 49; 50; 51; 55; 56; 58; 61; 62; 29:4; 5(2); 6; 15; 20; 23; 26(2); 30:11; 12; 17; 18; 31:2; 6(2); 8(2); 13; 17(2); 21; 32:5; 6(2); 17(3); 21(2); 27(2); 31; 34; 47; 51; 52; 33:6(2); 9; 11; 34:4; 7; 10; **Josh** 1:5(2); 7; 8; 9(2); 18; 2:4; 5; 14; 22; 3:4(2); 5:5; 6(2); 7; 6:10; 7:3(2); 12; 13; 19; 8:1; 4; 14; 17(2); 26; 35(2); 9:14; 18; 19; 26; 10:6; 8(2); 13(2); 19(2); 25; 11:6; 11; 19; 13:13; 33; 15:63; 16:10; 17:12; 13; 16; 17; 18:2; 20:5(2); 9; 21:44; 45; 22:3; 17; 19; 20(2); 22; 24; 26; 27; 28; 31; 33; 23:6; 7; 14(2); 24:10; 12; 13(3); 19; **Judg** 1:19; 21; 28; 32; 34; 2:2; 3; 10; 14; 17(2); 19; 20; 21; 22; 3:1; 22; 25; 28; 29; 4:6; 8(2); 9; 14; 16; 18; 5:23; 30(2); 6:10(2); 13; 14; 18; 23(2); 27; 39; 7:4(2); 8:1; 2; 19; 20; 23; 34; 9:15; 20; 28; 38; 41; 54; 10:6; 11; 11:2; 7; 10; 15; 17(2); 18; 20; 24; 26; 27; 28; 12:1; 2; 3; 6; 13:2; 3; 4(2); 6; 9; 14; 16(2); 23; 14:4; 6; 9; 14; 15; 16(3); 18(2); 15:1; 2; 11; 12; 13; 16:8; 9; 15(2); 17; 20; 18:1; 9; 25; 19:10; 12(2); 20; 23(2); 24; 25; 20:8; 13; 16; 34; 21:1; 5(2); 7; 8; 14; 17; 18; 22(2); **Ruth** 1:16; 20; 2:8(2); 9(2); 11; 13; 15; 16; 20; 22; 3:1; 2; 3; 10; 11; 13; 14; 17; 18; 4:4; 10; 14; **1Sa** 1:7; 8(2); 11; 13; 16; 22(2); 2:3; 12; 15; 16(2); 25; 31; 32; 33; 3:2; 5; 6; 7; 13; 14; 17; 4:7; 9; 15; 20(2); 5:7; 11; 12; 6:3(2); 6; 9(2); 12; 7:8; 8:3; 5; 7(2); 18; 9:2; 4(3); 7; 13; 20(2); 21; 10:1; 16; 21; 11:7; 11; 13; 12:4; 5; 14; 15; 17; 19; 20(2); 21; 22; 13:8; 11; 12; 13; 14(2); 14:1; 3; 9; 17; 27; 30; 34; 36; 37; 39; 45(2); 15:3; 9; 11; 17; 19; 26; 29(2); 16:7(2); 10; 11; 17:8; 29; 33; 39(2); 47; 18:17; 25; 26; 19:4(2); 6; 11; 20:2(2); 3; 5; 9; 12; 14(2); 15(2); 26(3); 27; 29; 30; 31; 37; 38; 39; 21:8; 11(2); 22:5; 15; 17(2); 23; 23:14; 17(2); 19; 24:7; 10; 11(2); 12; 13; 18; 21(2); 25:7; 11; 15; 19; 25(2); 28; 34; 26:1; 8; 9; 14; 15(2); 16(2); 20; 23; 28:6; 13; 18; 23; 29:3; 4(2); 5; 6(2); 7; 8; 9; 30:2; 10; 17; 21; 22(2); 23; 31:4; **2Sa** 1:10; 14; 20(2); 21; 22(2); 23; 2:19; 21; 26; 3:8; 11; 13; 22; 26; 29; 34; 37; 38; 4:11; 5:6; 8; 23; 6:10; 7:6; 7; 15; 9:3; 7; 10:3; 11:3; 9; 10(3); 11; 13; 20; 21; 25; 12:13; 17; 18; 23; 13:4; 12(2); 13; 14; 16; 20; 25(2); 26; 28(2); 30; 32; 33; 14:2; 7; 10; 11(2); 13; 14; 18; 19; 24(2); 28; 29(2); 15:11; 14; 27; 35; 16:17; 19; 17:6; 7; 8; 12; 13; 16; 17; 19; 20; 22(2); 23; 18:3(2); 11; 12; 14; 20; 29; 19:7(2); 10; 13(2); 19; 21; 22; 23; 25; 43; 20:3; 10; 21; 21:2; 17; 22:22; 23; 37; 38; 39; 42; 44; 23:5(2); 16; 17(2); 19(2); 23; 24:14; **1Kin** 1:4; 6; 8; 10; 11(2); 13; 18; 19; 26; 27; 51; 52; 2:4; 6; 8; 9; 16; 17; 20(2); 23; 26; 28; 32; 36; 42; 43; 3:7; 11; 13(2); 21; 5:3; 6; 6:6; 13; 7:31; 8:5; 8; 11; 19; 25; 41; 46; 56; 57; 9:5; 6; 12; 20; 21; 10:3(2); 7(2); 20; 11:2; 4; 6; 10(2); 11; 12; 13; 33; 34; 39; 41; 12:15; 16; 24; 31; 13:4; 8; 10; 16; 21; 22; 28; 33; 14:2; 4; 8; 29; 15:3; 5; 7; 14; 17; 23; 29; 31; 16:5; 11; 14; 20; 27; 17:1; 12; 13; 14; 16; 18:5; 10(3); 12; 13; 18; 21; 40; 44; 19:2; 4; 11(2); 12; 18(2); 20:7; 8; 9; 11; 28; 36; 21:4; 6; 15; 29; 22:3; 7; 8(2); 17; 18; 28; 33; 39; 43(2); 45; 48; 49; **2Kin** 1:3(2); 4; 6(3); 15; 16(2); 18; 2:2; 4; 6; 10(2); 16; 17; 18(2); 21; 3:2; 3; 11; 14(2); 17; 26; 4:2; 3; 6; 16; 24; 27; 28(2); 29(2); 30; 31; 39; 40; 5:12(2); 13; 17; 20; 26; 6:9; 10; 11; 16; 19; 22; 27; 32; 7:2; 9; 19; 8:19; 23; 9:3; 18; 20; 37; 10:4; 5; 19; 21(2); 29; 31; 34; 11:2; 6; 15; 12:3; 6; 7; 13; 15; 16; 19; 13:2; 6; 8; 11; 12; 23; 14:3; 4; 6(2); 11; 15; 18; 24; 26; 27; 28; 15:4; 6; 9; 16; 18; 20; 21; 24; 28; 35; 36; 16:2; 5; 19; 17:2; 9; 12; 14(2); 15; 19; 22; 25; 26(2); 34; 35; 37; 38; 40; 18:6; 7; 12(2); 22; 26; 27; 29(2); 30; 31; 32(2); 36(2); 19:3; 6; 10(2); 25; 32; 33; 20:1; 13; 15; 19; 20; 21:9; 17; 22; 25; 22:2; 13; 17; 20; 23:9; 22; 26; 28; 33; 24:4; 5; 7; 25:24; **1Chr** 4:10; 27; 5:1; 10:4; 13; 14; 11:5; 18; 19; 21; 25; 12:19; 33; 13:3; 13; 14:14; 15:13(2); 16:22; 30; 17:4; 5; 6; 13; 19:3; 21:3; 6; 13; 17(2); 24; 30; 22:8; 13; 18(2); 23:11; 26:10; 27:23; 24; 28:3; 20(2); 29:1; 25; **2Chr** 1:11; 4:18; 5:6; 9; 11; 14; 6:9; 16; 32; 36; 42; 7:2; 7; 18; 8:7; 8; 11; 15; 9:2; 6(2); 19; 20; 29; 10:15; 16; 11:4; 12:7(2); 12; 14; 15; 13:5; 7; 9; 10; 12(2); 14:11; 13; 15:7; 13; 17; 16:7; 8; 12; 17:3; 4; 18:6; 7; 17(2); 27; 30; 32; 19:6; 10(2); 20:6(3); 7; 10(2); 12; 15(2); 17(2); 32; 33(2); 37; 21:7; 12; 20; 22:11; 23:8; 14; 24:5; 6; 19; 22; 25; 25:2; 4(2); 7(2); 13; 15; 16; 20; 26; 26:18; 27:2; 28:1; 10; 13; 20; 21; 27; 29:7; 11; 34; 30:3(2); 5; 7; 8; 9; 17(2); 18; 19; 26; 32:7; 11; 12; 13; 15; 17(2); 25; 26; 33:10; 23; 34:21; 25; 33; 35:3; 15; 21(2); 22(2); 36:12; **Ezr** 2:59; 62; 63; 3:6; 13; 4:13; 14; 21; 22; 5:5; 16; 6:8; 7:24; 25; 26; 9:1; 9; 12; 14; 10:8; 13; **Neh** 1:7; 2:1; 2; 3; 16; 3:5; 4:5(2); 10; 11; 14; 5:9(2); 13; 14; 15; 18; 6:1; 9; 11; 12; 7:3; 4; 61; 64; 65; 8:9; 17; 9:16; 17; 19(2); 20; 21(2); 29(2); 30; 31; 32; 35; 10:30; 31; 39; 13:1; 2; 6; 10; 14; 18(2); 19; 24; 25; 26; **Est** 1:15; 16; 17; 19; 2:10(2); 20; 3:2; 4; 5; 8; 4:4; 11(2); 13; 16; 5:9; 6:1; 13; 7:4; 9:10; 15; 16; 27; 28; 10:2; **Job** 1:10; 12; 22; 2:10(2); 12; 3:4; 6(2); 10; 11(2); 16; 18; 21; 26; 4:6; 16; 21; 5:6; 17; 24; 6:10(2); 13; 29; 7:1(2); 8; 11; 16; 19; 21(2); 8:10; 12; 15(2); 18; 20; 9:5; 7; 11(2); 13; 15; 16; 18; 21; 24; 28; 32; 34; 35(2); 10:2; 7; 10; 14; 15; 19; 20; 21; 11:2; 11; 14; 15; 20; 12:3(2); 9; 11; 13:2; 11; 16; 20(2); 21; 14:2; 4; 7; 12(2); 16; 21(2); 15:6; 9(2); 15; 18; 22; 29; 30; 31; 32; 16:6; 13; 17; 18; 22; 17:2(2); 4; 18:5; 21; 19:3; 7; 22; 27; 20:4; 8; 13; 17; 18(2); 19; 20(2); 26; 21:4; 10(2); 14; 16; 29(2); 22:5; 7; 11; 12; 14; 20; 23:8; 11; 17; 24:1(2); 12; 13; 16; 18; 21(2); 25; 25:3; 5(2); 26:8; 27:4; 5; 6(2); 11; 14; 15; 19(2); 22; 28:7; 8; 13; 14(2); 17; 19; 29:16; 22; 24(2); 30:10; 20(2); 24; 25(2); 27; 31:3; 4; 15(2); 17; 20(2); 23; 31; 32; 34; 32:6; 9; 13; 14; 16; 21; 22; 33:7; 12; 13; 14; 21; 27; 33; 34:12; 19; 23; 27; 30; 31; 32; 33; 35:13; 14; 15(2); 36:4; 5; 6; 7; 12; 13; 19; 20; 21; 26; 32; 37:4; 21; 23; 24; 39:4; 16; 22; 40:5; 23; 41:9; 12; 33; 42:3(2); 7; 8; **Ps** 1:1; 3; 4; 5; 3:6; 4:4; 5:4; 5; 6:1; 7:12; 9:10; 12; 18(2); 19; 10:4(2); 6; 12; 13; 14:3; 4; 15:3; 4; 5; 16:2; 4; 8; 10; 17:1; 3; 5; 18:21; 22; 36; 38; 41; 43; 19:3; 13; 21:2; 7; 11; 22:2(2); 5; 11; 19; 24; 23:1; 24:4; 25:2(2); 7; 20; 26:1; 4; 5; 9; 27:3; 9(3); 12; 28:1; 3; 5(2); 30:1; 3; 12; 31:8; 17; 32:2; 5; 6; 9; 33:16; 34:5; 10; 20; 35:11; 15(2); 19; 20; 22(2); 24; 25(2); 36:4(2); 11(2); 12; 37:1; 7; 8; 10(2); 19; 21; 24; 25; 28; 33; 36(2); 38:1; 9; 13(2); 14; 21(2); 39:1; 6; 8; 9; 12; 40:4; 6(2); 9; 10(2); 11; 12; 41:2; 11; 44:3; 6; 9; 12; 17; 18; 21; 23; 46:2; 5; 49:9; 12; 16; 17; 20; 50:3; 8; 12; 51:11(2); 16(2); 17; 52:7; 53:3; 4; 54:t, 3; 55:1; 11; 12; 19; 23; 56:4; 8; 11; 13; 58:5; 8; 59:3; 5; 11; 13; 15; 60:10(2); 62:2; 6; 10(3); 64:4; 66:7; 9; 18; 20; 69:4; 5; 6(2); 14; 15(2); 17; 23; 27; 28; 33; 71:9(2); 12; 15; 18; 73:5; 74:9; 19(2); 21; 23; 75:4(2); 5(2); 77:2; 19; 78:4; 7; 8(3); 10; 22(2); 30; 32; 37; 38(2); 39; 42; 44; 50; 53; 56; 63; 67; 79:6(2); 8; 80:18; 81:5; 11; 82:5; 83:1(3); 85:6; 8; 86:14; 89:22; 30; 31; 33; 34; 35; 43; 48; 91:5; 7; 92:6; 94:7; 9(2); 10(2); 14; 95:8; 10; 11; 96:10; 100:3; 101:3; 4; 5; 7(2); 102:2; 17; 24; 103:2; 9; 10; 104:5; 9(2); 105:15; 28; 37; 106:7(2); 11; 13; 23; 24; 25; 34; 107:38; 108:11(2); 109:1; 14; 16; 17; 110:4; 112:6; 7; 8; 115:1(2); 5(2); 6(2); 7(2); 17; 118:6; 17; 18; 119:6; 8; 10; 11; 16; 19; 31; 36; 43; 46; 51; 60; 61; 80; 83; 85; 87; 102; 109; 110; 116; 121; 122; 133; 136; 141; 153; 155; 157; 158; 176; 121:3(2); 6; 124:1; 2; 6; 125:3; 127:5; 129:2; 7; 131:1; 132:3; 4; 10; 11; 135:16(2); 17; 137:6(2); 138:8; 139:4; 12; 15; 21(2); 140:8(2); 10; 11; 141:4(2); 5; 8; 143:2; 7; 146:3; 147:10(2); 20(2); 148:6; **Prov** 1:8; 10; 15; 28(2); 29; 3:1; 3; 5; 7; 11; 15; 21; 23; 24; 25; 27; 28; 29; 30; 31; 4:2; 5; 6(2); 12(2); 13; 14(2); 15; 16; 19; 21; 27; 5:6; 7; 8; 13; 17; 6:4; 20; 25; 27; 28; 29; 30; 33; 34; 35; 7:11; 19; 23; 25(2); 8:1; 10; 11; 26; 29; 33; 9:8; 18; 10:3; 19; 30; 11:4; 21; 12:3(2); 7; 27; 13:1; 8; 14:5; 6; 7; 10; 22; 15:7; 12; 16:5; 10; 29; 17:5; 7; 13; 26; 18:5; 19:2; 5(2); 9; 10; 18; 23; 24; 20:1; 4; 13; 19; 21; 22; 23; 21:13; 17; 26; 22:6; 20; 22; 24; 26; 28; 29; 23:3; 4; 5; 6; 7; 9; 10(2); 13(2); 17; 18; 20; 22; 23; 31; 35(2); 24:1; 7; 12(4); 14; 15(2); 17(2); 19; 21; 23; 28(2); 29; 25:6(2); 8(2); 9; 10; 27(2); 26:1; 2; 4; 7; 17; 19; 25; 27:1(2); 2(2); 10; 22; 24; 28:5; 13; 20; 21; 22; 27; 29:7; 19(2); 24; 30:2; 6; 7; 10; 11; 12; 15; 16(2); 18; 25; 30; 31:3; 4(2); 12; 18; 21; 27; **Eccl** 1:7; 8; 2:10(2); 21; 23; 4:3(2); 8; 10; 12; 16; 5:1; 2(2); 4; 5(2); 6; 8; 10; 12; 20; 6:2; 3; 5; 6; 7; 7:9; 10(2); 16; 17; 18; 20(2); 28(2); 8:3(2); 7; 11; 13(2); 17(2); 9:2; 5; 11; 12; 16; 10:4; 10; 15; 17; 20(3); 11:2; 4(2); 5(2); 6(2); 12:1; 2; **Song** 1:6(2); 8; 2:7; 3:1; 2; 4; 5; 5:6; 6:6; 7:2; 8:1; 4; **Is** 1:3(2); 6; 11; 15; 23; 2:4; 9; 3:7(2); 9; 5:4; 6; 12; 25; 6:9(2); 7:1; 4; 7; 8; 9(2); 12; 17; 25; 8:10; 11; 12; 19; 20; 9:1; 3; 12; 13; 17; 20; 21; 10:4; 7(2); 8; 9(3); 11; 24; 11:3; 9; 13(2); 12:2; 13:10(2); 17(2); 18; 22; 14:17; 20; 21; 29; 16:3; 6; 12; 17:8; 10; 14; 22:2; 4; 11; 14; 23:4; 13; 18; 24:9; 20; 26:10(2); 11; 14(2); 18; 27:4; 9; 11; 28:12; 15; 16; 18; 22; 25; 27; 28; 29:9(2); 12(2); 16; 17; 22; 30:1(2); 2; 5; 6; 9; 10(2); 14(2); 15; 20; 31:1; 2; 3(2); 4; 8(2); 32:3; 10; 33:1(2); 19(2); 20(2); 23(2); 24; 34:10; 35:4; 8(2); 9; 36:7; 11; 12; 14(2); 15; 16; 21(2); 37:3; 6; 10(2); 26; 33; 34; 38:1; 11; 18; 39:2; 4; 40:9; 16; 20(2); 21(4); 24(3); 26; 28(3); 31(2); 41:3; 7; 9; 10(2); 12; 13; 14; 17; 42:2; 3(2); 4; 8; 16(3); 20(2); 24(2); 25(2); 43:1; 2(2); 5; 6; 17; 18; 19; 22; 23(2); 25; 44:2; 8(3); 9(2); 18; 20; 21; 45:1; 4; 5; 13; 17; 18; 19(2); 21; 23; 46:2; 7(2); 10; 13(2); 47:3; 7; 8; 11(3); 14(2); 48:1; 6(2); 7(2); 8(3); 9; 10; 11; 16; 19; 21; 49:5; 10; 15(2); 23; 50:5; 6; 7(2); 51:6; 7; 9; 10; 14; 21; 52:12; 15(2); 53:3; 7(2); 54:1(2); 2; 4(4); 9; 10; 11; 14(2); 15; 55:2(2); 5(2); 8; 10; 11; 13; 56:5; 57:4; 10(2); 11(3); 12; 16; 58:1; 2; 3; 4; 6; 7(2); 11; 13; 59:1; 2; 6; 8(2); 21; 60:11; 12; 62:1(2); 6; 8; 12; 63:8; 13; 16; 19; 64:3; 4; 9; 65:1(3); 2; 5; 6; 8(2); 12(3); 17; 20; 22(2); 23; 25; 66:4(2); 9; 19; 24; **Jer** 1:7; 8; 17; 19; 2:2; 8(3); 11; 17; 19; 20; 23(2); 24; 27; 34; 35; 37; 3:1; 2; 4; 7; 8; 10; 12(2); 13; 19; 25; 4:1; 3; 6; 8; 11; 22; 27; 28; 29; 5:3(2); 4; 9(2); 10(2); 12; 13; 15; 18; 19; 21(2); 22(4); 28(2); 29(2); 6:8; 15; 16; 17; 19; 20; 25; 29; 7:4; 6(2); 9; 13(2); 16(2); 17; 19; 20; 22; 24(2); 26; 27(2); 28; 31; 8:2; 4(2); 6; 7; 12; 17; 19(2); 20; 22; 9:3(2); 4; 5; 9(2); 13; 23(2); 10:2(2); 4; 5(2); 7; 10; 11; 16; 20; 21(2); 23(2); 24; 25(2); 11:3; 8(2); 11(2); 12; 14(2); 19; 21(2); 12:4; 6; 13; 17; 13:1; 11; 12; 14; 15; 17; 21; 27; 14:9; 10(2); 11; 12(2); 13; 14; 15(2); 17; 18; 21(3); 22; 15:1; 7; 14; 15; 17; 19; 20; 16:2; 4; 5; 6; 8; 11; 12; 13(2); 17; 17:4; 6(2); 8(2); 11(2); 16; 17; 18(2); 23(2); 27(3); 18:10; 15; 17; 18(2); 23; 19:5; 15; 20:3; 9(2); 11(2); 14; 16; 17; 21:7; 10; 22:5; 6; 10; 11; 13; 15; 16; 17; 18(2); 21(2); 26; 27; 28; 30; 23:2; 10; 16(2); 20; 21(2); 23; 24(2); 29; 32(2); 38; 40; 24:2; 6(2); 25:3; 4; 6(2); 7; 8; 29; 33; 26:2; 4; 5; 16; 19; 24; 27:8(2); 9(2); 13; 14(2); 15; 16; 17; 18; 20; 28:15; 29:6; 8; 9; 11; 16; 19(2); 23; 27; 31; 32; 30:5; 10; 11(2); 14; 19(2); 24; 31:9; 12; 15; 32; 40; 32:4; 5; 23; 33(2); 35; 40(2); 33:3; 20; 21; 24; 25(2); 26; 34:3; 4; 14; 17; 18; 35:13; 14(2); 15(2); 16; 17(2); 19; 36:24; 25(2); 31; 37:4; 9(2); 14(2); 19; 20; 38:4; 5; 15(2); 16; 17; 18(2); 20; 23; 24; 25(2); 26; 27; 39:16; 17; 18; 40:3; 5; 7; 9; 14; 16; 41:8(2); 42:5; 10(2); 11(2); 13; 19; 21; 43:2(2); 4; 7; 44:3; 4; 5; 10; 16; 21(2); 23; 27; 45:5; 46:5; 6; 11; 15; 21; 27(2); 28(3); 47:3; 48:11(2); 27; 30(2); 49:9; 10(2); 12(2); 25; 36; 50:2; 5; 7; 13; 20; 24; 42; 51:3; 5; 6; 9; 19; 26; 39; 44; 50; 57; 64; **Lam** 1:9; 10; 14; 2:1; 2; 8; 14; 17; 18; 21; 3:2; 22(2); 31; 33; 36; 37; 38; 42; 43; 44; 49; 56; 57; 4:8; 12; 14; 15; 16(2); 17; 5:7; 12; **Eze** 1:9; 12; 17; 2:6(2); 8; 3:5; 6(2); 7(2); 9; 18; 19; 20(2); 21(2); 25; 26; 4:8; 14(2); 5:6; 7; 9(2); 6:10; 7:4; 7; 9; 12; 13(2); 19(2); 8:12; 18(2); 9:5; 6; 9; 10; 10:11(2); 16; 11:3; 11; 12; 12:2(2); 6; 9; 12; 13; 13:5; 6; 7(3); 9; 12; 19(2); 22(2); 14:23; 16:4(2); 16; 22; 28; 29; 31; 43(2); 47; 48; 56; 61; 17:9; 10; 12; 14; 18; 18:3; 6; 7; 8; 11; 12; 13; 14; 15(2); 16; 17(2); 18; 19; 20; 21; 22; 23; 24; 25(3); 28; 29(3); 30; 20:3; 7; 8(2); 9; 13; 14; 15; 16; 18; 21; 22; 24; 25(2); 31; 32; 38; 39; 44; 47; 48; 49; 21:5; 26; 22:24; 28; 30; 23:27; 48; 24:6; 7; 8; 12; 13(2); 14; 17(2); 19; 22; 23; 25; 25:10; 26:15; 19; 20; 28:2; 29:5; 30:21; 31:8(3); 32:7; 9; 27; 33:4; 5; 6(2); 8; 9; 12(2); 13; 15; 17(2); 20; 31; 32; 34:2; 3; 4; 8; 10; 35:6; 9; 36:22; 31; 32; 37:18; 38:14; 39:7; 41:6; 42:6; 14; 44:2; 8; 13; 18; 19; 31; 46:2; 9; 18(2); 20; 47:5(2); 11; 12; 48:11; 14; **Dan** 1:8(2); 2:5; 9; 10; 11; 18; 24; 30; 43(2); 44; 3:6; 11; 12(2); 14; 15; 16; 18(2); 24; 28; 4:7; 18; 19; 30; 5:8; 10; 15; 22; 23(2); 6:5; 8(2); 12(2); 13; 17; 22; 26; 7:14(2); 8:5; 22; 24; 9:11; 12; 13; 14; 18; 19; 26; 10:7; 12; 19; 11:4; 6; 12; 15; 17; 19; 21; 24; 25; 27; 29; 38; 42; 12:8; **Hos** 1:7; 9(2); 10; 2:2; 4; 6; 7(2); 8; 23(2); 3:3(2); 4:10(2); 14(2); 15(2); 5:3; 4(2); 6; 13; 6:6; 7:2; 8; 9(2); 10; 14; 16; 8:4(2); 6; 13; 9:1; 2; 3; 4(2); 12; 17; 10:3; 9; 11:3; 5; 9(4); 13:13; 14:3(2); **Joel** 1:16; 2:2; 7; 8; 13; 17; 21; 22; 3:21; **Amos** 1:3; 6; 9(2); 11; 13; 2:1; 4(2); 6; 11; 12; 14; 15; 3:6(2); 8; 10; 4:6; 7(2); 8(2); 9; 10; 11; 5:5(2); 11(2); 14; 18; 20(2); 21; 22; 23; 6:6; 10; 13; 7:3; 6; 8; 10; 13; 16(2); 8:2; 8; 11; 12; 9:1(2); 4; 7(2); 8; 9; 10; **Obad** 5(2); 8; 12; 13(2); 16; 18; **Jonah** 1:6; 13; 14(2); 3:7; 9; 10; 4:2; 10; 11; **Mic** 1:5(2); 10(2); 11; 2:3; 6(3); 7; 10; 3:1; 4; 5; 6(2); 11; 4:3; 12; 5:7; 15; 6:14(2); 15(3); 7:5(2); 8; 18; **Nah** 1:3; 9; 3:1; 17; 19; **Hab** 1:2(2); 5; 6; 12(2); 13; 17; 2:3(2); 4; 6(2); 7; 13; 3:17; **Zeph** 1:6; 12; 13(2); 2:1; 3:2(4); 3; 5(2); 7; 11; 13; 15; 16(2); **Hag** 1:2; 6(2); 2:3; 5; 17; 19; **Zec** 1:4(2); 6; 12; 3:2; 4:5; 6; 13; 7:6; 7; 10; 11; 13(2); 14; 8:11; 13; 14; 15; 9:5; 10:6; 10; 11:5(2); 6; 9; 12; 16; 12:7; 13:3; 14:2; 6; 7; 17; 18(3); 19; **Mal** 1:2; 8(2); 2:2(3); 6; 9; 10(2);

13; 15; 16; 3:5; 6(2); 7; 10(2); 11; 18; **Mt** 1:19; 20; 25; 2:6; 12; 18(2); 3:9; 10; 11; 4:4; 7; 5:17(2); 21; 27; 29; 30; 33; 34; 36; 39; 42; 46; 47; 6:1; 2; 3; 5; 7; 8; 13; 15; 16; 18; 19; 20; 25; 26(2); 28; 29; 30; 7:1(2); 3; 6; 19; 21; 22; 25; 26; 29; 8:8; 10(2); 20; 9:12; 13(2); 14; 24; 10:5(2); 13; 14; 20; 23; 24; 26(3); 28(2); 29(2); 31; 34(2); 37(2); 38(2); 11:6; 11; 17(2); 20; 12:2; 3; 4; 5; 7(2); 11; 16; 19; 20(2); 23; 24; 25; 30(2); 31; 32; 13:5; 11; 12; 13(2); 14(2); 17(2); 19; 21; 27; 34; 55(2); 56; 57; 58; 14:4; 16; 27; 15:2; 6; 11; 13; 17; 20; 23; 24; 26; 32; 16:3; 9; 11(2); 12; 17; 18; 22; 23; 28; 17:7; 12; 16; 19; 21; 24; 18:3; 10; 12; 13; 14; 16; 22; 25; 30; 33; 35; 19:4; 6; 8; 10; 14; 18(3); 20:13; 15; 22; 23; 26; 28; 21:21(2); 25; 29; 30; 32(2); 22:3; 8; 11; 12; 16; 17; 29; 31; 32; 23:3(2); 4; 8; 23; 30; 37; 39; 24:2(3); 6(2); 17; 20; 21; 23; 26(2); 29; 34; 35; 36; 39; 42; 43; 44; 50(2); 25:9(2); 12; 24(2); 26(2); 29; 43(3); 44; 45(2); 26:5; 11; 24; 29; 35; 39; 40; 41; 42; 70; 72; 74; 27:6; 13; 34; 28:5; 6; 10; **Mk** 1:7; 22; 34; 2:2; 4; 17; 18; 24; 26; 27; 3:12; 20; 4:5; 12(2); 13; 21; 22; 25; 27; 34; 38; 5:3; 7; 10; 19; 36; 39; 6:3(2); 4; 9; 11; 18; 19; 26; 34; 50; 52; 7:3; 4; 5; 18; 19; 24; 27; 8:17; 18(3); 21; 33; 9:1; 6; 18; 28; 30; 32; 37; 38(2); 39; 40; 41; 44(2); 46(2); 48(2); 10:9; 14; 15(2); 19(5); 27; 38; 40; 43; 45; 11:13; 16; 17; 23; 26; 31; 12:10; 14(2); 15; 24(2); 26; 27; 34; 13:2(2); 7(2); 11; 14; 15; 16; 18; 19; 21; 24; 30; 31; 32; 33; 35; 14:2; 7; 29; 31; 36; 37; 49; 56; 68; 71; 15:23; 16:6(2); 11; 14; 16; 18; **Lk** 1:13; 20(2); 22; 30; 34; 60; 2:10; 26; 37; 43; 45; 49; 50; 3:8; 9; 15; 16; 4:4; 12; 22; 35; 41; 42; 5:10; 19; 31; 32; 36; 6:2; 3; 4; 29; 30; 37(4); 39; 40; 41; 42; 43; 44; 46; 48; 49; 7:6(3); 9(2); 13; 23; 28; 30; 32(2); 45; 46; 8:10(2); 17(2); 18; 19; 28; 31; 47; 49; 50; 52(2); 9:5; 27; 33; 40; 45(2); 49; 50(2); 53; 55; 56; 58; 10:6; 7; 10; 20; 24(2); 40; 42; 11:4; 7; 8; 23(2); 35; 38; 40; 42; 44(2); 46; 52; 12:2(2); 4; 6(2); 7; 10; 15; 21; 26; 27(3); 29; 32; 33(2); 39; 40; 46(2); 47; 48; 56; 57; 59; 13:9; 14; 15; 16; 24; 25; 27; 34; 35; 14:5; 6; 8; 12; 26; 27; 28; 29; 30; 31; 33; 15:4; 8; 13; 28; 16:11; 12; 31; 17:8; 9; 17; 18; 20; 22; 23; 31(2); 18:1; 2; 4(2); 7; 11; 13; 16; 17; 20(4); 30; 19:3; 14; 21(2); 22(2); 23; 26; 27; 44(2); 48; 20:5; 7; 26; 38; 40; 21:6(2); 8(2); 9(2); 14; 15; 18; 21; 32; 33; 22:16; 18; 26; 27; 32; 34; 40; 42; 57; 58; 60; 67; 68; 23:28; 34; 40; 51; 24:3; 6; 11; 16; 18; 23; 24; 26; 32; 39; 41; **Jn** 1:3; 5; 8; 10; 11; 13; 20(2); 21; 25; 26; 27; 31; 33; 2:4; 9; 12; 16; 24; 25; 3:7; 8; 10; 11; 12; 15; 16; 17; 18(3); 24; 28; 34; 36(2); 4:2; 15; 18; 22; 29; 32; 35; 42; 48; 5:10; 13; 18; 23(2); 24; 28; 30; 31; 34; 38(2); 40; 41; 42; 43; 44; 45; 47; 6:7; 17; 20; 22; 24; 26; 27; 32; 36; 38; 42; 43; 46; 50; 58; 64(2); 70; 7:1; 6; 8(2); 10; 16; 19; 22; 23; 24; 25; 28(2); 30; 34; 35; 36; 39(2); 42; 45; 49; 8:6; 12; 13; 16; 20; 23; 24; 27; 29; 35; 40; 41; 43; 44; 45; 46; 47(2); 48; 49; 50; 55(2); 57; 9:8; 12; 16(2); 18; 21(2); 25; 27; 29; 30; 31; 32; 33; 39; 10:1; 5(2); 6; 8; 10; 12(2); 13; 16; 21; 25; 26(2); 33; 34; 37(2); 38; 11:4; 9(2); 15; 21; 30; 32; 37(2); 40; 50; 51; 52; 56; 12:5; 6; 8; 9; 15; 16; 30; 35; 37; 39; 40; 42; 44; 46; 47(3); 48; 49; 13:7; 8; 9; 10(2); 11; 16; 18; 36; 38; 14:1; 2; 5; 9; 10(2); 17; 18; 22(2); 24(3); 27(2); 30; 15:2; 6; 15(2); 16; 19; 20; 21; 22(2); 24(2); 16:1; 3; 4; 7(2); 9; 13; 16; 17; 19; 26; 30; 32; 17:9; 14(2); 15; 16(2); 25; 18:11; 17(2); 25(2); 26; 28; 30(2); 31; 36(3); 40; 19:10(2); 12; 21; 24; 31; 33; 36; 20:2; 5; 7; 9; 13; 14; 17(2); 24; 25; 27; 29; 30; 21:4; 6; 8; 11; 18; 23(3); 25; **Acts** 1:4; 5; 7; 2:7; 15; 24; 25; 27; 31; 34; 3:23; 4:18; 5:4(3); 7; 22; 28(2); 40; 42; 6:2; 10; 13; 7:5; 18; 19; 25; 32; 39; 40; 48; 50; 52; 53; 60; 8:21; 32; 9:21; 26; 38; 10:14; 15; 28; 41; 47; 11:8; 9; 12:9; 14; 19; 22; 23; 13:10; 11; 25(2); 27; 35; 39; 14:17; 18; 15:19; 38(2); 16:7; 21; 17:4; 5; 6; 12; 24; 27; 29; 18:9(2); 20; 19:2; 9; 26; 27; 30; 31; 32; 35; 20:10; 12; 16; 22; 27; 29; 31; 21:4; 12; 13; 14; 21; 34; 38; 22:9; 11; 18; 22; 23:5(2); 9; 21; 24:4; 25:7; 11; 16; 24; 27; 26:19; 25; 26; 29; 32; 27:7; 10; 12; 14; 15; 21; 24; 34; 39; 28:4; 19; 24; 25; 26(2); **Rom** 1:13; 16; 21; 28(2); 32; 2:4; 8; 13; 14(2); 21(2); 22; 26; 27; 28; 29(2); 3:3; 8; 10; 12; 17; 29; 4:2; 4; 5; 8; 10; 11; 12; 13; 16; 17; 19(2); 20; 23; 5:3; 5; 11; 13; 14; 15; 16; 6:3; 6; 12; 14(2); 15; 16; 7:1; 6; 7(3); 15(2); 16; 18; 19(2); 20; 8:1; 3; 4; 7; 9(2); 12; 15; 18; 20; 23; 24; 25; 26; 32(2); 9:1; 6(2); 8; 10; 11(2); 16; 21; 24; 25(2); 26; 30; 31; 32; 33; 10:2; 3; 6; 11; 14(2); 16; 18; 19; 20(2); 11:2(2); 4; 7; 8(2); 10; 18(2); 20; 21(2); 23; 25; 30; 31; 12:2; 3; 4; 11; 14; 16(2); 19; 21; 13:3(2); 4; 5; 9(5); 13(3); 14; 14:1; 3(4); 6(4); 13; 15(2); 16; 17; 20; 22; 23(2); 15:1; 3; 18(2); 20; 21(2); 31; 16:4; 18; **1Cor** 1:16; 17(2); 20; 21; 26(3); 28; 2:1; 2; 4; 5; 6; 8; 9; 12; 13; 14; 3:1; 2(2); 3; 4; 16; 4:3; 4; 6; 7(2); 14; 15; 18; 19; 20; 5:1; 2; 6(2); 8; 9; 10; 11(2); 12; 6:1; 2; 3; 5(2); 7(2); 9(3); 12(2); 13; 15; 16; 19(2); 7:1; 4(2); 5(2); 6; 10(2); 11; 12(3); 13(2); 15; 18(2); 21; 23; 27(2); 28(2); 30(3); 31; 35; 36; 38; 8:7; 8(2); 10; 9:1(4); 2; 4; 5; 6; 7(2); 8; 9; 12(2); 13; 16; 18; 21; 24; 26(2); 10:1; 5; 6; 13; 16(2); 18; 20(2); 23(2); 27; 28; 29; 33; 11:6; 7; 8; 14; 17(2); 20; 22(3); 29; 31; 32; 34; 12:1; 14; 15(3); 16(3); 13:1; 2; 3; 4(3); 5(3); 6; 14:2; 11; 16; 17; 20; 21; 22(4); 23; 24; 33; 34; 39; 15:9; 10(2); 13; 14; 15(2); 16(2); 17; 29; 32; 33; 34(2); 36; 37; 39; 46; 51; 58; 16:7; 12; 22; **2Cor** 1:8; 9; 12; 18; 19; 23; 24; 2:1; 4; 5(2); 11; 13; 17; 3:3(2); 5; 6; 7; 8; 13(2); 4:1; 2; 4; 5; 7; 8(2); 9(2); 16; 18(3); 5:1; 3; 4; 7; 12(2); 15; 19; 6:1; 3; 9; 12; 14; 17; 7:3; 7; 8; 9; 10; 12; 14; 8:5; 8; 10; 12(2); 13; 19; 21; 9:4; 5; 7; 12; 10:2; 3; 4; 8(2); 9; 12(2); 13; 14(2); 15; 16; 18; 11:4(3); 5; 6; 11; 17; 29(2); 31; 12:1; 4; 5; 6; 13; 14(3); 16; 18(2); 20(2); 21; 13:2; 3; 5; 6; 7; 10; **Gal** 1:1; 7; 10; 11; 16; 20; 2:5; 14(2); 15; 16(2); 20; 21; 3:1; 10; 12; 16; 20; 4:8; 12; 14; 17; 18; 21; 27(2); 30; 31; 5:1; 7; 8; 13; 15; 16; 18; 21; 26; 6:4; 7(2); 9(2); **Eph** 1:16; 21; 2:8; 9; 3:5; 13; 4:17; 20; 26(2); 30; 5:3; 4; 7; 15; 17; 18; 27; 6:4; 6; 7; 12; **Phil** 1:16; 22; 29; 2:4; 6; 12; 16; 21; 27; 30; 3:1; 9; 12; 13; 4:11; 17; **Col** 1:9; 23; 2:1; 8; 18; 19; 21(3); 23; 3:2; 9; 19; 21; 22; 23; **1Th** 1:5; 8(2); 2:1; 3; 4; 8; 9; 13; 15; 17; 19; 4:5(2); 7; 8; 9; 13(2); 15; 5:3; 4; 5; 6; 9; 19; 20; **2Th** 1:8(2); 2:2; 3; 5; 10; 12; 3:2; 6; 7; 8; 9(2); 10; 11; 13; 14; 15; **1Ti** 1:9; 20; 2:7; 9; 12; 14; 3:3(4); 5; 6; 8(3); 11; 4:14; 5:1; 8; 9; 13(2); 16; 18; 19; 6:1; 2; 3; 17; **2Ti** 1:7; 8; 9; 12; 16; 2:5; 9; 13; 14; 15; 20; 24; 4:3; 8; 16; **Titus** 1:6; 7(4); 11; 14; 2:3(2); 5; 9; 10; 3:5; 14; **Philem** 1:14; 16; 19; **Heb** 1:12; 14; 2:5; 8(2); 11; 16; 3:8; 10; 11; 15; 16; 17; 18(2); 19; 4:2(2); 6; 7; 8; 13; 15; 5:5; 12; 6:1; 10; 12; 7:6; 11; 16; 20; 21; 23; 27; 8:2; 4; 9(3); 11; 9:7; 8; 9; 11(2); 24; 10:1; 2; 4; 5; 8; 25; 35; 37; 39; 11:1; 3; 5(2); 7; 8; 13; 16; 23; 27; 31(2); 35; 38; 39; 40; 12:4; 5; 7; 8; 9; 18; 19; 20; 25(3); 26; 13:2; 6; 9(3); 16; 17; **Jas** 1:5; 7; 16; 20; 22; 23; 25; 26; 2:1; 4; 5; 6; 7; 11(2); 14; 16; 17; 21; 24; 25; 3:1; 2; 10; 14(2); 15; 4:1; 2(3); 3; 4; 11(2); 14; 17; 5:6; 9; 12; 17(2); **1Pet** 1:4; 8(2); 12; 14; 18; 23; 2:6; 10(2); 16; 18; 23(2); 3:1; 3; 4; 6; 7; 9; 14; 21; 4:4; 12; 16; 17; 5:2(2); 4; **2Pet** 1:12; 16; 21; 2:3(2); 4; 5; 10; 11; 12; 21; 3:8; 9(2); **1Jn** 1:6; 8; 10(2); 2:1; 2; 4(2); 11; 15(2); 16; 19(2); 21(2); 23; 27; 28; 3:1(2); 2; 6(2); 9; 10(3); 12; 13; 14; 18; 21; 4:1; 3(2); 6(2); 8(2); 10; 18; 20(2); 5:3; 6; 10(2); 12(2); 16(3); 17; 18(2); **2Jn** 1; 5; 7; 8; 9(2); 10(2); 12; **3Jn** 9; 10; 11(2); 13; **Jude** 5; 6; 9; 10; 19; **Rev** 1:17; 2:2(2); 3; 9; 11; 13; 21; 24(2); 3:2; 3(2); 4; 5; 8; 9; 17; 18; 4:8; 5:5; 6:6; 10; 7:1; 3; 8:12; 9:4(2); 5; 6; 20(3); 10:4; 11:2; 6; 9; 12:8; 11; 13:8; 15; 14:4; 15:4; 16:9; 11; 18; 20; 17:8(3); 10; 11; 18:4(2); 19:10; 20:4; 5; 15; 21:25; 22:9; 10

NOTHING

369, 408, 657, 1077, 1099, 1115, 1697, 2600, 3605, 3808, 3809, 3972, 4100, 4591, 7535, 8414, *114, 848, 3361, 3367, 3385, 3739, 3756, 3762, 3763, 3777, 3956, 4487, 5100*

Gen 11:6; 19:8; 26:29; 40:15; **Ex** 9:4; 12:10; 20; 16:18; 21:2; 22:3; 23:26; **Num** 6:4; 11:6; 16:26; 22:16; **Deut** 2:7; 20:16; 22:26; 28:55; **Josh** 11:15; **Judg** 3:2; 7:14; 14:6; **1Sa** 3:18; 20:2; 22:15; 25:21; 36; 27:1; 30:19; **2Sa** 12:3; 24:24; **1Kin** 4:27; 8:9; 10:21; 11:22; 18:43; 22:16; **2Kin** 10:10; 20:13; 15; 17; **2Chr** 5:10; 9:2; 14:11; 18:15; **Ezr** 4:3; **Neh** 2:2; 5:8; 12; 8:10; 9:21; **Est** 2:15; 5:13; 6:3; 10; **Job** 6:18; 8:9; 24:25; 26:7; 34:9; **Ps** 17:3; 19:6; 39:5; 49:17; 119:165; **Prov** 8:8; 9:13; 10:2; 13:4; 7; 20:4; 22:27; **Eccl** 2:24; 3:14; 22; 5:14; 15; 6:2; 7:14; **Is** 34:12; 39:2; 4; 6; 40:17(2); 23; 41:11; 12; 24; 29; 44:10; **Jer** 10:24; 13:7; 10; 32:17; 23; 38:14; 39:10; 42:4; 50:26; **Lam** 1:12; **Eze** 13:3; **Dan** 4:35; **Joel** 2:3; **Amos** 3:4; 5; 7; **Hag** 2:3; **Mt** 5:13; 10:26; 15:32; 17:20; 21:19; 23:16; 18; 26:62; 27:12; 19; 24; **Mk** 1:44; 4:22; 5:26; 6:8; 36; 7:15; 8:1; 2; 9:29; 11:13; 14:60; 61; 15:3; 4; 5; **Lk** 1:37; 4:2; 5:5; 6:35; 7:42; 8:17; 9:3; 10:19; 11:6; 12:2; 22:35; 23:9; 15; 41; **Jn** 3:27; 4:11; 5:19; 30; 6:12; 39; 63; 7:26; 8:28; 54; 9:33; 11:49; 12:19; 14:30; 15:5; 16:23; 24; 18:20; 21:3; **Acts** 4:14; 21; 10:20; 11:8; 12; 17:21; 19:36; 20:20; 21:24; 23:14; 29; 25:25; 26:31; 27:33; 28:17; **Rom** 14:14; **1Cor** 1:19; 4:4; 5; 7:19(2); 8:2; 4; 9:16; 13:2; 3; **2Cor** 6:10; 7:9; 8:15; 12:11(2); 13:8; **Gal** 2:6; 4:1; 5:2; 6:3; **Phil** 1:20; 28; 2:3; 4:6; **1Th** 4:12; **1Ti** 4:4; 5:21; 6:4; 7(2); **Titus** 1:15; 3:13; **Philem** 1:14; **Heb** 2:8; 7:14; 19; **Jas** 1:4; 6; **3Jn** 7; **Rev** 3:17

NOW

116, 227, 645, 1768, 2008, 2088, 3117, 3528, 3588, 3705, 4994, 6254, 6258, 6288, 6471, *737, 1160, 1161, 1211, 2235, 2236, 2532, 3063, 3568, 3570, 3765, 3767*

Gen 2:23; 3:1; 22; 4:11; 10:1; 11:6; 27; 12:1; 11; 19; 13:14; 15:5; 16:1; 2; 18:3; 11; 21; 27; 31; 19:2; 8; 9; 19; 20; 20:7; 21:23; 22:2; 12; 24:42; 49; 25:12; 26:22; 28; 29; 27:2; 3; 8; 9; 26; 36; 37; 43; 29:32; 34; 35; 30:20; 30(2); 31:12; 13; 16; 25; 28; 30; 34; 42; 44; 32:4; 10; 33:10; 15; 34:5; 35:22; 36:1; 37:3; 20; 32; 41:33; 42:1; 43:10; 11; 44:10; 30; 33; 45:5; 8; 19; 46:30; 34; 47:4; 29; 48:5; 10; 50:4; 5; 17(2); 21; **Ex** 1:1; 8; 2:15; 16; 3:1; 3; 9; 10; 18; 4:6; 12; 5:5; 18; 6:1; 7:11; 9:15; 18; 19; 10:11; 17; 11:2; 12:40; 16:36; 18:11; 19; 19:5; 21:1; 29:38; 32:10; 30; 32; 34; 33:5; 13(2); 34:9; **Num** 11:6; 23; 12:3; 6; 13; 13:20; 22; 14:15; 17; 19; 22; 25; 41; 16:1; 49; 20:10; 22:4; 6; 11; 19; 22; 29; 33; 34; 38; 24:11; 14; 17; 25:14; 31:17; 43; 32:1; **Deut** 2:13; 4:1; 32; 5:25; 6:1; 10:12; 22; 26:10; 31:19; 21; 32:39; **Josh** 1:1; 2; 2:12; 3:12; 5:5; 14; 6:1; 7:19; 8:11; 9:6; 11; 12; 17; 19; 23; 25; 10:1; 12:1; 13:1; 7; 14:10(2); 11; 12; 17:8; 18:21; 22:4(2); 7; 26; 31; 24:14; 23; **Judg** 1:1; 8; 10; 23; 3:1; 4:11; 6:13; 17; 39; 7:3; 8:2; 6; 10; 15; 9:16; 32; 38(2); 11:1; 7; 8; 13; 23; 25; 12:6; 13:3; 4; 7; 12; 14:2; 12; 15:3; 18; 16:9; 10; 27; 17:3; 13; 18:14; 19:9; 18; 22; 24; 20:3; 9; 13; 38; 21:1; **Ruth** 1:1; 2:2; 7; 3:2; 11; 12; 4:7; 18; **1Sa** 1:1; 9; 13; 2:12; 16; 22; 30; 3:7; 4:1; 15; 6:7; 8:2; 5; 9; 9:1; 3; 6(2); 9; 12; 13; 15; 10:19; 12:2; 7; 10; 13; 16; 13:12; 13; 14; 19; 14:1; 17; 30; 49; 15:1; 3; 25; 30; 16:12; 15; 16; 17; 17:1; 12; 17; 19; 29; 18:22; 19:2; 20:29; 31; 36; 21:3; 7; 22:6; 7; 12; 23:20; 24:20; 21; 25:3; 7(2); 10; 17; 21; 26(2); 27; 26:8; 11; 16; 19; 20; 27:1; 5; 28:3; 22; 29:1; 7; 10; 31:1; **2Sa** 1:1; 2:6; 7; 14; 3:1; 18; 4:11; 7:2; 8; 25; 28; 29; 9:6; 10; 12:10; 23; 28; 13:7; 13; 17; 20; 24; 25; 28(2); 33; 14:1; 2; 15(2); 17; 18; 21; 32; 15:34; 16:11; 17:1; 5; 9; 16; 17; 18:3(2); 18; 19; 19:7(2); 9; 10; 32; 20:6; 23; 21:2; 23:1; 24:2; 3; 10; 13; 14; 16; **1Kin** 1:1; 12; 18(2); 2:1; 9; 16; 24; 3:7; 5:4; 6; 8:25; 26; 9:11; 10:14; 12:4; 11; 16; 26; 13:6; 11; 14:14; 29; 15:1; 7; 31; 16:5; 14; 20; 27; 17:24; 18:3; 11; 14; 19; 43; 19:4; 20:31; 33; 21:7; 22:13; 23; 39; 45; **2Kin** 1:4; 5; 14; 18; 2:16; 3:1; 15; 23; 4:1; 9; 13; 26; 5:1; 6; 8; 15(2); 22; 6:1; 7:4; 9; 12; 19; 8:6; 9:12; 14; 26; 34; 10:2; 6; 10; 19; 34; 12:7; 13:8; 14; 19; 14:15; 19; 28; 15:36; 16:19; 18:1; 13; 19; 20; 21; 23; 25; 19:19; 25; 20:3; 21:17; 25; 22:14; 23:28; 24:5; 25:4; 11; **1Chr** 1:32; 43; 2:34; 42; 3:1; 5:1; 6:54; 7:1; 8:1; 9:2; 10:1; 11:15; 12:1; 14:1; 4; 17:1; 7; 23; 26; 27; 18:1; 9; 19:1; 10; 21:8; 12; 13; 15; 20; 22:5; 11; 14; 19; 23:3; 14; 24:1; 7; 25:9; 27:1; 28:8; 10; 29:2; 13; 17; 20; 29; **2Chr** 1:9; 10; 2:7; 13; 15; 3:3; 6:7; 16; 17; 40; 41; 7:1; 15; 16; 8:16; 9:13; 29; 10:4; 16; 12:15; 13:1; 8; 15:3; 18:1; 22; 30; 19:7; 20:10; 34; 21:1; 4; 23:12; 24:11; 17; 27; 25:3; 14; 19; 26; 27; 26:22; 27:7; 28:10; 11; 26; 29:5; 10; 11; 17; 31; 30:8; 31:1; 32:15; 32; 33:14; 18; 34:8; 22; 35:3; 26; 36:8; 22; **Ezr** 1:1; 2:1; 3:8; 4:1; 13; 14; 21; 22; 23; 5:16; 17; 6:6; 7:1; 11; 8:1; 33; 9:1; 8; 10; 12; 10:1; 2; 3; 11; 14; **Neh** 1:6(2); 10; 11; 2:1; 9; 4:3; 5:5; 18; 6:1; 7(2); 9; 7:1; 4; 9:1; 32; 10:1; 11:3; 12:1; 13:3; **Est** 1:1; 2:5; 12; 15; 3:4; 5:1; 6:4; 6; 9:1; 12; **Job** 1:6; 11; 2:5; 11; 3:13; 4:5; 12; 5:1; 6:3; 21; 28; 7:21; 8:6; 9:25; 12:7; 13:6; 18; 19; 14:16; 16:7; 19; 17:3; 10; 15; 19:6; 23; 22:21; 24:25; 30:1; 9; 16; 32:4; 14; 33:2; 34:16; 35:15; 37:21; 38:3; 40:7; 10; 15; 16; 42:5; 8; **Ps** 2:10; 12:5; 17:11; 20:6; 27:6; 37:25; 39:7; 41:8; 50:22; 71:18; 74:6; 115:2; 116:14; 18; 118:2; 3; 4; 25(2); 119:67; 122:8; 124:1; 129:1; **Prov** 5:7; 6:3; 7:12(2); 24; 8:32; **Eccl** 2:1; 16; 3:15; 9:6; 7; 15; 12:1; **Song** 3:2; 7:8; **Is** 1:18; 21; 5:1; 3; 5; 7:3; 13; 8:7; 16:14; 19:12; 22:1; 28:22; 29:22(2); 30:8; 31:3; 33:10(3); 36:1; 4; 5; 8; 10; 37:20; 26; 38:3; 42:14; 43:1; 19; 44:1; 47:8; 12; 13; 48:7; 16; 49:5; 19; 51:21; 52:5; 64:8; **Jer** 2:18; 4:12; 31; 5:1; 21; 24; 7:12; 13; 14:10; 17:15; 18:11(2); 13; 20:1; 25:5; 26:8; 13; 27:6; 16; 18; 28:7; 15; 29:1; 27; 30:6; 32:16; 36; 34:10; 15; 35:15; 36:15; 16; 17; 22; 37:3; 4; 19; 20; 38:7; 12; 25; 39:11; 15; 40:3; 4; 5; 7; 41:1; 9; 13; 42:15; 21; 22; 44:7; 45:3; 52:7; 12; **Eze** 1:1; 15; 4:14; 7:3; 8; 8:5; 8; 10:3; 16:8; 17:12; 18:14; 25; 19:5; 13; 22:2; 23:43; 26:2; 18; 27:2; 33:22; 38:12; 39:25; 41:12; 42:5; 15; 43:9; 46:12; 47:7; 48:1; **Dan** 1:6; 9; 18; 2:23(2); 3:15; 4:18; 37; 5:10; 12; 15; 16; 6:8; 10; 16; 8:18; 22; 9:15; 17; 22; 10:11; 14; 20; 11:2; 34; **Hos** 1:8; 2:7; 10; 4:16; 5:3; 7; 7:2; 8:8; 10; 13; 10:2; 3; 13:2; **Joel** 2:12; **Amos** 6:7; 7:16; **Jonah** 1:1; 17; 3:3; 4:3; **Mic** 4:9; 10; 11; 5:1; 4; 6:1; 5; 7:4; 10; **Nah** 1:13; **Hag** 1:5; 2:2; 3; 4; 11; 15; 18; **Zec** 1:4; 3:3; 8; 5:5; 8:11; 9:8; **Mal** 1:8; 9; 2:1; 3:10; 15; **Mt** 1:18; 22; 2:1; 3:10; 15; 4:12; 8:18; 9:18; 10:2; 11:2; 12; 14:15; 24; 15:32; 21:18; 22:25; 24:32; 26:6; 17; 20; 45; 48; 53; 59; 65; 69; 27:15; 42; 43; 45; 54; 62; 28:11; **Mk** 1:14; 16; 4:37; 5:11; 6:35(2); 8:2; 14; 10:30; 11:11; 12:20; 13:12; 28; 14:41; 15:6; 32; 42; 16:9; **Lk** 1:7; 57; 2:15; 29; 41; 3:1; 9; 21; 4:40; 5:4; 6:21(2); 25; 7:1; 6; 12; 39; 8:11; 22; 38; 9:7; 10:36; 38; 11:7; 39; 14:17; 15:25; 16:25; 18:22; 19:37; 42; 20:37; 21:30(2); 22:1; 36; 23:47; 24:1; **Jn** 1:44; 2:8; 10; 23; 4:6; 18; 23; 42; 43; 51; 5:2; 6; 25; 6:10; 16; 17; 7:2; 14; 8:5; 40; 52; 9:19; 21; 25; 31; 41; 11:1; 5; 18; 22; 30; 57; 12:27; 31(2); 13:1; 2; 7; 19; 23; 28; 31; 33; 36; 37; 14:29; 15:3; 22; 24; 16:5; 12; 19; 22; 29; 30; 31; 32; 17:5; 7; 11; 13; 18:14; 24; 36; 40; 19:23; 25; 28; 29; 41; 21:4; 6; 7; 10; 14; **Acts** 1:18; 2:6; 33; 37; 3:1; 17; 4:3; 13; 29; 5:24; 38; 7:4; 11; 34; 52; 8:14; 9:36; 10:5; 17; 33; 11:19; 12:1; 11; 18; 13:1; 11; 13; 34; 43; 15:10; 16:6; 36; 37; 17:1; 16; 30; 18:14; 20:22; 25; 32; 21:3; 22:1; 16; 23:15; 21; 24:13; 17; 25:1; 26:6; 17; 27:9(3); 22; **Rom** 1:10; 13; 3:19; 21; 4:4; 19; 23; 5:9; 11; 6:8; 19; 21; 22; 7:6; 17; 20; 8:1; 9; 22; 11:12; 30; 31; 13:11(2); 14:15; 15:5; 8; 13; 23; 25; 30; 33; 16:17; 25; 26; **1Cor** 1:10; 12; 2:12; 3:2; 8; 12; 4:7; 8(2); 18; 5:11; 6:7; 13; 7:1; 14; 25; 8:1; 9:25; 10:6; 11; 11:2; 17; 12:1; 4; 18; 20; 27; 13:12(2); 13; 14:6; 15:12; 20; 50; 16:1; 5; 7; 10; **2Cor** 1:21; 2:14; 3:17; 5:5; 16; 20; 6:2(2); 13; 7:9; 8:11; 14; 22; 9:10; 10:1; 12:6; 13:2; 7; **Gal** 1:9; 10; 20; 23; 2:20; 3:3; 16; 20; 4:1; 9; 20; 25; 28; 29; 5:19; **Eph** 2:2; 13; 19; 3:5; 10; 20; 4:9; 5:8; **Phil** 1:5; 20; 30; 2:12; 3:18; 4:10; 15; 20; **Col** 1:21; 24; 26; 3:8; **1Th** 3:6; 8; 11; 5:14; **2Th** 2:1; 6; 7; 16; 3:6; 12; 16; **1Ti** 1:5; 17; 4:1; 8; 5:5; **2Ti** 1:10; 3:8; 4:6; **Philem** 1:9; 11; 16; **Heb** 2:8; 7:4;

8:1; 6; 13; 9:5; 6; 24; 26; 10:18; 38; 11:1; 16; 12:11; 26; 13:20; **Jas** 2:11; 4:13; 16; 5:1; **1Pet** 1:6; 8; 12; 2:10(2); 25; 3:21; **2Pet** 2:3; 3:1; 7; 18; **1Jn** 2:8; 9; 18; 28; 3:2; 4:3; **2Jn** 5; **Jude** 24; 25; **Rev** 12:10

O

5599

Gen 17:18; 24:12; 42; 27:34; 38; 32:9; 43:20; 49:6; 18; **Ex** 4:10; 13; 15:6(2); 11; 16; 17(2); 32:4; 8; 34:9; **Num** 10:36; 12:13; 16:22; 21:17; 29; 24:5(2); **Deut** 3:24; 4:1; 5:1; 29; 6:3; 4; 9:1; 26; 20:3; 21:8; 26:10; 27:9; 32:1(2); 6; 29; 43; 33:23; 29(2); **Josh** 7:7; 8; 13; **Judg** 3:19; 5:3(2); 21; 31; 6:22; 13:8; 16:28(2); 21:3; **1Sa** 1:11; 4:9; 17:55; 20:12; 23:10; 11; 20; 26:17; **2Sa** 1:25; 7:18; 19(2); 22; 25; 27; 28; 29; 14:4; 9; 22; 15:31; 34; 16:4; 18:33(2); 19:4(2); 26; 20:1; 22:29; 50; 23:17; 24:10; **1Kin** 1:13; 20; 24; 3:7; 17; 26; 8:26; 28; 53; 12:16; 28; 13:2; 17:18; 20; 21; 18:26; 37; 19:4; 20:4; 21:20; 22:28; **2Kin** 1:11; 13; 4:40; 6:12; 26; 8:5; 9:5(2); 23; 13:14; 19:15; 19; 20:3; **1Chr** 16:13; 34; 35; 17:16; 17(2); 19; 20; 25; 27; 21:17; 29:11(2); 16; 18; **2Chr** 1:9; 6:14; 16; 17; 19; 41(2); 42; 10:16; 13:12; 14:11(2); 20:6; 12; 17; 20; 25:7; **Ezr** 9:6; 10; 15; **Neh** 1:5; 11; 4:4; 6:9; 13:14; 22; 29; 31; **Est** 7:3; **Job** 6:2; 7:7; 20; 16:18; 19:21; 33:31; 34:2; 37:14; **Ps** 2:10; 3:3; 7(2); 4:1; 2; 5:1; 3; 8; 10; 6:1; 2(2); 3; 4; 7:1; 3; 6; 8; 8:1; 9; 9:1; 2; 6; 13; 19; 20; 10:1; 12(2); 12:7; 13:1; 3; 16:1; 2; 17:1; 6; 7; 13; 14; 18:1; 15; 49; 19:14; 21:1; 22:2; 3; 19(2); 24:6; 7; 9; 25:1; 2; 4; 6; 7; 11; 17; 20; 22; 26:1; 2; 6; 27:7; 9; 11; 28:1; 29:1; 30:1; 2; 3; 4; 8; 10; 12; 31:1; 5; 9; 14; 17; 23; 33:1; 22; 34:3; 8; 9; 35:1; 22(2); 24; 36:5; 6; 7; 10; 38:1; 15(2); 21(2); 22; 39:12; 13; 40:5; 8; 9; 11; 13(2); 17; 41:10; 42:1; 5; 6; 11; 43:1(2); 3; 4; 5; 44:1; 4; 23; 45:3; 6; 10; 47:1; 48:9; 10; 50:7(2); 51:1; 10; 14; 15; 17; 52:1; 4; 54:1; 2; 6; 55:1; 9; 23; 56:1; 2; 7; 12; 57:1; 5; 7; 9; 11; 58:1(2); 6(2); 59:1; 3; 5; 8; 11; 17; 60:1(2); 10(2); 61:1; 5; 7; 62:12; 63:1; 64:1; 65:1; 2; 5; 66:8; 10; 67:3; 4; 5; 68:7; 9; 10; 24; 28; 32; 35; 69:1; 5; 6(2); 13(2); 16; 29; 70:1(2); 5(2); 71:1; 4; 5; 12(2); 17; 18; 19(2); 22(2); 72:1; 73:20; 74:1; 10; 18; 19; 21; 22; 75:1; 76:6; 77:13; 16; 78:1; 79:1; 8; 9; 12; 80:1; 3; 4; 7; 14; 19; 81:8(2); 82:8; 83:1(2); 13; 16; 84:1; 3; 8(2); 9; 12; 85:4; 7; 86:1; 2; 3; 4; 6; 8; 9; 11; 12; 14; 16; 87:3; 88:1; 13; 89:5; 8; 15; 51; 90:13; 14; 92:1; 5; 9; 93:3; 5; 94:1(2); 5; 12; 18; 95:1; 6; 96:1; 7; 9; 97:8; 98:1; 99:8; 101:1; 2; 102:1; 12; 24; 103:1; 2; 22; 104:1(2); 24; 35; 105:1; 6; 106:1; 4(2); 47; 107:1; 108:1; 3; 5; 11(2); 109:1; 21; 26(2); 113:1; 114:5; 115:1; 9; 10; 116:4; 7; 16; 19; 117:1; 118:1; 25(2); 29; 119:5; 8; 10; 12; 31; 33; 41; 52; 55; 57; 64; 65; 75; 89; 97; 107; 108; 137; 145; 149; 151; 156; 159; 169; 174; 120:2; 122:2; 123:1; 3; 125:4; 126:4; 130:1; 3; 132:8; 135:1; 9; 13(2); 19(2); 20; 136:1; 2; 3; 26; 137:5; 7; 8; 138:4; 8; 139:1; 4; 17; 19; 21; 23; 140:1; 4; 6; 7; 8; 141:3; 8; 142:5; 143:1; 7; 9; 11; 144:5; 9; 145:1; 10; 146:1; 10; 147:12(2); **Prov** 4:10; 5:7; 6:9; 7:24; 8:4; 5; 32; 24:15; 30:13; 31:4; **Eccl** 10:16; 17; 11:9; **Song** 1:5; 7; 8; 9; 2:7; 14; 3:5; 11; 4:11; 16; 5:1(2); 8; 9; 16; 6:1; 4; 13; 7:1; 6; 13; 8:1; 4; 12; **Is** 1:2(2); 2:5; 3:12; 5:3; 7:13; 8:8; 9; 10:5; 24; 30(2); 12:1; 14:12; 31(2); 16:9; 21:2(2); 10; 13; 23:4; 10; 12; 24:17; 25:1; 26:8; 13; 15; 17; 27:12; 33:2; 37:16; 17(2); 20; 38:3; 14; 16; 40:9(2); 27(2); 41:1; 43:12(2); 22(2); 44:1; 2; 21(2); 23(2); 45:15; 46:3; 8; 47:1(2); 5; 48:1; 12; 18; 49:1; 3; 13(3); 51:4; 9; 17; 52:1(2); 2(2); 54:1; 11; 62:6; 63:16; 17; 64:4; 8; 9; 12; **Jer** 2:4; 12; 28; 31; 3:14; 20; 4:1; 14; 19; 5:3; 15; 21; 6:1; 8; 18; 19; 23; 26; 7:29; 9:20; 10:1; 6; 7; 17; 23; 24; 11:5; 13; 20; 12:1; 3; 13:27; 14:7; 8; 9; 20; 22; 15:5; 15; 16; 16:19; 17:3; 13; 14; 18:6(2); 19; 19:3; 20:7; 12; 21:12; 13; 22:2; 23; 29; 30:10(2); 31:4; 7; 10; 21; 22; 23; 32:25; 34:4; 37:20; 42:19; 45:2; 46:11; 19; 27(2); 28; 47:6; 48:2; 19; 28; 32; 43; 46; 49:3; 4; 8; 16; 30; 50:11; 24; 31; 42; 51:13; 25; 62; **Lam** 1:9; 11; 20; 2:13(2); 18; 20; 3:55; 58; 59; 61; 64; 4:21; 22(2); 5:1; 19; 21; **Eze** 3:25; 7:7; 8:15; 17; 10:13; 11:4; 5; 12:25; 13:4; 11; 16:35; 18:25; 29; 30; 31; 20:31; 39; 44; 23:22; 26:3; 27:3(2); 8; 28:16; 22; 33:7; 8; 10; 11; 20; 34:9; 17; 35:3; 15; 36:8; 22; 32; 37:3; 4; 9; 12; 13; 38:3; 16; 39:1; 44:6; 45:9; **Dan** 2:4; 23; 29; 31; 37; 3:4; 9; 10; 12; 14; 16; 17; 18; 24; 4:9; 18; 22; 24; 27; 31; 5:10; 18; 22; 6:7; 8; 12; 13; 15; 20; 21; 22; 8:17; 9:4; 7; 8; 15; 16; 17; 18; 19(4); 22; 10:11; 16; 19; 12:4; 8; **Hos** 5:1(2); 3; 8; 6:4(2); 11; 8:5; 9:1; 14; 10:9; 13:9; 14(2); 14:1; **Joel** 1:11(2); 19; 2:17; 21; 3:4; 11; **Amos** 2:11; 3:1; 4:5; 12(2); 5:1; 25; 6:14; 7:2; 5; 12; 8:4; 14; 9:7; **Obad** 1:6; 14(2); 2:6; 4:2; 3; **Mic** 1:2; 13; 15; 2:7; 12; 3:1; 4:8; 10; 13; 5:1; 6:2; 3; 5; 8; 7:8; **Nah** 1:15; 3:18; **Hab** 1:2; 12(3); 3:2(2); **Zeph** 2:1; 5; 3:14(3); **Hag** 1:4; 2:4(2); 23; **Zec** 1:9; 12; 2:7; 10; 13; 3:2; 8; 4:7; 8:13; 9:9(2); 13(2); 11:1; 2; 7; 13:7; **Mal** 1:6; 2:1; **Mt** 7; 6:30; 8:26; 11:25; 12:34; 14:31; 15:22; 28; 16:3; 8; 17:17; 18:32; 20:30; 31; 23:37; 26:39; 42; **Mk** 9:19; 12:29; **Lk** 3:7; 5:8; 9:41; 10:21; 12:28; 13:34; 24:25; **Jn** 17:5; 25; **Acts** 1:1; 7:42; 13:10; 18:14; 25:26; 26:13; 19; **Rom** 2:1; 3; 7:24; 9:20; 11:33; **1Cor** 7:16(2); 15:55(2); **2Cor** 6:11;

Gal 3:1; **1Ti** 6:11; 20; **Heb** 1:8; 10:7; 9; **Jas** 2:20; **Rev** 4:11; 6:10; 11:17; 15:4; 16:5

OF

Gen 1:2(3); 6; 10; 14; 15; 17; 20; 24; 25; 26(2); 27; 28(2); 29(2); 30(2); 2:1; 4(2); 5(2); 6; 7(3); 9(5); 10; 11(2); 12; 13(2); 14(2); 15; 16(2); 17(4); 19(3); 20(2); 21; 23(3); 3:1(3); 2(3); 3(4); 6; 7; 8(4); 11; 12; 14(2); 17(6); 18; 19(2); 20; 21; 22(3); 23; 24(4); 4:2(2); 3(3); 4(3); 10; 14; 16(3); 17(2); 19(2); 20(2); 21; 22(2); 23; 25; 26; 5:1(3); 4; 8; 11; 14; 17; 20; 23; 27; 29(2); 31; 6:1; 2(3); 4(4); 5(3); 7(2); 8; 9; 13; 14; 15(4); 16; 17(2); 19(3); 20(5); 21; 7:2(2); 3(3); 4; 6; 7(2); 8(4); 10; 11(4); 13(2); 14; 15(2); 16; 18; 21; 22(2); 23; 25; 26; 27; 28; 29; 31(3); 32(6); 33(2); 34; 36(2); 38(2); 26:12(2); 13(4); 17(2); 19(3); 20(2); 21; 22(2); 24; 25(2); 28; 29(2); 31(3); 33; 34; 35; 36(2); 37(3); 27:1; 2(2); 3; 4(2); 5(2); 6; 7; 9; 11; 12; 14; 15; 16; 17; 19; 20; 21; 22; 23; 27; 28; 30(2); 31; 32(2); 33; 27; 29(2); 31; 6:1; 20(3); 4(4); 5(3); 7(2); 8; 9; 13; 14; 15(4); 16; 17(2); 19(3); 20(5); 21; 7:2(2); 3(3); 4; 6; 7(2); 8(4); 10; 11(4); 13(2); 14; 15(2); 16; 17(4); 18(3); 19; 20; 21(3); 22; 23; 24(4); 25(2); 26; 27(2); 28(4); 29(2); 30(4); 31; 32(4); 33(2); 34(2); 35(3); 36; 37; 38; 39(4); 40(2); 43(3); 37:1; 2(3); 3(2); 14(2); 20; 21; 22; 23(2); 25; 28(2); 31; 32; 36(2); 38:2; 7; 12(2); 19; 20; 21; 22; 27; 39:1(4); 2; 5; 11(2); 14; 19; 21(2); 22(2); 23; 40:1(3); 2; 3(2); 4; 5(4); 7; 8; 12; 14(2); 15(2); 17(3); 19; 20; 22; 23; 41:1(2); 2(4); 3(3); 5; 6(4); 8(3); 9; 16; 20(2); 24; 31; 33; 45:2; 8(2); 9; 10; 11; 12; 13(2); 14; 15(2); 16; 17(2); 18; 20(3); 21(2); 22(2); 23; 24(2); 25(4); 25(5); 26(6); 28; 29(2); 38:1(2); 2(2); 3; 5; 6; **Ex** 1:1(2); 5(2); 7; 9(2); 10; 12(2); 13; 14; 15(4); 16; 17; 18; 2:1(3); 3; 5; 6; 7; 10; 11; 13; 15(2); 16; 19(2); 23(5); 25; 3:14(4); 2(4); 4:5(4); 7(2); 8(2); 9(3); 10(5); 16(5); 17(3); 18(3); 19; 21; 22(4); 4:5(4); 7; 8(2); 9; 10(2); 11; 13; 15; 16(2); 17; 19(3); 20(2); 22(2); 23; 24(4); 25; 27; 28(2); 29(2); 30(2); 31(3); 32(2); 33(4); 35(3); 36; 9:1; 3(3); 4(3); 4(3); 5; 6; 7; 13; 27(2); 3; 4(2); 6; 7(3); 8(2); 10(2); 12; 13; 14(3); 15(6); 16(5); 17(3); 18(3); 19; 21; 22(4); 4:5(4); 7; 8(2); 2; 40(3); 41; 43(2); 46(4); 12:2(2); 3; 4(2); 5(4); 6(2); 7(3); 8; 11; 12(4); 13(2); 14; 15(2); 16(2); 17; 19; 20; 21(2); 22(4); 23; 25(2); 26; 27(2); 46:1; 2; 3(2); 5; 6; 8(2); 9; 10(2); 11; 12; 13(2); 14; 15(5); 16(5); 17(3); 18(3); 19; 21; 22(4); 23; 24(2); 25(2); 27(3); 28(2); 29(2); 30(2); 31(3); 32(2); 33(4); 35(3); 36; 9:1; 3; 4(3); 4; 7; 14; 15(2); 18; 22(2); 23(5); 24(4); 26(3); 29(2); 30(2); 31(3); 32(2); 33(4); 35(3); 36; 9:1; 3; 4; 5; 6; 7; 8; 9(3); 10; 17; 18; 19(2); 22(2); 23(2); 24(4); 26(3); 29(2); 30(2); 31(3); 32(2); 33(4); 35(3); 36; 9:1; 3; 4; 5; 6; 7; 8; 9(3); 10; 17; 18; 19(2); 22(2); 23(2); 24(4); 26(3); 27(3); 29(2); 30(4); 31; 33; 34(5); 35(2); 5:1(2); 2(3); 3(2); 4(2); 5; 6(2); 9(5); 11(2); 9; 13; 15(4); 16; 17(2); 6:3; 5; 6; **Lev** 1:1(2); 2(5); 3; 4(4); 5(2); 7; 9; 10(3); 11; 13; 14(3); 11; 12; 13(4); 14(3); 15; 16; 17; 2:1; 2; 3(2); 6; 7; 10; 13; 14(3); 4:2(4); 5(2); 6(2); 7(9); 8; 10(3); 11; 13(4); 14; 15(2); 16(2); 17; 18(7); 22(3); 23; 24; 25(6); 26(2); 27(3); 28; 29(2); 30(4); 31; 33; 34(5); 35(2); 5:1(2); 2(3); 3(2); 4(2); 5; 6(2); 9(5); 11(2); 9; 13(3); 15(4); 16; 4:2(4); 5; 6(2); 2; **Ex** 1:1(2); 5; 6; 7(3); 9(2); 10; 17; 18(2); 19(2); 22; 23(2); 10:1(2); 4(3); 5; 6; 7(4); 9; 10; 17; 18; 19(2); 12(2); 13(2); 14(4); 15; 16(2); 17(3); 18(3); 19; 21; 22(4); 4:5(4); 7; 8(2); 9; 10(2); 11; 13; 15; 2; 4(4); 6(4); 9(8); 11(3); 13(3); 14(2); 15(6); 16(2); 17(3); 22; 24; 25(2); 26; 27; 28; 29; 30; 31; 32; 33; 34; 35; 36; 37; 38; 39(4); 40(2); 41; 43(3); 44; 45(4); 46(2); 47; 50; 51(3); 12:3(3); 5(3); 5; 8(2); 9; 11; 12; 13(2); 14(2); 15(4); 16(2); 17(2); 18(5); 19(3); 6:1; 3; 4; 2(2); 4(5); 5; 8(3); 9; 11; 14; 16; 18(2); 19(5); 20(2); 21(3); 22; 24(2); 8:3; 5; 6(2); 7; 12; 13(4); 16(2); 20; 24(5); 25(3); 26; 29; 30; 7:2(2); 3(3); 8; 9; 11; 12; 14; 15(2); 16; 17; 18; 19(2); 20; 22; **Num** 1:2(2); 3; 4; 5; 6; 7; 8; 9; 10; 11; 12; 13; 14; 15; 16; 17; 18; 19; 20; 22; 24; 25; 26; 27; 28; 29(2); 30; 31; 32; 33; 34; 35; 36; 37; 38; 39(2); 40; 41(3); 43(3); 44; 45(4); 46(2); 27:2; 3(3); 5; 6(3); 9; 11; 15(2); 16(4); 17; 18; 19(2); 22(2); 23(3); 25; 27; 28(2); 29(2); 30(4); 31(3); 36(3); 38; 39(2); 40; 41(3); 43(3); 44; 45(4); 46(2); 27:2; 3(3);

23(2); 24(3); 25; 26; 27(2); 28(4); 29; 30(5); 31; 32(3); 34; **Num** 1:1(5); 2(5); 4(3); 5(4); 6(2); 7(2); 8(2); 9(2); 10(6); 11(2); 12(2); 13(2); 14(2); 15(2); 16(4); 18(3); 19; 20(3); 21(3); 22(5); 23(3); 24(4); 25(3); 26(4); 27(3); 28(4); 29(3); 30(4); 31(3); 32(6); 33(3); 34(4); 35(3); 36(4); 37(3); 38(4); 39(3); 40(4); 41(3); 42(4); 43(3); 44(2); 45(3); 47; 49(3); 50; 52; 53(5); 54; 2:2(4); 3(7); 4; 5(4); 7(4); 9; 10(5); 12(4); 13; 14(4); 15; 16; 17(3); 18(5); 19; 20(4); 21; 22(4); 23; 24(2); 25(5); 26; 27(4); 28; 29(4); 30; 31; 32(4); 33; 34(2); 3:1; 2(2); 3(2); 4(2); 6; 7(3); 8(5); 9(2); 12(3); 13; 14; 15(2); 16; 17; 18(2); 19; 20(3); 21(4); 22(3); 23; 24(4); 25(5); 26(3); 27(6); 28(2); 29(3); 30(5); 31; 32(4); 33(4); 34(2); 35(6); 36(3); 37; 38(4); 39(2); 40(4); 41(6); 42; 43(3); 45(4); 46(4); 47; 48; 49; 50(4); 51(2); 4:2(4); 3; 4(3); 5; 6(2); 7(2); 8(2); 9(2); 10; 11(2); 12(3); 14(3); 15(6); 16(4); 18(2); 22(3); 23; 24(2); 25(5); 26(4); 27(3); 28(6); 29(2); 30(2); 31(3); 32(3); 33(6); 34(3); 35; 36; 37(5); 38(3); 39; 40(2); 41(6); 42(4); 43; 44; 45(5); 46(3); 47(3); 48; 49(3); 5(2)(2); 4(2); 5; 6; 9(3); 10; 13; 14(4); 15(4); 17(2); 18; 19; 20; 21; 25; 26; 29(2); 30; 6:2(2); 3(3); 4(2); 5(4); 7; 8; 9(2); 10(2); 12(2); 13(4); 14(2); 15(3); 17(2); 18(6); 19(4); 21(3); 23; 27; 7:2(4); 3; 5(3); 7; 8(3); 9(2); 10; 11; 12(3); 13(4); 14(3); 15; 16; 17(4); 18(2); 19(4); 20(3); 21; 22; 23(4); 24(3); 25(4); 26(2); 27; 28; 29(4); 30(3); 31(6); 32(2); 33; 34; 35(4); 36(3); 37(2); 38(2); 39; 40; 41(4); 42(3); 43(6); 44(2); 45; 46; 47(4); 48(3); 49(4); 50(2); 51; 52; 53(4); 54(3); 55(6); 56(2); 57; 58; 59(4); 60(3); 61(4); 62(2); 63; 64; 65(4); 66(3); 67(4); 68(2); 69; 70; 71(4); 72(3); 73(4); 74(2); 75; 76; 77(4); 78(3); 79(4); 80(2); 81; 82; 83(4); 84(4); 85(2); 86(3); 87(2); 88(3); 89(3); 8:4(2); 6; 7; 9(3); 10; 11(3); 12; 14; 15(2); 16(5); 17(3); 18(2); 19(7); 20(3); 22; 24(2); 25; 26; 9:1(4); 2; 3(2); 4; 5; 6(3); 7(3); 10(4); 11; 12(3); 13; 14; 15(2); 16; 17(2); 18(3); 19(2); 20(2); 22; 23(5); 10:2(4); 3(2); 4(2); 8; 10(3); 11(2); 12(4); 13(4); 14(4); 15(4); 16(4); 17(2); 18(3); 19(4); 20(4); 22(4); 23(4); 24(4); 25(5); 26(4); 27(4); 28(2); 29(2); 31; 33(3); 34(2); 36; 11:1(2); 3(2); 4; 7; 8(3); 10(2); 11; 15; 16(4); 17(2); 18; 20; 22; 24(3); 25; 26(4); 28(3); 30; 31; 33; 34; 12:1; 3; 4; 5(2); 8; 9; 12(2); 16; 13(4); 15; 17; 18(2); 19(2); 21; 23; 25; 27(2); 29; 30(2); 34(3); 38(3); 39; 40; 41; 44(3); 15:2(2); 30(2); 4(4); 5(2); 6(3); 7(3); 9(3); 10(2); 13(2); 14; 15; 18; 19(2); 20(3); 21(2); 23; 24(2); 25(2); 26(2); 27; 29; 31; 32; 38(4); 39; 41(2); 16:6(2); 2(4); 3(2); 7; 8(4); 9(4); 10; 12; 13; 14(2); 15; 17; 18(2); 19(3); 22(2); 24; 25; 26(2); 27(2); 28; 29(2); 31; 34; 37(2); 38(3); 39; 40(4); 41(3); 42(2); 43; 47; 49; 50(2); 17:2(6); 3(3); 4; 5(2); 6(3); 7; 8(3); 9; 12; 13; 18; 19(3); 20; 21(3); 22(2); 23(3); 24(3); 26(4); 27(2); 28(3); 29(4); 30(3); 31; 32(4); 19:2(2); 4(3); 5; 6; 9(2); 10; 12; 13(4); 14(3); 15(3); 18(2); 20(2); 21; 22; 23(4); 24(2); 25(2); 26(4); 27; 28(2); 29(4); 30; 31; 32(4); 34; 22:1(2); 2; 3; 4(2); 6; 7; 8(2); 13(3); 15; 16(3); 17(4); 19(2); 20; 24; 25:1; 2; 3; 4(2); 5; 6(8); 7(4); 8(4); 11(4); 12; 13(2); 14(3); 15(3); 18(5); 26:1; 2(3); 3; 4(4); 5(6); 6(4); 7(2); 8; 9(2); 11; 12(7); 13(4); 14; 16(2); 17(2); 18; 19; 20; 21(2); 22; 23; 24; 25; 26(4); 27; 28; 29(6); 30(5); 31(4); 32(4); 33(4); 34(2); 35(7); 36(3); 37(4); 39(4); 40(4); 41; 42(4); 43(3); 5; 6; 8(2); 9; 11; 12(2); 13; 14; 15(7); 16(2); 17; 18; 19; 20(3); 23(4); 24(5); 25; 26(4); 28(3); 30; 29(3); 30(3); 32; 33(4); 34; 35(2); 36; 2:1(2); 4(2); 5; 6; 7; 8; 10(2); 14(2); 16; 17(2); 18; 19; 20(3); 21(4); 47; 62; 63(3); 16:1(3); 2; 3(2); 4; 5(3); 8(3); 9(3); 17:15; 2(10); 3(5); 4(3); 5; 6(3); 7(2); 8(3); 9(6); 11(4); 12(2); 13; 14; 15(6); 16(6); 17; 18; 18:1(3); 2; 3(2); 4; 5; 7(3); 10; 11(6); 12(2); 13(2); 14(3); 15(3); 16(6); 17(3); 19(4); 19:1(4); 8(4); 9(9); 10(2); 12; 14; 16(2); 17; 22; 23(3); 24(2); 27(2); 28; 29(2); 30; 31(2); 32(2); 39(3); 40(2); 41; 47(5); 48(3); 49(3); 50; 51(8); 20:2(3); 3; 4(5); 5; 6; 7; 8(6); 9(3); 21:1(7); 2(2); 3(2); 4(3); 9(4); 5(9); 6(10); 7; 8(3); 10(3); 11; 12; 13(2); 14(2); 15(2); 16(2); 17(2); 18(3); 19(4); 20(5); 21; 22(3); 23(2); 7:2(2); 8(4); 9(4); 10; 11; 12(2); 13(2); 14; 19(2); 20; 25(2); 26(2); 27; 28; 30(2); 31(4); 13:1(2); 3; 6;

27; 4:1; 2; 3; 4; 6; 9; 11; 12(3); 13; 15(3); 16(2); 17(2); 18(2); 19; 20(3); 23(2); 25(2); 28; 31; 32(2); 33(3); 34; 36(3); 37; 42; 43(3); 44; 45(2); 46(4); 47(3); 48; 49(2); 5:3; 4(2); 5(2); 6(3); 8; 9(2); 10; 11; 14(2); 15; 22(5); 23(3); 24(2); 25; 26(4); 28(3); 6:2; 3; 7; 9; 11; 12(3); 14(2); 15(2); 17; 18; 21; 7:4; 6; 7; 8(4); 13(4); 15(2); 18; 19; 22; 25; 8:3(2); 6; 7(4); 8(2); 9; 14(3); 15(2); 17; 20; 9:2(3); 4; 5(2); 7(2); 9(2); 10(3); 11(3); 12(2); 14; 15; 16; 17; 18(2); 19(2); 21; 23; 26; 27; 10:1(2); 3(2); 4(3); 6(3); 7(2); 8(3); 12; 13; 14; 16; 17(2); 18; 19; 21; 23; 26; 27; 10:1(2); 3(2); 4(3); 6(3); 7(2); 8(3); 12; 13; 14; 16; 17(2); 18; 19; 21; 23; 26; 27; 10:1(2); 3(2); 4(3); 6(3); 7(2); 8(3); 12; 13; 14; 16; 17(2); 18; 19; 21; 23; 26; 27; 28(2); 30(2); 12:1; 3(3); 5; 6(3); 11; 14; 15(2); 17(7); 21(2); 22; 25; 27(3); 28; 13:1; 3(2); 5(7); 6(2); 7(4); 9; 10(3); 12; 13(2); 16(2); 17:2; 18(2); 14:1; 7(2); 8; 9; 11; 12; 20; 21(2); 22; 23(5); 28(2); 29; 15:1; 2(3); 3; 7(3); 9; 11; 14(4); 15; 19(4); 16:1(3); 2; 3(6); 4; 5; 6(2); 10(3); 13; 15; 16(3); 17; 19(2); 21(2); 17:2(2); 3(2); 4; 6(3); 5(2); 6(3); 7; 8(2); 9; 10; 12; 13(3); 15; 16(3); 19; 20; 22(2); 19:2; 3; 4; 5; 6(2); 11; 12(3); 13; 14; 15(2); 20:1(3); 3; 6(2); 9(2); 11; 13; 14; 15(2); 16(2); 19(2); 21:3; 4; 5(2); 6; 8; 9(2); 12; 14; 15(2); 18; 19; 21:3; 4; 5(2); 6; 8; 9(2); 12; 14; 15(2); 18; 19; 26:2(4); 4(7); 5; 6(2); 7(3); 8; 9; 10; 11:3; 17; 18; 19; 26:2(4); 5; 7; 8; 10; 12; 14; 15(3); 17; 18(2); 19(2); 21(4); 22; 23; 25(2); 26(2); 27(2); 28(3); 29(4); 30; 31(3); 32; 33(3); 35; 36(4); 39; 40(2); 12:1(2); 2(2); 3; 4(3); 5(2); 6(2); 7(3); 8; 9; 10(2); 11(2); 12; 13; 14(4); 15(2); 16(3); 17(2); 18(2); 19; 20; 21; 22; 23(4); 24(2); 25; 27(3); 28; 29(3); 30(6); 31; 19:1(2); 3(2); 5; 9(3); 10(4); 12(2); 13; 14; 15(2); 16; 17(3); 19; 20(3); 21(3); 22(3); 23; 25; 27(2); 28(5); 29(2); 30(2); 31; 33(3); 34; 36(4); 3:1; 3(3); 7; 11; 14(2); 15(2); 17; 19; 20; 21; 4:1; 2; 3(6); 4(6); 5(2); 6(4); 8(2); 10; 11(2); 12(2); 14; 15(2); 16; 17; 19; 20; 21(2); 22; 23(3); 24(2); 25(2); 26(4); 28; 29(2); 30(3); 32:1; 3; 4; 5; 7(2); 8(4); 9; 10; 13(4); 14; 15; 18; 19(3); 20; 23(4); 24(3); 46; 49(3); 51(5); 52; 33:1(2); 3; 4(2); 5(2); 7(2); 8(2); 11(3); 12(2); 13(3); 15(2); 16(5); 17(5); 18; 19(4); 20(2); 21(3); 22; 23(2); 24; 26; 28(2); 29(2); 34:1(4); 2(2); 3(3); 5(3); 6(2); 8(3); 9(4); 11; 12; **Josh** 1:1(3); 2; 3; 4(2); 5; 6; 8(2); 9; 10; 12; 13; 14; 15; 18; 2:1(2); 2(3); 3; 5(2); 6(2); 9(2); 10(3); 11; 17; 18; 19(2); 20; 23; 24(2); 3:1; 3(2); 6(2); 7; 8(3); 9(2); 11(3); 12(3); 13(6); 14; 15(3); 16; 17(3); 4:2(3); 3(3); 4(3); 5(6); 7(5); 8(3); 9(3); 10; 11(2); 12(4); 13(4); 14(2); 17; 18(6); 19(3); 20; 21; 23; 24(2); 5:1(7); 2; 3(2); 4(3); 5; 6(4); 9(2); 10(3); 11(2); 12(6); 14(2); 15; 6:1(2); 2; 3; 4; 5(2); 6(4); 7; 8(3); 10; 11; 12; 13(3); 15; 18(2); 19(2); 20; 21; 24(2); 26; 7:1(9); 2; 4(2); 5(3); 6(2); 7; 9(2); 11; 12; 13(2); 15; 16; 17(3); 18(5); 19; 20; 21(4); 23(3); 24(3); 26(4); 8:1(2); 3(2); 8; 9; 10; 11(2); 12; 13(3); 14(2); 15; 19; 20(2); 21(2); 22(3); 23; 24(4); 25(2); 26; 27(2); 29(4); 30; 31(5); 32(4); 33(6); 34(2); 35(2); 9:1; 3; 5; 6; 7; 9(3); 10(3); 11; 12; 13(2); 14(2); 15; 16; 17; 18(3); 19; 20; 21(2); 23(4); 24(3); 26(3); 27(3); 10:1(2); 2; 3(5); 4; 5(6); 6(2); 7(6); 8; 11; 12(3); 13(2); 14; 18; 19; 20(3); 21(2); 22(3); 24(6); 25; 27(2); 28(3); 30(3); 32(2); 33; 35; 37; 39; 40(5); 41; 42; 11:1(4); 2(4); 3; 5; 6; 7(2); 8(2); 10; 11; 12(4); 13; 14; 15; 16(3); 17(2); 18; 19(4); 20(2); 21(2); 22(3); 23; 24; 25; 26; 27; 11:1; 2(4); 5(3); 6; 7; 9(2); 10; 11; 13(2); 14(2); 15(2); 16(2); 17(3); 18(3); 19; 20; 21(2); 22(3); 23(4); 24; 25(2); 26; 27(2); 29:4; 30; 31(5); 32(4); 33(6); 34(2); 35(2); 9:1; 3; 5; 6; 7; 9(3); 10(3); 11; 12; 13(2); 14(2); 15; 16; 17; 18(3); 19; 20; 21(2); 23(4); 24(3); 26(3); 27(3);

20; 21(5); 22(2); 24; 25(2); 26(2); 27(2); 28(2); 29; 30(2); 33(2); 34; 37; 38(2); 7:1(4); 3(2); 4(2); 5; 6(2); 8(2); 11; 12; 13(2); 14(3); 15(3); 17; 18(3); 19(2); 20(2); 22; 23(4); 24; 25(3); 8:1; 2(4); 3(2); 4; 5; 7; 8(2); 9; 10(3); 11(2); 12; 13; 14(4); 15(2); 16(3); 17(2); 18(2); 19; 22(2); 24; 25; 26(3); 28(2); 29; 30; 32(3); 33; 34(3); 35; 9:13(3); 4; 5; 8; 9; 13; 14(2); 18(2); 19; 20; 21; 25; 26; 29(2); 30; 31(2); 33; 34; 35(4); 36; 24(3); 25(2); 26(2); 27; 28(4); 30(3); 31; 35(3); 36(2); 37(2); 39; 40; 43; 44(2); 46(4); 47(2); 49(2); 51(2); 52; 53; 54; 55; 56; 57(4); 10:1(3); 4; 6(8); 7(4); 8(3); 9(2); 10; 11(2); 12; 14; 15; 16; 17(2); 18(3); 11:1(2); 2; 3; 4(2); 5(4); 6; 7(2); 8(3); 10; 11; 12; 13(4); 14(2); 15(3); 17(3); 18(7); 19(2); 21(4); 22; 23; 25(2); 27(3); 28(3); 29(4); 30; 31(2); 32; 33(3); 35; 36(4); 39; 40(2); 12:1(2); 2; 3(4); 5; 6(2); 7; 8; 9; 10(5); 11; 12(2); 13(4); 14(3); 15(2); 17(2); 18(5); 19; 20; 21(3); 22; 23(3); 24(2); 25(2); 26; 27; 29(3); 30(6); 31; 19:1(2); 3(2); 5; 9(3); 10(4); 12(2); 13; 14; 15(2); 16; 17(3); 19; 20(3); 21(3); 22(3); 23; 25; 27(2); 28(5); 29(2); 30(2); 31; 33(3); 34; 36(4); 49(4); 50(5); 51(3); 52; 15:1(2); 4; 5; 6(2); 8(2); 9(3); 10; 13(2); 14(2); 15(2); 17(2); 19(2); 20(2); 21(2); 22; 23; 24; 26; 27; 28; 29; 30; 31(2); 34; 35; 16:4; 7; 10; 12(3); 14; 18(3); 20; 17:2(2); 4(3); 5(4); 6(2); 7(2); 8; 10; 11; 12(3); 13(2); 17; 18; 19(2); 22(2); 23; 24; 25; 26; 28; 32; 33; 34; 35; 36; 37(4); 38; 42(3); 43(3); 44; 45(3); 46(2); 48(4); 21:1(2); 3; 5(2); 6; 7; 8(2); 9(2); 10(3); 12(3); 14(2); 15; 16(2); 17(2); 18(2); 19(4); 20; 21(5); 23(2); 24; **Ruth** 1:1(2); 2(5); 4:4(2); 5(2); 6(2); 7(2); 9(2); 13; 22(2); 2:1(4); 2; 3(3); 6(2); 9; 10; 11(2); 12(2); 13; 14; 16(2); 19; 20(3); 23(3); 3:2; 7(2); 9; 10; 11; 13(3); 15; 17; 4:1; 2(2); 3(3); 4; 5(5); 9(2); 10(4); 11; 12(3); 15(2); 17(2); 18; **1Sa** 1:1(6); 2(2); 3(4); 7; 9(2); 10; 11(3); 15; 16(3); 17(2); 20; 24(3); 27; 2:3(2); 4; 8(3); 9; 10(4); 12(2); 13; 15; 17(2); 20; 22(2); 23; 25; 27(2); 28(5); 29(2); 30(2); 31; 33(3); 34; 36(4); 3:1; 3(4); 4(3); 5; 7; 11; 14(2); 15(2); 17; 19; 20; 21; 4:1; 2; 3(6); 4(6); 5(2); 6(4); 8(2); 10; 11(2); 12(2); 14; 15(2); 16; 17; 19; 20; 21(2); 22; 23(3); 24(2); 25(2); 26(4); 28; 29(2); 30(3); 32(2); 5:1; 2(3); 3(2); 4; 6; 11(3); 12(2); 14(2); 15(2); 16(2); 17(2); 18(2); 19(3); 21; 22; 23(2); 24; 26; 28(2); 29(2); 34:1(4); 2(2); 3(3); 5(3); 6(2); 8(3); 9(4); 11; 12;

10; 11; 13; 18; 19; 21; 29; 30; 32(2); 34; 36; 37(2); 39; 14:1; 4; 7; 9; 11(2); 13; 15(2); 16(4); 17(2); 19(2); 20(3); 22; 25(2); 26; 27; 15:2(5); 3; 6(2); 10(2); 11; 13(2); 14; 23; 24(4); 25(2); 27; 28; 29; 30; 31; 32; 34; 35; 16:1(7); 3(2); 5(4); 6; 7; 8(3); 9; 10; 11; 15; 18; 19; 21(2); 22(2); 23(3); 17:4; 8(2); 9; 10; 12(2); 14(4); 15; 16; 18; 20; 21; 22; 23; 24; 25(3); 26; 27(7); 29; 18:1(2); 2(5); 3(3); 6; 7(3); 8; 9(3); 11; 12; 14(2); 17; 19(2); 22; 23; 27(3); 31; 32; 19:5(5); 9(6); 10; 11(2); 13(4); 14(3); 16(3); 17(3); 18; 19; 20(2); 21; 22; 24; 27; 28; 29; 32; 35; 37(2); 38; 40(2); 41(2); 42(4); 43(6); 20:1(3); 2(3); 3; 4; 5; 6; 7(2); 10; 11; 12(2); 13(2); 14; 15; 16; 17; 19(2); 21(2); 22(2); 23(2); 24; 21:1(2); 2(6); 3; 4(2); 5(2); 6(2); 7(4); 8(5); 9(3); 10(5); 11(2); 12(4); 13(3); 14(3); 16(4); 17(3); 18(2); 19(3); 20; 21(2); 22(2); 22:1(5); 3(2); 5(2); 6(2); 7; 8; 9(2); 11; 12; 13; 16(5); 17; 19; 21; 22; 31; 35; 36; 41; 43(2); 44(2); 46; 47(2); 51; 23:1(5); 2; 3(3); 4(2); 6(2); 7; 8; 9(3); 11(3); 12; 13(4); 14; 15(3); 16(3); 17(2); 18(2); 19; 20(6); 21; 22; 24(4); 26; 29(5); 30(2); 32(2); 33; 34(3); 36(2); 37; 24:1; 2(3); 3; 4(4); 5(3); 6; 7(4); 8; 9(3); 10; 11; 12; 13; 14(3); 16(3); 18; 19; 21; 22; 24(3); 1Kin 1:3; 5; 7; 8; 9(2); 11(2); 12; 19(2); 20(2); 25; 26; 27; 29; 30; 32; 33; 36(2); 37; 38; 39(2); 40; 41(3); 42; 44; 46; 47; 48; 50(2); 51; 52; 2:1; 2; 3(2); 4; 5(7); 7(3); 8(2); 10; 12; 13(2); 16; 20; 22; 24; 25(2); 26(2); 27(2); 28(2); 29(2); 30; 31; 32(6); 33(2); 34; 35(2); 39(5); 43; 45; 46(2); 3:1(5); 2; 3; 6; 7; 8; 11; 15(2); 17; 28(2); 4:2; 3(2); 4; 5(2); 6; 8; 9; 10(2); 11(3); 12; 13(4); 14; 15; 16; 17; 18; 19(6); 21(3); 22(2); 23; 25; 26; 29; 30; 33(6); 34(4); 5:1(3); 3(2); 4; 5(4); 6(2); 7(2); 8(2); 9; 10; 11; 12; 13; 15(6); 18; 19(2); 20; 21; 23; 24(4); 25; 26(6); 27(4); 29(2); 30; 31(3); 32(2); 33(3); 34(3); 36(2); 37(2); 38; 7:2(3); 6; 7(2); 8; 9(2); 10(3); 11; 12(5); 13; 14(3); 15(4); 16(4); 17(3); 19(2); 21; 22(2); 23; 24; 26(2); 27(3); 28; 29; 30(2); 31; 32(2); 33(2); 33(3); 34(3); 36(2); 37(2); 38; 7:2(3); 6; 7(2); 8; 9(2); 10(3); 11; 12(5); 14; 22(3); 23; 25(2); 28; 29(4); 11:1(2); 2(2); 4; 5(2); 6; 7(3); 9; 11; 12(2); 14; 15; 17; 18(3); 19(3); 20(2); 21; 23(2); 24; 25; 26(2); 27(2); 28(3); 29; 31(3); 32(2); 33(4); 34(2); 35; 39; 40(2); 41(4); 43; 12:2(3); 3; 4; 8; 14; 15; 16; 17(2); 19; 20(2); 21(4); 22(2); 23(4); 24(3); 24:3(2); 24:3(2); 4(3); 5(2); 6(3); 7; 8; 9; 11; 15(2); 17; 28(2); 4:2; 3(2); 4; 5(2); 6; 8; 9; 10(2); 11(3); 12; 13(4); 14; 15; 16; 17; 18; 19(6); 21(3); 22(2); 23; 25; 26; 29; 30; 33(6); 34(4); 5:1(3); 3(2); 4; 5(4); 6(2); 7(2); 8(2); 10; 12; 13; 15(2); 16; 17(2); 18; 19(2); 20(3); 21(2); 22; 23(5); 24(2); 25(7); 14:1(5); 2; 3; 6(3); 7(3); 8(3); 9(2); 10; 11(2); 13(6); 14(2); 15(6); 16; 17(5); 18(5); 20; 21(3); 23(5); 24; 25(8); 26; 27(3); 28(5); 29; 15:14(2); 2; 3; 5(2); 6(5); 7; 8(3); 9(3); 10; 11(5); 12(2); 13(3); 14(2); 15(5); 17(3); 18(3); 19(2); 20(7); 21(5); 23(3); 24(3); 25(4); 26(5); 27(3); 28(3); 29(4); 30(4); 31(5); 32(5); 33; 34; 35(2); 36(5); 37(2); 38; 16:1(4); 2; 3(4); 5(3); 6; 7(7); 8(3); 9(3); 10(3); 13; 14(3); 15(4); 17(2); 18(2); 19(5); 20; 17:1(3); 2(2); 3; 4(4); 5; 6(4); 7(5); 8(4); 9(2); 14; 16(2); 17; 18(2); 19(2); 20(3); 21(2); 22(2); 23(4); 25(2); 26(6); 27(4); 28; 29(2); 30(3); 31; 32(4); 33; 34; 36(2); 39(2); 18:1(5); 2; 3; 4; 5(2); 7; 8; 9(5); 10(4); 11(3); 12(2); 13(3); 14(3); 15(2); 16(4); 17(3); 18(2); 19; 21(2); 23; 24(3); 26(2); 28(2); 29; 30(2); 31(4); 32(4); 33(5); 34(4); 35(3); 37(3); 19:1; 2(2); 3(2); 4(2); 5; 8(2); 9(2); 10(2); 11; 12(3); 13(5); 14(3); 15(2); 16; 17(2); 18(3); 19; 21(2); 23; 24(3); 25(2); 26(2); 29(2); 30(2); 31(4); 32; 33(2); 34; 35(2); 36; 37(2); 38; 39(2); 40; 41(3); 42; 44; 46; 47; 48; 50(2); 51; 52; 53(4); 54(2); 55; 56(2); 59(2); 60; 63(3); 64(4); 65(2); 66; 9:1(2); 4; 5(2); 7(2); 9(2); 10(2); 11(2); 13; 14; 15(3); 16; 19(2); 20(3); 21(2); 22(4); 23; 24(2); 26(3); 27(2); 10:1(4); 2; 4; 5(4); 6(2); 7(2); 8(2); 9; 10; 11; 13; 15(6); 16(2); 18; 19(2); 20; 21; 23; 24(4); 25; 26(2); 27(4); 29(2); 30; 31(3); 32(2); 33(3); 34(3); 36(2); 37(2); 38; 7:2(3); 6; 7(2); 8; 9(2); 10(3); 11; 12(5); 14(2); 22(3); 23; 25(2); 28; 29(4); 11:1(2); 2(2); 4; 5(2); 6; 7(3); 9; 11; 12(2); 14; 15; 17; 18(3); 19(3); 20(2); 21; 23(2); 24; 25; 26(2); 27(2); 28(3); 29; 31(3); 32(2); 33(4); 34(2); 35; 39; 40(2); 41(4); 43;

14; 16; 17; 18(5); 19(5); 20; 21(3); 13:1(4); 2(3); 3(5); 4(2); 5(2); 6(2); 7(2); 8(5); 10(3); 11(3); 12(6); 13; 14(3); 16; 17(2); 18; 19; 20(2); 21(3); 22(2); 23; 24; 25(7); 14:1(5); 2; 3; 6(3); 7(3); 8(3); 9(2); 10; 11(2); 13(6); 14(2); 15(6); 16; 17(5); 18(5); 20; 21(3); 23(5); 24; 25(8); 26; 27(3); 28(5); 29; 15:14(2); 2; 3; 5(2); 6(5); 7; 8(3); 9(3); 10; 11(5); 12(2); 13(2); 14(5); 15(5); 17(3); 18(3); 19(2); 20(7); 21(5); 23(3); 24(3); 25(4); 26(5); 27(3); 28(3); 29(4); 30(4); 31(5); 32(5); 33(5); 34; 35(2); 36; 37(2); 39; 16:1(4); 2; 3(4); 5(3); 6; 7(7); 8(3); 9(3); 10(3); 13; 14(3); 15(4); 17(2); 18(2); 19(5); 20; 17:1(3); 2(2); 3; 4(4); 5; 6(4); 7(5); 8(4); 9(2); 14; 16(2); 17; 18(2); 19(2); 20(3); 21(2); 22(2); 23(4); 25(2); 26(6); 27(4); 28; 29(2); 30(3); 31; 32(4); 33; 34; 36(2); 39(2); 18:1(5); 2; 3; 4; 5(2); 7; 8; 9(5); 10(4); 11(3); 12(2); 13(3); 14(3); 15(2); 16(2); 17(3); 18(2); 19; 21(2); 23; 24(3); 26(2); 28(2); 29; 30(2); 31(4); 32(4); 33(5); 34(4); 35(3); 37(3); 19:1; 2(2); 3(2); 4(2); 5; 8(2); 9(2); 10(2); 11; 12(3); 13(5); 14(3); 15(2); 16; 17(2); 18(3); 19; 20; 21; 22:5(2); 6; 7(3); 8(6); 9(2); 10; 11(7); 12(8); 13(5); 14(6); 15(3); 16(6); 18(2); 19(10); 20; 21(4); 23(4); 26(2); 27; 28(2); 29(2); 30(3); 31(2); 32(3); 33(2); 34; 35; 40; 41; 44; 10:1; 2; 3; 7; 9; 10(2); 12(2); 13(3); 14(2); 11:3(2); 4; 5(3); 6; 7; 8; 9; 10(2); 11(2); 12(2); 13(2); 14; 15(4); 17(3); 18(4); 19(2); 20(2); 21; 22(4); 23(2); 24; 26(4); 28; 30; 31(3); 32(2); 34(2); 35(2); 37; 38(2); 39(2); 41; 42(2); 43; 44; 45; 46; 12:1(3); 2(3); 3(2); 7(2); 8(4); 14(4); 15; 16(2); 17; 18(3); 19(3); 20(3); 21(2); 22; 23(3); 24; 25(6); 26(2); 27(2); 28; 34(4); 35(4); 37(4); 38(4); 39(2); 40(3); 41(3); 42; 43(3); 44(4); 45(3); 46(3); 47(4); 48(4); 49(4); 50; 54(4); 55; 56(2); 57(3); 60(2); 61(6); 62(9); 63(7); 64; 65(9); 66(6); 67(2); 70(5); 71(4); 72(2); 74(2); 76(2); 77(4); 78(3); 80(2); 7:1; 2(5); 3(3); 4(2); 5(2); 6; 7(4); 8(2); 9(4); 10(2); 11(3); 12(2); 13(2); 14(2); 15(2); 16(2); 17(4); 19; 20; 21; 29(4); 30; 31(2); 33(2); 34; 35; 36; 38; 39; 40(5); 8:3; 6(4); 8; 9; 10; 11; 12; 13(4); 16; 18; 21; 25; 27; 28; 29; 34; 35; 40; 41; 44; 10:1; 2; 3; 7; 9; 10(2); 12(2); 13(3); 14(2); 11:3(2); 4; 5(3); 6; 7; 8; 9; 10(2); 11(2); 12(2); 13(2); 14; 15; 14:1; 15(4); 17(3); 18(4); 19(2); 20(2); 21; 22(4); 23(2); 24; 26(4); 28; 30; 31(3); 32(2); 34; 35; 36; 37(4); 38(2); 39(2); 41; 42(2); 43; 44; 45; 46; 12:1(3); 2(3); 3(2); 7(2); 8(4); 14(4); 15; 16(2); 17(4); 18(3); 20; 21(4); 22; 23(2); 24(5); 25(3); 26(6); 6:1; 2; 3(2); 15; 16; 17(2); 18(2); 19; 22(3); 24; 26; 27; 28; 29; 30; 31; 34; 35(3); 30:1(2); 5(2); 6(7); 7; 8; 10; 11(2); 12(4); 13; 15(2); 16(4); 17(2); 18(2); 19(2); 21(2); 22(2); 24(2); 25(4); 26(3); 31:1(3); 2(3); 3(2); 4(2); 5(5); 6(4); 7; 10(3); 11; 13(4); 14(3); 15; 16(2); 17(2); 18; 19(4); 20; 21(6); 22:1(4); 2; 3(2); 4(2); 5; 6(3); 7(8); 8(3); 9(2); 10; 11(3); 13(4); 14(3); 15(5); 17(6); 18; 19(5); 20; 21(6); 22(4); 24:3(2); 3(2); 4; 6(3); 7(3); 8(3); 9(2); 10; 11(3); 13(4); 14(3); 15(5); 16(2); 17(3); 18(2); 19(7); 20(2); 21(3); 22(4); 23(6); 24(2); 25(3); 26(2); 27(8); 28; 29;

15; 16; 17; 18(2); 3:1(2); 2(2); 3(2); 4(3); 6; 8; 9(2); 10; 11(4); 12(3); 13; 14; 15(3); 16; 17(2); 4:1; 2(2); 3(2); 5(5); 7; 8; 9(2); 10; 11; 12(3); 13(2); 16(2); 17; 18; 19; 20; 21; 22(5); 5:1(3); 2(9); 3; 4; 5; 6; 7(4); 8; 9(2); 10(2); 11; 12(5); 13(2); 14(3); 6:2; 3(2); 4; 5(3); 6; 7(4); 8; 9(2); 10(2); 11; 12(5); 13(2); 14(3); 15(2); 16; 17; 18(3); 20; 22(3); 14:1; 2; 3; 4; 5(2); 8(4); 9; 10; 14; 15; 15:12(2); 2(2); 15(3); 16; 13:1; 2(2); 3(3); 5(2); 6(2); 7(2); 8(2); 9(5); 10(5); 11; 12; 12(2); 13(2); 15(3); 16; 17; 18(3); 19; 21(2); 23; 24(3); 26(2); 28(2); 29; 30(2); 31(4); 32(4); 33(5); 34(2); 19:1; 2; 3; 4; 5; 7(3); 8(6); 9; 10; 11(4); 20:1(2); 4(3); 5(2); 6(2); 7(2); 9; 10; 11; 14(8); 15(2); 14:1; 2; 3; 4; 5(2); 8(4); 9; 10; 14; 15; 15:12(2); 2(2); 15(3); 16; 17; 18(3); 19(7); 20(2); 21(3); 22(4); 23(6); 24; 25:1; 2; 4; 5; 6(3); 7; 8; 9; 10; 11; 12(3); 13; 14; 15; 16(2); 17(3); 18(6); 19(2); 20(5); 21; 24:1; 2(2); 4; 5(3); 6(8); 7(4); 8(2); 9; 11; 12(5); 13; 14(5); 15; 16; 17; 18(2); 20(3); 21(3); 23(5); 24(2); 25:1; 2; 4; 5; 6(3); 7; 8; 9; 10; 11; 12(3); 13; 14; 15; 16(2); 17(3); 18(6); 19(2); 20(5); 21; 22(6); 23(4); Ezr 1:1(6); 2(3); 3(3); 4(2); 5(3); 6; 7(4); 8(3); 9(3); 10(2); 11(3); 2:1(4); 2(3); 3; 4; 5; 6(3); 7; 8; 9; 10; 11; 12; 13; 14; 15; 16(2); 17; 18; 19; 20; 21; 22; 23; 24; 25; 26; 27; 28; 29; 30; 31; 32; 33; 34; 35; 36(3); 37; 38; 39; 40(3); 41; 42(7); 43(3); 44(3); 45(3); 46(3); 47(3); 48(3); 49(3); 50(3); 51(3); 52(3); 53(3); 54(2); 55(4); 56(3); 57(5); 58; 59; 60(3); 61(7); 63; 65; 68(4); 69(3); 70; 3:1; 2(6); 3(2); 4(2); 5(4); 7(5); 8(8); 9(3); 10(5); 11(2); 12(3); 13(4); 4:1(3); 2(3); 3(4); 5(4); 6(3); 7(4); 8; 9; 10; 11; 12; 13(4); 14; 15; 16(2); 17; 18; 19; 20; 21; 22; 23; 24; 25; 26; 27; 28; 29; 30; 31; 32; 33; 34; 35; 36(3); 37; 38; 39; 40(3); 41; 42(7); 43(3); 44; Neh 1:1(2); 2(3); 3(2); 4; 5; 6(4); 9(2); 11(3); 2:1; 2; 3; 4; 5; 8(4); 9; 10(3); 13(2); 14; 15; 17; 18(2); 20; 3:1(3); 2(2); 3; 4(5); 5; 6(2); 7(3); 8(4); 9(3); 11(2); 12; 13; 14(3); 13; 14(3); 15(7); 16(5); 17(3); 18(3); 19(4); 20(4); 21(6); 22; 23(2); 24(3); 25(4); 27; 29(3); 30(3); 31(3); 32; 4:2(3); 4; 7; 8; 9; 10(2); 14(3); 15; 16; 17; 18(3); 6:1; 2(2); 7; 8; 10(5); 14; 15; 16; 17(2); 18(4); 7:2; 3(3); 5(2); 6(4); 7(3); 8; 9; 10; 11(3); 12; 13; 14; 15; 16; 17; 18; 19; 20; 21(2); 22; 23; 24; 25; 26; 27; 28; 29; 30; 31; 32; 33; 34; 35; 36; 37; 38; 39; 40; 41; 42; 43(4); 44; 45(6); 46(3); 47(3); 48(3); 49(3); 50(3); 51(3); 52(3); 53(3); 54(3); 55(3); 56(2); 57(4); 58(3); 59(5); 60; 61; 62(3); 63(6); 65; 67; 70(3); 71(5); 72(3); 73(2); 8:1(2); 2(2); 3(2); 4; 5; 8; 9; 10; 13(3); 14(2); 15; 16(6); 17(5);

18(2); 9:1(2); 2(2); 3(3); 4; 6(2); 7(3); 8; 9; 10; 11; 12; 14; 15; 17(2); 18; 19(2); 22(5); 23; 24(2); 25; 27(4); 28; 30(2); 32(2); 37; 38; 10:1; 9(3); 14; 28(3); 29(2); 30; 31(3); 32(3); 33(4); 34(3); 35(4); 36(6); 37(9); 38(3); 39(6); 11:1(3); 3(3); 4(13); 5(7); 6; 7(8); 9(2); 10(2); 11(7); 12(7); 13(5); 14(3); 15(5); 16(5); 17(6); 20(3); 22(9); 24(4); 25(2); 30; 31; 35; 36; 12:1; 7(3); 12(4); 13(2); 14(2); 15(2); 16(2); 17(3); 18(2); 19(2); 20(2); 21(2); 22(3); 23(5); 24(4); 25; 26(5); 27(3); 28(3); 29(3); 31(2); 32(2); 35(7); 36(2); 37(4); 38(3); 39(3); 40(3); 43; 44(3); 45(4); 46(4); 47(4); 13:1(3); 2; 4(3); 5(2); 6(3); 7(3); 8(2); 9(2); 10; 11; 12; 13(3); 14; 15; 16(3); 17; 19(2); 20(2); 22; 23(3); 24(2); 25; 26(2); 28(3); 29(2); 30; **Est** 1:1; 2; 3(3); 4(2); 5(2); 6(4); 7(2); 8; 10(2); 14; 15; 16; 17; 18(3); 19; 21; 22; 2:1; 3(4); 4; 5(3); 6(2); 8(3); 9(4); 11(2); 12(4); 13(2); 14(2); 15(5); 16; 17; 18; 20; 21(2); 23(2); 3:1; 5; 6(3); 7; 8; 9(3); 10; 12(4); 13(2); 14; 4:1; 5; 6; 7(3); 8(2); 9; 11(2); 5:1(2); 2; 3; 6(2); 8; 9; 11(4); 14; 6:1(2); 2(3); 4; 9(3); 10; 11; 13(2); 7:2(2); 7; 8(4); 9(2); 8:1; 2; 3; 5; 6; 7; 9; 11(2); 12(2); 13; 15(5); 17(3); 9:1(2); 2(2); 3(3); 5; 10(3); 11; 12(2); 15; 16; 17(3); 18(2); 19(4); 20; 21(2); 22(2); 24(2); 26(3); 28(2); 29(2); 30(3); 31(2); 32(2); 10:1; 2(7); 3(3); **Job** 1:1; 3(3); 5(2); 6; 10; 12; 15; 16; 17; 19; 21(2); 2:1; 7(2); 10(2); 11; 3:5(2); 6(2); 9(2); 10; 11; 14; 18; 25; 4:6; 9(2); 10(3); 11; 13; 15; 19; 5:1; 5; 6(2); 12; 13; 15; 17; 20; 21(2); 22(2); 23(2); 25; 26; 6:3; 4(2); 6; 10; 12(2); 14; 15; 16; 17; 18; 19(2); 22; 23; 26; 7:1; 2; 3; 4(2); 5; 8; 11(2); 20; 8:2; 6; 8(2); 9; 10; 13; 17; 19(2); 22; 9:2; 3; 6; 8; 9; 19(2); 23; 24(2); 28; 10:1(2); 3(2); 4; 5; 7; 15; 18; 21(2); 22(3); 11:2(2); 6(2); 20(2); 12:4; 5; 6; 7; 8; 9; 10(2); 12; 18; 20(2); 21; 22(2); 24(3); 13:4(2); 6; 12; 26; 27; 14:1(3); 4; 5; 7; 9; 12; 14; 15; 18; 19(3); 21; 15:5; 8; 11; 13; 14; 20; 22(2); 23; 26; 27; 30(2); 34(2); 16:5; 11; 16; 17:5; 6; 7; 11; 12; 16; 18:2; 4; 5(2); 7; 13(2); 14(2); 15; 18; 21(2); 19:7; 9; 11; 17; 20; 21; 28; 29(2); 20:3(2); 4; 5(2); 8; 11(2); 14; 15; 16; 17; 20; 21; 22(2); 23; 24; 25(2); 28(2); 29; 21:9; 12; 14; 16; 17; 20(2); 21; 24; 25; 28(2); 30(2); 33; 22:4; 6; 9; 11; 12(2); 14; 16; 18; 20; 24(2); 25; 30(2); 23:12(2); 15; 24:3; 4(2); 6; 8(2); 9; 12(2); 13; 15; 17(3); 18; 22; 24(3); 25:3; 4; 6; 26:9; 11; 14(3); 27:3; 8; 11; 13(3); 15; 21; 22; 23; 28:2(2); 3(2); 4; 5; 6(3); 12; 13; 16; 17(2); 18(3); 19; 20; 21(2); 24; 26; 28; 29:4(2); 6; 10; 13; 17(2); 24; 30:1; 2; 6(2); 8(2); 12; 14; 16; 18(2); 27; 31; 31:2(2); 3; 7; 13(2); 16; 19; 20; 23; 29; 31(2); 34(2); 37; 40(3); 32:2(4); 5; 6; 7; 8; 12; 18; 33:3(2); 4(2); 6; 8; 13(2); 15; 16; 19; 25; 30; 34:8; 10; 11; 16; 19(2); 21; 22(2); 26; 27; 28(2); 34; 36; 35:7; 8; 9(4); 11(2); 12(2); 36:6; 8; 16(2); 17; 19; 26; 27; 29(2); 30; 37:1; 2(2); 3; 4; 6; 7; 9(2); 10(2); 12; 14; 15; 16(2); 19; 22; 23; 24; 38:1; 3; 4; 7; 8; 13(3); 16(2); 17(3); 18; 21; 22(2); 23(2); 25(2); 27; 28; 29(2); 30; 31(2); 33; 34; 37; 39; 41; 39:1; 5; 7(2); 8; 17; 20; 24; 25; 28; 40:6; 7; 11; 16; 17; 18(2); 19(2); 20; 21; 22; 41:6; 9(2); 13; 14; 18; 19(2); 20(2); 21; 23; 24; 25; 26; 29; 31; 34; 42:4; 5(2); 7; 8; 10; 11(3); 12(2); 14(3); 15; 17; **Ps** 1:1(3); 2; 3; 5; 6(2); 2:2; 6; 8(2); 9; 10; 3:t, 2; 3; 4; 6(2); 7; 4:t, 1; 2; 5; 6; 5:t, 2; 5; 7; 8; 10; 6:t, 5; 7(2); 8(2); 7:2(2); 6(2); 7; 9; 10; 13; 17; 8:t, 2(3); 3; 4(2); 6; 7; 8(3); 9:t, 9; 12; 13(2); 14(2); 16; 18; 10:1; 3; 4; 5; 7; 8; 14; 15; 16; 17; 18; 11:t, 4; 6; 12:t, 1; 5(2); 6(2); 13:t, 3; 14:t, 2; 4; 5; 6; 7(3); 15:t; 16:t, 4; 5(2); 11(2); 17:t, 1; 4(3); 8(2); 12; 14(3); 18:(5); 2; 4(2); 5(2); 6; 7; 8(2); 10; 11; 12; 13; 15(4); 16; 18; 20; 21; 24; 30; 34; 35; 40; 43(2); 44; 45; 46; 19:t, 1; 4; 5; 6(2); 7(2); 8(2); 9(2); 11; 14(2); 20:t, 1(3); 2; 5; 6; 7; 21:t, 2; 3(2); 4(2); 7; 9; 10; 12; 22:t, 1; 3; 6(2); 9; 12; 14(2); 15; 16; 20; 21; 22; 23(2); 24; 25; 27(2); 23:t, 3; 4(2); 5; 6(2); 24:t, 3; 5; 6; 7; 8; 9; 10(3); 25:t, 5; 6; 7; 10; 14; 15; 17(2); 22; 26:t, 5; 7(2); 8; 10; 27:t, 1(2); 4(4); 5(2); 6; 9; 11; 12; 13(2); 14; 28:t, 2; 3; 4(2); 5(2); 6; 8; 29:t, 2; 3(2); 4(3); 5(2); 7(2); 8(2); 9(2); 30:(2); 4(2); 31:t, 2; 4; 5; 8; 10; 12; 13; 15; 19; 20(3); 22; 24; 32:t, 4; 5; 6; 7; 33:2; 4; 5(2); 6(3); 7; 8(2); 10(3); 11(2); 13; 14(2); 16; 18; 34:t, 6; 7; 11; 15; 16(2); 17; 18(2); 19(2); 20; 22(2); 35:t, 2; 5; 6; 12; 27; 28(2); 36:(2); 1(2); 3; 7(2); 8(3); 9; 11(2); 12; 37:t, 1(2); 4; 7(2); 11; 14; 16; 17; 18; 19; 20(2); 22(2); 23; 28; 30(2); 31(2); 37; 38; 39(3); 38:t, 3(2); 5; 8(2); 10; 39:t, 4; 8; 10; 40:t, 2(2); 5; 7(2); 12; 15; 41:t, 1; 2; 3; 5; 9; 13; 42:t, 4(2); 5; 6(2); 7; 8; 9(2); 11; 43:2(3); 4; 5; 44:t, 1; 3; 14; 15; 16(2); 19(2); 20; 21; 45:(2); 1(2); 2; 4; 5; 6; 7; 8(2); 9; 12; 13; 14; 16; 46:t, 2; 4(3); 5; 7(2); 8; 9; 11(2); 47:t, 1; 4; 5; 7; 8; 9(4); 48:t, 1(2); 2(3); 6; 7; 8(3); 9(2); 10(2); 11(2); 49:t, 1; 3(3); 5(2); 6; 7; 8; 15; 16; 19; 50:t, 1; 2(2); 9(2); 10; 11(2); 13(2); 15; 23; 51:t, 1; 12; 14(2); 17; 18; 19; 52:(2); 1; 5(3); 7; 8(2); 53:t, 2; 3; 4; 5; 6(3); 54:t, 2; 7; 55:t, 3(4); 4; 10; 14; 19; 21; 23; 56:t, 13; 57:t, 1; 3; 4; 58:t, 1; 2; 4; 5; 6; 8(2); 10; 59:t, 2; 5(2); 9; 10; 12(2); 13; 16(3); 17; 60:(3); 3; 4; 6; 7; 8; 11; 61:t, 2; 4; 5; 62:t, 3; 7; 9(2); 63:(2); 7; 9; 11; 64:t, 1; 2(3); 5; 6(2); 9(2); 65:t, 4(2); 5(4); 7(3); 8; 9(2); 12; 66:2; 3; 5(2); 8; 15(2); 19; 67:7; 68:t, 2; 5(2); 8(3); 10; 11; 12; 13; 15(3); 17(2); 19; 20; 21(2); 22; 23(2); 24; 26; 27(3); 29; 30(4); 31; 32; 33(2); 35(2); 69:t, 3; 4; 6(2); 9(2); 12; 13(2); 14(2); 16; 18; 20; 24; 26; 28(2); 30; 35; 36; 70:t, 3; 71:4(4); 6(2); 9; 16(3); 20; 22; 24; 72:4(2); 7; 8; 10(3); 13; 15(2); 16(4); 18; 20(2); 73:t, 1; 3; 10; 15; 17; 26; 74:t, 1; 2(2); 4; 7; 8; 11; 12(2); 13; 14; 17; 19(3); 20(3); 23(2); 75:t, 3; 8(4); 9; 10(2); 76:t, 3; 4; 5(2); 6; 9; 10(2); 12(2); 77:t, 2; 5(2); 10(2); 11(2); 12(2); 15; 18; 20; 78:t, 1; 2; 4; 7; 9(2); 10; 12(3); 14; 15; 16; 23; 24(2); 27; 28; 31(3); 38; 41; 43; 45; 49; 51(2); 54; 55; 60; 65(2); 67(2); 68; 72(2); 79:t, 2(4); 9(2); 10(2); 11(2); 13; 80:t, 1; 4(2); 5; 7; 8; 10; 13(2); 14; 16; 17(2); 19; 81:t, 1; 4(2); 5; 7(2); 10(2); 11; 15; 16(2); 82:t, 1; 2; 4(2); 5(2); 6(2); 7; 83:t, 4; 6(2); 7; 8; 9; 12; 84:t, 1; 2; 3; 5; 6; 7; 8(2); 9; 10(2); 12; 85:t, 1; 2; 3; 4; 11; 13; 86:t, 4; 6; 7; 14; 15; 16; 87:t, 2(2); 3(2); 4; 5; 88:(2); 1; 3; 9; 12; 89:t, 1(2); 5; 6; 7(2); 8; 9; 14; 15; 17; 18; 19; 22; 26; 27; 29; 34; 39; 42; 43; 45; 48; 50(2); 51; 90:(2); 3; 8; 10(2); 11; 17(3); 91:1(2); 2; 3; 8; 92:3; 4; 7; 9; 10; 11; 13(2); 93:2; 4(2); 94:2; 4; 7; 11; 12; 13; 16; 19; 20; 21; 22; 95:1; 4(2); 7(2); 8; 96:5; 7; 9; 12; 97:1; 2; 5(3); 7; 8(2); 10(3); 12; 98:2; 3(3); 5; 6; 99:8; 100:t, 3; 101:t, 1; 3; 6; 8(2); 102:t, 5(2); 6(2); 10; 15(2); 17; 19; 20; 21; 24; 25(3); 26; 28; 103:t, 7; 15; 17; 20; 21; 22; 104:3(2); 5; 7; 11; 12; 13; 14(2); 15; 16(3); 20; 24; 30; 31; 34; 35; 105:2; 3; 5; 6(2); 11(2); 16; 19; 20; 21(2); 23; 27; 30; 31; 33; 35; 36; 38; 40; 44(2); 106:2; 5(2); 7; 10(2); 11; 16; 17; 20; 22; 25; 28; 32; 38(3); 40; 41; 45; 46; 48; 107:2(2); 3; 6; 7; 8; 10; 11(2); 13; 14(2); 15; 16(2); 17(2); 18(2); 19; 21; 22; 24; 26; 28; 31; 32(2); 34; 37; 43; 108:t, 7; 8; 12; 109:t, 1; 2(2); 3; 10; 14(2); 15; 20(2); 24; 31; 110:t, 2(3); 3(4); 4; 5; 7; 111:1; 2(2); 4; 5; 6(2); 7; 10(2); 112:2; 4; 7; 10; 113:1(2); 2; 3(2); 7(2); 8; 9; 114:1(3); 7(3); 8; 115:4; 10; 12(3); 15; 16; 116:3(2); 4; 9; 13(2); 14; 15(2); 16; 17(2); 18; 19(2); 117:2; 118:3; 10; 11; 12(2); 15(3); 16(2); 17; 19; 20; 22; 26(3); 27; 119:1; 7; 13; 14; 18; 27(2); 29; 30; 32; 33; 35; 43(2); 46; 52; 53; 54; 61; 62; 63(2); 64; 72(2); 84; 88; 96; 108; 111; 115; 116; 119; 120(2); 123; 130; 134; 136; 144; 147; 152; 160; 161; 164; 172; 120:t, 4(2); 5; 121:t, 122:(2); 1; 4(3); 5(3); 6; 9(2); 123:t, 2(4); 4(2); 124:(2); 7(2); 8; 125:t, 3(2); 5; 126:t, 1; 127:t, 2; 3(2); 4(2); 5; 128:t, 2; 3; 5(3); 129:t, 4; 8(2); 130:t, 1; 2; 131:(2); 132:t, 2; 3; 5; 6(2); 8; 10; 11(2); 17; 133:(2); 2; 3(2); 134:t, 1(2); 3; 135:1(2); 2(3); 7(2); 8(2); 9; 11(3); 15(2); 19(2); 20; 21; 136:2; 3; 14; 19; 20; 26; 137:1; 3(4); 6; 7(2); 8; 138:t, 4(2); 5(2); 7(2); 8; 139:t, 9(2); 15; 16; 17; 140:t, 4; 6; 7(2); 8; 9(2); 12(2); 141:t, 2; 3; 4; 9(2); 142:t, 5; 7; 143:t, 5(2); 10; 11; 12; 144:t, 3(3); 7(2); 8; 9; 11(2); 12; 13; 145:t, 5(3); 6(2); 7(2); 8(2); 11(3); 12(2); 15; 16; 19; 21; 146:3; 5; 8; 9; 147:2; 4; 5; 10(2); 13; 14; 148:3; 4; 5; 11(2); 13; 14(4); 149:1; 2; 6; 8; 150:1; 3; **Prov** 1:1(3); 2; 3; 5; 6; 7(2); 8(2); 9; 17; 19(3); 21(2); 25; 29; 30; 31(2); 32(2); 33; 2:5(2); 6; 8(2); 12; 13(2); 14; 17(2); 19(2); 20(2); 22; 3:2; 3; 4; 9; 11(2); 14(2); 16; 17; 18; 25(3); 27; 31; 33(3); 35; 4:1; 3; 5; 9(2); 10; 11; 13; 14(2); 17(2); 18; 19; 21; 23(2); 26; 5:3; 6; 7; 8; 10; 13; 14; 15(2); 16; 18; 20; 21(2); 22; 23; 6:2(2); 3; 5(2); 9; 10; 20; 23(2); 24(2); 26(2); 31; 34(2); 7:2; 3; 6; 7; 10(2); 16(2); 18; 20; 21; 22; 24; 27; 8:2(2); 3; 4; 5; 6(2); 8; 12; 13; 16; 20(3); 22(2); 26(2); 27; 28; 29; 31(2); 34; 35; 9:3; 5(2); 6; 10(3); 11; 14(2); 18; 10:1(2); 2; 3(2); 4; 6(2); 7(2); 11(3); 13(3); 14; 15; 16(2); 17; 19; 20(2); 21(2); 22; 23; 24(2); 27(2); 28(2); 29(2); 31; 32(2); 11:3(2); 4; 5; 6; 7; 8; 11(2); 12(2); 13; 14; 20; 21; 22; 23(2); 26; 29; 30(2); 12:2(2); 3; 5(2); 6(2); 7; 8; 10(2); 11; 12(2); 13(2); 14(2); 15; 18(2); 19; 20(2); 23; 24; 25; 26; 27; 28; 13:2(2); 4(2); 8; 9(2); 12; 14(3); 15; 20; 22; 23(2); 25(2); 14:3(3); 4; 7(2); 8(2); 11(2); 12; 13; 17; 19; 20; 23; 24(2); 26(2); 27(3); 28(3); 29(2); 30(2); 33(2); 15:2(2); 3; 4; 6(2); 7(2); 8(2); 9; 11(2); 13; 14(2); 15(2); 16; 17; 19(3); 21(2); 22; 23; 24; 25(2); 26(2); 27; 28(2); 29; 30; 31; 33(2); 16:1(2); 2; 4; 6; 10; 11; 13; 14(2); 15(2); 17; 19; 21; 22(2); 23; 25; 26; 31(2); 33; 17:1; 2; 6(2); 8; 12; 14; 16; 18(2); 21; 23(2); 24(2); 27(2); 28; 18:4(2); 5; 7; 8(2); 10; 12; 14; 15(2); 19; 20(2); 21; 22; 19:3; 6; 7; 11; 12; 13(2); 14; 19; 21; 22; 23; 27; 28; 29; 20:2(2); 4; 5(2); 8; 10; 12; 15(2); 16; 17; 24; 27(3); 29(2); 30(2); 21:1(2); 2; 4; 5(2); 6(2); 7; 8; 9; 10; 12; 13; 15; 16(3); 20; 22(2); 25; 27; 31(2); 22:2; 4; 5; 8; 9; 11(2); 12(2); 14(2); 15(2); 17; 21(3); 23; 26(2); 23:3; 6; 9(2); 10; 12; 17; 20; 24(2); 29; 34(2); 24:2; 5; 6; 9; 10; 14; 15; 19; 20; 22; 23; 30(3); 33; 25:1(3); 2(2); 3; 6(2); 7; 11(2); 12(2); 13(3); 14; 17; 19(2); 22; 24; 26:6; 7(2); 9(2); 12(2); 22(2); 27:1; 6(2); 9; 10; 13; 16; 17; 19; 20; 23; 25; 26; 27; 28:2(2); 7; 17; 19; 21(2); 24; 25; 29:6; 7; 20(2); 25; 30:1(2); 2; 3; 4; 5; 7; 9; 17; 19(5); 20; 27; 33(3); 31:1; 2(2); 5(2); 6; 8; 9; 11(2); 12; 16; 21; 22; 23; 26; 27(2); 31(2); **Eccl** 1:1(2); 2(2); 3; 8; 10; 11(2); 13; 14; 16; 17; 2:2(2); 3(2); 5(2); 6; 7; 8(5); 10; 11; 16(2); 17; 20; 22(3); 24; 26; 3:8(2); 10; 13(2); 16(2); 18(2); 19; 20; 21(2); 4:1(2); 4(2); 6; 8(2); 14; 16(3); 5:1(2); 3(2); 6; 7; 8(2); 9; 11; 12(2); 15(2); 18(2); 19; 20(2); 6:2; 3; 7; 9(3); 12; 7:1(2); 2(3); 3; 4(4); 5(2); 6(2); 8; 9; 12; 13; 14(2); 15; 18(2); 25(3); 8:1(2); 2(2); 3; 4; 6; 8; 10; 11(2); 14(2); 15(2); 17; 9:1; 3(3); 5; 9(3); 11(2); 12; 17(2); 18; 10:1; 4; 12(2); 13(3); 14; 15(2); 17; 18; 20; 11:3; 5(3); 8; 9(3); 12:1; 3(2); 4(3); 5; 8; 10; 11(2); 12(2); 13(2); **Song** 1:1; 2; 3(2); 5(3); 6; 7; 8; 9; 10(2); 11(2); 13; 14(2); 17(2); 2:1(2); 3; 5; 7(2); 8; 12(3); 14(2); 17; 3:4; 5(2); 6(3); 7(2); 8; 9(2); 10(5); 11(4); 4:1; 2; 3(2); 4(2); 6(2); 8(3); 9(2); 10; 11(2); 13; 14; 15(2); 5:2(2); 4; 5; 7; 8(2); 12(2); 13; 15(2); 16; 6:2; 5; 6; 7; 9(2); 11(2); 12; 13; 7:1(3); 2; 4(3); 5; 7; 8(3); 9(2); 13; 8:1; 2(3); 4; 6; 7; 9(2); 11; 14; **Is** 1:1(4); 4(2); 6; 8(2); 9; 10(4); 11(7); 13; 15; 16; 19; 20; 21; 23(2); 24(4); 26; 28(2); 29; 31; 2:1; 2(2); 3(6); 5(2); 6(2); 7(4); 8(2); 10(2); 11(2); 12(2); 13(2); 16; 17(2); 19(4); 20(2); 21(4); 22; 3:1(3); 2; 3; 6(3); 7; 8; 9; 10; 11; 12; 14(2); 15(2); 16; 17(3); 18; 20; 22; 24(6); 4:1; 2(3); 4(5); 5(2); 6; 5:1; 2; 3(2); 7(4); 8; 9(2); 10(2); 12(2); 15; 16; 17; 18; 19(2); 22; 23; 24(4); 25(2); 26; 27(2); 29; 30; 6:3(2); 4(2); 5(4); 6; 8; 10; 12; 7:1(7); 2(3); 3(3); 4(4); 5; 6(2); 8(2); 9(2); 11; 13; 16; 17; 18(3); 19(2); 20(2); 22; 25(3); 8:2; 4(3); 6; 7(2); 8(2); 9; 11; 13; 14(4); 17; 18; 22; 9:1(4); 2(2); 4(4); 5(2); 6; 7(5); 9(2); 11; 13; 16(2); 18(2); 19(3); 20; 10:2; 3; 5; 6(2); 10(3); 12(4); 13(2); 14; 16(2); 17; 18(2); 19(2); 20(4); 21; 22(2); 23(2); 24(3); 26(4); 27; 29; 30; 31; 32(3); 33(2); 34; 11:1(3); 2(6); 3(4); 4(3); 5(2); 8; 9(2); 10(2); 11(2); 12(3); 13(2); 14(3); 15; 16(3); 12:3(2); 6(3); 13:1(2); 2; 4(6); 5(2); 6; 8; 9(2); 10; 11(2); 12; 13(4); 18; 19(2); 21(2); 22; 14:1; 2(2); 4; 5(2); 8; 9(2); 11; 12; 13(3); 14; 15; 17; 18(2); 19(3); 20; 21(2); 22; 23(3); 24; 27; 29(2); 30; 32(2); 15:1(3); 3; 4; 5(4); 6; 7; 8; 9(4); 16:1(3); 2(3); 3; 4(2); 5; 6(3); 7; 8(3); 9(2); 10; 14(2); 17:1; 2; 3(4); 4(2); 5; 6(3); 7; 8; 9(2); 10(3); 11(2); 12(4); 13(2); 14(2); 18:1; 2; 3; 4(2); 6(3); 7(5); 19:1(4); 3; 4(2); 6; 7; 11(5); 12; 13(3); 16(4); 17(4); 18(4); 19(2); 20(3); 22; 23; 24; 25(2); 20:1; 2; 4(2); 5(2); 6(2); 21:1(2); 3(3); 4; 7(3); 9(3); 10(4); 11(4); 13; 14(2); 15; 16(2); 17(5); 22:1(2); 2; 4(3); 5(6); 6; 7; 8(3); 9(3); 10; 11; 12; 14(2); 15; 18(2); 20; 21(2); 22(2); 24(4); 25; 23:1(3); 2(2); 3(3); 4; 5; 6; 7; 8; 9(3); 10; 12; 13; 14; 15(2); 17(3); 24:2(2); 4; 6; 8(3); 10; 11; 13(2); 14; 15(3); 16; 17; 18(4); 21(2); 23; 25:1; 2(3); 3; 4; 5(3); 6(6); 7; 8; 10; 11(2); 12(2); 26:1; 6(2); 7(2); 8(3); 9; 10(2); 11; 13; 15; 17; 18; 19; 21(2); 27:2; 5; 6(2); 7; 8; 9(2); 11; 12(3); 13(2); 28:1(4); 2(2); 3(2); 4; 5(4); 6; 7(3); 8; 13; 14; 17; 21; 22; 24; 28; 29; 29:4(5); 5(2); 6(3); 7(2); 8; 10; 11(2); 13; 14(2); 16(3); 18(4); 19; 21; 22; 23(4); 30:1(2); 2(2); 3(2); 5; 6(5); 9; 11(3); 12; 14(3); 15; 17(3); 18; 19; 20(2); 22(4); 23(3); 25(2); 26(6); 27(2); 28(3); 29(3); 30(3); 31; 32; 33(3); 31:1; 2(2); 4(4); 5; 6; 7(2); 8(2); 9; 32:2(2); 3(2); 4(2); 6(2); 7; 13(2); 14(3); 17(2); 20; 33:2; 3(2); 4(2); 6(3); 7; 12; 15(3); 16(2); 19(2); 20(3); 21; 23; 34:1; 2; 3; 4; 5; 6(5); 8(3); 11(2); 13; 14(3); 16(3); 35:2(4); 4; 5(2); 6; 7(2); 8; 10; 36:1(3); 2(3); 4; 6(2); 8; 9(3); 11; 13(2); 15(2); 16(4); 17(2); 18(5); 19(3); 20(3); 22(3); 37:1; 2(2); 3(3); 4(2); 5; 6(3); 8; 9; 10(3); 11; 12(2); 13(4); 14(2); 16(4); 17; 18(2); 19; 20; 21(3); 22(2); 23; 24(5); 25(2); 26; 27(2); 30(2); 31(2); 32(4); 33; 36(2); 37; 38(2); 38:1; 4; 5; 6(3); 8(2); 9(3); 10(4); 11(2); 12; 13; 15; 16; 17; 20(2); 21; 22; 39:1(2); 2(3); 5(2); 7(3); 8; 40:2; 3(2); 5(2); 6; 7; 8; 9; 12(2); 13; 14(2); 15(2); 21; 22; 23; 26; 28(3); 41:5; 6; 8; 9; 10; 12; 14(2); 16; 17; 18(3); 20(2); 21; 22; 24(2); 25; 28; 42:5; 6(2); 7; 9; 10; 11(2); 13; 22; 25(2); 43:3; 6; 13; 14; 15; 18; 20; 22; 23; 24; 28; 44:5(2); 6(2); 9; 11; 12; 13(2); 14; 19(2); 21; 23; 25; 26(3); 28; 45:1; 2(2); 3(3); 6; 9; 11(3); 13; 14(4); 15; 16(2); 19(2); 20(2); 22; 23; 25; 46:3(3); 6; 7; 9; 47:1(2); 4(2); 5(2); 7; 8; 9(3); 12; 13; 14; 48:1(7); 2(3); 3; 10; 13; 17; 18; 19; 20(3); 21; 49:1(2); 2; 5; 6(3); 7(4); 8(2); 10; 12; 15; 16; 17; 19(2); 23; 25(2); 26; 50:1(2); 4; 10(2); 11(2); 51:1; 3(2); 4; 7(2); 9(2); 10(2); 11; 12(3); 13(4); 15; 16(2); 17(4); 18; 20(4); 22(5); 23; 52:2(2); 7(2); 9; 10(3); 11(3); 12; 14; 53:1; 2; 3(2); 4; 5; 6; 8(3); 10; 11(2); 12; 54:1(2); 2(2); 4(2); 5(3); 6; 9(2); 10; 12(3); 13(2); 17(3); 55:3; 5(2); 11; 12; 13(2); 56:2; 3; 4; 5(2); 6(3); 7(2); 8; 9; 57:3(2); 4(2); 5; 6; 10(2); 11(2); 14(2); 15(3); 17(2); 19; 58:1; 2(3); 3; 4; 6; 8; 9(2); 11; 12(4); 13; 14(3); 59:5; 6(2); 7; 8; 13; 17(2); 19(3); 21(5); 60:1; 3; 5(2); 6(3); 7(3); 9(3); 10; 11; 13(3); 14(5); 15; 16(3); 20; 21(2); 61:1(2); 2(3); 3(5); 4; 5; 6(3); 10(2); 62:2; 3(3); 6; 8(2); 9; 10; 11(2); 12; 63:1; 3; 4(2); 7(4); 9(2); 11(3); 12; 14; 15(4); 16; 17; 18; 64:4; 7(2); 8; 65:1(2); 3; 4; 7; 9(3); 10(2); 14(3); 16(2); 19(2); 20; 21; 22(3); 23(2); 66:1; 2; 5; 6(2); 7; 11(2); 12; 14; 15; 16; 19; 20(3); 21; 24; **Jer** 1:1(4); 2(5); 3(8); 4; 5; 8; 11(2); 13; 14(2); 15(5); 16; 18(2); 2:1; 2(3); 3; 4(4); 6(7); 10; 13; 16(2); 18(4); 19; 20; 21; 26; 27; 28(2); 31(2); 34(2); 36(2); 3:4; 6; 8; 9; 14(2); 16(2); 17(3); 18(4); 19(2); 20; 21(2); 23(2); 24; 25; 4:1; 3; 4(5); 7; 8; 9(2); 11(2); 16; 17; 19(2); 21; 25; 26; 29; 30; 31(5); 5:1; 4(2); 5(2); 6(2); 11(2); 14; 15; 20; 22; 24; 27(2); 28(3); 6:1(5); 2; 4; 6(2); 9(2); 10; 11(4); 12; 13(2); 14(2); 17; 19; 22; 23; 24(2); 25; 26; 29; 7:2(3); 3(2); 4(3); 11; 12; 15(2); 17(2); 18; 19; 20(2); 21(2); 22(2); 24; 25(2); 28; 29; 30; 31(3); 32(3); 33(3); 34(6); 8:1(8); 2(2); 3(3); 5; 6; 7(2); 8(2); 9; 11(2); 12; 14; 15; 16(3); 19(4); 21(2); 22(2); 9:1(3); 2(2); 4; 6; 7(2); 10(3); 11(2); 12; 14; 15(3); 17; 19(2); 20(2); 22; 26(2); 10:1; 2(2); 3(4); 5; 7(2); 8; 9(4); 13(3); 15(2); 16(4); 17(2); 18; 20; 22(4); 23; 11:2(3); 3(2); 4(2); 6(3); 7(2); 8(2); 9(2); 10(3); 12(3); 13(3); 16(3); 17(5); 18; 19; 20; 21(3); 22; 23(3); 12:1(2); 3; 4(2); 5(2); 6; 7(2); 9; 12(3); 13(3); 14(2); 16(2); 13:2; 3; 4; 8; 9(2); 10; 11(3); 12; 13(2); 16; 18; 19(2); 22; 24; 25; 27; 14:1; 2; 8(2); 9; 14(2); 16(2); 17; 19; 20; 21; 22; 15:1; 3(2); 4(4); 7(2); 8(2); 9; 10(3); 11(2); 15; 16(2); 17(2); 21(4); 16:1; 4(4); 5; 7; 8; 9(7); 12; 13; 14(3); 15(2); 16(2); 18; 19(2); 17:1(5); 8; 10; 11; 12; 13(2); 15; 16; 17; 18; 19(4); 20(3); 21; 22; 24; 25(4); 26(4); 27(2); 18:4(2); 5; 6(2); 8; 10; 11(2); 12; 13; 14(2); 17; 18; 19; 21(2); 23; 19:1(4); 2(3); 3(5); 4(2); 5; 6(3); 7(4); 8; 9(3); 10; 11; 13(6); 14; 15(2); 20:1(2); 2(2); 3; 4(3); 5(4); 8; 9; 10; 12; 13(2); 18; 21:1(2); 2(2); 4(4); 6(2); 7(6); 8(2); 10(2); 11(3); 12(5); 13(2); 14; 22:1(2); 2(3); 3(2); 4(2); 6(2); 9; 11(4); 16; 18(2);

19(2); 23(2); 24(2); 25(5); 29; 30(2); 23:1; 2(2); 3(2); 7(3); 8(3); 9(4); 10(3); 12; 13; 14(3); 15(3); 16(5); 17; 18; 19(2); 20(2); 22; 26(3); 33; 34; 36(4); 38(3); 39; 24:1(6); 4; 5(4); 8(3); 9; 25:1(6); 2(2); 3(4); 5; 6; 7; 8; 9(2); 10(6); 11; 12(2); 14(2); 15(2); 16; 18; 19; 20(5); 21; 22(3); 24(2); 25(3); 26(4); 27(3); 28; 29(2); 30; 31; 32(2); 33(3); 34(3); 35; 36(4); 37(2); 38(3); 26:1(4); 2(2); 3(3); 5; 6; 7; 8; 9(2); 10(4); 13(2); 15; 16; 17(3); 18(6); 19(2); 20(4); 22; 23(2); 24(3); 27:1(4); 3(7); 4(2); 6(3); 7(2); 8(3); 9; 11(2); 12(3); 13; 14(2); 16(2); 17; 18(5); 19(2); 20(4); 21(6); 28:1(8); 2(4); 3(2); 4(5); 5(3); 6; 7; 8(4); 9(2); 11(5); 12(2); 13(2); 14(6); 16; 29:1(2); 2; 3(5); 4(2); 5; 7; 8(3); 11(2); 14; 16(4); 17; 18; 20(2); 21(8); 22(3); 25(3); 26(2); 27; 28; 29; 30; 31; 30:2; 3; 5(2); 6; 7(3); 9; 10; 11(2); 12(3); 13(4); 15; 16; 17; 18; 19(2); 21(4); 23(2); 24(2); 25; 26(3); 34:1(3); 2(4); 3(5); 6; 7(4); 9(2); 10; 12; 13(5); 14; 17; 18; 19(4); 204); 21(5); 22; 35:1(3); 2(3); 3(2); 4(4); 5(4); 6(4); 8(2); 11(5); 12; 13(4); 14(2); 16(3); 17(3); 18(4); 19(3); 36:1(3); 2(2); 3(5); 4(5); 6(4); 8(3); 9(4); 10(2); 11(2); 12(4); 14(4); 16; 19; 21; 23(5); 27(3); 28(5); 30(6); 45:1(5); 2; 46:1; 2(6); 10(5); 11; 12; 13(2); 16; 17; 18; 20; 21(3); 22; 24(3); 25(3); 26(5); 27; 28(2); 47:1; 2(2); 3(6); 4(3); 5; 6; 48:1(2); 2; 3; 5(3); 10; 13(3); 15(2); 16; 18; 19; 24(2); 25; 27; 28; 29(2); 31; 32(3); 33; 34(3); 36; 38; 41; 43; 44(2); 45(7); 46; 47(2); 49:2(2); 3; 5; 6(2); 7; 8(2); 12(2); 16(3); 18(2); 19(2); 20(3); 21; 22(5); 25(2); 26(2); 27(2); 28(3); 30(2); 32; 33; 34(4); 35(3); 36(2); 39; 50:1; 3; 4(2); 7(2); 8(4); 9(2); 11; 12; 13(2); 15; 16(2); 17(2); 18(4); 20(2); 21(2); 22(2); 23(2); 25(4); 26; 27; 28(5); 29; 30; 31; 33(3); 34(2); 35; 37; 38; 39(2); 40; 41; 42; 43(4); 44(2); 45(3); 46(2); 51:1; 2; 4; 5(4); 6(3); 7; 10; 11(4); 12(2); 13; 14; 16(3); 18(2); 19(4); 20; 23; 24; 26; 27; 28(2); 29(2); 30; 31; 32; 33(4); 34; 35(2); 41; 42; 43; 44(2); 45(3); 47(2); 49(2); 51; 53; 54(2); 55(2); 56(2); 57; 58(2); 59(4); 63(2); 64; 52:1(2); 2; 3(4); 4(6); 7; 8(2); 12(2); 15; 16(3); 17(4); 18; 19(3); 20(2); 21(2); 22(3); 24(2); 25(9); 26(2); 27(3); 29; 30(3); 31(9); 32; 33; 34(4);
Lam 1:1; 3(2); 4; 5; 6; 7(4); 12; 14; 15(2); 21; 2:1(3); 2(3); 3; 4(2); 5; 6(3); 7(4); 8(2); 10(3); 11(3); 12; 13(2); 14; 15(3); 17(2); 18(3); 19(4); 20(2); 21; 22; 3:1; 6; 12; 22; 26; 32; 33; 34; 36; 38(2); 39; 45; 48(3); 51(2); 55; 58; 62; 64; 65; 66; 4:1(2); 2(3); 3; 4(2); 6(5); 7; 9(2); 10(3); 12(3); 13(4); 16(2); 19; 20(2); 21(2); 22(3); 5:8; 9(3); 10; 11; 12; 15; 18(2); 21; Eze 1:1(3); 2(2); 3(4); 4(5); 5(3); 7(3); 8; 10(5); 11; 14(4); 14(2); 16(3); 18; 20; 21; 22(3); 24(5); 26(4); 27(5); 28(7); 2:1; 3(2); 6(4); 8; 9; 3:12(3); 4(2); 5(3); 6(2); 7(2); 10; 11(2); 12(3); 13(4); 14(2); 15(2); 16(2); 17(2); 22; 23(2); 25; 26; 4:1; 3(2); 9(3); 2(4); 26; 27(5); 28(7); 2:1; 3(2); 6(4); 4(2); 5(2); 6; 7; 8(2); 9; 10(2); 12(2); 14; 16(2); 5:1; 2(2); 3(2); 5(2); 6(3); 7(2); 10; 11(2); 12(3); 13(4); 14(2); 16(2); 17(2); 23:(4); 2:1; 3; 4(4); 5(6); 6(3); 6:1; 2; 13(3); 14; 15(2); 11:1; 1:1(2); 2; 4; 5(2); 6(4); 7(4); 8(1); 9; 10; 11(2); 13; 14(4); 15(2); 14:2; 14:2; 3; 7; 9;
Joel 1:1(2); 2(2); 3; 5(2); 6(2); 8; 9; 11; 12(2); 13(3); 14(2); 15; 16; 18(2); 19(2); 20(3); 2:1(2); 2(5); 3(4); 4(2); 7; 11; 13(2); 16(2); 17(2); 23; 24; 26; 27; 30; 31(2); 33; 37; 3:1; 2; 3; 4; 5(3);
Amos 1:1(7); 2(2); 3(2); 4(2); 5(4); 6; 7; 8; 9; 10; 11(3); 13; 15; 3:1(2); 2(2); 9; 12(5); 13; 15; 3:1(2); 2(2); 9; 12(5);
Obad 1; 3(2); 6; 7; 8(3); 9(2); 11; 12(4); 13(4); 14(3); 15; 17; 18(5); 19(5); 20(6); 21;
Jonah 1:1(2); 3(2); 5(3); 6; 7; 10; 4:2(2); 5(3); 6; 8;
Mic 1:1(3); 3(2); 5(6); 7(3); 9; 10; 11(4); 12(2); 13(4); 14(2); 15(2); 2:1; 4; 5; 7(2); 8; 9; 11(3); 12(6); 13; 3:1(3); 3; 7; 8(4); 9(4); 12(2); 4:1(3); 26; 4(2); 5(2); 8(4); 10(3); 12; 13(2); 5:1(2); 2(3); 4(4); 6(2); 7(3); 8(4); 9(4); 10(2); 11; 12; 13(3); 14(2); 6:2;

4(4); 5(3); 6; 7(5); 8; 9; 10(2); 11; 12; 13; 14; 16(4); 7:1; 2; 4(2); 5; 9; 10; 13(2); 14(3); 15(3); 17(4); 18(2); 19; 20; Nah 1:1(3); 3; 4; 6; 7; 8; 11; 14(3); 15; 2:2(2); 3(2); 6; 7; 8(2); 9(4); 10; 11(2); 13(2); 3:1; 2(5); 3(3); 4(4); 5; 10; 11; 12; 13(2); 16; 18; 19(2); Hab 1:2; 6; 7; 13; 14; 15; 2:8(5); 9; 11(2); 13(2); 14(2); 16; 17(6); 18(2); 19; 3:2(2); 3(4); 2(2); 23(5); 9; 16(2); Zeph 1:1(8); 3(2); 4(5); 5; 7(2); 8; 10; 11; 14(3); 15(5); 16; 18(3); 2:2(2); 3(2); 5(4); 7(3); 8(3); 9(6); 10(2); 11(2); 14(3); 3:8; 9; 10(2); 11(3); 12(2); 13; 14(2); 15(2); 17; 18(2); 20; Hag 1:1(6); 2; 3; 5; 7; 9(2); 11; 12(5); 14(9); 15(2); 2:1(2); 2(4); 3; 4(3); 5; 6; 7(2); 8; 9(4); 10(3); 11; 12; 13; 14; 15; 16(2); 17; 18(2); 20; Zec 1:1(4); 3(3); 4; 6(2); 7(5); 8(2); 9; 10(2); 11(2); 12; 13; 3:1; 2; 4; 5; 6; 7; 9(2); 10; 4:1(2); 2(3); 6(2); 7(3); 8(2); 9; 10(3); 11; 12; 14; 5:3; 4(4); 7(2); 8(2); 9; 11; 6:1; 5(2); 9; 10(7); 11(2); 12(3); 13(2); 14(2); 15(7); 7:1(3); 2(2); 5; 7(3); 8(3); 9; 11; 12; 13; 14(2); 15(2); 16(2); 17(2); 3:1(2); 2; 3(2); 4(2); 5; 6; 7(2); 10(2); 11(2); 12; 14; 16; 17; 4:1; 2(2); 3(2); 4; 5(2); 6(4); 7(4); 8(2); 9; 11; 6:1; 5(2); 9; 10(7); 11(2); 12(3); 13(2); 14(2); 15(7); 7:1(3); 2(2); 5; 7(3); 8(3); 9; 11; 12; 13; 14(2); 15(2); 16(2); 17(2); 8:3(3); 9(3); 10; 11(2); 12; 13; 14; 15(2); 16(2); 17(3); 18(2); 19(3); 20; 21(4); Mal 1:1(2); 3; 4(2); 5; 6; 7; 8; 9; 10; 11(3); 12; 13(2); 14; 2:2; 3; 4; 5; 6; 7(2); 8(3); 10; 11(2); 12(3); 13; 14(2); 15(2); 16(2); 3:1(2); 2; 3(2); 4(2); 5; 6; 7(2); 10(2); 11(2); 12; 14; 15; 16(2); 4:1(2); 2; 3; 4; 5(2); 6(2);
Mt 1:1(4); 3; 5(2); 6(2); 16(2); 18(2); 20(3); 22; 24; 2:1(2); 2; 4(2); 5; 6(3); 7; 12; 13; 15(3); 16(2); 19; 20; 21; 22(3); 3:1; 2; 3(3); 4; 6; 7(2); 9; 10; 13; 14; 16(2); 4:1(2); 3(2); 5; 6; 8(2); 13; 15(4); 16; 17; 18; 19; 21; 23(3); 25; 5:3; 9; 10; 11; 13(2); 14; 19(3); 20(2); 21(2); 22(3); 27; 29; 30; 31; 32; 35; 37; 42; 45; 6:1(2); 2; 5(2); 8; 16; 22(2); 23; 26; 27; 28; 29; 30; 31; 32(2); 33; 34; 7:4; 5(2); 9; 15; 16(2); 21; 24; 26; 27; 8:6; 11; 12(2); 14; 20(2); 21; 26; 27; 28; 29; 30; 31; 32(2); 33(4); 34; 9:3(3); 4(6); 7; 9; 10; 13; 14; 16(2); 4:1(2); 2; 9; 8(2); 13; 15(4); 16; 18; 19; 21; 23(3); 25; 5:3; 9; 10; 11; 13(2); 14; 19(3); 20(2); 21(2); 22(3); 27; 29; 30; 31; 32; 35; 37; 42; 45; 6:1(2); 2; 5(2); 8; 16; 22(2); 23; 26; 27; 28; 29; 30; 31; 32(2); 33; 34; 10:2(3); 3; 5(2); 6(2); 7; 12; 13; 15(3); 16(2); 19; 20; 21; 22(3); 3:1; 2; 3(3); 4; 6; 7(2); 9; 10; 13; 14; 16(2);
Dan 1:1(4); 2(7); 3(5); 4; 5(2); 6(2); 7(5); 8(3); 9; 10(2); 11; 13(3); 15(2); 16; 18(2); 20(2); 21; 2:1(2); 6; 7; 8; 9; 14; 16; 18(4); 19; 20; 23(2); 25(2); 26(2); 27(4); 28; 29; 30; 32(3); 33(4); 34(3); 35; Dan 1:1(4); 2(7); 3(5); 4; 5(2); 6(2); 7(5); 8(3); 9; 10(2); 11; 13(3); 15(2); 16; 18(4); 18(4); 20; 21(2); 22; 23(2); 24(2); 25(2); 26; 27(5); 28; 29(2); 30; 31; 32(3); 33(4); 34; 35; 36(2); 37(3); 39(2); 43; 44; 50(2); 51; 2:1; 2; 3; 4; 14; 19; 21; 23; 26; 29(2); 30; 31; 32(2); 34(2); 35(3); 39; 24:1; 3(4); 6(2); 8; 9; 12; 16(2); 17(2); 27; 30; 31(2); 32(2); 33(2); 35; 36(2); 37; 38(2); 39; 40; 41(2); 42(3); 43; 45; 50; 13:1; 5; 11(2); 14; 15; 18; 19; 21; 22(2); 24; 27; 30; 31(2); 32(2); 33(2); 35; 36(2); 37; 38(2); 39; 40; 41(2); 42; 43; 44; 45; 46; 47(2); 49; 50(2); 52(2); 58; 14:1(2); 6; 8; 13(2); 20; 24; 25; 27; 29; 31; 32(3); 34; 35(2); 36; 15:1; 2; 3; 6(2); 7; 9; 11; 14; 18; 19; 21; 22(3); 24(2); 27; 29; 31; 37; 39; 16:3(2); 4; 6(3); 8; 9; 10; 11(3); 12(5); 13(2); 14; 17; 20; 22; 23(2); 27(2); 28(2); 17:5; 9; 12(2); 13; 18; 19(2); 21(2); 23(2); 24(2); 25(2); 26; 27(2); 28(2); 18:1; 2; 3; 4; 6(2); 7; 10(2); 11; 12; 13(2); 14; 15; 16(2); 17; 23; 25(2); 26; 31(3); 32; 34(2); 37; 39; 40; 42; 43; 45; 22(2); 5; 13; 16(2); 27; 28; 29; 30; 31; 32(3); 34; 35(2); 36; 15:1; 2; 22(3); 23; 24(2); 27; 29; 31; 37; 39; 16:3(2); 4; 6(3); 8; 9; 10; 11(3); 12(5); 13(2); 14; 17; 20; 22; 23(2); 27(2); 28(2); 20:2; 3; 5(2); 6(2); 7; 10; 14(2); 15(2); 16; 17; 20; 22; 23(2); 25(2); 29; 30; 31; 36(2); 37(2); 38; 41(2); 42(3); 11:1; 2(2); 10; 11(2); 12(2); 19(3); 20; 23(2); 27; 28; 19:1; 7(2); 8(2); 13; 14(2); 21; 22; 23(2); 26; 28(2); 31; 32(2); 33; 34; 37; 40; 42; 43; 45; 22(2); 5; 13; 16(2); 27; 28; 29; 20; 21(2); 24; 26; 27; 8:6; 11; 12(2); 13; 14; 20; 21; 24; 25; 27; 31; 32; Mk 1:1(3); 3(2); 4(2); 5(4); 6; 7(2); 9(2); 10; 13; 14(2); 16; 19; 21; 24(2); 25; 26; 29(2); 30(2); 34; 2:3(2); 4; 5; 6; 9; 10; 14(2); 17; 18(4); 19; 21; 23; 26(2); 28(2); 3:5; 9; 11(7); 13; 21; 22; 28; 29; 33; 4:5; 4(2); 6; 9; 10; 11(2); 7:1(3); 5(2); 6; 7(4); 8(2); 10(3); 12(5); 13; 14(4); 15(2); 16(2); 18(2); 19(2); 20; 21(2); 22; 23; 24; 25; 26(2); 27; 29(2); 30; 34; 35; 36; 37; 38(2); 40; 42(2); 6:3(3); 6; 11; 14; 15; 21; 22(3); 23(2); 29; 33; 34; 43(2); 45; 46; 47(2); 49; 50(2); 5:2(2); 3; 5(2); 6(2); 7(4); 8(3); 9; 10(2); 11; 13(3); 15(2); 16; 18(2); 20(2); 21; 2:1(2); 6; 7; 8; 9; 14; 16; 18(4); 19; 20; 23(2); 25(2); 26(2); 27(4); 28; 29; 30; 32(3); 33(4); 34(3); 35; Dan 1:1(4); 2(7); 3(5); 4; 5(2); 6(2); 7(5); 8(3); 9; 10(2); 11; 13(3); 15(2); 16; Lk 1:5; 3; 4; 5(6); 6; 8; 9(2); 10(2); 11(3); 15; 16(2); 17(3); 19; 23; 26; 27(2); 29; 32(2); 33(3); 36; 38; 39; 40(2); 41(2); 42; 43; 44; 45; 48; 51; 52; 54; 59; 61; 65; 66(2); 67; 69; 70; 71; 15:2; 3; 9; 12; 17; 18; 21(2); 22; 26(2); 32; 35; 36; 38; 39; 40(2); 43(3); 45; 46(2); 47; 16:1; 2(3); 6; 9(2); 11; 12; 14; 19; 14; 15; 41; 42; 47; 10:1(2); 4; 6; 10; 14(2); 15; 23; 24; 25(2); 26; 33; 35; 38(2); 39(2); 44(2); 46(3); 47(2); 48; 49; 11:1(2); 3; 5; 9; 10(2); 13; 14; 15(2); 17(3); 19; 29; 30(2); 32; 12:2(2); 6; 8; 9; 10; 11; 14(2); 20(2); 24(2); 25; 27(3); 28; 32; 33; 36; 38; 39; 40(2); 43(3); 45; 46(2); 47; 48; 51; 52; 54; 59; 61; 65; 66(2); 67; 69; 70; 71; 15:2; 3; 9; 10; 11; 13; 16(2); 17(3); 19; 23; 26; 27(2); 31; 32;

33; 34; 35; 36(4); 37; 38; 39; 40; 41; 42; 43; 46; 3:1(8); 2(2); 3(2); 4(4); 6; 7(2); 8(2); 9; 14; 15; 16; 23(3); 24(5); 25(5); 26(5); 27(5); 28(5); 29(5); 30(5); 31(5); 32(5); 33(5); 34(5); 35(5); 36(5); 37(5); 38(4); 4:1; 2; 3; 4; 5(2); 6; 9(2); 14(2); 15; 17; 18(2); 19; 20; 22; 25(2); 26(2); 27(2); 29(2); 30; 31; 33; 34(2); 35(2); 37(2); 38; 40; 41(2); 43; 44; 5:1(2); 2; 3(2); 6; 9; 10; 12; 15(2); 17(4); 19; 24(2); 27; 29(2); 33(2); 34; 36(2); 6:1; 2; 4; 5(2); 13; 15; 16; 17(5); 19; 20; 22; 26; 30(2); 34; 35; 42; 44(2); 45(6); 49; 7:1; 3(2); 11; 12(3); 17; 18(2); 19; 21(2); 24; 27; 28(2); 29; 30(2); 31; 34(2); 35; 36; 37; 38; 39; 42; 44; 8:1(2); 2(2); 3(2); 4; 5; 10(2); 11; 12; 13; 14; 21; 22; 23; 24; 25; 26; 27; 28; 29(2); 32; 33; 35(2); 36; 37(2); 38; 41; 42; 43(2); 44(2); 46; 48; 49; 51; 9:2; 5; 7(2); 8(3); 9; 11(3); 17; 19; 20; 22(2); 26(5); 27(3); 29; 31; 35; 36; 38; 43; 44(2); 45; 46; 47; 52; 55(2); 56; 58(2); 60; 62; 10:2; 6; 7; 9; 10; 11(3); 19; 21; 22; 30; 34; 35; 36; 11:1; 5; 6; 8; 11(2); 15(2); 16; 20(2); 24; 26; 27; 28; 29; 30; 31(4); 32(2); 34(3); 36(3); 39(2); 41; 42(2); 44; 45; 46; 47; 48; 49(2); 50(3); 51(3); 52; 53; 54; 12:1(4); 4; 6; 7(2); 8(2); 9; 10; 13; 15(2); 16; 20; 25; 27; 28; 29; 30(2); 31; 39; 40; 42; 44; 46; 48(3); 54; 56(2); 57; 13:1; 7; 10; 11; 14; 15; 16; 18; 19(3); 20; 21; 25; 27; 28(2); 29; 31; 33; 35; 14:1(2); 5; 8(2); 10; 14; 15(2); 18; 19; 21(2); 24(2); 28; 32; 33; 15:4(2); 8; 10(2); 12(2); 15; 17; 19; 26; 16:2(2); 4; 5; 6; 7; 8(2); 9(2); 15; 16; 17; 20; 24; 28; 17:2; 6; 7; 11; 15; 20(3); 21; 22(3); 24(2); 25; 26(3); 28; 29; 30; 18:3; 8; 12; 16(2); 17; 24; 25; 29; 31; 34; 37; 38; 39; 19:3; 8; 9; 10; 11; 22; 29(2); 31; 34; 37(3); 38; 39; 44; 46(2); 47; 20:1; 4(2); 6; 10(2); 13; 15(2); 17; 20(2); 21(2); 26; 27; 32; 33; 34; 36(2); 37(3); 38(2); 39; 42; 45; 46; 21:3; 4(3); 5; 9; 16; 17; 18; 21; 22; 24(3); 25; 26; 27; 30; 31; 34; 35; 36; 37; 22:1; 3(2); 6; 7; 10; 11; 16; 18(3); 19; 21; 22; 23; 24; 25; 30; 39; 44; 47; 48; 50(2); 52; 53; 55; 58; 59(2); 61; 66; 69(3); 70; 71; 23:1; 3; 6; 8(2); 11; 15; 17; 22; 23(2); 26; 27(2); 28; 35; 37; 38(2); 39; 41; 45; 51(4); 52; 24:1; 3; 7(2); 10; 13; 14; 17; 18; 19; 22; 23; 24; 25; 31; 35(2); 36; 42(2); 44; 47; 48; 49(2); **Jn** 1:4; 7; 8; 12; 13(6); 14(3); 15(2); 16; 18; 19; 22; 23(2); 24; 29(2); 30; 34; 35; 36; 40; 42; 44(2); 45(3); 46; 47; 49(2); 51(2); 2:1(2); 3; 6(3); 8; 9(2); 11(2); 14; 15(2); 16; 17; 21(2); 25; 3:1(2); 3; 5(3); 6(2); 8; 10; 12; 13; 14; 18(2); 22; 25; 29(2); 31(2); 34; 36; 4:5(2); 7; 9(3); 10(2); 13; 14(2); 22; 30; 32; 34; 39(3); 41; 42(2); 46; 47(2); 52; 54; 5:1; 3(3); 4(2); 19; 25(2); 27; 29(2); 30(2); 31; 32(2); 36(2); 37; 39; 42; 44; 46; 6:1(2); 4; 7(2); 8; 11; 13; 14; 18; 22; 25; 26; 27; 28; 29; 33; 35; 38; 39; 40; 42; 45(2); 46; 48; 51(2); 53(2); 58; 60; 62; 64; 65; 66; 68; 69; 70; 71(3); 7:2; 7; 13(2); 14; 17(3); 18; 19; 22(2); 23; 25(2); 28; 31; 36; 37; 38(2); 39; 40(2); 41; 42(4); 43; 44; 48(2); 50; 52(2); 8:1; 12(2); 13; 14; 17; 18(2); 23(2); 26(2); 27; 28(2); 34; 39; 40; 41(2); 42; 44(4); 46(2); 47(2); 52; 54; 59(2); 9:3; 4; 5; 6(2); 7; 11; 16(2); 17; 18; 21; 22; 23; 31; 32; 33; 35; 40; 10:2; 5; 7; 14; 16; 18(2); 20; 21(2); 22; 25; 26; 28; 29; 32; 35; 36(2); 37; 39; 41; 11:1(2); 4(2); 8; 9; 11; 13(3); 19; 22; 27; 37(2); 39; 40; 42; 45; 46; 49; 51; 52; 55; 12:2; 3(4); 4; 7; 9; 11(2); 13(3); 15; 16; 17; 21(2); 23; 24; 30; 31(2); 34(3); 36; 38(2); 41; 42(2); 43(2); 49; 13:1(2); 2; 18; 21; 22; 23; 24; 26; 29(2); 31; 14:10; 17; 21; 30; 15:4; 15; 16; 19(3); 26(2); 16:2; 4; 5; 8(3); 9; 10; 11(2); 13(2); 14; 15; 17; 19; 21; 25; 33; 17:6; 7; 12(2); 14(2); 15; 16(2); 24; 18:3; 5; 7; 9; 12; 15; 17; 18; 19(2); 22(2); 23; 25; 26(2); 28; 32; 33; 34(2); 36(2); 37; 39; 19:2; 3; 5; 7; 14; 17; 19(2); 20; 21(3); 25(2); 29; 32(2); 34; 36; 38(5); 39; 40(2); 42; 20:1; 2; 12; 19(2); 24; 25(2); 30; 31; 21:1; 2(3); 6(2); 9; 10; 11; 12; 15; 16; 17; 24; **Acts** 1:1; 3(3); 4(2); 6; 8; 9; 11; 13(2); 14; 15(2); 16; 17; 18; 19; 20; 21; 22(2); 24(2); 25; 2:1; 2; 3(2); 5; 10(2); 11; 13; 14; 15; 17; 18; 19; 20; 21; 22(4); 23; 24(2); 28(2); 29; 30(2); 31(2); 33(3); 36; 37; 38(4); 42; 46; 3:1; 2(2); 5; 6(2); 10; 12; 13(5); 15; 16; 18; 19(2); 21(3); 22; 24; 25(3); 26; 4:1; 4(2); 6(2); 8(2); 9; 10(3); 11(2); 13(2); 15; 18; 19; 21; 22; 25; 26; 27(2); 30; 31; 32(5); 33(2); 34(2); 36(3); 5:2; 3(2); 7; 9(2); 12; 13; 14; 15(2); 16; 17; 19; 20; 21(2); 24(2); 30; 31; 32; 34; 35; 36; 37(2); 38; 39; 40; 41; 6:1(2); 2(2); 3(2); 4; 5(3); 7(3); 8; 9(5); 14; 15; 7:2; 3; 4(2); 8; 10(3); 11; 16(4); 17; 22; 23; 24; 29; 30(3); 31; 32(4); 34; 35; 36; 37(2); 40(3); 41; 42(4); 43(2); 44; 45(3); 46; 49; 52(4); 53; 55(3); 56(2); 58; 8:1; 3; 5; 7; 9; 10; 11; 12(2); 14; 16(2); 18; 20; 21; 22(2); 23(2); 24; 25(2); 26; 27(4); 32; 34(3); 37; 39(2); 9:1; 2(2); 11(2); 13; 15; 20; 24; 26; 27; 29; 31(2); 33; 36; 10:1; 3(2); 7(2); 12(3); 22(3); 28; 31; 32; 33; 34(2); 36(2); 38(2); 39(2); 41; 42(2); 43; 45(2); 48; 11:1; 2; 5; 6(2); 16; 20(2); 21; 22(2); 23(2); 24(2); 28(2); 30; 12:1; 2; 3; 4; 5; 7; 10; 11(5); 12(2); 13; 17; 18; 20; 22(2); 23(2); 24; 13:1; 5(2); 7(2); 10(4); 11; 12; 15(3); 16; 17(4); 18; 19; 20; 21(4); 22; 23; 24(2); 25; 26(3); 27; 28; 29; 31; 34; 36; 38; 39; 40; 42; 43(2); 44; 46(2); 47(2); 48; 49; 50(2); 51; 14:1(3); 3; 4; 5(2); 6(2); 11(2); 13; 14; 15; 19; 22(2); 26; 27; 15:1; 2; 3; 4(2); 5(3); 6; 7; 10; 11; 14; 15; 16; 17; 18; 20; 21; 22; 23; 26; 35; 36; 40; 16:1; 2; 3; 4; 6(2); 9; 12(2); 13; 14(4); 16; 17(2); 18(2); 19; 26; 27(2); 32; 33; 36; 39; 40(2); 17:1; 2; 4(3); 5(2); 6; 7; 8; 9(2); 10; 11; 12(3); 13(3); 18(3); 22(2); 24; 26(4); 27; 28; 29; 30; 32(3); 18:3; 8(2); 11; 12; 14; 15(3); 17(2); 18; 23; 25(3); 26; 19:4; 5; 8(2); 9(2); 10(2); 11; 12; 13(2); 14(2); 16; 17; 19(3); 20; 22; 25; 27; 28(2); 29; 31(2); 33; 34(2);

35(4); 37(2); 40; 20:4(4); 6; 7; 11; 16; 17; 19(2); 24(4); 25; 26; 27; 28; 30; 31; 32; 35; 38; 21:5; 6; 8(3); 11; 12; 13; 14; 16(3); 20(2); 21; 26(3); 27; 28; 30; 31; 32; 35(2); 36; 39(2); 22:3(3); 5; 8; 9; 10; 11(2); 12; 14(2); 15; 16; 18; 20(2); 30; 23:5(2); 6(3); 9; 10; 11(2); 12; 16; 17; 20; 21; 23; 27(2); 29(4); 34(2); 24:4; 5(3); 7; 8(2); 10; 14; 15(2); 16; 21; 22(2); 23; 25; 26; 25:2; 8; 9; 11(2); 15; 16; 18; 19(2); 20(3); 21; 23(2); 24; 25; 26; 26:2; 4; 5; 6(2); 7; 9(2); 10; 13; 16(2); 18(2); 20(2); 22; 25; 26(2); 31(2); 27:1; 2(3); 5(2); 6; 8; 10(2); 11; 12; 19; 21; 22(3); 23; 25; 29; 30(2); 32; 34(2); 35; 36; 41; 42; 44; 28:2(2); 3(2); 7(2); 8(3); 11; 15; 16; 17(3); 18; 19; 20; 21(3); 22; 23(4); 27(2); 28; 31; **Rom** 1:1(2); 3(2); 4(2); 6; 7; 8; 9(2); 10; 12; 16(3); 17; 18(2); 19; 20(2); 23; 24; 25; 27(2); 29; 30(2); 32(2); 2:2; 3; 4(2); 5(3); 9(3); 11; 13(2); 15; 16; 17; 18; 19(2); 20(4); 23; 24; 25; 26; 29(3); 3:1; 2; 3; 5; 7; 12; 13; 14; 17; 18; 20(2); 21; 22(2); 23(2); 25(2); 26; 27(2); 28; 29(3); 4:4(2); 6; 11(4); 12(4); 13(2); 14(2); 16(5); 17; 18; 19; 20; 5:2(2); 5; 10; 14(2); 15(2); 16; 17(3); 18(3); 19; 6:3; 4(2); 5(2); 6; 13(2); 16(2); 17(2); 18; 19(3); 20; 21; 23(2); 7:2; 4; 5; 6(2); 8; 22; 23(2); 24; 25(2); 8:2(3); 3; 4; 5(2); 7; 9(3); 10(2); 11; 13; 14(2); 15(2); 16; 17; 18; 19(3); 20; 21(3); 23(2); 27(2); 29; 33; 34; 35; 39; 9:4(2); 5; 6(2); 7; 8(3); 9; 11(3); 16(3); 21; 22; 23(2); 24(2); 26; 27(3); 29; 30; 31(2); 32; 33; 10:2; 3(2); 4; 5; 6; 8; 13; 14; 15(3); 17; 18; 20; 11:1(4); 2; 4(2); 5; 6(2); 8; 12(4); 13; 14; 15(3); 17(3); 20; 22; 24; 25(2); 26; 29; 33(3); 34; 36; 12:1; 2(2); 3(2); 5; 6; 13; 16(2); 17; 20; 21; 13:1(2); 2; 3(2); 4(2); 10; 11; 12(2); 14:7; 9; 10; 12(2); 14; 16; 17; 18; 20; 23(2); 15:1; 2; 3; 4; 5; 6; 7; 8(2); 12; 13(2); 14(2); 15(2); 16(3); 18(2); 19(3); 21; 26; 27; 29(3); 30; 31; 32; 33; 16:1; 2(3); 4; 5; 7; 10; 11(2); 16; 18; 20(2); 23(2); 24; 25(3); 26(3); S:1; **1Cor** 1:1(2); 2(2); 4; 6; 7; 8; 9; 10; 11(3); 12(5); 13; 14; 16; 17(3); 18(2); 19(2); 20(2); 21(2); 24(2); 25(2); 27(2); 28; 30(2); 2:1(3); 4(3); 5(2); 6(3); 7; 8(3); 9; 10; 11(4); 12(3); 14(2); 15; 16(2); 3:4(2); 10; 13; 16(2); 17(2); 19; 20; 4:1(5); 3(2); 5(3); 6(2); 13(2); 16; 17; 19; 20; 21; 5:4(2); 5(2); 8(2); 10(2); 6:1; 4; 9(2); 10; 11(3); 12; 15(3); 19(2); 7:4(2); 6; 7; 19(2); 23; 25(2); 31; 33; 34(2); 36; 40; 8:3; 4; 6; 7; 9; 10; 9:2; 5; 7(3); 9(2); 10; 12(2); 13(2); 14; 15; 16; 17; 18; 10:4; 5; 7; 8; 9(2); 10(2); 11; 16(5); 17; 18(2); 21(5); 27; 29(2); 30; 31; 32; 33; 11:1(2); 3(3); 7(2); 8(2); 10; 12(2); 16; 18; 22; 23; 24; 25; 27(3); 28(2); 32; 12:3; 4; 5; 6; 7; 8(2); 9; 10(4); 12; 15(2); 16(2); 18; 21(2); 22; 23; 27; 28(2); 29; 30; 13:1(2); 2; 13; 14:10(2); 11; 12(2); 16(2); 21; 24(2); 25(2); 26; 32; 33(3); 36; 37; 15:3; 5(2); 6(2); 7(2); 8(4); 9(2); 10(2); 12; 13; 15(2); 19; 20; 21; 32; 34; 37(2); 39(5); 40(2); 41(3); 42; 47; 49(2); 50; 52; 56(2); 58; 16:1; 2(2); 10; 15(3); 17(2); 19; 21; 23; **2Cor** 1:1(3); 3(3); 4; 5; 6; 7(3); 8(3); 9; 11; 12(2); 14; 16(2); 19; 20(2); 22; 24; 2:3(2); 4(2); 6; 9; 10; 11(2); 12; 13; 14; 15; 16(2); 17(4); 3:1(2); 2; 3(4); 5(3); 6(3); 7(4); 8; 9(2); 10; 12; 13(2); 14; 17; 18(2); 4:2(4); 4(5); 6(5); 7(3); 10(2); 11; 13; 15(2); 17; 5:1(2); 4; 5; 9; 10; 11; 14; 18(2); 19; 21; 6:1; 2(2); 4; 7(3); 16(2); 7:1(2); 4(2); 6; 10(2); 11; 12; 13; 14; 15; 8:1(3); 2(3); 3; 4; 5; 8(3); 9; 11(2); 16; 17; 19(3); 21(2); 23(4); 24(2); 9:2(3); 3; 4; 5(2); 7; 10; 12(2); 13(2); 14; 10:1; 2; 4(2); 5(2); 7; 8; 12; 13(2); 14; 15(2); 16; 11:7; 8; 10(3); 13; 14; 15; 17; 20; 22; 23; 24; 26(2); 28; 30; 31; 32; 12:1; 2; 3; 5(2); 6(2); 7(2); 9; 11; 12; 17(2); 18; 21; 13:1; 3; 4(2); 11(3); 14(3); S:1; **Gal** 1:1; 2; 4; 6; 7; 10; 11; 12(2); 13(2); 14(2); 19; 21; 22; 2:2; 4; 5; 6; 7(2); 8; 9; 12; 14(2); 15; 16(5); 17; 20(2); 21; 3:2(3); 5(2); 7(2); 9; 10(3); 11; 12; 13; 14(2); 15; 16(2); 17(2); 18(2); 19(2); 20; 21; 22; 26; 27; 4:1; 2; 3; 4(2); 5; 6; 7; 9; 11; 13; 14; 15; 19; 20; 23(2); 26; 28; 30(2); 31(2); 5:1; 4(2); 5; 8; 11; 15; 16; 18; 19; 21(2); 22; 26; 6:1; 2; 8(2); 10(2); 12; 14; 16; 17; 18; **Eph** 1:1(2); 3; 4; 5(2); 6(2); 7(2); 9; 10(2); 11(2); 12; 13(3); 14(3); 15; 16; 17(4); 18(4); 19(2); 23; 2:2(4); 3(4); 7; 8(2); 9; 12(2); 13; 14; 15(2); 19(2); 20; 22; 3:1; 2(3); 4; 5; 6(2); 7(3); 8(2); 9(2); 10; 12; 14; 15; 16; 19(2); 4:1(2); 3(2); 4; 6; 7(3); 9; 12(4); 13(7); 14(2); 16(3); 17; 18(3); 23; 25; 29(2); 30(2); 5:1; 4; 5(2); 6(3); 8; 9; 11; 12(2); 17; 20; 21; 23(3); 26; 30(3); 33; 6:4; 5; 6(2); 8; 9; 10; 11(2); 12(2); 13; 14; 15(2); 16(2); 17(3); 19; **Phil** 1:1; 3; 4; 6(2); 7(3); 8; 10; 11(2); 12; 14; 15(2); 16; 17(2); 19(2); 22; 25; 27(3); 28(3); 29; 2:1(2); 2(2); 3; 4; 6; 7(3); 8; 10(2); 11; 13; 15(2); 16(2); 17; 19; 22; 26; 30(2); 3:2(3); 5(5); 8(3); 9(3); 10(2); 11; 12; 14(2); 17; 18(3); 4:2; 3; 7; 8; 9; 10; 11; 15; 18(2); 22; 23; **Col** 1:1(2); 3; 4(2); 5(2); 6(2); 7(2); 9; 10(2); 12(2); 13(2); 14; 15(2); 18; 20; 22; 23; 24(2); 25(2); 27(3); 2:2(6); 3; 5; 8(2); 9; 10; 11(3); 12(2); 13; 14(2); 15; 16(3); 17(2); 18(2); 19; 20; 22; 23(3); 3:1; 6(2); 8; 10; 12(3); 14; 15; 16; 17; 22; 24(2); 25; 4:3(2); 9; 11(2); 12(3); 16; 18; **1Th** 1:1; 2; 3(4); 4; 5; 6(3); 8; 9(2); 2:2; 3(2); 4; 5; 6(4); 8(2); 9(2); 11; 12; 13(4); 14(4); 19(2); 3:2(2); 6(2); 13; 4:1; 3; 4; 5; 6; 9; 12; 15(2); 16(2); 5:1; 2; 5(4); 8(3); 18; 22; 23(2); 28; **2Th** 1:1; 3(2); 4; 5(4); 8; 9(2); 11(3); 12(2); 2:1; 2; 3(2); 4; 7(2); 8(2); 9; 10(2); 13(3); 14(2); 3:1; 5; 6(2); 8; 16; 17; 18; **1Ti** 1:1(2); 5(4); 7; 9(2); 11; 14; 15(2); 20; 2:1(2); 3; 4; 7; 3:1; 2(2); 3; 5(2); 6; 7(2); 8; 9; 10; 12; 13; 15(3); 16(2); 4:1; 3; 4; 5; 6(4); 8(2); 9; 10(2); 12; 14(2); 5:8; 9; 10; 17; 18; 22; 25; 6:1(2); 2; 3; 4; 5(3); 10(2); 11; 12; 13; 14; 15(2); 20; S:1; **2Ti** 1:1(3); 3; 4; 6(2); 7(4); 8(6); 10; 11; 13(2); 15; 16(2); 18; 2:2; 3; 4; 6; 8(2); 9; 14(2); 15; 17; 18; 19(2); 20(4); 22;

24; 25; 26(2); 3:2; 3; 4(2); 5; 6; 7; 8; 10; 11; 14(2); 16; 17; 4:2; 5(2); 6; 8; 15; 17(2); 19; S:1(2); **Titus** 1:1(4); 2; 3; 6(2); 7; 8(2); 10; 12(2); 14; 2:3; 5; 7; 8(2); 10; 11; 13; 14; 3:2; 4; 5(3); 7; 11; S:1(3); **Philem** 1:1; 4; 5; 6(2); 7; 9; 13; 14; 20; 25; **Heb** 1:2; 3(4); 5; 6; 7(2); 8(2); 9; 10(2); 13; 14; 2:2; 4; 6(2); 7; 9(2); 10; 11; 12; 14(3); 15; 16(2); 17; 3:1(2); 3; 5; 6; 8; 12(2); 13(2); 14(2); 16; 19; 4:1(3); 3; 4; 6; 8; 9; 11; 12(5); 13; 14; 15; 16(2); 5:2; 4; 6; 7; 9; 10(2); 11(2); 12(4); 13; 14(2); 6:1(4); 2(7); 4(2); 5(2); 6; 9; 10; 11(2); 12; 16; 17(2); 19; 20; 7:1(3); 2(4); 3(3); 4; 5(7); 6; 7; 8; 10; 11(2); 12(2); 13(2); 14(2); 15; 16(2); 17; 18; 19; 21; 22; 23; 28; 8:1(3); 2(2); 3; 5(2); 6; 8(2); 9(2); 10; 9:1; 3; 4(2); 5(2); 6; 7; 8; 10; 11(2); 12; 13(4); 14; 15(4); 16(2); 17(2); 19(2); 20; 21; 22; 23; 24(2); 25; 26(3); 28; 10:1(2); 2; 3; 4(2); 7(2); 10(2); 12; 18; 19; 21; 22; 23; 25(2); 26; 27; 29(4); 31; 32; 33; 34(2); 35; 36(2); 39(3); 11:1(2); 3(2); 4; 6; 7(4); 9(2); 11; 12(2); 13; 15; 18; 21(2); 22(3); 23(2); 24; 25(2); 26(2); 27; 28; 30; 32(6); 33; 34(4); 36(2); 38(2); 12:1; 2(3); 3; 5(2); 9(2); 10; 11; 13; 15(3); 16; 17; 19(2); 22(2); 23(3); 24(3); 27(2); 13:7(2); 11; 15(2); 20(3); 22; 24; **Jas** 1:1(2); 3; 5(2); 6; 7; 9; 10; 11(2); 12; 13; 14; 17(2); 18(4); 20(2); 21; 22; 23; 24; 25(2); 2:1(3); 4; 5(2); 9; 10; 11; 12; 15; 16; 23; 3:4; 6(3); 7(5); 8; 9; 10; 13(2); 17; 18(2); 4:1; 4(3); 10; 11(4); 5:3; 4(5); 5; 7(2); 8; 10(3); 11(4); 14(2); 15; 16; 17; 19; 20(2); **1Pet** 1:1; 2(4); 3(2); 5; 7(3); 8; 9(2); 10(2); 11(3); 13(2); 15; 17(2); 19(2); 20; 22; 23(3); 24(2); 25; 2:2; 4(2); 7; 8(2); 9(2); 10; 12; 13; 14(2); 15(2); 16(2); 25; 3:1; 3(5); 4(4); 7(2); 8(2); 12(2); 13; 14; 15; 16(2); 17; 20(2); 21(4); 22; 4:2(3); 3(3); 4(2); 7; 8; 10(2); 11(2); 13; 14(4); 15; 17(3); 19(2); 5:1(3); 2(2); 4; 5; 6; 10; 12; 14; **2Pet** 1:1(2); 2(2); 3; 4; 8; 11; 12; 16(2); 19; 20(2); 21(2); 2:2(3); 3(2); 4; 5(2); 6; 7; 9(2); 10(2); 12; 13; 14; 15(3); 16; 17; 18(2); 19(3); 20(2); 21; 3:1; 2(4); 4(2); 5(4); 7(2); 8; 10; 11; 12(2); 14; 15; 16; 17; 18; **1Jn** 1:1(2); 5; 7; 2:2; 5; 10; 14; 15; 16(5); 17; 19(3); 21; 27(2); 29; 3:1(2); 2; 4; 8(3); 9(2); 10(3); 12; 16; 17(2); 19; 22; 23; 4:1; 2(2); 3(2); 4; 5(2); 6(4); 7(2); 9; 13; 14; 15; 17; 5:1(2); 2; 3; 4; 5; 9(4); 10(2); 12; 13(4); 15; 18(2); 19; 20; **2Jn** 3; 4; 9(2); 11; 13; **3Jn** 3; 6; 7; 10; 11; 12(2); **Jude** 1(2); 3; 4(2); 5(2); 6; 7; 8; 9; 10; 11(3); 12(2); 13(2); 14(2); 15(2); 16; 17(2); 21(2); 22; 23; 24; **Rev** 1:1; 2(5); 3; 5(3); 7(2); 9(3); 10; 13(2); 14; 15; 16; 18(2); 20(2); 2:1(3); 5; 6; 7(4); 8; 9(2); 10(3); 11; 12; 14(2); 15; 16; 17; 18(3); 21; 22; 23; 24; 27(3); 3:1(2); 5(2); 7(2); 9(2); 10(2); 12(5); 14(4); 16; 17; 18(2); 4:1; 4; 5(3); 6(3); 8(2); 5:1; 5(4); 6(4); 7(2); 8(3); 9; 11(3); 6:1(3); 5; 6(3); 7; 8(2); 9(2); 11; 12; 13(2); 14; 15(2); 16(2); 17; 7:1(2); 2; 3; 4(4); 5(6); 6(6); 7(6); 8(6); 9; 13; 14(2); 15; 17(2); 8:1; 3; 4(3); 5; 7; 8; 9(2); 10(2); 11(3); 12(5); 13(5); 9:1; 2(4); 3(2); 4(2); 5; 7(2); 8(2); 9(4); 11; 13; 15; 16(3); 17(5); 18(2); 20(5); 21(4); 10:1; 7(3); 8; 10; 11:1; 4; 5; 6; 7; 8; 9; 11; 13(3); 15(3); 18; 19(2); 12:1; 4(2); 5; 6; 10(3); 11(2); 12(2); 14(2); 15(2); 16; 17(3); 13:1(3); 2(2); 3; 8(3); 10; 11; 12; 13; 14(2); 15(3); 17(2); 18(2); 14:2(3); 5; 6; 7(2); 8(3); 10(6); 11(2); 12(3); 14; 15(2); 17; 18(2); 19(3); 20(2); 15:1; 2(4); 3(4); 5(2); 6; 7(3); 8(2); 16:1(3); 2; 3; 4; 5; 6; 7; 9; 10(2); 11(3); 12(2); 13(6); 14(5); 17(2); 19(4); 21(4); 17:1(2); 2(3); 3(2); 4(2); 5(2); 6(3); 7(2); 8(3); 11; 14(2); 17; 18; 18:2(3); 3(6); 4(3); 9(2); 10; 11; 12(5); 13; 15(2); 18; 19; 22(4); 23(4); 24(3); 19:1; 2; 5; 6(3); 7; 8; 9(2); 10(4); 12; 13; 15(4); 16(2); 17(2); 18(6); 19; 20(2); 21(2); 20:1; 4(3); 5; 6(2); 7; 8(3); 9(3); 10; 12(2); 14; 15(2); 21:2; 3(2); 6(3); 9(2); 10; 11; 12(3); 14(3); 16; 17(2); 18(3); 19(3); 21(2); 22; 23(3); 24(3); 25; 26; 27; 22:1(5); 2(7); 3(2); 5; 6; 7(2); 8; 9(3); 10(2); 14; 16; 17; 18(2); 19(5); 21

OFF

5921, 6440, 114, 554, 568, 575, 595, 609, 631, 659, 660, 851, 1537, 1562, 1575, 1581, 1601, 1621, 3089, 3112, 4048, 4496

Gen 7:4; 8:3; 7; 8; 11(2); 13; 9:11; 11:8; 17:14; 22; 21:16; 22:4; 24:64; 27:40; 37:18; 38:14; 40:19(2); 41:42; 44:4; **Ex** 2:4; 3:5(2); 4:25; 9:15; 12:15; 19; 14:25; 20:18; 21; 23:23; 24:1; 30:33; 38; 31:14; 32:2; 3; 24; 33:5; 7; 34:34; **Lev** 1:15; 3:9; 4:8; 10; 31; 5:8; 6:11; 7:20; 21; 25; 27; 34; 8:28; 13:40; 41; 14:8; 9(2); 41; 16:12; 23; 17:4; 9; 10; 14; 18:29; 19:8; 20:3; 5; 6; 17; 18; 21:5; 22:3; 23:29; **Num** 2:2; 4:18; 7:89; 9:10; 13; 10:11; 12:10; 15:30; 31; 16:46; 19:13; 20; **Deut** 4:26; 6:15; 11:17; 12:29; 13:7; 19:1; 20:15; 21:4; 13; 23:1; 25:9; 12; 28:21; 63; 30:11; **Josh** 3:13; 16; 4:7(2); 5:9; 15; 7:9; 10:27; 11:21; 15:18; 23:4; 13; 15; 16; **Judg** 1:6; 7; 14; 4:15; 5:26; 13:20; 15:14; 16:12; 19; 21:6; **Ruth** 2:20; 4:7; 8; 10; **1Sa** 2:31; 33; 4:18; 5:4; 6:5(3); 17:39; 51; 19:24; 20:15(2); 24:4; 5; 11; 21; 25:23; 26:13; 28:9; 31:9(2); **2Sa** 4:12; 7:9; 10:4(2); 11:2; 24; 12:30; 15:17; 16:9; 20:22; **1Kin** 9:7; 11:16; 13:34(2); 14:10; 14; 15:21; 18:4; 20:11; 21:21; **2Kin** 1:16; 2:7; 4:25; 9:8; 16:17(3); 18:16; 23:27; **1Chr** 17:8; 19:4; 20:2; 28:9; **2Chr** 6:36; 11:14; 16:5; 20:25; 22:7; 26:21; 32:21; **Ezr** 3:13; 9:3; **Neh** 4:23(2); 5:10; 12:43; 13:25; **Est** 8:2; **Job** 2:12; 4:7; 6:9; 8:14; 9:27; 11:10; 15:4; 33(2); 17:11; 18:16; 21:21; 23:17; 24:24; 32:15; 36:20; 25; 39:25; 29; **Ps** 10:1; 12:3; 30:11; 31:22; 34:16; 36:3; 37:9; 22; 28; 34; 38; 38:11; 43:2; 44:9; 23; 54:5; 55:7; 60:1; 10; 65:5; 71:9; 74:1; 75:10; 76:12; 77:7; 83:4; 88:5; 14; 16; 89:38; 90:10;

94:14; 23(2); 101:5; 8; 108:11; 109:13; 15; 138:6; 139:2; 143:12; **Prov** 2:22; 17:14; 23:18; 24:14; 26:6; 27:10; 30:14; **Eccl** 7:24; **Song** 5:3; **Is** 6:6; 9:14; 10:7; 27(2); 11:13; 14:22; 25(2); 15:2; 17:13; 18:5; 20:2(2); 22:25; 23:7; 25:8(2); 27:11; 12; 29:20; 33:9; 13; 17; 34:4; 38:10; 12(2); 46:13; 47:11; 48:9; 19; 50:6; 53:8; 55:13; 56:5; 57:9; 19; 59:11; 14; 66:3; 19; **Jer** 7:28; 29; 9:21; 11:19; 23:23; 24:10; 28:10; 12; 16; 30:8; 31:10; 37; 33:24; 38:27; 44:7; 8; 11; 18; 46:27; 47:4; 5; 48:2; 25; 49:26; 30; 50:16; 30; 51:6; 50; 62; **Lam** 2:3; 7; 3:17; 31; 53; 54; **Eze** 6:12; 8:6; 10:18; 11:16; 12:27; 14:8; 13; 17; 19; 21; 17:4; 9; 17; 22; 18:17; 21:3; 4; 26; 23:34; 25:7; 13; 16; 26:16; 29:8; 30:15; 31:12; 35:7; 37:11; 44:19; **Dan** 4:14(2); 27; 9:7; 26; **Hos** 4:10; 8:3; 4; 5; 10:7; 15; 11:4; **Joel** 1:5; 9; 16; 2:20; 3:8; **Amos** 1:5; 8; 11; 2:3; 3:14; 5:7; 9:8; **Obad** 5; 9; 10; 14; **Mic** 2:8; 3:2(3); 3; 4:3; 7; 5:9; 10; 11; 12; 13; **Nah** 1:13; 14; 15; 2:13; 3:15; **Hab** 2:10; 3:17; **Zeph** 1:2; 3(2); 4; 11; 3:6; 7; **Zec** 5:3(2); 6:15; 9:6; 10(2); 10:6; 11:8; 9(2); 16; 13:2; 8; 14:2; **Mal** 2:12; **Mt** 5:30; 8:30; 10:14; 18:8; 26:51; 58; 27:31; 55; **Mk** 5:6; 6:11; 9:43; 45; 11:8; 13; 14:47; 54; 15:20; 40; **Lk** 9:5; 10:11; 14:32; 15:20; 16:23; 17:12; 18:13; 22:50; 54; 23:49; **Jn** 11:18; 18:10; 26; **Acts** 2:39; 7:33; 12:7; 13:51; 16:22; 22:23; 27:32(2); 28:5; **Rom** 11:17; 19; 20; 22; 13:12; **2Cor** 11:12; **Gal** 5:12; **Eph** 2:13; 17; 4:22; **Col** 2:11; 3:8; 9; **1Ti** 5:12; **Heb** 11:13; **2Pet** 1:9; 14; **Rev** 18:10; 15; 17

OFTEN

3740, 4178, 4212, 4437

Prov 29:1; **Mal** 3:16; **Mt** 23:37; **Mk** 5:4; **Lk** 5:33; 13:34; **1Cor** 11:26; **2Cor** 11:26; 27(2); **Phil** 3:18; **1Ti** 5:23; **Heb** 9:25; 26; **Rev** 11:6

OH

Gen 18:30; 32; 19:18; 20; 44:18; **Ex** 32:31; **Judg** 6:13; 15; **1Sa** 1:26; **2Sa** 15:4; 23:15; **1Chr** 4:10; 11:17; **Job** 6:8; 10:18; 11:5; 13:5; 14:13; 16:21; 19:23(2); 23:3; 29:2; 31:31; 35; **Ps** 6:4; 7:9; 14:7; 31:19; 53:6; 55:6; 81:13; 107:8; 15; 21; 31; **Is** 64:1; **Jer** 9:1; 2; 44:4

ON

Gen 2:2(2); 4:15; 16; 6:1; 6; 8:4; 5; 9; 14; 20; 12:8(3); 9; 13:3; 4; 14:15; 17:3; 18:5; 16; 19:2; 34; 20:9(2); 21:14; 33; 22:4; 9; 24:33; 45; 25:26; 28:12(2); 20; 29:1; 31:22; 32:1; 19; 33:4; 14; 16; 34:25; 37:23; 38:9; 19; 40:14; 16; 19; 41:45; 50; 43:31; 32; 44:14; 34; 46:20; 29(2); 48:16; 49:26(2); **Ex** 1:10; 2:6; 11; 4:3(2); 6:28; 8:4; 9:6; 12:7(2); 11; 18; 23; 29; 37; 14:16; 22(2); 29(2); 15:14; 19; 16:1; 5; 14; 22; 26; 27; 29(2); 30; 17:5; 9; 12(2); 18:13; 19:4; 16; 18; 20; 21:30; 22:30; 23:12; 24:6; 8; 17; 25:19(3); 20; 26; 26:10; 13(4); 18; 20; 35(2); 27:12; 13; 15; 21; 28:9; 10(2); 23; 24; 25; 27; 37; 29:9; 30; 31:17; 32:6; 15(3); 22; 26; 30; 33:4; 19; 34:21; 33; 35:2; 36:11; 37:7; 8(5); 9; 38:2; 7; 9; 15; 39:7; 17; 18; 19(2); 20; 31; 40:2; 17; 20; 24; 38; **Lev** 1:8; 9; 11; 12(2); 15; 16; 2:12; 3:4; 5(2); 4:12; 5:12; 6:10(2); 11; 12; 7:4; 16; 17; 18; 8:26; 28; 9:1; 14; 24; 11:2; 27; 34; 13:3(2); 5; 6; 21; 26; 31; 32; 34; 36; 51(2); 55; 14:9; 10; 23; 37; 15:6; 14; 23(2); 29; 16:4(2); 10; 23; 24; 29; 30; 32; 19:6; 7; 20:25; 21:10; 22:30; 23:6; 11; 21; 27; 35; 36; 39(2); 40; 24:6; 7; 25:9; **Num** 1:1; 18; 2:3; 10; 18; 25; 3:10; 13; 29; 35; 4:12; 6:9; 10; 23; 7:1; 11; 18; 24; 30; 36; 42; 48; 54; 60; 66; 72; 78; 8:17; 9:5; 6(2); 15; 10:5; 6; 11; 11:31(2); 14:5; 16:1; 27; 41; 46; 47; 17:8; 19:12(2); 19(3); 20:19; 21:13; 22:1; 24(2); 31; 41; 23:2; 14; 30; 24:20; 21; 28:9; 25; 29:1; 7; 12; 17; 20; 23; 26; 29; 32; 35; 30:8; 12; 31:19(2); 24; 32:19(2); 32; 33:3(2); 34:4(3); 9; 11; 15; 35:5(4); 14; **Deut** 1:1; 3; 5; 41; 2:28; 3:8; 4:15; 17; 18; 41; 46; 47; 49; 6:9; 7:25; 9:10; 10:2; 4; 11:30; 16:8; 21:19; 22; 22:5; 6; 28; 23:11; 26:7; 27:2; 28:1; 2; 30:7; 32:11; 13; 22; 41; 33:26; **Josh** 1:14; 15; 2:10; 19; 3:17(2); 4:14; 19; 22; 5:1; 10; 11; 12; 14; 6:7(2); 8; 9; 13(2); 15(2); 7:2; 7; 8:8; 9; 11; 12; 13(2); 19; 22(2); 24; 29; 33(2); 9:1; 12; 17; 10:26; 32; 35; 11:2(2); 3(2); 12:1(2); 3(2); 7(2); 13:16; 27; 32; 14:3; 9; 15:3; 7; 10(2); 16:1; 5; 6(2); 17:5; 7; 8; 9; 10(2); 18:5(2); 7; 12(2); 13; 15; 16(2); 20; 19:13(2); 14; 27; 34(2); 20:8; 22:4; 7; 20; 24:2; 8; 14; 15; 30; **Judg** 1:8; 2:9; 3:25; 4:15; 17; 23; 5:1; 10; 15; 17; 30; 6:32; 37; 38; 40; 7:1; 17; 18; 25; 8:11; 21; 26; 34; 9:8; 42; 48; 49; 10:4; 8; 11:18; 12:14; 13:5; 19; 20(2); 14:9; 15; 17; 18; 15:5; 18; 16:29; 19:1; 5; 8; 9; 14; 29; 20:30; 48; 21:4; 19(3); **Ruth** 1:7; 2:3; 9; 10; 3:15; **1Sa** 1:11; 2:26; 34; 5:3; 4; 5; 6:4(2); 7; 15; 7:6; 10; 9:20(4); 27(2); 10:3; 11:2; 7; 11; 12:11; 13:5; 14:1; 4(2); 16; 19; 24; 32; 40(2); 47; 15:12; 16; 18; 16:6; 7(4); 16; 17:3(4); 41; 18:10; 24; 19:23; 20:20; 21; 27; 41; 21:13; 22:18; 23:19; 21; 24; 26(2); 24:7; 25:13(3); 14; 18; 19; 20; 23; 41; 26:13; 25; 27:11; 28:8; 20; 22; 29:2(2); 30:1; 2; 31:7(2); 8; **2Sa** 1:2; 10; 11; 24; 2:13(2); 21; 25; 3:12; 29(4); 4:5; 7; 5:8; 10; 6:5(6); 8:7; 9:3; 6; 13; 11:13; 12:18; 30; 13:5; 19(4); 31; 14:2; 3; 4; 9(2); 12; 14; 22; 26; 30(2); 31; 33; 15:6; 18(2); 33; 16:2; 6(2); 12; 13; 17:12; 19:40(2); 20:8; 13; 21:10; 20(2); 22:4; 49; 23:1; 24:5; 20(2); **1Kin** 1:20; 27; 46; 48; 50; 51; 2:4; 5; 14; 15; 16; 19(2); 20; 24; 28; 37; 42; 3:6; 4:24(3); 29; 5:3; 4; 6:10; 15; 16; 7:3; 9; 28; 29; 35; 36(2); 39(3); 41; 43; 49(2); 8:20; 23; 25; 27; 50; 54; 66; 9:26; 10:9; 19(2); 20(2); 11:30; 12:32; 13:4; 14:23; 16:11; 24; 18:7; 23(2); 24(2); 25; 26; 33(3); 39; 46; 19:6; 15; 20:11; 20; 31; 32(2); 21:9; 12; 22:10(2); 19(3); 20(2); 24; 30; **2Kin** 1:4; 6; 9; 13; 16; 2:6; 8; 11; 15; 24; 3:11; 21; 22; 25; 4:8; 10; 11; 18; 20; 21; 31; 38; 5:2; 11; 18; 6:29; 31; 7:2; 17; 8:12; 15(2); 9:3; 6; 13; 17; 18; 19; 32; 33(2); 10:3; 15; 30; 11:5; 7; 9(2); 16; 19; 12:9; 15; 13:21; 23; 14:4; 20; 15:4; 12; 16:4; 14; 18:14; 20; 21(2); 23; 24; 26; 27; 19:22; 26; 20:5; 7; 23:8; 12; 13; 25:3; 8; 27; **1Chr** 4:10; 6:32; 39; 44; 49; 78(2); 10:5; 8; 12:18; 37; 40(4); 13:6; 14:2; 15:20; 21; 16:7; 18:7; 20:6(2); 21:17(3); 22:18; 23:28; 31; 26:30; 29:15; 21; 22; 23; 25; **2Chr** 2:4(3); 3:7; 13; 15; 16(2); 17(4); 4:6(2); 7(2); 8(2); 10; 12(2); 13(2); 6:10; 18; 7:6; 10; 22; 8:12; 13(3); 9:8; 18; 19(2); 10:12(2); 11:12; 14:7; 11; 16:7(2); 8; 17:19; 18:9; 18(2); 24; 29; 20:2; 19; 26; 29; 23:4; 8(2); 15; 24:25; 26:15; 27:3; 28:4; 29:17(2); 21; 22; 30:15; 32:15; 17; 18; 22; 33:14; 34:4; 35:1; 36:15(2); **Ezr** 4:10; 11; 16; 5:3; 6(2); 8; 6:13; 15; 7:9; 8:31; 33; 36; 10:9; **Neh** 2:14; 3:7; 13; 4:13; 17; 22; 6:14; 8:4(2); 13; 18; 9:10(2); 11; 32(6); 10:31(3); 12:31; 13:1; 15(2); 16; 19; 21(2); **Est** 1:2; 10; 11; 2:14; 21; 23; 3:6; 12; 4:1; 5:1(2); 6:1; 2; 4; 9; 11; 7:2; 10; 8:1; 9; 10(2); 13; 14; 9:1; 2; 10; 11; 15(2); 16; 17(2); 18(3); 25; **Job** 1:10; 4:13; 5:11; 9:11; 13:13; 15:26; 27; 16:16; 19; 17:9; 18:11; 19:10; 21:3; 6; 23:9(2); 24:20; 27:17; 20; 29:9; 14; 24; 31:2; 36:2; 7; 16; 17; 37:6; 38:26(2); 39:18; 21; 27; 28; 40:12; **Ps** 4:t; 6:t, 7:7; 12:8; 21:3; 22:8; 25:3; 5; 21; 27:14(2); 31:13; 35:17; 37:34; 48:2; 49:14; 52:9; 54:t; 55:t, 57:4; 63:6; 65:12; 66:6; 67:t, 68:18; 21; 25; 69:6; 29; 71:21; 75:5; 76:t, 78:53; 79:1; 81:3; 82:5; 83:14; 87:7; 91:14; 92:11; 93:4; 104:32; 107:41; 113:5; 118:6; 119:59; 84; 143; 124:1; 2; 142:4; 143:5(2); **Prov** 4:25; 5:5; 9:14; 15; 14:21; 31; 15:14; 20:22; 22:3; 27:12; 18; **Eccl** 2:3; 11(2); 4:1; **Song** 2:12; 3:1; 5:3; **Is** 7:25; 9:17; 20(2); 10:12; 11:8(2); 13:18; 14:1; 15:2; 3; 16:12; 18:3(2); 22:16; 24:18; 21; 25:6(2); 26:3; 5; 27:11(2); 28:1; 4; 20; 30:17; 31:1; 4; 32:15; 19; 33:5; 16; 36:5; 6; 8; 9; 11; 37:23; 27; 40:26; 42:25; 44:20; 47:1; 48:14(2); 49:10; 15; 18; 51:5; 9; 52:1(2); 53:6; 54:3(2); 8; 10; 56:2; 57:17; 58:4; 13; 59:17(2); 60:7; 10; 63:7(2); **Jer** 4:7; 5:9; 29; 6:23; 25; 7:29; 8:13(2); 21; 9:9; 10:25; 11:20; 12:15; 13:2; 27; 15:10(2); 17:11; 21; 22; 24; 25; 27; 18:3; 20:3; 10(2); 12; 22:4; 23:12; 25:29; 30; 30:6; 18; 31:29; 30; 32:29; 33:26; 36:22; 23(2); 38:22; 43:3; 12; 46:4; 48:11; 49:23; 24; 29; 50:6; 19; 52:23; **Lam** 1:2; 2:21; 4:6; **Eze** 1:8; 10(2); 23(2); 3:23; 4:6; 7:16; 10:3; 11:23; 16:11; 12; 15; 33; 18:2; 19:8; 21:16(2); 23:5(2); 7; 22; 24:3(2); 10; 17; 25:9; 26:17; 28:23; 31:4; 33:32; 36:3; 37:21; 39:6; 9; 11; 17; 40:2; 5; 10(4); 12(4); 21(2); 26(2); 34(2); 37(2); 39(2); 40; 41(2); 48(4); 49(2); 41:1(2); 2(2); 5; 10; 15(2); 16; 19(2); 20; 25(2); 26(3); 42:7; 9; 14; 43:20(2); 22; 44:19; 45:7(2); 46:1; 12; 19; 47:2; 7(2); 12(2); 48:16; 21(2); 30; **Dan** 3:27; 6:14; 7:5; 8:5; 18; 10:9; 11:17; 31; 12:5(2); **Hos** 4:8; 5:1; 6:3; 10:5; 8(2); 11:4; 6; 12:1; 6; **Joel** 2:5; 7; 32; **Amos** 1:7; 10; 2:7; 5:19; **Obad** 11; 12; 13(2); 21; **Jonah** 3:5; 4:5; 10; **Mic** 2:13; **Nah** 1:2; **Hab** 1:13; 2:9; 15; 16; 3:10; 19; **Zeph** 1:9; 12; **Zec** 1:12(2); 5:3(2); 10:5; 12:6(2); 13:9; 14:4; 13; **Mal** 1:10; **Mt** 1:18; 20; 4:5; 21; 5:14; 15; 28; 39; 45(4); 6:25; 9:2; 6; 27; 36; 10:29; 34; 12:1; 5; 10; 11(2); 12; 13:2; 14:3; 13; 19; 25; 26; 28; 29; 15:22; 32; 35; 16:19(2); 17:6; 15; 18:18(2); 19; 28; 33(2); 19:13; 15; 20:21(2); 23(2); 30; 31; 34; 21:7; 19; 38; 44(2); 46; 22:11; 40; 44; 23:4; 24:17; 20; 25:33(2); 34; 41; 26:5; 7; 12; 39; 45; 50; 55; 57; 64; 27:19; 25(2); 28; 30; 31; 38(2); 48; **Mk** 1:21; 2:10; 12; 21; 23; 24; 3:2; 4; 5; 9; 21; 34; 4:1; 5; 8; 16; 20; 21; 38; 5:19; 23; 6:9; 21; 47; 8:2; 6; 23; 33; 9:3; 20; 22; 40; 10:37(2); 40(2); 47; 48; 11:7; 12; 12:12; 36; 13:15; 14:2; 3; 6; 35; 41; 46; 51; 62; 65; 15:19; 20; 27(2); 29; 36; 40; 16:5; 18; 19; **Lk** 1:11; 25; 50; 59; 65; 78; 2:14; 4:9; 16; 20; 31; 40; 5:12; 17; 6:1; 2; 6; 7; 9; 20; 29; 48; 7:13; 16; 40; 8:8; 13; 15; 16; 22; 23; 32; 9:37; 10:11; 19; 31; 32(2); 33; 34; 35; 37; 11:33; 12:22; 49; 51; 13:7; 10; 13; 14(2); 15; 16; 14:1; 3; 5; 15:5; 20; 22(3); 16:24; 17:13; 16; 18:8; 32; 38; 39; 19:43; 20:1; 18; 19; 42; 21:12; 26; 35(2); 22:21; 30; 64; 69; 23:26; 30; 33(2); 39; 54; 24:49; **Jn** 1:12; 33; 2:11; 3:18; 36(2); 4:6; 35; 39; 5:9; 16; 24; 6:2; 19; 22; 25; 29; 35; 40; 47; 7:22; 23(2); 30; 31; 38; 39; 44; 48; 8:6; 8; 20; 30; 31; 9:6; 35; 36; 10:42; 11:45; 48; 12:11; 12; 15; 37; 42; 44(3); 46; 13:22; 23; 25; 14:12; 16:9; 17:4; 20; 19:2(2); 18; 19; 31; 37; 20:22; 21:1; 4; 6; 20; **Acts** 2:18(2); 21; 25; 30; 34; 3:4; 12; 4:3; 5; 22; 5:5; 15; 18; 30; 6:6; 15; 7:5; 6; 54; 55; 56; 8:17; 18; 19; 36; 39; 9:12; 14; 17; 21; 10:4; 7; 9(2); 19; 23; 39; 44; 45; 11:15(2); 17; 12:7; 8; 10; 13:3; 9; 11; 14; 15; 34; 36; 14:10; 23; 15:3; 16:13; 31; 17:5; 26; 18:8; 10; 19:4(2); 6; 16; 17; 20:7; 10; 37; 21:3; 5(2); 23; 27; 40; 22:16; 19; 30; 23:2; 24; 32; 25:6; 17(2); 23; 27:20; 33; 44(2); 28:3(2); 4; 8; **Rom** 4:5; 24; 9:15(2); 18; 23; 33; 10:6; 11; 14; 11:22; 12:7(2); 8; 20; 13:12; 14; 15:3; 24; 16:6; 19; **1Cor** 1:4; 11:10; 14:25; 15:53(2); 54(2); 16:6; 17; **2Cor** 1:11; 16; 4:8; 5:12; 6:7(2); 7:5; 8:1; 24; 10:7; 11:20; **Gal** 3:13; 14; 27; 6:16; **Eph** 1:10; 4:8; 24; 6:3; 11; 14; **Phil** 1:29; 2:4(2); 27(3); 4:8; **Col** 3:1; 2(3); 6; 10; 12; 14; **1Th** 5:8; **2Th** 1:8; **1Ti** 1:16; 18; 3:16; 4:14; 5:22; 6:12; 19; **2Ti** 1:6; 2:22; **Titus** 3:6; 13; **Philem** 1:18; **Heb** 1:3(2); 13; 2:16(2); 4:4; 5:2(2); 6:1; 2; 8:1; 4; 9:10; 10:12; 11:13; 12:25; **Jas** 3:6(2); 4:14; 5:5; 17; **1Pet** 1:17; 2:6; 24; 3:3; 22; 4:14(2); 16; **2Pet** 3:12; **1Jn** 3:23; 5:10; 13(2); **3Jn** 6; **Jude** 20; **Rev** 1:10; 3:3; 4:2; 4; 9; 10; 5:1(2); 10; 13; 6:2; 5; 8; 10(2); 16(2); 7:1(4); 11; 15; 16; 9:7; 17; 10:2; 11:10; 16; 13:13; 14(2); 14:1; 6; 14; 15; 16(2); 15:2; 17:8; 9; 18:19; 20; 19:4; 12; 16(2); 18; 19; 20:2; 6; 9; 11; 21:13(4); 22:2

ONE

259, 376, 428, 492, 802, 1397, 1571, 1668, 1836, 2063, 2088, 2297, 2298, 3605, 3627, 3671, 5315, 6918, *240, 243, 520, 846, 848, 1438, 1520, 2087, 2596, 3303, 3391, 3442, 3538, 3588, 3661, 3675, 3739, 3858, 3888, 3956, 4861, 5100, 5129*

Gen 1:9; 2:21; 24; 3:6; 22; 4:14; 19; 10:5; 8; 25; 11:1(2); 3; 6(2); 7; 13:11; 14:13; 15:3; 10; 19:9; 14; 20(2); 21:15; 22:2; 24:41; 25:23; 26:10; 26; 31; 27:29; 38; 45; 30:33; 35; 31:49; 32:8; 33:13; 34:14; 16; 22; 37:19; 38:28; 40:5; 41:5; 11; 22; 25; 26; 38; 42:1; 11; 13(2); 16; 19; 21; 27; 28; 32; 33; 43:33; 44:20; 28; 47:21; 48:1; 2; 22; 49:16; 28; **Ex** 1:15; 2:6; 11; 6:25; 8:31; 9:6; 7; 10:5; 19; 23; 11:1; 12:18; 30; 46; 48; 49; 14:7; 20; 28; 16:15; 22; 17:12(2); 18:3; 16; 21:18; 35; 23:29; 24:3; 25:12; 19(2); 20; 32; 33; 36; 26:2(4); 3(2); 4; 5(2); 6; 8(3); 10; 11; 13; 16; 17(2); 19; 21; 24; 25; 26; 27:9; 14; 28:10; 21; 29:1; 3; 15; 23(3); 39; 40; 30:13; 14; 31:14; 32:15; 33:7; 34:15; 35:21(2); 24; 36:2; 9(3); 10(2); 11; 12(2); 13(2); 15(3); 18; 21; 22(2); 24; 26; 29; 31; 33; 37:3; 6; 7; 8; 9; 18; 19; 22; 38:14; 26; 39:14; **Lev** 4:27; 5:4; 5; 7; 13; 6:18; 7:7; 10; 14; 8:26(2); 11:26; 12:8; 13:2; 14:5; 10(2); 12; 21(2); 22; 30; 31; 50; 15:15; 30; 16:5; 8; 27; 29; 17:15; 18:30; 19:8; 11; 34; 20:9; 22:28; 23:18; 19; 24:5; 22(2); 25:14; 17; 46; 48; 26:26; 37; **Num** 1:4; 41; 44; 2:16; 28; 34; 4:19; 30; 35; 39; 43; 47; 49; 5:2; 6:11; 14(3); 19(2); 7:3; 13(2); 14; 15(3); 16; 19(2); 20; 21(3); 22; 25(2); 26; 27(3); 28; 31(2); 32; 33(3); 34; 37(2); 38; 39(3); 40; 43; 44; 45(3); 46; 49(2); 50; 51(3); 52; 55(2); 56; 57(3); 58; 61(2); 62; 63(3); 64; 67(2); 68; 69(3); 70; 73(2); 74; 75(3); 76; 79(2); 80; 81(3); 82; 89; 8:12; 9:14; 10:4; 11:19; 26; 28; 12:12; 13:2; 23; 14:4; 15; 15:5; 11(2); 12; 15; 16(2); 24(2); 29; 16:3; 15(2); 22; 17:2; 3; 6(2); 18:11; 13; 19:3; 5; 16; 18(2); 21:8; 25:5; 6; 26:54; 28:4; 7; 11; 12(2); 13; 15; 19; 22; 27; 28(2); 29; 30; 29:2(2); 4(2); 5; 8(2); 9; 10; 11; 16; 19; 22; 25; 28; 31; 34; 36(2); 38; 31:28; 30; 34; 39; 47; 49; 34:18; 35:8; 15; 30; 36:7; 8; 9(2); **Deut** 1:22; 23; 35; 2:36; 4:4; 32; 42; 6:4; 12:14; 13:7; 12; 15:7; 17:6; 15; 18:10; 19:5; 11; 15; 21:1; 15; 23:16; 24:5; 25:5; 11(2); 28:7; 25; 57; 64; 32:30; 33:3; 8; **Josh** 9:2; 10:2; 42; 12:9(2); 10(2); 11(2); 12(2); 13(2); 14(2); 15(2); 16(2); 17(2); 18(2); 19(2); 20(2); 21(2); 22(2); 23(2); 24(2); 13:31; 17:14(2); 17; 20:4; 21:42; 22:7; 14; 23:10; 14(2); **Judg** 6:16; 29; 31; 7:5(2); 8:18; 9:2; 5; 18; 10:18; 11:35; 12:7; 16:5; 29; 17:5; 11; 18:19; 19:13; 20:1; 8; 11; 16; 31; 21:3; 6; 8; **Ruth** 1:4; 2:13; 20; 3:14; 4:1; **1Sa** 1:2; 24; 2:25; 34; 36(2); 3:11; 6:4; 17(5); 9:3; 10:3; 11; 12; 11:7; 13:1; 17; 14:4(2); 5; 16; 28; 40; 45; 16:18; 17:3; 7; 36; 18:7; 21; 19:22; 20:15; 41(2); 21:11; 22:2(3); 7; 20; 25:14; 26:15; 20; 22; 27:1; 29:5; **2Sa** 1:15; 2:13(2); 16; 21; 25; 27; 3:13; 29; 4:2; 10; 6:19(2); 20; 7:23; 8:2; 9:11; 10:4; 11:3; 25; 12:1(2); 3; 13:13; 30; 14:6; 11; 12; 13; 27; 15:2; 31; 17:12; 13; 22; 18:17; 19:7; 14; 20:11; 12; 19; 23:8; 9; 15; 24; 24:12; **1Kin** 1:48; 2:16; 20; 3:17(2); 23; 25; 4:22; 6:24(2); 25(2); 26; 27(3); 34; 7:7; 16; 17; 18; 23; 27; 34; 36; 37(3); 38(3); 42; 44; 8:56; 9:8; 10:14; 16; 17; 20; 11:13; 32; 36; 12:29; 30; 13:33; 14:21; 15:10; 16:11; 18:6; 23; 25; 40; 19:2; 20:20; 29(2); 22:8; 13(2); 20; 28; 38; **2Kin** 3:11; 23; 4:22(2); 39; 5:4; 6:3; 5; 12; 7:3; 6; 8; 9; 13; 8:26; 9:1; 11; 18; 10:21; 12:4; 9; 14:8; 11; 23; 17:27; 28; 18:24; 31(2); 19:22; 21:16; 22:1; 23:35; 24:18; 25:16; 17; **1Chr** 1:19; 9:31; 10:13; 11:11; 12; 17; 12:14; 25; 38; 16:3(2); 20; 17:5; 21; 21:10; 23:11; 24:5; 6(3); 17; 25:28; 26:12; 27:18; 29:7; **2Chr** 3:11(2); 12; 17; 4:15; 5:13(2); 6:29; 7:21; 9:6; 13; 15; 16; 19; 12:13; 16:13; 18:7; 8; 12(2); 19; 20:23; 22:2; 25:17; 21; 26:11; 28:6; 30:12; 17; 18; 31:16; 32:12; 34:1; 35:24; 36:11; **Ezr** 2:1; 26; 69(2); 3:1; 5; 5:14; 6:5; 8:34; 9:4; 11; 10:2; 13; **Neh** 1:2; 3:8; 28; 4:15; 17(2); 18; 19; 22; 23; 5:7; 18; 6:2; 7:3(2); 6; 30; 37; 63; 8:1; 16; 9:3; 10:28; 11:1; 3; 14; 20; 12:31; 13:10; 28; 30; **Est** 1:7; 3:13; 4:5; 11; 6:9; 7:9; 8:12; 9:19; 22; **Job** 1:1; 4; 8; 2:3; 10; 11; 12; 5:2; 6:10; 26; 9:3; 22; 12:4; 13:9; 14:3; 4; 16:21; 17:10; 19:11; 21:23; 23:13; 24:6; 17; 29:25; 31:15; 35; 33:23; 40:11; 12; 41:9; 16; 17; 32; 42:11; **Ps** 12:2; 14:3; 16:10; 27:4; 29:9; 32:6; 34:20; 35:14; 49:16; 50:21; 53:3(2); 58:8; 63:11; 64:6; 68:21; 30; 71:18; 22; 73:20; 75:7; 78:41; 65; 82:7; 83:5; 84:7; 89:10; 18; 19(3); 105:13(2); 37; 106:11; 115:8; 119:160; 162; 128:1; 135:18; 137:3; 141:7; 145:4; **Prov** 1:14; 19; 3:18; 6:11; 28; 8:30; 15:12; 16:5; 17:14; 19:25; 20:6; 21:5; 22:26; 24:34; 26:17; **Eccl** 1:4;

2:14; 3:19(3); 20; 4:8; 9; 10; 11; 12; 5:18; 6:6; 7:14; 27(2); 28; 8:9; 9:2; 3; 18; 10:3; 15; 12:11; **Song** 1:7; 2:10; 13; 4:2; 9(2); 6:6(2); 9(3); 8:10; 11; **Is** 1:4; 23; 24; 2:12(2); 20; 3:5(2); 4:1; 3; 5:10; 19; 24; 30; 6:2; 3; 6; 7:22; 9:14; 17; 10:14; 17(2); 20; 34; 12:6; 13:8; 14; 15(2); 14:18; 32; 15:3; 16:7; 17:7; 19:2(2); 17; 18; 20; 23:15; 27:12(2); 28:2; 29:4; 11; 19; 20; 23; 30:11; 12; 15; 17(2); 29(2); 31:1; 33:20; 34:15; 16; 36:9; 16(3); 37:23; 40:25; 26; 41:6(2); 14; 16; 20; 25; 27; 43:3; 7; 14; 15; 44:5; 45:11; 24; 46:7; 47:4; 9; 15; 48:17; 49:7(2); 26; 53:6; 54:5; 55:1; 5; 56:6; 11; 57:2; 15; 60:9; 14; 16; 22(2); 65:8; 66:8; 13; 17; 23(2); **Jer** 1:15; 3:14; 5:6; 8; 6:3; 13(2); 8:6; 10(2); 9:4; 5; 8; 20; 10:3; 11:8; 12:12; 13:14; 15:10; 16:12; 18:11; 12; 16; 19:8; 9; 11; 20:7; 11; 22:7; 23:17; 30; 35(2); 24:2; 25:5; 26; 33; 30:14; 16; 31:30; 32:19; 39(2); 34:10(2); 17; 35:2; 36:7; 16; 38:7; 46:16; 49:17; 50:13; 16(2); 29; 42; 51:5; 9; 31(3); 46; 56; 52:1; 20; 21; 22; **Eze** 1:6(2); 9(2); 11(2); 12; 15; 16; 23(3); 28; 3:13; 4:8; 9; 17; 7:16; 9:2; 10:7; 9(2); 10; 14; 19; 21(2); 22; 11:5; 19; 13:10; 14:7; 15:7; 16:15; 25; 44; 17:22; 18:10; 30; 19:3; 20:39; 21:16; 19; 22:6; 11; 23:2; 13; 24:23; 31:11; 33:20; 21; 24; 26; 30(2); 32; 34:23; 37:16; 17(3); 19(2); 22(2); 24; 39:7; 40:5(2); 6(2); 7(3); 8; 10(2); 12(2); 13; 26; 40; 42; 44; 49; 41:1; 2; 6; 11; 15; 19; 21; 24; 26; 42:4; 9; 12; 43:14(2); 45:7(2); 11; 15; 20; 46:12(2); 17; 22; 47:7; 14; 48:1; 8; 21; 31(3); 32(3); 33(3); 34(3); **Dan** 2:9; 43; 3:19; 4:13; 19; 23; 5:6; 7:3; 5; 13; 16; 8:3; 9; 13; 9:27; 10:13(2); 16; 18; 11:5; 7; 10; 27; 12:1; 5; 6; **Hos** 1:11; 4:3; 11:9; **Joel** 2:7; 8(2); **Amos** 3:5; 4:7(2); 8; 6:9; 12; 8:8; **Obad** 9; 11; **Jonah** 1:7; 3:8; **Mic** 2:4; 4:5; **Nah** 1:11; 2:4; **Hab** 1:12; 3:3; **Zeph** 2:11; 15; 3:9; **Hag** 2:1; 12; 13; 16(2); 22; **Zec** 3:9(2); 4:3; 5:3(2); 8:10; 21; 10:1; 11:6; 7; 8; 9; 16; 12:10(2); 13:4; 6; 14:7; 9(2); 13; 16; **Mal** 2:3; 10(2); 15(2); 16; 17; 3:16; **Mt** 3:3; 5:18(2); 19; 29; 30; 36; 6:24(2); 27; 29; 7:8; 21; 26; 29; 10:29; 42; 12:6; 11; 22; 29; 47; 13:19(2); 38; 46; 16:14; 17:4(3); 18:5; 6; 9; 10; 12; 14; 16; 24; 28; 35; 19:5; 6; 16; 17; 29; 20:12; 13; 21; 21:24; 35; 22:5; 35; 23:4; 8; 9; 10; 15; 24:2; 10(2); 31; 40; 41; 25:15(2); 18; 24; 29; 32; 40; 45; 26:14; 21; 22; 40; 47; 51; 73; 27:38; 48; **Mk** 1:3; 7; 22; 24; 2:3; 4:41; 5:22; 6:15; 7:14; 32; 8:14; 28; 9:5(3); 10; 17; 26; 37; 38; 42; 47; 49; 50; 10:8(2); 17; 18; 21; 37; 11:29; 12:6; 28; 29; 32; 13:1; 2; 14:10; 18; 19(2); 20; 37; 43; 47; 66; 69; 70; 15:6; 7; 21; 27; 36; **Lk** 2:3; 15; 36; 3:4; 16; 4:34; 40; 5:3; 6:9; 11; 29; 40; 7:8; 32; 36; 41; 8:25; 42; 49; 9:8; 19; 33(3); 43; 49; 10:42; 11:1; 4; 10; 45; 46; 12:1; 6; 13; 25; 27; 52; 13:10; 15; 23; 14:1; 15; 18; 15:4; 7; 8; 10; 19; 26; 16:5; 13(2); 17; 30; 31; 17:2; 15; 22; 24; 34(2); 35; 36; 18:10; 14; 19; 22; 19:26; 44; 20:1; 3; 21:6; 22:36; 47; 50; 59; 23:14; 17; 26; 33; 39; 24:17; 18; 32; **Jn** 1:23; 26; 40; 3:8; 20; 4:33; 37; 5:44; 45; 6:7; 8; 22; 40; 70; 71; 7:21; 50; 8:9(2); 18; 41; 50; 9:25; 32; 10:16(2); 30; 11:49; 50; 52; 12:2; 4; 48; 13:14; 21; 22; 23; 34(2); 35; 15:12; 17; 17:11; 21(2); 22(2); 23; 18:14; 17; 22; 25; 26; 37; 39; 19:18; 34; 20:12; 24; 21:25; **Acts** 1:14; 22; 2:1(2); 7; 12; 27; 38; 46; 3:14; 26; 4:24; 32(2); 5:12; 16; 25; 34; 7:24; 26(2); 52; 57; 8:6; 9; 9:11; 43; 10:2; 5; 6; 22; 28; 32; 11:28; 12:10; 20; 13:25; 35; 15:25; 39; 17:7; 26; 27; 18:7; 12; 19:9; 14; 29; 32; 34; 38; 20:31; 21:6; 7; 8; 16; 26; 34; 22:12; 14; 23:6; 17; 24:21; 25:19; 27:1; 2; 28:2; 13; 25; **Rom** 1:16; 27; 2:15; 28; 29; 3:10; 12; 30; 5:7; 12; 15(2); 16(2); 17(3); 18(2); 19(2); 9:10; 21; 10:4; 12:4; 5(3); 10(2); 16; 13:8; 14:2; 5(2); 12; 13; 19; 15:2; 5; 6(2); 7; 14; 16:16; **1Cor** 1:12; 3:4; 8; 4:6(2); 5:1; 5; 11; 6:5; 7; 16(2); 17; 7:5; 7; 17; 25; 8:4; 6(2); 9:24; 26; 10:8; 17(3); 11:5; 20; 21(2); 33; 12:8; 11; 12(3); 13(3); 14; 18; 19; 20; 25; 26(2); 14:23; 24(2); 26; 27; 31(2); 15:8; 39; 40; 41(2); 16:2; 16; 20; **2Cor** 2:7; 16; 5:10; 14; 10:11; 11:2; 24; 12:2; 5; 13:11; 12; **Gal** 3:10; 13; 16; 20(2); 28; 4:22; 24; 5:13; 14; 15(2); 17; 26(2); 6:1; 2; **Eph** 1:10; 2:14; 15; 16; 18; 4:2; 4(3); 5(3); 6; 7; 25; 32(2); 5:21; 31; 33; **Phil** 1:16; 27(2); 2:2(2); 3:13; **Col** 3:9; 13(2); 15; 16; 4:9; 12; **1Th** 2:11; 3:12; 4:4; 9; 18; 5:11; **2Th** 1:3; **1Ti** 2:5(2); 3:2; 4; 12; 5:9; 21; **2Ti** 2:19; **Titus** 1:6; 12; 3:3; **Philem** 1:9; **Heb** 2:6; 11; 3:13; 5:12; 13; 6:11; 10:12; 14; 24; 25; 11:12; 12:16; 13:14; **Jas** 2:10; 16; 19; 4:11; 12; 5:9; 16(2); 19; **1Pet** 1:22; 3:8(2); 4:9; 10; 5:5; 14; **2Pet** 3:8(3); **1Jn** 1:7; 2:13; 14; 20; 29; 3:11; 12; 23; 4:7(2); 11; 12; 5:1; 7; 8; 18; **2Jn** 5; **Rev** 1:13; 2:23; 4:2; 5:5; 8; 6:1(2); 4; 11; 7:13; 9:12; 11:10; 13:3; 14:14; 15:7; 17:1; 10; 12; 13; 18:8; 10; 17; 19; 21:9; 21

ONE'S

Eccl 7:1; **Acts** 16:26

ONES

1121

Gen 34:29; 43:8; 45:19; 46:5; 47:24; 50:8; 21; **Ex** 10:10; 24; **Num** 14:31; 31:9; 17; 32:16; 17; 24; 26; **Deut** 1:39; 2:34; 3:19; 20:14; 22:6; 29:11; **Josh** 1:14; 8:35; **Judg** 5:22; 18:21; **2Sa** 15:22; **1Chr** 16:13; **2Chr** 20:13; 31:18; **Ezr** 8:21; **Est** 8:11; **Job** 21:11; 38:41; 39:3; 4; 16; 30; **Ps** 10:10; 83:3; 137:9; **Prov** 1:22; 7:7; **Is** 5:17; 10:16; 33; 11:7; 13:3(2); 14:9; 24:21; 25:4; 5; 29:5; 32:11; 33:7; 57:15; **Jer** 2:33; 8:16; 14:3; 46:5; 48:4; 45; **Lam** 4:3; **Dan** 4:17; 8:8; 11:17; **Joel** 3:11; **Zec** 4:14; 13:7; **Mt** 10:42; 18:6; 10; 14; **Mk** 9:42; 10:42; **Lk** 17:2

ONLY

259, 389, 905, 910, 2108, 3162, 3173, 3535, 3697, 7535, *1520, 3439, 3440, 3441*

Gen 6:5; 7:23; 14:24; 19:8; 22:2; 12; 16; 24:8; 27:13; 34:22; 23; 41:40; 47:22; 26; 50:8; **Ex** 8:9; 11; 28; 9:26; 10:17(2); 24; 12:16; 21:19; 22:20; 27; **Lev** 21:23; 27:26; **Num** 1:49; 12:2; 14:9; 18:3; 20:19; 22:35; 31:22; 36:6; **Deut** 2:28; 35; 37; 3:11; 4:9; 12; 8:3; 10:15; 12:16; 23; 26; 15:5; 23; 20:20; 22:25; 28:13; 29; 33; 29:14; **Josh** 1:7; 17; 18; 6:15; 17; 24; 8:2; 27; 11:13; 22; 13:6; 14; 17:17; **Judg** 3:2; 6:37; 39; 40; 10:15; 11:34; 16:28; 19:20; **1Sa** 1:13; 23; 5:4; 7:3; 4; 12:24; 18:17; 20:14; 39; **2Sa** 13:32; 33; 17:2; 20:21; 23:10; **1Kin** 3:2; 3; 4:19; 8:39; 12:20; 14:8; 13; 15:5; 18:22; 19:10; 14; 22:31; **2Kin** 3:25; 10:23; 17:18; 19:19; 21:8; **1Chr** 22:12; **2Chr** 2:6; 6:30; 18:30; 33:17; **Ezr** 10:15; **Est** 1:16; **Job** 1:12; 15; 16; 17; 19; 13:20; 34:29; **Ps** 4:8; 51:4; 62:2; 4; 5; 6; 71:16; 72:18; 91:8; **Prov** 4:3; 5:17; 11:23; 13:10; 14:23; 17:11; 21:5(2); **Eccl** 7:29; **Song** 6:9; **Is** 4:1; 26:13; 28:19; 37:20; **Jer** 3:13; 6:26; 32:30(2); **Eze** 7:5; 14:16; 18; 44:20; **Amos** 3:2; 8:10; **Zec** 12:10; **Mt** 4:10; 5:47; 8:8; 10:42; 12:4; 14:36; 17:8; 21:19; 21; 24:36; **Mk** 2:7; 5:36; 6:8; 9:8; **Lk** 4:8; 7:12; 8:42; 50; 9:38; 24:18; **Jn** 1:14; 18; 3:16; 18; 5:18; 44; 11:52; 12:9; 13:9; 17:3; **Acts** 8:16; 11:19; 18:25; 19:27; 21:13; 25; 26:29; 27:10; **Rom** 1:32; 3:29; 4:9; 12; 16; 5:3; 11; 8:23; 9:10; 24; 13:5; 16:4; 27; **1Cor** 7:39; 9:6; 14:36; 15:19; **2Cor** 7:7; 8:10; 19; 21; 9:12; **Gal** 1:23; 2:10; 3:2; 4:18; 5:13; 6:12; **Eph** 1:21; **Phil** 1:27; 29; 2:12; 27; 4:15; **Col** 4:11; **1Th** 1:5; 8; 2:8; **2Th** 2:7; **1Ti** 1:17; 5:13; 6:15; 16; **2Ti** 2:20; 4:8; 11; **Heb** 9:10; 11:17; 12:26; **Jas** 1:22; 2:24; **1Pet** 2:18; **1Jn** 2:2; 4:9; 5:6; **2Jn** 1; **Jude** 4; 25; **Rev** 9:4; 15:4

OR

176, 854, 2008, 5704, *1161, 1535, 2228, 2532, 3361, 3383, 4253, 5037*

Gen 13:9; 17:12; 24:21; 49; 50; 26:11; 27:21; 30:1; 31:14; 24; 29; 39; 43; 50; 37:8; 32; 39:10; 41:44; 42:16; 44:8; 16; 19; **Ex** 4:11(4); 5:3; 10:15; 11:7; 12:5; 19; 16:4; 17:7; 19:12; 13(2); 20:4(3); 21:4; 6; 15; 16; 17; 18; 20; 21; 26; 27; 28; 29; 31; 32; 33(2); 36; 22:1(2); 4(2); 5; 6(2); 7; 9; 10(5); 14; 22; 23:4; 28:43; 29:34; 30:20; 33; 34:19; **Lev** 1:10; 14; 2:4; 3:1; 6; 4:23; 28; 5:1; 2(3); 3; 4(2); 6; 7; 11; 6:2(3); 3; 4(3); 5; 7:16; 21(2); 23(2); 26; 11:4; 32(3); 35; 36; 42; 12:6(2); 7; 8; 13:2(2); 16; 19; 24(2); 29(2); 30; 38; 42(2); 43; 47; 48(3); 49(4); 51(3); 52(3); 53(2); 55; 56(3); 57(2); 58(2); 59(4); 14:22; 30; 37; 15:3; 14; 23; 25; 29; 16:29; 17:3(3); 8(2); 10; 13(2); 15(2); 18:7; 9(2); 10; 17; 19:35; 20:2; 9(2); 17; 25(2); 27(2); 21:7; 11; 14(3); 18(3); 19(2); 20(6); 22:4(2); 5(2); 8; 10; 13; 16; 18; 19; 21(2); 22(5); 23(2); 24(3); 27(2); 28; 25:14; 35; 36; 47(3); 49(3); 26:15; 27:10; 12; 14; 20; 26; 27; 28; 30; 32; 33; **Num** 5:6; 14; 30; 6:2; 3(2); 7(2); 10; 9:10(2); 21; 22(3); 11:8; 22; 23; 13:18(2); 19(2); 20(2); 14:2; 15:3(4); 5; 6; 8(2); 11(3); 14; 30; 16:14; 29; 18:15; 17(2); 19:16(3); 18(3); 20:5(3); 17; 21:22; 22:18; 26; 23:8; 19; 24:13; 30:2; 5; 6; 10; 12; 13; 14; 32:19; 35:18; 20; 21; 22; 23; **Deut** 3:24; 4:16; 23; 25; 32; 34; 5:8(3); 21(4); 32; 7:14(2); 25; 8:2; 9:5; 12:17(5); 13:1(2); 2; 3; 5; 6(4); 7; 14:7; 21; 24; 26(4); 15:2; 12; 21(2); 17:1(2); 2; 3(2); 5(2); 6; 12; 20; 18:3; 10(5); 11(4); 20; 19:15(2); 21:18; 22:1; 2; 4; 6(3); 23:1; 3; 18; 24:3; 6; 7; 14; 27:15; 16; 22; 28:14; 51(3); 29:6; 18(3); 32:36; **Josh** 1:7; 5:13; 7:3; 8:17; 20; 22; 10:14; 19:2; 22:22; 23(3); 28; 29; 23:6; 24:15; **Judg** 2:22; 5:8; 30; 9:2; 11:25; 13:14; 14:3; 6; 18:19; 19:13; 20:28; 21:22; **Ruth** 1:16; 3:10; **1Sa** 2:14(3); 6:12; 12:3(3); 13:19; 14:6; 52; 16:7; 18:18; 20:2; 10; 12; 21:3; 8; 22:8; 15; 25:31; 36; 26:10(2); 18; 29:3; 30:2; **2Sa** 2:21; 3:29(4); 35; 14:19; 15:4; 21; 17:9; 19:35; 42; 20:20; 24:13(2); **1Kin** 3:7; 8:23; 37; 38; 46; 9:6; 15:17; 18:10; 27(3); 20:18; 39; 21:2; 6; 22:6; 15; **2Kin** 2:16; 21; 4:13; 6:27; 9:32; 12:13; 13:19; 17:34(2); 20:9; 22:2; 23:10; **1Chr** 21:12(2); **2Chr** 1:11; 6:28(3); 29(2); 36; 7:13(2); 8:15; 14:11; 15:13(2); 16:1; 18:5; 14; 30; 20:9(2); 32:15; 36:17(2); **Ezr** 7:24(2); 26(3); 9:12; 10:13; **Neh** 2:16; 5:8; 10:31(2); 13:20; 25; **Est** 4:11; 16; 8:6; 9:12; **Job** 3:12; 15; 16; 4:7; 6:5; 6; 12; 22; 23(2); 7:12; 8:3; 10:4; 11:10; 12:8; 13:9; 22; 15:3; 7; 16:3; 22:3; 11; 25:4; 28:16; 18; 31:5; 9; 13; 16; 17; 19; 24; 26; 27; 29; 34; 38; 39; 32:12; 34:13; 29; 33; 35:6; 7; 36:23; 29; 37:13(2); 38:5; 6; 8; 16; 17; 21; 22; 25; 28; 31; 32; 36; 37; 39; 39:1; 2; 5; 9; 10; 11; 13; 15; 40:9; 41:1; 2; 5; 7; 13; 20; **Ps** 18:31; 24:3; 32:9; 35:14; 44:20; 50:8; 13; 16; 66:t; 67:t; 68:t, 69:31; 75:t; 76:t; 83:t; 87:t, 88:t, 11; 89:8; 90:2; 92:t, 94:16; 108:t, 120:3; 131:1; 132:4; 139:7; 144:3; **Prov** 6:7; 7:22; 8:8; 23; 20:20; 22:26; 23:34; 28:24; 29:9; 30:4; 9; 32; **Eccl** 2:19; 25; 5:12; 9:1; 11:3; 6(2); 12:2(3); 6(4); 14; **Song** 2:9; 17; 6:12; 8:14; **Is** 1:11(2); 7:11; 10:14(2); 15(2); 17:6(2); 8; 19:15(2); 27:5; 7; 29:8; 16; 30:14; 38:14; 40:13; 18; 25; 41:22; 23; 42:19; 43:9; 44:10; 45:9; 10; 49:24; 50:1; 2; 57:11; 66:8; **Jer** 2:18; 32; 7:22; 11:14; 19; 13:23; 14:22; 15:5(2); 16:2; 7; 10(2); 18:14; 20:17; 21:13; 22:18(2); 23:33(2); 32:43; 34:9; 36:23; 37:18(2); 40:5; 42:6; 17; 44:14; 28; 48:24; **Eze** 2:5; 7; 3:11; 4:14; 14:7; 17; 19; 15:2; 3; 17:9; 15; 21:16(2); 22:14; 34:6; 44:22; 25(4); 31(2); 46:12; **Dan** 2:10(2); 4:19; 35; 6:4; 7; 12; 24; 11:29; **Joel** 1:2; **Amos** 3:12; 4:8; 5:19; 6:2; **Mic** 6:7; **Hag** 2:12(4); **Zec** 8:10; **Mal** 1:8; 2:13; 17; **Mt** 5:17; 18; 36; 6:24; 25; 31(2); 7:4; 9; 10; 16; 9:5; 10:11; 14; 19; 37(2); 11:3; 12:5; 25; 29; 33; 13:21; 15:4; 5; 6; 16:14; 26; 17:25(2); 18:8(3); 16(2); 20; 19:29(7); 21:25; 22:17; 23:17; 19; 24:23; 25:37; 38; 39(2); 44(5); 27:17; **Mk** 2:9; 3:4(2); 33; 4:17; 21; 30; 6:15; 56(2); 7:10; 11; 12; 8:37; 10:29(7); 11:30; 12:14; 15; 13:21; 35(3); **Lk** 2:24; 3:15; 5:23; 6:9(2); 7:19; 20; 8:16; 9:25; 11:11; 12; 12:11(2); 14; 29; 38; 41; 13:4; 15; 14:5; 12; 31; 32; 16:13; 17:7; 21; 23; 18:11; 29(4); 20:2; 4; 22; 22:27; **Jn** 2:6; 4:27; 6:19; 7:17; 48; 9:2; 21; 25; 13:29; 14:11; 18:34; **Acts** 1:7; 3:12(2); 4:7; 34; 5:38; 7:49; 8:34; 9:2; 10:14; 28(2); 11:8; 17:21; 29(2); 18:14; 19:12; 20:33(2); 23:9; 15; 29; 24:20; 23; 25:11; 26:31; 28:6; 17; 21; **Rom** 2:4; 15; 3:1; 4:9; 10; 13; 6:16; 8:35(6); 9:11; 10:7; 11:34; 35; 12:7(2); 8; 14:4; 8; 10; 13; 21(2); **1Cor** 1:13; 2:1; 3:22(7); 4:3; 21; 5:10(3); 11(5); 7:11; 15; 16; 8:5; 9:6; 7; 8; 10; 10:19; 31(2); 11:4; 5; 6; 22; 12:13(2); 26; 13:1; 14:6(3); 7(2); 23; 24; 27; 29; 36; 37; 15:11; 37; **2Cor** 1:6; 13; 17; 3:1(2); 5:9; 10; 13; 6:15; 8:23; 9:7; 10:12; 11:4(2); 12:2; 3; 6; 13:1; **Gal** 1:8; 10(2); 2:2; 3:2; 5; 15; 4:9; **Eph** 3:20; 5:3; 27(2); 6:8; **Phil** 1:18; 20; 27; 2:3; **Col** 1:16(3); 20; 2:16(4); 3:17; **1Th** 2:19(2); 5:10; **2Th** 2:2; 4; 15; **1Ti** 2:9(3); 5:4; 16; 19; **Titus** 1:6; 3:12; **Philem** 1:18; **Heb** 2:6; 10:28; 12:16; 20; **Jas** 2:3; 15; 4:13; 15; **1Pet** 1:11; 2:14; 3:3; 9; 4:15(3); **Rev** 2:5; 16; 3:15; 13:16; 17(3); 14:9; 20:4; 21:27

OTHER

251, 259, 269, 312, 317, 321, 428, 2063, 2088, 3541, 3671, 5048, 5676, 6311, 7453, 7605, 8145, *237, 240, 243, 244, 245, 492, 846, 1520, 1565, 2084, 2085, 2087, 2548, 3062, 3739, 4008*

Gen 4:19; 8:10; 12; 13:11; 20:16; 25:23; 28:17; 29:27; 30; 31:50; 32:8; 41:3(2); 19; 43:14; 22; 47:21; **Ex** 1:15; 4:7; 14:20; 17:12(2); 18:4; 7; 20:3; 23:13; 25:12; 19(2); 32; 33; 26:3; 13; 27; 27:15; 28:10(2); 25; 27(2); 29:19; 39; 41; 30:32; 32:15; 34:14; 36:10; 25; 32; 33; 37:3; 8; 18; 38:15; 39:20(2); **Lev** 5:7; 6:11; 7:24; 8:22; 11:23; 12:8; 13:26; 14:22; 31; 42(2); 15:15; 30; 16:8; 18:18; 20:24; 26; 25:53; **Num** 6:11; 8:12; 10:21; 11:26; 31; 21:13; 24:1; 28:4; 8; 32:38; 36:3; **Deut** 4:32; 5:7; 6:14; 7:4; 8:19; 11:16; 28; 30; 13:2; 6; 7; 13; 17:3; 18:20; 28:14; 36; 64(2); 29:26; 30:17; 31:18; 20; **Josh** 2:10; 7:7; 8:22; 11:19; 12:1; 13:27; 32; 14:3; 17:5; 20:8; 21:27; 22:4; 7; 23:16; 24:2(2); 3; 8; 14; 15; 16; **Judg** 2:12; 17; 19; 7:7; 25; 9:44; 10:8; 13; 11:18; 13:10; 16:17; 20; 29; 20:30; 31(2); **Ruth** 1:4; 2:22; **1Sa** 1:2; 3:10; 8:8; 14:1; 4(2); 5; 40; 17:3; 18:10; 19:21; 20:25; 21:9; 26:13; 19; 28:8; 30:20; 31:7(2); **2Sa** 1:24; 2:13(2); 4:2; 12:1; 13:16; 14:6; 17:9; 24:22; **1Kin** 3:22; 23; 25; 26; 6:24(2); 25; 26; 27(2); 34; 7:6; 7; 16; 17; 18; 20; 23; 9:6; 9; 10:20; 11:4; 10; 12:29; 14:9; 18:23; 20:29; **2Kin** 3:22; 5:17; 12:7; 17:7; 35; 37; 38; 22:17; **1Chr** 6:78; 9:32; 12:37; 23:17; **2Chr** 3:11(2); 12(3); 17; 7:19; 22; 9:19; 13:9; 20:1; 25:12; 28:25; 29:34; 30:23(2); 32:13; 17; 22; 34:12; 25; 35:13; **Ezr** 1:10; 2:31; **Neh** 3:11; 20; 4:16; 17; 5:5; 7:33; 34; 11:1; 12:38; **Est** 2:12; 9:16; **Job** 8:12; 24:24; **Ps** 73:5(2); 85:10; **Eccl** 3:19; 6:5; 7:14; **Is** 26:13; 49:20; **Jer** 1:16; 7:6; 9; 18; 11:10; 12:12; 13:10; 16:11; 13; 19:4; 13; 22:9; 24:2; 25:6; 33; 32:20; 29; 35:15; 36:16; 44:3; 5; 8; 15; **Eze** 1:23; 16:34; 21:16; 40:6; 40; 41:1; 2; 15; 19; 21; 24; 26; 42:14; 44:19; 45:7; 47:7; 48:8; 21; **Dan** 2:11; 44; 3:21; 29; 7:20; 8:3; 12:5(2); **Hos** 3:1; 9:1; 13:10; **Obad** 11; **Zec** 4:3; 11:7; 14; **Mt** 4:21; 5:39; 6:24(2); 8:18; 28; 12:13; 45; 13:8; 14:22; 16:5; 20:21; 21:36; 41; 22:4; 23:23; 24:31; 40; 41; 25:11; 16; 17; 20; 22; 27:61; 28:1; **Mk** 3:5; 4:8; 19; 35; 36; 5:1; 21; 6:45; 7:4; 8; 8:13; 10:37; 12:31; 32; 15:27; 41; **Lk** 3:18; 4:43; 5:7; 6:10; 29; 7:41; 8:8; 22; 10:1; 31; 32; 11:26; 42; 14:32; 16:13(2); 17:24; 34; 35; 36; 18:10; 11; 14; 22:65; 23:33; 40; 24:10; **Jn** 4:38; 6:22(2); 23; 25; 10:1; 16; 15:24; 18:16; 19:32; 20:2; 3; 4; 8; 12; 25; 30; 21:2; 8; 25; **Acts** 2:4; 40; 4:12(2); 5:29; 8:34; 15:2; 39; 17:9; 18; 19:39; 23:6; 26:22; 27:1; **Rom** 1:13; 8:39; 13:9; **1Cor** 1:16; 3:11; 7:5; 8:4; 9:5; 10:29; 11:21; 14:17; 21(2); 29; 15:37; **2Cor** 1:13; 2:16; 8:13; 10:15; 11:8; 12:13; 13:2; **Gal** 1:8; 9; 19; 2:13; 4:22; 5:17; **Eph** 3:5; 4:17; **Phil** 1:13; 17; 2:3; 3:4; 4:3; **2Th** 1:3; **1Ti** 1:3; 10; 5:22; **Jas** 5:12; **1Pet** 4:15; **2Pet** 3:16; **Rev** 2:24; 8:13; 17:10

OTHERS

312, 428, 243, 245, 2087, 3062, 3588, 3739

Job 8:19; 31:10; 34:24; 26; **Ps** 49:10; **Prov** 5:9; **Eccl** 7:22; **Is** 56:8; **Jer** 6:12; 8:10; **Eze** 9:5; 13:6; 10; **Dan** 7:19; 11:4; **Mt** 5:47; 15:30; 16:14; 20:3; 6; 21:8; 26:67; 27:42; **Mk** 6:15(2); 8:28; 11:8; 12:5; 9; 15:31; **Lk** 5:29; 8:3; 10; 9:8; 19; 11:16; 18:9; 20:16; 23:32; 35; 24:1; **Jn** 7:12; 41; 9:9; 16; 10:21; 12:29; 18:34; 19:18; **Acts** 2:13; 15:35; 17:32; 34; 28:9; **1Cor** 9:2; 12; 27; 14:19; **2Cor** 3:1; 8:8; **Eph** 2:3; **Phil** 2:4; **1Th** 2:6; 4:13; 5:6; **1Ti** 5:20; **2Ti** 2:2; **Heb** 9:25; 11:35; 36; **Jude** 23

OTHERWISE

176, 3808, 243, 247, 1490, 1893, 2085, 2088

2Sa 18:13; **1Kin** 1:21; **2Chr** 30:18; **Ps** 38:16; **Mt** 6:1; **Lk** 5:36; **Rom** 11:6(2); 22; **2Cor** 11:16; **Gal** 5:10; **Phil** 3:15; **1Ti** 5:25; 6:3; **Heb** 9:17

OUGHT

1697, 3972, 4465, 1163, 3762, 3784, 5100, 5534

Gen 20:9; 34:7; 39:6; 47:18; **Ex** 5:8; 11; 19; 12:46; 22:14; 29:34; **Lev** 4:2; 27; 11:25; 19:6; 25:14(2); 27:31; **Num** 15:24; 30; 30:6; **Deut** 4:2; 15:2; 26:14(2); **Josh** 21:45; **Ruth** 1:17; **1Sa** 12:4; 5; 25:7; 30:22; **2Sa** 3:35; 13:12; 14:10; 19; **1Chr** 12:32; 15:2; **2Chr** 13:5; **Neh** 5:9; **Ps** 76:11; **Mt** 5:23; 21:3; 23:23; **Mk** 7:12; 8:23; 11:25; 13:14; **Lk** 11:42; 12:12; 13:14; 16; 18:1; 24:26; **Jn** 4:20; 33; 13:14; 19:7; **Acts** 4:32; 5:29; 17:29; 19:36; 20:35; 21:21; 24:19(2); 25:10; 24; 26:9; 28:19; **Rom** 8:26; 12:3; 15:1; **1Cor** 8:2; 11:7; 10; **2Cor** 2:3; 7; 12:11; 14; **Eph** 5:28; 6:20; **Col** 4:4; 6; **1Th** 4:1; **2Th** 3:7; **1Ti** 5:13; **Titus** 1:11; **Philem** 1:18; **Heb** 2:1; 5:3; 12; **Jas** 3:10; 4:15; **2Pet** 3:11; **1Jn** 2:6; 3:16; 4:11; **3Jn** 8

OUR

2257

Gen 1:26(2); 5:29(2); 19:31; 32(2); 34; 23:6; 24:60; 29:26; 31:1(2); 14; 15; 16(2); 32; 33:12; 34:9; 14; 16; 17; 21; 31; 37:26; 27(3); 41:12; 42:13; 21; 32(2); 43:4; 7(2); 8; 18(2); 21(3); 22(3); 28; 44:8; 25; 26(2); 31; 46:34(2); 47:3; 18(4); 19(3); 25; **Ex** 1:10; 3:18; 5:3; 8; 21; 8:10; 26; 27; 10:9(6); 25; 26(2); 12:27; 17:3(2); 34:9(2); **Lev** 25:20; **Num** 11:6(2); 13:33; 14:3(2); 20:3; 4; 15(2); 16; 21:5; 27:3; 4(2); 31:49; 50; 32:16(2); 17; 18; 19; 26(4); 32; 36:2; 3(2); 4; **Deut** 1:6; 19; 20; 25; 28(2); 41; 2:1; 8; 29; 33; 36; 37; 3:3(2); 4:7; 5:2; 3; 24; 25; 27(2); 6:4; 20; 22; 23; 24(2); 25(2); 21:7(2); 20(2); 26:3; 7(5); 15; 29:15; 18; 29(2); 31:17; 32:3; 27; 31(2); **Josh** 2:11; 13; 14(2); 19; 20; 24; 5:13; 7:9; 9:11(2); 12(3); 13(2); 24; 17:4; 18:6; 21:2; 22:19; 24; 25; 27(5); 28(2); 29; 24:17(3); 18; 24; **Judg** 6:13; 9:3; 10:10; 11:2; 6; 8; 24; 13:23; 16:23(3); 24(4); 18:5; 19:19; 21:7; 18; 22; **Ruth** 2:20; 3:2; 4:3; **1Sa** 2:2; 4:3; 5:7; 10; 11; 7:8; 8:20(2); 9:6; 7; 8; 12:10; 19; 14:9; 10; 16:16; 17:9; 47; 20:29; 23:20; 25:14; 17; 30:23; **2Sa** 7:22; 10:12(2); 12:18; 18:12; 19:9; 41; 43(2); 22:32; **1Kin** 1:11; 43; 47; 8:21; 40; 53; 57(2); 58(2); 59; 61; 65; 12:4; 10; 20:31(2); **2Kin** 7:9; 18:22; 19:19; 22:13; **1Chr** 12:17; 19; 13:2(2); 3; 15:13; 16:14; 35; 17:20; 19:13(2); 28:2; 8; 29:10; 13; 15(2); 16; 18; **2Chr** 2:4; 5; 6:31; 10:4; 10; 13:10; 11; 12; 14:7; 11(2); 19:7; 20:6; 7; 9; 12(2); 28:13(3); 29:6(2); 9(4); 32:8(2); 11; 34:21; **Ezr** 4:3; 5:12; 7:27; 8:17; 18; 21(3); 22; 23; 25; 30; 31; 33; 9:6(3); 7(4); 8(4); 9(3); 10; 13(4); 15; 10:2; 3(2); 14(3); **Neh** 4:4; 9(2); 11; 15; 20; 2:5; 3(2); 4; 5(8); 8(2); 9(2); 16:2(2); 8:10; 9:9; 16; 32(6); 34(4); 36; 37(3); 38; 10:29; 30(2); 32; 33; 34(3); 35; 36(6); 37(5); 38; 39; 13:2; 4; 18; 27; **Job** 8:9; 17:16; 22:20; 28:22; 37:19; **Ps** 8:1; 9; 12:4(3); 17:11; 18:31; 20:5(2); 7; 22:4; 33:20(3); 21; 35:21; 40:3; 44:1(2); 5; 7; 9; 13; 18(2); 20(2); 24(2); 25(2); 46:1; 7; 11; 47:3; 4; 6; 48:1; 8; 14(2); 50:3; 59:11; 60:10; 12; 65:3; 5; 66:8; 9(2); 11; 12; 67:6; 68:19; 20; 74:9; 77:13; 78:3; 5; 79:4; 9(2); 10; 12; 80:6(2); 81:1; 3; 84:9; 85:4; 9; 12; 89:17(4); 18; 90:1; 8(2); 9(2); 10; 12(2); 14; 17(3); 92:13; 94:23; 95:1; 6; 7; 98:3; 99:5; 8; 9(2); 103:10(2); 12; 14; 105:7; 106:6; 7; 47; 108:11; 13; 113:5; 115:3; 116:5; 118:23; 122:2; 9; 123:2(2); 4; 124:1; 2; 4; 5; 7; 8; 126:2(2); 4; 135:2; 5; 136:23; 24; 137:2; 141:7; 144:12(2); 13(3); 14(2); 147:1; 5; 7; **Prov** 1:13; 7:18; **Song** 1:16; 17(2); 2:9; 12; 15; 7:13; 8:8; **Is** 1:10; 3:6; 4:1(3); 20:6; 25:9; 26:8; 12; 13; 28:15; 33:2; 20; 22(3); 35:2; 36:7; 37:20; 38:20; 40:3; 8; 42:17; 47:4; 52:10; 53:1; 3; 4(2); 5(3); 55:7; 58:3; 59:12(4); 13; 61:2; 6; 63:16(3); 17; 18; 64:6(2); 7; 8(2); 11(4); **Jer** 3:22; 23; 24(2); 25(6); 5:19; 24; 6:24; 8:14; 9:18(2); 19; 21(2); 11:21; 12:4; 14:7(2); 20:2(2); 22; 16:10(3); 19; 17:12; 18:12; 20:10; 21:13; 23:6; 36; 26:16; 19; 31:6; 33:16; 35:6; 8(5); 10; 36:15; 37:3; 42:2; 6(2); 20(2); 43:2; 44:17(4); 19; 25; 46:16(2); 50:28; 51:10(2); 51; **Lam** 3:40; 41(2); 44; 46; 4:17(3); 18(5); 19; 20; 5:1; 2(2); 3; 4(2); 5; 7; 9(2); 15(2); 16; 17(2)(2); 21; **Eze** 33:10(2); 21; 37:11(3); 40:1; **Dan** 1:13; 3:17; 9:6(3); 8(3); 9; 10; 12; 13(3); 14; 15; 16(2); 17; 18(3); **Hos** 7:5; 14:2; 3(2); **Joel** 1:16(2); **Amos** 6:13; **Mic** 2:4; 4:5; 11; 5:5(2); 6(2); 7:17; 19; 20; **Zec** 1:6(2); 9:7; **Mal** 2:10; **Mt** 3:9; 6:9; 11; 12(2); 8:17(2); 20:33; 21:42; 23:30; 25:8; 27:25; **Mk** 9:40; 11:10; 12:11; 29; **Lk** 1:55; 71; 72; 73; 74; 75; 78; 79; 3:8; 7:5; 11:2; 3; 4; 13:26; 17:5; 10; 23:41; 24:20; 22; 32; **Jn** 3:11; 4:12; 20; 6:31; 7:51; 8:39; 53; 9:20; 11:11; 48; 12:38; 14:23; 19:7; **Acts** 2:8; 11; 39; 3:12; 13; 25; 5:30; 7:2; 11; 12; 15; 19(2); 38; 39; 44; 45(2); 13:17; 14:17; 15:10; 25; 26; 36; 16:20; 17:20; 28; 19:25; 27; 20:21; 21:5(2); 6; 7; 15; 22:14; 24:6; 7; 26:5; 6; 7; 27:10; 19; 28:17; 25; **Rom** 1:3; 7; 3:5; 4:1; 12; 24; 25(2); 5:1; 5; 11; 21; 6:6; 11; 23; 7:5; 25; 8:16; 23; 26; 39; 9:10; 10:16; 12:7; 13:11; 15:4; 6; 16:1; 9; 18; 20; 24; **1Cor** 1:1; 2; 3; 7; 8; 9; 10; 2:7; 4:12; 5:4(2); 7; 6:11; 9:1; 10(2); 10:1; 6; 11; 12:23; 24; 15:3; 14; 31; 57; 16:12; 23; **2Cor** 1:1; 2; 3; 4; 5; 7; 8; 11; 12(3); 18; 22; 3:2(2); 5; 4:3; 6; 10; 11; 16; 17; 5:1; 2; 12; 6:11(2); 7:3; 4; 5; 12; 14; 8:9; 22; 23; 24; 9:3; 10:4; 8; 13; 14; 15(2); 16; 11:31; **Gal** 1:3; 4(2); 2:4; 3:24; 6:14; 18; **Eph** 1:2; 3; 14; 17; 2:3(2); 14; 3:11; 14; 5:20; 6:22; 24; **Phil** 1:2; 3:20; 21; 4:20; 23; **Col** 1:1; 2; 3; 7; 3:4; **1Th** 1:1; 2; 3(2); 5; 2; 1; 2; 3(2); 5:9; 23; 28; **2Th** 1:1; 2; 8; 10; 11; 12(2); 2:1(2); 14(2); 15; 16(2); 3:6; 12; 14; 18; **1Ti** 1:1(2); 2(2); 12; 14; 2:3; 6:3; 14; **2Ti** 1:2; 8; 9; 10; 4:15; **Titus** 1:3; 4; 2:10; 13; 3:4; 6; **Philem** 1:1(2); 2(2); 3; 25; **Heb** 1:3; 3:1; 14; 4:14; 15; 7:14; 10:22(2); 23; 12:2; 9; 10; 29; 13:15; 20; 23; **Jas** 2:1; 21; 3:6; **1Pet** 1:3; 2:24; 4:3; **2Pet** 1:1; 2; 8; 11; 14; 16; 3:15(2); 18; **1Jn** 1:1(2); 3; 9(2); 2:2; 3:5; 16; 19; 20(2); 21; 4:10; 17; 5:4; **2Jn** 12; **3Jn** 12; 14; **Jude** 4(2); 17; 21; 25; **Rev** 1:5; 5:10; 6:10; 7:3; 10; 12; 11:8; 15; 12:10(3); 19:1; 5; 22:21

OURS

2251, 2257

Gen 26:20; 31:16; 34:23; **Num** 32:32; **1Kin** 22:3; **Eze** 36:2; **Mk** 12:7; **Lk** 20:14; **1Cor** 1:2; **2Cor** 1:14; **Titus** 3:14; **1Jn** 2:2

OURSELVES

587, 846, 1438, 2249

Gen 37:10; 44:16; **Num** 32:17; **Deut** 2:35; 3:7; **1Sa** 14:8; **1Chr** 19:13; **Ezr** 4:3; 8:21; **Neh** 10:32; **Job** 34:4; **Ps** 83:12; 100:3; **Prov** 7:18; **Is** 28:15; 56:12; **Jer** 50:5; **Lk** 22:71; **Jn** 4:42; **Acts** 6:4; 23:14; **Rom** 8:23(3); 15:1; **1Cor** 11:31; **2Cor** 1:4; 9(2); 3:1; 5(2); 4:2; 5(2); 5:12; 13; 6:4; 7:1; 10:12(2); 14; 12:19; **Gal** 2:17; **1Th** 2:10; **2Th** 1:4; 3:7; 9; **Titus** 3:3; **Heb** 10:25; **1Jn** 1:8

OUT

4480, 1537

Gen 2:9; 10; 19; 23; 3:19; 24; 4:14; 16; 8:10; 19; 9:10; 10:11; 14; 12:1; 4; 13:1; 14:8; 17; 15:4; 7; 14; 17:6; 19:5; 6; 8; 12; 14(2); 24; 29; 30; 21:10; 17; 21; 22:11; 15; 23:4; 24:11; 13; 15; 29; 44; 63; 25:25; 26; 26:8; 27:3; 30; 28:10; 16; 29:2; 30:16(2); 31:13; 33; 32:25; 34:1; 6; 7; 24(2); 26(2); 35:9; 11; 37:14; 21; 22; 23; 28; 38:28(2); 29; 30; 39:12; 15; 18; 40:14; 15; 17; 41:2; 3; 14; 18; 33; 45; 46; 43:2; 23; 31; 44:4; 8(2); 16; 28; 45:1; 19; 24; 25; 46:26; 47:1; 10; 30; 48:12; 14; 22; 49:20; 50:24; **Ex** 1:5; 10(2); 2:10; 11; 13; 19; 3:2; 4; 8(2); 10; 11; 12; 17; 20; 4:6; 7; 9; 5:10; 6:1; 6(3); 7; 11; 13; 26; 27; 7:4; 5; 19; 8:6; 12; 13(3); 16; 17; 29; 30; 9:15; 29; 33; 10:5; 6; 11; 12; 18; 21; 11:1; 4; 8(3); 10; 12:5; 15; 17; 21; 22(2); 33(4); 39(2); 41; 42; 46; 51; 13:3(3); 4; 8; 9; 14; 16; 18; 14:8; 10; 11; 16; 21; 26; 30; 15:4; 8; 10; 20; 22; 16:1; 4; 6; 27; 29; 17:3; 6; 9(2); 14; 18:1; 7; 9; 10(2); 21; 25; 19:1; 3; 17; 20:2(2); 21:2; 3(2); 4; 5; 7; 11; 27; 22:6; 7; 23:13; 15; 16; 28; 29; 30; 31; 24:16; 25:32(3); 33; 35; 28:5; 29:23; 46; 32:1(2); 4; 7; 8(2); 11; 12; 19; 23; 24; 34(2); 37:7; 8; 9; 18(3); 19; **Lev** 1:1; 15; 2:14; 4:12(2); 18; 25; 30; 34; 5:9; 15; 18; 6:6; 12; 13; 7:14; 35; 8:26; 33; 9:9; 23; 24; 10:2; 4; 5; 7; 14; 11:45; 13:12; 20; 25; 56(4); 14:3; 8; 38; 41; 43; 45; 53; 15:2; 16; 25; 16:17; 18; 17:3; 13; 18:24; 25; 28(2); 19:36; 20:22; 23; 21:12; 22:33; 23:17; 43; 24:10; 23; 25:12; 28; 30; 31; 33; 38; 42; 51; 54; 55; 26:6; 13; 33; 45; 27:21; **Num** 1:1; 3:9; 5:2; 3; 4; 23; 25; 6:19; 9:1; 10:12; 33; 34; 11:15; 20(2); 24; 26; 12:4(2); 12; 14; 15; 13:16; 17; 14:44; 15:41; 16:13; 14; 27; 35; 37; 46; 17:9; 18:29(2); 20:5; 8; 10; 11; 16; 18; 20; 21:5; 13; 23; 26; 28; 32(2); 33; 22:5; 6; 11(2); 23; 32; 36; 23:7; 22; 24:7; 8; 17; 22; 26:4(2); 57; 29:4; 31:18; 20; **Deut** 1:22; 24; 27; 33; 44; 2:14; 23; 26; 32; 3:1; 8; 4:12; 15; 20(2); 33; 34; 36(2); 37(2); 38; 45; 46; 5:4; 6; 15(2); 20(2); 24; 26; 6:12(2); 12; 14; 15; 13:16; 17; 14:44; 15:41; 16:13; 14; 27; 35; 37; 46; 17:9; 18:29(2); 20:5; 8; 10; 11; 16; 18; 20; 21:5; 13; 23; 26; 28; 32(2); 33; 22:5; 6; 11(2); 23; 32; 36; 23:7; 22; 24:7; 8; 17; 22; 26:4(2); 57; 29:4; 31:18; 20; **Eccl** 1:13; 3:11; 4:14; 7:24; 25; 27; 8:12; 12:3; 9; 10; **Song** 3:6; 4:16; 8:11; **Is** 2:3; 5:2; 25; 8:8; 9:12; 17; 21; 10:4; 11:1(2); 16; 12:3; 9; 13; 14:19; 26; 27; 29; 15:4; 5; 16:2; 4; 8; 10(2); 18:2; 7; 19:23; 21:11; 22:16(2); 23:11; 24:18; 26:16; 17; 19; 21; 28:7(2); 27; 29:4(4); 9; 10; 18(2); 30:11(2); 13; 14; 31:3; 34:3(2); 11; 16; 35:6; 36:16; 18; 19; 20(2); 37:28; 32(2); 38:6; 40:12; 22(2); 26; 42:5(2); 7(2); 43:13; 25; 44:13(3);

22; 45:12; 23; 46:6; 7; 48:1; 3; 21(2); 51:17; 22; 52:11(2); 12; 53:2; 8; 12; 55:11; 12; 57:4; 14; 58:7; 10; 59:5; 21(3); 62:10; 12; 63:11; 65:2; 9(2); 66:5; 11; 20; Jer 1:5; 10; 14; 2:6; 13; 3:18; 4:1; 16; 5:6(2); 6:1(2); 4; 7(2); 11; 12; 7:15(2); 18; 20; 22; 25; 8:1(2); 9:8; 18; 19(2); 10:3; 12; 13; 17; 18; 22; 25; 11:4; 7; 12:3; 8; 14(2); 15; 14:16; 15:1; 6; 21(2); 16:9; 13; 14; 16; 17:8; 16; 19; 22; 18:21; 23; 19:13; 20:3; 8; 18; 21:9; 12(2); 22:3; 11; 14; 26; 28; 23:3; 7; 8; 16; 39; 24:5; 26:23; 27:10; 15; 30:7; 19; 31:32; 37; 32:4; 17; 21(2); 29; 37; 34:3; 13(2); 36:6; 11; 21; 30; 37:4; 5; 12; 17; 21; 38:8; 10; 13; 18; 23(2); 39:4(2); 7; 14; 40:12; 44:7; 17(2); 18; 19(2); 25; 28; 46:20; 47:2; 48:15; 31; 44; 45; 49:5; 20; 50:3; 8(2); 28; 45; 51:6; 15; 16; 25; 34; 44; 45; 55; 52:3; 7; 11; 25; 27; 31; Lam 1:10; 2:4; 8; 12; 19(2); 3:7; 8; 38; 55; 4:1; 3; 11; 5:8; Eze 1:4(3); 5; 13; 3:25; 4:12; 5:2; 12; 6:14; 7:8; 9:8; 10:7; 19; 11:7; 9; 17; 19; 12:5; 12; 14; 13:2; 17; 21; 23; 14:9; 13; 19; 15:7; 16:5; 15; 27; 36; 19:14; 20:8; 9; 10; 13; 14; 21; 28; 33(2); 34(4); 38(2); 41(2); 21:3; 4; 5; 19; 31; 22:15; 22; 31; 23:26; 34; 48; 24:6(2); 12; 25:7(2); 13; 16; 27:6; 33; 28:16; 29:4; 8; 30:13; 22; 25; 31:4; 11; 32:3; 7; 21; 33:21; 34:11; 12(3); 13; 25; 27; 35:3; 7; 11; 36:5; 20; 24; 26; 37:1; 12; 13; 23; 38:8(2); 12; 15; 39:3(2); 10(2); 14; 27; 29; 42:11; 14; 43:6; 11; 23; 25; 44:3; 45:14; 15(3); 46:9; 18(2); 20; 47:1; 2(2); 8; 12; 48:19; 30; Dan 2:34; 45; 3:15; 17; 5:2; 3; 13; 6:23(2); 7:17; 24; 25; 8:4; 7; 9; 22; 9:15; 11:7; 41; 44(2); Hos 1:11; 2:2; 10; 15; 17; 18; 4:2; 5:10; 7:5; 9:15; 10:11; 11:1; 11(2); 12:8; 13; 13:3(2); Joel 2:16; 28; 29; 3:7; 16; Amos 3:4; 12(2); 4:3; 11; 5:3; 6; 8; 6:4(2); 10(2); 7:11; 8:8; 9:3; 6; 7; 15; Obad 6; 8(2); Jonah 1:4; 2:1; 2; 4; 10; 4:5; Mic 1:3; 2:9; 13; 4:6; 9; 10; 5:2; 10; 12; 13; 14; 6:4(2); 7:2; 15; 17; Nah 1:6; 11; 14; 2:2; 9; Hab 1:2; 2:11(2); 3:4; 13; 14; Zeph 1:4; 17; 2:4; 13; 3:11; 15; 19; Hag 2:5; 16(2); Zec 1:21; 2:3; 13; 3:2; 4:1; 12; 5:9; 6:1; 12; 8:10; 23; 9:4; 7; 11; 10:4(4); 10(2); 11:6; 13:2(2); 14:8; Mal 2:8; 12; 13; 3:10; Mt 2:6; 15; 3:5; 16; 4:4; 5:13; 26; 29; 7:4(2); 5(4); 22; 8:12; 16; 28; 29; 31; 32; 34(2); 9:17; 32; 33; 34; 10:1; 8; 14; 11:7; 8; 9; 12:11; 14; 24; 26; 27(2); 28; 34; 35(2); 43; 44; 13:1; 41; 52; 14:13; 26; 29; 35; 15:11; 17; 18; 19; 22; 17:5; 18; 19; 21; 18:9; 28; 20:1; 3; 5; 6; 30; 21:12; 16; 17; 33; 39; 41; 22:10; 16; 24:1; 17; 27; 25:6; 8; 26:30; 51; 55; 71; 75; 27:23; 32; 53; 60; Mk 1:5; 10; 23; 25; 26; 29; 34; 35; 39; 45; 3:5; 15; 21; 22; 23; 4:3; 32; 5:2(2); 8; 10; 13; 14; 17; 30; 40; 6:1; 12; 13; 33; 34; 49; 54; 7:15; 19; 20; 21; 26; 29; 30; 8:23; 27; 9:7; 18; 24; 25; 26; 28; 38; 47; 10:26; 46; 47; 11:11; 15; 19; 12:1; 8; 13:1; 15; 14:26; 48; 68; 15:13; 14; 20; 21; 39; 46; 16:8; 9; 17; Lk 1:22; 42; 74; 2:1; 4; 4:14; 22; 29; 33; 35(2); 36; 37; 38; 41(2); 5:2; 3(2); 4; 17; 36; 6:12; 17; 19; 22; 42(4); 45(2); 7:12; 24; 25; 26; 8:2; 4; 5; 12; 27; 28; 29; 31; 33; 35(2); 38; 46; 54; 9:5; 35; 38; 39; 40; 49; 10:10; 35; 11:14(2); 15; 18; 19(2); 20; 24(2); 54; 12:54; 13:28; 31; 32; 33; 14:5; 7; 21; 23; 35; 15:28; 16:4; 17:24; 29; 19:22; 40; 45; 20:12; 15; 21:21; 37; 22:39; 52; 62; 23:18; 26; 24:31; 50; Jn 1:46; 2:8; 15(2); 4:30; 47; 54; 6:37; 7:38; 41; 42; 52; 8:9; 59; 9:22; 34; 35; 10:3; 9; 28; 29; 39; 11:11; 31; 55; 12:17; 31; 34; 42; 13:1; 30; 31; 15:19; 16:2; 27; 17:6; 8; 15; 18:16; 29; 38; 19:6; 12; 15; 34; 20:2; Acts 1:9; 18; 21; 2:5; 17; 18; 3:19; 4:15; 5:6; 9; 16; 6:3; 7:3; 4; 10; 12; 19; 21; 36; 40; 45; 57; 58; 8:7; 9; 39; 9:1; 28; 10:45; 12:9; 10; 11; 17; 13:17; 42; 50; 14:14; 19; 15:14; 24; 16:13; 18(2); 27(2); 30; 37(2); 39(2); 40; 17:2; 5; 19:12; 16; 28; 33; 34; 21:5; 28; 30; 38; 22:18; 23; 23:6; 24:7; 27:19; 29; 30(2); 38; 42; 28:3; 21; 23(2); Rom 2:18; 3:12; 11:24; 26; 33; 13:11; 1Cor 5:7; 10; 9:9; 14:36; 15:8; 2Cor 1:8; 16; 2:4; 4:6; 6:17; 8:11; 12:2; 3; Gal 2:4; 4:15; 30; Eph 4:29; Phil 1:12; 2:12; Col 2:14(2); 3:8; 1Th 1:8; 2Th 2:7; 1Ti 1:5; 5:18; 6:7; 2Ti 1:17; 2:22; 26; 3:11; 4:2; 17; Heb 3:16; 5:2; 7:5; 14; 8:9; 11:8(2); 15; 34; 12:13; Jas 2:25; 3:10; 11; 1Pet 2:9; 2Pet 2:9; 3:5; 1Jn 2:19(2); 4:1; 18; 3Jn 10; Jude 5; 13; 23; Rev 1:16; 2:5; 3:5(2); 12(2); 16; 4:5; 5:7; 9; 6:4; 14; 7:14; 8:4; 9:2; 3; 17; 18; 10:10; 11:2; 5; 7; 12:9(3); 15; 16; 13:1; 11; 14:10; 15; 17; 18; 20; 15:6; 16:1(2); 2; 3; 4; 7; 8; 10; 12; 13(3); 17(2); 21; 17:8; 18:4; 19:5; 15; 21; 20:7; 8; 9; 12; 21:2; 3; 10; 22:1; 19(2)

OUTSIDE

2351, 7097, *1623, 1855*

Judg 7:11; 17; 19; 1Kin 7:9; Eze 40:5; Mt 23:25; 26; Lk 11:39

OVER

413, 1157, 1541, 1591, 1869, 2498, 3148, 4136, 4480, 4605, 5048, 5226, 5227, 5414, 5462, 5534, 5674, 5676, 5736, 5848, 5921, 5922, 5924, 5975, 5980, 6440, 6743, 6903, 7235, *481, 495, 561, 1224, 1276, 1277, 1330, 1537, 1608, 1722, 1883, 1909, 1924, 2596, 2634, 2713, 3346, 3860, 3928, 4008, 4012, 4052, 4121, 4291, 5055, 5228, 5231, 5240*

Gen 1:18(2); 26(5); 28(3); 3:16; 4:7; 8:1; 9:14; 21:16(2); 24:2; 25:25; 27:29; 31:21; 52(2); 32:10; 16; 21; 22; 23(2); 31; 33:3; 14; 36:31; 37:8(2); 39:4; 5; 41:33; 34; 40; 41; 43; 45; 56; 42:6; 45:26; 47:6; 20; 26; 49:22; Ex 1:8; 11; 2:14; 5:14; 8:5(3); 6; 9; 10:12; 13; 14; 21; 12:13; 23; 27; 14:2; 7; 16; 21; 26; 27; 15:16(2); 16:18; 23; 18:21; 25; 25:27; 37; 26:12; 13; 35; 28:27; 30:6; 36:14; 37:9; 14; 39:20; 40:19; 24; 36; Lev 14:5; 6; 50; 16:21; 25:43; 46(2); 53; 26:16; 17; Num 1:50(3); 3:32; 49; 4:6; 5:30; 7:2; 8:2; 3; 10:10(2); 14; 15; 16; 18; 19; 20; 22; 23; 24; 25; 26; 27; 11:16; 14:14; 16:13; 22:5; 25:15; 27:16; 31:14(2); 48; 32:5; 7; 21; 27; 29; 30; 32; 33:51; 35:10; Deut 1:1; 13; 15(5); 2:13(2); 14; 18; 19; 24; 29; 3:18; 25; 27; 28; 29; 4:14; 21; 22(2); 26; 46; 9:1; 3; 11:30; 31; 12:10; 15:6(2); 17:14; 15(3); 21:6; 24:20; 27:2; 3; 4; 12; 28:23; 36; 63(2); 30:9(2); 13; 18; 31:2; 3(2); 13; 15; 32:11; 47; 49; 34:1; 4; 6; Josh 1:2; 11; 2:23; 3:1; 6; 11; 14; 16; 17(2); 4:1; 3; 5; 7; 8; 10; 11(2); 12; 13; 18; 22; 23(2); 5:1; 13; 7:7; 26; 8:31; 33(2); 9:1; 18:13; 17; 18; 22:11; 19; 24:11; Judg 3:28; 5:13(2); 6:33; 8:4; 22; 23(3); 9:2(2); 8(2); 9; 10; 11; 12; 13; 14; 15; 18; 22; 26; 10:9; 18; 11:8; 11; 29(3); 32; 12:1; 3; 5; 14:4; 15:11; 19:10; 12; 20:43; Ruth 2:5; 6; 3:9; 1Sa 2:1; 8:1; 7; 9; 11; 12(2); 19; 9:16; 17; 10:1; 19; 11:12; 12:1; 12; 13; 14; 13:1; 7; 14; 14:1; 4; 5(2); 6; 8; 23; 47; 15:1(2); 7; 17; 26; 35; 16:1; 17:50; 18:5; 13; 19:20; 22:2; 9; 23:17; 25:30; 26:13; 22; 27:2; 30:10; 2Sa 1:17(2); 24; 2:4; 7; 8; 9(6); 10; 11; 15; 29; 3:10(2); 17; 21; 33; 34; 4:12; 5:2(2); 3; 5(2); 12; 17; 23; 6:21(2); 7:8(2); 11; 26; 8:15; 16; 18; 10:17; 12:7; 15:22(2); 23(3); 16:9; 13; 17:16; 19; 20; 21; 22(2); 24; 18:1; 8; 24; 33; 19:10; 15; 17; 18(3); 22; 31(2); 33; 36; 37; 38; 39(2); 41; 20:21; 23(3); 24; 22:30; 23:3; 23; 24:5; 1Kin 1:34; 35(2); 2:11; 35; 37; 4:1; 4; 5; 6(2); 7; 21; 24(2); 5:7; 14; 16(2); 6:1; 7:20; 39; 8:7; 16; 9:23(2); 11:24; 25; 28; 37; 42; 12:17; 18; 20; 13:30; 14:2; 7; 14; 15:1; 9; 25(2); 33; 16:2; 8; 16; 18; 23; 29(2); 19:15; 16; 20:29; 22:31; 41; 51(2); 2Kin 2:8; 9; 14; 3:1; 5:11; 8:13; 20; 21; 9:3; 6(2); 12; 29; 10:5(2); 22; 36; 11:3; 4; 9; 10; 18; 19; 13:1; 10; 14; 15:5; 8; 17; 23; 27; 17:1; 18:18; 37; 19:2; 21:13; 25:19; 22; 1Chr 1:43; 5:11; 6:31; 8:32; 9:19(2); 20; 26; 31; 32; 38; 11:2; 3; 25; 12:4; 14(2); 15; 38; 14:2; 8; 14; 15:25; 17:7; 10; 18:14; 15; 17; 19:17; 21:16; 22:10; 23:1; 24:31(2); 26:20(2); 22; 26(2); 29; 32; 27:2; 4; 16; 25(2); 26; 27(2); 28(2); 29(2); 30(2); 31; 28:1(3); 4(2); 5; 29:3; 12; 26; 27; 30(3); 2Chr 1:9; 11; 13; 2:11; 4:10; 5:8; 6:5; 6; 36; 8:10; 9:8; 26; 30; 10:17; 18; 13:1; 5; 19:11; 20:6; 27; 31; 22:12; 23:14; 25:5(2); 26:21; 31:12; 14; 32:6; 11; 34:13; 36:4; 10; Ezr 4:10; 20(2); 9:6; Neh 2:7; 3:10; 16; 19; 23; 25; 26; 27; 28; 29; 30; 31; 5:15; 7:2; 3; 9:28; 37(3); 11:9; 21; 22; 12:8; 9; 24(2); 37; 38; 44; 13:13; 26; Est 1:3; 12; 5:1(2); 8:2; 9:1(2); Job 6:5; 7:12; 14:16; 16:11; 26:7; 34:13; 41:34; 42:11; Ps 8:6; 12:4; 13:2; 18:29; 19:13; 23:5; 25:2; 27:12; 30:1; 35:19; 24; 38:4; 16; 41:11; 42:7; 47:2; 8; 49:14; 60:8; 65:13; 66:12; 68:34; 78:50; 62; 83:18; 88:16; 91:11; 103:16; 19; 104:9; 106:41; 108:9(2); 109:6; 110:6; 118:18; 119:133; 124:4; 5; 145:9; Prov 17:2; 19:10; 11; 20:26; 22:7; 24:31; 25:28; 28:15; Eccl 1:12; 2:19; 7:14; 16(2); 17; 8:8; 9; Song 2:4; 11; Is 3:4; 12; 8:7(2); 8; 10:29; 11:15(2); 14:2; 15:2(2); 16:8; 19:4(2); 16; 22:15; 23:2; 6; 11; 12; 25:7(2); 26:13; 28:19; 31:5; 9; 35:8; 36:3; 22; 37:2; 40:19; 27; 41:2; 45:14(2); 47:2; 51:10; 23(2); 52:5; 54:9; 62:5(2); 63:19; Jer 1:10(2); 2:10; 5:6; 22; 6:17; 13:21; 15:3; 23:4; 31:28(2); 39; 32:41; 33:26; 40:5; 11; 41:2; 10; 43:10; 44:27; 48:32; 40; 49:19; 22; 50:44; Lam 2:17; 3:54; 5:8; Eze 1:20; 21; 22; 25; 26; 3:13; 9:1; 10:1; 2; 4; 18; 19; 11:22; 16:8; 27; 19:8; 20:33; 27:32; 29:15; 32:3; 8; 31; 34:23; 37:24; 40:18; 23; 41:6; 15; 16; 42:1; 3(2); 7; 10(2); 45:6; 7; 46:9; 47:5(2); 20; 48:13; 15; 18(2); 21(3); Dan 1:11; 2:38; 39; 48(2); 49; 3:12; 4:16; 17; 23; 25; 32; 5:5; 21; 6:1(2); 2; 3; 9:1; 11:39; 40; 43(2); Hos 10:5; 11; 12:4; Joel 2:17; Obad 12; Jonah 2:3; 4:6(2); Mic 3:6(2); 4:7; Nah 3:19; Hab 1:11; 14; 2:19; Zeph 3:17(2); Hag 1:10; Zec 1:21; 5:3; 9:14; 14:9; Mt 2:9; 9:1; 10:23; 14:34; 20:25; 21:2; 24:45; 47; 25:21(2); 23(2); 27:37; 45; 61; Mk 4:35; 5:1; 21; 6:7; 53; 10:42(2); 11:2; 12:41; 13:3; 15:26; 33; 39; Lk 1:33; 2:8; 4:10; 39; 6:38; 8:22; 26; 9:1; 10:19; 11:42; 44; 12:14; 42; 44; 15:7(2); 10; 19:14; 17; 19; 27; 30; 41; 22:25; 23:38; 44; Jn 6:1; 13; 17; 17:2; 18:1; Acts 6:3; 7:10; 11; 16; 27; 8:2; 16:9; 18:23; 19:13; 20:2; 15; 28; 21:2; 27:5; 7(2); Rom 1:28; 5:14; 6:9; 14; 7:1; 9:5; 21; 10:12; 15:12; 1Cor 7:37; 9:12; 2Cor 1:24; 3:13; 8:15; 11:2; Eph 1:22; 4:19; Col 2:15; 1Th 3:7; 5:12; 1Ti 2:12; Heb 2:7; 3:6; 9:5; 10:21; 13:7; 17; 24; Jas 5:14; 1Pet 3:12; 5:3; Jude 7; Rev 2:26; 6:8; 9:11; 11:6; 10; 13:7; 14:18; 15:2(4); 16:9; 17:18; 18:11; 20

PART

2505, 2506, 2513, 2673, 2677, 4481, 4490, 5337, 6418, 6447, 6504, 6626, 7117, *2819, 3307, 3310, 3313, 3348, 4119, 4403*

Gen 41:34; 47:24; 26; Ex 16:36; 19:17; 29:26; 40(2); Lev 1:16; 2:6; 16(2); 5:11; 16; 6:5; 20; 7:33; 8:29; 11:35; 37; 38; 13:41; 22:14; 23:13; 27:13; 15; 16; 19; 27; 31; Num 5:7; 15; 15:4; 5; 6; 7; 18:20(2); 26; 29; 22:41; 23:10; 13; 28:5(2); 7; 14(2); Deut 10:9; 12:12; 14:27; 29; 18:1; 33:21; Josh 14:4; 15:1; 5; 13; 18:7; 19:9; 22:25; 27; Ruth 1:17; 2:3; 3:13(4); 1Sa 9:8; 14:2; 23:20; 30:24(3); 2Sa 14:6; 18:2(3); 20:1; 1Kin 6:24(2); 31; 33; 2Kin 6:25; 7:5; 8; 11:5; 6(2); 18:23; 1Chr 12:29; 2Chr 23:4; 5(2); 29:16; Neh 1:9; 3:9; 12; 14; 15; 16; 17(2); 18; 5:11; 9:3(2); 10:32; Job 32:17; 41:6; Ps 5:9; 22:18; 51:6; 118:7; Prov 8:26; 31; 17:2; Is 7:18; 24:16; 36:8; 44:16(2); 19; Eze 4:11; 5:2(3); 12(3); 39:2; 45:11(2); 13(2); 14; 17; 46:14(2); Dan 1:2; 2:33(2); 41(2); 42(2); 5:5; 24; 11:31; Joel 2:20; Amos 7:4; Zec 13:9; Mk 4:38; 9:40; 13:27(2); Lk 10:42; 11:36; 39; 17:24(2); Jn 13:8; 19:23; Acts 1:8; 17; 25; 5:2(2); 3; 8:21; 14:4(2); 16:12; 19:32; 23:6; 9; 27:12; 41; Rom 11:25; 1Cor 12:24; 13:9(2); 10; 12; 15:6; 16:17; 2Cor 1:14; 2:5; 6:15; Eph 4:16; Titus 2:8; Heb 2:14; 7:2; 1Pet 4:14(2); Rev 6:8; 8:7; 8; 9(2); 10; 11; 12(5); 9:15; 18; 11:13; 12:4; 20:6; 21:8; 22:19

PARTS

905, 1335, 1506, 1697, 2506, 2677, 3027, 3411, 5409, 6310, 7098, *2825, 3313*

Gen 47:24; Ex 33:23; Lev 1:8; 22:23; Num 10:5; 11:1; 31:27; Deut 19:3; 30:4; Josh 18:5; 6; 9; 1Sa 5:9; 2Sa 19:43; 1Kin 6:38; 7:25; 16:21; 2Kin 11:7; 2Chr 4:4; Neh 11:1; Job 26:14; 38:36; 41:12; Ps 2:8; 51:6; 63:9; 65:8; 78:66; 136:13; 139:9; 15; Prov 18:8; 20:27; 30; 26:22; Is 3:17; 16:11; 44:23; Jer 31:33; 34:18; 19; Eze 26:20; 31:14; 16; 18; 32:18; 24; 37:11; 38:15; 39:2; 48:8; Zec 13:8; Mt 2:22; 12:42; Mk 8:10; Lk 11:31; Jn 19:23; Acts 2:10; 20:2; Rom 15:23; 1Cor 12:23; 24; Eph 4:9; Rev 16:19

PASS

935, 1980, 2498, 2499, 3615, 4569, 5674, 5709, 5964, 6213, 6452, *390, 1224, 1276, 1279, 1330, 3928, 5230*

Gen 4:3; 8; 14; 6:1; 7:10; 8:1; 6; 13; 9:14; 11:2; 12:11; 12; 14; 14:1; 15:17; 18:3; 5; 19:17; 29; 34; 20:13; 21:22; 22:1; 20; 24:14; 15; 22; 30; 43; 52; 25:11; 26:8; 32; 27:1; 30; 40; 29:10; 13; 23; 25; 30:25; 32; 41; 31:10; 52(2); 32:16; 33:14; 34:25; 35:17; 18; 22; 37:23; 38:1; 9; 24; 27; 28; 29; 39:5; 7; 10; 11; 13; 15; 18; 19; 40:1; 20; 41:1; 8; 13; 32; 42:35; 43:2; 21; 44:24; 31; 46:33; 47:24; 48:1; 50:20; Ex 1:10; 21; 2:11; 23; 3:21; 4:8; 9; 24; 6:28; 12:12; 13; 23(2); 25; 26; 29; 41(2); 51; 13:15; 17; 14:24; 15:16(2); 16:5; 10; 13; 22; 27; 17:11; 18:13; 19:16; 22:27; 32:19; 30; 33:7; 8; 9; 19; 22(2); 34:29; 40:17; Lev 9:1; 18:21; Num 5:27; 7:1; 10:11; 35; 11:23; 25; 16:31; 42; 17:5; 8; 20:17(2); 18; 21:8; 9; 22; 23; 22:41; 26:1; 27:7; 8; 32:27; 29; 30; 32; 33:55; 56; 34:4(2); Deut 1:3; 2:4; 16; 18; 24; 27; 28; 29; 30; 3:18; 5:23; 7:12; 9:1; 11; 11:13; 29; 31; 13:2; 18:10; 19; 22; 24:1; 27:2; 28:1; 15; 63; 29:19; 30:1; 31:21; 24; Josh 1:1; 11(2); 14; 2:5; 3:2; 6; 13; 14(2); 4:1; 5; 11; 18; 5:1; 8; 13; 6:5; 7(2); 8; 15; 16; 20; 8:5; 14; 24; 9:1; 16; 10:1; 11; 20; 24; 27; 11:1; 15:18; 17:13; 21:45; 22:19; 23:1; 14; 15; 24:29; Judg 1:14; 28; 2:4; 19; 3:27; 28; 6:7; 25; 7:9; 8:33; 9:42; 11:4; 17; 19; 20; 35; 39; 13:12; 17; 20; 14:11; 15; 17; 15:1; 17; 16:4; 16; 25; 19:1; 5; 12; 21:3; 4; Ruth 1:1; 19; 3:8; 1Sa 1:12; 20; 2:36; 3:2; 4:18; 5:10; 7:2; 8:1; 9:6; 26; 27; 10:5; 9; 11; 11:11; 13:10; 22; 14:1; 8; 19; 16:6; 8; 9; 10; 16; 23; 17:48; 18:1; 6; 10; 19; 30; 20:27; 35; 23:6; 23; 24:1; 5; 16; 25:30; 37; 38; 28:1; 30:1; 31:8; 2Sa 1:1; 2; 2:1; 23; 3:6; 4:4; 7:1; 4; 8:1; 10:1; 11:1; 2; 14; 16; 12:18; 31; 13:1; 23; 30; 36; 15:1; 7; 22; 32; 16:16; 17:9; 16; 21(2); 27; 19:25; 21:18; 1Kin 1:21; 2:39; 3:18; 5:7; 6:1; 8:10; 9:1; 10; 11:4; 15; 29; 12:2; 20; 13:4; 20; 23; 31; 32; 14:25; 15:21; 29; 16:11; 18; 31; 17:7; 17; 18:1; 6; 12; 17; 27; 29; 36; 44; 45; 19:17; 20:12; 26; 21:1; 15; 16; 27; 22:2; 32; 33; 2Kin 2:1; 9; 11; 3:5; 15; 20; 4:6; 25; 40; 5:7; 6:9; 20; 24; 30; 7:18; 8:3; 5; 15; 9:22; 10:7; 9; 25; 13:21; 14:5; 15:12; 16:3; 17:17; 18:1; 9; 19:1; 25; 35; 37; 20:4; 21:6; 22:3; 11; 23:10; 24:20; 25:1; 25; 27; 1Chr 10:8; 15:26; 29; 17:1; 3; 11; 18:1; 19:1; 20:1; 4; 2Chr 5:11; 13; 8:1; 10:2; 12:1; 2; 13:15; 16:5; 18:31; 32; 20:1; 21:19; 22:8; 24:4; 11; 23; 25:3; 14; 16; 33:6; 34:19; Neh 1:1; 4; 2:1; 14; 4:1; 7; 12; 15; 16; 6:1; 16; 7:1; 13:3; 19; Est 1:1; 2:8; 3:4; 5:1; Job 6:15; 11:16; 14:5; 19:8; 34:20; Ps 37:5; 7; 58:8; 78:13; 80:12; 89:41; 104:9; 136:14; 148:6; Prov 4:15(2); 8:29; 16:30; 19:11; 22:3; 27:12; Is 2:2; 3:24; 4:3; 7:1; 7; 18; 21; 22; 23; 8:8; 21(2); 10:12; 20; 27; 11:11; 14:3; 24; 16:12; 17:4; 21:1; 22:7; 20; 23:2; 6; 10; 12; 15; 17; 24:18; 21; 27:12; 13; 28:15; 18; 19; 21; 30:32; 31:9; 33:21; 34:10; 35:8; 36:1; 37:1; 26; 38; 42:9; 46:11; 47:2; 48:3; 5; 51:10; 65:24; 66:23; Jer 2:10; 3:9; 16; 4:9; 5:19; 22(2); 8:13; 9:10; 12:15; 16; 13:6; 15:2; 14; 16:10; 17:24; 20:3; 22:8; 25:12; 26:8; 27:8; 28:1; 9; 30:8; 31:28; 32:24; 35; 33:13; 35:11; 36:1; 9; 16; 23; 37:11; 39:4; 41:1; 4; 6; 13; 42:4; 7; 16; 43:1; 49:39; 51:43; 52:3; 4; 31; Lam 1:12; 2:15; 3:37; 44; 4:21; Eze 1:1; 3:16; 5:1; 14; 17; 8:1; 9:8; 10:6; 11:13; 12:25; 14:15(2); 16:21; 23; 20:1; 26; 31; 37; 21:7; 23:37; 24:14; 26:1; 29:11(2); 17; 30:20; 31:1; 32:1; 17; 19; 33:21; 28; 33; 37:2; 38:10; 18; 39:11; 15; 44:17; 46:21; 47:5; 9; 10; 22; 23; Dan 2:29(2); 45; 4:16; 23; 25; 32; 7:14; 8:2; 15; 11:10; 40; Hos 1:5; 10; 2:21; Joel 2:28; 32; 3:17; 18; Amos 5:5; 17; 6:2; 9; 7:2; 8; 8:2; 9;

Jonah 4:8; **Mic** 1:11; 2:8; 13; 4:1; 5:10; **Nah** 1:12; 15; 3:7; **Hab** 1:11; **Zeph** 1:8; 10; 12; 2:2; **Zec** 3:4; 6:15; 7:1; 13; 8:13; 20; 23; 9:8; 10:11; 12:9; 13:2(2); 3; 4; 8; 14:6; 7; 13; 16; **Mt** 5:18(2); 7:28; 8:28; 9:10; 11:1; 13:53; 19:1; 24:6; 34; 35(2); 26:1; 39; 42; **Mk** 1:9; 2:15; 23; 4:4; 35; 11:23; 13:29; 30; 31(2); 14:35; **Lk** 1:8; 23; 41; 59; 2:1; 15(2); 46; 3:21; 5:1; 12; 17; 6:1; 6; 12; 7:11; 8:1; 22; 40; 9:18; 28; 33; 37; 51; 57; 10:38; 11:1; 14; 27; 42; 12:55; 14:1; 16:17; 22; 26(2); 17:11; 14; 18:35; 36; 19:4; 15; 29; 20:1; 21:7; 9; 28; 31; 32; 33(2); 36; 24:4; 12; 15; 18; 30; 51; **Jn** 13:19; 14:29(2); 15:25; **Acts** 2:17; 21; 3:23; 4:5; 9:32; 37; 43; 11:26; 28; 14:1; 16:16; 18:27; 19:1; 21:1; 22:6; 17; 27:44; 28:8; 17; **Rom** 9:26; **1Cor** 7:36; 15:54; 16:5(2); **2Cor** 1:16; **1Th** 3:4; **Jas** 1:10; **1Pet** 1:17; **2Pet** 3:10; **Rev** 1:1

PASSED

1431, 2498, 5674, 5709, 5710, 6437, 6452, *492, 565, 1224, 1276, 1330, 1353, 3327, 3855, 3899, 3928, 4281*

Gen 12:6; 15:17; 31:21; 32:10; 22; 31; 33:3; 37:28; **Ex** 12:27; 34:6; **Num** 14:7; 20:17; 33:8; 51; **Deut** 2:8(2); 27:3; 29:16; **Josh** 2:23; 3:1; 4; 16; 17(2); 4:1; 7; 10; 11(2); 12; 13; 23; 5:1; 6:8; 10:29; 31; 34; 15:3(2); 4; 6; 7; 10(2); 11; 16:6; 18:9; 18; 19; 24:17; **Judg** 3:26; 8:4; 10:9; 11:29(3); 32; 12:3; 18:13; 19:14; **1Sa** 9:4(4); 27; 14:23; 15:12; 27:2; 29:2(2); **2Sa** 2:29; 10:17; 15:18(2); 22; 23(3); 17:22; 24; 24:5; **1Kin** 13:25; 19:11; 19; 20:39; **2Kin** 4:8(2); 31; 6:30; 14:9; **1Chr** 19:17; **2Chr** 9:22; 25:18; 30:10; **Job** 4:15; 9:26; 15:19; 28:8; **Ps** 18:12; 37:36; 48:4; 90:9; **Song** 3:4; **Is** 10:28; 40:27; 41:3; **Jer** 2:6; 11:15; 34:18; 19; 46:17; **Eze** 16:6; 8; 15; 25; 36:34; 47:5; **Dan** 3:27; 6:18; **Hos** 10:11; **Jonah** 2:3; **Mic** 2:13; **Nah** 3:19; **Hab** 3:10; **Zec** 7:14; **Mt** 9:1; 9; 20:30; 27:39; **Mk** 2:14; 5:21; 6:35; 48; 53; 9:30; 11:20; 15:21; 29; **Lk** 10:31; 32; 17:11; 19:1; **Jn** 5:24; 8:59; 9:1; **Acts** 9:32; 12:10; 14:24; 15:3; 17:1; 23; 19:1; 21; **Rom** 5:12; **1Cor** 10:1; **2Cor** 5:17; **Heb** 4:14; 11:29; **1Jn** 3:14; **Rev** 21:1; 4

PASSEST

5674

Deut 3:21; 30:18; **2Sa** 15:33; **1Kin** 2:37; **Is** 43:2

PASSETH

1980, 2498, 5674, *3855, 3928, 5235, 5242*

Ex 30:13; 14; 33:22; **Lev** 27:32; **Josh** 3:11; 16:2; 19:13; **1Kin** 9:8; **2Kin** 4:9; 12:4; **2Chr** 7:21; **Job** 9:11; 14:20; 30:15; 37:21; **Ps** 8:8; 78:39; 103:16; 144:4; **Prov** 10:25; 26:17; **Eccl** 1:4; **Is** 29:5; **Jer** 9:12; 13:24; 18:16; 19:8; **Eze** 35:7; **Hos** 13:3; **Mic** 7:18; **Zeph** 2:15; 3:6; **Zec** 9:8; **Lk** 18:37; **1Cor** 7:31; **Eph** 3:19; **Phil** 4:7; **1Jn** 2:17

PASSING

5674, *1330, 2064, 3881, 3928*

Judg 19:18; **2Sa** 1:26; 15:24; **2Kin** 6:26; **Ps** 84:6; **Prov** 7:8; **Is** 31:5; **Eze** 39:14; **Lk** 4:30; **Acts** 5:15; 8:40; 16:8; 27:8

PEOPLE'S

5971, *2992*

Lev 9:15; **Eze** 46:18; **Mt** 13:15; **Heb** 7:27

PEOPLES

2992

Rev 10:11; 17:15

PERHAPS

686, 3381, 5029

Acts 8:22; **2Cor** 2:7; **Philem** 1:15

PLACE

870, 1004, 1367, 3027, 3241, 3427, 3653, 4349, 4612, 4634, 4724, 4725, 4800, 5182, 5977, 6607, 7675, 7931, 8414, 8478, *201, 402, 1564, 1786, 3692, 3699, 4042, 5117, 5562, 5564, 5602*

Gen 1:9; 12:6; 13:3; 4; 14; 18:24; 26; 33; 19:12; 13; 14; 27; 20:11; 13; 21:31; 22:3; 4; 9; 14; 26:7(2); 28:11(3); 16; 17; 19; 29:3; 22; 30:25; 31:55; 32:2; 30; 33:17; 35:7; 13; 14; 15; 38:14; 21(2); 22(2); 39:20; 40:3; 13; 48:9; 50:19; **Ex** 3:5; 8; 10:23; 13:3; 15:17; 16:29(2); 17:7; 18:21; 23; 21:13; 23:20; 26:33; 34; 28:29; 35; 43; 29:30; 31; 31:11; 32:34; 33:21; 35:19; 38:24; 39:1; 41; **Lev** 1:16; 4:12; 24; 29; 33; 6:11; 16; 25; 26; 27; 30; 7:2; 6; 10:13; 14; 17; 18(2); 13:19; 23; 28; 14:13(2); 28; 40; 41; 42; 45; 16:2; 3; 16; 17; 20; 23; 24; 27; 24:9; **Num** 2:17; 9:17; 10:14; 29; 33; 11:3; 34; 13:24; 14:40; 18:10; 31; 19:9; 20:5(2); 21:3; 22:26; 23:3; 13; 27; 24:11; 25; 28:7; 32:1(2); 17; 33:54; **Deut** 1:31; 33; 2:37; 9:7; 11:5; 24; 12:3; 5; 11; 13; 14; 18; 21; 26; 14:23(2); 24; 25; 15:20; 16:2(2); 6(2); 7; 11(2); 15; 16; 17:8; 10; 18:6; 21:19; 23:12; 16; 26:2(2); 9; 27:15; 29:7; 31:11; **Josh** 1:3; 3:3; 4:3(2); 8; 9; 18; 5:9; 15; 7:26; 8:19; 9:27; 20:4; **Judg** 2:5; 6:26; 7:7; 21; 9:55; 11:19; 15:17; 19; 17:8; 9; 18:3; 10; 12; 19:16; 28; 20:22; 33; 36; 21:19; **Ruth** 1:7; 3:4; 4:10; **1Sa** 3:2; 9; 5:3; 11; 6:2; 9:12; 13; 14; 19; 22; 25; 10:5; 12; 13; 12:8; 14:9; 46; 15:12; 19:2; 20:19; 25; 27; 37; 41; 21:2; 23:22; 28; 26:5(2); 25; 27:5; 29:4; **2Sa** 2:16; 23(2); 5:20; 6:8; 17; 7:10(2); 11:16; 15:17; 19; 21; 17:9; 12; 18:18; 19:39; 22:20; 23:7; **1Kin** 3:4; 4:12; 28; 5:9; 6:16; 7:50; 8:6(2); 7; 8; 10; 13; 21; 29(2); 30(2); 35; 39; 43; 49; 10:19; 11:7; 13:8; 16; 22; 20:24; 21:19; 22:10; **2Kin** 5:11; 6:1; 2; 6; 8; 9; 10; 18:25; 22:16; 17; 19; 20; 23:15(3); **1Chr** 6:32; 49; 13:11; 14:11; 15:1; 3; 12; 16:27; 39; 17:9(2); 21:22; 25; 29; 23:32; 28:11; **2Chr** 1:3; 4; 13; 3:1; 4:22; 5:7(2); 8; 11; 6:2; 20(2); 21(2); 26; 30; 33; 39; 40; 41; 7:12; 15; 9:18; 18:9; 20:26; 24:11; 29:5; 7; 30:16; 27; 34:24; 25; 27; 28; 31; 35:5; 10; 15; 36:15; **Ezr** 1:4(2); 2:68; 5:15; 6:3; 5(2); 7; 8:17(2); 9:8; **Neh** 1:9; 2:3; 14; 3:16; 26; 31; 4:20; 8:7; 9:3; 13:11; **Est** 2:9; 4:14; 7:8; **Job** 2:11; 6:17; 7:10; 8:17; 18; 22; 9:6; 14:18; 16:18; 18:4; 21; 20:9; 26:7; 27:21; 23; 28:1; 6; 12; 20; 23; 36:16; 20; 37:1; 38:10; 12; 19; 39:28; 40:12; **Ps** 18:11; 19; 24:3; 26:8; 12; 32:7; 33:14; 37:10; 44:19; 46:4; 52:5; 66:12; 68:17; 74:7; 76:2; 79:7; 81:7; 90:1; 91:1; 103:16; 104:8; 118:5; 119:114; 132:5; **Prov** 1:21; 14:26; 15:3; 24:15; 25:6; 27:8; **Eccl** 1:5; 7; 3:16(2); 20; 6:6; 8:10; 10:4; 6; 11:3; **Is** 4:5; 6; 5:8; 7:23; 13:13; 14:2; 16:12; 18:4; 7; 22:23; 25; 25:5; 26:21; 28:8; 17; 25; 30:32; 32:2(2); 19; 33:16; 21; 34:14; 35:1; 45:19; 46:7(2); 13; 49:20(2); 54:2; 56:5; 57:15; 60:13(2); 65:10; 66:1; **Jer** 4:7; 26; 6:3; 7:3; 6; 7; 12; 14; 20; 32; 9:2; 13:7; 14:13; 16:2; 3; 9; 17:12; 18:14; 19:3; 4(2); 6; 7; 11; 12; 13; 22:3; 11; 12; 24:5; 27:22; 28:3(2); 4; 6; 29:10; 14; 32:37; 33:10; 12; 38:9; 40:2; 42:18; 22; 44:29; 51:37; 62; **Eze** 3:12; 6:13; 7:22; 10:11; 12:3(2); 16:24(2); 25; 31(2); 39; 17:16; 20:29; 21:19; 30; 26:5; 14; 37:14; 26; 38:15; 39:11; 41:4; 9; 11(2); 12; 13; 14; 15; 42:1; 10; 13(2); 14; 20; 43:7(2); 13; 21; 44:13; 45:3; 4(2); 46:19; 20; 47:10; 48:15; **Dan** 2:35; 8:11; 11:31; **Hos** 1:10; 4:16; 5:15; 9:13; 11:11; 13:13; **Joel** 3:7; **Amos** 8:3; **Mic** 1:3; 4; **Nah** 1:8; 2:11; 3:17; **Zeph** 1:4; 2:11; 15; **Hag** 2:9; **Zec** 6:12; 10:6; 10; 12:6; 14:10(2); **Mal** 1:11; **Mt** 8:32; 9:24; 12:6; 14:13; 15; 35; 17:20; 24:15; 26:36; 52; 27:33(2); 28:6; **Mk** 1:35; 5:13; 6:10(2); 31; 32; 35; 11:4; 12:1; 14:32; 15:22(2); 16:6; **Lk** 4:17; 37; 42; 8:33; 9:10; 12; 10:1; 32; 11:1; 33; 14:9; 16:28; 19:5; 22:40; 23:5; 33; **Jn** 4:20; 5:13; 6:10; 23; 8:37; 10:40; 11:6; 30; 41; 48; 14:2; 3; 18:2; 19:13; 17(2); 20; 41; 20:7; **Acts** 1:25; 2:1; 4:31; 6:13; 14; 7:7; 33; 49; 8:32; 12:17; 21:12; 28(2); 25:23; 27:8; 41; **Rom** 9:26; 12:19; 15:23; **1Cor** 1:2; 4:11; 11:20; 14:23; **2Cor** 2:14; **Gal** 2:5; **Eph** 4:27; **1Th** 1:8; **Heb** 2:6; 4:4; 5; 5:6; 8:7; 9:12; 25; 11:8; 12:17; **Jas** 2:3; 3:11; **2Pet** 1:19; **Rev** 2:5; 12:6; 8; 14; 16:16; 20:11

PLACED

776, 3240, 3427, 3947, 5414, 5975, 7760, 7931

Gen 3:24; 47:11; **1Kin** 12:32; **2Kin** 17:6; 24; 26; **2Chr** 1:14; 4:8; 17:2; **Job** 20:4; **Ps** 78:60; **Is** 5:8; **Jer** 5:22; **Eze** 17:5

PUT

Gen 2:8; 15; 3:15; 22; 8:9; 19:10; 24:2; 9; 47; 26:11; 27:15; 16; 28:11; 18; 20; 29:3; 30:40(2); 42; 31:34; 32:16; 33:2; 35:2; 37:34; 38:14; 19; 28; 39:4; 20; 40:3; 15; 41:10; 42(2); 42:17; 43:22; 44:1; 2; 46:4; 47:29; 48:18; 50:26; **Ex** 2:3; 3:5; 22; 4:4(2); 6(2); 7(2); 15; 21; 5:21; 8:23; 11:7; 12:15; 15:26; 16:33; 17:12; 14; 19:12; 21:12; 15; 16; 17; 29; 22:5; 8; 11; 19; 23:1; 24:6; 25:12; 14; 16; 21(2); 26; 26:11; 34; 35; 27:5; 7; 28:12; 23; 24; 25; 26; 27; 30; 37; 41; 29:3; 5; 6(2); 8; 9; 10; 12; 15; 17; 19; 20; 24; 30; 30:6; 18(2); 36; 31:6; 14; 15; 32:27; 33:4; 5; 22; 34:33; 35; 35:2; 34; 36:1; 2; 37:5; 13; 38:7; 39:7; 16; 17; 18; 19; 20; 25; 40:3; 5; 7; 13; 18; 19; 20(2); 22; 24; 26; 29; 30; **Lev** 1:4; 7; 2:1; 15; 4:7; 18; 25; 30; 34; 5:11(2); 6:10(3); 11(2); 12; 8:7(2); 8(2); 9(2); 13(2); 15; 23; 24; 26; 27; 9:9; 20; 10:1(2); 10; 11:32; 38; 13:45; 14:14; 17; 25; 28; 29; 34; 42; 15:19; 16:4(2); 13; 18; 23(2); 24; 32; 18:19; 19:14; 20; 20:2; 9; 10; 11; 12; 13; 15; 16; 25; 27; 21:7; 10; 22:14; 24:7; 12; 16(2); 17; 21; 26:8; 27:29; **Num** 1:51; 3:10; 38; 4:6(2); 7; 8; 10(2); 11; 12(2); 14(2); 5:2; 3(2); 4; 15; 17; 18; 6:18; 19; 27; 8:10; 11:17; 29; 15:34; 35; 38; 16:7(2); 14; 17; 18; 46(2); 47; 18:7; 19:17; 20:26; 28; 21:9; 23:5; 12; 16; 27:20; 35:16; 17; 18; 21; 30; 31; 36:3; 4; **Deut** 2:25; 7:15; 22; 10:2; 5; 11:29; 12:5; 7; 21; 13:5(2); 9; 16:9; 17:6(2); 7(2); 12; 18:18; 19:13; 19; 21:9; 13; 21; 22; 22:5; 19; 21; 22; 24; 29; 23:24; 24:7; 16(3); 25:6; 26:2; 28:48; 30:7; 31:19; 26; 32:30; 33:10; 14; **Josh** 1:18; 6:24; 7:6; 11; 10:24(2); 17:13; 24:7; 14; 23; **Judg** 1:28; 3:21; 5:26; 6:19(2); 21; 31; 37; 7:16; 8:27; 9:15; 26; 49; 10:16; 12:3; 14:12; 13; 16; 15:4; 15; 16:3; 21; 18:7; 21; 20:13(2); 20; 22; 30; 33; 21:5; **Ruth** 3:3; **1Sa** 1:14; 2:36; 4:2; 6:8; 15; 7:3; 4; 8:16; 11:11; 12; 13; 14:26; 27(2); 17:21; 38; 39; 40; 49; 54; 19:5; 13; 21:6; 22:17; 24:10; 28:3; 8; 21; 31:10; **2Sa** 1:24; 3:34; 6:6; 7:15; 8:2; 6; 14(2); 10:8; 9; 10; 12:13; 31; 13:17; 19; 14:2; 3; 19; 15:5; 17:23; 18:12; 19:21; 22; 20:3; 8; 21:9; **1Kin** 2:5; 8; 24; 26; 35(2); 5:3; 7:39; 51; 8:9; 9:3; 10:17; 24; 11:36; 12:4; 9; 29; 13:4(2); 14:21; 18:23(2); 25; 33; 42; 20:6; 24; 31; 32; 21:27; 22:10; 23; 27; 30; **2Kin** 2:20; 3:2; 21; 4:34; 6:7; 9:13; 10:7; 11:12; 12:9; 10; 13:16(3); 14:6(3); 12; 16:14; 17; 17:29; 18:11; 24; 19:28; 21:4; 7; 23:5; 24; 33(2); 25:7; **1Chr** 1:8; 5:20; 10:10; 11:19; 12:15; 13:9; 10; 18:6; 13; 19:9; 10; 16; 17; 19; 21:27; 27:24; **2Chr** 1:5; 2:14; 3:16(2); 4:6; 5:1; 10; 6:11; 20; 24; 9:16; 23; 10:4; 9; 11(2); 11:11; 12; 12:13; 15:8; 13; 16:10; 17:19; 18:22; 26; 29; 22:11; 23:7; 11; 25:22; 29:7; 33:7; 14; 34:10; 35:3; 24; 36:3; 7; 22; **Ezr** 1:1; 7; 2:62; 6:12; 7:27; 10:3; 19; **Neh** 2:12; 3:5; 4:23(2); 6:14; 19; 7:5; 64; **Est** 4:1; 11; 5:1; 8:3; 9:1; **Job** 1:11; 12; 2:5; 4:18; 11:14; 13:14; 17:3; 18:5; 6; 19:13; 21:17; 22:23; 23:6; 27:17; 29:14; 38:36; 41:2; **Ps** 2:12; 4:5; 7; 5:11; 7:1; 8:6; 9:5; 10; 20; 11:1; 16:1; 17:7; 18:22; 25:20; 27:9; 30:11; 31:1; 18; 35:4; 36:7; 40:3; 14; 44:7; 9; 53:5; 55:20; 56:4; 8; 11; 70:2; 71:1(2); 73:28; 78:66; 83:17; 88:8; 18; 118:8; 9; 119:31; 125:3; 146:3; **Prov** 4:24(2); 8:1; 13:9; 20:20; 23:2; 24:20; 25:6; 7; 8; 10; 30:5; **Eccl** 3:14; 10:10; 11:10; **Song** 5:3(2); 4; **Is** 1:16; 5:20(2); 10:13; 11:8; 20:2; 36:9; 37:29; 42:1; 43:26; 47:11; 50:1(2); 51:9; 16; 23; 52:1(2); 53:10; 54:4; 59:17(2); 21; 63:11; **Jer** 1:9(2); 3:1; 8; 19; 4:1; 7:21; 8:14; 12:13; 13:1(2); 2; 18:21; 20:2; 26:15; 19; 21; 24; 27:2; 8; 28:14; 29:26; 31:33; 32:14; 40; 37:4; 15; 18; 38:4; 7; 12; 15; 16; 25; 39:7; 18; 40:10; 43:3; 46:4; 47:6; 50:14; 42; 52:11(2); 27; **Eze** 3:25; 4:9; 8:3; 17; 10:7; 11:19; 14:3; 16:11; 12; 14; 17:2; 19:9; 22:26; 23:42; 24:17; 26:16; 29:4; 30:13; 21; 24; 25; 32:7; 25; 36:26; 27; 37:6; 14; 19; 38:4; 42:14; 43:9; 20; 44:19(2); 22; 45:19; **Dan** 5:19; 29; **Hos** 2:2; **Joel** 3:13; **Amos** 6:3; **Jonah** 3:5; **Mic** 2:12; 7:5; **Nah** 3:9; **Zeph** 3:19; **Hag** 1:6; **Mt** 1:19; 5:15; 31; 32; 6:25; 8:3; 9:16; 17(2); 25; 10:21; 12:18; 13:24; 31; 14:3; 5; 19:3; 6; 7; 8; 9(2); 13; 21:7; 22:34; 25:27; 26:52; 59; 27:1; 6; 28; 29; 31; 48; **Mk** 1:14; 41; 2:22; 4:21; 5:40; 6:9; 7:32; 33; 8:23; 25; 10:2; 4; 9; 11; 12; 16; 13:12; 14:1; 55; 15:17; 20; 36; **Lk** 1:52; 5:13; 38; 8:54; 9:62; 12:22; 14:7; 15:22(2); 16:4; 18; 18:33; 21:16; 23:32; **Jn** 5:7; 9:15; 22; 11:53; 12:6; 10; 42; 13:2; 16:2; 18:11; 31; 19:2(2); 19; 29(2); 20:25; **Acts** 1:7; 4:3; 5:18; 25; 34; 7:33; 9:40; 12:4; 19; 13:46; 15:9; 10; 26:10; 27:6; **Rom** 13:12; 14; 14:13; **1Cor** 5:13; 7:11; 12; 13:11; 15:24; 25; 27(3); 28; 53(2); 54(2); **2Cor** 3:13; 8:16; **Gal** 3:27; **Eph** 1:22; 4:22; 24; 31; 6:11; **Col** 3:8; 9; 10; 12; 14; **1Th** 2:4; **1Ti** 1:19; 4:6; **2Ti** 1:6; 2:14; **Titus** 3:1; **Philem** 1:18; **Heb** 2:5; 8(4); 13; 6:6; 8:10; 9:26; 10:16; **Jas** 3:3; **1Pet** 2:15; 3:18; **2Pet** 1:12; 14; **Jude** 5; **Rev** 2:24; 11:9; 17:17

PUTTEST

4916, 5414, 5596, 7673, 7760

Num 24:21; **Deut** 12:18; 15:10; **2Kin** 18:14; **Job** 13:27; **Ps** 119:119; **Hab** 2:15

PUTTETH

2590, 5414, 5844, 6605, 7760, 7971, 8213, *630, 649, 906, 1544, 1631, 1911, 5087*

Ex 30:33; **Num** 22:38; **Deut** 25:11; 27:15; **1Kin** 20:11; **Job** 15:15; 28:9; 33:11; **Ps** 15:5; 75:7; **Prov** 28:25; 29:25; **Song** 2:13; **Is** 57:13; **Jer** 43:12; **Lam** 3:29; **Eze** 14:4; 7; **Mic** 3:5; **Mt** 9:16; 24:32; **Mk** 2:22; 4:29; 13:28; **Lk** 5:36; 37; 8:16; 11:33; 16:18; **Jn** 10:4

PUTTING

5414, 7760, 7971, *555, 595, 659, 1745, 1746, 1878, 1936, 2007, 4261, 5087, 5279*

Gen 21:14; **Lev** 16:21; **Judg** 7:6; **Is** 58:9; **Mal** 2:16; **Acts** 9:12; 17; 19:33; **Rom** 15:15; **Eph** 4:25; **Col** 2:11; **1Th** 5:8; **1Ti** 1:12; **2Ti** 1:6; **1Pet** 3:3; 21; **2Pet** 1:13

RATHER

408, 977, *2228, 2309, 3123, 3304, 4056, 4133*

Josh 22:24; **2Sa** 10:3; **2Kin** 5:13; **Job** 7:15; 32:2; 36:21; **Ps** 52:3; 84:10; **Prov** 8:10; 16:16; 17:12; 22:1(2); **Jer** 8:3; **Mt** 10:6; 28; 18:8; 9; 25:9; 27:24; **Mk** 5:26; 15:11; **Lk** 10:20; 11:28; 41; 12:31; 51; 17:8; 18:14; **Jn** 3:19; **Acts** 5:29; **Rom** 3:8; 8:34; 11:11; 12:19; 14:13; **1Cor** 5:2; 6:7(2); 7:21; 9:12; 14:1; 5; 19; **2Cor** 2:7; 3:8; 5:8; 12:9; **Gal** 4:9; **Eph** 4:28; 5:4; 11; **Phil** 1:12; **1Ti** 1:4; 4:7; 6:2; **Philem** 1:9; **Heb** 11:25; 12:9; 13; 13:19; **2Pet** 1:10

REACH

1272, 1961, 4229, 5060, 5381, *2185, 5342*

Gen 11:4; **Ex** 26:28; 28:42; **Lev** 26:5(2); **Num** 34:11; 35:4; **Job** 20:6; **Is** 8:8; 30:28; **Jer** 48:32; **Zec** 14:5; **Jn** 20:27(2); **2Cor** 10:13

REACHED

4291, 5060, 6293, 6642, *190, 2185*

Gen 28:12; **Josh** 19:11(2); **Ruth** 2:14; **Dan** 4:11; 20; **2Cor** 10:14; **Rev** 18:5

REACHETH

4291, 5060, 6293, 7971

Num 21:30; **Josh** 19:22; 26; 27; 34(2); **2Chr** 28:9; **Ps** 36:5; 108:4; **Prov** 31:20; **Jer** 4:10; 18; 51:9; **Dan** 4:22

REACHING

5060, *1901*

2Chr 3:11(2); 12; **Phil** 3:13

SAID

559, 560, 1696, 1697, 4448, 4449, 5002, 6030, 7121, *669, 846, 2036, 2046, 2980, 3004, 4280, 4483, 5346*

Gen 1:3; 6; 9; 11; 14; 20; 24; 26; 28; 29; 2:18; 23; 3:1(2); 2; 3; 4; 9; 10; 11; 12; 13(2); 14; 16; 17; 22; 4:1; 6; 9(2); 10; 13; 15; 23; 25; 6:3; 7; 13; 7:1; 8:21; 9:1; 12; 17; 25; 26; 10:9; 11:3; 4; 6; 12:1; 7; 11; 18; 13:8; 14; 14:19; 21; 22; 15:2; 3; 5(2); 7; 8; 9; 13; 16:2; 5; 6; 8(2); 9; 10; 11; 13; 17:1; 9; 15; 17; 18; 19; 23; 18:3; 5(2); 6; 9(2); 10; 13; 15; 17; 20; 23; 26; 27; 28; 29(2); 30(2); 31(2); 32(2); 19:2(2); 5; 7; 9(2); 12; 14; 17; 18; 21; 31; 34; 20:2; 3; 4; 5(2); 6; 9; 10; 11; 13; 15; 16; 21:1; 6; 7(2); 10; 12(2); 16; 17; 24; 26; 29; 30; 22:1(2); 2; 5; 7(3); 8; 11(2); 12; 14; 16; 24:2; 5; 6; 12; 17; 18; 19; 23; 24; 25; 27; 31; 33(2); 34; 39; 40; 42; 45; 46; 47(2); 50; 54; 55; 56; 57; 58(2); 60; 65(2); 25:22; 23; 30; 31; 32; 33; 26:2; 7(2); 9(3); 10; 16; 22; 24; 27; 28(2); 32; 27:1(2); 2; 11; 13; 18(2); 19; 20(2); 21; 22; 24(2); 25; 26; 27; 31; 32(2); 33; 34; 35; 36(2); 37; 38; 39; 41; 42; 46; 28:1; 13; 16; 17; 29:4(2); 5(2); 6(2); 7; 8; 14; 15; 18; 19; 21; 25; 26; 32; 33; 34; 35; 30:1; 2; 3; 6; 8; 11; 13; 14; 15(2); 16; 18; 20; 23; 24; 25; 27; 28; 29; 31(2); 34; 31:3; 5; 8(2); 11; 12; 14; 16; 24; 26; 31(2); 35; 36; 43; 46; 48; 49; 51; 32:2; 8; 9; 16; 20; 26(2); 27(2); 28; 29(2); 33:5(2); 8(2); 9; 10; 12; 13; 15(2); 34:11; 13; 14; 30; 31; 35:1; 2; 10; 11; 17; 37:6; 8; 9; 10; 13(2); 14; 16; 17; 19; 21; 22; 26; 30; 32; 33; 35; 38:8; 11(2); 16(2); 17(2); 18(2); 21; 22(2); 23; 24; 25; 26; 29; 39:7; 8; 40:8(2); 9; 12; 16; 18; 41:15; 17; 25; 38; 39; 41; 44; 51; 54; 55; 42:1; 2; 4; 7(2); 9; 10; 12; 13; 14; 18; 21; 28; 31; 33; 36; 38; 43:2; 5; 6; 7; 8; 11; 16; 18; 20; 23; 27; 29(2); 31; 44:4; 7; 10; 15; 16; 17; 18; 20; 22; 25; 26; 27; 28; 45:3; 4(2); 17; 24; 27; 28; 46:2(2); 3; 30; 31; 47:1; 3(2); 4; 8; 9; 15; 16; 18; 23; 25; 29; 30(2); 31; 48:2; 3; 4; 8; 9(2); 11; 15; 18; 19; 21; 49:1; 29; 50:6; 11; 15; 18; 19; 24; **Ex** 1:9; 16; 18; 19; 2:6; 7; 8; 9; 10; 13; 14(2); 18; 19; 20; 22; 3:3; 4(2); 5; 6; 7; 11; 12; 13; 14(2); 15; 17; 4:1; 2(2); 3; 4; 6; 7; 10; 11; 13; 14; 18(2); 19; 21; 25; 26; 27; 5:2; 3; 4; 5; 17; 19; 21; 22; 6:1; 2; 26; 30; 7:1; 13; 14; 22; 8:8; 9; 10(2); 15; 16; 19(2); 20; 25; 26; 28; 29; 9:1; 8; 13; 22; 27; 29; 10:1; 3; 7; 8; 9; 10; 12; 16; 21; 24; 25; 28; 29; 11:1; 4; 9; 12:21; 31(2); 32; 33; 43; 13:3; 17; 14:5; 11; 13; 15; 25; 26; 15:9; 26; 16:3; 4; 6; 8; 15(2); 19; 23(2); 25; 28; 32; 33; 17:2(2); 3; 5; 9; 10; 14; 16; 18:3; 4; 6; 10; 14; 15; 17; 24; 19:8; 9; 10; 15; 21; 23; 24; 20:19; 20; 22; 23:13; 24:1; 3(2); 7(2); 8; 12; 14; 30:34; 32:1; 2; 4; 5; 7; 8; 9; 11; 17; 18; 21; 22; 23; 24; 26; 27; 29; 30; 31; 33; 33:1; 5; 12(2); 14; 15; 17; 18; 19; 20; 21; 34:1; 9; 10; 27; 35:1; 30; **Lev** 8:5; 31; 9:2; 6; 7; 10:3; 4; 5; 6; 19; 16:2; 17:12; 14; 20:24; 21:1; **Num** 3:40; 7:11; 9:7; 8; 10:29(2); 30; 31; 35; 36; 11:4; 11; 16; 21(2); 23; 27; 28; 29; 12:2; 6; 11; 14; 13:17; 27; 30; 31; 14:2; 4; 11; 13; 20; 31; 35; 41; 15:35; 16:3; 8; 12; 15; 16; 22; 28; 34; 40; 46; 17:10; 18:1; 24; 20:10; 18; 19; 20; 21:2; 7; 8; 14; 34; 22:4; 8; 9; 10; 12; 13; 14; 16; 18; 20; 28; 29; 30(2); 32; 34; 35; 37; 38; 23:1; 3; 4; 5; 7; 11; 12; 13; 15; 16; 17; 18; 19; 23; 25; 26; 27; 29; 30; 24:3(3); 4; 10; 12; 15(3); 16; 20; 21; 23; 25:4; 5; 26:65; 27:12; 18; 31:15; 21; 49; 32:5; 6; 16; 20; 29; 31; 36:2; 5; **Deut** 1:14; 20; 21; 22; 25; 27; 29; 39; 41; 42; 2:9; 13; 31; 3:2; 26; 4:10; 5:1; 24; 28(2); 9:3; 12; 25; 26; 10:1; 11; 11:25; 17:16; 18:2; 17; 29:2; 13; 31:2(2); 3; 7; 14; 16; 23; 32:20; 26; 46; 33:2; 7; 8; 9; 12; 13; 18; 20; 22; 23; 24; 34:4; **Josh** 1:3; 2:4; 9; 16; 17; 21; 24; 3:5; 7; 9; 10; 4:5; 5:2; 9; 13; 14(2); 15; 6:2; 6; 7; 16; 22; 7:3; 7; 10; 19; 20; 25; 8:1; 18; 9:6; 7; 8(2); 9; 19; 21; 24; 10:8; 12; 18; 22; 24; 25; 11:6; 23; 13:1; 14; 33; 14:6(2); 10; 12; 15:16; 18; 17:16; 18:3; 22:2; 21; 26; 28; 31; 23:2; 24:2; 16; 19; 21; 22(2); 23; 24; 27; **Judg** 1:2; 3; 7; 12; 14; 15; 20; 24; 2:1(2); 3; 15; 20; 3:19(2); 20; 24; 28; 4:6; 8; 9; 14; 18; 19; 20; 22; 5:23; 6:8; 10; 12; 13; 14; 15; 16; 17; 18; 20; 22; 23; 25; 27; 29(2); 30; 31; 36(2); 37; 39; 7:2; 4; 5; 7; 9; 13; 14; 15; 17; 8:1; 2; 3; 5; 6; 7; 15; 18; 19; 20; 21; 22; 23; 24; 9:3; 7; 8; 9; 10; 11; 12; 13; 14; 15; 28; 29; 36(2); 37; 38; 48; 54; 10:11; 15; 18; 11:2; 6; 7; 8; 9; 10; 15; 19; 30; 35; 36; 37; 38; 12:1; 2; 4; 5(3); 6(2); 13:3; 7; 8; 10; 11(2); 12; 13(2); 15; 16; 17; 18; 22; 23; 14:2; 3(2); 12; 13; 14; 15; 16(2); 18(2); 15:1; 2; 3; 6; 7; 10; 11(2); 12(2); 16; 18; 16:5; 6; 7; 9; 10; 11; 12; 13(2); 14; 15; 17; 20(2); 23; 24; 25; 26; 28; 30; 17:2(2); 3; 9(2); 10; 13; 18:2; 3; 4; 5; 6; 8; 9; 14; 18; 19; 23; 24; 25; 19:5; 6; 8; 9; 11; 12; 13; 17; 18; 20; 23; 28; 30; 20:3; 4; 18(2); 23; 28; 32(2); 39; 21:3; 5; 6; 8; 16; 17; 19; **Ruth** 1:8; 10; 11; 15; 16; 19; 20; 2:2(2); 4; 5; 6; 7; 8; 10; 11; 13; 14; 19(2); 20(2); 21(2); 22; 3:1; 5; 9; 10; 14; 15; 16; 17(2); 18; 4:1; 2; 3; 4; 5; 6; 8; 9; 11; 14; **1Sa** 1:8; 11; 14; 15; 17; 18; 22; 23; 26; 2:1; 15; 16; 20; 23; 27; 30; 3:5(2); 6; 8; 9; 11; 16; 17(3); 18; 4:3; 6; 7(2); 14; 16(2); 17; 20; 22; 5:7; 8; 11; 6:3; 4; 20; 7:5; 6; 8; 8:5; 6; 7; 11; 19; 22(2); 9:3; 5; 6; 7; 8; 10(2); 11; 12; 17; 18; 19; 21; 23(2); 24(2); 27; 10:1; 11; 12; 14(2); 15(2); 16; 18; 19; 24(2); 27; 11:1; 3; 5; 9; 10; 12(2); 13; 14; 12:1(2); 4; 5; 6; 10; 12; 19; 20; 13:9; 11(2); 12; 13; 19; 14:1; 6; 7; 8; 11; 12(2); 17; 18; 19; 28; 29; 33; 34; 36(3); 38; 40(2); 41; 42; 43(2); 45; 15:1; 6; 13; 14; 15; 16(3); 17; 18; 20; 22; 24; 26; 28; 30; 32(2); 33; 16:1; 2(2); 4; 5; 6; 7; 8; 9; 10; 11(3); 12; 15; 17; 18; 19; 17:8; 10; 17; 25; 28; 29; 32; 33; 34; 37(2); 39; 43; 44; 45; 55(2); 56; 58; 18:7; 8; 11; 17(2); 18; 21(2); 23; 25; 19:4; 14; 17(2); 22(2); 20:1; 2; 3; 4; 5; 9; 10; 11; 12; 18; 27; 29; 30; 32; 36; 37; 40; 42; 21:1; 2(2); 4; 5; 8; 9(2); 11; 14; 22:3; 5; 7; 9; 12; 13; 14; 16; 17; 18; 22; 23:2; 3; 4; 7; 9; 10; 11; 12(2); 17; 21; 24:4(2); 6; 9; 10; 16; 17; 25:5; 10; 13; 19; 21; 24; 32; 35; 39; 41; 26:6(2); 8; 9; 10; 14; 15; 17(2); 18; 21; 22; 25; 27:1; 5; 10(2); 28:1; 2(2); 7(2); 8; 9; 11(2); 13(2); 14(2); 15; 16; 21; 23; 29:3(2); 4; 6; 8; 9(2); 30:7; 13(2); 15(2); 20; 22; 23; 31:4; **2Sa** 1:3(2); 4; 5; 6; 8; 9; 13; 14; 15; 16; 2:1(3); 5; 14(2); 20; 21; 22; 26; 27; 3:7; 8; 13; 16; 21; 24; 28; 31; 33; 38; 4:8; 9; 5:2; 8(2); 19; 20; 23; 6:9; 20; 21; 7:2; 3; 18; 25; 9:1; 2(2); 3(2); 4(2); 6; 7; 8; 9; 11(2); 10:2; 3; 5; 11; 11:3; 5; 8; 10; 11; 12; 23; 25; 12:1; 5; 7; 13(2); 18; 19(2); 21; 22(2); 27; 13:4(2); 5; 6; 9; 10; 11; 15; 16; 17; 20; 24; 25; 26(2); 32; 35(2); 14:2; 4; 5; 7; 8; 9; 10; 11(2); 12(2); 13; 15; 17; 18(2); 19(2); 21; 22; 24; 30; 31; 15:2(2); 3; 4; 7; 9; 14; 15; 19; 21; 22; 25; 27; 31; 33; 16:2(2); 3(3); 4(2); 7; 9; 10(2); 11; 16; 17; 18; 20; 21; 17:1; 5; 7; 8; 14; 15; 20(2); 21; 29; 18:2; 4; 10; 11; 12; 14; 18; 19; 20; 21; 22(2); 23(2); 25; 26(2); 27(2); 28(2); 29; 30; 31; 32; 33; 19:5; 19; 21; 22; 23; 25; 26; 29(2); 30; 33; 34; 41; 43; 20:1; 4; 6; 9; 11; 17(2); 20; 21; 21:2; 3; 4(2); 6; 22:2; 23:1(2); 3; 15; 17; 24:2; 3; 10; 13; 14; 16; 17; 18; 21(2); 22; 23; 24; **1Kin** 1:2; 16; 17; 24(2); 28; 29; 31; 32; 33; 36; 39; 41; 42; 43; 48; 52; 53; 2:4; 13(2); 14(2); 15; 16; 17; 18; 20(2); 21; 22; 26; 30(3); 31(2); 36; 38(2); 42; 44; 3:5; 6; 11; 17; 22(2); 23; 24; 25; 26(2); 27; 5:7; 8:12; 15; 18; 23; 29; 9:3; 13; 10:6; 11:2; 11; 21; 22; 31; 12:5; 6; 9; 26; 28; 13:2; 6; 7; 8; 12; 13; 14(2); 15; 16; 17; 18; 26; 14:2; 5; 6; 17:1; 10; 11; 12; 13(2); 18; 19; 20; 21; 23; 24; 18:5; 7; 9; 10; 15; 17; 21; 22; 24; 25; 27; 30; 33; 34(2); 36; 39; 40; 41; 43(3); 44(2); 19:4; 5; 7; 9; 10; 11; 13; 14; 15; 20(2); 20:2; 4; 5; 7; 8; 9; 10; 11; 12; 14(3); 18; 22; 23; 28(2); 31; 32(2); 33(2); 34(2); 35; 36; 37; 39(2); 40; 42; 21:3; 4; 5; 6(2); 7; 15; 20; 22:3; 4(2); 5; 6(2); 7; 8(2); 9; 11; 14; 15; 16; 17(2); 18; 19; 20(3); 21; 22(3); 24; 25; 26; 28(2); 30; 32; 34; 49; **2Kin** 1:2; 3; 5; 6(2); 7; 8; 9; 10; 11(2); 12; 13; 15; 16; 2:2(2); 3(2); 4(2); 5; 6(2); 9(2); 10; 14; 15; 16(2); 17; 18; 19; 20; 21; 23; 3:7; 8; 10; 11(2); 12; 13(2); 14; 16; 23; 4:2(2); 3; 6(2); 7; 9; 12; 13; 14; 15; 16(2); 17; 19(2); 22; 23(2); 24; 25; 27; 28; 29; 30; 36(2); 38; 40; 41(2); 42; 43(2); 5:3; 4; 5; 7; 11; 13; 15; 16; 17; 19; 20; 21; 22; 23; 25(2); 26; 6:1; 3; 5; 6; 7; 11; 12; 13; 15; 17; 18; 19; 20; 21; 27; 28(2); 29; 31; 32; 33; 7:1; 2(2); 3; 6; 9; 12; 13; 17; 19(2); 8:5; 8; 9; 10; 12; 13; 14(2); 9:1; 5(3); 6; 11(2); 12(2); 15; 17(2); 18(2); 19; 21; 22; 23; 25; 27; 31; 32; 33; 34; 36; 10:4; 8; 9; 13; 14; 15; 16; 18; 20; 22; 23; 24; 25; 30; 11:12; 15(2); 12:4; 7; 13:14; 15; 16; 17(3); 18(2); 19; 14:27; 17:12; 23; 18:19; 22; 25; 26; 27; 19:3; 6; 15; 23; 20:1; 7; 8; 9; 14(3); 15; 16; 19(2); 21:4; 7; 22:8; 9; 15; 23:17; 18; 27(2); 24:13; 25:24; **1Chr** 10:4; 11:2; 5; 6; 17; 19; 12:17; 18; 13:2; 4; 14:10; 11; 14; 15:2; 12; 16:36; 17:1; 2; 16; 23; 19:2; 3; 5; 12; 21:2; 8; 11; 13; 15; 17; 22; 23; 24; 22:1; 5; 7; 11; 23:5; 25; 27:23; 28:2; 3; 6; 19; 20; 29:1; 10; 20; **2Chr** 1:7; 8; 11; 2:12; 6:1(2); 4; 8; 14; 20; 7:12; 8:11; 9:5; 10:5; 9; 12:5; 6; 13:4; 14:7; 11; 15:2; 16:7; 18:3; 4; 5(2); 6; 7(2); 8; 10; 13; 14(2); 15; 16(2); 17; 18; 19; 20(2); 21(2); 23; 24; 25; 27(2); 29; 31; 33; 19:2; 6; 20:6; 15; 20; 22:9; 23:3(2); 11; 13; 14(2); 24:5; 6; 20; 22; 25:9; 15; 16(2); 26:18; 23; 28:9; 13; 23; 29:5; 18; 31; 31:10; 33:4; 7; 34:15; 35:3; 23; **Ezr** 2:63; 4:2; 3; 5:3; 4; 9; 15; 8:28; 9:6; 10:2; 10; 12(2); **Neh** 1:3; 5; 2:2; 3; 4; 5; 6; 7; 17; 18; 19; 20; 4:2; 3; 10; 11; 12; 14; 19; 22; 5:2; 3; 4; 7; 8; 9; 12; 13(2); 6:10; 11; 7:3; 65; 8:9; 10; 9:5; 18; 13:11; 17; 21; **Est** 1:13; 2:2; 3:3; 8; 11; 5:3; 5(2); 6; 7; 8; 12; 14; 6:3(2); 4; 5(2); 6; 10(2); 13; 7:2; 3; 5; 6; 8; 9(2); 8:5; 7; 9:12; 13; **Job** 1:5; 7(2); 8; 9; 12; 14; 16; 17; 18; 21; 2:2(2); 3; 4; 6; 9; 10; 3:2; 3; 4:1; 6:1; 8:1; 9:1; 22; 11:1; 4; 12:1; 15:1; 16:1; 17:14; 18:1; 19:1; 20:1; 21:1; 22:1; 17; 23:1; 25:1; 26:1; 27:1; 28:28; 29:1; 18; 31:24; 31; 32:6; 7; 10; 17; 34:1; 5; 9; 31; 35:1; 36:1; 38:1; 11; 40:1; 3; 6; 42:1; 7; **Ps** 2:7; 10:6; 11; 13; 12:4; 14:1; 16:2; 18:t, 27:8; 30:6; 31:14; 22; 32:5; 35:21; 38:16; 39:1; 40:7; 41:4; 52:t, 53:1; 54:t, 55:6; 68:22; 74:8; 75:4; 77:10; 78:19; 82:6; 83:4; 12; 87:5; 89:2; 94:18; 95:10; 102:24; 106:23; 110:1; 116:11; 119:57; 122:1; 126:2; 137:7; 140:6; 142:5; **Prov** 4:4; 7:13; 25:7; **Eccl** 1:10; 2:1; 2; 15(2); 3:17; 18; 7:23; 8:14; 9:16; **Song** 2:10; 3:3; 7:8; **Is** 5:9; 6:3; 5; 7; 8; 9; 11; 7:3; 12; 13; 8:1; 3; 14:13; 18:4; 20:3; 21:6; 9; 12; 16; 22:4; 23:12; 24:16; 25:9; 28:12; 15; 29:13; 30:16; 32:5; 36:4; 7; 10; 11; 12; 13; 37:3; 6; 24; 38:1; 3; 10; 11; 21; 22; 39:3(3); 4; 5; 8(2); 40:6(2); 41:6; 9; 45:19; 47:10(2); 49:3; 4; 6; 14; 51:23; 63:8; 65:1; 66:5; **Jer** 1:6; 7; 9; 11; 12; 13; 14; 2:6; 8; 3:6; 7; 11; 19(2); 4:10; 11; 27; 5:4; 12; 6:6; 16; 17; 10:19; 11:5; 6; 9; 12:4; 13:6; 14:11; 13; 14; 15:1; 11; 16:14; 17:19; 18:10; 12; 18; 19:14; 20:3; 9; 21:3; 23:17; 25; 24:3(2); 25:5; 26:16; 28:5; 6; 15; 29:15; 32:6; 8; 25; 35:5; 6; 11; 18; 36:15; 16; 19; 37:14; 17(3); 18; 38:4; 5; 12; 14; 15; 17; 19; 20; 24; 25(2); 40:2; 3; 5; 14; 16; 41:6; 8; 42:2; 4; 5; 9; 19; 44:20; 24; 46:16; 50:7; 51:61; **Lam** 3:18; 54; 4:15; 20; **Eze** 2:1; 3; 3:1; 3; 4; 10; 22; 24; 4:13; 14; 15; 16; 6:10; 8:5; 6; 8; 9; 12; 13; 15; 17; 9:4; 5; 7; 8; 9; 10:2; 11:2; 5(2); 13; 15; 12:9; 13:12; 16:6(2); 20:7; 8; 13; 18; 21; 29; 49; 21:17; 23:36; 43; 24:19; 26:2; 27:3; 28:2; 29:3; 9; 35:10; 36:2; 20; 37:3; 4; 9; 11; 40:4; 45; 41:4; 22; 42:13; 43:7; 18; 44:2; 5; 46:20; 24; 47:6; 8; **Dan** 1:10; 11; 18; 2:3; 5; 7; 8; 10; 15; 20; 24; 25; 26; 27; 47; 3:9; 14; 16; 24(2); 25; 26; 28; 4:14; 19(2); 30; 5:7; 10; 13; 17; 6:5; 6; 12; 13; 15; 16; 20; 21; 7:2; 5; 23; 8:13; 14; 16; 17; 19; 9:4; 22; 10:11; 12; 16; 19(2); 20; 12:6; 8; 9; **Hos** 1:2; 4; 6; 9; 10(2); 2:5; 12; 3:1; 3; 12:8; **Joel** 2:32; **Amos** 1:2; 7:2; 5; 8(3); 12; 14; 15; 8:2(3); 9:1; **Jonah** 1:6; 7; 8; 9; 10; 11; 12; 14; 2:2; 4; 3:4; 10; 4:2; 4; 8; 9(2); 10; **Mic** 3:1; 7:10; **Hab** 2:2; **Zeph** 2:15; 3:7; 16; **Hag** 2:12; 13(2); 14; **Zec** 1:6; 9(2); 10; 11; 12; 14; 19; 21; 2:2(2); 4; 3:2; 4; 5; 4:2(2); 5(2); 11; 12; 13(2); 14; 5:2; 3; 5; 6(3); 8; 10; 11; 6:4; 5; 7; 11:9; 12; 13; 15; **Mal** 1:13; 3:7; 14; **Mt** 2:5; 8; 3:7; 15; 4:3; 4; 7; 5:21; 27; 31; 33; 38; 43; 8:8; 10; 13; 19; 21; 22; 32; 9:2; 3; 4; 11; 12; 15; 21; 22; 24; 28; 34; 11:3; 4; 25; 12:2; 3; 11; 23; 24; 25; 39; 47; 48; 49; 13:10; 11; 27; 28(2); 29; 37; 52; 54; 57; 14:2; 4; 8; 16; 18; 28; 29; 31; 15:3; 10; 12; 13; 15; 16; 24; 26; 27; 28; 32; 34; 16:2; 6; 8; 14; 16; 17; 23; 24; 17:4; 5; 7; 11; 17; 19; 20; 22; 24; 18:3; 21; 32; 19:4; 5; 11; 14; 16; 17; 18; 21; 23; 26; 27; 28; 20:4; 13; 17; 21; 22; 25; 32; 21:11; 13; 16; 19; 21; 23; 24; 27(2); 28; 29; 30(2); 38; 22:1; 13; 18; 24; 29; 37; 44; 24:2; 4; 25:8; 12; 21; 22; 23; 24; 26; 26:1; 5; 10; 15; 18; 21; 23; 25(3); 26; 33; 34; 35(2); 49; 50; 52; 55; 61(2); 62; 63; 64; 66; 71; 73; 75; 27:4; 6; 11; 13; 17; 21(2); 23; 25; 41; 43; 47; 49; 63; 65; 28:5; 6; 10; **Mk** 1:17; 37; 38; 2:5; 8; 14; 16; 19; 24; 25; 27; 3:21; 22; 23; 30; 32; 34; 4:2; 9; 11; 13; 21; 24; 26; 30; 39; 40; 41; 5:7; 8; 28; 30; 31; 34; 35; 41; 6:4; 10; 14; 15(2); 16; 18; 22(2); 24(2); 31; 35; 37; 7:6; 9; 10; 14; 20; 27; 28; 29; 8:5; 20; 21; 24; 34; 9:1; 5; 17; 21; 23; 24; 26; 29; 31; 36; 39; 10:3; 4; 5; 14; 18; 20; 21; 29; 36; 37; 38; 39(2); 51(2); 52; 11:5; 6; 14; 29; 33; 12:7; 15; 16; 17; 24; 32(2); 34; 35; 36(2); 38; 13:2; 14:2; 4; 6; 12; 16; 18; 19; 20; 22; 24; 29; 31; 36; 48; 61; 62; 67; 70; 72; 15:2; 12; 14; 31; 35; 39; 16:3; 7; 8; 15; **Lk** 1:13; 18; 19; 28; 30; 34; 35; 38; 42; 46; 60; 61; 2:10; 15; 24; 28; 34; 48; 49; 3:7; 12; 13; 14; 22; 4:3; 6; 8; 9; 12(2); 22; 23; 24; 43; 5:4; 5; 10; 20; 22; 24; 27; 31; 33; 34; 6:2; 3; 5; 8; 9; 10; 20; 7:9; 13; 14; 20; 22; 31; 40; 43(2); 44; 48; 50; 8:8; 10; 20; 21; 22; 25; 28; 30; 45(2); 46; 48; 52; 9:3; 7; 9; 12; 13(2); 14; 19; 20(2); 23; 33(2); 41; 43; 48; 49; 50; 54; 55; 57; 58; 59(2); 60; 61; 62; 10:2; 18; 21; 23; 26; 27; 28; 29; 30; 35; 37(2); 40; 41; 11:1; 2; 5; 15; 17; 27; 28; 39; 45; 46; 49; 53; 12:13; 14; 15; 18; 20; 22; 41; 42; 54; 13:2; 7; 8; 12; 14; 15; 17; 18; 20; 23(2); 32; 14:12; 15; 16; 18; 19; 20; 21; 22; 23; 25; 15:11; 12; 17; 21; 22; 27; 29; 31; 16:1; 2; 3; 5; 6(2); 7(3); 15; 24; 25; 27; 30; 31; 17:1; 5; 6; 13; 14; 17; 19; 20; 22; 37(2); 18:4; 6; 16; 19; 21; 22; 24; 26; 27; 28; 29; 31; 41; 42; 19:5; 8; 9; 12; 13; 17; 19; 24; 25; 32; 33; 34; 39; 40; 20:3; 8; 13; 16; 17; 23; 24; 25; 34; 39(2); 41; 42; 45; 21:3; 5; 8; 10; 22:9; 10; 13; 15; 17; 25; 31; 33; 34; 35(2); 36; 38(2); 40; 46; 48; 49; 51; 52; 56; 58(2); 60; 61; 67; 70(2); 71; 23:3; 4; 14; 22; 28; 34; 42; 43; 46(2); 24:5; 17; 18; 19(2); 23; 24; 25; 32; 38; 41; 44; 46; **Jn** 1:22; 23(2); 25; 30; 33; 38; 42; 46; 48; 50(2); 2:16; 18; 19; 20; 22(2); 3:2; 3; 7; 9; 10; 26; 27; 28; 4:10; 13; 17(3); 27; 32; 33; 42; 48; 52; 53; 5:10; 11; 12; 14; 18; 19; 6:6; 10; 12; 14; 25; 26; 28; 29; 30; 32; 34; 35; 36; 41; 42; 43; 53; 59; 60; 61; 65(2); 67; 7:3; 6; 9; 11; 12(2); 16; 20; 21; 25; 31; 33; 35; 36; 38; 40; 41(2); 42; 45; 52; 8:6; 7; 10; 11(2); 13; 14; 19; 21; 22; 23; 24; 25(2); 28; 31; 39; 41; 42; 48; 52; 57; 58; 9:7; 8; 9(3); 10; 11(2); 12(2); 15; 16(2); 17; 20; 23; 24; 25; 26; 28; 30; 34; 35; 36; 37; 38; 39; 40; 41; 10:7; 20; 21; 24; 26; 34; 36; 41; 11:4; 11; 12; 14; 16; 21; 25; 28; 34(2); 36; 37; 39; 40; 41; 42; 47; 49; 12:6; 7; 19; 29(2); 30; 33; 35; 39; 41; 44; 50; 13:7; 11; 12; 21(2); 27; 29; 31; 33; 36; 37;

14:23; 26; 28(2); 15:20; 16:4; 6; 15; 17; 18; 19(2); 29; 17:1; 18:4; 6; 7; 11; 20; 21(2); 25(2); 29; 30; 31(2); 33; 37; 38; 19:3; 21(2); 24; 30; 20:14; 20; 21; 22; 25(2); 26; 28; 21:6; 17(2); 20; 23; **Acts** 1:7; 11; 15; 24; 2:13; 14; 34; 37; 38; 3:4; 6; 22; 4:8; 19; 23; 24; 25; 32; 5:3; 8; 9; 19; 29; 35; 6:2; 11; 13; 7:1; 2; 3; 7; 33; 37; 56; 60; 8:20; 24; 29; 30; 31; 34; 36; 37(2); 9:5(2); 6(2); 10(2); 11; 15; 17; 21; 34; 40; 10:4(2); 14; 19; 21; 22; 28; 30; 31; 34; 11:8; 13; 16; 12:8; 11; 15(2); 17; 13:2; 10; 16; 22; 25; 34; 46; 14:10; 15:1; 7; 36; 16:18; 30; 31; 37; 17:18; 22; 28; 32; 18:6; 14; 19:2(2); 3(2); 4; 15; 25; 35; 20:10; 18; 35; 21:4; 11; 20; 37(2); 39; 22:8; 10(2); 13; 14; 19; 21; 22; 25; 27(2); 28; 23:1; 3; 4; 5; 7; 11; 14; 17; 18; 20; 35; 24:22; 25:5; 9; 10; 22(2); 24; 26:1; 15(2); 24; 25; 28; 29; 32; 27:10; 21; 31; 28:4; 6; 17; 21; 29; **Rom** 7:7; 9:12; 26; 29; **1Cor** 11:24; **2Cor** 6:16; 7:3; 9:3; 12:9; **Gal** 1:9; 2:14; **Titus** 1:12; **Heb** 1:5; 13; 3:10; 15; 4:3; 7; 5:5; 7:21; 10:7; 8; 9; 15; 30; 11:18; 12:21; 13:5; **Jas** 2:11(2); **Jude** 9; **Rev** 4:1; 5:14; 6:11; 16; 7:14(2); 10:8; 9(2); 11; 17:7; 19:3; 10; 21:5(2); 6; 22:6

SAIDST

559, 1696, *2046*

Gen 12:19; 26:9; 32:9; 12; 44:21; 23; **Ex** 32:13; **Judg** 9:38; **1Kin** 2:42; **Job** 35:2; 3; **Ps** 27:8; 89:19; **Is** 47:7; 57:10; **Jer** 2:20; 25; 22:21; **Lam** 3:57; **Eze** 25:3; **Hos** 13:10; **Jn** 4:18

SAITH

559, 1696, 5001, 5002, 6310, *2036, 2980, 3004, 5346*

Gen 22:16; 32:4; 41:55; 44:7; 45:9; **Ex** 4:22; 5:1; 10; 7:17; 8:1; 20; 9:1; 13; 10:3; 11:4; 32:27; **Num** 14:28; 20:14; 22:16; 24:13; 32:27; **Josh** 5:14; 7:13; 22:16; 24:2; **Judg** 6:8; 11:15; **1Sa** 2:27; 30(2); 9:6; 10:18; 15:2; 20:3; 24:13; **2Sa** 7:5; 8; 12:7; 11; 14:10; 17:5; 24:12; **1Kin** 2:30; 3:23(2); 11:31; 12:24; 13:2; 21; 14:7; 17:14; 20:2; 13; 14; 28; 32; 42; 21:19(2); 22:11; 14; 27; **2Kin** 1:4; 6; 16; 2:21; 3:16; 17; 4:43; 5:13; 7:1; 9:3; 6; 12; 18; 19; 26(2); 18:19; 29; 31; 19:3; 6; 20; 32; 33; 20:1; 5; 17; 21:12; 22:15; 16; 18; 19; **1Chr** 17:4; 7; 21:10; 11; **2Chr** 11:4; 12:5; 18:10; 13; 26; 20:15; 21:12; 24:20; 32:10; 34:23; 24; 26; 27; 36:23; **Ezr** 1:2; **Neh** 6:6; **Job** 28:14(2); 33:24; 35:10; 37:6; 39:25; **Ps** 12:5; 36:1; 50:16; **Prov** 9:4; 16; 20:14; 22:13; 23:7; 24:24; 26:13; 19; 28:24; 30:16; 20; **Eccl** 1:2; 4:8; 7:27; 10:3; 12:8; **Is** 1:11; 18; 24; 3:15; 16; 7:7; 10:8; 13; 24; 14:22(2); 23; 17:3; 6; 19:4; 22:14; 15; 25; 28:16; 29:11; 12; 22; 30:1; 12; 15; 31:9; 33:10; 36:4; 14; 16; 37:3; 6; 21; 33; 34; 38:1; 5; 39:6; 40:1; 25; 41:14; 21(2); 42:5; 22; 43:1; 10; 12; 14; 16; 44:2; 6; 16; 17; 24; 26; 27; 28; 45:1; 10; 11; 13; 14; 18; 48:17; 22; 49:5; 7; 8; 18; 22; 25; 50:1; 51:22; 52:3; 4; 5(2); 7; 54:1; 6; 8; 10; 17; 55:8; 56:1; 4; 8; 57:15; 19; 21; 59:20; 21(2); 65:7; 8(2); 13; 25; 66:1; 2; 9(2); 12; 17; 20; 21; 22; 23; **Jer** 1:8; 15; 19; 2:2; 3; 5; 9; 12; 19; 22; 29; 3:1; 10; 12(2); 13; 14; 16; 20; 4:1; 3; 9; 17; 5:9; 11; 14; 15; 18; 22; 29; 6:9; 12; 15; 16; 21; 22; 7:3; 11; 13; 19; 20; 21; 30; 32; 8:1; 3; 4; 12; 13; 17; 9:3; 6; 7; 9; 13; 15; 17; 22; 23; 24; 25; 10:2; 18; 11:3; 11; 21; 22; 12:14; 17; 13:1; 9; 11; 12; 13; 14; 25; 14:10; 15; 15:2; 3; 6; 9; 19; 20; 16:3; 5(2); 9; 11; 14; 16; 17:5; 21; 24; 18:6; 11; 13; 19:1; 3; 6; 11; 12; 15; 20:4; 21:4; 7; 8; 10; 12; 13; 14; 22:1; 3; 5; 6; 11; 14; 16; 18; 24; 30; 23:1; 2(2); 4; 5; 7; 11; 12; 15; 16; 23; 24(2); 28; 29; 30; 31(2); 32(2); 33; 38; 24:5; 8; 25:7; 8; 9; 12; 15; 27; 28; 29; 31; 32; 26:2; 4; 18; 27:2; 4; 8; 11; 15; 16; 19; 21; 22; 28:4; 11; 13; 14; 16; 29:4; 8; 9; 10; 11; 14(2); 16; 17; 19(2); 21; 23; 31; 32(2); 30:3(2); 5; 8; 10; 11; 12; 17; 18; 21; 31:1; 2; 7; 14; 15; 16(2); 17; 20; 23; 27; 28; 31; 32; 33; 34; 35; 36; 37(2); 38; 32:3; 5; 14; 15; 28; 30; 36; 42; 44; 33:2; 4; 10; 11; 12; 13; 14; 17; 20; 25; 34:2(2); 4; 5; 13; 17(2); 22; 35:13(2); 17; 18; 19; 36:29; 30; 37:7; 9; 38:2; 3; 17; 39:16; 17; 18; 42:9; 11; 15; 18; 43:10; 44:2; 7; 11; 25; 26; 29; 30; 45:2; 4; 5; 46:5; 8; 18; 23; 25; 26; 28; 47:2; 48:1; 12; 15; 25; 30; 35; 38; 40; 43; 44; 47; 49:1; 2(2); 5; 6; 7; 12; 13; 16; 18; 26; 28; 30; 31; 32; 35; 37; 38; 39; 50:4; 10; 18; 20; 21; 30; 31; 33; 35; 40; 51:1; 24; 25; 26; 33; 36; 39; 48; 52; 53; 57; 58; **Lam** 3:24; 37; **Eze** 2:4; 3:11; 27; 5:5; 7; 8; 11; 6:3; 11; 7:2; 5; 11:5; 7; 8; 16; 17; 21; 12:10; 19; 23; 25; 28(2); 13:3; 6; 7; 8(2); 13; 16; 18; 20; 14:4; 6; 11; 14; 16; 18; 20; 21; 23; 15:6; 8; 16:3; 8; 14; 19; 23; 30; 36; 43; 48; 58; 59; 63; 17:3; 9; 16; 19; 22; 18:3; 9; 23; 29; 30; 32; 20:3(2); 5; 27; 30; 31; 33; 36; 39; 40; 44; 47; 21:3; 7; 9; 13; 24; 26; 28; 22:3; 12; 19; 28; 31; 23:22; 28; 32; 34; 35; 46; 24:3; 6; 9; 14; 21; 25:3; 6; 8; 12; 13; 14; 15; 16; 26:3; 5; 7; 14; 15; 19; 21; 27:3; 28:2; 6; 10; 12; 22; 25; 29:3; 8; 13; 19; 20; 30:2; 6(2); 10; 13; 22; 31:10; 15; 18; 32:3; 8; 11; 14; 16; 31; 32; 33:11; 25; 27; 34:2; 8; 10; 11; 15; 17; 20; 30; 31; 35:3; 6; 11; 14; 36:2; 3; 4; 5; 6; 7; 13; 14; 15; 22; 23; 32; 33; 37; 37:5; 9; 12; 14; 19; 21; 38:3; 10; 14; 17; 18; 21; 39:1; 5; 8; 10; 13; 17; 20; 25; 29; 43:18; 19; 27; 44:6; 9; 12; 15; 27; 45:9(2); 15; 18; 46:1; 16; 47:13; 23; 48:29; **Hos** 2:13; 16; 21; 11:11; **Joel** 2:12; **Amos** 1:3; 5; 6; 8; 9; 11; 13; 15; 2:1; 3; 4; 6; 11; 16; 3:10; 11; 12; 13; 15; 4:3; 5; 6; 8; 9; 10; 11; 5:3; 4; 16; 17; 27; 6:8; 14; 7:3; 6; 11; 17; 8:3; 9; 11; 9:7; 8; 12; 13; 15; **Obad** 1; 3; 4; 8; **Mic** 2:3; 3:5; 4:6; 5:10; 6:1; **Nah** 1:12; 2:13; 3:5; **Hab** 2:19; **Zeph** 1:2; 3; 10; 2:9; 3:8; 20; **Hag** 1:5; 7; 8; 9; 13; 2:4(3); 6; 7; 8; 9(2); 11; 14; 17; 23(3); **Zec** 1:3(3); 4(2); 14; 16(2); 17; 2:5; 6(2); 8; 10; 3:7; 9; 10; 4:6; 5:4; 7:13; 8:2; 3; 4; 6(2); 7; 9; 11; 14(2); 17; 19; 20; 23; 10:12; 11:4; 6; 12:1; 4; 13:2; 7; 8; **Mal** 1:2(2); 4(2); 6; 8; 9; 10; 11; 13(2); 14; 2:2; 4; 8; 16(2); 3:1; 5; 7; 10; 11; 12; 13; 17; 4:1; 3; **Mt** 4:6; 9; 10; 19; 7:21; 8:4; 7; 20; 26; 9:6; 9; 28; 37; 12:13; 44; 13:14; 51; 15:34; 16:15; 17:25; 26(2); 18:22; 19:8; 18; 20; 20:6; 7; 8; 21; 23; 21:16; 31; 42; 22:8; 12; 20; 21; 43; 26:18; 31; 36; 38; 40; 45; 64; 27:22; **Mk** 1:41; 44; 2:10; 17; 3:3; 4; 5; 4:35; 5:19; 36; 39; 6:38; 50; 7:18; 34; 8:1; 12; 17; 29(2); 9:19; 35; 10:11; 23; 24; 27; 42; 11:2; 21; 22; 23(2); 33; 12:16; 43; 13:1; 14:13; 14; 27; 30; 32; 34; 37; 41; 45; 63; 15:28; 16:6; **Lk** 3:11; 5:39; 7:40; 11:24; 16:29; 18:6; 19:22; 20:42; 22:11; 24:36; **Jn** 1:21; 29; 36; 38; 39; 41; 43; 45; 46; 47; 48; 49; 51; 2:3; 4; 5(2); 7; 8; 10; 3:4; 4:7; 9; 10; 11; 15; 16; 19; 21; 25; 26; 28; 34; 49; 50; 5:6; 8; 6:5; 8; 20; 42; 7:50; 8:22; 25; 39; 11:7; 11; 23; 24; 27; 39; 40; 44; 12:4; 13:6; 8; 9; 10; 25; 14:5; 6; 8; 9; 22; 16:17; 18(2); 18:5; 17(2); 26; 38(2); 19:4; 5; 6; 9; 10; 14; 15; 24; 26; 27; 28; 35; 37; 20:2; 13; 15(2); 16(2); 17; 19; 22; 27; 29; 21:3; 5; 7; 10; 12; 15(3); 16(3); 17(2); 19; 21; 22; **Acts** 1:4; 2:17; 34; 7:48; 49; 12:8; 13:35; 15:17; 21:11; 22:2; **Rom** 3:19(2); 4:3; 9:15; 17; 25; 10:8; 11; 16; 19; 20; 21; 11:2; 4; 9; 12:19; 14:11; 15:10; 12; **1Cor** 1:12; 3:4; 6:16; 9:8; 10; 14:21; 34; 15:27; **2Cor** 6:2; 17; 18; **Gal** 3:16; 4:30; **Eph** 4:8; 5:14; **1Ti** 5:18; **Heb** 1:6; 7; 8; 3:7; 5:6; 8:5; 8(2); 9; 10; 13; 10:5; 16; 30; **Jas** 2:23; 4:5; 6; **1Jn** 2:4; 6; 9; **Rev** 1:8; 2:1; 7; 8; 11; 12; 17; 18; 29; 3:1; 6; 7; 13; 14; 22; 5:5; 14:13; 17:15; 18:7; 19:9(2); 22:9; 10; 20

SAME

428, 1459, 1791, 1797, 1931, 1933, 1992, 2063, 2088, 6106, 8478, *846, 1565, 2532, 3673, 3748, 3761, 3778, 4954, 5023, 5026, 5124, 5126, 5129, 5615, 5778*

Gen 2:13; 5:29; 6:4; 7:11; 10:12; 14:8; 15:18; 19:37; 38; 21:8; 23:2; 19; 24:14; 44; 25:30; 26:12; 24; 32; 32:13; 41:48; 44:6; 48:7; **Ex** 5:6; 12:6; 19:1; 25:31; 35(3); 36; 27:2; 28:8; 30:2; 37:17; 21(3); 22; 25; 38:2; 39:5; **Lev** 7:15; 16; 19:6; 22:30; 23:6; 28; 29; 30(2); **Num** 4:8; 6:11; 9:13; 10:32; 15:30; 32:10; **Deut** 9:20; 14:28; 27:11; 31:22; **Josh** 6:15; 11:16; 15:8; **Judg** 6:25; 7:4(2); 9; **1Sa** 4:12; 6:15; 16; 9:17; 10:12; 14:35; 17:23; 30; 31:6; **2Sa** 2:23; 5:7; 23:7; 8; **1Kin** 7:35; 8:64; 13:3; 9; **2Kin** 3:6; 8:22; 19:29; 33; **1Chr** 1:27; 4:33; 16:17; 17:3; **2Chr** 7:8; 13:9; 15:11; 16:10; 18:7; 20:26; 21:10; 27:5; 32:12; 30; 34:28; 35:16; **Ezr** 4:15; 5:3; 13; 16; 6:3; 10:23; **Neh** 4:22; 6:4; 10:37; **Est** 9:1; 17; 18; 21; **Job** 4:8; 13:2; **Ps** 68:23; 75:8; 102:27; 105:10; 113:3; **Prov** 28:24; **Eccl** 9:15; **Is** 7:20; 20:2; 37:30; 34; **Jer** 27:8; 28:1; 17; 31:1; 39:10; **Eze** 3:18; 10:16; 22; 21:26; 23:38; 39; 24:2(2); 38:10; 18; 44:3; **Dan** 3:6; 15; 4:33; 36; 5:5; 12; 7:21; 12:1; **Amos** 2:7; **Zeph** 1:9; **Zec** 6:10; **Mal** 1:11; **Mt** 3:4; 5:19; 46; 10:19; 12:50; 13:1; 20; 15:22; 18:1; 4; 28; 21:42; 22:23; 24:13; 25:16; 26:23; 44; 48; 55; 27:44; **Mk** 3:35; 4:35; 8:35; 9:35; 10:10; 13:13; 14:39; 44; **Lk** 2:8; 25; 6:33; 38; 7:21; 47; 9:24; 48; 10:7; 10; 12:12; 13:31; 16:1; 17:29; 20:17; 19; 47; 23:12; 40; 51; 24:13; 33; **Jn** 1:2; 7; 33(2); 3:2; 26; 4:53; 5:9; 11; 36; 7:18; 8:25; 10:1; 11:6; 49; 12:21; 48; 15:5; 18:13; 20:19; **Acts** 1:11; 22; 2:36; 41; 7:19; 35; 8:9; 35; 12:6; 13:33; 14:9; 15:27; 16:17; 18; 33; 18:3; 19:23; 21:9; 22:13; 24:20; 28:7; **Rom** 1:32; 2:1; 3; 8:20; 9:17; 21; 10:12; 12:4; 16; 13:3; **1Cor** 1:10(3); 7:20; 8:3; 9:8; 10:3; 4; 11:23; 25; 12:4; 5; 6; 8; 9(2); 25; 15:39; **2Cor** 1:6; 2:2; 3; 3:14; 18; 4:13; 6:13; 7:8; 8:6; 16; 19; 9:4; 5; 12:18(2); **Gal** 2:8; 10; 3:7; **Eph** 3:6; 4:10; 6:8; 9; 22; **Phil** 1:30; 2:2; 18; 3:1; 16(2); 4:2; **Col** 4:2; 8; **2Ti** 2:2; **Heb** 1:12; 2:14; 4:11; 6:11; 10:11; 11:9; 13:8; **Jas** 3:2; 10; 11; **1Pet** 2:7; 4:1; 4; 10; 5:9; **2Pet** 2:19; 3:7; **1Jn** 2:23; 27; **Rev** 3:5; 11:13; 14:10

SAW

2370, 2372, 4883, 7200, 7805, *991, 1492, 1689, 2147, 2300, 2334, 3708*

Gen 1:4; 10; 12; 18; 21; 25; 31; 3:6; 6:2; 5; 9:22; 23; 12:15; 16:4; 5; 18:2; 21:9; 19; 22:4; 24:30; 63; 64; 26:8; 28; 28:6; 29:10; 31; 30:1; 9; 31:10; 32:2; 25; 33:5; 34:2; 37:4; 18; 38:2; 14; 15; 39:3; 13; 40:16; 41:19; 22; 42:1; 7; 21; 35; 43:16; 29; 44:28; 45:27; 48:17; 49:15; 50:11; 15; 23; **Ex** 2:2; 5; 6; 12; 3:4; 8:15; 9:34; 10:23; 14:30; 31; 16:15; 18:14; 20:18(2); 24:10; 11; 32:1; 5; 19; 25; 33:10; 34:30; 35; **Lev** 9:24; **Num** 13:28; 32; 33; 20:29; 22:2; 23; 25; 27; 31; 33; 24:1; 2; 4; 16; 25:7; 32:1; 9; **Deut** 1:19; 4:12; 15; 7:19; 32:19; **Josh** 7:21; 8:14; 20; 21; **Judg** 1:24; 3:24; 9:36; 55; 11:35; 12:3; 14:1; 11; 16:1; 18; 24; 18:7; 26; 19:3; 17; 30; 20:36; 41; **Ruth** 1:18; 2:18; **1Sa** 5:7; 6:13; 9:17; 10:11; 14; 12:12; 13:6; 11; 14:52; 17:24; 42; 51; 55; 18:15; 28; 19:20; 22:9; 23:15; 25:23; 25; 26:3; 12; 28:5; 12; 13; 21; 31:5; 7; **2Sa** 1:7; 6:16; 10:6; 9; 14; 15; 19; 11:2; 12:19; 14:24; 28; 17:18; 23; 18:10(2); 26; 29; 20:12(2); 24:17; 20; **1Kin** 3:28; 12:16; 13:25; 16:18; 18:17; 39; 19:3; 22:17; 19; 32; **2Kin** 2:12(2); 15; 3:22; 26; 4:25; 5:21; 6:17; 20; 21; 9:22; 27; 11:1; 12:10; 13:4; 14:26; 16:10; 12; **1Chr** 10:5; 7; 15:29; 19:6; 10; 15; 16; 19; 21:16; 20; 21; 28; **2Chr** 7:3; 10:16; 12:7; 15:9; 18:18; 31; 22:10; 24:11; 25:21; 31:8; 32:2; **Neh** 6:16; 13:15; 23; **Est** 1:14; 3:5; 5:2; 9; 7:7; **Job** 2:13; 3:16; 20:9; 29:8; 11; 31:21; 32:5; 42:16; **Ps** 48:5; 73:3; 77:16(2); 95:9; 97:4; 114:3; **Prov** 24:32; **Eccl** 2:13; 24; 3:16; 4:7; 8:10; 9:11; **Song** 3:3; 6:9; **Is** 1:1; 2:1; 6:1; 10:15; 21:7; 41:5; 59:15; 16; **Jer** 3:7; 8; 39:4; 41:13; 44:17; **Lam** 1:7; **Eze** 1:1; 27(2); 28; 3:23; 8:4; 10; 10:15; 20; 22; 11:1; 16:6; 50; 19:5; 20:28; 23:11; 13; 14; 16; 41:8; 43:3(3); **Dan** 3:27; 4:5; 10; 13; 23; 5:5; 7:2; 7; 13; 8:2(3); 3; 4; 7; 10:7(2); 8; **Hos** 5:13(2); 9:10; 13; **Amos** 1:1; 9:1; **Jonah** 3:10; **Mic** 1:1; **Hab** 3:7; 10; **Hag** 2:3; **Zec** 1:8; 18; **Mt** 2:9; 10; 11; 16; 3:7; 16; 4:16; 18; 21; 8:14; 18; 34; 9:8; 9; 11; 22; 23; 36; 12:2; 22; 14:14; 26; 30; 15:31; 17:8; 18:31; 20:3; 21:15; 19; 20; 38; 22:11; 25:37; 38; 39; 44; 26:8; 71; 27:3; 24; 54; 28:17; **Mk** 1:10; 16; 19; 2:5; 12; 14; 16; 3:11; 5:6; 16; 22; 6:33; 34; 48; 49; 50; 7:2; 8:23; 25; 9:8; 14; 20; 25; 38; 10:14; 11:20; 12:34; 14:67; 69; 15:39; 16:4; 5; **Lk** 1:12; 29; 2:48; 5:2; 8; 20; 27; 7:13; 39; 8:28; 34; 36; 47; 9:32; 49; 54; 10:31; 33; 11:38; 13:12; 15:20; 17:14; 15; 18:15; 24; 43; 19:5; 7; 20:14; 21:1; 2; 22:49; 58; 23:8; 47; 24:24; **Jn** 1:32; 34; 38; 39; 47; 48; 50; 2:23; 5:6; 6:2; 5; 22; 24; 26; 8:10; 56; 9:1; 11:31; 32; 33; 12:41; 19:6; 26; 33; 35; 20:5; 8; 14; 20; 21:9; **Acts** 3:9; 12; 4:13; 6:15; 7:31; 55; 8:18; 39; 9:8; 35; 40; 10:3; 11; 11:5; 6; 12:3; 9; 16; 13:12; 36; 37; 45; 14:11; 16:19; 17:16; 21:27; 32; 22:9; 18; 26:13; 28:4; 6; 15; **Gal** 1:19; 2:7; 14; **Phil** 1:30; **Heb** 3:9; 11:23; **Rev** 1:2; 12; 17; 4:4; 5:1; 2; 6:1; 2; 9; 7:1; 2; 8:2; 9:1; 17; 10:1; 5; 11:11; 12:13; 13:1; 2; 3; 14:6; 15:1; 2; 16:13; 17:3; 6(2); 18:1; 18; 19:11; 17; 19; 20:1; 4(2); 11; 12; 21:1; 2; 22; 22:8

SAWEST

2370, 2372, 7200, *1492*

Gen 20:10; **1Sa** 19:5; 28:13; **2Sa** 18:11; **Ps** 50:18; **Is** 57:8; **Dan** 2:31; 34; 41(2); 43; 45; 4:20; 8:20; **Rev** 1:20(2); 17:8; 12; 15; 16; 18

SAY

559, 560, 1696, 1697, 4405, 7725, *471, 2036, 2046, 2980, 3004, 3056, 5335, 5346*

Gen 12:12; 13; 14:23; 20:13; 24:14(2); 43; 44; 26:7; 32:18; 20; 34:11; 12; 37:17; 20; 41:15; 43:7; 44:4; 16; 45:9; 17; 46:31; 33; 34; 50:17; **Ex** 3:13(3); 14; 15; 16; 18; 4:1; 12; 22; 23; 5:16; 17; 6:6; 29; 7:9; 16; 19; 8:1; 5; 16; 20; 9:13; 12:26; 27; 13:14; 14:3; 16:9; 19:3; 20:22; 21:5; 32:12; 33:5; **Lev** 1:2; 15:2; 17:2; 8; 18:2; 19:2; 20:2; 21:1; 22:3; 18; 23:2; 10; 25:2; 20; 27:2; **Num** 5:12; 19; 21; 22; 6:2; 8:2; 11:12; 18; 14:28; 15:2; 18; 18:26; 30; 21:27; 22:19; 20; 38; 23:16; 25:12; 28:2; 3; 33:51; 34:2; 35:10; **Deut** 1:42; 4:6; 5:27; 30; 6:21; 7:17; 8:17; 9:2; 28; 12:20; 13:12; 15:16; 17:14; 18:21; 20:3; 8; 21:7; 20; 22:14; 16; 25:7; 8; 9; 26:3; 5; 13; 27:14; 15; 16; 17; 18; 19; 20; 21; 22; 23; 24; 25; 26; 28:67(2); 29:22; 24; 25; 30:12; 13; 31:17; 32:27; 37; 40; 33:27; **Josh** 7:8; 13; 8:6; 9:11; 22:11; 27; 28(2); **Judg** 4:20(2); 7:4(2); 11; 18; 9:54; 12:6; 16:15; 18:8; 24; 21:22; **Ruth** 1:12; **1Sa** 2:36; 3:9; 8:7; 10:2; 11:9; 13:4; 14:9; 10; 34; 15:16; 16:2; 18:22; 25; 19:24; 20:6; 7; 21; 22; 25:6; **2Sa** 7:8; 20; 11:20; 21; 25; 13:5; 28; 14:12; 32; 15:10; 26; 34; 16:10; 17:9; 19:2; 13; 20:16; 21:4; 24:1; 12; **1Kin** 1:13; 25; 34; 36; 2:14(2); 16; 17; 20(2); 9:8; 12:10; 13:22; 14:5; 16:16; 18:44; 22:8; 27; **2Kin** 1:3; 6; 2:18; 4:13; 26; 28; 7:4; 13; 8:10; 9:3; 17; 37; 18:22; 19:6; 9; 22:18; **1Chr** 5:3; 16:31; 35; 17:7; 21:18; **2Chr** 7:21; 10:10; 18:7; 15; 26; 20:11; 21; 34:26; **Ezr** 8:17; 9:10; **Neh** 7:7; 9:8; **Est** 1:18; **Job** 6:22; 7:4; 13; 9:12; 20; 27; 10:2; 19:28; 20:7; 21:14; 28; 22:29; 23:5; 28:22; 32:11; 13; 33:27; 32; 34:18; 36:23; 37:19; 38:35; **Ps** 3:2; 4:6; 11:1; 13:4; 27:14; 35:3; 10; 25(2); 27; 40:15; 16; 41:8; 42:3; 9; 10; 58:11; 59:7; 64:5; 66:3; 70:3; 4; 73:11; 15; 79:10; 91:2; 94:7; 96:10; 106:48; 107:2; 115:2; 118:2; 3; 4; 122:8; 124:1; 129:1; 8; 130:6; 139:11; **Prov** 1:11; 3:28; 5:12; 7:4; 20:9; 22; 23:35; 24:29; 30:9; 15; **Eccl** 5:6; 6:3; 7:10; 8:4; 12:1; **Is** 2:3; 3:10; 5:19; 7:4; 8:12(2); 19; 9:9; 12:1; 4; 14:4; 10; 19:11; 20:6; 22:15; 29:15; 16(2); 30:10; 22; 33:24; 35:4; 36:4; 5; 7; 37:6; 9; 38:5; 15; 40:9; 41:26; 27; 42:17; 43:6; 9; 44:5; 19; 20; 45:9; 24; 48:5; 7; 20; 49:9; 20; 21; 51:16; 56:3; 12; 57:14; 58:3; 9; 62:11; 65:5; **Jer** 1:7; 2:23; 27; 31; 3:1; 12; 16; 4:5(2); 5:2; 15; 19; 24; 7:2; 10; 28; 8:4; 8; 10:11; 11:3; 13:12; 13; 18; 21; 22; 14:13; 15; 17; 15:2; 16:10; 11; 19; 17:15; 20; 19:3; 11; 20:10; 21:3; 8; 11; 13; 22:2; 8; 23:7; 17(2); 31; 33; 34; 35; 37; 38(3); 25:27; 28; 30; 26:4; 27:4(2); 31:7; 10; 29; 32:3; 36; 43; 33:10; 11; 36:29; 37:7; 38:22; 25; 26; 39:12; 42:13; 20;

43:2; 10; 45:3; 4; 46:14; 48:14; 17; 19; 50:2; 51:35(2); 62; 64; **Lam** 2:12; 16; **Eze** 2:4; 8; 3:18; 27; 6:3; 11; 8:12; 9:9; 11:3; 16; 17; 12:10; 11; 19; 23; 25; 27; 28; 13:2; 7; 11; 15; 18; 14:4; 6; 17; 16:3; 17:3; 9; 12; 18:19; 25; 19:2; 20:3; 5; 27; 30; 32; 47; 49; 21:3; 7; 9(2); 24; 28(2); 22:3; 24; 24:3; 25:3; 8; 26:17; 27:3; 28:2; 9; 12; 22; 29:3; 30:2; 32:2; 33:2; 8; 11; 12; 13; 14; 17; 20; 25; 27; 34:2; 35:3; 36:1; 3; 6; 13; 22; 35; 37:4; 9; 11; 12; 19; 21; 38:3; 11; 13; 14; 39:1; 44:5; 6; **Dan** 4:35; 5:11; **Hos** 2:1; 7; 23(2); 10:3; 8; 13:2; 14:2; 3; 8; **Joel** 2:17(2); 19; 3:10; **Amos** 3:9; 4:1; 5:16; 6:10(3); 13; 8:14; 9:10; **Mic** 2:4; 6; 3:11; 4:2; 11; **Nah** 3:7; **Hab** 2:1; 6; **Zeph** 1:12; **Hag** 1:2; **Zec** 1:3; 11:5; 12:5; 13:3; 5; 6; 9(2); **Mal** 1:2; 5; 6; 7(2); 12; 2:14; 17(2); 3:8; 13; **Mt** 3:9(2); 4:17; 5:11; 18; 20; 22(3); 26; 28; 32; 34; 39; 44; 6:2; 5; 16; 25; 29; 7:4; 22; 8:9; 10; 11; 9:5(2); 10:15; 23; 42; 11:7; 9; 11; 18; 19; 22; 24; 12:6; 31; 36; 13:17; 30; 51; 14:17; 15:5(2); 33; 16:2; 13; 14; 15; 18; 28; 17:10; 12; 20(2); 18:3; 10; 13; 18; 19; 22; 19:7; 9; 10; 23; 24; 28; 20:7; 22; 33; 21:3(2); 16; 21(2); 25(2); 26; 31(2); 41; 43; 22:21; 23; 42; 23:3; 16; 30; 36; 39(2); 24:2; 23; 26; 34; 47; 48; 25:12; 34; 40(2); 41; 45; 26:13; 18; 21; 22; 29; 34; 64; 27:22; 33; 46; 64; 28:13; **Mk** 1:44; 2:9(2); 11; 18; 3:28; 4:38; 5:41; 6:11; 37; 38; 7:2; 11(3); 8:12; 19; 27; 28; 29; 9:1; 6; 11; 13; 41; 10:15; 28; 29; 47; 11:3(2); 23(2); 24; 28; 31(2); 32; 12:14; 18; 35; 43; 13:5; 21; 30; 37(2); 14:9; 14; 18; 19; 25; 30; 58; 65; 69; **Lk** 3:8(2); 4:21; 23; 24; 5:23(2); 24; 6:27; 42; 46; 7:7; 8; 9; 14; 26; 28; 33; 34; 40(2); 47; 49; 9:18; 19(2); 20; 10:5; 9; 10; 12; 11:2; 5; 7; 8; 9; 18; 29; 51; 12:1; 4; 5; 8; 11; 12; 19; 22; 27; 37; 44; 45; 54; 55; 13:24; 25; 26; 27; 35(2); 14:9; 10; 17; 24; 15:7; 10; 18; 16:9; 17:6; 7; 8; 10; 21; 23; 18:17; 29; 19:26; 31; 20:5(2); 6; 41; 21:3; 32; 22:11; 16; 18; 37; 70; 23:29; 30; 43; **Jn** 1:38; 51; 3:3; 5; 11; 4:20; 35(2); 5:19; 24; 25; 34; 6:26; 32; 47; 53; 7:26; 8:4; 26; 34; 46; 48; 51; 54; 55; 58; 9:17; 19; 41; 10:1; 7; 36; 11:8; 12:24; 27; 49; 13:13; 16; 20; 21; 33; 38; 14:12; 16:12; 20; 23; 26; 20:13; 16; 17; 21:3; 18; **Acts** 1:19; 3:22; 4:14; 5:38; 6:14; 10:37; 13:15; 17:18; 21:23; 23:8; 18; 30; 24:20; 26:22; 28:26; **Rom** 3:5; 8; 26; 4:1; 9; 6:1; 7:7; 8:31; 9:1; 14; 19; 20; 30; 10:6; 18; 19; 11:1; 11; 19; 12:3; 15:8; **1Cor** 1:12; 15; 7:8; 26; 29; 9:8; 10:15; 19; 20; 28; 29; 11:22; 12:3; 15; 16; 21; 14:16; 23; 15:12; 35; 50; **2Cor** 5:8; 9:4; 6; 10:10; 11:16; 12:6; **Gal** 1:9; 3:17; 4:1; 5:2; 16; **Eph** 4:17; **Phil** 4:4; **Col** 1:20; 2:4; 4:17; **1Th** 4:15; 5:3; **1Ti** 1:7; **2Ti** 2:7; **Titus** 2:8; **Philem** 1:19; 21; **Heb** 5:11; 7:9; 9:11; 10:20; 11:14; 32; 13:6; **Jas** 1:13; 2:3(2); 14; 16; 18; 4:13; 15; **1Jn** 1:6; 8; 10; 4:20; 5:16; **Rev** 2:2; 9; 24; 3:9; 6:3; 5; 6; 7; 16:5; 7; 22:17(2)

SAYEST

559, *2036, 3004*

Ex 33:12; **Num** 22:17; **Ruth** 3:5; **1Kin** 18:11; 14; **2Kin** 18:20; **2Chr** 25:19; **Neh** 5:12; 6:8; **Job** 22:13; 35:14; **Ps** 90:3; **Prov** 24:12; **Is** 36:5; 40:27; 47:8; **Jer** 2:35(2); **Amos** 7:16; **Mt** 26:70; 27:11; **Mk** 5:31; 14:68; 15:2; **Lk** 8:45; 20:21; 22:60; 23:3; **Jn** 1:22; 8:5; 33; 52; 9:17; 12:34; 14:9; 18:34; 37; **Rom** 2:22; **1Cor** 14:16; **Rev** 3:17

SAYING

559, 560, 1697, 2420, *2036, 2981, 3004, 3007, 3056, 4487*

Gen 1:22; 2:16; 3:17; 5:29; 8:15; 9:8; 15:1; 4; 18; 17:3; 18:12; 13; 15; 19:15; 21:22; 22:20; 23:3; 5; 8; 10; 13; 14; 24:7; 30; 37; 26:11; 20; 27:6(2); 28:6; 20; 31:1; 11; 29; 32:4; 6; 17(2); 19; 34:4; 8; 20; 37:11; 15; 38:13; 21; 24; 25; 28; 39:12; 14; 17; 19; 40:7; 41:9; 16; 42:14; 22(2); 28; 29; 37; 43:3(2); 7; 44:1; 19; 32; 45:16; 26; 47:5; 48:20(2); 50:4(2); 5; 16(2); 25; **Ex** 1:22; 3:16; 5:6; 8; 10; 13; 15; 6:10; 12; 29; 7:8; 9; 16; 9:5; 11:8; 12:1; 3; 13:1; 8; 14; 19; 14:1; 12; 15:1; 24; 16:11; 12; 17:4; 7; 19:3; 12; 23; 20:1; 25:1; 30:11; 17; 22; 31; 31:1; 12; 13; 33:1; 35:4(2); 36:5; 6; 40:1; **Lev** 1:1; 4:1; 2; 5:14; 6:1; 8; 9; 19; 24; 25; 7:22; 23; 28; 29; 8:1; 31; 9:3; 10:3; 8; 16; 11:1; 2; 12:1; 2; 13:1; 14:1; 33; 35; 15:1; 17:1; 2; 18:1; 19:1; 20:1; 21:16; 17; 22:1; 17; 26; 23:1; 9; 23; 24; 26; 33; 34; 24:1; 13; 15; 25:1; 27:1; **Num** 1:1; 48; 2:1; 3:5; 11; 14; 44; 4:1; 17; 21; 5:1; 5; 11; 6:1; 22; 23(2); 7:4; 8:1; 5; 23; 9:1; 9; 10; 10:1; 11:13; 18; 20; 12:13; 13:1; 32; 14:7; 15; 17; 26; 40; 15:1; 17; 37; 16:5; 20; 23; 24; 26; 36; 41; 44; 17:1; 12; 18:25; 19:1; 2; 20:3; 7; 23; 21:21; 22:5; 10; 23:7; 26; 24:12; 25:10; 16; 26:1; 3; 52; 27:2; 6; 8; 15; 28:1; 30:1; 31:1; 3; 25; 32:2; 10; 25; 31; 33:50; 34:1; 13; 16; 35:1; 9; 36:5; 6; **Deut** 1:5; 6; 9; 16; 23; 28; 34; 37; 2:2; 4; 17; 26; 3:18; 21; 23; 5:5; 6:20; 9:4; 13; 23; 12:30; 13:2; 6; 12; 13; 15:9; 11; 18:16; 19:7; 20:5; 22:17; 27:1; 9; 11; 29:19; 31:10; 25; 32:48; 34:4; **Josh** 1:1; 10; 11; 12; 13; 16; 2:1; 2; 3; 3:3; 6; 8; 4:1; 3; 6; 15; 17; 21(2); 22; 6:10; 26; 7:2; 8:4; 9:11; 22(2); 10:3; 6; 17; 14:9; 17:4; 14; 17; 18:8; 20:1; 2; 21:2; 22:8; 15; 24(2); **Judg** 1:1; 4:6; 5:1; 6:13; 32; 7:2; 3; 24; 8:9; 15; 9:1; 31; 10:10; 11:12; 17; 13:6; 15:13; 16:2(2); 18; 19:22; 20:8; 12; 23; 28; 21:1; 5; 10; 18; 20; **Ruth** 2:15; 4:4; 17; **1Sa** 1:20; 4:21; 5:10; 6:2; 21; 7:3; 12; 9:15; 26; 10:2; 11:7; 13:3; 14:24; 28; 33; 15:10; 12; 16:22; 17:26; 27; 18:8; 22; 24; 19:2; 11; 15; 19; 20:16; 21; 42; 21:11; 23:1; 2; 19; 27; 24:1; 8; 9; 25:14; 40; 26:1; 6; 14; 19; 27:11(2); 12; 28:10; 12; 29:5; 30:8; 26; **2Sa** 1:16; 2:1; 4; 3:12(2); 14; 17; 18; 23; 35; 4:10; 5:1; 6; 19; 6:12; 7:4; 7; 26; 27; 11:6; 10; 15; 19; 13:7; 28; 30; 14:32; 15:8; 10; 13; 31; 17:4; 6(2); 16; 18:5; 12; 19:8; 9; 11(2); 20:18(2); 21:17; 24:11; 19; **1Kin** 1:5; 6; 11; 13; 17; 23; 30; 47; 51(2); 2:1; 4; 8; 23; 29; 30; 38; 39; 42; 5:2; 5; 8; 6:11; 8:15; 25; 47; 55; 9:5; 12:3; 7; 9; 10(2); 12; 14; 15; 16; 22; 23; 13:3; 4(2); 9; 18; 21; 27; 30; 31; 32; 15:18; 29; 16:1; 17:2; 8; 15; 18:1; 26; 31; 19:2; 20:4; 5(2); 13; 17; 21:2; 9; 10; 13; 14; 17; 19(2); 23; 28; 22:12; 13; 31; 36; **2Kin** 2:22; 3:7; 4:1; 31; 5:4; 6; 8; 10; 14; 22; 6:8; 9; 13; 26; 7:10; 12; 14; 18; 8:1; 2; 4; 6; 7; 8; 9; 9:12; 13; 18; 20; 36; 10:1; 5; 6; 8; 17; 11:5; 14:6; 8; 9(2); 15:12; 16:7; 15; 17:13; 26; 27; 35; 18:14; 28; 30; 32; 36; 19:9; 10(2); 20; 20:2; 4; 21:10; 22:3; 10; 12; 23:21; **1Chr** 4:9; 10; 11:1; 12:19; 13:12; 14:10; 16:18; 22; 17:3; 6; 24; 21:9; 10; 19; 22:8; 17; **2Chr** 2:3; 5:13; 6:4; 16; 37; 7:3; 18; 10:3; 6; 7; 9; 10(2); 12; 14; 16; 11:2; 3; 12:7; 16:2; 18:11; 12; 19(2); 30; 19:9; 20:2; 8; 37; 21:12; 25:4; 7; 17; 18(2); 30:6; 18; 32:4; 6; 9; 11; 12; 17; 34:16; 18; 20; 35:21; 36:22; **Ezr** 1:1; 5:11; 8:22; 9:1; 11; **Neh** 1:8; 6:2; 3; 7; 8; 9; 8:11; 15; 13:25; **Est** 1:21; **Job** 4:16; 8:18; 15:23; 24:15; 33:8; **Ps** 2:2; 22:7; 49:4; 71:11; 105:11; 15; 119:82; 137:3; **Prov** 1:21; **Eccl** 1:16; **Song** 5:2; **Is** 3:6; 7; 4:1; 6:8; 7:2; 5; 10; 8:5; 11; 14:8; 16; 24; 16:14; 18:2; 19:25; 20:2; 23:4; 29:11; 12; 30:21; 36:15; 18; 21; 37:9; 10(2); 15; 21; 38:4; 41:7; 13; 44:28; 45:14; 46:10; 56:3; 63:11; **Jer** 1:4; 11; 13; 2:1; 2; 27; 4:10; 31; 5:20; 6:14; 17; 7:1; 4; 23; 8:6; 11; 11:1; 4; 6; 7; 19; 21; 13:3; 8; 16:1; 18:1; 5; 11; 20:10; 15; 21:1; 22:18(2); 23:25; 33; 38; 24:4; 25:2; 26:1; 8; 9; 11; 12; 17; 18; 27:1; 9; 12; 14; 16(2); 28:1; 2; 11; 12; 13; 29:3; 22; 24; 25(2); 28; 30; 31; 30:1; 2; 17; 31:3; 34; 32:3; 6; 7; 13; 16; 26; 33:1; 19; 23; 24; 34:1; 5; 12; 13; 35:1; 6; 12; 15; 36:1; 5; 14; 17; 27; 29(2); 37:3; 6; 9; 13; 19; 38:1; 8; 10; 16; 39:11; 15; 16; 40:9; 15; 42:14; 20; 43:2; 8; 44:1; 4; 15; 20; 25(2); 26; 45:1; 48:39; 49:4; 14; 34; 50:5; 51:14; **Lam** 2:15; **Eze** 3:12; 16; 6:1; 7:1; 9:1; 11; 10:6; 11:14; 12:1; 8; 17; 21; 22; 26; 13:1; 6; 10; 14:2; 12; 15:1; 16:1; 44; 17:1; 11; 18:1; 2; 20:2; 5; 45; 21:1; 8; 18; 22:1; 17; 23; 28; 23:1; 24:1; 15; 20; 25:1; 26:1; 27:1; 32; 28:1; 11; 20; 29:1; 17; 30:1; 20; 31:1; 32:1; 17; 33:1; 10; 21; 23; 24; 30; 34:1; 35:1; 12; 36:16; 37:15; 18; 38:1; **Dan** 4:8; 23; 31; **Amos** 2:12; 3:1; 7:10; 8:5; **Jonah** 1:1; 3:1; 7; 4:2; **Mic** 2:11; **Hag** 1:1; 2; 3; 13; 2:1; 2; 10; 11; 20; 21; **Zec** 1:1; 4; 7; 14; 17; 21; 2:4; 3:4; 6; 4:4; 6(2); 8; 6:8; 9; 12(2); 7:3; 4; 5; 8; 9; 8:1; 18; 21; 23; **Mt** 1:20; 22; 2:2; 13; 15; 17; 20; 3:2; 3; 14; 17; 4:14; 5:2; 6:31; 8:2; 3; 6; 17; 25; 27; 29; 31; 9:14; 18; 27; 29; 30; 33; 10:5; 7; 11:17; 12:10; 17; 38; 13:3; 24; 31; 35; 36; 14:15; 26; 27; 30; 33; 15:1; 4; 7; 12; 22; 23; 25; 16:7; 13; 22; 17:9; 10; 14; 25; 18:1; 26; 28; 29; 19:3; 11; 22; 25; 20:12; 30; 31; 21:2; 4; 9; 10; 15; 20; 25; 37; 22:4; 16; 24; 31; 35; 42; 43; 23:2; 24:3; 5; 25:9; 11; 20; 37; 44; 45; 26:8; 17; 27; 39; 42; 44; 48; 65; 68; 69; 70; 74; 27:4; 9; 11; 19; 23; 24; 29; 40; 46; 54; 63; 28:9; 13; 15; 18; **Mk** 1:7; 11; 15; 24; 25; 27; 40; 2:12; 3:11; 33; 5:9; 12; 23; 6:2; 25; 7:29; 37; 8:15; 16; 26; 27; 32; 33; 9:7; 10; 11; 25; 32; 38; 10:22; 26; 33; 35; 49; 11:9; 17; 31; 12:6; 18; 26; 13:6; 14:44; 57; 60; 68; 71; 15:4; 9; 29; 34; 36; **Lk** 1:24; 29; 63; 66; 67; 2:13; 17; 50; 3:4; 10; 14; 16; 4:4; 34; 35; 36; 41; 5:8; 12; 13; 21; 26; 30; 7:4; 6; 16; 19; 20; 32; 39; 8:9; 24; 25; 30; 38; 49; 50; 54; 9:18; 22; 35; 38; 45(2); 10:17; 25; 11:45; 12:16; 17; 13:25; 31; 14:3; 5; 7; 30; 15:2; 3; 6; 9; 17:4; 18:2; 3; 13; 18; 34; 38; 41; 19:7; 14; 16; 18; 20; 30; 38; 42; 46; 20:2; 5; 14; 21; 28; 21:7; 8; 22:8; 19; 20; 42; 57; 59; 64; 66; 23:2(2); 3; 5; 18; 21; 35; 37; 39; 40; 47; 24:7; 23; 29; 34; **Jn** 1:15; 26; 32; 4:31; 37; 39; 42; 51; 6:52; 60; 7:15; 28; 36; 37; 40; 8:12; 51; 52; 55; 9:2; 19; 10:33; 11:3; 28; 31; 32; 12:21; 23; 28; 38; 15:20; 18:9; 22; 32; 40; 19:6; 8; 12; 13; 21:23; **Acts** 1:6; 2:7; 12; 40; 3:25; 4:16; 5:23; 25; 28; 6:5; 7:26; 27; 29; 32; 35; 40; 59; 8:10; 19; 26; 9:4; 10:3; 26; 11:3; 4; 7; 18; 12:7; 22; 13:15; 47; 14:11; 15; 15:5; 13; 24; 16:9; 15; 17; 20; 28; 35; 36; 17:7; 19; 18:13; 21; 19:4; 13; 21; 26; 28; 20:23; 21:14; 21; 40; 22:7; 18; 26; 23:9; 12; 23; 24:2; 9; 25:14; 26:14; 22; 31; 27:24; 33; 28:26; **Rom** 4:7; 11:2; 13:9; **1Cor** 11:25; 15:54; **Gal** 3:8; **1Ti** 1:15; 3:1; 4:9; **2Ti** 2:11; 18; **Titus** 3:8; **Heb** 2:6; 12; 4:7; 6:14; 8:11; 9:20; 12:26; **2Pet** 3:4; **Jude** 14; **Rev** 1:11; 17; 4:8; 10; 5:9; 12; 13; 6:1; 10; 7:3; 10; 12; 13; 8:13; 9:14; 10:4; 11:1; 12; 15; 17; 12:10; 13:4; 14; 14:7; 8; 9; 13; 18; 15:3; 16:1; 17; 17:1; 18:2; 4; 10; 16; 18; 19; 21; 19:1; 4; 5; 6; 17; 21:3; 9

SAYINGS

561, 1697, 2420, 6310, *3004, 3056, 4487*

Num 14:39; **Judg** 13:17; **1Sa** 25:12; **2Chr** 13:22; 33:19; **Ps** 49:13; 78:2; **Prov** 1:6; 4:10; 20; **Mt** 7:24; 26; 28; 19:1; 26:1; **Lk** 1:65; 2:51; 6:47; 7:1; 9:28; 44; **Jn** 10:19; 14:24; **Acts** 14:18; 19:28; **Rom** 3:4; **Rev** 19:9; 22:6; 7; 9; 10

SEE

2009, 2370, 2372, 2374, 4758, 5027, 7200, 7789, *308, 542, 991, 1227, 1492, 1689, 2234, 2300, 2334, 2396, 2400, 2477, 3070, 3467, 3700, 5461*

Gen 2:19; 8:8; 11:5; 12:12; 18:21; 19:21; 21:16; 27:1; 27; 31:5; 12; 50; 32:20; 34:1; 37:14; 20; 39:14; 41:41; 42:9; 12; 43:3; 5; 44:23; 26; 34; 45:12; 24; 28; 48:10; 11; **Ex** 1:16; 3:3; 4; 4:18; 21; 5:19; 6:1; 7:1; 10:5; 28; 29; 12:13; 13:17; 14:13(2); 16:7; 29; 32; 22:8; 23:5; 31:2; 33:12; 20(2); 23; 34:10; 35:30; **Lev** 13:8; 10; 15; 17; 30; 14:36(2); 20:17(2); **Num** 4:20; 11:15; 23; 13:18; 14:23(2); 22:41; 23:9; 13(3); 24:17; 27:12; 32:8; 11; **Deut** 1:35; 36; 3:25; 28; 4:28; 18:16; 22:1; 4; 23:14; 28:10; 34; 67; 68; 29:4; 22; 30:15; 32:20; 39; 52; 34:4; **Josh** 3:3; 6:2; 8:1; 8; 22:10; **Judg** 9:37; 14:8; 16:5; 21:21; **1Sa** 2:32; 3:2; 4:15; 6:9; 13; 10:24; 12:16; 17; 14:17; 29; 38; 15:35; 17:28; 19:3; 15; 20:29; 21:14; 23:22; 23; 24:11(3); 15; 25:35; 26:16; **2Sa** 3:13(2); 7:2; 13:5(2); 6; 14:24; 30; 32; 15:3; 28; 24:3; 13; **1Kin** 9:12; 12:16; 14:4; 17:23; 20:7; 22; 22:25; **2Kin** 2:10; 3:14; 17(2); 5:7; 6:17; 20; 32; 7:2; 13; 14; 19; 8:29; 9:16; 17; 34; 10:16; 19:16; 22:20; 23:17; **2Chr** 10:16; 18:16; 24; 20:17; 22:6; 24:5; 25:17; 29:8; 30:7; 34:28; **Ezr** 4:14; **Neh** 2:17; 4:11; 9:9; **Est** 3:4; 5:13; 8:6(2); **Job** 3:9; 6:21; 7:7; 8; 9:11; 25; 10:15; 17:15; 19:26; 27; 20:9; 17; 21:20; 22:11; 19; 23:9; 24:1; 15; 28:27; 31:4; 33:26; 28; 34:32; 35:5; 14; 36:25; 37:21; **Ps** 10:11; 14:2; 16:10; 22:7; 27:13; 31:11; 34:8; 12; 36:9; 37:34; 40:3; 41:6; 49:9; 19; 52:6; 53:2; 58:8; 59:10; 63:2; 64:5; 8; 66:5; 69:23; 32; 74:9; 86:17; 89:48; 91:8; 92:11; 94:7; 9; 97:6; 106:5; 107:24; 42; 112:8; 10; 115:5; 118:7; 119:74; 128:5; 6; 135:16; 139:16; 24; **Prov** 24:18; 29:16; **Eccl** 1:10; 2:3; 3:18; 22; 7:11; 8:16; **Song** 2:14; 6:11(2); 13; 7:12; **Is** 5:19; 6:9; 10; 13:1; 14:16; 18:3; 26:11(2); 29:18; 30:10; 20; 32:3; 33:17; 19; 20; 35:2; 37:17; 38:11; 40:5; 41:20; 42:18; 44:9; 18; 48:6; 49:7; 52:8; 10; 15; 53:2; 10; 11; 60:4; 5; 61:9; 62:2; 64:9; 66:14; 18; **Jer** 1:10; 11; 13; 2:10(2); 19; 23; 31; 3:2; 4:21; 5:1; 12; 21; 6:16; 7:12; 11:20; 12:4; 14:13; 17:6; 8; 20:12; 18; 22:10; 12; 23:24; 30:6(2); 42:14; 18; 51:61; **Lam** 1:11; 12; **Eze** 8:6; 13; 15; 12:2(2); 6; 12; 13; 13:9; 16; 23; 14:22; 23; 16:37; 20:48; 21:29; 32:31; 33:6; 39:21; **Dan** 1:10; 2:8; 3:25; 5:23; **Joel** 2:28; **Amos** 6:2; **Jonah** 4:5; **Mic** 6:9; 7:10; 16; **Hab** 1:1; 2:1; **Zeph** 3:15; **Hag** 2:3; **Zec** 2:2; 4:10; 5:2; 5; 9:5(2); 10:7; **Mal** 1:5; **Mt** 5:8; 16; 7:5; 8:4; 9:30; 11:4; 7; 8; 9; 12:38; 13:13; 14; 15; 16; 17(2); 15:31; 16:28; 22:11; 23:39; 24:2; 6; 15; 30; 33; 26:58; 64; 27:4; 24; 49; 28:1; 6; 7; 10; **Mk** 1:44; 4:12; 5:14; 15; 32; 6:38; 8:18; 24; 12:15; 13:1; 14; 26; 29; 14:62; 15:32; 36; 16:7; **Lk** 2:15; 26; 3:6; 6:42; 7:22; 24; 25; 26; 8:10; 16; 20; 35; 9:9; 27; 10:23(2); 24(2); 11:33; 12:54; 55; 13:28; 35; 14:18; 17:22(2); 23(2); 19:3; 4; 20:13; 21:20; 27; 30; 31; 23:8; 24:39(2); **Jn** 1:33; 39; 46; 50; 51; 3:3; 36; 4:29; 48; 6:19; 30; 62; 7:3; 8:51; 56; 9:15; 19; 25; 39(3); 41; 11:34; 40; 12:9; 21; 40; 14:19; 16:10; 16(2); 17(2); 19(2); 22; 18:26; 20:25; **Acts** 2:17; 27; 31; 33; 3:16; 7:56; 8:36; 13:35; 15:36; 19:21; 26; 20:25; 38; 22:11; 14; 23:22; 25:24; 28:20; 26; 27; **Rom** 1:11; 7:23; 8:25; 11:8; 10; 15:21; 24; **1Cor** 1:26; 8:10; 13:12; 16:7; 10; **2Cor** 8:7; **Gal** 1:18; 6:11; **Eph** 3:9; 5:15; 33; **Phil** 1:27; 2:23; 28; **1Th** 2:17; 3:6(2); 10; 5:15; **1Ti** 6:16; **2Ti** 1:4; **Heb** 2:8; 9; 3:19; 8:5; 10:25; 11:5; 12:14; 25; 13:23; **Jas** 2:24; **1Pet** 1:8; 22; 3:10; **2Pet** 1:9; **1Jn** 3:2; 5:16; **3Jn** 14; **Rev** 1:7; 12; 3:18; 6:1; 3; 5; 6; 7; 9:20; 11:9; 16:15; 18:7; 9; 19:10; 22:4; 9

SEEING

310, 518, 1768, 3282, 3588, 6493, 7200, *990, 991, 1063, 1492, 1512, 1893, 1894, 1897, 2334, 3708, 3754, 4275*

Gen 15:2; 18:18; 19:1; 22:12; 24:56; 26:27; 28:8; 44:30; **Ex** 4:11; 21:8; 22:10; 23:9; **Lev** 10:17; **Num** 15:26; 16:3; 35:23; **Josh** 17:14; 22:18; **Judg** 13:18; 17:13; 19:23; 21:7; 16; **Ruth** 1:21; 2:10; **1Sa** 16:1; 17:36; 18:23; 24:6; 25:26; 28:16; **2Sa** 13:39; 15:20; 18:22; 19:11; **1Kin** 1:48; 11:28; **2Kin** 10:2; **1Chr** 12:17; **2Chr** 2:6; **Ezr** 9:13; **Neh** 2:2; **Job** 14:5; 19:28; 21:22; 34; 24:1; 28:21; **Ps** 22:8; 50:17; **Prov** 3:29; 17:16; 20:12; **Eccl** 1:8; 2:16; 6:11; **Is** 21:3; 33:15; 42:20; 49:21; **Jer** 11:15; 47:7; **Eze** 16:30; 17:18; 21:4; 22:28; **Dan** 2:47; **Hos** 4:6; **Mt** 5:1; 9:2; 13:13; 14; **Mk** 4:12; 11:13; **Lk** 1:34; 5:12; 8:10; 23:40; **Jn** 2:18; 9:7; 21:21; **Acts** 2:15; 31; 3:3; 7:24; 8:6; 9:7; 13:11; 46; 16:27; 17:24; 25; 19:36; 24:2; 28:26; **Rom** 3:30; **1Cor** 14:16; **2Cor** 3:12; 4:1; 11:18; 19; **Col** 3:9; **2Th** 1:6; **Heb** 4:6; 14; 5:11; 6:6; 7:25; 8:4; 11:27; 12:1; **1Pet** 1:22; **2Pet** 2:8; 3:11; 14; 17

SEEM

1961, 3191, 4591, 4758, 5869, 7034, 7185, *1380*

Gen 27:12; **Deut** 15:18; 25:3; **Josh** 24:15; **1Sa** 24:4; **2Sa** 19:37; 38; **1Kin** 21:2; **1Chr** 13:2; **Ezr** 5:17; 7:18; **Neh** 9:32; **Est** 5:4; 8:5; **Jer** 40:4(2); **Nah** 2:4; **1Cor** 11:16; 12:22; **2Cor** 10:9; **Heb** 4:1; **Jas** 1:26

SEEMED

1961, 5869, *1096, 1380, 2107, 5316*

Gen 19:14; 29:20; **2Sa** 3:19(2); **Eccl** 9:13; **Jer** 18:4; 27:5; **Mt** 11:26; **Lk** 1:3; 10:21; 24:11; **Acts** 15:25; 28; **Gal** 2:6(2); 9

SEEMETH

5869, 6440, 7200, *1380*

Lev 14:35; **Num** 16:9; **Josh** 9:25; **Judg** 10:15; 19:24; **1Sa** 1:23; 3:18; 11:10; 14:36; 40; 18:23; **2Sa** 10:12; 15:26; 18:4; 24:22; **Est** 3:11; **Prov** 14:12; 16:25; 18:17; **Jer** 26:14; 40:4; 5; **Eze** 34:18; **Lk** 8:18; **Acts** 17:18; 25:27; **1Cor** 3:18; **Heb** 12:11

SEEMLY

5000

Prov 19:10; 26:1

SEEST

2372, 7200, 7210, *991, 2334*

Gen 13:15; 16:13; 31:43; **Ex** 10:28; **Deut** 4:19; 12:13; 20:1; 21:11; **Judg** 9:36; **1Kin** 21:29; **Job** 10:4; **Prov** 22:29; 26:12; 29:20; **Eccl** 5:8; **Is** 58:3; 7; **Jer** 1:11; 13; 7:17; 20:12; 24:3; 32:24; **Eze** 8:6; 40:4; **Dan** 1:13; **Amos** 7:8; 8:2; **Zec** 4:2; 5:2; **Mk** 5:31; 13:2; **Lk** 7:44; **Acts** 21:20; **Jas** 2:22; **Rev** 1:11

SEETH

2372, 7200, 7210, *991, 2334, 3708*

Gen 16:13; 44:31; **Ex** 4:14; 12:23; **Lev** 13:20; **Deut** 32:36; **1Sa** 16:7(2); **2Kin** 2:19; **Job** 8:17; 10:4; 11:11; 22:14; 28:10; 24; 34:21; 42:5; **Ps** 37:13; 49:10; 58:10; **Eccl** 8:16; **Is** 21:6; 28:4; 29:15; 23; 47:10; **Eze** 8:12; 9:9; 12:27; 18:14; 33:3; 39:15; **Mt** 6:4; 6; 18; **Mk** 5:38; **Lk** 16:23; **Jn** 1:29; 5:19; 6:40; 9:21; 10:12; 11:9; 12:45(2); 14:17; 19; 20:1; 6; 12; 21:20; **Rom** 8:24; **2Cor** 12:6; **1Jn** 3:17

SELF

846, 1683, 4572

Ex 32:13; **Jn** 5:30; 17:5; **1Cor** 4:3; **Philem** 1:19; **1Pet** 2:24

SENT

1980, 2904, 3947, 5414, 5674, 6680, 7725, 7964, 7971, 7972, *375, 628, 630, 649, 652, 657, 863, 1524, 1544, 1599, 1821, 3343, 3992, 4842, 4882*

Gen 3:23; 8:7; 8; 10; 12; 12:20; 19:13; 29; 20:2; 21:14; 24:59; 25:6; 26:27; 29; 31; 27:42; 28:5; 6; 31:4; 27; 42; 32:3; 5; 18; 23(2); 37:14; 32; 38:20; 23; 25; 41:8; 14; 42:4; 43:34; 44:3; 45:7; 8; 23; 24; 27; 46:5; 28; 50:16; **Ex** 2:5; 3:12; 13; 14; 15; 4:28; 5:22; 7:16; 9:7; 23; 27; 18:2; 24:5; **Num** 13:3; 16; 17; 14:36; 16:12; 28; 29; 20:14; 16; 21:6; 21; 32; 22:5; 10; 15; 40; 31:6; 32:8; **Deut** 2:26; 9:23; 24:4; 34:11; **Josh** 2:1; 3; 21; 6:17; 25; 7:2; 22; 8:3; 9; 10:3; 6; 11:1; 14:7; 11; 22:6; 7; 13; 24:5; 9; 12; **Judg** 1:23; 3:15; 18; 4:6; 5:15; 6:8; 14; 35(2); 7:8; 24; 9:23; 31; 11:12; 14; 17(2); 19; 28; 38; 12:9; 16:18; 18:2; 19:29; 20:6; 12; 21:10; 13; **1Sa** 4:4; 5:8; 10; 11; 6:21; 10:25; 11:7; 12:8; 11; 18; 13:2; 15:1; 18; 20; 16:12; 19; 20; 22; 17:31; 18:5; 19:11; 14; 15; 17; 20; 21(2); 20:22; 22:11; 25:5; 14; 32; 39; 40; 26:4; 30:26; 31:9; **2Sa** 2:5; 3:12; 14; 15; 21; 22; 23; 24; 26; 5:11; 8:10; 9:5; 10:2; 3(2); 4; 5; 6; 7; 16; 11:1; 3; 4; 5; 6(2); 14; 18; 22; 27; 12:1; 25; 27; 13:7; 14:2; 29(3); 32; 15:10; 12; 18:2; 29; 19:11; 14; 22:15; 17; 24:13; 15; **1Kin** 1:44; 53; 2:25; 29; 36; 42; 5:1; 2; 8; 14; 7:13; 8:66; 9:14; 27; 12:3; 18; 20; 14:6; 15:18; 19; 20; 18:10; 20; 19:2; 20:2; 5; 7; 10; 17; 34; 21:8; 11(2); 14; **2Kin** 1:2; 6; 9; 11; 13; 16; 2:2; 4; 6; 17; 3:7; 5:6; 8; 10; 22; 6:9; 10; 14; 23; 32(2); 7:14; 8:9; 9:19; 10:1; 5; 7; 21; 11:4; 12:18; 14:8; 9(2); 19; 16:7; 8; 10; 11; 17:4; 13; 25; 26; 18:14; 17; 27(2); 19:2; 4; 9; 16; 20; 20:12; 22:3; 15; 18; 23:1; 16; 24:2(2); **1Chr** 8:8; 10:9; 12:19; 14:1; 18:10; 19:2; 3; 4; 5; 6; 8; 16; 21:12; 14; 15; **2Chr** 2:3; 11; 13; 7:10; 8:18; 10:3; 18; 16:2; 3; 4; 17:7; 8; 24:19; 23; 25:13; 15; 17; 18(2); 27; 30:1; 32:21; 31; 34:8; 23; 26; 29; 35:21; 36:10; 15; **Ezr** 4:11; 14; 17; 18; 5:6; 7; 6:13; 7:14; 8:16; 17; **Neh** 2:9; 6:2; 3; 4; 5; 8; 12; 17; 19; **Est** 1:22; 3:13; 4:4; 5:10; 8:10; 9:20; 30; **Job** 1:4; 5; 22:9; 39:5; **Ps** 18:14; 16; 59:t; 77:17; 78:25; 45; 80:11; 105:17; 20; 26; 28; 106:15; 107:20; 111:9; 135:9; **Prov** 9:3; 17:11; **Is** 9:8; 20:1; 36:2; 12(2); 37:2; 4; 9; 17; 21; 39:1; 42:19; 43:14; 48:16; 55:11; 61:1; **Jer** 7:25; 14:3; 14; 15; 19:14; 21:1; 23:21; 32; 38; 24:5; 25:4; 17; 26:5; 12; 15; 22; 27:15; 28:9; 15; 29:1; 3; 9; 19; 20; 25; 28; 31; 35:15; 36:14; 21; 37:3; 7; 17; 38:14; 39:13; 14; 40:14; 42:9; 20; 21; 43:1; 2; 44:4; 49:14; **Lam** 1:13; **Eze** 2:9; 3:5; 6; 13:6; 23:16; 40(2); 31:4; **Dan** 3:2; 28; 5:24; 6:22; 10:11; **Hos** 5:13; **Joel** 2:25; **Amos** 4:10; 7:10; **Obad** 1; **Jonah** 1:4; **Mic** 6:4; **Hag** 1:12; **Zec** 1:10; 2:8; 9; 11; 4:9; 6:15; 7:2; 12; 9:11; **Mal** 2:4; **Mt** 2:8; 16; 10:5; 40; 11:2; 13:36; 14:10; 22; 23; 35; 15:24; 39; 20:2; 21:1; 34; 36; 37; 22:3; 4; 7; 16; 23:37; 27:19; **Mk** 1:43; 3:31; 4:36; 6:17; 27; 45; 46; 8:9; 26; 9:37; 12:2; 3; 4(2); 5; 6; **Lk** 1:19; 26; 53; 4:18; 26; 43; 7:3; 6; 10; 19; 20; 8:38; 9:2; 48; 52; 10:1; 16; 13:34; 14:17; 15:15; 19:14; 29; 32; 20:10(2); 11(2); 12; 20; 22:8; 35; 23:7; 11; 15; **Jn** 1:6; 8; 19; 22; 24; 33; 3:17; 28; 34; 4:34; 38; 5:23; 24; 30; 33; 36; 37; 38; 6:29; 38; 39; 40; 44; 57; 7:16; 18; 28; 29; 32; 33; 8:16; 18; 26; 29; 42; 9:4; 7; 10:36; 11:3; 42; 12:44; 45; 49; 13:16(2); 20; 14:24; 15:21; 16:5; 17:3; 18(2); 21; 23; 25; 18:24; 20:21; **Acts** 3:26; 5:21; 7:12; 14; 8:14; 9:17; 30; 38; 10:8; 17; 20; 21; 29(2); 33; 36; 11:11; 22; 30; 12:11; 13:3; 4; 15; 26; 15:27; 16:35; 36; 17:10; 14; 19:22; 31; 20:17; 23:30; 24:24; 26; 28:28; **Rom** 10:15; S:1; **1Cor** 1:17; 4:17; **2Cor** 8:18; 22; 9:3; 12:17; 18; **Gal** 4:4; 6; **Eph** 6:22; **Phil** 2:28; 4:16; 18; **Col** 4:8; **1Th** 3:2; 5; **2Ti** 4:12; **Philem** 1:12; **Heb** 1:14; **Jas** 2:25; **1Pet** 1:12; 2:14; **1Jn** 4:9; 10; 14; **Rev** 1:1; 5:6; 22:6; 16

SET

530, 631, 935, 1129, 1197, 1379, 1431, 2211, 2232, 2706, 2710, 3051, 3240, 3245, 3259, 3320, 3322, 3332, 3335, 3341, 3427, 3488, 3559, 3635, 4142, 4150, 4390, 4394, 4427, 4483, 4487, 4853, 5079, 5117, 5128, 5183, 5258, 5265, 5324, 5329, 5375, 5414, 5473, 5496, 5526, 5564, 5774, 5927, 5975, 6186, 6187, 6213, 6395, 6485, 6496, 6584, 6845, 6955, 6966, 7311, 7392, 7660, 7682, 7725, 7737, 7760, 7761, 7896, 7931, 7947, 7971, 8239, 8371, *321, 345, 377, 392, 461, 584, 630, 649, 816, 968, 1299, 1325, 1369, 1416, 1847, 1848, 1913, 1930, 1940, 2007, 2064, 2350, 2476, 2521, 2523, 2525, 2749, 3908, 4060, 4270, 4295, 4388, 4741, 4776, 4900, 4972, 5002, 5021, 5087, 5394, 5426*

Gen 1:17; 4:15; 6:16; 9:13; 17:21; 18:8; 19:16; 21:2; 28; 29; 24:33; 28:11; 12; 18; 22; 30:36; 38; 40; 31:17; 21; 37; 45; 35:14; 20; 41:33; 41; 43:9; 31; 32; 44:21; 47:7; 48:20; **Ex** 1:11; 4:20; 5:14; 7:23; 9:5; 13:12; 19:12; 23; 21:1; 23:31; 25:7; 30; 26:17; 35; 28:11; 17; 20; 31:5; 32:22; 35:9; 27; 33; 37:3; 39:10; 37; 40:2; 4(2); 5; 6; 7; 8; 18; 20; 21; 23; 28; 30; 33; **Lev** 17:10; 20:3; 5; 6; 24:6; 8; 26:1; 11; 17; **Num** 1:51; 2:9; 16; 17(2); 34; 4:15; 5:16; 18; 30; 7:1; 8:13; 10:17; 18; 21(2); 22; 25; 28; 35; 11:24; 21:8; 10; 22:1; 24:1; 27:16; 19; 22; 29:39; **Deut** 1:8; 21; 4:8; 44; 7:7; 11:26; 32; 14:24; 16:22; 17:14; 15(3); 19:14; 26:4; 10; 27:2; 4; 28:1; 36; 56; 30:1; 15; 19; 32:8; 22; 46; **Josh** 4:9; 6:26; 8:8; 12; 13; 19; 10:18; 18:1; 24:25; 26; **Judg** 1:8; 6:18; 7:5; 19; 22; 9:25; 33; 49; 15:5; 16:25; 18:30; 31; 20:22; 29; 36; 48; **Ruth** 2:5; 6; **1Sa** 2:8(2); 5:2; 3; 6:18; 7:12; 8:12; 9:20; 23; 24(2); 10:19; 12:13; 13:8; 15:11; 12; 17:2; 8; 18:5; 30; 22:9; 26:24(2); 28:22; **2Sa** 3:10; 6:3; 17; 7:12; 10:17; 11:15; 12:20; 30; 14:30(2); 31; 15:24; 18:1; 13; 19:28; 20:5; 23:23; **1Kin** 2:15; 19; 24; 5:5; 6:19; 27; 7:16; 21(3); 25; 39; 8:21; 9:6; 10:9; 12:29; 14:4; 15:4; 16:34; 20:12(2); 21:9; 10; 12; **2Kin** 4:4; 10; 38; 43; 44; 6:22; 8:12; 10:3; 12:4; 9; 17; 17:10; 18:23; 20:1; 21:7; 25:19; 28; **1Chr** 6:31; 9:22; 26; 31; 11:14; 25; 16:1; 19:10; 11; 17; 20:2; 21:18; 22:2; 19; 23:4; 31; 29:2; 3; **2Chr** 2:18(2); 3:5; 4:4; 7; 10; 19; 6:10; 13; 7:19; 9:8; 11:16; 13:3(2); 11; 14:10; 17:2; 19:5; 8; 20:3; 17; 22; 23:10; 14; 19; 20; 24:8; 13; 25:14; 29:25; 35; 31:3; 15; 18; 32:6; 33:7; 19; 34:12; 35:2; **Ezr** 2:68; 3:3; 5; 8; 9; 10; 4:10; 12; 13; 16; 5:11; 6:11; 18; 7:25; 9:9; **Neh** 1:9; 2:6; 3:1; 3; 6; 13; 14; 15; 4:9; 13(2); 5:7; 6:1; 7:1; 9:37; 10:33; 13:11; 19; **Est** 2:17; 3:1; 6:8; 8:2; **Job** 5:11; 6:4; 7:17; 20; 9:19; 14:13; 16:12; 19:8; 30:1; 13; 33:5; 34:14; 24; 36:16; 38:10; 33; **Ps** 2:2; 6; 3:6; 4:3; 8:1; 10:8; 12:5; 16:8; 17:11; 19:4; 20:5; 27:5; 31:8; 40:2; 50:21; 54:3; 57:4; 62:10; 69:29; 73:9; 18; 74:4; 17; 78:7; 8; 85:13; 86:14; 89:25; 42; 90:8; 91:14(2); 101:3; 102:13; 104:9; 109:6; 113:8; 118:5; 122:5; 132:11; 140:5; 141:2; 3; **Prov** 1:25; 8:23; 27; 22:28; 23:5; **Eccl** 3:11; 7:14; 8:11; 10:6; 12:9; **Song** 5:12; 14; 15; 7:2; 8:6; **Is** 3:24; 7:6; 9:11; 11:11; 12; 14:1; 17:10; 19:2; 21:6; 8; 22:7; 23:13; 27:4; 11; 36:8; 38:1; 41:19; 42:4; 25; 44:7; 45:20; 46:7; 49:22; 50:7; 57:7; 8; 62:6; 66:19; **Jer** 1:10; 15; 4:6; 5:26; 6:1; 17; 23; 27; 7:12; 30; 9:13; 10:20; 11:13; 21:8; 10; 23:4; 24:1; 6; 26:4; 31:21(2); 29; 30; 32:20; 29; 34; 34:16; 35:5; 38:22; 40:11; 42:15; 17; 43:10; 44:10; 11; 12; 49:38; 50:2; 9; 51:12(2); 27; 52:32; **Lam** 2:17; 3:6; 12; **Eze** 2:2; 3:24; 4:2(2); 3(2); 7; 5:5; 6:2; 7:20(2); 9:4; 12:6; 13:17; 14:3; 8; 15:7(2); 16:18; 19; 17:4; 5; 22; 18:2; 19:8; 20:46; 21:2; 15; 16; 22:7; 10; 23:24(2); 25; 41; 24:2; 3(2); 7; 8; 11; 25; 25:2; 4; 26:9; 20(2); 27:10; 28:2; 6; 14; 21; 29:2; 30:8; 14; 16; 31:4; 32:8; 23; 25; 33:2; 7; 34:23; 35:2; 37:1; 26; 38:2; 39:9; 15; 21; 40:2; 4; 44:8; **Dan** 1:11; 2:44; 49; 3:1; 2; 3(2); 5; 7; 12(2); 14; 18; 5:19; 6:1; 3; 14; 7:10; 8:18; 9:3; 10; 10:10; 12; 15; 11:11; 13; 17; 12:11; **Hos** 2:3(2); 4:8; 6:11; 8:1; 4; 11:8; **Joel** 2:5; **Amos** 7:8; 8:5; 9:4; **Obad** 4; **Nah** 3:6; 13; **Hab** 2:1; 9; **Zec** 3:5(2); 5:11; 6:11; 8:10; **Mal** 3:15; **Mt** 5:1; 14; 10:35; 18:2; 21:7; 25:33; 27:19; 37; **Mk** 1:32; 4:21; 6:41; 8:6(2); 7; 9:12; 36; 12:1; **Lk** 1:1; 2:34; 4:9; 18; 7:8; 9:16; 47; 51; 10:8; 34; 11:6; 19:35; 22:55; 23:11; **Jn** 2:6; 10; 3:33; 6:11; 8:3; 13:12; 19:29; **Acts** 4:7; 11; 5:27; 6:6; 13; 7:5; 26; 12:21; 13:9; 47; 15:16; 16:34; 17:5; 18:10; 19:27; 21:2; 22:30; 23:24; 26:32; **Rom** 3:25; 14:10; **1Cor** 4:9; 6:4; 10:27; 11:34; 12:18; 28; **Gal** 3:1; **Eph** 1:20; **Phil** 1:17; **Col** 3:2; **Titus** 1:5; **Heb** 2:7; 6:18; 8:1; 12:1; 2(2); 13:23; **Jas** 3:6; **Jude** 7; **Rev** 3:8; 21; 4:2; 10:2; 20:3

SETTING

5414, *1416, 3326*

Eze 43:8; **Mt** 27:66; **Lk** 4:40

SETTINGS

4396

Ex 28:17

SEVERAL

2669, *303, 1520, 2398*

Num 28:13; 21; 29; 29:10; 15; **2Kin** 15:5; **2Chr** 11:12; 26:21; 28:25; 31:19; **Mt** 25:15; **Rev** 21:21

SHALL

Gen 1:29; 2:23; 24(3); 3:1; 3(2); 4; 5(2); 15; 16(2); 18; 4:7; 12; 14(4); 15; 24; 5:29; 6:3(2); 15; 17; 19; 20; 21; 8:22; 9:2; 3; 4; 6; 11(2); 13; 14(2); 15; 16; 25; 26; 27(3); 12:3; 12(3); 13; 13:16; 15:4(3); 5; 8(2); 13(3); 14(2); 16; 16:10; 12; 17:5(2); 6; 10(2); 11(2); 12; 13; 14; 15; 16(2); 17(2); 19; 20; 21; 18:5; 10; 12; 13; 14; 17; 18(2); 19; 25; 28; 29; 30; 31; 32; 19:2; 20; 20:7; 13; 21:10; 12; 22:14; 17; 18; 23:6; 9; 24:7; 14(3); 43; 55; 25:23(3); 32; 26:2; 4; 11; 22; 27:12(2); 33; 37; 39; 40; 46; 28:14(2); 21; 22; 29:15; 30:3; 15; 24; 30; 31; 32; 33(3); 31:8(2); 32:4; 8; 19; 28; 34:10(2); 11; 12; 23; 30(2); 35:10(2); 11(2); 37:10; 20; 30; 38:18; 40:13; 14; 19(3); 41:16; 27; 30(3); 31(2); 36(2); 40; 44; 42:15(2); 16; 20(2); 33; 34(2); 38(2); 43:3; 5; 16; 44:10(2); 16(3); 17; 23; 29; 31(2); 32; 34(2); 45:6; 13(2); 18; 46:4; 33(3); 34; 47:19; 23; 24(3); 48:5; 6(2); 19(4); 20; 21; 49:1; 8(3); 9; 10(2); 12; 13(3); 16; 17(2); 19(2); 20(2); 25(2); 26; 27(3); 50:17; 25; **Ex** 1:16(2); 22(2); 2:7; 3:12(2); 13(3); 18(2); 21(2); 22(3); 4:8; 9(2); 15; 16(3); 21; 5:7; 8(2); 11; 18(2); 19; 6:1(2); 7; 12; 30; 7:1; 2; 4; 5; 9(2); 17; 18(3); 8:3(2); 4; 9; 11(2); 21; 22; 23; 26(2); 27; 28; 9:3; 4(2); 5; 9(2); 19(4); 28; 29(2); 10:5(3); 6; 7; 8; 14; 26(2); 11:1(2); 5; 6(2); 7; 8; 9; 12:2(2); 3; 4; 5(2); 6(2); 7(2); 8(2); 10(2); 11(2); 13(2); 14(3); 15(3); 16(3); 17(2); 18; 19(2); 20(2); 22(2); 24; 25(2); 26(2); 27; 43; 44; 45; 46(2); 47; 48(3); 49; 13:3; 5(2); 6; 7(3); 9; 11(3); 12; 14; 16; 19; 14:2; 4; 13; 14(2); 16; 17; 18; 15:9(2); 14(2); 15(3); 16(2); 18; 24; 16:4; 5(3); 6; 7; 8(2); 12(3); 25; 26(2); 17:4; 6; 18:19; 22(5); 23; 19:5; 6; 12; 13(4); 20:23(2); 21:2(2); 3(2); 4(2); 5; 6(4); 7; 8(2); 9; 10; 11; 12; 13; 15; 16; 17; 19(3); 20; 21; 22(2); 26; 27; 28(3); 29(2); 30; 31; 32(3); 33(2); 34(2); 35(2); 36(2); 22:1(2); 2; 3(2); 4; 5(4); 6; 7; 8; 9(3); 11(3); 12; 13; 14; 15; 16; 17; 19; 20; 22; 24(2); 27(2); 30; 31(3); 23:11; 15; 17; 18; 23; 25(2); 26; 28; 33; 24:2(3); 25:2; 3; 9; 10(2); 12; 15(2); 16; 17; 19; 20(3); 21; 23; 27; 31(2); 32; 34; 35; 36(2); 37; 38; 39; 26:2(2); 3(2); 6; 8(2); 12; 13; 16(2); 17; 20; 24(4); 25; 28; 31; 32; 33; 37; 27:1(2); 2; 7(2); 8; 9; 10(2); 11; 12; 13; 14; 15; 16(2); 17(2); 18; 19; 20(3); 21; 28:4(2); 5; 6; 7(2); 8; 12; 16(3); 17(2); 18; 20; 21(2); 28; 29; 30(2); 32(2); 35(2); 37; 38(3); 42; 43(2); 29:9; 10; 15; 19; 21; 26; 28(2); 29; 30; 32; 33(2); 34; 37(2); 42; 43; 46; 30:2(4); 4; 7(2); 8; 9(2); 10(2); 12; 13(2); 14; 15(2); 19; 20; 21(2); 25; 29; 31; 32(3); 33; 34; 36; 37(2); 38(2); 31:11; 13; 14(3); 15; 16; 32:1; 13; 23; 30; 34; 33:14; 16(2); 20; 22; 23; 34:3; 10; 13; 20; 23; 24; 25; 35:2(3); 3; 10; 40:9; 10; 15; **Lev** 1:2; 3; 4(2); 5(2); 6; 7; 8; 9(2); 10; 11(2); 12(2); 13(2); 14; 15(2); 16; 17(3); 2:1(2); 2(3); 3; 4; 5; 7; 8; 9(2); 10; 11(3); 12(2); 16; 3:1; 2(2); 3; 4; 5; 6; 7; 8(2); 9(2); 10; 11; 12; 13(2); 14; 15; 16; 17; 4:2(2); 4(2); 5; 6; 7(2); 8; 9; 10; 12(2); 14; 15(2); 16; 17; 18(2); 19; 20(4); 21; 23; 24; 25(2); 26(3); 28; 29; 30(2); 31(4); 32; 33; 34(2); 35(4); 5:1; 2; 3(2); 4(2); 5(3); 6(2); 7; 8(3); 9(2); 10(3); 11(3); 12(2); 13(3); 15; 16(4); 17; 18(3); 6:4(2); 5(2); 6; 7(2); 9; 10(3); 11; 12(4); 13(2); 14; 15(2); 16(3); 17; 18(3); 20; 21; 22(2); 23(2); 25; 26(2); 27(2); 28(2); 29; 30(2); 7:2(2); 3; 4; 5; 6(2); 7; 8; 9; 10; 11; 12; 13; 14(2); 15(2); 16(2); 17; 18(4); 19(3); 20; 21(2); 23; 24; 25; 26; 27; 29; 30(2); 31(2); 32; 33; 8:31; 32; 33(2); 35; 9:6; 10:7; 9; 13; 14; 15(2); 11:2; 3; 4; 8(2); 9(2); 10; 11(3); 12; 13(2); 20; 23; 24(2); 25; 26; 27; 28; 29; 31; 32(3); 33(2); 34(2); 35(3); 36(2); 37; 38; 39; 40(2); 41(2); 42; 43(2); 44(3); 45; 12:2(2); 3; 4(2); 5(2); 6; 7(2); 8(3); 13:2(2); 3(2); 4; 5(2); 6(3); 7; 8; 9; 10; 11(2); 13(2); 14; 15; 16; 17(2); 20; 21; 22; 23; 25(2); 26; 27(2); 28; 30(2); 31; 32; 33(2); 34(3); 36(2); 37; 39; 43; 44; 45(3); 46(4); 49; 50; 51; 52(2); 53; 54(2); 55; 56; 58(2); 14:2(2); 3(2); 4; 5; 6(2); 7(3); 8(3); 9(6); 10; 11; 12; 13(2); 14(2); 15; 16(2); 17; 18(2); 19(2); 20(3); 21; 22; 23; 24(2); 25(2); 26;

27; 28; 29; 30; 31; 35; 36(2); 37; 38; 39(2); 40(2); 41(2); 42(3); 44; 45(2); 46; 47(2); 48(2); 49; 50; 51; 52; 53(2); 15:3; 4; 5; 6; 7; 8; 9; 10(2); 11; 12(2); 13(2); 14; 15(2); 16; 17; 18(2); 19(2); 20(2); 21; 22; 23; 24(2); 25(2); 26(2); 27(2); 28(2); 29; 30(2); 31; 16:3; 4(5); 5; 6; 7; 8; 9; 10; 11(3); 12; 13; 14(2); 15(2); 17; 18(2); 19; 20; 21(2); 22(2); 23(3); 24; 25; 26; 27(2); 28(2); 29(2); 30; 31(2); 32(4); 33(3); 34; 17:4(2); 6; 7(2); 9; 12(2); 13; 14(2); 15(2); 16; 18:3(3); 4; 5(2); 6; 23; 26(2); 29(2); 30; 19:2; 3; 5; 6(2); 7; 8(2); 11; 12; 13; 15; 19(2); 20(2); 21; 22(2); 23:5; 24; 25; 26(2); 27; 28; 30; 33; 34; 35; 36; 37; 20:2(2); 8; 9(2); 10; 11(2); 12(2); 13(2); 14; 15(2); 16(2); 17(3); 18(3); 19; 20(3); 21(2); 22; 23; 24; 25(2); 26; 27(3); 21:1; 4; 5(2); 6(2); 7(2); 8; 9; 10; 11; 12; 13; 14(2); 15; 18; 21(2); 22; 23; 22:3; 4; 6(2); 7(2); 8; 9; 10(2); 11(2); 13(2); 14(2); 15; 19; 20(2); 21(2); 22; 23; 24(2); 25(2); 27(2); 28; 30(2); 31; 32; 23:2; 3(2); 2(2); 3(2); 4; 7(2); 8(2); 10(2); 11(2); 12; 13(2); 14(2); 15(2); 16(2); 17(2); 18(2); 19; 20; 21(2); 22; 23; 24; 25(2); 26; 27(3); 21:1; 4; 5(2); 6(2); 7(2); 8; 9; 10

15(2); 16(2); 24:27(2); **Judg** 1:1; 2; 2:2(2); 3(2); 4:9(2); 20; 5:11(2); 24(2); 6:15; 37; 7:4(5); 11; 17(2); 8:23(2); 9:33; 10:18; 11:9; 24; 31(2); 13:5(3); 7; 8(2); 12(2); 15; 22; 14:13; 16; 15:3; 18; 16:2; 7; 11; 17; 18:5; 10; 20:9; 18(2); 23; 28(2); 21:1; 5; 7; 11(2); 16; 22; **Ruth** 1:16; 2:2; 9; 3:1; 3; 4(2); 13; 4:12; 15; **1Sa** 1:11; 28; 2:9(2); 10(4); 25(2); 30; 31; 32(2); 33(3); 34(3); 35(2); 36(3); 3:9; 11; 14; 4:8; 5:7; 8; 6:2(2); 3(2); 4(2); 5(2); 9; 20; 8:9; 11(2); 17; 18(2); 9:7; 13(2); 17; 19; 10:2; 3; 5(2); 27; 11:7; 9(2); 10; 12; 13; 12:12; 14; 15; 17; 25(2); 13:14; 14:10; 37; 39; 45(2); 15:33; 16:16(2); 17:9; 25; 26; 27; 36; 47; 18:25; 19:6; 20:7; 10; 31; 32; 21:15; 23:2; 17(2); 20; 23; 24:4; 12; 13; 20; 25:6; 11; 29(2); 30(3); 31(2); 26:10(3); 27:1(3); 12; 28:8; 10; 11; 15; 19; 29:9; 30:8(2); 23; 24(2); **2Sa** 2:1(2); 26(2); 3:12; 39; 4:11; 5:8(2); 19; 24; 6:9; 22; 7:10; 12; 13; 14; 15; 16(2); 9:10(2); 11(2); 11; 11; 12:5; 6; 10; 11; 14; 23(2); 13:13; 14:7(2); 10; 11; 17; 18; 15:8(2); 10; 14; 15; 21; 25; 35; 36; 16:3; 10; 20; 17:2; 3; 6; 10; 12(3); 13; 19:21(2); 22; 37; 38(2); 20:6; 18; 21; 21:3(2); 4; 22:4; 44; 45(2); 46(2); 23:4; 6; 7(2); 24:13(2); **1Kin** 1:13(2); 17(2); 20; 21(3); 24(2); 30(2); 35(2); 52(3); 2:4; 24; 32; 33(2); 37(2); 44; 45(2); 3:5; 12; 13; 5:5; 6; 9; 8:19(2); 25; 29(2); 30; 33; 38; 42(2); 44; 47; 59; 9:3; 5; 6; 7; 8:3; 9; 11:2(2); 32; 38; 12:10; 24; 26; 27(2); 13:2(3); 3(2); 22; 14:3(2); 5(2); 11(2); 12; 13(2); 14(2); 15(3); 16; 16:4(2); 17:1; 4; 14(2); 18:12(3); 14; 31; 19:17(3); 20:6(3); 10; 14; 23; 25; 28; 36; 39; 40; 42; 21:19; 23; 24(2); 22:6(3); 12; 15(3); 16; 20; **2Kin** 1:2; 2:9; 10(2); 16; 21; 3:8; 17(3); 19(2); 4:2; 10(2); 23; 43(2); 5:8; 10; 17; 27; 6:8; 15; 21(2); 27; 31; 7:1; 4(3); 12; 18; 8:1; 8; 9; 10; 9:8; 10(2); 36; 37(2); 10:4; 10; 18; 19(2); 24; 30; 11:5(2); 6(2); 7; 8; 12:5; 14:6(2); 15:12; 16:15; 17:12; 35; 36(3); 37(2); 38(2); 39(2); 18:22; 29; 30; 9:6; 7(2); 10(2); 29(2); 30; 31(2); 32; 33(2); 20:8(2); 9; 17(2); 18(3); 21:12; 14; 22:17(2); 18; 20; 23:27; 25:24; **1Chr** 11:6; 19; 12:17; 13:12; 14:10; 15; 16:30; 33; 17:9(3); 11(2); 12; 13; 14; 27; 21:12; 22:9(3); 10(2); 23:26; 28:6; 21(2); **2Chr** 1:7; 12; 2:8; 9; 14; 6:9(2); 16; 21; 24; 29(3); 7:14; 15; 16; 18; 19; 21(2); 22; 8:11; 10:10; 11:4; 12:7; 8; 13:12; 15:7; 18:5(2); 11; 14(3); 15; 19; 19:9; 10(3); 11(2); 20:16; 17; 20(2); 23:3; 4(2); 5(2); 6(2); 7(2); 25:4(3); 8; 9; 26:18; 28:13; 30:9(2); 32:11; 12; 15; 17; 33:4; 34:25(2); 26; 28; 35:3; **Ezr** 4:21; 6:8; 11; 12; 7:18; 20; 21; 24; 9:10; **Neh** 2:6; 8; 4:3; 11; 12; 20; 5:8; 6:7; 9; 9:29; 10:38(2); 39; 13:25; 27; **Est** 1:15; 17(3); 18(2); 20(3); 4:11(2); 14(2); 5:3; 6(2); 8; 6:6; 9; 11; 7:2(2); 8:6; 9:12(2); 10:2; 2(2); **Job** 1:21; 2:10(2); 4:17(2); 5:19(2); 20; 23; 24; 25; 7:4; 7; 8; 9; 10(2); 13(2); 20; 21(2); 8:2; 10; 13; 14(2); 15(4); 18; 19; 22(2); 9:14; 19; 20(2); 31; 10:21; 11:3; 17; 19(2); 20(3); 12:2; 7(2); 8(2); 13:11; 16(2); 18; 19; 14:6; 12; 14; 22(2); 15:21; 22; 24(2); 29(3); 30(3); 31; 32(2); 33(2); 34(2); 16:3; 22(2); 17:5; 8(2); 9(2); 16(2); 18:4(2); 5(2); 6; 7(2); 9; 21(2); 20:8; 12; 24(2); 26(2); 21:8(2); 22:4; 6; 8; 11; 20; 25; 28; 23:8(2); 9(2); 19(2); 24:7(4); 8(2); 9; 10(2); 13(2); 14; 16; 17(2); 18; 19(3); 20(3); 21(3); 22(2); 20:8; 12; 24(2); 26(2); 21:8(2); 22:4; 6; 8; 11; 20; 25; 38; 23:8(2); 9(2); 19(2); 24(2); 24:7(4); 8(2); 9; 10(2); 13(2); 14; 16; 17(2); 18(3); 19(3); 20(3); 21; 22(3); 3; 24; 25(2); 29; 31(2); 32; 33; 34; 36:3(3); 4(3); 6; 7(2); 8; 9(2); **Deut** 1:17(3); 22(2); 28; 30; 35; 36; 38(2); 39(2); 2:4; 6(2); 25(2); 29; 3:18; 19; 20; 21; 22(2); 28(2); 4:2(2); 6; 10; 22; 25(3); 26(3); 27(3); 28; 5:25; 27; 32(2); 33(2); 6:6; 8; 10(2); 14; 16; 17; 25; 7:1; 2; 5(2); 12(2); 14; 16(2); 19; 23(2); 24(2); 25; 8:1; 9:3(2); 11:8; 13(2); 18; 19; 22; 23; 24(3); 25(3); 29; 31(2); 32; 12:1; 2(2); 3(2); 4; 5(2); 6; 7(2); 8; 11(3); 12; 14; 16(2); 18; 20; 22; 26; 27; 29; 13:4(2); 5; 8; 9; 11(2); 16(2); 17; 14:1; 4; 7; 8; 9(2); 11; 12; 19; 21; 23; 24; 25; 29(2); 15:2(2); 3; 4(2); 6(2); 10(2); 11; 16; 17; 18(2); 20; 22; 16:2; 4(2); 6; 7; 8; 15(2); 16(3); 17; 18; 19; 20; 22; 16:2; 4(2); 6; 7; 8; 15(2); 16(3); 17; 18; 19; 20; 21(2); 22; 23; 24(3); 25(3); 29; 30:2(3); 4(3); 5(2); 7(2); 8(2); 9; 11(2); 12(2); 15(2); 31(4; 23(4; 24(3); 32:6(2); 11; 15; 17; 22(2); 26; 29(2); 30; 33:52; 53; 54(5); 55(3); 56(2); 34:2; 3(2); 4(3); 5(2); 6(2); 7(2); 8(2); 9(3); 10; 11(3); 12(3); 13; 17; 18; 35:2; 3(2); 4(2); 5(3); 6(4); 7(3); 8(5); 11; 12; 13(2); 14(3); 15; 16; 17; 18; 19(2); 21(2); 24; 25(3); 26; 27; 28; 29; 30(2); 31(2); 32; 33; 34; 36:3(3); 4(3); 6; 7(2); 8; 9(2); **Deut** 1:17(3); 22(2); 28; 30; 35; 36; 38(2); 39(2); 2:4; 6(2); 25(2); 29; 3:18; 19; 20; 21; 22(2); 28(2); 4:2(2); 6; 10; 22; 25(3); 26(3); 27(3); 28; 5:25; 27; 32(2); 33(2); 6:6; 8; 10(2); 14; 16; 17; 25; 7:1; 2; 5(2); 12(2); 14; 16(2); 18; 23; 24; 25; 29(3); 15:2(3); 3; 4(2); 6; 10(2); 11; 16; 17; 18; 19; 22; 23; 24(3); 25(3); 29; 30(2); 23:1; 2(2); 3(2); 8; 10(2); 11(3); 13; 14; 16(2); 17; 22; 24:5(4); 6; 7; 8(2); 11; 13; 15; 16(3); 19; 20; 21; 25:1; 2(2); 5(2); 6(2); 8; 9(3); 10; 12; 19; 26:1; 2; 3; 4; 27:2(2); 4(2); 12; 13; 14; 15; 16; 17; 18; 19; 20; 21; 22; 23; 24; 25; 26; 28:1; 2; 4; 5; 7(2); 8(2); 9; 10(2); 11; 12; 13; 15(2); 17; 18; 20; 21; 22(2); 24(2); 26; 28; 29; 30; 31(4); 32(3); 33; 35; 36; 37; 38; 39; 40; 41; 42; 43; 44(2); 45(2); 46; 48(2); 49; 50; 51(2); 52(2); 53; 54(2); 55(2); 56; 57(3); 60; 62; 63(2); 64; 65(2); 66; 68(3); 29:19; 20(3); 21; 22(3); 24; 25; 30:1; 12; 13; 16; 28(1); 31:3; 4; 5; 11; 17(3); 18; 20(2); 21(3); 32:2(2); 20; 22(2); 24; 25; 35(2); 36; 37; 42; 46; 47; 33:3; 10(2); 12(3); 17; 19(3); 22; 25(2); 27(2); 28(3); 29; **Josh** 1:3; 4; 5; 8; 11; 14(2); 15; 18; 2:5; 14; 19(5); 3:3; 4; 8; 10; 13(4); 4:3(2); 7(2); 21; 22; 6:3; 4(3); 5(4); 10(3); 17(2); 19; 26(2); 7:8; 9(2); 14(7); 15(2); 25; 8:2(4); 5; 7; 8(3); 9:7; 23; 10:8; 14(5); 14; 19(3); 25; 4; 8; 10; 13(4); 4:3(2); 7(2); 9; 25:14; 9; 12; 15:4; 17:18(2); 18:4(2); 5(3); 6; 20:3; 4(3); 5; 6(3); 22:22; 25; 28; 34; 23:5(2); 10; 12; 13;

21; 146:10; 148:6; **Prov** 1:5; 9; 13(2); 28(3); 31; 32(2); 33(2); 2:11(2); 21(2); 22(2); 3:2; 6; 8; 10(2); 22; 23; 24; 26(2); 35(2); 4:6(2); 8(2); 9(2); 10; 12; 5:22(2); 23(2); 6:11; 15(2); 22(3); 29; 31(2); 33(2); 8:6; 7; 17; 35; 9:11(2); 10:7; 8; 9; 10; 24(2); 27; 28(2); 29; 30(2); 31; 11:3(2); 5(2); 6(2); 7; 9; 15; 18; 21(2); 25(2); 26(2); 27; 28(2); 29(2); 31; 12:3(2); 6; 7; 8(2); 11; 13; 14(2); 19; 21(2); 24(2); 25; 26; 14:3; 11(2); 14(2); 22; 26; 15:10; 27; 16:3; 5; 20; 21; 17:2(2); 5; 11; 13; 18:20(2); 21; 19:5(2); 8; 9(2); 15; 16; 19; 21; 20:2(2); 20:4; 17; 20; 21; 22; 21:7; 13(2); 15; 16; 17(2); 18; 28; 22:5; 8(2); 9; 10(2); 11; 13; 14; 15; 16; 18; 29(2); 23:11; 13; 15; 16; 18; 21(2); 24(2); 25(2); 33(2); 35; 24:4; 8; 12; 14(3); 16; 20(2); 22; 24(2); 25(2); 26; 34; 25:4; 5; 22; 26(2); 26; 27; 27:14; 28(2); 28:2; 8; 9; 10(2); 13(2); 14; 16; 17; 18(2); 19(2); 20(2); 22; 23; 25; 26; 27(2); 29:1; 14; 16; 17(2); 21; 23(2); 25; 30:17(2); 31:11; 25; 30; **Eccl** 1:9(2); 11(2); 2:16; 18; 19(2); 21; 3:14; 17; 22(2); 4:12; 15; 16; 5:10; 15(2); 16; 20; 6:4; 12; 7:18; 26(2); 8:1; 5; 7(2); 8; 12; 13(2); 15; 17(2); 9:5; 10:8(2); 9(2); 14(2); 20(2); 11:2; 3; 4(2); 6(2); 8; 12:3(2); 4(3); 5(5); 7(2); 14; **Song** 1:13; 5:3(2); 7; 8; 8:8(2); **Is** 1:18(2); 19; 20; 27; 28(2); 29(2); 30; 31(3); 2:2(4); 3(2); 4(5); 11(3); 12(2); 17(3); 18; 19; 20; 3:4; 5(2); 6; 7; 10(2); 11(2); 24(2); 25; 26(2); 4:1; 2(2); 3(2); 4(2); 5; 6; 5:5(2); 6(2); 9; 10(2); 14; 15(3); 16(2); 17(2); 24(2); 26; 27(3); 28; 29(5); 30; 6:8; 13(4); 7:7(2); 8; 9; 14(3); 15; 16(2); 17; 18(2); 19(2); 20(2); 21(2); 22(4); 23(3); 24; 25; 8:4(2); 7; 8(4); 9(3); 10(2); 12; 14; 15; 19; 21(4); 22(2); 9:1; 5; 6(2); 7; 9; 11; 12; 17(2); 18(3); 19(2); 20(4); 21; 10:3; 4(2); 11; 12; 15(2); 16(3); 17(2); 18(2); 19; 20(3); 21; 22(2); 23; 24(2); 25; 26(2); 27(3); 32(2); 33(3); 34(2); 11:1(2); 2; 3(2); 4(3); 5; 6(3); 7(3); 8(2); 9(2); 10(4); 11(3); 12(2); 13(4); 14(4); 15(3); 16(2); 12:3; 4; 13:6; 7(2); 8(5); 9(3); 10; 13; 14(2); 15(2); 16(2); 17(2); 18; 19(3); 20(4); 21(4); 22(5); 23(3); 24; 25; 20:4; 5; 6(2); 21:13; 16; 17; 22:7(3); 13; 14; 18; 19; 20; 24; 25; 22(4); 23; 24; 25(2); 23:5; 7; 15(3); 17(3); 18(3); 24:2; 3; 9(2); 13(2); 14(3); 18(3); 20(4); 21; 23(2); 23(2); 25:2; 3(2); 5; 6; 8; 9; 10(2); 11(2); 12; 26:1; 6; 11(2); 14(2); 19(1); 21(2); 27:12(2); 5; 6(2); 9(2); 10(3); 11; 12(3); 13(4); 28:2; 3; 4; 5; 9(2); 15(2); 16; 17(2); 18(4); 19; 20(4); 21(4); 22(1); 24(2); 3(2); 10; 16; 20; 24(2); 25; 27(2); 29(2); 30(3); 31(2); 32(2); 15:2(2); 3(2); 4(4); 5(4); 6; 7; 9; 16:2(2); 5(2); 6; 7(3); 10(3); 11; 12(3); 14(2); 17:1; 2(3); 3(2); 4(3); 5(3); 6; 7(2); 8(2); 9; 11; 13(4); 16(3); 17(3); 18(2); 19; 20(4); 21(4); 22(5); 23(3); 24; 25; 26; 27; 30:2(3); 2(3); 10; 11; 12(3); 13(4); 14; 15; 16; 17(2); 18(2); 19; 20:4; 5; 6(2); 21:13; 16; 17; 22:7(3); 13; 14; 18; 19; 20; 21; 22; 23; 24; 25; 27; 42:1; 2; 3(3); 4(2); 13(4); 17(2); 43:2(2); 10; 13; 17(2); 19(2); 20; 21; 44:4; 5(3); 7(3); 9; 11(3); 15; 19(2); 26; 28(2); 45:1; 9; 13(2); 14(6); 16(2); 17(2); 23(3); 24(3); 25(2); 46:7(2); 10; 13(2); 47:3(2); 7; 8(2); 9(2); 11(3); 13; 14(4); 15(4); 48:14; 15; 49:5(2); 7(3); 9(2); 10(4); 11; 12; 17(2); 19(2); 20; 22(3); 23; 24; 25(2); 50:7(2); 9(3); 11(4); 51:3(2); 4; 5(3); 6(5); 8(3); 11(4); 12(2); 19(2); 52:1; 3; 6(2); 8(4); 10; 12; 13(2); 15(4); 53:2(2); 8; 10(3); 11(4); 12; 54:3; 5; 10(3); 13(2); 14; 15(3); 17(2); 55:3; 5; 11(4); 12(3); 13(4); 56:5; 7; 12; 57:2(2); 12; 13(4); 14; 58:4; 8(4); 9(2); 10; 11; 12(2); 59:6(2); 8; 19(3); 20; 21; 60:2(3); 3; 4(2); 5(3); 6(4); 7(3); 9; 10(2); 11(2); 12(2); 13; 14(3); 18; 19(3); 20(4); 21(2); 22; 61:4(3); 5(2); 6(4); 7(4); 9(2); 62:2(2); 4(2); 5(2); 6; 8; 9(2); 63:3; 64:5; 65:9(2); 10; 12; 13(6); 14(3); 15(2); 16(2); 17; 19; 20(3); 21(2); 22(3); 23; 24; 25(4); 66:5(2); 8(2); 9(2); 12(2); 13; 14(3); 16; 17; 18(2); 19; 20; 22(2); 23(2); 24(4); **Jer** 1:7; 14; 15(2); 19(2); 2:3(2); 19(2); 24; 35; 3:1(2); 15; 16(6); 17(3); 18(2); 19; 4:2(2); 7; 9(4); 10; 11; 12(2); 13(2); 14; 17(4); 19(3); 29(2); 6:3(3); 9; 10; 11; 12; 15(2); 16; 21(2); 22; 23; 26; 30; 7:20(3); 23; 32(2); 33(2); 34; 8:1; 2(3); 3; 4(2); 10; 12; 13(3); 17; 9:7; 9(2); 22(2); 10:10(2); 11(2); 15; 21(2); 11:4; 11(2); 12(2); 22(2); 23; 12:4(2); 12(2); 13(2); 14; 17(4); 19(3); 29(2); 6:3(3); 9; 10; 11; 12; 15(2); 16; 21(2); 22; 23; 26; 30; 13:1; 2; 3; 6; 8; 9(2); 11; 13; 20:4(4); 5; 6; 10(2); 11(5); 21:3; 6; 7(2); 9(3); 10(2); 13(4); 12; 22:4; 5; 7; 22:4; 5; 7; 9(2); 11; 14; 16; 22(2); 28:9(2); 14; 29:7; 12(2); 13(2); 21; 22; 32(2); 30:3; 7; 8(2); 9; 10(3); 16(3); 18(2); 19(3); 20(2); 21(3); 22; 23; 24(2); 31:1; 5(2); 6(2);

8; 9(2); 12(4); 13; 14; 16(2); 17; 18; 22; 23(2); 24; 28; 29; 30(2); 33(2); 34(2); 36; 38; 39(2); 40(2); 32:3; 4(4); 5(3); 7; 15; 28; 29; 36; 38; 40; 43; 44; 33:9(3); 10(2); 11(2); 12; 13; 15; 16(3); 17; 18; 34:2; 3(2); 5; 20; 22; 35:6; 7(2); 15; 19; 36:29(2); 30(2); 37:7(2); 8; 9(2); 19; 38:2(4); 3(2); 17(2); 18(2); 20(3); 22(2); 23; 39:12; 16; 18; 40:9; 15; 42:4(2); 5; 14; 16(4); 17(3); 18(4); 20; 22; 43:10; 11; 12(3); 13(2); 44:12(4); 14(3); 26; 27; 28(3); 29(2); 46:6; 10(2); 14; 18; 19; 22(2); 23; 24(2); 26; 27(2); 47:2(4); 3; 48:2(2); 3; 5; 7; 8(4); 9; 12(2); 13; 18(2); 26(2); 30(2); 31; 33(2); 34; 36(2); 37(2); 38; 39(2); 40(2); 41; 42; 43; 44(2); 45(2); 49:2(3); 3; 4; 5(2); 10; 12; 13(2); 17(3); 18(2); 19; 20(2); 22(2); 26(2); 27; 28; 29(3); 32; 33(2); 36(2); 39; 50:3(4); 4(2); 5(2); 9(4); 10(2); 12(3); 13(3); 16(2); 19(2); 20(3); 30(2); 32(3); 34; 36(2); 37(2); 38; 39(4); 40(2); 41(2); 42(3); 44; 45(2); 51:2(3); 4; 14; 18; 26; 29(2); 31; 33; 35(2); 37; 38(2); 44(2); 46(3); 47(2); 48(2); 49; 52; 53; 56; 57; 58(4); 62(2); 63; 64(3); **Lam** 1:21; 2:13(3); 20(2); 4:15; 20; 21; 5:21; **Eze** 2:5; 3:10; 18; 19; 20(3); 21; 25(2); 4:3(2); 7; 10; 13; 16(2); 5:4; 10(2); 11; 12(3); 13(2); 15(2); 16(2); 17(2); 6:4(2); 6(2); 7(2); 8(2); 9(3); 10; 11; 12(3); 13(2); 14; 7:4(3); 9(2); 11(2); 13(3); 15(2); 16(2); 17(2); 18(3); 19(4); 21; 22(2); 24(2); 25(2); 26(4); 27(4); 8:18; 9:10; 11:10(2); 11(2); 12; 16; 18(2); 20; 12:11(2); 12(4); 13(2); 15(2); 16; 19; 20(3); 23; 24; 25(3); 28(2); 13:9(5); 11(4); 12; 13; 14(4); 21(2); 23(2); 14:8; 10(2); 16(3); 18(2); 20(2); 22(5); 23(2); 15:3; 5; 7(3); 16:16(2); 39(4); 40(2); 41; 42; 44; 53; 55(3); 17:9(3); 10(3); 15(3); 16; 17; 18; 20; 21(3); 23(3); 24; 18:3; 4; 9; 13(4); 17(2); 18; 19; 20(5); 21(2); 22(2); 24(3); 26; 27; 28(2); 30; 19:14; 20:11; 13; 20; 21; 31; 32; 38(2); 40; 42(2); 43(2); 44; 47(3); 48(2); 21:4; 5; 7(6); 12(3); 13; 19; 23; 24; 25; 26; 27; 29; 30; 32; 22:5; 14; 21; 22(2); 23:24(3); 25(5); 26; 29(4); 45; 47(2); 49(3); 24:12; 14(2); 16; 21; 22(2); 23(3); 24(2); 25; 26; 27(2); 25:4(3); 5; 11; 13; 14(2); 17(2); 26:2; 4; 5(2); 6(2); 8(2); 9(2); 10(3); 11(3); 12(3); 13; 15; 16(4); 17; 18(2); 19(3); 20(3); 27:27; 28; 29(2); 30(4); 31(2); 32; 34; 35(3); 36; 28:7(2); 8; 18; 19; 22(3); 23(2); 24(2); 25(3); 26(4); 29:4; 6; 9(2); 11(3); 12; 14; 15(3); 16(3); 19(2); 21; 30:3; 4(5); 5; 6(3); 7(2); 8(2); 9(2); 11(2); 13; 16(3); 17(2); 18(5); 19; 21; 24; 25(4); 26; 31:11; 13(2); 16; 32:3; 6; 7(2); 9; 10(3); 11; 12(2); 13; 15(4); 16(3); 20; 21; 27(2); 29; 31(2); 32; 33:4; 5(2); 8; 9; 12(3); 13(4); 15(2); 16(2); 18; 19; 25; 26; 27(2); 28(3); 29; 33; 34:10; 14(3); 22; 23(3); 25; 26; 27(4); 28(4); 29; 30; 35:6(2); 8; 9(2); 10; 15; 36:7; 8; 9; 10(2); 11(2); 12; 23(2); 25; 27; 28(2); 30; 31(2); 33(2); 34; 35; 36; 38(2); 37:5; 6(2); 13; 14(4); 17; 18; 19; 20; 22(3); 23(2); 24(3); 25(3); 26; 27(2); 28(2); 38:8; 10(2); 13; 16(2); 18(3); 19; 20(4); 21; 23; 39:6; 7; 9(3); 10(3); 11(4); 12; 13(3); 14(2); 15; 16(2); 18; 19; 20; 21; 22; 23; 28; 40:4; 42:13(2); 14(4); 43:7; 12; 13(3); 14(2); 15(2); 16; 17(4); 18; 21; 22; 24(2); 25; 26(2); 27(2); 44:2(4); 3(3); 9; 10; 11(3); 12; 13(2); 14; 15(2); 16(3); 17(3); 18(3); 19(3); 20(2); 21; 22(2); 23; 24(4); 25; 26; 27; 28(2); 29(2); 30(2); 31; 45:1(5); 2; 3; 4(3); 5; 6(2); 7(2); 8(3); 10; 11(2); 12(2); 13(2); 14; 16; 17(2); 19; 20; 21(2); 22; 23; 24; 25; 46:1(3); 2(6); 3; 4(2); 5(2); 6(2); 7(2); 8(3); 9(5); 10(2); 11; 12(5); 15; 16(2); 17(3); 18(2); 20(2); 24; 47:8; 9(7); 10(4); 11(2); 12(5); 13(3); 14(2); 15; 17; 18; 20; 21; 22(5); 23(2); 48:8(3); 9(2); 10(2); 11; 12; 13(2); 14; 15(2); 16; 17; 18(3); 19; 20(2); 21(3); 22; 23; 24; 28; 29; 31; 35; **Dan** 1:10; 2:5(2); 6; 9; 28; 29; 30; 39(2); 40(2); 41(2); 42; 43(2); 44(5); 45; 3:6; 10(2); 15(2); 29(2); 4:25(5); 26; 32(4); 5:7(3); 6:5; 7(2); 12(2); 26(2); 7:14(2); 17; 18; 23(4); 24(4); 25(3); 26(2); 27(2); 8:13; 14; 17; 19(2); 22; 23; 24(4); 25(5); 26; 9:25(2); 26(4); 27(4); 10:14; 20; 11:2(3); 3(2); 4(4); 5(3); 6(5); 7(5); 8(2); 9(2); 10(4); 11(4); 12(3); 13(3); 14(3); 15(3); 16(4); 17(4); 18(4); 19(2); 20(2); 21(3); 22(2); 23(3); 24(4); 25(4); 26(3); 27(4); 28(3); 29(2); 30(4); 31(4); 32(2); 33(2); 34(3); 35; 36(5); 37(2); 38(2); 39(4); 40(4); 41(3); 42(2); 43(2); 44(2); 45(3); 12:1(4); 2; 3; 4(2); 6; 7(3); 8; 10(4); 11(2); **Hos** 1:5; 10(3); 11(3); 2:6; 7(5); 10; 12; 15; 16; 17; 21(2); 22(2); 23; 3:4; 5(2); 4:3(3); 5; 9; 10(3); 13(2); 14; 19; 5:5(2); 6(2); 7; 9(2); 14; 6:2; 3(2); 4(2); 7:12; 16(2); 8:1; 2; 3; 6; 7(3); 8; 10; 11; 13; 14; 9:2(2); 3(3); 4(5); 6(4); 7; 11; 12; 13; 16; 17; 10:2(3); 3; 5(2); 6(3); 8(3); 10(2); 11(2); 14(2); 15(2); 11:5(2); 6(2); 8(4); 10(4); 11; 12:8; 14(2); 13:3; 8; 13; 14; 15(5); 16(4); 14:3; 5; 6(2); 7(3); 8; 9(4); **Joel** 1:15; 2:2; 3; 4; 5; 6(2); 7(4); 8(3); 9(4); 10(4); 11; 19; 20(2); 24(2); 26(2); 27(2); 28(4); 31; 32(5); 3:1; 8; 15(2); 16(2); 17(3); 18(6); 19(2); 20; **Amos** 1:2(2); 4; 5; 7; 8; 10; 12; 14; 15; 2:2(2); 5; 14(3); 15(3); 16; 3:5; 6(2); 11(3); 12; 14(2); 15(2); 4:2; 3(2); 5:2; 3(2); 4; 5(2); 6; 9; 11(2); 13; 14; 16(3); 17; 20; 6:7(2); 9(2); 10(4); 12; 14; 7:2; 3; 5; 6; 9(2); 11(2); 17(4); 8:3(3); 8(3); 9; 12(3); 13; 14; 9:1(2); 2; 3; 4; 5(4); 9; 10(2); 13(3); 14(3); 15; **Obad** 3; 8; 9; 10; 15(2); 16(4); 17(3); 18(3); 19(3); 20(2); 21(2); **Jonah** 1:11; 12; 3:4; **Mic** 1:4(2); 7(3); 11; 14; 15; 2:3(2); 4; 5; 6(2); 10; 11; 12; 13; 3:4; 6(6); 7(2); 12(2); 4:1(4); 2(2); 3(4); 4(2); 7; 8(2); 10; 12; 5:1; 2; 3; 4(3); 5(4); 6(2); 7; 8; 9(2); 10; 6:6(2); 7; 9; 11; 14; 16; 7:4; 8(2); 9; 10(4); 11; 12; 13; 16(3); 17(4); **Nah** 1:8; 9; 10; 12(2); 15; 2:3(2); 4(4); 5(4); 6(2); 7(3); 8(3); 13(2); 3:7(3); 12(2); 13(2); 15(3); 18; 19; **Hab** 1:2; 6; 7; 8(3); 9(3); 10(4); 11(2); 12; 17; 2:1; 3; 4; 6; 7(3); 8; 11(2); 13(2); 14; 16(2); 17; 19; 3:17(6); **Zeph** 1:8; 10(2); 12; 13(3); 14; 17(2); 18(3); 2:3; 4(3); 5; 6; 7(4); 9(3); 10; 11; 12; 14(5); 15; 3:8; 10; 12; 13(4); 16; **Hag** 2:7; 9; 12; 13(2); 22; **Zec** 1:16(2); 17(3); 2:4; 9(2); 11(2); 12(2); 3:9; 10; 4:7; 9; 10(2); 5:3(2); 4(3); 11; 6:12(2); 13(5); 14; 15(3); 8:3; 4; 5; 8(2); 12(4); 13(2); 16; 19; 20(2); 21; 22; 23(3); 9:1(2); 2; 4; 5(5); 6; 7(2); 8; 10(3); 14(4); 15(4); 16(2); 17; 10:1; 5(3); 6; 7(4); 8; 9(2); 10; 11(5); 12; 11:6; 16(3); 17(3); 12:2; 3; 5(2); 6(2); 7; 8(3); 9; 10(3); 11; 12; 13:1; 2(2); 3(4); 4(3); 5; 6(2); 7; 8(3); 9(2); 14:1; 2(3); 3; 4(4); 5(4); 6(2); 7(4); 8(3); 9(2); 10(2); 11(3); 12(4); 13(4); 14(2); 15(2); 16(2); 17(2); 18; 19; 20(2); 21(3); **Mal** 1:4(2); 5(2); 11(3); 2:3; 4; 3:1(3); 2; 3(2); 4; 7; 10; 11(2); 12(2); 17; 18; 4:1(4); 2(2); 3(3); 6; **Mt** 1:21(2); 23(3); 2:6(2); 23; 3:11; 4:4; 6(2); 5:4; 5; 6; 7; 8; 9; 11(2); 13; 18; 19(5); 20(2); 21(2); 22(5); 31; 32(2); 39; 41; 6:4; 6; 7; 18; 22; 23; 25(3); 30; 31(3); 33; 34; 7:2(2); 7(3); 8; 11; 16; 20; 21; 26; 8:8; 11(2); 12(2); 9:15(2); 18; 21; 10:11; 14; 15; 18; 19(3); 21(2); 22(2); 23; 25; 26(2); 29; 32; 33; 36; 39(2); 41(2); 42(2); 11:6; 10; 16; 22; 24; 29; 12:11(2); 18; 19(2); 20(2); 21; 25; 26; 27; 31(2); 32(2); 36(2); 39; 40; 41(2); 42(2); 45; 50; 13:12(3); 14(4); 40; 41(2); 42(2); 43; 49(2); 50(2); 15:5; 6; 13; 14; 16:4; 18; 19(2); 22; 25(2); 26(2); 27(2); 28; 17:11; 12; 17(2); 20(3); 22; 23(2); 18:3; 4; 5; 6; 15(2); 17; 18(4); 19(3); 21; 35; 19:5(3); 9(2); 16; 23; 27; 28(2); 29(2); 30(2); 20:7; 16; 18(2); 19(2); 22; 23(2); 26; 32; 21:2; 3; 13; 21(3); 22(2); 25; 26; 41; 43; 44(3); 22:9; 13; 24; 28; 23:11; 12(4); 14; 16(2); 18; 20; 21; 22; 34(2); 36; 39(2); 24:2(2); 3(2); 5(2); 6; 7(2); 9(3); 10(3); 11(2); 12(2); 13(2); 14(2); 15; 21(2); 22; 23; 24(3); 26; 27; 29(4); 30(3); 31(2); 33; 34; 35(2); 37; 39; 40(2); 41(2); 46; 47; 48; 49; 50; 51(2); 25:1; 29(3); 30; 31(2); 32(2); 33; 34; 37; 40; 41; 44; 45; 46; 26:13(2); 21; 23; 31(2); 33; 48; 52; 53; 54; 64; 27:22; 64; 28:7; 10; **Mk** 1:2; 8; 2:20(2); 3:28(2); 29; 35; 4:22; 24(2); 25(2); 30(2); 5:23; 28; 6:11(2); 24; 37; 7:11(2); 8:12; 35(3); 36(2); 37; 38(2); 9:1; 19(2); 31(2); 35; 37(2); 39; 41(2); 42; 43; 45; 49(2); 10:7; 8; 11; 12; 15(2); 17; 23; 30; 31; 33(3); 34(5); 35; 39(2); 40; 43(2); 44; 11:2; 17; 23(5); 24; 31; 32; 12:7; 9; 15(2); 23(2); 25; 40; 13:2(2); 4(3); 6(2); 7(2); 8(3); 9(3); 11(3); 12(3); 13(3); 14; 19(2); 21; 22(2); 24(2); 25(2); 26; 27(2); 29; 30; 31(2); 14:9(2); 13; 14(2); 18; 27(2); 29; 32; 44; 62; 15:12; 16:3; 7; 16(2); 17(3); 18(4); **Lk** 1:13; 14; 15(3); 16; 17; 18; 20(2); 32(3); 33(2); 34; 35(4); 37; 45; 48; 60; 66; 2:10; 12(2); 23; 34; 35; 3:5(4); 6; 10; 12; 14; 16; 4:4; 7; 10; 11; 5:35(2); 37; 6:21(2); 22(3); 25(2); 26; 35(2); 37(3); 38(3); 39; 40; 7:7; 23; 27; 31; 8:17(2); 18(2); 50; 9:24(2); 26(3); 27; 41; 44; 48(3); 10:6(2); 12; 14; 19; 25; 42; 11:5(2); 7; 9(3); 10; 11; 12; 13; 18; 19; 22; 29; 30; 31; 32(2); 36; 49; 51; 12:2(2); 3(2); 5; 8(2); 9; 10(3); 11(2); 12; 17; 20(2); 22(2); 29(2); 31; 37(2); 38; 42; 43; 45; 47; 48(2); 52; 53; 13:3; 5; 8; 18; 20; 24; 25; 26; 27; 28(2); 29(2); 30(2); 32; 35(2); 14:5; 11(2); 15; 24; 34; 15:7; 16:3; 12; 17:10; 21; 22(2); 23; 24; 26; 30; 31; 33(4); 34(3); 35(2); 36(2); 18:7; 8; 14(2); 17(2); 18; 24; 30; 31; 32(2); 33(2); 41; 19:26(2); 30; 31; 43(2); 44(2); 20:5; 13; 15; 16(2); 18(3); 35; 47; 21:6(2); 7(2); 8; 9; 10; 11(2); 12; 13; 14; 15; 16(2); 17; 18; 20; 23; 24(3); 25; 26; 27; 32; 33(2); 35; 36; 22:10; 11(2); 12; 18; 26; 34; 49; 69; 23:29; 30; 31; **Jn** 1:51; 3:12; 36; 4:13; 14(4); 21; 23; 5:24; 25(2); 28; 29; 43; 47; 6:5; 27; 28; 35(2); 37; 45; 51; 57; 58; 62; 68; 7:17; 34(2); 35; 36(2); 38; 41; 8:12(2); 21(2); 24(2); 28; 32(2); 33; 36(2); 51; 52; 55; 9:21; 10:9(2); 16(2); 28(2); 11:12; 23; 24; 25; 26; 48; 12:25(2); 26; 27; 31; 48; 13:21; 26; 32(2); 33; 35; 38; 14:12(2); 13; 14; 16; 17; 19; 20; 21; 26; 15:7(2); 8; 10; 16; 26; 27; 16:2; 4; 13(3); 14(3); 15(2); 16(2); 17(2); 19(2); 20(4); 22; 23(2); 24; 25(2); 26; 32(2); 33; 17:20; 18:11; 19:15; 24; 36; 37; 20:25; 21:6; 18; 21; 23; **Acts** 1:5; 8(2); 11; 2:17(4); 18; 20; 21(3); 26; 37; 38; 39; 3:19; 20; 22(3); 23(2); 25; 4:16; 5:9; 6:14(2); 7:3; 7(2); 37(2); 8:33; 9:6; 10:6; 32; 43; 11:14(2); 16; 13:22; 41; 15:11; 27; 29; 18:10; 19:39; 20:22; 25; 29; 30; 21:11(2); 22:10(2); 23:3; 24:15; 22; 26:2; 27:22; 25; 34; 28:26(3); **Rom** 1:17; 2:12(2); 13; 16; 26; 27; 3:3; 5; 6; 20; 30; 4:1; 18; 24; 5:9; 10; 17; 19; 6:1(2); 2; 5; 8; 14; 15; 7:3; 7; 24; 8:11; 13(2); 18; 21; 31; 32; 33; 35(2); 39; 9:7; 9; 12; 14; 20; 26(2); 27; 30; 33; 10:5; 6; 7; 11; 13(2); 14(3); 15; 11:15; 23; 24; 26(3); 27; 35; 13:2; 14:4; 10; 11(2); 12; 15:12(3); 21(2); 29; 16:20; **1Cor** 1:8; 3:8; 13(4); 14; 15(3); 17; 4:5; 17; 21; 6:2(2); 3; 5; 9; 10; 13; 15; 16; 7:28; 8:10; 11; 9:11; 11:22(2); 27(2); 12:15; 16; 13:8(3); 10; 12; 14:6(2); 7; 8; 9(2); 11(2); 16; 15:22; 24(2); 26; 28(2); 29; 37; 49; 51(2); 52(3); 54(3); 16:3; 4; 5; 12; **2Cor** 1:7; 13; 3:8; 16(2); 4:14(2); 5:3; 6:16; 18; 9:6(2); 10:15; 11:10; 15; 12:6; 20(2); 21; 13:1; 4; 6; 11; **Gal** 2:16; 3:8; 11; 12; 4:30; 5:2; 10; 16; 21; 6:4; 5; 7; 8(2); 9; **Eph** 5:14; 31(3); 6:8; 16; 21; **Phil** 1:19; 20(2); 22; 25; 2:23; 24; 3:15; 21; 4:7; 9; 19; **Col** 3:4(2); 24; 25; 4:7; 9; **1Th** 4:15; 16(2); 17(2); 5:3(2); **2Th** 1:7; 9; 10; 2:3; 8(3); 11; 3:3; **1Ti** 2:15; 3:5; 4:1; 6:15; **2Ti** 2:2; 11; 12; 21; 3:1; 2; 9(2); 12; 13; 4:1; 3; 4(2); 8; 18; **Titus** 3:12; **Philem** 1:22; **Heb** 1:5; 11(2); 12(2); 14; 2:3; 3:11; 4:3; 5; 6:6; 8:10; 11(2); 9:14; 28; 10:27; 29; 30; 37; 38(2); 11:18; 32; 12:9; 14; 20; 25; 13:6; **Jas** 1:5; 7; 10; 11; 12; 25; 2:10; 12; 13; 3:1; 4:10; 14; 15; 5:1; 3(2); 15(3); 20(2); **1Pet** 2:6; 12; 20; 4:5; 8; 13; 17; 18; 5:1; 4(2); **2Pet** 1:8; 10; 11; 2:1(2); 2(2); 3; 12; 13; 3:3; 10(3); 11; 12(2); **1Jn** 2:18; 24(2); 27; 28; 3:2(4); 19; 4:15; 5:16(3); **2Jn** 2; **3Jn** 14(2); **Rev** 1:7(2); 19; 2:10(2); 11; 23; 27(2); 3:4; 5; 10; 12; 5:10; 6:17; 7:15; 16(2); 17(3); 9:6(4); 10:7; 9(2); 11:2; 3; 7(3); 8; 9(2); 10(2); 15; 13:8; 10; 14:10(2); 15:4(2); 17:8(2); 13; 14(2); 16(3); 17; 18:7; 8(2); 9(2); 11; 15; 21(2); 22(3); 23(2); 19:15; 20:6(2); 7; 8; 10; 21:3(2); 4(3); 7(2); 8; 24; 25(2); 26; 27; 22:3(3); 4(2); 5(2); 12; 18(2); 19(2)

SHALT

Gen 2:17(2); 3:14(2); 15; 16; 17(2); 18; 19(2); 4:7(2); 12; 6:14(2); 15; 16(4); 18; 19; 21; 7:2; 12:2; 15:15(2); 16:11(2); 17:4; 9; 15; 19; 20:7(2); 13; 21:23; 30; 24:3; 4; 7; 8; 37; 38; 40; 41(2); 27:10; 40(4); 28:1; 6; 14; 22; 29:27; 30:31; 31:50(2); 52; 32:18; 35:17; 37:8(2); 40:13; 41:40; 43:9; 45:10(2); 47:30; 49:4; 50:5; **Ex** 3:14; 15; 18; 4:9; 12; 15; 16; 17(2); 22; 6:1; 7:2; 9; 15(2); 16; 17; 9:15; 10:28; 12:46; 13:5; 6; 8; 10; 12; 13(3); 14; 15:17; 17:6; 18:20(2); 21; 23(2); 19:3; 6; 12; 24; 20:3; 4; 5; 7; 9; 10; 13; 14; 15; 16; 17(2); 22; 24(2); 25; 26; 21:1; 14; 23; 22:18; 21; 25(2); 26; 28; 29(2); 30(2); 23:1; 2(2); 3; 4; 5; 6; 8; 9; 10(2); 11(2); 12(2); 14; 15(2); 18; 19(2); 22; 24(2); 27; 31; 32; 25:11(3); 12; 13; 14; 16; 17; 18(2); 21(2); 23; 24; 25(2); 26; 28; 29(2); 30; 31; 37; 26:1(2); 4(2); 5(2); 6; 7(2); 9(2); 10; 11; 14; 15; 17; 18; 19; 22; 23; 26; 29(2); 30; 31; 32; 33; 34; 35(2); 36; 37(2); 27:1; 2(2); 3(2); 4(2); 5; 6; 8; 9; 20; 28:2; 3; 9; 11(2); 12; 13; 14; 15(3); 17; 22; 23(2); 24; 25; 26(2); 27(2); 30; 31; 33; 36; 37; 39(3); 40(3); 41(2); 42; 29:1; 2; 3; 4(2); 5; 6; 7; 8; 9(2); 10; 11; 12; 13; 14; 15; 16(2); 17; 18; 19; 20; 21; 22; 24(2); 25; 26; 27; 31; 34; 35(2); 36(3); 37; 38; 39(2); 41(2); 30:1(2); 3(2); 4(2); 5; 6; 16(2); 18(3); 25; 26; 29; 30; 31; 35; 36; 37; 33:21; 23; 34:14; 17; 18(2); 20(3); 21(3); 22; 24; 25; 26(2); 40:2; 3; 4(2); 5; 6; 7(2); 8; 9(2); 10; 11; 12; 13; 14; 15; **Lev** 2:6; 8; 13(3); 14; 15; 6:21(2); 27; 9:3; 13:55; 57; 58; 17:8; 18:7(2); 8; 9; 10; 11; 12; 13; 14(2); 15(2); 16; 17(2); 18; 19; 20; 21(2); 22; 23; 19:9(2); 10(3); 12; 13; 14(2); 15(2); 16(2); 17(2); 18(2); 19(2); 27; 32; 34; 20:2; 16; 19; 21:8; 23:22(3); 24:5; 6; 7; 15; 25:3(2); 4; 5; 8; 9; 15; 16(2); 17; 35; 37; 39; 43(2); 44; **Num** 1:49; 50; 3:9; 10; 15; 41; 47(2); 48; 4:23; 29; 30; 7:5; 8:7; 8; 9(2); 10; 12; 13; 14; 15; 26; 10:2; 11:23; 14:15; 15:5; 6; 7; 10; 17:3; 4; 10; 18:10; 15(2); 16; 17(3); 20(2); 30; 20:8(2); 18; 20; 21:34; 22:12(2); 20; 35; 23:5; 13(2); 26:54(2); 27:7(2); 8; 13; 20; 28:3; 4(2); 7; 8(2); 21; 31:2; 30; **Deut** 1:37; 2:28; 3:2; 27; 28; 4:25; 29(2); 30; 40; 5:7; 8; 9; 11; 13; 14; 17; 18; 19; 20; 21(2); 31; 6:5; 7(2); 8; 9; 11; 13(2); 18; 21; 7:2(2); 3(3); 11; 14; 16(2); 17; 18(2); 21; 24; 25; 26(3); 8:2; 5; 6; 9(2); 10; 18; 9:3; 10:2; 20(3); 11:1; 20; 29; 12:5; 14(2); 18; 20; 21(2); 22; 24(2); 25(2); 26; 27(2); 31; 32; 13:3; 5; 8(3); 9; 10; 12; 14; 15; 16(2); 18; 14:3; 21(2); 22; 23; 25(2); 26(3); 27; 28(2); 15:1; 6(3); 7; 8(2); 10; 11; 12; 13; 14(2); 15; 17(2); 19(2); 20; 21; 22; 23(2); 16:2; 3(2); 6; 7(2); 8(2); 9; 10(2); 11; 12(2); 13; 14; 15(2); 18; 19(2); 20; 21(2); 22; 17:1; 5(2); 7; 8; 9; 10(2); 11(2); 12; 14(3); 15(2); 18:4; 9; 13; 14; 22; 19:2; 3; 7; 9(2); 13; 14(2); 19; 20:12; 13; 14(2); 15; 16; 17; 19(3); 20(2); 21:9(2); 12; 13; 14(3); 21; 23; 22:1(2); 2(2); 3(3); 4(2); 6; 7; 8; 9; 10; 11; 12; 21; 22; 24; 26; 23:6; 7(2); 12(2); 13(3); 15; 16; 18; 19; 20; 21(2); 22; 23; 24; 25; 24:4; 7; 10; 11; 12; 13; 14; 15; 17; 18; 19; 20; 21; 22; 25:4; 12; 13; 14; 15(2); 19(2); 26:2(4); 3; 5; 10; 11; 13; 16; 27:2; 3; 4; 5(2); 6(2); 7(2); 8; 10; 28:1; 2; 3(2); 6(2); 9; 12(2); 13(2); 14; 16(2); 19(2); 25(2); 29(3); 30(5); 31(2); 33; 34(2); 36(2); 37; 38(2); 39(2); 40(2); 41(2); 43; 44(2); 48; 49; 53; 64; 65; 66(2); 67(4); 68; 30:1; 2(2); 5; 8; 10; 17; 31:2; 3; 7; 11; 16; 23; 32:52(2); 33:29; 34:4; **Josh** 1:6; 8(3); 2:18(2); 3:8; 6:3; 8:2; 11:6; 17:17; 18(2); **Judg** 4:20; 6:14; 16; 23; 26; 7:5; 11; 9:33(2); 11:2; 30; 13:3; 5; 7; **Ruth** 2:21; 3:4(3); **1Sa** 2:16; 32; 3:9; 9:16; 10:2; 3(2); 4; 5(2); 6(2); 8(3); 14:44; 16:3(2); 16; 18:21; 19:11; 20:2; 8; 14; 15; 18; 19(2); 31; 22:16; 23; 23:17; 24:20; 26:25(2); 28:1; 2; 19; 30:8; **2Sa** 3:13; 5:2(2); 6; 23; 24; 7:5; 8; 12; 9:7; 10; 10:11; 11:25; 12:13; 13:13; 15:33; 35(2); 18:3; 20(3); 19:23; 38; 21:4; 17; **1Kin** 2:37(2); 42; 5:6; 9(3); 8:19; 44; 11:37(2); 12:10(2); 13:17; 14:5; 17:4; 19:16(2); 20:5; 13; 34; 39; 21:19(2); 22:11; 22; 25(2); **2Kin** 1:4(2); 6(2); 16(2); 4:4(3); 16; 5:10; 6:22; 7:2(2); 19(2); 8:13; 9:7; 10:5; 13:17; 19; 19:11; 20:1; 5; 9; 18; 22:20; **1Chr** 11:2(2); 5; 14:15(2); 17:4; 7; 19:12; 21:22; 22:8; 13; 28:3; **2Chr** 2:16(2); 6:9; 34; 7:17; 10:10(2); 16:9; 18:10; 21(2); 24(2); 21:15; 34:28; **Ezr** 4:13; 15; 16; 7:20; **Est** 4:13; 6:13(2); **Job** 5:21(2); 22(2); 23; 24(3); 25; 26; 7:21; 9:31; 11:15(3); 16; 17(2); 18(3); 19; 14:15; 17:4; 22:23(2); 24; 25; 26(2); 27(2); 28; 29; 35:14; 38:11; **Ps** 2:9(2); 5:3; 6; 12:7(2); 17:3; 21:9; 10; 12(2); 31:20(2); 32:7(2); 8; 36:8; 37:3(2); 10; 34; 50:15; 51:6; 19; 55:23; 59:8(2); 65:3; 67:4; 71:20(2); 21; 73:20; 24; 76:10; 81:9; 82:8; 89:2; 91:4; 5; 8; 13(2); 92:10; 102:12; 13; 26(2); 119:32; 128:2(2); 5; 6; 138:7; 142:7; **Prov** 2:5; 9; 3:4; 23; 24(2); 4:12; 9:12(2); 20:13; 22:24; 23:8; 14(2); 34; 35; 24:6; 25:22; 27:27; **Eccl** 11:1; 12:1; **Is** 1:26; 12:1; 14:4; 15; 20; 17:10(2); 11(2); 22:18; 23:12(2); 25:5; 29:4(2); 6; 30:19; 22(2); 23; 33:1(3); 19; 37:11; 38:1; 39:7;

41:12(2); 15(2); 16(3); 43:2; 44:21; 26; 28; 47:1; 5; 11(3); 12; 49:18; 20; 21; 23; 51:22; 53:10; 54:3; 4(4); 14(3); 17; 55:5; 58:9(2); 11; 12(2); 13; 14; 60:5; 16(3); 18; 62:2; 3; 4(2); 12; **Jer** 1:7(2); 2:36; 37(2); 3:19(2); 4:1; 2; 30; 5:19; 7:27(2); 28; 8:4; 13:12; 13; 14:17; 15:2; 19(2); 16:2(2); 8; 10; 11; 17:4; 18:22; 19:10; 11; 20:6(3); 21:8; 22:15; 22; 23; 23:33; 37; 25:27; 28; 26:4; 8; 28:13; 16; 29:24; 31:4(3); 5; 34:3(3); 4; 5; 14; 36:6; 29; 37:17; 38:17; 18; 23(3); 24; 26; 39:17; 18; 40:16; 45:4; 46:11(2); 48:2; 7; 49:12(2); 51:26; 61(2); 62; 63; 64; **Lam** 4:21(2); **Eze** 2:4; 7; 3:18; 25; 26(2); 27; 4:3; 4(2); 5; 6; 7(2); 8; 9(2); 10(2); 11(2); 12(2); 15; 5:2(3); 3; 8:6; 13; 15; 12:3; 4(2); 6(2); 16:41; 43; 61(2); 62; 21:7; 32(2); 22:2; 16(2); 23:27; 32(2); 33; 34(2); 24:13; 16; 27(2); 25:7; 26:14(2); 21(2); 27:34; 36(2); 28:8; 9; 10; 19(2); 29:5(2); 31:18(2); 32:28(2); 33:7; 8; 14; 35:4(2); 12; 15; 36:12(2); 14; 15(2); 38:8(2); 9(2); 11; 14; 15(2); 18; 20; 46:13(2); 14; **Dan** 4:26; 5:16(2); 12:13; **Hos** 2:16(2); 20; 3:3(3); 4:5; 6; 13:4; **Amos** 7:17; **Obad** 10; **Mic** 1:14; 2:5; 4:10(4); 13; 5:12; 13; 6:14(3); 15(5); **Nah** 3:11(3); **Hab** 2:7; **Zeph** 3:11(2); 15; **Zec** 2:11; 3:7(2); 4:7; 9; 13:3; **Mt** 1:21; 4:7; 10(2); 5:21; 26; 27; 33(2); 36; 43; 6:5; 7:5; 11:23; 12:37(2); 16:19(2); 17:27; 19:18(4); 19; 21; 22:37; 39; 26:34; 75; **Mk** 6:23; 10:21; 12:30; 31; 14:30; 72; **Lk** 1:13; 14; 20; 31(2); 76(2); 4:8(2); 12; 5:10; 6:42; 10:15; 27; 28; 12:59; 13:9; 14:10; 14(2); 17:4; 8; 18(2); 22:34; 61; 23:43; **Jn** 1:33; 42; 50; 13:7; 8; 36; 21:18(2); **Acts** 2:28; 13:11; 35; 16:31; 22:15; 23:5; 25:12; 22; **Rom** 2:3; 7:7; 10:9(3); 11:22; 12:20; 13:3; 9(6); **1Cor** 7:16(2); 9:9; 14:16; **Gal** 5:14; **1Ti** 4:6; 16; 5:18; **Heb** 1:12; **Jas** 2:8; **3Jn** 6; **Rev** 2:10; 3:3(2); 16:5; 18:14

SHE

Gen 2:23(2); 3:6; 12; 20; 4:1; 2; 17; 22; 25(2); 8:9; 11:30; 12:14; 16; 18; 19; 15:9; 16:1; 4(3); 5(2); 6; 8; 13(2); 17:16; 18:15; 19:26; 33(2); 35(2); 38; 20:2; 3; 5(3); 12(3); 16; 21:7; 9; 10; 14; 15; 16(3); 19(2); 22:20; 24:14(2); 16; 28(2); 29; 30; 32(2); 33(2); 34; 35(3); 30:1; 3(2); 4; 6; 8; 9(2); 11; 13; 15; 17; 18; 20; 21; 23; 24; 35; 31:35; 38; 32:14; 15; 34:1; 35:8; 16; 17; 18(2); 36:12; 14; 38:3; 4(2); 5(2); 14(3); 15; 16(2); 17; 18(2); 19; 24; 25(3); 26; 28; 29; 39:7; 10; 12; 13; 14; 16; 17; 19; 45:23; 46:15; 18; 25; **Ex** 1:16; 2:2(2); 3(3); 5(2); 6(3); 7; 8; 10(3); 22; 4:26; 6:20; 23; 25; 21:4; 7; 8; 11; **Lev** 12:2(2); 4(2); 5(3); 6; 7; 8(3); 15:19; 20(2); 22; 23; 25; 26(2); 28(3); 29; 18:7; 9; 11; 12; 13; 14; 15; 19; 19:20(2); 20:17; 18; 21:9(3); 22:12; 13; 26:43; **Num** 5:13(2); 14(2); 27; 28; 33; 26:59; 30:4(2); 5; 6(3); 7; 8(3); 10; 11; **Deut** 21:12; 13(2); 14; 22:19; 21(2); 24; 29; 24:1; 2(2); 4; 25:6; 28:57(2); **Josh** 2:6(2); 8; 9; 15(2); 16; 21(3); 6:17(2); 22; 23; 25(3); 15:18(3); **Judg** 1:14(3); 15; 4:4; 5; 6; 9; 18; 19; 5:24; 25(2); 26(4); 29; 8:31; 11:34; 36; 37; 38; 39(2); 13:9; 14; 14:3; 7; 17(3); 15:2; 16:8; 9; 14; 15; 16; 18; 19(2); 20; 19:3; 20:5; **Ruth** 1:3; 6(3); 7(2); 9; 15; 18(3); 20; 2:2; 3; 7(3); 10; 13; 14; 15; 16; 17(2); 18(5); 19(2); 23; 3:5; 6; 7; 9; 14(2); 15(2); 16(3); 17; 18; 4:13(2); **1Sa** 1:7(3); 10; 11; 12; 13(2); 18; 20; 22; 23; 24(2); 26; 2:5; 19; 21; 4:19(2); 20(2); 21; 22; 18:19; 21; 19:14; 25:3; 19(2); 20(3); 23; 35; 36; 41; 42; 28:12; 14; 24; 25; **2Sa** 4:4; 6:16; 11:4(3); 26; 27; 12:24; 13:2; 8; 9; 10; 11; 12; 14; 16; 18; 14:4; 5; 11; 27; 20:17; 18; 21:8(2); **1Kin** 1:17; 22; 28; 2:13; 14; 16; 19; 20; 21; 3:19; 20; 26; 27; 10:1; 2(3); 6; 13; 14:5(2); 6; 17; 15:13; 17:11; 12; 15(2); 18; 21:8; 9; 11; **2Kin** 2:24; 4:2; 5(2); 6; 7; 8; 9; 12; 13; 14; 15; 16; 21; 22; 23; 24; 25; 26; 27(2); 28; 36; 37; 5:2; 3; 6:28; 29; 8:2; 3; 6(2); 9:30; 31; 34; 11:1; 13; 14; 16(2); 22:14; 15; **1Chr** 1:32; 2:21; 26; 29; 35; 49; 4:17; 7:14; 16; 23; 15:29; **2Chr** 9:1(3); 5; 9(2); 12(4); 15; 16; 22:10; 11(2); 23:12; 13; 15; 34:22; 23; 36:21(2); **Est** 1:11; 15; 17; 19; 2:1; 7; 9; 10; 12; 13; 14(4); 15; 17; 20; 4:4; 8; 5:2; 12; **Job** 3:9; 16; 18(2); 28; 29; 30; 42:12; **Ps** 45:14; 46:5; 68:12; 80:11; 84:3; **Prov** 1:20; 21(2); 3:15; 18; 4:6(2); 8(2); 9(2); 13; 7:11; 12; 13; 21(2); 26; 8:2; 3; 9:1; 2(3); 3(2); 4; 13; 14; 16; 12:4; 23:22; 25; 28; 30:20; 23; 31:12; 13; 14(2); 15; 16(2); 17; 18; 19(2); 21; 22; 24; 25; 26; 27; 30; **Song** 6:9(2); 10; 8:5; 8(2); 9(2); **Is** 3:26; 8:3; 23:3; 17; 40:2; 49:15; 51:18(2); 66:7(3); 8; **Jer** 3:1; 6; 7(2); 9; 4:17; 6:6; 7; 11:15; 15:9(3); 33:16; 46:24; 50:9; 12; 14; 15(2); 29(2); 51:8; 9; 42; 53; **Lam** 1:1(3); 2(2); 3(2); 4; 7; 8(2); 9(3); 10; 11(2); 12(2); 13; 14(2); 16(2); 17; 18; 19(2); 20; 21:13; 22:1; 26:6; 35:25; 37:3; 40:10; 12; 45:11; 48:5; 8; 10; 58:5; 11; 61:8; 63:2; 64:8; 65:9; 68:2(2); 7; 73:20; 22; 77:4; 13; 78:21; 29; 53; 60; 72; 79:13; 80:12; 18; 81:12; 83:15; 90:11; 12; 102:4; 15; 103:5; 11; 12; 13; 15; 104:25; 106:9; 30; 32; 33; 107:2; 29; 30; 38; 109:17(2); 18; 115:8;

SO

Gen 1:7; 9; 11; 15; 24; 27; 30; 3:24; 6:22; 8:11; 11:8; 12:4; 19; 13:6; 16; 15:5; 18:5; 19:7; 11; 18; 20:17; 21:6; 22:8; 19; 24:46; 25:22; 27:1; 20; 23; 28:21; 29:26; 28; 30:33; 42; 31:21; 28; 36; 32:19; 23; 33:16; 34:12; 35:6; 37:14; 40:7; 41:4; 13; 21; 39; 57; 42:20(2); 34; 43:6; 11; 34; 44:5; 17; 45:8; 21; 47:13; 20; 28; 48:10; 18; 49:17; 50:3; 17; 26; **Ex** 1:10; 2:18; 4:26; 5:12; 22; 6:9; 7:6; 10; 20; 22; 8:7; 17; 18(2); 24; 26; 9:24; 10:10; 11; 15; 20; 11:10; 12:28; 36; 50; 14:4; 20; 25; 28; 15:22; 16:17; 30; 34; 17:6; 10; 18:22; 23; 24; 19:16; 25; 21:12; 22; 22:6; 25:9; 33; 27:8; 28:7; 30:21; 23; 32:21; 24; 33:16; 36:6; 13; 37:19; 39:32; 42; 43; 40:16; 33; **Lev** 4:20; 7; 8:34; 35; 36; 10:5; 13; 11:32; 14:13; 21; 16:4; 16; 24; 19:19; 20; 26:15; 27:12; 14; **Num** 1:19; 45; 54; 2:17; 34(2); 4:26; 5:4(2); 6:21; 8:3; 4; 7; 20; 22; 9:5; 14; 16; 20; 21; 12:7; 13:21; 33; 14:28; 15:12; 14; 15; 20; 16:27; 17:11(2); 20:8; 21:35; 22:30; 35; 25:8; 31:5; 32:23; 28; 31; 35:7; 16; 29; 33; 36:3; 4; 7; 10; **Deut** 1:11; 15; 43; 46; 2:5; 16; 3:3; 21; 29; 4:5; 7(2); 8(2); 7:4; 19; 8:5; 20; 9:3; 8; 15; 12:4; 10; 22; 30; 31; 13:5; 14:24; 17:7; 18:14; 19:10; 19; 20:18; 21:9; 21; 22:3; 5; 21; 22; 24; 26; 24:8; 25:9; 28:34; 54; 55; 63; 29:22; 30:17; 31:17; 32:12; 33:25; 34:5; 8; **Josh** 1:5; 17; 2:21; 23; 3:7; 4:8; 5:15; 6:11; 14; 20(2); 27; 7:4; 16; 22; 26; 8:3; 22(2); 35; 9:26; 10:1; 7; 13; 23; 39; 40; 11:7; 15(2); 16; 23; 14:5; 11; 12; 15:7; 16:4; 19:51; 21:40; 22:6; 25; 28; 23:15; 24:10; 25; 28; **Judg** 1:3; 7; 35; 2:14; 17; 3:14; 22; 30; 4:14; 15; 21; 23; 5:28; 31; 6:3; 20; 27; 38; 40; 7:1; 5; 8; 15; 17; 19; 8:18; 21; 28; 9:49; 10:9; 11:5; 10; 21; 23; 24; 32; 12:5; 13:19; 14:10(2); 15; 15:11; 16:9; 16; 30; 17:10; 18:21; 19:4; 21; 23; 24; 25; 30; 20:11; 36; 46; 21:14; 23; **Ruth** 1:17; 19; 22; 2:7; 17; 23; 4:8; 13; **1Sa** 1:7(2); 9; 18; 23; 2:3; 5; 14; 21; 3:9; 17; 4:4; 5; 5:7; 9; 11; 6:10; 7:13; 8:8; 9:10; 21; 24; 10:9; 11:7; 11(2); 12:18; 13:22; 14:15; 23; 24; 44; 45; 47; 15:6; 31; 33; 16:13; 23; 17:27; 50; 18:30; 19:12; 17; 18; 20:2; 13; 16; 24; 34; 21:6; 22:14; 23:5(2); 24:7; 25:12; 20; 21; 22; 25; 35; 26:7; 12; 24; 25; 27:1; 11(2); 28:23; 29:8; 11; 30:9; 10; 21; 23; 24; 25; 31:6; **2Sa** 1:2; 10; 2:2; 16; 28; 31; 3:9(2); 20; 30; 34; 35; 5:3; 9; 25; 6:10; 12; 13; 15; 19; 7:8; 17; 8:2; 9:11; 13; 10:14; 19; 11:12; 20(2); 22; 12:31; 13:2; 6; 8; 15; 20; 35; 38; 14:3; 7; 17; 23; 24; 25; 28; 33; 15:2; 5; 6; 9; 34; 37; 16:10(2); 19; 22; 23; 17:3; 12(2); 26; 18:6; 19:13; 14; 15; 20:2; 3; 5; 10(2); 18; 21; 22:4; 35; 37; 23:5; 24:8; 13; 15; 24; 25; **1Kin** 1:3; 6; 30; 36; 37; 38; 40; 45; 53; 2:7; 10; 23; 27; 34; 38; 46; 3:9; 12; 13; 4:1; 5:4; 10; 18; 6:7; 9; 14; 20; 21; 26; 27; 33; 38; 7:9; 18; 22; 40; 51; 8:11; 25; 46; 48; 54; 63; 9:25; 10:13; 23; 29; 11:19; 12:12; 16(2); 19; 32; 33; 13:4; 9; 14:4; 17; 18(2); 19:2; 7; 14; 17; 20:3; 21:11; 14; 22:35; **2Kin** 1:3; 18; 2:12; 20; 22; 23(2); 24; 3:15; 22(2); 23; 7:1; 10; 13:5; 16:3; 8; 17:7; 8; 9; 33; 19:2; 10; 12; 14; 16; 20; 22; 27; 20:11; 13; 24; 35; 21:11; 35; 22:24; 23:7; 11; 18; 22; 24:9; 14; 27:17; 44; 28:9; 14; **Rom** 1:15; 20; 4:18; 5:3; 11; 12; 15; 16; 18; 19; 21; 6:3; 4; 19; 7:2; 3(2); 8:5; 8; 9; 17; 9:16; 10:17; 11:5; 16; 26; 31; 12:5; 20; 14:12; 15:19; 20; **1Cor** 1:7; 2:11; 3:7; 15; 4:1; 5:1; 3; 6:5; 7:17(2); 26; 36; 37; 38; 40; 8:12; 9:14; 15; 24; 26(2); 11:12; 28; 12:12; 13:2; 14:9; 10; 12; 25; 15:11(2); 15; 22; 42; 45; 54; 16:1; **2Cor** 1:5; 7; 10; 2:7; 3:7; 4:12; 5:3; 7:7; 14; 8:6; 11; 9:7; 10:7; 11:3; 9; 22(3); 12:16; **Gal** 1:6; 9; 3:3; 4; 9; 4:3; 29; 31; 5:17; 6:2; **Eph** 2:15; 4:20; 21; 5:24; 28; 33; **Phil** 1:13; 20; 2:23; 3:17; 4:1; **Col** 2:6; 3:13; **1Th** 1:7; 8; 2:4; 8; 4:1; 14; 17; 5:2; **2Th** 1:4; 2:4; 3:17; **1Ti** 1:4; 3:11; 6:20; **2Ti** 3:8; **Heb** 1:4; 2:3; 3:11; 19; 4:7; 5:3; 5; 6:15; 7:9; 22; 9:28; 10:25; 33; 11:3; 12; 12:1(2); 20(2); 13:6; **Jas** 1:11; 2:12(2); 17; 26; 3:4; 5; 6; 10; 12; **1Pet** 1:15; 2:3; 15; 3:17; 4:10; 5:13; **2Pet** 1:11; **1Jn** 2:6; 4:11; 17; **Rev** 1:7; 2:15; 3:16; 8:12; 13:13; 16:7; 18(2); 17:3; 18:7; 17; 22:20

SOME

Gen 19:19; 27:3; 30:35; 33:15; 37:20(2); 47:2; **Ex** 16:17(2); 20; 27; 30:36; **Lev** 4:17; 18; 14:14; 15; 25; 27; 25:25; 27:16; **Num** 5:20; 21:1; 27:20; 31:3; **Deut** 24:1; **Josh** 8:22(2); **Judg** 21:13; **Ruth** 2:16; **1Sa** 8:11; 13:7; 24:10; 27:5; **2Sa** 11:17; 24; 17:9(3); 12; **1Kin** 14:13; **2Kin** 2:16(2); 5:13; 7:9; 13; 9:33; 17:25; **1Chr** 4:42; 9:29; 30; 12:19; **2Chr** 12:7; 16:10; 17:11; 20:2; **Ezr** 2:68; 70; 7:7; 10:44; **Neh** 2:12; 5:3; 5; 6:2; 7:70; 71; 73; 11:25; 12:44; 13:15; 19; **Job** 24:2; **Ps** 20:7(2); 69:20; **Prov** 4:16; **Jer** 49:9; **Eze** 6:8; **Dan** 8:10; 11:35; 12:2(2); **Amos** 4:11; **Obad** 5; **Mt** 13:4; 5; 7; 8(3); 23(3); 16:14(2); 28; 19:12(2); 23:34(2); 27:47; 28:11; 17; **Mk** 2:1; 4:4; 5; 7; 8(3); 20(3); 7:2; 8:28; 9:1; 12:5(2); 14:4; 65; 15:35; **Lk** 8:5; 6; 7; 9:7; 8; 19; 27; 11:15; 49; 13:1; 19:39; 21:5; 16; 23:8; **Jn** 3:25; 6:64; 7:12; 25; 41; 44; 9:9; 16; 40; 10:1; 11:37; 46; 13:29; 16:17; **Acts** 5:15; 8:9; 31; 34; 11:20; 13:11; 15:36; 17:4; 18(2); 21; 32; 18:23; 19:32(2); 21:34(2); 27:27; 34; 36; 44(2); 28:24(2); **Rom** 1:11; 13; 3:3; 8; 5:7; 11:14; 17; 15:15; 16:5; **1Cor** 4:18; 6:11; 8:7; 9:22; 10:7; 8; 9; 10; 12:28; 15:6; 12; 34; 35; 37; **2Cor** 3:1; 10:2; 12; **Gal** 1:7; **Eph** 4:11(4); **Phil** 1:15(2); **Col** 3:7; **1Th** 3:5; **2Th** 3:11; **1Ti** 1:3; 6; 19; 4:1; 5:15; 24(2); 25; 6:10; 21; **2Ti** 2:18; 20(2); **Heb** 3:4; 16; 4:6; 10:25; 11:40; 13:2; **1Pet** 4:12; **2Pet** 3:9; 16; **Jude** 22; **Rev** 2:10

SOMEBODY

5100

Lk 8:46; **Acts** 5:36

SOMETHING

4745, *5100*

1Sa 20:26; **Mk** 5:43; **Lk** 11:54; **Jn** 13:29; **Acts** 3:5; 23:15; 18; **Gal** 6:3

SOMETIME

4218

Col 1:21; **1Pet** 3:20

SOMEWHAT

3544, 3972, *3313*, *5100*

Lev 4:13; 22; 27; 13:6; 19; 21; 24; 26; 28; 56; **1Kin** 2:14; **2Kin** 5:20; **2Chr** 10:4; 9; 10; **Lk** 7:40; **Acts** 23:20; 25:26; **Rom** 15:24; **2Cor** 5:12; 10:8; **Gal** 2:6(2); **Heb** 8:3; **Rev** 2:4

SON'S

1121, 5220

Gen 11:31; 16:15; 21:23; 24:51; 27:25; 31; 30:14; 15(2); 16; 37:32; 33; **Ex** 10:2; **Lev** 18:10; 15; 17; **Deut** 6:2; **Judg** 8:22; **1Kin** 11:35; 21:29; **Prov** 30:4; **Jer** 27:7

SONS

1121, 1123, 2860, 3206, 3211, *5043*, *5206*, *5207*

Gen 5:4; 7; 10; 13; 16; 19; 22; 26; 30; 6:2; 4; 10; 18; 7:7; 13(2); 8:16; 18; 9:1; 8; 18; 19; 10:1(2); 2; 3; 4; 6; 7(2); 20; 25; 29; 31; 32; 11:11; 13; 15; 17; 19; 21; 23; 25; 19:12; 14(2); 23:3; 11; 16; 20; 25:3; 4; 6; 9; 10; 13; 16; 27:29; 29:34; 30:20; 35; 31:1; 17; 28; 55; 32:22; 34:5; 7; 13; 25; 27; 35:5; 22; 23; 24; 25; 26(2); 29; 36:5; 6; 10; 11; 12; 13(2); 14; 15(2); 16; 17(2); 18; 19; 20; 37:2(2); 35; 41:50; 42:1; 5; 11; 13; 32; 37; 44:27; 46:5; 7(2); 8; 9; 10; 11; 12(2); 13; 14; 15(2); 16; 17(2); 18; 19; 21; 22; 23; 24; 25; 27; 48:1; 5; 8; 9; 49:1; 2; 33; 50:12; 13; **Ex** 3:22; 4:20; 6:14; 15; 16; 17; 18; 19; 21; 22; 24; 10:9; 12:24; 18:3; 5; 6; 21:4; 22:29; 27:21; 28:1(2); 4; 40; 41; 43; 29:4; 8; 9(2); 10; 15; 19; 20; 21(3); 24; 27; 32; 35; 44; 30:19; 30; 31:10; 32:2; 26; 34:16(2); 20; 35:19; 39:27; 40:12; 14; 31; **Lev** 1:5; 7; 8; 11; 2:2; 3; 10; 3:2; 5; 8; 13; 6:9; 14; 16; 20; 22; 25; 7:10; 31; 33; 34; 35; 8:2; 6; 13; 14; 18; 22; 24; 30(2); 31(2); 36; 9:1; 9; 12; 18; 10:1; 4; 6; 9; 12; 14; 16; 13:2; 16:1; 17:2; 21:1; 24; 22:2; 18; 24:9; 26:29; **Num** 2:14; 18; 22; 3:2; 3; 9; 10; 17; 18; 19; 20; 25; 29; 36; 38; 48; 51; 4:2(2); 4; 5; 15(3); 19; 22; 27(2); 28; 29; 33; 34; 38; 41; 42; 45; 6:23; 7:7; 8; 9; 8:13; 19; 22; 10:8; 17(2); 13:33; 16:1(2); 7; 8; 10; 12; 27; 18:1(2); 2; 7; 8; 9; 11; 19; 21:29; 35; 26:8; 9; 12; 19; 20; 21; 23; 26; 28; 29; 30; 33; 35; 36; 37(2); 38; 40; 41; 42; 45; 47; 48; 27:3; 36:1; 3; 5; 11; 12; **Deut** 1:28; 2:33; 4:9(2); 11:6; 12:12; 31; 18:5; 21:5; 16; 23:17; 28:32; 41; 53; 31:9; 32:8; 19; **Josh** 7:24; 15:14; 17:3; 6(2); 24:32; **Judg** 1:20; 3:6; 8:19; 30; 9:2; 5; 18; 24; 10:4; 11:2(2); 12:9(2); 14; 17:5; 11; 18:30; 19:22; **Ruth** 1:1; 2; 3; 5; 11; 12; 4:15; **1Sa** 1:3; 4; 8; 2:12(2); 21; 22; 24; 29; 34; 3:13; 4:4; 11; 17; 8:1; 3; 5; 11; 12:2; 14:49; 16:1; 5; 10; 17:12; 13(2); 22:20; 28:19; 30:3; 6; 19; 31:2(2); 6; 7; 8; 12; **2Sa** 2:18; 3:2; 39; 4:2; 5; 9; 5:13; 6:3; 8:18; 9:10(2); 11; 13:23; 27; 29; 30; 32; 33; 35; 36; 14:6; 27; 15:27; 36; 16:10; 19:5; 17; 22; 21:6; 8(2); 16; 18; 23:6; 32; **1Kin** 1:9; 19; 25; 2:7; 4:3; 31; 11:20; 12:31; 13:11; 12; 13; 27; 31; 18:31; 20:35; 21:10; **2Kin** 2:3; 5; 7; 15; 4:1(2); 4; 5; 38(2); 5:22; 6:1; 9:26; 10:1; 2; 3; 6(2); 7; 8; 11:2; 15:12; 17:17; 19:37; 20:18; 25:7; **1Chr** 1:5; 6; 7; 8; 9(2); 17; 19; 23; 28; 31; 32(2); 33(2); 34; 35; 36; 37; 38; 39; 40(2); 41(2); 42(2); 2:1; 3; 4; 5; 6; 7; 8; 9; 16; 18; 23; 25; 27; 28(2); 30; 31(2); 32; 33(2); 34; 42(2); 43; 47; 50; 52; 54; 3:1; 9(2); 15; 16; 17; 19(2); 21(5); 22(2); 23; 24; 4:1; 4; 6; 7; 13(2); 15(2); 16; 17; 18; 19; 20(2); 21; 24; 26; 27; 42(2); 5:1(2); 3; 4; 18; 6:1; 2; 3; 16; 17; 18; 19; 22; 25; 26; 28; 29; 33; 44; 49; 50; 54; 57; 61; 62; 63; 66; 70; 71; 7:1; 2; 3(2); 4; 6; 7; 8(2); 10(2); 11; 12; 13(2); 14; 16; 17(2); 19; 20; 30; 31; 33; 34; 35; 36; 38; 39; 8:3; 6; 10; 12; 16; 18; 21; 25; 27; 35; 38(2); 39; 40(4); 9:5; 6; 7; 14; 30; 32; 41; 44(2); 10:2(2); 6; 7; 8; 12; 11:34; 44; 46; 12:3(2); 7; 14; 14:3; 15:5; 6; 7; 8; 9; 10; 17; 16:42; 17:11; 18:17; 21:20; 23:6; 8; 9; 10(2); 11; 12; 13(2); 14; 15; 16; 17(3); 18; 19; 20; 21(2); 22(2); 23; 24; 28; 32; 24:1(2); 3(2); 4(4); 5(2); 20(3); 21; 22; 23; 24(2); 25; 26(2); 27; 28; 30(2); 31; 25:1; 2(2); 3; 4; 5(2); 9; 10; 11; 12; 13; 14; 15; 16; 17; 18; 19; 20; 21; 22; 23; 24; 25; 26; 27; 28; 29; 30; 31; 26:1; 2; 4; 6; 7; 8(2); 9; 10; 11; 15; 19(2); 21(2); 22; 29; 27:32; 28:1; 4; 5(2); 29:24; **2Chr** 5:12; 11:14; 21; 13:5; 8; 9; 10; 21; 20:14; 21:2(2); 7; 17(2); 22:8; 11; 23:3; 11; 24:3; 7; 25; 27; 26:18; 28:8; 29:9; 11; 12(2); 13(2); 14(2); 21; 31:18; 19; 32:33; 34:12(2); 35:14(2); 15; 36:20; **Ezr** 3:9(5); 10; 6:10; 7:23; 8:2(3); 3(2); 4; 5; 6; 7; 8; 9; 10; 11; 12; 13; 14; 15; 18(2); 19(2); 9:2; 12(2); 10:2; 18(2); 20; 21; 22; 25; 26; 27; 28; 29; 30; 31; 33; 34; 43; **Neh** 3:3; 4:14; 5:2; 5; 10:9; 28; 30; 36; 11:6; 7; 22; 12:23; 28; 35; 13:25(2); 28; **Est** 9:10; 12; 13; 14; 25; **Job** 1:2; 4; 5; 6; 13; 18; 2:1; 14:21; 38:7; 32; 42:13; 16(2); **Ps** 4:2; 31:19; 33:13; 42:t; 44:t; 45:t; 46:t, 47:t; 48:t; 49:t, 57:4; 58:1; 77:15; 84:t; 85:t; 87:t; 88:t, 89:6; 106:37; 38; 144:12; 145:12; **Prov** 8:4; 31; **Eccl** 1:13; 2:3; 8; 3:10; 18; 19; 8:11; 9:3; 12; **Song** 2:3; **Is** 37:38; 39:7; 43:6; 45:11; 49:22; 51:18(2); 20; 52:14; 56:5; 6; 57:3; 60:4; 9; 10; 14; 61:5; 62:5; 8; **Jer** 3:24; 5:17; 6:21; 7:31; 11:22; 13:14; 14:16; 16:2; 3; 19:5; 9; 29:6(3); 32:19; 35; 35:3; 4; 5; 6; 8; 14; 16; 39:6; 40:8(2); 48:46; 49:1; 52:10; **Lam** 4:2; **Eze** 5:10(2); 14:16; 18; 22; 16:20; 20:31; 23:4; 10; 25; 37; 47; 24:21; 25; 40:46(2); 44:15; 46:16(2); 18; 48:11; **Dan** 5:21; 10:16; 11:10; **Hos** 1:10; **Joel** 1:12; 2:28; 3:8; **Amos** 2:11; 7:17; **Mic** 5:7; **Zec** 9:13(2); **Mal** 3:3; 6; **Mt** 20:20; 21; 21:28; 26:37; **Mk** 3:17; 28; 10:35; **Lk** 5:10; 11:19; 15:11; **Jn** 1:12; 21:2; **Acts** 2:17; 7:16; 29; 19:14; **Rom** 8:14; 19; **1Cor** 4:14; **2Cor** 6:18; **Gal** 4:5; 6; 22; **Eph** 3:5; **Phil** 2:15; **Heb** 2:10; 7:5; 11:21; 12:7; 8; **1Jn** 3:1; 2

SONS'

1121

Gen 6:18; 7:7; 8:16; 18; 46:7(2); 26; **Ex** 29:21; 28; 29; 39:41; **Lev** 8:27; 30(2); 10:13; 14; 15; **Deut** 4:9; **1Chr** 8:40; **Job** 42:16; **Eze** 46:17

SOUGHT

1158, 1245, 1875, 2713, 8446, *327*, *1567*, *1934*, *2212*

Gen 43:30; **Ex** 2:15; 4:19; 24; 33:7; **Lev** 10:16; **Num** 35:23; **Deut** 13:10; **Josh** 2:22; **Judg** 14:4; 18:1; **1Sa** 10:21; 13:14; 14:4; 19:10; 23:14; 27:4; **2Sa** 3:17; 4:8; 17:20; 21:2; **1Kin** 1:2; 3; 10:24; 11:40; **2Kin** 2:17; **1Chr** 15:13; 26:31; **2Chr** 1:5; 9:23; 14:7(2); 15:4; 15; 16:12; 17:3; 4; 22:9(2); 25:15; 20; 26:5(2); **Ezr** 2:62; **Neh** 7:64; 12:27; **Est** 2:2; 21; 3:6; 6:2; 9:2; **Ps** 34:4; 37:36; 77:2; 78:34; 86:14; 111:2; 119:10; 94; **Eccl** 2:3; 7:29; 12:9; 10; **Song** 3:1(2); 2; 5:6; **Is** 62:12; 65:1(2); 10; **Jer** 8:2; 10:21; 26:21; 44:30; 50:20; **Lam** 1:19; **Eze** 22:30; 26:21; 34:4; **Dan** 2:13; 4:36; 6:4; 8:15; **Obad** 6; **Zeph** 1:6; **Zec** 6:7; **Mt** 2:20; 21:46; 26:16; 59; **Mk** 11:18; 12:12; 14:1; 11; 55; **Lk** 2:44; 48; 49; 4:42; 5:18; 6:19; 11:16; 13:6; 19:3; 47; 20:19; 22:2; 6; **Jn** 5:16; 18; 7:1; 11; 30; 10:39; 11:8; 56; 19:12; **Acts** 12:19; 17:5; **Rom** 9:32; 10:20; **1Th** 2:6; **2Ti** 1:17; **Heb** 8:7; 12:17

SPAKE

559, 560, 981, 1696, 4449, 5002, 6030, 6032, *400*, *483*, *626*, *2036*, *2046*, *2551*, *2980*, *3004*, *4277*, *4377*, *4814*, *5537*

Gen 8:15; 9:8; 16:13; 18:29; 19:14; 21:22; 22:7; 23:3; 13; 24:7; 30; 27:5; 6; 29:9; 31:11; 29; 34:3; 4; 35:15; 39:10; 14; 17; 19; 41:9; 42:7; 14; 22; 23; 30; 37; 43:3; 27; 29; 44:6; 46:2; 47:5; 49:28; 50:4; 17; 21; **Ex** 1:15; 4:30; 5:10; 6:2; 9; 10; 12; 13; 27; 28; 29; 7:7; 8; 19; 8:1; 5; 12:1; 13:1; 14:1; 15:1; 16:9; 10; 11; 19:19; 25; 20:1; 25:1; 30:11; 17; 22; 31:1; 12; 33:11; 34:34; 35:4; 36:5; 40:1; **Lev** 1:1; 4:1; 5:14; 6:1; 8; 19; 24; 7:22; 28; 8:1; 10:3; 8; 12; 11:1; 12:1; 13:1; 14:1; 33; 15:1; 16:1; 17:1; 18:1; 19:1; 20:1; 21:16; 22:1; 17; 26; 23:1; 9; 23; 26; 33; 24:1; 13; 23; 25:1; 27:1; **Num** 1:1; 2:1; 3:1; 5; 11; 14; 44; 4:1; 17; 21; 5:1; 4; 5; 11; 6:1; 22; 7:4; 89; 8:1; 5; 23; 9:1; 4; 9; 10:1; 11:25; 12:1; 4; 13:1; 14:7; 26; 15:1; 17; 37; 16:5; 20; 23; 26; 36; 44; 17:1; 6; 12; 18:8; 20; 25; 19:1; 20:3; 7; 12; 23; 21:5; 16; 22:7; 24:12; 25:10; 16; 26:1; 3; 52; 27:6; 15; 28:1; 30:1; 31:1; 3; 25; 32:2; 25; 33:50; 34:1; 16; 35:1; 9; 36:1; **Deut** 1:1; 3; 6; 9; 43; 2:1; 2; 17; 4:12; 15; 45; 5:22; 28; 9:10; 13; 10:4; 13:2; 27:9; 28:68; 31:1; 30; 32:44; 48; **Josh** 1:1; 12; 3:6; 4:1; 8; 12; 15; 21; 7:2; 9:11; 22; 10:12; 14:10; 12; 17:14; 17; 20:1; 2; 21:2; 22:8; 15; 30; 23:14; 24:27; **Judg** 2:4; 8:8; 9; 9:3; 37; 15:13; 19:22; **Ruth** 4:1; **1Sa** 1:13; 7:3; 9:9; 17; 10:16; 16:4; 17:23; 26; 28; 30; 31; 18:23; 24; 19:1; 4; 20:26; 25:9; 40; 28:12; 17; 30:6; **2Sa** 3:19; 5:1; 6; 7:7; 12:18; 13:22; 14:4; 17:6; 20:18; 22:1; 23:2; 3; 24:17; **1Kin** 1:11; 42; 2:4; 27; 3:22; 26; 4:32; 33(2); 5:5; 6:12; 8:12; 15; 20; 12:3; 7; 10(2); 14; 15; 13:18; 26; 27; 31; 14:18; 15:29; 16:12; 34; 17:16; 20:28; 21:2; 6; 23; 22:13; 38; **2Kin** 1:9; 2:22; 5:13; 7:17; 8:1; 9:12; 36; 10:10(2); 17; 14:25; 15:12; 17:26; 18:28; 21:10; 22:19; 24:2; 25:28; **1Chr** 15:16; 17:6; 21:9; 19; **2Chr** 1:2; 6:4; 10:3; 7; 10(2); 15; 18:12; 19; 30:22; 32:6; 16; 19; 24; 33:10; 18; 34:22; 35:25; **Neh** 4:2; 8:1; 13:24; **Est** 3:4; 4:10; 8:3; **Job** 2:13; 3:2; 19:18; 29:22; 32:16; 35:1; **Ps** 18:t, 33:9; 39:3; 78:19; 99:7; 105:31; 34; 106:33; **Prov** 30:1; **Song** 2:10; 5:6; **Is** 7:10; 8:5; 11; 20:2; 65:12; 66:4; **Jer** 7:13; 22; 8:6; 14:14; 19:5; 20:8; 22:21; 25:2; 26:11; 12; 17; 18; 27:12; 16; 28:1; 11; 30:4; 31:20; 34:6; 36:2; 37:2; 38:8; 40:15; 43:2; 45:1; 46:13; 50:1; 51:12; 52:32; **Eze** 1:28; 2:2(2); 3:24; 10:2; 11:25; 24:18; **Dan** 1:3; 2:4; 3:9; 14; 19; 24; 26; 28; 4:19; 30; 5:7; 10; 13; 6:12; 16; 20; 7:2; 11; 20; 8:13; 9:6; 12; 10:16; **Hos** 12:4; 13:1; **Jonah** 2:10; **Hag** 1:13; **Zec** 1:21; 3:4; 4:4; 6; 6:8; **Mal** 3:16; **Mt** 9:18; 33; 12:22; 13:3; 33; 34(2); 14:27; 16:11; 17:5; 13; 21:45; 22:1; 23:1; 26:47; 28:18; **Mk** 3:9; 4:33; 34; 5:35; 7:35; 8:32; 9:18; 12:26; 14:31; 39; 43; **Lk** 1:42; 55; 64; 70; 2:38; 50; 4:36; 5:36; 6:39; 7:39; 8:4; 49; 9:11; 31; 34; 11:14; 27; 37; 12:16; 13:6; 14:3; 15:3; 18:1; 9; 19:11; 20:2; 21:5; 29; 22:47; 60; 65; 23:20; 24:6; 36; 44; **Jn** 1:15; 2:21; 6:71; 7:13; 39; 46; 8:12; 20; 27; 30; 9:22; 29; 10:6(2); 41; 11:13; 51; 56; 12:29; 36; 38; 41; 13:22; 24; 28; 17:1; 18:9; 16; 20; 32; 21:19; **Acts** 1:16; 2:31; 4:1; 31; 6:10; 7:6; 38; 8:6; 26; 9:29; 10:7; 15; 44; 11:20; 13:45; 14:1; 16:13; 32; 18:9; 25; 19:6; 8; 9; 20:38; 21:40; 22:2; 9; 26:24; 28:19; 21; 25; **1Cor** 13:11; 14:5; **2Cor** 7:14; **Gal** 4:15; **Heb** 1:1; 4:4; 7:14; 12:25; **2Pet** 1:21; **Rev** 1:12; 10:8; 13:11

SPAKEST

559, 1696, 1697

Judg 13:11; 17:2; **1Sa** 28:21; **1Kin** 8:24; 26; 53; **2Chr** 6:15; **Neh** 9:13; **Ps** 89:19; **Jer** 48:27

SPEAK

559, 560, 1680, 1696, 1897, 2790, 4405, 4448, 4449, 4911, 5608, 5790, 6030, 6315, 7878, *658*, *669*, *987*, *1097*, *2036*, *2046*, *2551*, *2635*, *2980*, *3004*, *4354*, *5350*

Gen 18:27; 30; 31; 32; 24:33; 50; 27:6; 31:24; 29; 32:4; 19; 37:4; 44:16; 18; 50:4; **Ex** 4:14; 15; 5:23; 6:11; 29; 7:2(2); 9; 11:2; 12:3; 14:2; 15; 16:12; 19:6; 9; 20:19(2); 23:2; 22; 25:2; 28:3; 29:42; 30:31; 31:13; 32:12; 34:34; 35; **Lev** 1:2; 4:2; 6:25; 7:23; 29; 9:3; 11:2; 12:2; 15:2; 16:2; 17:2; 18:2; 19:2; 21:1; 17; 22:2; 18; 23:2; 10; 24; 34; 24:15; 25:2; 27:2; **Num** 5:6; 12; 6:2; 23; 7:89; 8:2; 9:10; 12:6; 8(2); 14:15; 15:2; 18; 38; 16:24; 37; 17:2; 18:26; 19:2; 20:8; 21:27; 22:8; 35(2); 38; 23:5; 12; 24:13; 27:7; 8; 33:51; 35:10; **Deut** 3:26; 5:1; 27(2); 31; 9:4; 11:2; 18:18; 19; 20(3); 20:2; 5; 8; 25:8; 26:5; 27:14; 31:28; 32:1; **Josh** 4:10; 20:2; 22:24; **Judg** 5:10; 6:39; 9:2; 19:3; 30; 21:13; **1Sa** 3:9; 10; 25:17; 24; **2Sa** 3:19; 27; 7:17; 13:13; 14:3; 12; 13; 15(2); 18; 17:6; 19:7; 10; 11; 20:16; 18; **1Kin** 2:17; 18; 19; 12:7; 10; 23; 21:19(2); 22:13; 14; 24; **2Kin** 18:19; 26; 27; 19:10; **1Chr** 17:15; 18; **2Chr** 10:7; 11:3; 18:12; 13; 23; 32:17; **Neh** 13:24; **Est** 5:14; 6:4; **Job** 7:11; 8:2; 9:19; 35; 10:1; 11:5; 12:8; 13:3; 7; 13; 22; 16:4; 6; 18:2; 21:3; 27:4; 32:7; 20; 33:31; 32; 34:33; 36:2; 37:20(2); 41:3; 42:4; **Ps** 2:5; 5:6; 12:2(2); 17:10; 28:3; 29:9; 31:18; 35:20; 28; 38:12; 40:5; 41:5; 45:1; 49:3; 50:7; 52:3; 58:1; 59:12; 63:11; 69:12; 71:10; 73:8(2); 15; 75:5; 77:4; 85:8(2); 94:4; 109:20; 115:5; 7; 119:23; 46; 172; 120:7; 127:5; 135:16; 139:20; 145:5; 6; 11; 21; **Prov** 8:6; 7; 23:9; 16; **Eccl** 3:7; **Song** 7:9; **Is** 8:10; 20; 14:10; 19:18; 28:11; 29:4; 30:10; 32:4; 6; 36:11(2); 12; 37:10; 40:2; 41:1; 45:19; 50:4; 52:6; 56:3; 59:4; 63:1; **Jer** 1:6; 7; 17; 5:5; 14; 6:10; 7:27; 9:5(2); 22; 10:5; 11:2; 12:6; 13:12; 18:7; 9; 11; 20; 20:9; 22:1; 23:16; 28; 26:2(2); 8; 15; 27:9; 14; 28:7; 29:24; 32:4; 34:2; 3; 35:2; 38:20; 39:16; **Eze** 2:1; 7; 3:1; 4; 10; 11; 27; 11:5; 12:25(2); 14:4; 17:2; 20:3; 27; 49; 24:21; 27; 29:3; 31:2; 32:21; 33:2; 8; 10(2); 24; 30; 37:18; 39:17; **Dan** 2:9; 3:29; 7:25; 10:11; 19; 11:27; 36; **Hos** 2:14; **Hab** 2:3; **Zeph** 3:13; **Hag** 2:2; 21; **Zec** 2:4; 6:12; 7:3; 5; 8:16; 9:10; **Mt** 8:8; 10:19(2); 20; 27; 12:34; 36; 46; 47; 13:13; 15:31; **Mk** 1:34; 2:7; 7:37; 9:39; 12:1; 13:11(3); 14:71; 16:17; **Lk** 1:19; 20; 22; 4:41; 6:26; 7:15; 24; 11:53; 12:10; 13; 20:9; **Jn** 1:37; 40; 3:11; 4:26; 6:63; 7:17; 8:26; 28; 38; 9:21; 12:49; 50(2); 13:18; 14:10(2); 16:13(2); 25; 17:13; **Acts** 2:4; 6; 7; 11; 29; 4:17; 18; 20; 29; 5:20; 40; 6:11; 13; 10:32; 46; 11:15; 14:9; 18:9; 26; 21:37(2); 39; 23:5; 24:10; 26:1; 25; 26; 28:20; **Rom** 3:5; 6:19; 7:1; 11:13; 15:18; **1Cor** 1:10; 2:6; 7; 13; 3:1; 6:5; 7:6; 12; 35; 10:15; 12:30; 13:1; 14:6; 9; 18; 19; 21; 23; 27; 28; 29; 34; 35; 39; 15:34; **2Cor** 2:17; 4:13; 6:13; 7:3; 8:8; 11:17(2); 21(2); 23; 12:19; **Gal** 3:15; **Eph** 4:25; 5:12; 32; 6:20(2); **Phil** 1:14; 4:11; **Col** 4:3; 4; **1Th** 1:8; 2:2; 4; 16; **1Ti** 2:7; 5:14; **Titus** 2:1; 15; 3:2; **Heb** 2:5; 6:9; 9:5; **Jas** 1:19; 2:12; 4:11; **1Pet** 2:12; 3:10; 16; 4:11(2); **2Pet** 2:10; 12; 18; **1Jn** 4:5; **2Jn** 12; **3Jn** 14; **Jude** 8; 10; **Rev** 2:24; 13:15

SPEAKEST

1696, *2980*, *3004*

1Sa 9:21; **2Sa** 19:29; **2Kin** 6:12; **Job** 2:10; **Ps** 50:20; 51:4; **Is** 40:27; **Jer** 40:16; 43:2; **Eze** 3:18; **Zec** 13:3; **Mt** 13:10; **Lk** 12:41; **Jn** 16:29(2); 19:10; **Acts** 17:19

SPEAKETH

559, 981, 1696, 1897, 4448, 5046, 6315, 6963, *483, 1256, 2036, 2635, 2980, 3004*

Gen 45:12; **Ex** 33:11; **Num** 23:26; **Deut** 18:22; **1Kin** 20:5; **Job** 2:10; 17:5; 33:14; **Ps** 12:3; 15:2; 37:30; 41:6; 144:8; 11; **Prov** 2:12; 6:13; 19; 10:32; 12:17; 18; 14:25; 16:13; 19:5; 9; 21:28; 26:25; **Is** 9:17; 32:7; 33:15; **Jer** 9:8(2); 10:1; 28:2; 29:25; 30:2; **Eze** 10:5; **Amos** 5:10; **Hag** 1:2; **Zec** 6:12; 7:9; **Mt** 10:20; 12:32(2); 34; **Lk** 5:21; 6:45; **Jn** 3:31; 34; 7:18; 26; 8:44(2); 19:12; **Acts** 2:25; 8:34; **Rom** 10:6; **1Cor** 14:2(3); 3; 4; 5; 11(2); 13; **1Ti** 4:1; **Heb** 11:4; 12:5; 24; 25(2); **Jas** 4:11(2); **Jude** 16

SPEAKING

1696, 2790, 4405, 4449, *226, 987, 988, 2980, 3004, 4180, 4354, 5350, 5573*

Gen 24:15; 45; **Ex** 34:33; **Num** 7:89; 16:31; **Deut** 4:33; 5:26; 11:19; 20:9; 32:45; **Judg** 15:17; **Ruth** 1:18; **1Sa** 18:1; 24:16; **2Sa** 13:36; **2Chr** 36:12; **Est** 10:3; **Job** 1:16; 17; 18; 4:2; 32:15; **Ps** 34:13; 58:3; **Is** 58:9; 13; 59:13; 65:24; **Jer** 7:13; 25:3; 26:7; 8; 35:14; 38:4; 27; 43:1; **Eze** 43:6; **Dan** 7:8; 8:13; 18; 9:20; 21; **Mt** 6:7; **Lk** 5:4; **Acts** 1:3; 7:44; 13:43; 14:3; 20:30; 26:14; **1Cor** 12:3; 14:6; **2Cor** 13:3; **Eph** 4:15; 31; 5:19; **1Ti** 4:2; 5:13; **1Pet** 4:4; **2Pet** 2:16; 3:16; **Rev** 13:5

STAY

4102, 4223, 4937, 5564, 5702, 5975, 6117, 6438, 7503, 7901, 8172, 8551

Gen 19:17; **Ex** 9:28; **Lev** 13:5; 23; 28; 37; **Josh** 10:19; **Ruth** 1:13; **1Sa** 15:16; 20:38; **2Sa** 22:19; 24:16; **1Chr** 21:15; **Job** 37:4; 38:37; **Ps** 18:18; **Prov** 28:17; **Song** 2:5; **Is** 3:1(3); 10:20(2); 19:13; 29:9; 30:12; 31:1; 48:2; 50:10; **Jer** 4:6; 20:9; **Dan** 4:35; **Hos** 13:13

STAYED

309, 2342, 3176, 3322, 3607, 5564, 5975, 6113, 7896, 8156, 8555, *1907, 2722*

Gen 8:10; 12; 32:4; **Ex** 10:24; 17:12; **Num** 16:48; 50; 25:8; **Deut** 10:10; **Josh** 10:13; **1Sa** 20:19; 24:7; 30:9; **2Sa** 17:17; 24:21; 25; **1Kin** 22:35; **2Kin** 4:6; 13:18; 15:20; **1Chr** 21:22; **2Chr** 18:34; **Job** 38:11; **Ps** 106:30; **Is** 26:3; **Lam** 4:6; **Eze** 31:15; **Hag** 1:10(2); **Lk** 4:42; **Acts** 19:22

STEAD

8478, *5228*

Gen 22:13; 30:2; 36:33; 34; 35; 36; 37; 38; 39; **Ex** 29:30; **Lev** 6:22; 16:32; **Num** 32:14; **Deut** 2:12; 21; 22; 23; 10:6; **Josh** 5:7; **2Sa** 10:1; 16:8; **1Kin** 1:30; 35; 11:43; 14:20; 27; 31; 15:8; 24; 28; 16:6; 10; 28; 22:40; 50; **2Kin** 1:17; 3:27; 8:15; 24; 10:35; 12:21; 13:9; 24; 14:16; 29; 15:7; 10; 14; 22; 30; 38; 16:20; 19:37; 20:21; 21:18; 24; 26; 23:30; 24:6; 17; **1Chr** 1:44; 45; 46; 47; 48; 49; 50; 19:1; 29:28; **2Chr** 1:8; 9:31; 12:16; 14:1; 17:1; 21:1; 22:1; 24:27; 26:23; 27:9; 28:27; 32:33; 33:20; 25; 36:1; 8; **Job** 16:4; 33:6; 34:24; **Prov** 11:8; **Eccl** 4:15; **Is** 37:38; **Jer** 29:26; **2Cor** 5:20; **Philem** 1:13

SUCH

428, 492, 834, 1836, 1931, 1932, 1992, 2007, 2063, 2088, 2888, 3541, 3602, 3644, 3651, 3706, 6423, *1170, 3588, 3592, 3634, 3748, 3778, 5023, 5107, 5108, 5125, 5128, 5130*

Gen 4:20(2); 21; 27:4; 9; 14; 46; 30:32; 41:19; 38; 44:15; **Ex** 9:18; 24; 10:14(2); 11:6; 12:36; 18:21(2); 34:10; **Lev** 10:19; 11:34(2); 14:22; 30; 31; 20:6; 22:6; 27:9; **Num** 8:16; **Deut** 4:32; 5:29; 13:11; 14; 16:9; 17:4; 19:20; 25:16; **Judg** 3:2; 13:23; 18:23; 19:30; **Ruth** 4:1; **1Sa** 2:23; 4:7; 21:2(2); 25:17; **2Sa** 9:8; 12:8(2); 13:12; 18; 14:13; 16:2; 19:36; **1Kin** 10:10; 12; **2Kin** 6:8(2); 9; 7:19; 19:29; 21:12; 23:22; 25:15; **1Chr** 12:33; 36; 29:25; **2Chr** 1:12; 4:6; 9:9; 11; 11:16; 23:13; 24:12(2); 30:5; 35:18; **Ezr** 4:10; 11; 17; 6:21; 7:12; 25; 27; 8:31; 9:13; 10:3; **Neh** 6:8; 11; **Est** 2:9; 4:11; 14; 9:2; 27; **Job** 12:3; 14:3; 15:13; 16:2; 18:21; 23:14; **Ps** 25:10; 27:12; 34:18; 37:14; 22; 40:4; 16; 50:21; 55:20; 68:21; 70:4; 73:1; 103:18; 107:10; 125:5; 139:6; 144:15; **Prov** 11:20; 28:4; 30:20; 31:8; **Eccl** 4:1; **Is** 9:1; 10:20; 20:6; 37:30; 58:5; 66:8(2); **Jer** 2:10; 5:9; 29; 9:9; 15:2(4); 18:13; 21:7; 38:4; 43:11(3); 44:14; **Eze** 17:15; 18:14; **Dan** 1:4; 2:10; 10:15; 11:32; 12:1; **Amos** 5:16; **Mic** 5:15; **Zeph** 1:8; **Mt** 9:8; 18:5; 19:14; 24:21; 44; 26:18; **Mk** 4:18; 20; 33; 6:2; 7:8; 13; 9:37; 10:14; 13:7; 19; **Lk** 9:9; 10:7; 8; 11:41; 13:2; 18:16; **Jn** 4:23; 7:32; 8:5; 9:16; **Acts** 2:47; 3:6; 15:24; 16:24; 18:15; 21:25; 22:22; 25:18; 20; 26:29; 28:10; **Rom** 1:32; 2:2; 3; 16:18; **1Cor** 5:1; 5; 11; 6:11; 7:15; 28; 10:13; 11:16; 15:48(2); 16:16; 18; **2Cor** 2:6; 7; 3:4; 12; 10:11(3); 11:13; 12:2; 3; 5; 20(2); **Gal** 5:21(2); 23; 6:1; **Eph** 5:27; **Phil** 2:29; **1Th** 4:6; **2Th** 3:12; **1Ti** 6:5; **2Ti** 3:5; **Titus** 3:11; **Philem** 1:9; **Heb** 5:12; 7:26; 8:1; 11:14; 12:3; 13:5; 16; **Jas** 4:13; 16; **2Pet** 1:17; 3:14; **3Jn** 8; **Rev** 5:13; 16:18; 20:6

SURELY

199, 389, 403, 518, 551, 983, 3588, 3651, 3808, 7535, *230, 2229, 3843, 4135*

Gen 2:17; 3:4; 9:5; 18:18; 20:7; 11; 26:11; 28:16; 22; 29:14; 32; 30:16; 31:42; 32:12; 42:16; 43:10; 44:28; 46:4; 50:24; 25; **Ex** 2:14; 3:7; 16; 4:25; 11:1; 13:19; 18:18; 19:12; 13; 21:12; 15; 16; 17; 20; 22; 28; 36; 22:6; 14; 16; 19; 23; 23:4; 5; 33; 31:14; 15; 40:15; **Lev** 20:2; 9; 10; 11; 12; 13; 15; 16; 27; 24:16; 17; 27:29; **Num** 13:27; 14:23; 35; 15:35; 18:15; 22:33; 23:23; 26:65; 27:7; 32:11; 35:16; 17; 18; 21; 31; **Deut** 1:35; 4:6; 8:19; 13:9; 15; 15:8; 10; 16:15; 22:4; 23:21; 30:18; 31:18; **Josh** 14:9; **Judg** 3:24; 4:9; 6:16; 11:31; 13:22; 15:13; 20:39; 21:5; **Ruth** 1:10; **1Sa** 9:6; 14:39; 44; 15:32; 16:6; 17:25; 20:26; 31; 22:16; 22; 24:20; 25:21; 34; 28:2; 29:6; 30:8; **2Sa** 2:27; 9:7; 11:23; 12:5; 14; 15:21; 18:2; 20:18; 24:24; **1Kin** 2:37; 42; 8:13; 11:2; 11; 13:32; 18:15; 20:23; 25; 22:32; **2Kin** 1:4; 6; 16; 3:14; 23; 5:11; 8:10; 14; 9:26; 18:30; 23:22; 24:3; **Est** 6:13; **Job** 8:6; 13:3; 10; 14:18; 18:21; 20:20; 28:1; 31:36; 33:8; 34:12; 31; 35:13; 37:20; 40:20; **Ps** 23:6; 32:6; 39:6(2); 11; 62:9; 73:18; 76:10; 77:11; 85:9; 91:3; 112:6; 131:2; 132:3; 139:11; 19; 140:13; **Prov** 1:17; 3:34; 10:9; 22:16; 23:18; 30:2; 33; **Eccl** 4:16; 7:7; 8:12; 10:11; **Is** 7:9; 14:24; 16:7; 19:11; 22:14; 17; 18; 29:16; 36:15; 40:7; 45:14; 24; 49:4; 18; 53:4; 54:15; 60:9; 62:8; 63:8; **Jer** 2:35; 3:20; 4:10; 5:2; 4; 8:13; 16:19; 22:6; 22; 24:8; 26:8; 15; 31:18; 19; 20; 32:4; 34:3; 36:16; 37:9; 38:3; 15; 39:18; 44:25(3); 29; 46:18; 49:12; 20(2); 50:45(2); 51:14; 56; **Lam** 3:3; **Eze** 3:6; 18; 21; 5:11; 17:16; 19; 18:9; 13; 17; 19; 21; 28; 20:33; 31:11; 33:8; 13; 14; 15; 16; 27; 34:8; 36:5; 7; 38:19; **Hos** 5:9; 12:11; **Amos** 3:7; 5:5; 7:11; 17; 8:7; **Mic** 2:12(2); **Hab** 2:3; **Zeph** 2:9; 3:7; **Mt** 26:73; **Mk** 14:70; **Lk** 1:1; 4:23; **Jn** 17:8; **Heb** 6:14; **Rev** 22:20

TAKE

6, 270, 622, 680, 935, 962, 1197, 1497, 1692, 1898, 1961, 2095, 2254, 2388, 2502, 2846, 3051, 3212, 3318, 3381, 3423, 3615, 3920, 3947, 5253, 5267, 5312, 5375, 5376, 5381, 5414, 5493, 5496, 5535, 5674, 5709, 5749, 5927, 5978, 6331, 6679, 6901, 6902, 7061, 7126, 7200, 7311, 7760, 7896, 7901, 7997, 8175, 8551, 8610, *142, 353, 726, 851, 1209, 1949, 2507, 2722, 2902, 2983, 3335, 3880, 3911, 4014, 4084, 4355, 4648, 4815, 4838, 4868*

Gen 3:22; 6:21; 7:2; 12:19; 13:9; 14:21; 23(2); 24; 15:9; 19:15; 19; 21:30; 22:2; 23:13; 24:3; 4; 7; 37; 38; 40; 48; 51; 27:3(2); 46; 28:1; 2; 6(2); 30:15; 31:24; 29; 31; 32; 50; 33:11; 12; 34:9; 16; 17; 21; 38:23; 41:34; 42:33; 36; 43:11; 12; 13; 18; 44:29; 45:18; 19; **Ex** 2:9; 4:4; 9; 17; 6:7; 7:9; 15; 19; 8:8; 9:8; 10:17; 26; 28; 12:3; 4; 5; 7; 21; 22; 32; 15:14; 15; 16:16; 33; 17:5(2); 19:12; 20:7; 21:10; 14; 22:26; 23:8; 25; 25:2; 3; 26:5; 28:1; 5; 9; 29:1; 5; 7; 12; 13; 15; 16; 19; 20; 21; 22; 26; 31; 30:16; 23; 34; 33:23; 34:9; 12; 16; 35:5; 40:9; **Lev** 2:2; 9; 3:4; 9; 10; 15; 4:5; 8; 9; 19; 25; 30; 31; 34; 35; 5:12; 6:10; 15; 7:4; 8:2; 9:2; 3; 10:12; 14:4; 6; 10; 12; 14; 15; 21; 24; 25; 40; 42(2); 49; 51; 15:14; 29; 16:5; 7; 12; 14; 18; 18:17; 18; 20:14; 17; 21; 21:7(2); 13; 14(2); 22:5; 23:40; 24:5; 25:36; 46; **Num** 1:2; 49; 51; 3:40; 41; 45; 47(2); 4:2; 5; 9; 12; 13; 22; 5:17(2); 25; 26; 6:18; 19; 7:5; 8:6; 8(2); 10:6; 11:17; 16:3; 6; 7; 17; 37; 46; 17:2; 10; 18:26; 19:4; 6; 17; 18; 20:8; 25; 21:7; 23:12; 25:4; 26:2; 4; 27:18; 31:26; 29; 30; 34:18; 35:31; 32; **Deut** 1:7; 13; 40; 2:4; 24; 4:9; 15; 23; 34; 5:11; 7:3; 15; 25; 10:11; 11:16; 12:13; 19; 26; 30; 15:17; 16:19; 20:7; 14; 19; 21:3; 22:6; 7; 13; 15; 18; 30; 24:4; 6; 8; 17; 25:5; 7; 8; 26:2; 4; 27:9; 31:26; 32:41; **Josh** 3:6; 12; 4:2; 3; 5; 6:6; 18; 7:13; 14(2); 8:1; 2; 29; 9:11; 10:42; 11:12; 20:4; 22:5; 19; 23:11; **Judg** 4:6; 5:30; 6:20; 25; 26; 7:24; 14:3; 8; 15; 15:2; 19:30; 20:10; **Ruth** 2:10; 19; **1Sa** 2:16(2); 6:7; 8; 8:11; 13; 14; 15; 16; 17; 9:3; 5; 16:2; 17:17; 18; 46; 19:2; 14; 20; 20:21; 21:9(2); 23:23; 26; 24:11; 25:11; 39; 40; 26:11; **2Sa** 2:21; 4:11; 5:6; 12:4; 11; 28(2); 13:33; 15:20; 16:9; 19:19; 30; 20:6; 24:10; 22; **1Kin** 1:33; 2:4; 31; 8:25; 11:31; 34; 35; 37; 14:3; 10; 16:3; 18:40; 19:4; 10; 14; 20:6; 18(2); 24; 21:15; 16; 21; 22:3; 26; **2Kin** 2:1; 3; 5; 4:1; 29; 36; 5:15; 16; 20; 23; 6:2; 7; 32; 7:13; 8:8; 9:1; 3; 17; 25; 26; 10:6; 14; 12:5; 13:15; 18; 18:32; 19:30; 20:7; 18; **1Chr** 7:21; 17:13; 21:23; 24; 28:10; **2Chr** 6:16; 18:25; 19:6; 7; 20:25; 32:18; 33:8; **Ezr** 4:22; 5:14; 15; 9:12; **Neh** 5:2; 6:7; 10:30; 38; 13:25; **Est** 3:13; 4:4; 6:10; 8:11; **Job** 7:21; 9:18; 34; 10:20; 11:18; 13:14; 18:9; 21:12; 23:10; 24:2; 3; 9; 10; 27:20; 30:17; 31:36; 32:22; 36:17; 18; 21; 38:13; 20; 41:4; 42:8; **Ps** 2:2; 7:5; 13:2; 16:4; 27:10; 31:13; 35:2; 39:1; 50:9; 16; 51:11; 52:5; 58:9; 69:20; 24; 71:10; 11; 80:9; 81:2; 83:12; 89:33; 102:14; 24; 109:8; 116:13; 119:43; 139:9; 20; **Prov** 2:19; 4:13; 5:5; 22; 6:25; 27; 7:18; 20:16(2); 22:27; 25:4; 5; 27:13(2); 30:9; **Eccl** 5:15; 19; 7:18; 21; **Song** 2:15; 7:8; **Is** 1:25; 3:1; 6; 18; 4:1(2); 5:5; 23; 7:4; 8:1; 10; 10:2; 6(2); 13:8; 14:2(2); 4; 16:3; 18:4; 5; 23:16; 25:8; 27:5; 6; 9; 28:19; 30:1; 14(2); 33:23; 36:17; 37:31; 38:21; 39:7; 40:24(2); 44:15; 45:21; 47:2; 3; 56:4; 57:13; 14; 58:2; 9; 64:7; 66:21; **Jer** 2:22; 3:14; 4:4; 5:10; 7:29; 9:4; 10; 18; 13:4; 6; 21; 15:15; 19; 16:2; 17:21; 18:22; 19:1; 20:5; 10; 25:9; 10; 15; 28; 29:6(2); 32:3; 14; 24; 25; 28; 44; 33:26; 34:22; 36:2; 14; 26; 28; 37:8; 38:3; 10(2); 39:12; 43:9; 10; 44:12; 46:11; 49:29(2); 50:15; 51:8; 26; 36; **Lam** 2:13; **Eze** 4:1; 3; 9; 5:1(3); 2; 3; 4; 10:6; 11:18; 19; 14:5; 15:3; 16:16; 39; 17:22; 19:1; 21:26; 22:16; 23:25(2); 26; 29; 24:5; 8; 16; 25; 26:17; 27:2; 32; 28:12; 29:19(3); 30:4; 32:2; 33:2; 4; 6; 36:24; 26; 37:16(2); 19; 21; 38:12(2); 13(4); 39:10; 43:20; 21; 44:22(2); 45:9; 18; 19; 46:18; **Dan** 6:23; 7:18; 26; 11:15; 18; 31; **Hos** 1:2; 6; 2:9; 17; 4:10; 11; 5:14; 11:4; 14:2(2); **Amos** 3:5; 4:2; 5:1; 11; 12; 23; 6:10; 9:2; 3; **Jonah** 1:12; 4:3; **Mic** 2:2(2); 4; 6; 6:14; **Nah** 1:2; 2:9(2); **Hab** 1:10; 15; 2:6; **Zeph** 3:11; **Hag** 1:8; 2:23; **Zec** 1:6; 3:4; 6:10; 11; 8:23(2); 9:7; 11:15; 14:21; **Mal** 2:3; 15; 16; **Mt** 1:20; 2:13; 20; 5:40; 6:1; 25; 28; 31; 34(2); 9:6; 10:19; 11:12; 29; 15:26; 16:5; 6; 24; 17:25; 27(2); 18:10; 16; 23; 20:14; 22:13; 24:4; 17; 18; 25:28; 26:4; 26; 45; 52; 55; **Mk** 2:9; 11; 4:24; 6:8; 7:27; 8:14; 15; 34; 10:21; 12:19; 13:5; 9; 11; 15; 16; 23; 33; 14:1; 22; 36; 41; 44; 48; 15:24; 36; 16:18; **Lk** 1:25; 5:24; 6:4; 29; 8:18; 9:3; 23; 10:35; 11:35; 12:11; 15; 19; 22; 26; 14:9; 16:6; 7; 17:3; 31; 19:24; 20:20; 26; 28; 21:8; 34; 22:17; 36; **Jn** 2:16; 5:8; 11; 12; 6:7; 15; 7:30; 32; 10:17; 18; 39; 11:39; 48; 57; 16:15; 17:15; 18:31; 19:6; 38; 20:15; **Acts** 1:20; 25; 5:35; 12:3; 15:14; 37; 38; 20:13; 26; 28; 21:24; 22:26; 23:10; 24:8; 27:33; 34; **Rom** 11:21; 27; 15:24; **1Cor** 3:10; 6:7; 15; 8:9; 9:9; 10:12; 11:24; **2Cor** 8:4; 11:20; 12:10; **Gal** 5:15; **Eph** 6:13; 17; **Col** 4:17; **1Ti** 3:5; 4:16; **2Ti** 4:11; **Heb** 3:12; 7:5; 10:4; 11; **Jas** 5:10; **1Pet** 2:20(2); **2Pet** 1:19; **1Jn** 3:5; **Rev** 3:11; 5:9; 6:4; 10:8; 9; 22:17; 19(2)

TAKEN

247, 270, 622, 1197, 1497, 1639, 2254, 2388, 2502, 2974, 3289, 3381, 3885, 3920, 3921, 3947, 4672, 5267, 5312, 5337, 5375, 5381, 5493, 5674, 5709, 5927, 6001, 6213, 6679, 6813, 7092, 7287, 7311, 7628, 7725, 8610, *142, 353, 522, 642, 782, 851, 1096, 1723, 1808, 1869, 2021, 2221, 2638, 2639, 2983, 3880, 4014, 4084, 4356, 4815, 4912*

Gen 2:22; 23; 3:19; 23; 4:15; 12:15; 19; 14:14; 18:27; 31; 20:3; 21:25; 27:33; 35; 36; 30:15; 23; 31:1; 9; 16; 26; 34; **Ex** 14:11; 25:15; 40:36; 37(2); **Lev** 4:10; 31; 35; 6:2; 7:34; 14:43; 24:8; **Num** 3:12; 5:13; 8:16; 18; 9:17; 21(2); 22; 10:11; 17; 16:15; 18:6; 21:26; 31:26; 49; 53; 36:3(2); 4; **Deut** 4:20; 20:7; 21:10; 24:1; 5(2); 26:14; 28:31; **Josh** 7:11; 15; 16; 17; 18; 8:8; 21; 10:1; **Judg** 1:8; 11:36; 14:9; 15:6; 17:2; 18:24; **1Sa** 4:11; 17; 19; 21; 22; 7:14; 10:20; 21(2); 12:3(2); 4; 14:41; 42; 21:6(2); 30:2; 3; 5; 16; 19; **2Sa** 12:9; 10; 27; 16:8; 18:9; 18; 23:6; **1Kin** 7:8; 9:9; 16; 16:18; 21:19; 22:43; **2Kin** 2:9; 10; 16; 4:20; 6:22; 12:3; 13:25; 14:4; 18:10; 22; 24:7; **1Chr** 24:6(2); **2Chr** 15:8; 17; 17:2; 19:3; 20:33; 28:11; 18; 30:2; 32:12; **Ezr** 9:2; 10:2; 10; 14; 17; 18; 44; **Neh** 5:15; 6:18; **Est** 2:15; 16; 8:2; **Job** 1:21; 16:12; 19:9; 20:19; 22:6; 24:24; 27:2; 28:2; 30:16; 34:5; 20; **Ps** 9:15; 10:2; 40:12; 59:12; 83:3; 85:3; 119:53; 111; 143; **Prov** 3:26; 4:16; 6:2; 7:20; 11:6; **Eccl** 2:18; 3:14; 7:26; 9:12; **Is** 6:6; 7; 7:5; 8:4; 15; 10:27; 29; 16:10; 17:1; 21:3; 23:8; 24:18; 28:13; 33:20; 36:7; 41:9; 49:24; 25; 51:22; 52:5; 53:8; 57:1(2); 64:6; **Jer** 6:11; 24; 8:9; 21; 12:2; 16:5; 29:22; 34:3; 38:23; 28(2); 39:5; 40:1; 10; 48:1; 7; 33; 41; 44; 46; 49:20; 24; 30; 50:2; 9; 24; 45; 51:31; 41; 56; **Lam** 2:6; 4:20; **Eze** 12:13; 15:3; 16:17; 20; 37; 17:12; 13(3); 20; 18:8; 13; 17; 19:4; 8; 21:23; 24; 22:12(2); 25; 25:15; 27:5; 33:6; 36:3; **Dan** 5:2; 3; 6:23; 7:12; 8:11; 11:12; 12:11; **Hos** 4:3; **Joel** 3:5; **Amos** 3:4; 5; 12; 4:10; 6:13; **Mic** 2:9; 4:9; **Zeph** 3:15; **Zec** 14:2; **Mt** 4:24; 9:15; 13:12; 16:7; 21:43; 24:40; 41; 25:29; 27:59; 28:12; **Mk** 2:20; 4:25; 6:41; 9:36; **Lk** 1:1; 4:38; 5:5; 9; 18; 35; 36; 8:18; 37; 9:17; 10:42; 11:52; 17:34; 35; 36; 19:8; 26; **Jn** 7:44; 8:3; 4; 13:12; 19:31; 20:1; 2; 13; **Acts** 1:2; 9; 11; 22; 2:23; 8:7; 33(2); 17:9; 20:9; 21:6; 23:27; 27:17; 20; 33; 40; **Rom** 9:6; **1Cor** 5:2; 10:13; **2Cor** 3:16; **1Th** 2:17; **2Th** 2:7; **1Ti** 5:9; **2Ti** 2:26; **Heb** 5:1; **2Pet** 2:12; **Rev** 5:8; 11:17; 19:20

TAKETH

270, 1197, 2254, 2388, 2862, 3920, 3947, 5190, 5337, 5375, 5493, 5710, 5998, 6908, 7953, 8610, *142, 337, 851, 1405, 2018, 2638, 2983, 3880, 4301*

Ex 20:7; **Deut** 5:11; 10:17; 24:6; 25:11; 27:25; 32:11; **Josh** 7:14; 15:16; **Judg** 1:12; **1Sa** 17:26; **1Kin** 14:10; **Job** 5:5; 13; 9:12; 12:20; 24; 21:6; 27:8; 40:24; **Ps** 15:3; 5; 118:7; 137:9; 147:10; 11; 149:4; **Prov** 1:19; 16:32; 17:23; 25:20; 26:17; 30:28; **Eccl** 1:3; 2:23; 5:18; **Is** 13:14; 40:15; 44:14; 51:18; 56:6; **Eze** 16:32; 33:4; 5; **Amos** 3:12; **Mt** 4:5; 8; 9:16; 10:38; 12:45; 17:1; **Mk** 2:21; 4:15; 5:40; 9:2; 18; 14:33; **Lk** 6:29; 30; 8:12; 9:39; 11:22; 26; 16:3; **Jn** 1:29; 10:18; 15:2; 16:22; 21:13; **Rom** 3:5; **1Cor** 3:19; 11:21; **Heb** 5:4; 10:9

TAKING

3947, 4727, 8610, *142, 321, 353, 1325, 2983*

2Chr 19:7; **Job** 5:3; **Ps** 119:9; **Jer** 50:46; **Eze** 25:12; **Hos** 11:3; **Mt** 6:27; **Mk** 13:34; **Lk** 4:5; 12:25; 19:22; **Jn** 11:13; **Rom** 7:8; 11; **2Cor** 2:13; 11:8; **Eph** 6:16; **2Th** 1:8; **1Pet** 5:2; **3Jn** 7

TALK

1696, 1697, 1897, 5608, 6310, 7878, 8193, *2980, 3056*

Num 11:17; **Deut** 5:24; 6:7; **1Sa** 2:3; **2Kin** 18:26; **1Chr** 16:9; **Job** 11:2; 13:7; 15:3; **Ps** 69:26; 71:24; 77:12; 105:2; 119:27; 145:11; **Prov** 6:22; 14:23; 24:2; **Eccl** 10:13; **Jer** 12:1; **Eze** 3:22; **Dan** 10:17; **Mt** 22:15; **Jn** 14:30

TALKED

559, 1696, *2980, 3656, 4814, 4926*

Gen 4:8; 17:3; 35:13; 14; 45:15; **Ex** 20:22; 33:9; 34:29; 31; **Deut** 5:4; **Judg** 14:7; **1Sa** 14:19; 17:23; **1Kin** 1:22; **2Kin** 2:11; 6:33; 8:4; **2Chr** 25:16; **Jer** 38:25; **Dan** 9:22; **Zec** 1:9; 13; 19; 2:3; 4:1; 4; 5; 5:5; 10; 6:4; **Mt** 12:46; **Mk** 6:50; **Lk** 9:30; 24:14; 32; **Jn** 4:27; **Acts** 10:27; 20:11; 26:31; **Rev** 17:1; 21:9; 15

TALKING

1696, 4405, 7879, *2980, 3473, 4814*

Gen 17:22; **1Kin** 18:27; **Est** 6:14; **Job** 29:9; **Eze** 33:30; **Mt** 17:3; **Mk** 9:4; **Eph** 5:4; **Rev** 4:1

TELL

559, 1696, 3045, 5046, 5608, 8085, *226, 312, 518, 1334, 1492, 1583, 1650, 2036, 2046, 2980, 3004, 4302*

Gen 12:18; 15:5; 21:26; 22:2; 24:23; 49(2); 26:2; 29:15; 31:27; 32:5; 29; 37:16; 40:8; 43:6; 22; 45:13; 49:1; **Ex** 9:1; 10:2; 14:12; 19:3; **Lev** 14:35; **Num** 14:14; 21:1; 23:3; **Deut** 17:11; 32:7; **Josh** 7:19; **Judg** 14:16; 16:6; 10; 13; 20:3; **Ruth** 3:4; 4:4; **1Sa** 6:2; 9:8; 18; 19; 10:15; 14:43; 15:16; 17:55; 19:3; 20:9; 10; 22:22; 23:11; 27:11; **2Sa** 1:4; 20; 7:5; 12:18(2); 22; 13:4; 15:35; 17:16; 18:21; **1Kin** 1:20; 14:3; 7; 18:8; 11; 12; 14; 20:9; 11; 22:16; 18; **2Kin** 4:2; 7:9; 8:4; 9:12; 15; 20:5; 22:15; **1Chr** 17:4; 10; 21:10; **2Chr** 18:17; 34:23; **Job** 1:15; 16; 17; 19; 8:10; 12:7; 34:34; **Ps** 22:17; 26:7; 48:12; 13; 50:12; **Prov** 30:4; **Eccl** 6:12; 8:7; 10:14(2); 20; **Song** 1:7; 5:8; **Is** 5:5; 6:9; 19:12; 42:9; 45:21; 48:20; **Jer** 15:2; 19:2; 23:27; 28; 32; 28:13; 34:2; 35:13; 36:16; 17; 48:20; **Eze** 3:11; 12:23; 17:12; 24:19; **Dan** 2:4; 7; 9; 36; 4:9; **Joel** 1:3(2); **Jonah** 1:8; 3:9; **Mt** 8:4; 10:27; 16:20; 17:9; 18:15; 17; 21:5; 24(2); 27(2); 22:4; 17; 24:3; 26:63; 28:7; 9; 10; **Mk** 1:30; 5:19; 7:36; 8:26; 30; 9:9; 10:32; 11:29; 33(2); 13:4; 16:7; **Lk** 4:25; 5:14; 7:22; 42; 8:56; 9:21; 27; 10:24; 12:51; 59; 13:3; 5; 27; 32; 17:34; 18:8; 14; 19:40; 20:2; 7; 8; 22:34; 67(2); **Jn** 3:8; 12; 4:25; 8:14; 45; 10:24; 12:22; 13:19; 16:7; 18; 18:34; 20:15; **Acts** 5:8; 10:6; 11:14; 15:27; 17:21; 22:27; 23:17; 19; 22; **2Cor** 12:2(2); 3; **Gal** 4:16; 21; 5:21; **Phil** 3:18; **Heb** 11:32; **Rev** 17:7

TELLING

1696, 4557, 5608

Judg 7:15; **2Sa** 11:19; **2Kin** 8:5

THAN

518, 1768, 3588, 4480, 4481, 5921, 5973, 6440, *1883, 2228, 2260, 3844, 4133, 5228, 5245, 7508*

Gen 3:1; 4:13; 19:9; 25:23; 26:16; 29:19; 30; 34:19; 36:7; 37:3; 4; 38:26; 39:9; 41:40; 48:19; **Ex** 1:9; 14:12; 18:11; 30:15; 36:5; **Lev** 13:3; 4; 20; 21; 25; 26; 30; 31; 32; 34; 14:37; 27:8; **Num** 3:46; 13:31; 14:12; 22:15; 24:7; **Deut** 1:28; 4:38; 7:1; 7; 17; 9:1; 14; 11:23; 20:1; **Josh** 10:2; 11; **Judg** 2:19; 8:2; 11:25; 14:18(2); 15:2; 3; 16:30; **Ruth** 3:10; 12; 4:15; **1Sa** 1:8; 9:2(2); 10:23; 15:22(2); 28; 18:30; 24:17; 27:1; **2Sa** 1:23(2); 6:22; 13:14; 15; 16; 17:14; 18:8; 19:7; 43(2); 20:5; 6; 23:23; **1Kin** 1:37; 47(2); 2:32; 4:31(2); 12:10; 16:25; 33; 19:4; 20:23(2); 25; 21:2; **2Kin** 5:12; 6:16; 9:35; 21:9; **1Chr** 4:9; 11:21; 24:4; **2Chr** 10:10; 20:25; 21:13; 25:9; 29:34; 30:18; 32:7; 33:9; **Ezr** 8:15; 9:13; **Est** 1:19; 2:17; 4:13; 6:6; **Job** 3:21; 4:17(2); 6:3; 7:6; 15; 9:25; 11:6; 8; 9(2); 17; 15:10; 23:2; 12; 30:1; 8; 32:2; 4; 33:12; 25; 34:19; 23; 35:2; 5; 11(2); 36:21; 42:12; **Ps** 4:7; 8:5; 19:10(3); 37:16; 40:5; 12; 45:2; 51:7; 52:3(2); 55:21(2); 61:2; 62:9; 63:3; 69:4; 31; 73:7; 76:4; 84:10(2); 87:2; 89:27; 93:4(2); 105:24; 118:8; 9; 119:72; 98; 99; 100; 103; 130:6(2); 139:18; 142:6; **Prov** 3:14(2); 15; 5:3; 8:10; 11; 19(3); 11:24; 12:9; 26; 15:16; 17; 16:8; 16(2); 19; 32(2); 17:1; 10; 12; 18:19; 24; 19:1; 22; 21:3; 9; 19; 22:1(2); 25:7; 24; 26:12; 16; 27:3; 5; 10; 28:6; 23; 29:20; 30:2; **Eccl** 1:16; 2:9; 16; 24; 25; 3:22; 4:2; 3; 6; 9; 13; 5:1; 5; 8(2); 6:3; 5; 8; 9; 10; 7:1(2); 2; 3; 5; 8(2); 10; 19; 26; 8:15; 9:4; 16; 17; 18; **Song** 1:2; 4; 4:10(2); 5:9(2); **Is** 13:12(2); 28:20(2); 33:19; 40:17; 52:14(2); 54:1; 55:9(3); 56:5; 57:8; 65:5; **Jer** 3:11; 4:13; 5:3; 7:26; 8:3; 16:12; 20:7; 31:11; 46:23; **Lam** 4:6; 7(3); 8; 9; 19; **Eze** 3:9; 5:6(2); 7; 6:14; 8:15; 15:2(2); 16:47; 51; 52(2); 23:11(2); 28:3; 36:11; 42:5(3); 6; **Dan** 1:10; 15; 20; 2:30; 3:19; 7:20; 8:3; 11:2; 8; 13; **Hos** 2:7; 6:6; **Amos** 6:2(2); **Jonah** 4:3; 8; 11; **Mic** 7:4; **Nah** 3:8; **Hab** 1:8(2); 13(2); **Hag** 2:9; **Mt** 3:11; 5:37; 47; 6:25(2); 26; 10:15; 31; 37(2); 11:9; 11(2); 22; 24; 12:6; 12; 41; 42; 45(2); 18:8; 9; 13; 19:24; 21:36; 23:15; 26:53; 27:64; **Mk** 1:7; 4:31; 32; 6:11; 8:14; 9:43; 45; 47; 10:25; 12:31; 33; 43; 14:5; **Lk** 3:13; 16; 7:26; 28(2); 10:12; 14; 11:22; 26(2); 31; 32; 12:7; 23(2); 24; 14:8; 15:7; 16:8; 17; 17:2; 18:14; 25; 21:3; **Jn** 1:50; 3:19; 4:1; 12; 5:20; 36; 7:31; 8:53; 10:29; 12:43; 13:16(2); 14:12; 28; 15:13; 20; 21:15; **Acts** 4:19; 5:29; 15:28; 17:11; 20:35; 23:13; 21; 25:6; 26:22; 27:11; **Rom** 1:25; 3:9; 8:37; 12:3; 13:11; **1Cor** 1:25(2); 3:11; 7:9; 9:15; 10:22; 14:5; 18; 19; 15:10; **2Cor** 1:13; **Gal** 1:8; 9; 4:27; **Eph** 3:8; **Phil** 2:3; **1Ti** 1:4; 5:8; **2Ti** 3:4; **Philem** 1:21; **Heb** 1:4(2); 2:7; 9; 3:3(2); 4:12; 7:26; 9:23; 11:4; 25; 26; 12:24; **1Pet** 1:7; 3:17; **2Pet** 2:20; 21; **1Jn** 3:20; 4:4; **3Jn** 4; **Rev** 2:19

THAT

834, 2088, 3588, *1565, 3754*

Gen 1:4; 10; 12; 18; 20(2); 21(2); 25(2); 26; 28; 30; 31; 2:3; 4; 9; 11; 12; 13; 14; 17; 18; 19; 3:5; 6(2); 7; 11(2); 13; 4:3; 8; 14(2); 5:1; 5; 6:2(2); 3; 4; 5(2); 6; 7; 17; 21; 22; 7:2; 4; 5; 8(2); 10; 14; 16; 19; 21(2); 22; 23; 8:1; 6; 11; 17(3); 9:2; 3; 10(2); 12; 14; 16(2); 17; 18; 10:11; 11:2; 7; 12:1; 3(2); 5(2); 11(2); 12; 13; 14(2); 18(2); 20; 13:1; 6(2); 10; 14; 16; 14:2; 5; 7; 10; 13; 14; 17; 23(3); 24; 15:4; 7; 8; 13(2); 14; 17(2); 16:2; 4; 5; 10; 13(2); 17:12(2); 13(2); 14; 17(2); 18; 23(2); 18:5; 17; 18; 19(3); 24; 25(3); 19:5; 11(2); 14; 17; 21; 25; 29; 32; 33; 34(2); 35; 20:6; 7(2); 9(2); 10; 13; 16; 21:3; 6(2); 7; 8; 12; 22(3); 23(2); 30(2); 31; 22:1; 12; 14; 17; 20; 23:4; 6; 8; 9; 10; 11; 15; 17(2); 18; 20; 24:2(2); 3; 6; 7; 9; 11; 14(4); 15; 22; 30; 32; 36; 43; 49; 52; 54; 55; 56; 65; 66; 25:5; 11; 18; 26; 30; 26:1; 5; 8; 11; 12; 21; 22; 28; 29; 32; 27:1(2); 4(2); 7; 8; 10(2); 19; 20; 21; 25; 29(2); 30; 31; 33; 40; 45; 28:3; 4; 6(2); 7; 8; 11(2); 15; 18; 19(2); 20; 21; 22; 29:2; 7; 10; 12(2); 13; 19(2); 21; 23; 25; 31; 33; 30:1; 3; 9; 15; 16; 25(2); 27; 33(2); 35(4); 38; 41(2); 31:1(2); 5; 6; 10(2); 12; 16; 19; 20(2); 21; 22; 24; 26; 27; 29; 32; 35; 36; 37; 39; 43; 52(2); 32:2; 5; 7; 13(2); 19; 20; 21; 22; 23; 25; 29; 32; 33:9; 11; 13; 14; 15; 16; 34:5; 14(2); 15; 24(2); 25; 28(2); 29; 35:1; 2(2); 5; 6(2); 17; 18; 20; 22(2); 36:7; 16; 17; 18; 24(2); 29; 30; 31; 40; 37:4; 10; 22(2); 23(2); 38:1(2); 9(3); 14; 16(2); 18; 21(2); 22; 24; 26; 27; 28; 29; 30; 39:3(3); 4; 5(4); 6; 7; 8; 10; 11; 13; 14; 15(2); 18; 19; 22; 23(2); 40:1; 7; 15; 16; 20; 41:1; 8(2); 15(2); 21; 24; 27; 31; 32; 35; 36(2); 53; 57; 42:1; 2(2); 5; 6; 14(2); 16; 21; 23; 28; 29; 33; 34(2); 35; 43:7; 8; 12; 14; 15; 18(2); 21; 25; 32; 44:2; 7; 15(2); 17; 21; 27; 30; 31(2); 34; 45:1; 5; 8; 10; 11; 12(2); 13; 15; 24; 46:1; 26; 32; 34(2); 47:1; 13; 14; 17; 18(2); 19(2); 24; 26; 29; 48:1; 10; 17; 20; 49:1(2); 15(2); 17(2); 25; 26; 28; 29; 30; 32; 50:14; 15; **Ex** 1:5; 6; 10; 21; 22; 2:2; 7; 11; 12(2); 13; 18; 20(2); 23; 3:4; 8; 10; 11(2); 12; 14; 16; 18; 19; 20; 21; 22; 4:2; 5(2); 8; 9; 14; 21(2); 23; 24; 31(2); 5:1; 2; 9; 19; 22; 6:7; 11; 26; 27; 29(2); 7:2(2); 4; 5; 13; 16; 17(2); 18; 19(2); 20(2); 21; 25; 8:1; 8(2); 9; 10(2); 15; 16; 20; 22(3); 28; 29; 9:1; 4; 6; 13; 14(2); 15; 16; 17; 19; 20; 21; 22; 25; 28; 29(2); 30; 34; 10:1; 2(3); 3; 5(2); 6; 7(2); 8; 11(2); 12(2); 13(2); 15; 17; 20; 21; 25; 28; 11:5(2); 7(2); 8(2); 9; 10; 12:8; 10; 15; 16(2); 19(2); 22(2); 25; 27; 29(3); 33; 36; 37; 41; 42; 44; 48; 49(2); 51; 13:5; 8(2); 9; 12(3); 14; 15(2); 17(2); 14:2; 4(3); 5(2); 12(3); 15; 18; 20; 21; 24; 25(2); 26; 28; 30; 31; 15:7; 26(2); 16:4; 5(2); 6; 7(2); 8; 10; 12; 13; 14; 18(2); 22; 23(4); 25; 27; 29; 32; 17:2; 3; 6; 11; 16; 18:1(2); 8(2); 11; 13; 14(2); 17; 18; 19; 20; 22; 24; 19:8; 9; 12; 16(3); 20:4(3); 5; 6; 7; 10; 11; 12; 17; 20(2); 22; 26; 21:12(2); 14; 15; 16; 17; 19; 22; 26; 28; 29; 35; 36; 22:2; 6(2); 11; 13; 16; 20; 25; 26; 27(2); 31; 23:5; 11; 12; 13; 22; 24:7; 12; 25:2(2); 8; 9; 14; 21; 26; 28; 33; 35; 37; 40; 26:5(2); 10; 11; 12(2); 13(2); 33; 27:5; 20; 28:1; 3(3); 4; 28(2); 32; 35; 37; 38(2); 41; 43; 29:1; 13(3); 21; 22(2); 23; 27(2); 30(2); 32; 38; 46(3); 30:6(2); 12; 13(2); 14(2); 16; 20; 21; 29; 30; 38; 31:6(3); 7; 11; 13(3); 14(2); 32:1(2); 10(2); 13; 18(3); 19; 21; 22; 23; 25; 28; 29; 30; 33:5; 7; 8; 13(3); 16(3); 17; 22; 34:1; 3; 7; 10; 11; 19(2); 29(2); 32; 34; 35; 35:1; 10; 22; 24; 25(2); 34; 35(2); 36:1; 4; 8; 18; 19; 37:8; 13; 38:15; 22; 24; 25; 26(2); 39:5; 7; 21(2); 23; 32; 42; 40:4; 9; 13; 15; 16; 17; 37; **Lev** 1:5; 8; 12; 17; 2:8; 10; 3:3(2); 4; 5; 9(2); 10; 14(2); 15; 17; 4:3; 5; 8(2); 9; 16; 18; 35; 5:3; 4; 5(3); 8; 11; 13; 16; 6:2; 3(2); 4(3); 5; 7; 18; 22; 26; 27; 7:3; 4(2); 7; 8; 9(3); 14; 15; 16; 18(2); 19(2); 20(3); 21(2); 24(2); 25; 27(2); 29; 30; 33; 36; 38; 8:10; 16; 25; 26; 31; 32; 35; 9:1; 5; 6; 19; 10:3(2); 10; 11; 12(2); 20; 11:2; 3; 4(2); 9; 10(2); 12; 20; 21; 26; 27; 28; 29; 31; 34(2); 36; 39; 40(2); 41; 42; 43(2); 44; 45; 46(2); 47(2); 12:7; 13:4; 7; 8; 12; 13; 17; 24; 31(2); 33; 37; 39; 41; 47; 50; 51; 52; 54; 55; 57; 14:4; 5; 6; 7; 8(3); 9; 11(2); 14; 16; 17(2); 18(2); 19; 25; 27; 28(2); 29(2); 31; 32; 35; 36(3); 40; 41; 43; 46(2); 47(2); 15:4; 6(2); 7(2); 8(2); 9; 10(2); 11; 12; 13; 20(2); 22; 28; 31(2); 32; 33(4); 16:2(2); 13(3); 15(2); 16; 18; 26; 28; 29(2); 30(2); 17:3(2); 4(2); 5(2); 8; 9; 10(4); 11; 12; 13(2); 15(3); 18:6; 26; 28(2); 29; 30(2); 19:8(2); 13; 20; 25; 31; 34; 20:2(2); 3; 5(2); 6(2); 9; 10(2); 11; 14; 22; 24; 25; 26; 27(2); 21:2(2); 3; 7; 10(2); 17; 18(2); 19; 20; 21; 23; 22:2(2); 3(2); 4; 8; 11; 18; 20; 23(2); 24; 33; 23:12; 14; 15; 21; 28; 29(2); 30(2); 42; 43(2); 24:2; 7; 12; 14(2); 16(2); 17; 18; 21(2); 23(2); 25:5; 6; 7; 11(2); 25; 27; 28(2); 30(2); 33; 35; 36; 39; 44; 45(2); 47; 48; 49; 50(2); 51; 26:13; 15(2); 16; 17; 25; 36; 39; 40; 41; 44; 45; 27:8; 9; 15; 18; 19; 23; 28(2); **Num** 1:3; 5; 20; 21; 22(2); 23; 24; 25; 26; 27; 28; 29; 30; 31; 32; 33; 34; 35; 36; 37; 38; 39; 40; 41; 42; 43; 44; 45(2); 46; 50; 51; 53; 54; 2:4; 5; 6; 8; 9; 11; 13; 15; 16; 19; 21; 23; 24; 26; 27; 28; 30; 31; 32; 34; 3:1; 6; 10; 12; 13; 22(2); 32; 34; 36; 38(2); 39; 43; 46; 49(2); 51; 4:3; 15; 16; 19; 23; 25; 26; 30; 35; 36; 37(2); 38; 39; 40; 41(2); 42; 43; 44; 45; 46; 47; 48; 5:2(2); 3; 6(2); 17; 18; 19; 22; 24(2); 27(3); 6:4; 6; 11(2); 12; 20; 21(2); 7:1; 2(2); 5; 9; 10; 12; 88; 89; 8:11; 15; 17; 19; 20; 22; 24; 9:4; 5; 6(3); 7; 13(2); 14; 15; 17; 21(2); 22; 10:2; 5; 6; 9; 10; 11; 32; 35(2); 11:1; 4; 11; 12; 13; 16; 17; 20; 21; 25(2); 26; 29(2); 32(3); 34(2); 12:14; 13:2; 18; 19(2); 28; 31; 32(2); 14:1; 2; 3; 6; 14(4); 23; 29; 35; 37; 38; 42; 45; 15:4; 12; 13; 15; 16; 19; 23(2); 24; 26; 28; 29(3); 30(2); 31; 32; 33; 38(2); 39(2); 40; 16:7; 9; 11; 13(2); 14; 21; 28; 30(2); 31(2); 32; 33; 34; 35; 37; 39; 40(2); 42; 45; 49(2); 17:5; 8; 10; 18:2; 3; 5; 7; 11; 13; 15; 16; 23; 19:2; 3; 8; 9; 10(2); 11; 13(2); 14(2); 16; 18(2); 20(2); 21(3); 22; 20:3; 4; 14; 29; 21:1; 7; 8(2); 9; 13; 15; 16; 20; 27; 29; 32; 22:2; 4(2); 6(3); 19; 20; 24; 28; 34; 35(2); 36; 38(2); 40; 41(2); 23:12; 19(2); 26(2); 27; 28; 24:1; 9(2); 13; 19(2); 20; 25:4; 5; 9; 11; 14(2); 15; 26:1; 2; 7; 9; 10; 18; 22; 25; 27; 34; 37; 41; 43; 47; 50; 54; 57; 62; 63; 27:3; 11; 14; 17; 20; 29:40; 30:2; 5; 7; 8(2); 9; 14; 15; 31:8; 17; 18; 20; 23(2); 26; 27; 35; 36; 42; 43; 52; 32:1; 9; 11; 13; 24; 32; 33:55; 56; 34:2; 35:2; 6; 8(2); 11; 12; 15(2); 16; 20; 21(2); 23; 32(2); 33(2); 36:8(2); **Deut** 1:3(2); 9; 16(2); 17; 18; 19; 30; 31(2); 35; 36; 39; 41; 44; 46; 2:6(2); 17; 20; 25; 28(2); 30; 31; 34; 36; 3:4; 8(2); 12; 18(2); 19; 21(2); 23; 24; 25(2); 4:1; 2; 3; 4; 5; 7; 8; 10(4); 14(2); 15; 17(2); 18(2); 21(3); 22; 26; 32(2); 34; 35(2); 36; 39; 40(2); 42(2); 5:1; 5; 8(3); 9; 10; 11; 14(2); 15(2); 16(2); 21; 23; 24; 26; 27(2); 28; 29(3); 31; 33(3); 6:1; 2(2); 3(3); 18(3); 23; 24; 7:4; 6; 9(2); 10(2); 12; 15; 16; 20; 25; 8:1; 3(3); 5; 7; 11; 13; 15; 16(2); 18(2); 19; 9:3; 4; 5; 6; 7; 8; 11; 14; 19; 21; 24; 10:1; 2; 8; 10; 11; 14; 21; 11:6; 8; 9(2); 14(2); 15; 16; 17(2); 18; 21; 25; 29; 12:1; 3; 7; 8; 10; 11; 12; 13(2); 14; 18(2); 19; 23; 25(2); 28(2); 30(3); 13:3(2); 5(2); 10; 14; 15(2); 17; 18; 14:2; 6(2); 7(2); 9(2); 19; 21(3); 22; 23; 24; 26; 27; 29; 15:2; 3; 8; 9; 10(2); 14; 15; 18; 19; 16:3; 6; 11(2); 12; 13; 14; 20(2); 17:1; 2; 4; 5(5); 6; 9; 10(2); 12(3); 14; 16(2); 17; 18(2); 19; 20(3); 18:3; 8; 10(2); 12; 16(2); 17; 18; 19; 20(2); 22; 19:3; 4; 5; 10; 11; 12; 13; 14; 15; 16; 20:2; 4; 5; 6; 7; 8; 9; 11(2); 14; 16; 18; 20(2); 21:2; 3(2); 4; 6(3); 9; 11; 13; 15; 16(2); 17; 18; 21; 23(3); 22:5(2); 7(2); 8; 18(2); 21; 22; 23; 24(2); 25; 28; 29; 23:1; 8; 10(2); 13; 14; 16; 19; 20(2); 23; 24:1; 4(2); 7; 8(2); 9; 13; 14(2); 18; 19; 22; 25:1; 2; 6(2); 9(2); 10; 11; 15; 16(2); 18; 19; 26:2(2); 3(2); 9; 11; 12; 14; 15; 18; 19; 27:2; 3(2); 4; 15; 16; 17; 18; 19; 20; 21; 22; 23; 24; 25; 26; 28:1; 7; 8; 10; 13; 15; 20; 23(2); 34; 35; 43; 54(2); 55; 57; 58(2); 63; 29:2; 6(2); 9(2); 11; 12; 13(2); 15(2); 18; 19; 20(2); 21; 22(4); 23(2); 27; 29; 30:2; 3; 6; 7; 12(2); 13(2); 14; 16(2); 17; 18(2); 19(2); 20(4); 31:5; 6; 8; 12(3); 13; 14(2); 17(3); 18(2); 19; 20; 21; 25; 26; 28; 29; 32:6; 13; 17; 18(2); 21; 27; 29(3); 35; 36; 39(2); 41; 42; 48; 49; 33:11(3); 13; 16(2); 20; 34:1; 12; **Josh** 1:1; 3(2); 7(2); 8(2); 16; 18(2); 2:3; 5; 9(3); 10; 12; 13(2); 14; 19; 23; 3:2; 4; 7(2); 8; 10(2); 13(3); 15(2); 16(3); 17; 4:1; 6(2); 7; 10(2); 11; 14; 16(2); 18(2); 24(3); 5:1(2); 2; 4(2); 5(2); 6(4); 8; 12; 13; 6:5; 7; 8; 9; 15(2); 17(3); 20(2); 21; 22(2); 23(2); 24; 25; 26(2); 7:14; 15(3); 24; 26; 8:5(2); 8; 9; 11; 13(2); 14(2); 16; 17; 18(2); 20(2); 21(2); 22(2); 24; 25(3); 27; 29(2); 33(3); 34; 35(2); 9:2; 9; 10(2); 16(3); 24; 26; 27; 10:2; 4; 6; 10; 11; 14(2); 20; 24; 27; 28(2); 30; 32(2); 35(4); 37(3); 39; 40; 11:1; 2; 4; 10; 11; 13(2); 15; 16; 17; 19; 20(4); 21; 23; 12:4; 7; 13:2; 4; 9(2); 16(2); 17; 22; 25; 14:6; 8; 9; 11; 12(3); 14; 15:2; 4; 7; 8; 16; 18; 46; 16:1; 10; 17:7; 12; 13; 16; 18:6; 8(2); 13; 14; 16; 19:8; 11; 20:3(2); 4(3); 6(2); 9(2); 21:26; 44; 22:2(2); 10; 16(3); 18(2); 20; 23; 27(3); 28(2); 29(2); 30; 31; 34; 23:1(2); 3(2); 4(2); 6(2); 7(2); 10; 11; 12; 13; 14; 15; 24:5; 8; 15; 16; 17; 20; 22; 25; 26; 29; 31(2); 33; **Judg** 1:1; 3; 9; 10; 12; 14; 17; 21; 27; 28; 29; 35; 2:4; 5; 7(2); 10; 12; 14(2); 16; 18; 19; 20; 22; 3:2; 3; 18; 19(2); 22; 24; 27; 29; 30; 4:2; 4; 9; 12; 13; 15; 20; 23; 5:1; 5; 7(2); 9; 10(2); 11; 13; 14; 18; 21; 30; 31; 6:3; 8; 9; 11; 17; 21; 22; 25(3); 27(2); 28(2); 30(2); 31(2); 32; 37; 40; 7:1(2); 2; 4; 5(2); 6; 7; 9; 11; 13(3); 15; 17; 18; 19(2); 8:1; 3; 4; 5; 6; 10(2); 11; 15(2); 21; 24; 26(3); 28; 31; 33; 9:2(3); 6; 7; 16; 24; 25(2); 28;

32; 33(2); 34; 35; 38(2); 41; 42; 44(2); 45(2); 46; 47; 48(2); 49; 54; 55; 10:4; 8(2); 9; 18; 11:4; 5; 6; 8; 12; 21; 24; 26(2); 31; 35(2); 36; 37; 39; 40; 12:3; 5(2); 6; 14; 13:8; 10; 11; 13; 14(2); 16; 17; 20; 21; 14:3; 4(3); 9; 11; 13; 15(3); 17; 15:1; 2; 7; 11(2); 12(2); 14(2); 17(2); 19; 16:3; 4; 5; 7; 11; 16; 17; 18; 20; 25(2); 26(3); 27; 28; 30; 17:2; 6; 13; 18:1; 5; 7(2); 9; 10; 12; 14(2); 17(2); 19; 22; 23; 24; 26; 27; 28; 31; 19:1; 5; 9(2); 10; 12; 15; 18; 22(2); 23; 30(3); 20:2; 3; 4(2); 5; 10(2); 12; 13; 15(2); 17; 21; 26; 34; 35; 36; 38; 41; 46(3); 48(2); 21:3; 4; 5(2); 7(2); 8; 11(2); 12; 13; 14; 15; 16; 17(2); 18; 19; 22(2); 23; 24; 25; **Ruth** 1:1; 6(2); 9; 11; 13; 18; 19; 2:5; 6(2); 7; 9(3); 10; 11; 13(2); 16; 17; 18; 19; 22(2); 3:1; 4; 5; 6; 8; 11(2); 12; 13; 14; 15; 16; 4:3; 4; 9(3); 10; 11(2); 14; **1Sa** 1:4; 12; 17; 20; 22; 26; 2:4; 5(4); 13; 14(2); 15; 21; 22(2); 24; 30(3); 31(2); 34; 35(2); 36(3); 3:2(2); 4; 8; 9; 11; 12; 13; 14; 17(2); 20; 4:3; 4; 5; 6; 8; 9; 15; 16; 18; 19(2); 20; 5:5; 7; 9; 10; 11; 12; 6:5; 8; 9(3); 15; 7:2; 6; 7; 8; 10; 8:1; 7(2); 8; 9; 10; 11; 18(2); 20(2); 9:5; 6(2); 8; 9; 13; 16; 19; 20; 22; 24(3); 26(2); 27; 10:5(2); 7; 9(2); 11(3); 14; 16; 18; 24; 11:2; 3; 5; 9(2); 10; 11(3); 12(2); 12:1; 5; 6(2); 7; 12; 14; 17(2); 18; 19; 23; 13:3; 4(2); 6; 8; 10(2); 11(3); 14; 15; 16; 17; 18; 22(2); 14:1(3); 2; 3; 6(2); 7; 14; 17; 18; 19(2); 20; 21(3); 22; 23; 24(3); 27; 28; 31; 33; 34; 35; 37; 39; 43; 45; 48; 15:2; 3; 7; 9(3); 11; 25; 28; 29; 30; 35; 16:4; 6; 13; 16; 17; 18; 23; 17:10; 12; 13; 25(2); 26(3); 27; 28; 37; 41; 43; 46(2); 47; 48; 49; 18:1; 2; 4; 6; 9; 10; 15; 18; 19; 21(2); 23; 27; 28(2); 30(2); 19:1; 3; 10; 15; 17; 18; 22; 24(2); 20:1; 2; 3; 5; 6; 7; 9; 13; 14; 26; 27; 30; 33; 35; 21:6; 7(2); 9(3); 10; 15; 22:2(3); 4; 6(2); 7; 8(5); 11; 13(2); 17; 18(2); 21; 22(2); 23; 23:6; 7(2); 9; 10; 13; 15; 17; 22; 23; 25; 26; 28; 24:1; 4; 5; 6; 10; 11(2); 16; 18; 19; 20(2); 21(2); 25:4; 6(2); 7; 10; 11; 17; 20; 21(3); 22(2); 26; 27; 30; 31(3); 34; 35; 37; 38(2); 39(2); 42; 26:3; 4; 11(2); 14; 16(2); 27:1; 2; 4; 5; 6; 7; 28:1(2); 3; 7(3); 9; 14; 15; 21; 22; 25; 29:4; 7; 8; 9; 10; 30:1; 2; 4; 9(2); 10; 15; 16; 18; 19; 21(2); 22(3); 23(2); 24(2); 25(2); 31:5; 6; 7(4); 8; 11; **2Sa** 1:2(2); 4; 5(2); 6; 10(4); 11; 13; 15; 2:1; 3; 4(2); 5; 11; 16; 17; 23(2); 24; 26; 29; 31; 3:6; 8; 13; 19(2); 20; 21(3); 23; 24; 25(2); 27; 29(5); 31; 37(2); 38; 4:1; 2; 4(2); 10; 5:2; 8(2); 12(2); 14; 17; 20; 24; 6:2(2); 3; 9; 12; 13(2); 17; 7:2; 3; 4(2); 6; 9; 10; 11(2); 18; 22; 25; 28; 29; 8:1; 7; 9; 11; 9:1(2); 3; 8; 9; 10; 11; 12; 10:1; 3(2); 6; 9; 10; 12; 13; 14; 15; 16; 19(2); 11:1; 2; 12; 14; 15; 16(2); 20(2); 21; 22; 26; 27; 12:4(2); 5; 8; 14; 15; 18(3); 19(2); 21; 22; 31; 13:1; 2; 5; 6; 10; 15; 16; 17; 18; 19; 23; 27; 30; 32(2); 33; 34; 36; 14:1; 2; 7(2); 11; 13; 14; 15(2); 16; 18; 19; 20; 22(2); 26; 32; 15:1; 2(2); 4(2); 5; 6; 7; 11; 14; 17; 22; 30; 32; 35; 36; 16:2; 4(2); 12(2); 14; 16; 21(2); 17:2; 7; 8; 9(2); 10(2); 11(3); 12; 13; 14; 16; 21; 22(2); 23; 25; 27; 29; 18:1; 3; 7; 8; 9; 11; 12; 15; 19; 22; 28; 31; 32(2); 19:2(2); 3; 6(3); 7(2); 14; 19(3); 20; 22(2); 25; 26; 28; 34; 37; 38(2); 43; 20:8; 10; 11(2); 12(3); 15; 16; 19; 20; 21:3; 4(2); 5(3); 7; 13; 14(2); 17; 18; 20; 22:1; 18; 28; 31; 35; 37; 39; 40; 41(2); 48(2); 49(2); 23:3; 7; 8; 9; 10; 15; 16; 17(2); 24:2; 3; 5; 9; 10(2); 12; 13(2); 16; 17; 18; 21; 24; **1Kin** 1:2; 11; 12; 20; 21; 29; 35; 40; 41; 45(2); 49; 51; 2:1; 3(2); 4; 5(2); 7; 11; 15(3); 17; 25; 27; 29; 31; 37(2); 39; 41; 42(2); 43; 44; 46; 3:4(2); 6; 8; 9; 10; 12; 13(2); 16; 18(2); 23; 28; 4:12; 27; 29; 33(2); 5:1; 3; 4; 6(4); 7; 9; 15; 16; 6:1; 6; 7; 17; 22; 27; 7:3; 18; 19; 29; 40; 41; 42; 48; 51; 8:1; 4; 5(2); 8; 10; 11; 12; 16(2); 18; 19; 20; 23; 24; 25(3); 27; 29(2); 36; 40(2); 41; 43(4); 44; 46(2); 47; 50(2); 52(2); 54; 56(2); 58; 59; 60(3); 64(2); 65; 66; 9:2; 3; 4; 8; 11; 16; 19(2); 20; 21; 23(2); 25; 27; 10:2(2); 4; 6; 8; 11; 13; 14; 15; 27; 11:4; 7; 10(2); 17; 19; 21(3); 22; 25; 27; 28; 29(2); 30; 33(2); 36; 37; 38(3); 41; 42; 12:3; 6(2); 8; 9; 10(2); 13; 15; 16; 18; 20(3); 32(2); 13:2; 3; 4(2); 6; 9; 10; 11(2); 14; 17; 18; 20(2); 21; 23; 26; 31; 14:1; 2; 5; 6; 8; 9; 10(2); 11(2); 14; 22; 25; 28; 29; 15:5(2); 7; 11; 12; 17; 18(2); 19; 21; 23; 29(2); 31; 16:4(2); 7; 11(2); 14; 16(2); 18(2); 20; 22(2); 25; 27; 30; 31; 33; 17:3; 4; 5; 7; 10; 12(2); 14; 17(2); 24(2); 18:1; 4; 5; 7; 9; 10; 12; 17(2); 18; 24; 26; 27; 29(2); 30; 36(4); 37(3); 38; 44(2); 45; 19:1; 3; 4; 8; 13; 17(3); 20:4; 6; 9; 10; 11(2); 12; 13; 16; 25; 26; 28; 29; 30; 31; 37; 41; 21:1; 2; 3; 5; 8; 10; 13; 15(2); 16(2); 21(2); 24(2); 27; 22:2; 3; 7; 13(2); 14; 16(2); 17; 18; 20(2); 25; 31; 32; 33(2); 35; 39(2); 43; 45; 53; **2Kin** 1:2; 3; 4; 6(3); 16; 2:1; 3(2); 5(2); 8; 9; 11; 13; 14; 3:2; 5; 9; 10; 11; 14; 15; 17(2); 20; 21(2); 24; 26(2); 27; 4:1; 4; 6; 8(2); 9; 10; 11; 17(2); 18; 22; 25(2); 40; 41; 42; 43; 5:3; 4; 6; 7(2); 8(3); 15; 18; 20; 6:9; 12(2); 13; 16(2); 17; 20(2); 22; 24; 28; 29; 30; 7:9; 12; 13(3); 19; 8:3; 4; 5; 6(2); 10; 12; 13(2); 14; 15(2); 23; 9:7; 8(2); 22; 25; 37; 10:1; 5(4); 7; 9; 10(2); 11; 17; 19; 21(2); 22; 23; 24; 25; 29(2); 30(2); 34; 36; 11:1; 2; 5(2); 6; 7; 8; 9(3); 10; 15; 17; 12:2; 4(4); 6; 9(2); 10(3); 11(3); 12; 13; 14; 18(2); 19; 13:2; 5; 8; 11; 12; 21; 14:3; 5; 6; 9(3); 10; 14; 22; 24; 26; 27; 28; 15:3(2); 4; 5; 6; 9; 16(2); 18; 19; 21; 24; 26; 28; 31; 34(2); 36; 16:2; 6; 8; 10; 11; 16; 17; 18; 17:2(2); 7; 9; 14; 15(3); 25; 38; 18:1; 3(2); 4; 5(2); 9; 10; 12; 14; 15; 16; 20; 21; 22; 26; 27; 32; 35(2); 19:1; 4; 8; 19(2); 20; 21; 25(2); 29; 30; 31; 33; 35(2); 37; 20:3; 4; 8(2); 9(2); 12(2); 13(2); 15(2); 17(3); 18; 21:2; 7; 8(2); 11; 12; 15; 16; 17(2); 20; 21(2); 24; 22:2; 3; 4; 5; 7; 9(3); 11; 13(3); 15; 17; 19; 23:3; 4; 5; 7; 8;

10; 11; 12; 13; 15(2); 16; 17(3); 18; 19(2); 20; 22; 24(3); 25; 26; 28; 32(2); 33; 37(2); 24:3; 4; 5; 7; 9(2); 10; 16; 19(2); 20; 25:1; 10; 11(2); 13(2); 19(3); 22; 23; 25(3); 27(2); 28; **1Chr** 1:43; 2:9; 24; 55; 4:10(5); 21; 23; 33; 41; 43; 5:18; 20; 6:10(2); 31; 33; 49; 61; 7:21(2); 40; 9:2; 16; 28; 31; 33; 10:5; 7(3); 8; 11; 13; 11:2; 14; 17(2); 18; 19(2); 31; 12:1; 8; 15; 20; 22; 23; 24; 32; 38; 40; 13:2(3); 4; 6(2); 11; 12; 14; 14:2; 8; 11; 15; 15:12(2); 13; 26(2); 27; 29; 16:1; 7; 10; 12; 30; 32; 35; 39; 40; 41; 42; 17:1; 2; 3; 5; 7; 8; 10(2); 11(2); 13; 16; 20; 23; 24; 25; 27; 18:1; 7; 11; 19:1; 3(2); 6; 9; 10; 13; 14; 15; 16(2); 19; 20:1(2); 3; 4(2); 21:2; 5(2); 10; 12(2); 15; 17(3); 18; 22(2); 23; 24; 28(2); 29; 22:2; 5; 12; 19; 23:13; 24; 25; 29(2); 32; 25:7(2); 26:6; 28; 27:1; 6; 26; 28; 29(2); 28:1; 8; 12; 18; 29:3; 9; 11; 14; 16; 17; 21; 22; 27; 30; **2Chr** 1:3; 5; 7; 10(2); 11; 12; 13; 15; 2:6; 7(2); 8; 10; 12(2); 17; 3:1; 4; 15; 17(2); 4:11; 19; 20; 21; 5:1(2); 5; 6; 9; 11; 13; 14; 6:1; 4; 5(2); 6; 8; 10; 11; 14; 15; 16(2); 20(2); 31; 33(3); 34; 40; 7:7; 10; 11; 13; 15; 16; 17; 21(2); 8:2; 6(2); 7; 10; 11; 18; 9:1(2); 3; 6; 12; 13; 14; 23; 27; 10:2; 4; 6; 8(2); 9(2); 10(2); 15; 16; 17; 18(2); 11:1; 13; 12:2; 3; 5; 7; 8; 10; 12; 13:5; 9(2); 15; 18; 14:2; 8(2); 11; 13(2); 15:5(2); 8; 9; 13; 18(2); 16:1; 2; 3; 5; 7; 17:10(2); 18:2; 6; 12; 13; 15; 16; 17; 19(2); 24; 30; 31; 32(2); 33; 34; 19:2; 3; 10(2); 20:1; 2; 6; 12; 21; 29; 32; 37; 21:6; 7; 16; 17(2); 19; 22:1; 8(2); 10; 11(2); 23:4; 6; 8(3); 9; 14; 16; 19; 21; 24:2; 4; 5; 7; 9; 11(2); 20; 23; 26; 25:2; 3(2); 5; 10; 12; 13; 14(2); 16(2); 18(3); 19; 20; 24; 27; 26:2; 4(2); 7; 11; 13; 17; 18; 27:2(2); 28:1; 7; 9(2); 12; 15; 16; 22; 23; 29:2(2); 6; 10; 11; 16; 24; 29; 34; 36; 30:1; 3; 5; 6; 8; 9(2); 14; 17(2); 19; 21; 22; 25(3); 31:1; 4(2); 6; 10; 16; 19(2); 20; 21; 32:2(2); 4; 5; 7; 9; 10; 14(3); 18(2); 21; 23; 26; 31(3); 33:2; 8(2); 13; 15; 18; 22; 25; 34:2; 4(2); 9(2); 10(2); 12; 13; 14; 16; 17; 19; 21(4); 22(2); 23; 24; 25; 28; 30; 32; 33(2); 35:3; 6; 7; 12; 17(2); 18(2); 21; 22; 24(2); 26; 36:5; 8; 9; 12; 17; 20; 22(2); **Ezr** 1:1(2); 4; 6(2); 11; 2:1; 62; 63; 3:5(2); 7; 8; 12; 13; 4:1; 10; 11; 12; 13; 15(3); 16; 17; 19(2); 21; 22; 5:1; 4; 5; 6; 8; 10(2); 11; 12; 14; 15; 16; 17; 6:2; 8(2); 9; 10; 11; 12(2); 13; 7:11; 13; 16; 17; 18; 19; 21; 24; 25(3); 8:1; 17; 21; 22(2); 34; 35; 9:2; 4(2); 8; 12; 13(2); 14; 10:3; 5; 6; 7; 8(2); 13; 17; 18; 19; **Neh** 1:2(2); 3; 4; 5(2); 6; 8; 9; 2:1; 5(2); 7; 8(2); 10; 12; 14; 16; 17(2); 18; 19; 3:15; 16; 25; 26; 27; 4:1(2); 3; 7(3); 10; 12; 15(2); 16(2); 17(2); 18; 22; 23; 5:2(2); 3(2); 4(2); 9; 11; 12; 13; 14(2); 15; 17(2); 18; 19; 6:1(3); 2; 3; 6(2); 9; 11; 12(2); 13(3); 14; 16(3); 7:2; 5; 6(2); 64; 65; 72; 8:1; 2; 3(2); 9; 12; 14; 15; 17(2); 9:6(2); 10; 11; 15; 17; 18; 21; 23; 24; 28; 29; 32; 33; 35; 36; 10:1; 28; 30; 31(2); 36; 37(2); 39; 11:2; 3; 6; 12; 19; 23; 12:1; 31; 38; 40; 43(2); 44(2); 13:1(2); 2; 3; 7; 10(2); 14; 17; 19(4); 21; 22(2); 23; **Est** 1:2; 5; 8; 10; 13; 16; 17; 19(3); 22(2); 2:2; 3; 7; 8; 10; 12; 14; 15; 17; 3:1; 2; 4(2); 5; 6; 7(3); 9(2); 12(2); 14(2); 4:1; 7(2); 8(2); 11(2); 13; 16; 17; 5:1; 2(2); 4; 5(2); 8; 9(2); 12; 14; 6:1; 2; 3; 4; 8; 9; 10(2); 13; 14; 7:5; 7; 10; 8:1; 3; 6; 9(3); 11; 13(2); 14; 9:1(4); 5; 11(2); 15; 16; 18; 19; 20; 21; 22; 24; 25(2); 26; 27; 28(2); **Job** 1:1(2); 3; 5(2); 8(2); 10; 11; 12; 2:3(2); 4; 11; 13; 3:4; 6; 7; 8; 12; 15; 20; 25; 4:4; 8; 19; 5:1; 11(2); 12; 24; 25; 6:2; 6; 7; 8(3); 9(2); 11(2); 14; 26; 7:7; 8; 9; 12; 15; 17(2); 18; 20; 8:13; 22; 9:16; 26; 28; 32; 33; 10:3(2); 6; 7(2); 9; 13; 18; 20; 11:5; 6(4); 16; 12:5(2); 6; 9; 13:5; 9; 13; 18; 19; 28; 14:1; 5; 6; 7(2); 13(3); 15:7; 9; 13; 14(2); 17; 22; 23; 31; 16:3; 21; 17:3; 5; 9; 18:20(2); 21; 19:3; 4; 6; 8; 15; 23(2); 24; 25(2); 29; 20:5; 18; 20; 26; 21:3(2); 15; 18; 22; 29; 30; 22:2; 3(2); 11; 14; 23:3(2); 9; 10; 13; 14; 24:1; 7; 13; 21; 25:4; 6; 26:2(2); 3; 27:5; 7; 11; 15; 18; 28:11; 28; 29:2; 12(2); 13; 25; 30:1; 23; 25; 31; 31:6; 12; 15; 28; 29; 31; 34; 35(3); 38; 32:5; 12(2); 20; 33:12; 17; 20; 21(2); 27; 34:2; 9; 10(2); 17(2); 19; 23; 25; 28; 30; 32; 36; 35:2; 36:2; 4; 9; 10; 16; 24; 32; 37:2; 7; 12; 20; 24; 38:2; 13(2); 20(2); 34; 35; 39:2; 12; 15(2); 24; 40:2(2); 8; 11; 12; 14; 19; 23; 41:10; 11; 16; 17; 26; 42:2(2); 3(2); 7(2); 8; 11(2); **Ps** 1:1; 3; 2:4; 12; 3:1(2); 6; 4:3(2); 6; 7; 5:4; 6; 11(2); 7:1; 4(2); 6; 8; 8:2; 4(2); 9:10(2); 13(2); 14; 15; 17; 20; 10:2; 10; 18; 11:2; 5; 12:3; 5; 13:4; 14:1; 2; 3; 7; 15:2; 3; 4(2); 5(2); 16:3; 4; 17:1; 2; 3; 5; 7(2); 9; 12; 18:t; 12; 30; 32; 34; 36; 38; 39; 40(2); 47; 48; 20:6; 21:8; 22:3; 7; 8; 9; 23; 25; 26; 29(2); 31(2); 24:1; 4; 6(2); 25:3; 12(2); 14; 26:7; 27:4(2); 28:1; 30:3; 12; 31:4; 6; 11; 15; 19(2); 24; 32:6; 10; 11; 33:18(2); 34:7; 8(2); 9; 10; 12(2); 16; 18; 21; 22; 35:1(2); 3; 4(2); 8(2); 10(2); 11; 14; 19(2); 20; 26(2); 27; 36:1; 4; 10; 37:9; 13; 16; 22; 37; 38:12(2); 13; 14; 19; 20(2); 39:1; 4; 13; 40:4(2); 12; 14(2); 15; 16; 41:1; 7; 8; 10; 11; 42:4; 44:5; 7; 13; 16; 45:14; 46:5; 10; 48:13; 49:6; 9; 10; 11; 12; 20(2); 50:4; 5; 16; 21; 22; 23; 51:4; 8; 52:7; 53:1; 2(2); 3; 5; 6; 54:4; 55:6; 12(3); 18; 19; 56:2; 13; 57:2; 3; 4; 58:4; 8; 11(2); 59:1; 13(2); 60:4(2); 5; 12; 61:2; 5; 8; 62:11; 63:9; 11(2); 64:4; 8; 65:2; 4; 5; 8; 66:16; 67:2; 68:1; 4; 11; 12; 18; 20; 23; 28; 30; 33(2); 35; 69:4(3); 6(2); 9; 10; 12; 14; 22; 23; 31; 32; 34; 35; 36; 70:2(2); 3; 4; 71:6; 10; 13(2); 18; 24; 72:6; 9; 12; 73:25; 27(2); 28; 74:3; 9; 18(2); 23; 75:1; 76:11(2); 77:4; 14; 78:4; 5; 6; 7; 8; 11; 20; 35; 39(2); 44; 53; 60; 65; 79:4; 6(2); 11; 80:1(2); 12; 15; 81:5; 13; 83:2; 4; 16; 18(2); 84:4; 11; 12; 85:6; 9(2); 12; 86:2; 5; 17; 87:4; 5; 6; 88:4(2); 5; 89:7; 10; 15; 19; 23; 34;

35; 41; 48; 90:9; 12; 14; 91:1; 5; 6(2); 92:7; 11; 13; 15; 93:1; 94:9(2); 10(2); 11; 13; 95:10; 11; 96:10(2); 12; 97:7(2); 10; 98:7; 99:6; 7; 8; 100:3(2); 101:3; 5; 6(2); 7(2); 8; 102:4; 8; 11; 20; 103:1; 5; 6; 11; 13; 14; 17; 18; 20(2); 21; 104:5; 9(2); 14; 15; 26; 27; 28; 105:3; 5; 19; 34; 45; 106:3(2); 4; 5(3); 8; 10; 20; 23; 31; 32; 33; 40; 41; 46; 107:7; 8; 15; 21; 23(2); 29; 31; 34; 36; 38; 108:6; 13; 109:11; 15; 16(2); 20; 27(3); 31; 111:2; 5; 6; 10; 112:1(2); 113:6; 8; 114:5(2); 6; 115:8(2); 11; 13; 17; 118:2; 3; 4(2); 7(2); 13; 26; 119:2(2); 5; 11; 17; 18; 20; 21; 42; 53; 57; 63(2); 71(2); 73; 74; 75(2); 77; 79(2); 80; 84; 101; 106; 116; 118; 125; 132; 138; 148; 150; 152; 162; 120:5(2); 6; 121:3; 4; 122:3; 6; 123:1; 2; 4; 125:1; 4(2); 126:1; 5; 6; 127:1; 5; 128:1(2); 4(2); 129:5; 7; 130:4; 6(2); 131:2; 132:12; 133:2(2); 3; 134:3; 135:2; 5(2); 6; 18(2); 20; 136:5; 6; 7; 10; 137:3(2); 8; 9; 138:8; 139:14; 21(2); 140:9; 10; 12; 141:4; 10; 142:4; 7; 143:3; 7; 12; 144:3(2); 4; 10; 12(2); 13(2); 14(3); 15(3); 145:14(2); 18(2); 19; 20; 146:4; 5; 6; 8; 147:11(2); 148:4; 149:2; 150:6; **Prov** 1:12; 19; 29; 2:2; 7; 12; 19; 20; 3:13(2); 18(2); 4:18; 22; 5:2(2); 6; 13; 6:11; 17; 18(2); 19(2); 29; 32; 7:5; 23; 8:9(2); 11; 17(2); 21(2); 29; 32; 34; 36(2); 9:4; 7(2); 16; 18(2); 10:4; 5(3); 9(2); 10; 13(2); 17(2); 18(2); 19; 26; 11:12; 13; 15(2); 17; 18; 19; 20; 24(2); 25; 26(2); 27(2); 28; 29; 30; 12:1; 4; 8; 9(2); 11(2); 15; 17; 18; 20; 22; 27; 13:3(2); 6; 7(2); 11; 13; 18(2); 20; 23; 24(2); 14:2(2); 6; 13; 17; 21(2); 22(2); 29(2); 31(2); 33(2); 35; 15:5; 9; 10(2); 12; 14; 15; 18; 21; 24; 27(2); 31; 32(2); 16:5; 13; 17; 20; 22; 25; 26; 29; 32(3); 17:2; 5; 8; 9(2); 15(2); 19(2); 20(2); 21; 24; 25; 27; 28; 18:2; 9(2); 13; 17; 21; 24(2); 19:1(2); 2(2); 5; 6; 8(2); 9; 16(2); 17(2); 20; 21; 23; 25; 26(2); 27; 20:8; 16; 19(2); 25; 21:5; 6; 16; 17(2); 21; 28; 22:5; 8; 9; 11; 14; 16(2); 19; 21(3); 23; 26(2); 23:5; 6; 22; 24; 25; 30(2); 34(2); 24:8; 11(2); 12(2); 21; 24; 25; 26; 34; 25:7(2); 10; 13; 18; 20(2); 28(2); 26:6; 8(2); 10; 16; 17(2); 19; 24; 27; 28; 27:8(2); 10; 11(2); 13; 14; 18; 28:3; 4; 5; 6(2); 7; 8(2); 9; 11; 13; 14(2); 16(2); 17; 18; 19(2); 20; 21; 22(2); 23(2); 25(2); 26; 27(2); 29:1(2); 3; 4; 5; 14; 18; 20; 21; 27; 30:5; 11; 12; 15; 16(2); 17; 23; 31:1; 3; 6(2); 11; 18; 30; **Eccl** 1:9(4); 11(2); 13; 14; 15(2); 16; 17; 18; 2:3; 6; 7; 8; 9; 11(2); 12(2); 13; 14; 15; 16; 17; 18; 21; 24(3); 26(3); 3:2; 9(2); 11(2); 12; 13; 14(2); 15(3); 16(2); 18(3); 19(2); 21(2); 22(3); 4:1; 3; 4; 10; 14; 15; 16(2); 5:1; 4; 5(2); 6; 8; 10(2); 11; 16(2); 18(2); 6:2(2); 3(3); 8; 10(3); 11; 7:2; 10; 11; 12(2); 13; 14; 15(2); 18(2); 20; 21; 22; 24; 29; 8:2; 7; 8(3); 9; 12(2); 14(2); 15; 16(2); 17(2); 9:1(2); 2(4); 3(3); 4; 5; 6; 9; 11; 12(2); 15; 17; 10:1; 3(2); 8; 9; 20; 11:4(2); 5; 6; 8; 9; 12:3; 5; 10; **Song** 1:7; 2:7; 14; 15; 3:3; 4(2); 5; 6; 4:1; 2; 5; 16; 5:2; 7; 8(2); 9; 6:1; 5; 9; 10; 13; 7:3; 9(2); 8:1(2); 4; 5(2); 10; 12; 13; **Is** 1:4; 28; 29; 30; 2:1; 2; 8; 11; 12(2); 13; 14; 17; 20; 3:7; 10; 15; 18; 24; 4:1; 2(2); 3; 3(4); 5:2; 4(2); 6; 8(3); 11(3); 14; 16; 18; 19(3); 20(3); 21; 22; 30; 6:1; 4; 7:1; 8; 15; 16; 17(2); 18(4); 20; 21(2); 22(2); 23(2); 25; 8:6; 11; 17; 19(3); 21; 9:2(2); 9; 13; 15; 16; 10:1(2); 2(2); 12; 14(2); 15(3); 19; 20(3); 24; 27(2); 31; 11:10; 11(2); 16; 12:1; 4(2); 13:2; 3; 8; 14; 15(2); 14:3; 4; 6; 16(3); 17(2); 19(2); 21; 25; 26(2); 28; 29; 32; 15:7; 9; 16:2; 3; 12(2); 13(2); 14; 17:4(2); 5; 7; 8; 9; 12; 14(2); 18:2; 7; 19:3; 8(2); 9(2); 10; 13; 16; 17; 18; 19; 21; 23; 24; 20:1; 6; 21:3; 10; 14(2); 22:1; 2; 3; 7; 8; 9; 11; 12; 16(3); 20(2); 25(3); 23:1; 2; 13; 15(2); 16(2); 17; 18; 24:6; 8; 9; 10; 18(2); 21(3); 25:7; 9; 11; 26:1; 2; 5; 17; 19; 27:1(3); 2; 5; 6; 7(2); 9; 11(2); 12(2); 13(2); 28:1; 4; 5; 6(2); 8; 9; 13; 14; 16; 19; 20(2); 21; 29:4; 5; 7(3); 8; 11(2); 12; 15; 16(2); 18; 20; 21(2); 24(2); 30:1(3); 2; 5; 6; 8; 9(2); 14(2); 16; 18(3); 23(2); 24; 26; 31:1; 2; 3(2); 7; 32:3(2); 9; 11; 20(2); 33:1; 13(2); 15(4); 17; 18; 19; 20; 24; 34:1(2); 35:4; 36:1; 5; 6; 11; 12(2); 20(2); 22; 37:1; 4; 6; 8; 16; 20(2); 26(2); 30; 31; 32; 34; 38; 38:3; 7(2); 13; 18; 22; 39:1(2); 2(2); 4(2); 6(3); 7; 40:2(2); 3; 9(2); 11; 20(4); 22(2); 23; 26(2); 28; 29; 31; 41:3; 7(3); 11(2); 12(2); 20(2); 22; 23(4); 24; 26(5); 27; 28; 42:5(5); 7; 8; 10(2); 11; 16(2); 17(2); 18; 19(2); 43:1(2); 7; 8(2); 9; 10(2); 12; 13; 25; 26; 44:2; 3; 7; 8; 9(2); 10; 13; 18(2); 20; 24(4); 25(2); 26(2); 27; 28; 45:3(2); 6(2); 9(2); 10; 15; 16; 18(2); 19; 20(3); 21; 23; 24; 46:5; 10; 11; 12; 47:7; 8(3); 13; 48:4; 8(3); 9; 16; 17; 18; 49:5; 6(2); 7; 9(2); 10; 15; 17; 19; 20; 23(2); 25; 26(2); 50:2; 4(2); 6; 7; 8; 9; 10(3); 11(3); 51:1(2); 2; 6; 7; 9; 10; 12(3); 13; 14(3); 15; 16; 18(2); 22; 23(3); 52:5(2); 6(3); 7(5); 11; 15(2); 53:2; 54:1(2); 9(2); 10; 16(2); 17(2); 55:1(2); 2(3); 5(2); 10; 11(2); 13; 56:2(3); 3; 4(2); 5; 6(2); 8; 11; 57:1; 11; 13; 15(2); 19(2); 58:2; 5; 6(2); 7(4); 12; 59:1(2); 2; 5(2); 15(2); 16(2); 20; 21; 60:8; 11(2); 12; 14(2); 15; 16; 21; 61:1; 2; 3(3); 9(2); 11; 62:1; 6; 9(2); 63:1(3); 2; 5; 7; 8; 11(2); 12; 13(2); 64:1(3); 2; 4; 5(2); 7(2); 65:1(3); 2; 3(2); 5; 8; 10; 11(6); 12; 16(2); 18; 20; 24; 66:1; 2; 3(4); 4; 5(3); 6; 10(2); 11(2); 17; 18; 19(3); 23; 24; **Jer** 1:1; 7; 17; 2:2; 3; 5; 6(3); 8(2); 11; 13; 17; 19(3); 24(2); 28; 3:1; 6; 9; 13; 16; 17; 18; 4:4; 9(2); 11; 14; 16; 31(3); 5:1(2); 6; 7; 19; 22; 24; 26; 6:10; 11; 15(2); 27; 7:1; 2; 7; 8; 18; 22; 23(2); 25; 28; 32; 8:1; 3; 10; 12; 13; 16(2); 19; 9:1(2); 2(2); 10; 12(3); 17(2); 18; 24(3); 25; 26(2); 10:4; 11; 18; 23(2); 25(2); 11:1; 3; 4; 5; 7; 13; 14; 17; 19(3); 20(2); 21(2); 12:1; 4; 14; 15; 17; 13:4; 6; 11; 12; 13; 20(2); 23; 24; 26; 14:1; 8; 9; 15; 18(2); 22; 15:4; 9; 10; 13; 15; 18; 16:3(3);

10; 12; 13; 14(2); 15(2); 21; 17:4; 5; 7; 8; 11; 13(2); 16; 18; 20; 23; 18:4; 8(2); 10; 14; 16; 19; 20; 19:2; 6; 7; 8; 9; 10; 11; 15(2); 20:1; 2; 3; 6; 12; 16; 17; 18; 21:2(2); 4; 7; 9(3); 12(2); 22:2(2); 5; 10; 13(2); 14; 21; 23; 25; 26; 30; 23:1; 2; 5; 7; 14; 16; 17(2); 24; 25; 26; 28(2); 29; 30; 31; 32; 34(2); 39; 24:1; 2; 3; 5; 7; 8(2); 10; 25:1(2); 3; 5; 7; 12(2); 13(2); 16; 23; 24; 30; 31; 33; 26:2; 3; 8(2); 12; 13; 15; 20; 24; 27:5; 8(3); 10; 11; 13; 14; 15(3); 16; 18; 19; 21; 22; 28:1; 3; 4; 5; 6; 7; 8; 9; 12; 14; 29:1; 2; 4; 6(2); 8; 10; 11; 16(4); 17; 25; 26(3); 31; 32; 30:1; 2; 3(2); 4; 7(2); 8(2); 13; 16(3); 19; 20; 21; 31:4; 6; 8; 10; 11; 17; 19(2); 24; 27; 28; 30; 31; 32(2); 33; 37; 38; 32:1; 7; 8(2); 9; 11(2); 12(2); 14; 23; 24; 29; 31(2); 35; 39; 40(2); 42; 33:2; 9(2); 10; 11(2); 13; 14(2); 15; 20; 21; 22; 24; 26; 34:7; 8(2); 9(2); 10(2); 13; 18; 20; 21; 35:7; 8; 10; 11; 14; 17; 18; 36:1; 2; 3(3); 6; 7; 8; 9(2); 13; 23(3); 24; 25; 27; 28; 31; 37:5; 7; 10; 11; 15; 18; 20; 21(2); 38:1; 2(2); 4; 5; 6; 7; 9; 14; 16(2); 19; 21; 22; 25; 26; 27; 28; 39:4; 9(4); 14; 16; 17; 40:1(3); 6; 7(2); 10; 11(4); 13; 14; 15; 41:1; 2; 3(2); 5; 7(2); 8; 9; 10(2); 11(2); 12; 13(2); 14; 16(2); 42:3(2); 4; 6; 7; 10; 12; 16; 17(2); 19; 20; 22; 43:1; 3; 5; 6; 10; 13; 44:1; 2; 3; 4; 8(3); 10; 12; 13; 14(2); 15(3); 16; 20; 21; 22; 24; 25; 26(2); 27; 28(2); 29(3); 30(2); 45:1; 4(2); 46:7; 9(2); 10; 13; 25; 26; 47:1(2); 2(2); 4(2); 48:9; 10(2); 12(2); 17(2); 18; 19(2); 20; 28(2); 35(2); 36; 41; 44(2); 45; 49:2(2); 4; 5(2); 8; 12; 13; 16(2); 17; 19(3); 20(2); 22; 26; 31; 32; 34; 37; 39; 50:1; 4; 5; 7; 10; 12; 13; 14; 16; 20; 21; 28; 29(2); 30; 31; 33; 34; 37; 44(3); 45(2); 51:1(2); 2; 3(2); 4; 7; 12; 13; 24; 31; 32; 39; 44; 46(2); 47; 48; 50; 52; 60(2); 62(2); 63; 64; 52:2(2); 3; 4; 6; 14; 15(3); 17(2); 19(2); 20; 25(2); 31; 32; **Lam** 1:1(2); 6; 7; 8; 10(2); 12; 16; 17; 21(3); 2:4; 13; 15(2); 16; 17(2); 19; 22(2); 3:1; 6; 7; 22; 25(2); 26; 27; 30; 37; 44; 57; 62; 4:5(2); 6; 9(2); 12; 13; 14; 17; 18; 21; 5:8; 16; **Eze** 1:1; 18; 23; 25; 26; 28(2); 2:2(2); 3; 5; 8(2); 3:1; 2; 3; 10; 13; 15; 16; 21; 26; 27(2); 4:4; 9; 12; 14; 17; 5:5; 6; 7(2); 9; 13; 14(2); 15; 6:6; 7; 8(2); 9; 10(3); 12(3); 13; 14; 7:4; 7; 9(3); 13; 15(2); 16; 27; 8:1; 3; 4; 6(2); 9; 13; 17; 9:1; 4(3); 8; 10:1; 6; 7(2); 12; 15; 20(2); 11:2; 5; 10; 12(2); 13; 20; 24; 25; 12:4; 6; 10; 12(2); 14; 15; 16(2); 19(3); 20(2); 22(2); 25; 27(2); 13:2(2); 3; 6; 9(3); 11; 14(3); 15(2); 18(2); 19(3); 20; 21; 22; 23; 14:4(2); 5; 7; 8(2); 9; 10; 11(2); 15(2); 17(2); 19; 22(3); 23(2); 15:7; 16:5; 15; 21; 24; 25; 27; 31(2); 32; 33; 34; 37(3); 38; 44; 45; 46(2); 47; 52(2); 54(3); 57; 62; 63(2); 17:7; 8(3); 9; 14(3); 15(2); 16; 19(2); 20; 21(2); 24; 18:2; 4; 5; 8(2); 10(2); 11; 14; 15; 17(2); 18; 19; 20; 21(2); 22(2); 23(2); 24(4); 26; 27(2); 28; 32; 19:5; 9; 11; 14; 20:1; 6(2); 9; 12(3); 14; 15; 20(2); 22; 23; 25; 26(5); 27; 32(2); 38(2); 42; 43; 44; 48; 21:4; 5(2); 7; 10; 11; 14; 15; 19; 20; 23(2); 24(3); 26(2); 29; 22:3; 4; 5(2); 9; 10; 14; 16; 22; 24; 30(2); 23:7; 13(2); 14; 27; 37; 40; 43; 44; 45; 48; 49; 24:8(2); 11(3); 19; 21; 24(2); 25; 26(3); 27(2); 25:5; 7; 8; 10; 11; 12; 17; 26:1; 2(2); 6; 17(2); 18; 19; 20(3); 27:3; 7(2); 8; 27; 29; 28:3; 8; 9(2); 13; 14; 15; 17; 18; 19; 22; 23; 24(3); 25; 26(2); 29:3; 6; 9; 12(2); 15; 16; 18; 21(2); 30:5; 6; 7(2); 8; 9; 12; 19; 20; 22; 25; 26; 31:1; 9(2); 14(3); 16(2); 17(3); 18; 32:1; 15(3); 17; 18; 20; 21; 24; 25(2); 27; 28; 29(2); 30(2); 32; 33:5; 8; 11; 12(2); 13(2); 14; 15; 16(2); 19; 21(2); 22; 24; 27(3); 28; 29; 30; 32; 33; 34:2; 3; 4(4); 10; 12(2); 16(4); 19(2); 27(2); 30(2); 35:4; 5; 7(2); 8; 9; 12(2); 15; 36:3; 4(2); 7; 11; 18; 23; 28; 30; 31; 33; 34; 35; 36(4); 38; 37:6; 9; 13; 14; 25; 28; 38:7; 8; 10; 11(2); 12(3); 14; 16; 17; 18; 19; 20(3); 22; 23; 39:4; 6(2); 7; 9; 10(3); 11(2); 12; 13; 14; 15; 17(2); 21(2); 22(2); 23; 26; 28; 40:1; 4(3); 10(2); 12(2); 20; 21; 22; 24; 26; 34; 37; 39; 41; 47; 48(2); 49; 41:6; 9(2); 11(2); 12; 17; 18; 19; 22; 42:1; 7; 8; 12; 13; 43:1; 3(2); 8; 10; 11(2); 19; 27; 44:3; 5; 7; 9; 10; 14; 15; 17; 18; 22(2); 25; 27; 30; 31; 45:11; 13; 20(2); 22; 46:1; 2; 4; 8; 9(2); 12; 18; 20; 24; 47:2; 3; 5(2); 9(2); 10; 12; 22(2); 23; 48:9; 11; 12; 15; 18; 19; 22; 35; **Dan** 1:3; 5; 8(2); 13; 16; 18; 20(2); 2:8; 9; 10(2); 11(2); 13; 16(2); 18(2); 21; 25; 28; 29; 30(3); 34(2); 35(2); 40; 45(2); 46; 47; 3:3(2); 5(2); 7(2); 8; 10(2); 11; 15(3); 18; 19; 20; 22; 28(2); 29(2); 4:1; 2; 6; 9(2); 17(2); 19; 20; 22; 25(2); 26(2); 30; 32; 34; 37; 5:2; 3; 5; 6; 13; 14(2); 15; 16; 19; 21(2); 25; 29; 30; 6:2; 7; 8; 10; 12(2); 13(2); 15(2); 17; 22; 23; 25; 26(2); 7:7; 14(2); 16; 20(4); 22; 24; 8:1; 2; 4(2); 6; 7; 13; 21; 22; 9:2; 4(2); 7(3); 11(2); 12; 13; 15; 16; 17; 25; 26; 27; 10:7(2); 11; 12; 16; 21(2); 11:3; 6(3); 16; 24; 26; 30; 31; 32; 33; 36(2); 12:1(4); 2; 3(2); 5; 7(2); 11(2); 12; **Hos** 1:1; 5(2); 10; 2:3; 5(2); 6; 8; 12; 16(2); 18; 21; 23; 4:3; 4; 6; 14; 5:9; 10; 6:5; 8; 7:2; 7; 8:3; 4; 9:4; 10; 12; 10:5; 10; 11; 11:3; 4; 12:8; 9; 13:2; 3(2); 8; 10; 14:7; **Joel** 1:1; 4(3); 2:5; 11; 16; 17; 25; 26; 27(2); 28; 32; 3:1; 3; 6; 17; 18(2); 21; **Amos** 1:5; 8; 13; 2:7; 13; 15(3); 16(2); 3:1; 12; 14(2); 4:1; 2(2); 3; 13(2); 5:3(2); 8(2); 9(2); 10(2); 13; 14; 15; 18; 6:1; 3; 4; 5; 6; 7(2); 8; 9; 10(2); 7:2; 8:3; 4; 5(2); 6; 8; 9(2); 11; 13; 14; 9:1(3); 5(2); 6(2); 8; 11(2); 12(2); 13(2); **Obad** 3(2); 7(2); 8; 9; 11(2); 12; 14(2); 20; **Jonah** 1:2; 4; 5; 6(2); 7; 10; 11; 12; 2:8; 9(2); 3:2(2); 8; 9; 10(3); 4:2; 6; 7; 8(2); 11(2); **Mic** 1:1; 2; 4; 2:1; 4; 5; 6(2); 7(2); 8; 3:4; 5(3); 6(2); 9; 4:1; 6(4); 7(2); 11; 5:2; 3; 7; 10(2); 6:5; 10; 14; 16; 7:3; 5; 10; 11(2); 12; 13; 18; **Nah** 1:5; 7; 11; 14; 15(2); 2:1; 3:4; 7(2); 8(2); 19; **Hab** 1:3; 6(2); 8; 13(2); 14; 2:2(2); 6(3); 7(2); 8; 9(3); 12; 13; 15(3); 17; 18(2); 19; 3:8; 16; **Zeph** 1:5(4); 6(2); 8; 9; 10(2); 11; 12(4); 15; 17; 18; 2:5; 15(3); 3:1; 6(3); 8(2); 9; 11(2); 16; 18; 19(4); 20(2); **Hag** 1:2; 6; 9; 11; 2:3; 5; 13; 14; 18; 22; 23; **Zec** 1:8; 9; 10; 11; 13; 14; 15; 19; 21; 2:3; 7; 8; 9; 11(2); 3:2; 4; 7; 8; 9(2); 10; 4:1(2); 4; 5; 9; 14; 5:3(4); 4; 5(2); 6; 7; 10; 6:4; 7; 8; 15(2); 7:1; 11; 13; 14; 8:9(3); 10; 13; 16; 17; 20; 23(3); 9:7; 8(2); 12; 16; 11:1; 5; 9(4); 10; 11(3); 13; 14; 16(5); 17; 12:3(2); 4; 6; 7; 8(3); 9(3); 10; 11; 14; 13:1; 2(2); 3(3); 4(2); 7; 8; 14:4; 6(2); 7; 8(2); 9; 12; 13(2); 15; 16(2); 17; 18(2); 19; 20; 21(2); **Mal** 1:6; 7; 9; 10; 12; 13; 2:4(2); 12(2); 13; 15; 16(2); 17; 3:3; 5(2); 10(2); 14(2); 15(2); 16(3); 17(2); 18(2); 4:1(4); 2; 3; **Mt** 1:6; 20; 22; 2:2; 6; 8; 12; 15; 16(2); 17; 22; 23; 3:3; 9; 11; 4:3; 4; 12; 14; 17; 24(2); 5:4; 14; 15; 16; 17; 20; 21; 22; 23; 27; 28; 29(2); 30(2); 32(2); 33; 38; 39; 42(2); 43; 44(2); 45; 6:1; 2; 4; 5; 7; 16; 18; 23(2); 29; 32; 7:1; 3(2); 6; 8(3); 11; 12; 13; 14; 19; 21(2); 22; 23; 25; 26; 27; 8:4; 8; 10; 11; 16(2); 17; 24; 27; 28(2); 33; 34; 9:6(2); 12(3); 13; 16; 22; 26; 28; 30; 31; 38; 10:14; 15; 19; 20; 22; 25; 26(2); 27(2); 34; 37(2); 38; 39(2); 40(3); 41(2); 11:3; 8; 11(2); 15; 24; 25; 28; 12:1; 2; 3; 5; 6; 10; 11; 16; 17; 22; 30(2); 36(2); 45; 48; 13:2; 12; 17; 19; 20(2); 22(2); 23(2); 28; 32; 35; 37; 39; 41; 44(2); 46; 47; 52; 53; 54; 14:1; 15; 20; 21; 33; 35(3); 36; 15:4; 11(2); 12; 17; 28; 30; 31; 37; 38; 16:1; 11(3); 12; 13; 14; 15; 18; 20(2); 21(2); 23(2); 17:10; 12; 13; 18; 24; 27(2); 18:6(2); 7(2); 10(2); 11; 12; 13(2); 14; 16; 19(2); 25; 27; 28; 31; 32(2); 34; 19:1; 4; 12; 13; 16; 17; 21; 22; 23; 28; 29; 30; 20:1; 7; 9; 10; 14; 21; 22(2); 23; 25(2); 30; 32; 33; 21:4; 9(3); 12(2); 15; 31; 32; 34; 45; 22:3; 16; 21; 23; 31; 34; 46; 23:3; 11; 12; 13; 17; 18; 19; 21; 22(2); 26(2); 31; 35; 37; 39; 24:2; 4; 6; 13; 19(2); 20; 24; 32; 33; 36; 38(2); 43; 46; 47; 48; 50(2); 25:3; 9; 10; 16; 17; 18; 20; 22; 24; 25; 26; 29(3); 26:2; 4; 12; 13; 16; 17; 21; 23; 24(2); 29; 34; 41; 46; 48(2); 52; 53; 54; 55; 56; 57; 63; 68; 71; 73; 27:3; 4(3); 8; 9(2); 14; 15; 17; 18; 19; 20; 21; 24(2); 31; 33; 35; 39; 40; 46; 47(2); 54(2); 62; 63(2); 64; 28:5; 7; 10; 11; **Mk** 1:9; 14; 22; 27; 32(2); 34; 36; 38; 45; 2:1; 2; 8; 10(2); 12; 15; 16; 17(2); 21; 23; 24; 25; 3:2; 9; 10; 12; 14(2); 20; 24; 25; 29; 4:1; 8; 9; 10; 11; 12; 15; 22; 24; 25(3); 28; 31; 32; 37; 38; 40; 41; 5:4; 7; 10; 12; 14(2); 15; 16(2); 18(2); 23; 26; 29(2); 30; 32; 36; 38; 40; 43(2); 6:2; 5; 8; 10; 11; 12; 13; 14; 15(2); 20; 21; 22; 25; 36; 44; 55(2); 56; 7:2; 9; 11; 15(2); 18; 20(2); 26; 32; 34; 36; 8:8; 9; 21; 25; 27; 29; 30; 31; 32; 33(2); 9:1(2); 7; 9; 10; 11; 12; 13; 18; 23; 25; 26; 30; 31; 32; 33; 37; 39; 40; 42(2); 43; 45; 10:13(2); 17; 18; 22; 23; 24; 29; 31; 35; 36; 37; 38(2); 39(2); 42; 47; 48; 51(2); 11:3; 5; 9(3); 10; 15(2); 16; 23(2); 24; 25; 32; 12:2; 12; 14; 15; 17(2); 19; 26; 28; 34(2); 35; 41; 43; 44; 13:2; 11(3); 13; 14(2); 15; 16; 17(2); 18; 20; 24; 25; 28; 29; 30; 32(2); 14:4; 9; 12(2); 20; 21(2); 25(2); 28; 30; 35; 42; 44(2); 47; 58; 69; 70; 72; 15:5; 6; 7; 9; 10; 11; 12; 29(2); 32(2); 35; 39; 42; 16:1; 4; 7; 10; 11; 12; 16(2); 17; **Lk** 1:4; 7; 8; 19; 20; 21; 22; 23; 28; 35; 41; 43; 45; 49; 50; 57; 59; 61; 65; 66; 71(2); 74(2); 79; 2:1(2); 6(2); 18; 20; 23; 24; 26; 35; 38(2); 46; 47; 49(2); 3:7; 8; 11(3); 13; 20; 21; 4:3; 4; 6; 18; 20; 26; 29; 40; 41; 42; 5:1; 3; 7(2); 9; 17; 24(2); 25; 29; 31(2); 36; 6:1; 2; 4; 5; 6; 7; 12; 18; 21(2); 23; 24; 25(2); 28; 29(2); 30(2); 31; 32; 38; 40; 41(2); 42(3); 45(2); 48; 49(3); 7:3; 4; 6; 9; 10(2); 11; 14; 15; 16(2); 19; 20; 21(2); 22; 28(2); 29; 36; 37; 39; 43; 49(2); 8:1; 8; 10; 12; 14; 15; 16; 17(2); 18; 22; 31; 32; 34; 36; 38; 40; 41; 45; 46; 47; 53; 56; 9:5; 7(3); 8(2); 10; 11; 12; 17; 18; 19; 20; 21; 32(2); 37; 39; 45(2); 48(2); 50; 51; 54; 57; 10:2; 9; 11; 12(3); 16(4); 20; 21(2); 23; 24; 31; 36; 37; 38; 40(2); 42; 11:1; 4; 10(3); 11; 13; 18; 23(2); 26; 27; 28; 33; 35; 38; 40(3); 44; 48; 50; 52; 54; 12:1; 2(2); 3; 4(3); 9; 10; 13; 21; 26; 27; 30; 33(2); 36(2); 37; 39; 42; 43; 44(2); 45; 46; 47; 48; 51; 56; 58; 13:1(2); 2; 4(2); 9; 14; 17; 23; 32; 33; 34; 35; 14:1; 9; 10(3); 11; 12; 15(2); 17; 21; 23; 24; 29; 31; 33(2); 35; 15:4; 7(2); 10; 12; 14; 15; 16; 29; 31; 32; 16:1; 2; 4; 9; 10(3); 12(2); 15; 16; 18; 22; 24; 25; 26(2); 27; 28; 17:1; 2(2); 9(2); 10; 11; 12; 14; 15; 18; 24; 27; 29; 31(2); 34; 18:1; 3; 8; 9; 11; 12; 14(2); 15; 19; 22; 24(2); 26; 29; 31; 35; 37; 39; 41(2); 19:4; 7(2); 10; 11; 15(2); 21(2); 22(3); 23; 24(2); 26(3); 27; 32; 37; 38; 40; 43; 45(2); 20:1; 2; 6; 7; 10; 14; 17; 18; 19; 20(2); 21; 27; 28; 35; 37; 40; 41; 21:3; 4; 6; 8; 20; 21; 22; 23(2); 30; 31; 34; 35; 36(2); 37; 22:8; 9; 21; 22; 23; 25; 26(3); 27(4); 30; 31; 32; 34(2); 36(2); 37(2); 40; 47; 63; 64; 70; 23:2; 7(2); 14; 23; 24; 25; 26; 29; 48(2); 49; 53; 54; 24:10; 12; 13; 15; 16; 17; 21; 23(2); 25; 33; 37; 39; 44; 45; 47; **Jn** 1:3; 7; 8(2); 9(2); 12; 15; 21; 22(2); 25(2); 31; 33; 34; 39; 48; 2:9; 10; 14; 16; 17; 18; 22; 25; 3:2(2); 6(2); 7; 8; 11(2); 13; 15; 16(2); 17; 18(2); 19; 20; 21(3); 26; 28(2); 29; 31(3); 32; 33(2); 36(2); 4:1; 5; 9; 10; 11; 14(2); 15; 18; 19; 20; 24; 25; 26; 27; 29; 32; 34; 36(4); 37; 38; 39(2); 40; 42; 44; 45; 47(2); 50; 53; 54; 5:6(2); 10; 11; 12; 13(2); 15; 18; 20(2); 23(2); 24(2); 25; 28; 29(2); 32(2); 34; 36(3); 40; 42; 44; 45(2); 6:2; 5; 7; 11; 12(2); 13; 14(3); 15; 18; 22(4); 23; 24; 27; 28; 29; 30; 32; 35(2); 36; 37(2); 38; 39; 40(2); 42; 45; 46; 47; 48; 50; 51; 56; 57; 58(2); 61; 63(2); 64(2); 65; 66; 69(2); 71; 7:3(2); 4; 7; 16; 18(3); 23; 26; 28; 32; 33; 35; 36; 37; 38; 39(2); 42; 50; 8:5; 6; 7; 12; 16; 17; 18(2); 24(2); 25; 26; 27; 28(2); 29(2); 37; 38(2); 40; 47; 48; 50; 52; 54(2); 9:2; 3; 4; 8(2); 11; 13; 16; 17; 18(2); 20(2); 22(2); 24(2); 25; 29; 30; 31; 32(2); 35; 36; 37; 39(2); 10:1; 2; 8; 10(2); 12; 17; 21; 25; 33; 38(2); 41; 11:2; 4(2); 6; 7; 11(2); 13; 15; 16; 17; 20; 22; 24; 25; 27; 29; 30; 31; 37; 39; 40; 41; 42(3); 44; 49; 50(3); 51(3); 52(3); 53; 56; 57(2); 12:2; 6; 9(2); 10; 11; 12(2); 13; 16(2); 17; 18(2); 20; 23; 25(2); 29(2); 34; 35; 36; 38; 39; 40; 44(2); 45(2); 46; 48(3); 50; 13:1(2); 3(2); 5; 10; 15; 16(2); 18(2); 19(2); 20(3); 21; 24; 27; 29(3); 34(2); 35; 14:3; 9; 10(3); 11; 12(2); 13(2); 16; 20(2); 21(3); 22; 24; 29; 31(2); 15:2(3); 5; 8; 11(2); 12; 13; 15; 16(3); 17; 18; 20; 21; 23; 25(2); 16:1; 2(2); 4(2); 5; 7; 13; 15(2); 17; 18; 19(2); 20; 21; 23; 24; 26(2); 27; 30(3); 32; 33; 17:1; 2; 3; 7; 8(2); 11; 12(2); 13; 15(2); 19; 21(4); 22; 23(3); 24(2); 25; 26; 18:4; 8; 9; 13; 14(2); 15; 16(2); 17; 28; 32; 36; 37(3); 39(2); 19:4(2); 8; 10; 11; 13(2); 21; 24; 27(2); 28(2); 31(4); 33; 35(3); 36; 38; 20:3; 7; 8; 9; 14; 18(2); 29; 31(3); 21:3; 4; 7(2); 12; 14(2); 15; 16; 17; 20; 22(2); 23(4); 24; 25(2); **Acts** 1:1; 2; 4; 8; 16; 19(2); 21; 22(2); 25(2); 2:6; 14; 16; 20; 21; 24; 25; 29; 30(2); 31; 36(2); 39; 41; 44; 3:2; 10(2); 11; 17; 18; 19; 23(2); 24; 4:2; 5; 10; 13(2); 16(2); 17(2); 21; 23; 24(2); 29; 30; 32(2); 34(2); 5:5; 9; 15(2); 17; 21(2); 28; 32; 33; 40; 41; 6:2; 14; 15; 7:5; 6(2); 7; 12; 16; 19; 24; 25; 27; 36; 37; 38; 44(2); 45; 8:1; 4; 7(2); 8; 9; 11; 14; 15; 18; 19; 20; 23; 24; 26; 31; 37; 39; 9:2; 12; 14; 17(2); 20; 21(4); 22; 23; 26; 27; 35; 37; 38(2); 43; 10:2; 7; 14; 15; 22; 27; 28(3); 33(2); 34; 35; 37; 38; 42; 43; 45; 47; 11:1(2); 2; 9; 16; 17; 19; 22; 23; 26; 28; 12:1; 9; 10; 11; 15; 19; 13:1(2); 16; 20; 25; 27; 28; 29; 32; 33; 34; 38; 39; 40; 42; 46; 47; 14:1(2); 6; 9; 15(2); 17; 18; 21; 22; 27; 15:2; 4; 5; 7(2); 11; 17; 19; 20(2); 21; 24; 26; 29; 39; 16:2; 3; 4; 10; 12(2); 14; 19; 26; 27; 32; 38; 17:3(2); 6; 7; 11; 13; 15; 17; 22; 24(2); 27; 29; 31(2); 18:2; 5; 7; 14; 21; 28(2); 19:1; 4(2); 9; 10; 12; 16(2); 18; 22; 23; 25; 26(2); 27(2); 31; 34; 35(2); 36; 20:18; 20; 22; 23(2); 24; 25; 26; 29; 31; 34(2); 35; 38; 21:1; 4; 8; 11; 12; 21(2); 22; 23; 24(3); 25(2); 26; 28; 29; 31; 35; 38(2); 22:2; 6; 9(2); 11(2); 14(2); 17; 19(2); 20; 22; 24(2); 25(2); 26; 29; 23:2; 4; 5; 6; 8; 9; 12; 14; 15; 19; 20; 21; 22; 24; 27; 30; 34; 24:2(2); 4(2); 9; 10(2); 11(2); 14; 15; 21; 22; 23; 26(2); 25:3; 4(2); 16; 24; 25(2); 26; 26:5; 8; 9; 18(2); 20; 23(3); 26; 27; 29(2); 30; 27:1; 10; 13; 20; 24; 25; 27; 33; 43; 44; 28:1; 6; 8; 16; 17; 19; 20; 21; 22; 25; 28(2); 30; **Rom** 1:7; 8; 9; 11; 12(2); 13(2); 15; 16; 19; 20(2); 21; 26; 27(2); 32(2); 2:1(2); 2; 3(2); 4; 8; 9; 10; 18; 19; 21; 22(2); 23; 28; 29; 3:2; 4; 8(2); 9; 11(2); 12; 19(2); 22; 24; 25; 26; 28; 4:1; 4; 5(2); 9; 11(3); 12; 13; 16(3); 18(2); 21; 23; 24; 5:3; 8; 12; 14(2); 16; 20; 21; 6:1; 2; 3; 4; 6(3); 7; 8; 9; 10(2); 12; 13; 16; 17(2); 7:1(2); 3(2); 4(2); 6(2); 13(4); 14; 15(3); 16(2); 17(2); 18(3); 19(2); 20(3); 21; 24; 8:3; 4; 5(2); 8; 9; 11(3); 16; 17(2); 18; 22; 24; 25; 27; 28(2); 29; 32; 33; 34(3); 37; 38; 9:2; 3; 8; 11(2); 16(3); 17(2); 20(2); 23; 26; 30; 32; 10:1; 2; 4; 5; 6; 7; 8; 9(2); 12; 15; 19; 20(2); 11:7; 8(2); 10; 11; 19; 25(2); 31; 32; 12:1; 2(2); 3; 6; 7; 8(4); 9(2); 15(2); 13:1; 2; 3; 4(2); 8; 11(2); 14:1; 2; 3(3); 4; 6(4); 9; 13; 14(2); 18; 20; 22(2); 23; 15:1; 3; 4; 6; 8; 9; 12; 13; 14; 15; 16(2); 19; 21; 29; 30; 31(3); 32; 16:2(2); 5; 11; 18; 19; 25; **1Cor** 1:2(2); 5; 7; 8; 10(3); 11; 12; 14; 15; 18; 21(2); 26; 28; 29; 31(2); 2:5; 6(2); 9; 12(2); 15; 16; 3:7(3); 8(2); 11; 16(2); 18; 20; 4:2; 3; 4; 6(3); 7; 8; 9; 5:1(2); 2(2); 3; 5; 6; 7; 11; 12(2); 13(2); 6:2; 3(2); 5(2); 6; 8; 9; 15; 16; 17; 18(2); 19; 7:5(2); 7(2); 12; 13; 22(2); 25; 26(2); 29(2); 30(3); 31; 32(2); 33(2); 34(2); 35(3); 36; 37(2); 38(2); 40; 8:1; 2; 4(3); 5; 7; 9; 9:3; 9; 10(4); 13; 14; 15(2); 18(2); 19; 20(4); 21(3); 22(2); 23; 24(2); 25; 26; 27; 10:1(2); 4(3); 12; 13(2); 17; 19(2); 20(2); 25; 27; 28; 30; 33; 11:2; 3; 5(2); 13; 14; 17(2); 18; 19; 22; 23(2); 28(2); 29; 32; 34; 12:2; 3(3); 11; 12; 24; 25(2); 28; 13:2; 10(2); 14:1; 2; 3; 4(2); 5(5); 11(2); 12; 13(2); 16; 19; 21; 22(3); 23(2); 24; 25; 27; 30; 31; 37(2); 15:3(2); 4(2); 5; 6; 7; 9; 12(2); 15(2); 20; 23; 26; 27; 28(2); 36; 37(3); 46(3); 48(2); 50; 54; 58; 16:2; 4; 6(2); 10; 11; 15(2); 16(2); 17; 18; 19; **2Cor** 1:4; 7; 8(2); 9; 10; 11; 12; 14; 15; 17(2); 23; 24; 2:1; 2; 3; 4(2); 5; 7; 8; 9; 15(2); 3:5; 7; 10(2); 11(2); 12; 13(2); 17; 4:3; 7; 10; 11; 14; 15; 5:1; 3; 4(3); 5; 6; 9; 10(2); 12; 14; 15(2); 19; 21; 6:1; 3; 15; 7:3; 6(2); 7; 8; 9(3); 11; 12(3); 16; 8:2; 4; 6(2); 7; 9(2); 11(2); 12(2); 13; 14(3); 15(2); 19; 20; 9:2; 3; 4; 5(2); 8; 10; 10:2(2); 5; 7(2); 9; 11; 12; 15(2); 17; 18; 11:2; 3; 4; 7; 9; 12(3); 16; 17; 18; 28(2); 31; 12:4; 6(2); 8; 9; 13; 19; 20; 21; 13:2; 5; 6(2); 7(4); **Gal** 1:4; 6(2); 7; 8; 9; 11; 13; 16; 23; 2:2; 4(2); 5; 7; 8; 9(2); 10; 12; 13; 14; 16(2); 19; 3:1; 5; 7; 8; 10; 11; 12; 13; 14(2); 17(3); 22(2); 24; 25; 4:1; 5(2); 9; 15; 17; 21; 22; 27(2); 29(2); 5:2; 3(2); 7; 8; 10(2); 15; 17(2); 21; 24; 6:6(2); 7; 8(2); 13; 14; **Eph** 1:4; 10; 12; 13(3); 17; 18; 21(2); 23; 2:2; 7; 8; 10; 11(2); 12(2); 16; 17; 3:3; 6; 8; 10; 13; 16; 17(2); 19; 20(3); 4:1; 9(2); 10(3); 14; 16; 17; 18; 21; 22; 24; 28(3); 29(2); 5:5; 13; 14; 15; 26; 27(2); 28; 33; 6:3; 5; 8; 9; 11; 13; 19(2); 20; 21; 22(2); 24; **Phil** 1:6; 9; 10(3); 12; 13; 17; 19; 20(2); 25; 26; 27(2); 28; 2:2; 10; 11(2); 15; 16(2); 19; 22; 24; 25; 26(2); 28(2); 3:4; 8; 9; 10; 12(2); 18; 21; 4:2; 10; 11; 14; 15; 17; 22; **Col** 1:9; 10; 16(2); 18; 19; 21; 24; 28; 2:1; 2; 14; 3:9; 10; 24; 25; 4:1(2); 3; 4; 5; 6; 8; 12; 13(2); 16(2); 17; **1Th** 1:7(2); 8; 2:1; 2; 10; 12; 13; 16; 3:3(2); 4; 6; 10(2); 4:1; 3; 4; 6(2); 8; 9; 10; 11; 12(3); 13; 14; 15; 5:1;

2; 4(2); 7(2); 10; 14; 15(2); 21; 24; 27; **2Th** 1:3; 4(2); 5; 6; 8(2); 10(2); 11; 12; 2:2(2); 3(2); 4(4); 5; 6; 8; 10(2); 11; 12; 3:1; 2; 4; 6(2); 8; 10; 11; 12(2); 14(2); **1Ti** 1:3(2); 8; 9; 10(2); 12; 15; 16; 18; 20; 2:1; 2(2); 8; 9; 3:4; 13; 15; 4:1; 8(2); 10; 14; 15; 16; 5:3; 4; 5; 6; 7; 14; 16(3); 17; 18; 20(2); 21; 25; 6:1; 2; 5; 9; 14; 17(2); 18(2); 19; 20; **2Ti** 1:3; 4; 5(2); 6; 12(3); 14; 15; 18(2); 2:1; 2; 4(2); 6; 8; 10; 14; 15; 18; 19(2); 22; 23; 25; 26; 3:1; 3; 12; 15; 17; 4:8(2); 13; 16; 17(2); **Titus** 1:2; 5(2); 9; 13; 14; 15; 16; 2:2; 3; 4; 5; 8(3); 10; 11; 12; 13; 14; 3:4; 7; 8(2); 10; 11(2); 13; 14; 15(2); **Philem** 1:6; 8; 12; 13; 14; 15; 18; 21; 22; **Heb** 2:3; 6(2); 8(2); 9; 11; 14(3); 17; 18(2); 3:2; 4; 10; 16; 17; 18(2); 19; 4:2; 6; 10; 11; 13; 14(2); 16; 5:1; 2(2); 4; 5; 7(2); 9; 12; 13; 14; 6:7; 8; 9; 10; 11; 12; 18; 19; 7:2; 5(2); 6; 8(2); 11; 14; 15; 21; 25; 8:3; 4(2); 5; 7; 9; 10; 13(2); 9:4(2); 8; 9(2); 11; 15(2); 23; 25; 28; 10:2; 4; 9; 14; 15; 16; 20; 23; 26; 28; 30; 33; 34; 36; 37; 39; 11:3(2); 4; 5(2); 6(4); 13; 14(2); 15; 16; 17; 18; 19; 28; 31; 35; 40; 12:1; 2; 3; 10; 13; 17; 18(2); 19(2); 20; 21; 24(2); 25(4); 27(3); 13:3; 6; 9(2); 12; 15; 17(4); 19; 20(2); 21; 23; 24; **Jas** 1:3; 4; 5; 6; 7(2); 9; 10; 12(2); 18; 2:3; 5; 7; 11; 12; 13; 19; 20; 24; 3:1; 3; 6; 17; 18; 4:1; 3; 4; 5(2); 11; 12; 13; 14; 15(2); 17; 5:1; 11; 16; 17; 20; **1Pet** 1:4; 7(2); 10; 11; 12(2); 13; 18; 21(2); 22; 2:2; 3; 6; 9; 12; 14(2); 15; 21; 23; 24; 3:1; 3; 4; 7; 9(2); 10(2); 12; 13(2); 15(2); 16(2); 17; 18; 20; 4:1; 2; 4; 5; 6(2); 11; 13; 17(2); 19; 5:1; 4; 6; 9(2); 10; 12; 13; 14; **2Pet** 1:1; 3(2); 4(2); 8; 9(2); 14; 15; 19(2); 20; 2:1; 4; 6; 8; 10; 12; 13; 14; 17; 18; 22; 3:2; 3; 5; 6; 8; 9(2); 10; 11; 14(2); 15; 16; **1Jn** 1:1; 2; 3(2); 4; 5; 6; 8; 10; 2:1; 3; 4; 5; 6; 9; 10; 11(2); 13; 14; 15; 16; 17; 18(2); 19(2); 21; 22(3); 23; 24(2); 25; 26; 27; 28; 29(3); 3:1; 2; 3; 5; 7; 8(2); 10; 11(2); 12; 14(2); 15; 19; 22; 23; 24(2); 4:2(2); 3(4); 4(2); 6(2); 7; 8; 9(2); 10(2); 13; 14; 15; 16(2); 17; 18; 20; 21; 5:1(4); 2; 3; 4; 5(3); 6(2); 7; 8; 10(3); 11; 12(2); 13(4); 14(2); 15(3); 16(2); 18(3); 19; 20(4); **2Jn** 1; 4; 5(2); 6(2); 7; 8(2); 9; 11; 12; **3Jn** 2; 3; 4; 7; 8; 10; 11(4); 12; **Jude** 1; 3; 5(2); 15; 18; 24; **Rev** 1:2; 3(2); 5; 9; 12; 18; 2:1; 6; 7(2); 10; 11(2); 14; 15; 17(3); 20; 22; 23; 25; 26; 29; 3:1(3); 2; 5; 6; 7(4); 9; 10; 11(2); 12; 13; 15; 17; 18(4); 21; 22; 4:3; 9; 10(2); 5:1; 7; 12; 13(2); 14; 6:2; 4(3); 5; 8; 9; 10; 11(2); 16; 7:1; 15; 8:3; 9:4; 5(2); 17; 20; 10:6(4); 11:1; 6; 7; 10(2); 18(3); 12:6; 9; 12(2); 13; 14; 15; 13:6; 8; 10(2); 13; 14(3); 15(2); 17(2); 18; 14:3; 6; 7; 8; 12; 13; 15; 16; 18; 15:2; 5; 16:12; 14; 15; 17:1; 7; 8(3); 11; 14; 18; 18:4(2); 10(2); 14; 16(2); 19(2); 21; 24; 19:4; 5; 8; 10; 11; 12; 15; 17; 18(2); 19; 20(3); 21; 20:2; 3(2); 4; 6; 10; 11; 21:5; 6; 7; 10; 15; 17; 27; 22:7; 11(3); 14(2); 17(2); 18(2)

THE

3588

Gen 1:1(3); 2(6); 4(3); 5(5); 6(4); 7(5); 8(4); 9(3); 10(3); 11(4); 12(2); 13(3); 14(4); 15(3); 16(5); 17(3); 18(4); 19(3); 20(4); 21; 22(3); 23(3); 24(3); 25(3); 26(7); 27; 28(6); 29(4); 30(3); 31(3); 2:1(3); 2(2); 3; 4(7); 5(6); 6(3); 7(4); 8(2); 9(7); 10; 11(3); 12(2); 13(4); 14(4); 15(3); 16(3); 17(3); 18(2); 19(5); 20(3); 21(2); 22(3); 25; 3:1(5); 2(5); 3(4); 4(2); 5; 6(4); 7; 8(9); 9; 10; 11; 12(3); 13(4); 14(4); 15; 16; 17(4); 18(2); 19(2); 20; 21; 22(3); 23(3); 24(5); 4:1; 2; 3(3); 4(3); 6; 7; 8; 9; 10(2); 11; 12(2); 13; 14(3); 15(2); 16(4); 17(3); 19(4); 20; 21(2); 22; 26(2); 5:1(4); 2; 4; 5; 8; 11; 14; 17; 20; 23; 27; 29(2); 31; 6:1(2); 2(2); 3; 4(4); 5(3); 6(2); 7(6); 8(2); 9; 11(2); 12(2); 13(3); 14; 15(5); 16(4); 17(3); 18; 19; 20; 7:1(2); 2(2); 3(5); 4(3); 5; 6(2); 7(3); 8; 9(3); 10(3); 11(8); 12(2); 13(4); 14(2); 15(2); 16; 17(5); 18(5); 19(4); 20(2); 21(2); 22(2); 23(7); 24(2); 8:1(4); 2(4); 3(5); 4(5); 5(7); 6(3); 7(2); 8(3); 9(7); 10(2); 11(4); 12; 13(10); 14(4); 16; 17(3); 19(2); 20(2); 21(4); 22; 9:1; 2(7); 3; 4(2); 5(4); 6; 7; 10(5); 11(2); 12(2); 13(2); 14(3); 15; 16(4); 17(3); 18(3); 19(2); 21; 22(2); 23; 26; 27; 28; 29; 10:1(3); 2; 3; 4; 5(2); 6; 7(2); 8; 9(3); 10(2); 11; 12; 16(3); 17(3); 18(5); 19(2); 20; 21(4); 22; 23; 25(2); 29; 30; 31; 32(5); 11:1; 2(2); 4(2); 5(4); 6(2); 8(4); 9(7); 10(2); 27; 28(2); 29(5); 31(3); 32; 12:1; 3; 4; 5(3); 6(5); 7(2); 8(6); 9; 10(3); 12; 14(2); 15(2); 17; 13:1; 3(3); 4(5); 6; 7(5); 9(5); 10(5); 11(3); 12(3); 13(2); 14(2); 15; 16(4); 17(3); 18(2); 14:1; 2; 3(2); 4; 5(5); 6(2); 7(3); 8(7); 9; 10(3); 11; 13(3); 15; 16(3); 17(5); 18(2); 19; 20; 21(3); 22(4); 24(3); 15:1(2); 2; 4(2); 5; 6; 7(2); 10(2); 11(2); 12; 16(3); 17; 18(5); 19(3); 20(3); 21(4); 16:2(2); 3(2); 5; 7(5); 8; 9(2); 10(2); 11(3); 12; 13(2); 14; 17:1(2); 8(2); 11(2); 12; 14; 21; 23(3); 24; 25; 26; 27(3); 18:1(5); 2(2); 4; 6(2); 7; 8(2); 9; 10(2); 11; 13; 14(3); 16(2); 17; 18(2); 19(3); 20(2); 21; 22(2); 23(2); 24(3); 25(6); 26(3); 27; 28(2); 30; 31; 32; 33; 19:1(2); 2; 4(5); 5; 6(2); 8; 9(2); 10(3); 11(4); 12(2); 13(4); 14; 15(4); 16(5); 17(2); 19; 21; 22(2); 23(2); 24(2); 25(4); 27(3); 28(5); 29(6); 30; 31(5); 33; 34(3); 35; 36; 37(4); 38(4); 20:1; 3; 5; 6; 7; 8(2); 11; 12(2); 16; 18(3); 21:1(2); 2; 3; 8(2); 9(2); 10; 11; 12; 13(2); 14(3); 15(4); 16(2); 17(5); 18; 19(2); 20(2); 21(2); 22; 23(2); 28; 32(3); 33(3); 34; 22:2(2); 3(4); 4(2); 5(2); 6(3); 7(3); 9(4); 10; 11(2); 12; 13(2); 14(3); 15(3); 16; 17(5); 18(2); 21; 23:1(2); 2(2); 3; 5; 6; 7(3); 8; 9(2); 10(5); 11(4); 12(2); 13(4); 15; 16(4); 17(6); 18(3); 19(4); 20(3); 24:1; 3(6); 5(3); 7(2); 8; 9(2); 10(4); 11(4); 13(4); 14(2); 15; 16(2); 17; 20(2); 21(2); 22(2); 24(2); 26(2); 27(4); 28; 29(2); 30(6); 31(3); 32(4); 35; 37(2); 39; 40; 42; 43(2); 44(3); 45; 46; 47(3); 48(3); 49(2); 50(2); 51; 52(2); 53; 54(2); 55(2); 56; 57; 60(2); 61(3); 62(3); 63(3); 64; 65(3); 66; 25:3; 4(2); 6(3); 7(2); 8; 9(4); 10(2); 11(2); 12(2); 13(3); 16; 17(3); 18; 19; 20(4); 21(2); 22(2); 23(5); 25; 27(2); 29; 32; 26:1(4); 2(2); 3; 4(3); 7(4); 8; 10; 12(2); 13; 14; 15(3); 17; 18(5); 19; 20(4); 21; 22(3); 24(3); 25(2); 26; 28; 29(2); 31; 32(2); 33(2); 34(4); 27:2; 3; 5; 7; 9(2); 15; 16(4); 17(3); 20; 22(3); 27(4); 28(3); 30; 34; 39(3); 40; 41(2); 46(4); 28:1; 2(2); 4(2); 5(2); 6; 8; 9(3); 11(2); 12(3); 13(4); 14(8); 16; 17(2); 18(3); 19(3); 21; 22; 29:1(3); 2(3); 3(6); 5; 6; 7(2); 8(4); 10(5); 13; 14; 16(4); 20; 22(2); 23; 25; 26(2); 27; 31; 32; 33; 35; 30:2(2); 13; 14(2); 16(2); 17; 19; 24; 27; 30; 32(5); 33(2); 35(5); 36; 37(3); 38(5); 39(2); 40(6); 41(6); 42(3); 43; 31:1; 2; 3(2); 4; 5; 8(4); 9; 10(4); 11; 12(2); 13(3); 16; 18(2); 19; 20; 21(2); 22; 23; 24; 25(2); 26; 29(2); 33; 34(3); 35(2); 38; 39; 40(3); 42(4); 46; 48; 49; 53(4); 54(2); 55; 32:1; 2; 3(2); 6; 7(3); 8(2); 9; 10(3); 11(4); 12(2); 16; 17; 19(3); 20; 21(2); 22; 23; 24(2); 25(2); 26; 30(2); 31; 32(6); 33:1(2); 2; 3; 5(3); 6; 8; 10; 13(3); 14(2); 15(2); 17(2); 18(2); 19(2); 34:1(3); 2(3); 3(3); 5; 6; 7(3); 8; 10; 12; 13; 19(3); 20(2); 21(2); 22; 24(2); 25(4); 26(2); 27(3); 28(2); 29; 30(4); 35:1; 2; 3(2); 4(2); 5(3); 6(2); 7(2); 8; 12(2); 13; 14; 15(2); 17; 19; 20; 21; 22; 23; 24; 25; 26(2); 27; 28; 29; 36:1; 2(6); 5(2); 6(4); 7; 9(3); 10(5); 11; 12; 13(2); 14(3); 15(3); 16(3); 17(4); 18(3); 19; 20(3); 21(4); 22; 23; 24(4); 25(2); 26; 27; 28; 29(2); 30(2); 31(3); 32(2); 33; 34; 35(3); 37; 38; 39(4); 40(2); 43(4); 37:1(2); 2(5); 3; 5; 7; 8; 9(3); 10; 11; 13; 14(2); 15(2); 17; 22; 24; 27; 28(2); 29(2); 30; 31(3); 32; 35; 36(2); 38:7(3); 9(2); 10(2); 12(2); 14; 16; 17; 19; 20(4); 21(3); 22(2); 24; 25(2); 27; 28(2); 30; 39:1(3); 2(3); 3(2); 5(7); 6; 8; 11(3); 14; 17; 19; 20(3); 21(4); 22(5); 23(4); 40:1(3); 2(4); 3(5); 4(2); 5(5); 6; 7; 9; 10(2); 11(2); 12(2); 13; 15(3); 16(2); 17(3); 18(2); 19; 20(4); 21(2); 22; 23; 41:1(2); 2; 3(4); 4(2); 5; 6; 7(2); 8(3); 9; 10(3); 11; 12(2); 14; 17(2); 18; 19; 20(3); 21; 23; 24(3); 25; 26(3); 27(3); 28; 29; 30(4); 31(2); 32(2); 33; 34(4); 35(3); 36(5); 37(3); 38; 40; 41; 43(3); 44; 45(2); 46(2); 47(2); 48(8); 49(2); 50(2); 51(2); 52(3); 53(2); 54(3); 55(3); 56(7); 57; 42:5(3); 6(5); 7; 9(3); 12(2); 13(3); 15; 16; 18; 19(2); 21; 22; 25; 26; 27; 29; 30(4); 32(2); 33(4); 34; 35; 38(3); 43:1(2); 2; 3; 5; 6; 7(2); 8; 9; 11(3); 12(2); 13; 14; 15; 16; 17(3); 18(3); 19(3); 20; 21(2); 23; 24(2); 25; 26(3); 27; 32(4); 33(3); 44:1(2); 2(4); 3(2); 4(2); 8(2); 11; 12(3); 13; 14; 16(2); 17(2); 22; 24; 26; 28; 29; 30(2); 31(3); 32(2); 33(2); 34(2); 45:2(2); 6(3); 7; 8; 10; 12; 16; 17; 18(4); 19; 20(2); 21(3); 23(2); 24; 25; 26; 27(3); 46:1; 2(2); 3; 5(2); 6; 8(2); 9; 10(2); 11; 12(3); 13; 14; 15(2); 16; 17(2); 18; 19; 20(2); 21; 22(2); 23; 24; 25(2); 26(2); 27(3); 28; 31; 32; 34(2); 47:1(2); 4(4); 6(4); 9(8); 11(4); 13(5); 14(5); 15(4); 17(4); 18(2); 19; 20(4); 21(3); 22(3); 23(2); 24(3); 25; 26(4); 27(2); 28(2); 29; 31; 48:2; 3; 5; 6; 7(4); 10; 12; 14(2); 15; 16(5); 17; 18; 21; 22(2); 49:1; 3(3); 8; 9; 10(3); 11(3); 13(2); 15; 16; 17(3); 19; 22; 23; 24(5); 25(5); 26(7); 27(3); 28; 29(3); 30(5); 32(4); 33(2); 50:2(2); 3(2); 4(3); 5; 7(4); 8(2); 10; 11(7); 13(5); 15; 17(4); 19; 23(3); 24; 25; **Ex** 1:1(2); 5(2); 7(2); 9(2); 10; 12(3); 13(2); 14; 15(6); 16(3); 17(3); 18(3); 19(4); 20(2); 21; 22; 2:1; 2; 3(3); 5(5); 6(3); 7(2); 8(2); 9(2); 10(2); 12(2); 13(3); 14; 15(2); 16(2); 17; 19(3); 20; 21; 23(4); 25; 3:1(6); 2(5); 3; 4(3); 5; 6(4); 7(2); 8(9); 9(4); 10; 11; 12; 13(2); 14; 15(5); 16(3); 17(8); 18(6); 19; 20; 21(2); 22; 4:1; 2; 3(2); 4(2); 5(4); 6; 8(4); 9(6); 10; 11(5); 13; 14(3); 16; 19(2); 20(2); 21(2); 22; 24(3); 25; 26; 27(3); 28(3); 29(2); 30(5); 31(3); 5:1(2); 2(2); 3(5); 4(2); 5(2); 6(3); 7; 8(2); 9; 10(3); 12(2); 13; 14(2); 15(2); 16; 17; 18; 19(2); 20; 21(3); 22; 6:1; 2; 3; 4(2); 5(3); 6(4); 7(3); 8(3); 9; 10; 11; 12(2); 13(4); 14(4); 15(3); 16(4); 17; 18(3); 19(2); 20(2); 21; 22; 24(3); 25(4); 26(3); 27; 28(3); 29(2); 30; 7:1; 2; 3; 4(2); 5(3); 6; 8; 10; 11(3); 13; 14(2); 15(4); 16(3); 17(5); 18(6); 19(3); 20(8); 21(7); 22(2); 24(4); 25(2); 8:1(2); 3(2); 4; 5(5); 6(3); 7(2); 8(4); 9(2); 10; 11(2); 12(2); 13(6); 14; 15; 16(4); 17(5); 18; 19(3); 20(4); 21(3); 22(5); 24(5); 25; 26(5); 27(2); 28(2); 29(4); 30; 31(3); 32; 9:1(3); 3(8); 4(4); 5(3); 6(5); 7(4); 8(4); 9(2); 10; 11(5); 12(3); 13(4); 14; 15; 16; 18; 19(3); 20(4); 21(3); 22(4); 23(5); 24(2); 25(6); 26(2); 27; 28; 29(5); 30; 31(5); 32(2); 33(5); 34(3); 35(3); 10:1(2); 2(2); 3(2); 4; 5(6); 6(5); 7(2); 8; 9; 10; 11; 12(6); 13(5); 14(3); 15(11); 16; 17; 18; 19(4); 20(2); 21(2); 22; 23; 24; 25; 26(2); 27; 11:1; 2(2); 3(9); 4(2); 5(7); 6; 7(3); 8; 9(2); 10(2); 12:1(2); 2(3); 3(3); 4(5); 5(3); 6(5); 7(4); 8; 9; 10(2); 11; 12(5); 13(5); 14; 15(3); 16(2); 17(2); 18(5); 19(2); 21(2); 22(8); 23(8); 25(2); 27(7); 28(2); 29(8); 30(2); 31(2); 33(3); 34; 35(3); 36(5); 37; 39; 40(2); 41(6); 42(4); 43(3); 46(2); 47; 48(3); 49; 50(2); 51(4); 13:1; 2(3); 3(3); 4; 5(7); 6(2); 8; 9(2); 11(3); 12(4); 13; 14(2); 15(8); 16; 17(5); 18(6); 19(2); 20(2); 21(2); 22(4); 14:1; 2(3); 3(3); 4(2); 5(4); 7; 8(4); 9(3); 10(4); 11; 12(4); 13(4); 14; 15(2); 16(4); 17(2); 18(2); 19(4); 20(6); 21(5); 22(5); 23(3); 24(8); 25(4); 26(4); 27(8); 28(5); 29(4); 30(5); 31(5); 15:1(5); 2; 3(2); 4(2); 5(2); 6; 7; 8(6); 9(2); 10(2); 11; 12; 13; 14(2); 15(3); 16(2); 17(3); 18; 19(8); 20(3); 21(3); 22(3); 23(2); 24; 25(4); 26(4); 27; 16:1(6); 2(3); 3(6); 4(2); 5; 6(3); 7(4); 8(6); 9(3); 10(6); 11; 12(4); 13(5); 14(5); 15(3); 16(3); 17; 19; 20; 21; 22(3); 23(5); 24; 25(2); 26(2); 27(2); 28; 29(5); 30(2); 31(3); 32(5); 33; 34(2); 35(3); 36; 17:1(6); 2(2); 3(2); 4; 5(4); 6(5); 7(6); 9(3); 10(2); 12(6); 13(2); 14(3); 15; 16(2); 18:1(2); 3(2); 4(4); 5(2); 7; 8(5); 9(4); 10(7); 11(2); 12; 13(5); 14(3); 15; 16; 17; 19(2); 20(2); 21; 22(2); 24; 25; 26(2); 19:1(5); 2(3); 3(4); 4; 5; 6(2); 7(3); 8(5); 9(5); 10(2); 11(5); 12(4); 13(2); 14(3); 15(2); 16(7); 17(4); 18(4); 19(2); 20(6); 21(3); 22(3); 23(3); 24(4); 25; 20:2(3); 4(3); 5(5); 7(3); 8; 10(3); 11(5); 12(2); 18(7); 20; 21(2); 22(2); 21:1; 2; 4; 5; 6(3); 7; 9; 19; 22(2); 26(2); 28(3); 29(2); 30; 32(2); 34(4); 35(3); 36(2); 22:3; 4; 5(2); 6(4); 7(2); 8(4); 9(3); 11(2); 12; 14; 15; 17; 20; 21; 24; 26; 28(2); 29(2); 30; 31(2); 23:1; 5; 6; 7(2); 8(4); 9(2); 10; 11(4); 12(3); 13; 14; 15(3); 16(7); 17(2); 18(3); 19(4); 20(2); 23(6); 25(2); 26; 27; 28(3); 29(3); 30; 31(7); 24:1(2); 2(2); 3(7); 4(5); 5(2); 6(3); 7(5); 8(5); 9; 10(2); 11(2); 12(2); 13; 14; 15(2); 16(6); 17(7); 18(4); 25:1; 2; 3; 6; 7(2); 9(4); 10(3); 12(3); 14(5); 15(3); 16(2); 17(2); 18(2); 19(6); 20(5); 21(4); 22(5); 23(3); 25; 26(3); 27(4); 28(2); 29; 30; 31(2); 32(5); 33(3); 34; 35(5); 36; 37(2); 38(2); 40; 26:1; 2(3); 3; 4(7); 5(6); 6(2); 7; 8(3); 9(3); 10(6); 11(3); 12(6); 13(7); 14; 15; 16(2); 17(2); 18(3); 19; 20(3); 22(2); 23(3); 24(2); 26(3); 27(7); 28(3); 29(3); 30(3); 32; 33(8); 34(4); 35(9); 36(2); 37; 27:1(2); 2(3); 3; 4(2); 5(5); 6; 7(5); 8; 9(4); 10(3); 11(3); 12(3); 13(3); 14(2); 15; 16(2); 17(2); 18(4); 19(6); 20(3); 21(7); 28:1(2); 3(2); 4(2); 6; 7(2); 8(4); 9(2); 10(3); 11(5); 12(5); 14(3); 15(3); 16(2); 17(2); 18; 19; 20; 21(5); 22(2); 23(4); 24(4); 25(5); 26(5); 27(6); 28(8); 29(5); 30(7); 31(2); 32(4); 33(2); 34(2); 35(2); 36(2); 37(3); 38(4); 39(3); 41; 42(2); 43(4); 29:1(2); 3(3); 4(3); 5(8); 6(3); 7; 9(2); 10(4); 11(5); 12(7); 13(7); 14(3); 15(2); 16(2); 17(2); 18(4); 19(3); 20(9); 21(4); 22(10); 23(3); 24(3); 25(3); 26(3); 27(6); 28(4); 29; 30(3); 31(3); 32(7); 33; 34(5); 36; 37(2); 38(2); 39(3); 40(3); 41(5); 42(4); 43(2); 44(4); 45; 46(3); 30:2(5); 3(3); 4(4); 5; 6(5); 7; 8(2); 10(5); 11; 12(3); 13(4); 14; 15(3); 16(7); 17; 18(3); 20(4); 22; 24(2); 25(2); 26(4); 27(3); 28(2); 30; 31; 32; 34; 35(2); 36(3); 37(3); 31:1; 2(3); 3; 6(3); 7(7); 8(3); 9(2); 10(5); 11(2); 12; 13(2); 14; 15(4); 16(3); 17(3); 18; 32:1(5); 2(2); 3(2); 4; 5; 6(2); 7(2); 8(2); 9; 11(2); 12(4); 13; 14(2); 15(6); 16(5); 17(3); 18(3); 19(5); 20(4); 22(2); 23(2); 24; 25; 26(4); 27(2); 28(3); 29; 30(3); 31; 33; 34(3); 35(3); 33:1(4); 2(6); 3(2); 4; 5(3); 6(2); 7(9); 8(3); 9(5); 10(4); 11(4); 12; 16(3); 17; 19(2); 21; 22; 34:1(4); 2(4); 3(2); 4(4); 5(4); 6(3); 7(7); 8; 10(4); 11(6); 12(3); 14; 15(2); 18(4); 19; 20(2); 21; 22(4); 23(3); 24(3); 25(5); 26(4); 27(2); 28(5); 29(3); 30(2); 31(2); 32(2); 34(3); 35(4); 35:1(4); 2(2); 3; 4(4); 5(2); 8(2); 9(2); 10; 11; 12(5); 13(2); 14(4); 15(7); 16(2); 17(5); 18(4); 19(6); 20(3); 21(5); 22; 24(2); 25; 26; 27(3); 28(3); 29(4); 30(5); 31; 33; 34(2); 35(4); 36:1(4); 2(2); 3(5); 4(3); 5(4); 6(4); 7(2); 8(2); 9(3); 10(2); 11(6); 12(5); 13(2); 14(2); 15(3); 17(6); 18; 19; 20; 21(2); 22(2); 23(2); 24; 25(3); 27(2); 28(3); 29(2); 31(3); 32(6); 33(4); 34(3); 37; 38; 37:1(4); 3(3); 5(5); 6(3); 7(2); 8(5); 9(5); 10(4); 12; 13(3); 14(5); 15(2); 16(2); 17(3); 18(5); 19(3); 20; 21(4); 22; 24; 25(6); 26(3); 27(4); 28; 29(4); 38:1(4); 2(4); 3(8); 4(3); 5(3); 6; 7(5); 8(7); 9(4); 10(2); 11(4); 12(3); 13; 14(3); 15(2); 16(2); 17(7); 18(8); 19; 20(3); 21(8); 22(4); 23; 24(8); 25(4); 26(2); 27(6); 28(2); 29(2); 30(8); 31(8); 39:1(4); 2; 3(5); 4; 5(4); 6(2); 7(4); 8(3); 9(3); 10(2); 11; 12; 13; 14(5); 15(2); 16(3); 17(4); 18(5); 19(5); 20(6); 21(8); 22(2); 23(4); 24(2); 25(5); 26(3); 29; 30(4); 31(2); 32(6); 33(2); 34(4); 35(4); 36(3); 37(5); 38(5); 39(2); 40(9); 41(5); 42(3); 43(2); 40:1; 2(5); 3(4); 4(4); 5(7); 6(6); 7(4); 8(3); 9(3); 10(3); 11; 12(3); 13(2); 15; 16; 17(5); 18(3); 19(5); 20(6); 21(7); 22(6); 23(3); 24(6); 25(3); 26(4); 27; 28(3); 29(8); 30(4); 32(4); 33(6); 34(5); 35(6); 36(3); 37(2); 38(5); **Lev** 1:1(3); 2(5); 3(5); 4(2); 5(9); 6; 7(5); 8(7); 9(3); 10(3); 11(5); 12(4); 13(5); 14(2); 15(6); 16(4); 17(6); 2:1; 2(8); 3(4); 4; 7; 8(4); 9(4); 10(3); 11(2); 12(4); 13(2); 14(3); 16(6); 3:1(2); 2(7); 3(7); 4(6); 5(5); 6(2); 7; 8(5); 9(10); 10(6); 11(5); 12; 13(6); 14(5); 15(6); 16(6); 4:1; 2(3); 3(4); 4(8); 5(4); 6(6); 7(15); 8(7); 9(6); 10(5); 11(2); 12(5); 13(6); 14(5); 15(7); 16(4); 17(4); 18(13); 19; 20(3); 21(4); 22(2); 23; 24(5); 25(7); 26(4); 27(3); 28; 29(5); 30(7); 31(7); 33(4); 34(8); 35(10); 5:1; 2; 3; 6(4); 7(2); 8(2); 9(8); 10(3); 11; 12(5); 13(3); 14; 15(6); 16(7); 17(2); 18(3); 19; 6:1; 2; 4(2); 5(3); 6(3); 7(2); 8; 9(8); 10(6); 11(2); 12(6); 13(2); 14(5); 15(8); 16(5); 17(2); 18(4); 19; 20(5); 21(3); 22(2); 23; 24; 25(6); 26(5); 27(3); 28; 29(2); 30(5); 7:1(2); 2(5); 3(4); 4(6); 5(3); 6(2); 7(3); 8(4); 9(5); 10; 11(3); 12; 13(2); 14(5); 15(4); 16(4); 17(4); 18(4); 19(2); 20(4); 21(5); 22; 23; 24(3); 25(4); 28; 29(5); 30(6); 31(4); 32(3); 33(5); 34(6); 35(8); 36(3); 37(8); 38(5); 8:1; 2(3); 3(4); 4(5); 5(3); 7(6); 8(4); 9(5); 10(2); 11(3); 12; 13; 14(5); 15(7); 16(6); 17(3); 18(4); 19(2); 20(4); 21(6); 22(4); 23(4); 24(6); 25(8); 26(4); 27; 28(3); 29(4); 30(3); 31(6); 32(2); 33(4); 34; 35(5); 36(2); 9:1(2); 2; 3(3); 4(2); 5(4); 6(4); 7(5); 8(3); 9(8); 10(7); 11(3); 12(3); 13(4); 14(4); 15(5); 16(2); 17(4); 18(5); 19(8); 20(4); 21(3); 22(3); 23(6); 24(5); 10:1(2); 2(2); 3(2); 4(4); 5; 6(4); 7(6); 8; 9(2); 11(4); 12(4); 13(3); 14(3); 15(6); 16(3); 17(5); 18(3); 19(4); 11:1; 2(4); 3(3); 4(5); 5(3); 6(3); 7(3); 9(4); 10(4); 12; 13(4); 14(2); 16(4); 17(3); 18(3); 19(4); 21; 22(4); 24(2); 25(2); 26(3); 27; 28(2); 29(5); 30(5); 31; 32; 38; 39(2); 40(4); 41; 42(2); 44(2); 45(2); 46(5); 47(4); 12:1; 2(3); 3(2); 4(3); 5; 6(6); 7(3); 8(4); 13:1; 2(5); 3(9); 4(6); 5(6); 6(6); 7(4); 8(4); 9(2); 10(5); 11(2); 12(5);

13(3); 15(3); 16(2); 17(4); 18(2); 19(3); 20(5); 21(3); 22(2); 23(2); 24(2); 25(7); 26(4); 27(5); 28(5); 29(2); 30(5); 31(7); 32(6); 33(3); 34(7); 35(2); 36(4); 37(3); 38; 39(4); 40; 41; 42; 43(6); 44; 45(2); 46(3); 47(2); 48; 49(6); 50(3); 51(7); 52(2); 53(5); 54(3); 55(5); 56(7); 57(4); 58(3); 59(3); 14:1; 2(4); 3(5); 4; 5(2); 6(8); 7(3); 8; 9; 10(2); 11(6); 12(3); 13(8); 14(8); 15(3); 16(4); 17(9); 18(6); 19(3); 20(5); 22(2); 23(6); 24(6); 25(9); 26(3); 27(3); 28(9); 29(5); 30(3); 31(5); 32(2); 33; 34(3); 35(3); 36(7); 37(5); 38(5); 39(5); 40(4); 41(3); 42(2); 43(4); 44(4); 45(6); 46(3); 47(2); 48(7); 49; 50(2); 51(8); 52(8); 53(4); 54; 55; 57; 15:1; 2; 4; 5; 6(2); 7(3); 8(2); 9; 10(2); 11(2); 12(2); 14(6); 15(5); 16; 17(2); 18(2); 19; 21; 22; 23; 24; 25(5); 26(3); 27; 29(5); 30(6); 31; 32; 33(2); 16:1(4); 2(7); 3; 4(3); 5(3); 6; 7(5); 8(4); 9(2); 10(5); 11(4); 12(3); 13(7); 14(5); 15(8); 16(6); 17(4); 18(8); 19(3); 20(5); 21(8); 22(3); 23(4); 24(4); 25(3); 26(3); 27(7); 28; 29(3); 30(2); 32(5); 33(7); 34(2); 17:1; 2(3); 3(3); 4(6); 5(9); 6(9); 8(2); 9(4); 10(2); 11(6); 12; 13(3); 14(7); 15; 18:1; 2(2); 3(4); 4; 5; 6; 7(2); 8; 9(2); 10; 11; 12; 13; 14; 15; 16; 17; 18; 21(3); 24; 25(3); 27(3); 28(2); 29; 30; 19:1; 2(3); 3; 4; 5; 6(4); 7; 8(2); 9(3); 10(2); 12(2); 13(2); 14(3); 15(4); 16(2); 18(2); 21(4); 22(5); 23(2); 24(3); 25(4); 26; 27(2); 28(2); 29(2); 30; 31; 32(4); 34(3); 36(2); 37; 20:1; 2(5); 4(3); 6; 7; 8; 10(3); 11; 15; 16(2); 17; 18; 19; 22; 23(2); 24(5); 25; 26; 21:1(4); 5; 6(4); 8(2); 9(2); 10(3); 12(5); 15; 16; 17; 21(5); 22(3); 23(3); 24; 22:1; 2(3); 3(4); 4(2); 6(2); 7(2); 8(2); 9(6); 10(3); 11; 12(3); 13; 14(2); 15; 16(2); 17; 18(4); 19(3); 21; 22(3); 24; 25; 26; 27(3); 29; 30(3); 31; 32(2); 33(2); 23:1; 2(3); 3(4); 4(2); 5(3); 6(4); 7; 8(2); 9; 10(5); 11(5); 12(3); 13(4); 14; 15(5); 16(3); 17(2); 18(4); 19(2); 20(7); 21; 22(5); 23; 24(4); 25; 26; 27(2); 28; 30; 32(2); 33; 34(4); 35; 36(3); 37(3); 38(3); 39(7); 40(5); 41(3); 43(3); 44; 24:1; 2(3); 3(7; 4(3); 6(2); 7(2); 8(2); 9(3); 10(4); 11(5); 12(2); 13; 14(2); 15; 16(7); 22(2); 23(4); 25:1; 2(4); 3; 4(3); 5(2); 6(2); 7(2); 8(2); 9(6; 10(3); 11; 12(3); 13; 15(4); 16(7); 17; 18; 19; 20; 21; 22(3); 23(2); 24(2); 26; 27(4); 28(3); 30(4); 31(5); 32(5); 33(8); 34(4); 38(3); 40; 41; 42; 44; 45(2); 46; 27(1; 2(3); 3(3); 5(2); 6(2); 7(2); 8(2); 9(2); 10; 11(3); 12(2); 14(3); 15(2); 16(2); 17; 18(6); 19(3); 20(2); 21(5); 22(2); 23(5); 24(5); 25(3); 26(4); 28(3); 30(8); 31; 32(6); 33; 34(3); **Num** 1:1(8); 2(5); 4; 5(4); 6; 7; 8; 9; 10(3); 11; 12; 13; 14; 15; 16(3); 18(6); 19(2); 20(4); 21; 22(4); 23; 24(4); 25; 26(4); 27; 28(4); 29; 30(4); 31; 32(5); 33; 34(4); 35; 36(4); 37; 38(4); 39; 40(4); 41; 42(4); 43; 44(2); 45(2); 47(2); 48; 49(6); 50(6); 51(5); 52; 53(7); 54(2); 2:1; 2(4); 3(7); 5(3); 7(3); 9; 10(6); 12(4); 14(4); 16(4); 17(6); 18(6); 20(4); 22(4); 24(2); 25(6); 27(4); 28(6); 31; 32(3); 33(3); 34(3); 3:1(3); 2(3); 3(4); 4(5); 5; 6(2); 7(6); 8; 9; 10; 11; 12(3); 13(6); 14(6); 15(2); 16(2); 17; 18(2); 19; 20(4); 21(6); 22(2); 23(3); 24(5); 25(11); 26(9); 27(10); 28(4); 29(4); 30(6); 31(8); 32(7); 33(5); 34(2); 35(7); 36(8); 37(2); 38(9); 39(4); 40(5); 41(9); 42(3); 43(2); 44; 45(7); 46(4); 47(4); 48(2); 49(2); 50(5); 51(4); 4:1; 2(4); 3(4); 4(5); 5; 6(2); 7(5); 8(2); 9(3); 10; 11(2); 12(2); 13(2); 14(8); 15(9); 16(12); 17; 18(4); 19; 20; 21; 22(3); 23(4); 24(3); 25(4); 26(9); 27(4); 28(8); 29(2); 30(4); 31(7); 32(4); 33(8); 34(5); 35(4); 37(7; 38(2); 39(4); 40; 41(6); 42(3); 43; 44(3); 45(5); 46(4); 47(6; 48(2); 49(2); 50(5); 51(4); 4:1; 2(4); 3(4); 4(5); 5; 6(2); 7(5); 8(2); 9; 10; 11; 12; 13; 14(2); 15(9); 16(12); 17; 18(4); 19; 20; 21; 22(3); 23(4); 24(3); 25(4); 26(9); 27(4); 28(8); 29(2); 30(4); 31(7); 32(4); 33(8); 34(5); 35(4); 37(7; 38(2); 39(4); 40; 41(6); 42(3); 43; 44(3); 45(5); 46(4); 47(6; 5:1; 2(3); 3(2); 4(4); 5; 6(2); 7(2); 8(7); 9(3); 10; 11(2); 12(2); 13(2); 14(8); 15(9); 16(12); 17(18); 18; 20; 21; 22(3); 23(4); 24(3); 26(3); 28(8); 29(2); 30(4); 31(7); 32(4); 33(8); 34(5); 35(4); 37(7; 38(2); 39(4); 40; 41(6); 42(3); 43; 44(3); 45(5); 46(4); 47(6; 6:1; 2(3); 3(2); 4(4); 5; 6(2); 7(2); 8; 9; 10(3); 11; 12; 13; 14(2); 15(2); 16(2); 17; 18(2); 19; 20(4); 21(6); 22(2); 23(3); 24(5); 25(11); 26(9); 27(10); 28(4); 29(4); 30(6); 31(8); 32(7); 33(5); 34(2); 35(7); 36(8); 37(2); 38(9); 39(4); 40(5); 41(9); 42(3); 43(2); 44; 45(7); 46(4); 47(4); 48(2); 49(2); 50(5); 51(4); 7:1; 2(3); 3(2); 4(4); 5(7); 6(2); 7; 8(2); 9(3); 10; 11(2); 12(2); 13; 14(2); 15(9); 16; 17(2); 18; 19(2); 20; 21; 22; 23; 24; 25; 26; 27; 28; 29(3); 30:1; 2; 3; 34; 35(3); 36(3); 37(3); 39; 40; 41(3); 42(3); 43(3); 43; 45(7); 46(4); 47(4); 48(2); 49(2); 50(5); 51(4); 8(3); 9(3); 10; 11; 12; 14; 15; 16(2); 17; 18; 20; 21(3); 22(4); 23(3); 24; 25(5); 26; 27(4); 28(4); 30(4); 31; 6:1; 2; 3; 4(4); 5(7); 6(2); 7; 8(2); 9(3); 10; 11(2); 12(2); 13; 14(2); 15(9); 16; 17(2); 18; 19(2); 20; 21; 22; 23; 24; 25; 26; 27; 28; 29(3); 30:1; 2; 3; 34; 35(3); 36(3); 37(3); 39; 40; 41(3); 42(3); 43(3); 43; 45(7); 46(4); 47(4); 48(2); 49(2); 50(5); 51(4);

13(2); 14; 15(4); 16; 17; 18(2); 19(3); 20(3); 21(2); 22; 23(4); 24(6); 25(5); 26(4); 27; 28(3); 29(2); 30(4); 31(2); 32(3); 33; 35(4); 36(3); 37; 38(4); 39(2); 41(3); 16:15(2); 2(3); 3(4); 5; 7(3); 9(6); 10(2); 11; 12; 13; 14; 15; 16; 17; 18(3); 19(7); 20; 22(3); 23; 24(2); 25; 26(2); 27(2); 28; 29(3); 30(4); 31; 32(2); 33(3); 34(2); 35(2); 36(3); 37(5); 38(4); 39(3); 40(5); 41(6); 42(6); 43(2); 44; 46(4); 47(5); 48(3); 49(2); 50(4); 17:1; 2(3); 3(3); 4(5); 6(2); 7(3); 8(4); 9(3); 11; 12; 13(2); 18:1(4); 2; 3(5); 4(5); 5(5); 6(6); 7(3); 8(5); 9(2); 10; 11(3); 12(2); 13(2); 14(7); 15; 18:1(2); 2(3); 4; 5; 6; 7; 8(2); 9(4); 11; 13(3); 14(7); 15(2); 16(2); 17(7; 18; 19(2); 22(2); 23(3); 24(3); 27(3); 28(3); 29(2); 21:1(4); 2; 3(3); 8; 9(5); 10(5); 12; 13; 14; 24:1(3; 25:1; 2(4); 3(4); 4(6); 5(6); 6; 7(4); 8(2); 10; 11(2); 12; 13(3); 14; 16; 18(3); 19; 20(2); 21(2); 22:3(2); 23(9); 24(3); 25(5); 26(4); 27(3); 29; 31(2); 32(3); 33(3); 34(3); 35(5); 36(2); 38; 40; 41(4); 23:3; 5; 6; 7(3); 8; 9(5); 10(5); 12; 13; 14(2); 15; 16; 17(2); 19; 21(2); 22; 24(4); 26; 28; 24:1(2); 2; 3(2); 4(3); 6(5); 7; 8(2); 9(2); 11; 13(3); 14; 15(2); 16(5); 17(2); 19; 20(2); 21; 22; 24; 25:1(2); 2(3); 3(4); 4(7; 5; 6(8); 7(4); 8(6); 9; 10; 11(3); 13(3; 14(5); 15(3); 16; 17; 18(5); 26:14(2; 3); 4(2); 4(5); 5(6); 6(4); 7(2); 8; 9(4); 10(2); 11; 12(7); 13(4); 14(2; 15(7; 16(4); 17(4); 18(2); 19(2); 20(7); 21(5); 22; 23(4; 24(4); 25; 26(7); 27(2); 28; 29(5); 30(5); 31(4); 32(4); 33(3); 34; 35(7); 36(3); 37(3); 38(7; 39(4); 40(5); 41; 42(4); 44(7); 45(5); 46(2); 47(2); 48(5); 49(4); 50; 51(2); 52; 53(2); 54(2); 55:1; 56(2; 57(7); 58(12); 59(2); 61; 62(2); 63(3); 64(3); 65(4); 27:1(8; 2(6); 3(4); 4(2); 5; 6; 7(2); 8; 11(2); 12(3); 14(6); 15; 16(4); 17(2); 18(3); 19(2); 20(2); 21(5); 22(3); 23(2); 28:1; 2; 3(3); 4(3); 5; 6; 7(2); 29; 30; 31; 29:1(4; 2(2); 4; 5; 6(4); 7; 8(2); 10; 11(2); 13(2); 14(2); 15; 16(2); 17; 18(3); 19(5); 20(2); 21(5); 22(2); 23(3); 24(4); 25(2); 26(2); 36(2); 37(4); 38; 39; 40(2); 30:1(5; 2; 3; 5(2); 7; 8(2); 13(3); 14(2); 15; 16; 17(3); 18; 19(2); 21(2); 22(3); 24(4); 25(2); 26(2); 27(4); 28(4); 29(2); 30(4); 31; 32(2); 33(4); 34; 35; 36(2); 37(4; 38; 39; 40(2); 30:1(5; 2; 3; 5(2); 7; 8(2); 13(3); 14(2); 15; 16; 17(3); 18; 19(2); 21(2); 22(3); 24(4); 25(2); 26(2); 27(4); 28(4); 29(2); 30(4); 31; 32(2); 33(4);

16(3); 17(3); 18(4); 21(2); 22(2); 23(5); 24(4); 25(3); 26; 27; 28(3); 29(6); 15:1; 2(3); 4(3); 5(2); 6; 7; 9(3); 10; 11(2); 12; 14; 15(2); 17; 18; 19(4); 20(3); 21; 22(4); 23(2); 16:1(5); 2(6); 3(5); 4(3); 5(2); 6(6); 7(3); 8(2); 9(3); 10(4); 11(7; 13; 14(4); 15(5); 16(6); 17(2); 18(2; 19(4); 20(3); 21(2); 22(2); 23; 24(4); 31; 3(2); 4; 6(2); 7(5); 8(2); 9(4); 10(2); 11(6); 12(5); 13; 14(3); 15; 16(3); 18(3); 19(3); 20(5); 18:15(2; 2; 3(6); 4(3); 5(3); 6(3); 7(4); 8(9); 13; 14(3); 15; 16(3); 17; 18; 19; 27:1(3; 2(3); 4(2); 5(5); 6(4); 8(2); 9; 10; 11; 13; 14(2); 15(3); 17(5); 18; 20; 21; 4(2); 5(5); 6(4); 9; 10; 11; 2:1(3); 3(4); 4; 5(3); 6; 7; 8(2); 9(4); 11; 13; 14(2); 15(2); 16(2); 17(7; 18; 19(2); 20(2); 20; 21; 23(2); 22:4; 5(2); 6(7); 7(9; 8(2); 9(4); 10; 11; 12(2); 14(2); 15; 17; 20; 21; 22(2); 23(2); 23(6); 24(5); 25; 26(2); 27(6); 28(6); 30(8); 32(6); 35(3); 37(6); 39(6); 40(6); 41; 42; 43; 11:1(2); 2(7); 3(10); 2; 5; 6; 7(2); 8; 10(4); 11(3); 12(7; 13; 14(5); 15(2); 15(17); 16(6); 17; 19(2); 21(6); 22(4); 23(7; 24(2; 25:1(3); 2(3); 4(3); 5(2); 6(3); 7(4); 8; 9(2); 10(3); 11(4); 12(3); 13; 14(5; 16(7; 17(5); 18(15); 19(4; 20(11); 21(3); 22(2); 24(7); 25(2); 26(4; 27(2; 7:1(10); 2(3); 3(2); 4(2); 5(5); 6; 8(3); 9(4); 14(8); 15(3); 16(2); 17(5); 18(4); 19; 20; 21(4); 5(3); 6(2); 7(3); 8(4); 9(2); 10(4); 11(4); 12(2); 12(8); 14(5); 15(2); 16; 17; 18(4); 19(3); 20(6); 21(5); 22(3); 23; 24(8); 25; 26(2); 27(4); 29(6); 30; 31(6); 32(4); 33(10); 34(5); 35(4); 9:1(11); 3; 5; 6(2); 7(2); 9(3); 10(2); 11(2); 12; 13; 14(3); 15(2); 16; 17(2); 10:1; 2(2); 4; 5(7); 6(5); 7(2); 8; 10(2); 11(4); 12(7; 13(6); 14(3); 15; 17; 18(2); 19(2); 20(2); 21(3); 22(3); 23(6); 24(5); 25; 26(4); 27(6; 7:1(10); 2(3); 23(6); 24(5); 25; 27(4; 29(6); 30; 31(6); 32(4); 33(10); 34(5); 35(4); 9(1(11); 3; 5; 6(2); 7(2); 9(3); 10(2); 11(2); 12; 13; 14(3); 15(2); 16; 17(2);

11; 12; 13(2); 14(4); 15(3); 16(5); 24:1(2); 2(6); 3(3); 6(3); 7(4); 8(3); 9(2); 11(8); 12(3); 13; 14(5); 15(7); 16(2); 17(5); 18(5); 19(2); 20; 21(2); 22(2); 23(2); 24(2); 25; 26(4); 27(3); 28; 29(3); 30(3); 31(6); 32(6); 33; **Judg** 1:1(4); 2(2); 3; 4(3); 5(2); 8(4); 9(5); 10(2); 11(2); 13; 15(2); 16(7); 17(3); 18(3); 19(5); 20; 21(4); 22(2); 23(3); 24(4); 25(6); 26(5); 27(5); 28; 29(2); 30(3); 31(2); 32(4); 33(6); 34(4); 35(3); 36(4); 2:1(2); 2; 4(4); 5(2); 6(3); 7(7); 8(3); 9(4); 10(2); 11(3); 12(5); 13; 14(4); 15(4); 16(2); 17(3); 18(7); 19; 20(2); 21; 22(2); 23(2); 3:1(3); 2(3); 3(5); 4(3); 5(2); 7(5); 8(4); 9(5); 10(3); 11(4); 12(7); 13(2); 14(2); 15(4); 16; 17; 18(3); 19; 21; 22(6); 23(3); 24(2); 25(3); 26; 27(3); 28(3); 30(2); 31(2); 4:1(3); 2(4); 3(3); 4; 5(2); 6(4); 7(2); 9(3); 11(5); 12; 13(3); 14(3); 15(3); 16(6); 17(6); 18; 20(2); 21(3); 22(2); 23(2); 24(3); 5:1; 2(3); 3(2); 4(4); 5(3); 6(5); 7(2); 8; 9(3); 10; 11(9); 13(4); 14(2); 15(3); 16(4); 17; 18(3); 19(3); 20; 21(2); 22(4); 23(8); 24(3); 26(3); 30(3); 31(2); 6:1(5); 2(5); 3(4); 4(2); 5; 6(3); 7(3); 8(4); 9(3); 10(3); 11(4); 12(5); 13(5); 14(3); 15; 16(2); 19(3); 20(4); 21(11); 22(2); 23; 24(2); 25(5); 26(6); 27(3); 28(7); 29; 30(4); 33(5); 34(2); 37(4); 38(4); 39(3); 40(2); 7:1(7); 2(3); 3(3); 4(5); 5(4); 6(3); 7(4); 8(4); 9(3); 10; 11(4); 12(7); 13(2); 14(3); 15(6); 16(2); 17(2); 18(4); 19(8); 20(7); 21(2); 22(6); 22(2); 24(4); 25(5); 8:1(2); 2(3); 3; 4; 5(2); 6(2); 7(3); 8(2); 9; 10(3); 11(4); 12(2); 13(2); 14(3); 15(2); 16(4); 17(3); 18; 19(2); 20; 21(2); 22(2); 23; 24; 25; 26(4); 27(4); 28(2); 29; 32(3); 33; 34(3); 35(2); 9:1(3); 2(3); 4; 5(2); 6(4); 7; 8(2); 9; 10; 11(2); 12(2); 13(2); 14(3); 15(4); 16; 17; 18(2); 20(4); 23(2); 24(4); 25(3); 26(7); 27(3); 28(4); 30(7); 31(2); 32(4); 33(6); 34(4); 35(2); 36(4); 37(4); 38(4); 39(3); 40(2); 7:1(7); 2(3); 3(3); 4(5); 5(4); 6(3); 7(4); 8(4); 9(3); 10; 11(4); 12(7); 13(2); 14(3); 15(6); 16(2); 17(4); 18(5); 19; 20(6); 21(3); 22(4); 23; 24; 25(3); 26; 27(3); 28(7); 29; 30(4); 33(5); 34(2); 35(2); 37(4); 38(4); 39(3); 40(2); 41(3); 42(4); 21:1(2); 2(3); 4(2); 5(5); 6(4); 7(4); 8; 9(5); 10; 11(3); 12; 13(4); 14; 15; 22:1; 3; 4(3); 5(4); 6; 7; 8; 9(4); 10(3); 11(5); 13(4); 15(2); 16; 17; 18; 19; 20(2); 21(4); 22; 23; 24(2); 25(6); 26(2); 27(4); 28(4); 38:1; 39:3; 4; 7:1(7); 2(3); 6:1; 2(5); 3(4); 4; 5(2); 6(3); 9:1(3); 11(4); 12(3); 13; 14; 15(2); 16(4); 17; 18(3); 19; 20(2); 21; 22(4); 23(2); 24; 25(5); 26; 27(3); 28(4); 29; 30(3); 31(2); 4:1(3); 2(4); 3(3); 4; 5(2); 6(4); 7(2); 9(3); 11(5); 12; 13(3); 14(3); 15(3); 16(6); 17(6); 18; 20(2); 21(3); 22(2); 23(2); 24(3); **2Sa** 1:1(3); 2(3); 3; 4(4); 5; 6(2); 10(2); 11; 12(4); 13(2); 14; 15; 16; 18(4); 19(2); 20(5); 21(3); 22(6); 25(3); 26; 27(2); 2:1(3); 2(2); 3; 4(3); 5(2); 6; 7; 8(2); 9; 10; 11(2); 12(3); 13(9); 14; 15(2); 16; 17(2); 19(2); 21; 22; 23(6); 24(4); 25(2); 26(3); 27(2); 28; 29; 30; 31; 32(3); 3:1(3); 2(5); 6(3); 7; 8; 9(3); 10; 11(4); 12(3); 13(4); 14; 15(2); 16(4); 17; 18(4); 19(2); 20(7); 21(3); 23; 24(3); 25(3); 14:1(2); 2(2); 3(4); 4(3); 5; 6(2); 7; 8(4); 9(2); 10(2); 12(2); 14(3); 15(2); 16; 17(4); 18(4); 19(3); 15:1(2); 3; 4; 5(6); 6(4); 8(2); 9; 10; 11(3); 12(2); 13; 14(4); 16(2); 17; 18(4); 19(2); 20(2); 16:2(5); 3(5); 4; 6; 7; 8(4); 9(2); 10(7); 11; 12(3); 13; 14; 15(4); 16(2); 17(5); 18; 19; 20(3); 21(3); 22(4); 24; 25(4); 26(2); 27(2); 28(4); 29(4); 30(5); 31(2); 17:2(3); 3(3); 4; 5(3); 6; 7; 8(4); 9(2); 10(7); 11(2); 12(2); 13(3); 14; 15; 16(2); 17(3); 18(3); 19; 20(2); 21; 22(2); 23(2); 24(2); 25(5); 26(5); 27(7); 28(2); 29; 30(3); 20:1(4); 2(5); 3(3); 4(3); 5(2); 6(2); 8; 9; 10(3); 11(2); 12(2); 13(5); 14(3); 15(3); 17; 18(5); 19(2); 20(2); 21(3); 22(4); 23; 24(3); 25(4); 26(5); 27(3); 28(4); 30(3); 31(8); 32(5); 34; 35(4); 36(4); 37(5); 38(3); 39(4); 40(5); 41(2); 42(6); 43(2); 45(3); 46; 47(3); 48(7); 21:1; 2(2); 4(2); 5(5); 6; 7; 8(4); 9(2); 10(7); 11; 12(3); 3(4); 14; 15(3); 16; 3; 18; 19(5); 20(2); 21(4); 22; 23(2); 24; 25(2); 23(3); 24; 25(2); 26(2); 27(4); 4(5); 6(4); 5(2); 6(2); 7; 8; 9(4); 10(2); 11; 12; 14; 15(5); 16(2); 17; 18; **Ruth** 1:1(5); 2(5); 4(5); 5; 6(3); 7(3); 8(2); 9(2); 13(2); 17; 19; 20; 21(3); 22(3); 2:1; 2(2); 3(4); 4(3); 5; 6(4); 7(4); 9(4); 10; 11(2); 12(2); 14(3); 15; 16; 17; 18; 19; 20(4); 21; 23(2); 3:2; 3(2); 4; 6; 7(2); 8(10); 10(7); 11(6); 12(3); 13; 14(2); 16; 17(3); 18; **1Sa** 1:1(4); 2(4); 3(4); 4; 5; 6; 7(3); 9(4); 10; 11(3); 12; 13; 15; 16; 17; 18; 19(3); 20(2); 21(2); 23(2); 24(3); 25; 26(2); 27; 28(3); 2:1(2); 2; 3; 4(2); 5; 6(2); 7; 8(9); 9(2); 10(6); 11(3); 12(4); 13(4); 14(4); 15(4); 16; 17(5); 18; 19; 20(3); 21(3); 22(4); 24; 25(4); 26(2); 27(2); 28(4); 29(3); 31(2); 32(3); 33(3); 36; 3:1(4); 4; 6; 7(3); 8(4); 9; 10(7); 11(6); 12(4); 13; 14(6); 15(9); 16(3); 17(3); 18(10); 19(7); 20; 21(4); 7:1(7); 2(4); 3(6); 4(2); 5; 6(4); 7; 9(3); 10(4); 11(2); 12(6); 13(3); 14(5); 15(2); 16(3); 17(3); 18(10); 19(7); 20; 21(4); 7:1(7); 2(3); 6(2); 8(2); 9(3); 10(2); 11(4); 12; 14; 15(5); 16(2); 17; 18; 19(2); 21(2); 22(2); 23(3); 17:2(3); 3; 4(4); 5(3); 6; 7(3); 8(6); 9(6); 10(5); 11(5); 12(6); 12(5); 14(3); 15; 16(2); 17(3); 18; 19(4); 20; 21; 22(2); 23; 24(2); 25(2); 26(4); 27(4); 28(4); 29(4); 30(2); 31(5); 32(4); 33(5); 34(4); 35(3); 36(2); 37; 38(6); 39(2); 40(2); 41(2); 43(2); 45(4); 46(2); 47(4); 48(2); 49(6); 50(5); 51(3); 52(2); 15:1(4); 2(2); 4; 5; 6(5);

19(5); 20(3); 21; 22(2); 23(5); 25(4); 26(2); 27(3); 28(2); 29(2); 30; 31(2); 32(4); 33(2); 34(3); 36(4); 37(3); 38(5); 39(4); 40(4); 41(4); 42(2); 44(7); 45(4); 46(2); 47(4); 48(2); 49; 50(2); 51(3); 52; 53; 2:1; 2(2); 3(3); 4(2); 5(7); 6; 7(2); 8(4); 9; 10; 11; 12; 13(2); 15(3); 17(2); 18; 19(2); 20; 21; 22(4); 23; 24(2); 25(2); 26(4); 27(4); 28(4); 29(4); 30(4); 31(3); 32(6); 33(3); 34(2); 35(6); 36; 37(2); 38(3); 39(2); 42(4); 43(3); 44(3); 45(2); 46(4); 3:1(4); 2(3); 3(2); 4(2); 5; 8; 10(2); 11; 13; 15(3); 16; 17(2); 18(3); 19; 21(2); 22(6); 23(6); 24(2); 25(4); 26(5); 27(3); 28(4); 4:2(3); 3(3); 4(3); 5(4); 6(3); 7; 8; 9; 10(2); 11(3); 12(2); 13(4); 14; 15; 16; 17; 18; 19(6); 20(2); 21(5); 23; 24(4); 25; 28(3); 29(2); 30(4); 31(2); 33(3); 34(2); 5:1; 3(5); 4; 5(3); 6; 7(2); 8; 9(2); 12; 13; 14; 15; 16(4); 17(3); 18(2); 6:1(8); 2(5); 3(8); 4; 5(6); 6(8); 7(2); 8(7); 9(2); 11(2); 12(4); 14; 15(9); 16(6); 17(2); 19(5); 20(4); 21(3); 22(4); 23; 24(8); 25(2); 26(2); 27(2); 28(3); 29(3); 11:1(2); 2(3); 4(2); 5(4); 6(3); 7(4); 9(2); 10; 11(2); 12; 13; 14(3); 15(7); 2); 3; 4; 5(6); 6(8); 7(2); 8(7); 9(2); 11(2); 12(4); 14; 15(9); 16(6); 17(5); 18(5); 19(4); 20(6); 21(7); 22(2); 23(4); 24(3); 25(5); 26(2); 27(3); 28(4); 4:2(3); 3(3); 4(3); 5(4); 6(3); 7; 8; 9; 10(2); 11(3); 12(2); 13(4); 14; 15; 16; 17; 18; 19(6); 20(2); 21(5); 23; 24(4); 25; 28(3); 29(2); 30(4); 31(2); 33(3); 34(2); 49:7(4); 8(2); 9; 10; 11(2); 12(3); 13; 14; 15(5); 16(2); 17; 18; **2Sa** 1:1(3); 2(3); 3; 4(4); 5; 6(2); 10(2); 11; 12(4); 13(2); 14; 15; 16; 18(4); 19(2); 20(5); 21(3); 22(6); 25(3); 26; 27(2); 2:1(3); 2(2); 3; 4(3); 5(2); 6; 7; 8(2); 9; 10; 11(2); 12(3); 13(9); 14; 15(2); 16; 17(2); 19(2); 21; 22; 23(6); 24(4); 25(2); 26(3); 27(2); 28; 29; 30; 31; 32(3); 3:1(3); 2(5); 6(3); 7; 8; 9(3); 10; 11(4); 12(3); 13(4); 14; 15(2); 16(4); 17; 18(4); 19(2); 20(7); 21(3); 23; 24(3); 25(3); 14:1(2); 2(2); 3(4); 4(3); 5; 6(2); 7; 8(4); 9(2); 10(2); 12(2); 14(3); 15(2); 16; 17(4); 18(4); 19(3); 15:1(2); 3; 4; 5(6); 6(4); 8(2); 9; 10; 11(3); 12(2); 13; 14(4); 16(2); 17; 18(4); 19(2); 20(2); 16:2(5); 3(5); 4; 6; 7; 8(4); 9(2); 10(7); 11; 12(3); 13; 14; 15(4); 16(2); 17(5); 18; 19; 20(3); 21(3); 22(4); 24; 25(4); 26(2); 27(2); 28(4); 29(4); 30(5); 31(2); 17:2(3); 3(3); 4; 5(3); 6; 7; 8(4); 9(2); 10(7); 11(2); 12(2); 13(3); 14; 15; 16(2); 17(3); 18(3); 19; 20(2); 21; 22(2); 23(2); 24(2); 25(5); 26(5); 27(7); 28(2); 29; 30(3); 20:1(4); 2(5); 3(3); 4(3); 5(2); 6(2); 8; 9; 10(3); 11(2); 12(2); 13(5); 14(3); 15(3); 17; 18(5); 19(2); 20(2); 21(3); 22(4); 23; 24(3); 25(4); 26(5); 27(3); 28(4); 30(3); 31(8); 32(5); 34; 35(4); 36(4); 37(5); 38(3); 39(4); 40(5); 41(2); 42(6); 43(2); 45(3); 46; 47(3); 48(7); 21:1; 2(2); 4(2); 5(5); 6; 7; 8(4); 9(2); 10(7); 11; 12(3); 3(4); 14; 15(3); 16; 3; 18; 19(5); 20(2); 21(4); 22; 23(2); 24; 25(2); 23(3); 24; 25(2); 26(2); 27(4); 4(5); 6(4); 5(2); 6(2); 7; 8; 9(4); 10(2); 11; 12; 14; 15(5); 16(2); 17; 18; 19(3); 20:1; 2; 3; 4; 5; 6; 7(3); 8(2); 9(4); 10(3); 11; 12(3); 13(2); 14(5); 15(5); 16(3); 17(3); 19(4); 20(3); 21(3); 22(5); 23(4); 24; 25(2); 26(2); 27(4); 28(3); 29(5); 30(4); 31(3); 32; 33(2); 34; 35(5); 36(2); 37; 38(3); 39(4); 40; 41(3); 42; 43; 21:1(2); 2; 3(2); 4(3); **2Kin** 1:1; 2; 3(6); 4; 5; 6(3); 8; 9(3); 10; 11; 12; 13(3); 14(2); 15(3); 16(2); 17(4); 18(5); 2:1; 2(2); 3(3); 4(2); 5(3); 6(2); 7(2); 8; 12(2); 13(2); 14(4); 15(4); 16(2); 19(5); 21(4); 22(2); 23(2); 24(3); 3:1(2); 2(3); 2(2); 4(2); 5(2); 6; 7(2); 8(2); 9(5); 10(3); 11(5); 12(4); 13(6); 14(3); 15(3); 16; 17; 18(3); 19(4); 2(3); 4(2); 5(2); 6(7); 7(3); 9; 10(3); 11(5); 12(4); 13; 6(2); 17; 18(2); 19(3); 20(2); 21(5); 22(3); 23(4); 24(5); 25(2); 26; 27(2); 28(2); 29(2); 30(4); 31(4); 32(3); 33(3); 34(5); 35(7); 36(3); 37(2); 38(5); 39(7); 41(2); 42; 43(6); 44; 45(5); 46; 48; 49(2); 50; 51(2); 52(6); 53; **2Kin** 1:1; 2; 3(6); 4; 5; 6(3); 8; 9(3); 10; 11; 12; 13(3); 14(2); 15(3); 16(2); 17(4); 18(5); 2:1; 2(2); 3(3); 4(2); 5(3); 6(2); 7(2); 8; 12(2); 13(2); 14(4); 15(4); 16(2); 19(5); 21(4); 22(2); 23(2); 24(3); 3:1(2); 2(3); 2(2); 4(2); 5(2); 6; 7(2); 8(2); 9(5); 10(3); 11(5); 12(4); 13(6); 14(3); 15(3); 16; 17; 18(3); 19(4); 2(3); 4(2); 5(2); 6(7); 7(3); 9; 10(3); 11(5); 12(4); 13; 6(2); 17; 18(2); 19(3); 20(2); 21(5); 22(3); 23(4); 24(5); 25(2); 26; 27(2); 28(2); 29(2); 30(4); 31(3);

32(2); 33(5); 34(5); 36; 11:1(2); 2(4); 3(3); 4(9); 5(4); 6(5); 7(5); 8(3); 9(6); 10(4); 11(8); 12(4); 13(6); 14(7); 15(10); 16(4); 17(6); 18(8); 19(14); 20(5); 12:1; 2(3); 3(3); 4(11); 5(3); 6(4); 7(6); 8(4); 9(11); 10(6); 11(9); 12(4); 13(5); 14(3); 15(2); 16(4); 18(6); 19(5); 20; 21(3); 13:13; 14(3); 15(2); 16(3); 3(2); 4(3); 5(2); 6(9); 9(11); 10(6); 11(4); 12(5); 13; 14(3); 16(3); 14(6); 15(5); 16; 17(2); 18(5); 20; 21; 22; 23(3); 24(4); 25(9); 26(2); 27(4); 28(5); 29; 15:1; 3(2); 4(3); 5(7); 6(5); 7; 8(2); 9(4); 10(2); 11(5); 12(4); 13(2); 14(2); 15(5); 16(2); 17(2); 18(4); 19(3); 20(2); 21; 22; 23(9); 24(2); 26(5); 27(2); 28(4); 29(2); 30(4); 31(5); 32(3); 33; 34(2); 35(6); 36(5); 37(3); 38; 16:13(2); 2(2); 3(7); 4(2); 6(7); 7(4); 8(6); 9(3); 10(5); 11(2); 12(5); 13(2); 14(9); 15(13); 16; 17(5); 18(7); 19(5); 20; 17:1(2); 2(3); 4(3); 5(2); 6(5); 7(4); 8(5); 9(5); 11(4); 12; 13(5); 14(2); 15(2); 16(3); 17(3); 18(2); 19(3); 20(3); 21(3); 22(2); 23(2); 24(4); 25(3); 26(9); 27(5); 28(2); 29(3); 30(4); 31(2); 32(3); 33(4); 34(2); 35(3); 36(2); 37(6); 19:1(2); 2(6); 3(2); 4(7); 5; 6(4); 7; 8; 10(2); 11; 12(3); 13(4); 14(6); 15(4); 16(2); 17(2); 18(2); 19(2); 20(2); 21(2); 22(4); 23(8); 24(4); 25(6); 26(4); 27(7); 28(2); 29; 30(2); **1Chr** 1:5; 6; 7; 8; 9(2); 10; 12; 14(3); 15(3); 16(4); 17; 19(3); 23; 27; 28; 29; 31; 32(2); 33(2); 34; 35; 36; 37; 38; 39; 40(2); 41(2); 42(2); 43(5); 44; 45(2); 46(3); 48; 49; 50(3); 51; 54; 2:1; 3(6); 4; 5; 6; 7(3); 8; 9; 10; 13(2); 14(2); 15(2); 16; 17(2); 18; 21(2); 22; 23(4); 24(3); 25(3); 26; 22:1; 2(5); 3(7); 4(7); 5(12); 6; 7; 8(7); 9(10); 10(4); 11(4); 13(6); 14(7); 15(2); 16(5); 17; 18(4); 19(3); 20(2); 23:1(2); 2(13); 3(6); 4(13); 5(9); 6(3); 7(3); 8(4); 9(2); 10(3); 11(11); 12(11); 13(11); 14(3); 15(6); 16(8); 17(5); 18(2); 19(6); 20(3); 21(5); 22(5); 23(2); 24(12); 25(2); 26(3); 27(2); 28(5); 29(2); 30(3); 31; 32(2); 33(2); 34(2); 35(9); 36; 37(2); 24:2(8); 3(3); 4(2); 5(5); 7(5); 8; 9(2); 10(2); 11(4); 12(2); 13(3); 14(7); 15(2); 16(5); 17; 18(4); 19; 20(2); 22(2); 23(3); 24(3); 25(4); 26(7); 6:1; 2; 3(2); 10(2); 15(2); 16; 17(2); 18; 19(3); 22; 25; 26; 28(2); 29; 31(4); 32(5); 33(4); 34(4); 35(4); 37(4); 38(4); 39; 40; 41; 42(2); 7:1(6); 2(6); 3(4); 5(3); 6(6); 7(10); 8(4); 9(4); 10(5); 11(5); 12; 13(2); 15; 18; 20; 21; 22(3); 8:1(3); 2(2); 4(2); 5(2); 6(5); 7(6); 8(2); 9; 10(2); 11(7); 12(4); 13(8); 14(8); 15(6); 16(7); 17(2); 18(3); 9:1(2); 3(3); 4(5); 5; 6(3); 8(2); 9(2); 10(2); 11(6); 12(2); 13; 14(2); 16; 17; 18(4); 19(4); 20(5); 21(3); 22(2); 23(3); 25(2); 26(7); 27(3); 29(9); 31; 10:2(3); 4; 5; 6; 8(3); 9; 10(2); 12(4); 13(3); 14(2); 15(7); 16(4); 17(2); 18(2); 19; 11:1(2); 2(3); 3(4); 11; 13(2); 14(3); 15(3); 16(5); 17(8); 18(4); 20; 21(2); 23(2); 12:1(3); 13(2); 14(3); 15(3); 16(2); 17(4); 18(9); 21(4); 22(4); 23; 24(7); 25(6); 26; 27; 31; 33; 34; 35(3); 37(5); 38; 39(3); 40; 41(2); 42(2); 43(2); 5:1(7); 2(2); 3(2); 4; 6; 7(2); 8(3); 9(4); 6:2; 6; 7; 8(7); 9(4); 10(4); 11(4); 12(2); 13(2); 14(8); 15(6); 16; 17(2); 18(3); 19(12); 20(3); 21(4); 22(2); 23(6); 24(7); 25(6); 26(7); 27(3); 28(9); 29(3); 30; 31; 32(3); 33(3); 34(6); 37(4); 38(4); 39(3); 43(3); 44(5); 45(3); 46(3); 47(4); 48(3); 49(6); 49(6); 50; 54(2); 55(2); 56(4); 57(3); 60; 61(4); 62(5); 63(4); 64(2); 65(6); 66(4); 67; 70(4); 71(3); 72; 74; 76; 77(3); 78(4); 80; 7:1; 2(2); 3(2); 4; 5; 6; 7(2); 9(2); 10(2); 11(2); 12(2); 13(2); 14(3); 15(3); 16(2); 17(4); 19; 20; 21; 24(2); 28(4); 29(4); 30; 31(2); 33(2); 34; 35; 36; 38; 39; 40(5); 8:1(2); 2(2); 3; 5; 6(4); 8; 10; 12; 13(3); 16; 18; 21; 25; 27; 28; 29; 34; 35; 38; 39(3); 40(2); 9:1(2); 2(4); 3(3); 4(6); 5(2); 6; 7(4); 8(6); 9(2); 10; 11(7); 12(8); 13(4); 14(5); 14(5); 16(7); 17(2); 18(3); 19(12); 20(3); 21(4); 22(2); 23(6); 24(6); 26(3); 27(3); 28(3); 30(4); 31(6); 32(3); 33(4); 34; 35; 40; 41; 44; 10:1(3); 2(3); 5; 7(3); 8(3); 9(3); 10(2); 1; 12(4); 13(3); 14(3); 11:2(3); 4(3); 5(3); 6(2); 7(2); 8(9); 9(10); 11(4); 12(3); 13(3); 14(3); 15(6); 16(4); 17(2); 18(6); 19(2); 20(3); 21(3); 22(2); 23(3); 24(3); 25(2); 26(4); 27(2); 28(3); 29(4); 30(2); 31(4); 32(3); 33(5); 34; 35; 37(5); 38; 13:1; 2(4); 3(2); 4(4); 5(2); 6(3); 7(3); 9(3); 10(3); 11; 12; 13(4); 14(4); 14:2; 4; 8(2); 9(2); 10(2); 11(2); 12(3); 13; 14(3); 15(4); 16(2); 17(3); 15:1(2); 2(4); 3(2); 4(2); 5(2); 6(2); 7(2); 8(2); 9(2); 10(2); 11(2); 12(6); 13(3); 14(4); 15(6); 16(4); 17(5); 18(2); 19; 21; 22(2); 23; 24(2); 25(6); 26(4); 27(6); 28(4); 31(6); 32(3); 33(4); 34; 35; 40; 41; 44; 10:1(7); 2(2); 3; 4; 5(2); 6(2); 7(2); 8(3); 9; 11(5); 12(3); 13; 14(4); 14:2; 8(2); 9(4); 10; 11(5); 12(4); 14:2; 8(2); 9(4); 10; 11(5); 12(4); 9(9); 17; 20(5); 21(2); 22(3); 23(2); 24(2); 25(3); 26(4)

30(3); 22:1(4); 2(3); 3(4); 4; 5(2); 6; 7(2); 8(3); 10; 11(3); 12(3); 13(2); 14(2); 16(5); 17; 18(5); 19(10); 23:2(3); 3(2); 4(3); 5(2); 6; 7; 8(2); 9(3); 10(2); 11(2); 12; 13(3); 14(2); 15; 16(2); 17(3); 18(2); 19(5); 20(3); 21(2); 22; 23; 24(9); 25; 26(3); 27(2); 28(10); 29(4); 30; 31(6); 24:1(3); 2; 3(2); 4(6); 5(5); 6(10); 7(2); 8(2); 9(2); 10(4); 12(4); 14(2); 15(2); 16(2); 17(2); 18(2); 19(4); 20(4); 21(3); 23(4); 24(4); 25(8); 26(4); 27(3); 28(5); 29(5); 30(4); 31(5); 32(3); 33; 34(2); 36(2); 37(6); 9(2); 10; 11; 12; 13; 14; 15; 16; 17; 18; 19; 20; 21; 22; 23; 24; 25; 26; 27; 28; 29; 30; 31; 30; 31(5); 32(3); 33; 34; 35; 36; 37(6); 19:1(2); 2(6); 3(2); 4(7); 5; 6; 7(3); 8(4); 5; 6; 7; 9; 10; 11; 12(3); 14(3); 15(4); 16(3); 3(3); 4(7); 5; 6(4); 7; 8; 10(2); 11; 12(3); 13(4); 14(6); 8(3); 9(5); 10(4); 11(5); 17; 18(5); 19(4); 20(5); 21(4); 22(4); 23(4); 24(9); 25; 26(3); 27(2); 28(10); 2(10); 3(4); 4(3); 5(7); 6(2); 7(9); 8(6); 9(6); 10(4); 11(3); 12(4); 13(7); 14(5); 6:1(2); 3(3); 4(2); 5(3); 14(3); 15(4); 17(3); 18(2); 3:1(6); 3(6); 3(6); 4(7); 5; 6(2); 7(6); 8(5); 9(3); 10; 11(8); 12(6); 13; 14; 15(3); 16(4); 4:1(3); 2; 3(2); 4(5); 5(4); 6(5); 7(3); 8(3); 9(5); 10(4); 11(5); 12(2); 22(11); 5:1(9); 17(3); 18(2); 19(5); 20(3); 21(3); 22(11); 5:1(9); 2(10); 3(4); 4(3); 5(7); 6(2); 7(9); 8(6); 9(6); 10(4); 7(10); 8(4); 9(4); 10(5); 11(5); 12; 13(2); 15; 18; 20; 21; 22(2); 8:13(2); 4(2); 6(5); 7(6); 8(2); 9(4); 10(2); 11(7); 12(4); 13(8); 14(8); 15(6); 16(7); 17(2); 18(3); 9:1(2); 3(3); 4(5); 5; 6(3); 11(6); 12(2); 13(2); 14(2); 15; 16(2); 17; 18(4); 19(4); 20(5); 21(3); 22(3); 23(3); 25(2); 26(3); 27(3); 29(9); 31; 10:2(3); 4; 5; 6; 8(3); 9; 10(2); 12(4); 13(3); 14(2); 15(7); 15(7); 16(4); 17(2); 18(2); 19; 22; 25; 26; 28(2); 29; 30; 31(4); 32(4); 33(2); 34(6); 36; 37(3); 21:1; 2(2); 3(2); 5; 6(3); 7(4); 8(2); 9(3); 10(3); 11(8); 12(2); 13:1; 14(5); 14; 15; 16; 17; 18(5); 19(3); 20; 21(2); 14(4); 12(7); 13(4); 14(7); 15(6); 16(7); 17(3); 18(6); 19(2); 20; 21; 22(3); 23(2); 24(2); 25(3); 26(4); 27(3)

27(2); 36:1(3); 3(2); 4; 5(2); 7(3); 8(4); 9(2); 10(4); 12(5); 13; 14(7); 15; 16(3); 17(4); 18(7); 19(4); 20(3); 21(4); 22(6); 23(4); **Ezr** 1:1(6); 2(3); 3(3); 4(3); 5(6); 7(5); 8(3); 9; 11(2); 2:1(4); 3; 4; 5; 6(2); 7; 8; 9; 10; 11; 12; 13; 14; 15; 16; 17; 18; 19; 20; 21; 22; 23; 24; 25; 26; 27; 28; 29; 30; 31(2); 32; 33; 34; 35; 36(3); 37; 38; 39; 40(3); 41(2); 42(8); 43(4); 44(3); 45(4); 46(3); 47(3); 48(3); 49(3); 50(3); 51(3); 52(3); 53(3); 54(2); 55(4); 56(3); 57(4); 58(2); 60(3); 61(7); 62; 63(2); 64; 68(5); 69(2); 70(6); 3:1(4); 2(7); 3(3); 4(4); 5(5); 6(6); 7(4); 8(13); 10(9); 11(6); 12(6); 13(4); 5:2(6); 3(4); 5(4); 5(2); 6(3); 7(6); 8(3); 9(12); 10(6); 11(5); 12(6); 13(4); 14(3); 15(5); 16(3); 17(6); 18; 20; 22(2); 23(3); 24(4); 5:16(6); 2(4); 3(2); 4(2); 5(4); 6(6); 7; 8(5); 10(3); 11(3); 12(5); 13(3); 14(6); 15(2); 16(3); 17(4); 6:1(4); 2(3); 3(10); 4(2); 5(5); 7(5); 8(5); 9(4); 10(3); 12; 13(2); 14(8); 15(5); 16(7); 17(3); 18(4); 19(3); 20(4); 21(3); 22; 3:3(4); 4(2); 5(2); 6(4); 7(1); 4:2; 3; 3(3); 4(2); 5(4); 6(5); 7; 8(2); 9(2); 10(2); 11(2); 12; 13; 14; 15(4); 17(5); 18(4); 19; 20(4); 21; 22(5); 24(2); 25; 26; 28(5); 29(7); 30(7); 31(7); 33(11); 34; 35(4); 36(6); 9:1(14); 2(4); 3; 4(4); 5(2); 6; 7(5); 8(4); 9(4); 7(2); 8(4); 9(8); 10; 11(4); 12; 13; 14(4); 14(3); 15(3); 16(8); 17(3); 16; 17; 18; 20; 22(2); 23(2); 24(2); 25; 26; 27; 28; 29; 30; 31; 33; 34; 43; **Neh** 1:1(5); 2(2); 3(5); 4; 5; 6(4); 7(3); 8(2); 9(3); 11(4); 2:1(5); 2; 3(5); 4(3); 5(3); 6(3); 7(4); 8(10); 9(5); 10(5); 12(2); 13(6); 14(4); 15(5); 16(3); 17(3); 18(2); 19(5); 20; 3:1(6); 2(6); 3(6); 4(5); 5(2); 6(7); 7(6); 8(5); 9(3); 10(2); 11(5); 12(3); 13(7); 14(6); 15(2); 16(8); 17(4); 18(3); 19(6); 20(7); 21(6); 22(3); 23(2); 24(5); 25(8); 26(5); 27(3); 28(2); 29(4); 30(3); 31(7); 32(5); 4:1(2); 2(4); 3; 4; 5; 6(4); 7(5); 8(3); 9(4); 5(4); 6(2); 7(2); 8(4); 9(8); 10(2); 11(4); 12; 13; 14(4); 15(3); 16(9); 17(3); 18(6); 19(6); 20(2); 21(5); 22(4); 23(2); 5:1(2); 3; 4; 5; 7(2); 8(4); 9(10); 10(4); 11(3); 12(2); 13(9); 14(5); 15(8); 16(2); 17(3); 18(2); 5; 7(2); 8(9); 9(2); 10; 11(5); 12; 13(3); 14(7); 15(4); 16(2); 17(2); 18(3); 6:1(5); 2; 4; 5; 6(3); 7; 9; 10(8); 11; 14(3); 15(3); 16; 17(2); 18(4); 7:1(5); 2(2); 3(4); 4; 5(2); 6; 7; 9; 10(8); 11; 14(3); 15(3); 16; 17; 18; 19; 20; 21; 22; 23; 24; 25; 26; 27; 28; 29; 30; 31; 32; 33(2); 34; 35; 36; 37; 38; 39(3); 40; 41; 42; 43(3); 44(2); 45(6); 46(2); 47(8); 48(3); 49(3); 51(3); 52(3); 53(3); 54(3); 55(2); 56(2); 57(4); 58(3); 59(4); 60(2); 62(3); 63(6); 64; 65(2); 66; 70(5); 71(4); 72(2); 73(8); 8:1(7); 2(5); 3(9); 4(2); 5(4); 6(2); 7(4); 8(4); 9(10); 10(4); 11(3); 12(2); 13(9); 14(5); 15(2); 16(8); 17(6); 18(7); 9:1(2); 2(3); 3(5); 4(7); 5(7); 6(4); 7(3); 8(2); 10(4); 11(6); 12; 13(3); 14; 15(2); 16; 17(3); 273(3); 28(2); 29; 30(3); 32(6); 35; 36(3); 37; 10:1(2); 8; 9(3); 14; 15; 16; 17(2); 18; 19(6); 20; 21(2); 22(4); 23(4); 28(4); 29(4); 30(3); 31(2); **Est** 1:1; 2(3); 3(4); 4(2); 5(6); 6; 7(3); 8(4); 9(3); 10(6); 11(5); 12(3); 13(4); 14(5); 15(4); 16(8); 17(3); 18(4); 19(5); 20(2); 21(5); 22(3); 2:1; 2(2); 3(9); 4(4); 5(4); 6(2); 7; 8(6); 9(5); 11(2); 12(5); 13(4); 14(9); 15(8); 16(3); 17(4); 18(4); 19(3); 20; 21(4); 22(3); 23(3); 3(3); 6(4); 7(6); 8(4); 9(5); 10(4); 11(3); 12(9); 13(6); 14(2); 4:1(2); 2(3); 4; 5(6); 6(4); 7(6); 8(6); 9; 11(6); 12(4); 13(2); 14(3); 16(3); 5:1(8); 2(7); 3(3); 3(5); 4(5); 5(3); 6(4); 8(6); 9; 11(6); 12(4); 13(2); 14(2); 7:1(2); 2(2); 4; 5(2); 6(2); 7(4); 8(10); 9(6); 10(2); 11(5); 12(4); 13(3); 14(2); 7:1(2); 2(2); 4; 5(2); 6(2); 7(4); 8(5); 9(10); 10(2); 11(5); 12(4); 13(3); 14(2); **Job** 1:1; 3(3); 5(6); 6(2); 7(3); 8(2); 9; 10(4); 12(3); 14(2); 16(3); 17(5); 19(4); 20; 21(4); 2:1(3); 2(3); 3(2); 4; 6; 7(3); 8(3); 9; 10; 11(3); 3:3(2); 4; 5; 6(4); 8; 9(4); 10; 11(3); 12(2); 14; 17(2); 18(2); 19(2); 20; 22(4); 25; 4:1; 3; 4; 5; 6; 7; 8; 9(2); 10(6); 11(2); 13(2); 16; 17(2); 18; 5:1; 2; 3(2); 5(2); 6(2); 7; 8; 9; 10(2); 11(2); 12(2); 13(3); 14(3); 15(4); 16; 17(3); 18; 19; 20; 21(2); 22; 23(3); 24(2); 25(2); 26(3); 32:(2); 3; 4(4); 5; 6; 7:1; 2(2); 3; 8; 9(2); 11(2); 21(2); 8:1; 2; 3(2); 5(5); 6; 7; 9(3); 10(3); 13(2); 14; 17(2); 18; 20; 22(2); 9:5; 6; 8(2); 9; 10; 11(2); 13(2); 14; 17(2); 18; 19(2); 20; 22; 23(2); 24(4); 25; 13:2; 3; 6; 7; 9(3); 17(2); 20(4); 12:2; 4; 5; 6; 7(3); 8(3); 9(2); 10(2); 11(2); 12; 15(2); 16(2); 17; 18; 19; 20(4); 21(2); 22(2); 23; 24(2); 25(2); 13:2; 3; 6; 9(3); 10; 13(2); 14(2); 15; 16; 17; 19; 20(3); 21; 22; 23; 24; 25; 26; 29(2); 30(2); 32(2); 34(2); 16:5; 10; 11; 13; 15; 16(3); 18; 4(2); 5(3); 6; 7; 9(3); 10(3); 13(2); 14; 17(2); 18; 21(3); 19:9; 17; 20; 21; 24; 25(2); 28(2); 29(3);

20:1; 3(2); 5(4); 6(2); 8; 9; 10; 11(2); 14; 16(2); 17(3); 18; 19; 22(2); 23; 24(2); 25(2); 27(2); 28(2); 29(2); 21:7; 9; 12(3); 13; 14; 15; 16(2); 17(2); 18(2); 20(2); 21(2); 25; 26(2); 27; 28(4); 29; 30(3); 32(2); 33(2); 22:1; 3; 6; 7(2); 8(3); 9(2); 12(3); 13; 14; 15; 17; 18(2); 19(2); 20(2); 22; 23; 24(3); 25; 26; 28; 29; 30(3); 23:5; 7; 9(2); 10; 12(2); 14; 16; 17(2); 24:1; 2; 3(3); 4(4); 5(2); 6(3); 7(2); 8(3); 9(3); 10(2); 12(3); 13(3); 14(4); 15(3); 16(3); 17(4); 18(4); 19(2); 20(2); 21(2); 22; 24(3); 25:1; 5(2); 6; 26:2; 3; 5(2); 7(3); 8(2); 9; 10(2); 11; 12(3); 14; 27:2; 3(2); 7(2); 8(2); 10; 11(2); 13(3); 14; 16(2); 17(3); 18; 19; 20; 21; 28:1; 2(2); 3(2); 4(4); 5; 6(2); 7; 8(2); 9(3); 10; 11(2); 12; 13(3); 14(2); 15; 16(3); 17(3); 18; 19; 20; 21(3); 22; 23(2); 24(3); 25(3); 26(3); 28(2); 29:2; 4(2); 5; 6; 7(3); 8(2); 9; 10(2); 11(2); 12(2); 13(2); 15(2); 16(2); 17(3); 18; 19(2); 23(2); 24; 25(2); 30:1; 2; 3; 4; 6(4); 7(2); 8; 11; 12(2); 14; 15; 16; 17; 18(2); 19; 22; 23; 24; 25; 27; 28(4); 29; 30(3); 31; 31:2; 3(2); 7; 11; 13; 15(2); 16(3); 17; 20; 21(2); 22; 24; 26(2); 28(2); 29; 31; 32(3); 34(2); 35; 37; 38; 39(2); 40; 32:2(4); 5; 6(2); 8(2); 9; 18; 33:3; 4(3); 6; 8; 11; 15(2); 16; 18(2); 19; 22(2); 24; 25; 28(2); 30(3); 34:3(2); 8; 10; 11; 12; 13(2); 16; 19(4); 20(2); 21; 22; 25; 26; 28(4); 30(2); 36; 35:5(2); 8; 9(4); 10; 11(3); 12; 13; 36:6(3); 7(2); 12; 13; 14; 15; 16; 17(2); 19; 20; 26; 27(2); 28; 29(3); 30(2); 31; 32(2); 33(3); 37:2(2); 3(3); 4; 6(4); 7; 8; 9(3); 10(3); 11; 12(3); 14; 15; 16(3); 17(2); 18; 21(3); 22; 23; 38:1(2); 4(2); 5(2); 6(2); 7(2); 8(2); 9(2); 12(2); 13(3); 14; 15(2); 16(4); 17(3); 18(2); 19(2); 20(3); 21; 22(4); 23(2); 24(3); 25(2); 26(2); 27(3); 28(2); 29(2); 30(3); 31(2); 33(3); 34; 36(2); 37(2); 38(2); 39(4); 40; 41; 39:1(4); 2(3); 5(2); 6(2); 7(4); 8(2); 9; 10(3); 13(3); 14(2); 15(2); 18; 19; 20; 21(2); 22; 23(3); 24(3); 25(5); 26(2); 27; 28(4); 29; 30; 40:1; 2; 3; 6(2); 11; 12; 13; 16; 17; 19(2); 20(3); 21(3); 22(3); 41:6(2); 8; 9(2); 11; 13; 14; 18(2); 23; 24; 25; 26(4); 28; 29; 30; 31(2); 32; 34; 42:1; 5(2); 7(4); 8; 9(5); 10(3); 11(2); 12(2); 14(6); 15(2); **Ps** 1:1(6); 2(2); 3; 4(3); 5(4); 6(5); 2:1(2); 2(4); 4(2); 7(2); 8(3); 10; 11; 12(2); 3:3; 4; 5; 7(3); 8; 4:3(2); 5(2); 6; 7; 5:t; 2; 3(2); 5; 6(2); 7; 10; 12; 6:t; 5; 6; 8(2); 9(2); 7:3(3); 5(3); 6(2); 7(2); 8(2); 9(5); 10; 11(2); 12(3); 13(2); 15; 17:3; 8:t; 1(2); 2(3); 3(3); 4; 5; 6; 7(2); 8(6); 9; 9:t; 4; 5(2); 7; 8(2); 9(2); 11(2); 12(2); 13; 14(2); 15(4); 16(2); 17(2); 18(3); 19; 20; 10:2(3); 3(3); 4(2); 8(5); 9(2); 10; 12; 13; 14(3); 15(3); 16(2); 17(2); 18(4); 11:t; 1; 2(3); 3(2); 5(2); 6(2); 7(2); 12:t; 1(3); 3(2); 5(5); 6(2); 8(2); 13; 3; 6; 14:t; 1; 2(2); 4(2); 5(2); 7(3); 7(3); 15:2; 4; 5; 16:2; 3(3); 5(2); 6; 7(2); 8; 11; 17:1; 2; 3; 4(4); 8(3); 9; 11; 13; 14(2); 18(9); 10:3(3); 12(3); 13; 15(5); 18(2); 20(2); 21(2); 24(2); 25; 26(2); 27; 28; 30(2); 31; 35; 39; 40; 41; 42(4); 43(4); 44; 45; 46(2); 47; 48; 49; 19:t; 1(3); 4(4); 6(4); 7(6); 8(6); 9(4); 10; 13; 14(2); 20:t; 1(4); 2; 5(2); 6(2); 7(2); 9; 21:t; 2; 3; 7(4); 9(2); 10(2); 11; 12; 13(3); 15(5); 18(2); 20(2); 21(2); 24(2); 25; 26(2); 27; 28; 30:2(2); 31; 35; 39; 40; 41; 42(4); 43(4); 44; 45; 46(2); 47; 48; 49; 19:t; 14; 4(4); 4; 7(6); 8(6); 5; 16(2); 22:t; 1; 2; 3; 6; 7(2); 8; 9; 10; 14; 15; 16(2); 20:3; 21(3); 22(2); 23(3); 24(2); 25; 26(2); 27(5); 28(4); 29; 30; 23:1; 2; 3; 4(2); 5; 6(3); 6(4); 7; 8(2); 9; 10(2); 25:5(2); 7; 8(2); 9(2); 10(2); 12(2); 13; 14(2); 15(2); 17; 26:1; 5(2); 7; 8(2); 12(2); 27:1(3); 2; 4(6); 5(2); 6; 10; 12; 13(4); 14(2); 28:1; 2; 3(2); 4(2); 5(4); 6(2); 7(3); 8(4); 9; 31:t; 4; 6; 8(2); 13; 15; 17(2); 18(2); 19; 20(3); 21; 22; 23(4); 24; 32:2(3); 4; 10; 11(2); 12(2); 15(3); 16(4); 17(2); 18(3); 19(3); 1(2); 2; 3; 4; 6; 7(2); 8(2); 9; 10; 11(3); 12; 37:1(4); 5; 6(2); 7(2); 8(2); 9; 10; 11(3); 12(3); 13(2); 14(3); 16; 18(2); 20; 23; 24; 25(3); 26(4); 27(2); 28; 36:3(3); 1(2); 3; 4; 9; 10; 11(2); 12(3); 13; 14; 15; 16(5); 17(2); 18(2); 19(4); 117:1; 2(3); 118:1; 3; 4; 5(2); 6; 7; 8; 9; 10(2); 11(2); 12(3); 13; 14; 15(5); 16(4); 17(2); 18; 19(2); 20(2); 22(4); 23; 24(2); 26(4); 27(4); 29; 19:14(2); 3; 13; 14; 19; 20; 21; 25; 27; 29; 30; 32; 33(2); 35; 43; 49; 51; 53; 54; 55; 61(2); 64; 69; 72; 78; 83; 84; 85; 88; 90; 95; 97; 100; 108; 110; 111; 112; 115; 119(2); 122; 123; 130(2); 134; 142; 144; 147(2); 148; 155; 158; 160; 120:1; 4; 5; 121:1; 2; 5(2); 6(2); 7; 8; 122:1(2); 4(6); 5(2); 6; 9(2); 123:1; 2(5); 4(3); 124:1; 2; 4(2); 5; 6; 7(3); 8(2); 125:1; 2(2); 3(5); 5(2); 126:1(2); 2(2); 3; 4(2); 127:1(5); 2; 3(3); 4(2); 5(3); 128:1; 2; 3; 4(2); 5(3); 129:3; 4(3); 7; 8(4); 130:1; 2; 5; 6(3); 7(2); 131:3; 132:2(2); 3; 5(2); 6(2); 8; 10; 133:2(4); 3(5); 134:4(4); 2(2); 3; 135:14(4); 3(2); 4; 5; 6(2); 7(5); 8; 9; 11(2); 14; 15(3); 19(2); 20(3); 21(2); 136:1; 2; 3; 5; 6(4); 8; 13; 14; 15; 16; 19; 20; 26; 137:1; 2(2); 3; 4; 6; 7(3); 9; 138:1; 3; 4(3); 5(4); 6(3); 7(2); 8(4); 139:t; 9(4); 11(2); 12(5); 15(2); 17; 18; 19; 24; 140:t; 1(2); 4(3); 5(2); 6(2); 7(3); 8(2); 9(2); 10; 11(2); 12(2); 141:2(2); 3; 5; 7(2); 8; 9(3); 10; 142:t; 1(2); 3; 5(2); 7; 143:3(2); 5(2); 7; 8(2); 10; 144:1; 3; 5; 7; 10; 11; 14; 15; 145:3; 5; 6; 7; 9; 11; 12(2); 14; 15; 16; 17; 18; 19; 20(2); 21(2); 146:1(2); 2; 3; 5(4); 6(3); 7(2); 8(3); 9(5); 10(2); 11; 12; 14(2); 16; 18; 20; 148:1(4); 4; 5(2); 7(2); 11(2); 13(3); 14(4); 149:1(3); 2; 3(2); 4(2); 5; 6; 7(2); 9(2); 150:1(2); 3(3); 4; 5(2); 6(2); **Prov** 1:1(2); 2; 3; 4(2); 6(3); 7(3); 8(2); 11; 12(2); 15; 17(2); 19(3); 20; 21(4); 22; 29(2); 31; 32(3); 2:5(3); 6; 7; 8(2); 12(3); 13(2); 14(2); 16(2); 17(2); 18; 19; 20(3); 21(3); 22(3); 3:3; 4; 5; 7; 9(2); 11(2); 12(2); 13(2); 14(3); 15; 19(3); 20(3); 25(2); 26; 27; 31; 32(3); 33(6); 34(2); 35(2); 4:1; 3; 5; 7; 10; 11; 14(3); 17(2); 18(4); 19(2); 21; 23; 26; 27(2); 5:3; 6; 7; 8; 9; 10; 11; 13; 14(2); 16; 18; 19; 20; 21(3); 22(2); 23; 6:2(2); 3; 5(4); 6; 8(2); 10; 16; 20; 23(4); 24; 26(2); 31; 34(2); 7:2; 3; 5(2); 6; 7(2); 8(2); 9(3); 10; 12; 16; 18; 20; 148:1(4); 4; 5(2); 7(2); 8:2(4); 3(5); 4; 6; 8; 11; 13(4); 16(2); 20(3); 22(2); 23(2); 25(5); 26(5); 27(3); 28(3); 29(4); 31(2); 34(2); 35; 9:3(2); 5; 6(2); 10(5); 11; 14(3); 18(2); 10:1(2); 3(5); 4(4); 6(4); 7(4); 8(2); 11(3); 12; 14(2); 15(2); 17; 18(2); 20; 21(2); 22(2); 24(4); 28(4); 29(4); 30(3); 31(3); 32(4); 11:1; 2; 3(3); 4; 5(3); 6(2); 7; 8(2); 9; 10(3); 11(5); 13; 14(2); 17; 18; 20; 21(3); 23; 24; 27(2); 28(2); 13:2(3); 4(4); 6(2); 12:1; 2; 4(2); 6; 7; 8(2); 9(2); 10(2); 11(2); 13(3); 14; 16(6); 17; 21; 22(2); 23; 24(3); 15; 26:3(3); 27(2); 28(2); 13:2(3); 4(4); 6(2);

8(2); 9(4); 10; 12(2); 13(2); 14(3); 15; 19(2); 21; 22(3); 23(2); 25(4); 14:1; 2; 3(4); 4(3); 7(2); 8(3); 9; 10; 11(4); 12(2); 13(2); 14; 15(2); 16; 18(2); 19(5); 20(2); 21; 23(2); 24(3); 26(2); 27(3); 28(5); 30(4); 31(2); 32(2); 33(2); 35; 15:2(3); 3(4); 4; 6(4); 7; 8(5); 9(3); 10; 11(3); 12; 13(2); 14(2); 15(2); 16; 18(2); 19(5); 20(2); 21; 22; 23; 24(2); 25(5); 26(5); 29(4); 30(4); 31(3); 33(3); 16:15(3); 2(3); 3; 4(3); 5; 6(2); 7; 9; 10(2); 11(3); 12; 13; 14; 15(3); 17(2); 19(3); 20; 21(3); 22; 23(2); 24(2); 25(2); 28; 29; 31(2); 32; 33(4); 17:2(2); 3(4); 5; 6(2); 7; 9; 10(2); 11(3); 12; 13; 14; 15(3); 17(2); 18(2); 19; 20; 21(3); 22; 23(2); 24(2); 25(2); 27; 28(2); 19:1; 2; 3(2); 4; 6(2); 7(2); 11; 12(3); 13(2); 14(2); 16; 17(2); 21(2); 22; 23(2); 27(2); 28(2); 29; 20:2(2); 4(2); 5; 7; 8; 10; 12(3); 14; 15; 21(2); 22; 23; 24; 25; 26(2); 27(5); 28; 29(4); 30(4); 31(3); 33(3); 35; 15:2(3); 3; 4(3); 5; 6(2); 7; 8(3); 9(2); 10; 11(3); 12; 13; 14; 15(3); 16; 18(2); 19(5); 20; 21(3); 22; 23(3); 24; 25; 26; 28; 23:6; 8; 9(2); 10(3); 12; 13(3); 15; 22; 23; 24(2); 26; 27; 29; 30(4); 31(3); 33(3); 25:1; 2(3); 3(3); 4(3); 5(2); 6; 7(2); 8; 13; 15; 22; 23; 24(2); 26; 26:2(3); 3(3); 6(3); 7(3); 9(2); 13(3); 14(2); 15; 16; 17; 19; 20(2); 21(2); 22; 23; 24; 25(3); 26(4); 27(2); 28:1(2); 2(3); 3; 4(3); 5; 6; 7; 8; 9; 10(2); 11(2); 12; 14; 15; 16; 17(2); 23; 24(2); 25; 27; 28(2); 29:2(4); 4(2); 7; 8(3); 10(3); 13(3); 14; 15; 16(4); 17(4); 20; 21; 22; 23(3); 24; 25(3); 26(4); 27(2); 28:1(2); 2; 3; 4(3); 5; 6; 7(2); 9; 10(3); 11(2); 12; 14; 16; 17; 18(2); 19; 20; 21(2); 23; 24; 25(3); 26(4); 27(2); 28:1(2); 2; 3; 4(3); 5; 6; 7(2); 9; 10(3); 11(2); 12; 14; 16; 17; 18(2); 19; 20; 21(2); 23; 24; 25(3); 26(4); 27(2); 28:1(2); 2; 3; 4(4); 14(3); 15; 16(4); **Eccl** 1:1(3); 2; 3; 4; 5(2); 6(4); 7(5); 8(2); 9(2); 12; 13; 14(2); 2:3(3); 6; 8(4); 11(3); 12(2); 14(2); 15; 16(5); 17(2); 18(2); 19; 20(2); 22(2); 23; 24; 26; 3:1; 10(2); 11(4); 13(2); 16(3); 17(2); 18(2); 19(3); 20; 21(4); 4:1(4); 2(2); 3(2); 5; 6; 7; 10; 15(3); 16; 5:1(2); 3; 6(2); 7; 8(4); 9(4); 11(2); 12(2); 7:12(2); 6:1; 3; 5(2); 7(2); 8(4); 9(4); 11; 12(2); 7:12; 2(4); 3(3); 5(3); 6(3); 7; 8(4); 9; 10(2); 11; 12; 13; 14(5); 15; 16; 5:1(2); 3; 6:2; 7; 8(4); 9(4); 11; 12(2); 7:12; 2(4); 3(3); 5(3); 6(3); 7; 8(4); 9; 10(2); 11; 12; 13; 14(5); 15; 19(2); 25(2); 26(2); 27(2); 8:13(2); 9(3); 2(7); 3(4); 4; 5(3); 9; 6(2); 7; 10(2); 11; 12; 2(4); 3(3); 5(3); 6(3); 7; 9:1(3); 2; 3; 4(2); 5(3); 6(3); 7; 8(4); 9(4); 11; 12(2); 7:13; 14(5); 15; 19(2); 25(2); 26(2); 27(2); 8:13(2); 9(3); **Song** 1:1; 2; 3(4); 4(2); 5(2); 6(3); 7; 8(3); 12(2); 14; 17; 2:1(3); 2(2); 3(4); 4; 7(3); 8(3); 9(2); 11(2); 12(6); 13(3); 14(4); 15(3); 16; 17(3); 3:2(3); 3(2); 4; 5(2); 6(2); 7; 8; 9; 10(5); 11(4); 4:2; 4; 5; 6(4); 8(5); 10; 11(3); 14; 16; 5:2(3); 4(2); 5(2); 7(4); 10; 11; 12(2); 14; 15; 6:2(3); 3; 9(5); 10(3); 11(5); 12; 13(2); 7:1(3); 4(3); 5(3); 8(4); 9(3); 11(2); 12(4); 13; 8:1; 2; 5(2); 6(2); 7; 8; 11(2); 12; 13(2); 14; **Is** 1:1(3); 2; 3(2); 4(2); 5(2); 6(3); 8; 9; 10(3); 11(5); 13(3); 16; 17(3); 18; 19(2); 20(3); 21; 23(3); 24(3); 26(4); 28(4); 29(2); 31(2); 2:1(2); 2(6); 3(7); 4; 5(2); 6(4); 8; 9(2); 10(4); 11(3); 12(2); 13(2); 14(2); 16; 17(3); 18; 19(7); 20(2); 21(7); 3:1(6); 2(6); 3(5); 5(5); 6; 7; 8(2); 9; 10(2); 11(2); 12; 13(2); 14(6); 15(3); 16(2); 17(5); 18(3); 19(3); 20(6); 21; 22(4); 23(4); 25(2); 26; 4:2(4); 3; 4(7); 5(3); 6; 5:2(3); 5(2); 6; 7(4); 8(2); 9; 10; 11; 12(6); 15(4); 16; 17(3); 18(6); 19(3); 23; 24(8); 25(5); 27(2); 29; 30(5); 6:1(3); 2; 3; 4(4); 5(6); 7(4); 8(2); 9; 10; 11(3); 12; 13; 14; 15(3); 17(2); 18(6); 19; 20; 21(2); 7:1(5); 2(5); 3; 4; 5; 6(2); 7; 8; 9(2); 10; 11(3); 12; 14; 15(2); 16(4); 17(3); 18(6); 19(3); 20(8); 21; 22; 23(7); 24(5); 26(5); 25:3(3); 4(7); 5(6); 6(3); 7(3); 8(4); 9; 10(3); 11(2); 12(4); 26:1; 2(3); 4(2); 5(3); 6(5); 7(4); 8(3); 9(4);

10(4); 11(2); 15(4); 17; 18(3); 19(3); 20; 21(4); 27:1(4); 3; 4; 5(2); 6(2); 7(4); 9(2); 13(6); 28:1(4); 2(3); 3(2); 4(5); 5(2); 6(2); 7(4); 9(2); 12(3); 13(2); 14(2); 15; 16; 17(6); 18; 19(2); 20(2); 21(2); 22(2); 24(2); 25(6); 27(4); 28; 29; 29:1; 4(4); 5(3); 6(2); 7(2); 8(2); 10(4); 11(2); 12; 13(2); 14(2); 15(2); 16(3); 17; 18(5); 19(4); 20(2); 21(2); 22(2); 23(4); 30:1(2); 2(2); 3(3); 6(3); 7; 8; 9(2); 10(2); 11(3); 12; 14(5); 15(2); 16; 17(3); 18(2); 19(2); 20(3); 21(3); 22(2); 23(4); 24(5); 25(3); 26(11); 27(3); 28(6); 29(4); 30(4); 31(3); 32(2); 33(4); 31:1(2); 2(3); 3(2); 4(6); 5; 6; 8(4); 9(2); 32:2(3); 3(2); 4(2); 5(2); 6(6); 7(4); 8; 10(2); 12(3); 13(3); 14(4); 15(3); 16(2); 17(2); 19(2); 20(3); 33:2; 3(5); 4(3); 5; 6(7); 8(4); 9; 10; 12(3); 14(3); 15; 16; 17(2); 18(3); 20(3); 21; 22(3); 23(4); 24(2); 34:1(2); 2(3); 3; 4(5); 5; 6(3); 7; 8; 10(2); 11(5); 12(2); 13; 14(6); 15(2); 16(2); 17; 35:1(6); 16(4); 17(2); 18(2); 19(2); 20(3); 21; 22(6); 37:1(2); 26; 3(2); 4(7); 5; 6(4); 7; 8; 10(2); 11(5); 12(2); 13(4); 14; 14(6); 15(2); 16(2); 17(3); 18(2); 19(2); 20; 22(2); 23; 24; 28(3); 44:2(2); 3; 4(2); 5(4); 6(5); 7(2); 11; 12(4); 13(3); 14(4); 14; 15(4); 16; 17; 19(4); 20(5); 21; 22(3; 39:1; 2(6); 3; 5(2); 6(2); 7(2); 8(2); 40:2; 3(5); 4(2); 5(4); 6; 7(5); 8(3); 9(2); 10; 11; 12(7); 13(2); 14(2); 15(4); 16; 19(2); 21(3); 22(4); 23(3); 24(2); 25; 26; 27; 28(5); 29; 30(2); 31; 41:1; 2(4); 3; 4(5); 5(3); 7(5); 8; 9(3); 10; 13; 14(2); 15(2); 16(4); 17(3); 18(2); 19(2); 20(6); 23; 24; 28(3); 44:2(2); 3; 4(2); 5(4); 6(5); 7(2); 8; 9; 10(6); 11(7); 12(2); 13; 15(2); 16; 17; 19; 20; 21(2); 23; 24; 28(3); 44:2(2); 3; 4(2); 5; 6(3); 7(4); 8; 9; 10(6); 11(7); 47:1(3); 2(2); 4(4); 5(2); 6; 7(3); 8; 9(3); 12; 13(4); 14(3); 48:1(5); 2(3); 3(2); 5; 7(2); 8; 10; 12(2); 13(2); 14(2); 16(2); 17(4); 18(2); 19(3); 20(4); 21(5); 22(2); 49:1(3); 2; 4; 5(4); 6(5); 7(5); 8(4); 9(2); 10(2); 13; 14; 15; 16; 18; 19(2); 20(3); 22(3); 23(3); 24(3); 25(5); 26(2); 50:1(2); 2(3); 3; 4(4); 5; 6(2); 7; 9(2); 10(4); 11(2); 51:1(4); 3(4); 4; 5(2); 6(4); 7(2); 8(2); 9(4); 10(6); 11(2); 12; 13(8); 14(2); 17(5); 18(3); 19(2); 20(5); 22(5); 23(3); 52:1(3); 2; 3(2); 4(2); 5(2); 7(2); 8(3); 9; 10(6); 11(3); 12(2); 13; 15; 16(5); 17; 19(2); 20(2); 21; 22(3); 23(3); 24(2); **Jer** 1:1(4); 2(5); 3(7); 4(2); 5(3); 7; 8; 9(2); 10(2); 11(2); 12; 13(5); 14(4); 15(8); 16; 18(6); 19; 2:1(2); 2(2); 3(3); 4(4); 5; 6(7); 7(2); 8(2); 9(5); 10(4); 11(2); 12; 13; 15; 16(2); 17(2); 18(5); 19(2); 20; 21; 22; 24(2); 26(2); 27; 28(2); 29; 30; 31(3); 6:1(3); 3(2); 4(5); 6(7); 8(2); 10; 11(2); 12; 13; 15; 16(2); 17(2); 18(5); 19(2); 20; 21; 22; 24(2); 26(2); 28(7); 29; 30; 31(3); 6:1(3); 3(2); 4(5); 6; 7(2); 48:1(2); 2(3); 4(3); 5(2); 6(2); 7(3); 9; 10(2); 12(2); 13; 14; 15(3); 16; 17(2); 24(2); 25(2); 28(5); 29(2); 29:2; 30(4); 31(2); 32(3); 33(3); 34(2); 35(2); 36(2); 37(3); 38(3); 39; 40; 41(3); 42; 43(3); 44(6); 45(7); 46; 47(4); 49:1(2); 2(4); 3; 4; 5; 6(3); 7(2); 8(3); 10; 14(3); 16; 17; 18(3); 19(4); 20(5); 21(5); 22(4); 23(2); 25(2); 26(2); 27(2); 28(4); 29(2); 30(5); 31; 32(3); 35(2); 36(3); 37(3); 38(4); 39; 40(6); 41(3); 42(4); 44(2); 45(2); 46(4); 47(8); 48; 21:1(2); 2(2); 3(4); 4(4); 5; 6; 7(2); 9; 10; 11(2); 12(2); 13(3); 14(6); 16(2); 17; 18(2); 19(5); 20(3); 21(6); 23; 24(2); 26(4); 28(6); 29(2); 30(2); 31(2); 32(4); 22:12(2); 3; 4(3; 6; 7(4); 9(2); 12; 13; 14(2); 15(2); 16(3); 17(3); 18(4); 19; 21; 22(2); 23(2); 24; 25(4); 26(3); 27(2); 28(4); 29(2); 30(3); 31(2); 32(3); 33; 34(2); 35(2); 37(3); 38(4); 39; 40; 41; 42(4); 43(2); 44(10); 33:1(5); 2(4); 4(7); 5(2); 6; 7(3); 9(5); 10(3); 11(16); 12(2); 13(12); 14(4); 15(2); 16(2); 17(3); 18(2); 19(2); 20(3); 21(2); 22(5); 23(2); 24(2); 25(2); 26(2); 34:1(6); 2(5); 3(2); 4(4); 5(4); 6; 7(3); 8(4); 10(3); 11(6); 12(3); 13(5); 14; 15; 17(7); 18(5); 19(8); 20(5); 21; 22(4); 43:14(4); 3(4); 5(5); 6(7); 7(3); 8(4); 9(7); 10; 12; 13(3); 14; 15(3); 17; 18(2); 19; 20(2); 21(3); 22; 23(3); 24; 25(2); 26(3); 27(2); 28(4); 29(2); 30(3); 31(2); 32(3); 33; 34(2); 35(2); 36; 37; 38; 39(2); 40; 41(3); 42; 43(4); 44; 45(2); 46(4); 47(8); 48; 21:1(2); 2(2); 3; 4; 5(6); 6(3; 7(3); 8(4); 9(2); 10(2); 12; 13(3); 14; 15(3); 17; 18(2); 19; 20; 22(2); 23(5); 24(4); 25(3; 26; 29:1(6); 30:1(4); 31:1(3); 32:2(3); 33(2); 34(4); 35; 36; 37; 38; 39(2); 40(6); 41(2); 42:1(7); 2(3); 3(4); 4(2); 5(5); 6(6); 7(6); 8(4); 9(3);

18; 19(4); 21; 17:1(4); 2(2); 3(2); 4; 5(3); 6(4); 7(3); 8(3); 9; 10(4); 11(2); 12(2); 13(4); 15(2); 16; 17; 18; 19(2); 20(2); 19(7); 20(3); 21(3); 22(2); 24(4); 25(4); 26(8); 27(5); 18:1(2); 2; 3(2); 4(4); 5(2); 6(3); 8; 10; 11(3); 12; 13(3); 14(4); 15; 17(4); 18(6; 19; 21(4); 23; 19:1(5); 2(5); 3(5); 4(2); 5(6); 7(7); 8; 9(4); 10(3); 11; 12(2); 13(6); 14(4); 15(3); 20:1(4); 2(5); 3(3); 4(5); 5(6); 8(2); 10; 11; 12(3); 13(5); 14(2); 15; 16(5); 17; 18; 21:1(3); 2(4); 6; 7(10); 8(3); 9(4); 10(3); 11(4); 12(5); 13(3); 14(3); 22:1(3); 2(3); 3(7); 4(2); 5; 6(3); 7; 8; 9(2); 10; 11(2); 12(3); 13(5); 14(2); 15; 16(5); 17; 18; 19(6); 20(2); 21(2); 22(3); 23(6); 24(4); 24:4(4); 25:4(4); 26(7); 27(3); 28(2); 29(4); 30(4); 31(6); 33(3); 34(3); 35(3); 36(5); 37(3); 38(3); 26:1(4); 2(6); 3(2); 4; 5(2); 6(2); 7(5); 8(2); 10; 11; 12(3); 13(5); 14(2); 15; 16(5); 17; 18; 21:1(5); 2(4); 6; 7(10); 8(3); 9(4); 10(3); 11(4); 12:5; 13(3); 14(3); 15(5); 16(5); 17; 18(2); 19(3); 20(4); 2:1; 2(3); 3; 4; 5(4); 6(4); 7; 8; 9; 11; 14(4); 31:1(4); 3; 4; 5; 6(3); 7(4); 8(6); 9; 10(3); 11(2); 12(6); 13(2); 14(5); 15(2); 16(5); 17; 18(8); 19(6); 20(2); 21(2); 22(2); 23:5; 24; 25; 26(3); 27(6); 28(3); 29(2); 30(6); 31:1(2); 32(6); 37:1(6); 2(5); 3(6); 4; 6(3); 7; 9; 20(2); 21(3); 22:1(2); 23:1(2); 24(5); 26(3); 27(2); 28:1(6); 29:2; 30:1(2); 3(2); 4; 5(6); 6(2); 7; 8; 9; 10; 12(2); 13(3); 14; 16(3); 17(2); 18:1(6); 20(2); 21(8); 38:1(6); 2(5); 3(3); 4(8); 5(3); 6(6); 7; 8(2); 9(3); 10; 11(5); 12(2); 13; 14(6); 16(3); 17(4); 18(3); 19(3); 20(2); 22(4); 23(3); 26; 27(3); 39:1(2); 2(5); 3(6); 4(9); 5(3); 6; 7(3); 8(4); 9; 10(5); 11; 12(2); 13(2); 14(2); 15(3); 16(5); 17; 26:1(5); 2(2); 3(2); 4(2); 5(5); 6(3); 7(2); 8(3); 10(5); 11(3); 12(3); 13(2); 14(5); 15(2); 17; 18(3; 19(7); 10; 16; 17; 18; 19; 20(4); 21(5; 22(4); 23; 24; 25(2); 26(3); 27(2); 28(4); 29(2); 30(5); 31; 34:1(6); 2(5); 3(2); 4(4); 5(4); 6; 7(3); 8(4); 10(3); 11(6); 12(3); 13(5); 14; 15; 17(7); 18(5); 19(8); 20(5); 21; 22(4); 43:14(4); 3(4); 5(5); 6(7); 7(3); 8(4); 9(7); 3(3); 4(7); 5(2); 6; 7(3); 9(5); 10(3); 11(16); 12(2); 13(12); 14(4); 15(2); 16(2); 17(3); 18(2); 19(2); 20(3); 21(2); 22(2); 23(3); 26(2); 34:16(2); 3(2); 4(4); 5; 6(3); 7(4); 8; 9; 10; 11(5); 12(2); 13(2); 14(6); 16(3); 17(5); 18(3); 19(7); 20(5); 21(6); 22(2); 3:1(2); 3; 12; 13; 14; 18; 19(2); 22; 23(2); 24(3); 25(3); 26(2); 27; 29; 31; 32; 33; 34(2); 35(3); 36; 37; 38(2); 39; 40; 41; 45(3); 48(2); 50; 51; 53; 55; 57; 58; 62(2); 64; 66(2); 4:1(5); 2(4); 3(5); 4(4); 5; 6(5); 8; 9(3);

10(4); 11(2); 12(7); 13(5); 14; 15; 16(5); 19(4); 20(4); 21(2); 22; 5:6(3); 9(3); 10; 11(3); 12; 13(3); 14(3); 15; 16; 18(2); **Eze** 1:1(7); 2(3); 3(9); 4(5); 5(3); 7(3); 8; 10(7); 12; 13(6); 14(2); 15(3); 16(4); 19(5); 20(5); 21(5); 22(6); 23(3); 24(6); 25; 26(7); 27(5); 28(10); 2:2; 3; 4; 3:1; 4; 5; 7(2); 11(3); 12(3); 13(5); 14(4); 15(2); 16(3); 17(2); 18(3); 19; 21(2); 22(3); 23(5); 24; 26; 27; 4:1; 2; 3(2); 4(4); 5(5); 6(2); 7; 8; 9(2); 11; 13(3); 16; 5:1; 2; 3(2); 4(4); 13; 14(2); 15(2); 16(2); 17; 18(2); 19(6); 20(2); 21(2); 22(3); 23(2); 24(4); 26:1(4); 27:6(2); 8:1(7); 2(4); 3(10); 4(4); 5(7); 6(2); 7(3); 8(2); 9; 10(3); 11(4); 12(7); 14(4); 16(12); 17(4); 9:1; 2(4); 3(7); 4(8); 5(2); 6(3); 7(4); 8; 9(7); 10:1(5); 2(5); 3(6); 4(10); 5(5); 6(4); 7(4); 8(2); 10:1(5); 2(5); 3(6); 4(10); 5(5); 6(4); 7(5); 8(2); 9(2); 10(3); 11:1(8); 8(2); 3(2); 13(5); 14(2); 15(4); 16(4); 17(4); 18(2); 19; 21(2); 22(4); 23(7); 24(4); 25; 12:1(2); 2; 5; 6(3); 7(3); 8(3); 9(2); 10(3); 12(4); 13(2); 14; 15(3); 16(5); 17(2); 19(6); 20(3); 21(2); 22(3); 23(3); 24; 25(4); 26(2); 27(3); 28(3); 13:1(2); 2(3); 4(2); 5(6); 6(2); 7(3); 8; 10; 11(5); 12(2); 13(4); 14(6); 15(2); 16(4); 17(4); 18(2); 19; 21(2); 22(4); 23:7; 24(4); 25; 1:4(4); 5; 6(3); 7(2); 9; 10(2); 11(4); 12(3); 13(3); 14; 15(2); 16(4); 17; 18(2); 19; 21(2); 22(4); 23(7; 24(4); 25; 12:1(2); 2; 5; 6(3); 7(3); 8(3); 9(2); 10(3); 12(4); 13(2); 14; 48; 49(3); 53(4); 56; 57(4); 58; 59(3); 60; 62; 63; 17:1(2); 2; 3(4); 4; 5(2); 6; 7; 9(5); 10(2); 11(2); 12(4); 13(3); 14; 15; 16(4); 17; 18(2); 19; 21(2); 22(4); 23(4); 24(8); 18:1(2); 2(3); 3; 4(5); 6(3); 7(3); 8(4); 9(2); 10(2); 12; 13(3); 14; 15(3); 16(2); 17(2); 18(2); 19; 20(3); 22(2); 23(6); 24(6); 27(2); 28(4); 29(2); 30(3); 31(2); 32(3); 33; 34(2); 35(2); 36; 37(3); 38(4); 39; 40(6); 41(3); 42(4); 44(2); 45(2); 46(4); 47(8); 48; 21:1(2); 2(2); 4(4); 5; 6; 7(4); 9(2); 10(2); 12; 13(3); 14; 15(2); 16(2); 17; 18(4); 21; 22; 23; 25(3); 26(3); 27(5); 28(3); 29(5); 30; 32(3); 33(4); 34(5); 35(2); 36(2); 28:1(2); 2(6); 7(2); 8(4); 9; 10(4); 11(2); 12(3); 13(11); 14(4); 15; 16(5); 17; 18(5); 19; 20(2); 22(3; 23(4); 24(2); 25(5); 26; 29:1(6); 3(3); 4(3); 5(7); 6(8); 9; 10; 11(4); 12(9); 13; 14; 15(3); 17(3); 18; 19; 20(2); 21(5); 22(2); 23(2); 24(3); 25; 26; 27(8); 28(7); 29(3); 30(6); 31; 34:1(2); 2(6); 3(3); 4; 5(2); 6(3); 7(2); 8(3); 9(2); 10(4); 11; 12(2); 13(6); 14(2); 15; 16; 17; 18(4); 20(3); 21; 24(2); 25(4); 26(2); 27(6); 28(3); 29(3); 30(3); 31; 35:1(2); 2; 3; 4; 5(6); 6; 8; 9; 10; 11; 12(2); 14(2); 15(3); 36:1(3); 2(3); 3; 4(11); 5(5); 6(8); 7(2); 8; 9(3); 10; 17(2); 18(2); 19(2); 20(3); 21(2); 22(3); 23(5); 24; 26; 28; 29; 30(5); 32(3); 34(4); 35(2); 36(4); 37(2); 38(4); 37:16(2; 4(2); 5; 6; 7; 8(3); 9(4); 10; 11; 12(2); 13; 14(2); 16(3; 18; 19(5); 20; 21(3); 22(2); 23; 25; 26; 28(3); 38:1(2; 2(2); 3(5); 5(2); 6(7); 17(2); 18(3); 19(2; 20(3); 21; 22; 23(2); 19:1(2); 2(5); 3(3); 4(5); 5(2); 6(7; 7(6); 8(4); 9(3);

10(7); 11(4); 12(8); 13(11); 14(4); 15(3); 16(3); 17(2); 18(2); 19(2); 20(3); 43:1(3); 2(5); 3(7); 4(6); 5(5); 6(2); 7(7); 8; 9(2); 10(3); 11(11); 12(7); 13(10); 14(7); 15(2); 16(2); 17(5); 18(4); 19(4); 20(5); 21(5); 22(4); 23; 24(3); 25; 26; 27(4); 44:1(4); 2(3); 3(7); 4(7); 5(8); 6(3); 7(2); 8; 9(2); 10; 11(6); 12(2); 13(2); 14(3); 15(8); 17(4); 19(5); 21; 22(2); 23(4); 27(5); 29(3); 30(6); 31; 45:1(7); 2(2); 3(4); 4(7); 5(5); 6(5); 7(17); 8(4); 9(2); 11(8); 12; 13(3); 14(4); 15(3); 16(3); 17(10); 18(5); 19(11); 20(3); 21(4); 22(3); 23(4); 25(10); 46:1(8); 2(10); 3(6); 4(4); 5(3); 6(2); 7; 8(4); 9(14); 10(2); 11(4); 12(6); 13(2); 14(4); 15(3); 16(3); 17(2); 18(2); 19(7); 20(7); 21(4); 22(2); 23; 24(5); 47:1(12); 2(6); 3(5); 4(5); 5; 6(2); 7(4); 8(5); 9(2); 10(3); 11(2); 12(6); 13(4); 14; 15(5); 16(3); 17(6); 18(5); 19(5); 20(4); 21; 22(4); 23(2); 48:1(7); 2(3); 3(3); 4(3); 5(3); 6(3); 7(3); 8(9); 9(2); 10(8); 11(4); 12(3); 13(5); 14(3); 15(6); 16(5); 17(6); 18(7); 19(2); 20(4); 21(18); 22(9); 23(4); 24(3); 25(3); 26(3); 27(3); 28(6); 29(3); 30(3); 31(4); 32; 33; 34; 35(3); **Dan** 1:1(2); 2(7); 3(5); 4(4); 5(5); 6; 7(3); 8(5); 9(2); 10(5); 11(2); 13(4); 15(4); 16(2); 18(5); 19(2); 20(2); 21; 2:1(2); 2(7); 3(2); 4(4); 5(5); 6(4); 7(3); 8(3); 9(4); 10(4); 11(3); 12(2); 13(2); 14(3); 15(4); 16(3); 17; 18(3); 19(2); 20; 21(3); 22(3); 23; 24(6); 25(4); 26(3); 27(9); 28(3); 30(3); 31; 34; 35(11); 36(3); 37; 38(5); 39; 40; 41(5); 42(3); 43; 44(3); 45(11); 46; 47; 48(4); 49(5); 3:1(4); 2(13); 3(12); 5(4); 6(2); 7(8); 8; 9; 10(3); 11; 12(3); 13; 14; 15(5); 16; 17; 18; 19(2); 20(2); 21(2); 22(4); 23(2); 24(4); 25(5); 26(5); 27(4); 28(2); 29; 30(2); 4:1(2); 2(2); 5(2); 6(3); 7(6); 8(5); 9(5); 10(4); 11(5); 12(7); 13; 14(3); 15(8); 17(10); 18(5); 19(5); 20(4); 21(5); 22(2); 23(10); 24(4); 25(5); 26(3); 27; 28; 29(3); 30(5); 31(3); 32(4); 33(3); 34(3); 35(5); 36(2); 37; 5:1(2); 2(4); 3(4); 4; 5(8); 6(2); 7(9); 8(4); 10(5); 11(8); 12(3); 13(5); 14(2); 15(5); 16(4); 17(4); 18; 19; 21(6); 23(4); 24(2); 25; 26(2); 27; 28; 29(2); 30(2); 31(2); 6:1(2); 2(2); 3(3); 4(2); 5; 6; 7(7); 8(4); 9(2); 10; 12(7); 13(4); 14(3); 15(5); 16(3); 17(5); 18(2); 19(3); 20(4); 21; 22; 23(3); 24(6); 25; 26(3); 27(2); 28(3); 7:1(4); 2(3); 3; 4(4); 5(2); 6(2); 7(4); 8(4); 9(5); 10(2); 11(5); 12(2); 13(4); 15(2); 16(3); 17; 18(4); 19(4); 20(2); 21(2); 22(6); 23(3); 24(2); 25(4); 26(2); 27(7); 28(3); 8:1(3); 2(3); 3(4); 4; 5(5); 6(3); 7(5); 8(3); 9(3); 10(4); 11(4); 12(3); 13(5); 14; 15(3); 16(2); 17(3); 18; 19(4); 20(2); 21(4); 22; 23(3); 24(2); 25; 26(4); 27(2); 9:1(6); 2(7); 3; 4(3); 6(3); 7(3); 9; 10(3); 11(4); 12; 13(2); 14(3); 15; 16; 17(2); 18; 20(3); 21(5); 23(4); 24(3); 25(6); 26(7); 27(8); 10:1(5); 4(4); 6(4); 7(3); 9(3); 10; 11; 12; 13(4); 14(2); 15; 16(3); 17; 18; 20(2); 21; 11:1(2); 2(3); 4; 5(2); 6(7); 7(3); 8(2); 9(2); 11(5); 12; 13(3); 14(4); 15(5); 16; 17(2); 18(2); 19; 20(2); 21(3); 22(3); 23; 24(4); 25(4); 26; 27(2); 28; 29(4); 30(3); 31(3); 32(2); 33(2); 35(2); 36(3); 37(2); 38; 39(2); 40(7); 41(3); 42(2); 43(4); 44(2); 45(3); 12:1(3); 2(2); 3(3); 4(4); 5(6); 6(4); 7(5); 8; 9(3); 10(3); 11(3); 12; 13(3); **Hos** 1:1(6); 2(6); 3; 4(5); 5(2); 6; 7(2); 10(7); 11(4); 2:3; 4; 5; 9(2); 10; 12(2); 13(2); 14; 15(4); 16; 17; 18(9); 20; 21(3); 22(4); 23; 3:1(4); 3; 4; 5(4); 4:1(6); 3(6); 4; 5(3); 6; 8; 10; 11; 12; 13(4); 14; 15(2); 16; 19; 5:1; 2; 4(3); 5; 6; 7; 8(2); 9(2); 10(2); 11; 12; 13; 14; 6:1; 2; 3(5); 4; 5(3); 6; 7; 9(2); 10(2); 11; 7:1(4); 3(2); 4(2); 5(2); 6(2); 8; 10(2); 12(2); 16(4); 8:1(3); 3(2); 6(2); 7(4); 8; 10(3); 12; 13(2); 14; 9:2(3); 3; 4(4); 5(4); 6; 7(6); 8(3); 9; 10(3); 11(3); 13; 15; 16; 17; 10:1(3); 3; 4(2); 5(5); 7(2); 8(6); 9(3); 10; 11; 12; 13(2); 14(2); 15; 11:4; 5(2); 6; 7; 9(4); 10(3); 11(2); 12(2); 12:1(2); 2; 3(2); 4; 5(2); 7; 9(4); 10(3); 11(2); 12; 13; 13:2(4); 3(7); 4(2); 5(2); 7; 8(2); 12; 13(3); 14(2); 15(4); 16; 14:1; 2(2); 3(2); 5(2); 6; 7(4); 9(4); **Joel** 1:1(3); 2(2); 4(6); 5; 6(2); 7; 8; 9(6); 10(5); 11(4); 12(8); 13(4); 14(6); 15(4); 16(2); 17(4); 18(3); 19(6); 20(6); 2:1(5); 2(4); 3(2); 4(2); 5(4); 6; 7; 8; 9(4); 10(5); 11(3); 12; 13(2); 14; 15; 16(7); 17(7); 18; 19(2); 20(3); 21; 22(6); 23(6); 24(2); 25(5); 26(2); 27(2); 29(2); 30(2); 31(5); 32(5); 3:1; 2(2); 4; 6(3); 7; 8(4); 9(3); 10; 12(3); 13(4); 14(4); 15(3); 16(7); 17; 18(6); 19(2); 21; **Amos** 1:1(6); 2(4); 3(2); 4(2); 5(7); 6(3); 7(2); 8(5); 9(4); 10(2); 11(3); 12; 13(4); 14(5); 15; 2:1(4); 2(3); 3(4); 4(5); 5; 6(4); 7(7); 8(3); 9(4); 10(4); 11; 12(2); 14(4); 15(2); 16(2); 3:1(3); 2(2); 4; 5(2); 6(3); 7(2); 8(2); 9(8); 10; 11(2); 12(6); 13(3); 14(6); 15(5); 4:1(3); 2(2); 3(3); 5(2); 6; 7(3); 8; 9(2); 10(5); 11(2); 13(7); 5:2; 3(3); 4(2); 6(2); 7; 8(9); 9(4); 10; 11; 12(3); 13; 14(2); 15(5); 16(5); 17; 18(4); 19(2); 20(2); 22; 23(2); 25; 26(2); 27(2); 6:1(3); 2(2); 3(2); 4(5); 5(2); 6(2); 7(2); 8(5); 10(6); 11(3); 12(2); 14(5); 7:1(6); 2(2); 3(2); 4(3); 6(2); 7; 8(3); 9(4); 10(4); 11; 12; 13(2); 15(3); 16(3); 17(3); 8:1; 2(2); 3(3); 4(3); 5(5); 6(4); 7(2); 8(2); 9(4); 10(2); 11(5); 12(4); 13; 14(2); 9:1(8); 3(4); 4; 5(3); 6(7); 7(5); 8(7); 9(3); 10(3); 11(3); 12(3); 13(7); 14(4); 15; **Obad** 1(4); 2; 3(4); 4(3); 5; 6; 7(3); 8(3); 9(2); 11(4); 12(5); 13(4); 14(2); 15(3); 16; 17; 18(5); 19(6); 20(6); 21(3); **Jonah** 1:1(3); 3(5); 4(4); 5(6); 6; 7; 9(4); 10(4); 11(2); 12(2); 13(3); 14; 15(2); 16(3); 17(3); 2:1(2); 2(2); 3(4); 5(4); 6(3); 7; 9(2); 10(3); 3:1(3); 2; 3(2); 4; 5(3); 6; 7(2); 8; 10; 4:2(2); 4; 5(5); 6(2); 7(3); 8(3); 9; 10(3); **Mic** 1:1(4); 2(2); 3(3); 4(4); 5(5); 6(4); 7(6); 8(2); 9; 10(2); 11(2); 12(3); 13(6); 14(2); 15; 16; 2:1(2); 3; 4; 5(2); 7(3); 8(2); 9; 11(2); 12(5); 13(4); 3:1; 2(2); 3(3); 4; 5(2); 6(3); 7(2); 8(2); 9(2); 11(5); 12(4); 4:1(7); 2(7); 4(2); 5(3); 6; 7; 8(6); 10(4); 12(4); 13(3); 5:1(2); 2; 3(3); 4(7); 5(2); 6(5); 7(6); 8(6); 10(2); 11; 13(2); 14; 15; 6:1(3); 2(3); 4(2); 5(3); 6(2); 7(3); 8; 9(4); 10(4);

11(2); 12(2); 14(2); 15; 16(5); 7:1(4); 2(2); 3(3); 4(3); 5; 6(5); 7(2); 8; 9(3); 10(3); 11(2); 12(3); 13(2); 14(4); 15(2); 16; 17(3); 18(2); 19(2); 20(3); **Nah** 1:1(4); 2(3); 3(7); 4(3); 5(4); 6(2); 7(2); 8; 9(2); 11; 12; 14(4); 15(3); 2:1(2); 2(4); 3(5); 4(4); 5(2); 6(3); 7; 9(4); 10(3); 11(7); 12; 13(5); 3:1(2); 2(6); 3(3); 4(4); 5(3); 8(4); 10(2); 11; 12(3); 13(3); 14(3); 15(5); 16(2); 17(5); 18(2); 19(2); **Hab** 1:1(2); 4(3); 5; 6(4); 8(3); 9(3); 10(2); 13(2); 14(3); 15; 17; 2:1; 2(2); 3(2); 4; 8(5); 9; 11(4); 13(4); 14(6); 16(2); 17(5); 18(4); 19(3); 20(2); 3:1; 2(4); 3(3); 4(2); 5; 6(4); 7(3); 8(4); 9(3); 10(4); 11(3); 12(2); 13(6); 14(2); 15(2); 16(3); 17(8); 18(2); 19(2); **Zeph** 1:1(8); 2(2); 3(8); 4(5); 5(3); 6(2); 7(5); 8(4); 9(2); 10(5); 11; 12(2); 13; 14(6); 16(3); 17(2); 18(5); 2:2(7); 3(4); 4; 5(8); 6; 7(6); 8(3); 9(6); 10(2); 11(5); 13; 14(9); 15; 3:1; 2(2); 3(2); 4(2); 5(3); 6; 8(7); 9(3); 10(2); 11; 12(3); 13; 14; 15(4); 17(2); 18(2); 20(3); **Hag** 1:1(11); 2(4); 3(3); 5; 7; 8(3); 9; 10(2); 11(8); 12(12); 13(4); 14(11); 15(4); 2:1(6); 2(5); 4(5); 5; 6(5); 7(2); 8(3); 9(4); 10(6); 11(3); 12(2); 13; 14; 15(2); 16(2); 17(2); 18(5); 19(6); 20(4); 21(2); 22(7); 23(4); **Zec** 1:1(7); 2; 3(3); 4(3); 5; 6(2); 7(9); 8(2); 9; 10(4); 11(5); 12(3); 13(2); 14(2); 15(2); 16(2); 17(2); 19(2); 20; 21(4); 2:2(2); 3; 4; 5(3); 6(6); 7; 8(4); 9; 10(2); 11(3); 12(2); 13; 3:1(3); 2(4); 3; 4; 5(2); 6(2); 7; 8(2); 9(4); 10(3); 4:1; 2(3); 3(4); 4; 5; 6(3); 7; 8(2); 9(3); 10(6); 11(3); 12(2); 14(3); 5:2(2); 3(3); 4(7); 5; 6; 7(2); 8(4); 9(5); 10(2); 11; 6:1; 2(2); 3(2); 4; 5(5); 6(5); 7(4); 8(2); 9(2); 10(4); 11(3); 12(5); 13(4); 14(4); 15(5); 7:1(5); 2(2); 3(5); 4(2); 5(4); 7(6); 8(2); 9; 10(4); 11; 12(5); 13; 14(3); 8:1(2); 2; 3(5); 4(2); 5(3); 6(4); 7(3); 8; 9(8); 10; 11(3); 12(5); 13; 14(2); 15; 16(3); 17; 18(2); 19(11); 20(2); 21(3); 22(2); 23(3); 9:1(8); 3(3); 4(2); 5; 6(2); 8; 9; 10(7); 11(2); 12; 13(2); 14(5); 15(3); 16(3); 17(2); 10:1(5); 2(2); 3(5); 4(3); 5(5); 6(3); 7; 9; 10(2); 11(7); 12(2); 11:1; 2(4); 3(4); 4(3); 5; 6(6); 7(5); 9(2); 10; 11(4); 13(6); 14; 15(2); 16(4); 17(3); 12:1(8); 2(2); 3(2); 4(3); 5(3); 6(5); 7(6); 8(5); 9; 10(3); 11(2); 12(5); 13(3); 14; 13:1(2); 2(7); 3(2); 4; 6; 7(5); 8(3); 9(3); 14:1(3); 2(7); 3(2); 4(9); 5(8); 6; 7; 8(2); 9(2); 10(6); 12(3); 13(3); 14(2); 15(6); 16(4); 17(4); 18(5); 19(3); 20(7); 21(4); **Mal** 1:1(3); 2(2); 3(2); 4(5); 5(2); 6; 7(2); 8(3); 9; 10(2); 11(7); 12(3); 13(4); 14(4); 2:2; 3; 4; 5; 6; 7(4); 8(4); 9(2); 10; 11(3); 12(6); 13(3); 14(3); 15(3); 16(3); 17(4); 3:1(5); 2; 3(2); 4(3); 5(7); 6; 7(2); 10(4); 11(5); 12; 13; 14; 15; 16(3); 17; 18(2); 4:1(4); 2(2); 3(4); 4(2); 5(4); 6(6); **Mt** 1:1(4); 6(3); 11; 16; 17(3); 18(2); 20(3); 22(2); 24(2); 2:1(3); 2(2); 3; 4(2); 5; 6(3); 7(2); 8; 9(4); 10; 11(2); 13(4); 14; 15(3); 16(5); 17; 19; 20(3); 21(2); 22(2); 23; 3:1(2); 2; 3(5); 4; 5; 7(2); 10(4); 11; 12(2); 16(3); 4:1(3); 3(2); 4; 5(3); 6; 7; 8(4); 10; 11; 13(2); 14; 15(5); 16(2); 17; 18(2); 21; 22; 23(3); 24; 5:1; 3(2); 5(2); 7; 8; 9(2); 10; 12; 13(3); 14(2); 15; 17(2); 18; 19(4); 20(3); 21; 22(2); 23; 24; 25(5); 26; 32; 33; 35(3); 39; 40; 45(5); 46(2); 47; 6:2(3); 5(4); 7; 13(3); 16; 22(3); 23; 24(4); 25(2); 26(2); 28(2); 30(3); 32; 33; 34(5); 7:3(2); 4; 5(2); 6; 12(2); 13(3); 14(2); 19; 21(2); 25(3); 26; 27(4); 28; 29; 8:1; 4(2); 6; 8(2); 11(2); 12(2); 13(2); 15; 16(2); 17; 18; 20(4); 22; 24(3); 26(2); 27(3); 28(4); 29; 31(2); 32(4); 33(3); 34; 9:2(3); 3; 6(3); 8; 9; 10; 11; 13; 14(2); 15(5); 16(2); 17(3); 20; 22; 23(3); 24; 25(3); 26; 28(2); 33(3); 34(3); 35(4); 36; 37(2); 38(2); 10:2(4); 3(2); 4; 5(3); 6(2); 7; 8(3); 10; 13; 14; 15(2); 16; 17; 18; 20; 21(5); 22; 23(2); 24(2); 25(4); 27(2); 28(2); 29; 30; 35(2); 41(2); 42; 11:2(2); 5(7); 7(3); 11(2); 12(4); 13(2); 16; 19; 20; 21; 22; 23; 24(2); 25; 27(5); 12:1(3); 2(2); 4(3); 5(5); 6; 7; 8(2); 10; 11; 12; 13(2); 14; 17; 18; 19; 21; 22; 23(2); 24(3); 28(2); 29; 31(2); 32(3); 33(3); 34(3); 35(3); 36; 38(2); 39(2); 40(4); 41(2); 42(6); 43; 45(2); 46; 50(2); 13:1(3); 2(2); 4(2); 6; 7; 10; 11(2); 14; 18(2); 19(4); 20(3); 21; 22(5); 23(2); 24; 25; 26(2); 27(2); 28; 29(2); 30(5); 31; 32(5); 33(2); 34; 35(3); 36(5); 37(2); 38(8); 39(7); 40(3); 41; 43(3); 44(2); 45; 47(2); 48(2); 49(5); 50; 52; 55; 14:1(2); 2(2); 5; 6; 9(2); 10; 11; 12; 13(2); 15(3); 19(7); 20; 22(2); 23(2); 24(4); 25(3); 26(2); 28; 29(2); 30; 32(2); 33(2); 34; 35; 36; 15:2(2); 3; 4; 6; 9; 10; 11(2); 12; 14(4); 17(3); 18(3); 19; 20; 21; 22; 24(2); 26; 27(2); 29; 31(6); 32(2); 33; 35(2); 36(4); 37; 39(2); 16:1(2); 2; 3(6); 4(2); 5; 6(3); 9(2); 10(2); 11(3); 12(4); 13(2); 14(2); 16(3); 18; 19(2); 20; 21(2); 23; 26; 27(2); 28; 17:2(2); 5; 6; 9(4); 10; 12; 13(2); 14; 15(2); 18(2); 19; 22(2); 23; 25(3); 26; 27(2); 18:1(4); 2; 3; 4(2); 6(2); 7(2); 10; 11; 12(2); 13; 14; 16; 17(2); 20; 23; 26; 27(2); 28(2); 30; 34; 19:1; 3; 4; 8(2); 10(2); 12; 13; 14; 17; 20; 21; 22; 23; 24(2); 28(4); 30; 20:1(2); 2; 3(2); 4; 5; 6(2); 7; 8(5); 9; 10; 11(2); 12(2); 16(2); 17(2); 18(3); 19(2); 20; 21(3); 22(2); 23; 24(2); 25(2); 28; 30; 31(2); 21:1; 2; 3; 4; 5(2); 6; 7(2); 8(3); 9(5); 10; 11(2); 12(5); 13; 14(3); 15(5); 16; 17; 18(2); 19(2); 20(2); 21(2); 23(4); 25; 26; 28; 30; 31(5); 32(3); 34(4); 35; 36; 38(3); 39; 40(2); 41; 42(7); 43(2); 45; 46; 22:2; 3; 4; 6; 7; 8; 9(2); 10(2); 11(2); 13(2); 15; 16(3); 19; 21(2); 23(2); 25; 26(3); 27; 28(2); 29(2); 30(2); 31(2); 32(6); 33; 34(2); 36(2); 37; 38; 39; 40(2); 41; 42; 44; 23:1; 2(2); 5; 6(3); 7; 9; 13; 14; 15; 16(3); 17(3); 18(2); 19(3); 20; 21; 22; 23(3); 25(3); 26(2); 29(4); 30(3); 31(2); 32; 33; 35(6); 37; 39(2); 24:1(3); 3(5); 6; 8; 12; 13(2); 14(3); 15(3); 16; 17; 18; 20(2); 21(2); 22; 24; 26(2); 27(5); 28(2); 29(6); 30(6); 31(2); 32; 33; 36; 37(3); 38(4); 39(3); 40(3); 41(3); 43(3); 44; 49; 50; 51; 25:1(2); 4; 5; 6; 8(2); 9; 10(3); 11; 13(3); 14; 16(2); 18; 19; 21; 23; 24; 25; 27; 28; 30; 31(3); 32; 33(3);

34(4); 37; 40(2); 41(2); 45; 46; 26:2(3); 3(6); 5(2); 6(2); 9; 10; 11; 13; 14(2); 17(4); 18(3); 19(2); 20(2); 23(2); 24(2); 26; 27; 28(2); 29; 30; 31(3); 34; 35; 36; 37; 40; 41(2); 42; 44(2); 45(3); 47(3); 51; 52(2); 54; 55(2); 56(3); 57(3); 58(3); 59(2); 60; 61; 62; 63(4); 64(3); 65; 67; 69; 71; 72; 74(2); 75(2); 27:1(3); 2; 3(2); 4; 5(2); 6(4); 7; 8; 9(4); 10(2); 11(4); 12; 14; 15(2); 19; 20(2); 21(2); 23(2); 24(2); 25; 27(4); 29(2); 30(2); 31; 35; 37(2); 38(2); 40(3); 41(2); 42(2); 43; 44(2); 45(3); 46; 49; 50; 51(6); 52(2); 53(2); 54(3); 56(2); 57; 58(2); 59; 60(3); 61(2); 62(4); 64(6); 66(2); 28:1(6); 2(4); 4; 5(2); 6(2); 7; 8; 9; 11(4); 12(2); 14; 15(2); 16; 19(4); 20(2); **Mk** 1:1(3); 2; 3(4); 4(3); 5(2); 7; 8; 10(3); 12(2); 13(3); 14(2); 15(3); 16(2); 19(2); 20(2); 21(2); 22; 24; 26; 27; 28; 29(2); 31(2); 32; 33(2); 34; 35; 38; 42; 44; 45(2); 2:1; 2(2); 3; 4(5); 5(2); 6; 9(2); 10(3); 12; 13(2); 14(2); 16; 17(2); 18(4); 19(4); 20(2); 21(3); 22(4); 23(3); 24(2); 26(5); 27(2); 28(2); 3:1; 2; 3(2); 4; 5(3); 6(2); 7; 9; 11; 17(3); 18(2); 20; 22(3); 27; 28; 29; 32; 35(2); 4:1(5); 4(3); 6; 7; 10(2); 11(2); 14(2); 15(3); 16; 17; 18; 19(4); 20; 26(2); 27; 28(5); 29(3); 30; 31(3); 32(3); 33; 35(3); 36(2); 37(2); 38(2); 39(3); 41(2); 5:1(4); 2(2); 3; 4(2); 5(2); 7; 8; 10; 11; 12(2); 13(5); 14(3); 15(2); 16(2); 18(2); 19; 21(2); 22(2); 23; 27; 29; 30; 31; 33(2); 35(3); 36(3); 37; 38(4); 39; 40(4); 41(2); 42(2); 6:2(2); 3(3); 6; 7; 11(2); 14(2); 15; 16; 22(4); 23; 24(2); 25(3); 26; 27(2); 28(2); 30; 33; 35(2); 36(2); 39; 41(4); 43(2); 44; 45(3); 47(4); 48(4); 49; 51(2); 52(2); 53(2); 54; 56(3); 7:1(2); 3(4); 4(2); 5(3); 7; 8(3); 9; 10; 13; 14; 15(2); 17(3); 18; 19(2); 20(2); 21; 23; 24; 26(2); 27(3); 28(3); 29; 30(2); 31(4); 33; 35; 36(2); 37(2); 8:1; 2; 3; 4; 6(4); 8; 10; 11; 13(2); 14(2); 15(3); 19; 20; 23(3); 26(2); 27(2); 28(2); 29; 31(3); 33(2); 34; 35(2); 36; 38(3); 9:1; 7; 9(3); 10(2); 11; 12; 14; 15; 16; 17; 20(2); 22(2); 24(2); 25(2); 26; 27; 28; 31(3); 33(2); 34(2); 35(2); 36; 42; 43; 44; 45; 46; 47; 48; 50; 10:1(3); 2; 5; 6(2); 10(2); 14(2); 15; 17; 19; 21(2); 23; 24(2); 25(2); 29; 30; 31; 32(2); 33(4); 34; 35; 37; 38(2); 39(2); 41; 42; 44; 45; 46(2); 48; 49; 51; 52; 11:1; 2; 3; 4(2); 5; 7; 8(3); 9(2); 10(4); 11(3); 12; 13; 15(5); 16; 17; 18(2); 19; 20(3); 21; 23; 27(4); 30; 32; 12:1; 2(5); 4; 7(2); 8; 9(4); 10(4); 11; 12(2); 13(2); 14(2); 17(2); 18; 20; 21(2); 22(2); 23(2); 24(2); 25(2); 26(6); 27(4); 28(2); 29(3); 30(2); 31; 32(2); 33(4); 34; 35(3); 36(2); 37; 38(2); 39(3); 41(3); 43; 13:1; 3(2); 4; 7; 8; 9; 10; 11; 12(4); 13(2); 14(3); 15(2); 16; 18; 19(2); 20(3); 22; 24(2); 25(2); 26(2); 27(4); 28; 29; 32(3); 33; 34(2); 35(4); 14:1(4); 2(2); 3(3); 4; 5; 7; 8; 9; 10(2); 12(3); 13; 14(5); 16(2); 17(2); 20(2); 21(2); 23; 24; 25(3); 26; 27(2); 30; 31; 35(2); 38(2); 39; 41(4); 43(4); 47; 49(2); 51; 52; 53(4); 54(4); 55(2); 60(2); 61(2); 63; 64; 65(2); 66(3); 68(2); 72(4); 15:1(4); 2(2); 3; 7; 8; 9(2); 10; 11(2); 12(2); 14; 15; 16(3); 18; 19; 20; 21(2); 22(2); 25; 26(3); 27(2); 28(2); 29; 30; 31(2); 32(2); 33(3); 34; 37; 38(4); 39(3); 40(2); 42(4); 43(2); 44; 45(2); 46(3); 47; 16:1(2); 2(6); 3(3); 4; 5(2); 6; 8; 9(2); 12; 13; 14; 15(2); 18; 19(2); 20(2); **Lk** 1:2(2); 3; 4; 5(4); 6(2); 8(2); 9(4); 10(3); 11(3); 13; 15(3); 16(2); 17(8); 18; 19(2); 20; 21(2); 22; 23; 25(2); 26(2); 27(2); 28(2); 30; 32(4); 33; 34; 35(5); 36; 38(3); 39; 40; 41(3); 42; 43; 44(2); 45; 46; 48; 51(2); 52; 53(2); 58; 59(3); 65; 66(2); 67; 68; 69; 70(2); 71; 72; 73; 74; 75; 76(4); 77; 78(2); 79(2); 80(3); 2:1; 4(3); 6; 7; 8(2); 9(4); 10; 11(2); 12; 13(2); 14; 15(3); 16; 17; 18; 20(2); 21(4); 22(3); 23(4); 24(2); 25(3); 26(2); 27(6); 31; 32(2); 34; 35; 36(2); 37; 38; 39(2); 40(2); 41(2); 42(2); 43(2); 44; 46(3); 50; 3:1(4); 2(4); 3(3); 4(7); 5(2); 6; 7(2); 9(4); 10; 14; 15(2); 16(2); 17(2); 18; 19(2); 21(2); 22; 23(2); 24(5); 25(5); 26(5); 27(5); 28(5); 29(5); 30(5); 31(5); 32(5); 33(5); 34(5); 35(5); 36(5); 37(5); 38(4); 4:1(3); 2; 3(2); 5(3); 6(2); 8; 9(2); 12; 13(2); 14(3); 16(2); 17(4); 18(7); 19(2); 20(4); 22; 25(3); 27(3); 28; 29(3); 30; 31; 33; 34; 35(2); 36; 37(2); 38; 39; 40; 41; 42; 43; 44; 5:1(3); 2(2); 3(4); 4; 5(2); 7(2); 9(2); 10; 13; 14; 15; 16; 17(3); 19(4); 21(2); 24(3); 27; 32; 33(3); 34(3); 35(2); 36(4); 37(3); 39; 6:1(4); 2(2); 4(3); 5(2); 6; 7(2); 8(3); 9; 10(2); 15; 16(2); 17(3); 19; 20; 22; 23(2); 26; 29(3); 33; 35(4); 38; 39(3); 40; 41(2); 42(4); 45(4); 46; 48(3); 49(3); 7:1(2); 3(2); 6(2); 9; 10(2); 11; 12(4); 13; 14; 17; 18; 20; 22(7); 24(4); 28(2); 29(3); 30(2); 31(2); 32; 33; 34; 36(2); 37(2); 38(2); 39; 41(2); 44(2); 45; 47; 50; 8:1(3); 3; 5(3); 7; 10(2); 11(3); 12(3); 13(2); 15(2); 16; 19; 21; 22(2); 23; 24(3); 25; 26(2); 27(2); 29(5); 31; 32; 33(5); 34(2); 35(3); 36; 37(4); 38(2); 39; 40; 41(2); 42; 44; 45; 47(2); 49(3); 51(4); 54; 9:2(2); 5; 6(2); 7(2); 8; 10(2); 11(2); 12(4); 16(4); 18; 19(2); 20; 22(3); 24; 25; 26(2); 27; 29; 32; 34; 35; 36; 37(2); 38; 42(3); 43; 44(2); 47; 48; 51; 52; 56; 57; 58(2); 60(2); 62(2); 10:1; 2(4); 4; 6; 7(2); 9(2); 10(2); 11(2); 13; 14; 17(2); 19(2); 20; 21; 22(5); 23(2); 26; 27; 31; 32(2); 35(2); 36; 11:7; 13; 14(3); 15(2); 20(2); 24; 26(2); 27(3); 28; 29(3); 30(2); 31(7); 32(3); 33; 34(3); 35; 36(2); 38; 39(4); 42(2); 43(3); 44; 45; 46; 47(2); 48; 49; 50(4); 51(4); 52; 53(2); 12:1(3); 3(3); 4; 7; 8(2); 9; 10(2); 11; 12(2); 13(2); 15(2); 16; 22; 23(2); 24(2); 26; 27; 28(3); 30(2); 31; 32; 33; 36; 37; 38(2); 39(3); 40; 42; 45; 46(2); 48; 49; 53(10); 54(2); 55; 56(3); 58(6); 59; 13:1; 2; 4; 7(2); 10(2); 14(5); 15(3); 16; 17(2); 18; 19(3); 20; 21; 22; 24; 25(4); 28(2); 29(5); 31(2); 32; 33; 34; 35(3); 14:1(3); 2; 3(2); 5; 7; 8; 9; 10(2); 13(4); 14(2); 15; 18; 21(8); 22; 23(3); 28; 29; 32; 34; 35(2); 15:1; 2; 4(2); 8; 9; 10(2); 12(2); 13; 16(2); 21; 22(2); 23; 25(2); 26; 27;

30; 16:1; 3(2); 4; 5; 8(4); 9; 10; 11(2); 13(4); 14; 15; 16(3); 17; 21(3); 22(3); 24; 29; 30; 31(2); 17:1; 2; 5(2); 6(3); 7; 9; 11; 14; 17; 20(3); 21; 22(4); 24(4); 26(3); 27(3); 28; 29; 30(2); 31(3); 34(2); 35(2); 36(3); 37(2); 18:6(2); 8(2); 10(3); 11; 12; 13; 14; 16; 17; 20; 22; 24; 25; 27; 29; 30; 31(3); 32; 33; 34; 35; 36; 39; 43; 19:2(2); 3; 5; 8(3); 10; 11; 15(2); 16; 18; 23; 24; 29(2); 30(2); 31; 33(3); 34; 35; 36; 37(5); 38(4); 39(2); 40; 41; 42; 43; 44(2); 45; 46; 47(5); 48; 20:1(6); 4; 6; 9; 10(5); 13(2); 14(3); 15(3); 16; 17(5); 19(4); 20(2); 21(2); 25(2); 26; 27; 29; 30; 31(2); 32; 33; 34; 35(2); 36(4); 37(6); 38(2); 39; 42(2); 45(2); 46(5); 47; 21:1(2); 4(2); 5; 6(2); 8; 9; 12; 20; 21(3); 22; 23; 24(5); 25(6); 26(2); 27; 29(2); 31; 35(2); 36; 37(4); 38(3); 22:1(2); 2(2); 3(2); 4; 6(2); 7(2); 8; 10(2); 11(5); 13; 14(2); 16; 17; 18(3); 20(2); 21(2); 22; 24; 25(2); 26; 30; 31; 34; 37(2); 39; 40; 44; 47; 48; 49; 50(2); 52(3); 53(2); 54; 55(2); 56; 59; 60; 61(4); 63; 64; 66(4); 67; 69(3); 70; 23:1; 2; 3(2); 4(2); 5(2); 6; 10; 12; 13(3); 14; 17; 19; 22; 23(2); 26(2); 29(5); 30(2); 31; 33(5); 35(3); 36; 37(2); 38(2); 39; 40(2); 41; 44(3); 45(4); 46; 47; 48(2); 49; 51(4); 52; 54(2); 55(2); 56(2); 24:1(5); 2(2); 3(2); 5(3); 7(3); 9(3); 10(2); 12(2); 18(2); 19; 20; 21; 22; 24(2); 25; 27(3); 28; 29; 32(2); 33(2); 34; 35; 36; 44(4); 45; 46(2); 49(2); 53; **Jn** 1:1(4); 2(2); 4(2); 5(2); 7(2); 9(2); 10(3); 12; 13(3); 14(4); 17; 18(3); 19(2); 20; 23(5); 24; 29(4); 32; 33(4); 34; 35; 36; 37; 39; 40; 41(2); 42; 43; 44; 45(3); 48; 49(2); 50; 51(2); 2:1(2); 2; 3; 5; 6(3); 7(2); 8(2); 9(8); 10(2); 13; 14(2); 15(5); 17; 18; 20; 21; 22(3); 23(3); 3:1(2); 2; 3; 4; 5(2); 6(2); 8(3); 13; 14(3); 16; 17(3); 18(2); 19(2); 20(2); 21; 22; 25; 26; 28; 29(5); 31(2); 34(2); 35(2); 36(3); 4:1(2); 5; 6(2); 8; 9(3); 10; 11(2); 12; 14(2); 15; 17; 19; 20; 21(2); 22; 23(4); 25; 27; 28(3); 29; 30; 31; 33; 34; 35; 39(3); 40; 42(4); 45(4); 46; 47; 49; 50(2); 52(3); 53(3); 54; 5:1; 2(2); 3(2); 4(4); 7(3); 9(3); 10(2); 11; 14; 15(2); 16(2); 18(3); 19(3); 20(2); 21(3); 22(2); 23(4); 25(4); 26(2); 27; 28(3); 29(2); 30(2); 32; 33; 36(4); 37; 39; 42; 44; 45; 6:1(2); 4(2); 10(3); 11(4); 12; 13(2); 14(2); 16; 17; 18; 19(2); 21(3); 22(5); 23(2); 24; 25(2); 26(2); 27(3); 28; 29; 31; 32; 33(2); 35; 37; 38; 39(2); 40(3); 41(2); 42; 44(2); 45(2); 46(2); 49; 50; 51(4); 52; 53(2); 54; 57(2); 59; 62; 63(3); 64; 67; 68; 69(2); 71(2); 7:1; 2; 3; 4; 7(2); 10; 11(2); 12(2); 13; 14(3); 15; 17; 18; 19(2); 20; 22(2); 23(3); 24; 26(2); 28; 31; 32(4); 35(4); 37(2); 38; 39(2); 40(2); 41; 42(3); 43; 45(2); 46; 47; 48(2); 49; 8:1(2); 2(3); 3(2); 4; 5; 6; 8; 9(4); 10; 12(3); 13; 15; 16; 17; 18; 20(2); 22; 25(2); 26; 27; 28; 29; 32(2); 34; 35(3); 36; 39; 40; 41; 44(5); 45; 46; 48; 52(2); 53; 57; 59(2); 9:3; 4(2); 5(3); 6(5); 7; 8; 11; 13; 14(2); 15; 16(2); 17; 18(2); 22(3); 24(2); 30; 32(2); 35; 40; 10:1(3); 2(3); 3(2); 4; 5; 7(2); 8; 9; 10; 11(3); 12(6); 13(2); 14; 15(3); 19; 21(3); 22(2); 23; 24(2); 25; 31; 33; 35(2); 36(3); 37; 38(2); 40; 11:1; 2; 4(2); 6; 8; 9(3); 10; 15; 17; 19; 20; 24(2); 25(2); 27(3); 28; 30; 31(3); 33(2); 36; 37(2); 38; 39(2); 40; 41(3); 42; 45(2); 46; 47(2); 48; 49; 50(2); 52; 54(2); 55(3); 56(2); 57(2); 12:1(2); 2; 3(4); 5; 6(2); 7; 8; 9(2); 10; 11; 12(2); 13(3); 16; 17(2); 18; 19(2); 20; 21; 23(2); 24; 29; 31(2); 32; 34(3); 35(2); 36(2); 38(4); 42(3); 43(2); 46; 47(2); 48(3); 49; 50; 13:1(5); 2(2); 3; 5(2); 16; 18; 22; 26(2); 27; 28; 29(3); 30; 31; 33; 38; 14:4; 5; 6(4); 8; 9(2); 10(5); 11(3); 12; 13(2); 16; 17(2); 19; 22; 24(2); 26(3); 27; 28; 30; 31(3); 15:1(2); 3; 4(2); 5(3); 6; 9; 15; 16; 18; 19(5); 20(2); 24; 25; 26(4); 27; 16:2(2); 3; 4(2); 7(2); 8; 11; 13; 15; 16; 17; 20; 21(3); 23; 25(2); 26; 27; 28(4); 32(2); 33(2); 17:1; 3; 4(2); 5(2); 6(2); 8; 9; 11(2); 12(3); 13; 14(3); 15(2); 16(2); 18(2); 19; 21; 22; 23; 24(2); 25; 26; 18:1(2); 2; 3; 6; 9; 10(2); 11(2); 12(3); 13; 14(2); 15(3); 16(3); 17(2); 18; 19; 20(4); 22(3); 23; 24; 26(3); 27; 28(3); 31; 32; 33(3); 35; 36; 37(3); 38; 39(3); 19:2; 3; 5(3); 6; 7(2); 8; 9; 11; 12; 13(3); 14(4); 15; 17(2); 18; 19(4); 20(3); 21(5); 23(3); 24(2); 25(2); 26; 27; 28; 30(2); 31(5); 32(4); 34; 36; 38(3); 39; 40(4); 41(2); 42(2); 20:1(5); 2(3); 3; 4(2); 5; 6(2); 7(2); 8; 9(2); 10; 11(2); 12(5); 15; 18(2); 19(7); 20(2); 22; 24; 25(6); 26(2); 30; 31(2); 21:1(2); 2; 4(3); 6(4); 7(3); 8(2); 10; 11(2); 12(2); 14(2); 16; 17(2); 20; 23; 24; 25(3); **Acts** 1:1; 2(3); 3(2); 4(2); 5; 6; 7(3); 8(3); 12; 13(2); 14(2); 15(3); 16(2); 18(2); 19(2); 20; 21(2); 22; 24; 26(2); 2:1; 2; 4(2); 6; 9; 10; 11; 14; 15(2); 16; 17; 19; 20(3); 21(2); 22; 23; 24; 25; 28; 29; 30(2); 31; 33(4); 34(2); 36; 37(2); 38(4); 39(2); 41; 42; 43; 46; 47(3); 3:1(3); 2(3); 3; 6; 7; 8; 9; 10(2); 11(3); 12; 13(3); 14(2); 15(2); 16(2); 18; 19(3); 21(4); 22(2); 23; 24; 25(5); 4:1(5); 2(3); 3; 4(3); 5; 6(3); 7; 8(2); 9(2); 10(3); 11(3); 13; 14; 15; 17; 18; 19; 20; 21; 22; 23; 24; 25(3); 26(4); 27(2); 30; 31(3); 32(2); 33(3); 34(2); 35; 36(3); 37(2); 5:2(2); 3(3); 5; 6; 7; 8; 9(4); 10(2); 11; 12(3); 13(2); 14(2); 15(4); 16; 17(3); 18(2); 19(3); 20(3); 21(7); 22(2); 23(3); 24(4); 25(3); 26(3); 27(2); 29; 30; 32; 33; 34(4); 37(2); 40(2); 41(2); 42; 6:1(5); 2(4); 3; 4(2); 5(3); 6; 7(5); 8; 9(3); 10(2); 12(4); 13; 14; 15(2); 7:1; 2; 3; 4(2); 7; 8(3); 9; 10; 11; 13; 16(3); 17(3); 19(2); 22(2); 23; 24; 26; 28; 29; 30(2); 31(3); 32(4); 33(2); 34; 35(4); 36(3); 37(2); 38(5); 40; 41(2); 42(5); 43(2); 44(3); 45(4); 46; 48(2); 49(2); 51; 52(4); 53(2); 54; 55(3); 56(3); 58(2); 8:1(3); 3; 4; 5; 6(2); 9(2); 10(3); 12(3); 13; 14(2); 15; 16(2); 17; 18(2); 19; 20; 21; 22; 23(2); 24; 25(4); 26(4); 27(2); 28; 29; 30; 32(3); 33; 34(2); 35; 36; 37; 38(3); 39(4); 40; 9:1(3); 2; 4; 5(2); 6(2); 7; 8(2); 10; 11(3); 14; 15(3); 17(4); 19; 20(2); 21; 22(2); 23; 24; 25(2); 26; 27(4); 29(3); 30;

31(5); 32; 33; 35; 38; 39(3); 40; 41; 42; 10:1(2); 2; 3(2); 6; 7; 9(4); 11(2); 12(2); 15(2); 16; 17(2); 19(2); 21(2); 22(3); 23; 24; 30; 31; 32(2); 36(2); 37; 38(2); 39(2); 40; 41(2); 42(2); 43; 44(2); 45(4); 47; 48(2); 11:1(3); 2; 4(2); 5; 6(3); 9; 11; 12(2); 15(2); 16(3); 17(2); 18; 19(3); 20(2); 21(3); 22(2); 23(2); 24(2); 26(2); 28(3); 29(2); 30(2); 12:1(2); 2(2); 3(2); 4; 5; 6(4); 7(4); 8; 9; 10(5); 11(5); 12(3); 13(2); 14(2); 16; 17(4); 18; 19; 20(2); 22(2); 23(4); 24; 13:1(2); 2(3); 4; 5(3); 6; 7(3); 8(3); 9; 10(3); 11(4); 12(3); 14(2); 15(6); 17(3); 18(2); 19; 20(2); 21(3); 22; 24(2); 26(2); 27(2); 29; 30; 31; 32(2); 33(2); 34(2); 36; 38; 39; 40; 42(4); 43(3); 44(3); 45(2); 46(2); 47(4); 48(3); 49(3); 50(4); 51; 52(2); 14:1(4); 2(3); 3(2); 4(4); 5(2); 6; 7; 9; 11(4); 12; 13(3); 14(2); 15(2); 18; 19(2); 20(3); 21; 22(4); 23; 25; 26(2); 27(3); 28; 15:1(2); 2; 3(4); 4(2); 5(3); 6; 7(3); 8(2); 10(2); 11(2); 12(2); 14(2); 15(2); 16(2); 17(4); 18(2); 19; 21; 22(3); 23(3); 24; 26; 27; 28; 30(2); 31; 32; 33(2); 35(2); 36(2); 38; 39(2); 40(2); 41; 16:1; 2; 3; 4(3); 5(2); 6(3); 7; 9; 10(3); 11; 12; 13(3); 14(3); 15; 17(4); 18(3); 19(3); 20; 22(2); 23; 24(2); 25; 26(3); 27(4); 31; 32(2); 33(2); 35(2); 36(3); 38(2); 39; 40(3); 17:1; 2; 3; 4(2); 5(5); 6(3); 7; 8(3); 9; 10(3); 11(2); 13(3); 14(2); 16; 17(4); 18(3); 21; 22; 23; 24; 26(4); 27; 29(2); 30; 31(3); 32(2); 34(2); 18:3; 4(3); 5(2); 6; 7; 8(4); 9(2); 11; 12(3); 13; 14; 16; 17(4); 18; 19(2); 22; 23(2); 24; 25(6); 26(2); 27(2); 28(2); 19:1; 2; 4(2); 5(2); 6; 7; 8(4); 9(3); 10(3); 11; 12(3); 13(3); 14; 15; 16(2); 17(3); 19; 20; 21; 23; 24; 25; 27(3); 28; 29(2); 30(2); 31(2); 32(2); 33(4); 34(2); 35(6); 38(2); 41; 20:1(2); 3; 4; 6; 7(4); 8; 9; 12; 15(3); 16(2); 17(2); 18; 19(3); 21(2); 22(2); 23; 24(4); 25; 26; 27; 28(4); 29; 31; 32; 35(3); 38(2); 21:1; 3(2); 4; 5(2); 7; 8(4); 9; 11(5); 13(2); 14(2); 16; 17; 18(2); 19; 20(2); 21(3); 22; 24; 25; 26(5); 27(4); 28(4); 29(2); 30(4); 31(2); 32(2); 33; 34(4); 35(4); 36(2); 37(2); 38; 39; 40(4); 22:2(2); 3(4); 4; 5(4); 7; 9(2); 10; 11(2); 12(2); 13; 14(2); 16(2); 17; 20(2); 21; 22; 23; 24(2); 25; 26(2); 27; 28; 29; 30(4); 23:1; 2(2); 3(2); 5(2); 6(6); 7(3); 8(2); 9(2); 10(3); 11(2); 12; 14; 15(2); 16; 17(2); 18(2); 19(2); 20(2); 22(2); 23(2); 24; 26; 27; 28; 30(2); 31; 32(3); 33(2); 34(2); 24:1(3); 5(4); 6; 7; 9; 10(2); 12(4); 13; 14(4); 15(2); 18; 20; 21(2); 22(2); 24; 26; 27; 25:1; 2(3); 3; 6(2); 7; 8(3); 9; 10; 12; 14; 15(3); 16(4); 17(3); 18; 21; 22; 23(4); 24(2); 27; 26:1; 2(2); 3; 4(2); 5(2); 6(2); 7; 8; 9; 10(2); 12; 13(3); 14(3); 16; 17(2); 18; 19; 20(2); 21(2); 22; 23(4); 25; 26; 27; 30(2); 27:2; 3; 4; 5; 6; 7; 8(2); 9; 10; 11(4); 12(3); 13; 15(2); 16; 17(2); 18(2); 19(3); 21; 22; 23; 27(2); 29(2); 30(5); 31(3); 32(3); 33(2); 34; 37; 38(3); 39(3); 40(5); 41(5); 42(2); 43(2); 44(2); 28:1; 2(3); 3(2); 4(3); 5(2); 7(3); 8; 9; 11; 13(2); 15(2); 16(4); 17(5); 19; 20; 21; 23(3); 24; 25(2); 27; 28(2); 29; 31(2); **Rom** 1:1; 2; 3(2); 4(4); 5; 6; 7; 8; 9; 10; 11; 12; 14(4); 15; 16(4); 17(2); 18(2); 20(4); 23(2); 24; 25(3); 26; 27(3); 32(2); 2:1; 2; 3(2); 4(2); 5(2); 8; 9(2); 10(2); 12(2); 13(4); 14(5); 15(3); 16(2); 17; 18(2); 19; 20(4); 23(2); 24(2); 25(2); 26(3); 27(3); 28; 29(3); 3:1; 2; 3; 5; 6; 7; 12; 13; 17; 19(3); 20(4); 21(4); 22; 23; 24; 25(2); 26; 27; 28(2); 29(4); 30; 31(2); 4:1; 3; 4; 5; 6(2); 8(2); 9(2); 11(4); 12(3); 13(5); 14(2); 15; 16(6); 17; 18; 19; 20; 24; 5:2; 5(2); 6; 10; 11; 12; 13(2); 14(2); 15(5); 16(3); 17; 18(3); 19; 20(2); 6:4(3); 5(2); 6; 9; 12; 13; 14; 15; 17(2); 18; 19(2); 20; 21; 22; 23(2); 7:1(2); 2(4); 4(3); 5(3); 6(3); 7(3); 8(2); 9(2); 10; 11; 12(2); 13; 14; 16; 19(2); 22(2); 23(2); 24; 25(4); 8:1(2); 2(4); 3(4); 4(4); 5(6); 7(2); 8; 9(4); 10(2); 11(3); 12(2); 13(4); 14(2); 15(2); 16(2); 18(2); 19(4); 20(2); 21(4); 22; 23(4); 26(2); 27(5); 28; 29(2); 33; 34; 35; 36(2); 39; 9:1(2); 3; 4(7); 5(2); 6; 7; 8(6); 9; 11(2); 12(2); 17(2); 20; 21(3); 22; 23(2); 24(2); 26(3); 27(4); 28(3); 29; 30(2); 31(2); 32(2); 10:3; 4(2); 5(3); 6; 7(2); 8(2); 9(2); 10(2); 11; 12(3); 13(2); 15(2); 16; 17; 18(3); 11:1(2); 2; 4(3); 5; 7(2); 8; 11; 12(6); 13(2); 15(5); 16(4); 17(3); 18(3); 19; 21; 22; 24(2); 25(2); 26; 28(3); 29; 33(3); 34(2); 12:1; 2; 3(2); 4; 6(2); 11; 13; 16; 17; 19; 13:1(2); 2(2); 3(3); 4(3); 8; 10(2); 11; 12(4); 13; 14(3); 14:1; 6(6); 8(3); 9; 10; 11; 14; 17(2); 19; 20; 15:1(2); 3; 4; 5; 6; 7; 8(4); 9(2); 11; 12(2); 13(3); 15(2); 16(6); 18; 19(3); 20; 25; 26; 27; 29(3); 30(3); 31; 32; 33; 16:1; 2; 4(2); 5(2); 7; 8; 11(2); 12(3); 13; 14; 15; 16; 17; 18(2); 20(2); 22; 23(3); 24; 25(4); 26(5); S:1(2); **1Cor** 1:1; 2(2); 3; 4; 6; 7; 8(2); 9; 10(4); 11; 13; 16; 17(2); 18(3); 19(4); 20(4); 21(3); 22(2); 23(2); 24(2); 25(2); 26; 27(6); 28; 31; 2:1; 4; 5(2); 6(2); 7(3); 8(2); 9(2); 10(2); 11(4); 12(4); 13(2); 14(3); 16(3); 3:5; 6; 7; 10(2); 13(2); 16(2); 17(2); 19(2); 20(3); 22; 4:1(2); 4; 5(5); 9(2); 13(3); 15; 17; 19(3); 20; 21; 5:1; 4(2); 5(5); 6; 7; 8(3); 10(3); 6:1(2); 2(4); 4; 6; 9(2); 10; 11(3); 12; 13(6); 14; 15(3); 17; 18; 19(2); 7:1; 3(4); 4(4); 5; 8; 10(3); 11; 12(2); 13; 14(4); 15; 17; 19(2); 20; 22(2); 23; 25(2); 26; 28; 29; 31; 32(3); 33(2); 34(5); 35; 36; 39(3); 40; 8:3; 4(2); 6; 7; 8(2); 10(2); 11; 12; 13; 9:1; 2(2); 5(2); 7(3); 8(2); 9(4); 12; 13(4); 14(3); 16(2); 17; 18(3); 19; 20(5); 21; 22(2); 23; 24; 25; 26; 10:1(2); 2(2); 3; 4; 5; 6; 7; 10; 11(2); 13; 16(6); 18(3); 19; 20(2); 21(5); 22; 25; 26(3); 28(3); 29; 31; 32(3); 33; 11:2; 3(5); 6; 7(4); 8(4); 9(4); 10(2); 11(5); 12(4); 16; 17(2); 18; 20; 22; 23(3); 25(3); 26; 27(3); 29; 32(2); 34; 12:3(3); 4; 5; 6; 7(2); 8(4); 9(3); 10(2); 11; 12(2); 14; 15(4); 16(4); 17(4); 18(2); 19; 21(4); 22; 23; 24; 25(3); 26(2); 27; 28; 30; 31; 13:1; 2; 3; 6; 13; 14:2; 4; 5; 7; 8(2); 9(2); 10; 11(2); 12(2); 15(4); 16(3); 17; 19; 21(2); 23; 25; 27; 28; 29(2); 30; 32(3); 33(2);

34(2); 35; 36; 37(3); 15:1; 3; 4(2); 5; 6; 7; 9(3); 10(2); 12(2); 13; 15; 16; 20(2); 21(2); 23; 24(3); 26; 28; 29(3); 32(2); 34; 35; 39; 40(4); 41(3); 42(2); 45(2); 47(4); 48(2); 49(4); 50; 52(4); 54; 56(3); 57; 58(3); 16:1(3); 2(2); 7(2); 10(2); 11; 12; 13; 15(4); 17; 19(3); 20; 21; 22; 23; S:1(2); **2Cor** 1:1(3); 2; 3(3); 4; 5; 6(2); 7(2); 9(2); 11(2); 12(3); 13; 14(2); 17(2); 19; 20(2); 22(2); 2:2; 3; 4; 9; 10; 12; 14; 16(4); 17(2); 3:3(4); 6(5); 7(4); 8(2); 9(2); 10; 13(2); 14(3); 15; 16(2); 17(3); 18(5); 4:2(4); 4(5); 5; 6(5); 7(2); 10(4); 11; 13; 14; 15(3); 16; 18(4); 5:1; 5(3); 6(2); 8(2); 10(2); 11(2); 14; 16(2); 18; 19(2); 21; 6:1; 2(3); 3; 4; 6; 7(5); 13; 16(3); 17(2); 18; 7:1(2); 6; 7(2); 8; 10(2); 12(2); 13(2); 15; 8:1(2); 2(2); 4(4); 5(2); 6; 8(2); 9; 11; 16(2); 17; 18(3); 19(3); 21(3); 22; 23(3); 24(2); 9:1(2); 2; 3; 5(2); 9; 10(2); 12(3); 13(2); 14; 10:1; 2; 3(2); 4(2); 5(2); 7; 8; 12; 13(2); 14; 16(2); 17; 18; 11:3(2); 5; 7; 9; 10(2); 13; 15; 17; 18; 20; 22; 24; 25; 26(4); 28(2); 30; 31; 32(4); 33; 12:1; 2(3); 3(2); 6; 7(4); 8; 9; 11; 12; 14(5); 15(2); 18(2); 21; 13:1(2); 2; 4(2); 5; 8(2); 10(2); 11; 13; 14(5); S:1(2); **Gal** 1:1(2); 2(2); 3; 4; 6; 7; 10; 11; 12; 13(2); 14(2); 16; 19(2); 20; 21; 22; 23; 2:2; 5(2); 7(4); 8(4); 9(4); 10(2); 11; 12(2); 13; 14(6); 15; 16(8); 17; 18; 19(2); 20(4); 21(2); 3:1; 2(4); 3(2); 5(4); 7(2); 8(3); 10(5); 11(3); 12(2); 13(2); 14(4); 15; 16; 17(3); 18(2); 19(4); 21(3); 22(2); 23(2); 24; 26; 29; 4:1; 2(2); 3(2); 4(3); 5(2); 6; 9; 13(3); 15; 16; 21(2); 22(2); 23(3); 24(3); 26; 27; 28; 29(2); 30(6); 31(2); 5:1(2); 3; 4; 5(2); 7; 9; 10; 11(2); 13; 14; 16(3); 17(7); 18(2); 19(2); 21(2); 22(2); 24(2); 25(2); 6:1; 2; 6; 8(3); 10; 12(2); 13; 14(3); 16; 17(2); 18; S:1; **Eph** 1:1(3); 2; 3; 4(2); 5(2); 6(3); 7(2); 9; 10(2); 11(2); 12; 13(2); 14(4); 15(2); 17(4); 18(5); 19(2); 20(2); 22(2); 23; 2:2(6); 3(5); 7(2); 8; 11(3); 12(3); 13; 14; 15(2); 16(2); 18; 19(2); 20(3); 21(2); 22; 3:1; 2(2); 3; 4; 5(2); 6(3); 7(3); 8(3); 9(4); 10(4); 11; 12; 14; 15; 16(2); 18; 19(2); 20; 21; 4:1(3); 3(3); 7(2); 9(2); 10; 12(6); 13(7); 14; 15(2); 16(5); 17(2); 18(4); 21; 22(3); 23; 24; 26; 27; 28; 29(2); 30(2); 5:5; 6(2); 8; 9(2); 10; 11; 13; 14; 16(2); 17(2); 18; 19; 20(2); 21; 22; 23(7); 24(2); 25; 26(2); 29(2); 32; 33; 6:1; 2; 3; 4(2); 5; 6(3); 7; 8(2); 9; 10(2); 11(3); 12(2); 13(2); 14; 15(2); 16(3); 17(4); 18; 19(2); 21; 22; 23(3); S:1; **Phil** 1:1(3); 2; 5(2); 6; 7(2); 8; 10; 11(2); 12(3); 13; 14(3); 16; 17(3); 19(2); 22(2); 24; 27(3); 29; 30; 2:1; 2; 4; 6; 7(2); 8(2); 10(2); 11(2); 15(3); 16(2); 17; 18; 19; 21; 22(3); 24; 28(2); 29; 30; 3:1(2); 2; 3(3); 4(2); 5(5); 6(3); 8(3); 9(3); 10(2); 11(2); 14(3); 16(2); 18(2); 20(2); 21; 4:1; 2(2); 3(2); 4; 5; 7; 9; 10(2); 15(2); 18; 21; 22; 23; S:1; **Col** 1:1; 2(2); 3; 4(2); 5(4); 6(3); 8; 9(2); 10(2); 12(3); 13(2); 14; 15(3); 18(7); 19; 20; 22; 23(3); 24(2); 25(2); 26; 27(4); 2:1; 2(4); 3; 5(3); 6; 7; 8(3); 9(2); 10; 11(5); 12(3); 13; 14(2); 16(2); 17; 19(3); 20(3); 22(2); 23(3); 3:1; 2; 5; 6(2); 7; 9; 10(2); 12; 14; 15(2); 16(2); 17(3); 18; 20; 22; 23; 24(4); 25; 4:2; 3; 5; 7; 8; 11(2); 12; 14; 15(2); 16(3); 17(2); 18(2); S:1; **1Th** 1:1(5); 3; 5; 6(3); 8(2); 9; 10(2); 2:2; 4; 6; 8; 9; 13(3); 14(2); 15; 16(3); 17; 19; 3:2; 5; 8; 9; 12; 13(2); 4:1; 2; 3; 5(2); 6(2); 10; 15(4); 16(5); 17(4); 5:1(2); 2(3); 5(4); 7(2); 8(3); 12; 14(2); 18; 19; 23(2); 26; 27(2); 28; S:1(2); **2Th** 1:1(3); 2; 3; 4; 5(2); 7; 8; 9(3); 11(2); 12(3); 2:1; 2; 3; 4; 7(2); 8(3); 9; 10(2); 12; 13(4); 14(2); 15; 3:1(2); 3; 4(2); 5(3); 6(2); 16(2); 17(2); 18; S:1(2); **1Ti** 1:1; 2; 5(2); 7; 8; 9(3); 11(2); 12; 14; 15; 17(2); 18; 2:3; 4(2); 5; 7(2); 11; 12; 14(2); 3:1; 2; 5; 6(2); 7(2); 8; 9(2); 10; 12(2); 13(2); 15(5); 16(5); 4:1(3); 3; 5; 6(2); 8; 10(2); 12; 14(4); 16; 5:1; 2(2); 8; 9(2); 10(2); 11; 14(3); 16; 17(2); 18(4); 21(2); 25; 6:1(2); 2; 3(2); 5; 10(3); 12; 13; 14; 15(2); 16; 17; 19; 21; S:1(2); **2Ti** 1:1(2); 2; 5; 6(2); 7; 8(4); 9; 10(2); 11; 12; 13; 14; 16(2); 18(2); 2:1; 2(2); 4; 6(2); 7; 8(2); 9; 10(2); 14(3); 15; 18(3); 19(3); 21; 22; 24(2); 25(2); 26(2); 3:1; 5; 7(2); 8(2); 11; 14; 15; 17; 4:1(3); 2; 3; 4; 5; 6; 7; 8(2); 11; 13(3); 14(2); 17(5); 18; 19; 21; 22; S:1(5); **Titus** 1:1(3); 2; 3; 4(3); 5; 6; 7; 9(2); 10; 12; 13; 14; 15; 2:1; 2; 3; 4; 5; 8; 10; 11; 13(2); 3:4; 5(2); 7; 9; 10; 13; 15; S:1(3); **Philem** 1:2; 3; 5; 6(2); 7(2); 9; 13(2); 16(2); 20(2); 25; **Heb** 1:1(2); 2; 3(5); 4; 5; 6(3); 7; 8(2); 9; 10(5); 12; 13; 2:1(2); 2; 3(2); 4; 5(2); 6; 7(2); 9(3); 10; 12(2); 13; 14(4); 16(2); 17(2); 3:1(2); 3(2); 6(4); 7; 8(3); 12; 13; 14(2); 15; 17; 4:2(2); 3(3); 4(2); 9; 11; 12(5); 13; 14(2); 15; 16; 5:2(2); 3; 6; 7; 8; 9; 10; 12(3); 13; 6:1(3); 2(2); 4(2); 5(3); 6; 7(2); 10; 11(3); 12; 15; 16; 17(2); 18; 19(2); 20(2); 7:1(3); 3; 4(3); 5(6); 6; 7(2); 10; 11(5); 12(2); 13; 15; 16(2); 17; 18(2); 19(3); 21(2); 25; 26; 27; 28(5); 8:1(6); 2(3); 4; 5(4); 6; 7; 8(4); 9(5); 10(3); 11(3); 13; 9:1; 2(5); 3(3); 4(6); 5(2); 6(3); 7(4); 8(4); 9(3); 10; 12(2); 13(5); 14(3); 15(6); 16(2); 17; 18; 19(5); 20(2); 21(3); 22; 23(3); 24(4); 25(2); 26(5); 27; 28(2); 10:1(4); 2; 4; 5; 7(2); 8; 9(2); 10(3); 11; 12; 15; 16(2); 19(2); 20; 21; 23; 25(4); 26(2); 27; 29(4); 30(2); 31(2); 32; 34; 36(2); 38; 39(2); 11:1(2); 2; 3(2); 7(4); 9(3); 12(4); 13(2); 17; 19; 21(2); 22(2); 23; 24; 25(2); 26(4); 27(2); 28(3); 29(2); 30; 31(2); 32(2); 33; 34(5); 37; 38(2); 39; 12:1(2); 2(6); 5(3); 6; 7; 9; 11(2); 12(2); 13; 14; 15; 17; 18; 19(3); 20; 21; 22(3); 23(4); 24(3); 26(2); 27; 13:3; 4; 6; 7(3); 8; 9; 10; 11(4); 12(2); 13; 15(2); 17; 19(2); 20(5); 22; 24(2); S:1; **Jas** 1:1(2); 3; 6(2); 7; 9; 10(3); 11(6); 12(3); 17; 18; 20(2); 21; 22; 23; 25(2); 27(3); 2:1(2); 3(2); 5(2); 6(2); 7; 8(2); 9; 10; 11; 12; 16; 19; 21; 23(2); 25(2); 26(2); 3:1; 2(2); 3; 4(2); 5; 6(4); 7; 8; 9(2); 10; 11; 12; 14; 17; 18; 4:4(4); 5(2); 6(2); 7; 10(2); 11(4); 14; 15; 5:3(2); 4(5); 5; 6; 7(6); 8(2);

9(2); 10(3); 11(4); 12; 14(4); 15(3); 16; 17(2); 18(2); 19; 20(2); **1Pet** 1:1; 2(4); 3(3); 5(2); 7(2); 9(2); 10(2); 11(3); 12(4); 13(4); 14; 17(2); 19; 20(2); 21; 22(3); 23; 24(4); 25(4); 2:2(2); 3; 6; 7(5); 8; 9; 10; 11; 12(2); 13(2); 14(2); 15(2); 16; 17(2); 18(2); 24; 25; 3:1(4); 3; 4(4); 5(2); 7(3); 12(5); 15(2); 17; 18(4); 19; 20(3); 21(6); 22; 4:1(3); 2(4); 3(3); 4; 5(2); 6(3); 7; 8; 10(3); 11(2); 12; 14(2); 17(4); 18(3); 19(2); 5:1(3); 2(2); 3; 4; 5(3); 6; 8; 9(3); 10; 12; 13; **2Pet** 1:1; 2; 3; 4(3); 8; 10; 11; 12; 16; 17(2); 18; 19(2); 20; 21(3); 2:1(2); 2; 4; 5(5); 6; 7(2); 9(4); 10(2); 11; 12; 13(2); 15(4); 16(3); 17; 18(2); 19(2); 20(6); 21(2); 22(3); 3:2(5); 3; 4(4); 5(5); 6; 7(4); 8; 9; 10(8); 12(4); 15(2); 16; 17(2); 18; **1Jn** 1:1(2); 2(2); 3; 5; 6; 7(3); 8; 2:1(2); 2(3); 4; 5; 6; 7(3); 8(2); 9; 10; 11(3); 13; 14; 15; 19; 23; 24; 4:1(2); 3(3); 5; 5:1; 2; 3; 4(3); 5(2); 6(2); 7(3); 8(3); 9(3); 10(3); 13(4); 14; 15; 19; 20(2); **2Jn** 1(4); 2; 3; 4(3); 5(3); 6(2); 7(2); 9(4); 10(2); 12; 13(2); 14(2); 17(2); 18; 19; 20; 21(2); 22(3); **Jude** 1(2); 3(3); 4(2); 5(3); 6(2); 7(2); 8; 9(4); 11(3); 12; 13(2); 14(2); 17(2); 18; 19; 20; 21(2); 23(3); 24; 25; **Rev** 1:1; 2(2); 3(2); 4(2); 5(6); 7; 8(4); 9(4); 10(2); 11(3); 12; 13(5); 15; 16; 17(2); 18; 19(3); 20(8); 2:1(5); 5; 6(2); 7(2); 8(4); 9(2); 10; 11(3); 12; 13(5); 15; 16; 17(4); 18; 19(3); 20(8); 2:1(5); 6(2); 7(3); 8; 9; 10(4); 14(7); 15(2); 16; 17(4); 18(3); 19(3); 20(2); 21(4); 22; 4:1(2); 3; 3(7); 8; 9; 13(4); 14(3); 16(4); 17(3); 18(3); 19(5); 21

THEE

4571

Gen 3:11(2); 15; 16; 17; 18; 4:7; 12; 6:14; 18(2); 19; 20; 21(3); 7:1; 2; 8:16; 17(2); 12:1(2); 2(2); 3(3); 12(2); 13(2); 13:8(2); 9(2); 15; 17; 15:7(2); 16(2); 5(2); 6; 17:2(2); 4; 5; 6(3); 7(4); 8(2); 9; 10; 16; 18; 19; 20; 21; 18:3; 10; 14; 25(2); 19:5; 9; 17; 21; 22; 20:6(2); 7; 9; 15(2); 16(2); 21:12; 17; 22; 23(2); 22:2(2); 17; 23:6; 11(3); 13(2); 13; 40; 41; 43; 45; 50; 51; 25:30; 26:2; 3(3); 24(2); 28(3); 29(3); 27:3; 4; 7; 8; 10; 19; 21(2); 25; 28; 29(5); 37; 42(2); 45(2); 28:2; 3(3); 13; 14; 15(5); 22; 29:18; 19; 25; 27; 30:2; 14; 15; 16; 26(2); 27; 29; 30; 31; 31:3; 12; 13; 16; 27; 32; 35; 38; 39; 41; 42; 44; 48; 49; 50; 51; 52; 32:6; 9; 11; 12; 17(3); 26; 29; 33:5; 10; 11(2); 12; 14; 15; 35:1; 11; 12(2); 37:10; 13; 14; 16; 38:16(2); 17; 18; 25; 29; 39:9; 40:13; 14(2); 19(3); 41:15; 39; 41; 44; 42:37(2); 43:4; 9(2); 29; 44:8; 18; 32; 33; 45:11; 46:3; 4(2); 47:4; 5; 6; 29(2); 48:2; 4(4); 5(2); 9; 20(2); 22; 49:8; 25(2); 50:5; 6; 17(3); **Ex** 2:7(2); 9; 14; 3:10; 12(3); 18; 4:1; 5; 8; 12; 13; 14(2); 16; 18; 23; 5:3; 6:29; 7:1; 2; 15; 16; 8:4; 9(2); 11; 21; 29; 9:15; 16(2); 30; 10:17; 28; 11:8(2); 12:24; 48; 13:5(2); 7(2); 9(2); 11(3); 14; 14:12; 15:7; 11(2); 17; 26(2); 17:5; 6; 18:6; 14; 18(2); 19(2); 22(2); 23; 19:9(3); 24(2); 20:2; 4; 12; 24(2); 21:13; 22:25; 23:5; 7; 15; 20(3); 23(2); 25; 27(2); 28(2); 29(2); 30; 31; 33(2); 24:12; 25:9; 16; 21; 22(3); 40; 26:30; 27:8; 20; 28:1; 29:35; 42; 30:6; 23; 34; 36; 37; 31:6; 11; 32:4; 7; 8; 10; 21; 32; 34(2); 33:2; 3(2); 5(4); 12; 13(2); 14(2); 17; 18; 19(2); 22(2); 32:5; 6; 7; 9; 10; 11(2); 12; 14; 15; 16; 17; 21; 29:18; 22; 23; 32:5; 6; 8(3); 9; 10; 34:38; 39(2); **Lev** 9:2; 10:9; 14; 15; 19:13; 19; 33; 21:8; 24:2; 25:6(2); 8(2); 15; 16; 35(2); 36; 39(2); 40(2); 41; 47(2); **Num** 5:19; 20; 21; 6:24(2); 25(2); 26(2); 10:2; 3; 4; 29; 31; 32; 35(2); 11:15; 16; 17(3); 23; 12:11; 13; 14:12; 15; 17; 19; 16:10(2); 18:1(2); 2(4); 4; 7; 8(2); 9; 10; 11(2); 12; 19(4); 19:2; 20:17; 18; 21:7; 8; 29; 22:6; 9; 16(2); 17(2); 20(2); 28; 29; 30; 32; 33; 34; 35; 37(3); 38; 23:3; 11; 13; 26; 27(2); 24:9(2); 10; 11(2); 14; 22; 27:12; 18; **Deut** 1:21(2); 31; 38;

2:7(2); 9; 19; 25(4); 31; 3:25; 26; 27; 4:21; 23; 30; 31(2); 32; 35; 36(3); 37; 38(3); 40(4); 5:6; 8; 12; 15(2); 16(3); 27; 28; 31(2); 6:2; 3(2); 6; 10(2); 12; 15(2); 17; 18; 19; 20; 7:1(2); 2; 4; 6; 11; 12; 13(4); 15(3); 16(2); 19; 20; 22(2); 23; 24; 25; 8:1; 2(3); 3(4); 4; 5; 7; 10; 11; 14; 15(2); 16(4); 18; 9:3(2); 4(2); 5; 6; 12; 14; 10:12(2); 10; 12; 13; 21; 22; 11:29; 12:1; 7; 14; 15; 20; 21(3); 25(2); 28(3); 13:1; 2; 5(3); 6; 7(2); 10(2); 12; 17(3); 18; 14:2; 24(3); 27; 29(2); 15:4(2); 5; 6(3); 7; 9(2); 10; 11; 12(3); 13; 14; 15(2); 16(4); 18(5); 16:1; 4; 5; 9; 10; 15; 17; 18(2); 20; 20:1(2); 11(4); 12(2); 14; 15; 16; 17; 20; 21:1; 23; 22:2(2); 6; 7; 21; 23; 24(3); 27; 28; 29:1; 34:4; **Josh** 1:5(4); 7; 9(2); 17(2); 2:3; 14; 18; 19; 3:7(2); 5:2; 7:10; 13; 19; 25; 8:1; 2; 9:25; 10:8; 13:6; 14:6; 17:15; **Judg** 1:3; 24(2); 3:19; 20; 4:6; 7; 9; 14; 19; 20; 22; 5:14; 6:12; 14; 16; 18(3); 23; 39; 7:2; 4(6); 9; 9:31; 32; 33; 10:10; 15(2); 11:8; 17; 19; 24; 27; 36; 12:1(2); 13:4; 15(3); 17; 14:15; 16; 15:2; 12(2); 13(3); 16:5; 6(2); 9; 10; 12; 14; 15; 20; 28(2); 17:2; 3; 10; 18:3; 5; 19; 23; 24; 25; 19:6; 8; 11; 20; **Ruth** 1:10; 16(2); 17; 2:4; 9; 12; 19; 22; 3:1(2); 3(3); 4(2); 11; 13(3); 15; 4:4(3); 8; 12; 14; 15(3); **1Sa** 1:8; 14; 17; 23; 26; 2:2; 15; 20; 34; 36; 3:9; 17(4); 8(7); 8; 9:3; 16; 17; 19(2); 20; 23(3); 24(2); 26; 27; 10:1; 2; 3; 4(2); 6; 7(3); 8(3); 15; 11:1; 3; 12:10; 13:13; 14; 14:7(2); 36; 40; 15:1; 16; 17; 18; 23; 25; 26(2); 28; 30; 16:1; 2; 3(2); 15; 16(2); 22; 17:37; 45; 46(3); 18:17; 22(2); 19:2(2); 3; 4; 17; 20:4; 8; 9(3); 10; 12(2); 13(4); 21(2); 22(2); 23(2); 37; 42; 21:1; 2(2); 22:3; 5; 23:11; 12; 17(2); 24:4(2); 10(3); 12(3); 13; 15; 17; 19; 25:6(2); 8(2); 22; 29; 30(2); 32; 33; 34; 40(2); 26:6; 8; 11; 16; 18; 19; 22(2); 29:6(2); 8; 10; 30:7; 15; **2Sa** 1:4; 9; 16; 2:21(3); 22(2); 3:8; 12(2); 13(2); 21; 24; 25; 5:2; 24; 7:3; 8; 9(2); 11(3); 12; 15; 16; 20; 22(2); 24; 25; 26(2); 27(2); 9:7(2); 10:3(2); 11:12; 12:5(2); 7(3); 8(3); 11; 14; 13:5(3); 13(3); 14(2); 15(2); 17(3); 19; 32(2); 15:3(3); 4(2); 6; 10; 21; 27; 28; 18:2; 3; 12; 19; 24; 25; 26(2); 14:2; 5; 8; 10(2); 11; 12; 17; 18(2); 19; 32(2); 33:3; 37; 25:5(3); 34:3; 4; 5(3); 14(3); 36:2(3); 19; 28; 37:18; 20(3); 38:4; 10; 14; 15(2); 16(2); 20(4); 22(2); 25(5); 39:12; 16; 17; 18(2); 40:4(6); 5; 14; 15(3); 42:2(2); 5; 6; 43:2; 3; 44:16; 45:2; 5; 46:14(2); 27; 28(5); 48:2; 18; 27; 32; 43; 46; 49:5(2); 9; 15; 16(2); 50:21; 24; 31(2); 42; 51:14(2); 20(2); 21(2); 22(3); 23(3); 25(4); 26; 36; **Lam** 1:22; 2:13(5); 14(2); 15; 16; 17; 3:57; 4:21; 22; 5:21; **Eze** 2:1; 3; 4; 6; 8(2); 3:3; 4; 6(2); 7; 10; 11; 17; 22; 25(2); 27; 4:1(2); 3(2); 5; 6; 8(2); 9(2); 15; 5:1(3); 8(2); 9; 10(3); 11; 12(3); 14(2); 15(2); 17(3); 7(3); 8(4); 9(2); 8:6; 13; 15; 12:3; 6; 9; 16:4; 5(3); 6(4); 7; 8(5); 9(3); 10(4); 11; 14; 17; 19(2); 23; 24(2); 27(3); 31; 37; 38(2); 39(3); 40(3); 41(2); 42(2); 44; 57; 59; 60(2); 61; 62; 63; 20:47(2); 21:3(2); 4; 7; 16; 19; 29(3); 30; 31(3); 22:4; 5(2); 6; 7(3); 9(3); 10(2); 11; 12; 13; 14; 15(3); 23:22(2); 24(3); 25(2); 26; 27; 28; 29(2); 30; 34; 37; 38(2); 39(3); 40(3); 41(2); 42(2); 44; 57; 59; 60(2); 61; 62; 63; 20:47(2); 21:3(2); 4; 7; 16; 19; 29(3); 30; 31(3); 22:4; 5(2); 6; 7(3); 9(3); 10(2); 11; 12; 13; 14; 15(3); 16; 17; 26(2); 25:4(3); 7(5); 8(3); 10; 14; 15; 16; 17(3); 19(3); 20(2); 21; 27:5; 7; 8; 9(2); 10; 15; 21; 25; 26(2); 27(2); 30; 31(2); 32(2); 34; 35; 36; 28:3; 4; 7; 8; 9(2); 13; 14; 15; 16(3); 17(3); 18(4); 19(2); 22(2); 29:3; 4; 5(3); 7(2); 8(2); 10; 11; 14; 15; 16; 17; 30; 31(2); 32(2); 33; 34; 35; 36; 28:3; 4; 7; 8; 9(2); 13; 14; 15; 16(3); 17(3); 18(4); 19(2); 22(2); 30; 31; 32(2); 33; 34; 35; 36; 28:3; 4; 7; 8; 9(2); 13; 14; 15; 16(3); 17(3); 18(4); 19(2); 32:3; 4; 6; 17; 21; 27; 33:7; 30; 31(2); 35:3(3); 6(3); 9; 11; 14; 15; 36:12; 13; 37:16; 12; 19; 21; 22; 43(4); 44(3); 20:2; 22:11; 32; 33; 34; 64; 23:43; **Jn** 1:48(2); 50(2);

75:1(2); 76:10; 77:16(2); 79:6; 11; 12; 13; 80:14; 18; 81:7(3); 8; 9; 10; 16; 83:2; 5; 84:4; 5; 12; 85:6; 86:2; 3; 4; 5; 7; 8; 9; 12; 14; 87:3; 7; 88:1; 2; 9(2); 10; 13(2); 89:8(2); 90:8; 13; 91:3; 4; 7; 10; 11(2); 12; 94:20; 101:1; 102:1; 28; 103:4; 104:27; 105:11; 108:3(2); 114:5; 116:4; 7; 17; 19; 118:21; 25(2); 28(2); 119:7; 10; 11; 62; 63; 74; 76; 79; 108; 120; 126; 146; 164; 168; 169; 170; 175; 120:3(2); 121:3; 6; 7; 122:6; 8; 123:1; 128:2; 5; 130:1; 4; 134:3; 135:9; 137:5; 6; 8; 138:1(2); 4; 139:12(2); 14; 15; 18; 20; 21(2); 141:1(2); 2; 8(2); 142:5; 143:6(2); 8(2); 9; 144:9(2); 145:1; 2; 10(2); 15; 147:13; 14; **Prov** 1:10; 2:1; 11(2); 12; 16; 3:2; 3; 28; 29; 30; 4:6(2); 8(2); 9; 11(2); 24(2); 25; 5:17; 19; 6:22(3); 24; 25; 7:1; 5; 15(2); 9:8(2); 20:22; 22:18; 19(2); 20; 21(2); 27; 23:1; 7(2); 11; 22; 25; 25:7; 8; 10; 16; 17(2); 22; 27:2; 29:17; 30:6; 7; 9; 10; **Eccl** 2:1; 7:21; 8:2; 9:9; 10:4; 16; 11:9(2); **Song** 1:3; 4(3); 9; 11; 4:7; 6:1; 13; 7:5; 12; 13; 8:1(2); 2(3); 5(4); **Is** 1:25; 2:10; 3:12(2); 7:5; 11; 17; 8:1; 9:3; 10:24(2); 12:1; 6; 14:3; 8; 9(3); 10; 11(2); 16(3); 29; 16:4; 9; 19:12; 22:1; 3; 15; 16; 17(2); 18; 19(2); 24:17; 25:1; 3(2); 26:3(2); 8(2); 9(2); 13(2); 16; 20; 29:3(3); 11; 12; 30:19(2); 21; 22; 33:1(3); 2; 36:8(2); 11; 12; 37:9; 10; 22(3); 29; 30; 38:3(2); 6; 7; 18(2); 19; 39:3; 7; 40:9; 41:9(4); 10(4); 11(2); 12(2); 13(2); 14; 15; 42:6(3); 43:1(4); 2(3); 3; 4(2); 5(2); 23(2); 44:2(3); 8; 21; 22; 24; 45:2; 3(2); 4(2); 5; 14(5); 47:3; 5; 9(2); 10; 11(3); 13(2); 15(2); 48:5(2); 6; 9(2); 10(2); 17(2); 49:6; 7; 8(4); 15; 16; 17(2); 18(3); 19; 23; 25; 26; 51:16; 19(3); 23; 52:1; 14; 54:6; 7(2); 8(2); 9(2); 10(2); 14; 15; 17(2); 55:5(3); 57:8; 12; 13; 58:8; 9; 11; 12; 14(2); 59:12; 21; 60:1; 2(2); 4; 5(2); 6; 7(2); 9; 10(3); 11; 12; 13; 14(4); 15(2); 19(2); 62:4; 5(2); 64:4; 5; 7; 9; 11; 65:15; **Jer** 1:5(4); 7(2); 8(2); 10; 17(2); 18; 19(4); 2:2; 17; 19(3); 21; 22(2); 28(2); 31; 35; 3:19(2); 22; 4:14; 18; 30(2); 5:7; 6:8(2); 23; 26(2); 12:1(2); 3; 5(2); 6(3); 13:1; 6; 12; 20; 20(3); 21; 27; 14:7; 20; 22; 15:2; 5(2); 6(2); 11; 14; 19(2); 20(6); 21(2); 16:2; 10; 19; 17:4(2); 13; 16(2); 18:2; 20; 23; 19:2; 10; 20:4; 12; 15; 21:2; 13; 22:6; 7; 21; 23; 24; 25; 26(2); 23:33; 37; 25:15; 26(2); 27:2; 28:8; 15; 16; 29:22; 26; 30:2(2); 10; 11(6; 14(3); 15; 16(3); 17(3); 31:3(2); 4; 21(2); 23; 32:7(2); 8; 17; 20; 25; 33:3(2); 34:3; 4; 15(4); 36:2(3); 19; 28; 37:18; 20(3); 38:4; 10; 14; 15(2); 16(2); 19; 28; 37:18; 20(3); 40:4(2); 5; 44; 57; 59; 60(2); 61; 62; 63; 20:47(2); 21:3(2); 4; 7; 16; 19; 29(3); 30; 31(3); 22:11; 32; 33; 34; 64; 23:43; **Jn** 1:48(2); 50(2);

2:4; 3:3; 5; 7; 11; 26; 4:10(2); 26; 5:10; 12; 14; 6:30; 7:20; 8:10; 11; 9:26; 37; 10:33; 11:8; 22; 28; 40; 41; 13:8; 37; 38; 16:30; 17:1; 3; 4; 5; 7; 8; 11; 13; 21; 25(2); 18:26; 30; 34; 35; 19:10(2); 11(2); 21:3; 15; 16; 17; 18(3); 20; 22; 23; **Acts** 3:6; 5:9; 7:3(2); 27; 34; 35; 8:20; 22; 34; 9:5; 6; 17; 34; 10:6; 19; 20; 22(2); 32; 33(2); 11:14; 12:8; 13:11; 33; 47; 16:18; 17:32; 18:10(3); 21:21; 23; 24; 37; 39; 22:10(2); 14; 18; 19; 21; 23:3; 18(2); 20; 21; 30(2); 35; 24:2; 4(2); 8; 14; 19; 25; 25:26; 26:2; 3(2); 14; 16(3); 17(2); 24; 27:24(2); 28:21(2); 22; **Rom** 2:4; 27; 4:17; 9:17(2); 10:8; 11:18; 21; 22; 13:4; 15:3; 9; **1Cor** 4:7; 8:10; 12:21; **2Cor** 6:2(2); 12:9; **Gal** 3:8; **Eph** 5:14; 6:3; **Phil** 4:3; **1Ti** 1:3; 18(2); 3:14(2); 4:14(2); 16; 5:21; 6:13; 21; **2Ti** 1:3; 4; 5(2); 6(2); 14; 2:7; 3:15; 4:1; 11; 13; 21; **Titus** 1:5(2); 2:15; 3:12; 15; **Philem** 1:4; 7; 8; 9; 10; 11(2); 16; 18(2); 19; 20; 21; 23; **Heb** 1:5; 9; 2:12; 5:5; 6:14(2); 8:5; 13:5(2); **Jas** 2:18; **2Jn** 5(2); 13; **3Jn** 3; 13; 14(3); **Jude** 9; **Rev** 2:4; 5; 10; 14; 16; 20; 3:3(2); 8; 9; 10; 16; 18; 4:1; 11:17(2); 14:15; 15:4(2); 17:1; 7; 18:14(2); 22(3); 23(2); 21:9

THEIR

846

Gen 1:21; 25; 5:2; 6:20(2); 7:14; 8:19; 9:23(4); 10:5(3); 20(4); 30; 31(4); 32(2); 11:7; 12:5; 13:6; 14:6; 11(2); 24; 17:7; 8; 9; 23; 18:20; 22; 26; 19:10; 33; 35; 36; 20:8; 24:52; 59; 25:13(2); 16(4); 26:18; 31:38; 43; 53; 32:15; 33:2; 6; 34:13; 18; 20(2); 21; 23(2); 27; 28(3); 29(3); 35:4(3); 36:7(2); 19; 30; 40(3); 43(2); 37:2; 4; 12; 16; 21; 22; 25(2); 32; 40:1; 42:6; 24; 25; 26; 28; 29; 35(2); 36; 43:2; 11; 15; 24(2); 26; 27; 28; 44:3; 13; 45:25; 27; 46:5(3); 6(2); 17; 32(3); 47:1(2); 4; 9; 12; 17(2); 22(2); 30; 48:6(2); 49:5; 6(4); 7(2); 28; 50:8(3); 15; 17; **Ex** 1:11; 14(2); 2:11; 16; 17; 18; 23; 24; 3:7(3); 4:5; 31(2); 5:4; 5; 6; 10; 21; 6:4; 6; 14; 16; 17; 19; 25; 26; 7:11; 12; 19(4); 22; 8:7; 18; 26; 10:7; 23; 12:3; 34(4); 42; 51; 13:20; 14:10; 19; 22(2); 25; 26(2); 29(2); 16:1(2); 17:1; 18:7; 23; 19:7; 10; 14; 21:32; 22:23; 23:24(3); 26; 27; 32; 33; 25:20(3); 34(2); 36(2); 40; 26:21; 25; 29; 32; 37; 27:10(2); 11(2); 12(2); 14(2); 15(2); 16(2); 17(2); 18; 21; 28:10(2); 12; 20; 21; 38; 42; 29:10; 15; 19; 20(2); 25; 28(2); 45; 46(2); 30:12; 19(2); 21(3); 31:16; 32:3; 4; 15; 25(2); 32; 34; 33:6; 34:13(3); 15(2); 16(4); 35:17; 18; 25; 36:26; 30; 34; 36; 38(4); 37:9(3); 22(2); 38:10(3); 11(3); 12(3); 14(2); 15(2); 17(2); 19(5); 28; 39:13; 14; 40:15(3); 31(2); 36; 38; **Lev** 4:15; 6:17; 7:34; 36; 38; 8:14; 16; 18; 22; 24(3); 25; 28; 9:24; 10:5; 19(2); 11:8(2); 11(2); 21; 27; 35; 36; 37; 38; 13:38; 39; 15:31(2); 16:16(3); 21(2); 22; 27(3); 34; 17:5; 7(2); 18:3; 6; 9; 10; 29; 20:4; 5; 11; 12; 13; 16; 17; 18; 19; 20; 24; 27; 21:5(3); 6(3); 17; 22:16; 25; 23:4; 18(2); 24:14; 25:32; 33; 34(2); 45; 26:4; 13; 20; 36(2); 39(2); 40(3); 41(3); 43(2); 44(2); 45(3); **Num** 1:2(4); 3; 16; 17; 18(4); 20(4); 22(4); 24(3); 26(3); 28(3); 30(3); 32(3); 34(3); 36(3); 38(3); 40(3); 42(3); 45; 47; 52(2); 2:2; 3; 9; 10; 16; 17; 18; 24; 25; 31; 32(2); 34(3); 3:4; 10; 15(2); 17; 18; 19; 20(2); 31; 37(3); 39; 40; 45; 4:2(2); 22(2); 26(2); 27(3); 28; 29(2); 31(2); 32(6); 33; 34(2); 36; 38(2); 40(2); 42(2); 44; 46(2); 5:3; 7; 6:15(2); 7:2; 3; 7; 8; 9; 10; 11; 87; 8:7(2); 10; 12; 21; 22; 26(2); 9:17; 18; 20; 22; 10:6(2); 12; 13; 14; 18; 22; 25; 28; 11:10; 12; 33; 13:2; 4; 33; 14:1; 5; 6; 9; 23; 15:12; 25(3); 38(2); 16:15; 22; 26; 27(4); 32(2); 38; 45; 17:2(3); 3; 6(3); 10; 18:11; 17(2); 20; 21; 23; 20:6; 8(2); 11; 21:2; 3; 18; 22:7; 24:2; 8; 25:2(2); 18(2); 26:2; 12; 15; 20; 23; 26; 28; 35; 37; 38; 41; 42(2); 44; 48; 50; 55; 57; 59; 27:5; 7(2); 14; 19; 28:2; 14; 20; 28; 31; 29:3; 6(2); 9; 11; 14; 18(3); 19; 21(3); 24(3); 27(3); 30(3); 33(3); 37(3); 30:9; 31:9(4); 10(2); 29; 32:17; 38; 33:1; 2(4); 4(2); 12; 52(3); 34:14(4); 15; 35:2; 3(3); 7; 36:3; 4(2); 6; 11; 12(2); **Deut** 1:8; 25; 2:5; 9; 12; 21; 22; 23; 4:10; 37; 38; 5:29; 7:5(4); 10; 16; 24(2); 25; 9:5; 14; 27(2); 10:6; 11; 15; 11:4(2); 6(3); 9; 12:2; 3(4); 29; 30(2); 31(4); 13:13; 14:8(2); 18:2(2); 18; 19:1(2); 20:18(2); 21:5; 6; 23:3; 6(2); 8; 29:8; 17(2); 25; 28; 31:7; 11; 13; 19; 20; 21(2); 28; 32:5; 8; 20; 21; 27; 29; 30; 31; 32(3); 33; 35(2); 36; 37(2); 38(2); 33:29; **Josh** 1:6; 3:14; 4:6; 18; 21; 5:1; 6; 7(2); 8; 7:6; 8(2); 11; 12(3); 16; 8:13; 19; 33(2); 9:4; 5(2); 14; 16; 17(2); 10:5; 13; 19; 24; 40; 42; 11:4; 6(2); 9(2); 13; 17; 20; 21; 23(2); 12:1; 7; 13:8; 14; 15; 16; 23; 24; 25; 28(2); 29; 30; 31; 33; 14:2; 4(3); 15:1; 2; 5; 12; 20; 32; 36; 41; 44; 46; 51; 54; 57; 59; 60; 62; 16:4; 5(2); 8; 9; 17:2(2); 4; 18:2; 5(2); 7(2); 10; 11(2); 12; 20; 21; 24; 28(2); 19:1(2); 2; 6; 7; 8; 9; 10(2); 11; 15; 16(2); 17; 18; 22(2); 23(2); 24; 25; 30; 31(2); 32; 33; 38; 39(2); 40; 41; 47; 48(2); 49; 21:3(2); 7; 8; 19; 20; 26; 33(2); 40(2); 41; 42; 43; 44(4); 22:6; 7(2); 9; 14; 23:1; 2(4); 5; 7; 24:1(3); 8; **Judg** 1:4; 7(3); 2:2; 3; 4; 10; 12; 14(2); 17(2); 18(2); 19(3); 20; 22; 3:4; 6(5); 7; 25; 5:18; 20; 22; 6:5(3); 9; 7:2; 6(3); 8(2); 12; 19; 20(2); 8:3; 10; 21; 26; 28; 33; 34(2); 9:3; 24(2); 26; 27(2); 57; 10:12; 12:2; 13:20; 14:17; 19; 15:13; 16:18; 23; 24; 25; 18:1; 2(2); 8(2); 14; 16; 23; 26; 29; 19:14; 21; 22; 20:13; 22; 33(2); 42; 21:2; 6; 22(2); 23(2); **Ruth** 1:9; 14; **1Sa** 1:19; 2:20; 25; 33; 5:9; 6:6; 7; 10; 11; 13(2); 8:9; 22; 9:16; 10:4; 12; 21; 11:4; 12:9; 14:30; 46; 15:24; 17:1; 18(2); 51; 53; 18:27; 21:13; 22:17(2); 23:5; 25:12; 28:1; 23; 29:1; 30:2; 3(3); 4; 31:9; 13; **2Sa** 1:23(2); 2:26; 3:18; 30; 4:12(2); 5:21; 7:10; 23; 24; 10:3; 4(3); 18; 12:30; 13:31; 36; 15:11; 36; 17:8; 18:28; 20:2; 3; 22:46; 23:17; 19; **1Kin** 2:4(3); 15; 33; 4:8; 6:27; 7:25; 31; 33(4); 8:7; 23; 25; 34; 35; 37(2); 44; 45(3); 48(5); 49(3); 50; 66; 9:9(2); 21; 10:5; 29; 11:2; 8; 12:16; 27; 13:11; 12; 14:15(2); 22(2); 27; 30; 15:16; 32; 16:2; 13; 26; 18:28; 37; 39; 19:21; 20:6; 23; 24; 25; 32(2); 22:10; **2Kin** 1:14; 3:24; 27; 5:24; 6:20; 22; 23; 7:7(4); 15; 8:12(4); 21; 10:7; 11:12; 13:3; 5; 14:12; 16:15(2); 17:7; 9(2); 14(3); 15; 16; 17(2); 19; 23; 25; 29(2); 31; 33; 34(2); 40; 41(4); 18:12; 27(2); 35; 36; 37; 19:17; 18; 26; 21:8; 14(2); 15; 22:7; 17; 23:2; 3(2); 9; 14; 25:21; 23(2); 24; **1Chr** 1:29; 3:9; 19; 4:3; 27; 31; 32; 33(3); 38(3); 39; 41(3); 42; 5:7(2); 9; 10(2); 13(2); 15; 16; 20(2); 21(2); 22; 24(2); 25; 6:19; 32(2); 33; 44; 48; 54(3); 57; 60(2); 62; 63; 64; 65; 66; 7:2(2); 4(2); 5(2); 7(2); 9(3); 11; 21; 22; 28; 30; 32; 40; 8:28; 32; 9:1; 2(2); 6; 9(3); 13(2); 17; 19; 22(3); 23; 25(2); 26; 32; 34; 38(2); 10:7; 8; 9; 10; 12; 11:19(2); 21; 12:30; 32(2); 39; 13:2; 8; 14:12; 15:15; 16; 17; 18; 16:21; 38; 17:9; 22; 19:4(2); 7; 20:2; 21:16; 23:3(2); 11; 22; 24(2); 28; 32; 24:2; 3(2); 4(2); 19(3); 30; 31(2); 25:1; 3; 6; 7; 26:6; 8(2); 13; 27:1(2); 28:15; 18; 29:18; 20(2); 21; **2Chr** 1:17; 3:13(2); 4:4; 7; 16; 20; 5:8; 12(2); 13; 6:14; 16; 25; 26; 28(2); 34; 35(3); 36; 37; 38(5); 39(3); 7:3; 6(2); 10; 14(3); 22; 8:8; 14(3); 9:4(2); 6; 10:16; 11:13; 14(2); 16(2); 13:10; 16; 18; 14:4; 15:4; 12(3); 15(2); 17:14; 18:9; 19:4; 10; 20:13(3); 27; 33(2); 21:3; 22:5; 24:18(2); 24(2); 25:4; 5; 10; 15; 20; 26:11; 13; 28:6; 8; 15; 29:6(2); 15; 23; 24; 30; 34; 30:7; 16(2); 22; 27(2); 31:1; 2; 6; 15(2); 16(4); 17(3); 18(5); 19; 32:13; 17; 33:17; 34:5; 6; 25; 30; 32; 33(2); 35:2; 10(2); 11; 15(3); 25; 36:15; 17(2); **Ezr** 1:6; 2:59(2); 61; 62; 65(2); 66(2); 67(2); 69; 70(2); 3:8(2); 9(2); 10; 12; 4:5; 7; 9; 17; 23; 5:3; 5; 8; 10; 6:12; 13; 18(2); 20; 22; 7:13; 16; 17(2); 8:1; 19; 24; 26; 9:1; 2(2); 11; 11(2); 12(4); 10:16(2); 19(3); **Neh** 2:18; 3:5(3); 18; 23; 4:3; 4(2); 5(2); 13(4); 15; 5:1(2); 5; 6; 8; 11(4); 14; 15; 6:6; 9; 14; 16; 7:61(2); 63; 64; 67(2); 68(2); 69; 73(2); 8:6(3); 7; 12; 15; 16; 9:2(2); 3(3); 4; 6; 9; 11; 15(2); 16; 17(3); 20(2); 21(2); 23(2); 24(2); 26; 27(3); 28; 29; 35(2); 37; 10:10; 28(3); 29(2); 30; 11:3; 9; 12; 14(2); 19; 25; 30; 31; 12:7; 9; 24; 27; 42; 45; 13:11; 13(2); 24; 25(3); **Est** 1:17(2); 20; 22; 2:3; 12; 3:8; 12; 8:9(3); 11; 13; 9:2(2); 5; 10; 15; 16(4); 22; 27(3); 28; 31(3); **Job** 1:4(2); 5(2); 13; 18; 2:12(3); 3:8; 15; 4:21; 5:5; 12(2); 13; 15; 6:17; 18; 8:4; 8; 10; 11:3; 20; 12:18; 14:12; 15:18; 35; 16:10; 17:2; 4; 19:12; 15; 20:10; 21:8(4); 9; 10(2); 11(2); 13; 16(2); 17; 29; 22:6; 18; 24:5(2); 11(2); 18; 23; 27:23; 29:9(2); 10(3); 23; 25; 30:2; 4; 9(2); 12; 31:16; 39; 33:16; 34:24; 25; 36:9(2); 10; 11(2); 14; 15; 20; 37:8; 38:15; 40; 39:3(2); 4; 40:12; 13; 22; 42:15(2); **Ps** 2:3(2); 12; 4:7(2); 5:9(4); 10(2); 11; 7:7; 9:5; 6; 10; 15; 10:17; 11:2(2); 6; 16:4(3); 17:7; 10(2); 11; 14(3); 18:45; 19:3; 4(2); 21:10(2); 12; 22:13; 26:10; 28:3(2); 4(4); 8; 33:15(2); 19; 34:5; 15; 17; 35:6; 7; 16; 17; 21; 25; 36:7; 37:14; 15(3); 18; 39; 40:15; 44:1; 3(2); 12; 49:6(2); 8; 10; 11(5); 13(4); 14(2); 55:9; 15; 23; 56:5; 57:4; 58:4; 6(2); 59:7(2); 12(3); 62:4; 64:3(3); 8; 65:7; 68:27(2); 69:22(2); 23(2); 25(2); 27; 70:3; 72:14(2); 73:4(2); 7; 9(2); 17; 20; 74:4; 8; 76:5(2); 78:4; 5; 6; 7; 8(2); 12; 18(2); 28(2); 29; 30(3); 33(2); 35(2); 36(2); 37; 38; 44(2); 46(2); 47(2); 48(2); 50(2); 51; 53; 55; 57; 58(2); 63(2); 64(2); 79:3; 10; 12(2); 81:12(2); 14(2); 15; 83:11(2); 16; 85:2; 89:17; 32(2); 90:10; 16; 91:12; 93:3(2); 94:23(2); 95:10; 98:8; 99:8; 102:17; 28; 104:11; 12; 17; 21(2); 22; 27; 29(2); 105:14; 24; 25; 29(2); 30(2); 31; 32; 33(3); 35(2); 36(2); 37; 106:11; 15(2); 18; 20; 21; 25; 27; 29; 32; 35; 36; 37(2); 38(2); 39(2); 42(2); 43(2); 44(2); 107:5; 6(2); 12; 13(2); 14; 17(2); 18; 19(2); 20; 26; 27; 28(2); 30; 38; 109:10(2); 13; 25; 29; 115:2; 4; 7; 9(2); 10(2); 11(2); 119:70; 118; 123:2; 124:3; 6; 125:3; 4; 5; 129:3; 132:12; 135:12; 17; 136:10; 21; 140:2; 3(2); 9; 141:4; 5; 6; 10; 144:8; 11; 12; 145:15; 19; 147:3; 4; 149:2; 5; 6(2); 8(2); **Prov** 1:6; 15; 16; 18(2); 22; 31(2); 2:15; 4:16; 22; 8:21; 9:15; 10:15; 11:6; 20; 14:24; 17:6; 18:19; 20:29; 21:12; 22:23; 23:11(2); 24:2(2); 22; 25:27; 29:13; 16; 30:5; 11(2); 12(2); 13(2); 14; 25; 26; **Eccl** 2:3; 3:11; 4:1; 9; 5:11; 13; 9:1; 3; 6(3); **Is** 2:4(2); 7(4); 8(3); 3:4; 8(2); 9(3); 10; 12; 16; 17; 18(4); 5:12; 13(2); 14(3); 17; 21(2); 24(2); 25; 27(2); 28(3); 29; 6:10(5); 13; 8:12; 19; 21(2); 9:17(2); 10:2; 5; 13; 25; 29; 11:7; 14; 13:8; 10; 11(2); 16(4); 18(2); 20; 21; 22(2); 14:1; 2(2); 9; 21; 25; 15:2; 3(3); 4; 16:10(2); 18:2; 7; 20:4; 5(2); 21:14; 24:14; 25:11(2); 26:11; 14; 21; 28:25; 29:13(4); 14(2); 15(2); 19; 30:6(2); 7; 26; 31:3; 4; 33:2; 7; 9; 23; 24; 34:2; 3(4); 4; 7(2); 35:10; 36:12(2); 20; 21; 22; 37:18; 19; 27; 40:24; 26; 31; 41:1; 17; 29(2); 42:11; 15; 43:9; 14; 44:9(2); 18(2); 25; 45:12; 20; 46:1; 47:9; 49:9; 22(2); 23(2); 26(2); 50:2; 3; 51:7; 11; 52:15; 53:11; 54:17; 55:12; 56:7(2); 11; 57:2; 8; 58:1(2); 2; 59:5; 6(4); 7(3); 8; 18; 60:8; 9(2); 10; 11; 61:6; 7(2); 8; 9(2); 62:6; 63:3; 6; 8; 9; 10; 65:2; 4; 6; 7(2); 22; 23; 66:3(3); 4(2); 18(2); 24(2); **Jer** 1:8; 16(2); 17; 2:11(2); 26(4); 27(3); 3:17; 21(2); 24(4); 4:16; 5:3; 4; 5; 6(3); 16; 24; 27; 31; 6:3(2); 10; 12(2); 19; 23; 27; 7:18; 19; 24(2); 26(3); 28(2); 30; 31(2); 8:1; 7; 10(2); 12; 19; 9:3(2); 5; 8; 14(2); 16; 10:7; 9; 15; 21; 11:8(2); 10(2); 12; 14; 18; 22(2); 23; 12:2(2); 14; 13:10; 14:3(4); 4; 6; 10(3); 11; 12; 14; 16(4); 15:7; 8; 9; 16:3(2); 4; 7(2); 15(2); 17(2); 18(3); 17:1; 2(3); 23(2); 25; 18:8; 15; 16; 17; 21(6); 22; 23(3); 19:4; 5; 7(3); 9(4); 15; 20:4; 5; 11; 21:7(2); 22:9; 23:3; 8; 10(2); 11; 12(2); 16; 22(2); 26; 27(2); 31; 32(2); 24:5; 7(2); 9; 10; 25:12; 14(2); 36; 38; 26:3; 27:4; 8; 11(2); 29:23; 30:3; 9(2); 10; 20(2); 21(2); 31:12; 13(2); 17; 23; 32; 33(3); 34(2); 32:18; 22; 30(2); 32(4); 34; 35(2); 38; 39; 40; 44; 33:8(2); 12; 20; 26; 34:14; 16; 20(3); 21(2); 35:14; 16; 36:3(2); 6; 7; 15; 24; 31; 37:7; 38:18; 19; 23; 40:7; 8; 9; 41:5(3); 8; 42:17; 43:1(2); 44:3; 5(2); 9; 12; 15; 46:5; 10; 21(2); 25(2); 26; 27; 47:3; 5; 48:12; 13; 33; 34; 44; 49:1; 3; 7; 20; 21; 29(5); 32(3); 35; 37(2); 50:4; 5; 6(2); 7(2); 9; 27(2); 34(2); 37(2); 38; 42; 45; 51:5; 18; 24; 30(2); 39(2); 55; 56; **Lam** 1:11; 14; 19(2); 22; 2:10(2); 12(3); 15(2); 16; 18; 20; 3:14; 46; 60(2); 61(2); 62; 63(3); 64; 4:3; 7; 8(3); 10(2); 14; 20; 5:7; 8; 12; 14; **Eze** 1:5; 7(2); 8(4); 9; 10; 11(3); 13; 16(3); 17; 18(2); 20; 22; 23(2); 24(2); 25(2); 26; 2:3; 6(3); 3:8(2); 9; 4:4; 5; 12; 13; 17; 5:10; 16; 6:5; 9(4); 13(4); 14; 7:11; 18; 19(7); 20(2); 24(2); 27(2); 8:16(2); 17; 9:10(2); 10:8; 10; 11; 12(4); 16; 19; 21; 22(2); 11:19; 20; 21(4); 22; 12:3(2); 4(2); 5; 6; 7; 16; 19(2); 13:2; 3; 17; 14:3(4); 5(2); 10; 11(2); 14(2); 20(2); 22(2); 23(2); 16:39; 40; 45(2); 47(2); 53; 55(2); 19:4; 7(2); 8(2); 20:4; 8; 16(2); 18(3); 24(2); 26; 28(4); 30; 21:6; 14; 15(3); 23; 28; 29; 22:6; 10; 26; 31(2); 23:3(3); 4; 7; 8; 15(3); 17; 20; 24; 30; 36; 37(3); 39(2); 42(2); 45; 47(4); 24:25(6); 25:4(2); 26:10; 16(3); 17; 27:9; 11; 29; 30(2); 32; 35(2); 28:7; 25; 26; 29:7(2); 14; 16; 30:11; 13; 31:6(2); 14(4); 32:2; 10; 14(2); 24(2); 25(2); 26; 27(5); 29; 30(3); 33:2(2); 17; 29; 31(3); 34:10(2); 13; 14; 23; 24; 27(2); 30; 35:5(2); 36:5(2); 7; 12; 17(4); 18; 19(2); 23; 37:10; 20; 21; 23(5); 25(3); 27; 38:16; 39:22; 23(2); 24(2); 26(3); 27; 28(2); 40:16; 22(3); 41; 44; 41:16; 42:4; 11(3); 14; 43:7(4); 8(4); 9(2); 10; 11; 44:10(2); 12(2); 13(2); 18(2); 19(2); 20(3); 22; 28(2); 45:4; 8; 46:16; 18; 47:10(2); 12; 48:29; 34; **Dan** 1:15; 16; 2:30; 3:21(4); 27(2); 28(2); 29; 4:21; 6:24(3); 7:12(2); 8:23; 9:7; 11:8(3); 32; **Hos** 1:7; 2:5; 17; 3:5(2); 4:7; 8(2); 9(2); 12(3); 18; 19; 5:4(2); 5; 6(2); 7; 15(2); 7:2(3); 3(2); 6(2); 7(2); 10; 12; 14(2); 15; 16(3); 8:4(2); 13(2); 9:4(3); 6(2); 9(2); 10; 11; 12; 15(3); 16(2); 10:2(3); 8; 10; 11:3; 4; 6; 11; 12:11; 13:2(2); 6(2); 8; 16(2); 14:4; **Joel** 1:3(2); 17; 2:6; 7; 10; 17; 22; 3:6; 13; 15; 19; 21; **Amos** 1:13; 15; 2:4(2); 8; 3:10; 4:1; 5:12; 6:2; 4; 7:11; 8:7; 9:4; 15(2); **Obad** 12; 13(5); 17; **Jonah** 1:2; 2:8; 3:8; 10(2); 4:11(2); **Mic** 2:1(2); 9(2); 12; 13; 3:2(3); 3(2); 4; 5(2); 7; 4:3(2); 13(2); 6:12(2); 16; 7:4; 13; 16(4); 17; 19; **Nah** 2:2; 5; 7; 3:3(2); 17; **Hab** 1:7(2); 8(3); 9; 15(2); 16(4); 17; 2:15; 3:11; 14; **Zeph** 1:9; 12(2); 13(2); 17(2); 18(2); 2:7(2); 8; 10; 14; 3:6(3); 7(2); 13; **Hag** 1:12(2); 14; 2:14; 22; **Zec** 1:21; 2:9; 5:6; 9; 7:2; 11; 12; 8:8; 12; 9:16; 10:2; 5; 6; 7(3); 9; 11:3; 5; 6; 8; 16; 12:5(2); 12(2); 13(2); 14; 14:12(6); **Mal** 4:6; **Mt** 1:21; 2:11; 12; 3:6; 4:6; 20; 21(2); 22; 23; 6:2; 5; 7; 14; 15; 16(2); 7:6; 16; 20; 8:22; 33; 34; 9:2; 4; 29; 30; 35; 10:17; 21; 11:1; 5; 16; 12:9; 25; 13:15(5); 43; 54; 58; 14:14; 15:2; 8(3); 27; 17:6; 8; 25; 18:10; 31; 35; 19:12; 20:4; 8; 31; 34(2); 21:7; 8; 41; 22:5; 7; 16; 18; 22; 23:3; 4; 5(3); 25:1; 3; 4(2); 7; 26:43; 67; 27:39; **Mk** 1:5; 18; 19; 20; 23; 39; 2:5; 6; 3:4; 5; 4:12; 15; 5:17; 6:6; 8(2); 26; 52; 7:3; 6(2); 8:3; 9:34; 44; 46; 48; 10:42; 11:4; 7; 8; 12:12; 15; 44; 13:12; 14:40; 46; 56; 59; 65; 15:19; 29; 16:14; **Lk** 1:16; 20; 51; 52; 66; 77; 2:8; 39; 44; 3:15; 4:11; 15; 29; 5:2; 6; 7; 11; 15; 20; 22; 30; 6:1; 8; 17; 22; 23; 26; 7:21; 8:3; 12; 9:47; 60; 11:17; 48; 12:36; 42; 13:1; 14:4; 16:4; 8; 17:13; 19:32; 35; 36; 40; 20:23; 26; 21:1; 4; 12; 22:66; 23:25; 48; 24:5; 11; 16; 31(2); 45; **Jn** 3:19; 4:38; 8:9; 10:39; 11:19; 46; 12:40(4); 13:12; 15:22; 25; 17:19; 20; 18:6; 19:3; 31; 20:10; **Acts** 1:9; 19; 26; 2:37; 45; 46; 4:5; 23; 24; 29; 5:18; 6:1; 6; 7:19; 34; 39; 41; 54; 57; 58; 60; 8:17; 36; 9:24; 10:9; 11:18; 12:17; 20(2); 25; 13:3; 5; 18; 19; 22; 27; 33; 50; 51; 14:2; 3; 5; 11; 13; 14; 16; 15:3; 9; 13; 22; 26; 16:19; 22; 24; 33; 17:21; 26; 18:3; 19:18; 19; 21:21; 24; 22:22; 23; 30; 23:16; 28; 29; 25:19; 26:18; 27:13; 43; 28:6; 27(5); **Rom** 1:21(2); 24(2); 26; 27(2); 28; 2:15(3); 3:3; 13(3); 15; 16; 18; 10:3; 18(2); 11:9; 10(2); 11; 12; 24; 27; 30; 13:7; 15:27(3); 16:4; 5; 18; **1Cor** 3:19; 8:7; 12; 14:35; 16:19; **2Cor** 3:14; 15; 5:19; 6:16; 8:2(3); 3(2); 5; 14(2); 9:14; 11:15; **Gal** 2:13; **Eph** 4:17; 18; 5:24; 28(2); **Phil** 2:21; 3:19(2); **Col** 2:2; **1Th** 2:15; 16; 5:13; **2Th** 3:12; **1Ti** 3:11; 12(2); 4:2; 5:4; 12; 6:1; **2Ti** 2:17; 3:2; 9; 4:3; 4; 16; **Titus** 1:12; 15; 2:4(2); 5; 9; 3:13; **Heb** 2:10; 15; 3:10; 5:14; 7:5; 8:9; 10(2); 12(3); 10:16(2); 17; 11:16; 35; 12:10; 13:7; **Jas** 1:27; 3:3; **1Pet** 3:5; 12; 14; 4:14; 19; **2Pet** 2:2; 3; 8; 12; 13; 3:3; 16; **3Jn** 6; **Jude** 6(2); 13; 15(2); 16(2); 18; **Rev** 2:22; 3:4; 4:4; 10; 6:11(2); 14; 7:3; 9; 11; 14; 17; 9:4; 5; 7(2); 8; 9; 10(2); 17; 18; 19(4); 20; 21(4); 10:3; 4; 11:5(2); 6; 7; 8; 9(2); 11; 12; 16(2); 12:8; 11(2); 13:16(2); 14:1; 2; 5; 11; 13(2); 15:6; 16:10; 11(3); 17:13; 17(2); 18:11; 19; 19:19; 21; 20:4(2); 12; 13; 21:3; 4; 8; 24; 22:4

THEIRS

1992, 2007, 846, 1565, 3588

Gen 15:13; 34:23; 43:34; **Ex** 29:9; **Lev** 18:10; **Num** 16:26; 18:9(4); **Josh** 21:10; **1Chr** 6:54; **2Chr** 18:12; **Jer** 44:28; **Eze** 7:11; **Hab** 1:6; **Mt** 5:3; 10; **1Cor** 1:2; **2Ti** 3:9

THEM

846

Gen 1:14; 15; 17; 22; 26; 27; 28(2); 2:1; 19(2); 3:7; 21; 5:2(2); 6:1; 2; 4; 7; 13(2); 19; 20; 21; 7:13; 9:1; 19; 10:1; 11:3; 6; 8; 9; 29; 31; 12:3; 13:6; 14:8; 14; 15(3); 24; 15:5; 10; 11; 13(2); 18:2(2); 8(2); 16(2); 19:1(2); 3(2); 5(2); 6; 8(2); 9; 10; 12; 13; 17; 18; 20:14; 21:27(2); 31; 22:6; 8; 23:8; 24:28; 53; 56; 60; 25:6; 26; 26:15(2); 18(2); 27; 30; 31; 27:9; 13; 14; 15; 28:11; 29:4; 5; 6; 7; 9(2); 30:14; 35; 37; 40; 42; 31:5; 9; 32; 33; 34(3); 55; 32:2; 4; 16; 23(2); 33:3; 13; 34:8; 14; 21(3); 23; 35:4; 5; 36:7; 37:6; 13; 17(2); 18; 22; 38:26; 39:14; 40:3; 4(2); 5; 6(2); 8(2); 11; 17; 22; 41:3; 6; 8(2); 19; 21(2); 23; 27; 30; 35(2); 42:7(4); 9(2); 12; 14; 17; 18; 22; 23(2); 24(4); 25(2); 27; 28; 29; 36; 43:2; 11; 16; 23; 24; 27; 32; 34; 44:4(2); 6(2); 15; 45:1; 15; 21(2); 22; 24; 26; 27; 47:2; 6(3); 11; 17(2); 20; 21; 22(2); 24; 48:6; 9(2); 10(3); 12; 13(2); 16(2); 20; 49:7(2); 28(3); 29(2); 50:12; 19; 21(2); **Ex** 1:7; 10(2); 11(2); 12; 14; 16; 17; 18; 19; 21; 2:17(2); 25; 3:8(2); 9; 13(2); 16; 22; 4:20; 5:4; 5; 7; 8; 9; 13; 14; 21; 6:1(2); 3; 4(2); 13; 7:5; 6; 13; 22; 8:2; 14; 15; 19; 9:2(2); 12; 17; 19; 27; 10:2; 8; 10; 14(2); 19; 27; 12:3; 16; 21; 33; 36; 38; 42; 13:17; 21(3); 14:3; 4; 7; 9(2); 10; 13; 17; 19(2); 20; 22; 23; 25(2); 28(2); 29; 15:5; 7(2); 9(2); 10; 12; 13; 15; 16; 17(2); 19; 21; 25(2); 16:3; 4; 12; 15; 16; 20(2); 23; 17:2; 18:8(2); 11; 16; 20(2); 21; 22; 25; 19:10(2); 21; 22; 24; 25; 20:5(3); 6; 11; 21:1; 34; 22:11; 23; 23:23; 24(2); 29; 30; 31; 32; 24:12; 14; 25:3; 8(2); 12; 13; 14; 18; 28(2); 29; 40; 26:1; 24; 37(2); 27:6; 28:9; 11; 14; 25; 26; 27; 33; 40(2); 41(4); 42; 29:1(2); 2; 3(2); 4; 8; 9(2); 13(2); 17; 22; 24; 25(2); 29; 30; 33; 35; 46(2); 30:5; 12(3); 13; 14; 21; 29(2); 30; 31:5; 32:2(2); 3; 4; 8(2); 10(2); 12(3); 13; 18(3); 19; 21; 24(2); 25; 27; 31; 34; 34:31(2); 32; 33; 35:1(2); 23; 26; 29; 33; 35(2); 36:8(2); 14; 29; 36(2); 37:4; 7; 15; 28; 38:6; 25; 28; 39:7; 18; 19; 20; 43; 40:12; 14; 15; **Lev** 1:2; 12; 2:12; 3:4; 10; 15; 16; 4:2; 9; 10; 20(2); 35; 5:8; 6:10; 17; 18; 7:4; 5; 7; 34; 35; 36(2); 8:6; 10; 11; 13(3); 26; 27; 28(2); 9:2; 7; 13; 14; 22; 10:1(2); 2; 3; 4; 5; 11; 17; 11:1; 4(2); 9; 22; 24; 25; 26; 28; 31; 32; 33; 42; 43; 13:58; 14:6; 12; 23; 24; 40; 42; 45; 51; 15:2; 14; 15; 29; 31; 16:4; 7; 16; 21; 23; 28; 17:2; 5(2); 7; 8; 16; 18:2; 5; 29; 19:2; 10; 31(2); 37; 20:6; 8; 11(2); 12(2); 13(2); 16; 18; 22; 23; 27(2); 21:1; 23; 22:3; 9; 16(2); 18; 22; 25(2); 31; 23:2; 10; 20; 22; 43; 24:6; 12; 25:2; 18; 31; 44; 45; 46(2); 51; 26:3; 36(2); 39; 41(2); 43(2); 44(4); 27:2; **Num** 1:3; 19; 21; 22; 23; 25; 27; 29; 31; 33; 35; 37; 39; 41; 43; 47; 49; 2:4; 13; 15; 19; 21; 23; 26; 28; 30; 3:6; 15; 16; 22(2); 32; 34; 43; 47; 48; 49(2); 51; 4:8; 12(3); 19(2); 23; 26; 27; 29; 30; 36; 40; 44; 48; 5:3; 4; 12; 23; 6:2; 16; 19; 20; 23; 27; 7:1(2); 2; 3; 5(2); 6; 9; 13; 19; 25; 31; 37; 43; 49; 55; 61; 67; 73; 79; 8:6; 7(5); 8; 13; 15(2); 16; 17; 20; 21(3); 22; 9:8; 10:2(2); 3; 33(2); 34; 35; 11:1(2); 3; 4; 12(2); 16(2); 17; 21; 22(4); 24; 25; 26(2); 28; 29; 31; 32; 12:9; 13:2; 3; 17(2); 26(2); 14:2; 6; 9(2); 10; 11; 12(2); 13; 14(2); 16(2); 23; 28; 31; 40; 45(2); 15:2; 18; 25; 26; 29; 38(2); 39; 16:3(3); 7; 9; 15(2); 17; 18; 19; 21; 28; 30(2); 31; 32; 33(2); 34(2); 38(3); 45; 46; 49; 17:2; 4; 18:8; 11; 12(2); 18; 20; 24; 26(2); 30; 19:9; 10; 21; 20:6; 8; 10; 12; 13; 25; 26; 28; 21:1; 3; 16; 30(2); 33; 22:6(2); 8; 11(3); 12; 20; 23:11; 13(4); 21; 22; 25(2); 27; 24:8; 10; 25:4; 8; 11; 17; 26:3; 7; 10; 18; 22; 25; 27; 34; 37; 41; 43; 47; 50; 62(2); 64; 65(2); 27:3; 7(2); 17(4); 28:2; 3; 31; 30:12(3); 14(2); 15(2); 31:3; 6(2); 8; 13; 15; 27(2); 30; 36; 47; 51; 32:7; 8; 9; 13; 15; 17; 19; 20; 28; 29(2); 33; 41; 33:4; 51; 52; 55; 56; 34:2; 35:2; 3; 5; 6; 7; 8(2); 10; 15; 36:6; **Deut** 1:3; 8(2); 13; 15; 29; 39; 42; 2:5; 6(2); 9; 11; 12(4); 14; 15(2); 19(2); 20; 21(3); 22(2); 23; 3:4; 6; 14; 20; 22; 28; 4:1; 3; 6; 7; 9; 10; 13; 14; 19(2); 31; 37; 5:1(3); 9(3); 10; 22(2); 29(2); 30; 31(3); 6:1; 7(2); 8; 9; 7:2(5); 3; 5; 9; 10(2); 11; 12; 15(2); 16; 17; 18; 20; 21; 22; 23(2); 24; 25; 8:19(2); 9:3(4); 4(2); 5; 10; 12(2); 14; 17(2); 28(5); 10:2; 4; 11; 15(2); 11:4(2); 6; 9; 16; 18; 19(2); 20; 21; 22; 12:3; 18; 22(2); 29(2); 30; 13:2; 14:7(2); 17:3; 5; 19; 18:2; 3; 12; 18(2); 19:1; 9; 20:1; 3(2); 17; 19(4); 20; 21:5; 8; 10(2); 18; 22:1(2); 4(2); 19; 22; 24(2); 23:8; 24:8; 25:1; 5; 26:13(2); 16; 27:2; 3; 4; 5; 26; 28:13; 14; 25(2); 26; 31; 32; 39(2); 41; 55; 57; 61; 29:1; 2; 7; 9; 17; 25(2); 26(2); 28(2); 30:1; 7; 17; 20; 31:2; 3; 4(2); 5(2); 6; 7(2); 10; 16(2); 17(4); 20(2); 21(3); 23; 28; 32:11(2); 19; 20; 21(2); 23(2); 24; 26(2); 28; 30(2); 35; 38; 41; 46; 33:2(2); 11(2); 17; 27; **Josh** 1:2; 6; 14; 15; 2:4; 5(2); 6(2); 7(2); 8; 15; 16; 21; 22(2); 23; 4:3(3); 5; 7; 8(3); 12; 5:1; 5; 6; 7(2); 6:6; 8; 13; 23; 26; 7:2; 5(3); 11; 21(2); 23(3); 24; 25(2); 8:3; 4; 5; 6(2); 9; 11; 12; 15; 16; 20; 22(3); 24; 33(3); 35; 9:5; 8; 11(2); 15(4); 16(2); 18(2); 19(2); 20(3); 21(4); 22(2); 26(3); 27; 10:1; 8(3); 9; 10(4); 11; 18; 19(3); 20(2); 24; 25; 26(3); 27(2); 28; 39; 41; 11:4; 6(2); 7(2); 8(5); 9; 11; 12(3); 13; 14; 17(2); 20(2); 21; 12:6; 13:6; 8(2); 12; 14; 22(2); 33; 14:1; 3; 12; 15:63; 17:4; 13; 15; 18:1; 4(2); 7; 8; 10; 19:9(2); 47; 49; 20:4(2); 9; 21:2; 11; 21; 42; 44(2); 22:2; 4; 6(2); 7(2); 8; 12; 15; 30; 32; 33; 23:2; 5(2); 7(3); 12(2); 16; 24:5; 7(2); 8(2); 11; 12; 13; 25; **Judg** 1:1; 4; 22; 25; 28; 29; 30; 32; 33; 34; 2:3; 10; 12(3); 14(3); 15(2); 16(2); 17; 18(5); 19(2); 21; 22; 23(2); 3:1; 2; 4; 8; 9; 15; 23; 25; 27; 28; 4:2; 5:14; 21; 30; 31; 6:1; 2; 3; 4; 8; 9; 20; 35; 7:1; 4(2); 6; 17; 24; 8:2; 4; 8; 10; 11; 12; 16; 19; 20; 23; 24; 25; 34; 9:1; 7; 8; 9; 11; 13; 24; 25; 33; 38; 43(3); 44; 49(2); 51(2); 57; 10:7; 14; 16; 11:9; 11; 21; 24; 25; 26; 32(2); 33; 35; 12:2; 3; 13:1; 14:9(2); 12; 14; 18; 19(2); 15:3(2); 5; 7; 8; 11(2); 12; 16:3(3); 8; 12; 23; 25; 26; 17:4; 18:1(2); 2; 4; 6; 7; 8; 9; 18; 21; 27; 31; 19:6; 8; 14; 15; 23(2); 24(3); 25; 20:13; 20; 25; 28; 32; 34; 40; 41; 42(3); 43(2); 45(3); 48; 21:6; 7(2); 10; 12; 13; 14(2); 15; 16; 17; 18; 22(3); 23(3); **Ruth** 1:4; 5; 6; 9; 13(2); 19; 20; 2:9; 16(2); **1Sa** 2:8(3); 10; 16; 23; 25; 30; 34; 3:13; 5:6(3); 8; 6:6; 7; 10; 12; 15; 7:10; 11; 8:7; 8; 9(3); 11; 12; 14(2); 16; 21; 22; 9:4(2); 11; 12; 14; 20; 22(3); 26; 10:5; 6; 10; 18; 11:2; 7(2); 8; 11; 12; 12:5; 8; 9(2); 13:16; 19; 14:8; 9; 10; 11; 12; 21; 22; 32(2); 34(3); 36(2); 37; 47; 48(2); 15:3; 4; 6; 9; 15; 18; 16:5; 20; 17:3; 8; 23(2); 31; 36; 39(2); 40; 18:16; 27; 19:8; 20; 20:11; 21; 40; 21:13; 22:2; 4; 11; 23:5; 26; 24:7; 22; 25:7(2); 14; 15; 16; 18; 20; 29; 43; 26:12(2); 13; 27:5; 30:2; 8(2); 17(2); 19(2); 21; 22(2); 27(3); 28(3); 29(3); 30(3); 31; 31:7; 12; 13; **2Sa** 1:10; 11; 18; 2:5; 7; 14; 3:22; 36; 4:7; 9; 12(2); 5:3; 19; 20; 21; 23(2); 6:22; 7:10(2); 21; 8:1; 2(2); 4; 7; 10:4; 5; 9; 10; 16; 19; 11:23; 12:11; 17; 31(2); 13:9; 10; 11; 30; 14:6; 15:36(2); 16:1; 17:9; 17; 18(2); 20(2); 22; 18:1; 4; 14; 31; 19:3; 28; 20:3(3); 8; 19; 21:2(3); 6(2); 7; 9(2); 10(2); 12(2); 13; 22:15(2); 18; 23; 28; 31; 38(2); 39(2); 40; 41; 42; 43(3); 49; 23:6; 7; 18; 24:1; 12; **1Kin** 1:20; 33; 40; 2:7; 32; 5:3; 9(4); 14; 18; 6:12; 15; 16; 32(2); 35; 7:6(2); 15; 25; 37; 46; 8:21; 34; 35; 36; 37; 44; 46(3); 47(2); 48; 50(4); 52; 53; 9:6; 7; 9(3); 13; 21; 10:17; 29; 11:2; 18; 24; 12:5; 7(3); 9; 10; 14; 16; 17; 28; 13:11; 12; 14:15; 23; 27; 28(2); 15:18(2); 22; 18:4(2); 6; 13; 23(2); 26; 27; 28; 40(5); 19:2; 21; 20:15; 18(2); 19; 20; 23; 25; 27(2); 21:8; 11(2); 22:6; 10; 11; 13; 17; **2Kin** 1:2; 3; 5; 7; 12; 2:11; 12; 16; 18; 24(3); 3:9; 10; 13; 21; 24; 4:31; 33; 39(2); 44; 5:12; 22; 23(2); 24(2); 6:4; 11; 16; 18; 19(2); 21(3); 22(2); 23(2); 33; 7:10; 12; 15; 9:11; 17; 18; 19; 20; 10:1; 6(2); 7(2); 8; 14(4); 18; 22; 25(3); 26; 29; 32; 11:4(4); 5; 9; 15; 12:5(2); 7; 11; 13:3; 4; 7(2); 17; 18; 23(5); 14:27; 15:29; 16:17; 17:6; 7; 9; 10; 11; 12; 15(4); 16; 18; 20(3); 21; 22; 24; 25(2); 26(2); 27(2); 28; 29; 32(2); 35(4); 18:11; 12(2); 13; 18; 19; 23; 27; 19:6; 11; 12; 18; 20:13(3); 15; 21:3; 8(2); 9; 14; 21; 24; 22:5(2); 7; 9; 15; 23:4(2); 5; 12(2); 16; 19; 20; 24:2; 3; 16; 20; 25:13; 19; 20; 21(2); 22; 24(2); **1Chr** 2:6; 23; 53; 4:21; 41; 42; 5:11; 20(3); 25; 26(2); 6:55; 67; 78; 7:3; 4; 9; 40; 8:6; 7; 8; 32; 9:20; 25; 27(2); 28(2); 29; 10:7; 12; 11:3; 14; 20; 12:15; 17(2); 18(2); 19; 29; 32; 34; 39; 40; 13:2; 14:8; 10(2); 11; 14(3); 15:2; 12; 18; 16:10; 21; 41; 42; 17:9(2); 18:1; 4; 7; 11; 19:4(2); 5; 6; 10; 16; 17(2); 20:3; 21:2; 6; 10; 23:6; 22; 31; 24:3; 6; 19; 25:7; 26:30; 31; 27:23; 26; 29:8; **2Chr** 2:2; 11; 17; 18; 3:10; 15; 16(2); 4:4; 6(2); 7; 8; 9; 17; 5:12(2); 6:25(2); 26; 27; 28; 34; 36(3); 38; 7:6; 19; 20(2); 22(4); 8:2; 8(2); 18; 9:8(2); 16; 10:5; 7(2); 9; 10; 13; 14; 16; 17; 11:11; 12; 14; 16; 23; 12:5; 7(2); 10; 11(2); 13:7; 9; 13(2); 16; 17; 14:7; 9; 11; 13; 14(2); 15:4; 6; 9; 15(2); 16:8; 9; 17:8(2); 9; 14; 18:5; 9(2); 16; 31; 19:2; 4; 9; 10; 20:1; 10(2); 12; 16(2); 17; 23; 25(2); 27(2); 21:3; 22:8; 12; 23:3; 8; 14; 24:5; 13; 17; 19(3); 20; 23; 25:5(3); 10; 12(2); 13; 14(3); 20; 26:9; 14; 27:5; 28:5(2); 8; 9(3); 12; 13; 15(7); 23(2); 29:3; 4; 5; 8; 21; 23; 24; 34; 30:7; 9(2); 10(2); 12; 14; 17; 18; 31:1; 6; 7; 11; 32:1; 6(2); 18(2); 22; 26; 33:3; 8; 11; 15; 22; 25; 34:4(4); 12; 21; 23; 35:2; 11; 13; 15; 25; 36:7; 15; 17(2); 20; **Ezr** 1:5; 6; 7; 8; 9; 11; 2:63; 65; 3:3; 7(2); 4:2; 3; 4; 5; 20; 23; 5:1; 2(2); 3(2); 4; 5; 9; 10; 12; 14; 15; 6:5; 9; 20; 21; 22(2); 7:17; 24; 25(2); 8:1; 13; 14; 15; 17(2); 20; 22(2); 24; 25; 28; 29(2); 30; 33; 10:3; 6; 10; 14(2); 15; 16; 44; **Neh** 1:2; 5; 9(3); 2:9; 10; 17; 18; 20(2); 3:2; 4(3); 5; 7; 9; 10; 27; 29; 4:4; 8; 9(2); 11(2); 12; 14; 16; 21; 23; 5:2; 5; 7(2); 8; 10; 11(2); 12(3); 15; 6:3; 4; 8; 17; 7:3(3); 5; 65; 8:8; 10(2); 12; 16; 17; 9:1; 6; 10; 11; 12(2); 13(2); 14(2); 15(4); 17(2); 18; 19(4); 20(2); 21; 22(2); 23; 24(3); 26(2); 27(5); 28(4); 29(3); 30(3); 31(2); 34; 35(2); 10:31; 11:23; 12:9; 24; 27; 29; 31; 32; 36; 37; 38(3); 40; 43; 44; 47; 13:2(2); 10; 11(2); 13; 15; 17; 21(2); 25(4); 29; 30; **Est** 1:7; 2:3; 15; 3:4(2); 8; 11; 13; 4:7; 8; 15; 5:8; 11; 8:11(2); 17; 9:1(3); 2(2); 3; 5; 21; 22(2); 23; 24(3); 26; 27(2); 28; 31; **Job** 1:4; 5(2); 6; 14; 15(2); 16; 17; 2:1; 3:8; 4:19; 21; 5:4; 6:19; 8:4; 9:5; 12:15; 23(2); 24; 25; 14:21; 15:19; 17:4; 20:15(2); 21:8; 9; 17; 26; 29; 22:17; 19; 20; 24:5; 12; 17(2); 26:8; 29:22; 24; 30:5; 31; 32:8; 34:25; 26; 36:7; 9; 13; 31; 37:4; 12; 15; 21; 39:4; 14; 15(2); 40:13; 41:16; 42:9; 15; **Ps** 2:4; 5(2); 9(2); 5:6; 10(3); 11(3); 6:10; 7:1; 9:6; 10; 12; 13; 20; 10:2; 5; 12:7(2); 15:4; 17:7(2); 18:14(2); 17; 37; 38; 40; 41(2); 42(2); 19:4; 11(2); 13; 21:9(3); 12(2); 22:4; 18; 25; 24:6; 9; 25:3; 14(2); 28:1; 4(3); 5(2); 9(2); 29:6; 31:6; 15; 17; 19(2); 20(2); 33:6; 18(2); 19; 34:7(2); 9; 16(2); 17; 18; 19; 20; 22; 35:1(2); 3; 4(2); 5(2); 6; 19(2); 20; 24; 25(2); 26(2); 27(2); 36:8; 10; 37:40(4); 39:6; 40:5; 14(2); 15; 41:10; 42:4; 43:3(2); 44:2(2); 3(2); 5; 7; 13; 48:6; 49:7; 14(2); 50:21; 53:3; 5(2); 54:3; 4; 5; 55:15(3); 19; 23; 57:4; 58:7(2); 8; 9; 59:1; 8; 11(3); 12; 13(3); 14(2); 15; 60:4; 62:10; 63:11; 64:5; 6; 7; 8; 65:3; 5; 9; 68:1; 2; 3(2); 17; 18; 25; 69:6; 9; 11; 14; 22; 24(2); 27; 28; 70:2(2); 3; 71:13(2); 73:6(2); 10; 18(2); 27; 74:8; 75:8(2); 78:4; 5; 6(2); 11; 13; 14; 15; 24(2); 25; 27; 29; 31(2); 34; 38; 42; 45(3); 49(2); 52; 53; 54; 55(2); 66; 72(2); 79:3; 4; 80:5(2); 81:12; 16; 82:4; 83:4; 8; 9; 13; 15(2); 17(2); 84:5; 7; 11; 85:8; 9; 86:5; 14; 87:4; 88:4; 8; 89:7; 9; 11; 12; 23; 90:5; 94:23(3); 97:10; 99:3; 6(2); 7(2); 8(2); 101:3; 102:26(2); 103:11; 13; 17; 18; 104:8; 12; 22; 24; 27; 28; 105:3; 14; 17; 24; 27; 32; 37; 38(2); 40; 44; 106:8; 9; 10(3); 11; 15; 23(2); 26(2); 27; 29; 34; 36; 41(3); 42; 43; 45; 46(2); 107:3; 5; 6; 7; 13; 14; 19; 20(2); 22; 28; 30; 32; 34; 38; 40; 109:10; 15(2); 20; 25; 28(2); 29; 111:2; 5; 6; 115:8(3); 13; 118:4; 7(2); 10; 11; 12; 19; 119:63(2); 84; 93; 118; 129; 152; 165; 167; 125:4; 5; 126:1; 2; 127:5; 129:5; 6; 132:12; 135:18(3); 136:11; 139:16; 17; 18; 21; 22(2); 140:9; 10(2); 143:7; 12; 144:6(2); 145:15; 18; 19(2); 20; 146:8; 147:4; 11; 18; 20; 148:5; 6; 13; 149:3(2); 5; 9; **Prov** 1:12; 15; 32(2); 2:7; 3:3(2); 18; 21; 27; 4:21(2); 22; 5:6; 13; 17; 6:21(2); 7:3(2); 8:8; 9; 17; 10:26; 11:3(2); 6; 12:6; 20; 26; 14:3; 22; 19:7; 20:10; 12; 26; 21:6; 7; 22:2; 5; 18; 21; 23; 26(2); 24:1; 11; 21; 22; 25(2); 25:13; 27:3; 28:4; 13; 30:5; 7; 27; 31:29; **Eccl** 2:5; 10; 14; 3:12; 18; 19; 4:16; 5:11(2); 7:11; 12; 18; 8:11; 12; 9:1; 5; 11; 12; 10:15; 11:8; 12:1; **Song** 3:4; 4:2; 5:3; 6:6; **Is** 1:14; 23; 31; 2:9; 3:4; 9; 12; 4:2; 5:8; 11(2); 18; 20; 21; 22; 25(2); 26; 27; 30; 6:13; 7:19; 20; 8:7; 12; 15; 19; 20; 9:2; 10; 13; 16(2); 10:1; 6; 10; 15; 19; 20; 22; 11:6; 14(2); 13:2; 3; 8; 15; 17; 14:1(2); 2(4); 18; 20; 22; 25; 16:4; 17:2; 13; 14(2); 18:6(2); 19:3; 4; 12(2); 20(2); 22(2); 23:1; 13; 18; 24:8; 9; 25:11; 26:5; 11; 14; 16; 27:4(2); 6; 7; 11(5); 28:1; 6; 9; 13; 29:1; 15; 30:5; 6; 8; 22; 28; 31:1; 2; 4; 32:3(2); 33:4; 34:2(2); 7; 16; 17(2); 35:1; 4; 36:1; 4; 8; 37:6; 11; 12; 19; 38:21; 39:2(3); 4; 40:11; 22; 24(2); 26; 29; 41:1(2); 2; 3; 12(3); 15; 16(3); 17(2); 22(5); 27; 28(2); 42:5(2); 7; 9; 11; 12; 16(4); 22; 43:9(3); 44:7(2); 9; 11(2); 45:8; 16; 21(2); 47:6(2); 14; 48:3(2); 5(2); 6; 7(2); 13; 14; 21(2); 49:9; 10(4); 18(2); 26; 50:6; 9; 51:8(2); 17; 23(2); 52:4; 5(2); 15; 54:2; 56:5(2); 7(2); 57:6; 8; 13(2); 59:8; 12; 20; 21; 60:9; 14; 61:1; 3(2); 7; 8; 9(2); 62:12; 63:3(2); 6; 7; 9(4); 10; 11; 12(2); 13; 19; 65:1(2); 8; 21(2); 23; 66:4; 19(2); 21; **Jer** 1:16; 17(2); 2:3; 13; 25; 28; 37; 3:2; 4:12; 5:3(2); 5; 6(2); 7(2); 13(2); 14; 19; 6:10; 13(2); 15(2); 18; 21; 30(2); 7:16; 22(2); 23; 25; 27(2); 28; 31; 33; 8:2; 3(2); 4; 9; 10(2); 12; 13(3); 19; 9:2; 7(2); 9; 10; 13; 14; 15(2); 16(3); 18; 22; 25; 10:2; 5(2); 11; 14; 16; 18; 11:3; 4(2); 5; 6; 7; 8(3); 10; 11(2); 12; 14(2); 20; 22; 23; 12:2; 3(2); 4; 6; 14(2); 15(3); 13:10(2); 12; 13; 14(2); 19; 20; 21; 24; 14:10; 12(2); 13; 14(3); 15; 16(3); 17(2); 18; 15:1(2); 2; 3; 4; 7(2); 8; 9; 10; 16; 19(2); 16:3(2); 5; 6(2); 7(3); 8; 11(3); 15(2); 16(2); 21(2); 17:11(2); 18(4); 20; 18:8; 10; 15; 17(2); 19; 20(2); 22; 23(2); 19:7(2); 9(2); 11(2); 20:4(2); 5(3); 12; 21:3; 4; 7(2); 22:7; 9; 25(2); 23:2(2); 3(2); 4(2); 8; 12(2); 14; 15(2); 17; 21; 22; 32(4); 33; 24:1; 5; 6(6); 7; 8; 9(2); 10(2); 25:4; 6(2); 9(3); 10; 14(2); 16; 18; 26; 27; 28; 30(2); 31; 26:2; 3; 4; 5; 19; 27:2; 3; 4; 8; 15; 17; 18(2); 22(3); 28:3; 13; 29:5(2); 9; 17(2); 18(3); 19(2); 21(2); 22; 23; 28(2); 31; 30:3; 9; 16; 19(4); 20; 21; 31:4; 5; 8(3); 9(2); 13(2); 28(2); 32(3); 34(2); 32:13; 14; 18; 22(2); 23(2); 33(2); 35; 37(4); 39(3); 40(3); 41(3); 42(2); 44; 33:5; 6(2); 7; 8; 9; 11(2); 13; 24(2); 26; 34:8; 9; 10(2); 11; 13; 16; 20(2); 21; 22; 35:2(3); 4; 5; 15(2); 16; 17(3); 36:3; 6; 13; 14; 18(2); 25; 26; 31(2); 32; 37:5; 10; 38:4; 11; 26; 27; 39:4; 5; 10; 40:7; 9; 10; 11; 14; 41:5; 6(3); 7(2); 8(2); 9; 10; 18; 42:4; 9; 17(2); 43:1; 9; 10(2); 12(2); 44:4; 13; 21; 27(2); 30; 45:5; 46:5; 15; 21; 25; 26; 47:2; 48:39; 49:2; 11; 20(2); 29; 32; 36; 37(4); 50:6(2); 7(2); 20; 21; 27(2); 28; 33(3); 43; 44; 45(2); 51:1(2); 17; 19; 39; 40; 52:3; 17; 25; 26(2); 27(2); **Lam** 1:13; 17; 22; 2:2; 21; 3:20; 25; 64; 65(2); 66; 4:4; 15; 16(2); **Eze** 1:18; 19; 20; 21; 2:4(2); 5; 6; 7; 3:4; 6; 9; 11(3); 13; 15(2); 17; 25(2); 26; 27; 4:6; 9; 13; 5:2; 3; 4(3); 6; 12; 13(2); 16; 6:2; 10; 12; 14; 7:11(2); 16(2); 18; 19; 20; 22; 27(2); 8:11(2); 18; 9:1; 2; 7; 8; 10:1; 2; 13; 16(2); 17; 19(2); 11:4; 5; 16(3); 19(2); 20; 21; 22(2); 24; 25; 12:10(2); 11; 12; 14; 15(2); 16; 19; 23(2); 28; 13:2; 6; 11; 15; 17; 20(3); 14:3; 4(2); 15:7(3); 16:17; 18(2); 19; 20; 21(3); 27; 28; 33; 36; 37(4); 50; 53; 54; 61; 17:12(2); 18:19; 24; 26; 19:11; 12; 20:3; 4(3); 5(3); 6(3); 7; 8(2); 9(2); 10(2); 11(3); 12(3); 13(3); 14; 15(3); 17(3); 19; 21(4); 22; 23(3); 25; 26(2); 27; 28(2); 29; 38(2); 40(2); 21:23(2); 29; 22:26; 28(2); 30; 31(2); 23:4; 6; 7(2); 12; 15; 16(3); 17(2); 22; 23(3); 24; 27; 28(2); 36; 37(2); 43; 45; 46(2); 47(2); 24:3; 5; 20; 25; 27; 25:2; 10; 12; 17(2); 26:20(2); 27:31; 28:8; 18; 24(2); 25; 26(2); 29:12; 14; 15; 16; 21; 30:5; 9; 23; 26; 31:14; 16; 17; 18; 32:10; 12; 13(2); 15; 18(2); 20; 21; 22; 23; 24(2); 25(3); 26; 28; 29(2); 30(3); 31; 32; 33:2; 6; 7; 10; 11; 17; 25; 27; 31; 32(2); 33; 34:2; 3; 4; 6; 10(2); 11; 12;

13(4); 14; 15; 16; 20; 21; 23(3); 24; 25; 26; 27(2); 28(2); 29; 30; 35:11(2); 13; 36:12; 18; 19(2); 20; 23; 27; 37(2); 37:2; 4; 8(3); 10; 12; 17; 19(3); 21(3); 22(2); 23(2); 24(2); 26(5); 27; 28; 38:4(2); 5(2); 7; 8; 11(2); 15; 17; 39:6; 7; 9; 10(2); 12; 13(2); 18; 21; 23(2); 24(2); 26; 27(3); 28(3); 29; 40:4; 22; 26; 41:25; 42:9; 11; 12; 43:8(2); 9(2); 10; 11(2); 24(3); 44:11(2); 12(2); 14; 17; 19; 23; 28(2); 45:15; 46:10; 17; 18; 20; 23(2); 24; 48:10; 12; 18; **Dan** 1:4; 5(2); 12; 14(2); 16; 17; 18(2); 19(2); 20(2); 2:3; 21; 34; 35(2); 38; 3:14; 20; 27; 4:7; 19; 5:3; 23; 6:2; 24(3); 7:8; 16; 21; 24; 8:9; 10; 9:4(2); 7; 10:7; 11:7; 24; 30; 34; 35(3); 39; 12:2; **Hos** 1:6; 7(2); 10(2); 2:5; 7(3); 12(2); 13; 18(2); 23; 4:9(2); 12(2); 16; 5:2; 4; 5; 6; 7; 10(2); 6:5(2); 8; 7:2; 7; 12(3); 13(3); 8:4; 5; 10; 13; 9:2; 4; 6(3); 12(3); 14(2); 15(3); 17; 10:9; 10(2); 11:2(2); 3(2); 4(3); 6; 7; 11; 13:2(2); 7(2); 8(3); 14(2); 14:4; 9(2); **Joel** 2:3(5); 4; 10; 17(2); 3:2(2); 6; 7(2); 8; 9; **Amos** 1:6; 2:4; 9; 4:3; 9; 5:8; 11(2); 22; 6:1; 7; 7:8; 8:2; 3; 9:1(5); 2(2); 3(2); 4(2); 6; 14(2); 15(2); **Obad** 11; 18(2); **Jonah** 1:3; 5; 9; 10; 12; 13; 3:5(2); 7; 8; 10; **Mic** 2:1; 2(2); 6(2); 8; 12; 13(3); 3:2; 3(2); 4(2); 6; 4:4; 7; 12; 5:3; 6:11; 7:4; 13; 14; **Nah** 1:7; 2:2; 10; 11; 3:18; **Hab** 1:10; 12(2); 13; 14; 15(3); 16; 2:7; 17; 3:16; **Zeph** 1:5(2); 6; 13; 18(2); 2:7; 9(2); 11; 3:7; 8; 11; 13; 18; 19; **Hag** 2:22; **Zec** 1:3; 21; 2:9; 3:5; 6:6; 10; 11; 13; 7:14(2); 8:8; 9:8; 14; 15; 16; 10:1; 3; 5; 6(5); 8(3); 9; 10(4); 12; 11:5(3); 6; 8; 12; 13(2); 12:8(2); 13:9(3); 14:8(2); 13; 17; 21; **Mal** 1:4; 2:2; 5; 17; 3:3; 7; 16; 17; 4:1(2); **Mt** 2:4; 7; 8; 9; 3:7; 4:8; 16; 19; 21; 24; 5:2; 19; 21; 27; 33; 44(3); 46; 6:1; 8; 26; 7:6; 11; 12; 16; 20; 23; 24; 26; 29; 8:4; 10; 15; 26; 30; 32; 33; 9:12; 15(3); 18; 24; 28; 30; 36; 10:1(2); 5; 18; 21; 25; 26; 28; 29; 11:4; 5; 11; 25; 12:3; 4; 11; 15; 16; 25; 27; 39; 13:3; 4; 7; 10; 11(2); 13; 14; 15; 17(2); 24; 28(2); 29; 30(2); 31; 33; 34; 37; 39; 41; 42; 50; 51; 52; 54; 57; 14:6; 9; 14; 16(2); 18; 25; 27; 15:3; 10; 14; 30(3); 32; 34; 36; 16:1; 2; 4; 6; 8; 12; 15; 17:1; 2; 3; 5; 7; 9; 11; 12; 13; 20; 22; 27(2); 18:2; 8(2); 12; 17; 19; 20; 19:2; 4(3); 8; 11; 13(2); 14; 15; 26(2); 28; 20:2; 4; 6; 7; 8; 12; 13; 17; 23(2); 25(3); 31; 32; 34; 21:2(3); 3(2); 6; 7; 8; 12(2); 13; 14; 16; 17; 21; 24; 27; 31(2); 36; 37; 42; 45; 22:1; 3; 4; 6(2); 20; 21; 29; 35; 41; 43; 23:4(2); 13; 26; 30; 31; 34(3); 37; 24:2; 4; 16; 19(2); 39; 45; 25:2; 3; 9; 14; 16; 19; 20; 22; 32; 34; 40; 41; 45; 26:10; 15; 19; 22; 27; 31; 36; 38; 40; 43; 44; 45; 48; 51; 70; 71; 73; 27:6; 7; 10; 17; 21; 22; 26; 35; 47; 48; 65; 28:9; 10; 16; 18; 19; 20; **Mk** 1:17; 20; 22; 31; 32; 38; 44; 2:2(2); 8; 12; 13; 17; 19(3); 20; 25; 26; 27; 3:4; 5; 12; 14; 17; 23(2); 33; 34; 4:2(2); 9; 11(2); 12; 13; 21; 24; 33; 34; 35; 40; 5:10; 12; 13; 16; 19; 38; 39; 40(2); 43; 6:4; 5; 7(2); 8; 10; 11; 13; 22; 31; 33(2); 34(2); 36; 37(3); 38; 39; 41(3); 46; 48(4); 50(2); 51; 7:6; 9; 14; 18; 36(2); 8:1; 3(2); 5; 6(2); 7(2); 9; 13; 14; 15; 17; 21; 27; 29; 30; 31; 34; 9:1(2); 2(2); 3; 4; 7; 9; 12; 14(2); 16; 29; 31; 33; 35; 36(2); 10:1; 3; 5; 6; 11; 13(2); 14(2); 16(3); 24(2); 27; 32(2); 36; 38; 39; 40; 42(4); 11:2; 5(2); 6(2); 8; 15(2); 17; 22; 24(2); 29; 33; 12:1; 4; 6; 12; 15; 16; 17; 23; 24; 28(2); 38; 43; 13:5; 9; 12; 14; 17(2); 14:7; 10; 13; 16; 20; 22; 23; 24; 27; 34; 37; 40; 41; 44; 47; 48; 52; 69(2); 70; 15:6; 7; 8; 9; 11; 12; 14; 15; 24; 35; 16:6; 10; 12; 13; 14(2); 15; 17; 18; 19; 20; **Lk** 1:2; 22(2); 50; 52; 65; 66(2); 79; 2:7; 9(2); 10; 15; 17; 18; 19; 20; 34; 38; 46(2); 49; 50; 51(2); 3:11; 13; 14; 16; 4:6; 18; 20; 21; 23; 26; 27; 30; 31; 39; 40(3); 41(2); 42; 43; 5:2; 7; 14; 17; 22; 25; 29; 31; 34(2); 35; 36; 6:1; 2; 3; 4; 5; 9; 10; 13; 17; 19; 27; 28(2); 30; 31; 32(2); 33; 34; 39; 47; 7:6; 19; 22; 38(2); 42(2); 44; 8:21; 22; 25; 31; 32(3); 34; 36; 37; 54; 56; 9:1; 2; 3; 5; 10; 11(3); 13(2); 14; 15; 16; 17; 18; 20; 21(2); 23; 34; 45; 46(2); 48; 54; 55; 56; 61; 10:1; 2; 9; 18; 21; 24(2); 35; 11:2; 5; 13; 15; 17; 19; 31; 44(2); 47; 48; 49(2); 52; 53; 12:4; 6; 15; 16; 24; 37(2); 38; 42; 13:2; 4; 14; 23; 32; 34; 14:5; 7; 10; 15; 17; 19; 23; 25; 15:2; 3; 4; 6; 12(2); 16:15; 28; 29(2); 30; 17:14(2); 15; 20; 23(2); 27; 29; 37; 18:1; 7; 8; 15(2); 16(2); 29; 31; 34; 19:13(2); 24; 27(2); 32; 33; 40; 45(2); 46; 20:3; 8; 15; 17; 19; 23; 25; 33; 34; 41; 21:8; 10; 21(3); 23(2); 26; 29; 35; 22:4; 6; 10; 13; 15; 19; 23; 24(2); 25(3); 35; 36; 38; 40; 41; 45; 46; 47; 50; 55; 58; 67; 70; 23:1; 14; 17; 20; 22; 23; 25; 28; 34; 35; 51; 24:1; 4; 5; 10; 11(2); 13; 15; 17; 18; 19; 24; 25; 27; 29; 30(2); 33(2); 35; 36(2); 38; 40; 41; 43; 44; 46; 50(2); 51(2); **Jn** 1:12(2); 22; 26; 38(2); 39; 2:7(2); 8; 15; 16; 19; 22; 24; 3:22; 4:32; 34; 40; 52; 5:11; 17; 19; 21; 39; 6:2; 7(2); 11; 13(2); 17; 20; 26; 29; 31; 32; 35; 43; 53; 61; 70; 7:6; 9; 16; 21; 25; 33; 44; 45; 47; 50(2); 8:2; 6; 7; 12; 14; 21; 23; 25; 27; 28; 34; 39; 42; 47; 58; 59; 9:15; 16; 19; 20; 27; 30; 41; 10:3; 4; 6(2); 7; 8; 12; 16; 20; 25; 27; 28(2); 29(2); 32; 34; 35; 11:11; 14; 19; 37; 44; 46(2); 49(2); 12:2; 20; 23; 35; 36; 37; 40; 13:1; 5; 12; 17; 29; 14:21; 15:6(2); 22; 24; 16:4; 12; 19; 31; 17:6; 8(2); 9(2); 10; 12(3); 14(2); 15(2); 17; 18; 20; 22; 23(2); 26(3); 18:4; 5(2); 6; 7; 9; 18; 21(2); 29; 31; 38; 19:4; 5; 6; 15; 16; 24; 20:2; 13; 17; 19; 20; 21; 22(2); 23; 24; 25; 26; 21:3; 5; 6; 10; 12; 13; **Acts** 1:3; 4(2); 7; 10; 16; 2:3(2); 4; 6; 11; 14; 38; 41; 45; 3:2; 5(2); 8; 11; 4:1; 3(2); 4; 7; 8; 13; 14; 15; 16(2); 17; 18(2); 19; 21(3); 23; 24; 32(2); 33; 34(2); 35; 5:5; 9; 13(2); 15(2); 16; 18; 19; 21; 22; 24; 25; 26; 27(3); 32; 33; 35; 38; 40(2); 6:2; 6; 9; 7:6(2); 24; 25; 26(2); 34; 36; 39; 42; 43; 52; 8:3; 5; 7; 11; 14; 15; 16; 17; 18; 9:2; 21(2); 27; 28; 38; 39(2); 40; 10:7; 8(2); 20(2); 23(3); 24; 28; 44; 46; 48; 11:3; 4; 12; 15; 17; 20; 21; 23; 28; 12:10; 17(2); 20; 21; 25; 13:2; 3(2); 8; 13; 15; 17; 19; 20; 21; 22; 27; 31; 42; 43(2); 50; 51; 14:5(2); 18; 22; 23(2); 27; 15:2(2); 4; 5(2); 7; 8(2); 9; 12; 14; 19; 20; 21; 23; 32; 37; 38(3); 39; 16:4; 7; 10; 19; 20; 22(2); 23(3); 24; 25; 30; 33; 34(2); 37(2); 39(3); 40; 17:2(2); 4; 5(2); 6; 9; 12; 16; 17; 18; 33; 34; 18:2; 3; 6; 11; 16; 19; 20; 21; 26; 27; 19:2; 3; 6(2); 9; 12(2); 13(2); 16(3); 17; 19(3); 22; 38; 20:1; 2; 6; 7; 18; 30; 32; 34; 36; 21:1; 7; 16; 19; 23; 24(3); 26(2); 32; 40; 22:2; 5; 11; 19; 20; 30; 23:2; 10(2); 21(2); 24; 27; 31; 24:21; 22; 25:5; 6; 11; 26:10; 11(4); 13; 18(2); 20; 30; 27:9; 10; 21; 24; 33; 35; 42; 43; 28:3; 14; 17; 23; 27; **Rom** 1:19(2); 24; 26; 28; 32(2); 2:2; 3; 7; 8; 19; 3:2; 19; 22; 4:11(2); 12; 5:14; 7:1; 8:1; 28(2); 30(3); 9:25; 26; 10:2; 5; 15; 19; 20(2); 11:8; 9; 11; 12(2); 14(2); 15(2); 17(2); 22; 23; 27; 32; 12:14; 15(2); 15:3; 26; 27(2); 28; 31; 16:10; 11; 14; 15; 17(2); **1Cor** 1:2; 11; 18; 21; 24; 2:6; 9; 10; 14; 4:19; 5:12(2); 13; 6:4; 13; 15; 7:8; 9; 36; 8:9; 9:3; 20(2); 21(2); 10:4; 5; 7; 8; 9; 10; 11; 27; 11:2; 22; 12:18; 14:10; 22(4); 34; 35; 15:20; 16:3; 18; **2Cor** 1:4; 2:3; 13; 15(2); 4:3; 4(2); 5:12; 15; 19; 6:16(2); 17; 8:22; 24; 9:2; 13; 11:8; 12; 12:17; 13:2; **Gal** 1:17; 2:2(2); 12; 14; 3:10; 12(2); 22; 4:5; 8; 15; 17; 6:10; 16; **Eph** 2:10; 17; 4:18; 5:7; 11; 12; 6:4; 5; 9; 24; **Phil** 1:28; 3:8; 17; **Col** 2:1; 15(2); 3:7; 19; 4:5; 13(2); **1Th** 2:16; 4:12; 13; 14; 15; 17; 5:3; 12; 13; 14; **2Th** 1:6; 8; 10; 2:10; 11; 3:12; **1Ti** 1:10; 16; 18; 3:7; 10; 4:3; 15; 16(2); 5:4; 16(3); 20; 6:2(3); 17; **2Ti** 2:14(2); 19; 22; 25; 3:11; 14; 4:8; **Titus** 1:13; 15; 2:9; 3:1; 13; 15; **Heb** 1:12; 14; 2:1; 3; 4; 11; 15; 18; 3:17; 18; 4:2(3); 8; 5:2; 9; 14; 6:6; 7; 12; 16; 7:6; 8; 25(2); 8:8; 9(3); 10(2); 9:10; 28; 10:14; 16(2); 33; 39(2); 11:6; 13(3); 16; 28; 31; 12:9; 11; 19; 13:13(3); 7; 9; 17; 24; **Jas** 1:12; 2:5; 16(2); 25; 3:18; 5:3; 4; 11; 14; **1Pet** 1:11; 12; 2:7; 8; 14(2); 3:7; 12; 4:4; 6; 17; 19; **2Pet** 1:1; 12; 2:1; 4(2); 6(2); 8; 10; 11; 18; 19; 20; 21(2); 22; 3:16; **1Jn** 2:26; 4:4; 5; 5:16; **3Jn** 9; 10(2); **Jude** 1; 5; 7; 11; 15; 23; **Rev** 2:2(3); 9; 14; 15; 16; 22; 27; 3:9(2); 10; 4:8; 5:8; 11; 13; 6:8; 9; 10; 11(2); 7:4; 14; 15; 16; 17(2); 8:2; 12; 9:3; 4; 5(2); 6; 11; 16; 17(2); 19; 10:4; 11:1; 5(2); 6; 7(3); 10(2); 11(3); 12(2); 18(2); 12:4; 10; 12; 13:6; 7; 12; 14(2); 14:6; 9; 13; 15:1; 2; 16:2; 6; 14; 16; 17:14; 18:14; 19:15; 18(2); 20(2); 20:4(3); 8; 9; 10; 11; 13; 21:3(2); 14; 24; 22:5; 8; 9

THEMSELVES

853, 905, 1992, 3027, 5315, *240, 830, 846, 848, 1438, 3441*

Gen 3:7; 8; 13:11; 19:11; 21:28; 29; 30:40; 32:16; 33:6; 7(2); 34:30; 42:6; 43:26; 32(2); **Ex** 5:7; 11:8; 12:39; 18:26; 19:22; 26:9(2); 32:1; 7; 26; 33:6; 36:16(2); **Lev** 15:18; 22:2; **Num** 6:2(2); 8:7; 10:3; 4; 11:32; 16:3; 20:2; 27:3; **Deut** 7:20; 9:12; 31:14; 20; 32:5; 27; 31; **Josh** 8:27; 9:2; 10:5; 13; 16; 11:14; 22:12; 24:1; **Judg** 2:12; 17; 19; 5:2; 9; 7:2; 23; 24; 10:17; 12:1; 15:9; 20:2; 14; 20; 22(2); 30; 33; 37; **1Sa** 2:5; 3:13; 4:2; 8:4; 13:5; 6; 11; 14:11(2); 20; 22; 21:4; 22:2; 28:4; **2Sa** 2:25; 5:18; 22; 10:8; 15; 17; 16:14; 22:45; **1Kin** 8:2; 47; 18:23; 28; 20:12; **2Kin** 2:15; 7:12; 8:20; 17:17; 32; 19:29; **1Chr** 11:1; 10; 14; 12:8; 13:2; 14:9; 13; 15:14; 19:6; 7; 9; 11; 21:20; 29:24; **2Chr** 3:13; 5:3; 6:37; 7:3; 14; 12:6; 7(2); 13:7; 14:13; 15:10; 20:4; 25; 26; 21:8; 29:15; 29; 34(2); 30:3(2); 11; 15; 18; 24; 31:18; 32:8; 35:14(2); **Ezr** 3:1; 6:20; 21; 9:1; 2(2); 10:7; 9; **Neh** 4:2; 8:1; 16; 9:2; 25; 10:28; 11:2; 12:28; 30; 13:22; **Est** 8:11; 13; 9:2; 15; 16; 27; 31; **Job** 1:6; 2:1; 3:14; 6:4; 16:10; 24:4; 16; 29:8; 30:14; 34:22; 39:3; 41:23; 25; **Ps** 2:2; 3:6; 9:20; 18:44; 35:15(2); 26; 37:11; 38:16; 44:10; 49:6; 56:6(2); 57:6; 59:4; 64:5; 8; 66:3; 7; 80:6; 81:15; 94:4; 21; 97:7; 104:22; 106:28; 109:29; 140:8; **Prov** 23:5; 28:28; **Eccl** 3:18; 11:3; 12:3; **Is** 2:6; 3:9; 8:21; 10:31; 15:3; 22:7; 30:2; 46:2; 47:14; 48:2(2); 49:18; 56:6; 59:6; 60:4; 14; 66:17(2); **Jer** 2:24; 4:2; 5:7; 22; 7:19; 9:5; 11:17; 12:13; 16:6(2); 7; 25:14; 27:7; 30:8; 21; 34:10; 41:5; 49:29; 50:9; **Lam** 2:10; 4:14; **Eze** 6:9; 7:18; 10:17; 22; 14:18; 26:16; 27:30; 31; 31:14; 34:2; 8; 10; 27; 37:23; 43:26; 44:18; 25(2); 45:5; **Dan** 2:43; 10:7; 11:6; 14; **Hos** 1:11; 4:14; 7:14; 9:9; 10; 10:10; **Amos** 2:8; 6:4; 5; 6; 7; 9:3; **Mic** 3:4; **Hab** 1:7; 8; 2:13; **Zeph** 2:8; 10; **Zec** 4:12; 11:5; 12:3; 7; **Mt** 9:3; 14:2; 15; 16:7; 19:12; 21:25; 38; 23:4; **Mk** 1:27; 2:8; 4:17; 6:14; 30; 36; 51; 8:16; 9:2; 8; 10; 34; 10:26; 11:31; 12:7; 14:4; 15:31; 16:3; **Lk** 4:36; 7:30; 49; 18:9; 20:5; 14; 20; 22:23; 23:12; 24:12; **Jn** 6:52; 7:35; 11:55; 56; 12:19; 16:17; 17:13; 18:18; 28; 19:24; **Acts** 4:15; 5:36; 11:26; 15:32; 16:37; 18:6; 21:25; 23:12; 21; 24:15; 26:31; 27:40; 43; 28:4; 25; 29; **Rom** 1:22; 24; 27; 2:14; 10:3; 13:2; **1Cor** 6:9; 16:15; **2Cor** 5:15; 8:3; 10:12(5); 11:13; **Gal** 6:13; **Eph** 4:19; **Phil** 2:3; **1Th** 1:9; **1Ti** 1:10; 2:9; 3:13; 6:10; 19; **2Ti** 2:25; 26; 4:3; **Titus** 1:12; **Heb** 6:6; 9:23; **1Pet** 1:12; 3:5; **2Pet** 2:1; 13; 19; **Jude** 7; 10; 12; 19; **Rev** 6:15; 8:6

THEN

116, 176, 227, 233, 1571, 3117, 3588, *686, 1063, 1161, 1534, 1899, 2532, 3063, 3303, 3588, 3766, 3767, 5037, 5106, 5119*

Gen 3:5; 4:26; 8:9; 12:6; 13:7; 9(2); 11; 16; 18; 17:17; 18:15; 26; 19:15; 24; 20:9; 21:32; 22:4; 24:8; 41; 50; 25:1; 8; 34; 26:12; 26; 27:41; 45; 28:9; 21; 29:1; 8; 25; 30:14; 31:8(2); 16; 17; 25; 33; 54; 32:7; 8; 18; 33:6; 10; 34:16; 17; 35:2; 37:28; 38:11; 21; 39:9; 41:9; 14; 42:25; 34; 38; 43:9; 44:8; 11; 13; 18; 26; 32; 45:1; 47:1; 6; 23; 49:4; **Ex** 1:16(2); 2:7; 4:25; 26; 31; 5:15; 6:1; 12; 7:9; 11; 8:8; 19; 9:1; 10:16; 12:21; 44; 48; 13:13; 15:1; 15; 16:4; 6; 7; 17:8; 18:2; 23; 19:5; 21:3; 6; 8; 11; 13; 19; 23; 28; 30; 35; 22:3; 8; 11; 13; 23:22; 24:9; 29:7; 20; 34; 30:12; 32:24; 26; 34:20; 36:1; 40:34; 37; **Lev** 1:14; 3:7; 12; 4:3; 14; 28; 5:1; 3; 4; 7; 11; 12; 15; 6:4; 7:12; 10:3; 12:2; 4; 5; 8; 13:2; 4; 5; 8; 9; 13; 17; 21; 22; 25; 26; 27; 30(2); 31; 34; 36; 39; 43; 54; 56; 58; 14:4; 21; 36; 38; 40; 44; 48; 15:8; 13; 16; 28; 16:15; 17:15; 16; 19:23; 20:5; 22:14; 27; 23:10; 19; 25:2; 9; 21; 25; 27; 28; 29; 30; 33; 35; 41; 52; 54; 26:4; 18; 24; 28; 34(2); 41(2); 42; 27:4; 5; 6; 7; 8; 10; 11; 13; 14; 15; 16; 18; 19; 23; 27(2); 33; **Num** 2:7; 14; 17; 22; 29; 5:7; 15; 21; 25; 27; 28; 31; 6:9; 7:89; 8:8; 9:17; 19; 21; 10:4; 5; 6; 9; 11:10; 12:8; 14:5; 8; 13; 15; 45; 15:4; 9; 19; 24; 27; 16:3; 29; 30; 18:26; 30; 19:7; 12; 20:1; 19; 21:1; 2; 17; 22:31; 27:1; 8; 9; 10; 11; 30:4; 7; 8; 11; 12; 14; 15; 32:22; 29; 33:52; 55; 34:3; 35:11; 24; 36:3; 4; **Deut** 1:29; 41; 2:1; 32; 3:1; 20; 4:41; 5:25; 6:12; 21; 8:10; 14; 9:9; 23; 11:17; 23; 12:11; 21; 13:14; 14:25; 15:12; 17; 17:5; 8; 18:7; 19:9; 12; 17; 19; 20:10; 11; 12; 21:2; 12; 14; 16; 19; 22:2; 8; 15; 21; 22; 24; 25; 29; 23:9; 10; 24; 25; 24:1; 7; 25:1; 3; 7; 8; 9; 12; 26:13; 28:59; 29:20; 25; 30:3; 31:17; 20; 32:15; 33:28; **Josh** 1:8(2); 10; 15; 2:15; 20; 3:3; 4:4; 7; 22; 6:10; 7:21; 8:7; 21; 30; 10:12; 22; 29; 33; 14:6; 11; 12; 15:1; 17:15; 19:12; 29; 34; 20:5; 6; 21:1; 22:1; 7; 19; 21; 23:16; 24:9; 20; **Judg** 2:18; 3:23; 4:8(2); 21; 5:1; 8; 11; 13; 19; 22; 6:13; 17; 21(2); 24; 27; 30; 33; 37; 7:1; 11; 18; 24; 8:3; 7; 18; 21; 22; 9:12; 14; 15; 19(2); 23; 29; 33; 38; 50; 54; 10:17; 11:3; 11; 17; 18; 29; 31; 12:3; 4; 6(2); 7; 10; 13:6; 8; 21; 14:3; 5; 12; 13; 15:6; 9; 11; 16:1; 7; 8; 11; 17; 18; 23; 31; 17:13; 18:7; 14; 18; 19:26; 28; 20:1; 3; 26; 21:16; 19; 21; **Ruth** 1:6; 9; 18; 21; 2:5; 8; 10; 13; 3:1; 13; 18; 4:1; 4; 5; **1Sa** 1:8; 11; 17; 22; 2:16(2); 3:10; 16; 6:3; 4; 6; 9(2); 7:3; 4; 12; 8:4; 9:4; 7; 10; 18; 21; 10:1; 2; 3; 11; 25; 11:1; 3; 4; 14; 12:8; 14; 15; 21; 13:6; 14:8; 9; 10; 17; 28; 29; 33; 36; 40; 43; 46; 15:10; 14; 16; 19; 30; 32; 34; 16:8; 9; 13; 18; 17:9(2); 45; 18:3; 30; 19:5; 22; 20:4; 6; 7; 9; 10; 12; 13; 18; 19; 21; 30; 21:1; 14(2); 22:5; 7; 9; 11; 14; 15; 23:1; 3; 4; 10; 12; 13; 19; 24:2; 4; 25:11; 18; 31; 26:2; 6; 8; 13; 14; 15; 21; 25; 27:6; 28:7; 9; 11; 16(2); 20; 25; 29:3; 6; 30:4; 22; 23; 31:4; **2Sa** 1:11; 2:15; 20; 22; 26(2); 27; 3:8; 16; 18; 24; 5:1; 24(2); 6:20; 7:18; 8:6; 10; 9:5; 9; 11; 10:2; 5; 11(2); 14; 11:10; 11; 18; 21; 25; 12:18; 20(2); 21; 13:7; 15; 17; 18; 26; 28; 29; 31; 14:11; 12; 13; 17; 18; 31; 15:2; 8; 10; 19; 33; 34; 16:4; 9; 10; 20; 21; 17:5; 13; 15; 22; 24; 18:14; 19; 21; 22; 23; 19:6; 8; 12; 35; 40; 42; 43; 20:4; 16; 17; 18; 22; 21:1; 17; 18; 22:8; 43; 23:14(2); 24:6; **1Kin** 1:5; 13; 28; 31; 35; 2:12; 20; 23; 28; 29; 43; 3:14; 16; 23; 26; 27; 6:10; 12; 7:7; 38; 8:1; 12; 32; 34; 36; 39; 45; 49; 9:5; 7; 11; 24; 11:7; 22; 12:5; 7; 18; 25; 27; 13:15; 31; 15:18; 22; 16:1; 21; 18:21; 22; 38; 19:2; 5; 20; 21; 20:7; 14; 15; 33(2); 34; 36; 37; 39; 21:10; 13; 14; 22:6; 9; 47; 49; **2Kin** 1:1; 9; 10; 3:27; 4:3; 7; 14; 20; 24; 28; 29; 35; 37; 41; 5:13; 14; 17; 6:8; 31; 7:1; 2; 4; 9; 8:1; 16; 22; 9:3(2); 11; 13; 15; 19; 25; 10:4; 6; 12:7; 17; 13:17; 19; 14:8; 15:16; 16:5; 17:5; 27; 28; 18:24; 26; 28; 31; 37; 19:20; 20:2; 14; 19; 23:17; 24:1; **1Chr** 1:29; 2:24; 6:32; 9:36; 10:4; 7; 11:1; 16(2); 12:3; 18(2); 14:11; 15; 15:2; 16:7; 33; 17:2; 18:6; 19:5(2); 12(2); 15; 21:3; 16; 18; 22; 28; 22:1; 6; 13; 26:14; 28:2; 11; 29:5; 6; 9; 23; **2Chr** 1:2; 13; 2:6; 11; 3:1; 5:2; 11; 13; 6:1; 17; 23; 25; 27; 29; 30; 33; 35; 39; 7:4; 14; 18; 20; 8:12; 17; 10:18; 12:5; 13:15; 14:10; 16:2; 6; 10; 18:16; 20; 23; 25; 27; 20:2; 9; 14; 27; 37; 21:9; 23:11; 13; 14; 17; 24:17; 25:10; 16; 17; 26:1; 19; 28:12; 15; 29:12; 18; 20; 31; 30:15; 27; 31:1; 9; 11; 32:18; 33:13; 34:18; 29; 36:1; **Ezr** 1:5; 3:2; 9; 4:2; 4; 9; 13; 17; 24; 5:1; 2; 4; 5; 9; 16; 6:1; 13; 8:16; 21; 24; 31; 9:4; 10:5; 6; 9; 12; **Neh** 2:2; 4; 9; 14; 15; 17; 18; 20; 3:1; 4:7; 5:7; 8; 12(2); 6:5; 8; 8:10; 9:4; 5; 12:31; 13:9; 11; 12; 17; 21; 27; **Est** 1:13; 2:2; 13; 18; 19; 3:3; 5; 12; 4:4; 5; 13; 14; 15; 5:3; 5; 7; 9; 14(2); 6:3; 10; 11; 13; 7:3; 5; 6; 8(2); 9; 10; 8:4; 7; 9; 9:13; 29; **Job** 1:7; 9; 20; 2:9; 3:13; 4:1; 15; 6:10; 7:14; 8:1; 18; 9:1; 29; 35; 10:14; 18; 20; 11:1; 10; 11; 15; 13:20; 22; 15:1; 16:1; 22; 18:1; 19:1; 20:1; 21:34; 22:1; 24; 26; 29; 23:1; 25:1; 4; 27:12; 28:20; 27; 29:11; 18; 30:26; 31:1; 8; 10; 14; 22; 32:2; 5; 33:16; 24; 34:29(2); 36:9; 18; 37:8; 38:1; 21; 40:3; 6; 14; 41:10; 42:1; 11; **Ps** 2:5; 18:7; 15; 42; 19:13; 27:10; 39:3; 40:7; 43:4; 50:18; 51:13; 19(2); 55:6; 7; 12(2); 56:9; 67:6; 69:4; 73:17; 78:34; 65; 80:12; 89:19; 32; 96:12; 106:12; 30; 107:6; 13; 19; 28; 30; 116:4; 119:6; 92; 124:3; 4; 5; 126:2(2); 142:3; **Prov** 1:28; 2:5; 9; 3:23; 8:30; 11:2; 15:11; 18:3; 20:14; 24; 24:14; 32; **Eccl** 2:11;

13; 15(3); 4:7; 11; 8:15; 17; 9:16; 10:10; 12:7; **Song** 8:10; **Is** 5:17; 6:5; 6; 8; 11; 7:3; 8:3; 14:25; 32; 24:23; 28:18; 30:23; 31:8; 32:16; 33:23; 35:5; 6; 36:3; 9; 11; 13; 22; 37:21; 36; 38:2; 4; 39:3; 4; 5; 8; 40:18; 25; 41:1; 44:15; 48:18; 49:4; 21; 58:8; 9; 10; 14; 60:5; 63:11; 66:12; **Jer** 1:4; 6; 9; 12; 14; 2:21; 4:1; 10; 5:7; 19; 7:7; 34; 8:5; 22; 11:5; 6; 12; 15; 18; 12:5(2); 16; 13:7; 8; 13; 23; 14:11; 13; 14; 18(2); 15:1; 2; 19; 16:11; 17:25; 27; 18:3; 5; 10; 18; 19:10; 14; 20:2; 3; 9; 21:3; 22:4; 9; 15; 16; 22; 23:22; 33; 24:3; 25:17; 28; 26:6; 10; 11; 12; 16; 17; 27:7; 22; 28:5; 9; 10; 12; 15; 29:12; 30; 31:13; 36; 32:2; 8; 26; 33:21; 26; 34:6; 10; 35:3; 12; 36:4; 10; 12; 13; 18; 19; 27; 32; 37:5; 6; 12; 14; 17; 21; 38:1; 5; 6; 7; 10; 14; 15; 17(2); 18; 24; 26; 27; 39:4; 6; 9; 40:6; 8; 15; 41:2; 10; 12; 13; 16; 42:1; 4; 5; 8; 10; 16; 43:2; 8; 44:15; 17; 20; 47:2; 49:1; 2; 51:48; 62; 52:7; 9; 11; 15; **Lam** 3:54; **Eze** 3:3; 12; 15; 23; 24; 4:14; 15; 5:1; 4; 6:13; 7:26; 8:2; 5; 8; 12; 14; 15; 17; 9:6; 9; 10:1; 4; 6; 18; 11:2; 13; 22; 25; 12:4; 14:1; 13; 16:9; 53; 55; 61; 18:13; 19:5; 8; 20:2; 7; 8; 13; 21; 28; 29; 49; 21:4; 10; 22:3; 23:13; 18; 39; 43; 24:11; 20; 26:16; 28:25; 32:4; 14; 15; 33:4; 10; 23; 29; 33; 36:25; 31; 36; 37:9; 11; 14; 16; 39:15; 28; 40:6; 9; 13; 17; 19; 41:3; 42:1; 13; 14; 44:1; 2; 4; 46:2; 12(2); 17; 20; 21; 24; 47:2; 6; 8; **Dan** 1:10; 11; 13; 18; 2:2; 4; 14; 15; 16; 17; 19(2); 25; 35; 46; 48; 49; 3:2; 3; 4; 13(2); 19; 21; 24; 26(2); 28; 30; 4:7; 19; 5:3; 6; 8; 9; 13; 17; 24; 29; 6:3; 4; 5; 6; 11; 12; 13; 14; 15; 16; 18; 19; 21; 23; 25; 7:1; 11; 19; 8:3; 13; 14; 15; 10:5; 9; 12; 16; 18; 20; 11:10; 19; 20; 28; 12:5; 8; **Hos** 1:9; 11; 2:7(2); 3:1; 5:13; 6:3; 7:1; 10:3; 11:1; 10; **Joel** 2:18; 23; 3:17; **Amos** 6:2; 10; 7:2; 5; 8; 10; 14; 8:2; **Jonah** 1:5; 8; 10; 11; 16; 2:1; 4; 4:4; 10; **Mic** 3:4; 7; 5:3; 5; 7:10; **Hab** 1:11; **Zeph** 3:9; 11; **Hag** 1:3; 12; 13; 2:13; 14; **Zec** 1:9; 12; 18; 21; 2:2; 3:7; 4:5; 6; 11; 14; 5:1; 3; 5; 9; 10; 6:4; 8; 11; 7:4; 11:9; 14; 13:3; 6; 14:3; **Mal** 1:6; 3:4; 16; 18; **Mt** 1:19; 24; 2:7; 16; 17; 3:5; 13; 15; 4:1; 5; 10; 11; 5:24; 7:5; 11; 23; 8:26; 9:6; 14; 15; 29; 37; 11:20; 12:12; 13; 14; 22; 26; 28; 29; 38; 44; 45; 47; 13:19; 26; 27; 28; 36; 43; 52; 56; 14:33; 15:1; 12; 15; 21; 25; 28; 32; 16:6; 12; 20; 22; 24; 27; 17:4; 10; 13; 17; 19; 26; 18:16; 21; 27; 32; 19:7; 13; 23; 25; 27; 20:20; 21:1; 25; 22:8; 13; 15; 21; 35; 43; 45; 23:1; 32; 24:9; 10; 14; 16; 21; 23; 30(2); 40; 45; 25:1; 7; 16; 24; 27; 31; 34; 37; 41; 44; 45; 26:3; 14; 25; 31; 36; 38; 45; 50; 52; 54; 56; 65; 67; 74; 27:3; 9; 13; 16; 22; 25; 26; 27; 38; 58; 28:10; 16; **Mk** 2:20; 3:27; 31; 4:13; 28; 7:1; 5; 10:8; 21; 26; 28; 11:31; 12:18; 37; 13:14; 21; 26; 27; 14:63; 15:12; 14; 16:19; **Lk** 1:34; 2:28; 3:7; 10; 12; 5:35; 36; 6:9; 42; 7:6; 22; 31; 8:12; 19; 24; 33; 35; 37; 9:1; 12; 16; 46; 10:37; 11:13; 26; 45; 12:20; 26; 28; 41; 42; 13:7; 9; 15; 18; 23; 26; 14:10; 12; 16; 21; 15:1; 16:3; 7; 27; 17:1; 18:26; 28; 31; 19:15; 16; 23; 20:5; 9; 13; 17; 27; 39; 44; 45; 21:10; 20; 21; 27; 28; 22:3; 7; 36; 52; 54; 70(2); 23:4; 9; 30; 34; 24:12; 25; 45; **Jn** 1:21; 22; 25; 38; 2:10; 18; 20; 3:25; 4:5; 9; 11; 28; 30; 35; 45; 48; 52; 5:4; 12; 19; 6:5; 14; 21; 28; 30; 32; 34; 41; 42; 53; 67; 68; 7:6; 10; 11; 25; 28; 30; 33(2); 35; 45; 47; 8:12; 19; 21; 22; 25; 28(2); 31(2); 41; 48; 52; 57; 59; 9:12; 15; 19; 24; 26; 28; 10:7; 24; 31; 11:7; 12; 14; 16; 17; 20; 21; 31; 32; 36; 41; 45; 47; 53; 56; 12:1; 3; 4; 7; 16; 28; 35; 13:6; 14; 22; 25; 27; 30; 14:9; 16:17; 18:3; 6; 7; 10; 11; 12; 16; 17; 19; 27; 28; 29; 31; 33; 36; 37; 40; 19:1; 5; 10; 16; 20; 21; 23; 27; 32; 40; 20:2; 6; 8; 10; 19; 20; 21; 26; 27; 21:5; 9; 13; 20; 23; **Acts** 1:12; 2:38; 41; 3:6; 4:8; 5:9; 10; 17; 25; 26; 29; 34; 6:2; 9; 11; 7:1; 4; 14; 29; 32; 33; 42; 57; 8:5; 13; 17; 24; 29; 35; 9:13; 19; 25; 31; 39; 10:21; 23; 34; 46; 48; 11:16; 17; 18; 22; 25; 29; 12:3; 15; 13:9; 12; 16; 46; 14:13; 15:12; 22; 16:1; 29; 17:14; 18; 22; 29; 18:9; 17; 18; 19:3; 4; 13; 36; 21:13; 26; 33; 22:22; 27; 29; 23:3; 5; 17; 19; 22; 27; 31; 24:10; 25:2; 10; 12; 22; 26:1(2); 20; 28; 32; 27:20; 29; 32; 36; 28:1; **Rom** 3:1; 6; 9; 27; 31; 4:1; 9; 10; 5:9; 6:1; 15; 18; 21; 7:3; 7; 13; 16; 17; 21; 25; 8:8; 17; 25; 31; 9:14; 16; 19; 30; 10:14; 17; 11:1; 5; 6(2); 7; 11; 19; 12:6; 13:3; 14:12; 16; 15:1; **1Cor** 3:5; 7; 4:5; 5:10; 6:4; 15; 7:38; 9:18; 10:19; 12:28; 13:10; 12(2); 14:15; 26; 15:5; 7; 13; 14; 16; 18; 24; 28; 29; 54; **2Cor** 2:2; 3:12; 4:12; 5:14; 20; 6:1; 12:10; **Gal** 1:18; 2:1; 21; 3:9; 19; 21; 29; 4:7; 8; 15; 29; 31; 5:11; 16; 6:4; **Eph** 5:15; **Phil** 1:18; **Col** 3:1; 4; **1Th** 4:1; 17; 5:3; **2Th** 2:8; **1Ti** 2:13; 3:2; 10; **Heb** 3:12; 4:8; 14; 7:27; 8:7; 9:1; 9; 26; 10:2; 7; 9; 12:8; 26; **Jas** 1:15; 2:4; 24; 3:17; 4:14; **1Pet** 4:1; **2Pet** 3:6; 11; **1Jn** 1:5; 3:21; **Rev** 3:16; 22:9

THERE

2008, 8033, 8536, *846, 847, 1563, 1722, 1759, 1927, 5602*

Gen 1:3(2); 6; 14; 30; 2:5; 6; 8; 11; 12; 20; 4:26; 6:4; 7:9; 9:11; 11:2; 7; 9; 31; 12:7; 8; 10(2); 13:4(2); 7; 8; 18; 14:8; 10; 13; 18:24; 28(2); 29(2); 30(3); 31(2); 32; 19:1; 31; 21:31; 33; 22:2; 9; 23:13; 24:23; 33; 25:10; 24; 26:1; 8; 17; 19; 25(3); 28; 28:11; 29:2; 31:14; 46; 32:4; 13; 24; 29; 33:20; 35:1(2); 3; 7(2); 16; 36:31; 37:24; 28; 38:2; 21; 22; 39:9; 11(2); 20; 22; 40:8; 17; 41:2; 8; 12(2); 15; 18; 24; 29; 30; 39; 54; 42:1; 2; 16; 43:25; 30; 44:14; 45:1; 6(2); 11(2); 46:3; 47:13; 18; 48:7(2); 49:31(3); 50:5; 9; 10; **Ex** 1:8; 10; 2:1; 12; 5:9; 13; 16; 18; 7:19; 21; 8:10; 15; 18; 22; 24; 31; 9:3; 4; 7; 14; 22; 24(2); 26; 28; 29; 10:14; 15; 19; 21; 22; 26; 11:6(2); 12:16(2); 19; 30(3); 43; 13:3; 7(2); 14:11; 28; 15:25(2); 27; 16:14; 24; 26; 27; 17:1; 3; 6(2); 19:2; 13; 16; 21:30; 22:2; 3; 23:26; 24:10; 12; 25:22; 35; 26:17; 20; 27:9; 11; 28:32; 29:42; 43; 30:12; 34; 32:17; 24; 28; 33:20; 21; 34:2; 5; 28; 35:2; 36:30; 39:23; 40:30; **Lev** 6:27; 7:7; 8:31; 9:24; 10:2; 11:36; 13:10; 19; 21; 24(2); 26; 30; 31; 32; 37; 42; 14:35; 16:17; 23; 17:3; 8; 10; 13; 20:14; 21:1; 22:10; 13; 21; 23:27; 25:51; 52; **Num** 1:4; 53; 5:13; 6:5; 8:19; 9:6; 15; 17; 11:6; 16; 17; 26; 27; 31; 34; 12:6; 13:20; 28; 33; 14:35; 43; 16:35; 46; 18:5; 19:18; 20:1(2); 2; 4; 5; 26; 28; 21:5(2); 28; 32; 35; 22:5; 11; 29; 23:23(2); 24:17; 26:62; 64; 65; 31:5; 16; 49; 32:26; 33:9; 38; 35:6; **Deut** 1:2; 28; 35; 46; 2:36; 3:4; 24; 4:7; 8; 28; 32; 35; 39; 5:26; 29; 7:14; 24; 8:15; 10:5; 6(2); 11:17; 25; 12:5; 7; 11(2); 14(2); 21; 13:1; 12; 17; 14:23; 24; 26; 15:4; 7; 9; 21; 16:2; 4(2); 6; 11; 17:2; 8; 12; 18:7; 10; 20:5; 7; 8; 21:4; 22:26; 27; 23:10; 17; 25:1; 26:2; 5(2); 27:5; 7; 28:32; 36; 64; 65; 68; 29:18(2); 31:26; 32:12; 28; 36; 39(2); 33:19; 21; 26; 34:5; 10; **Josh** 1:5; 2:1; 2; 4; 11; 16; 22; 3:1; 4; 4:8; 9; 5:1; 13; 7:4; 13; 8:11; 14; 17; 32; 35; 9:23; 10:8; 14; 11:11; 19; 22(2); 13:1; 14:12; 17:1; 2; 5; 15; 18:1; 2; 10; 21:44; 45; 22:10; 17; 24:26; **Judg** 1:7; 2:5; 10; 3:29; 4:16; 17; 20; 5:8; 11; 14; 15; 16; 27; 6:11; 21; 24; 39; 40; 7:3(2); 4; 13; 8:10; 9:21; 36; 37; 51; 10:1; 11:3; 12:6; 13:2; 14:3; 8; 10; 15:19; 16:1; 9; 12; 17; 27(2); 17:1; 6; 7(2); 18:1; 2; 7; 10; 11; 14; 28; 19:1(2); 2; 4; 7; 10; 15; 16; 18; 19(3); 30; 20:16; 26; 27; 34; 38; 44; 21:1; 2; 3; 4; 5; 6; 8(2); 9(2); 17; 19; 25; **Ruth** 1:1; 2; 4; 11; 17; 3:12; 4:1; 4; 17; **1Sa** 1:1; 3; 11; 22; 28; 2:2(3); 27; 31; 32; 3:1; 4:4; 7; 10(2); 12; 16; 17; 5:11(2); 6:7; 14(2); 7:6; 14; 17(3); 9:1; 2; 4; 6; 7; 12; 10:3; 24; 26; 11:3; 13; 14; 15(3); 13:19; 22(2); 14:4; 6; 15; 17; 20; 25; 30; 34; 39; 45; 52; 16:11; 17:3; 4; 23; 29; 34; 46; 50; 18:10; 19:8; 16; 20:3; 6(2); 8; 12; 21; 29; 21:3; 4(2); 6(2); 7; 8; 9(2); 22:2; 8(2); 22; 23:22; 27; 24:11; 25:2; 7; 10; 13; 34; 26:15; 27:1; 5; 28:7; 10; 20; 30:17; 19; 31:12; **2Sa** 1:21(3); 2:4; 15; 17; 18(2); 23; 30; 3:1; 6; 27; 29; 38; 4:3; 5:13; 20; 21; 6:7(2); 7:22(2); 9:1; 2; 3; 10:18; 11:8; 17; 12:1; 4; 13:16; 30; 34; 38; 14:6; 11; 25(2); 27; 30; 32(2); 15:3; 13; 21; 28; 29; 35; 36; 16:14; 17:9; 12; 13(2); 22; 18:7(2); 8; 11; 13; 25; 19:7; 17; 18; 22; 20:1(2); 7; 21:1; 18; 19; 20; 22:9; 42; 23:9; 24:9; 13; 15; 25; **1Kin** 1:2; 14; 34; 52; 2:4; 33; 36; 3:2; 4; 12; 13; 16; 18; 4:34; 5:4; 6; 9; 12; 6:7; 18; 19; 7:4; 24; 29; 34; 35; 8:8; 9(2); 21; 23; 25; 29; 35; 37(4); 46; 56; 60; 64; 9:3(2); 5; 10:3; 5; 10; 12; 19; 20(2); 11:16; 36; 12:20; 13:1; 11; 17; 14:2; 13; 21; 24; 30; 15:6; 7; 16; 19; 32; 17:1; 4; 7; 9(2); 10; 17; 18:2; 10(2); 26; 29; 40; 41; 43; 44; 45; 19:3; 6; 9; 13; 20:1; 13; 17; 28; 30; 40; 21:13; 25; 22:7; 8; 21; 36; 47; **2Kin** 1:3; 6(2); 10; 14; 16; 2:11; 16; 21(2); 23; 24; 3:9; 11; 20; 27; 4:1; 6; 10; 11; 31; 38; 40; 41; 42; 5:8; 15; 17; 18; 22; 6:2; 10; 25; 26; 7:3; 4; 5(2); 10(2); 9:2; 10; 16; 17; 18; 23; 27; 32; 10:2; 8; 10; 21; 23; 11:16; 12:10; 13; 13:6; 14:9; 19; 26; 15:20; 16:6; 17:11; 18; 25; 27; 18:18; 19:3; 32; 20:13; 15; 22:7; 23:16; 20; 22; 25(2); 27; 34; 25:3; 23; **1Chr** 3:4; 4:23; 40; 41(3); 43; 5:22; 11:13; 12:8; 16; 17; 19; 20; 22; 39; 40; 13:10; 14:11; 12; 16:37; 17:20(2); 19:5; 20:2; 4; 5; 6; 21:14; 26; 28; 22:15; 16; 24:4(2); 26:31; 27:24; 28:21; 29:15; **2Chr** 1:3; 12; 5:9; 10; 6:5; 6; 14; 16; 20; 26; 28(4); 36; 7:7; 13; 16(2); 18; 8:2; 9:2; 4; 9; 11; 18; 19(2); 12:13; 15; 13:2; 7; 8; 17; 14:9; 14; 15:5; 19; 16:3(2); 18:6; 7; 20; 19:3; 7; 20:2(2); 6; 26; 21:12; 17; 23:15; 24:11; 25:7; 18; 27; 28:9; 10; 13; 18; 30:13; 17; 26(2); 32:4; 7; 14; 21; 25; 34:13; 35:18; 36:16; 23; **Ezr** 1:3; 2:63; 65(2); 4:20; 5:17(2); 6:2; 12; 7:7; 23; 8:15(2); 21; 25; 32; 9:14; 10:1; 2; 18; **Neh** 1:3; 9(2); 2:10; 11; 12; 14; 4:10; 5:1; 2; 3; 4; 17; 6:1; 7; 8; 11; 18; 7:65; 67; 8:17; 12:46; 13:16; 19; 26; **Est** 1:18; 19; 2:2; 5; 3:8; 12; 4:3; 11; 14; 6:3; 7:7; **Job** 1:1; 2; 6; 8; 13; 14; 16; 17; 18; 19; 2:1; 3; 3:3; 17(2); 18; 19; 4:16; 5:1; 4; 19; 6:6; 30; 7:1; 9:33; 10:7; 11:18; 12:14; 24; 14:7; 15:11; 17:2; 19:7; 29; 20:21; 21:33; 34; 22:29; 23:7; 8; 25:3; 28:1; 7; 30:26; 31:2; 32:5; 8; 12; 33:9; 23; 34:22; 35:12; 36:16; 18; 38:26; 39:30; 41:33; 42:11; **Ps** 3:2(2); 4:6; 5:9; 6:5; 7:2; 3; 14:1(2); 2; 3; 5; 16:11; 18:8; 41; 19:3; 6; 11; 22:11; 30:9; 32:2; 33:16; 34:9; 36:1; 12; 38:3(2); 7; 45:12; 46:4; 48:6; 50:22; 53:1(2); 2; 3; 5; 55:18; 58:11; 66:6; 68:27; 69:2; 20; 35; 71:11; 72:16; 73:4; 11; 25; 74:9(2); 75:8; 76:3; 79:3; 81:9; 86:8(2); 87:4; 6; 7; 91:10; 92:15; 104:26(2); 105:31; 37; 106:11; 107:12; 36; 40; 109:12(2); 112:4; 122:5; 130:4; 7; 132:17; 133:3; 135:17; 137:1; 3; 139:4; 8(2); 10; 16; 24; 142:4; 144:14(2); 146:3; **Prov** 7:10; 8:8; 24(2); 27; 9:18; 10:19; 11:10; 14; 24(2); 12:18; 21; 28; 13:7(2); 23; 14:9; 12; 23; 16:25; 27; 17:16; 18:24; 19:18; 21; 20:15; 21:20; 30; 22:13; 23:18; 24:6; 14; 20; 25:4; 26:12; 13; 20(2); 25; 28:12; 29:6; 9; 18; 20; 30:11; 12; 13; 14; 15; 18; 24; 29; 31; **Eccl** 1:9; 10; 11(2); 2:11; 16; 21; 24; 3:1; 12; 16(2); 17(2); 22; 4:1; 8(3); 16; 5:7; 8; 11; 13; 14; 6:1; 11; 7:11; 15(2); 20; 8:4; 6; 8(2); 9; 14(3); 16; 9:2; 3; 4; 10; 14(2); 15; 10:5; 11:3; 12:12; **Song** 4:4; 7; 6:6; 8; 7:12; 8:5(2); **Is** 1:6; 2:7(2); 3:24; 4:6; 5:6; 8; 6:12; 7:23; 25; 8:20; 9:7; 10:14; 11:1; 10; 16; 13:20(2); 21(3); 14:31; 15:6; 16:10(2); 17:9; 19:15; 19; 23; 22:18(2); 23:1; 10; 12; 24:11; 13; 27:10(2); 28:8; 10; 13; 29:2; 30:14; 25; 28; 33:21; 34:12; 14; 15(2); 35:8; 9(3); 37:3; 33; 39:2; 4; 8; 40:28; 41:17; 26(3); 28(2); 43:10(2); 11; 12; 13; 44:6; 8(2); 19; 20; 45:5(2); 6(2); 14(2); 18; 21(2); 22; 46:9(2); 47:1; 14; 48:16; 22; 50:2(3); 51:18(2); 52:1; 4; 53:2; 57:10; 21; 59:8; 11; 15; 16(2); 63:3; 5(2); 64:7; 65:9; 20; **Jer** 2:10; 25; 3:3; 6; 4:25; 5:1; 6:14; 20; 7:2; 32; 8:11; 13; 14; 22(3); 10:6; 7; 13; 14; 20; 11:23; 13:4; 6; 14:4; 5; 6; 19(2); 22; 16:13; 19; 17:25; 18:2; 12; 19:2; 11; 20:6(2); 22:1; 4; 26; 26:20; 27:22; 29:6; 30:13; 31:6; 17; 24; 32:5; 17; 27; 33:10; 20; 36:12; 22; 32; 37:10; 13; 16; 17(2); 20; 38:6; 9; 26; 28; 41:1; 3; 5; 42:14; 15; 16(3); 17; 43:2; 44:12; 14(2); 27; 28; 46:17; 47:7; 48:2; 38; 49:18; 23; 33(2); 36; 50:3; 20; 39; 40; 51:16; 17; 52:6; 23; 34; **Lam** 1:12; 17; 20; 21; 3:29; 4:15; 5:8; **Eze** 1:3; 25; 2:5; 10; 3:15; 22(2); 23; 4:14; 7:11; 25; 8:1; 4; 11; 14; 10:1; 8; 12:13; 24; 28; 13:10; 11; 13; 16; 20; 17:7; 20; 20:28(4); 35; 40(3); 43; 22:20; 25; 23:2; 3(2); 28:3; 24; 29:14; 30:13; 18; 32:22; 24; 26; 29; 30; 34:5; 8; 14; 26; 35:10; 37:2; 7; 8; 38:19; 39:11(2); 28; 40:3; 16; 17; 25; 26; 27; 29; 33; 49; 41:7; 25(2); 26; 42:13; 14; 45:2; 46:19; 21; 22; 23; 47:2; 9; 23; 48:35; **Dan** 2:9; 10(2); 11; 28; 41; 3:12; 29; 4:31; 5:11; 6:4; 7:8(2); 14; 8:3; 4; 7(2); 15; 10:8; 13; 17(2); 18; 21; 11:2; 14; 15; 12:1(2); 5; 11; **Hos** 1:10; 2:15; 4:1; 9; 6:7; 10; 7:7; 9; 9:12; 15; 10:9; 12:4; 11; 13:4; 8; **Joel** 2:2; 3:2; 12; 17; **Amos** 3:6; 11; 4:7; 5:2; 6; 6:9; 10; 12; 7:12(2); 8:3; **Obad** 7; 17; 18; **Jonah** 1:4; 4:5; **Mic** 3:7; 4:9; 10(2); 6:10; 7:1; 2; **Nah** 1:11; 2:9; 3:3(2); 15; 19; **Hab** 1:3; 2:19; 3:4; 17; **Zeph** 1:10; 14; 2:5; 15; 3:6(2); **Hag** 1:6; 2:14; 16(2); **Zec** 1:8; 5:7; 9; 11; 6:1; 8:4; 10(2); 20; 10:2; 11:3; 12:11; 13:1; 14:4; 9; 11; 18; 20; 21; **Mal** 1:10; 3:10(2); **Mt** 2:1; 13; 15; 18; 4:25; 5:23; 24; 6:21; 7:9; 13; 14; 8:2; 5; 12; 24; 26; 28; 30; 9:18; 10:11; 26; 11:11; 12:10; 11; 39; 45; 13:42; 50; 58; 14:23; 15:29; 16:4; 28; 17:3; 14; 18:20; 19:2; 12(3); 13; 17; 21:17; 33; 22:11; 13; 23; 25; 24:2; 7; 22; 23; 24; 28; 51; 25:6; 9; 25; 30; 26:5; 7; 13; 71; 27:36; 38; 45; 47; 55; 57; 61; 28:2; 7; 10; **Mk** 1:5; 7; 11; 13; 23; 35; 38; 40; 2:2; 6(2); 15; 3:1(2); 31; 4:1; 3; 22; 36; 37; 39; 5:2; 11(2); 22; 35; 6:5; 10; 31; 7:4; 15; 8:12; 9:1; 4; 7; 39; 10:17; 18; 29; 11:5; 27; 12:18; 20; 31; 32(2); 42; 13:2; 8(2); 21; 14:2; 3; 4; 13; 15; 51; 57; 66; 15:7; 33; 40; 16:7; **Lk** 1:5; 11; 33; 45; 61; 2:1; 6; 7; 8; 13; 25; 36; 4:14; 17; 33; 5:15; 17; 29; 6:6; 19; 7:12; 16; 28; 41; 8:23; 24; 27; 32(2); 41; 49; 9:4; 17; 27; 30; 34; 35; 46; 10:6; 31; 11:26; 29; 12:1; 2; 18; 34; 52; 54; 55; 13:1; 11; 14; 23; 28; 30(2); 31; 14:2; 22; 25; 15:10; 13; 14; 16:1; 19; 20; 26; 17:12; 17; 18; 21; 23; 34; 18:2; 3; 29; 19:2; 20:27; 29; 21:6; 7; 11; 18; 23; 25; 22:10; 12; 24; 43; 23:27; 32; 33; 44; 50; 24:18; **Jn** 1:6; 26; 46; 2:1(2); 6(2); 12; 3:1; 22; 23(2); 25; 4:6; 7; 35; 40; 46; 5:1; 2; 5; 32; 45; 6:3; 9; 10; 22(2); 23; 24; 64; 7:4; 12; 43; 8:44; 50; 9:16; 10:16; 19; 40; 42; 11:9; 10; 15; 31; 54; 12:2; 9; 20; 26; 28; 13:23; 14:3; 18:18; 19:25; 29; 34; 39; 41; 42; 21:2; 9; 11; 25; **Acts** 2:2; 3; 5; 41; 4:12(2); 34; 5:16; 34; 6:1; 9; 7:11; 12; 30; 8:1; 8; 9; 9:3; 10; 18; 33; 36; 38; 10:1; 13; 18; 11:11; 28(2); 12:18; 19; 13:1; 11; 25; 14:5; 7; 8; 19; 28; 15:5; 7; 33; 34; 16:1; 9; 13; 15; 26; 17:7; 14; 21; 18:11; 18; 19; 23; 19:2; 14; 21; 23; 35; 38; 40; 20:3; 4; 8; 9; 13; 22; 21:3; 4; 10(2); 16; 20; 40; 22:5; 6; 10; 12; 23:7; 8; 9; 10; 21; 24:11; 15; 25:5; 9; 11; 14(2); 20; 27:6; 12; 14; 22; 23; 34; 28:3; 12; 18; 23; **Rom** 2:11; 3:1; 10; 11(2); 12; 18; 20; 22; 4:15; 5:13; 8:1; 9:14; 26; 10:12; 11:5; 26; 13:1; 9; 14:14; 15:12; **1Cor** 1:10; 11; 3:3; 5:1; 6:5; 7; 7:34; 8:4; 5(2); 6; 7; 10:13; 11:18; 19; 12:4; 5; 6; 25; 13:8(3); 14:10; 23; 24; 28; 15:12; 13; 39; 40; 41; 44(2); 16:2; 9; **2Cor** 1:17; 3:17; 8:11(2); 12; 14; 12:7; 20; **Gal** 1:7; 3:21; 28(3); 5:23; **Eph** 4:4; 6:9; **Phil** 2:1; 4:8(2); **Col** 3:11; 25; **2Th** 2:3; 3:11; **1Ti** 1:10; 2:5; **2Ti** 2:20; 4:8; **Titus** 1:10; 3:12; **Philem** 1:23; **Heb** 3:12; 4:9; 13; 7:8; 11; 12; 15; 18; 8:4; 9:2; 16; 10:3; 18; 26; 11:12; 12:16; **Jas** 2:2(2); 3; 19; 3:16; 4:12; 13; **2Pet** 1:17; 2:1(2); 3:3; **1Jn** 2:10; 18; 4:18; 5:7; 8; 16; 17; **2Jn** 10; **Jude** 4; 18; **Rev** 2:14; 4:3; 5; 6; 6:4(2); 12; 7:4; 8:1; 3; 5; 7; 10; 9:2; 3; 10; 12; 10:6; 11:1; 13; 15; 19(2); 12:1; 3; 6; 7; 13:5; 14:8; 16:2; 17; 18(2); 21; 17:1; 10; 20:11; 21:1; 4(2); 9; 25(2); 27; 22:2; 3; 5(2)

THEREBY

2004, 5921, *846, 1223, 1722, 5026*

Gen 24:14; **Lev** 11:43; **Job** 22:21; **Prov** 20:1; **Eccl** 10:9; **Is** 33:21; **Jer** 18:16; 19:8; 51:43; **Eze** 12:5; 12; 33:12; 18; 19; **Zec** 9:2; **Jn** 11:4; **Eph** 2:16; **Heb** 12:11; 15; 13:2; **1Pet** 2:2

THEREFORE

1571, 1768, 1836, 2006, 2063, 3588, 3606, 3651, 5921, 6903, *235, 473, 686, 1063, 1160, 1211, 1223, 1352, 1360, 1519, 3756, 3767, 3844, 5105, 5106, 5124, 5607, 5620, 5628*

Gen 2:24; 3:23; 4:15; 11:9; 12:12; 19; 17:9; 18:5; 12; 19:8; 22; 20:6; 7; 8; 21:23; 23:15; 24:65; 25:30; 26:33; 27:3; 8; 28; 43; 29:15; 32; 33; 34; 35; 30:6; 15; 31:44; 48; 32:32; 33:10; 17; 34:21;

37:20; 38:29; 41:33; 42:21; 22; 44:30; 33; 45:5; 47:4; 50:5; 21; **Ex** 1:11; 20; 3:9; 10; 4:12; 5:8; 17; 18; 9:19; 10:17; 12:17; 13:10; 15; 15:23; 16:29; 19:5; 31:14; 32:10; 34; 33:5; 13; **Lev** 8:35; 9:8; 11:44; 45; 13:52; 16:4; 17:12; 14; 18:5; 25; 26; 30; 19:8; 37; 20:7; 22; 23; 25; 21:6; 8; 22:9(2); 31; 25:17; **Num** 3:12; 11:18; 14:16; 43; 16:38; 18:7; 24; 30; 20:12; 21:7; 22:5; 6; 17; 19; 34; 24:11; 14; 27:4; 31:17; 50; 35:34; **Deut** 2:4; 4:1; 6; 15; 37; 39; 40; 5:15; 25; 32; 6:3; 7:9; 11; 8:6; 9:3; 6; 26; 10:16; 19; 11:1; 8; 18; 14:7; 15:11; 15; 16:2; 15; 18:2; 23:14; 24:18; 22; 25:19; 26:16; 27:4; 10; 28:48; 29:9; 30:19; 31:19; 22; **Josh** 1:2; 2:12; 3:12; 4:17; 7:12; 14; 8:6; 9; 9:6; 11; 19; 23; 24; 10:5; 9; 13:7; 14:4; 12; 14; 17:1; 4; 18:6; 19:9; 47; 22:4; 26; 28; 23:6; 11; 15; 24:10; 14; 18; 23; 27; **Judg** 2:23; 3:8; 25; 6:32; 7:3; 8:7; 9:16; 32; 11:8; 13; 26; 13:4; 14:2; 15:2; 16:12; 17:3; 18:14; 19:7; 20:13; 42; 21:20; **Ruth** 3:3; 9; 4:8; **1Sa** 1:7; 13; 28; 3:9; 14; 5:5; 8; 10; 6:7; 8:9; 9:13; 10:12; 19; 22; 11:10; 12:7; 13; 16; 13:12(2); 14:41; 15:1; 25; 17:51; 18:13; 22; 19:2; 20:8; 29; 21:3; 22:1; 23:2; 20; 23; 28; 24:15; 21; 25:17; 26; 26:4; 8; 19; 20; 27:12; 28:2; 15; 18; 22; 31:4; **2Sa** 2:7; 4:11; 5:20; 6:21; 23; 7:8; 27; 29; 9:10; 12:10; 16; 19; 28; 13:13; 33; 14:15; 17; 21; 26; 29; 30; 32; 15:29; 35; 17:11; 16; 18:3; 19:7; 10; 20; 23; 27; 28; 22:25; 50; 23:17; 19; **1Kin** 1:12; 2:2; 6; 9; 19; 24; 33; 44; 3:9; 5:6; 8:25; 61; 9:9; 10:9; 11:40; 12:4; 18; 24; 13:26; 14:10; 12; 18:19; 23; 20:23; 28; 42; 22:19; 23; **2Kin** 1:4; 6; 14; 16; 2:17; 3:23; 4:33; 5:15; 27; 6:7; 11; 14; 7:4; 9; 12; 14; 9:26; 10:19; 12:7; 14:11; 15:16; 17:4; 18; 25; 26; 18:23; 19:18; 19; 26; 28; 32; 21:12; 22:17; 20; **1Chr** 10:14; 11:3; 7; 19; 14:11; 14; 16; 17:7; 23; 25; 27; 21:7; 12; 22:5; 16; 19; 23:11; 24:2; 28:8; 29:13; **2Chr** 2:7; 15; 6:10; 16; 19; 21; 41; 7:22; 9:8; 10:4; 12:5; 7; 14:7; 15:7; 16:7; 9; 17:5; 18:5; 12; 16; 18; 22; 31; 33; 19:2; 20:26; 28:11; 23; 30:7; 17; 32:15; 25; 34:25; 35:14; 24; 36:17; **Ezr** 2:62; 4:14; 5:17; 6:6; 9:12; 10:3; 11; **Neh** 2:20; 4:13; 20; 5:2; 6:7; 9; 13; 7:64; 9:27; 28; 30; 32; 13:8; 28; **Est** 1:12; 2:23; 3:8; 9:19; 26; **Job** 5:17; 6:3; 28; 7:11; 9:22; 10:15; 11:6; 17:4; 20:2; 21; 21:14; 22:10; 23:15; 32:10; 34:10; 25; 33; 35:14; 16; 37:24; 42:3; 8; **Ps** 1:5; 2:10; 7:7; 16:9; 18:24; 49; 21:12; 25:8; 26:1; 27:6; 28:7; 31:3; 36:7; 40:12; 42:6; 45:2; 7; 17; 46:2; 55:19; 59:5; 63:7; 73:6; 10; 78:21; 33; 91:14; 106:23; 26; 40; 107:12; 110:7; 116:2; 10; 118:7; 119:104; 119; 127; 128; 129; 140; 139:19; 143:4; **Prov** 1:31; 4:7; 5:7; 6:15; 34; 7:15; 24; 8:32; 17:11; 14; 20:4; 19; **Eccl** 2:1; 17; 20; 5:2; 8:6; 11; 11:10; **Song** 1:3; **Is** 1:24; 2:6; 9; 3:17; 5:13; 14; 24; 25; 7:14; 8:7; 9:11; 14; 17; 10:16; 24; 12:3; 13:7; 13; 15:4; 7; 16:7; 9; 17:10; 21:3; 22:4; 24:6(2); 25:3; 26:14; 27:9; 11; 28:16; 22; 29:14; 22; 30:3; 7; 13; 16(2); 18(2); 36:8; 37:19; 20; 27; 29; 33; 38:20; 42:25; 43:4; 12; 28; 47:8; 11; 50:7(2); 51:11; 21; 52:5; 6(2); 53:12; 57:10; 59:9; 16; 60:11; 61:7; 63:5; 10; 65:7; 12; 13; **Jer** 1:17; 2:19; 33; 3:3; 5:4; 27; 6:11; 15; 18; 21; 7:14; 16; 20; 27; 32; 8:10; 12; 9:7; 15; 10:21; 11:8; 11; 14; 21; 22; 12:8; 13:12; 24; 26; 14:10; 15; 17; 22; 15:6; 19; 16:13; 14; 21; 18:11; 13; 21; 19:6; 20:11; 22:18; 23:2; 7; 15; 30; 32; 38; 39; 25:8; 27; 30; 26:13; 27:9; 14; 28:16; 29:20; 27; 28; 32; 30:10; 16; 31:3; 12; 20; 32:23; 28; 36; 34:12; 17; 35:17; 19; 36:6; 14; 30; 37:20; 38:4; 40:3; 42:15; 22; 44:7; 11; 22; 23; 26; 48:11; 12; 31; 36; 49:2; 20; 26; 50:18; 30; 39; 45; 51:7; 36; 47; **Lam** 1:8; 9; 2:8; 3:21; 24; **Eze** 3:17; 4:7; 5:7; 8; 10; 11; 7:20; 8:18; 11:4; 7; 16; 17; 12:3; 23; 28; 13:8(2); 13; 23; 14:4; 6; 15:6; 16:27; 34; 37; 43; 50; 17:19; 18:30; 20:27; 21:4; 6; 12; 14; 24; 22:4; 13; 19(2); 31; 23:22; 31; 35(2); 24:9; 25:4; 7; 9; 13; 16; 26:3; 28:6; 7; 16; 18; 29:8; 10; 19; 30:22; 31:5; 10; 11; 32:3; 33:7; 10; 12; 34:7; 9; 20; 22; 35:6; 11; 36:3; 4; 5; 6; 7; 14; 22; 37:12; 38:14; 39:1; 23; 25; 41:7; 42:6; 44:2; 12; **Dan** 1:8; 19; 2:6; 9; 10; 24; 3:7; 19; 22; 29; 4:6; 8:8; 9:11; 14; 17; 23; 25; 10:8; 11:30; 44; **Hos** 2:2; 6; 9; 14; 4:3; 5; 7; 13; 14; 5:5; 10; 12; 6:5; 8:6; 9:9; 10:14; 12:6; 14; 13:3; 6; 7; **Joel** 2:12; **Amos** 2:14; 3:2; 11; 4:12; 5:11; 13; 16; 27; 6:7; 8; 7:16; 17; **Jonah** 4:2; 3; **Mic** 1:6; 8; 14; 2:3; 5; 3:6; 12; 5:3; 6:13; 16; 7:7; **Hab** 1:4(2); 15; 16; 17; **Zeph** 1:13; 2:9; 3:8; **Hag** 1:5; 10; **Zec** 1:3; 16; 7:12; 13; 8:19; 10:2; **Mal** 2:9; 15; 16; 3:6; **Mt** 3:8; 10; 5:19; 23; 48; 6:2; 8; 9; 22; 23; 25; 31; 34; 7:12; 24; 9:38; 10:16; 26; 31; 32; 12:27; 13:13; 18; 40; 52; 14:2; 18:4; 23; 26; 19:6; 27; 21:40; 43; 22:9; 17; 21; 28; 23:3; 14; 20; 24:15; 42; 44; 25:13; 27; 28; 27:17; 64; 28:19; **Mk** 1:38; 2:28; 6:14; 19; 8:38; 10:9; 11:24; 12:6; 9; 23; 24; 27; 37; 13:35; **Lk** 1:35; 3:8; 9; 4:7; 43; 6:36; 7:42; 8:18; 10:2(2); 40; 11:19; 34; 35; 36; 49; 12:3; 7; 22; 40; 13:14; 14:20; 15:28; 16:11; 27; 19:12; 20:15; 25; 29; 33; 44; 21:8; 14; 36; 23:16; 20; 22; **Jn** 1:31; 2:22; 3:29; 4:1; 6; 33; 5:10; 16; 18; 6:13; 15; 24; 30; 43; 45; 52; 60; 65; 7:3; 22; 40; 8:13; 24; 36; 47; 9:7; 8; 10; 16; 23; 41; 10:17; 19; 39; 11:3; 6; 33; 38; 54; 12:9; 17; 19; 21; 29; 39; 50; 13:11; 24; 31; 15:19; 16:15; 18; 22; 18:4; 8; 25; 31; 37; 39; 19:1; 4; 6; 8; 11; 13; 16; 24(2); 26; 30; 31; 38; 42; 20:3; 25; 21:6; 7; **Acts** 1:6; 2:26; 30; 33; 36; 3:19; 8:4; 22; 10:20; 29(2); 32; 33(2); 12:5; 13:38; 40; 14:3; 15:2; 10; 27; 16:11; 36; 17:12; 17; 20; 23; 19:32; 20:11; 28; 31; 21:22; 23; 23:15; 25:5; 17; 26:22; 28:20; 28; **Rom** 2:1; 21; 26; 3:20; 28; 4:16; 22; 5:1; 18; 6:4; 12; 8:1; 12; 9:18; 11:22; 12:1; 20; 13:2; 7; 10; 12; 14:8; 13; 19; 15:17; 28; 16:19; **1Cor** 3:21; 4:5; 5:7; 8; 13; 6:7; 20; 7:8; 26; 8:4; 9:26; 10:31; 11:20; 12:15; 16; 14:11; 23; 15:11; 58; 16:11; 18; **2Cor** 1:17; 4:1; 13(2); 5:6; 11; 17; 7:1; 13; 16; 8:7; 11; 9:5; 11:15; 12:9; 10; 13:10; **Gal** 2:17; 3:5; 7; 4:16; 5:1; 6:10; **Eph** 2:19; 4:1; 17; 5:1; 7; 24; 6:14; **Phil** 2:1; 23; 28; 29; 3:15; 4:1; **Col** 2:6; 16; 3:5; 12; **1Th** 3:7; 4:8; 5:6; **2Th** 2:15; **1Ti** 2:1; 8; 4:10; 5:14; **2Ti** 1:8; 2:1; 3; 10; 21; 4:1; **Philem** 1:12; 15; 17; **Heb** 1:9; 2:1; 4:1; 6; 9; 11; 16; 6:1; 7:11; 9:23; 10:19; 35; 11:12; 13:13; 15; **Jas** 4:4; 7; 17; 5:7; **1Pet** 2:7; 4:7; 5:6; **2Pet** 3:17; **1Jn** 2:24; 3:1; 4:5; **3Jn** 8; **Jude** 5; **Rev** 2:5; 3:3(2); 19; 7:15; 12:12; 18:8

THEREIN

413, 1459, 2004, 2007, 4393, 5921, 7130, 8033, 8432, *846, 1519, 1722, 3639, 5125, 5129*

Gen 9:7; 18:24; 23:11; 17; 20; 34:10(2); 21; 47:27; 49:32; **Ex** 2:3; 5:9; 16:24; 33; 21:33; 29:29; 30:18; 31:14; 35:2; 40:3; 7; 9; **Lev** 6:3; 7; 8:10; 10:1; 13:21; 37; 18:4; 30; 20:22; 22:21; 23:3; 7; 8; 21; 25; 35; 36; 25:19; 26:32; **Num** 4:16; 13:18; 20; 14:30; 16:7; 46; 28:18; 29:7; 35; 32:40; 33:53; 35:33; **Deut** 2:10; 20; 7:25; 8:12; 10:14; 11:31; 13:15; 15:21; 16:8; 17:14; 19; 20:11; 26:1; 28:30; 29:23; **Josh** 1:8(2); 6:17; 24; 10:28; 30; 32; 35; 37(2); 39; 11:11; 19:47; 50; 21:43; **Judg** 2:22; 8:25; 9:45; 16:30; 18:7; 28; **1Sa** 30:2; **2Sa** 12:31; **1Kin** 8:16; 11:24; 12:25; **2Kin** 2:20; 12:9; 13:6; 11; 15:16(2); **1Chr** 16:32; 21:22; **2Chr** 2:3; 5:10; 20:8(2); **Ezr** 4:19; 6:2; **Neh** 6:1; 7:4; 5; 8:3; 9:6(2); 13:1; 16; **Job** 3:7; 20:18; **Ps** 24:1; 37:29; 68:10; 69:34; 36; 96:12; 98:7; 104:26; 107:34; 111:2; 119:35; 146:6; **Prov** 15:4; 22:14; 26:27; **Eccl** 2:21; **Is** 5:2; 7:6; 24:6; 33:24; 34:1; 17; 35:8; 42:5; 10; 44:23; 51:3; 6; 59:8; **Jer** 4:29; 6:16(2); 8:16; 9:13; 12:4; 17:24; 23:12; 27:11; 36:2; 29; 32; 44:2; 47:2(2); 48:9; 50:3; 39; 40; 51:48; **Eze** 2:9; 10; 7:20; 12:19(2); 14:22; 20:47; 24:5; 6; 28:26; 30:12; 32:15; 37:25; 40:33; 42:14; 44:14; **Dan** 5:2; **Hos** 4:3; 14:9; **Amos** 6:8; 8:8; 9:5; **Mic** 1:2; 7:13; **Nah** 1:5; **Hab** 2:8; 17; 18; **Zec** 2:4; 6:6; 13:8(2); 14:21; **Mt** 23:21; **Mk** 10:15; 13:15; **Lk** 10:9; 18:17; 19:45; **Jn** 12:6; **Acts** 1:20; 14:15; 17:24; 27:6; **Rom** 1:17; 6:2; **1Cor** 7:24; **Eph** 6:20; **Phil** 1:18; **Col** 2:7; **Heb** 4:6; 10:8; 13:9; **Jas** 1:25; **2Pet** 2:20; 3:10; **Rev** 1:3; 10:6(3); 11:1; 13:12; 21:22

THEREOF

846, 1588, 3012

Gen 2:17; 19; 21; 3:5; 6; 4:4; 6:16; 9:4(2); 40:10; 18; 41:8; 45:16; 47:21; **Ex** 3:20; 5:8; 9:18; 10:26; 12:9; 43; 44; 45; 46; 48; 16:31; 19:18; 22:11; 12; 14; 15; 23:10; 25:9; 10(3); 12; 17(2); 19; 23(3); 25; 26; 29(4); 37(2); 38(2); 26:30; 27:1; 2; 3; 4; 10; 19(2); 28:7(2); 8; 16(2); 26; 27(2); 28; 32; 33; 29:33; 41; 30:2(4); 3(3); 4; 37; 35:12; 36:29; 37:6(2); 8; 10(3); 12; 13; 18(3); 24; 25; 26; 27(2); 38:1(3); 2(2); 3; 4; 39:5; 9(2); 20; 35; 36; 37(2); 40:4; 9; 18(2); **Lev** 1:15; 17; 2:2(3); 9; 16(3); 3:8; 9; 13; 14; 4:30(2); 31; 34; 35; 5:12; 6:15; 16; 20; 27(2); 29; 7:2; 3; 6; 19; 8:11; 9:13; 17; 11:39; 13:4; 18; 20; 14:45; 17:13; 14(2); 18:25; 19:23; 24; 25(2); 22:13; 14; 24; 23:10; 13(2); 24:5; 25:3; 7; 10; 12; 16; 27; 27:10; 13; 16; 21; 31; 33; **Num** 1:50(2); 2:6; 8; 11; 3:25; 26; 31; 36(4); 4:6; 8; 9; 10; 11; 14; 16; 31(3); 5:7(2); 26; 7:1(2); 13; 8:3; 4(2); 25; 9:3; 14; 11:7; 13:32; 18:28; 29(2); 30; 21:25; 32; 26:56; 28:7; 8; 9; 29:19; 32:33; 41; 42; 34:2; 4; 12; **Deut** 3:11; 12; 17; 9:21; 12:15; 13:15; 16(2); 15:23; 20:13; 14; 19; 26:14(3); 28:30; 31; 29:23; 33:16; **Josh** 6:2; 26; 7:14; 8:2(2); 9:1; 10:2; 28; 30(2); 37(2); 39(3); 11:10; 13:23(2); 15:7; 12; 47; 16:3; 8; 18:12; 14; 20; 19:14; 29; 33; 21:2; 11; 12; 22:7; 23:14; **Judg** 1:18(3); 26(2); 3:2; 5:23; 7:15; 8:14; 27; 14:9; 15:19; 17:4; **1Sa** 5:6; 6:8; 7:14; 17:51; 20:20; 28:24; **2Sa** 20:8; 23:16; **1Kin** 2:32; 3:27; 6:2(3); 3(2); 20; 38; 7:2(3); 6(2); 21(2); 26; 27; 30; 31; 35(2); 36(2); 8:7; 13:26; 15:21; 22; 16:34(2); 17:13; **2Kin** 2:12; 3:25; 4:39; 40; 42; 43; 44; 7:2; 19; 13:14; 15:16; 16:10; 17:24; 18:8; 19:23(2); 29; 22:16; 19; 23:6; **1Chr** 2:23; 6:55; 56; 7:28(4); 8:12; 9:27; 16:32; 21:27; 23:26; 28:11(4); 15(2); **2Chr** 3:7(2); 8; 4:1(3); 2; 22; 5:8; 13:11; 19(3); 16:6; 28:18(3); 29:18(2); 32:1; 34:24; 27; 36:19(2); **Ezr** 4:12; 16; 6:3(3); 9:9; 10:14; **Neh** 1:3; 2:3; 13; 17; 3:3(4); 6(4); 13(3); 14(3); 15(3); 4:6; 6:16; 9:36(2); 11:25(3); 27; 28; 30(2); 13:14; **Est** 1:22; 2:22; 3:12; 8:9(2); 9:18(2); **Job** 3:9; 4:12; 16; 9:6; 24; 11:9; 14:7; 8(2); 15:29; 24:2; 13(2); 26:5; 28:13; 15; 22; 23(2); 31:17; 38; 39(2); 36:27; 33; 38:5; 6(2); 9; 19; 20(2); 33; **Ps** 19:6; 24:1; 34:2; 46:3(2); 48:12; 50:1; 12; 55:10; 11; 60:2; 65:10(3); 71:15; 72:16; 74:6; 75:3; 8; 80:10; 89:9; 11; 96:11; 97:1; 98:7; 102:14; 103:16; 107:25; 29; 137:2; 7; **Prov** 1:19; 3:14; 12:28; 14:12; 16:25; 33; 18:21; 20:21; 21:22; 24:31(2); 25:8; 27:18; 28:2(2); **Eccl** 5:11; 13; 19; 6:2; 7:8; **Song** 1:12; 3:10(3); 4:16; 7:8; 8:6; 11; 12; **Is** 3:14; 4:4; 5:2; 5(2); 30; 6:13; 13:9; 10; 14:17; 15:8(2); 16:8; 17:6; 19:3(2); 10; 13; 14(2); 17; 19; 21:2; 22:11; 23:11; 13(2); 24:1; 5; 20; 27:10; 11; 28:25; 30:27; 33; 31:4; 33:20(2); 34:9(3); 10; 12; 13; 37:24(2); 30; 40:6; 16; 22; 41:9; 42:10; 11; 44:15; 16(2); 17; 19(2); 26; 48:19; 62:1(2); **Jer** 1:13; 15; 18(2); 2:7(2); 4:26; 5:1; 22; 31; 6:24; 11:19; 14:2; 8; 17:27; 19:8; 12; 20:5(2); 21:14; 23:14; 25:9; 18(2); 26:15; 29:7; 30:18; 31:23; 24; 35; 33:2; 12; 34:1; 18; 46:8; 22; 48:9; 38; 49:13; 17; 18; 21; 32; 50:29; 40; 51:28(2); 42; 52:21; **Lam** 2:2; 4:11; **Eze** 1:4; 5; 4:9(2); 5:3; 4; 7:12; 13; 14; 9:4; 10:7; 11:6; 9; 11; 18(2); 13:14(2); 14:13; 15:3; 17:6; 9(3); 12(2); 23; 19:7; 20:29; 22:21; 22; 25(2); 27; 23:34; 24:4; 11; 27:9; 31:15; 32:7; 12; 13; 38:13; 40:6; 9; 20(2); 21(4); 22; 24(2); 25; 26(2); 29(4); 31(2); 33(4); 34(2); 36(3); 37(2); 38; 41:2; 4; 12; 13; 15; 22(4); 42:7; 43:11(9); 12; 13(2); 16; 17(2); 20; 44:5; 14; 45:1; 2; 11; 46:8; 16; 47:11(2); 12(4); 48:10; 15; 16; 18; 21; **Dan** 1:5; 2:5; 6(2); 9; 26; 31; 36; 45; 3:1; 4:7; 9; 10; 11(2); 12(3); 18; 19(2); 20; 21; 23; 5:7; 8; 15; 16; 7:4; 9:26; **Hos** 2:9(2); 4:13; 8:14; 9:4; 10:5(3); 14:7; **Joel** 1:7; **Amos** 1:3; 6; 7; 9; 10; 11; 13; 14; 2:1; 3(2); 4; 6; 3:9(2); 8:10; 9:11; 14; **Jonah** 1:3; **Mic** 1:6(2); 7(3); 3:11(3); 5:6; 6:12(2); 16; **Nah** 1:8; 2:5; **Hab** 2:18; **Zeph** 1:13; 3:5; **Zec** 2:2(2); 3:9; 4:2; 3; 7; 11; 5:2(2); 4(2); 8; 7:7; 8:5; 9:1; 14:4; **Mal** 1:12; **Mt** 2:16; 6:34; 12:36; 13:32; 44; 14:13; 21:43; 22:7; 27:34; **Mk** 6:16; **Lk** 19:33; 21:20; 22:16; **Jn** 3:8; 4:12; 6:50; 7:7; **Acts** 15:16; **Rom** 6:12; 13:14; **1Cor** 9:7; 23; 10:26; 28; **2Ti** 3:5; **Heb** 7:18; **Jas** 1:11; **1Pet** 1:24; 5:2; **1Jn** 2:17; **Rev** 5:2; 5; 9; 16:12; 21; 21:15(2); 17; 23

THEREON

5921, *846, 1722, 1883, 1909, 1911, 1913, 1924, 1945, 2026*

Gen 35:14(2); **Ex** 17:12; 20:24; 26; 30:7; 9(2); 40:27; 35; **Lev** 2:1; 6; 15; 5:11; 6:12; 10:1; 11:38; **Num** 4:6; 7(2); 13; 5:15; 9:22; 16:18; **Deut** 27:6; **Josh** 8:29; 31; 22:23(2); **2Sa** 17:19; 19:26; **1Kin** 6:35; 13:13; **2Kin** 16:12; **1Chr** 12:17; 15:15; **2Chr** 3:5; 14; 33:16; **Ezr** 3:2; 3; 6:11; **Est** 5:14; 7:9; **Is** 30:12; 35:9; **Eze** 15:3; 40:39; 43:18(2); **Zec** 4:2; **Mt** 21:7; 19; 23:20; 22; **Mk** 11:13; 14:72; **Lk** 13:6; 19:35; **Jn** 12:14; 21:9; **1Cor** 3:10; **Rev** 5:3; 4; 6:4; 21:12

THERETO

5921, *1928*

Ex 25:24; 29:41; 30:38; **Lev** 5:16; 6:5; 18:23; 20:16; 27:27; 31; **Num** 3:36; 19:17; **Deut** 12:32; **Judg** 11:17; **1Chr** 22:14; **2Chr** 10:14; 21:11; **Ps** 119:9; **Is** 44:15; **Mk** 14:70; **Gal** 3:15

THEREUPON

2026

Ex 31:7; **Eze** 16:16; **Zeph** 2:7; **1Cor** 3:10; 14

THESE

411, 412, 428, 429, 438, 459, 479, 581, 1836, 1931, 1992, 2004, 2007, 2063, 2088, 4481, 5921, *846, 3588, 3778, 5023, 5025, 5118, 5128, 5130*

Gen 2:4; 6:9; 9:19; 10:1; 5; 20; 29; 31; 32(2); 11:10; 27; 14:2; 3; 13; 15:1; 10; 19:8; 20:8; 21:29; 30; 22:1; 20; 23; 23:1; 24:28; 25:4; 7; 12; 13; 16(2); 17; 19; 26:3; 4; 27:36; 42; 46; 29:13; 31:43(4); 32:17; 33:8; 34:21; 35:26; 36:1; 5; 9; 10; 12; 13(2); 14; 15; 16(2); 17(3); 18(2); 19(2); 20; 21; 23; 24; 25; 26; 27; 28; 29; 30; 31; 40; 43; 37:2; 38:25(2); 39:7; 17; 40:1; 42:36; 43:7; 16(2); 44:6; 7; 45:6; 46:8; 15; 18(2); 22; 25(2); 48:1; 8; 49:28; **Ex** 1:1; 4:9; 6:14(2); 15; 16; 19; 24; 25; 26; 27(2); 10:1; 11:8; 10; 14:20; 15:26; 19:6; 7; 20:1; 21:1; 11; 24:8; 25:39; 28:4; 30:34; 32:4; 8; 33:4; 34:1; 27(2); 35:1; **Lev** 2:8; 5:4; 5; 13; 17; 6:3; 11:2; 4; 9; 13; 21; 22; 24; 29; 31; 16:4; 18:24(2); 26; 27; 29; 30; 20:23; 21:14; 22:22; 25; 23:2; 4; 37; 25:54; 26:14; 23; 46; 27:34; **Num** 1:5; 16; 17; 44; 2:9; 32; 3:1; 2; 3; 17; 18; 20; 21; 27; 33; 35; 4:15; 37; 41; 45; 5:23; 13:4; 16; 14:22; 39; 15:13; 22; 16:14; 26; 28; 29; 30; 31; 38; 21:25; 22:9; 28; 32; 33; 24:10; 26:7; 14; 18; 22; 25; 27; 30; 34; 35; 36; 37(2); 41; 42(2); 47; 50; 51; 53; 57; 58; 63; 64; 27:1; 28:23; 29:39; 30:16; 31:16; 33:1; 2; 34:17; 19; 29; 35:13; 15; 24; 29; 36:13; **Deut** 1:1; 35; 2:7; 3:5; 21; 4:6; 30; 42; 45; 5:22; 6:1; 6; 24; 25; 7:12; 17; 8:2; 4; 9:4; 5; 10:21; 11:18; 22; 23; 12:1; 28; 30; 14:4; 7; 9; 12; 15:5; 16:12; 17:19; 18:12(2); 14; 19:9(2); 11; 20:15; 16; 22:17; 23:18; 25:3; 26:16; 27:4; 12; 13; 28:2; 15; 45; 65; 29:1; 18; 30:1; 7; 31:1; 3; 17; 28; 32:45; **Josh** 2:11; 4:6; 7; 21; 9:13(2); 10:16; 24; 42; 11:5; 14; 12:1; 7; 13:12; 32; 14:1; 10; 17:2; 3; 9; 19:8; 16; 31; 48; 51; 20:9; 21:3; 8; 9; 42(2); 22:3; 23:3; 4; 7(2); 12(2); 13; 24:26; 29; **Judg** 2:4; 3:1; 9:3; 13:23(2); 16:15; 18:14; 18; 19:13; 20:17; 25; 35; 44; 46; **Ruth** 3:17; 4:18; **1Sa** 4:8(2); 6:17; 10:7; 14:6; 8; 49; 16:10; 17:17; 18; 39; 18:26; 21:5; 12; 23:2; 24:7; 16; 25:37; 29:3(3); 4; 31:4; **2Sa** 3:5; 39; 5:14; 7:17; 21; 13:21; 14:19; 16:2; 21:22; 23:1; 8; 17(2); 22; 24:17; 23; **1Kin** 4:2; 8; 7:9; 45; 8:59; 9:13; 23; 10:8; 10; 11:2; 17:1; 17; 18:36; 20:19; 21:1; 22:11; 17; 23; **2Kin** 1:7; 13;

2:21; 3:10; 13; 6:20; 7:8; 10:9; 17:41; 18:27; 20:14; 21:11; 23:16; 17; 25:16; 17; 20; **1Chr** 1:23; 29; 31; 33; 43; 54; 2:1; 18; 23; 33; 50; 55; 3:1; 4; 5; 9; 4:2; 3; 4; 6; 12; 18; 22; 23; 31; 33; 38; 41; 5:14; 17; 24; 6:17; 19; 31; 33; 50; 54; 64; 65; 7:8; 11; 17; 29; 33; 40; 8:6(2); 10; 28(2); 32; 38(2); 40; 9:9; 22(2); 26; 33; 34(2); 44(2); 10:4; 11:10; 19(3); 24; 12:1; 14; 15; 23; 38; 14:4; 17:15; 19; 18:11; 20:8; 21:17; 23:9; 10; 24; 24:1; 19; 20; 30; 31; 25:5; 6; 26:8; 12; 19; 27:22; 31; 29:17; 19; **2Chr** 3:3; 13; 4:18; 5:5; 8:10; 9:7; 14:7; 8; 15:8; 17:14; 19; 18:10; 16; 22; 21:2; 24:26; 29:32; 32:1; 35:7; 36:18; **Ezr** 1:11; 2:1; 59; 62; 4:21; 5:9; 11; 15; 6:8(2); 7:1; 8:1; 13; 9:1; 14; 10:44; **Neh** 1:4; 10; 4:2; 5:6; 6:6; 7; 14; 16; 7:6; 61; 64; 10:8; 11:3; 7; 12:1; 7; 26; 13:26; **Est** 1:5; 2:1; 3:1; 4:11; 9:20; 26; 27; 28(2); 31; 32; **Job** 8:2; 10:13; 12:3; 9; 19:3; 26:14; 32:1; 5; 33:29; 42:7; **Ps** 15:5; 42:4; 50:21; 57:1; 73:12; 104:27; 107:24; 43; **Prov** 6:16; 24:23; 25:1; **Eccl** 7:10; 11:9; 12:12; **Is** 7:4; 34:16; 36:12; 20; 38:16(2); 39:3; 40:26; 42:16; 44:21; 45:7; 47:7; 9; 13; 48:14; 49:12(3); 18; 21(3); 51:19; 57:6; 60:8; 64:12; 65:5; **Jer** 2:34; 3:7; 12; 4:18; 5:4; 5; 9; 19; 25; 29; 7:2; 4; 10; 13; 27; 9:9; 24; 26; 10:11; 11:6; 13:22; 14:22; 16:10; 17:20; 20:1; 22:2; 5; 23:21; 24:5; 25:9; 11; 30; 26:7; 10; 15; 27:6; 12; 28:14; 29:1; 30:4; 15; 31:21; 32:14; 34:6; 7; 36:16; 17; 18; 24; 38:9; 12; 16; 24; 27; 43:1; 10; 45:1; 51:60; 61; 52:20; 22; **Lam** 1:16; 4:9; 5:17; **Eze** 1:21(2); 8:15; 10:17(2); 11:2; 14:3; 14; 16; 18; 16:5; 20; 30; 43; 17:12; 18; 18:10; 13; 23:10; 30; 24:19; 27:21; 24; 30:17; 35:10(2); 36:20; 37:3; 4; 5; 9; 11; 18; 40:24; 28; 29; 32; 33; 35; 46; 42:5; 9; 43:13; 18; 27; 46:22; 24; 47:8; 9; 48:1(2); 16; 29; 30; **Dan** 1:6; 17; 2:28; 40; 44(2); 3:12; 13; 21; 23; 27; 6:2; 5; 6; 11; 14; 15; 7:17; 10:21; 11:6; 27; 41; 12:6; 7; 8; **Hos** 2:12; 14:9; **Amos** 6:2; **Mic** 2:7; **Hab** 2:6; **Hag** 2:13; **Zec** 1:9(2); 10; 12; 19(2); 21(3); 3:7; 4:4; 5; 11; 12; 13; 14; 5:10; 6:4; 5; 8; 7:3; 8:6; 9(2); 10; 12; 15; 16; 17; 13:6; 14:15; **Mt** 1:20; 2:3; 3:9; 4:3; 9; 5:19; 37; 6:29; 32(2); 33; 7:24; 26; 28; 9:18; 10:2; 5; 42; 11:25; 13:34; 51; 53; 54; 56; 15:20; 18:6; 10; 14; 19:1; 20; 20:12; 21; 21:16; 23; 24; 27; 22:22; 40; 23:23; 36; 24:2; 3; 6; 8; 33; 34; 25:40; 45; 46; 26:1; 62; **Mk** 2:8; 4:11; 15; 16; 18; 20; 6:2; 7:23; 8:4; 9:42; 10:20; 11:28(2); 29; 33; 12:31; 40; 13:2; 4(2); 8; 29; 30; 14:60; 16:17; **Lk** 1:19; 20; 65; 2:19; 51; 3:8; 4:28; 5:27; 7:9; 18; 8:8; 13; 21; 9:28; 44; 10:1; 21; 36; 11:27; 42; 53; 12:27; 30(2); 31; 13:2; 7; 16; 17; 14:6; 15; 21; 15:26; 29; 16:14; 17:2; 18:21; 22; 34; 19:11; 15; 40; 20:2; 8; 16; 21:4; 6; 7(2); 9; 12; 22; 28; 31; 36; 23:31; 49; 24:9; 10; 14; 17; 18; 21; 26; 44; 48; **Jn** 1:28; 50; 2:16; 18; 3:2; 9; 10; 22; 5:3; 16; 19; 20; 34; 6:1; 5; 59; 7:1; 4; 9; 31; 8:20; 28; 30; 9:22; 40; 10:19; 21; 11:11; 12:16(3); 36; 41; 13:17; 14:12; 25; 15:11; 17; 21; 16:1; 3; 4(2); 6; 25; 33; 17:1; 11; 13; 20; 25; 18:1; 8; 19:24; 36; 20:18; 31; 21:1; 15; 24(2); **Acts** 1:9; 14; 21; 24; 2:7; 13; 15; 22; 3:24; 4:16; 5:5(2); 11; 24; 32; 35; 36; 38; 7:1; 50; 54; 8:24; 10:8; 44; 47; 11:12; 18; 22; 27; 12:17; 13:42; 14:15(2); 18; 15:17; 28; 16:17; 20; 38; 17:6; 7; 8; 11; 20; 18:1; 19:21; 28; 36; 37; 20:5; 24; 34; 21:12; 38; 23:22; 24:8; 9; 20; 22; 25:9; 11(2); 20; 26:16; 21; 26(2); 29; 27:31; 28:29; **Rom** 2:14; 8:31; 37; 9:8; 11:24; 31; 14:18; 15:23(2); **1Cor** 4:6; 14; 9:8; 15(2); 10:6; 11; 12:2; 11; 23; 13:13(2); **2Cor** 2:16; 7:1; 13:10; **Gal** 2:6; 4:24; 5:17; 19; **Eph** 5:6; **Phil** 4:8; **Col** 3:8; 14; 4:11; **1Th** 3:3; 4:18; **2Th** 2:5; **1Ti** 3:10; 14; 4:6; 11; 15; 5:7; 21; 6:2; 11; **2Ti** 1:12; 2:14; 21; 3:8; **Titus** 2:15; 3:8(2); **Heb** 1:2; 7:13; 9:6; 23(2); 10:18; 11:13; 39; **Jas** 3:10; **1Pet** 1:20; **2Pet** 1:4; 8; 9; 10; 12; 15; 2:12; 17; 3:11; 16; 17; **1Jn** 1:4; 2:1; 26; 5:7; 8; 13; **Jude** 8; 10; 12; 14; 16; 19; **Rev** 2:1; 8; 12; 18; 3:1; 7; 14; 7:1; 13; 14; 9:18; 20; 11:4; 6; 10; 14:4(3); 16:9; 17:13; 14; 16; 18:1; 15; 19:1; 9; 20; 21:5; 22:6; 8(2); 16; 18; 20

THEY

1992, *846*

Gen 2:4; 24; 25; 3:7(3); 8; 4:8; 5:2; 6:2(3); 4; 19; 7:14; 15; 16; 23(2); 8:17; 9:2; 23; 11:2(3); 3(3); 4; 6(3); 7; 8; 31(2); 12:5(4); 12(3); 20; 13:6(2); 11; 14:4(2); 7; 8; 10; 11; 12; 15:13; 14(2); 16; 18:5; 8; 9; 19; 21; 19:2; 3(2); 4; 5; 8; 9(3); 11(2); 16; 17; 33; 35; 20:11; 17; 21:30; 31; 32(2); 22:6; 8; 9; 19; 24:19; 41; 54(2); 57; 58; 59; 60; 61; 25:18; 25; 26:18; 20; 21; 22; 28; 30; 31(2); 32; 29:2; 3; 4; 5; 6; 8(2); 20; 30:38(2); 41; 31:23; 37; 43; 46(2); 54; 32:18; 33:4; 6(2); 7; 34:5; 7(2); 14; 22; 23; 25; 26; 27; 28; 29; 30; 31; 35:4; 5(2); 16; 36:7(2); 37:4; 5; 8; 16; 17; 18(2); 19; 23; 24; 25(2); 28(2); 31; 32(2); 38:21; 39:22; 40:4; 5; 6; 8; 15; 41:2; 14; 18; 21(3); 43; 42:7; 8; 10; 13; 20; 21; 23; 26; 28; 29; 35(3); 43:2(2); 7; 15; 18(2); 19(2); 24; 25(3); 26; 28(2); 32; 33; 34; 44:1; 3; 4; 7; 11; 13; 14; 45:3; 4; 24; 25; 27; 46:6(2); 28; 32(2); 47:1(2); 3; 4; 14; 17; 18; 22; 25; 27; 48:5; 9; 49:6(2); 26; 31(2); 50:8; 10(2); 11; 15; 16; 17(2); 18; 26; **Ex** 1:10(2); 11(2); 12(3); 14(2); 19; 2:16; 18; 19; 23; 3:13; 18; 4:1(2); 5; 8(2); 9; 18; 31(2); 5:1; 3; 8(3); 9; 10; 16; 19; 20(2); 21; 6:4; 9; 27; 7:6; 7; 10; 11; 12(2); 16; 17; 19; 24; 8:1; 8; 9; 11; 14; 17; 18; 20; 21; 26; 9:1; 10; 13; 19; 32; 10:3; 5(2); 6(2); 7; 8; 11; 12; 14(2); 15(2); 23; 12:3; 7(2); 8(2); 28; 33(2); 35; 36(3); 39(4); 50; 13:17(2); 20; 14:2; 3; 4; 5; 10; 11; 15; 17; 25; 15:5; 10; 16; 22(2); 23(3); 27(2); 16:1; 4; 5(3); 10; 15(2); 18(2); 20; 21; 22; 24; 27; 32; 35(3); 17:4; 7; 12; 18:7(2); 11; 16(2); 20(2); 22(3); 26(3); 19:1; 2; 13; 14; 17; 21; 20:18; 19; 21:28; 35(2); 22:23; 23:11; 33(2); 24:2; 7; 10; 11; 25:2; 10; 15; 37(2); 26:24(3); 25; 27:8; 20; 28:3; 4(2); 5; 6; 20; 21; 28; 30; 38; 41; 42; 43(4); 29:33(2); 46; 30:4; 12; 13; 15; 20(4); 21(2); 29; 30; 31:6; 11; 32:4; 6; 8(2); 13; 15; 17; 20; 22; 23; 24; 35; 33:4; 34:15; 30; 35:21(2); 22; 25; 36:3(2); 4; 5; 6; 7; 29; 39:1; 3; 4; 6; 7; 9; 10; 13; 15; 16; 17; 18; 19; 20; 21; 24; 25; 27; 30; 31; 32; 33; 43(2); 40:15; 32(3); 37; **Lev** 2:12; 4:13; 14; 24; 33; 6:16; 20; 7:2(2); 8:28; 9:5; 13; 20; 24; 10:2; 5; 7; 14; 15; 19; 11:8; 10; 11; 13(3); 28; 31; 32; 35(2); 42; 13:54; 14:36; 40(2); 41(2); 42; 15:18; 31(2); 16:1; 27; 17:5(2); 7(2); 18:17; 19:20; 20:12; 13; 14(2); 16; 17; 19; 20(2); 21; 23; 27; 21:5(2); 6(3); 7(2); 22:2(3); 9(3); 11; 15(2); 16; 18; 25; 23:17(3); 18; 20; 24:2; 9; 11; 12; 23; 25:31(2); 42(2); 45(2); 46; 55; 26:7; 17; 26; 36(2); 37; 39(2); 40(3); 41; 43(2); 44; 27:11; **Num** 1:1; 18(2); 46; 50(2); 54; 2:2; 3; 16; 17(2); 24; 31(2); 34(2); 3:4(2); 6; 7; 8; 9; 10; 13; 31; 4:5; 7; 8; 9(2); 10; 11; 12(2); 13; 14(3); 15(2); 19(2); 20(2); 25; 26; 37; 41; 49(2); 5:2; 3; 7(2); 9; 6:7; 27; 7:3(2); 5; 9; 11; 8:11; 16; 21; 22; 24; 25; 9:1; 4; 5; 6(2); 11; 12(2); 18(2); 20(2); 21(2); 22; 23(3); 10:3; 4; 6; 8; 10; 13; 21; 28; 33; 34; 11:13; 16; 17; 21; 25; 26(2); 32(2); 34; 12:2; 4; 5; 13:2; 18; 19(3); 21; 22; 23(3); 25; 26; 27; 31; 32(2); 14:4; 7; 9; 11; 12; 14(2); 23; 27; 31; 32; 35(2); 40; 44; 15:25; 32; 33; 34; 38(2); 16:2; 3; 16; 18; 22; 27; 29; 30; 33(2); 34; 37; 38(3); 39(2); 42; 45; 49; 17:5; 9; 10; 18:2; 3(3); 4; 6; 9; 12; 13; 15; 17; 21; 22; 23(2); 24(2); 19:2; 17; 20:2; 6; 27; 29; 21:3; 4; 6; 11; 12; 13; 16; 18; 27; 32; 33; 35(2); 22:3; 5(2); 6; 7; 12; 14; 15; 16; 39; 24:6; 25:2; 18(2); 26:7; 9; 10; 41; 50; 55; 57; 61; 62; 63; 64; 65; 27:2; 21(2); 28:19; 31; 29:8; 13; 30:9; 31:7(2); 8(2); 10(2); 11; 12; 49; 52; 32:1; 5; 9(3); 11; 12; 16; 30(2); 38; 33:3; 6; 7(2); 8; 9(2); 10; 11; 12; 13; 14; 15; 16; 17; 18; 19; 20; 21; 22; 23; 24; 25; 26; 27; 28; 29; 30; 31; 32; 33; 34; 35; 36; 37; 41; 42; 43; 44; 45; 46; 47; 48; 49; 34:29; 35:2; 3; 12; 36:2; 3(2); 4; 6(2); 12; **Deut** 1:22; 24; 25; 39(2); 2:4; 12; 15; 21; 22; 3:20; 4:9; 10(3); 45; 46; 47; 5:28(3); 29; 31; 6:8; 7:4(2); 20; 23; 9:12(2); 14; 29; 10:5; 7; 11; 11:4; 18; 30; 12:30; 31(2); 14:7(2); 12; 19; 15:6; 16:16; 18; 17:5; 9; 10(2); 11(3); 18:1; 2; 3; 8; 17(2); 19:14; 20:8; 9; 11; 18(2); 20; 21:2; 7; 15; 18; 20; 22:6; 17; 19; 21; 22; 24; 28; 23:3; 4(2); 25:1(2); 26:12; 28:7; 10; 22; 41; 46; 60; 29:22; 25; 26(2); 31:12(2); 16; 17(2); 18(2); 20(2); 21; 24; 30; 32:5(2); 7; 16(2); 17(2); 20; 21(2); 24; 27; 28; 29(3); 37; 33:3; 9; 10(2); 11; 17(2); 19(3); **Josh** 1:15; 16; 2:1; 3; 4; 7(2); 8; 13; 21; 22; 24; 3:1(2); 3; 6; 7; 13; 15; 4:8; 9; 14(2); 16; 18; 20; 5:4; 5(2); 6; 7(2); 8(3); 11; 12(2); 6:5; 11; 14(2); 15(2); 19; 20; 21; 23; 24(2); 7:3(2); 4; 5; 11(3); 12; 21; 22; 23; 24; 25; 26; 8:5; 6(3); 9; 13; 14; 15; 16; 17; 19(2); 20(2); 21; 22(3); 23; 24(3); 29; 31; 33; 9:2; 4(2); 6; 8; 9; 13; 16(4); 24; 26; 10:2; 5; 11(4); 20; 23; 24(2); 26; 27(2); 34; 35; 36; 37; 39; 11:4(2); 5; 7; 8(2); 11; 14(3); 19; 20(2); 14:4; 5; 16:10; 17:4; 10; 13; 16(2); 18(2); 18:4(2); 5; 19:2; 49; 50; 51; 20:3; 4; 5; 7; 8; 21:2; 9; 11; 12; 13; 20; 21; 27; 43; 22:6; 9; 10; 15(2); 28; 23:12; 13; 24:1; 2; 7; 8; 22; 30; 32; 33; **Judg** 1:4; 5(3); 6; 7; 10; 16; 17; 19; 20; 22; 24; 25(2); 28; 32; 34; 35; 2:3; 5(2); 9; 12; 13; 14; 15(2); 17(4); 19(2); 22; 3:4(2); 6; 12; 24(2); 25(3); 26; 28; 29; 4:12; 24; 5:7; 8; 11(2); 14; 19; 20; 23; 30(2); 6:3; 4; 5(4); 29(3); 35; 7:11; 19(2); 20; 21; 25(3); 8:1; 5; 18(3); 19; 24(2); 25(2); 28; 35; 9:3; 4; 7; 8; 9; 25; 27; 31; 34; 36; 41; 42; 46; 51; 55; 10:4; 8; 16; 11:2; 6; 13; 17; 18; 21; 22; 12:4; 6(2); 14:9; 11(2); 13; 14; 15; 15:6; 10; 11; 12; 13(2); 16:2; 7; 11; 23; 24(2); 25(3); 30; 17:4; 18:2(3); 3(3); 5; 7(2); 8; 9; 12(2); 13; 15; 19; 21; 22; 23(2); 26; 27(2); 28(2); 29; 31; 19:4; 5; 6; 8(2); 11; 14(2); 15; 21; 22; 25(2); 20:5; 6; 10(3); 22; 31; 32; 34; 36(3); 38; 39(2); 41; 42(2); 43; 45(2); 48(2); 21:5; 8; 12(2); 14(3); 17; 19; 20; 23(2); 24; **Ruth** 1:2; 4(2); 7; 9; 10; 11; 13; 14; 19(4); 22; 2:4; 9(2); 21; 22; 4:2; 17; **1Sa** 1:9(2); 19; 25; 2:4; 5(2); 12; 14; 15; 20; 22; 25; 27; 30; 34; 4:2(2); 4; 6(2); 7(2); 9; 10; 5:2; 3(2); 4; 7; 8(3); 9(2); 10(2); 11; 6:3; 4(2); 6(2); 11; 12; 13(2); 14; 16; 18; 19; 21; 7:6; 7; 10; 11; 13; 8:2; 6; 7(3); 8(3); 19; 9:4(4); 5; 10; 11(2); 12; 13; 14(2); 20; 25; 26(2); 27; 10:2; 4; 5; 10; 14; 21; 22; 23; 27; 11:5(2); 7; 9(2); 11(2); 15(2); 12:4; 5; 9(2); 10; 21; 13:5; 6; 21; 14:9; 10; 11; 13; 15; 16; 17; 20; 21; 22(2); 25; 30; 31; 33(2); 36; 15:3; 6; 9; 15; 18; 16:6; 17:11; 19; 24; 31; 51; 53; 18:6; 7; 8(2); 20; 27; 30; 19:1; 8; 20(2); 21(2); 22; 24; 20:11; 41; 21:11; 22:1; 4; 11; 17; 23:1(2); 12; 13; 18; 24; 25; 28; 25:7; 8; 9; 11; 13; 16; 26; 40; 43; 26:12(2); 19(3); 27:11; 28:4; 8; 25(2); 29:5; 30:2; 4; 10; 11(2); 12; 16(2); 19; 20; 21(3); 22(2); 24; 31:7(2); 8; 9; 10(2); 13; **2Sa** 1:12(2); 23(3); 2:3; 4(3); 13; 16(2); 24; 28; 29; 32(2); 3:21; 23; 32; 4:6(3); 7(2); 8; 12(2); 5:3; 8; 11; 17; 21; 6:3; 4; 6; 13; 17; 7:10; 8:14; 9:2; 10:5; 6; 13; 14; 15(2); 16; 19(2); 11:1; 10; 20; 12:18; 19; 20; 13:9; 30; 32; 14:6; 7(2); 11; 15:11(2); 24; 29; 30(2); 36; 16:22; 17:8(2); 10; 17(2); 18(2); 20(4); 21(2); 22; 29; 18:3(2); 17; 19:3; 8; 14; 17; 20:3; 7; 8; 14; 15(2); 18(3); 22(2); 21:5; 9(2); 13; 14(2); 22:18; 19; 39(2); 42; 45(2); 46; 23:6; 7; 9; 24:3; 5; 6(2); 7; 8(2); 13; 17; **1Kin** 1:1; 3; 7; 23; 25; 32; 39; 41; 44; 45; 53; 2:7; 39; 3:22; 24; 28(2); 4:21; 27; 28; 5:1; 6; 12; 14; 17; 18; 6:8; 10; 27; 7:28; 47; 8:1; 4; 8(3); 9; 25; 30; 33; 35(2); 36; 40(2); 42; 43; 46(2); 47(2); 50(2); 51; 52; 66; 9:8; 9(2); 12; 22; 28; 10:25; 29; 11:2(2); 18(3); 24; 29; 33; 41; 12:3; 7(2); 8; 13; 20; 24; 27; 13:11; 13; 20; 25; 27; 30; 14:15; 18; 19; 22(2); 23; 24; 29; 15:7; 8; 22; 23; 31; 16:5; 13(2); 14; 17; 20; 27; 18:6; 10(2); 26(3); 28; 29; 34(2); 39(2); 40; 19:10; 14; 21; 20:6(2); 12; 15; 16; 17; 18(2); 20; 23(2); 25; 29; 32; 33; 21:12; 13; 14; 22:1; 6; 32(2); 33; 37; 38; 39; 45; 48; **2Kin** 1:6; 8; 18; 2:2; 4; 6; 7; 8(2); 9; 11; 14; 15(2); 16; 17(3); 18; 20; 3:9; 21; 22; 23(2); 24(3); 25(3); 26; 27; 4:39; 40(4); 41; 42; 43(2); 44; 5:23; 24; 6:4(2); 14; 16(2); 18; 20(4); 22; 23(2); 25; 7:3; 4(2); 5(2); 6; 7; 8; 9; 10(3); 11; 12(3); 13(2); 14; 15; 8:23; 9:12; 13; 21; 27; 33; 35(2); 36; 37; 10:4; 7; 8; 13; 14; 16; 20; 21; 24; 25; 26; 27; 34; 35; 11:2; 7; 9; 12(2); 16; 17; 18; 19; 20; 12:10(2); 11(2); 14; 15(3); 19; 21; 13:5; 6; 8; 9; 12; 20; 21(3); 14:12; 15; 18; 19(2); 20; 28; 15:6; 7; 11; 15; 16; 21; 26; 31; 36; 16:5; 18; 19; 17:8; 9; 10; 11; 12; 14; 15(3); 16; 17; 19; 21; 22; 24; 25; 26(3); 28(2); 29; 32; 33(2); 34(3); 40(2); 41; 18:10; 12; 17(3); 18; 20; 27; 34; 35; 19:3; 18(2); 26(2); 31; 35(2); 37; 20:7; 14(2); 15(2); 18(2); 20; 21:8; 9; 14; 15; 17; 25; 22:7; 14; 17(2); 19; 20; 23:1; 9; 18; 28; 24:5; 25:1; 6(2); 7; 14(2); 23(2); 26; **1Chr** 4:14; 23; 28; 39; 40(2); 43; 5:10(2); 16; 19; 20(3); 21; 22; 23; 25; 6:31; 32(2); 33; 55; 56; 57; 65; 67(2); 7:2; 4; 21; 8:6; 9:1; 18; 23; 27; 28; 33; 38; 10:7(2); 8; 9(2); 10; 12; 11:3; 7; 14; 19; 12:1(2); 2; 15(2); 19; 21(2); 33; 39; 40; 13:2; 4; 7; 9; 14:11(2); 12(2); 16; 15:26; 16:1(2); 20; 17:9; 19:6; 7; 11; 14; 15; 16(2); 17; 19(2); 20:4; 8; 21:3(2); 5; 17(2); 22:4; 23:11; 24; 25; 26; 32; 24:4; 5; 25:8; 26:6; 8; 13; 14; 27; 31; 28:21; 29:8; 9(2); 21; 22; 29; **2Chr** 1:17(2); 2:17; 3:13; 4:6(2); 20; 5:5; 9(2); 10; 13; 6:21; 24; 26(2); 27; 31(2); 32; 34; 36(2); 37(2); 38(2); 7:3; 9(2); 22; 8:9; 15; 18; 9:24; 28; 29; 10:3; 7(2); 11:4; 17(2); 12:2; 6; 7(2); 8(2); 15; 13:11(2); 13; 14; 18; 14:1; 7; 10; 13(3); 14(2); 15; 15:4; 9(2); 10; 11(2); 12; 14; 15; 16:4; 6; 11; 14(2); 17:9; 10; 18:5; 9; 10; 14; 29; 31(2); 32; 19:8; 10; 20:2; 4; 8; 10(2); 11; 16; 20(2); 21; 22(2); 23; 24(2); 25(4); 26(2); 27; 28; 29; 34; 36; 37; 21:17; 20; 22:4; 9(4); 23:2(2); 6(3); 11; 15(2); 16; 20; 21; 24:7; 8; 9; 10; 11(2); 13; 14(3); 16; 18; 19(2); 21; 23; 24(2); 25(4); 26; 27; 25:10; 12; 13; 20; 21; 22; 26; 27(2); 28; 26:18; 20; 23(2); 27:7; 9; 28:5; 6; 15; 18; 23(2); 26; 27(2); 29:7; 15; 16; 17(4); 18; 19; 21; 22(5); 23(2); 24; 29; 30(2); 34; 30:1; 3; 5(3); 9; 10; 14(2); 15; 16(2); 18; 22; 23; 31:1; 4; 5; 6; 7; 8; 11; 18; 32:3; 18(2); 19; 21; 32; 33; 33:8; 10; 18; 19; 20; 34:4; 9(3); 10(2); 11; 13; 14; 16; 17; 22(2); 24; 25(2); 28; 33; 35:1; 6; 11; 12(3); 13(2); 14; 15; 24; 25; 27; 36:8; 16; 19; 20; **Ezr** 1:6; 2:59(3); 62(2); 63; 68; 69; 3:3(2); 4; 6; 7(2); 8; 10; 11(2); 4:2; 6; 11; 13; 15; 23; 5:5(2); 7; 11; 14; 6:3; 8; 9; 10; 13; 14(2); 18; 7:13; 8:17(2); 18; 36(2); 9:2; 10:5(2); 7(2); 17; 19(3); 44; **Neh** 1:3; 2:7; 18(2); 19; 3:1(3); 6; 8; 13; 4:2(4); 3; 5; 7; 11; 12(2); 17(2); 22; 5:8(2); 12(2); 6:2; 4; 9; 10(2); 13(2); 16(2); 19; 7:3; 5; 61(3); 64; 65; 67; 8:1; 4; 6; 8; 9; 12; 14; 15; 18; 9:3(2); 10; 11; 12; 15; 16; 18; 19; 21; 22; 23; 24(2); 25(2); 26(2); 27; 28(4); 29; 30; 35(2); 37; 10:28; 29; 11:30; 12:27; 37; 39; 43; 47; 13:1; 2; 3(2); 5; 9; 13; 15(2); 19; 21; 22(2); 29; **Est** 1:7; 8; 17; 2:3; 23; 3:4(2); 6; 7; 8; 9; 14; 4:12; 6:1; 9; 14; 7:8; 10; 8:7; 9:5; 10(2); 12; 14; 15; 16; 17; 18; 21; 22; 23; 26(2); 27; 31; 10:2; **Job** 1:15; 19; 2:11(2); 12(3); 13(2); 3:18; 22; 4:8; 9(2); 20(2); 21; 5:4; 14; 6:15; 17(3); 18; 20(3); 8:10; 22; 9:5; 25(2); 26; 11:6; 20; 12:6; 7(2); 15(2); 25; 14:12; 21; 15:24; 35; 16:10(3); 17:12; 16; 18:20(2); 19:15; 18; 19; 23; 24; 20:7; 21:11; 12; 13; 14; 18; 26; 30; 22:12; 24:1; 2; 3(2); 4; 5; 6(2); 7(2); 8; 9; 10(2); 13(2); 16(3); 17; 24(2); 27:13; 28:1; 4(2); 29:22; 23(2); 24(2); 30:1; 3; 5(2); 7(2); 8(2); 10(2); 11; 12(2); 13(3); 14(2); 15; 24; 31:13; 32:3; 4; 15(3); 16; 34:19; 20; 25; 27; 28; 35:9(2); 12; 36:7(2); 8; 9; 10; 11(2); 12(3); 13; 14; 27; 37:12; 38:14; 35; 40; 41; 39:2(2); 3(3); 4(2); 16; 41:6; 17(3); 23(2); 25; 42:11(2); **Ps** 2:12; 3:1(2); 5:9; 10; 9:3; 10; 15(2); 10:2; 11:2(2); 12:2(2); 14:1(2); 3(2); 4; 5; 17:10(2); 11(2); 14; 18:17; 18; 37; 38(2); 41; 44(2); 19:10; 20:8; 21:11(3); 22:4; 5(2); 7(3); 13; 16; 17; 18; 26; 29(2); 31; 23:4; 24:1; 25:6; 19(2); 27:2; 28:5; 31:4; 11; 13(2); 32:6; 9; 34:5; 10; 21; 35:7(2); 11; 12; 13; 15(2); 16; 20(2); 21; 36:8; 12; 37:2; 9; 19(2); 20(2); 22; 28; 40; 38:4; 12(2); 16(2); 19(2); 20; 39:6; 40:5(2); 12; 41:7; 8; 42:3; 10; 44:3; 10; 45:8; 15(2); 48:4; 5(3); 49:6; 11; 14; 19; 51:19; 53:1; 3; 4(2); 5; 54:3; 55:3(2); 10; 19(2); 21; 56:2; 5; 6(4); 7; 8; 57:6(3); 58:3(2); 4; 8; 59:t, 3; 4; 6(2); 7(2); 12; 13; 15; 62:4(4); 9; 63:10(2); 64:4(2); 5(3); 6(2); 7; 8; 9; 65:8; 12; 13(2); 66:4; 6; 68:24; 69:4(2); 12; 21(2); 23; 26(2); 35; 36; 71:10; 24(2); 72:5; 9; 16; 73:5(2); 7; 8(2); 9; 11; 12; 19(2); 27; 74:4; 6; 7(2); 8(2); 76:5; 77:16; 78:5; 7; 10; 17; 18; 19(2); 22; 29; 30; 32; 34(2); 35; 36(2); 37; 39; 40; 41; 42; 44; 53; 56; 57; 58; 79:1(2); 2; 3; 7; 12; 80:12; 16; 81:12; 82:5(3); 83:2; 3; 4; 5(2); 8; 10; 16; 84:4(2); 7; 86:17; 88:5; 17(2); 89:15; 16(2); 31; 51; 90:5(2); 10; 91:12; 92:7; 14(2); 94:4; 5; 6; 7; 11; 21; 95:10; 11; 97:7; 98:7; 99:6; 7; 101:6; 102:8; 26(2); 104:7(2); 8(2); 9(2); 11; 22; 28(2); 29(2); 30; 32;

105:12; 13; 18; 27; 28; 38; 41; 44; 45; 106:3; 7; 12(2); 13(2); 16; 19; 20; 21; 24(2); 28; 29; 32; 33; 34; 36; 37; 38; 39; 41; 42; 43; 107:4(2); 6; 7; 11; 12; 13; 18; 19; 23; 26(2); 27; 28; 30(2); 36; 38; 39; 43; 109:2; 3; 4; 5; 25(2); 27; 28; 111:8; 10; 115:5(4); 6(4); 7(5); 8; 118:11(2); 12(2); 119:2; 3(2); 74(2); 78; 86; 87; 91; 98; 111; 126; 136; 150(2); 155; 158; 165; 120:7; 122:1; 6; 124:3; 125:1; 126:2; 5; 127:1; 5(2); 129:1; 2(2); 3; 8; 130:6(2); 135:16(4); 17(2); 18; 137:3(2); 138:4; 5; 139:18; 20; 140:2; 3; 5(2); 8; 10; 141:6(2); 9; 142:3; 6; 144:5; 145:7; 11; 147:20; 148:5; **Prov** 1:9; 11; 18(2); 28(3); 29; 30(2); 31; 2:15; 19; 3:2; 22; 4:16(3); 17; 19(2); 22; 7:5; 8:9; 32; 36; 11:20; 12:22; 14:22; 15:22; 16:13; 17:15; 18:8; 21; 19:7; 21:7; 22:18; 23:3; 5; 30(2); 35(2); 26:22; 28:4; 5; 28; 30:24; 25; 26; 27; 31:5; **Eccl** 1:7; 16; 2:3; 3:18(2); 19; 4:1(2); 3; 9; 10; 11; 16; 5:1(2); 8; 11; 7:29; 8:10(2); 9:3(2); 5(2); 6; 11:3; 6; 8; 12:3; 5; **Song** 1:6; 3:8; 5:7(2); 6:5; 9; **Is** 1:2; 4(3); 6; 14; 18(3); 23; 28; 29; 31; 2:4(2); 6(2); 8; 19; 20; 3:9(3); 10; 12; 16; 5:6; 8; 11; 12; 13; 24; 26; 29(2); 30; 6:10; 13; 7:19; 22; 8:19; 20; 21(3); 22(2); 9:2; 3(2); 12; 13; 16; 18; 20(2); 21; 10:1; 2; 4(2); 18; 29(2); 11:9; 14(3); 13:2; 5; 8(3); 14; 17; 18; 14:1; 2(3); 7; 10; 16; 21; 15:3; 5(2); 7(3); 16:7; 8(3); 17:2; 3; 9; 18; 18:6; 19:2; 3; 6; 8(2); 9(2); 10; 12; 13(2); 14; 20; 21; 22; 20:5; 21:14; 15; 22:3; 9; 24; 23:5; 13(2); 24:5; 6; 9; 14(3); 22(2); 26:11(2); 14(4); 16(2); 19; 27:11; 13; 28:7(5); 12; 13; 29:9(2); 15; 23; 24(2); 30:1; 5; 6; 16; 18; 31:1(3); 3; 32:12; 33:1(2); 12; 17; 23(2); 34:12; 17(2); 35:2; 10; 36:5; 12; 19; 20; 21; 37:3; 19(2); 27(2); 32; 36(2); 38; 38:18; 39:3(2); 4(2); 7(2); 40:17; 24(3); 31(4); 41:6; 11(3); 12; 20; 22; 29; 42:9; 16(2); 17(2); 22(3); 24(2); 43:2; 9; 17(4); 21; 44:4; 9(4); 11(3); 18(3); 45:6; 14(5); 16(2); 20; 46:1(3); 8(3); 47:9; 14(2); 15(2); 48:2; 3(2); 7; 13; 21; 49:9; 10; 15; 17; 19; 21; 22; 23(2); 26; 50:9; 51:5; 6; 11; 20(2); 52:5; 6; 8(2); 15(3); 54:15; 56:10(3); 11(3); 12; 57:2; 6(2); 12; 58:2(3); 3; 12; 59:4(2); 5; 6; 7; 8(2); 19; 60:4(2); 6(3); 7; 11; 14(2); 21; 61:3; 4(3); 7(2); 9; 62:9(2); 12; 63:8; 10; 13; 15; 19; 65:11; 16; 21(2); 22(2); 22(2); 24(2); 25; 66:3; 4(2); 5; 17; 18; 19; 20; 24(2); **Jer** 1:15(2); 19(2); 2:5; 6; 8; 13; 15; 24(2); 26; 27(2); 28; 30; 3:1; 16(3); 17(2); 18; 21(2); 4:2; 17; 22(5); 23; 24; 29; 30; 5:2(2); 3(4); 4(2); 5; 7; 8; 10; 12; 15; 16; 17(4); 22(3); 23; 24; 26(3); 27; 28(6); 6:3(2); 9; 10(3); 14; 15(6); 16; 17; 19; 23(3); 28(3); 7:17; 18; 19(2); 24; 26(2); 27(2); 30; 31; 32; 8:1; 2(8); 4; 5(2); 6; 9(2); 11; 12(6); 16; 17; 19; 9:2; 3(4); 5(2); 6; 10(2); 13; 8; 11:8(2); 10(2); 11(2); 12(2); 14; 17; 19; 12:1; 2(3); 4; 5(2); 6(3); 10(2); 11; 13(3); 16(3); 17; 13:11(2); 12; 14:2; 3(3); 4; 6; 10(2); 12(2); 14; 15; 16(2); 18; 15:2; 7; 20(2); 16:4(5); 6; 10; 12; 16(2); 17; 18(2); 20; 21; 17:13(2); 15; 19; 23(2); 25; 26; 18:12; 15(2); 20:4; 10; 11(3); 21:6; 22:7; 8; 9(2); 11; 12; 18(2); 27(2); 28(2); 23:3; 4(2); 7; 8; 12; 14(3); 16(2); 17(2); 21(2); 22(2); 26; 27; 32; 24:2; 3; 7(2); 8; 10; 25:5; 16; 28; 30; 33(2); 26:3; 10; 23; 24; 27:10; 11; 14; 15; 16; 18; 22(2); 28:14(2); 29:6; 9; 17; 19; 23; 30:3; 9; 14; 16(2); 17; 19(2); 31:1; 9(2); 12(2); 15; 16; 23; 24; 29; 32; 33:3; 32:17; 32:14; 23(3); 24; 29; 31; 32(2); 33(2); 34; 35(3); 38; 39; 40; 33:5; 8(3); 9; 24(2); 34:5(2); 10; 11(2); 18(2); 22; 35:6; 14; 17(2); 36:3; 7; 9; 15; 16(2); 17; 18(2); 20; 21; 17:13(2); 15; 19; 23(2); 25; 26; 18:12; 15; 2:7; 20:22; 23; 25; 27; 39:1; 4; 5(2); 14; 16; 40:7; 8(2); 12; 41:1; 7; 12; 13; 17; 18; 42:5; 17; 43:3; 5; 7(3); 44:2; 3(4); 5; 6; 9; 10(2); 12(4); 14(2); 46:6(2); 12; 15; 16; 17; 21(2); 22(3); 23; 24; 25; 27; 29(3); 50:3(2); 4(2); 5; 6(3); 7; 9; 16(2); 20; 33; 36(2); 37(2); 38(2); 42(3); 57; 58; 64; 52:7; 9; 18(2); **Lam** 1:2; 6; 8; 10; 11(2); 14; 19(2); 21(3); 2:7; 8; 10(2); 12(2); 14; 15; 16(2); 3:6; 23; 53; 4:2; 3; 5(2); 7(2); 8; 9(2); 10; 14(2); 15(4); 16(4); 18; 19(2); 5:11; 13; **Eze** 1:5; 7; 8(2); 9(3); 10(3); 12(4); 16; 17(4); 18(2); 20; 24(3); 25; 2:3; 4; 5(4); 6; 7(3); 3:6; 7; 9; 11(2); 15; 25; 26; 27; 4:16(2); 17; 5:6(2); 12; 13; 17; 6:9(4); 10; 11; 13; 14; 7:14; 16; 18; 19(2); 20; 21; 24; 25; 26; 27; 8:6; 9; 12; 13; 16; 17(4); 18; 9:2; 6; 7; 8; 9; 10:10; 11(7); 17(2); 19; 20; 21; 22; 23; 15:7; 8; 16:33(2); 37; 39(2); 40(2); 41; 47; 50; 51; 52(2); 17:15; 21; 23; 18:22; 19:4; 9(2); 20:8(3); 9; 12; 13(3); 16; 20; 21; 24; 25; 26(2); 27; 28(4); 38(2); 49; 21:7; 23; 29(2); 22:7(3); 9(2); 10(2); 12; 18(2); 20; 25; 26(3); 28; 29; 23:3(3); 4(2); 8(2); 10(2); 13; 17; 24(2); 25(3); 26; 29; 29:3(3); 38(2); 39(3); 40; 43; 44(3); 45(2); 47; 49; 24:14; 25; 27; 25:3; 4(3); 6; 10(3); 11(2); 12; 17; 26:4; 14; 15; 16; 17(2); 21(2); 22(2); 29; 30; 31; 32; 33(2); 56; 24:1(2); 2; 3; 4; 5(2); 8; 11; 14; 15; 16; 17(2); 18(4); 20; 21; 28:3; 7(2); 8; 16; 17; 18; 19; 22; 24; 26; 28; 34(2); 35; 39(2); 10:4; 5(2); 6(2); 10(2); 16; 25; 27; 28; 39; 11:13; 31; 34; 41; 42; 53; 56(2);

23(2); 26(3); 28; 40:10; 22; 38; 41; 42(2); 49; 41:6(3); 42:6; 11(2); 13(2); 14(4); 43:7; 8(2); 10; 11(3); 18; 22(2); 24; 25; 26(2); 44:7; 10; 11(3); 12(2); 13(3); 15(2); 16(3); 17(3); 18(2); 19(5); 20(2); 21; 22(2); 23; 24(4); 25(2); 26; 29; 45:8; 46:6; 10(2); 15; 20(2); 47:9; 10; 11; 12(2); 22(2); 48:14; 19; **Dan** 1:4; 5; 16; 19; 2:2; 7; 13; 18; 43(2); 46; 3:3; 9; 12; 13; 19; 24; 25; 28; 4:6; 7; 25(3); 26; 32(2); 5:3; 4; 8; 15(2); 20; 21; 23; 29; 6:4; 12; 13; 16; 22; 23; 24(3); 7:5; 12; 13; 25; 26; 9:7; 11; 10:7; 11:2; 6(2); 14; 21; 22; 25; 26; 27; 31(2); 33(2); 34(2); 12:3(2); **Hos** 1:11; 2:4; 8; 17; 21; 22; 23; 4:2; 4; 7(2); 8(2); 10(3); 12; 13; 14(3); 18; 19; 5:4(2); 6(2); 7(2); 15(2); 6:7(2); 9; 7:1; 2(2); 3; 4; 6(2); 7; 10; 11(2); 12; 13(3); 14(4); 15; 16(2); 8:1; 4(4); 5; 7(2); 8; 9; 10(2); 12; 13(2); 9:3(2); 4(2); 5; 10(2); 12; 16(2); 8:1; 4(4); 5; 7; 10; 11:3; 12:2(2); 8; 11(2); 12:1; 2; 8; 11; 12:1; 2; 8; 11; 13:2(2); 36; 11:7; 8; 18; 19; 20; 21; 12:2; 3; 10(2); 14; 16; 24; 27; 36; 41; 45; 13:5(3); 6(3); 13(3); 15(2); 16(2); 17; 18; 31(2); 32(2); 34; 37(2); 38; 16:5; 7; 12; 14; 20; 28; 17:6; 8; 12(2); 9; 12(2); 14; 16; 22; 23(4); 27; 29(2); 30; 31; 32(2); 22:2(2); 9(2); 17; 18; 19; 22; 23; 24; 25; 29; 23:4; 12(2); 17(3); 18; 27; 28(2); 29; 30(2); 36(2); 38(2); 39(3); 40(2); 41; 43; 44; 28:1(2); 2; 4; 6(3); 10; 15; 17; 18; 21; 25(2); 27(2); 28; **Rom** 1:20; 21(2); 22; 28; 32; 3:9(2); 12(2); 13; 17; 4:7; 11; 14; 17; 5:17; 8:5(2); 8; 14; 23; 9:6; 7(2); 8; 36; 32(2); 10:1; 2; 3; 14(5); 15(2); 16; 18; 11:3(2); 8(2); 10; 11(2); 20; 22(3); 28(2); 31; 13:2; 6; 15:21(2); 27; 16:18; **1Cor** 2:8(2); 14(2); 3:20; 7:8; 9; 14; 29(2); 30(6); 31; 9:13(2); 14; 24; 25; 10:4; 5; 6; 11; 18; 20; 33; 11:19; 12:19; 20; 13:8(2); 14:7; 21; 23; 34; 35; 15:10; 11; 18; 23; 29(2); 35; 48(2); 16:4; 15; 17; 18; **2Cor** 5:15; 6:16; 8:3; 5; 23; 9:4; 5; 13; 10:10; 12; 11:12(2); 22(3); 23; 12:21; **Gal** 1:23; 24; 2:4; 6(2); 7; 9(2); 10; 12; 14; 4:17(2); 5:12; 21; 24; 6:12(2); 13(2); **Eph** 4:14; 5:31; **Phil** 3:18; 4:2; 22; **Col** 1:16; 20; 3:21; 4:9; **1Th** 1:9; 2:14; 15; 16; 5:3(2); 7(2); **2Th** 2:10(2); 11; 12; 3:12; **1Ti** 1:3; 7(2); 20; 2:15; 3:13; 5:7; 11(2); 12; 13(2); 17; 24; 25; 6:2(3); 9; 10; 17; 18(2); 19; **2Ti** 1:15; 2:10; 14; 16; 23; 26; 3:6; 9; 4:3(2); 4; **Titus** 1:10; 11; 13; 16(3); 2:3; 4; 10; 3:8; 9; 14; **Heb** 1:4; 11(2); 12; 14; 2:11; 3:10(2); 11; 16; 18; 19; 4:3; 5; 6; 6:6(2); 7:5(2); 23(2); 8:9; 10; 11; 9:15; 10:1; 2; 11:13; 14(2); 15(3); 16; 23(2); 29; 30; 35; 37(3); 38; 40; 12:10; 19; 20; 25; 13:10; 17(3); 24; **Jas** 2:7; 12; 3:3; 4(2); 4:1; 5:15; **1Pet** 1:12; 2:8; 12(3); 3:1; 2; 10; 16(2); 4:4; 6; **2Pet** 1:8; 21; 2:3; 10(2); 12; 13(3); 14; 18(2); 19(2); 20(2); 21; 3:4; 5; 16(2); **1Jn** 2:19(7); 4:1; 5(2); **3Jn** 7; **Jude** 10(3); 11; 12(2); 15; 18; 19; **Rev** 1:7; 15; 2:2; 9; 22; 24; 27; 3:4(2); 9; 4:4; 8(2); 11; 5:9; 6:4; 9; 10; 11(2); 7:13; 14; 15; 16; 8:7; 11; 9:4; 5(2); 8; 9; 10; 11; 19; 20; 21; 11(2); 8; 7; 9; 9; 10; 11; 12(2); 18; 12:6; 11(2); 13:4(2); 14; 14:3; 4(3); 5; 11; 12; 13; 15:3; 16:4; 6(2); 9; 10; 14; 15; 17(4); 18; 19; 18; 19; 19:3; 9; 20:4(2); 6; 9; 13; 21:3; 26; 27; 22:4; 5(2); 14(2)

THINE

1438, 2398, 3588, 4572, 4671, 4674, 4675

Gen 13:14; 14:20; 23; 15:4(3); 20:7; 21:18; 22:2; 12(2); 16; 30:27; 31:12; 32; 38:18; 40:13; 44:18; 46:4; 47:19; 48:6; 49:8; **Ex** 4:2; 4; 6; 7; 17; 21; 5:16; 7:15; 19; 8:3(2); 5; 9:14; 22; 10:12; 21; 13:9(2); 16(2); 14:16; 26; 15:7; 16; 17; 17:5; 20:24; 22:30; 23:1; 4; 12(2); 22(2); 27; 32:13; 34:9; **Lev** 2:13; 10:15; 18:10; 14; 19:17; 27:23; 27; **Num** 5:20; 10:35; 18:9; 11; 13(2); 14; 15; 16; 18(2); 20; 22:30(2); 32; 27:18; 20; **Deut** 2:24; 3:21; 27(2); 4:9; 19; 39; 5:14(2); 6:5; 6; 7; 8(2); 19; 7:13; 16; 17; 19; 24; 26; 8:2; 5; 14; 17; 9:4; 5; 26; 29; 10:21; 11:14; 19; 20; 12:17; 18; 13:6; 8; 9; 17; 14:23; 25; 26; 28; 29; 15:3(2); 7(2); 8; 9(2); 10(2); 11; 16; 16:10; 15(2); 18:4; 21; 19:13; 14; 21; 20:1; 13; 14; 21:10(2); 12; 13; 22:2; 8; 23:9; 14; 20; 24; 25; 24:19(2); 20; 25:12; 14; 19; 26:4; 11; 12; 16; 28:7; 8; 12; 20; 25; 31(4); 32(2); 34; 40; 48; 53(2); 55; 57; 67(2); 29:3; 30:4; 2; 6(2); 7; 9; 10; 17; 33:10; 29; 34:4; **Josh** 2:3; 17; 20; 6:2; 7:13; 8:18; 9:25; 10:8; 14:9; 17:18(2); **Judg** 4:7; 9; 14; 5:31; 6:39; 7:7; 9; 11; 8:6(2); 15; 9:29; 11:36; 12:1; 16:15; 18:19; 19:5; 6; 8; 9; 22; 20:28; **Ruth** 2:9; 10; 11; 13(2); 3:9(2); 4:11; 15; **1Sa** 1:11(3); 16; 18; 2:31(2); 32; 33(4); 36; 9:19; 20; 14:7; 19; 15:17; 28; 16:1; 17:28; 46; 20:3; 29; 30; 21:3; 8; 22:14; 23:4; 24:4(2); 10; 15; 18; 20; 25:6; 8(2); 24(3); 25; 26(2); 27; 28; 29; 31; 35; 41; 26:8(2); 21; 27:5; 28:16; 17; 21; 22; **2Sa** 1:14; 25; 3:21; 4:8; 5:19; 7:3; 9; 11; 16; 21; 11:10; 12:10; 11; 13:10; 14:7; 8; 12; 17; 19; 16:4; 17:11; 19:6; 27; 28; 20:17; 22:28; 24:13; 16; 17; **1Kin** 1:12; 13; 17; 53; 2:26; 37; 44(2); 3:11; 20; 26; 8:18(2); 24; 29; 31; 51; 52; 53; 11:22; 12:16; 13:8; 18; 14:12; 17:11; 19:10; 14; 20:4; 6(2); 13; 28; 21:7; 19; 22; 22:34; **2Kin** 4:2; 16; 29; 7:2; 19; 8:1; 8; 9:1; 10:5; 15(2); 13:16; 14:10; 19:16(2); 22; 20:1; 15; 17; 22:19; 20; **1Chr**

4:10; 12:18(2); 14:10; 17:2; 8; 10; 17; 19; 22; 21:12; 15; 17; 24; 29:11(3); 12(2); 14; 16(3); **2Chr** 1:11(2); 6:8(2); 15; 20; 22; 40(2); 42; 9:5; 10:16; 16:7; 8; 18:33; 19:3; 20:6; 25:15; 19(2); 26:18; 34:27; 28; **Ezr** 7:14; 25; **Neh** 1:6(2); 11; 6:8; **Job** 1:11; 12; 2:5; 6; 9; 5:25; 7:8; 17; 10:3; 7; 8; 13; 17; 11:4; 6; 13(2); 14; 17; 13:21; 24; 14:3; 15; 15:5; 6(2); 12; 22:5; 22; 30; 35:7; 40:14; 41:8; **Ps** 2:8; 6:1; 7:6; 8:2; 10:12; 17; 16:10; 17:2; 6; 20:4; 21:8(2); 9; 12; 13; 26:6; 8; 27:14; 28:9; 31:2; 5; 22; 37:4; 38:2; 3; 39:10; 44:3; 45:5; 10(2); 50:20; 21; 51:19; 56:7; 66:3; 68:9; 23; 69:9; 24; 71:2; 16; 74:1; 2; 4; 16(2); 22; 23; 77:15; 17; 79:1; 83:2; 84:3; 9; 85:3; 4; 5; 86:1; 16; 88:2; 89:10; 11(2); 38; 51(2); 90:7; 11; 91:8; 92:9(2); 93:5; 94:5; 102:2; 10; 103:3; 104:28; 106:5; 110:1; 2; 116:16; 119:91; 94; 173; 128:2; 3; 130:2; 132:10; 138:7; 8; 139:5; 16; 20; 144:6; 7; 145:16; **Prov** 2:2(2); 10; 3:1; 3; 5(2); 7; 9; 21; 27; 4:4; 9; 20; 21(2); 25(2); 5:1; 9; 15(2); 17; 6:4(2); 21; 25; 7:2; 3; 25; 20:13; 22:17(2); 23:4; 5; 12(2); 15; 17; 18; 19; 26(2); 33(2); 24:17(2); 27; 25:7; 10; 21; 27:2(2); 10; 30:32; **Eccl** 5:2; 6; 7:18; 22; 11:6; 9(2); **Song** 4:9; 10; 6:5; 7:4; 5(2); 8:6(2); **Is** 6:7; 12:1; 14:13; 26:11; 30:20; 21; 33:17; 18; 20; 37:17(2); 23; 38:1; 39:4; 6; 42:6; 43:24; 44:3; 45:14; 47:6; 8; 9; 10; 12; 48:8; 49:18; 20; 21; 51:22; 54:2; 5; 57:10; 58:7; 8; 13(3); 60:4; 5; 17; 20; 62:8; 63:2; 17; 19; 64:2; **Jer** 2:2; 19; 22; 37(2); 3:2; 13; 4:1; 14; 18; 5:3; 17(2); 6:9; 7:29; 9:6; 10:24; 13:22(2); 27(2); 15:14; 17:4(2); 18:23; 20:4; 6; 22:17(2); 25:28; 28:7; 30:14; 15(2); 16; 31:16; 17; 21; 32:7(2); 8(2); 19; 34:3; 36:14; 38:12; 17; 40:4; 42:2; 43:9; 49:16; 51:13; **Lam** 2:14; 16; 17(2); 18; 19; 21; 3:56; 4:22(2); **Eze** 3:10(2); 18; 20; 24; 4:7; 5:1; 9; 11; 6:11; 7:3; 4; 8; 9; 8:5; 10:2; 16:6; 7; 12(2); 15; 22; 27; 30; 31(2); 39; 41; 43(2); 46; 51(2); 52; 54; 58; 61; 21:14; 22:4; 14(2); 16; 23:25; 27; 31; 34; 24:16; 17; 26; 25:6; 27:6; 10; 11; 15; 28:2(2); 4; 5; 6; 17; 18; 33:8; 35:11(2); 37:17; 20; 38:4; 12; 39:3; 40:4(3); 44:5(2); 30; **Dan** 2:38; 3:17; 4:19; 27; 5:22; 9:16; 18(2); 19; 10:12; **Hos** 9:7; 13:9; 14:1; **Joel** 2:17; **Obad** 3; 15; **Jonah** 1:8; 2:7; **Mic** 4:10; 13; 5:9(3); 12; 13; 7:14; **Nah** 3:13; **Hab** 3:8(2); 11; 13; 15; **Zeph** 3:15; 16; **Zec** 3:4; 5:5; 13:6; **Mt** 5:25; 33; 43; 6:2; 4; 13; 17; 22; 23; 7:3; 4(2); 5; 9:6; 12:13; 18:9; 20:14; 15; 22:44; 25:25; **Mk** 2:11; 3:5; 9:47; 12:36; **Lk** 4:7; 5:24; 33; 6:41; 42(3); 7:44; 8:39; 11:34(2); 12:19; 58; 13:12; 15:31; 19:22; 42; 43; 20:43; 22:42; **Jn** 2:17; 8:10; 9:10; 17; 26; 17:5; 6; 9; 10(2); 11; 18:35; **Acts** 2:27; 4:30; 5:3; 4(3); 8:22; 37; 10:4; 31; 13:35; 23:35; **Rom** 10:6; 9; 11:3; 12:20; **1Cor** 10:29; **1Ti** 5:23; **Philem** 1:19; **Heb** 1:10; 13; **Rev** 3:18

THING

562, 1697, 3627, 3651, 3972, 4399, 4406, 4859, 5315, *1520, 3056, 4110, 4229, 4487, 5313*

Gen 1:24; 25; 26; 28; 30; 31; 6:7; 17; 19; 20; 7:8; 14; 21; 8:1; 17(2); 19; 21; 9:3; 14:23; 18:14; 17; 19:21; 22; 20:10; 21:11; 26; 22:12; 16; 24:50; 30:31(2); 34:7; 14; 19; 38:10; 39:9; 23; 41:28; 32; 37; 44:7; **Ex** 1:18; 2:14; 15; 9:5; 6; 10:15; 12:24; 16:14; 16; 32; 18:11; 14; 17; 18; 23; 20:4; 17; 22:9; 15; 29:1; 33:17; 34:10; 35:4; **Lev** 2:3; 10; 4:13; 5:2; 5; 16; 6:2; 4(2); 7; 7:19; 21(2); 8:5; 9:6; 11:10; 21; 35; 41; 43; 44; 12:4; 13:48; 49; 52; 53; 54; 57; 58; 59; 15:4; 6; 10; 20(2); 22; 23; 17:2; 19:8; 26; 20:17; 21; 25; 21:18; 22:4; 5; 10(2); 14(2); 23; 23:37; 27:23; 28(2); **Num** 4:15; 16:9; 13; 30; 17:13; 18:7; 14; 15; 20:19; 22:38; 30:1; 31:23; 32:20; 35:22; 36:6; **Deut** 1:14; 32; 4:18; 23; 25; 32(2); 5:8; 21; 7:26(2); 8:9; 12:32; 13:14; 17; 14:3; 19; 21; 15:10; 15; 16:4; 17:4; 5; 18:22(2); 22:20; 23:9; 14; 19; 24:10; 18; 22; 26:11; 31:13; 32:47(2); **Josh** 4:10; 6:18(2); 7:1(2); 11; 13(2); 15; 9:24; 14:6; 21:45; 22:20; 24; 33; 23:14(2); **Judg** 6:29(2); 8:27; 11:25; 37; 13:4; 7; 14(2); 18:7; 10; 19:19; 24; 20:9; 21:11; **Ruth** 3:18; **1Sa** 3:11; 17(2); 4:7; 8:6; 12:16; 14:12; 15:9; 18:20; 23; 20:2; 26; 39; 21:2; 22:15; 24:6; 25:15; 26:16; 28:10; 18; 30:19; **2Sa** 2:6; 3:13; 7:19; 11:11; 25; 27; 12:5; 6; 12; 21; 13:2; 12; 20; 33; 14:13(2); 15; 18; 20; 21; 15:11; 35; 36; 17:19; 24:3; **1Kin** 1:27; 3:10; 11; 10:3; 11:10; 12:24; 30; 13:33; 34; 14:5; 13; 15:5; 16:31; 20:9; 24; 33; **2Kin** 2:10; 3:18; 4:2; 5:13; 18(2); 6:11; 7:2; 19; 8:9; 13; 11:5; 17:12; 20:9; 10; **1Chr** 2:7; 11:19; 13:4; 17:17; 23; 21:3; 7; 8; 26:28; **2Chr** 9:20; 11:4; 16:10; 23:4; 19; 29:36; 30:4; **Ezr** 7:27; 9:3; 10:2; 13; **Neh** 2:19; 13:17; **Est** 2:4; 22; 5:14; 6:13; 8:5; **Job** 3:25; 4:12; 6:8; 21; 9:22; 12:10; 13:28; 14:4; 15:11; 22:28; 23:14; 26:3; 28:10; 11; 33:32; 39:8; 42:2; 7; 8; **Ps** 2:1; 27:4; 33:17; 34:10; 38:20; 69:34; 84:11; 89:34; 92:1; 101:3; 141:4; 145:16; 150:6; **Prov** 4:7; 18:22; 22:18; 25:2; 27:7; **Eccl** 1:9(2); 10; 3:1; 11; 14; 19; 5:2; 6:5; 7:8; 8:1; 3; 5; 15; 9:5; 6; 11:7; 12:14; **Is** 7:13; 15:6; 17:13; 19:7; 29:16; 21; 38:7; 40:15; 41:12; 43:19; 49:6; 52:11; 55:11; 64:6; 66:8; **Jer** 2:10; 19; 5:30; 7:23; 11:13; 14:14; 18:13; 22:4; 23:14; 31:22; 32:27; 33:14; 38:5; 14; 40:3; 16; 42:3; 4; 21; 44:4; 17; **Lam** 2:13(2); **Eze** 8:17; 14:9; 16:47; 34:18; 44:18; 29; 31; 47:9(2); 48:12; **Dan** 2:5; 8; 11; 15; 17; 3:29; 4:33; 5:15; 26; 6:12; 10:1(3); **Hos** 6:10; 8:3; 12; **Amos** 6:13; **Jonah** 3:7; **Mal** 1:14; **Mt** 8:33; 18:19; 19:16; 20:20; 21:24; 24:17; **Mk** 1:27; 4:22; 5:32; 7:18; 9:22; 10:21; 11:13; 13:15; 16:8; 18; **Lk** 1:35; 2:15; 6:9; 8:17; 9:21; 10:42; 12:11; 26; 18:22; 19:8; 20:3; 22:23; 35; **Jn** 1:3; 46; 5:14; 7:4; 9:25; 30; 14:14; 18:34; **Acts** 5:4; 10:14; 28; 12:12; 17:21; 25; 19:32; 39; 21:25; 34; 23:17; 25:8; 11; 26; 26:8; 10; 26; **Rom** 7:18; 8:33; 9:20; 13:6; 8; 14:14; 21; 22; **1Cor** 1:5; 10; 2:2; 3:7; 4:3; 8:2; 7; 9:11; 17; 10:19(2); 14:30; 35; **2Cor** 2:10(2); 3:5; 5:5; 6:3; 17; 7:11; 14; 8:7; 9:11; 10:5; 11:15; 12:8; **Gal** 4:18; 5:6; 6:15; **Eph** 4:28; 5:24; 27; 6:8; **Phil** 1:6; 3:13; 15; 16; 4:6; **1Th** 1:8; 5:18; **2Th** 1:6; **1Ti** 1:10; **2Ti** 1:14; **Titus** 2:8; **Philem** 1:6; **Heb** 10:29; 31; 11:40; 13:9; **Jas** 1:7; **1Pet** 4:12; **2Pet** 3:8; **1Jn** 2:8; 5:14; **Rev** 2:15; 9:4; 21:27

THINGS

1697, *18, 846, 3056, 4229, 4487, 5023*

Gen 7:23; 9:3; 15:1; 20:8; 22:1; 20; 24:1; 28; 53; 66; 29:13; 39:7; 40:1; 42:36; 45:23; 48:1; **Ex** 10:2; 12:36; 23:13; 25:22; 28:38; 29:33; 35; 40:4; **Lev** 2:8; 4:2; 13; 22; 27; 5:2; 5; 15; 17; 8:36; 10:19; 11:23; 29; 42; 14:11; 15:10; 27; 18:24; 20:23; 22:2(2); 3; 4; 6; 7; 12; 15; 16; 26:23; **Num** 1:50; 4:4; 15; 19; 20; 5:9; 10; 15:13; 18:8; 9; 19; 32; 29:39; 31:20; 35:29; **Deut** 1:18; 4:7; 9; 30; 6:11; 10:21; 12:8; 26; 18:12; 22:3; 25:16; 26:13; 28:47; 48; 57; 29:29(2); 30:1; 32:35; 33:13; 14; 15(2); 16; **Josh** 1:17; 2:11; 23; 11:1; 23:14; 15(2); 24:29; **Judg** 13:23(2); 18:27; **Ruth** 4:7; **1Sa** 2:23; 3:12; 17; 12:21; 24; 15:21; 19:7; 25:37; 26:25; **2Sa** 7:21; 23; 11:18; 12:8; 13:21; 14:20; 23:5; 17; 22; 24:12; 23; **1Kin** 4:33; 5:8; 7:51; 15:15(2); 17:17; 18:36; 21:1; 26; **2Kin** 8:4; 11:9; 12:4; 18(2); 14:3; 17:9; 11; 19:29; 20:13; 15; 23:17; 25:15; **1Chr** 4:22; 9:31; 11:19; 24; 17:19; 21:10; 23:13; 28; 26:20; 26; 28:12; 14; 29:2(5); 5(2); 14; 17; 19; **2Chr** 3:3; 4:6; 5:1; 12:12; 15:18; 19:3; 21:3; 23:8; 24:7; 29:33; 31:5; 6; 12; 14; 32:1; **Ezr** 1:6; 2:63; 7:1; 9:1; **Neh** 6:8; 16; 7:65; 9:6; 10:33; 12:47; 13:26; **Est** 2:1; 3; 9(2); 12; 3:1; 5:11; 9:20; **Job** 5:9(2); 6:7; 30; 8:2; 9:10; 10:13; 12:3; 22; 13:20; 26; 14:19; 16:2; 22:18; 23:14; 26:5; 33:29; 37:5; 41:30; 34; 42:3; **Ps** 8:6; 12:3; 15:5; 17:2; 31:18; 35:11; 38:12; 42:4; 45:1; 4; 50:21; 57:2; 60:3; 65:5; 71:19; 72:18; 78:12; 86:10; 87:3; 94:4; 98:1; 103:5; 104:25; 106:21; 22; 107:43; 113:6; 119:18; 128; 126:2; 3; 131:1; 148:10; **Prov** 2:12; 3:15; 6:16; 8:6(2); 11; 15:28; 16:4; 30; 22:20; 23:16; 33; 24:23; 26:10; 28:5; 10; 30:7; 15(2); 18; 21; 24; 29; **Eccl** 1:8; 11(2); 13; 6:11; 7:15; 25; 9:2; 3; 10:19; 11:9; **Is** 12:5; 25:1; 6(2); 29:16; 30:10(2); 32:8(2); 34:1; 38:16(2); 39:2; 40:26; 41:22(2); 23; 42:9(2); 16(2); 20; 43:9; 18(2); 44:7; 9; 24; 45:7; 11; 19; 46:9; 10; 47:7; 9; 13; 48:3; 6(2); 14; 51:19; 56:4; 61:11; 64:3; 11; 12; 65:4; 66:2(2); 8; **Jer** 2:8; 3:5; 7; 4:18; 5:9; 19; 25(2); 29; 8:13; 9:9; 24; 10:16; 13:22; 14:22; 16:18; 19; 17:9; 18:13; 20:1; 5; 21:14; 26:10; 30:15; 31:5; 33:3; 42:5; 44:18; 45:5; 51:19; **Lam** 1:7; 10; 11; 16; 2:14; 5:17; **Eze** 5:11; 7:20; 8:10; 11:5; 18; 21; 25; 16:16; 30; 43; 17:12; 15; 18; 18:10; 20:40; 22:8; 25; 26; 23:30; 24:19; 27:24; 37:23; 38:10; 20; 42:13(2); 14; 44:8; 13; 30; **Dan** 2:10; 22; 40; 7:8; 16; 20; 10:21; 11:36; 38; 43; 12:7; 8; **Hos** 2:18; 8:12; 9:3; 14:9; **Joel** 2:20; 21; 3:5; **Obad** 6(2); **Mic** 7:15; **Hab** 1:14; **Zeph** 1:2; **Zec** 4:10; 8:12; 16; 17; **Mt** 1:20; 2:3; 4:9; 6:8; 32(2); 33; 34; 7:11; 12; 9:18; 11:4; 25; 27; 12:34; 35(2); 13:3; 17(2); 34; 35; 41; 51; 52; 56; 15:18; 20; 16:21; 23; 17:11; 19:20; 26; 21:15; 22; 23; 24; 27; 22:4; 21(2); 23:20; 36; 24:2; 3; 6; 33; 34; 25:21(2); 23(2); 27:13; 19; 54; 28:11; 20; **Mk** 1:44; 2:8; 3:8; 4:2; 11; 19; 34; 5:19; 20; 26; 6:2; 20; 30; 34; 7:4; 8; 13; 15; 23; 37; 8:31; 33(2); 9:9; 12(2); 23; 10:27; 32; 11:11; 23; 24; 28(2); 29; 33; 12:17(2); 13:4(2); 7; 23; 29; 30; 14:36; 15:3; 4; **Lk** 1:1; 3; 4; 20; 45; 49; 53; 2:18; 19; 20; 33; 39; 3:18; 4:28; 5:26; 27; 6:46; 7:9; 18; 22; 8:8; 39(2); 9:9; 22; 36; 43; 10:1; 7; 8; 21; 22; 23; 24(2); 41; 11:27; 41(2); 53(2); 12:15; 20; 30(2); 31; 48; 13:2; 17(2); 14:6; 15; 17; 21; 15:26; 16:14; 25(2); 17:9; 10; 25; 18:22; 27; 31; 34(2); 19:11; 42; 20:2; 8; 25(2); 21:6; 7(2); 9; 22; 26; 28; 31; 36; 22:37; 65; 23:8; 14; 31; 48; 49; 24:9; 10; 14; 18; 19; 21; 26; 27; 35; 44; 48; **Jn** 1:3; 28; 50; 2:16; 18; 3:9; 10; 12(2); 22; 35; 4:25; 29; 45; 5:16; 19; 20; 34; 6:1; 59; 7:1; 4; 32; 8:26(2); 28; 29; 10:6; 41; 11:11; 45; 46; 12:16(3); 36; 41; 13:3; 17; 29; 14:25; 26(2); 15:11; 15; 17; 21; 16:1; 3; 4(2); 6; 12; 13; 15; 25; 30; 33; 17:7; 13; 18:4; 19:24; 28; 36; 20:18; 21:1; 17; 24(2); 25; **Acts** 1:3; 9; 2:44; 3:18; 21; 22; 4:20; 25; 32(2); 34; 5:5; 11; 24; 32; 7:1; 50; 54; 8:6; 12; 24; 9:16; 10:8; 12; 33; 39; 11:6; 18; 22; 12:17; 13:39; 45; 14:15(2); 15:4; 17; 20; 27; 28; 29; 16:14; 17:8; 11; 20(2); 22; 24; 25; 18:1; 17; 25; 19:8; 21; 36; 20:22; 24; 30; 35; 21:12; 19; 24; 25; 22:10; 23:22; 24:8; 9; 13; 14; 22; 25:9; 11; 18; 26:2; 9; 16(2); 22; 26(2); 27:11; 28:10; 24; 31; **Rom** 1:20(2); 23; 28; 30; 32; 2:1; 2; 3; 14; 18; 3:19; 4:17; 6:21(2); 8:5(2); 28; 31; 32; 37; 38(2); 10:5; 15; 11:36; 12:16; 17; 14:2; 18; 19(2); 20; 15:4; 17; 18; 27(2); **1Cor** 1:27(3); 28(4); 2:9; 10(2); 11(2); 12; 13(2); 14; 15; 3:21; 22(2); 4:5; 6; 13; 14; 6:3; 4; 12(3); 7:1; 32; 33; 34(2); 8:1; 4; 6(2); 10; 9:8; 11(2); 12; 13(2); 15(2); 22; 25; 10:6(2); 11; 20; 23(4); 33; 11:2; 12; 13:7(4); 11; 14:7; 26; 37; 40; 15:27(3); 28(2); 16:14; **2Cor** 1:13; 17; 2:9; 16; 4:2; 15; 18(4); 5:10; 17(2); 18; 6:4; 10; 7:11; 14; 16; 8:21; 22; 9:8; 10:7; 13; 15; 16; 11:6; 9; 28; 30; 12:19; 13:10; **Gal** 1:20; 2:18; 3:4; 10; 4:24; 5:17; 21; 6:6; **Eph** 1:10; 11; 22(2); 3:9; 4:10; 15; 5:6; 12; 13; 20; 6:9; 21; **Phil** 1:10; 12; 2:4(2); 10(3); 14; 21; 3:1; 7; 8(2); 13(2); 19; 21; 4:8(7); 9; 12; 13; 18; **Col** 1:16(2); 17(2); 18; 20(3); 2:17; 18; 23; 3:1; 2(2); 14; 20; 22; 4:9; **1Th** 2:14; 5:21; **2Th** 2:5; 3:4; **1Ti** 3:11; 14; 4:6; 8; 11; 15; 5:7; 13; 21; 6:2; 11; 13; 17; **2Ti** 1:12; 18; 2:2; 7; 10; 14; 3:14; 4:5; **Titus** 1:5; 11; 15; 2:1; 3; 7; 9; 10; 15; 3:8(2); **Heb** 1:2; 3; 2:1; 8(2); 10(2); 17(2); 3:4; 5; 4:13; 5:1; 8; 11; 6:9(2); 18; 7:13; 8:1; 5(2); 9:6; 11; 22; 23(2); 10:1(2); 11:1(2); 3(2); 7; 14; 20; 12:24; 27(3); 13:5; 18; **Jas** 2:16; 3:2; 5; 7; 10; 5:12; **1Pet** 1:12(2); 18; 4:7; 8; 11; **2Pet** 1:3; 8; 9; 10; 12; 15; 2:12; 3:4; 11; 14; 16(2); 17; **1Jn** 1:4; 2:1; 15; 20; 26; 27; 3:20; 22; 5:13; **2Jn** 8; 12; **3Jn** 2; 13; **Jude** 10(2); **Rev** 1:1; 2; 3; 19(3); 2:1; 8; 10; 12; 14(2); 18; 20(2); 3:1; 2; 7; 14; 4:1; 11; 7:1; 10:4; 6(3); 13:5; 18:1; 14; 15; 19:1; 20:12; 21:4; 5; 7; 22:6; 8(2); 16; 18; 19; 20

THIS

428, 1791, 1797, 1836, 1931, 1975, 1976, 1977, 1992, 2007, 2008, 2063, 2088, 2090, 2097, 3541, 3602, 3651, 3660, 6311, 6471, *737, 846, 1565, 3278, 3568, 3588, 3592, 3739, 3778, 3779, 4594, 5023, 5026, 5124, 5125, 5126, 5127, 5128, 5129, 5602*

Gen 2:23; 3:13; 14; 4:14; 5:1; 29; 6:15; 7:1; 9:12; 17; 11:6; 12:7; 12; 18; 15:2; 4; 7; 18; 17:10; 21; 18:25; 32; 19:5; 9; 12; 13; 14(2); 20; 21(2); 34; 37; 38; 20:5; 6; 10; 11; 13; 21:10(2); 26; 30; 22:14; 16; 23:19; 24:5; 7; 8; 12; 41; 42; 58; 65; 25:31; 32; 33; 26:3; 10; 11; 33; 28:15; 16; 17(3); 20; 22; 29:25; 27; 33; 34; 30:31; 31:1; 13; 38; 43; 48(2); 51(2); 52(5); 32:2; 10; 19; 32; 33:8; 34:4; 14; 15; 35:17; 20; 36:24; 37:6; 10; 19; 22; 32; 38:21; 22; 23; 28; 29; 39:9(2); 11; 19; 40:12; 14; 18; 41:9; 24; 28; 34; 38; 39; 42:13; 18; 21; 28; 32; 43:10; 11; 29; 44:5; 7; 15; 29; 45:17; 19; 23; 47:23; 26; 48:4; 9; 15; 18; 49:28; 50:11; 20; 24; **Ex** 1:18; 2:6; 9; 12; 14; 15; 3:3; 12(2); 15(2); 21; 4:17; 5:22; 23; 7:17; 23; 8:19; 23; 32; 9:5; 14; 16; 18; 27; 10:6; 7; 17(2); 12:2; 3; 12; 14; 17(2); 24; 25; 26; 42; 43; 13:3(2); 4; 5(2); 8; 10; 14; 14:5; 12; 15:1; 16:3(2); 8; 15; 16; 23; 32; 17:3; 4; 14; 18:14; 18(2); 23(2); 21:31; 25:3; 26:13; 28:17; 29:1; 38; 42; 30:13; 31; 32:1; 9; 12; 13; 21; 23; 24; 29; 31; 33:12; 13; 17; 34:11; 35:4; 37:8; 38:15; 21; 39:10; **Lev** 4:20; 6:9; 14; 20; 25; 7:1; 11; 35; 37; 8:5; 34; 9:6; 10:3; 19; 11:46; 12:7; 13:59; 14:2; 32; 54; 57; 15:3; 32; 16:29; 34; 17:2; 7; 23:27; 34; 24:10; 25:13; 26:16; 18; 27; **Num** 4:4; 24; 28; 31; 33; 5:19; 22; 29; 30; 31; 6:13; 20; 21; 23; 7:17; 23; 29; 35; 41; 47; 53; 59; 65; 71; 77; 83; 84; 88; 8:4; 24; 9:3; 11:6; 11; 12; 13; 14; 31; 13:17; 27; 14:2; 3; 8; 11; 13; 14(2); 15; 16; 19(2); 27; 29; 32; 35(2); 15:13; 16:6; 21; 45; 18:9; 11; 27; 19:2; 14; 20:4; 5; 10; 12; 13; 21:2; 5; 17; 22:1; 4; 6; 8; 17; 19; 24; 30; 23:23; 24:14; 23; 26:9; 27:12; 28:3; 10; 14; 17; 24; 29:7; 30:1; 31:21; 32:5; 15; 19; 20; 22; 32; 34:2; 6; 7; 9; 12; 13; 15; 35:5; 14; 36:6; **Deut** 1:1; 5(2); 6; 10; 31; 32; 35; 2:3; 7; 18; 22; 25; 30; 3:8; 12; 14; 18; 26; 27; 28; 4:4; 6(2); 8(2); 20; 22; 26; 32; 38; 39; 40; 41; 44; 46; 47; 49; 5:1; 3(2); 24; 25; 28; 6:6; 24; 7:11; 8:1; 11; 17; 18; 19; 9:1; 3; 4; 6; 7; 13; 27; 10:8; 13; 15; 11:2; 4; 5; 8; 13; 26; 27; 28; 32; 12:8; 13:11; 18; 15:2; 5; 10; 15; 17:18; 19; 18:3; 16; 19:4; 9; 20:3; 21:7; 20; 22:14; 16; 20; 26; 24:18; 22; 26:3; 9(2); 16; 17; 18; 27:1; 3; 4; 8; 9; 10; 26; 28:1; 13; 14; 15; 58(3); 61; 29:4; 7; 9; 10; 12; 14(2); 15(2); 18; 19; 20; 21; 24(2); 27(2); 28; 29; 30:2; 8; 10; 11(2); 15; 16; 18; 19; 31:2(2); 7; 9; 11; 12; 16; 19(2); 21; 22; 24; 26; 27; 30; 32:27; 29; 34; 44; 46(2); 47; 49; 33:1; 7; 34:4; 6; **Josh** 1:2(2); 4; 6; 8; 11; 13; 14; 15; 2:14; 17; 18; 20; 3:4; 7; 4:3; 6; 9; 22; 5:4; 9(2); 6:25; 26; 7:7; 25; 26(2); 8:20; 22; 28; 29; 33; 9:1; 12; 20; 24; 27; 10:13; 27; 11:6; 12:7; 13:2; 7; 13; 23; 28; 29; 14:10(2); 11; 12; 14; 15:1; 4; 12; 20; 63; 16:8; 10; 18:14; 19; 20; 28; 19:8; 16; 23; 31; 39; 48; 22:3; 7; 16(3); 17; 18; 22; 24; 29; 31(2); 23:8; 9; 13; 14; 15; 24:15; 27; **Judg** 1:21; 26; 2:2(2); 20; 4:14; 6:13; 14; 20; 24; 26; 29(2); 39(2); 7:4(2); 14; 8:9; 9:18; 19; 29; 38; 10:4; 15; 11:27; 37; 12:3; 13:23; 15:6; 7; 11; 18; 19; 16:18; 28; 18:3; 12; 24; 19:11; 23(2); 24; 30; 20:3; 9; 12; 16; 21:3; 6; 11; 22; **Ruth** 1:19; 2:5; 3:13; 18; 4:7(2); 9; 10; 12; 14; **1Sa** 1:3; 27; 2:20; 23; 34; 4:6; 14; 5:5; 6:9; 18; 20; 8:8; 11; 9:6; 13; 16; 17; 24; 10:11; 19; 27; 11:2; 13; 12:2; 5; 8; 16; 19; 20; 14:10; 28; 29; 33; 38(2); 45(2); 15:14; 16; 28; 16:8; 9; 12; 17:10; 17; 25; 26(2); 27; 32; 33; 36; 37; 46(2); 47; 55; 18:21; 24; 20:2; 3; 21; 21:5; 11; 15(2); 22:8; 13; 15; 23:26; 24:6; 10; 16; 18; 19; 25:21; 24; 25; 27; 31; 32; 33; 26:8; 16; 17; 19; 21; 24; 27:6; 28:10; 18(2); 29:3(2); 4; 5; 6; 8; 30:8; 15(2); 20; 24; 25; **2Sa** 1:17; 2:1; 5; 6(2); 3:8(2); 38; 39; 4:3; 8; 6:8; 7:6; 17; 19(2); 27; 28; 8:1; 10:1; 11:3; 11; 25; 12:5; 6; 11; 12; 14; 21; 13:1; 12; 16; 17; 20; 32; 14:3; 13; 15; 19; 20(2); 21; 15:1; 6; 20; 16:9; 11; 12; 17; 18; 17:1; 6; 7; 16; 18:18; 20(2); 31; 19:5(2); 6(3); 7; 14; 20; 21; 22(3); 35; 42; 21:18; 22:1; 23:5; 17(2); 24:3; **1Kin** 1:25; 27; 30; 41; 45; 48; 2:23; 24; 26; 3:6(2); 9; 10; 11; 17; 18; 19; 22; 23; 4:24(2); 5:7(2);

6:12; 7:8; 28; 37; 8:8; 24; 27; 29(2); 30; 31; 33; 35; 38; 42; 43; 54; 61; 9:3; 7; 8(3); 9; 13; 15; 21; 10:12; 11:10; 11; 27; 39; 12:6; 7(2); 9; 10; 19; 24; 27(2); 30; 13:3; 8; 16; 33; 34; 14:2; 15; 17:21; 24; 18:36; 37; 19:2; 20:6; 7; 9; 12; 13(2); 24; 28; 34; 39; 22:20; 27; **2Kin** 1:2; 2:19; 22; 3:16; 18; 23; 4:9; 12; 13; 16; 36; 43; 5:6; 7; 18(2); 20; 6:11; 18; 19(2); 24; 28; 31; 32; 33; 7:1; 2; 9; 18; 8:5(2); 8; 9; 13; 22; 9:1; 11; 25; 26; 27; 34; 36; 37; 10:2; 6; 27; 11:5; 14:7; 10; 15:12; 16:6; 17:12; 23; 34; 41; 18:19; 21; 22; 25(2); 30; 19:3; 21; 29(2); 31; 32; 33; 34; 20:6(2); 9; 17; 21:7; 15; 22:13(2); 16; 17; 19; 20; 23:3(2); 21; 23; 27; 24:3; **1Chr** 4:41; 43; 5:26; 11:11; 19; 13:11; 16:7; 17:5; 15; 17; 19; 26; 18:1; 19:1; 20:4; 21:3; 7; 8; 22; 22:1(2); 26:30; 27:6; 28:7; 8; 19(2); 29:5; 14; 16; 18; **2Chr** 1:10(2); 11; 2:4; 5:9; 6:15; 18; 20(2); 21; 22; 24; 26; 29; 32; 33; 34; 40; 7:12; 15; 16; 20; 21(3); 22; 8:8; 10:6; 7; 9; 19; 11:4; 14:11; 16:10; 18:19; 26; 19:10; 20:1; 2; 7; 9(2); 12; 15; 17; 26; 35; 21:10; 18; 23:4; 24:4; 18; 25:9; 16; 28:22; 29:9; 28; 30:9; 31:1; 10; 32:9; 15; 20; 30; 33:7; 14; 34:21; 24; 25; 27; 28; 31; 35:19; 20; 21; 25; **Ezr** 1:9; 3:12; 4:8; 10; 11(2); 13; 15(2); 16(3); 19; 21; 22; 5:3(3); 4(2); 5; 6(2); 8; 9; 12; 13; 17(2); 6:7(2); 8; 11(2); 12; 13; 15; 16; 17; 7:6; 11; 17; 24; 27; 8:1; 23; 35; 36; 9:2; 3; 7(2); 10; 13; 15(2); 10:2; 4; 5; 9; 13(2); 14; 15; **Neh** 1:11(2); 2:2; 18; 19; 3:7; 5:10; 11; 12; 13(2); 16; 18(2); 19; 6:4; 12; 16; 7:7; 8:9; 10; 9:1; 10; 18; 32; 36; 38; 13:4; 6; 14; 17; 18(2); 22; 27; **Est** 1:1; 17; 18; 4:14(2); 15; 5:4; 13; 6:3; 9; 7:6; 9:4; 13; 21; 26(2); 29; **Job** 1:3; 22; 2:10; 11; 3:1; 4:6; 5:27; 8:19; 9:22; 10:13; 12:9; 13:1; 17:8; 18:21; 19:26; 20:2; 4; 29; 21:2; 27:13; 31:11; 28; 33:12; 34:16; 35:2; 36:21; 37:1; 14; 38:2; 42:16; **Ps** 2:7; 7:3; 11:6; 12:7; 17:14; 18:t, 22:31; 24:6; 8; 10; 27:3; 32:6; 34:6; 35:22; 41:11; 44:17; 21; 48:14; 49:1; 13; 50:22; 51:4; 52:7; 56:9; 62:11; 68:16; 69:31; 32; 71:18; 73:16; 74:2; 18; 77:10; 78:21; 32; 54; 59; 80:14; 81:4; 5; 87:4; 5; 6; 92:6; 95:10; 102:18; 104:25; 109:20; 27; 113:2; 115:18; 118:20; 23; 24; 119:50; 56; 91; 121:8; 132:14; 149:9; **Prov** 6:3; 7:14; 22:19; **Eccl** 1:10; 13; 17; 2:1; 10; 15; 19; 21; 23; 24; 26; 4:4(2); 8; 16; 5:10; 16; 19; 6:2; 5; 9; 12; 7:6; 10; 18(2); 23; 27; 29; 8:9; 10; 14; 9:1(2); 3; 9; 13; 11:6; 12:13; **Song** 3:6; 5:16(2); 7:7; 8:5; **Is** 1:12; 3:6; 5:25; 6:7; 9; 10; 8:6; 11; 12; 20; 9:5; 7; 12; 16; 17; 21; 10:4; 12:5; 14:4; 16; 26(2); 28; 16:13; 17:14; 20:6; 22:14; 15; 23:7; 8; 13; 24:3; 25:6; 7; 9(2); 10; 26:1; 27:9(2); 28:11; 12(2); 14; 29; 29:11; 12; 13; 14; 30:7; 9; 12; 13; 21; 36:4; 6; 7; 10(2); 15; 37:3; 22; 30(2); 32; 33; 34; 35; 38:6(2); 7(2); 19; 39:6; 41:20; 42:22; 23; 43:9; 21; 45:21; 46:8; 47:8; 48:1; 6(2); 16; 20; 50:11; 51:21; 54:9; 17; 56:2; 12; 58:4; 5; 6; 59:21; 63:1(2); 66:2; 14; **Jer** 1:10; 18; 2:12; 17; 3:4; 10; 25; 4:8; 10; 11; 18; 28; 5:7; 9; 14(2); 20; 21; 23; 29; 6:6; 19; 21; 7:2; 3; 6; 7; 10; 11; 14; 16; 20; 23; 25; 28; 33; 8:3; 5; 9:9; 12; 15; 24; 10:18; 19; 11:2; 3; 5; 6; 7; 8; 14; 13:9; 10(2); 12; 13; 25; 14:10; 11; 13; 15; 17; 15:1; 20; 16:2; 3(2); 5; 6; 9; 10(2); 13; 21; 17:24; 25(2); 18:6; 19:3; 4(2); 6; 7; 8; 11(2); 12(2); 15; 20:5; 21:4; 6; 7; 8; 9; 10; 22:1; 3; 4(2); 5; 8(2); 11; 12; 16; 21; 28; 30; 23:6; 26; 32; 33; 38; 24:5; 6; 8; 25:3; 9; 11; 13; 15; 18; 26:1; 6(2); 9(2); 11(2); 12(2); 15; 16; 20(2); 27:1; 16; 17; 19; 22; 28:3(2); 4; 6; 7; 15; 16; 29:10; 16; 28; 29; 32; 30:17; 21; 31:23; 26; 33; 32:3; 8; 14(2); 15; 20(2); 22; 23; 28; 29(2); 31(2); 35; 36; 37; 41; 42(2); 43; 33:4; 5; 10; 12; 16; 24; 34:2; 8; 22; 35:14; 16; 36:1; 2; 7; 29(2); 37:8; 10; 18; 19; 38:2; 3; 4(4); 16; 17; 18; 21; 23; 39:16; 40:2(2); 3; 4; 16; 42:2; 10; 13; 18; 19; 21; 44:2; 4; 6; 7; 10; 22; 23(2); 29(2); 45:4; 46:7; 10; 50:17; 25; 51:6; 59; 62; 63; 52:28; **Lam** 2:15; 16; 20; 3:21; 5:17; **Eze** 1:5; 23; 28; 2:3; 3:1; 3; 4:3; 5:5; 6:10; 8:5; 15; 17; 10:15; 20; 11:2; 3; 6; 7; 11; 15; 12:10; 23; 16:20; 43; 44; 49; 17:7; 18:2; 3; 19:14; 20:27; 29; 31; 21:11; 26; 23:11; 38; 24:2(2); 24; 31:18; 32:16; 33:33; 36:22; 32; 35; 37; 39:8; 40:10(2); 12(2); 21; 26; 34; 37; 39; 41; 45; 48(2); 49; 41:4; 22; 43:12(2); 13; 44:2; 45:1; 2; 3; 13; 16; 46:3; 20; 47:6; 12; 13; 14; 15; 17; 18; 19; 20; 21; 48:10; 12; 29; **Dan** 1:14; 2:12; 18; 30; 31; 32; 36; 38; 47; 3:16; 29; 4:17; 18; 24(2); 28; 30; 5:7; 15; 22; 24; 25; 26; 6:3; 5; 28; 7:6; 7; 8; 16; 24; 8:16; 9:7; 13; 15; 10:8; 11; 17(2); 11:18; 12:5; **Hos** 5:1; 7:10; 16; **Joel** 1:2(2); 3:9; **Amos** 3:1; 4:1; 5; 12; 5:1; 7:3; 6(2); 8:4; 8; 9:12; **Obad** 20; **Jonah** 1:7; 8; 10; 12; 14; 4:2; **Mic** 1:5; 2:3(2); 10; 11; 3:9; 5:5; **Hab** 1:11; **Zeph** 1:4; 2:10; 15; **Hag** 1:2; 4; 2:3; 7; 9(2); 14(2); 15; 18; 19; **Zec** 2:4; 3:2; 4:6; 9; 5:3(2); 5; 6(2); 7; 8; 6:15; 8:6; 11; 12; 14:12; 15; 19; **Mal** 1:9; 13; 2:1; 4; 12; 13; 3:9; 4:3; **Mt** 1:18; 22; 3:3; 17; 6:9; 11; 7:12; 8:9(2); 27; 9:3; 28; 10:23; 11:10; 14; 16; 23; 12:6; 7; 23; 24; 32; 41; 42; 45; 13:15; 19; 22; 28; 40; 54(2); 55; 56; 14:2; 15; 15:8; 11; 12; 15; 16:18; 22; 17:5; 20; 21; 18:4; 19:5; 11; 26; 20:14; 21:4; 10; 11; 21(2); 23; 38; 42; 44; 22:20; 33; 38; 23:36; 24:14; 21; 34; 43; 26:8; 9; 12; 13(3); 26; 28; 29; 31; 34; 39; 42; 56; 61; 71; 27:8; 19; 24; 37; 47; 54; 28:14; 15(2); **Mk** 1:27(2); 2:7; 12; 4:13; 19; 41; 5:32; 39; 6:2(2); 3; 35; 7:6; 29; 8:12(2); 38; 9:7; 21; 29; 10:5; 7; 30; 11:3; 23; 28; 12:7; 10; 11; 16; 30; 31; 43; 13:19; 30; 14:4; 9(2); 22; 24; 27; 30(2); 36; 58; 69; 71; 15:39; **Lk** 1:18; 29; 34; 36; 43; 61; 66; 2:2; 11; 12; 15; 17; 34; 3:20; 4:3; 6; 21(2); 22; 23; 36; 5:6; 21; 6:3; 7:4; 8; 17; 27; 31; 39(2); 44; 45; 46; 49; 8:9; 11; 14; 25; 9:9; 13; 35; 45; 48; 54; 10:5; 11; 20; 28; 11:29; 30; 31; 32; 50; 51; 12:18; 20; 39; 41; 56; 13:6; 7; 8; 16(2); 14:9; 30; 15:2; 3; 24; 30; 32; 16:2; 8; 24; 26; 28; 17:6; 18; 25; 18:1; 5; 9; 11; 14; 23; 30; 34; 19:9(2); 14; 42; 20:2; 9; 14; 17; 19; 34; 21:3; 23; 32; 34; 22:15; 17; 19(2); 20; 23; 34; 37; 42; 53; 56; 59; 23:2; 4; 5; 14(2); 18; 38; 41; 47; 52; 24:21; **Jn** 1:15; 19; 30; 34; 2:11; 12; 19; 20; 22; 3:19; 29; 4:13; 15; 20; 21; 27; 29; 42; 54; 5:1; 28; 6:6; 14; 29; 34; 39; 40; 42; 50; 51; 52; 58(2); 60(2); 61; 7:8(2); 15; 25; 26; 27; 31; 36; 39; 40(2); 41; 46; 49; 8:4; 6; 23(2); 40; 9:2; 3; 8; 9; 16; 19; 20; 24; 29; 33; 39; 10:6; 16; 18; 41; 11:4; 9; 26; 37(2); 39; 47; 51; 12:5; 6; 7; 18(2); 25; 27(3); 30; 31(2); 33; 34; 13:1; 28; 35; 14:30; 15:12; 13; 25; 16:11; 17; 18; 30; 17:3; 18:17; 29; 34; 36(2); 37(2); 38; 40; 19:12; 20; 28; 38; 20:22; 30; 21:1; 14; 19(2); 21; 23; 24; **Acts** 1:6; 11; 16; 17; 18; 25; 2:6; 12; 14; 16; 29; 31; 32; 33; 37; 40; 3:12(2); 16(2); 4:7; 9; 10; 11; 17; 22; 5:4; 20; 24; 28(2); 37; 38(2); 6:3; 13(2); 14(2); 7:4; 6; 7; 29; 35; 37; 38; 40; 60(2); 8:10; 19; 21; 22; 29; 32; 34; 9:2; 13; 21(2); 22; 36; 10:16; 17; 30; 11:10; 13:17; 23; 26; 33; 34; 38; 48; 15:2; 6; 15; 16; 23; 16:18; 36; 17:3; 18; 19; 23; 30; 32; 18:10; 13; 18; 21; 25; 19:5; 10; 17; 25; 26; 27; 40(2); 20:26; 29; 21:11; 23; 28(3); 22:3(2); 4; 22; 26; 28; 23:1; 9; 13; 17; 18; 25; 27; 24:2; 5; 10; 14; 21(2); 25; 25:5; 24; 26:2; 16; 22; 26; 29; 31; 32; 27:10; 21; 23; 33; 34; 28:4; 9; 20(2); 22; 26; 27; **Rom** 1:26; 2:3; 3:26; 4:9; 5:2; 6:6; 7:24; 8:18; 9:9(2); 10; 17; 10:6; 11:5; 8; 25; 27; 12:2; 13:6(2); 9(2); 14:9; 13; 15:9; 28(2); 16:22; **1Cor** 1:12; 20(2); 2:6(2); 8; 3:12; 18; 19; 4:11; 13; 17; 5:2; 3; 10; 6:3; 4; 7:6; 7; 26; 29; 31(2); 35; 8:7; 9; 9:3; 10; 12(2); 17; 23; 10:28; 11:10; 17; 20; 22; 24(2); 25(2); 26(2); 27(2); 30; 14:21; 15:6; 19; 34; 50; 53(2); 54(2); 16:12; **2Cor** 1:12; 15; 2:1; 3; 6; 9; 3:10; 14; 15; 4:1; 4; 7; 5:1; 2; 4; 7:3; 11(2); 8:5; 7; 10; 14; 19; 20(2); 9:3; 4; 6; 12; 13; 10:7; 11; 11:10; 17; 12:8; 13; 13:1; 9; **Gal** 1:4; 3:2; 17; 4:25; 5:8; 14; 16; 6:16; **Eph** 1:21; 2:2; 3:1; 8; 14; 4:17; 5:5; 31; 32; 6:1; 12; **Phil** 1:6; 7; 9; 19; 22; 25; 2:5; 3:13; 15; **Col** 1:9; 27; 2:4; 3:20; 4:16; **1Th** 2:13; 3:5; 4:3; 15; 5:18; 27; **2Th** 1:11; 2:11; 3:10; 14; **1Ti** 1:9; 15; 16; 18; 2:3; 3:1; 4:9; 16; 6:7; 14; 17; **2Ti** 1:15; 2:4; 19; 3:1; 6; 4:10; **Titus** 1:5; 13; 2:12; 3:8; **Heb** 1:5; 3:3; 4:4; 5; 5:4; 6:3; 7:1; 4; 21; 24; 27; 8:1; 3; 10; 9:8; 11; 15; 20; 27; 10:12; 16; 11:5; 12:27; 13:19; **Jas** 1:3; 25; 26; 27; 2:5; 3:15; 4:15; **1Pet** 1:25; 2:19; 20; 3:5; 4:6; 16; 5:12; **2Pet** 1:5; 13; 14; 17; 18; 20; 3:1; 3; 5; 8; **1Jn** 1:5; 2:25; 3:3; 8; 10; 11; 17; 23; 4:3; 9; 17; 21; 5:2; 3; 4; 6; 9; 11(2); 14; 20; **2Jn** 6(2); 7; 10; **Jude** 4; 5; **Rev** 1:3; 2:6; 24; 4:1; 7:9; 11:5; 15; 18:18; 20:5; 14; 22:7; 9; 10; 18(2); 19(2)

THOSE

411, 428, 479, 582, 1768, 1931, 1992, 1994, 2007, 2088, *846, 1565, 3588, 3745, 5023, 5025, 5125, 5130*

Gen 6:4; 15:17; 19:25; 24:60; 33:5; 41:35; 42:5; 50:3; **Ex** 2:11; 4:21; 29:33; 35:35; **Lev** 11:27; 14:11; 42; 15:10; 27; 22:2; **Num** 1:21; 22; 23; 25; 27; 29; 31; 33; 35; 37; 39; 41; 43; 44; 45; 2:4; 5; 6; 8; 11; 12; 13; 15; 19; 21; 23; 26; 27; 28; 30; 32(2); 3:22(2); 34; 38; 43; 46; 4:36; 38; 40; 42; 44; 45; 46; 48; 9:7; 13:3; 14:22; 37; 18:16; 25:9; 26:18; 22; 25; 27; 34; 37; 43; 47; 54; 62; 33:55; **Deut** 7:22; 17:9; 18:9; 19:5; 17; 20; 26:3; 29:3; 29; 32:21; **Josh** 3:16; 4:20; 10:22; 23; 24; 11:1; 10; 12; 18; 17:12; 20:4; 6; 21:16; 24:17; **Judg** 2:16; 23; 7:8; 11:13; 12:5; 17:6; 18:1(2); 19:1; 20:27; 28; 21:25; **1Sa** 3:1; 7:16; 10:9; 11:6; 17:11; 28; 18:23; 19:7; 25:9; 12; 27:8; 28:1; 3; 9; 30:9; 20; 22; **2Sa** 5:14; 16:23; **1Kin** 2:7; 3:2; 4:27; 8:4; 9:21; 21:27; **2Kin** 4:4; 6:22; 10:32; 15:37; 17:9; 18:4; 20:1; 24:15; **1Chr** 4:23; 16:42; **2Chr** 14:6; 15:5; 17:19; 20:29; 32:13; 14; 24; **Ezr** 1:8; 2:1; 62; 3:3; 5:9; 14; 7:19; 8:35; 9:2; 4; 10:3; 8; **Neh** 4:17; 5:17; 6:17; 7:6; 64; 8:3; 10:1; 13:15; 23; **Est** 1:2; 2:21(2); 3:9; 9:5; 11; **Job** 5:11(2); 21:22; 24:13; 19; 27:15; **Ps** 5:11; 13:4; 17:7; 18:30; 39; 48; 21:8; 37:9; 40:16; 50:5; 61:5; 63:9; 68:6; 11; 69:6; 26; 70:4; 74:23; 79:11; 92:13; 102:20; 103:18; 106:46; 109:31; 119:79(2); 132; 123:4; 125:4; 139:21; 140:9; 143:3; 145:14; 147:11; **Prov** 1:12; 4:22; 8:17; 21; 22:23; 24:11; 26:28; 31:6; **Eccl** 1:11; 5:14; 7:28; 8:8; 12:3; **Song** 7:9; 8:12; **Is** 14:19; 27:7; 35:8; 38:1; 40:11; 56:8; 60:12; 64:5(2); 66:2(2); 19; **Jer** 3:16; 18; 4:12; 5:18; 8:16; 14:15; 21:7; 27:11; 31:29; 33; 36; 33:15; 16; 38:22; 39:9; 46:26; 49:5; 36; 50:4; 20; 52:15; **Lam** 2:22; 3:62; **Eze** 1:21(3); 18:11; 22:5(2); 28:26; 33:24; 34:27; 38:17; 39:10(2); 14; 40:25; 42:14; **Dan** 3:22; 4:37; 6:24; 10:2; 11:4; 14; **Joel** 2:16; 29; 3:1; **Obad** 14(2); **Zeph** 1:6; 9; **Hag** 2:16; 22; **Zec** 3:4; 4:10; 7:5; 8:23; 11:16; 13:6; 14:3; **Mal** 3:5; **Mt** 3:1; 4:24(3); 11:4; 13:17(2); 15:18; 30; 16:23; 21:40; 41; 22:7; 10; 24:19; 22(2); 29; 25:7; 19; 27:54; **Mk** 1:9; 44; 2:20; 6:55; 7:15; 8:1; 10:13; 11:23; 12:7; 13:17; 19; 20; 24; **Lk** 1:1; 4; 24; 39; 45; 2:1; 18; 33; 4:2; 5:35; 6:12; 32; 7:28; 8:12; 9:36(2); 10:24(2); 12:20; 37; 38; 13:4; 14:7; 24; 17:10; 19:27; 20:1; 21:23; 26; 23:14; **Jn** 2:14; 6:14; 8:10; 26; 29; 31; 10:32; 13:29; 17:11; 12; **Acts** 1:15; 2:18; 3:18; 24; 6:1; 7:41; 8:6; 9:37; 13:45; 16:3; 35; 17:11(2); 18:17; 20:2; 21:5; 15; 24; 26:16; 22; 27:11; 28:31; **Rom** 1:28; 4:17; 6:13; 21(2); 10:5; 15:17; 18; **1Cor** 8:4; 10; 12:22; 23; 14:23; **2Cor** 7:6; 11:28; **Eph** 5:12; **Phil** 3:7; 13(2); 4:3; 9; **Col** 2:18; 3:1; **1Ti** 4:10; 5:8; **2Ti** 2:25; 3:3; **Heb** 3:5; 5:14; 6:4; 7:21; 27; 8:10; 10:1; 3; 16; 12:27(2); 13:11; **Jas** 2:16; **2Pet** 2:6; 18; **1Jn** 3:22; **2Jn** 8; **Jude** 10(2); **Rev** 1:3; 2:10; 13; 4:9; 9:4; 6; 10:4; 13:14; 20:12

THOU

859, *4771*

Gen 2:16; 17(3); 3:9; 11(3); 12; 13; 14(4); 15; 16; 17(3); 18; 19(5); 4:6; 7(4); 10; 11; 12(2); 14; 6:14; 15; 16(4); 18(2); 19; 21(2); 7:1; 2; 8:16; 10:19(2); 30; 12:1; 11; 13; 18(2); 19; 13:9(2); 10; 14; 15; 14:23; 15:2; 3; 5; 15(2); 16:8(2); 11; 13; 17:1; 4; 8; 9(2); 15; 19; 18:5; 15; 23; 24; 28; 19:12(2); 15; 17(2); 19(2); 21; 22; 34; 20:3(2); 4; 6; 7(5); 9(3); 10(2); 13; 21:22; 23(3); 26; 29; 30; 22:2; 12(3); 16; 18; 23:6(2); 13; 24:3; 4; 5; 6(2); 7; 8; 14(2); 23; 31(2); 37; 38; 40; 41(3); 42; 44; 47; 58; 60(2); 25:18; 26:9; 10(2); 16; 29(2); 27:10; 18; 19; 20; 21; 24; 32; 33; 36; 38; 40(3); 43; 45; 28:1; 3; 4(2); 6; 13; 14; 15; 22; 29:14; 15(2); 25(2); 27; 30:15(2); 16; 26; 29; 30; 31(2); 31:13(2); 24; 26(2); 27; 28; 29(2); 30(3); 31; 32(2); 36; 37(2); 39; 41; 42; 43; 44(2); 50(2); 52; 32:10; 12; 17(2); 18; 26; 28; 29; 33:8; 9; 10; 35:1; 17; 37:8(2); 10; 15; 38:16(2); 17(2); 23; 29; 39:9; 17; 40:13(2); 41:15; 39; 40(2); 43:4; 5; 8; 9; 44:4; 18; 21; 23; 45:10(4); 11(2); 19; 46:30; 47:6; 8; 25; 30(2); 48:6; 49:3; 4(3); 6(2); 8; 9; 50:5; **Ex** 2:13; 14(2); 3:5; 10; 12; 14; 15; 18(2); 4:9(2); 10; 12; 13; 15; 16; 17(2); 21(2); 22; 23; 25; 26; 5:15; 22(2); 23; 6:1; 29; 7:2; 9; 15(2); 16(2); 17; 8:2; 10; 21; 22; 9:2; 14; 15; 17(2); 19; 29; 10:2; 3; 4; 7; 25; 28(2); 29; 12:44; 46; 13:5; 6; 8; 10; 12(2); 13(4); 14; 14:11(2); 15; 16; 15:7(2); 10; 12; 13(3); 16; 17(2); 26; 17:3; 5; 6; 18:14(2); 17; 18(3); 19(2); 20; 21; 23(2); 19:3; 6; 12; 23; 24(2); 20:3; 4; 5; 7; 9; 10(2); 13; 14; 15; 16; 17(2); 19; 22; 24; 25(4); 26; 21:1; 2; 14; 23; 22:18; 21; 23; 25(3); 26(2); 28; 29(2); 30(2); 23:1; 3; 4(2); 5(2); 6; 7; 8; 9; 10; 11(2); 12(2); 14; 15(3); 16(2); 18; 19(2); 22; 24(2); 27; 30; 31; 32; 33; 24:1; 12; 25:11(2); 12; 13; 14; 16; 17; 18(2); 21(2); 23; 24; 25(2); 26; 28; 29(2); 30; 31; 37; 40; 26:1(2); 4(2); 5(2); 6; 7(2); 9; 10; 11; 14; 15; 17; 18; 19; 22; 23; 26; 29(2); 30; 31; 32; 33(2); 34; 35(2); 36; 37(2); 27:1; 2(2); 3(2); 4(2); 5; 6; 8; 9; 20; 28:1; 2; 3; 9; 11(2); 12; 13; 14; 15(3); 17; 22; 23; 24; 25; 26(2); 27; 30; 31; 33; 36; 37; 39(3); 40(3); 41; 42; 29:1; 2; 3; 4; 5; 6; 7; 8; 9(2); 10; 11; 12; 13; 14; 15; 16(2); 17; 18; 19; 20; 21; 22; 24; 25; 26; 27; 31; 34; 35(2); 36(4); 37; 38; 39(2); 41; 30:1(2); 3(2); 4(2); 5; 6; 12(3); 16; 18(3); 23; 25; 26; 29; 30; 31; 35; 36; 37; 31:13; 32:7; 11; 13; 21; 22; 32(2); 33:1(2); 3; 12(5); 16; 17(2); 20; 21; 23; 34:1; 10; 11; 12(2); 14; 15(2); 16; 17; 18(3); 20(4); 21(3); 22; 24; 25; 26(2); 27; 40:2; 3; 4(2); 5; 6; 7; 8; 9; 10; 11; 12; 13; 14; 15(2); **Lev** 2:4; 6; 8; 13(3); 14(2); 15; 6:21(2); 27; 8:3; 9:3; 10:9; 14; 13:55; 57; 58; 17:8; 18:7(2); 8; 9; 10; 11; 12; 13; 14(2); 15(2); 16; 17(2); 18; 19; 20; 21(2); 22; 23; 19:9(2); 10(3); 12; 13; 14; 15(2); 16(2); 17(2); 18(2); 19(2); 27; 32; 34; 20:2; 16; 19; 21:8; 22:23; 23:22(4); 24:5; 6; 7; 15; 25:3(2); 4; 5; 8; 9; 14; 15; 16(2); 17; 35; 36; 37; 39; 43; 44; 27:12; **Num** 1:3; 49; 50; 3:9; 10; 15; 41; 47(2); 48; 4:23; 29; 30; 5:19(2); 20(2); 7:5; 8:2; 7; 8; 9(2); 10; 12; 13; 14; 15; 26; 10:2(2); 29; 31(2); 32; 11:11(2); 12(2); 15; 16; 17; 18; 21; 23; 29; 13:2; 27; 14:13; 14(3); 15; 17; 19; 15:5; 6; 7; 8; 10; 16:11; 13(2); 14(2); 15; 16(2); 17; 22; 37; 17:2; 3; 4; 10; 18:1(2); 2(2); 7; 10; 15(2); 16; 17(2); 20(2); 30; 20:8(4); 14; 18; 20; 21:2; 29; 34(2); 22:6(2); 12(2); 17; 20; 28; 29; 30; 32; 34; 35; 37; 23:5; 11(2); 13(2); 18; 27; 24:10; 11; 12; 21; 26:54(2); 27:7(2); 8; 13(2); 20; 28:3; 4(2); 7; 8(2); 21; 31:2; 26; 30; **Deut** 1:14; 31; 37; 2:4; 7; 18; 19; 28; 31; 37; 3:2(2); 21; 24; 27; 28; 4:9; 10; 19(2); 25; 29(3); 30(2); 33; 35; 36; 38; 40(2); 5:7; 8; 9; 11; 13; 14(3); 15; 17; 18; 19; 20; 21(2); 27(2); 31(2); 6:2(2); 5; 7(5); 8; 9; 10; 11(4); 12; 13; 18(2); 21; 7:1(2); 2(2); 3(3); 6; 11; 14; 15; 16(2); 17; 18; 19; 21; 22; 24(2); 25(2); 26(4); 8:2(2); 3; 5; 6; 9(3); 10(2); 11; 12; 13; 14; 17; 18; 19; 9:1; 2(2); 3; 4; 5; 6; 7(2); 12; 26(2); 28; 29; 10:2(2); 20(3); 11:1; 10(2); 14; 15; 19(4); 20; 29(2); 12:5; 13(2); 14(2); 15; 17(2); 18(4); 19(2); 20(2); 21(2); 22; 23(2); 24(2); 25(2); 26(2); 27(2); 28; 29(2); 30(2); 31; 32; 13:2; 3; 5; 6(2); 8(3); 9; 10; 12; 14; 15; 16; 18; 14:2; 3; 21(4); 22; 23(2); 24; 25; 26(4); 27; 28; 29; 15:1; 3; 5; 6(3); 7; 8; 9; 10(3); 11; 12; 13(2); 14(2); 15(2); 17(2); 18(2); 19(2); 20(2); 21; 22; 23(2); 16:2; 3(5); 4; 5; 6(2); 7(2); 8(2); 9(2); 10(2); 11(2); 12(3); 13(2); 14(2); 15(2); 18; 19(2); 20(2); 21(2); 22; 17:1; 4; 5; 7; 8; 9; 10(2); 11(2); 12; 14; 15(3); 18:4; 9(2); 13; 14; 16; 21; 22; 19:1; 2; 3; 7; 9(2); 13; 14(2); 19; 20:1(2); 10; 12; 13; 14(2); 15; 16; 17; 19(4); 20(3); 21:8; 9(2); 10(2); 11; 12; 13; 14(5); 21; 22; 23; 22:1(2); 2(3); 3(5); 4(2); 6; 7(2); 8(3); 9(2); 10; 11; 12(2); 21; 22; 24; 26; 23:6; 7(3); 12(2); 13(3); 15; 16; 18; 19; 20(4); 21(2); 22; 23(3); 24(3); 25(3); 24:4; 7; 8; 10(2); 11(2); 12; 13; 14; 15; 17; 18(2); 19(2); 20(2); 21(2); 22(2); 25:4; 12; 13; 14; 15(2); 18; 19(2); 26:1; 2(2); 3; 5; 10(2); 11(2); 12; 13(2); 14; 15(2); 16; 17; 18; 19; 27:2; 3(3); 4; 5(2); 6(2); 7; 8; 9; 10; 28:1; 2;

3(2); 6(4); 8; 9; 10; 12(2); 13(3); 14; 15; 16(2); 19(4); 20(4); 21; 22; 24; 25; 27; 29(3); 30(4); 31(2); 33(2); 34(2); 36(3); 37; 38; 39; 40(2); 41(2); 43; 44(2); 45(2); 47; 48; 49; 51; 52; 53; 58(2); 60; 61; 62; 63; 64(2); 65; 66; 67(4); 68; 29:12; 30:1; 2; 5; 6; 8; 10(2); 12; 13; 14; 16(2); 17; 18; 19; 20(4); 31:2; 3; 7(2); 11; 14; 16; 23; 32:14; 15(3); 18; 50; 52(2); 33:7; 8(2); 23; 29(2); 34:4; **Josh** 1:2; 6; 7(4); 8(4); 9(2); 16(2); 18; 2:17; 18(3); 20(2); 3:8; 5:13; 15; 6:3; 7:7; 9; 10; 13; 19; 25; 8:1; 2(2); 10:12(2); 11:6; 13:1; 6; 14:6; 9; 12; 15:18; 19; 17:14; 15; 17(2); 18(2); **Judg** 1:14; 15; 4:8(2); 9; 20; 22; 5:4(2); 12; 16; 21; 6:4; 12; 14; 16; 17; 18; 23; 26; 36(2); 37(2); 7:5; 10(2); 11; 8:1(3); 18; 21; 22(3); 9:8; 10; 12; 14; 32; 33(3); 36; 38(2); 10:15; 11:2(2); 8; 12(2); 23; 24; 25; 27; 30; 33; 35(2); 36; 12:1; 5; 13:3(2); 5; 7; 8; 11; 16(3); 18; 14:3; 16(2); 15:2; 11(2); 18; 16:6; 10(2); 13(3); 15(2); 17:2(2); 9; 18:3(2); 19; 23; 25; 19:9; 17(2); **Ruth** 1:15; 16(2); 17; 2:8; 9(2); 10; 11(3); 12; 13(2); 14; 19(2); 21; 22; 3:2; 4(3); 5; 9(2); 10(3); 11(2); 15; 16; 18; 4:4(2); 5(2); 6; 11; **1Sa** 1:8(2); 11; 14; 17; 23; 2:16; 32; 3:5; 6; 8; 9; 17; 4:20; 8:5; 9:16; 21; 27; 10:2(3); 3(2); 4; 5(3); 6; 7; 8(3); 12:4(2); 13:11(2); 13(2); 14; 14:37; 43; 44; 15:1; 7; 13; 17(2); 19; 23; 26; 28; 16:1; 3(2); 4; 16; 17:28(4); 33(2); 43; 45(2); 52; 56; 58(2); 18:17; 21; 19:3; 5(2); 11(2); 17; 20:2; 8(3); 13; 14; 15; 18; 19(3); 21; 23; 30(2); 31; 21:1; 9(2); 22:12; 13(2); 16(2); 18; 23(2); 23:17; 24:4; 9; 11(2); 14; 17(2); 18(3); 19; 20; 21(2); 25:6; 7; 17; 25; 31; 33; 34; 26:11; 14(2); 15(2); 16; 25(2); 27:8; 28:1(3); 2; 9(2); 12(2); 13; 15(2); 16; 18; 19; 21; 22(3); 29:4; 6; 7; 8; 9; 30:8; 13(2); 15(2); **2Sa** 1:3; 5; 8; 13; 14; 25; 26; 2:20; 26(2); 27; 3:7; 8; 13(3); 21; 24(2); 25(2); 34; 5:2(3); 6(2); 19; 23; 24(2); 25; 6:22; 7:5; 8; 9; 12; 18; 19; 20; 21; 22; 23; 24(2); 25(2); 27; 28(2); 29; 9:2; 7; 8; 10(2); 10:3; 11; 11:10(2); 11; 19; 21; 25(2); 12:7; 9(2); 10; 12; 13; 14; 21(3); 13:4(2); 12; 13; 16; 14:11; 13; 15:2; 19(2); 20(2); 27; 33(2); 34(2); 35(3); 16:2; 7(2); 8(3); 10; 17; 21; 17:3; 6; 8; 11; 18:3(3); 11(2); 13; 20(3); 21; 22(2); 19:5; 6(3); 7; 13(2); 14; 19; 23; 25; 28; 29(2); 33; 38; 20:4; 6; 9; 17; 19(2); 21:4; 17(2); 22:3; 26(2); 27(2); 28(2); 29; 36; 37; 40(2); 41; 44(2); 49(2); 24:13; **1Kin** 1:6; 11; 12; 13; 14; 16; 17; 18; 20(2); 24; 27; 42; 2:2; 3(3); 5; 8; 9(3); 13; 15; 22; 26(3); 31; 37(3); 42(3); 43; 44(2); 3:6(3); 7; 8; 11; 13; 14; 5:3; 6(3); 8; 9(3); 6:12(2); 8:18; 19; 24(2); 25(2); 26; 28; 29(2); 30(3); 32; 34(2); 35; 36(3); 39(4); 40; 43; 44(2); 45; 46; 48(2); 49; 51; 53(3); 9:3(2); 4; 13; 11:11; 22(2); 37; 38; 12:4; 7; 10(3); 13:8; 9; 14; 17(2); 18; 21; 14:2; 5; 6(2); 8; 9; 12; 16:2; 17:4; 13; 18(2); 20; 24; 18:7; 9; 11; 14; 17; 18(2); 36; 37(2); 19:9; 13; 15; 16(2); 20:5; 9; 13(2); 14; 22; 25; 34; 36(2); 39; 42; 21:5; 7; 10; 19(3); 20(2); 22; 29; 22:4(2); 11(2); 16; 19; 22; 25(2); 28; 30; **2Kin** 1:4(2); 6(3); 9; 16(3); 2:3; 5; 10(2); 23(2); 3:7(2); 4:1; 2; 4(3); 7; 13(2); 16(2); 23; 29; 40; 5:6; 8; 10; 13; 25; 6:9; 12; 22(3); 7:2; 19; 8:1(2); 10; 12(3); 13; 14; 9:2; 7; 18; 19; 25; 10:5(2); 30; 13:17(2); 19(4); 14:10(4); 17:26; 18:14; 19; 20(3); 21; 23; 24; 19:6; 10; 11(2); 15(3); 19(3); 20; 22(2); 23; 25(2); 28; 20:1; 5; 9; 18; 19; 22:18; 19(2); 20; 23:17; **1Chr** 4:10(2); 11:2(3); 5; 12:18; 14:10; 15(2); 17:4; 7(2); 8; 11; 16; 17; 18; 19; 21; 22(2); 23(2); 25(2); 26; 27; 19:3; 12; 21:22; 22:8(3); 11; 12; 13(2); 14; 28:3(2); 9(4); 20; 29:10; 11; 12; 17; **2Chr** 1:8; 9; 11(2); 2:3; 16(2); 6:8; 9; 15(2); 16(2); 17; 20(2); 21(2); 23; 25(2); 26; 27(3); 30(3); 31; 33; 34(2); 35; 36; 38(2); 39; 41; 7:17; 9:6; 10:4; 7; 10(3); 13:4; 14:11; 16:7; 8; 9(2); 18:3(2); 10; 12; 15; 21(2); 24(2); 27; 29; 33; 19:2; 3; 20:6(2); 7; 9; 10; 11; 12; 15; 37; 21:12; 15; 24:6; 25:8; 15; 16(3); 19(5); 26:18; 34:26; 27(2); 28; 35:21; **Ezr** 4:13; 15; 16; 7:14; 16; 17; 19; 20; 25; 9:11; 13; 14(2); 15; 10:12; **Neh** 1:6; 7; 8; 10; 2:2; 4; 5; 6; 5:12; 6:6(3); 7; 8(2); 14; 9:6(4); 7; 8; 10(2); 11(2); 12; 13; 15; 17(2); 19; 20; 21; 22; 23(2); 24; 27(3); 28(3); 29; 30(2); 31(2); 33(2); 34; 35(2); 36; 37; **Est** 3:3; 4:13; 14(3); 5:3; 14(2); 6:10(2); 13(2); **Job** 1:7; 8; 10(2); 2:2; 3(2); 9; 10; 4:2; 3(2); 4; 5(2); 5:1; 17; 21(2); 22(2); 23; 24(2); 25; 26; 27; 7:12; 14; 17(2); 18; 19; 20(2); 21(2); 8:2; 5; 6; 9:12; 28; 31; 10:2; 3(2); 4(2); 6; 7; 8; 9(2); 10; 11; 12; 13; 14(2); 15; 16(2); 17; 18; 11:3; 4; 7(2); 8(2); 13; 15(2); 16; 17(2); 18(3); 19; 13:22(2); 24; 25(2); 26; 27(2); 14:3; 5; 13(3); 15(2); 16(2); 17; 19(2); 20(2); 15:4; 5; 7(2); 8(2); 9(2); 13; 16:3; 7; 8; 18; 17:4(2); 14(2); 20:4; 22:3(2); 6; 7(2); 9; 11; 13; 15; 23(3); 24; 25; 26; 27(2); 28; 29; 26:2(2); 3(2); 4; 30:20(2); 21(2); 22(2); 23; 31:24; 33:5; 8; 12; 13; 32; 34:16; 17; 18; 32; 33(3); 35:2(2); 3; 5; 6(3); 7(2); 8; 14(3); 36:17; 21; 23; 24; 37:6; 15; 16; 18; 38:3; 4(2); 5; 11; 12; 16(2); 17; 18(2); 20(2); 21(2); 22(2); 31; 32(2); 33(2); 34; 35; 39; 39:1(2); 2(2); 10; 11(2); 12; 13; 19(2); 20; 40:7; 8(3); 9(2); 41:1(2); 2; 4; 5(2); 7; 42:2; 4; **Ps** 2:7; 9(2); 3:3; 7(2); 4:1; 6; 7; 8; 5:3; 4; 5; 6; 10; 11; 12(2); 6:3; 7:6; 7; 8:2(2); 3; 4(2); 5; 6(2); 9:2; 4(2); 5(3); 6(2); 10; 13; 10:1(2); 13; 14(3); 15(2); 17(3); 12:7(2); 13:1(2); 16:2(2); 5; 10(2); 11; 17:3(3); 6; 7; 14; 18:25(2); 26(2); 27; 28; 35; 36; 39(2); 40; 43(2); 48(2); 19:12; 21:2; 3(2); 4; 5; 6(2); 9; 10; 12(2); 13; 22:1(2); 2; 3(2); 4; 9(2); 10; 15; 19; 21; 23:4; 5(2); 25:5; 7; 17; 27:8; 9; 28:1; 30:1; 2; 3(2); 7(2); 10; 11(2); 31:2; 3; 4; 5; 7(2); 8; 14; 19(2); 20(2); 22; 32:5; 6; 7(3); 8; 35:17; 22; 36:6; 8; 37:1; 3(2); 10; 34; 38:15; 39:5; 9; 11(2); 40:5; 6(3); 9; 11; 17; 41:2; 3; 10; 11; 12; 42:5(3); 9; 11(3); 43:2(2); 5(2); 44:1; 2(2); 3; 4; 7; 9; 10; 11; 12; 13; 14; 19; 23; 24; 45:2; 7; 11; 16; 48:7; 49:16; 18; 50:15; 16(2); 17; 18(2); 19; 20(2); 21(2); 51:4(3); 6(2); 8; 14; 15; 16(2); 17; 18; 19; 52:1; 3; 4(2); 9; 53:5; 55:13; 23; 56:2; 8(2); 13(2); 57:5; 11; 59:5; 8(2); 16; 60:1(3); 2(2); 3(2); 4; 8; 10(2); 61:3; 5(2); 6; 62:5; 12; 63:1; 7; 65:2; 3; 4; 5; 8; 9(4); 10(4); 11; 66:3; 10(2); 11(2); 12(2); 67:4; 68:7(2); 9(2); 10; 18(3); 28; 30; 35; 69:5; 19; 26(2); 70:5; 71:3(3); 5(2); 6; 7; 17; 20; 21; 22; 23; 73:18(2); 20(2); 23; 24; 27; 74:1; 2(3); 11; 13(2); 14; 15(2); 16; 17(2); 76:4; 7(3); 8; 10; 77:4; 14(2); 15; 20; 79:5; 11; 80:1(2); 4; 5; 6; 8(2); 9; 12; 15; 17; 81:7; 8; 9; 82:8; 83:1; 18; 85:1(2); 2(2); 3(2); 5(2); 6; 86:2; 5; 7; 9; 10(2); 13; 15; 17; 88:5; 6; 7; 8(2); 10; 14(2); 18; 89:2; 9(2); 10(2); 11; 12; 13; 17; 19; 26; 38(2); 39(2); 40(2); 42(2); 43; 44; 45(2); 46; 47; 49; 90:1; 2(2); 3; 5; 8; 15; 17(2); 91:4; 5; 8; 9; 12; 13(2); 92:4; 8; 10; 93:2; 94:2; 12; 13; 97:9(2); 99:4(2); 8(3); 101:2; 102:10; 12; 13; 25; 26(2); 27; 104:1(2); 6; 8; 9; 20; 24; 26; 27; 28(2); 29(2); 30(2); 35; 106:4; 108:5; 11(2); 109:6; 21(2); 27; 28; 110:1; 2; 3; 4; 114:5(4); 7; 115:9; 116:8; 16; 118:13; 21; 28(2); 119:4; 12; 18; 21; 25; 26; 28; 32; 37; 49; 57; 65; 68; 75; 82; 84; 86; 90; 93; 98; 102; 114; 117; 118; 119; 132(2); 137; 138; 151; 152; 171; 120:3; 123:1; 128:2(2); 5; 6; 130:3; 4; 132:8; 137:8; 138:2; 3; 7(2); 139:1; 2(2); 3; 4; 5; 8(2); 13(2); 19; 140:6; 7; 142:3; 5; 7; 143:10; 144:3(2); 145:15; 16; **Prov** 1:10; 15; 2:1; 2; 3; 4; 5; 9; 20; 3:4; 15; 23; 24(3); 28; 31; 4:8; 12(3); 5:2; 6(2); 9; 11; 19; 20; 6:1(2); 2(2); 3; 6; 9(2); 22(3); 35; 7:4; 9:12(4); 14:7; 19:19(2); 20; 20:13(2); 22; 22:18; 21; 24; 25; 26; 27; 29; 23:1; 2; 5; 6(2); 8(2); 13; 14; 17; 19; 31; 34; 35; 24:1; 6; 10; 11; 12; 13; 14; 19; 21; 24; 25:7; 8; 16(2); 22; 26:4; 12; 27:1; 22; 23; 27; 29:20; 30:4; 6(2); 10; 32(2); 31:29; **Eccl** 5:1; 2; 4(2); 5(2); 6; 7; 8; 7:10(2); 16; 17(2); 18; 21; 22; 8:4; 9:9(2); 10; 10:17; 11:1; 2; 5(2); 6; 9; 12:1; **Song** 1:7(3); 8(2); 15(3); 16; 2:17; 4:1(3); 7; 9(2); 16; 5:9(2); 6:1; 4; 7:6; 8:1; 12; 13; 14; **Is** 1:26; 2:6; 3:6(2); 7:3; 16; 9:3; 4; 12:1(3); 6; 14:3; 4; 8; 10(2); 12(2); 13; 15; 19; 20(2); 29; 31; 16:4; 17:10(2); 11(2); 22:1; 2; 8; 16(3); 18; 23:2; 4; 12(3); 16(2); 25:1(2); 2; 4; 5; 26:3; 7; 12(2); 14; 15(4); 20; 27:8; 29:4; 6; 30:19; 22(2); 23; 33:1(4); 2; 19(3); 36:4; 5(3); 6; 7; 8; 9; 37:6; 10; 11(2); 16(3); 20(2); 21; 23(2); 24; 26(2); 29; 38:1; 12; 13; 16; 17(2); 39:7; 8; 40:27; 28(2); 41:8; 9(2); 10; 12; 14; 15; 16(2); 42:20; 43:1; 2(3); 4(2); 22(2); 23(2); 24(4); 26(2); 44:2; 17; 21(3); 26; 28; 45:3; 4; 5; 9; 10(2); 15; 47:1; 5(2); 6(2); 7(2); 8; 10(3); 11(3); 12(3); 13; 15; 48:4; 5; 6(2); 7(2); 8(3); 17; 18; 49:3; 6(2); 9; 18; 20(2); 21; 23; 51:9; 10; 12(2); 16; 17; 21; 22; 23; 53:10; 54:1(2); 3; 4(4); 6; 11; 14(3); 17; 55:5(2); 57:6(2); 7(2); 8(5); 9; 10(4); 11(3); 13; 58:3(2); 5; 7(4); 9(3); 10; 11; 12(2); 13; 14; 60:5; 15; 16(2); 18; 62:2; 3; 4(2); 8; 12; 63:2; 14; 16(2); 17; 19; 64:1(2); 3(2); 5(2); 7; 8(2); 12(2); 65:5; **Jer** 1:5; 7(2); 11; 12; 13; 17; 2:2; 17(2); 18(2); 19; 20(2); 21; 22; 23(3); 25; 27(2); 28; 33(2); 35(2); 36(3); 37(2); 3:1; 2(3); 3(2); 4(2); 5(2); 6; 7; 12; 13; 19; 22; 4:1(3); 2; 10; 14; 19; 30(6); 5:3(2); 15; 17; 19; 6:8; 27; 7:16; 17; 27(2); 28; 8:4; 10:6; 24; 11:3; 14; 15(2); 18; 21; 12:1; 2(2); 3(2); 5(4); 13:4; 12; 13; 21(2); 22; 25; 27; 14:7; 8; 9(2); 17; 19(2); 22(2); 15:2; 5; 6(2); 10; 14; 15; 17; 18; 19(5); 16:2(2); 8; 10; 11; 17:4(2); 14; 16; 17; 18:22; 23; 19:10; 20:6(5); 7(2); 21:8; 22:2; 6; 15(2); 21(2); 22; 23; 25; 23:33; 37; 24:3; 25:27; 28; 30; 26:4; 8; 9; 27:13; 28:6; 7; 13(2); 15; 16(2); 29:24; 25; 26; 27; 30:10; 13(2); 15; 31:4(2); 5; 18(3); 21; 22(2); 32:3; 17; 18; 22; 23(2); 24(2); 25; 33:3; 24; 34:3(2); 4; 5; 14; 36:6(3); 14; 17; 19; 29(3); 37:13; 17; 20; 38:15(2); 17(2); 18(2); 21; 23(2); 24; 25; 26; 39:17(2); 18(2); 40:14; 16(2); 43:2; 44:16; 45:3; 4; 5(2); 46:11(2); 19; 27; 28; 47:5; 6(2); 48:2; 7(2); 18; 27(2); 49:4; 12(3); 16(2); 50:24(4); 31; 51:13; 20; 26; 61; 62(2); 63(2); 64; **Lam** 1:10; 21(3); 22; 2:20; 21(2); 22; 3:17; 42; 43(3); 44; 45; 56; 57(2); 58(2); 59(2); 60; 61; 4:21; 5:19; 20; 21; 22(2); **Eze** 2:4; 6(2); 7; 8(2); 3:1; 5; 6; 18(2); 19(2); 20; 21(2); 25(2); 26; 27; 4:1; 3(2); 4(3); 5; 6(2); 7(2); 8(2); 9(3); 10(2); 11(2); 12(2); 15; 5:1; 2(3); 3; 11; 7:2; 7; 8:6(2); 12; 13; 15(2); 17; 9:8; 11; 11:13; 12:2; 3(2); 4(2); 5; 6(3); 9; 10; 13:2; 17(2); 16:4(3); 5(2); 6(2); 7(3); 8; 13(4); 15; 16; 17; 18; 19; 20(3); 21; 22(2); 24; 25; 26; 28(3); 29(2); 30; 31(2); 33; 34(2); 36; 37(3); 41; 43(2); 45(2); 47(2); 48(2); 51(2); 52(5); 54(3); 55; 58; 59; 61(2); 62; 63(2); 17:9; 19:1; 20:4(2); 21:6; 7(2); 14; 19(2); 25; 28(2); 30; 32(2); 22:2(4); 3; 4(4); 8; 12(2); 13; 16(2); 24; 23:21; 27; 28; 30(2); 31; 32(2); 33; 34(2); 35(2); 36; 40; 41; 24:13(2); 16; 19(2); 25; 27(2); 25:3; 6; 7; 26:14(2); 17; 20; 21(3); 27:2; 3(2); 7; 25; 33(2); 34; 36; 28:2(3); 3; 4; 5; 6; 8; 9(2); 10; 12; 13(2); 14(3); 15(2); 16; 17; 18; 19(2); 29:5(2); 7(2); 31:2; 10; 18(3); 32:2(3); 6; 9; 19(2); 28; 33:7(2); 8(2); 9(2); 10; 12; 14; 27; 30; 32; 35:4(2); 5; 6; 10; 11; 12(2); 15(2); 36:1; 12(2); 13; 14; 15(2); 37:3; 16; 18(2); 20; 38:7(3); 8(2); 9(3); 10; 11; 13(2); 14; 15(2); 16; 17; 39:1; 4(2); 5; 17; 40:4(2); 43:10; 19; 20(2); 21; 22; 23(2); 24; 25; 44:6; 45:3; 18; 20; 46:13(2); 14; 47:6; **Dan** 1:13; 2:23(2); 26; 30; 31; 34; 37; 38; 41(2); 43; 45; 47; 3:10; 12(2); 18; 4:18(2); 20; 22; 25; 26; 32; 35; 5:13; 16(3); 18; 22(2); 23(3); 27; 6:12; 13; 16; 20; 8:20; 26; 9:7; 23; 10:12; 19; 20; 12:4; 13(2); **Hos** 2:16; 20; 23(2); 3:3(3); 4:5; 6(3); 15; 5:3; 9:1(2); 14; 10:9; 13; 12:6; 13:4; 9; 10; 14:1; **Amos** 5:23; 7:8; 12; 16(2); 17; 8:2; **Obad** 2; 3; 4(2); 5; 10; 11(2); 12(3); 13(2); 14(2); 15; **Jonah** 1:6; 8(2); 10; 14; 2:2; 3; 6; 4:2; 4; 9; 10(2); **Mic** 1:11; 13; 14; 2:5; 7; 4:8; 9; 10(4); 13; 5:2(2); 12; 13; 6:1; 14(3); 15(4); 7:19; 20(2); **Nah** 1:14; 3:8; 11(3); 16; **Hab** 1:2(2); 3; 12(3); 13(2); 2:7; 8; 10; 15; 16(2); 3:8; 9; 12(2); 13(2); 14; 15; **Zeph** 3:7(2); 11(3); 15; 16; **Zec** 1:3; 12(2); 14; 2:2; 11; 3:7(3); 8; 4:2; 5; 7(2); 9; 13; 5:2; 6:10; 13:3(2); **Mal** 1:2; 2:14; **Mt** 1:20; 21; 2:6; 13; 3:14; 4:3; 6(2); 7; 9; 10(2); 5:21; 22; 23; 25(2); 26(2); 27; 33; 36(2); 42; 43; 6:2; 3; 5(2); 6(3); 17(2); 18; 7:3; 4; 5(2); 8:2(2); 3; 4; 8; 13; 19; 29(2); 31; 9:27; 11:3; 23; 25; 12:37(2); 13:10; 27; 28; 14:28; 31(2); 33; 15:5; 12; 22; 28; 16:14; 16; 17; 18; 19(2); 23(2); 17:4; 25; 27(3); 18:15; 28; 32(2); 33; 19:17(2); 18(4); 19; 21(3); 20:12; 13; 21; 30; 31; 21:16(2); 21(2); 23; 22:12; 16(3); 17; 37; 39; 44; 23:26; 37; 25:20; 21(3); 22; 23(2); 24(3); 25; 26(2); 27; 26:17; 25; 34; 39; 50; 53; 62; 63(2); 64; 68; 69; 70; 73; 75; 27:4; 11(2); 13; 19; 40(2); 46; **Mk** 1:11; 24(3); 40(2); 41; 44; 3:11; 4:38; 5:7(2); 8; 31(2); 35; 6:22; 23; 25; 7:11; 8:29; 33; 9:22; 23; 24; 25; 10:18; 19; 21(3); 35; 47; 48; 51; 11:21; 23(2); 28; 12:14(2); 30; 31; 32; 34; 36; 13:2; 14:12(2); 30; 36; 37(2); 60; 61; 67; 68; 70(2); 72; 15:2(2); 4; 29; 34; **Lk** 1:4(2); 13; 14; 20(2); 28(2); 30; 31; 42; 76(2); 2:29; 31; 48; 3:22; 4:3; 7; 8(2); 9; 11; 12; 34(3); 41; 5:10; 12(2); 13; 6:41; 42(4); 7:6; 19; 20; 43; 44(2); 45; 46; 8:28; 45; 9:54; 57; 60; 10:15; 21; 26; 27; 28(2); 35; 36; 37; 40; 41; 11:27; 45; 12:19; 20(2); 41; 58(3); 59(2); 13:9; 12; 15; 26; 14:8(2); 9; 10(2); 12; 13; 14(2); 22; 15:29; 30; 31; 16:2; 5; 7; 25(2); 27; 17:4; 6(2); 8; 18:19; 20; 22(3); 38; 39; 41; 19:17(3); 19; 21(4); 22(2); 23; 42(2); 44; 20:2; 21(2); 39; 42; 22:9; 32; 34(2); 42; 48; 58; 60; 61; 67; 70; 23:3(2); 37; 39; 40(2); 42; 43; 24:18; **Jn** 1:19; 21(2); 22(2); 25(2); 33; 38; 42(2); 48(2); 49(2); 50(2); 2:10; 18(2); 20; 3:2(2); 8; 10; 26; 4:9; 10(2); 11(2); 12; 17; 18(3); 19; 27(2); 5:6; 14; 6:25; 30(2); 68; 69; 7:3; 4; 20; 52; 8:5; 13; 25; 33; 48; 52(2); 53(2); 57(2); 9:17; 28; 34(2); 35; 37; 10:24(2); 33; 36; 11:3; 8; 21; 22; 26; 27; 32; 40(2); 41; 42(2); 12:34; 13:6; 7(2); 8(2); 27; 36(3); 38(2); 14:5; 9(2); 10; 22; 16:5; 29; 30(2); 17:2(2); 3; 4; 5; 6(2); 7; 8(2); 9; 11; 12; 15(2); 18; 21(2); 22; 23(3); 24(3); 25; 26; 18:9; 17; 21; 22; 23; 25; 33; 34; 35; 37(2); 19:9; 10(2); 11; 12(2); 20:13; 15(4); 29(2); 21:12; 15(2); 16(2); 17(4); 18(6); 22; **Acts** 1:6; 24(2); 2:27(2); 28(2); 34; 4:24; 27; 5:4(2); 7:28(2); 33; 8:20; 21; 23; 30(2); 37(2); 9:4; 5(2); 6(2); 17(2); 10:6; 15; 33(2); 11:3; 9; 14; 12:15; 13:10(3); 11; 33; 35; 47; 16:31; 17:19; 20; 21:20; 21; 22; 24; 37; 38; 22:7; 8(2); 14; 15(2); 16; 26; 27; 23:3(2); 4; 5; 11(2); 19; 20; 21; 22(2); 24:4; 10; 11; 25:9; 10; 12(2); 22; 26:1; 14; 15(2); 16; 24; 27(2); 28; 29; 27:24; 28:22; **Rom** 2:1(5); 3(2); 4; 17; 19; 21(4); 22(4); 23(2); 25(2); 3:4(2); 7:7; 9:19; 20(2); 10:9(2); 11:17; 18(2); 19; 20; 22(2); 24; 12:20; 13:3(2); 4; 9(6); 14:4; 10(2); 15; 22; **1Cor** 4:7(5); 7:16(4); 21(2); 27(2); 28(2); 9:9; 14:16(2); 17; 15:36(2); 37(2); **Gal** 2:14(2); 4:7; 27(2); 5:14; 6:1; **Eph** 5:14; 6:3; **Col** 4:17(2); **1Ti** 1:3; 18; 3:15(2); 4:6(3); 12; 16; 5:18; 21; 6:11; 12; 14; **2Ti** 1:6; 8(2); 13; 15; 18; 2:1; 2(2); 3; 3:10; 14(3); 15; 4:5; 13; 15; **Titus** 1:5; 2:1; 3:8; **Philem** 1:5; 12; 15; 17; 19; 21; **Heb** 1:5; 9; 10; 11; 12(2); 2:6(2); 7(2); 8; 5:5; 6; 7:17; 21; 8:5; 10:5(2); 6; 8; 12:5(2); **Jas** 2:3(2); 8; 11(3); 18; 19(2); 20; 22; 4:11(2); 12; **3Jn** 2; 3; 5(2); 6(2); **Rev** 1:11; 19; 20(2); 2:2(2); 4; 5(2); 6(2); 9; 10(2); 13(2); 14; 15; 20; 3:1(2); 3(3); 4; 8; 10; 11; 15(2); 16; 17(2); 18(3); 4:11(2); 5:9(2); 6:6; 10; 7:14; 10:11; 11:17; 18; 15:3; 4; 16:5(2); 6; 17:7; 8; 12; 15; 16; 18; 18:14; 20; 19:10; 22:9

THOUGH

518, 834, 1571, 1768, 3518, 3588, 3606, 3863, 6903, *1223, 1437, 1487, 1499, 1512, 2532, 2539, 2544, 2579, 3676, 3754*

Gen 31:30; 33:10; 40:10; **Lev** 5:17; 11:7; 25:35; **Num** 18:27; **Deut** 29:19; **Josh** 17:18(2); **Judg** 13:16; 15:3; 7; **Ruth** 2:13; **1Sa** 14:39; 20:20; 21:5; **2Sa** 1:21; 3:39; 4:6; 18:12; **1Kin** 2:28; **1Chr** 26:10; **2Chr** 30:19; **Neh** 1:9; 6:1; **Est** 9:1; **Job** 8:7; 9:15; 21; 10:19; 11:12; 13:15; 14:8; 16:6(2); 19:17; 26; 27; 20:6; 12(2); 13; 24:23; 27:8; 16; 30:24; 39:16; **Ps** 23:4; 27:3(2); 35:14; 37:24; 44:19; 46:2(2); 3(2); 49:18; 68:13; 78:23; 99:8; 138:6; 7; **Prov** 6:35; 11:21; 16:5; 27:22; 28:6; 29:19; **Eccl** 6:6; 8:12; 17(2); **Is** 1:18(2); 10:22; 12:1; 30:20; 35:8; 45:4; 5; 49:5; 63:16; **Jer** 2:22; 4:30(3); 5:2; 22(2); 11:11; 12:6; 14:7; 15:1; 22:24; 30:11; 32:5; 33; 37:10; 46:23; 49:16; 51:5; 53(2); **Lam** 3:32; **Eze** 2:6(2); 3:9; 8:18; 12:3; 13; 14:14; 16; 18; 20; 26:21; 28:2; 32:25; 26; 27; **Dan** 5:22; 9:9; **Hos** 4:15; 5:2; 7:13; 15; 8:10; 9:12; 16; 11:7; 13:15; **Amos** 5:22; 9:2(2); 3(2); 4; **Obad** 4(2); 16; **Mic** 5:2; **Nah** 1:12(2); **Hab** 1:5; 2:3; **Zec** 9:2; 10:6; 12:3; **Mt** 26:33; 35; 60; **Lk** 9:53; 11:8; 16:31; 18:4; 7; 24:28; **Jn** 4:2; 8:6; 14; 10:38; 11:25; 12:37; **Acts** 3:12; 13:28; 41; 17:25; 27; 23:15; 20; 27:30; 28:4; 17; **Rom** 4:11; 17; 7:3; 9:6; 27; **1Cor** 4:15; 18; 5:3; 7:29; 30(3); 8:5; 9:16; 19; 13:1; 2(2); 3(2); **2Cor** 4:16; 5:16; 20; 7:8(3);

12; 8:9; 10:3; 8; 14; 11:6; 21; 12:6; 11; 15; 13:4; 7; **Gal** 1:8; 3:15; 4:1; **Phil** 3:4; 12; **Col** 2:5; 20; **Philem** 1:8; **Heb** 5:8; 6:9; 7:5; 12:17; **Jas** 2:14; 3:4; **1Pet** 1:6; 7; 8; 4:12; **2Pet** 1:12; **2Jn** 5; **Jude** 5

THROUGH

413, 1119, 1157, 1234, 1811, 1856, 1870, 2864, 2944, 3027, 4480, 5674, 5921, 6440, 7130, 7751, 8432, *303, 1223, 1224, 1279, 1330, 1350, 1358, 1537, 1653, 1722, 1909, 2596, 2700, 4044, 4063*

Gen 6:13; 12:6; 13:17; 30:32; 41:36; **Ex** 10:15; 12:12; 23; 13:17; 18; 14:16; 24; 19:13; 21; 24; 21:6; 36:33; **Lev** 4:2; 13; 22; 27; 5:15; 18:21; 26:6; **Num** 13:32; 14:7; 15:27; 29; 20:17(3); 19; 20; 21; 21:22; 23; 24:8; 25:8(2); 31:16; 23(2); 33:8; **Deut** 1:19; 2:4; 7; 8; 18; 27; 28; 5:15; 8:15; 9:26; 15:17; 18:10; 29:16; 31:29; 32:47; 33:11; **Josh** 1:11; 2:15; 3:2; 18:4; 8; 9; 12; 24:17; **Judg** 2:22; 3:23; 5:6; 26; 28; 9:54; 11:16; 17; 18; 19; 20; 20:12; **1Sa** 9:4(4); 19:12; 31:4(2); **2Sa** 2:29(2); 4:7; 6:16; 12:31; 18:14; 20:14; 22:13; 30; 23:16; 24:2; 8; **2Kin** 1:2; 3:8; 26; 10:21; 16:3; 17:17; 21:6; 23:10; 24:20; **1Chr** 10:4; 11:18; **2Chr** 19:4; 23:20; 24:9; 30:10; 31:18; 32:4; 33:6; **Ezr** 6:14; **Neh** 9:11; **Est** 6:9; 11; **Job** 7:14; 14:9; 20:24; 22:13; 24:16; 26:12; 29:3; 7; 40:24; 41:2; **Ps** 8:8; 10:4; 18:29; 19:4; 21:7; 23:4; 32:3; 44:5(2); 60:12; 66:3; 6; 12(2); 68:7; 73:9; 78:13; 81:5; 84:6; 92:4; 106:9(2); 107:39; 108:13; 109:24; 110:5; 115:7; 119:98; 104; 136:14; 16; **Prov** 7:6; 8; 23; 11:9; 18:1; 24:3; **Eccl** 5:3; 10:18(2); **Song** 2:9; **Is** 8:8; 21; 9:19; 13:15; 14:19; 16:8; 21:1; 23:10; 27:4; 28:7(4); 15; 18; 30:31; 34:10; 43:2(3); 48:21; 60:15; 62:10(2); 63:13; **Jer** 2:6(5); 3:9; 5:1; 9:6; 10; 12; 12:12; 17:24; 32:35; 51:4; 52; 52:3; **Lam** 3:44; 4:9; 21; **Eze** 5:17; 6:8; 9:4(2); 5; 12:5; 7; 12; 14:5; 15(2); 17; 16:14; 21; 36; 40; 20:23; 26; 31; 23:37; 29:11(2); 12; 30:23; 33:28; 34:6; 36:19; 39:14; 15; 41:19; 46:19; 47:3; 4(2); **Dan** 8:25; 9:7; 11:2; 10; **Joel** 3:17; **Amos** 2:10; 5:17; **Jonah** 3:7; **Mic** 2:13; 5:8; **Nah** 1:12; 15; 3:4(2); **Hab** 1:6; 3:12; 14; 15(2); **Zec** 1:10; 11; 17; 4:10; 12; 5:6; 6:7(3); 7:14; 9:8; 15; 10:7; 11; 13:3; 9; **Mt** 6:19; 20; 9:34; 12:1; 43; 19:24; **Mk** 2:23; 6:55; 7:13; 31; 9:30; 10:25; 11:16; **Lk** 1:78; 2:35; 4:14; 30; 5:19; 6:1; 9:6; 10:17; 11:15; 18; 24; 12:39; 13:22; 17:1; 11; 18:25; 19:1; **Jn** 1:7; 3:17; 4:4; 8:59; 15:3; 17:11; 17; 19; 20; 20:31; **Acts** 1:2; 3:16; 17; 4:2; 8:18; 40; 10:43; 12:10; 13:6; 38; 14:22; 15:3; 11; 41; 16:4; 17:1; 18:27; 19:1; 21; 20:3; 21:4; **Rom** 1:8; 24; 2:23; 24; 3:7; 24; 25(2); 30; 31; 4:13(2); 20; 5:1; 9; 11; 15; 21; 6:11; 23; 7:25; 8:3; 13; 37; 11:11; 30; 31; 36; 12:3; 15:4; 13; 17; 19; 16:27; **1Cor** 1:1; 4:15; 8:11; 10:1; 13:12; 15:57; 16:5(2); **2Cor** 3:4; 4:15; 8:9; 9:11; 10:4; 11:3; 33; 12:7; 13:4; **Gal** 2:19; 3:8; 14(2); 4:7; 13; 5:5; 10; **Eph** 1:7; 2:7; 8; 18; 22; 4:6; 18; **Phil** 1:19; 2:3; 3:9; 4:7; 13; **Col** 1:14; 20; 22; 2:8; 12; **2Th** 2:13; 16; **1Ti** 6:10; **2Ti** 1:10; 3:15; **Titus** 1:3; 3:6; **Philem** 1:22; **Heb** 2:10; 14; 15; 3:13; 6:12; 9:14; 10:10; 20; 11:3; 11; 28; 29; 33; 39; 12:20; 13:20; 21; **1Pet** 1:2; 5; 6; 22; 4:11; **2Pet** 1:1; 2; 3; 4; 2:3; 18(2); 20; **1Jn** 4:9; **Rev** 8:13; 18:3; 22:14

THROUGHOUT

5921, *1223, 1330, 1519, 1722, 1909, 2596, 3650*

Gen 41:29; 46; 45:8; **Ex** 5:12; 7:19; 21; 8:16; 17; 9:9; 16; 22; 25; 11:6; 12:14; 29:42; 30:8; 10; 21; 31; 31:13; 16; 32:27; 34:3; 35:3; 36:6; 37:19; 40:15; 38; **Lev** 3:17; 7:36; 10:9; 17:7; 23:14; 21; 31; 25:9; 10; 30; **Num** 1:42; 52; 2:3; 9; 16; 24; 32; 3:39; 4:22; 38; 40; 42; 10:8; 25; 11:10; 15:38; 18:23; 26:2; 28:14; 21; 24; 29; 29:4; 10; 31:4; 35:29; **Deut** 16:18; 28:40; 52(2); **Josh** 2:22; 6:27; 16:1; 22:14; 24:3; **Judg** 6:35; 7:22; 24; 20:6; 10; **1Sa** 5:11; 11:7; 13:3; 19; 23:23; **2Sa** 8:14; 15:10; 19:9; **1Kin** 1:3; 6:38; 15:22; 18:6; 22:36; **2Kin** 17:5; **1Chr** 5:10; 6:54; 60; 62; 63; 7:40; 9:34; 12:30; 21:4; 12; 22:5; 26:6; 27:1; **2Chr** 8:6; 11:23; 16:9; 17:9; 19; 19:5; 20:3; 25:5; 26:14; 30:5; 6; 22; 31:20; 34:7; 36:22; **Ezr** 1:1; 10:7; **Est** 1:20; 3:6; 9:2; 4; 28; **Ps** 72:5; 102:24; 135:13; 145:13; **Jer** 17:3; **Eze** 38:21; **Mt** 4:24; **Mk** 1:28; 39; 14:9; **Lk** 1:65; 4:25; 7:17(2); 8:1; 39; 23:5; **Jn** 19:23; **Acts** 8:1; 9:31; 32; 42; 10:37; 11:28; 13:49; 14:24; 16:6; 19:26; 24:5; 26:20; **Rom** 1:8; 9:17; **2Cor** 8:18; **Eph** 3:21; **1Pet** 1:1

THUS

428, 1836, 2007, 2008, 2063, 2088, 2090, 3541, 3588, 3602, 3644, 3651, 3652, 3660, 3662, *2532, 2596, 3592, 3779, 5023, 5124, 5127*

Gen 2:1; 6:22; 19:36; 20:16; 21:32; 24:30; 25:22; 34; 31:8(2); 9; 40; 41; 32:4(2); 36:8; 37:35; 42:25; 45:9; **Ex** 3:14; 15; 4:22; 5:1; 10; 15; 7:17; 8:1; 20; 9:1; 13; 10:3; 11:4; 12:11; 50; 14:11; 30; 19:3; 20:22; 26:17; 24; 29:35; 32:27; 36:22; 29; 39:32; 40:16; **Lev** 15:31; 16:3; **Num** 4:19; 49; 8:7; 14; 26; 10:28; 11:15; 15:11; 18:26; 28; 20:14; 21; 21:31; 22:16; 23:5; 16; 32:8; **Deut** 7:5; 9:25; 20:15; 29:24; 32:6; **Josh** 2:4; 6:3; 7:10; 13; 20(2); 10:25; 16:5; 21:13; 42; 22:16; 24:2; **Judg** 6:8; 8:1; 28; 9:56; 11:15; 33; 13:18; 18:4(2); 20:43; **1Sa** 2:27; 9:9; 10:18; 11:9; 14:9; 10; 15:2; 18:25; 20:7; 22; 25:6; 26:18; **2Sa** 6:22; 7:5; 8; 11:25; 12:7; 11; 31; 15:26; 16:7; 17:15(4); 21; 18:14; 33; 24:12; **1Kin** 1:48; 2:30(3); 3:22; 5:11; 9:8; 11:31; 12:10(2); 24; 13:2; 21; 14:5(2); 7; 16:12; 17:14; 20:2; 5; 13; 14; 28; 42; 21:19(2); 22:11; 27; **2Kin** 1:4; 6; 11; 16; 2:21; 3:16; 17; 4:43; 5:4(2); 7:1; 9:3; 6; 12(3); 18; 19; 10:28; 16:16; 18:19; 29; 31; 19:3; 6(2); 10; 20; 32; 20:1; 5; 21:12; 22:15; 16; 18(2); **1Chr** 15:28; 17:4; 7(2); 18:6; 13; 21:10; 11; 24:4; 5; 29:26; **2Chr** 4:18; 5:1; 7:11; 21; 10:10(2); 11:4; 12:5; 13:18; 18:10; 26; 19:9; 20:15; 21:12; 24:11; 20; 22; 31:20; 32:10; 22; 34:23; 24; 26; 36:23; **Ezr** 1:2; 5:3; 7; 9; 11; 6:2; **Neh** 5:13; 13:18; 30; **Est** 1:18; 2:13; 6:9; 11; 9:5; **Job** 1:5; 27:12; **Ps** 38:14; 63:4; 73:15; 21; 106:20; 29; 39; 128:4; **Is** 7:7; 8:11; 10:24; 21:6; 16; 22:15; 24:13; 28:16; 29:22; 30:12; 15; 31:4; 36:4; 14; 16; 37:3; 6(2); 10; 21; 33; 38:1; 5; 42:5; 43:1; 14; 16; 44:2; 6; 24; 45:1; 11; 14; 18; 47:15; 48:17; 49:7; 8; 22; 25; 50:1; 51:22; 52:3; 4; 56:1; 4; 57:15; 65:8; 13; 66:1; 12; **Jer** 2:2; 5; 4:3; 27; 5:13; 14; 6:6; 9; 16; 21; 22; 7:3; 20; 21; 8:4; 9:7; 15; 17; 22; 23; 10:2; 11; 18; 11:3; 11; 21; 22; 12:14; 13:1; 9; 12; 13; 14:10(2); 15; 15:2; 19; 16:3; 5; 9; 17:5; 19; 21; 18:11; 13; 23; 19:1; 3; 11; 12; 15; 20:4; 21:3; 4; 8; 12; 22:1; 3; 6; 8; 11; 18; 30; 23:2; 15; 16; 35; 37; 38; 24:5; 8; 25:8; 15; 27; 28; 32; 26:2; 4; 18; 19; 27:2; 4(2); 16; 19; 21; 28:2; 11; 13; 14; 16; 29:4; 8; 10; 16; 17; 21; 24; 25; 31; 32; 30:2; 5; 12; 18; 31:2; 7; 15; 16; 18; 23; 35; 37; 32:3; 14; 15; 28; 36; 42; 33:2; 4; 10; 12; 17; 20; 24; 25; 34:2(2); 4; 13; 17; 35:8; 13; 17; 18; 19; 36:29; 30; 37:7(2); 9; 21; 38:2; 3; 4; 17; 39:16; 42:9; 15; 18; 43:7; 10; 44:2; 7; 11; 25; 30; 45:2; 4(2); 47:2; 48:1; 40; 47; 49:1; 7; 12; 28; 35; 50:18; 33; 51:1; 4; 33; 36; 58; 64(2); 52:27; **Eze** 1:11; 2:4; 3:11; 27; 4:13; 5:5; 7; 8; 13; 6:3; 11; 12; 7:2; 5; 11:5(2); 7; 16; 17; 12:10; 19; 23; 28; 13:3; 8; 13; 15; 18; 20; 14:4; 6; 21; 15:6; 16:3; 13; 19; 36; 59; 17:3; 9; 19; 22; 20:3; 5; 27; 30; 39; 47; 21:3; 9; 24; 26; 28; 22:3; 19; 28; 23:4; 7; 21; 22; 27; 28; 32; 35; 39; 46; 48; 24:3; 6; 9; 21; 24; 25:3; 6; 8; 12; 13; 15; 16; 26:3; 7; 15; 19; 27:3; 28:2; 6; 12; 22; 25; 29:3; 8; 13; 19; 30:2; 6; 10; 13; 19; 22; 31:7; 10; 15; 18; 32:3; 11; 33:10; 25; 27(2); 34:2; 10; 11; 17; 20; 30; 35:3; 7; 13; 14; 36:2; 3; 4; 5; 6; 7; 13; 22; 33; 37; 37:5; 9; 12; 19; 21; 38:3; 10; 14; 17; 23; 39:1; 16; 17; 20; 25; 43:18; 20; 44:6; 9; 45:9; 18; 46:1; 15; 16; 47:13; **Dan** 1:16; 2:24; 25; 4:10; 14; 6:6; 7:5; 23; 11:17; 39; **Hos** 10:4; **Amos** 1:3; 6; 9; 11; 13; 2:1; 4; 6; 11; 3:11; 12; 4:12; 5:3; 4; 16; 7:1; 4; 7; 11; 17; 8:1; **Obad** 1; **Mic** 2:3; 3:5; 5:6; **Nah** 1:12(2); **Hag** 1:2; 5; 7; 2:6; 11; **Zec** 1:3; 4; 14; 16; 17; 2:8; 3:7; 6:12; 7:9; 14; 8:2; 3; 4; 6; 7; 9; 14; 19; 20; 23; 11:4; **Mal** 1:4; 13; **Mt** 2:5; 3:15; 15:6; 26:54; **Mk** 2:7; **Lk** 1:25; 2:48; 9:34; 11:45; 17:30; 18:11; 19:28; 31; 22:51; 23:46; 24:36; 40; 46(2); **Jn** 4:6; 9:6; 11:43; 48; 13:21; 18:22; 20:14; **Acts** 19:41; 20:36; 21:11; 26:24; 30; 27:35; **Rom** 9:20; **1Cor** 14:25; **2Cor** 1:17; 5:14; **Phil** 3:15; **Heb** 6:9; 9:6; **Rev** 9:17; 16:5; 18:21

THY

4674, 4675

Gen 3:10; 14(2); 15(2); 16(4); 17(3); 19; 4:6; 9; 10; 11(2); 14; 6:18(3); 7:1; 8:16(3); 12:1(3); 2; 7; 13; 18; 19(2); 13:8; 15; 16(2); 14:20; 15:1(2); 5; 13; 15; 18; 16:5; 6(2); 9; 10; 11; 17:5(2); 7(2); 8; 9; 10; 12; 13(2); 15; 19; 18:3(2); 9; 10; 19:12(2); 15(2); 17; 19(3); 20:6; 13; 16; 21:12(3); 13; 22:2; 12; 16; 17(2); 18; 20; 23:6(2); 11; 15; 24:2; 5; 7; 14(3); 17; 19; 23; 40; 43; 44; 46; 51; 60; 25:23(2); 31; 26:3(2); 4(3); 9; 10; 24(2); 27:3(3); 6(2); 9; 10; 13; 19(2); 20; 29(2); 31; 32(2); 35(2); 37; 39; 40(3); 42; 44; 45; 28:2(2); 4; 13(2); 14(2); 29:15; 18; 30:14; 15; 27; 28; 29; 31; 32; 33; 34; 31:3(2); 8(2); 13; 30; 31; 32; 37(2); 38(3); 41(3); 32:4; 5; 6; 9(2); 10; 12; 18; 20; 27; 28; 29; 33:5; 10(2); 35:1; 10(3); 11; 12; 37:10(2); 13; 14; 32; 38:8(2); 11; 13; 18(3); 24; 39:19; 40:13; 19(2); 41:40; 42:10; 11; 13; 43:28; 44:7; 8; 9; 16; 18(2); 21; 23; 24; 27; 30; 31(2); 32; 33; 45:9; 10(4); 11; 17; 46:3; 30; 34; 47:3; 4(2); 5(2); 6; 15; 29(2); 48:1; 2; 4; 5; 6; 11(2); 18; 22; 49:4; 8(3); 18; 25; 26; 50:6; 16; 17(2); 18; **Ex** 2:9; 13; 3:5(2); 6; 18; 4:6; 7; 9; 10; 12; 14; 15; 16; 19; 23(2); 5:15; 16(2); 23(2); 7:1(2); 2; 9; 19; 8:2; 3(5); 4(2); 5; 9(3); 10; 11(3); 16; 21(3); 23; 9:3; 14(2); 15; 19; 30; 10:2(2); 4; 6(4); 29; 11:8; 12:24; 13:5; 7; 8; 9; 11; 13; 14; 14:16; 15:6(2); 7; 8; 10; 12; 13(3); 16; 17; 26; 17:5; 18:6(2); 20:2; 5; 7; 9; 10(8); 12(4); 16; 17(3); 24(3); 25; 26; 22:26; 28; 29(3); 30; 23:6; 10; 11(3); 12(2); 13; 16(2); 17; 19(2); 25(2); 26(2); 31; 33; 28:1; 2; 4; 41; 29:12; 26; 32:4; 7; 8; 11(2); 12(2); 13; 32; 33:1; 5; 13(4); 15; 16(3); 18; 34:9; 10; 16(2); 19; 20; 24(3); 26(2); **Lev** 2:5; 7; 13(3); 14(2); 5:15; 18; 6:6; 9:7(2); 10:9; 13(2); 14(4); 15; 16:2; 18:7(3); 8(2); 9(3); 10(2); 11(3); 12(2); 13(2); 14; 15(2); 16(2); 20; 21(2); 19:9(2); 10(2); 12; 13; 14; 15; 16(2); 17(2); 18(2); 19(2); 27; 29; 32; 20:19(2); 21:8; 17; 23:22(2); 25:3(2); 4(2); 5(2); 6(4); 7(2); 11; 14(2); 15; 17; 25; 35; 36(2); 37(2); 39; 43; 44(2); 47; 53; 27:2; 3(2); 4; 5; 6(2); 7; 8; 13; 15; 16; 17; 18; 19; 23; 25; 27; **Num** 5:19; 20; 21(3); 22(3); 11:11(2); 12; 15; 14:13; 14; 19; 20; 16:10; 11; 16; 18:1(3); 2(3); 3; 7; 8; 9; 11(3); 19(3); 20; 20:8; 14; 16; 17(2); 19; 21:22(2); 34; 22:32; 23:3; 15; 24:5(2); 11; 12; 14; 21(2); 27:13(2); 31:2; 49; 32:4; 5(2); 25; 27; 31; **Deut** 1:21(2); 31; 2:7(4); 27; 30(2); 3:2; 24(5); 4:3; 9(5); 10; 19; 21; 23; 24; 25; 29(3); 30; 31(2); 37; 40(3); 5:6; 9; 11; 12; 13; 14(10); 15(2); 16(5); 20; 21(3); 6:2(5); 3; 5(3); 7; 9(2); 10(2); 13; 15(2); 18; 20; 21; 7:1; 2; 3(2); 4; 6(2); 9; 12(2); 13(7); 16; 18; 19(2); 20; 21; 22; 23; 25; 8:2; 3; 4(2); 5; 6; 7; 10; 11; 13(4); 14; 16(2); 18(2); 19; 9:3(2); 4; 5(3); 6(2); 7; 12; 26(2); 27; 29(3); 10:9; 11; 12(5); 13; 14; 15; 20; 21(2); 22(2); 11:1; 10(2); 12(2); 14(2); 15(2); 20; 29; 12:1; 7; 13; 14(2); 15(3); 17(8); 18(8); 20(4); 21(5); 25; 26(2); 27(4); 28(2); 29; 31; 13:5; 6(7); 10; 12(2); 16; 17; 18(2); 14:2; 21(2); 22; 23(6); 24(2); 25; 26(3); 27; 28; 29(2); 15:3; 4; 5; 6; 7(5); 9(2); 10(2); 11(4); 12; 14(4); 15; 17(2); 18; 19(5); 20(2); 21; 22; 16:1(2); 2; 3; 4; 5(2); 6; 7(2); 8; 10(3); 11(7); 13(2); 14(6); 15(2); 16(2); 17; 18(3); 20; 21; 22; 17:1(2); 2(3); 5; 8(2); 12; 14; 15(3); 18:4(3); 5(2); 6; 9; 12; 13; 14; 15(2); 16; 19:1(2); 2(2); 3(2); 8(4); 9; 10(2); 14(2); 20:1; 13; 14; 16; 17; 21:1; 2(2); 5; 8(2); 10; 11; 13; 23(2); 22:1(2); 2(2); 3; 4; 5; 7; 8; 9(3); 12; 17; 23:5(3); 6; 7; 13; 14(3); 16; 18(2); 19; 20(2); 21(2); 23(3); 24(3); 25(2); 24:4; 9; 10; 13; 14(4); 18; 19(2); 21; 25:3; 13; 15(2); 16; 19(2); 26:1; 2(3); 3; 4; 5; 10(2); 11; 12; 13(3); 15(2); 16(2); 17; 19; 27:2; 3(2); 5; 6(2); 7; 9; 10; 28:1(2); 2; 4(5); 5(2); 7; 8(2); 9; 11(4); 12; 13; 15; 17(2); 18(4); 20; 23(2); 24; 26; 29; 31(2); 32(2); 33(2); 35(2); 36(2); 40; 42(2); 45; 46; 47; 48; 51(4); 52(6); 53(3); 55; 57; 58; 59(2); 62; 64; 65; 66(2); 29:5(2); 11(4); 12(2); 13; 30:1; 2(3); 3(3); 4; 5(3); 6(4); 7; 9(5); 10(3); 14(2); 16(2); 19; 20(4); 31:3; 6; 11; 12(2); 14; 16; 27(2); 32:6; 7(2); 50(2); 33:3(3); 8(3); 9(2); 10(2); 18(2); 25(3); 26; 27; 29(2); 34:4; **Josh** 1:5; 8(2); 9; 17; 18(2); 2:18(4); 19; 5:15(2); 7:9; 10; 8:1; 18; 9:8; 9(2); 24(2); 10:6(2); 14:9(2); 24:12(2); **Judg** 1:3; 5:12; 14; 6:14; 17; 25(2); 26; 30; 7:10; 8:15; 22(2); 9:38; 54; 11:10; 17; 19; 24; 36(2); 13:12; 16; 17(2); 14:3; 13; 15(2); 15:2; 18; 16:6; 15; 17:10; 18:19(2); 25(3); 19:19(2); 20; **Ruth** 1:10; 15(2); 16(2); 2:11(4); 12; 13; 14; 3:3; 9; 12; 17; 4:12; 15(2); **1Sa** 1:8; 14; 17; 18; 26; 2:1; 16; 27; 28; 29; 30(2); 31; 34; 3:9; 10; 4:17; 8:5(2); 9:20(2); 10:2; 12:19(2); 13:13(2); 14; 14:7; 28; 15:15; 21; 24; 30; 33(2); 16:11; 16; 19; 17:17(2); 18; 28; 32; 34; 36; 44; 55; 58; 19:11; 20:1; 3(2); 4; 6; 7; 8(3); 10; 15; 18; 22; 30; 31; 42; 22:14(2); 15; 16; 22; 23; 23:10; 11(2); 20; 24:9; 11(2); 16; 25:7; 8(3); 26; 28; 29(2); 33; 35(2); 26:15(2); 17; 24; 27:5; 28:1; 2; 17; 19; 21(2); 22; 29:6(3); 8; 10; 31:4; **2Sa** 1:16(3); 19; 26; 2:21(2); 22; 3:8; 12; 25(2); 34(2); 4:8; 5:1(2); 6:21; 7:9; 12(4); 16(2); 19(2); 20; 21(2); 23(3); 24; 25; 26(2); 27(2); 28(2); 29(3); 9:2; 6; 7(2); 8; 9; 10(4); 11; 10:3; 11:8(2); 10; 11; 21; 24(2); 25; 12:8(3); 9; 10; 11(3); 13; 13:5(2); 7; 20(3); 24(2); 35; 14:6; 11(2); 15; 17; 19(2); 20; 22(2); 31; 15:2; 3; 8; 15; 19; 20; 21; 27; 34(3); 16:3; 4; 8(2); 17(3); 19(2); 21(2); 17:8(2); 10; 18:28; 29; 19:5(6); 6; 7(2); 14; 19; 20; 26(2); 27; 28; 29; 35(2); 36; 37(2); 20:6; 22:36(2); 24:3; 10; 13(2); 23; **1Kin** 1:2; 12; 13; 14; 17(2); 19; 26(2); 27; 30; 47(2); 2:3; 4; 6; 7(2); 21; 37; 38; 39; 44; 3:6; 7; 8(2); 9(3); 12; 13; 14(2); 22(2); 23(2); 5:5(3); 6(2); 8; 6:12; 8:19(2); 23; 24(2); 25(2); 26(2); 28(2); 29; 30(3); 32; 33(2); 34; 35; 36(4); 38; 39; 41(2); 42(3); 43(4); 44(2); 48; 49; 50; 51; 52(2); 53; 9:3(2); 4; 5(2); 10:6(2); 7; 8(3); 9; 11:11; 12(3); 13; 37; 12:4(2); 7; 9; 10; 28; 13:6; 21; 22(2); 14:9; 12; 15:19(2); 16:3; 17:12; 13; 19; 23; 24; 18:8; 9; 10; 11; 12; 14; 18; 31; 36(2); 44; 19:2; 10(2); 14(2); 15; 16; 20:3(4); 4; 5(4); 6; 9; 31; 32; 33; 34; 39(2); 40(2); 42(3); 21:2; 5; 6; 19; 21; 22:4(2); 13; 23; 30; 49; **2Kin** 1:10; 12; 13(2); 14; 2:2; 3(2); 4; 5(2); 6; 9; 16(2); 3:7(2); 13(2); 4:1(2); 3; 4; 7(2); 24; 26; 29(2); 30; 36; 5:8; 10; 15; 17(2); 18(2); 25; 27; 6:3; 12; 22(2); 28; 29; 8:9; 13; 9:1; 7; 22; 10:5; 15; 30; 14:9; 10; 15:12; 16:7(2); 18:23; 24; 26; 27; 19:4(3); 10; 22; 23; 27(4); 28(4); 20:3; 5(3); 6; 17; 18; 22:9; 19; 20(2); **1Chr** 10:4; 11:1(2); 2; 12:18(2); 16:35(2); 17:11(4); 17; 18(2); 19; 21(2); 22; 23; 24(2); 25(2); 26; 27; 19:3; 21:8; 12; 17; 22:11; 12; 28:6; 9; 21; 29:13; 17; 18; 19(3); **2Chr** 1:9; 10; 2:8(2); 10; 14(2); 6:2; 9(2); 14; 15(2); 16(2); 17(2); 19(2); 20(2); 21(3); 23; 24(2); 25; 26; 27(4); 29; 30; 31; 32(4); 33(4); 34(2); 38; 39(2); 41(4); 42; 7:12; 17; 18(2); 9:5; 6; 7(3); 8(3); 10:4(2); 7; 9; 10; 14:11; 16:3(2); 7; 18:3; 12; 22; 29; 20:7(2); 8; 9(2); 11; 37; 21:12(2); 13(2); 14(4); 15(2); 25:18; 34:16; 27; 28(2); **Ezr** 4:11; 15; 7:14; 18; 19; 20; 25(2); 26; 9:10; 11; 14; **Neh** 1:6(2); 7; 8; 10(4); 11(4); 2:2; 5(2); 6; 9:5; 8; 14(2); 16; 17; 18; 19; 20(2); 25; 26(2); 27; 28; 29(3); 30(2); 31; 32; 34(3); 35; 13:22; **Est** 3:8; 4:14(2); 5:3; 6(2); 7:2(2); 3; 9:12(2); **Job** 1:11; 12; 18(2); 2:5; 4:4; 6(4); 5:24(2); 25; 26; 27; 8:2; 4; 5; 6; 7(2); 21(2); 10:5(2); 12; 17; 11:3; 14; 15; 16; 18; 13:21; 24; 14:13; 15:5; 10; 12; 13(2); 21:14; 22:3; 5; 6; 23; 25; 26(2); 27(2); 28; 30:21; 33:5; 6; 8; 31; 33; 34:33; 35:4; 6; 8(2); 36:16; 19; 37:17; 38:3; 11; 12; 21; 34; 39:9; 11; 12(2); 26; 27; 40:7; 11; 41:5; 42:7; **Ps** 2:8; 3:8(2); 4:6; 5:5; 7(4); 8(2); 11; 6:1; 4; 8:1(2); 3(2); 6; 9; 9:1; 2; 3; 10; 14(2); 19; 10:5; 14; 13:1; 5(2); 15:1(2); 16:11(2); 17:2; 4; 5; 7(2); 8; 13; 14(2); 15(2); 18:15(2); 35(3); 49; 19:11; 13; 14; 20:3(2); 4; 5(2); 21:1(2); 5; 6; 8; 12; 13; 22:22; 23:4(2); 24:6; 25:4(2); 5; 6(2); 7(2); 11; 26:3(2); 7; 8; 27:8; 9(2);

11; 28:2; 9; 30:7(2); 9; 31:1; 3; 7; 15; 16(3); 19; 20; 32:4; 33:22; 34:13(2); 35:3; 24; 28(2); 36:5(2); 6(2); 7(2); 8(2); 9; 10(2); 37:5; 6(2); 38:1(2); 2; 39:10; 12; 40:5(2); 8(2); 10(5); 11(3); 16; 41:12; 42:3; 7(3); 10; 43:3(4); 44:2; 3(2); 5; 8; 12(2); 17; 18; 22; 24; 26; 45:2; 3(4); 4(2); 6(2); 7(2); 8; 9(2); 10; 11(2); 12; 16(2); 17; 48:9(2); 10(3); 11; 50:7; 8(2); 9(2); 14; 16; 19(2); 20; 51:1(2); 4; 9; 11(2); 12(2); 13; 14; 15; 18; 52:2; 5; 9(2); 54:1(2); 5; 6; 55:22; 56:8(2); 12; 57:1; 5; 10(2); 11; 59:11; 16(2); 60:3; 5(2); 61:4(2); 5; 8; 63:2(2); 3; 4; 7; 8; 65:4(3); 8; 11(2); 66:3(2); 4; 13; 67:2(2); 68:7; 10(2); 23(2); 24; 28(2); 29; 35; 69:7; 13(2); 16(2); 17(2); 24; 27; 29; 70:4; 71:2; 8(2); 15(2); 16; 17; 18(2); 19; 22; 24; 72:1(2); 2(2); 73:15; 24; 28; 74:1; 2; 3; 4; 7(2); 10; 11(3); 13; 18; 19(2); 21; 75:1(2); 76:6; 7; 77:11; 12(2); 13; 14; 15; 18; 19(3); 20; 79:1; 2(2); 5; 6(2); 8; 9(2); 10; 11; 13(3); 80:2; 3; 4; 7; 15; 16; 17(2); 18; 19; 81:10(2); 83:1; 3(2); 15(2); 16; 84:1; 4; 10; 85:1; 2; 3; 6; 7(2); 86:2; 4; 8; 9; 11(3); 12; 13; 16(2); 88:5; 7(2); 11(2); 12(2); 14; 15; 16(2); 89:1; 2; 4(2); 5(2); 8; 10; 12; 13(2); 14(2); 15; 16(2); 17; 19; 39; 46; 49(2); 50; 90:4; 7; 8; 9; 11(2); 13; 14; 16(3); 91:4; 7(2); 9; 10; 11; 12; 92:1; 2(2); 4(2); 5(2); 93:2; 5; 94:5; 12; 18; 19; 97:8; 99:3; 102:2; 10; 12; 14; 15; 24; 25; 27; 28; 103:3; 4; 5(2); 104:7(2); 13; 24(2); 29; 30; 106:4(2); 5(2); 7(2); 47(2); 108:4(2); 5; 6(2); 109:1; 21(2); 26; 27; 28; 110:1; 2; 3(3); 5; 115:1(3); 116:7; 16(2); 119:4; 5; 6; 7; 8; 9; 10; 11; 12; 13; 14; 15(2); 16(2); 17(2); 18; 19; 20; 21; 22; 23(2); 24; 25; 26; 27(2); 28; 29; 30; 31; 32; 33; 34; 35; 36; 37; 38(3); 39; 40(2); 41(3); 42; 43; 44; 45; 46; 47; 48(2); 49; 50; 51; 52; 53; 54; 55(2); 56; 57; 58(2); 59; 60; 61; 62; 63; 64(2); 65(2); 66; 67; 68; 69; 70; 71; 72; 73(2); 74; 75; 76(3); 77(2); 78; 79; 80; 81(2); 82; 83; 84; 85; 86; 87; 88(2); 89; 90; 91; 92; 93; 94; 95; 96; 97; 98; 99; 100; 101; 102; 103; 104; 105; 106; 107; 108; 109; 110; 111; 112; 113; 114; 116; 117; 118; 119; 120; 122; 123(2); 124(3); 125(2); 126; 127; 128; 129; 130; 131; 132; 133; 134; 135(3); 136; 137; 138; 139; 140(2); 141; 142(2); 143; 144; 145; 146; 147; 148; 149(2); 150; 151; 152; 153; 154; 155; 156(2); 157; 158; 159(2); 160(2); 161; 162; 163; 164; 165; 166(2); 167; 168(2); 169; 170; 171; 172(2); 173; 174(2); 175; 176(2); 121:3; 5(3); 7; 8(2); 122:2; 7(2); 9; 128:3(3); 5; 6; 132:8(2); 9(2); 10; 11(2); 12(2); 135:13(2); 137:9; 138:2(6); 4; 7; 8; 139:7(2); 10(2); 14; 16; 17; 20; 140:13(2); 142:7; 143:1(2); 2(2); 5(2); 7; 8; 10(2); 11(2); 12(2); 144:5; 145:1; 2; 4(2); 5(2); 6(2); 7(2); 10(2); 11(2); 13(2); 146:10; 147:12; 13(2); 14; **Prov** 1:8(2); 9(2); 14; 15; 2:3; 10; 3:3; 6(2); 8(2); 9; 10(2); 22(2); 23(2); 24; 26(2); 28; 29; 4:7; 10; 12; 13; 23; 26(2); 27; 5:2; 8; 9; 10(2); 11(2); 16; 18(2); 6:1(2); 2(2); 3(2); 9; 11(2); 20(2); 21; 7:3; 4; 15; 9:11(2); 16:3(2); 19:18(2); 20; 22:18; 19; 25; 27; 28; 23:2; 8; 9; 16; 22(2); 25(2); 24:6; 10; 12; 13; 14(2); 27; 28(2); 34(2); 25:8; 9(2); 17(2); 27:10(3); 23(2); 26; 27(3); 29:17(2); 30:32; 31:3(2); 8; 9; **Eccl** 5:1; 2(2); 6(3); 7:9; 17; 21; 9:7(4); 8(2); 9(4); 10(2); 10:4; 16(2); 17(2); 20(2); 11:1; 6; 9(3); 10(2); 12:1(2); **Song** 1:2; 3(2); 4; 7(2); 8(2); 10(2); 2:14(4); 4:1(2); 2; 3(4); 4; 5; 9; 10(2); 11(3); 13; 5:9(2); 6:1(2); 5; 6; 7(2); 7:1(2); 2(2); 3; 4(2); 7(2); 8(2); 9; 8:5; 13; **Is** 1:22(2); 23; 25(2); 26(2); 2:6; 3:6; 12; 25(2); 4:1; 6:7(2); 7:3; 11; 17(2); 8:8; 10:22; 27(2); 30; 14:3(2); 9; 11(2); 19; 20(2); 30(2); 16:3; 9(2); 17:10(2); 11(2); 19:12; 20:2(3); 22:2; 3; 7; 18(2); 19(2); 21(3); 23:10; 25:1(2); 12; 26:8(2); 9; 11; 13; 16; 17; 19(2); 20(2); 29:4(3); 5; 30:19; 20(2); 22(2); 23(2); 33:6; 23; 36:8; 9; 11; 12; 37:4(3); 10; 23; 24; 28(4); 29(4); 38:3; 5(4); 17; 18; 19; 39:6; 7; 40:9; 41:10; 13(2); 14; 43:1; 3(3); 4; 5; 23(2); 24(2); 25(2); 27(2); 44:3; 22(2); 24; 27; 28; 45:3; 4; 9; 47:2; 3(2); 6; 7; 9; 10(3); 12(2); 13; 15(2); 48:4(2); 17(2); 18(2); 19(2); 49:16; 17(2); 19(3); 22(2); 23(2); 25; 26(2); 51:13; 15; 16; 20(2); 22(2); 23(2); 52:1(2); 2; 7; 8; 54:2(3); 3; 4(2); 5(2); 6; 8; 11(2); 12(3); 13(2); 15; 55:5; 57:6(2); 7; 8(2); 9(2); 10; 11; 12(2); 13; 58:1; 7(2); 8(3); 10(3); 11(2); 13(2); 14; 59:21(4); 60:1; 3(2); 4(3); 9(2); 10; 11; 14; 16(2); 17; 18(4); 19(3); 20(3); 21; 62:2(2); 3; 4(3); 5(2); 6; 8(2); 11; 63:2; 14; 15(6); 16; 17(3); 18(2); 19; 64:1; 2(2); 3; 5; 7(2); 8; 9; 10; 12; 66:9; **Jer** 1:9; 17; 2:2; 16; 17; 19(2); 20(2); 23; 25(2); 28(4); 33(2); 34; 36; 37; 3:2(2); 13(2); 4:7(2); 14; 18(3); 30(3); 5:7; 14; 17(7); 10:6; 17; 25(2); 11:13(2); 16; 20; 21; 12:1; 6(2); 13:1; 4; 20; 22(2); 25(2); 26(3); 27(2); 14:7; 9; 19; 21(3); 15:11; 13(4); 15(2); 16(3); 17; 17:3(4); 18:20; 23; 20:3; 4; 6; 12; 22:2(2); 7; 15; 17; 20(2); 21(3); 22(3); 23; 25; 26; 27:2; 13; 28:6; 29:25; 30:8(2); 10; 12(2); 13; 14(2); 15(2); 17; 31:4; 7; 16(2); 17; 21; 32:17; 21; 23(2); 34:5; 37:18; 38:16; 17; 20; 22(2); 23(2); 39:18(2); 40:2; 42:2; 3; 5; 45:5; 46:12(2); 15; 27; 47:6; 48:7(2); 18(2); 32(3); 46(2); 49:4; 11(2); 16(2); 50:31; 51:13; 36; **Lam** 1:10; 2:13; 14(2); 19(2); 3:23; 55; 65; 4:22; 5:19; **Eze** 2:1; 8; 3:3(2); 8(2); 9; 11; 19; 21; 26(2); 27; 4:3; 4; 6; 7; 8; 9; 10; 15; 5:1; 3; 11; 6:2; 11; 7:3; 4; 8; 9; 9:8(2); 11:15(3); 12:3; 4; 6(2); 18(2); 13:4; 17(2); 16:3(4); 4(2); 5; 6(2); 7; 8(2); 9; 11(2); 12; 13; 14(2); 15(2); 16(2); 17; 18; 20(3); 22(3); 23; 25(4); 26(2); 27; 29; 33(3); 34; 36(6); 37(3); 39(3); 43(2); 45(2); 46(3); 47; 48(2); 49; 51(2); 52(4); 53; 55(2); 56(3); 57(2); 58; 60; 61(4); 63(2); 19:2; 10(2); 20:46(2); 21:2(2); 6; 12; 16; 30; 32; 22:4(3); 12; 13(2); 15; 23:21(3); 22(2); 25(5); 26(2); 27(2); 28; 29(4); 31; 32; 33; 35(3); 40; 24:13(2); 14(2); 16; 17(3); 27; 25:2; 4(2); 6; 26:8; 9(2); 10(2); 11(3); 12(7); 13(2); 15; 18(2); 27:4(3); 5; 6; 7; 8(3); 9(2); 10(2); 11(4); 12(2); 13(2); 14; 15; 16(3); 17(2); 18(2); 19(2); 20; 21; 22(2); 23; 24(2); 25; 26; 27(10); 28; 33(3); 34(2); 28:4(2); 5(4); 7(2); 13(3); 15; 16; 17(3); 18(2); 21; 29:2; 4(6); 5; 7; 10; 31:2; 32:2(2); 5(2); 6; 8; 9; 10; 12; 33:2; 9; 12; 17; 30; 31; 32; 35:2; 4; 8(3); 9; 11; 12; 36:13; 14; 15; 37:18; 38:2; 4; 7; 9; 10; 13; 15; 39:3(3); 4; **Dan** 1:12; 13; 2:4; 28(3); 29(3); 30; 3:12; 18; 4:22(2); 25; 26; 27(2); 32; 5:10(2); 11(4); 16; 17(2); 18; 23(5); 26; 28; 6:16; 20; 9:5(2); 6(2); 11(2); 13; 15; 16(5); 17(3); 18(2); 19(3); 23; 24(2); 10:12(3); 14; 11:14; 12:1(2); 9; 13(2); **Hos** 2:6; 4:4; 5; 6(2); 6:5; 8:1; 5; 9:1; 10:13(2); 14(2); 12:6(2); 9; 13:4; 10(3); 14(2); 14:1; 8; **Joel** 2:17; 3:11; **Amos** 3:11(2); 4:12; 5:23(2); 6:10; 7:16; 17(4); 8:14; 9:15; **Obad** 4; 7(2); 9; 10(2); 12; 15; **Jonah** 1:6; 8; 2:3(2); 4(2); **Mic** 1:11; 16(2); 4:9; 13; 5:10(2); 11(2); 13(2); 14(2); 6:1; 8; 9; 13; 14; 7:4(2); 5(2); 10; 11; 14(2); 15; **Nah** 1:13; 14(3); 15(2); 2:1(3); 13(3); 3:5(4); 9; 12; 13(3); 14; 16; 17(2); 18(3); 19(3); **Hab** 1:13; 2:10(2); 15; 16(2); 3:2(2); 8(2); 9(2); 11; 13; **Zeph** 1:7; 3:11(2); 15; 17; **Zec** 3:8; 9:9; 11(2); 13(2); 11:1(2); 14:1; **Mal** 1:6; 8(2); 2:14(3); **Mt** 1:20; 4:6; 7; 10; 5:23(2); 24(4); 29(3); 30(3); 36; 39; 40(2); 43; 6:3(2); 4; 6(4); 9; 10(2); 17; 18(2); 22; 23; 7:3; 4; 5; 22(3); 8:4; 13; 9:2; 5; 6; 14; 18; 22; 11:10(2); 26; 12:2; 37(2); 47(2); 13:27; 15:2; 4; 28; 17:16; 18:8(2); 15(2); 33; 19:19(3); 20:14; 21(2); 21:5; 22:37(4); 39; 44; 23:37; 24:3; 25:21; 23; 25; 26:18; 42; 52; 73; **Mk** 1:2(2); 25; 44(2); 2:5; 9(2); 11(2); 18; 3:32(2); 5:9; 19; 23; 34(2); 35; 6:18; 7:5; 10(2); 29(2); 9:18; 38; 43; 45; 10:19; 21; 37(3); 52(2); 12:30(5); 31; 36; 14:70; **Lk** 1:13(2); 31; 36; 38; 42; 44; 61; 2:29(2); 30; 32; 35; 48; 4:8; 11; 12; 23; 35; 5:5; 14; 20; 23; 24; 6:10; 29(2); 30; 41; 42(2); 7:27(2); 48; 50; 8:20(2); 30; 48; 49; 9:40; 41; 49; 10:17; 21; 27(6); 11:2(3); 34(2); 36; 12:20; 13:26; 34; 14:12(4); 15:19(2); 21(2); 27(2); 29; 30(2); 32; 16:2; 6; 7; 25(2); 17:3; 19(2); 18:20(2); 42(2); 19:5; 16; 18; 20; 39; 42(2); 44(2); 20:43; 22:32(2); 23:42; 46; **Jn** 4:16; 18; 42; 50(2); 51; 53; 5:8; 10; 11; 12; 7:3; 8:13; 19; 11:23; 12:15; 28; 13:37; 38; 17:1(2); 6(2); 12; 14; 17(2); 26; 18:11; 19:26; 27; 20:27(2); 21:18; **Acts** 2:28; 35(2); 3:25; 4:25; 27; 28(2); 29(2); 30; 5:9; 7:3(2); 32; 33(2); 8:20; 21; 22; 9:13; 14; 15; 17; 34; 10:4; 31; 11:14; 12:8(2); 14:10; 16:31; 18:9; 22:13; 16; 18; 20; 23:5; 24:2; 4; 25; 26:16; **Rom** 2:5; 17; 23; 25; 3:4; 4:18; 8:36; 9:7; 10:8(2); 9; 11:3; 13:9; 14:10(2); 15(3); 21; 15:9; **1Cor** 7:16(2); 8:11; 14:16; 15:55(2); **Gal** 3:16; 5:14; **Eph** 6:2; **1Ti** 4:12; 15; 5:23; 6:20; **2Ti** 1:4; 5(2); 4:5; 9; 21; 22; **Philem** 1:2; 5; 6; 7; 13; 14(2); 21; **Heb** 1:8(2); 9(2); 12; 13; 2:7; 12; 10:7; 9; 11:18; **Jas** 2:8; 18(2); **2Jn** 4; 13; **3Jn** 2; 6; **Rev** 2:2(3); 4; 5; 9; 13; 19(3); 3:1; 2; 8; 9; 11; 15; 18; 4:11; 5:9; 10:9(2); 11:17; 18(3); 14:15; 18; 15:3(2); 4(2); 16:7; 18:10; 14; 23(2); 19:10(2); 22:9(2)

TILL

3588, 5647, 5704, 5705, 6440, *891, 1508, 1519, 2193, 3360, 3752, 3757*

Gen 2:5; 3:19; 23; 19:22; 29:8; 38:11; 17; **Ex** 15:16(2); 16:19; 24; 34:33; 40:37; **Num** 12:15; **Deut** 17:5; 28:45; **Josh** 5:6; 8; 8:6; 10:20; **Judg** 3:25; 6:4; 11:33; 16:3; 19:26; 21:2; **Ruth** 1:13; **1Sa** 10:8; 16:11; 22:3; **2Sa** 3:35; 9:10; **1Kin** 14:10; 18:28; **2Kin** 2:17; 4:20; 7:9; 10:17; 13:17; 19; 21:16; **2Chr** 26:15; 29:34; 36:16; **Ezr** 2:63; 5:5; 9:14; **Neh** 2:7; 4:11; 21; 7:65; 13:19; **Job** 7:19; 8:21; 14:6; 12; 14; 27:5; 32:4; **Ps** 10:15; 18:37; 68:30; **Prov** 7:23; 29:11; **Eccl** 2:3; **Song** 2:7; 3:5; **Is** 5:8; 11; 22:14; 30:17; 38:13; 42:4; 62:7(2); **Jer** 7:32; 9:16; 19:11; 23:20; 24:10; 27:11; 49:9; 37; 52:3; 11; **Lam** 3:50; **Eze** 4:8; 14; 24:13; 28:15; 34:21; 39:15; 19(2); 47:20; **Dan** 2:9; 34; 4:23; 25; 33; 5:21; 6:14; 7:4; 9; 11; 10:3; 11:36; 12:9; 13; **Hos** 5:15; 10:12; **Obad** 5; **Jonah** 4:5; **Zeph** 3:3; **Mt** 1:25; 2:9; 5:18(2); 26; 10:11; 23; 12:20; 13:33; 16:28; 18:21; 30; 34; 22:44; 23:39; 24:34; **Mk** 6:10; 9:1; 9; 12:36; 13:30; **Lk** 1:80; 9:27; 12:50; 59; 13:8; 21; 15:8; 17:8; 19:13; 20:43; 21:32; **Jn** 13:38; 21:22; 23; **Acts** 7:18; 8:40; 20:11; 21:5; 23:12; 21; 25:21; 28:23; **1Cor** 11:26; 15:25; **Gal** 3:19; **Eph** 4:13; **Phil** 1:10; **1Ti** 4:13; **Heb** 10:13; **Rev** 2:25; 7:3; 15:8; 20:3

TIME

116, 227, 268, 570, 1767, 2165, 2166, 3117, 3118, 4150, 4279, 5732, 5769, 6256, 6258, 6440, 6471, 6635, 7225, 7227, 7674, 8032, 8462, 8543, *744, 1074, 1208, 1597, 1909, 2119, 2121, 2235, 2250, 2540, 3195, 3379, 3568, 3598, 3819, 4218, 4287, 4340, 4455, 5119, 5550, 5551, 5610*

Gen 4:3; 17:21; 18:10; 14(2); 21:2; 22; 22:15; 24:11(2); 26:8; 29:7; 34; 30:33; 31:10; 38:1; 12; 27; 39:5; 11; 41:5; 43:10; 18; 20; 47:29; **Ex** 2:23; 8:32; 9:5; 14; 18; 27; 13:14; 21:19; 29; 36; 23:15; 34:18; 21; **Lev** 13:58; 15:25(2); 18:18; 25:32; 50; 26:5; **Num** 10:6; 13:20(2); 20:15; 22:4; 23:23; 26:10; 32:10; 35:26; **Deut** 1:9; 16; 18; 2:20; 34; 3:4; 8; 12; 18; 21; 23; 4:14; 5:5; 6:20; 9:19; 20; 10:1; 8; 10(2); 16:9; 19:4; 6; 14; 20:19; 32:35; **Josh** 2:5; 3:15; 4:6; 21; 5:2(2); 6:16; 26; 8:14; 10:27; 42; 11:6; 10; 18; 21; 22:24; 27; 28; 23:1; 24:2; **Judg** 3:29; 4:4; 9:8; 10:14; 11:4; 26; 12:6; 13:23; 14:4; 8; 15:1; 18:31; 20:15; 21:14; 22; 24; **Ruth** 4:7; **1Sa** 1:4; 20; 3:2; 8; 4:20; 7:2; 9:13; 16; 24; 11:9; 13:8; 14:18; 21; 18:19; 19:21; 20:12; 35; 26:8; 27:7; **2Sa** 2:11; 5:2; 7:6; 11; 11:1; 14:2; 29; 17:7; 20:5; 18; 23:8; 13; 20; 24:15; **1Kin** 1:6; 2:26; 8:65; 9:2; 11:29; 42; 14:1; 15:23; 18:29; 34(4); 36; 44; 19:2; 7; 20:6; **2Kin** 3:6; 4:16; 17; 5:26; 7:1; 18; 8:22; 10:6(2); 36; 16:6; 18:16; 20:12; 24:10; **1Chr** 9:20; 25(2); 11:2; 11; 12:22; 17:10; 20:1; 4; 21:28; 29:22; 27; **2Chr** 7:8; 13:18; 15:11; 16:7; 10; 18:34; 21:10; 19; 24:11; 25:27; 28:16; 22; 30:3; 5; 26; 35:17; **Ezr** 4:10; 11; 15; 17; 19; 5:3; 16; 7:12; 8:34; 10:13; **Neh** 2:6; 4:16; 22; 5:14; 6:1; 5; 9:27; 32; 12:44; 13:6; 21; **Est** 2:19; 4:14(2); 8:9; 9:27; **Job** 6:17; 7:1; 9:19; 14:13; 14; 15:32; 22:16; 30:3; 38:23; 39:1; 2; 18; **Ps** 4:7; 21:9; 27:5; 32:6; 37:19; 39; 41:1; 56:3; 69:13; 71:9; 78:38; 81:3; 15; 89:47; 102:13(2); 105:19; 113:2; 115:18; 119:126; 121:8; 129:1; 2; **Prov** 25:13; 19; 31:25; **Eccl** 1:10; 3:1; 2(4); 3(4); 4(4); 5(4); 6(4); 7(4); 8(4); 11; 17; 7:17; 8:5; 6; 9; 9:11; 12(2); **Song** 2:12; **Is** 11:11; 13:22; 16:13; 18:7; 20:2; 26:17; 28:19; 30:8; 33:2; 39:1; 42:14; 23; 44:8; 45:21(2); 48:6; 8; 16; 49:8; 60:22; **Jer** 1:13; 2:20; 27; 28; 3:4; 17; 4:11; 6:15; 8:1; 7; 12; 15; 10:15; 11:12; 14; 13:3; 14:8; 19; 15:11(2); 18:23; 27:7; 30:7; 31:1; 33:1; 15; 39:10; 46:17; 21; 49:8; 19; 50:4; 16; 20; 27; 31; 44; 51:6; 18; 33(2); **Lam** 5:20; **Eze** 4:10(2); 11(2); 7:7; 12; 16:8(2); 57; 21:14; 22:3; 26:20; 27:34; 30:3; 35:5(2); 38:10; 17; 18; **Dan** 2:8; 9; 16; 3:5; 7; 8; 15; 4:36; 7:12; 22; 25(2); 8:17; 19; 23; 9:21; 10:1; 11:24; 27; 29; 35(2); 40; 12:1(4); 4; 7; 9; 11; **Hos** 2:9; 9:10; 10:12; **Joel** 3:1; **Amos** 5:13(2); **Jonah** 3:1; **Mic** 2:3; 3:4; 5:3; **Nah** 1:9; **Hab** 2:3; **Zeph** 1:12; 3:19; 20(2); **Hag** 1:2(2); 4; **Zec** 10:1; 14:7; **Mal** 3:11; **Mt** 1:11; 2:7; 16; 4:6; 17; 5:21; 25; 27; 33; 8:29; 11:25; 12:1; 13:15; 30; 14:1; 15; 16:21; 18:1; 21:34; 24:21; 25:19; 26:16; 18; 42; 44; **Mk** 1:15; 4:12; 17; 6:35; 10:30; 11:13; 13:19; 33; 14:41; 72; **Lk** 1:10; 57; 4:5; 11; 27; 7:45; 8:13; 27; 9:51; 12:1; 56; 13:35; 14:17; 15:29; 16:16; 18:30; 19:44; 20:9; 21:8; 34; 37; 23:7; 22; **Jn** 1:18; 3:4; 5:6; 37; 6:66; 7:6(2); 8; 11:39; 14:9; 16:2; 4; 25; 21:14; 16; 17(2); **Acts** 1:6; 21; 7:13; 17; 20; 8:1; 11; 10:15; 11:8; 12:1; 13:18; 14:3; 28; 15:21; 17:21; 18:20; 23; 19:23; 20:16; 24:25; 27:9; **Rom** 3:26; 5:6; 8:18; 9:9; 11:5; 13:11(2); **1Cor** 4:5; 7:5; 29; 9:7; 15:8; 16:12(2); **2Cor** 6:2(2); 8:14; 12:14; 13:1; 2; **Gal** 1:13; 4:2; 4; 5:21; **Eph** 2:2; 11; 12; 5:16; **Col** 3:7; 4:5; **1Th** 2:5; 17; **2Th** 2:6; **1Ti** 2:6; 6:19; **2Ti** 4:3; 6; S:1; **Philem** 1:11; **Heb** 1:1; 5; 2:1; 4:7; 16; 5:12; 9:9; 10; 28; 11:32; **Jas** 4:14; **1Pet** 1:5; 11; 17; 2:10; 3:5; 4:2; 3; 17; 5:6; **2Pet** 1:21; 2:3; **1Jn** 2:18(2); 4:12; **Jude** 18; **Rev** 1:3; 10:6; 11:18; 12:12; 14(2); 14:15; 22:10

TIMES

865, 2165, 2166, 3027, 3117, 4150, 4151, 4489, 5732, 6256, 6471, 8543, *1074, 1441, 2034, 2540, 3999, 4218, 5151, 5550*

Gen 27:36; 31:7; 41; 33:3; 43:34; **Ex** 23:14; 17; **Lev** 4:6; 17; 8:11; 14:7; 16; 27; 51; 16:2; 14; 19; 19:26; 25:8; 26:18; 21; 24; 28; **Num** 14:22; 19:4; 22:28; 32; 33; 24:1; 10; **Deut** 1:11; 2:10; 4:42; 16:16; 18:10; 14; **Josh** 6:4; 15(2); **Judg** 13:25; 16:15; 20; 20:30; 31; **1Sa** 3:10; 18:10; 19:7; 20:25; 41; **2Sa** 3:17; **1Kin** 8:59; 9:25; 17:21; 18:43; 22:16; **2Kin** 4:35; 5:10; 14; 13:19; 25; 19:25; 21:6; **1Chr** 12:32; 21:3; 29:30; **2Chr** 8:13; 15:5; 18:15; 33:6; **Ezr** 10:14; **Neh** 4:12; 6:4; 9:28; 10:34; 13:31; **Est** 1:13; 9:31; **Job** 19:3; 24:1; **Ps** 9:9; 10:1; 12:6; 31:15; 34:1; 44:1; 62:8; 77:5; 106:3; 43; 119:20; 164; **Prov** 5:19; 17:17; 24:16; **Eccl** 8:12; **Is** 14:31; 33:6; 37:26; 46:10; **Jer** 8:7; **Eze** 12:27; **Dan** 1:20; 2:21; 3:19; 4:16; 23; 25; 32; 6:10; 13; 7:10; 25(2); 9:25; 11:6; 14; 12:7; **Mt** 16:3; 18:21; 22(2); **Lk** 17:4(2); 21:24; **Acts** 1:7; 3:19; 21; 11:10; 14:16; 17:26; 30; **Rom** 11:30; **2Cor** 11:24; **Gal** 1:23; 4:10; **Eph** 1:10; 2:3; **1Th** 5:1; **1Ti** 4:1; 6:15; **2Ti** 3:1; **Titus** 1:3; **Heb** 1:1; 13; **1Pet** 1:20; **Rev** 5:11; 12:14

TO

1519

Gen 1:14; 15; 16(2); 17; 18(2); 29; 30(3); 2:5(2); 9(2); 10; 15(2); 19; 20(3); 21; 3:6(3); 12; 16; 18; 21; 22; 23; 24; 4:3; 4; 5; 8; 11; 14; 23(2); 26(3); 6:1(2); 4; 16; 17; 19; 20; 21; 22; 7:2; 3; 4; 10; 8:1; 6; 7; 8; 11; 13; 9:8; 10; 11; 14; 15; 20; 10:8; 19; 21; 11:2; 3(2); 4; 5; 6(2); 7; 8; 31; 12:5; 10; 11(3); 12; 14; 19(2); 13:3; 6; 9(3); 15(2); 14:1; 7; 10; 17; 21; 22; 23; 15:3; 5; 6; 7(2); 15; 17; 16:2; 3(2); 6; 7; 9; 16; 17:1; 7(2); 8; 18:2; 5; 7; 10; 11; 14; 16; 19; 21; 25(2); 27; 31; 19:1(2); 5; 8; 9(2); 10(2); 11; 13; 17(2); 19; 20; 27; 29; 30; 31; 34; 20:3(2); 6; 9; 13(2); 16; 21:2; 3; 6; 17; 22; 23(2); 26; 22:1; 5; 9; 10; 14; 19; 20; 23; 23:2(2); 7(2); 8; 16; 24:4; 5; 8; 9; 10; 11(2); 13; 14(2); 15(2); 16(2); 17; 20; 21; 22; 23; 25; 27; 30; 32; 33; 36; 37; 38; 41; 43(4); 44; 48; 49(2); 52(2); 53(3); 56; 63; 65; 25:8; 11; 13; 16; 20(2); 22; 24; 30; 32(2); 33; 26:4; 7(2); 8; 11; 23; 26; 27; 31; 32; 34; 35; 27:1; 3; 4; 5(4); 8; 9; 10; 11; 12; 14; 20; 25(2); 29(2); 30; 37; 40; 42(2);

43(2); 45; 46; 28:2(2); 4(2); 5; 6(2); 7; 9; 11; 12; 13(2); 14(4); 15; 20(2); 21; 29:10; 13(3); 14; 19(2); 20; 23(2); 25(2); 26; 28; 29(2); 30:4; 9; 14; 15; 16; 18; 22; 24; 25(2); 32; 33; 34; 38(2); 41; 31:3; 4; 7; 9; 10; 18(2); 19; 20; 24(2); 26(2); 28; 29(2); 31; 32; 35; 36; 51; 52; 54; 32:3; 5; 6(3); 8; 9; 13; 30; 33:3(2); 4; 8; 11; 14; 17; 18; 34:1; 4; 6; 7; 8; 12; 14(2); 16; 17; 19; 21; 22(2); 25; 30(3); 35:1; 2; 3; 6; 12(2); 16(2); 17; 18; 19; 22; 26; 36:4; 12(2); 14; 40; 43; 37:7; 8; 9; 10(5); 12; 13; 14(2); 17; 18; 19; 22(2); 23; 25(3); 27; 28; 32; 35(2); 38:1(2); 8; 9(2); 11; 12; 13(2); 14(2); 15; 16; 20; 22; 23; 24; 25; 26; 27; 28; 29; 39:1; 3; 5; 7; 8; 10(4); 11(2); 13; 14(2); 15; 17(2); 18; 19(2); 22; 23(2); 40:1; 5; 7; 8; 9(2); 20; 22; 41:1; 8; 11; 12(4); 13(2); 15; 24; 25; 28; 32; 36; 43; 45; 52; 54; 55(2); 57(2); 42:3; 5; 6(2); 7; 9; 10; 12; 21; 24; 25(3); 27; 28; 30; 35; 37(2); 38; 43:2; 6; 7; 15; 16; 19; 20; 21(2); 22; 23; 26(2); 30; 33(2); 44:2; 7; 11; 13; 14; 24; 29; 30; 31(2); 32; 33; 34; 45:1; 4; 5; 7(2); 8; 9; 11; 21; 22(2); 23; 27; 46:1; 3; 5; 18; 22; 28; 29(2); 32; 33; 47:4; 6; 12; 21(2); 24; 48:1; 4; 7; 11; 12; 17; 22; 49:4(2); 15; 28; 29; 50:2; 7; 10; 11; 14; 20(3); 24(3); **Ex** 1:10; 11; 13; 15; 16; 21; 2:1; 4(2); 5(2); 7(2); 8; 11; 13; 14; 15; 16; 18(2); 21; 23; 3:1(3); 4; 6; 8(2); 13; 16; 18(2); 21; 4:8(2); 9; 14; 16(2); 18(2); 20; 21; 23; 24(2); 25; 27(2); 5:2; 7; 8; 10; 12; 14; 16; 17; 21(3); 23(3); 6:1; 3; 4; 7(2); 8(4); 13; 16; 17; 19; 20; 23; 25(2); 26(2); 27(2); 28; 7:1; 14; 15; 17; 18; 20; 23; 24; 8:2; 5; 9; 10(2); 13; 18; 20; 22; 23; 25; 26(2); 27; 28; 29(3); 31; 9:2; 5; 8; 16; 18(2); 10:3; 4(2); 5; 10; 26; 28; 12:2; 3(2); 4(2); 13(2); 14; 16; 21; 23(3); 24(2); 25(2); 26; 29; 35; 37; 41(2); 42(2); 48; 49; 51; 13:5; 6; 10; 11; 14; 15(2); 17(2); 21(3); 14:11(2); 12; 13(3); 20(2); 21; 23; 24; 27; 15:17; 21; 23; 26(2); 27; 16:3(3); 5; 8(2); 10; 13; 15(2); 16(2); 18; 21; 22; 23(3); 25(3); 27(2); 28; 32; 33; 34; 35; 17:1(2); 3; 4; 9; 10(2); 11; 16; 18:7; 8; 9; 12; 13(2); 14(2); 15; 18; 19; 21; 23(2); 24; 19:2; 3; 10(2); 12(2); 13; 16; 17; 20; 21; 22; 23; 24; 20:5; 8; 20; 21:6; 7; 8(2); 12; 14; 15; 16; 17; 19; 29(3); 31; 36; 22:5; 7; 8; 9; 10; 16; 17(2); 18; 19; 25(2); 26; 27; 29; 31; 23:1; 2(3); 4; 5; 20(2); 24; 27; 24:4; 12; 14; 25:7; 9; 20; 25; 27; 29; 35; 26:3(2); 7; 13; 28; 30; 27:3; 5; 7; 20(2); 21; 28:3; 8; 10; 11; 14; 21(2); 35; 36; 42; 43; 29:1(2); 10; 29(2); 30; 33(2); 35(2); 36; 41(2); 42; 44(2); 30:1; 4(2); 15; 16; 18; 20(3); 21(3); 37(2); 38; 31:4(2); 5(2); 10; 11; 14; 15(2); 16; 32:1; 5(2); 6(3); 12(2); 13; 14; 19; 20; 27; 28; 29(2); 30; 33:1(2); 5; 7; 8; 9; 11; 19; 22; 34:2; 7; 12; 24; 29; 30; 34; 35; 35:2(3); 9; 19(2); 21; 27; 29(2); 32(2); 33(2); 35; 36:1(3); 2(2); 3; 5; 6; 7; 12; 18; 29(2); 33(2); 34; 37:2; 3; 5; 9(2); 14; 15; 16; 21; 27(2); 29; 38:5; 7; 18; 21(2); 26; 30; 39:1; 3; 4; 5; 7; 14(3); 26; 30(2); 31; 32; 37; 41(2); 42; 40:4; 5; 16; 17; 30; 35; **Lev** 1:4; 9; 14; 2:2(2); 13; 4:2; 3; 5; 16; 23; 27; 28; 35; 5:4(2); 7; 10; 11; 12(2); 17; 6:2; 4; 5; 25; 30; 7:8; 35; 36; 38; 8:5; 11; 12; 15; 31; 34(2); 9:1; 4(2); 16; 10:7; 15; 17(2); 19; 11:1; 7; 8; 21; 31; 37; 45; 47; 12:2; 8; 13:12; 15; 19; 59(2); 14:4(2); 7; 8; 11; 14; 17; 18; 19; 21(2); 22; 25; 28; 29(2); 31(2); 32(2); 34; 35; 36(2); 38; 41; 49; 57; 15:1; 13; 14; 28; 29; 16:10(3); 17; 27; 30; 32; 34; 17:4; 5; 9; 11(2); 18:4; 6(3); 14; 17; 18(3); 19; 20; 21; 23(2); 19:4; 11; 20(2); 24; 29(3); 31; 20:2(2); 3(2); 5; 6; 9; 10; 11; 12; 13; 15; 16; 22; 24; 27; 21:4; 10; 11; 14; 17; 21(2); 24; 22:2; 8; 16; 18; 21(2); 33; 23:2; 11; 20; 22; 28; 37(2); 43; 24:2(2); 16(2); 17; 19; 20; 21; 23; 25:9; 15; 16(3); 25; 26(2); 27; 28(2); 30; 38(2); 39; 46; 47; 50(2); 26:1; 5; 8; 21; 37; 44(2); 27:8; 14; 16; 17; 18; 19; 20; 24(2); 25; 27(2); 29; **Num** 1:3(2); 18; 20(3); 22(3); 24(3); 26(3); 28(3); 30(3); 32(3); 34(3); 36(3); 38(3); 40(3); 42(3); 45(2); 50; 51(2); 54; 2:10; 18; 34(2); 3:3; 7; 8; 9; 10; 16; 20; 22; 34; 38; 46; 48(2); 51(2); 4:3; 7; 11; 14; 15(2); 16; 19(2); 20; 23(2); 24; 30; 31; 33; 37; 41; 45; 47; 49(3); 5:6; 8(2); 15; 19; 20; 21(2); 22(3); 24; 26; 27(2); 29; 6:2(2); 4; 10(2); 21; 7:1; 5(3); 7; 89; 8:7; 12; 15; 19(4); 20; 21; 22; 24; 26; 9:3(2); 5; 12; 13; 14(2); 20(2); 10:3; 7; 8; 9; 10; 11; 13; 14; 18; 22; 28; 30(2); 31(2); 33; 35; 11:4; 13; 14; 16; 18(2); 22(2); 23; 25; 12:8(2); 13:16; 17; 21; 26(4); 30; 31; 32; 14:3(2); 4; 7; 14(2); 16; 20; 22; 25; 28; 29; 30; 36(2); 38; 44; 15:3; 12(3); 24; 28; 34; 35; 39; 41; 16:5(3); 7; 9(5); 10; 12; 13; 16; 28; 31; 33; 40(3); 42; 17:2(2); 5(2); 6; 8; 10; 18:6(2); 7; 8; 11(2); 16(2); 19; 24(2); 28; 20:5(3); 8; 12; 17(2); 21; 21:3; 4; 5; 7; 8; 9; 15; 16; 18; 19(2); 20; 23(2); 29; 32; 33; 34; 22:2; 5(2); 11; 13(2); 14; 16(2); 18; 20; 23; 26(3); 30; 32; 36; 37(3); 38; 40(2); 41; 23:3(2); 11; 12; 14; 17; 20; 23; 24:1(2); 2; 10; 11(2); 12; 13; 14; 25; 25:1; 2; 26:1; 2(2); 18; 22; 25; 27; 37; 43; 47; 50; 53; 54(4); 55; 56; 59; 27:7; 8; 11; 14; 28:2; 7; 22; 30; 29:5; 9(2); 14; 15; 18; 21; 24; 27; 30; 33; 37; 40; 30:2(2); 13; 14; 31:4; 6(3); 13; 16; 21; 27; 28; 36; 50; 52; 32:2; 6(2); 8; 14; 19; 20; 27; 29; 33(2); 39; 33:2(2); 14; 53; 54(3); 55; 56(2); 34:4(5); 8; 9; 10; 11; 12; 13(2); 14(2); 18; 29; 35:2; 3; 5; 6; 7; 8; 11; 16; 17; 18; 21; 24; 25; 30(3); 31; 32(2); 36:2(3); 3(2); 5; 6(2); 7(2); 9(2); **Deut** 1:3; 5; 7(2); 8(2); 9; 14; 19; 27(2); 28; 30; 33(3); 35; 36(2); 38; 41(2); 45; 2:4; 15; 16; 18; 22; 24; 25; 27; 31(2); 32; 34; 3:1(2); 3; 7; 12; 18; 24(3); 28; 4:1; 5; 9; 10; 13; 14(2); 19; 20; 25(2); 26(2); 30; 34(2); 36; 38(3); 5:4; 5; 12; 15; 23; 30; 31; 32(3); 6:1(2); 2; 3; 10(4); 19; 20; 23; 24(2); 25; 7:1; 6; 9; 10(4); 11; 12(2); 13; 24; 25; 8:1; 2(3); 3; 6(2); 16; 18; 9:1(4); 4; 5;

6; 7; 8(2); 9; 10; 11; 18(2); 19; 20; 22; 23; 27(2); 28(2); 10:4; 6; 7; 8(4); 10; 11; 12(4); 13; 15; 20; 11:4(2); 8; 9(2); 10; 11; 13(3); 16; 21; 22(4); 25; 28; 29(2); 31(2); 32; 12:1(2); 5; 9(2); 10; 11(2); 13; 15; 19; 20; 21; 29; 30; 31(2); 32; 13:2; 3; 5(4); 9(2); 10; 12; 17; 18(3); 14:2; 23(2); 24(2); 15:4; 5(2); 11(2); 15; 18; 16:2; 6; 8; 9(3); 11; 17; 17:6(2); 7(2); 10(3); 11(4); 12; 16(4); 17(2); 19(3); 20(3); 18:5(2); 8; 9; 10; 14; 16; 19; 20(2); 22; 19:2; 3; 5(2); 8; 9(3); 14; 16; 19; 20:1; 4(2); 5; 9; 10; 18; 19(2); 21:1; 5(2); 10; 11; 12; 16; 22(2); 22:2; 4; 6; 7; 14; 16; 21(2); 22; 27; 23:2; 3; 4; 14(2); 19; 20(2); 21; 22; 24:1; 3; 4(2); 5; 6(2); 8(2); 10; 11; 16(3); 17; 18; 19; 22; 25:2(4); 5(2); 7(3); 8(2); 11; 19; 26:2; 3; 5; 13(3); 14(2); 16; 17(4); 18; 19; 27:12; 13; 18; 25; 26; 28:1(3); 7; 11; 12(2); 13(2); 14(4); 15(3); 20; 21; 25; 31(2); 44(2); 45; 50; 55; 56; 58; 63(7); 29:1; 4(3); 8(2); 13(4); 18; 19(3); 21; 22; 27; 29; 30:1(2); 2; 6; 10; 12; 16(4); 18(2); 19; 20(4); 31:4(2); 7(2); 11; 12; 13(2); 16; 21; 24; 28; 29(2); 32:8(2); 13; 16(2); 17(3); 21(4); 26; 30; 35; 40; 41; 43(2); 45; 46(2); 47; 33:7; 9; 17; 24; 34:1; 4; 5; 10; 11(4); **Josh** 1:1; 2(2); 5; 6; 7(4); 8(2); 11(3); 12(3); 18; 2:1; 2(2); 3(2); 5; 6; 7; 16; 20; 23; 3:1; 2; 5; 7; 8; 13; 14(2); 4:1; 6; 8; 10(2); 11; 13; 18; 21; 23; 5:1; 8; 13; 14; 6:5; 8; 15; 16; 17; 20; 25; 7:2; 3(2); 6; 7(3); 13; 14(2); 19; 8:1; 2; 3; 5; 8; 9; 10; 12; 14(2); 16; 20(3); 23; 24; 34; 9:1; 2; 3; 6(2); 10(3); 11(2); 12; 15; 16; 20; 24(2); 25; 10:1(3); 6(3); 10(2); 11(2); 12; 13; 15; 18; 19; 20; 21(2); 24; 25; 27; 28; 32(2); 33; 35(2); 37(2); 38; 39(5); 43; 11:1(4); 2; 3(3); 5; 6; 11; 14; 17; 20; 23(2); 12:3(2); 7(2); 13:1; 3; 4; 15; 31; 14:1; 4; 7; 11(2); 12; 15:1; 3(6); 6(2); 7; 8; 9(2); 10(2); 11(2); 12(2); 13(2); 15; 16(2); 17; 18(2); 20; 16:1; 2(2); 3(2); 5; 6(2); 7(3); 17:1; 4(2); 5; 7; 8; 13(2); 14; 15; 17(2); 18:3(2); 4(2); 6; 8(2); 9(2); 10; 11; 12; 13(2); 15; 16(4); 17(2); 19; 20; 21; 28; 19:1(2); 8(2); 10; 11(2); 12(2); 13(4); 14; 16; 17(2); 22; 23; 24; 26(2); 27(4); 29(4); 31; 32(2); 33; 34(5); 39; 40; 47; 48; 49; 50; 20:2; 21:2(2); 12; 13(2); 21; 27; 32; 33; 38; 43; 44; 45; 22:5(6); 7; 9(3); 10(2); 12(2); 13(2); 15(2); 16; 18(2); 23(3); 24(2); 26; 27(2); 28(3); 29; 31(2); 32; 33(2); 23:1; 4; 6(4); 7; 9; 12; 14; 15; 16; 24:1; 4; 5; 9; 15; 16; 22; 29; 33; **Judg** 1:1(2); 7; 9; 12(2); 13; 14(3); 23; 28(2); 34(2); 36; 2:1(2); 4; 6; 12; 19(3); 22; 3:1; 2; 4(2); 6(2); 9; 10; 18; 27; 28; 4:5; 7; 9; 10; 12; 17; 18(2); 19; 22; 5:3; 11; 16; 23(2); 26(2); 29; 30(2); 6:5; 7; 11; 22; 25; 29; 31; 35; 7:2; 3; 5; 6(2); 9; 10(2); 11; 17; 20; 22(2); 25; 8:1; 3; 4; 8; 27; 33; 35(2); 9:1; 3; 7; 8; 9; 10; 11; 13; 16; 21; 24; 26; 29(2); 31; 33; 36; 42; 48; 49; 50; 51(2); 52; 53; 10:1; 9; 12; 18(2); 11:3; 4; 5; 8; 9; 10; 12(2); 16; 20; 24; 27; 31; 32; 33; 34(2); 35; 36(2); 39(2); 40; 12:1(2); 3; 6; 13:5; 7(2); 9; 11; 12; 17; 20(2); 21(2); 23; 25; 14:1; 2; 3; 5(2); 8(2); 9; 10; 11(2); 15(2); 17(2); 19(2); 20; 15:1(3); 2; 4; 6; 10(4); 11(2); 12; 17; 16:1; 3; 4; 5; 6(2); 8; 16; 19(2); 21; 22; 23(2); 25; 17:3(2); 4; 8(3); 9; 11; 13; 18:1; 2(4); 7(2); 8; 9(3); 10; 14(2); 15; 17; 19(2); 22; 30; 19:1(2); 2; 3(3); 5(2); 7; 8; 9(3); 12; 13(2); 14; 15(3); 18(3); 22; 25(2); 27; 20:1; 3; 4(2); 5; 8; 9; 10(3); 13(2); 14(2); 18(2); 20(2); 21; 23; 25; 28(2); 31(3); 36; 39; 40(2); 47; 48(2); 21:1; 2; 3(2); 4; 5(3); 7; 8(4); 12; 13(3); 18; 19; 21(2); 22(2); 23; 24(3); **Ruth** 1:1(2); 7; 8; 12(2); 16(2); 17; 18; 19(3); 22; 2:2; 3; 8; 10; 12; 15; 18; 19(2); 20(2); 23; 3:2; 3; 6; 7; 8; 11; 13(2); 16(2); 17; 4:1; 4(2); 5; 6; 7(2); 10(2); 15; 17; **1Sa** 1:3(2); 4(2); 6; 7; 8(2); 12; 19(2); 20; 21; 25; 28(2); 2:6; 8(2); 10; 11(2); 15(2); 16; 19(3); 20; 24; 28(4); 29; 33(2); 35; 36(2); 3:2(2); 3; 6; 8; 11; 15; 17; 19; 20(2); 21; 4:1(2); 3; 4; 9; 12; 16; 18; 19; 5:3; 4(2); 10(5); 11; 12; 6:2(2); 3; 4(2); 7; 9(2); 10; 12(3); 13; 16; 18(2); 20(2); 21(2); 7:1; 2; 5; 6; 7; 8(2); 10; 14; 16(2); 17; 8:1; 4; 5; 6; 8; 11; 12(3); 13(3); 14; 15(2); 16; 19; 22; 9:3; 5(2); 6; 7(3); 8(2); 9(2); 10; 11(2); 12(3); 13(2); 14(2); 16(2); 17; 18; 19(2); 21; 26(2); 27(2); 10:1; 2(2); 3(3); 5(3); 8(4); 9(2); 10; 11(2); 13; 14(3); 17; 20; 21; 24; 25; 26; 11:3(2); 4; 9(2); 10; 11; 12; 13(2); 14(2); 15; 12:3; 7(2); 17; 19; 22; 23; 13:2; 4; 5; 7; 8(2); 9; 10(2); 12; 13; 14; 17; 18(3); 20(2); 21; 22; 23; 14:1(2); 4; 6(3); 7; 9; 12; 19; 20; 21; 25; 26; 27; 30; 31; 43; 45; 46; 15:1(2); 2; 5; 6; 7; 11; 12(3); 13; 15; 16; 21; 22(2); 27; 28; 32; 34(3); 35; 16:1; 2(2); 3; 4; 5(3); 6; 9; 10; 12(2); 13; 16(2); 17; 21; 22; 23; 17:1(2); 8(3); 9(2); 13(2); 15; 17(2); 20(2); 23; 25; 26(2); 27; 32; 33(3); 39; 40; 43; 44(3); 45(3); 46; 48(3); 49; 52(3); 54; 58; 18:1; 2; 4(4); 6(2); 8; 10; 11; 17(2); 18; 19(3); 21(2); 23(2); 25(3); 26; 27(2); 30; 19:1(2); 2(2); 4; 5; 7; 10(2); 11(4); 14; 15(2); 18(3); 20; 22(2); 23(2); 20:5(2); 6; 8; 9; 10; 12; 13(2); 17; 18(2); 19; 21; 24; 27(3); 28(2); 29; 30; 33(2); 35; 37; 38; 40; 41; 42; 21:1(2); 2; 6; 7; 10; 11; 14; 15; 22:1(2); 3; 8; 9(2); 11(2); 13; 15(2); 17(2); 18; 23:3; 4; 5; 6(3); 7; 8(4); 9; 10(3); 13; 15; 16; 18; 19(2); 20(3); 23(2); 24; 25; 26(2); 24:1; 2; 3(2); 4; 5; 6; 7; 8; 9; 10; 11; 16; 17; 25:1; 5(2); 6(3); 8(2); 9(2); 14; 17; 22; 23; 26(2); 29(2); 30(3); 32(2); 33; 34; 35(2); 36; 37; 38; 39(3); 40(5); 41(2); 44; 26:1; 2(2); 5; 6(5); 7; 8(2); 9; 10; 13; 14(3); 15(3); 16; 20(2); 23(2); 25(2); 27:1; 4; 8; 9; 10; 11(2); 12; 28:1(3); 2(2); 7(2); 8; 9(2); 10(2); 12; 14; 15(2); 17(3); 19; 29:1; 4(3); 5; 9(2); 11(3); 30:1(2); 3; 4; 7(2); 9; 11; 12; 13(2); 14; 15(3); 19(2); 21(5); 22; 24; 26(2); 27(3); 28(3); 29(3); 30(3); 31(3); 31:8(2); 9; 10; 11; 12; **2Sa** 1:1; 2(3); 14(2); 26; 2:1; 8; 10; 12; 14; 15; 19(2); 21(3); 22(3); 23(3); 24; 26; 29; 32; 3:5; 6; 7; 8(3); 9(3); 10(3); 12(2); 13; 14(2);

16; 17; 19(3); 20(2); 23; 24; 25(3); 27(2); 31(2); 35(3); 37; 39; 4:2; 3; 4(2); 5; 8(2); 10; 5:1; 2; 3(2); 4; 6; 8; 11; 13; 17(2); 19; 20; 24; 25; 6:2; 6(2); 8; 9; 19(3); 20(3); 21; 7:1; 3; 4; 5; 6; 7; 8; 11(2); 17(2); 19; 21(2); 22; 23(5); 24(2); 27(2); 29; 8:1; 2(4); 3; 5; 6; 7; 10(2); 9:9(3); 10; 11; 10:1; 2; 3(3); 4; 5; 14; 16; 17; 19(2); 11:1(2); 2(2); 6(2); 8(2); 9; 11(3); 12(3); 13(2); 14(2); 16; 27; 12:4(3); 5; 7; 9(2); 10; 14(2); 17(2); 18(2); 20; 22; 23(2); 27; 29; 13:1; 2(2); 4; 5; 6; 7(2); 8; 9; 10; 11; 12; 13; 23; 24; 25; 30(2); 33(2); 36; 37; 38; 39; 14:2(2); 3; 4(2); 6; 7; 8; 10; 11(2); 15; 16; 17; 19(2); 20(3); 22; 23(2); 24(2); 25(2); 29(3); 31; 32(3); 33(3); 15:1(2); 2; 3; 5(2); 6(2); 7; 8; 9; 13; 14; 15; 16; 19(2); 22; 26; 28; 29; 32(3); 34; 35; 16:2(2); 4; 5; 10; 11(2); 15; 16; 17(2); 20; 21; 17:6; 9; 11(2); 13; 14(2); 15; 17; 18; 20(3); 21; 23(2); 24; 25(2); 27(2); 29; 18:11; 17; 18; 21; 22; 24; 28; 32; 33; 19:5; 8; 11(6); 12; 13(2); 15(5); 16; 18(2); 19; 20(2); 21; 22(2); 24; 25(3); 26; 28; 31; 34; 37; 38; 40; 41; 42; 20:1(2); 2; 3(2); 4; 5; 6; 7; 9(2); 10(2); 13; 14; 15; 18; 19; 21; 22(3); 21:2(2); 9; 10; 16; 17; 18; 20; 22; 22:4; 7; 21(2); 25(2); 31; 35; 40; 42; 44; 51(2); 23:3; 5; 9; 10; 13; 16; 21; 23; 37; 24:1; 2(2); 4; 6(4); 7(4); 8; 13(2); 15(2); 16(2); 18; 19; 21(3); **1Kin** 1:3; 4; 5; 8; 21; 23; 31(2); 33(2); 35; 38(2); 43; 44; 47; 48; 51; 52; 53(2); 2:3(2); 4(2); 5(2); 6(2); 7; 8(4); 9(2); 13; 14; 17; 19(3); 21(2); 23; 24; 26(2); 28; 30; 32; 39; 40(3); 41; 42; 44(3); 3:4(2); 5; 6; 7; 9(2); 11; 12; 14; 15(2); 18; 21; 25(2); 28; 4:10; 11; 12(2); 13(2); 15; 24; 25; 28; 34; 5:2; 5; 6(2); 7; 8(2); 9; 10; 11(2); 14; 17; 18; 6:1(2); 3; 11; 12; 19; 38; 7:7; 8; 9; 14(2); 16; 18; 23; 32; 34; 36; 41; 42; 45; 50; 8:6; 10; 11; 13(2); 16(2); 17; 18; 25(2); 28(4); 30; 31(2); 32(3); 33; 36; 39(2); 43(3); 44; 46; 52; 53; 54; 56; 58(2); 61(2); 64; 9:1(2); 2; 3; 4(2); 5; 8; 10; 11; 12; 14; 15; 19; 21; 28(2); 10:1; 2(2); 6; 9(2); 10; 13; 14; 16; 17; 24(2); 27(2); 11:2; 4; 11; 13; 15(2); 17; 18(2); 19; 21(2); 22(2); 24; 25; 29; 31(2); 33(2); 36; 37; 38; 40; 12:1(3); 2; 5; 7; 9; 11; 12(2); 14(2); 16(2); 18(4); 20; 21(4); 23; 24(4); 26; 27(2); 28(2); 30; 13:1; 4(2); 5; 10; 11; 17(2); 20; 22; 23(2); 26; 27; 29(3); 31(2); 32; 34(2); 14:2(3); 3; 4(2); 5(2); 6(2); 8; 9(2); 12; 13; 15(2); 16; 17(2); 18; 21(2); 22; 24; 25; 15:4(2); 17(2); 18; 21; 25; 26; 27(2); 29(2); 30; 33; 34; 16:1; 2(3); 7; 8; 11(2); 12; 13(2); 15; 18; 19(2); 21; 23; 26(3); 29; 31(3); 33(2); 34; 17:1; 4; 7; 9(3); 10(3); 11(2); 15; 16; 17; 18(4); 24; 18:1(2); 2; 5; 6; 9; 10; 12; 15; 16(2); 17; 19; 27; 29(2); 31; 36; 40; 42(3); 43; 44; 45(2); 46; 19:2(2); 3(2); 9; 10; 14; 15(2); 16(2); 17; 20; 20:2; 4; 6; 9; 12; 22; 26(3); 30; 31; 32; 33(2); 35; 42; 43(2); 21:1; 2; 3; 4; 5; 8; 10; 14; 15(3); 16(4); 17; 18(2); 20(2); 22(2); 25; 26; 27; 28; 22:2(2); 4(3); 5; 6; 12; 13; 15(2); 17; 24; 25; 26; 29; 32(2); 33; 36(2); 37; 41; 42; 48(2); 51; 52; 53(2); **2Kin** 1:3(3); 6(2); 7; 9; 10; 16(2); 17; 2:1; 2(2); 3(2); 4(2); 5(2); 6; 7; 9; 11; 15(3); 18; 20; 22; 25(2); 3:1; 3; 5; 7(2); 10; 12; 13(4); 15; 20; 21(2); 23; 24; 26; 27; 4:1(2); 5; 6; 8(3); 10; 12; 13(3); 14; 16; 17; 18(2); 19(2); 20; 22; 23(2); 24; 25(3); 26; 27(3); 29; 31; 35; 37; 38; 39; 40(2); 44; 5:5; 6(2); 7(4); 8(2); 10; 11; 13; 14; 15; 16; 17; 18; 21; 22; 24; 26(3); 6:4; 7; 10; 18(2); 19(2); 20; 22; 23; 24; 28(2); 30; 31; 32(3); 7:1; 3; 5(2); 6(3); 8; 9; 10; 11; 12(2); 16; 17(2); 18(3); 8:1; 3(2); 5(5); 7; 9(2); 14(3); 15; 16; 17; 19(2); 21; 25; 26; 28; 29(2); 9:1; 2; 4; 5(2); 10; 11(2); 12; 15(3); 16(2); 17; 18(3); 19(2); 22; 23; 25; 26; 27(2); 28; 29; 30; 32(2); 35; 10:1(3); 2; 5; 6(4); 7(3); 9(2); 12; 13; 15(3); 17(3); 19(3); 21; 24; 25(4); 29(2); 30; 31(2); 32; 11:4; 9(3); 10; 11; 13; 19; 21; 12:1; 4(2); 5; 8(2); 11; 12(4); 14; 15; 17(2); 18; 20; 13:1; 2; 7; 10; 16; 21; 14:2; 3; 5; 6(3); 8; 9(4); 10; 11; 12(2); 13; 14; 19(2); 22; 23; 24; 25; 28; 15:1; 2; 3; 9; 12; 13; 14; 16; 17; 18; 19; 20(2); 23; 24; 27; 28; 29; 32; 33; 34; 37; 16:1; 2; 3(2); 5(2); 6(2); 7; 8; 9; 10(4); 11; 12; 15; 16; 17:1; 4(2); 5; 9; 11(2); 13(2); 14; 17(4); 23; 26; 31; 35(2); 36; 37; 18:1(2); 2; 3; 4; 6; 8; 9; 14(2); 16; 17(2); 18(2); 19; 22; 23(2); 25(2); 26; 27(4); 29; 31(2); 32; 37; 19:1; 2; 3(2); 4; 5; 6; 7(2); 9; 10; 11; 16; 20(2); 21; 23(2); 25(2); 34; 35; 37; 20:1; 2; 4(2); 10; 21:1; 6(2); 7(2); 8(3); 9; 11; 14; 15; 16(2); 19; 22:1; 2(2); 3(2); 4; 5(2); 6(2); 8; 9; 11; 13; 15; 17; 18(3); 23:3(4); 4; 5(5); 6; 8; 9; 10(2); 11; 15(2); 16; 19(4); 20; 23; 25(2); 29; 30; 31; 32; 33; 34(2); 35(5); 36; 37; 24:2(2); 3(2); 7; 8; 9; 12; 15(2); 16; 17; 18; 19; 20; 25:1; 6(2); 7; 11; 12; 13; 20(2); 23(2); 24(3); 25; 26; 27(2); 28; **1Chr** 1:10; 2:21; 23; 35(2); 4:27; 39(2); 42; 5:1; 18(3); 20; 26; 6:19; 32; 49(2); 56; 57; 62; 64; 7:2; 11; 15; 21; 22; 23; 40(2); 8:6; 9:1; 9; 22; 25(2); 27; 29; 32; 10:4; 8(2); 9(2); 11; 12; 13; 11:1; 3(3); 4; 5; 10(2); 13; 15(2); 18(2); 21; 23; 25; 31; 12:1(2); 8; 15; 16; 17(4); 18; 19(4); 20(2); 22(2); 23(6); 24; 31; 32(2); 33; 36; 38(3); 13:2; 3; 5; 6(4); 9; 10; 11; 12; 13(2); 14:1(2); 8; 11; 15(2); 16; 15:2(3); 3(2); 14; 15; 16(3); 19; 21; 25; 26; 29(2); 16:3(2); 4(3); 5; 7; 15; 17(2); 20(2); 21; 23; 25(2); 33; 35; 37; 38; 40(3); 41(2); 43(2); 17:1(2); 3(2); 4; 5(2); 6(2); 10; 11(2); 15(2); 17(2); 18; 19; 20; 21(3); 24; 25; 27; 18:1; 3; 5; 7; 10(3); 19:1; 2(4); 3(4); 5; 6(2); 7; 15; 16; 19; 20:1(2); 2; 3; 4; 21:1; 2(4); 3; 4; 6; 11; 12(2); 15(2); 17; 18(2); 21(3); 22; 23; 24; 25; 30; 22:2(3); 4; 5; 6; 7(2); 8; 9; 13; 17; 19(4); 23:4; 5; 11; 13(3); 28; 30(2); 31(2); 24:3; 4; 7(2); 8(2); 9(2); 10(2); 11(2); 12(2); 13(2); 14(2); 15(2); 16(2); 17(2); 18(2); 19(2); 25:1(2); 2; 3(2); 5(2); 6(2); 9(2); 10; 11; 12; 13; 14; 15; 16; 17; 18; 19; 20; 21; 22; 23; 24; 25; 26; 27;

28; 29; 30; 31; 26:12; 13; 14; 15(2); 16; 27; 31; 32; 27:1; 23; 24; 28:1; 2; 4(3); 5; 6; 7; 10; 11; 15; 20; 29:2(2); 3(2); 4; 5(2); 8; 9; 12(2); 14; 16; 17; 19(3); 20; 22(2); **2Chr** 1:2(3); 3; 4; 6; 8; 11; 13(2); 2:1; 2(3); 3(3); 4(5); 6(2); 7(2); 8; 9(2); 10; 11; 12; 14(4); 16(3); 18(3); 3:1; 2; 4; 8(2); 11(2); 12(2); 4:2; 6(2); 7; 11; 12(2); 13; 16; 5:2; 7; 11; 13(3); 14; 6:4; 5(2); 6; 7; 8(2); 16(3); 19(3); 20; 22; 23; 24; 25(2); 31; 33(2); 34; 38; 7:3; 6; 7; 10(2); 11; 12(2); 13; 17; 18; 20; 21; 8:1; 2(2); 3; 6; 8; 13; 14(4); 17(2); 18(2); 9:1(2); 5; 8(4); 11(2); 12(2); 13; 14; 15; 16; 18(2); 21; 23; 26; 10:1(3); 2; 3; 6(2); 7(2); 9(2); 11; 12(2); 15; 16(3); 18(4); 11:1(3); 2; 3; 4; 13; 14; 16(3); 18; 22(2); 12:1; 2; 4(2); 5(3); 7; 10; 13(2); 14; 13:1; 5(4); 8; 9; 11; 12; 13; 15; 14:4(2); 11; 15; 15:2; 5(2); 9; 12; 13; 16:1(2); 2; 5; 7; 9(2); 12(2); 17:4; 5; 7(7); 14; 15; 18:2(4); 3; 4; 5(2); 11; 12(3); 14(3); 15(2); 16; 17; 23; 24; 25(2); 28; 29(2); 31(3); 32; 33; 19:1(2); 2(2); 3; 4; 6; 8; 10; 20:1(2); 3; 4(2); 6; 7; 11(3); 12; 16; 17(2); 18; 19; 21; 22(2); 23(2); 24; 25; 27(3); 28; 31; 36(3); 37(2); 21:3; 4; 5; 6; 7(3); 11; 12; 13(2); 19; 20; 22:1; 2; 3; 4; 5; 6(2); 7(2); 8(2); 9(2); 23:2; 7; 8(3); 9; 10; 12; 13; 15; 17; 18; 24:1; 4(2); 5(3); 6(2); 9(2); 11(2); 12(3); 14(2); 17; 19(2); 22; 23(2); 25:1; 3(2); 5(3); 7(2); 8(2); 9(3); 10(3); 11; 13; 14(2); 16(2); 17; 18(4); 19(2); 21; 22(2); 23(2); 24; 27(2); 26:2; 3; 4; 5; 8(2); 11(2); 13; 14; 15(2); 16(2); 18(3); 19; 20; 23; 27:1; 2; 8; 28:1; 5; 7; 8; 9; 10; 13(3); 15(5); 16; 23; 25(2); 29:1; 2; 8(3); 10; 11(2); 15(2); 16(2); 17(2); 18; 20; 21; 24; 25; 27; 30; 32; 34; 30:1(4); 2; 3; 5(3); 6(2); 7; 10(2); 11; 12(2); 13; 16; 17; 19(2); 20; 22; 23; 24(2); 27; 31:1(2); 2(4); 3; 4; 7; 10(2); 11; 14; 15(4); 16; 17; 18; 19(3); 21; 32:1; 2; 3; 5; 6(2); 8(2); 9; 11(2); 13; 14; 15; 17(2); 18(2); 20; 21; 23(2); 24; 25; 30; 31(2); 33:1; 6(3); 7(2); 8(2); 9(2); 10(2); 11; 13; 14; 16; 18; 21; 34:1; 2(2); 3(2); 7; 8; 9(2); 10(2); 11(3); 12; 15(2); 16(2); 17; 19; 21; 22(3); 23; 25; 26; 28(2); 31(3); 32(3); 33(3); 35:2; 4(2); 5; 6; 7(2); 8(2); 10; 12(2); 13; 15; 16(3); 18; 20; 21(3); 22; 23; 24; 25; 26; 36:2; 4(2); 5; 6(2); 7; 9; 10; 11; 15; 18; 20(2); 21(2); 23; **Ezr** 1:2; 3; 5(2); 2:68(2); 3:1; 2; 4; 6; 7(5); 8; 9; 10; 4:2(2); 3(2); 5; 8; 12; 14; 17(2); 21(2); 22(2); 23(2); 5:2; 3(3); 5(2); 8; 9(2); 10; 13; 17(3); 6:5; 8; 9; 12(4); 13; 14(2); 17; 21; 22; 7:6; 8; 9(3); 10(3); 11; 13(2); 14(2); 15; 18(3); 20; 21; 22(3); 24; 26(3); 27; 28; 8:15(2); 17; 21; 22(2); 30(2); 31; 32; 36; 9:1(2); 6(2); 7(4); 8(3); 9(4); 11(2); 12; 10:3(3); 5(2); 8; 10; 13; 16; **Neh** 1:1; 4; 9; 11(3); 2:1; 4; 6; 7; 8(3); 9; 10; 11; 12; 13; 14(3); 16(5); 19; 3:2; 5; 16; 19(2); 21; 31; 4:1; 5; 6; 7(2); 8(3); 10; 11; 12; 14(2); 15(3); 16; 19(2); 22; 5:5(2); 8; 9; 11; 12; 13; 14; 19; 6:1; 2; 3; 6(2); 7(3); 10(2); 11; 14; 16; 19(2); 7:1; 3; 5; 6(2); 63; 70; 71; 8:1(2); 6; 7; 8; 12(4); 13; 15; 9:8(3); 12; 15(2); 16; 17(5); 19(2); 20; 23(2); 26(2); 27; 28; 36; 10:29(3); 31; 32; 33; 34(2); 35; 36(2); 37; 38; 11:1(3); 2; 3; 17; 12:22; 24(3); 27(3); 44; 45; 13:3; 5(2); 7; 10; 13(2); 19(2); 22(2); 24; 26; 27(2); 28; **Est** 1:1; 6; 7; 8(3); 9; 11(3); 12; 13; 15; 16(3); 17; 20(2); 21; 22(3); 2:3; 8(3); 9(2); 11; 12(4); 13; 14; 15; 18(2); 21; 22; 3:4(2); 6(2); 7(3); 8; 9(2); 11(3); 12(5); 13(5); 14; 15; 4:4(2); 5(3); 6; 7(3); 8(6); 11(4); 12; 13; 14(2); 16; 17; 5:1; 2; 3; 5(2); 6; 8(4); 12; 14(2); 6:1; 2; 3; 4(2); 6(4); 7; 8; 9(4); 10(2); 11; 12(2); 13; 14; 7:1; 2; 4(3); 5; 7(2); 8:3; 5(2); 6(2); 7; 9(6); 11(7); 13(2); 9:1(3); 2; 13(3); 14; 19; 21; 22(3); 23; 24(3); 27(2); 29; 30; 31; 10:3; **Job** 1:4(2); 5; 6; 7; 11; 15; 16; 17; 19; 2:1(2); 2; 3; 5; 8; 11(3); 3:8; 20; 23; 4:2; 12; 14; 20; 5:1; 4; 11(2); 26; 6:7; 9; 14; 18; 24; 26; 7:1; 3(2); 4; 9; 10; 20; 8:5; 8; 22; 9:14; 15; 18; 19; 26; 10:19; 21; 11:6; 12:3; 4; 5; 8; 22; 24; 25; 13:3(2); 6; 12; 23; 25; 26; 14:15; 18; 21; 15:8; 20; 24; 28; 16:8; 11; 12; 17:5; 14(2); 16; 18:11; 14; 19:3; 17; 20(2); 20:2; 3; 6; 10; 18; 23; 21:4; 13; 30(2); 31; 32; 22:3(2); 7(2); 14; 19; 23; 23:2; 3; 24:5; 7; 10; 12; 17; 21; 23; 25:5; 26:4; 10; 28:3; 11; 24; 25; 28; 29:7; 10; 11; 12; 13(2); 15(2); 16; 30:1; 6; 10; 21; 22(2); 23(2); 24; 29(2); 31; 31:3(2); 5; 7; 11; 12; 16; 23; 24; 28; 30(2); 32; 36; 39; 32:1; 10; 11(2); 19; 22; 33:1; 6; 22; 23; 24; 25; 30(2); 32(2); 34:4; 11(2); 16; 18(3); 19; 28; 31; 33; 35:2; 9; 36:2; 3; 6; 10; 27; 32; 37:6(3); 13; 15; 38:12; 14; 20(2); 26(2); 27(3); 34; 36; 40; 39:9; 11; 17; 21; 40:19; 41:10; 13; 16; 17; 31; 32(2); 42:7; 8; **Ps** 4:t; 5:t, 1; 6:t, 6; 7:2; 6; 8(2); 9; 17(2); 8:t, 6; 9:t, 2; 6; 8; 11; 20; 10:9; 14; 17; 18; 11:t, 1(2); 12:t; 13:t; 14:t, 2; 15:3; 4; 5; 16:2; 3(2); 10; 17:11; 14; 18:t, 3; 20(2); 24(2); 30; 34; 38; 41; 50(4); 19:t, 4; 5; 10; 20:t, 4; 21:t, 11; 22:t, 7; 11; 15; 19; 29; 30; 23:2; 25:7; 27:2; 4(2); 13; 28:1(2); 3; 4(3); 29:6; 9; 30:1; 3; 7; 8; 9; 12(2); 31:t, 2(2); 11; 13; 16; 18; 32:10; 33:10; 11; 19(2); 34:9; 16; 35:4(2); 11; 12; 23; 24; 26; 36:t, 2; 3(2); 10; 12; 37:5; 7; 8; 14(2); 32; 34; 38:(2); 17; 22; 39:(2); 1; 4; 11; 40:t, 4; 5; 8; 12; 13(2); 14(2); 41:t, 6(2); 13; 42:t, 4; 43:3; 44:t, 7; 9; 10; 13(2); 20; 25; 45:t, 17; 46:t, 9; 47:t, 6; 48:1; 10; 13; 49:t, 4; 7; 10; 11; 18; 19; 50:4(2); 8; 16(2); 19; 22; 23; 51:(2); 1; 6; 8; 52:(2); 3; 53:t, 2; 5; 54:(2); 2; 55:t, 1; 22; 56:t; 57:t; 58:t, 5; 7; 59:(2); 4; 5(2); 60:(2); 1; 2; 3; 4; 61:t, 2; 62:(2); 4; 9; 12(2); 63:2; 9; 64:t, 3; 8; 65:t, 4; 8; 66:t, 4; 8; 9; 12; 19; 67:t, 1; 68:t, 4; 16; 33; 69:t, 10; 11; 16; 20; 21; 23; 26; 70:(3); 1(2); 2; 71:1; 2; 3; 11; 13; 18(2); 72:3; 8; 15; 73:1(2); 10; 16; 24; 28(2); 74:7; 14(2); 75:t, 4; 9; 76:t, 7; 8; 9(2); 11; 12; 77:(2); 2; 6; 9; 78:1(2); 4(2); 5; 6(2); 10; 13(2); 16; 24; 25; 26; 48(2); 50(2); 52; 54(2); 55; 58(2); 63; 66; 71; 72; 79:2; 3; 4(2); 11(2); 13; 80:t, 3; 5; 7; 9; 19; 81:t, 11; 82:3; 83:9(2); 12; 17; 84:t, 7; 10; 85:t, 4; 5; 8(2); 86:5; 6; 11; 87:4; 88:t, 10; 15; 89:1; 4; 7(2); 8; 19; 29; 33; 39; 40; 41; 42; 43; 44(2); 90:2; 3; 11; 12; 15; 91:11; 92:1(2); 2; 15; 94:1(2); 2; 95:1; 7; 96:2; 4(2); 13; 98:9; 100:5; 101:3; 102:4; 5; 13; 18; 20(3); 21; 22; 103:8; 10; 17; 18(3); 104:9; 11; 14; 15(2); 23; 26; 29; 33; 105:8; 10; 13(2); 14; 22; 25(2); 39; 106:8; 23; 26; 27(2); 29; 45; 46; 47(2); 48; 107:4; 7; 8; 12; 15; 21; 23; 26(2); 27; 31; 36; 38; 40; 109:t, 12(2); 16; 26; 31; 111:4; 112:9; 113:3; 6; 9(2); 115:16; 116:17; 118:8(2); 9(2); 19; 119:4; 5; 9; 25; 27; 31; 35; 36; 38; 41; 42; 49; 58; 60; 62; 76; 91; 95; 103; 112; 121; 126; 128; 132; 135; 149; 154; 156; 159; 169; 170; 121:3; 122:4; 124:6; 125:4; 127:2(3); 130:2; 132:4(2); 17; 133:1; 2; 135:7; 136:3; 4; 5; 6; 7; 8; 9; 10; 13; 14; 16; 17; 25; 137:6; 7; 8; 139:t, 12; 140:t, 4; 11; 141:4(2); 143:1; 3(2); 8(2); 9; 10; 144:1(2); 4; 14; 145:3; 4; 8; 9; 12(2); 18; 146:4; 7; 147:1; 6; 8; 9(2); 18; 149:7; 8; 9; 150:2; **Prov** 1:2(2); 3; 4(3); 6; 16(2); 2:2; 7; 12; 13; 14; 16; 3:2; 8(2); 15; 18; 22; 27(2); 28; 32; 4:1; 8; 9(2); 16; 20; 22; 27(2); 5:1; 5; 13; 6:4(2); 6; 10; 18; 24; 26; 29; 30; 7:8; 15(2); 21; 22(2); 23; 24; 25; 27(2); 8:4; 7; 9(2); 11(2); 13; 21; 29; 9:4; 7; 9; 15; 16; 10:3; 16(2); 23(2); 26(3); 29(2); 11:1; 17; 18; 19(2); 20; 24; 29; 12:4; 6; 8; 20; 21; 22; 13:5; 14; 18; 19(3); 21; 22; 25; 14:8; 15; 22; 23; 27; 29; 34; 15:8; 18; 21; 24; 26; 28; 16:5; 7; 12(2); 16(3); 17; 19(2); 23; 24(2); 30(2); 32; 17:4(2); 15; 16(2); 21; 23; 25(2); 26(2); 18:5(2); 9; 18; 19; 19:6; 7; 10; 11; 23; 24; 27(2); 20:2; 3; 10; 13; 17; 25(2); 21:3(2); 5(2); 6; 7; 9; 15(3); 19; 20; 25; 22:1; 7; 9; 16(3); 19(2); 20; 21; 25; 27; 23:1; 2(2); 4; 7; 12; 21; 30; 24:1; 8; 9; 11(2); 12(2); 13; 20; 21; 23(2); 25; 29(4); 33; 25:2(2); 8(3); 9; 10; 13; 20; 21(2); 24; 25; 27(2); 26:4; 5; 8; 11(2); 15(2); 17; 21(3); 27:1; 4; 7; 14; 19(2); 21; 23(2); 24; 28:10; 17(2); 20; 21; 22; 29:7; 12; 15(2); 27(2); 30:14; 17; 23; 31:3; 4; 6; 8; 15(2); 19; 20(2); 25; 27; **Eccl** 1:5; 6; 11; 13(3); 16; 17(2); 2:1; 3(2); 6; 11; 12; 14; 15(2); 16; 20(2); 21; 26(5); 3:1(2); 2(4); 3(4); 4(4); 5(4); 6(4); 7(4); 8(2); 10(2); 11; 12(2); 14; 15; 20; 21; 22; 4:10(2); 14; 5:1(3); 2; 4; 6(2); 11; 12; 13; 15; 18(3); 19(4); 6:2(2); 6; 8; 7:2(5); 5(2); 9; 11; 12; 14; 25(4); 27; 8:1; 2; 3; 6; 8(2); 9; 11; 14(3); 15(3); 16(2); 17(3); 9:1; 2(8); 3; 4(2); 10; 11(6); 10:1; 3; 10(2); 15(2); 16; 11:2(2); 7; 12:5; 7; 10; **Song** 1:7; 9; 2:3; 4; 3:3; 4:6(2); 5:2; 5(2); 6; 6:2(3); 11(2); 7:7(2); 8; 9; 12; 8:2; 11; 13(2); 14(2); **Is** 1:11; 12(2); 14; 16; 17; 2:2; 3(2); 19; 20(3); 21(2); 22; 3:4; 8; 10; 12; 13(2); 15; 24; 4:1; 3; 5:1; 4; 5(2); 8(2); 22(2); 26; 7:1(2); 3; 7; 13; 15; 16; 18; 21; 22; 23; 8:2; 3; 4; 8; 10; 11; 12(2); 14(2); 19; 20(3); 21; 22; 9:3; 7(2); 16; 10:2(2); 3; 6(3); 7; 11; 12; 20; 26; 27; 28(2); 30; 31; 11:10; 11(2); 16; 13:5; 9; 10; 11; 14; 16; 18; 20; 22; 14:1; 2; 3(2); 9; 11; 12; 15(2); 16; 19; 24; 15:1(2); 2(3); 7; 16:1(2); 4; 10; 12(3); 17:4; 7(2); 8; 11(2); 12(2); 18:1; 2(2); 6; 7; 19:3(4); 14; 18; 19(2); 21; 22; 23; 20:4; 6; 21:2; 11; 14; 16; 22:1; 4; 5; 7; 8; 10; 12(4); 13; 20; 21(2); 23; 24; 23:1; 6; 7; 9(2); 11; 12; 13; 15(2); 17(2); 18(2); 24:2; 9; 16; 18; 20; 21; 25:2; 4(2); 11; 12(2); 26:5(2); 8(2); 10; 14; 21; 27:6; 7; 9; 12; 13(2); 28:1(2); 2; 6(3); 9; 11; 12(2); 17(2); 19; 21; 24; 26; 29:1(3); 11; 12; 14; 15; 20; 24; 30:1(2); 2(3); 4; 6; 7(2); 8; 10(2); 11; 13(2); 14(2); 21(2); 28(3); 29(2); 30; 31:1(2); 4; 9; 32:4; 5; 6(4); 7; 33:1(3); 4; 34:1; 2; 5; 10; 12; 14; 17; 35:4; 10; 36:1; 2; 4; 6; 7(3); 8(2); 10; 11; 12(4); 14; 16(2); 17; 22; 37:1; 3(2); 4; 5; 7(2); 9(2); 10; 11; 17; 21; 22; 24(2); 26(2); 35; 38; 38:4; 5; 10; 12; 13; 16; 17; 19; 20(2); 22; 39:1; 5; 6; 8; 40:2; 14; 16; 17; 18; 20; 22; 23; 25; 29(2); 41:1; 2(3); 6; 22; 23; 27(2); 42:1; 2; 5; 7(2); 8(2); 9; 10; 17; 23(2); 24; 25; 43:6(2); 14; 20(2); 23; 24; 28(2); 44:13; 15; 19(2); 26(2); 27; 28(2); 45:1(4); 9; 10; 11; 16; 18; 24; 46:1; 4(2); 5; 8; 11; 47:7; 8; 9; 11; 12; 14(2); 15; 48:3; 5(2); 17; 18; 20; 21; 49:5(3); 6(3); 7(3); 8(3); 9(2); 18; 20; 21; 22(2); 23; 50:1; 2(2); 4(3); 6(2); 8; 51:1(2); 4; 6; 8; 10; 13; 18; 23(2); 52:4; 5; 8; 53:1; 6; 7; 10(2); 54:3; 4; 16; 55:1; 4(2); 7; 10(2); 13; 56:1(2); 3; 6(4); 7; 8; 9; 10; 11; 12; 57:1(2); 6; 7; 8; 9; 11; 15(2); 18; 19(2); 21; 58:2(2); 4(3); 5(4); 6(3); 7(3); 10; 12; 14; 59:7(2); 18(4); 20; 60:3(2); 4; 8; 9(2); 13; 61:1(5); 2(2); 3(2); 11(2); 62:8; 11; 63:1; 5(2); 6; 7(3); 10; 12; 14(2); 17; 64:2(3); 7; 65:3(2); 5; 10; 12(2); 24; 66:2(2); 5; 6; 8; 9(3); 12; 15; 19(3); 20; 23(4); **Jer** 1:2; 7; 8; 10(6); 12; 19; 2:1; 7; 18(4); 24; 27(2); 28; 33; 36; 3:1; 3; 5; 9; 12; 13; 14; 15; 16(2); 17(2); 18; 4:3; 4; 7; 9; 11(4); 16; 22(2); 5:1; 3(2); 7; 19; 31; 6:1; 2; 6; 10; 13; 17; 19; 20(2); 7:1; 2; 3; 6; 7(2); 10; 12; 14(3); 16; 18(4); 19(2); 27; 30; 31; 34; 8:5; 6; 10(2); 14(2); 19; 9:3; 5(2); 6; 8; 12; 15; 21; 10:5; 7; 10; 13; 20(2); 22; 23; 24; 11:1; 2; 4; 5; 8; 10(3); 11; 13(4); 15; 17(2); 19; 12:9; 11; 12; 13; 14; 15(3); 16(3); 13:2; 4; 6(3); 7; 10(3); 11(2); 16; 18; 21; 23; 14:1; 3(2); 8; 10; 16(2); 15:2(5); 3(3); 4; 5; 8(2); 9; 10(2); 11; 13; 14; 18; 20(2); 16:5; 7(2); 8(3); 9; 10; 21(2); 17:3; 4; 10(3); 16; 21; 24(3); 27(2); 18:1; 2(2); 3; 4(2); 5; 7(3); 8; 9(2); 11(3); 15(3); 16; 18; 19(2); 20(2); 21(2); 22; 23; 19:5; 7(2); 9; 11; 12; 14(2); 20:3; 4(2); 5; 6(2); 15; 17; 18; 21:2; 3; 9; 14; 22:1; 3; 8; 16; 17(2); 20; 27(2); 23:3; 13; 21; 22; 27(3); 28; 32; 35(2); 37; 24:1; 6; 7; 9(2); 10; 25:1; 2; 4; 5; 6(3); 7(2); 12; 14(2); 15(2); 17; 18(2); 28(2); 29; 31(2); 32; 35(2); 26:2(2); 3; 4(2); 5(2); 6; 8(2); 11(2); 12(2); 15(2); 16(3); 17; 18; 19; 20; 21(2); 24(2); 27:2; 3(6); 4; 6; 8; 9(5); 10; 12(2); 16(3); 18(2); 20; 22(2); 28:1; 3; 4; 6; 9; 15; 29:1(4); 3; 4; 6; 7; 8(2); 10(2); 11; 14; 18(3); 19; 20; 24; 25(2); 27; 31(2); 32; 30:1; 3(3); 8; 11; 13; 21(2); 31:2(2); 6; 9(2); 12; 15; 17; 18; 21; 28(8); 32(2); 38; 39; 32:1; 4; 5; 7; 8(2); 11; 19(3); 22(2); 23(2); 24(2); 29(2); 30; 31; 32(2); 33; 34; 35(4); 37; 40; 41; 44; 33:2; 5(2); 7; 9; 11; 12; 14; 15; 17; 18(3); 21; 23; 26(2); 34:2; 3(2); 8; 9; 11; 12; 15; 16(2); 17(6); 20; 22(2); 35:2; 8; 9(2); 10; 11(2); 13(2); 14; 15(3); 19; 36:1; 3; 8; 9(3); 16; 20; 21; 23; 25; 26; 27; 29(2); 30(3); 32; 37:3; 7(4); 11; 12(2); 13; 14(3); 20(2); 38:2; 4; 8; 9(2); 11; 15; 16; 18; 19; 21; 22; 23(2); 25; 26(3); 27; 39:4; 5(2); 7(2); 9; 11; 12; 16; 40:1; 4(3); 5(2); 6; 7; 8(2); 9(2); 10; 12(2); 13(2); 14; 15; 41:1(2); 4; 5(2); 6(3); 10(3); 12; 13; 15; 17(2); 42:4(2); 5(3); 6; 7; 8; 9; 11(2); 12(2); 15(2); 16; 17(2); 21; 22(2); 43:1(2); 2(2); 3(2); 4; 5; 7; 11(3); 44:1; 3(4); 5(2); 7(3); 8; 11; 12(2); 14(4); 17(2); 18(3); 19(2); 20(3); 24; 25(3); 28; 45:3; 46:1; 3; 13; 16(3); 19; 47:1; 3; 4(2); 48:4; 9; 11; 12; 15; 16; 32; 33; 35(2); 39; 49:2; 3; 9; 10; 12; 14; 24; 28; 29; 34; 37; 39; 50:5(2); 6(2); 9; 16(2); 19; 21; 27; 28; 29(2); 33; 34; 39; 42; 51:9; 11; 16; 24; 27; 29; 30; 31(3); 33; 35(2); 40; 49; 53; 61(2); 62; 63; 52:1; 2; 3; 4; 9; 11; 15; 17; 26(2); 27; 31; **Lam** 1:2; 4; 11; 12; 14(2); 15; 17; 19; 21; 2:2; 4; 6; 8(2); 10; 12; 13(3); 14; 17; 20; 3:13; 14; 21; 25; 30; 32; 34; 35; 36; 37; 40; 64; 4:2; 3; 4; 8; 5:2(2); 6(3); 13; 19; **Eze** 1:1; 9; 11; 12; 20(2); 2:3(2); 3:2; 3; 5(2); 6(2); 11; 15; 16; 18(2); 26(2); 4:3; 4; 5; 8; 9; 10; 11; 5:1(2); 7; 13; 16; 6:3(4); 13; 7:3; 8; 9; 13; 14(2); 19; 21; 24; 27; 8:1; 3(3); 4; 7; 14; 17(4); 9:1; 3(2); 5; 8; 10:5; 6; 11; 16; 11:13; 16; 24; 12:2(2); 3; 12; 13(2); 14; 17; 23; 25; 26; 27; 13:5; 6; 13; 14; 16; 18(3); 19(3); 20(2); 21; 14:4(2); 7(2); 12; 15; 19; 21; 15:3(2); 6; 16:2; 4; 5(3); 7(2); 17; 20; 21(2); 23; 25(2); 26(2); 33(2); 34; 41; 42; 55(3); 17:9; 12(3); 17; 20; 24; 18:3; 6(2); 7(2); 9; 10; 12; 15; 16; 24; 30; 19:3; 6; 9; 12; 14(2); 20:1(2); 3; 4; 6; 8; 10; 12; 13; 21(2); 26(2); 28(2); 31; 32; 35; 37; 42(2); 44(2); 47(2); 21:3; 4; 7; 10; 11(2); 17; 19; 20(2); 21; 22(6); 23(2); 24(2); 28; 29; 30; 31; 32; 22:3; 4(2); 6(2); 9; 12; 18; 20(2); 27(3); 23:15(2); 17; 19; 21; 24; 27; 32; 37(2); 39(2); 40; 46; 48(2); 24:6(2); 7; 8(2); 9; 13; 14(3); 17; 19; 24; 26(2); 27; 25:4; 7(2); 14(2); 15; 26:1; 3(2); 5; 11; 13; 14; 15; 17(2); 20; 27:5; 7; 9; 19; 30; 28:8; 17; 18; 25; 29:4; 5(2); 6; 7; 14; 16; 17; 18; 21; 30:9; 10; 11; 13; 20; 21(5); 22; 31:1; 2; 14(3); 15(2); 16(2); 18; 32:1; 4; 6; 12; 14; 17; 20; 21; 24; 25; 27; 29; 30; 33:2; 8; 9; 12; 13(2); 21; 22; 27(2); 30(2); 33; 34:2; 5; 8; 10; 13; 15; 18(2); 25; 26; 28; 35:11(2); 12; 36:4(7); 5; 6(3); 8(2); 12; 15(2); 19(2); 20; 27; 28; 33; 37; 37:2; 5; 7; 9; 12; 17; 22; 38:9; 10; 11(2); 12(3); 13(5); 16; 18; 20; 39:2; 3; 4(2); 11; 13; 14(2); 17(2); 24(2); 28; 40:4(2); 13; 16(3); 23; 24; 26(2); 27; 28(2); 29; 31; 32; 33; 34; 35(2); 36; 37; 39; 40; 46(2); 48; 49; 41:1; 7(2); 16; 17; 42:11(2); 12; 14; 19; 20; 43:1; 3(3); 10; 14(2); 18(2); 19(2); 44:3; 6(2); 7(2); 11(2); 12; 13(3); 15(3); 16(2); 17; 19; 20; 23; 24; 25; 27; 30; 45:4; 8(2); 15; 17(2); 23; 25(4); 46:5(2); 7; 9; 11(5); 14; 17(3); 18; 20; 21; 47:3; 4(2); 5; 6(2); 9; 10(3); 11; 12; 13; 14; 15; 19(2); 21; 22(2); 23; 48:1(3); 28; **Dan** 1:2; 4; 7(3); 10; 11; 12(2); 14; 2:2(2); 3; 4; 5; 9; 12; 13; 14(2); 15(2); 17(2); 21; 24; 26(2); 28; 29(3); 30(2); 34; 35; 39; 43; 44; 45(2); 3:2(3); 4; 9; 13; 16(2); 17; 19; 20(2); 26; 4:2; 3; 6; 8; 11; 17(2); 18; 19(2); 20; 22; 25(2); 26; 27; 31; 32(2); 34; 35; 37; 5:1; 2; 7(2); 8; 16; 17(3); 28; 6:1; 3; 4; 6; 7(2); 8; 12; 14(2); 18; 20(3); 7:4; 5; 6; 11; 13; 22; 25; 26(2); 27; 8:2; 4; 6; 7(2); 10(2); 11; 12; 13(2); 15; 16; 23; 25; 9:2; 3; 4(2); 6(2); 7(2); 8(4); 9; 10; 16(2); 17; 21; 22; 23; 24(6); 25(2); 27; 10:6; 7; 12(2); 13; 14; 20; 11:1(2); 3; 4(2); 6(2); 10; 14; 15; 16; 17; 18(2); 21; 25; 27; 28; 34; 35(4); 36; 39; 44(2); 45; 12:1; 2(2); 3; 4(2); 6(2); 7; 12; **Hos** 1:2; 4; 5; 10; 2:1; 7; 9; 11; 13; 18; 21; 23; 3:1(2); 2; 4:6; 10(2); 12; 15; 17; 5:2; 4; 5; 6; 12; 13(2); 14; 15; 6:3; 7:10(2); 11(2); 16; 8:1; 5; 9; 11(2); 12; 13; 9:3; 4; 10; 12; 13; 10:1(2); 3; 6; 8(2); 11(2); 12(2); 11:2; 3; 4; 5; 7(2); 9; 12:2(2); 6; 7; 9; 14; 13:2; 6; 14:2; 3; 8; **Joel** 1:1; 19; 2:2; 9; 12; 13; 17; 23; 25; 28; 32; 3:4; 8(2); 11; 12(2); 18; 20; **Amos** 1:6(2); 9; 2:4; 7; 8; 10; 12; 3:10; 14; 4:1; 4; 7(3); 8; 10; 12; 5:2; 3; 5(2); 6; 7; 16(2); 18; 26; 27; 6:1(2); 2(2); 3; 5(2); 9; 10; 13; 7:2; 4; 10(2); 14; 8:4(2); 9(2); 12(4); 9:2; **Obad** 3; 5(2); 7; 9; 14; 21; **Jonah** 1:2; 3(4); 4; 5; 6; 7; 13(2); 17; 2:5; 6; 3:3; 4; 5; 7; 4:2; 3(2); 4; 6(2); 8(4); 9(3); **Mic** 1:1; 7(2); 9; 13(2); 14(2); 2:1; 6(2); 7; 3:1; 8(2); 4:1; 2(2); 8; 10(2); 5:2; 10; 6:8(3); 14; 7:1; 9; 11; 12(4); 15; 20(2); **Nah** 1:3; 2:5; 3:1; 7; **Hab** 1:3; 6; 8; 13; 17; 2:1; 6(2); 9(2); 10; 12; 15; 18; 19(2); 3:9; 14(2); 19(2); **Zeph** 1:8; 10; 12; 18; 2:15; 3:1(2); 2; 4; 5; 8(3); 9(2); 16(2); 18; 19; **Hag** 1:1; 4; 6; 8; 9; 2:2(3); 5; 16(3); 17; 21; **Zec** 1:6(3); 10(2); 11; 16; 21(4); 2:2(2); 3; 4; 9; 11; 3:1; 4; 7; 4:2; 4; 10; 5:3(2); 10; 11; 6:7(4); 14(4); 15; 7:1; 2; 3(2); 5(2); 9; 11; 13; 8:1; 10; 12; 13; 14(2); 15(2); 16; 19; 20; 21(3); 22(2); 23; 9:10(2); 12(2); 10:1; 6; 11:9; 13; 17; 12:9(2); 13:1(2); 2(2); 3; 4(2); 5; 8; 14:2; 5; 6; 7(2); 10; 13; 16(4); 17; 18; 19; **Mal** 1:1; 2:2(3); 5; 8; 15; 16; 3:1; 5(2); 10; 14; 16; 4:6(2); **Mt** 1:11; 12; 17; 18; 19(2); 20; 2:1; 2; 8; 12; 13(2); 16; 19; 22; 3:5; 7(3); 9(3); 11; 13(2); 14(2); 15(2); 4:1; 3; 16; 17(2); 5:13(2); 17(3); 22; 23; 24; 25(2); 28; 32; 39; 41; 42; 44; 45; 6:1; 5; 6; 16; 18; 24; 30(2); 7:2; 4; 5;

8; 11(2); 12(2); 13; 15; 22; 28; 8:4; 9(3); 10; 18; 20; 21; 25; 28; 29(2); 31; 33; 34; 9:2; 5(2); 6(2); 7; 10; 13(2); 14; 16; 24; 28(2); 29; 32; 10:1(2); 6; 13; 17; 21(3); 22; 28(2); 34(2); 35; 42; 11:1(3); 5; 7(2); 8; 9; 14; 15; 20; 23; 27; 12:1(2); 2; 4; 10; 12; 13; 18; 25; 32; 39; 42; 46(2); 47; 13:3; 9; 11(2); 12; 13; 17(2); 30(2); 31; 43; 48; 53; 14:4; 5; 7; 9; 11(2); 15; 16; 18; 19(4); 22(2); 23; 29(2); 30; 15:1; 5; 20; 26(3); 31(4); 32; 33; 35; 36(2); 16:3; 5(2); 11; 21; 22; 27; 17:4; 9; 14(3); 16; 17; 19; 20; 24(2); 27; 18:7; 8(2); 9(2); 11; 17(2); 21; 24; 25(3); 34; 19:1; 3; 5; 7(2); 8; 10; 11; 12; 14; 21; 24(2); 20:1; 15; 17; 18(2); 19(4); 20; 22(2); 23(3); 28(3); 21:1; 9; 14; 15; 19; 21; 28(2); 30; 33; 34; 43; 44; 46; 22:3(2); 5(2); 8; 9; 11; 13; 17; 23; 34; 46; 23:1(2); 4; 5; 7; 13; 15; 23(2); 34; 24:1(2); 6; 9; 17; 18; 19; 21; 31; 43; 45; 49(2); 25:1; 6; 9; 10(2); 11; 15(4); 27(2); 45(2); 26:1; 2; 8; 9; 16; 17(2); 18; 22; 26; 27; 37; 45; 49; 53; 55(2); 57; 58; 59(2); 61(2); 73; 74(2); 27:1(2); 2; 3; 4(2); 6; 7; 14; 15; 19; 24; 26; 31; 32; 33; 34; 46; 48; 49; 51; 58(2); 60; 28:1(2); 8; 9; 14; 20; **Mk** 1:7; 9; 17; 24(2); 34; 40(2); 44(2); 45(3); 2:2; 9(3); 10(2); 15; 17(2); 18; 23(2); 26(2); 3:4(4); 7; 9; 10; 14; 15(3); 21; 4:1; 3; 4; 9; 11; 21(2); 23; 24; 25; 33; 34; 41; 5:7; 14; 15; 16; 17(2); 19; 20; 32; 37; 38; 40; 43; 6:2; 7; 18; 21; 27; 28(2); 31; 34; 36; 37(2); 39; 41(3); 45(3); 46; 53; 55; 7:2; 4; 5; 11(2); 12; 16; 27(2); 30; 32; 34; 37(2); 8:1; 2; 3; 6(3); 7; 11; 13; 14; 22(2); 26(2); 31; 32; 9:5(2); 6; 14; 15; 18; 22; 23; 32; 33; 35; 41(2); 43(2); 45(2); 47(2); 10:2(2); 4(2); 7; 12; 13; 14; 17; 21; 24; 25(2); 28; 30; 32(2); 33(3); 40(3); 41; 42(2); 45(3); 46; 47; 49; 50; 11:1; 7; 13; 15(2); 21; 23; 27(2); 28; 12:1(2); 2; 12; 13; 14(2); 17(2); 23; 33(2); 36; 38; 13:5; 9(2); 12(3); 14; 15; 16; 17(2); 21; 22; 27; 29; 34(3); 14:1; 5; 8(2); 10; 11; 14; 19(2); 21; 22; 23; 32(2); 33(2); 40; 45; 48; 53; 55(2); 64; 65(4); 69(2); 70; 71(2); 72; 15:1; 8(2); 15(2); 18; 20; 21; 23; 36(2); 38; 45; 16:8; 9; 15; **Lk** 1:1; 3(2); 8; 9(2); 16; 17(4); 19(2); 20; 23(2); 25; 27(2); 38; 41; 43(2); 49; 50; 55(3); 56; 59(2); 62; 72(3); 73; 76; 77; 79(3); 2:1; 3; 5; 10; 14; 15(3); 22(4); 23; 24(2); 27; 29; 32; 38; 39(2); 41; 42; 44; 45; 46; 51; 3:7(4); 8(3); 11; 12; 14; 16; 21; 23; 4:6; 9; 10; 16(2); 18(7); 19; 20; 21; 31; 34(2); 41; 43; 5:1(2); 7; 11; 12; 14(2); 15(2); 17(2); 18(2); 21; 23(2); 24; 25; 26; 32(2); 6:1; 2; 4(2); 6; 8; 9(4); 11; 12(3); 17(2); 19; 26; 27; 29; 30; 31(2); 33(2); 34(4); 35; 38; 42(2); 47(2); 7:2; 4; 6; 7; 8(2); 10; 11; 12; 15(2); 19; 22; 24(2); 25; 26; 31; 32(2); 36; 38; 40; 42; 43; 44; 45; 47; 49; 50; 8:1; 4; 5; 8; 10(2); 14; 18(2); 19; 20; 22; 24; 25; 27; 28; 29; 31; 32; 35(2); 37; 39; 40; 49; 51; 53; 55; 9:1; 2(2); 9; 10; 12; 13; 14; 16(3); 17; 18; 21; 23; 28(2); 33(2); 37; 40; 42; 45; 51(3); 52; 53; 54; 56(3); 57; 58; 59; 62; 10:5; 6; 7; 15(2); 19; 22(2); 24(2); 25; 29; 30; 34(2); 35; 38; 40(2); 11:1(2); 4; 6(2); 10; 13(2); 14; 17; 26; 27; 29; 30; 31; 37(2); 42(2); 46; 53(3); 54; 12:1; 5; 12; 13; 17; 19; 25; 26; 28(2); 32; 37(2); 39; 41; 42; 45(3); 47; 48; 49; 50; 51; 54; 55; 58(3); 13:12; 14; 15; 24(2); 25(3); 26; 32(2); 33(2); 14:1(2); 3; 6; 7; 8; 9(2); 12; 17(2); 18; 19; 21; 23; 26; 28(2); 29(2); 30(2); 31(2); 35; 15:1; 12(2); 14; 15(2); 17(2); 18; 19; 20; 21; 22; 24; 25; 29; 16:3; 4; 7; 9; 11; 13; 17(2); 21; 22; 26(2); 27; 17:3; 4; 7; 10; 11(2); 14; 18(2); 22; 23; 31; 33; 18:1(3); 10; 13; 14; 16; 18; 25(2); 30; 31; 33; 35; 40; 19:3; 4(2); 5(2); 7; 8; 9; 10(2); 11; 12(2); 14; 15(3); 19; 24; 28; 29(2); 35; 37; 45; 47; 48; 20:1; 9(3); 10; 16; 18; 19; 22; 27; 30; 33; 35; 46; 21:7; 9; 12; 13; 14; 15; 16(2); 21; 23; 28(2); 29; 31; 34; 36(3); 38(2); 22:5; 6; 15; 23; 31; 33(2); 39; 44; 45; 47; 52; 23:2(3); 4(2); 5; 7; 8(2); 11; 15; 20(2); 25; 30(3); 32(2); 33; 36; 43; 48; 51; 56; 24:4; 5; 9; 11; 12; 13; 15; 17; 18; 20(2); 21; 24; 25; 26(2); 29; 30(2); 32(2); 33; 34; 46(2); 50; 51; 52; **Jn** 1:7; 8; 12(3); 19; 22; 27; 31; 33; 38; 42; 47; 2:2; 4; 7; 12; 13; 3:2; 13; 17; 20; 21; 23; 26(2); 33; 4:5(3); 7(2); 8; 10(2); 11; 15; 20; 23; 28; 32; 33(2); 34(2); 35; 38; 52; 5:1; 7; 10; 16; 18; 26(2); 27; 35; 36; 40; 45; 6:6; 11(2); 15; 17; 24; 31; 35; 37(2); 38; 44; 52; 68; 7:1; 4(2); 19; 20; 24; 25; 30; 32; 45; 50; 8:6; 26(3); 27; 31; 33; 37; 40; 41; 56; 59; 9:11; 13; 26(2); 10:3; 10(3); 18(2); 24; 29; 31; 39; 11:7; 8; 15; 19(2); 31; 38; 45; 46; 53(2); 54; 55(2); 56; 12:1; 5; 10; 12(2); 13; 20; 21; 29; 38; 47(2); 13:2; 3; 5(2); 6; 10(2); 12; 14; 15; 19; 24; 26(2); 29; 33; 35; 14:2; 18; 21; 26; 29(2); 15:25; 16:5; 10; 12; 13; 16; 17; 19; 28; 32; 17:1; 2; 4; 11; 13; 18:6; 13(2); 14; 20; 31(3); 36; 37; 19:4; 7; 10(2); 12; 16; 20; 21; 23; 27; 29; 33; 39; 40; 20:2(2); 3; 4; 8; 15; 16; 17(3); 21; 27; 21:1; 6; 9; 11; 14; 15; 16; 21; 22; 23; **Acts** 1:1; 3(2); 6; 7; 16; 19; 22; 25; 2:4; 7; 12; 14; 17; 21; 27; 28; 30(3); 37; 39(2); 45; 46; 47; 3:2; 3; 5; 12; 13; 14; 23; 26; 4:5; 9; 10; 15; 16(2); 17; 18; 19; 23; 24; 28(2); 30; 5:2; 3(3); 9; 13; 14; 20; 21(2); 28; 29; 31(3); 32; 33(2); 34; 35(2); 36(3); 38; 39; 40; 41; 42; 6:4(2); 7; 10; 12; 13; 7:5(3); 7; 13; 14; 17; 19; 23; 26; 30; 31; 33; 34; 35(2); 38(2); 39; 40; 42(2); 43; 44; 46; 54; 60; 8:2; 3; 5; 10(2); 11; 24; 25; 27(2); 29; 30; 32; 36; 38; 40; 9:2(2); 4; 5; 6; 10; 13; 14; 15; 23; 24; 26(3); 27(2); 29; 30(2); 32(2); 35; 37; 38(3); 40; 43; 10:2(2); 3; 5; 6; 8; 9; 11; 13; 21; 22(2); 28; 32; 33(2); 41(2); 42(3); 43; 48(2); 11:2; 3; 5; 13; 15; 18; 19; 20; 25(2); 26; 28; 29(2); 30; 12:1; 3; 4(4); 10; 11; 12; 13; 17(2); 19(2); 20; 13:2; 4; 5; 7; 8; 10; 11; 13(2); 14; 19; 22(2); 23; 24; 25; 26; 31; 34(2); 35; 42; 43(2); 44; 46(2); 47; 48; 14:1; 3; 5(2); 9; 11; 16; 20; 21(3); 22; 23; 24; 26(2); 15:2; 4; 5(3); 6; 10(2); 12; 14; 15; 19; 22(2); 24; 25; 28(3); 29; 30; 34; 37; 38(2); 16:1; 3; 4; 6; 7(2); 8; 9; 10(2); 11(2); 12; 13; 15(2); 16(2); 18(2); 20; 21(2); 22; 23; 30; 32; 36(2); 39; 17:1; 5(2); 7; 14(2); 15(2); 16; 18; 20; 21(2); 23; 25; 26; 29; 30; 18:1; 2; 5; 7; 9; 10; 12; 13(2); 14; 15; 19; 20; 22; 24; 26; 27(2); 19:1(2); 13; 17; 21(2); 27; 36(2); 40; 20:1; 3(2); 6; 7(2); 13(3); 14; 15; 16(2); 17; 18; 20; 21(2); 24; 26; 27; 28(2); 30; 31; 32(4); 34; 35(4); 21:1; 3; 4(2); 7; 12(2); 13(4); 15; 17; 21(3); 23; 25; 26; 31; 33; 34; 37; 39; 22:2; 3; 5(3); 6; 9; 10; 12; 17(2); 24; 25; 30; 23:2; 3(3); 9; 10(3); 14; 15(3); 17; 18(3); 19; 20(2); 22; 23(2); 29(3); 30(3); 31; 32(2); 33(2); 35; 24:2; 6(2); 8; 10; 11(2); 16; 17(2); 19; 23(3); 25; 27; 25:1; 3(2); 6; 9(2); 10(2); 11; 13; 15; 16(5); 17; 19; 20; 21(3); 22; 24; 25(2); 26(2); 27(3); 26:1; 3(2); 7; 9(2); 10; 11; 12; 14(2); 16; 18(3); 20(2); 21; 22; 23; 28; 29; 27:2; 3(2); 5; 12(4); 16; 21; 22; 27; 30; 31(2); 33; 34; 35(2); 39; 40; 42; 43(2); 44(2); 28:4; 6; 8(2); 13(2); 14; 15; 16(3); 17; 19(2); 20(2); 22; 23(2); **Rom** 1:1; 3; 4(2); 5; 7(3); 10; 11(2); 13; 14(4); 15(2); 16(3); 17; 22; 23(2); 24(2); 28(3); 30; 2:2; 4; 6(2); 7; 10(3); 16; 3:15; 19; 25(2); 26; 4:1; 2; 4; 5; 8; 9; 12; 13(2); 16(4); 18; 20; 21; 22; 23; 24; 5:7; 10; 14(2); 16; 18; 6:2; 11; 16(3); 19(3); 22; 7:1; 2; 3(2); 4(3); 5; 10(2); 18(2); 23; 8:1; 6(2); 7; 12(2); 15; 18; 20; 23; 27; 28(3); 29(2); 31; 33; 38; 39; 9:3; 4; 11; 15; 20; 21; 22(3); 26; 30; 31; 10:1; 2; 3; 4; 6; 7; 19; 21; 11:2; 4(2); 5; 11(2); 13; 14; 23; 24; 25; 35; 36(2); 12:2; 3(5); 6(3); 9; 10; 13(2); 16; 17; 13:2; 3(2); 4(2); 7(5); 8; 10; 11; 14; 14:1; 4(2); 6(3); 7(2); 9; 11(2); 12; 13; 14(3); 18; 21(2); 22; 15:1(2); 2; 5(2); 7; 8; 9; 12; 14; 15; 16; 17; 18(2); 20; 21; 22; 23; 24(3); 25; 26; 27; 28; 30; 16:17; 25(4); 26(2); 27; S:1; **1Cor** 1:1; 2(2); 17(2); 18; 19; 21; 27(2); 28(2); 2:1; 2; 6; 12; 3:2; 5; 8; 10; 18; 22; 4:5; 6(3); 7; 8; 9(3); 14; 18; 19; 5:5; 9; 11(2); 12(2); 6:1; 2; 3; 4(2); 5(2); 6; 7(2); 16; 7:1; 2; 5; 8; 9(2); 11; 12(2); 13; 15; 17; 25; 26; 27; 32; 39(2); 8:2; 6; 8; 9; 10(2); 13(2); 9:2; 3; 4(2); 5; 6; 15; 16; 20; 21(3); 22(2); 25; 27; 10:6; 7(2); 13(4); 15; 19; 20(2); 22; 27(2); 31; 32(3); 11:2; 6; 7; 10; 15; 16; 20; 22(3); 29; 33; 12:3; 7(2); 8(2); 9(2); 10(5); 11; 13; 21; 22; 23; 24; 13:3(2); 12; 14:3; 6; 8; 9; 12; 22(2); 28(2); 30; 32; 34(2); 35; 37; 39(2); 15:3; 4; 9; 24; 32; 34(2); 38; 54; 57; 16:1; 3; 7; 12(2); 15; 16; S:1; **2Cor** 1:2; 4; 8; 12; 13; 15; 16(3); 17; 23; 2:1; 3; 6; 7; 9; 10(2); 12(2); 14; 16(2); 3:1(2); 3; 4; 5; 7; 13; 16; 18; 4:2; 3; 6(2); 15; 5:2; 8(2); 10; 12(2); 13; 18(2); 19; 20; 21; 7:3(2); 9; 10(2); 11; 14(2); 8:1; 3; 4; 5; 7; 8; 10(2); 11; 12(2); 16; 19(2); 24; 9:1(3); 2; 5; 8(2); 9; 10; 11(2); 10:2(2); 4; 5; 6; 7; 13(3); 14; 15; 16(3); 11:1; 2(2); 7; 8; 9(2); 15; 32; 12:1(2); 2; 4; 6(2); 7(2); 11; 13(2); 14(4); 13:1; 2(2); 3; 7; 10(3); S:1; **Gal** 1:3; 4; 5; 10; 16; 17(2); 18(2); 2:1; 2; 3; 4; 5; 6(4); 8; 9(2); 10; 11(3); 14(2); 17; 19; 3:5; 6; 10; 16(3); 18; 19; 22; 24; 29; 4:5; 9(2); 15; 18; 20(2); 21; 24; 25; 5:3(2); 13; 17; 6:3; 8(2); 12(2); 13; 16; **Eph** 1:1(2); 2; 5(2); 6; 7; 9; 11; 12; 16; 19(2); 21; 22(2); 2:2(2); 7; 15; 17(2); 3:2; 7; 9; 10; 11; 16(2); 18; 19; 20(2); 4:3; 7; 14(2); 16; 19; 22; 27; 28(2); 29; 32; 5:2; 12; 19(2); 21; 24; 27; 28; 6:4; 5(2); 7(2); 11; 13(2); 16; 19; 20; 21; 23; **Phil** 1:1; 7; 14; 16(2); 19; 20; 21(3); 23(2); 24; 26; 28(2); 29(2); 30; 2:6; 11; 13(2); 19; 23; 25(3); 30; 3:1(3); 7; 13; 21(2); 4:11; 12(6); 17; 18; 19; S:1; **Col** 1:2; 3; 4; 9(2); 11; 12; 20; 22; 23; 25(3); 26; 27; 29; 2:2; 14(2); 17; 20; 22; 23; 3:9; 15; 16; 17; 21; 22; 23; 4:3; 4; 6; 10; 17(2); S:1; **1Th** 1:2; 7; 8(2); 9(2); 10(2); 2:2; 4; 8; 15; 16(4); 17; 3:1; 2(2); 4; 5; 6(2); 9; 12; 13; 4:1(2); 4; 9; 11(3); 13; 17; 5:9(2); 12; 13; 15; **2Th** 1:3; 6(2); 7; 10(2); 12; 2:13(3); 14; 3:7; 8; 9(2); S:1; **1Ti** 1:3; 4; 7; 10; 11(2); 15; 16(2); 18; 20; 2:4(2); 6; 12(3); 3:2(2); 3; 5; 8; 13; 14; 15; 4:1; 3(3); 4; 8; 13(3); 15(2); 5:4(2); 11; 13(2); 14(2); 24; 6:3(3); 16; 17; 18(2); 19; 20; S:1; **2Ti** 1:1; 2; 4; 5; 8; 9(2); 10; 12; 2:2(2); 4; 8; 14(2); 15(2); 20(2); 24; 25; 3:2; 7(2); 15; 4:3; 6; 8; 9; 10; 11; 12; 14; 16; 18; 21; **Titus** 1:1; 3; 4; 7(2); 9(2); 14; 2:3; 4(3); 5(2); 6; 8; 9(2); 11; 3:1(5); 2(2); 5; 7; 8; 12(3); 14; S:1; **Philem** 1:2(2); 3; 8; 11(3); 16; 19; S:1; **Heb** 1:5(2); 13; 14; 2:1(2); 3; 4; 5; 10; 11; 15; 17(3); 18; 3:2; 5; 7; 13; 15; 18(2); 4:1; 6; 7(2); 9; 11; 12; 13; 16; 5:1; 3; 5(2); 7; 11(2); 12; 14(2); 6:5; 6(3); 8; 10(2); 11; 13; 16; 17; 18(2); 7:2; 5(2); 13; 23; 25(3); 27; 8:3(2); 4; 5(3); 9(2); 10(2); 11; 12; 13; 9:9; 11(2); 13; 14(2); 19(2); 24; 26; 27; 28; 10:1; 2; 7; 9; 15; 19; 20; 24(2); 31; 32; 39; 11:6(2); 7; 8; 11; 15; 16; 19; 20; 24(2); 25(2); 29; 32; 34; 35; 12:11; 19; 22; 23(3); 24(2); 13:2; 8; 10; 14; 15(2); 16(2); 18; 19(2); 21(2); S:1; **Jas** 1:1; 5; 12; 19(3); 21; 26; 27(2); 2:3(2); 5; 8; 9; 16; 3:2; 10; 17; 4:2; 5; 7; 8(2); 9(2); 12(2); 13(3); 15; 17(3); 5:1; 16; 17; **1Pet** 1:1; 2; 3; 4; 5; 12; 13(2); 14; 17; 2:4; 5(2); 8; 13(2); 15; 18(3); 23; 24; 3:1; 7; 15(2); 18(2); 4:2(2); 3; 4; 5(2); 6(3); 9; 10; 11; 12; 19(2); 5:3; 5(2); 11; **2Pet** 1:1; 3; 5(2); 6(3); 7(2); 10; 12; 13; 15; 17; 2:4(2); 8; 9(3); 10; 12; 13; 17; 21(2); 22(3); 3:9(2); 11; 13; 15; 16; 18; **1Jn** 1:9(2); 2:6; 3:5; 16; 4:10; 11; 14; 16; 5:11; 14; **2Jn** 8; 12(3); **3Jn** 4; 5(2); 8(2); 9; 13; 14(2); **Jude** 1; 3(2); 4; 7; 13; 15(2); 24(2); 25; **Rev** 1:1(2); 4(2); 6; 8; 12; 13; 2:7(2); 12; 14(3); 17(2); 19; 20(4); 21; 23; 26; 27; 3:2; 7; 9(2); 10; 18; 20; 21(2); 4:3; 8; 9; 11; 5:2(2); 3(2); 4(3); 5(2); 9(3); 12; 6:2; 4(2); 8; 16; 17; 7:2(3); 10; 14; 8:2; 6; 13(2); 9:1; 5; 6; 9; 10; 14; 15; 10:4; 5; 7(2); 11:6(4); 9; 10; 12; 13; 17(2); 18; 12:2; 4(3); 5(2); 12; 14; 15; 17; 13:3; 4; 5; 6; 7(2); 12; 14(3); 15; 16; 14:4; 6(2); 7; 15(2); 18; 15:8; 16:1; 6; 8; 9; 14(2); 19; 17:17(2); 18:6(2); 17; 19:7; 8; 10; 17; 19; 20:8(3); 12; 13; 21:10; 15; 17; 23; 22:6; 8; 12; 14; 16

TOGETHER

259, 2298, 3162, *240, 260, 346, 846, 864, 1794, 1865, 1909, 1996, 1997, 1998, 2086, 2596, 2675, 3326, 3588, 3674, 4314, 4776, 4779, 4786, 4789, 4794, 4801, 4802, 4806, 4811, 4816, 4822, 4831, 4836, 4837, 4851, 4853, 4854, 4863, 4865, 4866, 4867, 4873, 4883, 4886, 4888, 4890, 4891, 4896, 4897, 4899, 4903, 4904, 4905, 4911, 4925, 4936, 4943, 4944, 4966*

Gen 1:9; 10; 3:7; 13:6(2); 14:3; 22:6; 8; 19; 25:22; 29:7; 8; 22; 34:30; 36:7; 42:17; 49:1; 2; **Ex** 2:13; 3:16; 4:29; 8:14; 15:8; 19:8; 21:18; 26:3; 6; 11; 24(2); 28:7; 30:35; 32:1; 26; 35:1; 36:18; 29; 39:4(2); **Lev** 8:3; 4; 24:10; 26:25; **Num** 1:18; 8:9; 10:7; 11:22; 14:35; 16:3; 11; 20:2; 8; 10; 21:16; 23; 24:10; 26:10; 27:3; **Deut** 4:10; 22:10; 11; 25:5; 11; 31:12; 33:5; 17; **Josh** 8:16; 9:2; 10:5; 6; 11:5(2); 17:10; 18:1; 22:12; **Judg** 4:13; 6:33; 38; 7:23; 24; 9:6; 47; 10:17(2); 11:20; 12:1; 4; 16:23; 18:22; 19:6; 29; 20:1; 11; 14; **1Sa** 5:11; 7:6; 7; 8:4; 10:17; 11:11; 13:4; 5; 11; 15:4; 17:1(2); 2; 10; 23:8; 25:1; 28:1; 4(2); 23; 29:1; 31:6; **2Sa** 2:13; 16; 25; 30; 6:1; 10:15; 17; 12:3; 28; 29; 14:6; 16; 20:14; 21:9; 23:9; 11; **1Kin** 3:18; 5:12; 10:26; 11:1; 18:20; 20:1; 22:6; **2Kin** 2:8; 3:10; 13; 9:25; 10:18; **1Chr** 10:6; 11:13; 13:5; 15:3; 16:35; 19:7; 22:2; 23:2; **2Chr** 12:5; 15:10; 18:5; 20:4; 24:5; 25:5; 28:24; 29:4; 30:3; 32:4; 6; 34:17; 29; **Ezr** 2:64; 3:1; 9; 11; 4:3; 6:20; 7:28; 8:15; 10:7; 9; **Neh** 4:6; 8; 6:2; 7; 10; 7:5; 66; 8:1; 13; 12:28; 13:11; **Est** 2:3; 8; 19; 4:16; 8:11; 9:2; 15; 16; 18; **Job** 2:11; 3:18; 6:2; 9:32; 10:8; 11:10; 16:10; 17:16; 19:12; 24:4; 30:7; 34:15; 38:7; 38; 40:13; 17; 41:15; 17; 23; **Ps** 2:2; 14:3; 31:13; 33:7; 34:3; 35:15(2); 26; 37:38; 40:14; 41:7; 47:9; 48:4; 49:2; 50:5; 55:14; 56:6; 71:10; 74:8; 83:5; 85:10; 88:17; 94:21; 98:8; 102:22; 104:22; 122:3; 133:1; 140:2; 147:2; **Prov** 22:2; 29:13; **Eccl** 3:5; 4:5; 11; **Is** 1:18; 28; 31; 8:10; 9:11; 21; 11:6; 7; 12; 14; 13:4; 18:6; 22:3(2); 9; 24:22; 25:11; 26:19; 27:4; 31:3; 34:4; 40:5; 41:1; 19; 20; 23; 43:9; 17; 26; 44:11(2); 45:8; 16; 20; 21; 46:2; 48:13; 49:18; 50:8; 52:8; 9; 54:15(2); 60:4; 5; 7; 13; 62:9; 65:7; 25; 66:17; **Jer** 3:18; 4:5; 6:11; 12; 21; 13:14; 31:8; 12; 13; 24; 41:1; 46:12; 21; 48:7; 49:3; 14; 50:4; 29; 33; 51:27; 38; 44; **Lam** 2:8; **Eze** 21:14; 17; 29:5; 37:7; **Dan** 2:35; 3:2; 3; 27; 6:6; 7; 11:6; **Hos** 1:11; 11:8; **Joel** 3:11; **Amos** 1:15; 3:3; **Mic** 2:12; **Nah** 1:10; 2:10; **Zeph** 2:1(2); **Zec** 10:4; 12:3; 14:14; **Mt** 1:18; 2:4; 13:2; 30(2); 18:20; 19:6; 22:10; 34; 41; 23:37; 24:28; 31; 26:3; 27:17; 62; **Mk** 1:33; 2:2; 15; 3:20; 6:30; 33; 7:1; 9:25; 10:9; 12:28; 13:27; 14:56; 59; 15:16; **Lk** 5:15; 6:38; 8:4; 9:1; 11:29; 12:1; 13:11; 34; 15:6; 9; 13; 17:35; 37; 22:55; 66; 23:12; 13; 48; 24:14; 15; 33; **Jn** 4:36; 6:13; 11:52; 53; 20:4; 7; 21:2; **Acts** 1:4; 6; 15; 2:6; 44; 3:1; 11; 4:6; 26; 27; 31; 5:9; 21; 10:24; 27; 12:12; 13:44; 14:1; 27; 15:6; 30; 16:22; 19:19; 25; 32; 20:7; 8; 21:22; 30; 23:12; 28:17(2); **Rom** 1:12; 3:12; 6:5; 8:17; 22; 28; 15:30; **1Cor** 1:10; 3:9; 5:4; 7:5; 11:17; 18; 20; 33; 34; 12:24; 14:23; 26; **2Cor** 1:11; 6:1; 14; **Eph** 1:10; 2:5; 6(2); 21; 22; 4:16; **Phil** 1:27; 3:17; **Col** 2:2; 13; 19; **1Th** 4:17; 5:10; 11; **2Th** 2:1; **Heb** 10:25; **Jas** 5:3; **1Pet** 3:7; 5:13; **Rev** 6:14; 16:16; 19:17; 19; 20:8

TOLD

559, 560, 1540, 1696, 4487, 5046, 5608, 6310, 7760, 8085, 8505, *312, 518, 1285, 1334, 1834, 2036, 2046, 2980, 3004, 3377, 4277, 4280, 4302*

Gen 3:11; 9:22; 14:13; 20:8; 22:3; 9; 20; 24:28; 33; 66; 26:32; 27:42; 29:12(2); 13; 31:20; 22; 37:5; 9; 10; 38:13; 24; 40:9; 41:8; 12; 24; 42:29; 43:7; 44:24; 45:26; 27; 47:1; 48:1; 2; **Ex** 4:28; 5:1; 14:5; 16:22; 18:8; 19:9; 24:3; **Lev** 21:24; **Num** 11:24; 27; 13:27; 14:39; 23:26; 29:40; **Deut** 17:4; **Josh** 2:2; 23; 9:24; 10:17; **Judg** 6:13; 7:13; 9:7; 25; 42; 47; 13:6(2); 23; 14:2; 6; 9; 16(2); 17(2); 16:2; 10; 13; 15; 17; 18; **Ruth** 3:16; **1Sa** 3:13; 18; 4:13; 14; 8:10; 9:15; 10:16(2); 25; 11:4; 5; 14:1; 33; 43; 15:12; 18:20; 24; 26; 19:2; 11; 18; 19; 21; 23:1; 7; 13; 22; 25; 24:1; 25:12; 14; 19; 36; 37; 27:4; **2Sa** 1:5; 6; 13; 2:4; 3:23; 4:10; 6:12; 10:5; 17; 11:5; 10; 18; 14:33; 15:31; 17:17(2); 18; 21; 18:10; 11; 25; 19:1; 8; 21:11; 24:13; **1Kin** 1:23; 51; 2:29; 39; 41; 8:5; 10:3(2); 7; 13:11(2); 25; 14:2; 18:13; 16; 19:1; 20:17; **2Kin** 1:7; 4:7; 27; 31; 5:4; 6:10; 13; 7:10; 11; 15; 8:6; 7; 14; 9:18; 20; 36; 10:8; 12:10; 11; 18:37; 23:17; **1Chr** 17:25; 19:5; 17; **2Chr** 2:2; 5:6; 9:2(2); 6; 20:2; 34:18; **Ezr** 8:17; **Neh** 2:12; 16; 18; **Est** 2:22; 3:4(2); 4:4; 7; 9; 12; 5:11; 6:2; 13; 8:1; **Job** 15:18; 37:20; **Ps** 44:1; 52:t, 78:3; 90:9; **Eccl** 6:6; **Is** 7:2; 36:22; 40:21; 44:8; 45:21; 52:15; **Jer** 36:20; 38:27; **Dan** 4:7; 8; 7:1; 16; 8:26; **Jonah** 1:10; **Hab** 1:5; **Zec** 10:2; **Mt** 8:33; 12:48; 14:12; 18:31; 24:25; 26:13; 28:7; **Mk** 5:14; 16; 33; 6:30; 9:12; 16:10; 13; **Lk** 1:45; 2:17; 18; 20; 8:20; 34; 36; 9:10; 36; 13:1; 18:37;

24:9; 10; 35; **Jn** 3:12; 4:29; 39; 51; 5:15; 8:40; 9:27; 10:25; 11:46; 14:2; 29; 16:4(2); 18:8; 20:18; **Acts** 5:22; 25; 9:6; 12:14; 16:36; 38; 22:10; 26; 23:16; 30; 27:25; **2Cor** 7:7; 13:2; **Gal** 5:21; **Phil** 3:18; **1Th** 3:4; **2Th** 2:5; **Jude** 18

TOO

1767, 3498, 7368, *1174*

Gen 18:14; **Ex** 12:4; 18:18; 36:7; **Num** 11:14; 16:3; 7; 22:6; **Deut** 1:17; 2:36; 12:21; 14:24(2); 17:8; **Josh** 17:15; 19:9; 47; 22:17; **Judg** 7:2; 4; 18:26; **Ruth** 1:12; **2Sa** 3:39; 10:11(2); 12:8; 22:18; **1Kin** 1:36; 8:64; 12:28; 19:7; **2Kin** 3:26; 6:1; **1Chr** 19:12(2); **2Chr** 29:34; **Est** 1:18; **Job** 42:3; **Ps** 18:17; 35:10; 38:4; 73:16; 131:1; 139:6; **Prov** 24:7; 30:18; **Is** 49:19; 20; **Jer** 32:17; 27; **Acts** 17:22

TOOK

270, 622, 680, 935, 1491, 1497, 1518, 2388, 3318, 3381, 3920, 3947, 4185, 5265, 5267, 5312, 5375, 5384, 5414, 5493, 5674, 5709, 5927, 6901, 6902, 7287, 7311, 7673, 7760, 8610, *142, 337, 353, 520, 539, 618, 643, 657, 1011, 1209, 1453, 1519, 1544, 1562, 1684, 1723, 1921, 1949, 1959, 2021, 2192, 2507, 2902, 2983, 3348, 3880, 4084, 4160, 4327, 4355, 4815, 4823, 4838, 4863*

Gen 2:15; 21; 3:6; 4:19; 5:24; 6:2; 8:9; 20; 9:23; 11:29; 31; 12:5; 14:11; 12; 15:10; 16:3; 17:23; 18:8; 20:2; 14; 21:14; 21; 27; 22:3; 6(2); 10; 13; 24:7; 10; 22; 61; 65; 67; 25:1; 20; 26; 26:34; 27:15; 36; 28:9; 11; 18; 29:23; 30:9; 37; 31:23; 45; 46; 32:13; 22; 23; 33:11; 34:2; 25; 26; 28; 29; 36:2; 6; 37:24; 31; 38:2; 6; 28; 39:20; 40:11; 41:42; 42:24; 30; 43:15(2); 34; 44:11; 46:1; 6; 47:2; 48:1; 13; 22; 50:25; **Ex** 2:1; 3; 9; 4:6; 20(2); 25; 6:20; 23; 25; 9:10; 10:19; 12:34; 13:19; 20; 22; 14:6; 7; 25; 15:20; 16:1; 17:12; 18:2; 12; 24:6; 7; 8; 32:20; 33:7; 34:4; 34; 40:20; **Lev** 6:4; 8:10; 15; 16; 23; 25; 26; 28; 29; 30; 9:15; 17; 10:1; **Num** 1:17; 3:49; 50; 7:6; 10:12; 13; 11:25; 16:1; 18; 39; 47; 17:9; 20:9; 21:1; 25; 32; 22:41; 23:7; 11; 18; 24:3; 15; 20; 21; 23; 25:7; 27:22; 31:9(2); 11; 27; 47; 51; 54; 32:39; 41; 42; 33:12; **Deut** 1:15; 23; 25; 2:1; 34; 35(2); 3:4(2); 7; 8; 14; 9:17; 21; 10:6; 22:14; 24:3; 29:8; **Josh** 2:4; 3:6; 4:8; 20; 6:12; 20; 7:1; 17; 21; 23; 24; 8:12; 19; 23; 27; 9:4; 12; 14; 10:27; 28; 32; 35; 37; 39; 11:10; 14; 16; 17; 19; 23; 15:17; 16:4; 19:47; 24:3; 26; **Judg** 1:13; 18; 3:6; 21; 25; 28; 4:21(2); 5:19; 6:27; 7:8; 24; 25; 8:12; 16; 21; 9:43; 45; 48(2); 50; 11:13; 15; 12:5; 6; 9; 13:19; 14:9; 19; 15:4; 15; 16:3; 12; 21; 29; 31; 17:2; 4; 18:17; 20; 27; 19:1; 15; 25; 28; 29; 20:6; 21:23; **Ruth** 1:4; 2:18; 4:2; 13; 16; **1Sa** 1:24; 2:14; 5:1; 2; 3; 6:10; 12; 15; 7:9; 12; 8:3; 9:22; 24; 10:1; 11:7; 14:32; 47; 52; 15:8; 21; 16:13; 20; 23; 17:20; 34; 40; 49; 51; 54; 57; 18:2; 19:13; 24:2; 25:18; 43; 26:12; 27:9; 28:24; 30:20; 31:4; 12; 13; **2Sa** 1:10; 11; 2:8; 32; 3:15; 27; 36; 4:4; 7; 10; 12; 5:7; 13; 6:6; 7:8; 15; 8:1; 4; 7; 8; 10:4; 11:4; 12:4; 26; 29; 30; 13:8; 9; 10; 11; 15:5; 17:19; 18:14; 17; 20:3; 9; 10; 21:8; 10; 12; 22:17; 23:16; **1Kin** 1:39; 3:1; 20; 4:15; 8:3; 11:18; 12:28; 13:29; 14:26(3); 15:12; 18; 22; 16:31; 17:19; 23; 18:4; 10; 26; 31; 40; 19:21; 20:34; 41; 22:46; **2Kin** 2:8; 12; 13; 14; 3:26; 27; 4:37; 5:5; 24; 6:7; 8; 7:14; 8:9; 15; 9:13; 10:7; 14; 15; 31; 11:2; 4; 9; 19; 12:9; 17; 18; 13:15; 18; 25; 14:7; 13; 14; 21; 15:29; 16:8; 9; 17; 17:6; 18:10; 13; 20:7; 23:11; 16; 19; 30; 34; 24:12; 25:6; 14; 15; 18; 19; 20; **1Chr** 2:19; 23; 4:18; 5:21; 7:15; 10:4; 9; 12; 11:5; 18; 14:3; 17:7; 13; 18:1; 4; 7; 19:4; 20:2; 23:22; 27:23; **2Chr** 5:4; 8:18; 10:6; 8; 11:18; 20; 21; 12:4; 9(2); 13:19; 14:3; 5; 15:8; 16:6; 17:6; 22:11; 23:1; 8; 20; 24:3; 11; 25:13; 17; 23; 24; 26:1; 28:8; 15; 21; 29:16; 30:14(2); 23; 32:3; 33:11; 15; 34:33; 35:24; 36:1; 4; **Ezr** 2:61; 5:14; 6:5; 8:30; **Neh** 2:1; 4:1; 5:12; 7:63; 9:25; **Est** 2:7; 3:10; 6:11; 8:2; 9:27; **Job** 1:15; 2:8; **Ps** 18:16; 22:9; 31:13; 48:6; 55:14; 56:t, 69:4; 71:6; 78:70; **Prov** 12:27; **Eccl** 2:20; **Song** 5:7; **Is** 8:2; 20:1; 36:1; 40:14; **Jer** 13:7; 25:17; 26:8; 27:20; 28:3; 10; 31:32; 32:10; 11; 35:3; 36:14; 21; 32; 37:13; 14; 17; 38:6; 11(2); 13; 14; 39:14; 40:2; 41:12; 16; 43:5; 50:33; 43; 52:9; 18; 19; 24; 25; 26; **Lam** 5:13; **Eze** 3:12; 14; 8:3; 10:7(2); 11:24; 16:50; 17:3; 5; 19:5; 23:10; 13; 29:7; 33:5; 43:5; **Dan** 1:16; 3:22; 5:20; 31; **Hos** 1:3; 12:3; 13:11; **Amos** 7:15; **Jonah** 1:15; **Zec** 11:7; 10; 13; **Mt** 1:24; 2:14; 21; 8:17; 9:25; 13:31; 33; 14:12; 19; 20; 15:36; 37; 39; 16:9; 10; 22; 18:28; 20:17; 21:35; 46; 22:6; 15; 24:39; 25:1; 3(2); 4; 15; 35; 38; 43; 26:26; 27; 37; 50; 27:1; 6; 7; 9; 24; 27; 30; 31; 48; 28:15; **Mk** 1:31; 2:12; 3:6; 4:36; 5:41; 6:29; 43; 7:33; 8:6; 8; 19; 20; 23; 32; 9:27; 36; 10:16; 32; 12:8; 20; 21; 14:22; 23; 46; 49; 15:20; 46; **Lk** 2:28; 5:25; 8:54; 9:10; 16; 28; 47; 10:34; 35; 13:19; 21; 14:4; 15:13; 18:31; 20:29; 30; 31; 22:17; 19; 54; 23:53; 24:30; 43; **Jn** 5:9; 6:11; 24; 8:59; 10:31; 11:41; 53; 12:3; 13; 13:4; 18:12; 19:1; 16; 23; 27; 38; 40; **Acts** 1:16; 3:7; 4:13; 5:33; 7:21; 43; 9:23; 25; 27; 10:26; 12:25; 13:29; 15:39; 16:3; 33; 17:5; 19; 18:17; 18; 26; 19:13; 20:14; 21:6; 11; 15; 26; 30; 32; 33; 23:18; 19; 31; 24:6; 7; 27:35; 36; 28:15; **1Cor** 11:23; 25; **Gal** 2:1; **Phil** 2:7; **Col** 2:14; **Heb** 2:14; 16(2); 8:9; 9:19; 10:34; **Rev** 5:7; 8:5; 10:10; 18:21

TOWARD

413, 681, 854, 1870, 4136, 5049, 5704, 5921, 5973, 5974, 6440, *1519, 1722, 1909, 2596, 4314, 5228*

Gen 2:14; 12:9; 13:12; 15:5; 18:2; 16; 22; 19:1; 28(2); 20:1; 25:18; 28:10; 30:40; 31:2; 5; 21; 48:13(2); **Ex** 9:8; 10; 22; 23; 10:21; 22; 16:10; 25:20; 26:35; 28:27; 34:8; 36:25; 39:20; **Lev** 9:22; 13:41; **Num** 2:3; 3:38; 16:42; 21:11; 20; 23:28; 24:1; 32:14; 34:15; **Deut** 4:41; 47; 28:54(3); 56(3); 57(2); **Josh** 1:4; 15; 3:16; 8:18(2); 12:1; 13:5; 15:4; 7(3); 21; 16:6; 18:13; 17; 18; 19:11; 12; 18; 27(2); 34; **Judg** 3:28; 4:6; 5:9; 11; 8:3; 13:20; 19:9; 18; 20:43; 45; **1Sa** 13:18; 17:30; 48; 20:12; 41; **2Sa** 14:1; 15:23; 24:5; 20; **1Kin** 7:9; 25(4); 8:22; 29(3); 30; 35; 38; 42; 44(2); 48; 14:13; 18:43; **2Kin** 3:14; 25:4; **1Chr** 9:24; 12:15(2); 26:17; **2Chr** 4:4(4); 6:13; 20; 21; 26; 34; 38(3); 16:9; 20:24; 24:16(2); 31:14; **Ezr** 3:11; **Neh** 3:26; 12:31; **Est** 1:13; 8:4; **Job** 2:12; 11:13; 39:26; **Ps** 5:7; 25:15; 28:2; 66:5; 85:4; 86:13; 98:3; 103:11; 116:12; 117:2; 138:2; **Prov** 14:35; 23:5; **Eccl** 1:6; 11:3(2); **Song** 7:4; 10; **Is** 7:1; 11:14; 29:13; 38:2; 49:23; 63:7; 15; 66:14(2); **Jer** 1:13; 3:12; 4:6; 11; 12:3; 15:1; 29:10; 11; 31:21; 40; 46:6; 49:36; **Lam** 2:19; **Eze** 1:23; 4:7; 6:2; 14; 8:3; 5(2); 14; 16(3); 9:2; 12:14; 16:42; 63; 17:6; 7(2); 21; 20:46(2); 21:2(2); 24:23; 33:25; 40:6; 20; 22; 23(2); 24(2); 27(2); 31; 32; 34; 37; 44(2); 45; 46; 41:11(3); 12; 14; 19(2); 42:1(2); 4; 7; 10; 11; 12(2); 15(2); 43:1; 4; 17; 44:1; 46:1; 12; 19; 47:1; 8; 15; 48:10(4); 17(4); 21(2); 28; **Dan** 4:2; 6:10; 8:8; 9(3); 18; 10:9; 15; 11:4; 19; 29; **Hos** 3:1; 5:1; **Joel** 2:20(2); **Jonah** 2:4; **Zec** 6:6; 8; 9:1; 14:4(4); 8(2); **Mt** 12:49; 14:14; 28:1; **Mk** 6:34; **Lk** 2:14; 12:21; 13:22; 24:29; **Jn** 6:17; **Acts** 1:10; 8:26; 20:21(2); 22:3; 24:15; 16(2); 27:12; 40; 28:14; **Rom** 1:27; 5:8; 11:22; 12:16; 15:5; **1Cor** 7:36; **2Cor** 1:16; 18; 2:8; 7:4; 7; 15; 9:8; 10:1; 13:4; **Gal** 2:8; **Eph** 1:8; 2:7; **Phil** 2:30; 3:14; **Col** 4:5; **1Th** 3:12(3); 4:10; 12; 5:14; **2Th** 1:3; **Titus** 3:4; **Philem** 1:5(2); **Heb** 6:1; 10; **1Pet** 2:19; 3:21; **1Jn** 3:21; 4:9

TWO

2677, 6471, 6771, 8147, *296, 1250, 1332, 1367, 1417*

Gen 1:16; 4:19; 5:18; 20; 26; 28; 6:19; 20; 7:2; 9(2); 15(2); 9:22; 10:25; 11:10; 19; 20; 21; 23; 32; 19:1; 8; 15; 16; 30(2); 22:3; 24:22; 25:23(2); 27:9; 36; 29:16; 31:33; 41; 32:7; 10; 14(2); 22(2); 33:1; 34:25; 40:2; 41:1; 50; 42:37; 44:27; 45:6; 46:27; 48:1; 5; 49:14; **Ex** 2:13; 4:9; 12:7; 22; 23; 16:22; 29; 18:3; 6; 21:21; 25:10; 12(2); 17; 18(2); 19; 22; 23; 35(3); 26:17; 19(4); 21(2); 23(2); 24; 25(2); 27; 27:7; 28:7(2); 9; 11; 12(2); 14; 23(3); 24(2); 25(3); 26(2); 27(2); 29:1; 3; 13; 22; 38; 30:2; 4(3); 23(2); 31:18; 32:15; 34:1; 4(2); 29; 36:22; 24(4); 26(2); 28(2); 30; 37:1; 3(2); 6; 7(2); 8; 10; 21(3); 25; 27(3); 38:29; 39:4; 16(4); 17(2); 18(3); 19(2); 20(2); **Lev** 3:4; 10; 15; 4:9; 5:7(2); 11(2); 7:4; 8:2; 16; 25; 12:5; 8(2); 14:4; 10; 22(2); 49; 15:14(2); 29(2); 16:1; 5; 7; 8; 23:13; 17(2); 18; 19; 20; 24:5; 6; **Num** 1:35(2); 39; 2:21(2); 26; 3:34; 39; 43(2); 46; 4:36; 40; 44; 6:10(2); 7:3; 7; 17; 23; 29; 35; 41; 47; 53; 59; 65; 71; 77; 83; 85; 89; 9:22; 10:2; 11:19; 26; 31; 13:23; 15:6; 16:2; 17; 35; 22:22; 26:10; 14(2); 34; 37; 28:3; 9(2); 11; 12; 19; 20; 27; 28; 29:3; 9; 13; 14(2); 17; 20; 23; 26; 29; 32; 31:27; 35; 40; 34:15; 35:5(4); 6; **Deut** 3:8; 21; 4:13; 47; 5:22; 9:10; 11; 15(2); 17(2); 10:1; 3(2); 14:6; 17:6; 18:3; 19:15; 21:15; 32:30; **Josh** 2:1; 4; 10; 23; 3:4; 6:22; 7:3; 21; 9:10; 14:3; 4; 15:60; 19:30; 21:16; 25; 27; 24:12; **Judg** 3:16; 5:30; 7:3; 25; 8:12; 9:44; 10:3; 11:37; 38; 39; 12:6; 15:4; 13; 16:3; 28; 29; 17:4; 19:10; 20:21; 45; **Ruth** 1:1; 2; 3; 5; 7; 8; 19; 4:11; **1Sa** 1:2; 3; 2:21; 34; 4:4; 11; 17; 6:7; 10; 10:2; 4; 11:11; 13:1; 2; 14:49; 15:4; 18:27; 23:18; 25:13; 18(3); 27:3; 28:8; 30:5; 10; 12; 18; 21; **2Sa** 1:1; 2:2; 10; 4:2; 8:2; 5; 12:1; 13:23; 14:6(2); 26; 28; 15:11; 27; 36; 16:1; 18:24; 21:8; 23:20; **1Kin** 2:5; 32; 39; 3:16; 18; 25; 5:12; 14; 6:23; 32; 34(3); 7:15; 16; 18; 20(2); 24; 26; 41(5); 42(3); 8:7; 9; 63; 9:10; 10:16; 19; 11:29; 12:28; 14:20; 15:25; 16:8; 21; 24; 29; 17:12; 18:21; 23; 32; 20:1; 15(2); 16; 27; 21:10; 13; 22:31; 51; **2Kin** 1:14; 2:6; 7; 8; 12; 24(2); 4:1; 5:17; 22(2); 23(5); 7:1; 14; 16; 18; 8:17; 26; 9:32; 10:4; 8; 14; 11:7; 15:2; 23; 27; 17:16; 18:23; 21:5; 19(2); 23:12; 25:4; 16; **1Chr** 1:19; 4:5; 5:21(2); 7:2; 7; 9; 11; 9:22; 11:21; 22; 12:28; 32; 15:6; 8; 18:5; 19:7; 24:17; 25:7; 29; 26:8; 17(2); 18; 32; **2Chr** 3:10; 15; 4:3; 12(4); 13(3); 5:10; 7:5; 8:10; 9:15; 18; 13:21; 14:8; 17:15; 16; 17; 21:5; 19; 20; 22:2; 24:3; 26:3; 12; 28:8; 29:32; 33:5; 21(2); 35:8; **Ezr** 2:3(2); 4; 6; 7; 10; 12(2); 14; 19; 24; 27; 28; 29; 31; 37; 38; 58; 60; 64; 65; 66; 6:17; 8:4; 9; 20; 27; 10:13; **Neh** 5:14; 6:15; 7:8(2); 9; 10; 11; 12; 17(2); 19; 28; 31; 33; 34; 40; 41; 60; 62; 66; 67; 68; 71(2); 72; 11:12; 13(2); 18; 19; 12:31; 40; 13:6; **Est** 2:21; 6:2; 9:27; **Job** 13:20; 42:7; **Prov** 30:7; 15; **Eccl** 4:9; 11; 12; **Song** 4:5(2); 6:13; 7:3(2); 8:12; **Is** 7:4; 21; 17:6; 22:11; 36:8; 45:1; 47:9; 51:19; **Jer** 2:13; 3:14; 24:1; 28:3; 11; 33:24; 39:4; 52:7; 20; 29; **Eze** 1:11(2); 23(2); 21:19; 21; 23:2; 35:10(2); 37:22(2); 40:9; 39(2); 40(2); 41:3; 18; 22; 23; 24(4); 43:14; 45:15; 46:19; 47:13; 48:17(4); **Dan** 5:31; 8:3(2); 6; 7; 14; 20; 9:25; 26; 12:5; 11; **Hos** 6:2; 10:10; **Amos** 1:1; 3:3; 12; 4:8; **Zec** 4:3; 11; 12(2); 14; 5:9; 6:1; 11:7; 13:8; **Mt** 2:16; 4:18; 21; 6:24; 8:28; 9:27; 10:10; 29; 11:2; 14:17; 19; 18:8(2); 9; 16(2); 19; 20; 20:21; 24; 30; 21:1; 28; 22:40; 24:40; 41; 25:15; 17(2); 22(3); 26:2; 37; 60; 27:38; **Mk** 5:13; 6:7(2); 9; 37; 38; 41(2); 9:43; 45; 47; 11:1; 4; 12:42; 14:1; 13; 15:27; 16:12; **Lk** 2:24; 3:11; 5:2; 7:19; 41; 9:3; 13; 16; 30; 32; 10:1(2); 35; 12:6; 52(2); 15:11; 16:13; 17:34; 35; 36; 18:10; 19:29; 21:2; 22:38; 23:32; 24:4; 13; **Jn** 1:35; 37; 40; 2:6; 4:40; 43; 6:7; 9; 8:17; 11:6; 19:18; 20:12; 21:2; 8; **Acts** 1:10; 23; 24; 7:29; 9:38; 10:7; 12:6(2); 19:10; 22; 34; 21:33; 23:23(3); 24:27; 27:37; 41; 28:30; **1Cor** 6:16; 14:27; 29; **2Cor** 13:1; **Gal** 4:22; 24; **Eph** 5:31; **Phil** 1:23; **1Ti** 5:19; **Heb** 6:18; 10:28; **Rev** 2:12; 9:12; 16; 11:2; 3(2); 4(2); 10; 12:6; 14; 13:5; 11

UNDER

413, 4295, 5921, 8460, 8478, *332, 506, 1640, 1722, 1772, 1909, 2662, 2709, 2736, 5259, 5270, 5273, 5284, 5293, 5295, 5299*

Gen 1:7; 9; 6:17; 7:19; 16:9; 18:4; 8; 19:8; 21:15; 24:2; 9; 35:4; 8; 39:23; 41:35; 47:29; 49:25; **Ex** 6:6; 7; 17:12; 14; 18:10; 20:4; 21:20; 23:5; 24:4; 10; 25:35(3); 26:19(3); 21(2); 25(2); 33; 27:5; 30:4; 36:24(3); 26(2); 30; 37:21(3); 27; 38:4; **Lev** 15:10; 22:27; 27:32; **Num** 3:36; 4:28; 33; 6:18; 7:8; 16:31; 22:27; 31:49; 33:1; **Deut** 2:25; 3:17; 4:11; 19; 49; 7:24; 9:14; 12:2; 25:19; 28:23; 29:20; **Josh** 7:21; 22; 11:3; 17; 12:3; 13:5; 16:10; 24:26; **Judg** 1:7; 3:16; 30; 4:5; 6:11; 19; 9:29; **Ruth** 2:12; **1Sa** 7:11; 14:2; 21:3; 4; 8; 22:6; 31:13; **2Sa** 2:23; 3:27; 4:6; 12:31(3); 18:2(3); 9(2); 22:10; 37; 39; 40; 48; **1Kin** 4:25(2); 5:3; 7:24; 30; 32; 44; 8:6; 13:14; 14:23; 18:23(2); 25; 19:4; 5; **2Kin** 8:20; 22; 9:13; 33; 13:5; 14:27; 16:4; 17; 17:7; 10; **1Chr** 10:12; 17:1; 24:19; 25:2; 3; 6; 26:28; 27:23; **2Chr** 4:3; 15; 5:7; 13:18; 21:8; 10(2); 26:11; 13; 28:4; 10; 31:13; **Neh** 2:14; 8:17; **Job** 9:13; 20:12; 26:5; 8; 28:5; 24; 30:7; 37:3; 40:21; 41:11; 30; **Ps** 8:6; 10:7; 17:8; 18:9; 36; 38; 39; 47; 36:7; 44:5; 45:5; 47:3(2); 91:1; 4; 13; 106:42; 140:3; 144:2; **Prov** 12:24; 22:27; **Eccl** 1:3; 9; 13; 14; 2:3; 11; 17; 18; 19; 20; 22; 3:1; 16; 4:1; 3; 7; 15; 5:13; 18; 6:1; 12; 7:6; 8:9; 15(2); 17; 9:3; 6; 9(2); 11; 13; 10:5; **Song** 2:3; 6; 4:11; 8:3; 5; **Is** 3:6; 10:4(2); 16; 14:11; 19; 25; 18:7; 24:5; 25:10; 28:3; 15; 34:15; 57:5(2); 58:5; **Jer** 2:20; 3:6; 13; 10:11; 12:10; 27:8; 11; 12; 33:13; 38:11; 12(2); 48:45; 52:20; **Lam** 1:15; 3:34; 66; 4:20; 5:5; 13; **Eze** 1:8; 23; 6:13(2); 10:2; 8; 20; 21; 17:6; 23; 20:37; 24:5; 31:6(2); 17; 32:27; 42:9; 46:23; 47:1(2); **Dan** 4:12; 14; 21; 7:27; 8:13; 9:12; **Hos** 4:12; 13; 14:7; **Joel** 1:17; **Amos** 2:13; **Obad** 7; **Jonah** 4:5; **Mic** 1:4; 4:4(2); **Zec** 3:10(2); **Mal** 4:3; **Mt** 2:16; 5:13; 15; 7:6; 8:8; 9(2); 23:37; **Mk** 4:21(2); 32; 6:11; 7:28; **Lk** 7:6; 8(2); 8:16; 11:33; 13:34; 17:24(2); **Jn** 1:48; 50; **Acts** 2:5; 4:12; 8:27; 23:12; 14; 27:4; 7; 16; 30; **Rom** 3:9; 13; 19; 6:14(2); 15(2); 7:14; 16:20; **1Cor** 6:12; 7:15; 9:20(3); 21; 27; 10:1; 14:34; 15:25; 27(3); 28; **2Cor** 11:32; **Gal** 3:10; 22; 23; 25; 4:2; 3; 4; 5; 21; 5:18; **Eph** 1:22; **Phil** 2:10; **Col** 1:23; **1Ti** 5:9; 6:1; **Heb** 2:8(4); 7:11; 9:15; 10:28; 29; **Jas** 2:3; **1Pet** 5:6; **Jude** 6; **Rev** 5:3; 13; 6:9; 11:2; 12:1

UNDERNEATH

4295, 8478

Ex 28:27; 39:20; **Deut** 33:27

UNLESS

Lev 22:6; **Num** 22:33; **2Sa** 2:27; **Ps** 27:13; 94:17; 119:92; **Prov** 4:16; **1Cor** 15:2

UNTIL

518, 834, 3588, 5704, *891, 1519, 2193, 3360*

Gen 8:5; 7; 24:19; 33; 26:13; 27:44; 45; 28:15; 29:8; 32:4; 24; 33:3; 14; 34:5; 39:16; 41:49; 46:34; 49:10; **Ex** 9:18; 10:26; 12:6; 10(2); 15; 18; 22; 16:20; 23; 35(2); 17:12; 23:18; 30; 24:14; 33:8; 34:34; 35; **Lev** 7:15; 8:33; 11:24; 25; 27; 28; 31; 32; 39; 40(2); 12:4; 14:46; 15:5; 6; 7; 8; 10(2); 11; 16; 17; 18; 19; 21; 22; 23; 27; 16:17; 17:15; 19:6; 13; 22:4; 6; 30; 23:14; 25:22(2); 28; **Num** 4:3; 23; 6:5; 9:15; 11:20; 14:19; 33; 19:7; 8; 10; 21; 22; 20:17; 21:22; 35; 23:24; 24:22; 32:13; 17; 18; 21; 35:12; 28; 32; **Deut** 1:31; 2:14(2); 15; 29; 3:3; 20(2); 7:20; 23; 24; 9:7; 21; 11:5; 16:4; 20:20; 22:2; 28:20(2); 21; 22; 24; 48; 51(2); 52; 61; 31:24; 30; **Josh** 1:15; 2:16; 22; 3:17; 4:10; 23(2); 5:1; 6:10; 7:6; 13; 8:24; 26; 29; 10:13; 26; 27; 33; 11:8; 14; 13:13; 20:6(2); 9; 22:17; 23:13; 15; **Judg** 4:24; 5:7; 6:18(2); 13:15; 18:30; 19:8; 25; 20:23; 26; **Ruth** 1:19; 2:7; 17; 21; 3:3; 13; 14; 18(2); **1Sa** 1:22; 23(2); 3:15; 7:11; 9:13; 11:11; 14:9; 24; 36; 15:7; 18; 35; 17:52; 19:2; 23; 20:41; 25:36; 30:4; **2Sa** 1:12; 4:3; 5:25; 10:5; 15:24; 28; 17:13; 19:7; 24; 21:10; 22:38; 23:10; **1Kin** 3:1; 2; 5:3; 6:22; 10:7; 11:16; 40; 15:29; 17:14; 18:26; 29; 22:11; 27; **2Kin** 6:25; 7:3; 8:6; 11; 10:8; 11; 17:20; 23;

18:32; 24:20; **1Chr** 5:22; 6:32; 12:22; 19:5; 28:20; **2Chr** 8:8; 16; 9:6; 16:12; 18:10; 26; 34; 21:15; 24:10; 29:28; 34: 31:1; 35:14; 36:16; 20; 21; **Ezr** 4:5; 21; 5:16; 8:29; 9:4; 10:14; **Neh** 7:3; 8:3; 12:23; **Job** 14:13; 26:10; **Ps** 36:2; 57:1; 71:18; 73:17; 94:13; 104:23; 105:19; 110:1; 112:8; 123:2; 132:5; **Prov** 7:18; **Song** 2:17; 3:4; 4:6; 8:4; **Is** 5:11; 6:11; 26:20; 32:15; 36:17; 39:6; 62:1; **Jer** 23:20; 27:7; 8; 22; 30:24(2); 32:5; 36:23; 37:21; 38:28; 44:27; 52:34; **Eze** 21:27; 33:22; 46:2; **Dan** 4:32; 7:22; 25; 9:27; **Hos** 7:4; **Mic** 5:3; 7:9; **Zeph** 3:8; **Mt** 1:17; 2:13; 15; 11:12; 13; 23; 13:30; 17:9; 18:22(2); 24:38; 39; 26:29; 27:64; 28:15; **Mk** 14:25; 15:33; **Lk** 1:20; 13:35; 15:4; 16:16; 17:27; 21:24; 22:16; 18; 23:44; 24:49; **Jn** 2:10; 9:18; **Acts** 1:2; 2:35; 3:21; 10:30; 13:20; 20:7; 21:26; 23:1; 14; **Rom** 5:13; 8:22; 11:25; **1Cor** 4:5; 16:8; **2Cor** 3:14; **Gal** 4:2; 19; **Eph** 1:14; **Phil** 1:5; 6; **2Th** 2:7; **1Ti** 6:14; **Heb** 1:13; 9:10; **Jas** 5:7; **2Pet** 1:19; **1Jn** 2:9; **Rev** 6:11; 17:17; 20:5

UNTO

¹⁵¹⁹

Gen 1:9; 28; 2:19; 22; 24; 3:1; 2; 4; 6; 9(2); 13; 14; 16; 17(2); 19(2); 21; 4:3; 4; 5; 6; 7; 9; 10; 12; 13; 15; 18; 19; 23(2); 6:1; 4; 13; 20; 21; 7:1; 5; 9; 15; 8:9(2); 12; 15; 20; 9:1; 8; 17; 24; 25; 10:1; 19(3); 21; 25; 30; 11:4; 31; 12:1(2); 4; 6(2); 7(4); 8(2); 11; 18; 13:3; 4; 8; 10; 14; 17; 18; 14:6; 14; 15; 21; 22; 15:1; 4; 5; 7; 9; 10; 13; 18(2); 16:2(2); 4; 5; 6; 9; 9; 10; 13; 17:1; 7; 8; 9; 15; 17; 18; 21; 23; 18:1; 6; 7(2); 9; 10; 13; 14; 21; 27; 29; 30; 31; 33; 19:3; 5(3); 6; 8(2); 12; 14(2); 16; 18; 19; 20; 21; 31(2); 34; 37; 38; 20:5; 6; 9(3); 10; 13(2); 14; 16(2); 17; 21:1; 21:1; 3; 5; 7; 9; 10; 12; 14; 17; 22; 23(3); 27; 29; 30; 22:1; 3; 5; 7; 11; 12; 15; 19; 20; 23:3; 5; 13; 14; 15; 16; 18; 20; 24:2; 3; 4(2); 5(3); 6; 7(4); 10; 12; 14; 20; 24(2); 25; 29(2); 30(2); 36; 38(2); 39; 40; 42; 45(2); 47; 48; 50; 54; 56; 58; 60; 65; 25:5; 6(2); 12; 17; 18; 23; 33(2); 26:1(2); 2; 3(3); 4; 9; 10; 16; 18; 19; 27; 32; 33(3); 9; 13; 14(2); 6(2); 13; 18; 19; 20; 21; 22; 26; 31(2); 32; 34; 37(2); 38; 39; 42; 28:1; 4; 5; 9(2); 22; 29:4; 5; 6; 15; 20; 21(2); 23; 24; 25; 30; 34; 30:1; 3; 4; 14; 15; 16; 17; 25(2); 27; 29; 30; 40; 31:3(2); 4; 5; 7; 11; 13; 24; 9; 10; 16; 18; 19; 27; 32; 33:13; 19; 13; 14(2); 18; 20; 22; 23; 28(2); 31; 33; 34; 36; 37; 43:2; 3(2); 5; 8; 9; 11; 13; 23; 29(2); 32; 34; 44:4(2); 6; 7; 8; 10; 15; 16; 17; 18; 21(2); 22; 23; 24; 25; 27; 32(2); 45:1; 3; 4; 5(2); 7; 9(2); 10; 11; 2(2); 13; 13(2); 23; 24; 26; 28; 46:1; 2; 15; 18; 20(2); 25(2); 28(2); 29; 30; 31(4); 34; 47:2 3(2); 4; 5(2); 8; 9(2); 15; 17; 18(2); 19; 23; 24; 29; 31(2); 48:2; 3(2); 4; 5(2); 7; 9(2); 10; 11; 13; 15; 17; 18; 21(2); 49:1; 2; 6; 10; 11(2); 13; 15; 26; 28; 29(2); 33; 50:4; 12; 15; 16; 17(3); 19; 20; 21; 24(2); Ex 1:9; 10; 18; 19(2); 2:9; 10; 11; 20; 23; 25; 3:2; 4; 8(3); 9; 10; 11(2); 12; 13(5); 14(3); 15(4); 16(2); 17(2); 18(2); 4:1(2); 2; 4; 5; 6; 9; 10(2); 11; 15; 16; 18(2); 19; 21; 22; 23; 30; 5:1; 3; 4(2); 15; 16; 21; 2; 6; 1; 10; 11(2); 13; 15; 26; 28; 29(2); 33; 50:4; 12; 15; 16; 17(3); 19; 20(2); 23; 24(2); 25(2); 20:4; 5; 6; 9; 20; 21; 24(2); 23; 24(2); 26; 21:6(2); 8; 9; 11; 31; 32; 34; 22:7; 8(2); 9; 10; 11; 12; 17; 20(2); 23; 26; 27; 29; 31; 23:13; 14; 22(2); 23; 27; 31(2); 33; 24:1(2); 5; 12; 14(3); 16; 25:1; 2; 22; 35; 33; 34; 26:24; 33; 27:21; 28:1(2); 3(2); 4; 12; 28; 29; 35; 41; 42; 43(3); 29:1(2); 4; 17(2); 18(2); 25; 28; 34; 35; 41; 42; 30:3; 10; 11; 12; 14; 15; 16; 17; 20; 22; 30(3); 32; 34(2); 36; 37; 38; 31:1; 12; 13; 14; 18; 32:1(2); 2(2); 3; 7; 9; 13(2); 14; 17; 19; 21(2); 23; 24; 25; 26(2); 27; 30(2); 31; 33; 34(2); 33:14; 1; 5(3); 7; 8; 11(2); 12(2); 15; 17; 34:1(2); 2; 4(2); 6(2); 7; 10; 11; 15; 19; 21(2); 24; 25; 26(2); 27; 30(2); 31; 32(3); 33; 34(2); 33:14; 1; 5; 6; 7; 28:1; 7; 8(2); 9; 11; 13(2); 14; 15; 18; 21(4); 22; 23; 29:3(3); 4(2); 8(2); 11; 13(2); 14(3); 15; 19; 21; 24; 26; 27; 28(2); 29; 31; 36; 38; 8(2); 9; 12; 14; 16(3); 17; 20; 21; 28; 29; 24:10; 11; 12(2); 16; 25:2; 7; 10; 13(2); 15; 17; 19; 20; 17:8(2); 13; 18; 28; 34; 37; 39; 41; 43; 44; 46; 52(2); 55; 18:1; 8; 18; 19; 19:4(2); 6; 11; 17(2); 20:2; 4; 5(2); 11; 12(2); 21; 22; 27; 29; 30(2); 31; 32; 36; 40(2); 21:1; 2(2); 5; 8; 11; 14; 22:2; 3; 5; 7; 8; 13; 15; 17; 22; 23:2; 3; 17(2); 24:4(3); 6(2); 16; 19; 21; 22(2); 25:5; 6; 7; 8; 11; 13; 15; 16; 19; 21; 22(2); 27(2); 31(2); 34; 35; 40(2); 26:1; 27:2; 5; 6(2); 8; 28:1; 7; 8(2); 9; 11; 13(2); 14; 15; 18; 21(4); 22; 23; 29:3(3); 4(2); 8(2); 30:13; 15; 17; 24; 25; 26; 31:4; **2Sa** 1:3(2); 4; 5; 7; 8; 9; 10; 13; 14; 16; 26; 2:1(2); 5(4); 6; 3:2; 7; 8; 12; 16; 21(2); 24; 38; 4:8; 9; 5:1; 6(2); 14; 19; 6:10; 12; 21; 23; 7:2; 4; 8; 9; 17; 20; 24; 27; 28; 8:10; 11; 15; 9:2(2); 3(2); 4(2); 6; 7; 9(2); 11; 12; 10:2(2); 3(3); 5; 13; 11:4(2); 7; 10(3); 11; 16; 19; 20(2); 23(3); 25(2); 12:13(2); 18; 4(2); 8; 11; 13(2); 14; 15(2); 18(2); 19; 21; 24; 31(2); 13:4(2); 5(2); 6; 10; 11(2); 13; 14; 15; 16(3); 17; 20; 22; 25; 26; 28; 29; 35; 39; 14:2; 3; 8; 9; 10; 15(2); 16(3); 17; 20; 21; 24; 29; 15:2; 8; 9; 10; 12(2); 15; 20; 21; 23; 27; 28; 33; 16:2; 3; 4; 8; 9; 17; 22:1; 42; 45(2); 50; 51; 23:10; 13; 16; 19; 24:3(2); 9; 10; 11; 12(2); 13(2); 14; 17; 18(2); 21; 22(2); 23(2); 24(2); 25; **1Kin** 1:2; 11; 13(3); 15(2); 16; 17(2); 27; 30; 33; 42; 51; 53; 2:5(2); 7; 9; 14; 16; 17; 18; 19(3); 20; 22; 26(2); 27; 28; 29; 30; 31; 36; 38; 39; 42(3); 3:2; 6; 11; 12; 13; 16; 26; 4:12; 21(2); 27; 28; 33; 5:1; 3; 5(3); 6(2); 7; 9(2); 6:12; 24; 7:8; 9; 48; 8:1; 2; 5; 6; 8; 15; 18(2); 19; 26; 28(2); 29; 33; 34(2); 40; 44; 46; 47; 48(3); 52(4); 54; 56; 58; 59; 63; 65; 66; 9:2; 3; 8; 13; 16; 21; 24; 25; 10:5; 12; 13; 11:2(3); 8; 9; 11; 14; 18; 22; 24; 35; 36; 38(2); 40; 12:3; 5; 7(2); 9; 10(5); 15(2); 16(2); 19; 23(2); 27(2); 28; 30; 32(3); 13:1; 2; 6; 7; 8; 11; 12; 13; 14; 15; 18(3); 20; 21; 22; 26(3); 34; 14:5(2); 27; 15:19; 20; 29; 17:1; 2; 5; 8; 13(2); 18(2); 19; 20; 21; 23; 18:1; 2; 5(3); 15; 17; 19; 20(2); 21; 22; 25; 30(3); 31; 40; 41; 44; 19:2; 5; 8; 9(2); 13; 15; 18; 20; 21(2); 20:2; 5; 6; 7; 8(2); 9; 10(2); 12; 13; 14; 22; 23; 25; 28; 31; 34; 35; 36; 39(2); 40; 42; 21:2(2); 3; 5; 6(3); 7; 8; 11(2); 19(2); 22; 22:3; 4; 5; 6; 8; 13(2); 14; 15; 16; 18; 22; 24; 26; 30; 34; 38; 49; **2Kin** 1:2; 3; 5(2); 6(4); 7; 9(2); 11(2); 12; 13(2); 16; 2:2(2); 3; 4; 5; 6; 9; 10; 16; 18(2); 19; 21; 22; 23(2); 3:3; 4; 13(2); 26; 4:1(2); 2; 6(2); 9; 13(2); 16; 17; 19; 22; 25; 26; 33; 36; 38; 42; 5:3; 5; 6; 7; 10; 13; 14; 17(2); 19; 25; 26; 27(2); 6:1; 2; 9; 11; 15; 18; 19; 21; 26; 28(2); 29; 33; 7:4; 5; 10; 12; 16; 20; 8:1; 3; 6; 8; 10(2); 12; 22; 9:1; 5; 6; 11(2); 20; 10:6; 10; 17; 18; 19; 22; 23; 27; 30(2); 11:15; 12:7; 13:4; 14; 15(2); 18; 23(2); 14:6; 7; 13; 25; 15:5; 12(2); 16:6; 9; 17:12; 23; 32; 34; 41; 48:4; 8; 11; 14; 19; 21; 22; 26; 27; 32; 19:3; 6; 9; 29; 20:1(2); 2; 5; 6; 8; 11; 12; 13; 14(3); 16; 17; 19; 21:15; 22:6; 8; 13(2); 14; 15; 17; 20; 23:1; 4; 5; 6; 21; 25; 35; 24:7; 25:2; 8; 17; 24; **1Chr** 1:19; 2:3; 9; 19; 3:1; 4; 5; 4:31; 33; 39; 41; 43; 5:1; 8; 9; 11; 23(2); 26(2); 6:48; 61; 63; 67; 71; 77; 7:28; 10:9; 14; 11:1; 2; 12:8; 16; 17(3); 18; 40; 13:2(4); 5; 9; 14:10; 14; 15:2; 3; 12(2); 16:8; 9(2); 16; 18; 23; 28(2); 29(2); 34; 40; 17:2; 5; 7; 15; 26; 18:3; 11; 19:2; 3(2); 11; 14; 20:8; 21:5; 8; 9; 10; 11; 13; 15; 17; 18; 22; 23; 26; 22:7; 8; 9; 23:13; 25; 26; 31(2); 26:6; 28:1; 3; 6; 29:1; 5; 12; 17; 18; 19; 21(2); 22; 24; **2Chr** 1:2; 5; 7(2); 8(2); 9; 12; 2:15; 3:1; 5:2; 3; 6; 7; 9; 6:14; 17; 19; 20; 21; 25; 27; 30(2); 31; 34; 36; 37; 40; 42; 7:8; 10; 12; 15; 21(2); 8:11; 12; 15; 16; 9:12; 26; 28; 10:5(2); 7; 9; 10(3); 15; 16; 19; 11:3; 4; 16; 23; 12:5; 13:7; 10; 11; 14; 14:7; 9; 11; 13; 15:2; 4; 11; 14; 19; 16:4; 7; 17:3; 16; 18:3; 4; 5; 7(2); 14; 17; 20; 23; 29; 19:4; 20:9; 15; 21; 24; 26; 28; 33; 21:10; 23:3; 14; 24:5; 6; 11; 17; 19; 20; 23; 25:12; 13; 14; 15(2); 16(2); 26:18(3); 21; 27:5; 28:9(2); 10; 13; 16; 20; 21; 23; 25; 29:5; 7; 11; 30; 31; 30:1; 5; 6; 8; 9(2); 10; 17; 21; 22; 27; 31:6; 16; 32:9(2); 13; 18; 23; 24(2); 25; 31; 33:3; 12; 13; 17; 22; 36:13; 22; **Ezr** 1:8; 11; 2:1(3); 63; 69; 3:3; 5; 6; 7(2); 8(2); 11; 4:1; 2(2); 3(3); 6; 7; 11(2); 12(2); 13; 15; 17(2); 18; 20; 23;

24; 5:1(2); 3; 4; 6; 7(2); 8; 9; 12; 14; 15; 6:5(2); 8; 10; 21; 22; 7:7; 11; 12; 15; 22; 26; 28; 8:17(3); 22; 25; 26; 28(3); 30; 31; 35(2); 36; 9:4; 5; 6; 7; 9; 11; 12(2); 10:1; 2; 4; 7(2); 9; 10; 11; **Neh** 1:3; 9(3); 2:1; 2; 3; 4; 5(3); 6; 7; 8; 17; 18; 20; 3:1(2); 2; 4(3); 5; 7(2); 8(3); 9; 10(2); 12; 13; 15; 16(2); 17; 20; 24(2); 26; 27; 31; 32; 4:6; 9; 12(2); 14; 15(2); 19; 20; 22; 5:5; 7; 8(3); 14; 15; 16; 17; 6:2; 3; 4; 5; 8; 10; 17(2); 18; 7:3; 6; 65; 70; 8:1; 3; 9(2); 10(3); 12; 13; 15; 17; 18(2); 9:4; 14; 27; 28; 29(2); 32; 34; 36; 37; 38; 10:28; 30; 35; 36; 37(2); 38; 39; 11:30; 12:37; 38; 39; 46; 47(2); 13:4; 6; 12; 13; 16; 17; 21; 25(2); 27; **Est** 1:1; 3; 5(2); 14; 15; 17; 18; 19; 2:2; 3(2); 8(2); 9; 13(2); 14; 15; 16; 18; 22; 3:3; 4(2); 8; 10; 11; 12; 14; 4:6; 7; 8(4); 10(2); 11(2); 16; 5:3; 4(2); 6; 12(2); 14(3); 6:3; 4; 5; 6(2); 11; 13; 14; 7:2; 5; 8:1(2); 2; 6; 7; 9(4); 13; 9:5; 12; 13; 20; 22; 23; 26; 27; 30; 10:3; **Job** 1:2; 7; 8; 12; 14; 2:2; 3; 6; 7; 9; 10; 13; 3:6; 20; 25; 5:7; 8(2); 6:22; 28; 7:4; 20; 8:5; 9:12; 16; 10:2; 3; 15; 11:7; 19; 12:8; 13:2; 12; 20; 27; 15:19; 16:20; 19:11; 20:6; 29; 21:14; 15; 33; 22:2(2); 17; 21; 26; 27; 28; 23:5; 28:28; 29:21; 30:20; 26; 31:10; 37(2); 32:12; 21; 33:22; 23; 24; 26(3); 31; 33; 34:2; 10; 11; 14; 15; 28; 31; 34; 36; 37; 35:3; 5; 6; 37:3; 14; 19; 38:17; 35; 41; 39:4; 13(2); 40:6; 7; 14; 19; 41:3(2); 42:4; 7; 8; 11; **Ps** 2:5; 7; 3:4; 8; 4:3; 5:2(2); 3; 7:t, 4; 10:14; 13:6; 16:2; 6; 17:1(2); 6; 18:t, 6; 39; 41; 44; 49(2); 19:2(2); 6; 22:5; 22; 24; 27; 31; 24:4; 25:1; 10; 16; 26:11; 27:6; 8; 12; 28:1; 2; 29:1(2); 2(2); 11; 30:2; 4; 8; 12; 31:22; 32:2; 5(2); 6(2); 9; 33:2; 3; 34:5; 11; 15; 18; 35:3; 10; 23; 36:5; 10; 37:5; 39:12; 40:1; 3; 5; 15; 41:2; 4; 8; 10; 42:3; 7; 8; 9; 10; 43:3; 4(2); 44:3; 25; 45:14(2); 46:9; 47:1; 6; 9; 48:10; 14; 50:1; 5; 14(2); 16; 51:t, 1; 12; 13; 18; 52:t, 54:5; 6; 55:2; 14; 56:1; 4; 9; 11; 12; 57:1(2); 2(2); 9; 10(2); 59:13; 17; 61:1; 2; 8; 62:11; 12; 65:1; 2; 4; 66:1; 3(2); 4; 15; 17; 67:1; 68:4; 20; 29; 31; 32(2); 34; 35; 69:1; 8(2); 13; 16; 18; 27; 70:5; 71:2; 7; 18; 19; 22; 23; 24; 72:1; 8; 74:3; 19; 20; 75:1(2); 4; 76:11(2); 77:1(3); 78:36; 46(2); 62; 79:2(2); 12; 80:6; 11(2); 81:1(2); 8(2); 12; 13; 15; 83:9(2); 85:1; 8; 86:3(2); 4; 5; 6; 8(2); 16(2); 88:2; 3; 8; 9; 13; 89:3; 6(2); 8; 26; 35; 49; 90:12; 16(2); 92:1(2); 94:15; 95:1; 2; 11; 96:1(2); 2; 7(2); 8(2); 98:1; 4; 5; 99:7; 100:1; 4; 101:1; 2; 102:1; 2; 12; 103:7(2); 17; 20; 104:8; 23; 33; 105:1; 2(2); 9; 10; 11; 106:1; 4; 25; 28; 31(2); 36; 37; 38; 47; 107:1; 6; 13; 18; 19; 28; 30; 108:3; 4; 109:4; 12; 17; 19; 25; 110:1; 111:5; 9; 112:4; 113:3; 5; 115:1(3); 8; 116:2; 7; 12; 14; 18; 118:1; 6; 18; 27; 29; 119:6; 15; 20; 25; 28; 31; 33; 36; 38; 41; 48; 49; 58; 59; 62; 65; 72; 76; 77; 79; 90; 103; 105(2); 107; 112; 116; 117; 124; 130; 132(2); 146; 149; 120:1; 3(2); 121:1; 122:1; 4(2); 123:1; 2(2); 125:3; 4; 5; 130:1; 132:2(2); 11; 135:3; 4; 12; 18; 136:1; 2; 22; 26; 138:1; 6; 139:6; 17; 140:6; 13; 141:1(4); 8; 142:1(2); 5; 6; 143:6; 7; 8; 9; 144:9(2); 10; 145:18; 146:2; 10; 147:1; 7(2); 19(2); 148:14; 149:1; 3; **Prov** 1:5; 9; 23(2); 33; 2:2; 10; 18(2); 19; 3:5; 15; 22; 28; 34; 4:4; 18; 20; 22; 5:1; 9(2); 6:16; 7:4; 13; 24; 8:4; 32; 11:27; 12:14; 15; 14:6; 12; 15:9; 10; 12; 16:3; 22; 25; 18:13; 19:17; 20:23; 22:17; 21; 23:12; 22; 24:11; 14; 24; 25:7; 26:4; 28:27; 29:17; 30:1(2); 5; 6; 10; 31:3; 6(2); 24; **Eccl** 1:6; 7; 2:3; 17; 18; 3:20; 5:4; 7:21; 8:4; 9; 14; 9:3; 13; 12:7; **Song** 1:13; 14; 2:10; 8:11; **Is** 1:4; 6; 9(2); 10; 11; 13; 14; 23; 2:2; 3:9(2); 11; 5:8; 11; 18; 20; 21; 22; 26; 30; 6:3; 6; 7:3; 4; 10; 8:1; 2; 3; 5; 19(4); 22; 9:6(2); 13; 10:1; 11; 21; 30; 12:5; 13:2; 15; 14:10(2); 15:4(2); 5; 8(2); 16:1; 8; 18:4; 6; 7; 19:11; 16; 17; 20(2); 21; 20:1; 21:2; 4; 6; 9; 10; 16; 22:11(2); 15(2); 24:16; 25:6; 26:15; 27:2; 12; 28:5; 13; 15; 29:2; 11; 15; 30:10(2); 18; 19; 22; 31:1; 4; 6; 7; 32:9; 33:2; 21; 34:17; 35:2; 36:2; 3; 4; 10; 11(2); 37:2; 3; 6(2); 14; 15; 21; 30; 38:1(3); 2; 5; 7; 15; 39:3(4); 40:2; 9; 18; 20; 41:9; 13; 42:3; 5; 10; 12; 16; 24; 44:5; 7; 17(2); 22; 45:9; 10(2); 14(3); 19; 20; 22; 23; 46:3; 7; 12; 47:15; 48:11; 12; 13; 16; 22; 49:1; 3; 6; 51:1; 2(2); 4(2); 7; 11; 16; 19; 52:7; 53:12; 54:9; 55:2; 3; 5; 7; 11; 56:4; 5; 8; 57:9; 18; 59:16; 20; 60:5(2); 7(2); 9; 10; 11; 13; 14; 19(2); 61:1; 3(2); 7; 62:11; 63:5; 65:1; 2; 11; 15; 66:1; 19; 20; 24; **Jer** 1:3(2); 4; 5; 7; 9; 11; 12; 13; 14; 16; 17; 2:3; 10; 17; 21; 27; 31(2); 3:1; 2; 4; 6; 7; 10; 11; 14; 17; 18; 22; 25; 4:1; 10; 12; 13; 18(2); 5:5(2); 13; 19; 24; 6:3; 4; 10; 12; 13(2); 19; 20; 7:9; 12; 13; 14(2); 18; 21; 22; 23; 25(2); 26; 27(2); 28; 8:4; 10(3); 10:1; 6; 7; 11; 11:2; 3; 5; 6; 7(2); 9; 11(2); 12(2); 13; 14; 17; 20; 12:6; 8; 9; 11; 13:1; 3; 6; 8; 11(2); 12(2); 13; 18; 27; 14:2; 10; 11; 13; 14(3); 17; 15:1; 2; 16; 18; 19(2); 20; 16:1; 10; 11; 12; 15; 19; 20; 17:15; 17; 19; 20; 24; 26; 27; 18:8; 19:2; 4; 5; 11; 12; 13(2); 20:3; 8; 12; 13; 15; 21:1(2); 3; 8; 9; 22:6(2); 8; 13; 21; 23:1; 5; 12; 14; 16(2); 17(2); 33; 38; 24:3; 4; 7; 10; 25:2; 3(3); 4; 5; 7; 15; 17; 27; 28; 30; 33; 26:2(2); 3; 4; 5; 8; 10; 11; 12; 14; 15; 16; 23; 27:1; 3; 4(2); 5(2); 9; 10; 14(3); 15; 16(2); 17; 28:1; 5; 12; 15; 29:1; 3; 4(2); 7; 9; 12(2); 19; 21; 25; 28; 30; 31; 30:2; 9; 15; 17; 21(2); 31:3; 6; 26; 32; 34; 38; 40(3); 32:6; 7; 8; 12; 16(2); 18; 20; 24; 25; 26; 29(2); 31; 33; 35; 37; 33:1; 3; 6; 9(2); 14; 15; 19; 22; 34:1; 6; 8(2); 14(2); 16; 17; 20; 35:1; 2(2); 5; 12; 14(3); 15(2); 16; 17(2); 18(2); 36:1; 2(2); 3; 4; 9; 13; 14(2); 15; 16; 18; 19; 32; 37:2; 3; 6; 7; 18; 19; 38:1; 4(2); 12; 14(2); 15(3); 16; 17(2); 19; 20(2); 24; 25(5); 26; 27; 39:12(2); 14; 15; 18; 40:1; 2; 4(3); 5; 6; 7; 9; 10; 12; 14; 15; 16; 41:1; 6; 8; 14; 42:1; 2(2); 4(3); 7; 9(2); 10; 12; 20(4); 21; 43:1; 2; 8; 10; 44:4; 5; 8(2); 10; 12; 15; 16(2); 17(2); 18; 19(2); 20; 23; 24; 25; 29; 45:1; 2; 4; 5; 48:1; 9; 12; 27; 34(3); 46; 49:2; 4; 14; 29; 31; 50:15; 27; 29; 44; 51:2; 6; 9; 24; 44; 48; 53; 52:5; 9; 22; 32; **Lam** 1:12(2); 21; 22(2); 2:1; 18; 3:10; 25; 41; 64; 65; 4:4; 15; 21; 5:4; 16; 21; **Eze** 1:3; 16; 2:1(2); 2(2); 3(2); 4(2); 7; 8; 9; 3:1(2); 3; 4(3); 6; 7(2); 10(2); 11(2); 16; 17; 18; 22; 24; 27; 4:3; 9; 15; 16; 5:15; 6:1; 10; 7:1; 2; 7; 27; 8:5; 6; 8; 9; 12; 13; 15; 17; 9:4; 7; 9; 10:2; 7; 13; 11:1; 2; 5; 14; 15(2); 25; 12:1; 6; 8; 9; 10; 11; 19; 21; 23; 28; 13:1; 2; 3; 11; 12; 15; 18; 14:1; 2; 4(2); 6; 10; 22; 15:1; 16:1; 3; 5; 6(2); 8; 20(2); 23; 24; 27; 29; 33; 34; 36; 37; 54; 60; 61; 17:1; 2; 3; 11; 18:1; 22; 19:4; 20:2; 3(2); 5(4); 6; 7; 8; 9; 15; 18; 23; 27(2); 29(2); 30; 31; 39; 45; 21:1; 7; 8; 18; 23; 29(2); 22:1; 4(2); 17; 23; 24; 28; 23:1; 16; 27; 30; 36(2); 37; 38; 40; 43; 44(4); 24:1; 3(2); 15; 18; 19; 20; 21; 24; 26; 27; 25:1; 3; 8; 10; 26:1; 2; 27:1; 3; 28:1; 2; 11; 12; 20; 24; 29:1; 4(2); 10; 17; 19; 30:1; 20; 31:1; 2; 4; 8; 14; 17; 18; 32:1; 2; 17; 18; 33:1; 2; 7; 8; 10; 11; 12; 14; 16; 21; 23; 25; 27; 31; 32; 34:1; 2(2); 18; 20; 35:1; 3; 6; 15; 36:1; 3; 6; 9; 11; 13; 16; 20; 22; 32; 37:3; 4(2); 5; 9(2); 11; 12; 15; 18; 19; 21; 25; 38:1; 7(2); 13; 14; 39:4; 11; 17; 24; 28; 40:4(2); 6; 14; 15; 19; 22; 45; 46; 41:4; 17; 20; 22; 42:13(2); 43:6; 7; 18; 19(2); 24; 44:2; 5(2); 11; 12; 13(2); 15(2); 16; 26; 27; 28; 30; 45:1; 4; 7; 46:4; 7; 12; 13; 14; 16; 20; 24; 47:1; 2; 6; 8; 10; 14(2); 18; 21; 22(2); 48:2; 3; 4; 5; 6; 7; 8(2); 9; 12; 14; 18; 23; 24; 25; 26; 27; 28; 29; **Dan** 1:1; 3; 7(2); 10; 21; 2:3; 5; 9; 19; 21; 23(2); 24(3); 25(2); 26; 27; 46; 47; 3:3; 14; 18; 24(2); 4:1(2); 6; 7; 11; 16; 18; 20; 22; 26; 27; 34(2); 35; 36(4); 5:13; 15; 17; 6:2; 6; 15(2); 16; 19; 20; 21; 25(2); 26; 7:5; 10; 16; 26; 8:1(3); 6; 7; 13; 14(2); 17; 9:3; 4; 6; 7(3); 25; 26; 10:1; 11(4); 12; 15; 16; 19(2); 20; 11:18; 12:7; **Hos** 1:1; 2; 4; 6; 10(2); 2:1; 14; 19(2); 20; 23; 3:1; 3; 4:12; 15; 5:4; 12; 14; 6:1; 3(2); 4(2); 7:7; 13(2); 14; 8:2; 11; 9:4(2); 10; 17; 10:1; 6; 15; 11:2; 4; 12:4; 14; 13:7; 14:1; 2; 5; **Joel** 1:14; 20; 2:13; 14; 19; 3:6; **Amos** 1:5; 2:7; 3:7; 4:6; 8(2); 9; 10(2); 11; 12(2); 13; 5:4; 15; 18; 25; 6:2; 10; 14; 7:1; 4; 8; 12; 15(2); 8:1; 2; 9:7; **Obad** 15; 20; **Jonah** 1:1; 3(2); 5; 6; 8; 9; 10; 11(3); 12(2); 14; 16; 2:1; 2; 7; 9; 10; 3:1; 2(2); 3; 6; 8; 10; 4:2(2); 9; **Mic** 1:9(2); 12; 15(2); 2:11; 3:4; 6(2); 8; 4:1; 8; 13(2); 5:2; 3; 4; 6:3; 5; 9; 7:7; 8; 10; 15; 18; 20; **Nah** 3:13; **Hab** 1:2; 10; 11; 16(2); 2:1; 5(2); 7; 15; 16; 19; 3:13; 16; **Zeph** 1:1; 2:5; 11; **Hag** 1:1; 9; 13; 2:20; **Zec** 1:1; 3(3); 4(2); 6; 7; 9; 14; 19; 2:2; 4; 5; 8; 11; 3:2; 4(2); 6; 4:2; 5; 6(2); 7; 8; 9; 11; 12; 5:2; 3; 5; 11; 6:4; 5; 8; 9; 12; 15; 7:1; 2; 3; 4; 5(2); 8; 8:3; 11; 15; 18; 9:9; 10; 12; 11:7; 12; 13(2); 15(2); 12:2; 13:3; 6; 14:5; 10(3); 17; 20; 21; **Mal** 1:6; 8; 9; 11(2); 14; 2:2; 4; 12; 3:3; 4; 7(2); 4:2; 4; **Mt** 1:17; 20(2); 24; 2:5; 11; 3:7; 9(2); 10; 11; 13; 15; 16; 4:6; 7; 9; 10; 11; 19; 24; 5:1; 15; 18; 20; 22; 26; 28; 32; 33; 34; 39; 44; 6:2; 5; 8; 16(2); 18(2); 25; 27; 29; 33; 34; 7:6; 7; 11; 14; 21; 23; 24; 26; 8:4(2); 5; 7; 10; 11; 13(2); 15; 16; 18; 19; 20; 21; 22; 26; 32; 9:2; 6; 8; 9; 11; 12; 15; 16; 18; 24; 28(2); 29; 37; 10:1; 15; 23; 42(2); 11:3; 4; 7; 9; 11; 16(2); 17(2); 21(2); 22; 23; 24; 25; 27; 28; 29; 12:2; 3; 6; 11; 20; 22; 25; 28; 31(3); 36; 39; 45; 47; 48; 13:2; 3; 10(2); 11(2); 17; 24(2); 27; 28(2); 31; 33(2); 34(2); 36(2); 37; 44; 45; 47; 51(2); 52(3); 57; 14:2; 4; 16; 17; 22; 25; 27; 28; 31; 35; 15:3; 8; 10; 12; 15(2); 22; 24; 28(2); 29; 30; 32; 33; 34; 16:2; 4; 6; 8; 15; 17(2); 18; 19; 21(2); 22; 23(2); 24; 28; 17:3; 4; 11; 12(2); 13; 20(4); 22; 26(2); 27; 18:1; 2; 3; 7; 10; 13; 17(2); 18; 19; 22(2); 23; 24; 31; 32; 34; 35; 19:3(2); 4; 7; 8; 9; 10; 11; 13; 14; 16; 17; 18; 20; 21; 23(2); 24; 26; 27; 28(2); 20:1; 4; 6; 7(2); 8(2); 12; 14(2); 17; 18(2); 21(2); 22; 23; 25; 28; 32; 33; 21:1(2); 2(2); 3; 5; 13; 16(2); 19; 21(3); 23; 24; 25; 27; 31(3); 32; 36; 37; 40; 41(2); 42; 43; 22:1; 2; 4; 12; 16; 17; 19; 20; 21(4); 24; 25; 26; 29; 31; 37; 39; 42; 43; 44; 23:13; 14; 15; 16; 23; 25; 27(2); 28; 29; 31; 34; 35; 36; 37; 38; 39; 24:2(2); 3; 4; 13; 14; 19; 23; 26; 27; 34; 47; 25:1; 8; 12; 14; 15; 20; 21; 22; 23; 26; 28; 29; 34; 36; 39; 40(4); 41; 44; 45; 26:1; 3; 7; 10; 13; 14; 15(2); 17; 18; 21; 22; 24; 25; 29; 31; 33; 34(2); 35; 36(2); 38(2); 40(2); 45; 50; 52; 58; 62; 63; 64(2); 68; 69; 71; 73; 75; 27:8; 11; 13; 15; 17(2); 19; 21(2); 22(2); 26; 27; 33; 45; 53; 55; 62; 64; 65; 28:5; 10; 11; 12; 18(2); 20; **Mk** 1:5; 13; 17; 31; 32; 37; 38; 40; 41; 44(2); 2:2; 3; 4; 5; 8; 11; 13; 14; 16; 17; 18; 19; 24; 25; 27; 3:3; 4; 5; 8; 13(2); 23(2); 28(2); 31; 32; 4:1; 2; 9; 11(3); 13; 21; 24(2); 33; 34; 35(2); 38; 39; 40; 5:1; 8; 11; 19; 21(3); 31; 34; 36; 39; 41(2); 6:2; 4; 7; 10; 11; 18; 22; 23(2); 24; 25; 30; 31; 33; 35; 37(2); 38; 45; 48(2); 50; 51; 7:1; 6; 9; 14(3); 18; 27(2); 28; 29; 31; 32; 34; 8:1(2); 12(2); 17; 19; 21; 22; 27; 29(2); 34(2); 9:1(2); 4; 13(2); 17; 19; 20; 21; 23; 25; 29; 31; 35; 36; 41; 10:1; 3; 5; 11; 14(2); 15; 18; 20; 21; 23; 24; 28; 29; 32; 33(2); 35; 36; 37(2); 38; 39(2); 42; 45; 49; 51(3); 52; 11:1; 2; 3; 5; 6; 11; 14; 17; 21; 22; 23(2); 24; 28; 29; 33(2); 12:1; 4; 6; 9; 13; 14; 15; 16(2); 17; 18; 19(2); 24; 26; 32; 34; 38; 43(3); 13:1; 2; 13; 19; 30; 37(2); 14:9; 10(2); 12; 13; 16; 18; 19; 20; 24; 25; 27; 29; 30(2); 34(2); 36; 37; 41; 48; 61; 65; 72; 15:2; 6; 8; 9; 11; 12(2); 14; 15; 22; 41(2); 43; 44; 46; 16:2; 6; 7; 12; 13; 14; 15; 19; **Lk** 1:2; 3; 11; 13; 18; 19(2); 22(2); 26; 28; 30; 32; 34; 35; 38; 61; 74; 77; 80; 2:4; 10; 11; 12; 15(2); 20; 26; 34; 38; 48; 49; 50; 51; 3:2; 8(2); 9; 11; 12; 13; 14; 16; 18; 4:3; 5; 6(2); 8; 9; 12; 17; 21; 23(2); 24; 26(3); 29; 39; 40; 42; 43; 5:4; 5; 7; 10; 14; 20; 22; 24(2); 27; 31; 33; 34; 36; 6:2; 5; 9; 10; 13; 23; 24; 25(2); 26; 27; 29; 35; 38; 39; 7:2; 3; 6; 7; 8; 9(2); 13; 14; 19; 20(2); 21; 22; 24; 26; 28; 32(2); 40(2); 43; 44; 47; 48; 8:3; 10; 21; 22(2); 25; 39(2); 47; 48; 9:3; 11; 12; 13; 20; 33; 43; 48; 50; 57; 58; 59; 60; 62; 10:2; 9(2); 11; 12; 13(2); 17; 18; 19; 20; 21; 23; 26; 28; 29; 35; 36; 37; 41; 11:1; 2; 5(3); 8; 9(2); 13; 17; 24; 27; 30; 39; 41; 42; 43; 44; 45; 46; 47; 51(2); 52; 53; 12:1; 4; 5; 8; 10; 11(2); 13; 14; 15; 16; 20; 22(2); 27; 31; 36(2); 37; 41(2); 44; 48; 13:2; 7; 8; 12; 14; 18; 23(2); 24; 25(2); 31; 32; 34; 35(2); 14:3; 7; 10; 15; 16; 18; 23; 24; 25; 15:1; 3; 6; 7; 10; 12; 16; 18; 21; 27; 31; 16:1(2); 2; 5(3); 6; 7; 9; 15; 28; 29; 30; 31; 17:1(2); 5; 6; 7; 8; 14(2); 19; 22; 24; 37(2); 18:1; 3; 7; 9; 13; 15; 16(2); 17; 19; 22(2); 29(2); 31(2); 32; 35; 40; 41; 42; 43; 19:5; 8; 9; 13; 15; 17; 22; 24; 25; 26(2); 31; 32; 33; 39; 40; 42; 46; 20:2; 3; 8; 15; 20; 22; 23; 25(3); 28(2); 34; 36; 38; 41; 42; 45; 21:3; 4; 10; 23; 32; 22:4; 6; 9; 10; 11(2); 13; 15; 16; 18; 19; 22; 25; 29(2); 33; 35; 36; 37; 38; 40; 43; 46; 47; 48; 49; 52; 61; 67; 70; 23:1; 7; 14(2); 15; 17; 18; 22; 25; 28; 42; 43(2); 52; 24:1; 5; 6; 9; 10; 12; 17; 18; 19(2); 25; 27; 28; 36(2); 38; 41; 44(2); 46; **Jn** 1:11; 22; 25; 29; 33; 38(2); 39; 41; 43; 45; 46(2); 48(2); 49; 50(2); 51(2); 2:3; 4; 5(2); 7; 8(2); 10; 16; 18(2); 19; 22; 24; 3:2; 3(2); 4; 5; 7; 9; 10; 11; 26(2); 34; 4:7; 8; 9; 10; 11; 13; 15; 16; 17; 19; 21; 25; 26(2); 30; 32; 34; 35; 36; 40; 42; 45; 47; 48; 49; 50(2); 52; 53; 5:6; 8; 10; 11; 12; 14(2); 19(2); 22; 24(2); 25; 29(2); 33(2); 6:5(2); 8; 12; 13; 16; 19; 20; 23; 25; 26; 27(2); 28; 29; 30; 32(2); 33; 34; 35; 36; 43; 45; 47; 53(2); 61; 63; 65(3); 67; 7:3; 6; 8(2); 9; 10; 21; 22; 26; 33(2); 35; 37; 45; 50; 52; 53; 8:1; 2; 3; 4; 7; 9; 10; 11; 12; 13; 14; 19; 21; 23; 24; 25(3); 28; 34; 39(2); 42; 48; 51; 52; 55; 57; 58(2); 9:7; 10; 11; 12; 15; 17; 24; 29; 30; 34; 35; 37; 40; 41; 10:1; 6(2); 7(2); 24; 26; 28; 35; 41; 11:3; 4; 8; 11; 14; 15; 16; 18; 21; 23; 24; 25; 27; 29; 31; 32; 34; 39; 40(2); 44; 49; 54; 12:16; 24; 25; 27; 32; 35; 50; 13:1(2); 6; 7; 8; 9; 12; 16; 20; 21; 25; 27; 28; 29; 33; 34; 36; 37; 38; 14:3; 5; 6(2); 8; 9; 10; 12(2); 22(3); 23(2); 25; 26; 27(2); 28(3); 15:3; 7; 11; 15; 20; 21; 22; 26; 16:1; 3; 4; 6; 7(2); 12; 14; 15; 17; 19; 20; 23; 25(2); 26; 29; 33; 17:6; 8; 26; 18:4; 5; 6; 11; 15; 16(2); 17; 21; 24; 25; 28; 29; 30(2); 31(2); 33; 35; 37(2); 38(3); 39(2); 19:4; 5; 6; 9; 10(2); 11; 14; 15; 16; 26; 27; 20:1; 2; 10; 13(2); 15(2); 16(2); 17(3); 18; 19(2); 20; 21; 22; 23; 25(2); 26; 28; 29; 21:3(2); 5; 6; 7(2); 10; 12; 15(2); 16(2); 17(4); 18; 19; 22; 23; **Acts** 1:2; 7; 8(2); 12; 19; 22; 2:3; 14(2); 29(2); 34; 37; 38; 39; 41; 3:5; 10; 11; 12; 14; 20; 22(4); 25; 26; 4:1; 3; 8; 10; 19(3); 23; 29; 35; 5:4(2); 8; 9; 16; 35; 38; 6:2; 7:2; 3; 13; 26; 31; 37(3); 38; 40; 41; 44; 45; 8:1; 5; 6; 14; 20; 26(3); 29; 35; 36; 9:1; 2; 4; 6; 11; 15(2); 17; 21; 27; 34; 38; 10:3; 4; 7; 8; 9; 11; 15; 19; 21; 28(2); 29; 32; 36; 41; 42; 11:4; 7; 11(2); 13; 17; 18; 19; 20; 21; 22; 23; 24; 26; 27; 29; 12:5; 8(2); 10(2); 15; 17(3); 21; 13:4; 6; 15; 20; 21; 22; 23; 31; 32(2); 33; 36; 38(2); 41; 47; 51; 14:3; 6(2); 13; 15(2); 18; 27; 15:2; 3; 7; 8; 13; 18; 20; 23; 25(2); 33; 36; 39; 40; 16:10; 13; 14; 17; 19; 25; 32; 37; 38; 17:2; 3; 5; 6; 10; 15(2); 18; 19; 23; 29; 31; 34; 18:2; 6(2); 14; 21; 26(2); 19:2(2); 3(3); 4; 12; 22; 24; 30; 31; 33; 20:1; 6; 7; 13; 18; 20; 22; 24; 27; 28; 34; 38; 21:1(3); 2; 8; 11; 18; 20; 31; 32; 37(2); 39; 40(2); 22:1; 4; 5(2); 6; 7(2); 8; 10; 13(2); 15; 18; 20; 21(2); 22; 25; 27; 23:3; 15; 17(2); 18(3); 21; 23; 24; 26; 24:2; 4; 8; 10(2); 14; 23; 25:6; 11(2); 12(2); 13; 14; 21; 22; 26; 26:1; 6; 7; 11; 14; 16(2); 17; 18; 19; 20; 22; 23; 28; 32(2); 27:1; 3; 8; 10; 21; 40; 28:17; 19; 21; 25; 26; 28(2); 30; **Rom** 1:1; 10; 11; 13; 16; 19; 26; 2:5; 8; 14; 3:2; 7; 22; 4:3; 6; 11; 5:5; 15; 16; 18; 21(2); 6:10(2); 11(2); 13(3); 16(2); 19(2); 22; 7:4; 5; 10; 13; 16; 9:12; 17; 19; 21(2); 23; 26; 29; 10:3; 10(2); 12; 18; 20; 21; 11:4; 8; 9; 11; 27; 35; 12:1; 3; 19; 13:1; 14:6; 8(2); 15:8; 9; 15; 19; 23; 25(2); 27; 29; 32; 16:1; 4; 5; 19(2); **1Cor** 1:2; 3; 8; 9; 11; 18; 23(2); 24; 30; 2:1; 7; 10; 14; 3:1(4); 10; 4:9; 11; 13; 17; 21; 5:5; 9; 11; 6:12; 17; 7:1; 3(2); 10; 27; 8:1; 4; 7(2); 9:2; 11; 15; 16; 17; 19; 20; 10:2; 11; 28(2); 11:13; 14; 17; 23; 34; 12:2; 21; 31; 14:2(2); 3; 6; 11(2); 21; 26; 34; 36; 37; 15:1(2); 2; 3; 6; 28(2); 16:3; 5; 9; 11; 12; 16; **2Cor** 1:1; 13; 15; 16; 20; 23; 2:3; 4(2); 12; 14; 15; 16(2); 3:15; 4:4; 11; 5:5; 11; 12; 15(2); 19(3); 6:11; 13; 18; 7:12(2); 8:2; 5; 17; 9:5; 12; 13(2); 15; 10:13; 14; 11:9; 12:9; 17; 19; 20; **Gal** 1:2; 6; 8(2); 9; 17; 20; 22; 2:2; 7(2); 9(3); 14; 19; 3:8; 23; 24; 4:8; 13; 5:2; 4; 13; 6:6; 10(2); 11; 14(2); S:1; **Eph** 1:5; 9; 14; 15; 17; 2:10; 16; 18; 21; 3:3; 5(2); 7; 8; 10; 14; 20; 21; 4:7; 8; 13(2); 16; 19; 29; 30; 5:10; 20; 22(2); 24; 31; 6:5; 9; 13; 19; 22; S:1; **Phil** 1:2; 11; 12(2); 29; 2:8; 19; 27; 30; 3:10; 11; 13; 15; 21(2); 4:5; 6; 16; 20; **Col** 1:2; 6; 8; 10; 11; 12; 20; 2:2; 3:18; 20; 23; 4:1; 3; 7; 8; 9; 10; 11(2); **1Th** 1:1(2); 5; 9; 2:1; 2; 8(2); 9(2); 12; 18; 3:6; 11; 4:7(2); 8; 9; 15(2); 5:1; 15; 23; 27; S:1; **2Th** 1:1; 2; 2:1; 3:9; **1Ti** 1:2; 6; 17; 18; 20; 2:4; 3:14(2); 16; 4:7; 8; 16(2); 6:16; **2Ti** 1:12; 14; 16; 18(2); 2:9; 15; 16; 21(2); 24; 3:9; 11; 15; 17; 4:4; 8; 9; 10(2); 18; S:1; **Titus** 1:3; 15(2); 16; 2:9; 14; 3:2; 8; 12(2); 13; **Philem** 1:1; 13; 16; 19; 21; 22; **Heb** 1:1; 2; 5; 8; 2:3; 5; 10;

12(2); 17; 3:6; 14; 4:2(2); 13; 16; 5:4; 5; 7; 9; 6:1; 6; 8; 11; 17; 7:3; 4; 19; 21; 25; 8:5; 9:20; 27; 28(2); 10:24; 29; 30; 39; 11:4; 26; 12:2; 4; 5(2); 9; 11; 18(2); 22(2); 13:6; 7; 13; 22; **Jas** 1:23; 2:2; 3; 16; 23; 4:6; 5:7; **1Pet** 1:2(2); 3; 5; 7; 10; 12(5); 13; 22; 25; 2:4; 7(2); 14(2); 24; 25; 3:5; 7(2); 12; 19; 22; 4:7; 12; 19; 5:5; 10; 12; **2Pet** 1:2; 3(2); 4; 11; 16; 19; 2:4; 6; 9; 21; 22; 3:1; 7; 12; 15(2); 16; **1Jn** 1:2(2); 3; 4; 5; 2:1; 7; 8; 12; 13(3); 14(2); 21; 26; 3:14; 5:13; 16(3); 17; **2Jn** 1; 5; 10; 12(2); **3Jn** 1; 9; 13; **Jude** 2; 3(3); 6; 11; 21; 24; **Rev** 1:1(3); 4; 5; 6; 11(8); 13; 15; 17; 2:1; 5; 7; 8; 10; 11; 14; 16; 17; 18(2); 20; 23; 24(2); 26; 29; 3:1; 6; 13; 14; 22; 4:3; 6; 5:5; 10; 13(2); 6:2; 4; 8; 11(2); 13; 7:10; 12; 13; 14; 17; 8:3; 9:1; 3; 7(2); 10; 19; 10:4; 8; 9(3); 11; 11:1; 2; 3; 12; 18; 12:5; 11; 12; 13; 13:2; 4(2); 5(2); 7; 15; 14:4; 6; 13; 14; 20; 15:7; 16:8; 14; 19; 17:1(2); 7; 13; 15; 17; 18:5; 6; 18; 19:1; 9(3); 10; 17; 20:4; 21:5; 6(2); 9; 11; 18; 22:6(2); 9; 10; 16; 18(3)

UP

4605, *507*

Gen 2:6; 21; 4:8; 7:11; 17(2); 8:7; 13; 13:1; 10; 14; 14:22; 17:22; 18:2; 16; 19:1; 2; 14; 27; 28; 30; 20:18; 21:14; 16; 18; 32; 22:3(2); 4; 13(2); 19; 23:3; 7; 24:16; 54; 63; 64; 25:8; 17; 34; 26:23; 31; 27:38; 28:12; 18(2); 29:11; 31:10; 12; 17; 21; 35; 45; 55; 32:22; 33:1; 5; 35:1; 3; 13; 14; 29; 37:25; 28; 35; 38:8; 12; 13; 39:15; 16; 18; 40:13; 19; 20; 41:2; 3; 4; 5; 6; 18; 19; 20; 21; 22; 23; 27; 34; 35; 44; 48(3); 43:2; 15; 29; 44:4; 17; 24; 30; 33; 34; 45:9; 25; 46:4; 5; 29; 31; 47:14; 48:17; 49:4(2); 9(2); 33(2); 50:5; 6; 7(2); 9; 14; 23; 25; **Ex** 1:8; 10; 2:17; 23; 3:8; 17; 7:12; 20; 8:3; 4; 5; 6; 7; 20; 9:10; 13; 16; 32; 10:12; 14; 12:6; 30; 31; 34; 38; 13:18; 19; 14:10; 16; 15:7; 16:13; 14; 23; 24; 33; 34; 17:3; 10; 11; 12; 19:3; 12; 13; 20(2); 23; 24(2); 20:25; 26; 22:2; 24:1; 2; 4; 9; 12; 13(2); 15; 18; 26:15; 30; 33; 29:27; 32:1(2); 4; 6(2); 8; 23; 30; 33:1(2); 3; 5; 8; 10; 12; 15; 34:2; 3; 4(2); 24; 35:21; 26; 36:2; 20; 40:2; 8(2); 17; 18(3); 21; 28; 33(2); 36; 37(2); **Lev** 6:10; 9:22; 11:45; 13:4; 5; 11; 21; 26; 31; 33; 37; 42; 50; 54; 14:38; 46; 19:16; 32; 22:30; 26:1(2); 38; **Num** 1:51; 6:26; 7:1; 9:15; 17; 21(2); 22; 10:11; 21; 35; 11:32; 13:17(2); 21; 30; 31(2); 32(2); 14:1; 13; 36; 37; 40(3); 42; 44; 15:19; 20; 16:2; 3; 12; 13; 14; 24; 25; 27; 30; 32; 34; 37; 45; 17:4; 7; 18:26; 19:9(2); 20:4; 5; 11; 25; 27; 21:3; 5; 17; 33; 22:4(2); 13; 14; 20; 21; 41; 23:7; 18(2); 24(2); 24:2; 3; 8; 9; 15; 20; 21; 23; 25; 25:4; 7; 26:10; 27:12; 31:52; 32:9; 11; 14; 33:38; **Deut** 1:21; 22; 24; 26; 28(2); 41(2); 42; 43; 2:13; 24; 3:1; 27(2); 4:19; 5:5; 6:7; 8:14; 9:1; 9; 23; 10:1; 3; 11:6; 17; 18; 19; 14:25; 28; 16:22; 17:8; 20; 18:15; 18; 19:11; 15; 16; 20:1; 22:4; 14; 19; 23:14; 24:5; 25:7(2); 9; 27:2; 4; 5; 28:7; 33; 43; 29:22; 30:12; 31:5; 16; 32:11; 17; 30; 34(2); 36; 38; 40; 49; 50; 33:2; 34:1; **Josh** 2:6; 8; 10; 3:6(2); 16; 4:5; 8; 9; 16; 17; 18(2); 19; 23(2); 5:1; 7; 13; 6:1; 5; 6; 12; 20; 26(2); 7:2(2); 3(2); 4; 10; 13; 16; 8:1; 3; 7; 10(2); 11; 14; 20; 31; 9:4; 10:4; 5; 6; 9; 10; 12; 33; 36; 11:6; 17; 12:7; 14:8; 15:3(2); 6(2); 7(2); 8(2); 15; 16:1; 17:15; 18:1; 11; 12(2); 17; 19:10; 11; 12; 47; 20:5; 22:12; 33; 24:17; 26; 32; **Judg** 1:1; 2; 3; 4; 16; 22; 36; 2:1(2); 4; 16; 18; 3:9; 15; 4:5; 10(2); 12; 14; 6:3(2); 5; 8; 13; 21; 35; 38; 7:1; 8:8; 11; 13; 20; 28; 9:7; 18; 32; 33; 34; 35; 43; 48; 51; 11:2; 13; 16; 31; 37; 12:3; 13:20; 14:2; 19; 15:5; 6; 9; 10(2); 13; 16:3; 5; 8; 18(2); 29; 31; 18:9; 12; 17; 30; 31; 19:5; 7; 9; 10; 17; 27; 28(3); 30; 20:3; 9; 18(3); 19; 23(3); 26; 28; 30; 31; 33; 38; 40(2); 21:2; 5(2); 8; 19; **Ruth** 1:9; 14; 2:15; 18; 3:14; 4:1; 5; 10; **1Sa** 1:3; 5; 6; 7; 9; 19; 21; 22(2); 24; 2:6; 7; 8(2); 14; 19; 35; 5:12; 6:9; 10; 13; 20; 21; 7:1; 7; 10; 8:8; 9:11; 13(2); 14(2); 19; 24; 26; 10:3; 18; 25; 11:1; 4; 12:6; 13:5; 15; 14:9; 10(2); 12(2); 13; 21; 46; 15:2; 6; 11; 12; 34; 16:13; 17:20; 23; 25(2); 19:15; 20:38; 21:12; 22:8; 23:11; 12; 19; 29; 24:7; 16; 22; 25:5; 13; 35; 26:19; 27:8; 28:8; 11(2); 14; 15; 25; 29:9; 10(2); 11(2); 30:4; **2Sa** 2:1(3); 2; 3; 22; 27; 32; 3:10; 32; 4:4; 12; 5:8; 17; 19(2); 22; 23; 6:2; 12; 15; 7:6; 12; 12:3(2); 11; 17; 13:29; 34; 36; 14:14; 15:2; 20; 24; 30(4); 17:16; 21; 18:9; 18; 24(2); 28(2); 31; 33; 19:34; 20:2; 3; 15; 19; 20; 21; 21:6; 8; 13; 22:9; 40; 49(2); 23:1; 8; 18; 24:9; 11; 18; 19; 22; **1Kin** 1:35; 40; 45; 49; 2:19; 34; 3:15; 6:8; 7:21(3); 8:1; 3; 4(2); 20; 35; 54; 9:16; 24; 10:5; 29; 11:14; 15; 23; 26; 27; 12:8; 10; 18; 24; 27; 28(2); 13:4; 29; 14:10; 14; 15; 16; 25; 15:4; 17; 16:17; 32; 34; 17:7; 19; 18:38; 41; 42(2); 43(2); 44; 46; 20:1; 22; 26; 33; 21:16; 21; 25; 22:6; 12; 20; 29; 35; 38; **2Kin** 1:3; 4; 6(2); 7; 9; 13; 14; 16; 2:1; 11; 13; 16; 23(4); 3:7; 8; 21; 22; 24; 4:21; 29; 34; 35; 36; 37; 6:7; 24; 7:5; 8:12; 9:1; 2; 8; 25; 27; 32; 10:1; 5; 6; 15; 12:10(2); 17(2); 13:21; 14:10; 11; 26; 15:14; 16; 16:5; 7(2); 9; 17:3; 4; 5(2); 7; 10; 36; 18:9; 13; 17(2); 25(2); 19:4; 14; 22; 23; 24; 26; 28; 20:5; 8; 17; 21:3(2); 22:4; 23:2; 9; 29; 24:1; 10; 25:4; 6; 27; **1Chr** 5:26; 11:6; 11; 20; 13:6(2); 14:2; 8; 10(2); 11; 14; 15:3; 12; 14; 16; 25; 28; 17:5; 11; 21:1; 16; 18(2); 19; 27; 25:5; 26:16; 28:2; **2Chr** 1:4; 6; 17; 2:16; 3:17; 5:2; 4; 5(2); 13; 6:10; 26; 7:13; 20; 8:11; 9:4; 10:8; 10; 18; 11:4; 12:2; 9; 13:4; 6; 16:1; 17:6; 18:2; 5; 11; 14; 19; 28; 34; 20:16; 19; 23; 21:4; 9; 16; 17; 24:7; 23; 25:14; 19; 21; 26:16; 19; 28:9; 12; 15; 24; 29:7; 20; 30:7; 27; 32:5(2); 25; 33:3; 14; 19; 34:30; 35:20; 36:6; 15; 22; 23; **Ezr** 1:1; 3; 5(2); 11(2); 2:1; 59; 63; 68; 3:2; 4:2; 12(2); 13; 16; 23; 5:2; 3; 9; 11; 6:1; 11; 7:6; 7; 9; 13; 28; 8:1; 9:5; 6(2); 9; 10:6; 10; **Neh** 2:1; 15; 17; 18; 3:1(2); 3; 6; 13; 14; 15; 19; 31; 32; 4:3; 7; 14; 5:2; 6:1; 10; 7:1; 5; 6; 61; 65; 8:5; 6; 9:3; 4; 5; 18; 10:38; 12:1; 31; 37(2); **Est** 2:7; 20; 5:9; 7:7; **Job** 1:5; 7; 16; 2:2; 12(2); 3:8; 10; 11; 4:15; 5:5(2); 11; 18; 6:3; 4; 7:9; 8:11; 9:7; 10:15; 18; 11:10; 15; 20; 12:14; 15; 13:19; 14:10; 11; 17(2); 15:30; 16:4; 8; 12; 17:8; 18:16; 19:8; 12; 20:6; 15; 27; 21:19; 22:22; 23; 24; 26; 29; 24:22; 26:8; 27:7; 16; 28:4; 5; 29:8; 30:4; 12; 20; 22; 28; 31:14; 18; 21; 29; 33:5; 34:7; 36:13; 37:7; 20; 38:3; 8; 10; 34; 39:4; 18; 27; 30; 40:7; 23(2); 41:10; 15; 25; 42:8; **Ps** 3:1; 3; 4:6; 5:3; 7:6; 9:13; 10:12; 14:4; 15:3; 16:4; 17:5; 7; 18:8; 35; 39; 48(2); 20:5; 21:9; 22:15; 24:4; 7(2); 9(2); 25:1; 27:2; 5; 6; 10; 12; 28:2; 5; 9; 30:1; 3; 31:8; 19; 33:7; 35:2; 11; 23; 25; 39:6; 40:2; 5; 12; 41:8; 9; 10; 44:5; 47:5; 53:4; 54:3; 56:1; 2; 57:3; 8; 59:1; 15; 63:4; 69:9; 15; 29; 71:6; 20; 74:3; 4; 5; 8; 15; 23; 75:3; 4; 5; 7; 77:9; 78:21; 38; 48; 80:2; 81:3; 12; 83:2; 86:4; 87:6; 88:8; 15; 89:2; 4; 42; 90:5; 6; 91:12; 92:11; 93:3(3); 94:2; 16(2); 18; 97:3; 102:10; 16; 104:8; 105:35; 106:9; 17; 18; 26; 30; 107:25; 26; 109:23; 110:7; 113:7; 119:48; 117; 121:1; 122:4; 123:1; 124:2; 3; 127:2(2); 129:6; 132:3; 134:2; 139:8; 21; 140:10; 141:2; 143:8; 144:12; 145:14; 147:2; 3; 6; **Prov** 1:12; 2:3; 7; 3:20; 7:1; 8:23; 30; 10:12; 14; 13:22; 15:1; 18; 16:27; 21:20; 22:6; 23:8; 24:16; 25:7; 26:9; 24; 28:25; 29:21; 22; 30:4; 13; 31; 32; 31:28; **Eccl** 2:26; 3:2; 3; 4:10(2); 15; 10:4; 12; 12:4; **Song** 2:7; 10; 3:5; 4:2; 12; 5:5; 6:6; 7:8; 12; 13; 8:4; 5(2); **Is** 1:2; 6; 2:3; 4; 12; 13; 14; 3:13; 14; 5:5; 6; 11; 13; 24; 26; 6:1; 7:1; 6; 8:7(2); 16; 9:11; 18(2); 10:15(2); 24; 26(2); 28; 29; 30; 11:12; 16; 13:2; 14; 17; 14:4; 8; 9(2); 22; 15:2; 5(3); 7; 18:3; 19:5; 6; 21:2; 22:1; 23:4(2); 13(2); 18; 24:10; 14; 18; 22; 25:8; 26:11; 27:9; 28:4; 7; 21; 30:26; 32:9; 13; 33:3; 10; 12; 34:3; 10; 13; 35:9; 36:1; 10(2); 37:4; 14; 23; 24; 25; 27; 29; 38:22; 39:6; 40:9(3); 15; 26; 31; 41:2; 25; 42:2; 11; 13; 15(2); 43:6; 44:4; 11; 26; 27; 45:8; 13; 20; 47:13; 48:13; 49:6; 18; 19; 21; 22(2); 23; 50:2; 9; 51:6; 8; 17; 18; 52:8; 53:2; 55:13(2); 57:7; 8(2); 14(3); 20; 58:1; 12; 59:19; 60:4; 7; 10; 61:1; 4; 62:10(3); 63:11; 64:7; 11; **Jer** 1:17; 2:6; 24; 3:2; 6; 4:3; 6; 7; 13; 29; 5:10; 17(3); 6:1; 4; 7:13; 16; 25; 29; 9:10(2); 12; 18; 21; 10:17; 20; 25; 11:7; 13; 14; 12:17; 13:19; 20; 14:2; 6; 15:9; 16:14; 15; 18:7; 15; 21; 20:9; 21:2; 22:20(2); 22; 23:4; 7; 8; 10; 24:6; 25:32; 26:5; 10; 17; 27:22; 29:15; 19; 22; 30:9; 13; 31:6; 21; 28; 40; 32:2; 3; 33; 33:1; 15; 34:21; 35:11; 15; 36:5; 20; 37:10; 11; 38:10; 13(2); 39:2; 5; 15; 42:10; 45:4; 46:4; 7; 8(2); 9; 11; 47:2; 6; 48:5(2); 15; 44; 49:5; 14; 19; 22; 28; 31; 50:2; 3; 9; 21; 26; 32; 38; 41; 44; 51:1(2); 3; 9; 11; 12(2); 14; 27(2); 34; 36; 42; 44; 53; 52:7; 9; 31; **Lam** 1:14(2); 19; 2:2; 5(2); 7; 10; 16; 17; 19; 22; 3:41; 62; 63; 4:5; 5:12; **Eze** 1:13; 19(2); 20; 21(2); 3:12; 14; 4:14; 7:11; 8:3; 5(2); 11; 9:3; 10:4; 15; 16(2); 17(2); 19(2); 11:1; 22; 23; 24(2); 13:5(2); 10; 14:3; 4; 7; 16:40; 17:9(2); 14; 17; 24; 18:6; 12; 15; 19:1; 3; 6; 12(2); 20:5(2); 6; 15; 23; 28; 42; 21:15; 22; 22:30; 23:22; 27; 46; 47; 24:8; 26:3(2); 8; 17; 19; 27:2; 30; 32; 28:2; 5; 12(2); 14; 17; 29:4; 30:21; 31:4; 10(3); 14(2); 32:2; 3; 33:25; 34:4; 16; 18; 23; 29; 36:3(2); 7; 13; 37:6; 8; 10; 12; 13; 38:11; 16; 18; 39:2; 15; 40:6; 22; 26; 31; 34; 37; 40; 49; 41:16; 43:5; 24; 44:12; 47:14; **Dan** 2:21; 44; 3:1; 2; 3(2); 5; 7; 12; 14; 18; 22; 24; 4:17; 34; 5:19; 20; 23; 6:23(2); 7:3; 4; 5; 8(2); 20; 8:3(2); 8; 22(2); 23; 25; 26; 27; 9:24; 10:5; 11:2(2); 3; 4(2); 6; 7; 10(2); 12; 14; 15; 20; 21; 23; 25(2); 12:1; 4; 7; 9; 11; **Hos** 1:11; 2:6; 15; 4:8; 15; 19; 6:1; 2; 8:4; 7; 8; 9; 9:6; 12; 16; 10:4; 8; 12; 11:8; 13:12; 15(2); 16; **Joel** 1:6; 10; 12; 20; 2:9; 20(2); 3:9(2); 12; **Amos** 1:6; 9; 13; 2:10; 11; 3:1; 5; 10; 4:10; 5:1; 2; 6:8; 10; 14; 7:1; 4; 8:4; 8; 10; 14; 9:2; 5; 7; 11(3); 15; **Obad** 1; 6; 14; 21; **Jonah** 1:2; 3; 12; 15; 17; 2:6; 4:6; 10; **Mic** 2:4; 8; 13(2); 3:10; 4:2; 3; 5:3; 9; 14; 6:4; 14; 7:3; 6; **Nah** 1:4; 9; 2:1; 7; 3:3; 15; **Hab** 1:3; 6; 9; 15; 2:4; 6; 7; 3:10; 16; **Zeph** 2:4; 3:8; **Hag** 1:8; 14; **Zec** 1:18; 21(2); 2:1; 13; 5:1; 5; 7; 9(2); 6:1; 12; 9:3; 13; 16; 10:11; 12; 11:16; 17; 14:10; 13; 16; 17; 18(2); 19; **Mal** 3:15; 17; 4:1; 2; **Mt** 3:9; 12; 16; 4:1; 5; 6; 8; 16; 5:1; 6:19; 20; 9:6; 16; 10:17; 19; 21(2); 11:5; 12:42; 13:4; 5; 6; 7; 26; 28; 29(2); 14:12; 19; 20; 23; 15:13; 29; 37; 16:9; 10; 24; 17:1; 8; 27(2); 19:20; 20:17; 18; 22:7; 24; 23:13; 32; 24:9; 43; 26:52; 27:37; 50; **Mk** 1:10; 31; 35; 2:4; 9; 11; 12; 21; 3:13; 26; 4:4; 5; 6; 7; 8; 27; 32; 5:29; 6:29; 41; 43; 51; 7:34; 8:8; 19; 20; 24; 25; 34; 9:2; 27; 10:16; 21; 32; 33; 11:20; 12:19; 13:9; 11; 12; 16; 14:42; 60; 15:37; 39; 41; 16:18; 19; **Lk** 1:66; 69; 2:4; 28; 42; 3:8; 20; 4:5; 11; 16(2); 25; 29; 5:23; 24; 25(2); 28; 6:8; 20; 7:15; 16; 8:6; 7; 8; 37; 9:16; 17; 23; 28; 51; 10:25; 34; 11:27; 31; 32; 12:19; 21; 13:11; 25; 14:10; 16:23; 17:6; 13; 18:10; 13; 21; 31; 19:4; 5; 20; 21; 22; 28; 20:28; 21:1; 12; 28(2); 22:45; 23:5; 46; 24:33; 50; 51; **Jn** 2:7; 13; 17; 19; 20; 3:13; 14(2); 4:14; 35; 5:1; 8; 9; 11; 12; 21; 6:3; 5; 12; 39; 40; 44; 54; 62; 7:8(2); 10(2); 14; 8:7; 10; 28; 59; 10:1; 31; 11:31; 41; 55; 12:20; 32; 34; 13:18; 17:1; 18:11; 30; 19:30; 21:11; **Acts** 1:2; 9; 10; 11(2); 13; 15; 22; 2:14(2); 24; 30; 32; 3:1; 6; 7; 8; 13; 22; 26; 4:24; 26; 5:5; 6; 10; 17; 30; 34; 36; 37; 6:12; 13; 7:20; 21; 37; 42; 43; 55; 8:31; 39; 9:40; 41; 10:4; 9; 16; 26(2); 40; 11:2; 10; 28; 12:7(2); 23; 13:1; 16; 22; 31; 33; 34; 43; 50; 14:2; 11; 20; 15:2; 5; 7; 16; 16:22; 17:13; 18:22; 20:9; 11; 32; 21:4; 12; 15(2); 27; 22:3; 13; 22; 24:11; 12; 25:9; 18; 26:10; 30; 27:15; 17; 27; 40(2); **Rom** 1:24; 26; 2:5; 4:24; 6:4; 8:11(2); 32; 9:17; 10:7; 14:4; 15:16; **1Cor** 4:6; 18; 19; 5:2; 6:14(2); 8:1; 10:7; 13:4; 15:15(2); 24; 35; 54; **2Cor** 2:7; 4:14(2); 5:4; 9:5; 12:2; 4; 14; **Gal** 1:17; 18; 2:1; 2; 3:23; **Eph** 2:6; 4:8; 10; 15; 6:4; **Col** 1:5; 24; 2:7; 18; **1Th** 2:16; 4:17; **1Ti** 2:8; 3:6; 16; 4:6; 5:10; 6:19; **2Ti** 1:6; 4:8; **Heb** 1:12; 5:7; 7:27(2); 11:17(2); 19; 12:12; 15; **Jas** 4:10; 5:15; **1Pet** 1:13; 21; 2:5(2); **2Pet** 1:13; 3:1; 10; **1Jn** 3:17; **Jude** 12; 20; **Rev** 4:1; 8:4; 7(2); 10:4; 5; 9; 10; 11:12(2); 12:5; 16; 13:1; 11; 14:11; 15:1; 16:12; 18:21; 19:3; 20:3; 9; 13(2)

UPON

5921, *1909*

Gen 1:2(2); 11; 15; 17; 25; 26; 28; 29; 30; 2:5; 21; 3:14; 4:15; 26; 6:12(2); 17; 7:3; 4; 6; 8; 10; 12; 14; 17; 18(2); 19; 21(2); 23; 24; 8:4; 17(2); 19; 9:2(5); 16(2); 17; 23; 11:4; 8; 9; 12:8; 11; 15:11; 12(2); 16:5; 17:17; 18:6; 19; 27; 31; 19:3; 9; 16(3); 23; 24(2); 25; 22:2; 6; 9; 12; 17; 24:15; 16; 18; 30; 47(2); 61; 26:7; 10; 25; 27:12; 13; 15; 16(2); 28:11; 18; 29:2; 3; 32; 30:3; 31:10; 12; 17; 34; 35; 46; 54; 32:31(2); 32; 34:25; 27; 35:5; 20; 37:22; 27; 34; 38:28; 29; 30; 39:5; 7; 40:6; 17; 41:3; 5; 17; 42; 42:1; 21; 43:18; 30; 44:21; 45:14(2); 15; 46:4; 47:31; 48:2; 14(2); 17; 18; 50:1(2); 23; **Ex** 1:16; 2:25; 3:6; 12; 22(2); 4:9(2); 20; 31; 5:3; 8; 9; 21; 7:4; 5; 17; 19(5); 8:3(2); 4(2); 5; 7; 14; 18(2); 21(3); 9:3(6); 9(2); 10(2); 11(2); 14(3); 19(2); 22(3); 23(2); 33; 10:6; 12; 13; 11:1(2); 5; 12:13(2); 23; 33; 34; 13:9; 16; 14:4(2); 17(4); 18(3); 22; 26(3); 29; 30; 31; 15:9; 15; 16; 19; 26(2); 16:14; 17:6; 18:8; 19:11; 16; 18; 20; 22; 24; 20:5; 12; 25; 21:14; 19; 22; 30; 22:3; 25; 24:11; 16; 25:11; 21; 22; 30; 26:4; 7; 32(2); 34; 27:2; 4; 7; 28:8; 12(2); 22; 23; 26; 29; 30(2); 33; 34; 35; 36; 37(2); 38(2); 41; 43(2); 29:5; 6(2); 7; 8; 10; 12; 13(2); 15; 16; 18; 19; 20(5); 21(5); 22; 25; 38; 30:1; 4; 7; 8; 10(2); 32; 33; 31:18; 32:16; 20; 21; 29(3); 34; 33:16; 21; 34:1; 7(2); 28; 35; 35:3; 36:17(2); 37:3(2); 13; 16; 27; 39:5; 15; 19; 24; 25; 30; 31; 43; 40:4; 13; 19; 20; 22; 23; 29; 38; **Lev** 1:4; 5; 7(2); 8(2); 11; 12; 13; 17(3); 2:1; 2; 9; 15; 3:2(2); 3; 5(2); 8(2); 9; 10; 11; 13(2); 14; 15; 16; 4:4; 7; 8; 9; 10; 15; 18; 19; 24; 25; 26; 29; 30; 31; 33; 34; 35; 5:9; 11; 6:9; 10; 12(2); 13; 15(2); 27; 7:2; 5; 20; 31; 8:7(2); 8; 9(3); 11; 12; 13(2); 14; 15(2); 16(2); 18; 19; 21; 22; 23(3); 24(4); 25; 26; 27(2); 28; 30(5); 9:9; 10; 12; 13; 14; 17; 18; 20(2); 24; 10:6; 7; 11:20; 21(2); 27; 29; 32; 37; 38; 41; 42(3); 44; 46; 13:25; 27; 29; 30; 43; 45; 50; 14:7; 14(3); 17(4); 18; 20; 25(3); 28(4); 29; 48; 15:8; 9; 20(2); 22; 24; 26; 16:2(2); 4; 8; 9; 13(2); 14; 15; 18; 19; 21(2); 22; 25; 17:6; 11; 18:25; 19:17; 19; 28; 20:9; 11; 12; 13; 16; 27; 21:5; 10; 12; 22:3; 22; 23:37; 24:4; 6; 7; 14; 25:21; 37; 26:21; 25; 30; 35; 36; 37; **Num** 1:53; 4:7; 8; 10; 11; 14(2); 25; 5:14(2); 15; 25; 26; 30(2); 6:5; 7; 19; 25; 26; 27; 7:9; 89; 8:7; 10; 12; 24; 25; 9:15; 18; 19; 20; 22; 10:34; 11:9(2); 11; 17(2); 25(2); 26; 29; 31; 12:3; 10; 11; 13:23; 14:18; 36; 37; 15:31; 32; 38; 39; 16:3; 4; 7; 22; 33; 45; 17:2; 3; 18:5; 17; 19:2; 13(2); 15; 18(4); 19; 20; 20:6; 26; 28; 21:8(2); 9; 15; 22:22; 30; 23:4; 24:2; 27:18; 20; 23; 30:14; 31:27; 33:4; 35:22; 23; **Deut** 1:36; 2:25; 4:7; 10; 13; 26; 30; 32; 36; 39; 40; 5:9; 6:8; 9; 22(3); 7:6; 7; 15(2); 16; 22; 8:4; 11:12; 18; 20(2); 21; 25(2); 29(2); 12:1; 2(2); 16; 19; 24; 27(2); 13:9; 17; 14:2; 15:23; 17:7; 18; 19:5; 10; 21:23; 22:6(2); 8; 12; 14; 19; 23:13; 19(2); 20(2); 24:15(2); 26:6; 27:3; 5; 8; 12; 13; 28:8; 15; 20; 24; 45; 46(2); 48; 56; 60; 61; 29:5(2); 20; 22; 27; 30:1; 3; 7; 18; 31:17; 32:2(2); 23(2); 24; 35; 42; 33:10; 16(2); 26; 28; 29; 34:9; **Josh** 1:3; 2:6; 8; 9; 15(2); 19(2); 3:13; 16; 4:5; 7:6(2); 10; 8:7; 20; 32; 9:4; 5(2); 20; 10:11; 12; 13; 18; 24(2); 26; 11:4; 7; 12:2; 13:9; 19:34; 20:8; 23:15(2); 24:7; **Judg** 3:10; 16; 22; 23; 4:16; 6:14; 20; 26; 28; 34; 37; 39(2); 40; 7:5; 6; 25; 8:21; 9:5; 18; 24(2); 33; 44; 49; 53; 57(2); 11:29; 37; 38; 12:1; 13:19; 14:6; 17; 19; 15:12; 14(2); 16; 16:3; 9; 12; 14; 17; 19; 20; 26; 27; 29; 30(2); 18:19; 25; 19:14; 20; 27; 28; 20:5; 37; 41; 48; **Ruth** 3:3; 15; 4:5; 10; **1Sa** 1:9; 11; 2:8; 10; 28; 34; 4:12; 13; 19; 5:3; 4(2); 6; 7(2); 6:8; 11; 7:10; 9:16; 24; 25; 10:1; 6; 10; 11:2; 6; 13:12; 13; 14:1; 13(2); 25; 32; 15:19; 27; 16:13; 16; 23; 17:5; 6; 38; 39; 49; 51; 18:4; 10; 17(2); 19:9; 20; 23; 20:9; 25(2); 31; 21:13; 22:17; 18(2); 24:2; 12; 13; 25:24(2); 39; 42; 26:12; 28:18; 23; 30:14(3); 16; 17; 31:2(2); 4; 5; **2Sa** 1:2; 6(2); 9(2); 10(2); 15; 16; 19; 21; 24; 4:11; 5:20; 23; 6:3; 8; 9:8; 11:2(2); 21; 23; 24; 12:16; 13:18; 29; 14:7; 15:14; 32; 16:1; 8; 22; 17:2; 12(2); 14; 18:9; 17; 28; 20:8(2); 12; 21:10(2); 22:7; 11(2); 28; 34; 24:15; 16; 20; **1Kin** 1:13; 17; 20; 24; 30; 33; 35; 38; 44; 47; 2:5; 12; 25; 29; 31; 32(2); 33(6); 34; 37; 44; 46; 3:4; 26; 5:5; 6:32(3); 35; 7:2(2); 3; 16; 17; 18(2); 19; 20(2); 22; 25(2); 29; 31; 38; 41; 42; 8:31; 32; 36; 9:5(2); 9(2); 21; 25(2); 10:20; 12:4;

9; 32; 33(2); 13:2(3); 3; 29; 14:10; 17:14; 19; 20; 21; 18:1; 26; 28; 42; 19:11; 19; 20:30; 31; 38; 21:4; 21; 27; 29; 22:17; **2Kin** 2:9; 16; 3:15; 22; 27; 4:4(2); 5(2); 21; 29; 31; 32; 33; 34(5); 35; 5:23; 6:26; 30(2); 7:6; 9; 17; 20; 8:1; 9:25; 37; 11:12; 12:11; 13:13; 16(3); 18; 16:13; 15(2); 17; 18:21(2); 23; 19:7; 21:12; 22:16(2); 20; 23:6; 16; 20(2); 24:3; 25:6; 17(2); **1Chr** 1:10; 5:16; 6:49; 9:27; 10:4; 12:8; 18; 19; 13:11; 14:11; 14; 17; 15:13; 15; 27; 16:8; 40; 19:17; 20:2; 21:14; 16; 26(2); 22:8; 28:2; 5; 19; 29:25; **2Chr** 1:6; 4:4(2); 13; 14; 6:13(2); 16; 20(2); 22; 23; 27; 7:3(2); 22; 9:19; 10:4; 9; 11; 12:7; 13:4; 10; 11; 18; 14:14; 15:1; 5; 17:10; 18:16; 18; 23; 19:2; 7; 10(2); 20:9; 12; 14; 22:8; 23:11; 20; 24:7; 9; 18; 20; 22; 27; 25:13; 28; 26:15; 16; 20; 28:11; 15; 29:8; 22(2); 23; 24; 27; 32:8; 12; 25(2); 26; 33:11; 34:4; 5; 21; 24(2); 25; 28(2); 35:3; 16; 36:17(2); **Ezr** 3:3(2); 5:5; 6:19; 7:6; 9(2); 17; 24; 26; 28; 8:18; 22; 31; 9:5; 13; **Neh** 2:8; 12; 18; 4:4; 12; 19; 5:4; 18; 19; 6:1; 14; 8:2; 4; 16; 9:1; 4; 10; 13; 32; 33; 10:34; 12:31(2); 38; 13:18(3); **Est** 1:6; 2:15; 17; 3:13; 4:5; 5:1; 6:8(2); 7:8; 8:7(2); 12(2); 14; 17; 9:2; 3; 13; 25; 27(3); 10:1(2); **Job** 1:12; 15; 17; 19; 20; 2:11; 12; 13; 3:4; 5; 6; 25; 4:5; 14; 5:10(2); 6:28; 7:1; 8; 17; 8:9; 15; 9:8; 33; 10:1; 3; 16; 17; 12:4; 21; 13:11; 27; 14:3; 22; 15:21; 26(2); 29; 16:9(2); 10(2); 13; 14(2); 15; 18:8; 15; 19:21(2); 25; 20:4; 22; 23(2); 25; 21:5; 9; 17; 22:28; 24:23; 25:3; 26:7; 9; 27:9; 10; 22; 28:9; 29:3; 4; 13; 19; 22; 30:12; 14(2); 15; 16(2); 22; 30; 31:1; 10; 36; 33:7; 15(2); 19; 27; 34:14; 21; 23; 36:28; 30; 37:12; 38:5; 24; 39:28; 40:4; 41:8; 30; 33; 42:11; **Ps** 2:6; 3:7; 8; 4:1; 4; 6; 5:t; 6:t, 2; 7:5; 16(2); 8:t; 9:t, 13; 11:2; 6; 12:t, 14:2; 4; 17:6; 18:3; 6; 10(2); 33; 21:5; 12; 22:t, 9; 10; 13; 17; 18; 29; 24:2(2); 25:16; 18; 27:2; 5; 7; 29:3(2); 10; 30:10; 31:9; 16; 17; 32:4; 33:14; 18(2); 22; 34:15; 35:8; 16; 36:4; 37:9; 12; 40:2; 12; 17; 41:2; 3; 43:4; 44:17; 45:t, 3; 9; 46:t, 47:8; 48:6; 49:4; 50:10; 15; 51:1; 19; 53:t, 2; 4; 54:7; 55:3; 4; 5; 10; 15; 16; 22; 56:t, 12; 59:9; 10; 60:t; 61:t, 62:1; 5; 10; 63:6; 64:8; 65:5; 12; 66:11; 67:1; 2; 4; 68:4; 33; 69:t, 9; 15; 24; 72:6; 16; 73:25; 74:5; 78:24; 27; 31; 49; 79:6(3); 80:t, 17(2); 18; 81:t; 84:t, 9; 86:5; 7; 16; 88:t, 7; 9; 89:19; 22; 90:17(2); 91:13; 14; 15; 92:3(3); 94:23; 99:6(2); 101:6; 102:7; 13; 103:17; 104:3; 27; 105:1; 16; 38; 106:29; 107:40; 109:25; 112:2; 8; 116:2; 3; 4; 13; 17; 118:5; 7; 119:49; 53; 87; 132; 135; 121:5; 123:2(2); 3(2); 125:3; 5; 128:6; 129:3; 6; 8; 132:11; 12; 18; 133:2(2); 3; 135:9(2); 137:2; 139:5; 140:10; 141:7; 144:9; 145:15; 18(2); 147:7; 8; 15; 149:5; 7(2); 9; 150:5(2); **Prov** 1:27; 28; 3:3; 18; 6:21; 28; 7:3(2); 8:27; 9:3; 10:6; 24; 11:26; 19:12; 17; 23:5; 31; 34; 24:25; 32; 25:12; 20; 22; 26:14(2); 27; 28:22; 30:19; 24; 32; **Eccl** 5:2; 7:20; 8:6; 14; 16; 9:12; 10:7(2); 11:1; 2; 3; **Song** 1:6(2); 2:8(2); 17; 3:8; 4:16; 5:5; 15; 6:13; 7:5; 8:5; 6(2); 9; 14; **Is** 1:25; 2:12(2); 13(2); 14(2); 15(2); 16(2); 3:26; 4:5(3); 5:6; 6:1; 7; 7:17(3); 19(2); 8:7; 17; 9:2; 6; 7(2); 8; 10:12; 20(2); 26; 11:2; 14(2); 12:4; 13:2; 14:13; 16; 25; 26(2); 15:9(3); 16:5; 18:2; 4; 6(2); 19:1; 8; 12; 20:3(2); 21:3; 8; 13; 22:22; 24; 25; 23:17; 24:17; 20; 21; 26:16; 28:4; 10(4); 13(4); 22; 27; 29:10; 30:6(2); 16(2); 17; 18; 25(2); 32; 32:11; 13(2); 15; 33:4; 20; 34:2(2); 5(2); 11; 35:10; 36:8; 12; 37:7; 38:21; 40:7; 22; 24; 31; 41:25(3); 42:1; 5; 25; 43:2; 22; 44:3(4); 19; 45:12; 46:1(2); 7; 47:6; 9; 11(3); 13; 48:2; 49:13; 16; 22; 50:10; 51:5; 6; 11; 52:7; 53:5; 55:6; 7; 56:7; 57:7; 58:14; 59:17; 21; 60:1; 2(2); 61:1; 62:6; 63:3; 64:7; 65:3; 7(2); 66:4; 12(2); 20(3); 24; **Jer** 1:14; 2:3; 15; 20; 34; 37; 3:6; 12; 21; 4:20; 29; 5:3; 10; 12; 15; 6:11(2); 12; 19; 21; 23; 26; 7:20(5); 8:2; 9:3; 22; 10:25(2); 11:8; 11; 16; 23; 12:12; 13:1; 4; 13; 16; 22; 26; 14:16; 22; 15:5; 8(3); 14; 16:4; 17; 17:1(2); 2; 18; 25; 18:22; 19:3; 13; 15(2); 22:2; 4; 23; 24; 30; 23:2; 12; 17; 19; 40; 24:6; 25:13; 26; 29; 30; 33; 26:15(3); 27:2; 5; 28:14; 29:12; 16; 17; 30:16; 18; 23; 31:5; 6; 19; 20; 26; 39; 32:19; 23; 29; 42(2); 33:17; 21; 35:17(2); 36:4; 6; 30; 31(3); 39:5; 16; 40:2; 3; 4; 42:12; 17; 18(2); 43:10; 44:2(2); 45:5; 46:16; 21; 47:5; 48:8; 18; 21(4); 22(3); 23(3); 24(3); 32(2); 37(2); 38; 43; 44(2); 49:5; 8; 36; 37; 50:15; 19; 35(4); 36(2); 37(4); 38(2); 42; 51:12; 13; 25; 35(2); 42; 47; 52; 56(2); 60; 64; 52:9; 22(2); 23; **Lam** 1:10; 14; 2:10(2); 11; 3:28; 47; 53; 55; 57; 4:19; 5:1; 18; **Eze** 1:3; 15; 17; 22; 26(2); 28; 2:1; 2; 3:14; 22; 24; 25; 4:1; 4(3); 5; 8; 9; 5:1(2); 13; 16(2); 17(2); 6:3; 12; 13; 14; 7:2; 3(3); 4; 8(2); 12; 14; 18(2); 26(2); 8:1; 10; 9:4; 6; 8(2); 10; 10:11; 11:5; 8; 13; 21; 23; 12:6; 7; 12; 13; 13:9; 15(2); 18; 14:9; 13(2); 17; 19; 21; 22(2); 16:5; 8; 11; 12; 14; 41; 43; 17:19; 20; 22; 18:6; 8; 11; 13(2); 15; 20(2); 19:9; 20:8; 13; 21; 21:12(4); 29; 31; 22:9; 20; 21; 22; 24; 31(2); 23:6; 8; 9; 10; 12(2); 14; 15(2); 16; 20; 23; 41; 42(2); 46; 49; 24:6; 7(2); 8; 11; 13; 17(2); 23(2); 25:7; 11; 12; 13; 14; 16; 17(2); 26:7; 14; 16; 19; 27:11(2); 29; 30; 28:7; 12; 14; 18; 23; 26; 29:5; 7; 8; 30:4; 9; 15; 25; 31:12; 13(2); 32:4(3); 5; 8; 11; 27; 33:2; 3; 4; 5; 10; 22; 26; 34:6(2); 13; 14(2); 36:10; 11; 12; 18(2); 25; 29; 37:1; 4; 6(2); 8; 9; 10; 16(2); 22; 38:12(2); 15; 20(2); 22(3); 39:2; 4; 5; 14; 17; 21; 25; 29; 40:1; 2; 4; 16; 17; 26; 31; 34; 37; 43; 41:25(2); 26; 43:3; 12; 14; 20; 24; 27(2); 44:4; 17; 18(2); 45:19(3); 22; 47:10; 12; **Dan** 1:13; 2:10; 28; 29; 34; 46; 3:27; 4:5; 13; 21; 24; 28; 33; 5:5; 6:10; 17; 23; 7:1; 2; 4; 6; 23; 8:7; 10; 17; 9:11; 12(2); 13; 14(2); 17; 24(2); 27; 10:7; 10(2); 16; 11:18; 24; 42; 12:6; 7; **Hos** 1:4; 6; 7; 2:4; 13; 23; 4:13(2); 5:1; 10; 7:9; 12; 14; 8:14; 9:1; 10:7; 11; 12; 14; 12:14; 13:13; 14:3; **Joel** 1:6; 2:2; 8; 9(2); 28; 29(2); 3:4; 7; **Amos** 1:12; 2:2; 5; 8; 3:5; 9; 14; 4:2; 7(3); 13; 5:2; 8; 11; 6:4(2); 12; 7:7; 8:2; 10(2); 9:1; 4; 6; 8; 9; 15; **Obad** 11; 15(2); 16; 17; **Jonah** 1:6(2); 7(2); 8; 12; 14; 2:10; 4:8; **Mic** 1:3; 2:1; 3:11(2); 4:11; 5:1; 7; 9; 15; 7:16; 19; **Nah** 1:15; 2:7; 3:3; 5; 6; 7; 18; 19; **Hab** 1:13; 2:1(2); 2; 3:1; 8; 19; **Zeph** 1:4(2); 5; 17; 2:2(2); 3:8(2); 9; **Hag** 1:9; 11(9); 2:15; **Zec** 1:7; 8; 16; 2:9; 3:5(2); 9; 4:2(2); 3(2); 11(2); 5:8; 11; 6:8; 11; 13(2); 9:9(2); 16; 10:6; 11:11; 17(2); 12:4; 10(3); 13:7; 14:4; 12; 17; 20; **Mal** 1:7; 2:2; 3; 3:16; **Mt** 3:16; 4:13; 6:19; 7:24; 25(2); 26; 27; 9:18; 10:13; 27; 11:29; 12:2; 18; 13:5; 16:18; 19:28; 20:25; 21:5; 23:9; 18; 35(2); 36; 24:2; 3; 25:31; 26:10; 27:29; 30; 35; 28:2; **Mk** 1:10; 3:10; 6:5; 17; 39; 48; 49; 7:30; 32; 8:23; 25; 10:16; 27; 34; 42; 11:7; 11; 13:2; 3; 14:67; 15:19; 24; **Lk** 1:12; 35; 58; 2:9; 25; 40; 3:22; 4:18; 5:1; 19; 24; 36; 6:10; 48(2); 49; 8:6; 43; 9:38; 10:6; 11:20; 22; 12:1; 3; 13:4; 17:31; 18:13; 19:35; 43; 44; 20:1; 18; 21:6; 23; 25; 34; 22:25; 56; 61; 23:26; 24:1; 49; **Jn** 1:32; 33; 36; 51; 4:27; 9:15; 11:38; 12:35; 18:4; 19:29; 31; **Acts** 1:8; 26; 2:3; 17; 43; 3:4; 4:1; 33; 5:11(2); 28; 6:12; 7:57; 59; 8:16; 24; 10:9; 11:6; 19; 12:7; 21(2); 13:11; 40; 15:10; 17; 28; 16:23; 18:6; 19:6; 13; 20:7; 21:35; 22:13; 24:7; 26:16; 27:26; 29; **Rom** 2:9; 3:22; 4:9(2); 5:12; 18(2); 9:28; 10:12; 13; 11:32; 13:4; 6; 15:20; **1Cor** 1:2; 3:12; 7:35(2); 9:16; 10:11; 12:23; 15:10; 16:2; **2Cor** 1:11; 23; 3:15; 5:2; 4; 8:4; 22; 11:28; 12:9; **Gal** 4:11; 6:16; **Eph** 2:20; 4:26; 5:6; **Phil** 1:3; 2:7; 17; 27; **Col** 3:5; **1Th** 2:16; 5:3(2); **1Ti** 4:15; **Heb** 6:7; 18; 8:6; 11:21; **Jas** 2:21; 4:3; 5:1; **1Pet** 4:14; 5:7; **2Pet** 2:1; 5; **1Jn** 1:1; 3:1; **Jude** 15; **Rev** 1:17; 2:24; 3:3; 10(2); 12(2); 4:3; 4; 5:7; 13; 7:10; 8:3; 7; 10(2); 9:3; 10:1; 2; 5(2); 8(2); 11:10; 11(2); 16; 12:1; 3; 13:1(3); 8; 14:14; 16:1; 2(3); 3; 4; 8; 10; 12; 18; 21; 17:1; 3; 5; 16; 18:24; 19:11; 14; 21; 20:3; 4(2); 21:5

US

2248

Gen 1:26; 3:22; 5:29; 11:3; 4(4); 7; 19:5; 13; 31; 32; 34; 20:9; 23:6(3); 24:23; 55; 65; 26:10(2); 16; 22; 28(3); 29; 31:14; 15; 37; 44; 50; 53; 32:18; 20; 33:12(2); 34:9(2); 10; 14; 16; 17; 21(4); 22(3); 23(2); 35:3; 37:8(2); 17; 20; 21; 27; 39:14(2); 17; 41:12(2); 13; 42:2; 21(2); 28; 30(2); 33; 43:2; 3; 4; 5; 7; 18(3); 44:25; 26(2); 27; 30; 31; 47:15; 19(2); 25; 50:15(2); **Ex** 1:10(2); 2:14; 19(2); 3:18(2); 5:3(3); 8; 16; 17; 21; 8:26; 27; 10:7; 25; 26; 13:14; 15; 16; 14:5; 11(3); 12(2); 25; 16:3; 7; 8; 17:2; 3(2); 7; 9; 19:23; 20:19(2); 24:14; 32:1(3); 23(3); 33:15; 16; 34:9(2); **Num** 10:29; 31(2); 32(2); 11:4; 13; 18(2); 12:2; 11; 13:27; 30; 14:3(2); 4(2); 8(3); 9(2); 16:13(3); 14(2); 34; 20:5(2); 14; 15; 16; 17; 21:5; 7; 22:4; 14; 27:4; 31:49; 32:5; 19; **Deut** 1:6; 14; 19; 20; 22(3); 25(3); 27(4); 41; 2:29; 30; 32; 33; 36(2); 37; 3:1; 5:2; 3(3); 24; 25; 27; 6:21; 23(3); 24(2); 25; 9:28; 13:2(2); 6; 13; 26:3; 6(3); 8; 9(2); 15; 29:7; 15(2); 29; 30:12(2); 13(2); 31:17(2); 33:4; **Josh** 1:16(2); 2:9; 14; 17; 18; 20; 24; 4:23; 5:6; 13; 7:7(2); 9; 25; 8:5; 6(2); 9:6; 7; 11(2); 20; 22(2); 25; 10:6(4); 17:4; 16; 21:2; 22:17; 19(2); 22; 23; 25; 26(2); 27(2); 28(2); 31; 34; 24:17(2); 18; 27(2); **Judg** 1:1; 24; 6:13(6); 8:1(2); 21; 22(2); 9:8; 10; 12; 14; 10:15(2); 11:8; 10; 19; 24; 12:1; 13:8(2); 15; 23(3); 14:15(2); 15:10(2); 11(2); 16:5; 24; 25; 18:19(2); 25; 19:11; 13; 28; 20:3; 8(2); 13; 18; 32(2); 39; 21:1; 22; **Ruth** 2:20; **1Sa** 4:3(5); 7; 8(2); 5:7(2); 10(2); 11; 6:2; 9(3); 20; 7:8(2); 12; 8:5(2); 6(2); 19; 20(2); 9:5(2); 6(2); 8; 9; 10; 27; 10:16; 19; 27; 11:1; 3(2); 10; 12; 14; 12:4(2); 10; 12; 19; 14:1; 6(2); 9; 10(2); 12; 17; 36(3); 17:9; 20:11; 42; 21:5; 23:19; 25:7; 15; 16; 40; 26:11; 27:11; 29:4(2); 9; 30:22; 23(3); **2Sa** 2:14; 5:2; 10:12; 11:23(2); 13:25; 26; 15:14(3); 19; 20; 17:5; 18:3(5); 19:9(2); 10; 42(2); 43; 20:6(2); 21:4; 5(2); 6; 17; 24:14; **1Kin** 3:18; 5:6; 8:57(3); 12:4; 9; 10; 18:23; 26; 20:23; 31; **2Kin** 1:6(2); 4:9; 10(3); 13; 6:1; 2(3); 11; 16; 7:4(3); 6(2); 9; 12; 13; 9:5; 12; 10:5; 14:8; 18:26; 30; 32; 19:19; 22:13(2); **1Chr** 13:2(2); 3(2); 15:13; 16:35(3); 19:13; **2Chr** 10:4; 9; 10; 13:10; 12; 14:7(3); 11; 20:9; 11(3); 12; 25:17; 29:10; 32:7; 8(2); 11; 34:21; **Ezr** 4:2(2); 3(2); 12; 14; 18; 5:11; 17; 8:17; 18(2); 21; 22; 23; 31(2); 9:8(3); 9(4); 13(3); 14(2); 10:3; 14; **Neh** 2:17; 18; 19(2); 20; 4:12(2); 15(2); 20(2); 22; 23; 5:8; 10; 17(2); 6:2; 7; 9; 10(2); 16; 9:32; 33; 37; 10:32; 13:18; **Job** 9:33(2); 15:9; 10; 21:14; 22:17; 31:15; 34:4(3); 37; 35:11(2); 37:19; **Ps** 2:3(2); 4:6(2); 12:4; 17:11; 20:9; 33:22; 34:3; 44:1; 5; 7(2); 9; 10(2); 11(2); 13(2); 14; 17; 19(2); 23; 26; 46:7; 11; 47:3; 4; 54:t, 60:1(3); 3; 10; 11; 62:8; 65:5; 66:10(2); 11; 12; 67:1(3); 6; 7; 68:19; 28; 74:1; 8; 9; 78:3; 79:4; 8(2); 9(2); 80:2; 3; 6; 7; 18; 19; 83:4; 12; 85:4(2); 5; 6; 7(2); 13; 90:12; 14; 15(2); 17(2); 95:1(2); 2; 6(2); 100:3; 103:10(2); 12; 106:47(2); 108:11; 12; 115:1(2); 12(2); 117:2; 118:27; 119:4; 122:1; 123:2; 3(2); 124:2; 3(2); 4; 6; 126:3; 136:23; 24; 137:3(5); 8; **Prov** 1:11(3); 12; 14(2); 7:18(2); **Eccl** 1:10; 12:13; **Song** 2:15; 5:9; 7:11(2); 12(2); **Is** 1:9; 18; 2:3(2); 5; 4:1; 6:8; 7:6(3); 8:10; 9:6(2); 14:8; 10; 17:14(2); 22:13; 25:9; 26:12(2); 13; 28:15; 29:15(2); 30:10(2); 11; 32:15; 33:2; 14(2); 21; 22; 36:11; 15; 18; 37:20; 41:1; 22(2); 43:9; 26; 50:8; 53:6; 59:9(2); 11; 12(2); 63:7; 16(2); 17; 64:6; 7(2); 12; **Jer** 2:6(2); 27; 3:25; 4:5; 8; 13; 5:12; 19; 24(2); 6:4(2); 5(2); 24; 26; 8:8; 14(4); 9:18; 19; 11:19(2); 14:7; 9(2); 19(2); 21(2); 16:10; 18:18(3); 21:2(4); 13; 26:16; 29:15; 28; 31:6; 35:6; 8; 9; 10; 11; 36:17; 37:3; 9; 38:16; 25(2); 40:10; 41:8; 42:2(2); 3; 5(2); 6; 20(2); 43:3(4); 44:16; 46:16; 48:2; 50:5; 51:9; 10; **Lam** 3:40; 41; 43; 45; 46; 47; 4:17(2); 19(2); 5:1; 4; 8(2); 16; 20(2); 21; 22(2); **Eze** 8:12; 11:3; 15; 24:19(2); 33:10; 24; 35:12; 37:18; **Dan** 1:12; 2:23; 3:17(2); 9:7; 8; 10; 11; 12(3); 13; 14; 16; **Hos** 6:1(3); 2(2); 3; 10:3; 8(2); 12:4; 14:2; 3; **Amos** 4:1; 6:13; 9:10; **Obad** 1; **Jonah** 1:6; 7(2); 8(2); 11; 14(2); **Mic** 3:11(2); 4:2(2); 5:1; 6; 7:19; **Zec** 1:6(2); 8:21; **Mal** 1:2; 9; 2:10; **Mt** 1:23; 3:15; 6:11; 12; 13(2); 8:25; 29; 31(2); 9:27; 13:36; 56; 15:15; 23; 17:4(2); 20:7; 12; 30; 31; 21:25; 38(2); 22:17; 25; 24:3; 25:8; 9; 11; 26:46; 63; 68; 27:4; 25; 49; **Mk** 1:24(2); 38; 4:35; 5:12; 6:3; 9:5(2); 22(2); 38(2); 40; 10:35; 37; 12:7; 19; 13:4; 14:15; 42; 15:36; 16:3; **Lk** 1:1; 2; 69; 71; 74; 78; 2:15(2); 48; 4:34(2); 7:5; 16; 20; 8:22; 9:33(2); 49; 50(2); 10:11; 17; 11:1; 3; 4(4); 45; 12:41; 13:25; 15:23; 16:26(2); 17:13; 19:14; 20:2; 6; 14; 22; 28; 22:8; 67; 23:18; 30(2); 39; 24:22; 24; 29; 32(3); **Jn** 1:14; 22; 2:18; 4:12; 25; 6:34; 52; 8:5; 9:34; 10:24(2); 11:7; 15; 16; 50; 14:8(2); 9; 22; 31; 16:17; 17:21; 18:31; 19:24; **Acts** 1:17; 21(2); 22(2); 2:29; 3:4; 12; 4:17; 5:28; 6:14; 7:27; 38; 40(3); 10:41; 42; 11:13; 15; 17; 13:33; 47; 14:11; 17; 15:7; 8; 9; 24; 25; 28; 36; 16:9; 10; 14; 15(2); 16; 17(2); 21; 37(4); 17:27; 20:5; 14; 21:5; 11; 16; 17; 18; 23:9; 24:4; 7; 25:24; 27:2; 6; 7; 20; 28:2(2); 7(2); 10(2); 15(2); **Rom** 3:8; 4:16; 24; 5:5; 8(2); 6:3; 8:4; 18; 26; 31(2); 32(2); 34; 35; 37; 39; 9:24; 29; 12:6(2); 7; 13:12(2); 13; 14:7; 12; 13; 19; 15:2; 7; 16:6; **1Cor** 1:18; 30; 2:10; 12; 4:1; 6; 8; 9; 5:7; 8; 6:14; 7:15; 8:6; 8; 10:8; 9; 15:32; 57; 16:16; **2Cor** 1:4; 5; 8; 10(2); 11(2); 14; 19; 20; 21(2); 22; 2:11; 14(2); 3:3; 6; 4:7; 12; 14(2); 17; 5:5(2); 14; 18(2); 19; 20; 21; 6:12; 7:1; 2; 6; 7; 9; 8:4(2); 5; 7; 19(2); 20(2); 9:11; 10:2; 8; 13; **Gal** 1:4; 23; 2:4; 3:13(2); 24; 4:26; 5:1; 25; 26; 6:9; 10; **Eph** 1:3; 4; 5; 6; 8; 9; 2:4; 5; 6(2); 7; 14; 3:20; 4:7; 5:2(2); **Phil** 3:15; 16(2); 17; **Col** 1:8; 12; 13(2); 2:14(2); 4:3(2); **1Th** 1:6; 9; 10; 2:8; 13; 15; 16; 18; 3:6(4); 4:1; 7; 8; 5:6(2); 8; 9; 10; 25; **2Th** 1:7; 2:2; 16(2); 3:1; 6; 7; 9; **1Ti** 6:8; 17; **2Ti** 1:7; 9(3); 14; 2:12; **Titus** 2:12; 14(2); 3:5; 6; 15; **Heb** 1:2; 2:3; 4:1(2); 2; 11; 14; 16; 6:1; 18; 20; 7:26; 9:12; 24; 10:15; 20; 22; 23; 24; 11:40(2); 12:1(4); 9; 10; 28; 13:13; 15; 18; **Jas** 1:18; 3:3; 4:5; **1Pet** 1:3; 12; 2:21(2); 3:18; 21; 4:1; 3; 17; 5:10; **2Pet** 1:1; 3(2); 4; 3:2; **1Jn** 1:2; 3; 7; 8; 9(2); 10; 2:19(5); 25; 3:1(2); 16; 18; 20; 21; 23; 24(2); 4:6(2); 7; 9; 10; 11; 12(2); 13(2); 16; 19; 5:11; 14; 15; 20; **2Jn** 2(2); **3Jn** 9; 10; **Rev** 1:5(2); 6; 5:9; 10; 6:16(2); 19:7

USE

559, 3231, 3947, 4399, 4911, 4912, 5172, 5656, 7080, *1838*, *1908*, *5195*, *5382*, *5530*, *5532*, *5540*

Lev 7:24; 19:26; **Num** 10:2; 15:39; **Deut** 26:14; **2Sa** 1:18; **1Chr** 12:2; 28:15; **Jer** 23:31; 31:23; 46:11; **Eze** 12:23; 16:44; 18:2; 3; 21:21; **Mt** 5:44; 6:7; **Lk** 6:28; **Acts** 14:5; **Rom** 1:26; 27; **1Cor** 7:21; 31; **2Cor** 1:17; 3:12; 13:10; **Gal** 5:13; **Eph** 4:29; **1Ti** 1:8; 3:10; 5:23; **2Ti** 2:21; **Heb** 5:14; **1Pet** 4:9

USED

3928, 6213, *390*, *1096*, *1247*, *1387*, *1510*, *1722*, *3096*, *4238*, *5530*

Ex 21:36; **Lev** 7:24; **Judg** 14:10; 20; **2Kin** 17:17; 21:6; **2Chr** 33:6(2); **Jer** 2:24; **Eze** 22:29; 35:11; **Hos** 12:10; **Mk** 2:18; **Acts** 8:9; 19:19; 27:17; **Rom** 3:13; **1Cor** 9:12; 15; **1Th** 2:5; **1Ti** 3:13; **Heb** 10:33

USES

5532

Titus 3:14

USING

671, *2192*

Col 2:22; **1Pet** 2:16

VERY

199, 430, 552, 651, 898, 899, 1199, 1419, 1767, 1851, 1854, 1942, 3190, 3304, 3453, 3559, 3960, 3966, 4213, 4295, 4592, 4605, 4801, 5464, 5690, 5704, 6106, 6621, 6985, 7023, 7230, 7260, 7690, *85*, *230*, *662*, *846*, *927*, *957*, *1565*, *1582*, *1646*, *1888*, *2236*, *2532*, *2566*, *2735*, *3029*, *3827*, *4036*, *4118*, *4119*, *4184*, *4185*, *4186*, *4708*, *4970*, *5228*

Gen 1:31; 4:5; 12:14; 13:2; 18:20; 21:11; 24:16; 26:13; 27:21; 24; 33; 34:7; 41:19; 31; 49; 47:13; 50:9; 10; **Ex** 1:20; 8:28; 9:3; 16; 18; 24; 10:14;

11:3; 12:38; 30:36; **Num** 6:9; 11:33; 12:3; 13:28; 16:15; 22:17; 32:1; **Deut** 9:20; 21; 20:15; 27:8; 28:43(2); 54; 30:14; 32:20; **Josh** 1:7; 3:16; 8:4; 9:9; 13; 22; 10:20; 27; 11:4; 13:1; 22:8(2); 23:6; **Judg** 3:17; 11:33; 35; 13:6; 18:9; **Ruth** 1:20; **1Sa** 2:17; 22; 4:10; 5:9; 11; 14:15; 20; 31; 18:8; 15; 19:4; 20:7; 23:22; 25:2; 15; 34; 36; 26:4; **2Sa** 1:26; 2:17; 3:8; 11:2; 12:15; 13:3; 21; 36; 18:17; 19:32(2); 24:10; **1Kin** 1:4; 6; 15; 7:34; 10:2(2); 10; 19:10; 14; 21:26; **2Kin** 14:26; 17:18; 21:16; **1Chr** 9:13; 18:8; 21:8; 13; 23:17; **2Chr** 6:18; 7:8; 9:1; 14:13; 16:8; 14; 20:35; 24:24; 30:13; 32:29; 33:14; 36:14; **Ezr** 10:1(2); **Neh** 1:7; 2:2; 4:7; 5:6; 8:17; **Est** 1:12; **Job** 1:3; 2:13; 15:10; 32:6; **Ps** 5:9; 35:8; 46:1; 50:3; 71:19; 79:8; 89:2; 92:5; 93:5; 104:1; 105:12; 119:107; 138; 140; 142:6; 146:4; 147:15; **Prov** 17:9; 27:15; **Is** 1:9; 5:1; 10:25; 16:6; 14; 24:16; 29:17; 30:19; 31:1; 33:17; 40:15; 47:6; 48:8; 52:13; 64:9; 12; **Jer** 2:12; 4:19; 5:11; 12:1; 14:17; 18:13; 20:15; 24:2(2); 3(2); 27:7; 40:12; 46:20; **Lam** 5:22; **Eze** 2:3; 16:47; 27:25; 33:32; 37:2(2); 40:2; 47:7; 9; **Dan** 2:12; 6:19; 7:20; 8:8; 11:25; **Joel** 2:11(2); **Amos** 5:20; **Jonah** 4:1; **Hab** 2:13(2); **Zec** 1:15; 8:4; 9:2; 5; 14:4; **Mt** 10:30; 15:28; 17:18; 18:31; 21:8; 24:24; 26:7; 37; **Mk** 8:1; 14:3; 33; 16:2; 4; **Lk** 1:3; 9:5; 10:11; 12:7; 59; 18:23(2); 24; 19:17; 48; 24:1; **Jn** 7:26; 8:4; 12:3; 14:11; **Acts** 9:22; 10:10; 24:2; 25:10; **Rom** 10:20; 13:6; **1Cor** 4:3; **2Cor** 9:2; 11:5; 12:11; 15; **Phil** 1:6; **1Th** 5:13; 23; **2Ti** 1:17; 18; **Heb** 10:1; **Jas** 3:4; 5:11

WAS

1961, *2258*

Gen 1:2(2); 3; 4; 7; 9; 10; 11; 12(2); 15; 18; 21; 24; 25; 30; 31; 2:5(2); 10; 19; 20; 23; 3:1; 6(2); 10(2); 20; 23; 4:2(2); 5; 18; 19; 20; 21(2); 22; 26; 5:24; 32; 6:5(2); 9; 11(2); 12; 7:6(2); 12; 17(2); 22(2); 23(2); 8:1; 2; 11; 13; 14; 9:19; 21(2); 10:9; 10; 19; 25(3); 30; 11:1; 10; 29; 30; 12:4; 6; 10(2); 11; 14(2); 15; 18; 13:2; 6(2); 7; 10; 14; 14:10; 14; 18; 15:12; 17; 16:1; 4; 5; 14; 16; 17:1; 24(2); 25(2); 26; 18:10; 15; 19:22; 23; 20:16; 21:3; 5(2); 8(2); 11; 15; 20; 22:20; 24; 23:1; 17(3); 24:1; 15; 16; 29; 33; 36; 67; 25:1; 8; 10; 17; 20; 21(2); 26(2); 27(2); 29; 30; 26:1(2); 7; 8; 28; 34; 27:1; 30; 28:7; 11; 17; 19; 29:2; 12(2); 16(2); 17(2); 25; 31(2); 33; 34; 30:2; 29; 30; 37; 31:1(2); 2; 22(2); 31; 36; 39; 40; 48; 32:7(2); 24; 25; 34:19; 24; 28(2); 29; 35:3; 4; 5; 8(2); 16; 17; 18; 19; 29; 36:12; 22; 24; 32; 35; 39(2); 37:1; 2(3); 3; 15; 23(2); 24(2); 29; 38:1; 2; 5; 6; 7; 12; 13; 14(2); 16; 21(2); 22; 24; 25; 29; 30; 39:1; 2(3); 3; 5; 6; 11; 13; 19; 20; 21; 22; 23(2); 40:2; 3; 9; 10; 11; 15; 16(2); 17; 20; 41:7; 8(2); 10; 12; 13; 24; 32; 37; 46; 48; 49; 53; 54(2); 55; 56; 57; 42:1; 5; 6(2); 27; 35; 43:1; 12(2); 18; 21; 26; 34; 44:3; 12; 14; 45:8; 16; 47:13(2); 14; 18; 28; 48:7; 14(2); 49:7(2); 15(2); 26; 32; 33; 50:9; 11; 15; 26; **Ex** 1:5; 7; 14; 15; 2:2; 11; 12; 21; 3:2; 6; 4:6; 7; 14; 5:13; 19; 6:3; 7:7; 15; 21(2); 22; 8:15; 19; 24; 9:7(2); 11; 24(2); 25; 26; 31(3); 33; 35; 10:13; 15; 22; 11:3; 6; 12:29; 30(3); 34; 39; 40; 13:17; 14:5(2); 20; 15:23; 16:14; 15; 20; 24; 31(2); 17:1; 18:3; 4(2); 11; 19:16; 18; 20:21; 22:13; 24:10; 17; 18; 25:40; 26:30; 27:8; 29:33; 31:17; 32:16; 33:7; 8; 34:28; 34; 35:23; 24; 36:7; 9; 12; 15(2); 21; 37:1; 6; 10; 22; 25(3); 38:1(2); 18(3); 21; 23; 24(2); 25; 29; 39:4; 5(2); 9(2); 10(2); 19; 23; 32; 40:17; 35; 36; 37; 38(2); **Lev** 4:10; 6:2; 3; 4; 27; 8:4; 10; 16; 21; 25; 26; 29; 30; 9:8; 15; 18; 10:16(2); 18; 20; 13:18; 14:6; 48; 15:10; 16:27; 17:15; 19:20; 21:10; 24:10; 11; 25:33; 50; 51; 27:24; **Num** 1:44; 3:16; 21; 27; 33; 35; 6:12; 7:9; 10; 12; 13(2); 17; 19; 23; 25(2); 29; 31; 35; 37(2); 41; 43; 47; 49(2); 53; 55; 59; 61(2); 65; 67(2); 71; 73(2); 77; 79(2); 83; 84(2); 86; 88(2); 89(2); 8:4(2); 9:14; 15(2); 16; 17; 20(2); 21(4); 22; 10:11; 14; 15; 16; 17; 18; 19; 20; 22; 23; 24; 25(2); 26; 27; 34; 11:1; 2; 4; 7; 8; 10(2); 18; 25; 26; 33(3); 12:3; 9; 10; 15(2); 13:20; 22; 24; 14:16; 15:34; 16:15; 31; 42; 47; 48; 50; 17:6; 8; 19:13; 20:1; 2; 13; 29; 21:4; 24; 26; 35; 22:3(2); 4; 22(2); 26; 27; 30(2); 36; 24:10; 20; 25:3; 8; 11; 13; 14(3); 15(3); 18; 26:46; 59; 60; 62; 64; 65; 27:3; 13; 28:6; 31:14; 16; 26; 32; 36(2); 37; 38; 39; 40; 41; 43; 52; 32:1; 10; 13(2); 39; 33:14; 39; 35:23; 25(2); 26; 36:2; **Deut** 1:34; 37; 2:14; 15; 20; 36; 3:3; 4; 8; 11(2); 13; 26; 4:21; 35; 8:2; 15; 9:8; 9; 10; 19(2); 20; 21; 28; 10:6; 11:6; 19:6; 21:15; 22:27; 26:5; 29:27; 32:12; 50; 33:5; 16; 21; 34:7(2); 9; **Josh** 1:5; 17; 2:2; 5; 15; 3:7; 4:10; 5:1; 13; 6:1; 21; 24; 27(2); 7:1; 16; 17; 18; 22; 26; 8:11; 13; 17; 25; 29; 33; 35; 9:5; 10; 24; 10:2(2); 14; 17; 11:10; 11; 19; 20; 22; 12:4; 13:1; 16; 23(2); 25; 29; 30; 33; 14:2; 7(2); 11(2); 15(2); 15:1(2); 2; 5(2); 9(2); 11; 12; 15; 16:5(2); 17:1(3); 2; 7; 9; 10(2); 18:1; 12; 14(2); 15; 17; 19; 20(2); 19:1; 9(2); 10; 18; 25; 33; 41; 21:10; 22:14; 17; 24:26; 33; **Judg** 1:10; 11; 17; 19; 22; 23; 28; 36; 2:14; 15; 18; 19; 20; 3:8; 17; 20; 24; 25; 27; 30; 31; 4:1; 2; 11; 12; 16; 17; 21; 22; 5:8(2); 14; 15; 6:3; 6; 11; 21; 22; 27; 28(5); 30; 34; 35; 38; 40(2); 7:8; 13(2); 15; 8:3(2); 11; 13; 20; 26(2); 28(2); 31; 32; 33; 9:5; 6; 25; 30; 44; 45; 47; 51; 55; 10:2; 5; 7; 9; 16; 11:1(2); 5; 18; 34; 39; 12:5; 7; 10; 12; 15; 13:2(3); 6(2); 9; 16; 21; 14:4; 8; 19; 20; 15:14; 18; 19; 16:2; 4; 9; 16; 20; 22; 27; 29; 17:1(2); 6(2); 7(2); 11(2); 12; 18:1; 7; 20; 28(3); 29(2); 31; 19:1(2); 2; 10; 11; 15; 16; 26(2); 27; 29; 30(2); 20:1; 3; 4; 27; 34(2); 38; 41; 21:25(2); **Ruth** 1:1; 2; 3; 4; 5; 7; 18; 19; 2:1; 3(2); 5; 6; 14; 15; 17; 18; 3:7; 8; 4:3; 7(2); 9(2); 13; **1Sa** 1:1(2); 2; 4; 10; 13; 18; 20; 24; 2:13(2); 17; 22; 26; 3:1(2); 2; 3(2); 7; 19; 20; 4:2; 6; 10(2); 11; 15; 18; 19(2); 21; 5:3; 4(2); 6; 7; 9(2); 11(2); 6:1; 4; 9; 14; 15; 7:2(2); 10; 13; 14; 17(2); 8:1; 2; 9:1(2); 2(3); 5; 9; 10; 24; 10:9; 20; 21(2); 23; 11:6; 11; 12:8; 12; 15; 13:3; 4; 7; 19; 22(2); 14:3; 4(2); 5; 14; 15(2); 18; 19; 20(2); 25; 27; 35; 39; 42; 43; 50(2); 51(2); 52; 15:9(2); 12; 16:12; 23(3); 17:3; 4; 5(2); 7; 12(2); 14; 20; 28; 40; 42; 50; 51; 18:1; 4; 5; 6; 8; 10; 12(3); 14; 15; 19; 28; 29; 30; 19:7; 8; 9; 16; 19; 20; 21; 23; 20:19; 24; 25; 27(2); 30; 33; 34; 37; 41; 21:1; 6(3); 7(2); 12; 22:2(3); 4; 6; 9; 22; 23:7(2); 13(2); 15(2); 24:1(2); 3; 25:2(3); 3(4); 7; 20; 21; 36(2); 37; 39; 44; 26:4; 12; 16; 21; 24; 27:4(2); 7; 28:3; 5; 14; 20(2); 21; 30:3; 6(2); 19; 25; 31:3; 4; 5; **2Sa** 1:1; 2; 10(4); 26; 2:10; 11(2); 16; 17(2); 18; 32; 3:1; 2; 6; 7; 8; 22(2); 23; 26; 27; 35; 37; 4:1; 2(2); 4(3); 5:2; 4; 10; 13; 6:3; 4; 7; 8; 9; 12; 13; 14; 20; 21; 7:9; 19; 8:16(2); 17; 18; 9:2(2); 6; 12; 13; 10:9; 17; 11:1; 2; 4; 7; 26; 27; 12:3; 4(2); 5; 15; 18(2); 19; 21(2); 22; 30(2); 13:1; 2(2); 3(2); 6; 8; 15; 19; 21; 38; 39(2); 14:1; 6; 25(2); 26(2); 27(2); 15:2; 5; 12; 17; 30; 32; 16:1; 5; 16; 23(2); 17:6; 19; 22; 23(2); 25(2); 27; 18:6; 7; 8; 9(2); 14; 29; 33; 19:1; 2(2); 16; 18; 25; 32(2); 39; 20:1; 8; 10; 13; 17; 23(2); 24(2); 25; 26; 21:1; 7; 11; 14; 16; 18(2); 19(2); 20(3); 22:8; 10; 11; 19; 24; 42; 23:1; 2; 8; 9; 10; 11(2); 14(2); 16; 18; 19(2); 23; 24; 24:1; 2; 11; 16; 25(2); **1Kin** 1:1; 4; 6; 15; 23; 51; 2:5; 10; 12; 15(2); 26; 29(2); 34; 41(2); 46; 3:2; 4; 12; 15; 17; 18(3); 21(2); 26; 28; 4:1; 4; 5(2); 6(2); 15; 16; 19(3); 22; 31(2); 5:1; 12; 13; 14; 6:2; 3(2); 6(3); 7(5); 8; 17; 18(3); 20(2); 22; 24; 25; 26(2); 37; 38(2); 7:1; 2; 3; 4; 5; 6(2); 7; 8; 10; 12; 14(3); 16(2); 20; 22(2); 23(2); 24; 25; 26(2); 27; 28; 29; 31(2); 32; 33; 35; 38; 47; 48; 51; 8:9; 17; 18(2); 54; 57; 64(3); 9:1; 25; 10:2(2); 3; 5; 6; 7; 14; 19; 20; 21; 11:4(3); 9(2); 14; 15(2); 20; 21; 25; 26; 27; 28(2); 30; 40; 42; 43; 12:2(2); 15; 18; 20(2); 21; 13:5; 6(2); 9; 17; 24(2); 26; 14:6; 8; 21(2); 28; 30; 31(2); 15:2; 3; 5; 6; 7; 10; 11; 14; 16; 22; 23; 24; 32; 16:6; 9; 18; 28; 17:1; 10; 11; 17(2); 18:2; 3; 4; 7; 13; 26(3); 29(2); 30; 38; 45(2); 46; 19:6; 11(2); 12; 13; 19; 20:12; 16; 29(2); 36; 40(2); 41; 21:1; 11; 15(2); 16; 25; 22:13; 33; 35; 37; 42(2); 43; 47(2); 50; **2Kin** 1:2(2); 7; 8; 2:17; 23; 3:4; 5; 9; 20(2); 26; 27; 4:8(2); 18; 31; 32(2); 36; 38; 41; 5:1(3); 8; 11; 14; 6:5(2); 11; 13; 15; 17; 25(2); 26; 7:5; 7; 10; 15; 16; 8:5; 6; 7(2); 11; 17; 18; 24; 26(2); 27; 29; 9:15; 16; 21; 30; 33; 34; 10:5(2); 12; 15; 21(2); 22; 30; 36; 11:1; 2; 3; 14; 16; 20; 21; 12:1; 2; 6; 9; 10(3); 12; 13; 16(2); 18; 13:2; 3; 11; 13; 14; 19; 21; 23; 14:2(2); 3; 5; 9(3); 12; 16; 20; 21; 24; 25; 26(2); 15:2(2); 3; 5(2); 9; 12; 18; 24; 28; 33(2); 34; 38; 16:2(2); 8; 10; 12; 14; 20; 17:2; 7; 18(2); 23; 25; 18:2(2); 3; 5; 7; 9; 10; 15; 18; 36; 37; 19:2; 8; 37; 20:1; 4; 13(2); 21:1(2); 2; 15; 16; 18; 19(2); 20; 26; 22:1(2); 2; 7(2); 9; 19; 23:2; 11; 15; 22; 23; 25; 26; 31(2); 32; 36(2); 37; 24:8(2); 9; 10; 18(2); 19; 25:2; 3; 4; 13; 16; 17(2); 19; 21; 30; **1Chr** 1:19(3); 39; 43; 44; 45; 46(2); 47; 48; 49; 50(3); 2:3; 17; 19; 21; 24; 26(2); 29; 34; 42; 45(2); 49; 3:10; 4:3; 9; 11; 40; 41; 5:1(2); 2; 6; 7; 20; 22; 6:54; 7:2; 9; 15(2); 16; 24; 25; 40; 8:29; 34; 37; 9:17; 20(2); 21; 27; 31; 35; 40; 10:3; 4; 5; 11:2; 6; 9; 12(2); 13(2); 16(2); 18; 20; 21(2); 23; 25; 12:3; 14; 18; 22; 27; 40; 13:4; 10; 11; 12; 14:2; 8; 15:22(2); 27; 16:39; 17:13; 17; 18:15; 16; 17; 19:10; 17; 20:1; 2; 4; 5(2); 6(3); 21:5; 6; 7; 15; 20; 30; 22:7; 23:1; 3; 8; 11; 13; 16; 28; 24:21; 25; 29; 25:1; 7; 26:1; 10; 20; 24; 28; 31; 27:2; 3; 4(2); 5; 6(2); 7; 8; 9; 10; 11; 12; 13; 14; 15; 16; 24; 25(2); 26; 27(2); 28(2); 29(2); 30(2); 31(2); 32(2); 33(2); 34(2); 29:27; **2Chr** 1:1(2); 3(2); 6; 11; 13; 2:14; 3:3(2); 4(3); 6; 8; 9; 11(2); 12(2); 15(2); 4:3(2); 4; 5; 6; 11; 19; 5:1; 3; 10; 13; 6:7; 8(2); 7:7(2); 8:16(3); 9:1(2); 2; 4; 5; 6; 9; 13; 19; 20; 31; 10:2; 15; 18; 11:1; 12:13(2); 16; 13:2(2); 7; 13; 14; 14:1; 2; 5; 14; 15:4; 5; 6; 8; 9; 15; 17; 19; 16:3; 6; 10(2); 12(2); 14; 17:3; 6; 15; 16; 18; 18:14; 32; 20:25; 26; 29; 30; 31(2); 32; 21:1; 3; 4; 5; 6; 17(2); 20; 22:2(2); 3; 6; 7(2); 8; 9; 10; 11; 12; 23:15; 18; 19; 21; 24:1(2); 2; 4; 11(2); 13; 15(2); 25:1(2); 2; 3; 10(2); 14; 15; 18(3); 22; 26:1; 3(2); 4; 13; 15(2); 16(2); 19(2); 20; 21(3); 27:1(2); 2; 8; 28:1(2); 5; 7; 9(3); 29:1(2); 2; 6; 8; 25; 28; 32; 34; 35; 36; 30:5; 12; 17; 18; 26(2); 27; 31:1; 12(2); 14; 20; 32:2(2); 4; 5; 14; 15; 21; 23; 24; 25(2); 31(2); 33:1; 2; 12; 13(2); 19(2); 21; 22; 34:1; 2; 3; 9; 14; 16; 17; 27; 30; 35:10; 16; 18; 19; 24; 26; 36:2; 5(2); 8; 9(2); 10; 11; 12; 16; **Ezr** 1:6; 2:61; 64; 3:1; 3; 6; 11; 12; 13; 4:7; 14; 15; 20; 23; 5:5; 7; 11; 14(2); 17; 6:1; 2(2); 15(2); 7:6; 8; 28(2); 8:22; 23; 31; 33(3); 34; 35; 10:9; **Neh** 1:1; 11; 2:1; 2; 10; 11; 12; 14(2); 18; 3:16; 25; 4:1; 3; 6; 15; 18; 5:1; 6; 14; 18(3); 6:1; 6; 10; 13; 15; 16; 18; 7:1; 2; 4; 7; 63; 64; 66; 72; 8:1; 3; 5; 17; 18; 10:29; 11:9(2); 11; 14; 17; 22; 23; 24; 12:8; 37; 43; 13:1; 4; 5; 6; 13(2); 26(2); 28; **Est** 1:2; 8; 10; 11; 12; 13; 14; 2:1(2); 5(2); 7; 8(2); 12; 13; 15; 16; 20; 22; 23(3); 3:4; 5; 12(2); 14; 15(2); 4:1; 3; 4; 5(2); 6; 8; 5:2(2); 9; 6:2; 4; 7:6; 7; 8(2); 10; 8:1; 9; 13; 14; 15; 9:1; 4; 11; 14; 22; 32; 10:3; **Job** 1:1(3); 3(2); 5; 6; 13; 16; 17; 18; 2:1; 11; 13; 3:3(2); 25; 26(2); 4:4; 12; 16(2); 8:7; 15:7; 19; 16:12; 17:6; 20:4; 22:16; 23:17; 29:4(2); 5; 13; 14; 15(2); 16; 19; 20(2); 30:2; 25(2); 31:18; 23; 25; 32:1; 2(2); 3; 5(2); 6; 12; 33:27; 42:7; **Ps** 4:1; 7:4; 18:7; 9; 12; 18; 23; 41; 22:9; 10; 30:7; 31:11; 13; 32:4; 33:9; 35:13; 37:36; 38:13; 14; 39:2(2); 3(2); 9; 50:21; 51:5; 53:5; 55:12(2); 13; 18; 21; 63:t, 66:14; 17; 68:8; 9; 11; 14; 69:10; 12; 20; 73:3; 16; 21(2); 22(2); 74:5; 76:8; 77:3(2); 18; 78:8; 21(2); 30; 35; 37; 59; 62; 79:3; 81:4; 87:4; 5; 6; 95:10; 97:8; 105:17; 18; 37; 38; 106:9; 11; 18; 30; 31; 38; 40; 107:12; 114:2; 3; 116:6; 10; 119:67; 158; 122:1; 124:1; 2; 3; 126:2; 139:15(2); 16; 142:t, 3; 4; **Prov** 4:3; 5:14; 8:23(2); 24; 25; 27; 30(2); 23:35; 24:31(2); **Eccl** 1:10; 12; 2:3; 9; 10; 11(2); 15; 24; 3:16(2); 4:1; 5:6; 7:23; 9:14; 15; 12:7; 9; 10(2); **Song** 2:3; 4; 3:4; 5:6; 6:12; 8:10; 11; **Is** 1:21; 6:4; 7:2(2); 9:1; 10:14; 26; 11:16; 14:28; 21:3(2); 14; 22:14; 25; 23:13; 26:16; 28:13; 36:3; 21; 22; 37:2; 8; 38; 38:1; 8; 9; 20; 39:1; 2(3); 41:28(2); 43:10; 12; 13; 47:6; 48:8; 16; 49:21; 50:2(2); 5; 52:14; 53:3; 5(3); 7(2); 8(3); 9; 12; 57:17(2); 59:15; 16(2); 17; 63:3; 5(2); 8; 9; 10; 65:1; 2; 66:7; **Jer** 2:2; 3; 3:21; 4:23; 25; 26; 7:12; 8:16; 11:19; 13:7(2); 20; 14:4; 5; 6; 15:9; 16; 17:16; 18:4; 20:1; 2; 7; 8; 9(2); 14; 22:15; 16(2); 25:1; 26:20; 21; 24; 28:1; 31:11; 15; 18; 19(3); 26; 32; 32:1; 2(2); 8; 9; 11(2); 33:1; 35:4(2); 36:22; 23(3); 37:5; 11; 13(3); 16; 38:6(2); 7; 27; 28(3); 39:2; 15; 40:5; 41:7; 9; 44:6(2); 46:2; 5; 21; 48:13; 27(2); 49:12; 21; 51:5; 59; 52:1(2); 2; 5; 6(2); 7(2); 8; 12; 17; 19(2); 20; 21(3); 22(2); 27; 34; **Lam** 1:1(2); 2:5; 12; 3:10; 14; 4:6; 7; 20; 5:10; **Eze** 1:1; 2; 3; 4; 5; 7; 12; 13(2); 16(2); 20(3); 21; 22; 25(2); 26(3); 28(2); 2:9(2); 10(2); 3:3; 14; 22; 8:3; 4; 14; 9:2; 3(2); 8; 10:1; 4(2); 5; 7(2); 9; 13; 14(2); 17; 19; 21; 22; 11:22; 12:7; 13:10; 15:5(2); 16:3; 4; 8; 13; 14; 15; 19; 36; 45; 49(2); 56; 57; 17:7; 8; 19:4; 5; 7; 8; 10; 11; 12(2); 21:22; 22:10; 23:5; 11; 13; 17(2); 18(2); 40; 42; 43; 24:18; 25:3(2); 26:2; 27:7(2); 12; 16; 18; 20; 28:13(2); 15; 17; 29:18(2); 30:22; 31:3(2); 5; 7(2); 8; 32:15; 25; 33:22(4); 24; 34:4(4); 6; 8; 16(4); 35:10; 15; 36:17; 23; 35; 36; 37:1(2); 7(2); 8; 40:1(2); 2; 3(2); 6(2); 7(2); 9; 12(2); 13; 18; 21; 23; 25; 27; 29; 33; 36; 40; 43; 44(2); 47; 48; 49; 41:1; 2; 6; 7(2); 9(4); 10; 11(3); 12(3); 15; 18(2); 19(2); 22; 42:1(2); 2(2); 3(2); 4; 6; 7(2); 8; 9; 11; 12; 43:2; 3; 44:1; 46:19(2); 21; 23(2); 47:5; 48:35; **Dan** 1:4; 19; 2:1; 3; 12; 14; 19; 26; 31(2); 32; 34; 35(2); 45; 3:1; 19(3); 22; 24; 27; 4:4; 8; 10; 11; 12(2); 19(2); 20; 21; 31; 33(3); 36(2); 5:2; 3; 6; 9(2); 11; 13; 20(2); 21(4); 24(2); 25; 30; 6:2; 3(2); 4(2); 10; 14; 17; 22; 23(3); 7:4(3); 6; 7; 9(2); 10; 11; 14; 15; 19; 20; 22; 8:2(2); 3; 4; 5; 7(3); 8(2); 11(2); 12; 17; 18(2); 26; 27(2); 9:1; 20; 21; 10:1(4); 2; 4; 6; 8(2); 9; 19; 12:1(2); 6; 7; **Hos** 1:10; 2:3; 7; 7:1; 8:6; 9:8; 10:14; 11:1; 4; 12:13; 13:6; **Amos** 1:1; 2:9(2); 4:7; 7:1; 14(3); **Jonah** 1:4(2); 5(2); 11; 13; 17; 2:6; 3:3; 4:1; 2(2); 6; **Mic** 4:7; **Nah** 3:8(3); 9; 10; **Hab** 3:2; 3; 4(2); 8(3); 9; 14; **Zeph** 3:18; 19; **Hag** 2:15; 18; **Zec** 1:15; 3:3; 5:7; 9; 7:7; 14; 8:2(2); 9; 10(2); 10:2; 3; 11:11(2); 13; 13:6; **Mal** 1:2; 13; 2:5(2); 6(2); 3:16; **Mt** 1:16; 18(3); 19; 22(2); 2:1; 3; 9; 15(2); 16(2); 17(2); 18; 19; 22; 23; 3:3; 4; 16; 4:1; 2; 12; 14; 5:1; 21; 27; 6:29; 7:25; 27; 8:1; 3; 5; 13; 14; 16; 17; 23; 24(2); 26; 28; 30; 33; 9:20; 22; 28; 33(2); 36; 10:3; 11:14; 12:3; 4; 9; 10; 13; 17; 22; 40; 13:6; 19; 26; 33; 35; 47; 48; 54; 14:6; 9; 11; 14; 15; 23(2); 24(2); 29; 30; 15:28; 37; 16:20; 17:2(2); 18; 25; 18:11; 24; 27; 31(2); 34(2); 19:8; 20:8; 21:4(2); 10(2); 23(2); 25; 33; 22:7; 10; 12; 31; 35; 46; 24:21; 25:6; 10; 25; 35(3); 36(2); 42(2); 43; 26:3; 6; 20; 56; 71(2); 27:1; 3; 8; 9(3); 12; 15; 19; 24; 35; 45; 51; 54; 56; 57(2); 61; 63; 28:2; 3; 5; **Mk** 1:6; 9; 13(2); 14; 23; 33; 42; 45; 2:1(2); 2; 3; 4; 25; 27; 3:1; 5; 4:1(2); 6(2); 10; 15; 22; 35; 36; 37; 38; 39; 5:2; 5; 11; 14(2); 15; 16; 18; 21(2); 26; 29(2); 33; 36; 39; 40; 42; 6:2; 14(2); 20; 21; 26; 34; 35; 47(2); 48; 52; 55; 7:17; 26; 30; 32; 35; 8:8; 25; 9:2; 7; 26; 28; 33; 10:1; 14; 17; 22; 47; 11:11; 12; 13; 18; 19; 27; 30; 32; 12:11; 13:19; 14:1; 4; 32; 45; 49; 66; 15:7; 25; 26; 28(2); 33(2); 38; 39; 40; 41; 42(2); 46; 47; 16:1; 4(2); 6; 9; 11; 14; 19; **Lk** 1:5(3); 7; 9; 12; 26; 27(2); 29; 36; 41; 64; 66; 67; 80; 2:2(2); 4; 6; 7; 13; 17; 20; 21(3); 25(4); 26; 36(2); 37; 40; 42; 51; 3:21; 23(2); 24(5); 25(5); 26(5); 27(5); 28(5); 29(5); 30(5); 31(5); 32(5); 33(5); 34(5); 35(5); 36(5); 37(5); 38(4); 4:1; 16; 17(2); 25(2); 26(2); 27; 29; 32; 33; 38; 40; 41; 42; 5:3; 9; 10; 12; 17(2); 18; 29; 36; 6:3; 6(2); 10; 13; 16; 48; 49; 7:2(2); 4; 6; 12(3); 15; 37; 41; 8:5; 6; 20; 24; 29(2); 32; 34; 35; 36(2); 40; 41; 47(2); 53; 56; 9:7(4); 8; 17; 18; 29(2); 36(2); 42; 45; 51; 53; 10:32; 33; 36; 40; 11:1; 14(3); 30; 50; 12:27; 13:10; 11(2); 13; 21; 14:2; 30; 15:6; 20; 24(2); 25; 28; 30; 32(3); 16:1(2); 19(2); 20(2); 22(2); 17:10; 15; 16; 20; 26; 28; 18:2; 3; 23(2); 24; 34; 35; 40; 19:2(3); 3(2); 4; 7; 10; 11; 15; 22; 29; 37; 41; 20:4; 6; 7; 21:5; 37; 22:14; 22; 23; 24; 37; 39; 40; 41; 44; 45; 47; 53; 56; 59; 66; 23:7; 8(2); 19; 25; 38; 44(2); 45(2); 47(2); 50(2); 51; 53(2); 54; 55; 24:6; 10; 12; 13; 18; 19; 23; 35; 44; 51; **Jn** 1:1(3); 2; 3(2); 4(2); 6(2); 8(2); 9; 10(2); 14; 15(2); 17; 28; 30; 39; 40; 44; 2:1(2); 2; 9(2); 13; 17; 20; 22; 23; 25; 3:1; 23(2); 24; 26; 4:6(2); 45; 46(2); 47(2); 51; 53; 54; 5:1; 4; 5; 9(2); 10; 13(2); 15; 18; 35; 6:4; 10; 16; 17(2); 21; 22; 24; 62; 71; 7:2; 12; 30; 39(2); 42; 43; 8:4; 9; 20; 44; 56; 58; 9:1; 2; 8; 13; 14; 16; 19; 20; 22; 24; 25; 32(2); 10:19; 22(2); 11:1; 2(2);

6(2); 15; 18; 20; 30(2); 32(2); 33; 38; 39; 41; 44(2); 55; 12:1; 2; 3; 5; 6(2); 9; 12; 16; 17; 21; 13:1; 3; 5; 12; 21; 23; 30; 31; 16:4; 17:5; 12; 18:1; 10; 13(2); 14(2); 15; 16; 18; 28; 37; 40; 19:8; 14; 19; 20(3); 23; 29; 31(2); 32; 33; 41(3); 42; 20:1; 7; 14; 24; 21:4(2); 7(2); 11; 12; 14; 17; **Acts** 1:2; 9; 16; 17; 19; 22; 23; 26; 2:1; 6; 16; 24; 26; 31; 3:2; 10; 11; 13; 20; 4:3; 4; 11; 14; 21; 22(2); 31; 32; 33; 34; 35; 36; 5:4(3); 7(2); 36; 6:1; 7:2; 4; 9; 12; 13(2); 20(2); 21; 22(2); 23; 24; 29; 38; 58; 8:1(3); 8; 9(2); 13; 16; 18; 28; 32(2); 33; 40; 9:9; 10; 18; 19(2); 24; 26(2); 28; 33; 36(2); 37; 38(2); 39(2); 42; 10:1; 4; 7; 16(2); 18; 22; 25; 29; 30; 37; 38; 42; 45; 11:2; 5; 10; 11; 17; 21; 22; 23; 24(2); 12:5(2); 6; 9(2); 11; 12; 15; 18(3); 20(2); 23; 25; 13:1(2); 6; 7; 12; 29; 31; 32; 36; 43; 46; 49; 14:4; 5; 12; 13; 15:5; 37; 39; 16:1(3); 2; 3; 13; 15; 19; 26; 33; 35; 17:1; 2; 13; 16; 34; 18:3; 5(2); 12; 14; 25; 27(2); 28; 19:1; 16; 17(2); 29; 32; 34; 20:1; 3; 9(2); 11; 20; 21:3; 8; 11; 30; 31; 33; 35(2); 37; 40; 22:3; 6; 17(2); 20(2); 28; 29(2); 30; 23:5; 7; 12; 27(2); 30; 31; 34(2); 24:2; 24; 25:1; 7; 15; 19; 23(3); 26:4; 19; 26; 27:1; 8; 9(3); 12; 15; 20; 25; 27; 33; 39; 41; 42; 28:1; 6; 7; 9; 11; 16; 17; 18; 19; **Rom** 1:3; 13; 21; 27; 4:3; 9; 10(2); 13; 18; 19; 20; 21; 22; 23(2); 25(2); 5:13; 14; 16(2); 6:4; 17; 7:8; 9; 10; 13; 8:3; 20; 9:12; 25; 26; 10:20(2); 15:8; 20; 21; 16:25; **1Cor** 1:6; 13; 2:3; 4; 7:20; 10:4; 5; 11:9; 23; 13:11; 15:4; 5; 6; 7; 8; 10(3); 45(2); 46; 16:12; 17; S:1; **2Cor** 1:15; 17; 18; 19(3); 2:6; 12; 3:7(2); 10; 11; 5:19; 7:7; 13; 8:9; 11; 19; 9:2; 11:5; 9(3); 25(2); 33; 12:4; 7; 13; 13:4; S:1; **Gal** 1:11; 12; 22; 2:3(2); 7(2); 8; 9; 10; 11(2); 13; 3:6; 17(2); 19(3); 24; 4:4; 14; 23(3); 28; 29(2); **Eph** 3:5; 7; **Phil** 2:5; 7; 26; 27; 30; S:1; **Col** 1:23; 2:14(2); **1Th** 2:1; 3; S:1; **2Th** 1:10; 2:5; S:1; **1Ti** 1:11; 13; 14; 2:13; 14(2); 3:16; 4:14; S:1; **2Ti** 1:9; 14; 16; 17; 2:8; 3:9; 4:17; S:1(2); **Titus** 1; **Philem** 1:11; **Heb** 2:2; 3; 9; 3:2(2); 3; 5; 10; 17(2); 4:2; 6; 15; 5:4; 7(2); 6:18; 7:4; 10; 11; 20; 22; 28; 8:5(2); 6; 9:2(2); 4; 8(2); 9; 18; 23; 28; 10:29; 11:4; 5(2); 8; 11(2); 17; 18; 19; 21; 23(3); 24; 38; 12:2; 17; 20; 21; **Jas** 1:24; 2:21; 22; 23(3); 25; 5:17; **1Pet** 1:11; 12; 20(2); 2:22; 23; 3:20; 4:6; **2Pet** 1:9; 2:16; 22; 3:6; **1Jn** 1:1; 2(3); 3:5; 8; 12; 4:9; **Jude** 3(2); **Rev** 1:4; 8; 9; 10; 16; 18; 2:8; 13(2); 4:1(2); 2(2); 3(2); 6; 7(2); 8; 5:3; 4; 11; 12; 6:2; 4(3); 8(2); 11; 12; 7:2; 8:1; 3(2); 7(2); 8; 12(2); 9:1; 3; 4; 5(2); 9; 10; 18; 10:1(2); 4; 10(2); 11:1; 8; 13; 19(2); 12:4(2); 5(2); 7; 8; 9(2); 13; 17; 13:2; 3; 5(2); 7(2); 12; 14:5; 16; 20; 15:5; 8(2); 16:8; 10; 12; 18(2); 19; 21; 17:4; 5; 8(2); 11; 18:1; 16; 24; 19:8; 11; 13; 20; 20:4; 10; 11; 12; 15(2); 21:1; 11; 18(2); 19; 21(2); 22:2

WAY

734, 776, 935, 1870, 2008, 2088, 3212, 3541, 4499, 5265, 5410, 7125, 7971, 8582, *1545, 1624, 1722, 3112, 3319, 3598, 3938, 4105, 4206, 4311, 5158*

Gen 3:24(2); 6:12; 12:19; 14:11; 16:7; 18:16; 19; 33; 21:16; 24:27; 40; 42; 48; 56; 61; 62; 25:34; 28:20; 32:1; 33:16; 35:3; 16; 19; 38:14; 16; 21; 42:25; 38; 45:21; 23; 24; 48:7(3); 49:17; **Ex** 2:12(2); 4:24; 5:20; 13:17; 18; 21; 18:8; 20; 27; 23:20; 32:8; 33:3; 13; **Num** 13:17; 14:25; 20:17; 19; 21:1; 4(2); 22; 33; 22:22; 23(3); 26; 31; 32; 34; 24:25; **Deut** 1:2; 19; 22; 31; 33(2); 40; 2:1; 8(2); 27; 3:1; 6:7; 8:2; 9:12; 16; 11:19; 28; 30; 13:5; 14:24; 17:16; 19:3; 6; 22:4; 6; 23:4; 24:9; 25:17; 18; 27:18; 28:7; 25; 68; 31:29; **Josh** 1:8; 2:7; 16; 22; 3:4(2); 5:4; 5; 7; 8:15; 20(2); 10:10; 12:3; 23:14; 24:17; **Judg** 2:17; 19; 22; 5:10; 8:11; 9:25; 18:5; 6; 22; 26; 19:5; 9; 14; 27; 20:42; **Ruth** 1:7; 12; **1Sa** 1:18; 6:9; 12(2); 9:6; 8; 12:23; 13:17; 18(2); 15:2; 20; 17:52; 20:22; 24:3; 7; 25:12; 26:3; 25; 28:22; 30:2; **2Sa** 2:24; 13:30; 34; 15:2; 23; 16:13; 18:23; 19:36; 22:31; 33; **1Kin** 1:49; 2:2; 4; 8:25; 32; 36; 11:29; 13:9; 10(2); 12(2); 17; 24(2); 25; 26; 28; 33; 15:26; 34; 16:2; 19; 26; 18:6(2); 7; 19:15; 20:38; 22:24; 52(3); **2Kin** 2:23; 3:8(2); 20; 4:29; 5:19; 6:19; 7:15; 8:18; 27; 9:27; 10:12; 11:16; 19; 16:3; 19:28; 33; 21:21; 22; 22:2; 25:4(2); **2Chr** 6:16; 23; 27; 34; 11:17; 18:23; 20:32; 21:6; 13; **Ezr** 8:21; 22; 31; **Neh** 8:10; 12; 9:12; 19(2); **Est** 4:17; **Job** 3:23; 6:18; 8:19; 12:24; 16:22; 17:9; 18:10; 19:8; 12; 21:29; 31; 22:15; 23:10; 11; 24:4; 18; 24; 28:23; 26; 29:25; 31:7; 36:23; 38:19; 24; 25; **Ps** 1:1; 6(2); 2:12; 5:8; 18:30; 32; 25:8; 9; 12; 27:11; 32:8; 35:3; 6; 36:4; 37:5; 7; 23; 34; 44:18; 49:13; 67:2; 77:13; 19; 78:50; 80:12; 85:13; 86:11; 89:41; 101:2; 6; 102:23; 107:4; 7; 40; 110:7; 119:1; 9; 14; 27; 29; 30; 32; 33; 37; 101; 104; 128; 139:24(2); 142:3; 143:8; 146:9; **Prov** 1:15; 31; 2:8; 12; 20; 3:23; 4:11; 14; 19; 5:8; 6:23; 7:8; 27; 8:2; 13; 20; 22; 9:6; 10:17; 29; 11:5; 20; 12:15; 26; 28; 13:6; 15; 14:8; 12; 15:9; 10; 19(2); 24; 16:9; 17; 25; 29; 31; 19:3; 20:14; 24; 21:2; 8; 16; 29; 22:5; 6; 23:19; 26:13; 28:10; 29:27; 30:19(4); 20; **Eccl** 9:7; 10:3; 11:5; 12:5; **Song** 1:8; **Is** 3:12; 8:11; 9:1; 15:5; 26:7; 8; 28:7(2); 30:11; 21; 35:8(2); 37:29; 34; 40:3; 14; 27; 41:3; 42:16; 43:16; 19; 48:15; 17; 49:11; 51:10; 53:6; 55:7; 56:11; 57:10; 14(2); 17; 59:8; 62:10; 65:2; **Jer** 2:17; 18(2); 23; 33; 36; 3:21; 4:7; 18; 5:4; 5; 6:16; 25; 27; 10:2; 23; 12:1; 18:11; 15; 21:8(2); 23:12; 22; 25:5; 35; 26:3; 28:11; 31:9; 21; 32:39; 35:15; 36:3; 7; 39:4(2); 42:3; 48:19; 50:5; 52:7(2); **Eze** 3:18; 19; 7:27; 8:5(2); 9:2; 10; 11:21; 13:22; 14:22; 16:25; 27; 31; 43; 18:25(2); 29; 21:16; 19; 20; 21; 22:31; 23:13; 31; 33:8; 9(2); 11; 17(2); 20; 36:17(2); 19; 42:1; 4; 11; 12(2); 43:2; 4; 44:1; 3(2); 4; 46:2; 8(2); 9(5); 47:2(3); 15; 48:1; **Dan** 12:9; 13; **Hos** 2:6; 6:9; 10:13; 13:7; **Amos** 2:7; **Jonah** 3:8; 10; **Nah** 1:3; 2:1; **Zec** 10:2; **Mal** 2:8; 3:1; **Mt** 2:12; 3:3; 4:15; 5:24; 25; 7:13; 14; 8:4; 13; 28; 30; 10:5; 11:10; 13:4; 19; 25; 15:32; 20:4; 14; 17; 30; 21:8(2); 19; 32; 22:16; 22; 27:65; **Mk** 1:2; 3; 44; 2:11; 4:4; 15; 7:29; 8:3; 27; 9:33; 34; 10:17; 21; 32; 52(2); 11:2; 4; 8(2); 12:12; 14; 16:7; **Lk** 1:79; 3:4; 4:30; 5:19; 7:22; 27; 8:5; 12; 39; 9:57; 10:4; 31; 12:58; 14:32; 15:20; 17:19; 18:35; 19:4; 32; 36; 20:21; 22:4; 24:32; 35; **Jn** 1:23; 4:28; 50(2); 8:21; 9:7; 10:1; 11:28; 14:4; 5; 6; 16:5; 18:8; **Acts** 8:26; 36; 39; 9:2; 15; 17(2); 27; 15:3; 16:17; 18:25; 26; 19:9; 23; 21:5(2); 22:4; 24:14; 22; 25; 25:3; 26:13; **Rom** 3:2; 12; 17; 14:13; 15:24; **1Cor** 10:13; 12:31; 16:7; **2Cor** 1:16; **Phil** 1:18; **Col** 2:14; **1Th** 3:11; **2Th** 2:7; **Heb** 5:2; 9:8; 10:20; 12:13; **Jas** 1:24; 2:25; 5:20; **2Pet** 2:2; 15(2); 21; 3:1; **Jude** 11; **Rev** 16:12

WAYS

734, 1870, 1979, 4546, 4570, 7339, *296, 684, 3598, 4197*

Gen 19:2; **Lev** 20:4; 26:22; **Num** 30:15; **Deut** 5:33; 8:6; 10:12; 11:22; 19:9; 26:17; 28:7; 9; 25; 29; 30:16; 32:4; **Josh** 22:5; **1Sa** 8:3; 5; 18:14; **2Sa** 22:22; **1Kin** 2:3; 3:14; 8:39; 58; 11:33; 38; 22:43; **2Kin** 17:13; **2Chr** 6:30; 31; 7:14; 13:22; 17:3; 6; 21:12(2); 22:3; 27:6; 7; 28:2; 26; 32:13; 34:2; **Job** 4:6; 13:15; 21:14; 22:3; 28; 24:13; 23; 26:14; 30:12; 31:4; 34:11; 21; 27; 40:19; **Ps** 10:5; 18:21; 25:4; 39:1; 51:13; 81:13; 84:5; 91:11; 95:10; 103:7; 119:3; 5; 15; 26; 59; 168; 125:5; 128:1; 138:5; 139:3; 145:17; **Prov** 1:19; 2:13; 15; 3:6; 17(2); 31; 4:26; 5:6; 21; 6:6; 7:25; 8:32; 9:15; 10:9; 14:2; 12; 14; 16:2; 7; 25; 17:23; 19:16; 22:25; 23:26; 28:6; 18; 31:3; 27; **Eccl** 11:9; **Song** 3:2; **Is** 2:3; 42:24; 45:13; 49:9; 55:8(2); 9(2); 57:18; 58:2; 13; 63:17; 64:5; 66:3; **Jer** 2:23; 33; 3:2; 13; 6:16; 7:3; 5; 23; 12:16; 15:7; 16:17; 17:10; 18:11; 15; 23:12; 26:13; 32:19(2); **Lam** 1:4; 3:9; 11; 40; **Eze** 7:3; 4; 8; 9; 14:23; 16:47(2); 61; 18:23; 25; 29(2); 30; 20:43; 44; 21:19; 21; 24:14; 28:15; 33:11; 20; 36:31; 32; **Dan** 4:37; 5:23; **Hos** 4:9; 9:8; 12:2; 14:9; **Joel** 2:7; **Mic** 4:2; **Nah** 2:4; **Hab** 3:6; **Hag** 1:5; 7; **Zec** 1:4; 6; 3:7; **Mal** 2:9; **Mt** 8:33; 22:5; **Mk** 11:4; **Lk** 1:76; 3:5; 10:3; 10; **Jn** 11:46; **Acts** 2:28; 13:10; 14:16; **Rom** 3:16; 11:33; **1Cor** 4:17; **Heb** 3:10; **Jas** 1:8; 11; **2Pet** 2:2; **Rev** 15:3; 16:1

WE

587, *2249*

Gen 3:2; 11:4; 13:8; 19:2; 5; 9; 13; 32(2); 34; 20:13; 24:25; 50; 57; 26:16; 22; 28(2); 29(2); 32; 29:4; 5; 8(2); 27; 31:15; 49; 32:6; 34:14; 15(2); 16(4); 17(2); 37:7; 20(2); 26; 32; 38:23; 40:8; 41:11(2); 12; 38; 42:2; 11(2); 21(3); 31(3); 32; 43:4; 5; 7(2); 8(3); 10(2); 18; 20; 21(3); 22(2); 44:8(3); 9; 16(5); 20(2); 22; 24(2); 26(4); 46:34; 47:3; 4(2); 15; 18; 19(4); 25; 50:15; 17; 18; **Ex** 1:9; 3:18(2); 5:3; 8:26(2); 27; 10:9(3); 25; 26(4); 12:33; 14:5(2); 12(3); 15:24; 16:3(3); 7; 8; 17:2; 19:8; 20:19(2); 24:3; 7; 14; 32:1; 23; 33:16; **Lev** 25:20(2); **Num** 9:7(3); 10:29(2); 31; 32; 11:5(2); 13; 20; 12:11(2); 13:27; 28; 30; 31(2); 32(2); 33(3); 14:2(2); 7; 40(2); 16:12; 14; 17:12(3); 13; 20:3; 4; 10; 15; 16(2); 17(5); 19; 21:7(2); 22(4); 30(2); 22:6; 31:50; 32:5; 16; 17(2); 18; 19; 31; 32; **Deut** 1:19(3); 22(3); 28(3); 41(2); 2:1(2); 8(2); 13; 14(2); 33; 34(2); 35(2); 3:1; 3; 4(2); 6(2); 7; 8; 12; 29; 4:7; 5:24(2); 25(3); 26; 27; 6:21; 25; 12:8; 18:21; 26:7; 29:7; 8; 16(2); 29; 30:12; 13; **Josh** 1:16(2); 17(2); 2:10; 11; 14; 17; 18; 19; 20; 4:23; 5:1; 6:17; 7:7; 8:5; 6(2); 9:6; 7; 8; 9; 11; 12(2); 13; 19(2); 20(3); 22; 24; 25; 10:4; 22:17; 23; 24; 26; 27; 28(2); 29; 31; 24:15; 16; 17(2); 18; 21; 22; 24(2); **Judg** 1:3; 24(2); 8:6; 15; 25; 9:28(2); 38; 10:10(2); 15(2); 11:6; 8; 10; 19; 24; 12:1; 13:8; 12(2); 15; 17; 22(2); 14:13; 15(2); 15:10; 12(2); 13(2); 16:2; 5(3); 18:5(3); 9(2); 19:12(2); 18; 22; 20:8(2); 9(2); 10; 13; 21:7(3); 16; 18; 22(2); **Ruth** 1:10; 4:11; **1Sa** 5:8; 6:2(2); 4; 9; 7:6; 8:19; 20; 9:6; 7(3); 10:14(2); 11:1; 3(2); 10; 12; 12:10(3); 19(2); 14:8(2); 9(2); 10; 12; 15:15; 16:11; 17:9; 10; 20:42; 23:3(2); 25:7; 8; 15(4); 16; 30:14(2); 22(2); **2Sa** 5:1; 7:22; 11:23; 12:18(2); 13:25; 14:7(2); 14; 15:14; 16:20; 17:6; 12(2); 13; 18:3; 19:6; 10; 42; 43(2); 20:1(2); 21:4; 5; 6; **1Kin** 3:18(2); 8:47(2); 12:4; 9; 16(2); 17:12; 18:5(2); 20:23(2); 25(2); 31; 22:3; 7; 8; 15(2); **2Kin** 2:16; 3:8; 11; 6:1; 2(2); 15; 28(2); 29(2); 7:3(2); 4(7); 9(4); 10; 12(2); 10:4; 5(2); 13(2); 18:22; 26; **1Chr** 11:1; 12:18; 13:3; 15:13; 16:35; 17:20; 29:13; 14(2); 15; 16; **2Chr** 2:16(2); 6:37(2); 10:4; 9; 16(2); 13:10; 11; 14:7(2); 11(2); 18:3; 5; 6; 7; 14; 20:9; 12(2); 25:9; 28:13; 29:18; 19; 31:10; **Ezr** 4:2(2); 3; 14(2); 16; 5:4; 8; 9; 10(2); 11; 7:24; 8:15; 21; 22; 23; 31; 32; 9:7(2); 9; 10(2); 14; 15(3); 10:2; 4; 12; 13(2); **Neh** 1:6; 7; 2:17(2); 20; 4:1; 4; 6; 9; 10; 11; 15; 19; 21; 5:2(3); 3(2); 4; 5; 8; 12(2); 16; 9:33; 36(2); 37; 38; 10:30; 31(2); 32; 34; 37; 39; 13:27; **Est** 1:15; 7:4(2); **Job** 2:10(2); 4:2; 5:27; 8:9; 9:32; 15:9; 18:2; 3; 19:28; 21:14; 15(3); 28:22; 31:31(2); 32:13; 36:26; 37:5; 19(2); 23; 38:35; **Ps** 12:4; 20:5(2); 7; 8; 9; 21:13; 33:21; 22; 35:25(2); 36:9; 44:1; 5(2); 8; 17(2); 20; 22(2); 46:2; 48:8(2); 9; 55:14; 60:12; 65:4; 66:6; 12; 74:9; 75:1(2); 78:3; 4; 79:4; 8; 13(2); 80:3; 7; 14; 18(2); 19; 90:7(2); 9; 10; 12; 14; 15; 95:7; 100:3(2); 103:14; 106:6(3); 108:13; 115:18; 118:24; 26; 123:3; 124:7; 126:1; 3; 129:8; 132:6(2); 7(2); 137:1(3); 2; 4; **Prov** 1:13(2); 24:12; **Song** 1:4(3); 11; 6:1; 13; 8:8(2); 9(2); **Is** 1:9(2); 2:3; 4:1; 5:19(2); 9:10(2); 14:10; 16:6; 20:6(2); 22:13; 24:16; 25:9(3); 26:1; 8; 13; 17; 18(4); 28:15(4); 30:16(2); 33:2; 36:7; 11; 38:20; 41:22; 23(2); 26(2); 42:24; 46:5; 51:23; 53:2(2); 3(2); 4; 5; 6(2); 56:12; 58:3(2); 59:9(2); 10(5); 11(2); 12; 63:19; 64:3; 5(2); 6(2); 8(2); 9(2); **Jer** 2:31(2); 3:22; 25(3); 4:13; 5:12; 6:16; 17; 24; 7:10; 8:8; 14(2); 15; 20; 9:19(3); 13:12; 14:7; 9; 19; 20(2); 22; 15:2; 16:10; 18:12(2); 20:10(3); 26:19; 30:5; 35:6; 8(2); 9; 10; 11(2); 36:16; 38:4; 25; 41:8; 42:2(2); 3(2); 5; 6(3); 13; 14(3); 20; 44:16; 17(4); 18(2); 19(2); 25(2); 48:14; 29; 50:7; 51:9; 51(2); **Lam** 2:16(4); 3:22; 42; 4:17; 18; 20(2); 5:3; 4; 5; 6; 7; 9; 16; 21; **Eze** 11:3; 20:32; 21:10; 33:10(2); 24; 35:10; 37:11; **Dan** 2:4; 7; 23; 36; 3:16; 17; 18; 24; 6:5(2); 9:5; 6; 8; 9; 10; 11; 13(2); 14; 15(2); 18; **Hos** 6:2; 3(2); 8:2; 10:3(2); 14:2; 3(2); **Amos** 6:10; 13; 8:5(2); 6; **Obad** 1; **Jonah** 1:6; 7; 8; 11; 14(2); 3:9; **Mic** 2:4; 4:2; 5; 5:5; **Hab** 1:12; **Zec** 1:11; 8:23(2); **Mal** 1:4(2); 6; 7; 2:10(2); 17; 3:7; 8; 13; 14(2); 15; **Mt** 2:2; 3:9; 6:12; 31(3); 7:22; 8:25; 29; 9:14; 11:3; 17(2); 12:38; 13:28; 14:17; 15:33; 16:7; 17:19; 27; 19:27(2); 20:18; 22; 21:25; 26(2); 27; 22:16; 23:30(2); 25:37; 38; 39; 44; 26:17; 65; 27:42; 63; 28:13; 14; **Mk** 1:24; 2:12; 4:30(2); 38; 5:9; 12; 6:37; 8:16; 9:28; 38(2); 10:28; 33; 35(2); 37; 39; 11:31; 32; 33; 12:14; 15(2); 14:12; 58; 63; 15:32; **Lk** 1:71; 74; 3:8; 10; 12; 14; 4:23; 34; 5:5; 26; 7:19; 20; 32(2); 8:24; 9:12; 13(2); 49(2); 54; 10:11; 11:4; 13:26; 15:32; 17:10(2); 18:28; 31; 19:14; 20:5; 6; 21; 22:8; 9; 49; 71(2); 23:2; 41(2); 24:21; **Jn** 1:14; 16; 22; 41; 45; 3:2; 11(3); 4:22(2); 42(2); 6:5; 28(2); 30; 42; 68; 69; 7:27; 35; 8:33; 41(2); 48; 52; 9:20; 21(2); 24; 28; 29(2); 31; 40; 41; 10:33; 11:16; 47; 48; 12:21; 34; 13:29; 14:5(2); 23; 16:18; 30(2); 17:11; 22; 18:30; 19:7; 15; 20:2; 25; 21:3; 24; **Acts** 2:8(2); 11; 32; 37; 3:12; 15; 4:9; 12; 16(2); 20(2); 5:23(3); 28; 29; 32; 6:2; 3; 4; 11; 14; 7:40; 10:33; 39; 47; 11:12; 13:32; 46; 14:15; 22; 15:10; 11(2); 19; 20; 24(2); 27; 36; 16:10; 11; 12; 13(2); 16; 28; 17:19; 20; 28(2); 29(2); 32; 19:2; 13; 25; 40(2); 20:6(2); 13; 14; 15(3); 21:1(2); 2; 3(2); 4; 5(4); 6(2); 7(2); 8(2); 10; 12(2); 14; 15; 16; 17; 23(2); 25; 23:9; 14(3); 15; 24:2; 3; 5; 6; 8; 26:14; 27:1; 2; 3; 4(2); 5(2); 7(2); 15; 16; 18; 19; 20; 26; 27; 29; 37; 28:10; 11; 12; 13(2); 14(2); 16; 21; 22(2); **Rom** 1:5; 2:2; 3:5; 8(2); 9(2); 19; 28; 31(2); 4:1; 9; 24; 5:1; 2(2); 3; 6; 8; 9; 10(3); 11(2); 6:1(2); 2; 4(2); 5(2); 6; 8(3); 15(2); 7:4; 5; 6(3); 7; 14; 8:12; 15; 16; 17(2); 22; 23; 24; 25(3); 26(3); 28; 31; 36(2); 37; 9:14; 29; 30; 10:8; 12:4; 5; 13:11; 14:8(6); 10; 15:1; 4; **1Cor** 1:23; 2:6; 7; 12(2); 13; 16; 3:9; 4:8; 9; 10(3); 11; 12(2); 13(2); 6:3; 8:1(2); 4; 6(2); 8(4); 9:4; 5; 6; 11(2); 12(3); 25; 10:6; 16(2); 17(2); 22(2); 11:16; 31(2); 32(3); 12:13(3); 23(2); 13:9(2); 12; 15:11; 15(2); 19(2); 30; 32; 49(2); 51(2); 52; **2Cor** 1:4(2); 6(3); 8(3); 9(2); 10; 12; 13; 14; 24; 2:11; 15; 16; 17(2); 3:1(2); 4; 5; 12(2); 18; 4:1(3); 5; 7; 8(2); 11; 13(2); 16; 18; 5:1(2); 2; 3; 4(2); 6(3); 7; 8; 9(2); 10; 11(2); 12; 13(2); 14; 16(3); 20(2); 21; 6:1; 9; 7:2(3); 5(2); 13(2); 14; 8:1; 4; 5; 6; 18; 22(2); 9:4(2); 10:2; 3(2); 7; 11(4); 12; 13; 14(3); 15; 11:4; 6; 12; 21; 12:18(2); 19(3); 13:4(2); 6; 7(2); 8; 9(3); **Gal** 1:8(2); 9; 2:4; 5; 9; 10; 15; 16(2); 17(2); 3:14; 23; 24; 25; 4:3(2); 5; 28; 31; 5:5; 25; 6:9(2); 10; **Eph** 1:4; 7; 11; 12; 2:3; 5; 10(2); 18; 3:12; 20; 4:13; 14; 25; 5:30; 6:12; **Phil** 3:3; 16; 20; **Col** 1:3; 4; 9(2); 14; 28(2); **1Th** 1:2; 5; 7; 8; 9; 2:2(2); 4(2); 5; 6(2); 7; 8; 9(2); 10; 11; 13; 17; 18; 3:1(2); 3; 4(3); 6; 7; 8; 9(2); 10; 12; 4:1; 2; 6; 10; 11; 14; 15(2); 17(2); 5:5; 10(2); 12; 14; **2Th** 1:3; 4; 11; 2:1; 13; 3:2; 4(2); 6; 7; 8(2); 9; 10(2); 11; 12; **1Ti** 1:8; 2:2; 4:10(2); 6:7(2); **2Ti** 2:11(2); 12(3); 13; **Titus** 2:12; 3:3; 5; 7; **Philem** 1:7; **Heb** 2:1(3); 3(2); 5; 8; 9; 3:6(2); 14(2); 19; 4:3; 13; 14; 15(2); 16; 5:11; 6:3; 9(2); 11; 18; 19; 7:19; 8:1(2); 9:5; 10:10; 26(2); 30; 39; 11:3; 12:1; 9(3); 10; 25(2); 28(2); 13:6; 10; 14(2); 18(2); **Jas** 1:18; 3:1; 2; 3(2); 9(2); 4:13; 15; 5:11; 17; **1Pet** 2:24; 4:3; **2Pet** 1:16(2); 18(2); 19; 3:13; **1Jn** 1:1(3); 2; 3(2); 4; 5; 6(3); 7(2); 8(3); 9; 10(3); 2:1; 3(3); 5(2); 18; 28; 3:1; 2(5); 11; 14(3); 16(2); 19(2); 21; 22(3); 23; 24; 4:6(2); 9; 10; 11; 12; 13(2); 14; 16; 17(2); 19; 21; 5:2(3); 3; 9; 14(2); 15(5); 18; 19(2); 20(3); **2Jn** 4; 5(2); 6; 8(3); **3Jn** 8(2); 12; 14; **Rev** 5:10; 7:3; 11:17

WENT

236, 935, 980, 1718, 1961, 1980, 3212, 3318, 3381, 5066, 5075, 5265, 5375, 5437, 5493, 5674, 5927, 5954, 6743, 6805, 6923, 7121, 7126, 7272, 7311, 7725, 7751, 8582, 305, 402, 424, 549, 565, 589, 1279, 1330, 1353, 1525, 1531, 1607, 1684, 1821, 1831, 1910, 2021, 2064, 2212, 2597, 2718, 3596, 3598, 3854, 3899, 3987, 4013, 4105, 4160, 4198, 4254, 4281, 4334, 4344, 4848, 4897, 4905, 5217, 5221, 5298

Gen 2:6; 10; 4:16; 7:7; 9; 15; 16(2); 18; 8:7; 18; 19; 9:18; 23; 10:11; 11:31; 12:4; 5; 10; 13:1; 3; 5; 14:8; 11; 17; 24; 15:17; 16:4; 17:22; 18:16; 22; 33; 19:6; 14; 28; 30; 33; 21:16; 19; 22:3; 6; 8; 13; 19; 23:10; 18; 24:10; 16; 45; 61; 63; 25:22; 34; 26:1; 13; 23; 26; 27:5; 14; 22; 28:5; 9; 10(2); 29:1; 10; 23; 30; 30:4; 14; 16; 31:19; 33(2); 32:1; 21; 34:1; 6; 24(2); 26; 35:3; 13; 22; 36:6; 37:12; 17; 38:1; 2; 9; 11; 12; 19; 39:11; 41:45; 46(2); 42:3; 43:15; 31; 44:28; 45:25; 46:29; 47:10; 49:4; 50:7(2); 9; 14; 18; **Ex** 2:1; 8; 11; 13; 4:18; 27; 29; 5:1; 10; 7:10; 23; 8:12; 30; 9:33; 10:6; 14; 18; 11:8; 12:28; 38; 41; 13:18; 21; 14:8; 19(3); 22; 23; 15:19(2); 20; 22(2); 16:27; 17:10; 18:7; 27; 19:3; 14; 20; 25; 24:9; 13; 18; 32:15; 33:7; 8; 34:4; 34; 35; 38:26; 40:32; 36; **Lev** 9:8; 23; 10:2; 5; 16:23; 24:10; **Num** 8:22; 10:14; 33; 34; 11:8; 24; 26; 31; 13:21; 26; 31; 14:24; 38; 16:25; 33; 17:8; 20:6; 15; 27; 21:16; 18; 23; 33(2); 22:14; 21; 22; 23; 26; 32; 35; 36; 39; 23:3; 24:1; 25(2); 25:8; 26:4; 31:13; 21; 27; 28; 36; 32:9; 39; 41; 42; 33:1; 3; 8; 23; 29; 33; 38; **Deut** 1:19; 24; 31; 33; 43; 2:13; 3:1; 5; 10:3; 22; 26:5; 29:26; 31:1; 14; 33:2; 34:1; **Josh** 2:1; 5(2); 22; 3:2; 6; 5:13; 6:1; 9; 13(2); 20; 23; 7:2; 4; 8:9; 10; 11; 13; 14; 17; 9:4; 10:5; 9; 24; 36; 11:4; 14:8; 15:3(2); 4; 6(2); 7; 8(2); 9; 10; 11(2); 15; 16:6(2); 7(2); 8; 17:7; 18:8(2); 9; 12(2); 13; 15(2); 17(2); 18; 19:11; 47(2); 22:6; 24:4; 11; 17; **Judg** 1:3; 4; 9; 10; 11; 16(2); 17; 22; 26; 2:6; 15; 17; 3:10; 13; 19; 22; 23; 27; 28; 4:9; 10(2); 14; 18; 21; 6:19; 33; 7:11; 8:8; 11; 27; 29; 33; 9:1; 5; 6; 7; 8; 21; 26; 27(2); 35; 39; 42; 50; 52; 11:3; 5; 11; 18; 38; 40; 12:1; 13:11; 20; 14:1; 5; 7; 9; 10; 18; 19(2); 15:4; 8; 9; 11; 16:1(2); 3; 14; 19; 17:10; 18:11; 12; 14; 17(2); 18; 20; 26(2); 19:2; 3; 14(2); 15; 18; 27; 20:1; 18; 20; 23; 25; 26; 30; 31; 21:23; 24; **Ruth** 1:1; 7(2); 19; 21; 2:3; 18; 3:6; 7; 15; 4:1; 13; **1Sa** 1:3; 7; 18; 21; 22; 2:11; 20; 3:3; 5; 6; 8; 9; 4:1; 5:12; 6:12(3); 7:7; 11; 16; 9:9; 10; 11; 14; 26; 10:14; 26(2); 11:15; 13:7; 10; 20; 23; 14:16; 19; 21; 46(2); 15:34(2); 16:13; 17:4; 7; 12; 13(2); 15; 20; 35; 41; 18:5; 13; 16; 27; 30(2); 19:8; 12; 18; 22; 23(2); 20:11; 35; 42; 21:10; 22:1; 3; 23:5; 13; 16; 18; 24; 25; 26; 28; 29; 24:2; 3; 7; 8; 22; 25:1; 12; 13; 42(2); 26:2; 13; 25; 27:8; 28:8; 25; 29:11; 30:2; 9; 21; 22(2); 31:3; 12; **2Sa** 1:4; 2:2; 12; 13; 15; 24; 29; 32; 3:16; 19; 21; 4:5; 5:6; 10; 17; 6:2; 4; 12; 7:18; 23; 8:3; 6; 14; 10:16; 11:9; 10; 13(2); 17; 21; 22; 12:16; 17; 24; 29; 13:8; 9; 19; 37; 38; 14:23; 15:9; 11(2); 16; 17; 24; 30(5); 16:13(3); 22; 17:17(2); 18(2); 21; 25; 18:6; 9(2); 24; 33(2); 19:17; 18; 19; 31; 39; 40(2); 20:2; 3; 5; 7(2); 8(2); 13; 14(2); 22; 21:12; 15; 22:9; 23:13; 17; 20; 21; 24:4; 7; 19; 20; **1Kin** 1:15; 38; 49; 50; 2:8; 19; 34; 40(2); 46; 3:4; 6:8; 8:66; 10:5; 13; 16; 17; 29; 11:5; 6; 24; 29; 12:1; 25; 30; 13:10; 12(2); 14; 19; 28; 14:4; 28; 15:17; 16:10; 17; 18; 31; 17:5(2); 10; 15; 18:2(2); 6(2); 16(2); 42(2); 43; 45; 19:3; 4; 8; 13; 21; 20:1; 16; 17; 21; 26; 27; 39; 43; 21:27; 22:24(2); 29; 30; 36; 48; **2Kin** 1:9; 13; 15; 2:1; 2; 6; 7; 8; 11(2); 13; 14; 21; 23; 25; 3:6; 7; 9; 12; 24; 25; 4:5; 18; 21(2); 25; 31; 33; 34; 35; 37(2); 39; 5:4; 11; 12; 14; 25(2); 26; 27; 6:4; 23; 24; 7:8(3); 15; 16; 8:2; 3; 29(2); 9:4; 6; 16; 18; 21(2); 24; 35; 10:9; 23; 24; 25; 11:16; 18; 12:17; 18; 13:5; 14:11; 15:14; 15:14; 16:9; 10; 17:5; 15; 18:7; 17; 19:1; 14; 35; 36; 22:14; 23:2; 29(2); 24:12; 25:4; **1Chr** 2:21; 4:39; 42; 5:18; 25; 6:15; 7:23(2); 10:3; 11:4; 6; 15; 22; 23; 12:15; 17; 20; 33; 36; 13:6; 14:8(2); 17; 15:25; 16:20; 17:21; 18:3; 6; 13; 19:5; 16; 21:4; 19; 21; 27:1; 29:30; **2Chr** 1:3; 6; 8:3; 17; 18; 9:4; 11:17; 16; 12:12; 14:10; 15:2; 5; 17:9; 18:2; 12; 23; 28; 29; 19:2; 4; 20:20(2); 21; 21:9; 22:5; 6; 7; 23:2; 17; 25:11; 21; 26:6; 11; 16; 17; 28:9; 29:16; 18; 20; 30:6; 31:1; 34:22; 30; 35:20; **Ezr** 2:1; 59; 4:23; 5:8; 7:6; 7; 8:1; 10:6; **Neh** 2:13; 14; 15; 16; 7:6; 61; 8:12; 16; 9:11; 24; 12:1; 31; 32; 37; 38; **Est** 2:14; 3:15; 4:1; 6; 17; 5:9; 7:7; 8; 8:14; 15; 9:4; **Job** 1:4; 12; 2:7; 18:20; 29:7; 30:28; 31:34; 42:9; **Ps** 18:8; 42:4; 66:6; 12; 68:25; 73:17; 77:17; 81:5; 105:13; 106:32; 39; 114:1; 119:67; 133:2; **Prov** 7:8; 24:30; **Eccl** 2:20; **Song** 5:7; 6:11; **Is** 7:1; 8:3; 37:1; 14; 36; 37; 48:3; 51:23; 52:4; 57:17; 60:15; **Jer** 3:8; 7:24; 11:10; 13:5; 7; 18:3; 22:11; 26:21; 28:4; 11; 31:2; 36:12; 20; 37:4; 12; 38:8; 11; 39:4(2); 40:6; 41:6(2); 12; 14; 44:3; 51:59; 52:7(2); **Eze** 1:9(2); 12(3); 13(2); 17(3); 19(2); 20; 21(2); 24; 3:14; 23; 8:10; 11; 9:2; 7; 10:2; 3; 4; 6; 7; 11(4); 16(2); 19; 22; 12:7; 23:44(2); 24:12; 25:3; 27:33; 31:15; 17; 36:20; 21; 22; 39:23; 40:6; 22; 49; 41:3; 7; 44:10(2); 15; 47:3; 48:11(3); **Dan** 2:13; 16; 17; 24(2); 6:10; 18(2); 19; **Hos** 1:3; 2:13; 5:13; 9:10; 12; **Amos** 5:3(2); 19; **Jonah** 1:3(2); 2:6; 3:3; 4:5; **Nah** 3:10; **Hab** 3:5(2); 11; **Zec** 2:3(2); 5:5; 6:7; 8:10; 10:2; **Mt** 2:9; 3:5; 16; 4:23; 24; 5:1; 8:32; 33; 9:25; 26; 32; 35; 11:7; 8; 9; 12:1; 9; 14; 13:1; 2; 3; 25; 36; 46; 14:12; 14; 23; 25; 15:21; 29; 18:13; 28; 30; 19:22; 20:1;

3; 4; 5; 6; 21:6; 9; 12; 17; 29; 30; 33; 22:5; 10; 15; 22; 24:1; 25:1; 10(2); 16; 18; 25; 26:14; 30; 39; 42; 44; 58; 75; 27:5; 53; 58; 66; 28:9; 16; **Mk** 1:5; 20; 21; 35; 45; 2:12; 13; 23(2); 26; 3:6; 19; 21; 4:3; 5:13; 14; 24; 6:1; 6; 12; 24; 27; 51; 7:24; 8:27; 10:22; 32; 46; 11:4; 9; 11; 15; 19; 12:1; 12; 13:1; 14:10; 16; 26; 35; 39; 68; 15:43; 16:8; 10; 12; 13; 20; **Lk** 1:9; 39; 2:1; 3; 4; 41; 42; 44; 51; 4:14; 16; 30; 37; 42; 5:15; 19; 27; 6:1; 4; 12; 19; 7:6; 11(2); 17; 24; 25; 26; 36; 8:1; 2; 5; 22; 27; 33; 34; 35; 37; 39; 42; 9:6; 10; 28; 52; 56; 57; 10:30; 34; 38; 11:37; 13:22; 14:1; 25; 15:15; 16:30; 17:11; 14; 19; 21:37; 22:4; 13; 39; 47; 62; 23:52; 24:13; 15; 24; 28; 29; **Jn** 2:12; 13; 4:28; 30; 43; 45; 47; 50; 5:1; 4; 6:1; 3; 16; 17; 21; 22; 66; 7:10; 14; 53; 8:1; 9; 59; 9:7; 11; 10:40; 11:20; 28; 31; 46; 54; 55; 12:11; 13; 13:3; 30; 18:1; 4; 6; 15; 16; 28; 29; 38; 19:4; 9; 17; 20:3; 5; 6; 8; 10; 21:3; 11; 23; **Acts** 1:10; 13; 21; 3:1; 4:23; 5:26; 7:15; 8:4; 5; 27; 36; 38; 39; 9:1; 17; 29; 39; 10:9(2); 21; 23; 27; 38; 12:9; 10; 17; 19; 13:11; 14; 14:1; 25; 15:24; 38; 41; 16:4; 13; 16; 40; 17:2; 10; 18:22; 23; 19:8; 12; 20:10; 13; 21:2; 5; 15; 16; 18; 31; 22:5; 26; 23:16; 19; 24:11; 25:6; 26(2); 21; 28:14; **Rom** 10:18; **2Cor** 2:13; 8:17; **Gal** 1:17(2); 18; 2:1; 2; **1Ti** 1:18; **Heb** 9:6; 7; 11:8(2); **1Pet** 3:19; **1Jn** 2:19(2); **3Jn** 7; **Rev** 1:16; 6:2; 4; 10:9; 12:17; 16:2; 20:9

WERE

1961, 2258

Gen 1:5; 7(2); 8; 13; 19; 23; 31; 2:1; 4; 25(2); 3:7(2); 4:8; 5:2; 4; 5; 8; 11; 14; 17; 20; 23; 27; 31; 6:1; 2; 4(2); 7:10; 11(2); 18; 19(2); 20; 23(2); 8:2; 3; 5; 7; 8; 9; 11; 13; 9:18; 23; 29; 10:1; 5; 18; 21; 25; 29; 31; 11:32; 13:13; 14:3; 5; 13; 17; 17:23(2); 27; 18:11; 19:11; 36; 20:8; 21:16; 23:1; 17(3); 20; 24:10; 32; 54; 63; 25:3; 4; 24(2); 26:35; 27:1; 15; 23; 42; 29:2; 3; 30:35(2); 42(2); 31:10; 19; 34:5(2); 7(2); 14; 25; 35:2; 4(2); 5; 6; 22; 26; 28; 36:5; 7(2); 11; 12; 13; 14; 15; 16; 18; 22; 25; 37:7; 27; 38:27; 39:20; 22; 40:5; 6; 7; 10; 41:21; 48; 50; 53; 42:28; 35; 43:18(2); 34; 44:3; 4; 45:3; 46:12; 15; 20; 21; 22(2); 25; 26; 27(3); 31; 48:5; 10; 49:24; 50:3; 4; 23; **Ex** 1:5; 7; 12; 5:12; 14; 19; 6:4; 16; 18; 20; 7:20(3); 25; 8:18; 9:26; 32(2); 34; 10:6; 8; 11; 14(2); 12:33; 37; 39; 14:10; 11; 21; 22; 29; 15:8(2); 23; 27; 17:12(2); 19:1; 2(2); 16; 21:3; 29; 22:21; 23:9; 24:10(2); 28:32; 32:3; 15(3); 16; 25; 34:1; 30; 35:22; 25; 36:6; 9; 15; 29; 30(2); 36; 38; 37:9; 13; 14; 16; 17; 20; 22; 25; 38:2; 9; 10(2); 11(2); 12; 14; 15; 16; 17(2); 19; 20; 25; 27; 39:13; 14; 40:37; **Lev** 8:20; 10:1; 12; 16; 14:35; 18:27; 28; 30; 19:34; 26:37; **Num** 1:1; 16; 20; 21(2); 22(2); 23(2); 24; 25(2); 26; 27(2); 28; 29(2); 30; 32(2); 33(2); 34; 35(2); 36; 37(2); 38; 39(2); 40; 41(2); 42; 43(2); 44; 45(3); 46(2); 47; 2:4(2); 6(2); 8(2); 9(2); 11(2); 13(2); 15(2); 16(2); 19(2); 21(2); 23(2); 24(2); 26(2); 28(2); 30(2); 31(2); 32(3); 33; 3:3; 17; 22(3); 28; 34(2); 39(2); 43(2); 49(2); 4:2; 4:36(2); 37(2); 38; 40(2); 41; 42; 43; 44; 49; 41:2; 6; 8; 9; 11; 16; 20; 21; 22; 25(3); 26; 42:3(2); 5(2); 6; 8(2); 10; 11(2); 12; 43:3; 46:22(2); 47:3; 4(2); 5; 7; **Dan** 1:6; 20; 2:34; 42; 3:20; 21(2); 27; 4:10; 12; 21; 33; 5:3; 6; 9; 12; 6:18; 7:4; 7; 8(2); 9; 10; 12; 19; 20; 8:10; 3; 10; 13; **Hos** 2:23; 4:7; 5:10; 8:12; 9:10; 12:8; 13:6(2); **Amos** 4:7; 8; 11; **Obad** 7; **Jonah** 1:5(2); 10; 2:5; **Mic** 1:13; **Nah** 3:9(2); 10(2); **Hab** 3:6; **Hag** 2:16(3); **Zec** 1:8(2); 6:1; 2; 7:3; 8:9; 13; 10(2); **Mt** 1:11; 12; 2:11; 13; 16; 3:6; 16; 4:18; 24(3); 5:12; 7:28; 8:16(2); 32; 9:25; 30; 31; 36; 11:20; 21; 12:1; 3; 4; 23; 13:2; 6; 54; 57; 14:20; 21; 26; 32; 33; 34; 35; 36; 15:1; 12; 30; 37; 38; 16:5; 17:6; 14; 23; 24; 18:6(3); 31; 19:12(2); 15; 20(2); 22; 20:12; 21:15; 22:25; 23:5; 30; 32; 34:5(2); 36:19; 31; 37:2(2); 40:7; 10(2); 12; 15; 16(3); 17(2); 21(2); 22(2); 25; 26(2); 29; 30; 31(2); 33(2); 34(2); 37(2); 38; 39; 40(2); 41; 42; 43; 44; 49; 41:2; 6; 8; 9; 11; 16; 20; 21; 22; 25(3); 26; 42:3(2); 5(2); 6; 8(2); 10; 11(2); 12; 43:3; 46:22(2); 47:3; 4(2); 5; 7; **Dan** 1:6; 20; 2:34; 42; 3:20; 21(2); 27; 4:10; 12; 21; 33; 5:3; 6; 9; 12; 6:18; 7:4; 7; 8(2); 9; 10; 12; 19; 20; 8:10; 3; 10; 13; **Hos** 2:23; 4:7; 5:10; 8:12; 9:10; 12:8; 13:6(2); **Amos** 4:7; 8; 11; **Obad** 7; **Jonah** 1:5(2); 10; 2:5; **Mic** 1:13; **Nah** 3:9(2); 10(2); **Hab** 3:6; **Hag** 2:16(3); **Zec** 1:8(2); 6:1; 2; 7:3; 8:9; 13; 10(2); **Mt** 1:11; 12; 2:11; 13; 16; 3:6; 16; 4:18; 24(3); 5:12; 7:28; 8:16(2); 32; 9:25; 30; 31; 36; 11:20; 21; 12:1; 3; 4; 23; 13:2; 6; 54; 57; 14:20; 21; 26; 32; 33; 34; 35; 36; 15:1; 12; 30; 37; 38; 16:5; 17:6; 14; 23; 24; 18:6(3); 31; 19:12(2); 15; 20(2); 22; 20:12; 21:15; 22:25; 23:5; 30; 32; 24:6; 9; 21(2); 38; 26:20; 51; 57; 71; 27:17; 33; 38; 44; 52; 54(2); 55; 28:11(2); 12; 15; **Mk** 1:5; 16; 19; 22; 27; 29; 32(2); 34; 36; 2:2; 6; 12; 15; 26; 4:10; 33; 34; 36; 5:13(2); 15; 40; 42; 6:2; 3; 31; 33; 34; 42; 44; 50; 51; 54; 55; 56(2); 7:35; 37; 8:8; 9; 9:4; 6; 9; 15; 32(2); 10:24; 26; 32(3); 11:12; 14; 20; 41; 13:22; 14:4; 11; 21; 35; 40; 53; 15:32; 40; 44; 16:5; 8; **VM; Lk** 1:2; 6; 7; 10; 23; 45; 65; 2:6(2); 8; 9; 15; 18; 21; 22; 33; 47; 48; 3:15(2); 21; 4:2; 20(2); 25; 27; 28; 32; 36; 5:2(2); 7; 9; 10; 17(2); 26(2); 8; 4; 11; 18(2); 7:10; 20; 21; 24; 39; 8:1; 4(2); 23(2); 30; 33; 35(2); 37; 38; 40; 45; 56; 9:10; 14; 17; 18; 30; 32(3); 37; 43; 11:29; 12; 13:1; 2; 4; 17(2); 14:7; 17; 24; 16:14; 16; 17:22(2); 9; 12; 14; 17; 27; 18:9; 34; 19:32; 33; 48; 20:29; 22:5; 44; 49; 52; 55; 23:5;

6; 12(2); 23; 32; 33; 39; 48; 24:4; 5; 10; 16; 21; 22; 24; 31; 33; 35; 37; 44; 53; **Jn** 1:3; 13; 24(2); 28; 2:6; 3:19; 23; 4:8; 40; 5:35; 6:2; 11; 12; 19; 22(2); 26; 64; 65; 7:10(2); 8:33; 39; 42; 9:10; 33; 40; 41; 10:6; 41; 11:25; 31; 52; 57; 12:12; 16; 20; 13:1; 14:2; 15:19; 16:19; 17:6; 18:30; 36; 19:11; 28; 36; 20:19(2); 20; 26; 21:2; 6; 8(2); 9; 11; **Acts** 1:6; 13; 15; 2:1; 2; 4; 5; 6; 7; 8; 12(2); 37; 41(2); 43; 44; 3:10; 4:6(2); 13; 26; 27; 31(2); 32; 34(2); 5:12(2); 14; 16(2); 17(2); 21; 33; 36; 37; 41; 6:1; 7; 10; 7:16; 30; 54; 8:1; 4; 7(3); 12; 13; 14; 15; 16; 39; 9:2; 8; 19; 21; 23; 26; 31(2); 10:12; 17; 18; 21; 27; 38; 45; 11:1; 2; 10; 11; 19; 20(2); 26; 12:3; 10; 12; 16; 13:1; 5; 42; 45(2); 48(2); 52; 14:6; 27; 15:4(2); 10; 30; 33; 16:2; 3; 4(2); 5; 6; 7; 12; 14; 26(3); 32; 38; 17:11(2); 12; 14; 21; 18:3; 5; 8; 14; 19:3; 5; 7; 9; 12; 14; 21; 28; 31; 32; 20:8(2); 12; 16; 18; 34; 21:1; 5; 8; 17; 18; 24; 27(2); 30; 38; 22:5; 9(2); 11; 23:6; 9; 13; 24:9; 25:17; 26:10; 14; 29; 31; 27:4; 7; 11; 17; 27; 30; 36; 37; 39(2); 28:1; 7; 9; 10; 14; 17; 24; **Rom** 1:21; 3:2; 4:2; 17; 5:6; 8; 10(2); 19; 6:3(2); 17; 20(2); 7:5(2); 6; 9:3; 25; 32; 11:7; 19; 20; 15:4(2); 16:7; **1Cor** 1:9; 13; 3:2; 4:9; 5:3; 6:11; 7:7; 14; 9:15; 10:1; 2; 5; 6; 7; 9; 10; 11:5; 12:2(2); 17(4); 19(2); 15:11; **2Cor** 1:8; 3:14; 5:1; 14; 7:5(4); 8; 9(2); 13; 8:3; 11:17; 12:12; 13; 13:2; **Gal** 1:17; 22; 2:2; 6; 12(2); 3:16; 23; 4:3(2); 5; 5:12; **Eph** 1:13; 2:1; 3; 5; 12; 13; 17(2); 5:8; **Phil** 3:7; 12; 4:10; 18; **Col** 1:16(2); 21; **1Th** 1:5; 7; 2:2(2); 4; 7; 8(2); 3:4; 7; **2Th** 3:10; **Titus** 3:3; **Philem** 1:14; **Heb** 2:15; 3:5; 4:3; 5:8; 6:4(2); 7:11; 21; 23(2); 8:4; 9:6; 9; 15; 10:32; 33(2); 11:3(2); 13(2); 23; 29; 30; 34; 35; 37(4); **Jas** 5:3; **1Pet** 1:18; 2:8; 10; 21; 24; 25; 3:20(2); **2Pet** 1:16; 18; 21; 2:1; 18; 3:2; 4; 5; **1Jn** 2:19(2); 3:12; **Jude** 4; 17; **Rev** 1:14(2); 4:1; 4; 5; 6; 8; 11; 6:1; 9; 11(2); 14; 7:4(2); 5(3); 6(3); 7(3); 8(3); 8:2; 5; 7; 8; 9(2); 10; 11; 9:2; 7(4); 8; 9; 10; 15(2); 16; 17; 19; 20; 10:1; 11:13(2); 15; 18; 19; 12:9; 14; 13:2; 3; 14:3(2); 4(2); 15:2; 8; 16:9; 18(2); 20; 17:8; 18:14; 15; 19; 23(2); 24; 19:6; 12(2); 14; 20; 21(2); 20:4; 5; 12(3); 13(3); 14; 21:1; 19; 21(2); 22:2

WHAT

335, 349, 375, 376, 834, 853, 1571, 1697, 1768, 2088, 3602, 3605, 3964, 4100, 4310, 4479, *686, 1063, 2228, 2245, 3588, 3634, 3697, 3699, 3739, 3745, 3748, 3779, 4169, 4214, 4217, 4459, 5100, 5101*

Gen 2:19; 3:13; 4:10; 9:24; 12:18; 15:2; 20:9(2); 10; 21:17; 29; 23:15; 24:65; 25:32; 26:10; 27:37; 46; 29:15; 25; 30:31; 31:26; 32; 36(2); 37; 43; 32:27; 33:8; 15; 34:11; 37:10; 15; 20; 26; 38:16; 18; 39:8; 41:25; 28; 55; 42:28; 44:15; 16(2); 46:33; 47:3; **Ex** 2:4; 3:13(2); 4:2; 12; 15; 6:1; 10:2; 26; 12:26; 13:14; 15:24; 16:7; 8; 15; 17:4; 18:14; 19:4; 23:11; 32:1; 21; 23; 33:5; **Lev** 15:9; 17:3; 22:4; 25:20; **Num** 9:8; 10:32; 13:18; 19(2); 20; 15:34; 16:11; 21:14; 22:9; 19; 28; 23:11; 17; 23; 24:13; 14; 26:10; 31:50; **Deut** 1:22(2); 33; 3:24; 4:3; 7; 8; 6:20; 7:18; 8:2; 10:12; 11:4; 5; 6; 12:32; 20:5; 6; 7; 8; 24:9; 25:17; 29:24; 32:20; **Josh** 2:10; 4:6; 21; 5:14; 7:8; 9; 19; 9:3; 15:18; 22:16; 24; 24:7; **Judg** 1:14; 7:11; 8:2; 3; 18; 9:48; 10:18; 11:12; 13:8; 17; 14:6; 18(2); 15:11; 16:5; 18:3(2); 8; 14; 18; 23; 24(3); 19:24; 20:12; 21:8; **Ruth** 2:18; 3:4; 4:5; **1Sa** 1:23; 3:17; 18; 4:6; 14; 16; 5:8; 6:2; 4; 9:7(2); 10:2; 8; 11; 15; 11:5; 13:11; 14:40; 43; 15:14; 16; 16:3; 17:26; 29; 18:8; 18; 19:3; 20:1(3); 10; 32; 21:2; 3(2); 22:3; 25:17; 26:18(2); 28:2; 9; 13; 14; 15; 29:3; 8(2); **2Sa** 3:24; 7:18; 20; 23; 9:8; 12:21; 14:5; 15:2; 21; 35; 16:2; 10; 20; 17:5; 18:4; 21; 29; 19:18; 22; 27; 28; 35(2); 37; 21:3; 4; 11; 24:13; 17; 22; **1Kin** 1:16; 2:5(2); 9; 3:5; 8:38; 9:13; 11:22; 12:9; 16; 13:12(2); 14:3; 14; 16:5; 17:18; 18:9; 13; 19:9; 13; 20; 20:22; 22:14; **2Kin** 1:7; 2:9; 3:13; 4:2(2); 13; 14; 43; 6:28; 33; 7:12; 8:13; 14; 9:18; 19; 22; 18:19; 19:11; 20:8; 14; 15; 22:19; 23:17; **1Chr** 12:32; 17:16; 18; 21; 21:12; 17; 29:14; **2Chr** 1:7; 6:29(2); 10:6; 9; 16; 18:13; 19:6; 10; 20:12; 24:11; 25:9; 32:13; 35:21; **Ezr** 5:4; 6:8; 8:17; 9:10; **Neh** 2:4; 12; 16; 19; 4:2; 20; 13:17; **Est** 1:15; 2:1(2); 11; 15; 4:5; 5:3(2); 6(2); 6:3; 6; 7:2(2); 8:1; 9:5; 12(3); **Job** 2:10; 6:11(2); 17; 25; 7:17; 20; 9:12; 11:8(2); 13:2; 13; 15:9(2); 12; 14; 16:3; 6; 21:15(2); 21; 31; 22:17; 23:5; 13; 27:8; 31:2(2); 14(2); 32:11; 34:4; 7; 33; 35:3(2); 6(2); 7(2); 37:19; 38:24; 39:18; 40:4; **Ps** 8:4; 11:3; 25:12; 30:9; 34:12; 39:4; 7; 44:1; 46:8; 50:16; 56:3; 4; 11; 66:16; 85:8; 89:48; 114:5; 116:12; 118:6; 120:3(2); 144:3; **Prov** 4:19; 10:32; 23:1; 25:8; 27:1; 30:4(2); 31:2(3); **Eccl** 1:3; 2:2; 3; 12; 22; 3:9; 22; 5:11; 16; 6:8(2); 11; 12(2); 7:10; 8:4; 10:14(2); 11:2; 5; **Song** 5:9(2); 6:13; 8:8; **Is** 1:11; 3:15; 5:4; 5; 10:3; 14:32; 19:12; 21:6; 11(2); 22:1; 16; 33:13; 36:4; 37:11; 38:15; 22; 39:3; 4; 40:6; 18; 41:22(2); 45:9; 10(2); 52:5; 64:4; **Jer** 1:11; 13; 2:5; 18(2); 23; 4:30; 5:15; 31; 6:18; 20; 7:12; 17; 8:6; 9; 9:12; 11:15; 13:21; 16:10(2); 18:7; 9; 23:25; 28; 33(2); 35(2); 37(2); 24:3; 32:24; 33:24; 37:18; 38:25(2); 48:19; **Lam** 2:13(3); 5:1; **Eze** 2:8; 8:6; 12; 12:9; 22; 15:2; 17:12; 18:2; 19:2; 20:29; 21:13; 24:19; 27:32; 33:30; 37:18; 47:23; **Dan** 2:22; 23; 28; 29(2); 45; 3:5; 15; 4:35; 8:19; 10:14; 12:8; **Hos** 6:4(2); 9:5; 14; 10:3; 14:8; **Joel** 3:4; **Amos** 4:13; 5:18; 7:8; 8:2; **Jonah** 1:6; 8(3); 11; 4:5; **Mic** 1:5(2); 6:1; 3; 5(2); 8(2); **Nah** 1:9; **Hab** 2:1(2); 18; **Zec** 1:9(2); 19; 21; 2:2(2); 4:2; 4; 5; 11; 12; 13; 5:2; 5; 6; 6:4; 13:6; **Mal** 1:13; 3:13; 14; **Mt** 2:7; 5:46; 47; 6:3; 8; 25(3); 31(2); 7:2(2); 9; 8:27; 29; 33; 9:13; 10:19(2); 27(2); 11:7; 8; 9; 12:3; 7; 11; 16:26(2); 17:25; 18:31; 19:6; 16; 20; 27; 20:15; 21; 22; 32; 21:16; 23; 24; 27; 28; 40; 22:17; 42; 24:3; 42; 43; 26:8; 15; 40; 62; 65; 66; 70; 27:4; 22; 23; **Mk** 1:24; 27(2); 2:25; 3:8; 4:24(2); 30; 41; 5:7; 9; 14; 33; 6:2; 10; 24; 30(2); 8:36; 37; 9:6; 9; 10; 16; 33; 10:3; 9; 17; 32; 36; 38; 51; 11:5; 24; 28; 29; 33; 12:9; 13:1(2); 4; 11; 37; 14:8; 36(2); 40; 60; 63; 64; 68; 15:12; 14; 24; **Lk** 1:29; 66; 3:10; 12; 14; 4:34; 36; 5:19; 22; 6:3; 11; 32; 33; 34; 7:22; 24; 25; 26; 31; 39; 8:9; 25; 28; 30; 34; 35; 36; 47; 56; 9:25; 33; 55; 10:25; 26; 12:11(2); 12; 17; 22(2); 29(2); 39; 49; 57; 13:18; 14:31; 15:4; 8; 26; 16:3; 4; 18:6; 18; 36; 41; 19:48; 20:2; 8; 13; 15; 17; 21:7; 14; 22:49; 60; 71; 23:22; 31; 34; 47; 24:17; 19; 35; **Jn** 1:21; 22; 38; 2:4; 18; 25; 3:32; 4:22(2); 27; 5:12; 19(2); 6:6; 9; 28; 30(2); 62; 7:36; 51; 8:5; 9:17; 21; 26; 10:6; 11:46; 47; 56; 12:6; 27; 33; 49(2); 13:7; 12; 28; 15:7; 15; 16:17; 18(2); 18:21(2); 29; 32; 35; 38; 19:22; 21:19; 21; 22; 23; **Acts** 2:12; 37; 4:7(2); 9; 16; 5:7; 35; 7:40; 49(2); 8:30; 36; 9:6(2); 10:4; 6; 15; 17; 21; 29; 11:9; 17; 12:18; 13:12; 14:11; 15:12; 16:30; 17:18; 19; 20; 19:3; 35; 20:18; 21:13; 19; 22; 33; 22:10; 15; 26; 23:19; 30; 34; 28:22; **Rom** 3:1(2); 3; 5; 9; 19; 27; 4:1; 3; 21; 6:1; 15; 21; 7:7; 15(2); 8:3; 24; 26; 27; 31; 9:14; 22; 30; 10:8; 11:2; 4; 7; 15; 12:2; **1Cor** 2:11; 3:13; 4:7; 21; 5:12; 6:16; 19; 7:16; 36; 9:18; 10:15; 19; 11:22(2); 14:6; 7; 9; 15; 16; 36; 15:2; 10; 29; 32; 35; **2Cor** 1:13; 6:14(2); 15(2); 16; 7:11(7); 11:12; 12:13; **Gal** 4:30; **Eph** 1:18(2); 19; 3:9; 18; 4:9; 5:10; 17; **Phil** 1:18; 22; 3:7; **Col** 1:27; 2:1; **1Th** 1:5; 9; 2:19; 3:9; 4:2; **2Th** 2:6; **1Ti** 1:7; **2Ti** 2:7; 3:11; **Heb** 2:6; 7:11; 11:32; 12:7; 13:6; **Jas** 1:24; 2:14; 16; 4:14(2); **1Pet** 1:11(2); 2:20; 4:17; **2Pet** 3:11; **1Jn** 3:1; 2; **Jude** 10; **Rev** 1:11; 2:7; 11; 17; 29; 3:3; 6; 13; 22; 7:13; 18:18

WHATSOEVER

376, 834, 853, 1401, 1697, 1768, 3605, 3627, 4100, *302, 1221, 1437, 1487, 3588, 3697, 3739, 3745, 3748, 3956, 4219, 5100*

Gen 2:19; 8:19; 19:12; 31:16; 39:22; **Ex** 13:2; 21:30; 29:37; 30:29; **Lev** 5:3; 4; 6:27; 7:27; 11:3; 9; 12; 27; 32(2); 33; 42(3); 13:58; 15:26; 17:8; 10; 13; 21:18; 22:5; 18; 20; 23:29; 30; 27:32; **Num** 5:10; 18:13; 19:22; 22:17; 23:3; 30:12; **Deut** 2:37; 12:8; 15; 20; 21; 14:10; 26(2); **Judg** 10:15; 11:31; **1Sa** 14:36; 20:4; 25:8; **2Sa** 3:36; 15:15; 19:38; **1Kin** 8:37(2); 10:13; 20:6; **2Chr** 6:28(2); 9:12; **Ezr** 7:18; 20; 21; 23; **Est** 2:13; **Job** 37:12; 41:11; **Ps** 1:3; 8:8; 115:3; 135:6; **Eccl** 2:10; 3:14; 8:3; 9:10; **Jer** 1:7; 42:4; 44:17; **Mt** 5:37; 7:12; 10:11; 14:7; 15:5; 17; 16:19(2); 17:12; 18:18(2); 20:4; 7; 21:22; 23:3; 28:20; **Mk** 6:22; 23; 7:11; 18; 9:13; 10:21; 35; 11:23; 13:11; **Lk** 4:23; 9:4; 10:5; 8; 10; 35; 12:3; **Jn** 2:5; 5:4; 11:22; 12:50; 14:13; 26; 15:14; 16; 16:13; 23; 17:7; **Acts** 3:22; 4:28; **Rom** 14:23; 15:4; 16:2; **1Cor** 10:25; 27; 31; **Gal** 2:6; 6:7; **Eph** 5:13; 6:8; **Phil** 4:8(6); 11; **Col** 3:17; 23; **1Jn** 3:22; 5:4; 15; **3Jn** 5; **Rev** 18:22; 21:27

WHEN

310, 518, 834, 1767, 1768, 1961, 3117, 3588, 3644, 4481, 4970, 5704, 5750, 5921, 6256, 6310, *1437, 1722, 1875, 1893, 2259, 2531, 3326, 3588, 3698, 3704, 3752, 3753, 3756, 4218, 5613*

Gen 2:4; 3:6; 4:8; 12; 5:2; 6:1; 4; 7:6; 9:14; 12:4; 11; 12; 14; 14:14; 15:11; 12; 17; 16:4; 5; 6; 16; 17:1; 24; 25; 18:2; 19:15; 17; 23; 29(2); 33(2); 35(2); 20:13; 21:5; 24:19; 30(2); 36; 41; 43; 52; 64; 25:20; 24; 26; 26:8; 34; 27:1; 5; 34; 40; 28:6; 29:10; 13; 31; 30:1; 9; 25; 30; 33; 38(2); 42; 31:49; 32:2; 17; 19; 25; 33:18; 34:2; 7; 25; 35:1; 7; 9; 17; 22; 37:4; 18; 23; 38:5; 9; 15; 25; 28; 39:13; 15; 19; 40:13; 14; 16; 41:21; 46; 55; 42:1; 21; 35; 43:2; 16; 21; 26; 44:4(2); 24; 30; 31; 45:27; 46:33; 47:15; 18; 48:7(2); 17; 49:33; 50:4; 11; 15; 17; **Ex** 1:10; 16; 2:2; 3; 5; 6; 11; 12; 13; 15; 18; 3:4; 12; 13; 21; 4:6; 14; 21; 31; 5:13; 6:28; 7:5; 7; 9; 8:9; 15; 9:34; 10:13; 11:1; 12:13(2); 23; 25; 26; 27; 44; 48; 13:5; 8; 11; 14; 15; 17(2); 14:10; 18; 27; 15:23; 25; 16:3(2); 8; 14; 15; 18; 21; 32; 17:11(2); 18:1; 14; 16; 19:1; 9; 13; 19; 20:18; 22:27; 23:16; 28:29; 30; 35(2); 43(2); 29:30; 36; 30:7; 8; 12(3); 15; 20(2); 31:18; 32:1; 5; 17; 25; 34; 33:4; 8; 34:24; 29(2); 30; 34; 40:32(2); 36; **Lev** 2:1; 8; 4:14; 22; 5:3; 4; 5; 6:20; 21; 27; 7:35; 9:24; 10:9; 20; 11:31; 32; 12:6; 13:2; 3; 9; 14; 20; 14:34; 57(2); 15:2; 13; 23; 31; 16:1; 17; 20; 23; 18:28; 19:9; 23; 20:4; 22:7; 16; 27; 29; 23:10; 12; 22(2); 39; 43; 24:16; 25:2; 26:17; 25; 26; 35; 36; 37; 44; 27:2; 14; 21; **Num** 1:51(2); 3:4; 4:5; 15; 19; 20; 5:6; 21; 27; 29; 30; 6:2; 7; 13; 7:84; 89; 8:2; 9:17; 19; 20; 21; 22; 10:3; 5; 6; 7; 28; 34; 35; 36; 11:1; 2; 9; 25; 12:12; 15:2; 8; 18; 19; 28; 16:4; 42; 18:26; 30; 32; 19:14; 20:3; 16; 29; 21:1; 8; 9; 22:25; 27; 36; 23:17; 24:1; 20; 23; 25:7; 26:9; 10; 61; 64; 27:13; 28:26; 30:6; 32:1; 8; 9; 33:39; 51; 34:2; 35:10; 19; 21; 36:4; **Deut** 1:19; 41; 2:8; 12; 16; 19; 22; 4:10; 19; 25; 30; 5:23; 28; 6:7(4); 10; 11; 20; 7:1; 2; 8:10; 12; 13; 9:9; 23; 11:19(4); 29; 12:10(2); 20; 25; 28; 29; 13:18; 14:24; 15:4; 10; 13; 18; 16:3; 17:14; 18; 18:9; 22; 19:1; 5; 20:1; 2; 9; 10; 13; 19; 21:9; 10; 16; 18; 22:8; 14; 26; 23:4; 9; 11(2); 13; 21; 24; 25; 24:1; 2; 5; 10; 13; 19; 20; 21; 25:4; 11; 17; 18; 19; 26:1; 7; 12; 27:2; 3; 4; 12; 28:6(2); 19(2); 29:7; 19; 22; 25; 30:1; 31:11; 20; 21; 24; 32:8(2); 19; 36; 33:5; 34:7; **Josh** 2:5; 10; 14; 18; 3:3; 8; 14; 4:1; 6; 7; 11; 18; 21; 5:1; 8; 13; 6:5(2); 8; 16; 18; 20(2); 7:8; 21; 8:5; 8; 13; 14; 20; 21; 24(2); 9:1; 3; 22; 10:1; 12; 20; 24; 11:1; 5; 14:7; 17:13; 19:49; 20:4; 22:7; 10; 12; 28; 30; 23:16; 24:7; **Judg** 1:14; 25; 28; 2:4; 6; 18; 19; 21; 3:9; 15; 18; 24(2); 27; 4:1; 18; 20; 22; 5:2; 4(2); 26; 31; 6:3; 7; 22; 28; 29; 7:13; 15; 17; 18; 8:1; 3; 7; 9; 12; 9:7; 22; 30; 33; 36; 46; 55; 11:5; 7; 13; 16; 31; 35; 12:2; 3; 5; 13:17; 20; 14:11; 15:5; 14; 17; 19; 16:2; 9; 15; 16; 18; 24; 25; 17:3; 18:2; 3; 10; 22; 26; 19:1; 3; 5; 7; 9; 11; 14; 15; 17; 25; 29; 20:10; 39; 40; 41; 21:22; **Ruth** 1:1; 18; 19; 2:9; 15; 3:4; 7; 15; 16; 4:13; **1Sa** 1:4; 7; 20; 24; 2:13; 19; 27; 3:2; 12; 4:2; 3(2); 5; 6; 13(2); 14; 18; 19; 5:2; 3; 4; 7; 6:6; 16; 7:7(2); 8:1; 6; 9:5; 9; 14; 17; 25; 10:2; 5; 7; 9; 10; 11; 13; 14; 20; 21(2); 23; 11:6; 8; 12:8; 9; 12(2); 13:1; 6; 14:17; 22; 26; 27; 52; 15:2; 6; 12; 17; 16:6; 16; 23; 17:11; 24; 28; 31; 35; 42; 48; 51; 55; 18:1; 6; 15; 19; 26; 19:14; 16; 20; 21; 20:12; 15; 19(2); 24; 37; 21:6; 22:1; 6; 17; 22; 23:6; 25; 24:1; 8; 16; 18; 25:9; 15; 23; 30; 31; 37; 39; 40; 26:20; 28:5; 6; 12; 22; 30:1; 12; 16; 21; 26; 31:5; 7; 8; 11; **2Sa** 1:1; 2; 7; 2:10; 24; 30; 3:13; 23; 26; 27; 28; 35; 4:1; 4; 7; 10; 11; 5:2; 4; 17; 23; 24; 6:6; 13; 7:1; 12; 8:5; 9; 13; 9:2; 6; 10:5; 6; 7; 9; 14; 15; 17; 19; 11:1; 7; 10; 13; 16; 19; 20; 26; 27; 12:19; 20; 21; 13:5; 6; 11; 21; 28(2); 14:4; 26; 29; 33; 15:2; 5; 32; 16:1; 5; 7; 16; 17:6; 9; 20(2); 23; 27; 18:5; 29; 19:3; 25; 39; 20:8; 12(2); 13; 17; 21:12; 21; 22:5; 23:4; 9; 24:8; 11; 16; 17; **1Kin** 1:21; 23; 41; 2:7; 8; 3:21(2); 5:7; 6:7; 7:24; 8:9(2); 10; 21; 30(2); 33; 35(2); 42; 53; 54; 9:1; 10; 10:1; 2; 4; 11:4; 15; 21; 24; 29; 12:2; 16; 20; 21; 13:4; 24; 26; 31; 14:5; 6; 12; 17; 21; 28; 15:21; 29; 16:11; 18; 17:10; 18:4; 10; 12; 13; 17; 29; 39; 19:3; 13; 15; 20:12; 21:15; 16; 27; 22:25; 32; 33; 42; **2Kin** 1:5; 2:1; 9; 10; 14; 15; 17; 18; 3:5; 15; 20; 21; 24; 26; 4:4; 6; 10; 12; 15; 18; 20; 25; 27; 32; 36; 5:6; 7; 8; 13; 18(2); 21; 24; 26; 6:4; 15; 18; 20; 21; 23; 30; 32; 7:5; 8; 12; 17; 8:6; 17; 26; 29; 9:2; 5; 15; 22; 25; 27; 30; 34; 10:7; 15; 17; 24; 11:1; 13; 14; 21; 12:10; 13:21; 14:2; 15:2; 33; 16:2; 12; 18:2; 17; 18; 32; 19:1; 9; 35; 21:1; 19; 22:1; 11; 19; 23:29; 31; 36; 24:8; 18; 25:23; **1Chr** 1:44; 45; 46; 47; 48; 49; 50; 2:19; 21; 5:7; 6:15; 7:23; 10:5; 7; 8; 9; 11; 11:2; 12:15; 19; 13:9; 14:8; 12; 15; 15:26; 16:2; 19; 20; 17:11; 18:5; 9; 19:6; 8; 10; 15; 16; 17; 19; 20:7; 21:28; 23:1; **2Chr** 4:3; 5:10(2); 11; 13; 6:21; 26(2); 27; 29; 7:1; 3; 6; 9:1(2); 3; 10:2; 16; 11:1; 12:1; 7; 11; 12; 13; 13:7; 14; 15:4; 8; 9; 16:5; 18:14; 24; 31; 32; 19:8; 20:9; 10; 21; 22; 23; 24; 25; 29; 31; 21:4; 5; 20; 22:2; 6; 7; 8; 9; 10; 23:7(2); 12; 15; 24:1; 11; 14; 15(2); 22; 25; 25:1; 3; 26:3; 16; 27:1; 8; 28:1; 29:1; 22; 27; 29; 31:1; 8; 32:2; 21; 33:1; 12; 21; 34:1; 7; 8; 9; 14; 19; 27; 35:20; 36:2; 5; 9; 10; 11; **Ezr** 2:68; 3:1; 10; 11; 12; 4:1; 23; 9:1; 3; 10:1(2); 6; **Neh** 1:4; 2:3; 6; 10; 19; 4:1; 7; 12; 15; 5:6; 6:1; 16; 7:1; 73; 8:5; 9; 9:18; 27; 28; 10:38; 13:3; 19; **Est** 1:2; 4; 5; 10; 17; 20; 2:1; 7; 8(2); 12; 15; 19; 20; 23; 3:4; 5; 4:1; 5:2; 9; 10; 9:1; 25; **Job** 1:5; 6; 13; 2:1; 11; 12; 3:11; 22; 4:13; 5:21; 6:5; 17; 7:4(2); 13; 11:3; 16:22; 17:16; 20:23; 21:6; 21; 22:29; 23:10; 15; 27:8; 9; 28:26; 29:2; 3(2); 4; 5(2); 6; 7(2); 11(2); 30:26(2); 31:13; 14(2); 21; 26; 29; 32:5; 16; 33:15; 34:29(2); 36:13; 20; 37:4; 15; 17; 38:4; 7; 8; 9; 38; 40; 41; 39:1(2); 2; 41:25; 42:10; **Ps** 2:12; 3:t, 4:1(2); 3; 8:3; 9:3; 12; 10:9; 12:8; 13:4; 14:7; 17:15; 20:9; 21:12; 22:9; 24; 27:2; 7; 8; 10; 28:2(2); 30:9; 31:22; 32:3; 6; 34:t, 35:13; 37:33; 34; 38:16; 39:11; 41:5; 6; 42:2; 4; 49:5; 16(2); 17; 18; 50:18; 51:t, 4(2); 52:t, 53:6; 54:t, 56:t, 6; 9; 57:t, 58:7; 10; 59:t, 60:(2); 61:2; 63:t, 6; 65:9; 66:14; 68:7(2); 9; 14; 69:10; 71:9; 18; 23; 72:12; 73:3; 16; 20(2); 75:2; 76:7; 9; 78:34; 42; 59; 81:5; 87:6; 89:9; 90:4; 92:7(2); 94:8; 18; 95:9; 101:2; 102:t, 2(2); 16; 22; 105:12; 13; 38; 106:44; 109:7; 23; 25; 28; 114:1; 119:6; 7; 32; 74; 82; 84; 171; 120:7; 122:1; 124:2; 3; 126:1; 137:1; 138:3; 4; 139:15; 16; 18; 141:1; 6; 7; 142:t, 3; **Prov** 1:26; 27(2); 2:10; 3:24; 25; 27; 28; 4:8; 12(2); 5:11; 6:3; 9; 22(3); 30; 8:24(2); 27(2); 28(2); 29(2); 11:2; 7; 10(2); 13:12; 14:7; 16:7; 17:14; 28; 18:3; 20:14; 21:11(2); 27; 22:6; 23:1; 16; 22; 31(3); 35; 24:14; 17(2); 25:8; 26:25; 28:1; 12(2); 28(2); 29:2(2); 16; 30:22(2); 23; 31:23; **Eccl** 4:10; 5:1; 4; 11; 8:7; 16; 9:12; 10:3; 16; 17; 12:1; 3; 4; 5; **Song** 5:6; 8:1; 8; **Is** 1:12; 15(2); 2:19; 21; 3:6; 4:4; 5:4; 6:13; 8:19; 21; 9:1; 3; 10:12; 18; 13:19; 16:12; 17:5; 18:3(2); 5; 20:1; 24:13(2); 23; 25:4; 26:9; 11; 16; 27:8; 9; 11; 28:4; 15; 18; 25; 29:8(2); 23; 30:19; 21(2); 25; 29(2); 31:3; 4; 32:7; 19; 33:1(2); 37:1; 9; 36; 38:9; 41:17; 28; 43:2(2); 12; 48:7; 13; 21; 50:2(2); 52:8; 53:2; 10; 54:6; 57:13; 20; 58:7; 59:19; 64:2; 3; 65:12(2); 66:4(2); 14; **Jer** 2:2; 7; 17; 20; 26; 3:8; 16; 4:30; 5:7; 19; 6:14; 15; 8:11; 12; 18; 10:13; 11:15; 12:1; 13:21; 27; 14:12(2); 16:10; 17:6; 8; 18:22; 21:1; 22:23; 23:33; 25:12; 26:8; 10; 21(2); 27:20; 28:9; 29:13; 31:2; 23; 35; 32:16; 34:1; 7; 10; 14; 18; 35:11; 36:11; 13; 16; 23; 37:5; 11; 13;

16; 38:7; 28; 39:4; 5; 40:1; 7; 11; 41:7; 11; 13; 42:6; 18; 20; 43:1; 11; 44:19; 45:1; 51:16; 55; 59; 61; 63; 52:1; **Lam** 1:7; 2:12(2); 3:8; 37; 4:15; **Eze** 1:9; 12; 17(2); 19(2); 21(3); 24(2); 25; 28; 2:2; 9; 3:18; 20; 27; 4:6; 5:2; 13; 15; 16; 6:8; 13; 8:7; 8; 10:3; 5; 6; 9; 11; 16(2); 17(2); 19; 11:13; 12:15; 13:12; 14:9; 13; 21; 23; 15:5(2); 7; 16:6(3); 8; 22; 53; 55; 61; 63; 17:10; 18; 18:19; 24; 26; 27; 19:5; 20:5(2); 28; 31(2); 41; 42; 44; 21:7; 25; 29; 22:28; 23:5; 11; 14; 39; 24:24; 25; 25:3(3); 17; 26:10; 15(2); 19(2); 20; 27:33; 34; 28:22; 25; 26; 29:7(2); 16; 30:4; 8(2); 18; 25; 31:5; 15; 16; 32:7; 9; 10; 15(2); 33:2; 3; 8; 13; 14; 18; 29; 33; 34:5; 27; 35:11; 14; 36:17; 20(2); 23; 37:8; 13; 18; 28; 38:14; 16; 18; 39:15; 26; 27; 42:14; 15; 43:3; 18; 23; 27; 44:7; 10; 15; 17; 19; 21; 45:1; 46:8; 9; 10(2); 12; 47:3; 7; 48:11; **Dan** 3:7; 5:20; 6:10; 14; 20; 8:2; 8; 15; 17; 23; 10:9; 11; 15; 19; 20; 11:4; 12; 34; 12:7(2); **Hos** 1:8; 2:15; 4:14(2); 5:13; 6:11; 7:1; 12; 14; 9:12; 10:10; 11:1; 10; 13:1(2); **Joel** 2:8; 3:1; **Amos** 3:4; 4:7; 9; 7:2; 8:5; **Jonah** 2:7; 4:2; 7; 8; **Mic** 2:1; 5:5(2); 6(2); 7:1; 8(2); **Nah** 1:12; 3:17; **Hab** 1:13; 2:1; 3:16(2); **Zeph** 3:20; **Hag** 1:9; 2:5; 16(2); **Zec** 7:2; 5; 6(2); 7(2); 8:14; 9:1; 13; 12:2; 13:3(2); 4; 14:3; **Mal** 2:17; 3:2; 17; **Mt** 1:18; 2:1; 3; 4; 7; 8; 9; 10; 11(2); 13; 14; 16; 19; 22; 3:7; 16; 4:2; 3; 12; 5:1; 11; 6:2; 3; 5; 6(2); 7; 16; 17; 7:28; 8:1; 5; 10; 14; 16; 18; 23; 28; 32; 34; 9:8; 11; 12; 15; 22; 23; 25; 27; 28; 31; 33; 36; 10:1; 12; 14; 19; 23; 11:1; 2; 12:2; 3; 9; 15; 24; 43; 44; 13:4; 6; 19; 21; 26; 32; 44; 46; 48; 53; 54; 14:5; 6; 13(2); 15; 23(2); 26; 29; 30; 32; 34; 35; 15:2; 31; 16:2; 5; 8; 13; 17:6; 8; 14; 24; 25; 27; 18:24; 31; 19:1; 22; 25; 28; 20:2; 8; 9; 10; 11; 24; 30; 21:1; 10; 15; 19; 20; 23; 32; 34; 38; 40; 45; 46; 22:7; 11; 22; 25; 33; 34; 23:15; 24:3; 15; 32; 33; 46; 50; 25:31; 37; 38; 39; 44; 26:1; 6; 8; 10; 20; 29; 30; 71; 27:1; 2; 3; 12; 17; 19; 24; 26; 29; 33; 34; 47; 50; 54; 57; 59; 28:11; 12; 17; **Mk** 1:19; 26; 29; 32; 37; 2:4(2); 5; 8; 16; 17; 20; 25; 3:5; 8; 11; 21; 4:6; 10; 15; 16; 17; 29; 31; 32; 34; 35; 36; 5:2; 6; 18; 21; 22; 27; 39; 40; 6:2; 11; 16; 20; 21; 22; 29; 34; 35; 38; 41; 46; 47; 49; 53; 54; 7:2; 4; 14; 17; 30; 8:17; 19; 20; 23; 33; 34; 38; 9:8; 14; 15; 20; 25; 28; 36; 10:14; 17; 41; 47; 11:1; 11; 12; 13; 19; 24; 25; 12:14; 23; 25; 34; 13:4(2); 7; 11; 14; 28; 29; 33; 35; 14:11; 12; 23; 26; 40; 67; 72; 15:15; 20; 24; 33; 35; 39; 41; 42; 45; 16:1; 4; 9; 11; **Lk** 1:9; 12; 22; 29; 41; 2:2; 17; 21; 22; 27; 39; 42; 43; 45; 48; 3:21; 4:2; 13; 17; 25(2); 28; 35; 40; 42; 5:4; 6; 8; 11; 12; 19; 20; 22; 35; 6:3; 13; 22(2); 26; 42; 48; 7:1; 3; 4; 6; 9; 12; 13; 20; 24; 37; 39; 42; 8:4; 8; 13; 14; 16; 27; 28; 34; 40; 45; 47; 50; 51; 9:5; 10; 11; 12; 26; 32; 36; 37; 51; 54; 10:31; 32; 33; 35(2); 11:1; 2; 14; 21; 22; 24; 25; 29; 33; 34(2); 36; 38; 12:1; 11; 36(2); 37; 40; 43; 46(2); 54; 55; 58; 13:12; 17; 25; 28; 35; 14:7; 8; 10(2); 12; 13; 15; 15:5; 6; 9; 14; 17; 20; 16:4; 9; 17:7; 10; 14; 15; 20(2); 22; 30; 18:8; 15; 22; 23; 24; 40; 43; 19:5; 7; 15; 28; 29; 37; 41; 20:13; 14; 16; 37; 21:7(2); 9; 20; 28; 30; 31; 22:7; 10; 14; 32; 35; 40; 45; 49; 53; 55; 64; 23:6; 8; 13; 33; 42; 46; 47; 24:6; 23; 40; **Jn** 1:19; 42; 48; 2:3; 9; 10; 15; 22; 23(2); 3:4; 4:1; 21; 23; 25; 40; 45; 47; 52; 54; 5:6; 7; 25; 6:5; 11; 12; 14; 15; 16; 19; 22; 24; 25(2); 60; 61; 7:9; 10; 27; 31; 40; 8:3; 7; 10; 28; 44; 9:4; 6; 14; 35; 10:4; 11:4; 6; 17; 28; 31; 32; 33; 43; 12:12; 14; 16; 17; 41; 13:1; 19; 21; 26(2); 31; 14:29; 15:26; 16:4; 8; 13; 21; 25; 18:1; 22; 38; 19:6; 8; 13; 23; 26; 30; 33; 20:1; 14; 19; 20(2); 22; 24; 21:4; 7; 15; 18(2); 19; **Acts** 1:6; 9; 13; 2:1; 6; 37; 3:12; 13; 19; 4:7; 13; 15; 21; 24; 31; 5:7; 21; 22; 23; 24; 27; 33; 40; 6:1; 6; 7:2; 4; 5; 12; 17; 21; 23; 30; 31; 54; 60; 8:12; 13; 14; 15; 18; 25; 39; 9:8; 19; 26; 30; 37; 39; 40; 41; 10:4; 7; 8; 32; 11:2; 6; 18; 20; 23; 26; 12:4; 6; 10; 11; 12; 14; 16; 19; 25; 13:3; 5; 6; 12; 13; 14; 17; 19; 22; 24; 29; 42; 43; 45; 48; 14:5; 11; 14; 21; 23; 25; 27; 15:2; 4; 7; 30(2); 31; 16:6; 15; 19; 23; 34; 35; 38; 40; 17:1; 6; 8; 9; 13; 16; 32; 18:5; 6; 12; 14; 20; 22; 26; 27(2); 19:5; 6; 9; 21; 28; 30; 34; 35; 41; 20:2; 3; 7; 11; 14; 18; 36; 21:3; 5; 6; 7; 11; 12; 14; 17; 19; 20; 27(2); 32; 34; 35; 40(2); 22:2; 11; 17; 20; 26; 23:6; 7; 10; 12; 16; 28; 30; 33; 34(2); 35; 24:2; 22(2); 24; 25; 25:1; 6; 7; 12; 14; 15; 17; 18; 21; 23; 25; 26:10; 14; 30; 31; 27:1; 4; 5; 7; 9(2); 13; 15; 17; 20; 27; 28; 30; 35(2); 38; 39; 40; 28:1; 3; 4; 6; 9; 10; 15(2); 16; 17; 18; 19; 23; 25; 29; **Rom** 1:21; 2:14; 16; 3:4; 4:10; 19; 5:6; 10; 13; 6:20; 7:5; 9; 21; 9:10; 11:27; 13:11; 15:28; 29; **1Cor** 2:1; 5:4; 8:12; 9:18; 27; 11:18; 20; 24; 25; 32; 33; 34; 13:10; 11(2); 14:16; 26; 15:24(2); 27; 28; 54; 16:2; 3; 5; 12; **2Cor** 1:17; 2:3; 12; 3:15; 16; 7:5; 7; 10:2; 6; 11(2); 15; 11:9; 12:10; 20; 21; 13:9; **Gal** 1:15; 2:7; 9; 11; 12; 14; 4:3; 4; 8; 18; 6:3; **Eph** 1:20; 2:5; 3:4; 4:8; **Phil** 2:19; 28; 4:15; **Col** 3:4; 7; 4:16; **1Th** 2:6; 13; 3:1; 4; 5; 6; 5:3; **2Th** 1:7; 10; 2:5; 3:10; **1Ti** 1:3; 5:11; **2Ti** 1:5; 17; 4:3; 13; S:1; **Titus** 3:12; **Heb** 1:3; 6; 3:9; 16; 5:7; 12; 6:13; 7:10; 27; 8:5; 8; 9; 9:6; 19; 10:5; 8; 11:8; 11; 17; 21; 22; 23; 24; 31; 12:5; 17; **Jas** 1:2; 12; 13; 14; 15(2); 2:21; 25; **1Pet** 1:11; 2:20(2); 23(2); 3:20; 4:13; 5:4; **2Pet** 1:16; 17; 18; 2:18; **1Jn** 2:28; 3:2; 5:2; **3Jn** 3; **Jude** 3; 9; 12; **Rev** 1:17; 4:9; 5:8; 6:1; 3; 5; 7; 9; 12; 13; 14; 8:1; 9:5; 10:3(2); 4; 7; 11:7; 12:13; 17:6; 8; 10; 18:9; 18; 20:7; 22:8

WHENCE

335, 370, 834, 1992, 2088, 8033, *3606, 3739, 4159*

Gen 3:23; 16:8; 24:5; 29:4; 42:7; **Num** 11:13; 23:13; **Deut** 9:28; 11:10; **Josh** 2:4; 9:8; 20:6; **Judg** 13:6; 17:9; 19:17; **1Sa** 25:11; 30:13; **2Sa** 1:3; 13; **2Kin** 5:25; 6:27; 20:14; **Neh** 4:12; **Job** 1:7; 2:2; 10:21; 16:22; 28:20; **Ps** 121:1; **Eccl** 1:7; **Is** 30:6; 39:3; 47:11; 51:1(2); **Jer** 29:14; **Jonah** 1:8; **Nah** 3:7; **Mt** 12:44; 13:27; 54; 56; 15:33; 21:25; **Mk** 6:2; 8:4; 12:37; **Lk** 1:43; 11:24; 13:25; 27; 20:7; **Jn** 1:48; 2:9; 3:8; 4:11; 6:5; 7:27(2); 28; 8:14(2); 9:29; 30; 19:9; **Acts** 14:26; **Phil** 3:20; **Heb** 11:15; 19; **Jas** 4:1; **Rev** 2:5; 7:13

WHERE

335, 346, 349, 370, 375, 413, 575, 645, 657, 833, 834, 1768, 2088, 3027, 5921, 8033, 8478, 8536, *296, 1330, 1337, 1722, 2596, 3606, 3699, 3739, 3757, 3837, 4226, 5101, 5117*

Gen 2:11; 3:9; 4:9; 13:3; 10; 14; 18:9; 19:5; 27; 20:15; 21:17; 22:7; 27:33; 31:13(2); 33:19; 35:13; 14; 15; 27; 37:16; 38:21; 39:20; 40:3; 43:30; **Ex** 2:20; 5:11; 9:26; 12:13; 30; 15:27; 18:5; 20:21; 24; 27:18; 29:42; 30:6; 36; **Lev** 4:12(2); 24; 33; 6:25; 7:2; 14:13; **Num** 9:17; 13:22; 17:4; 22:26; 33:14; 54; **Deut** 1:31; 8:15; 11:10; 30; 18:6; 23:16; 32:37; **Josh** 4:3(2); 8; 9; **Judg** 5:27; 6:13; 9:38; 17:8; 9; 18:10; 19:26; 20:22; **Ruth** 1:7; 16; 17; 2:19(2); 3:4; **1Sa** 3:3; 6:14; 9:10; 18; 10:5; 14; 14:11; 19:3; 22; 20:19; 23:22; 23; 24:3; 26:5(2); 16; 30:9; 31; **2Sa** 2:23; 9:4; 11:16; 15:32; 16:3; 17:12; 20; 18:7; 21:12; 19; 20; 23:11; **1Kin** 4:28; 7:7; 8; 13:25; 17:19; 21:19; **2Kin** 2:14; 4:8; 6:1; 2; 6; 13; 18:34(2); 19:13; 23:7; 8; **1Chr** 11:4; 13; 13:2; 20:6; **2Chr** 3:1; 25:4; 36:20; **Ezr** 1:4; 6:1; 3; **Neh** 10:39; 13:5; **Est** 1:6; 7:5; **Job** 4:7; 9:24; 10:22; 12:24; 14:10; 15:23; 17:15; 20:7; 21:28(2); 23:3; 9; 28:1; 12(2); 20; 34:22; 35:10; 36:16; 38:4; 19(3); 26; 39:30; 40:20; **Ps** 19:3; 26:8; 42:3; 10; 53:5; 63:1; 69:2(2); 79:10; 81:5; 84:3; 89:49; 104:17; 107:40; 115:2; **Prov** 11:14; 14:4; 15:17; 26:20(2); 29:18; **Eccl** 1:5; 8:4; 10; 11:3; **Song** 1:7(2); **Is** 7:23; 10:3; 19:12(2); 29:1; 30:32; 33:18(3); 35:7; 36:19(2); 37:13; 49:21; 50:1; 51:13; 57:8; 63:11(2); 15; 64:11; 66:1(2); **Jer** 2:6(2); 8; 28; 3:2; 6:16; 7:12; 13:7; 20; 16:13; 17:15; 22:26; 35:7; 36:19; 37:19; 38:9; 39:5; 42:14; 52:9; **Lam** 2:12; **Eze** 3:15; 6:13; 8:3; 11:16; 17; 13:12; 17:10; 16; 20:38; 21:30; 34:12; 40:38; 42:13; 43:7; 46:20(2); 24; **Dan** 8:17; **Hos** 1:10; 13:10; **Joel** 2:17; **Amos** 3:5; **Mic** 7:10; **Nah** 2:11(2); 3:17; **Zeph** 3:19; **Zec** 1:5; **Mal** 1:6(2); 2:17; **Mt** 2:2; 4; 9; 6:19(2); 20(2); 21; 8:20; 13:5; 18:20; 25:24(2); 26(2); 26:17; 57; 28:6; 16; **Mk** 2:4; 4:5; 15; 5:40; 6:55; 9:44; 46; 48; 11:4; 13:14; 14:12; 14(2); 15:47; 16:6; 20; **Lk** 4:16; 17; 8:25; 9:6; 58; 10:33; 12:17; 33; 34; 17:17; 37; 22:9; 10; 11(2); **Jn** 1:28; 38; 39; 3:8; 4:20; 46; 6:23; 62; 7:11; 34; 36; 42; 8:10; 19; 9:12; 10:40; 11:6; 30; 32; 34; 41; 57; 12:1; 26; 14:3; 17:24; 18:1; 19:18; 20; 41; 20:2; 12; 13; 15; 19; **Acts** 1:13; 2:2; 4:31; 7:29; 33; 8:4; 11:11; 12:12; 15:36; 16:13; 17:1; 30; 20:6; 8; 21:28; 25:10; 27:41; 28:14; 22; **Rom** 3:27; 4:15; 5:20; 9:26; 15:20; **1Cor** 1:20(3); 4:17; 12:17(2); 19; 15:55(2); **2Cor** 3:17; **Gal** 4:15; **Phil** 4:12; **Col** 3:1; 11; **1Ti** 2:8; **Heb** 9:16; 10:18; **Jas** 3:16; **1Pet** 4:18; **2Pet** 3:4; **Rev** 2:13(3); 11:8; 12:6; 14; 17:15; 20:10

WHEREAS

518, 834, 1768, 3282, 3588, 6258, 8478, *1722, 3699, 3748, 3759*

Gen 31:37; **Deut** 19:6; 28:62; **1Sa** 24:17; **2Sa** 7:6; 15:20; **1Kin** 8:18; 12:11; **2Kin** 13:19; **2Chr** 10:11; 28:13; **Job** 22:20; **Eccl** 4:14; **Is** 37:21; 60:15; **Jer** 4:10; **Eze** 13:7; 16:7; 34; 35:10; 36:34; **Dan** 2:41; 43; 4:23; 26; 8:22; **Mal** 1:4; **Jn** 9:25; **1Cor** 3:3; **Jas** 4:14; **1Pet** 2:12; 3:16; **2Pet** 2:11

WHEREBY

834, 4100, 4482, *1223, 1722, 2596, 3588, 3606, 3739, 3757, 4012, 4314, 5101*

Gen 15:8; 44:5; **Lev** 22:5; **Num** 5:8; 17:5; **Deut** 7:19; 28:20; **1Sa** 20:33; **Ps** 45:5; 8; 68:9; **Jer** 3:8; 17:19; 23:6; 33:8(3); **Eze** 18:31; 20:25; 39:26; 40:49; 46:9; 47:13; **Zeph** 2:8; **Lk** 1:18; 78; **Acts** 4:12; 11:14; 19:40; **Rom** 8:15; 14:21; **Eph** 3:4; 4:14; 30; **Phil** 3:21; **Heb** 12:28; **2Pet** 1:4; 3:6; **1Jn** 2:18

WHEREFORE

199, 389, 1836, 2063, 2088, 3588, 3651, 4069, 4100, 5921, 8478, *686, 1065, 1161, 1223, 1302, 1352, 1355, 1519, 1752, 1909, 2443, 3303, 3606, 3739, 3767, 5101, 5124, 5484, 5620*

Gen 10:9; 16:14; 18:13; 21:10; 31; 24:31; 26:27; 29:25; 31:27; 30; 32:29; 38:10; 40:7; 43:6; 44:4; 7; 47:19; 22; 50:11; **Ex** 2:13; 5:4; 14; 15; 22; 6:6; 14:11; 15; 17:2(2); 3; 20:11; 31:16; 32:12; **Lev** 10:17; 13:25; 25:18; **Num** 9:7; 11:11(2); 12:8; 14:3; 41; 16:3; 20:5; 21; 21:5; 14; 27; 22:32; 37; 25:12; 32:5; 7; **Deut** 7:12; 10:9; 19:7; 29:24; **Josh** 5:9; 7:5; 7; 10; 26; 9:11; 22; 10:3; **Judg** 2:3; 10:13; 11:27; 12:1; 3; 15:19; 18:12; **Ruth** 1:7; **1Sa** 1:20; 2:17; 29; 30; 4:3; 6:5; 6; 9:21; 14:27; 15:19; 16:19; 18:15; 21; 27; 19:5; 24; 20:27; 31; 32; 21:14; 23:25; 28; 24:9; 19; 25:8; 36; 26:15; 18; 27:6; 28:9; 16; 29:7; 10; **2Sa** 2:16; 22; 23; 3:7; 5:8; 7:22; 10:4; 11:20; 12:9; 23; 14:13; 31; 32; 15:19; 16:10; 18:22; 19:12; 25; 35; 42; 21:3; 24:21; **1Kin** 1:2; 11; 41; 11:11; 12:15; 16:16; 20:9; 22:34; **2Kin** 4:23; 31; 5:7; 8; 7:7; 9:11; 36; 17:26; 19:4; **1Chr** 13:11; 19:4; 21:4; 29:10; **2Chr** 5:3; 19:7; 22:4; 25:10; 15; 28:5; 29:8; 34; 33:11; **Neh** 2:2; **Est** 3:6; 9:26; **Job** 3:20; 10:2; 18; 13:14; 24; 18:3; 21:7; 32:6; 33:1; 42:6; **Ps** 10:13; 44:24; 49:5; 79:10; 89:47; 115:2; **Prov** 17:16; **Eccl** 3:22; 4:2; 5:6; **Is** 5:4; 10:12; 16:11; 24:15; 28:14; 29:13; 30:12; 37:4; 50:2; 55:2; 58:3(2); 63:2; **Jer** 2:9; 29; 31; 5:6; 14; 19; 12:1(2); 13:22; 16:10; 20:18; 22:8; 28; 23:12; 27:17; 30:6; 32:3; 37:15; 40:15; 44:6; 7; 46:5; 49:4; 51:52; **Lam** 3:39; 5:20; **Eze** 5:11; 7:24; 13:20; 16:35; 18:32; 20:10; 25; 30; 21:7; 23:9; 24:6; 33:25; 36:18; 43:8; **Dan** 3:8; 4:27; 6:9; 8:26; 10:20; **Joel** 2:17; **Jonah** 1:14; **Hab** 1:13; **Mal** 2:14; 15; **Mt** 6:30; 7:20; 9:4; 12:12; 31; 14:31; 18:8; 19:6; 23:31; 34; 24:26; 26:50; 27:8; **Lk** 7:7; 47; 19:23; **Jn** 9:27; **Acts** 1:21; 6:3; 10:21; 13:35; 15:19; 19:32; 38; 20:26; 22:24; 30; 23:28; 24:26; 25:26; 26:3; 27:25; 34; **Rom** 1:24; 5:12; 7:4; 12; 9:32; 13:5; 15:7; **1Cor** 4:16; 8:13; 10:12; 14; 11:27; 33; 12:3; 14:13; 22; 39; **2Cor** 2:8; 5:9; 16; 6:17; 7:12; 8:24; 11:11; **Gal** 3:19; 24; 4:7; **Eph** 1:15; 2:11; 3:13; 4:8; 25; 5:14; 17; 6:13; **Phil** 2:9; 12; **Col** 2:20; **1Th** 2:18; 3:1; 4:18; 5:11; **2Th** 1:11; **2Ti** 1:6; **Titus** 1:13; **Philem** 1:8; **Heb** 2:17; 3:1; 7; 10; 7:25; 8:3; 10:5; 11:16; 12:1; 12; 28; 13:12; **Jas** 1:19; 21; 4:6; **1Pet** 1:13; 2:1; 6; 4:19; **2Pet** 1:10; 12; 3:14; **1Jn** 3:12; **3Jn** 10; **Rev** 17:7

WHEREIN

834, 1459, 2004, 2098, 4100, 8033, 8432, *1223, 1519, 1722, 1909, 3739, 3757, 4012*

Gen 1:30; 6:17; 7:15; 17:8; 21:23; 28:4; 36:7; 37:1; **Ex** 1:14; 6:4; 12:7; 18:11; 20; 22:27; 33:16; **Lev** 4:23; 5:18; 6:28; 11:32; 36; 13:46; 52; 54; 57; 18:3; **Num** 12:11(2); 19:2; 31:10; 33:55; 35:33; 34; **Deut** 8:9; 15; 12:2; 7; 17:1; 28:52; **Josh** 8:24; 10:27; 22:19; 33; 24:17; **Judg** 16:5; 6; 15; 18:6; **1Sa** 6:15; 14:38; **2Sa** 7:7; **1Kin** 2:26; 8:21; 36; 50; 13:31; **2Kin** 12:2; 14:6; 17:29; 18:19; 23:23; **2Chr** 3:3; 6:11; 27; 8:1; 33:19; **Ezr** 5:7; **Neh** 6:6; 9:12; 19; 13:15; **Est** 5:11; 8:11; 9:22; **Job** 3:3; 6:16; 24; 38:26; **Ps** 74:2; 90:15(2); 104:20; 25; 142:3; 143:8; **Eccl** 2:19(2); 22; 3:9; 8:9; **Is** 2:22; 14:3; 33:21; 36:4; 47:12; 65:12; **Jer** 5:17; 7:14; 12:5; 16:19; 20:14(2); 22:28; 31:9; 36:14; 41:9; 42:3; 48:38; 51:43; **Eze** 20:34; 41; 43; 23:19; 26:10; 32:6; 37:23; 25; 42:14; 44:19; **Hos** 2:13; 8:8; **Jonah** 4:11; **Mic** 6:3; **Zeph** 3:11; **Zec** 9:11; **Mal** 1:2; 6; 7; 2:17; 3:7; 8; **Mt** 11:20; 25:13; **Mk** 2:4; **Lk** 1:4; 25; 11:22; 23:53; **Jn** 19:41; **Acts** 2:8; 7:4; 10:12; **Rom** 2:1; 5:2; 7:6; **1Cor** 7:20; 24; 15:1; **2Cor** 11:12; 12:13; **Eph** 1:6; 8; 2:2; 5:18; **Phil** 4:10; **Col** 2:12; **2Ti** 2:9; **Heb** 6:17; 9:2; 4; **1Pet** 1:6; 3:20; 4:4; 5:12; **2Pet** 3:12; 13; **Rev** 2:13; 18:19

WHEREOF

834, *1537, 1909, 3739, 4012, 5101*

Gen 3:11; **Lev** 6:30; 13:24; 27:9; **Num** 5:3; 7:19; 25; 37; 49; 61; 67; 73; 79; 21:16; **Deut** 13:2; 28:27; 68; **Josh** 14:12; 20:2; 22:9; **1Sa** 10:16; 13:2; **2Sa** 12:30; **2Kin** 13:14; 17:12; **2Chr** 3:8; 6:20; 24:14; 33:4; **Neh** 12:31; **Job** 6:4; **Ps** 46:4; 57:6; 126:3; **Eccl** 1:10; **Song** 4:2; 6:6; **Jer** 32:36; 43; 42:16; **Eze** 32:15; 39:8; **Dan** 9:2; **Hos** 2:12; **Lk** 23:14; **Acts** 2:32; 3:15; 17:19; 31; 21:24; 24:8; 13; 25:11; 26:2; **Rom** 4:2; 6:21; 15:17; **1Cor** 7:1; **2Cor** 9:5; **Eph** 3:7; **Phil** 3:4; **Col** 1:5; 23; 25; **1Ti** 1:7; 6:4; **Heb** 2:5; 10:15; 12:8; 13:10; **1Jn** 4:3

WHERESOEVER

413, 834, 1768, 3605, 3606, 8033, *302, 1437, 3699*

Lev 13:12; **2Kin** 8:1; 12:5; **1Chr** 17:6; **Jer** 40:5; **Dan** 2:38; **Mt** 24:28; 26:13; **Mk** 9:18; 14:9; 14; **Lk** 17:37

WHEREUNTO

834, 8033, *1519, 3739, 5101*

Num 36:3; 4; **Deut** 4:26; **2Chr** 8:11; **Est** 10:2; **Ps** 71:3; **Jer** 22:27; **Eze** 5:9; 20:29; **Mt** 11:16; **Mk** 4:30; **Lk** 7:31; 13:18; 20; **Acts** 5:24; 13:2; 27:8; **Gal** 4:9; **Col** 1:29; **2Th** 2:14; **1Ti** 2:7; 4:6; 6:12; **2Ti** 1:11; **1Pet** 2:8; 3:21; **2Pet** 1:19

WHEREUPON

413, 834, 4100, 5921, *1722, 3606, 3739*

Lev 11:35; **Judg** 16:26; **1Kin** 7:48; 12:28; **2Chr** 12:6; **Job** 38:6; **Eze** 9:3; 23:41; 24:25; 40:41; 42; **Amos** 4:7; **Mt** 14:7; **Acts** 24:18; 26:12; 19; **Heb** 9:18

WHETHER

176, 335, 518, 996, 3588, 3808, 4100, 4480, 5704, 5750, *1437, 1487, 1520, 1535, 2273, 3379, 3739, 4220, 5037, 5101*

Gen 18:21; 24:21; 27:21; 31:39; 37:14; 32; 42:16; 43:6; **Ex** 4:18; 12:19; 16:4; 19:13; 21:31; 22:4; 8; 9; 34:19; **Lev** 3:1; 5:1; 2; 7:26; 11:32; 35; 13:47; 48(2); 52; 55; 15:3; 16:29; 17:15; 18:9; 22:28; 27:12; 14; 26; 30; 33; **Num** 9:21; 22; 11:23; 13:18; 19(2); 20(2); 15:30; 18:15; **Deut** 4:32; 8:2; 13:3; 18:3; 22:6; 24:14; **Josh** 24:15; **Judg** 2:22; 3:4; 9:2; 18:5; **Ruth** 3:10; **2Sa** 12:22; 15:21; **1Kin** 20:18(2); 33; **2Kin** 1:2; **2Chr** 14:11; 15:13(2); **Ezr** 2:59; 5:17; 7:26; **Neh** 7:61; **Est** 3:4; 4:11; 14; **Job** 34:29; 33(2); 37:13; **Prov** 20:11(2); 29:9; **Eccl** 2:19; 5:12; 11:6(2); 12:14(2); **Song** 6:11; 7:12; **Jer** 30:6; 42:6(2); **Eze** 2:5(2); 7(2); 3:11(2); 44:31; **Mt** 9:5; 21:31; 23:17; 19; 26:63; 27:21; 49; **Mk** 2:9; 3:2; 15:36; 44; **Lk** 3:15; 5:23; 6:7; 14:28; 31; 22:27; 23:6; **Jn** 7:17(2); 9:25; **Acts** 1:24; 4:19; 5:8; 9:2; 10:18; 17:11; 19:2; 25:20; **Rom** 6:16; 12:6; 14:8(3); **1Cor** 1:16; 3:22; 7:16(2); 8:5; 10:31; 12:13(2); 26; 13:8(3); 14:7; 15:11; **2Cor** 1:6(2); 2:9; 5:9; 10; 13(2); 8:23; 12:2(2); 3; 13:5; **Eph** 6:8; **Phil** 1:18; 20; 27; **Col** 1:16; 20; **1Th** 5:10; **2Th** 2:15; **1Pet** 2:13; **1Jn** 4:1

WHICH

227, 428, 589, 595, 834, 1768, 1931, 1958, 1961, 1992, 2004, 2088, 2098, 3426, 3588, 3605, 3651, 4100, 4310, 4480, *302, 846, 1536, 2076, 2532, 3583, 3588, 3634, 3699, 3735, 3739, 3745, 3748, 5101*

Gen 1:7(2); 21; 29(2); 2:2(2); 3; 11; 14; 22; 3:1; 3; 17; 24; 4:11; 5:29; 6:2; 4; 15; 7:23; 8:6; 7; 12; 9:4; 12; 15; 17; 11:5; 6; 13:4; 5; 15; 18; 14:2; 3; 6; 7; 15; 17; 20; 24(2); 16:15; 17:10; 12; 21; 18:8; 10; 13; 17; 19; 21; 27; 19:5; 8; 14; 15; 19; 21; 25; 29; 20:3; 13; 21:2; 9; 25; 29; 22:2; 3; 9; 17; 23:9(2); 16; 17(3); 24:7(2); 24; 42; 48; 60; 25:6; 7; 9; 10; 26:2; 3; 15; 18(2); 32; 35; 27:8; 15; 17; 27; 45; 46; 28:4; 9; 15; 22; 29:27; 30:26; 30; 37; 38; 31:1; 10; 12; 16; 18(2); 39; 43; 51; 32:8; 9; 10; 12; 13; 32(2); 33:5; 8; 18; 34:1; 7; 28(2); 35:3; 4(3); 6; 12; 19; 26; 27; 36:5; 6; 37:6; 38:10; 14; 39:1; 6; 17; 19; 23; 40:5; 20; 41:28; 36; 43; 48(2); 50; 42:9; 38; 43:2; 26; 32; 44:5; 8; 45:6; 27(2); 46:5; 6; 8; 15; 20; 22; 25; 26; 27(2); 31; 47:14; 22; 26; 48:5; 6; 15; 16; 22; 49:1; 30(2); 50:3; 5; 10; 11; 13; 15; 24; **Ex** 1:1; 8; 15; 3:7; 16; 20; 4:9; 18; 19; 21; 28; 30; 5:8; 14; 6:7; 8; 27; 7:15; 17; 8:3; 12; 22; 9:3; 19; 10:2; 5(3); 6; 15; 19; 21; 12:10; 16; 19; 25; 39; 13:3; 5; 8; 12; 14:13; 19; 31; 15:7; 13; 16; 17(2); 25; 26(2); 16:1; 5; 8; 15; 16(2); 23(3); 26; 32; 18:3; 9; 19:6; 7; 22; 20:2; 12; 21:1; 22:9; 13; 23:16(2); 20; 28; 24:3; 5; 8; 12; 25:3; 16; 22(2); 40; 26:10; 13; 30; 27:21; 28:4; 8; 24; 26; 38; 29:27(4); 35; 38; 30:37; 32:1; 2; 3; 4; 7; 8(2); 11; 14; 20; 23; 32; 34; 35; 33:1(2); 7(2); 34:1; 10; 11; 34; 35:1; 4; 25; 29; 36:3; 4; 5; 12; 17; 25; 37:16; 38:8; 39:19; **Lev** 1:8; 12; 2:10; 11; 3:4; 5; 10; 15; 4:2; 3; 7(2); 9; 13; 14; 18(2); 22; 27; 28(2); 5:6; 7; 8; 10; 17; 6:2; 3; 4(4); 5; 10; 15; 20; 7:4; 8; 11; 21; 24; 25; 36; 38; 8:5; 30; 32; 36; 9:5; 6; 8; 12; 15; 18(2); 19; 24; 10:1; 6; 11; 14; 16; 11:2; 10; 13; 21; 23; 26; 34(2); 36; 37; 39; 13:18; 58; 14:32; 34; 37; 40; 15:12; 16:2; 6; 9; 10; 11(2); 23; 17:2; 5; 8; 13; 15(2); 18:5; 24; 27; 30; 19:22(2); 36; 20:8; 23; 24; 25; 21:3; 8; 22:2; 3; 6; 8; 15; 18; 24; 32; 23:2; 4; 10; 37; 38; 25:2; 5; 11; 25; 28; 31; 38; 42; 44; 45; 26:13; 22; 32; 40; 46; 27:11; 22(2); 26; 29; 34; **Num** 1:17; 44; 2:12; 32; 3:3; 26; 39; 46; 4:26; 37; 5:7; 9; 18; 6:5; 18; 21; 8:4; 10:4; 25; 29; 11:5; 12; 17; 20; 12:3; 13:2; 16; 24; 32(2); 33; 14:6; 7; 8; 11; 15; 16; 22(2); 23; 27(2); 29; 30; 31(2); 34; 36; 38; 40; 45; 15:2; 22; 39; 41; 16:11; 12; 40; 18:9; 12; 13; 15; 16; 19; 21; 24; 26; 28; 19:2(2); 15; 20:12; 24; 21:1; 11; 13; 20; 30; 34; 22:5; 11; 20; 30; 36(2); 23:12; 24:4(2); 6; 12; 16(2); 25:18; 26:4; 9; 27:12; 17(5); 28:3; 6; 23; 30:1; 8(2); 14; 16; 31:12; 14; 21(2); 28; 30; 32; 36; 38; 39; 40; 41; 42; 47; 48; 49; 32:4; 7; 9; 11; 24; 38; 39; 33:1; 4; 6; 7; 36; 40; 55; 34:13(2); 17; 35:4; 6(2); 7; 8(2); 11; 13; 14; 25; 31; 34; 36:6; 13; **Deut** 1:1; 4(2); 8; 14; 18; 19; 20; 25; 30; 35; 38; 39(2); 44; 2:4; 8; 11; 12; 14; 22; 23(2); 29(3); 35; 36; 3:2; 4; 9; 12(2); 13; 16; 19; 20(2); 28; 4:1(2); 2(2); 6; 8; 9; 13; 19; 21; 23(2); 28; 31; 32; 40(2); 42; 44; 45; 47; 48(2); 5:1; 6; 16; 28; 31(2); 33(2); 6:1; 2; 6; 10(2); 11(3); 12; 14; 17; 18(2); 20; 23; 7:8; 9; 11; 12; 13; 15; 16; 19; 8:1(2); 2; 3; 10; 11; 14; 16; 18; 20; 9:3; 5; 9; 10; 12(2); 16; 18; 21; 23; 26(2); 28; 29; 10:2; 4; 5; 11; 13; 17; 21; 11:2(2); 3; 7; 8; 9; 12; 13; 17; 21; 22; 27; 28(2); 30; 31; 32; 12:1(2); 2; 5; 9; 10; 11(2); 14; 15; 17; 18; 21(2); 25; 26(2); 28(2); 31; 13:2; 5(2); 6(2); 7; 10; 12; 13; 18(2); 14:4; 12; 23; 24; 25; 29(2); 15:3; 4; 5; 7; 8; 20; 16:2; 4; 5; 6; 7; 10; 11; 15; 16; 17; 18; 20(2); 21; 22; 17:2; 3; 5; 8; 10(2); 11(3); 14; 15; 18; 18:6; 7; 8; 9; 14; 17; 19; 20(2); 21; 22; 19:2; 3; 4; 8; 9; 10; 14(2); 16; 17; 20; 20:1; 14; 15(2); 16; 18; 20; 21:1; 2; 3(3); 4; 9; 16(2); 18; 23; 22:3; 5; 9; 28; 23:13; 15; 16; 23(2); 24:3; 4(2); 5; 25:6(2); 15; 19; 26:1; 2(2); 3; 10; 11; 12; 13; 15; 19; 27:1; 2; 3; 4; 10; 28:1; 8; 11; 13; 14; 15; 33; 34; 36(2); 45; 48; 50; 51; 52; 53; 54; 56; 57; 60; 61; 64; 67; 29:1(2); 3; 12; 16; 17; 22; 23; 25; 29; 30:1; 5; 7; 8; 10; 11; 20; 31:5; 7; 9; 11; 13; 16; 18; 20; 21(2); 23; 25; 29; 32:15; 21(2); 38; 46(2); 49(2); 52; 34:4; 11; 12; **Josh** 1:2; 6; 7; 11; 13; 14; 15(2); 2:3; 6; 7; 17; 18; 20; 3:4; 16; 4:9; 10; 20; 23; 5:1(2); 6(2); 6:25; 7:2; 11; 14(3); 8:27; 31; 32; 33; 35; 9:1; 10; 13; 20; 27; 10:11; 20; 24; 27; 32; 12:1; 2(2); 4; 7(2); 9; 13:3(2); 8; 10; 12; 21(2); 30; 32; 14:1(2); 15; 15:7; 8; 9; 10; 13; 25; 49; 54; 60; 17:5; 18:2; 3; 7; 13; 14; 16; 17; 28; 19:50; 51; 20:7; 21:4; 9; 10; 11; 20; 40; 43; 45; 22:4; 5; 9; 17; 28; 30; 23:13; 14; 15(2); 16(2); 24:5; 8; 12; 13(3); 14; 15; 17; 18; 23; 27; 30; 31; 32(2); 33; **Judg** 1:16; 26; 2:1; 10(2); 12; 16; 17; 20; 21; 3:1; 4; 16; 20; 31; 4:2; 11(2); 14; 6:2; 8; 11; 13; 26; 8:27; 35; 9:2; 4; 13; 24(2); 56; 10:4(2); 8; 14; 11:24; 28; 36; 39; 12:5; 13:8; 14:19; 15:19; 16:8; 24; 29(2); 30(2); 17:2; 6; 18:5; 16; 24; 27(2); 31; 19:10; 14; 16; 19; 20:9; 13; 15; 18; 31; 36; 42; 46; 21:12; 14; 19; 25; **Ruth** 1:22; 2:9; 11; 4:3; 11; 12; 14; 15(2); **1Sa** 1:27; 2:20; 29; 32; 35; 3:11; 12; 13; 4:4; 6:4; 7; 8; 17; 18; 7:14; 8:8; 18; 9:22; 23(2); 24(2); 10:2; 4; 11:11; 12:7; 8; 16; 17; 21; 13:5; 13; 14; 14:2; 4; 14(2); 21; 22; 30; 39; 15:2; 14; 20; 21; 16:4; 16; 19; 17:1; 31; 40; 20:23; 27; 36; 37; 22:9; 14; 23:13; 19; 24:4; 25:7; 27; 32; 33; 34; 35; 44; 26:1; 3; 28:21; 29:1; 3; 4; 30:10; 14; 17; 20; 21; 23; 27(3); 28(3); 29(3); 30(3); 31; 31:11; **2Sa** 2:15; 16; 32; 3:8; 14; 26; 4:8; 5:6; 6:4; 21; 22; 7:12; 23; 8:11(2); 9:3; 10:12; 12:3; 13:10; 23; 14:7; 13; 14; 15:4; 7; 16; 18; 16:11; 21; 23; 17:10; 18; 25; 18:18; 28; 19:5; 16; 19; 38; 20:5; 8; 21:12; 16; 18; 22:44; 23:15; 24:2; 24; **1Kin** 1:8; 9; 48; 2:4; 8; 24; 27; 31; 44; 46; 3:8; 13; 21; 28; 4:2; 7; 11; 12; 13(2); 19; 20; 34; 5:3; 7; 8; 16(2); 6:1; 2; 12(2); 20; 38; 7:8; 17; 20; 41; 45; 51; 8:1; 2; 9; 15; 21; 26; 28; 29(2); 34; 36; 38; 40; 43; 44; 48(4); 51; 56; 58; 63; 9:1; 3; 6; 7(2); 8; 12; 13; 15; 19; 20; 23; 24; 25; 26; 10:3; 5; 7; 8; 9; 10; 13; 24; 11:2; 8; 9; 10; 11; 13; 18; 23; 32; 33; 36; 12:4; 8(2); 9; 15; 17; 21; 28; 31; 32; 33(2); 13:3; 4(2); 5; 11; 12; 21; 22; 26(2); 32(2); 14:2; 8; 15; 18; 20; 21; 22; 24; 26; 27; 15:3; 5; 11; 15(2); 20; 23; 27; 29; 30(2); 16:12; 13(2); 15; 19(2); 24; 27; 32; 34; 17:9; 16; 18:3; 19; 26(2); 19:3; 18(2); 20:19; 34; 21:1; 4; 11; 15; 18; 25; 22:13; 16; 24; 38; 39; 43; 46; **2Kin** 1:4; 6; 7; 16; 17; 18; 2:15; 22; 3:3; 8; 11; 4:4; 9; 5:20; 6:10; 11; 7:13; 15; 8:21; 29; 9:5; 15; 19; 27; 36; 10:5; 6; 10(2); 17; 30; 31; 33; 11:2; 16; 12:2; 20; 13:2(2); 11; 25; 14:3; 5; 6; 11; 15; 21; 24; 25(2); 28; 15:3; 9; 12; 15; 18; 24; 28; 34; 16:2; 7; 14; 19; 17:2; 7; 8; 13(2); 15; 19; 22; 25; 26; 29; 32; 34; 37; 18:3; 6; 9; 14; 16; 17; 18; 21; 27; 37; 19:2; 4; 6(2); 12(2); 15; 16; 20; 28; 29; 20:3; 11; 17; 18; 19; 21:2; 3; 4; 7(2); 8; 11; 15; 16; 20; 25; 22:2; 4(2); 5; 13; 16; 18(2); 20; 23:2; 8; 10; 11; 12(2); 13(2); 15; 16; 17; 19; 24; 27(2); 32; 37; 24:2; 4; 9; 13; 19; 25:4; 8; 16; 19(2); **1Chr** 1:46; 2:3; 19; 42; 55; 3:1; 4:10; 11; 18; 6:61; 65; 9:22; 25; 10:13(2); 11:4; 5; 12:31; 32; 33; 13:2; 6; 14:4; 15:3; 16:15; 16; 40; 17:11; 19:13; 18; 20:4; 21:19; 23; 24; 29; 22:13; 23:4; 5; 29(2); 25:2; 26:22; 26(2); 27:1; 31; 29:3; 17; 19; **2Chr** 1:3; 4; 6; 14; 2:5; 9; 11; 14; 15; 3:5; 4:3; 12(2); 13; 5:2; 3; 6; 10; 12; 6:4; 9; 14; 15(2); 16; 17; 18; 19; 20; 21; 25; 27; 31; 32; 33; 34(2); 36; 38(3); 39; 7:6; 7; 14; 19; 20(2); 21; 22; 8:2; 4; 7; 12; 9:2; 4; 5; 7; 8; 10; 12; 14; 18; 10:8; 9; 15; 11:1; 10; 15; 19; 20; 12:4; 9; 10; 13; 13:4; 8; 10; 14:2; 15:8; 11; 16:14(2); 17:2; 18:23; 20:2; 11; 22; 25; 32; 21:6; 9; 13; 22:6; 23:9; 19; 24:2; 20; 22; 25:2; 9; 13; 15(2); 21; 26:4; 23; 27:2; 28:1; 6; 11; 15; 23; 29:2; 6; 19; 32; 30:7; 8; 16; 31:6; 10; 12; 19; 20; 32:3; 19; 21; 33:2; 3; 7(3); 8; 11; 22(2); 34:2; 9; 11; 24; 26; 31; 35:3(2); 26; 36:5; 8(2); 9; 12; 14; 23; **Ezr** 1:2; 3(2); 5; 7; 2:1; 2; 59; 61; 68; 4:2; 12; 15; 18; 20; 24; 5:2; 6; 8; 11; 14; 16; 17; 6:5(3); 6; 9(2); 12; 13; 15; 18; 21; 7:6; 8; 13; 14; 15; 16; 17; 20; 21; 25; 27(2); 8:25; 35; 9:11(3); 10:14; **Neh** 1:2; 6(2); 7; 2:8; 13; 18; 3:25; 4:2; 3; 12; 14; 17; 23; 5:8; 18; 6:6; 7:5; 61; 63; 72; 8:1; 4; 9; 14; 9:5; 15; 23; 26; 29; 35; 10:29; 12:8; 37; 13:5; 15; 16; **Est** 1:1; 2; 9; 13; 14(2); 18; 20; 2:4; 6; 9; 14; 16; 21; 3:3; 13; 4:6; 16; 6:8(2); 7:9; 8:2; 5(2); 8; 9; 11; 12; 9:13; 22; 25; 26(2); **Job** 3:3; 14; 16; 21; 22; 25(2); 4:14; 19; 21; 5:1; 9; 11; 6:6; 16; 26; 9:5(2); 6; 7; 8; 9; 10; 11:6; 14:19; 15:9; 14; 16; 17; 18; 28(2); 16:8; 20:7; 9; 11; 18; 19; 20; 21:27; 22:15; 16; 17; 23:5; 24:11; 16; 19; 25:6; 27:11; 13; 28:7(2); 29:16; 32:19; 33:27; 34:8; 32; 35:5; 36:16; 24; 28; 37:5; 16; 18; 21; 38:23; 24; 39:14; 40:15; 41:1; 42:3; 8; **Ps** 1:4; 3:2; 7:t, 10; 15; 8:3; 9:11; 13; 15; 16; 17:7; 13; 14(2); 18:17; 19:5; 21:11; 25:3; 28:3; 31:18; 19(2); 32:8; 9; 35:7; 10; 27; 40:5(2); 41:9; 44:10; 45:1; 51:8; 58:5; 7; 8; 59:12; 60:10(2); 61:7; 65:6; 7; 9; 66:9; 14; 20; 68:6; 16; 28; 33; 69:4; 22; 71:20; 23; 74:2(2); 78:3; 5; 6; 45(2); 54; 60; 68; 69; 79:10; 80:12; 15; 81:10; 83:10; 85:12; 86:17; 89:49; 90:5; 91:9; 94:20; 102:18; 104:8; 10; 12; 15; 16; 105:8; 9; 106:21; 36; 107:25; 37; 109:19; 114:8; 115:15; 118:20; 22; 24; 27; 119:21; 39; 47; 48; 49; 85; 165; 121:2; 125:1; 129:6; 8; 134:1; 135:21; 136:13; 16; 17; 138:8; 139:16; 140:2; 141:5; 9; 144:1; 146:6(2); 7(2); 147:9; 148:6; **Prov** 1:19; 2:16; 17; 6:7; 7:5; 9:5; 11:22; 12:27; 14:12; 33; 19:17; 20:25; 22:28; 23:5; 8; 24:13; 25:1; 27:16; 28:3; 30:18(2); 21; 24; 29; 30; 31:3; **Eccl** 1:3; 9(3); 10; 15(2); 2:3; 12; 16; 18; 20; 3:2; 10; 15(3); 19; 4:2(2); 3; 15; 5:4; 13; 15; 18(2); 6:1; 10; 12; 7:13; 19; 24; 28; 8:7; 12; 13; 14; 15; 9:9(2); 10:5(2); 20; 12:5; 10; 11; **Song** 1:1; 3:7; 4:2; 5; 6:6; 7:2; 4; 13; 8:6; 12; **Is** 1:1; 29; 2:8; 20; 3:12; 5:23; 6:6; 8:18; 10:1; 3; 11:10; 11; 16; 13:1; 17; 14:12; 15:7; 17:2; 8; 9; 12; 18:1; 19:15; 16; 17; 21:10; 22:3; 15; 26:2; 27:13; 28:1; 2; 4(2); 14; 29; 29:11; 30:10; 24; 31; 32; 31:7; 36:3; 37:4; 12(2); 17; 22; 29; 30; 38:3; 8(2); 39:6; 7; 8; 42:5; 43:16; 17; 44:2; 14; 45:3; 46:3(2); 47:11; 48:1(2); 14; 17(2); 49:20; 50:1; 51:10; 12; 17; 23; 52:15(2); 55:2(3); 11; 56:8; 11; 57:16; 59:5; 21; 61:9; 62:2; 6; 8; 63:7; 64:3; 65:2; 4(2); 5; 7; 18; 66:4; 22; **Jer** 2:11(2); 3:6; 15; 5:17; 21(2); 22; 7:10; 11; 12; 14(2); 30; 31(2); 8:3; 17; 9:13; 14; 24; 25; 10:1; 11:4(2); 5; 8; 10(2); 11; 17; 12:14; 13:4; 6; 10(3); 15:4; 14(2); 18; 17:4(2); 16; 19; 18:1; 14; 19:2; 3; 5; 20:2; 5; 16; 21:1; 4; 13; 22:6; 11(2); 28; 23:4; 7; 8(2); 27(2); 40; 24:2; 8; 25:2; 13(2); 22; 26; 27; 29; 26:2; 3; 4; 19; 27:3; 8; 9; 18; 20; 28:1; 6; 9; 29:1; 8; 19; 21; 22; 23; 27; 31:2; 21; 32; 35(2); 32:1; 2; 8; 11(2); 14(2); 20; 22; 32; 34; 35(2); 33:3; 4; 9; 10; 12; 14; 24; 34:1; 5; 8; 10; 14; 15; 18(2); 19; 21; 35:1; 4(2); 15; 16; 36:3; 4; 6; 21; 27; 28; 32; 37:2; 7; 19; 38:3; 7; 20; 39:10; 40:1; 4; 7; 10; 15; 41:9; 13; 17; 42:5; 8; 16; 21; 43:1; 9; 44:1(2); 3; 9; 14(2); 15; 20; 22; 45:4(2); 46:1; 2(2); 49:28; 31(2); 50:3; 51:12; 25; 44; 59; 52:2; 7; 12(2); 19(2); 20; 25(2); **Lam** 1:12; 2:3; 17; 5:18; **Eze** 1:2; 23(2); 3:20; 23; 4:10; 14; 5:9; 16(2); 6:9(3); 7:13(2); 8:3; 14; 17; 9:2; 3; 6; 11; 10:22; 11:1; 3; 23; 12:2; 28; 13:11; 16(2); 17; 14:7; 15:2; 6; 16:14; 17; 19; 27; 32; 36; 45; 51; 52; 57; 59; 17:3; 18:5; 14; 18; 19; 21; 27; 19:14; 20:6; 11; 13; 15(2); 21; 28; 32; 42; 21:14; 22:4; 5; 13(2); 23:6; 24; 42; 24:21; 27; 25:9; 26:6; 17(2); 27:3; 7(2); 27; 29:3; 16; 30:22; 32:9; 23; 24(2); 27; 29; 30; 33:14; 16; 19; 29; 34:4(4); 16(4); 19(2); 35:11; 12; 36:4; 5; 21; 22; 23(2); 37:1; 19; 38:8; 12; 17; 39:19; 28; 40:2; 6(3); 40; 44; 46; 41:1; 6; 9(2); 15; 42:1; 3(2); 11; 13; 14; 43:3; 19; 44:1; 10; 13; 45:4; 14; 46:19(2); 47:8; 9; 14; 16(2); 22; 48:8; 11(2); 22; 29; **Dan** 1:2; 5; 8; 10; 15; 2:14; 26; 27; 34; 39; 44; 3:2; 12; 14; 15; 18; 29; 4:5; 20; 21; 24; 5:2(2); 3; 13; 23; 6:1; 8; 12; 13; 15; 24; 26; 7:6; 11; 14(2); 17(2); 19(2); 20; 23; 8:1; 2; 3; 6; 9; 13; 16; 20; 26; 9:1; 6; 10; 12; 14; 18; 10:4; 10; 21; 11:4; 7; 16; 24; 12:1; 6; 7; **Hos** 1:3; 10; 2:8; 23; 5:9; **Joel** 1:4(3); 2:25; **Amos** 1:1; 4; 7; 10; 12; 2:4; 3:1; 4:1(3); 3; 5:1; 3; 26; 6:1; 13(2); 9:10; 12; 15; **Obad** 20; **Jonah** 1:9; 4:10(2); **Mic** 1:1; 2:3; 5:3; 6:14; 7:10; 14; 20; **Nah** 3:17; **Hab** 1:1; 5; 6; 2:4; 6; 17; **Zeph** 1:1; 9; 2:3; **Hag** 1:11; 2:14; **Zec** 1:6; 7; 12; 19; 21(2); 2:8; 4:2; 10; 12; 6:5; 6; 10; 7:3; 7; 12; 8:9; 10:5; 11:10; 16; 12:1; 13:6; 14:4; 7; 16; **Mal** 1:13; 14; 2:11; 4:4; **Mt** 1:20; 22; 23; 2:9; 15; 16; 17; 20; 23; 3:10; 4:13; 14; 16(2); 24(2); 5:6; 10; 12; 16; 44; 45; 46; 48; 6:1; 4; 6(2); 9; 18(2); 27; 30; 7:6; 11; 13; 14; 15; 21; 24; 26; 8:17; 9:8; 16; 20; 10:20; 28(2); 32; 33; 11:4; 10; 14; 21; 23(2); 12:2; 4(2); 10; 17; 50; 13:14; 17(2); 19(2); 23; 24; 31; 32; 33; 35(2); 41; 44; 48; 52(2); 14:9; 15:1; 11(2); 13; 18; 20; 27; 16:8; 17; 28; 17:5; 18:6; 10; 11; 12; 13; 14; 19; 23; 24; 28; 19:4; 9; 12(3); 18; 28; 20:1; 12; 21:4; 21; 24; 33; 41; 42; 22:2; 4; 8; 11; 21; 23; 31; 35; 36; 23:9; 16; 24; 26; 27; 31; 37; 24:16; 17; 18; 25:1; 24; 28; 29; 26:25; 28; 51; 62; 75; 27:3; 9; 17; 22; 35; 44; 52; 55; 56; 60; 28:5; **Mk** 1:2; 44; 2:3; 24; 26(2); 3:1; 3; 17; 19; 22; 34; 4:16; 18; 20; 22; 25; 31; 5:25; 35; 41; 6:2; 26; 7:1; 4; 13; 15; 20; 9:1; 17; 39; 10:42; 11:21; 23; 25; 26; 12:10; 18; 25; 28; 38; 40; 42; 43; 13:19; 32; 14:18; 24; 32; 60; 15:7; 22; 28; 34; 39; 41; 43; 46; 16:6; 14; **Lk** 1:1; 2; 20; 35; 45; 70; 73; 2:4; 10; 11; 15(2); 17; 18; 21; 24; 31; 33; 34; 37; 50; 3:9; 13; 19; 22; 23; 24(5); 25(5); 26(5); 27(5); 28(5); 29(5); 30(5); 31(5); 32(5); 33(5); 34(5); 35(5); 36(5); 37(5); 38(4); 4:22; 33; 5:3; 7; 9; 10; 17; 18; 21; 6:2; 3; 4; 8; 16; 17; 27(2); 28; 32; 33; 45(2); 46; 48; 49; 7:25; 27; 37; 39; 41; 42; 47; 8:2; 3; 13(2); 14(2); 15; 16; 18; 20; 21; 26; 27; 36; 43; 9:27; 30; 31; 36; 43; 46; 61; 10:11; 13; 15; 23; 24(2); 30; 36; 39; 42; 11:2; 5; 27; 33; 35; 40(2); 44; 50; 51; 12:1; 3; 5; 15; 20; 24; 25; 26; 28; 33; 47; 13:11; 14; 19; 21; 30(2); 34; 14:2; 5; 7; 24; 28; 15:4; 6; 7; 9; 30; 16:1; 10; 12(2); 15(2); 19; 20; 21; 26; 17:7; 10(2); 12; 31; 18:2; 7; 9; 27; 34; 39; 19:2; 10; 20; 26; 27; 30; 42; 20:17; 20; 25(2); 27; 35; 46; 47; 21:6(2); 15; 21(2); 22; 26; 22:1; 19; 20; 23; 24; 28; 49; 52; 23:27; 29(2); 33; 39; 48; 55; 24:1; 10; 12; 13; 14; 18; 19; 21; 22; 23; 24; 44(2); **Jn** 1:9; 13; 18; 24; 29; 30; 33; 38; 40; 41; 42; 2:9; 10; 22; 23; 3:6(2); 13; 29; 4:5; 9; 12; 25; 29; 39; 53; 5:2; 5; 12; 15; 23; 28; 30; 32; 36; 37; 39; 44; 6:1; 2; 9; 13; 22; 27(3); 33; 39(2); 40; 41; 44; 46; 50; 51(2); 58; 7:31; 39; 8:9; 26; 31; 38(2); 40; 46; 53; 9:1; 7; 8; 39(2); 40; 10:6; 16; 29; 32; 11:2; 16; 27; 31; 33; 37; 42; 45(2); 12:1; 4; 21; 38; 49; 13:1; 14:24(2); 26; 15:3; 24; 26; 17:4; 5; 6; 8; 9; 20; 22; 24; 18:1; 2; 5; 9(2); 11; 13; 14; 16; 21; 22; 32; 19:17; 24; 32; 39; 20:8; 16; 30; 21:10; 20(2); 24;

25(2); **Acts** 1:2; 4; 7; 11(2); 12; 16(2); 21; 24; 25; 2:7; 16; 22; 33; 3:2; 10(2); 11; 16; 18; 20; 21; 23; 25; 4:4; 11(2); 14; 20; 21; 24; 32; 36; 5:9; 16; 17; 6:9; 10; 11; 13; 14; 7:3; 17; 18; 20; 34; 35; 37; 38; 40; 43; 45; 52(2); 8:1; 6(2); 9; 13; 14; 24; 26; 32; 9:7; 11; 19; 21; 22; 30; 32; 33; 36(2); 39; 10:2; 7; 17(2); 18; 21; 36; 37(2); 39; 42; 44; 45; 47; 11:6; 13; 19; 20; 22; 28; 29; 30; 12:9; 10; 13:1; 7; 22; 27; 31; 32; 39; 40; 41; 45; 14:3; 13; 14; 15; 26; 15:1; 5; 8; 10; 16; 19; 23; 24; 29; 31; 16:1; 2; 3; 4; 12; 13; 14(2); 16; 17; 21; 17:5; 12; 21; 31; 34; 18:27; 19:4; 10; 13; 14; 19; 24; 26; 31; 35; 37; 38; 20:19; 24; 28(2); 32(2); 38; 21:8; 9; 20; 21; 23; 25; 27; 38; 39; 22:1; 3; 5; 10; 12; 29; 23:13; 21; 24:14(2); 15; 24; 25:5; 7(2); 16; 19; 24; 26:3; 4; 5; 7(2); 10; 13; 16(2); 18; 22; 27:8; 11; 12; 16; 17; 39; 43; 28:9; 11; 24; 31; **Rom** 1:2; 3; 19; 26; 27(2); 28; 32; 2:2; 3; 14; 15; 19; 20; 21; 27; 28(2); 29; 3:22; 26; 30; 4:11; 12; 14; 16(2); 17; 18; 5:5; 15; 17; 6:17; 7:2; 5; 10; 13(2); 15; 16; 18; 19; 23; 8:1; 18; 23; 26; 39; 9:6; 8; 23; 25(2); 30(2); 31; 10:5(2); 6; 8; 11:2; 7; 14; 22; 24(2); 12:1; 9(2); 14; 13:3; 4; 14:3; 19; 22; 15:17; 18; 22; 26; 31; 16:1(2); 10; 11; 12; 14; 15; 17(2); 19; 25; **1Cor** 1:2; 4; 11; 18; 24; 27; 28(2); 2:7; 8; 9; 11; 12; 13(3); 3:10; 11; 14; 17; 4:6; 17; 19; 6:16; 19(2); 20; 7:13; 35; 8:10(3); 9:13(2); 14; 24; 10:16(2); 18; 19; 20; 30; 11:19; 23(2); 24; 12:6; 22; 23; 24; 13:10(2); 14:22; 15:1(2); 2; 3; 10(2); 18; 27; 29; 31; 36; 37; 46(3); 57; 16:17; **2Cor** 1:1(2); 4; 6(2); 8; 9; 21; 2:2; 4; 6; 14; 17; 3:7; 10; 11(2); 13(2); 14; 4:4; 11; 14; 16; 17; 18(4); 5:2; 12; 15(2); 7:14; 8:11; 16; 19; 20; 22; 9:2; 6(2); 11; 14; 10:2; 8; 13; 11:4(2); 9(2); 12; 17; 28; 30; 31; 12:4; 6; 21(2); 13:2; 3; 7; 10; **Gal** 1:2; 7; 8; 11; 17; 20; 22; 23(2); 2:2(2); 4; 10; 12; 18; 20; 3:7; 9; 10; 16; 17; 21; 23; 4:8; 14; 24(3); 25; 26(2); 27; 5:6; 12; 19; 21(2); 6:1; **Eph** 1:1; 9; 10(2); 14; 20; 21; 23; 2:10; 11; 17; 3:2; 5; 9; 11; 13; 19; 4:15; 16; 22; 24; 28; 29; 5:4; 12; 6:2; 17; 20; **Phil** 1:1; 6; 11; 12; 23; 28; 30; 2:5; 9; 13; 21; 3:3; 6; 9(3); 12; 13(2); 17; 4:3; 7; 9; 13; 18; 21; **Col** 1:2; 4; 5; 6; 12; 23(3); 24(2); 25; 26; 27; 29; 2:10; 14; 17; 18; 19; 22; 23; 3:1; 5(2); 6; 7; 10; 14; 15; 25; 4:1; 3; 9; 11(2); 15(2); 17; **1Th** 1:1; 10; 2:4; 13(2); 14; 3:10; 4:5; 10; 13(2); 14; 15(2); 17; 5:12; 15; 21; **2Th** 1:5(2); 2:15; 16; 3:4; 6; 11; 17; **1Ti** 1:1; 4(2); 6; 11; 14; 16; 18; 19; 2:10; 3:7; 13; 15; 4:3(2); 8; 14; 5:13; 6:3; 9; 10; 15; 16; 20; 21; S:1; **2Ti** 1:1; 5; 6; 9; 12(2); 13(2); 14(2); 15; 2:10; 3:6; 11; 14; 15(2); 4:8; **Titus** 1:1; 2; 3; 11; 2:1; 3:5; 6; 8; **Philem** 1:5; 6; 8; 11; **Heb** 1:5; 13; 2:1; 3; 11; 13; 3:5; 4:3; 15; 5:8; 12; 6:7; 8; 10; 18; 19(2); 7:2; 13; 14; 19; 28(2); 8:1; 2; 6; 13; 9:2; 3; 4; 5; 7; 9(2); 10; 15; 20; 24; 10:1; 8; 10; 11; 20; 27; 32; 35; 11:3(2); 4; 7(2); 8; 10; 12; 29; 12:1; 5; 9; 11; 13; 14; 19; 20; 23; 27; 28; 13:3; 7; 9; 10; 21; **Jas** 1:1; 12; 21; 2:5; 7; 16; 23; 3:4; 9; 5:4(2); 11; 20; **1Pet** 1:3; 10; 11; 12(2); 15; 23; 25; 2:7(3); 8; 10(2); 11; 12; 3:4(2); 13; 19; 20; 4:11; 12; 5:1; 2; **2Pet** 1:18; 2:11; 15; 3:1; 2; 7; 10; 16(2); **1Jn** 1:1(4); 2; 3; 5; 2:7(2); 8; 24(2); 27; 3:24; 5:9; 16; **2Jn** 2; 5; 8; **3Jn** 6; 10; 11(2); **Jude** 3; 6; 10; 15(2); 17; **Rev** 1:1(2); 3; 4(5); 7; 8(3); 11; 19(3); 20(2); 2:2(2); 6; 7; 8; 9; 10; 12; 15; 17; 20; 23; 24; 25; 3:2; 4; 9; 10; 11; 12(2); 4:1(3); 5; 8; 5:6; 8; 13; 6:9; 7:4; 9; 10; 13; 14; 17; 8:2; 3; 4; 6; 9; 13; 9:4; 11; 13; 14(2); 15; 18; 20(2); 10:4; 5; 6; 8(3); 11:2; 8; 11; 16; 17; 18; 12:4; 9; 10; 13; 16; 17; 13:2; 4; 12; 14(2); 14:3; 4(2); 10; 13; 17; 18; 16:2(2); 5; 9; 14; 17:1; 7; 9(2); 12(2); 15; 16; 18(2); 18:6; 14; 15; 19:2; 9; 14; 20; 21; 20:2; 4; 8; 12(2); 13(2); 21:8(2); 9; 12; 24; 27; 22:2; 6; 8; 9; 11; 19; 20

WHILE

518, 3117, 3541, 3588, 4705, 5704, 5750, 5751, 7350, *891, 1722, 2193, 2250, 2540, 3153, 3397, 3588, 3641, 3739, 3752, 3753, 3819, 4340, 5099, 5550, 5613*

Gen 8:22; 19:16; 25:6; 29:9; 45:1; 46:29; **Ex** 33:22(2); 34:29; **Lev** 4:27; 14:46; 26:43; **Num** 11:33; 15:32; 23:15; 25:11; **Deut** 19:6; 31:27; **Josh** 14:10; **Judg** 3:26; 11:26; 14:17; 15:1; 16:27; **1Sa** 2:13; 7:2; 9:27; 14:19; 20:14; 22:4; 25:7; 16; 27:11; **2Sa** 3:6; 35; 7:19; 12:18; 21; 22; 13:30; 15:8; 12; 17:2; 18:14; 19:32; 24:13; **1Kin** 1:14; 22; 42; 3:20; 6:7; 12:6; 17:7; 18:45; **2Kin** 6:33; **1Chr** 12:1; 17:17; 21:12; **2Chr** 10:6; 14:7; 15:2; 26:19; 34:3; **Neh** 7:3; **Est** 2:21; 6:14; **Job** 1:16; 17; 18; 20:23; 24:24; 27:3; **Ps** 7:2; 31:13; 37:10; 39:1; 3; 42:3; 10; 49:18; 63:4; 69:3; 78:30; 88:15; 104:33; 146:2(2); **Prov** 8:26; 19:18; 31:15; **Eccl** 9:3; 12:1; 2; **Song** 1:12; **Is** 10:25; 28:4; 29:17; 55:6(2); 63:18; 65:24; **Jer** 13:16; 15:9; 33:1; 39:15; 40:5; 51:33; **Lam** 1:19; **Eze** 9:8; **Dan** 4:31; **Hos** 1:4; **Nah** 1:10(2); **Hag** 2:6; **Zec** 14:12; **Mt** 1:20; 9:18; 12:46; 13:21; 25; 29; 14:22; 17:5; 22; 22:41; 25:5; 10; 26:36; 47; 73; 27:63; 28:13; **Mk** 1:35; 2:19; 5:35; 6:31; 45; 12:35; 14:32; 43; 15:44; **Lk** 1:8; 2:6; 5:34; 8:13; 49; 9:34; 43; 10:13; 14:32; 18:4; 22:47; 58; 60; 24:15; 32(2); 41; 44; 51; **Jn** 4:31; 5:7; 7:33; 9:4; 12:35(2); 36; 13:33; 14:19; 16:16(2); 17(2); 18; 19(2); 17:12; **Acts** 1:9; 10; 9:39; 10:10; 17; 19; 44; 15:7; 17:16; 18:18; 19:1; 20:11; 22:17; 24:20; 25:8; 27:33; 28:6; **Rom** 2:15; 5:8; 7:3; **1Cor** 3:4; 8:13; 16:7; **2Cor** 4:18; **Gal** 2:17; **1Ti** 5:6; 6:10; **Heb** 3:13; 15; 9:8; 17; 10:37; **1Pet** 3:2; 20; 5:10; **2Pet** 2:13; 19

WHITHER

413, 575, 834, 5921, 8033, *3699, 3739, 3757, 4226*

Gen 16:8; 20:13; 28:15; 32:17; 37:30; **Ex** 21:13; 34:12; **Lev** 18:3; 20:22; **Num** 13:27; 15:18; 35:25; 26; **Deut** 1:28; 3:21; 4:5; 14; 27; 6:1; 7:1; 11:8; 10; 11; 29; 12:29; 21:14; 23:12; 20; 28:21; 37; 63; 30:1; 3; 16; 18; 31:13; 16; 32:47; 50; **Josh** 2:5; **Judg** 19:17; **Ruth** 1:16; **1Sa** 10:14; 27:10; **2Sa** 2:1; 13:13; 15:20; 17:18; **1Kin** 2:36; 42; 8:47; 18:10; 12; 21:18; **2Kin** 5:25; **2Chr** 6:37; 38; 10:2; **Neh** 2:16; **Ps** 122:4; 139:7(2); **Eccl** 9:10; **Song** 6:1(2); **Is** 20:6; **Jer** 8:3; 15:2; 16:15; 19:14; 22:12; 23:3; 8; 24:9; 29:7; 14; 18; 30:11; 32:37; 40:4; 12; 42:22; 43:5; 44:8; 45:5; 46:28; 49:36; **Eze** 1:12; 4:13; 6:9; 10:11; 12:16; 29:13; 36:20; 21; 22; 37:21; 47:9; **Dan** 9:7; **Joel** 3:7; **Zec** 2:2; 5:10; **Lk** 10:1; 24:28; **Jn** 3:8; 6:21; 7:35; 8:14(2); 21; 22; 12:35; 13:33; 36(2); 14:4; 5; 16:5; 18:20; 21:18(2); **Heb** 6:20; 11:8; **1Jn** 2:11

WHO

428, 430, 589, 834, 1768, 1931, 1992, 4479, *841, 846, 2532, 3588, 3739, 3745, 3748, 3778, 5100, 5101*

Gen 3:11; 12:7; 14:12; 21:7; 26; 24:15; 27; 27:18; 32; 33; 30:2; 33:5; 35:3; 36:1; 19; 20; 35; 42:30; 43:22; 48:8; 14; 49:9; 25(2); **Ex** 2:14; 3:11; 4:11(2); 28; 5:2; 20; 6:12; 10:8; 12:27; 40; 15:11(2); 18:10(2); 21:8; 32:26; **Lev** 5:8; 12:7; 27:12; **Num** 6:21; 7:2; 9:6; 11:4; 18; 12:7; 14:36; 16:5(2); 21:26; 23:10; 24:9; 23; 25:6; 26:9; 47; 63; 27:21; 31:27; **Deut** 1:33; 2:25; 4:7; 46; 5:3; 26; 8:15(2); 16; 9:2; 21:1; 30:12; 13; 33:9; 26; 29(2); **Josh** 9:8; 11:8; 12:2; 13:12; 15:19; 17:16(2); 21:10; **Judg** 1:1; 2:7; 3:9; 19; 6:29; 35; 7:1; 8:34; 9:28(2); 38; 11:39; 15:6; 17:4; 5; 7; 18:2; 3; 29; 19:1; 21:5; **Ruth** 2:3; 20; 3:9; 16; **1Sa** 2:25; 4:8; 6:20; 10:12; 19; 11:12; 14:17; 45; 16:16; 17:25; 26; 18:18; 20:10; 22:14; 23:22; 25:10(2); 26:6; 9; 14; 15; 30:23; 24; **2Sa** 1:8; 24(2); 4:5; 9; 10; 6:20; 7:18; 10:18; 11:21; 12:22; 16:10; 22:4; 32(2); 23:1; 20; **1Kin** 1:20; 27; 2:24; 32; 3:9; 8:23; 24; 50; 9:9; 12:2; 9; 18; 13:26; 14:8(2); 14; 16(2); 17:1; 19:19; 20:14; 21:11; 22:20; 52; **2Kin** 4:5; 7:17; 8:14; 9:31; 32(2); 10:9; 13; 29; 13:6; 11; 14:24; 15:9; 18; 24; 28; 17:36; 18:35; 23:15; 16; **1Chr** 2:7; 22; 4:22; 5:8; 10; 6:39; 7:24; 31; 8:12; 13(2); 9:1; 18; 31; 33; 11:10; 12; 22; 12:18; 16:41; 17:16; 19:7; 21:16; 22:9; 24:28; 25:1; 3; 9; 27:6; 29:5; 14; **2Chr** 1:10; 2:6(2); 12; 6:4; 8:8; 10:2; 17:16; 18:19; 19:6; 20:7; 34; 35; 22:9; 26:1; 5; 28:5; 30:7; 32:4; 14; 31; 34:26; 35:21; 36:13; 17; 23; **Ezr** 1:3; 3:12; 5:3; 9; 12; **Neh** 1:11; 3:3; 6:10; 11; 7:7; 9:7; 27(2); 32; 13:26; **Est** 2:6; 15; 22; 4:11; 14; 6:2; 4; 7:5; 9; **Job** 3:8; 15; 4:2; 7; 5:10; 9:4; 12(2); 19; 24; 11:10; 12:3; 4; 9; 13:19; 14:4; 16:9; 17:3; 15; 21:31(2); 23:13; 24:25; 26:14; 27:2(2); 30:4; 34:7; 13(2); 29(2); 35:10; 11; 36:22; 23(2); 38:2; 5(2); 6; 8; 25; 28; 29; 36(2); 37(2); 41; 39:5(2); 41:10; 11; 13(2); 14; 33; 42:3; **Ps** 4:6; 6:5; 8:1; 12:4(2); 14:4; 15:1(2); 16:7; 17:9; 18:t; 3; 31(2); 19:12; 24:3(2); 4; 8; 10; 34:t; 35:10; 37:7(2); 39:6; 42:11; 43:5; 53:4; 59:7; 60:9(2); 64:3; 5; 65:5; 68:19; 71:19(2); 72:18; 73:12; 76:7; 77:13; 78:6; 83:12; 84:6; 89:6(2); 8; 90:11; 94:16(2); 103:3(2); 4(2); 5; 104:2(2); 3(3); 4; 5; 105:17; 106:2(2); 108:10(2); 11; 113:5(2); 6; 119:1; 38; 124:1; 2; 6; 8; 130:3; 135:8; 9; 10; 136:4; 23; 25; 137:7; 8; 140:4; 144:2; 10; 147:8(3); 17; **Prov** 2:13; 14; 9:15; 18:14; 20:6; 9; 25; 21:24; 23:29(6); 24:22; 26:18; 27:4; 30:4(4); 9; 31:10; **Eccl** 2:19; 25(2); 3:21; 22; 4:3; 13; 6:12(2); 7:13; 24; 8:1(2); 4; 7; 10; 10:14; 11:5; 12:7; **Song** 3:6; 6:10; 8:2; 5; **Is** 1:12; 6:8; 14:6; 27(2); 23:8; 24:18; 27:4; 29:15(2); 22; 33:14(2); 36:20; 37:2; 40:12; 13; 14; 26; 41:2; 4; 26; 42:19(2); 23(2); 24; 43:9; 13; 44:7; 10; 45:21(2); 49:21(2); 50:8(2); 9; 10; 51:12; 19; 53:1; 8; 60:8; 63:1; 65:16; 66:8(2); **Jer** 1:16; 2:24; 9:12(2); 10:7; 15:5(3); 17:9; 18:13; 20:1; 15; 21:13(2); 23:18(2); 26:20; 23; 30:21; 36:32; 46:7; 49:4; 19(4); 50:44(4); 52:25; **Lam** 2:13; 3:37; **Eze** 10:7; **Dan** 1:10; 2:23; 3:15; 28; 6:27; **Hos** 3:1; 7:4; 14:9; **Joel** 2:11; 14; **Amos** 1:1; 3:8(2); 10; 5:7; **Obad** 3; **Jonah** 3:9; **Mic** 3:2(2); 3; 5:8; 6:9; 7:18; **Nah** 1:6(2); 3:7; **Hab** 2:5; **Zeph** 3:18; **Hag** 2:3; **Zec** 4:7; 10; **Mal** 1:10; 3:2(2); **Mt** 1:16; 3:7; 10:2; 4; 11; 12:48(2); 13:9; 43; 46; 18:1; 19:25; 21:10; 23; 24:45; 25:14; 26:3; 68; 27:57; **Mk** 1:19; 24; 2:7; 3:33; 4:16; 5:3; 30; 31; 9:34; 10:26; 11:28; 13:34; 15:7; 21; 41; 16:3; **Lk** 1:36; 3:7; 4:34; 5:12; 21(2); 7:2; 39; 49; 8:45(2); 9:9; 31; 10:22(2); 29; 12:14; 42; 16:11; 12; 14; 18:26; 30; 19:3; 20:2; 22:64; 23:7; 19; 51; **Jn** 1:19; 22; 27; 4:10; 5:13; 6:60; 64(2); 7:20; 49; 8:25; 9:2; 19; 21; 36; 12:34; 38; 13:11; 24; 25; 18:18; 21:12; **Acts** 1:23; 3:3; 4:25; 36; 5:36; 7:27; 35; 38; 46; 53; 8:15; 27; 33; 9:5; 10:32; 38; 41; 11:14; 17; 23; 13:7; 9; 31; 43; 14:8; 9; 16; 19; 15:17; 27; 38; 16:24; 17:10; 18:27; 19:15; 21:4; 32; 33; 37; 22:8; 23:18; 33; 24:1; 6; 19; 26:15; 28:7; 10; 18; **Rom** 1:18; 25(2); 32; 2:6; 7; 27; 3:5; 19; 4:12(2); 16; 17; 18; 25; 5:14; 7:4; 24; 8:1; 4; 20; 28; 31; 33; 34(3); 35; 9:4; 5; 19; 20; 10:6; 7; 16; 11:4; 34(2); 35; 14:2; 4; 20; 16:4; 5; 6; 7(2); 12; 22; **1Cor** 1:8; 30; 2:16; 3:5(2); 4:5; 7; 17(2); 6:4; 9:7(3); 10:13; 14:8; **2Cor** 1:4; 10; 19;

22; 2:2; 16; 3:6; 4:4; 6; 5:5; 18; 21; 8:10; 19; 10:1; 11:29(2); **Gal** 1:1; 4; 15; 2:3; 4; 6(2); 9; 15; 20; 3:1; 4:23; 5:7; 6:10; 13; **Eph** 1:3; 11; 12; 19; 2:1; 4; 11; 13; 14; 3:8; 9; 4:6; 19; 5:5; **Phil** 2:6; 20; 3:19; 21; **Col** 1:7; 8; 13; 15; 18; 24; 2:12; 3:4; 4:7; 9; 11; 12; **1Th** 2:12; 15; 4:8; 5:8; 10; 24; **2Th** 1:7; 9; 2:4; 7; 12; 3:3; **1Ti** 1:12; 13; 2:4; 6; 4:10; 5:17; 6:13(2); 15; 16; 17; **2Ti** 1:9; 10; 2:2; 4; 18; 26; 4:1; **Titus** 1:11; 2:14; **Heb** 1:1; 3; 7; 14; 2:9; 11; 15; 3:2; 3; 5:2; 7; 14; 6:4; 12; 18; 7:1; 5; 9; 16; 26; 27; 28; 8:1; 5; 9:14; 10:29; 39; 11:11; 27; 33; 12:2; 16; 25; 13:7; **Jas** 3:13; 4:12(2); 5:4; 10; **1Pet** 1:5; 10; 17; 20; 21; 2:9; 22; 23; 24; 3:5; 13; 22; 4:5; 5:1; 10; **2Pet** 2:1; 15; 18; **1Jn** 2:22; 3:12; 4:21; 5:5; **2Jn** 7; **3Jn** 9; **Jude** 4; 18; 19; **Rev** 1:2; 5; 9; 2:1; 13; 14; 18; 4:9; 5:2; 6:17; 10:6; 12:5; 13:4(2); 14:11; 15:4; 7; 18:8; 9

WHOM

413, 428, 834, 853, 1768, 1922, 1992, 2006, 2098, 3487, 3588, 4310, 4479, 5921, 5973, 6440, *846, 3588, 3739, 5101*

Gen 2:8; 3:12; 4:25; 6:7; 10:14; 15:14; 21:3; 22:2; 24:3; 14; 40; 44; 47; 25:12; 30:26; 41:38; 43:27; 29; 44:10; 16; 45:4; 46:18; 48:9; 15; 49:8; **Ex** 4:13; 6:5; 26; 14:13; 18:9; 22:9; 23:27; 28:3; 32:13; 33:12; 19(2); 35:21; 23; 24; 36:1; **Lev** 6:5; 13:45; 14:32; 15:18; 16:32(2); 17:7; 22:5; 25:27; 55; 26:45; 27:24(2); **Num** 3:3; 4:41; 45; 46; 5:7; 11:16; 21; 12:1; 12; 16:5; 7; 17:5; 22:6(2); 23:8(2); 26:5; 59; 64; 27:18; 34:29; 36:6; **Deut** 4:46; 7:19; 9:2(2); 17:15; 19:4; 17; 21:8; 24:11; 28:55; 29:26(2); 31:4; 32:17(2); 20; 37; 33:8(2); 34:10; **Josh** 2:10; 4:4; 5:6; 7; 10:11; 25; 13:8; 21; 24:15; 17; **Judg** 4:22; 7:4; 8:15; 18; 12:9; 14:20; 21:23; **Ruth** 2:19(2); 4:1(2); 12; **1Sa** 2:33; 6:20; 9:17; 20; 10:24; 12:3(2); 13(2); 16:3; 17:28; 45; 21:9; 24:14(2); 25:11; 25; 28:8; 11; 29:5; 30:13; 21; **2Sa** 7:7; 15; 23; 14:7; 15:33; 16:18; 19; 17:3; 19:10; 20:3; 21:6; 8(2); 23:8(2); **1Kin** 2:5; 5:5; 7:8; 9:21; 10:26; 11:20; 34; 13:23; 17:1; 20; 18:15; 31; 20:14; 42; 21:25; 26; 22:8; **2Kin** 3:14; 5:16; 6:19; 22; 8:5; 10:24; 16:3; 17:8; 11; 15; 27; 28; 33; 34; 35; 18:20; 19:4; 10; 22(2); 21:2; 9; 23:5; 25:22; **1Chr** 1:12; 2:21; 5:6; 25; 6:31; 7:14; 21; 9:22; 11:10; 11; 17:6; 21(2); 26:32; 29:1; 8; **2Chr** 1:11; 2:7; 8:8; 9:25; 17:19; 18:7; 20:10; 22:7; 23:18; 28:3; 33:2; 9; **Ezr** 2:1; 65; 4:10; 5:14; 8:20; 10:44; **Neh** 1:10; 7:6; 67; 8:10; 9:37; **Est** 2:6; 7; 4:5; 11; 6:6(2); 7; 9(2); 11; 13; **Job** 3:23; 5:17; 9:15; 15:19; 19:19; 27; 25:3; 26:4; 30:2; **Ps** 10:3; 16:3; 18:2; 43; 27:1(2); 32:2; 33:12; 41:9; 45:16; 47:4; 65:4; 69:26(2); 73:25; 80:17; 86:9; 88:5; 89:21; 94:1(2); 12; 95:11; 104:26; 105:26; 106:34; 38; 107:2; 144:2; 146:3; **Prov** 3:12(2); 27; 25:7; 30:31; **Eccl** 4:8; 5:19; 6:2; 8:14(2); 9:9; **Song** 1:7; 3:1; 2; 3(2); 4; **Is** 6:8; 8:12; 18; 10:3; 19:25; 22:16; 23:2; 28:9(2); 12; 31:6; 36:5; 37:4; 10; 23(2); 40:14; 18; 25; 41:8; 9; 42:1(2); 24; 43:10; 44:1; 2; 46:5; 47:15; 49:3; 7(2); 50:1(2); 51:18; 19; 53:1; 57:4(2); 11; 66:13; **Jer** 1:2; 6:10; 7:9; 8:2(5); 9:12; 16; 11:12; 14:16; 18:8; 19:4; 20:6; 23:9; 24:5; 25:15; 17; 26:5; 27:5; 29:1; 3; 4; 20; 22; 30:9; 17; 33:5; 34:11; 16; 37:1; 38:9; 39:17; 40:5; 41:2; 9; 10; 16(2); 18; 42:6; 9; 11; 44:3; 50:20; 52:28; **Lam** 1:10; 14; 2:20; 4:20; **Eze** 9:6; 11:1; 7; 15; 13:22; 16:20; 37; 20:9; 23:7; 9; 22; 28(2); 37; 40(2); 24:21; 28:25; 31:2; 18; 32:19; 38:17; **Dan** 1:4(2); 7; 11; 2:24; 3:12; 17; 4:8; 5:11(2); 12; 13; 19(4); 6:2; 16; 20; 7:8; 20; 9:21; 11:21; 38; 39; **Hos** 13:10; **Joel** 2:32; 3:2; **Amos** 6:1; 7:2; 5; **Nah** 3:19; **Zeph** 3:18; **Zec** 1:4; 10; 7:14; 12:10; **Mal** 1:4; 2:14; 3:1(2); **Mt** 1:16; 3:17; 7:9; 11:10; 12:18(2); 27; 16:13; 15; 17:5; 25; 18:7; 19:11; 20:23; 23:35; 24:45; 46; 26:24; 27:9; 15; 17; **Mk** 1:11; 3:13; 6:16; 8:27; 29; 10:40; 13:20; 14:21; 71; 15:12; 40; 16:9; **Lk** 6:13; 14; 34; 47; 7:4; 27; 43; 47; 8:2; 35; 38; 9:9; 18; 20; 10:22; 11:19; 12:5; 37; 42; 43; 48; 13:4; 16; 17:1; 19:15; 22:22; 23:25; **Jn** 1:15; 26; 30; 33; 45; 47; 3:26; 34; 4:18; 5:21; 38; 45; 6:29; 68; 7:25; 28; 8:53; 54; 10:35; 36; 11:3; 12:1; 9; 38; 13:18; 22; 23; 24; 26; 14:17; 26; 15:26; 17:3; 11; 24; 18:4; 7; 19:26; 37; 20:2; 15; 21:7; 20; **Acts** 1:2; 3; 2:24; 36; 3:2; 13; 15; 16; 21; 4:10(2); 22; 27; 5:25; 30; 32; 36; 6:3; 6; 7:7; 35; 39; 45; 52; 8:10; 34; 9:5; 37; 10:21; 39; 13:22; 25; 37; 14:23; 15:17; 24; 17:3; 7; 23; 31; 18:26; 19:13; 16; 25; 27; 20:25; 21:16; 29; 22:5; 8; 23:29; 24:6; 8; 25:15; 16; 18; 19; 24; 26; 26:15; 17; 26; 27:23; 28:4; 8; 15; 23; **Rom** 1:5; 6; 9; 3:25; 4:6; 8; 17; 24; 5:2; 11; 6:16(2); 8:29; 30(3); 9:4; 5; 15(2); 18(2); 24; 10:14(2); 11:36; 13:7(4); 14:15; 15:21; 16:4; **1Cor** 1:9; 3:5; 7:39; 8:6(2); 11; 10:11; 15:6; 15; **2Cor** 1:10; 2:3; 10(2); 4:4; 8:22; 10:18; 11:4; 12:17; **Gal** 1:5; 2:5; 3:19; 4:19; 6:14; **Eph** 1:7; 11; 13(2); 2:3; 21; 22; 3:12; 15; 4:16; 6:22; **Phil** 2:15; 3:8; 18; **Col** 1:14; 27; 28; 2:3; 11; 4:8; 10; **1Th** 1:10; **2Th** 2:8; **1Ti** 1:15; 20(2); 6:16(2); **2Ti** 1:3; 12; 15; 2:17; 3:14; 4:15; 18; **Philem** 1:10; 12; 13; **Heb** 1:2(2); 2:10(2); 3:17; 18; 4:6; 13; 5:11; 6:7; 7:2; 4; 8; 13; 11:18; 38; 12:6(2); 7; 13:21; 23; **Jas** 1:17; **1Pet** 1:8(2); 12; 2:4; 4:11; 5:8; 9; **2Pet** 1:17; 2:2; 17; 19; **1Jn** 4:20(2); **2Jn** 1; **3Jn** 1; 6; **Jude** 13; **Rev** 7:2; 17:2; 20:8

WHOSE

834, 853, 1768, 1931, 3588, 4310, *846, 2532, 3588, 3739, 5100, 5101*

Gen 1:11; 12; 7:22; 11:4; 16:1; 17:14; 22:24; 24:23; 37; 47; 32:17(2); 38:1; 2; 6; 25(2); 44:17; 49:22; **Ex** 34:14; 35:21; 26; 29; 36:2(2); **Lev** 13:40; 14:32; 15:32; 16:27; 21:10; 22:4; 24:10; **Num** 24:3; 15; **Deut** 8:9(2); 19:1; 28:49; 29:18; **Josh** 24:15; **Judg** 4:2; 6:10; 8:31; 13:2; 16:4; 17:1; **Ruth** 2:2; 5; 12; 3:2; **1Sa** 9:1; 2; 10:26; 12:3(3); 17:4; 12; 55; 56; 58; 25:2; **2Sa** 3:7; 12; 6:2; 9:2; 12; 13:1; 3; 14:27; 16:5; 8; 17:10; 25; 20:1; 21:16; 19; **1Kin** 3:26; 8:39; 11:26; **2Kin** 7:2; 17; 8:1; 5; 12:15; 18:22(2); **1Chr** 2:16; 26; 34; 7:2; 15; 8:29; 38; 9:35; 44; 12:8; 13:6; 20:5; 6; 26:7; **2Chr** 6:30; 16:9; 28:9; **Ezr** 1:5; 5:14; 7:15; 8:13; **Est** 2:5; **Job** 1:1; 3:23; 4:19; 5:5; 8:14(2); 12:6; 10; 22:16; 26:4; 30:1; 38:29; 39:6; **Ps** 15:4; 17:14; 26:10; 32:1(2); 2; 9; 33:12; 38:14; 57:4; 78:8; 83:18; 84:5(2); 105:18; 144:8; 11; 15; 146:5; **Prov** 2:15; 26:26; 30:14; **Eccl** 2:21; 7:26; **Is** 1:30; 2:22; 5:28; 6:13; 10:10; 14:2; 18:2; 7; 23:7; 8(2); 26:3; 28:1; 30:13; 31:9; 36:7(2); 43:14; 45:1; 51:7; 15; 57:15; 20; 58:11; **Jer** 5:15; 17:5; 7; 19:13; 22:25; 32:29; 33:5; 37:13; 44:28; 46:7; 18; 48:15; 49:12; 51:57; **Eze** 3:6; 11:21; 17:6; 16(2); 20:9; 14; 22; 21:25; 27; 29; 23:20(2); 24:6(2); 32:23; 40:3; 45; 46; 42:15; 43:4; 47:12; **Dan** 2:11; 26; 31; 3:1; 27; 4:8; 19; 20; 21(2); 34; 37; 5:23(2); 7:9; 19; 20; 27; 10:1; 5; **Joel** 1:6; **Amos** 2:9; 5:27; **Obad** 3; **Jonah** 1:7; 8; **Mic** 5:2; **Nah** 3:8; **Zec** 6:12; 11:5; **Mt** 3:11; 12; 10:3; 22:20; 28; 42; **Mk** 1:7; 7:25; 12:16; 23; **Lk** 1:27; 2:25; 3:16; 17; 6:6; 12:20; 13:1; 20:24; 33; 24:18; **Jn** 1:6; 27; 4:46; 6:42; 10:12; 11:2; 18:26; 19:24; 20:23(2); **Acts** 7:58; 10:5; 6; 32; 11:13; 12:12; 25; 13:6; 25; 15:37; 16:14; 18:7; 27:23; 28:7; 11; **Rom** 2:29; 3:8; 14; 4:7(2); 9:5; **2Cor** 8:18; 11:15; **Gal** 3:1; **Phil** 3:19(3); 4:3; **2Th** 2:9; **Titus** 1:11; **Heb** 3:6; 17; 6:8; 7:6; 11:10; 12:26; 13:7; 11; **1Pet** 2:24; 3:3; 6; **2Pet** 2:3; **Jude** 12; **Rev** 9:11; 13:8; 12; 17:8; 20:11

WHOSO

376, 834, 1768, 3605, 4310, 4479, *302, 3588, 3739*

Gen 9:6; **Lev** 11:27; 22:4; **Num** 35:30; **Deut** 19:4; **2Chr** 23:14; **Ps** 50:23; 101:5; 107:43; **Prov** 1:33; 6:32; 8:35; 9:4; 16; 12:1; 13:13; 16:20; 17:5; 13; 18:22; 20:2; 20; 21:13; 23; 25:14; 26:27; 27:18; 28:7; 10; 13; 18; 24; 26; 29:3; 24; 25; **Eccl** 7:26; 8:5; 10:8; 9; **Dan** 3:6; 11; **Zec** 14:17; **Mt** 18:5; 6; 19:9; 23:20; 21; 24:15; **Mk** 7:10; **Jn** 6:54; **Jas** 1:25; **1Jn** 2:5; 3:17

WHOSOEVER

376, 834, 3605, 4310, *302, 1437, 1536, 3588, 3739, 3745, 3748, 3956*

Gen 4:15; **Ex** 12:15; 19; 19:12; 22:19; 30:33(2); 38; 31:14; 15; 32:24; 33; 35:2; 5; **Lev** 7:25; 11:24; 25; 31; 15:5; 10; 19; 21; 22; 27; 17:14; 18:29; 19:20; 20:2; 21:17; 22:3; 5; 21; 24:15; **Num** 5:2; 15:14; 17:13; 19:13; 16; 31:19(2); **Deut** 18:19; **Josh** 1:18; 2:19(2); 20:9; **Judg** 7:3; **1Sa** 11:7; **2Sa** 5:8; 14:10; 17:9; **1Kin** 13:33; **2Kin** 10:19; 21:12; **1Chr** 11:6; 26:28; **2Chr** 13:9; 15:13; 23:7; **Ezr** 1:4; 6:11; 7:26; 10:8; **Est** 4:11; **Prov** 6:29; 20:1; 27:16; **Is** 54:15; 59:8; **Jer** 19:3; **Eze** 33:4; **Dan** 5:7; 6:7; **Joel** 2:32; **Mt** 5:19(2); 21; 22(3); 28; 31; 32(2); 39; 41; 7:24; 10:14; 32; 33; 42; 11:6; 12:32(2); 50; 13:12(2); 15:5; 16:25(2); 18:4; 19:9; 20:26; 27; 21:44; 23:12; 16(2); 18(2); **Mk** 3:35; 6:11; 8:34; 35(2); 38; 9:37(2); 41; 42; 10:11; 15; 43; 44; 11:23; **Lk** 6:47; 7:23; 8:18(2); 9:5; 24(2); 26; 48(2); 12:8; 10; 14:11; 27; 33; 16:18(2); 17:33(2); 18:17; 20:18; **Jn** 3:15; 16; 4:13; 14; 5:4; 8:34; 11:26; 12:46; 16:2; 19:12; **Acts** 2:21; 10:43; 13:26; **Rom** 2:1; 9:33; 10:11; 13; 13:2; **1Cor** 11:27; **Gal** 5:4; 10; **Jas** 2:10; 4:4; **1Jn** 2:23; 3:4; 6(2); 9; 10; 15; 4:15; 5:1; 18; **2Jn** 9; **Rev** 14:11; 20:15; 22:15; 17

WHY

4069, 4100, 4101, 5922, *1063, 1302, 1519, 2444, 3754, 5101*

Gen 4:6(2); 12:18; 19; 25:22; 27:45; 42:1; 47:15; **Ex** 1:18; 2:20; 3:3; 5:22; 14:5; 17:2; 18:14; 32:11; **Num** 11:20; 20:4; 27:4; **Deut** 5:25; **Josh** 5:4; 7:25; 17:14; **Judg** 2:2; 5:16; 17; 28(2); 6:13; 8:1; 9:28; 11:7; 26; 13:18; 15:10; 21:3; **Ruth** 1:11; 21; 2:10; **1Sa** 1:8(3); 2:23; 6:3; 17:8; 28; 19:17(2); 20:2; 8; 21:1; 22:13; 27:5; 28:12; 15; **2Sa** 3:24; 7:7; 11:10; 21; 13:4; 26; 16:9; 17; 18:11; 19:10; 11; 29; 36; 41; 43; 20:19; 24:3; **1Kin** 1:6; 13; 2:22; 43; 9:8; 14:6; 21:5; **2Kin** 1:5; 7:3; 8:12; 12:7; 14:10; **1Chr** 17:6; 21:3(2); **2Chr** 7:21; 24:6; 20; 25:15; 16; 19; 32:4; **Ezr** 4:22; 7:23; **Neh** 2:2; 3; 6:3; 13:11; 21; **Est** 3:3; 4:5; **Job** 3:11(2); 12(2); 23; 7:20; 21; 9:29; 15:12; 19:22; 28; 21:4; 24:1; 27:12; 31:1; 33:13; **Ps** 2:1; 10:1(2); 22:1(2); 42:5(2); 9(2); 11(2); 43:2(2); 5(2); 44:23; 52:1; 68:16; 74:1(2); 11; 80:12; 88:14(2); **Prov** 5:20; 22:27; **Eccl** 2:15; 7:16; 17; **Song** 1:7; **Is** 1:5; 40:27; 63:17; **Jer** 2:14; 33; 36; 8:5; 14; 19; 22; 14:8; 9; 19; 15:18; 26:9; 27:13; 29:27; 30:15; 36:29; 46:15; 49:1; **Eze** 18:19; 31; 33:11; **Dan** 1:10; 2:15; **Jonah** 1:10; **Mic** 4:9; **Hab** 1:3; **Hag** 1:9; **Mal** 2:10; **Mt** 6:28; 7:3; 8:26; 9:11; 14; 13:10; 15:2; 3; 16:8; 17:10; 19; 19:7; 17; 20:6; 21:25; 22:18; 26:10; 27:23; 46; **Mk** 2:7; 8; 18; 24; 4:40; 5:35; 39; 7:5; 8:12; 17; 9:11; 28; 10:18; 11:3; 31; 12:15; 14:4; 6; 15:14; 34; **Lk** 2:48; 5:30; 33; 6:2; 41; 46; 12:26; 57; 13:7; 18:19; 19:31; 33; 20:5; 23; 22:46; 23:22; 24:5; 38(2); **Jn** 1:25; 4:27; 7:19; 45; 8:43; 46; 9:30; 10:20; 12:5; 13:37; 18:21; 23; 20:13; 15; **Acts** 1:11; 3:12(2); 4:25; 5:3; 4; 7:26; 9:4; 14:15; 15:10; 22:7; 16; 26:8; 14; **Rom** 3:7; 8:24; 9:19; 20; 14:10(2); **1Cor** 4:7; 6:7(2); 10:29; 30; 15:29; 30; **Gal** 2:14; 5:11; **Col** 2:20

WILL

14, 165, 2654, 3045, 5314, 5315, 6634, 7470, 7522, *210, 1012, 1013, 1014, 1106, 1479, 2107, 2133, 2307, 2308, 2309, 3195*

Gen 2:18; 3:15; 16; 6:7; 13; 18; 7:4(2); 8:21(2); 9:5(3); 11; 15; 16; 11:6; 12:1; 2(2); 3; 7; 12(2); 13:9(2); 15; 16; 17; 14:23(2); 15:14; 16:10; 12(2); 17:2(2); 6(2); 7; 8(2); 16(2); 19; 20(3); 21; 18:5; 10; 14; 19; 21(2); 26; 28; 29; 30(2); 31; 32(2); 19:2; 9(2); 13; 14; 21; 32; 20:11; 21:6; 13; 18; 24; 22:2; 5; 8; 17(2); 23:13(2); 24:3; 5; 7; 8; 14; 19; 33; 39; 40; 44; 46; 49; 57; 58; 26:3(4); 4(2); 24; 27:9; 12; 25; 41; 45; 28:13; 15(3); 20(3); 22; 29:18; 27; 32; 34; 35; 30:13; 20; 28; 31; 32; 31:3; 52; 32:9; 11; 12; 20(3); 26; 33:12; 13; 14; 34:11; 12; 15(2); 16(4); 17(3); 22; 23; 35:3; 12(2); 37:13; 20(2); 35; 38:17; 41:32; 40; 42:34; 36; 37; 43:4; 5; 8; 9; 44:9; 26; 31; 45:11; 18; 28; 46:3; 4(2); 31; 47:16; 18; 19; 25; 30(2); 48:4(3); 9; 49:7; 50:5; 15(2); 21; 24; 25; **Ex** 2:9; 3:3; 10; 12; 17; 19; 20(3); 21; 4:1(2); 8(2); 9; 12; 14; 15(2); 21; 23; 5:2; 10; 6:1; 6(3); 7(2); 8(2); 7:3; 17; 8:2; 8; 21; 22; 23; 26; 27; 28; 29; 9:14; 15; 18; 28; 29; 30; 10:4; 9(2); 10; 29; 11:1(2); 4; 8; 12:12(3); 13; 23(3); 25; 48; 13:19; 14:3; 4(2); 13; 17(2); 15:1; 2(2); 9(4); 26; 16:4(2); 23(2); 17:6; 9; 14; 16; 18:19; 19:5; 8; 11; 20:7; 19; 24(2); 21:5; 13; 22; 22:23; 24; 27; 23:7; 21; 22; 23; 25; 26; 27(3); 28; 29; 30; 31(2); 33; 24:3; 7; 12; 25:22(3); 29:42; 43; 44(2); 45(2); 30:6; 36; 32:10; 13(2); 30; 33; 34; 33:1; 2(2); 3; 5; 14; 17; 19(6); 22(2); 23; 34:1; 7; 10(2); 24; **Lev** 1:3; 2:1; 9:4; 10:3(2); 16:2; 17:10(2); 19:5; 20:3(2); 5(2); 6(2); 24; 22:18(2); 19; 29(2); 32; 23:30; 25:21; 26:4; 6(2); 9; 11; 12(2); 14(2); 15; 16(2); 17; 18(2); 19(2); 21(2); 22; 23(2); 24(2); 25(2); 27; 28(2); 30; 31(2); 32; 33(2); 36; 42(3); 44(2); 45; 27:13; 15; 19; 20; 31; **Num** 6:27; 9:8(2); 14; 10:29(2); 30(2); 32; 11:17(3); 18; 21; 12:6(2); 8; 14:8; 11(2); 12(2); 14; 15; 24; 28; 31; 35; 40; 43; 15:3; 14; 16:5(3); 12; 14; 17:4; 5; 20:17(4); 19(3); 21:2; 16; 22(3); 22:8; 17(2); 19; 34; 23:3(3); 27(2); 24:13; 14; 32:15; 16; 17; 18; 19; 20(2); 21; 23(2); 25; 27; 29; 30; 31; 32; 33:55; **Deut** 1:13; 17; 22; 36; 39; 41; 2:5; 9; 19; 25; 27(2); 28; 3:2; 4:10; 31; 5:11; 25; 27; 31; 7:4(2); 10(2); 13(2); 15(3); 16; 20; 22; 9:14; 10:2; 11:14; 15; 23; 28; 12:20; 30; 15:16; 17:12(2); 14; 18:15; 18(2); 19(2); 20:12(2); 21:14; 18(2); 20; 23:21; 25:7; 9; 28:1; 27; 55; 59; 60; 61; 63; 29:20; 30:3(2); 4(2); 5(2); 6; 7; 9(2); 31:3(2); 6; 8(2); 16(2); 17(3); 18; 20; 23; 29(3); 32:1; 3; 7(2); 20(2); 21(2); 23(2); 24; 41(2); 42; 43(3); 33:16; 34:4; **Josh** 1:5(2); 16(2); 17; 18; 2:12; 13; 14; 17; 19; 20; 3:5; 7(2); 10; 7:12; 8:5(2); 6(3); 7; 18; 9:20(2); 11:6; 13:6; 14:12; 15:16; 18:4; 22:18(2); 23:13; 24:15(2); 18; 19; 20; 21; 24(2); **Judg** 1:3; 12; 24; 2:1; 3; 21; 22; 4:7(2); 8(2); 9; 22; 5:3(2); 6:16; 18; 31(3); 37; 39; 7:4; 7; 8:7; 9; 23; 25; 10:13; 18; 11:24; 31; 12:1; 13:16; 14:12(2); 15:1; 7(2); 12; 13(2); 16:5; 17; 20; 17:3; 10; 13; 19:12(2); 24; 20:8(2); 9(2); 10; 28; 21:7; 22; **Ruth** 1:10; 11; 16(2); 17(2); 3:4; 5; 11; 13(3); 18(2); 4:4; **1Sa** 1:11; 22(2); 2:9; 15; 16; 30; 31; 35(2); 3:11; 12(2); 13; 6:5; 7:3; 5; 8; 8:11(2); 12(2); 13; 14; 15; 16; 17; 18; 19; 9:8; 13; 16; 19(2); 10:2; 4; 6; 8; 11:1; 2; 3; 10; 12:3; 10; 14; 15; 16; 17; 22; 23; 13:12; 14:6; 8(2); 9(2); 10; 12; 40; 15:16; 26; 29; 16:1; 2; 3; 11; 17:9; 25(2); 32; 37; 44; 46(3); 47; 18:11; 17; 21; 19:3(3); 20:2(2); 4; 13; 18; 20; 21; 22:3; 7; 23:4; 11(3); 12(2); 23(2); 24:4; 10; 19; 25:8; 28; 26:6(2); 8; 21; 27:11; 28:2; 19; 23; 30:15; 22; 24; **2Sa** 2:6; 26; 3:13; 18; 21(2); 5:19; 6:21; 22(2); 7:10(2); 11; 12(2); 13; 14(2); 27; 9:7(2); 10:2; 11; 11:11; 12; 12:11(2); 12; 18; 22; 13:13; 14:7; 8; 15(2); 16; 17; 15:8; 21; 25; 28; 34(2); 16:12(2); 18(2); 19; 17:1; 2(3); 3; 8; 9(2); 12; 13; 18:2; 3(2); 4; 19:7(2); 26; 33; 36; 38(2); 20:21; 21:4(2); 6(2); 22:3; 4; 29; 50; 24:24(2); **1Kin** 1:5; 14; 30; 51; 52; 2:8; 17; 18; 20; 26; 30; 38; 3:14; 5:5; 6; 8; 9(2); 6:12; 13(2); 8:27; 9:5; 6; 7(2); 11:2; 11(2); 12(2); 13(2); 31(2); 34(2); 35(2); 36; 37; 38(2); 39; 12:4; 7; 11(2); 14(2); 13:7; 8(2); 16; 14:10(3); 16:3(2); 18:1; 15; 23; 24; 19:20; 20:6; 9; 13; 22; 25; 28; 31; 34(2); 21:2(2); 4; 6(2); 7; 21(3); 22; 29(2); 22:14; 21; 22(2); 30; **2Kin** 2:2; 3; 4; 5; 6; 3:7; 18; 4:30; 5:5; 11; 16; 17; 20; 6:3; 11; 19; 28; 7:4; 9; 12; 9:8; 9; 26; 10:5(2); 6; 18:14; 21; 23; 30; 32; 19:4(2); 7(2); 23(2); 28(2); 34; 20:5; 6(3); 8; 9; 21:4; 7; 8(2); 13(2); 14; 22:16; 20(2); 23:27(2); **1Chr** 12:19; 14:10; 16:18; 17:9(2); 10(2); 11(2); 12; 13(2); 14; 19:2; 12; 21:3; 24(2); 22:5; 9(2); 10(2); 28:6; 7; 9(2); 20(2); 21; **2Chr** 1:12; 2:10; 16(2); 6:18; 7:14(3); 18; 20(3); 10:4; 7; 11(2); 14(2); 12:7(2); 15:2(2); 18:3; 5; 13; 20; 21; 29(2); 20:17; 21:14; 28:23; 30:6; 9; 33:7; 8(2); 34:24; 28(2); **Ezr** 4:3; 13; 7:18; 26; 10:4; **Neh** 1:8; 9(2); 2:19; 20(2); 4:2(4); 12; 5:8; 12(3); 6:10(2); 11; 10:39; 13:21; **Est** 3:9; 4:16(2); 5:8; 7:8; **Job** 1:11; 2:4; 5; 5:1; 6:24; 7:11(3); 8:20(2); 9:3; 12; 13; 18; 23; 27(2); 10:1(2); 2; 15; 11:11; 13:7; 8(2); 10; 13; 15(2); 19; 20; 22; 14:7(2); 9; 14; 15; 15:17(2); 17:3; 18:2(2); 19:2; 5; 22:4(2); 23:6; 24:25; 27:5; 6; 9; 10(2); 11(2); 30:24; 32:10; 14; 17(2); 20(2); 33:12; 26(2); 28; 31; 34:12(2); 23; 31; 32; 33; 35:3; 4; 13(2); 36:2; 3(2); 19; 37:4; 23; 38:3; 39:9; 10; 12; 40:4; 5(2); 7; 14; 41:3(2); 4; 12; 42:4(2); 8; **Ps** 2:7; 3:6; 4:2(2); 3; 6; 8; 5:2; 3(2); 6; 7(2); 6:9; 7:12; 17(2); 9:1(2); 2(2); 9; 10; 14; 10:4; 11; 12:4; 5(2); 13:6; 16:4; 7; 17:15; 18:1; 2; 3; 28; 49; 20:5(2); 6; 7; 21:13; 22:22(2); 25; 23:4; 6; 25:8; 9(2); 14; 26:4; 5; 6(2); 11; 12; 27:3; 4; 6(3); 8; 10; 12; 28:1; 7; 29:11(2); 30:1; 12; 31:7; 32:5; 8(2); 34:1; 11; 35:18(2); 37:33; 38:18(2); 39:1(2); 40:8; 41:1; 2(2); 3; 42:6; 8; 9; 43:4(2); 44:5(2); 6; 45:17; 46:2; 10(2); 48:8; 14; 49:4(2); 15; 18; 50:7(2); 8; 9; 13; 15; 21; 23; 51:13; 52:9(2); 54:6(2); 55:16; 17; 23; 56:3; 4(2); 10(2); 11; 12; 57:1; 2; 7; 8; 9(2); 58:5; 59:9; 16(2); 17; 60:6(2); 8; 9(2); 61:2; 4(2); 8; 62:3; 63:1; 4(2); 7; 66:13(2); 15(2); 16; 18; 68:16; 22(2); 69:30(2); 35(2); 71:14(2); 16(2); 22(2); 73:15; 75:2; 9(2); 10; 77:7(2); 10; 11(2); 12; 78:2(2); 4; 79:13(2); 80:18(2); 81:8; 10; 82:2; 5; 84:4; 11(2); 85:8(3); 86:7; 11; 12(2); 87:4; 89:1(2); 4; 23; 25; 27; 28; 29; 32; 33; 34; 35; 91:2(2); 14(2); 15(3); 16; 92:4; 94:8; 14(2); 16(2); 95:7; 101:1(2); 2(2); 3; 4; 5(2); 8; 102:17; 103:9(2); 104:33(2); 34; 105:11; 107:43; 108:1; 2; 3(2); 7(2); 9(2); 10(2); 109:30(2); 110:4; 111:1; 5; 112:5; 115:12(3); 13; 18; 116:2; 9; 13; 14; 17(2); 18; 118:6; 10; 11; 12; 19(2); 21; 24; 28(2); 119:7; 8; 15; 16(2); 32; 45; 46(2); 47; 48(2); 62; 69; 74; 78; 93; 95; 106(2); 115; 117; 134; 145; 121:1; 3(2); 122:8; 9; 132:3; 4; 7(2); 11(2); 12; 14; 15(2); 16; 17; 18; 135:14(2); 138:1(2); 2; 8; 139:14; 140:12; 143:10; 144:9(2); 145:1(2); 2(2); 5; 6; 19(3); 20; 146:2(2); 149:4; **Prov** 1:5(2); 22; 23(2); 26(2); 28; 3:28; 6:26; 34; 35(2); 7:20; 8:6; 21; 9:8; 9(2); 10:3; 8; 12:2; 14:5(2); 15:12; 25(2); 16:14; 18:14; 19:6; 17; 24; 25(2); 20:3; 4; 5; 6; 22; 21:1; 22:6; 23; 23:9; 35; 24:29(2); 26:27; 27:22; 28:8; 21; 29:19(2); 31:12; **Eccl** 2:1; 4:10; 13; 5:12; 7:2; 23; 10:11; 12; 11:9; **Song** 1:4(3); 11; 3:2(2); 4:6; 6:13; 7:8(2); 12; 8:9(2); **Is** 1:5; 15(2); 24; 25; 26; 2:3(2); 3:4; 7; 14; 17(2); 18; 4:1; 5; 5:1; 5(3); 6(2); 26(2); 6:8; 7:9; 12(2); 13; 8:17(2); 9:7; 10(2); 14; 10:3(3); 6(2); 12; 12:1; 2; 13:11(3); 12; 13; 17; 14:1(2); 13(3); 14(2); 22; 23(2); 25; 30; 15:9; 16:9(2); 18:4(2); 19:2; 3; 4; 21:12; 22:4; 17(2); 18; 19; 20; 21(2); 22; 23; 23:17; 25:1(2); 7; 8(2); 9(2); 26:1; 9(2); 10(3); 11; 13; 27:3(2); 11(2); 28:11; 17; 28; 29:2; 3(3); 14; 30:6; 9; 16(2); 18(2); 19(2); 32; 31:2(3); 4; 5(3); 32:6(3); 33:10(3); 21; 22; 35:4(2); 36:6; 8; 15; 18; 37:4(2); 7(2); 24(2); 29(2); 35; 38:5; 6(2); 7; 8; 12; 13; 20; 40:10; 18(2); 20; 25; 41:10(3); 13(2); 14; 15; 17(2); 18(2); 19(2); 27; 42:6(2); 8; 14(2); 15(3); 16(4); 21; 23(2); 43:2; 4; 5; 6; 13; 19(2); 25; 44:2; 3(2); 15; 26; 27; 45:1; 2(2); 3; 13; 46:4(4); 5; 10; 11(2); 13; 47:3(2); 48:6; 9(2); 11(2); 14; 49:3; 6; 8; 11; 13; 15; 22; 25(2); 26; 50:7; 8; 9; 51:3(2); 4; 23; 52:12(2); 53:12; 54:7; 8; 11; 12; 55:3; 7(2); 56:5(2); 7; 8; 12(2); 57:12; 16(2); 18(2); 19; 58:14; 59:2; 18(2); 60:7; 12; 13; 15; 17(3); 22; 61:8(2); 10; 11; 62:1(2); 8; 63:3(2); 6(2); 7; 8; 65:6(2); 7; 8; 9; 12; 19; 24(2); 66:2; 4(2); 12; 13; 15; 16; 18; 19(2); 21; 22; **Jer** 1:12; 15; 16; 2:9(2); 20; 24; 25; 27; 29; 31; 35; 3:5(2); 12(2); 14(2); 15; 22; 4:6; 12; 27; 28(2); 30(2); 5:1; 5(2); 14; 15; 18; 22; 31; 6:11; 12; 16; 17; 19; 21; 7:3; 7; 9; 14; 15; 16; 23; 27(2); 34; 8:10; 13; 17(2); 9:4(2); 5(2); 7; 10; 11(2); 15; 16(2); 25; 10:18(2); 11:4; 8; 11(2); 14; 22; 23; 12:14; 15(2); 16; 17(2); 13:9; 13; 14(2); 17; 24; 26; 14:10; 12(3); 13; 16; 22; 15:3; 4; 6; 7(3); 9; 11; 13; 14; 19; 20; 21(2); 16:9; 13(2); 15; 16(2); 18; 21(2); 17:3; 4; 27(2); 18:2; 8; 10; 12(2); 14; 17(2); 19:3; 7(3); 8; 9; 11; 12; 15; 20:4(2); 5(2); 9; 10(2); 21:2; 4(2); 5; 6; 7; 14(2); 22:5; 6; 7; 14; 21; 25; 26; 23:2; 3(2); 4; 5; 12; 15; 33; 34; 39(2); 40; 24:5; 6(4); 7(2); 8; 9; 10; 25:6; 9(3); 10; 12(2); 13; 14; 16; 27; 29; 31(2); 26:3; 4; 6(2); 13; 27:8(3); 11; 13(2); 22; 28:3; 4(2); 11; 16; 29:10; 12; 14(4); 17(2); 18(2); 21; 32(2); 30:3(2); 8(2); 9; 10; 11(3); 16; 17(2); 18; 19(2); 20; 21; 22; 31:1; 4; 8; 9(2); 10; 13(2); 14; 20; 27; 28; 31; 33(3); 34(2); 37; 32:3; 28; 37(3); 38; 39; 40(3); 41(2); 42; 44; 33:3; 6(3); 7(2); 8(2); 11; 14; 15; 22; 26(3); 34:2; 5; 17; 18; 20; 21; 22(2); 35:6; 13; 17; 36:3; 7(2); 16; 31(2); 38:14; 16(2); 25; 39:16; 17; 18; 40:4; 10(2); 15; 42:4(3); 6; 10(3); 12; 13; 14(2); 17; 20; 43:10(2); 12; 44:11; 12; 13; 16; 17; 25(2); 27; 29; 30; 45:4(2); 5(2); 46:8(3); 25; 26; 27; 28(3); 47:4; 6; 48:12; 31(2); 32; 35; 44; 47; 49:2; 5; 6; 8(2); 9; 11; 15; 16; 19(3); 27; 32(2); 35; 36(2); 37(3); 38(2); 39; 50:9; 18; 19; 20; 31; 32; 42; 44(3); 51:1; 2; 6; 14; 20(2); 21(2); 22(3); 23(3); 24; 25(2); 36(2); 39(2); 40; 44(2); 47; 52; 57; 64; **Lam** 3:24; 31; 32; 4:16; 22(3); **Eze** 2:1; 5(2); 7(2); 3:7(2); 11(2); 18; 20; 22; 26; 27; 4:8; 13; 16; 5:2; 8; 9(2); 10(2); 11(2); 12(2); 13(2); 14; 16(3); 17(2); 6:3(2); 4; 5(2); 8; 12; 14;

7:3(3); 4(2); 8(3); 9(2); 21; 22; 24(2); 27(2); 8:18(3); 9:10(2); 11:7; 8; 9(2); 10; 11; 16; 17(2); 19(4); 20; 21; 12:3; 13(2); 14(2); 16; 23; 25(3); 13:13; 14; 15(2); 18(2); 19; 20(2); 21; 23; 14:4; 7; 8(3); 9(2); 13(4); 15:3; 6; 7; 8; 16:27; 37(3); 38(2); 39; 41; 42(3); 43; 53; 59; 60(2); 61; 62; 17:19; 20(3); 22(4); 23; 18:21; 30; 31; 20:3; 8; 31; 32; 33; 34(2); 35(2); 36; 37(2); 38(2); 39; 40(2); 41(2); 47; 21:3(2); 4; 17(2); 23; 27(2); 30; 31(2); 22:14; 15(2); 19; 20(2); 21; 23:22(2); 24; 25; 27; 28; 30; 31; 43; 46(2); 48; 24:9; 14(4); 21; 25:4; 5; 7(5); 9; 10; 11; 13(3); 14; 16(2); 17; 26:3; 4; 7; 13; 14; 21; 28:7; 16(2); 17(2); 18(2); 22; 23; 29:4(3); 5; 8; 10; 12(3); 13; 14(2); 15; 19; 21(2); 30:10; 12(2); 13(3); 14(3); 15(2); 16; 19; 22(2); 23(2); 24(2); 25; 26; 32:3; 4(4); 5; 6; 7(2); 8; 9; 10; 12; 13; 14; 33:6; 8; 11; 20; 27; 28; 31; 33; 34:10(2); 11; 12(2); 13(2); 14; 15(2); 16(5); 20; 22(2); 23; 24; 25(2); 26(2); 29; 35:3(2); 4; 6; 7; 8; 9; 10; 11(2); 14; 15; 36:9; 10; 11(3); 12; 15; 23; 24(2); 25(2); 26(4); 27; 28; 29(3); 30; 33; 36; 37(2); 37:5; 6(2); 12; 19(2); 21(2); 22; 23(3); 26(3); 27; 38:4(2); 11(2); 16; 21; 22(2); 23(2); 39:2(3); 3(2); 4; 6; 7(2); 11; 21; 25(2); 29; 43:7; 9; 27; 44:14; **Dan** 2:4; 5; 7; 9; 24; 25; 36; 3:17; 18; 4:17; 25; 32; 35; 5:12; 17; 21; 6:16; 8:4; 19; 10:20; 21; 11:2; 3; 16; 36; **Hos** 1:4(2); 5; 6(2); 7(3); 9; 2:4; 5; 6; 7; 9(2); 10; 11; 12(2); 13; 14; 15; 17; 18(3); 19(2); 20; 21(2); 23(3); 3:3; 4:5; 6(2); 7; 9; 14; 16; 5:4; 10; 12; 14(3); 15(2); 6:1(2); 2(2); 7:12(3); 8:5; 10; 13; 14; 9:5; 9(2); 12; 15(2); 16; 17; 10:11; 11:9(3); 11; 12:2(2); 9; 13:7(2); 8(3); 10; 14(4); 14:2; 3(2); 4(2); 5; **Joel** 1:19; 2:14; 18; 19(3); 20(2); 21; 23; 25; 28; 29; 30; 3:2(3); 4(2); 7(2); 8; 12; 16; 21; **Amos** 1:2; 3; 4; 5; 6; 7; 8(2); 9; 10; 11; 12; 13; 14; 2:1; 2; 3(2); 4; 5; 6; 7; 3:2; 4(2); 7; 8; 14; 15; 4:2; 12(2); 5:15; 17; 21; 22(2); 23; 27; 6:8; 11; 12; 14; 7:8(2); 9; 8:2; 5; 7; 9(2); 10(3); 11; 9:1; 2; 3(2); 4(2); 8(2); 9(2); 11(3); 14; 15; **Obad** 4; **Jonah** 1:6; 2:4; 9(2); 3:9; **Mic** 1:3; 6(3); 7; 8(3); 15; 2:11; 12(3); 3:4(2); 11; 4:2(2); 5(2); 6(2); 7; 13(3); 5:3; 10(2); 11; 12; 13; 14(2); 15; 6:2; 7; 13; 14; 7:7(3); 9(2); 15; 19(3); **Nah** 1:2; 3; 8; 9; 12; 13(2); 14(2); 2:13(2); 3:5(2); 6(2); 7; **Hab** 1:5(2); 2:1(3); 3(2); 3:16; 18(2); 19(2); **Zeph** 1:2; 3(3); 4(2); 8; 9; 12(3); 17; 2:5; 11(2); 13(2); 3:5; 9; 11; 12; 17(4); 18; 19(3); 20(2); **Hag** 1:8(2); 2:6; 7(2); 9; 19; 21; 22(3); 23(2); **Zec** 1:3; 9; 2:5(2); 9; 10; 11; 3:4; 7; 8; 9(2); 5:4; 6:15; 8:3; 7; 8(2); 11; 12; 13; 21; 23; 9:4(2); 6; 7; 8; 10; 12; 10:6(4); 8; 9; 10(2); 12; 11:6(3); 7; 9; 16; 12:2; 3; 4(3); 6; 9; 10; 13:2(2); 7; 9(5); 14:2; 12; 17; 18; **Mal** 1:4(2); 5; 8; 9(2); 10; 2:2(4); 3; 12; 13; 3:1; 5(2); 7; 8; 10; 11; 17; 4:5; **Mt** 2:13; 3:12(2); 4:9; 19; 5:40; 6:10; 14; 15; 21; 24(2); 7:9; 10; 21; 22; 23; 24; 8:3; 7; 19; 9:13; 15; 38; 10:17(2); 32; 33; 11:14; 27; 28; 12:7; 11; 18; 29; 44; 50; 13:30; 35(2); 15:32; 16:2; 3; 18; 19; 24; 25(2); 18:14; 16; 26; 29; 20:4; 14; 15; 26; 27; 32; 21:3; 24(2); 25; 29; 31; 37; 40; 41(2); 44; 23:4; 24:28; 25:21; 23; 26:15(2); 18; 29; 31; 32; 33; 35; 39; 42; 27:17; 21; 42; 43; 49; 63; 28:14; **Mk** 1:17; 41; 2:20; 22; 3:27(2); 35; 4:13; 6:22; 23; 25; 8:3; 34; 35; 9:50; 10:43; 44; 11:3; 26; 29(2); 31; 12:6; 9(2); 14:7; 15; 25; 27; 28; 29; 31; 36; 58(2); 15:9; 12; 36; **Lk** 2:14; 3:17(3); 4:6(2); 23; 5:5; 13; 35; 37; 6:9; 47; 7:42; 9:5; 23; 24(2); 57; 61; 10:22; 35; 11:2; 8(2); 11(2); 12; 24; 49; 12:5; 18(3); 19; 28; 34; 36; 37; 44; 46(3); 47(2); 48; 49; 55; 13:24; 31; 14:5; 15:18(2); 16:11; 13(2); 30; 31; 17:1; 7; 8; 22; 37; 18:5; 8; 19:14; 22; 20:3; 5; 6; 13(2); 18; 21:6; 7; 15; 22:16; 18; 42; 67; 68; 23:16; 22; 25; **Jn** 1:13(2); 2:19; 4:25; 34; 48; 5:20; 21; 30(2); 40; 43; 45; 6:37; 38(2); 39; 40(2); 44; 51(2); 54; 67; 7:17(2); 31; 35(2); 8:22; 44; 9:27; 31; 10:5(2); 11:22; 48; 56; 12:26; 28; 32; 13:37; 14:3; 13; 14; 16; 18(2); 21(2); 23(3); 26; 30; 15:7; 20(2); 21; 26; 16:2; 3; 7(2); 8; 13(2); 22; 23; 26; 17:24; 26; 18:39; 20:15; 25; 21:22; 23; **Acts** 2:17; 18; 19; 3:23; 5:38; 6:4; 7:7; 34; 43; 49; 9:16; 13:22; 34; 36; 15:16(4); 17:18; 31; 32; 18:6; 15; 21(2); 21:14; 22; 22:14; 18; 21; 23:14; 21; 35; 24:22; 25; 26:16; 27:10; 28:28; **Rom** 1:10; 2:6; 18; 4:8; 5:7; 7:18; 8:27; 9:9; 15(4); 18(2); 19; 25; 28(2); 10:19(2); 12:2; 19; 15:9; 18; 24; 28; 32; **1Cor** 1:1; 19(2); 4:5(2); 19(3); 21; 6:12; 14; 7:36; 37(2); 39; 8:13; 9:17; 10:13(2); 11:34; 12:11; 14:15(4); 21(2); 23; 25; 35; 15:35; 16:3; 5; 6; 7; 8; 12(2); **2Cor** 1:1; 10; 6:16(2); 17; 18; 8:5; 11; 10:11; 13; 11:9; 12; 18; 30; 12:1; 5(2); 6; 9; 14; 15; 21; 13:2; **Gal** 1:4; 5:10; **Eph** 1:1; 5; 9; 11; 5:17; 6:6; 7; **Phil** 1:6; 15; 18; 2:13; 20; 23; **Col** 1:1; 9; 2:23; 4:12; **1Th** 4:3; 14; 5:18; 24; **2Th** 2:7; 3:4; **1Ti** 2:4; 8; 5:11; 14; 6:9; **2Ti** 1:1; 2:12; 16; 17; 25; 26; 3:12; 4:3(2); 18; **Titus** 3:8; **Philem** 1:19; **Heb** 1:5; 2:4; 12(2); 13; 3:7; 15; 4:7; 6:3; 14(2); 7:21; 8:8; 10(3); 12(2); 10:7; 9; 10; 16(3); 17; 30; 36; 37(2); 13:4; 5; 6; 21; 23; **Jas** 1:18; 2:18; 4:4; 7; 8; 13; 15; **1Pet** 2:15; 3:10; 13; 17; 4:2; 3; 19; **2Pet** 1:12; 15; 21; 3:10; **1Jn** 2:17; 5:14; **3Jn** 10; 13; **Jude** 5; **Rev** 2:5(2); 7; 10; 16(2); 17(2); 22; 23(2); 24; 26; 28; 3:3(2); 5(2); 9(2); 10; 12(3); 16; 20(2); 21; 4:1; 11:3; 5(2); 6; 17:1; 7; 17; 21:3; 6; 7; 9; 22:17

WILLING

14, 2655, 5068, 5071, 5081, *830, 1014, 2106, 2309, 2843, 4288, 4289*

Gen 24:5; 8; **Ex** 35:5; 21; 22; 29(2); **1Chr** 28:9; 21; 29:5; **Job** 39:9; **Ps** 110:3; **Is** 1:19; **Mt** 1:19; 26:41; **Mk** 15:15; **Lk** 10:29; 22:42; 23:20; **Jn** 5:35; **Acts** 24:27; 25:9; 27:43; **Rom** 9:22; **2Cor** 5:8; 8:3; 12; **1Th** 2:8; **1Ti** 6:18; **Heb** 6:17; 13:18; **2Pet** 3:9

WILLINGLY

2656, 2974, 3820, 5068, 5071, 5414, *1595, 1596, 1635, 2309, 2596*

Ex 25:2; **Judg** 5:2; 9; 8:25; **1Chr** 29:6; 9(2); 14; 17(2); **2Chr** 17:16; 35:8; **Ezr** 1:6; 3:5; 7:16; **Neh** 11:2; **Prov** 31:13; **Lam** 3:33; **Hos** 5:11; **Jn** 6:21; **Rom** 8:20; **1Cor** 9:17; **Philem** 1:14; **1Pet** 5:2; **2Pet** 3:5

WITH

5973, *4862*

Gen 3:6; 12; 4:8; 5:22; 24; 6:3; 9; 11; 13(2); 14; 16; 18(2); 19; 7:7; 13; 23; 8:1; 16; 17(2); 18; 9:4; 8; 9(2); 10(3); 11; 12; 11:31; 12:4; 13; 17; 13:1; 5; 14:2(2); 5; 8; 9(3); 13; 17; 24; 15:14; 18; 16:6; 11; 17:3; 4; 12; 13; 19(2); 21; 22; 23; 27(2); 18:11; 16; 23; 25; 33; 19:1; 9(2); 11; 30; 32; 33; 34(2); 35; 36; 20:16(2); 21:6; 10(2); 19; 20; 22; 23(3); 22:3; 5; 23:4(2); 8; 16; 24:15; 32; 40; 45; 49; 54; 55; 58; 25:30; 26:3; 8; 10; 15; 20(2); 24; 28(2); 27:15; 34; 35; 37; 44; 28:4; 15; 20; 29:6; 9(2); 14; 19; 25; 27; 30; 30:8(2); 15; 16(2); 20(2); 29; 33; 31:3; 5; 6; 21; 23; 25; 26; 27(4); 32(2); 36; 38; 42; 50; 32:4; 6; 7; 9; 10; 11; 15; 20; 24; 25; 28(2); 33:1; 5; 7; 10; 11; 13(2); 15(2); 34:2; 5; 6; 7; 8; 9; 10; 16; 20; 21; 22; 23; 26; 31(2); 35:2; 3; 6; 13; 14; 15; 22; 37:2(3); 14(2); 25; 38:14; 24; 25; 39:2; 3; 7; 8; 10; 12; 14(2); 15; 18; 21; 23; 40:4; 7; 14; 41:6; 10; 12; 23; 27; 42:4; 6; 13; 24; 25; 26; 32; 33; 38(2); 43:3; 4; 5; 6; 8; 16(2); 19; 32(2); 34; 44:1; 9; 10; 16; 23; 26(2); 29; 30; 31(2); 33; 34; 45:1; 5; 15; 23(2); 46:1; 4; 6; 7(2); 15; 26; 47:12; 17; 29; 30; 48:1; 12; 21; 22(2); 49:12(2); 25; 29; 30; 50:7; 9; 10; 13; 14; **Ex** 1:1; 7; 10; 11; 13; 14(2); 20; 2:3(2); 21; 24(3); 3:2; 8; 12; 17; 18; 20; 4:12; 15(2); 5:3(3); 15; 6:1(2); 4; 6(2); 7:11; 17; 22; 8:2; 5; 7; 17; 18; 9:9; 10; 15; 24; 10:9(6); 10; 24; 26(2); 12:8(2); 9(4); 10; 11; 22; 38; 48; 13:5; 7(2); 9; 13; 19(2); 14:6; 8; 11; 15:8; 10; 19(2); 20(2); 16:3; 12; 18; 20; 31; 17:2(2); 3; 5; 8; 9(2); 10; 13; 16; 18:5; 6; 12; 18; 19; 22; 19:9; 17; 24; 20:19(2); 22; 23; 21:3; 6; 8; 9; 14; 18(2); 20; 22; 29; 22:14; 15; 16; 19; 24; 30(3); 23:1; 5; 11(2); 18; 32(2); 24:2; 3; 8; 14; 25:2; 11; 13; 14; 20; 22(2); 24; 28(2); 33(2); 34; 39; 26:1(2); 6; 29(2); 31; 32; 36; 37; 27:2; 6; 8; 16; 17; 28:1; 3; 6; 11(2); 15; 21(2); 28; 41; 29:2(2); 3; 4; 5; 9; 12; 14; 21(2); 34; 40(2); 43; 30:3; 5; 6; 10; 20; 28; 34; 36; 31:3; 6; 8; 9; 18(2); 32:4; 11(2); 33:3; 9; 12; 14; 15; 16; 22; 34:3; 5; 10; 12; 15; 20; 25; 27(2); 28; 29(2); 31; 32; 33; 34; 35; 35:12; 14; 16; 23; 24; 25; 31; 35; 36:8; 13; 34(2); 35; 36; 38(2); 37:2; 4; 9(2); 11; 15; 26; 28; 38:2; 6; 7; 17; 23; 39:3; 6; 14; 21; 23; 37(2); 40:3; 12; 14; **Lev** 1:12; 13; 16; 17; 2:2; 4(2); 5; 7; 11; 13(2); 16; 3:4; 10; 15; 4:9; 11(2); 12; 20(3); 25; 30; 34; 5:4(2); 15; 16; 18; 6:6; 10; 16; 17; 21; 7:4; 10; 12(4); 13; 17; 19; 24; 30; 8:2; 6; 7(3); 13; 15; 17; 30(2); 31; 32; 9:4; 11; 13; 10:9; 14; 15(2); 16; 11:43(2); 44; 13:57; 14:10; 16; 21; 27; 31; 37; 52(6); 15:3; 17; 18(2); 24; 33; 16:3; 4(2); 10; 14(2); 15(2); 19; 24; 17:13; 15; 18:20(2); 22(2); 23; 19:13; 19(2); 20; 22; 26; 33; 34; 20:2; 5; 10(2); 11; 12; 13(2); 14; 15; 18; 20; 24; 27; 21:9; 22:6; 8; 11; 14; 23:13; 17; 18(2); 20(2); 24:23; 25:6; 23; 35(2); 36; 40; 41; 43; 45; 46; 50(2); 52; 53(2); 54; 26:9; 39; 40; 42(3); 44; **Num** 1:2; 4; 5; 2:2; 17; 31; 3:1; 4:5; 8; 11; 12; 32(2); 5:7; 13(2); 19(2); 20; 21; 23; 6:15(2); 17; 20; 7:13; 19; 25; 31; 37; 43; 49; 55; 61; 67; 73; 79; 87; 89; 8:8(2); 26; 9:11; 10:3; 4; 8; 9; 10; 29; 32; 11:15; 16; 17(2); 18; 33; 12:8; 13:23; 27; 31; 14:8; 9; 10; 12; 21; 24; 27; 43; 15:4; 5; 6; 9(2); 14; 15; 16; 24; 35; 36; 16:2; 10; 13; 14; 18; 22; 30; 17:4; 13; 18:1(2); 2(2); 7; 11(2); 19(2); 19:4; 5; 12; 16; 20:3; 11; 13; 18; 20(2); 21:18; 24; 22:7; 8; 9; 12; 13; 14; 20; 21; 22; 27; 35(2); 39; 40; 23:13; 17; 21; 24:8; 25:1; 14; 18; 26:3; 10; 27:21; 28:5; 9; 12(2); 13; 20; 28; 29:3; 9; 14; 30:2; 8; 10; 31:6; 8; 10; 14(2); 17; 18; 23; 35; 32:19; 29; 30; 33; 33:1; 3; 34:2; 12; 35:7; 16; 17; 18; 21; 23; 25; **Deut** 1:16; 37; 2:5; 7; 9; 19; 24; 26; 3:5; 13; 26; 27; 4:11(2); 21; 23; 29(2); 37; 40(2); 5:2; 3(2); 4; 16; 22; 23; 24; 29(2); 33; 6:3(2); 5(3); 18; 21; 7:2; 3; 5(2); 8; 9; 23; 25; 8:3; 16; 9:8; 9; 10(2); 15; 20; 21; 26; 10:9; 12(2); 14; 22; 11:2; 9; 10; 13(2); 12:3; 12; 23; 25(2); 28(2); 13:3(2); 10; 15(2); 16; 14:27; 29; 15:3; 16; 19; 16:3; 4; 10; 18; 17:5; 19; 18:1; 6; 11; 13; 19:5(2); 13; 20:1; 4; 12; 13; 20; 21:3; 21; 22:2; 3(3); 6; 7; 9; 10; 21; 22(2); 23; 24; 25(2); 28; 29; 23:4(2); 11; 16; 23; 25; 24:5; 12; 25:3; 11; 26:5; 8(5); 9; 15; 16(2); 27:1; 2; 3; 4; 14; 20; 21; 22; 23; 28:22(7); 27(4); 28; 30; 32; 35; 40; 47(2); 68; 29:1(2); 10; 12(2); 14; 15(4); 25; 30:2(2); 6(2); 10(2); 31:6; 7; 8; 16(2); 20; 23; 27; 32:12; 14(2); 15; 16(2); 21(4); 22; 24(4); 25; 34; 39; 42(2); 43; 33:2; 8(2); 17; 20; 21(2); 23(2); 24; 34:4; **Josh** 1:5(2); 9; 17(2); 2:6; 14; 19; 3:7(2); 4:3; 8; 5:6; 13; 6:4; 5(2); 8; 9(2); 10; 13(2); 16; 17; 20(2); 21; 24; 27; 7:12; 15(2); 24; 25(3); 8:1; 5; 11; 24; 35; 9:2(3); 6; 7; 11(2); 15(2); 16; 10:1; 4(2); 7; 10; 11(2); 15; 20; 24; 28; 29; 30; 31; 32; 34; 35; 36; 37; 38; 39; 43; 11:4(2); 6; 7; 9; 10; 11(2); 12; 14; 18; 19; 21; 13:8; 21; 22; 14:4; 8; 12; 15:32; 36; 41; 44; 45; 46; 47(2); 51; 54; 57; 59; 60; 62; 63; 16:9; 18:24; 28; 19:15; 16; 22; 30; 31; 38; 46; 47; 48; 21:2; 8; 11; 13(2); 14(2); 15(2); 16(3); 17(2); 18(2); 19; 21(2); 22(2); 23(2); 24(2); 25(2); 26; 27(2); 28(2); 29(2); 30(2); 31(2); 32(3); 33; 34(2); 35(2); 36(2); 37(2); 38(2); 39(2); 41; 42; 22:5(2); 8(8); 14; 15; 18; 24; 27(3); 30; 23:4; 12; 24:6; 8; 12(2); 25; **Judg** 1:3(3); 8; 16; 17; 18(3); 19; 21; 22; 25; 2:1; 2; 18; 3:27; 31; 4:6; 7; 8(2); 9(2); 10(2); 13; 15; 18; 5:15; 26; 6:5; 12; 13; 16; 17; 26; 39; 7:1; 2; 4(3); 5; 10; 11; 16; 18(2); 19; 8:1(2); 4; 7(2); 10; 15; 16; 9:1(2); 16; 19(2); 23; 26; 32; 33; 34; 35; 38; 39; 44; 45; 48(2); 52; 11:3; 6; 8; 11; 12; 33; 34(2); 38; 39; 12:1(2); 2; 4; 13:9; 19; 14:7; 11; 15; 18; 15:1; 5; 6; 8; 13; 14; 16(2); 16:3; 7; 8; 9; 11; 13; 14(3); 15; 16; 21; 29(2); 30(2); 17:2; 10; 11; 18:4; 7; 11; 16; 17(2); 19; 23; 25; 27(2); 28; 19:3; 4; 5; 10(2); 19; 20; 24; 29; 20:1; 37; 38; 40; 43; 48; 21:5; 10(2); 12; **Ruth** 1:6; 7; 8(3); 10; 11; 18; 20; 22; 2:4; 6; 19(2); 22; 23; 3:1; 2; **1Sa** 1:24(2); 2:4; 13(2); 18; 19; 22; 26(2); 29; 3:14; 19; 4:4; 5; 8; 12(2); 19; 5:6; 7; 8; 9; 12; 6:11; 15; 19; 7:3; 10; 9:3; 5; 19; 24; 25; 10:5; 6; 7; 26; 11:1; 2; 7; 10; 12:2; 7; 20; 24; 13:2(2); 4; 5; 15; 16; 22(3); 14:2; 7; 17; 18; 20; 21(4); 27; 28; 32; 33; 34(2); 43; 45; 15:6; 8; 25; 26; 30; 16:1; 2; 5; 16; 18; 19; 20; 23; 17:5; 9; 19; 20; 23; 25; 28; 32; 33; 37; 38(2); 39; 43; 45(3); 47; 50(2); 57; 18:1; 6(3); 10; 11; 12; 14; 22; 28; 19:3; 8(2); 9(2); 10; 13; 16; 20:5; 8(2); 13(2); 16; 35(2); 41; 21:1; 8; 22:2; 3; 4; 6; 8; 17; 19(2); 23(2); 23:5(2); 6; 19; 23(2); 24:7; 8; 18; 25:7; 15; 16; 25; 26; 29; 31; 33; 39; 42; 26:2; 6(2); 8; 27:2(2); 3(3); 5; 28:1(2); 8; 12; 14(2); 19(2); 23; 29:2; 3; 4(3); 6; 8; 9; 10(2); 30:1; 3; 4; 9; 14; 21; 22(2); 23; 31:5; **2Sa** 1:2; 11; 17; 21; 24; 2:3(2); 23; 3:8; 12(2); 13; 16; 17; 20(2); 21; 22(2); 23; 27; 31(2); 5:3; 10; 6:2(2); 12; 14(2); 15(2); 7:3; 7(2); 9; 12; 14(2); 22; 29; 8:2(3); 10(2); 11; 10:13; 17; 19; 11:1; 4; 5; 9; 11; 13; 17; 12:3(2); 9(2); 11; 17; 24; 30; 13:11; 14; 18; 20; 24; 26(2); 27; 28; 31; 14:2; 17; 19; 15:11; 12; 14(2); 19(2); 20(2); 22; 23; 24; 27; 30; 31; 32; 33; 35; 36; 16:1; 10; 14; 15; 17; 18; 21; 23(2); 17:2; 8; 10; 12; 16; 22; 24; 29; 18:1; 2; 5(2); 14; 27; 19:4; 7; 16; 17(2); 22; 25; 31; 33(2); 34; 36(2); 37; 38; 40; 41; 20:8; 9; 15; 16; 21:15(2); 16; 17; 18; 19; 22:26(2); 27(2); 40; 23:5(2); 6; 7(2); 9; 21(2); 24:2; **1Kin** 1:1; 7(2); 8; 14; 21; 22; 23; 31; 33; 34; 37(2); 40(3); 41; 44; 49; 51; 2:4(2); 8(3); 9; 10; 32; 43; 3:1; 6; 17; 18; 4:13; 5:6; 6:8; 9; 10; 12; 15(3); 16; 18; 20; 21(2); 22(2); 28; 29; 30; 32; 35; 36; 7:2; 3; 5; 7; 9; 12; 14; 18; 26; 31; 49; 8:5; 9; 15(2); 21; 23(2); 24(3); 25; 46; 48(2); 54; 55; 57(2); 61; 62; 65; 9:11(2); 16; 27; 10:1; 2(3); 18; 22; 26; 11:1; 4; 9; 16; 17; 18; 21; 22; 29; 38; 43; 12:6; 8(2); 10; 11(3); 14(2); 18; 21; 13:7; 8; 15; 16(3); 18; 19; 14:3; 6; 8; 20; 22; 31(2); 15:3; 8; 14; 19; 20; 22; 24(2); 16:2; 6; 7; 13; 17; 18; 26; 28; 17:18; 20; 18:4; 13; 28; 32; 33; 35; 45; 19:1; 10; 14; 19(2); 21; 20:1; 20; 21; 34(2); 38; 21:8(2); 13; 22:4; 11; 13; 27(2); 31(2); 40; 44; 49; 50(2); **2Kin** 1:8; 9; 11; 13; 14; 15(2); 2:1; 16; 3:4; 7; 12; 13; 17; 19; 20; 26; 4:13; 26(3); 5:1; 3; 5; 9(2); 23; 26; 6:1; 3; 4; 8; 15; 16(2); 18(2); 22(2); 32; 33; 7:2; 19; 8:2; 4; 9; 12(2); 21; 24(2); 28; 9:13; 15; 18; 19; 24; 28; 10:2(2); 6; 13; 15; 16; 23; 25; 31; 35; 11:3; 4(2); 8(2); 9; 11; 14; 15; 20; 12:15; 21; 13:9; 13(2); 19; 23; 14:10; 15; 16(2); 20; 22; 29(2); 15:7(2); 16; 19; 22; 25(2); 38(2); 16:15; 20(2); 17:15; 18; 35; 36; 38; 18:7; 17; 26; 27; 28; 31; 37; 19:1; 2; 6; 23; 24; 32; 37; 20:3; 21; 21:6; 11; 18; 22:7; 14; 17; 23:2; 3; 11; 14; 18; 24; 25(3); 24:4; 6; 25:7; 9; 10; 11; 17; 24; 25(2); 28; **1Chr** 2:23(2); 4:9; 10; 23; 5:10; 18; 19(2); 20; 6:32; 33; 57(2); 58(2); 59(2); 60(3); 64; 67(2); 68(2); 69(2); 70(2); 71(2); 72(2); 73(2); 74(2); 75(2); 76(3); 77(2); 78(2); 79(2); 80(2); 81(2); 7:4; 23; 28; 8:12; 32; 9:20; 25; 38; 11:3; 9; 10(2); 13; 19; 23(2); 42; 12:2; 19; 27; 33; 34(2); 37; 38; 39; 13:1(2); 2; 8(7); 14; 14:1; 12; 15:15; 16(2); 18; 19; 20; 21; 24; 25; 27(2); 28(5); 16:5(3); 6; 16; 38; 41; 42(3); 17:2; 6; 8; 11; 20; 18:10(2); 11; 19:14; 17; 19; 20:3(4); 4; 5; 21:7; 20; 21; 22:11; 13; 15; 16; 18; 23:2; 5; 24:5; 25:1(3); 3; 6; 7; 9; 26:16; 27:32; 28:1(3); 9(2); 20; 21(2); 29:2; 6; 8; 9(2); 17; 21; 22; 30; **2Chr** 1:1; 3; 14; 2:3(2); 7(2); 8; 12; 13; 14(2); 3:4; 5(2); 6; 7; 8; 9; 10; 4:5; 9; 20; 5:10; 12(3); 13(2); 6:4(2); 11; 14; 15(3); 16; 18; 36; 38(2); 41; 7:3; 6; 8; 18; 8:5; 18; 9:1(3); 17; 18; 21; 25; 31; 10:6; 8(2); 10; 11(2); 14(2); 18; 12:1; 3(2); 16; 13:3(2); 8; 9; 11; 12(2); 14; 17; 19(3); 14:1; 9; 11(3); 13; 15:2(2); 6; 9(2); 12(2); 14(4); 15(2); 16:3; 8; 10(2); 13; 14; 17:3; 8(2); 9; 14; 15; 16; 17(2); 18; 18:1; 2(2); 3(2); 10; 12; 26(2); 30(3); 19:6; 7; 9; 11; 20:1; 13; 17(2); 18; 19; 21; 25; 27; 28; 35; 36; 37; 21:1(2); 3; 4; 7; 9(2); 14; 18; 22:1; 5; 6; 7; 9; 12; 23:1; 3; 7(2); 8; 13(2); 14; 18(2); 21; 24:21; 24; 25:2; 7(3); 13; 16; 19; 24; 28; 26:2; 13; 17; 19; 23(2); 27:5; 9; 28:5; 9; 10(2); 15; 18(2); 27; 29:8; 10; 18(2); 24; 25(3); 26(2); 27(2); 29; 30(2); 35; 30:6; 21(2); 23; 25; 31:9; 21; 32:3; 7(3); 8(2); 9; 18; 21(2); 33; 33:6(2); 11; 20; 34:6; 25; 31(2);

35:12; 13; 21(3); 22; 36:10; 17; 19; 23; **Ezr** 1:3; 4(4); 5; 6(5); 11; 2:2; 63(2); 3:9(2); 10(2); 11; 12; 13; 4:2; 3; 5:2; 8; 6:4; 12; 16; 22; 7:13; 16; 17(2); 18; 28; 8:1; 3; 4; 5; 6; 7; 8; 9; 10; 11; 12; 13; 14; 17; 18; 19; 24; 33(2); 9:2; 11(3); 14(2); 10:3; 4; 12; 14; 16; 17; **Neh** 1:3; 2:3; 9; 12(2); 13; 17; 3:1; 4:13; 17(3); 22; 5:7; 6:5; 7:7; 65; 8:2; 6(2); 9:1(2); 4; 6; 8; 13; 24(2); 10:32; 38; 11:25; 12:1; 24; 27(5); 35; 36; 40; 41; 42; 43; 13:2(2); 9; 11; 17; 25; **Est** 1:6; 10; 11; 2:6(2); 9; 12(3); 13; 20; 3:1; 11; 12; 4:1(2); 2; 13; 5:9; 12(2); 14; 6:14; 7:1; 8:3; 8(2); 10; 15(2); 9:5; 29; 30; **Job** 1:4; 15; 17; 2:7; 10; 11; 13; 3:14; 15(2); 4:2; 18; 5:14; 23(2); 7:5; 14; 8:21(2); 22; 9:2; 3; 14; 17; 18; 30; 35; 10:2; 11(2); 13; 12:2; 5; 12; 13; 16; 18; 13:3; 17; 19; 14:3; 5; 15:2; 3(2); 10; 11(2); 20; 27; 16:5; 8; 9; 10; 14; 16; 21; 17:2; 3(2); 18:6; 19:2; 4; 6; 16; 20; 22; 24; 20:11; 26; 21:8; 24; 25; 22:4; 16; 18; 21; 23:4; 6; 7; 14; 24:8; 14; 22; 25:2; 4; 26:10; 12; 27:11; 13; 14; 28:14; 16(2); 19; 22; 29:5; 6; 30:1; 21; 30:1; 5; 13; 18(2); 20; 32:14; 33:19(2); 23; 26; 29; 30; 34:8(2); 9; 23; 35:4; 36:4; 7; 18; 32; 37:8; 30; 32; 39:4; 10; 19; 24; 40:2; 9; 10(2); 15; 22; 24; 41:1(2); 2; 4; 5(2); 7:12; 15; 28; 42:8; 11; **Ps** 2:9; 11(2); 3:4; 4:4; 5:4; 9; 12(2); 6:6(2); 7:4; 11; 14; 8:5; 9:1; 6; 10:14; 12:2(3); 4; 13:6; 15:3; 17:10; 14; 15; 18:25(2); 26(2); 32; 39; 20:6; 21:3; 6; 22:13; 23:4; 5; 25:14; 19; 26:4(2); 5; 7; 9(2); 27:7; 28:3(2); 7; 29:11; 30:11; 31:9; 10(2); 32:7; 8; 9; 33:2(2); 3; 34:3; 35:1(2); 13; 16(2); 19; 26; 36:8; 9; 37:12; 24; 38:7; 39:1(2); 2; 3; 11; 12; 42:4(4); 8; 10; 44:1; 2; 9; 19; 45:3; 7; 12; 15; 46:3; 7; 11; 47:1; 5(2); 7; 48:7; 50:5; 18(2); 51:7; 12; 19(2); 54:t; 4; 55:18; 20; 58:9; 59:7; 60:(2); 5; 10; 62:4; 63:5(2); 64:7; 65:4; 6; 9; 10; 11; 13(2); 66:13; 15(2); 17(2); 68:6; 13(2); 19; 25; 27; 30(2); 69:10; 28; 30(2); 71:8(2); 13; 22(2); 72:2(2); 19; 73:7; 19; 23; 24; 74:6; 75:5; 77:1(2); 6; 15; 78:8; 14(2); 36(2); 37; 47(2); 58(2); 62; 71; 80:5; 10; 16; 81:2; 16(2); 83:5; 7; 8; 15(2); 16; 85:5; 86:12; 87:4; 88:4; 7; 89:1; 3; 10; 20; 21; 24; 28; 32(2); 38; 45; 90:5; 14; 91:4; 8; 15; 16; 92:3; 10; 93:1(2); 94:20; 95:2(2); 10; 96:13(2); 98:5(2); 6; 9(2); 100:2(2); 4(2); 101:2; 6; 102:9; 103:4; 5; 10; 104:1; 2(2); 6(2); 13; 28; 105:9; 18; 25; 37; 40; 43(2); 106:4(2); 5; 6; 29; 32; 33; 38; 39(2); 43; 107:9; 12; 22; 108:1; 6; 11; 109:2; 3; 14; 112(2); 113:8(2); 116:7; 118:7; 27; 119:2; 7; 10; 13; 17; 34; 58; 65; 69; 78; 93; 98; 124; 145; 120:4; 6; 123:3; 4(2); 125:5; 126:2(2); 6(2); 127:5; 128:2; 130:4; 7(2); 132:9; 15; 16; 18; 136:12(2); 138:1; 3; 139:3; 18; 21; 22; 141:4; 142:1(2); 7; 143:2; 147:7; 8; 14; 20; 149:3; 4; 8(2); 150:3(2); 4(2); **Prov** 1:11; 13; 15; 31; 2:1; 16; 3:5; 9(2); 10(2); 14; 17; 18; 19; 20; 22; 6:1; 2(2); 12; 13(3); 22; 25; 32; 7:1; 5; 10; 13; 14; 16(3); 17; 18; 20; 21(2); 8:12; 18; 24; 30; 31; 10:4; 10; 18; 22; 11:2; 9; 10; 14; 18; 15:16; 16:7; 8; 19(2); 17:1; 14; 18:1; 3; 20(2); 19:2; 7; 23; 20:8; 13; 17; 18; 19(2); 21:9; 19; 27; 22:24(2); 23:1; 7; 11; 13; 14; 21; 24:1; 4; 21; 28; 31; 25:9; 24; 26:17; 23; 24; 27:14; 22; 28:4; 20; 23; 29:3; 9; 24; 30:8; 16; 19; 22; 28; 31:13; 16; 17; 21; 26; **Eccl** 1:8(2); 11; 16; 2:1; 3; 9; 4:6(2); 8; 15; 5:2; 10(2); 11; 17; 6:3; 4(2); 10; 7:1; 8:12; 13; 15; 16; 9:7(2); 9; 10; 11:5; 12:14; **Song** 1:2; 6; 10(2); 11; 2:3; 5(2); 13; 3:6(2); 10; 11; 4:8(2); 9(2); 13(2); 14(2); 5:1(3); 2(2); 5(2); 12; 14(2); 6:1; 4; 10; 7:1; 2; 8:9; **Is** 1:4; 6; 7; 13; 20; 22(2); 3:10; 11; 14; 16(2); 17; 5:2; 13; 18(2); 20; 22; 26; 6:2(3); 4; 6; 10(3); 7:2(2); 10; 11; 14; 16(2); 17; 5:2; 13; 22; 26; 6:2(3); 4; 6; 10(3); 7:2(2); 9; 14; 22:2; 6; 12; 17; 21(2); 23:17; 24:2(12); 9; 12; 25:5; 11; 26:9(2); 17; 18; 19; 27:1; 5(2); 8; 28:1; 5; 8; 29:16; 9(2); 14; 17:5; 10; 18:1; 5; 19; 20; 21; 3(2); 8(3); 10(2); 11; 14; 3:13; 14; 6; 2(2); 8:1; 10; 11; 9:5(2); 7(2); 10; 12; 10:22; 24; 33; 34; 11:4(4); 6(2); 15; 12:1; 13:10; 16; 20; 14:1; 10; 14; 18; 15:16; 16:7; 8; 19(2); 17:1; 14; 18:1; 3; 20(3); 19:2; 7; 22; 24:(2); 9; 12; 25:5; 11; 26:9(2); 15(2); 2; 8; 11; 12(2); 17(2); 18; 28(2); 29:3; 6(3); 9(2); 30(2); 31; 24(2); 31:8; 32:7; 33:12(5); 5; 14(2); 21; 34:3; 6(4); 7(4); 14; 15; 35:2(4); 4(2); 45:9(2); 17; 47:6; 12(2); 15; 48:10; 20; 49:4(2); 18(2); 23; 25(2); 26(3); 50:3; 5; 11; 51:21; 52:8; 12; 53:3; 5; 9(2); 12(3); 54:1; 9; 15(2); 56:12; 57:5; 8; 9; 15; 58:4; 14; 59:3(2); 6; 12; 17; 21; 60:7; 9; 61:8; 10(4); 62:11; 63:1; 3; 11; 12(2); 64:11; 65:6(3); 16(3); 11(2); 15(4); 16; **Jer** 1:8; 19; 2:9(2); 22; 29; 35; 3:1; 2(3); 9(2); 10; 15; 18; 20; 4:8; 30(3); 5:17; 18; 6:3; 11(3); 12; 26; 28; 8:8; 19(2); 9:4; 8; 15; 18(2); 25; 10:3; 4(4); 13; 24; 11:5; 10; 15; 16; 19; 12:1(2); 5(2); 6; 13; 12:2; 13; 7; 11; 16; 17; 14:17; 17:1(2); 8; 18:6; 17; 18; 19; 23:5; 10; 24:7(3); 10(2); 1; 14; 17; 26:8; 18; 17(3); 18(2); 21; 15:6; 7; 11; 14; 17; 20; 16:8; 18; 17:1(2); 21; 15:6; 7; 11; 14; 17; 20; 16:8; 18; 17:1(2); 21; 18:12; 14; 17; 20; 16:8; 40:4(2); 5; 6; 9; 41:1; 10(2); 3(2); 5(2); 6; 8; 9; 11; 41:1; 2(2); 3(2); 9; 43:10; 2; 3; 27; 35; 38(3); 41; 45; 46; 11:2; 22; 25; 28; 23:15; 19; 21; 27; 32; 24:12(3); 7; 12; 18(2); 24; 26; 25:5; 12; 23(2); 24(2); 26:8; 9; 12; 13; 24; 30; 27:3; 10; 18; 19; 24; 29; 41; 28:10(2); 14; 16; 20(2); 27(3); 31; **Rom** 1:4; 9; 12; 27; 29;

2:11; 3:13; 5:1; 6:4; 6; 8(2); 7:18; 21; 25(2); 8:16; 17(2); 18; 25; 26; 32; 9:14; 22; 10:9; 10(2); 11:17; 12:8(3); 10; 15(2); 18; 21; 14:15(2); 20; 15:6; 10; 13; 14; 24; 30; 32(2); 33; 16:14; 15; 16; 20; 24; **1Cor** 1:2; 17; 2:1; 3; 4; 13; 3:2(2); 9; 19; 4:3; 8; 12; 21; 5:4; 8(3); 9; 10(3); 11; 6:6; 7; 9; 20; 7:5; 12; 13; 23; 24; 8:7; 9:13; 23; 10:5; 13; 20; 11:5; 32; 12:26(2); 30; 13:1; 14:5(2); 6; 15(4); 16; 18; 19; 21; 23; 39; 15:10; 32; 35; 16:4; 6; 7; 10; 11; 12; 14; 16; 19; 20; 21; 23; 24; **2Cor** 1:1; 12; 17; 2:1; 4; 7; 3:3(2); 18; 4:14; 5:1; 2; 8; 6:1; 14(3); 15(2); 16; 7:3; 4; 8; 15; 8:4; 18; 19(2); 22; 9:4; 10:2; 12; 11:1(2); 2; 4; 9; 25; 32; 12:16; 18; 13:4; 11; 12; 14; **Gal** 1:2; 16; 18; 2:1(2); 3; 5; 12; 13(2); 20; 3:9; 4:18; 20; 25; 30; 5:1; 24; 6:11; 18; **Eph** 1:3; 13; 2:5; 19; 3:12; 16; 18; 19; 4:2(2); 14; 19; 25; 28; 31; 5:6; 7; 11; 18(2); 26; 6:2; 3; 5; 6; 7; 9; 14; 15; 18(2); 23; 24; **Phil** 1:1; 4; 11; 20; 23; 25; 27; 2:6; 12; 17; 18; 22(2); 23; 29; 4:3(3); 6; 9; 14; 15; 21; 23; **Col** 1:9; 11(2); 2:4; 5; 7; 11; 12(2); 13; 19; 20; 22; 3:1; 4; 9; 16; 22; 4:2; 6(2); 9; 18; **1Th** 1:6; 2:2; 4; 17; 3:4; 13; 4:11; 14; 16(3); 17(2); 18; 5:3; 10; 26; 28; **2Th** 1:6; 7(2); 9; 11; 2:5; 8(2); 9; 10; 3:1; 8; 10; 12; 14; 16; 17; 18; **1Ti** 1:10; 14; 2:9(2); 10; 11; 15; 3:4; 6; 4:2; 3; 4; 14; 5:2; 6:6; 10; 21; **2Ti** 1:3; 4; 9; 2:4; 10; 11(2); 12; 22; 3:6(2); 4:2; 11(2); 13(2); 16; 17; 22(2); **Titus** 2:15; 3:15(2); **Philem** 1:13; 19; 25; **Heb** 1:9; 2:4(2); 7; 9; 3:10; 17(2); 4:2; 13; 15; 5:2; 7; 7:21; 8:8(3); 9; 10; 9:4; 11; 19; 21; 22; 23(2); 24; 25; 10:1; 16; 22(2); 11:7; 9(2); 25; 31(2); 37; 12:1(2); 7(2); 14; 17; 18; 20; 28; 13:3; 5; 9(3); 12; 16; 17(2); 23; 25; **Jas** 1:6; 11; 17; 18; 21; 2:2; 3; 4; 13(2); 4:4; 5:14; **1Pet** 1:7; 8; 12; 18; 19; 22; 2:15; 18; 20; 3:2; 6; 7; 15; 4:1; 4; 13; 5:5; 13; 14(2); **2Pet** 1:1; 18; 2:3; 6; 7; 8; 13(2); 14; 16; 17; 20; 3:6; 8; 10(2); 12; 17; **1Jn** 1:1; 2; 3(3); 6; 7; 2:1; 19; **2Jn** 2; 3; 12; **3Jn** 10; 13; **Jude** 9; 12; 14; 23; 24; **Rev** 1:7; 12; 13(2); 2:12; 16; 22; 23; 27; 3:4; 17; 18; 20(2); 21(2); 4:1; 5:1; 2; 12; 6:8(5); 10; 7:2; 9; 10; 8:3; 4; 5; 7; 8; 13; 9:19; 10:1; 3; 11:6; 12:1; 2; 5; 9; 17(2); 13:4; 7; 10(2); 14:1; 2; 4; 7; 9; 10; 15; 18; 15:2; 6; 8; 16:8; 9; 16; 21; 19:2; 13; 15(2); 17; 20(3); 21(2); 20:4; 6; 21:3(3); 8; 9; 15; 16; 19; 22:12; 21

<hr>

WITHIN

413, 990, 996, 1004, 1157, 2315, 2436, 4481, 5704, 5705, 5750, 5921, 5978, 6441, 7130, 7146, 8432, 8537, *1223*, *1722*, *1787*, *2080*, *2081*, *2082*, *4314*

Gen 6:14; 9:21; 18:12; 24; 26; 25:22; 39:11; 40:13; 19; **Ex** 20:10; 25:11; 26:33; 37:2; **Lev** 10:18; 13:55; 14:41; 16:2; 12; 15; 25:29(2); 30; 26:25; **Num** 4:10; 18:7; **Deut** 5:14; 12:12; 17; 18; 14:27; 28; 19; 15:7; 22; 16:5; 11; 14; 17:2; 8; 23:10; 24:14; 26:12; 28:43; 31:12; 32:25; **Josh** 1:11; 19:1; 9; 21:41; **Judg** 7:16; 9:51; 11:18; 26; 14:12; 15:1; **1Sa** 13:11; 14:14; 25:36; 37; 26:7; **2Sa** 7:2; 20:4; **1Kin** 6:15; 16; 18; 19; 21; 23; 27; 29; 30; 7:8; 9; 31; **2Kin** 4:27; 6:30; 7:11; 11:8; **2Chr** 4:15; 10:8; 9; **Neh** 4:22; 6:10; **Job** 6:4; 14:22; 19:27; 20:13; 14; 24:11; 32:18; **Ps** 36:1; 39:3; 40:8; 10; 42:6; 11; 43:5; 45:13; 51:10; 55:4; 94:19; 101:2; 7; 103:1; 109:22; 122:2; 7(2); 8; 142:3; 143:4(2); 147:13; **Prov** 22:18; 26:24; **Eccl** 9:14; **Song** 4:1; 3; 6:7; **Is** 7:8; 16:14; 21:16; 26:9; 56:5; 60:18; 63:11; **Jer** 4:14; 23:9; 28:3; 11; **Lam** 1:20; **Eze** 1:27; 2:10; 3:24; 7:15; 11:19; 12:24; 36:24; 27; 40:7; 8; 16; 43; 41:9; 17; 44:17; **Dan** 6:12; 11:20; **Hos** 11:3(4); 4; **Jonah** 2:7; **Mic** 3:3; 5:6; **Zeph** 3:3; **Zec** 12:1; **Mt** 3:9; 9; 21; 23:25; 26; 27; 28; **Mk** 2:8; 7:21; 23; 14:4; 58; **Lk** 3:8; 7:39; 49; 11:7; 40; 12:17; 16:3; 17:21; 18:4; 19:44; 24:32; **Jn** 20:26; **Acts** 5:23; **Rom** 8:23; **1Cor** 5:12; **2Cor** 7:5; **Heb** 6:19; **Rev** 4:8; 5:1

<hr>

WITHOUT

268, 369, 413, 657, 1004, 1097, 1107, 1115, 1372, 1768, 2351, 2435, 2600, 2963, 3808, 4682, 5493, 5703, 5704, 5769, 7367, 8267, 8414, 8549, *35*, *77*, *88*, *89*, *112*, *175*, *186*, *267*, *275*, *278*, *280*, *282*, *298*, *299*, *361*, *369*, *379*, *427*, *448*, *459*, *460*, *504*, *505*, *563*, *671*, *678*, *729*, *772*, *784*, *794*, *801*, *815*, *817*, *820*, *866*, *870*, *880*, *886*, *895*, *1432*, *1500*, *1618*, *1622*, *1854*, *1855*, *2673*, *3326*, *3361*, *3367*, *3672*, *3756*, *3924*, *4160*, *5565*

Gen 1:2; 6:14; 9:22; 19:16; 24:11; 31; 37:33; 41:44; 49; **Ex** 12:5; 21:11; 25:11; 26:35; 27:21; 29:1; 14; 33:7(2); 37:2; 40:22; **Lev** 1:3; 10; 3:1; 6; 4:3; 12; 21; 23; 28; 32; 5:15; 18; 6:6; 11; 8:17; 9:2; 3; 11; 10:12; 13:46; 55; 14:10(2); 40; 41; 16:27; 22:19; 23:12; 18; 24:3; 14; 26:43; **Num** 5:3; 4; 6:14(3); 15:24; 35; 36; 19:2; 3; 9; 20:19; 28:3; 9; 11; 19; 31; 29:2; 8; 13; 17; 20; 23; 26; 29; 32; 36; 31:13; 19; 35:5; 22(2); 26; 27; **Deut** 8:9; 23:12; 25:5; 32:4; 25; **Josh** 3:10; 6:23; **Judg** 2:23; 6:5; 7:12; 11:30; **Ruth** 4:14; **1Sa** 19:5; 30:8; **2Sa** 23:4; **1Kin** 6:6; 29; 30; 7:9; 8:8; 22:1; **2Kin** 10:24; 11:15; 16:18; 18:25; 23:4; 6; 25:16; **1Chr** 2:30; 32; 21:24; 22:3; 14; **2Chr** 5:9; 12:3; 15:3(3); 21:20; 24:8; 32:3; 5; 33:14; **Ezr** 6:9; 7:22; 10:13; **Neh** 13:20; **Job** 2:3; 4:20; 21; 5:9; 6:6; 7:6; 8:11(2); 9:10; 17; 10:22; 11:15; 12:25; 24:7; 10; 26:2; 30:28; 31:19; 39; 33:9; 34:6; 20; 24; 35(2); 35:16; 36:12; 38:2; 39:16; 41:33; 42:3; **Ps** 7:4; 25:3; 31:11; 35:7(2); 19; 59:4; 69:4; 105:34; 109:3;

119:78; 161; **Prov** 1:11; 20; 3:30; 5:23; 6:15; 7:12; 11:22; 15:22; 16:8; 19:2; 22:13; 23:29; 24:27; 28; 25:14; 28; 29:1; **Eccl** 10:11; **Song** 6:8; 8:1; **Is** 5:9; 14; 6:11(2); 10:4; 33:7; 36:10; 45:17; 52:3; 4; 55:1(2); **Jer** 2:15; 32; 4:7; 23; 5:21; 9:11; 21; 15:13; 21:4; 22:13; 26:9; 32:43; 33:10(5); 12(2); 34:22; 44:19; 22; 46:19; 48:9; 49:31; 51:29; 37; 52:20; **Lam** 1:6; 3:49; 52; **Eze** 2:10; 7:15; 14:23; 17:9; 33:15; 38:11; 40:19; 40; 44; 41:9; 17(2); 25; 42:7; 43:21; 22; 23(2); 25; 45:18; 23; 46:2; 4(2); 6(2); 13; 47:2; **Dan** 2:34; 45; 8:25; 11:18; **Hos** 3:4(6); 7:1; 11; **Joel** 1:6; **Zec** 2:4; **Mt** 5:22; 10:29; 12:46; 47; 13:34; 57; 15:16; 26:69; **Mk** 1:45; 3:31; 32; 4:11; 34; 6:4; 7:15; 18(2); 11:4; 14:58; **Lk** 1:10; 74; 6:49; 8:20; 11:40; 13:25; 20:28; 29; 22:35; **Jn** 1:3; 8:7; 15:5; 25; 18:16; 19:23; 20:11; **Acts** 5:23; 26; 9:9; 10:29; 12:5; 14:17; 25:17; **Rom** 1:9; 20; 31(2); 2:12(2); 3:3; 21; 28; 4:6; 5:6; 7:8; 9; 10:14; 11:29; 12:9; **1Cor** 4:8; 5:12; 13; 6:18; 7:32; 35; 9:18; 21(4); 11:11(2); 14:7; 10; 16:10; **2Cor** 7:5; 10:13; 15; 11:28; **Eph** 1:4; 2:12(2); 3:21; 5:27; **Phil** 1:10; 14; 2:14; 15; **Col** 2:11; 4:5; **1Th** 1:3; 2:13; 4:12; 5:17; **1Ti** 2:8; 3:7; 16; 5:21; 6:14; **2Ti** 1:3; 3:3; **Philem** 1:14; **Heb** 4:15; 7:3(3); 7; 20; 21; 9:7; 14; 18; 22; 28; 10:23; 28; 11:6; 40; 12:8; 14; 13:5; 11; 12; 13; **Jas** 2:13; 18; 20; 26(2); 3:17(2); **1Pet** 1:17; 19(2); 3:1; 4:9; **2Pet** 2:17; 3:14; **Jude** 12(3); **Rev** 11:2; 14:5; 10; 20; 22:15

WORSE

2196, 5062, 7451, 7489, *1640, 2276, 5302, 5501*

Gen 19:9; **2Sa** 19:7; **1Kin** 16:25; **2Kin** 14:12; **1Chr** 19:16; 19; **2Chr** 6:24; 25:22; 33:9; **Jer** 7:26; 16:12; **Dan** 1:10; **Mt** 9:16; 12:45; 27:64; **Mk** 2:21; 5:26; **Lk** 11:26; **Jn** 2:10; 5:14; **1Cor** 8:8; 11:17; **1Ti** 5:8; **2Ti** 3:13(2); **2Pet** 2:20

WORST

7451

Eze 7:24

WOULD

14, 305, 2654, 2974, 3863, 4310, 5315, 5414, 6634, *1096, 2172, 2309, 3195, 3785*

Gen 2:19; 21:7; 30:34; 42:21; 22; 43:7; 44:22; **Ex** 2:4; 8:32; 9:35; 10:20; 27; 11:10; 13:15; 16:3; **Num** 11:29(2); 14:2(2); 20:3; 21:23; 22:18; 29(2); 24:13; **Deut** 1:26; 43; 45; 2:30; 3:26; 5:29; 7:8; 8:20; 9:25; 10:10; 23:5; 21; 28:56; 67(2); 32:26(2); 29; **Josh** 5:6(2); 7:7; 17:12; 24:10; **Judg** 1:27; 34; 35; 2:17; 3:4; 8:19; 24(2); 9:29(2); 11:17(2); 13:23(3); 14:6; 15:1; 19:10; 25; 20:13; **Ruth** 1:13(2); **1Sa** 2:16; 25; 13:13; 15:9; 18:2; 20:9; 22:17; 22; 26:23; 31:4; **2Sa** 2:21; 4:6; 10; 6:10; 11:20; 12:8; 17; 18; 13:14; 16; 25; 14:16; 29(2); 15:4; 18:11; 12; 33; 23:15; 16; 17; **1Kin** 8:12; 13:33; 18:32; 20:33; 21:4; 22:18; 49; **2Kin** 2:1; 3:14; 5:3(2); 7:2; 8:19; 13:23; 14:11; 27; 17:14; 18:12; 24:4; **1Chr** 10:4; 11:17; 18; 19; 13:4; 19:19; 27:23; **2Chr** 6:1; 10:16; 12:12; 15:13; 18:17; 21:7; 24:19; 25:20; 33:10; 35:22; **Ezr** 10:8; 19; **Neh** 6:11; 14; 9:24; 29; 30; 10:30; 31(2); **Est** 3:4; 6:6; 8:11; 9:5; 27; **Job** 5:8(2); 6:3; 8; 9(2); 10; 7:16; 8:6; 9:15(2); 16; 21(2); 35; 11:5; 6; 12; 13:3; 5; 16:5; 23:4; 5(3); 6; 27:22; 30:1; 31:12; 35(2); 36; 37(2); 32:22; 34:27; 36:16; 41:32; **Ps** 22:8; 35:25; 40:5; 50:12; 51:16; 55:6; 7; 8; 12; 56:1; 2; 57:3; 69:4; 81:11(2); 106:23; 107:8; 15; 21; 31; 119:57; 142:4; **Prov** 1:25; 30; **Song** 3:4; 8:1; 2(3); 7(2); **Is** 27:4(3); 28:12; 30:15; 42:24; 54:9; **Jer** 8:18; 10:7; 13:11; 18:10; 22:24; 29:19; 36:25(2); 38:26; 49:9; 51:9; **Lam** 4:12; **Eze** 3:6; 6:10; 13:6; 20:8; 13; 15; 21; 23; 38:17; **Dan** 1:8; 2:8; 16(2); 18; 5:19(4); 7:19; 9:2; **Hos** 7:1; 11:7; **Obad** 5(2); **Jonah** 3:10; 4:5; **Zec** 7:13(2); **Mal** 1:10; **Mt** 2:18; 5:42; 7:12; 8:34; 11:21; 23; 12:7; 38; 14:5; 7; 16:1; 18:23; 30; 22:3; 23:30; 37(2); 24:43(3); 27:15; 34; **Mk** 3:2; 13; 5:10; 6:19; 26; 48; 7:24; 26; 9:30; 10:35; 36; 11:16; **Lk** 1:62; 74; 5:3; 6:7; 31; 7:3; 36; 39; 8:31; 32; 41; 9:53; 10:1; 2; 12:39(2); 13:34(2); 15:16; 28; 16:26(2); 18:4; 13; 15; 19:27; 40; 22:49; 24:28; **Jn** 1:43; 4:10; 40; 47; 5:46; 6:6; 11; 15; 7:1; 44; 8:39; 42; 9:27; 12:21; 14:2; 28; 15:19; 18:30; 36; **Acts** 2:30; 5:24; 7:5; 25(2); 26; 39; 8:31; 9:38; 10:10; 11:23; 12:6; 14:13; 16:3; 27; 17:20; 18:14; 19:30; 31; 33; 20:16; 21:14; 22:30; 23:12; 15; 20; 28; 24:6; 25:3; 4; 20; 22; 26:5; 29; 27:30; 28:18; **Rom** 1:13; 5:7; 7:15; 16; 19(2); 20; 21; 11:25; 16:19; **1Cor** 2:8; 4:8; 18; 7:7; 32; 10:1; 20; 11:3; 31; 12:1; 14:5; **2Cor** 1:8; 2:1; 8; 5:4; 8:4; 6; 9:5; 10:9; 11:1; 12:6; 20(2); **Gal** 1:7; 2:10; 3:2; 8; 4:15; 17; 5:12; 17; **Eph** 3:16; **Phil** 1:12; **Col** 1:27; 2:1; 4:3; **1Th** 2:9; 12; 18; 4:1; 13; **2Th** 1:11; 3:10; **Philem** 1:13; 14; **Heb** 4:8; 10:2; 11:32; 12:17; **1Jn** 2:19; **2Jn** 12; **3Jn** 10; **Rev** 3:15; 13:15

WOULDEST

3426, *2309*

Gen 30:15; 31:30; 31; **Ex** 7:16; 23:5; **Deut** 8:2; 21:11; 28:62; **Josh** 15:18; **2Sa** 14:11; 18:13; **1Kin** 1:16; 18:9; **2Kin** 4:13; 5:13; 6:22; **1Chr** 4:10(2); **2Chr** 6:20; 20:10; **Ezr** 9:14; **Neh** 2:5; **Job** 8:5; 14:13(3); **Is** 48:8; 64:1(2); **Lk** 16:27; **Jn** 4:10; 11:40; 21:18(2); **Acts** 23:20; 24:4; **Heb** 10:5; 8

YE

859, *5210*

Gen 3:1; 3(3); 4; 5(2); 4:23; 9:4; 7; 17:10; 11; 18:5(3); 19:2; 8; 22:5; 24:49; 26:27(2); 29:4; 5; 7; 31:6; 32:4; 19(2); 20; 34:9; 10(2); 11; 12; 15; 17; 30; 40:7; 42:1; 7; 9(2); 12; 14; 15(2); 16(2); 19(2); 20; 22; 33; 34(3); 36(2); 38(2); 43:3; 5; 6(2); 7; 27; 29; 44:4; 5; 10; 15(2); 19; 23; 27; 29(2); 45:4; 5; 9; 13(3); 17; 18; 19; 24; 46:34(2); 47:23; 24; 49:2; 50:17; 20; 21; 25; **Ex** 1:16(2); 18; 22(2); 2:18; 20; 3:12; 18; 21(2); 22(2); 4:15; 5:4; 5; 7; 8(2); 11(2); 14; 17(3); 18; 19; 21; 6:7; 8:25; 28(2); 9:28; 30; 10:2; 11(2); 24; 11:7; 12:3; 5; 6; 10(2); 11(2); 13; 14(2); 15(2); 17(2); 18; 20(2); 22; 24; 25(2); 26; 27; 31(2); 32; 46; 13:3; 4; 19; 14:2; 13(3); 14; 15:21; 16:3; 6; 7(2); 8; 12(3); 16; 23(2); 25; 26; 28; 29; 17:2(2); 19:4; 5(2); 6; 12; 20:20; 22; 23(2); 22:21; 22; 31(3); 23:9(2); 25; 24:1; 14; 25:2; 3; 9; 19; 30:9(2); 32; 37; 31:13(2); 14; 32:30; 33:5; 34:13; 35:1; 3; 5; **Lev** 1:2; 2:11(2); 12; 3:17; 7:23; 24; 26; 32; 8:32; 33; 35(2); 9:3; 6; 10:6; 7(2); 9(2); 10; 11; 13; 14; 17; 18; 11:2; 3; 4; 8(2); 9(2); 11(2); 13; 21; 22; 24; 33; 39; 42; 43(3); 44(3); 45; 14:34; 15:31; 16:29; 30; 31; 17:14; 18:3(4); 4; 5; 24; 26; 28; 30(3); 19:2; 3; 4; 5(2); 6; 9; 11; 12; 15; 19; 23(2); 25; 26(2); 27; 28; 30; 33; 34; 35; 36; 37; 20:7; 8; 15; 22; 23; 24; 25(2); 26(2); 22:19; 20; 22; 24(2); 25; 28; 29; 30; 31; 32; 23:2; 3; 4; 6; 7(2); 8(2); 10(2); 12(2); 14(2); 15(2); 16(2); 17; 18; 19; 21(2); 22; 24; 25(2); 27; 28; 31; 32(2); 35; 36(3); 37; 38; 39(2); 40(2); 41(2); 42; 24:22; 25:2; 9; 10(3); 11; 12; 13; 14; 17; 18(2); 19; 20; 22(2); 23; 24; 44; 45; 46(2); 26:1(2); 2; 3; 5; 6; 7; 10; 12; 13; 14; 15(3); 16; 17(2); 18; 21; 23; 25(2); 26; 27; 29(2); 34; 35; 37; 38; **Num** 1:2; 4:18; 27; 32; 5:3(2); 6:23; 9:3(2); 14; 10:5; 6; 7(2); 9(4); 10; 11:18(3); 19; 20; 12:4; 8; 13:2; 20; 14:9(2); 28; 30; 31(2); 34(3); 41; 42; 43(2); 15:2; 12(2); 14; 15; 18; 19(2); 20(3); 21; 22; 29; 39(3); 40; 16:3(2); 7(2); 8; 10; 11; 17; 26; 28; 30; 41; 18:3; 5; 7; 26(2); 28(3); 29; 30; 31(2); 32(4); 19:3; 20:4; 5; 8; 10; 12(2); 24; 21:5; 17; 22:19; 25:5; 27:8; 9; 10; 11; 14; 28:2; 3; 11; 18; 19; 20; 23; 24; 25(2); 26(3); 27; 31; 29:1(2); 2; 7(3); 8; 12(3); 13; 17; 35(2); 36; 39; 31:4; 15; 19; 23(2); 24(3); 32:6; 7; 14; 15(2); 20(2); 22; 23(2); 29; 33:51; 52; 53; 54(4); 55(3); 34:2; 6; 7; 8; 10; 13; 18; 35:2; 4; 5; 6(3); 7(2); 8(3); 10; 11; 13(2); 14(2); 31; 32; 33(2); 34; **Deut** 1:6; 10; 11; 14; 17(3); 18; 19; 20; 22; 26; 27; 31(2); 32; 33; 39; 41(3); 42; 43; 45; 46(2); 2:3; 4(2); 6(4); 24; 3:18; 19; 20; 22; 4:1; 2(3); 4; 5(2); 11; 12(2); 14(2); 15(2); 16; 20; 22; 23; 25; 26(3); 27; 28; 5:1; 5; 23(2); 24; 28; 32(2); 33(4); 6:1(2); 3; 14; 16(2); 17; 7:5(2); 7(2); 12; 25; 8:1(2); 19; 20(2); 9:7(2); 8; 16(2); 18; 21; 22; 23(2); 24; 10:19(2); 11:2; 5; 8(3); 9; 10; 11; 13; 16; 17; 18; 19; 22; 23; 25; 27; 28(2); 31(2); 32; 12:1(2); 2(2); 3(2); 4; 5; 6; 7(4); 8; 9; 10(2); 11(2); 12(2); 16(2); 13:3; 4(2); 13; 14:1(2); 4; 6; 7; 8; 9(2); 10; 11; 12; 20; 21; 17:16; 18:15; 19:19; 20:2; 3(2); 18; 22:24(2); 23:4; 24:8; 9; 25:17; 27:2; 4(2); 12; 28:62(2); 63; 68; 29:2; 6(3); 7; 9(2); 10; 16(2); 17; 30:18(2); 31:5; 13(2); 19; 27; 29(2); 32:1; 3; 6; 43; 46; 47(2); 51(2); **Josh** 1:11; 14; 15; 2:5; 10(3); 12; 13; 14; 16; 3:3(2); 4(3); 8(2); 10; 4:3(3); 6; 7; 17; 22; 23; 24; 6:3(2); 4; 5; 10(2); 18(3); 22; 7:12; 13; 14; 8:2; 4(2); 7; 8(3); 9:6; 7; 8(2); 11; 22(2); 23; 10:19; 25; 18:3; 6; 22:2; 3; 4; 16(3); 18(2); 19; 24; 25(2); 27; 31(2); 23:3; 5; 6(2); 7; 8; 11; 12; 13; 14; 16(2); 24:6; 7; 8; 11; 13(5); 14; 15(2); 19; 20; 22(2); 27; **Judg** 2:2(4); 5:2; 3(2); 9; 10(2); 23(2); 6:10(2); 31(2); 7:17; 18; 8:15; 18; 19; 24; 9:7; 15; 16(3); 18; 19(2); 48; 10:12; 13; 14; 11:7(3); 9; 26; 12:2; 3(2); 4; 14:12; 13(2); 15; 18(2); 15:7; 10; 12; 18:6; 8; 9; 10(2); 14(2); 18; 24(3); 19:24; 20:7; 21:11(2); 21; 22(2); **Ruth** 1:8; 9; 11; 13(2); 21; 4:2; 9; 10; **1Sa** 2:23; 24; 29; 4:9(2); 6:3(2); 5(2); 6; 8; 21; 7:3; 8:17; 18(2); 22; 9:13(3); 19; 10:14; 19(2); 24; 11:9(2); 10; 12:1; 5; 11; 12(2); 13(2); 14(2); 15; 17(2); 20; 21(2); 25(3); 14:33; 38; 40; 15:6; 32; 17:8(2); 9; 25; 18:25; 21:14(2); 15; 22:7; 13; 23:21(2); 23; 25:6; 13; 26:16(2); 27:10; 29:10; 30:23; **2Sa** 1:21; 24; 2:5(2); 6; 7; 3:17; 38; 7:7; 11:15(2); 20(3); 21; 13:28; 15:10(2); 36(2); 16:10; 19:10; 11; 12(3); 13; 22(2); 42; 43(2); 21:3; 4; 24:2; **1Kin** 1:34; 35; 45; 9:6(2); 11:2; 12:6; 9; 24; 18:18; 21; 24; 25; 20:28; 33; 22:3; **2Kin** 1:3; 5; 2:3; 5; 16; 3:17(4); 19; 6:2; 11; 19; 32; 7:1; 9:11; 10:6(3); 8; 9; 13; 11:5; 6; 8(2); 12:7; 17:12; 13; 27; 35; 36(3); 37(2); 38(2); 39; 18:19; 22(2); 31(2); 32; 19:6; 10; 29(2); 22:13; 18; **1Chr** 12:17(2); 15:12(3); 13; 16:9; 10; 13(2); 15; 19; 28; 35; 17:6; 22:19; 28:8; **2Chr** 7:19; 10:6; 9; 11:4; 12:5; 13:5; 8(2); 9; 11; 12(2); 15:2(4); 7; 18:14; 25; 27; 30; 19:6(2); 9; 10(2); 20:15(2); 16(2); 17(2); 20(3); 23:4; 7; 24:5; 20(3); 28:9; 10; 11; 13(2); 29:5; 8; 11; 31; 30:6; 7(2); 8; 9(2); 32:10(2); 12; 13; 34:23; 26; **Ezr** 4:2; 3; 18; 21; 22; 6:6; 8; 7:25; 8:28; 29(2); 9:11; 12; 10:10; **Neh** 1:8; 9; 2:17; 19(2); 20; 4:12; 14; 20(2); 5:7; 8; 9(2); 11; 8:10; 11; 13:17; 18; 21(2); 25; **Est** 4:16; 8:8; **Job** 6:21(2); 26; 27(2); 12:2; 13:2; 4(2); 5; 7; 8(2); 9; 10; 16:2; 4; 17:10; 18:2; 19:2; 3(3); 5; 21; 22; 28; 29(2); 21:27; 28; 29(2); 34; 27:12(2); 32:6; 11; 13; 34:2(2); 10; 18; 42:7; 8; **Ps** 2:10(2); 12; 4:2(3); 6:8; 11:1; 14:6; 22:23(3); 24:7(3); 9(2); 27:8; 29:1; 30:4; 31:23; 24; 32:9; 11(2); 33:1; 34:9; 11; 47:1; 7; 48:13(2); 49:1(2); 50:22; 58:1(3); 2(2); 62:3(3); 8; 66:1; 8; 16; 68:13(2); 16(2); 26; 32; 34; 82:2; 6; 7; 90:3; 94:8(3); 95:7; 96:7; 97:7; 10; 12; 99:5; 100:1; 3; 103:20; 21(3); 104:35; 105:2; 3; 6(2); 45; 106:1; 48; 111:1; 112:1; 113:1(2); 9; 114:6(3); 115:11; 15; 116:19; 117:1(2); 2; 119:115; 134:1(2); 135:1(3); 2; 20; 21; 139:19; 146:1; 10; 147:1; 20; 148:1(2); 2(2); 3(2); 4(2); 7; 14; 149:1; 9; 150:1; 6; **Prov** 1:22(2); 24; 25; 4:1; 2; 5:7; 7:24; 8:5(3); 32; **Song** 1:5; 2:7(2); 3:3; 5(2); 11; 5:8(2); 6:13; 8:4; **Is** 1:5(2); 10(2); 12; 15(2); 19(2); 20(2); 29(3); 30; 2:3; 5; 22; 3:10; 14; 15(2); 6:9(2); 7:9(2); 13(2); 8:9(5); 12(2); 10:3(3); 12:3; 4; 13:2; 6; 16:1; 7; 18:2; 3(3); 19:11; 21:5; 12(2); 13(2); 22:9(2); 10(2); 11(2); 14; 23:1; 2; 6(2); 14; 24:15; 26:2; 4; 19; 27:2; 12(2); 28:12; 14; 15; 18; 22; 23; 29:1; 9; 30:12; 15(2); 16(2); 17(2); 21(3); 22; 29; 31:6; 32:9(2); 10(2); 11(2); 20; 33:11(2); 13(2); 34:1(2); 16; 35:3; 36:4; 7; 13; 16(2); 37:6; 10; 30(2); 40:1(2); 2; 3; 18(2); 21(3); 25; 41:14; 23; 24; 42:10; 17; 18(3); 43:10(2); 12; 18; 19; 44:8(2); 23(3); 26; 45:8; 11; 17; 19; 20; 21; 22; 46:5; 8; 12; 48:1; 6; 14; 16(2); 20(4); 49:1; 50:1; 11(4); 51:1(4); 7(3); 52:3(2); 9; 11(5); 12; 55:1(2); 2(2); 6(2); 12; 56:1; 9(2); 12; 57:3; 4(3); 14(2); 58:3; 4(3); 6; 61:6(3); 7; 62:6; 10; 11; 65:11; 12(3); 13(3); 14; 15; 18; 66:1; 5; 10(3); 11(2); 12(2); 13; 14; **Jer** 2:4; 7(2); 12(2); 29(2); 31; 3:13; 16; 20; 22; 4:4; 5(2); 10; 16; 5:1(2); 10; 14; 19(3); 22(2); 31; 6:1; 4; 6; 16(2); 18; 7:2; 4; 5(2); 6; 8; 9(2); 12; 13(3); 14; 23(2); 8:8; 9:4(2); 17; 20; 10:1; 11; 11:2; 4; 6; 13; 12:9; 13:15; 16; 17; 23; 14:13(2); 16:12(2); 13(3); 17:4; 20(2); 22(2); 24; 27; 18:6; 11; 13; 19:3; 20:13; 21:3; 4; 11; 22:3; 4; 5; 10; 26(2); 30; 23:2; 17; 20; 35; 36(2); 38(3); 25:3; 4; 5; 7(2); 8; 27; 28; 29(2); 34(3); 26:4; 5; 11; 12; 15(3); 27:4; 9(2); 10; 13; 14; 15(2); 29:5; 6(2); 7; 8; 12(2); 13(2); 15; 19; 20(2); 26; 28; 30:6; 22; 24; 31:6; 7(2); 10; 32:5(2); 36; 43; 33:10; 20; 34:14; 15(2); 16; 17; 35:5; 6(2); 7(4); 13; 14; 15(3); 18; 36:19; 37:7; 10; 18; 40:3; 10(3); 42:9; 10; 11; 13; 15(2); 16(3); 18(3); 19(2); 20(2); 21; 22(2); 44:2; 3; 7; 8(4); 9; 21(2); 22; 23(2); 25(2); 26; 29; 46:3; 4; 9(2); 14(2); 48:14; 17(2); 20; 26; 28; 49:3; 5; 8; 14; 28; 30; 50:2; 11(4); 14; 29; 45; 51:3(2); 27; 45(2); 46; 50; **Lam** 1:12; 4:15; **Eze** 5:7; 6:3; 7; 8(2); 13; 7:4; 9; 9:5(2); 7; 11:5; 6(2); 7; 8; 10(2); 11; 12(2); 17; 12:20; 22; 13:2; 5; 7(3); 8; 9; 11; 12; 14(3); 18(2); 19; 20(2); 21; 22; 23(2); 14:8; 22(2); 23(2); 15:7; 17:12; 21; 18:2(2); 3; 19; 25; 31(2); 32; 20:3; 7; 18; 20; 29; 30(2); 31(3); 32; 34; 38; 39(4); 41; 42; 43(4); 44(2); 21:24(3); 22:19; 21; 22(2); 23:40; 49(2); 24:21; 22(2); 23(2); 24(2); 25:5; 30:2; 33:10; 11(3); 20(2); 25(2); 26(4); 34:3(4); 4(6); 7; 9; 18(2); 19(2); 21(2); 31; 35:9; 13; 36:1; 3(2); 4; 6; 8(2); 9; 11; 22(2); 23; 25; 27; 28(2); 30; 31; 37:4; 5; 6(2); 13; 14(2); 39:17; 18; 19(3); 20; 44:6; 7(2); 8(2); 28; 30; 45:1(2); 6; 10; 13(2); 14; 20; 21; 47:13; 14; 18; 21; 22; 23; 48:8; 9; 20; 29; **Dan** 1:10; 2:5(2); 6(2); 8(2); 9(3); 3:5(2); 14; 15(5); 26; **Hos** 1:9; 10(2); 2:1; 4:1; 15(2); 18; 5:1(4); 8; 9:5; 10:13(3); 14:3; **Joel** 1:2(2); 3; 5(2); 11(3); 13(3); 14; 2:1; 12; 19; 22; 23; 26; 27; 3:4(3); 5; 6(2); 7; 9; 11; 13; 17; **Amos** 2:11; 12; 3:13; 4:1; 3(2); 5; 6; 8; 9; 10; 11(2); 5:1; 4(2); 6; 7; 11(5); 14(2); 22; 25; 26(2); 6:2(2); 3; 12; 13; 8:4; 9:7; **Obad** 1; 16; **Mic** 1:2; 10(2); 11; 2:3(2); 6; 8; 9(2); 10; 3:1; 6(2); 9; 6:1; 2(2); 5; 9; 16(2); 7:5(2); **Nah** 1:9; 2:9; **Hab** 1:5(2); **Zeph** 1:11; 2:3(3); 12(2); 3:8; **Hag** 1:4; 6(6); 9(3); 2:3; 4; 5(2); 17; **Zec** 1:3; 4(2); 2:9; 3:10; 6:15(2); 7:5(2); 6(3); 7; 8:9; 13(2); 15; 16(2); 9:12; 10:1; 11:2; 12; 14:5(3); **Mal** 1:2; 5; 6; 7(3); 8(2); 10; 12(2); 13(4); 2:1; 2(3); 4; 8(3); 9; 13; 14; 16; 17(3); 3:1(2); 6; 7(2); 8(2); 9(2); 10; 12; 13; 14; 18; 4:2; 3; 4; **Mt** 2:8; 3:2; 3; 5:11; 13; 14; 20; 21; 27; 33; 38; 39; 43; 45; 46(2); 47(2); 48; 6:1(2); 7; 8(3); 9; 14; 15; 16; 24; 25(3); 26; 28; 30; 32; 33; 7:1; 2(3); 6; 7; 11; 12(2); 13; 16; 20; 23; 8:26(2); 9:4; 6; 13; 28; 38; 10:5; 7; 8; 11(2); 12; 14; 16; 18; 19(2); 20; 22; 23(2); 27(3); 31(2); 11:4; 7; 8; 9; 14; 17(2); 28; 29; 12:3; 5; 7(2); 34; 13:14(2); 17(2); 18; 29(2); 30; 51; 14:16; 15:3; 5; 6; 7; 16; 17; 34; 16:2; 3(3); 8(3); 9(2); 10; 11(2); 15; 17:5; 20(2); 18:3(2); 10; 12; 18(2); 35; 19:4; 28(2); 20:4; 6; 7(2); 22(3); 23; 25; 32; 21:2; 3; 5; 13; 16; 21(3); 22(2); 24; 25; 28; 32(4); 42; 22:9(2); 18(2); 29; 31; 42; 23:3; 8(2); 10; 13(3); 14(2); 15(2); 16; 17; 19; 23(2); 24; 25; 27; 28(2); 29; 31(2); 32; 33(3); 34(2); 35; 37; 39(2); 24:2; 6(2); 9; 15; 20; 32; 33(2); 42; 44(2); 25:6; 9; 13; 30; 34; 35(3); 36(3); 40(2); 41; 42(2); 43(3); 45(2); 26:2; 10; 11(2); 15; 27; 31; 36; 38; 40; 41; 55(2); 64; 65; 66; 27:17; 21; 24; 65(2); 28:5(2); 7; 13; 19; **Mk** 1:3; 15; 17; 2:8; 10; 25; 4:13(2); 24(2); 40(2); 5:39; 6:10(2); 11; 31; 37; 38; 7:8(2); 9(2); 11; 12; 13(2); 18(2); 8:5; 17(4); 18(3); 19; 20; 21; 29; 9:16; 33; 41; 50; 10:36; 38(3); 39(2); 42; 11:2(2); 3(2); 5; 17; 24(4); 25(2); 26; 31; 12:10; 15;

24(2); 26; 27; 13:7(2); 9(2); 11(4); 13; 14; 18; 23; 28; 29(2); 33(2); 35(2); 14:6; 7(4); 13; 14; 27; 32; 34; 38(2); 48; 49; 62; 64(2); 71; 15:9; 12(2); 16:6; 7; 15; **Lk** 2:12; 49(2); 3:4; 4:23; 5:22; 24; 30; 34; 6:2; 3; 20; 21(4); 22; 23; 24; 25(2); 31(2); 32(2); 33(2); 34(3); 35(2); 36; 37(3); 38; 46; 7:22; 24; 25; 26; 32(2); 33; 34; 8:18; 9:4; 5; 13; 20; 55(2); 10:2; 5; 8; 10; 11; 23; 24(2); 11:2; 9; 13; 18; 39; 40; 41; 42(2); 43; 44; 46(3); 47; 48(3); 52(3); 12:1; 3(2); 5; 7; 11(3); 12; 22(2); 24; 26(2); 28; 29(4); 30; 31; 33; 36; 40(2); 51; 54(2); 55(2); 56(3); 57; 13:2; 3(2); 4; 5(2); 25(2); 26; 27(2); 28; 32; 34; 35(2); 16:9; 11; 12; 13; 15; 17:6(2); 10(2); 22(2); 19:30(2); 31(2); 33; 46; 20:5; 23; 21:6; 8(2); 9; 14; 16; 17; 19; 20; 30; 31(3); 36(2); 22:10; 11; 26; 28; 30; 35; 40; 46(2); 51; 52; 53; 67; 68; 70; 23:14(2); 24:5; 17(2); 38; 39; 41; 48; 49(2); **Jn** 1:26; 38; 51; 3:7; 11; 12(2); 28; 4:20; 21; 22(2); 32; 35; 38(2); 48(2); 5:20; 33; 34; 35; 37; 38(2); 39(2); 40(2); 42; 43(2); 44; 45; 46(2); 47(2); 6:26(3); 29; 36; 53(2); 62; 67; 7:8; 19; 21; 22; 23; 28(3); 34(2); 36(2); 45; 47; 8:14; 15; 19(3); 21(2); 22; 23(2); 24(3); 28(2); 31(2); 32; 33; 36; 37(2); 38(2); 39(2); 40; 41; 42; 43(2); 44(2); 45; 46; 47(2); 49; 54; 55; 9:19; 27(3); 30; 41(3); 10:20; 25; 26(2); 32; 34; 36; 38(2); 11:15; 34; 39; 49; 56; 12:8(2); 19(2); 35; 36(2); 13:10; 11; 12; 13(2); 14; 15; 17(3); 19; 33(2); 34(2); 35(2); 14:1; 3; 4(2); 7(3); 13; 14; 15; 17; 19(2); 20(2); 24; 28(3); 29; 15:3; 4(2); 5(2); 7(3); 8(2); 9; 10(2); 12; 14(2); 16(3); 17; 18; 19(2); 27(2); 16:1; 4; 10; 12; 16(2); 17(2); 19(3); 20(2); 22; 23(2); 24(2); 26; 27; 31; 32; 33(2); 18:4; 7; 8; 29; 31; 39(2); 19:4; 6; 35; 20:22; 23(2); 31(2); 21:5; 6; 10; **Acts** 1:4; 5; 8(2); 11(3); 2:14(2); 15; 22(2); 23; 33; 36; 38; 3:12(3); 13; 14; 16; 17; 19; 22; 25; 4:7; 8; 10; 19; 5:8; 9; 25; 28(2); 30; 35(2); 39(2); 6:3; 7:4; 26(2); 37; 42(2); 43(2); 49; 51(3); 52; 8:24(2); 10:21(2); 28; 29; 37; 11:16; 13:15(2); 16; 25; 39; 41(2); 46; 14:15(2); 15:1(2); 7; 10; 24; 29(4); 16:15; 17:22(2); 23; 18:14; 15; 19:2(2); 3; 15; 25; 26; 35; 36; 37; 39; 20:18; 25; 34; 35; 21:13; 22:1; 3; 23:15(2); 25:24; 27:21; 31; 33; 28:26(2); **Rom** 1:6; 11; 6:3; 11; 12; 13; 14; 16(4); 17(2); 18; 19; 20(2); 21(2); 22; 7:1; 4(2); 8:9; 13(4); 15(2); 9:26; 11:2; 25(2); 30; 12:1; 2(2); 13:5; 6; 14; 14:1; 15:6; 7; 10; 11(2); 13; 14; 30; 16:2(2); 17; **1Cor** 1:5; 7; 8; 9; 10(2); 13; 26; 30; 3:2(2); 3(2); 4; 5; 9(2); 16(2); 17; 23; 4:6; 8(4); 10(3); 15(2); 16; 21; 5:2; 4; 6; 7(2); 10; 12; 6:2(2); 3; 4; 7(3); 8; 9; 11(3); 15; 16; 19(3); 20; 7:1; 5(2); 23(2); 35; 8:12(2); 9:1; 2; 13; 24(2); 10:1; 7; 10; 13(2); 15; 20; 21(2); 27; 31(2); 11:1; 2; 17; 18; 20; 22(2); 25(2); 26(2); 33; 34; 12:2(3); 27; 14:1; 5(2); 9(3); 12(3); 18; 20; 23; 26; 31; 15:1(2); 2(3); 11; 17; 58(2); 16:1; 3; 6; 13; 15; 16; 18; 20; **2Cor** 1:7(2); 11; 13(2); 14(2); 15; 24; 2:4(2); 7; 8; 9; 10; 3:2; 3; 5:12; 20; 6:1; 11; 12(2); 13; 14; 16; 17; 18; 7:3; 9(4); 11(2); 15; 8:7(2); 9(2); 11; 13; 24; 9:3; 4; 5; 8; 10:7; 11:1; 4(4); 7; 19(2); 20; 12:11; 13; 19; 20; 13:3; 5(3); 6; 7(2); 9; **Gal** 1:6; 9; 13; 3:1; 2; 3(2); 4; 7; 26; 28; 29(2); 4:6; 8(2); 9(3); 10; 12(2); 13; 14; 15(2); 17; 21(2); 5:2; 4; 7(2); 10; 13; 15(2); 16; 17(2); 18(2); 6:1; 2; 11; **Eph** 1:13(4); 18; 2:2; 5; 8; 11; 12; 13; 19; 22; 3:2; 4(2); 13; 17; 19; 4:1(2); 4; 17; 20; 21; 22; 24; 26; 30; 32; 5:1; 5; 7; 8(2); 15; 17; 6:4; 9; 11; 13; 16; 21; 22; **Phil** 1:7; 10(2); 12; 27; 30; 2:2(2); 12; 15(2); 18; 22; 26; 28(2); 3:15; 17; 4:9; 10(2); 14(2); 15(2); 16; **Col** 1:4; 5; 6; 7; 9; 10; 23(2); 2:1; 6(2); 7; 10; 11; 12; 20(2); 3:1; 3; 4; 7(2); 8; 9; 13; 15(2); 17; 23; 24(2); 4:1; 6(2); 10; 12; 16; **1Th** 1:5; 6; 9; 2:2; 5; 8; 9; 10; 11; 12; 13(3); 14(2); 19; 20; 3:4; 6; 8; 4:1(3); 2; 3; 9(2); 10(2); 11; 12(2); 13; 5:1; 4; 5; 11; **2Th** 1:4; 5(2); 12; 2:2; 5; 6; 15; 3:4; 6; 7; 13; **Heb** 3:7; 15; 4:7; 5:11; 12(2); 6:10(2); 12; 10:25; 29; 32(2); 33(2); 34(2); 36(3); 12:3; 4; 5; 7; 8(2); 17; 18; 22; 25; 13:5; 23; **Jas** 1:2; 4; 22; 2:3; 4; 6; 7; 8(2); 9(2); 12; 16(2); 24; 3:14; 4:2(5); 3(3); 4(2); 5; 8(2); 13; 14; 15; 16; 5:1; 3; 5(2); 6; 8; 9; 11; 12; 16; **1Pet** 1:6(2); 8(3); 15; 16; 17; 18(2); 22(2); 2:2; 3; 5; 9(2); 15; 20(4); 21(2); 24; 25; 3:1; 6(2); 7; 8; 9(2); 13; 14(2); 17; 4:4; 7; 13(2); 14(2); 5:4; 5; 10; 12; 14; **2Pet** 1:4; 8; 10(2); 12; 15; 19(2); 3:2; 11; 14(2); 17(3); **1Jn** 1:3; 2:1; 7(2); 13(3); 14(3); 18; 20(2); 21(2); 24(3); 27(3); 29(2); 3:5; 11; 15; 4:2; 3; 4; 5:13(3); **2Jn** 6(2); **3Jn** 12; **Jude** 3; 5; 17; 20; **Rev** 2:10(2); 25; 12:12(2); 18:4(2); 20; 19:5(2); 18

YEA

637, 834, 1571, 3588, *235, 1161, 2228, 2532, 3304, 4483*

Gen 3:1; 17:16; 20:6; 27:33; **Lev** 25:35; **Num** 10:32; **Deut** 33:3; **Judg** 5:29; **1Sa** 15:20; 21:5; 24:11; **2Sa** 19:30; 22:39; **2Kin** 2:3; 5; 16:3; **1Chr** 16:21; **2Chr** 26:20; **Ezr** 9:2; **Neh** 5:15; 16; 6:10; 9:18; 21; **Est** 5:12; **Job** 1:15; 17; 2:4; 5:19; 6:10; 27; 29; 9:10; 11:15; 18; 19; 12:3; 14:10; 15:4; 6; 15; 18:5; 19:18; 20:8; 25; 21:7; 22:25; 25:5; 28:27; 30:2; 8; 9; 31:8; 11; 32:12; 33:14; 22; 34:12; 36:7; 40:5; 41:24; **Ps** 7:4; 5; 8:7; 16:6; 18:10; 14; 48; 19:10; 23:4; 25:3; 27:6; 29:5; 10; 31:9; 35:10; 15; 21; 27; 37:10; 36; 40:8; 41:9; 43:4; 44:22; 57:1; 58:2; 59:16; 68:3; 16; 18; 72:11; 78:19; 38; 41; 83:11; 17; 84:2; 3; 85:12; 90:17; 93:4; 94:23; 102:13; 26; 105:12; 14; 106:24; 37; 109:30; 116:5; 118:11; 119:34; 103; 127; 128:6; 137:1; 138:5; 139:12; 144:15; **Prov** 2:3; 9; 3:24; 6:16; 7:26; 8:18; 19; 16:4; 22:10; 23:16; 34; 24:5; 29:17; 30:15; 18; 29; 31:20; **Eccl** 1:16; 2:18; 23; 3:19; 4:3; 8(2); 6:6; 7:18; 8:17; 9:3; 10:3; 12:9; **Song** 1:16; 5:1; 16; 6:9; 8:1; **Is** 1:15; 5:10; 29; 14:8; 19:21; 24:16; 26:8; 9; 11; 29:5; 30:33; 32:13; 40:24(3); 41:10(2); 23; 26(3); 42:13; 43:7; 13; 44:8; 12; 15(2); 16; 19; 45:21; 46:6; 7; 11; 47:3; 48:8(3); 15; 49:15; 55:1; 56:9; 11; 59:15; 60:12; 66:3; **Jer** 2:37; 5:28; 8:7; 12:2(2); 6; 14:5; 18; 23:11; 26; 27:21; 31:3; 19; 32:41; 46:16; 51:44; **Lam** 1:8; **Eze** 6:14; 16:6; 8; 9; 28; 52; 17:10; 22:2; 21; 29; 23:36; 26:18; 28:26; 32:10; 28; 34:6; 36:12; 37:27; 39:13; **Dan** 8:11; 9:11; 21; 10:19; 11:22; 24; 26; **Hos** 2:19; 4:3; 7:9; 8:10; 9:12; 16; 12:4; 11; **Joel** 1:16; 18; 2:3; 19; 3:4; **Amos** 8:6; **Obad** 13; 16; **Jonah** 3:8; **Mic** 3:7; **Nah** 1:5; **Hab** 2:5; **Zeph** 2:1; **Hag** 2:19; **Zec** 7:12; 8:22; 10:7; 14:5; 21; **Mal** 2:2; 3:15(2); 4:1; **Mt** 5:37(2); 9:28; 11:9; 13:51; 21:16; 26:60; **Lk** 2:35; 7:26; 11:28; 12:5; 57; 14:26; 24:22; **Jn** 11:27; 16:2; 32; 21:15; 16; **Acts** 3:16; 24; 5:8; 7:43; 20:34; 22:27; **Rom** 3:4; 31; 8:34; 14:4; 15:20; **1Cor** 1:28; 2:10; 4:3; 9:16; 15:15; 16:6; **2Cor** 1:17(2); 18; 19(2); 20; 5:16; 7:11(6); 13; 8:3; **Gal** 4:17; **Phil** 1:18; 2:17; 3:8; **2Ti** 3:12; **Philem** 1:20; **Heb** 11:36; **Jas** 2:18; 5:12(2); **1Pet** 5:5; **2Pet** 1:13; **3Jn** 12; **Rev** 14:13

YES

3304, 3483

Mt 17:25; **Mk** 7:28; **Rom** 3:29; 10:18

YET

227, 389, 518, 559, 637, 1297, 1571, 2008, 2962, 3588, 3651, 5704, 5750, 6258, 7535, *188, 235, 1063, 1161, 2089, 2236, 2532, 2579, 2596, 3195, 3305, 3364, 3369, 3380, 3764, 3765, 3768*

Gen 6:3; 7:4; 8:10; 12; 15:16; 18:22; 29; 32; 20:12; 21:26; 25:6; 27:30; 29:7; 9; 27; 30; 31:14; 30; 37:5; 8; 9; 38:5; 40:13; 19; 23; 43:6; 7; 27; 28; 44:4; 14; 45:3; 6; 11; 26; 28; 46:30; 48:7; **Ex** 4:18; 5:11; 18; 9:17; 30; 34; 10:7; 11:1; 21:22; 32:32; 33:12; 36:3; **Lev** 5:17; 11:7; 21; 13:40; 41; 25:22; 51; 26:18; 24; 44; **Num** 9:10; 11:33; 19:13; 22:15; 20; 30:16; 32:14; 15; **Deut** 1:32; 9:29; 12:9; 14:8; 20:6; 22:17; 29:4; 31:27; 32:52; **Josh** 3:4; 13:1; 2; 14:11; 17:12; 13; 18:2; **Judg** 1:35; 2:10; 17; 6:24; 31; 7:4; 8:4; 20; 9:5; 10:13; 15:7; 17:4; 19:19; 20:28; 21:14; **Ruth** 1:11; **1Sa** 3:6; 7(2); 8:9; 10:22; 12:20; 13:7; 21; 15:30; 16:11; 18:29; 20:14; 23:4; 22; 24:11; 25:29; **2Sa** 1:9; 3:35; 5:13; 22; 6:22; 7:19; 9:1; 3(2); 12:18; 22; 14:14; 18:12; 14; 22; 19:28(2); 35; 21:15; 20; 23:5; **1Kin** 1:14; 22; 42; 8:28; 47; 11:17; 12:2; 5; 6; 14:8; 19:18; 20:6; 32; 22:8; 43; **2Kin** 3:17; 4:6; 6:33; 8:19; 22; 13:23; 14:3; 4; 17:13; 19:30; **1Chr** 12:1; 14:13; 17:17; 20:6; 26:10; 29:1; **2Chr** 1:11; 6:16; 26; 37; 10:6; 13:6; 14:7; 16:8; 12; 18:7; 20:33; 24:19; 27:2; 28:22; 30:18; 32:15; 16; 33:17; 34:3; **Ezr** 3:6; 5:16; 9:9; 15; 10:2; **Neh** 1:9; 2:16; 5:5; 18; 6:4; 9:19; 28; 29; 30(2); 13:18; 26; **Est** 2:20; 5:13; 6:14; 8:3; **Job** 1:16; 17; 18; 3:26; 5:7; 6:10; 8:7; 12; 9:15; 16; 21; 31; 10:8; 15; 13:15; 14:9; 19:26; 20:7; 14; 21:32; 22:18; 24:12; 23; 29:5; 32:3; 33:14; 35:14; 15; 36:2; **Ps** 2:6; 37:10; 25; 36; 40:17; 42:5; 8; 11; 43:5; 44:17; 49:13; 55:21; 68:13; 71:14; 78:17; 30; 56; 90:10; 94:7; 107:41; 119:51; 83; 109; 110; 141; 143; 157; 129:2; 138:6; 139:16(2); 141:5; **Prov** 6:10; 8:26; 9:9; 11:24; 13:7(2); 19:7; 19; 23:35; 24:33; 27:22; 30:12; 25; 26; 27; 31:15; **Eccl** 1:7; 2:3; 19; 21; 4:2; 3; 8; 6:2; 6; 7; 7:28; 8:12; 17(2); 9:11(3); 15; 11:8; **Is** 6:13; 10:22; 25; 32; 14:1; 15; 17:6; 26:10; 27:10; 28:4; 12; 29:2; 17; 30:20; 31:2; 42:25(2); 44:1; 11; 46:7; 10; 49:4; 5; 15; 53:4; 7; 10; 56:8; 57:10; 58:2; 65:24; **Jer** 2:9; 11; 21; 22; 32; 35; 3:1; 8; 10; 4:27; 5:22(2); 28; 7:26; 9:20; 11:8; 12:1; 14:9; 15; 15:1; 9; 10; 18:23; 22:6; 24; 23:21(2); 32; 25:7; 27:15; 30:11; 31:5; 23; 39; 32:33; 33:1; 34:4; 36:24; 37:10; 40:5; 44:28; 46:28; 48:47; 51:33; 53; **Lam** 3:32; 4:17; **Eze** 2:5; 3:19; 6:8; 7:13; 8:6; 13; 15; 11:16; 12:13; 14:22; 15:5; 16:28; 29; 47; 18:19; 25; 29; 20:15; 27; 23:19; 44; 24:16; 26:21; 28:2; 9; 29:13; 18; 31:18; 32:24; 25; 33:17; 20; 36:37; 44:11; **Dan** 4:23; 5:17; 7:12; 9:13; 10:9; 14; 11:2; 27; 33; 35; 45; **Hos** 1:4; 10; 3:1(2); 4:4; 15; 5:13; 7:9; 13; 15; 9:12; 16; 11:12; 12:8; 9; 13:4; **Amos** 2:9(2); 4:6; 7; 8; 9; 10; 11; 6:10; 9:9; **Jonah** 2:4; 6; 3:4; 4:2; **Mic** 1:15; 3:11; 5:2; 6:10; **Nah** 1:12; 2:8; 3:10; **Hab** 2:3; 3:18; **Hag** 2:4; 6; 17; 19(2); **Zec** 1:17(4); 8:4; 20; 11:15; 13:3; **Mal** 1:2(2); 2:14(2); 15; 17; 3:8; 13; **Mt** 6:25; 26; 29; 10:10; 12:46; 13:21; 15:16; 17; 27; 16:9; 17:5; 19:20; 24:6; 32; 26:33; 35; 47; 60; 27:63; **Mk** 5:35; 6:26; 7:28; 8:17(2); 11:13; 12:6; 13:7; 28; 14:29; 43; 15:5; **Lk** 3:20; 8:49; 9:42; 11:8; 12:27; 14:22; 32; 35; 15:20; 29; 18:5; 22; 19:30; 22:37; 47; 60; 23:15; 24:6; 41; 44; **Jn** 2:4; 3:24; 4:21; 27; 35; 7:6; 8(2); 19; 30; 33; 39(2); 8:14; 16; 20; 55; 57; 9:30; 11:25; 30; 12:35; 37; 13:33; 14:9; 19; 25; 16:12; 32; 19:41; 20:1; 5; 9; 17; 29; 21:11; 23; **Acts** 7:5(2); 8:16; 9:1; 10:44; 13:27; 28; 18:18; 19:37; 22:3; 24:11; 25:8; 28:4; 17; **Rom** 3:7; 4:11; 12; 19; 5:6; 7; 8; 8:24; 9:11; 19; 11:30; 16:19; **1Cor** 2:6; 15; 3:2; 3; 15; 4:4; 15; 5:10; 7:10; 25; 8:2; 9:2; 19; 12:20; 31; 14:19; 21; 15:10; 17; **2Cor** 1:10; 23; 4:8; 16; 5:16; 6:8; 9; 10(3); 8:9; 9:3; 11:6; 16; 12:5; 13:4; **Gal** 1:10; 2:20; 3:4; 15; 5:11(2); **Eph** 5:29; **Phil** 1:9; 22; 2:25; **Col** 1:21; 2:5; **1Th** 2:6; **2Th** 2:5; 3:15; **2Ti** 2:5; 13; **Philem** 1:9; **Heb** 2:8; 4:15; 5:8; 7:10; 15; 9:8(2); 25; 10:37; 11:4; 7; 12:4; 26; 27; **Jas** 2:10; 11; 3:4; 4:2; **1Pet** 1:8; 4:16; **1Jn** 3:2; **Jude** 9; **Rev** 6:11; 8:13; 9:20; 17:8; 10; 12

YOU

5209

Gen 1:29(2); 9:2(2); 3(2); 7; 9(2); 10(2); 11; 12(2); 15; 17:10(2); 11; 12; 18:4; 19:2; 7; 8(2); 14; 22:5; 23:4(2); 9; 26:27; 27:45; 31:29; 34:8; 9; 10(2); 15(2); 16(2); 35:2; 37:6; 40:8; 41:55; 42:2; 14; 16(2); 22; 34; 38; 43:3; 5; 14; 23(2); 44:17(2); 23; 45:4; 5; 7(2); 8; 12; 17; 18; 19; 46:33; 47:16; 23(2); 48:21(2); 49:1(2); 50:4; 20; 21; 24(2); 25; **Ex** 3:13; 14; 15; 16(2); 17; 19; 20; 4:15; 5:4; 10; 11; 18; 21; 6:6(3); 7(3); 8(2); 7:4; 9(2); 8:28; 9:8; 28; 10:5(2); 10(3); 16; 24; 11:1(3); 9; 12:2(2); 13(4); 14; 16(2); 21; 22; 23; 25; 26; 31; 49; 13:3; 19(2); 14:13; 14; 16:4; 6; 8; 15; 23; 29(2); 32(2); 18:10; 19:4(2); 20:20; 22; 23; 22:24; 23:13; 24:8; 14(2); 26:33; 29:42; 30:32; 36; 31:13(2); 14; 32:29; 35:2; 5; 10; **Lev** 1:2; 8:33; 34; 9:4; 6; 10:7; 17; 11:4; 5; 6; 7; 8; 10; 11; 12; 20; 23; 26; 27; 28; 29; 31; 35; 38; 45; 14:34; 16:29(2); 30(2); 31; 34; 17:8; 10; 11; 12(2); 13; 18:3; 6; 24; 26; 27; 28(2); 30; 19:23; 25; 28; 34(3); 36; 20:8; 14; 22(2); 23; 24(3); 25; 26; 21:8; 22:20; 25; 32; 33; 23:10; 11; 15; 21; 27; 28; 32; 36; 40; 25:2; 6; 10; 11; 12; 21; 38(2); 44; 45(2); 46; 26:1(2); 4; 6; 7; 8(3); 9(4); 11(2); 12; 13(2); 16(2); 17(4); 18; 21; 22(3); 24(2); 25(2); 26; 28(2); 30; 33(2); 36; 38; 39; **Num** 1:4; 5; 9:8; 10; 14; 10:8; 9; 10; 29; 11:18; 20(2); 12:6; 13:17; 14:25(2); 28; 29; 30; 32; 42; 43(2); 15:2; 14(2); 15(2); 16(2); 18; 23; 39; 41; 16:3; 6; 7; 8; 9(3); 17; 24; 26; 45; 17:4; 5; 18:4; 6; 7; 26; 27; 20:10; 22:8; 13(2); 19; 25:18(2); 28:19; 22; 30; 31; 29:1; 5; 8; 32:21; 23; 24; 29(2); 30(2); 33:52; 53; 55(2); 56; 34:2; 7; 17; 35:11(2); 12; 29; **Deut** 1:7; 8; 9(2); 10; 11(3); 13(2); 15; 17; 18; 20; 22; 23; 29; 30(3); 33(3); 40(2); 42; 43; 44(3); 45; 2:3; 4; 5; 13; 3:18(2); 19; 20(2); 22; 4:1(2); 2(2); 3; 4; 5; 8; 12; 13(2); 14; 15; 16; 20(2); 23(2); 26; 27(2); 34; 5:4; 5(2); 30; 32; 33(2); 6:1; 14; 15; 20; 7:4; 7(2); 8(3); 14; 21; 8:19; 9:8(2); 9; 10; 16(2); 19(2); 23(2); 24; 25; 10:4; 15; 11:4; 5; 8; 13; 14; 17(2); 22; 23; 25(4); 26; 27; 28; 31; 32; 12:9; 10(2); 11; 12; 32; 13:1; 3; 5(3); 7; 11; 13; 14; 14:7; 8; 10; 19; 15:4; 7; 16:11; 17:2; 7; 16; 18:10; 19:19; 20; 20:4(3); 18; 21:9; 21; 22:21; 24; 23:4; 10; 16; 24:7; 8; 26:11; 27:1; 4; 28:54; 56; 63(6); 68; 29:4; 5(2); 10; 14; 18(2); 22; 30:18; 19(2); 31:5; 19; 27; 29(2); 32:38; 46; 47; **Josh** 1:3; 11(2); 13(3); 14; 15(2); 2:9(2); 10; 11; 12(2); 16(2); 3:4; 5; 10(2); 11; 12; 4:2; 3(2); 5(2); 6; 23; 5:9; 6:10; 16; 7:12(2); 13; 8:8; 9:7; 11; 12; 22; 23; 24(3); 18:3; 4; 6; 7; 8; 20:2(2); 22:2(2); 4(2); 5; 16; 19; 25; 27; 28; 23:3(2); 4; 5(2); 7; 9(3); 10(3); 12(2); 13(3); 14(2); 15(5); 16(3); 24:5; 7; 8(3); 9; 10(2); 11; 12(3); 13; 15(2); 20(3); 22; 23; 27; **Judg** 2:1(3); 3(2); 6:8(2); 9(4); 10; 7:7; 8:2; 3; 5; 19; 23(3); 24; 9:2(4); 7; 15; 17(2); 19; 10:11; 12(2); 13; 14; 12:2; 14:12(2); 15:7; 19:9(2); 23; 24; 20:12; 21:21; **Ruth** 1:8; 9(2); 2:4; 7; **1Sa** 4:9; 6:3(2); 4; 5; 21; 7:3(2); 5; 8:11; 18(2); 9:12; 13; 10:2; 15; 18(2); 19; 11:2; 10(2); 12:1; 2(3); 3; 5; 7(2); 11; 12; 13; 14; 15; 17; 22; 23(2); 24; 14:9; 12; 29; 15:6(2); 17:8(2); 47; 18:23; 22:3; 7(2); 8(2); 23:22; 23; 25:5; 19; 30:24; 26; **2Sa** 1:21; 24; 2:6(2); 3:17; 31; 4:11; 7:23; 13:28(2); 15:27; 28; 16:10; 20; 17:21; 18:2; 4; 19:22; 20:16; 21:3; 4; **1Kin** 1:33; 9:6; 11:2; 12:11(3); 14(2); 28; 18:25; 20:7; 22:28; **2Kin** 1:6; 7(2); 2:18; 5:7; 6:19; 7:12; 10:2(3); 23; 11:5; 7; 17:13; 36; 37; 38; 39; 18:27; 29(2); 30; 32(2); 22:15; 18; 25:24; **1Chr** 12:17; 13:2; 22:18(2); 28:8; **2Chr** 7:19; 10:11(3); 14(2); 12:5; 13:8(2); 9; 12; 15:2(3); 19:6; 7; 10(2); 11(2); 20:15; 17(2); 23:4; 24:20; 28:10(3); 11; 29:11; 30:6; 8; 9; 32:11; 14; 15(3); 34:23; 26; 36:23; **Ezr** 1:3; 4:2; 5:3; 9; 7:21; 24; **Neh** 1:8; 9; 4:12; 5:10; 11; 6:3; 13:21; 27; **Est** 8:8; **Job** 6:28; 29; 12:2; 3(2); 13:2; 9; 10; 11(2); 16:4(2); 5; 17:10(2); 27:5; 11; 32:6; 12(2); 21; 42:8(3); **Ps** 34:11; 50:22; 62:3; 82:6; 115:14(2); 118:26; 127:2; 129:8(2); **Prov** 1:23(3); 27; 4:2; 8:4; **Song** 2:7; 3:5; 5:8; 8:4; **Is** 1:15; 16(2); 5:3; 5; 7:13; 14; 8:19; 21:10; 22:14; 28:19; 29:10; 11; 30:11; 13; 16; 18(2); 20; 31:7; 32:11(2); 33:11; 35:4; 36:12; 14(2); 15; 17; 18; 40:21; 41:24; 42:9; 23; 43:12; 46:4(2); 50:1; 10; 51:2; 12; 52:12; 55:3; 12; 59:2(2); 61:6; 65:12; 66:5(2); 13; **Jer** 2:7; 9; 3:12; 14(3); 15(2); 4:8; 5:15; 18; 25; 6:17; 7:3; 7; 13(2); 14; 15; 23(2); 25; 8:17(2); 10:1; 11:4; 14:13; 14; 15:14; 16:13(2); 18:6; 11(2); 21:4; 5; 8; 9; 14; 23:2; 16(2); 17; 33; 38; 39(4); 40; 25:3; 4; 5; 6; 27; 26:4; 5; 13; 14; 15; 27:9; 10(3); 14(2); 15(2); 16(2); 29:7; 8(2); 9; 10(3); 11(2); 12; 14(5); 16; 21; 27; 31(2); 34:16; 17(2); 21; 35:14; 15(2); 18; 37:7(2); 10; 19(2); 38:5; 40:3; 9; 42:4(4); 10(5); 11(3); 12(3); 16(2); 18; 19(2); 21(2); 44:4; 7(2); 10; 11; 23; 29(3); 49:3; 30(3); 31; 50:12; **Lam** 1:12; 18; **Eze** 5:7(2); 16(2); 17; 6:3; 7; 9; 11:7; 8; 9(3); 10; 11; 12; 15; 17(3); 19; 13:8; 12; 15; 18; 14:22; 23; 18:30; 31(2); 20:3; 20; 31(2); 33; 34(2); 35(2); 36; 37(2); 38; 39; 41(4); 42; 44; 22:19; 20(3); 21(2); 22; 23:49; 24:24; 33:20; 30; 34:3; 17; 18; 36:2; 3(2); 7; 9(2); 10; 11(3); 12; 13;

23; 24(3); 25(2); 26(3); 27(2); 29(2); 32; 33(2); 36; 37:5; 6(4); 12(2); 13; 14(2); 39:17; 19; 43:27; 44:6; 45:9; 47:14; 21; 22(5); **Dan** 2:9; 3:4; 15; 4:1; 6:25; **Hos** 5:1; 13(2); 10:12; 15; 14:2; **Joel** 2:19(2); 20; 23(2); 25(2); 26; 3:13; **Amos** 2:10(2); 13; 3:1; 2(2); 4:2(2); 5; 6; 7; 9; 10; 11; 5:1; 14; 18(2); 27; 6:14(2); **Jonah** 1:12(2); **Mic** 1:2; 11; 2:4; 10; 3:1(2); 6(2); 9; **Hab** 1:5; **Zeph** 2:2(2); 5; 3:20(3); **Hag** 1:4; 6; 10; 13; 2:3; 4; 5(2); 15; 17; 19; **Zec** 1:3; 2:6; 8(2); 4:9; 6:7; 15; 7:10; 8:13; 14; 17; 23(2); 9:12; 11:7; 9; **Mal** 1:2; 6; 9; 10(2); 2:1; 2; 3; 4; 9; 3:5; 7; 10(2); 12; 4:2; 5; **Mt** 3:7; 9; 11(2); 4:19; 5:11(3); 12; 18; 20; 22; 28; 32; 34; 39; 44(5); 46; 6:2; 5; 14; 16; 25; 27; 29; 30; 33; 7:2; 6; 7(2); 9; 12; 15; 23; 8:10; 11; 9:29; 10:13; 14; 15; 16; 17(2); 19(2); 20; 23(2); 27; 40; 42; 11:9; 11; 17(2); 21; 22(2); 24; 28; 29; 12:6; 11; 28; 31; 36; 13:11; 17; 15:7; 16:11; 28; 17:12; 17(2); 20(2); 18:3; 10; 13; 18; 19(2); 35; 19:8; 9; 23; 24; 28; 20:4; 26(2); 27; 32; 21:2; 3; 21; 24(2); 27; 31(2); 32; 43(2); 22:31; 23:3; 11; 13; 14; 15; 16; 23; 25; 27; 29; 34; 35; 36; 38; 39; 24:2; 4; 9(2); 23; 25; 26; 34; 47; 25:9; 12(2); 34; 40; 45; 26:11; 13; 15; 21(2); 29(2); 32; 55; 64; 27:17; 21; 28:7(2); 14; 20(2); **Mk** 1:8(2); 17; 3:28; 4:11; 24(2); 6:11(3); 7:6; 14; 8:12; 9:1; 13; 19(2); 41(2); 10:3; 5; 15; 29; 36; 43(2); 44; 11:2; 3; 23; 24; 25; 29(2); 33; 12:43; 13:5; 9; 11(3); 21; 23; 30; 36; 37; 14:7; 9; 13; 15; 18(2); 25; 28; 49; 15:9; 16:7(2); **Lk** 2:10; 11; 12; 3:7; 8; 13; 16(2); 4:24; 25; 6:9; 22(3); 24; 25(2); 26(2); 27(2); 28(2); 31; 32; 33; 38(2); 47; 7:9; 26; 28; 32(2); 8:10; 9:5; 27; 41(2); 48; 10:3; 6; 8(2); 9; 10; 11(2); 12; 13; 14; 16(2); 19(2); 20; 24; 11:5; 8; 9(3); 11; 20; 41; 42; 43; 44; 46; 47; 51; 52; 12:4; 5(2); 8; 11; 12; 14; 22; 25; 27; 28; 31; 32; 37; 44; 51; 13:3; 5; 15; 24; 25(2); 27(2); 28; 35(2); 14:5; 24; 28; 33; 15:4; 7; 10; 16:9(2); 12; 26(2); 17:6; 7; 10; 21; 23; 34; 18:8; 14; 17; 29; 19:26; 30; 31; 40; 20:3; 8; 21:3; 12(3); 13; 15; 16; 32; 34; 22:10; 12; 15; 16; 18; 19; 20; 26; 27; 29; 31(2); 35; 37; 53; 67; 68; 23:14; 15; 24:6; 36; 44(2); 49; **Jn** 1:26; 51; 2:5; 3:12(2); 4:35; 38; 5:19; 24; 25; 38; 42(2); 45(2); 6:26; 27; 32(3); 36; 47; 53(2); 61; 63; 64; 65; 70(2); 7:7; 19(2); 22; 33; 8:7; 24; 25; 26; 32; 34; 36; 37; 40; 45; 46; 51; 55; 58; 9:27; 10:1; 7; 25; 26; 32; 12:8; 24; 35(2); 13:12; 15(2); 16; 18; 19; 20; 21(2); 33(2); 34(2); 14:2(2); 3(2); 9; 10; 12; 16(2); 17(2); 18(2); 20; 25(2); 26(2); 27(3); 28(2); 29; 30; 15:3; 4; 7(2); 9; 11(2); 12; 14; 15(3); 16(3); 17; 18(2); 19(2); 20(2); 21; 26; 16:1; 2(2); 3; 4(4); 5; 6; 7(4); 12; 13(2); 14; 15; 20; 22(2); 23(2); 25(3); 26(2); 27; 33; 18:8; 39(2); 19:4; 20:19; 21(2); 26; **Acts** 1:7; 8; 11; 2:14; 22(2); 29; 38; 39; 3:14; 16; 20; 22(2); 26(3); 4:10(2); 11; 19; 5:28; 38; 6:3; 7:37; 43; 10:29; 13:26(2); 32; 34; 38(2); 40; 41; 46(2); 14:15(2); 15:24; 25; 27; 28; 16:36; 17:3; 23; 18:14; 21; 19:13; 20:18; 20(3); 26; 27; 28; 29; 32(3); 35; 22:1; 25; 23:15; 24:21; 25:5; 26; 26:8; 27:22(2); 34(2); 28:20(3); 28; **Rom** 1:7; 8; 9; 10; 11(2); 12(2); 13(3); 15; 2:24; 6:14; 17; 8:9; 10; 11(2); 10:19(2); 11:13; 12:1; 3; 14; 18; 15:5; 13; 14; 15(2); 22; 23; 24(3); 28; 29; 30; 32(2); 33; 16:1; 2; 16; 17; 19; 20; 21; 22; 23(2); 24; 25; **1Cor** 1:3; 4; 6; 8; 10(2); 11(2); 12; 13; 14; 2:1(2); 2; 3; 3:1; 2; 3; 16; 18; 4:3; 6; 8; 14(2); 15; 16; 17(2); 18; 19; 21; 5:1; 2; 9; 11; 6:1; 2; 5; 7; 11; 19; 7:5; 28; 32; 35; 9:2; 11; 12; 23; 10:13(2); 27(2); 28; 11:2(2); 3; 14; 17(2); 18; 19(2); 22(3); 23; 24; 30; 12:1; 3; 21; 31; 14:6(3); 25; 26; 36(2); 37; 15:1(2); 2; 3; 12; 51; 16:2; 5; 6; 7(2); 10; 12; 13; 15; 19(2); 20; 23; 24; **2Cor** 1:2; 7; 8; 13; 15; 16(3); 18; 19; 21; 23; 2:1; 2; 3(3); 4(2); 5; 8; 9; 3:1(2); 4:12; 14; 5:12(2); 20(2); 6:1; 11; 17; 18; 7:3(2); 4(2); 7; 8(2); 11; 12(3); 13; 14(2); 15(2); 16; 8:1; 6; 10; 16; 17; 22; 23; 9:1; 2; 3; 4; 5; 8; 14(3); 10:1(3); 2; 9; 13; 14(2); 15; 16; 11:2(3); 6; 7; 8; 9(2); 11; 20(4); 12:11; 12; 13; 14(3); 15(2); 16(2); 17(2); 18; 19; 20(2); 21; 13:1; 2(2); 3; 4; 5; 11; 13; 14; **Gal** 1:3; 6; 7; 8(2); 9; 11; 20; 2:5; 3:1(2); 2; 5(2); 27; 4:11(2); 12; 13; 15; 16; 17(2); 18; 19; 20(2); 5:2(2); 4(2); 7; 8; 10(2); 12; 21(2); 6:11; 12; 13; **Eph** 1:2; 16(2); 17; 2:1; 17; 3:1; 13; 16; 4:1; 6; 31; 32; 5:3; 6; 33; 6:13; 21; 22; **Phil** 1:2; 3; 4; 6; 7(2); 8; 24; 25; 26; 27; 28; 29; 2:5; 13; 17; 19; 25; 26; 3:1(2); 15; 18(2); 4:9; 18; 21; 22; 23; **Col** 1:2; 3; 5; 6(2); 7; 9; 21; 22; 24; 25; 27; 2:1; 4; 5; 8; 13(2); 16; 18; 3:13; 16; 4:7; 8; 9(2); 10(2); 12(3); 13; 14; 16; 18; **1Th** 1:1; 2(2); 5(2); 8; 9; 2:1; 2; 6; 7; 8(2); 9(2); 10; 11; 12; 13; 17; 18; 3:2(2); 4(2); 5; 6(2); 7; 9; 11; 12(2); 4:1(2); 2; 4; 6; 9; 10; 11; 13; 15; 5:1; 4; 12(4); 14; 18; 23; 24; 27; 28; **2Th** 1:2; 3(2); 4; 6; 7; 10; 11(2); 12; 2:1; 3; 5(2); 13(2); 14; 17; 3:1; 3(2); 4(2); 6; 7; 8; 9; 10(2); 11; 16(2); 18; **2Ti** 4:22; **Titus** 2:8; 3:15; **Philem** 1:3; 6; 22; **Heb** 3:12; 13; 4:1; 5:12; 6:9; 11; 9:20; 12:5; 7; 15; 13:7(2); 17(2); 19(2); 21(2); 22(2); 23; 24(2); 25; **Jas** 1:5; 26; 2:6(2); 16; 3:13; 4:1; 7; 8; 10; 5:1; 3; 4; 6; 13; 14; 19; **1Pet** 1:2; 4; 10; 12(2); 13; 15; 20; 25; 2:7; 9; 11; 12; 3:13; 15(2); 16; 4:4; 12(2); 14; 15; 5:1; 2; 5; 6; 7; 10(2); 12; 13(2); 14; **2Pet** 1:2; 8(2); 11; 12; 13(2); 16; 2:1; 3; 13; 3:1; 15; **1Jn** 1:2; 3; 4; 5; 2:1; 7; 8(2); 12(2); 13(3); 14(3); 21; 24(2); 26(2); 27(4); 3:7; 13; 4:4; 5:13; **2Jn** 3; 10; 12(2); **Jude** 2; 3(3); 5; 12; 18; 24(2); **Rev** 1:4; 2:10; 13; 23; 24(2); 12:12; 18:6; 20; 22:16; 21

YOUR

5315, 546, 1438, 2398, 2596, 3588, 3844, 5209, 5212, 5213, 5216

Gen 3:5; 9:2; 5(2); 9; 17:11; 12; 13; 18:4; 5(2); 19:2(3); 8; 23:8; 31:5; 6; 7; 9; 29; 34:8; 9; 11; 16; 35:2; 37:7; 42:15; 16(2); 19(3); 20(2); 33(2); 34(2); 43:3; 5; 7(2); 11; 12(3); 13; 14; 23(4); 27; 29; 44:10; 17; 23; 45:4; 7; 12; 17; 18(2); 19(3); 20; 46:33; 47:3; 16(2); 23; 24(4); 48:21; 49:2; 50:4; 21; **Ex** 3:13; 15; 16; 22(2); 5:4; 11; 13(2); 14; 19(2); 6:7; 8:25; 28; 10:8; 10; 16; 17; 24(3); 12:4; 5; 11(5); 14; 15; 17(2); 19; 20; 21; 23; 26; 32(2); 14:14; 16:7; 8(2); 9; 12; 16; 32; 33; 19:15; 20:20; 22:24(2); 23:21; 25; 31; 29:42; 30:8; 10; 15; 16; 31; 31:13; 32:2(3); 13(2); 30; 34:23; 35:3; **Lev** 1:2; 3:17(2); 6:18; 7:26; 32; 8:33; 10:4; 6(3); 9; 11:44; 45; 14:34; 16:29(2); 30; 31; 17:11; 15; 18:2; 4; 26; 30; 19:2; 3; 4; 5; 9; 10; 25; 27; 28; 31; 33; 34; 36; 20:7; 24; 25; 22:3(2); 19; 24; 25; 29; 33; 23:3; 10; 14(3); 17; 21(2); 22(2); 27; 28; 31(2); 32(2); 38(3); 40; 41; 43(2); 24:3; 22(2); 25:9; 17; 19; 24; 38(2); 45(2); 46(3); 55; 26:1(2); 5(3); 6; 7; 8; 12; 13(2); 15; 16(2); 17; 18; 19(3); 20(2); 21; 22(3); 24; 25; 26(3); 28; 29(2); 30(4); 31(3); 32; 33(2); 34; 35; 37; 38; 39; **Num** 9:10; 10:8; 9(3); 10(7); 11:20; 14:29(2); 31; 32; 33(3); 34; 42; 15:2; 3; 14; 15; 20; 21(2); 23; 39(2); 40; 41(3); 18:1; 6; 7(2); 23; 26; 27; 28; 29; 31(3); 22:13; 28:11; 26; 29:7; 39(7); 31:19; 20; 24; 32:6; 8; 14; 22; 23; 24(3); 33:54(2); 55(2); 34:3(2); 4; 6; 7; 8; 9; 10; 12; 35:29(2); **Deut** 1:7; 8; 10; 11; 12(3); 13; 15(2); 16(2); 26; 27; 30(2); 32; 33; 34; 35; 37; 39(2); 40; 42; 45; 2:4; 24; 3:18(2); 19(4); 20(2); 21; 22; 26; 4:1; 2; 3; 4; 6(2); 21; 23; 26; 34(2); 5:1; 22; 23(2); 28; 30; 32; 33(2); 6:1; 16; 17; 7:8; 14; 8:1; 20(2); 9:16; 17; 18; 21; 23; 10:16; 17; 11:2(2); 7; 9(2); 13(3); 14; 16; 18(4); 19; 21(3); 22; 24(2); 25; 27; 28; 31; 12:4; 5(2); 6(8); 7(3); 9; 10(2); 11(6); 12(6); 13:3(4); 4; 5; 14:1(2); 20:3(2); 4(2); 18; 28:68; 29:2; 5; 6; 10(5); 11(2); 22; 30:18; 31:5; 12; 13; 26; 28(2); 29; 32:17; 38; 46(2); 47(2); **Josh** 1:3; 4; 11; 13; 14(4); 15(3); 2:9; 11; 16; 21; 3:3(2); 9; 4:5; 6; 21; 22; 23(2); 24; 6:10(2); 7:14; 8:7(2); 9:11; 10:19(3); 24; 25; 15:4; 18:3; 20:3; 22:3(2); 4(4); 5(3); 8(3); 19; 24; 25; 27; 23:3(2); 4; 5(3); 8; 10; 11; 13(4); 14(3); 15(2); 16; 24:2; 3; 6(2); 7; 8; 11; 14; 15; 19(2); 23; 27; **Judg** 2:1; 3; 3:28(2); 6:10; 7:15; 8:3; 7; 9:2(2); 15; 18; 10:14; 11:9; 18:6; 10; 19:5; 9; 30; 20:7; **Ruth** 1:11; 12; 13; **1Sa** 2:3; 23; 6:4; 5(4); 6; 7:3(2); 8:11; 13; 14(3); 15(2); 16(4); 17; 18; 10:19(5); 11:2; 12:1; 6; 7; 8(2); 11; 12(2); 14; 15; 16; 17; 20; 24; 25; 17:8; 9; 26:16; **2Sa** 1:24; 2:5; 7(2); 3:31; 4:11; 10:5; 15:27; **1Kin** 1:33; 8:61; 9:6; 11:2; 12:11; 14(2); 16; 24; 18:24; 25; **2Kin** 2:3; 5; 3:17(2); 18; 9:15; 10:2; 3(2); 6; 24; 12:7; 17:13(2); 39(2); 18:32; 19:6; 23:21; **1Chr** 15:12; 16:18; 19:5; 22:18; 19(3); 28:8(2); 29:20; **2Chr** 10:11; 14; 16; 11:4; 13:12; 15:7(2); 18:14; 19:10(2); 20:20; 24:5; 28:9(2); 10; 11; 29:5; 8; 30:7(2); 8(2); 9(3); 32:14; 15; 33:8; 35:3(2); 4(2); 5; 6; **Ezr** 4:2; 6:6; 7:17; 18; 8:28; 9:12(3); 10:11; **Neh** 4:14(5); 5:8; 8:9; 10(2); 11; 9:5; 13:18; 25(2); **Job** 6:22; 25; 27; 13:5(2); 12(2); 13; 17; 16:4; 5; 18:3; 21:2; 5(2); 27; 34; 32:11(2); 14; 42:8; **Ps** 4:4(2); 5; 11:1; 22:26; 24:7; 9; 31:24; 47:1; 58:2; 9; 62:8; 10; 69:32; 75:5; 76:11; 78:1; 95:8; 9; 105:11; 115:14; 134:2; 146:3; **Prov** 1:26(2); 27(2); **Is** 1:7(4); 11; 12; 14(2); 15(2); 16; 18; 3:14; 8:13(2); 10:3; 23:7; 14; 28:18(2); 22; 29:10(2); 16; 30:3(2); 15; 31:7; 32:11; 33:4; 11; 35:4; 36:17; 37:6; 40:1; 9; 26; 41:21(2); 24; 26; 43:14(2); 15(2); 46:1; 4; 50:1(4); 11; 51:2; 6; 52:12; 55:2(2); 3(2); 8(2); 9(2); 58:3(2); 4; 59:2(3); 3(4); 61:5(3); 7; 65:7(2); 15; 66:5(2); 14(2); 20; 22(2); **Jer** 2:5; 9; 30(3); 3:18; 22; 4:3; 4(2); 5:19; 25(2); 6:16; 20(2); 7:3(2); 5(2); 6; 7; 11; 14; 15; 21(2); 22; 23; 25; 9:20(2); 11:4(2); 5; 7; 12:13; 13:16(2); 17; 18(2); 20; 16:9(2); 11; 12; 13; 17:1; 22(2); 18:11(2); 21:4; 12; 14; 23:2; 39; 25:4; 5(2); 6; 7(2); 34(2); 26:11; 13(3); 14; 15; 27:4; 9(5); 10; 12; 16; 29:6(2); 8(3); 13; 14; 16; 21; 30:22; 34:13; 14; 35:6; 7; 15(3); 18; 37:19; 38:5; 40:10(2); 42:4(2); 9; 12; 13; 15; 20(2); 21; 44:3; 7; 8; 9(3); 10; 21(3); 22(2); 25(5); 46:4; 48:6; 50:12; 51:24; 46; 50; **Eze** 5:16; 6:3; 4(4); 5(2); 6(5); 9:5; 11:5; 6; 7; 11; 12:11; 25; 13:19(2); 20(2); 21(3); 23; 14:6(3); 16:45(2); 55; 18:25; 29; 30(2); 31; 20:5; 7; 18; 19; 20; 27; 30; 31(3); 32; 36; 39(2); 40(3); 41; 42; 43(4); 44(2); 21:24(4); 23:48; 49(2); 24:21(5); 22; 23(5); 33:11; 25(2); 26; 34:18(3); 19(2); 21; 31; 35:13(2); 36:8(2); 11(2); 22; 24; 25(2); 26; 28(2); 29; 31(5); 32(2); 33; 37:12(2); 13(2); 14; 25; 43:27(2); 44:6; 7; 30(2); 45:9; 12; 47:14; **Dan** 1:10(4); 2:5; 47; 10:21; **Hos** 1:9; 2:1(2); 2; 4:13(2); 14(2); 5:13; 6:4; 9:10; 10:12; 15; **Joel** 1:2(2); 3(2); 5; 13; 14; 2:12; 13(3); 14; 23; 26; 27; 28(4); 3:4(2); 5; 7(2); 8(2); 10(2); 17; **Amos** 2:11(2); 3:2; 4:2; 4(2); 6(2); 9(4); 10(4); 5:11; 12(2); 21(2); 22(2); 26(3); 6:2; 8:10(2); **Mic** 2:3; 10; 3:12; **Hab** 1:5; **Zeph** 3:20(2); **Hag** 1:4; 5; 7; 2:3; 17; **Zec** 1:2; 4(3); 5; 6; 6:15; 7:10; 8:9; 13; 14; 16; 17; **Mal** 1:5; 9(2); 10; 13; 2:2; 3(3); 13; 15; 16; 17; 3:7; 11(3); 13; 4:3; **Mt** 5:12; 16(3); 20; 37; 44; 45; 47; 48; 6:1(2); 8; 14; 15(2); 21(2); 25(2); 26; 32; 7:6; 11(2); 9:4; 11; 29; 10:9; 10; 13(2); 14(2); 20; 29; 30; 11:29; 12:27(2); 13:16(2); 15:3; 6; 17:20; 24; 18:14; 35; 19:8(2); 20:26; 27; 23:8; 9(2); 10; 11; 32; 34; 38; 24:20; 42; 25:8; 26:45; 27:65; **Mk** 2:8; 6:11; 7:9; 13; 8:17; 10:5; 43; 11:2; 25(2); 26(2); 13:18; 14:41; 16:7; **Lk** 3:14; 4:21; 5:4; 22; 6:22; 23; 24; 27; 35(2); 36; 38; 7:22; 8:25; 9:3; 5; 44; 10:3; 6; 10; 11; 20; 11:13(2); 19(2); 39; 46; 47; 48; 12:7; 22; 30; 32; 34(2); 35(2); 13:35; 16:11; 12; 15; 19:30; 21:14; 15; 18; 19(2); 28(2); 30; 34; 22:53; 23:28; 24:38; **Jn** 4:35; 6:49; 58; 7:6; 8:17; 21; 24(2); 38; 41; 42; 44(2); 54; 56; 9:19; 41; 10:34; 11:15; 12:30; 13:14(2); 14:1; 26; 27; 15:11; 16; 16:6; 20; 22(2); 24; 18:31; 19:14; 15; 20:17(2); **Acts** 2:17(4); 39; 3:17; 19; 22(2); 5:28; 7:37(2); 43; 51; 52; 13:41; 15:24; 17:23; 28; 18:6(2); 15; 19:37; 20:30; 24:22; 27:34; **Rom** 1:8; 6:12; 13(2); 19(3); 22; 8:11; 11:25; 28; 31; 12:1(2); 2; 16; 14:16; 15:24; 30; 16:19(2); 20; **1Cor** 1:4; 26; 2:5; 4:6; 5:6; 6:5; 8; 15; 19(2); 20(2); 7:5; 14; 35; 9:11; 14:34; 15:14; 17(2); 31; 34; 58; 16:3(2); 14; 17; **2Cor** 1:6(2); 14; 24(2); 2:8; 10; 4:5; 15; 5:11; 13; 6:12; 7:7(3); 13; 8:7; 8; 9; 14(2); 19; 24(2); 9:2(2); 5; 10(3); 13(2); 10:6; 8; 15; 11:3; 12:19; 13:5(2); 9; **Gal** 4:6; 15; 16; 6:13; 18; **Eph** 1:13; 15; 18; 3:13; 17; 4:4; 23; 26; 29; 5:19; 22; 25; 6:1; 4; 5(2); 9; 14; 15; 22; **Phil** 1:5; 9; 19; 25; 26; 27(2); 28; 2:12; 17; 19; 20; 25; 30; 4:5; 6; 7; 10; 17; 19; **Col** 1:4; 8; 21; 2:5(2); 13(2); 18; 3:2; 3; 5; 8; 15; 16; 18; 19; 20; 21; 22; 4:1; 6; 8(2); **1Th** 1:3; 4; 5; 8; 2:14; 17; 3:2; 5; 6; 7; 9; 10(2); 13; 4:3; 11(2); 5:23; **2Th** 1:3; 4(2); 2:17; 3:5; **Philem** 1:22; 25; **Heb** 3:8; 9; 15; 4:7; 6:10; 9:14; 10:34; 35; 12:3; 13; 13:5; 17; **Jas** 1:3; 21; 22; 2:2; 3:14; 4:1(2); 3; 8(2); 9(2); 14; 16; 5:1; 2(2); 3(2); 4; 5; 8; 12(2); 16; **1Pet** 1:7; 9(2); 13; 14; 17; 18(2); 21; 22; 2:12(2); 16; 18; 20; 25; 3:1; 2; 7; 15; 16; 4:14; 5:7; 8; 9; **2Pet** 1:5; 10; 19; 3:1; 17; **1Jn** 1:4; 2:12; **2Jn** 10; **Jude** 12; 20; **Rev** 1:9; 2:23; 16:1

YOURS

5212, 5216

Gen 45:20; **Deut** 11:24; **Josh** 2:14; **2Chr** 20:15; **Jer** 5:19; **Lk** 6:20; **Jn** 15:20; **1Cor** 3:21; 22; 8:9; 16:18; **2Cor** 12:14

YOURSELVES

853, 859, 3027, 5315, 5869, *240, 846, 1438, 5210, 5213, 5216*

Gen 18:4; 45:5; 49:1; 2; **Ex** 19:12; 30:37; 32:29; **Lev** 11:43(2); 44(2); 18:24; 30; 19:4; 20:7; **Num** 11:18; 16:3; 21; 31:3; 18; 19; **Deut** 2:4; 4:15; 16; 23; 25; 11:16; 23; 14:1; 31:14; 29; **Josh** 2:16; 3:5; 6:18(2); 7:13; 8:2; 23:7; 11; 16; 24:22; **Judg** 15:12; **1Sa** 2:29; 4:9(2); 10:19; 14:34; 16:5; **1Kin** 18:25; 20:12; **2Kin** 17:35; **1Chr** 15:12; **2Chr** 20:17; 29:5; 31; 30:8; 32:11; 35:4; 6; **Ezr** 10:11; **Neh** 13:25; **Job** 19:3; 5; 27:12; 42:8; **Is** 8:9(3); 29:9; 45:20; 46:8; 48:14; 49:9; 50:1; 11; 52:3; 57:4; 5; 61:6; **Jer** 4:4; 5; 6:1; 8:14; 13:18; 17:21; 25:34; 26:15; 37:9; 44:8; 50:14; **Eze** 14:6; 18:30; 32; 20:7; 18; 31; 43; 36:31; 39:17(2); 44:8; **Hos** 10:12; **Joel** 1:13; 3:11(2); **Amos** 3:9; 5:26; **Zeph** 2:1; **Zec** 7:6(2); **Mt** 3:9; 6:19; 20; 16:8; 23:13; 15; 31; 25:9; **Mk** 6:31; 9:33; 50; 13:9; **Lk** 3:8; 11:46; 52; 12:33; 36; 57; 13:28; 16:9; 15; 17:3; 14; 21:34; 22:17; 23:28; **Jn** 3:28; 6:43; 16:19; **Acts** 2:22; 40; 5:35; 13:46; 15:29; 20:10; 28; 34; **Rom** 6:11; 13; 16; 12:19; **1Cor** 5:13; 6:7; 7:5; 11:13; 16:16; **2Cor** 7:11(2); 11:19; 13:5; **Eph** 2:8; 5:19; 21; 22; **Col** 3:18; **1Th** 2:1; 3:3; 4:9; 5:2; 11; 13; 15; **2Th** 3:6; 7; **Heb** 10:34; 13:3; 17; **Jas** 2:4; 4:7; 10; **1Pet** 1:14; 2:13; 4:1; 8; 5:5; 6; **1Jn** 5:21; **2Jn** 8; **Jude** 20; 21; **Rev** 19:17

New Strong's™
Concise Dictionary
of the Words in the
Hebrew Bible

with their Renderings in the
King James Version

Read this first!

How to Use the Hebrew and Aramaic Dictionary

For many people Strong's unique system of numbers continues to be *the* bridge between the original languages of the Bible and the English of the *King James Version* (AV). In order to enhance the strategic importance of *Strong's Hebrew and Aramaic Dictionary* for Bible students, it has been significantly improved in this brand-new, up-to-date edition. It is now completely re-typeset with modern, larger typefaces that are kind to the eye, and all known errors in the original typesetting have been corrected, bringing this pivotal work to a new level of usefulness and accuracy.

1. What the Dictionary Is

Strong's Hebrew and Aramaic Dictionary is a fully integrated companion to the main concordance. Its compact entries contain a wealth of information about the words of the Bible in their original language. You can enrich your study of the Bible enormously if you will invest the time to understand the various elements included in each entry and their significance. The example that follows identifies many of these entry elements; and the following sections on the transliteration, abbreviations, and special symbols used offer fuller explanations. While no dictionary designed for readers who do not know biblical Hebrew can explain all that a faithful student of the language would know, this *Dictionary* gives the serious student of the English Bible the basic information needed to pursue infinitely deeper and broader studies of God's Word. Vast amounts of biblical insight can be gained by using this *Concordance* alone or in conjunction with other time-proven biblical reference works, such as Thomas Nelson's *Vine's Complete Expository Dictionary of Old and New Testament Words* and *Nelson's New Illustrated Bible Dictionary*.

2. Using the Dictionary with the Main Concordance

To use this *Dictionary*, locate the number given next to the biblical reference for any particular entry in the main concordance. For example, under "SHADY," you find *Strong's* number 6628 next to the first Bible reference shown, "Job 40:21." Since the reference is in the Old Testament (and since this numeral is set in regular type [and not in italic type]), you know that it refers to the *Hebrew and Aramaic Dictionary*. You may view that enlarged entry, here, or on page 118 in this *Dictionary*. The enlarged example that follows, together with the following sections of explanation, identify the kinds of information such entries provide.

3. Using the Dictionary to Do Word Studies

Careful Bible students do word studies, and *The New Strong's™ Exhaustive Concordance* with this revised, newly-typeset *Hebrew and Aramaic Dictionary* offers unique assistance. Consider the word "love" as found the King James Bible. By skimming the main concordance, you find these numbers for Hebrew (and Aramaic) words that the King James Bible translates with the English word "love": 157, 160, 2836, 7355, 1730, 7474, 5691, 5690. Now for any one Bible reference in this entry there is only one Hebrew word cited, and you may be interested only in establishing the precise meaning for just that word in that occurrence. If so, it will be very helpful for you to observe that same Hebrew word in *each* of its occurrences in the Bible. In that way, you develop an idea of its possible range of meanings, and you help clarify what it probably meant precisely in the specific Bible reference you are studying.

But don't overlook exploring each Hebrew (and Aramaic) word translated as "love." You may wish to take notes as you look up each occurrence of the word that goes with 157, and then each occurrence of the word that goes with 160, and so forth. This method gives you an excellent basis for understanding all that the Hebrew Bible (the Old Testament) signifies with the King James Version's word "love."

Now see the *Dictionary* entry 157 itself, and notice that after the symbol :— all the words and word prefixes and suffixes are listed. These show you that this one Hebrew word, 'ahab, is translated into several different, but related words in the King James Bible: beloved, love, loved, lovely, lover, like, befriend. This list tells you the range of uses of the one Hebrew word in the King James Bible. This information can help you distinguish between the nuances of meaning found where this and the other Hebrew words are translated by these same words and similar ones in the King James Bible.

These three ways of using the *Dictionary* in conjunction with the main concordance show you only a sampling of the many ways *The New Strong's™ Exhaustive Concordance* can enrich your study of the Bible. And they show you why it is important that you take the time to become familiar with each feature in the *Dictionary* as illustrated in the example on the following page.

An Example
from the
Hebrew and Aramaic Dictionary

Strong's number, corresponding to the numbers at the ends of the context lines in the main concordance.

An unnumbered cross-reference entry.

The word as it appears in the original Hebrew (or Aramaic) spelling.

The degree symbol denotes the presence of a textual variation. (See "Special Symbols")

The Hebrew (or Aramaic) word represented in English letters in **bold** type (the transliteration).

Strong's syllable-by-syllable pronunciation in *italics*, with the emphasized syllable marked by the accent.

Information regarding relationship to other Hebrew (or Aramaic) words, usually cited by Strong's numbers. Sometimes a word may refer to a Greek entry (shown by *italic* numbers) or it may come from another language.

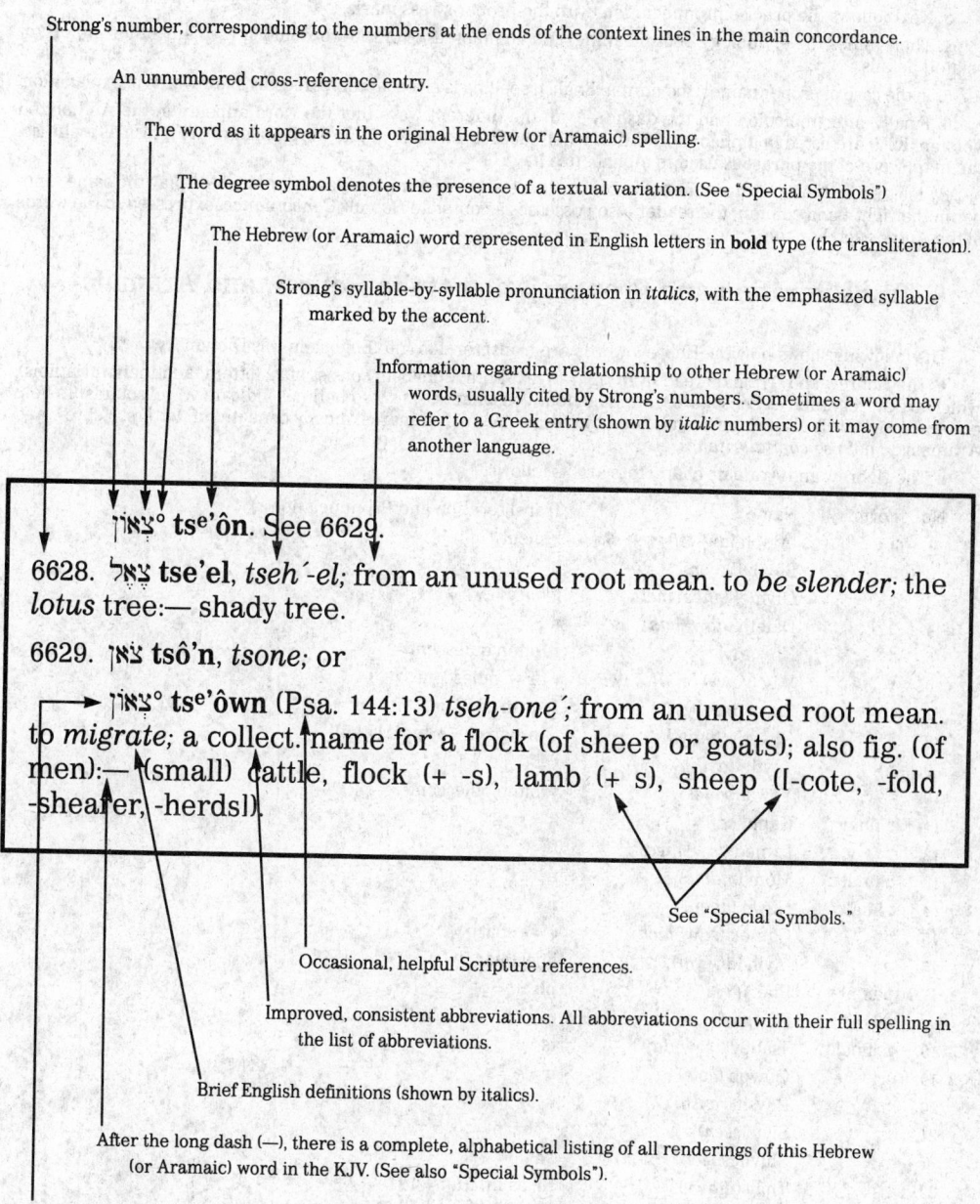

צֹאון° **tse'ôn.** See 6629.

6628. צֶאֱל **tse'el,** *tseh´-el;* from an unused root mean. to *be slender;* the *lotus* tree:— shady tree.

6629. צֹאן **tsô'n,** *tsone;* or

צְאֹון° **tse'ôwn** (Psa. 144:13) *tseh-one´;* from an unused root mean. to *migrate;* a collect. name for a flock (of sheep or goats); also fig. (of men):— (small) cattle, flock (+ -s), lamb (+ s), sheep ([-cote, -fold, -shearer, -herds]).

See "Special Symbols."

Occasional, helpful Scripture references.

Improved, consistent abbreviations. All abbreviations occur with their full spelling in the list of abbreviations.

Brief English definitions (shown by italics).

After the long dash (—), there is a complete, alphabetical listing of all renderings of this Hebrew (or Aramaic) word in the KJV. (See also "Special Symbols").

Note that Hebrew (or Aramaic) spelling variations are conveniently indented for easy comparison.

Plan of the Hebrew and Aramaic Dictionary

1. All the original words are presented in their alphabetical order (according to Hebrew and Aramaic). They are numbered for easy matching between this Dictionary and the main part of the Concordance. Many reference books also use these same numbers created by Dr. Strong.

2. Immediately after each word, the exact equivalent of each sound (phoneme) is given in English characters, according to the transliteration system given below.

3. Next follows the precise pronunciation, with the proper stress mark.

4. Then comes the etymology, root meaning, and common uses of the word, along with any other important related details.

5. In the case of proper names, the normal English spelling is given, accompanied by a few words of explanation.

6. Finally, after the colon and the dash (:—), all the different ways that the word appears in the Authorized Version (KJV) are listed in alphabetical order. When the Hebrew or Aramaic word appears in English as a phrase, the main word of the phrase is used to alphabetize it.

By looking up these words in the main concordance and by noting the passages which display the same number in the right-hand column, the reader also possesses a complete *Hebrew Concordance*, expressed in the words of the Authorized Version.

Transliteration and Pronunciation of the Hebrew and Aramaic

The following shows how the Hebrew words are transliterated into English in this Dictionary.

1. The Hebrew and Aramaic read *from right to left*. Both alphabets consist of 22 letters (and their variations), which are all regarded as *consonants*, although four consonants (א ה ו י) sometimes indicate vowel sounds. To help enunciation, vowels are primarily indicated by certain "points" or marks, mostly beneath the letters. Hebrew and Aramaic do not use *capitals, italics,* etc.

2. The Hebrew and Aramaic characters are as follows:

No.	Form	Name	Transliteration and Pronunciation
1.	א	'Aleph (*aw´-lef*)	', silent
2.	ב	Bêyth (*bayth*)	**b**
3.	ג	Gîymel (*ghee´-mel*)	**g** hard = γ
4.	ד	Dâleth (*daw´-leth*)	**d**
5.	ה	Hê' (*hay*)	**h**, often quiescent
6.	ו	Vâv (*vawv*) or Wâw (*waw*)	**v** or **w**, quiescent
7.	ז	Zayin (*zah´-yin*)	**z**, as in *zeal*
8.	ח	Chêyth (*khayth*)	German **ch** = χ (nearly *kh*)
9.	ט	Têyth (*tayth*)	**ṭ** = **T**
10.	י	Yôwd (*yode*)	**y**, often quiescent
11.	כ final ך	Kaph (*caf*)	**k** = כ
12.	ל	Lâmed (*law´-med*)	**l**
13.	מ final ם	Mêm (*mame*)	**m**
14.	נ final ן	Nûwn (*noon*)	**n**
15.	ס	Çâmek (*saw´-mek*)	**ç** = *s* sharp = שׂ
16.	ע	'Ayin (*ah´-yin*)	' peculiar [1]
17.	פ final ף	Phê' (*fay*)	**ph** = *f* = φ
	פ	Pê' (*pay*)	**p**
18.	צ, final ץ	Tsâdêy (*tsaw-day´*)	**ts**
19.	ק	Qôwph (*cofe*)	**q** = *k* = כ
20.	ר	Rêysh (*raysh*)	**r**
21.	שׂ	Sîyn (*seen*)	*s* sharp = ס = σ
	שׁ	Shîyn (*sheen*)	**sh**
22.	ת	Thâv (*thawv*)	**th**, as in *THin* = θ
	ת	Tâv (*tawv*)	**t** = ט = τ

---

[1] The letter *'Ayin*, because Westerners find it difficult to pronounce accurately (it is a deep guttural sound, like that made in *gargling*), is generally passed over silently in reading. We have represented it to the eye (but not exactly to the ear) by the Greek *rough breathing* mark (') in order to distinguish it from *'Aleph*, which is likewise treated as silent, being similarly represented by the Greek *smooth breathing* (').

3. The vowel points are as follows:

Form[2]	Name	Transliteration and Pronunciation
בָ	Qâmêts (*caw-mates*)	â, as in *All*
בַ	Pattach (*pat´-takh*)	a, as in *mAn*
בֲ	Shevâ'-Pattach (*she-vaw´ pat´-takh*)	ă, as in *hAt*
בֵ	Tsêrêy (*tsay-ray*)	ê, as in *thEy* = η
בֶ	Çegôwl (*seg-ole*)	e, as in *thEir*
		e, as in *mEn* = ε
בֱ	Sheva'-Çegôwl (*she-vaw´ seg-ole*)	ĕ, as in *mEt*
בְ	Sheva' (*she-vaw*)[3]	obscure, as in *avErage*
		silent, as *e* in *madE*
בִ	Chîyriq (*khee´-rik*)	î, as in *machIne*[4]
		i, as in *supplIant* (*misery, hit*)
בֹ	Chôwlem (*kho´-lem*)[5]	ô, as in *no* = ω
בָ	Short Qâmêts (*caw-mates*)[6]	o, as in *nor* = o
בֳ	Sheva-Qâmêts (*she-vaw´ caw-mates*)	ŏ, as in *not*
ו	Shûwrêq * (*shoo-rake*)[7]	û, as in *crUel*
בֻ	Qïbbûts * (*kib´-boots*)[7]	u, as in *fUll, rude*

4. A point in the heart of a letter is called *Dâgêsh´*, and is of two kinds, which must be carefully distinguished.

a. Dâgêsh *lenè* occurs only in the letters ב, ג, ד, כ, פ, ת (technically vocalized *Begad´-Kephath*), when they *begin* a clause or sentence, or are preceded by a consonant *sound*; and simply has the effect of removing their aspiration.[8]

b. Dâgêsh *fortè* may occur in any letter except א, ה, ח, ע or ר; it is equivalent to *doubling* the letter, and at the same time it removes the aspiration of a Begad-Kephath letter.[9]

5. The *Maqqêph´* (-), like a *hyphen*, unites words only for purposes of pronunciation (by removing the primary accent from all except the last word), but it does not affect their meaning or grammatical construction.

Special Symbols

+ (*addition*) denotes a rendering in the A.V. of one or more Hebrew or Aramaic words in connection with the one under consideration. For example, in 2 Kgs. 4:41, No. 1697, דָּבָר (**dâbâr**) is translated as "harm," in connection with No. 7451. Literally, it is "bad thing."

× (*multiplication*) denotes a rendering in the A.V. that results from an idiom peculiar to the Hebrew or Aramaic. For example, in Psa. 132:15, the whole Hebrew phrase in which בָּרֵךְ, **bârak** (1288) appears is a means of expressing a verb root emphatically, i. e. "blessing, I will bless" = "I will abundantly bless."

° (*degree*), attached to a Hebrew word, denotes a corrected vowel pointing which is different from the Biblical text. (This mark is set in Hebrew Bibles over syllables in which the vowels of the margin have been inserted instead of those which properly belong to the text.)

For example, see the difference between the Hebrew text and the scribes' marginal note in Ezek. 40:15 for No. 2978, translated "entrance."

( ) (*parentheses*), in the renderings from the A.V., denote a word or syllable which is sometimes given in connection with the principal word to which it is attached. In Num. 34:6, the only occurrence of "western" in the A. V., the underlying Hebrew word is יָם (**yâm**, No. 3220), which is usually translated "sea."

[ ] (*brackets*), in the rendering from the A.V., denote the inclusion of an additional word in the Hebrew or Aramaic. For example, No. 3117, יוֹם (**yôwm**), is translated as "birthday" in Gen. 40:20, along with No. 3205. So, two Hebrew words are translated by one English word.

Italics, at the end of a rendering from the A.V., denote an explanation of the variations from the usual form.

---

[2] The same Hebrew/Aramaic consonant (ב) is shown here in order to show the position of the vowel points, whether below, above, or in the middle of Hebrew or Aramaic consonants.

[3] *Silent Sheva'* is not represented by any mark in our method of transliteration, since it is understood whenever there is no other vowel point.

[4] *Chîyriq* is long only when it is followed by a quiescent *yôwd* (either expressed or implied).

[5] *Chôwlem* is written *fully* only over *Vâv* or *Wâw* (וֹ), which is then quiescent (w); but when used "defectively" (without the *Vâv* or *Wâw*) it may be written either over the left-hand corner of the letter to which it belongs, or over the right-hand corner of the following one.

[6] Short *Qâmêts* is found only in *unaccented syllables ending with a consonant sound.*

[7] *Shûwrêq* is written only in the heart of *Vâv* or *Wâw*. Sometimes it is said to be "defectively" written (without the *Vâv* or *Wâw*), and then takes the form of *Qibbûts*, which in such cases is called *vicarious.*

[8] In our system of transliteration Dâgêsh *lenè* is represented only in the letters פ and ת, because elsewhere it does not affect the pronunciation.

[9] A point in the heart of ה is called *Mappiyq* (*map-peek*). It occurs only in the final vowel-less letter of a few words, and we have represented it by *hh*. A Dâgêsh *fortè* in the heart of ו may easily be distinguished from the vowel *Shûwrêq* by noticing that in the former case the letter has a proper vowel point accompanying it.

It should be noted that both kinds of Dâgêsh are often omitted in writing (being *implied*), but (in the case at least of Dâgêsh *fortè*) the word is usually pronounced the same as if it were present.

Abbreviations

abb. = abbreviated
    abbreviation
abstr. = abstract
    abstractly
act. = active (voice)
    actively
acc. = accusative (case) [1]
adj. = adjective
    adjectivally
adv. = adverb
    adverbial
    adverbially
aff. = affix [2]
    affixed
affin. = affinity
alt. = alternate
    alternately
anal. = analogy
appar. = apparent
    apparently
arch. = architecture
    architectural
    architecturally
art. = article [3]
artif. = artificial
    artificially
Ass. = Assyrian
A.V. = Authorized Version
    (King James Version)
Bab. = Babylon
    Babylonia
    Babylonian
caus. = causative [4]
    causatively
cerem. = ceremony
    ceremonial
    ceremonially
Chald. = Chaldee (Aramaic)
    Chaldaism
    (Aramaism)
Chr. = Christian
collat. = collateral
    collaterally
collect. = collective
    collectively
comp. = compare [5]
    comparison
    comparative
    comparatively
concr. = concrete
    concretely
conjec. = conjecture
    conjectural
    conjecturally
conjug. = conjugation [6]
    conjugational
    conjugationally
conjunc. = conjunction
    conjunctional
    conjunctionally
constr. = construct [7]
    construction
    constructive
    constructively

contr. = contracted [8]
    contraction
correl. = correlated
    correlation
    correlative
    correlatively
corresp. = corresponding
    correspondingly
dat. = dative (case) [9]
def. = definite [10]
    definitely
demonstr. = demonstrative [11]
denom. = denominative [12]
    denominatively
der. = derived
    derivation
    derivative
    derivatively
desc. = descended
    descendant
    descendants
dimin. = diminutive [13]
dir. = direct
    directly
E. = East
    Eastern
eccl. = ecclesiastical
    ecclesiastically
e.g. = for example
Eg. = Egypt
    Egyptian
    Egyptians
ellip. = ellipsis [14]
    elliptical
    elliptically
emphat. = emphatic
    emphatically
equiv. = equivalent
    equivalently
err. = error
    erroneous
    erroneously
espec. = especially
etym. = etymology [15]
    etymological
    etymologically
euphem. = euphemism [16]
    euphemistic
    euphemistically
euphon. = euphonious [17]
    euphonically
extens. = extension [18]
    extensive
extern. = external
    externally
fem. = feminine (gender)
fig. = figurative
    figuratively
for. = foreign
    foreigner
freq. = frequentative
    frequentatively
fut. = future

gen. = general
    generally
    generic
    generical
    generically
Gr. = Greek
    Graecism
gut. = guttural [19]
Heb. = Hebrew
    Hebraism
i.e. = that is
ident. = identical
    identically
immed. = immediate
    immediately
imper. = imperative [20]
    imperatively
imperf. = imperfect [21]
impers. = impersonal
    impersonally
impl. = implied
    impliedly
    implication
incept. = inceptive [22]
    inceptively
incl. = including
    inclusive
    inclusively
indef. = indefinite
    indefinitely
ind. = indicative [23]
    indicatively
indiv. = individual
    individually
infer. = inference
    inferential
    inferentially
infin. = infinitive
inhab. = inhabitant
    inhabitants
ins. = inserted
intens. = intensive
    intensively
interch. = interchangeable
intern. = internal
    internally
interj. = interjection [24]
    interjectional
    interjectionally
interrog. = interrogative [25]
    interrogatively
intr. = intransitive [26]
    intransitively
invol. = involuntary
    involuntarily
irreg. = irregular
    irregularly
Isr. = Israelite
    Israelites
    Israelitish
Lat. = Latin
Levit. = Levitical
    Levitically

lit. = literal
    literally
marg. = margin
    marginal reading
masc. = masculine (gender)
mean. = meaning
ment. = mental
    mentally
metaph. = metaphorical
    metaphorically
mid. = middle (voice) [27]
modif. = modified
    modification
mor. = moral
    morally
mult. = multiplicative [28]
nat. = natural
    naturally
neg. = negative
    negatively
neut. = neuter (gender)
obj. = object
    objective
    objectively
obs. = obsolete
ord. = ordinal [29]
or. = origin
orig. = original
    originally
orth. = orthography [30]
    orthographical
    orthographically
Pal. = Palestine
part. = participle
pass. = passive (voice)
    passively
patron. = patronymic [31]
    patronymical
    patronymically
perh. = perhaps
perm. = permutation [32] (of
    adjacent letters)
pers. = person
    personal
    personally
Pers. = Persia
    Persian
    Persians
phys. = physical
    physically
plur. = plural
poet. = poetry
    poetical
    poetically
pos. = positive
    positively
pref. = prefix
    prefixed
prep. = preposition
    prepositional
    prepositionally
prim. = primitive
prob. = probable
    probably

prol. = prolonged [33]
    prolongation
pron. = pronoun
    pronominal
    pronominally
prop. = properly
prox. = proximate
    proximately
recip. = reciprocal
    reciprocally
redupl. = reduplicated [34]
    reduplication
refl. = reflexive [35]
    reflexively
reg. = regular
rel. = relative
    relatively
relig. = religion
    religious
    religiously
Rom. = Roman
second. = secondary
    secondarily
signif. = signification
    signifying
short. = shorter
    shortened
sing. = singular
spec. = specific
    specifically
streng. = strengthening
subdiv. = subdivision
    subdivisional
    subdivisionally
subj. = subjectively
    subjective
    subject
substit. = substituted
suff. = suffix
superl. = superlative [36]
    superlatively
symb. = symbolic
    symbolical
    symbolically
tech. = technical
    technically
term. = termination
tran. = transitive [37]
    transitively
transc. = transcription
transm. = transmutation [38]
transp. = transposed [39]
    transposition
typ. = typical
    typically
uncert. = uncertain
    uncertainly
var. = various
    variation
voc. = vocative (case) [40]
vol. = voluntary
    voluntarily

---

[1] often indicating the direct object of an action verb

[2] part of a word which, when attached to the beginning of the word is called a prefix; if attaching within a word, an infix; and if at the end, a suffix

[3] "the" is the definite article; "a" and "an" are indefinite articles

[4] expressing or denoting causation

[5] the comparative of an adjective or adverb expresses a greater degree of an attribute, e.g. "higher"; "more slowly"

[6] a systematic array of various verbal forms

[7] the condition in Hebrew and Aramaic when two adjacent nouns are combined semantically as follows, e.g. "sword" + "king" = "(the) sword of (the) king" or "(the) king's sword". These languages tend to throw the stress of the entire noun phrase toward the end of the whole expression.

[8] a shortened form of a word. It is made by omitting or combining some elements or by reducing vowels or syllables. e.g. "is not" becomes "isn't".

[9] often the indirect object of an action verb

[10] the definite article ("the")

[11] demonstrative pronouns which point (show), e.g. "this," "that"

[12] derived from a noun

[13] a grammatical form which expresses smallness and/or endearment

[14] a construction which leaves out understood words

[15] the historical origin of a word

[16] the use of a pleasant, polite, or harmless-sounding word or phrase to hide harsh, rude, or infamous truths, e.g. "to pass away" = "to die"

[17] a linguistic mechanism to make pronunciation easier, e.g. "an" before "hour" instead of "a"

[18] when a general term can denote an entire class of things

[19] speech sounds which are produced deep in the throat

[20] the mood which expresses a command

[21] used of a tense which expresses a continuous but unfinished action or state

[22] used of a verbal aspect which denotes the beginning of an action

[23] used of the mood which expresses a verbal action as actually occurring (not hypothetical)

[24] an exclamation which expresses emotion

[25] indicating a question

[26] referring to verbs which do not govern direct objects

[27] reflexive

[28] capable of multiplying or tending to multiply

[29] This shows the position or the order within a series, e.g. "second"; the corresponding cardinal number is "two".

[30] the written system of spelling in a given language

[31] a name derived from that of a paternal ancestor, often created by an affix in various languages

[32] a rearrangement

[33] lengthening a pronunciation

[34] the repetition of a letter or syllable to form a new, inflected word

[35] denoting action by the subject upon itself

[36] expressing the highest degree of comparison of the quality indicated by an adjective or an adverb, e.g. "highest"; "most timely"

[37] expressing an action directed toward a person or a thing (the direct object)

[38] the change of one grammatical element to another

[39] switching word order

[40] an inflection which is used when one is addressing a person or a thing directly, e.g. "John, come here!"

HEBREW AND ARAMAIC DICTIONARY OF THE OLD TESTAMENT

א

1. אָב *'âb*, awb; a prim. word; *father* in a lit. and immed., or fig. and remote application):— chief, (fore-) father (l-less]), × patrimony, principal. Comp. names in "Abi-".

2. אַב *'ab* (Chald.), ab; corresp. to 1:— father.

3. אֵב *'êb*, abe; from the same as 24; a *green* plant:— greenness, fruit.

4. אֵב *'êb* (Chald.), abe; corresp. to 3:— fruit.

אֹב *'ôb*. See 178.

5. אֲבַגְתָא *'Ăbagthâ*, ab-ag-thaw'; of for. or.; *Abagtha*, a eunuch of Xerxes:— Abagtha.

6. אָבַד *'âbad*, aw-bad'; a prim. root; prop. to *wander* away, i.e. *lose* oneself; by impl. to *perish* (caus. *destroy*):— break, destroy (-uction), + not escape, fail, lose, (cause to, make) perish, spend, × and surely, take, be undone, × utterly, be void of, have no way to flee.

7. אֲבַד *'ăbad* (Chald.), ab-ad'; corresp. to 6:— destroy, perish.

8. אֹבֵד *'ôbêd*, o-bade'; act. of part. of 6; (concr.) *wretched* or (abstr.) *destruction*:— perish.

9. אֲבֵדָה *'ăbêdâh*, ab-ay-daw'; from 6; concr. something *lost*; abstr. *destruction*, i.e. Hades:— lost. Comp. 10.

10. אֲבֵדָה *'ăbaddôh*, ab-ad-do'; the same as 9, miswritten for 11; a *perishing*:— destruction.

11. אֲבַדֹּן *'ăbaddôwn*, ab-ad-done'; intens. from 6; abstr. a *perishing*; concr. Hades:— destruction.

12. אַבְדָן *'abdân*, ab-dawn'; from 6; a *perishing*:— destruction.

13. אׇבְדָן *'obdân*, ob-dawn'; from 6; a *perishing*:— destruction.

14. אָבָה *'âbâh*, aw-baw'; a prim. root; to *breathe* after, i.e. (fig.) to *be acquiescent*:— consent, rest content, be willing.

15. אָבֶה *'âbeh*, aw-beh'; from 14; *longing*:— desire.

16. אֵבֶה *'êbeh*, ay-beh'; from 14 (in the sense of *bending* toward); the *papyrus*:— swift.

17. אֲבוֹי *'ăbôwy*, ab-o'ee; from 14 (in the sense of *desiring*); *want*:— sorrow.

18. אֵבוּס *'êbûwç*, ay-booce'; from 75; a *manger* or *stall*:— crib.

19. אִבְחָה *'ibchâh*, ib-khaw'; from an unused root (appar. mean. to *turn*); *brandishing* of a sword:— point.

20. אֲבַטִּיחַ *'ăbaṭṭîyach*, ab-at-tee'-akh; of uncert. der.; a *melon* (only. plur.):— melon.

21. אֲבִי *'Ăbîy*, ab-ee'; from 1; *fatherly*; *Abi*, Hezekiah's mother:— Abi.

22. אֲבִיאֵל *'Ăbîy'êl*, ab-ee-ale'; from 1 and 410; *father* (i.e. *possessor*) *of God*; *Abiel*, the name of two Isr.:— Abiel.

23. אֲבִיאָסָף *'Ăbîy'âçâph*, ab-ee-aw-

sawf'; from 1 and 622; *father of gathering* (i.e. *gatherer*); *Abiasaph*, an Isr.:— Abiasaph.

24. אָבִיב *'âbîyb*, aw-beeb'; from an unused root (mean. to *be tender*); *green*, i.e. a young *ear* of grain; hence, the name of the month *Abib* or *Nisan*:— Abib, ear, green ears of corn.

25. אֲבִי גִבְעוֹן *'Ăbîy Gib'ôwn*, ab-ee' ghib-one'; from 1 and 1391; *father* (i.e. *founder*) *of Gibon; Abi-Gibon*, perh. an Isr.:— father of Gibeon.

26. אֲבִיגַיִל *'Ăbîygayil*, ab-ee-gah'-yil, or short.

אֲבִיגַל *'Ăbîygal*, ab-ee-gal'; from 1 and 1524; *father* (i.e. *source*) *of joy; Abigail* or *Abigal*, the name of two Israelitesses:— Abigal.

27. אֲבִידָן *'Ăbîydân*, ab-ee-dawn'; from 1 and 1777; *father of judgment* (i.e. *judge*); *Abidan*, an Isr.:— Abidan.

28. אֲבִידָע *'Ăbîydâ'*, ab-ee-daw'; from 1 and 3045; *father of knowledge* (i.e. *knowing*); *Abida*, a son of Abraham by Keturah:— Abida, Abidah.

29. אֲבִיָּה *'Ăbîyâh*, ab-ee-yaw'; or prol.

אֲבִיָּהוּ *'Ăbîyâhûw*, ab-ee-yaw'-hoo; from 1 and 3050; *father* (i.e. *worshipper*) *of Jah; Abijah*, the name of several Isr. men and two Israelitesses:— Abiah, Abijah.

30. אֲבִיהוּא *'Ăbîyhûw'*, ab-ee-hoo'; from 1 and 1931; *father* (i.e. *worshipper*) *of Him* (i.e. *God*); *Abihu*, a son of Aaron:— Abihu.

31. אֲבִיהוּד *'Ăbîyhûwd*, ab-ee-hood'; from 1 and 1935; *father* (i.e. *possessor*) *of renown; Abihud*, the name of two Isr.:— Abihud.

32. אֲבִיהַיִל *'Ăbîyhayil*, ab-ee-hah'-yil; or (more correctly)

אֲבִיחַיִל *'Ăbîychayil*, ab-ee-khah'-yil; from 1 and 2428; *father* (i.e. *possessor*) *of might; Abihail* or *Abichail*, the name of three Isr. and two Israelitesses:— Abihail.

33. אֲבִי הָעֶזְרִי *'Ăbîy hâ-'Ezrîy*, ab-ee' haw-ez-ree'; from 44 with the art. ins.; *father of the Ezrite*; an *Abiezrite* or desc. of Abiezer:— Abiezrite.

34. אֶבְיוֹן *'ebyôwn*, eb-yone'; from 14, in the sense of *want* (espec. in feeling); *destitute*:— beggar, needy, poor (man).

35. אֲבִיוֹנָה *'ăbîyôwnâh*, ab-ee-yo-naw'; from 14; provocative of *desire*; the *caper berry* (from its *stimulative* taste):— desire.

אֲבִיחַיִל *'Ăbîychayil*. See 32.

36. אֲבִיטוּב *'Ăbîyṭûwb*, ab-ee-toob'; from 1 and 2898; *father of goodness* (i.e. *good*); *Abitub*, an Isr.:— Abitub.

37. אֲבִיטַל *'Ăbîyṭal*, ab-ee-tal'; from 1 and 2919; *father of dew* (i.e. *fresh*); *Abital*, a wife of King David:— Abital.

38. אֲבִיָּם *'Ăbîyâm*, ab-ee-yawm'; from 1 and 3220; *father of* (the) *sea* (i.e. *seaman*); *Abijam* (or *Abijah*), a king of Judah:— Abijam.

39. אֲבִימָאֵל *'Ăbîymâ'êl*, ab-ee-maw-ale'; from 1 and an elsewhere unused (prob. for.) word; *father of Mael* (appar. some Arab tribe); *Abimael*, a son of Joktan:— Abimael.

40. אֲבִימֶלֶךְ *'Ăbîymelek*, ab-ee-mel'-ek; from 1 and 4428; *father of* (the) *king; Abimelek*, the name of two Philistine kings and of two Isr.:— Abimelech.

41. אֲבִינָדָב *'Ăbîynâdâb*, ab-ee-naw-dawb'; from 1 and 5068; *father of generosity* (i.e. *liberal*); *Abinadab*, the name of four Isr.:— Abinadab.

42. אֲבִינֹעַם *'Ăbîynô'am*, ab-ee-no'-am; from 1 and 5278; *father of pleasantness* (i.e. *gracious*); *Abinoam*, an Isr.:— Abinoam.

אֲבִינֵר *'Ăbîynêr*. See 74.

43. אֶבְיָסָף *'Ebyâçâph*, eb-yaw-sawf'; contr. from 23; *Ebjasaph*, an Isr.:— Ebiasaph.

44. אֲבִיעֶזֶר *'Ăbîy'ezer*, ab-ee-ay'-zer; from 1 and 5829; *father of help* (i.e. *helpful*); *Abiezer*, the name of two Isr.:— Abiezer.

45. אֲבִי־עַלְבוֹן *'Ăbîy-'albôwn*, ab-ee-al-bone'; from 1 and an unused root of uncert. der.; prob. *father of strength* (i.e. *valiant*); *Abialbon*, an Isr.:— Abialbon.

46. אָבִיר *'âbîyr*, aw-beer'; from 82; *mighty* (spoken of God):— mighty (one).

47. אַבִּיר *'abbîyr*, ab-beer'; from 46:— angel, bull, chiefest, mighty (one), stout [-hearted], strong (one), valiant.

48. אֲבִירָם *'Ăbîyrâm*, ab-ee-rawm'; from 1 and 7311; *father of height* (i.e. *lofty*); *Abiram*, the name of two Isr.:— Abiram.

49. אֲבִישַׁג *'Ăbîyshag*, ab-ee-shag'; from 1 and 7686; *father of error* (i.e. *blundering*); *Abishag*, a concubine of David:— Abishag.

50. אֲבִישׁוּעַ *'Ăbîyshûwa'*, ab-ee-shoo'-ah; from 1 and 7771; *father of plenty* (i.e. *prosperous*); *Abishua*, the name of two Isr.:— Abishua.

51. אֲבִישׁוּר *'Ăbîyshûwr*, ab-ee-shoor'; from 1 and 7791; *father of* (the) *wall* (i.e. perh. *mason*); *Abishur*, an Isr.:— Abishur.

52. אֲבִישַׁי *'Ăbîyshay*, ab-ee-shah'ee; or (short.)

אַבְשַׁי *'Abshay*, ab-shah'ee; from 1 and 7862; *father of a gift* (i.e. prob. *generous*); *Abishai*, an Isr.:— Abishai.

53. אֲבִישָׁלוֹם *'Ăbîyshâlôwm*, ab-ee-shaw-lome'; or (short.)

אַבְשָׁלוֹם *'Abshâlôwm*, ab-shaw-lome'; from 1 and 7965; *father of peace* (i.e. *friendly*); *Abshalom*, a son of David; also (the fuller form) a later Isr.:— Abishalom, Absalom.

54. אֶבְיָתָר *'Ebyâthâr*, ab-yaw-thawr'; contr. from 1 and 3498; *father of abundance* (i.e. *liberal*); *Ebjathar*, an Isr.:— Abiathar.

1

55. אָבַך **'âbak**, *aw-bak´*; a prim. root; prob. to *coil* upward:— mount up.

56. אָבַל **'âbal**, *aw-bal´*; a prim. root; to *bewail*:— lament, mourn.

57. אָבֵל **'âbêl**, *aw-bale´*; from 56; *lamenting*:— mourn (-er, -ing).

58. אָבֵל **'âbêl**, *aw-bale´*; from an unused root (mean. to be grassy); a *meadow*:— plain. Comp. also the prop. names beginning with Abel-.

59. אָבֵל **'Âbêl**, *aw-bale´*; from 58; a *meadow*; *Abel*, the name of two places in Pal.:— Abel.

60. אֵבֶל **'êbel**, *ay´-bel*; from 56; *lamentation*:— mourning.

61. אֲבָל **'âbâl**, *ab-awl´*; appar. from 56 through the idea of *negation*; *nay* (i.e. *truly* or *yet*):— but, indeed, nevertheless, verily.

62. אָבֵל בֵּית־מַעֲכָה **'Âbêl Bêyth-Mä'akâh**, *aw-bale´ bayth ma-a-kaw´*; from 58 and 1004 and 4601; *meadow of Beth-Maakah*; *Abel of Beth-maakah*, a place in Pal.:— Abel-beth-maachah, Abel of Beth-maachah.

63. אָבֵל הַשִּׁטִּים **'Âbêl hash-Shiṭṭiym**, *aw-bale´ hash-shit-teem´*; from 58 and the plur. of 7848, with the art. ins.; *meadow of the acacias*; *Abel hash-Shittim*, a place in Pal.:— Abel-shittim.

64. אָבֵל כְּרָמִים **'Âbêl Kᵉrâmiym**, *aw-bale´ ker-aw-meem´*; from 58 and the plur. of 3754; *meadow of vineyards*; *Abel-Keramim*, a place in Pal.:— plain of the vineyards.

65. אָבֵל מְחוֹלָה **'Âbêl Mᵉchôwlâh**, *aw-bale´ mekh-o-law´*; from 58 and 4246; *meadow of dancing*; *Abel-Mecholah*, a place in Pal.:— Abel-meholah.

66. אָבֵל מַיִם **'Âbêl Mayim**, *aw-bale´ mah´-yim*; from 58 and 4325; *meadow of water*; *Abel-Majim*, a place in Pal.:— Abel-maim.

67. אָבֵל מִצְרַיִם **'Âbêl Mitsrayim**, *aw-bale´ mits-rah´-yim*; from 58 and 4714; *meadow of Egypt*; *Abel-Mitsrajim*, a place in Pal.:— Abel-mizraim.

68. אֶבֶן **'eben**, *eh´-ben*; from the root of 1129 through the mean. to *build*; a *stone*:— + carbuncle, + mason, + plummet, [chalk-, hail-, head-, sling-] stone (-ny), (divers) weight (-s).

69. אֶבֶן **'eben** (Chald.), *eh´-ben*; corresp. to 68:— stone.

70. אֹבֶן **'ôben**, *o´-ben*; from the same as 68; a *pair of stones* (only dual); a potter's *wheel* or a midwife's *stool* (consisting alike of two horizontal disks with a support between):— wheel, stool.

71. אֲבָנָה **'Âbânâh**, *ab-aw-naw´*; perh. fem. of 68; *stony*; *Abanah*, a river near Damascus:— Abana. Comp. 549.

72. אֶבֶן הָעֵזֶר **'Eben hâ-'êzer**, *eh´-ben haw-e´-zer*; from 68 and 5828 with the art. ins.; *stone of the help*; *Eben-ha-Ezer*, a place in Pal.:— Ebenezer.

73. אַבְנֵט **'abnêṭ**, *ab-nate´*; of uncert. der.; a *belt*:— girdle.

74. אַבְנֵר **'Abnêr**, *ab-nare´*; or (fully)

אֲבִינֵר **'Ăbîynêr**; from 1

and 5216; *father of light* (i.e. *enlightening*); *Abner*, an Isr.:— Abner.

75. אָבַס **'âbaç**, *aw-bas´*; a prim. root; to *fodder*:— fatted, stalled.

76. אַבְעֲבֻעָה **'āba'bû'âh**, *ab-ah-boo-aw´*; (by redupl.) from an unused root (mean. to *belch* forth); an inflammatory *pustule* (as *eruption*):— blains.

77. אָבַק **'Ebets**, *eh´-bets*; from an unused root prob. mean. to *gleam*; *conspicuous*; *Ebets*, a place in Pal.:— Abez.

78. אִבְצָן **'Ibtsân**, *ib-tsawn´*; from the same as 76; *splendid*; *Ibtsan*, an Isr.:— Ibzan.

79. אָבַק **'âbaq**, *aw-bak´*; a prim. root, prob. to *float* away (as vapor), but used only as denom. from 80; to *bedust*, i.e. *grapple*:— wrestle.

80. אָבָק **'âbâq**, *aw-bawk´*; from root of 79; light *particles* (as *volatile*):— (small) dust, powder.

81. אֲבָקָה **'ăbâqâh**, *ab-aw-kaw´*; fem. of 80:— powder.

82. אָבַר **'âbar**, *aw-bar´*; a prim. root; to *soar*:— fly.

83. אֵבֶר **'êber**, *ay-ber´*; from 82; a *pinion*:— [long-] wing (-ed).

84. אֶבְרָה **'ebrâh**, *eb-raw´*; fem. of 83:— feather, wing.

85. אַבְרָהָם **'Abrâhâm**, *ab-raw-hawm´*; contr. from 1 and an unused root (prob. mean. to be *populous*); *father of a multitude*; *Abraham*, the later name of Abram:— Abraham.

86. אַבְרֵךְ **'abrêk**, *ab-rake´*; prob. an Eg. word mean. *kneel*:— bow the knee.

87. אַבְרָם **'Abrâm**, *ab-rawm´*; contr. from 48; *high father*; *Abram*, the original name of Abraham:— Abram.

אַבְשַׁי **'Abshay**. See 52.

אַבְשָׁלוֹם **'Abshâlôwm**. See 53.

88. אֹבֹת **'Ôbôth**, *o-both´*; plur. of 178; *water-skins*; *Oboth*, a place in the Desert:— Oboth.

89. אָגֵא **'Âgê'**, *aw-gay´*; of uncert. der. [comp. 90]; *Agë*, an Isr.:— Agee.

90. אֲגַג **'Ăgag**, *ag-ag´*; or

אֲגָג **'Ăgâg**, *Ag-awg´*; of uncert. der. [comp. 89]; *flame*; *Agag*, a title of Amalekitish kings:— Agag.

91. אֲגָגִי **'Ăgâgîy**, *ag-aw-ghee´*; patrial or patron. from 90; an *Agagite* or descendent (subject) of Agag:— Agagite.

92. אֲגֻדָּה **'ăguddâh**, *ag-ood-daw´*; fem. pass. part. of an unused root (mean. to *bind*); a *band, bundle, knot,* or *arch*:— bunch, burden, troop.

93. אֱגוֹז **'ĕgôwz**, *eg-oze´*; prob of Pers. or.; a *nut*:— nut.

94. אָגוּר **'Âgûwr**, *aw-goor´*; pass. part. of 103; *gathered* (i.e. *received* among the sages); *Agur*, a fanciful name for Solomon:— Agur.

95. אֲגוֹרָה **'ăgôwrâh**, *ag-o-raw´*; from the same as 94; prop. something *gathered*, i.e. perh. a *grain* or *berry*; used only of a small (silver) *coin*:— piece [of] silver.

96. אֵגֶל **'egel**, *eh´-ghel*; from an unused root (mean. to *flow* down or together as drops); a *reservoir*:— drop.

97. אֶגְלַיִם **'Eglayim**, *eg-lah´-yim*; dual of 96; a *double pond*; *Eglajim*, a place in Moab:— Eglaim.

98. אֲגַם **'ăgam**, *ag-am´*; from an unused root (mean. to *collect* as water); a *marsh*; hence, a *rush* (as growing in swamps); hence, a *stockade* of reeds:— pond, pool, standing [water].

99. אָגֵם **'âgêm**, *aw-game´*; prob. from the same as 98 (in the sense of *stagnant* water); fig. *sad*:— pond.

100. אַגְמוֹן **'agmôwn**, *ag-mone´*; from the same as 98; a marshy *pool* [others from a different root, a *kettle*]; by impl. a *rush* (as growing there); collect. a rope of rushes:— bulrush, caldron, hook, rush.

101. אַגָּן **'aggân**, *ag-gawn´*; prob. from 5059; a *bowl* (as *pounded* out hollow):— basin, cup, goblet.

102. אַגָּף **'aggâph**, *ag-gawf´*; prob. from 5062 (through the idea of *impending*); a *cover* or *heap*; i.e. (only plur.) *wings* of an army, or *crowds* of troops:— bands.

103. אָגַר **'âgar**, *aw-gar´*; a prim. root; to *harvest*:— gather.

104. אִגְּרָא **'iggᵉrâ'** (Chald.), *ig-er-aw´*; of Pers. or.; an *epistle* (as carried by a state courier or postman):— letter.

105. אִגַּרְטָל **'ăgarṭâl**, *ag-ar-tawl´*; of uncert. der.; a *basin*:— charger.

106. אֶגְרֹף **'egrôph**, *eg-rofe´*; from 1640 (in the sense of *grasping*); the *clenched hand*:— fist.

107. אִגֶּרֶת **'iggereth**, *ig-eh´-reth*; fem. of 104; an *epistle*:— letter.

108. אֵד **'êd**, *ade* from the same as 181 (in the sense of *enveloping*); a *fog*:— mist, vapor.

109. אָדַב **'âdab**, *aw-dab´*; a prim. root; to *languish*:— grieve.

110. אַדְבְּאֵל **'Adbᵉ'êl**, *ad-beh-ale´*; prob. from 109 (in the sense of *chastisement*) and 410; *disciplined of God*; *Adbeël*, a son of Ishmael:— Adbeel.

111. אֲדַד **'Ădad**, *ad-ad´*; prob. an orth. var. for 2301; *Adad* (or Hadad), an Edomite:— Hadad.

112. אִדּוֹ **'Iddôw**, *id-do´*; of uncert. der.; *Iddo*, an Isr.:— Iddo.

אֱדוֹם **'Ĕdôwm**. See 123.

אֱדוֹמִי **'Ĕdôwmîy**. See 130.

113. אָדוֹן **'âdôwn**, *aw-done´*; or (short).

אָדֹן **'âdôn**, *aw-done´*; from an unused root (mean. to *rule*); *sovereign*, i.e. *controller* (human or divine):— lord, master, owner. Comp. also names beginning with "Adoni-".

114. אַדּוֹן **'Addôwn**, *ad-done´*; prob. intens. for 113; *powerful*; *Addon*, appar. an Isr.:— Addon.

115. אֲדוֹרַיִם **'Ădôwrayim**, *ad-o-rah´-yim*; dual from 142 (in the sense of *eminence*); *double mound*; *Adorajim*, a place in Pal.:— Adoraim.

116. אֱדַיִן **'ĕdayin** (Chald.), *ed-ah´-yin*; of uncert. der.; *then* (of time):— now, that time, then.

117. אַדִּיר **'addîyr**, *ad-deer´*; from 142; *wide* or (gen.) *large*; fig. *powerful*:— excellent, famous, gallant, glorious,

goodly, lordly, mighty (-ier, one), noble, principal, worthy.

118. אֲדַלְיָא **'Ădalyâ**, ad-al-yaw'; of Pers. der.; Adalja, a son of Haman:— Adalia.

119. אָדַם **'âdam**, aw-dam'; to show blood (in the face), i.e. flush or turn rosy:— be (dyed, made) red (ruddy).

120. אָדָם **'âdâm**, aw-dawm'; from 119; ruddy, i.e. a human being (an individual or the species, mankind, etc.):— × another, + hypocrite, + common sort, × low, man (mean, of low degree), person.

121. אָדָם **'Âdâm**, aw-dawm'; the same as 120; Adam the name of the first man, also of a place in Pal.:— Adam.

122. אָדֹם **'âdôm**, aw-dome'; from 119; rosy:— red, ruddy.

123. אֱדֹם **'Ědôm**, ed-ome'; or (fully)

אֱדוֹם **'Ědôwm**, ed-ome'; from 122; red [see Gen. 25:25]; Edom, the elder twin-brother of Jacob; hence, the region (Idumæa) occupied by him:— Edom, Edomites, Idumea.

124. אֹדֶם **'ôdem**, o'-dem; from 119; redness, i.e. the ruby, garnet, or some other red gem:— sardius.

125. אֲדַמְדָּם **'ădamdâm**, ad-am-dawm'; redupl. from 119; reddish:— (somewhat) reddish.

126. אַדְמָה **'Admâh**, ad-maw'; contr. for 127; earthy; Admah, a place near the Dead Sea:— Admah.

127. אֲדָמָה **'ădâmâh**, ad-aw-maw'; from 119; soil (from its gen. redness):— country, earth, ground, husband [-man] (-ry), land.

128. אֲדָמָה **'Ădâmâh**, ad-aw-maw'; the same as 127; Adamah, a place in Pal.:— Adamah.

אֲדָמִי **'admôwnîy**. See 132.

129. אֲדָמִי **'Ădâmîy**, ad-aw-mee'; from 127; earthy; Adami, a place in Pal.:— Adami.

130. אֱדֹמִי **'Ědômîy**, ed-o-mee'; or (fully)

אֱדוֹמִי **'Ědôwmîy**, ed-o-mee'; patron. from 123; an Edomite, or desc. from (or inhab. of) Edom:— Edomite. See 726.

131. אֲדֻמִּים **'Ădummîym**, ad-oom-meem'; plur. of 121; red spots; Adummim, a pass in Pal.:— Adummim.

132. אַדְמֹנִי **'admônîy**, ad-mo-nee'; or (fully)

אַדְמוֹנִי **'admôwnîy**, ad-mo-nee'; from 119; reddish (of the hair or the complexion):— red, ruddy.

133. אַדְמָתָא **'Admâthâ**, ad-maw-thaw'; prob. of Pers. der.; Admatha, a Pers. nobleman:— Admatha.

134. אֶדֶן **'eden**, eh'-den; from the same as 113 (in the sense of strength); a basis (of a building), a column, etc.):— foundation, socket.

אָדוֹן **'âdôn**. See 113.

135. אַדָּן **'Addân**, ad-dawn'; intens. from the same as 134; firm; Addan, an Isr.:— Addan.

136. אֲדֹנָי **'Ădônây**; am em-

phat. form of 113; the Lord (used as a proper name of God only):— (my) Lord.

137. אֲדֹנִי־בֶזֶק **'Ădônîy-Bezeq**, ad-o''-nee-beh'-zek; from 113 and 966; lord of Bezek; Adoni-Bezek; a Canaanitish king:— Adoni-bezek.

138. אֲדֹנִיָּה **'Ădônîyâh**, ad-o-nee-yaw'; or (prol.)

אֲדֹנִיָּהוּ **'Ădônîyâhûw**, ad-o-nee-yaw'-hoo; from 113 and 3050; lord (i.e. worshipper) of Jah; Adonijah, the name of three Isr.:— Adonijah.

139. אֲדֹנִי־צֶדֶק **'Ădônîy-Tsedeq**, ad-o''-nee-tseh'-dek; from 113 and 6664; lord of justice; Adoni-Tsedek, a Canaanitish king:— Adonizedec.

140. אֲדֹנִיקָם **'Ădônîyqâm**, ad-o-nee-kawm'; from 113 and 6965; lord of rising (i.e. high); Adonikam, the name of one or two Isr.:— Adonikam.

141. אֲדֹנִירָם **'Ădônîyrâm**, ad-o-nee-rawm'; from 113 and 7311; lord of height; Adoniram, an Isr.:— Adoniram.

142. אָדַר **'âdar**, aw-dar'; a prim. root; to expand, i.e. be great or (fig.) magnificent:— (become) glorious, honourable.

143. אֲדָר **'Ădâr**, ad-awr'; prob. of for. der.; perh. mean. fire; Adar, the 12th Heb. month:— Adar.

144. אֲדָר **'Ădâr** (Chald.), ad-awr'; corresp. to 143:— Adar.

145. אֶדֶר **'eder**, eh'-der; from 142; amplitude, i.e. (concr.) a mantle; also (fig.) splendor:— goodly, robe.

146. אַדָּר **'Addâr**, ad-dawr'; intens. from 142; ample; Addar, a place in Pal.; also an Isr.:— Addar.

147. אִדַּר **'iddar** (Chald.), id-dar'; intens. from a root corresp. to 142; ample, i.e. a threshing- floor:— threshing-floor.

148. אֲדַרְגָּזֵר **'ădargâzêr** (Chald.), ad-ar''-gaw-zare'; from the same as 147 and 1505; a chief diviner, or astrologer:— judge.

149. אַדְרַזְדָּא **'adrazdâ** (Chald.), ad-raz-daw'; prob. of Pers. or.; quickly or carefully:— diligently.

150. אַדַרְכֹּן **'ădarkôn**, ad-ar-kone'; of Pers. or.; a daric or Pers. coin:— dram.

151. אֲדֹרָם **'Ădôrâm**, ad-o-rawm'; contr. for 141; Adoram (or Adoniram), an Isr.:— Adoram.

152. אַדְרַמֶּלֶךְ **'Adrammelek**, ad-ram-meh'-lek; from 142 and 4428; splendor of (the) king; Adrammelek, the name of an Ass. idol, also of a son of Sennacherib:— Adrammelech.

153. אֶדְרָע **'edra'** (Chald.), ed-raw'; an orth. var. for 1872; an arm, i.e. (fig.) power:— force.

154. אֶדְרֶעִי **'edre'îy**, ed-reh'-ee; from the equiv. of 153; mighty; Edrei, the name of two places in Pal.:— Edrei.

155. אַדֶּרֶת **'addereth**, ad-deh'-reth; fem. of 117; something ample (as a large vine, a wide dress); also the same as 145:— garment, glory, goodly, mantle, robe.

156. אָדַשׁ **'âdash**, aw-dash'; a prim. root; to tread out (grain):— thresh.

157. אָהַב **'âhab**, aw-hab'; or

אָהֵב **'âhêb**, aw-habe'; a prim. root; to have affection for (sexually or otherwise):— (be-) love (-d, -ly, -r), like, friend.

158. אַהַב **'ahab**, ah'-hab; from 157; affection (in a good or a bad sense):— love (-r).

159. אֹהַב **'ôhab**, o'-hab; from 156; mean. the same as 158:— love.

160. אַהֲבָה **'ahăbâh**, ă-hab-aw'; fem. of 158 and mean. the same:— love.

161. אֹהַד **'Ôhad**, o'-had; from an unused root mean. to be united; unity; Ohad, an Isr.:— Ohad.

162. אֲהָהּ **'ăhâhh**, ă-haw'; appar. a prim. word expressing pain exclamatorily; Oh!:— ah, alas.

163. אַהֲוָא **'Ăhăvâ'**, ă-hav-aw'; prob. of for. or.; Ahava, a river of Bab.:— Ahava.

164. אֵהוּד **'Êhûwd**, ay-hood'; from the same as 161; united; Ehud, the name of two or three Isr.:— Ehud.

165. אֱהִי **'ĕhîy**, e-hee'; appar. an orth. var. for 346; where:— I will be (Hos. 13:10, 14) [which is often the rendering of the same Heb. form from 1961].

166. אָהַל **'âhal**, aw-hal'; a prim. root; to be clear:— shine.

167. אָהַל **'âhal**, aw-hal'; a denom. from 168; to tent:— pitch (remove) a tent.

168. אֹהֶל **'ôhel**, o'-hel; from 166; a tent (as clearly conspicuous from a distance):— covering, (dwelling) (place), home, tabernacle, tent.

169. אֹהֶל **'Ôhel**, o'-hel; the same as 168; Ohel, an Isr.:— Ohel.

170. אָהֳלָה **'Ohŏlâh**, ŏ-hol-aw'; in form a fem. of 168, but in fact for

אָהֳלָהּ **'Ohŏláhh**, ŏ-hol-aw'; from 168; her tent (i.e. idolatrous sanctuary); Oholah, a symbol. name for Samaria:— Aholah.

171. אָהֳלִיאָב **'Ohŏlîy'âb**, ŏ''-hol-e-awb'; from 168 and 1; tent of (his) father; Oholiab, an Isr.:— Aholiab.

172. אָהֳלִיבָה **'Ohŏlîybâh**, ŏ''-hol-ee-baw'; (similarly with 170) for

אָהֳלִיבָהּ **'Ohŏlîybâhh**, ŏ''-hol-e-baw'; from 168; my tent (is) in her; Oholibah, a symb. name for Judah:— Aholibah.

173. אָהֳלִיבָמָה **'Ohŏlîybâmâh**, ŏ''-hol-ee-baw-maw'; from 168 and 1116; tent of (the) height; Oholibamah, a wife of Esau:— Aholibamah.

174. אֲהָלִים **'ăhâlîym**, ă-haw-leem'; or (fem.)

אֲהָלוֹת **'ăhâlôwth**, ă-haw-loth' (only used thus in the plur.); of for. or.; aloe wood (i.e. sticks):— (tree of lign-) aloes.

175. אַהֲרוֹן **'Ahărôwn**, a-har-one'; of uncert. der.; Aharon, the brother of Moses:— Aaron.

176. אוֹ **'ôw**, o; presumed to be the "constr." or genitival form of

אַו **'av**, av; short. for 185; desire (and so prob. in Prov. 31:4); hence, (by way of alternative) or, also if:— also, and, either, if, at the least, × nor, or, otherwise, then, whether.

177. אוּאֵל **'Ûw'êl**, oo-ale´; from 176 and 410; *wish of God*; *Uel*, an Isr.:— Uel.

178. אוֹב **'ôwb**, obe; from the same as 1 (appar. through the idea of *prattling* a father's name); prop. a *mumble*, i.e. a water- *skin* (from its hollow sound); hence, a *necromancer* (ventriloquist, as from a jar):— bottle, familiar spirit.

179. אוֹבִיל **'Ôwbîyl**, o-beel´; prob. from 56; *mournful*; *Obil*, an Ishmaelite:— Obil.

180. אוֹבָל **'ûwbâl**, oo-bawl´; or (short.)

אֻבָל **'ûbâl**, oo-bawl´; from 2986 (in the sense of 2988); a *stream*:— river.

181. אוּד **'ûwd**, ood; from an unused root mean. to *rake* together; a *poker* (for *turning* or *gathering* embers):— (fire-) brand.

182. אוֹדוֹת **'ôwdôwth**, o-dôth´; or (short.)

אֹדוֹת **'ôdôwth**, o-dôth´ (only thus in the plur.); from the same as 181; *turnings* (i.e. *occasions*); (adv.) on *account* of:— (be-) cause, concerning, sake.

183. אָוָה **'âvâh**, aw-vaw´; a prim. root; to *wish* for:— covet, (greatly) desire, be desirous, long, lust (after).

184. אָוָה **'âvâh**, aw-vaw´; a prim. root; to *extend* or *mark* out:— point out.

185. אַוָּה **'avvâh**, av-vaw´; from 183; *longing*:— desire, lust after, pleasure.

186. אוּזַי **'Ûwzay**, oo-zah´-ee; perh. by perm. for 5813, *strong*; *Uzai*, an Isr.:— Uzai.

187. אוּזָל **'Ûwzâl**, oo-zâwl´; of uncert. der.; *Uzal*, a son of Joktan:— Uzal.

188. אוֹי **'ôwy**, ō´-ee; prob. from 183 (in the sense of *crying* out after); *lamentation*; also interj. Oh!:— alas, woe.

189. אֱוִי **'Ĕvîy**, ev-ee´; prob. from 183; *desirous*; *Evi*, a Midianitish chief:— Evi.

אוֹיֵב **'ôwyêb**. See 341.

190. אוֹיָה **'ôwyâh**, o-yaw´; fem. of 188:— woe.

191. אֱוִיל **'ĕvîyl**, ev-eel´; from an unused root (mean. to *be perverse*); (fig.) *silly*:— fool (-ish) (man).

192. אֱוִיל מְרֹדַךְ **'Ĕvîyl Merôdak**, ev-eel´ mer-o-dak´; of Chald. der. and prob. mean. *soldier of Merodak*; *Evil-Merodak*, a Bab. king:— Evil-merodach.

193. אוּל **'ûwl**, ool; from an unused root mean. to *twist*, i.e. (by impl.) *be strong*; the *body* (as being *rolled* together); also *powerful*:— mighty, strength.

194. אוּלַי **'ûwlay**, oo-lah´ee; or (short.)

אֻלַי **'ûlay**, oo-lah´ee; from 176; *if not*; hence, *perhaps*:— if so be, may be, peradventure, unless.

195. אוּלַי **'Ûwlay**, oo-lah´ee; of Pers. der.; the *Ulai* (or Eulæus), a river of Pers.:— Ulai.

196. אֱוִילִי **'ĕvîlîy**, ev-ee-lee´; from 191; *silly*, *foolish*; hence, (mor.) *impious*:— foolish.

197. אוּלָם **'ûwlâm**, oo-lawm´; or (short.)

אֻלָם **'ûlâm**, oo-lawm´; from 481 (in the sense of *tying*); a *vestibule* (as *bound* to the building):— porch.

198. אוּלָם **'Ûwlâm**, oo-lawm´; appar. from 481 (in the sense of *dumbness*);

solitary; *Ulam*, the name of two Isr.:— Ulam.

199. אוּלָם **'ûwlâm**, oo-lawm´; appar. a var. of 194; *however* or *on the contrary*:— as for, but, howbeit, in very deed, surely, truly, wherefore.

200. אֻלֶת **'ivveleth**, iv-veh´-leth; from the same as 191; *silliness*:— folly, foolishly (-ness).

201. אוֹמָר **'Ôwmâr**, o-mawr´; from 559; *talkative*; *Omar*, a grandson of Esau:— Omar.

202. אוֹן **'ôwn**, ōne; prob. from the same as 205 (in the sense of *effort*, but successful); *ability*, *power*, (fig.) *wealth*:— force, goods, might, strength, substance.

203. אוֹן **'Ôwn**, ōne; the same as 202; *On*, an Isr.:— On.

204. אוֹן **'Ôwn**, ōne; or (short.);

אֹן **'Ôn**, ōne; of Eg. der.; *On*, a city of Egypt:— On.

205. אָוֶן **'âven**, aw-ven´; from an unused root perh. mean. prop. to *pant* (hence, to *exert* oneself, usually in vain; to *come* to naught); strictly *nothingness*; also *trouble*, *vanity*, *wickedness*; spec. an *idol*:— affliction, evil, false, idol, iniquity, mischief, mourners (-ing), naught, sorrow, unjust, unrighteous, vain ,vanity, wicked (-ness). Comp. 369.

206. אָוֶן **'Âven**, aw´-ven; the same as 205; *idolatry*; *Aven*, the contemptuous synonym of three places, one in Cæle-Syria, one in Egypt (On), and one in Pal. (Bethel):— Aven. See also 204, 1007.

207. אוֹנוֹ **'Ôwnôw**, o-no´; or (short.)

אֹנוֹ **'Ônôw**, o-no´; prol. from 202; *strong*; *Ono*, a place in Pal.:— Ono.

208. אוֹנָם **'Ôwnâm**, o-nawm´; a var. of 209; *strong*; *Onam*, the name of an Edomite and of an Isr.:— Onam.

209. אוֹנָן **'Ôwnân**, o-nawn´; a var. of 207; *strong*; *Onan*, a son of Judah:— Onan.

210. אוּפָז **'Ûwphâz**, oo-fawz´; perh. a corruption of 211; *Uphaz*, a famous gold region:— Uphaz.

211. אוֹפִיר **'Ôwphîyr**, o-feer´; or (short.)

אֹפִיר **'Ôphîyr**, o-feer´; and

אוֹפִר **'Ôwphir**, o-feer´; of uncert. der.; *Ophir*, the name of a son of Joktan, and of a gold region in the East:— Ophir.

212. אוֹפָן **'ôwphân**, o-fawn´; or (short.)

אֹפָן **'ôphân**, o-fawn´; from an unused root mean. to *revolve*; a *wheel*:— wheel.

אוֹפִר **'Ôwphîr**. See 211.

213. אוּץ **'ûwts**, oots; a prim. root; to *press*; (by impl.) to *be close, hurry, withdraw*:— (make) haste (-n, -y), labor, be narrow.

214. אוֹצָר **'ôwtsâr**, o-tsawr´; from 686; a *depository*:— armory, cellar, garner, store (-house), treasure (-house) (-y).

215. אוֹר **'ôwr**, ore; a prim. root; to *be* (caus. *make*) *luminous* (lit. and metaph.):— × break of day, glorious, kindle, (be, en-, give, show) light (-en, -ened), set on fire, shine.

216. אוֹר **'ôwr**, ore; from 215; *illumination* or (concr.) *luminary* (in every sense, incl. *lightning*, *happiness*, etc.):— bright, clear, + day, light (-ning), morning, sun.

217. אוּר **'ûwr**, oor; from 215; *flame*, hence, (in the plur.) the *East* (as being the region of light):— fire, light. See also 224.

218. אוּר **'Ûwr**, oor; the same as 217; *Ur*, a place in Chaldæa; also an Isr.:— Ur.

219. אוֹרָה **'ôwrâh**, o-raw´; fem. of 216; *luminousness*, i.e. (fig.) *prosperity*; also a plant (as being *bright*):— herb, light.

220. אֲוֵרָה **'ăvêrâh**, av-ay-raw´; by transp. for 723; a *stall*:— cote.

221. אוּרִי **'Ûwrîy**, oo-ree´; from 217; *fiery*; *Uri*, the name of three Isr.:— Uri.

222. אוּרִיאֵל **'Ûwrîy'êl**, oo-ree-ale´; from 217 and 410; *flame of God*; *Uriel*, the name of two Isr.:— Uriel.

223. אוּרִיָה **'Ûwrîyâh**, oo-ree-yaw´; or (prol.)

אוּרִיָהוּ **'Ûwrîyâhûw**, oo-ree-yaw´-hoo; from 217 and 3050; *flame of Jah*; *Urijah*, the name of one Hittite and five Isr.:— Uriah, Urijah.

224. אוּרִים **'Ûwrîym**, oo-reem´; plur. of 217; *lights*; *Urim*, the oracular brilliancy of the figures in the high-priest's breastplate:— Urim.

אוֹרְנָה **'Owrenâh**. See 728.

225. אוּת **'ûwth**, ooth; a prim. root; prop. to *come*, i.e. (impl.) to *assent*:— consent.

226. אוֹת **'ôwth**, ōth; prob. from 225 (in the sense of *appearing*); a *signal* (lit. or fig.), as a *flag*, *beacon*, *monument*, *omen*, *prodigy*, *evidence*, etc.:— mark, miracle, (en-) sign, token.

227. אָז **'âz**, awz; a demonstr. adv.; *at that time* or *place*; also a conjunc., *therefore*:— beginning, for, from, hitherto, now, of old, once, since, then, at which time, yet.

228. אֲזָא **'ăzâ'** (Chald.), az-zaw´; or

אֲזָה **'ăzâh** (Chald.), az-aw´; to *kindle*; (by impl.) to *heat*:— heat, hot.

229. אֶזְבַּי **'Ezbay**, ez-bah´ee; prob. from 231; *hyssop-like*; *Ezbai*, an Isr.:— Ezbai.

230. אֲזַד **'ăzad** (Chald.), az-zawd´; of uncert. der.; *firm*:— be gone.

231. אֵזוֹב **'êzôwb**, ay-zobe´; prob. of for. der.; *hyssop*:— hyssop.

232. אֵזוֹר **'êzôwr**, ay-zore´; from 246; something *girt*; a *belt*, also a *band*:— girdle.

233. אֲזַי **'ăzay**, az-ah´ee; prob. from 227; *at that time*:— then.

234. אַזְכָּרָה **'azkârâh**, az-kaw-raw´; from 2142; a *reminder*; spec. *remembrance-offering*:— memorial.

235. אָזַל **'âzal**, aw-zal´; a prim. root; to *go away*, hence, to *disappear*:— fail, gad about, go to and fro [but in Ezek. 27:19 *the word is rendered by many* "from Uzal," *by others* "yarn"], be gone (spent).

236. אֲזַל **'ăzal** (Chald.), az-al´; the same as 235; to *depart*:— go (up).

237. אֵזֶל **'ezel**, eh´-zel; from 235; *depar-

ture; Ezel, a memorial stone in Pal.:— Ezel.

238. אָזַן **'âzan**, *aw-zan´*; a prim. root; prob. to *expand;* but used only as a denom. from 241; to *broaden out the ear* (with the hand), i.e. (by impl.) to *listen:*— give (perceive by the) ear, hear (-ken). See 239.

239. אָזַן **'âzan**, *aw-zan´*; a prim. root [rather ident. with 238 through the idea of *scales* as if two ears]; to *weigh,* i.e. (fig.) *ponder:*— give good head.

240. אָזֵן **'âzên**, *aw-zane´*; from 238; a *spade* or *paddle* (as having a *broad* end):— weapon.

241. אֹזֶן **'ôzen**, *o´-zen;* from 238; *broadness,* i.e. (concr.) the *ear* (from its form in man):— + advertise, audience, + displease, ear, hearing, + show.

242. אֹזֶן שֶׁאֵרָה **'Uzzên She'ërâh**, *oozzane´ sheh-er-aw´;* from 238 and 7609; *plat of Sheerah* (i.e. settled by him); *Uzzen-Sheërah*, a place in Pal.:— Uzzen-sherah.

243. אַזְנוֹת תָּבוֹר **'Aznôwth Tâbôwr**, *aznôth´ taw-bore´;* from 238 and 8396; *flats* (i.e. *tops) of Tabor* (i.e. situated on it); *Aznoth-Tabor*, a place in Pal.:— Aznoth-tabor.

244. אָזְנִי **'Oznîy**, *oz-nee´;* from 241; *having* (quick) *ears; Ozni*, an Isr.; also an *Oznite* (collect.), his desc.:— Ozni, Oznites.

245. אֲזַנְיָה **'Ăzanyâh**, *az-an-yaw´;* from 238 and 3050; *heard by Jah; Azanjah*, an Isr.:— Azaniah.

246. אֲזִקִּים **'ăziqqîym**, *az-ik-keem´;* a var. for 2131; *manacles:*— chains.

247. אָזַר **'âzar**, *aw-zar´;* a prim. root; to *belt:*— bind (compass) about, gird (up, with).

248. אֶזְרוֹעַ **'ezrôwa'**, *ez-ro-´ă;* a var. for 2220; the *arm:*— arm.

249. אֶזְרָח **'ezrâch**, *ez-rawkh´;* from 2224 (in the sense of *springing up*); a spontaneous *growth,* i.e. *native* (tree or persons):— bay tree, (home-) born (in the land), of the (one's own) country (nation).

250. אֶזְרָחִי **'Ezrâchîy**, *ez-raw-khee´;* patron. from 2246; an *Ezrachite* or desc. of Zerach:— Ezrahite.

251. אָח **'âch**, *awkh;* a prim. word; a *brother* (used in the widest sense of lit. relationship and metaph. affinity or resemblance [like 1]):— another, brother (-ly), kindred, like, other. Compare also the proper names beginning with "Ah-" or "Ahi-".

252. אָח **'ach** (Chald.), *akh;* corresp. to 251:— brother.

253. אָח **'âch**, *awkh;* a var. for 162; *Oh!* (expressive of grief or surprise):— ah, alas.

254. אָח **'âch**, *awkh;* of uncert. der.; a fire-*pot* or chafing-dish:— hearth.

255. אֹחַ **'ôach**, *o´-akh;* prob. from 253; a *howler* or lonesome wild animal:— doleful creature.

256. אַחְאָב **'Ach'âb**, *akh-awb´;* once (by contr.)

אֶחָב **'Echâb** (Jer. 29:22), *ekh-awb´;*

from 251 and 1; *brother* [i.e. *friend*] of (his) *father; Achab*, the name of a king of Israel and of a prophet at Bab.:— Ahab.

257. אַחְבָּן **'Achbân**, *akh-bawn´;* from 251 and 995; *brother* (i.e. *possessor) of understanding; Achban*, an Isr.:— Ahban.

258. אָחַד **'âchad**, *aw-khad´;* perh. a prim. root; to *unify,* i.e. (fig.) *collect* (one's thoughts):— go one way or other.

259. אֶחָד **'echâd**, *ekh-awd´;* a numeral from 258; prop. *united,* i.e. *one;* or (as an ord.) *first:*— a, alike, alone, altogether, and, any (-thing), apiece, a certain, [dai-]ly, each (one), + eleven, every, few, first, + highway, a man, once, one, only, other, some, together.

260. אָחוּ **'âchûw**, *aw´-khoo;* of uncert. (perh. Eg.) der.; a *bulrush* or any marshy grass (particularly that along the Nile):— flag, meadow.

261. אֵחוּד **'Êchûwd**, *ay-khood´;* from 258; *united; Echud*, the name of three Isr.:— Ehud.

262. אַחְוָה **'achvâh**, *akh-vaw´;* from 2331 (in the sense of 2324); an *utterance:*— declaration.

263. אַחֲוָה **'achăvâh** (Chald.), *akh-av-aw´;* corresp. to 262; *solution* (of riddles):— showing.

264. אַחֲוָה **'achăvâh**, *akh-av-aw´;* from 251; *fraternity:*— brotherhood.

265. אֲחוֹחַ **'Ăchôwach**, *akh-o´-akh;* by redupl. from 251; *brotherly; Achoach*, an Isr.:— Ahoah.

266. אֲחוֹחִי **'Ăchôwchîy**, *akh-o-khee´;* patron. from 264; an *Achochite* or desc. of Achoach:— Ahohite.

267. אֲחוּמַי **'Ăchûwmay**, *akh-oo-mah´-ee;* perh. from 251 and 4325; *brother* (i.e. *neighbour) of water; Achumai*, an Isr.:— Ahumai.

268. אָחוֹר **'âchôwr**, *aw-khore´;* or (short.)

אָחֹר **'âchôr**, *aw-khore´;* from 299; the *hinder* part; hence, (adv.) *behind, backward;* also (as facing north) the *West:*— after (-ward), back (part, -side, -ward), hereafter, (be-) hind (-er part), time to come, without.

269. אָחוֹת **'âchôwth**, *aw-khôth´;* irreg. fem. of 251; a *sister* (used very widely [like 250], lit. and fig.):— (an-) other, sister, together.

270. אָחַז **'âchaz**, *aw-khaz´;* a prim. root; to *seize* (often with the accessory idea of holding in possession):— + be affrighted, bar, (catch, lay, take) hold (back), come upon, fasten, handle, portion, (get, have or take) possess (-ion).

271. אָחָז **'Âchâz**, *aw-khawz´;* from 270; *possessor; Achaz*, the name of a Jewish king and of an Isr.:— Ahaz.

272. אֲחֻזָּה **'ăchuzzâh**, *akh-ooz-zaw´;* fem. pass. part. from 270; something *seized,* i.e. a *possession* (espec. of land):— possession.

273. אַחְזַי **'Achzay**, *akh-zah´ee;* from 270; *seizer; Achzai*, an Isr.:— Ahasai.

274. אֲחַזְיָה **'Ăchazyâh**, *akh-az-yaw´;* or (prol.)

אֲחַזְיָהוּ **'Ăchazyâhûw**, *akh-az-yaw´-hoo;* from 270 and 3050; *Jah has seized; Achazjah*, the name of a Jewish and an Isr. king:— Ahaziah.

275. אֲחֻזָּם **'Ăchuzzâm**, *akh-ooz-zawm´;* from 270; *seizure; Achuzzam*, an Isr.:— Ahuzam.

276. אֲחֻזַּת **'Ăchuzzath**, *akh-ooz-zath´;* a var. of 272; *possession; Achuzzath*, a Philistine:— Ahuzzath.

277. אֲחִי **'Ăchîy**, *akh-ee´;* from 251; *brotherly; Achi*, the name of two Isr.:— Ahi.

278. אֵחִי **'Êchîy**, *ay-khee´;* prob. the same as 277; *Echi*, an Isr.:— Ehi.

279. אֲחִיאָם **'Ăchîy'âm**, *akh-ee-awm´;* from 251 and 517; *brother of* (the) *mother* (i.e. *uncle); Achiam*, an Isr.:— Ahiam.

280. אֲחִידָה **'ăchîydâh** (Chald.), *akh-ee-daw´;* corresp. to 2420, an *enigma:*— hard sentence.

281. אֲחִיָּה **'Ăchîyâh**, *akh-ee-yaw´;* or (prol.)

אֲחִיָּהוּ **'Ăchîyâhûw**, *akh-ee-yaw´-hoo;* from 251 and 3050; *brother* (i.e. *worshipper) of Jah; Achijah*, the name of nine Isr.:— Ahiah, Ahijah.

282. אֲחִיהוּד **'Ăchîyhûwd**, *akh-ee-hood´;* from 251 and 1935; *brother* (i.e. *possessor) of renown; Achihud*, an Isr.:— Ahihud.

283. אַחְיוֹ **'Achyôw**, *akh-yo´;* prol. from 251; *brotherly; Achio*, the name of three Isr.:— Ahio.

284. אֲחִיחֻד **'Ăchîychud**, *akh-ee-khood´;* from 251 and 2330; *brother of a riddle* (i.e. *mysterious); Achichud*, an Isr.:— Ahihud.

285. אֲחִיטוּב **'Ăchîytûwb**, *akh-ee-toob´;* from 251 and 2898; *brother of goodness; Achitub*, the name of several priests:— Ahitub.

286. אֲחִילוּד **'Ăchîylûwd**, *akh-ee-lood´;* from 251 and 3205; *brother of one born; Achilud*, an Isr.:— Ahilud.

287. אֲחִימוֹת **'Ăchîymôwth**, *akh-ee-môth´;* from 251 and 4191; *brother of death; Achimoth*, an Isr.:— Ahimoth.

288. אֲחִימֶלֶךְ **'Ăchîymelek**, *akh-ee-meh´-lek;* from 251 and 4428; *brother of* (the) *king; Achimelek*, the name of an Isr. and of a Hittite:— Ahimelech.

289. אֲחִימַן **'Ăchîyman**, *akh-ee-man´;* or

אֲחִימָן **'Ăchîymân**, *akh-ee-mawn´;* from 251 and 4480; *brother of a portion* (i.e. *gift); Achiman*, the name of an Anakite and of an Isr.:— Ahiman.

290. אֲחִימַעַץ **'Ăchîyma'ats**, *akh-ee-mah´-ats;* from 251 and the equiv. of 4619; *brother of anger; Achimaats*, the name of three Isr.:— Ahimaaz.

291. אַחְיָן **'Achyân**, *akh-yawn´;* from 251; *brotherly; Achjan*, an Isr.:— Ahian.

292. אֲחִינָדָב **'Ăchîynâdâb**, *akh-ee-nawdawb´;* from 251 and 5068; *brother of liberality; Achinadab*, an Isr.:— Ahinadab.

293. אֲחִינֹעַם **'Ăchîynô'am**, *akh-ee-no´-am;* from 251 and 5278; *brother of pleasantness; Achinoam*, the name of two Israelitesses:— Ahinoam.

294. אֲחִיסָמָךְ 'Ăchîyçâmâk, *akh-ee-saw-mawk'*; from 251 and 5564; *brother of support*; *Achisamak*, an Isr.:— Ahisamach.

295. אֲחִיעֶזֶר 'Ăchîy'ezer, *akh-ee-eh'-zer*; from 251 and 5828; *brother of help*; *Achiezer*, the name of two Isr.:— Ahiezer.

296. אֲחִיקָם 'Ăchîyqâm, *akh-ee-kawm'*; from 251 and 6965; *brother of rising* (i.e. *high*); *Achikam*, an Isr.:— Ahikam.

297. אֲחִירָם 'Ăchîyrâm, *akh-ee-rawm'*; from 251 and 7311; *brother of height* (i.e. *high*); *Achiram*, an Isr.:— Ahiram.

298. אֲחִירָמִי 'Ăchîyrâmîy, *akh-ee-raw-mee'*; patron. from 297; an *Achiramite* or desc. (collect.) of Achiram:— Ahiramites.

299. אֲחִירַע 'Ăchîyra', *akh-ee-rah'*; from 251 and 7451; *brother of wrong*; *Achira*, an Isr.:— Ahira.

300. אֲחִישַׁחַר 'Achiyshachar, *akh-ee-shakh'-ar*; from 251 and 7837; *brother of* (the) *dawn*; *Achishachar*, an Isr.:— Ahishar.

301. אֲחִישָׁר 'Ăchîyshâr, *akh-ee-shawr'*; from 251 and 7891; *brother of* (the) *singer*; *Achishar*, an Isr.:— Ahishar.

302. אֲחִיתֹפֶל 'Ăchîythôphel, *akh-ee-tho'-fel*; from 251 and 8602; *brother of folly*; *Achithophel*, an Isr.:— Ahithophel.

303. אֶחְלָב 'Achlâb, *akh-lawb'*; from the same root as 2459; *fatness* (i.e. *fertile*); *Achlab*, a place in Pal.:— Ahlab.

304. אַחְלַי 'Achlay, *akh-lah'ee*; the same as 305; *wishful*; *Achlai*, the name of an Israelitess and of an Isr.:— Ahlai.

305. אַחְלַי 'achălay, *akh-al-ah'ee*; or

אַחֲלֵי 'achălêy, *akh-al-ay'*; prob. from 253 and a var. of 3863; *would that!*:— O that, would God.

306. אַחְלָמָה 'achlâmâh, *akh-law'-maw*; perh. from 2492 (and thus *dream*-*stone*); a gem, prob. the *amethyst*:— amethyst.

307. אַחְמְתָא 'Achmᵉthâ', *akh-me-thaw'*; of Pers. der.; *Achmetha* (i.e. *Ecbatana*), the summer capital of Persia:— Achmetha.

308. אֲחַסְבַּי 'Ăchaçbay, *akh-as-bah'ee*; of uncert. der.; *Achasbai*, an Isr.:— Ahasbai.

309. אָחַר 'âchar, *aw-khar'*; a prim. root; to *loiter* (i.e. *be behind*); by impl. to *procrastinate*:— continue, defer, delay, hinder, be late (slack), stay (there), tarry (longer).

310. אַחַר 'achar, *akh-ar'*; from 309; prop. the *hind* part; gen. used as an adv. or conjunc., *after* (in various senses):— after (that, -ward), again, at, away from, back (from, -side), behind, beside, by, follow (after, -ing), forasmuch, from, hereafter, hinder end, + out (over) live, + persecute, posterity, pursuing, remnant, seeing, since, thence [-forth], when, with.

311. אַחַר 'achar (Chald.), *akh-ar'*; corresp. to 310; *after*:— [here-] after.

312. אַחֵר 'achêr, *akh-air'*; from 309; prop. *hinder*; gen. *next, other*, etc.:—

(an-) other man, following, next, strange.

313. אַחֵר 'Achêr, *akh-air'*; the same as 312; *Acher*, an Isr.:— Aher.

314. אַחֲרוֹן 'achărôwn, *akh-ar-one'*; or (short.)

אַחֲרֹן 'achărôn, *akh-ar-one'*; from 309; *hinder*; gen. *late* or *last*; spec. (as facing the east) *western*:— after (-ward), to come, following, hind (-er, -ermost, -most), last, latter, rereward, ut(ter)most.

315. אַחְרַח 'Achrach, *akh-rakh'*; from 310 and 251; *after* (his) *brother*; *Achrach*, an Isr.:— Aharah.

316. אַחְרְחֵל 'Ăcharchêl, *akh-ar-kale'*; from 310 and 2426; *behind* (the) *intrenchment* (i.e. *safe*); *Acharchel*, an Isr.:— Aharhel.

317. אָחֳרִי 'ochŏriy (Chald.), *okh-or-ee'*; from 311; *other*:— (an-) other.

318. אָחֳרִין 'ochŏrêyn (Chald.), *okh-or-ane'*; or (short.)

אָחֳרִן 'ochŏrên (Chald.), *okh-or-ane'*; from 317; *last*:— at last.

319. אַחֲרִית 'achăriyth, *akh-ar-eeth'*; from 310; the *last* or *end*, hence, the *future*; also *posterity*:— (last, latter) end (time), hinder (utter) -most, length, posterity, remnant, residue, reward.

320. אַחֲרִית 'achăriyth (Chald.), *akh-ar-eeth'*; from 311; the same as 319; *later*:— latter.

321. אָחֳרָן 'ochŏrân (Chald.), *okh-or-awn'*; from 311; the same as 317; *other*:— (an-) other.

אָחֳרֵן 'ochŏrên. See 318.

322. אֲחֹרַנִּית 'ăchôrannîyth, *akh-o-ran-neeth'*; prol. from 268; *backwards*:— back (-ward), again.

323. אֲחַשְׁדַּרְפָּן 'ăchashdarpan, *akh-ash-dar-pan'*; of Pers. der.; a *satrap* or governor of a main province (of Persia):— lieutenant.

324. אֲחַשְׁדַּרְפָּן 'ăchashdarpan (Chald.), *akh-ash-dar-pan'*; corresp. to 323:— prince.

325. אֲחַשְׁוֵרוֹשׁ 'Ăchashvêrôwsh, *akh-ash-vay-rosh'*; or (short.)

אֲחַשְׁרֹשׁ 'Achashrôsh, *akh-ash-rosh'* (Esth. 10:1); of Pers. or.; *Achashverosh* (i.e. Ahasuerus or Artaxerxes, but in this case Xerxes), the title (rather than name) of a Pers. king:— Ahasuerus.

326. אֲחַשְׁתָּרִי 'ăchashtâriy, *akh-ash-taw-ree'*; prob. of Pers. der.; an *achastarite* (i.e. *courier*); the designation (rather than name) of an Isr.:— Haakashtari [includ. the art.].

327. אֲחַשְׁתָּרָן 'ăchastârân, *akh-ash-taw-rawn'*; of Pers. or.; a *mule*:— camel.

328. אַט 'at, *at*; from an unused root perh. mean. to *move softly*; (as a noun) a *necromancer* (from their soft incantations), (as an adv.) *gently*:— charmer, gently, secret, softly.

329. אָטָד 'âṭâd, *aw-tawd'*; from an unused root prob. mean. to *pierce* or *make fast*; a *thorn*-tree (espec. the *buckthorn*):— Atad, bramble, thorn.

330. אֵטוּן 'êṭûwn, *ay-toon'*; from an unused root (prob. mean. to *bind*); prop. *twisted* (yarn), i.e. *tapestry*:— fine linen.

331. אָטַם 'âṭam, *aw-tam'*; a prim. root; to *close* (the lips or ears); by anal. to *contract* (a window by bevelled jambs):— narrow, shut, stop.

332. אָטַר 'âṭar, *aw-tar'*; a prim. root; to *close* up:— shut.

333. אָטֵר 'Âṭêr, *aw-tare'*; from 332; *maimed*; *Ater*, the name of three Isr.:— Ater.

334. אִטֵּר 'iṭṭêr, *it-tare'*; from 332; *shut* up, i.e. *impeded* (as to the use of the right hand):— + left-handed.

335. אֵי 'ay, *ah'ee*; perh. from 370; *where?* hence, *how?*:— how, what, whence, where, whether, which (way).

336. אִי 'îy, *ee*; prob. ident. with 335 (through the idea of a *query*); *not*:— island (Job 22:30).

337. אִי 'îy, *ee*; short. from 188; *alas!*:— woe.

338. אִי 'îy, *ee*; prob. ident. with 337 (through the idea of a *doleful* sound); a *howler* (used only in the plur.), i.e. any solitary wild creature:— wild beast of the islands.

339. אִי 'îy, *ee*; from 183; prop. a *habitable* spot (as *desirable*); dry *land*, a *coast*, an *island*:— country, isle, island.

340. אָיַב 'âyab, *aw-yab'*; a prim. root; to *hate* (as one of an opposite tribe or party); hence, to *be hostile*:— be an enemy.

341. אֹיֵב 'ôyêb, *o-yabe'*; or (fully)

אוֹיֵב 'ôwyêb, *o-yabe'*; act. part. of 340; *hating*; an *adversary*:— enemy, foe.

342. אֵיבָה 'êybâh, *ay-baw'*; from 340; *hostility*:— enmity, hatred.

343. אֵיד 'êyd, *ade*; from the same as 181 (in the sense of *bending* down); *oppression*; by impl. *misfortune, ruin*:— calamity, destruction.

344. אַיָּה 'ayâh, *ah-yaw'*; perh. from 337; the *screamer*, i.e. a *hawk*:— kite, vulture.

345. אַיָּה 'Ayâh, *ah-yaw'*; the same as 344; *Ajah*, the name of two Isr.:— Aiah, Ajah.

346. אַיֵּה 'ayêh, *ah-yay'*; prol. from 335; *where?*:— where.

347. אִיּוֹב 'Îyôwb, *ee-yobe'*; from 340; *hated* (i.e. *persecuted*); *Ijob*, the patriarch famous for his patience:— Job.

348. אִיזֶבֶל 'Îyzebel, *ee-zeh'-bel*; from 336 and 2083; *chaste*; *Izebel*, the wife of king Ahab:— Jezebel.

349. אֵיךְ 'êyk, *ake*; also

אֵיכָה 'êykâh, *ay-kaw'*; and

אֵיכָכָה 'êykâkâh, *ay-kaw'-kah*; prol. from 335; *how?* or *how!*; also *where*:— how, what.

350. אִי־כָבוֹד 'Îy-kâbôwd, *ee-kaw-bode'*; from 336 and 3519; (there is) *no glory*, i.e. *inglorious*; *Ikabod*, a son of Phineas:— I-chabod.

351. אֵיכֹה 'êykôh, *ay-kō*; prob. a var. for

349, but not as an interrogative; *where*:— where.

אֵיכָה **'êykâh**;

אֵיכָכָה **'êykâkâh**. See 349.

352. אֵיל **'ayîl**, *ah´-yil*; from the same as 193; prop. *strength*; spec. a *chief* (politically); also a *ram* (from his strength); an *oak* or other strong tree:— mighty (man), lintel, oak, post, ram, tree.

353. אֵיל **'êyâl**, *eh-yawl´*; a var. of 352; *strength*:— strength.

354. אֵיל **'ayâl**, *ah-yawl´*; an intens. form of 352 (in the sense of *ram*); a *stag* or male deer:— hart.

355. אֵילָה **'ayâlâh**, *ah-yaw-law´*; fem. of 354; a *doe* or female deer:— hind.

356. אֵילוֹן **'Êylôwn**, *ay-lone´*; or (short.)

אֵילֹן **'Êlôn**, *ay-lone´*; or

אֵילוֹן **'Êylôn**; from 352; *oak-grove*; *Elon*, the name of a place in Pal., and also of one Hittite, two Isr.:— Elon.

357. אַיָּלוֹן **'Ayâlôwn**, *ah-yaw-lone´*; from 354; *deer-field*; *Ajalon*, the name of five places in Pal.:— Aijalon, Ajalon.

358. אֵילוֹן בֵּית חָנָן **'Êylôwn Bêyth Chânân**, *ay-lone´ bayth chaw-nawn´*; from 356, 1004, and 2603; *oak-grove of* (the) *house of favor*; *Elon of Beth-chanan*, a place in Pal.:— Elon-beth-hanan.

359. אֵילוֹת **'Êylôwth**, *ay-lôth´*; or

אֵילַת **'Êylath**, *ay-lath´*; from 352; *trees* or a *grove* (i.e. palms); *Eloth* or *Elath*, a place on the Red Sea:— Elath, Eloth.

360. אֵילוּת **'êyâlûwth**, *eh-yaw-looth´*; fem. of 353; *power*; by impl. *protection*:— strength.

361. אֵילָם **'êylâm**, *ay-lawm´*; or (short.)

אֵלָם **'êlâm**, *ay-lawm´*; or (fem.)

אֵלַמָּה **'êlammâh**, *ay-lam-maw´*; prob. from 352; a *pillar-space* (or colonnade), i.e. a *pale* (or portico):— arch.

362. אֵלִם **'Êylim**, *ay-leem´*; plur. of 352; *palm-trees*; *Elim*, a place in the Desert:— Elim.

363. אִילָן **'îylân** (Chald.), *ee-lawn´*; corresp. to 356; a *tree*:— tree.

364. אֵיל פָּארָן **'Êyl Pâ'rân**, *ale paw-rawn´*; from 352 and 6290; *oak of Paran*; *El-Paran*, a portion of the district of Paran:— El-paran.

אֵילֹן **'Êylôn**. See 356.

365. אַיֶּלֶת **'ayeleth**, *ah-yeh´-leth*; the same as 355; a *doe*:— hind, Aijeleth.

אַיִם **'ayim**. See 368.

366. אָיֹם **'âyôm**, *aw-yome´*; from an unused root (mean. to *frighten*); *frightful*:— terrible.

367. אֵימָה **'êymâh**, *ay-maw´*; or (short.)

אֵמָה **'êmah**, *ay-maw´*; from the same as 366; *fright*; concr. an *idol* (as a bugbear):— dread, fear, horror, idol, terrible, terror.

368. אֵימִים **'Êymîym**, *ay-meem´*; plur. of 367; *terrors*; *Emim*, an early Canaanitish (or Moabitish) tribe:— Emims.

369. אַיִן **'ayin**, *ah´-yin*; as if from a prim.

root mean. to *be nothing* or *not exist*; a *non-entity*; gen. used as a neg. particle:— else, except, fail, [father-]less, be gone, in[-curable], neither, never, no (where), none, nor, (any, thing), not, nothing, to nought, past, un[-searchable], well-nigh, without. Comp. 370.

370. אַיִן **'ayin**, *ah´-yin*; prob. ident. with 369 in the sense of *query* (comp. 336); *where*? (only in connection with prep. pref., *whence*):— whence, where.

371. אַיִן **'îyn**, *een*; appar. a short. form of 369; but (like 370) interrog.; is it *not*?:— not.

372. אִיעֶזֶר **'Îy'ezer**, *ee-eh´-zer*; from 336 and 5828; *helpless*; *Iezer*, an Isr.:— Jeezer.

373. אִיעֶזְרִי **'Îy'ezrîy**, *ee-ez-ree´*; patron. from 372; an *Iezrite* or desc. of Iezer:— Jezerite.

374. אֵיפָה **'êyphâh**, *ay-faw´*; or (short.)

אֵפָה **'êphâh**, *ay-faw´*; of Eg. der.; an *ephah* or measure for grain; hence, a *measure* in gen.:— ephah, (divers) measure (-s).

375. אֵיפֹה **'êyphôh**, *ay-fo´*; from 335 and 6311; *what place?*; also (of time) *when?*; or (of means) *how?*:— what manner, where.

376. אִישׁ **'îysh**, *eesh*; contr. for 582 [or perh. rather from an unused root mean. to *be extant*]; a *man* as an individual or a male person; often used as an adjunct to a more def. term (and in such cases frequently not expressed in translation):— also, another, any (man), a certain, + champion, consent, each, every (one), fellow, [foot-, husband-] man, (good-, great, mighty) man, he, high (degree), him (that is), husband, man [-kind], + none, one, people, person, + steward, what (man) soever, whoso (-ever), worthy. Comp. 802.

377. אִישׁ **'îysh**, *eesh*; denom. from 376; to *be a man*, i.e. act in a manly way:— show (one) self a man.

378. אִישׁ־בֹּשֶׁת **'Îysh-Bôsheth**, *eesh-bo´-sheth*; from 376 and 1322; *man of shame*; *Ish-Bosheth*, a son of King Saul:— Ish-bosheth.

379. אִישְׁהוֹד **'Îyshhôwd**, *eesh-hode´*; from 376 and 1935; *man of renown*; *Ishod*, an Isr.:— Ishod.

380. אִישׁוֹן **'îyshôwn**, *ee-shone´*; dimin. from 376; the *little man* of the eye; the *pupil* or *ball*; hence, the *middle* (of night):— apple [of the eye], black, obscure.

אִישׁ־חַי **'Îysh-Chay**. See 381.

381. אִישׁ־חַיִל **'Îysh-Chayil**, *eesh-khah´-yil*; from 376 and 2428; *man of might*; by defect. transc. (2 Sam. 23:20)

אִישׁ־חַי **'Îysh-Chay**, *eesh-khah´-ee*; as if from 376 and 2416; *living man*; *Ish-chail* (or *Ish-chai*), an Isr.:— a valiant man.

382. אִישׁ־טוֹב **'Îysh-Tôwb**, *eesh-tobe´*; from 376 and 2897; *man of Tob*; *Ish-Tob*, a place in Pal.:— Ish-tob.

אִישַׁי **'Îshay**. See 3448.

אִיתוֹן **'îythôwn**. See 2978.

383. אִיתַי **'îythay** (Chald.), *ee-thah´ee*; corresp. to 3426; prop. *entity*; used only as a particle of affirmation, there *is*:— art thou, can, do ye, have, it be, there is (are), × we will not.

384. אִיתִיאֵל **'Îythîy'êl**, *eeth-ee-ale´*; perh. from 837 and 410; *God has arrived*; *Ithiel*, the name of an Isr., also of a symb. person:— Ithiel.

385. אִיתָמָר **'Îythâmâr**, *eeth-aw-mawr´*; from 339 and 8558; *coast of* the *palm-tree*; *Ithamar*, a son of Aaron:— Ithamar.

386. אֵיתָן **'êythân**, *ay-thawn´*; or (short.)

אֵתָן **'êthân**, *ay-thawn´*; from an unused root (mean. to *continue*); *permanence*; hence, (concr.) *permanent*; spec. a *chieftain*:— hard, mighty, rough, strength, strong.

387. אֵיתָן **'Êythân**, *ay-thawn´*; the same as 386; *permanent*; *Ethan*, the name of four Isr.:— Ethan.

388. אֵיתָנִים **Êythânîym**, *ay-thaw-neem´*; plur. of 386; always with the art.; the *permanent* brooks; *Ethanim*, the name of a month:— Ethanim.

389. אַךְ **'ak**, *ak*; akin to 403; a particle of affirmation, *surely*; hence, (by limitation) *only*:— also, in any wise, at least, but, certainly, even, howbeit, nevertheless, notwithstanding, only, save, surely, of a surety, truly, verily, + wherefore, yet (but).

390. אַכַּד **'Akkad**, *ak-kad´*; from an unused root prob. mean. to *strengthen*; a *fortress*; *Accad*, a place in Bab.:— Accad.

391. אַכְזָב **'akzâb**, *ak-zawb´*; from 3576; *falsehood*; by impl. *treachery*:— liar, lie.

392. אַכְזִיב **'Akzîyb**, *ak-zeeb´*; from 391; *deceitful* (in the sense of a winter-torrent which *fails* in summer); *Akzib*, the name of two places in Pal.:— Achzib.

393. אַכְזָר **'akzâr**, *ak-zawr´*; from an unused root (appar. mean. to *act harshly*); *violent*; by impl. *deadly*; also (in a good sense) *brave*:— cruel, fierce.

394. אַכְזָרִי **'akzârîy**, *ak-zaw-ree´*; from 393; *terrible*:— cruel (one).

395. אַכְזְרִיּוּת **'akzerîyûwth**, *ak-ze-ree-ooth´*; from 394; *fierceness*:— cruel.

396. אֲכִילָה **'ăkîylâh**, *ak-ee-law´*; fem. from 398; something *eatable*, i.e. *food*:— meat.

397. אָכִישׁ **'Âkîysh**, *aw-keesh´*; of uncert. der.; *Akish*, a Philistine king:— Achish.

398. אָכַל **'âkal**, *aw-kal´*; a prim. root; to *eat* (lit. or fig.):— × at all, burn up, consume, devour (-er, up), dine, eat (-er, up), feed (with), food, × freely, × in ... wise (-deed, plenty), (lay) meat, × quite.

399. אֲכַל **'ăkal** (Chald.), *ak-al´*; corresp. to 398:— + accuse, devour, eat.

400. אֹכֶל **'ôkel**, *o´-kel*; from 398; *food*:— eating, food, meal [-time], meat, prey, victuals.

401. אֻכָל **'Ûkâl**, *oo-kawl´*; or

אֻכָּל **'Ukkâl**, *ook-kawl´*; appar. from 398; *devoured*; *Ucal*, a fancy name:— Ucal.

402. אָכְלָה **'oklâh**, *ok-law´*; fem. of 401;

food:— consume, devour, eat, food, meat.

403. אָכֵן **'âkên,** *aw-kane´*; from 3559 [comp. 3651]; *firmly;* fig. *surely;* also (advers.) *but:*— but, certainly, nevertheless, surely, truly, verily.

404. אָכַף **'âkaph,** *aw-kaf´;* a prim. root; appar. mean. *to curve* (as with a burden); to *urge:*— crave.

405. אֶכֶף **'ekeph,** *eh´-kef;* from 404; a *load;* by impl. a *stroke* (others *dignity*):— hand.

406. אִכָּר **'ikkâr,** *ik-kawr´;* from an unused root mean. to *dig;* a *farmer:*— husbandman, ploughman.

407. אַכְשָׁף **'Akshâph,** *ak-shawf´;* from 3784; *fascination; Acshaph,* a place in Pal.:— Achshaph.

408. אַל **'al,** *al;* a neg. particle [akin to 3808]; *not* (the qualified negation, used as a deprecative); once (Job 24:25) as a noun, *nothing:*— nay, neither, + never, no, nor, not, nothing [worth], rather than.

409. אַל **'al** (Chald.), *al;* corresp. to 408:— not.

410. אֵל **'êl,** *ale;* short. from 352; *strength;* as adj. *mighty;* espec. the *Almighty* (but used also of any *deity*):— God (god), × goodly, × great, idol, might (-y one), power, strong. Comp. names in "-el."

411. אֵל **'êl,** *ale;* a demonstr. particle (but only in a plur. sense) *these* or *those:*— these, those. Comp. 428.

412. אֵל **'êl** (Chald.), *ale;* corresp. to 411:— these.

413. אֵל **'êl,** *ale;* (but only used in the short. constr. form

     אֶל **'el,** *el);* a prim. particle; prop. denoting motion *towards,* but occasionally used of a quiescent position, i.e. *near, with* or *among;* often in general, *to:*— about, according to, after, against, among, as for, at, because (-fore, -side), both ... and, by, concerning, for, from, × hath, in (-to), near, (out) of, over, through, to (-ward), under, unto, upon, whether, with (-in).

414. אֵלָא **'Êlâ,** *ay-law´;* a var. of 424; *oak; Ela,* an Isr.:— Elah.

415. אֵל אֱלֹהֵי יִשְׂרָאֵל **'Êl 'ĕlôhêy Yisrâ'êl,** *ale el-o-hay´ yis-raw-ale´;* from 410 and 430 and 3478; the *mighty God of Jisrael; El-Elohi-Jisrael,* the title given to a consecrated spot by Jacob:— El-elohe-israel.

416. אֵל בֵּית־אֵל **'Êl Bêyth-'Êl,** *ale bayth-ale´;* from 410 and 1008; the *God of Bethel; El-Bethel,* the title given to a consecrated spot by Jacob:— El-beth-el.

417. אֶלְגָּבִישׁ **'elgâbîysh,** *el-gaw-beesh´;* from 410 and 1378; *hail* (as if a *great pearl*):— great hail [-stones].

418. אַלְגּוּמִּים **'algûwmmîym,** *al-goom-meem´;* by transp. for 484; sticks of *algum* wood:— algum [trees].

419. אֶלְדָּד **'Eldâd,** *el-dâd´;* from 410 and 1730; *God has loved; Eldad,* an Isr.:— Eldad.

420. אֶלְדָּעָה **'Eldâ'âh,** *el-daw-aw´;* from 410 and 3045; *God of knowledge; Eldaah,* a son of Midian:— Eldaah.

421. אָלָה **'âlâh,** *aw-law´;* a prim. root [rather ident. with 422 through the idea of *invocation*]; to *bewail:*— lament.

422. אָלָה **'âlâh,** *aw-law´;* a prim. root; prop. to *adjure,* i.e. (usually in a bad sense) *imprecate:*— adjure, curse, swear.

423. אָלָה **'âlâh,** *aw-law´;* from 422; an *imprecation:*— curse, cursing, execration, oath, swearing.

424. אֵלָה **'êlâh,** *ay-law´;* fem. of 352; an *oak* or other strong tree:— elm, oak, teil tree.

425. אֵלָה **'Êlâh,** *ay-law´;* the same as 424; *Elah,* the name of an Edomite, of four Isr., and also of a place in Pal.:— Elah.

426. אֱלָהּ **'ĕlâhh** (Chald.), *el-aw´;* corresp. to 433; *God:*— God, god.

427. אַלָּה **'allâh,** *al-law´;* a var. of 424:— oak.

428. אֵלֶּה **'êl-leh,** *ale´-leh;* prol. from 411; *these* or *those:*— an(the) other; one sort, so, some, such, them, these (same), they, this, those, thus, which, who (-m).

429. אֵלֶּה **'êlleh** (Chald.), *ale´-leh;* corresp. to 428:— these.

אֱלֹהַּ **'ĕlôahh.** See 433.

430. אֱלֹהִים **'ĕlôhîym,** *el-o-heem´;* plur. of 433; *gods* in the ordinary sense; but spec. used (in the plur. thus, espec. with the art.) of the supreme *God;* occasionally applied by way of deference to *magistrates;* and sometimes as a superlative:— angels, × exceeding, God (gods) (-dess, -ly), × (very) great, judges, × mighty.

431. אֲלוּ **'ălûw** (Chald.), *al-oo´;* prob. prol. from 412; *lo!:*— behold.

432. אִלּוּ **'illûw,** *il-loo´;* prob. from 408; *nay,* i.e. (softened) *if:*— but if, yea though.

433. אֱלוֹהַּ **'ĕlôwahh,** *el-o´-ah;* rarely (short.)

     אֱלֹהַּ **'ĕlôahh,** *el-o´-ah;* prob. prol. (emphat.) from 410; a *deity* or the *Deity:*— God, god. See 430.

434. אֱלוּל **'ĕlûwl,** *el-ool´;* for 457; good for *nothing:*— thing of nought.

435. אֱלוּל **'Ĕlûwl,** *el-ool´;* prob. of for. der.; *Elul,* the sixth Jewish month:— Elul.

436. אֵלוֹן **'êlôwn,** *ay-lone´;* prol. from 352; an *oak* or other strong tree:— plain. See also 356.

437. אַלּוֹן **'allôwn,** *al-lone´;* a var. of 436:— oak.

438. אַלּוֹן **'Allôwn,** *al-lone´;* the same as 437; *Allon,* an Isr., also a place in Pal.:— Allon.

439. אַלּוֹן בָּכוּת **'Allôwn Bâkûwth,** *al-lone´ baw-kooth´;* from 437 and a var. of 1068; *oak of weeping; Allon-Bakuth,* a monumental tree:— Allon-bachuth.

440. אֱלוֹנִי **'Êlôwnîy,** *ay-lo-nee´;* or rather (short.)

     אֵלֹנִי **'Êlônîy,** *ay-lo-nee´;* patron. from 438; an *Elonite* or desc. (collect.) of Elon:— Elonites.

441. אַלּוּף **'allûwph,** *al-loof´;* or (short.)

     אַלֻּף **'allûph,** *al-loof´;* from 502; *familiar;* a *friend,* also *gentle;* hence, a *bullock* (as being tame; applied, although masc., to a *cow*); and so, a *chieftain* (as notable, like neat cattle):— captain, duke, (chief) friend, governor, guide, ox.

442. אָלוּשׁ **'Âlûwsh,** *aw-loosh´;* of uncert. der.; *Alush,* a place in the Desert:— Alush.

443. אֶלְזָבָד **'Elzâbâd,** *el-zaw-bawd´;* from 410 and 2064; *God has bestowed; Elzabad,* the name of two Isr.:— Elzabad.

444. אָלַח **'âlach,** *aw-lakh´;* a prim. root; to *muddle,* i.e. (fig. and intr.) to *turn* (morally) *corrupt:*— become filthy.

445. אֶלְחָנָן **'Elchânân,** *el-khaw-nawn´;* from 410 and 2603; *God (is) gracious; Elchanan,* an Isr.:— Elkanan.

אֱלִי **'Êlîy.** See 1017.

446. אֱלִיאָב **'Ĕlîy'âb,** *el-ee-awb´;* from 410 and 1; *God of (his) father; Eliab,* the name of six Isr.:— Eliab.

447. אֱלִיאֵל **'Ĕlîy'êl,** *el-ee-ale´;* from 410 repeated; *God of (his) God; Eliel,* the name of nine Isr.:— Eliel.

448. אֱלִיאָתָה **'Ĕlîy'âthâh,** *el-ee-aw-thaw´;* or (contr.)

     אֱלִיָתָה **'Ĕlîyâthâh,** *el-ee-aw-thaw´;* from 410 and 225; *God of (his) consent; Eliathah,* an Isr.:— Eliathah.

449. אֱלִידָד **'Ĕlîydâd,** *el-ee-dawd´;* from the same as 419; *God of (his) love; Elidad,* an Isr.:— Elidad.

450. אֶלְיָדָע **'Elyâdâ',** *el-yaw-daw´;* from 410 and 3045; *God (is) knowing; Eljada,* the name of two Isr. and of an Aramaean leader:— Eliada.

451. אַלְיָה **'alyâh,** *al-yaw´;* from 422 (in the orig. sense of *strength*); the *stout* part, i.e. the fat *tail* of the Oriental sheep:— rump.

452. אֵלִיָּה **'Êlîyâh,** *ay-lee-yaw´;* or prol.

     אֵלִיָּהוּ **'Êlîyâhûw,** *ay-lee-yaw´-hoo;* from 410 and 3050; *God of Jehovah; Elijah,* the name of the famous prophet and of two other Isr.:— Elijah, Eliah.

453. אֱלִיהוּ **'Êlîyhûw,** *el-ee-hoo´;* or (fully)

     אֱלִיהוּא **'Êlîyhûw',** *el-ee-hoo´;* from 410 and 1931; *God of him; Elihu,* the name of one of Job's friends, and of three Isr.:— Elihu.

454. אֶלְיְהוֹעֵינַי **'Ely°hôw'êynay,** *el-ye-ho-ay-nah´ee;* or (short.)

     אֶלְיוֹעֵינַי **'Elyôw'êynay,** *el-yo-ay-nah´ee;* from 413 and 3068 and 5869; *toward Jehovah (are) my eyes; Eljehoenai* or *Eljoenai,* the name of seven Isr.:— Elihoenai, Elionai.

455. אֶלְיַחְבָּא **'Elyachbâ',** *el-yakh-baw´;* from 410 and 2244; *God will hide; Eljachba,* an Isr.:— Eliahbah.

456. אֱלִיחֹרֶף **'Êlîychôreph,** *el-ee-kho´-ref;* from 410 and 2779; *God of autumn; Elichoreph,* an Isr.:— Elihoreph.

457. אֱלִיל **'ĕlîyl,** *el-eel´;* appar. from 408; good for *nothing,* by anal. *vain* or *vanity;* spec. an *idol:*— idol, no value, thing of nought.

458. אֱלִימֶלֶךְ **'Ĕlîymelek**, *el-ee-meh´-lek*; from 410 and 4428; *God of* (the) *king; Elimelek*, an Isr.:— Elimelech.

459. אִלֵּין **'illêyn** (Chald.), *il-lane´*; or short.

אִלֵּן **'illên**, *il-lane´*; prol. from 412; *these:*— the, these.

460. אֶלְיָסָף **'Ĕlyâçâph**, *el-yaw-sawf´*; from 410 and 3254; *God* (is) *gatherer; Eljasaph*, the name of two Isr.:— Eliasaph.

461. אֱלִיעֶזֶר **'Ĕlîy'ezer**, *el-ee-eh´-zer*; from 410 and 5828; *God of help; Eliezer*, the name of a Damascene and of ten Isr.:— Eliezer.

462. אֱלִיעֵינַי **'Ĕlîy'êynay**, *el-ee-ay-nah´ee*; prob. contr. for 454; *Elienai*, an Isr.:— Elienai.

463. אֱלִיעָם **'Ĕlîy'âm**, *el-ee-awm´*; from 410 and 5971; *God of* (the) *people; Eliam*, an Isr.:— Eliam.

464. אֱלִיפַז **'Ĕlîyphaz**, *el-ee-faz´*; from 410 and 6337; *God of gold; Eliphaz*, the name of one of Job's friends, and of a son of Esau:— Eliphaz.

465. אֱלִיפָל **'Ĕlîyphâl**, *el-ee-fawl´*; from 410 and 6419; *God of judgment; Eliphal*, an Isr.:— Eliphal.

466. אֱלִיפְלֵהוּ **'Ĕlîyphᵉlêhûw**, *el-ee-fe-lay´-hoo*; from 410 and 6395; *God of his distinction; Eliphelehu*, an Isr.:— Elipheleh.

467. אֱלִיפֶלֶט **'Ĕlîyphelet**, *el-ee-feh´-let*; or (short.)

אֶלְפֶלֶט **'Elpelet**, *el-peh´-let*; from 410 and 6405; *God of deliverance; Eliphalet* or *Elpelet*, the name of six Isr.:— Eliphalet, Eliphelet, Elpalet.

468. אֱלִיצוּר **'Ĕlîytsûwr**, *el-ee-tsoor´*; from 410 and 6697; *God of* (the) *rock; Elitsur*, an Isr.:— Elizur.

469. אֱלִיצָפָן **'Ĕlîytsâphân**, *el-ee-tsaw-fawn´*; or (short.)

אֶלְצָפָן **'Eltsâphân**, *el-tsaw-fawn´*; from 410 and 6845; *God of treasure; Elitsaphan* or *Eltsaphan*, an Isr.:— Elizaphan, Elzaphan.

470. אֱלִיקָא **'Ĕlîyqâ**, *el-ee-kaw´*; from 410 and 6958; *God of rejection; Elika*, an Isr.:— Elika.

471. אֶלְיָקִים **'Ĕlyâqîym**, *el-yaw-keem´*; from 410 and 6965; *God of raising; Eljakim*, the name of four Isr.:— Eliakim.

472. אֱלִישֶׁבַע **'Ĕlîysheba'**, *el-ee-sheh´-bah*; from 410 and 7651 (in the sense of 7650); *God of* (the) *oath; Elisheba*, the wife of Aaron:— Elisheba.

473. אֱלִישָׁה **'Ĕlîyshâh**, *el-ee-shaw´*; prob. of for. der.; *Elishah*, a son of Javan:— Elishah.

474. אֱלִישׁוּעַ **'Ĕlîyshûwa**, *el-ee-shoo´-ah*; from 410 and 7769; *God of supplication* (or *of riches*); *Elishua*, a son of King David:— Elishua.

475. אֶלְיָשִׁיב **'Ĕlyâshîyb**, *el-yaw-sheeb´*; from 410 and 7725; *God will restore; Eljashib*, the name of six Isr.:— Eliashib.

476. אֱלִישָׁמָע **'Ĕlîyshâmâ**, *el-ee-shaw-maw´*; from 410 and 8085; *God of hear-*

ing; Elishama, the name of seven Isr.:— Elishama.

477. אֱלִישָׁע **'Ĕlîyshâ'**, *el-ee-shaw´*; contr. for 474; *Elisha*, the famous prophet:— Elisha.

478. אֱלִישָׁפָט **'Ĕlîyshâphât**, *el-ee-shaw-fawt´*; from 410 and 8199; *God of judgment; Elishaphat*, an Isr.:— Elishaphat.

אֱלִיָּתָה **'Ĕlîyâthâh**. See 448.

479. אִלֵּךְ **'illêk** (Chald.), *il-lake´*; prol. from 412; *these:*— these, those.

480. אֲלַי **'al'lay**, *al-le-lah´ee*; by redupl. from 421; *alas!*— woe.

481. אָלַם **'âlam**, *aw-lam´*; a prim. root; to *tie* fast; hence, (of the mouth) to be *tongue-tied:*— bind, be dumb, put to silence.

482. אֵלֶם **'êlem**, *ay´-lem*; from 481; *silence* (i.e. mute justice):— congregation. Comp. 3128.

אֵלָם **'êlâm**. See 361.

אֻלָם **'âlûm**. See 485.

483. אִלֵּם **'illêm**, *il-lame´*; from 481; *speechless:*— dumb (man).

484. אַלְמֻגִּים **'almuggiym**, *al-moog-gheem´*; prob. of for. der. (used thus only in the plur.); *almug* (i.e. prob. sandal-wood) *sticks:*— almug trees. Comp. 418.

485. אֲלֻמָּה **'ălummâh**, *al-oom-maw´*; or (masc.)

אֱלֻם **'âlûm**, *aw-loom´*; pass. part. of 481; something *bound*; a *sheaf:*— sheaf.

486. אַלְמוֹדָד **'Almôwdâd**, *al-mo-dawd´*; prob. of for. der.; *Almodad*, a son of Joktan:— Almodad.

487. אַלַּמֶּלֶךְ **'Allammelek**, *al-lam-meh´-lek*; from 427 and 4428; *oak of* (the) *king; Allammelek*, a place in Pal.:— Alammelech.

488. אַלְמָן **'almân**, *al-mawn´*; prol. from 481 in the sense of *bereavement; discarded* (as a divorced person):— forsaken.

489. אַלְמֹן **'almôn**, *al-mone´*; from 481 as in 488; *bereavement:*— widowhood.

490. אַלְמָנָה **'almânâh**, *al-maw-naw´*; fem. of 488; a *widow*; also a *desolate* place:— desolate house (palace), widow.

491. אַלְמָנוּת **'almânûwth**, *al-maw-nooth´*; fem. of 488; concr. a *widow*; abstr. *widowhood:*— widow, widowhood.

492. אַלְמֹנִי **'almônîy**, *al-mo-nee´*; from 489 in the sense of *concealment; some* one (i.e. *so and so*, without giving the name of the person or place):— one, and such.

אִלֵּן **'illên**. See 459.

אֵלֹנִי **'Êlônîy**. See 440.

493. אֶלְנַעַם **'Elna'am**, *el-nah´-am*; from 410 and 5276; *God* (is his) *delight; El-naam*, an Isr.:— Elnaam.

494. אֶלְנָתָן **'Elnâthân**, *el-naw-thawn´*; from 410 and 5414; *God* (is the) *giver; Elnathan*, the name of four Isr.:— Elnathan.

495. אֶלָּסָר **'Ellâçâr**, *el-law-sawr´*; prob. of for. der.; *Ellasar*, an early country of Asia:— Ellasar.

496. אֶלְעָד **'El'âd**, *el-awd´*; from 410 and 5749; *God has testified; Elad*, an Isr.:— Elead.

497. אֶלְעָדָה **'El'âdâh**, *el-aw-daw´*; from 410 and 5710; *God has decked; Eladah*, an Isr.:— Eladah.

498. אֶלְעוּזַי **'El'ûwzay**, *el-oo-zah´ee*; from 410 and 5756 (in the sense of 5797); *God* (is) *defensive; Eluzai*, an Isr.:— Eluzai.

499. אֶלְעָזָר **'El'âzâr**, *el-aw-zawr´*; from 410 and 5826; *God* (is) *helper; Elazar*, the name of seven Isr.:— Eleazar.

500. אֶלְעָלֵא **'El'âlê**, *el-aw-lay´*; or (more prop.)

אֶלְעָלֵה **'El'âlêh**, *el-aw-lay´*; from 410 and 5927; *God* (is) *going up; Elale* or *Elaleh*, a place east of the Jordan:— Elealeh.

501. אֶלְעָשָׂה **'El'âsâh**, *el-aw-saw´*; from 410 and 6213; *God has made; Elasah*, the name of four Isr.:— Elasah, Eleasah.

502. אָלַף **'âlaph**, *aw-laf´*; a prim. root, to *associate* with; hence, to *learn* (and caus. to *teach*):— learn, teach, utter.

503. אָלַף **'âlaph**, *aw-laf´*; denom. from 505; caus. to *make a thousandfold:*— bring forth thousands.

504. אֶלֶף **'eleph**, *eh´-lef*; from 502; a *family*; also (from the sense of *yoking* or *taming*) an *ox* or *cow:*— family, kine, oxen.

505. אֶלֶף **'eleph**, *eh´-lef*; prop. the same as 504; hence, (the ox's head being the first letter of the alphabet, and this eventually used as a numeral) a *thousand:*— thousand.

506. אֲלַף **'ălaph** (Chald.), *al-af´*; or

אֶלֶף **'eleph** (Chald.), *eh´-lef*; corresp. to 505:— thousand.

507. אֶלֶף **'Eleph**, *eh´-lef*; the same as 505; *Eleph*, a place in Pal.:— Eleph.

אַלּוּף **'allûph**. See 441.

אֶלְפֶלֶט **'Elpelet**. See 467.

508. אֶלְפַּעַל **'Elpa'al**, *el-pah´-al*; from 410 and 6466; *God* (is) *act; Elpaal*, an Isr.:— Elpaal.

509. אָלַץ **'âlats**, *aw-lats´*; a prim. root; to *press:*— urge.

אֶלְצָפָן **'Eltsâphân**. See 469.

510. אַלְקוּם **'alqûwm**, *al-koom´*; prob. from 408 and 6965; a *non-rising* (i.e. *resistlessness*):— no rising up.

511. אֶלְקָנָה **'Elqânâh**, *el-kaw-naw´*; from 410 and 7069; *God has obtained; Elkanah*, the name of several Isr.:— Elkanah.

512. אֶלְקֹשִׁי **'Elqôshîy**, *el-ko-shee´*; patrial from a name of uncert. der.; an *Elkoshite* or native of Elkosh:— Elkoshite.

513. אֶלְתּוֹלַד **'Eltôwlad**, *el-to-lad´*; prob. from 410 and a masc. form of 8435 [comp. 8434]; *God* (is) *generator; Eltolad*, a place in Pal.:— Eltolad.

514. אֶלְתְּקֵא **'Eltᵉqê**, *el-te-kay´*; or (more prop.)

אֶלְתְּקֵה **'Eltᵉqêh**, *el-te-kay´*; of uncert. der.; *Eltekeh* or *Elteke*, a place in Pal.:— Eltekeh.

515. אלתקן 'Elt°qôn, *el-te-kone'*; from 410 and 8626; *God* (is) *straight*; *Eltekon*, a place in Pal.:— Eltekon.

516. אל תשחת 'Al tashchêth, *al tash-kayth'*; from 408 and 7843; *Thou must not destroy*; prob. the opening words of a popular song:— Al-taschith.

517. אם 'êm, *ame*; a prim. word; a *mother* (as the *bond* of the family); in a wide sense (both lit. and fig. llike 1l:— dam, mother, × parting.

518. אם 'îm, *eem*; a prim. particle; used very widely as demonstr., *lo!*; interrog., *whether?*; or conditional, *if, although*; also *Oh that!, when*; hence, as a neg., *not*:— (and, can-, doubtless, if, that) (not), + but, either, + except, + more (-over if, than), neither, nevertheless, nor, oh that, or, + save (only, -ing), seeing, since, sith, + surely (no more, none, not), though, + of a truth, + unless, + verily, when, whereas, whether, while, + yet.

519. אמה 'âmâh, *aw-maw'*; appar. a prim. word; a *maid-servant* or female slave:— (hand-) bondmaid (-woman), maid (-servant).

אמה 'êmâh. See 367.

520. אמה 'ammâh, *am-maw'*; prol. from 517; prop. a *mother* (i.e. *unit* of measure, or the *fore-arm* (below the elbow), i.e. a *cubit*; also a door-*base* (as a *bond* of the entrance):— cubit, + hundred lby *exchange for* 3967l, measure, post.

521. אמה 'ammâh (Chald.), *am-maw'*; corresp. to 520:— cubit.

522. אמה 'Ammâh, *am-maw'*; the same as 520; *Ammah*, a hill in Pal.:— Ammah.

523. אמה 'ummâh, *oom-maw'*; from the same as 517; a *collection*, i.e. community of persons:— nation, people.

524. אמה 'ummâh (Chald.), *oom-maw'*; corresp. to 523:— nation.

525. אמון 'âmôwn, *aw-mone'*; from 539, prob. in the sense of *training*; *skilled*, i.e. an architect llike 542l:— one brought up.

526. אמן 'Âmôwn, *aw-mone'*; the same as 525; *Amon*, the name of three Isr.:— Amon.

527. אמון 'âmôwn, *aw-mone'*; a var. for 1995; a *throng* of people:— multitude.

528. אמון 'Âmôwn, *aw-mone'*; of Eg. der.; *Amon* (i.e. Ammon or Amn), a deity of Egypt (used only as an adjunct of 4996):— multitude, populous.

529. אמון 'êmûwn, *ay-moon'*; from 539; *established*, i.e. (fig.) *trusty*; also (abstr.) *trustworthiness*:— faith (-ful), truth.

530. אמונה 'ĕmûwnâh, *em-oo-naw'*; or (short.)

אמנה 'ĕmûnâh, *em-oo-naw'*; fem. of 529; lit. *firmness*; fig. *security*; mor. *fidelity*:— faith (-ful, -ly, -ness, lmanl), set office, stability, steady, truly, truth, verily.

531. אמוץ 'Âmôwts, *aw-mohts'*; from 553; *strong*; *Amots*, an Isr.:— Amoz.

532. אמי 'Âmiy, *aw-mee'*; an abbrev. for 526; *Ami*, an Isr.:— Ami.

533. אמיץ 'ammîyts, *am-meets'*; or (short.)

אמץ 'ammîts, *am-meets'*; from 553; *strong* or (abstr.) *strength*:— courageous, mighty, strong (one).

534. אמיר 'âmîyr, *aw-meer'*; appar. from 559 (in the sense of *self-exaltation*); a *summit* (of a tree or mountain:— bough, branch.

535. אמל 'âmal, *aw-mal'*; a prim. root; to *droop*; by impl. to *be sick*, to *mourn*:— languish, be weak, wax feeble.

536. אמלל 'umlal, *oom-lal'*; from 535; *sick*:— weak.

537. אמלל 'ămêlâl, *am-ay-lawl'*; from 535; *languid*:— feeble.

538. אמם 'Âmâm, *am-awm'*; from 517; *gathering*-spot; *Amam*, a place in Pal.:— Amam.

539. אמן 'âman, *aw-man'*; a prim. root; prop. to *build up* or *support*; to *foster* as a parent or nurse; fig. to *render* (or *be*) *firm* or faithful, to *trust* or believe, to *be permanent* or quiet; mor. to *be true* or certain; once (Isa. 30:21; interch. for 541) to *go to the right hand*:— hence, assurance, believe, bring up, establish, + fail, be faithful (of long continuance, stedfast, sure, surely, trusty, verified), nurse, (-ing father), (put), trust, turn to the right.

540. אמן 'ăman (Chald.), *am-an'*; corresp. to 539:— believe, faithful, sure.

541. אמן 'âman, *aw-man'*; denom. from 3225; to take the *right hand* road:— turn to the right. See 539.

542. אמן 'âmân, *aw-mawn'*; from 539 (in the sense of *training*); an *expert*:— cunning workman.

543. אמן 'âmên, *aw-mane'*; from 539; *sure*; abstr. *faithfulness*; adv. *truly*:— Amen, so be it, truth.

544. אמן 'ômen, *oh-men'*; from 539; *verity*:— truth.

545. אמנה 'omnâh, *om-naw'*; fem. of 544 (in the spec. sense of *training*); *tutelage*:— brought up.

546. אמנה 'omnâh, *om-naw'*; fem. of 544 (in its usual sense); adv. *surely*:— indeed.

547. אמנה 'ôm°nâh, *om-me-naw'*; fem. act. part. of 544 (in the orig. sense of *supporting*); a *column*:— pillar.

548. אמנה 'ămânâh, *am-aw-naw'*; fem. of 543; something *fixed*, i.e. a *covenant*, an *allowance*:— certain portion, sure.

549. אמנה 'Ămânâh, *am-aw-naw'*; the same as 548; *Amanah*, a mountain near Damascus:— Amana.

אמנה 'ĕmûnâh. See 530.

550. אמנון 'Amnôwn, *am-nohn'*; or

אמינון 'Ămîynôwn, *am-ee-nohn'*; from 539; *faithful*; *Amnon* (or Aminon), a son of David:— Amnon.

551. אמנם 'omnâm, *om-nawm'*; adv. from 544; *verily*:— indeed, no doubt, surely, (it is, of a) true (-ly, -th).

552. אמנם 'umnâm, *oom-nawm'*; an

אמנון 'Âmîynôwn. See 550.

553. אמץ 'âmats, *aw-mats'*; a prim. root; to *be alert*, phys. (on foot) or ment. (in courage):— confirm, be courageous (of good courage, stedfastly minded, strong, stronger), establish, fortify, harden, increase, prevail, strengthen (self), make strong (obstinate, speed).

554. אמץ 'âmôts, *aw-mohts'*; prob. from 553; of a *strong color*, i.e. *red* (others *fleet*):— bay.

555. אמץ 'ômets, *o'-mets*; from 553; *strength*:— stronger.

אמץ 'ammîts. See 533.

556. אמצה 'amtsâh, *am-tsaw'*; from 553; *force*:— strength.

557. אמצי 'Amtsîy, *am-tsee'*; from 553; *strong*; *Amtsi*, an Isr.:— Amzi.

558. אמציה 'Ămatsyâh, *am-ats-yaw'*; or

אמציהו 'Ămatsyâhûw, *am-ats-yaw'-hoo*; from 553 and 3050; *strength of Jah*; *Amatsjah*, the name of four Isr.:— Amaziah.

559. אמר 'âmar, *aw-mar'*; a prim. root; to *say* (used with great latitude):— answer, appoint, avouch, bid, boast self, call, certify, challenge, charge, + (at the, give) command (-ment), commune, consider, declare, demand, × desire, determine, × expressly, × indeed, × intend, name, × plainly, promise, publish, report, require, say, speak (against, of), × still, × suppose, talk, tell, term, × that is, × think, use lspeechl, utter, × verily, × yet.

560. אמר 'ămar (Chald.), *am-ar'*; corresp. to 559:— command, declare, say, speak, tell.

561. אמר 'êmer, *ay'-mer*; from 559; something *said*:— answer, × appointed unto him, saying, speech, word.

562. אמר 'ômer, *o'-mer*; the same as 561:— promise, speech, thing, word.

563. אמר 'immar (Chald.), *im-mar'*; perh. from 560 (in the sense of *bringing forth*); a *lamb*:— lamb.

564. אמר 'Immêr, *im-mare'*; from 559; *talkative*; *Immer*, the name of five Isr.:— Immer.

565. אמרה 'imrâh, *im-raw'*; or

אמרה 'emrâh, *em-raw'*; fem. of 561, and mean. the same:— commandment, speech, word.

566. אמרי 'Imrîy, *im-ree'*; from 564; *wordy*; *Imri*, the name of two Isr.:— Imri.

567. אמר 'Ĕmôrîy, *em-o-ree'*; prob. a patron. from an unused name derived from 559 in the sense of *publicity*, i.e. prominence; thus, a *mountaineer*; an *Emorite*, one of the Canaanitish tribes:— Amorite.

568. אמריה 'Ămaryâh, *am-ar-yaw'*; or prol.

אמריהו 'Ămaryâhûw, *am-ar-yaw'-hoo*; from 559 and 3050; *Jah has said* (i.e. promised); *Amarjah*, the name of nine Isr.:— Amariah.

569. אמרפל 'Amrâphel, *am-raw-fel'*; of uncert. (perh. for.) der.; *Amraphel*, a king of Shinar:— Amraphel.

orth. var. of 551:— in (very) deed; of a surety.

Hebrew

570. אמש **'emesh**, *eh´-mesh;* time *past,* i.e. *yesterday* or *last night:*— former time, yesterday (-night).

571. אמת **'emeth**, *eh´-meth;* contr. from 539; *stability;* fig. *certainty, truth, trustworthiness:*— assured (-ly), establishment, faithful, right, sure, true (-ly, -th), verity.

572. אמתחת **'amtêchath**, *am-taykh´-ath;* from 4969; prop. something *expansive,* i.e. a *bag:*— sack.

573. אמתי **'Ămittay**, *am-it-tah´ee;* from 571; *veracious; Amittai,* an Isr.:— Amittai.

574. אמתני **'emtâniy** (Chald.), *em-tawnee´;* from a root corresp. to that of 4975; well-*loined* (i.e. burly) or *mighty:*— terrible.

575. אן **'ân**, *awn;* or

אנה **'ânâh**, *aw-naw´;* contr. from 370; *where?;* hence, *whither?, when?;* also *hither* and *thither:*— + any (no) whither, now, where, whither (-soever).

אן **'Ôn**. See 204.

576. אנא **'ănâ'** (Chald.), *an-aw´;* or

אנה **'ănâh**, *an-aw´;* corresp. to 589; *I:*— I, as for me.

577. אנא **'ânnâ'**, *awn-naw´;* or

אנה **'ânnâh**, *awn-naw´;* appar. contr. from 160 and 4994; *oh now!:*— I (me) beseech (pray) thee, O.

אנה **'ânâh**. See 576.

אנה **'ânâh**. See 575.

578. אנה **'ânâh**, *aw-naw´;* a prim. root; to *groan:*— lament, mourn.

579. אנה **'ânâh**, *aw-naw´;* a prim. root [perh. rather ident. with 578 through the idea of *contraction* in anguish]; to *approach;* hence, to *meet* in various senses:— befall, deliver, happen, seek a quarrel.

אנה **'ânnâh**. See 577.

580. אנו **'ănûw**, *an-oo´;* contr. for 587; *we:*— we.

או **'Ônôw**. See 207.

581. אנון **'innûwn** (Chald.), *in-noon´;* or (fem.)

אנין **'inniyn** (Chald.), *in-neen´;* corresp. to 1992; *they:*— × are, them, these.

582. אנוש **'ěnôwsh**, *en-oshe´;* from 605; prop. a *mortal* (and thus differing from the more dignified 120); hence, a *man* in gen. (singly or collect.):— another, × [blood-] thirsty, certain, chap [-man]; divers, fellow, × in the flower of their age, husband, (certain, mortal) man, people, person, servant, some (× of them), + stranger, those, + their trade. It is often unexpressed in the English Version, espec. when used in apposition with another word. Comp. 376.

583. אנוש **'Ěnôwsh**, *en-ohsh´;* the same as 582; *Enosh,* a son of Seth:— Enos.

584. אנח **'ânach**, *aw-nakh´;* a prim. root; to *sigh:*— groan, mourn, sigh.

585. אנחה **'ănâchâh**, *an-aw-khaw´;* from 584; *sighing:*— groaning, mourn, sigh.

586. אנחנא **'ănachnâ'** (Chald.), *an-akhnaw´;* or

אנחנה **'ănachnâh** (Chald.), *an-akhnaw´;* corresp. to 587; *we:*— we.

587. אנחנו **'ănachnûw**, *an-akh´-noo;* appar. from 595; *we:*— ourselves, us, we.

588. אנחרת **'Ănâchărâth**, *an-aw-kharawth´;* prob. from the same root as 5170; a *gorge* or narrow pass; *Anacharath,* a place in Pal.:— Anaharath.

589. אני **'ăniy**, *an-ee´;* contr. from 595; *I:*— I, (as for) me, mine, myself, we, × which, × who.

590. אני **'ŏniy**, *on-ee´;* prob. from 579 (in the sense of *conveyance*); a *ship* or (collect.) a *fleet:*— galley, navy (of ships).

591. אניה **'ŏniyâh**, *on-ee-yaw´;* fem. of 590; a *ship:*— ship (I-men).

592. אניה **'ăniyâh**, *an-ee-yaw´;* from 578; *groaning:*— lamentation, sorrow.

אנין **'inniyn**. See 581.

593. אניעם **'Ăniy`âm**, *an-ee-awm´;* from 578 and 5971; *groaning of* (the) *people; Aniam,* an Isr.:— Aniam.

594. אנך **'ănâk**, *an-awk´;* prob. from an unused root mean. to *be narrow;* according to most a plumb-*line,* and to others a *hook:*— plumb-line.

595. אנכי **'ânôkiy**, *aw-no-kee´* (sometimes *aw-no´-kee*); a prim. pron.; *I:*— I, me, × which.

596. אנן **'ânan**, *aw-nan´;* a prim. root; to *mourn,* i.e. *complain:*— complain.

597. אנס **'ânaç**, *aw-nas´;* to *insist:*— compel.

598. אנס **'ănaç** (Chald.), *an-as´;* corresp. to 597; fig. to *distress:*— trouble.

599. אנף **'ânaph**, *aw-naf´;* a prim. root; to *breathe hard,* i.e. *be enraged:*— be angry (displeased).

600. אנף **'ănaph** (Chald.), *an-af´;* corresp. to 639 (only in the plur. as a sing.); the *face:*— face, visage.

601. אנפה **'ănâphâh**, *an-aw-faw´;* from 599; an unclean bird, perh. the *parrot* (from its *irascibility*):— heron.

602. אנק **'ânaq**, *aw-nak´;* a prim. root; to *shriek:*— cry, groan.

603. אנקה **'ănâqâh**, *an-aw-kaw´;* from 602; *shrieking:*— crying out, groaning, sighing.

604. אנקה **'ănâqâh**, *an-aw-kaw´;* the same as 603; some kind of lizard, prob. the *gecko* (from its *wail*):— ferret.

605. אנש **'ânash**, *aw-nash´;* a prim. root; to *be frail, feeble,* or (fig.) *melancholy:*— desperate (-ly wicked), incurable, sick, woeful.

606. אנש **'ěnâsh** (Chald.), *en-awsh´;* or

אנש **'ěnash** (Chald.), *en-ash´;* corresp. to 582; a *man:*— man, + whosoever.

אנת **'ant**. See 859.

607. אנתה **'antâh** (Chald.), *an-taw´;* corresp. to 859; *thou:*— as for thee, thou.

608. אנתון **'antûwn** (Chald.), *an-toon´;* plur. of 607; *ye:*— ye.

609. אסא **'Âçâ'**, *aw-saw´;* of uncert. der.; *Asa,* the name of a king and of a Levite:— Asa.

610. אסוך **'âçûwk**, *aw-sook´;* from 5480; *anointed,* i.e. an oil-*flask:*— pot.

611. אסון **'âçôwn**, *aw-sone´;* of uncert. der.; *hurt:*— mischief.

612. אסור **'êçûwr**, *ay-soor´;* from 631; a *bond* (espec. *manacles* of a prisoner):— band, + prison.

613. אסור **'ěçûwr** (Chald.), *es-oor´;* corresp. to 612:— band, imprisonment.

614. אסיף **'âçiyph**, *aw-seef´;* or

אסף **'âçiph**, *aw-seef´;* from 622; *gathered,* i.e. (abstr.) a *gathering* in of crops:— ingathering.

615. אסיר **'âçiyr**, *aw-sere´;* from 631; *bound,* i.e. a *captive:*— (those which are) bound, prisoner.

616. אסיר **'açç̂iyr**, *as-sere´;* for 615:— prisoner.

617. אסיר **'Açç̂iyr**, *as-sere´;* the same as 616; *prisoner; Assir,* the name of two Isr.:— Assir.

618. אסם **'âçâm**, *aw-sawm´;* from an unused root mean. to *heap* together; a *storehouse* (only in the plur.):— barn, storehouse.

619. אסנה **'Açnâh**, *as-naw´;* of uncert. der.; *Asnah,* one of the Nethinim:— Asnah.

620. אסנפר **'Oçnappar** (Chald.), *os-nappar´;* of for. der.; *Osnappar,* an Ass. king:— Asnapper.

621. אסנת **'Âçěnath**, *aw-se-nath´;* of Eg. der.; *Asenath,* the wife of Joseph:— Asenath.

622. אסף **'âçaph**, *aw-saf´;* a prim. root; to *gather* for any purpose; hence, to *receive, take away,* i.e. remove (destroy, leave behind, put up, restore, etc.):— assemble, bring, consume, destroy, fetch, gather (in, together, up again), × generally, get (him), lose, put all together, receive, recover [another from leprosy], (be) rereward, × surely, take (away, into, up), × utterly, withdraw.

623. אסף **'Âçâph**, *aw-sawf´;* from 622; *collector; Asaph,* the name of three Isr., and of the family of the first:— Asaph.

אסף **'âçiph**. See 614.

624. אסף **'âçuph**, *aw-soof´;* pass. part. of 622; *collected* (only in the plur.), i.e. a *collection* (of offerings):— threshold, Asuppim.

625. אסף **'ôçeph**, *o´-sef;* from 622; a *collection* (of fruits):— gathering.

626. אספה **'ăçêphâh**, *as-ay-faw´;* from 622; a *collection* of people (only adv.):— × together.

627. אספה **'ăçuppâh**, *as-up-paw´;* fem. of 624; a *collection* of (learned) men (only in the plur.):— assembly.

628. אספסף **'ăçp̂ěçuph**, *as-pes-oof´;* by redupl. from 624; *gathered up together,* i.e. a promiscuous *assemblage* (of people):— mixt multitude.

629. אספרנא **'oçparnâ'** (Chald.), *os-parnaw´;* of Pers. der.; *diligently:*— fast, forthwith, speed (-ily).

630. אספתא **'Açpâthâ'**, *as-paw-thaw´;* of Pers. der.; *Aspatha,* a son of Haman:— Aspatha.

631. אָסַר **'âçar**, aw-sar´; a prim. root; to *yoke* or *hitch*; by anal. to *fasten* in any sense, to *join* battle:— bind, fast, gird, harness, hold, keep, make ready, order, prepare, prison (-er), put in bonds, set in array, tie.

632. אֵסֶר **'êçâr**, es-sawr´; or

אִסָּר **'içâr**, is-sawr´; from 631; an *obligation* or *vow* (of abstinence):— binding, bond.

633. אֱסָר **'êçâr** (Chald.), es-sawr´; corresp. to 632 in a legal sense; an *interdict*:— decree.

634. אֵסַר־חַדּוֹן **'Êçar-Chaddôwn**, ay-sar´ chad-dohn´; of for. der.; *Esar-chaddon*, an Ass. king:— Esar-haddon.

635. אֶסְתֵּר **'Eçtêr**, es-tare´; of Pers. der.; *Ester*, the Jewish heroine:— Esther.

636. אָע **'â** (Chald.), aw; corresp. to 6086; a *tree* or *wood*:— timber, wood.

637. אַף **'aph**, af; a prim. particle; mean. *accession* (used as an adv. or conjunc.); *also* or *yea*; adversatively *though*:— also, + although, and (furthermore, yet), but, even, + how much less (more, rather than), moreover, with, yea.

638. אַף **'aph** (Chald.), af; corresp. to 637:— also.

639. אַף **'aph**, af; from 599; prop. the *nose* or *nostril*; hence, the *face*, and occasionally a *person*; also (from the rapid breathing in passion) *ire*:— anger (-gry), + before, countenance, face, + forebearing, forehead, + [long-] suffering, nose, nostril, snout, × worthy, wrath.

640. אָפַד **'âphad**, aw-fad´; a prim. root [rather a denom. from 646]; to *gird on* (the ephod):— bind, gird.

אֵפֹד **'êphôd**. See 646.

641. אֵפֹד **'Êphôd**, ay-fode´; the same as 646 short.; *Ephod*, an Isr.:— Ephod.

642. אֲפֻדָּה **'êphuddâh**, ay-food-daw´; fem. of 646; a *girding on* (of the ephod); hence, gen. a *plating* (of metal):— ephod, ornament.

643. אַפֶּדֶן **'appeden**, ap-peh´-den; appar. of for. der.; a *pavilion* or palace-tent:— palace.

644. אָפָה **'âphâh**, aw-faw´; a prim. root; to *cook*, espec. to *bake*:— bake (-r, [-meats]).

אֵפָה **'êphâh**. See 374.

645. אֵפוֹ **'êphôw**, ay-fo´; or

אֵפוֹא **'êphôw'**, ay-fo´; from 6311; strictly a demonstr. particle, *here*; but used of time, *now* or *then*:— here, now, where?

646. אֵפוֹד **'êphôwd**, ay-fode´; rarely

אֵפֹד **'êphôd**, ay-fode´; prob. of for. der.; a *girdle*; spec. the *ephod* or high-priest's shoulder-piece; also gen. an *image*:— ephod.

647. אֲפִיחַ **'Aphîyach**, af-ee´-akh; perh. from 6315; *breeze*; *Aphiach*, an Isr.:— Aphiah.

648. אָפִיל **'âphîyl**, aw-feel´; from the same as 651 (in the sense of *weakness*); *unripe*:— not grown up.

649. אַפַּיִם **'Appayim**, ap-pah´-yim; dual of 639; *two nostrils*; *Appajim*, an Isr.:— Appaim.

650. אָפִיק **'âphîyq**, aw-feek´; from 622; prop. *containing*, i.e. a *tube*; also a *bed* or *valley* of a stream; also a *strong* thing or a *hero*:— brook, channel, mighty, river, + scale, stream, strong piece.

אוֹפִיר **'Ôphîyr**. See 211.

651. אָפֵל **'âphêl**, aw-fale´; from an unused root mean. to *set* as the sun; *dusky*:— very dark.

652. אֹפֶל **'ôphel**, o´fel; from the same as 651; *dusk*:— darkness, obscurity, privily.

653. אֲפֵלָה **'âphêlâh**, af-ay-law´; fem. of 651; *duskiness*, fig. *misfortune*; concr. *concealment*:— dark, darkness, gloominess, × thick.

654. אֶפְלָל **'Ephlâl**, ef-lawl´; from 6419; *judge*; *Ephlal*, an Isr.:— Ephlal.

655. אֹפֶן **'ôphen**, o´-fen; from an unused root mean. to *revolve*; a *turn*, i.e. a *season*:— + fitly.

אוֹפָן **'ôphân**. See 212.

656. אָפֵס **'âphêç**, aw-face´; a prim. root; to *disappear*, i.e. *cease*:— be clean gone (at an end, brought to nought), fail.

657. אֶפֶס **'epheç**, eh´-fes; from 656; *cessation*, i.e. an *end* (espec. of the earth); often used adv. *no further*; also (like 6466) the *ankle* (in the dual), as being the extremity of the leg or foot:— ankle, but (only), end, howbeit, less than nothing, nevertheless (where), no, none (beside), not (any, -withstanding), thing of nought, save (-ing), there, uttermost part, want, without (cause).

658. אֶפֶס דַּמִּים **'Epheç Dammîym**, eh´-fes dam-meem´; from 657 and the plur. of 1818; *boundary of blood*-drops; *Ephes-Dammim*, a place in Pal.:— Ephes-dammim.

659. אָפַע **'êpha'**, eh´-fah; from an unused root prob. mean. to *breathe*; prop. a *breath*, i.e. *nothing*:— of nought.

660. אֶפְעֶה **'eph'eh**, ef-eh´; from 659 (in the sense of *hissing*); an *asp* or other venomous serpent:— viper.

661. אָפַף **'âphaph**, aw-faf´; a prim. root; to *surround*:— compass.

662. אָפַק **'âphaq**, aw-fak´; a prim. root; to *contain*, i.e. (reflex.) *abstain*:— force (oneself), restrain.

663. אֲפֵק **'Âphêq**, af-ake´; or

אֲפִיק **'Âphîyq**, af-eek´; from 662 (in the sense of *strength*); *fortress*; *Aphek* (or *Aphik*), the name of three places in Pal.:— Aphek, Aphik.

664. אֲפֵקָה **'Âphêqâh**, af-ay-kaw´; fem. of 663; *fortress*; *Aphekah*, a place in Pal.:— Aphekah.

665. אֵפֶר **'êpher**, ay´-fer; from an unused root mean. to *bestrew*; *ashes*:— ashes.

666. אֲפֵר **'âphêr**, af-ayr´; from the same as 665 (in the sense of *covering*); a *turban*:— ashes.

667. אֶפְרֹחַ **'ephrôach**, ef-ro´-akh; from 6524 (in the sense of *bursting* the shell); the *brood* of a bird:— young (one).

668. אַפִּרְיוֹן **'appiryôwn**, ap-pir-yone´; prob. of Eg. der.; a *palanquin*:— chariot.

669. אֶפְרַיִם **'Ephrayim**, ef-rah´-yim; dual of a masc. form of 672; *double fruit*; *Ephrajim*, a son of Joseph; also the tribe descended from him, and its territory:— Ephraim, Ephraimites.

670. אֲפָרְסַי **'Âphârᵉçay** (Chald.), af-aw-re-sah´ee; of for. or. (only in the plur.); an *Apharesite* or inhab. of an unknown region of Assyria:— Apharsite.

671. אֲפַרְסְכַי **'Âpharçᵉkay** (Chald.), af-ar-sek-ah´ee; or

אֲפַרְסַתְכַי **'Âpharçathkay** (Chald.), af-ar-sath-kah´ee; of for. or. (only in the plur.); an *Apharsekite* or *Apharsathkite*, an unknown Ass. tribe:— Apharsachites, Apharsathchites.

672. אֶפְרָת **'Ephrâth**, ef-rawth´; or

אֶפְרָתָה **'Ephrâthâh**, ef-raw´-thaw; from 6509; *fruitfulness*; *Ephrath*, another name for Bethlehem; once (Psa. 132:6) perh. for *Ephraim*; also of an Isr. woman:— Ephrath, Ephratah.

673. אֶפְרָתִי **'Ephrâthîy**, ef-rawth-ee´; patrial from 672; an *Ephrathite* or an *Ephraimite*:— Ephraimite, Ephrathite.

674. אַפְּתֹם **'appᵉthôm** (Chald.), ap-pe-thome´; of Pers. or.; *revenue*; others *at the last*:— revenue.

675. אֶצְבּוֹן **'Etsbôwn**, ets-bone´; or

אֶצְבֹּן **'Etsbôn**, ets-bone´; of uncert. der.; *Etsbon*, the name of two Isr.:— Ezbon.

676. אֶצְבַּע **'etsba'**, ets-bah´; from the same as 6648 (in the sense of *grasping*); something to *seize* with, i.e. a *finger*; by anal. a *toe*:— finger, toe.

677. אֶצְבַּע **'etsba'** (Chald.), ets-bah´; corresp. to 676:— finger, toe.

678. אָצִיל **'âtsîyl**, aw-tseel´; from 680 (in its second. sense of *separation*); an *extremity* (Isa. 41:9), also a *noble*:— chief man, noble.

679. אַצִּיל **'atstsîyl**, ats-tseel´; from 680 (in its primary sense of *uniting*); a *joint* of the hand (i.e. *knuckle*); also (according to some) a *party-wall* (Ezek. 41:8):— [arm] hole, great.

680. אָצַל **'âtsal**, aw-tsal´; a prim. root; prop. to *join*; used only as a denom. from 681; to *separate*; hence, to *select*, *refuse*, *contract*:— keep, reserve, straiten, take.

681. אֵצֶל **'êtsel**, ay´-tsel; from 680 (in the sense of *joining*); a *side*; (as a prep.) *near*:— at, (hard) by, (from) (beside), near (unto), toward, with. See also 1018.

682. אָצֵל **'Âtsêl**, aw-tsale´; from 680; *noble*; *Atsel*, the name of an Isr., and of a place in Pal.:— Azal, Azel.

683. אֲצַלְיָהוּ **'Atsalyâhûw**, ats-al-yaw´-hoo; from 680 and 3050 prol.; *Jah has reserved*; *Atsaljah*, an Isr.:— Azaliah.

684. אֹצֶם **'Ôtsem**, o´-tsem; from an unused root prob. mean. to *be strong*; *strength* (i.e. *strong*); *Otsem*, the name of two Isr.:— Ozem.

685. אֶצְעָדָה **'ets'âdâh**, ets-aw-daw´; a

var. from 6807; prop. a *step-chain;* by anal. a *bracelet:*— bracelet, chain.

686. אָצַר **'âtsar**, *aw-tsar';* a prim. root; to *store* up:— (lay up in) store, (make) treasure (-r).

687. אֹצָר **'Etser**, *ay'-tser;* from 686; *treasure; Etser*, an Idumæan:— Ezer.

688. אֶקְדָּח **'eqdâch**, *ek-dawkh';* from 6916; *burning,* i.e. a *carbuncle* or other fiery gem:— carbuncle.

689. אַקּוֹ **'aqqôw**, *ak-ko';* prob. from 602; *slender,* i.e. the *ibex:*— wild goat.

690. אֲרָא **'Ărâ**, *ar-aw';* prob. for 738; *lion; Ara*, an Isr.:— Ara.

691. אֲרִאֵל **'er'êl**, *er-ale';* prob. for 739; a *hero* (collect.):— valiant one.

692. אַרְאֵלִי **'Ar'êlîy**, *ar-ay-lee';* from 691; *heroic; Areli* (or an *Arelite,* collect.), an Isr. and his desc.:— Areli, Arelites.

693. אָרַב **'ârab**, *aw-rab';* a prim. root; to *lurk:*— (lie in) ambush (-ment), lay (lie in) wait.

694. אָרָב **'Ărâb**, *ar-awb';* from 693; *am-bush; Arab*, a place in Pal.:— Arab.

695. אֶרֶב **'ereb**, *eh'-reb;* from 693; *am-buscade:*— den, lie in wait.

696. אֹרֶב **'ôreb**, *o'-reb;* the same as 695:— wait.

אַרְבֵּאל **'Arbê'l**. See 1009.

697. אַרְבֶּה **'arbeh**, *ar-beh';* from 7235; a *locust* (from its rapid *increase*):— grasshopper, locust.

698. אֲרֻבָּה **'orôbah**, *or-ob-aw';* fem. of 696 (only in the plur.); *ambuscades:*— spoils.

699. אֲרֻבָּה **'ărubbâh**, *ar-oob-baw';* fem. part. pass. of 693 (as if for *lurking*); a *lattice;* (by impl.) a *window, dove-cot* (because of the pigeon-holes), *chimney* (with its apertures for smoke), *sluice* (with openings for water):— chimney, window.

700. אֲרֻבּוֹת **'Ărubbôwth**, *ar-oob-both';* plur. of 699; *Arubboth*, a place in Pal.:— Aruboth.

701. אַרְבִּי **'Arbîy**, *ar-bee';* patrial from 694; an *Arbite* or native of Arab:— Arbite.

702. אַרְבַּע **'arba'**, *ar-bah';* masc.

אַרְבָּעָה **'arbâ'âh**, *ar-baw-aw';* from 7251; *four:*— four.

703. אַרְבַּע **'arba'** (Chald.), *ar-bah';* cor-resp. to 702:— four.

704. אַרְבַּע **'Arba'**, *ar-bah';* the same as 702; *Arba*, one of the Anakim:— Arba.

אַרְבָּעָה **'arbâ'âh**. See 702.

705. אַרְבָּעִים **'arbâ'îym**, *ar-baw-eem';* multiple of 702; *forty:*— forty.

706. אַרְבַּעְתַּיִם **'arba'tayim**, *ar-bah-tah'-yim;* dual of 702; *fourfold:*— fourfold.

707. אָרַג **'ârag**, *aw-rag';* a prim. root; to *plait* or *weave:*— weaver (-r).

708. אֶרֶג **'ereg**, *eh'-reg;* from 707; a *weaving;* a *braid;* also a *shuttle:*— beam, weaver's shuttle.

709. אַרְגֹּב **'Argôb**, *ar-gobe';* from the same as 7263; *stony; Argob*, a district of Pal.:— Argob.

710. אַרְגְּמָן **'arg°vân**, *arg-ev-awn';* a var. for 713; *purple:*— purple.

711. אַרְגְּוָן **'arg°vân** (Chald.), *arg-ev-awn';* corresp. to 710:— purple.

712. אַרְגָּז **'argâz**, *ar-gawz';* perh. from 7264 (in the sense of being *suspended*); a *box* (as a pannier):— coffer.

713. אַרְגָּמָן **'argâmân**, *ar-gaw-mawn';* of for. or.; *purple* (the color or the dyed stuff):— purple.

714. אַרְדְּ **'Ard**, *ard;* from an unused root prob. mean. to *wander; fugitive; Ard*, the name of two Isr.:— Ard.

715. אַרְדּוֹן **'Ardôwn**, *ar-dohn';* from the same as 714; *roaming; Ardon*, an Isr.:— Ardon.

716. אַרְדִּי **'Ardîy**, *ar-dee';* patron. from 714; an *Ardite* (collect.) or desc. of Ard:— Ardites.

717. אָרָה **'ârâh**, *aw-raw';* a prim. root; to *pluck:*— gather, pluck.

718. אֲרוּ **'ărûw** (Chald.), *ar-oo';* prob. akin to 431; *lo!:*— behold, lo.

719. אַרְוַד **'Arvad**, *ar-vad';* prob. from 7300; a *refuge* for the *roving; Arvad*, an island-city of Pal.:— Arvad.

720. אֲרוֹד **'Ărôwd**, *ar-ode';* an orth. var. of 719; *fugitive; Arod*, an Isr.:— Arod.

721. אַרְוָדִי **'Arvâdîy**, *ar-vaw-dee';* pa-trial from 719; an *Arvadite* or citizen of Arvad:— Arvadite.

722. אֲרוֹדִי **'Ărôwdîy**, *ar-o-dee';* patron. from 721; an *Arodite* or desc. of Arod:— Arodi, Arodites.

723. אֻרְוָה **'urvâh**, *oor-vaw';* or

אֲרָיָה **'ărâyâh**, *ar-aw-yah';* from 717 (in the sense of *feeding*); a *herding-place* for an animal:— stall.

724. אֲרוּכָה **'ărûwkâh**, *ar-oo-kaw';* or

אֲרֻכָה **'ărûkâh**, *ar-oo-kaw';* fem. pass. part. of 748 (in the sense of *restor-ing* to soundness); *wholeness* (lit. or fig.):— health, made up, perfected.

725. אֲרוּמָה **'Ărûwmâh**, *ar-oo-maw';* a var. of 7316; *height; Arumah*, a place in Pal.:— Arumah.

726. אֲרוֹמִי **'Ărôwmîy**, *ar-o-mee';* a clerical err. for 130; an *Edomite* (as in the marg.):— Syrian.

727. אָרוֹן **'ârôwn**, *aw-rone';* or

אָרֹן **'ârôn**, *aw-rone';* from 717 (in the sense of *gathering*); a *box:*— ark, chest, coffin.

728. אֲרַוְנָה **'Ăravnâh**, *ar-av-naw';* or (by transp.)

אוֹרְנָה° **'Ôwrnâh**, *ore-naw';* or

אׇרְנִיָה° **'Arnîyah**, *ar-nee-yaw';* all by orth. var. for 771; *Aravnah* (or *Arnijah* or *Ornah*), a Jebusite:— Araunah.

729. אָרַז **'âraz**, *aw-raz';* a prim. root; to *be firm;* used only in the pass. part. as a denom. from 730; of *cedar:*— made of cedar.

730. אֶרֶז **'erez**, *eh-rez';* from 729; a *ce-dar* tree (from the tenacity of its roots):— cedar (tree).

731. אַרְזָה **'arzâh**, *ar-zaw';* fem. of 730; *cedar paneling:*— cedar work.

732. אָרַח **'ârach**, *aw-rakh';* a prim. root; to *travel:*— go, wayfaring (man).

733. אָרַח **'Ârach**, *aw-rakh';* from 732;

way-faring; Arach, the name of three Isr.:— Arah.

734. אֹרַח **'ôrach**, *o'-rakh;* from 732; a well-trodden *road* (lit. or fig.); also a *caravan:*— manner, path, race, rank, traveller, troop, lby-, high-l way.

735. אֹרַח **'ôrach** (Chald.), *o'-rakh;* cor-resp. to 734; a *road:*— way.

736. אֹרְחָה **'ôr°châh**, *o-rekh-aw';* fem. act. part. of 732; a *caravan:*— (travel-ling) company.

737. אֲרֻחָה **'ărûchâh**, *ar-oo-khaw';* fem. pass. part. of 732 (in the sense of *ap-pointing*); a *ration* of food:— allowance, diet, dinner, victuals.

738. אֲרִי **'ăriy**, *ar-ee';* or (prol.)

אַרְיֵה **'aryêh**, *ar-yay';* from 717 (in the sense of *violence*); a *lion:*— (young) lion, + pierce lfrom the marg.l.

739. אֲרִיאֵל **'ăriy'êl**, *ar-ee-ale';* or

אֲרִאֵל **'ărî'êl**, *ar-ee-ale';* from 738 and 410; *lion of God,* i.e. *heroic:*— lion-like men.

740. אֲרִיאֵל **'Ărî'êl**, *ar-ee-ale';* the same as 739; *Ariel*, a symb. name for Jerusa-lem, also the name of an Isr.:— Ariel.

741. אֲרִאֵיל **'ărî'êyl**, *ar-ee-ale';* either by transp. for 739 or, more prob. an orth. var. for 2025; the *altar* of the Temple:— altar.

742. אֲרִידַי **'Ărîyday**, *ar-ee-dah'-ee;* of Pers. or.; *Aridai*, a son of Haman:— Ari-dai.

743. אֲרִידָתָא **'Ărîydâthâ**, *ar-ee-daw-thaw';* of Pers. or.; *Aridatha*, a son of Haman:— Aridatha.

אַרְיֵה **'aryêh**. See 738.

744. אַרְיֵה **'aryêh** (Chald.), *ar-yay';* cor-resp. to 738:— lion.

745. אַרְיֵה **'Aryêh**, *ar-yay';* the same as 738; *lion; Arjeh*, an Isr.:— Arieh.

אֲרָיָה **'ărâyâh**. See 723.

746. אַרְיוֹךְ **'Aryôwk**, *ar-yoke';* of for. or.; *Arjok*, the name of two Babylonians:— Arioch.

747. אֲרִיסַי **'Ărîyçay**, *ar-ee-sah'-ee;* of Pers. or.; *Arisai*, a son of Haman:— Ar-isai.

748. אָרַךְ **'ârak**, *aw-rak';* a prim. root; to *be* (caus. *make*) *long* (lit. or fig.):— de-fer, draw out, lengthen, (be, become, make, pro-) long, + (out-, over-) live, tarry (long).

749. אֲרַךְ **'ărak** (Chald.), *ar-ak';* prop. corresp. to 748, but used only in the sense of *reaching* to a given point; to *suit:*— be meet.

750. אָרֵךְ **'ârêk**, *aw-rake';* from 748; *long:*— long l-suffering, -wingedl, pa-tient, slow lto angerl.

751. אֶרֶךְ **'Erek**, *eh'-rek;* from 748; *length; Erek*, a place in Bab.:— Erech.

752. אָרֹךְ **'ârôk**, *aw-roke';* from 748; *long:*— long.

753. אֹרֶךְ **'ôrek**, *o'rek';* from 748; *length:*— + for ever, length, long.

754. אַרְכָּא **'arkâ'** (Chald.), *ar-kaw';* or

אַרְכָה **'arkâh** (Chald.), *ar-kaw';* from 749; *length:*— lengthening, pro-longed.

755. אַרְכֻּבָה 'arkûbâh (Chald.), ar-koo-baw'; from an unused root corresp. to 7392 (in the sense of bending the knee); the knee:— knee.

אַרְכָה 'ărûkâh. See 724.

756. אַרְכְּוַי 'Arkᵉvay (Chald.), ar-kev-ah´ee; patrial from 751; an Arkevite (collect.) or native of Erek:— Archevite.

757. אַרְכִּי 'Arkîy, ar-kee´; patrial from another place (in Pal.) of similar name with 751; an Arkite or native of Erek:— Archi, Archite.

758. אֲרָם 'Arâm, arawm´; from the same as 759; the highland; Aram or Syria, and its inhab.; also the name of a son of Shem, a grandson of Nahor, and of an Isr.:— Aram, Mesopotamia, Syria, Syrians.

759. אַרְמוֹן 'armôwn, ar-mone´; from an unused root (mean. to be elevated); a citadel (from its height):— castle, palace. Comp. 2038.

760. אֲרַם צוֹבָה 'Aram Tsôwbâh, ar-am´ tso-baw´; from 758 and 6678; Aram of Tsoba (or Cœle-Syria):— Aram-zobah.

761. אֲרַמִּי 'Ărammîy, ar-am-mee´; patrial from 758; an Aramite or Aramæan:— Syrian, Aramitess.

762. אֲרָמִית 'Arâmîyth, ar-aw-meeth´; fem. of 761; (only adv.) in Aramæan:— in the Syrian language (tongue), in Syriack.

763. אֲרַם נַהֲרַיִם 'Aram Nahărayim, ar-am´ nah-har-ah´-yim; from 758 and the dual of 5104; Aram of (the) two rivers (Euphrates and Tigris) or Mesopotamia:— Aham-naharaim, Mesopotamia.

764. אַרְמֹנִי 'Armônîy, ar-mo-nee´; from 759; palatial; Armoni, an Isr.:— Armoni.

765. אֲרָן 'Ărân, ar-awn´; from 7442; stridulous; Aran, an Edomite:— Aran.

766. אֹרֶן 'ôren, o´-ren; from the same as 765 (in the sense of strength); the ash tree (from its toughness):— ash.

767. אֹרֶן 'Ôren, o´-ren; the same as 766; Oren, an Isr.:— Oren.

אָרוֹן 'ârôn. See 727.

768. אַרְנֶבֶת 'arnebeth, ar-neh´-beth; of uncert. der.; the hare:— hare.

769. אַרְנוֹן 'Arnôwn, ar-nohn´; or

אַרְנֹן 'Arnôn, ar-nohn´; from 7442; a brawling stream; the Arnon, a river east of the Jordan; also its territory:— Arnon.

אַרְנִיָה° 'Arnîyah. See 728.

770. אַרְנָן 'Arnân, ar-nawn´; prob. from the same as 769; noisy; Arnan, an Isr.:— Arnan.

771. אָרְנָן 'Ornân, or-nawn´; prob. from 766; strong; Ornan, a Jebusite:— Ornan. See 728.

772. אֲרַע 'ăra' (Chald.), ar-ah´; corresp. to 776; the earth; by impl. (fig.) low:— earth, interior.

773. אַרְעִית 'ar'îyth (Chald.), arh-eeth´; fem. of 772; the bottom:— bottom.

774. אַרְפָּד 'Arpâd, ar-pawd´; from 7502;

spread out; Arpad, a place in Syria:— Arpad, Arphad.

775. אַרְפַּכְשַׁד 'Arpakshad, ar-pak-shad´; prob. of for. or.; Arpakshad, a son of Noah; also the region settled by him:— Arphaxad.

776. אֶרֶץ 'erets, eh´-rets; from an unused root prob. mean. to be firm; the earth (at large, or partitively a land):— × common, country, earth, field, ground, land, × nations, way, + wilderness, world.

777. אַרְצָא 'artsâ', ar-tsaw´; from 776; earthiness; Artsa, an Isr.:— Arza.

778. אֲרַק 'ăraq (Chald.), ar-ak´; by transm. for 772; the earth:— earth.

779. אָרַר 'ârar, aw-rar´; a prim. root; to execrate:— × bitterly curse.

780. אֲרָרַט 'Ărârat, ar-aw-rat´; of for. or.; Ararat (or rather Armenia):— Ararat, Armenia.

781. אָרַשׂ 'âras, aw-ras´; a prim. root; to engage for matrimony:— betroth, espouse.

782. אֲרֶשֶׁת 'ăresheth, ar-eh´-sheth; from 781 (in the sense of desiring to possess); a longing for:— request.

783. אַרְתַּחְשַׁסְתָּא 'Artachshastâ' (Chald.), ar-takh-shas-taw´; or

אַרְתַּחְשַׁשְׁתְּא 'Artachshast' (Chald.), ar-takh-shast´; or by perm.

אַרְתַּחְשַׁשְׂתְּא 'Artachshaçt' (Chald.), ar-takh-shast´; of for. or.; Artachshasta (or Artaxerxes), a title (rather than name) of several Pers. kings:— Artaxerxes.

784. אֵשׁ 'êsh, aysh; a prim. word; fire (lit. or fig.):— burning, fiery, fire, flaming, hot.

785. אֵשׁ 'êsh (Chald.), aysh; corresp. to 784:— flame.

786. אִשׁ 'îsh, eesh; ident. (in or. and formation) with 784; entity; used only adv., there is or are:— are there, none can. Comp. 3426.

787. אֹשׁ 'ôsh (Chald.), ohsh; corresp. (by transp. and abb.) to 803; a foundation:— foundation.

788. אַשְׁבֵּל 'Ashbêl, ash-bale´; prob. from the same as 7640; flowing; Ashbel, an Isr.:— Ashbel.

789. אַשְׁבֵּלִי 'Ashbêlîy, ash-bay-lee´; patron. from 788; an Ashbelite (collect.) or desc. of Ashbel:— Ashbelites.

790. אֶשְׁבָּן 'Eshbân, esh-bawn´; prob. from the same as 7644; vigorous; Eshban, an Idumæan:— Eshban.

791. אַשְׁבֵּעַ 'Ashbêa', ash-bay´-ah; from 7650; adjurer; Asbea, an Isr.:— Ashbea.

792. אֶשְׁבַּעַל 'Eshba'al, esh-bah´-al; from 376 and 1168; man of Baal; Eshbaal (or Ishbosheth), a son of King Saul:— Eshbaal.

793. אֶשֶׁד 'eshed, eh´-shed; from an unused root mean. to pour; an outpouring:— stream.

794. אֲשֵׁדָה 'ăshêdâh, ash-ay-daw´; fem. of 793; a ravine:— springs.

795. אַשְׁדּוֹד 'Ashdôwd, ash-dode´; from 7703; ravager; Ashdod, a place in Pal.:— Ashdod.

796. אַשְׁדּוֹדִי 'Ashdôwdiy, ash-do-dee´; patrial from 795; an Ashdodite (often collect.) or inhab. of Ashdod:— Ashdodites, of Ashdod.

797. אַשְׁדּוֹדִית 'Ashdôwdîyth, ash-do-deeth´; fem. of 796; (only adv.) in the language of Ashdod:— in the speech of Ashdod.

798. אַשְׁדּוֹת הַפִּסְגָּה 'Ashdôwth hap-Piçgâh, ash-doth´ hap-pis-gaw´; from the plur. of 794 and 6449 with the art. interposed; ravines of the Pisgah; Ash-doth-Pisgah, a place east of the Jordan:— Ashdoth-pisgah.

799. אֶשְׁדָּת 'eshdâth, esh-dawth´; from 784 and 1881; a fire-law:— fiery law.

800. אֶשָּׁה 'eshshâh, esh-shaw´; fem. of 784; fire:— fire.

801. אִשָּׁה 'ishshâh, ish-shaw´; the same as 800, but used in a liturgical sense; prop. a burnt-offering; but occasionally of any sacrifice:— (offering, sacrifice), (made) by fire.

802. אִשָּׁה 'ishshâh, ish-shaw´; fem. of 376 or 582; irreg. plur.

נָשִׁים nâshîym, naw-sheem´; a woman (used in the same wide sense as 582):— [adulterless, each, every, female, × many, + none, one, + together, wife, woman. [Often unexpressed in English.]

803. אָשֻׁיָה° 'ăshûwyâh, ash-oo-yah´; fem. pass. part. from an unused root mean. to found; foundation:— foundation.

804. אַשּׁוּר 'Ashshûwr, ash-shoor´; or

אַשֻּׁר 'Ashshûr, ash-shoor´; appar. from 833 (in the sense of successful); Ashshur, the second son of Shem; also his desc. and the country occupied by them (i.e. Assyria), its region and its empire:— Asshur, Assur, Assyria, Assyrians. See 838.

805. אַשּׁוּרִי 'Ashûwrîy, ash-oo-ree´; or

אַשּׁוּרִי 'Ashshûwrîy, ash-shoo-ree´; from a patrial word of the same form as 804; an Ashurite (collect.) or inhab. of Ashur, a district in Pal.:— Asshurim, Ashurites.

806. אַשְׁחוּר 'Ashchûwr, ash-khoor´; prob. from 7835; black; Ashchur, an Isr.:— Ashur.

807. אֲשִׁימָא 'Ăshîymâ', ash-ee-maw´; of for. or.; Ashima, a deity of Hamath:— Ashima.

אֲשֵׁירָה 'ăshêyrâh. See 842.

808. אָשִׁישׁ 'âshîysh, aw-sheesh´; from the same as 784 (in the sense of pressing down firmly; comp. 803); a (ruined) foundation:— foundation.

809. אֲשִׁישָׁה 'ăshîyshâh, ash-ee-shaw´; fem. of 808; something closely pressed together, i.e. a cake of raisins or other comfits:— flagon.

810. אֶשֶׁךְ 'eshek, eh´-shek; from an unused root (prob. mean. to bunch together); a testicle (as a lump):— stone.

811. אֶשְׁכּוֹל 'eshkôwl, esh-kole´; or

אֶשְׁכֹּל 'eshkôl, esh-kole´; prob. prol. from 810; a bunch of grapes or other fruit:— cluster (of grapes).

812. אֶשְׁכֹּל 'Eshkôl, esh-kole´; the same

as 811; *Eshcol*, the name of an Amorite, also of a valley in Pal.:— Eshcol.

813. אַשְׁכְּנַז **'Ashk^enaz**, *ash-ken-az'*; of for. or.; *Ashkenaz*, a Japhethite, also his desc.:— Ashkenaz.

814. אֶשְׁכָּר **'eshkâr**, *esh-kawr'*; for 7939; a *gratuity*:— gift, present.

815. אֵשֶׁל **'êshel**, *ay'-shel*; from a root of uncert. signif.; a *tamarisk* tree; by extens. a *grove* of any kind:— grove, tree.

816. אָשָׁם **'âsham**, *aw-sham'*; or

אָשֵׁם **'âshêm**, *aw-shame'*; a prim. root; to *be guilty*; by impl. to *be punished* or *perish*:— × certainly, be (-come, made) desolate, destroy, × greatly, be (-come, found, hold) guilty, offend (acknowledge offence), trespass.

817. אָשָׁם **'âshâm**, *aw-shawm'*; from 816; *guilt*; by impl. a *fault*; also a *sin-offering*:— guiltiness, (offering for) sin, trespass (offering).

818. אָשֵׁם **'âshêm**, *aw-shame'*; from 816; *guilty*; hence, *presenting a sin-offering*:— one which is faulty, guilty.

819. אַשְׁמָה **'ashmâh**, *ash-maw'*; fem. of 817; *guiltiness*, a *fault*, the *presentation of a sin-offering*:— offend, sin, (cause of) trespass (-ing, offering).

אַשְׁמוּרָה **'ashmûwrâh**. See 821.

820. אַשְׁמָן **'ashmân**, *ash-mawn'*; prob. from 8081; a *fat* field:— desolate place.

821. אַשְׁמֻרָה **'ashmûrâh**, *ash-moo-raw'*; or

אַשְׁמוּרָה **'ashmûwrâh**, *ash-moo-raw'*; or

אַשְׁמֹרֶת **'ashmôreth**, *ash-mo'-reth*; fem. from 8104; a night *watch*:— watch.

822. אֶשְׁנָב **'eshnâb**, *esh-nawb'*; appar. from an unused root (prob. mean. to *leave small spaces between two things*); a latticed *window*:— casement, lattice.

823. אַשְׁנָה **'Ashnâh**, *ash-naw'*; prob. a var. for 3466; *Ashnah*, the name of two places in Pal.:— Ashnah.

824. אֶשְׁעָן **'Esh'ân**, *esh-awn'*; from 8172; *support*; *Eshan*, a place in Pal.:— Eshean.

825. אַשָּׁף **'ashshâph**, *ash-shawf'*; from an unused root (prob. mean. to *lisp*, i.e. *practice enchantment*); a *conjurer*:— astrologer.

826. אַשָּׁף **'ashshâph** (Chald.), *ash-shawf'*; corresp. to 825:— astrologer.

827. אַשְׁפָּה **'ashpâh**, *ash-paw'*; perh. (fem.) from the same as 825 (in the sense of *covering*); a *quiver* or arrow-case:— quiver.

828. אַשְׁפְּנַז **'Ashp^enaz**, *ash-pen-az'*; of for. or.; *Ashpenaz*, a Bab. eunuch:— Ashpenaz.

829. אֶשְׁפָּר **'eshpâr**, *esh-pawr'*; of uncert. der.; a measured *portion*:— good piece (of flesh).

830. אַשְׁפֹּת **'ashpôth**, *ash-pohth'*; or

אַשְׁפּוֹת **'ashpôwth**, *ash-pohth'*; or (contr.)

שְׁפֹת **sh^ephôth**, *shef-ohth'*; plur. of a noun of the same form as 827, from

8192 (in the sense of *scraping*); a heap of *rubbish* or *filth*:— dung (hill).

831. אַשְׁקְלוֹן **'Ashq^elôwn**, *ash-kel-one'*; prob. from 8254 in the sense of *weighing*-place (i.e. *mart*); *Ashkelon*, a place in Pal.:— Ashkelon, Askalon.

832. אֶשְׁקְלוֹנִי **'Eshq^elôwnîy**, *esh-kel-o-nee'*; patrial from 831; an *Ashkelonite* (collect.) or inhab. of Ashkelon:— Eshkalonites.

833. אָשַׁר **'âshar**, *aw-shar'*; or

אָשֵׁר **'âshêr**, *aw-share'*; a prim. root; to *be straight* (used in the widest sense, espec. to *be level, right, happy*); fig. to *go forward, be honest, prosper*:— (call, be) bless (-ed, happy), go, guide, lead, relieve.

834. אֲשֶׁר **'âsher**, *ash-er'*; a prim. rel. pron. (of every gender and number); *who, which, what, that*; also (as adv. and conjunc.) *when, where, how, because, in order that*, etc.:— × after, × alike, as (soon as), because, × every, for, + forasmuch, + from whence, + how (-soever), × if, (so) that ([thing] which, wherein), × though, + until, + whatsoever, when, where (+ -as, -in, -of, -on, -soever, -with), which, whilst, + whither (-soever), who (-m, -soever, -se). [As it is indeclinable, it is often accompanied by the personal pron. expletively, used to show the connection.]

835. אֶשֶׁר **'esher**, *eh'-sher*; from 833; *happiness*; only in masc. plur. constr. as interj., how *happy*!:— blessed, happy.

836. אָשֵׁר **'Âshêr**, *aw-share'*; from 833; *happy*; *Asher*, a son of Jacob, and the tribe descended from him, with its territory; also a place in Pal.:— Asher.

837. אֹשֶׁר **'ôsher**, *o'-sher*; from 833; *happiness*:— happy.

838. אָשׁוּר **'âshshûwr**, *aw-shoor'*; or

אַשֻׁר **'ashshûr**, *ash-shoor'*; from 833 in the sense of *going*; a *step*:— going, step.

839. אָשֻׁר **'âshûr**, *ash-oor'*; contr. for 8391; the *cedar* tree or some other light elastic wood:— Ashurite.

אַשּׁוּר **'Ashshûr**. See 804, 838.

840. אֲשַׂרְאֵל **'Ăsar'êl**, *as-ar-ale'*; by orth. var. from 833 and 410; *right of God*; *Asarel*, an Isr.:— Asareel.

841. אֲשַׂרְאֵלָה **'Ăsar'êlâh**, *as-ar-ale'-aw*; from the same as 840; *right toward God*; *Asarelah*, an Isr.:— Asarelah. Comp. 3480.

842. אֲשֵׁרָה **'âshêrâh**, *ash-ay-raw'*; or

אֲשֵׁירָה **'âshêyrâh**, *ash-ay-raw'*; from 833; *happy*; *Asherah* (or Astarte) a Phœnician goddess; also an *image* of the same:— grove. Comp. 6253.

843. אָשֵׁרִי **'Âshêrîy**, *aw-shay-ree'*; patron. from 836; an *Asherite* (collect.) or desc. of Asher:— Asherites.

844. אַשְׂרִיאֵל **'Asrîy'êl**, *as-ree-ale'*; an orth. var. for 840; *Asriel*, the name of two Isr.:— Ashriel, Asriel.

845. אַשְׂרִאֵלִי **'Asrî'êlîy**, *as-ree-ale-ee'*; patron. from 844; an *Asrielite* (collect.) or desc. of Asriel:— Asrielites.

846. אֻשַּׁרְנָא **'ushsharnâ'** (Chald.), *oosh-*

ar-naw'; from a root corresp. to 833; a *wall* (from its uprightness):— wall.

847. אֶשְׁתָּאֹל **'Eshtâ'ôl**, *esh-taw-ole'*; or

אֶשְׁתָּאוֹל **'Eshtâ'ôwl**, *esh-taw-ole'*; prob. from 7592; *intreaty*; *Eshtaol*, a place in Pal.:— Eshtaol.

848. אֶשְׁתָּאֻלִי **'Eshtâ'ûlîy**, *esh-taw-oo-lee'*; patrial from 847; an *Eshtaolite* (collect.) or inhab. of Eshtaol:— Eshtaulites.

849. אֶשְׁתַּדּוּר **'eshtaddûwr** (Chald.), *esh-tad-dure'*; from 7712 (in a bad sense); *rebellion*:— sedition.

850. אֶשְׁתּוֹן **'Eshtôwn**, *esh-tone'*; prob. from the same as 7764; *restful*; *Eshton*, an Isr.:— Eshton.

851. אֶשְׁתְּמֹעַ **'Esht^emôa**, *esh-tem-o'-ah*; or

אֶשְׁתְּמוֹעַ **'Esht^emôwa**, *esh-tem-o'-ah*; or

אֶשְׁתְּמֹה **'Esht^emôh**, *esh-tem-o'*; from 8085 (in the sense of *obedience*); *Eshtemoa* or *Eshtemoh*, a place in Pal.:— Eshtemoa, Eshtemoh.

אָת **'ath**. See 859.

852. אָת **'âth** (Chald.), *awth*; corresp. to 226; a *portent*:— sign.

853. אֵת **'êth**, *ayth*; appar. contr. from 226 in the demonstr. sense of *entity*; prop. *self* (but gen. used to point out more def. the obj. of a verb or prep., *even or namely*):— [as such unrepresented in English].

854. אֵת **'êth**, *ayth*; prob. from 579; prop. *nearness* (used only as a prep. or an adv.), *near*; hence, gen. *with, by, at, among*, etc.:— against, among, before, by, for, from, in (-to), (out) of, with. [Often with another prep. prefixed.]

855. אֵת **'êth**, *ayth*; of uncert. der.; a *hoe* or other digging implement:— coulter, plowshare.

אַתָּה **'âttâ**. See 859.

אָתָא **'âthâ'**. See 857.

856. אֶתְבַּעַל **'Ethba'al**, *eth-bah'-al*; from 854 and 1168; *with Baal*; *Ethbaal*, a Phœnician king:— Ethbaal.

857. אָתָה **'âthâh**, *aw-thaw'*; or

אָתָא **'âthâ'**, *aw-thaw'*; a prim. root [collat. to 225 contr.]; to *arrive*:— (be-, things to) come (upon), bring.

858. אָתָה **'âthâh** (Chald.), *aw-thaw'*; or

אָתָא **'âthâ'** (Chald.), *aw-thaw'*; corresp. to 857:— (be-) come, bring.

859. אַתָּה **'attâh**, *at-taw'*; or (short.);

אַתָּ **'attâ**, *at-taw'*; or

אָת **'ath**, *ath*; fem. (irreg.) sometimes

אַתִּי **'attîy**, *at-tee'*; plur. masc.

אַתֶּם **'attem**, *at-tem'*; fem.

אַתֶּן **'atten**, *at-ten'*; or

אַתֵּנָה **'attênâh**, *at-tay'-naw*; or

אַתֵּנָּה **'attênnâh**, *at-tane'-naw*; a prim. pron. of the second pers.; *thou* and *thee*, or (plur.) *ye* and *you*:— thee, thou, ye, you.

860. אָתוֹן **'âthôwn**, *aw-thone'*; prob. from the same as 386 (in the sense of

patience); a female *ass* (from its docility):— (she) ass.

861. אַתּוּן 'attûwn (Chald.), *at-toon´*; prob. from the corresp. to 784; prob. a *fire-place*, i.e. *furnace*:— furnace.

862. אָתִיק 'attûwq, *at-tooke´*; or

אַתִּיק 'attîyq; *at-teek´*; from 5423 in the sense of *decreasing*; a *ledge* or offset in a building:— gallery.

אֵתִי 'attîy. See 859.

863. אִתַּי 'Ittay, *it-tah´ee*; or

אִיתַי 'Iythay, *ee-thah´ee*; from 854; *near*; *Ittai* or *Ithai*, the name of a Gittite and of an Isr.:— Ithai, Ittai.

864. אֵתָם 'Êthâm, *ay-thawm´*; of Eg. der.; *Etham*, a place in the Desert:— Etham.

אֵתֶן 'attem. See 859.

865. אֶתְמוֹל 'ethmôwl, *eth-mole´*; or

אִתְמוֹל 'ithmôwl, *ith-mole´*; or

אֶתְמוּל 'ethmûwl, *eth-mool´*; prob. from 853 or 854 and 4136; *heretofore*; def. *yesterday*:— + before (that) time, + heretofore, of late (old), + times past, yesterlday!

אֵתֶן 'atten. See 859.

866. אֶתְנָה 'ethnâh, *eth-naw´*; from 8566; a *present* (as the price of harlotry):— reward.

אֶתְנֶה 'attênâh or

אֶתְנֶּה 'attênnâh. See 859.

867. אֶתְנִי 'Ethnîy, *eth-nee´*; perh. from 866; *munificence*; *Ethni*, an Isr.:— Ethni.

868. אֶתְנַן 'ethnan, *eth-nan´*; the same as 866; a *gift* (as the price of harlotry or idolatry):— hire, reward.

869. אֶתְנָן 'Ethnan, *eth-nan´*; the same as 868 in the sense of 867; *Ethnan*, an Isr.:— Ethnan.

870. אֲתַר 'âthar (Chald.), *ath-ar´*; from a root corresp. to that of 871; a *place*; (adv.) *after*:— after, place.

871. אֲתָרִים 'Athârîym, *ath-aw-reem´*; plur. from an unused root (prob. mean. to *step*); *places*; *Atharim*, a place near Pal.:— spies.

בּ

872. בְּאָה bᵉâh, *bĕ-aw´*; from 935, an *entrance* to a building:— entry.

873. בְּאוּשׁ bi'ûwsh (Chald.), *be-oosh´*; from 888; *wicked*:— bad.

874. בָּאַר bâ'ar, *baw-ar´*; a prim. root; to *dig*; by anal. to *engrave*; fig. to *explain*:— declare, (make) plain (-ly).

875. בְּאֵר bᵉêr, *bĕ-ayr´*; from 874; a *pit*; espec. a *well*:— pit, well.

876. בְּאֵר Bᵉêr, *bĕ-ayr´*; the same as 875; *Beër*, a place in the Desert, also one in Pal.:— Beer.

877. בֹּאר bô'r, *bore*; from 874; a *cistern*:— cistern.

878. בְּאֵרָא Bᵉêrâ, *bĕ-ay-raw´*; from 875; a *well*; *Beëra*, an Isr.:— Beera.

879. בְּאֵר אֵלִים Bᵉêr 'Êlîym, *bĕ-ayr´ ay-leem´*; from 875 and the plur. of 410; *well of heroes*; *Beër-Elim*, a place in the Desert:— Beer-elim.

880. בְּאֵרָה Bᵉêrâh, *bĕ-ay-raw´*; the same as 878; *Beërah*, an Isr.:— Beerah.

881. בְּאֵרוֹת Bᵉêrôwth, *bĕ-ay-rohth´*; fem. plur. of 875; *wells*; *Beëroth*, a place in Pal.:— Beeroth.

882. בְּאֵרִי Bᵉêrîy, *bĕ-ay-ree´*; from 875; *fountained*; *Beëri*, the name of a Hittite and of an Isr.:— Beeri.

883. בְּאֵר לַחַי רֹאִי Bᵉêr la-Chay Rô'îy, *bĕ-ayr´ lakh-ah´ee ro-ee´*; from 875 and 2416 (with pref.) and 7203; *well of a living* (One) *my seer*; *Beër-Lachai-Roï*, a place in the Desert:— Beer-lahai-roi.

884. בְּאֵר שֶׁבַע Bᵉêr Sheba', *be-ayr´ sheh´-bah*; from 875 and 7651 (in the sense of 7650); *well of an oath*; *Beër-Sheba*, a place in Pal.:— Beer-shebah.

885. בְּאֵרֹת בְּנֵי־יַעֲקָן Bᵉêrôth Bᵉnêy-Ya'âqan, *bĕ-ay-roth´ be-nay´ yah-a-kan´*; from the fem. plur. of 875, and the plur. contr. of 1121, and 3292; *wells of* (the) *sons of Jaakan*; *Beëroth-Bene-Jaakan*, a place in the Desert:— Beeroth of the children of Jaakan.

886. בְּאֵרֹתִי Bᵉêrôthîy, *bĕ-ay-ro-thee´*; patrial from 881; a *Beërothite* or inhab. of Beëroth:— Beerothite.

887. בָּאַשׁ bâ'ash, *baw-ash´*; a prim. root; to *smell* bad; fig. to *be offensive* mor.:— (make to) be abhorred (had in abomination, loathsome, odious), (cause a, make to) stink (-ing savour), × utterly.

888. בְּאֵשׁ bᵉêsh (Chald.), *bĕ-aysh´*; corresp. to 887:— displease.

889. בְּאֹשׁ bᵉôsh, *bĕ-oshe´*; from 877; a *stench*:— stink.

890. בָּאְשָׁה bo'shâh, *bosh-aw´*; fem. of 889; *stink-weed* or any other noxious or useless plant:— cockle.

891. בְּאֻשִׁים bᵉushîym, *bĕ-oo-sheem´*; plur. of 889; *poison-berries*:— wild grapes.

892. בָּבָה bâbâh, *baw-baw´*; fem. act. part. of an unused root mean. to *hollow* out; something *hollowed* (as a *gate*), i.e. the *pupil* of the eye:— apple [of the eye].

893. בֵּבַי Bêbay, *bay-bah´ee*; prob. of for. or.; *Bebai*, an Isr.:— Bebai.

894. בָּבֶל Bâbel, *baw-bel´*; from 1101; *confusion*; *Babel* (i.e. Babylon), incl. Babylonia and the Bab. empire:— Babel, Babylon.

895. בָּבֶל Bâbel (Chald.), *baw-bel´*; corresp. to 894:— Babylon.

896. בַּבְלִי Bablîy (Chald.), *bab-lee´*; patrial from 895; a *Babylonian*:— Babylonia.

897. בַּג bag, *bag*; a Pers. word; *food*:— spoil [from the marg. for 957.]

898. בָּגַד bâgad, *baw-gad´*; a prim. root; to *cover* (with a garment); fig. to *act covertly*; by impl. to *pillage*:— deal deceitfully (treacherously, unfaithfully), offend, transgress (-or), (depart), treacherous (dealer, -ly, man), unfaithful (-ly, man), × very

899. בֶּגֶד beged, *behg´-ed*; from 898; a *covering*, i.e. clothing; also *treachery* or *pillage*:— apparel, cloth (-es, ing), garment, lap, rag, raiment, robe, × very [treacherously], vesture, wardrobe.

900. בֹּגְדוֹת bôgᵉdôwth, *bohg-ed-ōhth´*; fem. plur. act. part. of 898; *treacheries*:— treacherous.

901. בָּגוֹד bâgôwd, *baw-gode´*; from 898; *treacherous*:— treacherous.

902. בִּגְוַי Bigvay, *big-vah´ee*; prob. of for. or.; *Bigvai*, an Isr.:— Bigvai.

903. בִּגְתָא Bigthâ', *big-thaw´*; of Pers. der.; *Bigtha*, a eunuch of Xerxes:— Bigtha.

904. בִּגְתָן Bigthân, *big-thawn´*; or

בִּגְתָנָא Bigthânâ', *big-thaw´naw*; of similar der. to 903; *Bigthan* or *Bigthana*, a eunuch of Xerxes:— Bigthan, Bigthana.

905. בַּד bad, *bad*; from 909; prop. *separation*; by impl. a *part* of the body, *branch* of a tree, *bar* for carrying; fig. *chief* of a city; espec. (with prep. pref.) as adv., *apart*, *only*, *besides*:— alone, apart, bar, besides, branch, by self, of each alike, except, only, part, staff, strength.

906. בַּד bad, *bad*; perh. from 909 (in the sense of *divided* fibres); flaxen *thread* or yarn; hence, a *linen garment*:— linen.

907. בַּד bad, *bad*; from 908; a *brag* or *lie*; also a *liar*:— liar, lie.

908. בָּדָא bâdâ', *baw-daw´*; a prim. root; (fig.) to *invent*:— devise, feign.

909. בָּדַד bâdad, *baw-dad´*; a prim. root; to *divide*, i.e. (reflex.) be *solitary*:— alone.

910. בָּדָד bâdâd, *baw-dawd´*; from 909; *separate*; adv. *separately*:— alone, desolate, only, solitary.

911. בְּדַד Bᵉdad, *bed-ad´*; from 909; *separation*; *Bedad*, an Edomite:— Bedad.

912. בֵּדְיָה Bêdᵉyâh, *bay-dĕ-yaw´*; prob. short. form 5662; *servant of Jehovah*; *Bedejah*, an Isr.:— Bedeiah.

913. בְּדִיל bᵉdîyl, *bed-eel´*; from 914; *alloy* (because *removed* by smelting); by anal. *tin*:— + plummet, tin.

914. בָּדַל bâdal, *baw-dal´*; a prim. root; to *divide* (in var. senses lit. or fig., *separate*, *distinguish*, *differ*, *select*, etc.):— (make, put) difference, divide (asunder), (make) separate (self, -ation), sever (out), × utterly.

915. בָּדָל bâdâl, *baw-dawl´*; from 914; a *part*:— piece.

916. בְּדֹלַח bᵉdôlach, *bed-o´-lakh*; prob. from 914; something in *pieces*, i.e. *bdellium*, a (fragrant) gum (perh. *amber*); others a *pearl*:— bdellium.

917. בְּדָן Bᵉdân, *bed-awn´*; prob. short. for 5658; *servile*; *Bedan*, the name of two Isr.:— Bedan.

918. בָּדַק bâdaq, *baw-dak´*; a prim. root; to *gap* open; used only as a denom. from 919; to *mend* a breach:— repair.

919. בֶּדֶק bedeq, *beh´-dek*; from 918; a *gap* or *leak* (in a building or a ship):— breach, + calker.

920. בִּדְקַר Bidqar, *bid-car´*; prob. from 1856 with prep. pref.; *by stabbing*, i.e. *assassin*; *Bidkar*, an Isr.:— Bidkar.

921. בְּדַר bᵉdar (Chald.), *bed-ar´*; cor-

resp. (by transp.) to 6504; to *scatter:*— scatter.

922. בֹהוּ **bôhûw**, *bo´-hoo;* from an unused root (mean. to *be empty*); a *vacuity,* i.e. (superficially) an undistinguishable *ruin:*— emptiness, void.

923. בהט **bahaṭ**, *bah´-hat;* from an unused root (prob. mean. to *glisten*); white *marble* or perh. *alabaster:*— red [marble].

924. בהילו **b**ᵉ**hîylûw** (Chald.), *bĕ-hee-loo´;* from 927; a *hurry;* only adv. *hastily:*— in haste.

925. בהיר **bâhîyr**, *baw-here´;* from an unused root (mean. to *be bright*); *shining:*— bright.

926. בהל **bâhal**, *baw-hal´;* a prim. root; to *tremble* inwardly (or *palpitate*), i.e. (fig.) *be* (caus. *make*) (suddenly) *alarmed* or *agitated;* by impl. to *hasten* anxiously:— be (make) affrighted (afraid, amazed, dismayed, rash), (be, get, make) haste (-n, -y, -ily), (give) speedy (-ily), thrust out, trouble, vex.

927. בהל **b**ᵉ**hal** (Chald.), *bĕ-hal´;* corresp. to 926; to *terrify, hasten:*— in haste, trouble.

928. בהלה **behâlâh**, *beh-haw-law´;* from 926; *panic, destruction:*— terror, trouble.

929. בהמה **b**ᵉ**hêmâh**, *bĕ-hay-maw´;* from an unused root (prob. mean. to *be mute*); prop. a *dumb beast;* espec. any large quadruped or *animal* (often collect.):— beast, cattle.

930. בהמות **b**ᵉ**hêmôwth**, *bĕ-hay-môhth´;* in form a plur. of 929, but really a sing. of Eg. der.; a *water-ox,* i.e. the *hippopotamus* or Nile-horse:— Behemoth.

931. בהן **bôhen**, *bo´-hen;* from an unused root appar. mean. to *be thick;* the *thumb* of the hand or *great toe* of the foot:— thumb, great toe.

932. בהן **Bôhan**, *bo´han;* an orth. var. of 931; *thumb, Bohan,* an Isr.:— Bohan.

933. בהק **bôhaq**, *bo´-hak;* from an unused root mean. to *be pale;* white *scurf:*— freckled spot.

934. בהרת **bôhereth**, *bo-heh´-reth;* fem. act. part. of the same as 925; a *whitish* spot on the skin:— bright spot.

935. בא **bôw´**, *bo;* a prim. root; to *go* or *come* (in a wide variety of applications):— abide, apply, attain, × be, befall, + besiege, bring (forth, in, into, to pass), call, carry, × certainly, (cause, let, thing for) to come (against, in, out, upon, to pass), depart, × doubtless again, + eat, + employ, (cause to) enter (in, into, -tering, -trance, -try) be fallen, fetch, + follow, get, give, go (down, in, to war), grant, + have, × indeed, [in-]vade, lead, lift [up], mention, pull in, put, resort, run (down), send, set, × (well) stricken [in age], × surely, take (in), way.

בוב **bûwb**. See 892, 5014.

936. בוז **bûwz**, *booz;* a prim. root; to *disrespect:*— contemn, despise, × utterly.

937. בוז **bûwz**, *booz;* from 936; *disrespect:*— contempt (-uously), despised, shamed.

938. בוז **Bûwz**, *booz;* the same as 937;

Buz, the name of a son of Nahor, and of an Isr.:— Buz.

939. בוזה **bûwzâh**, *boo-zaw´;* fem. pass. part. of 936; something *scorned;* an obj. of *contempt:*— despised.

940. בוזי **Bûwziy**, *boo-zee´;* patron. from 938; a *Buzite* or desc. of Buz:— Buzite.

941. בוזי **Bûwzîy**, *boo-zee´;* the same as 940; *Buzi,* an Isr.:— Buzi.

942. בוי **Bavvay**, *bav-vah´ee;* prob. of Pers. or.; *Bavvai,* an Isr.:— Bavai.

943. בוך **bûwk**, *book;* a prim. root; to *involve* (lit. or fig.):— be entangled, (perplexed).

944. בול **bûwl**, *bool;* for 2981; *produce* (of the earth, etc.):— food, stock.

945. בול **Bûwl**, *bool;* the same as 944 (in the sense of *rain*); *Bul,* the eighth Heb. month:— Bul.

בום **bûwm**. See 1116.

946. בונה **Bûwnâh**, *boo-naw´;* from 995; *discretion; Bunah,* an Isr.:— Bunah.

בוני **Bûwnîy**. See 1138.

947. בוס **bûwç**, *boos;* a prim. root; to *trample* (lit. or fig.):— loath, tread (down, under [foot]), be polluted.

948. בוץ **bûwts**, *boots;* from an unused root (of the same form) mean. to *bleach,* i.e. (intr.) *be white;* prob. *cotton* (of some sort):— fine (white) linen.

949. בוצץ **Bôwtsêts**, *bo-tsates´;* from the same as 948; *shining; Botsets,* a rock near Michmash:— Bozez.

950. בוקה **bûwqâh**, *boo-kaw´;* fem. pass. part. of an unused root (mean. to *be hollow*); *emptiness* (as adj.):— empty.

951. בוקר **bôwkêr**, *bo-kare´;* prop. act. part. from 1239 as denom. from 1241; a *cattle-tender:*— herdman.

952. בור **bûwr**, *boor;* a prim. root; to *bore,* i.e. (fig.) *examine:*— declare.

953. בור **bôwr**, *bore;* from 952 (in the sense of 877); a *pit hole* (espec. one used as a *cistern* or a *prison*):— cistern, dungeon, fountain, pit, well.

954. בוש **bûwsh**, *boosh;* a prim. root; prop. to *pale,* i.e. by impl. to *be ashamed;* also (by impl.) to *be disappointed,* or *delayed:*— (be, make, bring to, cause, put to, with, a-) shamed (-d), be (put to) confounded (-fusion), become dry, delay, be long.

955. בושה **bûwshâh**, *boo-shaw´;* fem. part. pass. of 954; *shame:*— shame.

956. בות **bûwth** (Chald.), *booth;* appar. denom. from 1005; to *lodge* over night:— pass the night.

957. בז **baz**, *baz;* from 962; *plunder:*— booty, prey, spoil (-ed).

958. בזא **bâzâ´**, *baw-zaw´;* a prim. root; prob. to *cleave:*— spoil.

959. בזה **bâzâh**, *baw-zaw´;* a prim. root; to *disesteem:*— despise, disdain, contemn (-ptible), + think to scorn, vile person.

960. בזה **bâzôh**, *baw-zo´;* from 959; *scorned:*— despise.

961. בזה **bizzâh**, *biz-zaw´;* fem. of 957; *booty:*— prey, spoil.

962. בזז **bâzaz**, *baw-zaz´;* a prim. root;

---

to *plunder:*— catch, gather, (take) for a prey, rob (-ber), spoil, take (away, spoil), × utterly.

963. בזיון **bizzâyôwn**, *biz-zaw-yone´;* from 959; *disesteem:*— contempt.

964. בזיותיה **bizyôwth**ᵉ**yâh**, *biz-yo-thĕ-yaw´;* from 959 and 3050; *contempts of Jah; Bizjothjah,* a place in Pal.:— Bizjothjah.

965. בזק **bâzâq**, *baw-zawk´;* from an unused root mean. to *lighten; a flash* of lightning:— flash of lightning.

966. בזק **Bezeq**, *beh´-zek;* from 965; *lightning; Bezek,* a place in Pal.:— Bezek.

967. בזר **bâzar**, *baw-zar´;* a prim. root; to *disperse:*— scatter.

968. בזתא **Bizthâ´**, *biz-thaw´;* of Pers. or.; *Biztha,* a eunuch of Xerxes:— Biztha.

969. בחון **bâchôwn**, *baw-khone´;* from 974; an *assayer* of metals:— tower.

970. בחור **bâchûwr**, *baw-khoor´;* or

בחר **bâchûr**, *baw-khoor´;* pass. part. of 977; prop. *selected,* i.e. a *youth* (often collect.):— (choice) young (man), chosen, × hole.

בחורות **b**ᵉ**chûrôwth**. See 979.

בחורים **Bachûwrîym**. See 980.

971. בחין **bachîyn**, *bakh-een´;* another form of 975; a *watch-tower* of besiegers:— tower.

972. בחיר **bâchîyr**, *baw-kheer´;* from 977; *select:*— choose, chosen one, elect.

973. בחל **bâchal**, *baw-khal´;* a prim. root; to *loathe:*— abhor, get hastily [from the marg. for 926].

974. בחן **bâchan**, *baw-khan´;* a prim. root; to *test* (espec. metals); gen. and fig. to *investigate:*— examine, prove, tempt, try (trial).

975. בחן **bachan**, *bakh´-an;* from 974 (in the sense of keeping a *look-out*); a watch-*tower:*— tower.

976. בחן **bôchan**, *bo´-khan;* from 974; *trial:*— tried.

977. בחר **bâchar**, *baw-khar´;* a prim. root; prop. to *try,* i.e. (by impl.) *select:*— acceptable, appoint, choose (choice), excellent, join, be rather, require.

בחר **bâchûr**. See 970.

978. בחרומי **Bachărûwmiy**, *bakh-ar-oo-mee´;* patrial from 980 (by transp.); a *Bacharumite* or inhab. of Bachurim:— Baharumite.

979. בחרות **b**ᵉ**chûrôwth**, *bekh-oo-rothe´;* or

בחרות **b**ᵉ**chûrôwth**, *bekh-ooroth´;* fem. plur. of 970; also (masc. plur.)

בחרים **b**ᵉ**chûrîym**, *bekh-oo-reem´; youth* (collect. and abstr.):— young men, youth.

980. בחרים **Bachûrîym**, *bakh-oo-reem´;* or

בחרים **Bachûwrîym**, *bakh-oo-reem´;* masc. plur. of 970; *young men; Bachurim,* a place in Pal.:— Bahurim.

981. בטא **bâṭâ´**, *baw-taw´;* or

בטה **bâṭâh**, *baw-taw´;* a prim. root;

to *babble;* hence, to *vociferate* angrily:— pronounce, speak (unadvisedly).

982. בָּטַח **bâṭach**, *baw-takh´;* a prim. root; prop. to *hie* for refuge [but not so *precipitately* as 2620]; fig. to *trust, be confident* or *sure:*— be bold (confident, secure, sure), careless (one, woman), put confidence, (make to) hope, (put, make to) trust.

983. בֶּטַח **beṭach**, *beh´takh;* from 982; prop. a place of *refuge;* abstr. *safety,* both the fact (*security*) and the feeling (*trust*); often (adv. with or without prep.) *safely:*— assurance, boldly, (without) care (-less), confidence, hope, safe (-ly, -ty), secure, surely.

984. בֶּטַח **Beṭach**, *beh´-takh; the same as* 983; *Betach, a place in Syria:*— Betah.

985. בִּטְחָה **biṭchâh**, *bit-khaw´;* fem. of 984; *trust:*— confidence.

986. בִּטָּחוֹן **biṭṭâchôwn**, *bit-taw-khone´;* from 982; *trust:*— confidence, hope.

987. בַּטֻּחוֹת **baṭṭuchôwth**, *bat-too-khôth´; fem. plur. from* 982; *security:*— secure.

988. בָּטֵל **bâṭêl**, *baw-tale´;* a prim. root; to *desist* from labor:— cease.

989. בְּטֵל **beṭêl** (Chald.), *bet-ale´;* corresp. to 988; to *stop:*— (cause, make to), cease, hinder.

990. בֶּטֶן **beṭen**, *beh´-ten;* from an unused root prob. mean. to *be hollow;* the *belly,* espec. the *womb;* also the *bosom* or *body* of anything:— belly, body, + as they be born, + within, womb.

991. בֶּטֶן **Beṭen**, *beh´-ten; the same as* 990; *Beten, a place in Pal.:*— Beten.

992. בֹּטֶן **bôṭen**, *bo´-ten;* from 990; (only in plur.) a *pistachio*-nut (from its form):— nut.

993. בְּטֹנִים **Beṭônîym**, *bet-o-neem´;* prob. plur. from 992; *hollows; Betonim,* a place in Pal.:— Betonim.

994. בִּי **bîy**, *bee;* perh. from 1158 (in the sense of *asking*); prop. a *request;* used only adv. (always with "my Lord"); *Oh that!; with leave,* or *if it please:*— alas, O, oh.

995. בִּין **bîyn**, *bene;* a prim. root; to *separate* mentally (or *distinguish*), i.e.(gen.) *understand:*— attend, consider, be cunning, diligently, direct, discern, eloquent, feel, inform, instruct, have intelligence, know, look well to, mark, perceive, be prudent, regard, (can) skill (-full), teach, think, (cause,make to, get, give, have) understand (-ing), view, (deal) wise (-ly, man).

996. בֵּין **bêyn**, *bane* (sometimes in the plur. masc. or fem.); prop. the constr. contr. form of an otherwise unused noun from 995; a *distinction;* but used only as a prep. *between* (repeated before each noun, often with other particles); also as a conj., *either ... or:*— among, asunder, at, between (-twixt ... and), + from (the widest), × in, out of, whether (it be ... or), within.

997. בֵּין **bêyn** (Chald.), *bane;* corresp. to 996:— among, between.

998. בִּינָה **bîynâh**, *bee-naw´;* from 995; *understanding:*— knowledge, mean-

ing, × perfectly, understanding, wisdom.

999. בִּינָה **bîynâh** (Chald.), *bee-naw´;* corresp. to 998:— knowledge.

1000. בֵּיצָה **bêytsâh**, *bay-tsaw´;* from the same as 948; an *egg* (from its whiteness):— egg.

1001. בִּירָא **bîyrâ** (Chald.), *bee-raw´;* corresp. to 1002; a *palace:*— palace.

1002. בִּירָה **bîyrâh**, *bee-raw´;* of for. or.; a *castle* or *palace:*— palace.

1003. בִּירָנִית **bîyrânîyth**, *bee-raw-neeth´;* from 1002; a *fortress:*— castle.

1004. בַּיִת **bayith**, *bah´-yith;* prob. from 1129 abb.; a *house* (in the greatest var. of applications, espec. *family,* etc.):— court, daughter, door, + dungeon, family, + forth of, × great as would contain, hangings, homeborn], [winter]house (-hold), inside (-ward), palace, place, + prison, + steward, + tablet, temple, web, + within (-out).

1005. בַּיִת **bayith** (Chald.), *bah-yith;* corresp. to 1004:— house.

1006. בַּיִת **Bayith**, *bah´-yith; the same as* 1004; *Bajith,* a place in Pal.:— Bajith.

1007. בֵּית אָוֶן **Bêyth 'Âven**, *bayth aw´ven;* from 1004 and 205; *house of vanity; Beth-Aven,* a place in Pal.:— Beth-aven.

1008. בֵּית־אֵל **Bêyth-'Êl**, *bayth-ale´;* from 1004 and 410; *house of God; Beth-El,* a place in Pal.:— Beth-el.

1009. בֵּית אַרְבֵּאל **Bêyth 'Arbê'l**, *bayth arbale´;* from 1004 and 695 and 410; *house of God's ambush; Beth-Arbel,* a place in Pal.:— Beth-Arbel.

1010. בֵּית בַּעַל מְעוֹן **Bêyth Ba'al Me'ôwn**, *bayth bah´-al mě-own´;* from 1004 and 1168 and 4583; *house of Baal of* (the) *habitation of* [appar. by transp.]; or (short.)

בֵּית מְעוֹן **Bêyth Me'ôwn**, *bayth mě-own´; house of habitation of* (Baal); *Beth-Baal-Meön,* a place in Pal.:— Beth-baal-meon. Comp. 1186 and 1194.

1011. בֵּית בִּרְאִי **Bêyth Bir'îy**, *bayth bir-ee´;* from 1004 and 1254; *house of a creative one; Beth-Biri,* a place in Pal.:— Beth-birei.

1012. בֵּית בָּרָה **Bêyth Bârâh**, *bayth bawraw´;* prob. from 1004 and 5679; *house of* (the) *ford; Beth-Barah,* a place in Pal.:— Beth-barah.

1013. בֵּית־גָּדֵר **Bêyth-Gâdêr**, *bayth-gawdare´;* from 1004 and 1447; *house of* (the) *wall; Beth-Gader,* a place in Pal.:— Beth-gader.

1014. בֵּית גָּמוּל **Bêyth Gâmûwl**, *bayth gaw-mool´;* from 1004 and the pass. part. of 1576; *house of* (the) *weaned; Beth-Gamul,* a place E. of the Jordan:— Beth-gamul.

1015. בֵּית דִּבְלָתַיִם **Bêyth Diblâthayim**, *bayth dib-law-thah´-yim;* from 1004 and the dual of 1690; *house of* (the) *two figcakes; Beth-Diblathajim,* a place E. of the Jordan:— Beth-diblathaim.

1016. בֵּית־דָּגוֹן **Bêyth-Dâgôwn**, *bayth-daw-gohn´;* from 1004 and 1712; *house of Dagon; Beth-Dagon,* the name of two places in Pal.:— Beth-dagon.

1017. בֵּית הָאֱלִי **Bêyth hâ-'Ĕlîy**, *bayth haw-el-ee´;* patrial from 1008 with the art. interposed; a *Beth-elite,* or inhab. of Bethel:— Bethelite.

1018. בֵּית הָאָצֵל **Bêyth hâ-'Êtsel**, *bayth haw-ay´-tsel;* from 1004 and 681 with the art. interposed; *house of the side; Beth-ha-Etsel,* a place in Pal.:— Beth-ezel.

1019. בֵּית הַגִּלְגָּל **Bêyth hag-Gilgâl**, *bayth hag-gil gawl´;* from 1004 and 1537 with the article interposed; *house of Gilgal* (or *rolling*); *Beth-hag-Gilgal,* a place in Pal.:— Beth-gilgal.

1020. בֵּית הַיְשִׁמוֹת **Bêyth ha-Yeshîymôwth**, *bayth hah-yesh-ee-môth´;* from 1004 and the plur. of 3451 with the art. interposed; *house of the deserts; Beth-ha-Jeshimoth,* a town E. of the Jordan:— Beth-jeshimoth.

1021. בֵּית הַכֶּרֶם **Bêyth hak-Kerem**, *bayth hak-keh´-rem;* from 1004 and 3754 with the art. interposed; *house of the vineyard; Beth-hak-Kerem,* a place in Pal.:— Beth-haccerem.

1022. בֵּית הַלַּחְמִי **Bêyth hal-Lachmîy**, *bayth hal-lakh-mee´;* patrial from 1035 with the art. ins.; a *Beth-lechemite,* or native of Bethlechem:— Bethlehemite.

1023. בֵּית הַמֶּרְחָק **Bêyth ham-Merchâq**, *bayth ham-mer-khawk´;* from 1004 and 4801 with the art. interposed; *house of the breadth; Beth-ham-Merchak,* a place in Pal.:— place that was far off.

1024. בֵּית הַמַּרְכָּבוֹת **Bêyth ham-Markâbôwth**, *bayth ham-mar-kaw-both´;* or (short.)

בֵּית מַרְכָּבוֹת **Bêyth Markâbôwth**, *bayth mar-kaw-both´;* from 1004 and the plur. of 4818 (with or without the art. interposed); *place of* (the) *chariots; Beth-ham-Markaboth* or *Beth-Mark-aboth,* a place in Pal.:— Beth-mar-caboth.

1025. בֵּית הָעֵמֶק **Bêyth hâ-'Êmeq**, *bayth haw-ay´-mek;* from 1004 and 6010 with the art. interposed; *house of the valley; Beth-ha-Emek,* a place in Pal.:— Beth-emek.

1026. בֵּית הָעֲרָבָה **Bêyth hâ-'Ărâbâh**, *bayth haw-ar-aw-baw´;* from 1004 and 6160 with the art. interposed; *house of the Desert; Beth-ha-Arabah,* a place in Pal.:— Beth-arabah.

1027. בֵּית הָרָם **Bêyth hâ-Râm**, *bayth haw-rawm´;* from 1004 and 7311 with the art. interposed; *house of the height; Beth-ha-Ram,* a place E. of the Jordan:— Beth-aram.

1028. בֵּית הָרָן **Bêyth hâ-Rân**, *bayth haw-rawn´;* prob. for 1027; *Beth-ha-Ran,* a place E. of the Jordan:— Beth-haran.

1029. בֵּית הַשִּׁטָּה **Bêyth hash-Shiṭṭâh**, *bayth hash-shit-taw´;* from 1004 and 7848 with the art. interposed; *house of the acacia; Beth-hash-Shittah,* a place in Pal.:— Beth-shittah.

1030. בֵּית הַשִּׁמְשִׁי **Bêyth hash-Shimshîy**, *bayth hash-shim-shee´;* patrial from 1053 with the art. ins.; a *Beth-shim-shite,* or inhab. of Bethshemesh:— Bethshemite.

1031. בֵּית חָגְלָה **Bêyth Choglâh**, *bayth chog-law´;* from 1004 and the same as

2295; *house of a partridge; Beth-Choglah*, a place in Pal.:— Beth-hoglah.

1032. בֵּית חוֹרוֹן **Bêyth Chôwrôwn**, *bayth kho-rone´;* from 1004 and 2356; *house of hollowness; Beth-Choron*, the name of two adjoining places in Pal.:— Beth-horon.

בֵּית חָנָן **Bêyth Chânân**. See 358.

1033. בֵּית כַּר **Bêyth Kar**, *bayth kar;* from 1004 and 3733; *house of pasture; Beth-Car*, a place in Pal.:— Beth-car.

1034. בֵּית לְבָאוֹת **Bêyth Lᵉbâ'ôwth**, *bayth leb-aw-ôth´;* from 1004 and the plural of 3833; *house of lionesses; Beth-Lebaoth*, a place in Pal.:— Beth-lebaoth. Comp. 3822.

1035. בֵּית לֶחֶם **Bêyth Lechem**, *bayth leh´-khem;* from 1004 and 3899; *house of bread; Beth-Lechem*, a place in Pal.:— Beth-lehem.

1036. בֵּית לְעַפְרָה **Bêyth lᵉ-'Aphrâh**, *bayth lĕ-af-raw´;* from 1004 and the fem. of 6083 (with prep. interposed); *house to* (i.e. *of*) *dust; Beth-le-Aphrah*, a place in Pal.:— house of Aphrah.

1037. בֵּית מִלֹּא **Bêyth Millôw'**, *bayth mil-lo´;* or

בֵּית מִלֹּא **Bêyth Millô'**, *bayth mil-lo´;* from 1004 and 4407; *house of* (the) *rampart; Beth-Millo*, the name of two citadels:— house of Millo.

1038. בֵּית מַעֲכָה **Bêyth Ma'ăkâh**, *bayth mah-ak-aw´;* from 1004 and 4601; *house of Maakah; Beth-Maakah*, a place in Pal.:— Beth-maachah.

1039. בֵּית נִמְרָה **Bêyth Nimrâh**, *bayth nim-raw´;* from 1004 and the fem. of 5246; *house of* (the) *leopard; Beth-Nimrah*, a place east of the Jordan:— Beth-nimrah. Comp. 5247.

1040. בֵּית עֵדֶן **Bêyth 'Êden**, *bayth ay´-den;* from 1004 and 5730; *house of pleasure; Beth-Eden*, a place in Syria:— Beth-eden.

1041. בֵּית עַזְמָוֶת **Bêyth 'Azmâveth**, *bayth az-maw´-veth;* from 1004 and 5820; *house of Azmaveth*, a place in Pal.:— Beth-az-maveth. Comp. 5820.

1042. בֵּית עֲנוֹת **Bêyth 'Ânôwth**, *bayth an-ôth´;* from 1004 and a plur. from 6030; *house of replies; Beth-Anoth*, a place in Pal.:— Beth-anoth.

1043. בֵּית עֲנָה **Bêyth 'Ănâth**, *bayth an-awth´;* an orth. var. for 1042; *Beth-Anath*, a place in Pal.:— Beth-anath.

1044. בֵּית עֵקֶד **Bêyth 'Êqed**, *bayth ay´-ked;* from 1004 and a der. of 6123; *house of* (the) *binding* (for sheep-shearing); *Beth-Eked*, a place in Pal.:— shearing house.

1045. בֵּית עַשְׁתָּרוֹת **Bêyth 'Ashtârôwth**, *bayth ash-taw-rôth´;* from 1004 and 6252; *house of Ashtoreths; Beth-Ashtaroth*, a place in Pal.:— house of Ashtaroth. Comp. 1203, 6252.

1046. בֵּית פֶּלֶט **Bêyth Peleṭ**, *bayth peh´-let;* from 1004 and 6412; *house of escape; Beth-Palet*, a place in Pal.:— Beth-palet.

1047. בֵּית פְּעוֹר **Bêyth Pᵉ'ôwr**, *bayth pĕore´;* from 1004 and 6465; *house of Peor; Beth-Peor*, a place E. of the Jordan:— Beth-peor.

1048. בֵּית פַּצֵּץ **Bêyth Patstsêts**, *bayth pats-tsates´;* from 1004 and a der. from 6327; *house of dispersion; Beth-Patstsets*, a place in Pal.:— Beth-pazzez.

1049. בֵּית צוּר **Bêyth Tsûwr**, *bayth tsoor´;* from 1004 and 6697; *house of* (the) *rock; Beth-Tsur*, a place in Pal.:— Beth-zur.

1050. בֵּית רְחוֹב **Bêyth Rᵉchôwb**, *bayth rĕ-khobe´;* from 1004 and 7339; *house of* (the) *street; Beth-Rechob*, a place in Pal.:— Beth-rehob.

1051. בֵּית רָפָא **Bêyth Râphâ'**, *bayth raw-faw´;* from 1004 and 7497; *house of* (the) *giant; Beth-Rapha*, an Isr.:— Beth-rapha.

1052. בֵּית שְׁאָן **Bêyth Shᵉ'ân**, *bayth shĕ-awn´;* or

בֵּית שָׁן **Bêyth Shân**, *bayth shawn´;* from 1004 and 7599; *house of ease; Beth-Shean* or *Beth-Shan*, a place in Pal.:— Beth-shean, Beth-Shan.

1053. בֵּית שֶׁמֶשׁ **Bêyth Shemesh**, *bayth sheh´-mesh;* from 1004 and 8121; *house of* (the) *sun; Beth-Shemesh*, a place in Pal.:— Beth-shemesh.

1054. בֵּית תַּפּוּחַ **Bêyth Tappûwach**, *bayth tap-poo´-akh;* from 1004 and 8598; *house of* (the) *apple; Beth-Tappuach*, a place in Pal.:— Beth-tappuah.

1055. בִּיתָן **bîythân**, *bee-thawn´;* prob. from 1004; a *palace* (i.e. *large house*):— palace.

1056. בָּכָא **Bâkâ'**, *baw-kaw´;* from 1058; *weeping; Baca*, a valley in Pal.:— Baca.

1057. בָּכָא **bâkâ'**, *baw-kaw´;* the same as 1056; the *weeping* tree (some gum-distilling tree, perh. the *balsam*):— mulberry tree.

1058. בָּכָה **bâkâh**, *baw-kaw´;* a prim. root; to *weep;* gen. to *bemoan:*— × at all, bewail, complain, make lamentation, × more, mourn, × sore, × with tears, weep.

1059. בֶּכֶה **bekeh**, *beh´-keh;* from 1058; a *weeping:*— × sore.

1060. בְּכוֹר **bᵉkôwr**, *bek-ore´;* from 1069; *firstborn;* hence, *chief:*— eldest (son), firstborn (-ling).

1061. בִּכּוּר **bikkûwr**, *bik-koor´;* from 1069; the *first-fruits* of the crop:— first fruit (-ripe [fig.]), hasty fruit.

1062. בְּכוֹרָה **bᵉkôwrâh**, *bek-o-raw´;* or (short.)

בְּכֹרָה **bᵉkôrâh**, *bek-o-raw´;* fem. of 1060; the *firstling* of man or beast; abstr. *primogeniture:*— birthright, firstborn (-ling).

1063. בִּכּוּרָה **bikkûwrâh**, *bik-koo-raw´;* fem. of 1061; the *early* fig:— firstripe (fruit).

1064. בְּכוֹרַת **Bᵉkôwrath**, *bek-o-rath´;* fem. of 1062; *primogeniture; Bekorath*, an Isr.:— Bechorath.

1065. בְּכִי **bᵉkîy**, *bek-ee´;* from 1058; a *weeping;* by anal. a *dripping:*— overflowing, × sore, (continual) weeping, wept.

1066. בֹּכִים **Bôkîym**, *bo-keem´;* plur. act. part. of 1058; (with the art.) the *weepers; Bo-kim*, a place in Pal.:— Bochim.

1067. בְּכִירָה **bᵉkîyrâh**, *bek-ee-raw´;* fem.

from 1069; the *eldest* daughter:— firstborn.

1068. בְּכִית **bᵉkîyth**, *bek-eeth´;* from 1058; a *weeping:*— mourning.

1069. בָּכַר **bâkar**, *baw-kar´;* a prim. root; prop. to *burst* the womb, i.e. (caus.) *bear* or *make early fruit* (of woman or tree); also (as denom. from 1061) to *give the birthright:*— make firstborn, be firstling, bring forth first child (new fruit).

1070. בֶּכֶר **beker**, *beh´-ker;* from 1069 (in the sense of *youth*); a young *camel:*— dromedary.

1071. בֶּכֶר **Beker**, *beh´-ker;* the same as 1070; *Beker*, the name of two Isr.:— Becher.

1072. בִּכְרָה **bikrâh**, *bik-raw´;* fem. of 1070; a young *she-camel:*— dromedary.

בְּכֹרָה **bᵉkôrâh**. See 1062.

1073. בַּכֻּרָה **bakkûrâh**, *bak-koo-raw´;* by orth. var. for 1063; a *first-ripe* fig:— firstripe.

1074. בֹּכְרוּ **Bôkᵉrûw**, *bo-ker-oo´;* from 1069; *first-born; Bokeru*, an Isr.:— Bocheru.

1075. בִּכְרִי **Bikrîy**, *bik-ree´;* from 1069; *youth-ful; Bikri*, an Isr.:— Bichri.

1076. בַּכְרִי **Bakrîy**, *bak-ree´;* patron. from 1071; a *Bakrite* (collect.) or desc. of Beker:— Bachrites.

1077. בַּל **bal**, *bal;* from 1086; prop. a *failure;* by impl. *nothing;* usually (adv.) *not* at all; also *lest:*— lest, neither, no, none (that ...), not (any), nothing.

1078. בֵּל **Bêl**, *bale;* by contr. for 1168; *Bel*, the Baal of the Babylonians:— Bel.

1079. בָּל **bâl** (Chald.), *bawl;* from 1080; prop. *anxiety,* i.e. (by impl.) the *heart* (as its seat):— heart.

1080. בְּלָא **bᵉlâ'** (Chald.), *bel-aw´;* corresp. to 1086 (but used only in a ment. sense); to *afflict:*— wear out.

1081. בַּלְאֲדָן **Bal'ădân**, *bal-ad-awn´;* from 1078 and 113 (contr.); *Bel* (is his) *lord; Baladan*, the name of a Bab. prince:— Baladan.

1082. בָּלַג **bâlag**, *baw-lag´;* a prim. root; to *break off* or *loose* (in a favorable or unfavorable sense), i.e. *desist* (from grief) or *invade* (with destruction):— comfort, (recover) strength (-en).

1083. בִּלְגָּה **Bilgâh**, *bil-gaw´;* from 1082; *desistance; Bilgah*, the name of two Isr.:— Bilgah.

1084. בִּלְגַּי **Bilgay**, *bil-gah´-ee;* from 1082; *desistant; Bilgai*, an Isr.:— Bilgai.

1085. בִּלְדַּד **Bildad**, *bil-dad´;* of uncert. der.; *Bildad*, one of Job's friends:— Bildad.

1086. בָּלָה **bâlâh**, *baw-law´;* a prim. root; to *fail;* by impl. to *wear out, decay* (caus. *consume, spend*):— consume, enjoy long, become (make, wax) old, spend, waste.

1087. בָּלֶה **bâleh**, *baw-leh´;* from 1086; *worn out:*— old.

1088. בָּלָה **Bâlâh**, *baw-law´;* fem. of 1087; *failure; Balah*, a place in Pal.:— Balah.

1089. בָּלַהּ **bâlahh**, *baw-lah´;* a prim. root [rather by transp. for 926]; to *pal-*

pitate; hence, (caus.) to *terrify:*— trouble.

1090. בִּלְהָה **Bilhâh,** *bil-haw´;* from 1089; *timid; Bilhah,* the name of one of Jacob's concubines; also of a place in Pal.:— Bilhah.

1091. בִּלְהָה **ballâhâh,** *bal-law-haw´;* from 1089; *alarm;* hence, *destruction:*— terror, trouble.

1092. בִּלְהָן **Bilhân,** *bil-hawn´;* from 1089; *timid; Bilhan,* the name of an Edomite and of an Isr.:— Bilhan.

1093. בְּלוֹ **bᵉlôw** (Chald.), *bel-o´;* from a root corresp. to 1086; *excise* (on articles consumed):— tribute.

1094. בְּלוֹא **bᵉlôw´,** *bel-o´;* or (fully)

בְּלוֹי **bᵉlôwy,** *bel-o´-ee;* from 1086; (only in plur. constr.) *rags:*— old.

1095. בֵּלְטְשַׁאצַּר **Bêlṭᵉsha'tstsar,** *bale-tesh-ats-tsar´;* of for. der.; *Belteshatstsar,* the Bab. name of Daniel:— Belteshazzar.

1096. בֵּלְטְשַׁאצַּר **Bêlṭᵉsha'tstsar** (Chald.), *bale-tesh-ats-tsar´;* corresp. to 1095:— Belteshazzar.

1097. בְּלִי **bᵉlîy,** *bel-ee´;* from 1086; prop. *failure,* i.e. *nothing* or *destruction;* usually (with prep.) *without, not yet, because not, as long as,* etc.:— corruption, iglnorantlyl, for lack of, where no ... is, so that no, none, not, unlawaresl, without.

1098. בְּלִיל **bᵉliyl;** from 1101; *mixed,* i.e. (spec.) *feed* (for cattle):— corn, fodder, provender.

1099. בְּלִימָה **bᵉliymâh,** *bel-ee-mah´;* from 1097 and 4100; (as indef.) *nothing whatever:*— nothing.

1100. בְּלִיַּעַל **bᵉliyaʿal,** *bel-e-yah´-al;* from 1097 and 3276; *without profit, worthlessness;* by extens. *destruction, wickedness* (often in connection with 376, 802, 1121, etc.):— Belial, evil, naughty, ungodly (men), wicked.

1101. בָּלַל **bâlal,** *baw-lal´;* a prim. root; to *overflow* (spec. with oil); by impl. to *mix;* also (denom. from 1098) to *fodder:*— anoint, confound, × fade, mingle, mix (self), give provender, temper.

1102. בָּלַם **bâlam,** *baw-lam´;* a prim. root; to *muzzle:*— be held in.

1103. בָּלַס **bâlaç,** *baw-las´;* a prim. root; to *pinch* sycamore figs (a process necessary to ripen them):— gatherer.

1104. בָּלַע **bâla',** *baw-lah´;* a prim. root; to *make away with* (spec. by *swallowing);* gen. to *destroy:*— cover, destroy, devour, eat up, be at end, spend up, swallow down (up).

1105. בֶּלַע **bela',** *beh´-lah;* from 1104; a *gulp;* fig. *destruction:*— devouring, that which he hath swallowed up.

1106. בֶּלַע **Bela',** *beh´-lah;* the same as 1105; *Bela,* the name of a place, also of an Edomite and of two Isr.:— Bela.

1107. בִּלְעֲדֵי **bil'ädêy,** *bil-ad-ay´;* or

בַּלְעֲדֵי **bal'ädêy,** *bal-ad-ay´;* constr. plur. from 1077 and 5703, *not till,* i.e. (as prep. or adv.) *except, without, besides:*— beside, not (in), save, without.

1108. בַּלְעִי **Bal'îy,** *bal-ee´;* patron. from

1106: a *Belaite* (collect.) or desc. of Bela:— Belaites.

1109. בִּלְעָם **Bil'âm,** *bil-awm´;* prob. from 1077 and 5971; *not* (of the) *people,* i.e. *foreigner; Bilam,* a Mesopotamian prophet; also a place in Pal.:— Balaam, Bileam.

1110. בָּלַק **bâlaq,** *baw-lak´;* a prim. root; to *annihilate:*— (make) waste.

1111. בָּלָק **Bâlâq,** *baw-lawk´;* from 1110; *waster; Balak,* a Moabitish king:— Balak.

1112. בֵּלְשַׁאצַּר **Bêlsha'tstsar,** *bale-shats-tsar´;* or

בֵּלְשַׁאצַּר **Bêl'shatstsar,** *bale-shats-tsar´;* of for. or. (comp. 1095); *Belshatstsar,* a Bab. king:— Belshazzar.

1113. בֵּלְשַׁאצַּר **Bêlsha'tstsar** (Chald.), *bale-shats-tsar´;* corresp. to 1112:— Belshazzar.

1114. בִּלְשָׁן **Bilshân,** *bil-shawn´;* of uncert. der.; *Bilshan,* an Isr.:— Bilshan.

1115. בִּלְתִּי **biltîy,** *bil-tee´;* constr. fem. of 1086 (equiv. to 1097); prop. a *failure of,* i.e. (used only as a neg. particle, usually with prep. pref.) *not, except, without, unless, besides, because not, until,* etc.:— because unlsatiablel, beside, but, + continual, except, from, lest, neither, no more, none, not, nothing, save, that no, without.

1116. בָּמָה **bâmâh,** *baw-maw´;* from an unused root (mean. to *be high);* an *elevation:*— height, high place, wave.

1117. בָּמָה **Bâmâh,** *baw-maw´;* the same as 1116; *Bamah,* a place in Pal.:— Bamah. See also 1120.

1118. בִּמְהָל **Bimhâl,** *bim-hawl´;* prob. from 4107 with prep. pref.; *with pruning; Bimhal,* an Isr.:— Bimhal.

1119. בְּמוֹ **bᵉmôw,** *bem-o´;* prol. for prep. pref.; *in, with, by,* etc.:— for, in into, through.

1120. בָּמוֹת **Bâmôwth,** *baw-mōth´;* plur. of 1116; *heights;* or (fully)

בָּמוֹת בַּעַל **Bâmôwth Ba'al,** *baw-mōth´ bah´-al;* from the same and 1168; *heights of Baal; Bamoth* or *Bamoth-Baal,* a place E. of the Jordan:— Bamoth, Bamoth-baal.

1121. בֵּן **bên,** *bane;* from 1129; a *son* (as a *builder* of the family name), in the widest sense (of lit. and fig. relationship, incl. *grandson, subject, nation, quality* or *condition,* etc., (like 1, 251, etc.)):— + afflicted, age, [Ahoh-] [Ammon-] [Hachmon-] [Lev-lite, [anoint-] ed one, appointed to, (+) arrow, [Assyr-] [Babylon-] [Egypt-] [Grec-lian, one born, bough, branch, breed, + (young) bullock, + (young) calf, × came up in, child, colt, × common, × corn, daughter, × of first , + firstborn, foal, + very fruitful, + postage, × in, + kid, + lamb, (+) man, meet, + mighty, + nephew, old, (+) people, + rebel, + robber, × servant born, × soldier, son, + spark, + steward, + stranger, × surely, them of, + tumultuous one, + valiant [-estl, whelp, worthy, young (one), youth.

1122. בֵּן **Bên,** *bane;* the same as 1121; *Ben,* an Isr.:— Ben.

1123. בֵּן **bên** (Chald.), *bane;* corresp. to 1121:— child, son, young.

1124. בְּנָא **bᵉnâ'** (Chald.), *ben-aw´;* or

בְּנָה **bᵉnâh** (Chald.), *ben-aw´;* corresp. to 1129; to *build:*— build, make.

1125. בֶּן־אֲבִינָדָב **Ben-'Äbîynâdâb,** *ben-ab-ee´-naw-dawb;* from 1121 and 40; (the) *son of Abinadab; Ben-Abinadab,* an Isr.:— the son of Abinadab.

1126. בֶּן־אוֹנִי **Ben-'Ôwnîy,** *ben-o-nee´;* from 1121 and 205; *son of my sorrow; Ben-Oni,* the orig. name of Benjamin:— Ben-oni.

1127. בֶּן־גֶּבֶר **Ben-Geber,** *ben-gheh´-ber;* from 1121 and 1397; *son of* (the) *hero; Ben-Geber,* an Isr.:— the son of Geber.

1128. בֶּן־דֶּקֶר **Ben-Deqer,** *ben-deh´-ker;* from 1121 and a der. of 1856; *son of piercing* (or *of a lance); Ben-Deker,* an Isr.:— the son of Dekar.

1129. בָּנָה **bânâh,** *baw-naw´;* a prim. root; to *build* (lit. and fig.):— (begin to) build (-er), obtain children, make, repair, set (up), × surely.

1130. בֶּן־הֲדַד **Ben-Hädad,** *ben-had-ad´;* from 1121 and 1908; *son of Hadad; Ben-Hadad,* the name of several Syrian kings:— Ben-hadad.

1131. בִּנּוּי **Binnûwy,** *bin-noo´-ee;* from 1129; *built* up; *Binnui,* an Isr.:— Binnui.

1132. בֶּן־זוֹחֵת **Ben-Zôwchêth,** *ben-zo-khayth´;* from 1121 and 2105; *son of Zocheth; Ben-Zocheth,* an Isr.:— Ben-zoketh.

1133. בֶּן־חוּר **Ben-Chûwr,** *ben-khoor´;* from 1121 and 2354; *son of Chur; Ben-Chur,* an Isr.:— the son of Hur.

1134. בֶּן־חַיִל **Ben-Chayil,** *ben-khah´-yil;* from 1121 and 2428; *son of might; Ben-Chail,* an Isr.:— Ben-hail.

1135. בֶּן־חָנָן **Ben-Chânân,** *ben-khaw-nawn´;* from 1121 and 2605; *son of Chanan; Ben-Chanan,* an Isr.:— Ben-ha-nan.

1136. בֶּן־חֶסֶד **Ben-Cheçed,** *ben-kheh´-sed;* from 1121 and 2617; *son of kindness; Ben-Chesed,* an Isr.:— the son of Hesed.

1137. בָּנִי **Bânîy,** *baw-nee´;* from 1129; *built; Bani,* the name of five Isr.:— Bani.

1138. בֻּנִּי **Bunniy,** *boon-nee´;* or (fuller)

בּוּנִי **Bûwnîy,** *boo-nee´;* from 1129; *built; Bunni* or *Buni,* an Isr.:— Bunni.

1139. בְּנֵי־בְרַק **Bᵉnêy-Bᵉraq,** *ben-ay´-ber-ak´;* from the plur. constr. of 1121 and 1300; *sons of lightning, Bene-berak,* a place in Pal.:— Bene-barak.

1140. בִּנְיָה **binyâh,** *bin-yaw´;* fem. from 1129; a *structure:*— building.

1141. בְּנָיָה **Bᵉnâyâh,** *ben-aw-yaw´;* or (prol.)

בְּנָיָהוּ **Bᵉnâyâhûw,** *ben-aw-yaw´-hoo;* from 1129 and 3050; *Jah has built; Benajah,* the name of twelve Isr.:— Benaiah.

1142. בְּנֵי יַעֲקָן **Bᵉnêy Yaʿäqan,** *ben-ay´ yah-ak-awn´;* from the plur. of 1121 and 3292; *sons of Yaakan; Bene-Jaakan,* a place in the Desert:— Bene-jaakan.

1143. בֵּנַיִם **bênayim,** bay-nah´-yim; dual of 996; a *double interval,* i.e. the space between two armies:— + champion.

1144. בִּנְיָמִן **Binyâmîyn,** bin-yaw-mene´; from 1121 and 3225; *son of* (the) *right hand; Binjamin,* youngest son of Jacob; also the tribe descended from him, and its territory:— Benjamin.

1145. בֶּן־יְמִינִי **Ben-yᵉmîynîy,** ben-yem-ee-nee´; sometimes (with the art. ins.)

בֶּן־הַיְמִינִי **Ben-ha-yᵉmîynîy,** ben-hah-yem-ee-nee´; with 376 ins. (1 Sam. 9:1)

בֶּן־אִישׁ יְמִינִי **Ben-'Îysh Yᵉmîynîy,** ben-eesh´ yem-ee-nee´; *son of a man of Jemini;* or short. (1 Sam. 9:4; Esth. 2:5)

אִישׁ יְמִינִי **'Îysh Yᵉmîynîy,** eesh yem-ee-nee´; *a man of Jemini,* or (1 Sam. 20:1) simply

יְמִינִי **Yᵉmîynîy,** yem-ee-nee´; *a Jeminite;* (plur.

בֶּן־יְמִינִי **Bᵉnîy Yᵉmîynîy,** ben-ay´ yem-ee-nee´; patron. from 1144; a *Benjaminite,* or descendent of Benjamin:— Benjamite, of Benjamin.

1146. בִּנְיָן **binyân,** bin-yawn´; from 1129; an *edifice:*— building.

1147. בִּנְיָן **binyân** (Chald.), bin-yawn´; corresp. to 1146:— building.

1148. בְּנִינוּ **Bᵉnîynûw,** ben-ee-noo´; prob. from 1121 with pron. suff.; *our son; Beninu,* an Isr.:— Beninu.

1149. בְּנַס **bᵉnaç** (Chald.), ben-as´; of uncert. affin.; to *be enraged:*— be angry.

1150. בִּנְעָא **Bin'á',** bin-aw´; or

בִּנְעָה **Bin'âh,** bin-aw´; of uncert. der.; *Bina* or *Binah,* an Isr.:— Binea, Bineah.

1151. בֶּן־עַמִּי **Ben-'Ammîy,** ben-am-mee´; from 1121 and 5971 with pron. suff.; *son of my people; Ben-Ammi,* a son of Lot:— Ben-ammi.

1152. בְּסוֹדְיָה **Bᵉçôwdᵉyâh,** bes-o-deh-yaw´; from 5475 and 3050 with prep. pref.; *in* (the) *counsel of Jehovah; Besodeiah,* an Isr.:— Besodeiah.

1153. בְּסַי **Bᵉçay,** bes-ah´-ee; from 947; *domineering; Besai,* one of the Nethinim:— Besai.

1154. בֶּסֶר **beçer,** beh´-ser; from an unused root mean. to *be sour;* an *immature* grape:— unripe grape.

1155. בֹּסֶר **bôçer,** bo´ser; from the same as 1154:— sour grape.

1156. בְּעָא **bᵉ'â'** (Chald.), beh-aw´; or

בְּעָה **bᵉ'âh** (Chald.), beh-aw´; corresp. to 1158; to *seek* or *ask:*— ask, desire, make [petition], pray, request, seek.

1157. בְּעַד **bᵉ'ad,** beh-ad´; from 5704 with prep. pref.; *in up to* or *over against;* gen. *at, beside, among, behind, for,* etc.:— about, at, by (means of), for, over, through, up (-on), within.

1158. בְּעָה **bâ'âh,** baw-aw´; a prim. root; to *gush* over, i.e. to *swell;* (fig.) to *desire* earnestly; by impl. to *ask:*— cause, inquire, seek up, swell out.

1159. בְּעוּ **bâ'ûw** (Chald.), baw-oo´; from 1156; a *request:*— petition.

1160. בְּעוֹר **Bᵉ'ôwr,** beh-ore´; from 1197

(in the sense of *burning*); a *lamp; Beör,* the name of the father of an Edomitish king; also of that of Balaam:— Beor.

1161. בְּעוּתִים **bi'ûwthîym,** be-oo-theme´; masc. plur. from 1204; *alarms:*— terrors.

1162. בֹּעַז **Bô'az,** bo´-az; from an unused root of uncert. mean.; *Boaz,* the ancestor of David; also the name of a pillar in front of the temple:— Boaz.

1163. בָּעַט **bâ'at,** baw-at´; a prim. root; to *trample* down, i.e. (fig.) *despise:*— kick.

1164. בְּעִי **bᵉ'îy,** beh-ee´; from 1158; a *prayer:*— grave.

1165. בְּעִיר **bᵉ'îyr,** beh-ere´; from 1197 (in the sense of *eating*); *cattle:*— beast, cattle.

1166. בָּעַל **bâ'al,** baw-al´; a prim. root; to *be master;* hence, (as denom. from 1167) to *marry:*— have dominion (over), be husband, marry (-ried, × wife).

1167. בַּעַל **ba'al,** bah´-al; from 1166; a *master;* hence, a *husband,* or (fig.) *owner* (often used with another noun in modifications of this latter sense):— + archer, + babbler, + bird, captain, chief man, + confederate, + have to do, + dreamer, those to whom it is due, + furious, those that are given to it, great, + hairy, he that hath it, have, + horseman, husband, lord, man, + married, master, person, + sworn, they of.

1168. בַּעַל **Ba'al,** bah´-al; the same as 1167; *Baal,* a Phœnician deity:— Baal, [plur.] Baalim.

1169. בְּעֵל **bᵉ'êl** (Chald.), beh-ale´; corresp. to 1167:— + chancellor.

1170. בַּעַל בְּרִית **Ba'al Bᵉrîyth,** bah´-al ber-eeth´; from 1168 and 1285; *Baal of* (the) *covenant; Baal-Berith,* a special deity of the Shechemites:— Baal-berith.

1171. בַּעַל גָּד **Ba'al Gâd,** bah´-al gawd; from 1168 and 1409; *Baal of Fortune; Baal-Gad,* a place in Syria:— Baal-gad.

1172. בַּעֲלָה **ba'âlâh,** bah-al-aw´; fem. of 1167; a *mistress:*— that hath, mistress.

1173. בַּעֲלָה **Ba'âlâh,** bah-al-aw´; the same as 1172; *Baalah,* the name of three places in Pal.:— Baalah.

1174. בַּעַל חָמוֹן **Ba'al Hâmôwn,** bah´-al haw-mone´; from 1167 and 1995; *possessor of a multitude; Baal-Hamon,* a place in Pal.:— Baal-hamon.

1175. בְּעָלוֹת **Bᵉ'âlôwth,** beh-aw-loth´; plur. of 1172; *mistresses; Beäloth,* a place in Pal.:— Bealoth, in Aloth [by mistake for a plur. from 5927 with prep. pref.].

1176. בַּעַל זְבוּב **Ba'al Zᵉbûwb,** bah´-al zeb-oob´; from 1168 and 2070; *Baal of* (the) *Fly; Baal-Zebub,* a special deity of the Ekronites:— Baal-zebub.

1177. בַּעַל חָנָן **Ba'al Chânân,** bah´-al khaw-nawn´; from 1167 and 2603; *possessor of grace; Baal-Chanan,* the name of an Edomite, also of an Isr.:— Baal-hanan.

1178. בַּעַל חָצוֹר **Ba'al Châtsôwr,** bah´-al khaw-tsore´; from 1167 and a modif. of 2691; *possessor of a village; Baal-Chatsor,* a place in Pal.:— Baal-hazor.

1179. בַּעַל חֶרְמוֹן **Ba'al Chermôwn,** bah´-al kher-mone´; from 1167 and 2768; *possessor of Hermon; Baal-Chermon,* a place in Pal.:— Baal-hermon.

1180. בַּעֲלִי **Ba'âlîy,** bah-al-ee´; from 1167 with pron. suff.; *my master; Baali,* a symb. name for Jehovah:— Baali.

1181. בַּעֲלֵי בָּמוֹת **Ba'âlêy Bâmôwth,** bah-al-ay´ baw-môth´; from the plur. of 1168 and the plur. of 1116; *Baals of* (the) *heights; Baale-Bamoth,* a place E. of the Jordan:— lords of the high places.

1182. בְּעֶלְיָדָע **Bᵉ'elyâdâ',** beh-el-yaw-daw´; from 1168 and 3045; *Baal has known; Beëljada,* an Isr.:— Beeliada.

1183. בְּעַלְיָה **Bᵉ'alyâh,** beh-al-yaw´; from 1167 and 3050; *Jah* (is) *master; Bealjah,* an Isr.:— Bealiah.

1184. בַּעֲלֵי יְהוּדָה **Ba'âlêy Yᵉhûwdâh,** bah-al-ay´ yeh-hoo-daw´; from the plural of 1167 and 3063; *masters of Judah; Baale-Jehudah,* a place in Pal.:— Baale of Judah.

1185. בַּעֲלִיס **Ba'âlîç,** bah-al-ece´; prob. from a der. of 5965 with prep. pref.; *in exultation; Baalis,* an Ammonitish king:— Baalis.

1186. בַּעַל מְעוֹן **Ba'al Mᵉ'ôwn,** bah-al meh-one´; from 1168 and 4583; *Baal of* (the) *habitation* (of) [comp. 1010]; *Baal-Meön,* a place E. of the Jordan:— Baal-meon.

1187. בַּעַל פְּעוֹר **Ba'al Pᵉ'ôwr,** bah´-al peh-ore´; from 1168 and 6465; *Baal of Peor; Baal-Peör,* a Moabitish deity:— Baal-peor.

1188. בַּעַל פְּרָצִים **Ba'al Pᵉrâtsîym,** bah´-al per-aw-tseem´; from 1167 and the plur. of 6556; *possessor of breaches; Baal-Peratsim,* a place in Pal.:— Baal-perazim.

1189. בַּעַל צְפוֹן **Ba'al Tsᵉphôwn,** bah´-al tsef-one´; from 1168 and 6828 (in the sense of *cold*) [according to others an Eg. form of *Typhon,* the destroyer]; *Baal of winter; Baal-Tsephon,* a place in Eqypt:— Baal-zephon.

1190. בַּעַל שָׁלִשָׁה **Ba'al Shâlîshâh,** bah´-al shaw-lee-shaw´; from 1168 and 8031; *Baal of Shalishah, Baal-Shalishah,* a place in Pal.:— Baal-shalisha.

1191. בַּעֲלָה **Ba'âlâth,** bah-al-awth´; a modif. of 1172; *mistress-ship; Baalath,* a place in Pal.:— Baalath.

1192. בַּעֲלַת בְּאֵר **Ba'âlath Bᵉ'êr,** bah-al-ath´ beh-ayr´; from 1172 and 875; *mistress of a well; Baalath-Beër,* a place in Pal.:— Baalath-beer.

1193. בַּעַל תָּמָר **Ba'al Tâmâr,** bah´-al taw-mawr´; from 1167 and 8558; *possessor of* (the) *palm-tree; Baal-Tamar,* a place in Pal.:— Baal-tamar.

1194. בְּעֹן **Bᵉ'ôn,** beh-ohn´; prob. a contr. of 1010; *Beön,* a place E. of the Jordan:— Beon.

1195. בַּעֲנָא **Ba'ánâ',** bah-an-aw´; the same as 1196; *Baana,* the name of four Isr.:— Baana, Baanah.

1196. בַּעֲנָה **Ba'ánâh,** bah-an-aw´; from a der. of 6031 with prep. pref.; *in affliction; Baanah,* the name of four Isr.:— Baanah.

1197. בָּעַר **bâ'ar,** baw-ar´; a prim. root;

to *kindle*, i.e. *consume* (by fire or by eating); also (as denom. from 1198) to *be* (-*come*) *brutish*:— be brutish, bring (put, take) away, burn, (cause to) eat (up), feed, heat, kindle, set (Ion fire), waste.

1198. בָּעַר **ba'ar**, *bah'-ar*; from 1197; prop. *food* (as *consumed*); i.e. (by exten.) of cattle *brutishness*; (concr.) *stupid*:— brutish (person), foolish.

1199. בְּעֵרָא **Bâ'ărâ'**, *bah-ar-aw'*; from 1198; *brutish: Baara*, an Isr. woman:— Baara.

1200. בְּעֵרָה **bᵉ'êrâh**, *bĕ-ay-raw'*; from 1197; a *burning*:— fire.

1201. בַּעְשָׁא **Ba'shâ'**, *bah-shaw'*; from an unused root mean. to *stink; offensiveness; Basha*, a king of Israel:— Baasha.

1202. בַּעֲשֵׂיָה **Ba'ăsêyâh**, *bah-as-ay-yaw'*; from 6213 and 3050 with a prep. pref.; *in* (the) *work of Jah; Baasejah*, an Isr.:— Baaseiah.

1203. בְּעֶשְׁתְּרָה **Bᵉ'eshtᵉrâh**, *beh-esh-ter-aw'*; from 6251 (as sing. of 6252) with prep. pref.; *with Ashtoreth; Beështerah*, a place E. of the Jordan:— Beeshterah.

1204. בָּעַת **bâ'ath**, *baw-ath'*; a prim. root; to *fear*:— affright, be (make) afraid, terrify, trouble.

1205. בְּעָתָה **bᵉ'âthâh**, *beh-aw-thaw'*; from 1204; *fear*:— trouble.

1206. בֹּץ **bôts**, *botse*; prob. the same as 948; *mud* (as *whitish* clay):— mire.

1207. בִּצָּה **bitstsâh**, *bits-tsaw'*; intens. from 1206; a *swamp*:— fen, mire (-ry place).

1208. בָּצוֹר° **bâtsôwr**, *baw-tsore'*; from 1219; *inaccessible*, i.e. *lofty*:— vintage [by confusion with 1210].

1209. בֵּצַי **Bêtsay**, *bay-tsah'-ee*; perh. the same as 1153; *Betsai*, the name of two Isr.:— Bezai.

1210. בָּצִיר **bâtsiyr**, *haw-tseer'*; from 1219; *clipped*, i.e. the *grape crop*:— vintage.

1211. בֶּצֶל **betsel**, *beh'-tsel*; from an unused root appar. mean. to *peel*; an *onion*:— onion.

1212. בְּצַלְאֵל **Bᵉtsal'êl**, *bets-al-ale'*; prob. from 6738 and 410 with prep. pref.; *in* (the) *shadow* (i.e. *protection*) *of God; Betsalel*, the name of two Isr.:— Bezaleel.

1213. בַּצְלוּת **Batslûwth**, *bats-looth'*; or

בַּצְלִית **Batslîyth**, *bats-leeth'*; from the same as 1211; a *peeling; Batsluth* or *Batslith*, an Isr.:— Bazlith, Bazluth.

1214. בָּצַע **bâtsa'**, *baw-tsah'*; a prim. root to *break* off, i.e. (usually) *plunder*; fig. to *finish*, or (intr.) *stop*:— (be) covet (-ous), cut (off), finish, fulfill, gain (greedily), get, be given to [covetousness], greedy, perform, be wounded.

1215. בֶּצַע **betsa'**, *beh'-tsah*; from 1214; *plunder*; by extens. *gain* (usually unjust):— covetousness, (dishonest) gain, lucre, profit.

1216. בָּצֵק **bâtsêq**, *baw-tsake'*; a prim. root; perh. to *swell* up, i.e. *blister*:— swell.

1217. בָּצֵק **bâtsêq**, *baw-tsake'*; from

1216; *dough* (as *swelling* by fermentation):— dough, flour.

1218. בָּצְקָה **Botsqath**, *bots-cath'*; from 1216; a *swell* of ground; *Botscath*, a place in Pal.:— Bozcath, Boskath.

1219. בָּצַר **bâtsar**, *baw-tsar'*; a prim. root; to *clip* off; spec. (as denom. from 1210) to *gather* grapes; also to be *isolated* (i.e. *inaccessible* by height or fortification):— cut off, (de-) fenced, fortify, (grape) gather (-er), mighty things, restrain, strong, wall (up), withhold.

1220. בֶּצֶר **betser**, *beh'-tser*; from 1219; strictly a *clipping*, i.e. *gold* (as *dug* out):— gold defence.

1221. בֶּצֶר **Betser**, *beh'-tser*; the same as 1220, an *inaccessible* spot; *Betser*, a place in Pal.; also an Isr.:— Bezer.

1222. בְּצַר **bᵉtsar**, *bets-ar'*; another form for 1220; *gold*:— gold.

1223. בָּצְרָה **botsrâh**, *bots-raw'*; fem. from 1219; an *enclosure*, i.e. *sheepfold*:— Bozrah.

1224. בָּצְרָה **Botsrâh**; *bots-raw'*; the same as 1223; *Botsrah*, a place in Edom:— Bozrah.

1225. בִּצָּרוֹן **bitstsârôwn**, *bits-tsaw-rone'*; masc. intens. from 1219; a *fortress*:— stronghold.

1226. בַּצֹּרֶת **batstsôreth**, *bats-tso'-reth*; fem. intens. from 1219; *restraint* (of rain), i.e. *drought*:— dearth, drought.

1227. בַּקְבּוּק **Baqbûwq**, *bak-book'*; the same as 1228; *Bakbuk*, one of the *Nethinim*:— Bakbuk.

1228. בַּקְבֻּק **baqbûk**, *bak-book'*; from 1238; a *bottle* (from the gurgling in *emptying*):— bottle, cruse.

1229. בַּקְבֻּקְיָה **Baqbuqyâh**, *bak-book-yaw'*; from 1228 and 3050; *emptying* (i.e. *wasting*) *of Jah; Bakbukjah*, an Isr.:— Bakbukiah.

1230. בַּקְבַּקַּר **Baqbaqqar**, *bak-bak-kar'*; redupl. from 1239; *searcher; Bakbakkar*, an Isr.:— Bakbakkar.

1231. בֻּקִּי **Buqqiy**, *book-kee'*; from 1238; *wasteful; Bukki*, the name of two Isr.:— Bukki.

1232. בֻּקִּיָּה **Buqqîyâh**, *book-kee-yaw'*; from 1238 and 3050; *wasting of Jah; Bukkijah*, an Isr.:— Bukkiah.

1233. בְּקִיעַ **bᵉqîya'**, *bek-ee'-ah*; from 1234; a *fissure*:— breach, cleft.

1234. בָּקַע **bâqa'**, *baw-kah'*; a prim. root; to *cleave*; gen. to *rend, break, rip* or *open*— make a breach, break forth (into, out, in pieces, through, up), be ready to burst, cleave (asunder), cut out, divide, hatch, rend (asunder), rip up, tear, win.

1235. בֶּקַע **beqa'**, *beh'-kah*; from 1234; a *section* (half) of a shekel, i.e. a *beka* (a weight and a coin):— bekah, half a shekel.

1236. בִּקְעָא **biq'â'** (Chald.), *bik-aw'*; corresp. to 1237:— plain.

1237. בִּקְעָה **biq'âh**, *bik-aw'*; from 1234; prop. a *split*, i.e. a wide level *valley* between mountains:— plain, valley.

1238. בָּקַק **bâqaq**, *baw-kak'*; a prim. root; to *pour* out, i.e. to *empty*, fig. to *depopulate*; by anal. to *spread* out (as a

fruitful vine):— (make) empty (out), fail, × utterly, make void.

1239. בָּקַר **bâqar**, *baw-kar*; a prim. root; prop. to *plow*, or (gen.) *break* forth, i.e. (fig.) to *inspect, admire, care for, consider*:— (make) inquire (-ry), (make) search, seek out.

1240. בְּקַר **bᵉqar** (Chald.), *bek-ar'*; corresp. to 1239:— inquire, make search.

1241. בָּקָר **bâqâr**, *baw-kawr'*; from 1239; a *beeve* or animal of the ox kind of either gender (as used for *plowing*); collect. a *herd*:— beeve, bull (+ -ock), + calf, + cow, great [cattle], + heifer, herd, kine, ox.

1242. בֹּקֶר **bôqer**, *bo'-ker*; from 1239; prop. *dawn* (as the *break* of day); gen. *morning*:— (+) day, early, morning, morrow.

1243. בַּקָּרָה **baqqârâh**, *bak-kaw-raw'*; intens. from 1239; a *looking after*:— seek out.

1244. בִּקֹּרֶת **biqqôreth**, *bik-ko'-reth*; from 1239; prop. *examination*, i.e. (by impl.) *punishment*:— scourged.

1245. בָּקַשׁ **bâqash**, *baw-kash'*; a prim. root; to *search* out (by any method, spec. in worship or prayer); by impl. to *strive after*:— ask, beg, beseech, desire, enquire, get, make inquisition, procure, (make) request, require, seek (for).

1246. בַּקָּשָׁה **baqqâshâh**, *bak-kaw-shaw'*; from 1245; a *petition*:— request.

1247. בַּר **bar** (Chald.), *bar*; corresp. to 1121; a *son, grandson*, etc.:— × old, son.

1248. בַּר **bar**, *bar*; borrowed (as a title) from 1247; the *heir* (apparent to the throne):— son.

1249. בַּר **bar**, *bar*; from 1305 (in its various senses); *beloved*; also *pure, empty*:— choice, clean, clear, pure.

1250. בָּר **bâr**, *bawr*; or

בַּר **bar**, *bar*; from 1305 (in the sense of *winnowing*); *grain* of any kind (even while standing in the field); by extens. the open *country*:— corn, wheat.

1251. בַּר **bar** (Chald.), *bar*; corresp. to 1250; a *field*:— field.

1252. בֹּר **bôr**, *bore*; from 1305; *purity*:— cleanness, pureness.

1253. בֹּר **bôr**, *bore*; the same as 1252; vegetable *lye* (from its *cleansing*); used as a *soap* for washing, or a *flux* for metals:— × never so, purely.

1254. בָּרָא **bârâ'**, *baw-raw'*; a prim. root; (absolutely) to *create*; (qualified) to *cut* down (a wood), *select, feed* (as formative processes):— choose, create (creator), cut down, dispatch, do, make (fat).

1255. בְּרֹאדַךְ בַּלְאֲדָן **Bᵉrô'dak Bal'ădân**, *ber-o-dak' bal-ad-awn'*; a var. of 4757; *Berodak-Baladan*, a Bab. king:— Berodach-baladan.

בְּרָאִי **Bir'îy**. See 1011.

1256. בְּרָאיָה **Bᵉrâ'yâh**, *ber-aw-yaw'*; from 1254 and 3050; *Jah has created; Berajah*, an Isr.:— Beraiah.

1257. בַּרְבֻּר **barbûr**, *bar-boor'*; by redupl. from 1250; a *fowl* (as fattened on *grain*):— fowl.

1258. בָּרַד **bârad**, *baw-rad´*; a prim. root, to *hail*:— hail.

1259. בָּרָד **bârâd**, *baw-rawd´*; from 1258; *hail*:— hail (Istones]).

1260. בֶּרֶד **Bered**, *beh´red*; from 1258; *hail*; *Bered*, the name of a place south of Pal., also of an Isr.:— Bered.

1261. בָּרֹד **bârôd**, *baw-rode´*; from 1258; *spotted* (as if with *hail*):— grisled.

1262. בָּרָה **bârâh**, *baw-raw´*; a prim. root, to *select*; also (as denom. from 1250) to *feed*; also (as equiv. to 1305) to *render clear* (Eccl. 3:18):— choose, (cause to) eat, manifest, (give) meat.

1263. בָּרוּךְ **Bârûwk**, *baw-rook´*; pass. part. from 1288; *blessed*; *Baruk*, the name of three Isr.:— Baruch.

1264. בְּרוֹם **berôwm**, *ber-ome´*; prob. of for. or.; *damask* (stuff of variegated thread):— rich apparel.

1265. בְּרוֹשׁ **berôwsh**, *ber-ôsh´*; of uncert. der.; a *cypress* (?) tree; hence, a *lance* or a *musical* instrument (as made of that wood):— fir (tree).

1266. בְּרוֹת **berôwth**, *ber-ôth´*; a var. of 1265; the *cypress* (or some elastic tree):— fir.

1267. בָּרוּת **bârûwth**, *baw-rooth´*; from 1262; *food*:— meat.

1268. בֵּרוֹתָה **Bêrôwthâh**, *bay-ro-thaw´*; or

בֵּרֹתַי **Bêrôthay**, *bay-ro-tha´-ee*; prob. from 1266; *cypress* or *cypresslike*; *Berothah* or *Berothai*, a place north of Pal.:— Berothah, Berothai.

1269. בִּרְזוֹת **Birzôwth**, *beer-zoth´*; prob. fem. plur. from an unused root (appar. mean. to *pierce*); *holes*; *Birzoth*, an Isr.:— Birzavith [from the marg.].

1270. בַּרְזֶל **barzel**, *bar-zel´*; perh. from the root of 1269; *iron* (as *cutting*); by extens. an iron *implement*:— (ax) head, iron.

1271. בַּרְזִלַּי **Barzillay**, *bar-zil-lah´-ee*; from 1270; *iron-hearted*; *Barzillai*, the name of three Isr.:— Barzillai.

1272. בָּרַח **bârach**, *baw-rakh´*; a prim. root; to *bolt*, i.e. fig. to *flee* suddenly:— chase (away); drive away, fain, flee (away), put to flight, make haste, reach, run away, shoot.

בָּרִיחַ **bârîach**. See 1281.

1273. בַּרְחֻמִי **Barchûmíy**, *bar-khoo-mee´*; by transp. for 978; a *Barchumite*, or native of *Bachurim*:— Barhumite.

1274. בְּרִי **beríy**, *ber-ee´*; from 1262; *fat*:— fat.

1275. בֵּרִי **Bêríy**, *bay-ree´*; prob. by contr. from 882; *Beri*, an Isr.:— Beri.

1276. בֵּרִי **Bêríy**, *bay-ree´*; of uncert. der.; (only in the plur. and with the art.) the *Berites*, a place in Pal.:— Berites.

1277. בָּרִיא **bârîy'**, *baw-ree´*; from 1254 (in the sense of 1262); *fatted* or *plump*:— fat (Ifleshedl, -ter), fed, firm, plenteous, rank.

1278. בְּרִיאָה **berîy'âh**, *ber-ee-aw´*; fem. from 1254; a *creation*, i.e. a *novelty*:— new thing.

1279. בִּרְיָה **biryâh**, *beer-yaw´*; fem. from 1262; *food*:— meat.

1280. בְּרִיחַ **berîyach**, *ber-ee´-akh*; from 1272; a *bolt*:— bar, fugitive.

1281. בָּרִיחַ **bârîyach**, *baw-ree´-akh*; or (short.)

בָּרִחַ **bâriach**, *baw-ree´-akh*; from 1272; a *fugitive*, i.e. the *serpent* (as *fleeing*), and the *constellation* by that name:— crooked, noble, piercing.

1282. בָּרִיחַ **Bârîyach**, *baw-ree´-akh*; the same as 1281; *Bariach*, an Isr.:— Bariah.

1283. בְּרִיעָה **Berîy'âh**, *ber-ee´-aw*; appar. from the fem. of 7451 with prep. pref.; *in trouble*; *Beriah*, the name of four Isr.:— Beriah.

1284. בְּרִיעִי **Berîy'íy**, *ber-ee-ee´*; patron. from 1283; a *Beriite* (collect.) or desc. of Beriah:— Beerites.

1285. בְּרִית **berîyth**, *ber-eeth´*; from 1262 (in the sense of *cutting* [like 1254]); a *compact* (because made by passing between *pieces* of flesh):— confederacy, [con-Ifederf-ate], covenant, league.

1286. בְּרִית **Berîyth**, *ber-eeth´*; the same as 1285; *Berith*, a Shechemitish deity:— Berith.

1287. בֹּרִית **bôrîyth**, *bo-reeth´*; fem. of 1253; vegetable *alkali*:— sope.

1288. בָּרַךְ **bârak**, *baw-rak´*; a prim. root; to *kneel*; by impl. to *bless* God (as an act of adoration), and (vice-versa) man (as a benefit); also (by euphem.) to *curse* (God or the king, as treason):— × abundantly, × altogether, × at all, blaspheme, bless, congratulate, curse, × greatly, × indeed, kneel (down), praise, salute, × still, thank.

1289. בְּרַךְ **berak** (Chald.), *ber-ak´*; corresp. to 1288:— bless, kneel.

1290. בֶּרֶךְ **berek**, *beh´-rek*; from 1288; a *knee*:— knee.

1291. בְּרַךְ **berek** (Chald.), *beh´-rek*; corresp. to 1290:— knee.

1292. בָּרַכְאֵל **Bârak'êl**, *baw-rak-ale´*; from 1288 and 410; *God has blessed*; *Barakel*, the father of one of Job's friends:— Barachel.

1293. בְּרָכָה **berâkâh**, *ber-aw-kaw´*; from 1288; *benediction*; by impl. *prosperity*:— blessing, liberal, pool, present.

1294. בְּרָכָה **Berâkâh**, *ber-aw-kaw´*; the same as 1293; *Berakah*, the name of an Isr., and also of a valley in Pal.:— Berachah.

1295. בְּרֵכָה **berêkâh**, *ber-ay-kaw´*; from 1288; a *reservoir* (at which camels *kneel* as a resting-place):— (fish-) pool.

1296. בֶּרֶכְיָה **Berekyâh**, *beh-rek-yaw´*; or

בֶּרֶכְיָהוּ **Berekyâhûw**, *beh-rek-yaw´-hoo*; from 1290 and 3050; *knee* (i.e. *blessing*) of *Jah*; *Berekjah*, the name of six Isr.:— Berachiah, Berechiah.

1297. בְּרַם **beram** (Chald.), *ber-am´*; perh. from 7313 with prep. pref.; prop. *highly*, i.e. *surely*; but used adversatively, *however*:— but, nevertheless, yet.

1298. בֶּרַע **Bera'**, *beh´-rah*; of uncert. der.; *Bera*, a Sodomitish king:— Bera.

1299. בָּרַק **bâraq**, *baw-rak´*; a prim. root; to *lighten* (lightning):— cast forth.

1300. בָּרָק **bârâq**, *baw-rawk´*; from 1299; *lightning*; by anal. a *gleam*; concr. a *flashing* sword:— bright, glitter (-ing sword), lightning.

1301. בָּרָק **Bârâq**, *baw-rawk´*; the same as 1300; *Barak*, an Isr.:— Barak.

1302. בַּרְקוֹס **Barqôwç**, *bar-kose´*; of uncert. der.; *Barkos*, one of the Nethinim:— Barkos.

1303. בַּרְקָן **barqân**, *bar-kwan´*; from 1300; a *thorn* (perh. as burning *brightly*):— brier.

1304. בָּרֶקֶת **bârᵉqath**, *baw-reh´-keth*; or

בָּרְקַת **bârᵉkath**, *baw-rek-ath´*; from 1300; a *gem* (as *flashing*), perh. the *emerald*:— carbuncle.

1305. בָּרַר **bârar**, *baw-rar´*; a prim. root; to *clarify* (i.e. *brighten*), *examine*, *select*:— make bright, choice, chosen, cleanse (be clean), clearly, polished, (shew self) pure (-ify), purge (out).

1306. בִּרְשַׁע **Birsha'**, *beer-shah´*; prob. from 7562 with a prep. pref.; *with wickedness*; *Birsha*, a king of Gomorrah:— Birsha.

1307. בֵּרֹתִי **Bêrôthíy**, *bay-ro-thee´*; patrial from 1268; a *Berothite*, or inhab. of Berothai:— Berothite.

1308. בְּשׂוֹר **Besôwr**, *bes-ore´*; from 1319; *cheerful*; *Besor*, a stream of Pal.:— Besor.

1309. בְּשׂוֹרָה **besôwrâh**, *bes-o-raw´*; or (short.)

בְּשֹׂרָה **besôrâh**, *bes-o-raw´*; fem. from 1319; glad *tidings*; by impl. *reward for good news*:— reward for tidings.

1310. בָּשַׁל **bâshal**, *baw-shal´*; a prim. root; prop. to *boil up*; hence, to *be done* in cooking; fig. to *ripen*:— bake, boil, bring forth, is ripe, roast, seethe, sod (be sodden).

1311. בָּשֵׁל **bâshêl**, *baw-shale´*; from 1310; *boiled*:— × at all, sodden.

1312. בִּשְׁלָם **Bishlâm**, *bish-lawm´*; of for. der.; *Bishlam*, a Pers.:— Bishlam.

1313. בָּשָׂם **bâsâm**, *baw-sawm´*; from an unused root mean. to *be fragrant*; [comp. 5561] the *balsam* plant:— spice.

1314. בֶּשֶׂם **besem**, *beh´-sem*; or

בֹּשֶׂם **bôsem**, *bo´-sem*; from the same as 1313; *fragrance*; by impl. *spicery*; also the *balsam* plant:— smell, spice, sweet (odour).

1315. בָּשְׂמַת **Bosmath**, *bos-math´*; fem. of 1314 (the second form); *fragrance*; *Bosmath*, the name of a wife of Esau, and of a daughter of Solomon:— Bashemath, Basmath.

1316. בָּשָׁן **Bâshân**, *baw-shawn´*; of uncert. der.; *Bashan* (often with the art.), a region E. of the Jordan:— Bashan.

1317. בָּשְׁנָה **boshnâh**, *bosh-naw´*; fem. from 954; *shamefulness*:— shame.

1318. בָּשַׁס **bâshaç**, *baw-shas´*; a prim. root; to *trample* down:— tread.

1319. בָּשַׂר **bâsar**, *baw-sar´*; a prim. root; prop. to *be fresh*, i.e. *full* (rosy, (fig.) *cheerful*); to *announce* (glad news):— messenger, preach, publish, shew forth, (bear, bring, carry, preach, good, tell good) tidings.

1320. בָּשָׂר **bâsâr**, *baw-sawr´*; from 1319;

flesh (from its *freshness*); by extens. *body, person;* also (by euphem.) the *pudenda* of a man:— body, [fat, lean] flesh [-ed], kin, [man-] kind, + nakedness, self, skin.

1321. בְּשַׂר **bᵉsar** (Chald.), *bes-ar´;* corresp. to 1320:— flesh.

בְּשֹׂרָה **bᵉsôrâh.** See 1309.

1322. בֹּשֶׁת **bôsheth,** *bo´-sheth;* from 954; *shame* (the feeling and the condition, as well as its cause); by impl. (spec.) an *idol:*— ashamed, confusion, + greatly, (put to) shame (-ful thing).

1323. בַּת **bath,** *bath;* from 1129 (as fem. of 1121); a *daughter* (used in the same wide sense as other terms of relationship, lit. and fig.):— apple [of the eye], branch, company, daughter, × first, × old, + owl, town, village.

1324. בַּת **bath,** *bath;* prob. from the same as 1327; a *bath* or Heb. measure (as a means of *division*) of liquids:— bath.

1325. בַּת **bath** (Chald.), *bath;* corresp. to 1324:— bath.

1326. בָּתָה **bâthâh,** *baw-thaw´;* prob. an orth. var. for 1327; *desolation:*— waste.

1327. בַּתָּה **battâh,** *bat-taw´;* fem. from an unused root (mean. to *break* in pieces); *desolation:*— desolate.

1328. בְּתוּאֵל **Bᵉthûw'êl,** *beth-oo-ale´;* appar. from the same as 1326 and 410; *destroyed of God; Bethuel,* the name of a nephew of Abraham, and of a place in Pal.:— Bethuel. Comp. 1329.

1329. בְּתוּל **Bᵉthûwl,** *beth-ool´;* for 1328; *Bethul* (i.e. *Bethuel*), a place in Pal.:— Bethuel.

1330. בְּתוּלָה **bᵉthûwlâh,** *beth-oo-law´;* fem. pass. part. of an unused root mean. to *separate;* a *virgin* (from her *privacy*); sometimes (by continuation) a *bride;* also (fig.) a *city* or *state:*— maid, virgin.

1331. בְּתוּלִים **bᵉthûwlîym,** *beth-oo-leem´;* masc. plur. of the same as 1330; (collect. and abstr.) *virginity;* by impl. and concr. the *tokens* of it:— × maid, virginity.

1332. בִּתְיָה **Bithyâh,** *bith-yaw´;* from 1323 and 3050; *daughter* (i.e. *worshipper*) *of Jah; Bithjah,* an Eg. woman:— Bithiah.

1333. בָּתַק **bâthaq,** *baw-thak´;* a prim. root; to *cut* in pieces:— thrust through.

1334. בָּתַר **bâthar,** *baw-thar´;* a prim. root, to *chop* up:— divide.

1335. בֶּתֶר **bether,** *beh´-ther;* from 1334; a *section:*— part, piece.

1336. בֶּתֶר **Bether,** *beh´-ther;* the same as 1335; *Bether,* a (craggy) place in Pal.:— Bether.

1337. בַּת רַבִּים **Bath Rabbîym,** *bath rab-beem´;* from 1323 and a masc. plur. from 7227; the *daughter* (i.e. *city*) *of Rabbah:*— Bath-rabbim.

1338. בִּתְרוֹן **Bithrôwn,** *bith-rone´;* from 1334; (with the art.) the *craggy spot; Bithron,* a place E. of the Jordan:— Bithron.

1339. בַּת־שֶׁבַע **Bath-Sheba',** *bath-sheh´-bah;* from 1323 and 7651 (in the sense of

7650); *daughter of an oath; Bath-Sheba,* the mother of Solomon:— Bath-sheba.

1340. בַּת־שׁוּעַ **Bath-Shûwa',** *bath-shoo´-ah;* from 1323 and 7771; *daughter of wealth; Bath-shuä,* the same as 1339:— Bath-shua.

ג

1341. גֵּא **gê',** *gay´;* for 1343; *haughty:*— proud.

1342. גָּאָה **gâ'âh,** *gaw-aw´;* a prim. root; to *mount* up; hence, in gen. to *rise,* (fig.) be *majestic:*— gloriously, grow up, increase, be risen, triumph.

1343. גֵּאֶה **gê'eh,** *gay-eh´;* from 1342; *lofty;* fig. *arrogant:*— proud.

1344. גֵּאָה **gê'âh,** *gay-aw´;* fem. from 1342; *arrogance:*— pride.

1345. גְּאוּאֵל **Gᵉ'ûw'êl,** *gheh-oo-ale´;* from 1342 and 410; *majesty of God; Geüel,* an Isr.:— Geuel.

1346. גַּאֲוָה **ga'ävâh,** *gah-av-aw´;* from 1342; *arrogance* or *majesty;* by impl. (concr.) *ornament:*— excellency, haughtiness, highness, pride, proudly, swelling.

1347. גָּאוֹן **gâ'ôwn,** *gaw-ohn´;* from 1342; the same as 1346:— arrogancy, excellency (-lent), majesty, pomp, pride, proud, swelling.

1348. גֵּאוּת **gê'ûwth,** *gay-ooth´;* from 1342; the same as 1346:— excellent things, lifting up, majesty, pride, proudly, raging.

1349. גַּאֲיוֹן **ga'äyôwn,** *gah-äh-yone´;* from 1342: *haughty:*— proud.

1350. גָּאַל **gâ'al,** *gaw-al´;* a prim. root, to *redeem* (according to the Oriental law of kinship), i.e. to *be the next of kin* (and as such to *buy back* a relative's property, *marry* his widow, etc.):— × in any wise, × at all, avenger, deliver, (do, perform the part of near, next) kinsfolk (-man), purchase, ransom, redeem (-er), revenger.

1351. גָּאַל **gâ'al,** *gaw-al´;* a prim. root, [rather ident. with 1350, through the idea of *freeing,* i.e. *repudiating*]; to *soil* or (fig.) *desecrate:*— defile, pollute, stain.

1352. גֹּאֶל **gô'el,** *go´-el;* from 1351; *profanation:*— defile.

1353. גְּאֻלָּה **gᵉullâh,** *gheh-ool-law´;* fem. pass. part. of 1350; *redemption* (incl. the right and the object); by impl. *relationship:*— kindred, redeem, redemption, right.

1354. גַּב **gab,** *gab;* from an unused root mean. to *hollow* or *curve;* the *back* (as *rounded* [comp. 1460 and 1479]; by anal. the *top* or *rim,* a *boss,* a *vault, arch* of eye, *bulwarks,* etc.:— back, body, boss, eminent (higher) place, [eye] brows, nave, ring.

1355. גַּב **gab** (Chald.), *gab;* corresp. to 1354:— back.

1356. גֵּב **gêb,** *gabe;* from 1461; a *log* (as *cut* out); also *well* or *cistern* (as *dug*):— beam, ditch, pit.

1357. גֵּב **gêb,** *gabe;* prob. from 1461 [comp. 1462]; a *locust* (from its *cutting*):— locust.

1358. גֹּב **gôb** (Chald.), *gobe;* from a root corresp. to 1461; a *pit* (for wild animals) (as *cut* out):— den.

1359. גֹּב **Gôb,** *gobe;* or (fully)

גּוֹב **Gôwb,** *gobe;* from 1461; *pit; Gob,* a place in Pal.:— Gob.

1360. גֶּבֶא **gebe',** *geh´-beh;* from an unused root mean. prob. to *collect;* a *reservoir;* by anal. a *marsh:*— marish, pit.

1361. גָּבַהּ **gâbahh,** *gaw-bah´;* a prim. root; to *soar,* i.e. be *lofty;* fig. to be *haughty:*— exalt, be haughty, be (make) high (-er), lift up, mount up, be proud, raise up great height, upward.

1362. גָּבָהּ **gâbâhh,** *gaw-bawh´;* from 1361; *lofty* (lit. or fig.):— high, proud.

1363. גֹּבַהּ **gôbahh,** *go´-bah;* from 1361; *elation, grandeur, arrogance:*— excellency, haughty, height, high, loftiness, pride.

1364. גָּבֹהַּ **gâbôahh,** *gaw-bo´-ah;* or (fully)

גָּבוֹהַּ **gâbôwahh,** *gaw-bo´-ah;* from 1361; *elevated* (or *elated*), *powerful, arrogant:*— haughty, height, high (-er), lofty, proud, × exceeding proudly.

1365. גַּבְהוּת **gabhûwth,** *gab-hooth´;* from 1361; *pride:*— loftiness, lofty.

1366. גְּבוּל **gᵉbûwl,** *gheb-ool´;* or (short.)

גְּבֻל **gᵉbul,** *gheb-ool´;* from 1379; prop. a *cord* (as *twisted*), i.e. (by impl.) a *boundary;* by extens. the *territory* inclosed:— border, bound, coast, × great, landmark, limit, quarter, space.

1367. גְּבוּלָה **gᵉbûwlâh,** *gheb-oo-law´;* or (short.)

גְּבֻלָה **gᵉbulâh,** *gheb-oo-law´;* fem. of 1366; a *boundary, region:*— border, bound, coast, landmark, place.

1368. גִּבּוֹר **gibbôwr,** *ghib-bore´;* or (short.)

גִּבֹּר **gibbôr,** *ghib-bore´;* intens. from the same as 1397; *powerful;* by impl. *warrior, tyrant:*— champion, chief, × excel, giant, man, mighty (man, one), strong (man), valiant man.

1369. גְּבוּרָה **gᵉbûwrâh,** *gheb-oo-raw´;* fem. pass. part. from the same as 1368; *force* (lit. or fig.); by impl. *valor, victory:*— force, mastery, might, mighty (act, power), power, strength.

1370. גְּבוּרָה **gᵉbûwrâh** (Chald.), *gheb-oo-raw´;* corresp. to 1369; *power:*— might.

1371. גִּבֵּחַ **gibbêach,** *ghib-bay´-akh;* from an unused root mean. to be *high* (in the forehead); *bald* in the forehead:— forehead bald.

1372. גַּבַּחַת **gabbachath,** *gab-bakh´-ath;* from the same as 1371; *baldness* in the forehead; by anal. a *bare spot* on the right side of cloth:— bald forehead, × without.

1373. גַּבַּי **Gabbay,** *gab-bah´-ee;* from the same as 1354; *collective; Gabbai,* an Isr.:— Gabbai.

1374. גֵּבִים **Gêbîym,** *gay-beem´;* plur. of 1356; *cisterns; Gebim,* a place in Pal.:— Gebim.

1375. גְּבִיעַ **gᵉbîya',** *gheb-ee-ah;* from an unused root (mean. to be *convex*); a *goblet;* by anal. the *calyx* of a flower:—house, cup, pot.

1376. גְּבִיר **geꞏbîyr**, *gheb-eer´;* from 1396; a *master:*— lord.

1377. גְּבִירָה **geꞏbîyrâh**, *gheb-ee-raw´;* fem. of 1376; a *mistress:*— queen.

1378. גָּבִישׁ **gâbîysh**, *gaw-beesh´;* from an unused root (prob. mean. to *freeze*); *crystal* (from its resemblance to *ice*):— pearl.

1379. גָּבַל **gâbal**, *gaw-bal´;* a prim. root; prop. to *twist* as a rope; only (as a denom. from 1366) to *bound* (as by a line):— be border, set (bounds about).

1380. גְּבַל **Geꞏbal**, *gheb-al´;* from 1379 (in the sense of a *chain* of hills); a *mountain; Gebal*, a place in Phœnicia:— Gebal.

1381. גְּבָל **Geꞏbâl**, *gheb-awl´;* the same as 1380; *Gebal*, a region in Idumæa:— Gebal.

גְּבֻלָה **geꞏbûlâh**. See 1367.

1382. גְּבָלִי **Gibliy**, *ghib-lee´;* patrial from 1380; a *Gebalite*, or inhab. of Gebal:— Giblites, stone-squarer.

1383. גַּבְלֻת **gablûth**, *gab-looth´;* from 1379; a twisted *chain* or *lace:*— end.

1384. גִּבֵּן **gibbên**, *gib-bane´;* from an unused root mean. to be *arched* or contracted; *hunch-backed:*— crookbackt.

1385. גְּבִנָה **geꞏbînâh**, *gheb-ee-naw´;* fem. from the same as 1384; *curdled* milk:— cheese.

1386. גַּבְנֹן **gabnôn**, *gab-nohn´;* from the same as 1384; a *hump* or *peak* of hills:— high.

1387. גֶּבַע **Geba'**, *gheh´-bah;* from the same as 1375, a *hillock; Geba*, a place in Pal.:— Gaba, Geba, Gibeah.

1388. גִּבְעָא **Gib'â'**, *ghib-aw´;* by perm. for 1389; a *hill; Giba*, a place in Pal.:— Gibeah.

1389. גִּבְעָה **gib'âh**, *ghib-aw´;* fem. from the same as 1387; a *hillock:*— hill, little hill.

1390. גִּבְעָה **Gib'âh**, *ghib-aw´;* the same as 1389; *Gibah;* the name of three places in Pal.:— Gibeah, the hill.

1391. גִּבְעוֹן **Gib'ôwn**, *ghib-ohn´;* from the same as 1387; *hilly; Gibon*, a place in Pal.:— Gibeon.

1392. גִּבְעֹל **gib'ôl**, *ghib-ole´;* prol. from 1375; the *calyx* of a flower:— bolled.

1393. גִּבְעֹנִי **Gib'ôniy**, *ghib-o-nee´;* patrial from 1391; a *Gibonite*, or inhab. of Gibon:— Gibeonite.

1394. גִּבְעַת **Gib'ath**, *ghib-ath´;* from the same as 1375; *hilliness; Gibath:*— Gibeath.

1395. גִּבְעָתִי **Gib'âthiy**, *ghib-aw-thee´;* patrial from 1390; a *Gibathite*, or inhab. of Gibath:— Gibeathite.

1396. גָּבַר **gâbar**, *gaw-bar´;* a prim. root; to be *strong;* by impl. to *prevail, act insolently:*— exceed, confirm, be great, be mighty, prevail, put to more [strength], strengthen, be stronger, be valiant.

1397. גֶּבֶר **geber**, *gheh´-ber;* from 1396; prop. a *valiant* man or *warrior;* gen. a

person simply:— every one, man, × mighty.

1398. גֶּבֶר **Geber**, *gheh´-ber;* the same as 1397; *Geber*, the name of two Isr.:— Geber.

1399. גֶּבַר **geꞏbar**, *gheb-ar´;* from 1396; the same as 1397; a *person:*— man.

1400. גְּבַר **geꞏbar** (Chald.), *gheb-ar´;* corresp. to 1399:— certain, man.

1401. גִּבָּר **gibbâr** (Chald.), *ghib-bawr´;* intens. of 1400; *valiant*, or *warrior:*— mighty.

1402. גִּבָּר **Gibbâr**, *ghib-bawr´;* intens. of 1399; *Gibbar*, an Isr.:— Gibbar.

גְּבוּרָה **geꞏbûrâh**. See 1369.

1403. גַּבְרִיאֵל **Gabriy'êl**, *gab-ree-ale´;* from 1397 and 410; *man of God; Gabriel*, an archangel:— Gabriel.

1404. גְּבֶרֶת **geꞏbereth**, *gheb-eh´-reth;* fem. of 1376; *mistress:*— lady, mistress.

1405. גִּבְּתוֹן **Gibbeꞏthôwn**, *ghib-beth-one´;* intens. from 1389; a *hilly* spot; *Gibbethon*, a place in Pal.:— Gibbethon.

1406. גָּג **gâg**, *gawg;* prob. by redupl. from 1342; a *roof;* by anal. the *top* of an altar:— roof (of the house), (house) top (of the house).

1407. גַּד **gad**, *gad;* from 1413 (in the sense of *cutting*); *coriander* seed (from its furrows):— coriander.

1408. גַּד **Gad**, *gad;* a var. of 1409; *Fortune*, a Bab. deity:— that troop.

1409. גָּד **gâd**, *gawd;* from 1464 (in the sense of *distributing*); *fortune:*— troop.

1410. גָּד **Gâd**, *gawd;* from 1464; Gad, a son of Jacob, incl. his tribe and its territory; also a prophet:— Gad.

1411. גְּדָבָר **geꞏdâbâr** (Chald.), *ghed-aw-bawr´;* corresp. to 1489; a *treasurer:*— treasurer.

1412. גֻּדְגֹּדָה **Gudgôdâh**, *gud-go´-daw;* by redupl. from 1413 (in the sense of *cutting*) *cleft; Gudgodah*, a place in the Desert:— Gudgodah.

1413. גָּדַד **gâdad**, *gaw-dad´;* a prim. root [comp. 1464]; to *crowd;* also to *gash* (as if by *pressing* into):— assemble (selves by troops), gather (selves together, self in troops), cut selves.

1414. גְּדַד **geꞏdad** (Chald.), *ghed-ad´;* corresp. to 1413; to *cut* down:— hew down.

גְּדֻדָה **geꞏdûdâh**. See 1417.

1415. גָּדָה **gâdâh**, *gaw-daw´;* from an unused root (mean. to *cut* off); a *border* of a river (as *cut* into by the stream):— bank.

גַּדָּה **Gaddâh**. See 2693.

1416. גְּדוּד **geꞏdûwd**, *ghed-ood´;* from 1413; a *crowd* (espec. of soldiers):— army, band (of men), company, troop (of robbers).

1417. גְּדוּד **geꞏdûwd**, *ghed-ood´;* or (fem.)

גְּדֻדָה **geꞏdûddâh**, *ghed-oo-daw´;* from 1413; a *furrow* (as *cut*):— furrow.

1418. גְּדוּדָה **geꞏdûwdâh**, *ghed-oo-daw´;* fem. pass. part. of 1413; an *incision:*— cutting.

1419. גָּדוֹל **gâdôwl**, *gaw-dole´;* or (short.)

גָּדֹל **gâdôl**, *gaw-dole´;* from 1431;

great (in any sense); hence, *older;* also *insolent:*— + aloud, elder (-est), + exceeding (-ly), + far, (man of) great (man, matter, thing, -er, -ness), high, long, loud, mighty, more, much, noble, proud thing, × sore, (×) very.

1420. גְּדוּלָה **geꞏdûwlâh**, *ghed-oo-law´;* or (short.)

גְּדֻלָּה **geꞏdullâh**, *ghed-ool-law´;* or (less accurately)

גְּדוּלָּה **geꞏdûwllâh**, *ghed-ool-law´;* fem. of 1419; *greatness;* (concr.) *mighty acts:*— dignity, great things (-ness), majesty.

1421. גִּדּוּף **giddûwph**, *ghid-doof´;* or (short.)

גִּדֻּף **giddûph**, *ghid-doof´;* and (fem.)

גִּדּוּפָה **giddûwphâh**, *ghid-doo-faw´;* or

גִּדֻּפָה **giddûphâh**, *ghid-doo-faw´;* from 1422; *vilification:*— reproach, reviling.

1422. גְּדוּפָה **geꞏdûwphâh**, *ghed-oo-faw´;* fem. pass. part. of 1442; a *revilement:*— taunt.

גְּדוֹר **Geꞏdôwr**. See 1446.

1423. גְּדִי **geꞏdiy**, *ghed-ee´;* from the same as 1415; a *young goat* (from *browsing*):— kid.

1424. גָּדִי **Gâdiy**, *gaw-dee´;* from 1409; *fortunate; Gadi*, an Isr.:— Gadi.

1425. גָּדִי **Gâdiy**, *gaw-dee´;* patron. from 1410; a *Gadite* (collect.) or desc. of Gad:— Gadites, children of Gad.

1426. גַּדִּי **Gaddiy**, *gad-dee´;* intens. for 1424; *Gaddi*, an Isr.:— Gaddi.

1427. גַּדִּיאֵל **Gaddiy'êl**, *gad-dee-ale´;* from 1409 and 410; *fortune of God; Gaddiel*, an Isr.:— Gaddiel.

1428. גִּדְיָה **gidyâh**, *ghid-yaw´;* or

גִּדְיָה **gadyâh**, *gad-yaw´;* the same as 1415; a *river brink:*— bank.

1429. גְּדִיָּה **geꞏdiyâh**, *ghed-ee-yaw´;* fem. of 1423; a *young female goat:*— kid.

1430. גָּדִישׁ **gâdîysh**, *gaw-deesh´;* from an unused root (mean. to *heap* up); a *stack* of sheaves; by anal. a *tomb:*— shock (stack) (of corn), tomb.

1431. גָּדַל **gâdal**, *gaw-dal´;* a prim. root; prop. to *twist* [comp. 1434], i.e. to be (caus. *make*) *large* (in various senses, as in body, mind, estate or honor, also in pride):— advance, boast, bring up, exceed, excellent, be (-come, do, give, make, wax), great (-er, come to … estate, + things), grow (up), increase, lift up, magnify (-ifical), be much set by, nourish (up), pass, promote, proudly [spoken], tower.

1432. גָּדֵל **gâdêl**, *gaw-dale´;* from 1431; *large* (lit. or fig.):— great, grew.

1433. גֹּדֶל **gôdel**, *go´-del;* from 1431; *magnitude* (lit. or fig.):— greatness, stout (-ness).

1434. גְּדִל **geꞏdîl**, *ghed-eel´;* from 1431 (in the sense of *twisting*); *thread*, i.e. a *tassel* or *festoon:*— fringe, wreath.

1435. גִּדֵּל **Giddêl**, *ghid-dale´;* from 1431; *stout; Giddel*, the name of one of the

Nethinim, also of one of "Solomon's servants":— Giddel.

נָדֹל **gâdôl.** See 1419.

גְּדֻלָּה **gᵉdullâh.** See 1420.

1436. גְּדַלְיָה **Gᵉdalyâh,** *ghed-al-yaw´;* or (prol.)

גְּדַלְיָהוּ **Gᵉdalyâhûw,** *ghed-al-yaw´-hoo;* from 1431 and 3050; *Jah has become great; Gedaljah,* the name of five Isr.:— Gedaliah.

1437. גְּדַלְתִּי **Giddaltiy,** *ghid-dal´-tee;* from 1431; *I have made great; Giddalti,* an Isr.:— Giddalti.

1438. גָּדַע **gâda´,** *gaw-dah´;* a prim. root; to *fell* a tree; gen. to *destroy* anything:— cut (asunder, in sunder, down, off), hew down.

1439. גִּדְעוֹן **Gid´ôwn,** *ghid-ohn´;* from 1438; *feller* (i.e. *warrior*); *Gidon,* an Isr.:— Gideon.

1440. גִּדְעֹם **Gid´ôm,** *ghid-ohm´;* from 1438; a *cutting* (i.e. *desolation*); *Gidom,* a place in Pal.:— Gidom.

1441. גִּדְעֹנִי **Gid´ôniy,** *ghid-o-nee´;* from 1438; *warlike* [comp. 1439]; *Gidoni,* an Isr.:— Gideoni.

1442. גָּדַף **gâdaph,** *gaw-daf´;* a prim. root; to *hack* (with words), i.e. *revile:*— blaspheme, reproach.

גִּדֻּף **giddûph,** and

גִּדֻּפָה **giddûphâh.** See 1421.

1443. גָּדַר **gâdar,** *gaw-dar´;* a prim. root; to *wall* in or around:— close up, fence up, hedge, inclose, make up [a wall], mason, repairer.

1444. גֶּדֶר **geder,** *gheh´-der;* from 1443; a *circumvallation:*— wall.

1445. גֶּדֶר **Geder,** *gheh´-der;* the same as 1444; *Geder,* a place in Pal.:— Geder.

1446. גְּדֹר **Gᵉdôr,** *ghed-ore´;* or (fully)

גְּדוֹר **Gᵉdôwr,** *ghed-ore´;* from 1443; *inclosure; Gedor,* a place in Pal.; also the name of three Isr.:— Gedor.

1447. גָּדֵר **gâdêr,** *gaw-dare´;* from 1443; a *circumvallation;* by impl. an *inclosure:*— fence, hedge, wall.

1448. גְּדֵרָה **gᵉdêrâh,** *ghed-ay-raw´;* fem. of 1447; *inclosure* (espec. for flocks):— [sheep-] cote (fold) hedge, wall.

1449. גְּדֵרָה **Gᵉdêrâh,** *ghed-ay-raw´;* the same as 1448; (with the art.) *Gederah,* a place in Pal.:— Gederah, hedges.

1450. גְּדֵרוֹת **Gᵉdêrôwth,** *ghed-ay-rohth´;* plur. of 1448; *walls; Gederoth,* a place in Pal.:— Gederoth.

1451. גְּדֵרִי **Gᵉdêriy,** *ghed-ay-ree´;* patrial from 1445; a *Gederite,* or inhab. of Geder:— Gederite.

1452. גְּדֵרָתִי **Gᵉdêrâthiy,** *ghed-ay-raw-thee´;* patrial from 1449; a *Gederathite,* or inhab. of Gederah:— Gederathite.

1453. גְּדֵרֹתַיִם **Gᵉdêrôthayim,** *ghed-ay-ro-thah´-yim;* dual of 1448; *double wall; Gederothajim,* a place in Pal.:— Gederothaim.

1454. גֵּה **gêh,** *gay;* prob. a clerical err. for 2088; *this:*— this.

1455. גָּהָה **gâhâh,** *gaw-haw´;* a prim. root; to *remove* (a bandage from a wound, i.e. *heal* it):— cure.

1456. גֵּהָה **gêhâh,** *gay-haw´;* from 1455; a *cure:*— medicine.

1457. גָּהַר **gâhar,** *gaw-har´;* a prim. root; to *prostrate* oneself:— cast self down, stretch self.

1458. גַּו **gav,** *gav;* another form for 1460; the *back:*— back.

1459. גַּו **gav** (Chald.), *gav;* corresp. to 1460; the *middle:*— midst, same, there(where-) in.

1460. גֵּו **gêv,** *gave;* from 1342 [corresp. to 1354]; the *back;* by anal. the *middle:*— + among, back, body.

1461. גּוּב **gûwb,** *goob;* a prim. root; to *dig:*— husbandman.

1462. גּוֹב **gôwb,** *gobe;* from 1461; the *locust* (from its *grubbing* as a larvae):— grasshopper, × great.

1463. גּוֹג **Gôwg,** *gohg;* of uncert. der.; *Gog,* the name of an Isr., also of some northern nation:— Gog.

1464. גּוּד **gûwd,** *goode;* a prim. root [akin to 1413]; to *crowd* upon, i.e. *attack:*— invade, overcome.

1465. גֵּוָה **gêvâh,** *gay-vaw´;* fem. of 1460; the *back,* i.e. (by extens.) the *person:*— body.

1466. גֵּוָה **gêvâh,** *gay-vaw´;* the same as 1465; *exaltation;* (fig.) *arrogance:*— lifting up, pride.

1467. גֵּוָה **gêvâh** (Chald.), *gay-vaw´;* corresp. to 1466:— pride.

1468. גּוּז **gûwz,** *gooz;* a prim. root [comp. 1494]; prop. to *shear* off; but used only in the (fig.) sense of *passing* rapidly:— bring, cut off.

1469. גּוֹזָל **gôwzâl,** *go-zawl´;* or (short.)

גֹּזָל **gôzâl,** *go-zawl´;* from 1497; a *nestling* (as being comp. *nude* of feathers):— young (pigeon).

1470. גּוֹזָן **Gôwzân,** *go-zawn´;* prob. from 1468; a *quarry* (as a place of *cutting* stones); *Gozan,* a province of Assyria:— Gozan.

1471. גּוֹי **gôwy,** *go´-ee;* rarely (short.)

גֹּי **gôy,** *go´-ee;* appar. from the same root as 1465 (in the sense of *massing*); a foreign *nation;* hence, a *Gentile;* also (fig.) a *troop* of animals, or a *flight* of locusts:— Gentile, heathen, nation, people.

1472. גְּוִיָּה **gᵉviyâh,** *ghev-ee-yaw´;* prol. for 1465; a *body,* whether alive or dead:— (dead) body, carcase, corpse.

1473. גּוֹלָה **gôwlâh,** *go-law´;* or (short.)

גֹּלָה **gôlâh,** *go-law´;* act. part. fem. of 1540; *exile;* concr. and collect. *exiles:*— (carried away) captive (-ity), removing.

1474. גּוֹלָן **Gôwlân,** *go-lawn´;* from 1473; *captive; Golan,* a place E. of the Jordan:— Golan.

1475. גּוּמָּץ **gûwmmâts,** *goom-mawts´;* of uncert. der.; a *pit:*— pit.

1476. גּוּנִי **Gûwniy,** *goo-nee´;* prob. from 1598; *protected; Guni,* the name of two Isr.:— Guni.

1477. גּוּנִי **Gûwniy,** *goo-nee´;* patron. from 1476; a *Gunite* (collect. with art. pref.) or desc. of Guni:— Gunites.

1478. גָּוַע **gâva´,** *gaw-vah´;* a prim. root;

to *breathe* out, i.e. (by impl.) *expire:*— die, be dead, give up the ghost, perish.

1479. גּוּף **gûwph,** *goof;* a prim. root; prop. to *hollow* or *arch,* i.e. (fig.) *close;* to *shut:*— shut.

1480. גּוּפָה **gûwphâh,** *goo-faw´;* from 1479; a *corpse* (as *closed* to sense):— body.

1481. גּוּר **gûwr,** *goor;* a prim. root; prop. to *turn* aside from the road (for a lodging or any other purpose), i.e. *sojourn* (as a guest); also to *shrink, fear* (as in a *strange* place); also to *gather* for hostility (as *afraid*):— abide, assemble, be afraid, dwell, fear, gather (together), inhabitant, remain, sojourn, stand in awe, (be) stranger, × surely.

1482. גּוּר **gûwr,** *goor;* or (short.)

גֻּר **gûr,** *goor;* perh. from 1481; a *cub* (as still *abiding* in the lair), espec. of the lion:— whelp, young one.

1483. גּוּר **Gûwr,** *goor;* the same as 1482; *Gur,* a place in Pal.:— Gur.

1484. גּוֹר **gôwr,** *gore;* or (fem.)

גֹּרָה **gôrâh,** *go-raw´;* a var. of 1482:— whelp.

1485. גּוּר־בַּעַל **Gûwr-Ba'al,** *goor-bah´-al;* from 1481 and 1168; *dwelling of Baal; Gur-Baal,* a place in Arabia:— Gur-baal.

1486. גּוֹרָל **gôwrâl,** *go-rawl´;* or (short.)

גֹּרָל **gôrâl,** *go-ral´;* from an unused root mean. to be *rough* (as stone); prop. a *pebble,* i.e. a *lot* (small stones being used for that purpose); fig. a *portion* or *destiny* (as if determined by lot):— lot.

1487. גּוּשׁ **gûwsh,** *goosh;* or rather (by perm.)

גִּישׁ **gîysh,** *gheesh;* of uncert. der.; a *mass* of earth:— clod.

1488. גֵּז **gêz,** *gaze;* from 1494; a *fleece* (as *shorn*); also mown *grass:*— fleece, mowing, mown grass.

1489. גִּזְבָּר **gizbâr,** *ghiz-bawr´;* of for. der.; *treasurer:*— treasurer.

1490. גִּזְבָּר **gizbâr** (Chald.), *ghiz-bawr´;* corresp. to 1489:— treasurer.

1491. גָּזָה **gâzâh,** *gaw-zaw´;* a prim. root [akin to 1468]; to *cut off,* i.e. *portion* out:— take.

1492. גַּזָּה **gazzâh,** *gaz-zaw´;* fem. from 1494; a *fleece:*— fleece.

1493. גִּזוֹנִי **Gizôwniy,** *ghee-zo-nee´;* patrial from the unused name of a place appar. in Pal.; a *Gizonite* or inhab. of Gizoh:— Gizonite.

1494. גָּזַז **gâzaz,** *gaw-zaz´;* a prim. root [akin to 1468]; to *cut off;* spec. to *shear* a flock or *shave* the hair; fig. to *destroy* an enemy:— cut off (down), poll, shave, [sheep-] shear (-er).

1495. גָּזֵז **Gâzêz,** *gaw-zaze´;* from 1494; *shearer; Gazez,* the name of two Isr.:— Gazez.

1496. גָּזִית **gâziyth,** *gaw-zeeth´;* from 1491; something *cut,* i.e. *dressed* stone:— hewed, hewn stone, wrought.

1497. גָּזַל **gâzal,** *gaw-zal´;* a prim. root; to *pluck* off; spec. to *flay, strip* or *rob:*— catch, consume, exercise [robbery],

Hebrew

pluck (off), rob, spoil, take away (by force, violence), tear.

1498. גָּזֵל **gâzêl**, *gaw-zale´;* from 1497; *robbery,* or (concr.) *plunder:*— robbery, thing taken away by violence.

1499. גֵּזֶל **gêzel**, *ghe´-zel;* from 1497; *plunder,* i.e. *violence:*— violence, violent perverting.

גֹּזָל **gôzâl**. See 1469.

1500. גְּזֵלָה **gᵉzêlâh**, *ghez-ay-law´;* fem. of 1498 and mean. the same:— that (he had robbed) [which he took violently away], spoil, violence.

1501. גָּזָם **gâzâm**, *gaw-zawm´;* from an unused root mean. to *devour;* a kind of *locust:*— palmer-worm.

1502. גַּזָּם **Gazzâm**, *gaz-zawm´;* from the same as 1501; *devourer;* Gazzam, one of the Nethinim:— Gazzam.

1503. גֶּזַע **geza´**, *geh´-zah;* from an unused root mean. to *cut down* (trees); the *trunk* or *stump* of a tree (as felled or as planted):— stem, stock.

1504. גָּזַר **gâzar**, *gaw-zar´;* a prim. root; to *cut* down or off; (fig.) to *destroy, divide, exclude,* or *decide:*— cut down (off), decree, divide, snatch.

1505. גְּזַר **gᵉzar** (Chald.), *ghez-ar´;* corresp. to 1504; to *quarry; determine:*— cut out, soothsayer.

1506. גֶּזֶר **gezer**, *gheh´-zer;* from 1504; something *cut* off; a *portion:*— part, piece.

1507. גֶּזֶר **Gezer**, *gheh´-zer;* the same as 1506; *Gezer,* a place in Pal.:— Gazer, Gezer.

1508. גִּזְרָה **gizrâh**, *ghiz-raw´;* fem. of 1506; the *figure* or person (as if *cut* out); also an *inclosure* (as *separated*):— polishing, separate place.

1509. גְּזֵרָה **gᵉzêrâh**, *ghez-ay-raw´;* from 1504; a *desert* (as *separated*):— not inhabited.

1510. גְּזֵרָה **gᵉzêrâh** (Chald.), *ghez-ay-raw´;* from 1505 (as 1504); a *decree:*— decree.

1511. גִּזְרִי **Gizrîy** (in the marg.), *ghiz-ree´;* patrial from 1507; a *Gezerite* (collect.) or inhab. of Gezer; but better (as in the text) by transp.

גִּרְזִי° **Girzîy**, *gher-zee´;* patrial of 1630; a *Girzite* (collect.) or member of a native tribe in Pal.:— Gezrites.

גִּיחוֹן **Gîchôwn**. See 1521.

1512. גָּחוֹן **gâchôwn**, *gaw-khone´;* prob. from 1518; the external *abdomen, belly* (as the *source* of the fetus [comp. 1521]):— belly.

גֵּחֲזִי **Gêchăzîy**. See 1522.

גָּחֹל **gâchol**. See 1513.

1513. גַּחַל **gechel**, *geh´-khel;* or (fem.)

גַּחֶלֶת **gacheleth**, *gah-kheh´-leth;* from an unused root mean. to *glow* or *kindle;* an *ember:*— (burning) coal.

1514. גַּחַם **Gacham**, *gah´-kham;* from an unused root mean. to *burn; flame; Gacham,* a son of Nahor:— Gaham.

1515. גַּחַר **Gachar**, *gah´-khar;* from an unused root mean. to *hide; lurker; Gachar,* one of the Nethinim:— Gahar.

גוֹי **gôy**. See 1471.

1516. גַּיְא **gay'**, *gah´-ee;* or (short.)

גַּי **gay**, *gah´-ee;* prob. (by transm.) from the same root as 1466 (abb.); a *gorge* (from its *lofty* sides; hence, narrow, but not a gully or winter-torrent):— valley.

1517. גִּיד **gîyd**, *gheed;* prob. from 1464; a *thong* (as *compressing*); by anal. a *tendon:*— sinew.

1518. גִּיחַ **gîyach**, *ghee´-akh;* or (short.)

גֹּחַ **gôach**, *go´-akh;* a prim. root; to *gush* forth (as water), gen. to *issue:*— break forth, labor to bring forth, come forth, draw up, take out.

1519. גִּיחַ **gîyach** (Chald.), *ghee´-akh;* or (short.)

גּוּחַ **gûwach** (Chald.), *goo´-akh;* corresp. to 1518; to *rush* forth:— strive.

1520. גִּיחַ **Gîyach**, *ghee´-akh;* from 1518; a *fountain; Giach,* a place in Pal.:— Giah.

1521. גִּיחוֹן **Gîychôwn**, *ghee-khone´;* or (short.)

גִּחוֹן **Gichôwn**, *ghee-khone´;* from 1518; *stream; Gichon,* a river of Paradise; also a valley (or pool) near Jerusalem:— Gihon.

1522. גֵּיחֲזִי **Gêychăzîy**, *gay-khah-zee´;* or

גֵּחֲזִי **Gêchăzîy**, *gay-khah-zee´;* appar. from 1516 and 2372; *valley of a visionary; Gechazi,* the servant of Elisha:— Gehazi.

1523. גִּיל **gîyl**, *gheel;* or (by perm.)

גּוּל° **gûwl**, *gool;* a prim. root; prop. to *spin* round (under the influence of any violent emotion), i.e. usually *rejoice,* or (as *cringing*) *fear:*— be glad, joy, be joyful, rejoice.

1524. גִּיל **gîyl**, *gheel;* from 1523; a *revolution* (of time, i.e. an *age*); also *joy:*— × exceedingly, gladness, × greatly, joy, rejoice (-ing), sort.

1525. גִּילָה **gîylâh**, *ghee-law´;* or

גִּילַת **gîylath**, *ghee-lath´;* fem. of 1524; *joy:*— joy, rejoicing.

גִּילֹה **Gîylôh**. See 1542.

1526. גִּילֹנִי **Gîylônîy**, *ghee-lo-nee´;* patrial from 1542; a *Gilonite* or inhab. of Giloh:— Gilonite.

1527. גִּינַת **Gîynath**, *ghee-nath´;* of uncert. der.; *Ginath,* an Isr.:— Ginath.

1528. גִּיר **gîyr** (Chald.), *gheer;* corresp. to 1615; *lime:*— plaster.

גֵּיר **gêyr**. See 1616.

1529. גֵּישָׁן **Gêyshân**, *gay-shawn´;* from the same as 1487; *lumpish; Geshan,* an Isr.:— Geshan.

1530. גַּל **gal**, *gal;* from 1556; something *rolled,* i.e. a *heap* of stone or dung (plural *ruins*), by anal. a *spring* of water (plur. *waves*):— billow, heap, spring, wave.

1531. גֹּל **gôl**, *gole;* from 1556; a *cup* for oil (as *round*):— bowl.

גֵּלָא **gᵉlâ'**. See 1541.

1532. גַּלָּב **gallâb**, *gal-lawb´;* from an unused root mean. to *shave;* a *barber:*— barber.

1533. גִּלְבֹּעַ **Gilbôa'**, *ghil-bo´-ah;* from

1530 and 1158; *fountain of ebullition; Gilboa,* a mountain of Pal.:— Gilboa.

1534. גַּלְגַּל **galgal**, *gal-gal´;* by redupl. from 1556; a *wheel;* by anal. a *whirlwind;* also *dust* (as *whirled*):— heaven, rolling thing, wheel.

1535. גַּלְגַּל **galgal** (Chald.), *gal-gal´;* corresp. to 1534; a *wheel:*— wheel.

1536. גִּלְגָּל **gilgâl**, *ghil-gawl´;* a var. of 1534:— wheel.

1537. גִּלְגָּל **Gilgâl**, *ghil-gawl´;* the same as 1536 (with the art. as a prop. noun); *Gilgal,* the name of three places in Pal.:— Gilgal. See also 1019.

1538. גֻּלְגֹּלֶת **gulgôleth**, *gul-go´-leth;* by redupl. from 1556; a *skull* (as *round*); by impl. a *head* (in enumeration of persons):— head, every man, poll, skull.

1539. גֶּלֶד **geled**, *ghe´-led;* from an unused root prob. mean. to *polish;* the (human) *skin* (as *smooth*):— skin.

1540. גָּלָה **gâlâh**, *gaw-law´;* a prim. root; to *denude* (espec. in a disgraceful sense); by impl. to *exile* (captives being usually *stripped*); fig. to *reveal:*— + advertise, appear, bewray, bring, (carry, lead, go) captive (into captivity), depart, disclose, discover, exile, be gone, open, × plainly, publish, remove, reveal, × shamelessly, shew, × surely, tell, uncover.

1541. גְּלָה **gᵉlâh** (Chald.), *ghel-aw´;* or

גְּלָא **gᵉlâ'** (Chald.), *ghel-aw´;* corresp. to 1540:— bring over, carry away, reveal.

גֹּלָה **gôlâh**. See 1473.

1542. גִּלֹה **Gîloh**, *ghee-lo´;* or (fully)

גִּילֹה **Gîylôh**, *ghee-lo´;* from 1540; *open; Giloh,* a place in Pal.:— Giloh.

1543. גֻּלָּה **gullâh**, *gool-law´;* fem. from 1556; a *fountain, bowl* or *globe* (all as *round*):— bowl, pommel, spring.

1544. גִּלּוּל **gillûwl**, *ghil-lool´;* or (short.)

גִּלֻּל **gillûl**, *ghil-lool´;* from 1556; prop. a *log* (as *round*); by impl. an *idol:*— idol.

1545. גְּלוֹם **gᵉlôwm**, *ghel-ome´;* from 1563; *clothing* (as *wrapped*):— clothes.

1546. גָּלוּת **gâlûwth**, *gaw-looth´;* fem. from 1540; *captivity;* concr. *exiles* (collect.):— (they that are carried away) captives (-ity).

1547. גָּלוּת **gâlûwth** (Chald.), *gaw-looth´;* corresp. to 1546:— captivity.

1548. גָּלַח **gâlach**, *gaw-lakh´;* a prim. root; prop. to be *bald,* i.e. (caus.) to *shave;* fig. to *lay waste:*— poll, shave (off).

1549. גִּלָּיוֹן **gillâyôwn**, *ghil-law-yone´;* or

גִּלְיוֹן **gilyôwn**, *ghil-yone´;* from 1540; a *tablet* for writing (as *bare*); by anal. a *mirror* (as a *plate*):— glass, roll.

1550. גָּלִיל **gâlîyl**, *gaw-leel´;* from 1556; a *valve* of a folding door (as *turning*); also a *ring* (as *round*):— folding, ring.

1551. גָּלִיל **Gâlîyl**, *gaw-leel´;* or (prol.)

גָּלִילָה **Gâlîylâh**, *gaw-lee-law´;* the same as 1550; a *circle* (with the art.); *Galil* (as a special *circuit*) in the North of Pal.:— Galilee.

1552. גְּלִילָה **gᵉlîylâh**, *ghel-ee-law´;* fem.

of 1550; a *circuit* or *region:*— border, coast, country.

1553. גְּלִילוֹת **Geliylôwth**, *ghel-ee-lowth´;* plur. of 1552; *circles; Geliloth,* a place in Pal.:— Geliloth.

1554. גַּלִּים **Galliym**, *gal-leem´;* plur. of 1530; *springs; Gallim,* a place in Pal.:— Gallim.

1555. גָּלְיָת **Golyath**, *gol-yath´;* perh. from 1540; *exile; Goljath,* a Philistine:— Goliath.

1556. גָּלַל **gâlal**, *gaw-lal´;* a prim. root; to *roll* (lit. or fig.):— commit, remove, roll (away, down, together), run down, seek occasion, trust, wallow.

1557. גָּלָל **gâlâl**, *gaw-lawl´;* from 1556; *dung* (as in balls):— dung.

1558. גָּלָל **gâlâl**, *gaw-lawl´;* from 1556; a *circumstance* (as *rolled* around); only used adv., on *account* of:— because of, for (sake).

1559. גָּלָל **Gâlâl**, *gaw-lawl´;* from 1556, in the sense of 1560; *great; Galal,* the name of two Isr.:— Galal.

1560. גְּלָל **gelâl** (Chald.), *ghel-awl´;* from a root corresp. to 1556; *weight* or *size* (as if *rolled*):— great.

1561. גֵּלֶל **gêlel**, *gay´-lel;* a var. of 1557; *dung* (plur. *balls* of dung):— dung.

1562. גִּלֲלַי **Gilălay**, *ghe-lal-ah´-ee;* from 1561; *dungy; Gilalai,* an Isr.:— Gilalai.

1563. גָּלַם **gâlam**, *gaw-lam´;* a prim. root; to *fold:*— wrap together.

1564. גֹּלֶם **gôlem**, *go´-lem;* from 1563; a *wrapped* (and unformed *mass,* i.e. as the *embryo*):— substance yet being unperfect.

1565. גַּלְמוּד **galmûwd**, *gal-mood´;* prob. by prol. from 1563; *sterile* (as *wrapped* up too hard); fig. *desolate:*— desolate, solitary.

1566. גָּלַע **gâla'**, *gaw-lah´;* a prim. root; to *be obstinate:*— (inter-) meddle (with).

1567. גַּלְעֵד **Gal'êd**, *gal-ade´;* from 1530 and 5707; *heap of testimony; Galed,* a memorial cairn E. of the Jordan:— Galeed.

1568. גִּלְעָד **Gil'âd**, *ghil-awd´;* prob. from 1567; *Gilad,* a region E. of the Jordan; also the name of three Isr.:— Gilead, Gileadite.

1569. גִּלְעָדִי **Gil'âdîy**, *ghil-aw-dee´;* patron. from 1568; a *Giladite* or desc. of Gilad:— Gileadite.

1570. גָּלַשׁ **gâlash**, *gaw-lash´;* a prim. root; prob. to *caper* (as a goat):— appear.

1571. גַּם **gam**, *gam;* by contr. from an unused root mean. to *gather;* prop. *assemblage;* used only adv. *also, even, yea, though;* often repeated as correl. *both … and:*— again, alike, also, (so much) as (soon), both (so) … and, but, either … or, even, for all, (in) likewise (manner), moreover, nay … neither, one, then (-refore), though, what, with, yea.

1572. גָּמָא **gâmâ'**, *gaw-maw´;* a prim. root (lit. or fig.) to *absorb:*— swallow, drink.

1573. גֹּמֶא **gôme'**, *go´-meh;* from 1572;

prop. an *absorbent,* i.e. the *bulrush* (from its *porosity*); spec. the *papyrus:*— (bul-) rush.

1574. גֹּמֶד **gômed**, *go´-med;* from an unused root appar. mean. to *grasp;* prop. a *span:*— cubit.

1575. גַּמָּד **Gammâd**, *gam-mawd´;* from the same as 1574; a *warrior* (as *grasping* weapons):— Gammadims.

1576. גְּמוּל **gemûwl**, *ghem-ool´;* from 1580; *treatment,* i.e. an *act* (of good or ill); by impl. *service* or *requital:*— + as hast served, benefit, desert, deserving, that which he hath given, recompense, reward.

1577. גָּמוּל **Gâmûwl**, *gaw-mool´;* pass. part. of 1580; *rewarded; Gamul,* an Isr.:— Gamul. See also 1014.

1578. גְּמוּלָה **gemûwlâh**, *ghem-oo-law´;* fem. of 1576; mean. the same:— deed, recompense, such a reward.

1579. גִּמְזוֹ **Gimzôw**, *ghim-zo´;* of uncert. der.; *Gimzo,* a place in Pal.:— Gimzo.

1580. גָּמַל **gâmal**, *gaw-mal´;* a prim. root; to *treat* a person (well or ill), i.e. *benefit* or *requite;* by impl. (of *toil*), to *ripen,* i.e. (spec.) to *wean:*— bestow on, deal bountifully, do (good), recompense, requite, reward, ripen, + serve, mean, yield.

1581. גָּמָל **gâmâl**, *gaw-mawl´;* appar. from 1580 (in the sense of *labor* or *burden-bearing*); a *camel:*— camel.

1582. גְּמַלִּי **Gemalliy**, *ghem-al-lee´;* prob. from 1581; *camel-driver; Gemalli,* an Isr.:— Gemalli.

1583. גַּמְלִיאֵל **Gamliy'êl**, *gam-lee-ale´;* from 1580 and 410; *reward of God; Gamliel,* an Isr.:— Gamaliel.

1584. גָּמַר **gâmar**, *gaw-mar´;* a prim. root; to *end* (in the sense of *completion* or *failure*):— cease, come to an end, fail, perfect, perform.

1585. גְּמַר **gemar** (Chald.), *ghem-ar´;* corresp. to 1584:— perfect.

1586. גֹּמֶר **Gômer**, *go´-mer;* from 1584; *completion; Gomer,* the name of a son of Japheth and of his desc.; also of a Hebrewess:— Gomer.

1587. גְּמַרְיָה **Gemaryâh**, *ghem-ar-yaw´;* or

גְּמַרְיָהוּ **Gemaryâhûw**, *ghem-ar-yaw´-hoo;* from 1584 and 3050; *Jah has perfected; Gemarjah,* the name of two Isr.:— Gemariah.

1588. גַּן **gan**, *gan;* from 1598; a *garden* (as *fenced*):— garden.

1589. גָּנַב **gânab**, *gaw-nab´;* a prim. root; to *thieve* (lit. or fig.); by impl. to *deceive:*— carry away, × indeed, secretly bring, steal (away), get by stealth.

1590. גַּנָּב **gannâb**, *gaw-nab´;* from 1589; a *stealer:*— thief.

1591. גְּנֵבָה **genêbâh**, *ghen-ay-baw´;* from 1589; *stealing,* i.e. (concr.) something *stolen:*— theft.

1592. גְּנֻבַת **Genûbath**, *ghen-oo-bath´;* from 1589; *theft; Genubath,* an Edomitish prince:— Genubath.

1593. גַּנָּה **gannâh**, *gan-naw´;* fem. of 1588; a *garden:*— garden.

1594. גִּנָּה **ginnâh**, *ghin-naw´;* another form for 1593:— garden.

1595. גֶּנֶז **genez**, *gheh´-nez;* from an unused root mean. to *store; treasure;* by impl. a *coffer:*— chest, treasury.

1596. גְּנַז **genaz** (Chald.), *ghen-az´;* corresp. to 1595; *treasure:*— treasure.

1597. גִּנְזַךְ **ginzak**, *ghin-zak´;* prol. from 1595; a *treasury:*— treasury.

1598. גָּנַן **gânan**, *gaw-nan´;* a prim. root; to *hedge* about, i.e. (gen.) *protect:*— defend.

1599. גִּנְּתוֹן **Ginnethôwn**, *ghin-neth-ône´;* or

גִּנְּתוֹ **Ginnethôw**, *ghin-neth-o´;* from 1598; *gardener; Ginnethon* or *Ginnetho,* an Isr.:— Ginnetho, Ginnethon.

1600. גָּעָה **gâ'âh**, *gaw-aw´;* a prim. root; to *bellow* (as cattle):— low.

1601. גֹּעָה **Gô'âh**, *go-aw´;* fem. act. part. of 1600; *lowing; Goah,* a place near Jerusalem:— Goath.

1602. גָּעַל **gâ'al**, *gaw-al´;* a prim. root; to *detest;* by impl. to *reject:*— abhor, fail, lothe, vilely cast away.

1603. גַּעַל **Ga'al**, *gah´-al;* from 1602; *loathing; Gaal,* an Isr.:— Gaal.

1604. גֹּעַל **gô'al**, *go´-al;* from 1602; *abhorrence:*— loathing.

1605. גָּעַר **gâ'ar**, *gaw-ar´;* a prim. root; to *chide:*— corrupt, rebuke, reprove.

1606. גְּעָרָה **ge'ârâh**, *gheh-aw-raw´;* from 1605; a *chiding:*— rebuke (-ing), reproof.

1607. גָּעַשׁ **gâ'ash**, *gaw-ash´;* a prim. root to *agitate* violently:— move, shake, toss, trouble.

1608. גַּעַשׁ **Ga'ash**, *ga´-ash;* from 1607; a *quaking; Gaash,* a hill in Pal.:— Gaash.

1609. גַּעְתָּם **Ga'tâm**, *gah-tawm´;* of uncert. der.; *Gatam,* an Edomite:— Gatam.

1610. גַּף **gaph**, *gaf;* from an unused root mean. to *arch; the back;* by extens. the *body* or *self:*— + highest places, himself.

1611. גַּף **gaph** (Chald.), *gaf;* corresp. to 1610; a *wing:*— wing.

1612. גֶּפֶן **gephen**, *gheh´-fen;* from an unused root mean. to *bend;* a *vine* (as *twining*), espec. the grape:— vine, tree.

1613. גֹּפֶר **gôpher**, *go´-fer;* from an unused root, prob. mean. to *house in;* a kind of tree or wood (as used for *building*), appar. the *cypress:*— gopher.

1614. גָּפְרִית **gophrîyth**, *gof-reeth´;* prob. fem. of 1613; prop. cypress-*resin;* by anal. *sulphur* (as equally inflammable):— brimstone.

1615. גִּר **gir**, *gheer;* perh. from 3564; *lime* (from being *burned* in a kiln):— chalk [-stone].

1616. גֵּר **gêr**, *gare;* or (fully)

גֵּיר **gêyr**, *gare;* from 1481; prop. a *guest;* by impl. a *foreigner:*— alien, sojourner, stranger.

גּוּר **gûr**. See 1482.

1617. גֵּרָא **Gêrâ'**, *gay-raw´;* perh. from 1626; a *grain; Gera,* the name of six Isr.:— Gera.

1618. גָּרָב **gârâb**, *gaw-rawb'*; from an unused root mean. to *scratch; scurf* (from *itching*):— scab, scurvy.

1619. גָּרָב **Gârêb**, *gaw-rabe'*; from the same as 1618; *scabby; Gareb*, the name of an Isr., also of a hill near Jerusalem:— Gareb.

1620. גַּרְגַּר **gargar**, *gar-gar'*; by redupl. from 1641; a *berry* (as if a pellet of *rumination*):— berry.

1621. גַּרְגְּרוֹת **gargᵉrôwth**, *gar-gher-owth'*; fem. plur. from 1641; the *throat* (as used in *rumination*):— neck.

1622. גִּרְגָּשִׁי **Girgâshîy**, *ghir-gaw-shee'*; patrial from an unused name [of uncert. der.]; a *Girgashite*, one of the native tribes of Canaan:— Girgashite, Girgasite.

1623. גָּרַד **gârad**, *gaw-rad'*; a prim. root; to *abrade*:— scrape.

1624. גָּרָה **gârâh**, *gaw-raw'*; a prim. root; prop. to *grate*, i.e. (fig.) to *anger*:— contend, meddle, stir up, strive.

1625. גֵּרָה **gêrâh**, *gay-raw'*; from 1641; the *cud* (as *scraping* the throat):— cud.

1626. גֵּרָה **gêrâh**, *gay-raw'*; from 1641 (as in 1625); prop. (like 1620) a *kernel* (round as if *scraped*), i.e. a *gerah* or small weight (and coin):— gerah.

גֹּרָה **gôrâh**. See 1484.

1627. גָּרוֹן **gârôwn**, *gaw-rone'*; or (short.) גָּרֹן **gârôn**, *gaw-rone'*; from 1641; the *throat* [comp. 1621] (as *roughened* by swallowing):— × aloud, mouth, neck, throat.

1628. גְּרוּת **gêrûwth**, *gay-rooth'*; from 1481; a (temporary) *residence*:— habitation.

1629. גָּרַז **gâraz**, *gaw-raz'*; a prim. root; to *cut off*:— cut off.

1630. גְּרִזִים **Gᵉrîzîym**, *gher-ee-zeem'*; plur. of an unused noun from 1629 [comp. 1511], *cut up* (i.e. *rocky*); *Gerizim*, a mountain of Pal.:— Gerizim.

1631. גַּרְזֶן **garzen**, *gar-zen'*; from 1629; an *axe*:- - ax.

1632. גָּרֹל **gârôl**, *gaw-role'*; from the same as 1486; *harsh*:— man of great [as in the marg. which reads 1419].

גֹּרָל **gôrâl**. See 1486.

1633. גָּרַם **gâram**, *gaw-ram'*; a prim. root; to *be spare* or *skeleton-like*; used only as a denom. from 1634; (caus.) to *bone*, i.e. *denude* (by extens. *crunch*) the bones:— gnaw the bones, break.

1634. גֶּרֶם **gerem**, *gheh'-rem*; from 1633; a *bone* (as the *skeleton* of the body); hence, *self*, i.e. (fig.) *very*:— bone, strong, top.

1635. גֶּרֶם **gerem** (Chald.), *gheh'-rem*; corresp. to 1634; a *bone*:— bone.

1636. גַּרְמִי **Garmîy**, *gar-mee'*; from 1634; *bony*, i.e. *strong*:— Garmite.

1637. גֹּרֶן **gôren**, *go'-ren*; from an unused root mean. to *smooth*; a *threshing-floor* (as made *even*); by anal. any open *area*:— (barn, corn, threshing-) floor, (threshing-, void) place.

גָּרֹן **gârôn**. See 1627.

1638. גָּרַס **gâraç**, *gaw-ras'*; a prim. root; to *crush*; also (intr. and fig.) to *dissolve*:— break.

1639. גָּרַע **gâra'**, *gaw-rah'*; a prim. root; to *scrape* off; by impl. to *shave, remove, lessen,* or *withhold*:— abate, clip, (di-) minish, do (take) away, keep back, restrain, make small, withdraw.

1640. גָּרַף **gâraph**, *gaw-raf'*; a prim. root; to *bear* off violently:— sweep away.

1641. גָּרַר **gârar**, *gaw-rar'*; a prim. root; to *drag* off roughly; by impl. to *bring up* the cud (i.e. *ruminate*); by anal. to *saw*:— catch, chew, × continuing, destroy, saw.

1642. גְּרָר **Gᵉrâr**, *gher-awr'*; prob. from 1641; a *rolling* country; *Gerar*, a Philistine city:— Gerar.

1643. גֶּרֶשׂ **geres**, *gheh'-res*; from an unused root mean. to *husk*; a *kernel* (collect.), i.e. *grain*:— beaten corn.

1644. גָּרַשׁ **gârash**, *gaw-rash'*; a prim. root; to *drive* out from a possession; espec. to *expatriate* or *divorce*:— cast up (out), divorced (woman), drive away (forth, out), expel, × surely put away, trouble, thrust out.

1645. גֶּרֶשׁ **geresh**, *gheh'-resh*; from 1644; *produce* (as if *expelled*):— put forth.

1646. גְּרֻשָׁה **gᵉrushâh**, *gher-oo-shaw'*; fem. pass. part. of 1644; (abstr.) *dispossession*:— exaction.

1647. גֵּרְשֹׁם **Gêrᵉshôm**, *gay-resh-ome'*; for 1648; *Gereshom*, the name of four Isr.:— Gershom.

1648. גֵּרְשׁוֹן **Gêrᵉshôwn**, *gay-resh-one'*; or גֵּרְשׁוֹם **Gêrᵉshôwm**, *gay-resh-ome'*; from 1644; a *refugee; Gereshon* or *Gereshom*, an Isr.:— Gershon, Gershom.

1649. גֵּרְשֻׁנִּי **Gêrᵉshunnîy**, *gay-resh-oon-nee'*; patron. from 1648; a *Gereshonite* or desc. of Gereshon:— Gershonite, sons of Gershon.

1650. גְּשׁוּר **Gᵉshûwr**, *ghesh-oor'*; from an unused root (mean. to *join*); *bridge; Geshur*, a district of Syria:— Geshur, Geshurite.

1651. גְּשׁוּרִי **Gᵉshûwrîy**, *ghe-shoo-ree'*; patrial from 1650; a *Geshurite* (also collect.) or inhab. of Geshur:— Geshuri, Geshurites.

1652. גָּשַׁם **gâsham**, *gaw-sham'*; a prim. root; to *shower* violently:— (cause to) rain.

1653. גֶּשֶׁם **geshem**, *gheh'-shem*; from 1652; a *shower*:— rain, shower.

1654. גֶּשֶׁם **Geshem**, *gheh'-shem*; or (prol.) גַּשְׁמוּ **Gashmûw**, *gash-moo'*; the same as 1653; *Geshem* or *Gashmu*, an Arabian:— Geshem, Gashmu.

1655. גֶּשֶׁם **geshem** (Chald.), *gheh'-shem*; appar. the same as 1653; used in a peculiar sense, the *body* (prob. for the [fig.] idea of a *hard* rain):— body.

1656. גֹּשֶׁם **gôshem**, *go'-shem*; from 1652; equiv. to 1653:— rained upon.

גַּשְׁמוּ **Gashmûw**. See 1654.

1657. גֹּשֶׁן **Gôshen**, *go'-shen*; prob. of Eg. or.; *Goshen*, the residence of the Isr. in Egypt; also a place in Pal.:— Goshen.

1658. גִּשְׁפָּא **Gishpâ'**, *ghish-paw'*; of uncert. der.; *Gishpa*, an Isr.:— Gispa.

1659. גָּשַׁשׁ **gâshash**, *gaw-shash'*; a prim. root; appar. to *feel* about:— grope.

1660. גַּת **gath**, *gath*; prob. from 5059 (in the sense of *treading* out grapes); a *wine-press* (or vat for holding the grapes in pressing them):— (wine-) press (fat).

1661. גַּת **Gath**, *gath*; the same as 1660; *Gath*, a Philistine city:— Gath.

1662. גַּת־הַחֵפֶר **Gath-ha-Chêpher**, *gath-hah-khay'-fer*; or (abridged) גִּתָּה־חֵפֶר **Gittâh-Chêpher**, *ghit-taw-khay'-fer*; from 1660 and 2658 with the art. ins.; *wine-press of* (the) *well; Gath-Chepher*, a place in Pal.:— Gath-kephr, Gittah-kephr.

1663. גִּתִּי **Gittîy**, *ghit-tee'*; patrial from 1661; a *Gittite* or inhab. of Gath:— Gittite.

1664. גִּתַּיִם **Gittayim**, *ghit-tah'-yim*; dual of 1660; *double wine-press; Gittajim*, a place in Pal.:— Gittaim.

1665. גִּתִּית **Gittîyth**, *ghit-teeth'*; fem. of 1663; a *Gittite* harp:— Gittith.

1666. גֶּתֶר **Gether**, *gheh'-ther*; of uncert. der.; *Gether*, a son of Aram, and the region settled by him:— Gether.

1667. גַּת־רִמּוֹן **Gath-Rimmôwn**, *gath-rim-mone'*; from 1660 and 7416; *wine-press of* (the) *pomegranate; Gath-Rimmon*, a place in Pal.:— Gath-rimmon.

ד

1668. דָּא **dâ'** (Chald.), *daw*; corresp. to 2088; *this*:— one ... another, this.

1669. דָּאַב **dâ'ab**, *daw-ab'*; a prim. root; to *pine*:— mourn, sorrow (-ful).

1670. דְּאָבָה **dᵉ'âbâh**, *dĕh-aw-baw'*; from 1669; prop. *pining*; by anal. *fear*:— sorrow.

1671. דְּאָבוֹן **dᵉ'âbôwn**, *dĕh-aw-bone'*; from 1669; *pining*:— sorrow.

1672. דָּאַג **dâ'ag**, *daw-ag'*; a prim. root; *be anxious*:— be afraid (careful, sorry), sorrow, take thought.

1673. דֹּאֵג **Dô'êg**, *do-ayg'*; or (fully) דּוֹאֵג **Dôw'êg**, *do-ayg'*; act. part. of 1672; *anxious; Doëg*, an Edomite:— Doeg.

1674. דְּאָגָה **dᵉ'âgâh**, *dĕh-aw-gaw'*; from 1672; *anxiety*:— care (-fulness), fear, heaviness, sorrow.

1675. דָּאָה **dâ'âh**, *daw-aw'*; a prim. root; to *dart*, i.e. *fly* rapidly:— fly.

1676. דָּאָה **dâ'âh**, *daw-aw'*; from 1675; the *kite* (from its rapid *flight*):— vulture. See 7201.

1677. דֹּב **dôb**, *dobe*; or (fully) דּוֹב **dôwb**, *dobe*; from 1680; the *bear* (as slow):— bear.

1678. דֹּב **dôb** (Chald.), *dobe*; corresp. to 1677:— bear.

1679. דֹּבֶא **dôbe'**, *do'-beh*; from an unused root (comp. 1680) (prob. mean. to *be sluggish*, i.e. *restful*); *quiet*:— strength.

1680. דְּבַב **dâbab**, *daw-bab´*; a prim. root (comp. 1679); to *move* slowly, i.e. *glide*:— cause to speak.

1681. דִּבָּה **dibbâh**, *dib-baw´*; from 1680 (in the sense of *furtive* motion); *slander*:— defaming, evil report, infamy, slander.

1682. דְּבוֹרָה **dᵉbôwrâh**, *deb-o-raw´*; or (short.)

דְּבֹרָה **dᵉbôrâh**, *deb-o-raw´*; from 1696 (in the sense of *orderly* motion); the *bee* (from its *systematic* instincts):— bee.

1683. דְּבוֹרָה **Dᵉbôwrâh**, *deb-o-raw´*; or (short.)

דְּבֹרָה **Dᵉbôrâh**, *deb-o-raw´*; the same as 1682; *Deborah*, the name of two Hebrewesses:— Deborah.

1684. דְּבַח **dᵉbach** (Chald.), *deb-akh´*; corresp. to 2076; to *sacrifice* (an animal):— offer [sacrifice].

1685. דְּבַח **dᵉbach** (Chald.), *deb-akh´*; from 1684; a *sacrifice*:— sacrifice.

1686. דִּבְיוֹן **dibyôwn**, *dib-yone´*; in the marg. for the textual reading

חֲרִיוֹן° **cheryôwn**, *kher-yone´*; both (in the plur. only and) of uncert. der.; prob. some cheap vegetable, perh. a bulbous root:— dove's dung.

1687. דְּבִיר **dᵉbîyr**, *deb-eer´*; or (short.)

דְּבִר **dᵉbir**, *deb-eer´*; from 1696 (appar. in the sense of *oracle*); the *shrine* or innermost part of the sanctuary:— oracle.

1688. דְּבִיר **Dᵉbîyr**, *deb-eer´*; or (short.)

דְּבִר **Dᵉbîr** (Josh. 13:26 [but see 3810]), *deb-eer´*; the same as 1687; *Debir*, the name of an Amoritish king and of two places in Pal.:— Debir.

1689. דִּבְלָה **Diblâh**, *dib-law´*; prob. an orth. err. for 7247; *Diblah*, a place in Syria:— Diblath.

1690. דְּבֵלָה **dᵉbêlâh**, *deb-ay-law´*; from an unused root (akin to 2082) prob. mean. to *press* together; a *cake* of pressed figs:— cake (lump) of figs.

1691. דִּבְלַיִם **Diblayim**, *dib-lah´-yim*; dual from the masc. of 1690; *two cakes*; *Diblajim*, a symb. name:— Diblaim.

דִּבְלָתָיְמָה **Diblâthayim**. See 1015.

1692. דָּבַק **dâbaq**, *daw-bak´*; a prim. root; prop. to *impinge*, i.e. *cling* or *adhere*; fig. to *catch* by pursuit:— abide fast, cleave (fast together), follow close (hard after), be joined (together), keep (fast), overtake, pursue hard, stick, take.

1693. דְּבַק **dᵉbaq** (Chald.), *deb-ak´*; corresp. to 1692; to *stick* to:— cleave.

1694. דֶּבֶק **debeq**, *deh´-bek*; from 1692; a *joint*; by impl. *solder*:— joint, solder.

1695. דָּבֵק **dâbêq**, *daw-bake´*; from 1692; *adhering*:— cleave, joining, stick closer.

1696. דָּבַר **dâbar**, *daw-bar´*; a prim. root; perh. prop. to *arrange*; but used fig. (of words), to *speak*; rarely (in a destructive sense) to *subdue*:— answer, appoint, bid, command, commune, declare, destroy, give, name, promise, pronounce, rehearse, say, speak, be spokesman, subdue, talk,

teach, tell, think, use [entreaties], utter, × well, × work.

1697. דָּבָר **dâbâr**, *daw-baw´*; from 1696; a *word*; by impl. a *matter* (as *spoken* of) or *thing*; adv. a *cause*:— act, advice, affair, answer, × any such (thing), + because of, book, business, care, case, cause, certain rate, + chronicles, commandment, × commune (-ication), + concern [-ing], + confer, counsel, + dearth, decree, deed, × disease, due, duty, effect, + eloquent, errand, [evil favoured-] ness, + glory, + harm, hurt, + iniquity, + judgment, language, + lying, manner, matter, message, [no] thing, oracle, × ought, × parts, + pertaining, + please, portion, + power, promise, provision, purpose, question, rate, reason, report, request, × (as hast) said, sake, saying, sentence, + sign, + so, some [uncleanness], somewhat to say, + song, speech, × spoken, talk, task, + that, × there done, thing (concerning), thought, + thus, tidings, what [-soever], + wherewith, which, word, work.

1698. דֶּבֶר **deber**, *deh´-ber*; from 1696 (in the sense of *destroying*); a *pestilence*:— murrain, pestilence, plague.

1699. דֹּבֶר **dôber**, *do´-ber*; from 1696 (in its original sense); a *pasture* (from its *arrangement* of the flock):— fold, manner.

דְּבִיר **dᵉbîr** or

דְּבִר **Dᵉbîr**. See 1687, 1688.

1699´. דִּבֵּר **dibbêr**, *dib-bare´*; for 1697:— word.

1700. דִּבְרָה **dibrâh**, *dib-raw´*; fem. of 1697; a *reason*, *suit* or *style*:— cause, end, estate, order, regard.

1701. דִּבְרָה **dibrâh** (Chald.), *dib-raw´*; corresp. to 1700:— intent, sake.

דְּבֹרָה **dᵉbôrâh** or

דְּבוֹרָה **Dᵉbôrâh**. See 1682, 1683.

1702. דֹּבְרָה **dôbᵉrâh**, *do-ber-aw´*; fem. act. part. of 1696 in the sense of *driving* [comp. 1699]; a *raft*:— float.

1703. דַּבָּרָה **dabbârâh**, *dab-baw-raw´*; intens. from 1696; a *word*:— word.

1704. דִּבְרִי **Dibrîy**, *dib-ree´*; from 1697; *wordy*; *Dibri*, an Isr.:— Dibri.

1705. דָּבְרַת **Dâbᵉrath**, *daw-ber-ath´*; from 1697 (perh. in the sense of 1699); *Daberath*, a place in Pal.:— Dabareh, Daberath.

1706. דְּבַשׁ **dᵉbash**, *deb-ash´*; from an unused root mean. to *be gummy*; *honey* (from its *stickiness*); by anal. *syrup*:— honey [-comb].

1707. דַּבֶּשֶׁת **dabbesheth**, *dab-beh´-sheth*; intens. from the same as 1706; a sticky *mass*, i.e. the *hump* of a camel:— hunch [of a camel].

1708. דַּבֶּשֶׁת **Dabbesheth**, *dab-beh´-sheth*; the same as 1707; *Dabbesheth*, a place in Pal.:— Dabbesheth.

1709. דָּג **dâg**, *dawg*; or (fully)

דָּאג° **dâ'g** (Neh. 13:16), *dawg*; from 1711; a *fish* (as *prolific*); or perh. rather from 1672 (as *timid*); but still better from 1672 (in the sense of *squirming*, i.e. moving by the vibratory

action of the tail); a *fish* (often used collect.):— fish.

1710. דָּגָה **dâgâh**, *daw-gaw´*; fem. of 1709, and mean. the same:— fish.

1711. דָּגָה **dâgâh**, *daw-gaw´*; a prim. root; to *move rapidly*; used only as a denom. from 1709; to *spawn*, i.e. *become numerous*:— grow.

1712. דָּגוֹן **Dâgôwn**, *daw-gohn´*; from 1709; the *fish-god*; *Dagon*, a Philistine deity:— Dagon.

1713. דָּגַל **dâgal**, *daw-gal´*; a prim. root; to *flaunt*, i.e. *raise a flag*; fig. to *be conspicuous*:— (set up, with) banners, chiefest.

1714. דֶּגֶל **degel**, *deh´-gel*; from 1713; a *flag*:— banner, standard.

1715. דָּגָן **dâgân**, *daw-gawn´*; from 1711; prop. *increase*, i.e. *grain*:— corn ([floor]), wheat.

1716. דָּגַר **dâgar**, *daw-gar´*; a prim. root, to *brood* over eggs or young:— gather, sit.

1717. דַּד **dad**, *dad*; appar. from the same as 1730; the *breast* (as the seat of *love*, or from its shape):— breast, teat.

1718. דָּדָה **dâdâh**, *daw-daw´*; a doubtful root; to *walk gently*:— go (softly, with).

1719. דְּדָן **Dᵉdân**, *ded-awn´*; or (prol.)

דְּדָנֶה **Dᵉdâneh** (Ezek. 25:13), *deh-daw´-neh*; of uncert. der.; *Dedan*, the name of two Cushites and of their territory:— Dedan.

1720. דְּדָנִים **Dᵉdânîym**, *ded-aw-neem´*; plur. of 1719 (as patrial); *Dedanites*, the desc. or inhab. of Dedan:— Dedanim.

1721. דֹּדָנִים **Dôdânîym**, *do-daw-neem´*; or (by orth. err.)

רֹדָנִים **Rôdânîym** (1 Chron. 1:7), *ro-daw-neem´*; a plur. of uncert. der.; *Dodanites*, or desc. of a son of Javan:— Dodanim.

1722. דְּהַב **dᵉhab** (Chald.), *deh-hab´*; corresp. to 2091; *gold*:— gold (-en).

1723. דַּהֲוָא° **Dahăvâ'** (Chald.), *dah-hav-aw´*; of uncert. der.; *Dahava*, a people colonized in Samaria:— Dehavites.

1724. דָּהַם **dâham**, *daw-ham´*; a prim. root (comp. 1740); to *be dumb*, i.e. (fig.) *dumb-founded*:— be astonished.

1725. דָּהַר **dâhar**, *daw-har´*; a prim. root; to *curvet* or move irregularly:— pause.

1726. דַּהֲהַר **dahăhar**, *dah-hah-har´*; by redupl. from 1725; a *gallop*:— pransing.

דֹּאֵג **Dôw'êg**. See 1673.

1727. דּוּב **dûwb**, *doob*; a prim. root; to *mope*, i.e. (fig.) *pine*:— sorrow.

דּוּב **dôwb**. See 1677.

1728. דַּוָּג **davvâg**, *dav-vawg´*; an orth. var. of 1709 as a denom. [1771]; a *fisherman*:— fisher.

1729. דּוּגָה **dûwgâh**, *doo-gaw´*; fem. from the same as 1728; prop. *fishery*, i.e. a *hook* for fishing:— fish [hook].

1730. דּוֹד **dôwd**, *dode*; or (short.)

דֹּד **dôd**, *dode*; from an unused root mean. prop. to *boil*, i.e. (fig.) to *love*; by impl. a *love-token*, *lover*, friend; spec. an *uncle*:— (well-) beloved, father's brother, love, uncle.

1731. דּוּד **dûwd**, *dood;* from the same as 1730; a *pot* (for *boiling*); also (by resemblance of shape) a *basket*:— basket, caldron, kettle, (seething) pot.

1732. דְּוִד **Dâvid**, *daw-veed´;* rarely (fully)

דָּוִיד **Dâvîyd**, *daw-veed´;* from the same as 1730; *loving; David*, the youngest son of Jesse:— David.

1733. דּוֹדָה **dôwdâh**, *do-daw´;* fem. of 1730; an *aunt*:— aunt, father's sister, uncle's wife.

1734. דּוֹדוֹ **Dôwdôw**, *do-do´;* from 1730; *loving; Dodo*, the name of three Isr.:— Dodo.

1735. דּוֹדָוָהוּ **Dôwdâvâhûw**, *do-daw-vaw´-hoo;* from 1730 and 3050; *love of Jah; Dodavah*, an Isr.:— Dodavah.

1736. דּוּדַי **dûwday**, *doo-dah´-ee;* from 1731; a *boiler* or *basket;* also the *mandrake* (as *aphrodisiac*):— basket, mandrake.

1737. דּוֹדַי **Dôwday**, *do-dah´-ee;* formed like 1736; *amatory; Dodai*, an Isr.:— Dodai.

1738. דָּוָה **dâvâh**, *daw-vaw´;* a prim. root; to *be sick* (as if in menstruation):— infirmity.

1739. דָּוֶה **dâveh**, *daw-veh´;* from 1738; *sick* (espec. in menstruation):— faint, menstruous cloth, she that is sick, having sickness.

1740. דּוּחַ **dûwach**, *doo´-akh;* a prim. root; to *thrust* away; fig. to *cleanse*:— cast out, purge, wash.

1741. דְּוַי **deʹvay**, *dev-ah´-ee;* from 1739; *sickness;* fig. *loathing*:— languishing, sorrowful.

1742. דַּוָּי **davvây**, *dav-voy´;* from 1739; *sick;* fig. *troubled*:— faint.

דָּוִיד **Dâvîyd**. See 1732.

1743. דּוּךְ **dûwk**, *dook;* a prim. root; to *bruise* in a mortar:— beat.

1744. דּוּכִיפַת **dûwkîyphath**, *doo-kee-fath´;* of uncert. der.; the *hoopoe* or else the *grouse*:— lapwing.

1745. דּוּמָה **dûwmâh**, *doo-maw´;* from an unused root mean. to *be dumb* (comp. 1820); *silence;* fig. *death*:— silence.

1746. דּוּמָה **Dûwmâh**, *doo-maw´;* the same as 1745; *Dumah*, a tribe and region of Arabia:— Dumah.

1747. דּוּמִיָּה **dûwmîyâh**, *doo-me-yaw´;* from 1820; *stillness;* adv. *silently;* abstr. *quiet, trust*:— silence, silent, waiteth.

1748. דּוּמָם **dûwmâm**, *doo-mawm´;* from 1826; *still;* adv. *silently*:— dumb, silent, quietly wait.

דּוּמֶשֶׂק° **Dûwmesheq**. See 1833.

1749. דּוֹנַג **dôwnag**, *do-nag´;* of uncert. der.; *wax*:— wax.

1750. דּוּץ **dûwts**, *doots;* a prim. root; to *leap*:— be turned.

1751. דּוּק **dûwq** (Chald.), *dook;* corresp. to 1854; to *crumble*:— be broken to pieces.

1752. דּוּר **dûwr**, *dure;* a prim. root;

prop. to *gyrate* (or move in a circle), i.e. to *remain*:— dwell.

1753. דּוּר **dûwr** (Chald.), *dure;* corresp. to 1752; to *reside*:— dwell.

1754. דּוּר **dûwr**, *dure;* from 1752; a *circle, ball* or *pile*:— ball, turn, round about.

1755. דּוֹר **dôwr**, *dore;* or (short.)

דֹּר **dôr**, *dore;* from 1752; prop. a *revolution* of time, i.e. an *age* or generation; also a *dwelling*:— age, × evermore, generation, [n-lever, posterity.

1756. דּוֹר **Dôwr**, *dore* or (by perm.)

דֹּאר **Dôʹr** (Josh. 17:11; 1 Kings 4:11), *dore;* from 1755; *dwelling; Dor*, a place in Pal.:— Dor.

1757. דּוּרָא **Dûwrâ'** (Chald.), *doo-raw´;* prob. from 1753; *circle* or *dwelling; Dura*, a place in Bab.:— Dura.

1758. דּוּשׁ **dûwsh**, *doosh;* or

דּוֹשׁ **dôwsh**, *dōsh;* or

דִּישׁ **dîysh**, *deesh;* a prim. root; to *trample* or *thresh*:— break, tear, thresh, tread out (down), at grass [Jer. 50:11, *by mistake for* 1877].

1759. דּוּשׁ **dûwsh** (Chald.), *doosh;* corresp. to 1758; to *trample*:— tread down.

1760. דָּחָה **dâchâh**, *daw-khaw´;* or

דָּחַח **dâchach** (Jer. 23:12), *daw-khakh´;* a prim. root; to *push* down:— chase, drive away (on), overthrow, outcast, × sore, thrust, totter.

1761. דַּחֲוָה **dachăvâh** (Chald.), *dakh-av-aw´;* from the equiv. of 1760; prob. a musical *instrument* (as being *struck*):— instrument of music.

1762. דְּחִי **deʹchîy**, *deh-khee´;* from 1760; a *push*, i.e. (by impl.) a *fall*:— falling.

1763. דְּחַל **deʹchal** (Chald.), *deh-khal´;* corresp. to 2119; to *slink*, i.e. (by impl.) to *fear*, or (caus.) be *formidable*:— make afraid, dreadful, fear, terrible.

1764. דֹּחַן **dôchan**, *do´-khan;* of uncert. der.; *millet*:— millet.

1765. דָּחַף **dâchaph**, *daw-khaf´;* a prim. root; to *urge*, i.e. *hasten*:— (be) haste (-ned), pressed on.

1766. דָּחַק **dâchaq**, *daw-khak´;* a prim. root; to *press*, i.e. *oppress*:— thrust, vex.

1767. דַּי **day**, *dahee;* of uncert. der.; *enough* (as noun or adv.), used chiefly with prep. in phrases:— able, according to, after (ability), among, as (oft as), (more than) enough, from, in, since, (much as is) sufficient (-ly), too much, very, when.

1768. דִּי **dîy** (Chald.), *dee;* appar. for 1668; *that*, used as rel., conjunc., and espec. (with prep.) in adv. phrases; also as prep. *of*:— × as, but, for (-asmuch +), + now, of, seeing, than, that, therefore, until, + what (-soever), when, which, whom, whose.

1769. דִּיבוֹן **Dîybôwn**, *dee-bome´;* or (short.)

דִּיבֹן **Dîybôn**, *dee-bone´;* from 1727; *pining; Dibon*, the name of three places in Pal.:— Dibon. [Also, *with* 1410 *added*, Dibon-gad.]

1770. דִּיג **dîyg**, *deeg;* denom. from 1709; to *fish*:— fish.

1771. דַּיָּג **dayâg**, *dah-yawg´;* from 1770; a *fisherman*:— fisher.

1772. דַּיָּה **dayâh**, *dah-yaw´;* intens. from 1675; a *falcon* (from its *rapid* flight):— vulture.

1773. דְּיוֹ **deʹyôw**, *deh-yo´;* of uncert. der.; *ink*:— ink.

1774. דִּי זָהָב **Dîy zâhâb**, *dee zaw-hawb´;* as if from 1768 and 2091; *of gold; Dizahab*, a place in the Desert:— Dizahab.

1775. דִּימוֹן **Dîymôwn**, *dee-mone´;* perh. for 1769; *Dimon*, a place in Pal.:— Dimon.

1776. דִּימוֹנָה **Dîymôwnâh**, *dee-mo-naw´;* fem. of 1775; *Dimonah*, a place in Pal.:— Dimonah.

1777. דִּין **dîyn**, *deen;* or (Gen. 6:3)

דּוּן **dûwn**, *doon;* a prim. root [comp. 113]; to *rule;* by impl. to *judge* (as umpire); also to *strive* (as at law):— contend, execute (judgment), judge, minister judgment, plead (the cause), at strife, strive.

1778. דִּין **dîyn** (Chald.), *deen;* corresp. to 1777; to *judge*:— judge.

1779. דִּין **dîyn**, *deen;* or (Job 19:29)

דּוּן **dûwn**, *doon;* from 1777; *judgement* (the suit, justice, sentence or tribunal); by impl. also *strife*:— cause, judgement, plea, strife.

1780. דִּין **dîyn** (Chald.), *deen;* corresp. to 1779:— judgement.

1781. דַּיָּן **dayân**, *dah-yawn´;* from 1777; a *judge* or *advocate*:— judge.

1782. דַּיָּן **dayân** (Chald.), *dah-yawn´;* corresp. to 1781:— judge.

1783. דִּינָה **Dîynâh**, *dee-naw´;* fem. of 1779; *justice; Dinah*, the daughter of Jacob:— Dinah.

1784. דִּינַי **Dîynay** (Chald.), *dee-nah´-ee;* patrial from an uncert. prim.; a *Dinaite* or inhab. of some unknown Ass. province:— Dinaite.

דִּיפַת **Dîyphath**. See 7384.

1785. דָּיֵק **dâyêq**, *daw-yake´;* from a root corresp. to 1751; a *battering-tower*:— fort.

1786. דַּיִשׁ **dayîsh**, *dah-yish´;* from 1758; *threshing*-time:— threshing.

1787. דִּישׁוֹן **Dîyshôwn**,

דִּישֹׁן **Dîyshôn**,

דִּשׁוֹן **Dîshôwn**, or

דִּשֹׁן **Dîshôn**, *dee-shone´;* the same as 1788; *Dishon*, the name of two Edomites:— Dishon.

1788. דִּישׁוֹן **dîyshôn**, *dee-shone´;* from 1758; the *leaper*, i.e. an *antelope*:— pygarg.

1789. דִּישָׁן **Dîyshân**, *dee-shawn´;* another form of 1787; *Dishan*, an Edomite:— Dishan, Dishon.

1790. דַּךְ **dak**, *dak;* from an unused root (comp. 1794); *crushed*, i.e. (fig.) *injured*:— afflicted, oppressed.

1791. דֵּךְ **dêk** (Chald.), *dake;* or

דָּךְ **dâk** (Chald.), *dawk;* prol. from 1668; *this*:— the same, this.

1792. דָּכָא **dâkâ'**, *daw-kaw´;* a prim. root (comp. 1794); to *crumble;* tran. to *bruise* (lit. or fig.):— beat to pieces, break (in pieces), bruise, contrite, crush, destroy, humble, oppress, smite.

1793. דָּכָא **dakkâ'**, *dak-kaw'*; from 1792; *crushed* (lit. *powder*, or fig. *contrite*):— contrite, destruction.

1794. דָּכָה **dâkâh**, *daw-kaw'*; a prim. root (comp. 1790, 1792); to *collapse* (phys. or ment.):— break (sore), contrite, crouch.

1795. דַּכָּה **dakkâh**, *dak-kaw'*; from 1794 like 1793; *mutilated:*— + wounded.

1796. דֳכִי **dŏkiy**, *dok-ee'*; from 1794; a *dashing* of surf:— wave.

1797. דִּכֵּן **dikkên** (Chald.), *dik-kane'*; prol. from 1791; *this:*— same, that, this.

1798. דְכַר **dᵉkar** (Chald.), *dek-ar'*; corresp. to 2145; prop. a *male*, i.e. of sheep:— ram.

1799. דִּכְרוֹן **dikrôwn** (Chald.), *dik-rone'*; or

דָּכְרָן **dokrân**, *dok-rawn'* (Chald.); corresp. to 2146; a *register:*— record.

1800. דַּל **dal**, *dal*; from 1809; prop. *dangling*, i.e. (by impl.) *weak* or *thin:*— lean, needy, poor (man), weaker.

1801. דָּלַג **dâlag**, *daw-lag'*; a prim. root; to *spring:*— leap.

1802. דָּלָה **dâlâh**, *daw-law'*; a prim. root (comp. 1809); prop. to *dangle*, i.e. to *let down* a bucket (for *drawing* out water); fig. to *deliver:*— draw (out), × enough, lift up.

1803. דַּלָּה **dallâh**, *dal-law'*; from 1802; prop. something *dangling*, i.e. a loose *thread* or *hair*; fig. *indigent:*— hair, pining sickness, poor (-est sort).

1804. דָּלַח **dâlach**, *daw-lakh'*; a prim. root; to *roil* water:— trouble.

1805. דְּלִי **dᵉliy**, *del-ee'*; or

דֳלִי **dŏliy**, *dol-ee'*; from 1802; a *pail* or *jar* (for *drawing* water):— bucket.

1806. דְּלָיָה **Dᵉlâyâh**, *del-aw-yaw'*; or (prol.)

דְּלָיָהוּ **Dᵉlâyâhûw**, *del-aw-yaw'-hoo*; from 1802 and 3050; *Jah has delivered*; *Delajah*, the name of five Isr.:— Dalaiah, Delaiah.

1807. דְּלִילָה **Dᵉlîylâh**, *del-ee-law'*; from 1809; *languishing*; *Delilah*, a Philistine woman:— Delilah.

1808. דָּלִיָּה **dâliyâh**, *daw-lee-yaw'*; from 1802; something *dangling*, i.e. a *bough:*— branch.

1809. דָּלַל **dâlal**, *daw-lal'*; a prim. root (comp. 1802); to *slacken* or *be feeble*; fig. to *be oppressed:*— bring low, dry up, be emptied, be not equal, fail, be impoverished, be made thin.

1810. דִּלְעָן **Dil'ân**, *dil-awn'*; of uncert. der.; *Dilan*, a place in Pal.:— Dilean.

1811. דָּלַף **dâlaph**, *daw-laf'*; a prim. root; to *drip*; by impl. to *weep:*— drop through, melt, pour out.

1812. דֶּלֶף **deleph**, *deh'-lef*; from 1811; a *dripping:*— dropping.

1813. דַּלְפוֹן **Dalphôwn**, *dal-fone'*; from 1811; *dripping*; *Dalphon*, a son of Haman:— Dalphon.

1814. דָּלַק **dâlaq**, *daw-lak'*; a prim. root;

to *flame* (lit. or fig.):— burning, chase, inflame, kindle, persecute (-or), pursue hotly.

1815. דְּלַק **dᵉlaq** (Chald.), *del-ak'*; corresp. to 1814:— burn.

1816. דַּלֶּקֶת **dalleqeth**, *dal-lek'-keth*; from 1814; a *burning* fever:— inflammation.

1817. דֶּלֶת **deleth**, *deh'-leth*; from 1802; something *swinging*, i.e. the *valve* of a door:— door (two-leaved), gate, leaf, lid. [In Psa. 141:3, *dâl*, irreg.]

1818. דָּם **dâm**, *dawm*; from 1826 (comp. 119); *blood* (as that which when shed causes *death*) of man or an animal; by anal. the *juice* of the grape; fig. (espec. in the plur.) *bloodshed* (i.e. *drops* of blood):— blood (-y, -guiltiness, [-thirsty], + innocent.

1819. דָּמָה **dâmâh**, *daw-maw'*; a prim. root; to *compare*; by impl. to *resemble*, *liken*, *consider:*— compare, devise, (be) like (-n), mean, think, use similitudes.

1820. דָּמָה **dâmâh**, *daw-maw'*; a prim. root; to *be dumb* or *silent*; hence, to *fail* or *perish*; trans. to *destroy:*— cease, be cut down (off), destroy, be brought to silence, be undone, × utterly.

1821. דְּמָה **dᵉmâh** (Chald.), *dem-aw'*; corresp. to 1819; to *resemble:*— be like.

1822. דֻּמָּה **dummâh**, *doom-maw'*; from 1820; *desolation*; concr. *desolate:*— destroy.

1823. דְּמוּת **dᵉmûwth**, *dem-ooth'*; from 1819; *resemblance*; concr. *model*, *shape*; adv. *like:*— fashion, like (-ness, as), manner, similitude.

1824. דְּמִי **dᵉmiy**, *dem-ee'*; or

דֳמִי **dŏmiy**, *dom-ee'*; from 1820; *quiet:*— cutting off, rest, silence.

1825. דִּמְיוֹן **dimyôwn**, *dim-yone'*; from 1819; *resemblance:*— × like.

1826. דָּמַם **dâmam**, *daw-mam'*; a prim. root [comp. 1724, 1820]; to *be dumb*; by impl. to *be astonished*, to *stop*; also to *perish:*— cease, be cut down (off), forbear, hold peace, quiet self, rest, be silent, keep (put to) silence, be (stand) still, tarry, wait.

1827. דְּמָמָה **dᵉmâmâh**, *dem-aw-maw'*; fem. from 1826; *quiet:*— calm, silence, still.

1828. דֹּמֶן **dômen**, *do'-men*; of uncert. der.; *manure:*— dung.

1829. דִּמְנָה **Dimnâh**, *dim-naw'*; fem. from the same as 1828; a *dung-heap*; *Dimnah*, a place in Pal.:— Dimnah.

1830. דָּמַע **dâma'**, *daw-mah'*; a prim. root; to *weep:*— × sore, weep.

1831. דֶּמַע **dema'**, *dah'-mah*; from 1830; a *tear*; fig. *juice:*— liquor.

1832. דִּמְעָה **dim'âh**, *dim-aw'*; fem. of 1831; *weeping:*— tears.

1833. דְּמֶשֶׁק **dᵉmesheq**, *dem-eh'-shek*; by orth. var. from 1834; *damask* (as a fabric of Damascus):— in Damascus.

1834. דַּמֶּשֶׂק **Dammeseq**, *dam-meh'-sek*; or

דּוּמֶשֶׂק° **Dûwmeseq**, *doo-meh'-sek*; or

דַּרְמֶשֶׂק **Darmeseq**, *dar-meh'-sek*;

of for. or.; *Damascus*, a city of Syria:— Damascus.

1835. דָּן **Dân**, *dawn*; from 1777; *judge*; *Dan*, one of the sons of Jacob; also the tribe descended from him, and its territory; likewise a place in Pal. colonized by them:— Dan.

1836. דֵּן **dên** (Chald.), *dane*; an orth. var. of 1791; *this:*— [afore-] time, + after this manner, here [-after], one ... another, such, there [-fore], these, this (matter), + thus, where [-fore], which.

דָּנִאֵל **Dânî'êl**. See 1841.

1837. דַּנָּה **Dannâh**, *dan-naw'*; of uncert. der.; *Dannah*, a place in Pal.:— Dannah.

1838. דִּנְהָבָה **Dinhâbâh**, *din-haw-baw'*; of uncert. der.; *Dinhabah*, an Edomitish town:— Dinhaban.

1839. דָּנִי **Dâniy**, *daw-nee'*; patron. from 1835; a *Danite* (often collect.) or desc. (or inhab.) of Dan:— Danites, of Dan.

1840. דָּנִיֵּאל **Dânîyê'l**, *daw-nee-yale'*; in Ezek.

דָּנִיֵאל **Dânî'êl**, *daw-nee-ale'*; from 1835 and 410; *judge of God*; *Daniel* or *Danijel*, the name of two Isr.:— Daniel.

1841. דָּנִיֵּאל **Dânîyê'l** (Chald.), *daw-nee-yale'*; corresp. to 1840; *Danijel*, the Heb. prophet:— Daniel.

1842. דָּן יַעַן **Dân Ya'an**, *dawn yah'-an*; from 1835 and (appar.) 3282; *judge of purpose*; *Dan-Jaan*, a place in Pal.:— Dan-jaan.

1843. דֵּעַ **dêa'**, *day'-ah*; from 3045; *knowledge:*— knowledge, opinion.

1844. דֵּעָה **dê'âh**, *day-aw'*; fem. of 1843; *knowledge:*— knowledge.

1845. דְּעוּאֵל **Dᵉ'ûw'êl**, *deh-oo-ale'*; from 3045 and 410; *known of God*; *Deüel*, an Isr.:— Deuel.

1846. דָּעַך **dâ'ak**, *daw-ak'*; a prim. root; to *be extinguished*; fig. to *expire* or *be dried up:*— be extinct, consumed, put out, quenched.

1847. דַּעַת **da'ath**, *dah'-ath*; from 3045; *knowledge:*— cunning, [ig-]norantly, know (-ledge), [un-] awares (wittingly).

1848. דֳּפִי **dŏphiy**, *dof-ee'*; from an unused root (mean. to *push* over); a *stumbling*-block:— slanderest.

1849. דָּפַק **dâphaq**, *daw-fak'*; a prim. root; to *knock*; by anal. to *press* severely:— beat, knock, overdrive.

1850. דָּפְקָה **Dophqâh**, *dof-kaw'*; from 1849; a *knock*; *Dophkah*, a place in the Desert:— Dophkah.

1851. דַּק **daq**, *dak*; from 1854; *crushed*, i.e. (by impl.) *small* or *thin:*— dwarf, lean [-fleshed], very little thing, small, thin.

1852. דֹּק **dôq**, *doke*; from 1854; something *crumbling*, i.e. *fine* (as a *thin* cloth):— curtain.

1853. דִּקְלָה **Diqlâh**, *dik-law'*; of for. or.; *Diklah*, a region of Arabia:— Diklah.

1854. דָּקַק **dâqaq**, *daw-kak'*; a prim. root [comp. 1915]; to *crush* (or intr.) *crumble:*— beat in pieces (small), bruise, make dust, (into) × powder, (be, very) small, stamp (small).

Hebrew

1855. דְּקַק **d°qaq** (Chald.), *dek-ak´;* corresp. to 1854; to *crumble* or (trans.) *crush:*— break to pieces.

1856. דָּקַר **dâqar**, *daw-kar´;* a prim. root; to *stab;* by anal. to *starve;* fig. to *revile:*— pierce, strike (thrust) through, wound.

1857. דֶּקֶר **Deqer**, *deh´-ker;* from 1856; a *stab; Deker*, an Isr.:— Dekar.

1858. דַּר **dar**, *dar;* appar. from the same as 1865; prop. a *pearl* (from its sheen as rapidly *turned*); by anal. *pearl-stone*, i.e. mother-of-pearl or alabaster:— × white.

1859. דָּר **dâr** (Chald.), *dawr;* corresp. to 1755; an *age:*— generation.

דֹּר **dôr**. See 1755.

1860. דְּרָאוֹן **d°râ'ôwn**, *der-aw-one´;* or

דֵּרָאוֹן **dêrâ'ôwn**, *day-raw-one´;* from an unused root (mean. to *repulse*); an obj. of *aversion:*— abhorring, contempt.

1861. דָּרְבֹּון **dorbôwn**, *dor-bone´* [also *dor-bawn´*]; of uncert. der.; a *goad:*— goad.

1862. דַּרְדַּע **Darda'**, *dar-dah´;* appar. from 1858 and 1843; *pearl of knowledge; Darda*, an Isr.:— Darda.

1863. דַּרְדַּר **dardar**, *dar-dar´;* of uncert. der.; a *thorn:*— thistle.

1864. דָּרוֹם **dârôwm**, *daw-rome´;* of uncert. der.; the *south;* poet. the *south wind:*— south.

1865. דְּרוֹר **d°rôwr**, *der-ore´;* from an unused root (mean. to *move rapidly*); *freedom;* hence, *spontaneity* of outflow, and so *clear:*— liberty, pure.

1866. דְּרוֹר **d°rôwr**, *der-ore´;* the same as 1865, applied to a bird; the *swift*, a kind of swallow:— swallow.

1867. דָּרְיָוֶשׁ **Dâr°yâvêsh**, *daw-reh-yaw-vaysh´;* of Pers. or.; *Darejavesh*, a title (rather than name) of several Pers. kings:— Darius.

1868. דָּרְיָוֶשׁ **Dâr°yâvêsh** (Chald.), *daw-reh-yaw-vaysh´;* corresp. to 1867:— Darius.

1869. דָּרַךְ **dârak**, *daw-rak´;* a prim. root; to *tread;* by impl. to *walk;* also to *string* a bow (by treading on it in bending):— archer, bend, come, draw, go (over), guide, lead (forth), thresh, tread (down), walk.

1870. דֶּרֶךְ **derek**, *deh´-rek;* from 1869; a *road* (as *trodden*); fig. a *course* of life or *mode* of action, often adv.:— along, away, because of, + by, conversation, custom, [east-] ward, journey, manner, passenger, through, toward, [high-] [path-] way [-side], whither [-soever].

1871. דַּרְכְּמוֹן **dark°môwn**, *dar-kem-one´;* of Pers. or.; a "*drachma*," or coin:— dram.

1872. דְּרָע **d°râ'** (Chald.), *der-aw´;* corresp. to 2220; an *arm:*— arm.

1873. דָּרַע **Dâra'**, *daw-rah´;* prob. contr. from 1862; *Dara*, an Isr.:— Dara.

1874. דַּרְקוֹן **Darqôwn**, *dar-kone´;* of uncert. der.; *Darkon*, one of "Solomon's servants":— Darkon.

1875. דָּרַשׁ **dârash**, *daw-rash´;* a prim. root; prop. to *tread* or *frequent;* usually

to *follow* (for pursuit or search); by impl. to *seek* or *ask;* spec. to *worship:*— ask, × at all, care for, × diligently, inquire, make inquisition, [necro-] mancer, question, require, search, seek [for, out], × surely.

1876. דְּשָׁא **dâshâ'**, *daw-shaw´;* a prim. root; to *sprout:*— bring forth, spring.

1877. דֶּשֶׁא **deshe'**, *deh´-sheh;* from 1876; a *sprout;* by anal. *grass:*— (tender) grass, green, (tender) herb.

1878. דָּשֵׁן **dâshên**, *daw-shane´;* a prim. root; to *be fat;* tran. to *fatten* (or regard as fat); spec. to *anoint;* fig. to *satisfy;* denom. (from 1880) to *remove* (fat) *ashes* (of sacrifices):— accept, anoint, take away the (receive) ashes (from), make (wax) fat.

1879. דָּשֵׁן **dâshên**, *daw-shane´;* from 1878; *fat;* fig. *rich*, *fertile:*— fat.

1880. דֶּשֶׁן **deshen**, *deh´-shen;* from 1878; the *fat;* abstr. *fatness*, i.e. (fig.) *abundance;* spec. the (fatty) *ashes* of sacrifices:— ashes, fatness.

1881. דָּת **dâth**, *dawth;* of uncert. (perh. for.) der.: a *royal edict* or *statute:*— commandment, commission, decree, law, manner.

1882. דָּת **dâth** (Chald.), *dawth;* corresp. to 1881:— decree, law.

1883. דֶּתֶא **dethe'** (Chald.), *deh´-thay;* corresp. to 1877:— tender grass.

1884. דְּתָבָר **d°thâbâr** (Chald.), *deth-aw-bawr´;* of Pers. or.; mean. one *skilled in law;* a *judge:*— counsellor.

1885. דָּתָן **Dâthân**, *daw-thawn´;* of uncert. der.; *Dathan*, an Isr.:— Dathan.

1886. דֹּתָן **Dôthân**, *do´-thawn;* or (Chaldaizing dual)

דֹּתַיִן **Dôthayin** (Gen. 37:17), *do-thah´-yin;* of uncert. der.; *Dothan*, a place in Pal.:— Dothan.

ה

1887. הֵא **hê'**, *hay;* a prim. particle; *lo!:*— behold, lo.

1888. הֵא **hê'** (Chald.), *hay;* or

הָא **hâ'** (Chald.), *haw;* corresp. to 1887:— even, lo.

1889. הֶאָח **he'âch**, *heh-awkh´;* from 1887 and 253; *aha!:*— ah, aha, ha.

הָאֲרָרִי **Hâ'ârâriy**. See 2043.

1890. הַבְהָב **habhâb**, *hab-hawb´;* by redupl. from 3051; *gift* (in sacrifice), i.e. *holocaust:*— offering.

1891. הָבַל **hâbal**, *haw-bal´;* a prim. root; to *be vain* in act, word, or expectation; spec. to *lead astray:*— be (become, make) vain.

1892. הֶבֶל **hebel**, *heh´-bel;* or (rarely in the abs.)

הֲבֵל **hâbêl**, *hab-ale´;* from 1891; *emptiness* or *vanity;* fig. something *transitory* and *unsatisfactory;* often used as an adv.:— × altogether, vain, vanity.

1893. הֶבֶל **Hebel**, *heh´-bel;* the same as 1892; *Hebel*, the son of Adam:— Abel.

1894. הֹבֶן **hôben**, *ho´-ben;* only in plur., from an unused root mean. to *be hard; ebony:*— ebony.

1895. חָבַר **hâbar**, *haw-bar´;* a prim. root of uncert. (perh. for.) der.; to *be a horoscopist:*— + (astro-)loger.

1896. הֵגֵא **Hêgê'**, *hay-gay´;* or (by perm.)

הֵגַי **Hêgay**, *hay-gah´-ee;* prob. of Pers. or.; *Hege* or *Hegai*, a eunuch of Xerxes:— Hegai, Hege.

1897. הָגָה **hâgâh**, *haw-gaw´;* a prim. root [comp. 1901]; to *murmur* (in pleasure or anger); by impl. to *ponder:*— imagine, meditate, mourn, mutter, roar, × sore, speak, study, talk, utter.

1898. הָגָה **hâgâh**, *haw-gaw´;* a prim. root; to *remove:*— stay, take away.

1899. הֶגֶה **hegeh**, *heh´-geh;* from 1897; a *muttering* (in sighing, thought, or as thunder):— mourning, sound, tale.

1900. הָגוּת **hâgûwth**, *haw-gooth´;* from 1897; *musing:*— meditation.

1901. הָגִיג **hâgîyg**, *haw-gheeg´;* from an unused root akin to 1897; prop. a *murmur*, i.e. *complaint:*— meditation, musing.

1902. הִגָּיוֹן **higgâyôwn**, *hig-gaw-yone´;* intens. from 1897; a *murmuring* sound, i.e. a musical notation (prob. similar to the modern *affettuoso* to indicate solemnity of movement); by impl. a *machination:*— device, Higgaion, meditation, solemn sound.

1903. הָגִין **hâgîyn**, *haw-gheen´;* of uncert. der.; perh. *suitable* or *turning:*— directly.

1904. הָגָר **Hâgâr**, *haw-gawr´;* of uncert. (perhaps for.) der.; *Hagar*, the mother of Ishmael:— Hagar.

1905. הַגְרִי **Hagrîy**, *hag-ree´;* or (prol.)

הַגְרִיא **Hagrîy'**, *hag-ree´;* perh. patron. from 1904; a *Hagrite* or member of a certain Arabian clan:— Hagarene, Hagarite, Haggeri.

1906. הֵד **hêd**, *hade;* for 1959; a *shout:*— sounding again.

1907. הַדָּבָר **haddâbâr** (Chald.), *had-daw-bawr´;* prob. of for. origin; a *vizier:*— counsellor.

1908. הֲדַד **Hădad**, *had-ad´;* prob. of for. or. [comp. 111]; *Hadad*, the name of an idol, and of several kings of Edom:— Hadad.

1909. הֲדַרְעֶזֶר **Hădad'ezer**, *had-ad-eh´-zer;* from 1908 and 5828; *Hadad (is his) help; Hadadezer*, a Syrian king:— Hadadezer. Comp. 1928.

1910. הֲדַדְרִמּוֹן **Hădadrimmôwn**, *had-ad-rim-mone´;* from 1908 and 7417; *Hadad-Rimmon*, a place in Pal.:— Hadad-rimmon.

1911. הָדָה **hâdâh**, *haw-daw´;* a prim. root [comp. 3034]; to *stretch forth* the hand:— put.

1912. הֹדוּ **Hôdûw**, *ho´-doo;* of for. or.; *Hodu* (i.e. Hindü-stan):— India.

1913. הֲדוֹרָם **Hădôwrâm**, *had-o-rawm´;* or

הֲדֹרָם **Hădôrâm**, *had-o-rawm´;* prob. of for. der.; *Hadoram*, a son of Joktan, and the tribe descended from him:— Hadoram.

1914. הִדַּי **Hidday**, *hid-dah´-ee;* of uncert. der.; *Hiddai*, an Isr.:— Hiddai.

1915. הָדַךְ **hâdak**, *haw-dak´*; a prim. root [comp. 1854]; to *crush* with the foot:— tread down.

1916. הֲדֹם **hădôm**, *had-ome´*; from an unused root mean. to *stamp* upon; a foot-*stool*:— [foot-] stool.

1917. הַדָּם **haddâm** (Chald.), *had-dawm´*; from a root corresp. to that of 1916; something *stamped* to pieces, i.e. a *bit*:— piece.

1918. הֲדַס **hădaç**, *had-as´*; of uncert. der.; the *myrtle*:— myrtle (tree).

1919. הֲדַסָּה **Hădaççâh**, *had-as-saw´*; fem. of 1918; *Hadassah* (or Esther):— Hadassah.

1920. הָדַף **hâdaph**, *haw-daf´*; a prim root; to *push* away or down:— cast away (out), drive, expel, thrust (away).

1921. הָדַר **hâdar**, *haw-dar´*; a prim. root; to *swell* up (lit. or fig., act. or pass.); by impl. to *favor* or *honour*, *be high* or *proud*:— countenance, crooked place, glorious, honour, put forth.

1922. הֲדַר **hădar** (Chald.), *had-ar´*; corresp. to 1921; to *magnify* (fig.):— glorify, honour.

1923. הֲדַר **hădar** (Chald.), *had-ar´*; from 1922; *magnificence*:— honour, majesty.

1924. הֲדַר **Hădar**, *had-ar´*; the same as 1926; *Hadar*, an Edomite:— Hadar.

1925. הֶדֶר **heder**, *heh´-der*; from 1921; *honour*; used (fig.) for the *capital* city (Jerusalem):— glory.

1926. הָדָר **hâdâr**, *haw-dawr´*; from 1921; *magnificence*, i.e. ornament or splendor:— beauty, comeliness, excellency, glorious, glory, goodly, honour, majesty.

1927. הֲדָרָה **hădârâh**, *had-aw-raw´*; fem. of 1926; *decoration*:— beauty, honour.

הֲדֹרָם **Hădôrâm**. See 1913.

1928. הֲדַרְעֶזֶר **Hădar'ezer**, *had-ar-eh´-zer*; from 1924 and 5828; *Hadar* (i.e. *Hadad*, 1908) is his *help*; *Hadarezer* (i.e. Hadadezer, 1909), a Syrian king:— Hadarezer.

1929. הָהּ **hâhh**, *haw*; a short. form of 162; *ah!* expressing grief:— woe worth.

1930. הוֹ **hôw**, *ho*; by perm. from 1929; *oh!*:— alas.

1931. הוּא **hûw'**, *hoo*; of which the fem. (beyond the Pentateuch) is

הִיא **hîy'**, *he*; a prim. word, the third pers. pron. sing., *he* (*she* or *it*); only expressed when emphat. or without a verb; also (intens.) *self*, or (espec. with the art.) the *same*; sometimes (as demonstr.) *this* or *that*; occasionally (instead of copula) *as* or *are*:— he, as for her, him (-self), it, the same, she (herself), such, that (... it), these, they, this, those, which (is), who.

1932. הוּא **hûw'** (Chald.), *hoo*; or (fem.)

הִיא **hîy'** (Chald.), *he*; corresp. to 1931:— × are, it, this.

1933. הָוָא **hâvâ'**, *haw-vaw´*; or

הָוָה **hâvâh**, *haw-vaw´*; a prim. root [comp. 183, 1961] supposed to mean prop. to *breathe*; to *be* (in the sense of existence):— be, × have.

1934. הֲוָא **hăvâ'** (Chald.), *hav-aw´*; or

הֲוָה **hăvâh** (Chald.), *hav-aw´*; corresp. to 1933; to *exist*; used in a great variety of applications (espec. in connection with other words):— be, become, + behold, + came (to pass), + cease, + cleave, + consider, + do, + give, + have, + judge, + keep, + labour, + mingle (self), + put, + see, + seek, + set, + slay, + take heed, tremble, + walk, + would.

1935. הוֹד **hôwd**, *hode*; from an unused root; *grandeur* (i.e. an imposing form and appearance):— beauty, comeliness, excellency, glorious, glory, goodly, honour, majesty.

1936. הוֹד **Hôwd**, *hode*; the same as 1935; *Hod*, an Isr.:— Hod.

1937. הוֹדְוָה **Hôwd°vâh**, *ho-dev-aw´*; a form of 1938; *Hodevah* (or Hodevjah), an Isr.:— Hodevah.

1938. הוֹדְוָיָה **Hôwdavyâh**, *ho-dav-yaw´*; from 1935 and 3050; *majesty of Jah*; *Hodavjah*, the name of three Isr.:— Hodaviah.

1939. הוֹדַיְוָהוּ **Howday°vâhûw**, *ho-dah-yeh-vaw´-hoo*; a form of 1938; *Hodajvah*, an Isr.:— Hodaiah.

1940. הוֹדִיָה **Hôwdîyâh**, *ho-dee-yaw´*; a form for the fem. of 3064; a *Jewess*:— Hodiah.

1941. הוֹדִיָה **Hôwdîyâh**, *ho-dee-yaw´*; a form of 1938; *Hodijah*, the name of three Isr.:— Hodijah.

הַוָּה **hăvâh**. See 1933.

הַוָּה **hăvâh**. See 1934.

1942. הַוָּה **havvâh**, *hav-vaw´*; from 1933 (in the sense of eagerly *coveting* and *rushing* upon; by impl. of *falling*); *desire*; also *ruin*:— calamity, iniquity, mischief, mischievous (thing), naughtiness, naughty, noisome, perverse thing, substance, very wickedness.

1943. הֹוָה **hôvâh**, *ho-vaw´*; another form for 1942; *ruin*:— mischief.

1944. הוֹהָם **Hôwhâm**, *ho-hawm´*; of uncert. der.; *Hoham*, a Canaanitish king:— Hoham.

1945. הוֹי **hôwy**, *hoh´-ee*; a prol. form of 1930 [akin to 188]; *oh!*:— ah, alas, ho, O, woe.

1946. הוּךְ **hûwk** (Chald.), *hook*; corresp. to 1981; to *go*; caus. to *bring*:— bring again, come, go (up).

1947. הוֹלֵלָה **hôwlêlâh**, *ho-lay-law´*; fem. act. part. of 1984; *folly*:— madness.

1948. הוֹלֵלוּת **hôwlêlûwth**, *ho-lay-looth´*; from act. part. of 1984; *folly*:— madness.

1949. הוּם **hûwm**, *hoom*; a prim. root [comp. 2000]; to *make an uproar*, or *agitate* greatly:— destroy, move, make a noise, put, ring again.

1950. הוֹמָם **Hôwmâm**, *ho-mawm´*; from 2000; *raging*; *Homam*, an Edomitish chieftain:— Homam. Comp. 1967.

1951. הוּן **hûwn**, *hoon*; a prim. root; prop. to *be naught*, i.e. (fig.) to *be* (caus. *act*) *light*:— be ready.

1952. הוֹן **hôwn**, *hone*; from the same as 1951 in the sense of 202; *wealth*; by impl. *enough*:— enough, + for nought, riches, substance, wealth.

1953. הוֹשָׁמָע **Hôwshâmâ'**, *ho-shaw-maw´*; from 3068 and 8085; *Jehovah has heard*; *Hoshama*, an Isr.:— Hoshama.

1954. הוֹשֵׁע **'Hôwshêä'**, *ho-shay´-ah*; from 3467; *deliverer*; *Hosheä*, the name of five Isr.:— Hosea, Hoshea, Oshea.

1955. הוֹשַׁעְיָה **Hôwshi'yâh**, *ho-shee-yaw´*; from 3467 and 3050; *Jah has saved*; *Hoshajah*, the name of two Isr.:— Hoshaiah.

1956. הוֹתִיר **Hôwthîyr**, *ho-theer´*; from 3498; *he has caused to remain*; *Hothir*, an Isr.:— Hothir.

1957. הָזָה **hâzâh**, *haw-zaw´*; a prim. root [comp. 2372]; to *dream*:— sleep.

1958. הִי **hîy**, *he*; for 5092; *lamentation*:— woe.

הִיא **hîy'**. See 1931, 1932.)

1959. הֵידָד **hêydâd**, *hay-dawd´*; from an unused root (mean. to *shout*); *acclamation*:— shout (-ing).

1960. הֻיְּדָה **huy°dâh**, *hoo-yed-aw´*; from the same as 1959; prop. an *acclaim*, i.e. a *choir* of singers:— thanksgiving.

1961. הָיָה **hâyâh**, *haw-yaw´*; a prim. root [comp. 1933]; to *exist*, i.e. *be* or *become*, *come to pass* (always emphat., and not a mere copula or auxiliary):— beacon, × altogether, be (-come), accomplished, committed, like), break, cause, come (to pass), do, faint, fall, + follow, happen, × have, last, pertain, quit (one-) self, require, × use.

1962. הַיָה **hayâh**, *hah-yaw´*; another form for 1943; *ruin*:— calamity.

1963. הֵיךְ **hêyk**, *hake*; another form for 349; *how?*:— how.

1964. הֵיכָל **hêykâl**, *hay-kawl´*; prob. from 3201 (in the sense of *capacity*); a large public building, such as a *palace* or *temple*:— palace, temple.

1965. הֵיכַל **hêykal** (Chald.), *hay-kal´*; corresp. to 1964:— palace, temple.

1966. הֵילֵל **hêylêl**, *hay-lale´*; from 1984 (in the sense of *brightness*); the *morning-star*:— lucifer.

1967. הֵימָם **Hêymâm**, *hay-mawm´*; another form for 1950; *Hemam*, an Idumæan:— Hemam.

1968. הֵימָן **Hêymân**, *hay-mawn´*; prob. from 539; *faithful*; *Heman*, the name of at least two Isr.:— Heman.

1969. הִין **hîyn**, *heen*; prob. of Eg. or.; a *hin* or liquid measure:— hin.

1970. הָכַר **hâkar**, *haw-kar´*; a prim. root; appar. to *injure*:— make self strange.

1971. הַכָּרָה **hakkârâh**, *hak-kaw-raw´*; from 5234; *respect*, i.e. partiality:— shew.

הַל **hal**. See 1973.

1972. הָלָא **hâlâ'**, *haw-law´*; prob. denom. from 1973; to *remove* or be *remote*:— cast far off.

1973. הָלְאָה **hâl°âh**, *haw-leh-aw´*; from the prim. form of the art. [הַל hal]; to the *distance*, i.e. *far away*; also (of time) *thus far*:— back, beyond, (hence-) forward, hitherto, thenceforth, yonder.

1974. הִלּוּל **hillûwl,** *hil-lool´;* from 1984 (in the sense of *rejoicing*); a *celebration* of thanksgiving for harvest:— merry, praise.

1975. הַלָּז **hallâz,** *hal-lawz´;* from 1976; *this* or *that:*— side, that, this.

1976. הַלָּזֶה **hallâzeh,** *hal-law-zeh´;* from the art. [see 1973] and 2088; *this very:*— this.

1977. הַלֵּזוּ **hallêzûw,** *hal-lay-zoo´;* another form of 1976; *that:*— this.

1978. הָלִיךְ **hâlîyk,** *haw-leek´;* from 1980; a *walk,* i.e. (by impl.) a *step:*— step.

1979. הֲלִיכָה **hălîykâh,** *hal-ee-kaw´;* fem. of 1978; a *walking;* by impl. a *procession* or *march,* a *caravan:*— company, going, walk, way.

1980. הָלַךְ **hâlak,** *haw-lak´;* akin to 3212; a prim. root; to *walk* (in a great variety of applications, lit. and fig.):— (all) along, apace, behave (self), come, (on) continually, be conversant, depart, + be eased, enter, exercise (self), + follow, forth, forward, get, go (about, abroad, along, away, forward, on, out, up and down), + greater, grow, be wont to haunt, lead, march, × more and more, move (self), needs, on, pass (away), be at the point, quite, run (along), + send, speedily, spread, still, surely, + tale-bearer, + travel (-ler), walk (abroad, on, to and fro, up and down, to places), wander, wax, [way-] faring man, × be weak, whirl.

1981. הֲלַךְ **hălak** (Chald.), *hal-ak´;* corresp. to 1980 [comp. 1946]; to *walk:*— walk.

1982. הֵלֶךְ **hêlek,** *hay´-lek;* from 1980; prop. a *journey,* i.e. (by impl.) a *wayfarer;* also a *flowing:*— × dropped, traveller.

1983. הֲלָךְ **hălâk** (Chald.), *hal-awk´;* from 1981; prop. a *journey,* i.e. (by impl.) *toll* on goods at a road:— custom.

1984. הָלַל **hâlal,** *haw-lal´;* a prim. root; to *be clear* (orig. of sound, but usually of color); to *shine;* hence, to *make a show,* to *boast;* and thus to *be* (clamorously) *foolish;* to *rave;* caus. to *celebrate;* also to *stultify:*— (make) boast (self), celebrate, commend, (deal, make), fool (-ish, -ly), glory, give [light], be (make, feign self) mad (against), give in marriage, [sing, be worthy of] praise, rage, renowned, shine.

1985. הִלֵּל **Hillêl,** *hil-layl´;* from 1984; *praising* (namely God); *Hillel,* an Isr.:— Hillel.

1986. הָלַם **hâlam,** *haw-lam´;* a prim. root; to *strike* down; by impl. to *hammer, stamp, conquer, disband:*— beat (down), break (down), overcome, smite (with the hammer).

1987. הֵלֶם **Hêlem,** *hay´-lem;* from 1986; *smiter; Helem,* the name of two Isr.:— Helem.

1988. הֲלֹם **hălôm,** *hal-ome´;* from the art. [see 1973]; *hither:*— here, hither (-to], thither.

1989. הַלְמוּת **halmûwth,** *hal-mooth´;* from 1986; a *hammer* (or *mallet*):— hammer.

1990. הָם **Hâm,** *hawm;* of uncert. der.; *Ham,* a region of Pal.:— Ham.

1991. הֵם **hêm,** *haym;* from 1993; *abundance,* i.e. *wealth:*— any of theirs.

1992. הֵם **hêm,** *haym;* or (prol.)

הֵמָּה **hêmmâh,** *haym´-maw;* masc. plur. from 1931; *they* (only used when emphat.):— it, like, × (how, so) many (soever, more as) they (be), (the) same, × so, × such, their, them, these, they, those, which, who, whom, withal, ye.

1993. הָמָה **hâmâh,** *haw-maw´;* a prim. root [comp. 1949]; to *make a loud sound* (like the English "hum"); by impl. to *be in great commotion* or *tumult,* to *rage, war, moan, clamor:*— clamorous, concourse, cry aloud, be disquieted, loud, mourn, be moved, make a noise, rage, roar, sound, be troubled, make in tumult, tumultuous, be in an uproar.

1994. הִמּוֹ **himmôw** (Chald.), *him-mo´;* or (prol.)

הִמּוֹן **himmôwn** (Chald.), *him-mone´;* corresp. to 1992; *they:*— × are, them, those.

1995. הָמוֹן **hâmôwn,** *haw-mone´;* or

הָמֹן **hâmôn** (Ezek. 5:7), *haw-mone´;* from 1993; a *noise, tumult, crowd;* also *disquietude, wealth:*— abundance, company, many, multitude, multiply, noise, riches, rumbling, sounding, store, tumult.

הַמֹּלֶכֶת **ham-môleketh.** See 4447.

1996. הֲמוֹן גּוֹג **Hămôwn Gôwg,** *ham-one´-gohg;* from 1995 and 1463; the *multitude of Gog;* the fanciful name of an emblematic place in Pal.:— Hamon-gog.

1997. הֲמוֹנָה **Hămôwnâh,** *ham-o-naw´;* fem. of 1995; *multitude; Hamonah,* the same as 1996:— Hamonah.

הֲמוּנֶךְ **hămûwnêk.** See 2002.

1998. הֶמְיָה **hemyâh,** *hem-yaw´;* from 1993; *sound:*— noise.

1999. הֲמֻלָּה **hămullâh,** *ham-ool-law´;* or (too fully)

הֲמוּלָּה **hămûwllâh** (Jer. 11:16), *ham-ool-law´;* fem. pass. part. of an unused root mean. to *rush* (as rain with a windy roar); a *sound:*— speech, tumult.

הַמֶּלֶךְ **ham-melek.** See 4429.

2000. הָמַם **hâmam,** *haw-mam´;* a prim. root [comp. 1949, 1993]; prop. to *put in commotion;* by impl. to *disturb, drive, destroy:*— break, consume, crush, destroy, discomfit, trouble, vex.

הָמֹן **hâmôn.** See 1995.

2001. הָמָן **Hâmân,** *haw-mawn´;* of for. der.; *Haman,* a Pers. vizier:— Haman.

2002. הַמְנִיךְ **hamnîyk** (Chald.), *ham-neek´;* but the text is

הֲמוּנֶךְ **hămûwnêk,** *ham-oo-nayk´;* of for. or.; a *necklace:*— chain.

2003. הָמָס **hâmâç,** *haw-mawce´;* from an unused root appar. mean. to *crackle;* a dry *twig* or *brushwood:*— melting.

2004. הֵן **hên,** *hane;* fem. plur. from 1931; *they* (only used when emphat.):— × in, such like, (with) them, thereby, therein, (more than) they, wherein, in which, whom, withal.

2005. הֵן **hên,** *hane;* a prim. particle; *lo!;* also (as expressing surprise) *if:*— behold, if, lo, though.

2006. הֵן **hên** (Chald.), *hane;* corresp. to 2005: *lo!* also *there* [-fore], [un-] *less, whether, but, if:*— (that) if, or, whether.

2007. הֵנָּה **hênnâh,** *hane´-naw;* prol. for 2004; *themselves* (often used emphat. for the copula, also in indirect relation):— × in, × such (and such things), their, (into) them, thence, therein, these, they (had), on this side, those, wherein.

2008. הֵנָּה **hênnâh,** *hane´-naw;* from 2004; *hither* or *thither* (but used both of place and time):— here, hither [-to], now, on this (that) side, + since, this (that) way, thitherward, + thus far, to ... fro, + yet.

2009. הִנֵּה **hinnêh,** *hin-nay´;* prol. for 2005; *lo!:*— behold, lo, see.

2010. הֲנָחָה **hănâchâh,** *han-aw-khaw´;* from 5117; *permission* of rest, i.e. *quiet:*— release.

2011. הִנֹּם **Hinnôm,** *hin-nome´;* prob. of for. or.; *Hinnom,* appar. a Jebusite:— Hinnom.

2012. הֵנַע **Hêna',** *hay-nah´;* prob. of for. der.; *Hena,* a place appar. in Mesopotamia:— Hena.

2013. הָסָה **hâçâh,** *haw-saw´;* a prim. root; to *hush:*— hold peace (tongue), (keep) silence, be silent, still.

2014. הֲפֻגָה **hăphûgâh,** *haf-oo-gaw´;* from 6313; *relaxation:*— intermission.

2015. הָפַךְ **hâphak,** *haw-fak´;* a prim. root; to *turn* about or over; by impl. to *change, overturn, return, pervert:*— × become, change, come, be converted, give, make [a bed], overthrow (-turn), perverse, retire, tumble, turn (again, aside, back, to the contrary, every way).

2016. הֶפֶךְ **hephek,** *heh´-fek;* or

הֵפֶךְ **hêphek,** *hay´-fek;* from 2015; a *turn,* i.e. the *reverse:*— contrary.

2017. הֹפֶךְ **hôphek,** *ho´-fek;* from 2015; an *upset,* i.e. (abstr.) *perversity:*— turning of things upside down.

2018. הֲפֵכָה **hăphêkâh,** *haf-ay-kaw´;* fem. of 2016; *destruction:*— overthrow.

2019. הֲפַכְפַּךְ **hăphakpak,** *haf-ak-pak´;* by redupl. from 2015; *very perverse:*— froward.

2020. הַצָּלָה **hatstsâlâh,** *hats-tsaw-law´;* from 5337; *rescue:*— deliverance.

2021. הֹצֶן **hôtsen,** *ho´-tsen;* from an unused root mean. appar. to *be sharp* or *strong;* a *weapon* of war:— chariot.

2022. הַר **har,** *har;* a short. form of 2042; a *mountain* or *range* of hills (sometimes used fig.):— hill (country), mount (-ain), × promotion.

2023. הֹר **Hôr,** *hore;* another form of 2022; *mountain; Hor,* the name of a peak in Idumæa and of one in Syria:— Hor.

2024. הָרָא **Hârâ',** *haw-raw´;* perh. from 2022; *mountainousness; Hara,* a region of Media:— Hara.

2025. הַרְאֵל **har'êl,** *har-ale´;* from 2022

and 410; *mount of God;* fig. the *altar* of burnt-offering:— altar. Comp. 739.

2026. הָרַג **hârag**, *haw-rag´*; a prim. root; to *smite* with deadly intent:— destroy, out of hand, kill, murder (-er), put to [death], make [slaughter], slay (-er), × surely.

2027. הֶרֶג **hereg**, *heh´-reg;* from 2026; *slaughter:*— be slain, slaughter.

2028. הֲרֵגָה **hărêgâh**, *har-ay-gaw´;* fem. of 2027; *slaughter:*— slaughter.

2029. הָרָה **hârâh**, *haw-raw´;* a prim. root; to *be* (or *become) pregnant, conceive* (lit. or fig.):— been, be with child, conceive, progenitor.

2030. הָרֶה **hâreh**, *haw-reh´;* or

הָרִי **hârîy** (Hos. 14:1), *haw-ree´;* from 2029; *pregnant:*— (be, woman) with child, conceive, × great.

2031. הַרְהֹר **harhôr** (Chald.), *har-hor´;* from a root corresp. to 2029; a mental *conception:*— thought.

2032. הֵרוֹן **hêrôwn**, *hay-rone´;* or

הֵרָיוֹן **hêrâyôwn**, *hay-raw-yone´;* from 2029; *pregnancy:*— conception.

2033. הֲרוֹרִי **Hărôwrîy**, *har-o-ree´;* another form for 2043; a *Harorite* or mountaineer:— Harorite.

2034. הֲרִיסָה **hărîyçâh**, *har-ee-saw´;* from 2040; something *demolished:*— ruin.

2035. הֲרִיסוּת **hărîyçûwth**, *har-ee-sooth´;* from 2040; *demolition:*— destruction.

2036. הֹרָם **Hôrâm**, *ho-rawm´;* from an unused root (mean. to *tower* up); *high; Horam,* a Canaanitish king:— Horam.

2037. הָרֻם **Hârûm**, *haw-room´;* pass. part. of the same as 2036; *high; Harum,* an Isr.:— Harum.

2038. הַרְמוֹן **harmôwn**, *har-mone´;* from the same as 2036; a *castle* (from its height):— palace.

2039. הָרָן **Hârân**, *haw-rawn´;* perh. from 2022; *mountaineer; Haran,* the name of two men:— Haran.

2040. הָרַס **hâraç**, *haw-ras´;* a prim. root; to *pull* down or in pieces, *break, destroy:*— beat down, break (down, through), destroy, overthrow, pluck down, pull down, ruin, throw down, × utterly.

2041. הֶרֶס **hereç**, *heh´-res;* from 2040; *demolition:*— destruction.

2042. הָרָר **hârâr**, *haw-rawr´;* from an unused root mean. to *loom* up; a *mountain:*— hill, mount (-ain).

2043. הֲרָרִי **Hărârîy**, *hah-raw-ree´;* or

הָרָרִי **Hârârîy** (2 Sam. 23:11), *haw-raw-ree´;* or

הָאֲרָרִי **Hâ'rârîy** (2 Sam. 23:34, last clause), *haw-raw-ree´;* appar. from 2042; a *mountaineer:*— Hararite.

2044. הָשֵׁם **Hâshêm**, *haw-shame´;* perh. from the same as 2828; *wealthy; Hashem,* an Isr.:— Hashem.

2045. הַשְׁמָעוּת **hâshmâ'ûwth**, *hashmaw-ooth´;* from 8085; *announcement:*— to cause to hear.

2046. הִתּוּךְ **hittûwk**, *hit-took´;* from 5413; a *melting:*— is melted.

2047. הֲתָךְ **Hăthâk**, *hath-awk´;* prob. of for. or.; *Hathak,* a Pers. eunuch:— Hatach.

2048. הָתַל **hâthal**, *haw-thal´;* a prim. root; to *deride;* by impl. to *cheat:*— deal deceitfully, deceive, mock.

2049. הָתֹל **hâthôl**, *haw-thole´;* from 2048 (only in plur. collect.); a *derision:*— mocker.

2050. הָתַת **hâthath**, *haw-thath´;* a prim. root; prop. to *break* in upon, i.e. to *assail:*— imagine mischief.

ו

2051. וְדָן **Vᵉdân**, *ved-awn´;* perh. for 5730; *Vedan* (or Aden), a place in Arabia:— Dan also.

2052. וְהֵב **Vâhêb**, *vaw-habe´;* of uncert. der.; *Vaheb,* a place in Moab:— what he did.

2053. וָו **vâv**, *vaw;* prob. a *hook* (the name of the sixth Heb. letter):— hook.

2054. וָזָר **vâzâr**, *vaw-zawr´;* presumed to be from an unused root mean. to *bear* guilt; *crime:*— × strange.

2055. וַיְזָתָא **Vayᵉzâthâ'**, *vah-yez-aw´-thaw;* of for. or.; *Vajezatha,* a son of Haman:— Vajezatha.

2056. וָלָד **vâlâd**, *vaw-lawd´;* for 3206; a *boy:*— child.

2057. וַנְיָה **Vanyâh**, *van-yaw´;* perh. for 6043; *Vanjah,* an Isr.:— Vaniah.

2058. וָפְסִי **Vophçîy**, *vof-see´;* prob. from 3254; *additional; Vophsi,* an Isr.:— Vophsi.

2059. וַשְׁנִי **Vashnîy**, *vash-nee´;* prob. from 3461; *weak; Vashni,* an Isr.:— Vashni.

2060. וַשְׁתִּי **Vashtîy**, *vash-tee´;* of Pers. or.; *Vashti,* the queen of Xerxes:— Vashti.

ז

2061. זְאֵב **zᵉ'êb**, *zeh-abe´;* from an unused root mean. to *be yellow;* a *wolf:*— wolf.

2062. זְאֵב **Zᵉ'êb**, *zeh-abe´;* the same as 2061; *Zeëb,* a Midianitish prince:— Zeeb.

2063. זֹאת **zô'th**, *zothe´;* irreg. fem. of 2089; *this* (often used adv.):— hereby (-in, -with), it, likewise, the one (other, same), she, so (much), such (deed), that, therefore, these, this (thing), thus.

2064. זָבַד **zâbad**, *zaw-bad´;* a prim. root; to *confer:*— endure.

2065. זֶבֶד **zebed**, *zeh´-bed;* from 2064; a *gift:*— dowry.

2066. זָבָד **Zâbâd**, *zaw-bawd´;* from 2064; *giver; Zabad,* the name of seven Isr.:— Zabad.

2067. זַבְדִּי **Zabdîy**, *zab-dee´;* from 2065; *giving; Zabdi,* the name of four Isr.:— Zabdi.

2068. זַבְדִּיאֵל **Zabdîy'êl**, *zab-dee-ale´;* from 2065 and 410; *gift of God; Zabdiel,* the name of two Isr.:— Zabdiel.

2069. זְבַדְיָה **Zᵉbadyâh**, *zeb-ad-yaw´;* or

זְבַדְיָהוּ **Zᵉbadyâhûw**, *zeb-ad-yaw´-hoo;* from 2064 and 3050; *Jah has given;*

Zebadjah, the name of nine Isr.:— Zebadiah.

2070. זְבוּב **zᵉbûwb**, *zeb-oob´;* from an unused root (mean. to *flit*); a *fly* (espec. one of a stinging nature):— fly.

2071. זָבוּד **Zâbûwd**, *zaw-bood´;* from 2064; *given; Zabud,* an Isr.:— Zabud.

2072. זַבּוּד **Zabbûwd**, *zab-bood´;* a form of 2071; *given; Zabbud,* an Isr.:— Zabbud.

2073. זְבוּל **zᵉbûwl**, *ze-bool´;* or

זְבֻל **zᵉbûl**, *zeb-ool´;* from 2082; a *residence:*— dwell in, dwelling, habitation.

2074. זְבוּלוּן **Zᵉbûwlûwn**, *zeb-oo-loon´;* or

זְבֻלוּן **Zᵉbûlûwn**, *zeb-oo-loon´;* or

זְבוּלֻן **Zᵉbûwlûn**, *zeb-oo-loon´;* from 2082; *habitation; Zebulon,* a son of Jacob; also his territory and tribe:— Zebulun.

2075. זְבוּלֹנִי **Zᵉbûwlônîy**, *zeb-oo-lo-nee´;* patron. from 2074; a *Zebulonite* or desc. of Zebulun:— Zebulonite.

2076. זָבַח **zâbach**, *zaw-bakh´;* a prim. root; to *slaughter* an animal (usually in sacrifice):— kill, offer, (do) sacrifice, slay.

2077. זֶבַח **zebach**, *zeh´-bakh;* from 2076; prop. a *slaughter,* i.e. the *flesh* of an animal; by impl. a *sacrifice* (the victim or the act):— offer (-ing), sacrifice.

2078. זֶבַח **Zebach**, *zeh´-bakh;* the same as 2077; *sacrifice; Zebach,* a Midianitish prince:— Zebah.

2079. זַבַּי **Zabbay**, *zab-bah´-ee;* prob. by orth. err. for 2140; *Zabbai* (or Zaccai), an Isr.:— Zabbai.

2080. זְבִידָה **Zᵉbîydâh**, *zeb-ee-daw´;* fem. from 2064; *giving; Zebidah,* an Israelitess:— Zebudah.

2081. זְבִינָא **Zᵉbîynâ'**, *zeb-ee-naw´;* from an unused root (mean. to *purchase*); *gainfulness; Zebina,* an Isr.:— Zebina.

2082. זָבַל **zâbal**, *zaw-bal´;* a prim. root; appar. prop. to *inclose,* i.e. to *reside:*— dwell with.

2083. זְבֻל **Zᵉbûl**, *zeb-ool´;* the same as 2073; *dwelling; Zebul,* an Isr.:— Zebul. Comp. 2073.

זְבֻלוּן **Zᵉbûlûwn**. See 2074.

2084. זְבַן **zᵉban** (Chald.), *zeb-an´;* corresp. to the root of 2081; to *acquire* by purchase:— gain.

2085. זָג **zâg**, *zawg;* from an unused root prob. mean. to *inclose; the skin* of a grape:— husk.

2086. זֵד **zêd**, *zade´;* from 2102; *arrogant:*— presumptuous, proud.

2087. זָדוֹן **zâdôwn**, *zaw-done´;* from 2102; *arrogance:*— presumptuously, pride, proud (man).

2088. זֶה **zeh**, *zeh;* a prim. word; the masc. demonstr. pron., *this* or *that:*— he, × hence, × here, it (-self), × now, × of him, the one ... the other, × than the other, (× out of) the [self] same, such (an one) that, these, this (hath, man), on this side ... on that side, × thus, very, which. Comp. 2063, 2090, 2097, 2098.

2089. זֶה **zeh** (1 Sam. 17:34), *zeh*; by perm. for 7716; a *sheep*:— lamb.

2090. זֹה **zôh**, *zo*; for 2088; *this* or *that*:— as well as another, it, this, that, thus and thus.

2091. זָהָב **zâhâb**, *zaw-hawb'*; from an unused root mean. to *shimmer*; *gold*, fig. something *gold-colored* (i.e. *yellow*), as *oil*, a *clear sky*:— gold (-en), fair weather.

2092. זָהַם **zâham**, *zaw-ham'*; a prim. root; to *be rancid*, i.e. (tran.) to *loathe*:— abhor.

2093. זַהַם **Zaham**, *zah'-ham*; from 2092; *loathing*; *Zaham*, an Isr.:— Zaham.

2094. זָהַר **zâhar**, *zaw-har'*; a prim. root; to *gleam*; fig. to *enlighten* (by caution):— admonish, shine, teach, (give) warn (-ing).

2095. זְהַר **z°har** (Chald.), *zeh-har'*; corresp. to 2094; (pass.) *be admonished*:— take heed.

2096. זֹהַר **zôhar**, *zo'-har*; from 2094; *brilliancy*:— brightness.

2097. זוֹ **zôw**, *zo*; for 2088; *this* or *that*:— that, this.

2098. זוּ **zûw**, *zoo*; for 2088; *this* or *that*:— that, this, × wherein, which, whom.

2099. זִו **Zîv**, *zeev*; prob. from an unused root mean. to *be prominent*; prop. *brightness* [comp. 2122], i.e. (fig.) the month of *flowers*; *Ziv* (corresp. to Ijar or May):— Zif.

2100. זוּב **zûwb**, *zoob*; a prim. root; to *flow* freely (as water), i.e. (spec.) to *have a* (sexual) *flux*; fig. to *waste* away; also to *overflow*:— flow, gush out, have a (running) issue, pine away, run.

2101. זוֹב **zôwb**, *zobe*; from 2100; a seminal or menstrual *flux*:— issue.

2102. זוּד **zûwd**, *zood*; or (by perm.) זִיד **zîyd**, *zeed*; a prim. root; to *seethe*; fig. to *be insolent*:— be proud, deal proudly, presume, (come) presumptuously, sod.

2103. זוּד **zûwd** (Chald.), *zood*; corresp. to 2102; to *be proud*:— in pride.

2104. זוּזִים **Zûwzîym**, *zoo-zeem'*; plur. prob. from the same as 2123; *prominent*; *Zuzites*, an aboriginal tribe of Pal.:— Zuzims.

2105. זוֹחֵת **Zôwchêth**, *zo-khayth'*; of uncert. or.; *Zocheth*, an Isr.:— Zoheth.

2106. זָוִית **zâvîyth**, *zaw-veeth'*; appar. from the same root as 2099 (in the sense of *prominence*); an *angle* (as *projecting*), i.e. (by impl.) a *corner-column* (or *anta*):— corner (stone).

2107. זוּל **zûwl**, *zool*; a prim. root [comp. 2151]; prob. to *shake* out, i.e. (by impl.) to *scatter* profusely; fig. to *treat lightly*:— lavish, despise.

2108. זוּלָה **zûwlâh**, *zoo-law'*; from 2107; prob. *scattering*, i.e. *removal*; used adv. *except*:— beside, but, only, save.

2109. זוּן **zûwn**, *zoon*; a prim. root; perh. prop. to *be plump*, i.e. (tran.) to *nourish*:— feed.

2110. זוּן **zûwn** (Chald.), *zoon*; corresp. to 2109:— feed.

2111. זוּעַ **zûwâ'**, *zoo'-ah*; a prim. root; prop. to *shake* off, i.e. (fig.) to *agitate* (as with fear):— move, tremble, vex.

2112. זוּעַ **zûwa'** (Chald.), *zoo'-ah*; corresp. to 2111; to *shake* (with fear):— tremble.

2113. זְוָעָה **z°vâ'âh**, *zev-aw-aw'*; from 2111; *agitation, fear*:— be removed, trouble, vexation. Comp. 2189.

2114. זוּר **zûwr**, *zoor*; a prim. root; to *turn* aside (espec. for lodging); hence, to *be a foreign, strange, profane*; spec. (act. part.) to *commit adultery*:— (come) from) another (man, place), fanner, go away, (e-) strange (-r, thing, woman).

2115. זוּר **zûwr**, *zoor*; a prim. root [comp. 6695]; to *press* together, *tighten*:— close, crush, thrust together.

2116. זוּרה **zûwreh**, *zoo-reh'*; from 2115; *trodden* on:— that which is crushed.

2117. זָזָא **Zâzâ'**, *zaw-zaw'*; prob. from the root of 2123; *prominent*; *Zaza*, an Isr.:— Zaza.

2118. זָחַח **zâchach**, *zaw-khakh'*; a prim. root; to *shove* or *displace*:— loose.

2119. זָחַל **zâchal**, *zaw-khal'*; a prim. root; to *crawl*; by impl. to *fear*:— be afraid, serpent, worm.

2120. זֹחֶלֶת **Zôcheleth**, *zo-kheh'-leth*; fem. act. part. of 2119; *crawling* (i.e. *serpent*); *Zocheleth*, a boundary stone in Pal.:— Zoheleth.

2121. זֵידוֹן **zêydôwn**, *zay-dohn'*; from 2102; *boiling* of water, i.e. *wave*:— proud.

2122. זִיו **zîyv** (Chald.), *zeev*; corresp. to 2099; (fig.) *cheerfulness*:— brightness, countenance.

2123. זִיז **zîyz**, *zeez*; from an unused root appar. mean. to *be conspicuous*; *fulness* of the breast; also a moving *creature*:— abundance, wild beast.

2124. זִיזָא **Zîyzâ'**, *zee-zaw'*; appar. from the same as 2123; *prominence*; *Ziza*, the name of two Isr.:— Ziza.

2125. זִיזָה **Zîyzâh**, *zee-zaw'*; another form for 2124; *Zizah*, an Isr.:— Zizah.

2126. זִינָא **Zîynâ'**, *zee-naw'*; from 2109; *well-fed*; or perh. an orth. err. for 2124; *Zina*, an Isr.:— Zina.

2127. זִיעַ **Zîya'**, *zee'-ah*; from 2111; *agitation*; *Zia*, an Isr.:— Zia.

2128. זִיף **Zîyph**, *zeef*; from the same as 2203; *flowing*; *Ziph*, the name of a place in Pal.; also of an Isr.:— Ziph.

2129. זִיפָה **Zîyphâh**, *zee-faw'*; fem. of 2128; a *flowing*; *Ziphah*, an Isr.:— Ziphah.

2130. זִיפִי **Zîyphiy**, *zee-fee'*; patrial from 2128; a *Ziphite* or inhab. of *Ziph*:— Ziphim, Ziphite.

2131. זִיקָה **zîyqâh** (Isa. 50:11), *zee-kaw'* (fem.); and

זִק **ziq**, *zeek*; or

זֵק **zêq**, *zake*; from 2187; prop. what *leaps* forth, i.e. *flash* of fire, or a burning *arrow*; also (from the orig. sense of the root) a *bond*:— chain, fetter, firebrand, spark.

2132. זַיִת **zayith**, *zay'-yith*; prob. from an unused root [akin to 2099]; an *olive* (as yielding *illuminating* oil), the tree, the branch or the berry:— olive (tree, -yard), Olivet.

2133. זֵיתָן **Zêythân**, *zay-thawn'*; from 2132; *olive* grove; *Zethan*, an Isr.:— Zethan.

2134. זַךְ **zak**, *zak*; from 2141; *clear*:— clean, pure.

2135. זָכָה **zâkâh**, *zaw-kaw'*; a prim. root [comp. 2141]; to *be translucent*; fig. to *be innocent*:— be (make) clean, cleanse, be clear, count pure.

2136. זְכָו **zâkâw** (Chald.), *zaw-koo*; from a root corresp. to 2135; *purity*:— innocency.

2137. זְכוּכִית **z°kûwkîyth**, *zek-oo-keeth'*; from 2135; prop. *transparency*, i.e. *glass*:— crystal.

2138. זָכוּר **zâkûwr**, *zaw-koor'*; prop. pass. part. of 2142, but used for 2145; a *male* (of man or animals):— males, men-children.

2139. זַכּוּר **Zakkûwr**, *zaw-koor'*; from 2142; *mindful*; *Zakkur*, the name of seven Isr.:— Zaccur, Zacchur.

2140. זַכַּי **Zakkay**, *zak-kah'-ee*; from 2141; *pure*; *Zakkai*, an Isr.:— Zaccai.

2141. זָכַךְ **zâkak**, *zaw-kak'*; a prim. root [comp. 2135]; to *be transparent* or *clean* (phys. or mor.):— be (make) clean, be pure (-r).

2142. זָכַר **zâkar**, *zaw-kar'*; a prim. root; prop. to *mark* (so as to be recognized), i.e. to *remember*; by impl. to *mention*; also (as denom. from 2145) to *be male*:— × burn [incense], × earnestly, be male, (make) mention (of), be mindful, recount, record (-er), remember, make to be remembered, bring (call, come, keep, put) to (in) remembrance, × still, think on, × well.

2143. זֵכֶר **zêker**, *zay'-ker*; or

זֶכֶר **zeker**, *zeh'-ker*; from 2142; a *memento*, abstr. *recollection* (rarely if ever); by impl. *commemoration*:— memorial, memory, remembrance, scent.

2144. זֶכֶר **Zeker**, *zeh'-ker*; the same as 2143; *Zeker*, an Isr.:— Zeker.

2145. זָכָר **zâkâr**, *zaw-kawr'*; from 2142; prop. *remembered*, i.e. a *male* (of man or animals, as being the most noteworthy sex):— × him, male, man (child, -kind).

2146. זִכְרוֹן **zikrôwn**, *zik-rone'*; from 2142; a *memento* (or memorable thing, day or writing):— memorial, record.

2147. זִכְרִי **Zikriy**, *zik-ree'*; from 2142; *memorable*; *Zicri*, the name of twelve Isr.:— Zichri.

2148. זְכַרְיָה **Z°karyâh**, *zek-ar-yaw'*; or

זְכַרְיָהוּ **Z°karyâhûw**, *zek-ar-yaw'-hoo*; from 2142 and 3050; *Jah has remembered*; *Zecarjah*, the name of twenty-nine Isr.:— Zachariah, Zechariah.

2149. זֻלּוּת **zullûwth**, *zool-looth'*; from 2151; prop. a *shaking*, i.e. perh. a *tempest*:— vilest.

2150. זַלְזַל **zalzal**, *zal-zal'*; by redupl. from 2151; *tremulous*, i.e. a *twig*:— sprig.

2151. זָלַל **zâlal**, *zaw-lal'*; a prim. root

[comp. 2107]; to *shake* (as in the wind), i.e. to *quake*; fig. to *be loose* morally, *worthless* or *prodigal*:— blow down, glutton, riotous (eater), vile.

2152. זַלְעֵפֶה zal'âphâh, zal-aw-faw'; or

זִלְעֵפָף zil'âphâph, zil-aw-faw'; from 2196; a *glow* (of wind or anger); also a *famine* (as *consuming*):— horrible, horror, terrible.

2153. זִלְפָּה Zilpâh, zil-paw'; from an unused root appar. mean. to *trickle*, as myrrh; fragrant *dropping*; Zilpah, Leah's maid:— Zilpah.

2154. זִמָּה zimmâh, zim-maw'; or

זַמָּה zammâh, zam-maw'; from 2161; a *plan*, espec. a bad one:— heinous crime, lewd (-ly, -ness), mischief, purpose, thought, wicked (device, mind, -ness).

2155. זִמָּה Zimmâh, zim-maw'; the same as 2154; *Zimmah*, the name of two Isr.:— Zimmah.

2156. זְמוֹרָה zᵉmôwrâh, zem-o-raw'; or

זְמֹרָה zᵉmôrâh, zem-o-raw' (fem.); and

זְמֹר zᵉmôr, zem-ore' (masc.); from 2168; a *twig* (as *pruned*):— vine, branch, slip.

2157. זַמְזֹם Zamzôm, zam-zome'; from 2161; *intriguing*; a Zamzumite, or native tribe of Pal.:— Zamzummim.

2158. זָמִיר zâmîyr, zaw-meer'; or

זָמִר zâmir, zaw-meer'; and (fem.)

זְמִרָה zᵉmîrâh, zem-ee-raw'; from 2167; a *song* to be accompanied with instrumental music:— psalm (-ist), singing, song.

2159. זָמִיר zâmîyr, zaw-meer'; from 2168; a *twig* (as *pruned*):— branch.

2160. זְמִירָה Zᵉmîyrâh, zem-ee-raw'; fem. of 2158; *song*; Zemirah, an Isr.:— Zemira.

2161. זָמַם zâmam, zaw-mam'; a prim. root; to *plan*, usually in a bad sense:— consider, devise, imagine, plot, purpose, think (evil).

2162. זָמָם zâmâm, zaw-mawm'; from 2161; a *plot*:— wicked device.

2163. זָמַן zâman, zaw-man'; a prim. root; to *fix* (a time):— appoint.

2164. זְמַן zᵉman (Chald.), zem-an'; corresp. to 2163; to *agree* (on a time and place):— prepare.

2165. זְמָן zᵉmân, zem-awn'; from 2163; an *appointed* occasion:— season, time.

2166. זְמָן zᵉmân (Chald.), zem-awn'; from 2165; the same as 2165:— season, time.

2167. זָמַר zâmar, zaw-mar'; a prim. root [perh. ident. with 2168 through the idea of *striking* with the fingers]; prop. to *touch* the strings or parts of a musical instrument, i.e. *play* upon it; to make *music*, accompanied by the voice; hence, to *celebrate* in song and music:— give praise, sing forth praises, psalms.

2168. זָמַר zâmar, zaw-mar'; a prim. root [comp. 2167, 5568, 6785]; to *trim* (a vine):— prune.

2169. זֶמֶר zemer, zeh'-mer; appar. from

2167 or 2168; a *gazelle* (from its lightly *touching* the ground):— chamois.

2170. זְמָר zᵉmâr (Chald.), zem-awr'; from a root corresp. to 2167; instrumental *music*:— musick.

זָמִיר zâmîr. See 2158.

זְמֹר zᵉmôr. See 2156.

2171. זַמָּר zammâr (Chald.), zam-mawr'; from the same as 2170; an instrumental *musician*:— singer.

2172. זִמְרָה zimrâh, zim-raw'; from 2167; a *musical* piece or *song* to be accompanied by an instrument:— melody, psalm.

2173. זִמְרָה zimrâh, zim-raw'; from 2168; *pruned* (i.e. *choice*) fruit:— best fruit.

זְמִרָה zᵉmîrâh. See 2158.

זְמֹרָה zᵉmôrâh. See 2156.

2174. זִמְרִי Zimrîy, zim-ree'; from 2167; *musical*; Zimri, the name of five Isr., and of an Arabian tribe:— Zimri.

2175. זִמְרָן Zimrân, zim-rawn'; from 2167; *musical*; Zimran, a son of Abraham by Keturah:— Zimran.

2176. זִמְרָת zimrâth, zim-rawth'; from 2167; instrumental *music*; by impl. *praise*:— song.

2177. זַן zan, zan; from 2109; prop. *nourished* (or fully *developed*), i.e. a *form* or *sort*:— divers kinds, × all manner of store.

2178. זַן zan (Chald.), zan; corresp. to 2177; *sort*:— kind.

2179. זָנַב zânab, zaw-nab'; a prim. root mean. to *wag*; used only as a denom. from 2180; to *curtail*, i.e. *cut off* the rear:— smite the hindmost.

2180. זָנָב zânâb, zaw-nawb'; from 2179 (in the orig. sense of *flapping*); the *tail* (lit. or fig.):— tail.

2181. זָנָה zânâh, zaw-naw'; a prim. root [highly-*fed* and therefore *wanton*]; to *commit adultery* (usually of the female, and less often of simple fornication, rarely of involuntary ravishment); fig. to *commit idolatry* (the Jewish people being regarded as the spouse of Jehovah):— (cause to) commit fornication, × continually, × great, (be an, play the) harlot, (cause to be, play the) whore, (commit, fall to) whoredom, (cause to) go a-whoring, whorish.

2182. זָנוֹחַ Zânôwach, zaw-no'-akh; from 2186; *rejected*; Zanoach, the name of two places in Pal.:— Zanoah.

2183. זָנוּן zânûwn, zaw-noon'; from 2181; *adultery*; fig. *idolatry*:— whoredom.

2184. זְנוּת zᵉnûwth, zen-ooth'; from 2181; *adultery*, i.e. (fig.) *infidelity*, *idolatry*:— whoredom.

2185. זֹנוֹת zônôwth, zo-noth'; regarded by some as if from 2109 or an unused root, and applied to military *equipments*; but evidently the fem. plur. act. part. of 2181; *harlots*:— armour.

2186. זָנַח zânach, zaw-nakh'; a prim. root mean. to *push* aside, i.e. *reject*, *forsake*, *fail*:— cast away (off), remove far away (off).

2187. זָנַק zânaq, zaw-nak'; a prim. root; prop. to *draw together* the feet (as an

animal about to dart upon its prey), i.e. to *spring* forward:— leap.

2188. זֵעָה zê'âh, zay-aw'; from 2111 (in the sense of 3154); *perspiration*:— sweat.

2189. זַעֲוָה za'ăvâh, zah-av-aw'; by transp. for 2113; *agitation*, *maltreatment*:— × removed, trouble.

2190. זַעֲוָן Za'ăvân, zah-av-awn'; from 2111; *disquiet*; Zaavan, an Idumæan:— Zaavan.

2191. זְעֵיר zᵉ'êyr, zeh-ayr'; from an unused root [akin (by perm.) to 6819], mean. to *dwindle*; *small*:— little.

2192. זְעֵיר zᵉ'êyr (Chald.), zeh-ayr'; corresp. to 2191:— little.

2193. זָעַךְ zâ'ak, zaw-ak'; a prim. root; to *extinguish*:— be extinct.

2194. זָעַם zâ'am, zaw-am'; a prim. root; prop. to *foam* at the mouth, i.e. to *be enraged*:— abhor, abominable, (be) angry, defy, (have) indignation.

2195. זַעַם za'am, zah'-am; from 2194; strictly *froth* at the mouth, i.e. (fig.) *fury* (espec. of God's displeasure with sin):— angry, indignation, rage.

2196. זָעַף zâ'aph, zaw-af'; a prim. root; prop. to *boil up*, i.e. (fig.) to *be peevish* or *angry*:— fret, sad, worse liking, be wroth.

2197. זַעַף za'aph, zah'-af; from 2196; *anger*:— indignation, rage (-ing), wrath.

2198. זָעֵף zâ'êph, zaw-afe'; from 2196; *angry*:— displeased.

2199. זָעַק zâ'aq, zaw-ak'; a prim. root; to *shriek* (from anguish or danger); by anal. (as a herald) to *announce* or *convene* publicly:— assemble, call (together), (make a) cry (out), come with such a company, gather (together), cause to be proclaimed.

2200. זְעִיק zᵉ'îq (Chald.), zeh-eek'; corresp. to 2199; to *make an outcry*:— cry.

2201. זַעַק za'aq, zah'-ak; and (fem.)

זְעָקָה zᵉ'âqâh, zeh-aw-kaw'; from 2199; a *shriek* or *outcry*:— cry (-ing).

2202. זִפְרֹן Ziphrôn, zi-frone'; from an unused root (mean. to *be fragrant*); *Ziphron*, a place in Pal.:— Ziphron.

2203. זֶפֶת zepheth, zeh'-feth; from an unused root (mean. to *liquify*); *asphalt* (from its tendency to *soften* in the sun):— pitch.

זִיק zîq or

זֵק zêq. See 2131.

2204. זָקֵן zâqên, zaw-kane'; a prim. root; to *be old*:— aged man, be (wax) old (man).

2205. זָקֵן zâqên, zaw-kane'; from 2204; *old*:— aged, ancient (man), elder (-est), old (man, men and ... women), senator.

2206. זָקָן zâqân, zaw-kawn'; from 2204; the *beard* (as indicating *age*):— beard.

2207. זֹקֶן zôqen, zo'-ken; from 2204; old *age*:— age.

2208. זָקֻן zâqûn, zaw-koon'; prop. pass. part. of 2204 (used only in the plur. as a noun); *old age*:— old age.

2209. זִקְנָה ziqnâh, zik-naw'; fem. of 2205; *old age*:— old (age).

Hebrew

2210. זָקַף **zâqaph**, *zaw-kaf´*; a prim. root; to *lift*, i.e. (fig.) *comfort*:— raise (up).

2211. זְקַף **z⁰qaph** (Chald.), *zek-af´*; corresp. to 2210; to *hang*, i.e. *impale*:— set up.

2212. זָקַק **zâqaq**, *zaw-kak´*; a prim. root; to *strain*, (fig.) *extract, clarify*:— fine, pour down, purge, purify, refine.

2213. זֵר **zêr**, *zare*; from 2237 (in the sense of *scattering*); a *chaplet* (as *spread* around the top), i.e. (spec.) a border *moulding*:— crown.

2214. זָרָא **zârâ**, *zaw-raw´*; from 2114 (in the sense of *estrangement*) [comp. 2219]; *disgust*:— loathsome.

2215. זָרַב **zârab**, *zaw-rab´*; a prim. root; to *flow* away:— wax warm.

2216. זְרֻבָּבֶל **Z⁰rubbâbel**, *zer-oob-baw-bel´*; from 2215 and 894; *descended of* (i.e. from) *Babylon*, i.e. *born there*; *Zerubbabel*, an Isr.:— Zerubbabel.

2217. זְרֻבָּבֶל **Z⁰rubbâbel** (Chald.), *zer-oob-baw-bel´*; corresp. to 2216:— Zerubbabel.

2218. זֶרֶד **Zered**, *zeh´-red*; from an unused root mean. to *be exuberant* in growth; lined with *shrubbery*; *Zered*, a brook E. of the Dead Sea:— Zared, Zered.

2219. זָרָה **zârâh**, *zaw-raw´*; a prim. root [comp. 2114]; to *toss* about; by impl. to *diffuse, winnow*:— cast away, compass, disperse, fan, scatter (away), spread, strew, winnow.

2220. זְרוֹעַ **z⁰rôwa**, *zer-o´-ah*; or (short.) זְרֹעַ **z⁰rôa**, *zer-o´-ah*; and (fem.) זְרוֹעָה **z⁰rôw‘âh**, *zer-o-aw´*; or זְרֹעָה **z⁰rô‘âh**, *zer-o-aw´*; from 2232; the *arm* (as *stretched* out), or (of animals) the *foreleg*; fig. *force*:— arm, + help, mighty, power, shoulder, strength.

2221. זֵרוּעַ **zêrûwa**, *zay-roo´-ah*; from 2232; something *sown*, i.e. a *plant*:— sowing, thing that is sown.

2222. זַרְזִיף **zarzîyph**, *zar-zeef´*; by redupl. from an unused root mean. to *flow*; a *pouring rain*:— water.

זְרֹעָה **z⁰rôw‘âh**. See 2220.

2223. זַרְזִיר **zarzîyr**, *zar-zeer´*; by redupl. from 2115; prop. *tightly girt*, i.e. prob. a *racer*, or some fleet animal (as being *slender* in the waist):— + greyhound.

2224. זָרַח **zârach**, *zaw-rakh´*; a prim. root; prop. to *irradiate* (or shoot forth beams), i.e. to *rise* (as the sun); spec. to *appear* (as a symptom of leprosy):— arise, rise (up), as soon as it is up.

2225. זֶרַח **zerach**, *zeh´-rakh*; from 2224; a *rising* of light:— rising.

2226. זֶרַח **Zerach**, *zeh´-rakh*; the same as 2225; *Zerach*, the name of three Isr., also of an Idumæan and an Ethiopian prince:— Zarah, Zerah.

2227. זַרְחִי **Zarchîy**, *zar-khee´*; patron. from 2226; a *Zarchite* or desc. of Zerah:— Zarchite.

2228. זְרַחְיָה **Z⁰rachyâh**, *zer-akh-yaw´*; from 2225 and 3050; *Jah has risen*; *Zerachjah*, the name of two Isr.:— Zerahiah.

2229. זָרַם **zâram**, *zaw-ram´*; a prim. root; to *gush* (as water):— carry away as with a flood, pour out.

2230. זֶרֶם **zerem**, *zeh´-rem*; from 2229; a *gush* of water:— flood, overflowing, shower, storm, tempest.

2231. זִרְמָה **zirmâh**, *zir-maw´*; fem. of 2230; a *gushing* of fluid (semen):— issue.

2232. זָרַע **zâra**, *zaw-rah´*; a prim. root; to *sow*; fig. to *disseminate, plant, fructify*:— bear, conceive seed, set with, sow (-er), yield.

2233. זֶרַע **zera**, *zeh´-rah*; from 2232; *seed*; fig. *fruit, plant, sowing-time, posterity*:— × carnally, child, fruitful, seed (-time), sowing-time.

2234. זְרַע **z⁰ra** (Chald.), *zer-ah´*; corresp. to 2233; *posterity*:— seed.

זְרֹעַ **z⁰rôa**. See 2220.

2235. זֵרֹעַ **zêrôa**, *zay-ro´-ah*; or זֵרָעֹן **zêrâ‘ôn**, *zay-raw-ohn´*; from 2232; something *sown* (only in the plur.), i.e. a *vegetable* (as food):— pulse.

זֵרֹעָה **z⁰rô‘âh**. See 2220.

2236. זָרַק **zâraq**, *zaw-rak´*; a prim. root; to *sprinkle* (fluid or solid particles):— be here and there, scatter, sprinkle, strew.

2237. זָרַר **zârar**, *zaw-rar´*; a prim. root [comp. 2114]; perh. to *diffuse*, i.e. (spec.) to *sneeze*:— sneeze.

2238. זֶרֶשׁ **Zeresh**, *zeh´-resh*; of Pers. or.; *Zeresh*, Haman's wife:— Zeresh.

2239. זֶרֶת **zereth**, *zeh´-reth*; from 2219; the *spread* of the fingers, i.e. a *span*:— span.

2240. זַתּוּא **Zattûw**, *zat-too´*; of uncert. der.; *Zattu*, an Isr.:— Zattu.

2241. זֵתָם **Zêthâm**, *zay-thawm´*; appar. a var. for 2133; *Zetham*, an Isr.:— Zetham.

2242. זֵתַר **Zêthar**, *zay-thar´*; of Pers. or.; *Zethar*, a eunuch of Xerxes:— Zethar.

ח

2243. חֹב **chôb**, *khobe*; by contr. from 2245; prop. a *cherisher*, i.e. the *bosom*:— bosom.

2244. חָבָא **châbâ**, *khaw-baw´*; a prim. root [comp. 2245]; to *secrete*:— × held, hide (self), do secretly.

2245. חָבַב **châbab**, *khaw-bab´*; a prim. root [comp. 2244, 2247]; prop. to *hide* (as in the bosom), i.e. to *cherish* (with affection):— love.

2246. חֹבָב **Chôbâb**, *kho-bawb´*; from 2245; *cherished*; *Chobab*, father-in-law of Moses:— Hobab.

2247. חָבָה **châbah**, *khaw-baw´*; a prim. root [comp. 2245]; to *secrete*:— hide (self).

2248. חֲבוּלָה **châbûwlâh** (Chald.), *khab-oo-law´*; from 2255; prop. *overthrown*, i.e. (morally) *crime*:— hurt.

2249. חָבוֹר **Châbôwr**, *khaw-bore´*; from 2266; *united*; *Chabor*, a river of Assyria:— Habor.

2250. חֲבוּרָה **chabbûwrâh**, *khab-boo-raw´*; or

חַבֻּרָה **chabbûrâh**, *khab-boo-raw´*; or

חֲבֻרָה **chăbûrâh**, *khab-oo-raw´*; from 2266; prop. *bound* (with stripes), i.e. a *weal* (or black-and-blue mark itself):— blueness, bruise, hurt, stripe, wound.

2251. חָבַט **châbat**, *khaw-bat´*; a prim. root; to *knock* out or off:— beat (off, out), thresh.

2252. חֲבַיָּה **Chăbayâh**, *khab-ah-yaw´*; or

חֲבָיָה **Chăbâyâh**, *khab-aw-yaw´*; from 2247 and 3050; *Jah has hidden*; *Chabajah*, an Isr.:— Habaiah.

2253. חֶבְיוֹן **chebyôwn**, *kheb-yone´*; from 2247; a *concealment*:— hiding.

2254. חָבַל **châbal**, *khaw-bal´*; a prim. root; to *wind* tightly (as a rope), i.e. to *bind*; spec. by a *pledge*; fig. to *pervert, destroy*; also to *writhe* in pain (espec. of parturition):— × at all, band, bring forth, (deal) corrupt (-ly), destroy, offend, lay to (take a) pledge, spoil, travail, × very, withhold.

2255. חֲבַל **chăbal** (Chald.), *khab-al´*; corresp. to 2254; to *ruin*:— destroy, hurt.

2256. חֶבֶל **chebel**, *kheh´-bel*; or

חֵבֶל **chêbel**, *khay-bel´*; from 2254; a *rope* (as *twisted*), espec. a measuring *line*; by impl. a *district* or *inheritance* (as *measured*); or a *noose* (as of *cords*); fig. a *company* (as if *tied* together); also a *throe* (espec. of *parturition*); also *ruin*:— band, coast, company, cord, country, destruction, line, lot, pain, pang, portion, region, rope, snare, sorrow, tackling.

2257. חֲבַל **chăbal** (Chald.), *khab-al´*; from 2255; *harm* (personal or pecuniary):— damage, hurt.

2258. חֲבֹל **chăbôl**, *khab-ole´*; or (fem.)

חֲבֹלָה **chăbôlâh**, *khab-o-law´*; from 2254; a *pawn* (as security for debt):— pledge.

2259. חֹבֵל **chôbêl**, *kho-bale´*; act. part. from 2254 (in the sense of handling *ropes*); a *sailor*:— pilot, shipmaster.

2260. חִבֵּל **chibbêl**, *khib-bale´*; from 2254 (in the sense of furnished with *ropes*); a *mast*:— mast.

2261. חֲבַצֶּלֶת **chăbatstseleth**, *khab-ats-tseh´-leth*; of uncert. der.; prob. *meadow-saffron*:— rose.

2262. חֲבַצַּנְיָה **Chăbatstsanyâh**, *khab-ats-tsan-yaw´*; of uncert. der.; *Chabatstsanjah*, a Rechabite:— Habazaniah.

2263. חָבַק **châbaq**, *khaw-bak´*; a prim. root; to *clasp* (the hands or in embrace):— embrace, fold.

2264. חִבֻּק **chibbûq**, *khib-book´*; from 2263; a *clasping* of the hands (in idleness):— fold.

2265. חֲבַקּוּק **Chăbaqqûwq**, *khab-ak-kook´*; by redupl. from 2263; *embrace*; *Chabakkuk*, the prophet:— Habakkuk.

2266. חָבַר **châbar**, *khaw-bar´*; a prim. root; to *join* (lit. or fig.); spec. (by means of spells) to *fascinate*:— charm (-er), be compact, couple (together), have fellowship with, heap up, join (self, together), league.

2267. חֶבֶר **cheber**, *kheh´-ber*; from 2266; a *society*; also a *spell*:— + charmer (-ing), company, enchantment, × wide.

2268. חֶבֶר **Cheber**, *kheh´-ber*; the same as 2267; *community*; *Cheber*, the name of a Kenite and of three Isr.:— Heber.

2269. חֲבַר **chăbar** (Chald.), *khab-ar´*; from a root corresp. to 2266; an *associate*:— companion, fellow.

2270. חָבֵר **châbêr**, *khaw-bare´*; from 2266; an *associate*:— companion, fellow, knit together.

2271. חַבָּר **chabbâr**, *khab-bawr´*; from 2266; a *partner*:— companion.

2272. חֲבַרְבֻּרָה **chăbarbûrâh**, *khab-arboo-raw´*; by redupl. from 2266; a *streak* (like a *line*), as on the tiger:— spot.

2273. חֲבְרָה **chabrâh** (Chald.), *khabraw´*; fem. of 2269; an *associate*:— other.

2274. חֶבְרָה **chebrâh**, *kheb-raw´*; fem. of 2267; *association*:— company.

2275. חֶבְרוֹן **Chebrôwn**, *kheb-rone´*; from 2267; seat of *association*; *Chebron*, a place in Pal.; also the name of two Isr.:— Hebron.

2276. חֶבְרוֹנִי **Chebrôwnîy**, *kheb-ro-nee´*; or

חֶבְרֹנִי **Chebrônîy**, *kheb-ro-nee´*; patron. from 2275; *Chebronite* (collect.), an inhab. of Chebron:— Hebronites.

2277. חֶבְרִי **Chebrîy**, *kheb-ree´*; patron. from 2268; a *Chebrite* (collect.) or desc. of Cheber:— Heberites.

2278. חֲבֶרֶת **chăbereth**, *khab-eh´-reth*; fem. of 2270; a *consort*:— companion.

2279. חֹבֶרֶת **chôbereth**, *kho-beh´-reth*; fem. act. part. of 2266; a *joint*:— which coupleth, coupling.

2280. חָבַשׁ **châbash**, *khaw-bash´*; a prim. root; to *wrap* firmly (espec. a turban, compress, or *saddle*); fig. to *stop*, to *rule*:— bind (up), gird about, govern, healer, put, saddle, wrap about.

2281. חָבֵת **châbêth**, *khaw-bayth´*; from an unused root prob. mean. to *cook* [comp. 4227]; something *fried*, prob. a griddle-*cake*:— pan.

2282. חַג **chag**, *khag*; or

חָג **châg**, *khawg*; from 2287; a *festival*, or a *victim* therefore:— (solemn) feast (day), sacrifice, solemnity.

2283. חָגָא **châgâ'**, *khaw-gaw´*; from an unused root mean. to *revolve* [comp. 2287]; prop. *vertigo*, i.e. (fig.) *fear*:— terror.

2284. חָגָב **châgâb**, *khaw-gawb´*; of uncert. der.; a *locust*:— locust.

2285. חָגָב **Chăgâb**, *khaw-gawb´*; the same as 2284; *locust*; *Chagab*, one of the Nethinim:— Hagab.

2286. חֲגָבָא **Chăgâbâ'**, *khag-aw-baw´*; or

חֲגָבָה **Chăgâbâh**, *khag-aw-baw´*; fem. of 2285; *locust*; *Chagaba* or *Chagabah*, one of the Nethinim:— Hagaba, Hagabah.

2287. חָגַג **châgag**, *khaw-gag´*; a prim. root [comp. 2283, 2328]; prop. to move in a *circle*, i.e. (spec.) to *march* in a sacred procession, to *observe* a festival; by impl. to *be giddy*:— celebrate, dance, (keep, hold) a (solemn) feast (holiday), reel to and fro.

2288. חֲגָו **chăgâv**, *khag-awv´*; from an unused root mean. to *take refuge*; a *rift* in rocks:— cleft.

2289. חָגוֹר **châgôwr**, *khaw-gore´*; from 2296; *belted*:— girded with.

2290. חֲגוֹר **chăgôwr**, *khag-ore´*; or

חֲגֹר **chăgôr**, *khag-ore´*; and (fem.)

חֲגוֹרָה **chăgôwrâh**, *khag-o-raw´*; or

חֲגֹרָה **chăgôrâh**, *khag-o-raw´*; from 2296; a *belt* (for the waist):— apron, armour, gird (-le).

2291. חַגִּי **Chaggîy**, *khag-ghee´*; from 2287; *festive*, *Chaggi*, an Isr.; also (patron.) a *Chaggite*, or desc. of the same:— Haggi, Haggites.

2292. חַגַּי **Chaggay**, *khag-gah´-ee*; from 2282; *festive*; *Chaggai*, a Heb. prophet:— Haggai.

2293. חֲגִיָּה **Chaggîyâh**, *khag-ghee-yaw´*; from 2282 and 3050; *festival of Jah*; *Chaggijah*, an Isr.:— Haggiah.

2294. חַגִּית **Chaggîyith**, *khag-gheeth´*; fem. of 2291; *festive*; *Chaggith*, a wife of David:— Haggith.

2295. חָגְלָה **Choglâh**, *khog-law´*; of uncert. der.; prob. a *partridge*; *Choglah*, an Israelitess:— Hoglah. See also 1031.

2296. חָגַר **châgar**, *khaw-gar´*; a prim. root; to *gird* on (as a belt, armor, etc.):— be able to put on, be afraid, appointed, gird, restrain, × on every side.

2297. חַד **chad**, *khad*; abridged from 259; *one*:— one.

2298. חַד **chad** (Chald.), *khad*, corresp. to 2297; as card. *one*; as art. *single*; as an ord. *first*; adv. *at once*:— a, first, one, together.

2299. חַד **chad**, *khad*; from 2300; *sharp*:— sharp.

2300. חָדַד **châdad**, *khaw-dad´*; a prim. root; to *be* (caus. *make*) *sharp* or (fig.) *severe*:— be fierce, sharpen.

2301. חֲדַד **Chădad**, *khad-ad´*; from 2300; *fierce*; *Chadad*, an Ishmaelite:— Hadad.

2302. חָדָה **châdâh**, *khaw-daw´*; a prim. root; to *rejoice*:— make glad, be joined, rejoice.

2303. חַדּוּד **chaddûwd**, *khad-dood´*; from 2300; a *point*:— sharp.

2304. חֶדְוָה **chedvâh**, *khed-vaw´*; from 2302; *rejoicing*:— gladness, joy.

2305. חֶדְוָה **chedvâh** (Chald.), *khed-vaw´*; corresp. to 2304:— joy.

2306. חֲדִי **chădîy** (Chald.), *khad-ee´*; corresp. to 2373; a *breast*:— breast.

2307. חָדִיד **Châdîyd**, *khaw-deed´*; from 2300; a *peak*; *Chadid*, a place in Pal.:— Hadid.

2308. חָדַל **châdal**, *khaw-dal´*; a prim. root; prop. to *be flabby*, i.e. (by impl.) *desist*; (fig.) *be lacking* or *idle*:— cease,

end, fail, forbear, forsake, leave (off), let alone, rest, be unoccupied, want.

2309. חֶדֶל **chedel**, *kheh´-del*; from 2308; *rest*, i.e. the state of the *dead*:— world.

2310. חָדֵל **châdêl**, *khaw-dale´*; from 2308; *vacant*, i.e. *ceasing* or *destitute*:— he that forbeareth, frail, rejected.

2311. חַדְלַי **Chadlay**, *khad-lah´-ee*; from 2309; *idle*; *Chadlai*, an Isr.:— Hadlai.

2312. חֵדֶק **chêdeq**, *khay´-dek*; from an unused root mean. to *sting*; a *prickly* plant:— brier, thorn.

2313. חִדֶּקֶל **Chiddeqel**, *khid-deh´-kel*; prob. of for. or.; the *Chiddekel* (or Tigris) river:— Hiddekel.

2314. חָדַר **châdar**, *khaw-dar´*; a prim. root; prop. to *inclose* (as a room), i.e. (by anal.) to *beset* (as in a siege):— enter a privy chamber.

2315. חֶדֶר **cheder**, *kheh´-der*; from 2314; an *apartment* (usually lit.):— [bed] inner) chamber, innermost (-ward) part, parlour, + south, × within.

2316. חֲדַר **Chădar**, *khad-ar´*; another form for 2315; *chamber*; *Chadar*, an Ishmaelite:— Hadar.

2317. חַדְרָךְ **Chadrâk**, *khad-rawk´*; of uncert. der.; *Chadrak*, a Syrian deity:— Hadrach.

2318. חָדַשׁ **châdash**, *khaw-dash´*; a prim. root; to *be new*; caus. to *rebuild*:— renew, repair.

2319. חָדָשׁ **châdâsh**, *khaw-dawsh´*; from 2318; *new*:— fresh, new thing.

2320. חֹדֶשׁ **chôdesh**, *kho´-desh*; from 2318; the *new* moon; by impl. a *month*:— month (-ly), new moon.

2321. חֹדֶשׁ **Chôdesh**, *kho´-desh*; the same as 2320; *Chodesh*, an Israelitess:— Hodesh.

2322. חֲדָשָׁה **Chădâshâh**, *khad-aw-shaw´*; fem. of 2319; *new*; *Chadashah*, a place in Pal.:— Hadashah.

2323. חֲדַת **chădath** (Chald.), *khad-ath´*; corresp. to 2319; *new*:— new.

2324. חֲוָא **chăvâ'** (Chald.), *khav-aw´*; corresp. to 2331; to *show*:— shew.

2325. חוּב **chûwb**, *khoob*; also

חָיַב **châyab**, *khaw-yab´*; a prim. root; prop. perh. to *tie*, i.e. (fig. and refl.) to *owe*, or (by impl.) to *forfeit*:— make endanger.

2326. חוֹב **chôwb**, *khobe*; from 2325; *debt*:— debtor.

2327. חוֹבָה **chôwbâh**, *kho-baw´*; fem. act. part. of 2247; *hiding* place; *Chobah*, a place in Syria:— Hobah.

2328. חוּג **chûwg**, *khoog*; a prim. root [comp. 2287]; to describe a *circle*:— compass.

2329. חוּג **chûwg**, *khoog*; from 2328; a *circle*:— circle, circuit, compass.

2330. חוּד **chûwd**, *khood*; a prim. root; prop. to *tie* a knot, i.e. (fig.) to *propound* a riddle:— put forth.

2331. חָוָה **châvâh**, *khaw-vah´*; a prim. root; [comp. 2324, 2421]; prop. to *live*; by impl. (intens.) to *declare* or *show*:— show.

2332. חַוָּה **Chavvâh**, *khav-vaw´*; caus.

from 2331; *life-giver; Chavvah* (or Eve), the first woman:— Eve.

2333. חַוָּה **chavvâh**, *khav-vaw´*; prop. the same as 2332 (*life-giving*, i.e. *living-place*); by impl. an encampment or *village*:— (small) town.

2334. חַוֹּת יָעִיר **Chavvôwth Yâ'îyr**, *khav-vothe´ yaw-eer´*; from the plural of 2333 and a modif. of 3265; *hamlets of Jair*, a region of Pal.:— [Bashan-] Havoth-jair.

2335. חוֹזַי **Chôwzay**, *kho-zah´-ee*; from 2374; *visionary; Chozai*, an Isr.:— the seers.

2336. חוֹחַ **chôwach**, *kho´-akh*; from an unused root appar. mean. to *pierce*; a *thorn*; by anal. a *ring* for the nose:— bramble, thistle, thorn.

2337. חָוָח **châvâch**, *khaw-vawkh´*; perh. the same as 2336; a *dell* or *crevice* (as if *pierced* in the earth):— thicket.

2338. חוּט **chûwṭ** (Chald.), *khoot*; corresp. to the root of 2339, perhaps as a denom.; to *string* together, i.e. (fig.) to *repair*:— join.

2339. חוּט **chûwṭ**, *khoot*; from an unused root prob. mean. to *sew*; a *string*; by impl. a measuring *tape*:— cord, fillet, line, thread.

2340. חִוִּי **Chivvîy**, *khiv-vee´*; perh. from 2333; a *villager*; a *Chivvite*, one of the aboriginal tribes of Pal.:— Hivite.

2341. חֲוִילָה **Chăvîylâh**, *khav-ee-law´*; prob. from 2342; *circular; Chavilah*, the name of two or three eastern regions; also perh. of two men:— Havilah.

2342. חוּל **chûwl**, *khool*; or

חִיל **chîyl**, *kheel*; a prim. root; prop. to *twist* or *whirl* (in a circular or spiral manner), i.e. to *dance*, to *writhe* in pain (espec. of parturition) or fear; fig. to *wait*, to *pervert*:— bear, (make to) bring forth, (make to) calve, dance, drive away, fall grievously (with pain), fear, form, great, grieve, (be) grievous, hope, look, make, be in pain, be much (sore) pained, rest, shake, shapen, (be) sorrow (-ful), stay, tarry, travail (with pain), tremble, trust, wait carefully (patiently), be wounded.

2343. חוּל **Chûwl**, *khool*; from 2342; a *circle; Chul*, a son of Aram; also the region settled by him:— Hul.

2344. חוֹל **chôwl**, *khole*; from 2342; *sand* (as *round* or whirling particles):— sand.

2345. חוּם **chûwm**, *khoom*; from an unused root mean. to *be warm*, i.e. (by impl.) *sunburnt* or *swarthy* (blackish):— brown.

2346. חוֹמָה **chôwmâh**, *kho-maw´*; fem. act. part. of an unused root appar. mean. to *join*; a *wall* of protection:— wall, walled.

2347. חוּס **chûwç**, *khoos*; a prim. root; prop. to *cover*, i.e. (fig.) to *compassionate*:— pity, regard, spare.

2348. חוֹף **chôwph**, *khofe*; from an unused root mean. to *cover*; a *cove* (as a *sheltered* bay):— coast [of the seal, haven, shore, [sea-] side.

2349. חוּפָם **Chûwphâm**, *khoo-fawm´*; from the same as 2348; *protection; Chupham*, an Isr.:— Hupham.

2350. חוּפָמִי **Chûwphâmiy**, *khoo-faw-mee´*; patron. from 2349; a *Chuphamite* or desc. of Chupham:— Huphamites.

2351. חוּץ **chûwts**, *khoots*; or (short.)

חֻץ **chûts**, *khoots*; (both forms fem. in the plur.) from an unused root mean. to *sever*; prop. *separate* by a wall, i.e. *outside, outdoors*:— abroad, field, forth, highway, more, out (-side, -ward), street, without.

2352. חוּר **chûwr**, *khoor*; or (short.)

חֻר **chûr**, *khoor*; from an unused root prob. mean. to *bore*; the *crevice* of a serpent; the *cell* of a prison:— hole.

2353. חוּר **chûwr**, *khoor*; from 2357; *white* linen:— white.

2354. חוּר **Chûwr**, *khoor*; the same as 2353 or 2352; *Chur*, the name of four Isr. and one Midianite:— Hur.

2355. חוֹר **chôwr**, *khore*; the same as 2353; *white* linen:— network. Comp. 2715.

2356. חוֹר **chôwr**, *khore*; or (short.)

חֹר **chôr**, *khore*; the same as 2352; a *cavity, socket, den*:— cave, hole.

2357. חָוַר **châvar**, *khaw-var´*; a prim. root; to *blanch* (as with shame):— wax pale.

2358. חִוָּר **chivvâr** (Chald.), *khiv-vawr´*; from a root corresp. to 2357; *white*:— white.

2359. חוֹרוֹן **Chôwrôwn**. See 1032.

חוֹרִי **chôwrîy**. See 2753.

2359. חוּרִי **Chûwrîy**, *khoo-ree´*; prob. from 2353; *linen*-worker; *Churi*, an Isr.:— Huri.

2360. חוּרַי **Chûwray**, *khoo-rah´ee*; prob. an orth. var. for 2359; *Churai*, an Isr.:— Hurai.

2361. חוּרָם **Chûwrâm**, *khoo-rawm´*; prob. from 2353; *whiteness*, i.e. noble; *Churam*, the name of an Isr. and two Syrians:— Huram. Comp. 2438.

2362. חַוְרָן **Chavrân**, *khav-rawn´*; appar. from 2357 (in the sense of 2352); *cavernous; Chavran*, a region E. of the Jordan:— Hauran.

2363. חוּשׁ **chûwsh**, *koosh*; a prim. root; to *hurry*; fig. to *be eager* with excitement or enjoyment:— (make) haste (-n), ready.

2364. חוּשָׁה **Chûwshâh**, *khoo-shaw´*; from 2363; *haste; Chushah*, an Isr.:— Hushah.

2365. חוּשַׁי **Chûwshay**, *khoo-shah´-ee*; from 2363; *hasty; Chushai*, an Isr.:— Hushai.

2366. חוּשִׁים **Chûwshîym**, *khoo-sheem´*; or

חֻשִׁים **Chûshîym**, *khoo-sheem´*; or

חֻשִׁם **Chushîm**, *khoo-sheem´*; plur. from 2363; *hasters; Chushim*, the name of three Isr.:— Hushim.

2367. חוּשָׁם **Chûwshâm**, *khoo-shawm´*; or

חֻשָׁם **Chushâm**, *khoo-shawm´*; from 2363; *hastily; Chusham*, an Idumæan:— Husham.

2368. חוֹתָם **chôwthâm**, *kho-thawm´*; or

חֹתָם **chôthâm**, *kho-thawm´*; from 2856; a *signature*-ring:— seal, signet.

2369. חוֹתָם **Chôwthâm**, *kho-thawm´*; the same as 2368; *seal; Chotham*, the name of two Isr.:— Hotham, Hothan.

2370. חֲזָא **chăzâ'** (Chald.), *khaz-aw´*; or

חֲזָה **chăzâh** (Chald.), *khaz-aw´*; corresp. to 2372; to *gaze* upon; ment. to *dream, be usual* (i.e. *seem*):— behold, have [a dream], see, be wont.

2371. חֲזָאֵל **Chăzâ'êl**, *khaz-aw-ale´*; or

חֲזָהאֵל **Chăzâh'êl**, *khaz-aw-ale´*; from 2372 and 410; *God has seen; Chazaël*, a king of Syria:— Hazael.

2372. חָזָה **châzâh**, *khaw-zaw´*; a prim. root; to *gaze* at; ment. to *perceive, contemplate* (with pleasure); spec. to *have a vision of*:— behold, look, prophesy, provide, see.

2373. חָזֶה **châzeh**, *khaw-zeh´*; from 2372; the *breast* (as most *seen* in front):— breast.

2374. חֹזֶה **chôzeh**, *kho-zeh´*; act. part. of 2372; a *beholder* in vision; also a *compact* (as *looked upon* with approval):— agreement, prophet, see that, seer, [star-] gazer.

חֲזָהאֵל **Chăzâh'êl**. See 2371.

2375. חֲזוֹ **Chăzow**, *khaz-o´*; from 2372; *seer; Chazo*, a nephew of Abraham:— Hazo.

2376. חֵזֶו **chêzev** (Chald.), *khay´-zev*; from 2370; a *sight*:— look, vision.

2377. חָזוֹן **châzôwn**, *khaw-zone´*; from 2372; a *sight* (ment.), i.e. a *dream, revelation*, or *oracle*:— vision.

2378. חָזוֹת **châzôwth**, *khaw-zooth´*; from 2372; a *revelation*:— vision.

2379. חֲזוֹת **chăzôwth** (Chald.), *khaz-oth´*; from 2370; a *view*:— sight.

2380. חָזוּת **châzûwth**, *khaw-zooth´*; from 2372; a *look*; hence, (fig.) striking *appearance, revelation*, or (by impl.) *compact*:— agreement, notable (one), vision.

2381. חֲזִיאֵל **Chăzîy'êl**, *khaz-ee-ale´*; from 2372 and 410; *seen of God; Chaziel*, a Levite:— Haziel.

2382. חֲזָיָה **Chăzâyâh**, *khaz-aw-yaw´*; from 2372 and 3050; *Jah has seen; Chazajah*, an Isr.:— Hazaiah.

2383. חֶזְיוֹן **Chezyôwn**, *khez-yone´*; from 2372; *vision; Chezjon*, a Syrian:— Hezion.

2384. חִזָּיוֹן **chizzâyôwn**, *khiz-zaw-yone´*; from 2372; a *revelation*, espec. by *dream*:— vision.

2385. חֲזִיז **chăzîyz**, *khaw-zeez´*; from an unused root mean. to *glare*; a *flash* of lightning:— bright cloud, lightning.

2386. חֲזִיר **chăzîyr**, *khaw-zeer´*; from an unused root prob. mean. to *inclose*; a *hog* (perh. as *penned*):— boar, swine.

2387. חֵזִיר **Chêzîyr**, *khay-zeer´*; from the same as 2386; perh. *protected; Chezir*, the name of two Isr.:— Hezir.

2388. חָזַק **châzaq**, *khaw-zak´*; a prim. root; to *fasten* upon; hence, to *seize*, be *strong* (fig. *courageous*, caus. *strengthen, cure, help, repair, fortify*), *obstinate;* to *bind, restrain, conquer:*— aid, amend, × calker, catch, cleave, confirm, be constant, constrain, continue, be of good (take) courage (-ous, -ly), encourage (self), be established, fasten, force, fortify, make hard, harden, help, (lay) hold (fast), lean, maintain, play the man, mend, become (wax) mighty, prevail, be recovered, repair, retain, seize, be (wax) sore, strengthen (self), be stout, be (make, shew, wax) strong (-er), be sure, take (hold), be urgent, behave self valiantly, withstand.

2389. חָזָק **châzâq,** *khaw-zawk';* from 2388; *strong* (usually in a bad sense, *hard, bold, violent*):— harder, hottest, + impudent, loud, mighty, sore, stiff [-hearted], strong (-er).

2390. חָזֵק **châzêq,** *khaw-zake';* from 2388; *powerful:*— × wax louder, stronger.

2391. חֵזֶק **chêzeq,** *khay'-zek;* from 2388; *help:*— strength.

2392. חֹזֶק **chôzeq,** *kho'-zek;* from 2388; *power:*— strength.

2393. חֶזְקָה **chezqâh,** *khez-kaw';* fem. of 2391; *prevailing power:*— strength (-en self), (was) strong.

2394. חָזְקָה **chozqâh,** *khoz-kaw';* fem. of 2392; *vehemence* (usually in a bad sense):— force, mightily, repair, sharply.

2395. חִזְקִי **Chizqiy,** *khiz-kee';* from 2388; *strong; Chizki,* an Isr.:— Hezeki.

2396. חִזְקִיָּה **Chizqîyâh,** *khiz-kee-yaw';* or

חִזְקִיָּהוּ **Chizqîyâhûw,** *khiz-kee-yaw'-hoo;* also

יְחִזְקִיָּה **Yᵉchizqîyâh,** *yekh-iz-kee-yaw';* or

יְחִזְקִיָּהוּ **Yᵉchizqîyâhûw,** *yekh-iz-kee-yaw'-hoo;* from 2388 and 3050; *strengthened of Jah; Chizkijah,* a king of Judah, also the name of two other Isr.:— Hezekiah, Hizkiah, Hizkijah. Comp. 3169.

2397. חָח **châch,** *khawkh;* once (Ezek. 29:4)

חָחִי **châchiy,** *khakh-ee';* from the same as 2336; a *ring* for the nose (or lips):— bracelet, chain, hook.

2398. חָטָא **châtâ',** *khaw-taw';* a prim. root; prop. to *miss;* hence, (fig. and gen.) to *sin;* by infer. to *forfeit, lack, expiate, repent,* (caus.) *lead astray, condemn:*— bear the blame, cleanse, commit [sin], by fault, harm he hath done, loss, miss, (make) offend (-er), offer for sin, purge, purify (self), make reconciliation, (cause, make) sin (-ful, -ness), trespass.

2399. חֵטְא **chêt',** *khate;* from 2398; a *crime* or its *penalty:*— fault, × grievously, offence, (punishment of) sin.

2400. חַטָּא **chattâ',** *khat-taw';* intens. from 2398; a *criminal,* or one accounted *guilty:*— offender, sinful, sinner.

2401. חֲטָאָה **chătâ'âh,** *khat-aw-aw';* fem. of 2399; an *offence,* or a *sacrifice* for it:— sin (offering), sinful.

2402. חֲטָאָה **chattâ'âh** (Chald.), *khat-taw-aw';* corresp. to 2401; an *offence,* and the *penalty* or *sacrifice* for it:— sin (offering).

2403. חַטָּאָה **chattâ'âh,** *khat-taw-aw';* or

חַטָּאת **chattâ'th,** *khat-tawth';* from 2398; an *offence* (sometimes habitual *sinfulness*), and its penalty, occasion, sacrifice, or expiation; also (concr.) an *offender:*— punishment (of sin), purifying (-fication for sin), sin (-ner, offering).

2404. חָטַב **châtab,** *khaw-tab';* a prim. root; to *chop* or *carve* wood:— cut down, hew (-er), polish.

2405. חֲטֻבָה **chătûbâh,** *khat-oo-baw';* fem. pass. part. of 2404; prop. a *carving;* hence, a *tapestry* (as figured):— carved.

2406. חִטָּה **chittâh,** *khit-taw';* of uncert. der.; *wheat,* whether the grain or the plant:— wheat (-en).

2407. חַטּוּשׁ **Chattûwsh,** *khat-toosh';* from an unused root of uncert. signif.; *Chattush,* the name of four or five Isr.:— Hattush.

2408. חֲטִי **chătiy** (Chald.), *khat-ee';* from a root corresp. to 2398; an *offence:*— sin.

2409. חַטָּיָא **chattâyâ'** (Chald.), *khat-taw-yaw';* from the same as 2408; an *expiation:*— sin offering.

2410. חֲטִיטָא **Chătîyta',** *khat-ee-taw';* from an unused root appar. mean. to *dig out; explorer; Chatita,* a temple porter:— Hatita.

2411. חַטִּיל **Chattîyl,** *khat-teel';* from an unused root appar. mean. to *wave; fluctuating; Chattil,* one of "Solomon's servants":— Hattil.

2412. חֲטִיפָא **Chătîyphâ',** *khat-ee-faw';* from 2414; *robber; Chatipha,* one of the Nethinim:— Hatipha.

2413. חָטַם **châtam,** *khaw-tam';* a prim. root; to *stop:*— refrain.

2414. חָטַף **châtaph,** *khaw-taf';* a prim. root; to *clutch;* hence, to *seize* as a prisoner:— catch.

2415. חֹטֵר **chôter,** *kho'-ter;* from an unused root of uncert. signif.; a *twig:*— rod.

2416. חַי **chay,** *khah'-ee;* from 2421; *alive;* hence, *raw* (flesh); *fresh* (plant, water, year), *strong;* also (as noun, espec. in the fem. sing. and masc. plur.) *life* (or living thing), whether lit. or fig.:— + age, alive, appetite, (wild) beast, company, congregation, life (-time), live (-ly), living (creature, thing), maintenance, + merry, multitude, + (be) old, quick, raw, running, springing, troop.

2417. חַי **chay** (Chald.), *khah'-ee;* from 2418; *alive;* also (as noun in plur.) *life:*— life, that liveth, living.

2418. חֲיָא **chăyâ'** (Chald.), *khah-yaw';* or

חֲיָה **chăyâh** (Chald.), *khah-yaw';* corresp. to 2421; to *live:*— live, keep alive.

2419. חִיאֵל **Chîy'êl,** *khee-ale';* from 2416 and 410; *living of God; Chiel,* an Isr.:— Hiel.

2420. חִידָה **chîydâh,** *khee-daw';* from 2330; a *puzzle,* hence, a *trick, conundrum,* sententious *maxim:*— dark saying (sentence, speech), hard question, proverb, riddle.

2421. חָיָה **châyâh,** *khaw-yaw';* a prim. root [comp. 2331, 2421]; to *live,* whether lit. or fig.; caus. to *revive:*— keep (leave, make) alive, × certainly, give (promise) life, (let, suffer to) live, nourish up, preserve (alive), quicken, recover, repair, restore (to life), revive, (× God) save (alive, life, lives), × surely, be whole.

2422. חָיֶה **châyeh,** *khaw-yeh';* from 2421; *vigorous:*— lively.

2423. חֵיוָא **chêyvâ'** (Chald.), *khay-vaw';* from 2418; an *animal:*— beast.

2424. חַיּוּת **chayûwth,** *khah-yooth';* from 2421; *life:*— × living.

2425. חָיַי **châyay,** *khaw-yah'-ee;* a prim. root [comp. 2421]; to *live;* caus. to *revive:*— live, save life.

2426. חֵיל **chêyl,** *khale;* or (short.)

חֵל **chêl,** *khale;* a collat. form of 2428; an *army;* also (by anal.) an *intrenchment:*— army, bulwark, host, + poor, rampart, trench, wall.

חִיל **chîyl.** See 2342.

2427. חִיל **chîyl,** *kheel;* and (fem.)

חִילָה **chîylâh,** *khee-law';* from 2342; a *throe* (espec. of childbirth):— pain, pang, sorrow.

2428. חַיִל **chayil,** *khah'-yil;* from 2342; prob. a *force,* whether of men, means or other resources; an *army, wealth, virtue, valor, strength:*— able, activity, (+) army, band of men (soldiers), company, (great) forces, goods, host, might, power, riches, strength, strong, substance, train, (+) valiant (-ly), valour, virtuous (-ly), war, worthy (-ily).

2429. חַיִל **chayil** (Chald.), *khah'-yil;* corresp. to 2428; an *army,* or *strength:*— aloud, army, × most [mighty], power.

2430. חֵילָה **chêylâh,** *khay-law';* fem. of 2428; an *intrenchment:*— bulwark.

2431. חֵילָם **Chêylâm,** *khay-lawm';* or

חֵלָאם **Chêlâ'm,** *khay-lawm';* from 2428; *fortress; Chelam,* a place E. of Pal.:— Helam.

2432. חִילֵן **Chîylên,** *khee-lane';* from 2428; *fortress; Chilen,* a place in Pal.:— Hilen.

2433. חִין **chîyn,** *kheen;* another form for 2580; *beauty:*— comely.

2434. חַיִץ **chayits,** *khah'-yits;* another form for 2351; a *wall:*— wall.

2435. חִיצוֹן **chîytsôwn,** *khee-tsone';* from 2434; prop. the (outer) *wall side;* hence, *exterior;* fig. *secular* (as opposed to sacred):— outer, outward, utter, without.

2436. חֵיק **chêyq,** *khake;* or

חֵק **chêq,** *khake;* and

חוֹק **chôwq,** *khoke;* from an unused root, appar. mean. to *inclose;* the *bosom* (lit. or fig.):— bosom, bottom, lap, midst, within.

2437. חִירָה **Chîyrâh,** *khee-raw';* from

2357 in the sense of *splendor; Chirah*, an Adullamite:— Hirah.

2438. חִירָם **Chîyrâm**, *khee-rawm´*; or

חִירוֹם **Chîyrôm**, *khee-rome´*; another form of 2361; *Chiram* or *Chirom*, the name of two Tyrians:— Hiram, Huram.

2439. חִישׁ **chîysh**, *kheesh;* another form of 2363; to *hurry:*— make haste.

2440. חִישׁ **chîysh**, *kheesh;* from 2439; prop. a *hurry;* hence, (adv.) *quickly:*— soon.

2441. חֵךְ **chêk**, *khake;* prob. from 2596 in the sense of *tasting;* prop. the *palate* or inside of the mouth; hence, the *mouth* itself (as the organ of speech, taste and kissing):— (roof of the) mouth, taste.

2442. חָכָה **châkâh**, *khaw-kaw´;* a prim. root [appar. akin to 2707 through the idea of *piercing*]; prop. to *adhere* to; hence, to *await:*— long, tarry, wait.

2443. חַכָּה **chakkâh**, *khak-kaw´;* prob. from 2442; a *hook* (as *adhering*):— angle, hook.

2444. חֲכִילָה **Chakîylâh**, *khak-ee-law´;* from the same as 2447; *dark; Chakilah*, a hill in Pal.:— Hachilah.

2445. חַכִּים **chakkîym** (Chald.), *khak-keem´;* from a root corresp. to 2449; *wise*, i.e. a *Magian:*— wise.

2446. חֲכַלְיָה **Chăkalyâh**, *khak-al-yaw´;* from the base of 2447 and 3050; *darkness* (of) *Jah; Chakaljah*, an Isr.:— Hachaliah.

2447. חַכְלִיל **chaklîyl**, *khak-leel´;* by redupl. from an unused root appar. mean. to *be dark;* darkly *flashing* (only of the eyes); in a good sense, *brilliant* (as stimulated by wine):— red.

2448. חַכְלִלוּת **chaklîlûwth**, *khak-lee-looth´;* from 2447; *flash* (of the eyes); in a bad sense, *blearedness.*— redness.

2449. חָכַם **châkam**, *khaw-kam´;* a prim. root, to *be wise* (in mind, word or act):— × exceeding, teach wisdom, be (make self, shew self) wise, deal (never so) wisely, make wiser.

2450. חָכָם **châkâm**, *khaw-kawm´;* from 2449; *wise*, (i.e. intelligent, skilful or artful):— cunning (man), subtil, (un-)wise [hearted], man).

2451. חָכְמָה **chokmâh**, *khok-maw´;* from 2449; *wisdom* (in a good sense):— skilful, wisdom, wisely, wit.

2452. חָכְמָה **chokmâh** (Chald.), *khok-maw´;* corresp. to 2451; *wisdom:*— wisdom.

2453. חַכְמוֹנִי **Chakmôwnîy**, *khak-mo-nee´;* from 2449; *skilful; Chakmoni*, an Isr.:— Hachmoni, Hachmonite.

2454. חָכְמוֹת **chokmôwth**, *khok-môth´;* or

חַכְמוֹת **chakmôwth**, *khak-môth´;* collat. forms of 2451; *wisdom*, every wise [woman]:— wisdom.

חֵל **chêl**. See 2426.

2455. חֹל **chôl**, *khole;* from 2490; prop. *exposed;* hence, *profane:*— common, profane (place), unholy.

2456. חָלָא **châlâ'**, *khaw-law´;* a prim.

---

root [comp. 2470]; to *be sick:*— be diseased.

2457. חֶלְאָה **chel'âh**, *khel-aw´;* from 2456; prop. *disease;* hence, *rust:*— scum.

2458. חֶלְאָה **Chel'âh**, *khel-aw´;* the same as 2457; *Chelah*, an Israelitess:— Helah.

2459. חֶלֶב **cheleb**, *kheh´-leb;* or

חֵלֶב **chêleb**, *khay´-leb;* from an unused root mean. to *be fat; fat*, whether lit. or fig.; hence, the *richest* or *choice* part:— × best, fat (-ness), × finest, grease, marrow.

2460. חֵלֶב **Chêleb**, *khay´-leb;* the same as 2459; *fatness; Cheleb*, an Isr.:— Heleb.

2461. חָלָב **châlâb**, *khaw-lawb´;* from the same as 2459; *milk* (as the *richness* of kine):— + cheese, milk, sucking.

2462. חֶלְבָּה **Chelbâh**, *khel-baw´;* fem. of 2459; *fertility; Chelbah*, a place in Pal.:— Helbah.

2463. חֶלְבּוֹן **Chelbôwn**, *khel-bone´;* from 2459; *fruitful; Chelbon*, a place in Syria:— Helbon.

2464. חֶלְבְּנָה **chelbᵉnâh**, *khel-ben-aw´;* from 2459; *galbanum*, an odorous gum (as if *fatty*):— galbanum.

2465. חֶלֶד **cheled**, *kheh´-led;* from an unused root appar. mean. to *glide* swiftly; *life* (as a *fleeting* portion of time); hence, the *world* (as *transient*):— age, short time, world.

2466. חֵלֶד **Chêled**, *khay´-led;* the same as 2465; *Cheled*, an Isr.:— Heled.

2467. חֹלֶד **chôled**, *kho´-led;* from the same as 2465; a *weasel* (from its *gliding* motion):— weasel.

2468. חֻלְדָּה **Chuldâh**, *khool-daw´;* fem. of 2467; *Chuldah*, an Israelitess:— Huldah.

2469. חֶלְדַּי **Chelday**, *khel-dah´-ee;* from 2466; *worldliness; Cheldai*, the name of two Isr.:— Heldai.

2470. חָלָה **châlâh**, *khaw-law´;* a prim. root [comp. 2342, 2470, 2490]; prop. to *be rubbed* or *worn;* hence, (fig.) to *be weak, sick, afflicted;* or (caus.) to *grieve, make sick;* also to *stroke* (in flattering), *entreat:*— beseech, (be) diseased, (put to) grief, be grieved, (be) grievous, infirmity, intreat, lay to, put to pain, × pray, make prayer, be (fall, make) sick, sore, be sorry, make suit (× supplication), woman in travail, be (become) weak, be wounded.

2471. חַלָּה **challâh**, *khal-law´;* from 2490; a *cake* (as usually *punctured*):— cake.

2472. חֲלֹם **chălôm**, *khal-ome´;* or (short.)

חֲלֹם **chălôm**, *khal-ome´;* from 2492; a *dream:*— dream (-er).

2473. חֹלוֹן **Chôlôwn**, *kho-lone´;* or (short.)

חֹלֹן **Chôlôn**, *kho-lone´;* prob. from 2344; *sandy; Cholon*, the name of two places in Pal.:— Holon.

2474. חַלּוֹן **challôwn**, *khal-lone´;* a *window* (as *perforated*):— window.

2475. חֲלוֹף **chălôwph**, *khal-ofe´;* from

2498; prop. *surviving;* by impl. (collect.) *orphans:*— × destruction.

2476. חֲלוּשָׁה **chălûwshâh**, *khal-oo-shaw´;* fem. pass. part. of 2522; *defeat:*— being overcome.

2477. חֲלַח **Chălach**, *khal-akh´;* prob. of for. or.; *Chalach*, a region of Assyria:— Halah.

2478. חַלְחוּל **Chalchûwl**, *khal-khool´;* by redupl. from 2342; *contorted; Chalchul*, a place in Pal.:— Halhul.

2479. חַלְחָלָה **chalchâlâh**, *khal-khaw-law´;* fem. from the same as 2478; *writhing* (in childbirth); by impl. *terror:*— (great, much) pain.

2480. חָלַט **châlat**, *khaw-lat´;* a prim. root; to *snatch* at:— catch.

2481. חֲלִי **chălîy**, *khal-ee´;* from 2470; a *trinket* (as *polished*):— jewel, ornament.

2482. חֲלִי **Chălîy**, *khal-ee´;* the same as 2481; *Chali*, a place in Pal.:— Hali.

2483. חֳלִי **chŏlîy**, *khol-ee´;* from 2470; *malady, anxiety, calamity:*— disease, grief, (is) sick (-ness).

2484. חֶלְיָה **chelyâh**, *khel-yaw´;* fem. of 2481; a *trinket:*— jewel.

2485. חָלִיל **châlîyl**, *khaw-leel´;* from 2490; a *flute* (as *perforated*):— pipe.

2486. חֲלִילָה **châlîylâh**, *khaw-lee´-law;* or

חֲלִלָה **châlîlâh**, *khaw-lee´-law;* a directive from 2490; lit. *for a profaned thing;* used (interj.) *far be it!:*— be far, (× God) forbid.

2487. חֲלִיפָה **chălîyphâh**, *khal-ee-faw´;* from 2498; *alternation:*— change, course.

2488. חֲלִיצָה **chălîytsâh**, *khal-ee-tsaw´;* from 2503; *spoil:*— armour.

2489. חֵלְכָא **chêlkâ'**, *khay-lek-aw´;* or

חֵלְכָה **chêlᵉkâh**, *khay-lek-aw´;* appar. from an unused root prob. mean. to *be dark* or (fig.) *unhappy;* a *wretch*, i.e. *unfortunate:*— poor.

2490. חָלַל **châlal**, *khaw-lal´;* a prim. root [comp. 2470]; prop. to *bore*, i.e. (by impl.) to *wound*, to *dissolve;* fig. to *profane* (a person, place or thing), to *break* (one's word), to *begin* (as if by an "opening wedge"); denom. (from 2485) to *play* (the flute):— begin (× men began), defile, × break, defile, × eat (as common things), × first, × gather the grape thereof, × take inheritance, pipe, player on instruments, pollute, (cast as) profane (self), prostitute, slay (slain), sorrow, stain, wound.

2491. חָלָל **châlâl**, *khaw-lawl´;* from 2490; *pierced* (espec. to death); fig. *polluted:*— kill, profane, slain (man), × slew, (deadly) wounded.

חֲלִלָה **châlîlâh**. See 2486.

2492. חָלַם **châlam**, *khaw-lam´;* a prim. root; prop. to *bind* firmly, i.e. (by impl.) to *be* (caus. to *make*) *plump;* also (through the fig. sense of *dumbness*) to *dream:*— (cause to) dream (-er), be in good liking, recover.

2493. חֵלֶם **chêlem** (Chald.), *khay´-lem;* from a root corresp. to 2492; a *dream:*— dream.

2494. חלם **Chêlem**, *khay'lem;* from 2492; a *dream; Chelem*, an Isr.:— Helem. Comp. 2469.

2495. חלמות **challâmûwth**, *khal-law-mooth';* from 2492 (in the sense of *insipidity*); prob. *purslain:*— egg.

2496. חלמיש **challâmîysh**, *khal-law-meesh';* prob. from 2492 (in the sense of *hardness*); *flint:*— flint (-y), rock.

2497. חלן **Chêlôn**, *khay-lone';* from 2428; *strong; Chelon*, an Isr.:— Helon.

2498. חלף **châlaph**, *khaw-laf';* a prim. root; prop. to *slide* by, i.e. (by impl.) to *hasten* away, *pass* on, *spring* up, *pierce* or *change:*— abolish, alter, change, cut off, go on forward, grow up, be over, pass (away, on, through), renew, sprout, strike through.

2499. חלף **châlaph** (Chald.), *khal-af';* corresp. to 2498; to *pass* on (of time):— pass.

2500. חלף **chêleph**, *khay'-lef;* from 2498; prop. *exchange;* hence, (as prep.) *instead* of:— × for.

2501. חלף **Cheleph**, *kheh'-lef;* the same as 2500; *change; Cheleph*, a place in Pal.:— Heleph.

2502. חלץ **châlats**, *khaw-lats';* a prim. root; to *pull* off; hence, (intens.) to *strip*, (reflex.) to *depart;* by impl. to *deliver*, *equip* (for fight); *present, strengthen:*— arm (self), (go, ready) armed (× man, soldier), deliver, draw out, make fat, loose, (ready) prepared, put off, take away, withdraw self.

2503. חלץ **Chelets**, *kheh'-lets;* or

חלץ **Chêlets**, *khay'-lets;* from 2502; perh. *strength; Chelets*, the name of two Isr.:— Helez.

2504. חלץ **châlâts**, *khaw-lawts';* from 2502 (in the sense of *strength*); only in the dual; the *loins* (as the seat of vigor):— loins, reins.

2505. חלק **châlaq**, *khaw-lak';* a prim. root; to *be smooth* (fig.); by impl. (as smooth stones were used for *lots*) to *apportion* or *separate:*— deal, distribute, divide, flatter, give, (have, impart (-ner), take away a portion, receive, separate self, (be) smooth (-er).

2506. חלק **chêleq**, *khay'-lek;* from 2505; prop. *smoothness* (of the tongue); also an *allotment:*— flattery, inheritance, part, × partake, portion.

2507. חלק **Chêleq**, *khay'-lek;* the same as 2506; *portion; Chelek*, an Isr.:— Helek.

2508. חלק **châlâq** (Chald.), *khal-awk';* from a root corresp. to 2505; a *part:*— portion.

2509. חלק **châlâq**, *khaw-lawk';* from 2505; *smooth* (espec. of tongue):— flattering, smooth.

2510. חלק **Châlâq**, *khaw-lawk';* the same as 2509; *bare; Chalak*, a mountain of Idumæa:— Halak.

2511. חלק **challâq**, *khal-lawk';* from 2505; *smooth:*— smooth.

2512. חלק **challûq**, *khal-look';* from 2505; *smooth:*— smooth.

2513. חלקה **chelqâh**, *khel-kaw';* fem. of 2506; prop. *smoothness;* fig. *flattery;*

also an *allotment:*— field, flattering (-ry), ground, parcel, part, piece of land (ground), plat, portion, slippery place, smooth (thing).

2514. חלקה **chălaqqâh**, *khal-ak-kaw';* fem. from 2505; *flattery:*— flattery.

2515. חלקה **chăluqqâh**, *khal-ook-kaw';* fem. of 2512; a *distribution:*— division.

2516. חלקי **Chelqîy**, *khel-kee';* patron. from 2507; a *Chelkite* or desc. of Chelek:— Helkites.

2517. חלקי **Chelqay**, *khel-kah'ee;* from 2505; *apportioned; Chelkai*, an Isr.:— Helkai.

2518. חלקיה **Chilqîyâh**, *khil-kee-yaw';* or

חלקיהו **Chilqîyâhûw**, *khil-kee-yaw'-hoo;* from 2506 and 3050; *portion* (of) *Jah; Chilhijah*, the name of eight Isr.:— Hilkiah.

2519. חלקלקה **chălaqlaqqâh**, *khal-ak-lak-kaw';* by redupl. from 2505; prop. something *very smooth;* i.e. a *treacherous* spot; fig. *blandishment:*— flattery, slippery.

2520. חלקת **Chelqath**, *khel-kath';* a form of 2513; *smoothness; Chelkath*, a place in Pal.:— Helkath.

2521. חלקת הצרים **Chelqath hats-Tsûrîym**, *khel-kath' hats-tsoo-reem';* from 2520 and the plur. of 6697, with the art. ins.; *smoothness of the rocks; Chelkath Hats-tsurim*, a place in Pal.:— Helkath-hazzurim.

2522. חלש **châlash**, *khaw-lash';* a prim. root; to *prostrate;* by impl. to *overthrow, decay:*— discomfit, waste away, weaken.

2523. חלש **challâsh**, *khal-lawsh';* from 2522; *frail:*— weak.

2524. חם **châm**, *khawm;* from the same as 2346; a *father-in-law* (as in *affinity*):— father in law.

2525. חם **châm**, *khawm;* from 2552; *hot:*— hot, warm.

2526. חם **Châm**, *khawm;* the same as 2525; *hot* (from the tropical habitat); *Cham*, a son of Noah; also (as a patron.) his desc. or their country:— Ham.

2527. חם **chôm**, *khome;* from 2552; *heat:*— heat, to be hot (warm).

2528. חמא **chêmâ'** (Chald.), *khem-aw';* or

חמה **chămâh** (Chald.), *kham-aw';* corresp. to 2534; *anger:*— fury.

חמא **chêmâ'**. See 2534.

2529. חמאה **chem'âh**, *khem-aw';* or (short.)

חמה **chêmâh**, *khay-maw';* from the same root as 2346; curdled *milk* or *cheese:*— butter.

2530. חמד **châmad**, *khaw-mad';* a prim. root; to *delight* in:— beauty, greatly beloved, covet, delectable thing, (× great) delight, desire, goodly, lust, (be) pleasant (thing), precious (thing).

2531. חמד **chemed**, *kheh'-med;* from 2530; *delight:*— desirable, pleasant.

2532. חמדה **chemdâh**, *khem-daw';* fem. of 2531; *delight:*— desire, goodly, pleasant, precious.

2533. חמדן **Chemdân**, *khem-dawn';* from 2531; *pleasant; Chemdan*, an Idumæan:— Hemdan.

2534. חמה **chêmâh**, *khay-maw';* or (Dan. 11:44)

חמא **chêmâ'**, *khay-maw';* from 3179; *heat;* fig. *anger, poison* (from its *fever*):— anger, bottles, hot displeasure, furious (-ly, -ry), heat, indignation, poison, rage, wrath (-ful). See 2529.

2535. חמה **chammâh**, *kham-maw';* from 2525; *heat;* by impl. the *sun:*— heat, sun.

2536. חמואל **Chammûw'êl**, *kham-moo-ale';* from 2535 and 410; *anger of God; Chammuel*, an Isr.:— Hamuel.

2537. חמוטל **Chămûwṭal**, *kham-oo-tal';* or

חמיטל **Chămîyṭal**, *kham-ee-tal';* from 2524 and 2919; *father-in-law of dew; Chamutal* or *Chamital*, an Israelitess:— Hamutal.

2538. חמול **Châmûwl**, *khaw-mool';* from 2550; *pitied; Chamul*, an Isr.:— Hamul.

2539. חמולי **Châmûwliy**, *khaw-moo-lee';* patron. from 2538: a *Chamulite* (collect.) or desc. of Chamul:— Hamulites.

2540. חמון **Chammôwn**, *kham-mone';* from 2552; *warm* spring; *Chammon*, the name of two places in Pal.:— Hammon.

2541. חמוץ **châmôwts**, *khaw-motse';* from 2556; prop. *violent;* by impl. a *robber:*— oppressed.

2542. חמוק **chammûwq**, *kham-mook';* from 2559; a *wrapping*, i.e. *drawers:*— joints.

2543. חמור **chămôwr**, *kham-ore';* or (short.)

חמר **chămôr**, *kham-ore';* from 2560; a male *ass* (from its dun *red*):— (he) ass.

2544. חמור **Chămôwr**, *kham-ore';* the same as 2543; *ass; Chamor*, a Canaanite:— Hamor.

2545. חמות **chămôwth**, *kham-ōth';* or (short.)

חמה **chămôth**, *kham-ōth';* fem. of 2524; a *mother-in-law:*— mother in law.

2546. חמט **chômeṭ**, *kho'-met;* from an unused root prob. mean. to *lie low;* a *lizard* (as *creeping*):— snail.

2547. חמטה **Chumṭâh**, *khoom-taw';* fem. of 2546; *low; Chumtah*, a place in Pal.:— Humtah.

2548. חמיץ **châmîyts**, *khaw-meets';* from 2556; *seasoned*, i.e. *salt* provender:— clean.

2549. חמישי **chămîyshîy**, *kham-ee-shee';* or

חמשי **chamishshîy**, *kham-ish-shee';* ord. from 2568; *fifth;* also a *fifth:*— fifth (part).

2550. חמל **châmal**, *khaw-mal';* a prim. root; to *commiserate;* by impl. to *spare:*— have compassion, (have) pity, spare.

2551. חמלה **chemlâh**, *khem-law';* from 2550; *commiseration:*— merciful, pity.

2552. חָמַם **châmam**, *khaw-mam'*; a prim. root; to *be hot* (lit. or fig.):— enflame self, get (have) heat, be (wax) hot, (be, wax) warm (self, at).

2553. חַמָּן **chammân**, *kham-mawn'*; from 2535; a *sun-pillar*:— idol, image.

2554. חָמַס **châmaç**, *khaw-mas'*; a prim. root; to *be violent*; by impl. to *maltreat*:— make bare, shake off, violate, do violence, take away violently, wrong, imagine wrongfully.

2555. חָמָס **châmâç**, *khaw-mawce'*; from 2554; *violence*; by impl. *wrong*; by meton. unjust *gain*:— cruel (-ty), damage, false, injustice, × oppressor, unrighteous, violence (against, done), violent (dealing), wrong.

2556. חָמֵץ **châmêts**, *khaw-mates'*; a prim. root; to *be pungent*; i.e. in taste (*sour*, i.e. lit. *fermented*, or fig. *harsh*), in color (*dazzling*):— cruel (man), dyed, be grieved, leavened.

2557. חָמֵץ **châmêts**, *khaw-mates'*; from 2556; *ferment*, (fig.) *extortion*:— leaven, leavened (bread).

2558. חֹמֶץ **chômets**, *kho'-mets*; from 2556; *vinegar*:— vinegar.

2559. חָמַק **châmaq**, *khaw-mak'*; a prim. root; prop. to *enwrap*; hence, to *depart* (i.e. turn about):— go about, withdraw self.

2560. חָמַר **châmar**, *khaw-mar'*; a prim. root; prop. to *boil up*; hence, to *ferment* (with scum); to *glow* (with redness); as denom. (from 2564) to *smear* with pitch:— daub, befoul, be red, trouble.

2561. חֶמֶר **chemer**, *kheh'-mer*; from 2560; *wine* (as *fermenting*):— × pure, red wine.

2562. חֲמַר **chămar** (Chald.), *kham-ar'*; corresp. to 2561; *wine*:— wine.

חֲמֹר **chămôr**. See 2543.

2563. חֹמֶר **chômer**, *kho'mer*; from 2560; prop. a *bubbling* up, i.e. of water, a *wave*; or mire or clay (cement); also a *heap*; hence, a *chomer* or dry measure:— clay, heap, homer, mire, motion, mortar.

2564. חֵמָר **chêmâr**, *khay-mawr'*; from 2560; *bitumen* (as *rising* to the surface):— slime (-pit).

2565. חֲמֹרָה **chămôrâh**, *kham-o-raw'*; from 2560 [comp. 2563]; a *heap*:— heap.

2566. חַמְרָן **Chamrân**, *kham-rawn'*; from 2560; *red*; *Chamran*, an Idumæan:— Amran.

2567. חָמַשׁ **châmash**, *khaw-mash'*; a denom. from 2568; to *tax a fifth*:— take up the fifth part.

2568. חָמֵשׁ **châmêsh**, *khaw-maysh'*; masc.

חֲמִשָּׁה **chămishshâh**, *kham-ish-shaw'*; a prim. numeral; *five*:— fifteenl, fifth, five (× apiece).

2569. חֹמֶשׁ **chômesh**, *kho'-mesh*; from 2567; a *fifth* tax:— fifth part.

2570. חֹמֶשׁ **chômesh**, *kho'-mesh*; from an unused root prob. mean. to *be stout*; the *abdomen* (as *obese*):— fifth [rib].

2571. חָמֻשׁ **châmush**, *khaw-moosh'*; pass. part. of the same as 2570;

staunch, i.e. able-bodied *soldiers*:— armed (men), harnessed.

חֲמִשָּׁה **chămishshâh**. See 2568.

חֲמִשִּׁי **chămishshiy**. See 2549.

2572. חֲמִשִּׁים **chămishshiym**, *kham-ish-sheem'*; multiple of 2568; *fifty*:— fifty.

2573. חֵמֶת **chêmeth**, *khay'-meth*; from the same as 2346; a skin *bottle* (as *tied* up):— bottle.

2574. חֲמָת **Chămâth**, *kham-awth'*; from the same as 2346; *walled*; *Chamath*, a place in Syria:— Hamath, Hemath.

חֲמֹת **chămôth**. See 2545.

2575. חַמַּת **Chammath**, *kham-math'*; a var. for the first part of 2576; *hot springs*; *Chammath*, a place in Pal.:— Hammath.

2576. חַמֹּת דֹּאר **Chammôth Dô'r**, *khammoth' dore*; from the plur. of 2535 and 1756; *hot springs of Dor*; *Chammath-Dor*, a place in Pal.:— Hamath-Dor.

2577. חֲמָתִי **Chămâthiy**, *kham-aw-thee'*; patrial from 2574; a *Chamathite* or native of *Chamath*:— Hamathite.

2578. חֲמָת צֹובָה **Chămath Tsôwbâh**, *kham-ath' tso-baw'*; from 2574 and 6678; *Chamath of Tsobah*; *Chamath-Tsobah*; prob. the šame as 2574:— Hamath-Zobah.

2579. חֲמַת רַבָּה **Chămath Rabbâh**, *kham-ath' rab-baw'*; from 2574 and 7237; *Chamath of Rabbah*; *Chamath-Rabbah*, prob. the same as 2574.

2580. חֵן **chên**, *khane*; from 2603; *graciousness*, i.e. subj. (*kindness, favor*) or obj. (*beauty*):— favour, grace (-ious), pleasant, precious, [well-] favoured.

2581. חֵן **Chên**, *khane*; the same as 2580; *grace*; *Chen*, a fig. name for an Isr.:— Hen.

2582. חֵנָדָד **Chênâdâd**, *khay-nawdawd'*; prob. from 2580 and 1908; *favor of Hadad*; *Chenadad*, an Isr.:— Henadad.

2583. חָנָה **chânâh**, *khaw-naw'*; a prim. root [comp. 2603]; prop. to *incline*; by impl. to *decline* (of the slanting rays of evening); spec. to *pitch* a tent; gen. to *encamp* (for abode or siege):— abide (in tents), camp, dwell, encamp, grow to an end, lie, pitch (tent), rest in tent.

2584. חַנָּה **Channâh**, *khan-naw'*; from 2603; *favored*; *Channah*, an Israelitess:— Hannah.

2585. חֲנֹךְ **Chănôwk**, *khan-oke'*; from 2596; *initiated*; *Chanok*, an antediluvian patriarch:— Enoch.

2586. חָנוּן **Chânûwn**, *khaw-noon'*; from 2603; *favored*; *Chanun*, the name of an Ammonite and of two Isr.:— Hanun.

2587. חַנּוּן **channûwn**, *khan-noon'*; from 2603; *gracious*:— gracious.

2588. חָנוּת **chânûwth**, *khaw-nooth'*; from 2583; prop. a *vault* or *cell* (with an arch); by impl. a *prison*:— cabin.

2589. חַנּוֹת **channôwth**, *khan-nôth'*; from 2603 (in the sense of *prayer*); *supplication*:— be gracious, intreated.

2590. חָנַט **chânat**, *khaw-nat'*; a prim. root; to *spice*; by impl. to *embalm*; also to *ripen*:— embalm, put forth.

2591. חִנְטָא **chinṭâ'** (Chald.), *khint-taw'*; corresp. to 2406; *wheat*:— wheat.

2592. חַנִּיאֵל **Channiy'êl**, *khan-nee-ale'*; from 2603 and 410; *favor of God*; *Channiel*, the name of two Isr.:— Hanniel.

2593. חָנִיךְ **chânîyk**, *kaw-neek'*; from 2596; *initiated*; i.e. *practiced*:— trained.

2594. חֲנִינָה **chănîynâh**, *khan-ee-naw'*; from 2603; *graciousness*:— favour.

2595. חֲנִית **chănîyth**, *khan-eeth'*; from 2583; a *lance* (for *thrusting*, like *pitching* a tent):— javelin, spear.

2596. חָנַךְ **chânak**, *khaw-nak'*; a prim. root; prop. to *narrow* (comp. 2614); fig. to *initiate* or *discipline*:— dedicate, train up.

2597. חֲנֻכָּא **chănukkâ'** (Chald.), *chanook-kaw'*; corresp. to 2598; *consecration*:— dedication.

2598. חֲנֻכָּה **chănukkâh**, *khan-ook-kaw'*; from 2596; *initiation*, i.e. *consecration*:— dedicating (-tion).

2599. חֲנֹכִי **Chănôkiy**, *khan-o-kee'*; patron. from 2585; a *Chanokite* (collect.) or desc. of Chanok:— Hanochites.

2600. חִנָּם **chinnâm**, *khin-nawm'*; from 2580; *gratis*, i.e. devoid of cost, reason or advantage:— without a cause (cost, wages), causeless, to cost nothing, free (-ly), innocent, for nothing (nought), in vain.

2601. חֲנַמְאֵל **Chănam'êl**, *khan-am-ale'*; prob. by orth. var. for 2606; *Chanamel*, an Isr.:— Hanameel.

2602. חֲנָמָל **chănâmâl**, *khan-aw-mawl'*; of uncert. der.; perh. the *aphis* or plant-louse:— frost.

2603. חָנַן **chânan**, *khaw-nan'*; a prim. root [comp. 2583]; prop. to *bend* or *stoop* in kindness to an inferior; to *favor*, *bestow*; caus. to *implore* (i.e. move to favor by petition):— beseech, × fair, (be, find, shew) favour (-able), be (deal, give, grant (gracious -ly), intreat, (be) merciful, have (shew) mercy (on, upon), have pity upon, pray, make supplication, × very.

2604. חֲנַן **chănan** (Chald.), *khan-an'*; corresp. to 2603; to *favor* or (caus.) to *entreat*:— shew mercy, make supplication.

2605. חָנָן **Chânân**, *khaw-nawn'*; from 2603; *favor*; *Chanan*, the name of seven Isr.:— Canan.

2606. חֲנַנְאֵל **Chănan'êl**, *khan-an-ale'*; from 2603 and 410; *God has favored*; *Chananel*, prob. an Isr., from whom a tower of Jerusalem was named:— Hananeel.

2607. חֲנָנִי **Chănâniy**, *khan-aw-nee'*; from 2603; *gracious*; *Chanani*, the name of six Isr.:— Hanani.

2608. חֲנַנְיָה **Chănanyâh**, *khan-an-yaw'*; or

חֲנַנְיָהוּ **Chănanyâhûw**, *khan-an-yaw'-hoo*; from 2603 and 3050; *Jah has favored*; *Chananjah*, the name of thirteen Isr.:— Hananiah.

2609. חָנֵס **Chânêç**, *khaw-nace'*; of Eg. der.; *Chanes*, a place in Egypt:— Hanes.

2610. חָנֵף **chânêph**, *khaw-nafe'*; a prim.

root; to *soil*, espec. in a mor. sense:— corrupt, defile, × greatly, pollute, profane.

2611. חָנֵף **chânêph**, *khaw-nafe'*; from 2610; *soiled* (i.e. with sin), *impious:*— hypocrite (-ical).

2612. חָנֵף **chôneph**, *kho'-nef*; from 2610; *moral filth*, i.e. *wickedness:*— hypocrisy.

2613. חֲנֻפָה **chănûphâh**, *khan-oo-faw'*; fem. from 2610; *impiety:*— profaneness.

2614. חָנַק **chânaq**, *khaw-nak'*; a prim. root [comp. 2596]; to *be narrow*; by impl. to *throttle*, or (reflex.) to *choke* oneself to death (by a rope):— hang self, strangle.

2615. חַנָּתֹן **Channâthôn**, *khan-naw-thone'*; prob. from 2603; *favored; Channathon*, a place in Pal.:— Hannathon.

2616. חָסַד **châcad**, *khaw-sad'*; a prim. root; prop. perh. to *bow* (the neck only [comp. 2603] in courtesy to an equal), i.e. to *be kind*; also (by euphem. [comp. 1288], but rarely) to *reprove:*— shew self merciful, put to shame.

2617. חֶסֶד **checed**, *kheh'-sed*; from 2616; *kindness*; by impl. (toward God) *piety*; rarely (by opposition) *reproof*, or (subj.) *beauty:*— favour, good deed (-liness, -ness), kindly, (loving-) kindness, merciful (kindness), mercy, pity, reproach, wicked thing.

2618. חֶסֶד **Checed**, *kheh'-sed*; the same as 2617; *favor; Chesed*, an Isr.:— Hesed.

2619. חֲסַדְיָה **Chăcadyâh**, *khas-ad-yaw'*; from 2617 and 3050; *Jah has favored; Chasadjah*, an Isr.:— Hasadiah.

2620. חָסָה **châçâh**, *khaw-saw'*; a prim. root; to *flee for protection* [comp. 982]; fig. to *confide in:*— have hope, make refuge, (put) trust.

2621. חֹסָה **Chôçâh**, *kho-saw'*; from 2620; *hopeful; Chosah*, an Isr.; also a place in Pal.:— Hosah.

2622. חָסוּת **châçûwth**, *khaw-sooth'*; from 2620; *confidence:*— trust.

2623. חָסִיד **châçîyd**, *khaw-seed'*; from 2616; prop. *kind*, i.e. (relig.) *pious* (a saint), by impl. *godly* (man), good, holy (one), merciful, saint, [un-] godly.

2624. חֲסִידָה **chăçîydâh**, *khas-ee-daw'*; fem. of 2623; the *kind* (maternal) bird, i.e. a *stork:*— × feather, stork.

2625. חָסִיל **châçîyl**, *khaw-seel'*; from 2628; the *ravager*, i.e. a *locust:*— caterpillar.

2626. חָסִין **chăçîyn**, *khas-een'*; from 2630; prop. *firm*, i.e. (by impl.) *mighty:*— strong.

2627. חַסִּיר **chaççîyr** (Chald.), *khas-seer'*; from a root corresp. to 2637; *deficient:*— wanting.

2628. חָסַל **châçal**, *khaw-sal'*; a prim. root; to *eat off:*— consume.

2629. חָסַם **châçam**, *khaw-sam'*; a prim. root; to *muzzle*; by anal. to *stop* the nose:— muzzle, stop.

2630. חָסַן **châçan**, *khaw-san'*; a prim. root; prop. to *(be) compact*; by impl. to *hoard:*— lay up.

2631. חֲסַן **chăçan** (Chald.), *khas-an'*;

corresp. to 2630; to *hold* in occupancy:— possess.

2632. חֵסֶן **chêçen** (Chald.), *khay'-sen*; from 2631; *strength:*— power.

2633. חֹסֶן **chôçen**, *kho'-sen*; from 2630; *wealth:*— riches, strength, treasure.

2634. חָסֹן **châçôn**, *khaw-sone'*; from 2630; *powerful:*— strong.

2635. חֲסַף **chăçaph** (Chald.), *khas-af'*; from a root corresp. to that of 2636; a *clod:*— clay.

2636. חַסְפַּס **chaçpaç**, *khas-pas'*; redupl. from an unused root mean. appar. to *peel*; a *shred* or *scale:*— round thing.

2637. חָסֵר **châçêr**, *khaw-sare'*; a prim. root; to *lack*; by impl. to *fail, want, lessen:*— be abated, bereave, decrease, (cause to) fail, (have) lack, make lower, want.

2638. חָסֵר **châçêr**, *khaw-sare'*; from 2637; *lacking*; hence, *without:*— destitute, fail, lack, have need, void, want.

2639. חֶסֶר **checer**, *kheh'-ler*; from 2637; *lack*; hence, *destitution:*— poverty, want.

2640. חֹסֶר **chôçer**, *kho'-ser*; from 2637; *poverty:*— in want of.

2641. חַסְרָה **Chaçrâh**, *khas-raw'*; from 2637; *want; Chasrah*, an Isr.:— Hasrah.

2642. חֶסְרֹון **cheçrôwn**, *khes-rone'*; from 2637; *deficiency:*— wanting.

2643. חַף **chaph**, *khaf*; from 2653 (in the mor. sense of *covered* from soil); *pure:*— innocent.

2644. חָפָא **châphâ'**, *khaw-faw'*; an orth. var. of 2645; prop. to *cover*, i.e. (in a sinister sense) to *act covertly:*— do secretly.

2645. חָפָה **châphâh**, *khaw-faw'*; a prim. root (comp. 2644, 2653); to *cover*; by impl. to *veil*, to *incase, protect:*— ceil, cover, overlay.

2646. חֻפָּה **chuppâh**, *khoop-paw'*; from 2645; a *canopy:*— chamber, closet, defence.

2647. חֻפָּה **Chuppâh**, *khoop-paw'*; the same as 2646; *Chuppah*, an Isr.:— Huppah.

2648. חָפַז **châphaz**, *khaw-faz'*; a prim. root; prop. to *start* up suddenly, i.e. (by impl.) to *hasten* away, to *fear:*— (make) haste (away), tremble.

2649. חִפָּזֹון **chippâzôwn**, *khip-paw-zone'*; from 2648; *hasty flight:*— haste.

2650. חֻפִּים **Chuppîym**, *khoop-peem'*; plur. of 2646 [comp. 2349]; *Chuppim*, an Isr.:— Huppim.

2651. חֹפֶן **chôphen**, *kho'-fen*; from an unused root of uncert. signif.; a *fist* (only in the dual):— fists, (both) hands, hand (-ful).

2652. חָפְנִי **Chophnîy**, *khof-nee'*; from 2651; perh. *pugilist; Chophni*, an Isr.:— Hophni.

2653. חָפַף **chôphaph**, *khaw-faf'*; a prim. root (comp. 2645, 3182); to *cover* (in protection):— cover.

2654. חָפֵץ **châphêts**, *khaw-fates'*; a prim. root; prop. to *incline* to; by impl. (lit. but rarely) to *bend*; fig. to *be pleased* with, *desire:*— × any at all,

(have, take) delight, desire, favour, like, move, be (well) pleased, have pleasure, will, would.

2655. חָפֵץ **châphêts**, *khaw-fates'*; from 2654; *pleased* with:— delight in, desire, favour, please, have pleasure, whosoever would, willing, wish.

2656. חֵפֶץ **chêphets**, *khay'-fets*; from 2654; *pleasure*; hence, (abstr.) *desire*; concr. a *valuable* thing; hence, (by extens.) a *matter* (as something in mind):— acceptable, delight (-some), desire, things desired, matter, pleasant (-ure), purpose, willingly.

2657. חֶפְצִי־בָהּ **Chephtsîy bâhh**, *kheftsee'-baw*; from 2656 with suffixes; *my delight (is) in her; Cheptsi-bah*, a fanciful name for Pal.:— Hephzi-bah.

2658. חָפַר **châphar**, *khaw-far'*; a prim. root; prop. to *pry* into; by impl. to *delve*, to *explore:*— dig, paw, search out, seek.

2659. חָפֵר **châphêr**, *khaw-fare'*; a prim. root [perhaps rath. the same as 2658 through the idea of *detection*]: to *blush*; fig. to *be ashamed, disappointed*; caus. to *shame, reproach:*— be ashamed, be confounded, be brought to confusion (unto shame), come (be put to) shame, bring reproach.

2660. חֵפֶר **Chêpher**, *khay'-fer*; from 2658 or 2659; a *pit* or *shame; Chepher*, a place in Pal.; also the name of three Isr.:— Hepher.

2661. חֲפֹר **chăphôr**, *khaf-ore'*; from 2658; a *hole*; only in connection with 6512, which ought rather to be joined as one word, thus

חֲפַרְפֵּרָה **chăpharpêrâh**, *khaf-ar-pay-raw'*; by redupl. from 2658; a *burrower*, i.e. probe. a *rat:*— + mole.

2662. חֶפְרִי **Chephrîy**, *khef-ree'*; patron. from 2660; a *Chephrite* (collect.) or desc. of *Chepher:*— Hepherites.

2663. חֲפָרַיִם **Chăphârayim**, *khaf-aw-rah'-yim*; dual of 2660; *double pit; Chapharajim*, a place in Pal.:— Haphraim.

חֲפַרְפֵּרָה **chăpharpêrâh**. See 2661.

2664. חָפַשׂ **châphas**, *khaw-fas'*; a prim. root; to *seek*; caus. to *conceal* oneself (i.e. let be sought), or *mask:*— change, (make) diligent (search), disguise self, hide, search (for, out).

2665. חֵפֶשׂ **chêphes**, *khay'-fes*; from 2664; something *covert*, i.e. a *trick:*— search.

2666. חָפַשׁ **châphash**, *khaw-fash'*; a prim. root; to *spread loose*; fig. to *manumit:*— be free.

2667. חֹפֶשׁ **Chôphesh**, *kho'-fesh*; from 2666; something *spread loosely*, i.e. a *carpet:*— precious.

2668. חֻפְשָׁה **chuphshâh**, *khoof-shaw'*; from 2666; *liberty* (from slavery):— freedom.

2669. חָפְשׁוּת **chôphshûwth**, *khof-shooth'*; and

חָפְשִׁית **chophshîyth**, *khof-sheeth'*; from 2666; *prostration* by sickness (with 1004, a *hospital*):— several.

2670. חָפְשִׁי **chophshîy**, *khof-shee'*; from 2666; *exempt* (from bondage, tax or care):— free, liberty.

Hebrew

2671. חֵץ **chêts**, *khayts*; from 2686; prop. a *piercer*, i.e. an *arrow*; by impl. a *wound*; fig. (of God) thunder-*bolt*; (by interchange for 6086) the *shaft* of a spear:— + archer, arrow, dart, shaft, staff, wound.

חֵץ **chûts**. See 2351.

2672. חָצַב **châtsab**, *khaw-tsab´*; or

חָצֵב **châtsêb**, *khaw-tsabe´*; a prim. root; to *cut* or *carve* (wood), stone or other material); by impl. to *hew, split, square, quarry, engrave*:— cut, dig, divide, grave, hew (out, -er), make, mason.

2673. חָצָה **châtsâh**, *khaw-tsaw´*; a prim. root [comp. 2686]); to *cut* or *split* in two; to *halve*:— divide, × live out half, reach to the midst. part.

2674. חָצוֹר **Châtsôwr**, *khaw-tsore´*; a collect. form of 2691; *village; Chatsor*, the name (thus simply) of two places in Pal. and of one in Arabia:— Hazor.

2675. חֲצוֹר חֲדַתָּה **Châtsôwr Chădattâh**, *khaw-tsore´ khad-at-taw´*; from 2674 and a Chaldaizing form of the fem. of 2319 [comp. 2323]; *new Chatsor*, a place in Pal.:— Hazor, Hadattah [as if *two places*].

2676. חָצוֹת **châtsôwth**, *khaw-tsoth´*; from 2673; the *middle* (of the night):— mid [-night].

2677. חֵצִי **chêtsiy**, *khay-tsee´*; from 2673; the *half* or *middle*:— half, middle, mid [-night], midst, part, two parts.

2678. חֵצִי **chitstsiy**, *khits-tsee´*; or

חֵצִי **chêtsiy**, *khay-tsee´*; prol. from 2671; an *arrow*:— arrow.

2679. חֲצִי הַמְּנֻחוֹת **Châtsiy ham-Mᵉnûchôwth**, *chat-tsee´ ham-men-oo-khoth´*; from 2677 and the plur. of 4496, with the art. interposed; *midst of the resting-places; Chatsi-ham-Menuchoth*, an Isr.:— half of the Manahethites.

2680. חֲצִי הַמְּנַחְתִּי **Châtsiy ham-Mᵉnachtiy**, *khat-see´ ham-men-akh-tee´*; patron. from 2679; a *Chatsi-ham-Men-achtite* or desc. of Chatsi-ham-Menuchoth:— half of the Manahethites.

2681. חָצִיר **châtsîyr**, *khaw-tseer´*; a collat. form of 2691; a *court* or *abode*:— court.

2682. חָצִיר **châtsîyr**, *khaw-tseer´*; perh. orig. the same as 2681, from the *greenness* of a courtyard; *grass*; also a *leek* (collect.):— grass, hay, herb, leek.

2683. חֵצֶן **chêtsen**, *khay´-tsen*; from an unused root mean. to hold *firmly*; the *bosom* (as *comprised* between the arms):— bosom.

2684. חֹצֶן **chôtsen**, *kho´tsen*; a collat. form of 2683, and mean. the same:— arm, lap.

2685. חֲצַף **chătsaph** (Chald.), *khats-af´*; a prim. root; prop. to *shear* or cut close; fig. to *be severe*:— hasty, be urgent.

2686. חָצַף **châtsats**, *khaw-tsats´*; a prim. root [comp. 2673]; prop. to *chop* into, pierce or sever; hence, to *curtail*, to *distribute* (into ranks); as denom. from 2671, to *shoot* an arrow:— archer, × bands, cut off in the midst.

2687. חָצָץ **châtsâts**, *khaw-tsawts´*; from 2687; prop. something *cutting*; hence, *gravel* (as *grit*); also (like 2671) an *arrow*:— arrow, gravel (stone).

2688. חַצְצוֹן תָּמָר **Chatsᵉtsôwn Tâmâr**, *khats-ets-one´ taw-mawr´*; or

חַצְצֹן תָּמָר **Chatsătsôn Tâmâr**, *khats-ats-one´ taw-mawr´*; from 2686 and 8558; *division* [i.e. perh. *rowl* of (the) *palm-tree; Chatsetson-tamar*, a place in Pal.:— Hazezon-tamar.

2689. חֲצֹצְרָה **châtsôtsᵉrâh**, *khats-o-tser-aw´*; by redupl. from 2690; a *trumpet* (from its *sundered* or *quavering* note):— trumpet (-er).

2690. חָצַר **châtsar**, *khaw-tsar´*; a prim. root; prop. to *surround* with a stockade, and thus *separate* from the open country; but used only in the redupl. form

חֲצֹצֵר **châtsôtsêr**, *khast-o-tsare´*; or (2 Chron. 5:12)

חַצֹּרֵר **châtsôrêr**, *khats-o-rare´*; as denom. from 2689; to *trumpet*, i.e. blow on that instrument:— blow, sound, trumpeter.

2691. חָצֵר **châtsêr**, *khaw-tsare´* (masc. and fem.); from 2690 in its orig. sense; a *yard* (as *inclosed* by a fence); also a *hamlet* (as similarly *surrounded* with walls):— court, tower, village.

2692. חֲצַר אַדָּר **Châtsar 'Addâr**, *khats-ar´ addawr´*; from 2691 and 146; (the) *village of Addar; Chatsar-Addar*, a place in Pal.:— Hazar-addar.

2693. חֲצַר נַּדָּה **Châtsar Gaddâh**, *khats-ar´ gad-daw´*; from 2691 and a fem. of 1408; (the) *village of* (female) *Fortune; Chatsar-Gaddah*, a place in Pal.:— Hazar-gaddah.

2694. חֲצַר הַתִּיכוֹן **Châtsar hat-Tîykôwn**, *khats-ar´ hat-tee-kone´*; from 2691 and 8484 with the art. interposed; *village of the middle; Chatsar-hat-Tikon*, a place in Pal.:— Hazar-hatticon.

2695. חֶצְרוֹ **Chetsrôw**, *khets-ro´*; by an orth. var. for 2696; *inclosure; Chetsro*, an Isr.:— Hezro, Hezrai.

2696. חֶצְרוֹן **Chetsrôwn**, *khets-rone´*; from 2691; *court-yard; Chetsron*, the name of a place in Pal.; also of two Isr.:— Hezron.

2697. חֶצְרוֹנִי **Chetsrôwnîy**, *khets-ro-nee´*; patron. from 2696; a *Chetsronite* or (collect.) desc. of Chetsron:— Hezronites.

2698. חֲצֵרוֹת **Châtsêrowth**, *khats-ay-roth´*; fem. plur. of 2691; *yards; Chatseroth*, a place in Pal.:— Hazeroth.

2699. חֲצֵרִים **Châtsêrîym**, *khats-ay-reem´*; plur. masc. of 2691; *yards; Chatserim*, a place in Pal.:— Hazerim.

2700. חֲצַרְמָוֶת **Châtsarmâveth**, *khats-ar-maw´-veth*; from 2691 and 4194; *village of death; Chatsarmaveth*, a place in Arabia:— Hazarmaveth.

2701. חֲצַר סוּסָה **Châtsar Çûwçâh**, *khats-ar´ soo-saw´*; from 2691 and 5484; *village of cavalry; Chatsar-Susah*, a place in Pal.:— Hazar-susah.

2702. חֲצַר סוּסִים **Châtsar Çûwçîym**, *khats-ar´ soo-seem´*; from 2691 and the

plur. of 5483; *village of horses; Chatsar-Susim*, a place in Pal.:— Hazar-susim.

2703. חֲצַר עֵינוֹן **Châtsar 'Êynôwn**, *khats-ar´ ay-nône´*; from 2691 and a der. of 5869; *village of springs; Chatsar-Enon*, a place in Pal.:— Hazar-enon.

2704. חֲצַר עֵינָן **Châtsar 'Êynân**, *khats-ar´ ay-nawn´*; from 2691 and the same as 5881; *village of springs; Chatsar-Enan*, a place in Pal.:— Hazar-enan.

2705. חֲצַר שׁוּעָל **Châtsar Shûw'âl**, *khats-ar´ shoo-awl´*; from 2691 and 7776; *village of* (the) *fox; Chatsar-Shual*, a place in Pal.:— Hazar-shual.

חֵק **chêq**. See 2436.

2706. חֹק **chôq**, *khoke*; from 2710; an *enactment*; hence, an *appointment* (of time, space, quantity, labor or usage):— appointed, bound, commandment, convenient. custom, decree (-d), due, law, measure, × necessary, ordinance (-nary), portion, set time, statute, task.

2707. חָקָה **châqah**, *khaw-kaw´*; a prim. root; to *carve*; by impl. to *delineate*; also to *intrench*:— carved work, portrayed, set a print.

2708. חֻקָּה **chuqqâh**, *khook-kaw´*; fem. of 2706, and mean. substantially the same:— appointed, custom, manner, ordinance, site, statute.

2709. חֲקוּפָא **Chăqûwphâ´**, *khak-oo-faw´*; from an unused root prob. mean. to *bend; crooked; Chakupha*, one of the Nethinim:— Hakupha.

2710. חָקַק **châqaq**, *khaw-kak´*; a prim. root; prop. to *hack*, i.e. *engrave* (Judg. 5:14; to *be a scribe* simply); by impl. to *enact* (laws being *cut* in stone or metal tablets in primitive times) or (gen.) *prescribe*:— appoint, decree, governor, grave, lawgiver, note, pourtray, print, set.

2711. חֵקֶק **chêqeq**, *khay´-kek*; from 2710; an *enactment*, a *resolution*:— decree, thought.

2712. חֻקֹּק **Chuqqôq**, *Khook-koke´*; or (fully)

חוּקֹק **Chûwqôq**, *khoo-koke´*; from 2710; *appointed; Chukkok* or *Chukok*, a place in Pal.:— Hukkok, Hukok.

2713. חָקַר **châqar**, *khaw-kar´*; a prim. root; prop. to *penetrate*; hence, to *examine* intimately:— find out, (make) search (out), seek (out), sound, try.

2714. חֵקֶר **chêqer**, *khay´-ker*; from 2713; *examination, enumeration, deliberation*:— finding out, number, [un-] search (-able, -ed, out, -ing).

2715. חֹר **chôr**, *khore*; or (fully)

חוֹר **chôwr**, *khore*; from 2787; prop. *white* or *pure* (from the *cleansing* or *shining* power of fire [comp. 2751]; hence, (fig.) *noble* (in rank):— noble.

חֻר **chûr**. See 2352.

2716. חֶרֶא **chere´**, *kheh´-reh*; from an unused (and vulgar) root prob. mean. to *evacuate* the bowels: *excrement*:— dung. Also

חֲרִי° **chăriy**, *khar-ee´*,

2717. חָרֵב **chârab**, *khaw-rab´*; or

חָרֵב **chârêb**, *khaw-rabe´*; a prim.

root; to *parch* (through drought) i.e. (by anal.) to *desolate, destroy, kill:*— decay, (be) desolate, destroy (-er), (be) dry (up), slay, × surely, (lay, lie, make) waste.

2718. חֲרַב **chărab** (Chald.), *khar-ab´;* a root corresp. to 2717; to *demolish:*— destroy.

2719. חֶרֶב **chereb**, *kheh´-reb;* from 2717; *drought;* also a *cutting* instrument (from its *destructive* effect), as a *knife, sword,* or other sharp implement:— axe, dagger, knife, mattock, sword, tool.

2720. חָרֵב **chârêb**, *khaw-rabe´;* from 2717; *parched* or *ruined:*— desolate, dry, waste.

2721. חֹרֶב **chôreb**, *kho´-reb;* a collat. form of 2719; *drought* or *desolation:*— desolation, drought, dry, heat, × utterly, waste.

2722. חֹרֵב **Chôrêb**, *kho-rabe´;* from 2717; *desolate; Choreb,* a (gen.) name for the Sinaitic mountains:— Horeb.

2723. חָרְבָּה **chorbâh**, *khor-baw´;* fem. of 2721; prop. *drought,* i.e. (by impl.) a *desolation:*— decayed place, desolate (place, -tion), destruction, (laid) waste (place).

2724. חֲרָבָה **chârâbâh**, *khaw-raw-baw´;* fem. of 2720; a *desert:*— dry (ground, land).

2725. חֲרָבוֹן **chărâbôwn**, *khar-aw-bone´;* from 2717; *parching heat:*— drought.

2726. חַרְבוֹנָא **Charbôwnâ´**, *khar-bo-naw´;* or

חַרְבוֹנָה **Charbôwnâh**, *khar-bo-naw´;* of Pers. or.; *Charbona* or *Charbonah,* a eunuch of Xerxes:— Harbona, Harbonah.

2727. חָרַג **chârag**, *khaw-rag´;* a prim. root; prop. to *leap* suddenly, i.e. (by impl.) to *be dismayed:*— be afraid.

2728. חַרְגֹּל **chargôl**, *khar-gole´;* from 2727; the *leaping* insect, i.e. a *locust:*— beetle.

2729. חָרַד **chârad**, *khaw-rad´;* a prim. root; to *shudder* with terror; hence, to *fear;* also to *hasten* (with anxiety):— be (make) afraid, be careful, discomfit, fray (away), quake, tremble.

2730. חָרֵד **chârêd**, *khaw-rade´;* from 2729; *fearful;* also *reverential:*— afraid, trembling.

2731. חֲרָדָה **chărâdâh**, *khar-aw-daw´;* fem. of 2730; *fear, anxiety:*— care, × exceedingly, fear, quaking, trembling.

2732. חֲרָדָה **Chărâdâh**, *khar-aw-daw´;* the same as 2731; *Charadah,* a place in the Desert:— Haradah.

2733. חֲרֹדִי **Chărôdîy**, *khar-o-dee´;* patrial from a der. of 2729 [comp. 5878]; a *Charodite,* or inhab. of *Charod:*— Harodite.

2734. חָרָה **chârâh**, *khaw-raw´;* a prim. root [comp. 2787]; to *glow* or *grow warm;* fig. (usually) to *blaze* up, of anger, zeal, jealousy:— be angry, burn, be displeased, × earnestly, fret self, grieve, be (wax) hot, be incensed, kindle, × very, be wroth. See 8474.

2735. חֹר הַגִּדְגָּד **Chôr hag-Gidgâd**, *khore hag-ghid-gawd´;* from 2356 and a col-

lat. (masc.) form of 1412, with the art. interposed; *hole of the cleft; Chor-hag-Gidgad,* a place in the Desert:— Horhagidgad.

2736. חַרְהֲיָה **Charhăyâh**, *khar-hah-yaw´;* from 2734 and 3050; *fearing Jah; Charhajah,* an Isr.:— Harhaiah.

2737. חָרוּז **chârûwz**, *khaw-rooz´;* from an unused root mean. to *perforate;* prop. *pierced,* i.e. a *bead* of pearl, gems or jewels (as strung):— chain.

2738. חָרוּל **chârûwl**, *khaw-rool´;* or (short.)

חָרֻל **chârûl**, *khaw-rool´;* appar. a pass. part. of an unused root prob. mean. to *be prickly;* prop. *pointed,* i.e. a *bramble* or other thorny weed:— nettle.

חֹרוֹן **chôrôwn**. See 1032, 2772.

2739. חֲרוּמַף **Chărûwmaph**, *khar-oo-maf´;* from pass. part. of 2763 and 639; *snub-nosed; Charumaph,* an Isr.:— Harumaph.

2740. חָרוֹן **chârôwn**, *khaw-rone´;* or (short.)

חָרֹן **chârôn**, *khaw-rone´;* from 2734; a *burning* of anger:— sore displeasure, fierce (-ness), fury, (fierce) wrath (-ful).

2741. חֲרוּפִי **Chărûwphiy**, *khar-oo-fee´;* a patrial from (prob.) a collat. form of 2756; a *Charuphite* or inhab. of Charuph (or Chariph):— Haruphite.

2742. חָרוּץ **chârûwts**, *khaw-roots´;* or

חָרֻץ **chârûts**, *khaw-roots´;* pass. part. of 2782; prop. *incised* or (act.) *incisive;* hence, (as noun masc. or fem.) a *trench* (as dug), *gold* (as mined), a *threshing-sledge* (having sharp teeth); (fig.) *determination;* also *eager:*— decision, diligent, (fine) gold, pointed things, sharp, threshing instrument, wall.

2743. חָרוּץ **Chârûwts**, *khaw-roots´;* the same as 2742; *earnest; Charuts,* an Isr.:— Haruz.

2744. חַרְחוּר **Charchûwr**, *khar-khoor´;* a fuller form of 2746; *inflammation; Charchur,* one of the Nethinim:— Harhur.

2745. חַרְחַס **Charchaç**, *khar-khas´;* from the same as 2775; perh. *shining; Charchas,* an Isr.:— Harhas.

2746. חַרְחֻר **charchûr**, *khar-khoor´;* from 2787; *fever* (as *hot*):— extreme burning.

2747. חֶרֶט **cheret**, *kheh´-ret;* from a prim. root mean. to *engrave;* a *chisel* or *graver;* also a *style* for writing:— graving tool, pen.

חָרִט **chârit**. See 2754.

2748. חַרְטֹם **chartôm**, *khar-tome´;* from the same as 2747; a *horoscopist* (as *drawing* magical lines or circles):— magician.

2749. חַרְטֹם **chartôm** (Chald.), *khar-tome´;* the same as 2748:— magician.

2750. חֳרִי **chŏrîy**, *khor-ee´;* from 2734; a *burning* (i.e. intense) anger:— fierce, × great, heat.

חֲרִי° **chăriy**. See 2716.

2751. חֳרִי **chŏrîy**, *kho-ree´;* from the same as 2353; *white* bread:— white.

2752. חֹרִי **Chôrîy**, *kho-ree´;* from 2356; *cave-dweller* or troglodyte; a *Chorite* or aboriginal Idumæan:— Horims, Horites.

2753. חֹרִי **Chôrîy**, *kho-ree´;* or

חוֹרִי **Chôwrîy**, *kho-ree´;* the same as 2752; *Chori,* the name of two men:— Hori.

2754. חָרִיט **chârîyṭ**, *khaw-reet´;* or

חָרִט **chârit**, *khaw-reet´;* from the same as 2747; prop. *cut* out (or *hollow*), i.e. (by impl.) a *pocket:*— bag, crisping pin.

2755. חֲרִי־יוֹנִים **chărêy-yôwnîym**, *khar-ay´-yo-neem´;* from the plur. of 2716 and the plur. of 3123; *excrements of doves* [or perh. rather the plur. of a single word

חַרְאִיוֹן **chârâ'yôwn**, *khar-aw-yone´;* of similar or uncert. deriv.], prob. a kind of *vegetable:*— doves' dung.

2756. חָרִיף **Chârîyph**, *khaw-reef´;* from 2778; *autumnal; Chariph,* the name of two Isr.:— Hariph.

2757. חָרִיץ **chârîyts**, *khaw-reets´;* or

חָרִץ **chârits**, *khaw-reets´;* from 2782; prop. *incisure* or (pass.) *incised* [comp. 2742]; hence, a *threshing-sledge* (with *sharp* teeth): also a *slice* (as cut):— + cheese, harrow.

2758. חָרִישׁ **chârîysh**, *khaw-reesh´;* from 2790; *plowing* or its season:— earing (time), ground.

2759. חֲרִישִׁי **chărîyshiy**, *khar-ee-shee´;* from 2790 in the sense of *silence; quiet,* i.e. *sultry* (as fem. noun, the *sirocco* or hot east wind):— vehement.

2760. חָרַךְ **chârak**, *khaw-rak´;* a prim. root; to *braid* (i.e. to *entangle* or snare) or *catch* (game) in a net:— roast.

2761. חֲרַךְ **chărak** (Chald.), *khar-ak´;* a root prob. allied to the equiv. of 2787; to *scorch:*— singe.

2762. חֶרֶךְ **cherek**, *kheh´-rek;* from 2760; prop. a *net,* i.e. (by anal.) *lattice:*— lattice.

חָרֻל **chârûl**. See 2738.

2763. חָרַם **charam**, *khaw-ram´;* a prim. root; to *seclude;* spec. (by a ban) to *devote* to relig. uses (espec. destruction); phys. and refl. to *be blunt* as to the nose:— make accursed, consecrate, (utterly) destroy, devote, forfeit, have a flat nose, utterly (slay, make away).

2764. חֵרֶם **chêrem**, *khay´-rem;* or (Zech. 14:11)

חֶרֶם **cherem**, *kheh´-rem;* from 2763; phys. (as *shutting in*) a *net* (either lit. or fig.); usually a *doomed* object; abstr. *extermination:*— (ac-) curse (-d, -d thing), dedicated thing, things which should have been utterly destroyed, (appointed to) utter destruction, devoted (thing), net.

2765. חֳרֵם **Chŏrêm**, *khor-ame´;* from 2763; *devoted; Chorem,* a place in Pal.:— Horem.

2766. חָרִם **Chârîm**, *khaw-reem´;* from

2763; *snub-nosed; Charim*, an Isr.:— Harim.

2767. חָרְמָה **Chormâh**, *khor-maw´*; from 2763; *devoted; Chormah*, a place in Pal.:— Hormah.

2768. חֶרְמוֹן **Chermôwn**, *kher-mone´*; from 2763; *abrupt; Chermon*, a mount of Pal.:— Hermon.

2769. חֶרְמוֹנִים **Chermôwnîym**, *kher-mo-neem´*; plur. of 2768; *Hermons*, i.e. its peaks:— the Hermonites.

2770. חֶרְמֵשׁ **chermêsh**, *kher-mashe´*; from 2763; a *sickle* (as *cutting*):— sickle.

2771. חָרָן **Chârân**, *kaw-rawn´*; from 2787; *parched; Charan*, the name of a man and also of a place:— Haran.

חֹרָן **chârôn**. See 2740.

2772. חֹרִי **Chôrônîy**, *kho-ro-nee´*; patrial from 2773; a *Choronite* or inhab. of Choronaim:— Horonite.

2773. חֹרֹנָיִם **Chôrônayim**, *kho-ro-nah´-yim*; dual of a der. from 2356; *double cave-town; Choronajim*, a place in Moab:— Horonaim.

2774. חַרְנֶפֶר **Charnepher**, *khar-neh´fer*; of uncert. der.; *Charnepher*, an Isr.:— Harnepher.

2775. חֶרֶס **chereç**, *kheh´-res*; or (with a directive enclitic)

חֶרְסָה **charçâh**, *khar´-saw*; from an unused root mean. to *scrape*; the *itch*; also [perh. from the mediating idea of 2777] the *sun*:— itch, sun.

2776. חֶרֶס **Chereç**, *kheh´-res*; the same as 2775; *shining; Cheres*, a mountain in Pal.:— Heres.

2777. חַרְסוּת **charçûwth**, *khar-sooth´*; from 2775 (appar. in the sense of a red *tile* used for scraping); a *potsherd*, i.e. (by impl.) a *pottery*; the name of a gate at Jerusalem:— east.

2778. חָרַף **châraph**, *khaw-raf´*; a prim. root; to *pull* off, i.e. (by impl.) to *expose* (as by *stripping*); spec. to *betroth* (as if a surrender); fig. to carp at, i.e. *defame*; denom.ˡ(from 2779) to spend the *winter*:— betroth, blaspheme, defy, jeopard, rail, reproach, upbraid.

2779. חֹרֶף **chôreph**, *kho´-ref*; from 2778; prop. the *crop* gathered, i.e. (by impl.) the *autumn* (and winter) season; fig. *ripeness* of age:— cold, winter (I-house), youth.

2780. חָרֵף **Chârêph**, *khaw-rafe´*; from 2778; *reproachful; Chareph*, an Isr.:— Hareph.

2781. חֶרְפָּה **cherpâh**, *kher-paw´*; from 2778; *contumely, disgrace*, the *pudenda*:— rebuke, reproach (-fully), shame.

2782. חָרַץ **chârats**, *khaw-rats´*; a prim. root; prop. to *point* sharply, i.e. (lit.) to *wound*; fig. to *be alert*, to *decide*:— bestir self, decide, decree, determine, maim, move.

2783. חֲרַץ **chărats** (Chald.), *khar-ats´*; from a root corresp. to 2782 in the sense of *vigor*; the *loin* (as the seat of strength):— loin.

חָרֻץ **chârûts**. See 2742.

2784. חַרְצֻבָּה **chartsubbâh**, *khar-tsoob-*

baw´; of uncert. der.; a *fetter*; fig. a *pain*:— band.

חָרִץ **chârits**. See 2757.

2785. חַרְצָן **chartsan**, *khar-tsan´*; from 2782; a *sour grape* (as sharp in taste):— kernel.

2786. חָרַק **châraq**, *khaw-rak´*; a prim. root; to *grate* the teeth:— gnash.

2787. חָרַר **chârar**, *khaw-rar´*; a prim. root; to *glow*, i.e. lit. (to *melt, burn, dry* up) or fig. (to *show* or *incite passion*):— be angry, burn, dry, kindle.

2788. חָרֵר **chârêr**, *khaw-rare´*; from 2787; *arid*:— parched place.

2789. חֶרֶשׂ **cheres**, *kheh´-res*; a collat. form mediating between 2775 and 2791; a piece of *pottery*:— earth (-en), (pot-) sherd, + stone.

2790. חָרַשׁ **chârash**, *khaw-rash´*; a prim. root; to *scratch*, i.e. (by impl.) to *engrave, plow*; hence, (from the use of tools) to *fabricate* (of any material); fig. to *devise* (in a bad sense); hence, (from the idea of secrecy) to *be silent*, to *let alone*; hence, (by impl.) to *be deaf* (as an accompaniment of dumbness):— × altogether, cease, conceal, be deaf, devise, ear, graven, imagine, leave off speaking, hold peace, plow (-er, man), be quiet, rest, practise secretly, keep silence, be silent, speak not a word, be still, hold tongue, worker.

2791. חֶרֶשׁ **cheresh**, *kheh´-resh*; from 2790; *magical craft*; also *silence*:— cunning, secretly.

2792. חֶרֶשׁ **Cheresh**, *kheh´-resh*; the same as 2791; *Cheresh*, a Levite:— Heresh.

2793. חֹרֶשׁ **chôresh**, *kho´-resh*; from 2790; a *forest* (perh. as furnishing material for fabric):— bough, forest, shroud, wood.

2794. חֹרֵשׁ **chôrêsh**, *kho-rashe´*; act. part. of 2790; a *fabricator* or mechanic:— artificer.

2795. חֵרֵשׁ **chêrêsh**, *khay-rashe´*; from 2790; *deaf* (whether lit. or spir.):— deaf.

2796. חָרָשׁ **chârâsh**, *khaw-rawsh´*; from 2790; a *fabricator* or any material:— artificer, (+) carpenter, craftsman, engraver, maker, + mason, skilful, (+) smith, worker, workman, such as wrought.

2797. חַרְשָׁא **Charshâ´**, *khar-shaw´*; from 2792; *magician; Charsha*, one of the Nethinim:— Harsha.

2798. חֲרָשִׁים **Chărâshîym**, *khar-aw-sheem´*; plur. of 2796; *mechanics*, the name of a valley in Jerusalem:— Charashim, craftsmen.

2799. חֲרֹשֶׁת **chărôsheth**, *khar-o´-sheth*; from 2790; *mechanical work*:— carving, cutting.

2800. חֲרֹשֶׁת **Chărôsheth**, *khar-o´-sheth*; the same as 2799; *Charosheth*, a place in Pal.:— Harosheth.

2801. חָרַת **chârath**, *khaw-rath´*; a prim. root; to *engrave*:— graven.

2802. חֶרֶת **Chereth**, *kheh´-reth*; from 2801 [but equiv. to 2793]; *forest; Chereth*, a thicket in Pal.:— Hereth.

2803. חָשַׁב **châshab**, *khaw-shab´*; a

prim. root; prop. to *plait* or interpenetrate, i.e. (lit.) to *weave* or (gen.) to *fabricate*; fig. to *plot* or contrive (usually in a malicious sense); hence, (from the ment. effort) to *think, regard, value, compute*:— (make) account (of), conceive, consider, count, cunning (man, work, workman), devise, esteem, find out, forecast, hold, imagine, impute, invent, be like, mean, purpose, reckon (-ing be made), regard, think.

2804. חֲשַׁב **châshab** (Chald.), *khash-ab´*; corresp. to 2803; to *regard*:— repute.

2805. חֵשֶׁב **chêsheb**, *khay´-sheb*; from 2803; a *belt* or strap (as being interlaced):— curious girdle.

2806. חַשְׁבַּדָּנָה **Chashbaddânâh**, *khash-bad-daw´-naw*; from 2803 and 1777; *considerate judge; Chasbaddanah*, an Isr.:— Hasbadana.

2807. חֲשֻׁבָה **Chăshûbâh**, *khash-oo-baw´*; from 2803; *estimation; Cashubah*, an Isr.:— Hashubah.

2808. חֶשְׁבּוֹן **cheshbôwn**, *khesh-bone´*; from 2803; prop. *contrivance*; by impl. *intelligence*:— account, device, reason.

2809. חֶשְׁבּוֹן **Cheshbôwn**, *khesh-bone´*; the same as 2808; *Cheshbon*, a place E. of the Jordan:— Heshbon.

2810. חִשָּׁבוֹן **chishshâbôwn**, *khish-shaw-bone´*; from 2803; a *contrivance*, i.e. actual (a warlike *machine*) or ment. (a *machination*):— engine, invention.

2811. חֲשַׁבְיָה **Chăshabyâh**, *khash-ab-yaw´*; or

חֲשַׁבְיָהוּ **Chăshabyâhûw**, *khash-ab-yaw´-hoo*; from 2803 and 3050; *Jah has regarded; Chashabjah*, the name of nine Isr.:— Hashabiah.

2812. חֲשַׁבְנָה **Chăshabnâh**, *khash-ab-naw´*; fem. of 2808; *inventiveness; Chashnah*, an Isr.:— Hashabnah.

2813. חֲשַׁבְנְיָה **Chăshabnᵉyâh**, *khash-ab-neh-yaw´*; from 2808 and 3050; *thought of Jah; Chashabnejah*, the name of two Isr.:— Hashabniah.

2814. חָשָׁה **châshâh**, *khaw-shaw´*; a prim. root; to *hush* or keep quiet:— hold peace, keep silence, be silent, still.

2815. חַשּׁוּב **Chashshûwb**, *khash-shoob´*; from 2803; *intelligent; Chashshub*, the name of two or three Isr.:— Hashub, Hasshub.

2816. חֲשׁוֹךְ **chăshôwk** (Chald.), *khash-oke´*; from a root corresp. to 2821; the *dark*:— darkness.

2817. חֲשׂוּפָא **Chăsûwphâ´**, *khas-oo-faw´*; or

חֲשֻׂפָא **Chăsûphâ´**, *khas-oo-faw´*; from 2834; *nakedness; Chasupha*, one of the Nethinim:— Hashupha, Hasupha.

חָשׁוּק **châshûwq**. See 2838.

2818. חֲשַׁח **chăshach** (Chald.), *khash-akh´*; a collat. root to one corresp. to 2363 in the sense of *readiness*; to be *necessary* (from the idea of *convenience*) or (tran.) to *need*:— careful, have need of.

2819. חַשְׁחוּת **chashchûwth**, *khash-khooth´*; from a root corresp. to 2818; *necessity*:— be needful.

חֲסֵיכָה chăshêykăh. See 2825.

חֻסִּים Chûshîym. See 2366.

2820. חָשַׂךְ châsak, *khaw-sak´*; a prim. root; to *restrain* or (reflex.) *refrain*; by impl. to *refuse, spare, preserve*; also (by interch. with 2821) to *observe*:— assuage, × darken, forbear, hinder, hold back, keep (back), punish, refrain, reserve, spare, withhold.

2821. חָשַׁךְ châshak, *khaw-shak´*; a prim. root; to *be dark* (as *withholding* light); tran. to *darken*:— be black, be (make) dark, darken, cause darkness, be dim, hide.

2822. חֹשֶׁךְ chôshek, *kho-shek´*; from 2821; the *dark*; hence, (lit.) *darkness*; fig. *misery, destruction, death, ignorance, sorrow, wickedness*:— dark (-ness), night, obscurity.

2823. חָשֹׁךְ châshôk, *khaw-shoke´*; from 2821; *dark* (fig. i.e. *obscure*):— mean.

2824. חֶשְׁכָה cheshkâh, *khesh-kaw´*; from 2821; *darkness*:— dark.

2825. חֲשֵׁכָה chăshêkâh, *khash-ay-kaw´*; or

חֲשֵׁיכָה chăshêykâh, *khash-ay-kaw´*; from 2821; *darkness*; fig. *misery*:— darkness.

2826. חָשַׁל châshal, *khaw-shal´*; a prim. root; to *make* (intrans. *be*) *unsteady*, i.e. *weak*:— feeble.

2827. חֲשַׁל chăshal (Chald.), *khash-al´*; a root corresp. to 2826; to *weaken*, i.e. *crush*:— subdue.

2828. חָשֻׁם Châshûm, *khaw-shoom´*; from the same as 2831; *enriched*; *Chashum*, the name of two or three Isr.:— Hashum.

חֻשָׁם Chûshâm. See 2367.

חֻשִׁם Chûshim. See 2366.

2829. חַשְׁמוֹן Cheshmôwn, *khesh-mone´*; the same as 2831; *opulent*; *Cheshmon*, a place in Pal.:— Heshmon.

2830. חַשְׁמַל chashmal, *khash-mal´*; of uncert. der.; prob. *bronze* or polished spectrum metal:— amber.

2831. חַשְׁמָן chashmân, *khash-man´*; from an unused root (prob. mean. *firm* or *capacious* in resources); appar. *wealthy*:— princes.

2832. חַשְׁמֹנָה Chashmônâh, *khash-mo-naw´*; fem. of 2831; *fertile*; *Chasmonah*, a place in the Desert:— Hashmonah.

2833. חֹשֶׁן chôshen, *kho´-shen*; from an unused root prob. mean. to *contain* or *sparkle*; perh. a *pocket* (as holding the Urim and Thummim), or *rich* (as containing gems), used only of the *gorget* of the high priest:— breastplate.

2834. חָשַׂף châsaph, *khaw-saf´*; a prim. root; to *strip* off, i.e. gen. to *make naked* (for exertion or in disgrace), to *drain* away or *bail* up (a liquid):— make bare, clean, discover, draw out, take, uncover.

2835. חָשִׂף châsiph, *khaw-seef´*; from 2834; prop. *drawn off*, i.e. separated; hence, a small *company* (as divided from the rest):— little flock.

2836. חָשַׁק châshaq, *khaw-shak´*; a prim. root; to *cling*, i.e. *join*, (fig.) to *love, delight* in; ellip. (or by interch. for

2820) to *deliver*:— have a delight, (have a) desire, fillet, long, set (in) love.

2837. חֵשֶׁק chêsheq, *khay´-shek*; from 2836; *delight*:— desire, pleasure.

2838. חָשֻׁק châshûq, *khaw-shook´*; or

חָשׁוּק châshûwq, *khaw-shook´*; pass. part. of 2836; *attached*, i.e. a fence-*rail* or rod connecting the posts or pillars:— fillet.

2839. חִשֻּׁק chishshûq, *khish-shook´*; from 2836; *conjoined*, i.e. a wheel-*spoke* or rod connecting the hub with the rim:— felloe.

2840. חִשֻּׁר chishshûr, *khish-shoor´*; from an unused root mean. to *bind together*; *combined*, i.e. the *nave* or hub of a wheel (as holding the spokes together):— spoke.

2841. חַשְׁרָה chashrâh, *khash-raw´*; from the same as 2840; prop. a *combination* or gathering, i.e. of watery *clouds*:— dark.

חֲשֻׂפָא Chăsûphâ'. See 2817.

2842. חָשַׁשׁ châshash, *khaw-shash´*; by var. for 7179; dry *grass*:— chaff.

2843. חוּשָׁתִי Chûshâthîy, *khoo-shaw-thee´*; patron. from 2364; a *Chushathite* or desc. of Chushah:— Hushathite.

2844. חַת chath, *khath*; from 2865; concr. *crushed*; also *afraid*; abstr. *terror*:— broken, dismayed, dread, fear.

2845. חֵת Chêth, *khayth*; from 2865; *terror*; *Cheth*, an aboriginal Canaanite:— Heth.

2846. חָתָה châthâh, *khaw-thaw´*; a prim. root; to *lay hold* of; espec. to *pick up* fire:— heap, take (away).

2847. חִתָּה chittâh, *khit-taw´*; from 2865; *fear*:— terror.

2848. חִתּוּל chittûwl, *khit-tool´*; from 2853; *swathed*, i.e. a *bandage*:— roller.

2849. חַתְחַת chathchath, *khath-khath´*; from 2844; *terror*:— fear.

2850. חִתִּי Chittîy, *khit-tee´*; patron. from 2845; a *Chittite*, or desc. of Cheth:— Hittite, Hittites.

2851. חִתִּית chittîyth, *khit-teeth´*; from 2865; *fear*:— terror.

2852. חָתַךְ châthak, *khaw-thak´*; a prim. root; prop. to *cut* off, i.e. (fig.) to *decree*:— determine.

2853. חָתַל châthal, *khaw-thal´*; a prim. root; to *swathe*:— × at all, swaddle.

2854. חֲתֻלָּה chăthullâh, *khath-ool-law´*; from 2853; a *swathing* cloth (fig.):— swaddling band.

2855. חֶתְלֹן Chethlôn, *kheth-lone´*; from 2853; *enswathed*; *Chethlon*, a place in Pal.:— Hethlon.

2856. חָתַם châtham, *khaw-tham´*; a prim. root; to *close up*; espec. to *seal*:— make an end, mark, seal (up), stop.

2857. חֲתַם chătham (Chald.), *khath-am´*; a root corresp. to 2856; to *seal*:— seal.

חֹתָם chôthâm. See 2368.

2858. חֹתֶמֶת chôthemeth, *kho-the-meth´*; fem. act. part. of 2856; a *seal*:— signet.

2859. חָתַן châthan, *khaw-than´*; a prim. root; to *give* (a daughter) *away* in mar-

riage; hence, (gen.) to *contract affinity* by marriage:— join in affinity, father in law, make marriages, mother in law, son in law.

2860. חָתָן châthân, *khaw-thawn´*; from 2859; a *relative* by marriage (espec. through the bride); fig. a *circumcised child* (as a species of relig. espousal):— bridegroom, husband, son in law.

2861. חֲתֻנָּה chăthunnâh, *khath-oon-naw´*; from 2859; a *wedding*:— espousal.

2862. חָתַף châthaph, *khaw-thaf´*; a prim. root; to *clutch*:— take away.

2863. חֶתֶף chetheph, *kheh´-thef*; from 2862; prop. *rapine*; fig. *robbery*:— prey.

2864. חָתַר châthar, *khaw-thar´*; a prim. root; to *force* a passage, as by burglary; fig. with oars:— dig (through), row.

2865. חָתַת châthath, *khaw-thath´*; a prim. root; prop. to *prostrate*; hence, to *break* down, either (lit.) by violence, or (fig.) by confusion and fear:— abolish, affright, be (make) afraid, amaze, beat down, discourage, (cause to) dismay, go down, scare, terrify.

2866. חֲתַת chăthath, *khath-ath´*; from 2865; *dismay*:— casting down.

2867. חֲתַת Chăthath, *khath-ath´*; the same as 2866; *Chathath*, an Isr.:— Hathath.

ט

2868. שְׁאֵב ţe°êb (Chald.), *teh-abe´*; a prim. root; to *rejoice*:— be glad.

2869. טָב ţâb (Chald.), *tawb*; from 2868; the same as 2896; *good*:— fine, good.

2870. טָבְאֵל Ţâbe°êl, *taw-beh-ale´*; from 2895 and 410; *pleasing* (to) *God*; *Tabeël*, the name of a Syrian and of a Persian:— Tabeal, Tabeel.

2871. טָבוּל ţâbûwl, *taw-bool´*; pass. part. of 2881; prop. *dyed*, i.e. a *turban* (prob. as of *colored* stuff):— dyed attire.

2872. טַבּוּר ţabbûwr, *tab-boor´*; from an unused root mean. to *pile up*; prop. *accumulated*; i.e. (by impl.) a *summit*:— middle, midst.

2873. טָבַח ţâbach, *taw-bakh´*; a prim. root; to *slaughter* (animals or men):— kill, (make) slaughter, slay.

2874. טֶבַח ţebach, *teh´-bakh*; from 2873; prop. something *slaughtered*; hence, a *beast* (or *meat*, as butchered); abstr. *butchery* (or concr. a place of slaughter):— × beast, slaughter, × slay, × sore.

2875. טֶבַח Ţebach, *teh´-bakh*; the same as 2874; *massacre*; *Tebach*, the name of a Mesopotamian and of an Isr.:— Tebah.

2876. טַבָּח ţabbâch, *tab-bawkh´*; from 2873; prop. a *butcher*; hence, a *lifeguardsman* (because acting as an executioner); also a *cook* (as usually slaughtering the animal for food):— cook, guard.

2877. טַבָּח ţabbâch (Chald.), *tab-bawkh´*; the same as 2876; a *lifeguardsman*:— guard.

2878. טִבְחָה ţibehâh, *tib-khaw´*; fem. of 2874 and mean. the same:— flesh, slaughter.

2879. מְבָחָה **ṭabbâchâh**, *tab-baw-khaw´*; fem. of 2876; a female *cook*:— cook.

2880. מִבְחַת **Ṭibchath**, *tib-khath´*; from 2878; *slaughter; Tibchath*, a place in Syria:— Tibhath.

2881. טָבַל **ṭâbal**, *taw-bal´*; a prim. root; to *dip*, plunge.

2882. טְבַלְיָהוּ **Ṭebalyâhûw**, *teb-al-yaw´-hoo;* from 2881 and 3050; *Jah has dipped; Tebaljah*, an Isr.:— Tebaliah.

2883. טָבַע **ṭâba'**, *taw-bah´*; a prim. root; to *sink*:— drown, fasten, settle, sink.

2884. טַבָּעוֹת **Ṭabbâ'ôwth**, *tab-baw-othe´*; plur. of 2885; *rings; Tabbaoth*, one of the Nethinim:— Tabbaoth.

2885. טַבַּעַת **ṭabba'ath**, *tab-bah´-ath*; from 2883; prop. a *seal* (as *sunk* into the wax), i.e. *signet* (for sealing); hence, (gen.) a *ring* of any kind:— ring.

2886. טַבְרִמּוֹן **Ṭabrimmôwn**, *tab-rim-mone´*; from 2895 and 7417; *pleasing* (to) *Rimmon; Tabrimmon*, a Syrian:— Tabrimmon.

2887. טֵבֵת **Ṭêbeth**, *tay´-beth;* prob. of for. der.; *Tebeth*, the tenth Heb. month:— Tebeth.

2888. טַבַּת **Ṭabbath**, *tab-bath´;* of uncert. der.; *Tabbath*, a place E. of the Jordan:— Tabbath.

2889. טָהוֹר **ṭâhôwr**, *taw-hore´;* or

טָהֹר **ṭâhôr**, *taw-hore´;* from 2891; *pure* (in a physical, chemical, ceremonial or moral sense):— clean, fair, pure (-ness).

2890. טְהוֹר **ṭehôwr**, *teh-hore´;* from 2891; *purity*:— pureness.

2891. טָהֵר **ṭâhêr**, *taw-hare´;* a prim. root; prop. to *be bright;* i.e. (by impl.) to *be pure* (phys. *sound, clear, unadulterated;* Levit. *uncontaminated;* mor. *innocent* or *holy*):— be (make, make self, pronounce) clean, cleanse (self), purge, purify (-ier, self).

2892. טֹהַר **ṭôhar**, *to´-har;* from 2891; lit. *brightness;* ceremonial *purification*:— clearness, glory, purifying.

2893. טָהֳרָה **ṭohŏrâh**, *toh-or-aw´;* fem. of 2892; ceremonial *purification;* moral *purity*:— × is cleansed, cleansing, purification (-fying).

2894. טוּא **ṭûw'**, *too;* a prim. root; to *sweep away*:— sweep.

2895. טוֹב **ṭowb**, *tobe;* a prim. root, to *be* (tran. *do* or *make) good* (or *well*) in the widest sense:— be (do) better, cheer, be (do, seem) good, (make) goodly, × please, (be, do, go, play) well.

2896. טוֹב **ṭôwb**, *tobe;* from 2895; *good* (as an adj.) in the widest sense; used likewise as a noun, both in the masc. and the fem., the sing. and the plur. (*good,* a *good* or *good* thing, a *good* man or woman; the *good, goods* or *good* things, *good* men or women), also as an adv. (*well*):— beautiful, best, better, bountiful, cheerful, at ease, × fair (word), (be in) favour, fine, glad, good (deed, -lier, -liest, -ly, -ness, -s), graciously, joyful, kindly, kindness, liketh (best), loving, merry, × most, pleasant, + pleaseth, pleasure, precious, prosperity, ready, sweet, wealth, welfare, (be) well (l-favoured).

2897. טוֹב **Ṭôwb**, *tobe;* the same as 2896; *good; Tob*, a region appar. E. of the Jordan:— Tob.

2898. טוּב **ṭûwb**, *toob;* from 2895; *good* (as a noun), in the widest sense, espec. *goodness* (superl. concr. the *best*), *beauty, gladness, welfare*:— fair, gladness, good (-ness, thing, -s), joy, go well with.

2899. טוֹב אֲדֹנִיָּהוּ **Ṭôwb Ădônîyâhûw**, *tobe ado-nee-yah´-hoo;* from 2896 and 138; *pleasing* (to) *Adonijah; Tob-Adonijah*, an Isr.:— Tob-adonijah.

2900. טוֹבִיָּה **Ṭôwbîyâh**, *to-bee-yaw´;* or

טוֹבִיָּהוּ **Ṭôwbîyâhûw**, *to-bee-yaw´-hoo;* from 2896 and 3050; *goodness of Jehovah; Tobijah*, the name of three Isr. and of one Samaritan:— Tobiah, Tobijah.

2901. טָוָה **ṭâvâh**, *taw-vaw´;* a prim. root; to *spin*:— spin.

2902. טוּחַ **ṭûwach**, *too´-akh;* a prim. root; to *smear;* espec. with lime:— daub, overlay, plaister, smut.

2903. טוֹפָפָה **ṭôwphâphâh**, *to-faw-faw´;* from an unused root mean. to *go around* or *bind;* a *fillet* for the forehead:— frontlet.

2904. טוּל **ṭûwl**, *tool;* a prim. root; to *pitch* over or *reel;* hence, (tran.) to *cast* down or out:— carry away, (utterly) cast (down, forth, out), send out.

2905. טוּר **ṭûwr**, *toor;* from an unused root mean. to *range* in a reg. manner; a *row;* hence, a *wall*:— row.

2906. טוּר **ṭûwr** (Chald.), *toor;* corresp. to 6697; a *rock* or hill:— mountain.

2907. טוּשׂ **ṭûws**, *toos;* a prim. root; to *pounce* as a bird of prey:— haste.

2908. טְוָת **ṭevâth** (Chald.), *tev-awth´;* from a root corresp. to 2901; *hunger* (as *twisting*):— fasting.

2909. טָחָה **ṭâchâh**, *taw-khaw´;* a prim. root; to *stretch* a bow, as an archer:— [bow-] shot.

2910. טוּחָה **ṭûwchâh**, *too-khaw´;* from 2909 (or 2902) in the sense of *overlaying;* (in the plur. only) the *kidneys* (as being *covered*); hence, (fig.) the inmost *thought*:— inward parts.

2911. טְחוֹן **ṭechôwn**, *tekh-one´;* from 2912; a hand *mill;* hence, a *millstone*:— to grind.

2912. טָחַן **ṭâchan**, *taw-khan´;* a prim. root; to *grind* meal; hence, to *be a concubine* (that being their employment):— grind (-er).

2913. טַחֲנָה **ṭachănâh**, *takh-an-aw´;* from 2912; a hand *mill;* hence, (fig.) *chewing*:— grinding.

2914. טְחֹר **ṭechôr**, *tekh-ore´;* from an unused root mean. to *burn;* a *boil* or ulcer (from the inflammation); espec. a tumor in the anus or pudenda (the piles):— emerod.

2915. טִיחַ **ṭîyach**, *tee´akh;* from (the equiv. of) 2902; *mortar* or *plaster*:— daubing.

2916. טִיט **ṭîyṭ**, *teet;* from an unused root mean. appar. to *be sticky* [rather perh. a denom. from 2894, through the idea of dirt to *be swept* away]; *mud* or *clay;* fig. *calamity*:— clay, dirt, mire.

2917. טִין **ṭîyn** (Chald.), *teen;* perh. by interchange, for a word corresp. to 2916; *clay*:— miry.

2918. טִירָה **ṭîyrâh**, *tee-raw´;* fem. of (an equiv. to) 2905; a *wall;* hence, a *fortress* or a *hamlet*:— (goodly) castle, habitation, palace, row.

2919. טַל **ṭal**, *tal;* from 2926; *dew* (as *covering* vegetation):— dew.

2920. טַל **ṭal** (Chald.), *tal;* the same as 2919:— dew.

2921. טָלָא **ṭâlâ'**, *taw-law´;* a prim. root; prop. to *cover* with pieces; i.e. (by impl.) to *spot* or *variegate* (as tapestry):— clouted, with divers colours, spotted.

2922. טְלָא **ṭelâ'**, *tel-aw´;* appar. from 2921 in the (orig.) sense of *covering* (for protection); a *lamb* [comp. 2924]:— lamb.

2923. טְלָאִים **Ṭelâ'îym**, *tel-aw-eem´;* from the plur. of 2922; *lambs; Telaim*, a place in Pal.:— Telaim.

2924. טָלֶה **ṭâleh**, *taw-leh´;* by var. for 2922; a *lamb*:— lamb.

2925. טַלְטֵלָה **ṭalṭêlâh**, *tal-tay-law´;* from 2904; *overthrow* or *rejection*:— captivity.

2926. טָלַל **ṭâlal**, *taw-lal´;* a prim. root; prop. to *strew* over, i.e. (by impl.) to *cover* in or *plate* (with beams):— cover.

2927. טְלַל **ṭelal** (Chald.), *tel-al´;* corresp. to 2926; to *cover* with shade:— have a shadow.

2928. טֶלֶם **Ṭelem**, *teh´-lem;* from an unused root mean. to *break* up or treat violently; *oppression; Telem*, the name of a place in Idumæa, also of a temple doorkeeper:— Telem.

2929. טַלְמוֹן **Ṭalmôwn**, *tal-mone´;* from the same as 2728; *oppressive; Talmon*, a temple doorkeeper:— Talmon.

2930. טָמֵא **ṭâmê'**, *taw-may´;* a prim. root; to *be foul*, espec. in a cerem. or mor. sense (*contaminated*):— defile (self), pollute (self), be (make, make self, pronounce) unclean, × utterly.

2931. טָמֵא **ṭâmê'**, *taw-may´;* from 2930; *foul* in a relig. sense:— defiled, + infamous, polluted (-tion), unclean.

2932. טֻמְאָה **ṭum'âh**, *toom-aw´;* from 2930; relig. *impurity*:— filthiness, unclean (-ness).

2933. טָמָה **ṭâmâh**, *taw-maw´;* a collat. form of 2930; to *be impure* in a relig. sense:— be defiled, be reputed vile.

2934. טָמַן **ṭâman**, *taw-man´;* a prim. root; to *hide* (by *covering* over):— hide, lay privily, in secret.

2935. טֶנֶא **ṭene'**, *teh´-neh;* from an unused root prob. mean. to *weave;* a *basket* (of interlaced osiers):— basket.

2936. טָנַף **ṭânaph**, *taw-naf´;* a prim. root; to *soil*:— defile.

2937. טָעָה **ṭâ'âh**, *taw-aw´;* a prim. root; to *wander;* caus. to *lead astray*:— seduce.

2938. טָעַם **ṭâ'am**, *taw-am´;* a prim. root; to *taste;* fig. to *perceive*:— × but, perceive, taste.

2939. טְעַם **t^e'am** (Chald.), *teh-am´*; corresp. to 2938; to *taste*; caus. to *feed*:— make to eat, feed.

2940. טַעַם **ṭa'am**, *tah´-am*; from 2938; prop. a *taste*, i.e. (fig.) *perception*; by impl. *intelligence*; tran. a *mandate*:— advice, behaviour, decree, discretion, judgment, reason, taste, understanding.

2941. טְעַם **ṭa'am** (Chald.), *tah´-am*; from 2939; prop. a *taste*, i.e. (as in 2940) a judicial *sentence*:— account, × to be commanded, commandment, matter.

2942. טְעֵם **t^e'êm** (Chald.), *teh-ame´*; from 2939, and equiv. to 2941; prop. *flavor*; fig. *judgment* (both subj. and obj.); hence, *account* (both subj. and obj.):— + chancellor, + command, commandment, decree, + regard, taste, wisdom.

2943. טָעַן **ṭâ'an**, *taw-an´*; a prim. root; to *load* a beast:— lade.

2944. טָעַן **ṭâ'an**, *taw-an´*; a prim. root; to *stab*:— thrust through.

2945. טַף **ṭaph**, *taf*; from 2952 (perh. referring to the *tripping* gait of children); a *family* (mostly used collect. in the sing.):— (little) children (ones), families.

2946. טָפַח **ṭâphach**, *taw-fakh´*; a prim. root; to *flatten* out or *extend* (as a tent); fig. to *nurse* a child (as *promotive* of growth); or perh. a denom. from 2947, from *dandling* on the palms:— span, swaddle.

2947. טֶפַח **ṭêphach**, *tay´-fakh*; from 2946; a *spread* of the hand, i.e. a *palmbreadth* (not "span" of the fingers); arch. a *corbel* (as a supporting palm):— coping, hand-breadth.

2948. טֹפַח **ṭôphach**, *to´-fakh*; from 2946 (the same as 2947):— hand-breadth (broad).

2949. טִפֻּח **ṭippûch**, *tip-pookh´*; from 2946; *nursing*:— span long.

2950. טָפַל **ṭâphal**, *taw-fal´*; a prim. root; prop. to *stick* on as a patch; fig. to *impute* falsely:— forge (-r), sew up.

2951. טִפְסַר **ṭiphçar**, *tif-sar´*; of for. der.; a military *governor*:— captain.

2952. טָפַף **ṭâphaph**, *taw-faf´*; a prim. root; appar. to *trip* (with short steps) coquettishly:— mince.

2953. טְפַר **t^ephar** (Chald.), *tef-ar´*; from a root corresp. to 6852, and mean. the same as 6856; a finger-*nail*; also a *hoof* or *claw*:— nail.

2954. טָפַשׁ **ṭâphash**, *taw-fash´*; a prim. root; prop. appar. to *be thick*; fig. to *be stupid*:— be fat.

2955. טָפַת **Ṭâphath**, *taw-fath´*; prob. from 5197; a *dropping* (of ointment); *Taphath*, an Israelitess:— Taphath.

2956. טָרַד **ṭârad**, *taw-rad´*; a prim. root; to *drive* on; fig. to *follow* close:— continual.

2957. טְרַד **t^erad** (Chald.), *ter-ad´*; corresp. to 2956; to *expel*:— drive.

2958. טְרוֹם **t^erôwm**, *ter-ome´*; a var. of 2962; *not yet*:— before.

2959. טָרַח **ṭârach**, *taw-rakh´*; a prim. root; to *overburden*:— weary.

2960. טֹרַח **ṭôrach**, *to´-rakh*; from 2959; a *burden*:— cumbrance, trouble.

2961. טָרִי **ṭâriy**, *taw-ree´*; from an unused root appar. mean. to *be moist*; prop. *dripping*; hence, *fresh* (i.e. recently made such):— new, putrefying.

2962. טֶרֶם **ṭerem**, *teh´-rem*; from an unused root appar. mean. to *interrupt* or *suspend*; prop. *non-occurrence*; used adv. *not yet* or *before*:— before, ere, not yet.

2963. טָרַף **ṭâraph**, *taw-raf´*; a prim. root; to *pluck off* or *pull* to pieces; caus. to *supply* with food (as in morsels):— catch, × without doubt, feed, ravin, rend in pieces, × surely, tear (in pieces).

2964. טֶרֶף **ṭereph**, *teh´-ref*; from 2963; something *torn*, i.e. a fragment, e.g. a *fresh* leaf, *prey*, *food*:— leaf, meat, prey, spoil.

2965. טָרָף **ṭârâph**, *taw-rawf´*; from 2963; recently *torn* off, i.e. *fresh*:— pluckt off.

2966. טְרֵפָה **t^erêphâh**, *ter-ay-faw´*; fem. (collect.) of 2964; *prey*, i.e. flocks devoured by animals:— ravin, (that which was) torn (of beasts, in pieces).

2967. טַרְפְּלַי **Ṭarp^elay** (Chald.), *tar-pel-ah´-ee*; from a name of for. der.; a *Tarpelite* (collect.) or inhab. of Tarpel, a place in Assyria:— Tarpelites.

2968. יָאַב **yâ'ab**, *yaw-ab´*; a prim. root; to *desire*:— long.

2969. יָאָה **yâ'âh**, *yaw-aw´*; a prim. root; to *be suitable*:— appertain.

יְאוֹר **y^e'ôwr**. See 2975.

2970. יַאֲזַנְיָה **Ya'ăzanyâh**, *yah-az-an-yaw´*; or

יַאֲזַנְיָהוּ **Ya'ăzanyâhûw**, *yah-az-an-yaw´-hoo*; from 238 and 3050; *heard of Jah*; *Jaazanjah*, the name of four Isr.:— Jaazaniah. Comp. 3153.

2971. יָאִיר **Yâ'iyr**, *yaw-ere´*; from 215; *enlightener*; *Jaïr*, the name of four Isr.:— Jair.

2972. יָאִרִי **Yâ'iriy**, *yaw-ee-ree´*; patron. from 2971; a *Jairite* or desc. of Jair:— Jairite.

2973. יָאַל **yâ'al**, *yaw-al´*; a prim. root; prop. to *be slack*, i.e. (fig.) to *be foolish*:— dote, be (become, do) foolish (-ly).

2974. יָאַל **yâ'al**, *yaw-al´*; a prim. root [prob. rather the same as 2973 through the idea of mental *weakness*]; prop. to *yield*, espec. *assent*; hence, (pos.) to *undertake* as an act of volition:— assay, begin, be content, please, take upon, × willingly, would.

2975. יְאֹר **y^e'ôr**, *yeh-ore´*; of Eg. or.; a *channel*, e.g. a fosse, canal, shaft; spec. the *Nile*, as the one river of Egypt, incl. its collat. trenches; also the *Tigris*, as the main river of Assyria:— brook, flood, river, stream.

2976. יָאַשׁ **yâ'ash**, *yaw-ash´*; a prim. root; to *desist*, i.e. (fig.) to *despond*:— (cause to) despair, one that is desperate, be no hope.

2977. יֹאשִׁיָּה **Yô'shiyâh**, *yo-shee-yaw´*; or

יֹאשִׁיָּהוּ **Yô'shiyâhûw**, *yo-she-yaw´-hoo*; from the same root as 803 and 3050; *founded of Jah*; *Joshijah*, the name of two Isr.:— Josiah.

2978. יְאִתוֹן **y^e'ithôwn**, *yeh-ee-thone´*; from 857; an *entry*:— entrance.

2979. יְאָתְרַי **Y^e'âth^eray**, *yeh-aw-ther-ah´ee*; from the same as 871; *stepping*; *Jeätherai*, an Isr.:— Jeaterai.

2980. יָבַב **yâbab**, *yaw-bab´*; a prim. root; to *bawl*:— cry out.

2981. יְבוּל **y^ebûwl**, *yeb-ool´*; from 2986; *produce*, i.e. a *crop* or (fig.) *wealth*:— fruit, increase.

2982. יְבוּס **Y^ebûwç**, *yeb-oos´*; from 947; *trodden*, i.e. threshing-place; *Jebus*, the aboriginal name of Jerusalem:— Jebus.

2983. יְבוּסִי **Y^ebûwçiy**, *yeb-oo-see´*; patrial from 2982; a *Jebusite* or inhab. of Jebus:— Jebusite (-s).

2984. יִבְחַר **Yibchar**, *yib-khar´*; from 977; *choice*; *Jibchar*, an Isr.:— Ibhar.

2985. יָבִין **Yâbiyn**, *yaw-bene´*; from 995; *intelligent*; *Jabin*, the name of two Canaanitish kings:— Jabin.

יָבֵשׁ **Yâbêysh**. See 3003.

2986. יָבַל **yâbal**, *yaw-bal´*; a prim. root; prop. to *flow*; caus. to *bring* (espec. with pomp):— bring (forth), carry, lead (forth).

2987. יְבַל **y^ebal** (Chald.), *yeb-al´*; corresp. to 2986; to *bring*:— bring, carry.

יוֹבֵל **yôbêl**. See 3104.

2988. יָבָל **yâbâl**, *yaw-bawl´*; from 2986; a *stream*:— [water-] course, stream.

2989. יָבָל **Yâbâl**, *yaw-bawl´*; the same as 2988; *Jabal*, an antediluvian:— Jabal.

יוֹבֵל **yôbêl**. See 3104.

2990. יָבֵּל **yabbêl**, *yab-bale´*; from 2986; having *running* sores:— wen.

2991. יִבְלְעָם **Yibl^e'âm**, *yib-leh-awm´*; from 1104 and 5971; *devouring people*; *Jibleäm*, a place in Pal.:— Ibleam.

2992. יָבַם **yâbam**, *yaw-bam´*; a prim. root of doubtful mean.; used only as a denom. from 2993; to *marry* a (deceased) brother's widow:— perform the duty of a husband's brother, marry.

2993. יָבָם **yâbâm**, *yaw-bawm´*; from (the orig. of) 2992; a *brother-in-law*:— husband's brother.

2994. יְבֵמֶת **y^ebêmeth**, *yeb-ay´-meth*; fem. part. of 2992; a *sister-in-law*:— brother's wife, sister in law.

2995. יַבְנְאֵל **Yabn^e'êl**, *yab-neh-ale´*; from 1129 and 410; *built of God*; *Jabneël*, the name of two places in Pal.:— Jabneel.

2996. יַבְנֶה **Yabneh**, *yab-neh´*; from 1129; a *building*; *Jabneh*, a place in Pal.:— Jabneh.

2997. יִבְנְיָה **Yibn^eyâh**, *yib-neh-yaw´*; from 1129 and 3050; *built of Jah*; *Jibnejah*, an Isr.:— Ibneiah.

2998. יִבְנִיָּה **Yibniyâh**, *yib-nee-yaw´*; from 1129 and 3050; *building of Jah*; *Jibnijah*, an Isr.:— Ibnijah.

2999. יַבֹּק **Yabbôq**, *yab-boke´*; prob.

Hebrew

from 1238; *pouring* forth; *Jabbok*, a river E. of the Jordan:— Jabbok.

3000. בְּרֶכְיָהוּ **Y^eberekyâhûw**, *yeb-eh-rek-yaw´-hoo*; from 1288 and 3050; *blessed of Jah*; *Jeberekjah*, an Isr.:— Jeberechiah.

3001. בֹּשׁ **yâbêsh**, *yaw-bashe´*; a prim. root; to *be ashamed*, *confused* or *disappointed*; also (as failing) to *dry* up (as water) or *wither* (as herbage):— be ashamed, clean, be confounded, (make) dry (up), (do) shame (-fully), × utterly, wither (away).

3002. בֹּשׁ **yâbêsh**, *yaw-bashe´*; from 3001; *dry*:— dried (away), dry.

3003. בֹּשׁ **Yâbêsh**, *yaw-bashe´*; the same as 3002 (also

יָבֵישׁ **Yâbêysh**, *yaw-bashe´*; often with the addition of 1568, i.e. *Jabesh of Gilad*); *Jabesh*, the name of an Isr. and of a place in Pal.:— Jabesh (I-Gilead).

3004. יַבָּשָׁה **yabbâshâh**, *yab-baw-shaw´*; from 3001; *dry ground*:— dry (ground, land).

3005. יִבְשָׂם **Yibsâm**, *yib-sawm´*; from the same as 1314; *fragrant*; *Jibsam*, an Isr.:— Jibsam.

3006. יַבֶּשֶׁת **yabbesheth**, *yab-beh´-sheth*; a var. of 3004; *dry ground*:— dry land.

3007. יַבֶּשֶׁת **yabbesheth** (Chald.), *yab-beh´-sheth*; corresp. to 3006; *dry* land:— earth.

3008. יִגְאָל **Yig'âl**, *yig-awl´*; from 1350; *avenger*; *Jigal*, the name of three Isr.:— Igal, Igeal.

3009. יָגַב **yâgab**, *yaw-gab´*; a prim. root; to *dig* or *plow*:— husbandman.

3010. יָגֵב **yâgêb**, *yaw-gabe´*; from 3009; a plowed *field*:— field.

3011. יָגְבְּהָה **Yogb^ehâh**, *yog-beh-haw´*; fem. from 1361; *hillock*; *Jogbehah*, a place E. of the Jordan:— Jogbehah.

3012. יִגְדַּלְיָהוּ **Yigdalyâhûw**, *yig-dal-yaw´-hoo*; from 1431 and 3050; *magnified of Jah*; *Jigdaljah*, an Isr.:— Igdaliah.

3013. יָגָה **yâgâh**, *yaw-gaw´*; a prim. root; to *grieve*:— afflict, cause grief, grieve, sorrowful, vex.

3014. יָגָה **yâgâh**, *yaw-gaw´*; a prim. root (prob. rather the same as 3013 through the common idea of *dissatisfaction*); to *push* away:— be removed.

3015. יָגוֹן **yâgôwn**, *yaw-gohn´*; from 3013; *affliction*:— grief, sorrow.

3016. יָגוֹר **yâgôwr**, *yaw-gore´*; from 3025; *fearful*:— afraid, fearest.

3017. יָגוּר **Yâgûwr**, *yaw-goor´*; prob. from 1481; a *lodging*; *Jagur*, a place in Pal.:— Jagur.

3018. יְגִיעַ **y^egîya'**, *yeg-ee´-ah*; from 3021; *toil*; hence, a *work*, *produce*, *property* (as the result of labor):— labour, work.

3019. יָגִיעַ **yâgîya'**, *yaw-ghee´-ah*; from 3021; *tired*:— weary.

3020. יָגְלִי **Yoglîy**, *yog-lee´*; from 1540; *exiled*; *Jogli*, an Isr.:— Jogli.

3021. יָגַע **yâga'**, *yaw-gah´*; a prim. root; prop. to *gasp*; hence, to *be exhausted*, to *tire*, to *toil*:— faint, (make to) labour, (be) weary.

3022. יָגַע **yâgâ'**, *yaw-gaw´*; from 3021; *earnings* (as the product of toil):— that which he laboured for.

3023. יָגֵעַ **yâgêa'**, *yaw-gay´-ah*; from 3021; *tired*; hence, (tran.) *tiresome*:— full of labour, weary.

3024. יְגִעָה **y^egî'âh**, *yeg-ee-aw´*; fem. of 3019; *fatigue*:— weariness.

3025. יָגֹר **yâgôr**, *yaw-gore´*; a prim. root; to *fear*:— be afraid, fear.

3026. יְגַר שָׂהֲדוּתָא **Y^egar Sahădûwthâ'** (Chald.), *yegar´ sah-had-oo-thaw´*; from a word derived from an unused root (mean. to *gather*) and a der. of a root corresp. to 7717; *heap of the testimony*; *Jegar-Sahadutha*, a cairn E. of the Jordan:— Jegar-Sahadutha.

3027. יָד **yâd**, *yawd*; a prim. word; a *hand* (the *open* one [indicating *power*, *means*, *direction*, etc.], in distinction from 3709, the *closed* one); used (as noun, adv., etc.) in a great variety of applications, both lit. and fig., both prox. and remote [as follows]:— (+ be) able, × about, + armholes, at, axletree, because of, beside, border, × bounty, + broad, [broken-] handed, × by, charge, coast, + consecrate, + creditor, custody, debt, dominion, × enough, + fellowship, force, × from, hand [-staves, -y work], × he, himself, × in, labour, + large, ledge, [left-] handed, means, × mine, ministry, near, × of, × order, ordinance, × our, parts, pain, power, × presumptuously, service, side, sore, state, stay, draw with strength, stroke, + swear, terror, × thee, × by them, × themselves, × thine own, × thou, through, × throwing, + thumb, times, × to, × under, × us, × wait on, [way-] side, where, + wide, × with (him, me, you), work, + yield, × yourselves.

3028. יַד **yad** (Chald.), *yad*; corresp. to 3027:— hand, power.

3029. יְדָא **y^edâ'** (Chald.), *yed-aw´*; corresp. to 3034; to *praise*:— (give) thank (-s).

3030. יִדְאֲלָה **Yid'âlâh**, *yid-al-aw´*; of uncert. der.; *Jidalah*, a place in Pal.:— Idalah.

3031. יִדְבָּשׁ **Yidbâsh**, *yid-bawsh´*; from the same as 1706; perh. *honeyed*; *Jidbash*, an Isr.:— Idbash.

3032. יָדַד **yâdad**, *yaw-dad´*; a prim. root; prop. to *handle* [comp. 3034], i.e. to *throw*, e.g. lots:— cast.

3033. יְדִדוּת **y^edîdûwth**, *yed-ee-dooth´*; from 3039; prop. *affection*; concr. a *darling* object:— dearly beloved.

3034. יָדָה **yâdâh**, *yaw-daw´*; a prim. root; used only as denom. from 3027; lit. to *use* (i.e. hold out) *the hand*; phys. to *throw* (a stone, an arrow) at or away; espec. to *revere* or *worship* (with extended hands); intens. to *bemoan* (by wringing the hands):— cast (out), (make) confess (-ion), praise, shoot, (give) thank (-ful, -s, -sgiving).

3035. יִדּוֹ **Yiddôw**, *yid-do´*; from 3034; *praised*; *Jiddo*, an Isr.:— Iddo.

3036. יָדוֹן **Yâdôwn**, *yaw-done´*; from 3034; *thankful*; *Jadon*, an Isr.:— Jadon.

3037. יַדּוּעַ **Yaddûwa'**, *yad-doo´-ah*;

from 3045; *knowing*; *Jadduä*, the name of two Isr.:— Jaddua.

3038. יְדוּתוּן **Y^edûwthûwn**, *yed-oo-thoon´*; or

יְדֻתוּן **Y^edùthûwn**, *yed-oo-thoon´*; or

יְדִיתוּן **Y^edîythûwn**, *yed-ee-thoon´*; prob. from 3034; *laudatory*; *Jeduthun*, an Isr.:— Jeduthun.

3039. יְדִיד **y^edîyd**, *yed-eed´*; from the same as 1730; *loved*:— amiable, (well-) beloved, loves.

3040. יְדִידָה **Y^edîydâh**, *yed-ee-daw´*; fem. of 3039; *beloved*; *Jedidah*, an Israelitess:— Jedidah.

3041. יְדִידְיָה **Y^edîyd^eyâh**, *yed-ee-deh-yaw´*; from 3039 and 3050; *beloved of Jah*; *Jedidejah*, a name of Solomon:— Jedidiah.

3042. יְדָיָה **Y^edâyâh**, *yed-aw-yaw´*; from 3034 and 3050; *praised of Jah*; *Jedajah*, the name of two Isr.:— Jedaiah.

3043. יְדִיעֲאֵל **Y^edîy'â'êl**, *yed-ee-ah-ale´*; from 3045 and 410; *knowing God*; *Jediaël*, the name of three Isr.:— Jediael.

3044. יִדְלָף **Yidlâph**, *yid-lawf´*; from 1811; *tearful*; *Jidlaph*, a Mesopotamian:— Jidlaph.

3045. יָדַע **yâda'**, *yaw-dah´*; a prim. root; to *know* (prop. to ascertain by *seeing*); used in a great variety of senses, fig., lit., euphem. and infer. (incl. *observation*, *care*, *recognition*; and caus. *instruction*, *designation*, *punishment*, etc.) [as follow]:— acknowledge, acquaintance (-ted with), advise, answer, appoint, assuredly, be aware, [un-] awares, can [-not], certainly, for a certainty, comprehend, consider, × could they, cunning, declare, be diligent, (can, cause to) discern, discover, endued with, familiar friend, famous, feel, can have, be [ig-] norant, instruct, kinsfolk, kinsman, (cause to, let, make) know, (come to give, have, take) knowledge, have [knowledge], (be, make, make to be, make self) known, + be learned, + lie by man, mark, perceive, privy to, × prognosticator, regard, have respect, skilful, shew, can (man of) skill, be sure, of a surety, teach, (can) tell, understand, have [understanding], × will be, wist, wit, wot.

3046. יְדַע **y^eda'** (Chald.), *yed-ah´*; corresp. to 3045:— certify, know, make known, teach.

3047. יָדָע **Yâdâ'**, *yaw-daw´*; from 3045; *knowing*; *Jada*, an Isr.:— Jada.

3048. יְדַעְיָה **Y^eda'yâh**, *yed-ah-yaw´*; from 3045 and 3050; *Jah has known*; *Jedajah*, the name of two Isr.:— Jedaiah.

3049. יִדְּעֹנִי **yidd^e'ônîy**, *yid-deh-o-nee´*; from 3045; prop. a *knowing* one; spec. a *conjurer*; (by impl.) a *ghost*:— wizard.

3050. יָהּ **Yâhh**, *yaw*; contr. for 3068, and mean. the same; *Jah*, the sacred name:— Jah, the Lord, most vehement. Comp. names in "-iah," "-jah."

3051. יָהַב **yâhab**, *yaw-hab´*; a prim. root; to *give* (whether lit. or fig.); gen. to *put*; imper. (refl.) *come*:— ascribe, bring, come on, give, go, set, take.

3052. יְהַב **yᵉhab** (Chald.), *yeh-hab´*; corresp. to 3051:— deliver, give, lay, + prolong, pay, yield.

3053. יְהַב **yᵉhâb**, *ye-hawb´*; from 3051; prop. what is *given* (by Providence), i.e. a *lot*:— burden.

3054. יָהַד **yâhad**, *yaw-had´*; denom. from a form corresp. to 3061; to *Judaize*, i.e. become Jewish:— become Jews.

3055. יְהֻד **yᵉhûd**, *yeh-hood´*; a briefer form of one corresp. to 3061; *Jehud*, a place in Pal.:— Jehud.

3056. יֶהְדַי **Yehday**, *yeh-dah´-ee*; perh. from a form corresp. to 3061; *Judaistic*; *Jehdai*, an Isr.:— Jehdai.

3057. יְהֻדִיָּה **Yᵉhûdîyâh**, *yeh-hoo-dee-yaw´*; fem. of 3064; *Jehudijah*, a Jewess:— Jehudijah.

3058. יֵהוּא **Yêhûw´**, *yay-hoo´*; from 3068 and 1931; *Jehovah* (is) *He*; *Jehu*, the name of five Isr.:— Jehu.

3059. יְהוֹאָחָז **Yᵉhôw´âchâz**, *yeh-ho-aw-khawz´*; from 3068 and 270; *Jehovah-seized*; *Jehoächaz*, the name of three Isr.:— Jehoahaz. Comp. 3099.

3060. יְהוֹאָשׁ **Yᵉhôw´âsh**, *yeh-ho-awsh´*; from 3068 and (perh.) 784; *Jehovah-fired*; *Jehoäsh*, the name of two Isr. kings:— Jehoash. Comp. 3101.

3061. יְהוּד **Yᵉhûwd** (Chald.), *yeh-hood´*; contr. from a form corresp. to 3063; prop. *Judah*, hence, *Judea*:— Jewry, Judah, Judea.

3062. יְהוּדָאִי **Yᵉhûwdâ´îy** (Chald.), *yeh-hoo-daw-ee´*; patrial from 3061; a *Jehudaïte* (or *Judaïte*), i.e. *Jew*:— Jew.

3063. יְהוּדָה **Yᵉhûwdâh**, *yeh-hoo-daw´*; from 3034; *celebrated*; *Jehudah* (or *Judah*), the name of five Isr.; also of the tribe descended from the first, and of its territory:— Judah.

3064. יְהוּדִי **Yᵉhûwdîy**, *yeh-hoo-dee´*; patron. from 3063; a *Jehudite* (i.e. *Judaite* or *Jew*), or desc. of Jehudah (i.e. Judah):— Jew.

3065. יְהוּדִי **Yᵉhûwdîy**, *yeh-hoo-dee´*; the same as 3064; *Jehudi*, an Isr.:— Jehudi.

3066. יְהוּדִית **Yᵉhûwdîyth**, *yeh-hoo-deeth´*; fem. of 3064; the *Jewish* (used adv.) language:— in the Jews' language.

3067. יְהוּדִית **Yᵉhûwdîyth**, *yeh-ho-deeth´*; the same as 3066; *Jewess*; *Jehudith*, a Canaanitess:— Judith.

3068. יְהוָה **Yᵉhôvâh**, *yeh-ho-vaw´*; from 1961; (the) self-*Existent* or *Eternal*; *Jehovah*, Jewish national name of God:— Jehovah, the Lord. Comp. 3050, 3069.

3069. יְהוִה **Yᵉhôvih**, *yeh-ho-vee´*; a var. of 3068 [used after 136, and pronounced by Jews as 430, in order to prevent the repetition of the same sound, since they elsewhere pronounce 3068 as 136]:— God.

3070. יְהוָה יִרְאֶה **Yᵉhôvâh Yir´eh**, *yeh-ho-vaw´ yir-eh´*; from 3068 and 7200; *Jehovah will see* (to it); *Jehovah-Jireh*, a symb. name for Mt. Moriah:— Jehovah-jireh.

3071. יְהוָה נִסִּי **Yᵉhôvâh Niççîy**, *yeh-ho-vaw´ nis-see´*; from 3068 and 5251 with the pron. suff.; *Jehovah* (is) *my banner*;

Jehovah-Nissi, a symb. name of an altar in the Desert:— Jehovah-nissi.

3072. יְהוָה צִדְקֵנוּ **Yᵉhôvâh Tsidqênûw**, *ye-ho-vaw´ tsid-kay´-noo*; from 3068 and 6664 with pron. suff.; *Jehovah* (is) *our right*; *Jehovah-Tsidkenu*, a symb. epithet of the Messiah and of Jerusalem:— the Lord our righteousness.

3073. יְהוָה שָׁלוֹם **Yᵉhôvâh Shâlôwm**, *yeh-ho-vaw´ shaw-lome´*; from 3068 and 7965; *Jehovah* (is) *peace*; *Jehovah-Shalom*, a symb. name of an altar in Pal.:— Jehovah-shalom.

3074. יְהוָה שָׁמָּה **Yᵉhôvâh Shâmmâh**, *yeh-ho-vaw´ shawm´-maw*; from 3068 and 8033 with directive enclitic; *Jehovah* (is) *thither*; *Jehovah-Shammah*, a symbol. title of Jerusalem:— Jehovah-shammah.

3075. יְהוֹזָבָד **Yᵉhôwzâbâd**, *yeh-ho-zaw-bawd´*; from 3068 and 2064; *Jehovah-endowed*; *Jehozabad*, the name of three Isr.:— Jehozabad. Comp. 3107.

3076. יְהוֹחָנָן **Yᵉhôwchânân**, *yeh-ho-khaw-nawn´*; from 3068 and 2603; *Jehovah-favored*; *Jehochanan*, the name of eight Isr.:— Jehohanan, Johanan. Comp. 3110.

3077. יְהוֹיָדָע **Yᵉhôwyâdâ´**, *yeh-ho-yaw-daw´*; from 3068 and 3045; *Jehovah-known*; *Jehojada*, the name of three Isr.:— Jehoiada. Comp. 3111.

3078. יְהוֹיָכִין **Yᵉhôwyâkîyn**, *yeh-ho-yaw-keen´*; from 3068 and 3559; *Jehovah will establish*; *Jehojakin*, a Jewish king:— Jehoiachin. Comp. 3112.

3079. יְהוֹיָקִים **Yᵉhôwyâqîym**, *yeh-ho-yaw-keem´*; from 3068 abb. and 6965; *Jehovah will raise*; *Jehojakim*, a Jewish king:— Jehoiakim. Comp. 3113.

3080. יְהוֹיָרִיב **Yᵉhôwyârîyb**, *yeh-ho-yaw-reeb´*; from 3068 and 7378; *Jehovah will contend*; *Jehojarib*, the name of two Isr.:— Jehoiarib. Comp. 3114.

3081. יְהוּכַל **Yᵉhûwkal**, *yeh-hoo-kal´*; from 3201; *potent*; *Jehukal*, an Isr.:— Jehucal. Comp. 3116.

3082. יְהוֹנָדָב **Yᵉhôwnâdâb**, *yeh-ho-naw-dawb´*; from 3068 and 5068; *Jehovah-largessed*; *Jehonadab*, the name of an Isr. and of an Arab:— Jehonadab, Jonadab. Comp. 3122.

3083. יְהוֹנָתָן **Yᵉhôwnâthân**, *yeh-ho-naw-thawn´*; from 3068 and 5414; *Jehovah-given*; *Jehonathan*, the name of four Isr.:— Jonathan. Comp. 3129.

3084. יְהוֹסֵף **Yᵉhôwçêph**, *yeh-ho-safe´*; a fuller form of 3130; *Jehoseph* (i.e. *Joseph*), a son of Jacob:— Joseph.

3085. יְהוֹעַדָּה **Yᵉhôw´addâh**, *yeh-ho-ad-daw´*; from 3068 and 5710; *Jehovah-adorned*; *Jehoäddah*, an Isr.:— Jehoada.

3086. יְהוֹעַדִּין **Yᵉhôw´addîyn**, *yeh-ho-ad-deen´*; or

יְהוֹעַדָּן **Yᵉhôw´addân**, *yeh-ho-ad-dawn´*; from 3068 and 5727; *Jehovah-pleased*; *Jehoäddin* or *Jehoäddan*, an Israelitess:— Jehoaddan.

3087. יְהוֹצָדָק **Yᵉhôwtsâdâq**, *yeh-ho-tsaw-dawk´*; from 3068 and 6663; *Jehovah-righted*; *Jehotsadak*, an Isr.:— Jehozadek, Josedech. Comp. 3136.

3088. יְהוֹרָם **Yᵉhôwrâm**, *yeh-ho-rawm´*; from 3068 and 7311; *Jehovah-raised*; *Jehoram*, the name of a Syrian and of three Isr.:— Jehoram, Joram. Comp. 3141.

3089. יְהוֹשֶׁבַע **Yᵉhôwsheba´**, *yeh-ho-sheh´-bah*; from 3068 and 7650; *Jehovah-sworn*; *Jehosheba*, an Israelitess:— Jehosheba. Comp. 3090.

3090. יְהוֹשַׁבְעַת **Yᵉhôwshab´ath**, *yeh-ho-shab-ath´*; a form of 3089; *Jehoshabath*, an Israelitess:— Jehoshabeath.

3091. יְהוֹשׁוּעַ **Yᵉhôwshûw´a**, *yeh-ho-shoo´-ah*; or

יְהוֹשֻׁעַ **Yᵉhôwshú´a**, *yeh-ho-shoo´-ah*; from 3068 and 3467; *Jehovah-saved*; *Jehoshuä* (i.e. *Joshua*), the Jewish leader:— Jehoshua, Jehoshuah, Joshua. Comp. 1954, 3442.

3092. יְהוֹשָׁפָט **Yᵉhôwshâphât**, *yeh-ho-shaw-fawt´*; from 3068 and 8199; *Jehovah-judged*; *Jehoshaphat*, the name of six Isr.; also of a valley near Jerusalem:— Jehoshaphat. Comp. 3146.

3093. יָהִיר **yâhîyr**, *yaw-here´*; prob. from the same as 2022; *elated*; hence, *arrogant*:— haughty, proud.

3094. יְהַלֶּלְאֵל **Yᵉhallel´êl**, *yeh-hal-lel-ale´*; from 1984 and 410; *praising God*; *Jehallelel*, the name of two Isr.:— Jehaleleel, Jehalelel.

3095. יַהֲלֹם **yahâlôm**, *yah-hal-ome´*; from 1986 (in the sense of *hardness*); a precious stone, prob. *onyx*:— diamond.

3096. יַהַץ **Yahats**, *yah´-hats*; or

יַהְצָה **Yahtsâh**, *yah´-tsaw*; or (fem.)

יַהְצָה **Yahtsâh**, *yah-tsaw´*; from an unused root mean. to *stamp*; perh. *threshing*-floor; *Jahats* or *Jahtsah*, a place E. of the Jordan:— Jahaz, Jahazah, Jahzah.

3097. יוֹאָב **Yôw´âb**, *yo-awb´*; from 3068 and 1; *Jehovah-fathered*; *Joäb*, the name of three Isr.:— Joab.

3098. יוֹאָח **Yôw´âch**, *yo-awkh´*; from 3068 and 251; *Jehovah-brothered*; *Joach*, the name of four Isr.:— Joah.

3099. יוֹאָחָז **Yôw´âchâz**, *yo-aw-khawz´*; a form of 3059; *Joächaz*, the name of two Isr.:— Jehoahaz, Joahaz.

3100. יוֹאֵל **Yôw´êl**, *yo-ale´*; from 3068 and 410; *Jehovah* (is his) *God*; *Joël*, the name of twelve Isr.:— Joel.

3101. יוֹאָשׁ **Yôw´âsh**, *yo-awsh´*; or

יֹאָשׁ **Yô´âsh** (2 Chron. 24:1), *yo-awsh´*; a form of 3060; *Joäsh*, the name of six Isr.:— Joash.

3102. יוֹב **Yôwb**, *yobe*; perh. a form of 3103, but more prob. by err. transc. for 3437; *Job*, an Isr.:— Job.

3103. יוֹבָב **Yôwbâb**, *yo-bawb´*; from 2980; *howler*; *Jobab*, the name of two Isr. and of three foreigners:— Jobab.

3104. יוֹבֵל **yôwbêl**, *yo-bale´*; or

יֹבֵל **yôbêl**, *yob-ale´*; appar. from 2986; the *blast* of a horn (from its *continuous* sound); spec. the *signal* of the silver trumpets; hence, the *instrument* itself and the festival thus introduced:— jubile, ram's horn, trumpet.

3105. יוּבָל **yûwbal**, yoo-bal´; from 2986; a stream:— river.

3106. יוּבָל **Yûwbâl**, yoo-bawl´; from 2986; stream; Jubal, an antediluvian:— Jubal.

3107. יוֹזָבָד **Yôwzâbâd**, yo-zaw-bawd´; a form of 3075; Jozabad, the name of ten Isr.:— Josabad, Jozabad.

3108. יוֹזָכָר **Yôwzâkâr**, yo-zaw-kawr´; from 3068 and 2142; Jehovah-remembered; Jozacar, an Isr.:— Jozachar.

3109. יוֹחָא **Yôwchâ'**, yo-khaw´; prob. from 3068 and a var. of 2421; Jehovah-revived; Jocha, the name of two Isr.:— Joha.

3110. יוֹחָנָן **Yôwchânân**, yo-khaw-nawn´; a form of 3076; Jochanan, the name of nine Isr.:— Johanan.

יוּטָה **Yûwṭâh**. See 3194.

3111. יוֹיָדָע **Yôwyâdâ'**, yo-yaw-daw´; a form of 3077; Jojada, the name of two Isr.:— Jehoiada, Joiada.

3112. יוֹיָכִין **Yôwyâkiyn**, yo-yaw-keen´; a form of 3078; Jojakin, an Isr. king:— Jehoiachin.

3113. יוֹיָקִים **Yôwyâqîym**, yo-yaw-keem´; a form of 3079; Jojakim, an Isr.:— Joiakim. Comp. 3137.

3114. יוֹיָרִיב **Yôwyârîyb**, yo-yaw-reeb´; a form of 3080; Jojarib, the name of four Isr.:— Joiarib.

3115. יוֹכֶבֶד **Yôwkebed**, yo-keh´-bed; from 3068 contr. and 3513; Jehovah-gloried; Jokebed, the mother of Moses:— Jochebed.

3116. יוּכַל **Yûwkal**, yoo-kal´; a form of 3081; Jukal, an Isr.:— Jucal.

3117. יוֹם **yôwm**, yome; from an unused root mean. to be hot; a day (as the warm hours), whether lit. (from sunrise to sunset, or from one sunset to the next), or fig. (a space of time defined by an associated term), loften used adv.l:— age, + always, + chronicles, continually (-ance), daily, (lbirthl, each, to) day, (now a, two) days (agone), + elder, × end, + evening, + (for) ever (-lasting, -more), × full, life, as (so) long as (... live), (even) now, + old, + outlived, + perpetually, presently, + remaineth, × required, season, × since, space, then, (process ofl time, + as at other times, + in trouble, weather, (as) when, (a, the, within a) while (that), × whole (+ age), (full) year (-ly), + younger.

3118. יוֹם **yôwm** (Chald.), yome; corresp. to 3117; a day:— day (by day), time.

3119. יוֹמָם **yôwmâm**, yo-mawm´; from 3117; daily:— daily, (by, in the) day (-time).

3120. יָוָן **Yâvân**, yaw-vawn´; prob. from the same as 3196; effervescing (i.e. hot and active); Javan, the name of a son of Joktan, and of the race (Ionians, i.e. Greeks) descended from him, with their territory; also of a place in Arabia:— Javan.

3121. יָוֵן **yâvên**, yaw-ven´; from the same as 3196; prop. dregs (as effervescing); hence, mud:— mire, miry.

3122. יוֹנָדָב **Yôwnâdâb**, yo-naw-dawb´; a

form of 3082; Jonadab, the name of an Isr. and of a Rechabite:— Jonadab.

3123. יוֹנָה **yôwnâh**, yo-naw´; prob. from the same as 3196; a dove (appar. from the warmth of their mating):— dove, pigeon.

3124. יוֹנָה **Yôwnâh**, yo-naw´; the same as 3123; Jonah, an Isr.:— Jonah.

3125. יְוָנִי **Yᵉvâniy**, yev-aw-nee´; patron. from 3121; a Jevanite, or desc. of Javan:— Grecian.

3126. יוֹנֵק **yôwnêq**, yo-nake´; act. part. of 3243; a sucker; hence, a twig (of a tree felled and sprouting):— tender plant.

3127. יוֹנֶקֶת **yôwneqeth**, yo-neh´-keth; fem. of 3126; a sprout:— (tender) branch, young twig.

3128. יוֹנַת אֵלֶם רְחֹקִים **Yôwnath 'êlem rᵉchôqîym**, yo-nath´ ay´-lem rekh-o-keem´; from 3123 and 482 and the plur. of 7350; dove of (the) silence (i.e. dumb Israel) of (i.e. among) distances (i.e. strangers); the title of a ditty (used for a name of its melody):— Jonath-elem-rechokim.

3129. יוֹנָתָן **Yôwnâthân**, yo-naw-thawn´; a form of 3083; Jonathan, the name of ten Isr.:— Jonathan.

3130. יוֹסֵף **Yôwçêph**, yo-safe´; future of 3254; let him add (or perh. simply act. part. adding); Joseph, the name of seven Isr.:— Joseph. Comp. 3084.

3131. יוֹסִפְיָה **Yôwçiphyâh**, yo-sif-yaw´; from act. part. of 3254 and 3050; Jah (is) adding; Josiphjah, an Isr.:— Josiphiah.

3132. יוֹעֵאלָה **Yôwê'lâh**, yo-ay-law´; perh. fem. act. part. of 3276; furthermore; Joelah, an Isr.:— Joelah.

3133. יוֹעֵד **Yôwê'd**, yo-ade´; appar. the act. part. of 3259; appointer; Joed, an Isr.:— Joed.

3134. יוֹעֶזֶר **Yôwe'zer**, yo-eh´-zer; from 3068 and 5828; Jehovah (is his) help; Joezer, an Isr.:— Joezer.

3135. יוֹעָשׁ **Yôw'âsh**, yo-awsh´; from 3068 and 5789; Jehovah-hastened; Joash, the name of two Isr.:— Joash.

3136. יוֹצָדָק **Yôwtsâdâq**, yo-tsaw-dawk´; a form of 3087; Jotsadak, an Isr.:— Jozadak.

3137. יוֹקִים **Yôwqîym**, yo-keem´; a form of 3113; Jokim, an Isr.:— Jokim.

3138. יוֹרֶה **yôwreh**, yo-reh´; act. part. of 3384; sprinkling; hence, a sprinkling (or autumnal showers):— first rain, former lrainl.

3139. יוֹרָה **Yôwrâh**, yo-raw´; from 3384; rainy; Jorah, an Isr.:— Jorah.

3140. יוֹרַי **Yôwray**, yo-rah´-ee; from 3384; rainy; Jorai, an Isr.:— Jorai.

3141. יוֹרָם **Yôwrâm**, yo-rawm´; a form of 3088; Joram, the name of three Isr. and one Syrian:— Joram.

3142. יוֹשָׁב חֶסֶד **Yûwshab Cheçed**, yoo-shab´ kheh´-sed; from 7725 and 2617; kindness will be returned; Jushab-Chesed, an Isr.:— Jushab-hesed.

3143. יוֹשִׁבְיָה **Yôwshîbyâh**, yo-shib-yaw´; from 3427 and 3050; Jehovah will cause to dwell; Josibjah, an Isr.:— Josibiah.

3144. יוֹשָׁה **Yôwshâh**, yo-shaw´; prob. a form of 3145; Joshah, an Isr.:— Joshah.

3145. יוֹשַׁוְיָה **Yôwshavyâh**, yo-shav-yaw´; from 3068 and 7737; Jehovah-set; Joshavjah, an Isr.:— Joshaviah. Comp. 3144.

3146. יוֹשָׁפָט **Yôwshâphâṭ**, yo-shaw-fawt´; a form of 3092; Joshaphat, an Isr.:— Joshaphat.

3147. יוֹתָם **Yôwthâm**, yo-thawm´; from 3068 and 8535; Jehovah (is) perfect; Jotham, the name of three Isr.:— Jotham.

3148. יוֹתֵר **yôwthêr**, yo-thare´; act. part. of 3498; prop. redundant; hence, over and above, as adj., noun, adv. or conjunc. las followsl:— better, more (-over), over, profit.

3149. יְזַוְאֵל **Yᵉzav'êl**, yez-av-ale´; from an unused root (mean. to sprinkle) and 410; sprinkled of God; Jezavel, an Isr.:— Jeziel lfrom the marg.l.

3150. יִזִיָּה **Yizzîyâh**, yiz-zee-yaw´; from the same as the first part of 3149 and 3050; sprinkled of Jah; Jizzijah, an Isr.:— Jeziah.

3151. יָזִיז **Yâziyz**, yaw-zeez´; from the same as 2123; he will make prominent; Jaziz, an Isr.:— Jaziz.

3152. יִזְלִיאָה **Yizliy'ah**, yiz-lee-aw´; perh. from an unused root (mean. to draw up); he will draw out; Jizliah, an Isr.:— Jezliah.

3153. יְזַנְיָה **Yᵉzanyâh**, yez-an-yaw´; or

יְזַנְיָהוּ **Yᵉzanyâhûw**, yez-an-yaw´-hoo; prob. for 2970; Jezanjah, an Isr.:— Jezaniah.

3154. יֶזַע **yeza'**, yeh´-zah; from an unused root mean. to ooze; sweat, i.e. (by impl.) a sweating dress:— any thing that causeth sweat.

3155. יִזְרָח **Yizrâch**, yiz-rawkh´; a var. for 250; a Jizrach (i.e. Ezrahite or Zarchite) or desc. of Zerach:— Izrahite.

3156. יִזְרַחְיָה **Yizrachyâh**, yiz-rakh-yaw´; from 2224 and 3050; Jah will shine; Jizrachjah, the name of two Isr.:— Izrahiah, Jezrahiah.

3157. יִזְרְעֶאל **Yizrᵉê'l**, yiz-reh-ale´; from 2232 and 410; God will sow; Jizreël, the name of two places in Pal. and of two Isr.:— Jezreel.

3158. יִזְרְעֵאלִי **Yizrᵉê'liy**, yiz-reh-ay-lee´; patron. from 3157; a Jizreëlite or native of Jizreel:— Jezreelite.

3159. יִזְרְעֵאלִית **Yizrᵉê'liyth**, yiz-reh-ay-leeth´; fem. of 3158; a Jezreëlitess:— Jezreelitess.

3160. יְחֻבָּה **Yᵉchubbâh**, yekh-oob-baw´; from 2247; hidden; Jechubbah, an Isr.:— Jehubbah.

3161. יָחַד **yâchad**, yaw-khad´; a prim. root; to be (or become) one:— join, unite.

3162. יַחַד **yachad**, yakh´-ad; from 3161; prop. a unit, i.e. (adv.) unitedly:— alike, at all (once), both, likewise, only, (al-) together, withal.

3163. יַחְדּוֹ **Yachdôw**, yakh-doe´; from 3162 with pron. suff.; his unity, i.e. (adv.) together; Jachdo, an Isr.:— Jahdo.

3164. יַחְדִּיאֵל **Yachdîy'êl**, yakh-dee-ale´; from 3162 and 410; *unity of God; Jach-diël*, an Isr.:— Jahdiel.

3165. יַחְדִּיָּהוּ **Yechdîyâhûw**, yekh-dee-yaw´-hoo; from 3162 and 3050; *unity of Jah; Jechdijah*, the name of two Isr.:— Jehdeiah.

יַחֲוְאֵל **Yechav'êl**. See 3171.

3166. יַחֲזִיאֵל **Yachăzîy'êl**, yakh-az-ee-ale´; from 2372 and 410; *beheld of God; Jachaziël*, the name of five Isr.:— Jahaziel, Jahziel.

3167. יַחְזְיָה **Yachzeyâh**, yakh-zeh-yaw´; from 2372 and 3050; *Jah will behold; Jachzejah*, an Isr.:— Jahaziah.

3168. יְחֶזְקֵאל **Yechezqê'l**, yekh-ez-kale´; from 2388 and 410; *God will strengthen; Jechezkel*, the name of two Isr.:— Ezekiel, Jehezekel.

3169. יְחִזְקִיָּה **Yechizqîyâh**, yekh-iz-kee-yaw´; or

יְחִזְקִיָּהוּ **Yechizqîyâhûw**, yekh-iz-kee-yaw´-hoo; from 3388 and 3050; *strengthened of Jah; Jechizkijah*, the name of five Isr.:— Hezekiah, Jehizkiah. Comp. 2396.

3170. יַחְזֵרָה **Yachzêrâh**, yakh-zay-raw´; from the same as 2386; perh. *protection; Jachzerah*, an Isr.:— Jahzerah.

3171. יְחִיאֵל **Yechîy'êl**, yekh-ee-ale´; or (2 Chron. 29:14)

יְחִיאֵל **Yechav'êl**, yekh-av-ale´; from 2421 and 410; *God will live; Jechiël* (or *Jechavel*), the name of eight Isr.:— Jehiel.

3172. יְחִיאֵלִי **Yechîy'êlîy**, yekh-ee-ay-lee´; patron. from 3171; a *Jechiëlite* or desc. of Jechiel:— Jehieli.

3173. יָחִיד **yâchîyd**, yaw-kheed´; from 3161; prop. *united*, i.e. *sole*; by impl. *beloved*; also *lonely*; (fem.) the *life* (as not to be replaced):— darling, desolate, only (child, son), solitary.

3174. יְחִיָּה **Yechîyâh**, yekh-ee-yaw´; from 2421 and 3050; *Jah will live; Jechijah*, an Isr.:— Jehiah.

3175. יָחִיל **yâchîyl**, yaw-kheel´; from 3176; *expectant*:— should hope.

3176. יָחַל **yâchal**, yaw-chal´; a prim. root; to *wait*; by impl. to *be patient, hope*:— (cause to, have, make to) hope, be pained, stay, tarry, trust, wait.

3177. יַחְלְאֵל **Yachle'êl**, yakh-leh-ale´; from 3176 and 410; *expectant of God; Jachleël*, an Isr.:— Jahleel.

3178. יַחְלְאֵלִי **Yachle'êlîy**, yakh-leh-ay-lee´; patron. from 3177; a *Jachleëlite* or desc. of Jachleel:— Jahleelites.

3179. יָחַם **yâcham**, yaw-kham´; a prim. root; prob. to *be hot*; fig. to *conceive*:— get heat, be hot, conceive, be warm.

3180. יַחְמוּר **yachmûwr**, yakh-moor´; from 2560; a kind of *deer* (from the color; comp. 2543):— fallow deer.

3181. יַחְמַי **Yachmay**, yakh-mah´-ee; prob. from 3179; *hot; Jachmai*, an Isr.:— Jahmai.

3182. יָחֵף **yâchêph**, yaw-khafe´; from an unused root mean. to *take off the shoes; unsandalled*:— barefoot, being unshod.

3183. יַחְצְאֵל **Yachtse'êl**, yakh-tseh-ale´;

from 2673 and 410; *God will allot; Jachtseël*, an Isr.:— Jahzeel. Comp. 3185.

3184. יַחְצְאֵלִי **Yachtse'êlîy**, yakh-tseh-ay-lee´; patron. from 3183; a *Jachtseëlite* (collect.) or desc. of Jachtseel:— Jahzeelites.

3185. יַחְצִיאֵל **Yachtsîy'êl**, yakh-tsee-ale´; from 2673 and 410; *allotted of God; Jachtsiël*, an Isr.:— Jahziel. Comp. 3183.

3186. יָחַר **yâchar**, yaw-khar´; a prim. root; to *delay*:— tarry longer.

3187. יָחַשׂ **yâchas**, yaw-khas´; a prim. root; to *sprout*; used only as denom. from 3188; to *enroll* by pedigree:— (number after, number throughout the) genealogy (to be reckoned), be reckoned by genealogies.

3188. יַחַשׂ **yachas**, yakh´-as; from 3187; a *pedigree* or family list (as *growing* spontaneously):— genealogy.

3189. יַחַת **Yachath**, yakh´-ath; from 3161; *unity; Jachath*, the name of four Isr.:— Jahath.

3190. יָטַב **yâṭab**, yaw-tab´; a prim. root; to *be* (caus.) *make well*, lit. (*sound, beautiful*) or fig. (*happy, successful, right*):— be accepted, amend, use aright, benefit, be (make) better, seem best, make cheerful, be comely, + be content, diligent (-ly), dress, earnestly, find favour, give, be glad, do (be, make) good (l-ness'l), be (make) merry, please (+ well), shew more [kindness], skilfully, × very small, surely, make sweet, thoroughly, tire, trim, very, be (can, deal, entreat, go, have) well [said, seen].

3191. יְטַב **yeṭab** (Chald.), yet-ab´; corresp. to 3190:— seem good.

3192. יָטְבָה **Yoṭbâh**, yot-baw´; from 3190; *pleasantness; Jotbah*, a place in Pal.:— Jotbah.

3193. יָטְבָתָה **Yoṭbâthâh**, yot-baw´-thaw; from 3192; *Jotbathah*, a place in the Desert:— Jotbath, Jotbathah.

3194. יֻטָּה **Yuṭṭâh**, yoo-taw´; or

יוּטָה **Yûwṭâh**, yoo-taw´; from 5186; *extended; Juttah* (or *Jutah*), a place in Pal.:— Juttah.

3195. יְטוּר **Yeṭûwr**, yet-oor´; prob. from the same as 2905; *encircled* (i.e. *inclosed*); *Jetur*, a son of Ishmael:— Jetur.

3196. יַיִן **yayin**, yah´-yin; from an unused root mean. to *effervesce; wine* (as fermented); by impl. *intoxication*:— banqueting, wine, wine [-bibber].

3197. יָך **yak**, yak; by err. transc. for 3027; a *hand* or *side*:— [way-] side.

3198. יָכַח **yâkach**, yaw-kahh´; a prim. root; to *be right* (i.e. *correct*); recip. to *argue*; caus. to *decide, justify* or *convict*:— appoint, argue, chasten, convince, correct (-ion), daysman, dispute, judge, maintain, plead, reason (together), rebuke, reprove (-r), surely, in any wise.

יְכִלְיָה **Yekîyleyâh**. See 3203.

3199. יָכִין **Yâkîyn**, yaw-keen´; from

3559; *he* (or *it*) *will establish; Jakin*, the name of three Isr. and of a temple pillar:— Jachin.

3200. יָכִינִי **Yâkîynîy**, yaw-kee-nee´; patron. from 3199; a *Jakinite* (collect.) or desc. of Jakin:— Jachinites.

3201. יָכֹל **yâkôl**, yaw-kole´; or (fuller)

יָכוֹל **yâkôwl**, yaw-kole´; a prim. root; to *be able*, lit. (*can, could*) or mor. (*may, might*):— be able, any at all (ways), attain, can (away with, l-notl), could, endure, might, overcome, have power, prevail, still, suffer.

3202. יְכֵל **yekêl** (Chald.), yek-ale´; or

יְכִיל **yekîyl** (Chald.), yek-eel´; corresp. to 3201:— be able, can, couldest, prevail.

3203. יְכָלְיָה **Yekolyâh**, yek-ol-yaw´; and

יְכָלְיָהוּ **Yekolyâhûw**, yek-ol-yaw´-hoo; or (2 Chron. 26:3)

יְכִילְיָה **Yekîyleyâh**, yek-ee-leh-yaw´; from 3201 and 3050; *Jah will enable; Jekoljah* or *Jekiljah*, an Israelitess:— Jecholiah, Jecoliah.

3204. יְכָנְיָה **Yekonyâh**, yek-on-yaw´; and

יְכָנְיָהוּ **Yekonyâhûw**, yek-on-yaw´-hoo; or (Jer. 27:20)

יְכוֹנְיָה **Yekôwneyâh**, yek-o-neh-yaw´; from 3559 and 3050; *Jah will establish; Jekonjah*, a Jewish king:— Jeconiah. Comp. 3659.

3205. יָלַד **yâlad**, yaw-lad´; a prim. root; to *bear* young; caus. to *beget*; medically, to *act as midwife*; spec. to *show lineage*:— bear, beget, birth (l-dayl), born, (make to) bring forth (children, young), bring up, calve, child, come, be delivered (of a child), time of delivery, gender, hatch, labour, (do the office of a) midwife, declare pedigrees, be the son of, (woman in, woman that) travail (-eth, -ing woman).

3206. יֶלֶד **yeled**, yeh´-led; from 3205; something *born*, i.e. a *lad* or *offspring*:— boy, child, fruit, son, young man (one).

3207. יַלְדָּה **yaldâh**, yal-daw´; fem. of 3206; a *lass*:— damsel, girl.

3208. יַלְדוּת **yaldûwth**, yal-dooth´; abstr. from 3206; *boyhood* (or *girlhood*):— childhood, youth.

3209. יִלּוֹד **yillôwd**, yil-lode´; pass. from 3205; *born*:— born.

3210. יָלוֹן **Yâlôwn**, yaw-lone´; from 3885; *lodging; Jalon*, an Isr.:— Jalon.

3211. יָלִיד **yâlîyd**, yaw-leed´; from 3205; *born*:— (home-l) born, child, son.

3212. יָלַך **yâlak**, yaw-lak´; a prim. root [comp. 1980]; to *walk* (lit. or fig.); caus. to *carry* (in various senses):— × again, away, bear, bring, carry (away), come (away), depart, flow, + follow (-ing), get (away, hence, him), (cause to, make) go (away, ing, -ne, one's way, out), grow, lead (forth), let down, march, prosper, + pursue, cause to run, spread, take away (l-journeyl), vanish, (cause to) walk (-ing), wax, × be weak.

3213. יָלַל **yâlal**, yaw-lal´; a prim. root; to *howl* (with a wailing tone) or *yell* (with a boisterous one):— (make to) howl, be howling.

3214. לְל yᵉlêl, *yel-ale´*; from 3213; a *howl*:— howling.

3215. יְלָלָה yᵉlâlâh, *yel-aw-law´*; fem. of 3214; a *howling*:— howling.

3216. יְלַע yâla', *yaw-lah´*; a prim. root; to *blurt* or utter inconsiderately:— devour.

3217. יַלֶּפֶת yallepheth, *yal-leh´-feth*; from an unused root appar. mean. to *stick* or *scrape*; *scurf* or *tetter*:— scabbed.

3218. יֶלֶק yekeq, *yeh´-lek*; from an unused root mean. to *lick* up; a *devourer*; spec. the young *locust*:— cankerworm, caterpillar.

3219. יַלְקוּט yalqûwt, *yal-koot´*; from 3950; a travelling *pouch* (as if for gleanings):— scrip.

3220. יָם yâm, *yawm*; from an unused root mean. to *roar*; a *sea* (as breaking in *noisy* surf) or large body of water; spec. (with the art.), the *Mediterranean*; sometimes a large *river*, or an artificial *basin*; locally, the *west*, or (rarely) the *south*:— sea (×-faring man, l-shore), south, west (-ern, side, -ward).

3221. יָם yâm (Chald.), *yawm*; corresp. to 3220:— sea.

3222. יֵם yêm, *yame*; from the same as 3117; a *warm* spring:— mule.

3223. יְמוּאֵל Yᵉmûw'êl, *yem-oo-ale´*; from 3117 and 410; *day of God; Jemuel*, an Isr.:— Jemuel.

3224. יְמִימָה Yᵉmîymâh, *yem-ee-maw´*; perh. from the same as 3117; prop. *warm*, i.e. *affectionate*; hence, *dove* [comp. 3123]; *Jemimah*, one of Job's daughters:— Jemimah.

3225. יָמִין yâmîyn, *yaw-meen´*; from 3231; the *right* hand or side (leg, eye) of a person or other object (as the *stronger* and more dexterous); locally, the *south*:— + left-handed, right (hand, side), south.

3226. יָמִין Yâmîyn, *yaw-meen´*; the same as 3225; *Jamin*, the name of three Isr.:— Jamin. See also 1144.

3227. יְמִינִי yᵉmîynîy, *yem-ee-nee´*; for 3225; *right*:— (on the) right (hand).

3228. יְמִינִי Yᵉmîynîy, *yem-ee-nee´*; patron. from 3226; a *Jeminite* (collect.) or desc. of Jamin:— Jaminites. See also 1145.

3229. יִמְלָא Yimlâ', *yeem-law´*; or

יִמְלָה Yimlâh, *yim-law´*; from 4390; *full*; *Jimla* or *Jimlah*, an Isr.:— Imla, Imlah.

3230. יַמְלֵךְ Yamlêk, *yam-lake´*; from 4427; *he will make king*; *Jamlek*, an Isr.:— Jamlech.

3231. יָמַן yâman, *yaw-man´*; a prim. root; to *be* (phys.) *right* (i.e. firm); but used only as denom. from 3225 and tran. to *be right-handed* or *take the right-hand* side:— go (turn) to (on, use) the right hand.

3232. יִמְנָה Yimnâh, *yim-naw´*; from 3231; *prosperity* (as betokened by the *right* hand); *Jimnah*, the name of two Isr.; also (with the art.) of the posterity of one of them:— Imna, Imnah, Jimnah, Jimnites.

3233. יְמָנִי yᵉmânîy, *yem-aw-nee´*; from 3231; *right* (i.e. at the right hand):— (on the) right (hand).

3234. יִמְנָע Yimnâ', *yim-naw´*; from 4513; *he will restrain*; *Jimna*, an Isr.:— Imna.

3235. יָמַר yâmar, *yaw-mar´*; a prim. root; to *exchange*; by impl. to *change places*:— boast selves, change.

3236. יִמְרָה Yimrâh, *yim-raw´*; prob. from 3235; *interchange*; *Jimrah*, an Isr.:— Imrah.

3237. יָמַשׁ yâmash, *yaw-mash´*; a prim. root; to *touch*:— feel.

3238. יָנָה yânâh, *yaw-naw´*; a prim. root; to *rage* or *be violent*; by impl. to *suppress*, to *maltreat*:— destroy, (thrust out by) oppress (-ing, -ion, -or), proud, vex, do violence.

3239. יָנוֹחַ Yânôwach, *yaw-no´-akh*; or (with enclitic)

יָנוֹחָה Yânôwchâh, *yaw-no´-khaw*; from 3240; *quiet*; *Janoäch* or *Janochah*, a place in Pal.:— Janoah, Janohah.

יָנוּם Yânûm. See 3241.

3240. יָנַח yânach, *yaw-nakh´*; a prim. root; to *deposit*; by impl. to *allow to stay*:— bestow, cast down, lay (down, up), leave (off), let alone (remain), pacify, place, put, set (down), suffer, withdraw, withhold. (The Hiphil forms with the *dagesh* are here referred to, in accordance with the older grammarians; but if any distinction of the kind is to be made, these should rather be referred to 5117, and the others here.)

3241. יָנִים Yânîym, *yaw-neem´*; from 5123; *asleep*; *Janim*, a place in Pal.:— Janum [from the marg.].

3242. יְנִיקָה yᵉnîqâh, *yen-ee-kaw´*; from 3243; a *sucker* or sapling:— young twig.

3243. יָנַק yânaq, *yaw-nak´*; a prim. root; to *suck*; caus. to *give milk*:— milch, nurse (-ing mother), (give, make to) suck (-ing child, -ling).

3244. יַנְשׁוּף yanshûwph, *yan-shoof´*; or

יַנְשׁוֹף yanshôwph, *yan-shofe´*; appar. from 5398; an unclean (aquatic) bird; prob. the *heron* (perh. from its *blowing* cry, or because the *night* heron is meant [comp. 5399]):— (great) owl.

3245. יָסַד yâçad, *yaw-sad´*; a prim. root; to *set* (lit. or fig.); intens. to *found*; refl. to *sit* down together, i.e. *settle*, *consult*:— appoint, take counsel, establish, (lay the, lay for a) found (-ation), instruct, lay, ordain, set, × sure.

3246. יְסֻד yᵉçûd, *yes-ood´*; from 3245; a *foundation* (fig. i.e. *beginning*):— × began.

3247. יְסוֹד yᵉçôwd, *yes-ode´*; from 3245; a *foundation* (lit. or fig.):— bottom, foundation, repairing.

3248. יְסוּדָה yᵉçûwdâh, *yes-oo-daw´*; fem. of 3246; a *foundation*:— foundation.

3249. יָסוּר yâçûwr, *yaw-soor´*; from 5493; *departing*:— they that depart.

3250. יִסּוֹר yiççôwr, *yis-sore´*; from 3256; a *reprover*:— instruct.

3251. יָסַךְ yâçak, *yaw-sak´*; a prim. root; to *pour* (intr.):— be poured.

3252. יִסְכָּה Yiçkàh, *yis-kaw´*; from an unused root mean. to *watch*; *observant*; *Jiskah*, sister of Lot:— Iscah.

3253. יִסְמַכְיָהוּ Yiçmakyâhûw, *yis-mak-yaw-hoo´*; from 5564 and 3050; *Jah will sustain*; *Jismakjah*, an Isr.:— Ismachiah.

3254. יָסַף yâçaph, *yaw-saf´*; a prim. root; to *add* or *augment* (often adv. to *continue* to do a thing):— add, × again, × any more, × cease, × come more, + conceive again, continue, exceed, × further, × gather together, get more, give more-over, × henceforth, increase (more and more), join, × longer (bring, do, make, much, put), × (the, much, yet) more (and more), proceed (further), prolong, put, be [strong-] er, × yet, yield.

3255. יְסַף yᵉçaph (Chald.), *yes-af´*; corresp. to 3254:— add.

3256. יָסַר yâçar, *yaw-sar´*; a prim. root; to *chastise*, lit. (with blows) or fig. (with words); hence, to *instruct*:— bind, chasten, chastise, correct, instruct, punish, reform, reprove, sore, teach.

3257. יָע yâ', *yaw*; from 3261; a *shovel*:— shovel.

3258. יַעְבֵּץ Ya'bêts, *yah-bates´*; from an unused root prob. mean. to *grieve*; *sorrowful*; *Jabets*, the name of an Isr., and also of a place in Pal.:— Jabez.

3259. יָעַד yâ'ad, *yaw-ad´*; a prim. root; to *fix* upon (by agreement or appointment); by impl. to *meet* (at a stated time), to *summon* (to trial), to *direct* (in a certain quarter or position), to *engage* (for marriage):— agree,(make an) appoint (-ment, a time), assemble (selves), betroth, gather (selves, together), meet (together), set (a time).

יְעְדּוֹ Yᵉ'dôw. See 3260.

3260. יֶעְדִּי Yᵉ'dîy, *yed-ee´*; from 3259; *appointed*; *Jedi*, an Isr.:— Iddo [from the marg.] See 3035.

3261. יָעָה yâ'âh, *yaw-aw´*; a prim. root; appar. to *brush* aside:— sweep away.

3262. יְעוּאֵל Yᵉ'ûw'êl, *yeh-oo-ale´*; from 3261 and 410; *carried away of God*; *Jeüel*, the name of four Isr.:— Jehiel, Jeiel, Jeuel. Comp. 3273.

3263. יְעוּץ Yᵉ'ûwts, *yeh-oots´*; from 5779; *counsellor*; *Jeüts*, an Isr.:— Jeuz.

3264. יָעוֹר yâ'ôwr, *yaw-ore´*; a var. of 3293; a *forest*:— wood.

3265. יָעוּר Yâ'ûwr, *yaw-oor´*; appar. pass. part. of the same as 3293; *wooded*; *Jaür*, an Isr.:— Jair [from the marg.].

3266. יְעוּשׁ Yᵉ'ûwsh, *yeh-oosh´*; from 5789; *hasty*; *Jeüsh*, the name of an Edomite and of four Isr.:— Jehush, Jeush. Comp. 3274.

3267. יָעַז yâ'az, *yaw-az´*; a prim. root; to *be bold* or *obstinate*:— fierce.

3268. יַעֲזִיאֵל Ya'ăzîy'êl, *yah-az-ee-ale´*; from 3267 and 410; *emboldened of God*; *Jaaziël*, an Isr.:— Jaaziel.

3269. יַעֲזִיָהוּ Ya'ăzîyâhûw, *yah-az-ee-yaw´-hoo*; from 3267 and 3050; *emboldened of Jah*; *Jaazijah*, an Isr.:— Jaaziah.

3270. יַעֲזֵיר Ya'äzêyr, *yah-az-ayr´*; or

יַעְזֵר **Ya'zêr**, *yah-zare´*; from 5826; *helpful*; *Jaazer* or *Jazer*, a place E. of the Jordan:— Jaazer, Jazer.

3271. יָעַט **yâ'at**, *yaw-at´*; a prim. root; to *clothe*:— cover.

3272. יְעַט **ye'at** (Chald.), *yeh-at´*; corresp. to 3289; to *counsel*; refl. to con-sult:— counsellor, consult together.

3273. יְעִיאֵל **Ye'iy'êl**, *yeh-ee-ale´*; from 3261 and 410; *carried away of God*; *Jeïel*, the name of six Isr.:— Jeiel, Je-hiel. Comp. 3262.

יָעִיר **Yâ'îyr**. See 3265.

3274. יְעִישׁ **Ye'îysh**, *yeh-eesh´*; from 5789; *hasty*; *Jeïsh*, the name of an Edomite and of an Isr.:— Jeush [from the marg.]. Comp. 3266.

3275. יָעְכָּן **Ya'kân**, *yah-kawn´*; from the same as 5912; *troublesome*; *Jakan*, an Isr.:— Jachan.

3276. יָעַל **yâ'al**, *yaw-al´*; a prim. root; prop. to *ascend*; fig. to *be valuable* (obj. *useful*, subj. *benefited*):— × at all, set forward, can do good, (be, have) profit (-able).

3277. יָעֵל **yâ'êl**, *yaw-ale´*; from 3276; an *ibex* (as *climbing*):— wild goat.

3278. יָעֵל **Yâ'êl**, *yaw-ale´*; the same as 3277; *Jaël*, a Canaanite:— Jael.

3279. יַעְלָא **Ya'älâ'**, *yah-al-aw´*; or

יַעְלָה **Ya'älâh**, *yah-al-aw´*; the same as 3280 or direct from 3276; *Jaala* or *Jaalah*, one of the Nethinim:— Jaala, Jaalah.

3280. יַעְלָה **ya'älâh**, *yah-al-aw´*; fem. of 3277:— roe.

3281. יַעְלָם **Ya'lâm**, *yah-lawm´*; from 5956; *occult*; *Jalam*, an Edomite:— Jalam.

3282. יַעַן **ya'an**, *yah´-an*; from an un-used root mean. to *pay attention*; prop. *heed*; by impl. *purpose* (sake or ac-count); used adv. to indicate the *reason* or *cause*:— because (that), forasmuch (+ as), seeing then, + that, + whereas, + why.

3283. יָעֵן **yâ'ên**, *yaw-ane´*; from the same as 3282; the *ostrich* (prob. from its *answering* cry:— ostrich.

3284. יַעֲנָה **ya'änâh**, *yah-an-aw´*; fem. of 3283, and mean. the same:— + owl.

3285. יַעֲנַי **Ya'änay**, *yah-an-ah´ee*; from the same as 3283; *responsive*; *Jaanai*, an Isr.:— Jaanai.

3286. יָעַף **yâ'aph**, *yaw-af´*; a prim. root; to *tire* (as if from wearisome *flight*):— faint, cause to fly, (be) weary (self).

3287. יָעֵף **yâ'êph**, *yaw-afe´*; from 3286; *fatigued*; fig. *exhausted*:— faint, weary.

3288. יְעָף **ye'âph**, *yeh-awf´*; from 3286; *fatigue* (adv. utterly *exhausted*):— swiftly.

3289. יָעַץ **yâ'ats**, *yaw-ats´*; a prim. root; refl. to *deliberate* or *re-solve*:— advertise, take advice, advise (well), consult, (give, take) counsel (-lor), determine, devise, guide, pur-pose.

3290. יַעֲקֹב **Ya'äqôb**, *yah-ak-obe´*; from 6117; *heel*-catcher (i.e. supplanter); *Jaakob*, the Isr. patriarch:— Jacob.

3291. יַעֲקֹבָה **Ya'äqôbâh**, *yah-ak-o´-baw*; from 3290; *Jaakobah*, an Isr.:— Jaako-bah.

3292. יַעֲקָן **Ya'äqân**, *yah-ak-awn´*; from the same as 6130; *Jaakan*, an Idumæan:— Jaakan. Comp. 1142.

3293. יַעַר **ya'ar**, *yah´-ar* from an unused root prob. mean. to *thicken* with ver-dure; a *copse* of bushes; hence, a *forest*; hence, *honey* in the *comb* (as hived in trees):— [honey-] comb, forest, wood.

3294. יַעְרָה **Ya'râh**, *yah-raw´*; a form of 3295; *Jarah*, an Isr.:— Jarah.

3295. יַעֲרָה **ya'ärâh**, *yah-ar-aw´*; fem. of 3293, and mean. the same:— [honey-] comb, forest.

3296. יַעֲרֵי אֹרְגִים **Ya'ärêy 'Oregîym**, *yah-ar-ay´ o-reg-eem´*; from the plural of 3293 and the masc. plur. act. part. of 707; *woods of weavers*; *Jaare-Oregim*, an Isr.:— Jaare-oregim.

3297. יְעָרִים **Ye'ârîym**, *yeh-aw-reem´*; plur. of 3293; *forests*; *Jeärim*, a place in Pal.:— Jearim. Comp. 7157.

3298. יַעֲרֶשְׁיָה **Ya'äreshyâh**, *yah-ar-esh-yaw´*; from an unused root of uncert. signif. and 3050; *Jaareshjah*, an Isr.:— Jaresiah.

3299. יַעֲשׂוּ **Ya'äsûw**, *yah-as-oo´*; from 6213; *they will do*; *Jaasu*, an Isr.:— Jaasau.

3300. יַעֲשִׂיאֵל **Ya'äsîy'êl**, *yah-as-ee-ale´*; from 6213 and 410; *made of God*; *Jaasiel*, an Isr.:— Jaasiel, Jasiel.

3301. יִפְדְּיָה **Yiphdeyâh**, *yif-deh-yaw´*; from 6299 and 3050; *Jah will liberate*; *Jiphdejah*, an Isr.:— Iphedeiah.

3302. יָפָה **yâphâh**, *yaw-faw´*; a prim. root; prop. to *be bright*, i.e. (by impl.) *beautiful*:— be beautiful, be (make self) fair (-r), deck.

3303. יָפֶה **yâpheh**, *yaw-feh´*; from 3302; *beautiful* (lit. or fig.):— + beautiful, beauty, comely, fair (-est, one), + goodly, pleasant, well.

3304. יְפֵה־פִיָּה **yephêh-phîyâh**, *yef-eh´ fee-yaw´*; from 3302 by redupl.; *very beautiful*:— very fair.

3305. יָפוֹ **Yâphôw**, *yaw-fo´*; or

יָפוֹא **Yâphôw'** (Ezra 3:7), *yaw-fo´*; from 3302; *beautiful*; *Japho*, a place in Pal.:— Japha, Joppa.

3306. יָפַח **yâphach**, *yaw-fakh´*; a prim. root; prop. to *breathe* hard, i.e. (by impl.) to *sigh*:— bewail self.

3307. יָפֵחַ **yâphêach**, *yaw-fay´-akh*; from 3306; prop. *puffing*, i.e. (fig.) *medi-tating*:— such as breathe out.

3308. יֳפִי **yŏphîy**, *yof-ee´*; from 3302; *beauty*:— beauty.

3309. יָפִיעַ **Yâphîya'**, *yaw-fee´-ah*; from 3313; *bright*; *Japhia*, the name of a Ca-naanite, an Isr., and a place in Pal.:— Japhia.

3310. יַפְלֵט **Yaphlêṭ**, *yaf-late´*; from 6403; *he will deliver*; *Japhlet*, an Isr.:— Japhlet.

3311. יַפְלֵטִי **Yaphlêṭîy**, *yaf-lay-tee´*; pa-tron. from 3310; a *Japhletite* or desc. of Japhlet:— Japhleti.

3312. יְפֻנֶּה **Yephunneh**, *yef-oon-neh´*; from 6437; *he will be prepared*; *Jephun-*

neh, the name of two Isr.:— Jephun-neh.

3313. יָפַע **yâpha'**, *yaw-fah´*; a prim. root; to *shine*:— be light, shew self, (cause to) shine (forth).

3314. יִפְעָה **yiph'âh**, *yif-aw´*; from 3313; *splendor* or (fig.) *beauty*:— brightness.

3315. יֶפֶת **Yepheth**, *yeh´-feth*; from 6601; *expansion*; *Jepheth*, a son of Noah; also his posterity:— Japheth.

3316. יִפְתָּח **Yiphtâch**, *yif-tawkh´*; from 6605; *he will open*; *Jiphtach*, an Isr.; also a place in Pal.:— Jephthah, Jiphtah.

3317. יִפְתַּח־אֵל **Yiphtach-'êl**, *yif-tach-ale´*; from 6605 and 410; *God will open*; *Jiphtach-el*, a place in Pal.:— Jiphthah-el.

3318. יָצָא **yâtsâ'**, *yaw-tsaw´*; a prim. root; to *go* (caus. *bring*) *out*, in a great variety of applications, lit. and fig., di-rect and proxim.:— × after, appear, × assuredly, bear out, × begotten, break out, bring forth (out, up), carry out, come (abroad, out, thereat, without), + be condemned, depart (-ing, -ure), draw forth, in the end, escape, exact, fail, fall (out), fetch forth (out), get away (forth, hence, out), (able to, cause to, let) go abroad (forth, on, out), going out, grow, have forth (out), issue out, lay (lie) out, lead out, pluck out, pro-ceed, pull out, put away, be risen, × scarce, send with commandment, shoot forth, spread, spring out, stand out, × still, × surely, take forth (out), at any time, × to [and frol, utter.

3319. יְצָא **yetsâ'** (Chald.), *yets-aw´*; cor-resp. to 3318:— finish.

3320. יָצַב **yâtsab**, *yaw-tsab´*; a prim. root; to *place* (any thing so as to stay); refl. to *station*, *offer*, *continue*:— pre-sent selves, remaining, resort, set (selves), (be able to, can, with-) stand (fast, forth, -ing, still, up).

3321. יְצֵב **yetsêb** (Chald.), *yets-abe´*; corresp. to 3320; to *be firm*; hence, to *speak surely*:— truth.

3322. יָצַג **yâtsag**, *yaw-tsag´*; a prim. root; to *place* permanently:— estab-lish, leave, make, present, put, set, stay.

3323. יִצְהָר **yitshâr**, *yits-hawr´*; from 6671; *oil* (as producing *light*); fig. *anointing*:— + anointed oil.

3324. יִצְהָר **Yitshâr**, *yits-hawr´*; the same as 3323; *Jitshar*, an Isr.:— Izhar.

3325. יִצְהָרִי **Yitshârîy**, *yits-haw-ree´*; pa-tron. from 3324; a *Jitsharite* or desc. of Jitshar:— Izeharites, Izharites.

3326. יָצוּעַ **yâtsûwa'**, *yaw-tsoo´-ah*; pass. part. of 3331; *spread*, i.e. a *bed*; (arch.) an *extension*, i.e. *wing* or *lean-to* (a sin-gle story or collect.):— bed, chamber, couch.

3327. יִצְחָק **Yitschâq**, *yits-khawk´*; from 6711; *laughter* (i.e. *mockery*); *Jitschak* (or Isaac), son of Abraham:— Isaac. Comp. 3446.

3328. יִצְהָר **Yitschar**, *yits-khar´*; from the same as 6713; *he will shine*; *Jit-schar*, an Isr.:— and Zehoar [from the marg.].

3329. יָצִיא **yâtsîy'**, *yaw-tsee´*; from 3318;

Hebrew

issue, i.e. offspring:— those that came forth.

3330. יַצִּיב **yatstsîyb** (Chald.), *yatstseeb´;* from 3321; *fixed, sure;* concr. *certainty:*— certain (-ty), true, truth.

3331. יָצַע **yâtsa',** *yaw-tsah´;* a prim. root; to *strew* as a surface:— make [one's] bed, × lie, spread.

3332. יָצַק **yâtsaq,** *yaw-tsak´;* a prim. root; prop. to *pour* out (tran. or intr.); by impl. to *melt* or *cast* as metal; by extens. to *place* firmly, to *stiffen* or grow hard:— cast, cleave fast, be (as) firm, grow, be hard, lay out, molten, overflow, pour (out), run out, set down, stedfast.

3333. יְצֻקָה **y͏eᵉtsuqâh,** *yets-oo-kaw´;* pass. part. fem. of 3332; *poured* out, i.e. *run* into a mould:— when it was cast.

3334. יָצַר **yâtsar,** *yaw-tsar´;* a prim. root; to *press* (intr.), i.e. *be narrow;* fig. *be in distress:*— be distressed, be narrow, be straitened (in straits), be vexed.

3335. יָצַר **yâtsar,** *yaw-tsar´;* prob. ident. with 3334 (through the *squeezing* into shape); ([comp.](3331)); to *mould* into a form; espec. as a *potter;* fig. to *determine* (i.e. form a resolution):— × earthen, fashion, form, frame, make (-r), potter, purpose.

3336. יֵצֶר **yêtser,** *yay´-tser;* from 3335; a *form;* fig. *conception* (i.e. *purpose*):— frame, thing framed, imagination, mind, work.

3337. יֵצֶר **Yêtser,** *yay-tser;* the same as 3336; *Jetser,* an Isr.:— Jezer.

3338. יָצֻר **yâtsûr,** *yaw-tsoor´;* pass. part. of 3335; *structure,* i.e. *limb* or *part:*— member.

3339. יִצְרִי **Yitsrîy,** *yits-ree´;* from 3335; *formative; Jitsri,* an Isr.:— Isri.

3340. יִצְרִי **Yitsrîy,** *yits-ree´;* patron. from 3337; a *Jitsrite* (collect.) or desc. of Jetser:— Jezerites.

3341. יָצַת **yâtsath,** *yaw-tsath´;* a prim. root; to *burn* or *set on fire;* fig. to *desolate:*— burn (up), be desolate, set (on) fire ([fire]), kindle.

3342. יֶקֶב **yeqeb,** *yeh´-keb;* from an unused root mean. to *excavate;* a *trough* (as dug out); spec. a wine-*vat* (whether the lower one, into which the juice drains; or the upper, in which the grapes are crushed):— fats, presses, press-fat, wine (-press).

3343. יְקַבְצְאֵל **y͏eᵉqabts͏eᵉ'êl,** *yek-ab-tseh-ale´;* from 6908 and 410; *God will gather; Jekabtseël,* a place in Pal.:— Jekabzeel. Comp. 6909.

3344. יָקַד **yâqad,** *yaw-kad´;* a prim. root; to *burn:*— (be) burn (-ing), × from the hearth, kindle.

3345. יְקַד **y͏eᵉqad** (Chald.), *yek-ad´;* corresp. to 3344:— burning.

3346. יְקֵדָא **y͏eᵉqêdâ'** (Chald.), *yek-ay-daw´;* from 3345; a *conflagration:*— burning.

3347. יָקְדְעָם **Yoqd͏eᵉ'âm,** *yok-deh-awm´;* from 3344 and 5971; *burning of* (the) *people; Jokdeäm,* a place in Pal.:— Jokdeam.

3348. יָקֶה **Yâqeh,** *yaw-keh´;* from an unused root prob. mean. to *obey; obedient; Jakeh,* a symb. name (for Solomon):— Jakeh.

3349. יִקָּהָה **yiqqâhâh,** *yik-kaw-haw´;* from the same as 3348; *obedience:*— gathering, to obey.

3350. יְקוֹד **y͏eᵉqôwd,** *yek-ode´;* from 3344; a *burning:*— burning.

3351. יְקוּם **y͏eᵉqûwm,** *yek-oom´;* from 6965; prop. *standing* (extant), i.e. by impl. a *living thing:*— (living) substance.

3352. יָקוֹשׁ **yâqôwsh,** *yaw-koshe´;* from 3369; prop. *entangling;* hence, a *snarer:*— fowler.

3353. יָקוּשׁ **yâqûwsh,** *yaw-koosh´;* pass. part. of 3369; prop. *entangled,* i.e. by impl. (intr.) a *snare,* or (tran.) a *snarer:*— fowler, snare.

3354. יְקוּתִיאֵל **Y͏eᵉqûwthîy'êl,** *yek-ooth-ee-ale´;* from the same as 3348 and 410; *obedience of God; Jekuthiël,* an Isr.:— Jekuthiel.

3355. יׇקְטָן **Yoqtân,** *yok-tawn´;* from 6994; *he will be made little; Joktan,* an Arabian patriarch:— Joktan.

3356. יָקִים **Yâqîym,** *yaw-keem´;* from 6965; *he will raise; Jakim,* the name of two Isr.:— Jakim. Comp. 3079.

3357. יַקִּיר **yaqqîyr,** *yak-keer´;* from 3365; *precious:*— dear.

3358. יַקִּיר **yaqqîyr** (Chald.), *yak-keer´;* corresp. to 3357:— noble, rare.

3359. יְקַמְיָה **Y͏eᵉqamyâh,** *yek-am-yaw´;* from 6965 and 3050; *Jah will rise; Jekamjah,* the name of two Isr.:— Jekamiah. Comp. 3079.

3360. יְקַמְעָם **Y͏eᵉqam'âm,** *yek-am´-awm;* from 6965 and 5971; (the) *people will rise; Jekamam,* an Isr.:— Jekameam. Comp. 3079, 3361.

3361. יׇקְמְעָם **Yoqm͏eᵉ'âm,** *yok-meh-awm´;* from 6965 and 5971; (the) *people will be raised; Jokmeäm,* a place in Pal.:— Jokmeam. Comp. 3360, 3362.

3362. יׇקְנְעָם **Yoqn͏eᵉ'âm,** *yok-neh-awm´;* from 6969 and 5971; (the) *people will be lamented; Jokneäm,* a place in Pal.:— Jokneam.

3363. יָקַע **yâqa',** *yaw-kah´;* a prim. root; prop. to *sever* oneself, i.e. (by impl.) to *be dislocated;* fig. to *abandon;* caus. to *impale* (and thus allow to drop to pieces by *rotting*):— be alienated, depart, hang (up), be out of joint.

3364. יָקַץ **yâqats,** *yaw-kats´;* a prim. root; to *awake* (intr.):— (be) awake (-d).

3365. יָקַר **yâqar,** *yaw-kar´;* a prim. root; prop. appar. to *be heavy,* i.e. (fig.) *valuable;* caus. to *make rare* (fig. to *inhibit*):— be (make) precious, be prized, be set by, withdraw.

3366. יְקָר **y͏eᵉqâr,** *yek-awr´;* from 3365; *value,* i.e. (concr.) *wealth;* abstr. *costliness, dignity:*— honour, precious (things), price.

3367. יְקָר **y͏eᵉqâr** (Chald.), *yek-awr´;* corresp. to 3366:— glory, honour.

3368. יָקָר **yâqâr,** *yaw-kawr´;* from 3365; *valuable* (obj. or subj.):— brightness,

clear, costly, excellent, fat, honourable women, precious, reputation.

3369. יָקֹשׁ **yâqôsh,** *yaw-koshe´;* a prim. root; to *ensnare* (lit. or fig.):— fowler (lay a) snare.

3370. יׇקְשָׁן **Yoqshân,** *yok-shawn´;* from 3369; *insidious; Jokshan,* an Arabian patriarch:— Jokshan.

3371. יׇקְתְאֵל **Yoqth͏eᵉ'êl,** *yok-theh-ale´;* prob. from the same as 3348 and 410; *veneration of God* [comp. 3354]; *Joktheël,* the name of a place in Pal., and of one in Idumæa:— Joktheel.

יָרָא **yârâ'.** See 3384.

3372. יָרֵא **yârê',** *yaw-ray´;* a prim. root; to *fear;* mor. to *revere;* caus. to *frighten:*— affright, be (make) afraid, dread (-ful), (put in) fear (-ful, -fully, -ing), (be had in) reverence (-end), × see, terrible (act, -ness, thing).

3373. יָרֵא **yârê',** *yaw-ray´;* from 3372; *fearing;* mor. *reverent:*— afraid, fear (-ful).

3374. יִרְאָה **yir'âh,** *yir-aw´;* fem. of 3373; *fear* (also used as infin.); mor. *reverence:*— × dreadful, × exceedingly, fear (-fulness).

3375. יִרְאוֹן **Yir'ôwn,** *yir-ohn´;* from 3372; *fearfulness; Jiron,* a place in Pal:— Iron.

3376. יִרְאִיָּה **Yir'îyâyh,** *yir-ee-yaw´;* from 3373 and 3050; *fearful of Jah; Jirijah,* an Isr.:— Irijah.

3377. יָרֵב **Yârêb,** *yaw-rabe´;* from 7378; *he will contend; Jareb,* a symb. name for Assyria:— Jareb. Comp. 3402.

3378. יְרֻבַּעַל **Y͏eᵉrubba'al,** *yer-oob-bah´-al;* from 7378 and 1168; *Baal will contend; Jerubbaal,* a symbol. name of Gideon:— Jerubbaal.

3379. יָרׇבְעָם **Yârob'âm,** *yaw-rob-awm´;* from 7378 and 5971; (the) *people will contend; Jarobam,* the name of two Isr. kings:— Jeroboam.

3380. יְרֻבֶּשֶׁת **Y͏eᵉrubbesheth,** *yer-oob-beh´-sheth;* from 7378 and 1322; *shame* (i.e. the idol) *will contend; Jerubbesheth,* a symbol. name for Gideon:— Jerubbesheth.

3381. יָרַד **yârad,** *yaw-rad´;* a prim. root; to *descend* (lit. to go *downwards;* or conventionally to a lower region, as the shore, a boundary, the enemy, etc.; or fig. to *fall*); caus. to *bring down* in all the above applications):— × abundantly, bring down, carry down, cast down, (cause to) come (-ing) down, fall (down), get down, go (-ing) down (-ward), hang down, × indeed, let down, light (down), put down (off), (cause to, let) run down, sink, subdue, take down.

3382. יֶרֶד **Yered,** *yeh´-red;* from 3381; a *descent; Jered,* the name of an antediluvian, and of an Isr.:— Jared.

3383. יַרְדֵּן **Yardên,** *yar-dane´;* from 3381; a *descender; Jarden,* the principal river of Pal.:— Jordan.

3384. יָרָה **yârâh,** *yaw-raw´;* or (2 Chron. 26:15)

יָרָא **yârâ',** *yaw-raw´;* a prim. root; prop. to *flow* as water (i.e. to *rain*); tran. to *lay* or *throw* (espec. an arrow, i.e. to *shoot*); fig. to *point out* (as if by *aiming* the finger), to *teach*:— (+) archer, cast, direct, inform, instruct, lay, shew, shoot, teach (-er,-ing), through.

3385. יְרוּאֵל **Yᵉrûw'êl**, yer-oo-ale´; from 3384 and 410; *founded of God; Jeruel*, a place in Pal.:— Jeruel.

3386. יְרוֹחַ **Yârôwach**, yaw-ro´-akh; perh. denom. from 3394; (born at the) new moon; *Jaroäch*, an Isr.:— Jaroah.

3387. יָרוֹק **yârôwq**, yaw-roke´; from 3417; *green*, i.e. an herb:— green thing.

3388. יְרוּשָׁא **Yᵉrûwshâ'**, yer-oo-shaw´; or

יְרוּשָׁה **Yᵉrûwshâh**, yer-oo-shaw´; fem. pass. part. of 3423; *possessed; Jerusha* or *Jerushah*, an Israelitess:— Jerusha, Jerushah.

3389. יְרוּשָׁלַםִ **Yᵉrûwshâlaim**, yer-oo-shaw-lah´-im; rarely

יְרוּשָׁלַיִם **Yᵉrûwshâlayim**, yer-oo-shaw-lah´-yim; a dual (in allusion to its two main hills [the true pointing, at least of the former reading, seems to be that of 3390]; prob. from (the pass. part. of) 3384 and 7999; *founded peaceful; Jerushalaïm* or *Jerushalem*, the capital city of Pal.:— Jerusalem.

3390. יְרוּשָׁלֵם **Yᵉrûwshâlêm** (Chald.), yer-oo-shaw-lame´; corresp. to 3389:— Jerusalem.

3391. יֶרַח **yerach**, yeh´-rakh; from an unused root of uncert. signif.; a *lunation*, i.e. *month*:— month, moon.

3392. יֶרַח **Yerach**, yeh´-rakh; the same as 3391; *Jerach*, an Arabian patriarch:— Jerah.

3393. יְרַח **yᵉrach** (Chald.), yeh-rakh´; corresp. to 3391; a *month*:— month.

3394. יָרֵחַ **yârêach**, yaw-ray´-akh; from the same as 3391; the *moon*:— moon.

יְרֵחוֹ **Yᵉrêchôw**. See 3405.

3395. יְרֹחָם **Yᵉrôchâm**, yer-o-khawm´; from 7355; *compassionate; Jerocham*, the name of seven or eight Isr.:— Jeroham.

3396. יְרַחְמְאֵל **Yᵉrachmᵉ'êl**, yer-akh-meh-ale´; from 7355 and 410; *God will compassionate; Jerachmeël*, the name of three Isr.:— Jerahmeel.

3397. יְרַחְמְאֵלִי **Yᵉrachmᵉ'êliy**, yer-akh-meh-ay-lee´; patron. from 3396; a *Jerachmeëlite* or desc. of Jerachmeel:— Jerahmeelites.

3398. יַרְחָא **Yarchâ'**, yar-khaw´; prob. of Eg. or.; *Jarcha*, an Eg.:— Jarha.

3399. יָרַט **yârat**, yaw-rat´; a prim. root; to *precipitate* or *hurl* (rush) headlong; (intr.) to *be rash*:— be perverse, turn over.

3400. יְרִיאֵל **Yᵉriy'êl**, yer-ee-ale´; from 3384 and 410; *thrown of God; Jeriël*, an Isr.:— Jeriel. Comp. 3385.

3401. יָרִיב **yârîyb**, yaw-rebe´; from 7378; lit. *he will contend*; prop. adj. *contentious*; used as noun, an *adversary*:— that content (-eth), that strive.

3402. יָרִיב **Yârîyb**, yaw-rebe´; the same as 3401; *Jarib*, the name of three Isr.:— Jarib.

3403. יְרִיבַי **Yᵉrîybay**, yer-eeb-ah´ee; from 3401; *contentious; Jeribai*, an Isr.:— Jeribai.

3404. יְרִיָּה **Yᵉrîyâh**, yer-ee-yaw´; or

יְרִיָּהוּ **Yᵉrîyâhûw**, yer-ee-yaw´-hoo; from 3384 and 3050; *Jah will throw; Jerijah*, an Isr.:— Jeriah, Jerijah.

3405. יְרִיחוֹ **Yᵉrîychôw**, yer-ee-kho´; or

יְרֵחוֹ **Yᵉrêchôw**, yer-ay-kho´; or var. (1 Kings 16:34)

יְרִיחֹה **Yᵉrîychôh**, yer-ee-kho´; perh. from 3394; *its month*; or else from 7306; *fragrant; Jericho* or *Jerecho*, a place in Pal.:— Jericho.

3406. יְרִימוֹת **Yᵉriymôwth**, yer-ee-mohth´; or

יְרֵמוֹת **Yᵉrêymôwth**, yer-ay-mohth´; or

יְרֵמוֹת **Yᵉrêmôwth**, yer-ay-mohth´; fem. plur. from 7311; *elevations; Jerimoth* or *Jeremoth*, the name of twelve Isr.:— Jeremoth, Jerimoth, and Ramoth [from the marg.].

3407. יְרִיעָה **yᵉrîy'âh**, yer-ee-aw´; from 3415; a *hanging* (as *tremulous*):— curtain.

3408. יְרִיעוֹת **Yᵉriy'ôwth**, yer-ee-ohth´; plur. of 3407; *curtains; Jerioth*, an Israelitess:— Jerioth.

3409. יָרֵךְ **yârêk**, yaw-rake´; from an unused root mean. to *be soft*; the *thigh* (from its fleshy *softness*); by euphem. the *generative parts*; fig. a *shank*, *flank*, *side*:— × body, loins, shaft, side, thigh.

3410. יַרְכָּא **yarkâ'** (Chald.), yar-kaw´; corresp. to 3411; a *thigh*:— thigh.

3411. יְרֵכָה **yᵉrêkâh**, yer-ay-kaw´; fem. of 3409; prop. the *flank*; but used only fig., the *rear* or *recess*:— border, coast, part, quarter, side.

3412. יַרְמוּת **Yarmûwth**, yar-mooth´; from 7311; *elevation; Jarmuth*, the name of two places in Pal.:— Jarmuth.

יְרֵמוֹת **Yᵉrêmôwth**. See 3406.

3413. יְרֵמַי **Yᵉrêmay**, yer-ay-mah´-ee; from 7311; *elevated; Jeremai*, an Isr.:— Jeremai.

3414. יִרְמְיָה **Yirmᵉyâh**, yir-meh-yaw´; or

יִרְמְיָהוּ **Yirmᵉyâhûw**, yir-meh-yaw´-hoo; from 7311 and 3050; *Jah will rise; Jirmejah*, the name of eight or nine Isr.:— Jeremiah.

3415. יָרַע **yâra'**, yaw-rah´; a prim. root; prop. *to be broken up* (with any violent action) i.e. (fig.) to *fear*:— be grievous [only Isa. 15:4; the rest belong to 7489].

3416. יִרְפְּאֵל **Yirpᵉ'êl**, yir-peh-ale´; from 7495 and 410; *God will heal; Jirpeël*, a place in Pal.:— Irpeel.

3417. יָרַק **yâraq**, yaw-rak´; a prim. root; to *spit*:— × but, spit.

3418. יֶרֶק **yereq**, yeh´-rek; from 3417 (in the sense of *vacuity* of color); prop. *pallor*, i.e. hence, the yellowish *green* of young and sickly vegetation; concr. *verdure*, i.e. grass or vegetation:— grass, green (thing).

3419. יָרָק **yârâq**, yaw-rawk´; from the same as 3418; prop. *green*; concr. a *vegetable*:— green, herbs.

יַרְקוֹן **Yarqôwn**. See 4313.

3420. יֵרָקוֹן **yêrâqôwn**, yay-raw-kone´; from 3418; *paleness*, whether of per-

sons (from fright), or of plants (from drought):— greenish, yellow.

3421. יָרְקְעָם **Yorqᵉ'âm**, yor-keh-awm´; from 7324 and 5971; *people will be poured forth; Jorkeäm*, a place in Pal.:— Jorkeam.

3422. יְרַקְרַק **yᵉraqraq**, yer-ak-rak´; from the same as 3418; *yellowishness*:— greenish, yellow.

3423. יָרַשׁ **yârash**, yaw-rash´; or

יָרֵשׁ **yârêsh**, yaw-raysh´; a prim. root; to *occupy* (by *driving* out previous tenants, and *possessing* in their place); by impl. to *seize*, to *rob*, to *inherit*; also to *expel*, to *impoverish*, to *ruin*:— cast out, consume, destroy, disinherit, dispossess, drive (-ing) out, enjoy, expel, × without fail, (give to, leave for) inherit (-ance, -or) + magistrate, be (make) poor, come to poverty, (give to, make to) possess, get (have) in (take) possession, seize upon, succeed, × utterly.

3424. יְרֵשָׁה **yᵉrêshâh**, yer-ay-shaw´; from 3423; *occupancy*:— possession.

3425. יְרֻשָּׁה **yᵉrushâh**, yer-oosh-shaw´; from 3423; something *occupied*; a *conquest*; also a *patrimony*:— heritage, inheritance, possession.

3426. יֵשׁ **yêsh**, yaysh; perh. from an unused root mean. to *stand out*, or *exist*; *entity*; used adv. or as a copula for the substantive verb (1961); there *is* or *are* (or any other form of the verb to *be*, as may suit the connection):— (there) are, (he, it, shall, there, there may, there shall, there should) be, thou do, had, hast, (which) hath, (I, shalt, that) have, (he, it, there) is, substance, it (there) was, (there) were, ye will, thou wilt, wouldest

3427. יָשַׁב **yâshab**, yaw-shab´; a prim. root; prop. to *sit* down (spec. as judgement in ambush, in quiet); by impl. to *dwell*, to *remain*; caus. to *settle*, to *marry*:— (make to) abide (-ing), continue, (cause to, make to) dwell (-ing), ease self, endure, establish, × fail, habitation, haunt, (make to) inhabit (-ant), make to keep [house], lurking, × marry (-ing), (bring again to) place, remain, return, seat, set (-tle), (down-) sit (-down, still, -ting down, -ting [place], -uate), take, tarry.

3428. יֶשֶׁבְאָב **Yesheb'âb**, yeh-sheb-awb´; from 3427 and 1; *seat of* (his) *father; Jeshebab*, an Isr.:— Jeshebeab.

3429. יֹשֵׁב בַּשֶּׁבֶת **Yôshêb bash-Shebeth**, yo-shabe´ bash-sheh´-beth; from the act. part. of 3427 and 7674, with a prep. and the art. interposed; *sitting in the seat; Josheb-bash-Shebeth*, an Isr.:— that sat in the seat.

3430. יִשְׁבּוֹ בְּנֹב **Yishbôw bᵉ-Nôb**, yish-bo´ beh-nobe´; from 3427 and 5011, with a pron. suff. and a prep. interposed; *his dwelling* (is) *in Nob; Jishbo-be-Nob*, a Philistine:— Ishbi-benob [from the marg.].

3431. יִשְׁבַּח **Yishbach**, yish-bakh´; from 7623; *he will praise; Jishbach*, an Isr.:— Ishbah.

3432. יָשׁוּבִי **Yâshûbiy**, yaw-shoo-bee´; patron. from 3437; a *Jashubite*, or desc. of Jashub:— Jashubites.

Hebrew

3433. יֹשְׁבֵי לֶחֶם **Yâshûbiy Lechem**, yaw-shoo-bee´ leh´-khem; from 7725 and 3899; returner of bread; Jashubi-Lechem, an Isr.:— Jashubi-lehem. [Prob. the text should be pointed

יֹשְׁבֵי לֶחֶם **Yôsheᵇbêy Lechem**, yo-sheh-bay´ leh´-khem, and rendered "(they were) inhab. of Lechem," i.e. of Bethlehem (by contr.). Comp. 3902l.

3434. יָשָׁבְעָם **Yâshob'âm**, yaw-shob-awm´; from 7725 and 5971; people will return; Jashobam, the name of two or three Isr.:— Jashobeam.

3435. יִשְׁבָּק **Yishbâq**, yish-bawk´; from an unused root corresp. to 7662; he will leave; Jishbak, a son of Abraham:— Ishbak.

3436. יָשָׁבְקָשָׁה **Yoshbeᵇqâshâh**, yosh-bek-aw-shaw´; from 3427 and 7186; a hard seat; Joshbekashah, an Isr.:— Joshbekashah.

3437. יָשׁוּב **Yâshûwb**, yaw-shoob´; or

יָשִׁיב **Yâshîyb**, yaw-sheeb´; from 7725; he will return; Jashub, the name of two Isr.:— Jashub.

3438. יִשְׁוָה **Yishvâh**, yish-vaw´; from 7737; he will level; Jishvah, an Isr.:— Ishvah, Isvah.

3439. יְשׁוֹחָיָה **Yᵉshôwchâyâh**, yesh-o-khaw-yaw´; from the same as 3445 and 3050; Jah will empty; Jeshochajah, an Isr.:— Jeshoaiah.

3440. יִשְׁוִי **Yishvîy**, yish-vee´; from 7737; level; Jishvi, the name of two Isr.:— Ishuai, Ishvi, Isui, Jesui.

3441. יִשְׁוִי **Yishvîy**, yish-vee´; patron. from 3440; a Jishvite (collect.) or desc. of Jishvi:— Jesuites.

3442. יֵשׁוּעַ **Yêshûwa'**, yay-shoo´-ah; for 3091; he will save; Jeshua, the name of ten Isr., also of a place in Pal.:— Jeshua.

3443. יֵשׁוּעַ **Yêshûwa'** (Chald.), yay-shoo´-ah; corresp. to 3442:— Jeshua.

3444. יְשׁוּעָה **yᵉshûw'âh**, yesh-oo´-aw; fem. pass. part. of 3467; something saved, i.e. (abstr.) deliverance; hence, aid, victory, prosperity:— deliverance, health, help (-ing), salvation, save, saving (health), welfare.

3445. יֶשַׁח **yeshach**, yeh´-shakh; from an unused root mean. to gape (as the empty stomach); hunger:— casting down.

3446. יִשְׂחָק **Yischâq**, yis-khawk´; from 7831; he will laugh; Jischak, the heir of Abraham:— Isaac. Comp. 3327.

3447. יָשַׁט **yâshat**, yaw-shat´; a prim. root; to extend:— hold out.

3448. יִשַׁי **Yîshay**, yee-shah´-ee; by Chald.

אִישַׁי **Îyshay**, ee-shah´-ee; from the same as 3426; extant; Jishai, David's father:— Jesse.

יָשִׁיב **Yâshîyb**. See 3437.

3449. יִשִּׁיָּה **Yishshîyâh**, yish-shee-yaw´; or

יִשִּׁיָּהוּ **Yishshîyâhûw**, yish-shee-yaw´-hoo; from 5383 and 3050; Jah will lend; Jishshijah, the name of five Isr.:— Ishiah, Isshiah, Ishijah, Jesiah.

3450. יְשִׂימָאֵל **Yᵉsîymâ'êl**, yes-eem-aw-

ale´; from 7760 and 410; God will place; Jesimaël, an Isr.:— Jesimael.

3451. יְשִׁימָה **yᵉshîymâh**, yesh-ee-maw´; from 3456; desolation:— let death seize [from the marg.].

3452. יְשִׁימוֹן **yᵉshîymôwn**, yesh-ee-mone´; from 3456; a desolation:— desert, Jeshimon, solitary, wilderness.

יְשִׁימוֹת **yᵉshîymôwth**. See 1020, 3451.

3453. יָשִׁישׁ **yâshîysh**, yaw-sheesh´; from 3486; an old man:— (very) aged (man), ancient, very old.

3454. יְשִׁישַׁי **Yᵉshîyshay**, yesh-ee-shah-ee; from 3453; aged; Jeshishai, an Isr.:— Jeshishai.

3455. יָשַׂם **yâsam**, yaw-sam´; a prim. root; to place; intr. to be placed:— be put (set).

3456. יָשַׁם **yâsham**, yaw-sham´; a prim. root; to lie waste:— be desolate.

3457. יִשְׁמָא **Yishmâ'**, yish-maw´; from 3456; desolate; Jishma, an Isr.:— Ishma.

3458. יִשְׁמָעֵאל **Yishmâ'ê'l**, yish-maw-ale´; from 8085 and 410; God will hear; Jishmaël, the name of Abraham's oldest son, and of five Isr.:— Ishmael.

3459. יִשְׁמָעֵאלִי **Yishmâ'ê'lîy**, yish-maw-ay-lee´; patron. from 3458; a Jishmaëlite or desc. of Jishmael:— Ishmaelite.

3460. יִשְׁמַעְיָה **Yishma'yâh**, yish-mah-yaw´; or

יִשְׁמַעְיָהוּ **Yishma'yâhûw**, yish-mah-yaw´-hoo; from 8085 and 3050; Jah will hear; Jishmajah, the name of two Isr.:— Ishmaiah.

3461. יִשְׁמְרַי **Yishmᵉray**, yish-mer-ah´-ee; from 8104; preservative; Jishmerai, an Isr.:— Ishmerai.

3462. יָשֵׁן **yâshên**, yaw-shane´; a prim. root; prop. to be slack or languid, i.e. (by impl.) sleep (fig. to die); also to grow old, stale or inveterate:— old (store), remain long, (make to) sleep.

3463. יָשֵׁן **yâshên**, yaw-shane´; from 3462; sleepy:— asleep, (one out of) sleep (-eth, -ing), slept.

3464. יָשֵׁן **Yâshên**, yaw-shane´; the same as 3463; Jashen, an Isr.:— Jashen.

3465. יָשָׁן **yâshân**, yaw-shawn´; from 3462; old:— old.

3466. יְשָׁנָה **Yᵉshânâh**, yesh-aw-naw´; fem. of 3465; Jeshanah, a place in Pal.:— Jeshanah.

3467. יָשַׁע **yâsha'**, yaw-shah´; a prim. root; prop. to be open, wide or free, i.e. (by impl.) to be safe; caus. to free or succor:— × at all, avenging, defend, deliver (-er), help, preserve, rescue, be safe, bring (having) salvation, save (-iour), get victory.

3468. יֶשַׁע **yesha'**, yeh´-shah; or

יֵשַׁע **yêsha'**, yay´-shah; from 3467; liberty, deliverance, prosperity:— safety, salvation, saving.

3469. יִשְׁעִי **Yish'îy**, yish-ee´; from 3467; saving; Jishi, the name of four Isr.:— Ishi.

3470. יְשַׁעְיָה **Yᵉsha'yâh**, yesh-ah-yaw´; or

יְשַׁעְיָהוּ **Yᵉsha'yâhûw**, yesh-ah-yaw´-hoo; from 3467 and 3050; Jah has saved; Jeshajah, the name of seven Isr.:— Isaiah, Jesaiah, Jeshaiah.

3471. יָשְׁפֵה **yâshᵉphêh**, yaw-shef-ay´; from an unused root mean. to polish; a gem supposed to be jasper (from the resemblance in name):— jasper.

3472. יִשְׁפָּה **Yishpâh**, yish-paw´; perh. from 8192; he will scratch; Jishpah, an Isr.:— Ispah.

3473. יִשְׁפָּן **Yishpân**, yish-pawn´; prob. from the same as 8227; he will hide; Jishpan, an Isr.:— Ishpan.

3474. יָשַׁר **yâshar**, yaw-shar´; a prim. root; to be straight or even; fig. to be (caus. to make) right, pleasant, prosperous:— direct, fit, seem good (meet), + please (will), be (esteem, go) right (on), bring (look, make, take the) straight (way), be upright (-ly).

3475. יֵשֶׁר **Yêsher**, yay´-sher; from 3474; the right; Jesher, an Isr.:— Jesher.

3476. יֹשֶׁר **yôsher**, yo´-sher; from 3474; the right:— equity, meet, right, upright (-ness).

3477. יָשָׁר **yâshâr**, yaw-shawr´; from 3474; straight (lit. or fig.):— convenient, equity, Jasher, just, meet (-est), + pleased well right (-eous), straight, (most) upright (-ly, -ness).

3478. יִשְׂרָאֵל **Yisrâ'êl**, yis-raw-ale´; from 8280 and 410; he will rule (as) God; Jisraël, a symb. name of Jacob; also (typ.) of his posterity:— Israel.

3479. יִשְׂרָאֵל **Yisrâ'êl** (Chald.), yis-raw-ale´; corresp. to 3478:— Israel.

3480. יְשַׂרְאֵלָה **Yᵉsar'êlâh**, yes-ar-ale´-aw; by var. from 3477 and 410 with directive enclitic; right towards God; Jesarelah, an Isr.:— Jesharelah. Comp. 841.

3481. יִשְׂרְאֵלִי **Yisrᵉ'êlîy**, yis-reh-ay-lee´; patron. from 3478; a Jisreëlite or desc. of Jisrael:— of Israel, Israelite.

3482. יִשְׂרְאֵלִית **Yisrᵉ'êlîyth**, yis-reh-ay-leeth´; fem. of 3481; a Jisreëlitess or female desc. of Jisrael:— Israelitish.

3483. יִשְׁרָה **yishrâh**, yish-raw´; fem. or 3477; rectitude:— uprightness.

3484. יְשֻׁרוּן **Yᵉshûrûwn**, yesh-oo-roon´; from 3474; upright; Jeshurun, a symbol. name for Israel:— Jeshurun.

3485. יִשָּׂשכָר **Yissâskâr**, yis-saw-kawr´; (strictly yis-saws-kawr´); from 5375 and 7939; he will bring a reward; Jissaskar, a son of Jacob:— Issachar.

3486. יָשֵׁשׁ **yâshêsh**, yaw-shaysh´; from an unused root mean. to blanch; gray-haired, i.e. an aged man:— stoop for age.

3487. יָת **yath** (Chald.), yath; corresp. to 853; a sign of the object of a verb:— + whom.

3488. יְתִב **yᵉthîb** (Chald.), yeth-eeb´; corresp. to 3427; to sit or dwell:— dwell, (be) set, sit.

3489. יָתֵד **yâthêd**, yaw-thade´; from an unused root mean. to pin through or fast; a peg:— nail, paddle, pin, stake.

3490. יָתוֹם **yâthôwm**, yaw-thome´; from an unused root mean. to be lonely; a *bereaved* person:— fatherless (child), orphan.

3491. יתור **yâthûwr**, *yaw-thoor'*; pass. part. of 3498; prop. what is *left*, i.e. (by impl.) a *gleaning*:— range.

3492. יתיר **Yattîyr**, *yat-teer'*; from 3498; *redundant*; *Jattir*, a place in Pal.:— Jattir.

3493. יתיר **yattîyr** (Chald.), *yat-teer'*; corresp. to 3492; *preeminent*; adv. *very*:— exceeding (-ly), excellent.

3494. יתלה **Yithlâh**, *yith-law'*; prob. from 8518; it *will hang*, i.e. *be high*; *Jithlah*, a place in Pal.:— Jethlah.

3495. יתמה **Yithmâh**, *yith-maw'*; from the same as 3490; *orphanage*; *Jithmah*, an Isr.:— Ithmah.

3496. יתניאל **Yathnîy'êl**, *yath-nee-ale'*; from an unused root mean. to *endure*, and 410; *continued of God*; *Jathniël*, an Isr.:— Jathniel.

3497. יתנן **Yithnân**, *yith-nawn'*; from the same as 8577; *extensive*; *Jithnan*, a place in Pal.:— Ithnan.

3498. יתר **yâthar**, *yaw-thar'*; a prim. root; to *jut* over or *exceed*; by impl. to *excel*; (intr.) to *remain* or *be left*; caus. to *leave, cause to abound, preserve*:— excel, leave (a remnant), left behind, too much, make plenteous, preserve, (be, let) remain (-der, -ing, -nant), reserve, residue, rest.

3499. יתר **yether**, *yeh'-ther*; from 3498; prop. an *overhanging*, i.e. (by impl.) an *excess, superiority, remainder*; also a small *rope* (as hanging free):— + abundant, cord, exceeding, excellency (-ent), what they leave, that hath left, plentifully , remnant, residue, rest, string, with.

3500. יתר **Yether**, *yeh'-ther*; the same as 3499; *Jether*, the name of five or six Isr. and of one Midianite:— Jether, Jethro. Comp. 3503.

3501. יתרא **Yithrâ'**, *yith-raw'*; by var. for 3502; *Jithra*, an Isr. (or Ishmaelite):— Ithra.

3502. יתרה **yithrâh**, *yith-raw'*; fem. of 3499; prop. *excellence*, i.e. (by impl.) *wealth*:— abundance, riches.

3503. יתרו **Yithrôw**, *yith-ro'*; from 3499 with pron. suff.; *his excellence*; *Jethro*, Moses' father-in-law:— Jethro. Comp. 3500.

3504. יתרון **yithrôwn**, *yith-rone'*; from 3498; *preeminence, gain*:— better, excellency (-leth), profit (-able).

3505. יתרי **Yithrîy**, *yith-ree'*; patron. from 3500; a *Jithrite* or desc. of *Jether*:— Ithrite.

3506. יתרן **Yithrân**, *yith-rawn'*; from 3498; *excellent*; *Jithran*, the name of an Edomite and of an Isr.:— Ithran.

3507. יתרעם **Yithr'ʻâm**, *yith-reh-awm'*; from 3499 and 5971; *excellence of people*; *Jithreäm*, a son of David:— Ithream.

3508. יתרת **yôthereth**, *yo-theh'-reth*; fem. act. part. of 3498; the *lobe* or *flap* of the liver (as if redundant or outhanging):— caul.

3509. יתת **Yᵉthêyth**, *yeh-thayth'*; of uncert. der.; *Jetheth*, an Edomite:— Jetheth.

כ

3510. כאב **kâ'ab**, *kaw-ab'*; a prim. root; prop. to feel *pain*; by impl. to *grieve*; fig. to *spoil*:— grieving, mar, have pain, make sad (sore), (be) sorrowful.

3511. כאב **kᵉ'êb**, *keh-abe'*; from 3510; *suffering* (phys. or ment.), *adversity*:— grief, pain, sorrow.

3512. כאה **kâ'âh**, *kaw-aw'*; a prim. root; to *despond*; caus. to *deject*:— broken, be grieved, make sad.

3513. כבד **kâbad**, *kaw-bad'*; or

כבד **kâbêd**, *kaw-bade'*; a prim. root; to *be heavy*, i.e. in a bad sense (*burdensome, severe, dull*) or in a good sense (*numerous, rich, honorable*); caus. to *make weighty* (in the same two senses):— abounding with, more grievously afflict, boast, be chargeable, × be dim, glorify, be (make) glorious (things), glory, (very) great, be grievous, harden, be (make) heavy, be heavier, lay heavily, (bring to, come to, do, get, be had in) honour (self), (be) honourable (man) , lade, × more be laid, make self many, nobles, prevail, promote (to honour), be rich, be (go) sore, stop.

3514. כבד **kôbed**, *ko'-bed*; from 3513; *weight, multitude, vehemence*:— grievousness, heavy, great number.

3515. כבד **kâbêd**, *kaw-bade'*; from 3513; *heavy*; fig. in a good sense (*numerous*) or in a bad sense (*severe, difficult, stupid*):— (so) great, grievous, hard (-ened), (too) heavy (-ier), laden, much, slow, sore, thick.

3516. כבד **kâbêd**, *kaw-bade'*; the same as 3515; the *liver* (as the *heaviest* of the viscera):— liver.

כבד **kâbôd**. See 3519.

3517. כבדה **kᵉbêdûth**, *keb-ay-dooth'*; fem. of 3515; *difficulty*:— × heavily.

3518. כבה **kâbâh**, *kaw-baw'*; a prim. root; to *expire* or (caus.) to *extinguish* (fire, light, anger):— go (put) out, quench.

3519. כבוד **kâbôwd**, *kaw-bode'*; rarely

כבד **kâbôd**, *kaw-bode'*; from 3513; prop. *weight*, but only fig. in a good sense, *splendor* or *copiousness*:— glorious (-ly), glory, honour (-able).

3520. כבודה **kᵉbûwddâh**, *keb-ood-daw'*; irreg. fem. pass. part. of 3513; *weightiness*, i.e. *magnificence, wealth*:— carriage, all glorious, stately.

3521. כבול **Kâbûwl**, *kaw-bool'*; from the same as 3525 in the sense of *limitation*; *sterile*; *Cabul*, the name of two places in Pal.:— Cabul.

3522. כבון **Kabbôwn**, *kab-bone'*; from an unused root mean. to *heap* up; *hilly*; *Cabon*, a place in Pal.:— Cabbon.

3523. כביר **kᵉbîyr**, *keb-eer'*; from 3527 in the orig. sense of *plaiting*; a *matrass* (of intertwined materials):— pillow.

3524. כביר **kabbîyr**, *kab-beer'*; from 3527; *vast*, whether in extent (fig. of power, *mighty*; of time, *aged*), or in

number, *many*:— + feeble, mighty, most, much, strong, valiant.

3525. כבל **kebel**, *keh'-bel*; from an unused root mean. to *twine* or braid together; a *fetter*:— fetter.

3526. כבס **kâbaç**, *kaw-bas'*; a prim. root; to *trample*; hence, to *wash* (prop. by stamping with the feet), whether lit. (incl. the *fulling* process) or fig.:— fuller, wash (-ing).

3527. כבר **kâbar**, *kaw-bar'*; a prim. root; prop. to *plait* together, i.e. (fig.) to *augment* (espec. in number or quantity, to *accumulate*):— in abundance, multiply.

3528. כבר **kᵉbâr**, *keb-awr'*; from 3527; prop. *extent* of time, i.e. a *great while*; hence, *long ago, formerly, hitherto*:— already, (seeing that which), now.

3529. כבר **Kᵉbâr**, *keb-awr'*; the same as 3528; *length*; *Kebar*, a river of Mesopotamia:— Chebar. Comp. 2249.

3530. כברה **kibrâh**, *kib-raw'*; fem. of 3528; prop. *length*, i.e. a *measure* (of uncert. dimension):— × little.

3531. כברה **kᵉbârâh**, *keb-aw-raw'*; from 3527 in its orig. sense; a *sieve* (as netted):— sieve.

3532. כבש **kebes**, *keh-bes'*; from an unused root mean. to *dominate*; a *ram* (just old enough to *butt*):— lamb, sheep.

3533. כבש **kâbash**, *kaw-bash'*; a prim. root; to *tread* down; hence, neg. to *disregard*; pos. to *conquer, subjugate, violate*:— bring into bondage, force, keep under, subdue, bring into subjection.

3534. כבש **kebesh**, *keh'-besh*; from 3533; a *footstool* (as trodden upon):— footstool.

3535. כבשה **kibsâh**, *kib-saw'*; or

כבשה **kabsâh**, *kab-saw'*; fem. of 3532; a *ewe*:— (ewe) lamb.

3536. כבשן **kibshân**, *kib-shawn'*; from 3533; a smelting *furnace* (as *reducing* metals):— furnace.

3537. כד **kad**, *kad*; from an unused root mean. to *deepen*; prop. a *pail*; but gen. of earthenware; a *jar* for domestic purposes:— barrel, pitcher.

3538. כדב **kᵉdab** (Chald.), *ked-ab'*; from a root corresp. to 3576; *false*:— lying.

3539. כדכד **kadkôd**, *kad-kobe'*; from the same as 3537 in the sense of *striking fire* from a metal forged; a *sparkling gem*, prob. the ruby:— agate.

3540. כדרלעמר **Kᵉdorlâʻômer**, *ked-or-law-o'-mer*; of for. or.; *Kedorlaomer*, an early Pers. king:— Chedorlaomer.

3541. כה **kôh**, *ko*; from the pref. *k* and 1931; prop. *like this*, i.e. by impl. (of manner) *thus* (or *so*); also (of place) *here* (or *hither*); or (of time) *now*:— also, here, + hitherto, like, on the other side, so (and much), such, on that manner, (on) this (manner, side, way, way and that way), + mean while, yonder.

3542. כה **kâh** (Chald.), *kaw*; corresp. to 3541:— hitherto.

3543. כהה **kâhâh**, *kaw-haw'*; a prim. root; to *be weak*, i.e. (fig.) to *despond* (caus. *rebuke*), or (of light, the eye) to *grow dull.*— darken, be dim, fail, faint, restrain, × utterly.

3544. כֵּהֶה **kêheh**, *kay-heh´*; from 3543; *feeble, obscure:*— somewhat dark, darkish, wax dim, heaviness, smoking.

3545. כֵּהָה **kêhâh**, *kay-haw´*; fem. of 3544; prop. a *weakening;* fig. *alleviation*, i.e. cure:— healing.

3546. כְּהַל **kᵉhal** (Chald.), *keh-hal´;* a root corresp. to 3201 and 3557; to be *able:*— be able, could.

3547. כָּהַן **kâhan**, *kaw-han´;* a prim. root, appar. mean. to *mediate* in relig. services; but used only as denom. from 3548; to *officiate* as a priest; fig. to *put on regalia:*— deck, be (do the office of a, execute the, minister in the) priest ('s office).

3548. כֹּהֵן **kôhên**, *ko-hane´;* act. part. of 3547; lit. one *officiating*, a *priest;* also (by courtesy) an *acting priest* (although a layman):— chief ruler, × own, priest, prince, principal officer.

3549. כָּהֵן **kâhên** (Chald.), *kaw-hane´;* corresp. to 3548:— priest.

3550. כְּהֻנָּה **kᵉhunnâh**, *keh-hoon-naw´;* from 3547; *priesthood:*— priesthood, priest's office.

3551. כַּו **kav** (Chald.), *kav;* from a root corresp. to 3854 in the sense of *piercing;* a *window* (as a perforation):— window.

3552. כּוּב **Kûwb**, *koob;* of for. der.; *Kub*, a country near Egypt:— Chub.

3553. כּוֹבַע **kôwba'**, *ko´-bah;* from an unused root mean. to be *high* or *rounded;* a *helmet* (as *arched*):— helmet. Comp. 6959.

3554. כָּוָה **kâvâh**, *kaw-vaw´;* a prim. root; prop. to *prick* or *penetrate;* hence, to *blister* (as smarting or eating into):— burn.

     כּוֹחַ **kôwach**. See 3581.

3555. כְּוִיָּה **kᵉvîyâh**, *kev-ee-yaw´;* from 3554; a *branding:*— burning.

3556. כּוֹכָב **kôwkâb**, *ko-kawb´;* prob. from the same as 3522 (in the sense of *rolling*) or 3554 (in the sense of *blazing*); a *star* (as *round* or as *shining*); fig. a *prince:*— star (-gazer).

3557. כּוּל **kûwl**, *kool;* a prim. root; prop. to *keep in;* hence, to *measure;* fig. to *maintain* (in various senses):— (be able to, can) abide, bear, comprehend, contain, feed, forbearing, guide, hold (-ing in), nourish (-er), be present, make provision, receive, sustain, provide sustenance (victuals).

3558. כּוּמָז **kûwmâz**, *koo-mawz´;* from an unused root mean. to *store* away; a *jewel* (prob. gold beads):— tablet.

3559. כּוּן **kûwn**, *koon;* a prim. root; prop. to *be erect* (i.e. stand perpendicular); hence, (caus.) to *set up*, in a great variety of applications, whether lit. (*establish, fix, prepare, apply*), or fig. (*appoint, render sure, proper* or *prosperous*):— certain (-ty), confirm, direct, faithfulness, fashion, fasten, firm, be fitted, be fixed, frame, be meet, ordain, order, perfect, (make) preparation, prepare (self), provide, make provision, (be, make) ready, right, set

(aright, fast, forth), be stable , (e-) stablish, stand, tarry, × very deed.

3560. כּוּן **Kûwn**, *koon;* prob. from 3559; *established; Kun*, a place in Syria:— Chun.

3561. כַּוָּן **kavvân**, *kav-vawn´;* from 3559; something *prepared*, i.e. a sacrificial *wafer:*— cake.

3562. כּוֹנַנְיָהוּ **Kôwnanyâhûw**, *ko-nan-yaw´-hoo;* from 3559 and 3050; *Jah has sustained; Conanjah*, the name of two Isr.:— Conaniah, Cononiah. Comp. 3663.

3563. כּוֹס **kôwç**, *koce;* from an unused root mean. to *hold* together; a *cup* (as a container), often fig. a *lot* (as if a potion); also some unclean bird, prob. an *owl* (perh. from the cup-like cavity of its eye):— cup, (small) owl. Comp. 3599.

3564. כּוּר **kûwr**, *koor;* from an unused root mean. prop. to *dig* through; a *pot* or *furnace* (as if excavated):— furnace. Comp. 3600.

     כּוּר **kôwr**. See 3733.

3565. כּוֹר עָשָׁן **Kôwr 'Âshân**, *kore aw-shawn´;* from 3564 and 6227; *furnace of smoke; Cor-Ashan*, a place in Pal.:— Chor-ashan.

3566. כּוֹרֶשׁ **Kôwresh**, *ko´-resh;* or (Ezra 1:1 llast timel, 2)

     כֹּרֶשׁ **Kôresh**, *ko´-resh;* from the Pers.; *Koresh* (or Cyrus), the Pers. king:— Cyrus.

3567. כּוֹרֶשׁ **Kôwresh** (Chald.), *ko´-resh;* corresp. to 3566:— Cyrus.

3568. כּוּשׁ **Kûwsh**, *koosh;* prob. of for. or.; *Cush* (or Ethiopia), the name of a son of Ham, and of his territory; also of an Isr.:— Chush, Cush, Ethiopia.

3569. כּוּשִׁי **Kûwshîy**, *koo-shee´;* patron. from 3568; a *Cushite*, or desc. of Cush:— Cushi, Cushite, Ethiopian (-s).

3570. כּוּשִׁי **Kûwshîy**, *koo-shee´;* the same as 3569; *Cushi*, the name of two Isr.:— Cushi.

3571. כּוּשִׁית **Kûwshîyth**, *koo-sheeth´;* fem. of 3569; a *Cushite woman:*— Ethiopian.

3572. כּוּשָׁן **Kûwshân**, *koo-shawn´;* perh. from 3568; *Cushan*, a region of Arabia:— Cushan.

3573. כּוּשַׁן רִשְׁעָתַיִם **Kûwshan Rish'âthâyim**, *koo-shan´ rish-aw-thah´-yim;* appar. from 3572 and the dual of 7564; *Cushan of double wickedness; Cushan-Rishathajim*, a Mesopotamian king:— Chushan-rishathaim.

3574. כּוֹשָׁרָה **kôwshârâh**, *ko-shaw-raw´;* from 3787; *prosperity;* in plur. *freedom:*— × chain.

3575. כּוּת **Kûwth**, *kooth;* or (fem.)

     כּוּתָה **Kûwthâh**, *koo-thaw´;* of for. or.; *Cuth* or *Cuthah*, a province of Assyria:— Cuth.

3576. כָּזַב **kâzab**, *kaw-zab´;* a prim. root; to *lie* (i.e. *deceive*), lit. or fig.:— fail, (be found a, make a) liar, lie, lying, be in vain.

3577. כָּזָב **kâzâb**, *kaw-zawb´;* from 3576; *falsehood;* lit. (*untruth*) or fig. (*idol*):— deceitful, false, leasing, + liar, lie, lying.

3578. כֹּזְבָא **Kôzᵉbâ'**, *ko-zeb-aw´;* from 3576; *fallacious; Cozeba*, a place in Pal.:— Choseba.

3579. כָּזְבִּי **Kozbîy**, *koz-bee´;* from 3576; *false; Cozbi*, a Midianitess:— Cozbi.

3580. כְּזִיב **Kᵉzîyb**, *kez-eeb´;* from 3576; *falsified; Kezib*, a place in Pal.:— Chezib.

3581. כֹּחַ **kôach**, *ko´-akh;* or (Dan. 11:6)

     כּוֹחַ **kôwach**, *ko´-akh;* from an unused root mean. to *be firm; vigor*, lit. (*force*, in a good or a bad sense) or fig. (*capacity, means, produce*); also (from its hardiness) a large *lizard:*— ability, able, chameleon, force, fruits, might, power (-ful), strength, substance, wealth.

3582. כָּחַד **kâchad**, *kaw-khad´;* a prim. root; to *secrete*, by act or word; hence, (intens.) to *destroy:*— conceal, cut down (off), desolate, hide.

3583. כָּחַל **kâchal**, *kaw-khal´;* a prim. root; to *paint* (with stibium):— paint.

3584. כָּחַשׁ **kâchash**, *kaw-khash´;* a prim. root; to *be untrue*, in word (to *lie, feign, disown*) or deed (to *disappoint, fail, cringe*):— deceive, deny, dissemble, fail, deal falsely, be found liars, (be-) lie, lying, submit selves.

3585. כַּחַשׁ **kachash**, *kakh´-ash;* from 3584; lit. a *failure* of flesh, i.e. *emaciation;* fig. *hypocrisy:*— leanness, lies, lying.

3586. כֶּחָשׁ **kechâsh**, *kekh-awsh´;* from 3584; *faithless:*— lying.

3587. כִּי **kîy**, *kee;* from 3554; a *brand* or *scar:*— burning.

3588. כִּי **kîy**, *kee;* a prim. particle lthe full form of the prepositional prefixl indicating *causal* relations of all kinds, antecedent or consequent; (by impl.) very widely used as a rel. conjunc. or adv. las belowl; often largely modif. by other particles annexed:— and, + (for-asmuch, inasmuch, where-) as, assured l-lyl, + but, certainly, doubtless, + else, even, + except, for, how, (because, in, so, than) that, + nevertheless, now, rightly, seeing, since, surely, then, therefore, + (al-) + though, + till, truly, + until, when, whether, while, whom, yea, yet.

3589. כִּיד **kîyd**, *keed;* from a prim. root mean. to *strike;* a *crushing;* fig. *calamity:*— destruction.

3590. כִּידוֹד **kîydôwd**, *kee-dode´;* from the same as 3589 lcomp. 3539l; prop. something *struck* off, i.e. a *spark* (as struck):— spark.

3591. כִּידוֹן **kîydôwn**, *kee-dohn´;* from the same as 3589; prop. something to *strike* with, i.e. a *dart* (perh. smaller than 2595):— lance, shield, spear, target.

3592. כִּידוֹן **Kîydôwn**, *kee-dohn´;* the same as 3591; *Kidon*, a place in Pal.:— Chidon.

3593. כִּידוֹר **kîydôwr**, *kee-dore´;* of uncert. der.; perh. *tumult:*— battle.

3594. כִּיּוּן **Kîyûwn**, *kee-yoon´;* from 3559; prop. a *statue*, i.e. idol; but used (by euphem.) for some heathen deity (perh. corresp. to Priapus or Baal-peor):— Chiun.

3595. כִּיוֹר **kîyôwr**, *kee-yore'*; or

כִּיֹר **kîyôr**, *kee-yore'*; from the same as 3564; prop. something *round* (as *excavated* or *bored*), i.e. a chafing-dish for coals or a *caldron* for cooking; hence, (from similarity of form) a *washbowl*; also (for the same reason) a *pulpit* or platform:— hearth, laver, pan, scaffold.

3596. כִּילַי **kîylay**, *kee-lah'-ee*; or

כֵּלַי **kêlay**, *kay-lah'-ee*; from 3557 in the sense of *withholding; niggardly*:— churl.

3597. כֵּילַף **kêylaph**, *kay-laf'*; from an unused root mean. to *clap* or strike with noise; a *club* or sledge-hammer:— hammer.

3598. כִּימָה **Kîymâh**, *kee-maw'*; from the same as 3558; a *cluster* of stars, i.e. the *Pleiades*:— Pleiades, seven stars.

3599. כִּיס **kîyç**, *keece*; a form for 3563; a *cup*; also a *bag* for money or weights:— bag, cup, purse.

3600. כִּיר **kîyr**, *keer*; a form for 3564 (only in the dual); a cooking *range* (consisting of two parallel stones, across which the boiler is set):— ranges for pots.

כִּיֹר **kîyôr**. See 3595.

3601. כִּישׁוֹר **kîyshôwr**, *kee-shore'*; from 3787; lit. a *director*, i.e. the *spindle* or shank of a distaff (6418), by which it is twirled:— spindle.

3602. כָּכָה **kâkâh**, *kaw'-kaw*; from 3541; *just so*, referring to the previous or following context:— after that (this) manner, this matter, (even) so, in such a case, thus.

3603. כִּכָּר **kikkâr**, *kik-kawr'*; from 3769; a *circle*, i.e. (by impl.) a circumjacent *tract* or region, expec. the *Ghôr* or valley of the Jordan; also a (round) *loaf*; also a *talent* (or large [round] coin):— loaf, morsel, piece, plain, talent.

3604. כִּכָּר **kikkêr** (Chald.), *kik-kare'*; corresp. to 3603; a *talent*:— talent.

3605. כֹּל **kôl**, *kole*; or (Jer. 33:8)

כּוֹל **kôwl**, *kole*; from 3634; prop. the *whole*; hence, *all, any* or *every* (in the sing. only, but often in a plur. sense):— (in) all (manner, [ye]), altogether, any (manner), enough, every (one, place, thing), howsoever, as many as, [no-] thing, ought, whatsoever, (the) whole, whoso (-ever).

3606. כֹּל **kôl** (Chald.), *kole*; corresp. to 3605:— all, any, + (forasmuch) as, + be-(for this) cause, every, + no (manner, -ne), + there (where) -fore, + though, what (where, who) -soever, (the) whole.

3607. כָּלָא **kâlâ'**, *kaw-law'*; a prim. root; to *restrict*, by act (*hold* back or in) or word (*prohibit*):— finish, forbid, keep (back), refrain, restrain, retain, shut up, be stayed, withhold.

3608. כֶּלֶא **kele'**, *keh'-leh*; from 3607; a *prison*:— prison. Comp. 3610, 3628.

3609. כִּלְאָב **Kil'âb**, *kil-awb'*; appar. from 3607 and 1; *restraint of* (his) *father; Kilab*, an Isr.:— Chileab.

3610. כִּלְאַיִם **kil'ayim**, *kil-ah'-yim*; dual of 3608 in the orig. sense of *separation; two heterogeneities*:— divers seeds (-e kinds), mingled (seed).

3611. כֶּלֶב **keleb**, *keh'-leb*; from an unused root means. to *yelp*, or else to *attack*; a *dog*; hence, (by euphem.) a male *prostitute*:— dog.

3612. כָּלֵב **Kâlêb**, *kaw-labe'*; perh. a form of 3611, or else from the same root in the sense of *forcible; Caleb*, the name of three Isr.:— Caleb.

3613. כָּלֵב אֶפְרָתָה **Kâlêb 'Ephrâthâh**, *kaw-labe' ef-raw'-thaw*; from 3612 and 672; *Caleb-Ephrathah*, a place in Egypt (if the text is correct):— Caleb-ephrathah.

3614. כָּלִבּוֹ **Kâlibbôw**, *kaw-lib-bo'*; prob. by err. transc. for

כָּלֵבִי **Kâlêbiy**, *kaw-lay-bee'*; patron. from 3612; a *Calebite* or desc. of Caleb:— of the house of Caleb.

3615. כָּלָה **kâlâh**, *kaw-law'*; a prim. root; to *end*, whether intr. (to *cease, be finished, perish*) or tran. (to *complete, prepare, consume*):— accomplish, cease, consume (away), determine, destroy (utterly), be (when ... were) done, (be an) end (of), expire, (cause to) fail, faint, finish, fulfil, × fully, × have, leave (off), long, bring to pass, wholly reap, make clean riddance, spend, quite take away, waste.

3616. כָּלֶה **kâleh**, *kaw-leh'*; from 3615; *pining*:— fail.

3617. כָּלָה **kâlâh**, *kaw-law'*; from 3615; a *completion;* adv. *completely;* also *destruction*:— altogether, (be, utterly) consume (-d), consummation (-ption), was determined, (full, utter) end, riddance.

3618. כַּלָּה **kallâh**, *kal-law'*; from 3634; a *bride* (as if *perfect*); hence, a *son's wife*:— bride, daughter-in-law, spouse.

כְּלוּא **kᵉlûw'**. See 3628.

3619. כְּלוּב **kᵉlûwb**, *kel-oob'*; from the same as 3611; a bird-*trap* (as furnished with a *clap*-stick or treadle to spring it); hence, a *basket* (as resembling a wicker cage):— basket, cage.

3620. כְּלוּב **Kᵉlûwb**, *kel-oob'*; the same as 3619; *Kelub*, the name of two Isr.:— Chelub.

3621. כְּלוּבַי **Kᵉlûwbay**, *kel-oo-bay'-ee*; a form of 3612; *Kelubai*, an Isr.:— Chelubai.

3622. כְּלוּהַי **Kᵉlûwhay**, *kel-oo-hah'-ee*; from 3615; *completed; Keluhai*, an Isr.:— Chelluh.

3623. כְּלוּלָה **kᵉlûwlâh**, *kel-oo-law'*; denom. pass. part. from 3618; *bridehood* (only in the plur.):— espousal.

3624. כֶּלַח **kelach**, *keh'-lakh*; from an unused root mean. to *be complete; maturity*:— full (old) age.

3625. כֶּלַח **Kelach**, *keh'-lakh*; the same as 3624; *Kelach*, a place in Assyria:— Calah.

3626. כָּל־חֹזֶה **Kol-Chôzeh**, *kol-kho-zeh'*; from 3605 and 2374; *every seer; Col-Chozeh*, an Isr.:— Col-hozeh.

3627. כְּלִי **kᵉlîy**, *kel-ee'*; from 3615; something *prepared*, i.e. any *appara-*

tus (as an implement, utensil, dress, vessel or weapon):— armour (l-bearerl), artillery, bag, carriage, + furnish, furniture, instrument, jewel, that is made of, × one from another, that which pertaineth, pot, + psaltery, sack, stuff, thing, tool, vessel, ware, weapon, + whatsoever.

3628. כְּלִיא **kᵉlîy**, *kel-ee'*; or

כְּלוּא **kᵉlûw'**, *kel-oo'*; from 3607 [comp. 3608]; a *prison*:— prison.

3629. כִּלְיָה **kilyâh**, *kil-yaw'*; fem. of 3627 (only in the plur.); a *kidney* (as an essential *organ*); fig. the *mind* (as the interior self):— kidneys, reins.

3630. כִּלְיוֹן **Kilyôwn**, *kil-yone'*; a form of 3631; *Kiljon*, an Isr.:— Chilion.

3631. כִּלְיוֹן **killâyôwn**, *kil-law-yone'*; from 3615; *pining, destruction*:— consumption, failing.

3632. כָּלִיל **kâlîyl**, *kaw-leel'*; from 3634; *complete;* as noun, the *whole* (spec. a sacrifice *entirely consumed*); as adv. *fully*:— all, every whit, flame, perfect (-ion), utterly, whole burnt offering (sacrifice), wholly.

3633. כַּלְכֹּל **Kalkôl**, *kal-kole'*; from 3557; *sustenance; Calcol*, an Isr.:— Calcol, Chalcol.

3634. כָּלַל **kâlal**, *kaw-lal'*; a prim. root; to *complete*:— (make) perfect.

3635. כְּלַל **kᵉlal** (Chald.), *kel-al'*; corresp. to 3634; to *complete*:— finish, make (set) up.

3636. כְּלָל **Kᵉlâl**, *kel-awl'*; from 3634; *complete; Kelal*, an Isr.:— Chelal.

3637. כָּלַם **kâlam**, *kaw-lawm'*; a prim. root; prop. to *wound;* but only fig., to *taunt* or *insult*:— be (make) ashamed, blush, be confounded, be put to confusion, hurt, reproach, (do, put to) shame.

3638. כִּלְמָד **Kilmâd**, *kil-mawd'*; of for. der.; *Kilmad*, a place appar. in the Ass. empire:— Chilmad.

3639. כְּלִמָּה **kᵉlimmâh**, *kel-im-maw'*; from 3637; *disgrace*:— confusion, dishonour, reproach, shame.

3640. כְּלִמּוּת **kᵉlimmûwth**, *kel-im-mooth'*; from 3639; *disgrace*:— shame.

3641. כַּלְנֶה **Kalneh**, *kal-neh'*; or

כַּלְנֵה **Kalnêh**, *kal-nay'*; also

כַּלְנוֹ **Kalnôw**, *kal-no'*; of for. der.; *Calneh* or *Calno*, a place in the Ass. empire:— Calneh, Calno. Comp. 3656.

3642. כָּמַהּ **kâmahh**, *kaw-mah'*; a prim. root; to *pine* after:— long.

3643. כִּמְהָם **Kimhâm**, *kim-hawm'*; from 3642; *pining; Kimham*, an Isr.:— Chimham.

3644. כְּמוֹ **kᵉmôw**, *kem-o'*; or

כָּמוֹ **kâmôw**, *kaw-mo'*; a form of the pref. *k*, but used separately [comp. 3651]; *as, thus, so*:— according to, (such) as (it were, well as), in comp. of, like (as, to, unto), thus, when, worth.

3645. כְּמוֹשׁ **Kᵉmôwsh**, *kem-oshe'*; or (Jer. 48:7)

כְּמִישׁ **Kᵉmîysh**, *kem-eesh'*; from an unused root mean. to *subdue;* the *powerful; Kemosh,* the god of the Moabites:— Chemosh.

3646. כַּמּוֹן **kammôn,** *kam-mone´;* from an unused root mean. to *store* up or *preserve; "cummin"* (from its use as a condiment):— cummin.

3647. כָּמַס **kâmaç,** *kaw-mas´;* a prim. root; to *store* away, i.e. (fig.) in the memory:— lay up in store.

3648. כָּמַר **kâmar,** *kaw-mar´;* a prim. root; prop. to *intertwine* or *contract,* i.e. (by impl.) to *shrivel* (as with heat); fig. to *be* deeply *affected* with passion (love or pity):— be black, be kindled, yearn.

3649. כָּמָר **kâmâr,** *kaw-mawr´;* from 3648; prop. an *ascetic* (as if *shrunk* with self-maceration), i.e. an idolatrous *priest* (only in plur.):— Chemarims (idolatrous) priests.

3650. כִּמְרִיר **kimrîyr,** *kim-reer´;* redupl. from 3648; *obscuration* (as if from *shrinkage* of light, i.e. an eclipse (only in plur.):— blackness.

3651. כֵּן **kên,** *kane;* from 3559; prop. *set* upright, hence, (fig. as adj.) *just;* but usually (as adv. or conjunc.) *rightly* or *so* (in various applications to manner, time and relation; often with other particles):— + after that (this, -ward, -wards), as ... as, + [for-] asmuch as yet, + be (for which) cause, + following, howbeit, in (the) like (manner, -wise), × the more, right, (even) so, state, straightway, such (thing), surely, + there (where-)fore, this, thus, true, well, × you.

3652. כֵּן **kên** (Chald.), *kane;* corresp. to 3651; *so:*— thus.

3653. כֵּן **kên,** *kane;* the same as 3651, used as a noun; a *stand,* i.e. pedestal or station:— base, estate, foot, office, place, well.

3654. כֵּן **kên,** *kane;* from 3661 in the sense of *fastening;* a *gnat* (from infixing its sting; used only in plur. [and irreg. in Exod. 8:17,18; Heb. 13:14]):— lice, × manner.

3655. כָּנָה **kânâh,** *kaw-naw´;* a prim. root; to *address* by an additional name; hence, to *eulogize:*— give flattering titles, surname (himself).

3656. כַּנֶּה **Kanneh,** *kan-neh´;* for 3641; *Canneh,* a place in Assyria:— Canneh.

3657. כַּנָּה **kannâh,** *kaw-naw´;* from 3661; a *plant* (as set):— × vineyard.

3658. כִּנּוֹר **kinnôwr,** *kin-nore´;* from a unused root mean. to *twang;* a *harp:*— harp.

3659. כָּנְיָהוּ **Konyâhûw,** *kon-yaw´-hoo;* for 3204; *Conjah,* an Isr. king:— Coniah.

3660. כְּנֵמָא **keᵉnêmâ'** (Chald.), *ken-ay-maw´;* corresp. to 3644; *so* or *thus:*— so, (in) this manner (sort), thus.

3661. כָּנַן **kânan,** *kaw-nan´;* a prim. root; to *set* out, i.e. *plant:*— × vineyard.

3662. כְּנָנִי **Keᵉnâniy,** *ken-aw-nee´;* from 3661; *planted; Kenani,* an Isr.:— Chenani.

3663. כְּנַנְיָה **Keᵉnanyâh,** *ken-an-yaw´;* or

כְּנַנְיָהוּ **Keᵉnanyâhûw,** *ken-an-yaw´-hoo;* from 3661 and 3050; *Jah has

planted; Kenanjah, an Isr.:— Chenaniah.

3664. כָּנַס **kânaç,** *kaw-nas´;* a prim. root; to *collect;* hence, to *enfold:*— gather (together), heap up, wrap self.

3665. כָּנַע **kâna',** *kaw-nah´;* a prim. root; prop. to *bend* the knee; hence, to *humiliate, vanquish:*— bring down (low), into subjection, under, humble (self), subdue.

3666. כִּנְעָה **kin'âh,** *kin-aw´;* from 3665 in the sense of *folding* [comp. 3664]; a *package:*— wares.

3667. כְּנַעַן **Keᵉna'an,** *ken-ah´-an;* from 3665; *humiliated; Kenaan,* a son a Ham; also the country inhabited by him:— Canaan, merchant, traffick.

3668. כְּנַעֲנָה **Keᵉna'ănâh,** *ken-ah-an-aw´;* fem. of 3667; *Kenaanah,* the name of two Isr.:— Chenaanah.

3669. כְּנַעֲנִי **Keᵉna'ăniy,** *ken-ah-an-ee´;* patrial from 3667; a *Kenaanite* or inhab. of Kenaan; by impl. a *pedlar* (the Canaanites standing for their neighbors the Ishmaelites, who conducted mercantile caravans):— Canaanite, merchant, trafficker.

3670. כָּנַף **kânaph,** *kaw-naf´;* a prim. root; prop. to *project* laterally, i.e. prob. (refl.) to *withdraw:*— be removed.

3671. כָּנָף **kânâph,** *kaw-nawf´;* from 3670; an *edge* or *extremity;* spec. (of a bird or army) a *wing,* (of a garment or bed-clothing) a *flap,* (of the earth) a *quarter,* (of a building) a *pinnacle:*— + bird, border, corner, end, feather [-ed], × flying, + (one an-) other, overspreading, × quarters, skirt, × sort, uttermost part, wing ([-ed]).

3672. כִּנְּרוֹת **Kinneᵉrôwth,** *kin-ner-ōth´;* or

כִּנֶּרֶת **Kinnereth,** *kin-neh´-reth;* respectively plur. and sing. fem. from the same as 3658; perh. *harp*-shaped; *Kinneroth* or *Kinnereth,* a place in Pal.:— Chinnereth, Chinneroth, Cinneroth.

3673. כְּנַשׁ **kânash** (Chald.), *kaw-nash´;* corresp. to 3664; to *assemble:*— gather together.

3674. כְּנָת **keᵉnâth,** *ken-awth´;* from 3655; a *colleague* (as having the same title):— companion.

3675. כְּנָת **keᵉnâth** (Chald.), *ken-awth´;* corresp. to 3674:— companion.

3676. כֵּס **kêç,** *kace;* appar. a contr. for 3678, but prob. by err. transc. for 5251:— sworn.

3677. כֶּסֶא **keçe',** *keh´-seh;* or

כֶּסֶה **keçeh,** *keh´-seh;* appar. from 3680; prop. *fulness* or the *full moon,* i.e. its festival:— (time) appointed.

3678. כִּסֵּא **kiççê',** *kis-say´;* or

כִּסֵּה **kiççêh,** *kis-say´;* from 3680; prop. *covered,* i.e. a *throne* (as canopied):— seat, stool, throne.

3679. כַּסְדַּי **Kaçday,** *kas-dah´-ee;* for 3778:— Chaldean.

3680. כָּסָה **kâçâh,** *kaw-saw´;* a prim. root; prop. to *plump,* i.e. *fill up* hollows; by impl. to *cover* (for clothing or secrecy):— clad self, close, clothe, con-

ceal, cover (self), (flee to) hide, overwhelm. Comp. 3780.

כֶּסֶה **keçeh.** See 3677.

כִּסֵּה **kiççêh.** See 3678.

3681. כָּסוּי **kâçûwy,** *kaw-soo´-ee;* pass. part. of 3680; prop. *covered,* i.e. (as noun) a *covering:*— covering.

3682. כְּסוּת **keᵉçûwth,** *kes-ooth´;* from 3680; a *cover* (garment); fig. a *veiling:*— covering, raiment, vesture.

3683. כָּסַח **kâçach,** *kaw-sakh´;* a prim. root; to *cut off:*— cut down (up).

3684. כְּסִיל **keᵉçîyl,** *kes-eel´;* from 3688; prop. *fat,* i.e. (fig.) stupid or *silly:*— fool (-ish).

3685. כְּסִיל **Keᵉçîyl,** *kes-eel´;* the same as 3684; any notable *constellation;* spec. *Orion* (as if a *burly* one):— constellation, Orion.

3686. כְּסִיל **Keᵉçîyl,** *kes-eel´;* the same as 3684; *Kesil,* a place in Pal.:— Chesil.

3687. כְּסִילוּת **keᵉçîylûwth,** *kes-eel-ooth´;* from 3684; *silliness:*— foolish.

3688. כָּסַל **kâçal,** *kaw-sal´;* a prim. root; prop. to *be fat,* i.e. (fig.) *silly:*— be foolish.

3689. כֶּסֶל **keçel,** *keh´-sel;* from 3688; prop. *fatness,* i.e. by impl. (lit.) the *loin* (as the seat of the leaf *fat)* or (gen.) the *viscera;* also (fig.) *silliness* or (in a good sense) *trust:*— confidence, flank, folly, hope, loin.

3690. כִּסְלָה **kiçlâh,** *kis-law´;* fem. of 3689; in a good sense, *trust;* in a bad one, *silliness:*— confidence, folly.

3691. כִּסְלֵו **Kiçlêv,** *kis-lave´;* prob. of for. or.; *Kisleu,* the 9th Heb. month:— Chisleu.

3692. כִּסְלוֹן **Kiçlôwn,** *kis-lone´;* from 3688; *hopeful; Kislon,* an Isr.:— Chislon.

3693. כְּסָלוֹן **Keᵉçâlôwn,** *kes-aw-lone´;* from 3688; *fertile; Kesalon,* a place in Pal.:— Chesalon.

3694. כְּסֻלּוֹת **Keᵉçullôwth,** *kes-ool-lōth´;* fem. plur. of pass. part. of 3688; *fattened; Kesulloth,* a place in Pal.:— Chesulloth.

3695. כַּסְלֻחִים **Kaçlúchîym,** *kas-loo´-kheem;* a plur. prob. of for. der.; *Casluchim,* a people cognate to the Eg.:— Casluhim.

3696. כִּסְלֹת תָּבֹר **Kiçlôth Tâbôr,** *kis-lōth´ taw-bore´;* from the fem. plur. of 3689 and 8396; *flanks of Tabor; Kisloth-Tabor,* a place in Pal.:— Chisloth-tabor.

3697. כָּסַם **kâçam,** *kaw-sam´;* a prim. root; to *shear:*— × only, poll. Comp. 3765.

3698. כֻּסֶּמֶת **kuççemeth,** *koos-seh´-meth;* from 3697; *spelt* (from its bristliness as if just *shorn):*— fitches, rie.

3699. כָּסַס **kâçaç,** *kaw-sas´;* a prim. root; to *estimate:*— make count.

3700. כָּסַף **kâçaph,** *kaw-saf´;* a prim. root; prop. to *become pale,* i.e. (by impl.) to *pine* after; also to *fear:*— [have] desire, be greedy, long, sore.

3701. כֶּסֶף **keçeph,** *keh´-sef;* from 3700; *silver* (from its *pale* color); by impl. *money:*— money, price, silver (-ling).

3702. כְּסַף **kᵉçaph** (Chald.), *kes-af´*; corresp. to 3701:— money, silver.

3703. כַּסְפְּיָא **Kâçiphyâ'**, *kaw-sif-yaw´*; perh. from 3701; *silvery*; *Casiphja*, a place in Bab.:— Casiphia.

3704. כֶּסֶת **keçeth**, *keh´-seth*; from 3680; a *cushion* or pillow (as *covering* a seat or bed):— pillow.

3705. כְּעַן **kᵉ'an** (Chald.), *keh-an´*; prob. from 3652; *now*:— now.

3706. כְּעֶנֶת **kᵉ'eneth** (Chald.), *keh-eh´-neth*; or

כְּעֶת **kᵉ'eth** (Chald.), *keh-eth´*; fem. of 3705; *thus* (only in the formula "and *so forth*"):— at such a time.

3707. כָּעַס **kâ'aç**, *kaw-as´*; a prim. root; to *trouble*; by impl. to *grieve, rage, be indignant*:— be angry, be grieved, take indignation, provoke (to anger, unto wrath), have sorrow, vex, be wroth.

3708. כַּעַס **ka'aç**, *kah´-as*; or (in Job)

כַּעַס **ka'as**, *kah´-as*; from 3707; *vexation*:— anger, angry, grief, indignation, provocation, provoking, × sore, sorrow, spite, wrath.

כְּעֶת **kᵉ'eth**. See 3706.

3709. כַּף **kaph**, *kaf*; from 3721; the hollow *hand* or palm (so of the *paw* of an animal, of the *sole*, and even of the *bowl* of a dish or sling, the *handle* of a bolt, the *leaves* of a palm-tree); fig. *power*:— branch, + foot, hand (I-full, -dle, I-led), hollow, middle, palm, paw, power, sole, spoon.

3710. כֵּף **kêph**, *kafe*; from 3721; a hollow *rock*:— rock.

3711. כָּפָה **kâphâh**, *kaw-faw´*; a prim. root; prop. to *bend*, i.e. (fig.) to *tame* or *subdue*:— pacify.

3712. כִּפָּה **kippâh**, *kip-paw´*; fem. of 3709; a *leaf* of a palm-tree:— branch.

3713. כְּפוֹר **kᵉphôwr**, *kef-ore´*; prop. a *cover*, i.e. (by impl.) a *tankard* (or *covered* goblet); also white *frost* (as *covering* the ground):— bason, hoar (-y) frost.

3714. כָּפִיס **kâphiyç**, *kaw-fece´*; from an unused root mean. to *connect*; a *girder*:— beam.

3715. כְּפִיר **kᵉphiyr**, *kef-eer´*; from 3722; a *village* (as *covered* in by walls); also a young *lion* (perh. as *covered* with a mane):— (young) lion, village. Comp. 3723.

3716. כְּפִירָה **Kᵉphiyrâh**, *kef-ee-raw´*; fem. of 3715; the *village* (always with the art.); *Kephirah*, a place in Pal.:— Chephirah.

3717. כָּפַל **kâphal**, *kaw-fal´*; a prim. root; to *fold* together; fig. to *repeat*:— double.

3718. כֶּפֶל **kephel**, *keh´-fel*; from 3717; a *duplicate*:— double.

3719. כָּפַן **kâphan**, *kaw-fan´*; a prim. root; to *bend*:— bend.

3720. כָּפָן **kâphân**, *kaw-fawn´*; from 3719; *hunger* (as making to *stoop* with emptiness and pain):— famine.

3721. כָּפַף **kâphaph**, *kaw-faf´*; a prim. root; to *curve*:— bow down (self).

3722. כָּפַר **kâphar**, *kaw-far´*; a prim.

root; to *cover* (spec. with bitumen); fig. to *expiate* or *condone*, to *placate* or *cancel*:— appease, make (an atonement, cleanse, disannul, forgive, be merciful, pacify, pardon, to *pitch*, purge (away), put off, (make) reconcile (-liation).

3723. כְּפָר **kâphâr**, *kaw-fawr´*; from 3722; a *village* (as *protected* by walls):— village. Comp. 3715.

3724. כֹּפֶר **kôpher**, *ko´-fer*; from 3722; prop. a *cover*, i.e. (lit.) a *village* (as *covered* in); (spec.) *bitumen* (as used for *coating*), and the *henna* plant (as used for *dyeing*); fig. a *redemption*-price:— bribe, camphire, pitch, ransom, satisfaction, sum of money, village.

3725. כִּפֻּר **kippûr**, *kip-poor´*; from 3722; *expiation* (only in plur.):— atonement.

3726. כְּפַר הָעַמֹּנִי **Kᵉphar hâ-'Ammôwniy**, *kef-ar´ haw-am-mo-nee´*; from 3723 and 5984, with the art. interposed; *village of the Ammonite; Kefar ha-Ammoni*, a place in Pal.:— Chefar-haamonai.

3727. כַּפֹּרֶת **kappôreth**, *kap-po´-reth*; from 3722; a *lid* (used only of the *cover* of the sacred Ark):— mercy seat.

3728. כָּפַשׁ **kâphash**, *kaw-fash´*; a prim. root; to *tread* down; fig. to *humiliate*:— cover.

3729. כְּפַת **kᵉphath** (Chald.), *kef-ath´*; a root of uncert. correspondence; to *fetter*:— bind.

3730. כַּפְתֹּר **kaphtôr**, *kaf-tore´*; or (Am. 9:1)

כַּפְתּוֹר **kaphtôwr**, *kaf-tore´*; prob. from an unused root mean. to *encircle*; a *chaplet*; but used only in an architectonic sense, i.e. the *capital* of a column, or a wreath-like *button* or *disk* on the candelabrum:— knop, (upper) lintel.

3731. כַּפְתֹּר **Kaphtôr**, *kaf-tore´*; or (Am. 9:7)

כַּפְתּוֹר **Kaphtôwr**, *kaf-tore´*; appar. the same as 3730; *Caphtor* (i.e. a *wreath*-shaped island), the orig. seat of the Philistines:— Caphtor.

3732. כַּפְתֹּרִי **Kaphtôriy**, *kaf-to-ree´*; patrial from 3731; a *Caphtorite* (collect.) or native of *Caphtor*:— Caphthorim, Caphtorim (-s).

3733. כַּר **kar**, *kar*; from 3769 in the sense of *plumpness*; a *ram* (as *full-grown* and *fat*), incl. a *battering-ram* (as *butting*); hence, a *meadow* (as for *sheep*); also a *pad* or camel's saddle (as *puffed out*):— captain, furniture, lamb, (large) pasture, ram. See also 1033, 3746.

3734. כֹּר **kôr**, *kore*; from the same as 3564; prop. a deep round *vessel*, i.e. (spec.) a *cor* or measure for things dry:— cor, measure. Chald. the same.

3735. כְּרָא **kârâ'** (Chald.), *kaw-raw´*; prob. corresp. to 3738 in the sense of *piercing* (fig.); to *grieve*:— be grieved.

3736. כַּרְבֵּל **karbêl**, *kar-bale´*; from the same as 3525; to *gird* or *clothe*:— clothed.

3737. כַּרְבְּלָא **karbᵉlâ'** (Chald.), *kar-bel-aw´*; from a verb corresp. to that of 3736; a *mantle*:— hat.

3738. כָּרָה **kârâh**, *kaw-raw´*; a prim. root; prop. to *dig*; fig. to *plot*; gen. to *bore* or *open*:— dig, × make (a banquet), open.

3739. כָּרָה **kârâh**, *kaw-raw´*; usually assigned as a prim. root, but prob. only a special application of 3738 (through the common idea of *planning* impl. in a bargain); to *purchase*:— buy, prepare.

3740. כֵּרָה **kêrâh**, *kay-raw´*; from 3739; a *purchase*:— provision.

3741. כָּרָה **kârâh**, *kaw-raw´*; fem. of 3733; a *meadow*:— cottage.

3742. כְּרוּב **kᵉrûwb**, *ker-oob´*; of uncert. der.; a *cherub* or imaginary figure:— cherub, [plur.] cherubims.

3743. כְּרוּב **Kᵉrûwb**, *ker-oob´*; the same as 3742; *Kerub*, a place in Bab.:— Cherub.

3744. כָּרוֹז **kârôwz** (Chald.), *kaw-roze´*; from 3745; a *herald*:— herald.

3745. כְּרַז **kᵉraz** (Chald.), *ker-az´*; prob. of Gr. or. (κηρύσσω); to *proclaim*:— make a proclamation.

3746. כָּרִי **kâriy**, *kaw-ree´*; perh. an abridged plur. of 3733 in the sense of *leader* (of the flock); a *life-guardsman*:— captains, Cherethites [from the marg.].

3747. כְּרִית **Kᵉriyth**, *ker-eeth´*; from 3772; a *cut*; *Kerith*, a brook of Pal.:— Cherith.

3748. כְּרִיתוּת **kᵉriythûwth**, *ker-ee-thooth´*; from 3772; a *cutting* (of the matrimonial bond), i.e. *divorce*:— divorce (-ment).

3749. כַּרְכֹּב **karkôb**, *kar-kobe´*; expanded from the same as 3522; a *rim* or top margin:— compass.

3750. כַּרְכֹּם **karkôm**, *kar-kome´*; prob. of for. or.; the *crocus*:— saffron.

3751. כַּרְכְּמִישׁ **Karkᵉmiysh**, *kar-kem-eesh´*; of for. der.; *Karkemish*, a place in Syria:— Carchemish.

3752. כַּרְכַּס **Karkaç**, *kar-kas´*; of Pers. or.; *Karkas*, a eunuch of Xerxes:— Carcas.

3753. כַּרְכָּרָה **karkârâh**, *kar-kaw-raw´*; from 3769; a *dromedary* (from its *rapid* motion as if dancing):— swift beast.

3754. כֶּרֶם **kerem**, *keh´-rem*; from an unused root of uncert. mean.; a *garden* or *vineyard*:— vines, (increase of the) vineyard (-s), vintage. See also 1021.

3755. כֹּרֵם **kôrêm**, *ko-rame´*; act. part. of an imaginary denom. from 3754; a *vinedresser*:— vine dresser [as one or two words].

3756. כַּרְמִי **Karmiy**, *kar-mee´*; from 3754; *gardener*; *Karmi*, the name of three Isr.:— Carmi.

3757. כַּרְמִי **Karmiy**, *kar-mee´*; patron. from 3756; a *Karmite* or desc. of *Karmi*:— Carmites.

3758. כַּרְמִיל **karmiyl**, *kar-mele´*; prob. of for. or.; *carmine*, a deep red:— crimson.

3759. כַּרְמֶל **karmel**, *kar-mel´*; from 3754; a *planted field* (garden, orchard, vineyard or park); by impl. garden *pro-*

duce:— full (green) ears (of corn), fruitful field (place), plentiful (field).

3760. כַּרְמֶל **Karmel**, *kar-mel'*; the same as 3759; *Karmel*, the name of a hill and of a town in Pal.:— Carmel, fruitful (plentiful) field, (place).

3761. כַּרְמְלִי **Karmᵉlîy**, *kar-mel-ee'*; patron. from 3760; a *Karmelite* or inhab. of Karmel (the town):— Carmelite.

3762. כַּרְמְלִית **Karmᵉlîyth**, *kar-meleeth'*; fem. of 3761; a *Karmelitess* or female inhab. of Karmel:— Carmelitess.

3763. כְּרָן **Kᵉrân**, *ker-awn'*; of uncert. der.; *Keran*, an aboriginal Idumæan:— Cheran.

3764. כָּרְסֵא **korçê'** (Chald.), *kor-say'*; corresp. to 3678; a *throne*:— throne.

3765. כִּרְסֵם **kirçêm**, *kir-same'*; from 3697; to *lay waste*:— waste.

3766. כָּרַע **kâra'**, *kaw-rah'*; a prim. root; to *bend* the knee; by impl. to *sink*, to *prostrate*:— bow (down, self), bring down (low), cast down, couch, fall, feeble, kneeling, sink, smite (stoop) down, subdue, × very.

3767. כָּרָע **kârâ'**, *kaw-raw'*; from 3766; the *leg* (from the knee to the ankle) of men or locusts (only in the dual):— leg.

3768. כַּרְפַּס **karpaç**, *kar-pas'*; of for. or.; *byssus* or fine vegetable wool:— green.

3769. כָּרַר **kârar**, *kaw-rar'*; a prim. root; to *dance* (i.e. *whirl*):— dance (-ing).

3770. כֶּרֶשׂ **kᵉrês**, *ker-ace'*; by var. from 7164; the *paunch* or belly (as *swelling* out):— belly.

כֹּרֶשׂ **Kôresh**. See 3567.

3771. כַּרְשְׁנָא **Karshᵉnâ'**, *kar-shen-aw'*; of for. or.; *Karshena*, a courtier of Xerxes:— Carshena.

3772. כָּרַת **kârath**, *kaw-rath'*; a prim. root; to *cut* (off, down or asunder); by impl. to *destroy* or *consume*; spec. to *covenant* (i.e. make an alliance or bargain, orig. by cutting flesh and passing between the pieces):— be chewed, be con- [feder-] ate, covenant, cut (down, off), destroy, fail, feller, be freed, hew (down), make a league ([covenant]), × lose, perish, × utterly, × want.

3773. כָּרֻתָה **kâruthâh**, *kaw-rooth-aw'*; pass. part. fem. of 3772; something *cut*, i.e. a hewn *timber*:— beam.

3774. כְּרֵתִי **Kᵉrêthîy**, *ker-ay-thee'*; prob. from 3772 in the sense of *executioner*; a *Kerethite* or *life-guardsman* [comp. 2876] (only collect. in the sing. as plur.):— Cherethims, Cherethites.

3775. כֶּשֶׂב **keseb**, *keh'-seb*; appar. by transp. for 3532; a young *sheep*:— lamb, sheep.

3776. כִּשְׂבָּה **kisbâh**, *kis-baw'*; fem. of 3775; a young *ewe*:— lamb.

3777. כֶּשֶׂד **Kesed**, *keh'-sed*; from an unused root of uncert. mean.; *Kesed*, a relative of Abraham:— Chesed.

3778. כַּשְׂדִּי **Kasdîy**, *kas-dee'*; (occasionally with enclitic)

כַּשְׂדִּימָה **Kasdîymâh**, *kas-dee'-maw*; toward (the) *Kasdites* (into Chaldea), patron. from 3777 (only in the plur.); a *Kasdite*, or desc. of Kesed; by impl. a *Chaldæan* (as if so descended);

also an *astrologer* (as if proverbial of that people:— Chaldeans, Chaldees, inhabitants of Chaldea.

3779. כַּשְׂדָּי **Kasday** (Chald.), *kas-dah'-ee*; corresp. to 3778; a *Chaldæan* or inhab. of Chaldæa; by impl. a *Magian* or professional astrologer:— Chaldean.

3780. כָּשָׂה **kâsâh**, *kaw-saw'*; a prim. root; to *grow fat* (i.e. be covered with flesh):— be covered. Comp. 3680.

3781. כַּשִּׂיל **kashshîyl**, *kash-sheel'*; from 3782; prop. a *feller*, i.e. an *axe*:— ax.

3782. כָּשַׁל **kâshal**, *kaw-shal'*; a prim. root; to *totter* or *waver* (through weakness of the legs, espec. the ankle); by impl. to *falter*, *stumble*, faint or fall:— bereave [from the marg.], cast down, be decayed, (cause to) fail, (cause, make to) fall (down, -ing), feeble, be (the) ruin (-ed, of), (be) overthrown, (cause to) stumble, × utterly, be weak.

3783. כִּשָּׁלוֹן **kishshâlôwn**, *kish-shaw-lone'*; from 3782; prop. a *tottering*, i.e. *ruin*:— fall.

3784. כָּשַׁף **kâshaph**, *kaw-shaf'*; a prim. root; prop. to *whisper* a spell, i.e. to *inchant* or practise magic:— sorcerer, (use) witch (-craft).

3785. כֶּשֶׁף **kesheph**, *keh'-shef*; from 3784; *magic*:— sorcery, witchcraft.

3786. כַּשָּׁף **kashshâph**, *kash-shawf'*; from 3784; a *magician*:— sorcerer.

3787. כָּשֵׁר **kâshêr**, *kaw-share'*; a prim. root; prop. to *be straight* or *right*; by impl. to *be acceptable*; also to *succeed* or *prosper*:— direct, be right, prosper.

3788. כִּשְׁרוֹן **kishrôwn**, *kish-rone'*; from 3787; *success*, *advantage*:— equity, good, right.

3789. כָּתַב **kâthab**, *kaw-thab'*; a prim. root; to *grave*, by impl. to *write* (describe, inscribe, prescribe, subscribe):— describe, record, prescribe, subscribe, write (-ing, -ten).

3790. כְּתַב **kᵉthab** (Chald.), *keth-ab'*; corresp. to 3789:— write (-ten).

3791. כְּתָב **kâthâb**, *kaw-thawb'*; from 3789; something *written*, i.e. a *writing*, *record* or *book*:— register, scripture, writing.

3792. כְּתָב **kᵉthâb** (Chald.), *keth-awb'*; corresp. to 3791:— prescribing, writing (-ten).

3793. כְּתֹבֶת **kᵉthôbeth**, *keth-o'-beth*; from 3789; a *letter* or other *mark* branded on the skin:— × any [mark].

3794. כִּתִּי **Kittîy**, *kit-tee'* or

כִּתִּיִּי **Kittîyîy**, *kit-tee-ee'*; patrial from an unused name denoting Cyprus (only in the plur.); a *Kittite* or Cypriote; hence, an *islander* in gen., i.e. the Greeks or Romans on the shores opposite Pal.:— Chittim, Kittim.

3795. כָּתִית **kâthîyth**, *kaw-theeth'*; from 3807; *beaten*, i.e. pure (oil):— beaten.

3796. כֹּתֶל **kôthel**, *ko'-thel*; from an unused root mean. to *compact*; a *wall* (as *gathering* inmates):— wall.

3797. כְּתַל **kᵉthal** (Chald.), *keth-al'*; corresp. to 3796:— wall.

3798. כָּתְלִישׁ **Kithlîysh**, *kith-leesh'*; from

3796 and 376; *wall of a man*; *Kithlish*, a place in Pal.:— Kithlish.

3799. כָּתַם **kâtham**, *kaw-tham'*; a prim. root; prop. to *carve* or *engrave*, i.e. (by impl.) to *inscribe* indelibly:— mark.

3800. כֶּתֶם **kethem**, *keh'-them*; from 3799; prop. something *carved* out, i.e. *ore*; hence, *gold* (pure as orig. mined):— [most] fine, (pure) gold (-en wedge).

3801. כְּתֹנֶת **kᵉthôneth**, *keth-o'-neth*; or

כֻּתֹּנֶת **kuttôneth**, *koot-to'-neth*; from an unused root mean. to *cover* [comp. 3802]; a *shirt*:— coat, garment, robe.

3802. כָּתֵף **kâthêph**, *kaw-thafe'*; from an unused root mean. to *clothe*; the *shoulder* (proper, i.e. upper end of the arm; as being the spot where the garments hang); fig. *side-piece* or lateral projection of anything:— arm, corner, shoulder (-piece), side, undersetter.

3803. כָּתַר **kâthar**, *kaw-thar'*; a prim. root; to *enclose*; hence, (in a friendly sense) to *crown*, (in a hostile one) to *besiege*; also to *wait* (as restraining oneself):— beset round, compass about, be crowned, inclose round, suffer.

3804. כֶּתֶר **kether**, *keh'-ther*; from 3803; prop. a *circlet*, i.e. a *diadem*:— crown.

3805. כֹּתֶרֶת **kôthereth**, *ko-theh'-reth*; fem. act. part. of 3803; the *capital* of a column:— chapiter.

3806. כָּתַשׁ **kâthash**, *kaw-thash'*; a prim. root; to *butt* or *pound*:— bray.

3807. כָּתַת **kâthath**, *kaw-thath'*; a prim. root; to *bruise* or violently *strike*:— beat (down, to pieces), break in pieces, crushed, destroy, discomfit, smite, stamp.

ל

3808. לֹא **lô'**, *lo*; or

לוֹא **lôw'**, *lo*; or

לֹה **lôh** (Deut. 3:11), *lo*; a prim. particle; *not* (the simple or abs. negation); by impl. *no*; often used with other particles (as follows):— × before, + or else, ere, + except, ig[-norant], much, less, nay, neither, never, no ([-ne], -r, [-thing], (× as though ..., [can-], for) not (out of), of nought, otherwise, out of, + surely, + as truly as, + of a truth, + verily, for want, + whether, without.

3809. לָא **lâ'** (Chald.), *law*; or

לָה **lâh** (Chald.) (Dan. 4:32), *law*; corresp. to 3808:— or even, neither, no (-ne, -r), ([can-]) not, as nothing, without.

לֻא **lû'**. See 3863.

3810. לֹא דְבַר **Lô' Dᵉbar**, *lo deb-ar'*; or

לוֹ דְבַר **Lôw Dᵉbar** (2 Sam. 9:4,5), *lo deb-ar'*; or

לִדְבִר **Lidbîr** (Josh. 13:26), *lid-beer'*; [prob. rather

לֹדְבַר **Lôdᵉbar**, *lo-deb-ar'*]; from 3808 and 1699; *pastureless*; *Lo-Debar*, a place in Pal.:— Debir, Lo-debar.

3811. לָאָה **lâ'âh**, *law-aw'*; a prim. root; to *tire*; (fig.) to *be* (or *make*) *dis-*

gusted:— faint, grieve, lothe, (be, make) weary (selves).

3812. לֵאָה **Lê'âh**, lay-aw´; from 3811; weary; Leah, a wife of Jacob:— Leah.

לְאוֹם **le'ôwm**. See 3816.

3813. לָאָט **lâ'aṭ**, law-at´; a prim. root; to muffle:— cover.

3814. לָאט **lâ'ṭ**, lawt; from 3813 (or perh. for act. part. of 3874); prop. muffled, i.e. silently:— softly.

3815. לָאֵל **Lâ'êl**, law-ale´; from the prep. pref. and 410; (belonging) to God; Lael, an Isr.:— Lael.

3816. לְאֹם **le'ôm**, leh-ome´ or

לְאוֹם **le'ôwm**, leh-ome´; from an unused root mean. to gather; a community:— nation, people.

3817. לְאֻמִּים **Le'ummîym**, leh-oom-meem´; plur. of 3816; communities; Leümmim, an Arabian:— Leummim.

3818. לֹא עַמִּי **Lô' 'Ammîy**, lo am-mee´; from 3808 and 5971 with pron. suff.; not my people; Lo-Ammi, the symbol. name of a son of Hosea:— Lo-ammi.

3819. לֹא רֻחָמָה **Lô' Rûchâmâh**, lo roo-khaw-maw´; from 3808 and 7355; not pitied; Lo-Ruchamah, the symbol. name of a son of Hosea:— Lo-ruhamah.

3820. לֵב **lêb**, labe; a form of 3824; the heart; also used (fig.) very widely for the feelings, the will and even the intellect; likewise for the center of anything:— + care for, comfortably, consent, × considered, couragl-eousl, friend l-lyl, lbroken-l, lhard-l, lmerry-l, lstiff-l, lstout-l, double) heart (l-edl), × heed, × l, kindly, midst, mind (-ed), × regard (l-edl), × themselves, × unawares, understanding, × well, willingly, wisdom.

3821. לֵב **lêb** (Chald.), labe; corresp. to 3820:— heart.

3822. לְבָאוֹת **Le'bâ'ôwth**, leb-aw-ôth´; plur. of 3833; lionesses; Lebaoth, a place in Pal.:— Lebaoth. See also 1034.

3823. לָבַב **lâbab**, law-bab´; a prim. root; prop. to be enclosed (as if with fat); by impl. (as denom. from 3824) to unheart, i.e. (in a good sense) transport (with love), or (in a bad sense) stultify; also (as denom. from 3834) to make cakes:— make cakes, ravish, be wise.

3824. לְבָב **lêbâb**, lay-bawb´; from 3823; the heart (as the most interior organ); used also like 3820:— + bethink themselves, breast, comfortably, courage, (faintl, ltender-l heart (l-edl), midst, mind, × unawares, understanding.

3825. לְבַב **le'bab** (Chald.), leb-ab´; corresp. to 3824:— heart.

לִבִּבָה **le'bîbâh**. See 3834.

3826. לִבָּה **libbâh**, lib-baw´; fem. of 3820; the heart:— heart.

3827. לַבָּה **labbâh**, lab-baw´; for 3852; flame:— flame.

3828. לְבוֹנָה **le'bôwnâh**, leb-o-naw´; or

לְבֹנָה **le'bonâh**, leb-o-naw´; from 3836; frankincense (from its whiteness or perh. that of its smoke):— (frank-) incense.

3829. לְבֹנָה **Le'bôwnâh**, leb-o-naw´; the same as 3828; Lebonah, a place in Pal.:— Lebonah.

3830. לְבוּשׁ **le'bûwsh**, leb-oosh´; or

לְבֻשׁ **le'bûsh**, leb-oosh´; from 3847; a garment (lit. or fig.); by impl. (euphem.) a wife:— apparel, clothed with, clothing, garment, raiment, vestment, vesture.

3831. לְבוּשׁ **le'bûwsh** (Chald.), leb-oosh´; corresp. to 3830:— garment.

3832. לָבַט **lâbaṭ**, law-bat´; a prim. root; to overthrow; intr. to fall:— fall.

לֻבִּי **Lubbîy**. See 3864.

3833. לָבִא **lâbîy'**, law-bee´; or (Ezek. 19:2)

לְבִיא **le'bîyâ'**, leb-ee-yaw´; irreg. masc. plur.

לְבָאִים **le'bâ'îym**, leb-aw-eem´; irreg. fem. plur.

לְבָאוֹת **le'bâ'ôwth**, leb-aw-ôth´; from an unused root mean. to roar; a lion (prop. a lioness as the fiercer lalthough not a roarer; comp. 738l):— (great, old, stout) lion, lioness, young llionl.

3834. לְבִיבָה **lâbîybâh**, law-bee-baw´; or rather

לְבִבָה **le'bibâh**, leb-ee-baw´; from 3823 in its orig. sense of fatness (or perh. of folding); a cake (either as fried or turned):— cake.

3835. לָבַן **lâban**, law-ban´; a prim. root; to be (or become) white; also (as denom. from 3843) to make bricks:— make brick, be (made, make) white (-r).

3836. לָבָן **lâbân**, law-bawn´; or (Gen. 49:12)

לָבֵן **lâbên**, law-bane´; from 3835; white:— white.

3837. לָבָן **Lâbân**, law-bawn´; the same as 3836; Laban, a Mesopotamian; also a place in the Desert:— Laban.

לַבֵּן **Labbên**. See 4192.

3838. לְבָנָא **Le'bânâ'**, leb-aw-naw´; or

לְבָנָה **Le'bânâh**, leb-aw-naw´; the same as 3842; Lebana or Lebanah, one of the Nethinim:— Lebana, Lebanah.

3839. לִבְנֶה **libneh**, lib-neh´; from 3835; some sort of whitish tree, perh. the storax:— poplar.

3840. לִבְנָה **libnâh**, lib-naw´; from 3835; prop. whiteness, i.e. (by impl.) transparency:— paved.

3841. לִבְנָה **Libnâh**, lib-naw´; the same as 3839; Libnah, a place in the Desert and one in Pal.:— Libnah.

3842. לְבָנָה **le'bânâh**, leb-aw-naw´; from 3835; prop. (the) white, i.e. the moon:— moon. See also 3838.

3843. לְבֵנָה **le'bênâh**, leb-ay-naw´; from 3835; a brick (from the whiteness of the clay):— (altar ofl brick, tile.

לְבֹנָה **le'bônâh**. See 3828.

3844. לְבָנוֹן **Le'bânôwn**, leb-aw-nohn´; from 3825; (the) white mountain (from its snow); Lebanon, a mountain range in Pal.:— Lebanon.

3845. לִבְנִי **Libnîy**, lib-nee´; from 3835; white; Libni, an Isr.:— Libni.

3846. לִבְנִי **Libnîy**, lib-nee´; patron. from 3845; a Libnite or desc. of Libni (collect.):— Libnites.

3847. לָבֵשׁ **lâbash**, law-bash´; or

לָבֵשׁ **lâbêsh**, law-bashe´; a prim. root; prop. wrap around, i.e. (by impl.) to put on a garment or clothe (oneself, or another), lit. or fig.:— (in) apparel, arm, array (self), clothe (self), come upon, put (on, upon), wear.

3848. לְבֵשׁ **le'bash** (Chald.), leb-ash´; corresp. to 3847:— clothe.

לְבוּשׁ **le'bûsh**. See 3830.

3849. לֹג **lôg**, lohg; from an unused root appar. mean. to deepen or hollow llike 3537l; a log or measure for liquids:— log lof oill.

3850. לֹד **Lôd**, lode; from an unused root of uncert. signif.; Lod, a place in Pal.:— Lod.

לִדְבִר **Lidbîr**. See 3810.

3851. לַהַב **lahab**, lah´-hab; from an unused root mean. to gleam; a flash; fig. a sharply polished blade or point of a weapon:— blade, bright, flame, glittering.

3852. לֶהָבָה **lehâbâh**, leh-aw-baw´; or

לַהֶבֶת **lahebeth**, lah-eh´-beth; fem. of 3851, and mean. the same:— flame (-ming), head lof a spearl.

3853. לְהָבִים **Le'hâbîym**, leh-haw-beem´; plur. of 3851; flames; Lehabim, a son of Mizrain, and his desc.:— Lehabim.

3854. לַהַג **lahag**, lah´-hag; from an unused root mean. to be eager; intense mental application:— study.

3855. לַהַד **Lahad**, lah´-had; from an unused root mean. to glow lcomp. 3851l or else to be earnest lcomp. 3854l; Lahad, an Isr.:— Lahad.

3856. לָהַהּ **lâhahh**, law-hah´; a prim. root mean. prop. to burn, i.e. (by impl.) to be rabid (fig. insane); also (from the exhaustion of frenzy) to languish:— faint, mad.

3857. לָהַט **lâhaṭ**, law-hat´; a prim. root; prop. to lick, i.e. (by impl.) to blaze:— burn (up), set on fire, flaming, kindle.

3858. לַהַט **lahaṭ**, lah´-hat; from 3857; a blaze; also (from the idea of enwrapping) magic (as covert):— flaming, enchantment.

3859. לָהַם **lâham**, law-ham´; a prim. root; prop. to burn in, i.e. (fig.) to rankle:— wound.

3860. לָהֵן **lâhên**, law-hane´; from the pref. prep. mean. to or for and 2005; prop. for if; hence, therefore:— for them lby mistake for prep. suff.l.

3861. לָהֵן **lâhên** (Chald.), law-hane´; corresp. to 3860; therefore; also except:— but, except, save, therefore, wherefore.

3862. לַהֲקָה **lahăqâh**, lah-hak-aw´; prob. from an unused root mean. to gather; an assembly:— company.

לוֹא **lôw'**. See 3808.

3863. לוּא **lûw'**, loo; or

לֻא **lû'**, loo; or

לוּ **lûw**, loo; a conditional particle; if; by impl. (interj. as a wish) would *that!:*— if (haply), peradventure, I pray thee, though, I would, would God (that).

3864. לוּב **Lûwbîy**, *loo-bee´;* or

לֻבִּי **Lubbîy** (Dan. 11:43) *loob-bee´;* patrial from a name prob. derived from an unused root mean. to *thirst,* i.e. a *dry* region; appar. a *Libyan* or inhab. of interior Africa (only in plur.):— Lubim (-s), Libyans.

3865. לוּד **Lûwd**, *lood;* prob. of for. der.; *Lud,* the name of two nations:— Lud, Lydia.

3866. לוּדִי **Lûwdîy**, *loo-dee´;* or

לוּדִי **Lûwdîyîy**, *loo-dee-ee´;* patrial from 3865; a *Ludite* or inhab. of Lud (only in plural):— Ludim, Lydians.

3867. לָוָה **lâvâh**, *law-vaw´;* a prim. root; prop. to *twine,* i.e. (by impl.) to *unite,* to *remain;* also to *borrow* (as a form of *obligation*) or (caus.) to *lend:*— abide with, borrow (-er), cleave, join (self), lend (-er).

3868. לוּז **lûwz**, *looz;* a prim. root; to *turn* aside [comp. 3867, 3874 and 3885], i.e. (lit.) to *depart,* (fig.) be *perverse:*— depart, froward, perverse (-ness).

3869. לוּז **lûwz**, *looz;* prob. of for. or.; some kind of *nut*-tree, perh. the *almond:*— hazel.

3870. לוּז **Lûwz**, *looz;* prob. from 3869 (as growing there); *Luz,* the name of two places in Pal.:— Luz.

3871. לוּחַ **lûwach**, *loo´-akh;* or

לֻחַ **lûach**, *loo´-akh;* from a prim. root; prob. mean. to *glisten;* a *tablet* (as *polished*), of stone, wood or metal:— board, plate, table.

3872. לוּחִית **Lûwchîyth**, *loo-kheeth´;* or

לֻחוֹת **Lûchôwth** (Jer. 48:5), *loo-khoth´;* from the same as 3871; *floored;* *Luchith,* a place E. of the Jordan:— Luhith.

3873. לוֹחֵשׁ **Lôwchêsh**, *lo-khashe´;* act. part. of 3907; (the) *enchanter; Lochesh,* an Isr.:— Hallohesh, Haloshesh [includ. *the art.*].

3874. לוּט **lûwṭ**, *loot;* a prim. root; to *wrap* up:— cast, wrap.

3875. לוּט **lôwṭ**, *lote;* from 3874; a *veil:*— covering.

3876. לוֹט **Lôwṭ**, *lote;* the same as 3875; *Lot,* Abraham's nephew:— Lot.

3877. לוֹטָן **Lôwṭân**, *lo-tawn´;* from 3875; *covering; Lotan,* an Idumæan:— Lotan.

3878. לֵוִי **Lêvîy**, *lay-vee´;* from 3867; *attached; Levi,* a son of Jacob:— Levi. See also 3879, 3881.

3879. לֵוִי **Lêvîy** (Chald.), *lay-vee´;* corresp. to 3880:— Levite.

3880. לִוְיָה **livyâh**, *liv-yaw´;* from 3867; something *attached,* i.e. a *wreath:*— ornament.

3881. לֵוִיִּי **Lêvîyîy**, *lay-vee-ee´;* or

לֵוִי **Lêvîy**, *lay-vee´;* patron. from 3878; a *Levite* or desc. of Levi:— Levite.

3882. לִוְיָתָן **livyâthân**, *liv-yaw-thawn´;* from 3867; a *wreathed* animal, i.e. a *serpent* (espec. the *crocodile* or some other large sea-monster); fig. the con-

stellation of the *dragon;* also as a symbol of *Babylon:*— leviathan, mourning .

3883. לוּל **lûwl**, *lool;* from an unused root mean. to *fold* back; a *spiral* step:— winding stair. Comp. 3924.

3884. לוּלֵא **lûwlê´**, *loo-lay´;* or

לוּלֵי **lûwlêy**, *loo lay´;* from 3863 and 3808; *if not:*— except, had not, if (... not), unless, were it not that.

3885. לוּן **lûwn**, *loon;* or

לִין **lîyn**, *leen;* a prim. root; to *stop* (usually over night); by impl. to *stay* permanently; hence, (in a bad sense) to *be obstinate* (espec. in words, to *complain*):— abide (all night), continue, dwell, endure, grudge, be left, lie all night, (cause to) lodge (all night, in, -ing, this night), (make to) murmur, remain, tarry (all night, that night).

3886. לוּעַ **lûwa´**, *loo´-ah;* a prim. root; to *gulp;* fig. to be *rash:*— swallow down (up).

3887. לוּץ **lûwts**, *loots;* a prim. root; prop. to *make mouths* at, i.e. to *scoff;* hence, (from the effort to pronounce a foreign language) to *interpret,* or (gen.) *intercede:*— ambassador, have in derision, interpreter, make a mock, mocker, scorn (-er, -ful), teacher.

3888. לוּשׁ **lûwsh**, *loosh;* a prim. root; to *knead:*— knead.

3889. לוּשׁ **Lûwsh**, *loosh;* from 3888; *kneading; Lush,* a place in Pal.:— Laish [from the marg.]. Comp. 3919.

3890. לְוָת **lᵉvâth** (Chald.), *lev-awth´;* from a root corresp. to 3867; prop. *adhesion,* i.e. (as prep.) *with:*— × thee.

לֻחוֹת **Lûchôwth**. See 3872.

לָז **lâz** and

לָזֶה **lâzeh**. See 1975 and 1976.

3891. לְזוּת **lᵉzûwth**, *lez-ooth´;* from 3868; *perverseness:*— perverse.

3892. לַח **lach**, *lakh;* from an unused root mean. to *be new; fresh,* i.e. unused or undried:— green, moist.

3893. לֵחַ **lêach**, *lay´-akh;* from the same as 3892; *freshness,* i.e. vigor:— natural force.

לֻחַ **lûach**. See 3871.

3894. לָחוּם **lâchûwm**, *law-khoom´;* or

לָחֻם **lâchûm**, *law-khoom´;* pass. part. of 3898; prop. *eaten,* i.e. *food;* also *flesh,* i.e. *body:*— while ... is eating, flesh.

3895. לְחִי **lᵉchîy**, *lekh-ee´;* from an unused root mean. to *be soft;* the *cheek* (from its *fleshiness*); hence, the *jaw*-bone:— cheek (bone), jaw (bone).

3896. לֵחִי **Lechîy**, *lekh´-ee;* a form of 3895; *Lechi,* a place in Pal.:— Lehi. Comp. also 7437.

3897. לָחַךְ **lâchak**, *law-khak´;* a prim. root; to *lick:*— lick (up).

3898. לָחַם **lâcham**, *law-kham´;* a prim. root; to *feed* on; fig. to *consume;* by impl. to *battle* (as *destruction*):— devour, eat, × ever, fight (-ing), overcome, prevail, (make) war (-ring).

3899. לֶחֶם **lechem**, *lekh´-em;* from 3898; *food* (for man or beast), espec. *bread,* or *grain* (for making it):— ([shew-])

bread, × eat, food, fruit, loaf, meat, victuals. See also 1036.

3900. לֶחֶם **lᵉchem** (Chald.), *lekh-em´;* corresp. to 3899:— feast.

3901. לָחֶם **lâchem**, *law-khem´;* from 3898, *battle:*— war.

לָחֻם **lâchûm**. See 3894.

3902. לַחְמִי **Lachmîy**, *lakh-mee´;* from 3899; *foodful; Lachmi,* a Philis.; or rather prob. a brief form (or perh. err. transc.) for 1022:— Lahmi. See also 3433.

3903. לַחְמָס **Lachmâç**, *lakh-maws´;* prob. by err. transc. for

לַחְמָם **Lachmâm**, *lakh-mawm´;* from 3899; *food-like; Lachmam* or *Lachmas,* a place in Pal.:— Lahmam.

3904. לֶחֱנָה **lᵉchênâh** (Chald.), *lekh-ay-naw´;* from an unused root of uncert. mean.; a *concubine:*— concubine.

3905. לָחַץ **lâchats**, *law-khats´;* a prim. root; prop. to *press,* i.e. (fig.) to *distress:*— afflict, crush, force, hold fast, oppress (-or), thrust self.

3906. לַחַץ **lachats**, *lakh´-ats;* from 3905; *distress:*— affliction, oppression.

3907. לָחַשׁ **lâchash**, *law-khash´;* a prim. root; to *whisper;* by impl. to *mumble* a spell (as a magician):— charmer, whisper (together).

3908. לַחַשׁ **lachash**, *lakh´-ash;* from 3907; prop. a *whisper,* i.e. by impl. (in a good sense) a private *prayer,* (in a bad one) an *incantation;* concr. an *amulet:*— charmed, earring, enchantment, orator, prayer.

3909. לָט **lâṭ**, *lawt;* a form of 3814 or else part. from 3874; prop. *covered,* i.e. *secret;* by impl. *incantation;* also *secrecy* or (adv.) *covertly:*— enchantment, privily, secretly, softly.

3910. לֹט **lôṭ**, *lote;* prob. from 3874; a *gum* (from its *sticky* nature), prob. *ladanum:*— myrrh.

3911. לְטָאָה **lᵉṭâ´âh**, *let-aw-aw´;* from an unused root mean. to *hide;* a kind of *lizard* (from its *covert* habits):— lizard.

3912. לְטוּשִׁם **Lᵉṭûwshîm**, *let-oo-sheem´;* masc. plur. of pass. part. of 3913; *hammered* (i.e. *oppressed*) ones; *Letushim,* an Arabian tribe:— Letushim.

3913. לָטַשׁ **lâṭash**, *law-tash´;* a prim. root; prop. to *hammer* out (an edge), i.e. to *sharpen:*— instructer, sharp (-en), whet.

3914. לֹיָה **lôyâh**, *lo-yaw´;* a form of 3880; a *wreath:*— addition.

3915. לַיִל **layil**, *lah´-yil;* or (Isa. 21:11)

לֵיל **lêyl**, *lale;* also

לַיְלָה **laylâh**, *lah´-yel-aw;* from the same as 3883; prop. a *twist* (away of the light), i.e. *night;* fig. *adversity:*— ([mid-]) night (season).

3916. לֵילְיָא **leylᵉyâ´** (Chald.), *lay-leh-yaw´;* corresp. to 3915:— night.

3917. לִילִית **lîylîyth**, *lee-leeth´;* from 3915; a *night* spectre:— screech owl.

3918. לַיִשׁ **layish**, *lah´-yish;* from 3888 in the sense of *crushing;* a *lion* (from his destructive *blows*):— (old) lion.

3919. לַיִשׁ **Layish**, *lah´-yish;* the same as

3918; *Laïsh*, the name of two places in Pal.:— Laish. Comp. 3889.

3920. לָכַד **lâkad**, *law-kad'*; a prim. root; to *catch* (in a net, trap or pit); gen. to *capture* or occupy; also to *choose* (by lot); fig. to *cohere*:— × at all, catch (self), be frozen, be holden, stick together, take.

3921. לֶכֶד **leked**, *leh'ked*; from 3920; something to *capture* with, i.e. a *noose*:— being taken.

3922. לֵכָה **Lêkâh**, *lay-kaw'*; from 3212; a *journey*; *Lekah*, a place in Pal.:— Lecah.

3923. לָחִישׁ **Lâchîysh**, *law-keesh'*; from an unused root of uncert. mean.; *Lakish*, a place in Pal.:— Lachish.

3924. לֻלָאָה **lûlâ'âh**, *loo-law-aw'*; from the same as 3883; a *loop*:— loop.

3925. לָמַד **lâmad**, *law-mad'*; a prim. root; prop. to *goad*, i.e. (by impl.) to *teach* (the rod being an Oriental *incentive*):— [un-] accustomed, × diligently, expert, instruct, learn, skilful, teach (-er, ing).

לִמֻּד **limmûd**. See 3928.

3926. לְמוֹ **lᵉmôw**, *lem-o'*; a prol. and separable form of the pref. prep.; *to* or *for*:— at, for, to, upon.

3927. לְמוּאֵל **Lᵉmûw'êl**, *lem-oo-ale'*; or

לְמוֹאֵל **Lᵉmôw'êl**, *lem-o-ale'*; from 3926 and 410; (belonging) *to God*; *Lemuël* or *Lemoël*, a symbol. name of Solomon:— Lemuel.

3928. לִמּוּד **limmûwd**, *lim-mood'*; or

לִמֻּד **limmûd**, *lim-mood'*; from 3925; *instructed*:— accustomed, disciple, learned, taught, used.

3929. לֶמֶךְ **Lemek**, *leh'mek*; from an unused root of uncert. mean.; *Lemek*, the name of two antediluvian patriarchs:— Lamech.

3930. לֹע **lôa'**, *lo'ah*; from 3886; the *gullet*:— throat.

3931. לָעַב **lâ'ab**, *law-ab'*; a prim. root; to *deride*:— mock.

3932. לָעַג **lâ'ag**, *law-ag'*; a prim. root; to *deride*; by impl. (as if imitating a foreigner) to *speak unintelligibly*:— have in derision, laugh (to scorn), mock (on), stammering.

3933. לַעַג **la'ag**, *lah'ag*; from 3932; *derision, scoffing*:— derision, scorn (-ing).

3934. לָעֵג **lâ'êg**, *law-ayg'*; from 3932; a *buffoon*; also a *foreigner*:— mocker, stammering.

3935. לַעְדָּה **La'dâh**, *lah-daw'*; from an unused root of uncert. mean.; *Ladah*, an Isr.:— Laadah.

3936. לַעְדָּן **La'dân**, *lah-dawn'*; from the same as 3935; *Ladan*, the name of two Isr.:— Laadan.

3937. לָעַז **lâ'az**, *law-az'*; a prim. root; to *speak in a foreign tongue*:— strange language.

3938. לָעַט **lâ'at**, *law-at'*; a prim. root; to *swallow* greedily; caus. to *feed*:— feed.

3939. לַעֲנָה **la'ănâh**, *lah-an-aw'*; from an unused root supposed to mean to *curse; wormwood* (regarded as *poisonous*, and therefore *accursed*):— hemlock, wormwood.

3940. לָפִיד **lappîyd**, *lap-peed'*; or

לַפִּד **lappîd**, *lap-peed'*; from an unused root prob. mean. to *shine*; a *flambeau, lamp* or *flame*:— (fire-) brand, (burning) lamp, lightning, torch.

3941. לַפִּידוֹת **Lappîydôwth**, *lap-pee-dôth'*; fem. plur. of 3940; *Lappidoth*, the husband of Deborah:— Lappidoth.

3942. לִפְנַי **liphnay**, *lif-nah'ee*; from the pref. prep. (*to* or *for*) and 6440; *anterior*:— before.

3943. לָפַת **lâphath**, *law-fath'*; a prim. root; prop. to *bend*, i.e. (by impl.) to *clasp*; also (refl.) to *turn around or aside*:— take hold, turn aside (self).

3944. לָצוֹן **lâtsôwn**, *law-tsone'*; from 3887; *derision*:— scornful (-ning).

3945. לָצַץ **lâtsats**, *law-tsats'*; a prim. root; to *deride*:— scorn.

3946. לַקּוּם **Laqqûwm**, *lak-koom'*; from an unused root thought to mean to *stop* up by a barricade; perh. *fortification*; *Lakkum*, a place in Pal.:— Lakum.

3947. לָקַח **lâqach**, *law-kakh'*; a prim. root; to *take* (in the widest variety of applications):— accept, bring, buy, carry away, drawn, fetch, get, infold, × many, mingle, place, receive (-ing), reserve, seize, send for, take (away, -ing, up), use, win.

3948. לֶקַח **leqach**, *leh'-kakh*; from 3947; prop. something *received*, i.e. (ment.) *instruction* (whether on the part of the teacher or hearer); also (in an act. and sinister sense) *inveiglement*:— doctrine, learning, fair speech.

3949. לִקְחִי **Liqchîy**, *lik-khee'*; from 3947; *learned*; *Likchi*, an Isr.:— Likhi.

3950. לָקַט **lâqat**, *law-kat'*; a prim. root; prop. to *pick up*, i.e. (gen.) to *gather*; spec. to *glean*:— gather (up), glean.

3951. לֶקֶט **leqet**, *leh'-ket*; from 3950; the *gleaning*:— gleaning.

3952. לָקַק **lâqaq**, *law-kak'*; a prim. root; to *lick* or *lap*:— lap, lick.

3953. לָקַשׁ **lâqash**, *law-kash'*; a prim. root; to *gather* the *after crop*:— gather.

3954. לֶקֶשׁ **leqesh**, *leh'-kesh*; from 3953; the *after crop*:— latter growth.

3955. לְשַׁד **lᵉshad**, *lesh-ad'*; from an unused root of uncert. mean.; appar. *juice*, i.e. (fig.) *vigor*; also a sweet or fat *cake*:— fresh, moisture.

3956. לָשׁוֹן **lâshôwn**, *law-shone'*; or

לָשֹׁן **lâshôn**, *law-shone'*; also (in plur.) fem.

לְשֹׁנָה **lᵉshônâh**, *lesh-o-naw'*; from 3960; the *tongue* (of man or animals), used lit. (as the instrument of licking, eating, or speech), and fig. (speech, an ingot, a fork of flame, a cove of water):— + babbler, bay, + evil speaker, language, talker, tongue, wedge.

3957. לִשְׁכָּה **lishkâh**, *lish-kaw'*; from an unused root of uncert. mean.; a *room* in a building (whether for storage, eating, or lodging):— chamber, parlour. Comp. 5393.

3958. לֶשֶׁם **leshem**, *leh'-shem*; from an unused root of uncert. mean.; a *gem*, perh. the *jacinth*:— ligure.

3959. לֶשֶׁם **Leshem**, *leh'-shem*; the same as 3958; *Leshem*, a place in Pal.:— Leshem.

3960. לָשַׁן **lâshan**, *law-shan'*; a prim. root; prop. to *lick*; but used only as a denom. from 3956; to *wag the tongue*, i.e. to *calumniate*:— accuse, slander.

3961. לִשָּׁן **lishshân** (Chald.), *lish-shawn'*; corresp. to 3956; *speech*, i.e. a *nation*:— language.

3962. לֶשַׁע **Lesha'**, *leh'-shah*; from an unused root thought to mean to *break* through; a boiling *spring*; *Lesha*, a place prob. E. of the Jordan:— Lasha.

3963. לֶתֶךְ **lethek**, *leh'-thek*; from an unused root of uncert. mean.; a *measure* for things dry:— half homer.

מ

מ **ma-**, or

מ **mâ-**. See 4100.

3964. מָא **mâ'** (Chald.), *maw*; corresp. to 4100; (as indef.) *that*:— + what.

3965. מַעֲבוּס **ma'âbûwç**, *mah-ab-ooce'*; from 75; a *granary*:— storehouse.

3966. מְעֹד **mᵉôd**, *meh-ode'*; from the same as 181; prop. *vehemence*, i.e. (with or without prep.) *vehemently*; by impl. *wholly, speedily*, etc. (often with other words as an intens. or superl.; espec. when repeated):— diligently, especially, exceeding (-ly), far, fast, good, great (-ly), × louder and louder, might (-ily, -y), (so) much, quickly, (so) sore, utterly, very (+ much, sore), well.

3967. מֵאָה **mê'âh**, *may-aw'*; or

מֵאיָה **mê'yâh**, *may-yaw'*; prop. a prim. numeral; a *hundred*; also as a multiplicative and a fraction:— hundred ([-foldl, -th), + sixscore.

3968. מֵאָה **Mê'âh**, *may-aw'*; the same as 3967; *Meäh*, a tower in Jerusalem:— Meah.

3969. מְאָה **mᵉâh** (Chald.), *meh-aw'*; corresp. to 3967:— hundred.

3970. מַאֲוַי **ma'ăvay**, *mah-av-ah'ee*; from 183; a *desire*:— desire.

מֹאל **môw'l**. See 4136.

3971. מְאוּם **m'ûwm**, *moom*; usually

מוּם **mûwm**, *moom*; as if pass. part. from an unused root prob. mean. to *stain*; a *blemish* (phys. or mor.):— blemish, blot, spot.

3972. מְאוּמָה **mᵉûwmâh**, *meh-oo'-maw*; appar. a form of 3971; prop. a *speck* or *point*, i.e. (by impl.) *something*; with neg. *nothing*:— fault, + no (-ught), ought, somewhat, any ([no-l) thing.

3973. מָאוֹס **mâ'ôwç**, *maw-oce'*; from 3988; *refuse*:— refuse.

3974. מָאוֹר **mâ'ôwr**, *maw-ore'*; or

מָאֹר **mâ'ôr**, *maw-ore'*; also (in plur.) fem.

מְאוֹרָה **mᵉôwrâh**, *meh-o-raw'*; or

מְאֹרָה **mᵉôrâh**, *meh-o-raw'*; from 215; prop. a *luminous* body or *luminary*, i.e. (abstr.) *light* (as an element); fig. *brightness*, i.e. *cheerfulness*; spec. a *chandelier*:— bright, light.

3975. מְאוּרָה **mᵉ'ûwrâh**, *meh-oo-raw*; fem. pass. part. of 215; something *lighted*, i.e. an *aperture*; by impl. a *crevice* or *hole* (of a serpent):— den.

3976. מאזן **mô'zên**, *mo-zane*; from 239; (only in the dual) a pair of *scales*:— balances.

3977. מאזן **mô'zên** (Chald.), *mo-zane*; corresp. to 3976:— balances.

3978. מאיה **mê'yâh**. See 3967.

3979. מַאֲכָל **ma'ăkâl**, *mah-ak-awl*; from 398; an *eatable* (includ. provender, flesh and fruit):— food, fruit, (bake-l) meat (-s), victual.

3979. מַאֲכֶלֶת **ma'ăkeleth**, *mah-ak-eh´leth*; from 398; something to *eat* with, i.e. a *knife*:— knife.

3980. מַאֲכֹלֶת **ma'ăkôleth**, *mah-ak-o´leth*; from 398; something *eaten* (by fire), i.e. *fuel*:— fuel.

3981. מַאֲמָץ **ma'ămâts**, *mah-am-awts´*; from 553; *strength*, i.e. (plur.) *resources*:— force.

3982. מַאֲמַר **ma'ămar**, *mah-am-ar´*; from 559; something (authoritatively) *said*, i.e. an *edict*:— commandment, decree.

3983. מֵאמַר **mê'mar** (Chald.), *may-mar´*; corresp. to 3982:— appointment, word.

3984. מָאן **mâ'n** (Chald.), *mawn*; prob. from a root corresp. to 579 in the sense of an *inclosure* by sides; a *utensil*:— vessel.

3985. מָאֵן **mâ'ên**, *maw-ane´*; a prim. root; to *refuse*:— refuse, × utterly.

3986. מָאֵן **mâ'ên**, *maw-ane´*; from 3985; *unwilling*:— refuse.

3987. מֵאֵן **mê'ên**, *may-ane´*; from 3985; *refractory*:— refuse.

3988. מָאַס **mâ'ac**, *maw-as´*; a prim. root; to *spurn*; also (intr.) to *disappear*:— abhor, cast away (off), contemn, despise, disdain, (become) loathe (some), melt away, refuse, reject, reprobate, × utterly, vile person.

3989. מַאֲפֶה **mâ'ăpheh**, *mah-af-eh´*; from 644; something *baked*, i.e. a *batch*:— baken.

3990. מַאֲפֵל **ma'ăphêl**, *mah-af-ale´*; from the same as 651; something *opaque*:— darkness.

3991. מַאְפֵלְיָה **ma'phêlᵉyâh**, *mah-af-ay-leh-yaw´*; prol. fem. of 3990; *opaqueness*:— darkness.

3992. מָאַר **mâ'ar**, *maw-ar´*; a prim. root; to *be bitter* or (caus.) to *embitter*, i.e. *be painful*:— fretting, picking.

מָאוֹר **mâ'ôr**. See 3974.

3993. מַאֲרָב **ma'ărâb**, *mah-ar-awb´*; from 693; an *ambuscade*:— lie in ambush, ambushment, lurking place, lying in wait.

3994. מְאֵרָה **mᵉ'êrâh**, *meh-ay-raw´*; from 779; an *execration*:— curse.

מְאֹרָה **mᵉ'ôrâh**. See 3974.

3995. מִבְדָּלָה **mibdâlâh**, *mib-daw-law´*; from 914; a *separation*, i.e. (concr.) a *separate* place:— separate.

3996. מָבוֹא **mâbôw'**, *maw-bo´*; from 935; an *entrance* (the place or the act); spec. (with or without 8121) *sunset* or the *west*; also (adv. with prep.) *towards*:— by which came, as cometh, in coming, as men enter into, entering, entrance into, entry, where goeth, going down, + westward. Comp. 4126.

3997. מְבוֹאָה **mᵉbôw'âh**, *meb-o-aw´*; fem. of 3996; a *haven*:— entry.

3998. מְבוּכָה **mᵉbûwkâh**, *meb-oo-kaw´*; from 943; *perplexity*:— perplexity.

3999. מַבּוּל **mabbûwl**, *mab-bool´*; from 2986 in the sense of *flowing*; a *deluge*:— flood.

4000. מָבוֹן **mâbôwn**, *maw-bone´*; from 995; *instructing*:— taught.

4001. מְבוּסָה **mᵉbûwçâh**, *meb-oo-saw´*; from 947; a *trampling*:— treading (trodden) down (under foot).

4002. מַבּוּעַ **mabbûwa'**, *mab-boo´-ah*; from 5042; a *fountain*:— fountain, spring.

4003. מְבוּקָה **mᵉbûwqâh**, *meb-oo-kah´*; from the same as 950; *emptiness*:— void.

4004. מִבְחוֹר **mibchôwr**, *mib-khore´*; from 977; *select*, i.e. well fortified:— choice.

4005. מִבְחָר **mibchâr**, *mib-khawr´*; from 977; *select*, i.e. best:— choice (-st), chosen.

4006. מִבְחָר **Mibchâr**, *mib-khawr´*; the same as 4005; *Mibchar*, an Isr.:— Mibhar.

4007. מַבָּט **mabbâṭ**, *mab-bawt´*; or

מֶבָּט **mebbâṭ**, *meb-bawt´*; from 5027; something *expected*, i.e. (abstr.) *expectation*:— expectation.

4008. מִבְטָא **mibṭâ'**, *mib-taw´*; from 981; a rash *utterance* (hasty vow):— (that which ...) uttered (out of).

4009. מִבְטָח **mibṭâch**, *mib-tawkh´*; from 982; prop. a *refuge*, i.e. (obj.) *security*, or (subj.) *assurance*:— confidence, hope, sure, trust.

4010. מַבְלִיגִית **mabliygîyth**, *mab-leeg-eeth´*; from 1082; *desistance* (or rather *desolation*):— comfort self.

4011. מִבְנֶה **mibneh**, *mib-neh´*; from 1129; a *building*:— frame.

4012. מְבֻנַּי **Mᵉbunnay**, *meb-oon-hah´-ee*; from 1129; *built* up; *Mebunnai*, an Isr.:— Mebunnai.

4013. מִבְצָר **mibtsâr**, *mib-tsawr´*; also (in plur.) fem. (Dan. 11:15)

מִבְצָרָה **mibtsârâh**, *mib-tsaw-raw´*; from 1219; a *fortification*, *castle*, or *fortified* city; fig. a *defender*:— (de-, most) fenced, fortress, (most) strong (hold).

4014. מִבְצָר **Mibtsâr**, *mib-tsawr´*; the same as 4013; *Mibtsar*, an Idumæan:— Mibzar.

מִבְצָרָה **mibtsârâh**. See 4013.

4015. מִבְרָח **mibrâch**, *mib-rawkh´*; from 1272; a *refugee*:— fugitive.

4016. מָבֻשׁ **mâbush**, *maw-boosh´*; from 954; (plur.) the (male) *pudenda*:— secrets.

4017. מִבְשָׂם **Mibsâm**, *mib-sawm´*; from the same as 1314; *fragrant*; *Mibsam*, the name of an Ishmaelite and of an Isr.:— Mibsam.

4018. מְבַשְּׁלָה **mᵉbashshᵉlâh**, *meb-ash-shel-aw´*; from 1310; a cooking *hearth*:— boiling-place.

מַג **Mâg**. See 7248, 7249.

4019. מַגְבִּישׁ **Magbîysh**, *mag-beesh´*; from the same as 1378; *stiffening*; *Magbish*, an Isr., or a place in Pal.:— Magbish.

4020. מִגְבָּלָה **migbâlâh**, *mig-baw-law´*; from 1379; a *border*:— end.

4021. מִגְבָּעָה **migbâ'âh**, *mig-baw-aw´*; from the same as 1389; a *cap* (as hemispherical):— bonnet.

4022. מֶגֶד **meged**, *meh´-ghed*; from an unused root prob. mean. to *be eminent*; prop. a *distinguished* thing; hence, something *valuable*, as a product or fruit:— pleasant, precious fruit (thing).

4023. מְגִדּוֹן **Mᵉgiddôwn** (Zech. 12:11), *meg-id-dône´*; or

מְגִדּוֹ **Mᵉgiddôw**, *meg-id-do´*; from 1413; *rendezvous*; *Megiddon* or *Megiddo*, a place in Pal.:— Megiddo, Megiddon.

4024. מִגְדּוֹל **Migdôwl**, *mig-dole´*; or

מִגְדֹּל **Migdôl**, *mig-dole´*; prob. of Eg. or.; *Migdol*, a place in Egypt:— Migdol, tower.

4025. מַגְדִּיאֵל **Magdîy'êl**, *mag-dee-ale´*; from 4022 and 410; *preciousness of God*; *Magdiël*, an Idumæan:— Magdiel.

4026. מִגְדָּל **migdâl**, *mig-dawl´*; also (in plur.) fem.

מִגְדָּלָה **migdâlâh**, *mig-daw-law´*; from 1431; a *tower* (from its size or height); by anal. a *rostrum*; fig. a (pyramidal) *bed* of flowers:— castle, flower, tower. Comp. the names following.

מִגְדֹּל **Migdôl**. See 4024.

מִגְדָּלָה **migdâlâh**. See 4026.

4027. מִגְדַּל־אֵל **Migdal-'Êl**, *mig-dal-ale´*; from 4026 and 410; *tower of God*; *Migdal-El*, a place in Pal.:— Migdal-el.

4028. מִגְדַּל־גָּד **Migdal-Gâd**, *migdal-gawd´*; from 4026 and 1408; *tower of Fortune*; *Migdal-Gad*, a place in Pal.:— Migdal-gad.

4029. מִגְדַּל־אֵדֶר **Migdal-'Êder**, *mig-dal´-ay-der*; from 4026 and 5739; *tower of a flock*; *Migdal-Eder*, a place in Pal.:— Migdal-eder, tower of the flock.

4030. מִגְדָּנָה **migdânâh**, *mig-daw-naw´*; from the same as 4022; *preciousness*, i.e. a *gem*:— precious thing, present.

4031. מָגוֹג **Mâgôwg**, *maw-gogue´*; from 1463; *Magog*, a son of Japheth; also a barbarous northern region:— Magog.

4032. מָגוֹר **mâgôwr**, *maw-gore´*; or (Lam. 2:22)

מָגוּר **mâgûwr**, *maw-goor´*; from 1481 in the sense of *fearing*; a *fright* (obj. or subj.):— fear, terror. Comp. 4036.

4033. מָגוּר **mâgûwr**, *maw-goor´*; or

מָגֻר **mâgûr**, *maw-goor´*; from 1481 in the sense of *lodging*; a temporary *abode*; by extens. a permanent *residence*:— dwelling, pilgrimage, where sojourn, be a stranger. Comp. 4032.

4034. מְגוֹרָה **m^egôwrâh**, *meg-o-raw´*; fem. of 4032; *affright:*— fear.

4035. מְגוּרָה **m^egûwrâh**, *meg-oo-raw´*; fem. of 4032 or of 4033; a *fright;* also a *granary:*— barn, fear.

4036. מָגוֹר מִסָּבִיב **Mâgôwr miç-Çâbîyb**, *maw-gore´ mis-saw-beeb´*; from 4032 and 5439 with the prep. ins.; *affright from around; Magor-mis-Sabib,* a symbol. name of Pashur:— Magor-missabib.

4037. מַגְזֵרָה **magzêrâh**, *mag-zay-raw´*; from 1504; a *cutting* implement, i.e. a *blade:*— axe.

4038. מַגָּל **maggâl**, *mag-gawl´*; from an unused root mean. to *reap;* a *sickle:*— sickle.

4039. מְגִלָּה **m^egillâh**, *meg-il-law´*; from 1556; a *roll:*— roll, volume.

4040. מְגִלָּה **m^egillâh** (Chald.), *meg-il-law´*; corresp. to 4039:— roll.

4041. מַגַּמָּה **m^egammâh**, *meg-am-maw´*; from the same as 1571; prop. *accumulation,* i.e. *impulse* or *direction:*— sup up.

4042. מָגַן **mâgan**, *maw-gan´*; a denom. from 4043; prop. to *shield; encompass* with; fig. to *rescue,* to *hand* safely *over* (i.e. *surrender):*— deliver.

4043. מָגֵן **mâgên**, *maw-gane´*; also (in plur.) fem.

מְגִנָּה **m^eginnâh**, *meg-in-naw´*; from 1598; a *shield* (i.e. the small one or *buckler*); fig. a *protector;* also the scaly *hide* of the crocodile:— × armed, buckler, defence, ruler, + scale, shield.

4044. מְגִנָּה **m^eginnâh**, *meg-in-naw´*; from 4042; a *covering* (in a bad sense), i.e. *blindness* or *obduracy:*— sorrow. See also 4043.

4045. מִגְעֶרֶת **mig'ereth**, *mig-eh´-reth;* from 1605; *reproof* (i.e. *curse):*— rebuke.

4046. מַגֵּפָה **maggêphâh**, *mag-gay-faw´*; from 5062; a *pestilence;* by anal. *defeat:*— (× be) plague (-d), slaughter, stroke.

4047. מַגְפִּיעָשׁ **Magpîy'âsh**, *mag-pee-awsh´*; appar. from 1479 or 5062 and 6211; *exterminator of* (the) *moth; Magpiash,* an Isr.:— Magpiash.

4048. מָגַר **mâgar**, *maw-gar´*; a prim. root; to *yield up;* intens. to *precipitate:*— cast down, terror.

4049. מְגַר **m^egar** (Chald.), *meg-ar´*; corresp. to 4048; to *overthrow:*— destroy.

4050. מְגֵרָה **m^egêrâh**, *meg-ay-raw´*; from 1641; a *saw:*— axe, saw.

4051. מִגְרוֹן **Migrôwn**, *mig-rone´*; from 4048; *precipice; Migron,* a place in Pal.:— Migron.

4052. מִגְרָעָה **migrâ'âh**, *mig-raw-aw´*; from 1639; a *ledge* or offset:— narrowed rest.

4053. מִגְרָפָה **migrâphâh**, *mig-raw-faw´*; from 1640; something *thrown off* (by the spade), i.e. a *clod:*— clod.

4054. מִגְרָשׁ **migrâsh**, *mig-rawsh´*; also (in plur.) fem. (Ezek. 27:28)

מִגְרָשָׁה **migrâshâh**, *mig-raw-shaw´*; from 1644; a *suburb* (i.e. open country whither flocks are driven for

---

pasture); hence, the *area* around a building, or the *margin* of the sea:— cast out, suburb.

4055. מַד **mad**, *mad;* or

מֵד **mêd**, *made;* from 4058; prop. *extent,* i.e. *height;* also a *measure;* by impl. a *vesture* (as measured); also a *carpet:*— armour, clothes, garment, judgment, measure, raiment, stature.

4056. מַדְבַּח **madbach** (Chald.), *mad-bakh´;* from 1684; a sacrificial *altar:*— altar.

4057. מִדְבָּר **midbâr**, *mid-bawr´;* from 1696 in the sense of *driving;* a *pasture* (i.e. open field, whither cattle are driven); by impl. a *desert;* also *speech* (incl. its organs):— desert, south, speech, wilderness.

4058. מָדַד **mâdad**, *maw-dad´*; a prim. root; prop. to *stretch;* by impl. to *measure* (as if by *stretching* a line); fig. to be *extended:*— measure, mete, stretch self.

4059. מִדַּד **middad**, *mid-dad´;* from 5074; *flight:*— be gone.

4060. מִדָּה **middâh**, *mid-daw´;* fem. of 4055; prop. *extension,* i.e. height or breadth; also a *measure* (incl. its standard); hence, a *portion* (as measured) or a *vestment;* spec. *tribute* (as measured):— garment, measure (-ing, meteyard, piece, size, (great) stature, tribute, wide.

4061. מִדָּה **middâh** (Chald.), *mid-daw´* or

מִנְדָּה **mindâh** (Chald.), *min-daw´;* corresp. to 4060; *tribute* in money:— toll, tribute.

4062. מַדְהֵבָה **madhêbâh**, *mad-hay-baw´;* perh. from the equiv. of 1722; *goldmaking,* i.e. *exactress:*— golden city.

4063. מֶדַו **medev**, *meh´-dev;* from an unused root mean. to *stretch;* prop. *extent,* i.e. *measure;* by impl. a *dress* (as measured):— garment.

4064. מַדְוֶה **madveh**, *mad-veh´;* from 1738; *sickness:*— disease.

4065. מַדּוּחַ **maddûwach**, *mad-doo´-akh;* from 5080; *seduction:*— cause of banishment.

4066. מָדוֹן **mâdôwn**, *maw-dohn´;* from 1777; a *contest* or quarrel:— brawling, contention (-ous), discord, strife. Comp. 4079, 4090.

4067. מָדוֹן **mâdôwn**, *maw-dohn´;* from the same as 4063; *extensiveness,* i.e. *height:*— stature.

4068. מָדוֹן **Mâdôwn**, *maw-dohn´;* the same as 4067; *Madon,* a place in Pal.:— Madon.

4069. מַדּוּעַ **maddûwa'**, *mad-doo´-ah;* or

מַדֻּעַ **maddûa'**, *mad-doo´-ah;* from 4100 and the pass. part. of 3045; *what* (is) *known?;* i.e. (by impl.) (adv.) *why?:*— how, wherefore, why.

4070. מְדוֹר **m^edôwr** (Chald.), *med-ore´;* or

מְדֹר **m^edôr** (Chald.), *med-ore´;* or

מְדָר **m^edâr** (Chald.), *med-awr´;* from 1753; a *dwelling:*— dwelling.

4071. מְדוּרָה **m^edûwrâh**, *med-oo-raw´;* or

מְדֻרָה **m^edûrâh**, *med-oo-raw´;* from 1752 in the sense of *accumulation;* a *pile* of fuel:— pile (for fire).

4072. מִדְחֶה **midcheh**, *mid-kheh´;* from 1760; *overthrow:*— ruin.

4073. מִדְחָפָה **m^edachphâh**, *med-akh-faw´;* from 1765; a *push,* i.e. *ruin:*— overthrow.

4074. מָדַי **Mâday**, *maw-dah´-ee;* of for. der.; *Madai,* a country of central Asia:— Madai, Medes, Media.

4075. מָדַי **Mâday**, *maw-dah´-ee;* patrial from 4074; a *Madian* or native of Madai:— Mede.

4076. מָדַי **Mâday** (Chald.), *maw-dah´-ee;* corresp. to 4074:— Mede (-s).

4077. מָדַי **Mâday** (Chald.), *maw-dah´-ee;* corresp. to 4075:— Median.

4078. מַדַּי **madday**, *mad-dah´-ee;* from 4100 and 1767; *what* (is) *enough,* i.e. *sufficiently:*— sufficiently.

4079. מִדְיָן **midyân**, *mid-yawn´;* a var. for 4066:— brawling, contention (-ous).

4080. מִדְיָן **Midyân**, *mid-yawn´;* the same as 4079; *Midjan,* a son of Abraham; also his country and (collect.) his desc.:— Midian, Midianite.

4081. מִדִּין **Middîyn**, *mid-deen´;* a var. for 4080:— Middin.

4082. מְדִינָה **m^edîynâh**, *med-ee-naw´;* from 1777; prop. a *judgeship,* i.e. *jurisdiction;* by impl. a *district* (as ruled by a judge); gen. a *region:*— (× every) province.

4083. מְדִינָה **m^edîynâh** (Chald.), *med-ee-naw´;* corresp. to 4082:— province.

4084. מִדְיָנִי **Midyânîy**, *mid-yaw-nee´;* patron. or patrial from 4080; a *Midjanite* or descend. (native) of Midjan:— Midianite. Comp. 4092.

4085. מְדֹכָה **m^edôkâh**, *med-o-kaw´;* from 1743; a *mortar:*— mortar.

4086. מַדְמֵן **Madmên**, *mad-mane´;* from the same as 1828; *dunghill; Madmen,* a place in Pal.:— Madmen.

4087. מַדְמֵנָה **madmênâh**, *mad-may-naw´;* fem. from the same as 1828; a *dunghill:*— dunghill.

4088. מַדְמֵנָה **Madmênâh**, *mad-may-naw´;* the same as 4087; *Madmenah,* a place in Pal.:— Madmenah.

4089. מַדְמַנָּה **Madmannâh**, *mad-man-naw´;* a var. for 4087; *Madmannah,* a place in Pal.:— Madmannah.

4090. מְדָן **m^edân**, *med-awn´;* a form of 4066:— discord, strife.

4091. מְדָן **M^edân**, *med-awn´;* the same as 4090; *Medan,* a son of Abraham:— Medan.

4092. מְדָנִי **M^edânîy**, *med-aw-nee´;* a var. of 4084:— Midianite.

4093. מַדָּע **maddâ'**, *mad-daw´;* or

מַדָּע **madda'**, *mad-dah´;* from 3045; *intelligence* or *consciousness:*— knowledge, science, thought.

מֹדָע **môdâ'**. See 4129.

מַדֻּעַ **madûa'**. See 4069.

4094. מַדְקָרָה **madqârâh**, *mad-kaw-raw´*; from 1856; a *wound*:— piercing.

מְדֹר **meᵈdôr.** See 4070.

4095. מַדְרֵגָה **madrêgâh**, *mad-ray-gaw´*; from an unused root mean. to *step*; prop. a *step*; by impl. a *steep* or inaccessible place:— stair, steep place.

מְדוּרָה **meᵈdûrâh.** See 4071.

4096. מִדְרָךְ **midrâk**, *mid-rawk´*; from 1869; a *treading*, i.e. a place for stepping on:— [foot-] breadth.

4097. מִדְרָשׁ **midrâsh**, *mid-rawsh´*; from 1875; prop. an *investigation*, i.e. (by impl.) a *treatise* or elaborate compilation:— story.

4098. מִדְשָׁה **meᵈdushshâh**, *med-oosh-shaw´*; from 1758; a *threshing*, i.e. (concr. and fig.) *down-trodden* people:— threshing.

4099. מְדָתָא **Meᵈdâthâ**, *med-aw-thaw´*; of Pers. or.; *Medatha*, the father of Haman:— Hammedatha [incl. the art.].

4100. מָה **mâh**, *maw*; or

מַה **mah**, *mah*; or

מָ **mâ**, *maw*; or

מַ **ma**, *mah*; also

מֶה **meh**, *meh*; a prim. particle; prop. interrog. *what?* (incl. *how? why? when?*); but also exclamation, *what!* (incl. *how!*), or indef. *what* (incl. *whatever*, and even rel. *that which*); often used with prefixes in various adv. or conjunc. senses:— how (long, oft, [-soever]) [no-] thing, what (end, good, purpose, thing), whereby (-fore, -in, -to, -with), (for) why.

4101. מָה **mâh** (Chald.), *maw*; corresp. to 4100:— how great (mighty), that which, what (-soever), why.

4102. מָהַהּ **mâhahh**, *maw-hah´*; appar. a denom. from 4100; prop. to *question* or *hesitate*, i.e. (by impl.) to *be reluctant*:— delay, linger, stay selves, tarry.

4103. מְהוּמָה **meᵈhûwmâh**, *meh-hoo-maw´*; from 1949; *confusion* or *uproar*:— destruction, discomfiture, trouble, tumult, vexation, vexed.

4104. מְהוּמָן **Meᵈhûwmân**, *meh-hoo-mawn´*; of Pers. or.; *Mehuman*, a eunuch of Xerxes:— Mehuman.

4105. מְהֵיטַבְאֵל **Meᵈhêyṭabʼêl**, *meh-hay-tab-ale´*; from 3190 (augmented) and 410; *bettered of God*; *Mehetabel*, the name of an Edomitish man and woman:— Mehetabeel, Mehetabel.

4106. מָהִיר **mâhîyr**, *maw-here´*; or

מָהִר **mâhir**, *maw-here´*; from 4116; *quick*; hence, *skilful*:— diligent, hasty, ready.

4107. מָהַל **mâhal**, *maw-hal´*; a prim. root; prop. to *cut down* or *reduce*, i.e. by impl. to *adulterate*:— mixed.

4108. מַהְלֵךְ **mahlêk**, *mah-lake´*; from 1980; a *walking* (plur. collect.), i.e. *access*:— place to walk.

4109. מַהֲלָךְ **mahălâk**, *mah-hal-awk´*; from 1980; a *walk*, i.e. a *passage* or a *distance*:— journey, walk.

4110. מַהֲלָל **mahălâl**, *mah-hal-awl´*; from 1984; *fame*:— praise.

4111. מַהֲלַלְאֵל **Mahălalʼêl**, *mah-hal-al-ale´*; from 4110 and 410; *praise of God*; *Mahalalel*, the name of an antediluvian patriarch and of an Isr.:— Mahalaleel.

4112. מַהֲלֻמָּה **mahălummâh**, *mah-hal-oom-maw´*; from 1986; a *blow*:— stripe, stroke.

4113. מַהֲמֹרָה **mahămôrâh**, *mah-ham-o-raw´*; from an unused root of uncert. mean.; perh. an *abyss*:— deep pit.

4114. מַהְפֵּכָה **mahpêkâh**, *mah-pay-kaw´*; from 2015; a *destruction*:— when ... overthrew, overthrow (-n).

4115. מַהְפֶּכֶת **mahpeketh**, *mah-peh´-keth*; from 2015; a *wrench*, i.e. the *stocks*:— prison, stocks.

4116. מָהַר **mâhar**, *maw-har´*; a prim. root; prop. to *be liquid* or *flow easily*, i.e. (by impl.); to *hurry* (in a good or a bad sense); often used (with another verb) adv. *promptly*:— be carried headlong, fearful, (cause to make, in, make) haste (-n, -ily), (be) hasty, (fetch, make ready) × quickly, rash, × shortly, (be so) × soon, make speed, × speedily, × straightway, × suddenly, swift.

4117. מָהַר **mâhar**, *maw-har´*; a prim. root (perh. rather the same as 4116 through the idea of *readiness* in assent); to *bargain* (for a wife), i.e. to *wed*:— endow, × surely.

4118. מַהֵר **mahêr**, *mah-hare´*; from 4116; prop. *hurrying*; hence, (adv.) *in a hurry*:— hasteth, hastily, at once, quickly, soon, speedily, suddenly.

מָהִר **mâhir.** See 4106.

4119. מֹהַר **môhar**, *mo´-har*; from 4117; a *price* (for a wife):— dowry.

4120. מְהֵרָה **meᵈhêrâh**, *meh-hay-raw´*; fem. of 4118; prop. a *hurry*; hence, (adv.) *promptly*:— hastily, quickly, shortly, soon, make (with) speed (-ily), swiftly.

4121. מַהֲרַי **Mahăray**, *mah-har-ah´-ee*; from 4116; *hasty*; *Maharai*, an Isr.:— Maharai.

4122. מַהֵר שָׁלָל חָשׁ בַּז **Mahêr Shâlâl Châsh Baz**, *mah-hare´ shaw-lawl´ khawsh baz*; from 4118 and 7998 and 2363 and 957; *hasting* (is he [the enemy] to the) *booty*, *swift* (to the) *prey*; *Maher-Shalal-Chash-Baz*; the symb. name of the son of Isaiah:— Maher-shalal-hash-baz.

4123. מַהֲתַלָּה **mahăthallâh**, *mah-hath-al-law´*; from 2048; a *delusion*:— deceit.

4124. מוֹאָב **Môwʼâb**, *mo-awb*; from a prol. form of the prep. pref. m- and 1; *from* (her [the mother's]) *father*; *Moäb*, an incestuous son of Lot; also his territory and desc.:— Moab.

4125. מוֹאָבִי **Môwʼâbîy**, *mo-aw-bee´*; fem.

מוֹאָבִיָּה **Môwʼâbîyah**, *mo-aw-bee-yaw´*; or

מוֹאָבִית **Môwâbîyth**, *mo-aw-beeth´*; patron. from 4124; a *Moäbite* or *Moäbitess*, i.e. a desc. from *Moab*:— (woman) of Moab, Moabite (-ish, -ss).

מוֹאל **môwʼl.** See 4136.

4126. מוֹבָא **môwbâ´**, *mo-baw´*; by transp. for 3996; an *entrance*:— coming.

4127. מוּג **mûwg**, *moog*; a prim. root; to *melt*, i.e. lit. (to *soften*, *flow down*, *disappear*), or fig. (to *fear*, *faint*):— consume, dissolve, (be) faint (-hearted), melt (away), make soft.

4128. מוּד **mûwd**, *mood*; a prim. root; to *shake*:— measure.

4129. מוֹדַע **môwdaʼ**, *mo-dah´*; or rather

מֹדָע **môdâ´**, *mo-daw´*; from 3045; an *acquaintance*:— kinswoman.

4130. מוֹדַעַת **môwdaʼath**, *mo-dah´-ath*; from 3045; *acquaintance*:— kindred.

4131. מוֹט **môwṭ**, *mote*; a prim. root; to *waver*; by impl. to *slip*, *shake*, *fall*:— be carried, cast, be out of course, be fallen in decay, × exceedingly, fall (-ing down), be (re-) moved, be ready, shake, slide, slip.

4132. מוֹט **môwṭ**, *mote*; from 4131; a *wavering*, i.e. *fall*; by impl. a *pole* (as shaking); hence, a *yoke* (as essentially a bent pole):— bar, be moved, staff, yoke.

4133. מוֹטָה **môwṭâh**, *mo-taw´*; fem. of 4132; a *pole*; by impl. an *ox-bow*; hence, a *yoke* (either lit. or fig.):— bands, heavy, staves, yoke.

4134. מוּךְ **mûwk**, *mook*; a prim. root; to *become thin*, i.e. (fig.) be *impoverished*:— be (waxen) poor (-er).

4135. מוּל **mûwl**, *mool*; a prim. root; to *cut short*, i.e. *curtail* (spec. the prepuce, i.e. to *circumcise*); by impl. to *blunt*; fig. to *destroy*:— circumcise (-ing), selves, cut down (in pieces), destroy, × must needs.

4136. מוּל **mûwl**, *mool*; or

מוֹל **môwl** (Deut. 1:1), *mole*; or

מוֹאל **môwʼl** (Neh. 12:38), *mole*; or

מֻל **mûl** (Num. 22:5), *mool*; from 4135; prop. *abrupt*, i.e. a *precipice*; by impl. the *front*; used only adv. (with prep. pref.) *opposite*:— (over) against, before, [fore-] front, from, [God-] ward, toward, with.

4137. מוֹלָדָה **Môwlâdâh**, *mo-law-daw´*; from 3205; *birth*; *Moladah*, a place in Pal.:— Moladah.

4138. מוֹלֶדֶת **môwledeth**, *mo-leh´-deth*; from 3205; *nativity* (plur. *birth-place*); by impl. *lineage*, *native country*; also *offspring*, *family*:— begotten, born, issue, kindred, native (-ity).

4139. מוּלָה **mûwlâh**, *moo-law´*; from 4135; *circumcision*:— circumcision.

4140. מוֹלִיד **Môwlîyd**, *mo-leed´*; from 3205; *genitor*; *Molid*, an Isr.:— Molid.

מוּם **muwm.** See 3971.

° מוֹמֻכָן **Môwmukân.** See 4462.

4141. מוּסָב **mûwçâb**, *moo-sawb´*; from 5437; a *turn*, i.e. *circuit* (of a building):— winding about.

4142. מוּסַבָּה **mûwçabbâh**, *moo-sab-baw´*; or

מֻסַבָּה **mûçabbâh**, *moo-sab-baw´*; fem. of 4141; a *reversal*, i.e. the *backside* (of a gem), *fold* (of a double-leaved door), *transmutation* (of a name):— being changed, inclosed, be set, turning.

4143. מוּסָד **mûwçâd**, *moo-sawd´*; from 3245; a *foundation*:— foundation.

4144. מוֹצָד **môwçâd**, *mo-sawd´*; from 3245; a *foundation:*— foundation.

4145. מוּצָדָה **mûwçâdâh**, *moo-saw-daw´*; fem. of 4143; a *foundation;* fig. an *appointment:*— foundation, grounded. Comp. 4328.

4146. מוֹסָדָה **môwçâdâh**, *mo-saw-daw´*; or

מֹסָדָה **môçâdâh**, *mo-saw-daw´*; fem. of 4144; a *foundation:*— foundation.

4147. מוֹסֵר **môwçêr**, *mo-sare´*; also (in plur.) fem.

מֹסֵרָה **môwçêrâh**, *mo-say-raw´*; or

מֹסְרָה **môç'râh**, *mo-ser-aw´*; from 3256; prop. *chastisement*, i.e. (by impl.) a *halter;* fig. *restraint:*— band, bond.

4148. מוּסָר **mûwçâr**, *moo-sawr´*; from 3256; prop. *chastisement;* fig. *reproof, warning* or *instruction;* also *restraint:*— bond, chastening (-ethl), chastisement, check, correction, discipline, doctrine, instruction, rebuke.

4149. מֹסְרָה **Môwçêrâh**, *mo-say-raw´*; or (plur.)

מֹסְרוֹת **Môç'rôwth**, *mo-ser-othe´* fem. of 4147; *correction* or *corrections; Moserah* or *Moseroth*, a place in the Desert:— Mosera, Moseroth.

4150. מוֹעֵד **môw'êd**, *mo-ade´*; or

מֹעֵד **mô'êd**, *mo-ade´*; or (fem.)

מוֹעָדָה **môw'âdâh** (2 Chron. 8:13), *mo-aw-daw´*; from 3259; prop. an *appointment*, i.e. a fixed *time* or season; spec. a *festival;* conventionally a *year;* by impl. an *assembly* (as convened for a def. purpose); tech. the *congregation;* by extens. the *place of meeting;* also a *signal* (as appointed beforehand):— appointed (sign, time), (place of, solemn) assembly, congregation, (set, solemn) feast, (appointed, due) season, solemn (-ity), synagogue, (set) time (appointed).

4151. מוֹעָד **môw'âd**, *mo-awd´*; from 3259; prop. an *assembly* [as in 4150]; fig. a *troop:*— appointed time.

4152. מוּעָדָה **mûw'âdâh**, *moo-aw-daw´*; from 3259; an *appointed* place, i.e. *asylum:*— appointed.

4153. מוֹעַדְיָה **Môw'adyâh**, *mo-ad-yaw´*; from 4151 and 3050; *assembly of Jah; Moädjah*, an Isr.:— Moadiah. Comp. 4573.

4154. מוּעֶדֶת **mûw'edeth**, *moo-ay´-deth;* fem. pass. part. of 4571; prop. *made to slip*, i.e. *dislocated:*— out of joint.

4155. מוּעָף **mûw'âph**, *moo-awf´*; prop. *covered*, i.e. *dark;* abstr. *obscurity*, i.e. *distress:*— dimness.

4156. מוֹעֵצָה **môw'êtsâh**, *mo-ay-tsaw´*; from 3289; a *purpose:*— counsel, device.

4157. מוּעָקָה **mûw'âqâh**, *moo-aw-kaw´*; from 5781; *pressure*, i.e. (fig.) *distress:*— affliction.

4158. מוֹפָעַת° **Môwpha'ath** (Jer. 48:21), *mo-fah´-ath;* or

מֵיפַעַת **Mêyphaath**, *may-fah´-ath;* or

מֵפַעַת **Mêphaath**, *may-fah´-ath;*

from 3313; *illuminative; Mophaath* or *Mephaath*, a place in Pal.:— Mephaath.

4159. מֹפֵת **môwphêth**, *mo-faith´;* or

מֹפֵת **môphêth**, *mo-faith´;* from 3302 in the sense of *conspicuousness;* a *miracle;* by impl. a *token* or *omen:*— miracle, sign, wonder (-ed at).

4160. מוּץ **mûwts**, *moots;* a prim. root; to *press*, i.e. (fig.) to *oppress:*— extortioner.

4161. מוֹצָא **môwtsâ'**, *mo-tsaw´;* or

מֹצָא **môtsâ'**, *mo-tsaw´;* from 3318; a *going forth*, i.e. (the act) an *egress*, or (the place) an *exit;* hence, a *source* or *product;* spec. *dawn*, the *rising* of the sun (the *East*), *exportation, utterance,* a *gate*, a *fountain*, a *mine*, a *meadow* (as producing grass):— brought out, bud, that which came out, east, going forth, goings out, that which (thing that) is gone out, outgoing, proceeded out, spring, vein, [water-] course, [springs].

4162. מוֹצָא **Môwtsâ'**, *mo-tsaw´;* the same as 4161; *Motsa*, the name of two Isr.:— Moza.

4163. מוֹצָאָה **môwtsâ'âh**, *mo-tsaw-aw´;* fem. of 4161; a *family descent;* also a *sewer* [marg.; comp. 6675]:— draught house; going forth.

4164. מוּצָק **mûwtsaq**, *moo-tsak´;* or

מוּצָק **mûwtsâq**, *moo-tsawk´;* from 3332; *narrowness;* fig. *distress:*— anguish, is straitened, straitness.

4165. מוּצָק **mûwtsâq**, *moo-tsawk´;* from 5694; prop. *fusion*, i.e. lit. a *casting* (of metal); fig. a *mass* (of clay):— casting, hardness.

4166. מוּצָקָה **mûwtsâqâh**, *moo-tsaw-kaw´;* or

מֻצָקָה **mûtsâqâh**, *moo-tsaw-kaw´;* from 3332; prop. something *poured* out, i.e. a *casting* (of metal); by impl. a *tube* (as cast):— when it was cast, pipe.

4167. מוּק **mûwq**, *mook;* a prim. root; to *jeer*, i.e. (intens.) *blaspheme:*— be corrupt.

4168. מוֹקֵד **môwqêd**, *mo-kade´;* from 3344; a *fire* or *fuel;* abstr. a *conflagration:*— burning, hearth.

4169. מוֹקְדָה° **môwq'dâh**, *mo-ked-aw´;* fem. of 4168; *fuel:*— burning.

4170. מוֹקֵשׁ **môwqêsh**, *mo-kashe´;* or

מֹקֵשׁ **môqêsh**, *mo-kashe´;* from 3369; a *noose* (for catching animals) (lit. or fig.); by impl. a *hook* (for the nose):— be ensnared, gin, (is) snare (-d), trap.

4171. מוּר **mûwr**, *moor;* a prim. root; to *alter;* by impl. to *barter*, to *dispose of:*— × at all, (ex-) change, remove.

4172. מוֹרָא **môwrâ'**, *mo-raw´;* or

מֹרָא **môrâ'**, *mo-raw´;* or

מוֹרָה **môrâh** (Psa. 9:20), *mo-raw´;* from 3372; *fear;* by impl. a *fearful thing* or *deed:*— dread, (that ought to be) fear (-ed), terribleness, terror.

4173. מוֹרַג **môwrag**, *mo-rag´;* or

מֹרַג **môrag**, *mo-rag´;* from an unused root mean. to *triturate;* a *threshing sledge:*— threshing instrument.

4174. מוֹרָד **môwrâd**, *mo-rawd´;* from 3381; a *descent;* arch. an ornamental *appendage*, perh. a *festoon:*— going down, steep place, thin work.

4175. מוֹרֶה **môwreh**, *mo-reh´;* from 3384; an *archer;* also *teacher* or *teaching;* also the *early rain* [see 3138]:— (early) rain.

4176. מוֹרֶה **Môwreh**, *mo-reh´;* or

מֹרֶה **Môreh**, *mo-reh´;* the same as 4175; *Moreh*, a Canaanite; also a hill (perh. named from him):— Moreh.

4177. מוֹרָה **môwrâh**, *mo-raw´;* from 4171 in the sense of *shearing;* a *razor:*— razor.

4178. מוֹרָט **môwrât**, *mo-rawt´;* from 3399; *obstinate*, i.e. *independent:*— peeled.

4179. מוֹרִיָּה **Môwrîyâh**, *mo-ree-yaw´;* or

מֹרִיָּה **Môrîyâh**, *mo-ree-yaw´;* from 7200 and 3050; *seen of Jah; Morijah*, a hill in Pal.:— Moriah.

4180. מוֹרָשׁ **môwrâsh**, *mo-rawsh´;* from 3423; a *possession;* fig. *delight:*— possession, thought.

4181. מוֹרָשָׁה **môwrâshâh**, *mo-raw-shaw´;* fem. of 4180; a *possession:*— heritage, inheritance, possession.

4182. מוֹרֶשֶׁת גַּת **Môwresheth Gath**, *mo-reh´-sheth gath;* from 3423 and 1661; *possession of Gath; Moresheth-Gath*, a place in Pal.:— Moresheth-gath.

4183. מוֹרַשְׁתִּי **Mowrashtîy**, *mo-rash-tee´;* patrial from 4182; a *Morashtite* or inhab.   of   Moresheth-Gath:— Morashthite.

4184. מוּשׁ **mûwsh**, *moosh;* a prim. root; to *touch:*— feel, handle.

4185. מוּשׁ **mûwsh**, *moosh;* a prim. root [perh. rather the same as 4184 through the idea of *receding* by *contact*]; to *withdraw* (both lit. and fig.), whether intr. or tran.):— cease, depart, go back, remove, take away.

4186. מוֹשָׁב **môwshâb**, *mo-shawb´;* or

מֹשָׁב **môshâb**, *mo-shawb´;* from 3427; a *seat;* fig. a *site;* abstr. a *session;* by extens. an *abode* (the place or the time); by impl. *population:*— assembly, dwell in, dwelling (-place), wherein (that) dwelt (in), inhabited place, seat, sitting, situation, sojourning.

4187. מוּשִׁי **Mûwshiy**, *moo-shee´;* or

מֻשִׁי **Mushshiy**, *mush-shee´;* from 4184; *sensitive; Mushi*, a Levite:— Mushi.

4188. מוּשִׁי **Mûwshiy**, *moo-shee´;* patron. from 4187; a *Mushite* (collect.) or desc. of Mushi:— Mushites.

4189. מוֹשְׁכָה **môwsh'kâh**, *mo-shek-aw´;* act. part. fem. of 4900; something *drawing*, i.e. (fig.) a *cord:*— band.

4190. מוֹשָׁעָה **môwshâ'âh**, *mo-shaw-aw´;* from 3467; *deliverance:*— salvation.

4191. מוּת **mûwth**, *mooth;* a prim. root; to *die* (lit. or fig.); caus. to *kill:*— × at all, × crying, (be) dead (body, man, one), (put to, worthy of) death, destroy (-er), (cause to, be like to, must) die, kill, necro [-mancer], × must needs, slay, × surely, × very suddenly, × in [no] wise.

4192. מוּת **Mûwth** (Psa. 48:14), *mooth;* or

מות לבן **Mûwth lab-bên**, *mooth lab-bane´*; from 4191 and 1121 with the prep. and art. interposed; "*To die for the son*", prob. the title of a popular song:— death, Muthlabben.

4193. מוֹה **môwth** (Chald.), *mohth;* corresp. to 4194; *death:*— death.

4194. מָוֶת **mâveth**, *maw´-veth;* from 4191; *death* (nat. or violent); concr. the *dead*, their place or state (*hades*); fig. *pestilence, ruin:*— (be) dead (l-lyl), death, die (-d).

מות לבן **Mûwth lab-bên**. See 4192.

4195. מוֹתָר **môwthar**, *mo-thar´;* from 3498; lit. *gain;* fig. *superiority:*— plenteousness, preeminence, profit.

4196. מוֹבֵּחַ **mizbêach**, *miz-bay´-akh;* from 2076; an *altar:*— altar.

4197. מֶזֶג **mezeg**, *meh´-zeg;* from an unused root mean. to *mingle* (water with wine); *tempered* wine:— liquor.

4198. מָזֶה **mâzeh**, *maw-zeh´;* from an unused root mean. to *suck* out; *exhausted:*— burnt.

4199. מִזָּה **Mizzâh**, *miz-zaw´;* prob. from an unused root mean. to *faint* with fear; *terror; Mizzah*, an Edomite:— Mizzah.

4200. מֶזֶו **mezev**, *meh´-zev;* prob. from an unused root mean. to *gather* in; a *granary:*— garner.

4201. מְזוּזָה **mᵉzûwzâh**, *mez-oo-zaw´;* or
מְזֻזָה **mᵉzûzâh**, *mez-oo-zaw´;* from the same as 2123; a *door-post* (as *prominent*):— (door, side) post.

4202. מָזוֹן **mâzôwn**, *maw-zone´;* from 2109; *food:*— meat, victual.

4203. מָזוֹן **mâzôwn** (Chald.), *maw-zone´;* corresp. to 4202:— meat.

4204. מָזוֹר **mâzôwr**, *maw-zore´;* from 2114 in the sense of *turning aside* from truth; *treachery*, i.e. a *plot:*— wound.

4205. מָזוֹר **mâzôwr**, *maw-zore´;* or
מָזוֹר **mâzôr**, *maw-zore´;* from 2115 in the sense of *binding* up; a *bandage*, i.e. remedy; hence, a *sore* (as needing a compress):— bound up, wound.

מְזֻזָה **mᵉzûzâh**. See 4201.

4206. מָזִיחַ **mâzîyach**, *maw-zee´-akh;* or
מֵזַח **mêzach**, *may-zakh´;* from 2118; a *belt* (as movable):— girdle, strength.

4207. מַזְלֵג **mazlêg**, *maz-layg´;* or (fem.)
מִזְלָגָה **mizlâgâh**, *miz-law-gaw´;* from an unused root mean. to *draw* up; a *fork:*— fleshhook.

4208. מַזָּלָה **mazzâlâh**, *maz-zaw-law´;* appar. from 5140 in the sense of *raining;* a *constellation*, i.e. Zodiacal sign (perh. as affecting the weather):— planet. Comp. 4216.

4209. מְזִמָּה **mᵉzimmâh**, *mez-im-maw´;* from 2161; a *plan*, usually evil (*machination*), sometimes good (*sagacity*):— (wicked) device, discretion, intent, witty invention, lewdness, mischievous (device), thought, wickedly.

4210. מִזְמוֹר **mizmôwr**, *miz-more´;* from 2167; prop. instrumental *music;* by impl. a *poem* set to notes:— psalm.

4211. מַזְמֵרָה **mazmêrâh**, *maz-may-*

raw´; from 2168; a *pruning-knife:*— pruning-hook.

4212. מְזַמְּרָה **mᵉzammᵉrâh**, *mez-am-mer-aw´;* from 2168; a *tweezer* (only in the plur.):— snuffers.

4213. מִזְעָר **miz´âr**, *miz-awr´;* from the same as 2191; *fewness;* by impl. as superl. *diminutiveness:*— few, × very.

מָזֹר **mâzôr**. See 4205.

4214. מִזְרֶה **mizreh**, *miz-reh´;* from 2219; a winnowing *shovel* (as scattering the chaff):— fan.

4215. מְזָרֶה **mᵉzâreh**, *mez-aw-reh´;* appar. from 2219; prop. a *scatterer*, i.e. the north *wind* (as dispersing clouds; only in plur.):— north.

4216. מַזָּרָה **Mazzârâh**, *maz-zaw-raw´;* appar. from 5144 in the sense of *distinction;* some noted *constellation* (only in the plur.), perh. collect. the *zodiac:*— Mazzoroth. Comp. 4208.

4217. מִזְרָח **mizrâch**, *miz-rawkh´;* from 2224; *sunrise*, i.e. the *east:*— east (side, -ward), (sun-) rising (of the sun).

4218. מִזְרָע **mizrâ'**, *miz-raw´;* from 2232; a planted *field:*— thing sown.

4219. מִזְרָק **mîzrâq**, *miz-rawk´;* from 2236; a *bowl* (as if for sprinkling):— bason, bowl.

4220. מֵחַ **mêach**, *may´-akh;* from 4229 in the sense of *greasing; fat;* fig. *rich:*— fatling (one).

4221. מֹחַ **môach**, *mo´-akh;* from the same as 4220; *fat*, i.e. marrow:— marrow.

4222. מָחָא **mâchâ'**, *maw-khaw´;* a prim. root; to *rub* or *strike* the hands together (in exultation):— clap.

4223. מְחָא **mᵉchâ'** (Chald.), *mekh-aw´;* corresp. to 4222; to *strike* in pieces; also to *arrest;* spec. to *impale:*— hang, smite, stay.

4224. מַחֲבֵא **machăbê'**, *makh-ab-ay´;* or
מַחֲבֹא **machăbô'**, *makh-ab-o´;* from 2244; a *refuge:*— hiding (lurking) place.

4225. מַחְבֶּרֶה **machbereth**, *makh-beh´-reth;* from 2266; a *junction*, i.e. seam or sewed piece:— coupling.

4226. מְחַבְּרָה **mᵉchabbᵉrâh**, *mekh-ab-ber-aw´;* from 2266; a *joiner*, i.e. brace or cramp:— coupling, joining.

4227. מַחֲבַת **machăbath**, *makh-ab-ath´;* from the same as 2281; a *pan* for baking in:— pan.

4228. מַחֲגֹרֶת **machăgôreth**, *makh-ag-o´-reth;* from 2296; a *girdle:*— girding.

4229. מָחָה **mâchâh**, *maw-khaw´;* a prim. root; prop. to *stroke* or *rub;* by impl. to *erase;* also to *smooth* (as if with oil), i.e. *grease* or make fat; also to *touch*, i.e. reach to:— abolish, blot out, destroy, full of marrow, put out, reach unto, × utterly, wipe (away, out).

4230. מְחוּגָה **mᵉchûwgâh**, *mekk-oo-gaw´;* from 2328; an instrument for marking a circle, i.e. *compasses:*— compass.

4231. מָחוֹז **mâchôwz**, *maw-khoze´;* from an unused root mean. to *enclose;* a *harbor* (as shut in by the shore):— haven.

4232. מְחוּיָאֵל **Mᵉchûwyâ'êl**, *mekh-oo-yaw-ale´;* or
מְחִיָּיאֵל **Mᵉchîyyâ'êl**, *mekh-ee-yaw-ale´;* from 4229 and 410; *smitten of God; Mechujael* or *Mechijael*, an antediluvian patriarch:— Mehujael.

4233. מַחֲוִים **Machăvîym**, *makh-av-eem´;* appar. a patrial, but from an unknown place (in the plur. only for a sing.); a *Machavite* or inhab. of some place named Machaveh:— Mahavite.

4234. מָחוֹל **mâchôwl**, *maw-khole´;* from 2342; a (round) *dance:*— dance (-cing).

4235. מָחוֹל **Mâchôwl**, *maw-khole´;* the same as 4234; *dancing; Machol*, an Isr.:— Mahol.

מְחוֹלָה **mᵉchôwlâh**. See 65, 4246.

4236. מַחֲזֶה **machăzeh**, *makh-az-eh´;* from 2372; a *vision:*— vision.

4237. מֶחֱזָה **mechĕzâh**, *mekh-ez-aw´;* from 2372; a *window:*— light.

4238. מַחֲזִיאוֹת **Machăzîy'ôwth**, *makh-az-ee-oth´;* fem. plur. from 2372; *visions; Machazioth*, an Isr.:— Mahazioth.

4239. מְחִי **mᵉchîy**, *mekh-ee´;* from 4229; a *stroke*, i.e. battering-*ram:*— engines.

4240. מְחִידָא **Mᵉchîydâ'**, *mek-ee-daw´;* from 2330; *junction; Mechida*, one of the Nethinim:— Mehida.

4241. מִחְיָה **michyâh**, *mikh-yaw´;* from 2421; *preservation of life;* hence, *sustenance;* also the live flesh, i.e. the *quick:*— preserve life, quick, recover selves, reviving, sustenance, victuals.

מְחִיָּיאֵל **Mᵉchîyyâ'êl**. See 4232.

4242. מְחִיר **mᵉchîyr**, *mekk-eer´;* from an unused root mean. to *buy; price, payment, wages:*— gain, hire, price, sold, worth.

4243. מְחִיר **Mᵉchîyr**, *mekh-eer´;* the same as 4242; *price; Mechir*, an Isr.:— Mehir.

4244. מַחְלָה **Machlâh**, *makh-law´;* from 2470; *sickness; Machlah*, the name appar. of two Israelitesses:— Mahlah.

4245. מַחֲלֶה **machăleh**, *makh-al-eh´;* or (fem.)
מַחֲלָה **machălâh**, *makk-al-aw´;* from 2470; *sickness:*— disease, infirmity, sickness.

4246. מְחוֹלָה **mᵉchôwlâh**, *mek-o-law´;* fem. of 4284; a *dance:*— company, dances (-cing).

4247. מְחִלָּה **mᵉchillâh**, *mekh-il-law´;* from 2490; a *cavern* (as if excavated):— cave.

4248. מַחְלוֹן **Machlôwn**, *makh-lone´;* from 2470; *sick; Machlon*, an Isr.:— Mahlon.

4249. מַחְלִי **Machliy**, *makh-lee´;* from 2470; *sick; Machli*, the name of two Isr.:— Mahli.

4250. מַחְלִי **Machliy**, *makh-lee´;* patron. from 4249; a *Machlite* or (collect.) desc. of Machli:— Mahlites.

4251. מַחְלֻי **machlûy**, *makh-loo´-ee;* from 2470; a *disease:*— disease.

4252. מַחֲלָף **machălâph**, *makh-al-awf´;* from 2498; a (sacrificial) *knife* (as *gliding* through the flesh):— knife.

4253. מַחְלָפָה **machlâphâh**, *makh-law-*

faw´; from 2498; a *ringlet* of hair (as *gliding* over each other):— lock.

4254. מחלצה **machălâtsâh**, *makh-al-aw-tsaw´*; from 2502; a *mantle* (as easily *drawn off*):— changeable suit of apparel, change of raiment.

4255. מחלקה **machlᵉqâh** (Chald.), *makh-lek-aw´*; corresp. to 4256; a *section* (of the Levites):— course.

4256. מחלקה **machălôqeth**, *makh-al-o´-keth*; from 2505; a *section* (of Levites, people or soldiers):— company, course, division, portion. See also 5555.

4257. מחלת **Machălath**, *makh-al-ath´*; from 2470; *sickness*; *Machalath*, prob. the title (initial word) of a popular song:— Mahalath.

4258. מחלת **Machălath**, *makh-al-ath´*; the same as 4257; *sickness*; *Machalath*, the name of an Ishmaelitess and of an Israelitess:— Mahalath.

4259. מחלתי **Mᵉchôlâthiy**, *mekh-o-law-thee´*; patrial from 65; a *Mecholathite* or inhab. of Abel-Mecholah:— Mecholathite.

4260. מחמאה **machămâ'âh**, *makh-am-aw-aw´*; a denom. from 2529; something *buttery* (i.e. unctuous and pleasant), as (fig.) *flattery*:— × than butter.

4261. מחמד **machmâd**, *makh-mawd´*; from 2530; *delightful*; hence, a *delight*, i.e. object of affection or desire:— beloved, desire, goodly, lovely, pleasant (thing).

4262. מחמד **machmûd**, *makh-mood´*; or

מחמוד **machmûwd**, *makh-mood´*; from 2530; *desired*; hence, a *valuable*:— pleasant thing.

4263. מחמל **machmâl**, *makh-mawl´*; from 2550; prop. *sympathy*; (by paronomasia with 4261) *delight*:— pitieth.

4264. מחנה **machăneh**, *makh-an-eh´*; from 2583; an *encampment* (of travellers or troops); hence, an *army*, whether lit. (of soldiers) or fig. (of dancers, angels, cattle, locusts, stars; or even the sacred courts):— army, band, battle, camp, company, drove, host, tents.

4265. מחנה־דן **Machănêh-Dân**, *makh-an-ay´-dawn*; from 4264 and 1835; *camp of Dan*; *Machaneh-Dan*, a place in Pal.:— Mahaneh-dan.

4266. מחנים **Machănayim**, *makh-an-ah´-yim*; dual of 4264; *double camp*; *Machanajim*, a place in Pal.:— Mahanaim.

4267. מחנק **machănaq**, *makh-an-ak´*; from 2614; *choking*:— strangling.

4268. מחסה **machăçeh**, *makh-as-eh´*; or

מחסה **machçeh**, *makh-seh´*; from 2620; a *shelter* (lit. or fig.):— hope, (place of) refuge, shelter, trust.

4269. מחסום **machçôwm**, *makh-sohm´*; from 2629; a *muzzle*:— bridle.

4270. מחסור **machçôwr**, *makh-sore´*; or

מחסר **machçôr**, *makh-sore´*; from 2637; *deficiency*; hence, *impoverishment*:— lack, need, penury, poor, poverty, want.

4271. מחסיה **Machçêyâh**, *makh-say-yaw´*; from 4268 and 3050; *refuge of* (i.e.

in) *Jah*; *Machsejah*, an Isr.:— Maaseiah.

4272. מחץ **mâchats**, *maw-khats´*; a prim. root; to *dash* asunder; by impl. to *crush*, *smash* or violently *plunge*; fig. to *subdue* or *destroy*:— dip, pierce (through), smite (through), strike through, wound.

4273. מחץ **machats**, *makh´-ats*; from 4272; a *contusion*:— stroke.

4274. מחצב **machtsêb**, *makh-tsabe´*; from 2672; prop. a *hewing*; concr. a *quarry*:— hewed (-n).

4275. מחצה **mechĕtsâh**, *mekh-ets-aw´*; from 2673; a *halving*:— half.

4276. מחצית **machătsiyth**, *makh-ats-eeth´*; from 2673; a *halving* or the *middle*:— half (so much), mid (-day).

4277. מחק **mâchaq**, *maw-khak´*; a prim. root; to *crush*:— smite off.

4278. מחקר **mechqâr**, *mekh-kawr´*; from 2713; prop. *scrutinized*, i.e. (by impl.) a *recess*:— deep place.

4279. מחר **mâchar**, *maw-khar´*; prob. from 309; prop. *deferred*, i.e. the *morrow*; usually (adv.) *tomorrow*; indef. *hereafter*:— time to come, tomorrow.

4280. מחראה **machărâ'âh**, *makh-ar-aw-aw´*; from the same as 2716; a *sink*:— draught house.

4281. מחרשה **machărêshâh**, *makh-ar-ay-shaw´*; from 2790; prob. a *pick-axe*:— mattock.

4282. מחרשה **machăresheth**, *makh-ar-eh´-sheth*; from 2790; prob. a *hoe*:— share.

4283. מחרת **mochŏrâth**, *mokh-or-awth´*; or

מחרתם **mochŏrâthâm** (1 Sam. 30:17), *mokh-or-aw-thawm´*; fem. from the same as 4279; the *morrow* or (adv.) *tomorrow*:— morrow, next day.

4284. מחשבה **machăshâbâh**, *makh-ash-aw-baw´*; or

מחשבת **machăshebeth**, *makh-ash-eh´-beth*; from 2803; a *contrivance*, i.e. (concr.) a *texture*, *machine*, or (abstr.) *intention*, *plan* (whether bad, a *plot*; or good, *advice*):— cunning (work), curious work, device (-sed), imagination, invented, means, purpose, thought.

4285. מחשך **machshâk**, *makh-shawk´*; from 2821; *darkness*; concr. a *dark place*:— dark (-ness, place).

4286. מחשף **machsôph**, *makh-sofe´*; from 2834; a *peeling*:— made appear.

4287. מחת **Machath**, *makh´-ath*; prob. from 4229; *erasure*; *Machath*, the name of two Isr.:— Mahath.

4288. מחתה **mᵉchittâh**, *mekh-it-taw´*; from 2846; prop. a *dissolution*; concr. a *ruin*, or (abstr.) *consternation*:— destruction, dismaying, ruin, terror.

4289. מחתה **machtâh**, *makh-taw´*; the same as 4288 in the sense of *removal*; a *pan* for live coals:— censer, firepan, snuffdish.

4290. מחתרת **machtereth**, *makh-teh´-reth*; from 2864; a *burglary*; fig. *unexpected examination*:— breaking up, secret search.

4291. מטא **mᵉtâ'** (Chald.), *met-aw´*; or

מטה **mᵉtâh** (Chald.) *met-aw´*; appar. corresp. to 4672 in the intr. sense of being found *present*; to *arrive*, *extend* or *happen*:— come, reach.

4292. מטאטא **mat'ătê'**, *mat-at-ay´*; appar. a denom. from 2916; a *broom* (as removing *dirt* [comp. Engl. "to dust"], i.e. remove dust]):— besom.

4293. מטבח **matbêach**, *mat-bay´-akh*; from 2873; *slaughter*:— slaughter.

4294. מטה **matteh**, *mat-teh´*; or (fem.)

מטה **mattâh**, *mat-taw´*; from 5186; a *branch* (as *extending*); fig. a *tribe*; also a *rod*, whether for chastising (fig. *correction*), ruling (a *sceptre*), throwing (a *lance*), or walking (a *staff*; fig. a *support* of life, e.g. bread):— rod, staff, tribe.

4295. מטה **mattâh**, *mat´-taw*; from 5786 with directive enclitic appended; *downward*, *below* or *beneath*; often adv. with or without prefixes:— beneath, down (-ward), less, very low, under (-neath).

4296. מטה **mittâh**, *mit-taw´*; from 5186; a *bed* (as *extended*) for sleeping or eating; by anal. a *sofa*, *litter* or *bier*:— bed (-chamber), bier.

4297. מטה **mutteh**, *moot-teh´*; from 5186; a *stretching*, i.e. *distortion* (fig. *iniquity*):— perverseness.

4298. מטה **muttâh**, *moot-taw´*; from 5186; *expansion*:— stretching out.

4299. מטוה **matveh**, *mat-veh´*; from 2901; something *spun*:— spun.

4300. מטיל **mᵉtiyl**, *met-eel´*; from 2904 in the sense of *hammering* out; an iron *bar* (as *forged*):— bar.

4301. מטמון **matmôwn**, *mat-mone´*; or

מטמן **matmôn**, *mat-mone´*; or

מטמן **matmûn**, *mat-moon´*; from 2934; a *secret* storehouse; hence, a *secreted* valuable (buried); gen. *money*:— hidden riches, (hid) treasure (-s).

4302. מטע **mattâ'**, *mat-taw´*; from 5193; something *planted*, i.e. the place (a *garden* or vineyard), or the thing (a *plant*, fig. of men); by impl. the act, *planting*:— plant (-ation, -ing).

4303. מטעם **mat'am**, *mat-am´*; or (fem.)

מטעמה **mat'ammâh**, *mat-am-maw´*; from 2938; a *delicacy*:— dainty (meat), savoury meat.

4304. מטפחת **mitpachath**, *mit-pakh´-ath*; from 2946; a wide *cloak* (for a woman):— vail, wimple.

4305. מטר **mâtar**, *maw-tar´*; a prim. root; to *rain*:— (cause to) rain (upon).

4306. מטר **mâtâr**, *maw-tawr´*; from 4305; *rain*:— rain.

4307. מטרא **mattârâ'**, *mat-taw-raw´*; or

מטרה **mattârâh**, *mat-taw-raw´*; from 5201; a *jail* (as a *guard*-house); also an *aim* (as being closely *watched*):— mark, prison.

4308. מטרד **Matrêd**, *mat-rade´*; from 2956; *propulsive*; *Matred*, an Edomitess:— Matred.

4309. מטרי **Matriy**, *mat-ree´*; from 4305; *rainy*; *Matri*, an Isr.:— Matri.

4310. מי **mîy**, *me*; an interrog. pron. of

Hebrew

persons, as 4100 is of things, *who?* (occasionally, by a peculiar idiom, of things); also (indef.) *whoever;* often used in oblique constr. with pref. or suff.:— *any* (man), × he, × him, + O that! what, which, who (-m, -se, soever), + would to God.

4311. מֵידְבָא **Mêydebâ'**, *may-deb-aw';* from 4325 and 1679; *water of quiet; Medeba,* a place in Pal.:— Medeba.

4312. מֵידָד **Mêydâd**, *may-dawd';* from 3032 in the sense of *loving; affectionate; Medad,* an Isr.:— Medad.

4313. מֵי הַיַּרְקוֹן **Mêy hay-Yarqôwn**, *may hah'-ee-yar-kone';* from 4325 and 3420 with the art. interposed; *water of the yellowness; Me-haj-Jarkon,* a place in Pal.:— Me-jarkon.

4314. מֵי זָהָב **Mêy Zâhâb**, *may zaw-hawb';* from 4325 and 2091; *water of gold; Me-Zahab,* an Edomite:— Mezahab.

4315. מֵיטָב **mêytâb**, *may-tawb';* from 3190; the *best* part:— best.

4316. מִיכָא **Mîykâ'**, *mee-kaw';* a var. for 4318; *Mica,* the name of two Isr.:— Micha.

4317. מִיכָאֵל **Mîykâ'êl**, *me-kaw-ale';* from 4310 and (the pref. der.) 3588 and 410; *who* (is) *like God?; Mikael,* the name of an archangel and of nine Isr.:— Michael.

4318. מִיכָה **Mîykâh**, *mee-kaw';* an abbrev. of 4320; *Micah,* the name of seven Isr.:— Micah, Micaiah, Michah.

4319. מִיכָהוּ **Mîykâhûw**, *me-kaw'-hoo;* a contr. for 4321; *Mikehu,* an Isr. prophet:— Micaiah (2 Chron. 18:8).

4320. מִיכָיָה **Mîykâyâh**, *me-kaw-yaw';* from 4310 and (the pref. der. from) 3588 and 3050; *who* (is) *like Jah?; Micajah,* the name of two Isr.:— Micah, Michaiah. Comp. 4318.

4321. מִיכָיְהוּ **Mîykâyehûw**, *me-kaw-yeh-hoo';* or

מְכָיְהוּ **Mîkâyehûw** (Jer. 36:11), *me-kaw-yeh-hoo';* abbrev. for 4322; *Mikajah,* the name of three Isr.:— Micah, Micaiah, Michaiah.

4322. מִיכָיָהוּ **Mîykâyâhûw**, *me-kaw-yaw'-hoo;* for 4320; *Mikajah,* the name of an Isr. and an Israelitess:— Michaiah.

4323. מִיכָל **mîykâl**, *me-kawl';* from 3201; prop. a *container,* i.e. a *streamlet:*— brook.

4324. מִיכָל **Mîykâl**, *me-kawl';* appar. the same as 4323; *rivulet; Mikal,* Saul's daughter:— Michal.

4325. מַיִם **mayim**, *mah'-yim;* dual of a prim. noun (but used in a sing. sense); *water;* fig. *juice;* by euphem. *urine, semen:*— + piss, wasting, water (-ing, l-course, -flood, -springl).

4326. מִיָּמִן **Mîyâmin**, *me-yaw-meem';* a form for 4509; *Mijamin,* the name of three Isr.:— Miamin, Mijamin.

4327. מִין **mîyn**, *meen;* from an unused root mean. to *portion* out; a *sort,* i.e. *species:*— kind. Comp. 4480.

4328. מְיֻסָּדָה **meyuçẓâdâh**, *meh-yoos-saw-daw';* prop. fem. pass. part. of

3245; something *founded,* i.e. a *foundation:*— foundation.

4329. מֵיצַך **mêyçâk**, *may-sawk';* from 5526; a *portico* (as *covered*):— covert.

מֵיפַעַת **Mêypha'ath**. See 4158.

4330. מִיץ **mîyts**, *meets;* from 4160; *pressure:*— churning, forcing, wringing.

4331. מֵישָׁא **Mêyshâ'**, *may-shaw';* from 4185; *departure; Mesha,* a place in Arabia; also an Isr.:— Mesha.

4332. מִישָׁאֵל **Mîyshâ'êl**, *mee-shaw-ale';* from 4310 and 410 with the abbrev. insep. rel. Isee 8341 interposed; *who* (is) *what God* (is)?; *Mishaël,* the name of three Isr.:— Mishael.

4333. מִישָׁאֵל **Mîyshâ'êl** (Chald.), *mee-shaw-ale';* corresp. to 4332; *Mishaël,* an Isr.:— Mishael.

4334. מִישׁוֹר **mîyshôwr**, *mee-shore';* or

מִישֹׁר **mîyshôr**, *mee-shore';* from 3474; a *level,* i.e. a *plain* (often used Iwith the art. pref.l as a prop. name of certain districts); fig. *concord;* also *straightness,* i.e. (fig.) *justice* (sometimes adv. *justly*):— equity, even place, plain, right (-eously), (made) straight, uprightness.

4335. מֵישַׁך **Mêyshak**, *may-shak';* borrowed from 4336; *Meshak,* an Isr.:— Meshak.

4336. מֵישַׁך **Mêyshak** (Chald.), *may-shak';* of for. or. and doubtful signif.; *Meshak,* the Bab. name of 4333:— Meshak.

4337. מֵישָׁע **Mêyshâ'**, *may-shah';* from 3467; *safety; Mesha,* an Isr.:— Mesha.

4338. מֵישַׁע **Mêysha'**, *may-shaw';* a var. for 4337; *safety; Mesha,* a Moabite:— Mesha.

4339. מֵישָׁר **mêyshâr**, *may-shawr';* from 3474; *evenness,* i.e. (fig.) *prosperity* or *concord;* also *straightness,* i.e. (fig.) *rectitude* (only in plur. with sing. sense; often adv.):— agreement, aright, that are equal, equity, (things that are) right (-eously, things), sweetly, upright (-ly, -ness).

4340. מֵיתָר **mêythâr**, *may-thar';* from 3498; a *cord* (of a tent) Icomp. 3499I or the *string* (of a bow):— cord, string.

4341. מַכְאֹב **mak'ôb**, *mak-obe';* sometimes

מַכְאוֹב **mak'ôwb**, *mak-obe';* also (fem. Isa. 53:3)

מַכְאֹבָה **mak'ôbâh**, *mak-o-baw';* from 3510; *anguish* or (fig.) *affliction:*— grief, pain, sorrow.

4342. מַכְבִּיר **makbîyr**, *mak-beer';* tran. part. of 3527; *plenty:*— abundance.

4343. מַכְבְּנָא **Makbênâ'**, *mak-bay-naw';* from the same as 3522; *knoll; Macbena,* a place in Pal. settled by him:— Machbenah.

4344. מַכְבַּנַּי **Makbannay**, *mak-ban-nah'-ee;* patrial from 4343; a *Macbannite* or native of Macbena:— Machbanai.

4345. מַכְבֵּר **makbêr**, *mak-bare';* from 3527 in the sense of *covering* Icomp. 3531I; a *grate:*— grate.

4346. מַכְבָּר **makbâr**, *mak-bawr';* from

3527 in the sense of *covering;* a *cloth* (as *netted* Icomp. 4345I):— thick cloth.

4347. מַכָּה **makkâh**, *mak-kaw';* or (masc.)

מַכֶּה **makkeh**, *mak-keh';* (plur. only) from 5221; a *blow* (in 2 Chron. 2:10, of the flail); by impl. a *wound;* fig. *carnage,* also *pestilence:*— beaten, blow, plague, slaughter, smote, × sore, stripe, stroke, wound (l-edl).

4348. מִכְוָה **mikvâh**, *mik-vaw';* from 3554; a *burn:*— that burneth, burning.

4349. מָכוֹן **mâkôwn**, *maw-kone';* from 3559; prop. a *fixture,* i.e. a *basis;* gen. a *place,* espec. as an *abode:*— foundation, habitation, (dwelling-, settled) place.

4350. מְכוֹנָה **mekôwnâh**, *mek-o-naw';* or

מְכֹנָה **mekônâh**, *mek-o-naw';* fem. of 4349; a *pedestal,* also a *spot:*— base.

4351. מְכוּרָה **mekûwrâh**, *mek-oo-raw';* or

מְכֹרָה **mekôrâh**, *mek-o-raw';* from the same as 3564 in the sense of *digging; origin* (as if a mine):— birth, habitation, nativity.

4352. מָכִי **Mâkîy**, *maw-kee';* prob. from 4134; *pining; Maki,* an Isr.:— Machi.

4353. מָכִיר **Mâkiyr**, *maw-keer';* from 4376; *salesman; Makir,* an Isr.:— Machir.

4354. מָכִירִי **Mâkîyrîy**, *maw-kee-ree';* patron. from 4353; a *Makirite* or descend. of Makir:— of Machir.

4355. מָכַך **mâkak**, *maw-kak';* a prim. root; to *tumble* (in ruins); fig. to *perish:*— be brought low, decay.

4356. מִכְלָאָה **miklâ'âh**, *mik-law-aw';* or

מִכְלָה **miklâh**, *mik-law';* from 3607; a *pen* (for flocks):— Isheep-I fold. Comp. 4357.

4357. מִכְלָה **miklâh**, *mik-law';* from 3615; *completion* (in plur. concr. adv. *wholly*):— perfect. Comp. 4356.

4358. מִכְלֹל **miklôwl**, *mik-lole';* from 3634; *perfection* (i.e. concr. adv. *splendidly*):— most gorgeously, all sorts.

4359. מִכְלָל **miklâl**, *mik-lawl';* from 3634; *perfection* (of beauty):— perfection.

4360. מִכְלֻל **miklul**, *mik-lool';* from 3634; something *perfect,* i.e. a splendid *garment:*— all sorts.

4361. מַכֹּלֶת **makkôleth**, *mak-ko'-leth;* from 398; *nourishment:*— food.

4362. מִכְמָן **mikmân**, *mik-man';* from the same as 3646 in the sense of *hiding; treasure* (as *hidden*):— treasure.

4363. מִכְמָס **Mikmâç** (Ezra 2:27; Neh. 7:31), *mik-maws';* or

מִכְמָשׁ **Mikmâsh**, *mik-mawsh';* or

מִכְמַשׁ **Mikmash** (Neh. 11:31), *mik-mash';* from 3647; *hidden; Mikmas* or *Mikmash,* a place in Pal.:— Mikmas, Mikmash.

4364. מַכְמָר **makmâr**, *mak-mawr';* or

מִכְמֹר **mikmôr**, *mik-more';* from 3648 in the sense of *blackening* by heat; a (hunter's) *net* (as *dark* from concealment):— net.

4365. מִכְמֶרֶת **mikmereth,** *mik-meh´-reth;* or

מִכְמֹרֶת **mikmôreth,** *mik-mo´-reth;* fem. of 4364; a (fisher's) *net:*— drag, net.

מִכְמָשׁ **Mikmâsh.** See 4363.

4366. מִכְמְתָת **Mikmᵉthâth,** *mik-meth-awth´;* appar. from an unused root mean. to *hide; concealment; Mikmethath,* a place in Pal.:— Michmethah.

4367. מַכְנַדְבַי **Maknadbay,** *mak-nad-bah´-ee;* from 4100 and 5068 with a particle interposed; *what* (is) *like* (a) *liberal* (man)?; *Maknadbai,* an Isr.:— Machnadebai.

מְכוֹנָה **mᵉkônâh.** See 4350.

4368. מְכֹנָה **Mᵉkônâh,** *mek-o-naw´;* the same as 4350; a *base; Mekonah,* a place in Pal.:— Mekonah.

4369. מְכֻנָה **mᵉkûnâh,** *mek-oo-naw´;* the same as 4350; a *spot:*— base.

4370. מִכְנָס **miknâç,** *mik-nawce´;* from 3647 in the sense of *hiding;* (only in dual) *drawers* (from *concealing* the private parts):— breeches.

4371. מֶכֶס **mekeç,** *meh´-kes;* prob. from an unused root mean. to *enumerate;* an *assessment* (as based upon a *census*):— tribute.

4372. מִכְסֶה **mikçeh,** *mik-seh´;* from 3680; a *covering,* i.e. weather-*boarding:*— covering.

4373. מִכְסָה **mikçâh,** *mik-saw´;* fem. of 4371; an *enumeration;* by impl. a *valuation:*— number, worth.

4374. מִכְסֶה **mᵉkaçceh,** *mek-as-seh´;* from 3680; a *covering,* i.e. *garment;* spec. a *coverlet* (for a bed), an *awning* (from the sun); also the *omentum* (as covering the intestines):— clothing, to cover, that which covereth.

4375. מַכְפֵּלָה **Makpêlâh,** *mak-pay-law´;* from 3717; a *fold; Makpelah,* a place in Pal.:— Machpelah.

4376. מָכַר **mâkar,** *maw-kar´;* a prim. root; to *sell,* lit. (as merchandise, a daughter in marriage, into slavery) or fig. (to *surrender*):— × at all, sell (away, -er, self).

4377. מֶכֶר **meker,** *meh´-ker;* from 4376; *merchandise;* also *value:*— pay, price, ware.

4378. מַכָּר **makkâr,** *mak-kawr´;* from 5234; an *acquaintance:*— acquaintance.

4379. מִכְרֶה **mikreh,** *mik-reh´;* from 3738; a *pit* (for salt):— [salt-] pit.

4380. מְכֵרָה **mᵉkêrâh,** *mek-ay-raw´;* prob. from the same as 3564 in the sense of *stabbing;* a *sword:*— habitation.

מְכֹרָה **mᵉkôrâh.** See 4351.

4381. מִכְרִי **Mikrîy,** *mik-ree´;* from 4376; *salesman; Mikri,* an Isr.:— Michri.

4382. מְכֵרָתִי **Mᵉkêrâthîy,** *mek-ay-raw-thee´;* patrial from an unused name (the same as 4380) of a place in Pal.; a *Mekerathite,* or inhab. of Mekerah:— Mecherathite.

4383. מִכְשׁוֹל **mikshôwl,** *mik-shole´;* or

מִכְשֹׁל **mikshôl,** *mik-shole´;* masc. from 3782; a *stumbling-block,* lit. or fig. (*obstacle, enticement* [spec. an idol], *scruple*):— caused to fall, offence, × [no-] thing offered, ruin, stumblingblock.

4384. מַכְשֵׁלָה **makshêlâh,** *mak-shay-law´;* fem. from 3782; a *stumbling-block,* but only fig. (*fall, enticement* [idol]):— ruin, stumbling-block.

4385. מִכְתָּב **miktâb,** *mik-tawb´;* from 3789; a thing *written,* the *characters,* or a *document* (letter, copy, edict, poem):— writing.

4386. מְכִתָּה **mᵉkittâh,** *mek-it-taw´;* from 3807; a *fracture:*— bursting.

4387. מִכְתָּם **Miktâm,** *mik-tawm´;* from 3799; an *engraving,* i.e. (techn.) a *poem:*— Michtam.

4388. מַכְתֵּשׁ **maktêsh,** *mak-taysh´;* from 3806; a *mortar;* by anal. a *socket* (of a tooth):— hollow place, mortar.

4389. מַכְתֵּשׁ **Maktêsh,** *mak-taysh´;* the same as 4388; *dell;* the *Maktesh,* a place in Jerusalem:— Maktesh.

מוּל **mûl.** See 4136.

4390. מָלֵא **mâlê,** *maw-lay´;* or

מָלָא **mâlâ'** (Esth. 7:5), *maw-law´;* a prim. root; to *fill* or (intr.) *be full* of, in a wide application (lit. and fig.):— accomplish, confirm, + consecrate, be at an end, be expired, be fenced, fill, fulfil, (be, become, × draw, give in, go) full (-ly, -ly set, tale), [over-] flow, fulness, furnish, gather (selves, together), presume, replenish, satisfy, set, space, take a [hand-] full, + have wholly.

4391. מְלָא **mᵉlâ'** (Chald.), *mel-aw´;* corresp. to 4390; to *fill:*— fill, be full.

4392. מָלֵא **mâlê',** *maw-lay´;* from 4390; *full* (lit. or fig.) or *filling* (lit.); also (concr.) *fulness;* adv. *fully:*— × she that was with child, fill (-ed, -ed with), full (-ly), multitude, as is worth.

4393. מְלֹא **mᵉlô',** *mel-o´;* rarely

מְלוֹא **mᵉlôw',** *mel-o´;* or

מְלוֹ **mᵉlôw** (Ezek. 41:8), *mel-o´;* from 4390; *fulness* (lit. or fig.):— × all along, × all that is (there-) in, fill, (× that whereof ... was) full, fulness, [hand-] full, multitude.

מְלֹא **Millô'.** See 4407.

4394. מִלֻּא **millu',** *mil-loo´;* from 4390; a *fulfilling* (only in plur.), i.e. (lit.) a *setting* (of gems), or (tech.) *consecration* (also concr. a dedicatory *sacrifice*):— consecration, be set.

4395. מְלֵאָה **mᵉlê'âh,** *mel-ay-aw´;* fem. of 4392; something *fulfilled,* i.e. *abundance* (of produce):— (first of ripe) fruit, fulness.

4396. מִלֻּאָה **millu'âh,** *mil-loo-aw´;* fem. of 4394; a *filling,* i.e. *setting* (of gems):— inclosing, setting.

4397. מַלְאָךְ **mal'âk,** *mal-awk´;* from an unused root mean. to *despatch* as a deputy; a *messenger;* spec. of God, i.e. an *angel* (also a prophet, priest or teacher):— ambassador, angel, king, messenger.

4398. מַלְאַךְ **mal'ak** (Chald.), *mal-ak´;* corresp. to 4397; an *angel:*— angel.

4399. מְלָאכָה **mᵉlâ'kâh,** *mel-aw-kaw´;* from the same as 4397; prop. *deputyship,* i.e. ministry; gen. *employment* (never servile) or work (abstr. or concr.); also *property* (as the result of *labor*):— business, + cattle, +industrious, occupation, (+ -pied), + officer, thing (made), use, (manner of) work ([-man], -manship).

4400. מַלְאֲכוּת **mal'ăkûwth,** *mal-ak-ooth´;* from the same as 4397; a *message:*— message.

4401. מַלְאָכִי **Mal'âkîy,** *mal-aw-kee´;* from the same as 4397; *ministrative; Malaki,* a prophet:— Malachi.

4402. מִלֵּאת **millê'th,** *mil-layth´;* from 4390; *fulness,* i.e. (concr.) a *plump* socket (of the eye):— × fitly.

4403. מַלְבּוּשׁ **malbûwsh,** *mal-boosh´;* or

מַלְבֻּשׁ **malbûsh,** *mal-boosh´;* from 3847; a *garment,* or (collect.) *clothing:*— apparel, raiment, vestment.

4404. מַלְבֵּן **malbên,** *mal-bane´;* from 3835 (denom.); a *brick-kiln:*— brickkiln.

4405. מִלָּה **millâh,** *mil-law´;* from 4448 (plur. masc. as if from

מִלֶּה **milleh,** *mil-leh´;* a *word;* collect. a *discourse;* fig. a *topic:*— + answer, by-word, matter, any thing (what) to say, to speak (-ing), speak, talking, word.

4406. מִלָּה **millâh** (Chald.), *mil-law´;* corresp. to 4405; a *word, command, discourse,* or *subject:*— commandment, matter, thing, word.

מְלוֹ **mᵉlôw.** See 4393.

מְלוֹא **mᵉlôw'.** See 4393.

4407. מִלּוֹא **millôw',** *mil-lo´;* or

מִלֹּא **millô'** (2 Kings 12:20) *mil-lo´;* from 4390; a *rampart* (as *filled* in), i.e. the *citadel:*— Millo. See also 1037.

4408. מַלּוּחַ **mallûwach,** *mal-loo´-akh;* from 4414; *sea-purslain* (from its *saltness*):— mallows.

4409. מַלּוּךְ **Mallûwk,** *mal-luke´;* or

מַלּוּכִי **Mallûwkîy** (Neh. 12:14) *mal-loo-kee´;* from 4427; *regnant; Malluk,* the name of five Isr.:— Malluch, Melichu [from the marg.].

4410. מְלוּכָה **mᵉlûwkâh,** *mel-oo-kaw´;* fem. pass. part. of 4427; something *ruled,* i.e. a *realm:*— kingdom, king's, × royal.

4411. מָלוֹן **mâlôwn,** *maw-lone´;* from 3885; a *lodgment,* i.e. *caravanserai* or *encampment:*— inn, place where ... lodge, lodging (place).

4412. מְלוּנָה **mᵉlûwnâh,** *mel-oo-naw´;* fem. from 3885; a *hut,* a *hammock:*— cottage, lodge.

4413. מַלּוֹתִי **Mallôwthiy,** *mal-lo´-thee;* appar. from 4448; *I have talked* (i.e. *loquacious*); *Mallothi,* an Isr.:— Mallothi.

4414. מָלַח **mâlach,** *maw-lakh´;* a prim. root; prop. to *rub* to pieces or pulverize; intr. to *disappear* as dust; also (as denom. from 4417) to *salt* whether intern. (to *season* with salt) or extern. (to *rub* with salt):— × at all, salt, season, temper together, vanish away.

4415. מְלַח **mᵉlach** (Chald.), *mel-akh´;*

corresp. to 4414; to *eat* salt, i.e. (gen.) *subsist*:— + have maintenance.

4416. מְלַח **m°lach** (Chald.), *mel-akh´;* from 4415; *salt:—* + maintenance, salt.

4417. מֶלַח **melach,** *meh´-lakh;* from 4414; prop. *powder,* i.e. (spec.) *salt* (as easily pulverized and dissolved:— salt (l-pit]).

4418. מֶלַח **mâlâch,** *maw-lawkh´;* from 4414 in its orig. sense; a *rag* or old garment:— rotten rag.

4419. מַלָּח **mallâch,** *mal-lawkh´;* from 4414 in its second. sense; a *sailor* (as following "the salt"):— mariner.

4420. מְלֵחָה **m°lêchâh,** *mel-ay-khaw´;* from 4414 (in its denom. sense); prop. *salted* (i.e. land [776 being understood], i.e. a *desert:—* barren land (-ness), salt [land].

4421. מִלְחָמָה **milchâmâh,** *mil-khaw-maw´;* from 3898 (in the sense of *fighting*); a *battle* (i.e. the *engagement*); gen. *war* (i.e. *warfare*):— battle, fight (-ing), war (l-rior]).

4422. מָלַט **mâlaṭ,** *maw-lat´;* a prim. root; prop. to *be smooth,* i.e. (by impl.) to *escape* (as if by *slipperiness*); caus. to *release* or *rescue;* spec. to *bring forth* young, *emit* sparks:— deliver (self), escape, lay, leap out, let alone, let go, preserve, save, × speedily, × surely.

4423. מֶלֶט **meleṭ,** *meh´-let;* from 4422, *cement* (from its plastic *smoothness*):— clay.

4424. מְלַטְיָה **M°latyâh,** *mel-at-yaw´;* from 4423 and 3050; (whom) *Jah has delivered; Melatjah,* a Gibeonite:— Melatiah.

4425. מְלִילָה **m°liylâh,** *mel-ee-law´;* from 4449 (in the sense of *cropping* [comp. 4135l); a *head* of grain (as *cut* off):— ear.

4426. מְלִיצָה **m°liytsâh,** *mel-ee-tsaw´;* from 3887; an *aphorism;* also a *satire:—* interpretation, taunting.

4427. מָלַךְ **mâlak,** *maw-lak´;* a prim. root; to *reign;* incept. to *ascend the throne;* caus. to *induct* into royalty; hence, (by impl.) to *take counsel:—* consult, × indeed, be (make, set a, set up) king, be (make) queen, (begin to, make to) reign (-ing), rule, × surely.

4428. מֶלֶךְ **melek,** *meh´-lek;* from 4427; a *king:—* king, royal.

4429. מֶלֶךְ **Melek,** *meh´-lek;* the same as 4428; *king; Melek,* the name of two Isr.:— Melech, Hammelech [by incl. the art.].

4430. מֶלֶךְ **melek** (Chald.), *meh´-lek;* corresp. to 4428; a *king:—* king, royal.

4431. מְלַךְ **m°lak** (Chald.), *mel-ak´;* from a root corresp. to 4427 in the sense of *consultation; advice:—* counsel.

4432. מֹלֶךְ **Môlek,** *mo´-lek;* from 4427; *Molek* (i.e. king), the chief deity of the Ammonites:— Molech. Comp. 4445.

4433. מַלְכָּא **malkâ´** (Chald.), *mal-kaw´;* corresp. to 4436; a *queen:—* queen.

4434. מַלְכֹּדֶת **malkôdeth,** *mal-ko´-deth;* from 3920; a *snare:—* trap.

4435. מִלְכָּה **Milkâh,** *mil-kaw´;* a form of

4436; *queen; Milcah,* the name of a Hebrewess and of an Isr.:— Milcah.

4436. מַלְכָּה **malkâh,** *mal-kaw´;* fem. of 4428; a *queen:—* queen.

4437. מַלְכוּ **malkûw** (Chald.), *mal-koo´;* corresp. to 4438; *dominion* (abstr. or concr.):— kingdom, kingly, realm, reign.

4438. מַלְכוּת **malkûwth,** *mal-kooth´;* or מַלְכֻת **malkûth,** *mal-kooth´;* or (in plur.)

מַלְכִיָּה **malkûyâh,** *mal-koo-yâh´;* from 4427; a *rule;* concr. a *dominion:—* empire, kingdom, realm, reign, royal.

4439. מַלְכִּיאֵל **Malkiy'êl,** *mal-kee-ale´;* from 4428 and 410; *king of* (i.e. appointed by) *God; Malkiël,* an Isr.:— Malchiel.

4440. מַלְכִּיאֵלִי **Malkiy'êliy,** *mal-kee-ay-lee´;* patron. from 4439; a *Malkielite* or desc. of Malkiel:— Malchielite.

4441. מַלְכִּיָּה **Malkîyâh,** *mal-kee-yaw´;* or מַלְכִּיָּהוּ **Malkîyâhûw** (Jer. 38:6), *mal-kee-yaw´-hoo;* from 4428 and 3050; *king of* (i.e. appointed by) *Jah; Malkijah,* the name of ten Isr.:— Malchiah, Malchijah.

4442. מַלְכִּי־צֶדֶק **Malkîy-Tsedeq,** *mal-kee-tseh´-dek;* from 4428 and 6664; *king of right; Malki-Tsedek,* an early king in Pal.:— Melchizedek.

4443. מַלְכִּירָם **Malkîyrâm,** *mal-kee-rawm´;* from 4428 and 7311; *king of a high one* (i.e. of exaltation); *Malkiram,* an Isr.:— Malchiram.

4444. מַלְכִּישׁוּעַ **Malkîyshûwa',** *mal-kee-shoo´-ah;* from 4428 and 7769; *king of wealth; Malkishua,* an Isr.:— Malchishua.

4445. מַלְכָּם **Malkâm,** *mal-kawm´;* or מַלְכּוֹם **Milkôwm,** *mil-kome´;* from 4428 for 4432; *Malcam* or *Milcom,* the national idol of the Ammonites:— Malcham, Milcom.

4446. מְלֶכֶת **m°leketh,** *mel-eh´-keth;* from 4427; a *queen:—* queen.

4447. מֹלֶכֶת **Môleketh,** *mo-leh´-keth;* fem. act. part. of 4427; *queen; Moleketh,* an Israelitess:— Hammoleketh [incl. the art.].

4448. מָלַל **mâlal,** *maw-lal´;* a prim. root; to *speak* (mostly poet.) or *say:—* say, speak, utter.

4449. מְלַל **m°lal** (Chald.), *mel-al´;* corresp. to 4448; to *speak:—* say, speak (-ing).

4450. מִילָלַי **Mîlălay,** *mee-lal-ah´-ee;* from 4448; *talkative; Milalai,* an Isr.:— Milalai.

4451. מַלְמָד **malmâd,** *mal-mawd´;* from 3925; a *goad* for oxen:— goad.

4452. מָלַץ **mâlats,** *maw-lats´;* a prim. root; to *be smooth,* i.e. (fig.) *pleasant:—* be sweet.

4453. מֶלְצָר **Meltsâr,** *mel-tsawr´;* of Pers. der.; the *butler* or other officer in the Bab. court:— Melzar.

4454. מָלַק **mâlaq,** *maw-lak´;* a prim. root; to *crack* a joint; by impl. to *wring* the neck of a fowl (without separating it):— wring off.

4455. מַלְקוֹחַ **malqôwach,** *mal-ko´-akh;* from 3947; *tran.* (in dual) the *jaws* (as taking food); intr. *spoil* [and captives] (as taken):— booty, jaws, prey.

4456. מַלְקוֹשׁ **malqôwsh,** *mal-koshe´;* from 3953; the spring *rain* (comp. 3954); fig. *eloquence:—* latter rain.

4457. מֶלְקָח **melqâch,** *mel-kawkh´;* or מַלְקָח **malqâch,** *mal-kawkh´;* from 3947; (only in dual) *tweezers:—* snuffers, tongs.

4458. מֶלְתָּחָה **meltâchâh,** *mel-taw-khaw´;* from an unused root mean. to *spread* out; a *wardrobe* (i.e. room where clothing is *spread*):— vestry.

4459. מַלְתָּעָה **maltâ'âh,** *mal-taw-aw´;* transp. for 4973; a *grinder,* i.e. back *tooth:—* great tooth.

4460. מַמְּגֻרָה **mamm°gûrâh,** *mam-meg-oo-raw´;* from 4048 (in the sense of *depositing*); a *granary:—* barn.

4461. מֵמַד **mêmad,** *may-mad´;* from 4058; a *measure:—* measure.

4462. מְמוּכָן **M°mûwkân,** *mem-oo-kawn´;* or (transp.)

מוֹמֻכָן **Môwmûkân** (Esth. 1:16), *mo-moo-kawn´;* of Pers. der.; *Memucan* or *Momucan,* a Pers. satrap:— Memucan.

4463. מָמוֹת **mâmôwth,** *maw-mothe´;* from 4191; a mortal *disease;* concr. a *corpse:—* death.

4464. מַמְזֵר **mamzêr,** *mam-zare´;* from an unused root mean. to *alienate;* a *mongrel,* i.e. born of a Jewish father and a heathen mother:— bastard.

4465. מִמְכָּר **mimkâr,** *mim-kawr´;* from 4376; *merchandise;* abstr. a *selling:—* × ought, (that which cometh of) sale, that which ... sold, ware.

4466. מִמְכֶּרֶת **mimkereth,** *mim-keh´-reth;* fem. of 4465; a *sale:—* + sold as.

4467. מַמְלָכָה **mamlâkâh,** *mam-law-kaw´;* from 4427; *dominion,* i.e. (abstr.) the estate (*rule*) or (concr.) the country (*realm*):— kingdom, king's, reign, royal.

4468. מַמְלָכוּת **mamlâkûwth,** *mam-law-kooth´;* a form of 4467 and equiv. to it:— kingdom, reign.

4469. מַמְסָךְ **mamçâk,** *mam-sawk´;* from 4537; *mixture,* i.e. (spec.) wine *mixed* (with water or spices):— drink-offering, mixed wine.

4470. מֶמֶר **memer,** *meh´-mer;* from an unused root mean. to *grieve; sorrow:—* bitterness.

4471. מַמְרֵא **Mamrê',** *mam-ray´;* from 4754 (in the sense of *vigor*); *lusty; Mamre,* an Amorite:— Mamre.

4472. מַמְרֹר **mamrôr,** *mam-rore´;* from 4843; a *bitterness,* i.e. (fig.) calamity:— bitterness.

4473. מִמְשַׁח **mimshach,** *mim-shakh´;* from 4886, in the sense of *expansion; outspread* (i.e. with outstretched wings):— anointed.

4474. מִמְשָׁל **mimshâl,** *mim-shawl´;* from 4910; a *ruler* or (abstr.) *rule:—* dominion, that ruled.

4475. מֶמְשָׁלָה **memshâlâh,** *mem-shaw-law´;* fem. of 4474; *rule;* also (concr. in plur.) a *realm* or a *ruler*:— dominion, government, power, to rule.

4476. מִמְשָׁק **mimshâq**, *mim-shawk´*; from the same as 4943; a *possession*:— breeding.

4477. מַמְתַּק **mamtaq**, *mam-tak´*; from 4985; something *sweet* (lit. or fig.):— (most) sweet.

4478. מָן **mân**, *mawn*; from 4100; lit. a *whatness* (so to speak), i.e. *manna* (so called from the question about it):— manna.

4479. מָן **mân** (Chald.), *mawn*; from 4101; *who* or *what* (prop. interrog., hence, also indef. and rel.):— what, who (-msoever, + -so).

4480. מִן **min**, *min*; or

מִנִּי **minnîy**, *min-nee´*; or

מִנֵּי **minnêy** (constr. plur.) *min-nay´*; (Isa. 30:11); for 4482; prop. a *part* of; hence, (prep.), *from* or *out of* in many senses (as follows):— above, after, among, at, because of, by (reason of), from (among), in, × neither, × nor, (out) of, over, since, × then, through, × whether, with.

4481. מִן **min** (Chald.), *min*; corresp. to 4480:— according, after, + because, + before, by, for, from, × him, × more than, (out) of, part, since, × these, to, upon, + when.

4482. מֵן **mên**, *mane*; from an unused root mean. to *apportion*; a *part*; hence, a musical *chord* (as parted into strings):— in [the same] (Psa. 68:23), stringed instrument (Psa. 150:4), whereby (Psa. 45:8 [*defective plur.*]).

4483. מְנָא **m°nâ´** (Chald.), *men-aw´*; or

מְנָה **m°nâh** (Chald.) *men-aw´*; corresp. to 4487; to *count, appoint*:— number, ordain, set.

4484. מְנֵא **menê´** (Chald.), *men-ay´*; pass. part. of 4483; *numbered*:— Mene.

4485. מַנְגִּינָה **mangîynâh**, *man-ghee-naw´*; from 5059; a *satire*:— music.

מִנְדָּה **mindâh**. See 4061.

4486. מַנְדַּע **manda'** (Chald.), *man-dah´*; corresp. to 4093; *wisdom* or *intelligence*:— knowledge, reason, understanding.

מְנָה **m°nâh**. See 4483.

4487. מָנָה **mânâh**, *maw-naw´*; a prim. root; prop. to *weigh* out; by impl. to *allot* or constitute officially; also to *enumerate* or enroll:— appoint, count, number, prepare, set, tell.

4488. מָנֶה **mâneh**, *maw-neh´*; from 4487; prop. a fixed *weight* or measured amount, i.e. (techn.) a *maneh* or *mina*:— maneh, pound.

4489. מֹנֶה **môneh**, *mo-neh´*; from 4487; prop. something *weighed* out, i.e. (fig.) a *portion* of time, i.e. an *instance*:— time.

4490. מָנָה **mânâh**, *maw-naw´*; from 4487; prop. something *weighed* out, i.e. (gen.) a *division*; spec. (of food) a *ration*; also a *lot*:— such things as belonged, part, portion.

4491. מִנְהָג **minhâg**, *min-hawg´*; from 5090; the *driving* (of a chariot):— driving.

4492. מִנְהָרָה **minhârâh**, *min-haw-raw´*; from 5102; prop. a *channel* or *fissure*, i.e. (by impl.) a *cavern*:— den.

4493. מָנוֹד **mânôwd**, *maw-node´*; from 5110 a *nodding* or *toss* (of the head in derision):— shaking.

4494. מָנוֹחַ **mânôwach**, *maw-no´-akh*; from 5117; *quiet*, i.e. (concr.) a *settled spot*, or (fig.) a *home*:— (place of) rest.

4495. מָנוֹחַ **Mânôwach**, *maw-no´-akh*; the same as 4494; *rest*; *Manoäch*, an Isr.:— Manoah.

4496. מְנוּחָה **m°nûwchâh**, *men-oo-khaw´*; or

מְנֻחָה **m°nûchâh**, *men-oo-khaw´*; fem. of 4495; *repose* or (adv.) *peacefully*; fig. *consolation* (spec. *matrimony*); hence, (concr.) an *abode*:— comfortable, ease, quiet, rest (-ing place), still.

4497. מָנוֹן **mânôwn**, *maw-nohn´*; from 5125; a *continuator*, i.e. *heir*:— son.

4498. מָנוֹס **mânôwç**, *maw-noce´*; from 5127; a *retreat* (lit. or fig.); abstr. a *fleeing*:— × apace, escape, way to flee, flight, refuge.

4499. מְנוּסָה **m°nuwçâh**, *men-oo-saw´*; or

מְנֻסָה **m°nûçâh**, *men-oo-saw´*; fem. of 4498; *retreat*:— fleeing, flight.

4500. מָנוֹר **mânôwr**, *maw-nore´*; from 5214; a *yoke* (prop. for *plowing*), i.e. the *frame* of a loom:— beam.

4501. מְנוֹרָה **m°nôwrâh**, *men-o-raw´*; or

מְנֹרָה **m°nôrâh**, *men-o-raw´*; fem. of 4500 (in the orig. sense of 5216); a *chandelier*:— candlestick.

4502. מִנְּזָר **minn°zâr**, *min-ez-awr´*; from 5144; a *prince*:— crowned.

4503. מִנְחָה **minchâh**, *min-khaw´*; from an unused root mean. to *apportion*, i.e. *bestow*; a *donation*; euphem. *tribute*; spec. a sacrificial *offering* (usually bloodless and voluntary):— gift, oblation, (meat) offering, present, sacrifice.

4504. מִנְחָה **minchâh** (Chald.), *min-khaw´*; corresp. to 4503; a sacrificial *offering*:— oblation, meat offering.

מְנֻחָה **m°nûchâh**. See 4496.

מְנֻחוֹת **M°nûchôwth**. See 2679.

4505. מְנַחֵם **M°nachêm**, *men-akh-ame´*; from 5162; *comforter*; *Menachem*, an Isr.:— Menahem.

4506. מָנַחַת **Mânachath**, *maw-nakh-ath*; from 5117; *rest*; *Manachath*, the name of an Edomite and of a place in Moab:— Manahath.

מָנַחְתִּי **M°nachtîy**. See 2680.

4507. מְנִי **M°nîy**, *men-ee´*; from 4487; the *Apportioner*, i.e. Fate (as an idol):— number.

מִנִּי **minnîy**. See 4480, 4482.

4508. מִנִּי **Minnîy**, *min-nee´*; of for. der.; *Minni*, an Armenian province:— Minni.

מְנָיוֹת **m°nâyôwth**. See 4521.

4509. מִנְיָמִין **Minyâmîyn**, *min-yaw-meen´*; from 4480 and 3225; *from* (the) *right hand*; *Minjamin*, the name of two Isr.:— Miniamin. Comp. 4326.

4510. מִנְיָן **minyân** (Chald.), *min-yawn´*; from 4483; *enumeration*:— number.

4511. מִנִּית **Minnîyth**, *min-neeth´*; from the same as 4482; *enumeration*; *Minnith*, a place E. of the Jordan:— Minnith.

4512. מִנְלֶה **minleh**, *min-leh´*; from 5239; *completion*, i.e. (in produce) *wealth*:— perfection.

מְנֻחָה **m°nûçâh**. See 4499.

4513. מָנַע **mâna'**, *maw-nah´*; a prim. root; to *debar* (neg. or pos.) from benefit or injury:— deny, keep (back), refrain, restrain, withhold.

4514. מַנְעוּל **man'ûwl**, *man-ool´*; or

מַנְעֻל **man'ûl**, *man-ool´*; from 5274; a *bolt*:— lock.

4515. מַנְעָל **man'âl**, *man-awl´*; from 5274; a *bolt*:— shoe.

4516. מַנְעַם **man'am**, *man-am´*; from 5276; a *delicacy*:— dainty.

4517. מְנַעְנַע **m°na'na'**, *men-ah-ah´*; from 5128; a *sistrum* (so called from its *rattling* sound):— cornet.

4518. מְנַקִּית **m°naqqîyth**, *men-ak-keeth´*; from 5352; a *sacrificial basin* (for holding blood):— bowl.

מְנֹרָה **m°nôrâh**. See 4501.

4519. מְנַשֶּׁה **M°nashsheh**, *men-ash-sheh´*; from 5382; *causing to forget*; *Menashsheh*, a grandson of Jacob, also the tribe descended from him, and its territory:— Manasseh.

4520. מְנַשִּׁי **M°nashshiy**, *men-ash-shee´*; from 4519; a *Menashshite* or desc. of Menashsheh:— of Manasseh, Manassites.

4521. מְנָת **m°nâth**, *men-awth´*; from 4487; an *allotment* (by courtesy, law or providence):— portion.

4522. מַס **maç**, *mas*; or

מִס **miç**, *mees*; from 4549; prop. a *burden* (as causing to faint), i.e. a *tax* in the form of forced *labor*:— discomfited, levy, task [-master], tribute (-tary).

4523. מָס **mâç**, *mawce*; from 4549; *fainting*, i.e. (fig.) *disconsolate*:— is afflicted.

4524. מֵסַב **mêçab**, *may-sab´*; plur. masc.

מְסִבִּים **m°çibbîym**, *mes-ib-beem´*; or fem.

מְסִבּוֹת **m°çibbôwth**, *mes-ib-bohth´*; from 5437; a *divan* (as enclosing the room); abstr. (adv.) *around*:— that compass about, (place) round about, at table.

מֻסַבָּה **mûçabbâh**. See 4142.

4525. מַסְגֵּר **maçgêr**, *mas-gare´*; from 5462; a *fastener*, i.e. (of a person) a *smith*, (of a thing) a *prison*:— prison, smith.

4526. מִסְגֶּרֶת **miçgereth**, *mis-gheh´-reth*; from 5462; something *enclosing*, i.e. a *margin* (of a region, of a panel); concr. a *stronghold*:— border, close place, hole.

4527. מַסַּד **maççad**, *mas-sad´*; from 3245; a *foundation*:— foundation.

מוֹסָדָה **môçâdâh**. See 4146.

4528. מִסְדְּרוֹן **miçd°rôwn**, *mis-der-ohn´*; from the same as 5468; a *colonnade* or *internal portico* (from its *rows* of pillars):— porch.

4529. מָסָה **mâçâh**, *maw-saw´*; a prim. root; to *dissolve*:— make to consume away, (make to) melt, water.

4530. מִסָּה **miççâh**, *mis-saw´*; from 4549 (in the sense of *flowing*); *abundance*, i.e. (adv.) *liberally*:— tribute.

4531. מַסָּה **maççâh**, *mas-saw´*; from 5254; a *testing*, of men (judicial) or of God (querulous):— temptation, trial.

4532. מַסָּה **Maççâh**, *mas-saw´*; the same as 4531; *Massah*, a place in the Desert:— Massah.

4533. מַסְוֶה **maçveh**, *mas-veh´*; appar. from an unused root mean. to *cover*; a *veil*:— vail.

4534. מְסוּכָה **mᵉçûwkâh**, *mes-oo-kaw´*; for 4881; a *hedge*:— thorn hedge.

4535. מַסָּח **maççâch**, *mas-sawkh´*; from 5255 in the sense of *staving off*; a *cordon*, (adv.) or (as a) military *barrier*:— broken down.

4536. מִסְחָר **miççhâr**, *mis-khawr´*; from 5503; *trade*:— traffic.

4537. מָסַךְ **mâçak**, *maw-sak´*; a prim. root; to *mix*, espec. wine (with spices):— mingle.

4538. מֶסֶךְ **meçek**, *meh´-sek*; from 4537; a *mixture*, i.e. of wine with spices:— mixture.

4539. מָסָךְ **mâçâk**, *maw-sawk´*; from 5526; a *cover*, i.e. *veil*:— covering, curtain, hanging.

4540. מְסֻכָּה **mᵉçukkâh**, *mes-ook-kaw´*; from 5526; a *covering*, i.e. garniture:— covering.

4541. מַסֵּכָה **maççêkâh**, *mas-say-kaw´*; from 5258; prop. a *pouring* over, i.e. *fusion* of metal (espec. a *cast* image); by impl. a *libation*, i.e. league; concr. a *coverlet* (as if *poured* out):— covering, molten (image), vail.

4542. מִסְכֵּן **miçkên**, *mis-kane´*; from 5531; *indigent*:— poor (man).

4543. מִסְכְּנָה **miçkᵉnâh**, *mis-ken-aw´*; by transp. from 3664; a *magazine*:— store (-house), treasure.

4544. מִסְכְּנֻת **miçkênûth**, *mis-kay-nooth´*; from 4542; *indigence*:— scarceness.

4545. מַסֶּכֶת **maççeketh**, *mas-seh´-keth*; from 5259 in the sense of *spreading* out; something *expanded*, i.e. the *warp* in a loom (as *stretched* out to receive the woof):— web.

4546. מְסִלָּה **mᵉçillâh**, *mes-il-law´*; from 5549; a *thoroughfare* (as *turnpiked*), lit. or fig.; spec. a *viaduct*, a *staircase*:— causeway, course, highway, path, terrace.

4547. מַסְלוּל **maçlûwl**, *mas-lool´*; from 5549; a *thoroughfare* (as turnpiked):— highway.

4548. מַסְמֵר **maçmêr**, *mas-mare´*; or

מִסְמֵר **miçmêr**, *mis-mare´*; also (fem.)

מַסְמְרָה **maçmᵉrâh**, *mas-mer-aw´*; or

מִסְמְרָה **miçmᵉrâh**, *mis-mer-aw´*; or even

מַשְׂמְרָה **masmᵉrâh** (Eccles. 12:11),

mas-mer-aw´; from 5568; a *peg* (as *bristling* from the surface):— nail.

4549. מָסַס **mâçaç**, *maw-sas´*; a prim. root; to *liquefy*; fig. to *waste* (with disease), to *faint* (with fatigue, fear or grief):— discourage, faint, be loosed, melt (away), refuse, × utterly.

4550. מַסַּע **maçça'**, *mas-sah´*; from 5265; a *departure* (from *striking* the tents), i.e. march (not necessarily a single day's travel); by impl. a *station* (or point of *departure*):— journey (-ing).

4551. מַסָּע **maççâ'**, *maw-saw´*; from 5265 in the sense of *projecting*; a *missile* (spear or arrow); also a *quarry* (whence stones are, as it were, *ejected*):— before it was brought, dart.

4552. מִסְעָד **miç'âd**, *mis-awd´* from 5582; a *balustrade* (for stairs):— pillar.

4553. מִסְפֵּד **miçpêd**, *mis-pade´*; from 5594; a *lamentation*:— lamentation, one mourneth, mourning, wailing.

4554. מִסְפּוֹא **miçpôw'**, *mis-po´*; from an unused root mean. to *collect*; *fodder*:— provender.

4555. מִסְפָּחָה **miçpâchâh**, *mis-paw-khaw´*; from 5596; a *veil* (as *spread* out):— kerchief.

4556. מִסְפַּחַת **miçpachath**, *mis-pakh´-ath*; from 5596; *scruf* (as *spreading* over the surface):— scab.

4557. מִסְפָּר **miçpâr**, *mis-pawr´*; from 5608; a *number*, def. (arithmetical) or indef. (large, *innumerable*; small, a *few*); also (abstr.) *narration*:— + abundance, account, × all, × few, [in-]finite, (certain) number (-ed), tale, telling, + time.

4558. מִסְפָּר **Miçpâr**, *mis-pawr´*; the same as 4457; *number*; *Mispar*, an Isr.:— Mizpar. Comp. 4559.

מִסְפְּרוֹת **Mocᵉrowth**. See 4149.

4559. מִסְפֶּרֶת **Miçpereth**, *mis-peh´-reth*; fem. of 4457; *enumeration*; *Mispereth*, an Isr.:— Mispereth. Comp. 4458.

4560. מָסַר **mâçar**, *maw-sar´*; a prim. root; to *sunder*, i.e. (tran.) *set apart*, or (reflex.) *apostatize*:— commit, deliver.

4561. מֹסָר **môçâr**, *mo-sawr´*; from 3256; *admonition*:— instruction.

4562. מָסֹרֶת **mâçôreth**, *maw-so´-reth*; from 631; a *band*:— bond.

4563. מִסְתּוֹר **miçtôwr**, *mis-tore´*; from 5641; a *refuge*:— covert.

4564. מַסְתֵּר **maçtêr**, *mas-tare´*; from 5641; prop. a *hider*, i.e. (abstr.) a *hiding*, i.e. *aversion*:— hid.

4565. מִסְתָּר **miçtâr**, *mis-tawr´*; from 5641; prop. a *concealer*, i.e. a *covert*:— secret (-ly, place).

מְעָא **mᵉ'â**. See 4577.

4566. מַעְבָּד **ma'bâd**, *mah-bawd´*; from 5647; an *act*:— work.

4567. מַעְבָּד **ma'bâd** (Chald.), *mah-bawd´*; corresp. to 4566; an *act*:— work.

4568. מַעֲבֶה **ma'âbeh**, *mah-ab-eh´*; from 5666; prop. *compact* (part of soil), i.e. *loam*:— clay.

4569. מַעֲבָר **ma'âbâr**, *mah-ab-awr´*; or fem.

מַעֲבָרָה **ma'âbârâh**, *mah-ab-aw-raw´*; from 5674; a *crossing*-place (of a river, a *ford*; of a mountain, a *pass*); abstr. a *transit*, i.e. (fig.) *overwhelming*:— ford, place where ... pass, passage.

4570. מַעְגָּל **ma'gâl**, *mah-gawl´*; or fem.

מַעְגָּלָה **ma'gâlâh**, *mah-gaw-law´*; from the same as 5696; a *track* (lit. or fig.); also a *rampart* (as *circular*):— going, path, trench, way (l-side).

4571. מָעַד **mâ'ad**, *maw-ad´*; a prim. root; to *waver*:— make to shake, slide, slip.

מוֹעֵד **môʿêd**. See 4150.

4572. מַעֲדַי **Ma'aday**, *mah-ad-ah´-ee*; from 5710; *ornamental*; *Maadai*, an Isr.:— Maadai.

4573. מַעַדְיָה **Ma'adyâh**, *mah-ad-yaw´*; from 5710 and 3050; *ornament of Jah*; *Maadjah*, an Isr.:— Maadiah. Comp. 4153.

4574. מַעֲדָן **ma'âdân**, *mah-ad-awn´*; or (fem.)

מַעֲדַנָּה **ma'âdannâh**, *mah-ad-an-naw´*; from 5727; a *delicacy* or (abstr.) *pleasure* (adv. *cheerfully*):— dainty, delicately, delight.

4575. מַעֲדַנָּה **ma'âdannâh**, *mah-ad-an-naw´*; by tran. from 6029; a *bond*, i.e. *group*:— influence.

4576. מַעְדֵּר **ma'dêr**, *mah-dare´*; from 5737; a (weeding) *hoe*:— mattock.

4577. מְעָה **mᵉ'âh** (Chald.), *meh-aw´*; or

מְעָא **mᵉ'â'** (Chald.), *meh-aw´*; corresp. to 4578; only in plur. the *bowels*:— belly.

4578. מֵעֶה **mê'âh**, *may-aw´*; from an unused root prob. mean. to *be soft*; used only in plur. the *intestines*, or (collect.) the *abdomen*, fig. *sympathy*; by impl. a *vest*; by extens. the *stomach*, the *uterus* (or of men, the seat of generation), the *heart* (fig.):— belly, bowels, × heart, womb.

4579. מֵעָה **mê'âh**, *may-aw´*; fem. of 4578; the *belly*, i.e. (fig.) interior:— gravel.

4580. מָעוֹג **mâ'owg**, *maw-ogue´*; from 5746; a *cake* of bread (with 3934 a *table-buffoon*, i.e. *parasite*):— cake, feast.

4581. מָעוֹז **mâ'owz**, *maw-oze´* (also

מָעוּז **mâ'ûwz**, *maw-ooz´*); or

מָעֹז **mâ'oz**, *maw-oze´* (also

מָעֻז **mâ'ûz**, *maw-ooz´*); from 5810; a *fortified* place; fig. a *defence*:— force, fort (-ress), rock, strength (-en), (× most) strong (hold).

4582. מָעוֹךְ **Mâ'owk**, *maw-oke´*; from 4600; *oppressed*; *Maok*, a Philistine:— Maoch.

4583. מָעוֹן **mâ'own**, *maw-ohn´*; or

מָעִין **mâ'iyn** (1 Chron. 4:41), *maw-een´*; from the same as 5772; an *abode*, of God (the Tabernacle or the Temple), men (their home) or animals (their lair); hence, a *retreat* (asylum):— den, dwelling (l-l place), habitation.

4584. מָעוֹן **Mâ'own**, *maw-ohn´*; the same as 4583; a *residence*; *Maon*, the name of an Isr. and of a place in Pal.:— Maon, Maonites. Comp. 1010, 4586.

4585. מְעוֹנָה **mᵉ'ôwnâh**, *meh-o-naw´*; or

מְעֹנָה **meʿônâh**, *meh-o-naw'*; fem. of 4583, and mean. the same:— den, habitation, (dwelling) place, refuge.

4586. מְעוּנִי **Meʿûwnîy**, *meh-oo-nee'*; or מְעִינִי° **Meʿîynîy**, *meh-ee-nee'*; prob. patrial from 4584; a Meünite, or inhab. of Maon (only in plur.):— Mehunim (-s), Meunim.

4587. מְעֹנֹתַי **Meʿôwnôthay**, *meh-o-no-thah'-ee*; plur. of 4585; *habitative*; Meonothai, an Isr.:— Meonothai.

4588. מָעוּף **mâʿûwph**, *maw-off'*; from 5774 in the sense of *covering* with shade [comp. 4155]; *darkness*:— dimness.

4589. מָעוֹר **mâʿôwr**, *maw-ore'*; from 5783; *nakedness*, i.e. (in plur.) the *pudenda*:— nakedness.

מָעֹז **mâʿôz**. See 4581.

מָעֻז **mâʿûz**. See 4581.

4590. מַעַזְיָה **Maʿazyâh**, *mah-az-yaw'*; or מַעַזְיָהוּ **Maʿazyâhûw**, *mah-az-yaw'-hoo*; prob. from 5756 (in the sense of *protection*) and 3050; *rescue of Jah*; Maazjah, the name of two Isr.:— Maaziah.

4591. מָעַט **mâʿaṭ**, *maw-at'*; a prim. root; prop. to *pare off*, i.e. *lessen*; intr. to *be* (or caus. to *make*) *small* or *few* (or fig. *ineffective*):— suffer to decrease, diminish, (be, × borrow a, give, make) few (in number, -ness), gather least (little), be (seem) little, (× give the) less, be minished, bring to nothing.

4592. מְעַט **meʿaṭ**, *meh-at'*; or מְעָט **meʿâṭ**, *meh-awt'*; from 4591; a *little* or *few* (often adv. or compar.):— almost, (some, very) few (-er, -est), lightly, little (while), (very) small (matter, thing), some, soon, × very.

4593. מָעֹט **mâʿôṭ**, *maw-ote'*; pass. adj. of 4591; *thinned* (as to the edge), i.e. *sharp*:— wrapped up.

4594. מַעֲטֶה **maʿăṭeh**, *mah-at-eh'*; from 5844; a *vestment*:— garment.

4595. מַעֲטָפָה **maʿăṭâphâh**, *mah-at-aw-faw'*; from 5848; a *cloak*:— mantle.

4596. מְעִי **meʿîy**, *meh-ee'*; from 5753; a *pile* of rubbish (as *contorted*), i.e. a *ruin* (comp. 5856):— heap.

4597. מָעַי **Mâʿay**, *maw-ah'-ee*; prob. from 4578; *sympathetic*; Maai, an Isr.:— Maai.

4598. מְעִיל **meʿîyl**, *meh-eel'*; from 4603 in the sense of *covering*; a *robe* (i.e. upper and outer *garment*):— cloke, coat, mantle, robe.

מֵעִים **mêʿîym**. See 4578.

מְעִין **meʿîyn** (Chald.). See 4577.

4599. מַעְיָן **maʿyân**, *mah-yawn'*; or מַעְיְנוֹ **maʿyeʿnôw** (Psa. 114:8) *mah-yen-o'*; or (fem.) מַעְיָנָה **maʿyânâh**, *mah-yaw-naw'*; from 5869 (as a denom. in the sense of a *spring*); a *fountain* (also collect.), fig. a *source* (of satisfaction):— fountain, spring, well.

מְעִינִי° **Meʿîynîy**. See 4586.

4600. מָעַךְ **mâʿak**, *maw-ak'*; a prim. root; to *press*, i.e. to *pierce, emasculate, handle*:— bruised, stuck, be pressed.

4601. מַעֲכָה **Maʿăkâh**, *mah-ak-aw'*; or מַעֲכָא **maʿăkâth** (Josh. 13:13), *mah-ak-awth'*; from 4600; *depression*; Maakah (or Maakath), the name of a place in Syria, also of a Mesopotamian, of three Isr., and of four Israelitesses and one Syrian woman:— Maachah, Maachathites. See also 1038.

4602. מַעֲכָתִי **Maʿăkâthîy**, *mah-ak-aw-thee'*; patrial from 4601; a *Maakathite*, or inhab. of Maakah:— Maachathite.

4603. מָעַל **mâʿal**, *maw-al'*; a prim. root; prop. to *cover up*; used only fig. to *act covertly*, i.e. *treacherously*:— transgress, (commit, do a) trespass (-ing).

4604. מַעַל **maʿal**, *mah'-al*; from 4603; *treachery*, i.e. sin:— falsehood, grievously, sore, transgression, trespass, × very.

4605. מַעַל **maʿal**, *mah'al*; from 5927; prop. the *upper* part, used only adv. with pref. *upward, above, overhead, from the top*, etc.:— above, exceeding (-ly), forward, on (× very) high, over, up (-on, -ward), very.

מֵעַל **mêʿal**. See 5921.

4606. מֵעָל **mêʿal** (Chald.), *may-awl'*; from 5954; (only in plur. as sing.) the *setting* (of the sun):— going down.

4607. מֹעַל **môʿal**, *mo'-al*; from 5927; a *raising* (of the hands):— lifting up.

4608. מַעֲלֶה **maʿăleh**, *mah-al-eh'*; from 5927; an *elevation*, i.e. (concr.) *acclivity* or *platform*; abstr. (the relation or state) a *rise* or (fig.) *priority*:— ascent, before, chiefest, cliff, that goeth up, going up, hill, mounting up, stairs.

4609. מַעֲלָה **maʿălâh**, *mah-al-aw'*; fem. of 4608; *elevation*, i.e. the act (lit. a *journey* to a higher place, fig. a *thought* arising), or (concr.) the condition (lit. a *step* or *grade*-mark, fig. a *superiority* of station); spec. a climactic *progression* (in certain Psalms):— things that come up, (high) degree, deal, go up, stair, step, story.

4610. מַעֲלֵה עַקְרַבִּים **Maʿăleh ʿAqrabbîym**, *mah-al-ay' ak-rab-beem'*; from 4608 and (the plur. of) 6137; *Steep of Scorpions*, a place in the Desert:— Maaleh-accrabim, the ascent (going up) of Akrabbim.

4611. מַעֲלָל **maʿălâl**, *mah-al-awl'*; from 5953; an *act* (good or bad):— doing, endeavour, invention, work.

4612. מַעֲמָד **maʿămâd**, *mah-am-awd'*; from 5975; (fig.) a *position*:— attendance, office, place, state.

4613. מָעֳמָד **moʿŏmâd**, *moh-om-awd'*; from 5975; lit. a *foothold*:— standing.

4614. מַעֲמָסָה **maʿămâçâh**, *mah-am-aw-saw'*; from 6006; *burdensomeness*:— burdensome.

4615. מַעֲמָק **maʿămâq**, *mah-am-awk'*; from 6009; a *deep*:— deep, depth.

4616. מַעַן **maʿan**, *mah'-an*; from 6030; prop. *heed*, i.e. *purpose*; used only adv., *on account of* (as a motive or an aim), teleologically *in order that*:— because of, to the end (intent) that, for (to, ... 's sake), + lest, that, to.

4617. מַעֲנֶה **maʿăneh**, *mah-an-eh'*; from 6030; a *reply* (favorable or contradictory):— answer, × himself.

4618. מַעֲנָה **maʿănâh**, *mah-an-aw'*; from 6031, in the sense of *depression* or *tilling*; a *furrow*:— + acre, furrow.

מְעֹנָה **meʿônâh**. See 4585.

4619. מַעַץ **Maʿats**, *mah'-ats*; from 6095; *closure*; Maats, an Isr.:— Maaz.

4620. מַעֲצֵבָה **maʿătsêbâh**, *mah-ats-ay-baw'*; from 6087; *anguish*:— sorrow.

4621. מַעֲצָד **maʿătsâd**, *mah-ats-awd'*; from an unused root mean. to *hew*; an *axe*:— ax, tongs.

4622. מַעְצוֹר **maʿtsôwr**, *mah-tsore'*; from 6113; obj. a *hindrance*:— restraint.

4623. מַעְצָר **maʿtsâr**, *mah-tsawr'*; from 6113; subj. *control*:— rule.

4624. מַעֲקֶה **maʿăqeh**, *mah-ak-eh'*; from an unused root mean. to *repress*; a *parapet*:— battlement.

4625. מַעֲקָשׁ **maʿăqâsh**, *mah-ak-awsh'*; from 6140; a *crook* (in a road):— crooked thing.

4626. מַעַר **maʿar**, *mah'-ar*; from 6168; a *nude* place, i.e. (lit.) the *pudenda*, or (fig.) a vacant *space*:— nakedness, proportion.

4627. מַעֲרָב **maʿărâb**, *mah-ar-awb'*; from 6148, in the sense of *trading*; *traffic*; by impl. mercantile *goods*:— market, merchandise.

4628. מַעֲרָב **maʿărâb**, *mah-ar-awb'*; or (fem.)

4629. מַעֲרָבָה **maʿărâbâh**, *mah-ar-aw-baw'*; from 6150, in the sense of *shading*; the *west* (as a region of the *evening* sun):— west.

4629. מַעֲרֶה **maʿăreh**, *mah-ar-eh'*; from 6168; a *nude* place, i.e. a *common*:— meadows.

4630. מַעֲרָה° **maʿărâh**, *mah-ar-aw'*; fem. of 4629; an *open* spot:— army [from the marg.].

4631. מְעָרָה **meʿârâh**, *meh-aw-raw'*; from 5783; a *cavern* (as dark):— cave, den, hole.

4632. מְעָרָה **Meʿârâh**, *meh-aw-raw'*; the same as 4631; *cave*; Meärah, a place in Pal.:— Mearah.

4633. מַעֲרָךְ **maʿărâk**, *mah-ar-awk'*; from 6186; an *arrangement*, i.e. (fig.) mental *disposition*:— preparation.

4634. מַעֲרָכָה **maʿărâkâh**, *mah-ar-aw-kaw'*; fem. of 4633; an *arrangement*; concr. a *pile*; spec. a military *array*:— army, fight, be set in order, ordered place, rank, row.

4635. מַעֲרֶכֶת **maʿăreketh**, *mah-ar-eh'-keth*; from 6186; an *arrangement*, i.e. (concr.) a *pile* (of loaves):— row, shewbread.

4636. מַעֲרֹם **maʿărôm**, *mah-ar-ome'*; from 6191, in the sense of *stripping*; *bare*:— naked.

4637. מַעֲרָצָה **maʿărâtsâh**, *mah-ar-aw-tsaw'*; from 6206; *violence*:— terror.

4638. מַעֲרָת **Maʿărâth**, *mah-ar-awth'*; a form of 4630; *waste*; Maarath, a place in Pal.:— Maarath.

4639. מַעֲשֶׂה **maʿăseh**, *mah-as-eh'*; from 6213; an *action* (good or bad); gen. a

Hebrew

transaction; abstr. activity; by impl. a *product* (spec. a *poem*) or (gen.) *property:*— act, art, + bakemeat, business, deed, do (-ing), labour, thing made, ware of making, occupation, thing offered, operation, possession, × well, (handy-, needle-, net-l) work (ing, -manship), wrought.

4640. מַעֲשַׂי **Ma'say**, *mah-as-ah'ee;* from 6213; *operative; Maasai,* an Isr.:— Maasai.

4641. מַעֲשֵׂיָה **Ma'ăsêyâh**, *mah-as-ay-yaw';* or

מַעֲשֵׂיָהוּ **Ma'ăsêyâhûw**, *mah-as-ay-yaw'-hoo;* from 4639 and 3050; *work of Jah; Maasejah,* the name of sixteen Isr.:— Maaseiah.

4642. מַעֲשֵׁקָּה **ma'ăshaqqâh**, *mah-ash-ak-kaw';* from 6231; *oppression:*— oppression, × oppressor.

4643. מַעֲשֵׂר **ma'ăsêr**, *mah-as-ayr';* or

מַעֲשַׂר **ma'ăsar**, *mah-as-ar';* and (in plur.) fem.

מַעֲשְׂרָה **ma'asrâh**, *mah-as-raw';* from 6240; a *tenth;* espec. a *tithe:*— tenth (part), tithe (-ing).

4644. מֹף **Môph**, *mofe;* of Eg. or.; *Moph,* the capital of Lower Egypt:— Memphis. Comp. 5297.

מְפִיבֹשֶׁת **Mᵉphibôsheth**. See 4648.

4645. מִפְגָּע **miphgâ'**, *mif-gaw';* from 6293; an *object of attack:*— mark.

4646. מַפָּח **mappâch**, *map-pawkh';* from 5301; a *breathing out* (of life), i.e. expiring:— giving up.

4647. מַפֻּחַ **mappûach**, *map-poo'-akh;* from 5301; the *bellows* (i.e. *blower*) of a forge:— bellows.

4648. מְפִיבֹשֶׁת **Mᵉphiybôsheth**, *mef-ee-bo'-sheth;* or

מְפִבֹשֶׁת **Mᵉphibôsheth**, *mef-ee-bo'-sheth;* prob. from 6284 and 1322; *dispeller of shame* (i.e. of Baal); *Mephibosheth,* the name of two Isr.:— Mephibosheth.

4649. מֻפִּים **Muppìym**, *moop-peem';* a plur. appar. from 5130; *wavings; Muppim,* an Isr.:— Muppim. Comp. 8206.

4650. מֵפִיץ **mêphìyts**, *may-feets';* from 6327; a *breaker,* i.e. *mallet:*— maul.

4651. מַפָּל **mappâl**, *map-pawl';* from 5307; a *falling off,* i.e. chaff; also something *pendulous,* i.e. a flap:— flake, refuse.

4652. מִפְלָאָה **miphlâ'âh**, *mif-law-aw';* from 6381; a *miracle:*— wondrous work.

4653. מִפְלַגָּה **miphlaggâh**, *mif-lag-gaw';* from 6385; a *classification:*— division.

4654. מַפָּלָה **mappâlâh**, *map-paw-law';* or

מַפֵּלָה **mappêlâh**, *map-pay-law';* from 5307; something *fallen,* i.e. a *ruin:*— ruin (-ous).

4655. מִפְלָט **miphlât**, *mif-lawt';* from 6403; an *escape:*— escape.

4656. מִפְלֶצֶת **miphletseth**, *mif-leh'-tseth;* from 6426; a *terror,* i.e. an *idol:*— idol.

4657. מִפְלָשׂ **miphlâs**, *mif-lawce';* from

an unused root mean. to *balance;* a *poising:*— balancing.

4658. מַפֶּלֶת **mappeleth**, *map-peh'-leth;* from 5307; *fall,* i.e. *decadence;* concr. a *ruin;* spec. a *carcase:*— carcase, fall, ruin.

4659. מִפְעָל **miph'âl**, *mif-awl';* or (fem.)

מִפְעָלָה **miph'âlâh**, *mif-aw-law';* from 6466; a *performance:*— work.

4660. מַפָּץ **mappâts**, *map-pawts';* from 5310; a *smiting* to pieces:— slaughter.

4661. מַפֵּץ **mappêts**, *map-pates';* from 5310; a *smiter,* i.e. a *war club:*— battle ax.

4662. מִפְקָד **miphqâd**, *mif-kawd';* from 6485; an *appointment,* i.e. *mandate;* concr. a designated *spot;* spec. a *census:*— appointed place, commandment, number.

4663. מִפְקָד **Miphqâd**, *mif-kawd';* the same as 4662; *assignment; Miphkad,* the name of a gate in Jerusalem:— Miphkad.

4664. מִפְרָץ **miphrâts**, *mif-rawts';* from 6555; a *break* (in the shore), i.e. a *haven:*— breach.

4665. מִפְרֶכֶת **miphreketh**, *mif-reh'-keth;* from 6561; prop. a *fracture,* i.e. *joint* (*vertebra*) of the neck:— neck.

4666. מִפְרָשׂ **miphrâs**, *mif-rawce';* from 6566; an *expansion:*— that which ... spreadest forth, spreading.

4667. מִפְשָׂעָה **miphsâ'âh**, *mif-saw-aw';* from 6585; a *stride,* i.e. (by euphem.) the *crotch:*— buttocks.

מֹפֵת **môphêth**. See 4159.

4668. מִפְתֵּחַ **maphtêach**, *maf-tay'-akh;* from 6605; an *opener,* i.e. a *key:*— key.

4669. מִפְתָּח **miphtâch**, *mif-tawkh';* from 6605; an *aperture,* i.e. (fig.) *utterance:*— opening.

4670. מִפְתָּן **miphtân**, *mif-tawn';* from the same as 6620; a *stretcher,* i.e. a *sill:*— threshold.

4671. מֹץ **môts**, *motes;* or

מוֹץ **môwts** (Zeph. 2:2), *motes;* from 4160; *chaff* (as *pressed* out, i.e. *winnowed* or [rather] *threshed* loose):— chaff.

4672. מָצָא **mâtsâ'**, *maw-tsaw';* a prim. root; prop. to *come forth* to, i.e. *appear* or *exist;* tran. to *attain,* i.e. *find* or *acquire;* fig. to *occur, meet* or *be present:*— + be able, befall, being, catch, × certainly, (cause to) come (on, to, to hand), deliver, be enough (cause to) find (-ing, occasion, out), get (hold upon), × have (here), be here, hit, be left, light (up-) on, meet (with), × occasion serve, (be) present, ready, speed, suffice, take hold on.

מֹצָא **môtsâ'**. See 4161.

4673. מַצָּב **matstsâb**, *mats-tsawb';* from 5324; a *fixed spot;* fig. an *office,* a military *post:*— garrison, station, place where ... stood.

4674. מֻצָּב **mutstsâb**, *moots-tsawb';* from 5324; a *station,* i.e. military *post:*— mount.

4675. מַצָּבָה **matstsâbâh**, *mats-tsaw-baw';* or

מַצָּבָה **mitstsâbâh**, *mits-tsaw-baw';* fem. of 4673; a military *guard:*— army, garrison.

4676. מַצֵּבָה **matstsêbâh**, *mats-tsay-baw';* fem. (caus.) part. of 5324; something *stationed,* i.e. a *column* or (memorial *stone*); by anal. an *idol:*— garrison, (standing) image, pillar.

4677. מְצֹבָיָה **Mᵉtsôbâyâh**, *mets-o-baw-yaw';* appar. from 4672 and 3050; *found of Jah; Metsobajah,* a place in Pal.:— Mesobaite.

4678. מַצֶּבֶת **matstsebeth**, *mats-tseh'-beth;* from 5324; something *stationary,* i.e. a monumental *stone;* also the *stock* of a tree:— pillar, substance.

4679. מְצַד **mᵉtsad**, *mets-ad';* or

מְצָד **mᵉtsâd**, *mets-awd';* or (fem.)

מְצָדָה **mᵉtsâdâh**, *mets-aw-daw';* from 6679; a *fastness* (as a *covert* of ambush):— castle, fort, (strong) hold, munition.

מְצֻדָה **mᵉtsûdâh**. See 4686.

4680. מָצָה **mâtsâh**, *maw-tsaw';* a prim. root; to *suck* out; by impl. to *drain,* to *squeeze* out:— suck, wring (out).

4681. מֹצָה **Môtsâh**, *mo-tsaw';* act. part. fem. of 4680; *drained; Motsah,* a place in Pal.:— Mozah.

4682. מַצָּה **matstsâh**, *mats-tsaw';* from 4711 in the sense of *greedily* devouring for sweetness; prop. *sweetness;* concr. *sweet* (i.e. not soured or bittered with yeast); spec. an *unfermented cake* or loaf, or (ellip.) the festival of *Passover* (because no leaven was then used):— unleavened (bread, cake), without leaven.

4683. מַצָּה **matstsâh**, *mats-tsaw';* from 5327; a *quarrel:*— contention, debate, strife.

4684. מַצְהָלָה **matshâlâh**, *mats-haw-law';* from 6670; a *whinnying* (through impatience for battle or lust):— neighing.

4685. מָצוֹד **mâtsôwd**, *maw-tsode';* or (fem.)

מְצוֹדָה **mᵉtsôwdâh**, *mets-o-daw';* or

מְצֹדָה **mᵉtsôdâh**, *mets-o-daw';* from 6679; a *net* (for *capturing* animals or fishes); also (by interch. for 4679) a *fastness* or (besieging) *tower:*— bulwark, hold, munition, net, snare.

4686. מָצוּד **mâtsûwd**, *maw-tsood';* or (fem.)

מְצוּדָה **mᵉtsûwdâh**, *mets-oo-daw';* or

מְצֻדָה **mᵉtsûdâh**, *mets-oo-daw';* for 4685; a *net,* or (abstr.) *capture;* also a *fastness:*— castle, defence, fort (-ress), (strong) hold, be hunted, net, snare, strong place.

4687. מִצְוָה **mitsvâh**, *mits-vaw';* from 6680; a *command,* whether human or divine (collect. the *Law*):— (which was) commanded (-ment), law, ordinance, precept.

4688. מְצוֹלָה **mᵉtsôwlâh**, *mets-o-law';* or

מְצֹלָה **mᵉtsôlâh**, *mets-o-law';* also

מְצוּלָה **mᵉtsûwlâh**, *mets-oo-law';* or

מְצֻלָה **m°tsûlâh**, *mets-oo-law´;* from the same as 6683; a *deep place* (of water or mud):— bottom, deep, depth.

4689. מָצוֹק **mâtsôwq**, *maw-tsoke´;* from 6693; a *narrow* place, i.e. (abstr. and fig.) *confinement* or *disability:*— anguish, distress, straitness.

4690. מָצוּק **mâtsûwq**, *maw-tsook´;* or

מָצֻק **mâtsûq**, *maw-tsook´;* from 6693; something *narrow*, i.e. a *column* or *hill*top:— pillar, situate.

4691. מְצוּקָה **m°tsûwqâh**, *mets-oo-kaw´;* or

מְצֻקָה **m°tsûqâh**, *mets-oo-kaw´;* fem. of 4690; *narrowness*, i.e. (fig.) *trouble:*— anguish, distress.

4692. מָצוֹר **mâtsôwr**, *maw-tsore´;* or

מָצוּר **mâtsûwr**, *maw-tsoor´;* from 6696; something *hemming* in, i.e. (obj.) a *mound* (of besiegers), (abstr.) a *siege*, (fig.) *distress*; or (subj.) a *fastness:*— besieged, bulwark, defence, fenced, fortress, siege, strong (hold), tower.

4693. מָצוֹר **mâtsôwr**, *maw-tsore´;* the same as 4692 in the sense of a *limit; Egypt* (as the *border* of Pal.):— besieged places, defence, fortified.

4694. מְצוּרָה **m°tsûwrâh**, *mets-oo-raw´;* or

מְצֻרָה **m°tsûrâh**, *mets-oo-raw´;* fem. of 4692; a *hemming* in, i.e. (obj.) a *mound* (of siege), or (subj.) a *rampart* (of protection), (abstr.) *fortification:*— fenced (city), fort, munition, strong hold.

4695. מַצּוּת **matstsûwth**, *mats-tsooth´;* from 5327; a *quarrel:*— that contended.

4696. מֶצַח **mêtsach**, *may´-tsakh;* from an unused root mean. to *be clear,* i.e. *conspicuous;* the *forehead* (as open and *prominent*):— brow, forehead, + impudent.

4697. מִצְחָה **mitschâh**, *mits-khaw´;* from the same as 4696; a *shin-piece* of armor (as *prominent*), only plur.:— greaves.

מְצֻלָּה **m°tsôlâh**. See 4688.

מְצֻלָּה **m°tsûlâh**. See 4688.

4698. מְצִלָּה **m°tsillâh**, *mets-il-law´;* from 6750; a *tinkler*, i.e. a *bell:*— bell.

4699. מְצֻלָּה **m°tsullâh**, *mets-ool-law´;* from 6751; *shade:*— bottom.

4700. מְצֵלֶת **m°tsêleth**, *mets-ay´-leth;* from 6750; (only dual) double *tinklers,* i.e. *cymbals:*— cymbals.

4701. מִצְנֶפֶת **mitsnepheth**, *mits-neh´-feth;* from 6801; a *tiara*, i.e. official *turban* (of a king or high priest):— diadem, mitre.

4702. מַצָּע **matstsâ'**, *mats-tsaw´;* from 3331; a *couch:*— bed.

4703. מִצְעָד **mits'âd**, *mits-awd´;* from 6805; a *step;* fig. *companionship:*— going, step.

4704. מִצְעִירָה **mits°°îyrâh**, *mits-tseh-ee-raw´;* fem. of 4705; prop. *littleness;* concr. *diminutive:*— little.

4705. מִצְעָר **mits'âr**, *mits-awr´;* from 6819; *petty* (in size or number); adv. a *short* (time):— little one (while), small.

4706. מִצְעָר **Mits'âr**, *mits-awr´;* the same

as 4705; *Mitsar*, a peak of Lebanon:— Mizar.

4707. מִצְפֶּה **mitspeh**, *mits-peh´;* from 6822; an *observatory*, espec. for military purposes:— watch tower.

4708. מִצְפֶּה **Mitspeh**, *mits-peh´;* the same as 4707; *Mitspeh*, the name of five places in Pal.:— Mizpeh, watch tower. Comp. 4709.

4709. מִצְפָּה **Mitspah**, *mits-paw´;* fem. of 4708; *Mitspah*, the name of two places in Pal.:— Mitspah. [This seems rather to be only an orthographic var. of 4708 when "in pause".]

4710. מִצְפֻּן **mitspûn**, *mits-poon´;* from 6845; a *secret* (place or thing, perh. *treasure*):— hidden thing.

4711. מָצַץ **mâtsats**, *maw-tsats´;* a prim. root; to *suck:*— milk.

מוּצָקָה **mûtsâqâh**. See 4166.

4712. מֵצַר **mêtsar**, *may-tsar´;* from 6896; something *tight,* i.e. (fig.) *trouble:*— distress, pain, strait.

מָצֻק **mâtsûq**. See 4690.

מְצֻקָה **m°tsûqâh**. See 4691.

מְצֻרָה **m°tsûrâh**. See 4694.

4713. מִצְרִי **Mitsrîy**, *mits-ree´;* from 4714; a *Mitsrite*, or inhab. of Mitsrajim:— Egyptian, of Egypt.

4714. מִצְרַיִם **Mitsrayim**, *mits-rah´-yim;* dual of 4693; *Mitsrajim*, i.e. Upper and Lower *Egypt:*— Egypt, Egyptians, Mizraim.

4715. מִצְרֵף **mitsrêph**, *mits-rafe´;* from 6884; a *crucible:*— fining pot.

4716. מַק **maq**, *mak;* from 4743; prop. a *melting,* i.e. (fig.) *putridity:*— rottenness, stink.

4717. מַקָּבָה **maqqâbâh**, *mak-kaw-baw´;* from 5344; prop. a *perforatrix*, i.e. a *hammer* (as *piercing*):— hammer.

4718. מַקֶּבֶת **maqqebeth**, *mak-keh´-beth;* from 5344; prop. a *perforator*, i.e. a *hammer* (as *piercing*); also (intr.) a *perforation,* i.e. a *quarry:*— hammer, hole.

4719. מַקֵּדָה **Maqqêdâh**, *mak-kay-daw´;* from the same as 5348 in the denom. sense of *herding* (comp. 5349); *fold; Makkedah*, a place in Pal.:— Makkedah.

4720. מִקְדָּשׁ **miqdâsh**, *mik-dawsh´;* or

מִקְּדָשׁ **miqq°dâsh** (Exod. 15:17), *mik-ked-awsh´;* from 6942; a *consecrated* thing or place, espec. a *palace, sanctuary* (whether of Jehovah or of idols) or *asylum:*— chapel, hallowed part, holy place, sanctuary.

4721. מַקְהֵל **maqhêl**, *mak-hale´;* or (fem.)

מַקְהֵלָה **maqhêlâh**, *mak-hay-law´;* from 6950; an *assembly:*— congregation.

4722. מַקְהֵלוֹת **Maqhêlôth**, *mak-hay-loth´;* plur. of 4721 (fem.); *assemblies; Makheloth*, a place in the Desert:— Makheloth.

4723. מִקְוֶה **miqveh**, *mik-veh´;* or

מִקְוֵה **miqvêh** (1 Kings 10:28) *mik-vay´;* or

מִקְוֵא° **miqvê'** (2 Chron. 1:16), *mik-*

vay´; from 6960; something *waited* for, i.e. *confidence* (obj. or subj.); also a *collection,* i.e. (of water) a *pond*, or (of men and horses) a *caravan* or *drove:*— abiding, gathering together, hope, linen yarn, plenty [of water], pool.

4724. מִקְוָה **miqvâh**, *mik-vaw´;* fem. of 4723; a *collection,* i.e. (of water) a *reservoir:*— ditch.

4725. מָקוֹם **mâqôwm**, *maw-kome´;* or

מָקֹם **mâqôm**, *maw-kome´;* also (fem.)

מְקוֹמָה **m°qôwmâh**, *mek-o-mah´;* or

מְקֹמָה **m°qômâh**, *mek-o-mah´;* from 6965; prop. a *standing,* i.e. a *spot;* but used widely of a *locality* (gen. or spec.); also (fig.) of a *condition* (of body or mind):— country, × home, × open, place, room, space, × whither [-soever].

4726. מָקוֹר **mâqôwr**, *maw-kore´;* or

מָקֹר **mâqôr**, *maw-kore´;* from 6979; prop. something *dug,* i.e. a (gen.) *source* (of water, even when naturally flowing; also of tears, blood [by euphem. of the female *pudenda*]; fig. of happiness, wisdom, progeny):— fountain, issue, spring, well (-spring).

4727. מִקָּח **miqqâch**, *mik-kawkh´;* from 3947; *reception:*— taking.

4728. מַקָּחָה **maqqâchâh**, *mak-kaw-khaw´;* from 3947; something *received,* i.e. *merchandise* (purchased):— ware.

4729. מִקְטָר **miqtâr**, *mik-tawr´;* from 6999; something to *fume* (incense) on, i.e. a *hearth* place:— to burn ... upon.

מְקַטְּרָה **m°qatt°râh**. See 6999.

4730. מִקְטֶרֶת **miqtereth**, *mik-teh´-reth;* fem. of 4729; something to *fume* (incense) in, i.e. a *coal-pan:*— censer.

4731. מַקֵּל **maqqêl**, *mak-kale;* or (fem.)

מַקְּלָה **maqq°lâh**, *mak-law´;* from an unused root mean. appar. to *germinate;* a *shoot,* i.e. *stick* (with leaves on, or for walking, striking, guiding, divining):— rod, ([hand-]) staff.

4732. מִקְלוֹת **Miqlôwth**, *mik-lohth´;* (or perh. *mik-kel-ohth´*); plur. of (fem.) 4731; *rods; Mikloth*, a place in the Desert:— Mikloth.

4733. מִקְלָט **miqlât**, *mik-lawt´;* from 7038 in the sense of *taking* in; an *asylum* (as a *receptacle*):— refuge.

4734. מִקְלַעַת **miqla'ath**, *mik-lah´-ath;* from 7049; a *sculpture* (prob. in bas-relief):— carved (figure), carving, graving.

מָקֹם **mâqôm**. See 4725.

מְקֹמָה **m°qômâh**. See 4725.

4735. מִקְנֶה **miqneh**, *mik-neh´;* from 7069; something *bought,* i.e. *property,* but only live *stock;* abstr. *acquisition:*— cattle, flock, herd, possession, purchase, substance.

4736. מִקְנָה **miqnâh**, *mik-naw´;* fem. of 4735; prop. a *buying,* i.e. *acquisition;* concr. a piece of *property* (land or living); also the *sum* paid:— (he that is) bought, possession, piece, purchase.

4737. מִקְנֵיָהוּ **Miqnêyâhûw**, *mik-nay-*

yaw´-hoo; from 4735 and 3050; *posses-sion of Jah; Miknejah,* an Isr.:— Mikneiah.

4738. מִקְסָם **miqçâm**, *mik-sawm´*; from 7080; an *augury:*— divination.

4739. מָקָץ **Mâqats**, *maw-kats´*; from 7112; *end; Makats,* a place in Pal.:— Makaz.

4740. מִקְצוֹעַ **maqtsôwa´**, *mak-tso´-ah;* or

מִקְצֹעַ **maqtsôa´**, *mak-tso´-ah;* or (fem.)

מִקְצֹעָה **maqtsô´âh**, *mak-tso-aw´;* from 7106 in the denom. sense of *bend-ing;* an *angle* or recess:— corner, turning.

4741. מַקְצֻעָה **maqtsû´âh**, *mak-tsoo-aw´;* from 7106; a *scraper,* i.e. a carving *chisel:*— plane.

4742. מִקְצֹעָה **m°quts´âh**, *mek-oots-aw´;* from 7106 in the denom. sense of *bend-ing;* an *angle:*— corner.

4743. מָקַק **mâqaq**, *maw-kak´;* a prim. root; to *melt;* fig. to *flow, dwindle, van-ish:*— consume away, be corrupt, dissolve, pine away.

4744. מָקוֹר **mâqôr**. See 4726.

4745. מִקְרָא **miqrâ´**, *mik-raw´;* from 7121; *something called* out, i.e. a public *meeting* (the act, the persons, or the place); also a *rehearsal:*— assembly, calling, convocation, reading.

4745. מִקְרֶה **miqreh**, *mik-reh´;* from 7136; *something met* with, i.e. an *acci-dent* or *fortune:*— something befallen, befalleth, chance, event, hap (-peneth).

4746. מְקָרֶה **m°qâreh**, *mek-aw-reh´;* from 7136; prop. something *meeting,* i.e. a *frame* (of timbers):— building.

4747. מְקֵרָה **m°qêrâh**, *mek-ay-raw´;* from the same as 7119; a *cooling* off:— × summer.

4748. מֹקֵשׁ **môqêsh**. See 4170.

4748. מִקְשֶׁה **miqsheh**, *mik-sheh´;* from 7185 in the sense of *knotting* up round and hard; something *turned* (rounded), i.e. a *curl* (of tresses):— × well [set] hair.

4749. מִקְשָׁה **miqshâh**, *mik-shaw´;* fem. of 4748; *rounded* work, i.e. moulded by *hammering* (repoussé:— beaten (out of one piece, work), upright, whole piece.

4750. מִקְשָׁה **miqshâh**, *mik-shaw´;* de-nom. from 7180; lit. a *cucumbered* field, i.e. a *cucumber* patch:— garden of cucumbers.

4751. מַר **mar**, *mar;* or (fem.)

מָרָה **mârâh**, *maw-raw´;* from 4843; *bitter* (lit. or fig.); also (as noun) *bitterness,* or (adv.) *bitterly:*— + angry, bitter (-ly, -ness), chafed, discontented, × great, heavy.

4752. מַר **mar**, *mar;* from 4843 in its orig. sense of *distillation;* a *drop:*— drop.

4753. מֹר **môr**, *mor;* or

מוֹר **môwr**, *more;* from 4843; *myrrh* (as *distilling* in drops, and also as *bitter*):— myrrh.

4754. מָרָא **mârâ´**, *maw-raw´;* a prim. root; to *rebel;* hence, (through the idea

of *maltreating)* to *whip,* i.e. *lash* (self with wings, as the ostrich in run-ning):— be filthy, lift up self.

4755. מָרָא **Mârâ´**, *maw-raw´;* for 4751 fem.; *bitter; Mara,* a symbol. name of Naomi:— Mara.

4756. מָרֵא **mârê´** (Chald.), *maw-ray´;* from a root corresp. to 4754 in the sense of *domineering;* a *master:*— lord, Lord.

4757. מְרֹאדַךְ בַּלְאָדָן **M°rô'dak Bal'âdân**, *mer-o-dak´ bal-aw-dawn´;* of for. der.; *Merodak-Baladan,* a Bab. king:— Merodach-baladan. Comp. 4781.

4757. מֹרָא **môrâ´**. See 4172.

4758. מַרְאֶה **mar'eh**, *mar-eh´;* from 7200; a *view* (the act of seeing); also an *ap-pearance* (the thing seen), whether (real) a *shape* (espec. if handsome, comeliness; often plur. the *looks*), or (ment.) a *vision:*— × apparently, ap-pearance (-reth), × as soon as beautiful (-ly), countenance, fair, favoured, form, goodly, to look (up) on (to), look [-eth], pattern, to see,.seem, sight, visage, vision.

4759. מַרְאָה **mar'âh**, *mar-aw´;* fem. of 4758; a *vision;* also (caus.) a *mirror:*— looking glass, vision.

4760. מֻרְאָה **mur'âh**, *moor-aw´;* appar. fem. pass. caus. part. of 7200; some-thing *conspicuous,* i.e. the *craw* of a bird (from its *prominence*):— crop.

4760. מַרְאוֹן **M°r'ôwn**. See 8112.

4761. מַרְאָשָׁה **mar'âshâh**, *mar-aw-shaw´;* denom. from 7218; prop. *head-ship,* i.e. (plur. for collect.) *dominion:*— principality.

4762. מַרְאֵשָׁה **Mar'êshâh**, *mar-ay-shaw´;* or

מַרְשָׁה **Marêshâh**, *mar-ay-shaw´;* formed like 4761; *summit; Mareshah,* the name of two Isr. and of a place in Pal.:— Mareshah.

4763. מְרַאֲשָׁה **m°ra'ăshâh**, *mer-ah-ash-aw´;* formed like 4761; prop. a *head-piece,* i.e. (plur. for adv.) *at* (or *as*) the *head-rest* (or pillow):— bolster, head, pillow. Comp. 4772.

4764. מֵרָב **Mêrâb**, *may-rawb´;* from 7231; *increase; Merab,* a daughter of Saul:— Merab.

4765. מַרְבַד **marbad**, *mar-bad´;* from 7234; a *coverlet:*— covering of tapestry.

4766. מַרְבֶּה **marbeh**, *mar-beh´;* from 7235; prop. *increasing;* as noun, *great-ness,* or (adv.) *greatly:*— great, in-crease.

4767. מִרְבָּה **mirbâh**, *meer-baw´;* from 7235; *abundance,* i.e. a great quan-tity:— much.

4768. מַרְבִּית **marbîyth**, *mar-beeth´;* from 7235; a *multitude;* also *offspring;* spec. *interest* (on capital):— greatest part, greatness, increase, multitude.

4769. מַרְבֵּץ **marbêts**, *mar-bates´;* from 7257; a *reclining* place, i.e. *fold* (for flocks):— couching place, place to lie down.

4770. מַרְבֵּק **marbêq**, *mar-bake´;* from an unused root mean. to *tie* up; a *stall* (for cattle):— × fat (-ted), stall.

4773. מֹרַג **môrag**. See 4173.

4771. מַרְגֹּעַ **margôwa´**, *mar-go-ah;* from 7280; a *resting* place:— rest.

4772. מַרְגְּלָה **marg°lâh**, *mar-ghel-aw´;* denom. from 7272; (plur. for collect.) a *footpiece,* i.e. (adv.) *at the foot,* or (di-rect.) the *foot* itself:— feet. Comp. 4763.

4773. מַרְגֵּמָה **margêmâh**, *mar-gay-maw´;* from 7275; a *stone-heap:*— sling.

4774. מַרְגֵּעָה **margê´âh**, *mar-gay-aw´;* from 7280; *rest:*— refreshing.

4775. מָרַד **mârad**, *maw-rad´;* a prim. root; to *rebel:*— rebel (-lious).

4776. מְרַד **m°rad** (Chald.), *mer-ad´;* from a root corresp. to 4775; *rebel-lion:*— rebellion.

4777. מֶרֶד **mered**, *meh´-red;* from 4775; *rebellion:*— rebellion.

4778. מֶרֶד **Mered**, *meh´-red;* the same as 4777; *Mered,* an Isr.:— Mered.

4779. מָרָד **mârâd** (Chald.), *maw-rawd´;* from the same as 4776; *rebellious:*— re-bellious.

4780. מַרְדּוּת **mardûwth**, *mar-dooth´;* from 4775; *rebelliousness:*— × rebel-lious.

4781. מְרֹדָךְ **M°rôdâk**, *mer-o-dawk´;* of for. der.; *Merodak,* a Bab. idol:— Mero-dach. Comp. 4757.

4782. מָרְדְּכַי **Mord°kay**, *mor-dek-ah´-ee;* of for. der.; *Mordecai,* an Isr.:— Morde-cai.

4783. מֻרְדָּף **murdâph**, *moor-dawf´;* from 7291; *persecuted:*— persecuted.

4784. מָרָה **mârâh**, *maw-raw´;* a prim. root; to *be* (caus. *make*) *bitter* (or un-pleasant); (fig.) to *rebel* (or resist; caus. to *provoke*):— bitter, change, be dis-obedient, disobey, grievously, provo-cation, provoke (-ing), (be) rebel (against, -lious).

4785. מָרָה **Mârâh**, *maw-raw´;* the same as 4751 fem.; *bitter; Marah,* a place in the Desert:— Marah.

4785. מֹרֶה **Môreh**. See 4175.

4786. מֹרָה **môrâh**, *mo-raw´;* from 4843; *bitterness,* i.e. (fig.) *trouble:*— grief.

4787. מָרָה **morrâh**, *mor-raw´;* a form of 4786; *trouble:*— bitterness.

4788. מָרוּד **mârûwd**, *maw-rood´;* from 7300 in the sense of *maltreatment;* an *outcast;* (abstr.) *destitution:*— cast out, misery.

4789. מֵרוֹז **Mêrôwz**, *may-roze´;* of un-cert. der.; *Meroz,* a place in Pal.:— Meroz.

4790. מְרוֹחַ **m°rôwach**, *mer-o-akh´;* from 4799; *bruised,* i.e. *emasculated:*— bro-ken.

4791. מָרוֹם **mârôwm**, *maw-rome´;* from 7311; *altitude,* i.e. concr. (an *elevated place*), abstr. (*elevation,* fig. (*elation*), or adv. (*aloft*):— (far) above, dignity, haughty, height, (most, on) high (one, place), loftily, upward.

4792. מֵרוֹם **Mêrôwm**, *may-rome´;* formed like 4791; *height; Merom,* a lake in Pal.:— Merom.

4793. מֵרוֹץ **mêrôwts**, *may-rotes´;* from 7323; a *run* (the trial of speed):— race.

4794. מְרוּצָה mᵉrûwtsâh, *mer-oo-tsaw*; or

מְרֻצָה mᵉrûtsâh, *mer-oo-tsaw*; fem. of 4793; a *race* (the act), whether the manner or the progress:— course, running. Comp. 4835.

4795. מָרוּק mârûwq, *maw-rook*; from 4838; prop. *rubbed*; but used abstr. a *rubbing* (with perfumery):— purification.

מְרוֹר mᵉrôwr. See 4844.

מְרוֹרָה mᵉrôwrâh. See 4846.

4796. מָרוֹת Mârôwth, *maw-rohth*; plur. of 4751 fem.; *bitter* springs; *Maroth*, a place in Pal.:— Maroth.

4797. מִרְזַח mirzach, *meer-zakh*; from an unused root mean. to *scream*; a *cry*, i.e. (of joy), a *revel*:— banquet.

4798. מַרְזֵחַ marzêach, *mar-zay'-akh*; formed like 4797; a *cry*, i.e. (of grief) a *lamentation*:— mourning.

4799. מָרַח mârach, *maw-rakh*; a prim. root; prop. to *soften* by rubbing or pressure; hence, (medicinally) to *apply* as an emollient:— lay for a plaister.

4800. מֶרְחָב merchâb, *mer-khawb*; from 7337; *enlargement*, either lit. (an *open space*, usually in a good sense), or fig. (*liberty*):— breadth, large place (room).

4801. מֶרְחָק merchâq, *mer-khawk*; from 7368; *remoteness*, i.e. (concr.) a *distant* place; often (adv.) *from afar*:— (a-, dwell in, very) far (country, off). See also 1023.

4802. מַרְחֶשֶׁת marchesheth, *mar-kheh'-sheth*; from 7370; a *stew-pan*:— frying-pan.

4803. מָרַט mârat, *maw-rat'*; a prim. root; to *polish*; by impl. to *make bald* (the head), to *gall* (the shoulder); also, to *sharpen*:— bright, furbish, (have his) hair (be) fallen off, peeled, pluck off (hair).

4804. מְרַט mᵉrat (Chald.), *mer-at'*; corresp. to 4803; to *pull* off:— be plucked.

4805. מְרִי mᵉriy, *mer-ee'*; from 4784; *bitterness*, i.e. (fig.) *rebellion*; concr. *bitter*, or *rebellious*:— bitter, (most) rebel (-lion, -lious).

4806. מְרִיא mᵉriy', *mer-ee'*; from 4754 in the sense of *grossness*, through the idea of *domineering* (comp. 4756); *stall-fed*; often (as noun) a *beeve*:— fat (fed) beast (cattle, -ling).

4807. מְרִיב בַּעַל Mᵉrîyb Ba'al, *mer-eeb' bah'-al*; from 7378 and 1168; *quarreller of Baal*; *Merib-Baal*, an epithet of Gideon:— Merib-baal. Comp. 4810.

4808. מְרִיבָה mᵉrîybâh, *mer-ee-baw'*; from 7378; *quarrel*:— provocation, strife.

4809. מְרִיבָה Mᵉrîybâh, *mer-ee-baw'*; the same as 4808; *Meribah*, the name of two places in the Desert:— Meribah.

4810. מְרִי בַּעַל Mᵉrîy Ba'al, *mer-ee' bah'-al*; from 4805 and 1168; *rebellion of* (i.e. *against*) *Baal*; *Meri-Baal*, an epithet of Gideon:— Meri-baal. Comp. 4807.

4811. מְרָיָה Mᵉrâyâh, *mer-aw-yaw'*; from 4784; *rebellion*; *Merajah*, an Isr.:— Meraiah. Comp. 3236.

4812. מְרָיוֹת Mᵉrâyôwth, *mer-aw-yohth'*; plur. of 4811; *rebellious*; *Merajoth*, the name of two Isr.:— Meraioth.

4813. מִרְיָם Miryâm, *meer-yawm'*; from 4805; *rebelliously*; *Mirjam*, the name of two Israelitesses:— Miriam.

4814. מְרִירוּת mᵉrîyrûwth, *mer-ee-rooth'*; from 4843; *bitterness*, i.e. (fig.) *grief*:— bitterness.

4815. מְרִירִי mᵉrîyriy, *mer-ee-ree'*; from 4843; *bitter*, i.e. *poisonous*:— bitter.

4816. מֹרֶךְ môrek, *mo'-rek*; perh. from 7401; *softness*, i.e. (fig.) *fear*:— faintness.

4817. מֶרְכָּב merkâb, *mer-kawb'*; from 7392; a *chariot*; also a *seat* (in a vehicle):— chariot, covering, saddle.

4818. מֶרְכָּבָה merkâbâh, *mer-kaw-baw'*; fem. of 4817; a *chariot*:— chariot. See also 1024.

4819. מַרְכֹּלֶת markôleth, *mar-ko'-leth*; from 7402; a *mart*:— merchandise.

4820. מִרְמָה mirmâh, *meer-maw'*; from 7411 in the sense of *deceiving*; *fraud*:— craft, deceit (-ful, -fully), false, feigned, guile, subtilly, treachery.

4821. מִרְמָה Mirmâh, *meer-maw'*; the same as 4820; *Mirmah*, an Isr.:— Mirma.

4822. מְרֵמוֹת Mᵉrêmôwth, *mer-ay-mohth'*; plur. from 7311; *heights*; *Meremoth*, the name of two Isr.:— Meremoth.

4823. מִרְמָס mirmâç, *meer-mawce'*; from 7429; *abasement* (the act or the thing):— tread (down)-ing, (to be) trodden (down) under foot.

4824. מֵרֹנֹתִי Mêrônôthîy, *may-ro-no-thee'*; patrial from an unused noun; a *Meronothite*, or inhab. of some (otherwise unknown) *Meronoth*:— Meronothite.

4825. מֶרֶס Mereç, *meh'-res*; of for. der.; *Meres*, a Pers.:— Meres.

4826. מַרְסְנָא Marçᵉnâ', *mar-sen-aw'*; of for. der.; *Marsena*, a Pers.:— Marsena.

4827. מֵרַע mêra', *may-rah'*; from 7489; used as (abstr.) noun, *wickedness*:— do mischief.

4828. מֵרֵעַ mêrêa', *may-ray'-ah*; from 7462 in the sense of *companionship*; a *friend*:— companion, friend.

4829. מִרְעֶה mir'eh, *meer-eh'*; from 7462 in the sense of *feeding*; *pasture* (the place or the act); also the *haunt* of wild animals:— feeding place, pasture.

4830. מִרְעִית mir'îyth, *meer-eeth'*; from 7462 in the sense of *feeding*; *pasturage*; concr. a *flock*:— flock, pasture.

4831. מַרְעֲלָה Mar'ălâh, *mar-al-aw'*; from 7477; perh. *earthquake*; *Maralah*, a place in Pal.:— Maralah.

4832. מַרְפֵּא marpê', *mar-pay'*; from 7495; prop. *curative*, i.e. lit. (concr.) a *medicine*, or (abstr.) a *cure*; fig. (concr.) *deliverance*, or (abstr.) *placidity*:— ([in-]l) cure (-able), healing (-lth), remedy, sound, wholesome, yielding.

4833. מִרְפָּשׂ mirpâs, *meer-paws'*; from 7515; *muddled* water:— that which ... have fouled.

4834. מָרַץ mârats, *maw-rats'*; a prim. root; prop. to *press*, i.e. (fig.) to *be pungent* or *vehement*; to *irritate*:— embolden, be forcible, grievous, sore.

4835. מְרֻצָה mᵉrûtsâh, *mer-oo-tsaw'*; from 7533; *oppression*:— violence. See also 4794.

4836. מַרְצֵעַ martsêa', *mar-tsay'-ah*; from 7527; an *awl*:— aul.

4837. מַרְצֶפֶת martsepheth, *mar-tseh'-feth*; from 7528; a *pavement*:— pavement.

4838. מָרַק mâraq, *maw-rak'*; a prim. root; to *polish*; by impl. to *sharpen*; also to *rinse*:— bright, furbish, scour.

4839. מָרָק mârâq, *maw-rawk'*; from 4838; *soup* (as if a *rinsing*):— broth. See also 6564.

4840. מֶרְקָח merqâch, *mer-kawkh'*; from 7543; a *spicy* herb:— × sweet.

4841. מֶרְקָחָה merqâchâh, *mer-kaw-khaw'*; fem. of 4840; abstr. a *seasoning* (with spicery); concr. an *unguent-kettle* (for preparing spiced oil):— pot of ointment, × well.

4842. מִרְקַחַת mirqachath, *meer-kakh'-ath*; from 7543; an aromatic *unguent*; also an *unguent-pot*:— prepared by the apothecaries' art, compound, ointment.

4843. מָרַר mârar, *maw-rar'*; a prim. root; prop. to *trickle* [see 4752]; but used only as a denom. from 4751; to *be* (caus. *make*) *bitter* (lit. or fig.):— (be, be in, deal, have, make) bitter (-ly, -ness), be moved with choler, (be, have sorely, it) grieved (-eth), provoke, vex.

4844. מְרֹר mᵉrôr, *mer-ore'*; or

מְרוֹר mᵉrôwr, *mer-ore'*; from 4843; a *bitter* herb:— bitter (-ness).

4845. מְרֵרָה mᵉrêrâh, *mer-ay-raw'*; from 4843; *bile* (from its bitterness):— gall.

4846. מְרֹרָה mᵉrôrâh, *mer-o-raw'*; or

מְרוֹרָה mᵉrôwrâh, *mer-o-raw'*; from 4843; prop. *bitterness*; concr. a *bitter thing*; spec. *bile*; also *venom* (of a serpent):— bitter (thing), gall.

4847. מְרָרִי Mᵉrâriy, *mer-aw-ree'*; from 4843; *bitter*; *Merari*, an Isr.:— Merari. See also 4848.

4848. מְרָרִי Mᵉrâriy, *mer-aw-ree'*; from 4847; a *Merarite* (collect.), or desc. of Merari:— Merarites.

מַרְשָׁה Mârêshâh. See 4762.

4849. מִרְשַׁעַת mirsha'ath, *meer-shah'-ath*; from 7561; a female *wicked doer*:— wicked woman.

4850. מְרָתַיִם Mᵉrâthayim, *mer-aw-thah'-yim*; dual of 4751 fem.; *double bitterness*; *Merathajim*, an epithet of Bab.:— Merathaim.

4851. מַשׁ Mash, *mash*; of for. der.; *Mash*, a son of Aram, and the people desc. from him:— Mash.

4852. מֵשָׁא Mêshâ', *may-shaw'*; of for. der.; *Mesha*, a place in Arabia:— Mesha.

4853. מַשָּׂא massâ', *mas-saw'*; from 5375; a *burden*; spec. *tribute*, or (abstr.) *porterage*; fig. an *utterance*, chiefly a *doom*, espec. *singing*; ment. *desire*:—

מֹרִיָּה Môrîyâh. See 4179.

burden, carry away, prophecy, × they set, song, tribute.

4854. מַשָּׂא **Massâ'**, *mas-saw'*; the same as 4853; *burden*; *Massa*, a son of Ishmael:— Massa.

4855. מַשָּׁא **mashshâ'**, *mash-shaw'*; from 5383; a *loan*; by impl. *interest* on a debt:— exaction, usury.

4856. מַשָּׂא **massô'**, *mas-so'*; from 5375; *partiality* (as a *lifting* up):— respect.

4857. מַשְׁאָב **mash'âb**, *mash-awb'*; from 7579; a *trough* for cattle to drink from:— place of drawing water.

מַשְׁאָה **m͏eshô'âh**. See 4875.

4858. מַשָּׂאָה **massâ'âh**, *mas-saw-aw'*; from 5375; a *conflagration* (from the *rising* of smoke):— burden.

4859. מַשָּׁאָה **mashshâ'âh**, *mash-shaw-aw'*; fem. of 4855; a *loan*:— × any [-thing], debt.

מַשֻּׁאָה **mashshû'âh**. See 4876.

4860. מַשָּׁאוֹן **mashshâ'ôwn**, *mash-shaw-ohn'*; from 5377; *dissimulation*:— deceit.

4861. מִשְׁאָל **Mish'âl**, *mish-awl'*; from 7592; *request*; *Mishal*, a place in Pal.:— Mishal, Misheal. Comp. 4913.

4862. מִשְׁאָלָה **mish'âlâh**, *mish-aw-law'*; from 7592; a *request*:— desire, petition.

4863. מִשְׁאֶרֶת **mish'ereth**, *mish-eh'-reth*; from 7604 in the orig. sense of *swelling*; a *kneading-trough* (in which the dough *rises*):— kneading trough, store.

4864. מַשְׂאֵת **mas'êth**, *mas-ayth'*; from 5375; prop. (abstr.) a *raising* (as of the hands in prayer), or *rising* (of flame); fig. an *utterance*; concr. a *beacon* (as *raised*); a *present* (as taken), *mess*, or *tribute*; fig. a *reproach* (as a *burden*):— burden, collection, sign of fire, (great) flame, gift, lifting up, mess, oblation, reward.

מֹשָׁב **môshâb**. See 4186.

מְשׁוּבָה **m͏eshûbâh**. See 4878.

4865. מִשְׁבְּצָה **mishb͏etsâh**, *mish-bets-aw'*; from 7660; a *brocade*; by anal. a (reticulated) *setting* of a gem:— ouch, wrought.

4866. מִשְׁבֵּר **mishbêr**, *mish-bare'*; from 7665; the *orifice* of the womb (from which the fetus *breaks* forth):— birth, breaking forth.

4867. מִשְׁבָּר **mishbâr**, *mish-bawr'*; from 7665; a *breaker* (of the sea):— billow, wave.

4868. מִשְׁבָּת **mishbâth**, *mish-bawth'*; from 7673; *cessation*, i.e. destruction:— sabbath.

4869. מִשְׂגָּב **misgâb**, *mis-gawb'*; from 7682; prop. a *cliff* (or other *lofty* or *inaccessible* place); abstr. *altitude*; fig. a *refuge*:— defence, high fort (tower), refuge.

4869'. מִשְׂגָּב **misgâb**, *mis-gawb'*; *Misgab*, a place in Moab:— Misgab.

4870. מִשְׁגֶּה **mishgeh**, *mish-gay'*; from 7686; an *error*:— oversight.

4871. מָשָׁה **mâshâh**, *maw-shaw'*; a prim. root; to *pull* out (lit. or fig.):— draw (out).

4872. מֹשֶׁה **Môsheh**, *mo-sheh'*; from 4871; *drawing* out (of the water), i.e. *rescued*; *Mosheh*, the Isr. lawgiver:— Moses.

4873. מֹשֶׁה **Môsheh** (Chald.), *mo-sheh'*; corresp. to 4872:— Moses.

4874. מַשֶּׁה **mashsheh**, *mash-sheh'*; from 5383; a *debt*:— + creditor.

4875. מְשׁוֹאָה **m͏eshôw'âh**, *meh-o-aw'*; or מְשֹׁאָה **m͏eshô'âh**, *mesh-o-aw'*; from the same as 7722; (a) *ruin*, abstr. (the act) or concr. (the wreck):— desolation, waste.

4876. מַשְׁאָה **mashshûw'âh**, *mash-shoo-aw'*; or מַשֻּׁאָה **mashshû'âh**, *mash-shoo-aw'*; for 4875; *ruin*:— desolation, destruction.

4877. מְשׁוֹבָב **M͏eshôwbâb**, *mesh-o-bawb'*; from 7725; *returned*; *Meshobab*, an Isr.:— Meshobab.

4878. מְשׁוּבָה **m͏eshûbâh**, *mesh-oo-baw'*; or מְשֻׁבָה **m͏eshûbâh**, *mesh-oo-baw'*; from 7725; *apostasy*:— backsliding, turning away.

4879. מְשׁוּגָה **m͏eshûwgâh**, *mesh-oo-gaw'*; from an unused root mean. to *stray*; *mistake*:— error.

4880. מָשׁוֹט **mâshôwṭ**, *maw-shote'*; or מִשּׁוֹט **mishshôwṭ**, *mish-shote'*; from 7751; an *oar*:— oar.

4881. מְשׂוּכָה **m͏esûwkâh**, *mes-oo-kaw'*; or מְשֻׂכָה **m͏esûkâh**, *mes-oo-kaw'*; from 7753; a *hedge*:— hedge.

4882. מְשׁוּסָה **m͏eshûwçâh**, *mesh-oo-saw'*; from an unused root mean. to *plunder*; *spoilation*:— spoil.

4883. מַשּׂוֹר **massôwr**, *mas-sore'*; from an unused root mean. to *rasp*; a *saw*:— saw.

4884. מְשׂוּרָה **m͏esûwrâh**, *mes-oo-raw'*; from an unused root mean. appar. to *divide*; a *measure* (for liquids):— measure.

4885. מָשׂוֹשׂ **mâsôws**, *maw-soce'*; from 7797; *delight*, concr. (the cause or object) or abstr. (the feeling):— joy, mirth, rejoice.

4886. מָשַׁח **mâshach**, *maw-shakh'*; a prim. root; to *rub* with oil, i.e. to *anoint*; by impl. to *consecrate*; also to *paint*:— anoint, paint.

4887. מְשַׁח **m͏eshach** (Chald.), *mesh-akh'*; from a root corresp. to 4886; *oil*:— oil.

4888. מִשְׁחָה **mishchâh**, *meesh-khaw'*; or מָשְׁחָה **moshchâh**, *mosh-khaw'*; from 4886; *unction* (the act); by impl. a *consecratory gift*:— (to be) anointed (-ing), ointment.

4889. מַשְׁחִית **mashchîyth**, *mash-kheeth'*; from 7843; *destructive*, i.e. (as noun) *destruction*, lit. (spec. a *snare*) or fig. (*corruption*):— corruption, (to) destroy (-ing), destruction, trap, × utterly.

4890. מִשְׂחָק **mischâq**, *mis-khawk'*; from 7831; a *laughing-stock*:— scorn.

4891. מִשְׁחָר **mishchâr**, *mish-khawr'*; from 7836 in the sense of day *breaking*; *dawn*:— morning.

4892. מַשְׁחֵת **mashchêth**, *mash-khayth'*; for 4889; *destruction*:— destroying.

4893. מִשְׁחָת **mishchâth**, *mish-khawth'*; or מָשְׁחָת **moshchâth**, *mosh-khawth'*; from 7843; *disfigurement*:— corruption, marred.

4894. מִשְׁטוֹחַ **mishṭôwach**, *mish-to'-akh*; or מִשְׁטַח **mishṭach**, *mish-takh'*; from 7849; a *spreading*-place:— (to) spread (forth, -ing, upon).

4895. מַשְׂטֵמָה **masṭêmâh**, *mas-tay-maw'*; from the same as 7850; *enmity*:— hatred.

4896. מִשְׂטָר **mishṭâr**, *mish-tawr'*; from 7860; *jurisdiction*:— dominion.

4897. מֶשִׁי **meshîy**, *meh'-shee*; from 4871; *silk* (as *drawn* from the cocoon):— silk.

מוּשִׁי **Mushîy**. See 4187.

4898. מְשֵׁיזַבְאֵל **M͏eshêyzab'êl**, *mesh-ay-zab-ale'*; from an equiv. to 7804 and 410; *delivered of God*; *Meshezabel*, an Isr.:— Meshezabeel.

4899. מָשִׁיחַ **mâshîyach**, *maw-shee'-akh*; from 4886; *anointed*; usually a *consecrated* person (as a king, priest, or saint); spec. the *Messiah*:— anointed, Messiah.

4900. מָשַׁךְ **mâshak**, *maw-shak'*; a prim. root; to *draw*, used in a great variety of applications (incl. to *sow*, to *sound*, to *prolong*, to *develop*, to *march*, to *remove*, to *delay*, to *be tall*. etc.):— draw (along, out), continue, defer, extend, forbear, × give, handle, make (pro-, sound) long, × sow, scatter, stretch out.

4901. מֶשֶׁךְ **meshek**, *meh'shek*; from 4900; a *sowing*; also a *possession*:— precious, price.

4902. מֶשֶׁךְ **Meshek**, *meh'-shek*; the same in form as 4901, but prob. of for. der.; *Meshek*, a son of Japheth, and the people desc. from him:— Mesech, Meshech.

4903. מִשְׁכַּב **mishkab** (Chald.), *mish-kab'*; corresp. to 4904; a *bed*:— bed.

4904. מִשְׁכָּב **mishkâb**, *mish-kawb'*; from 7901; a *bed* (fig. a *bier*); abstr. *sleep*; by euphem. carnal *intercourse*:— bed ([-chamber]), couch, lieth (lying) with.

מְשֻׂכָה **m͏esûkâh**. See 4881.

4905. מַשְׂכִּיל **maskîyl**, *mas-keel'*; from 7919; *instructive*, i.e. a *didactic* poem:— Maschil.

מַשְׂכִּים **maskîym**. See 7925.

4906. מַשְׂכִּית **maskîyth**, *mas-keeth'*; from the same as 7906; a *figure* (carved on stone, the wall, or any object); fig. *imagination*:— conceit, image (-ry), picture, × wish.

4907. מִשְׁכַּן **mishkan** (Chald.), *mish-kan'*; corresp. to 4908; *residence*:— habitation.

4908. מִשְׁכָּן **mishkân**, *mish-kawn'*; from 7931; a *residence* (incl. a shepherd's *hut*, the *lair* of animals, fig. the *grave*; also the *Temple*; spec. the *Tabernacle* (prop. its wooden *walls*):— dwelleth, dwelling (place), habitation, tabernacle, tent.

4909. מַשְׂכֹּרֶת **maskôreth**, *mas-koh´-reth*; from 7936; *wages* or a *reward*:— reward, wages.

4910. מָשַׁל **mâshal**, *maw-shal´*; a prim. root; to *rule*:— (have, make to have) dominion, governor, × indeed, reign, (bear, cause to, have) rule (-ing, -r), have power.

4911. מָשַׁל **mâshal**, *maw-shal´*; denom. from 4912; to *liken*. i.e. (tran.) to use fig. language (an allegory, adage, song or the like); intr. to *resemble*:— be (-come) like, compare, use (as a) proverb, speak (in proverbs), utter.

4912. מָשָׁל **mâshâl**, *maw-shawl´*; appar. from 4910 in some orig. sense of *superiority* in mental action; prop. a pithy *maxim*, usually of metaph. nature; hence, a *simile* (as an adage, poem, discourse):— byword, like, parable, proverb.

4913. מָשָׁל **Mâshâl**, *maw-shawl´*; for 4861; *Mashal*, a place in Pal.:— Mashal.

4914. מְשׁוֹל **mᵉshôl**, *mesh-ol´*; from 4911; a *satire*:— byword.

4915. מֹשֵׁל **môshel**, *mo´-shel*; (1) from 4910; *empire*; (2) from 4911; a *parallel*:— dominion, like.

מִשְׁלוֹשׁ **mishlôwsh**. See 7969.

4916. מִשְׁלוֹחַ **mishlôwach**, *mish-lo´-akh*; or

מִשְׁלֹחַ **mishlôach**, *mish-lo´-akh*; also

מִשְׁלָח **mishlâch**, *mish-lawkh´*; from 7971; a *sending* out, i.e. (abstr.) *presentation* (favorable), or *seizure* (unfavorable); also (concr.) a place of *dismissal*, or a *business* to be discharged:— to lay, to put, sending (forth), to set.

4917. מִשְׁלַחַת **mishlachath**, *mish-lakh´-ath*; fem. of 4916; a *mission*, i.e. (abstr.) and favorable) *release*, or (concr. and unfavorable) an *army*:— discharge, sending.

4918. מְשֻׁלָּם **Mᵉshullâm**, *mesh-ool-lawm´*; from 7999; *allied*; *Meshullam*, the name of seventeen Isr.:— Meshullam.

4919. מְשִׁלֵּמוֹת **Mᵉshillêmôwth**, *mesh-il-lay-mohth´*; plur. from 7999; *reconciliations*; *Meshillemoth*, an Isr.:— Meshillemoth. Comp. 4921.

4920. מְשֶׁלֶמְיָה **Mᵉshelemyâh**, *mesh-eh-lem-yaw´*; or

מְשֶׁלֶמְיָהוּ **Mᵉshelemyâhûw**, *mesh-eh-lem-yaw´-hoo*; from 7999 and 3050; *ally of Jah*; *Meshelemjah*, an Isr.:— Meshelemiah.

4921. מְשִׁלֵּמִית **Mᵉshillêmîyth**, *mesh-il-lay-meeth´*; from 7999; *reconciliation*; *Meshillemith*, an Isr.:— Meshillemith. Comp. 4919.

4922. מְשֻׁלֶּמֶת **Mᵉshullemeth**, *mesh-ool-leh´-meth*; fem. of 4918; *Meshullemeth*, an Israelitess:— Meshullemeth.

4923. מְשַׁמָּה **mᵉshammâh**, *mesh-am-maw´*; from 8074; a *waste* or *amazement*:— astonishment, desolate.

4924. מַשְׁמָן **mashmân**, *mash-mawn´*; from 8080; *fat*, i.e. (lit. and abstr.) *fatness*; but usually (fig. and concr.) a *rich*

dish, a *fertile* field, a *robust* man:— fat (one, -ness, -test, -test place).

4925. מִשְׁמַנָּה **Mishmannâh**, *mish-man-naw´*; from 8080; *fatness*; *Mashmannah*, an Isr.:— Mishmannah.

4926. מִשְׁמָע **mishmâ´**, *mish-maw´*; from 8085; a *report*:— hearing.

4927. מִשְׁמָע **Mishmâ´**, *mish-maw´*; the same as 4926; *Mishma*, the name of a son of Ishmael, and of an Isr.:— Mishma.

4928. מִשְׁמַעַת **mishma´ath**, *mish-mah´-ath*; fem. of 4926; *audience*, i.e. the royal *court*; also *obedience*, i.e. (concr.) a *subject*:— bidding, guard, obey.

4929. מִשְׁמָר **mishmâr**, *mish-mawr´*; from 8104; a *guard* (the man, the post, or the *prison*); fig. a *deposit*; also (as observed) a *usage* (abstr.), or an *example* (concr.):— diligence, guard, office, prison, ward, watch.

4930. מַשְׂמְרָה **masmᵉrâh**, *mas-mer-aw´*; for 4548 fem.; a *peg*:— nail.

4931. מִשְׁמֶרֶת **mishmereth**, *mish-meh´-reth*; fem. of 4929; *watch*, i.e. the act (custody) or (concr.) the *sentry*, the post; obj. *preservation*, or (concr.) *safe*; fig. *observance*, i.e. (abstr.) *duty*, or (obj.) a *usage* or *party*:— charge, keep, to be kept, office, ordinance, safeguard, ward, watch.

4932. מִשְׁנֶה **mishneh**, *mish-neh´*; from 8138; prop. a *repetition*, i.e. a *duplicate* (copy of a document), or a *double* (in amount); by impl. a *second* (in order, rank, age, quality or location):— college, copy, double, fatlings, next, second (order), twice as much.

4933. מְשִׁסָּה **mᵉshiççâh**, *mesh-is-saw´*; from 8155; *plunder*:— booty, spoil.

4934. מִשְׁעוֹל **mish´ôwl**, *mish-ole´*; from the same as 8168; a *hollow*, i.e. a narrow passage:— path.

4935. מִשְׁעִי **mish´îy**, *mish-ee´*; prob. from 8159; *inspection*:— to supple.

4936. מִשְׁעָם **Mish´âm**, *mish-awm´*; appar. from 8159; *inspection*; *Misham*, an Isr.:— Misham.

4937. מִשְׁעֵן **mish´ên**, *mish-ane´*; or

מִשְׁעָן **mish´ân**, *mish-awn´*; from 8172; a *support* (concr.), i.e. (fig.) a *protector* or *sustenance*:— stay.

4938. מִשְׁעֵנָה **mish´ênâh**, *mish-ay-naw´*; or

מִשְׁעֶנֶת **mish´eneth**, *mish-eh´-neth*; fem. of 4937; *support* (abstr.), i.e. (fig.) *sustenance* or (concr.) a *walking-stick*:— staff.

4939. מִשְׂפָּח **mispâch**, *mis-pawkh´*; from 5596; *slaughter*:— oppression.

4940. מִשְׁפָּחָה **mishpâchâh**, *mish-paw-khaw´*; from 8192 [comp. 8198]; a *family*, i.e. circle of relatives; fig. a *class* (of persons), a *species* (of animals) or *sort* (of things); by extens. a *tribe* or *people*:— family, kind (-red).

4941. מִשְׁפָּט **mishpât**, *mish-pawt´*; from 8199; prop. a *verdict* (favorable or unfavorable) pronounced judicially, esp. a *sentence* or formal decree (human or [participant's] divine *law*, indiv. or collect.), incl. the act, the place, the suit, the crime, and the penalty; abstr. *jus-

tice*, incl. a participant's *right* or *privilege* (statutory or customary), or even a *style*:— + adversary, ceremony, charge, × crime, custom, desert, determination, discretion, disposing, due, fashion, form, to be judged, judgment, just (-ice, -ly), (manner of) law (-ful), manner, measure, (due) order, ordinance, right, sentence, usest, × worthy, + wrong.

4942. מִשְׁפָּת **mishpâth**, *mish-pawth´*; from 8192; a *stall* for cattle (only dual):— burden, sheepfold.

4943. מֶשֶׁק **mesheq**, *meh´-shek*; from an unused root mean. to *hold*; *possession*:— + steward.

4944. מַשָּׁק **mashshâq**, *mash-shawk´*; from 8264; a *traversing*, i.e. rapid *motion*:— running to and fro.

4945. מַשְׁקֶה **mashqeh**, *mash-keh´*; from 8248; prop. *causing to drink*, i.e. a *butler*; by impl. (intr.), *drink* (itself); fig. a *well-watered* region:— butler (-ship), cupbearer, drink (-ing), fat pasture, watered.

4946. מַשְׁקוֹל **mishqôwl**, *mish-kole´*; from 8254; *weight*:— weight.

4947. מַשְׁקוֹף **mashqôwph**, *mash-kofe´*; from 8259 in its orig. sense of *overhanging*; a *lintel*:— lintel.

4948. מִשְׁקָל **mishqâl**, *mish-kawl´*; from 8254; *weight* (numerically estimated); hence, *weighing* (the act):— (full) weight.

4949. מִשְׁקֶלֶת **mishqeleth**, *mish-keh´-leth*; or

מִשְׁקֹלֶת **mishqôleth**, *mish-ko´-leth*; fem. of 4948 or 4947; a *weight*, i.e. a *plummet* (with line attached):— plummet.

4950. מִשְׁקָע **mishqâ´**, *mish-kaw´*; from 8257; a *settling* place (of water), i.e. a pond:— deep.

4951. מִשְׂרָה **misrâh**, *mis-raw´*; from 8280; *empire*:— government.

4952. מִשְׁרָה **mishrâh**, *mish-raw´*; from 8281 in the sense of *loosening*; *maceration*, i.e. steeped *juice*:— liquor.

4953. מַשְׁרוֹקִי **mashrôwqiy** (Chald.), *mash-ro-kee´*; from a root corresp. to 8319; a (musical) *pipe* (from its *whistling* sound):— flute.

4954. מִשְׁרָעִי **Mishrâ´iy**, *mish-raw-ee´*; patrial from an unused noun from an unused root; prob. mean. to *stretch* out; *extension*; a *Mishraite*, or inhab. (collect.) of Mishra:— Mishraites.

4955. מִשְׂרָפָה **misrâphâh**, *mis-raw-faw´*; from 8313; *combustion*, i.e. *cremation* (of a corpse), or *calcination* (of lime):— burning.

4956. מִשְׂרְפוֹת מַיִם **Misrᵉphôwth Mayim**, *mis-ref-ohth´ mah´-yim*; from the plur. of 4955 and 4325; *burnings of water*; *Misrephoth-Majim*, a place in Pal.:— Misrephoth-maim.

4957. מַשְׂרֵקָה **Masrêqâh**, *mas-ray-kaw´*; a form for 7796 used denom.; *vineyard*; *Masrekah*, a place in Idumæa:— Masrekah.

4958. מַשְׂרֵת **masrêth**, *mas-rayth´*; appar. from an unused root mean. to *perforate*, i.e. hollow out; a *pan*:— pan.

4959. מָשַׁשׁ **måshash**, *maw-shash´*; a prim. root; to *feel* of; by impl. to *grope*:— feel, grope, search.

4960. מִשְׁתֶּה **mishteh**, *mish-teh´*; from 8354; *drink*, by impl. *drinking* (the act); also (by impl.) a *banquet* or (gen.) feast:— banquet, drank, drink, feast ([l-ed], -ing).

4961. מִשְׁתֶּה **mishteh** (Chald.), *mish-teh´*; corresp. to 4960; a *banquet*:— banquet.

4962. מַת **math**, *math*; from the same as 4970; prop. an *adult* (as of full length); by impl. a *man* (only in the plur.):— + few, × friends, men, persons, × small.

4963. מַתְבֵּן **mathbên**, *math-bane´*; denom. from 8401; *straw* in the heap:— straw.

4964. מֶתֶג **metheg**, *meh-theg*; from an unused root mean. to *curb*; a *bit*:— bit, bridle.

4965. מֶתֶג הָאַמָּה **Metheg hâ-'Ammâh**, *meh´-theg haw-am-maw´*; from 4964 and 520 with the art. interposed; *bit of the metropolis*; *Metheg-ha-Ammah*, an epithet of Gath:— Metheg-ammah.

4966. מָתוֹק **mâthôwq**, *maw-thoke´*; or

מָתוּק **mâthûwq**, *maw-thook´*; from 4985; *sweet*:— sweet (-er, -ness).

4967. מְתוּשָׁאֵל **Mᵉthûwshâ'êl**, *meth-oo-shaw-ale´*; from 4962 and 410, with the rel. interposed; *man who* (is) *of God*; *Methushaël*, an antediluvian patriarch:— Methusael.

4968. מְתוּשֶׁלַח **Mᵉthûwshelach**, *meth-oo-sheh´-lakh*; from 4962 and 7973; *man of a dart*; *Methushelach*, an antediluvian patriarch:— Methuselah.

4969. מָתַח **mâthach**, *maw-thakh´*; a prim. root; to *stretch* out:— spread out.

4970. מָתַי **mâthay**, *maw-thah´ee*; from an unused root mean. to *extend*; prop. *extent* (of time); but used only adv. *when* (either rel. or interrog.):— long, when.

מֵתִים **mᵉthîym**. See 4962.

4971. מַתְכֹּנֶת **mathkôneth**, *math-ko´-neth*; or

מַתְכֻּנֶת **mathkûneth**, *math-koo´-neth*; from 8505 in the transferred sense of *measuring*; *proportion* (in size, number or ingredients):— composition, measure, state, tale.

4972. מַתְלָאָה **mattᵉlâ'âh**, *mat-tel-aw-aw´*; from 4100 and 8513; *what a trouble!*:— what a weariness.

4973. מְתַלְּעָה **mᵉthallᵉ'âh**, *meth-al-leh-aw´*; contr. from 3216; prop. a *biter*, i.e. a *tooth*:— cheek (jaw) tooth, jaw.

4974. מְתֹם **mᵉthôm**, *meth-ohm´*; from 8552; *wholesomeness*; also (adv.) *completely*:— men [by reading 4962], soundness.

מֶתֶן **Methen**. See 4981.

4975. מֹתֶן **môthen**, *mo´-then*; from an unused root mean. to *be slender*; prop. the *waist* or small of the back; only in plur. the *loins*:— + greyhound, loins, side.

4976. מַתָּן **mattân**, *mat-tawn´*; from 5414; a *present*:— gift, to give, reward.

4977. מַתָּן **Mattân**, *mat-tawn´*; the same

as 4976; *Mattan*, the name of a priest of Baal, and of an Isr.:— Mattan.

4978. מַתְּנָא **mattᵉnâ'** (Chald.), *mat-ten-aw´*; corresp. to 4979:— gift.

4979. מַתָּנָה **mattânâh**, *mat-taw-naw´*; fem. of 4976; a *present*; spec. (in a good sense), a sacrificial *offering*, (in a bad sense) a *bribe*:— gift.

4980. מַתָּנָה **Mattânâh**, *mat-taw-naw´*; the same as 4979; *Mattanah*, a place in the Desert:— Mattanah.

4981. מִתְנִי **Mithnîy**, *mith-nee´*; prob. patrial from an unused noun mean. *slenderness*; a *Mithnite*, or inhab. of Methen:— Mithnite.

4982. מַתְּנַי **Mattᵉnay**, *mat-ten-ah´ee*; from 4976; *liberal*; *Mattenai*, the name of three Isr.:— Mattenai.

4983. מַתַּנְיָה **Mattanyâh**, *mat-tan-yaw´*; or

מַתַּנְיָהוּ **Mattanyâhûw**, *mat-tan-yaw´-hoo*; from 4976 and 3050; *gift of Jah*; *Mattanjah*, the name of ten Isr.:— Mattaniah.

מַתְּנַיִם **mothnayim**. See 4975.

4984. מִתְנַשֵּׂא **mithnassê´**, *mith-nas-say´*; from 5375; (used as abstr.) supreme *exaltation*:— exalted.

4985. מָתַק **mâthaq**, *maw-thak´*; a prim. root; to *suck*, by impl. to *relish*, or (intr.) *be sweet*:— be (made, × take) sweet.

4986. מֶתֶק **metheq**, *meh´-thek*; from 4985; fig. *pleasantness* (of discourse):— sweetness.

4987. מֹתֶק **môtheq**, *mo´-thek*; from 4985; *sweetness*:— sweetness.

4988. מָתָק **mâthâq**, *maw-thawk´*; from 4985; a *dainty*, i.e. (gen.) *food*:— feed sweetly.

4989. מִתְקָה **Mithqâh**, *mith-kaw´*; fem. of 4987; *sweetness*; *Mithkah*, a place in the Desert:— Mithcah.

4990. מִתְרְדָת **Mithrᵉdâth**, *mith-red-awth´*; of Pers. or.; *Mithredath*, the name of two Pers.:— Mithredath.

4991. מַתָּת **mattâth**, *mat-tawth´*; fem. of 4976 abb.; a *present*:— gift.

4992. מַתַּתָּה **Mattattâh**, *mat-tat-taw´*; for 4993; *gift of Jah*; *Mattattah*, an Isr.:— Mattathah.

4993. מַתִּתְיָה **Mattithyâh**, *mat-tith-yaw´*; or

מַתִּתְיָהוּ **Mattithyâhûw**, *mat-tith-yaw´-hoo*; from 4991 and 3050; *gift of Jah*; *Mattithjah*, the name of four Isr.:— Mattithiah.

נ

4994. נָא **nâ´**, *naw*; a prim. particle of incitement and entreaty, which may usually be rendered *I pray, now* or *then*; added mostly to verbs (in the imperative or future), or to interj., occasionally to an adv. or conjunc.:— I beseech (pray) thee (you), go to, now, oh.

4995. נָא **nâ´**, *naw*; appar. from 5106 in the sense of *harshness* from refusal; prop. *tough*, i.e. *uncooked* (flesh):— raw.

4996. נֹא **Nô´**, *no*; of Eg. or.; *No* (i.e.

Thebes), the capital of Upper Egypt:— No. Comp. 528.

4997. נֹאד **nô'd**, *node*; or

נֹאוד **nô'wd**, *node*; also (fem.)

נֹאדָה **nô'dâh**, *no-daw´*; from an unused root of uncert. signif.; a (skin or leather) *bag* (for fluids):— bottle.

נֹאדְרִי **ne'dârîy**. See 142.

4998. נָאָה **nâ'âh**, *naw-aw´*; a prim. root; prop. to *be at home*, i.e. (by impl.) to be *pleasant* (or *suitable*), i.e. *beautiful*:— be beautiful, become, be comely.

4999. נָאָה **nâ'âh**, *naw-aw´*; from 4998; a *home*; fig. a *pasture*:— habitation, house, pasture, pleasant place.

5000. נָאוֶה **nâ'veh**, *naw-veh´*; from 4998 or 5116; *suitable*, or *beautiful*:— becometh, comely, seemly.

5001. נָאַם **nâ'am**, *naw-am´*; a prim. root; prop. to *whisper*, i.e. (by impl.) to *utter* as an oracle:— say.

5002. נְאֻם **nᵉ'ûm**, *neh-oom´*; from 5001; an *oracle*:— (hath) said, saith.

5003. נָאַף **nâ'aph**, *naw-af´*; a prim. root; to *commit adultery*; fig. to *apostatize*:— adulterer (-ess), commit (-ing) adultery, woman that breaketh wedlock.

5004. נִאֻף **ni'ûph**, *nee-oof´*; from 5003; *adultery*:— adultery.

5005. נַאֲפוּף **na'äphûwph**, *nah-af-oof´*; from 5003; *adultery*:— adultery.

5006. נָאַץ **nâ'ats**, *naw-ats´*; a prim. root; to *scorn*; or (Eccles. 12:5) by interchange for 5132, to *bloom*:— abhor, (give occasion to) blaspheme, contemn, despise, flourish, × great, provoke.

5007. נְאָצָה **nᵉ'âtsâh**, *neh-aw-tsaw´*; or

נֶאָצָה **ne'âtsâh**, *neh-aw-tsaw´*; from 5006; *scorn*:— blasphemy.

5008. נָאַק **nâ'aq**, *naw-ak´*; a prim. root; to *groan*:— groan.

5009. נְאָקָה **nᵉ'âqâh**, *neh-aw-kaw´*; from 5008; a *groan*:— groaning.

5010. נָאַר **nâ'ar**, *naw-ar´*; a prim. root; to *reject*:— abhor, make void.

5011. נֹב **Nôb**, *nobe*; the same as 5108; *fruit*; *Nob*, a place in Pal.:— Nob.

5012. נָבָא **nâbâ'**, *naw-baw´*; a prim. root; to *prophesy*, i.e. speak (or sing) by inspiration (in prediction or simple discourse):— prophesy (-ing), make self a prophet.

5013. נְבָא **nᵉbâ'** (Chald.), *neb-aw´*; corresp. to 5012:— prophesy.

5014. נָבַב **nâbab**, *naw-bab´*; a prim. root; to *pierce*; to *be hollow*, or (fig.) *foolish*:— hollow, vain.

5015. נְבוֹ **Nᵉbôw**, *neb-o´*; prob. of for. der.; *Nebo*, the name of a Bab. deity, also of a mountain in Moab, and of a place in Pal.:— Nebo.

5016. נְבוּאָה **nᵉbûw'âh**, *neb-oo-aw´*; from 5012; a *prediction* (spoken or written):— prophecy.

5017. נְבוּאָה **nᵉbûw'âh** (Chald.), *neb-oo-aw´*; corresp. to 5016; inspired *teaching*:— prophesying.

5018. נְבוּזַרְאֲדָן **Nᵉbûwzar'ädân**, *neb-oo-*

zar-ad-awn´; of for. or.; *Nebuzaradan*, a Bab. general:— Nebuzaradan.

5019. נְבֻכַדְנֶאצַּר **Nᵉbûwkadne'tstsar**, *neb-oo-kad-nets-tsar´*; or

נְבֻכַדְנֶאצַּר **Nᵉbûkadne'tstsar** (2 Kings 24:1, 10), *neb-oo-kad-nets-tsar´*; or

נְבוּכַדְנֶצַּר **Nᵉbûwkadnetstsar** (Esth. 2:6; Dan. 1:18), *neb-oo-kad-nets-tsar´*; or

נְבוּכַדְרֶאצַּר **Nᵉbûwkadre'tstsar**, *neb-oo-kad-rets-tsar´*; or

נְבוּכַדְרֶאצּוֹר **Nᵉbûwkadre'tstsôwr** (Ezra 2:1; Jer. 49:28), *neb-oo-kad-rets-tsore´*; or for. der.; *Nebukadnetstsar* (or *-retstsar*, or *-retstsor*), king of Bab.:— Nebuchadnezzar, Nebuchadrezzar.

5020. נְבוּכַדְרֶצַּר **Nᵉbûwkadnetstsar** (Chald.), *neb-oo-kad-nets-tsar´*; corresp. to 5019:— Nebuchadnezzar.

5021. נְבוּשַׁזְבָּן **Nᵉbûwshazbân**, *neb-oo-shaz-bawn´*; of for. der.; *Nebushazban*, Nebuchadnezzar's chief eunuch:— Nebushazban.

5022. נָבוֹת **Nâbôwth**, *naw-both´*; fem. plur. from the same as 5011; *fruits*; *Naboth*, an Isr.:— Naboth.

5023. נְבִזְבָּה **nᵉbizbâh** (Chald.), *neb-iz-baw´*; of uncert. der.; a *largess*:— reward.

5024. נָבַח **nâbach**, *naw-bakh´*; a prim. root; to *bark* (as a dog):— bark.

5025. נֹבַח **Nôbach**, *no´-bach*; from 5024; a *bark*; *Nobach*, the name of an Isr., and of a place E. of the Jordan:— Nobah.

5026. נִבְחַז **Nibchaz**, *nib-khaz´*; of for. or.; *Nibchaz*, a deity of the Avites:— Nibhaz.

5027. נָבַט **nâbat**, *naw-bat´*; a prim. root; to *scan*, i.e. look intently at; by impl. to *regard* with pleasure, favor or care:— (cause to) behold, consider, look (down), regard, have respect, see.

5028. נְבָט **Nᵉbât**, *neb-awt´*; from 5027; *regard*; *Nebat*, the father of Jeroboam I:— Nebat.

5029. נְבִיא **nᵉbiy'** (Chald.), *neb-ee´*; corresp. to 5030; a *prophet*:— prophet.

5030. נָבִיא **nâbiy'**, *naw-bee´*; from 5012; a *prophet* or (gen.) *inspired* man:— prophecy, that prophesy, prophet.

5031. נְבִיאָה **nᵉbiy'âh**, *neb-ee-yaw´*; fem. of 5030; a *prophetess* or (gen.) *inspired* woman; by impl. a *poetess*; by association a *prophet's wife*:— prophetess.

5032. נְבָיוֹת **Nᵉbâyôwth**, *neb-aw-yoth´*; or

נְבָיֹת **Nᵉbâyôth**, *neb-aw-yoth´*; fem. plur. from 5107; *fruitfulnesses*; *Nebajoth*, a son of Ismael, and the country settled by him:— Nebaioth, Nebajoth.

5033. נֵבֶךְ **nêbek**, *nay´-bek*; from an unused root mean. to *burst* forth; a *fountain*:— spring.

5034. נָבֵל **nâbêl**, *naw-bale´*; a prim. root; to wilt; gen. to *fall* away, *fail*, *faint*; fig. to be *foolish* or (mor.) *wicked*; caus. to *despise*, *disgrace*:— disgrace, dishonour, lightly esteem, fade (away, -ing), fall (down, -ling, off), do foolishly,

come to nought, × surely, make vile, wither.

5035. נֶבֶל **nebel**, *neh´-bel*; or

נֵבֶל **nêbel**, *nay´-bel*; from 5034; a skin-*bag* for liquids (from *collapsing* when empty); hence, a *vase* (as similar in shape when full); also a *lyre* (as having a body of like form):— bottle, pitcher, psaltery, vessel, viol.

5036. נָבָל **nâbâl**, *naw-bawl´*; from 5034; *stupid*; *wicked* (espec. *impious*):— fool (-ish, -ish man, -ish woman), vile person.

5037. נָבָל **Nâbâl**, *naw-bawl´*; the same as 5036; *dolt*; *Nabal*, an Isr.:— Nabal.

5038. נְבֵלָה **nᵉbêlâh**, *neb-ay-law´*; from 5034; a *flabby* thing, i.e. a *carcase* or *carrion* (human or bestial, often collect.); fig. an *idol*:— (dead) body, (dead) carcase, dead of itself, which died, (beast) that (which) dieth of itself.

5039. נְבָלָה **nᵉbâlâh**, *neb-aw-law´*; fem. of 5036; *foolishness*, i.e. (mor.) *wickedness*; concr. a *crime*; by extens. *punishment*:— folly, vile, villany.

5040. נַבְלוּת **nablûwth**, *nab-looth´*; from 5036; prop. *disgrace*, i.e. the (female) *pudenda*:— lewdness.

5041. נְבַלָּט **Nᵉballât**, *neb-al-lawt´*; appar. from 5036 and 3909; *foolish secrecy*; *Neballat*, a place in Pal.:— Neballat.

5042. נָבַע **nâba'**, *naw-bah´*; a prim. root; to *gush* forth; fig. to *utter* (good or bad words); spec. to *emit* (a foul odor):— belch out, flowing, pour out, send forth, utter (abundantly).

5043. נֶבְרְשָׁא **nebrᵉshâ'** (Chald.), *neb-reh-shaw´*; from an unused root mean. to *shine*; a *light*; plur. (collect.) a *chandelier*:— candlestick.

5044. נִבְשָׁן **Nibshân**, *nib-shawn´*; of uncert. der.; *Nibshan*, a place in Pal.:— Nibshan.

5045. נֶגֶב **negeb**, *neh´-gheb*; from an unused root mean. to *be parched*; the *south* (from its drought); spec. the *Negeb* or southern district of Judah, occasionally, *Egypt* (as south to Pal.):— south (country, side, -ward).

5046. נָגַד **nâgad**, *naw-gad´*; a prim. root; prop. to *front*, i.e. stand boldly out opposite; by impl. (caus.), to *manifest*; fig. to *announce* (always by word of mouth to one present); spec. to *expose*, *predict*, *explain*, *praise*:— bewray, × certainly, certify, declare (-ing), denounce, expound, × fully, messenger, plainly, profess, rehearse, report, shew (forth), speak, × surely, tell, utter.

5047. נְגַד **nᵉgad** (Chald.), *neg-ad´*; corresp. to 5046; to *flow* (through the idea of *clearing* the way):— issue.

5048. נֶגֶד **neged**, *neh´-ghed*; from 5046; a *front*, i.e. part opposite; spec. a *counterpart*, or *mate*; usually (adv., espec. with prep.) *over against* or *before*:— about, (over) against, × aloof, × far (off), × from, over, presence, × other side, sight, × to view.

5049. נֶגֶד **neged** (Chald.), *neh´-ghed*; corresp. to 5048; *opposite*:— toward.

5050. נָגַהּ **nâgahh**, *naw-gäh´*; a prim.

root; to *glitter*; caus. to *illuminate*:— (en-) lighten, (cause to) shine.

5051. נֹגַהּ **nôgahh**, *no´-gäh*; from 5050; *brilliancy* (lit. or fig.):— bright (-ness), light, (clear) shining.

5052. נֹגַהּ **Nôgahh**, *no´-gäh*; the same as 5051; *Nogah*, a son of David:— Nogah.

5053. נֹגַהּ **nôgahh** (Chald.), *no´-gäh*; corresp. to 5051; *dawn*:— morning.

5054. נְגֹהָה **nᵉgôhâh**, *neg-o-haw´*; fem. of 5051; *splendor*:— brightness.

5055. נָגַח **nâgach**, *naw-gakh´*; a prim. root; to *but* with the horns; fig. to *war* against:— gore, push (down, -ing).

5056. נַגָּח **naggâch**, *nag-gawkh´*; from 5055; *butting*, i.e. *vicious*:— used (wont) to push.

5057. נָגִיד **nâgîyd**, *naw-gheed´*; or

נָגִד **nâgîd**, *naw-gheed´*; from 5046; a *commander* (as occupying the *front*), civil, military or religious; gen. (abstr. plur.), *honorable* themes:— captain, chief, excellent thing, (chief) governor, leader, noble, prince, (chief) ruler.

5058. נְגִינָה **nᵉgîynâh**, *neg-ee-naw´*; or

נְגִינַת **nᵉgîynath** (Psa. 61:title), *neg-ee-nath´*; from 5059; prop. instrumental *music*; by impl. a stringed *instrument*; by extens. a *poem* set to music; spec. an *epigram*:— stringed instrument, musick, Neginoth [plur.], song.

5059. נָגַן **nâgan**, *naw-gan´*; a prim. root; prop. to *thrum*, i.e. *beat* a tune with the fingers; expec. to *play* on a stringed instrument; hence, (gen.), to *make music*:— player on instruments, sing to the stringed instruments, melody, ministrel, play (-er, -ing).

5060. נָגַע **nâga'**, *naw-gah´*; a prim. root; prop. to *touch*, i.e. *lay the hand upon* (for any purpose; euphem. to *lie with* a woman; by impl. to *reach* (fig. to *arrive*, *acquire*); violently, to *strike* (punish, defeat, destroy, etc.):— beat, (× be able to) bring (down), cast, come (nigh), draw near (nigh), get up, happen, join, near, plague, reach (up), smite, strike, touch.

5061. נֶגַע **nega'**, *neh´-gah*; from 5060; a *blow* (fig. *infliction*); also (by impl.) a *spot* (concr. a *leprous* person or dress):— plague, sore, stricken, stripe, stroke, wound.

5062. נָגַף **nâgaph**, *naw-gaf´*; a prim. root; to *push*, *gore*, *defeat*, *stub* (the toe), *inflict* (a disease):— beat, dash, hurt, plague, slay, smite (down), strike, stumble, × surely, put to the worse.

5063. נֶגֶף **negeph**, *neh´-ghef*; from 5062; a *trip* (of the foot); fig. an *infliction* (of disease):— plague, stumbling.

5064. נָגַר **nâgar**, *naw-gar´*; a prim. root; to *flow*; fig. to *stretch* out; caus. to *pour* out or down; fig. to *deliver* over:— fall, flow away, pour down (out), run, shed, spilt, trickle down.

5065. נָגַשׂ **nâgas**, *naw-gas´*; a prim. root; to *drive* (an animal, a workman, a debtor, an army); by impl. to *tax*, *harass*, *tyrannize*:— distress, driver, exact (-or), oppress (-or), × raiser of taxes, taskmaster.

Hebrew

5066. נָגַשׁ **nâgash**, *naw-gash´*; a prim. root; to *be* or *come* (caus. *bring*) *near* (for any purpose); euphem. to *lie with* a woman; as an enemy, to *attack*; relig. to *worship*; caus. to *present*; fig. to *adduce* an argument; by reversal, to *stand back*:— (make to) approach (nigh), bring (forth, hither, near), (cause to) come (hither, near, nigh), give place, go hard (up), (be, draw, go) near (nigh), offer, overtake, present, put, stand.

5067. נֵד **nêd**, *nade*; from 5110 in the sense of *piling* up; a *mound*, i.e. *wave*:— heap.

5068. נָדַב **nâdab**, *naw-dab´*; a prim. root; to *impel*; hence, to *volunteer* (as a soldier), to *present* spontaneously:— offer freely, be (give, make, offer self) willing (-ly).

5069. נְדַב **nᵉdab** (Chald.), *ned-ab´*; corresp. to 5068; *be* (or *give*) *liberal* (-ly):— (be minded of ... own) freewill (offering), offer freely (willingly).

5070. נָדָב **Nâdâb**, *naw-dawb´*; from 5068; *liberal*; *Nadab*, the name of four Isr.:— Nadab.

5071. נְדָבָה **nᵉdâbâh**, *ned-aw-baw´*; from 5068; prop. (abstr.) *spontaneity*, or (adj.) *spontaneous*; also (concr.) a *spontaneous* or (by infer., in plur.) *abundant* gift:— free (-will) offering, freely, plentiful, voluntary (-ily, offering), willing (-ly, offering).

5072. נְדַבְיָה **Nᵉdabyâh**, *ned-ab-yaw´*; from 5068 and 3050; *largess of Jah*; *Nedabjah*, an Isr.:— Nedabiah.

5073. נִדְבָּךְ **nidbâk** (Chald.), *nid-bawk´*; from a root mean. to *stick*; a *layer* (of building materials):— row.

5074. נָדַד **nâdad**, *naw-dad´*; a prim. root; prop. to *wave* to and fro (rarely to *flap* up and down); fig. to *rove, flee*, or (caus.) to *drive away*:— chase (away), × could not, depart, flee (× apace, away), (re-) move, thrust away, wander (abroad, -er, -ing).

5075. נְדַד **nᵉdad** (Chald.), *ned-ad´*; corresp. to 5074; to *depart*:— go from.

5076. נָדֻד **nâdûd**, *naw-dood´*; pass. part. of 5074; prop. *tossed*; abstr. a *rolling* (on the bed):— tossing to and fro.

5077. נָדָה **nâdâh**, *naw-daw´*; or

נָדָא **nâdâ'** (2 Kings 17:21), *naw-daw´*; a prim. root; prop. to *toss*; fig. to *exclude*, i.e. *banish, postpone, prohibit*:— cast out, drive, put far away.

5078. נֵדֶה **nêdeh**, *nay´-deh*; from 5077 in the sense of freely *flinging* money; a *bounty* (for prostitution):— gifts.

5079. נִדָּה **niddâh**, *nid-daw´*; from 5074; prop. *rejection*; by impl. *impurity*, espec. pers. (menstruation) or mor. (idolatry, incest):— × far, filthiness, flowers, menstruous (woman), put apart, × removed (woman), separation, set apart, unclean (-ness, thing, with filthiness).

5080. נָדַח **nâdach**, *naw-dakh´*; a prim. root; to *push off*; used in a great variety of applications, lit. and fig. (to expel, mislead, strike, inflict, etc.):— banish, bring, cast down (out), chase, compel, draw away, drive (away, out, quite),

fetch a stroke, force, go away, outcast, thrust away (out), withdraw.

5081. נָדִיב **nâdîyb**, *naw-deeb´*; from 5068; prop. *voluntary*, i.e. generous; hence, *magnanimous*; as noun, a *grandee* (sometimes a *tyrant*):— free, liberal (things), noble, prince, willing (hearted).

5082. נְדִיבָה **nᵉdîybâh**, *ned-ee-baw´*; fem. of 5081; prop. *nobility*, i.e. *reputation*:— soul.

5083. נָדָן **nâdân**, *naw-dawn´*; prob. from an unused root mean. to *give*; a *present* (for prostitution):— gift.

5084. נָדָן **nâdân**, *naw-dawn´*; of uncert. der.; a *sheath* (of a sword):— sheath.

5085. נִדְנֶה **nidneh** (Chald.), *nid-neh´*; from the same as 5084; a *sheath*, fig. the *body* (as the receptacle of the soul):— body.

5086. נָדַף **nâdaph**, *naw-daf´*; a prim. root; to *shove* asunder, i.e. *disperse*:— drive (away, and fro), thrust down, shaken, tossed to and fro.

5087. נָדַר **nâdar**, *naw-dar´*; a prim. root; to *promise* (pos., to do or give something to God):— (make a) vow.

5088. נֶדֶר **neder**, *neh´-der*; or

נֵדֶר **nêder**, *nay´-der*; from 5087; a *promise* (to God); also (concr.) a thing *promised*:— vow (I-edl).

5089. נֹהַּ **nôahh**, *no´-ăh*; from an unused root mean. to *lament*; *lamentation*:— wailing.

5090. נָהַג **nâhag**, *naw-hag´*; a prim. root; to *drive* forth (a person, an animal or chariot), i.e. *lead, carry away*; refl. to *proceed* (i.e. impel or guide oneself); also (from the *panting* induced by effort) to *sigh*:— acquaint, bring (away), carry away, drive (away), lead (away, forth), (be) guide, lead (away, forth).

5091. נָהָה **nâhâh**, *naw-haw´*; a prim. root; to *groan*, i.e. *bewail*; hence, (through the idea of *crying* aloud), to *assemble* (as if on proclamation):— lament, wail.

5092. נְהִי **nᵉhiy**, *neh-hee´*; from 5091; an *elegy*:— lamentation, wailing.

5093. נִהְיָה **nihyâh**, *nih-yaw´*; fem. of 5092; *lamentation*:— doleful.

5094. נְהִיר **nᵉhîyr** (Chald.), *neh-heere´*; or

נְהִירוּ **nehîyrûw** (Chald.), *neh-hee-roo´*; from the same as 5105; *illumination*, i.e. (fig.) *wisdom*:— light.

5095. נָהַל **nâhal**, *naw-hal´*; a prim. root; prop. to run with a *sparkle*, i.e. *flow*; hence, (tran.), to *conduct*, and (by infer.) to *protect, sustain*:— carry, feed, guide, lead (gently, on).

5096. נַהֲלָל **Nahâlâl**, *nah-hal-awl´*; or

נַהֲלֹל **Nahâlôl**, *nah-hal-ole´*; the same as 5097; *Nahalal* or *Nahalol*, a place in Pal.:— Nahalal, Nahallal, Nahalol.

5097. נַהֲלֹל **nahâlôl**, *nah-hal-ole´*; from 5095; *pasture*:— bush.

5098. נָהַם **nâham**, *naw-ham´*; a prim. root; to *growl*:— mourn, roar (-ing).

5099. נַהַם **naham**, *nah´-ham*; from 5098; a *snarl*:— roaring.

5100. נְהָמָה **nᵉhâmâh**, *neh-haw-maw´*; fem. of 5099; *snarling*:— disquietness, roaring.

5101. נָהַק **nâhaq**, *naw-hak´*; a prim. root; to *bray* (as an ass), *scream* (from hunger):— bray.

5102. נָהַר **nâhar**, *naw-har´*; a prim. root; to *sparkle*, i.e. (fig.) *be cheerful*; hence, (from the *sheen* of a running stream) to *flow*, i.e. (fig.) *assemble*:— flow (together), be lightened.

5103. נְהַר **nᵉhar** (Chald.), *neh-har´*; from a root corresp. to 5102; a *river*, espec. the Euphrates:— river, stream.

5104. נָהָר **nâhâr**, *naw-hawr´*; from 5102; a *stream* (incl. the *sea*; expec. the Nile, Euphrates, etc.); fig. *prosperity*:— flood, river.

5105. נְהָרָה **nᵉhârâh**, *neh-haw-raw´*; from 5102 in its orig. sense; *daylight*:— light.

5106. נוּא **nûw'**, *noo*; a prim. root; to *refuse, forbid, dissuade*, or *neutralize*:— break, disallow, discourage, make of none effect.

5107. נוּב **nûwb**, *noob*; a prim. root; to *germinate*, i.e. (fig.) to (caus. *make*) *flourish*; also (of words), to *utter*:— bring forth (fruit), make cheerful, increase.

5108. נוֹב **nôwb**, *nobe*; or

נֵיב **nêyb**, *nabe*; from 5107; *produce*, lit. or fig.:— fruit.

5109. נוֹבַי **Nôwbay**, *no-bah´ee*; from 5108; *fruitful*; *Nobai*, an Isr.:— Nebai [from the marg.].

5110. נוּד **nûwd**, *nood*; a prim. root; to *nod*, i.e. waver; fig. to *wander, flee, disappear*; also (from *shaking* the head in sympathy), to *console, deplore*, or (from *tossing* the head in scorn) *taunt*:— bemoan, flee, get, mourn, make to move, take pity, remove, shake, skip for joy, be sorry, vagabond, way, wandering.

5111. נוּד **nûwd** (Chald.), *nood*; corresp. to 5116; to *flee*:— get away.

5112. נוֹד **nôwd**, *node* [only defect.

נֹד **nôd**, *node*] from 5110; *exile*:— wandering.

5113. נוֹד **Nôwd**, *node*; the same as 5112; *vagrancy*; *Nod*, the land of Cain:— Nod.

5114. נוֹדָב **Nôwdâb**, *no-dawb´*; from 5068; *noble*; *Nodab*, an Arab tribe:— Nodab.

5115. נָוָה **nâvâh**, *naw-vaw´*; a prim. root; to *rest* (as at home); caus. (through the impl. idea of *beauty* [comp. 5116]), to *celebrate* (with praises):— keep at home, prepare an habitation.

5116. נָוֶה **nâveh**, *naw-veh´*; or (fem.)

נָוָה **nâvâh**, *naw-vaw´*; from 5115; (adj.) *at home*; hence, (by impl. of satisfaction) *lovely*; also (noun) a *home*, of God (temple), men (residence), flocks (pasture), or wild animals (den):— comely, dwelling (place), fold, habitation, pleasant place, sheepcote, stable, tarried.

5117. נוּחַ **nûwach**, *noo´-akh*; a prim. root; to *rest*, i.e. *settle* down; used in a great variety of applications, lit. and fig., intr., tran. and caus. (to *dwell, stay, let fall, place, let alone, withdraw, give comfort*, etc.):— cease, be confederate, lay, let down, (be) quiet, remain, (cause to, be at, give, have, make to) rest, set down. Comp. 3241.

5118. נוּחַ **nûwach**, *noo´-akh*; or

נֹחַ **nôwach**, *no´-akh*; from 5117; *quiet*:— rest (-ed, -ing place).

5119. נוֹחָה **Nôwchâh**, *no-chaw´*; fem. of 5118; *quietude*; *Nochah*, an Isr.:— Nohah.

5120. נוּט **nûwṭ**, *noot*; to *quake*:— be moved.

5121. נָוִית **Nâvîyth**, *naw-veeth´*; from 5115; *residence*; *Navith*, a place in Pal.:— Naioth [*from the marg.*].

5122. נְוָלוּ **nᵉvâlûw** (Chald.), *nev-aw-loo´*; or

נְוָלִי **nᵉvâlîy** (Chald.), *nev-aw-lee´*; from an unused root prob. mean. to be *foul*; a *sink*:— dunghill.

5123. נוּם **nûwm**, *noom*; a prim. root; to *slumber* (from drowsiness):— sleep, slumber.

5124. נוּמָה **nûwmâh**, *noo-maw´*; from 5123; *sleepiness*:— drowsiness.

5125. נוּן **nûwn**, *noon*; a prim. root; to *resprout*, i.e. propagate by shoots; fig., to be *perpetual*:— be continued.

5126. נוּן **Nûwn**, *noon*; or

נוֹן **Nôwn** (1 Chron. 7:27), *nohn*; from 5125; *perpetuity*; *Nun* or *Non*, the father of Joshua:— Non, Nun.

5127. נוּס **nûwç**, *noos*; a prim. root; to *flit*, i.e. *vanish* away (subside, escape; caus. chase, impel, deliver):— × abate, away, be displayed, (make to) flee (away, -ing), put to flight, × hide, lift up a standard.

5128. נוּעַ **nûwa'**, *noo´-ah*; a prim. root; to *waver*, in a great variety of applications, lit. and fig. (as subjoined):— continually, fugitive, × make, to [go] up and down, be gone away, (be) move (-able, -d), be promoted, reel, remove, scatter, set, shake, sift, stagger, to and fro, be vagabond, wag, (make) wander (up and down).

5129. נוֹעַדְיָה **Nôw'adyâh**, *no-ad-yaw´*; from 3259 and 3050; *convened of Jah*; *Noadjah*, the name of an Isr., and a false prophetess:— Noadiah.

5130. נוּף **nûwph**, *noof*; a prim. root; to *quiver* (i.e. *vibrate* up and down, or *rock* to and fro); used in a great variety of applications (incl. *sprinkling, beckoning, rubbing, bastinadoing, sawing, waving*, etc.):— lift up, move, offer, perfume, send, shake, sift, strike, wave.

5131. נוֹף **nôwph**, *nofe*; from 5130; *elevation*:— situation. Comp. 5297.

5132. נוּץ **nûwts**, *noots*; a prim. root; prop. to *flash*; hence, to *blossom* (from the brilliancy of color); also, to *fly away* (from the quickness of motion):— flee away, bud (forth).

5133. נוֹצָה **nôwtsâh**, *no-tsaw´*; or

נֹצָה **nôtsâh**, *no-tsaw´*; fem. act. part. of 5327 in the sense of *flying*; a

pinion (or wing feather); often (collect.) *plumage*:— feather (-s), ostrich.

5134. נוּק **nûwq**, *nook*; a prim. root; to *suckle*:— nurse.

5135. נוּר **nûwr** (Chald.), *noor*; from an unused root (corresp. to that of 5216) mean. to *shine*; *fire*:— fiery, fire.

5136. נוּשׁ **nûwsh**, *noosh*; a prim. root; to *be sick*, i.e. (fig.) *distressed*:— be full of heaviness.

5137. נָזָה **nâzâh**, *naw-zaw´*; a prim. root; to *spirt*, i.e. *besprinkle* (espec. in expiation):— sprinkle.

5138. נָזִיד **nâzîyd**, *naw-zeed´*; from 2102; something *boiled*, i.e. *soup*:— pottage.

5139. נָזִיר **nâzîyr**, *naw-zeer´*; or

נָזִר **nâzir**, *naw-zeer´*; from 5144; *separate*, i.e. consecrated (as *prince*, a *Nazirite*); hence, (fig. from the latter) an *unpruned* vine (like an unshorn Nazirite):— Nazarite [*by a false alliteration with Nazareth*], separate (-d), vine undressed.

5140. נָזַל **nâzal**, *naw-zal´*; a prim. root; to *drip*, or *shed* by trickling:— distil, drop, flood, (cause to) flow (-ing), gush out, melt, pour (down), running water, stream.

5141. נֶזֶם **nezem**, *neh´-zem*; from an unused root of uncert. mean.; a *nose-ring*:— earring, jewel.

5142. נְזַק **nᵉzaq** (Chald.), *nez-ak´*; corresp. to the root of 5143; to *suffer* (caus. *inflict*) *loss*:— have (en-) damage, hurt (-ful).

5143. נֵזֶק **nêzeq**, *nay´zek*; from an unused root mean. to *injure*; *loss*:— damage.

5144. נָזַר **nâzar**, *naw-zar´*; a prim. root; to *hold aloof*, i.e. (intr.) *abstain* (from food and drink, from impurity, and even from divine worship [i.e. *apostatize*]; spec. to *set apart* (to sacred purposes), i.e. *devote*:— consecrate, separate (-ing, self).

5145. נֶזֶר **nezer**, *neh´-zer*; or

נֵזֶר **nêzer**, *nay´-zer*; from 5144; prop. something *set apart*, i.e. (abstr.) *dedication* (of a priest or Nazirite); hence, (concr.) unshorn *locks*; also (by impl.) a *chaplet* (espec. of royalty):— consecration, crown, hair, separation.

5146. נֹחַ **Nôach**, *no´-akh*; the same as 5118; *rest*; *Noach*, the patriarch of the flood:— Noah.

5147. נַחְבִּי **Nachbîy**, *nakh-bee´*; from 2247; *occult*; *Nachbi*, an Isr.:— Nakbi.

5148. נָחָה **nâchâh**, *naw-khaw´*; a prim. root; to *guide*; by impl. to *transport* (into exile, or as colonists):— bestow, bring, govern, guide, lead (forth), put, straiten.

5149. נְחוּם **Nᵉchûwm**, *neh-khoom´*; from 5162; *comforted*; *Nechum*, an Isr.:— Nehum.

5150. נִחוּם **nichûwm**, *nee-khoom´*; or

נִחֻם **nichûm**, *nee-khoom´*; from 5162; prop. *consoled*; abstr. *solace*:— comfort (-able), repenting.

5151. נַחוּם **Nachûwm**, *nakh-oom´*; from 5162; *comfortable*; *Nachum*, an Isr. prophet:— Nahum.

5152. נָחוֹר **Nâchôwr**, *naw-khore´*; from the same as 5170; *snorer*; *Nachor*, the name of the grandfather and a brother of Abraham:— Nahor.

5153. נָחוּשׁ **nâchûwsh**, *naw-khoosh´*; appar. pass. part. of 5172 (perh. in the sense of *ringing*, i.e. bell-metal; or from the *red* color of the throat of a serpent [5175, as denom.] when hissing); *coppery*, i.e. (fig.) *hard*:— of brass.

5154. נְחוּשָׁה **nᵉchûwshâh**, *nekh-oo-shaw´*; or

נְחֻשָׁה **nᵉchûshâh**, *nekh-oo-shaw´*; fem. of 5153; *copper*:— brass, steel. Comp. 5176.

5155. נְחִילָה **Nᵉchîylâh**, *nekh-ee-law´*; prob. denom. from 2485; a *flute*:— [*plur.*] Nehiloth.

5156. נְחִיר **nᵉchiyr**, *nekh-eer´*; from the same as 5170; a *nostril*:— [*dual*] nostrils.

5157. נָחַל **nâchal**, *naw-khal´*; a prim. root; to *inherit* (as a [fig.] mode of descent), or (gen.) to *occupy*; caus. to *bequeath*, or (gen.) *distribute, instate*:— divide, have ([inheritance]), take as an heritage, (cause to, give to, make to) inherit, (distribute for, divide [for, for an, by] give for, have, leave for, take [for] inheritance, (have in, cause to, be made to) possess (-ion).

5158. נַחַל **nachal**, *nakh´-al*; or (fem.)

נַחְלָה **nachlâh** (Psa. 124:4), *nakh´-law*; or

נַחֲלָה **nachălâh** (Ezek. 47:19; 48:28), *nakh-al-aw´*; from 5157 in its orig. sense; a *stream*, espec. a winter *torrent*; (by impl.) a (narrow) *valley* (in which a brook runs); also a *shaft* (of a mine):— brook, flood, river, stream, valley.

5159. נַחֲלָה **nachălâh**, *nakh-al-aw´*; from 5157 (in its usual sense); prop. something *inherited*, i.e. (abstr.) *occupancy*, or (concr.) an *heirloom*; gen. an *estate, patrimony* or *portion*:— heritage, to inherit, inheritance, possession. Comp. 5158.

5160. נַחֲלִיאֵל **Nachălîy'êl**, *nakh-al-ee-ale´*; from 5158 and 410; *valley of God*; *Nachaliel*, a place in the Desert:— Nahaliel.

5161. נֶחֱלָמִי **Nechĕlâmîy**, *nekh-el-aw-mee´*; appar. a patron. from an unused name (appar. pass. part. of 2492); *dreamed*; a *Nechelamite*, or desc. of Nechlam:— Nehelamite.

5162. נָחַם **nâcham**, *naw-kham´*; a prim. root; prop. to *sigh*, i.e. *breathe* strongly; by impl. to *be sorry*, i.e. (in a favorable sense) to *pity, console* or (refl.) *rue*; or (unfavorably) to *avenge* (oneself):— comfort (self), ease [one's self], repent (-er,-ing, self).

5163. נַחַם **Nacham**, *nakh´-am*; from 5162; *consolation*; *Nacham*, an Isr.:— Naham.

5164. נֹחַם **nôcham**, *no´-kham*; from 5162; *ruefulness*, i.e. *desistance*:— repentance.

5165. נֶחָמָה **nechâmâh**, *nekh-aw-maw´*; from 5162; *consolation*:— comfort.

5166. נְחֶמְיָה **Nᵉchemyâh**, *nekh-em-yaw´*;

from 5162 and 3050; *consolation of Jah; Nechemjah*, the name of three Isr.:— Nehemiah.

5167. נַחֲמָנִי **Nachămânîy**, *nakh-am-aw-nee'*; from 5162; *consolatory; Nachamani*, an Isr.:— Nahamani.

5168. חֵנוּ **nachnûw**, *nakh-noo'*; for 587; *we:—* we.

5169. חָץ **nâchats**, *naw-khats'*; a prim. root; to *be urgent:—* require haste.

5170. נַחַר **nachar**, *nakh'-ar;* and (fem.)

נַחֲרָה **nachărâh**, *nakh-ar-aw';* from an unused root mean. to *snort* or *snore*; a *snorting:—* nostrils, snorting.

5171. נַחֲרַי **Nachăray**, *nakh-ar-ah'-ee;* or

נַחְרַי **Nachray**, *nakh-rah'-ee;* from the same as 5170; *snorer; Nacharai* or *Nachrai*, an Isr.:— Naharai, Nahari.

5172. נָחַשׁ **nâchash**, *naw-khash';* a prim. root; prop. to *hiss*, i.e. *whisper* a (magic) spell; gen. to *prognosticate:—* × certainly, divine, enchanter, (use) × enchantment, learn by experience, × indeed, diligently observe.

5173. נַחַשׁ **nachash**, *nakh'-ash;* from 5172; an *incantation* or *augury:—* enchantment.

5174. נְחָשׁ **nᵉchâsh** (Chald.), *nekh-awsh';* corresp. to 5154; *copper:—* brass.

5175. נָחָשׁ **nâchâsh**, *naw-khawsh';* from 5172; a *snake* (from its *hiss*):— serpent.

5176. נָחָשׁ **Nâchâsh**, *naw-khawsh';* the same as 5175; *Nachash*, the name of two persons appar. non-Isr.:— Nahash.

נְחֻשָׁה **nᵉchûshâh**. See 5154.

5177. נַחְשׁוֹן **Nachshôwn**, *nakh-shone';* from 5172; *enchanter; Nachshon*, an Isr.:— Naashon, Nahshon.

5178. נְחֹשֶׁת **nᵉchôsheth**, *nekh-o'-sheth;* for 5154; *copper*, hence, something made of that metal, i.e. *coin*, a *fetter;* fig. *base* (as compared with gold or silver):— brasen, brass, chain, copper, fetter (of brass), filthiness, steel.

5179. נְחֻשְׁתָּא **Nᵉchushtâ'**, *nekh-oosh-taw';* from 5178; *copper; Nechushta*, an Israelitess:— Nehushta.

5180. נְחֻשְׁתָּן **Nᵉchushtân**, *nekh-oosh-tawn';* from 5178; something made of *copper*, i.e. the copper *serpent* of the Desert:— Nehushtan.

5181. נָחַת **nâchath**, *naw-khath';* a prim. root; to *sink*, i.e. *descend;* caus. to *press* or *lead* down:— be broken, (cause to) come down, enter, go down, press sore, settle, stick fast.

5182. נְחַת **nᵉchath** (Chald.), *nekh-ath';* corresp. to 5181; to *descend;* caus. to *bring away, deposit, depose:—* carry, come down, depose, lay up, place.

5183. נַחַת **nachath**, *nakh'-ath;* from 5182; a *descent*, i.e. imposition, unfavorable (*punishment*) or favorable (*food*); also (intr.; perh. from 5117), *restfulness:—* lighting down, quiet (-ness), to rest, be set on.

5184. נַחַת **Nachath**, *nakh'-ath;* the same as 5183; *quiet; Nachath*, the name of an Edomite and of two Isr.:— Nahath.

5185. נָחֵת **nâchêth**, *naw-khayth';* from 5181; *descending:—* come down.

5186. נָטָה **nâṭâh**, *naw-taw';* a prim. root; to *stretch* or spread out; by impl. to *bend* away (incl. mor. deflection); used in a great variety of application (as follows):— + afternoon, apply, bow (down, -ing), carry aside, decline, deliver, extend, go down, be gone, incline, intend, lay, let down, offer, outstretched, overthrown, pervert, pitch, prolong, put away, shew, spread (out), stretch (forth, out), take (aside), turn (aside, away), wrest, cause to yield.

5187. נָטִיל **nᵉṭîyl**, *net-eel';* from 5190; *laden:—* that bear.

5188. נְטִיפָה **nᵉṭîyphâh**, *net-ee-faw';* from 5197; a *pendant* for the ears (espec. of pearls):— chain, collar.

5189. נְטִישָׁה **nᵉṭîyshâh**, *net-ee-shaw';* from 5203; a *tendril* (as an offshoot):— battlement, branch, plant.

5190. נָטַל **nâṭal**, *naw-tal';* a prim. root; to *lift;* by impl. to *impose:—* bear, offer, take up.

5191. נְטַל **nᵉṭal** (Chald.), *net-al';* corresp. to 5190; to *raise:—* take up.

5192. נֵטֶל **nêṭel**, *nay'-tel;* from 5190; a *burden:—* weighty.

5193. נָטַע **nâṭa'**, *naw-tah';* a prim. root; prop. to *strike* in, i.e. *fix;* spec. to *plant* (lit. or fig.):— fastened, plant (-er).

5194. נֶטַע **neṭa'**, *neh'-tah;* from 5193; a *plant;* collect. a *plantation;* abstr. a *planting:—* plant.

5195. נָטִיע **nâṭiya'**, *naw-tee'-ah;* from 5193; a *plant:—* plant.

5196. נְטָעִים **Nᵉṭâ'îym**, *net-aw-eem';* plur. of 5194; *Netaim*, a place in Pal.:— plants.

5197. נָטַף **nâṭaph**, *naw-taf';* a prim. root; to *ooze*, i.e. *distil* gradually; by impl. to *fall in drops;* fig. to *speak* by inspiration:— drop (-ping), prophesy (-et).

5198. נָטָף **nâṭâph**, *naw-tawf';* from 5197; a *drop;* spec. an aromatic *gum* (prob. *stacte*):— drop, stacte.

5199. נְטֹפָה **Nᵉṭôphâh**, *net-o-faw';* from 5197; *distillation; Netophah*, a place in Pal.:— Netophah.

5200. נְטֹפָתִי **Nᵉṭôphâthîy**, *net-o-faw-thee';* patron. from 5199; a *Netophathite*, or inhab. of Netophah:— Netophathite.

5201. נָטַר **nâṭar**, *naw-tar';* a prim. root; to *guard;* fig., to *cherish* (anger):— bear grudge, keep (-er), reserve.

5202. נְטַר **nᵉṭar** (Chald.), *net-ar';* corresp. to 5201; to *retain:—* keep.

5203. נָטַשׁ **nâṭash**, *naw-tash';* a prim. root; prop. to *pound*, i.e. *smite;* by impl. (as if beating out, and thus expanding) to *disperse;* also, to *thrust* off, down, out or upon (incl. *reject, let alone, permit, remit*, etc.):— cast off, drawn, let fall, forsake, join [battle], leave (off), lie still, loose, spread (self) abroad, stretch out, suffer.

5204. נִי **nîy**, *nee;* a doubtful word; appar. from 5091; *lamentation:—* wailing.

5205. נִיד **nîyd**, *need;* from 5110; *motion* (of the lips in speech):— moving.

5206. נִידָה **nîydâh**, *nee-daw';* fem. of 5205; *removal*, i.e. *exile:—* removed.

5207. נִיחוֹחַ **nîchôwach**, *nee-kho'-akh;* or

נִיחֹחַ **nîychôach**, *nee-kho'-akh;* from 5117; prop. *restful*, i.e. *pleasant;* abstr. *delight:—* sweet (odour).

5208. נִיחוֹחַ **nîychôwach** (Chald.), *nee-kho'-akh;* or (short.)

נִיחֹחַ **nîychôach** (Chald.), *nee-kho'-akh;* corresp. to 5207; *pleasure:—* sweet odour (savour).

5209. נִין **nîyn**, *neen;* from 5125; *progeny:—* son.

5210. נִינְוֵה **Nîynᵉvêh**, *nee-nev-ay';* of for. or.; *Nineveh*, the capital of Assyria:— Nineveh.

5211. נִיס **niyç**, *neece;* from 5127; *fugitive:—* that fleeth.

5212. נִיסָן **Nîyçân**, *nee-sawn';* prob. of for. or.; *Nisan*, the first month of the Jewish sacred year:— Nisan.

5213. נִיצוֹץ **niytsôwts**, *nee-tsotes';* from 5340; a *spark:—* spark.

5214. נִיר **nîyr**, *neer;* a root prob. ident. with that of 5216, through the idea of the *gleam* of a fresh furrow; to *till* the soil:— break up.

5215. נִיר **nîyr**, *neer;* or

נִר **nîr**, *neer;* from 5214; prop. *plowing*, i.e. (concr.) freshly *plowed land:—* fallow ground, ploughing, tillage.

5216. נִיר **nîyr**, *neer* or

נִר **nîr**, *neer;* also

נֵיר **nêyr**, *nare;* or

נֵר **nêr**, *nare;* or (fem.)

נֵרָה **nêrâh**, *nay-raw';* from a prim. root [see 5214; 5135] prop. mean. to *glisten;* a *lamp* (i.e. the burner) or *light* (lit. or fig.):— candle, lamp, light.

5217. נָכָא **nâkâ'**, *naw-kaw';* a prim. root; to *smite*, i.e. *drive away:—* be viler.

5218. נְכֵא **nâkê'**, *naw-kay';* or

נָכָא **nâkâ'**, *naw-kaw';* from 5217; *smitten*, i.e. (fig.) *afflicted:—* broken, stricken, wounded.

5219. נְכֹאת **nᵉkô'th**, *nek-ohth';* from 5218; prop. a *smiting*, i.e. (concr.) an aromatic *gum* [perh. *styrax* (as powdered):— spicery (-ces).

5220. נֶכֶד **neked**, *neh'-ked;* from an unused root mean. to *propagate; offspring:—* nephew, son's son.

5221. נָכָה **nâkâh**, *naw-kaw';* a prim. root; to *strike* (lightly or severely, lit. or fig.):— beat, cast forth, clap, give [wounds], × go forward, × indeed, kill, make [slaughter], murderer, punish, slaughter, slay (-er, -ing), smite (-r, -ing), strike, be stricken, (give) stripes, × surely, wound.

5222. נֵכֶה **nêkeh**, *nay-keh';* from 5221; a *smiter*, i.e. (fig.) *traducer:—* abject.

5223. נָכֵה **nâkeh**, *naw-keh';* smitten, i.e. (lit.) *maimed*, or (fig.) *dejected:—* contrite, lame.

5224. נְכוֹ **Nᵉkôw**, *nek-o';* prob. of Eg. or.;

Neko, an Eg. king:— Necho. Comp. 6549.

5225. נָכוֹן **Nâkôwn**, *naw-kone'*; from 3559; *prepared; Nakon*, prob. an Isr.:— Nachon.

5226. נֵכַח **nêkach**, *nay'-kakh*; from an unused root mean. to *be straightforward*; prop. the *fore* part; used adv., *opposite*:— before, over against.

5227. נֹכַח **nôkach**, *no'-kakh*; from the same as 5226; prop., the *front* part; used adv. (espec. with prep.), *opposite, in front of, forward, in behalf of*:— (over) against, before, direct l-lyl, for, right (on).

5228. נָכֹחַ **nâkôach**, *naw-ko'-akh*; from the same as 5226; *straightforward*, i.e. (fig.), *equitable, correct*, or (abstr.), *integrity*:— plain, right, uprightness.

5229. נְכֹחָה **nekôchâh**, *nek-o-khaw'*; fem. of 5228; prop. *straightforwardness*, i.e. (fig.) *integrity*, or (concr.) a *truth*:— equity, right (thing), uprightness.

5230. נָכַל **nâkal**, *naw-kal'*; a prim. root; to *defraud*, i.e. *act treacherously*:— beguile, conspire, deceiver, deal subtilly.

5231. נֵכֶל **nêkel**, *nay'-kel*; from 5230; *deceit*:— wile.

5232. נְכַס **nekaç** (Chald.), *nek-as'*; corresp. to 5233:— goods.

5233. נֶכֶס **nekeç**, *neh'-kes*; from an unused root mean. to *accumulate; treasure*:— riches, wealth.

5234. נָכַר **nâkar**, *naw-kar'*; a prim. root; prop. to *scrutinize*, i.e. look intently at; hence (with recognition impl.), to *acknowledge, be acquainted with, care for, respect, revere*, or (with suspicion impl.), to *disregard, ignore, be strange toward, reject, resign, dissimulate* (as if ignorant or disowning):— acknowledge, × could, deliver, discern, dissemble, feign self to be another, know, take knowledge (notice), perceive, regard, (have) respect, behave (make) self strange (-ly).

5235. נֶכֶר **neker**, *neh'-ker*; or נֹכֶר **nôker**, *no'-ker*; from 5234; something *strange*, i.e. unexpected *calamity*:— strange.

5236. נֵכָר **nêkâr**, *nay-kawr'*; from 5234; *foreign*, or (concr.) a *foreigner*, or (abstr.) *heathendom*:— alien, strange (+ -er).

5237. נָכְרִי **nokriy**, *nok-ree'*; from 5235 (second form); *strange*, in a variety of degrees and applications (*foreign, non-relative, adulterous, different, wonderful*):— alien, foreigner, outlandish, strange (-r, woman).

5238. נְכֹת **nekôth**, *nek-ôth'*; prob. for 5219; *spicery*, i.e. (gen.) *valuables*:— precious things.

5239. נָלָה **nâlâh**, *naw-law'*; appar. a prim. root; to *complete*:— make an end.

5240. נְמִבְזֶה **nemibzeh**, *nem-ib-zeh'*; from 959, *despised*:— vile.

5241. נְמוּאֵל **Nemûw'êl**, *nem-oo-ale'*; appar. for 3223; *Nemuel*, the name of two Isr.:— Nemuel.

5242. נְמוּאֵלִי **Nemûw'êlîy**, *nem-oo-ay-*

lee'; from 5241; a *Nemuelite*, or desc. of Nemuel:— Nemuelite.

5243. נָמַל **nâmal**, *naw-mal'*; a prim. root; to *become clipped* or (spec.) *circumcised*:— (branch to) be cut down (off), circumcise.

5244. נְמָלָה **nemâlâh**, *nem-aw-law'*; fem. from 5243; an *ant* (prob. from its almost *bisected* form):— ant.

5245. נְמַר **nemar** (Chald.), *nem-ar'*; corresp. to 5246:— leopard.

5246. נָמֵר **nâmêr**, *naw-mare'*; from an unused root mean. prop. to *filtrate*, i.e. *be limpid* [comp 5247 and 5249]; and thus to *spot* or *stain* as if by dripping; a *leopard* (from its stripes):— leopard.

נמרד **Nimrôd**. See 5248.

5247. נִמְרָה **Nimrâh**, *nim-raw'*; from the same as 5246; *clear* water; *Nimrah*, a place E. of the Jordan:— Nimrah. See also 1039, 5249.

5248. נִמְרוֹד **Nimrôwd**, *nim-rode'*; or נִמְרֹד **Nimrôd**, *nim-rode'*; prob. of for. or.; *Nimrod*, a son of Cush:— Nimrod.

5249. נִמְרִים **Nimriym**, *nim-reem'*; plur. of a masc. corresp. to 5247; *clear* waters; *Nimrim*, a place E. of the Jordan:— Nimrim. Comp. 1039.

5250. נִמְשִׁי **Nimshîy**, *nim-shee'*; prob. from 4871; *extricated; Nimshi*, the (grand-) father of Jehu:— Nimshi.

5251. נֵס **nêç**, *nace*; from 5264; a *flag*; also a *sail*; by impl. a *flagstaff*; gen. a *signal*; fig. a *token*:— banner, pole, sail, (en-) sign, standard.

5252. נְסִבָּה **necibbâh**, *nes-ib-baw'*; fem. pass. part. of 5437; prop. an *environment*, i.e. *circumstance* or *turn* of affairs:— cause.

5253. נָסַג **nâçag**, *naw-sag'*; a prim. root; to *retreat*:— departing away, remove, take (hold), turn away.

נְסָה **necâh**. See 5375.

5254. נָסָה **nâçâh**, *naw-saw'*; a prim. root; to *test*; by impl. to *attempt*:— adventure, assay, prove, tempt, try.

5255. נָסַח **nâçach**, *naw-sakh'*; a prim. root; to *tear away*:— destroy, pluck, root.

5256. נְסַח **neçach** (Chald.), *nes-akh'*; corresp. to 5255:— pull down.

5257. נְסִיךְ **neçîyk**, *nes-eek'*; from 5258; prop. something *poured* out, i.e. a *libation*; also a molten *image*; by impl. a *prince* (as anointed):— drink offering, duke, prince (-ipal).

5258. נָסַךְ **nâçak**, *naw-sak'*; a prim. root; to *pour* out, espec. a libation, or to *cast* (metal); by anal. to *anoint* a king:— cover, melt, offer, (cause to) pour (out), set (up).

5259. נָסַךְ **nâçak**, *naw-sak'*; a prim. root [prob. ident. with 5258 through the idea of fusion]; to *interweave*, i.e. (fig.) to *overspread*:— that is spread.

5260. נְסַךְ **neçak** (Chald.), *nes-ak'*; corresp. to 5258; to *pour* out a libation:— offer.

5261. נְסַךְ **neçak** (Chald.), *nes-ak'*; corresp. to 5262; a *libation*:— drink offering.

5262. נֶסֶךְ **neçek**, *neh'-sek*; or נֵסֶךְ **nêçek**, *nay'-sek*; from 5258; a *libation*; also a *cast idol*:— cover, drink offering, molten image.

נִסְמָן **niçmân**. See 5567.

5263. נָסַס **nâçaç**, *naw-sas'*; a prim. root; to *wane*, i.e. *be sick*:— faint.

5264. נָסַס **nâçaç**, *naw-sas'*; a prim. root; to *gleam* from afar, i.e. to *be conspicuous* as a signal; or rather perh. a denom. from 5251 land ident. with 5263, through the idea of a flag as *fluttering* in the windl; to *raise a beacon*:— lift up as an ensign.

5265. נָסַע **nâça'**, *naw-sah'*; a prim. root; prop. to *pull* up, espec. the tent-pins, i.e. *start* on a journey:— cause to blow, bring, get, (make to) go (away, forth, forward, onward, out), (take) journey, march, remove, set aside (forward), × still, be on his (go their) way.

5266. נָסַק **nâçaq**, *naw-sak'*; a prim. root; to *go up*:— ascend.

5267. נְסַק **neçaq** (Chald.), *nes-ak'*; corresp. to 5266:— take up.

5268. נִסְרֹךְ **Niçrôk**, *nis-roke'*; of for. or.; *Nisrok*, a Bab. idol:— Nisroch.

5269. נֵעָה **Nê'âh**, *nay-aw'*; from 5128; *motion; Neäh*, a place in Pal.:— Neah.

5270. נֹעָה **Nô'âh**, *no-aw'*; from 5128; *movement; Noah*, an Israelitess:— Noah.

5271. נָעוּר **nâ'ûwr**, *naw-oor'*; or נָעֻר **nâ'ûr**, *naw-oor'*; and (fem.) נְעֻרָה **ne'ûrâh**, *neh-oo-raw'*; prop. pass. part. from 5288 as denom.; (only in plur. collect. or emphat.) *youth*, the state (*juvenility*) or the persons (*young people*):— childhood, youth.

5272. נְעִיאֵל **Ne'îy'êl**, *neh-ee-ale'*; from 5128 and 410; *moved of God; Neiel*, a place in Pal.:— Neiel.

5273. נָעִים **nâ'îym**, *naw-eem'*; from 5276; *delightful* (obj. or subj., lit. or fig.):— pleasant (-ure), sweet.

5274. נָעַל **nâ'al**, *naw-al'*; a prim. root; prop. to *fasten* up, i.e. with a bar or cord; hence, (denom. from 5275), to *sandal*, i.e. furnish with slippers:— bolt, inclose, lock, shoe, shut up.

5275. נַעַל **na'al**, *nah'-al*; or (fem.) נַעֲלָה **na'ălâh**, *nah-al-aw'*; from 5274; prop. a sandal *tongue*; by extens. a *sandal* or slipper (sometimes as a symbol of occupancy, a refusal to marry, or of something valueless):— dryshod, (pair of) shoe (l-latchetl, -s).

5276. נָעֵם **nâ'êm**, *naw-ame'*; a prim. root; to *be agreeable* (lit. or fig.):— pass in beauty, be delight, be pleasant, be sweet.

5277. נַעַם **Na'am**, *nah'-am*; from 5276; *pleasure; Naam*, an Isr.:— Naam.

5278. נֹעַם **no'am**, *no'-am*; from 5276; *agreeableness*, i.e. *delight, suitableness, splendor* or *grace*:— beauty, pleasant (-ness).

5279. נַעֲמָה **Na'ămâh**, *nah-am-aw'*; fem. of 5277; *pleasantness; Naamah*, the name of an antediluvian woman, of an Ammonitess, and of a place in Pal.:— Naamah.

Hebrew

5280. נַעֲמִי **Na'âmîy**, *nah-am-ee'*; patron. from 5283; a *Naamanite*, or desc. of Naaman (collect.):— Naamites.

5281. נָעֳמִי **No'ŏmîy**, *no-ŏm-ee'*; from 5278; *pleasant; Noomi*, an Israelitess:— Naomi.

5282. נַעֲמָן **na'ămân**, *nah-am-awn'*; from 5276; *pleasantness* (plur. as concr.):— pleasant.

5283. נַעֲמָן **Na'ămân**, *nah-am-awn'*; the same as 5282; *Naaman*, the name of an Isr. and of a Damascene:— Naaman.

5284. נַעֲמָתִי **Na'ămâthîy**, *nah-am-aw-thee'*; patrial from a place corresp. in name (but not ident.) with 5279; a *Naamathite*, or inhab. of Naamah:— Naamathite.

5285. נַעֲצוּץ **na'ătsûwts**, *nah-ats-oots'*; from an unused root mean. to *prick*; prob. a *brier*; by impl. a *thicket* of thorny bushes:— thorn.

5286. נָעַר **nâ'ar**, *naw-ar'*; a prim. root; to *growl*:— yell.

5287. נָעַר **nâ'ar**, *naw-ar'*; a prim. root [prob. ident. with 5286, through the idea of the *rustling* of mane, which usually accompanies the lion's roar]; to *tumble* about:— shake (off, out, self), overthrow, toss up and down.

5288. נַעַר **na'ar**, *nah'-ar*; from 5287; (concr.) a *boy* (as act.), from the age of infancy to adolescence; by impl. a *servant*; also (by interch. of sex), a *girl* (of similar latitude in age):— babe, boy, child, damsel [from the marg.], lad, servant, young (man).

5289. נַעַר **na'ar**, *nah'-ar*; from 5287 in its der. sense of *tossing* about; a *wanderer*:— young one.

5290. נֹעַר **nô'ar**, *no'-ar*; from 5287; (abstr.) *boyhood* [comp. 5288]:— child, youth.

נָעֻר **nâ'ûr**. See 5271.

5291. נַעֲרָה **na'ărâh**, *nah-ar-aw'*; fem. of 5288; a *girl* (from infancy to adolescence):— damsel, maid (-en), young (woman).

5292. נַעֲרָה **Na'ărâh**, *nah-ar-aw'*; the same as 5291; *Naarah*, the name of an Israelitess, and of a place in Pal.:— Naarah, Naarath.

נְעֻרָה **n^e'ûrâh**. See 5271.

5293. נַעֲרַי **Na'ăray**, *nah-ar-ah'-ee*; from 5288; *youthful; Naarai*, an Isr.:— Naarai.

5294. נְעַרְיָה **N^e'aryâh**, *neh-ar-yaw'*; from 5288 and 3050; *servant of Jah; Nearjah*, the name of two Isr.:— Neariah.

5295. נַעֲרָן **Na'ărân**, *nah-ar-awn'*; from 5288; *juvenile; Naaran*, a place in Pal.:— Naaran.

5296. נְעֹרֶת **n^e'ôreth**, *neh-o'-reth*; from 5287; *something shaken* out, i.e. *tow* (as the refuse of flax):— tow.

נַעֲרָתָה **Na'ărâthâh**. See 5292.

5297. נֹף **Nôph**, *nofe*; a var. of 4644; *Noph*, the capital of Upper Egypt:— Noph.

5298. נֶפֶג **Nepheg**, *neh'-feg*; from an unused root prob. mean. to *spring forth*; a

sprout; *Nepheg*, the name of two Isr.:— Nepheg.

5299. נָפָה **nâphâh**, *naw-faw'*; from 5130 in the sense of *lifting*; a *height*; also a *sieve*:— border, coast, region, sieve.

5300. נְפוּשְׁסִים **N^ephûwsh^eçîym**, *nef-oo-shes-eem'*; for 5304; *Nephushesim*, a Temple-servant:— Nephisesim [from the marg.].

5301. נָפַח **nâphach**, *naw-fakh'*; a prim. root; to *puff*, in various applications (lit., to *inflate*, *blow* hard, *scatter*, *kindle*, *expire*; fig., to *disesteem*):— blow, breath, give up, cause to lose [life], seething, snuff.

5302. נֹפַח **Nôphach**, *no'-fakh*; from 5301; a *gust; Nophach*, a place in Moab:— Nophah.

5303. נְפִיל **n^ephîyl**, *nef-eel'*; or

נְפִל **n^ephîl**, *nef-eel'*; from 5307; prop., a *feller*, i.e. a *bully* or *tyrant*:— giant.

5304. נְפִיסִים **N^ephîyçîym**, *nef-ee-seem'*; plur. from an unused root mean. to *scatter*; *expansions; Nephisim*, a Temple-servant:— Nephusim [from the marg.].

5305. נָפִישׁ **Nâphîysh**, *naw-feesh'*; from 5314; *refreshed; Naphish*, a son of Ishmael, and his posterity:— Naphish.

5306. נֹפֶךְ **nôphek**, *no'-fek*; from an unused root mean. to *glisten*; *shining*; a gem, prob. the *garnet*:— emerald.

5307. נָפַל **nâphal**, *naw-fal'*; a prim. root; to *fall*, in a great variety of applications (intr. or caus., lit. or fig.):— be accepted, cast (down, self, [lots], out), cease, die, divide (by lot), (let) fail, (cause to, let, make, ready to) fall (away, down, -en, -ing), fell (-ing), fugitive, have [inheritance], inferior, be judged [by mistake for 6419], lay (along), (cause to) lie down, light (down), be (× hast) lost, lying, overthrow, overwhelm, perish, present (-ed, -ing), (make to) rot, slay, smite out, × surely, throw down.

5308. נְפַל **n^ephal** (Chald.), *nef-al'*; corresp. to 5307:— fall (down), have occasion.

5309. נֶפֶל **nephel**, *neh'-fel*; or

נֵפֶל **nêphel**, *nay'-fel*; from 5307; something *fallen*, i.e. an *abortion*:— untimely birth.

נְפִל **n^ephîl**. See 5303.

5310. נָפַץ **nâphats**, *naw-fats'*; a prim. root; to *dash* to pieces, or *scatter*:— be beaten in sunder, break (in pieces), broken, dash (in pieces), cause to be discharged, be dispersed, be overspread, scatter.

5311. נֶפֶץ **nephets**, *neh'-fets*; from 5310; a *storm* (as dispersing):— scattering.

5312. נְפַק **n^ephaq** (Chald.), *nef-ak'*; a prim. root; to *issue*; caus. to *bring out*:— come (go, take) forth (out).

5313. נִפְקָא **niphqâ'** (Chald.), *nif-kaw'*; from 5312; an *outgo*, i.e. *expense*:— expense.

5314. נָפַשׁ **nâphash**, *naw-fash'*; a prim. root; to *breathe*; pass., to *be breathed* upon, i.e. (fig.) *refreshed* (as if by a current of air):— (be) refresh selves (-ed).

5315. נֶפֶשׁ **nephesh**, *neh'-fesh*; from 5314; prop. a *breathing* creature, i.e. *animal* of (abstr.) *vitality*; used very widely in a lit., accommodated or fig. sense (bodily or ment.):— any, appetite, beast, body, breath, creature, × dead (-ly), desire, × [dis-] contented, × fish, ghost, + greedy, he, heart (-y), (hath, × jeopardy of) life (× in jeopardy), lust, man, me, mind, mortally, one, own, person, pleasure, (her-, him-, my-, thy-) self, them (your)-selves, + slay, soul, + tablet, they, thing, (× she) will, × would have it.

5316. נֶפֶת **nepheth**, *neh'-feth*; for 5299; a *height*:— country.

5317. נֹפֶת **nôpheth**, *no'-feth*; from 5130 in the sense of *shaking* to pieces; a *dripping*, i.e. of *honey* (from the comb):— honeycomb.

5318. נְפְתּוֹחַ **Nephtôwach**, *nef-to'-akh*; from 6605; *opened*, i.e. a *spring; Nephtoach*, a place in Pal.:— Neptoah.

5319. נַפְתּוּל **naphtûwl**, *naf-tool'*; from 6617; prop. *wrestled*; but used (in the plur.) tran., a *struggle*:— wrestling.

5320. נַפְתֻּחִים **Naphtûchîym**, *naf-too-kheem'*; plur. of for. or., *Naphtuchim*, an Eg. tribe:— Naphtuhim.

5321. נַפְתָּלִי **Naphtâlîy**, *naf-taw-lee'*; from 6617; *my wrestling; Naphtali*, a son of Jacob, with the tribe desc. from him, and its territory:— Naphtali.

5322. נֵץ **nêts**, *nayts*; from 5340; a *flower* (from its *brilliancy*); also a *hawk* (from it *flashing* speed):— blossom, hawk.

5323. נָצָא **nâtsâ'**, *naw-tsaw'*; a prim. root; to *go away*:— flee.

5324. נָצַב **nâtsab**, *naw-tsab'*; a prim. root; to *station*, in various applications (lit. or fig.):— appointed, deputy, erect, establish, × Huzzah [by mistake for a proper name], lay, officer, pillar, present, rear up, set (over, up), settle, sharpen, stablish, (make to) stand (-ing, still, up, upright), best state.

נְצִיב **n^etsîb**. See 5333.

5325. נִצָּב **nitstsâb**, *nits-tsawb'*; pass. part. of 5324; *fixed*, i.e. a *handle*:— haft.

5326. נִצְבָּה **nitsbâh** (Chald.), *nits-baw'*; from a root corresp. to 5324; *fixedness*, i.e. *firmness*:— strength.

5327. נָצָה **nâtsâh**, *naw-tsaw'*; a prim. root; prop. to *go forth*, i.e. (by impl.) to *be expelled*, and (consequently) *desolate*; caus. to *lay waste*; also (spec.), to *quarrel*:— be laid waste, ruinous, strive (together).

5328. נִצָּה **nitstsâh**, *nits-tsaw'*; fem. of 5322; a *blossom*:— flower.

נְצוּרָה **n^etsûwrâh**. See 5341.

5329. נָצַח **nâtsach**, *naw-tsakh'*; a prim. root; prop. to *glitter* from afar, i.e. to *be eminent* (as a superintendent, espec. of the Temple services and its music); also (as denom. from 5331), to *be permanent*:— excel, chief musician (singer), oversee (-r), set forward.

5330. נְצַח **n^etsach** (Chald.), *nets-akh'*; corresp. to 5329; to *become chief*:— be preferred.

5331. נֶצַח **netsach**, *neh'-tsakh*; or

נֶצַח **nêtsach**, *nay'-tsakh*; from 5329; prop. a *goal*, i.e. the bright object at a distance travelled toward; hence, (fig.) *splendor*, or (subj.) *truthfulness*, or (obj.) *confidence*; but usually (adv.), *continually* (i.e. to the most distant point of view):— alway (-s), constantly, end, (+ n-) ever (more), perpetual, strength, victory.

5332. נֶצַח **nêtsach**, *nay'-tsakh*; prob. ident. with 5331, through the idea of *brilliancy* of color; *juice* of the grape (as blood red):— blood, strength.

5333. נְצִיב **n°tsîyb**, *nets-eeb'*; or

נְצִב **n°tsib**, *nets-eeb'*; from 5324; something *stationary*, i.e. a *prefect*, a military *post*, à *statue*:— garrison, officer, pillar.

5334. נְצִיב **N°tsîyb**, *nets-eeb'*; the same as 5333; *station*; Netsib, a place in Pal.:— Nezib.

5335. נְצִיחַ **N°tsîyach**, *nets-ee'-akh*; from 5329; *conspicuous*; Netsiach, a Temple-servant:— Neziah.

5336. נָצִיר **nâtsîyr**, *naw-tsere'*; from 5341; prop. *conservative*; but used pass., *delivered*:— preserved.

5337. נָצַל **nâtsal**, *naw-tsal'*; a prim. root; to *snatch* away, whether in a good or a bad sense:— × at all, defend, deliver (self), escape, × without fail, part, pluck, preserve, recover, rescue, rid, save, spoil, strip, × surely, take (out).

5338. נְצַל **n°tsal** (Chald.), *nets-al'*; corresp. to 5337; to *extricate*:— deliver, rescue.

5339. נִצָּן **nitstsân**, *nits-tsawn'*; from 5322; a *blossom*:— flower.

5340. נָצַץ **nâtsats**, *naw-tsats'*; a prim. root; to *glare*, i.e. *be bright*-colored:— sparkle.

5341. נָצַר **nâtsar**, *naw-tsar'*; a prim. root; to *guard*, in a good sense (to *protect, maintain, obey*, etc.) or a bad one (to *conceal*, etc.):— besieged, hidden thing, keep (-er, -ing), monument, observe, preserve (-r), subtil, watcher (-man).

5342. נֵצֶר **nêtser**, *nay'-tser*; from 5341 in the sense of *greenness* as a striking color; a *shoot*; fig. a *descendant*:— branch.

5343. נְקֵא **n°qê'** (Chald.), *nek-ay'*; from a root corresp. to 5352; *clean*:— pure.

5344. נָקַב **nâqab**, *naw-kab'*; a prim. root; to *puncture*, lit. (to *perforate*, with more or less violence) or fig. (to *specify, designate, libel*):— appoint, blaspheme, bore, curse, express, with holes, name, pierce, strike through.

5345. נֶקֶב **neqeb**, *neh'keb*; a *bezel* (for a gem):— pipe.

5346. נֶקֶב **Neqeb**, *neh'-keb*; the same as 5345; *dell*; Nekeb, a place in Pal.:— Nekeb.

5347. נְקֵבָה **n°qêbâh**, *nek-ay-baw'*; from 5344; *female* (from the sexual form):— female.

5348. נָקֹד **nâqôd**, *naw-kode'*; from an unused root mean. to *mark* (by *puncturing* or *branding*); *spotted*:— speckled.

5349. נֹקֵד **nôqêd**, *no-kade'*; act. part.

from the same as 5348; a *spotter* (of sheep or cattle), i.e. the owner or tender (who thus marks them):— herdman, sheepmaster.

5350. נִקֻּד **niqqud**, *nik-kood'*; from the same as 5348; a *crumb* (as *broken* to spots); also a *biscuit* (as *pricked*):— cracknel, mouldy.

5351. נְקֻדָּה **n°quddâh**, *nek-ood-daw'*; fem. of 5348; a *boss*:— stud.

5352. נָקָה **nâqâh**, *naw-kaw'*; a prim. root; to *be* (or *make*) *clean* (lit. or fig.); by impl. (in an adverse sense) to *be bare*, i.e. *extirpated*:— acquit × at all, × altogether, be blameless, cleanse, (be) clear (-ing), cut off, be desolate, be free, be (hold) guiltless, be (hold) innocent, × by no means, be quit, be (leave) unpunished, × utterly, × wholly.

5353. נְקוֹדָא **N°qôwdâ'**, *nek-o-daw'*; fem. of 5348 (in the fig. sense of *marked*); *distinction*; Nekoda, a Temple-servant:— Nekoda.

5354. נָקַט **nâqat**, *naw-kat'*; a prim. root; to *loathe*:— weary.

5355. נָקִי **nâqîy**, *naw-kee'*; or

נָקִיא **nâqîy'** (Joel 4:19; Jonah 1:14), *naw-kee'*; from 5352; *innocent*:— blameless, clean, clear, exempted, free, guiltless, innocent, quit.

5356. נִקָּיוֹן **niqqâyôwn**, *nik-kaw-yone'*; or

נִקָּיוֹן **niqqâyôn**, *nik-kaw-yone'*; from 5352; *clearness* (lit. or fig.):— cleanness, innocency.

5357. נָקִיק **nâqîyq**, *naw-keek'*; from an unused root mean. to *bore*; a *cleft*:— hole.

5358. נָקַם **nâqam**, *naw-kam'*; a prim. root; to *grudge*, i.e. *avenge* or *punish*:— avenge (-r, self), punish, revenge (self), × surely, take vengeance.

5359. נָקָם **nâqâm**, *naw-kawm'*; from 5358; *revenge*:— + avenged, quarrel, vengeance.

5360. נְקָמָה **n°qâmâh**, *nek-aw-maw'*; fem. of 5359; *avengement*, whether the act or the passion:— + avenge, revenge (-ing), vengeance.

5361. נָקַע **nâqa'**, *naw-kah'*; a prim. root; to *feel aversion*:— be alienated.

5362. נָקַף **nâqaph**, *naw-kaf'*; a prim. root; to *strike* with more or less violence (*beat, fell, corrode*); by impl. (of attack) to *knock together*, i.e. *surround* or *circulate*:— compass (about, -ing), cut down, destroy, go round (about), inclose, round.

5363. נֹקֶף **nôqeph**, *no'-kef*; from 5362; a *threshing* (of olives):— shaking.

5364. נִקְפָּה **niqpâh**, *nik-paw'*; from 5362; prob. a *rope* (as *encircling*):— rent.

5365. נָקַר **nâqar**, *naw-kar'*; a prim. root; to *bore* (*penetrate, quarry*):— dig, pick out, pierce, put (thrust) out.

5366. נְקָרָה **n°qârâh**, *nek-aw-raw'*; from 5365, a *fissure*:— cleft, clift.

5367. נָקַשׁ **nâqash**, *naw-kash'*; a prim. root; to *entrap* (with a noose), lit. or fig.:— catch, (lay a) snare.

5368. נְקַשׁ **n°qash** (Chald.), *nek-ash'*;

corresp. to 5367; but used in the sense of 5362; to *knock*:— smote.

נֵר **nêr**,

נִר **nîr**. See 5215, 5216.

5369. נֵר **Nêr**, *nare*; the same as 5216; *lamp*; Ner, an Isr.:— Ner.

5370. נֵרְגַל **Nêrgal**, *nare-gal'*; of for. or.; *Nergal*, a Cuthite deity:— Nergal.

5371. נֵרְגַל שַׁרְאֶצֶר **Nêrgal Shar'etser**, *nare-gal' shar-eh'-tser*; from 5370 and 8272; *Nergal-Sharetser*, the name of two Bab.:— Nergal-sharezer.

5372. נִרְגָּן **nirgân**, *neer-gawn'*; from an unused root mean. to *roll to pieces*; a *slanderer*:— talebearer, whisperer.

5373. נֵרְד **nêrd**, *nayrd*; of for. or.; *nard*, an aromatic:— spikenard.

5374. נֵרָה **nêrâh**. See 5216.

5374. נֵרִיָּה **Nêrîyâh**, *nay-ree-yaw'*; or

נֵרִיָּהוּ **Nêrîyâhûw**, *nay-ree-yaw'-hoo*; from 5216 and 3050; *light of Jah*; Nerijah, an Isr.:— Neriah.

5375. נָשָׂא **nâsâ'**, *naw-saw'*; or

נָסָה **nâçâh** (Psa. 4:6 [7]) *naw-saw'*; a prim. root; to *lift*, in a great variety of applications, lit. and fig., absol. and rel. (as follows):— accept, advance, arise, (able to, [armour], suffer to) bear (-er, up), bring (forth), burn, carry (away), cast, contain, desire, ease, exact, exalt (self), extol, fetch, forgive, furnish, further, give, go on, help, high, hold up, honorable (+ man), lade, lay, lift (self) up, lofty, marry, magnify, × needs, obtain, pardon, raise (up), receive, regard, respect, set (up), spare, stir up, + swear, take (away, up), × utterly, wear, yield.

5376. נְשָׂא **n°sâ'** (Chald.), *nes-aw'*; corresp. to 5375:— carry away, make insurrection, take.

5377. נָשָׁא **nâshâ'**, *naw-shaw'*; a prim. root; to *lead astray*, i.e. (ment.) to *delude*, or (mor.) to *seduce*:— beguile, deceive, × greatly, × utterly.

5378. נָשָׁא **nâshâ'**, *naw-shaw'*; a prim. root [perh. ident. with 5377, through the idea of *imposition*]; to *lend* on interest; by impl. to *dun* for debt:— × debt, exact, giver of usury.

נָשִׂיא **nâsî'**. See 5387.

נְשֻׁאָה **n°sû'âh**. See 5385.

5379. נִשֵּׂאת **nissê'th**, *nis-sayth'*; pass. part. fem. of 5375; something *taken*, i.e. a *present*:— gift.

5380. נָשַׁב **nâshab**, *naw-shab'*; a prim. root; to *blow*; by impl. to *disperse*:— (cause to) blow, drive away.

5381. נָשַׂג **nâsag**, *naw-sag'*; a prim. root; to *reach* (lit. or fig.):— ability, be able, attain (unto), (be able to, can) get, lay at, put, reach, remove, wax rich, × surely, (over-) take (hold of, on, upon).

5382. נָשָׁה **nâshâh**, *naw-shaw'*; a prim. root; to *forget*; fig. to *neglect*; caus. to *remit, remove*:— forget, deprive, exact.

5383. נָשָׁה **nâshâh**, *naw-shaw'*; a prim. root [rather ident. with 5382, in the sense of 5378]; to *lend* or (by reciprocity) *borrow* on security or interest:— creditor, exact, extortioner, lend, usurer, lend on (taker of) usury.

5384. נֶשֶׁה **nâsheh**, *naw-sheh´*; from 5382, in the sense of *failure; rheumatic* or *crippled* (from the incident to Jacob):— which shrank.

5385. נְשׂוּאָה **n°sûw'âh**, *nes-oo-aw´*; or rather,

נְשֻׂאָה **n°sû'âh**, *nes-oo-aw´*; fem.. pass. part. of 5375; something *borne,* i.e. a *load*:— carriage.

5386. נְשִׁי **n°shîy**, *nesh-ee´*; from 5383; a *debt*:— debt.

5387. נָשִׂיא **nâsîy'**, *naw-see´*; or

נָשִׂא **nâsî'**, *naw-see´*; from 5375; prop. an *exalted* one, i.e. a *king* or *sheik*; also a rising *mist*:— captain, chief, cloud, governor, prince, ruler, vapour.

5388. נְשִׁיָּה **n°shîyâh**, *nesh-ee-yaw´*; from 5382; *oblivion*:— forgetfulness.

5389. נָשִׁין **nâshîym**. See 802.

נָשִׁין **nâshîyn** (Chald.), *naw-sheen´*; irreg. plur. fem. of 606:— women.

5390. נְשִׁיקָה **n°shîyqâh**, *nesh-ee-kaw´*; from 5401; a *kiss*:— kiss.

5391. נָשַׁךְ **nâshak**, *naw-shak´*; a prim. root; to *strike* with a sting (as a serpent); fig. to *oppress* with interest on a loan:— bite, lend upon usury.

5392. נֶשֶׁךְ **neshek**, *neh´-shek*; from 5391; *interest* on a debt:— usury.

5393. נִשְׁכָּה **nishkâh**, *nish-kaw´*; for 3957; a *cell*:— chamber.

5394. נָשַׁל **nâshal**, *naw-shal´*; a prim. root; to *pluck* off, i.e. *divest, eject,* or *drop*:— cast (out), drive, loose, put off (out), slip.

5395. נָשַׁם **nâsham**, *naw-sham´*; a prim. root; prop. to *blow* away, i.e. *destroy*:— destroy.

5396. נִשְׁמָא **nishmâ'** (Chald.), *nish-maw´*; corresp. to 5397; *vital breath*:— breath.

5397. נְשָׁמָה **n°shâmâh**, *nesh-aw-maw´*; from 5395; a *puff,* i.e. *wind,* angry or vital *breath, divine inspiration, intellect,* or (concr.) an *animal*:— blast, (that) breath (-eth), inspiration, soul, spirit.

5398. נָשַׁף **nâshaph**, *naw-shaf´*; a prim. root; to *breeze,* i.e. *blow* up fresh (as the wind):— blow.

5399. נֶשֶׁף **nesheph**, *neh´-shef*; from 5398; prop. a *breeze,* i.e. (by impl.) *dusk* (when the evening breeze prevails):— dark, dawning of the day (morning), night, twilight.

5400. נָשַׂק **nâsaq**, *naw-sak´*; a prim. root; to *catch* fire:— burn, kindle.

5401. נָשַׁק **nâshaq**, *naw-shak´*; a prim. root [ident. with 5400, through the idea of *fastening* up; comp. 2388, 2836]; to *kiss,* lit. or fig. (*touch*); also (as a mode of *attachment*), to *equip* with weapons:— armed (men), rule, kiss, that touched.

5402. נֶשֶׁק **nesheq**, *neh´-shek*; or

נֶשֶׁק **nêsheq**, *nay´-shek*; from 5401; military *equipment,* i.e. (collect.) *arms* (offensive or defensive), or (concr.) an *arsenal*:— armed men, armour (-y), battle, harness, weapon.

5403. נְשַׁר **n°shar** (Chald.), *nesh-ar´*; corresp. to 5404; an *eagle*:— eagle.

5404. נֶשֶׁר **nesher**, *neh´-sher*; from an unused root mean. to *lacerate;* the *eagle* (or other large bird of prey):— eagle.

5405. נָשַׁת **nâshath**, *naw-shath´*; a prim. root; prop. to *eliminate,* i.e. (intr.) to *dry* up:— fail.

5406. נִשְׁתְּוָן **n°thîbâh**. See 5410.

5406. נִשְׁתְּוָן **nisht°vân**, *nish-tev-awn´*; prob. of Pers. or.; an *epistle*:— letter.

5407. נִשְׁתְּוָן **nisht°vân** (Chald.), *nish-tev-awn´*; corresp. to 5406:— letter.

נְתוּן **Nâthûwn**. See 5411.

5408. נָתַח **nâthach**, *naw-thakh´*; a prim. root; to *dismember*:— cut (in pieces), divide, hew in pieces.

5409. נֵתַח **nêthach**, *nay´-thakh;* from 5408; a *fragment*:— part, piece.

5410. נָתִיב **nâthîyb**, *naw-theeb´;* or (fem.)

נְתִיבָה **n°thîybâh**, *neth-ee-baw´;* or

נְתִבָה **n°thîbâh** (Jer. 6:16), *neth-ee-baw´;* from an unused root mean. to *tramp;* a (beaten) *track*:— path (I-wayl), × travel I-lerl, way.

5411. נָתִין **Nâthîyn**, *naw-theen´;* or

נָתוּן **Nâthûwn** (Ezra 8:17), *naw-thoon´* (the proper form, as pass. part.), from 5414; one *given,* i.e. (in the plur. only) the *Nethinim,* or Temple-servants (as *given* to that duty):— Nethinims.

5412. נְתִין **N°thîyn** (Chald.), *netheen´;* corresp. to 5411:— Nethinims.

5413. נָתַךְ **nâthak**, *naw-thak´;* a prim. root; to *flow* forth (lit. or fig.); by impl. to *liquefy*:— drop, gather (together), melt, pour (forth, out).

5414. נָתַן **nâthan**, *naw-than´;* a prim. root; to *give,* used with greatest latitude of application (put, make, etc.):— add, apply, appoint, ascribe, assign, × avenge, × be (Ihealed]), bestow, bring (forth, hither), cast, cause, charge, come, commit, consider, count, + cry, deliver (up), direct, distribute, do, × doubtless, × without fail, fasten, frame, × get, give (forth, over, up), grant, hang (up), × have, × indeed, lay (unto charge, up), (give) leave, lend, let (out), + lie, lift up, make, + O that, occupy, offer, ordain, pay, perform, place, pour, print, × pull, put (forth), recompense, render, requite, restore, send (out), set (forth), shew, shoot forth (up), + sing, + slander, strike, Isub-] mit, suffer, × surely, × take, thrust, trade, turn, utter, + weep, × willingly, + withdraw, + would (to) God, yield.

5415. נְתַן **n°than** (Chald.), *neth-an´;* corresp. to 5414; *give:*— bestow, give, pay.

5416. נָתָן **Nâthân**, *naw-thawn´;* from 5414; *given; Nathan,* the name of five Isr.:— Nathan.

5417. נְתַנְאֵל **N°than'êl**, *neth-an-ale´;* from 5414 and 410; *given of God; Nethanel,* the name of ten Isr.:— Nethaneel.

5418. נְתַנְיָה **N°thanyâh**, *neth-an-yaw´;* or

נְתַנְיָהוּ **N°thanyâhûw**, *neth-an-*

yaw´-hoo; from 5414 and 3050; *given of Jah; Nethanjah,* the name of four Isr.:— Nethaniah.

5419. נְתַן־מֶלֶךְ **N°than-Melek**, *neth-an´ meh´-lek;* from 5414 and 4428; *given of* (the) *king; Nethan-Melek,* an Isr.:— Nathan-melech.

5420. נָתַס **nâthaç**, *naw-thas´;* a prim. root; to *tear* up:— mar.

5421. נָתַע **nâtha'**, *naw-thah´;* for 5422; to *tear* out:— break.

5422. נָתַץ **nâthats**, *naw-thats´;* a prim. root; to *tear* down:— beat down, break down (out), cast down, destroy, overthrow, pull down, throw down.

5423. נָתַק **nâthaq**, *naw-thak´;* a prim. root; to *tear* off:— break (off), burst, draw (away), lift up, pluck (away, off), pull (out), root out.

5424. נֶתֶק **netheq**, *neh´-thek;* from 5423; *scurf:*— (dry) scall.

5425. נָתַר **nâthar**, *naw-thar´;* a prim. root; to *jump,* i.e. *be* violently *agitated;* caus., to *terrify, shake* off, *untie:*— drive asunder, leap, (let) loose, × make, move, undo.

5426. נְתַר **n°thar** (Chald.), *neth-ar´;* corresp. to 5425:— shake off.

5427. נֶתֶר **nether**, *neh´-ther;* from 5425; mineral *potash* (so called from *effervescing* with acid):— nitre.

5428. נָתַשׁ **nâthash**, *naw-thash´;* a prim. root; to *tear* away:— destroy, forsake, pluck (out, up, by the roots), pull up, root out (up), × utterly.

ס

5429. סְאָה **ç°âh**, *seh-aw´;* from an unused root mean. to *define;* a *seah,* or certain measure (as *determinative*) for grain:— measure.

5430. סְאוֹן **ç°'ôwn**, *seh-own´;* from 5431; perh. a military *boot* (as a protection from *mud:*— battle.

5431. סָאַן **çâ'an**, *saw-an´;* a prim. root; to *be miry;* used only as denom. from 5430; to *shoe,* i.e. (act. part.) a *soldier* shod:— warrior.

5432. סַאסְּאָה **ça'ç°'âh**, *sah-seh-aw´;* for 5429; *measurement,* i.e. *moderation:*— measure.

5433. סָבָא **çâbâ'**, *saw-baw´;* a prim. root; to *quaff* to satiety, i.e. *become tipsy:*— drunkard, fill self, Sabean, Iwine-Ibibber.

5434. סְבָא **Ç°bâ'**, *seb-aw´;* of for. or.; *Seba,* a son of Cush, and the country settled by him:— Seba.

5435. סֹבֶא **çôbe'**, *so´-beh;* from 5433; *potation,* concr. (*wine*), or abstr. (*carousal*):— drink, drunken, wine.

5436. סְבָאִי **Ç°bâ'îy**, *seb-aw-ee´;* patrial from 5434; a *Sebaite,* or inhab. of Seba:— Sabean.

5437. סָבַב **çâbab**, *saw-bab´;* a prim. root; to *revolve, surround,* or *border;* used in various applications, lit. and fig. (as follows):— bring, cast, fetch, lead, make, walk, × whirl, × round about, be about on every side, apply, avoid, beset (about), besiege, bring again, carry (about), change, cause to come about, × circuit, (fetch a) compass (about, round), drive, environ, × on every side, beset (close, come, compass, go, stand) round about, inclose, remove, return, set, sit down, turn (self) (about, aside, away, back).

5438. כבה çibbāh, sib-baw'; from 5437; a (providential) turn (of affairs):— cause.

5439. כביב çâbîyb, saw-beeb'; or (fem.)

כביבה çᵉbîybâh, seb-ee-baw'; from 5437; (as noun) a circle, neighbour, or environs; but chiefly (as adv., with or without prep.) around:— (place, round) about, circuit, compass, on every side.

5440. כבך çâbak, saw-bak'; a prim. root; to entwine:— fold together, wrap.

5441. כבך çôbek, so'-bek; from 5440; a copse:— thicket.

5442. כבך çᵉbâk, seb-awk'; from 5440, a copse:— thick (-et).

5443. כבבא çabbᵉkâ' (Chald.), sab-bek-aw'; or

כבבא sabbᵉkâ' (Chald.), sab-bek-aw'; from a root corresp. to 5440; a lyre:— sackbut.

5444. כבבי Çibbᵉkay, sib-bek-ah'-ee; from 5440; copse-like; Sibbecai, an Isr.:— Sibbechai, Sibbechai.

5445. כבל çâbal, saw-bal'; a prim. root; to carry (lit. or fig.), or (refl.) be burdensome; spec. to be gravid:— bear, be a burden, carry, strong to labour.

5446. כבל çᵉbal (Chald.), seb-al'; corresp. to 5445; to erect:— strongly laid.

5447. כבל çêbel, say'-bel; from 5445; a load (lit. or fig.):— burden, charge.

5448. כבל çôbel, so'-bel; (only in the form

כבל çubbâl, soob-bawl'); from 5445; a load (fig.):— burden.

5449. כבל çabbâl, sab-bawl'; from 5445; a porter:— (to bear, bearer of) burden (-s).

5450. כבלה çᵉbâlâh, seb-aw-law'; from 5447; porterage:— burden.

5451. כבלה Çibbôleth, sib-bo'-leth; for 7641; an ear of grain:— Sibboleth.

5452. כבר çᵉbar (Chald.), seb-ar'; a prim. root; to bear in mind, i.e. hope:— think.

5453. כברים Çibrayim, sib-rah'-yim; dual from a root corresp. to 5452; double hope; Sibrajim, a place in Syria:— Sibraim.

5454. כבתא Çabtâ', sab-taw'; or

כבתה Çabtâh, sab-taw'; prob. of for. der.; Sabta or Sabtah, the name of a son of Cush, and the country occupied by his posterity:— Sabta, Sabtah.

5455. כבתכא Çabtᵉkâ', sab-tek-aw'; prob. of for. der.; Sabteca, the name of a son of Cush, and the region settled by him:— Sabtecha, Sabtechah.

5456. כגד çâgad, saw-gad'; a prim. root; to prostrate oneself (in homage):— fall down.

5457. כגד çᵉgîd (Chald.), seg-eed'; corresp. to 5456:— worship.

5458. כגור çᵉgôwr, seg-ore'; from 5462; prop. shut up, i.e. the breast (as inclos-

ing the heart); also gold (as gen. shut up safely):— caul, gold.

5459. כגלה çᵉgullâh, seg-ool-law'; fem. pass. part. of an unused root mean. to shut up; wealth (as closely shut up):— jewel, peculiar (treasure), proper good, special.

5460. כגן çᵉgan (Chald.), seg-an'; corresp. to 5461:— governor.

5461. כגן çâgân, saw-gawn'; from an unused root mean. to superintend; a præfect of a province:— prince, ruler.

5462. כגר çâgar, saw-gar'; a prim. root; to shut up; fig. to surrender:— close up, deliver (up), give over (up), inclose, × pure, repair, shut (in, self, out, up, up together), stop, × straitly.

5463. כגר çᵉgar (Chald.), seg-ar'; corresp. to 5462:— shut up.

5464. כגריד çagrîyd, sag-reed'; prob. from 5462 in the sense of sweeping away; a pouring rain:— very rainy.

5465. כד çad, sad; from an unused root mean. to estop; the stocks:— stocks.

5466. כדין çâdîyn, saw-deen'; from an unused root mean. to envelop; a wrapper, i.e. shirt:— fine linen, sheet.

5467. כדם Çᵉdôm, sed-ome'; from an unused root mean. to scorch; burnt (i.e. volcanic or bituminous) district; Sedom, a place near the Dead Sea:— Sodom.

5468. כדר çeder, seh'-der; from an unused root mean. to arrange; order:— order.

5469. כהר çahar, sah'-har; from an unused root mean. to be round; roundness:— round.

5470. כהר çôhar, so'-har; from the same as 5469; a dungeon (as surrounded by walls):— prison.

5471. כוא Çôw', so; of for. der.; So, an Eg. king:— So.

5472. כוג çûwg, soog; a prim. root; prop. to flinch, i.e. (by impl.) to go back, lit. (to retreat) or fig. (to apostatize):— backslider, drive, go back, turn (away, back).

5473. כוג çûwg, soog; a prim. root (prob. rather ident. with 5472 through the idea of shrinking from a hedge; comp. 7735); to hem in, i.e. bind:— set about.

כוג° çûwg. See 5509.

5474. כוגר çûwgar, soo-gar'; from 5462; an inclosure, i.e. cage (for an animal):— ward.

5475. כוד çôwd, sode; from 3245; a session, i.e. company of persons (in close deliberation); by impl. intimacy, consultation, a secret; by impl. assembly, counsel, inward, secret (counsel).

5476. כודי Çôwdîy, so-dee'; from 5475; a confidant; Sodi, an Isr.:— Sodi.

5477. כוח Çûwach, soo'-akh; from an unused root mean. to wipe away; sweeping; Suach, an Isr.:— Suah.

5478. כוחה çûwchâh, soo-khaw'; from the same as 5477; something swept away, i.e. filth:— torn.

כוט çûwṭ. See 7750.

5479. כוטי Çôwṭay, so-tah'-ee; from

7750; roving; Sotai, one of the Nethinim:— Sotai.

5480. כוך çûwk, sook; a prim. root; prop. to smear over (with oil), i.e. anoint:— anoint (self), × at all.

כולאה çôwlᵉlâh. See 5550.

5481. כומפוניה çûwmpôwnᵉyâh (Chald.), soom-po-neh-yaw'; or

כומפניה çûwmpônᵉyâh (Chald.), soom-po-neh-yaw'; or

כיפניא çîyphônᵉyâ' (Dan. 3:10) (Chald.), see-fo-neh-yaw'; of Gr. or. (συμφωνία); a bagpipe (with a double pipe):— dulcimer.

5482. כונה Çᵉvênêh, sev-ay-nay' (rather to be written

כונה Çᵉvênâh, sev-ay'-naw; for

כון Çᵉvên, sev-ane'; i.e. to Seven); of Eg. der.; Seven, a place in Upper Egypt:— Syene.

5483. כוס çûwç, soos; or

כס çûç, soos; from an unused root mean. to skip (prop. for joy); a horse (as leaping); also a swallow (from its rapid flight):— crane, horse (I-back, -hoof). Comp. 6571.

5484. כוסה çûwçâh, soo-saw'; fem. of 5483; a mare:— company of horses.

5485. כוסי Çûwçîy, soo-see'; from 5483; horse-like; Susi, an Isr.:— Susi.

5486. כוף çûwph, soof; a prim. root; to snatch away, i.e. terminate:— consume, have an end, perish, × be utterly.

5487. כוף çûwph (Chald.), soof; corresp. to 5486; to come to an end:— consume, fulfill.

5488. כוף çûwph, soof; prob. of Eg. or.; a reed, espec. the papyrus:— flag, Red (seal, weed. Comp. 5489.

5489. כוף Çûwph, soof; for 5488 (by ellip. of 3220); the Reed (Sea):— Red Sea.

5490. כוף çôwph, sofe; from 5486; a termination:— conclusion, end, hinder part.

5491. כוף çôwph (Chald.), sofe; corresp. to 5490:— end.

5492. כופה çûwphâh, soo-faw'; from 5486; a hurricane:— storm, tempest, whirlwind, Red sea.

5493. כור çûwr, soor; or

כור sûwr (Hosea 9:12), soor; a prim. root; to turn off (lit. or fig.):— be [-head], bring, call back, decline, depart, eschew, get [you], go (aside), × grievous, lay away (by), leave undone, be past, pluck away, put (away, down), rebel, remove (to and fro), revolt, × be sour, take (away, off), turn (aside, away, in), withdraw, be without.

5494. כור çûwr, soor; prob. pass. part. of 5493; turned off, i.e. deteriorated:— degenerate.

5495. כור Çûwr, soor; the same as 5494; Sur, a gate of the Temple:— Sur.

5496. כות çûwth, sooth; perh. denom. from 7898; prop. to prick, i.e. (fig.) stimulate; by impl. to seduce:— entice, move, persuade, provoke, remove, set on, stir up, take away.

5497. כות çûwth, sooth; prob. from the

same root as 4533; *covering*, i.e. *clothing*:— clothes.

5498. חָחַב **çâchab**, *saw-khab´*; a prim. root; to *trail* along:— draw (out), tear.

5499. סְחָבָה **çᵉchâbâh**, *seh-khaw-baw´*; from 5498; a *rag*:— cast clout.

5500. סָחָה **çâchâh**, *saw-khaw´*; a prim. root; to *sweep* away:— scrape.

5501. סְחִי **çᵉchîy**, *seh-khee´*; from 5500; *refuse* (as *swept off*):— offscouring.

סְחִישׁ **çâchîysh**. See 7823.

5502. סָחַף **çâchaph**, *saw-khaf´*; a prim. root; to *scrape* off:— sweep (away).

5503. סָחַר **çâchar**, *saw-khar´*; a prim. root; to *travel* round (spec. as a *pedlar*); intens. to *palpitate*:— go about, merchant (-man), occupy with, pant, trade, traffick.

5504. סַחַר **çachar**, *sakh´-ar*; from 5503; *profit* (from trade):— merchandise.

5505. סָחַר **çâchar**, *saw-khar´*; from 5503; an *emporium*; abstr. *profit* (from trade):— mart, merchandise.

5506. סְחֹרָה **çᵉchôrâh**, *sekh-o-raw´*; from 5503; *traffic*:— merchandise.

5507. סֹחֵרָה **çôchêrâh**, *so-khay-raw´*; prop. act. part. fem. of 5503; something *surrounding* the person, i.e. a *shield*:— buckler.

5508. סֹחֵרֶת **çôchereth**, *so-kheh´-reth*; similar to 5507; prob. a (black) *tile* (or *tessara*) for laying borders with:— black marble.

סֵט **çêt**. See 7750.

5509. סִיג **çîyg**, *seeg*; or

סוּג **çùwg** (Ezek. 22:18), *soog*; from 5472 in the sense of *refuse*; *scoria*:— dross.

5510. סִיוָן **çîyvân**, *see-vawn´*; prob. of Pers. or.; *Sivan*, the third Heb. month:— Sivan.

5511. סִיחוֹן **çîychôwn**, *see-khone´*; or

סִיחֹן **çîychôn**, *see-khone´*; from the same as 5477; *tempestuous*; *Sichon*, an Amoritish king:— Sihon.

5512. סִין **çîyn**, *seen*; of uncert. der.; *Sin*, the name of an Eg. town and (prob.) desert adjoining:— Sin.

5513. סִינִי **çîynîy**, *see-nee´*; from an otherwise unknown name of a man; a *Sinite*, or desc. of one of the sons of Canaan:— Sinite.

5514. סִינַי **çîynay**, *see-nah´-ee*; of uncert. der.; *Sinai*, a mountain of Arabia:— Sinai.

5515. סִינִים **çîynîym**, *see-neem´*; plur. of an otherwise unknown name; *Sinim*, a distant Oriental region:— Sinim.

5516. סִיסְרָא **çîyçᵉrâ**, *see-ser-aw´*; of uncert. der.; *Sisera*, the name of a Canaanitish king and of one of the Nethinim:— Sisera.

5517. סִיעָא **çîy'â**, *see-ah´*; or

סִיעֲהָא **çîy'ähâ'**, *see-ah-haw´*; from an unused root mean. to *converse*; *congregation*; *Sia* or *Siaha*, one of the Nethinim:— Sia, Siaha.

סִיפֹנְיָא **çîyphônᵉyâ'**. See 5481.

5518. סִיר **çîyr**, *seer*; or (fem.)

סִירָה **çîyrâh**, *see-raw´*; or

סִרָה **çîrâh** (Jer. 52:18), *see-raw´*; from a prim. root mean. to *boil* up; a *pot*; also a *thorn* (as springing up rapidly); by impl. a *hook*:— caldron, fishhook, pan, ([wash-]) pot, thorn.

5519. סָךְ **çâk**, *sawk*; from 5526; prop. a *thicket* of men, i.e. a *crowd*:— multitude.

5520. סֹךְ **çôk**, *soke*; from 5526; a *hut* (as of entwined boughs); also a *lair*:— covert, den, pavilion, tabernacle.

5521. סֻכָּה **çukkâh**, *sook-kaw´*; fem of 5520; a *hut* or *lair*:— booth, cottage, covert, pavilion, tabernacle, tent.

5522. סִכּוּת **çikkûwth**, *sik-kooth´*; fem. of 5519; an (idolatrous) *booth*:— tabernacle.

5523. סֻכּוֹת **Çukkôwth**, *sook-kohth´*; or

סֻכֹּת **Çukkôth**, *sook-kohth´*; plur. of 5521; *booths*; *Succoth*, the name of a place in Egypt and of three in Pal.:— Succoth.

5524. סֻכּוֹת בְּנוֹת **Çukkôwth Bᵉnôwth**, *sook-kohth´ ben-ohth´*; from 5523 and the (irreg.) plur. of 1323; *booths of* (the) *daughters*; *brothels*, i.e. idolatrous *tents* for impure purposes:— Succothbenoth.

5525. סֻכִּי **Çukkîy**, *sook-kee´*; patrial from an unknown name (perh. 5520); a *Sukkite*, or inhab. of some place near Egypt (i.e. *hut-dwellers*):— Sukkiims.

5526. סָכַךְ **çâkak**, *saw-kak´*; or

שָׂכַךְ **sâkak** (Exod. 33:22), *saw-kak´*; a prim. root; prop. to *entwine* as a screen; by impl. to *fence* in, *cover* over, (fig.) *protect*:— cover, defence, defend, hedge in, join together, set, shut up.

5527. סְכָכָה **Çᵉkâkâh**, *sek-aw-kaw´*; from 5526; *inclosure*; *Secacah*, a place in Pal.:— Secacah.

5528. סָכַל **çâkal**, *saw-kal´*; for 3688; to *be silly*:— do (make, play the, turn into) fool (-ish, -ishly, -ishness).

5529. סֶכֶל **çekel**, *seh´-kel*; from 5528; *silliness*; concr. and collect. *dolts*:— folly.

5530. סָכָל **çâkâl**, *saw-kawl´*; from 5528; *silly*:— fool (-ish), sottish.

5531. סִכְלוּת **çiklûwth**, *sik-looth´*; or

שִׂכְלוּת **siklûwth** (Eccl. 1:17) *sik-looth´*; from 5528; *silliness*:— folly, foolishness.

5532. סָכַן **çâkan**, *saw-kan´*; a prim. root; to *be familiar* with; by impl. to *minister* to, *be serviceable* to, *be customary*:— acquaint (self), be advantage, × ever, (be, [un-]) profit (-able), treasurer, be the wont.

5533. סָכַן **çâkan**, *saw-kan´*; prob. a denom. from 7915; prop. to *cut*, i.e. *damage*; also to *grow* (caus. *make*) *poor*:— endanger, impoverish.

5534. סָכַר **çâkar**, *saw-kar´*; a prim. root; to *shut* up; by impl. to *surrender*:— stop, give over. See also 5462, 7936.

5535. סָכַת **çâkath**, *saw-kath´*; a prim. root; to *be silent*; by impl. to *observe* quietly:— take heed.

סֻכֹּת **Çukkôth**. See 5523.

5536. סַל **çal**, *sal*; from 5549; prop. a *willow twig* (as *pendulous*), i.e. an *osier*;

but only as woven into a *basket*:— basket.

5537. סָלָא **çâlâ'**, *saw-law´*; a prim. root; to *suspend* in a balance, i.e. *weigh*:— compare.

5538. סִלָּא **Çillâ'**, *sil-law´*; from 5549; an *embankment*; *Silla*, a place in Jerusalem:— Silla.

5539. סָלַד **çâlad**, *saw-lad´*; a prim. root; prob. to *leap* (with joy), i.e. *exult*:— harden self.

5540. סֶלֶד **Çeled**, *seh´-led*; from 5539; *exultation*; *Seled*, an Isr.:— Seled.

5541. סָלָה **çâlâh**, *saw-law´*; a prim. root; to *hang* up, i.e. *weigh*, or (fig.) *contemn*:— tread down (under foot), value.

5542. סֶלָה **Çelâh**, *seh´-law*; from 5541; *suspension* (of music), i.e. *pause*:— Selah.

5543. סַלּוּ **Çallûw**, *sal-loo´*; or

סַלּוּא **Çallûw'**, *sal-loo´*; or

סָלוּא **Çâlûw**, *sal-loo´*; or

סַלַּי **Çallay**, *sal-lah´-ee*; from 5541; *weighed*; *Sallu* or *Sallai*, the name of two Isr.:— Sallai, Sallu, Salu.

5544. סִלּוֹן **çillôwn**, *sil-lone´*; or

סַלּוֹן **çallôwn**, *sal-lone´*; from 5541; a *prickle* (as if *pendulous*):— brier, thorn.

5545. סָלַח **çâlach**, *saw-lakh´*; a prim. root; to *forgive*:— forgive, pardon, spare.

5546. סַלָּח **çallâch**, *saw-lawkh´*; from 5545; *placable*:— ready to forgive.

סַלַּי **Çallay**. See 5543.

5547. סְלִיחָה **çᵉlîychâh**, *sel-ee-khaw´*; from 5545; *pardon*:— forgiveness, pardon.

5548. סַלְכָה **Çalkâh**, *sal-kaw´*; from an unused root. mean. to *walk*; *walking*; *Salcah*, a place E. of the Jordan:— Salcah, Salchah.

5549. סָלַל **çâlal**, *saw-lal´*; a prim. root; to *mound* up (espec. a turnpike); fig. to *exalt*; refl. to *oppose* (as by a dam):— cast up, exalt (self), extol, make plain, raise up.

5550. סֹלְלָה **çôlᵉlâh**, *so-lel-aw´*; or

סוֹלְלָה **çôwlᵉlâh**, *so-lel-aw´*; act. part. fem. of 5549, but used pass.; a military *mound*, i.e. *rampart* of besiegers:— bank, mount.

5551. סֻלָּם **çullâm**, *sool-lawm´*; from 5549; a *stair-case*:— ladder.

5552. סַלְסִלָּה **çalçillâh**, *sal-sil-law´*; from 5541; a *twig* (as *pendulous*):— basket.

5553. סֶלַע **çela'**, *seh´-lah*; from an unused root mean. to be *lofty*; a *craggy rock*, lit. or fig. (a *fortress*):— (ragged) rock, stone (-ny), strong hold.

5554. סֶלַע **Çela'**, *seh´-lah*; the same as 5553; *Sela*, the rock-city of Idumaea:— rock, Sela (-h).

5555. סֶלַע הַמַּחְלְקוֹת **Çela' hammachlᵉqôwth**, *seh´-lah ham-makh-lek-ôth´*; from 5553 and the plur. of 4256 with the art. interposed; *rock of the divisions*; *Sela-ham-Machlekoth*, a place in Pal.:— Sela-hammalekoth.

5556. סָלְעָם **çol'âm**, *sol-awm´*; appar.

from the same as 5553 in the sense of *crushing* as with a rock, i.e. consuming; a kind of *locust* (from its *destructiveness*):— bald locust.

5557. צָלַף **çâlaph**, *saw-laf´*; a prim. root; prop. to *wrench*, i.e. (fig.) to *subvert*:— overthrow, pervert.

5558. סֶלֶף **çeleph**, *seh´-lef*; from 5557; *distortion*, i.e. (fig.) *viciousness*:— perverseness.

5559. סְלִק **çeliq** (Chald.), *sel-eek´*; a prim. root; to *ascend*:— come (up).

5560. סֹלֶת **çôleth**, *so´-leth*; from an unused root mean. to *strip*; *flour* (as *chipped off*):— (fine) flour, meal.

5561. סַם **çam**, *sam*; from an unused root mean. to *smell* sweet; an *aroma*:— sweet (spice).

5562. סְמַגַּר נְבוֹ **Çamgar Nᵉbôw**, *sam-gar´ neb-o´*; of for. or.; *Samgar-Nebo*, a Bab. general:— Samgar-nebo.

5563. סְמָדַר **çemâdar**, *sem-aw-dar´*; of uncert. der.; a vine *blossom*; used also adv. *abloom*:— tender grape.

5564. סָמַך **çâmak**, *saw-mak´*; a prim. root; to *prop* (lit. or fig.); refl. to *lean* upon or *take hold* of (in a favorable or unfavorable sense):— bear up, establish, (up-) hold, lay, lean. lie hard, put, rest self, set self, stand fast, stay (self), sustain.

5565. סְמַכְיָהוּ **Çᵉmakyâhûw**, *sem-ak-yaw´-hoo*; from 5564 and 3050; *supported of Jah*; *Semakjah*, an Isr.:— Semachiah.

5566. סֶמֶל **çemel**, *seh´-mel*; or

סֵמֶל **çêmel**, *say´-mel*; from an unused root mean. to *resemble*; a *likeness*:— figure, idol, image.

5567. סָמַן **çâman**, *saw-man´*; a prim. root; to *designate*:— appointed.

5568. סָמַר **çâmar**, *saw-mar´*; a prim. root; to *be erect*, i.e. bristle as hair:— stand up, tremble.

5569. סָמָר **çâmâr**, *saw-mar´*; from 5568; *bristling*, i.e. *shaggy*:— rough.

5570. סְנָאָה **Çᵉnâʾah**, *sen-aw-aw´*; from an unused root mean. to *prick*; *thorny*; *Senaah*, a place in Pal.:— Senaah, Hassenaah [with the art.].

הַסְּנָאָה **çᵉnûʾah**. See 5574.

5571. סַנְבַלַּט **Çanballaṭ**, *san-bal-lat´*; of for. or.; *Sanballat*, a Pers. satrap of Samaria:— Sanballat.

5572. סְנֶה **çᵉneh**, *sen-eh´*; from an unused root mean. to *prick*; a *bramble*:— bush.

5573. סֶנֶה **Çeneh**, *seh-neh´*; the same as 5572; *thorn*; *Seneh*, a crag in Pal.:— Seneh.

סַנָּה **Çannâh**. See 7158.

5574. סְנוּאָה **Çᵉnûʾah**, *sen-oo-aw´*; or

הַסְּנָאָה **Çᵉnûʾah**, *sen-oo-aw´*; from the same as 5570; *pointed*; (used with the art. as a proper name) *Senuah*, the name of two Isr.:— Hasenuah [incl. the art.], Senuah.

5575. סַנְוֵר **çanvêr**, *san-vare´*; of uncert. der.; (in plur.) *blindness*:— blindness.

5576. סַנְחֵרִיב **Çanchêrîyb**, *san-khay-*

reeb´; of for. or.; *Sancherib*, an Ass. king:— Sennacherib.

5577. סַנְסִן **çançin**, *san-seen´*; from an unused root mean. to *be pointed*; a *twig* (as *tapering*):— bough.

5578. סַנְסַנָּה **Çançannâh**, *san-san-naw´*; fem. of a form of 5577; a *bough*; *Sansannah*, a place in Pal.:— Sansannah.

5579. סְנַפִּיר **çᵉnappîyr**, *sen-ap-peer´*; of uncert. der.; a *fin* (collect.):— fins.

5580. סָס **çâç**, *sawce*; from the same as 5483; a *moth* (from the *agility* of the fly):— moth.

סָס **çûç**. See 5483.

5581. סִסְמַי **Çiçmay**, *sis-mah´-ee*; of uncert. der.; *Sismai*, an Isr.:— Sisamai.

5582. סָעַד **çâʿad**, *saw-ad´*; a prim. root; to *support* (mostly fig.):— comfort, establish, hold up, refresh self, strengthen, be upholden.

5583. סְעַד **çᵉʿad** (Chald.), *seh-ad´*; corresp. to 5582; to *aid*:— helping.

5584. סָעָה **çâʿâh**, *saw-aw´*; a prim. root; to *rush*:— storm.

5585. סָעִיף **çâʿîyph**, *saw-eef´*; from 5586; a *fissure* (of rocks); also a *bough* (as *subdivided*):— (outmost) branch, clift, top.

5586. סָעַף **çâʿaph**, *saw-af´*; a prim. root; prop. to *divide* up; but used only as denom. from 5585, to *disbranch* (a tree):— top.

5587. סָעִף **çâʿiph**, *saw-eef´*; or

שָׂעִף **sâʿiph**, *saw-eef´*; from 5586; *divided* (in mind), i.e. (abstr.) a *sentiment*:— opinion.

5588. סֵעֵף **çêʿêph**, *say-afe´*; from 5586; *divided* (in mind), i.e. (concr.) a *skeptic*:— thought.

5589. סְעַפָּה **çᵉʿappâh**, *seh-ap-paw´*; fem. of 5585; a *twig*:— bough, branch. Comp. 5634.

5590. סָעַר **çâʿar**, *saw-ar´*; a prim. root; to *rush* upon; by impl. to *toss* (tran. or intr., lit. or fig.):— be (toss with) tempest (-uous), be sore troubled, come out as a (drive with the, scatter with a) whirlwind.

5591. סַעַר **çaʿar**, *sah´-ar*; or (fem.)

סְעָרָה **çᵉʿârâh**, *seh-aw-raw´*; from 5590; a *hurricane*:— storm (-y), tempest, whirlwind.

5592. סַף **çaph**, *saf*; from 5605, in its orig. sense of *containing*; a *vestibule* (as a *limit*); also a *dish* (for holding blood or wine):— bason, bowl, cup, door (post), gate, post, threshold.

5593. סַף **Çaph**, *saf*; the same as 5592; *Saph*, a Philistine:— Saph. Comp. 5598.

5594. סָפַד **çâphad**, *saw-fad´*; a prim. root; prop. to *tear* the hair and *beat* the breasts (as Orientals do in grief); gen. to *lament*; by impl. to *wail*:— lament, mourn (-er), wail.

5595. סָפָה **çâphâh**, *saw-faw´*; a prim. root; prop. to *scrape* (lit. to *shave*; but usually fig.) together (i.e. to *accumulate* or *increase*) or away (i.e. to *scatter*, *remove*, or *ruin*; intr. to *perish*):— add, augment, consume, destroy, heap, join, perish, put.

5596. סָפַח **çâphach**, *saw-fakh´*; or

שָׂפַח **sâphach** (Isa. 3:17) *saw-fakh´*; a prim. root; prop. to *scrape* out, but in certain peculiar senses (of *removal* or *association*):— abiding, gather together, cleave, smite with the scab.

5597. סַפַּחַת **çappachath**, *sap-pakh´-ath*; from 5596; the *mange* (as making the hair fall off):— scab.

5598. סִפַּי **Çippay**, *sip-pah´-ee*; from 5592; *bason-like*; *Sippai*, a Philistine:— Sippai. Comp. 5593.

5599. סָפִיחַ **çâphîyach**, *saw-fee´-akh*; from 5596; something (spontaneously) *falling* off, i.e. a *self-sown crop*; fig. a *freshet*:— (such) things as (which) grow (of themselves), which groweth of its own accord (itself).

5600. סְפִינָה **çᵉphîynâh**, *sef-ee-naw´*; from 5603; a (sea-going) *vessel* (as *ceiled* with a deck):— ship.

5601. סַפִּיר **çappîyr**, *sap-peer´*; from 5608; a *gem* (perh. as used for *scratching* other substances), prob. the *sapphire*:— sapphire.

5602. סֵפֶל **çêphel**, *say´-fel*; from an unused root mean. to *depress*; a *basin* (as *deepened* out):— bowl, dish.

5603. סָפַן **çâphan**, *saw-fan´*; a prim. root; to *hide* by covering; spec. to *roof* (pass. part. as noun, a *roof*) or *paneling*; fig. to *reserve*:— cieled, cover, seated.

5604. סִפֻּן **çippûn**, *sip-poon´*; from 5603; a *wainscot*:— cieling.

5605. סָפַף **çâphaph**, *saw-faf´*; a prim. root; prop. to *snatch* away, i.e. *terminate*; but used only as denom. from 5592 (in the sense of a *vestibule*), to *wait at* (the) *threshold*:— be a doorkeeper.

5606. סָפַק **çâphaq**, *saw-fak´*; or

שָׂפַק **sâphaq** (1 Kings 20:10; Job 27:23; Isa. 2:6), *saw-fak´*; a prim. root; to *clap* the hands (in token of compact, derision, grief, indignation, or punishment); by impl. of satisfaction, to *be enough*; by impl. of excess, to *vomit*:— clap, smite, strike, suffice, wallow.

5607. סֵפֶק **çêpheq**, *say´-fek*; or

שֶׂפֶק **sepheq** (Job 20:22; 36:18) *seh´-fek*; from 5606; *chastisement*; also *satiety*:— stroke, sufficiency.

5608. סָפַר **çâphar**, *saw-far´*; a prim. root; prop. to *score* with a mark as a tally or record, i.e. (by impl.) to *inscribe*, and also to *enumerate*; intens. to *recount*, i.e. *celebrate*:— commune, (ac-) count; declare, number, + penknife, reckon, scribe, shew forth, speak, talk, tell (out), writer.

5609. סְפַר **çᵉphar** (Chald.), *sef-ar´*; from a root corresp. to 5608; a *book*:— book, roll.

5610. סְפָר **çᵉphâr**, *sef-awr´*; from 5608; a *census*:— numbering.

5611. סְפָר **Çᵉphâr**, *sef-awr´*; the same as 5610; *Sephar*, a place in Arabia:— Sephar.

5612. סֵפֶר **çêpher**, *say´-fer*; or (fem.)

סִפְרָה **çiphrâh** (Psa. 56:8 [9]), *sif-raw´*; from 5608; prop. *writing* (the art or a document); by impl. a *book*:— bill, book, evidence, × learn [-ed] (-ing), letter, register, scroll.

5613. כְּפַר **çâphêr** (Chald.), *saw-fare´*; from the same as 5609; a *scribe* (secular or sacred):— scribe.

5614. סְפָרָד **Çᵉphârâd**, *sef-aw-rawd´*; of for. der.; *Sepharad*, a region of Assyria:— Sepharad.

5612. סִפְרָה **çiphrâh**. See 5612.

5615. סְפֹרָה **çᵉphôrâh**, *sef-o-raw´*; from 5608; a *numeration*:— number.

5616. סְפָרְוִי **Çᵉpharvîy**, *sef-ar-vee´*; patrial from 5617; a *Sepharvite* or inhab. of Sepharvaim:— Sepharvite.

5617. סְפַרְוַיִם **Çᵉpharvayim** (dual), *sef-ar-vah´-yim*; or

סְפָרִים° **Çᵉphârîym** (plur.), *sef-aw-reem´*; of for. der.; *Sepharvajim* or *Sepharim*, a place in Assyria:— Sepharvaim.

5618. סֹפֶרֶת **Çôphereth**, *so-feh´-reth*; fem. act. part. of 5608; a *scribe* (prop. female); *Sophereth*, a temple servant:— Sophereth.

5619. סָקַל **çâqal**, *saw-kal´*; a prim. root; prop. to *be weighty*; but used only in the sense of *lapidation* or its contrary (as if a delapidation):— (cast, gather out, throw) stone (-s), × surely.

5620. סַר **çar**, *sar*; from 5637 contr.; *peevish*:— heavy, sad.

5621. סְרָב **çârâb**, *saw-rawb´*; from an unused root mean. to *sting*; a *thistle*:— brier.

5622. סַרְבַּל **çarbal** (Chald.), *sar-bal´*; of uncert. der.; a *cloak*:— coat.

5623. סַרְגּוֹן **Çargôwn**, *sar-gone´*; of for. der.; *Sargon*, an Ass. king:— Sargon.

5624. סֶרֶד **Çered**, *seh´-red*; from a prim. root mean. to *tremble*; *trembling*; *Sered*, an Isr.:— Sered.

5625. סַרְדִּי **Çardîy**, *sar-dee´*; patron. from 5624; a *Seredite* (collect.) or desc. of Sered:— Sardites.

5626. סִרָה **Çirâh**, *see-raw´*; from 5493; *departure*; *Sirah*, a cistern so-called:— Sirah. See also 5518.

5627. סָרָה **çârâh**, *saw-raw´*; from 5493; *apostasy*, *crime*; fig. *remission*:— × continual, rebellion, revolt [-ed], turn away, wrong.

5628. סָרַח **çârach**, *saw-rakh´*; a prim. root; to *extend* (even to *excess*):— exceeding, hand, spread, stretch self, banish.

5629. סֶרַח **çerach**, *seh´-rakh*; from 5628; a *redundancy*:— remnant.

5630. סִריֹן **çiyrôn**, *sir-yone´*; for 8302; a *coat of mail*:— brigandine.

5631. סָרִיס **çârîyç**, *saw-reece´*; or

סָרִס **çâriç**, *saw-reece´*; from an unused root mean. to *castrate*; a *eunuch*; by impl. *valet* (espec. of the female apartments), and thus, a *minister* of state:— chamberlain, eunuch, officer. Comp. 7249.

5632. סָרֵךְ **çârêk** (Chald.), *saw-rake´*; of for. or.; an *emir*:— president.

5633. סֶרֶן **çeren**, *seh´-ren*; from an un-

used root of uncert. mean.; an *axle*; fig. a *peer*:— lord, plate.

5634. סַרְעַפָּה **çar'appâh**, *sar-ap-paw´*; for 5589; a *twig*:— bough.

5635. סָרַף **çâraph**, *saw-raf´*; a prim. root; to *cremate*, i.e. to *be* (near) *of kin* (such being privileged to kindle the pyre):— burn.

5636. סַרְפַּד **çarpâd**, *sar-pawd´*; from 5635; a *nettle* (as stinging like a *burn*):— brier.

5637. סָרַר **çârar**, *saw-rar´*; a prim. root; to *turn away*, i.e. (mor.) *be refractory*:— × away, backsliding, rebellious, revolter (-ing), slide back, stubborn, withdrew.

5638. סְתָו **çᵉthâv**, *seth-awv´*; from an unused root mean. to *hide*; *winter* (as the dark season):— winter.

5639. סְתוּר **Çᵉthûwr**, *seth-oor´*; from 5641; *hidden*; *Sethur*, an Isr.:— Sethur.

5640. סָתַם **çâtham**, *saw-tham´*; or

סָתַם **çâtham** (Num. 24:15), *saw-tham´*; a prim. root; to *stop up*; by impl. to *repair*; fig. to *keep secret*:— closed up, hidden, secret, shut out (up), stop.

5641. סָתַר **çâthar**, *saw-thar´*; a prim. root; to *hide* (by covering), lit. or fig.:— be absent, keep close, conceal, hide (self), (keep) secret, × surely.

5642. סְתַר **çᵉthar** (Chald.), *seth-ar´*; corresp. to 5641; to *conceal*; fig. to *demolish*:— destroy, secret thing.

5643. סֵתֶר **çêther**, *say´-ther*; or (fem.)

סִתְרָה **çithrâh** (Deut. 32:38), *sith-raw´*; from 5641; a *cover* (in a good or a bad, a lit. or a fig. sense):— backbiting, covering, covert, × disguise [-th], hiding place, privily, protection, secret (-ly, place).

5644. סִתְרִי **Çithrîy**, *sith-ree´*; from 5643; *protective*; *Sithri*, an Isr.:— Zithri.

ע

5645. עָב **'âb**, *awb* (masc. and fem.); from 5743; prop. an *envelope*, i.e. *darkness* (or *density*, 2 Chron. 4:17); spec. a (scud) *cloud*; also a *copse*:— clay, (thick) cloud, × thick, thicket. Comp. 5672.

5646. עָב **'âb**, *awb*; or

עֹב **'ôb**, *obe*; from an unused root mean. to *cover*; prop. equiv. to 5645; but used only as an arch. term, an *architrave* (as *shading* the pillars):— thick (beam, plant).

5647. עָבַד **'âbad**, *aw-bad´*; a prim. root; to *work* (in any sense); by impl. to *serve*, *till*, (caus.) *enslave*, etc.:— × be, keep in bondage, be bondmen, bond-service, compel, do, dress, ear, execute, + husbandman, keep, labour (-ing man, bring to pass, (cause to, make to) serve (-ing, self), (be, become) servant (-s), do (use) service, till (-er), transgress [from marg.], (set a) work, be wrought, worshipper.

5648. עֲבַד **'ᵃbad** (Chald.), *ab-bad´*; corresp. to 5647; to *do*, *make*, *prepare*, *keep*, etc.:— × cut, do, execute, go on, make, move, work.

5649. עֲבַד **'ᵃbad** (Chald.), *ab-bad´*; from 5648; a *servant*:— servant.

5650. עֶבֶד **'ebed**, *eh´-bed*; from 5647; a *servant*:— × bondage, bondman, [bond-] servant, (man-) servant.

5651. עֶבֶד **'Ebed**, *eh´-bed*; the same as 5650; *Ebed*, the name of two Isr.:— Ebed.

5652. עֲבָד **'ᵃbâd**, *ab-awd´*; from 5647; a *deed*:— work.

5653. עַבְדָּא **'Abdâ**, *ab-daw´*; from 5647; *work*; *Abda*, the name of two Isr.:— Abda.

5654. עֹבֵד אֱדוֹם **'Ôbêd 'Edôwm**, *o-bade´ ed-ome´*; from the act. part. of 5647 and 123; *worker of Edom*; *Obed-Edom*, the name of five Isr.:— Obed-edom.

5655. עַבְדְּאֵל **'Abdᵉ'êl**, *ab-deh-ale´*; from 5647 and 410; *serving God*; *Abdeel*, an Isr.:— Abdeel. Comp. 5661.

5656. עֲבֹדָה **'ᵃbôdâh**, *ab-o-daw´*; or

עֲבוֹדָה **'ᵃbôwdâh**, *ab-o-daw´*; from 5647; *work* of any kind:— act, bondage, + bondservant, effect, labour, ministering (-try), office, service (-ile, -itude), tillage, use, work, × wrought.

5657. עֲבֻדָּה **'ᵃbuddâh**, *ab-ood-daw´*; pass. part. of 5647; something *wrought*, i.e. (concr.) *service*:— household, store of servants.

5658. עַבְדּוֹן **'Abdôwn**, *ab-dohn´*; from 5647; *servitude*; *Abdon*, the name of a place in Pal. and of four Isr.:— Abdon. Comp. 5683.

5659. עַבְדוּת **'abdûwth**, *ab-dooth´*; from 5647; *servitude*:— bondage.

5660. עַבְדִּי **'Abdîy**, *ab-dee´*; from 5647; *serviceable*; *Abdi*, the name of two Isr.:— Abdi.

5661. עַבְדִּיאֵל **'Abdîy'êl**, *ab-dee-ale´*; from 5650 and 410; *servant of God*; *Abdiel*, an Isr.:— Abdiel. Comp. 5655.

5662. עֹבַדְיָה **'Ôbadyâh**, *o-bad-yaw´*; or

עֹבַדְיָהוּ **'Ôbadyâhûw**, *o-bad-yaw´-hoo*; act. part. of 5647 and 3050; *serving Jah*; *Obadjah*, the name of thirteen Isr.:— Obadiah.

5663. עֶבֶד מֶלֶךְ **'Ebed Melek**, *eh´-bed meh´-lek*; from 5650 and 4428; *servant of a king*; *Ebed-Melek*, a eunuch of Zedekeah:— Ebed-melech.

5664. עֶבֶד נְגוֹ **'Ăbêd Nᵉgôw**, *ab-ade´ neg-o´*; the same as 5665; *Abed-Nego*, the Bab. name of one of Daniel's companions:— Abed-nego.

5665. עֲבֵד נְגוֹא **'Ăbêd Nᵉgôw** (Chald.), *ab-ade´ neg-o´*; of for. or.; *Abed-Nego*, the name of Azariah:— Abed-nego.

5666. עָבָה **'âbâh**, *aw-baw´*; a prim. root; to *be dense*:— be (grow) thick (-er).

5667. עֲבוֹט **'ᵃbôwṭ**, *ab-ote´*; or

עֲבֹט **'ᵃbôṭ**, *ab-ote´*; from 5670; a *pawn*:— pledge.

5668. עָבוּר **'âbûwr**, *aw-boor´*; or

עָבֻר **'âbur**, *aw-boor´*; pass. part. of 5674; prop. *crossed*, i.e. (abstr.) *transit*; used only adv. on *account* of, in *order* that:— because of, for (... 's sake), (intent) that, to.

5669. עָבוּר **'âbûwr**, *aw-boor´*; the same

as 5668; *passed,* i.e. *kept* over; used only of *stored* grain:— old corn.

5670. עבט **'âbaṭ,** *aw-bat';* a prim. root; to *pawn;* caus. to *lend* (on security); fig. to *entangle:*— borrow, break lranksl, fetch la pledgel, lend, × surely.

5671. עבטיט **'abṭîyṭ,** *ab-teet';* from 5670; something *pledged,* i.e. (collect.) *pawned* goods:— thick clay lby a false etym.l.

5672. עבי **'ăbîy,** *ab-ee';* or

עבי **'ŏbîy,** *ob-ee';* from 5666; *density,* i.e. *depth* or *width:*— thick (-ness). Comp. 5645.

5673. עבידה **'ăbîydâh** (Chald.), *ab-ee-daw';* from 5648; *labor* or *business:*— affairs, service, work.

5674. עבר **'âbar,** *aw-bar';* a prim. root; to *cross* over; used very widely of any *transition* (lit. or fig.; tran., intr., intens., or caus.); spec. to *cover* (in copulation):— alienate, alter, × at all, beyond, bring (over, through), carry over, (over-) come (on, over), conduct (over), convey over, current, deliver, do away, enter, escape, fail, gender, get over, (make) go (away, beyond, by, forth, his way, in, on, over, through), have away (more), lay, meddle, overrun, make partition, (cause to, give, make to, over) pass (-age, along, away, beyond, by, -enger, on, out, over, through), (cause to, make) + proclaim (-amation), perish, provoke to anger, put away, rage, + raiser of taxes, remove, send over, set apart, + shave, cause to (make) sound, × speedily, × sweet smelling, take (away), (make to) transgress (-or), translate, turn away, lway-l faring man, be wrath.

5675. עבר **'ăbar** (Chald.), *ab-ar';* corresp. to 5676:— beyond, this side.

5676. עבר **'êber,** *ay'-ber;* from 5674; prop. a region *across;* but used only adv. (with or without a prep.) on the *opposite* side (espec. of the Jordan; usually mean. the *east*):— × against, beyond, by, × from, over, passage, quarter, (other, this) side, straight.

5677. עבר **'Êber,** *ay'-ber;* the same as 5676; *Eber,* the name of two patriarchs and four Isr.:— Eber, Heber.

5678. עברה **'ebrâh,** *eb-raw';* fem. of 5676; an *outburst* of passion:— anger, rage, wrath.

5679. עברה **'ăbârâh,** *ab-aw-raw';* from 5674; a *crossing-*place:— ferry, plain lfrom the marg.l.

5680. עברי **'Ibrîy,** *ib-ree';* patron. from 5677; an *Eberite* (i.e. Hebrew) or desc. of Eber:— Hebrew (-ess, woman).

5681. עברי **'Ibrîy,** *ib-ree';* the same as 5680; *Ibri,* an Isr.:— Ibri.

5682. עברים **'Ăbârîym,** *ab-aw-reem';* plur. of 5676; regions *beyond; Abarim,* a place in Pal.:— Abarim, passages.

5683. עברן **'Ebrôn,** *eb-rone';* from 5676; *transitional; Ebron,* a place in Pal.:— Hebron. lPerh. a clerical err. for 5658.l

5684. עברנה **'Ebrônâh,** *eb-raw-naw';* fem. of 5683; *Ebronah,* a place in the Desert:— Ebronah.

5685. עבש **'âbash,** *aw-bash';* a prim. root; to *dry* up:— be rotten.

5686. עבת **'âbath,** *aw-bath';* a prim. root; to *interlace,* i.e. (fig.) to *pervert:*— wrap up.

5687. עבת **'âbôth,** *aw-both';* or

עבות **'âbôwth,** *aw-both';* from 5686; *intwined,* i.e. *dense:*— thick.

5688. עבת **'ăbôth,** *ab-oth';* or

עבות **'ăbôwth,** *ab-oth';* or (fem.)

עבתה **'ăbôthâh,** *ab-oth-aw';* the same as 5687; something *intwined,* i.e. a *string, wreath* or *foliage:*— band, cord, rope, thick bough (branch), wreathen (chain).

5689. עגב **'âgab,** *aw-gab';* a prim. root; to *breathe* after, i.e. to *love* (sensually):— dote, lover.

5690. עגב **'egeb,** *eh'-gheb;* from 5689; *love* (concr.), i.e. *amative* words:— much love, very lovely.

5691. עגבה **'ăgâbâh,** *ag-aw-baw';* from 5689; *love* (abstr.), i.e. *amorousness:*— inordinate love.

5692. עגה **'uggâh,** *oog-gaw';* from 5746; an *ash-cake* (as *round*):— cake (upon the hearth).

5693. עגול **'âgôwl.** See 5696.

5693. עגור **'âgûwr,** *aw-goor';* pass. part. lbut with act. sensel of an unused root mean. to *twitter;* prob. the *swallow:*— swallow.

5694. עגיל **'âgîyl,** *aw-gheel';* from the same as 5696; something *round,* i.e. a *ring* (for the ears):— earring.

5695. עגל **'êgel,** *ay-ghel;* from the same as 5696; a (male) *calf* (as *frisking* round), espec. one nearly grown (i.e. a *steer*):— bullock, calf.

5696. עגל **'âgôl,** *aw-gole';* or

עגול **'âgôwl,** *aw-gole';* from an unused root mean. to *revolve, circular:*— round.

5697. עגלה **'eglâh,** *eg-law';* fem. of 5695; a (female) *calf,* espec. one nearly grown (i.e. a *heifer*):— calf, cow, heifer.

5698. עגלה **'Eglâh,** *eg-law';* the same as 5697; *Eglah,* a wife of David:— Eglah.

5699. עגלה **'ăgâlâh,** *ag-aw-law';* from the same as 5696; something *revolving,* i.e. a wheeled *vehicle:*— cart, chariot, wagon.

5700. עגלון **'Eglôwn,** *eg-lawn';* from 5695; *vituline; Eglon,* the name of a place in Pal. and of a Moabitish king:— Eglon.

5701. עגם **'âgam,** *aw-gam';* a prim. root; to *be sad:*— grieve.

5702. עגן **'âgan,** *aw-gan';* a prim. root; to *debar,* i.e. from marriage:— stay.

5703. עד **'ad,** *ad;* from 5710; prop. a (peremptory) *terminus,* i.e. (by impl.) *duration,* in the sense of *advance* or *perpetuity* (substantially as a noun, either with or without a prep.):— eternity, ever (-lasting, -more), old, perpetually, + world without end.

5704. עד **'ad,** *ad;* prop. the same as 5703 (used as a prep., adv. or conjunc.; espec. with a prep.); *as far* (or *long,* or *much*) *as,* whether of space (*even unto*)

or time (*during, while, until*) or degree (*equally with*):— against, and, as, at, before, by (that), even (to), for (-asmuch as), lhither-l to, + how long, into, as long (much) as, (so) that, till, toward, until, when, while, (+ as) yet.

5705. עד **'ad** (Chald.), *ad;* corresp. to 5704:— × and, at, for, lhither-l to, on, till, (un-) to, until, within.

5706. עד **'ad,** *ad;* the same as 5703 in the sense of the *aim* of an attack; *booty:*— prey.

5707. עד **'êd,** *ayd;* contr. from 5749 ; concr. a *witness;* abstr. *testimony;* spec. a *recorder,* i.e. *prince:*— witness.

5708. עד **'êd,** *ayd;* from an unused root mean. to *set* a period lcomp. 5710, 5749l; the *menstrual* flux (as periodical); by impl. (in plur.) *soiling:*— filthy.

5709. עד **'ôd.** See 5750.

5709. ערא **'ădâ'** (Chald.), *ad-aw';* or

עדה **'ădâh** (Chald.), *ad-aw';* corresp. to 5710:— alter, depart, pass (away), remove, take (away).

5710. עדד **'Ôdêd.** See 5752.

5710. עדה **'âdâh,** *aw-daw';* a prim. root; to *advance,* i.e. *pass* on or *continue;* caus. to *remove;* spec. to *bedeck* (i.e. bring an ornament upon):— adorn, deck (self), pass by, take away.

5711. עדה **'Âdâh,** *aw-daw';* from 5710; *ornament; Adah,* the name of two women:— Adah.

5712. עדה **'êdâh,** *ay-daw';* fem. of 5707 in the orig. sense of *fixture;* a stated *assemblage* (spec. a *concourse,* or gen. a *family* or *crowd*):— assembly, company, congregation, multitude, people, swarm. Comp. 5713.

5713. עדה **'êdâh,** *ay-daw';* fem. of 5707 in its techn. sense; *testimony:*— testimony, witness. Comp. 5712.

5714. עדו **'Iddôw,** *id-do';* or

עדוא **'Iddôw',** *id-do';* or

עדיא° **'Iddîy',** *id-dee';* from 5710; *timely; Iddo* (or *Iddi*), the name of five Isr.:— Iddo. Comp. 3035, 3260.

5715. עדות **'êdûwth,** *ay-dooth';* fem. of 5707; *testimony:*— testimony, witness.

5716. עדי **'ădîy,** *ad-ee';* from 5710 in the sense of *trappings; finery;* gen. an *outfit;* spec. a *headstall:*— × excellent, mouth, ornament.

5717. עדיאל **'Ădîy'êl,** *ad-ee-ale';* from 5716 and 410; *ornament of God; Adiel,* the name of three Isr.:— Adiel.

5718. עדיה **'Ădâyâh,** *ad-aw-yaw';* or

עדיהו **'Ădâyâhûw,** *ad-aw-yaw'-hoo;* from 5710 and 3050; *Jah has adorned; Adajah,* the name of eight Isr.:— Adaiah.

5719. עדין **'ădîyn,** *aw-deen';* from 5727; *voluptuous:*— given to pleasures.

5720. עדין **'Ădîyn,** *aw-deen';* the same as 5719; *Adin,* the name of two Isr.:— Adin.

5721. עדינא **'Ădîynâ',** *ad-ee-naw';* from 5719; *effeminacy; Adina,* an Isr.:— Adina.

5722. עדינו **'ădîynôw,** *ad-ee-no';* prob.

from 5719 in the orig. sense of *slender* (i.e. a *spear*); *his spear*:— Adino.

5723. עֲדִיתַיִם **'Ădiythayim**, *ad-ee-thah´-yim*; dual of a fem. of 5706; *double prey*; *Adithajim*, a place in Pal.:— Adithaim.

5724. עַדְלַי **'Adlay**, *ad-lah´-ee*; prob. from an unused root of uncert. mean.; *Adlai*, an Isr.:— Adlai.

5725. עֲדֻלָּם **'Ădullâm**, *ad-ool-lawm´*; prob. from the pass. part. of the same as 5724; *Adullam*, a place in Pal.:— Adullam.

5726. עֲדֻלָּמִי **'Ădullâmiy**, *ad-ool-law-mee´*; patrial from 5725; an *Adullamite* or native of Adullam:— Adullamite.

5727. עָדַן **'âdan**, *aw-dan´*; a prim. root; to be *soft* or *pleasant*; fig. and refl. to *live voluptuously*:— delight self.

5728. עֲדֶן **'âden**, *ad-en´*; or

עֲדֶנָּה **'âdennâh**, *ad-en´-naw*; from 5704 and 2004; *till now*:— yet.

5729. עֶדֶן **'Eden**, *eh´-den*; from 5727; *pleasure*; *Eden*, a place in Mesopotamia:— Eden.

5730. עֵדֶן **'êden**, *ay´-den*; or (fem.)

עֶדְנָה **'ednâh**, *ed-naw´*; from 5727; *pleasure*:— delicate, delight, pleasure. See also 1040.

5731. עֵדֶן **'Êden**, *ay´-den*; the same as 5730 (masc.); *Eden*, the region of Adam's home:— Eden.

5732. עִדָּן **'iddân** (Chald.), *id-dawn´*; from a root coresp. to that of 5708; a set *time*; tech. a *year*:— time.

5733. עַדְנָא **'Adnâ**, *ad-naw´* from 5727; *pleasure*; *Adna*, the name of two Isr.:— Adna.

5734. עַדְנָה **'Adnâh**, *ad-naw´*; from 5727; *pleasure*; *Adnah*, the name of two Isr.:— Adnah.

5735. עֲדְעָדָה **'Ăd'âdâh**, *ad-aw-daw´*; from 5712; *festival*; *Adadah*, a place in Pal.:— Adadah.

5736. עָדַף **'âdaph**, *aw-daf´*; a prim. root; to be (caus. *have*) *redundant*:— be more, odd number, be (have) over (and above), overplus, remain.

5737. עָדַר **'âdar**, *aw-dar´*; a prim. root; to *arrange*, as a battle, a vineyard (to *hoe*); hence, to *muster* and so to *miss* (or *find wanting*):— dig, fail, keep (rank), lack.

5738. עֶדֶר **'Eder**, *eh´-der*; from 5737; an *arrangement* (i.e. drove); *Eder*, an Isr.:— Ader.

5739. עֵדֶר **'êder**, *ay´-der*; from 5737; an *arrangement*, i.e. *muster* (of animals):— drove, flock, herd.

5740. עֵדֶר **'Êder**, *ay´-der*; the same as 5739; *Eder*, the name of an Isr. and of two places in Pal.:— Edar, Eder.

5741. עַדְרִיאֵל **'Adriy'êl**, *ad-ree-ale´*; from 5739 and 410; *flock of God*; *Adriel*, an Isr.:— Adriel.

5742. עָדָשׁ **'âdâsh**, *aw-dawsh´*; from an unused root of uncert. mean.; a *lentil*:— lentile.

עַוָּא **'Avvâ**. See 5755.

5743. עוּב **'ûwb**, *oob*; a prim. root; to be *dense* or *dark*, i.e. to *becloud*:— cover with a cloud.

5744. עוֹבֵד **'Ôwbêd**, *o-bade´*; act. part. of 5647; *serving*; *Obed*, the name of five Isr.:— Obed.

5745. עוֹבָל **'Ôwbâl**, *o-bawl´*; of for. der.; *Obal*, a son of Joktan:— Obal.

5746. עוּג **'ûwg**, *oog*; a prim. root; prop. to *gyrate*; but used only as a denom. from 5692, to *bake* (round cakes on the hearth):— bake.

5747. עוֹג **'Ôwg**, *ogue*; prob. from 5746; *round*; *Og*, a king of Bashan:— Og.

5748. עוּגָב **'ûwgâb**, *oo-gawb´*; or

עֻגָּב **'uggâb**, *oog-gawb´*; from 5689 in the orig. sense of *breathing*; a *reed-instrument* of music:— organ.

5749. עוּד **'ûwd**, *ood*; a prim. root; to *duplicate* or *repeat*; by impl. to *protest*, *testify* (as by reiteration); intens. to *encompass*, *restore* (as a sort of re-dupl.):— admonish, charge, earnestly, lift up, protest, call (take) to record, relieve, rob, solemnly, stand upright, testify, give warning, (bear, call to, give, take to) witness.

5750. עוֹד **'ôwd**, *ode*; or

עֹד **'ôd**, *ode*; from 5749; prop. *iteration* or *continuance*; used only adv. (with or without prep.), *again*, *repeatedly, still, more*:— again, × all life long, at all, besides, but, else, further (-more), henceforth, (any) longer, (any) more (-over), × once, since, (be) still, when, (good, the) while (having being), (as, because, whether, while) yet (within).

5751. עוֹד **'ôwd** (Chald.), *ode*; coresp. to 5750:— while.

5752. עוֹדֵד **'Ôwdêd**, *o-dade´*; or

עֹדֵד **'Ôdêd**, *o-dade´*; from 5749; *reiteration*; *Oded*, the name of two Isr.:— Oded.

5753. עָוָה **'âvâh**, *aw-vaw´*; a prim. root; to *crook*, lit. or fig. (as follows):— do amiss, bow down, make crooked, commit iniquity, pervert, (do) perverse (-ly), trouble, × turn, do wickedly, do wrong.

5754. עַוָּה **'avvâh**, *av-vaw´*; intens. from 5753 abb.; *overthrow*:— × overturn.

5755. עִוָּה **'Ivvâh**, *iv-vaw´*; or

עַוָּא **'Avvâ** (2 Kings 17: 24) *av-vaw´*; for 5754; *Ivvah* or *Avva*, a region of Assyria:— Ava, Ivah.

עָוֹן **'âvôwn**. See 5771.

5756. עוּז **'ûwz**, *ooz*; a prim. root; to be *strong*; caus. to *strengthen*, i.e. (fig.) to *save* (by flight):— gather (self, self to flee), retire.

5757. עַוִּי **'Avviy**, *av-vee´*; patrial from 5755; an *Avvite* or native of Avvah (only plur.):— Avims, Avites.

5758. עִוְיָא **'ivyâ'** (Chald.), *iv-yaw´*; from a root coresp. to 5753; *perverseness*:— iniquity.

5759. עֲוִיל **'ăviyl**, *av-eel´*; from 5764; a *babe*:— young child, little one.

5760. עֲוִיל **'ăviyl**, *av-eel´*; from 5765; *perverse* (morally):— ungodly.

5761. עַוִּים **'Avviym**, *av-veem´*; plur. of 5757; *Avvim* (as inhabited by Avvites), a place in Pal. (with the art. pref.):— Avim.

5762. עַוִּית **'Ăviyth**, *av-veeth´*; or [perh.

עַיּוֹת **'Ayôwth**, *ah-yôth´*, as if plur. of 5857]

עַוִּית **'Ăyûwth**, *ah-yôth´*; from 5753; *ruin*; *Avvith* (or *Avvoth*), a place in Pal.:— Avith.

5763. עוּל **'ûwl**, *ool*; a prim. root; to *suckle*, i.e. *give milk*:— milch, (ewe great) with young.

5764. עוּל **'ûwl**, *ool*; from 5763; a *babe*:— sucking child, infant.

5765. עָוַל **'âval**, *aw-val´*; a prim. root; to *distort* (morally):— deal unjustly, unrighteous.

עוֹל **'ôwl**. See 5923.

5766. עֶוֶל **'evel**, *eh´-vel*; or

עָוֶל **'âvel**, *aw´-vel*; and (fem.)

עַוְלָה **'avlâh**, *av-law´*; or

עוֹלָה **'ôwlâh**, *o-law´*; or

עֹלָה **'ôlâh**, *o-law´*; from 5765; (moral) *evil*:— iniquity, perverseness, unjust (-ly), unrighteousness (-ly), wicked (-ness).

5767. עַוָּל **'avvâl**, *av-vawl´*; intens. from 5765; *evil* (morally):— unjust, unrighteous, wicked.

עוֹלָה **'ôwlâh**. See 5930.

5768. עוֹלֵל **'ôwlêl**, *o-lale´*; or

עֹלָל **'ôlâl**, *o-lawl´*; from 5763; a *suckling*:— babe, (young) child, infant, little one.

5769. עוֹלָם **'ôwlâm**, *o-lawm´*; or

עֹלָם **'ôlâm**, *o-lawm´*; from 5956; prop. *concealed*, i.e. the *vanishing point*; gen. time *out of mind* (past or future), i.e. (practically) *eternity*; freq. adv. (espec. with prep. pref.) *always*:— alway (-s), ancient (time), any more, continuance, eternal, (for, [n-]) ever (-lasting, -more, of old), lasting, long (time), (of) old (time), perpetual, at any time, (beginning of the) world (+ without end). Comp. 5331, 5703.

5770. עָוַן **'âvan**, *aw-van´*; denom. from 5869; to *watch* (with jealousy):— eye.

5771. עָוֹן **'âvôn**, *aw-vone´*; or

עָווֹן **'âvôwn** (2 Kings 7:9; Psa. 51:5 [7]), *aw-vone´*; from 5753; *perversity*, i.e. (moral) *evil*:— fault, iniquity, mischief, punishment (of iniquity), sin.

5772. עוֹנָה **'ôwnâh**, *o-naw´*; from an unused root appar. mean. to *dwell* together; sexual (*cohabitation*):— duty of marriage.

5773. עַוְעֶה **'av'eh**, *av-eh´*; from 5753; *perversity*:— × perverse.

5774. עוּף **'ûwph**, *oof*; a prim. root; to *cover* (with wings or obscurity); hence, (as denom. from 5775) to *fly*; also (by impl. of dimness) to *faint* (from the darkness of swooning):— brandish, be (wax) faint, flee away, fly (away), × set, shine forth, weary.

5775. עוֹף **'ôwph**, *ofe*; from 5774; a *bird* (as *covered* with feathers, or rather as *covering* with wings), often collect.:— bird, that flieth, flying, fowl.

5776. עוֹף **'ôwph** (Chald.), *ofe*; coresp. to 5775:— fowl.

5777. עוֹפֶרֶת **'ôwphereth**, *o-feh´-reth*; or

עֹפֶרֶת **'ôphereth**, o-feh´-reth; fem. part. act. of 6080; *lead* (from its *dusty* color):— lead.

5778. עֹפַי **'Ôwphay**, o-fah´-ee; from 5775; *birdlike; Ephai*, an Isr.:— Ephai [from marg.].

5779. עוץ **'ûwts**, oots; a prim. root; to *consult*:— take advice [counsell together].

5780. עוץ **'Ûwts**, oots; appar. from 5779; *consultation; Uts*, a son of Aram, also a Seirite, and the regions settled by them.:— Uz.

5781. עוק **'ûwq**, ook; a prim. root; to *pack*:— be pressed.

5782. עור **'ûwr**, oor; a prim. root [rather ident. with 5783 through the idea of *opening* the eyes]; to *wake* (lit. or fig.):— (a-) wake (-n, up), lift up (self), × master, raise (up), stir up (self).

5783. עור **'ûwr**, oor; a prim. root; to (*be*) *bare*:— be made naked.

5784. עור **'ûwr** (Chald.), oor; *chaff* (as the *naked* husk):— chaff.

5785. עור **'ôwr**, ore; from 5783; *skin* (as *naked*); by impl. *hide, leather*:— hide, leather, skin.

5786. עור **'âvar**, aw-var´; a prim. root [rather denom. from 5785 through the idea of a *film* over the eyes]; to *blind*:— blind, put out. See also 5895.

5787. עור **'ivvêr**, iv-vare´; intens. from 5786; *blind* (lit. or fig.):— blind (men, people).

עורב **'ôwrêb**. See 6159.

5788. עורון **'ivvârôwn**, iv-vaw-rone´; and (fem.)

עוֶרֶת **'avvereth**, av-veh´-reth; from 5787; *blindness*:— blind (-ness).

5789. עוש **'ûwsh**, oosh; a prim. root; to *hasten*:— assemble self.

5790. עות **'ûwth**, ooth; for 5789; to *hasten*, i.e. *succor*:— speak in season.

5791. עות **'âvath**, aw-vath´; a prim. root; to *wrest*:— bow self, (make) crooked, falsifying, overthrow, deal perversely, pervert, subvert, turn upside down.

5792. עוָתָה **'avvâthâh**, av-vaw-thaw´; from 5791; *oppression*:— wrong.

5793. עותי **'Ûwthay**, oo-thah´-ee; from 5790; *succoring; Uthai*, the name of two Isr.:— Uthai.

5794. עז **'az**, az; from 5810; *strong, vehement, harsh*:— fierce, + greedy, mighty, power, roughly, strong.

5795. עז **'êz**, aze; from 5810; a she-*goat* (as *strong*), but masc. in plur. (which also is used ellipt. for *goat's hair*):— (she) goat, kid.

5796. עז **'êz** (Chald.), aze; corresp. to 5795:— goat.

5797. עז **'ôz**, oze; or (fully)

עוז **'ôwz**, oze; from 5810; *strength* in various applications (*force, security, majesty, praise*):— boldness, loud, might, power, strength, strong.

5798. עזא **'Uzzâ'**, ooz-zaw´; or

עזה **'Uzzâh**, ooz-zaw´; fem. of 5797; *strength; Uzza* or *Uzzah*, the name of five Isr.:— Uzza, Uzzah.

5799. עזאזל **'ăzâ'zêl**, az-aw-zale´; from 5795 and 235; *goat of departure*; the *scapegoat*:— scapegoat.

5800. עזב **'âzab**, aw-zab´; a prim. root; to *loosen*, i.e. *relinquish, permit*, etc.:— commit self, fail, forsake, fortify, help, leave (destitute, off), refuse, × surely.

5801. עזבון **'izzâbôwn**, iz-zaw-bone´; from 5800 in the sense of *letting go* (for a price, i.e. *selling*); *trade*, i.e. the place (*mart*) or the payment (*revenue*):— fair, ware.

5802. עזבוק **'Azbûwq**, az-book´; from 5794 and the root of 950; *stern depopulator; Azbuk*, an Isr.:— Azbuk.

5803. עזגד **'Azgâd**, az-gawd´; from 5794 and 1409; *stern troop; Azgad*, an Isr.:— Azgad.

5804. עזה **'Azzâh**, az-zaw´; fem. of 5794; *strong; Azzah*, a place in Pal.:— Azzah, Gaza.

5805. עזובה **'ăzûwbâh**, az-oo-baw´; fem. pass. part. of 5800; *desertion* (of inhabitants):— forsaking.

5806. עזובה **'Azûwbâh**, az-oo-baw´; the same as 5805; *Azubah*, the name of two Israelitesses:— Azubah.

5807. עזוז **'ĕzûwz**, ez-ooz´; from 5810; *forcibleness*:— might, strength.

5808. עזוז **'izzûwz**, iz-zooz´; from 5810; *forcible*; collect. and concr. an *army*:— power, strong.

5809. עזור **'Azzûwr**, az-zoor´; or

עזור **'Azzûr**, az-zoor´; from 5826; *helpful; Azzur*, the name of three Isr.:— Azur, Azzur.

5810. עזז **'âzaz**, aw-zaz´; a prim. root; to *be stout* (lit. or fig.):— harden, impudent, prevail, strengthen (self), be strong.

5811. עזז **'Azâz**, aw-zawz´; from 5810; *strong; Azaz*, an Isr.:— Azaz.

5812. עזזיהו **'Ăzazyâhûw**, az-az-yaw´-hoo; from 5810 and 3050; *Jah has strengthened; Azazjah*, the name of three Isr.:— Azaziah.

5813. עזי **'Uzzîy**, ooz-zee´; from 5810; *forceful; Uzzi*, the name of six Isr.:— Uzzi.

5814. עזיא **'Uzzîyâ'**, ooz-zee-yaw´; perh. for 5818; *Uzzija*, an Isr.:— Uzzia.

5815. עזיאל **'Ăzîy'êl**, az-ee-ale´; from 5756 and 410; *strengthened of God; Aziël*, an Isr.:— Aziel. Comp. 3268.

5816. עזיאל **'Uzzîy'êl**, ooz-zee-ale´; from 5797 and 410; *strength of God; Uzziël*, the name of six Isr.:— Uzziel.

5817. עזיאלי **'Ozzîy'êlîy**, oz-zee-ay-lee´; patron. from 5816; an *Uzziëlite* (collect.) or desc. of Uzziel:— Uzzielites.

5818. עזיה **'Uzzîyâh**, ooz-zee-yaw´; or

עזיהו **'Uzzîyâhûw**, ooz-zee-yaw´-hoo; from 5797 and 3050; *strength of Jah; Uzzijah*, the name of five Isr.:— Uzziah.

5819. עזיזא **'Ăzîyzâ'**, az-ee-zaw´; from 5756; *strengthfulness; Aziza*, an Isr.:— Aziza.

5820. עזמוה **'Azmâveth**, az-maw´-veth; from 5794 and 4194; *strong* (one) *of death; Azmaveth*, the name of three

Isr. and of a place in Pal.:— Azmaveth. See also 1041.

5821. עזן **'Azzân**, az-zawn´; from 5794; *strong* one; *Azzan*, an Isr.:— Azzan.

5822. עזניה **'oznîyâh**, oz-nee-yaw´; prob. fem. of 5797; prob. the *sea-eagle* (from its *strength*):— ospray.

5823. עזק **'âzaq**, aw-zak´; a prim. root; to *grub over*:— fence about.

5824. עזקא **'izqâ'** (Chald.), iz-kaw´; from a root corresp. to 5823; a *signet-ring* (as engraved):— signet.

5825. עזקה **'Ăzêqâh**, az´-ay-kaw´; from 5823; *tilled; Azekah*, a place in Pal.:— Azekah.

5826. עזר **'âzar**, aw-zar´; a prim. root; to *surround*, i.e. *protect* or *aid*:— help, succour.

5827. עזר **'Ezer**, eh´-zer; from 5826; *help; Ezer*, the name of two Isr.:— Ezer. Comp. 5829.

5828. עזר **'êzer**, ay´-zer; from 5826; *aid*:— help.

5829. עזר **'Êzer**, ay´-zer; the same as 5828; *Ezer*, the name of four Isr.:— Ezer. Comp. 5827.

עזר **'Azzûr**. See 5809.

5830. עזרא **'Ezrâ'**, ez-raw´; a var. of 5833; *Ezra*, an Isr.:— Ezra.

5831. עזרא **'Ezrâ'** (Chald.), ez-raw´; corresp. to 5830; *Ezra*, an Isr.:— Ezra.

5832. עזראל **'Ăzar'êl**, az-ar-ale´; from 5826 and 410; *God has helped; Azarel*, the name of five Isr.:— Azarael, Azareel.

5833. עזרה **'ezrâh**, ez-raw´; or

עזרה **'ezrâth** (Psa. 60:11 [13]; 108:12 [13]), ez-rawth´; fem. of 5828; *aid*:— help (-ed, -er).

5834. עזרה **'Ezrâh**, ez-raw´; the same as 5833; *Ezrah*, an Isr.:— Ezrah.

5835. עזרה **'ăzârâh**, az-aw-raw´; from 5826 in its orig. mean. of *surrounding*; an *inclosure*; also a *border*:— court, settle.

5836. עזרי **'Ezrîy**, ez-ree´; from 5828; *helpful; Ezri*, an Isr.:— Ezri.

5837. עזריאל **'Azrîy'êl**, az-ree-ale´; from 5828 and 410; *help of God; Azriël*, the name of three Isr.:— Azriel.

5838. עזריה **'Ăzaryâh**, az-ar-yaw´; or

עזריהו **'Ăzaryâhûw**, az-ar-yaw´-hoo; from 5826 and 3050; *Jah has helped; Azarjah*, the name of nineteen Isr.:— Azariah.

5839. עזריה **'Ăzaryâh** (Chald.), az-ar-yaw´; corresp. to 5838; *Azarjah*, one of Daniel's companions:— Azariah.

5840. עזריקם **'Azrîyqâm**, az-ree-kawm´; from 5828 and act. part. of 6965; *help of an enemy; Azrikam*, the name of four Isr.:— Azrikam.

5841. עזתי **'Azzâthîy**, az-zaw-thee´; patrial from 5804; an *Azzathite* or inhab. of Azzah:— Gazathite, Gazite.

5842. עט **'êt**, ate; from 5860 (contr.) in the sense of *swooping*, i.e. *side-long stroke*; a *stylus* or marking stick:— pen.

5843. עֵטָא **'êtâ'** (Chald.), *ay-taw'*; from 3272; *prudence*:— counsel.

5844. עָטָה **'âṭâh**, *aw-taw'*; a prim. root; to *wrap*, i.e. *cover*, *veil*, *clothe*, or *roll*:— array self, be clad, (put a) cover (-ing, self), fill, put on, × surely, turn aside.

5845. עָטִין **'âṭîyn**, *at-een'*; from an unused root mean. appar. to *contain*; a *receptacle* (for milk, i.e. *pail*; fig. *breast*):— breast.

5846. עֲטִישָׁה **'âṭîyshâh**, *at-ee-shaw'*; from an unused root mean. to *sneeze*; *sneezing*:— sneezing.

5847. עֲטַלֵּף **'ăṭallêph**, *at-al-lafe'*; of uncert. der.; a *bat*:— bat.

5848. עָטַף **'âṭaph**, *aw-taf'*; a prim. root; to *shroud*, i.e. *clothe* (whether tran. or reflex.); hence, (from the idea of *darkness*) to *languish*:— cover (over), fail, faint, feebler, hide self, be overwhelmed, swoon.

5849. עָטַר **'âṭar**, *aw-tar'*; a prim. root; to *encircle* (for attack or protection); espec. to *crown* (lit. or fig.):— compass, crown.

5850. עֲטָרָה **'ăṭârâh**, *at-aw-raw'*; from 5849 a *crown*:— crown.

5851. עֲטָרָה **'Ăṭârâh**, *at-aw-raw'*; the same as 5850; *Atarah*, an Israelitess:— Atarah.

5852. עֲטָרוֹת **'Ăṭârôwth**, *at-aw-rôth'*; or

עֲטָרֹת **'Ăṭârôth**, *at-aw-rôth'*; plur. of 5850; *Ataroth*, the name (thus simply) of two places in Pal.:— Ataroth.

5853. עֲטְרוֹת אַדָּר **'Aṭrôwth 'Addâr**, *at-rôth' ad-dawr'*; from the same as 5852 and 146; *crowns of Addar*; *Atroth-Addar*, a place in Pal.:— Ataroth-adar (-addar).

5854. עֲטְרוֹת בֵּית יוֹאָב **'Aṭrôwth Bêyth Yôw'âb**, *at-rôth' bayth yo-awb'*; from the same as 5852 and 1004 and 3097; *crowns of* (the) *house of Joäb*; *Atroth-beth-Joäb*, a place in Pal.:— Ataroth, the house of Joab.

5855. עֲטְרוֹת שׁוֹפָן **'Aṭrôwth Shôwphân**, *at-rôth' sho-fawn'*; from the same as 5852 and a name otherwise unused [being from the same as 8226] mean. *hidden*; *crowns of Shophan*; *Atroth-Shophan*, a place in Pal.:— Atroth, Shophan [as if two places].

5856. עִי **'îy**, *ee*; from 5753; a *ruin* (as if overturned):— heap.

5857. עַי **'Ay**, *ah'ee*; or (fem.)

עַיָּא **'Ayâ'** (Neh. 11:31), *ah-yaw'*; or

עַיָּת **'Ayâth** (Isa. 10:28), *ah-yawth'*; for 5856; *Ai*, *Aja* or *Ajath*, a place in Pal.:— Ai, Aija, Aijath, Hai.

5858. עֵיבָל **'Êybâl**, *ay-bawl'*; perh. from an unused root prob. mean. to *be bald*, *bare*; *Ebal*, a mountain of Pal.:— Ebal.

עִיָה **'Ayâh**. See 5857.

5859. עִיּוֹן **'Îyôwn**, *ee-yone'*; from 5856; *ruin*; *Ijon*, a place in Pal.:— Ijon.

5860. עִיט **'îyṭ**, *eet*; a prim. root; to *swoop* down upon (lit. or fig.):— fly, rail.

5861. עַיִט **'ayiṭ**, *ah'-yit*; from 5860; a *hawk* or other bird of prey:— bird, fowl, ravenous (bird).

5862. עֵיטָם **'Êyṭâm**, *ay-tawm'*; from

5861; *hawk-ground*; *Etam*, a place in Pal.:— Etam.

5863. עִיֵּי הָעֲבָרִים **'Îyêy hâ-'Ăbârîym**, *ee-yay' haw-ab-aw-reem'*; from the plur. of 5856 and the plur. of the act. part. of 5674 with the art. interposed; *ruins of the passers*; *Ije-ha-Abarim*, a place near Pal.:— Ije-abarim.

5864. עִיִּים **'Îyîym**, *ee-yeem'*; plur. of 5856; *ruins*; *Ijim*, a place in the Desert:— Iim.

5865. עֵילוֹם **'êylôwm**, *ay-lome'*; for 5769:— ever.

5866. עִילַי **'Îylay**, *ee-lah'-ee*; from 5927; *elevated*; *Ilai*, an Isr.:— Ilai.

5867. עֵילָם **'Êylâm**, *ay-lawm'*; or

עוֹלָם **'Ôwlâm** (Ezra 10:2; Jer. 49:36), *o-lawm'*; prob. from 5956; *hidden*, i.e. *distant*; *Elam*, a son of Shem, and his desc., with their country; also of six Isr.:— Elam.

5868. עֲיָם **'ăyâm**, *ah-yawm'*; of doubtful or. and authenticity; prob. mean. *strength*:— mighty.

5869. עַיִן **'ayin**, *ah'-yin*; prob. a prim. word; an *eye* (lit. or fig.); by anal. a *fountain* (as the *eye* of the landscape):— affliction, outward appearance, + before, + think best, colour, conceit, + be content, countenance, + displease, eye (l-browl, l-dl, -sight), face, + favour, fountain, furrow lfrom the marg.l, × him, + humble, knowledge, look, (+ well), × me, open (-ly), + (not) please, presence, + regard, resemblance, sight, × thee, × them, + think, × us, well, × you (-rselves).

5870. עַיִן **'ayin** (Chald.), *ah'-yin*; corresp. to 5869; an *eye*:— eye.

5871. עַיִן **'Ayin**, *ah'-yin*; the same as 5869; *fountain*; *Ajin*, the name (thus simply) of two places in Pal.:— Ain.

5872. עֵין גְּדִי **'Êyn Gedîy**, *ane geh'-dee*; from 5869 and 1423; *fountain of a kid*; *En-Gedi*, a place in Pal.:— En-gedi.

5873. עֵין גַּנִּים **'Êyn Gannîym**, *ane gan-neem'*; from 5869 and the plur. of 1588; *fountain of gardens*; *En-Gannim*, a place in Pal.:— En-gannim.

5874. עֵין־דֹּאר **'Êyn-Dò'r**, *ane-dore'*; or

עֵין דּוֹר **'Êyn Dôwr**, *ane dore*; or

עֵין־דֹּר **'Êyn-Dòr**, *ane-dore'*; from 5869 and 1755; *fountain of dwelling*; *En-Dor*, a place in Pal.:— En-dor.

5875. עֵין הַקּוֹרֵא **'Êyn haq-Qôwrê'**, *ane-hak-ko-ray'*; from 5869 and the act. part. of 7121; *fountain of One calling*; *En-hak-Korè*, a place near Pal.:— En-hakhore.

עֵינוֹן **'Êynôwn**. See 2703.

5876. עֵין חֲדָּה **'Êyn Chaddâh**, *ane khad-daw'*; from 5869 and the fem. of a der. from 2300; *fountain of sharpness*; *En-Chaddah*, a place in Pal.:— En-haddah.

5877. עֵין חָצוֹר **'Êyn Châtsôwr**, *ane khaw-tsore'*; from 5869 and the same as 2674; *fountain of a village*; *En-Chatsor*, a place in Pal.:— En-hazor.

5878. עֵין חֲרֹד **'Êyn Chărôd**, *ane khar-ode'*; from 5869 and a der. of 2729; *foun-*

tain of trembling; *En-Charod*, a place in Pal.:— well of Harod.

5879. עֵינַיִם **'Êynayim**, *ay-nah'-yim*; or

עֵינָם **'Êynâm**, *ay-nawm'*; dual of 5869; *double fountain*; *Enajim* or *Enam*, a place in Pal.:— Enaim, openly (Genesis 38:21).

5880. עֵין מִשְׁפָּט **'Êyn Mishpâṭ**, *ane mish-pawt'*; from 5869 and 4941; *fountain of judgment*; *En-Mishpat*, a place near Pal.:— En-mishpat.

5881. עֵינָן **'Êynân**, *ay-nawn'*; from 5869; *having eyes*; *Enan*, an Isr.:— Enan. Comp. 2704.

5882. עֵין עֶגְלַיִם **'Êyn 'Eglayim**, *ane eg-lah'-yim*; from 5869 and the dual of 5695; *fountain of two calves*; *En-Eglajim*, a place in Pal.:— En-eglaim.

5883. עֵין רֹגֵל **'Êyn Rôgêl**, *ane ro-gale'*; from 5869 and the act. part. of 7270; *fountain of a traveller*; *En-Rogel*, a place near Jerusalem:— En-rogel.

5884. עֵין רִמּוֹן **'Êyn Rimmôwn**, *ane rim-mone'*; from 5869 and 7416; *fountain of a pomegranate*; *En-Rimmon*, a place in Pal.:— En-rimmon.

5885. עֵין שֶׁמֶשׁ **'Êyn Shemesh**, *ane sheh'-mesh*; from 5869 and 8121; *fountain of* (the) *sun*; *En-Shemesh*, a place in Pal.:— En-shemesh.

5886. עֵין תַּנִּים **'Êyn Tannîym**, *ane tan-neem'*; from 5869 and the plur. of 8565; *fountain of jackals*; *En-Tannim*, a pool near Jerusalem:— dragon well.

5887. עֵין תַּפּוּחַ **'Êyn Tappûwach**, *ane tap-poo'-akh*; from 5869 and 8598; *fountain of an apple tree*; *En-Tappuäch*, a place in Pal.:— En-tappuah.

5888. עָיֵף **'âyêph**, *aw-yafe'*; a prim. root; to *languish*:— be wearied.

5889. עָיֵף **'âyêph**, *aw-yafe'*; from 5888; *languid*:— faint, thirsty, weary.

5890. עֵיפָה **'êyphâh**, *ay-faw'*; fem. from 5774; *obscurity* (as if from *covering*):— darkness.

5891. עֵיפָה **'Êyphâh**, *ay-faw'*; the same as 5890; *Ephah*, the name of a son of Midian, and of the region settled by him; also of an Isr. and of an Israelitess:— Ephah.

5892. עִיר **'îyr**, *eer*; or (in the plur.)

עָר **'âr**, *awr*; or

עָיַר **'âyar** (Judg. 10:4), *aw-yar'*; from 5782 a *city* (a place guarded by *waking* or a watch) in the widest sense (even of a mere *encampment* or *post*):— Ai [from marg.], city, court [from marg.], town.

5893. עִיר **'Îyr**, *eer*; the same as 5892; *Ir*, an Isr.:— Ir.

5894. עִיר **'îyr** (Chald.), *eer*; from a root corresp. to 5782; a *watcher*, i.e. an *angel* (as guardian):— watcher.

5895. עַיִר **'ayir**, *ah'-yeer*; from 5782 in the sense of *raising* (i.e. *bearing* a burden); prop. a young *ass* (as just broken to a load); hence, an ass-*colt*:— (ass) colt, foal, young ass.

5896. עִירָא **'Îyrâ'**, *ee-raw'*; from 5782; *wakefulness*; *Ira*, the name of three Isr.:— Ira.

5897. עִירָד **'Îyrâd**, *ee-rawd'*; from the

same as 6166; *fugitive; Irad*, an antediluvian:— Irad.

5898. עִיר הַמֶּלַח **'Îyr ham-Melach**, *eer ham-meh´-lakh;* from 5892 and 4417 with the art. of substance interp.; *city of* (the) *salt; Ir-ham-Melach*, a place near Pal.:— the city of salt.

5899. עִיר הַתְּמָרִים **'Îyr hat-Tᵉmârîym**, *eer hat-tem-aw-reem´;* from 5892 and the plur. of 8558 with the art. interpolated; *city of the palmtrees; Ir-hat-Temarim*, a place in Pal.:— the city of palmtrees.

5900. עִירוּ **'Îyrûw**, *ee-roo´;* from 5892; a *citizen; Iru*, an Isr.:— Iru.

5901. עִירִי **'Îyriy**, *ee-ree´;* from 5892; *urbane; Iri*, an Isr.:— Iri.

5902. עִירָם **'Îyrâm**, *ee-rawm´;* from 5892; *city-wise; Iram*, an Idumæan:— Iram.

5903. עֵירֹם **'êyrôm**, *ay-rome´;* or

עֵרֹם **'êrôm**, *ay-rome´;* from 6191; *nudity:*— naked (-ness).

5904. עִיר נָחָשׁ **'Îyr Nâchâsh**, *eer nawkhawsh´;* from 5892 and 5175; *city of a serpent; Ir-Nachash*, a place in Pal.:— Ir-nahash.

5905. עִיר שֶׁמֶשׁ **'Îyr Shemesh**, *eer shehmesh;* from 5892 and 8121; *city of* (the) *sun; Ir-Shemesh*, a place in Pal.:— Ir-shemesh.

5906. עַיִשׁ **'Ayish**, *ah´-yish;* or

עָשׁ **'Âsh**, *awsh;* from 5789; the constellation of the Great Bear (perh. from its *migration* through the heavens):— Arcturus.

עָיָה **'Ayâth**. See 5857.

5907. עַכְבּוֹר **'Akbôwr**, *ak-bore´;* prob. for 5909; *Akbor*, the name of an Idumæan and two Isr.:— Achbor.

5908. עַכָּבִישׁ **'akkâbîysh**, *ak-kawbeesh´;* prob. from an unused root in the lit. sense of *entangling; a spider* (as *weaving* a network):— spider.

5909. עַכְבָּר **'akbâr**, *ak-bawr´;* prob. from the same as 5908 in the second. sense of *attacking; a mouse* (as *nibbling*):— mouse.

5910. עַכּוֹ **'Akkôw**, *ak-ko´;* appar. from an unused root mean. to *hem* in; *Akko* (from its situation on a *bay*):— Accho.

5911. עָכוֹר **'Âkôwr**, *aw-lore´;* from 5916; *troubled; Akor*, the name of a place in Pal.:— Achor.

5912. עָכָן **'Âkân**, *aw-kawn´;* from an unused root mean. to *trouble; troublesome; Akan*, an Isr.:— Achan. Comp. 5917.

5913. עָכַס **'âkaç**, *aw-kas´;* a prim. root; prop. to *tie*, spec. with fetters; but used only as denom. from 5914; to *put on anklets:*— make a tinkling ornament.

5914. עֶכֶס **'ekeç**, *eh´-kes;* from 5913; a *fetter;* hence, an *anklet:*— stocks, tinkling ornament.

5915. עַכְסָה **'Akçâh**, *ak-saw´;* fem. of 5914; *anklet; Aksah*, an Israelitess:— Achsah.

5916. עָכַר **'âkar**, *aw-kar´;* a prim. root; prop. to *roil* water; fig. to *disturb* or *afflict:*— trouble, stir.

5917. עָכָר **'Âkâr**, *aw-kawr´;* from 5916;

troublesome; Akar, an Isr.:— Achar. Comp. 5912.

5918. עָכְרָן **'Okrân**, *ok-rawn´;* from 5916; *muddler; Okran*, an Isr.:— Ocran.

5919. עַכְשׁוּב **'akshûwb**, *ak-shoob´;* prob. from an unused root mean. to *coil;* an *asp* (from lurking *coiled* up):— adder.

5920. עַל **'al**, *al;* from 5927; prop. the *top;* spec. the *Highest* (i.e. *God*); also (adv.) *aloft, to Jehovah:*— above, high, Most High.

5921. עַל **'al**, *al;* prop. the same as 5920 used as a prep. (in the sing. or plur. often with pref., or as conjunc. with a particle following); *above, over, upon,* or *against* (yet always in this last relation with a downward aspect) in a great variety of applications (as follow):— above, according to (-ly), after, (as) against, among, and, × as, at, because of, beside (the rest of), between, beyond the time, × both and, by (reason of), × had the charge of, concerning for, in (that), (forth, out) of, (from) (off), (up-) on, over, than, through (-out), to, touching, × with.

5922. עַל **'al** (Chald.), *al;* corresp. to 5921:— about, against, concerning, for, [there-]fore, from, in, × more, of, (there-, up-) on, (in-) to, + why with.

5923. עֹל **'ôl**, *ole;* or

עוֹל **'ôwl**, *ole;* from 5953; a *yoke* (as *imposed* on the neck), lit. or fig.:— yoke.

5924. עֵלָּא **'êllâ** (Chald.), *ale-law´;* from 5922; *above:*— over.

5925. עֻלָּא **'Ullâ**, *ool-law´;* fem. of 5923; *burden; Ulla*, an Isr.:— Ulla.

5926. עִלֵּג **'illêg**, *il-layg´;* from an unused root mean. to *stutter; stuttering:*— stammerer.

5927. עָלָה **'âlâh**, *aw-law´;* a prim. root; to *ascend*, intr. (*be high*) or act. (*mount*); used in a great variety of senses, primary and second., lit. and fig. (as follow):— arise (up), (cause to) ascend up, at once, break [the day] (up), bring (up), (cause to) burn, carry up, cast up, + shew, climb (up), (cause to, make to) come (up), cut off, dawn, depart, exalt, excel, fall, fetch up, get up, (make to) go (away, up); grow (over), increase, lay, leap, levy, lift (self) up, light, [make] up, × mention, mount up, offer, make to pay, + perfect, prefer, put (on), raise, recover, restore, (make to) rise (up), scale, set (up), shoot forth (up), (begin to) spring (up), stir up, take away (up), work.

5928. עֲלָה **'âlâh** (Chald.), *al-aw´;* corresp. to 5930; a *holocaust:*— burnt offering.

5929. עָלֶה **'âleh**, *aw-leh´;* from 5927; a *leaf* (as *coming up* on a tree); collect. *foliage:*— branch, leaf.

5930. עֹלָה **'ôlâh**, *o-law´;* or

עוֹלָה **'ôwlâh**, *o-law´;* fem. act. part. of 5927; a *step* or (collect. *stairs*, as *ascending*); usually a *holocaust* (as *going up* in smoke):— ascent, burnt offering (sacrifice), go up to. See also 5766.

5931. עִלָּה **'illâh** (Chald.), *il-law´;* fem. from a root corresp. to 5927; a *pretext* (as *arising* artificially):— occasion.

5932. עַלְוָה **'alvâh**, *al-vaw´;* for 5766; *moral perverseness:*— iniquity.

5933. עַלְוָה **'Alvâh**, *al-vaw´;* or

עַלְיָה **'Alyâh**, *al-yaw´;* the same as 5932; *Alvah* or *Aljah*, an Idumæan:— Aliah, Alvah.

5934. עֶלֶן **'âlûwm**, *aw-loom´;* pass. part. of 5956 in the denom. sense of 5958; (only in plur. as abstr.) *adolescence;* fig. *vigor:*— youth.

5935. עַלְוָן **'Alvân**, *al-vawn´;* or

עַלְיָן **'Alyân**, *al-yawn´;* from 5927; *lofty; Alvan* or *Aljan*, an Idumæan:— Alian, Alvan.

5936. עֲלוּקָה **'ălûwqâh**, *al-oo-kaw´;* fem. pass. part. of an unused root mean. to *suck;* the *leech:*— horse-leech.

5937. עָלַז **'âlaz**, *aw-laz´;* a prim. root; to *jump* for joy, i.e. *exult:*— be joyful, rejoice, triumph.

5938. עָלֵז **'âlêz**, *aw-laze´;* from 5937; *exultant:*— that rejoiceth.

5939. עֲלָטָה **'ălâṭâh**, *al-aw-taw´;* fem. from an unused root mean. to *cover; dusk:*— dark, twilight.

5940. עֱלִי **'ĕlîy**, *el-ee´;* from 5927; a *pestle* (as *lifted*):— pestle.

5941. עֵלִי **'Êlîy**, *ay-lee´;* from 5927; *lofty; Eli*, an Isr. high-priest:— Eli.

5942. עִלִּי **'illîy**, *il-lee´;* from 5927; *high;* i.e. comparative:— upper.

5943. עִלַּי **'illay** (Chald.), *il-lah´-ee;* corresp. to 5942; *supreme* (i.e. *God*):— (most) high.

עֲלִיָה° **'Alyâh**. See 5933.

5944. עֲלִיָּה **'ălîyâh**, *al-ee-yaw´;* fem. from 5927; something *lofty*, i.e. a *stairway;* also a *second-story* room (or even one on the roof); fig. the *sky:*— ascent, (upper) chamber, going up, loft, parlour.

5945. עֶלְיוֹן **'elyôwn**, *el-yone´;* from 5927; an *elevation*, i.e. (adj.) *lofty* (comp.); as title, the *Supreme:*— (Most, on) high (-er, -est), upper (-most).

5946. עֶלְיוֹן **'elyôwn** (Chald.), *el-yone´;* corresp. to 5945; the *Supreme:*— Most high.

5947. עַלִּיז **'allîyz**, *al-leez´;* from 5937; *exultant:*— joyous, (that) rejoice (-ing).

5948. עֲלִיל **'ălîyl**, *al-eel´;* from 5953 in the sense of *completing;* prob. a *crucible* (as *working* over the metal):— furnace.

5949. עֲלִילָה **'ălîylâh**, *al-ee-law´;* or

עֲלִלָה **'ălîlâh**, *al-ee-law´;* from 5953 in the sense of *effecting;* an *exploit* (of God), or a *performance* (of man, often in a bad sense); by impl. an *opportunity:*— act (-ion), deed, doing, invention, occasion, work.

5950. עֲלִילִיָּה **'ălîylîyâh**, *al-ee-lee-yaw´;* for 5949; (miraculous) *execution:*— work.

עָלָן **'Alyân**. See 5935.

5951. עֲלִיצוּת **'ălîytsûwth**, *al-ee-tsooth´;* from 5970; *exultation:*— rejoicing.

5952. עִלִּית **'allîyth** (Chald.), *al-leeth´;* from 5927; a *second-story* room:— chamber. Comp. 5944.

Hebrew

5953. עֲלַל 'âlal, aw-lal´; a prim. root; to effect thoroughly; spec. to glean (also fig.); by impl. (in a bad sense) to overdo, i.e. maltreat, be saucy to, pain, impose (also lit.):— abuse, affect, × child, defile, do, glean, mock, practise, thoroughly, work (wonderfully).

5954. עֲלַל 'âlal (Chald.), al-al´; corresp. to 5953 (in the sense of thrusting oneself in), to enter; caus. to introduce:— bring in, come in, go in.

עֹלָל 'ôlâl. See 5768.

עֲלִילָה 'ălîlâh. See 5949.

5955. עֹלֵלָה 'ôlêlâh, o-lay-law´; fem. act. part. of 5953; only in plur. gleanings; by extens. gleaning-time:— (gleaning) (of the) grapes, grapegleanings.

5956. עָלַם 'âlam, aw-lam´; a prim. root; to veil from sight, i.e. conceal (lit. or fig.):— × any ways, blind, dissembler, hide (self), secret (thing).

5957. עֲלַם 'âlam (Chald.), aw-lam´; corresp. to 5769; remote time, i.e. the future or past indefinitely; often adv. forever:— for (In-) ever (lasting), old.

5958. עֶלֶם 'elem, eh´-lem; from 5956; prop. something kept out of sight [comp. 5959], i.e. a lad:— young man, stripling.

עֹלָם 'ôlâm. See 5769.

5959. עַלְמָה 'almâh, al-maw´; fem. of 5958; a lass (as veiled or private):— damsel, maid, virgin.

5960. עַלְמֹן 'Almôwn, al-mone´; from 5956; hidden; Almon, a place in Pal.:— Almon. See also 5963.

5961. עֲלָמוֹת 'Ălâmôwth, al-aw-môth´; plur. of 5959; prop. girls, i.e. the soprano or female voice, perh. falsetto:— Alamoth.

עַלְמוּת 'almûwth. See 4192.

5962. עֵלְמָי 'Almîy (Chald.), al-mee´; patrial from a name corresp. to 5867 contr.; an Elamite or inhab. of Elam:— Elamite.

5963. עַלְמֹן דִּבְלָתָיְמָה 'Almôn Diblâthâyᵉmâh, al-mone´ dib-law-thaw´-yem-aw; from the same as 5960 and the dual of 1690 [comp. 1015] with enclitic of direction; Almon toward Diblathajim; Almon-Diblathajemah, a place in Moab:— Almon-dilathaim.

5964. עָלֶמֶת 'Ălemeth, aw-leh´-meth; from 5956; a covering; Alemeth, the name of a place in Pal. and of two Isr.:— Alameth, Alemeth.

5965. עָלַס 'âlaç, aw-las´; a prim. root; to leap for joy, i.e. exult, wave joyously:— × peacock, rejoice, solace self.

5966. עָלַע 'âla', aw-lah´; a prim. root; to sip up:— suck up.

5967. עֲלַע 'âla' (Chald.), al-ah´; corresp. to 6763; a rib:— rib.

5968. עָלַף 'âlaph, aw-laf´; a prim. root; to veil or cover; fig. to be languid:— faint, overlaid, wrap self.

5969. עֻלְפֶה 'ulpeh, ool-peh´; from 5968; an envelope, i.e. (fig.) mourning:— fainted.

5970. עָלַץ 'âlats, aw-lats´; a prim. root; to jump for joy, i.e. exult:— be joyful, rejoice, triumph.

5971. עַם 'am, am; from 6004; a people (as a congregated unit); spec. a tribe (as those of Israel); hence, (collect.) troops or attendants; fig. a flock:— folk, men, nation, people.

5972. עַם 'am (Chald.), am; corresp. to 5971:— people.

5973. עִם 'im, eem; from 6004; adv. or prep., with (i.e. in conjunction with), in varied applications; spec. equally with; often with prep. pref. (and then usually unrepresented in English):— accompanying, against, and, as (× long as), before, beside, by (reason of), for all, from (among, between), in, like, more than, of, (un-) to, with (-al).

5974. עִם 'îm (Chald.), eem; corresp. to 5973:— by, from, like, to (-ward), with.

5975. עָמַד 'âmad, aw-mad´; a prim. root; to stand, in various relations (lit. and fig., intr. and tran.):— abide (behind), appoint, arise, cease, confirm, continue, dwell, be employed, endure, establish, leave, make, ordain, be [over], place, (be) present (self), raise up, remain, repair, + serve, set (forth, over, -tle, up), (make to, make to be at a, with-) stand (by, fast, firm, still, up), (be at a) stay (up), tarry.

5976. עָמַד 'âmad, aw-mad´; for 4571; to shake:— be at a stand.

5977. עֹמֶד 'ômed, o´-med; from 5975; a spot (as being fixed):— place, (+ where) stood, upright.

5978. עִמָּד 'immâd, im-mawd´; prol. for 5973; along with:— against, by, from, in, + me, + mine, of, + that I take, unto, upon, with (-in.)

עָמַד 'ammûd. See 5982.

5979. עֶמְדָּה 'emdâh, em-daw´; from 5975; a station, i.e. domicile:— standing.

5980. עֻמָּה 'ummâh, oom-maw´; from 6004; conjunction, i.e. society; mostly adv. or prep. (with prep. pref.), near, beside, along with:— (over) against, at, beside, hard by, in points.

5981. עֻמָּה 'Ummâh, oom-maw´; the same as 5980; association; Ummah, a place in Pal.:— Ummah.

5982. עַמּוּד 'ammûwd, am-mood´; or
עַמֻּד 'ammûd, am-mood´; from 5975; a column (as standing); also a stand, i.e. platform:— × apiece, pillar.

5983. עַמּוֹן 'Ammôwn, am-mone´; from 5971; tribal, i.e. inbred; Ammon, a son of Lot; also his posterity and their country:— Ammon, Ammonites.

5984. עַמּוֹנִי 'Ammôwnîy, am-mo-nee´; patron. from 5983; an Ammonite or (adj.) Ammonitish:— Ammonite (-s).

5985. עַמּוֹנִית 'Ammôwnîyth, am-mo-neeth´; fem. of 5984; an Ammonitess:— Ammonite (-ss).

5986. עָמוֹס 'Âmôwç, aw-moce´; from 6006; burdensome; Amos, an Isr. prophet:— Amos.

5987. עָמוֹק 'Âmôwq, aw-moke´; from 6009; deep; Amok, an Isr.:— Amok.

5988. עַמִּיאֵל 'Ammîy'êl, am-mee-ale´; from 5971 and 410; people of God; Ammiël, the name of three or four Isr.:— Ammiel.

5989. עַמִּיהוּד 'Ammîyhûwd, am-mee-hood´; from 5971 and 1935; people of splendor; Ammihud, the name of three Isr.:— Ammihud.

5990. עַמִּיזָבָד 'Ammîyzâbâd, am-mee-zaw-bawd´; from 5971 and 2064; people of endowment; Ammizabad, an Isr.:— Ammizabad.

5991. עַמִּיחוּר 'Ammîychûwr, am-mee-khoor´; from 5971 and 2353; people of nobility; Ammichur, a Syrian prince:— Ammihud [from the marg.].

5992. עַמִּינָדָב 'Ammîynâdâb, am-mee-naw-dawb´; from 5971 and 5068; people of liberality; Amminadab, the name of four Isr.:— Amminadab.

5993. עַמִּי נָדִיב 'Ammîy Nâdîyb, am-mee naw-deeb´; from 5971 and 5081; my people (is) liberal; Ammi-Nadib, prob. an Isr.:— Amminadib.

5994. עֲמִיק 'âmîyq (Chald.), am-eek´; corresp. to 6012; profound, i.e. unsearchable:— deep.

5995. עָמִיר 'âmîyr, aw-meer´; from 6014; a bunch of grain:— handful, sheaf.

5996. עַמִּישַׁדַּי 'Ammîyshadday, am-mee-shad-dah´ee; from 5971 and 7706; people of (the) Almighty; Ammishaddai, an Isr.:— Ammishaddai.

5997. עָמִית 'âmîyth, aw-meeth´; from a prim. root mean. to associate; companionship; hence, (concr.) a comrade or kindred man:— another, fellow, neighbour.

5998. עָמַל 'âmal, aw-mal´; a prim. root; to toil, i.e. work severely and with irksomeness:— [take] labour (in).

5999. עָמָל 'âmâl, aw-mawl´; from 5998; toil, i.e. wearing effort; hence, worry, wheth. of body or mind:— grievance (-vousness), iniquity, labour, mischief, miserable (-sery), pain (-ful), perverseness, sorrow, toil, travail, trouble, wearisome, wickedness.

6000. עָמָל 'Âmâl, aw-mawl´; the same as 5999; Amal, an Isr.:— Amal.

6001. עָמֵל 'âmêl, aw-male´; from 5998; toiling; concr. a laborer; fig. sorrowful:— that laboureth, that is a misery, had taken [labour], wicked, workman.

6002. עֲמָלֵק 'Ămâlêq, am-aw-lake´; prob. of for. or.; Amalek, a desc. of Esau; also his posterity and their country:— Amalek.

6003. עֲמָלֵקִי 'Ămâlêqîy, am-aw-lay-kee´; patron. from 6002; an Amalekite (or collect. the Amalekites) or desc. of Amalek:— Amalekite (-s).

6004. עָמַם 'âmam, aw-mam´; a prim. root; to associate; by impl. to overshadow (by huddling together):— become dim, hide.

6005. עִמָּנוּאֵל 'Immânûw'êl, im-maw-noo-ale´; from 5973 and 410 with a pron. suff. ins.; with us (is) God; Immanuel, a typical name of Isaiah's son:— Immanuel.

6006. עָמַס 'âmaç, aw-mas´; or
עָמַשׂ 'âmas, aw-mas´; a prim. root; to load, i.e. impose a burden (or fig. infliction):— be borne, (heavy) burden (self), lade, load, put.

6007. עֲמַסְיָה 'Ămaçyâh, am-as-yaw´;

from 6006 and 3050; *Jah has loaded;* *Amasjah,* an Isr.:— Amasiah.

6008. עמעד **'Am'âd**, *am-awd´;* from 5971 and 5703; *people of time; Amad,* a place in Pal.:— Amad.

6009. עמק **'âmaq**, *aw-mak´;* a prim. root; to *be* (caus. *make*) deep (lit. or fig.):— (be, have, make, seek) deep (-ly), depth, be profound.

6010. עמק **'êmeq**, *ay´-mek;* from 6009; a *vale* (i.e. broad *depression*):— dale, vale, valley [often *used as a part of proper names*]. See also 1025.

6011. עמק **'ômeq**, *o´-mek;* from 6009; *depth:*— depth.

6012. עמק **'âmêq**, *aw-make´;* from 6009; *deep* (lit. or fig.):— deeper, depth, strange.

6013. עמק **'âmôq**, *aw-moke´;* from 6009; *deep* (lit. or fig.):— (× exceeding) deep (thing).

6014. עמר **'âmar**, *aw-mar´;* a prim. root; prop. appar. to *heap;* fig. to *chastise* (as if *piling* blows); spec. (as denom. from 6016) to *gather* grain:— bind sheaves, make merchandise of.

6015. עמר **'âmar** (Chald.), *am-ar´;* corresp. to 6785; *wool:*— wool.

6016. עמר **'ômer**, *o´-mer;* from 6014; prop. a *heap,* i.e. a *sheaf;* also an *omer,* as a dry measure:— omer, sheaf.

6017. עמרה **'Âmôrâh**, *am-o-raw´;* from 6014; a (ruined) *heap; Amorah,* a place in Pal.:— Gomorrah.

6018. עמרי **'Omrîy**, *om-ree´;* from 6014; *heaping; Omri,* an Isr.:— Omri.

6019. עמרם **'Amrâm**, *am-rawm´;* prob. from 5971 and 7311; *high people; Amram,* the name of two Isr.:— Amram.

6020. עמרמי **'Amrâmîy**, *am-raw-mee´;* patron. from 6019; an *Amramite* or desc. of Amram:— Amramite.

עמס **'âmas**. See 6006.

6021. עמשא **'Âmâsâ**, *am-aw-saw´;* from 6006; *burden; Amasa,* the name of two Isr.:— Amasa.

6022. עמשי **'Âmâsay**, *am-aw-sah´-ee;* from 6006; *burdensome; Amasai,* the name of three Isr.:— Amasai.

6023. עמשסי **'Âmashçay**, *am-ash-sah´-ee;* prob. from 6006; *burdensome; Amashsay,* an Isr.:— Amashai.

6024. ענב **'Ânâb**, *an-awb´;* from the same as 6025; *fruit; Anab,* a place in Pal.:— Anab.

6025. ענב **'ênâb**, *ay-nawb´;* from an unused root prob. mean. to *bear* fruit; a *grape:*— (ripe) grape, wine.

6026. ענג **'ânag**, *aw-nag´;* a prim. root; to *be soft* or *pliable,* i.e. (fig.) *effeminate* or luxurious:— delicate (-ness), (have) delight (self), sport self.

6027. ענג **'ôneg**, *o´-neg;* from 6026; *luxury:*— delight, pleasant.

6028. ענג **'ânôg**, *aw-nogue´;* from 6026; *luxurious:*— delicate.

6029. ענד **'ânad**, *aw-nad´;* a prim. root; to *lace* fast:— bind, tie.

6030. ענה **'ânâh**, *aw-naw´;* a prim. root; prop. to *eye* or (gen.) to *heed,* i.e. *pay attention;* by impl. to *respond;* by ex-

tens. to *begin* to speak; spec. to *sing, shout, testify, announce:*— give account, afflict [by *mistake for* 6031], (cause to, give) answer, bring low [by *mistake for* 6031], cry, hear, Leannoth, lift up, say, × scholar, (give a) shout, sing (together by course), speak, testify, utter, (bear) witness. See also 1042, 1043.

6031. ענה **'ânâh**, *aw-naw´;* a prim. root [possibly rather ident. with 6030 through the idea of *looking* down or *browbeating*]; to *depress* lit. or fig., tran. or intr. (in various applications, as follows):— abase self, afflict (-ion, self), answer [by *mistake for* 6030], chasten self, deal hardly with, defile, exercise, force, gentleness, humble (self), hurt, ravish, sing [by *mistake for* 6030], speak [by *mistake for* 6030], submit self, weaken, × in any wise.

6032. ענה **'ânâh** (Chald.), *an-aw´;* corresp. to 6030:— answer, speak.

6033. ענה **'ânâh** (Chald.), *an-aw´;* corresp. to 6031:— poor.

6034. ענה **'Ânâh**, *an-aw´;* prob. from 6030; an *answer; Anah,* the name of two Edomites and one Edomitess:— Anah.

6035. ענו **'ânâwv**, *aw-nawv´;* or [by intermixture with 6041]

 עניו **'ânâyv**, *aw-nawv´;* from 6031; *depressed* (fig.), in mind (*gentle*) or circumstances (*needy,* espec. *saintly*):— humble, lowly, meek, poor. Comp. 6041.

6036. ענוב **'Ânûwb**, *aw-noob´;* pass. part. from the same as 6025; *borne* (as fruit); *Anub,* an Isr.:— Anub.

6037. ענוה **'anvâh**, *an-vaw´;* fem. of 6035; *mildness* (royal); also (concr.) *oppressed:*— gentleness, meekness.

6038. ענוה **'ănâvâh**, *an-aw-vaw´;* from 6035; *condescension,* human and subj. (*modesty*), or divine and obj. (*clemency*):— gentleness, humility, meekness.

6039. ענוה **'ênûwth**, *en-ooth´;* from 6031; *affliction:*— affliction.

6040. עני **'ŏnîy**, *on-ee´;* from 6031; *depression,* i.e. misery:— afflicted (-ion), trouble.

6041. עני **'ânîy**, *aw-nee´;* from 6031; *depressed,* in mind or circumstances [practically the same as 6035, although the marg. constantly disputes this, making 6035 subj. and 6041 obj.]:— afflicted, humble, lowly, needy, poor.

6042. עני **'Unnîy**, *oon-nee´;* from 6031; *afflicted; Unni,* the name of two Isr.:— Unni.

6043. עניה **'Ânâyâh**, *an-aw-yaw´;* from 6030; *Jah has answered; Anajah,* the name of two Isr.:— Anaiah.

עניו **'ânâyv** See 6035.

6044. ענים **'Ânîym**, *aw-neem´;* for plur. of 5869; *fountains; Anim,* a place in Pal.:— Anim.

6045. ענין **'inyân**, *in-yawn´;* from 6031; *ado,* i.e. (gen.) *employment* or (spec.) an *affair:*— business, travail.

6046. ענם **'Ânêm**, *aw-name´;* from the dual of 5869; *two fountains; Anem,* a place in Pal.:— Anem.

6047. ענם **'Ânâmim**, *an-aw-meem´;* as if plur. of some Eg. word; *Anamim,* a son of Mizraim and his desc., with their country:— Anamim.

6048. ענמלך **'Ânammelek**, *an-am-meh´-lek;* of for. or.; *Anammelek,* an Ass. deity:— Anammelech.

6049. ענן **'ânan**, *aw-nan´;* a prim. root; to *cover;* used only as a denom. from 6051, to *cloud* over; fig. to *act covertly,* i.e. practise magic:— × bring, enchanter, Meonemin, observe (-r of) times, soothsayer, sorcerer.

6050. ענן **'ânan** (Chald.), *an-an´;* corresp. to 6051:— cloud.

6051. ענן **'ânân**, *aw-nawn´;* from 6049; a *cloud* (as *covering* the sky), i.e. the *nimbus* or thunder-cloud:— cloud (-y).

6052. ענן **'Ânân**, *aw-nawn´;* the same as 6051; *cloud; Anan,* an Isr.:— Anan.

6053. עננה **'ănânâh**, *an-aw-naw´;* fem. of 6051; *cloudiness:*— cloud.

6054. ענני **'Ânânîy**, *aw-naw-nee´;* from 6051; *cloudy; Anani,* an Isr.:— Anani.

6055. עניה **'Ânanyâh**, *an-an-yaw´;* from 6049 and 3050; *Jah has covered; Ananjah,* the name of an Isr. and of a place in Pal.:— Ananiah.

6056. ענף **'ănaph** (Chald.), *an-af´;* or

ענף **'eneph** (Chald.), *eh´-nef;* corresp. to 6057:— bough, branch.

6057. ענף **'ânâph**, *aw-nawf´;* from an unused root mean. to *cover;* a *twig* [as *covering* the limbs]:— bough, branch.

6058. ענף **'ânêph**, *aw-nafe´;* from the same as 6057; *branching:*— full of branches.

6059. ענק **'ânaq**, *aw-nak´;* a prim. root; prop. to *choke;* used only as a denom. from 6060, to *collar,* i.e. adorn with a necklace; fig. to *fit out* with supplies:— compass about as a chain, furnish, liberally.

6060. ענק **'ânâq**, *aw-nawk´;* from 6059; a *necklace* (as if *strangling*):— chain.

6061. ענק **'Ânâq**, *aw-nawk´;* the same as 6060; *Anak,* a Canaanite:— Anak.

6062. ענקי **'Ânâqîy**, *aw-naw-kee´;* patron. from 6061; an *Anakite* or desc. of Anak:— Anakim.

6063. ענר **'Ânêr**, *aw-nare´;* prob. for 5288; *Aner,* a Amorite, also a place in Pal.:— Aner.

6064. ענש **'ânash**, *aw-nash´;* a prim. root; prop. to *urge;* by impl. to *inflict* a penalty, spec. to *fine:*— amerce, condemn, punish, × surely.

6065. ענש **'ănash** (Chald.), *an-ash´;* corresp. to 6066; a *mulct:*— confiscation.

6066. ענש **'ônesh**, *o´-nesh;* from 6064; a *fine:*— punishment, tribute.

ענת **'eneth** See 3706.

6067. ענת **'Ânâth**, *an-awth´;* from 6030; *answer; Anath,* an Isr.:— Anath.

6068. ענתות **'Ânâthôwth**, *an-aw-thoth´;* plur. of 6067; *Anathoth,* the name of two Isr., also of a place in Pal.:— Anathoth.

6069. ענתתי **'Anthôthîy**, *an-tho-thee´;* or

ענתותי **'Ann^ethôwthîy**, *an-ne-tho-thee´;* patrial from 6068; a *Antothite* or inhab. of Anathoth:— of Anathoth, Anethothite, Anetothite, Antothite.

6070. עֲנְתֹתִיָּה **'Anthôthîyâh**, *an-tho-thee-yaw'*; from the same as 6068 and 3050; *answers of Jah*; *Anthothijah*, an Isr.:— Antothijah.

6071. עָסִיס **'âçîyç**, *aw-sees'*; from 6072; *must* or fresh grape-juice (as just *trodden* out):— juice, new (sweet) wine.

6072. עָסַס **'âçaç**, *aw-sas'*; a prim. root; to *squeeze* out juice; fig. to *trample*:— tread down.

6073. עֲפֶא **'ôphe**, *of-eh'*; from an unused root mean. to *cover*; a *bough* (as covering the tree):— branch.

6074. עֳפִי **'ôphîy** (Chald.), *of-ee'*; corresp. to 6073; a *twig*; bough, i.e. (collect.) *foliage*:— leaves.

6075. עָפַל **'âphal**, *aw-fal'*; a prim. root; to *swell*; fig. *be elated*:— be lifted up, presume.

6076. עֹפֶל **'ôphel**, *o'-fel*; from 6075; a *tumor*; also a *mound*, i.e. *fortress*:— emerod, fort, strong hold, tower.

6077. עֹפֶל **'Ôphel**, *o'-fel*; the same as 6076; *Ophel*, a ridge in Jerusalem:— Ophel.

6078. עָפְנִי **'Ophnîy**, *of-nee'*; from an unused noun [denoting a place in Pal.; from an unused root of uncert. mean.]; an *Ophnite* (collect.) or inhab. of Ophen:— Ophni.

6079. עַפְעַף **'aph'aph**, *af-af'*; from 5774; an *eyelash* (as *fluttering*); fig. morning *ray*:— dawning, eye-lid.

6080. עָפַר **'âphar**, *aw-far'*; a prim. root: mean. either to *be gray* or perh. rather to *pulverize*; used only as denom. from 6083, to *be dust*:— cast [dust].

6081. עֵפֶר **'Épher**, *ay'-fer*; prob. a var. of 6082; *gazelle*; *Epher*, the name of an Arabian and of two Isr.:— Epher.

6082. עֹפֶר **'ôpher**, *o'-fer*; from 6080; a *fawn* (from the *dusty* color):— young roe [hart].

6083. עָפָר **'âphâr**, *aw-fawr'*; from 6080; *dust* (as *powdered* or *gray*); hence, *clay, earth, mud*:— ashes, dust, earth, ground, morter, powder, rubbish.

עָפְרָה **'Aphrâh**. See 1036.

6084. עָפְרָה **'Ophrâh**, *of-raw'*; fem. of 6082; *female fawn*; *Ophrah*, the name of an Isr. and of two places in Pal.:— Ophrah.

6085. עֶפְרוֹן **'Ephrôwn**, *ef-rone'*; from the same as 6081; *fawn-like*; *Ephron*, the name of a Canaanite and of two places in Pal.:— Ephron, Ephrain [from the marg.].

עֹפְרֶת **'ôphereth**. See 5777.

6086. עֵץ **'êts**, *ates*; from 6095; a *tree* (from its *firmness*); hence, *wood* (plur. *sticks*):— + carpenter, gallows, helve, + pine, plank, staff, stalk, stick, stock, timber, tree, wood.

6087. עָצַב **'âtsab**, *aw-tsab'*; a prim. root; prop. to *carve*, i.e. *fabricate* or *fashion*; hence, (in a bad sense) to *worry, pain* or *anger*:— displease, grieve, hurt, make, be sorry, vex, worship, wrest.

6088. עֲצַב **'átsab** (Chald.), *ats-ab'*; corresp. to 6087; to *afflict*:— lamentable.

6089. עֶצֶב **'etseb**, *eh'-tseb*; from 6087; an earthen *vessel*; usually (painful) *toil*; also a *pang* (whether of body or mind):— grievous, idol, labor, sorrow.

6090. עֹצֶב **'ôtseb**, *o'-tseb*; a var. of 6089; an *idol* (as fashioned); also *pain* (bodily or mental):— idol, sorrow, × wicked.

6091. עָצָב **'âtsâb**, *aw-tsawb'*; from 6087; an (idolatrous) *image*:— idol, image.

6092. עָצֵב **'âtsêb**, *aw-tsabe'*; from 6087; a (hired) *workman*:— labour.

6093. עִצָּבוֹן **'itstsâbôwn**, *its-tsaw-bone'*; from 6087; *worrisomeness*, i.e. *labor* or *pain*:— sorrow, toil.

6094. עַצֶּבֶת **'atstsebeth**, *ats-tseh'-beth*; from 6087; an *idol*; also a *pain* or *wound*:— sorrow, wound.

6095. עָצָה **'âtsâh**, *aw-tsaw'*; a prim. root; prop. to *fasten* (or *make firm*), i.e. to *close* (the eyes):— shut.

6096. עָצֶה **'âtseh**, *aw-tseh'*; from 6095; the *spine* (as giving *firmness* to the body):— backbone.

6097. עֵצָה **'êtsâh**, *ay-tsaw'*; fem. of 6086; *timber*:— trees.

6098. עֵצָה **'êtsâh**, *ay-tsaw'*; from 3289; *advice*; by impl. *plan*; also *prudence*:— advice, advisement, counsel (l-lorl), purpose.

6099. עָצוּם **'âtsûwm**, *aw-tsoom'*; or

עָצֻם **'âtsûm**, *aw-tsoom'*; pass. part. of 6105; *powerful* (spec. a *paw*); by impl. *numerous*:— + feeble, great, mighty, must, strong.

6100. עֶצְיוֹן גֶּבֶר **'Etsyôwn** (short.

'Etsyôn) **Geber**, *ets-yone' gheh'ber*; from 6096 and 1397; *backbone-like of a man*; *Etsjon-Geber*, a place on the Red Sea:— Ezion-gaber, Ezion-geber.

6101. עָצַל **'âtsal**, *aw-tsal'*; a prim. root; to *lean* idly, i.e. to *be indolent* or *slack*:— be slothful.

6102. עָצֵל **'âtsêl**, *aw-tsale'*; from 6101; *indolent*:— slothful, sluggard.

6103. עַצְלָה **'atslâh**, *ats-law'*; fem. of 6102; (as abstr.) *indolence*:— slothfulness.

6104. עַצְלוּת **'atslûwth**, *ats-looth'*; from 6101; *indolence*:— idleness.

6105. עָצַם **'âtsam**, *aw-tsam'*; a prim. root; to *bind* fast, i.e. *close* (the eyes); intr. to *be* (caus. *make*) *powerful* or *numerous*; denom. (from 6106) to *crunch* the bones:— break the bones, close, be great, be increased, be (wax) mighty (-ier), be more, shut, be (-come, make) strong (-er).

6106. עֶצֶם **'etsem**, *eh'tsem*; from 6105; a *bone* (as *strong*); by extens. the *body*; fig. the *substance*, i.e. (as pron.) *self-same*:— body, bone, × life, (self-) same, strength, × very.

6107. עֶצֶם **'Etsem**, *eh'-tsem*; the same as 6106; *bone*; *Etsem*, a place in Pal.:— Azem, Ezem.

6108. עֹצֶם **'ôtsem**, *o'-tsem*; from 6105; *power*; hence, *body*:— might, strong, substance.

עָצֻם **'âtsûm**. See 6099.

6109. עָצְמָה **'otsmâh**, *ots-maw'*; fem. of

6108; *powerfulness*; by extens. *numerousness*:— abundance, strength.

6110. עָצֻמָה **'atstsûmâh**, *ats-tsoo-maw'*; fem. of 6099; a *bulwark*, i.e. (fig.) *argument*:— strong.

6111. עַצְמוֹן **'Atsmôwn**, *ats-mone'*; or

עַצְמֹן **'Atsmôn**, *ats-mone'*; from 6107; *bone-like*; *Atsmon*, a place near Pal.:— Azmon.

6112. עֵצֶן **'Êtsen**, *ay'-tsen*; from an unused root mean. to *be sharp* or *strong*; a *spear*:— Eznite [from the marg.].

6113. עָצַר **'âtsar**, *aw-tsar'*; a prim. root; to *inclose*; by anal. to *hold back*; also to *maintain, rule, assemble*:— × be able, close up, detain, fast, keep (self close, still), prevail, recover, refrain, × reign, restrain, retain, shut (up), slack, stay, stop, withhold (self).

6114. עֶצֶר **'etser**, *eh'-tser*; from 6113; *restraint*:— + magistrate.

6115. עֹצֶר **'ôtser**, *o'-tser*; from 6113; *closure*; also *constraint*:— × barren, oppression, × prison.

6116. עֲצָרָה **'âtsârâh**, *ats-aw-raw'*; or

עֲצֶרֶת **'âtsereth**, *ats-eh'-reth*; from 6113; an *assembly*, espec. on a *festival* or *holiday*:— (solemn) assembly (meeting).

6117. עָקַב **'âqab**, *aw-kab'*; a prim. root; prop. to *swell* out or up; used only as denom. from 6119, to *seize by the heel*; fig. to *circumvent* (as if *tripping* up the heels); also to *restrain* (as if holding by the heel):— take by the heel, stay, supplant, × utterly.

6118. עֵקֶב **'êqeb**, *ay'-keb*; from 6117 in the sense of 6119; a *heel*, i.e. (fig.) the *last* of anything (used adv. *for ever*); also *result*, i.e. *compensation*; and so (adv. with prep. or rel.) on *account of*:— × because, by, end, for, if, reward.

6119. עָקֵב **'âqêb**, *aw-kabe'*; or (fem.)

עִקְּבָה **'iqqebâh**, *ik-keb-aw'*; from 6117; a *heel* (as *protuberant*); hence, a *track*; fig. the *rear* (of an army):— heel, [horse-] hoof, last, lier in wait [by mistake for 6120], (foot-) step.

6120. עָקֵב **'âqêb**, *aw-kabe'*; from 6117 in its denom. sense; a *lier in wait*:— heel [by mistake for 6119].

6121. עָקֹב **'âqôb**, *aw-kobe'*; from 6117; in the orig. sense, a *knoll* (as *swelling* up); in the denom. sense (tran.) *fraudulent* or (intr.) *tracked*:— crooked, deceitful, polluted.

6122. עָקְבָה **'oqbâh**, *ok-baw'*; fem. of an unused form from 6117 mean. a *trick*; *trickery*:— subtilty.

6123. עָקַד **'âqad**, *aw-kad'*; a prim. root; to *tie* with thongs:— bind.

עֶקֶד **'Êqed**. See 1044.

6124. עָקֹד **'âqôd**, *aw-kode'*; from 6123; *striped* (with *bands*):— ring straked.

6125. עָקָה **'âqâh**, *aw-kaw'*; from 5781; *constraint*:— oppression.

6126. עַקּוּב **'Aqqûwb**, *ak-koob'*; from 6117; *insidious*; *Akkub*, the name of five Isr.:— Akkub.

6127. עָקַל **'âqal**, *aw-kal'*; a prim. root; to *wrest*:— wrong.

6128. עֲקַלְקַל **'äqalqal**, ak-al-kal´; from 6127; *winding*:— by [-way], *crooked* way.

6129. עֲקַלָּתוֹן **'äqallâthôwn**, ak-al-law-thone´; from 6127; *tortuous*:— crooked.

6130. עֲקָן **'Âqân**, aw-kawn´; from an unused root mean. to *twist*; *tortuous*; *Akan*, an Idumæan:— Akan. Comp. 3292.

6131. עָקַר **'âqar**, aw-kar´; a prim. root; to *pluck* up (espec. by the roots); spec. to *hamstring*; fig. to *exterminate*:— dig down, hough, pluck up, root up.

6132. עֲקַר **'äqar** (Chald.), ak-ar´; corresp. to 6131:— pluck up by the roots.

6133. עֵקֶר **'êqer**, ay´-ker; from 6131; fig. a *transplanted* person, i.e. naturalized citizen:— stock.

6134. עֵקֶר **'Êqer**, ay´-ker; the same as 6133; *Eker*, an Isr.:— Eker.

6135. עָקָר **'âqâr**, aw-kawr´; from 6131; *sterile* (as if *extirpated* in the generative organs):— (× male or female) barren (woman).

6136. עִקַּר **'iqqar** (Chald.), ik-kar´; from 6132; a *stock*:— stump.

6137. עַקְרָב **'aqrâb**, ak-rawb´; of uncert. der.; a *scorpion*; fig. a *scourge* or knotted whip:— scorpion.

6138. עֶקְרוֹן **'Eqrôwn**, ek-rone´; from 6131; *eradication*; *Ekron*, a place in Pal.:— Ekron.

6139. עֶקְרוֹנִי **'Eqrôwniy**, ek-ro-nee´; or

עֶקְרֹנִי **'Eqrôniy**, ek-ro-nee´; patrial from 6138; an *Ekronite* or inhab. of Ekron:— Ekronite.

6140. עָקַשׁ **'âqash**, aw-kash´; a prim. root; to *knot* or *distort*; fig. to *pervert* (act or declare perverse):— make crooked, (prove, that is) perverse (-rt).

6141. עִקֵּשׁ **'iqqêsh**, ik-kashe´; from 6140; *distorted*; hence, *false*:— crooked, froward, perverse.

6142. עִקֵּשׁ **'Îqqêsh**, ik-kashe´; the same as 6141; *perverse*; *Ikkesh*, an Isr.:— Ikkesh.

6143. עִקְּשׁוּת **'iqqᵉshûwth**, ik-kesh-ooth´; from 6141; *perversity*:— × froward.

עָר **'âr**. See 5892.

6144. עָר **'Âr**, awr; the same as 5892; a *city*; *Ar*, a place in Moab:— Ar.

6145. עָר **'âr**, awr; from 5782; a *foe* (as *watchful* for mischief):— enemy.

6146. עָר **'âr** (Chald.), awr; corresp. to 6145:— enemy.

6147. עֵר **'Êr**, ayr; from 5782; *watchful*; *Er*, the name of two Isr.:— Er.

6148. עָרַב **'ârab**, aw-rab´; a prim. root; to *braid*, i.e. *intermix*; tech. to *traffic* (as if by barter); also to *give* or *be security* (as a kind of exchange):— engage, (inter-) meddle (with), mingle (self), mortgage, occupy, give pledges, be (-come, put in) surety, undertake.

6149. עָרֵב **'ârêb**, aw-rabe´ a prim. root [rather ident. with 6148 through the idea of close *association*]; to *be agreeable*:— be pleasant (-ing), take pleasure in, be sweet.

6150. עָרַב **'ârab**, aw-rab´; a prim. root [rather ident. with 6148 through the idea of *covering* with a texture]; to *grow dusky* at sundown:— be darkened, (toward) evening.

6151. עֲרַב **'ärab** (Chald.), ar-ab´; corresp. to 6148; to *commingle*:— mingle (self), mix.

6152. עֲרָב **'Ârâb**, ar-awb´ or

עֲרַב **'Ärab**, ar-ab´; from 6150 in the fig. sense of *sterility*; *Arab* (i.e. *Arabia*), a country E. of Pal.:— Arabia.

6153. עֶרֶב **'ereb**, eh´-reb; from 6150; *dusk*:— + day, even (-ing, tide), night.

6154. עֵרֶב **'êreb**, ay´-reb; or

עֶרֶב **'ereb** (1 Kings 10:15), (with the art. pref.), eh´-reb; from 6148; the *web* (or transverse threads of cloth); also a *mixture*, (or *mongrel* race):— Arabia, mingled people, mixed (multitude), woof.

6155. עֲרָב **'ârâb**, aw-rawb´; from 6148; a *willow* (from the use of osiers as wattles):— willow.

6156. עָרֵב **'ârêb**, aw-rabe´; from 6149; *pleasant*:— sweet.

6157. עָרֹב **'ârôb**, aw-robe´; from 6148; a *mosquito* (from its *swarming*):— divers sorts of flies, swarm.

6158. עֹרֵב **'ôrêb**, o-rabe´; or

עוֹרֵב **'ôwrêb**, o-rabe´; from 6150; a *raven* (from its *dusky* hue):— raven.

6159. עֹרֵב **'Ôrêb**, o-rabe´; or

עוֹרֵב **'Ôwrêb**, o-rabe´; the same as 6158; *Oreb*, the name of a Midianite and of a cliff near the Jordan:— Oreb.

6160. עֲרָבָה **'ärâbâh**, ar-aw-baw´; from 6150 (in the sense of *sterility*); a *desert*; espec. (with the art. pref.) the (gen.) sterile valley of the Jordan and its continuation to the Red Sea:— Arabah, champaign, desert, evening, heaven, plain, wilderness. See also 1026.

6161. עֲרֻבָּה **'ärubbâh**, ar-oob-baw´; fem. pass. part. of 6148 in the sense of a *bargain* or *exchange*; something given as *security*, i.e. (lit.) a *token* (of safety) or (metaph.) a *bondsman*:— pledge, surety.

6162. עֲרָבוֹן **'ärâbôwn**, ar-aw-bone´; from 6148 (in the sense of *exchange*); a *pawn* (given as security):— pledge.

6163. עֲרָבִי **'Ärâbîy**, ar-aw-bee´; or

עַרְבִי **'Arbîy**, ar-bee´; patrial from 6152; an *Arabian* or inhab. of Arab (i.e. Arabia):— Arabian.

6164. עַרְבָתִי **'Arbâthiy**, ar-baw-thee´; patrial from 1026; an *Arbathite* or inhab. of (Beth-) Arabah:— Arbahite.

6165. עָרַג **'ârag**, aw-rag´; a prim. root; to *long for*:— cry, pant.

6166. עֲרָד **'Ärâd**, ar-awd´; from an unused root mean. to *sequester* itself; *fugitive*; *Arad*, the name of a place near Pal., also of a Canaanite and an Isr.:— Arad.

6167. עֲרָד **'ärâd** (Chald.), ar-awd´; corresp. to 6171; an *onager*:— wild ass.

6168. עָרָה **'ârâh**, aw-raw´; a prim. root; to *be* (caus. *make*) *bare*; hence, to *empty*, *pour* out, *demolish*:— leave destitute, discover, empty, make naked, pour (out), rase, spread self, uncover.

6169. עָרָה **'ârâh**, aw-raw´; fem. from 6168; a *naked* (i.e. level) plot:— paper reed.

6170. עֲרוּגָה **'ärûgâh**, ar-oo-gaw´; or

עֲרֻגָה **'ärûgâh**, ar-oo-gaw´; fem. pass. part. of 6165; something *piled* up (as if [fig.] raised by mental aspiration), i.e. a *parterre*:— bed, furrow.

6171. עָרוֹד **'ârôwd**, aw-rode´; from the same as 6166; an *onager* (from his *lonesome* habits):— wild ass.

6172. עֶרְוָה **'ervâh**, er-vaw´; from 6168; *nudity*, lit. (espec. the *pudenda*) or fig. (*disgrace*, *blemish*):— nakedness, shame, unclean (-ness).

6173. עַרְוָה **'arvâh** (Chald.), ar-vaw´; corresp. to 6172; *nakedness*, i.e. (fig.) *impoverishment*:— dishonour.

6174. עָרוֹם **'ârôwm**, aw-rome´; or

עָרֹם **'ârôm**, aw-rome´; from 6191 (in its orig. sense); *nude*, either partially or totally:— naked.

6175. עָרוּם **'ârûwm**, aw-room´; pass. part. of 6191; *cunning* (usually in a bad sense):— crafty, prudent, subtil.

6176. עֲרוֹעֵר **'ärôw'êr**, ar-o-ayr´; or

עַרְעָר **'ar'âr**, ar-awr´; from 6209 redupl.; a *juniper* (from its *nudity* of situation):— heath.

6177. עֲרוֹעֵר **'Ärôw'êr**, ar-o-ayr´; or

עֲרֹעֵר **'Ärô'êr**, ar-o-ayr´; or

עַרְעוֹר **'Är'ôwr**, ar-ore´; the same as 6176; *nudity* of situation; *Aroër*, the name of three places in or near Pal.:— Aroer.

6178. עֲרוּץ **'ärûwts**, aw-roots´; pass. part. of 6206; *feared*, i.e. (concr.) a *horrible* place or *chasm*:— cliffs.

6179. עֵרִי **'Êrîy**, ay-ree´; from 5782; *watchful*; *Eri*, an Isr.:— Eri.

6180. עֵרִי **'Êrîy**, ay-ree´; patron. of 6179; a *Erite* (collect.) or desc. of Eri:— Erites.

6181. עֶרְיָה **'eryâh**, er-yaw´; for 6172; *nudity*:— bare, naked, × quite.

6182. עֲרִיסָה **'äriyçâh**, ar-ee-saw´; from an unused root mean. to *comminute*; *meal*:— dough.

6183. עָרִיף **'âriyph**, aw-reef´; from 6201; the *sky* (as *drooping* at the horizon):— heaven.

6184. עָרִיץ **'âriyts**, aw-reets´; from 6206; *fearful*, i.e. *powerful* or *tyrannical*:— mighty, oppressor, in great power, strong, terrible, violent.

6185. עֲרִירִי **'äriyrîy**, ar-e-ree´; from 6209; *bare*, i.e. destitute (of children):— childless.

6186. עָרַךְ **'ârak**, aw-rak´; a prim. root; to *set in a row*, i.e. *arrange*, put in *order* (in a very wide variety of applications):— put (set) (the battle, self) in array, compare, direct, equal, esteem, estimate, expert [in war], furnish, handle, join [battle], ordain, (lay, put, reckon up, set) (in) order, prepare, tax, value.

6187. עֵרֶךְ **'êrek**, eh´rek; from 6186; a *pile*, *equipment*, *estimate*:— equal, estimation, (things that are set in) order, price, proportion, × set at, suit, taxation, × valuest.

Hebrew

6188. עָרֵל **'ârêl,** aw-rale'; a prim. root; prop. to strip; but used only as denom. from 6189; to expose or remove the prepuce, whether lit. (to go naked) or fig. (to refrain from using):— count uncircumcised, foreskin to be uncovered.

6189. עָרֵל **'ârêl,** aw-rale'; from 6188; prop. exposed, i.e. projecting loose (as to the prepuce) used only tech. uncircumcised (i.e. still having the prepuce uncurtailed):— uncircumcised (person).

6190. עָרְלָה **'orlâh,** or-law'; fem. of 6189; the prepuce:— foreskin, + uncircumcised.

6191. עָרַם **'âram,** aw-ram'; a prim. root; prop. to be (or make) bare; but used only in the der. sense (through the idea perh. of smoothness) to be cunning (usually in a bad sense):— × very, beware, take crafty [counsell], be prudent, deal subtilly.

6192. עָרַם **'âram,** aw-ram'; a prim. root; to pile up:— gather together.

6193. עֹרֶם **'ôrem,** o'-rem; from 6191; a stratagem:— craftiness.

עָרַם **'Êrôm.** See 5903.

עָרֹם **'ârôm.** See 6174.

6194. עָרֵם **'ârêm** (Jer. 50:26), aw-rame'; or (fem.)

עֲרֵמָה **'ârêmâh,** ar-ay-maw'; from 6192; a heap; spec. a sheaf:— heap (of corn), sheaf.

6195. עָרְמָה **'ormâh,** or-maw'; fem. of 6193; trickery; or (in a good sense) discretion:— guile, prudence, subtilty, wilily, wisdom.

עֲרֵמָה **'ârêmâh.** See 6194.

6196. עַרְמוֹן **'armôwn,** ar-mone'; prob. from 6191; the plane tree (from its smooth and shed bark):— chestnut tree.

6197. עֵרָן **'Êrân,** ay-rawn'; prob. from 5782; watchful; Eran, an Isr.:— Eran.

6198. עֵרָנִי **'Êrâniy,** ay-raw-nee'; patron. from 6197; an Eranite or desc. (collect.) of Eran:— Eranites.

עָרוֹעֵר **'Ar'ôwr.** See 6177.

6199. עַרְעָר **'ar'âr,** ar-awr'; from 6209; naked, i.e. (fig.) poor:— destitute. See also 6176.

עֲרֹעֵר **'Arô'êr.** See 6177.

6200. עֲרֹעֵרִי **'Arô'êriy,** ar-o-ay-ree'; patron. from 6177; an Aroërite or inhab. of Aroër:— Aroerite.

6201. עָרַף **'âraph,** aw-raf'; a prim. root; to droop; hence, to drip:— drop (down).

6202. עָרַף **'âraph,** aw-raf'; a prim. root [rather ident. with 6201 through the idea of sloping]; prop. to bend downward; but used only as a denom. from 6203, to break the neck; hence, (fig.) to destroy:— that is beheaded, break down, break (cut off, strike off) neck.

6203. עֹרֶף **'ôreph,** o-ref'; from 6202; the nape or back of the neck (as declining); hence, the back generally (whether lit. or fig.):— back [stiff-] neck ([-ed).

6204. עָרְפָּה **'Orpâh,** or-paw'; fem. of 6203; mane; Orpah, a Moabitess:— Orpah.

6205. עֲרָפֶל **'ărâphel,** ar-aw-fel'; prob. from 6201; gloom (as of a lowering sky):— (gross, thick) dark (cloud, -ness).

6206. עָרַץ **'ârats,** aw-rats'; a prim. root; to awe or (intr.) to dread; hence, to harass:— be affrighted (afraid, dread, feared, terrified), break, dread, fear, oppress, prevail, shake terribly.

6207. עָרַק **'âraq,** aw-rak'; a prim. root; to gnaw, i.e. (fig.) eat (by hyperbole); also (part.) a pain:— fleeing, sinew.

6208. עַרְקִי **'Arqiy,** ar-kee'; patrial from an unused name mean. a tush; an Arkite or inhab. of Erek:— Arkite.

6209. עָרַר **'ârar,** aw-rar'; a prim. root; to bare; fig. to demolish:— make bare, break, raise up [perh. by clerical err. for razel, × utterly.

6210. עֶרֶשׂ **'eres,** eh'res; from an unused root mean. perh. to arch; a couch (prop. with a canopy):— bed (-stead), couch.

6211. עָשׁ **'âsh,** awsh; from 6244; a moth:— moth. See also 5906.

6211'. עֲשַׂב **'ăsab** (Chald.), as-ab'; 6212:— grass.

6212. עֶשֶׂב **'eseb,** eh'seb; from an unused root mean. to glisten (or be green); grass (or any tender shoot):— grass, herb.

6213. עָשָׂה **'âsâh,** aw-saw'; a prim. root; to do or make, in the broadest sense and widest application (as follows):— accomplish, advance, appoint, apt, be at, become, bear, bestow, bring forth, bruise, be busy, × certainly, have the charge of, commit, deal (with), deck, + displease, do, (ready) dress (-ed), (put in) execute (-ion), exercise, fashion, + feast, [fight-]ing man, + finish, fit, fly, follow, fulfil, furnish, gather, get, go about, govern, grant, great, + hinder, hold ([a feast]), × indeed, + be industrious, + journey, keep, labour, maintain, make, be meet, observe, be occupied, offer, + officer, pare, bring (come) to pass, perform, practise, prepare, procure, provide, put, requite, × sacrifice, serve, set, shew, × sin, spend, × surely, take, × throughly, trim, × very, + vex, be [warr-] ior, work (-man), yield, use.

6214. עֲשָׂהאֵל **'Asâh'êl,** as-aw-ale'; from 6213 and 410; God has made; Asahel, the name of four Isr.:— Asahel.

6215. עֵשָׂו **'Êsâv,** ay-sawv'; appar. a form of the pass. part. of 6213 in the orig. sense of handling; rough (i.e. sensibly felt); Esau, a son of Isaac, incl. his posterity:— Esau.

6216. עָשׁוֹק **'ashôwq,** aw-shoke'; from 6231; oppressive (as noun, a tyrant):— oppressor.

6217. עָשׁוּק **'âshûwq,** aw-shook'; or

עָשֻׁק **'âshûq,** aw-shook'; pass. part. of 6231; used in plur. masc. as abstr. tyranny:— oppressed (-ion). [Doubtful.]

6218. עָשׂוֹר **'âsôwr,** aw-sore'; or

עָשֹׂר **'âsôr,** aw-sore'; from 6235; ten; by abbrev. ten strings, and so a decachord:— (instrument of) ten (strings, -th).

6219. עָשׁוֹת **'âshôwth,** aw-shōth'; from 6245; shining, i.e. polished:— bright.

6220. עַשְׁוָת **'Ashvâth,** ash-vawth'; for 6219; bright; Ashvath, an Isr.:— Ashvath.

6221. עֲשִׂיאֵל **'Asîy'êl,** as-ee-ale'; from 6213 and 410; made of God; Asiël, an Isr.:— Asiel.

6222. עֲשָׂיָה **'Asâyâh,** aw-saw-yaw'; from 6213 and 3050; Jah has made; Asajah, the name of three or four Isr.:— Asaiah.

6223. עָשִׁיר **'âshîyr,** aw-sheer'; from 6238; rich, whether lit. or fig. (noble):— rich (man).

6224. עֲשִׂירִי **'ăsîyrîy,** as-ee-ree'; from 6235; tenth; by abb. tenth month or (fem.) part:— tenth (part).

6225. עָשַׁן **'âshan,** aw-shan'; a prim. root; to smoke, whether lit. or fig.:— be angry, (be on a) smoke.

6226. עָשֵׁן **'âshên,** aw-shane'; from 6225; smoky:— smoking.

6227. עָשָׁן **'âshân,** aw-shawn'; from 6225; smoke, lit. or fig. (vapor, dust, anger):— smoke (-ing).

6228. עָשָׁן **'Âshân,** aw-shawn'; the same as 6227; Ashan, a place in Pal.:— Ashan.

6229. עָשַׂק **'âsaq,** aw-sak'; a prim. root (ident. with 6231); to press upon, i.e. quarrel:— strive with.

6230. עֵשֶׂק **'Êseq,** ay'sek; from 6229; strife:— Esek.

6231. עָשַׁק **'âshaq,** aw-shak'; a prim. root (comp. 6229); to press upon, i.e. oppress, defraud, violate, overflow:— get deceitfully, deceive, defraud, drink up, (use) oppress ([-ion], -or), do violence (wrong).

6232. עֵשֶׁק **'Êsheq,** ay-shek'; from 6231; oppression; Eshek, an Isr.:— Eshek.

6233. עֹשֶׁק **'ôsheq,** o'-shek; from 6231; injury, fraud, (subj.) distress, (concr.) unjust gain:— cruelly, extortion, oppression, thing [deceitfully gotten].

עָשֻׁק **'âshûq.** See 6217.

6234. עָשְׁקָה **'oshqâh,** osh-kaw'; fem. of 6233; anguish:— oppressed.

6235. עֶשֶׂר **'eser,** eh'ser; masc.

עֲשָׂרָה **'ăsârâh,** as-aw-raw'; from 6237; ten (as an accumulation to the extent of the digits):— ten, [fif-, seven-] teen.

6236. עֲשַׂר **'ăsar** (Chald.), as-ar'; masc.

עֲשְׂרָה **'ăsrâh** (Chald.), as-raw'; corresp. to 6235; ten:— ten, + twelve.

6237. עָשַׂר **'âsar,** aw-sar'; a prim. root (ident. with 6238); to accumulate; but used only as denom. from 6235; to tithe, i.e. take or give a tenth:— × surely, give (take) the tenth, (have, take) tithe (-ing, -s), × truly.

6238. עָשַׁר **'âshar,** aw-shar'; a prim. root; prop. to accumulate; chiefly (spec.) to grow (caus. make) rich:— be (-come, en-, make, make self, wax) rich, make [1 Kings 22:48 marg.]. See 6240.

6239. עֹשֶׁר **'ôsher,** o'-sher; from 6238; wealth:— × far [richer], riches.

6240. עָצָר **'âsâr**, *aw-sawr'*; for 6235; *ten* (only in combination), i.e. *teen;* also (ord.) *-teenth:*— leigh-, fif-, four-, nine-, seven-, six-, thir-lteen (-th), + eleven (-th), + sixscore thousand, + twelve (-th).

עָצֹר **'âsôr**. See 6218.

6241. עִצָּרוֹן **'issârôwn**, *is-saw-rone';* or עִצָּרֹן **'issârôn**, *is-saw-rone';* from 6235; (fractional) a *tenth* part:— tenth deal.

6242. עֶצְרִים **'esrîym**, *es-reem';* from 6235; *twenty;* also (ord.) *twentieth:*— lsix-l score, twenty (-ieth).

6243. עֶצְרִין **'esrîyn** (Chald.), *es-reen';* corresp. to 6242:— twenty.

6244. עָשֵׁשׁ **'âshêsh**, *aw-shaysh';* a prim. root; prob. to *shrink,* i.e. *fail:*— be consumed.

6245. עָשַׁת **'âshath**, *aw-shath';* a prim. root; prob. to *be sleek,* i.e. *glossy;* hence, (through the idea of *polishing*) to *excogitate* (as if *forming* in the mind):— shine, think.

6246. עֲשַׁת **'âshith** (Chald.), *ash-eeth';* corresp. to 6245; to *purpose:*— think.

6247. עֶשֶׁת **'esheth**, *eh'-sheth;* from 6245; a *fabric:*— bright.

6248. עַשְׁתּוּת **'ashtûwth**, *ash-tooth';* from 6245; *cogitation:*— thought.

6249. עַשְׁתֵּי **'ashtêy**, *ash-tay';* appar. masc. plur. constr. of 6247 in the sense of an *afterthought* (used only in connection with 6240 in lieu of 259) *eleven* or (ord.) *eleventh:*— + eleven (-th).

6250. עַשְׁתֹּנָה **'eshtônâh**, *esh-to-naw';* from 6245; *thinking:*— thought.

6251. עַשְׁתְּרָה **'asht^erâh**, *ash-ter-aw';* prob. from 6238; *increase:*— flock.

6252. עַשְׁתָּרוֹת **'Ashtârôwth**, *ash-taw-rôth';* or עַשְׁתָּרֹת **'Ashtârôth**, *ash-taw-rôth';* plur. of 6251; *Ashtaroth,* the name of a Sidonian deity, and of a place E. of the Jordan:— Ashtaroth, Astaroth. See also 1045, 6253, 6255.

6253. עַשְׁתֹּרֶת **'Ashtôreth**, *ash-to'reth;* prob. for 6251; *Ashtoreth,* the Phœnician goddess of love (and *increase*):— Ashtoreth.

6254. עַשְׁתְּרָתִי **'Asht^erâthiy**, *ash-ter-aw-thee';* patrial from 6252; an *Ashterathite* or inhab. of Ashtaroth:— Ashterathite.

6255. עַשְׁתְּרֹת קַרְנַיִם **'Asht^erôth Qarnayim**, *ash-ter-ôth' kar-nah'-yim;* from 6252 and the dual of 7161; *Ashtaroth of* (the) *double horns* (a symbol of the deity); *Ashteroth-Karnaïm,* a place E. of the Jordan:— Ashteroth Karnaim.

6256. עֵת **'êth**, *ayth;* from 5703; *time,* espec. (adv. with prep.) *now, when,* etc.:— + after, lal-lways, × certain, + continually, + evening, long, (due) season, so llongl as, leven-, evening-, noon-l tide, (lmeal-l), what) time, when.

6257. עָתַד **'âthad**, *aw-thad';* a prim. root; to *prepare:*— make fit, be ready to become.

עָתֻד **'attûd**. See 6260.

6258. עַתָּה **'attâh**, *at-taw';* from 6256; at

this time, whether adv., conjunc. or expletive:— henceforth, now, straightway, this time, whereas.

6259. עָתוּד **'âthûwd**, *aw-thood';* pass. part. of 6257; *prepared:*— ready.

6260. עָתוּד **'attûwd**, *at-tood';* or עָתֻד **'attûd**, *at-tood';* from 6257; *prepared,* i.e. *full grown;* spoken only (in plur.) of *he-goats,* or (fig.) *leaders* of the people:— chief one, (he) goat, ram.

6261. עִתִּי **'ittiy**, *it-tee';* from 6256; *timely:*— fit.

6262. עַתַּי **'Attay**, *at-tah'ee;* for 6261; *Attai,* the name of three Isr.:— Attai.

6263. עֲתִיד **'âthîyd** (Chald.), *ath-eed';* corresp. to 6264; *prepared:*— ready.

6264. עָתִיד **'âthîyd**, *aw-theed';* from 6257; *prepared;* by impl. *skilful;* fem. plur. the *future;* also *treasure:*— things that shall come, ready, treasures.

6265. עֲתָיָה **'Âthâyâh**, *ath-aw-yaw';* from 5790 and 3050; *Jah has helped;* Athajah, an Isr.:— Athaiah.

6266. עָתִיק **'âthîyq**, *aw-theek';* from 6275; prop. *antique,* i.e. *venerable* or *splendid:*— durable.

6267. עַתִּיק **'attîyq**, *at-teek';* from 6275; *removed,* i.e. *weaned;* also *antique:*— ancient, drawn.

6268. עַתִּיק **'attîyq** (Chald.), *at-teek';* corresp. to 6267; *venerable:*— ancient.

6269. עֲתָךְ **'Âthâk**, *ath-awk';* from an unused root mean. to *sojourn; lodging; Athak,* a place in Pal.:— Athach.

6270. עַתְלַי **'Athlay**, *ath-lah'ee;* from an unused root mean. to *compress; constringent; Athlai,* an Isr.:— Athlai.

6271. עֲתַלְיָה **'Âthalyâh**, *ath-al-yaw';* or עֲתַלְיָהוּ **'Âthalyâhûw**, *ath-al-yaw'-hoo;* from the same as 6270 and 3050; *Jah has constrained; Athaljah,* the name of an Israelitess and two Isr.:— Athaliah.

6272. עָתַם **'âtham**, *aw-tham';* a prim. root; prob. to *glow,* i.e. (fig.) *be desolated:*— be darkened.

6273. עָתְנִי **'Otniy**, *oth-nee';* from an unused root mean. to *force; forcible; Othni,* an Isr.:— Othni.

6274. עָתְנִיאֵל **'Othniy'êl**, *oth-nee-ale';* from the same as 6273 and 410; *force of God; Othniël,* an Isr.:— Othniel.

6275. עָתַק **'âthaq**, *aw-thak';* a prim. root; to *remove* (intr. or tran.) fig. to *grow old;* spec. to *transcribe:*— copy out, leave off, become (wax) old, remove.

6276. עָתֵק **'âthêq**, *aw-thake';* from 6275; *antique,* i.e. *valued:*— durable.

6277. עָתָק **'âthâq**, *aw-thawk';* from 6275 in the sense of *license; impudent:*— arrogancy, grievous (hard) things, stiff.

6278. עֵת קָצִין **'Êth Qâtsîyn**, *ayth kaw-tseen';* from 6256 and 7011; *time of a judge; Eth-Katsin,* a place in Pal.:— Ittah-kazin [by incl. directive encliticl.

6279. עָתַר **'âthar**, *aw-thar';* a prim. root lrather denom. from 6281l; to *burn incense* in worship, i.e. *intercede* (recip. *listen* to prayer):— intreat, (make) pray (-er).

6280. עָתַר **'âthar**, *aw-thar';* a prim. root; to *be* (caus. *make*) *abundant:*— deceitful, multiply.

6281. עֶתֶר **'Ether**, *eh'ther;* from 6280; *abundance; Ether,* a place in Pal.:— Ether.

6282. עָתָר **'âthâr**, *aw-thawr';* from 6280; *incense* (as increasing to a *volume* of smoke); hence, (from 6279) a *worshipper:*— suppliant, thick.

6283. עֲתֶרֶת **'âthereth**, *ath-eh'-reth;* from 6280; *copiousness:*— abundance.

פ

פֹּא **pô'**. See 6311.

6284. פָּאָה **pâ'âh**, *paw-aw';* a prim. root; to *puff,* i.e. *blow* away:— scatter into corners.

6285. פֵּאָה **pê'âh**, *pay-aw';* fem. of 6311; prop. *mouth* in a fig. sense, i.e. *direction, region, extremity:*— corner, end, quarter, side.

6286. פָּאַר **pâ'ar**, *paw-ar';* a prim. root; to *gleam,* i.e. (caus.) *embellish;* fig. to *boast;* also to *explain* (i.e. make clear) oneself; denom. from 6288, to *shake* a *tree:*— beautify, boast self, go over the boughs, glorify (self), glory, vaunt self.

6287. פְּאֵר **p^e'êr**, *peh-ayr';* from 6286; an *embellishment,* i.e. fancy *head-dress:*— beauty, bonnet, goodly, ornament, tire.

6288. פְּאֹרָה **p^e'ôrâh**, *peh-o-raw';* or פֹּארָה **pô'râ'h**, *po-raw';* or פֻּרָה **pu'râh**, *poo-raw';* from 6286; prop. *ornamentation,* i.e. (plur.) *foliage* (incl. the limbs) as *bright green:*— bough, branch, sprig.

6289. פָּארוּר **pâ'rûwr**, *paw-roor';* from 6286; prop. *illuminated,* i.e. a *glow;* as noun, a *flush* (of anxiety):— blackness.

6290. פָּארָן **Pâ'rân**, *paw-rawn';* from 6286; *ornamental; Paran,* a desert of Arabia:— Paran.

6291. פַּג **pag**, *pag;* from an unused root mean. to *be torpid,* i.e. *crude;* an *unripe* fig:— green fig.

6292. פִּגּוּל **piggûwl**, *pig-gool';* or פִּגֻּל **piggûl**, *pig-gool';* from an unused root mean. to *stink;* prop. *fetid,* i.e. (fig.) *unclean* (ceremonially):— abominable (-tion, thing).

6293. פָּגַע **pâga'**, *paw-gah';* a prim. root; to *impinge,* by accident or violence, or (fig.) by *importunity:*— come (betwixt), cause to entreat, fall (upon), make intercession, -intercessor, intreat, lay, light lupon, meet (together), pray, reach, run.

6294. פֶּגַע **pega'**, *peh'-gah;* from 6293; *impact* (casual):— chance, occurrent.

6295. פַּגְעִיאֵל **Pag'îy'êl**, *pag-ee-ale';* from 6294 and 410; *accident of God; Pagiël,* an Isr.:— Pagiel.

6296. פָּגַר **pâgar**, *paw-gar';* a prim. root; to *relax,* i.e. *become exhausted:*— be faint.

6297. פֶּגֶר **peger**, *peh'gher;* from 6296; a *carcase* (as *limp*), whether of man or beast; fig. an idolatrous *image:*— carcase (carcass), corpse, dead body.

6298. פָּגַשׁ **pâgash**, *paw-gash';* a prim.

Hebrew

root; to *come in contact with*, whether by accident or violence; fig. to *concur*:— meet (with, together).

6299. פָּדָה **pâdâh**, *paw-daw´*; a prim. root; to *sever*, i.e. *ransom*; gen. to *release, preserve*:— × at all, deliver, × by any means, ransom, (that are to be, let be) redeem (-ed), rescue, × surely.

6300. פְּדַהְאֵל **Pᵉdah'êl**, *ped-ah-ale´*; from 6299 and 410; *God has ransomed; Pedahel*, an Isr.:— Pedahel.

6301. פְּדָהצוּר **Pᵉdâhtsûwr**, *ped-aw-tsoor´*; from 6299 and 6697; a *rock* (i.e. God) *has ransomed; Pedahzur*, an Isr.:— Pedahzur.

6302. פָּדוּי **pâdûwy**, *paw-doo´-ee*; pass. part. of 6299; *ransomed* (and so occurring under 6299); as abstr. (in plur. masc.) a *ransom*:— (that are) to be (that were) redeemed.

6303. פָּדוֹן **Pâdôwn**, *paw-done´*; from 6299; *ransom; Padon*, one of the Nethinim:— Padon.

6304. פְּדוּת **pᵉdûwth**; or

פְּדֻת **pᵉdûth**, *ped-ooth´*; from 6929; *distinction*; also *deliverance*:— division, redeem, redemption.

6305. פְּדָיָה **Pᵉdâyâh**, *ped-aw-yaw´*; or

פְּדָיָהוּ **Pᵉdâyâhûw**, *ped-aw-yaw´-hoo*; from 6299 and 3050; *Jah has ransomed; Pedajah*, the name of six Isr.:— Pedaiah.

6306. פִּדְיוֹם **pidyôwm**, *pid-yome´*; or

פִּדְיֹם **pidyôm**, *pid-yome´*; also

פִּדְיוֹן **pidyôwn**, *pid-yone´*; or

פִּדְיֹן **pidyôn**, *pid-yone´*; from 6299; a *ransom*:— ransom, that were redeemed, redemption.

6307. פַּדָּן **Paddân**, *pad-dawn´*; from an unused root mean. to *extend*; a *plateau*; or

פַּדַּן אֲרָם **Paddan 'Ărâm**, *pad-dan´ ar-awm´*; from the same and 758; the *table-land* of *Aram; Paddan* or *Paddan-Aram*, a region of Syria:— Padan, Padan-aram.

6308. פָּדַע **pâda'**, *paw-dah´*; a prim. root; to *retrieve*:— deliver.

6309. פֶּדֶר **peder**, *peh´der*; from an unused root mean. to be *greasy; suet*:— fat.

6304a. פְּדֻת **pᵉdûth**. See 6304.

6310. פֶּה **peh**, *peh*; from 6284; the *mouth* (as the means of *blowing*), whether lit. or fig. (particularly *speech*); spec. *edge, portion* or *side*; adv. (with prep.) *according to*:— accord (-ing as, -ing to), after, appointment, assent, collar, command (-ment), × eat, edge, end, entry, + file, hole, × in, mind, mouth, part, portion, × (should) say (-ing), sentence, skirt, sound, speech, × spoken, talk, tenor, × to, + two-edged, wish, word.

6311. פֹּה **pôh**, *po*; or

פֹּא **pô'** (Job 38:11), *po*; or

פּוֹ **pôw**, *po*; prob. from a prim. inseparable particle פ **p** (of demonstr. force) and 1931; *this place* (French *ici*), i.e. *here* or *hence*:— here, hither, the one (other, this, that) side.

פּוֹא **pôw'**. See 375.

6312. פּוּאָה **Pûw'âh**, *poo-aw´* or

פֻּוָּה **Puvvâh**, *poov-vaw´*; from 6284; a *blast; Puâh* or *Puvvah*, the name of two Isr.:— Phuvah, Pua, Puah.

6313. פּוּג **pûwg**, *poog*; a prim. root; to *be sluggish*:— cease, be feeble, faint, be slacked.

6314. פּוּגָה **pûwgâh**, *poo-gaw´*; from 6313; *intermission*:— rest.

6315a. פֻּוָּה **Puvvâh**. See 6312.

6315. פּוּחַ **pûwach**, *poo´akh*; a prim. root; to *puff*, i.e. blow with the breath or air; hence, to *fan* (as a breeze), i.e. to *utter*, to *kindle* (a fire), to *scoff*:— blow (upon), break, puff, bring into a snare, speak, utter.

6316. פּוּט **Pûwṭ**, *poot*; of for. or.; *Put*, a son of Ham, also the name of his desc. or their region, and of a Pers. tribe:— Phut, Put.

6317. פּוּטִיאֵל **Pûwṭiy'êl**, *poo-tee-ale´*; from an unused root (prob. mean. to *disparage*) and 410; *contempt of God; Putiël*, an Isr.:— Putiel.

6318. פּוֹטִיפַר **Pôwṭiyphar**, *po-tee-far´*; of Eg. der.; *Potiphar*, an Eg.:— Potiphar.

6319. פּוֹטִי פֶרַע **Pôwṭiy Phera'**, *po-tee feh´-rah*; of Eg. der.; *Poti-Phera*, an Eg.:— Poti-pherah.

6320. פּוּךְ **pûwk**, *pook*; from an unused root mean. to *paint; dye* (spec. *stibium* for the eyes):— fair colours, glistering, paint (-ed) (-ing).

6321. פּוֹל **pôwl**, *pole*; from an unused root mean. to be *thick*; a *bean* (as *plump*):— beans.

6322. פּוּל **Pûwl**, *pool*; of for. or.; *Pul*, the name of an Ass. king and of an Ethiopian tribe:— Pul.

6323. פּוּן **pûwn**, *poon*; a prim. root mean. to *turn*, i.e. be *perplexed*:— be distracted.

6324. פּוּנִי **Pûwniy**, *poo-nee´*; patron. from an unused name mean. a *turn*; a *Punite* (collect.) or desc. of an unknown Pun:— Punites.

6325. פּוּנֹן **Pûwnôn**, *poo-none´*; from 6323; *perplexity; Punon*, a place in the Desert:— Punon.

6326. פּוּעָה **Pûw'âh**, *poo-aw´*; from an unused root mean. to *glitter; brilliancy; Puäh*, an Israelitess:— Puah.

6327. פּוּץ **pûwts**, *poots*; a prim. root; to *dash* in pieces, lit. or fig. (espec. to *disperse*):— break (dash, shake) in (to) pieces, cast (abroad), disperse (selves), drive, retire, scatter (abroad), spread abroad.

6328. פּוּק **pûwq**, *pook*; a prim. root; to *waver*:— stumble, move.

6329. פּוּק **pûwq**, *pook*; a prim. root [rather ident. with 6328 through the idea of *dropping* out; comp. 5312]; to *issue*, i.e. *furnish*; caus. to *secure*; fig. to *succeed*:— afford, draw out, further, get, obtain.

6330. פּוּקָה **pûwqâh**, *poo-kaw´*; from 6328; a *stumbling-block*:— grief.

6331. פּוּר **pûwr**, *poor*; a prim. root; to *crush*:— break, bring to nought, × utterly take.

6332. פּוּר **Pûwr**, *poor*; also (plur.)

פּוּרִים **Pûwriym**, *poo-reem´*; or

פֻּרִים **Pûriym**, *poo-reem´*; from 6331; a *lot* (as by means of a *broken* piece):— Pur, Purim.

6333. פּוּרָה **pûwrâh**, *poo-raw´*; from 6331; a *wine-press* (as *crushing* the grapes):— winepress.

6334. פּוֹרָתָא **Pôwrâthâ'**, *po-raw-thaw´*; of Pers. or.; *Poratha*, a son of Haman:— Poratha.

6335. פּוּשׁ **pûwsh**, *poosh*; a prim. root; to *spread*; fig. *act proudly*:— grow up, be grown fat, spread selves, be scattered.

6336. פּוּתִי **Pûwthiy**, *poo-thee´*; patron. from an unused name mean. a *hinge*; a *Puthite* (collect.) or desc. of an unknown Puth:— Puhites [as if from 6312].

6337. פָּז **pâz**, *pawz*; from 6338; *pure* (gold); hence, *gold* itself (as refined):— fine (pure) gold.

6338. פָּזַז **pâzaz**, *paw-zaz´*; a prim. root; to *refine* (gold):— best [gold].

6339. פָּזַז **pâzaz**, *paw-zaz´*; a prim. root [rather ident. with 6338]; to *solidify* (as if by *refining*); also to *spring* (as if *separating* the limbs):— leap, be made strong.

6340. פָּזַר **pâzar**, *paw-zar´*; a prim. root; to *scatter*, whether in enmity or bounty:— disperse, scatter (abroad).

6341. פַּח **pach**, *pakh*; from 6351; a (metallic) *sheet* (as *pounded* thin); also a spring *net* (as spread out like a *lamina*):— gin, (thin) plate, snare.

6342. פָּחַד **pâchad**, *paw-khad´*; a prim. root; to *be startled* (by a sudden alarm); hence, to *fear* in general:— be afraid, stand in awe, (be in) fear, make to shake.

6343. פַּחַד **pachad**, *pakh´-ad*; from 6342; a (sudden) *alarm* (prop. the object feared, by impl. the feeling):— dread (-ful), fear, (thing) great [fear, -ly feared], terror.

6344. פַּחַד **pachad**, *pakh´-ad*; the same as 6343; a *testicle* (as a cause of *shame* akin to fear):— stone.

6345. פַּחְדָּה **pachdâh**, *pakh-daw´*; fem. of 6343; *alarm* (i.e. *awe*):— fear.

6346. פֶּחָה **pechâh**, *peh-khaw´*; of for. or.; a *prefect* (of a city or small district):— captain, deputy, governor.

6347. פֶּחָה **pechâh** (Chald.), *peh-khaw´*; corresp. to 6346:— captain, governor.

6348. פָּחַז **pâchaz**, *paw-khaz´*; a prim. root; to *bubble up* or *froth* (as boiling water), i.e. (fig.) to be *unimportant*:— light.

6349. פַּחַז **pachaz**, *pakh´-az*; from 6348; *ebullition*, i.e. froth (fig. lust):— unstable.

6350. פַּחֲזוּת **pachăzûwth**, *pakh-az-ooth´*; from 6348; *frivolity*:— lightness.

6351. פָּחַח **pâchach**, *paw-khakh´*; a prim. root; to *batter* out; but used only as denom. from 6341, to *spread a net*:— be snared.

6352. פֶּחָם **pechâm**, *peh-khawm´*; perh.

from an unused root prob. mean. to *be black*; a *coal*, whether charred or live:— coals.

6353. פְּחָר **pechâr** (Chald.), *peh-khawr´*; from an unused root prob. mean. to *fashion*; a *potter*:— potter.

6354. פָּחַת **pachath**, *pakh´-ath*; prob. from an unused root appar. mean. to *dig*; a *pit*, espec. for catching animals:— hole, pit, snare.

6355. פַּחַת מוֹאָב **Pachath Môw'âb**, *pakh´-ath mo-awb´*; from 6354 and 4124; *pit of Moäb*; Pachath-Moäb, an Isr.:— Pahath-moab.

6356. פֶּחֶתֶת **pechetheth**, *pekh-eh´-theth*; from the same as 6354; a *hole* (by mildew in a garment):— fret inward.

6357. פִּטְדָה **pitdâh**, *pit-daw´*; of for. der.; a *gem*, prob. the *topaz*:— topaz.

6358. פָּטוּר **pâṭûwr**, *paw-toor´*; pass. part. of 6362; *opened*, i.e. (as noun) a *bud*:— open.

6359. פָּטִיר **pâṭîyr**, *paw-teer´*; from 6362; *open*, i.e. *unoccupied*:— free.

6360. פַּטִּישׁ **paṭṭîysh**, *pat-teesh´*; intens. from an unused root mean. to *pound*; a *hammer*:— hammer.

6361. פַּטִּישׁ **paṭṭîysh** (Chald.), *pat-teesh´*; from a root corresp. to that of 6360; a *gown* (as if *hammered* out wide):— hose.

6362. פָּטַר **pâṭar**, *paw-tar´*; a prim. root; to *cleave* or burst through, i.e. (caus.) to *emit*, whether lit. or fig. (*gape*):— dismiss, free, let (shoot) out, slip away.

6363. פֶּטֶר **peṭer**, *peh´-ter*; or

פִּטְרָה **pitrâh**, *pit-raw´*; from 6362; a *fissure*, i.e. (concr.) *firstling* (as *opening* the matrix):— firstling, openeth, such as open.

6364. פִּי־בֶסֶת **Pîy-Beçeth**, *pee beh´-seth*; of Eg. or.; *Pi-Beseth*, a place in Egypt:— Pi-beseth.

6365. פִּיד **pîyd**, *peed*; from an unused root prob. mean. to *pierce*; (fig.) *misfortune*:— destruction, ruin.

6366. פֵּיָה **pêyâh**, *pay-aw´*; or

פִּיָּה **pîyâh**, *pee-yaw´*; fem. of 6310; an *edge*:— (two-) edge (-d).

6367. פִּי הַחִירֹת **Piy ha-Chîrôth**, *pee hah-khee-rôth´*; from 6310 and the fem. plur. of a noun (from the same root as 2356), with the art. interpolated; *mouth of the gorges*; Pi-ha-Chiroth, a place in Egypt:— Pi-hahiroth. [In Num. 14:19 without Pi-.]

6368. פִּיחַ **pîyach**, *pee´-akh*; from 6315; a *powder* (as easily *puffed* away), i.e. *ashes* or *dust*:— ashes.

6369. פִּיכֹל **Pîykôl**, *pee-kole´*; appar. from 6310 and 3605; *mouth of all*; Picol, a Philistine:— Phichol.

6370. פִּילֶגֶשׁ **pîylegesh**, *pee-leh´-ghesh*; or

פִּלֶגֶשׁ **pîlegesh**, *pee-leh´-ghesh*; of uncert. der.; a *concubine*; also (masc.) a *paramour*:— concubine, paramour.

6371. פִּימָה **pîymâh**, *pee-maw´*; prob. from an unused root mean. to *be plump*; *obesity*:— collops.

6372. פִּינְחָס **Pîynechâç**, *pee-nekh-aws´*;

appar. from 6310 and a var. of 5175; *mouth of a serpent*; Pinechas, the name of three Isr.:— Phinehas.

6373. פִּינֹן **Pîynôn**, *pee-none´*; prob. the same as 6325; Pinon, an Idumæan:— Pinon.

6374. פִּיפִיָּה **pîyphîyâh**, *pee-fee-yaw´*; for 6366; an *edge* or *tooth*:— tooth, × two-edged.

6375. פִּיק **pîyq**, *peek*; from 6329; a *tottering*:— smite together.

6376. פִּישׁוֹן **Pîyshôwn**, *pee-shone´*; from 6335; *dispersive*; Pishon, a river of Eden:— Pison.

6377. פִּיתוֹן **Pîythôwn**, *pee-thone´*; prob. from the same as 6596; *expansive*; Pithon, an Isr.:— Pithon.

6378. פַּךְ **pak**, *pak*; from 6379; a *flask* (from which a liquid may *flow*):— box, vial.

6379. פָּכָה **pâkâh**, *paw-kaw´*; a prim. root; to *pour*:— run out.

6380. פֹּכֶרֶת צְבָיִים **Pôkereth Tsᵉbâyîym**, *po-keh´-reth tseb-aw-yeem´*; from the act. part. (of the same form as the first word) fem. of an unused root (mean. to *entrap*) and plur. of 6643; *trap of gazelles*; Pokereth-Tsebajim, one of the "servants of Solomon":— Pochereth of Zebaim.

6381. פָּלָא **pâlâ'**, *paw-law´*; a prim. root; prop. perh. to *separate*, i.e. *distinguish* (lit. or fig.); by impl. to *be* (caus. *make*) *great*, *difficult*, *wonderful*:— accomplish, (arise ... too, be too) hard, hidden, things too high, (be, do, do a, shew) marvelous (-ly, -els, things, work), miracles, perform, separate, make singular, (be, great, make) wonderful (-ers, -ly, things, works), wondrous (things, works, -ly).

6382. פֶּלֶא **pele'**, *peh´-leh*; from 6381; a *miracle*:— marvellous thing, wonder (-ful, -fully).

6383. פִּלְאִי **pil'îy**, *pil-ee´*; or

פָּלִיא **pâlîy'**, *paw-lee´*; from 6381; *remarkable*:— secret, wonderful.

6384. פַּלֻּאִי **Pallû'îy**, *pal-loo-ee´*; patron. from 6396; a *Palluïte* (collect.) or desc. of Pallu:— Palluites.

פְּלָאיָה **Pᵉlâ'yâh**. See 6411.

פִּלְאֶצֶר **Pil'eçer**. See 8407.

6385. פָּלַג **pâlag**, *paw-lag´*; a prim. root; to *split* (lit. or fig.):— divide.

6386. פְּלַג **pᵉlag** (Chald.), *pel-ag´*; corresp. to 6385:— divided.

6387. פְּלַג **pᵉlag** (Chald.), *pel-ag´*; from 6386; a *half*:— dividing.

6388. פֶּלֶג **peleg**, *peh´-leg*; from 6385; a *rill* (i.e. small *channel* of water, as in irrigation):— river, stream.

6389. פֶּלֶג **Peleg**, *peh´-leg*; the same as 6388; *earthquake*; Peleg, a son of Shem:— Peleg.

6390. פְּלַגָּה **pᵉlaggâh**, *pel-ag-gaw´*; from 6385; a *runlet*, i.e. *gully*:— division, river.

6391. פְּלֻגָּה **pᵉluggâh**, *pel-oog-gaw´*; from 6385; a *section*:— division.

6392. פְּלֻגָּה **pᵉluggâh** (Chald.), *pel-oog-gaw´*; corresp. to 6391:— division.

פִּלֶגֶשׁ **pîlegesh**. See 6370.

6393. פְּלָדָה **pᵉlâdâh**, *pel-aw-daw´*; from an unused root mean. to *divide*; a *cleaver*, i.e. iron *armature* (of a chariot):— torch.

6394. פִּלְדָּשׁ **Pildâsh**, *pil-dawsh´*; of uncert. der.; *Pildash*, a relative of Abraham:— Pildash.

6395. פָּלָה **pâlâh**, *paw-law´*; a prim. root; to *distinguish* (lit. or fig.):— put a difference, show marvellous, separate, set apart, sever, make wonderfully.

6396. פַּלּוּא **Pallû'**, *pal-loo´*; from 6395; *distinguished*; Pallu, an Isr.:— Pallu, Phallu.

6397. פְּלוֹנִי **Pᵉlôwnîy**, *pel-o-nee´*; patron. from an unused name (from 6395) mean. *separate*; a *Pelonite* or inhab. of an unknown Palon:— Pelonite.

6398. פָּלַח **pâlach**, *paw-lakh´*; a prim. root; to *slice*, i.e. *break* open or *pierce*:— bring forth, cleave, cut, shred, strike through.

6399. פְּלַח **pᵉlach** (Chald.), *pel-akh´*; corresp. to 6398; to *serve* or *worship*:— minister, serve.

6400. פֶּלַח **pelach**, *peh´-lakh*; from 6398; a *slice*:— piece.

6401. פִּלְחָא **Pilchâ'**, *pil-khaw´*; from 6400; *slicing*; Pilcha, an Isr.:— Pilcha.

6402. פָּלְחָן **polchân** (Chald.), *pol-khawn´*; from 6399; *worship*:— service.

6403. פָּלַט **pâlaṭ**, *paw-lat´*; a prim. root; to *slip* out, i.e. *escape*; caus. to *deliver*:— calve, carry away safe, deliver, (cause to) escape.

6404. פֶּלֶט **Peleṭ**, *peh´-let*; from 6403; *escape*; Pelet, the name of two Isr.:— Pelet. See also 1046.

פָּלֵט **pâlêṭ**. See 6412.

6405. פַּלֵּט **palleṭ**, *pal-late´*; from 6403; *escape*:— deliverance, escape.

פְּלֵטָה **pᵉlêṭâh**. See 6413.

6406. פֶּלֶט **Palṭîy**, *pal-tee´*; from 6403; *delivered*; Palti, the name of two Isr.:— Palti, Phalti.

6407. פַּלְטִי **Palṭîy**, *pal-tee´*; patron. from 6406; a *Paltite* or desc. of Palti:— Paltite.

6408. פִּלְטַי **Pilṭay**, *pil-tah´-ee*; for 6407; *Piltai*, an Isr.:— Piltai.

6409. פַּלְטִיאֵל **Palṭîy'êl**, *pal-tee-ale´*; from the same as 6404 and 410; *deliverance of God*; Paltiël, the name of two Isr.:— Paltiel, Phaltiel.

6410. פְּלַטְיָה **Pᵉlaṭyâh**, *pel-at-yaw´*; or

פְּלַטְיָהוּ **Pᵉlaṭyâhûw**, *pel-at-yaw´-hoo*; from 6403 and 3050; *Jah has delivered*; Pelatjah, the name of four Isr.:— Pelatiah.

פָּלִיא **pâlîy'**. See 6383.

6411. פְּלָיָה **Pᵉlâyâh**, *pel-aw-yaw´*; or

פְּלָאיָה **Pᵉlâ'yâh**, *pel-aw-yaw´*; from 6381 and 3050; *Jah has distinguished*; Pelajah, the name of three Isr.:— Pelaiah.

6412. פָּלִיט **pâlîyṭ**, *paw-leet´*; or

פָּלֵיט **pâlêyṭ**, *paw-late´*; or

פָּלֵט **pâlêṭ**, *paw-late´*; from 6403; a

Hebrew

refugee:— (that have) escape (-d, -th), fugitive.

6413. פְּלֵיטָה **p^elêytâh**, *pel-ay-taw'*; or

פְּלֵטָה **p^elêtâh**, *pel-ay-taw'*; fem. of 6412; *deliverance*; concr. an *escaped* portion:— deliverance, (that is) escape (-d), remnant.

6414. פָּלִיל **pâlîyl**, *paw-leel'*; from 6419; a *magistrate*:— judge.

6415. פְּלִילָה **p^elîylâh**, *pel-ee-law'*; fem. of 6414; *justice*:— judgment.

6416. פְּלִילִי **p^elîylîy**, *pel-ee-lee'*; from 6414; *judicial*:— judge.

6417. פְּלִילִיָּה **p^elîylîyâh**, *pel-ee-lee-yaw'*; fem. of 6416; *judicature*:— judgment.

6418. פֶּלֶךְ **pelek**, *peh'-lek*; from an unused root mean. to *be round*; a *circuit* (i.e. *district*); also a *spindle* (as *whirled*); hence, a *crutch*:— (di-) staff, part.

6419. פָּלַל **pâlal**, *paw-lal'*; a prim. root; to *judge* (officially or mentally); by extens. to *intercede, pray*:— intreat, judge (-ment), (make) pray (-er, -ing), make supplication.

6420. פָּלָל **Pâlâl**, *paw-lawl'*; from 6419; *judge; Palal*, an Isr.:— Palal.

6421. פְּלַלְיָה **P^elalyâh**, *pel-al-yaw'*; from 6419 and 3050; *Jah has judged; Pelaljah*, an Isr.:— Pelaliah.

6422. פַּלְמוֹנִי **palmôwnîy**, *pal-mo-nee'*; prob. for 6423; a *certain* one, i.e. *so-and-so*:— certain.

פְּלֹאשֵׁר **Piln^eeçer**. See 8407.

6423. פְּלֹנִי **p^elônîy**, *pel-o-nee'*; from 6395; *such* a one, i.e. a specified *person*:— such.

פִּלְנֶצֶר **Pilneçer**. See 8407.

6424. פָּלַס **pâlaç**, *paw-las'*; a prim. root; prop. to *roll* flat, i.e. *prepare* (a road); also to *revolve*, i.e. *weigh* (mentally):— make, ponder, weigh.

6425. פֶּלֶס **peleç**, *peh'-les*; from 6424; a *balance*:— scales, weight.

פְּלֶצֶר **P^eleçer**. See 8407.

6426. פָּלַץ **pâlats**, *paw-lats'*; a prim. root; prop. perh. to *rend*, i.e. (by impl.) to *quiver*:— tremble.

6427. פַּלָּצוּת **pallâtsûwth**, *pal-law-tsooth'*; from 6426; *affright*:— fearfulness, horror, trembling.

6428. פָּלַשׁ **pâlash**, *paw-lash'*; a prim. root; to *roll* (in dust):— roll (wallow) self.

6429. פְּלֶשֶׁת **P^elesheth**, *pel-eh'-sheth*; from 6428; *rolling*, i.e. *migratory; Pelesheth*, a region of Syria:— Palestina, Palestine, Philistia, Philistines.

6430. פְּלִשְׁתִּי **P^elishtîy**, *pel-ish-tee'*; patrial from 6429; a *Pelishtite* or inhab. of Pelesheth:— Philistine.

6431. פֶּלֶת **Peleth**, *peh'-leth*; from an unused root mean. to *flee; swiftness; Peleth*, the name of two Isr.:— Peleth.

6432. פְּלֵתִי **P^elêthîy**, *pel-ay-thee'*; from the same form as 6431; a *courier* (collect.) or official *messenger*:— Pelethites.

6433. פֻּם **pùm** (Chald.), *poom*; prob. for 6310; the *mouth* (lit. or fig.):— mouth.

6434. פֵּן **pên**, *pane*; from an unused

root mean. to *turn*; an *angle* (of a street or wall):— corner.

6435. פֶּן **pên**, *pane*; from 6437; prop. *removal*; used only (in the constr.) adv. as conjunc. *lest*:— (lest) (peradventure), that ... not.

6436. פַּנַּג **Pannag**, *pan-nag'*; of uncert. der.; prob. *pastry*:— Pannag.

6437. פָּנָה **pânâh**, *paw-naw'*; a prim. root; to *turn*; by impl. to *face*, i.e. *appear, look*, etc.:— appear, at [even-] tide, behold, cast out, come on, × corner, dawning, empty, go away, lie, look, mark, pass away, prepare, regard, (have) respect (to), (re-) turn (aside, away, back, face, self), × right [early].

פָּנֶה **pâneh**. See 6440.

6438. פִּנָּה **pinnâh**, *pin-naw'*; fem. of 6434; an *angle*; by impl. a *pinnacle*; fig. a *chieftain*:— bulwark, chief, corner, stay, tower.

6439. פְּנוּאֵל **P^enûw'êl**, *pen-oo-ale'*; or (more prop.)

פְּנִיאֵל **P^enîy'êl**, *pen-ee-ale'*; from 6437 and 410; *face of God; Penuël* or *Peniël*, a place E. of Jordan; also (as Penuel) the name of two Isr.:— Peniel, Penuel.

פְּנִי **pânîy**. See 6443.

6440. פָּנִים **pânîym**, *paw-neem'*; plur. (but always as sing.) of an unused noun

[פָּנֶה **pâneh**, *paw-neh'*; from 6437]; the *face* (as the part that *turns*); used in a great variety of applications (lit. and fig.); also (with prep. pref.) as a prep. (*before*, etc.):— + accept, a-(be-)fore (-time), against, anger, × as (long as), at, + battle, + because (of), + beseech, countenance, edge, + employ, endure, + enquire, face, favour, fear of, for, forefront (-part), form (-er time, -ward), from, front, heaviness, × him (-self), + honourable, + impudent, + in, it, look [-eth] (-s), × me, + meet, × more than, mouth, of, off, (of) old (time), × on, open, + out of, over against, the partial, person, + please, presence, propect, was purposed, by reason, of, + regard, right forth, + serve, × shewbread, sight, state, straight, + street, × thee, × them (-selves), through (+ -out), till, time (-s) past, (un-) to (-ward), + upon, upside (+ down), with (+ -in, + -stand), × ye, × you.

6441. פְּנִימָה **p^enîymâh**, *pen-ee'-maw*; from 6440 with directive enclitic; *faceward*, i.e. *indoors*:— (with-) in (-ner part, -ward).

6442. פְּנִימִי **p^enîymîy**, *pen-ee-mee'*; from 6440; *interior*:— (with-) in (-ner, -ward).

6443. פָּנִין **pânîyn**, *paw-neen'*; or

פְּנִי **pânîy**, *paw-nee'*; from the same as 6434; prob. a *pearl* (as *round*):— ruby.

6444. פְּנִנָּה **P^eninnâh**, *pen-in-naw'*; prob. fem. from 6443 contr.; *Peninnah*, an Israelitess:— Peninnah.

6445. פָּנַק **pânaq**, *paw-nak'*; a prim. root; to *enervate*:— bring up.

6446. פַּס **paç**, *pas*; from 6461; prop. the *palm* (of the hand) or *sole* (of the foot) [comp. 6447]; by impl. (plur.) a *long and sleeved* tunic (perh. simply a *wide* one;

from the orig. sense of the root, i.e. of *many breadths*):— (divers) colours.

6447. פַּס **paç** (Chald.), *pas*; from a root corresp. to 6461; the *palm* (of the hand, as being *spread* out):— part.

6448. פָּסַג **pâçag**, *paw-sag'*; a prim. root; to *cut up*, i.e. (fig.) *contemplate*:— consider.

6449. פִּסְגָּה **Piçgâh**, *pis-gaw'*; from 6448; a *cleft; Pisgah*, a mountain E. of Jordan:— Pisgah.

6450. פַּס דַּמִּים **Paç Dammîym**, *pas dammeem'*; from 6446 and the plur. of 1818; *palm* (i.e. *dell*) *of bloodshed; Pas-Dammim*, a place in Pal.:— Pas-dammim. Comp. 658.

6451. פִּסָּה **piççâh**, *pis-saw'*; from 6461; *expansion*, i.e. *abundance*:— handful.

6452. פָּסַח **pâçach**, *paw-sakh'*; a prim. root; to *hop*, i.e. (fig.) *skip* over (or *spare*); by impl. to *hesitate*; also (lit.) to *limp*, to *dance*:— halt, become lame, leap, pass over.

6453. פֶּסַח **Peçach**, *peh'-sakh*; from 6452; a *pretermission*, i.e. *exemption*; used only tech. of the Jewish *Passover* (the festival or the victim):— passover (offering).

6454. פָּסֵחַ **Pâçêach**, *paw-say'-akh*; from 6452; *limping; Paseäch*, the name of two Isr.:— Paseah, Phaseah.

6455. פִּסֵּחַ **piççêach**, *pis-say'-akh*; from 6452; *lame*:— lame.

6456. פְּסִיל **p^eçîyl**, *pes-eel'*; from 6458; an *idol*:— carved (graven) image, quarry.

6457. פָּסַךְ **Pâçak**, *paw-sak'*; from an unused root mean. to *divide; divider; Pasak*, an Isr.:— Pasach.

6458. פָּסַל **pâçal**, *paw-sal'*; a prim. root; to *carve*, whether wood or stone:— grave, hew.

6459. פֶּסֶל **peçel**, *peh'-sel*; from 6458; an *idol*:— carved (graven) image.

6460. פְּסַנְטֵרִין **p^eçantêrîyn** (Chald.), *pesan-tay-reen'*; or

פְּסַנְתֵּרִין **p^eçantêrîyn**, *pes-an-tay-reen'*; a transliteration of the Gr. ψαλτήριον *psaltěriŏn*; a *lyre*:— psaltery.

6461. פָּסַס **pâçaç**, *paw-sas'*; a prim. root; prob. to *disperse*, i.e. (intr.) *disappear*:— cease.

6462. פִּסְפָּה **Piçpâh**, *pis-paw'*; perh. from 6461; *dispersion; Pispah*, an Isr.:— Pispah.

6463. פָּעָה **pâ'âh**, *paw-aw'*; a prim. root; to *scream*:— cry.

6464. פָּעוּ **Pâ'ûw**, *paw-oo'*; or

פָּעִי **Pâ'îy**, *paw-ee'*; from 6463; *screaming; Paü* or *Paï*, a place in Edom:— Pai, Pau.

6465. פְּעוֹר **P^e'ôwr**, *peh-ore'*; from 6473; a *gap; Peör*, a mountain E. of Jordan; also (for 1187) a deity worshipped there:— Peor. See also 1047.

פָּעִי **Pâ'îy**. See 6464.

6466. פָּעַל **pâ'al**, *paw-al'*; a prim. root; to *do* or *make* (systematically and habitually), espec. to *practise*:— commit, [evil-] do (-er), make (-r), ordain, work (-er), wrought.

6467. פֹּעַל **pô'al**, *po'-al*; from 6466; an

act or *work* (concr.):— act, deed, do, getting, maker, work.

6468. פְּעֻלָּה **pᵉˁullâh**, *peh-ool-law´*; fem. pass. part. of 6466; (abstr.) *work*:— labour, reward, wages, work.

6469. פְּעֻלְּתַי **Pᵉˁull'thay**, *peh-ool-leh-thah´-ee*; from 6468; *laborious*; *Peüllethai*, an Isr.:— Peulthai.

6470. פָּעַם **pâ'am**, *paw-am´*; a prim. root; to *tap*, i.e. *beat regularly*; hence, (gen.) to *impel* or *agitate*:— move, trouble.

6471. פַּעַם **pa'am**, *pah´-am*; or (fem.)

פַּעֲמָה **pa'ămâh**, *pah-am-aw´*; from 6470; a *stroke*, lit. or fig. (in various applications, as follow):— anvil, corner, foot (-step), going, [hundred-] fold, × now, (this) + once, order, rank, step, + thrice, (loften-l), second, this, two) time (-s), twice, wheel.

6472. פַּעֲמֹן **pa'ămôn**, *pah-am-one´*; from 6471; a *bell* (as *struck*):— bell.

6473. פָּעַר **pâ'ar**, *paw-ar´*; a prim. root; to *yawn*, i.e. *open* wide (lit. or fig.):— gape, open (wide).

6474. פְּעָרַי **Pa'ăray**, *pah-ar-ah´-ee*; from 6473; *yawning*; *Paarai*, an Isr.:— Paarai.

6475. פָּצָה **pâtsâh**, *paw-tsaw´*; a prim. root; to *rend*, i.e. *open* (espec. the mouth):— deliver, gape, open, rid, utter.

6476. פָּצַח **pâtsach**, *paw-tsakh´*; a prim. root; to *break* out (in joyful sound):— break (forth, forth into joy), make a loud noise.

6477. פְּצִירָה **pᵉtsiyrâh**, *pets-ee-raw´*; from 6484; *bluntness*:— + file.

6478. פָּצַל **pâtsal**, *paw-tsal´*; a prim. root; to *peel*:— pill.

6479. פְּצָלָה **pᵉtsâlâh**, *pets-aw-law´*; from 6478; a *peeling*:— strake.

6480. פָּצַם **pâtsam**, *paw-tsam´*; a prim. root; to *rend* (by earthquake):— break.

6481. פָּצַע **pâtsa'**, *paw-tsah´*; a prim. root; to *split*, i.e. *wound*:— wound.

6482. פֶּצַע **petsa'**, *peh´-tsah*; from 6481; a *wound*:— wound (-ing).

פְּצָצֵ֫ם **Patstsets**. See 1048.

6483. פִּצְצֵץ **Pitstsêts**, *pits-tsates´*; from an unused root mean. to *dissever*; *dispersive*; *Pitstsets*, a priest:— Apses [incl. *the art.*].

6484. פָּצַר **pâtsar**, *paw-tsar´*; a prim. root; to *peck at*, i.e. (fig.) *stun* or *dull*:— press, urge, stubbornness.

6485. פָּקַד **pâqad**, *paw-kad´*; a prim. root; to *visit* (with friendly or hostile intent); by anal. to *oversee, muster, charge, care for, miss, deposit*, etc.:— appoint, × at all, avenge, bestow, (appoint to have the, give a) charge, commit, count, deliver to keep, be empty, enjoin, go see, hurt, do judgment, lack, lay up, look, make, × by any means, miss, number, officer, (make) overseer, have (the) oversight, punish, reckon, (call to) remember (-brance), set (over), sum, × surely, visit, want.

פִּקֻּד **piqqûd**. See 6490.

6486. פְּקֻדָּה **pᵉquddâh**, *pek-ood-daw´*; fem. pass. part. of 6485; *visitation* (in

many senses, chiefly official):— account, (that have the) charge, custody, that which ... laid up, numbers, office (-r), ordering, oversight, + prison, reckoning, visitation.

6487. פִּקָּדוֹן **piqqâdôwn**, *pik-kaw-done´*; from 6485; a *deposit*:— that which was delivered (to keep), store.

6488. פְּקִדֻת **pᵉqiduth**, *pek-ee-dooth´*; from 6496; *supervision*:— ward.

6489. פְּקוֹד **Pᵉqôwd**, *pek-ode´*; from 6485; *punishment*; *Pekod*, a symbol. name for Bab.:— Pekod.

6490. פִּקּוּד **piqqûwd**, *pik-kood´*; or

פִּקֻּד **piqqûd**, *pik-kood´*; from 6485; prop. *appointed*, i.e. a *mandate* (of God; plur. only, collect. for the *Law*):— commandment, precept, statute.

6491. פָּקַח **pâqach**, *paw-kakh´*; a prim. root; to *open* (the senses, espec. the eyes); fig. to *be observant*:— open.

6492. פֶּקַח **Peqach**, *peh´-kakh*; from 6491; *watch*; *Pekach*, an Isr. king:— Pekah.

6493. פִּקֵּחַ **piqqêach**, *pik-kay´-akh*; from 6491; *clear-sighted*; fig. *intelligent*:— seeing, wise.

6494. פְּקַחְיָה **Pᵉqachyâh**, *pek-akh-yaw´*; from 6491 and 3050; *Jah has observed*; *Pekachjah*, an Isr. king:— Pekahiah.

6495. פְּקַח-קוֹחַ **pᵉqach-qôwach**, *pek-akh-ko´-akh*; from 6491 redoubled; *opening* (of a dungeon), i.e. *jail-delivery* (fig. *salvation* from sin):— opening of the prison.

6496. פָּקִיד **pâqîyd**, *paw-keed´*; from 6485; a *superintendent* (civil, military, or religious):— which had the charge, governor, office, overseer, [that] was set.

6497. פֶּקַע **peqa'**, *peh´-kah*; from an unused root mean. to *burst*; only used as an arch. term of an ornament similar to 6498, a *semi-globe*:— knop.

6498. פַּקֻּעָה **paqqu'âh**, *pak-koo-aw´*; from the same as 6497; the *wild cucumber* (from *splitting* open to shed its seeds):— gourd.

6499. פַּר **par**, *par*; or

פָּר **pâr**, *pawr*; from 6565; a *bullock* (appar. as *breaking* forth in wild strength, or perh. as *dividing* the hoof):— (+ young) bull (-ock), calf, ox.

6500. פָּרָא **pârâ'**, *paw-raw´*; a prim. root; to *bear fruit*:— be fruitful.

6501. פֶּרֶא **pere'**, *peh´-reh*; or

פֶּרֶה **pereh** (Jer. 2:24), *peh´-reh*; from 6500 in the second. sense of *running* wild; the *onager*:— wild (ass).

פֹּרָאה **pôrâ'h**. See 6288.

6502. פִּרְאָם **Pir'âm**, *pir-awm´*; from 6501; *wildly*; *Piram*, a Canaanite:— Piram.

6503. פַּרְבָּר **Parbâr**, *par-bawr´*; or

פַּרְוָר **Parvâr**, *par-vawr´*; of for. or.; *Parbar* or *Parvar*, a quarter of Jerusalem:— Parbar, suburb.

6504. פָּרַד **pârad**, *paw-rad´*; a prim. root; to *break* through, i.e. *spread* or *separate* (oneself):— disperse, divide,

be out of joint, part, scatter (abroad), separate (self), sever self, stretch, sunder.

6505. פֶּרֶד **pered**, *peh´-red*; from 6504; a *mule* (perh. from his *lonely* habits):— mule.

6506. פִּרְדָּה **pirdâh**, *pir-daw´*; fem. of 6505; a *she-mule*:— mule.

6507. פְּרֻדָה **pᵉrûdâh**, *per-oo-daw´*; fem. pass. part. of 6504; something *separated*, i.e. a *kernel*:— seed.

6508. פַּרְדֵּס **pardêç**, *par-dace´*; of for. or.; a *park*:— forest, orchard.

6509. פָּרָה **pârâh**, *paw-raw´*; a prim. root; to *bear fruit* (lit. or fig.):— bear, bring forth (fruit), (be, cause to be, make) fruitful, grow, increase.

6510. פָּרָה **pârâh**, *paw-raw´*; fem. of 6499; a *heifer*:— cow, heifer, kine.

6511. פָּרָה **Pârâh**, *paw-raw´*; the same as 6510; *Parah*, a place in Pal.:— Parah.

פָּרֶה **pereh**. See 6501.

6512. פֵּרָה **pêrâh**, *pay-raw´*; from 6331; a *hole* (as *broken*, i.e. *dug*):— + mole. Comp. 2661.

6513. פֻּרָה **Pûrâh**, *poo-raw´*; for 6288; *foliage*; *Purah*, an Isr.:— Phurah.

6514. פְּרוּדָא **Pᵉrûwdâ'**, *per-oo-daw´*; or

פְּרִידָא **Pᵉrîydâ'**, *per-ee-daw´*; from 6504; *dispersion*; *Peruda* or *Perida*, one of "Solomon's servants":— Perida, Peruda.

פְּרוֹ° **pᵉrôwziy**. See 6521.

6515. פָּרוּחַ **Pârûwach**, *paw-roo´-akh*; pass. part. of 6524; *blossomed*; *Paruäch*, an Isr.:— Paruah.

6516. פַּרְוַיִם **Parvayim**, *par-vah´-yim*; of for. or.; *Parvajim*, an Oriental region:— Parvaim.

6517. פָּרוּר **pârûwr**, *paw-roor´*; pass. part. of 6565 in the sense of *spreading* out [comp. 6524]; a *skillet* (as *flat* or *deep*):— pan, pot.

פַּרְוַר **Parvâr**. See 6503.

6518. פָּרָז **pârâz**, *paw-rawz´*; from an unused root mean. to *separate*, i.e. *decide*; a *chieftain*:— village.

6519. פְּרָזָה **pᵉrâzâh**, *per-aw-zaw´*; from the same as 6518; an *open country*:— (unwalled) town (without walls), unwalled village.

6520. פְּרָזוֹן **pᵉrâzôwn**, *per-aw-zone´*; from the same as 6518; *magistracy*, i.e. *leadership* (also concr. *chieftains*):— village.

6521. פְּרָזִי **pᵉrâziy**, *per-aw-zee´*; or

פְּרוֹזִי **pᵉrôwziy**, *per-o-zee´*; from 6519; a *rustic*:— village.

6522. פְּרִזִּי **Pᵉrîzziy**, *per-iz-zee´*; for 6521; *inhab. of the open country*; a *Perizzite*, one of the Canaanitish tribes:— Perizzite.

6523. פַּרְזֶל **parzel** (Chald.), *par-zel´*; corresp. to 1270; *iron*:— iron.

6524. פָּרַח **pârach**, *paw-rakh´*; a prim. root; to *break* forth as a bud, i.e. *bloom*; gen. to *spread*; spec. to *fly* (as extending the wings); fig. to *flourish*:— × abroad, × abundantly, blossom, break forth (out), bud, flourish, make fly, grow, spread, spring (up).

6525. פֶּרַח **perach**, *peh´-rakh;* from 6524; a *calyx* (nat. or artif.); gen. *bloom:*— blossom, bud, flower.

6526. פִּרְחַח **pirchach**, *pir-khakh´;* from 6524; *progeny,* i.e. a *brood:*— youth.

6527. פָּרַט **pârat**, *paw-rat´;* a prim. root; to *scatter* words, i.e. *prate* (or *hum*):— chant.

6528. פֶּרֶט **peret**, *peh´-ret;* from 6527; a *stray* or *single* berry:— grape.

6529. פְּרִי **peʳriy**, *per-ee´;* from 6509; *fruit* (lit. or fig.):— bough, ([first-]) fruit ([-full]), reward.

פְּרִידָא **Peʳriydâ'**. See 6514.

פְּרִיּם **Peʳriym**. See 6332.

6530. פְּרִיץ **peʳriyts**, *per-eets´;* from 6555; *violent,* i.e. a *tyrant:*— destroyer, ravenous, robber.

6531. פֶּרֶךְ **perek**, *peh´-rek;* from an unused root mean. to *break* apart; *fracture,* i.e. *severity:*— cruelty, rigour.

6532. פֹּרֶכֶת **pôreketh**, *po-reh´-keth;* fem. act. part. of the same as 6531; a *separatrix,* i.e. (the sacred) *screen:*— vail.

6533. פָּרַם **pâram**, *paw-ram´;* a prim. root; to *tear:*— rend.

6534. פַּרְמַשְׁתָּא **Parmashtâ'**, *par-mash-taw´;* of Pers. or.; *Parmashta,* a son of Haman:— Parmasta.

6535. פַּרְנַךְ **Parnak**, *par-nak´;* of uncert. der.; *Parnak,* an Isr.:— Parnach.

6536. פָּרַס **pâraç**, *paw-ras´;* a prim. root; to *break* in pieces, i.e. (usually without violence) to *split, distribute:*— deal, divide, have hoofs, part, tear.

6537. פְּרַס **peʳraç** (Chald.), *per-as´;* corresp. to 6536; to *split* up:— divide, [U-] pharsin.

6538. פֶּרֶס **pereç**, *peh´-res;* from 6536; a *claw;* also a kind of *eagle:*— claw, ossifrage.

6539. פָּרַס **Pâraç**, *paw-ras´;* of for. or.; *Paras* (i.e. *Persia*), an E. country, incl. its inhab.:— Persia, Persians.

6540. פָּרַס **Pâraç** (Chald.), *paw-ras´;* corresp. to 6539:— Persia, Persians.

6541. פַּרְסָה **parçah**, *par-saw´;* fem. of 6538; a *claw* or split *hoof:*— claw, [cloven-] footed, hoof.

6542. פַּרְסִי **Parçiy**, *par-see´;* patrial from 6539; a *Parsite* (i.e. *Persian*), or inhab. of Peres:— Persian.

6543. פַּרְסִי **Parçiy** (Chald.), *par-see´;* corresp. to 6542:— Persian.

6544. פָּרַע **pâra'**, *paw-rah´;* a prim. root; to *loosen;* by impl. to *expose, dismiss;* fig. *absolve, begin:*— avenge, avoid, bare, go back, let, (make) naked, set at nought, perish, refuse, uncover.

6545. פֶּרַע **pera'**, *peh´-rah;* from 6544; the *hair* (as *dishevelled*):— locks.

6546. פִּרְעָה **par'âh**, *par-aw´;* fem. of 6545 (in the sense of *beginning*); *leadership* (plur. concr. *leaders*):— + avenging, revenge.

6547. פַּרְעֹה **Par'ôh**, *par-o´;* of Eg. der.; *Paroh,* a gen. title of Eg. kings:— Pharaoh.

6548. פַּרְעֹה חָפְרַע **Par'ôh Chophra'**, *par-*

o´ khof-rah´; of Eg. der.; *Paroh-Chophra,* an Eg. king:— Pharaoh-hophra.

6549. פַּרְעֹה נְכֹה **Par'ôh Neʳkôh**, *par-o´ nek-o´;* or

פַּרְעֹה נְכוֹ **Par'ôh Neʳkôw**, *par-o´ nek-o´;* of Eg. der.; *Paroh-Nekoh* (or *-Neko*), an Eg. king:— Pharaoh-necho, Pharaoh-nechoh.

6550. פַּרְעֹשׁ **par'ôsh**, *par-oshe´;* prob. from 6544 and 6211; a *flea* (as the *isolated insect*):— flea.

6551. פַּרְעֹשׁ **Par'ôsh**, *par-oshe´;* the same as 6550; *Parosh,* the name of our Isr.:— Parosh, Pharosh.

6552. פִּרְעָתוֹן **Pir'âthôwn**, *pir-aw-thone´;* from 6546; *chieftaincy; Pirathon,* a place in Pal.:— Pirathon.

6553. פִּרְעָתוֹנִי **Pir'âthôwnîy**, *pir-aw-tho-nee´;* or

פִּרְעָתֹנִי **Pir'âthônîy**, *pir-aw-tho-nee´;* patrial from 6552; a *Pirathonite* or inhab. of Pirathon:— Pirathonite.

6554. פַּרְפַּר **Parpar**, *par-par´;* prob. from 6565 in the sense of *rushing; rapid; Parpar,* a river of Syria:— Pharpar.

6555. פָּרַץ **pârats**, *paw-rats´;* a prim. root; to *break* out (in many applications, dir. and indirect, lit. and fig.):— × abroad, (make a) breach, break (away, down, -er, forth, in, up), burst out, come (spread) abroad, compel, disperse, grow, increase, open, press, scatter, urge.

6556. פֶּרֶץ **perets**, *peh´-rets;* from 6555; a *break* (lit. or fig.):— breach, breaking forth (in), × forth, gap.

6557. פֶּרֶץ **Perets**, *peh´-rets;* the same as 6556; *Perets,* the name of two Isr.:— Perez, Pharez.

6558. פַּרְצִי **Partsiy**, *par-tsee´;* patron. from 6557; a *Partsite* (collect.) or desc. of Perets:— Pharzites.

6559. פְּרָצִים **Peʳrâtsîym**, *per-aw-tseem´;* plur. of 6556; *breaks; Peratsim,* a mountain in Pal.:— Perazim.

6560. פֶּרֶץ עֻזָּא **Perets 'Uzzâ'**, *peh´-rets ooz-zaw´;* from 6556 and 5798; *break of Uzza; Perets-Uzza,* a place in Pal.:— Perez-uzza.

6561. פָּרַק **pâraq**, *paw-rak´;* a prim. root; to *break* off or *crunch;* fig. to *deliver:*— break (off), deliver, redeem, rend (in pieces), tear in pieces.

6562. פְּרַק **peʳraq** (Chald.), *per-ak´;* corresp. to 6561; to *discontinue:*— break off.

6563. פֶּרֶק **pereq**, *peh´-rek;* from 6561; *rapine;* also a *fork* (in roads):— crossway, robbery.

6564. פָּרָק **pârâq**, *paw-rawk´;* from 6561; *soup* (as full of *crumbed* meat):— broth. See also 4832.

6565. פָּרַר **pârar**, *paw-rar´;* a prim. root; to *break* up (usually fig., i.e. to *violate, frustrate:*— × any ways, break (asunder), cast off, cause to cease, × clean, defeat, disannul, disappoint, dissolve, divide, make of none effect, fail, frustrate, bring (come) to nought, × utterly, make void.

6566. פָּרַשׂ **pâras**, *paw-ras´;* a prim. root; to *break* apart, *disperse,* etc.:— break,

chop in pieces, lay open, scatter, spread (abroad, forth, selves, out), stretch (forth, out).

6567. פָּרַשׁ **pârash**, *paw-rash´;* a prim. root; to *separate,* lit. (to *disperse*) or fig. (to *specify*); also (by impl.) to *wound:*— scatter, declare, distinctly, shew, sting.

6568. פְּרַשׁ **peʳrash** (Chald.), *per-ash´;* corresp. to 6567; to *specify:*— distinctly.

6569. פֶּרֶשׁ **peresh**, *peh´-resh;* from 6567; *excrement* (as *eliminated*):— dung.

6570. פֶּרֶשׁ **Peresh**, *peh´-resh;* the same as 6569; *Peresh,* an Isr.:— Peresh.

6571. פָּרָשׁ **pârâsh**, *paw-rawsh´;* from 6567; a *steed* (as *stretched* out to a vehicle, not single nor for mounting [comp. 5483]); also (by impl.) a *driver* (in a chariot), i.e. (collect.) *cavalry:*— horseman.

6572. פַּרְשֶׁגֶן **parshegen**, *par-sheh´-ghen;* or

פַּתְשֶׁגֶן **pathshegen**, *path-sheh´-ghen;* of for. or.; a *transcript:*— copy.

6573. פַּרְשֶׁגֶן **parshegen** (Chald.), *par-sheh´-ghen;* corresp. to 6572:— copy.

6574. פַּרְשְׁדֹן **parsheʳdôn**, *par-shed-one´;* perh. by compounding 6567 and 6504 (in the sense of *straddling* [comp. 5676]; the *crotch* (or *anus*):— dirt.

6575. פָּרָשָׁה **pârâshâh**, *paw-raw-shaw´;* from 6567; *exposition:*— declaration, sum.

6576. פַּרְשֵׁז **parshêz**, *par-shaze´;* a root appar. formed by compounding 6567 and that of 6518 [comp. 6574]; to *expand:*— spread.

6577. פַּרְשַׁנְדָּתָא **Parshandâthâ'**, *par-shan-daw-thaw´;* of Pers. or.; *Parshandatha,* a son of Haman:— Parshandatha.

6578. פְּרָת **Peʳrâth**, *per-awth´;* from an unused root mean. to *break* forth; *rushing; Perath* (i.e. *Euphrates*), a river of the East:— Euphrates.

פֹּרָת **pôrâth**. See 6509.

6579. פַּרְתַּם **partam**, *par-tam´;* of Pers. or.; a *grandee:*— (most) noble, prince.

6580. פַּשׁ **pash**, *pash;* prob. from an unused root mean. to *disintegrate; stupidity* (as a result of *grossness* or of *degeneracy*):— extremity.

6581. פָּשָׂה **pâsâh**, *paw-saw´;* a prim. root; to *spread:*— spread.

6582. פָּשַׁח **pâshach**, *paw-shakh´;* a prim. root; to *tear* in pieces:— pull in pieces.

6583. פַּשְׁחוּר **Pashchûwr**, *pash-khoor´;* prob. from 6582; *liberation; Pashchur,* the name of four Isr.:— Pashur.

6584. פָּשַׁט **pâshat**, *paw-shat´;* a prim. root; to *spread* out (i.e. *deploy* in hostile array); by anal. to *strip* (i.e. *unclothe, plunder, flay,* etc.):— fall upon, flay, invade, make an invasion, pull off, put off, make a road, run upon, rush, set, spoil, spread selves (abroad), strip (off, self).

6585. פָּשַׂע **pâsa'**, *paw-sah´;* a prim. root; to *stride* (from *spreading* the legs), i.e. *rush* upon:— go.

6586. פָּשַׁע **pâsha'**, *paw-shah´;* a prim. root [rather ident. with 6585 through the idea of *expansion*]; to *break* away (from just authority), i.e. *trespass, apostatize, quarrel:*— offend, rebel, revolt, transgress (-ion, -or).

6587. פֶּשַׂע **pesa'**, *peh´-sah;* from 6585; a *stride:*— step.

6588. פֶּשַׁע **pesha'**, *peh´-shah;* from 6586; a *revolt* (national, moral, or religious):— rebellion, sin, transgression, trespass.

6589. פָּשַׂק **pâsaq**, *paw-sak´;* a prim. root; to *dispart* (the feet or lips), i.e. *become licentious:*— open (wide).

6590. פְּשַׁר **p^eshar** (Chald.), *pesh-ar´;* corresp. to 6622; to *interpret:*— make [interpretations], interpreting.

6591. פְּשַׁר **p^eshar** (Chald.), *pesh-ar´;* from 6590; an *interpretation:*— interpretation.

6592. פֵּשֶׁר **pêsher**, *pay´-sher;* corresp. to 6591:— interpretation.

6593. פִּשְׁתֶּה **pishteh**, *pish-teh´;* from the same as 6580 as in the sense of *comminuting; linen* (i.e. the thread, as *carded*):— flax, linen.

6594. פִּשְׁתָּה **pishtâh**, *pish-taw´;* fem. of 6593; *flax;* by impl. a *wick:*— flax, tow.

6595. פַּת **path**, *path;* from 6626; a *bit:*— meat, morsel, piece.

6596. פֹּת **pôth**, *pohth;* or

פֹּתָה **pothâh** (Ezek. 13:19), *po-thaw´;* from an unused root mean. to *open;* a *hole,* i.e. *hinge* or the female *pudenda:*— hinge, secret part.

פְּתָאָי **p^ethâ'îy.** See 6612.

6597. פִּתְאֹם **pith'ôwm**, *pith-ome´;* or

פִּתְאֹם **pith'ôm**, *pith-ome´;* from 6621; *instantly:*— straightway, sudden (-ly).

6598. פַּתְבַּג **pathbag**, *pathbag´;* of Pers. or.; a *dainty:*— portion (provision) of meat.

6599. פִּתְגָם **pithgâm**, *pith-gawm´;* of Pers. or.; a (judicial) *sentence:*— decree, sentence.

6600. פִּתְגָם **pithgâm** (Chald.), *pithgawm´;* corresp. to 6599; a *word, answer, letter* or *decree:*— answer, letter, matter, word.

6601. פָּתָה **pâthâh**, *paw-thaw´;* a prim. root; to *open,* i.e. *be* (caus. *make*) *roomy;* usually fig. (in a mental or moral sense) to *be* (caus. *make*) *simple* or (in a sinister way) *delude:*— allure, deceive, enlarge, entice, flatter, persuade, silly (one).

6602. פְּתָאֵל **P^ethûw'êl**, *peth-oo-ale´;* from 6601 and 410; *enlarged of God;* *Pethuël,* an Isr.:— Pethuel.

6603. פִּתּוּחַ **pittûwach**, *pit-too´-akh;* or

פִּתֻּחַ **pittuach**, *pit-too´-akh;* pass. part. of 6605; *sculpture* (in low or high relief or even intaglio):— carved (work) (are, en-) grave (-ing, -n).

6604. פְּתוֹר **P^ethôwr**, *peth-ore´;* of for. or.; *Pethor,* a place in Mesopotamia:— Pethor.

6605. פָּתַח **pâthach**, *paw-thakh´;* a prim. root; to *open* wide (lit. or fig.); spec. to *loosen, begin, plow, carve:*— appear, break forth, draw (out), let go free, (en-) grave (-n), loose (self), (be, be set)

open (-ing), put off, ungird, unstop, have vent.

6606. פְּתַח **p^ethach** (Chald.), *peth-akh´;* corresp. to 6605; to *open:*— open.

6607. פֶּתַח **pethach**, *peh´-thakh;* from 6605; an *opening* (lit.), i.e. *door* (*gate*) or *entrance* way:— door, entering (in), entrance (-ry), gate, opening, place.

6608. פֵּתַח **pêthach**, *pay´-thakh;* from 6605; *opening* (fig.) i.e. *disclosure:*— entrance.

פָּתוּחַ **pâthûach.** See 6603.

6609. פְּתִחָה **p^ethichâh**, *peth-ee-khaw´;* from 6605; something *opened,* i.e. a *drawn* sword:— drawn sword.

6610. פִּתְחוֹן **pithchôwn**, *pith-khone´;* from 6605; *opening* (the act):— open (-ing).

6611. פְּתַחְיָה **P^ethachyâh**, *peth-akhyaw´;* from 6605 and 3050; *Jah has opened; Pethachjah,* the name of four Isr.:— Pethakiah.

6612. פְּתִי **p^ethîy**, *peth-ee´;* or

פְּתִי **pethîy**, *peh´-thee;* or

פְּתָאִי **p^ethâ'îy**, *peth-aw-ee´;* from 6601; *silly* (i.e. *seducible*):— foolish, simple (-icity, one).

6613. פְּתַי **p^ethay** (Chald.), *peth-ah´-ee;* from a root corresp. to 6601; *open,* i.e. (as noun) *width:*— breadth.

6614. פְּתִיגִיל **p^ethîygîyl**, *peth-eeg-eel´;* of uncert. der.; prob. a figured *mantle* for holidays:— stomacher.

6615. פְּתַיּוּת **p^ethayûwth**, *peth-ah-yooth´;* from 6612; *silliness* (i.e. *seducibility*):— simple.

6616. פָּתִיל **pâthîyl**, *paw-theel´;* from 6617; *twine:*— bound, bracelet, lace, line, ribband, thread, wire.

6617. פָּתַל **pâthal**, *paw-thal´;* a prim. root; to *twine,* i.e. (lit.) to *struggle* or (fig.) *be* (morally) *tortuous:*— (shew self) froward, shew self unsavoury, wrestle.

6618. פְּתַלְתֹּל **p^ethaltôl**, *peth-al-tole´;* from 6617; *tortuous* (i.e. *crafty*):— crooked.

6619. פִּתֹם **Pîthôm**, *pee-thome´;* of Eg. der.; *Pithom,* a place in Egypt:— Pithom.

6620. פֶּתֶן **pethen**, *peh´-then;* from an unused root mean. to *twist;* an *asp* (from its *contortions*):— adder.

6621. פֶּתַע **petha'**, *peh´-thah;* from an unused root mean. to *open* (the eyes); a *wink,* i.e. *moment* [comp. 6597] (used only [with or without prep.] adv. *quickly* or *unexpectedly*):— at an instant, suddenly, × very.

6622. פָּתַר **pâthar**, *paw-thar´;* a prim. root; to *open up,* i.e. (fig.) *interpret* (a dream):— interpret (-ation, -er).

6623. פִּתְרוֹן **pithrôwn**, *pith-rone´;* or

פִּתְרֹן **pithrôn**, *pith-rone´;* from 6622; *interpretation* (of a dream):— interpretation.

6624. פַּתְרוֹס **Pathrôwç**, *path-roce´;* of Eg. der.; *Pathros,* a part of Egypt:— Pathros.

6625. פַּתְרֻסִי **Pathrûçîy**, *path-roo-see´;*

patrial from 6624; a *Pathrusite,* or inhab. of Pathros:— Pathrusim.

פַּתְשֶׁגֶן **pathshegen.** See 6572.

6626. פָּתַת **pâthath**, *paw-thath´;* a prim. root; to *open,* i.e. *break:*— part.

צ

6627. צָאָה **tsâ'âh**, *tsaw-aw´;* from 3318; *issue,* i.e. (human) *excrement:*— that (which) cometh from (out).

צֹאָה **tsô'âh.** See 6675.

צֹאוֹן **ts^e'ôwn.** See 6629.

6628. צֶאֱל **tse'el**, *tseh´-el;* from an unused root mean. to *be slender;* the *lotus tree:*— shady tree.

6629. צֹאן **tsô'n**, *tsone;* or

צְאוֹן **ts^e'ôwn** (Psa. 144:13) *tsehone´;* from an unused root mean. to *migrate;* a collect. name for a *flock* (of sheep or goats); also fig. (of men):— (small) cattle, flock (+ -s), lamb (+ -s), sheep ([-cote, -fold, -shearer, -herds]).

6630. צַאֲנָן **Tsa'ănân**, *tsah-an-awn´;* from the same as 6629 used denom.; *sheep* pasture; *Zaanan,* a place in Pal.:— Zaanan.

6631. צֶאֱצָא **tse'ětsâ'**, *tseh-ets-aw´;* from 3318; *issue,* i.e. *produce, children:*— that which cometh forth (out), offspring.

6632. צָב **tsâb**, *tsawb;* from an unused root mean. to *establish;* a *palanquin* or *canopy* (as a *fixture*); also a species of *lizard* (prob. as clinging *fast*):— covered, litter, tortoise.

6633. צָבָא **tsâbâ'**, *tsaw-baw´;* a prim. root; to *mass* (an army or servants):— assemble, fight, perform, muster, wait upon, war.

6634. צְבָא **ts^ebâ'** (Chald.), *tseb-aw´;* corresp. to 6633 in the fig. sense of *summoning* one's wishes; to *please:*— will, would.

6635. צָבָא **tsâbâ'**, *tsaw-baw´;* or (fem.)

צְבָאָה **ts^ebâ'âh**, *tseb-aw-aw´;* from 6633; a *mass* of persons (or fig. things), espec. reg. organized for war (an *army*); by impl. a *campaign,* lit. or fig. (spec. *hardship, worship*):— appointed time, (+) army, (+) battle, company, host, service, soldiers, waiting upon, war (-fare).

6636. צְבֹאִים **Ts^ebô'iym**, *tseb-o-eem´;* or (more correctly)

צְבִיִּים **Ts^ebîyîym**, *tseb-ee-yeem´;* or

צְבִיִּם **Ts^ebîyîm**, *tseb-ee-yeem´;* plur. of 6643; *gazelles; Tseboïm* or *Tsebijim,* a place in Pal.:— Zeboiim, Zeboim.

6637. צֹבֵבָה **Tsôbêbâh**, *tso-bay-baw´;* fem. act. part. of the same as 6632; the *canopier* (with the art.); *Tsobebah,* an Israelitess:— Zobebah.

6638. צָבָה **tsâbâh**, *tsaw-baw´;* a prim. root; to *amass,* i.e. *grow turgid;* spec. to *array* an army against:— fight, swell.

6639. צָבֶה **tsâbeh**, *tsaw-beh´;* from 6638; *turgid:*— swell.

צֹבָה **Tsôbâh.** See 6678.

6640. צְבוּ **ts^ebûw** (Chald.), *tseb-oo´-*

from 6634; prop. *will;* concr. an *affair* (as a matter of *determination*):— purpose.

6641. צָבֻעַ **tsâbûwa'**, *tsaw-boo´-ah;* pass. part. of the same as 6648; *dyed* (in stripes), i.e. the *hyena:*— speckled.

6642. צָבַט **tsâbaṭ**, *tsaw-bat´;* a prim. root; to *grasp,* i.e. *hand* out:— reach.

6643. צְבִי **ts⁰bîy**, *tseb-ee´;* from 6638 in the sense of *prominence; splendor* (as *conspicuous*); also a *gazelle* (as *beautiful*):— beautiful (-ty), glorious (-ry), goodly, pleasant, roe (-buck).

6644. צִבְיָא **Tsibyâ'**, *tsib-yaw´;* for 6645; *Tsibja,* an Isr.:— Zibia.

6645. צִבְיָה **Tsibyâh**, *tsib-yaw´;* for 6646; *Tsibjah,* an Israelitess:— Zibiah.

6646. צְבִיָּה **ts⁰bîyâh**, *tseb-ee-yaw´;* fem. of 6643; a *female* gazelle:— roe.

צְבֹיִים **Ts⁰bîyîym**. See 6636.

צְבֹאִים **Ts⁰bâyîm**. See 6380.

6647. צְבַע **ts⁰ba'** (Chald.), *tseb-ah´;* a root corresp. to that of 6648; to *dip:*— wet.

6648. צֶבַע **tseba'**, *tseh´-bah;* from an unused root mean. to *dip* (into coloring fluid); a *dye:*— divers, colours.

6649. צִבְעוֹן **Tsib'ôwn**, *tsib-one´;* from the same as 6648; *variegated; Tsibon,* an Idumæan:— Zibeon.

6650. צְבֹעִים **Ts⁰bô'îym**, *tseb-o-eem´;* plur. of 6641; *hyenas; Tseboïm,* a place in Pal.:— Zeboim.

6651. צָבַר **tsâbar**, *tsaw-bar´;* a prim. root; to *aggregate:*— gather (together), heap (up), lay up.

6652. צִבֻּר **tsibbûr**, *tsib-boor´;* from 6551; a *pile:*— heap.

6653. צֶבֶת **tsebeth**, *tseh´-beth;* from an unused root appar. mean. to *grip;* a *lock* of stalks:— handful.

6654. צַד **tsad**, *tsad;* contr. from an unused root mean. to *sidle* off; a *side;* fig. an *adversary:*— (be-) side.

6655. צַד **tsad** (Chald.), *tsad;* corresp. to 6654; used adv. (with prep.) at or upon the *side* of:— against, concerning.

6656. צְדָא **ts⁰dâ'** (Chald.), *tsed-aw´;* from an unused root corresp! to 6658 in the sense of *intentness;* a (sinister) *design:*— true.

6657. צְדָד **Ts⁰dâd**, *tsed-awd´;* from the same as 6654; a *siding; Tsedad,* a place near Pal.:— Zedad.

6658. צָדָה **tsâdâh**, *tsaw-daw´;* a prim. root; to *chase;* by impl. to *desolate:*— destroy, hunt, lie in wait.

צֵדָה **tsêdâh**. See 6720.

6659. צָדוֹק **Tsâdôwq**, *tsaw-doke´;* from 6663; *just; Tsadok,* the name of eight or nine Isr.:— Zadok.

6660. צְדִיָּה **ts⁰dîyâh**, *tsed-ee-yaw´;* from 6658; *design* [comp. 6656]:— lying in wait.

6661. צִדִּים **Tsiddîym**, *tsid-deem´;* plur. of 6654; *sides; Tsiddim* (with the art.), a place in Pal.:— Ziddim.

6662. צַדִּיק **tsaddîyq**, *tsad-deek´;* from 6663; *just:*— just, lawful, righteous (man).

צִדֹנִי **Tsîdôniy**. See 6722.

6663. צָדַק **tsâdaq**, *tsaw-dak´;* a prim. root; to *be* (caus. *make*) *right* (in a moral or forensic sense):— cleanse, clear self, (be, do) just (-ice, -ify, -ify self), (be, turn to) righteous (-ness).

6664. צֶדֶק **tsedeq**, *tseh´-dek;* from 6663; the *right* (nat., mor. or legal); also (abstr.) *equity* or (fig.) *prosperity:*— × even, (× that which is altogether) just (-ice), ((un-) right (-eous) (cause, -ly, -ness).

6665. צִדְקָה **tsidqâh** (Chald.), *tsid-kaw´;* corresp. to 6666; *beneficence:*— righteousness.

6666. צְדָקָה **ts⁰dâqâh**, *tsed-aw-kaw´;* from 6663; *rightness* (abstr.), subj. (*rectitude*), obj. (*justice*), mor. (*virtue*) or fig. (*prosperity*):— justice, moderately, right (-eous) (act, -ly, -ness).

6667. צִדְקִיָּה **Tsidqîyâh**, *tsid-kee-yaw´;* or

צִדְקִיָּהוּ **Tsidqîyâhûw**, *tsid-kee-yaw´-hoo;* from 6664 and 3050; *right of Jah; Tsidkijah,* the name of six Isr.:— Zedekiah, Zidkijah.

6668. צָהַב **tsâhab**, *tsaw-hab´;* a prim. root; to *glitter,* i.e. *be golden* in color:— × fine.

6669. צָהֹב **tsâhôb**, *tsaw-obe´;* from 6668; *golden* in color:— yellow.

6670. צָהַל **tsâhal**, *tsaw-hal´;* a prim. root; to *gleam,* i.e. (fig.) *be cheerful;* by transf. to *sound* clear (of various animal or human expressions):— bellow, cry aloud (out), lift up, neigh, rejoice, make to shine, shout.

6671. צָהַר **tsâhar**, *tsaw-har´;* a prim. root; to *glisten;* used only as denom. from 3323, to *press* out oil:— make oil.

6672. צֹהַר **tsôhar**, *tso´-har;* from 6671; a *light* (i.e. *window*): dual *double light,* i.e. *noon:*— midday, noon (-day, -tide), window.

6673. צַו **tsav**, *tsav;* or

צָו **tsâv**, *tsawv;* from 6680; an *injunction:*— commandment, precept.

6674. צוֹא **tsôw'**, *tso;* or

צֹא **tsô'**, *tso;* from an unused root mean. to *issue; soiled* (as if *excrementitious*):— filthy.

6675. צוֹאָה **tsôw'âh**, *tso-aw´;* or

צֹאָה **tsô'âh**, *tso-aw´;* fem. of 6674; *excrement;* gen. *dirt;* fig. *pollution:*— dung, filth (-iness). [*Marg.* for 2716.]

6676. צַוָּאר **tsavva'r** (Chald.), *tsav-var´;* corresp. to 6677:— neck.

6677. צַוָּאר **tsavvâ'r**, *tsav-vawr´;* or

צַוָּאר **tsavvâr** (Neh. 3:5), *tsav-vawr´;* or

צַוָּרֹן **tsavvârôn** (Cant. 4:9), *tsav-vaw-rone´;* or (fem.)

צַוָּארָה **tsavvâ'râh** (Mic. 2:3) *tsav-vaw-raw´;* intens. from 6696 in the sense of *binding;* the back of the *neck* (as that on which burdens are *bound*):— neck.

6678. צוֹבָא **Tsôwbâ'**, *tso-baw´;* or

צוֹבָה **Tsôwbâh**, *tso-baw´;* or

צֹבָה **Tsôbâh**, *tso-baw´;* from an unused root mean. to *station;* a *station;*

Zoba or Zobah, a region of Syria:— Zoba, Zobah.

6679. צוּד **tsûwd**, *tsood;* a prim. root; to *lie* alongside (i.e. in wait); by impl. to *catch* an animal (fig. men); (denom. from 6718) to *victual* (for a journey):— chase, hunt, sore, take (provision).

6680. צָוָה **tsâvâh**, *tsaw-vaw´;* a prim. root; (intens.) to *constitute, enjoin:*— appoint, (for-) bid, (give a) charge, (give a, give in, send with) command (-er, -ment), send a messenger, put, (set) in order.

6681. צָוַח **tsâvach**, *tsaw-vakh´;* a prim. root; to *screech* (exultingly):— shout.

6682. צְוָחָה **ts⁰vâchâh**, *tsev-aw-khaw´;* from 6681; a *screech* (of anguish):— cry (-ing).

6683. צוּלָה **tsûwlâh**, *tsoo-law´;* from an unused root mean. to *sink; an abyss* (of the sea):— deep.

6684. צוּם **tsûwm**, *tsoom;* a prim. root; to *cover* over (the mouth), i.e. to *fast:*— × at all, fast.

6685. צוֹם **tsôwm**, *tsome;* or

צֹם **tsôm**, *tsome;* from 6684; a *fast:*— fast (-ing).

6686. צוּעָר **Tsûw'âr**, *tsoo-awr´;* from 6819; *small; Tsuär,* an Isr.:— Zuar.

6687. צוּף **tsûwph**, *tsoof;* a prim. root; to *overflow:*— (make to over-) flow, swim.

6688. צוּף **tsûwph**, *tsoof;* from 6687; *comb* of honey (from *dripping*):— honeycomb.

6689. צוּף **Tsûwph**, *tsoof;* or

צוֹפַי **Tsôwphay**, *tso-fah´-ee;* or

צִיף **Tsîyph**, *tseef;* from 6688; *honey-comb; Tsuph* or *Tsophai* or *Tsiph,* the name of an Isr. and of a place in Pal.:— Zophai, Zuph.

6690. צוֹפַח **Tsôwphach**, *tso-fakh´;* from an unused root mean. to *expand, breadth; Tsophach,* an Isr.:— Zophah.

צוֹפַי **Tsôwphay**. See 6689.

6691. צוֹפַר **Tsôwphar**, *tso-far´;* from 6852; *departing; Tsophar,* a friend of Job:— Zophar.

6692. צוּץ **tsûwts**, *tsoots;* a prim. root; to *twinkle,* i.e. *glance;* by anal. to *blossom* (fig. *flourish*):— bloom, blossom, flourish, shew self.

6693. צוּק **tsûwq**, *tsook;* a prim. root; to *compress,* i.e. (fig.) *oppress, distress:*— constrain, distress, lie sore, (op-) press (-or), straiten.

6694. צוּק **tsûwq**, *tsook;* a prim. root [rather ident. with 6693 through the idea of *narrowness* (of orifice)]; to *pour* out, i.e. (fig.) *smelt, utter:*— be molten, pour.

6695. צוֹק **tsôwq**, *tsoke;* or (fem.)

צוּקָה **tsûwqâh**, *tsoo-kaw´;* from 6693; a *strait,* i.e. (fig.) *distress:*— anguish, × troublous.

6696. צוּר **tsûwr**, *tsoor;* a prim. root; to *cramp,* i.e. *confine* (in many applications, lit. and fig., formative or hostile):— adversary, assault, beset, besiege, bind (up), cast, distress, fashion, fortify, inclose, lay siege, put up in bags.

6697. צוּר **tsûwr**, *tsoor;* or

צֻר **tsûr**, *tsoor;* from 6696; prop. a *cliff* (or sharp rock, as *compressed*); gen. a *rock* or *boulder;* fig. a *refuge;* also an *edge* (as *precipitous*):— edge, × (mighty) God (one), rock, × sharp, stone, × strength, × strong. See also 1049.

6698. צוּר **Tsûwr**, *tsoor;* the same as 6697; *rock; Tsur*, the name of a Midianite and of an Isr.:— Zur.

צוֹר **Tsôwr**. See 6865.

צַוָּר **tsavvâr**. See 6677.

6699. צוּרָה **tsûwrâh**, *tsoo-raw´;* fem. of 6697; a *rock* (Job 28:10); also a *form* (as if *pressed* out):— form, rock.

צֻרֹן **tsavvârôn**. See 6677.

6700. צוּרִיאֵל **Tsûwrîy'êl**, *tsoo-ree-ale´;* from 6697 and 410; *rock of God; Tsuriël*, an Isr.:— Zuriel.

6701. צוּרִישַׁדָּי **Tsûwrîyshadday**, *tsoo-ree-shad-dah´-ee;* from 6697 and 7706; *rock of (the) Almighty; Tsurishaddai*, an Isr.:— Zurishaddai.

6702. צוּת **tsûwth**, *tsooth;* a prim. root; to *blaze:*— burn.

6703. צַח **tsach**, *tsakh;* from 6705; *dazzling*, i.e. *sunny, bright,* (fig.) *evident:*— clear, dry, plainly, white.

צְחֵא **Tsîchâ'**. See 6727.

6704. צָחֵה **tsâcheh**, *tsee-kheh´;* from an unused root mean. to *glow; parched:*— dried up.

6705. צָחַח **tsâchach**, *tsaw-khakh´;* a prim. root; to *glare,* i.e. *be dazzling white:*— be whiter.

6706. צְחִיַח **tseᵉchîyach**, *tsekh-ee-´akh;* from 6705; *glaring,* i.e. *exposed* to the bright sun:— higher place, top.

6707. צְחִיחָה **tseᵉchîychâh**, *tsekh-ee-khaw´;* fem. of 6706; a *parched* region, i.e. the *desert:*— dry land.

6708. צְחִיחִי **tseᵉchîychîy**, *tsekh-ee-khee´;* from 6706; *bare* spot, i.e. in the *glaring* sun:— higher place.

6709. צַחֲנָה **tsachănâh**, *tsakh-an-aw´;* from an unused root mean. to *putrefy; stench:*— ill savour.

6710. צַחְצָחָה **tsachtsâchâh**, *tsakh-tsaw-khaw´;* from 6705; a *dry* place, i.e. *desert:*— drought.

6711. צָחַק **tsâchaq**, *tsaw-khak´;* a prim. root; to *laugh* outright (in merriment or scorn); by impl. to *sport:*— laugh, mock, play, make sport.

6712. צְחֹק **tseᵉchôq**, *tsekh-oke´;* from 6711; *laughter* (in pleasure or derision):— laugh (-ed to scorn).

6713. צַחַר **tsachar**, *tsakh-´ar;* from an unused root mean. to *dazzle; sheen,* i.e. *whiteness:*— white.

6714. צֹחַר **Tsôchar**, *tso´-khar;* from the same as 6713; *whiteness; Tsochar,* the name of a Hittite and of an Isr.:— Zohar. Comp. 3328.

6715. צָחֹר **tsâchôr**, *tsaw-khore´;* from the same as 6713; *white:*— white.

6716. צִי **tsîy**, *tsee;* from 6680; a *ship* (as a *fixture*):— ship.

6717. צִיבָא **Tsîybâ'**, *tsee-baw´;* from the

same as 6678; *station; Tsiba,* an Isr.:— Ziba.

6718. צַיִד **tsayid**, *tsah-´yid;* from a form of 6679 and mean. the same; the *chase;* also *game* (thus taken); (gen.) *lunch* (espec. for a journey):— × catcheth, food, × hunter, (that which he took in) hunting, venison, victuals.

6719. צַיָּד **tsayâd**, *tsah-´yawd;* from the same as 6718; a *huntsman:*— hunter.

6720. צֵידָה **tsêydâh**, *tsay-daw´;* or

צֵדָה **tsêdâh**, *tsay-daw´;* fem. of 6718; *food:*— meat, provision, venison, victuals.

6721. צִידוֹן **Tsîydôwn**, *tsee-done´;* or

צִידֹן **Tsîydôn**, *tsee-done´;* from 6679 in the sense of *catching* fish; *fishery; Tsidon,* the name of a son of Canaan, and of a place in Pal.:— Sidon, Zidon.

6722. צִידֹנִי **Tsîydônîy**, *tsee-do-nee´;* patrial from 6721; a *Tsidonian* or inhab. of Tsidon:— Sidonian, of Sidon, Zidonian.

6723. צִיָּה **tsîyâh**, *tsee-yaw´;* from an unused root mean. to *parch; aridity;* concr. a *desert:*— barren, drought, dry (land, place), solitary place, wilderness.

6724. צִיּוֹן **tsîyôwn**, *tsee-yone´;* from the same as 6723; a *desert:*— dry place.

6725. צִיּוּן **tsîyûwn**, *tsee-yoon´;* from the same as 6723 in the sense of *conspicuousness* [comp. 5329]; a *monumental* or *guiding* pillar:— sign, title, waymark.

6726. צִיּוֹן **Tsîyôwn**, *tsee-yone´;* the same (reg.) as 6725; *Tsijon* (as a permanent *capital*), a mountain of Jerusalem:— Zion.

6727. צִיחָא **Tsîychâ'**, *tsee-khaw´;* or

צִחָא **Tsîchâ'**, *tsee-khaw´;* as if fem. of 6704; *drought; Tsicha,* the name of two Nethinim:— Ziha.

6728. צִיִּי **tsîyîy**, *tsee-ee´;* from the same as 6723; a *desert-dweller,* i.e. *nomad* or *wild beast:*— wild beast of the desert, that dwell in (inhabiting) the wilderness.

6729. צִינֹק **tsîynôq**, *tsee-noke´;* from an unused root mean. to *confine;* the *pillory:*— stocks.

6730. צִיעֹר **Tsîy'ôr**, *tsee-ore´;* from 6819; *small; Tsior,* a place in Pal.:— Zior.

6731. צִיף° **Tsîyph**. See 6689.

6731. צִיץ **tsîyts**, *tseets;* or

צִץ **tsits**, *tseets;* from 6692; prop. *glistening,* i.e. a burnished *plate;* also a *flower* (as *bright* colored); a *wing* (as *gleaming* in the air):— blossom, flower, plate, wing.

6732. צִיץ **Tsîyts**, *tseets;* the same as 6731; *bloom; Tsits,* a place in Pal.:— Ziz.

6733. צִיצָה **tsîytsâh**, *tsee-tsaw´;* fem. of 6731; a *flower:*— flower.

6734. צִיצִת **tsîytsîth**, *tsee-tseeth´;* fem. of 6731; a *floral* or *wing*-like projection, i.e. a *fore-lock* of hair, a *tassel:*— fringe, lock.

6734. צִיקְלַג° **Tsîyqᵉlag**. See 6860.

6735. צִיר **tsîyr**, *tseer;* from 6696; a *hinge* (as *pressed* in turning); also a *throe* (as a physical or mental *pressure*); also a

herald or errand-doer (as *constrained* by the principal):— ambassador, hinge, messenger, pain, pang, sorrow. Comp. 6736.

6736. צִיר **tsîyr**, *tseer;* the same as 6735; a *form* (of beauty; as if *pressed* out, i.e. *carved*); hence, an (idolatrous) *image:*— beauty, idol.

6737. צִיר **tsâyar**, *tsaw-yar´;* a denom. from 6735 in the sense of *ambassador;* to *make an errand,* i.e. *betake* oneself:— make as if ... had been ambassador.

6738. צֵל **tsêl**, *tsale;* from 6751; *shade,* whether lit. or fig.:— defence, shade (-ow).

6739. צְלָא **tseᵉlâ'** (Chald.), *tsel-aw´;* prob. corresp. to 6760 in the sense of *bowing; pray:*— pray.

6740. צָלָה **tsâlâh**, *tsaw-law´;* a prim. root; to *roast:*— roast.

6741. צִלָּה **Tsillâh**, *tsil-law´;* fem. of 6738; *Tsillah,* an antediluvian woman:— Zillah.

6742. צְלוּל **tseᵉlûwl**, *tsel-ool´;* from 6749 in the sense of *rolling;* a (round or flattened) *cake:*— cake.

6743. צָלַח **tsâlach**, *tsaw-lakh´;* or

צָלֵחַ **tsâlêach**, *tsaw-lay´-akh;* a prim. root; to *push* forward, in various senses (lit. or fig., tran. or intr.):— break out, come (mightily), go over, be good, be meet, be profitable, (cause to, effect, make to, send) prosper (-ity, -ous, -ously).

6744. צְלַח **tseᵉlach** (Chald.), *tsel-akh´;* corresp. to 6743; to *advance* (tran. or intr.):— promote, prosper.

6745. צֵלָחָה **tsêlâchâh**, *tsay-law-khaw´;* from 6743; something *protracted* or flattened out, i.e. a *platter:*— pan.

6746. צְלֹחִית **tseᵉlôchîyth**, *tsel-o-kheeth´;* from 6743; something *prolonged* or tall, i.e. a *vial* or salt-*cellar:*— cruse.

6747. צַלַּחַת **tsallachath**, *tsal-lakh´-ath;* from 6743; something *advanced* or *deep,* i.e. a *bowl;* fig. the *bosom:*— bosom, dish.

6748. צָלִי **tsâlîy**, *tsaw-lee´;* pass. part. of 6740; *roasted:*— roast.

6749. צָלַל **tsâlal**, *tsaw-lal´;* a prim. root; prop. to *tumble* down, i.e. *settle* by a waving motion:— sink. Comp. 6750, 6751.

6750. צָלַל **tsâlal**, *tsaw-lal´;* a prim. root [rather ident. with 6749 through the idea of *vibration*]; to *tinkle,* i.e. *rattle* together (as the ears in *reddening* with shame, or the teeth in *chattering* with fear):— quiver, tingle.

6751. צָלַל **tsâlal**, *tsaw-lal´;* a prim. root [rather ident. with 6749 through the idea of *hovering* over (comp. 6754)]; to *shade,* as twilight or an opaque object:— begin to be dark, shadowing.

6752. צֵלֶל **tsêlel**, *tsay´-lel;* from 6751; *shade:*— shadow.

6753. צְלֶלְפּוֹנִי **Tseᵉlelpôwnîy**, *tsel-el-po-nee´;* from 6752 and the act. part. of 6437; *shade-facing; Tselelponi,* an Israelitess:— Hazelelponi [incl. the art.].

6754. צֶלֶם **tselem**, *tseh´-lem;* from an

unused root mean. to *shade;* a *phantom,* i.e. (fig.) *illusion, resemblance;* hence, a representative *figure,* espec. an *idol:*— image, vain shew.

6755. צֶלֶם **tselem** (Chald.), *tseh´-lem;* or צְלֵם **ts⁰lem** (Chald.), *tsel-em´;* corresp. to 6754; an idolatrous *figure:*— form, image.

6756. צַלְמוֹן **Tsalmôwn,** *tsal-mone´;* from 6754; *shady; Tsalmon,* the name of a place in Pal. and of an Isr.:— Zalmon.

6757. צַלְמָוֶת **tsalmâveth,** *tsal-maw´-veth;* from 6738 and 4194; *shade of death,* i.e. the *grave* (fig. *calamity*):— shadow of death.

6758. צַלְמֹנָה **Tsalmônâh,** *tsal-mo-naw´;* fem. of 6757; *shadiness; Tsalmonah,* a place in the Desert:— Zalmonah.

6759. צַלְמֻנָּע **Tsalmunnâ´,** *tsal-moon-naw´;* from 6738 and 4513; *shade has been denied; Tsalmunna,* a Midianite:— Zalmunna.

6760. צָלַע **tsâla',** *tsaw-lah´;* a prim. root; prob. to *curve;* used only as denom. from 6763, to *limp* (as if *one-sided*):— halt.

6761. צֶלַע **tsela',** *tseh´-lah;* from 6760; a *limping* or *fall* (fig.):— adversity, halt (-ing).

6762. צֶלַע **Tsela',** *tseh´-lah;* the same as 6761; *Tsela,* a place in Pal.:— Zelah.

6763. צֵלָע **tsêlâ,** *tsay-law´;* or (fem.) צַלְעָה **tsal'âh,** *tsal-aw´;* from 6760; a *rib* (as *curved*), lit. (of the body) or fig. (of a door, i.e. *leaf*) hence, a *side,* lit. (of a person) or fig. (of an object or the sky, i.e. *quarter*); arch. a (espec. floor or ceiling) *timber* or *plank* (single or collect., i.e. a *flooring*):— beam, board, chamber, corner, leaf, plank, rib, side (chamber).

6764. צֶלֶף **Tsâlâph,** *tsaw-lawf´;* from an unused root of unknown mean.; *Tsalaph,* an Isr.:— Zalaph.

6765. צְלָפְחָד **Ts⁰lophchâd,** *tsel-of-chawd´;* from the same as 6764 and 259; *Tselophchad,* an Isr.:— Zelophehad.

6766. צֶלְצַח **Tseltsakh,** *tsel-tsakh´;* from 6738 and 6703; *clear shade; Tseltsach,* a place in Pal.:— Zelzah.

6767. צְלָצַל **ts⁰lâtsal,** *tsel-aw-tsal´;* from 6750 redupl.; a *clatter,* i.e. (abstr.) *whirring* (of wings); (concr.) a *cricket;* also a *harpoon* (as *rattling*), a *cymbal* (as *clanging*):— cymbal, locust, shadowing, spear.

6768. צֶלֶק **Tseleq,** *tseh´-lek;* from an unused root mean. to *split; fissure; Tselek,* an Isr.:— Zelek.

6769. צִלְּתַי **Tsill⁰thay,** *tsil-leth-ah´-ee;* from the fem. of 6738; *shady; Tsillethai,* the name of two Isr.:— Zilthai.

צֹם **tsôm.** See 6685.

6770. צָמֵא **tsâmê,** *tsaw-may´;* a prim. root; to *thirst* (lit. or fig.):— (be a-, suffer) thirst (-y).

6771. צָמֵא **tsâmê,** *tsaw-may´;* from 6770; *thirsty* (lit. or fig.):— (that) thirst (-eth, -y).

6772. צָמָא **tsâmâ',** *tsaw-maw´;* from 6770; *thirst* (lit. or fig.):— thirst (-y).

6773. צִמְאָה **tsim'âh,** *tsim-aw´;* fem. of

6772; *thirst* (fig. of *libidinousnes*):— thirst.

6774. צִמָּאוֹן **tsimmâ'ôwn,** *tsim-maw-one´;* from 6771; a *thirsty* place, i.e. *desert:*— drought, dry ground, thirsty land.

6775. צָמַד **tsâmad,** *tsaw-mad´;* a prim. root; to *link,* i.e. *gird;* fig. to *serve,* (mentally) *contrive:*— fasten, frame, join (self).

6776. צֶמֶד **tsemed,** *tseh´-med;* a *yoke* or *team* (i.e. *pair*); hence, an *acre* (i.e. day's task for a yoke of cattle to plow):— acre, couple, × together, two lassesl, yoke (of oxen).

6777. צַמָּה **tsammâh,** *tsam-maw´;* from an unused root mean. to *fasten on;* a *veil:*— locks.

6778. צַמֻּק **tsammûwq,** *tsam-mook´;* from 6784; a *cake* of *dried* grapes:— bunch (cluster) of raisins.

6779. צָמַח **tsâmach,** *tsaw-makh´;* a prim. root; to *sprout* (tran. or intr., lit. or fig.):— bear, bring forth, (cause to, make to) bud (forth), (cause to, make to) grow (again, up), (cause to) spring (forth, up).

6780. צֶמַח **tsemach,** *tseh´-makh;* from 6779; a *sprout* (usually concr.), lit. or fig.:— branch, bud, that which (where) grew (upon), spring (-ing).

6781. צָמִיד **tsâmîyd,** *tsaw-meed´;* or צָמִד **tsâmid,** *tsaw-meed´;* from 6775; a *bracelet* or *arm-clasp;* gen. a *lid:*— bracelet, covering.

6782. צַמִּים **tsammiym,** *tsam-meem´;* from the same as 6777; a *noose* (as *fastening*); fig. *destruction:*— robber.

6783. צְמִיתֻת **ts⁰miythûth,** *tsem-eethooth´;* or צְמִתֻת **ts⁰mithûth,** *tsem-eethooth´;* from 6789; *excision,* i.e. *destruction;* used only (adv.) with pref. to *extinction,* i.e. *perpetually:*— ever.

6784. צָמַק **tsâmaq,** *tsaw-mak´;* a prim. root; to *dry* up:— dry.

6785. צֶמֶר **tsemer,** *tseh´-mer;* from an unused root prob. mean. to *be shaggy; wool:*— wool (-len).

6786. צְמָרִי **Ts⁰mâriy,** *tsem-aw-ree´;* patrial from an unused name of a place in Pal.; a *Tsemarite* or branch of the Canaanites:— Zemarite.

6787. צְמָרַיִם **Ts⁰mârayim,** *tsem-awrah´-yim;* dual of 6785; *double fleece; Tsemarajim,* a place in Pal.:— Zemaraim.

6788. צַמֶּרֶת **tsammereth,** *tsam-meh´-reth;* from the same as 6785; *fleeciness,* i.e. *foliage:*— highest branch, top.

6789. צָמַת **tsâmath,** *tsaw-math´;* a prim. root; to *extirpate* (lit. or fig.):— consume, cut off, destroy, vanish.

צְמִתֻת **ts⁰mithûth.** See 6783.

6790. צִן **Tsin,** *tseen;* from an unused root mean. to *prick;* a *crag; Tsin,* a part of the Desert:— Zin.

6791. צֵן **tsên,** *tsane;* from an unused root mean. to *be prickly;* a *thorn;* hence, a cactus-*hedge:*— thorn.

6792. צֹנֵא **tsônê',** *tso-nay´;* or

6772; *thirst* (fig. of *libidinousnes*):—

6793. צִנָּה **tsinnâh,** *tsin-naw´;* fem. of 6791; a *hook* (as *pointed*); also a (large) *shield* (as if guarding by *prickliness*); also *cold* (as *piercing*):— buckler, cold, hook, shield, target.

6794. צִנּוּר **tsinnûwr,** *tsin-noor´;* from an unused root perh. mean. to *be hollow;* a *culvert:*— gutter, water-spout.

6795. צָנַח **tsânach,** *tsaw-nakh´;* a prim. root; to *alight;* (tran.) to *cause to descend,* i.e. *drive* down:— fasten, light lfrom offl.

6796. צָנִין **tsâniyn,** *tsaw-neen´;* or צָנִן **tsânin,** *tsaw-neen´;* from the same as 6791; a *thorn:*— thorn.

6797. צָנִיף **tsâniyph,** *tsaw-neef´;* or צָנֹף **tsânôwph,** *tsaw-nofe´;* or (fem.) צְנִיפָה **tsâniyphâh,** *tsaw-nee-faw´;* from 6801; a *head-dress* (i.e. piece of cloth *wrapped* around):— diadem, hood, mitre.

6798. צָנַם **tsânam,** *tsaw-nam´;* a prim. root; to *blast* or *shrink:*— withered.

6799. צְנָן **Ts⁰nân,** *tsen-awn´;* prob. for 6630; *Tsenan,* a place near Pal.:— Zenan.

צָנִן **tsânin.** See 6796.

6800. צָנַע **tsâna',** *tsaw-nah´;* a prim. root; to *humiliate:*— humbly, lowly.

6801. צָנַף **tsânaph,** *tsaw-naf´;* a prim. root; to *wrap,* i.e. *roll* or *dress:*— be attired, × surely, violently turn.

6802. צְנֵפָה **ts⁰nêphâh,** *tsen-ay-faw´;* from 6801; a *ball:*— × toss.

6803. צִנְצֶנֶת **tsintseneth,** *tsin-tseh´-neth;* from the same as 6791; a *vase* (prob. a vial *tapering* at the top):— pot.

6804. צַנְתָּרָה **tsantârâh,** *tsan-taw-raw´;* prob. from the same as 6794; a *tube:*— pipe.

6805. צָעַד **tsâ'ad,** *tsaw-ad´;* a prim. root; to *pace,* i.e. *step* regularly; (upward) to *mount;* (along) to *march;* (down and caus.) to *hurl:*— bring, go, march (through), run over.

6806. צַעַד **tsa'ad,** *tsah´-ad;* from 6804; a *pace* or regular *step:*— pace, step.

6807. צְעָדָה **ts⁰'âdâh,** *tseh-aw-daw´;* fem. of 6806; a *march;* (concr.) an (ornamental) *ankle-chain:*— going, ornament of the legs.

6808. צָעָה **tsâ'âh,** *tsaw-aw´;* a prim. root; to *tip* over (for the purpose of *spilling* or *pouring* out), i.e. (fig.) *depopulate;* by impl. to *imprison* or *conquer;* (refl.) to *lie down* (for coitus, sexual intercourse):— captive exile, travelling, (cause to) wander (-er).

צָעוּר **tsâ'ôwr.** See 6810.

6809. צָעִיף **tsâ'iyph,** *tsaw-eef´;* from an unused root mean. to *wrap* over; a *veil:*— vail.

6810. צָעִיר **tsâ'iyr,** *tsaw-eer´;* or צָעוֹר **tsâ'ôwr,** *tsaw-ore´;* from 6819; *little;* (in number) *few;* (in age) *young,* (in value) *ignoble:*— least, little (one), small (one), + young (-er, -est).

6811. צָעִיר **Tsâ'iyr,** *tsaw-eer´;* the same

as 6810; *Tsaïr*, a place in Idumæa:— Zair.

6812. צְעִירָה **tseʻîyrâh**, *tseh-ee-raw´*; fem. of 6810; *smallness* (of age), i.e. *juvenility:*— youth.

6813. צָעַן **tsâʻan**, *tsaw-an´*; a prim. root; to *load* up (beasts), i.e. to *migrate:*— be taken down.

6814. צֹעַן **Tsôʻan**, *tso´-an;* of Eg. der.; *Tsoän*, a place in Egypt:— Zoan.

6815. צַעֲנִים **Tsaʻănannîym**, *tsah-an-an-neem´;* or (dual)

צַעֲנַיִם **Tsaʻănayim**, *tsah-an-ah´-yim;* plur. from 6813; *removals; Tsaanannim* or *Tsaanajim*, a place in Pal.:— Zaannannim, Zaanaim.

6816. צַעְצֻעַ **tsaʻtsûaʻ**, *tsah-tsoo´-ah;* from an unused root mean. to *bestrew* with carvings; *sculpture:*— image [work].

6817. צָעַק **tsâʻaq**, *tsaw-ak´;* a prim. root; to *shriek;* (by impl.) to *proclaim* (an assembly):— × at all, call together, cry (out), gather (selves) (together).

6818. צְעָקָה **tsaʻăqâh**, *tsah-ak-aw´;* from 6817; a *shriek:*— cry (-ing).

6819. צָעַר **tsâʻar**, *tsaw-ar´;* a prim. root; to *be small*, i.e. (fig.) *ignoble:*— be brought low, little one, be small.

6820. צֹעַר **Tsôʻar**, *tso´ar;* from 6819; *little; Tsoär*, a place E. of the Jordan:— Zoar.

6821. צָפַד **tsâphad**, *tsaw-fad´;* a prim. root; to *adhere:*— cleave.

6822. צָפָה **tsâphâh**, *tsaw-faw´;* a prim. root; prop. to *lean* forward, i.e. to *peer* into the distance; by impl. to *observe, await:*— behold, espy, look up (well), wait for, (keep the) watch (-man).

6823. צָפָה **tsâphâh**, *tsaw-faw´;* a prim. root [prob. rather ident. with 6822 through the idea of *expansion* in outlook, transferring to act]; to *sheet* over (espec. with metal):— cover, overlay.

6824. צָפָה **tsâphâh**, *tsaw-faw´;* from 6823; an *inundation* (as *covering*):— × swimmest.

6825. צְפוֹ **Tsephôw**, *tsef-o´;* or

צְפִי **Tsephîy**, *tsef-ee´;* from 6822; *observant; Tsepho* or *Tsephi*, an Idumæan:— Zephi, Zepho.

6826. צִפּוּי **tsippûwy**, *tsip-poo´-ee;* from 6823; *encasement* (with metal):— covering, overlaying.

6827. צְפוֹן **Tsephôwn**, *tsef-one´;* prob. for 6837; *Tsephon*, an Isr.:— Zephon.

6828. צָפוֹן **tsâphôwn**, *tsaw-fone´;* or

צָפֹן **tsâphôn**, *tsaw-fone´;* from 6845; prop. *hidden*, i.e. *dark;* used only of the *north* as a quarter (*gloomy* and *unknown*):— north (-ern, side, -ward, wind).

6829. צָפוֹן **Tsâphôwn**, *tsaw-fone´;* the same as 6828; *boreal; Tsaphon*, a place in Pal.:— Zaphon.

6830. צְפוֹנִי **tsephôwnîy**, *tsef-o-nee´;* from 6828; *northern:*— northern.

6831. צְפוֹנִי **Tsephôwnîy**, *tsef-o-nee´;* patron. from 6827; a *Tsephonite*, or (collect.) desc. of Tsephon:— Zephonites.

6832. צְפוּעַ **tsephûwaʻ**, *tsef-oo´-ah;* from

the same as 6848; *excrement* (as *protruded*):— dung.

6833. צִפּוֹר **tsippôwr**, *tsip-pore´;* or

צִפֹּר **tsippôr**, *tsip-pore´;* from 6852; a little *bird* (as *hopping*):— bird, fowl, sparrow.

6834. צִפּוֹר **Tsippôwr**, *tsip-pore´;* the same as 6833; *Tsippor*, a Moabite:— Zippor.

6835. צַפַּחַת **tsappachath**, *tsap-pakh´-ath;* from an unused root mean. to *expand;* a *saucer* (as *flat*):— cruse.

6836. צְפִיָּה **tsephîyâh**, *tsef-ee-yaw´;* from 6822; *watchfulness:*— watching.

6837. צִפְיוֹן **Tsiphyôwn**, *tsif-yone´;* from 6822; *watch*-tower; *Tsiphjon*, an Isr.:— Ziphion. Comp. 6827.

6838. צַפִּיחִת **tsappîychîth**, *tsap-pee-kheeth´;* from the same as 6835; a flat thin *cake:*— wafer.

6839. צֹפִים **Tsôphîym**, *tso-feem´;* plur. of act. part. of 6822; *watchers; Tsophim*, a place E. of the Jordan:— Zophim.

6840. צָפִן **tsâphîn**, *tsaw-feen´;* from 6845; a *treasure* (as *hidden*):— hid.

6841. צְפִיר **tsephîyr** (Chald.), *tsef-eer´;* corresp. to 6842; a he-*goat:*— he [goat].

6842. צָפִיר **tsâphîyr**, *tsaw-feer´;* from 6852; a male *goat* (as *prancing*):— (he) goat.

6843. צְפִירָה **tsephîyrâh**, *tsef-ee-raw´;* fem. formed like 6842; a *crown* (as *encircling* the head); also a *turn* of affairs (i.e. *mishap*):— diadem, morning.

6844. צָפִית **tsâphîyth**, *tsaw-feeth´;* from 6822; a *sentry:*— watchtower.

6845. צָפַן **tsâphan**, *tsaw-fan´;* a prim. root; to *hide* (by *covering* over); by impl. to *hoard* or *reserve;* fig. to *deny;* spec. (favorably) to *protect*, (unfavorably) to *lurk:*— esteem, hide (-den one, self), lay up, lurk (be set) privily, (keep) secret (-ly, place).

6846. צְפַנְיָה **Tsephanyâh**, *tsef-an-yaw´;* or

צְפַנְיָהוּ **Tsephanyâhûw**, *tsef-an-yaw´-hoo;* from 6845 and 3050; *Jah has secreted; Tsephanjah*, the name of four Isr.:— Zephaniah.

6847. צָפְנַת פַּעְנֵחַ **Tsophnath Paʻnêach**, *tsof-nath´ pah-nay´-akh;* of Eg. der.; *Tsophnath-Paneäch*, Joseph's Eg. name:— Zaphnath-paaneah.

6848. צֶפַע **tsepha**, *tseh´-fah;* or

צִפְעֹנִי **tsiphʻônîy**, *tsif-o-nee´;* from an unused root mean. to *extrude;* a *viper* (as *thrusting* out the tongue, i.e. *hissing*):— adder, cockatrice.

6849. צְפִיעָה **tsephîʻâh**, *tsef-ee-aw´;* fem. from the same as 6848; an *outcast* thing:— issue.

צִפְעֹנִי **tsiphʻônîy**. See 6848.

6850. צָפַף **tsâphaph**, *tsaw-faf´;* a prim. root; to *coo* or *chirp* (as a bird):— chatter, peep, whisper.

6851. צַפְצָפָה **tsaphtsâphâh**, *tsaf-tsaw-faw´;* from 6687; a *willow* (as growing in *overflowed* places):— willow tree.

6852. צָפַר **tsâphar**, *tsaw-far´;* a prim.

root; to *skip* about, i.e. *return:*— depart early.

6853. צְפַר **tsephar** (Chald.), *tsef-ar´;* corresp. to 6833; a *bird:*— bird.

צִפֹּר **tsippôr**. See 6833.

6854. צְפַרְדֵּעַ **tsephardêaʻ**, *tsef-ar-day´-ah;* from 6852 and a word elsewhere unused mean. a *swamp;* a *marsh-leaper*, i.e. *frog:*— frog.

6855. צִפֹּרָה **Tsippôrâh**, *tsip-po-raw´;* fem. of 6833; *bird; Tsipporah*, Moses' wife:— Zipporah.

6856. צִפֹּרֶן **tsippôren**, *tsip-po´-ren;* from 6852 (in the denom. sense [from 6833] of *scratching*); prop. a *claw*, i.e. (human) *nail;* also the *point* of a style (or pen, tipped with adamant):— nail, point.

6857. צְפַת **Tsephath**, *tsef-ath´;* from 6822; *watch*-tower; *Tsephath*, a place in Pal.:— Zephath.

6858. צֶפֶת **tsepheth**, *tseh´-feth;* from an unused root mean. to *encircle;* a *capital* of a column:— chapiter.

6859. צְפָתָה **Tsephâthâh**, *tsef-aw´-thaw;* the same as 6857; *Tsephathah*, a place in Pal.:— Zephathah.

צִיץ **tsîts**. See 6732.

6860. צִקְלַג **Tsiqlâg**, *tsik-lag´;* or

צִיקְלַג **Tsîyqelag** (1 Chron. 12:1, 20), *tsee-kel-ag´;* of uncert. der.: *Tsiklag* or *Tsikelag*, a place in Pal.:— Ziklag.

6861. צִקְלֹן **tsiqlôn**, *tsik-lone´;* from an unused root mean. to *wind;* a *sack* (as *tied* at the mouth):— husk.

6862. צַר **tsar**, *tsar;* or

צָר **tsâr**, *tsawr;* from 6887; *narrow;* (as a noun) a *tight* place (usually fig., i.e. *trouble*); also a *pebble* (as in 6864); (tran.) an *opponent* (as *crowding*):— adversary, afflicted (-tion), anguish, close, distress, enemy, flint, foe, narrow, small, sorrow, strait, tribulation, trouble.

6863. צֵר **Tsêr**, *tsare;* from 6887; *rock; Tser*, a place in Pal.:— Zer.

6864. צֹר **tsôr**, *tsore;* from 6696; a *stone* (as if *pressed* hard or to a point); (by impl. of use) a *knife:*— flint, sharp stone.

6865. צֹר **Tsôr**, *tsore;* or

צוֹר **Tsôwr**, *tsore;* the same as 6864; a *rock; Tsor*, a place in Pal.:— Tyre, Tyrus.

צוּר **tsûr**. See 6697.

6866. צָרַב **tsârab**, *tsaw-rab´;* a prim. root; to *burn:*— burn.

6867. צָרֶבֶת **tsârebeth**, *tsaw-reh´-beth;* from 6686; *conflagration* (of fire or disease):— burning, inflammation.

6868. צְרֵדָה **Tserêdâh**, *tser-ay-daw´;* or

צְרֵדָתָה **Tserêdâthâh**, *tser-ay-daw´-thaw;* appar. from an unused root mean. to *pierce; puncture; Tseredah*, a place in Pal.:— Zereda, Zeredathah.

6869. צָרָה **tsârâh**, *tsaw-raw´;* fem. of 6862; *tightness* (i.e. fig. *trouble*); tran. a female *rival:*— adversary, adversity, affliction, anguish, distress, tribulation, trouble.

6870. צְרוּיָה **Tsᵉrûwyâh**, tser-oo-yaw´; fem. pass. part. from the same as 6875; *wounded; Tserujah*, an Israelitess:— Zeruiah.

6871. צְרוּעָה **Tsᵉrûwʻâh**, tser-oo-aw´; fem. pass. part. of 6879; *leprous; Tseruäh*, an Israelitess:— Zeruah.

6872. צְרוֹר **tsᵉrôwr**, tser-ore´; or (short.)

צְרֹר **tsᵉrôr**, tser-ore´; from 6887; a *parcel* (as *packed* up); also a *kernel* or *particle* (as if a *package*):— bag, × bendeth, bundle, least grain, small stone.

6873. צָרַח **tsârach**, tsaw-rakh´; a prim. root; to *be clear* (in tone, i.e. *shrill*), i.e. to *whoop*:— cry, roar.

6874. צְרִי **Tsᵉrîy**, tser-ee´; the same as 6875; *Tseri*, an Isr.:— Zeri. Comp. 3340.

6875. צְרִי **tsᵉrîy**, tser-ee´; or

צֳרִי **tsŏrîy**, tsor-ee´; from an unused root mean. to *crack* las by *pressure*l, hence, to *leak; distillation*, i.e. *balsam*:— balm.

6876. צֹרִי **Tsôrîy**, tso-ree´; patrial from 6865; a *Tsorite* or inhab. of Tsor (i.e. *Syrian*):— (man) of Tyre.

6877. צְרִיחַ **tsᵉrîyach**, tser-ee´-akh; from 6873 in the sense of *clearness* of vision; a *citadel*:— high place, hold.

6878. צֹרֶךְ **tsôrek**, tso´-rek; from an unused root mean. to *need; need*:— need.

6879. צָרַע **tsâraʻ**, tsaw-rah´; a prim. root; to *scourge*, i.e. (intr. and fig.) to *be stricken with leprosy*:— leper, leprous.

6880. צִרְעָה **tsirʻâh**, tsir-aw´; from 6879; a *wasp* (as *stinging*):— hornet.

6881. צָרְעָה **Tsorʻâh**, tsor-aw´; appar. another form for 6880; *Tsorah*, a place in Pal.:— Zareah, Zorah, Zoreah.

6882. צָרְעִי **Tsorʻîy**, tsor-ee´; or

צָרְעָתִי **Tsorʻâthîy**, tsor-aw-thee´; patrial from 6881; a *Tsorite* or *Tsorathite*, i.e. inhab. of Tsorah:— Zorites, Zareathites, Zorathites.

6883. צָרַעַת **tsâraʻath**, tsaw-rah´-ath; from 6879; *leprosy*:— leprosy.

6884. צָרַף **tsâraph**, tsaw-raf´; a prim. root; to *fuse* (metal), i.e. *refine* (lit. or fig.):— cast, (re-) fine (-ėr), founder, goldsmith, melt, pure, purge away, try.

6885. צֹרְפִי **Tsôrᵉphiy**, tso-ref-ee´; from 6884; *refiner; Tsorephi* (with the art.), an Isr.:— goldsmith's.

6886. צָרְפַת **Tsârᵉphath**, tsaq-ref-ath´; from 6884; *refinement; Tsarephath*, a place in Pal.:— Zarephath.

6887. צָרַר **tsârar**, tsaw-rar´; a prim. root; to *cramp*, lit. or fig., tran. or intr. (as follows):— adversary, (be in) afflict (-ion), beseige, bind (up), (be in, bring) distress, enemy, narrower, oppress, pangs, shut up, be in a strait (trouble), vex.

6888. צְרֵרָה **Tsᵉrêrâh**, tser-ay-raw´; appar. by err. transc. for 6868; *Tsererah* for *Tseredah*:— Zererath.

6889. צֶרֶת **Tsereth**, tseh´-reth; perh. from 6671; *splendor; Tsereth*, an Isr.:— Zereth.

6890. צֶרֶת הַשַּׁחַר **Tsereth hash-Shachar**, tseh´-reth hash-shakh´-ar; from the same as 6889 and 7837 with the art. interposed; *splendor of the dawn; Tsereth-hash-Shachar*, a place in Pal.:— Zareth-shahar.

6891. צָרְתָן **Tsârᵉthân**, tsaw-reth-awn´; perh. for 6868; *Tsarethan*, a place in Pal.:— Zarthan.

ק

6892. קֵא **qêʼ**, kay; or

קִיא **qîyʼ**, kee; from 6958; *vomit*:— vomit.

6893. קָאָה **qâʼath**, kaw-ath´; from 6958; prob. the *pelican* (from *vomiting*):— cormorant.

6894. קַב **qab**, kab; from 6895; a *hollow*, i.e. vessel used as a (dry) *measure*:— cab.

6895. קָבַב **qâbab**, kaw-bab´; a prim. root; to *scoop* out, i.e. (fig.) to *malign* or *execrate* (i.e. *stab* with words):— × at all, curse.

6896. קֵבָה **qêbâh**, kay-baw´; from 6895; the *paunch* (as a *cavity*) or first stomach of ruminants:— maw.

6897. קֹבָה **qôbâh**, ko´-baw; from 6895; the *abdomen* (as a cavity):— belly.

6898. קֻבָּה **qubbâh**, koob-baw´; from 6895; a *pavilion* (as a domed *cavity*):— tent.

6899. קִבּוּץ **qibbûwts**, kib-boots´; from 6908; a *throng*:— company.

6900. קְבוּרָה **qᵉbûwrâh**, keb-oo-raw´; or

קְבֻרָה **qᵉbûrâh**, keb-oo-raw´; fem. pass. part. of 6912; *sepulture*; (concr.) a *sepulchre*:— burial, burying place, grave, sepulchre.

6901. קָבַל **qâbal**, kaw-bal´; a prim root; to *admit*, i.e. *take* (lit. or fig.):— choose, (take) hold, receive, (under-) take.

6902. קְבַל **qᵉbal** (Chald.), keb-al´; corresp. to 6901; to *acquire*:— receive, take.

6903. קְבֵל **qᵉbêl** (Chald.), keb-ale´; or

קֳבֵל **qôbêl** (Chald.), kob-ale´; (corresp. to 6905; (adv.) *in front of*; usually (with other particles) *on account of, so as, since, hence*:— + according to, + as, + because, before, + for this cause, + forasmuch as, + by this means, over against, by reason of, + that, + therefore, + though, + wherefore.

6904. קֹבֶל **qôbel**, ko´-bel; from 6901 in the sense of *confronting* (as standing *opposite* in order to receive); a *battering-ram*:— war.

6905. קָבָל **qâbâl**, kaw-bawl´; from 6901 in the sense of *opposite* lsee 6904l; the *presence*, i.e. (adv.) *in front of*:— before.

6906. קָבַע **qâbaʻ**, kaw-bah´; a prim. root; to *cover*, i.e. (fig.) *defraud*:— rob, spoil.

6907. קֻבַּעַת **qubbaʻath**, koob-bah´-ath; from 6906; a *goblet* (as deep like a *cover*):— dregs.

6908. קָבַץ **qâbats**, kaw-bats´; a prim. root; to *grasp*, i.e. *collect*:— assemble (selves), gather (bring) (together, selves together, up), heap, resort, × surely, take up.

6909. קַבְצְאֵל **Qabtsᵉʼêl**, kab-tseh-ale´; from 6908 and 410; *God has gathered; Kabtseël*, a place in Pal.:— Kabzeel. Comp. 3343.

6910. קְבֻצָה **qᵉbûtsâh**, keb-oo-tsaw´; fem. pass. part. of 6908; a *hoard*:— × gather.

6911. קְבֻצַיִם **Qîbtsayim**, kib-tsah´-yim; dual from 6908; a *double heap; Kibtsajim*, a place in Pal.:— Kibzaim.

6912. קָבַר **qâbar**, kaw-bar´; a prim. root; to *inter*:— × in any wise, bury (-ier).

6913. קֶבֶר **qeber**, keh´-ber; or (fem.)

קִבְרָה **qibrâh**, kib-raw´; from 6912; a *sepulchre*:— burying place, grave, sepulchre.

קְבֻרָה **qᵉbûrâh**. See 6900.

6914. קִבְרוֹת הַתַּאֲוָה **Qibrôwth hat-Taʼăvâh**, kib-roth´ hat-tah-av-aw´; from the fem. plur. of 6913 and 8378 with the art. interposed; *graves of the longing; Kibroth-hat-Taavh*, a place in the Desert:— Kibroth-hattaavah.

6915. קָדַד **qâdad**, kaw-dad´; a prim. root; to *shrivel* up, i.e. *contract* or *bend* the body (or neck) in deference:— bow (down) (the) head, stoop.

6916. קִדָּה **qiddâh**, kid-daw´; from 6915; *cassia* bark (as in *shrivelled* rolls):— cassia.

6917. קָדוּם **qâdûwm**, kaw-doom´; pass. part. of 6923; a *pristine* hero:— ancient.

6918. קָדוֹשׁ **qâdôwsh**, kaw-doshe´; or

קָדֹשׁ **qâdôsh**, kaw-doshe´; from 6942; *sacred* (cerem. or mor.); (as noun) *God* (by eminence), an *angel*, a *saint*, a *sanctuary*:— holy (One), saint.

6919. קָדַח **qâdach**, kaw-dakh´; a prim. root; to *inflame*:— burn, kindle.

6920. קַדַּחַת **qaddachath**, kad-dakh´-ath; from 6919; *inflammation*, i.e. febrile disease:— burning ague, fever.

6921. קָדִים **qâdîym**, kaw-deem´; or

קָדִם **qâdîm**, kaw-deem´; from 6923; the *fore* or front part; hence, (by orientation) the *East* (often adv. *eastward*, for brevity the *east wind*):— east (-ward, wind).

6922. קַדִּישׁ **qaddîysh** (Chald.), kad-deesh´; corresp. to 6918:— holy (One), saint.

6923. קָדַם **qâdam**, kaw-dam´; a prim. root; to *project* (one self), i.e. *precede*; hence, to *anticipate, hasten, meet* (usually for help):— come (go, Ifleel) before, + disappoint, meet, prevent.

6924. קֶדֶם **qedem**, keh´-dem; or

קֵדְמָה **qêdmâh**, kayd´-maw; from 6923; the *front*, of place (absolutely, the *fore part*, rel. the *East*) or time (*antiquity*); often used adv. (*before, anciently, eastward*):— aforetime, ancient (time), before, east (end, part, side, -ward), eternal, × ever (-lasting), forward, old, past. Comp. 6926.

6925. קֳדָם **qŏdâm** (Chald.), kod-awm´; or

קְדָם **qᵉdâm** (Chald.) (Dan. 7:13), ked-awm´; corresp. to 6924; *before*:— before, × from, × I (thought), × me, + of, × it pleased, presence.

קָדִים **qâdîm.** See 6921.

6926. קִדְמָה **qidmâh,** kid-maw´; fem. of 6924; *the* forward *part* (or rel.) *East* (often adv. *on* (the) *east* or *in front*):— east (-ward).

6927. קַדְמָה **qadmâh,** kad-maw´; from 6923; *priority* (in time); also used adv. (*before*):— afore, antiquity, former (old) estate.

6928. קַדְמָה **qadmâh** (Chald.), kad-maw´; corresp. to 6927; *former time*:— afore I-timel, ago.

קִדְמָה **qêdmâh.** See 6924.

6929. קֵדְמָה **Qêdᵉmâh,** kayd´-maw; from 6923; *precedence*; *Kedemah,* a son of Ishmael:— Kedemah.

6930. קַדְמוֹן **qadmôwn,** kad-mone´; from 6923; *eastern*:— east.

6931. קַדְמוֹנִי **qadmôwniy,** kad-mo-nee´; or

קַדְמֹנִי **qadmôniy,** kad-mo-nee´; from 6930; (of time) *anterior* or (of place) *oriental*:— ancient, they that went before, east, (thing of) old.

6932. קְדֵמוֹת **Qᵉdêmôwth,** ked-ay-mothe´; from 6923; *beginnings*; *Kedemoth,* a place in eastern Pal.:— Kedemoth.

6933. קַדְמַי **qadmay** (Chald.), kad-mah´-ee; from a root corresp. to 6923; *first*:— first.

6934. קַדְמִיאֵל **Qadmîy'êl,** kad-mee-ale´; from 6924 and 410; *presence of God*; *Kadmiël,* the name of three Isr.:— Kadmiel.

קַדְמֹנִי **qadmôniy.** See 6931.

6935. קַדְמֹנִי **Qadmôniy,** kad-mo-nee´; the same as 6931; *ancient,* i.e. aboriginal; *Kadmonite* (collect.), the name of a tribe in Pal.:— Kadmonites.

6936. קָדְקֹד **qodqôd,** kod-kode´; from 6915; the *crown* of the head (as the part most *bowed*):— crown (of the head), pate, scalp, top of the head.

6937. קָדַר **qâdar,** kaw-dar´; a prim. root; to *be ashy,* i.e. *dark*-colored; by impl. to *mourn* (in sackcloth or sordid garments):— be black (-ish), be (make) dark (-en), × heavily, (cause to) mourn.

6938. קֵדָר **Qêdâr,** kay-dawr´; from 6937; *dusky* (of the skin or the tent); *Kedar,* a son of Ishmael; also (collect.) *bedawin* (as his desc. or representatives):— Kedar.

6939. קִדְרוֹן **Qidrôwn,** kid-rone´; from 6937; *dusky place*; *Kidron,* a brook near Jerusalem:— Kidron.

6940. קַדְרוּת **qadrûwth,** kad-rooth´; from 6937; *duskiness*:— blackness.

6941. קְדֹרַנִּית **qᵉdôranniyth,** ked-o-ran-neeth´; adv. from 6937; *blackish ones* (i.e. *in sackcloth*); used adv. in *mourning* weeds:— mournfully.

6942. קָדַשׁ **qâdash,** kaw-dash´; a prim. root; to *be* (caus. *make, pronounce* or *observe* as) *clean* (cerem. or mor.):— appoint, bid, consecrate, dedicate, defile, hallow, (be, keep) holy (-er, place), keep, prepare, proclaim, purify, sanctify (-ied one, self), × wholly.

6943. קֶדֶשׁ **Qedesh,** keh´-desh; from

6942; a *sanctum*; *Kedesh,* the name of four places in Pal.:— Kedesh.

6944. קֹדֶשׁ **qôdesh,** ko´-desh; from 6942; a *sacred* place or thing; rarely abstr. *sanctity*:— consecrated (thing), dedicated (thing), hallowed (thing), holiness, (× most) holy (× day, portion, thing), saint, sanctuary.

6945. קָדֵשׁ **qâdêsh,** kaw-dashe´; from 6942; a (quasi) *sacred* person, i.e. (tech.) a (male) *devotee* (by prostitution) to licentious idolatry:— sodomite, unclean.

6946. קָדֵשׁ **Qâdêsh,** kaw-dashe´; the same as 6945; *sanctuary*; *Kadesh,* a place in the Desert:— Kadesh. Comp. 6947.

קָדֹשׁ **qâdôsh.** See 6918.

6947. קָדֵשׁ בַּרְנֵעַ **Qâdêsh Barnêa',** kaw-dashe´ bar-nay´-ah; from the same as 6946 and an otherwise unused word (appar. compounded of a correspondent to 1251 and a der. of 5128) mean. *desert of a fugitive*; *Kadesh of* (the) *Wilderness of Wandering*; *Kadesh-Barneä,* a place in the Desert:— Kadesh-barnea.

6948. קְדֵשָׁה **qᵉdêshâh,** ked-ay-shaw´; fem. of 6945; a female *devotee* (i.e. *prostitute*):— harlot, whore.

6949. קָהָה **qâhâh,** kaw-haw´; a prim. root; to *be dull*:— be set on edge, be blunt.

6950. קָהַל **qâhal,** kaw-hal´; a prim. root; to *convoke*:— assemble (selves) (together), gather (selves) (together).

6951. קָהָל **qâhâl,** kaw-hawl´; from 6950; *assemblage* (usually concr.):— assembly, company, congregation, multitude.

6952. קְהִלָּה **qᵉhillâh,** keh-hil-law´; from 6950; an *assemblage*:— assembly, congregation.

6953. קֹהֶלֶת **qôheleth,** ko-heh´-leth; fem. of act. part. from 6950; a (female) *assembler* (i.e. *lecturer*): abstr. *preaching* (used as a "nom de plume", *Koheleth*):— preacher.

6954. קְהֵלָתָה **Qᵉhêlâthâh,** keh-hay-law´-thaw; from 6950; *convocation*; *Kehelathah,* a place in the Desert:— Kehelathah.

6955. קְהָת **Qᵉhâth,** keh-hawth´; from an unused root mean. to *ally* oneself; *allied*; *Kehath,* an Isr.:— Kohath.

6956. קְהָתִי **Qᵉhâthiy,** ko-haw-thee´; patron. from 6955; a *Kohathite* (collect.) or desc. of Kehath:— Kohathites.

6957. קַו **qav,** kav; or

קָו **qâv,** kawv; from 6960 [comp. 6961]; a *cord* (as *connecting*), espec. for measuring; fig. a *rule*; also a *rim,* a musical *string* or *accord*:— line. Comp. 6978.

6958. קוֹא **qôw',** ko; or

קָיָה **qâyâh** (Jer. 25:27), kaw-yaw´; a prim. root; to *vomit*:— spue (out), vomit (out, up, up again).

6959. קוֹבַע **qôwba',** ko´-bah or ko-bah´; a form collat. to 3553; a *helmet*:— helmet.

6960. קָוָה **qâvâh,** kaw-vaw´; a prim.

root; to *bind* together (perh. by *twisting*), i.e. *collect*; (fig.) to *expect*:— gather (together), look, patiently, tarry, wait (for, on, upon).

6961. קָוֶה **qâveh,** kaw-veh´; from 6960; a (measuring) *cord* (as if for *binding*):— line.

קֹוַח **qôwach.** See 6495.

6962. קוּט **qûwt,** koot; a prim. root; prop. to *cut off,* i.e. (fig.) *detest*:— be grieved, loathe self.

6963. קוֹל **qôwl,** kole; or

קֹל **qôl,** kole; from an unused root mean. to *call* aloud; a *voice* or *sound*:— + aloud, bleating, crackling, cry (+ out), fame, lightness, lowing, noise, + hold peace, [pro-] claim, proclamation, + sing, sound, + spark, thunder (-ing), voice, + yell.

6964. קוֹלָיָה **Qôwlâyâh,** ko-law-yaw´; from 6963 and 3050; *voice of Jah*; *Kolajah,* the name of two Isr.:— Kolaiah.

6965. קוּם **qûwm,** koom; a prim. root; to *rise* (in various applications, lit., fig., intens. and caus.):— abide, accomplish, × be clearer, confirm, continue, decree, × be dim, endure, × enemy, enjoin, get up, make good, help, hold, (help to) lift up (again), make, × but newly, ordain, perform, pitch, raise (up), rear (up), remain, (a-) rise (up) (again, against), rouse up, set (up), (e-) stablish, (make to) stand (up), stir up, strengthen, succeed, (as-, make) sure (-ly), (be) up (-hold, -rising).

6966. קוּם **qûwm** (Chald.), koom; corresp. to 6965:— appoint, establish, make, raise up self, (a-) rise (up), (make to) stand, set (up).

6967. קוֹמָה **qôwmâh,** ko-maw´; from 6965; *height*:— × along, height, high, stature, tall.

6968. קוֹמְמִיּוּת **qôwmᵉmîyûwth,** ko-mem-ee-yooth´; from 6965; *elevation,* i.e. (adv.) *erectly* (fig.):— upright.

6969. קוּן **qûwn,** koon; a prim. root; to *strike* a musical note, i.e. *chant* or *wail* (at a funeral):— lament, mourning woman.

6970. קוֹעַ **Qôwa',** ko´-ah; prob. from 6972 in the orig. sense of *cutting* off; *curtailment*; *Koä,* a region of Bab.:— Koa.

6971. קוֹף **qôwph,** kofe; or

קֹף **qôph,** kofe; prob. of for. or.; a *monkey*:— ape.

6972. קוּץ **qûwts,** koots; a prim. root; to *clip* off; used only as denom. from 7019; to *spend the harvest* season:— summer.

6973. קוּץ **qûwts,** koots; a prim. root [rather ident. with 6972 through the idea of *severing* oneself from (comp. 6962)]; to *be* (caus. *make*) *disgusted* or *anxious*:— abhor, be distressed, be grieved, loathe, vex, be weary.

6974. קוּץ **qûwts,** koots; a prim. root [rather ident. with 6972 through the idea of *abruptness* in starting up from sleep (comp. 3364)]; to *awake* (lit. or fig.):— arise, (be) (a-) wake, watch.

6975. קוֹץ **qôwts,** kotse; or

Hebrew

קוץ **qôts**, *kotse;* from 6972 (in the sense of *pricking*); a *thorn.*— thorn.

6976. קוֹץ **Qôwts**, *kotse;* the same as 6975; *Kots,* the name of two Isr.:— Koz, Hakkoz [incl. *the art.*].

6977. קְוֻצָּה **qᵉvutstsâh**, *kev-oots-tsaw´;* fem. pass. part. of 6972 in its orig. sense; a *forelock* (as *shorn*):— lock.

6978. קַו־קַו **qav-qav**, *kav-kav´;* from 6957 (in the sense of a *fastening*); *stalwart:*— × meted out.

6979. קוּר **qûwr**, *koor;* a prim. root; to *trench;* by impl. to *throw forth;* also (denom. from 7023) to *wall up,* whether lit. (to *build* a wall) or fig. (to *estop*):— break down, cast out, destroy, dig.

6980. קוּר **qûwr**, *koor;* from 6979; (only plur.) *trenches,* i.e. a *web* (as if so formed):— web.

6981. קוֹרֵא **Qôwrê'**, *ko-ray´;* or

קֹרֵא **Qôrê'** (1 Chron. 26:1), *ko-ray´;* act. part. of 7121; *crier; Korè,* the name of two Isr.:— Kore.

6982. קוֹרָה **qôwrâh**, *ko-raw´;* or

קֹרָה **qôrâh**, *ko-raw´;* from 6979; a *rafter* (forming *trenches* as it were); by impl. a *roof:*— beam, roof.

6983. קוֹשׁ **qôwsh**, *koshe;* a prim. root; to *bend;* used only as denom. for 3369, to *set a trap:*— lay a snare.

6984. קוּשָׁיָהוּ **Qûwshâyâhûw**, *koo-shaw-yaw´-hoo;* from the pass. part. of 6983 and 3050; *entrapped of Jah; Kushajah,* an Isr.:— Kushaiah.

6985. קַט **qat**, *kat;* from 6990 in the sense of *abbreviation;* a *little,* i.e. (adv.) *merely:*— very.

6986. קֶטֶב **qeteb**, *keh´-teb;* from an unused root mean. to *cut off; ruin:*— destroying, destruction.

6987. קֹטֶב **qôteb**, *ko´-teb;* from the same as 6986; *extermination:*— destruction.

6988. קְטוֹרָה **qᵉtôwrâh**, *ket-o-raw´;* from 6999; *perfume:*— incense.

6989. קְטוּרָה **Qᵉtûwrâh**, *ket-oo-raw´;* fem. pass. part. of 6999; *perfumed; Keturah,* a wife of Abraham:— Keturah.

6990. קָטַט **qâtat**, *kaw-tat´;* a prim. root; to *clip off,* i.e. (fig.) *destroy:*— be cut off.

6991. קָטַל **qâtal**, *kaw-tal´;* a prim. root; prop. to *cut off,* i.e. (fig.) *put to death:*— kill, slay.

6992. קְטַל **qᵉtal** (Chald.), *ket-al´;* corresp. to 6991; to *kill:*— slay.

6993. קֶטֶל **qetel**, *keh´-tel;* from 6991; a *violent death:*— slaughter.

6994. קָטֹן **qâtôn**, *kaw-tone´;* a prim. root [rather denom. from 6996]; to *diminish,* i.e. *be* (caus. *make*) *diminutive* or (fig.) *of no account:*— be a (make) small (thing), be not worthy.

6995. קֹטֶן **qôten**, *ko´-ten;* from 6994; a *pettiness,* i.e. the *little finger:*— little finger.

6996. קָטָן **qâtân**, *kaw-tawn´;* or

קָטֹן **qâtôn**, *kaw-tone´;* from 6962; *abbreviated,* i.e. *diminutive,* lit. (in quantity, size or number) or fig. (in age or importance):— least, less (-er), little

(one), small (-est, one, quantity, thing), young (-er, -est).

6997. קָטָן **Qâtân**, *kaw-tawn´;* the same as 6996; *small; Katan,* an Isr.:— Hakkatan [incl. *the art.*].

6998. קָטַף **qâtaph**, *kaw-taf´;* a prim. root; to *strip* off:— crop off, cut down (up), pluck.

6999. קָטַר **qâtar**, *kaw-tar´;* a prim. root [rather ident. with 7000 through the idea of *fumigation* in a *close* place and perh. thus *driving* out the occupants]; to *smoke,* i.e. turn into fragrance by fire (espec. as an act of worship):— burn (incense, sacrifice) (upon), (altar for) incense, kindle, offer (incense, a sacrifice).

7000. קָטַר **qâtar**, *kaw-tar´;* a prim. root; to *inclose:*— join.

7001. קְטַר **qᵉtar** (Chald.), *ket-ar´;* from a root corresp. to 7000; a *knot* (as *tied* up), i.e. (fig.) a *riddle;* also a *vertebra* (as if a knot):— doubt, joint.

7002. קִטֵּר **qittêr**, *kit-tare´;* from 6999; *perfume:*— incense.

7003. קִטְרוֹן **Qitrôwn**, *kit-rone´;* from 6999; *fumigative; Kitron,* a place in Pal.:— Kitron.

7004. קְטֹרָה **qᵉtôrâh**, *ket-o´-reth;* from 6999; a *fumigation:*— (sweet) incense, perfume.

7005. קַטָּת **Qattâth**, *kat-tawth´;* from 6996; *littleness; Kattath,* a place in Pal.:— Kattath.

7006. קָיָה **qâyâh**, *kaw-yaw´;* a prim. root; to *vomit:*— spue.

7007. קַיִט **qâyit** (Chald.), *kah´-yit;* corresp. to 7019; *harvest:*— summer.

7008. קִיטוֹר **qîytôwr**, *kee-tore´;* or

קִיטֹר **qîytôr**, *kee-tore´;* from 6999; a *fume,* i.e. *cloud:*— smoke, vapour.

7009. קִים **qîym**, *keem;* from 6965; an *opponent* (as *rising* against one), i.e. (collect.) *enemies:*— substance.

7010. קְיָם **qᵉyâm** (Chald.), *keh-yawm´;* from 6966; an *edict* (as *arising* in law):— decree, statute.

7011. קַיָּם **qayâm** (Chald.), *kah-yawm´;* from 6966; *permanent* (as *rising* firmly):— stedfast, sure.

7012. קִימָה **qîymâh**, *kee-maw´;* from 6965; an *arising:*— rising up.

· קִימוֹשׁ **Qîymôwsh**. See 7057.

7013. קַיִן **qayin**, *kah´-yin;* from 6969 in the orig. sense of *fixity;* a *lance* (as *striking fast*):— spear.

7014. קַיִן **Qayin**, *kah´-yin;* the same as 7013 (with a play upon the affinity to 7069); *Kajin,* the name of the first child, also of a place in Pal., and of an Oriental tribe:— Cain, Kenite (-s).

7015. קִינָה **qîynâh**, *kee-naw´;* from 6969; a *dirge* (as accompanied by *beating* the breasts or on instruments):— lamentation.

7016. קִינָה **Qîynâh**, *kee-naw´;* the same as 7015; *Kinah,* a place in Pal.:— Kinah.

7017. קֵינִי **Qêynîy**, *kay-nee´;* or

קִינִי **Qîynîy** (1 Chron. 2:55) *kee-nee´;* patron. from 7014; a *Kenite* or member of the tribe of Kajin:— Kenite.

7018. קֵינָן **Qêynân**, *kay-nawn´;* from the same as 7064; *fixed; Kenan,* an antediluvian:— Cainan, Kenan.

7019. קַיִץ **qayits**, *kah´-yits;* from 6972; *harvest* (as the crop), whether the product (grain or fruit) or the (dry) season:— summer (fruit, house).

7020. קִיצוֹן **qîytsôwn**, *kee-tsone´;* from 6972; *terminal:*— out(utter-) most.

7021. קִיקָיוֹן **qîyqâyôwn**, *kee-kaw-yone´;* perh. from 7006; the *gourd* (as *nauseous*):— gourd.

7022. קִיקָלוֹן **qîyqâlôwn**, *kee-kaw-lone´;* from 7036; intense *disgrace:*— shameful spewing.

7023. קִיר **qîyr**, *keer;* or

קִר **qîr** (Isa. 22:5), *keer;* or (fem.)

קִירָה **qîyrâh**, *kee-raw´;* from 6979; a *wall* (as built in a *trench*):— + mason, side, town, × very, wall.

7024. קִיר **Qîyr**, *keer;* the same as 7023; *fortress; Kir,* a place in Ass.; also one in Moab:— Kir. Comp. 7025.

7025. קִיר חֶרֶשׂ **Qîyr Cheres**, *keer kheh´-res;* or (fem. of the latter word)

קִיר חֲרֶשֶׂת **Qîyr Chäreseth**, *keer khar-eh´-seth;* from 7023 and 2789; *fortress of earthenware; Kir-Cheres* or *Kir-Chareseth,* a place in Moab:— Kir-haraseth, Kir-hareseth, Kir-haresh, Kir-heres.

7026. קֵירֹס **Qêyrôç**, *kay-roce´;* or

קֵרֹס **Qêrôç**, *kay-roce´;* from the same as 7166; *ankled; Keros,* one of the Nethinim:— Keros.

7027. קִישׁ **Qîysh**, *keesh;* from 6983; a *bow; Kish,* the name of five Isr.:— Kish.

7028. קִישׁוֹן **Qîyshôwn**, *kee-shone´;* from 6983; *winding; Kishon,* a river of Pal.:— Kishon, Kison.

7029. קִישִׁי **Qîyshîy**, *kee-shee´;* from 6983; *bowed; Kishi,* an Isr.:— Kishi.

7030. קִיתָרֹס **qîythârôç** (Chald.), *kee-thaw-roce´;* of Gr. or. (κίθαρις); a *lyre:*— harp.

7031. קַל **qal**, *kal;* contr. from 7043; *light;* (by impl.) *rapid* (also adv.):— light, swift (-ly).

7032. קָל **qâl** (Chald.), *kawl;* corresp. to 6963:— sound, voice.

קֹל **qôl.** See 6963.

7033. קָלָה **qâlâh**, *kaw-law´;* a prim. root [rather ident. with 7034 through the idea of *shrinkage* by heat]; to *toast,* i.e. *scorch* partially or slowly:— dried, loathsome, parch, roast.

7034. קָלָה **qâlâh**, *kaw-law´;* a prim. root; to *be light* (as impl. in *rapid* motion), but fig. only (*be* [caus. *hold*] in *contempt*):— base, contemn, despise, lightly esteem, set light, seem vile.

7035. קָלַהּ **qâlahh**, *kaw-lah´;* for 6950; to *assemble:*— gather together.

7036. קָלוֹן **qâlôwn**, *kaw-lone´;* from 7034; *disgrace;* (by impl.) the *pudenda:*— confusion, dishonour, ignominy, reproach, shame.

7037. קַלַּחַת **qallachath**, *kal-lakh´-ath;* appar. but a form for 6747; a *kettle:*— caldron.

7038. קְלַט **qâlaṭ**, *kaw-lat´;* a prim. root; to *maim:*— lacking in his parts.

7039. קְלִי **qâliy**, *kaw-lee´;* or

קָלִיא **qâliy'**, *kaw-lee´;* from 7033; *roasted* ears of grain:— parched corn.

7040. קְל **Qallay**, *kal-lah´-ee;* from 7043; *frivolous; Kallai*, an Isr.:— Kallai.

7041. קֵלָיָה **Qêlâyâh**, *kay-law-yaw´;* from 7034; *insignificance; Kelajah*, an Isr.:— Kelaiah.

7042. קְלִיטָא **Qᵉlîyṭâ'**, *kel-ee-taw´;* from 7038; *maiming; Kelita*, the name of three Isr.:— Kelita.

7043. קָלַל **qâlal**, *kaw-lal´;* a prim. root; to *be* (caus. *make*) *light*, lit. (*swift, small, sharp*, etc.) or fig. (*easy, trifling, vile*, etc.):— abate, make bright, bring into contempt, (ac-) curse, despise, (be) ease (-y, -ier), (be a, make, make somewhat, move, seem a, set) light (-en, -er, -ly, -ly afflict, -ly esteem, thing), × slight [-ly], be swift (-er), (be, be more, make, re-) vile, whet.

7044. קְלָל **qâlâl**, *kaw-lawl´;* from 7043; *brightened* (as if *sharpened*):— burnished, polished.

7045. קְלָלָה **qᵉlâlâh**, *kel-aw-law´;* from 7043; *vilification:*— (ac-) curse (-d, -ing).

7046. קָלַס **qâlaç**, *kaw-las´;* a prim. root; to *disparage*, i.e. *ridicule:*— mock, scoff, scorn.

7047. קֶלֶס **qeleç**, *keh´-les;* from 7046; a *laughing-stock:*— derision.

7048. קַלָּסָה **qallâçâh**, *kal-law-saw´;* intens. from 7046; *ridicule:*— mocking.

7049. קָלַע **qâla'**, *kaw-lah´;* a prim. root; to *sling;* also to *carve* (as if a *circular* motion, or into *light* forms):— carve, sling (out).

7050. קֶלַע **qela'**, *keh´-lah;* from 7049; a *sling;* also a (door) *screen* (as if *slung* across), or the *valve* (of the door) itself:— hanging, leaf, sling.

7051. קַלָּע **qallâ'**, *kal-law´;* intens. from 7049; a *slinger:*— slinger.

7052. קְלֹקֵל **qᵉlôqêl**, *kel-o-kale´;* from 7043; *insubstantial:*— light.

7053. קִלְשׁוֹן **qillᵉshôwn**, *kil-lesh-one´;* from an unused root mean. to *prick;* a *prong*, i.e. hay-fork:— fork.

7054. קָמָה **qâmâh**, *kaw-maw´;* fem. of act. part. of 6965; something that *rises*, i.e. a *stalk* of grain:— (standing) corn, grown up, stalk.

7055. קְמוּאֵל **Qᵉmûw'êl**, *kem-oo-ale´;* from 6965 and 410; *raised of God; Kemuël*, the name of a rel. of Abraham, and of two Isr.:— Kemuel.

7056. קָמוֹן **Qâmôwn**, *kaw-mone´;* from 6965; an *elevation; Kamon*, a place E. of the Jordan:— Camon.

7057. קִמּוֹשׁ **qimmôwsh**, *kim-moshe´;* or

קִימוֹשׁ **qîymôwsh**, *kee-moshe´;* from an unused root mean. to *sting;* a *prickly* plant:— nettle. Comp. 7063.

7058. קֶמַח **qemach**, *keh´-makh;* from an unused root prob. mean. to *grind; flour:*— flour, meal.

7059. קָמַט **qâmaṭ**, *kaw-mat´;* a prim. root; to *pluck*, i.e. *destroy:*— cut down, fill with wrinkles.

7060. קָמַל **qâmal**, *kaw-mal´;* a prim. root; to *wither:*— hew down, wither.

7061. קָמַץ **qâmats**, *kaw-mats´;* a prim. root; to *grasp* with the hand:— take an handful.

7062. קֹמֶץ **qômets**, *ko´mets;* from 7061; a *grasp*, i.e. *handful:*— handful.

7063. קִמָּשׁוֹן **qimmâshôwn**, *kim-maw-shone´;* from the same as 7057; a *prickly* plant:— thorn.

7064. קֵן **qên**, *kane;* contr. from 7077; a *nest* (as *fixed*), sometimes incl. the *nestlings;* fig. a *chamber* or *dwelling:*— nest, room.

7065. קָנָא **qânâ'**, *kaw-naw´;* a prim. root; to *be* (caus. *make*) *zealous*, i.e. (in a bad sense) *jealous* or *envious:*— (be) envy (-ious), be (move to, provoke to) jealous (-y), × very, (be) zeal (-ous).

7066. קְנָא **qᵉnâ'** (Chald.), *ken-aw´;* corresp. to 7069; to *purchase:*— buy.

7067. קַנָּא **qannâ'**, *kan-naw´;* from 7065; *jealous:*— jealous. Comp. 7072.

7068. קִנְאָה **qin'âh**, *kin-aw´;* from 7065; *jealousy* or *envy:*— envy (-ied), jealousy, × sake, zeal.

7069. קָנָה **qânâh**, *kaw-naw´;* a prim. root; to *erect*, i.e. *create;* by extens. to *procure*, espec. by purchase (caus. *sell*); by impl. to *own:*— attain, buy (-er), teach to keep cattle, get, provoke to jealousy, possess (-or), purchase, recover, redeem, × surely, × verily.

7070. קָנֶה **qâneh**, *kaw-neh´;* from 7069; a *reed* (as *erect*); by resemblance a *rod* (espec. for measuring), *shaft, tube, stem*, the *radius* (of the arm), *beam* (of a steelyard):— balance, bone, branch, calamus, cane, reed, × spearman, stalk.

7071. קָנָה **Qânâh**, *kaw-naw´;* fem. of 7070; *reediness; Kanah*, the name of a stream and of a place in Pal.:— Kanah.

7072. קַנּוֹא **qannôw'**, *kan-no´;* for 7067; *jealous* or *angry:*— jealous.

7073. קְנַז **Qᵉnaz**, *ken-az´;* prob. from an unused root mean. to *hunt; hunter; Kenaz*, the name of an Edomite and of two Isr.:— Kenaz.

7074. קְנִזִּי **Qᵉnizzîy**, *ken-iz-zee´;* patron. from 7073, a *Kenizzite* or desc. of Kenaz:— Kenezite, Kenizzites.

7075. קִנְיָן **qinyân**, *kin-yawn´;* from 7069; *creation*, i.e. (concr.) *creatures;* also *acquisition, purchase, wealth:*— getting, goods, × with money, riches, substance.

7076. קִנָּמוֹן **qinnâmôwn**, *kin-naw-mone´;* from an unused root (mean. to *erect*); *cinnamon* bark (as in *upright* rolls):— cinnamon.

7077. קָנַן **qânan**, *kaw-nan´;* a prim. root; to *erect;* but used only as denom. from 7064; to *nestle*, i.e. *build* or *occupy* as a nest:— make ... nest.

7078. קֶנֶץ **qenets**, *keh´-nets;* from an unused root prob. mean. to *wrench; perversion:*— end.

7079. קְנָת **Qᵉnâth**, *ken-awth´;* from 7069; *possession; Kenath*, a place E. of the Jordan:— Kenath.

7080. קָסַם **qâçam**, *kaw-sam´;* a prim.

root; prop. to *distribute*, i.e. *determine* by lot or magical scroll; by impl. to *divine:*— divine (-r, -ation), prudent, soothsayer, use [divination].

7081. קֶסֶם **qeçem**, *keh´-sem;* from 7080; a *lot;* also *divination* (incl. its *fee*), or *acle:*— (reward of) divination, divine sentence, witchcraft.

7082. קָסַס **qâçaç**, *kaw-sas´;* a prim. root; to *lop* off:— cut off.

7083. קֶסֶת **qeçeth**, *keh´-seth;* from the same as 3563 (or as 7185); prop. a *cup*, i.e. an *ink-stand:*— inkhorn.

7084. קְעִילָה **Qᵉʻîylâh**, *keh-ee-law´;* perh. from 7049 in the sense of *inclosing; citadel; Keïlah*, a place in Pal.:— Keilah.

7085. קַעֲקַע **qaʻăqa'**, *kah-ak-ah´;* from the same as 6970; an *incision* or *gash:*— + mark.

7086. קְעָרָה **qᵉʻârâh**, *keh-aw-raw´;* prob. from 7167; a *bowl* (as *cut* out hollow):— charger, dish.

קוֹף **qôph**. See 6971.

7087. קָפָא **qâphâ'**, *kaw-faw´;* a prim. root; to *shrink*, i.e. *thicken* (as unracked wine, curdled milk, clouded sky, frozen water):— congeal, curdle, dark°, settle.

7088. קָפַד **qâphad**, *kaw-fad´;* a prim. root; to *contract*, i.e. *roll together:*— cut off.

7089. קְפָדָה **qᵉphâdâh**, *kef-aw-daw´;* from 7088; *shrinking*, i.e. *terror:*— destruction.

7090. קִפּוֹד **qippôwd**, *kip-pode´;* or

קִפֹּד **qippôd**, *kip-pode´;* from 7088; a species of *bird*, perh. the *bittern* (from its *contracted* form):— bittern.

7091. קִפּוֹז **qippôwz**, *kip-poze´;* from an unused root mean. to *contract*, i.e. *spring* forward; an *arrow-snake* (as *darting* on its prey):— great owl.

7092. קָפַץ **qâphats**, *kaw-fats´;* a prim. root; to *draw together*, i.e. *close;* by impl. to *leap* (by *contracting* the limbs); spec. to *die* (from *gathering* up the feet):— shut (up), skip, stop, take out of the way.

7093. קֵץ **qêts**, *kates;* contr. from 7112: an *extremity;* adv. (with prep. pref.) *after:*— + after, (utmost) border, end, [in-] finite, × process.

קֹץ **qôts**. See 6975.

7094. קָצַב **qâtsab**, *kaw-tsab´;* a prim. root; to *clip*, or (gen.) *chop:*— cut down, shorn.

7095. קֶצֶב **qetseb**, *keh´-tseb;* from 7094; *shape* (as if *cut* out); *base* (as if there *cut* off):— bottom, size.

7096. קָצָה **qâtsâh**, *kaw-tsaw´;* a prim. root; to *cut* off; (fig.) to *destroy;* (partially) to *scrape* off:— cut off, cut short, scrape (off).

7097. קָצֶה **qâtseh**, *kaw-tseh´;* or (neg. only)

7098. קֵצֶה **qêtseh**, *kay´-tseh;* from 7096; an *extremity* (used in a great variety of applications and idioms; comp. 7093):— × after, border, brim, brink, edge, end, [in-] finite, frontier, outmost coast, quarter, shore, (out-) side, × some, ut(-ter-) most (part).

7098. קָצָה **qâtsâh**, *kaw-tsaw´*; fem. of 7097; a *termination* (used like 7097):— coast, corner, (selv-) edge, lowest, (uttermost) part.

7099. קֶצֶב **qetsev**, *keh´-tsev;* and (fem.)

קִצְוָה **qitsvâh**, *kits-vaw´;* from 7096; a *limit* (used like 7097, but with less variety):— end, edge, uttermost part.

7100. קֶצַח **qetsach**, *keh´-tsakh;* from an unused root appar. mean. to *incise; fennel-flower* (from its *pungency*):— fitches.

7101. קָצִין **qâtsîyn**, *kaw-tseen´;* from 7096 in the sense of *determining;* a *magistrate* (as *deciding*) or other *leader:*— captain, guide, prince, ruler. Comp. 6278.

7102. קְצִיעָה **qᵉtsîy'âh**, *kets-ee-aw´;* from 7106; *cassia* (as *peeled;* plur. the *bark*):— cassia.

7103. קְצִיעָה **Qᵉtsîy'âh**, *kets-ee-aw´;* the same as 7102; *Ketsiah,* a daughter of Job:— Kezia.

7104. קְצִיץ **Qᵉtsîyts**, *kets-eets´;* from 7112; *abrupt; Keziz,* a valley in Pal.:— Keziz.

7105. קָצִיר **qâtsîyr**, *kaw-tseer´;* from 7114; *severed,* i.e. *harvest* (as *reaped*), the crop, the time, the reaper, or fig.; also a *limb* (of a tree, or simply *foliage*):— bough, branch, harvest (man).

7106. קָצַע **qâtsa'**, *kaw-tsah´;* a prim. root; to *strip off,* i.e. (partially) *scrape;* by impl. to *segregate* (as an angle):— cause to scrape, corner.

7107. קָצַף **qâtsaph**, *kaw-tsaf´;* a prim. root; to *crack off,* i.e. (fig.) *burst out* in rage:— (be) anger (-ry), displease, fret self, (provoke to) wrath (come), be wroth.

7108. קְצַף **qᵉtsaph** (Chald.), *kets-af´;* corresp. to 7107; to *become enraged:*— be furious.

7109. קְצַף **qᵉtsaph** (Chald.), *kets-af´;* from 7108; *rage:*— wrath.

7110. קֶצֶף **qetseph**, *keh´-tsef;* from 7107; a *splinter* (as *chipped* off); fig. *rage* or *strife:*— foam, indignation, × sore, wrath.

7111. קְצָפָה **qᵉtsâphâh**, *kets-aw-faw´;* from 7107; a *fragment:*— bark [-ed].

7112. קָצַץ **qâtsats**, *kaw-tsats´;* a prim. root; to *chop off* (lit. or fig.):— cut (asunder, in pieces, in sunder, off), × utmost.

7113. קְצַץ **qᵉtsats** (Chald.), *kets-ats´;* corresp. to 7112:— cut off.

7114. קָצַר **qâtsar**, *kaw-tsar´;* a prim. root; to *dock off,* i.e. *curtail* (tran. or intr., lit. or fig.); espec. to *harvest* (grass or grain):— × at all, cut down, much discouraged, grieve, harvestman, lothe, mourn, reap (-er), (be, wax) short (-en, -er), straiten, trouble, vex.

7115. קֹצֶר **qôtser**, *ko´-tser;* from 7114; *shortness* (of spirit), i.e. *impatience:*— anguish.

7116. קָצֵר **qâtsêr**, *kaw-tsare´;* from 7114; *short* (whether in size, number,

life, strength or temper):— few, hasty, small, soon.

7117. קְצָת **qᵉtsâth**, *kets-awth´;* from 7096; a *termination* (lit. or fig.); also (by impl.) a *portion;* adv. (with prep. pref.) *after:*— end, part, × some.

7118. קְצָת **qᵉtsâth** (Chald.), *kets-awth´;* corresp. to 7117:— end, partly.

7119. קַר **qar**, *kar;* contr. from an unused root mean. to *chill; cool;* fig. *quiet:*— cold, excellent [from the marg.].

קִר **qîr**. See 7023.

7120. קֹר **qôr**, *kore;* from the same as 7119; *cold:*— cold.

7121. קָרָא **qârâ'**, *kaw-raw´;* a prim. root [rather ident. with 7122 through the idea of *accosting* a person met]; to *call* out to (i.e. prop. *address* by name, but used in a wide variety of applications):— bewray [self], that are bidden, call (for, forth, self, upon), cry (unto), (be) famous, guest, invite, mention, (give) name, preach, (make) proclaim (-ation), pronounce, publish, read, renowned, say.

7122. קָרָא **qârâ'**, *kaw-raw´;* a prim. root: to *encounter,* whether accidentally or in a hostile manner:— befall, (by) chance, (cause to) come (upon), fall out, happen, meet.

7123. קְרָא **qᵉrâ'** (Chald.), *ker-aw´;* corresp. to 7121:— call, cry, read.

7124. קֹרֵא **qôrê'**, *ko-ray´;* prop. act. part. of 7121; a *caller,* i.e. *partridge* (from its *cry*):— partridge. See also 6981.

7125. קִרְאָה **qîr'âh**, *keer-aw´;* from 7122; an *encountering,* accidental, friendly or hostile (also adv. *opposite*):— × against (he come), help, meet, seek, × to, × in the way.

7126. קָרַב **qârab**, *kaw-rab´;* a prim. root; to *approach* (caus. *bring near*) for whatever purpose:— (cause to) approach, (cause to) bring (forth, near), (cause to) come (near, nigh), (cause to) draw near (nigh), go (near), be at hand, join, be near, offer, present, produce, make ready, stand, take.

7127. קְרֵב **qᵉrêb** (Chald.), *ker-abe´;* corresp. to 7126:— approach, come (near, nigh), draw near.

7128. קְרָב **qᵉrâb**, *ker-awb´;* from 7126; hostile *encounter:*— battle, war.

7129. קְרָב **qᵉrâb** (Chald.), *ker-awb´;* corresp. to 7128:— war.

7130. קֶרֶב **qereb**, *keh´-reb;* from 7126; prop. the *nearest* part, i.e. the *center,* whether lit., fig. or adv. (espec. with prep.):— × among, × before, bowels, × unto charge, + eat (up), × heart, × him, × in, inward (× -ly, part, -s, thought), midst, + out of, purtenance, × therein, × through, × within self.

7131. קָרֵב **qârêb**, *kaw-rabe´;* from 7126; *near:*— approach, come (near, nigh), draw near.

קָרֹב **qârôb**. See 7138.

7132. קְרָבָה **qᵉrâbâh**, *ker-aw-baw´;* from 7126; *approach:*— approaching, draw near.

7133. קָרְבָּן **qorbân**, *kor-bawn´;* or

קֻרְבָּן **qurbân**, *koor-bawn´;* from 7126; something *brought near* the altar, i.e. a sacrificial *present:*— oblation, that is offered, offering.

7134. קַרְדֹּם **qardôm**, *kar-dome´;* perh. from 6923 in the sense of *striking* upon; an *axe:*— ax.

7135. קָרָה **qârâh**, *kaw-raw´;* fem. of 7119; *coolness:*— cold.

7136. קָרָה **qârâh**, *kaw-raw´;* a prim. root; to *light upon* (chiefly by accident); caus. to *bring about;* spec. to *impose* timbers (for roof or floor):— appoint, lay (make) beams, befall, bring, come (to pass unto), floor, [hap] was, happen (unto), meet, send good speed.

7137. קָרֶה **qâreh**, *kaw-reh´;* from 7136; an (unfortunate) *occurrence,* i.e. some accidental (ceremonial) *disqualification:*— uncleanness that chanceth.

קֹרָה **qôrâh**. See 6982.

7138. קָרוֹב **qârôwb**, *kaw-robe´;* or

קָרֹב **qârôb**, *kaw-robe´;* from 7126; *near* (in place, kindred or time):— allied, approach, at hand, + any of kin, kinsfolk (-sman), (that is) near (of kin), neighbour, (that is) next, (them that come) nigh (at hand), more ready, short (-ly).

7139. קָרַח **qârach**, *kaw-rakh´;* a prim. root; to *depilate:*— make (self) bald.

7140. קֶרַח **qerach**, *keh´-rakh;* or

קֹרַח **qôrach**, *ko´-rakh;* from 7139; *ice* (as if *bald,* i.e. *smooth*); hence, *hail;* by resemblance, rock *crystal:*— crystal, frost, ice.

7141. קֹרַח **Qôrach**, *ko´rakh;* from 7139; *ice; Korach,* the name of two Edomites and three Isr.:— Korah.

7142. קֵרֵחַ **qêrêach**, *kay-ray´-akh;* from 7139; *bald* (on the back of the head):— bald (head).

7143. קָרֵחַ **Qârêach**, *kaw-ray´-akh;* from 7139; *bald; Kareäch,* an Isr.:— Careah, Kareah.

7144. קׇרְחָה **qorchâh**, *kor-khaw´;* or

קׇרְחָא **qorchâ'** (Ezek. 27:31), *korkhaw´;* from 7139; *baldness:*— bald (-ness), × utterly.

7145. קׇרְחִי **Qorchîy**, *kor-khee´;* patron. from 7141; a *Korchite* (collect.) or desc. of Korach:— Korahite, Korathite, sons of Kore, Korhite.

7146. קׇרַחַת **qârachath**, *kaw-rakh´-ath;* from 7139; a *bald spot* (on the back of the head); fig. a *threadbare* spot (on the back side of the cloth):— bald head, bare within.

7147. קְרִי **qᵉrîy**, *ker-ee´;* from 7136; hostile *encounter:*— contrary.

7148. קָרִיא **qârîy'**, *kaw-ree´;* from 7121; *called,* i.e. *select:*— famous, renowned.

7149. קִרְיָא **qiryâ'** (Chald.), *keer-yaw´;* or

קִרְיָה **qiryâh** (Chald.), *keer-yaw´;* corresp. to 7151:— city.

7150. קְרִיאָה **qᵉrîy'âh**, *ker-ee-aw´;* from 7121; a *proclamation:*— preaching.

7151. קִרְיָה **qiryâh**, *kir-yaw´;* from 7136 in the sense of *flooring,* i.e. *building;* a *city:*— city.

7152. קְרִיּוֹת **Qᵉriyôwth**, *ker-ee-yōth´;*

plur. of 7151; *buildings; Kerioth*, the name of two places in Pal.:— Kerioth, Kirioth.

7153. קִרְיַת עַרְבַּע **Qiryath 'Arba'**, *keer-yath' ar-bah';* or (with the art. interposed)

קִרְיַת הָאַרְבַּע **Qiryath hâ-'Arba'** (Neh. 11:25), *keer-yath' haw-ar-bah';* from 7151 and 704 or 702; *city of Arba*, or *city of the four* (giants); *Kirjath-Arba* or *Kirjath-ha-Arba*, a place in Pal.:— Kirjath-arba.

7154. קִרְיַת בַּעַל **Qiryath Ba'al**, *keer-yath' bah'-al;* from 7151 and 1168; *city of Baal; Kirjath-Baal*, a place in Pal.:— Kirjath-baal.

7155. קִרְיַת חֻצוֹת **Qiryath Chûtsôwth**, *keer-yath' khoo-tsôth';* from 7151 and the fem. plur. of 2351; *city of streets; Kirjath-Chutsoth*, a place in Moab:— Kirjath-huzoth.

7156. קִרְיָתַיִם **Qiryâthayim**, *keer-yaw-thah'-yim;* dual of 7151; *double city; Kirjathaim*, the name of two places in Pal.:— Kiriathaim, Kirjathaim.

7157. קִרְיַת יְעָרִים **Qiryath Yᵉ'ârîym**, *keer-yath' yeh-aw-reem';* or (Jer. 26:20) with the art. interposed; or (Josh. 18:28) simply the former part of the word; or

קִרְיַת עָרִים **Qiryath 'Ârîym**, *keer-yath' aw-reem';* from 7151 and the plur. of 3293 or 5892; *city of forests*, or *city of towns; Kirjath-Jeärim* or *Kirjath-Arim*, a place in Pal.:— Kirjath, Kirjath-jearim, Kirjath-arim.

7158. קִרְיַת סַנָּה **Qiryath Çannâh**, *keer-yath' san-naw';* or

קִרְיַת סֵפֶר **Qiryath Çépher**, *keer-yath' say-fer;* from 7151 and a simpler fem. from the same as 5577, or (for the latter name) 5612; *city of branches*, or *of a book; Kirjath-Sannah* or *Kirjath-Sepher*, a place in Pal.:— Kirjath-sannah, Kirjath-sepher.

7159. קָרַם **qâram**, *kaw-ram';* a prim. root;— *to cover*:— cover.

7160. קָרַן **qâran**, *kaw-ran';* a prim. root; *to push* or gore; used only as denom. from 7161, *to shoot out horns;* fig. *rays*:— have horns, shine.

7161. קֶרֶן **qeren**, *keh'-ren;* from 7160; a *horn* (as *projecting);* by impl. a *flask, cornet;* by resembl. an elephant's *tooth* (i.e. *ivory),* a *corner* (of the altar); a *peak* (of a mountain), a *ray* (of light); fig. *power*:— × hill, horn.

7162. קֶרֶן **qeren** (Chald.), *keh'-ren;* corresp. to 7161; a *horn* (lit. or for sound):— horn, cornet.

7163. קֶרֶן הַפּוּךְ **Qeren Hap-pûwk**, *keh'-ren hap-pook';* from 7161 and 6320; *horn of cosmetic; Keren-hap-Puk*, one of Job's daughters:— Keren-happuch.

7164. קָרַס **qâraç**, *kaw-ras';* a prim. root; prop. to *protrude;* used only as denom. from 7165 (for alliteration with 7167), to *hunch,* i.e. be hump-backed:— stoop.

7165. קֶרֶס **qereç**, *keh'-res;* from 7164; a *knob* or belaying-pin (from its swelling form):— tache.

קָרֵס **Qêrôç**. See 7026.

7166. קַרְסֹל **qarçôl**, *kar-sole';* from 7164;

an *ankle* (as a *protuberance* or joint):— foot.

7167. קָרַע **qâra'**, *kaw-rah';* a prim. root; to *rend,* lit. or fig. (*revile, paint* the eyes, as if enlarging them):— cut out, rend, × surely, tear.

7168. קֶרַע **qera'**, *keh'-rah;* from 7167; a *rag*:— piece, rag.

7169. קָרַץ **qârats**, *kaw-rats';* a prim. root; to *pinch,* i.e. (partially) to *bite* the lips, *blink* the eyes (as a gesture of malice), or (fully) to *squeeze* off (a piece of clay in order to mould a vessel from it):— form, move, wink.

7170. קְרַץ **qᵉrats** (Chald.), *ker-ats';* corresp. to 7171 in the sense of a *bit* (to "eat the *morsels* of" any one, i.e. *chew* him up [fig.] by *slander):— + accuse.

7171. קֶרֶץ **qerets**, *keh'-rets;* from 7169; *extirpation* (as if by *constriction):— destruction.

7172. קַרְקַע **qarqa'**, *kar-kah';* from 7167; *floor* (as if a *pavement* of pieces or *tesseræ),* of a building or the sea:— bottom, (× one side of the) floor.

7173. קַרְקַע **Qarqa'**, *kar-kah';* the same as 7172; *ground-floor; Karka* (with the art. pref.), a place in Pal.:— Karkaa.

7174. קַרְקֹר **Qarqôr**, *kar-kore';* from 6979; *foundation; Karkor*, a place E. of the Jordan:— Karkor.

7175. קֶרֶשׁ **qeresh**, *keh'-resh;* from an unused root mean. to *split* off; a *slab* or *plank;* by impl. a *deck* of a ship:— bench, board.

7176. קֶרֶת **qereth**, *keh'-reth;* from 7136 in the sense of *building;* a *city*:— city.

7177. קַרְתָּה **Qartâh**, *kar-taw';* from 7176; *city; Kartah*, a place in Pal.:— Kartah.

7178. קַרְתָּן **Qartân**, *kar-tawn';* from 7176; *city-plot; Kartan*, a place in Pal.:— Kartan.

7179. קַשׁ **qash**, *kash;* from 7197; *straw* (as *dry):— stubble.

7180. קִשֻּׁא **qishshû'**, *kish-shoo';* from an unused root (mean. to *be hard);* a *cucumber* (from the difficulty of *digestion):— cucumber.

7181. קָשַׁב **qâshab**, *kaw-shab';* a prim. root; to *prick up* the ears, i.e. *hearken*:— attend, (cause to) hear (-ken), give heed, incline, mark (well), regard.

7182. קֶשֶׁב **qesheb**, *keh'-sheb;* from 7181; a *hearkening*:— × diligently, hearing, much heed, that regarded.

7183. קַשָּׁב **qashshâb**, *kash-shawb';* or

קַשֻּׁב **qashshûb**, *kash-shoob';* from 7181; *hearkening*:— attent(-ive).

7184. קָשָׂה **qâsâh**, *kaw-saw';* or

קַשְׂוָה **qasvâh**, *kas-vaw';* from an unused root mean. to *be round;* a *jug* (from its shape):— cover, cup.

7185. קָשָׁה **qâshâh**, *kaw-shaw';* a prim. root; prop. to *be dense,* i.e. *tough* or *severe* (in various applications):— be cruel, be fiercer, make grievous, be [ask a], be in, have, seem, would] hard (-en, [labour], -ly, thing), be sore, (be, make) stiff (-en, [-necked]).

7186. קָשֶׁה **qâsheh**, *kaw-sheh';* from

7185; *severe* (in various applications):— churlish, cruel, grievous, hard (I-hearted), thing), heavy, + impudent, obstinate, prevailed, rough (-ly), sore, sorrowful, stiff (I-necked), stubborn, + in trouble.

7187. קְשׁוֹט **qᵉshôwṭ** (Chald.), *kesh-ote';* or

קְשֹׁט **qᵉshôṭ** (Chald.), *kesh-ote';* corresp. to 7189; *fidelity*:— truth.

7188. קָשַׁח **qâshach**, *kaw-shakh';* a prim. root; to *be* (caus. *make) unfeeling*:— harden.

7189. קֹשֶׁט **qôsheṭ**, *ko'-sheṭ;* or

קֹשְׁט **qôshṭ**, *kôshṭ;* from an unused root mean. to *balance; equity* (as evenly *weighed),* i.e. *reality*:— certainty, truth.

קֹשֹׁט **qôshôṭ**. See 7187.

7190. קְשִׁי **qᵉshîy**, *kesh-ee';* from 7185; *obstinacy*:— stubbornness.

7191. קִשְׁיוֹן **Qishyôwn**, *kish-yone';* from 7190; *hard ground; Kishjon*, a place in Pal.:— Kishion, Keshon.

7192. קְשִׂיטָה **qᵉsîyṭah**, *kes-ee-taw';* from an unused root (prob. mean. to *weigh* out); an *ingot* (as def. *estimated* and stamped for a coin):— piece of money (silver).

7193. קַשְׂקֶשֶׂת **qasqeseth**, *kas-keh'-seth;* by redupl. from an unused root mean. to *shale* off as bark; a *scale* (of a fish); hence, a *coat* of *mail* (as composed of or covered with jointed *plates* of metal):— mail, scale.

7194. קָשַׁר **qâshar**, *kaw-shar';* a prim. root: to *tie*, phys. (*gird, confine, compact)* or ment. (in *love, league):— bind (up), (make a) conspire (-acy, -ator), join together, knit, stronger, work [treason].

7195. קֶשֶׁר **qesher**, *keh'-sher;* from 7194; an (unlawful) *alliance*:— confederacy, conspiracy, treason.

7196. קִשֻּׁר **qishshûr**, *kish-shoor';* from 7194; an (ornamental) *girdle* (for women):— attire, headband.

7197. קָשַׁשׁ **qâshash**, *kaw-shash';* a prim. root; to *become sapless* through drought; used only as denom. from 7179; to *forage* for straw, stubble or wood; fig. to *assemble*:— gather (selves) (together).

7198. קֶשֶׁת **qesheth**, *keh'-sheth;* from 7185 in the orig. sense (of 6983) of *bending,* a *bow,* for *shooting* (hence, fig. *strength)* or the *iris*:— × arch (-er), + arrow, bow (I-man, -shot]).

7199. קַשָּׁת **qashshâth**, *kash-shawth';* intens. (as denom.) from 7198; a *bowman*:— × archer.

ר

7200. רָאָה **râ'âh**, *raw-aw';* a prim. root; to *see*, lit. or fig. (in numerous applications, dir. and impl., tran. intr. and caus.):— advise self, appear, approve, behold, × certainly, consider, discern, (make to) enjoy, have experience, gaze, take heed, × indeed, × joyfully, lo, look (on, one another, one on another, one upon another, out, up, upon), mark, meet, × be near, perceive, present, provide, regard, (have) respect, (fore-, cause to, let) see (-r, -m, one another), shew (self), × sight of others, (e-) spy, stare, × surely, × think, view, visions.

7201. רָאָה **râ'âh**, *raw-aw´;* from 7200; a *bird* of prey (prob. the *vulture*, from its sharp *sight*):— glede. Comp. 1676.

7202. רָאֶה **râ'eh**, *raw-eh´;* from 7200; *seeing*, i.e. experiencing:— see.

7203. רֹאֶה **rô'eh**, *ro-eh´;* act. part. of 7200; a *seer* (as often rendered); but also (abstr.) a *vision*:— vision.

7204. רֹאֵה **Rô'êh**, *ro-ay´;* for 7203; *prophet; Roëh,* an Isr.:— Haroeh (incl. the art.).

7205. רְאוּבֵן **Re'ûwbên**, *reh-oo-bane´;* from the imper. of 7200 and 1121; *see* ye a *son; Reüben,* a son of Jacob:— Reuben.

7206. רְאוּבֵנִי **Re'ûwbênîy**, *reh-oob-ay-nee´;* patron. from 7205; a *Reübenite* or desc. of Reüben:— children of Reuben, Reubenites.

7207. רַאֲוָה **ra'ăvâh**, *rah-av-aw´;* from 7200; *sight,* i.e. *satisfaction*:— behold.

7208. רְאוּמָה **Re'ûwmâh**, *reh-oo-maw´;* fem. pass. part. of 7213; *raised; Reümah,* a Syrian woman:— Reumah.

7209. רְאִי **re'îy**, *reh-ee´;* from 7200; a *mirror* (as *seen*):— looking glass.

7210. רֳאִי **rŏ'îy**, *ro-ee´;* from 7200; *sight,* whether abstr. (*vision*) or concr. (a *spectacle*):— gazingstock, look to, (that) see (-th).

7211. רְאָיָה **Re'âyâh**, *reh-aw-yaw´;* from 7200 and 3050; *Jah has seen; Reäjah,* the name of three Isr.:— Reaia, Reaiah.

7212. רְאִיַּת **re'îyath**, *reh-eeth´;* from 7200; *sight*:— beholding.

7213. רָאַם **râ'am**, *raw-am´;* a prim. root; to *rise*:— be lifted up.

7214. רְאֵם **re'êm**, *reh-ame´;* or

רְאֵים **re'êym**, *reh-ame´;* or

רֵים **rêym**, *rame;* or

רֵם **rêm**, *rame;* from 7213; a wild *bull* (from its *conspicuousness*):— unicorn.

7215. רָאמָה **râ'mâh**, *raw-maw´;* from 7213; something *high* in value, i.e. perh. *coral*:— coral.

7216. רָאמוֹת **Râ'môwth**, *raw-môth´;* or

רָאמֹת **Râmôth**, *raw-môth´;* plur. of 7215; *heights; Ramoth,* the name of two places in Pal.:— Ramoth.

7217. רֵאשׁ **rê'sh** (Chald.), *raysh;* corresp. to 7218; the *head;* fig. the *sum*:— chief, head, sum.

7218. רֹאשׁ **rô'sh**, *roshe;* from an unused root appar. mean. to *shake;* the *head* (as most easily *shaken*), whether lit. or fig. (in many applications, of place, time, rank, etc.):— band, beginning, captain, chapiter, chief (-est place, man, things), company, end, × every (man), excellent, first, forefront, ((be-)) head, height, (on) high (-est part, (priest)), × lead, × poor, principal, ruler, sum, top.

7219. רֹאשׁ **rô'sh**, *roshe;* or

רוֹשׁ **rôwsh** (Deut. 32:32), *roshe;*

appar. the same as 7218; a poisonous *plant,* prob. the *poppy* (from its conspicuous *head*); gen. *poison* (even of serpents):— gall, hemlock, poison, venom.

7220. רֹאשׁ **Rô'sh**, *roshe;* prob. the same as 7218; *Rosh,* the name of an Isr. and of a for. nation:— Rosh.

רֵאשׁ **rê'sh**. See 7389.

7221. רִאשָׁה **rî'shâh**, *ree-shaw´;* from the same as 7218; a *beginning*:— beginning.

7222. רֹאשָׁה **rô'shâh**, *ro-shaw´;* fem. of 7218; the *head*:— head (-stone).

7223. רִאשׁוֹן **rî'shôwn**, *ree-shone´;* or

רִאשֹׁן **rî'shôn**, *ree-shone´;* from 7221; *first,* in place, time or rank (as adj. or noun):— ancestor, (that were) before (-time), beginning, eldest, first, fore (-father) (-most), former (thing), of old time, past.

7224. רִאשֹׁנִי **rî'shônîy**, *ree-sho-nee´;* from 7223; *first*:— first.

7225. רֵאשִׁית **rê'shîyth**, *ray-sheeth´;* from the same as 7218; the *first,* in place, time, order or rank (spec. a *firstfruit*):— beginning, chief (-est), first (-fruits, part, time), principal thing.

7226. רַאֲשֹׁת **ra'ăshôth**, *rah-ash-ōth´;* from 7218; a *pillow* (being for the *head*):— bolster.

7227. רַב **rab**, *rab;* by contr. from 7231; *abundant* (in quantity, size, age, number, rank, quality):— (in) abound (-undance, -ant, -antly), captain, elder, enough, exceedingly, full, great (-ly, man, one), increase, long (enough, (time)), (do, have) many (-ifold, things, a time), ((ship-)) master, mighty, more, (too, very) much, multiply (-tude), officer, often (-times), plenteous, populous, prince, process (of time), suffice (-ient).

7228. רַב **rab**, *rab;* by contr. from 7232; an *archer* (or perh. the same as 7227):— archer.

7229. רַב **rab** (Chald.), *rab;* corresp. to 7227:— captain, chief, great, lord, master, stout.

רִב **rîb**. See 7378.

7230. רֹב **rôb**, *robe;* from 7231; *abundance* (in any respect):— abundance (-antly), all, × common (sort), excellent, great (-ly, ness, number), huge, be increased, long, many, more in number, most, much, multitude, plenty (-ifully), × very (age).

7231. רָבַב **râbab**, *raw-bab´;* a prim. root; prop. to *cast together* (comp. 7241), i.e. *increase,* espec. in number; also (as denom. from 7233) to *multiply by the myriad*:— increase, be many (-ifold), be more, multiply, ten thousands.

7232. רָבַב **râbab**, *raw-bab´;* a prim. root (rather ident. with 7231 through the idea of *projection*); to *shoot* an arrow:— shoot.

7233. רְבָבָה **re'bâbâh**, *reb-aw-baw´;* from 7231; *abundance* (in number), i.e. (spec.) a *myriad* (whether def. or indef.):— many, million, × multiply, ten thousand.

7234. רָבַד **râbad**, *raw-bad´;* a prim. root; to *spread*:— deck.

7235. רָבָה **râbâh**, *raw-baw´;* a prim. root; to *increase* (in whatever respect):— ((bring in)) abundance (× -antly), + archer (by *mistake* for 7232), be in authority, bring up, × continue, enlarge, excel, exceeding (-ly), be full of, (be, make) great (-er, -ly, × -ness), grow up, heap, increase, be long, (be, give, have, make, use) many (a time), (any, be, give, give the, have) more (in number), (ask, be, be so, gather, over, take, yield) much (greater, more), (make to) multiply, nourish, plenty (-eous), × process (of time), sore, store, thoroughly, very.

7236. רְבָה **re'bâh** (Chald.), *reb-aw´;* corresp. to 7235:— make a great man, grow.

7237. רַבָּה **Rabbâh**, *rab-baw´;* fem. of 7227; *great; Rabbah,* the name of two places in Pal., East and West:— Rabbah, Rabbath.

7238. רְבוּ **re'bûw** (Chald.), *reb-oo´;* from a root corresp. to 7235; *increase* (of dignity):— greatness, majesty.

7239. רִבּוֹ **ribbôw**, *rib-bo´;* from 7231; or

רִבּוֹא **ribbôw'**, *rib-bo´;* from 7231; a *myriad,* i.e. indef. *large number*:— great things, ten (eight)-een, (forl-ty, + sixscore, + threescore, × twenty, (twen)-ty) thousand.

7240. רִבּוֹ **ribbôw** (Chald.), *rib-bo´;* corresp. to 7239:— × ten thousand times ten thousand.

7241. רָבִיב **râbîyb**, *raw-beeb´;* from 7231; a *rain* (as an *accumulation* of drops):— shower.

7242. רָבִיד **râbîyd**, *raw-beed´;* from 7234; a *collar* (as *spread* around the neck):— chain.

7243. רְבִיעִי **re'bîy'îy**, *reb-ee-ee´;* or

רְבִעִי **re'bî'îy**, *reb-ee-ee´;* from 7251; *fourth;* also (fractionally) a *fourth*:— foursquare, fourth (part).

7244. רְבִיעַי **re'bîy'ay** (Chald.), *reb-ee-ah´-ee;* corresp. to 7243:— fourth.

7245. רַבִּית **Rabbîyth**, *rab-beeth´;* from 7231; *multitude; Rabbith,* a place in Pal.:— Rabbith.

7246. רָבַךְ **râbak**, *raw-bak´;* a prim. root; to *soak* (bread in oil):— baken, (that which is) fried.

7247. רִבְלָה **Riblâh**, *rib-law´;* from an unused root mean. to *be fruitful; fertile; Riblah,* a place in Syria:— Riblah.

7248. רַב־מָג **Rab-Mâg**, *rab-mawg´;* from 7227 and a for. word for a Magian; *chief Magian; Rab-Mag,* a Bab. official:— Rab-mag.

7249. רַב־סָרִיס **Rab-Çârîyç**, *rab-saw-reece´;* from 7227 and a for. word for a eunuch; *chief chamberlain; Rab-Saris,* a Bab. official:— Rab-saris.

7250. רָבַע **râba'**, *raw-bah´;* a prim. root; to *squat* or *lie* out flat, i.e. (spec.) in copulation:— let gender, lie down.

7251. רָבַע **râba'**, *raw-bah´;* a prim. root (rather ident. with 7250 through the idea of *sprawling* "at all fours" (or possibly the reverse is the order of deriv.); comp. 702); prop. to *be four* (sided);

7252. רֶבַע **reba'**, *reh'-bah*; from 7250; *prostration* (for sleep):— lying down.

7253. רֶבַע **reba'**, *reh'-bah*; from 7251; a *fourth* (part or side):— fourth part, side, square.

7254. רֶבַע **Reba'**, *reh'-bah*; the same as 7253; *Reba*, a Midianite:— Reba.

7255. רֹבַע **rôba'**, *ro'-bah*; from 7251; a *quarter*:— fourth part.

7256. רִבֵּעַ **ribbêa'**, *rib-bay'-ah*; from 7251; a desc. of the *fourth* generation, i.e. *great great grandchild*:— fourth.

רְבִיעִי rᵉbîy'îy. See 7243.

7257. רָבַץ **râbats**, *raw-bats'*; a prim. root; to *crouch* (on all four legs folded, like a recumbent animal); by impl. to *recline, repose, brood, lurk, imbed*:— crouch (down), fall down, make a fold, lay, (cause to, make to) lie (down), make to rest, sit.

7258. רֶבֶץ **rebets**, *reh'-bets*; from 7257; a *couch* or place of repose:— where each lay, lie down in, resting place.

7259. רִבְקָה **Ribqâh**, *rib-kaw'*; from an unused root prob. mean. to *clog* by tying up the fetlock; *fettering* (by beauty); *Ribkah*, the wife of Isaac:— Rebekah.

7260. רַבְרַב **rabrab** (Chald.), *rab-rab'*; from 7229; *huge* (in size); *domineering* (in character):— (very) great (things).

7261. רַבְרְבָן **rabrᵉbân** (Chald.), *rab-reb-awn'*; from 7260; a *magnate*:— lord, prince.

7262. רַבְשָׁקֵה **Rabshâqêh**, *rab-shaw-kay'*; from 7227 and 8248; *chief butler*; *Rabshakeh*, a Bab. official:— Rabshakeh.

7263. רֶגֶב **regeb**, *reh'-gheb*; from an unused root mean. to *pile* together; a *lump* of clay:— clod.

7264. רָגַז **râgaz**, *raw-gaz'*; a prim. root; to *quiver* (with any violent emotion, espec. anger or fear):— be afraid, stand in awe, disquiet, fall out, fret, move, provoke, quake, rage, shake, tremble, trouble, be wroth.

7265. רְגַז **rᵉgaz** (Chald.), *reg-az'*; corresp. to 7264:— provoke unto wrath.

7266. רְגַז **rᵉgaz** (Chald.), *reg-az'*; from 7265; violent *anger*:— rage.

7267. רֹגֶז **rôgez**, *ro'-ghez*; from 7264; *commotion, restlessness* (of a horse), *crash* (of thunder), *disquiet, anger*:— fear, noise, rage, trouble (-ing), wrath.

7268. רַגָּז **raggâz**, *rag-gawz'*; intens. from 7264; *timid*:— trembling.

7269. רָגְזָה **rogzâh**, *rog-zaw'*; fem. of 7267; *trepidation*:— trembling.

7270. רָגַל **râgal**, *raw-gal'*; a prim. root; to *walk* along; but only in spec. applications, to *reconnoiter*, to be a *tale-bearer* (i.e. *slander*); also (as denom. from 7272) to *lead about*:— backbite, search, slander, (e-) spy (out), teach to go, view.

7271. רְגַל **rᵉgal** (Chald.), *reg-al'*; corresp. to 7272:— foot.

7272. רֶגֶל **regel**, *reh'-gel*; from 7270; a *foot* (as used in *walking*); by impl. a *step*; by euphem. the *pudenda*:— × be

able to endure, × according as, × after, × coming, × follow, ((broken-)) foot ((-ed, -stool)), × great toe, × haunt, × journey, leg, + piss, + possession, time.

7273. רַגְלִי **raglîy**, *rag-lee'*; from 7272; a *footman* (soldier):— (on) foot (-man).

7274. רֹגְלִים **Rôgᵉliym**, *ro-gel-eem'*; plur. of act. part. of 7270; *fullers* (as *tramping* the cloth in washing); *Rogelim*, a place E. of the Jordan:— Rogelim.

7275. רָגַם **râgam**, *raw-gam'*; a prim. root (comp. 7263, 7321, 7551); to *cast* together (stones), i.e. to *lapidate*:— × certainly, stone.

7276. רֶגֶם **Regem**, *reh'-gem*; from 7275; stone-*heap*; *Regem*, an Isr.:— Regem.

7277. רִגְמָה **rigmâh**, *rig-maw'*; fem. of the same as 7276; a *pile* (of stones), i.e. (fig.) a *throng*:— council.

7278. רֶגֶם מֶלֶךְ **Regem Melek**, *reh'-gem meh'-lek*; from 7276 and 4428; *king's heap*; *Regem-Melek*, an Isr.:— Regem-melech.

7279. רָגַן **râgan**, *raw-gan'*; a prim. root; to *grumble*, i.e. *rebel*:— murmur.

7280. רָגַע **râga'**, *raw-gah'*; a prim. root; prop. to *toss* violently and suddenly (the sea with waves, the skin with boils); fig. (in a favorable manner) to *settle*, i.e. *quiet*; spec. to *wink* (from the motion of the eye-lids):— break, divide, find ease, be a moment, (cause, give, make to) rest, make suddenly.

7281. רֶגַע **rega'**, *reh'-gah*; from 7280. a *wink* (of the eyes), i.e. a very *short space* of time:— instant, moment, space, suddenly.

7282. רָגֵעַ **râgêa'**, *raw-gay'-ah*; from 7280; *restful*, i.e. *peaceable*:— that are quiet.

7283. רָגַשׁ **râgash**, *raw-gash'*; a prim. root; to *be tumultuous*:— rage.

7284. רְגַשׁ **rᵉgash** (Chald.), *reg-ash'*; corresp. to 7283; to *gather* tumultuously:— assemble (together).

7285. רֶגֶשׁ **regesh**, *reh'-ghesh*; or (fem.)

רִגְשָׁה **rigshâh**, *rig-shaw'*; from 7283; a tumultuous *crowd*:— company, insurrection.

7286. רָדַד **râdad**, *raw-dad'*; a prim. root; to *tread* in pieces, i.e. (fig.) to *conquer*, or (spec.) to *overlay*:— spend, spread, subdue.

7287. רָדָה **râdâh**, *raw-daw'*; a prim. root; to *tread* down, i.e. *subjugate*; spec. to *crumble* off:— (come to, make to) have dominion, prevail against, reign, (bear, make to) rule (-r, over), take.

7288. רַדַּי **Radday**, *rad-dah'-ee*; intens. from 7287; *domineering*; *Raddai*, an Isr.:— Raddai.

7289. רָדִיד **râdîyd**, *raw-deed'*; from 7286 in the sense of *spreading*; a *veil* (as expanded):— vail, veil.

7290. רָדַם **râdam**, *raw-dam'*; a prim. root; to *stun*, i.e. *stupefy* (with sleep or death):— (be fast a-, be in a deep, cast into a dead, that) sleep (-er, -eth).

7291. רָדַף **râdaph**, *raw-daf'*; a prim. root; to *run after* (usually with hostile intent; fig. [of time] *gone by*):— chase,

put to flight, follow (after, on), hunt, (be under) persecute (-ion, -or), pursue (-r).

7292. רָהַב **râhab**, *raw-hab'*; a prim. root; to *urge* severely, i.e. (fig.) *importune, embolden, capture, act insolently*:— overcome, behave self proudly, make sure, strengthen.

7293. רַהַב **rahab**, *rah'-hab*; from 7292; *bluster* (-er):— proud, strength.

7294. רַהַב **Rahab**, *rah'-hab*; the same as 7293; *Rahab* (i.e. *boaster*), an epithet of Egypt:— Rahab.

7295. רָהָב **râhâb**, *raw-hawb'*; from 7292; *insolent*:— proud.

7296. רֹהָב **rôhab**, *ro'-hab*; from 7292; *pride*:— strength.

7297. רָהָה **râhâh**, *raw-haw'*; a prim. root; to *fear*:— be afraid.

7298. רַהַט **rahat**, *rah'-hat*; from an unused root appar. mean. to *hollow out*; a *channel* or watering-box; by resemblance a *ringlet* of hair (as forming parallel lines):— gallery, gutter, trough.

7299. רֵו **rêv** (Chald.), *rave*; from a root corresp. to 7200; *aspect*:— form.

רוּב° **rûwb**. See 7378.

7300. רוּד **rûwd**, *rood*; a prim. root; to *tramp* about, i.e. *ramble* (free or disconsolate):— have the dominion, be lord, mourn, rule.

7301. רָוָה **râvâh**, *raw-vaw'*; a prim. root; to *slake* the thirst (occasionally of other appetites):— bathe, make drunk, (take the) fill, satiate, (abundantly) satisfy, soak, water (abundantly).

7302. רָוֶה **râveh**, *raw-veh'*; from 7301; *sated* (with drink):— drunkenness, watered.

7303. רֹוהֲגָה **Rôwhăgâh**, *ro-hag-aw'*; from an unused root prob. mean. to *cry* out; *outcry*; *Rohagah*, an Isr.:— Rohgah.

7304. רָוַח **râvach**, *raw-vakh'*; a prim. root [rather ident. with 7306]; prop. to *breathe* freely, i.e. *revive*; by impl. to *have ample room*:— be refreshed, large.

7305. רֶוַח **revach**, *reh'-vakh*; from 7304; *room*, lit. (an *interval*) or fig. (*deliverance*):— enlargement, space.

7306. רוּחַ **rûwach**, *roo'-akh*; a prim. root; prop. to *blow*, i.e. *breathe*; only (lit.) to *smell* or (by impl.) *perceive* (fig. to *anticipate, enjoy*):— accept, smell, × touch, make of quick understanding.

7307. רוּחַ **rûwach**, *roo'-akh*; from 7306; *wind*; by resemblance *breath*, i.e. a sensible (or even violent) *exhalation*; fig. *life, anger, unsubstantiality*; by extens. a *region* of the sky; by resemblance *spirit*, but only of a rational being (incl. its expression and functions):— air, anger, blast, breath, × cool, courage, mind, × quarter, × side, spirit ((-ual)), tempest, × vain, ((whirl-)) wind (-y).

7308. רוּחַ **rûwach** (Chald.), *roo'-akh*; corresp. to 7307:— mind, spirit, wind.

7309. רְוָחָה **rᵉvâchâh**, *rev-aw-khaw'*; fem. of 7305; *relief*:— breathing, respite.

7310. רְוָיָה **rᵉvâyâh**, *rev-aw-yaw´*; from 7301; *satisfaction:*— runneth over, wealthy.

7311. רוּם **rûwm**, *room;* a prim. root; to *be high;* act. to *rise* or *raise* (in various applications, lit. or fig.):— bring up, exalt (self), extol, give, go up, haughty, heave (up), (be, lift up on, make on, set up on, too) high (-er, one), hold up, levy, lift (-er) up, (be) lofty, (× a-) loud, mount up, offer (up), + presumptuously, (be) promote (-ion), proud, set up, tall (-er), take (away, off, up), breed worms.

7312. רוּם **rûwm**, *room;* or

רֻם **rûm**, *room;* from 7311; (lit.) *elevation* or (fig.) *elation:*— haughtiness, height, × high.

7313. רוּם **rûwm** (Chald.), *room;* corresp. to 7311; (fig. only):— extol, lift up (self), set up.

7314. רוּם **rûwm** (Chald.), *room;* from 7313; (lit.) *altitude:*— height.

7315. רוֹם **rôwm**, *rome;* from 7311; *elevation,* i.e. (adv.) *aloft:*— on high.

7316. רוּמָה **Rûwmâh**, *roo-maw´;* from 7311; *height; Rumah,* a place in Pal.:— Rumah.

7317. רוֹמָה **rôwmâh**, *ro-maw´;* fem. of 7315; *elation,* i.e. (adv.) *proudly:*— haughtily.

7318. רוֹמָם **rôwmâm**, *ro-mawm´;* from 7426; *exaltation,* i.e. (fig. and spec.) *praise:*— be extolled.

7319. רוֹמְמָה **rôwmᵉmâh**, *ro-mem-aw´;* fem. act. part. of 7426; *exaltation,* i.e. *praise:*— high.

7320. רוֹמַמְתִּי עֶזֶר **Rôwmamtîy 'Ezer** (or

לְמַמְתִּי **Rômamtîy**), *ro-mam´-tee eh´-zer;* from 7311 and 5828; *I have raised* up a *help; Romamti-Ezer,* an Isr.:— Romamti-ezer.

7321. רוּעַ **rûwa'**, *roo-ah´;* a prim. root; to *mar* (espec. by breaking); fig. to *split* the ears (with sound), i.e. *shout* (for alarm or joy):— blow an alarm, cry (alarm, aloud, out), destroy, make a joyful noise, smart, shout (for joy), sound an alarm, triumph.

7322. רוּף **rûwph**, *roof;* a prim. root; prop. to *triturate* (in a mortar), i.e. (fig.) to *agitate* (by concussion):— tremble.

7323. רוּץ **rûwts**, *roots;* a prim. root; to *run* (for whatever reason, espec. to *rush*):— break down, divide speedily, footman, guard, bring hastily, (make) run (away, through), post, stretch out.

7324. רוּק **rûwq**, *rook;* a prim. root; to *pour* out (lit. or fig.), i.e. *empty:*— × arm, cast out, draw (out), (make) empty, pour forth (out).

7325. רוּר **rûwr**, *roor;* a prim. root; to *slaver* (with spittle), i.e. (by anal.) to *emit* a fluid (ulcerous or natural):— run.

7326. רוּשׁ **rûwsh**, *roosh;* a prim. root; to *be destitute:*— lack, needy, (make self) poor (man).

רוֹשׁ **rôwsh**. See 7219.

7327. רוּת **Rûwth**, *rooth;* prob. for 7468; *friend; Ruth,* a Moabitess:— Ruth.

7328. רָז **râz** (Chald.), *rawz;* from an un-

used root prob. mean. to *attenuate,* i.e. (fig.) *hide;* a *mystery:*— secret.

7329. רָזָה **râzâh**, *raw-zaw´;* a prim. root; to *emaciate,* i.e. *make* (become) *thin* (lit. or fig.):— famish, wax lean.

7330. רָזֶה **râzeh**, *raw-zeh´;* from 7329; *thin:*— lean.

7331. רְזוֹן **Rᵉzôwn**, *rez-one´;* from 7336; *prince; Rezon,* a Syrian:— Rezon.

7332. רָזוֹן **râzôwn**, *raw-zone´;* from 7329; *thinness:*— leanness, × scant.

7333. רָזוֹן **râzôwn**, *raw-zone´;* from 7336; a *dignitary:*— prince.

7334. רָזִי **râzîy**, *raw-zee´;* from 7329; *thinness:*— leanness.

7335. רָזַם **râzam**, *raw-zam´;* a prim. root; to *twinkle* the eye (in mockery):— wink.

7336. רָזַן **râzan**, *raw-zan´;* a prim. root; prob. to *be heavy,* i.e. (fig.) *honorable:*— prince, ruler.

7337. רָחַב **râchab**, *raw-khab´;* a prim. root; to *broaden* (intr. or tran., lit. or fig.):— be an en- (make) large (-ing), make room, make (open) wide.

7338. רַחַב **rachab**, *rakh´-ab;* from 7337; a *width:*— breadth, broad place.

7339. רְחֹב **rᵉchôb**, *rekh-obe´;* or

רְחוֹב **rᵉchôwb**, *rekh-obe´;* from 7337; a *width,* i.e. (concr.) *avenue* or *area:*— broad place (way), street. See also 1050.

7340. רְחֹב **Rᵉchôb**, *rekh-obe´;* or

רְחוֹב **Rᵉchôwb**, *rekh-obe´;* the same as 7339; *Rechob,* the name of a place in Syria, also of a Syrian and an Isr.:— Rehob.

7341. רֹחַב **rôchab**, *ro´-khab;* from 7337; *width* (lit. or fig.):— breadth, broad, largeness, thickness, wideness.

7342. רָחָב **râchâb**, *raw-khawb´;* from 7337; *roomy,* in any (or every) direction, lit. or fig.:— broad, large, at liberty, proud, wide.

7343. רָחָב **Râchâb**, *raw-khawb´;* the same as 7342; *proud; Rachab,* a Canaanitess:— Rahab.

7344. רְחֹבוֹת **Rᵉchôbôwth**, *rekh-o-both´;* or

רְחֹבֹת **Rᵉchôbôth**, *rekh-o-both´;* plur. of 7339; *streets; Rechoboth,* a place in Assyria and one in Pal.:— Rehoboth.

7345. רְחַבְיָה **Rᵉchabyâh**, *rekh-ab-yaw´;* or

רְחַבְיָהוּ **Rᵉchabyâhûw**, *rek-ab-yaw´-hoo;* from 7337 and 3050; *Jah has enlarged; Rechabjah,* an Isr.:— Rehabiah.

7346. רְחַבְעָם **Rᵉchab'âm**, *rekh-ab-awm´;* from 7337 and 5971; a *people has enlarged; Rechabam,* an Isr. king:— Rehoboam.

רְחֹבוֹת **Rᵉchôbôth**. See 7344.

7347. רֵחֶה **rêcheh**, *ray-kheh´;* from an unused root mean. to *pulverize;* a *millstone:*— mill (stone).

רְחוֹב **Rᵉchôwb**. See 7339, 7340.

7348. רְחוּם **Rᵉchûwm**, *rekh-oom´;* a

form of 7349; *Rechum,* the name of a Pers. and of three Isr.:— Rehum.

7349. רַחוּם **rachûwm**, *rakh-oom´;* from 7355; *compassionate:*— full of compassion, merciful.

7350. רָחוֹק **râchôwq**, *raw-khoke´;* or

רָחֹק **râchôq**, *raw-khoke´;* from 7368; *remote,* lit. or fig., of place or time; spec. *precious;* often used adv. (with prep.):— (a-) far (abroad, off), long ago, of old, space, great while to come.

7351. רְחִיט **rᵉchîyt**, *rekh-eet´;* from the same as 7298; a *panel* (as resembling a *trough*):— rafter.

7352. רַחִיק **rachîyq** (Chald.), *rakh-eek´;* corresp. to 7350:— far.

7353. רָחֵל **râchêl**, *raw-kale´;* from an unused root mean. to *journey;* a *ewe* [the *females* being the predominant element of a flock] (as a good *traveller*):— ewe, sheep.

7354. רָחֵל **Râchêl**, *raw-khale´;* the same as 7353; *Rachel,* a wife of Jacob:— Rachel.

7355. רָחַם **râcham**, *raw-kham´;* a prim. root; to *fondle;* by impl. to *love,* espec. to *compassionate:*— have compassion (on, upon), love, (find, have, obtain, shew) mercy (-iful, on, upon), (have) pity, Ruhamah, × surely.

7356. רַחַם **racham**, *rakh´-am;* from 7355; *compassion* (in the plur.); by extens. the *womb* (as *cherishing* the fetus); by impl. a *maiden:*— bowels, compassion, damsel, tender love, (great, tender) mercy, pity, womb.

7357. רַחַם **Racham**, *rakh´-am;* the same as 7356; *pity; Racham,* an Isr.:— Raham.

7358. רֶחֶם **rechem**, *rekh´-em;* from 7355; the *womb* [comp. 7356]:— matrix, womb.

7359. רֶחֶם **rᵉchêm** (Chald.), *rekh-ame´;* corresp. to 7356; (plur.) *pity:*— mercy.

7360. רָחָם **râchâm**, *raw-khawm´;* or (fem.)

רָחָמָה **râchâmâh**, *raw-khaw-maw´;* from 7355; a kind of *vulture* (supposed to be *tender* toward its young):— gier-eagle.

7361. רַחֲמָה **rachămâh**, *rakh-am-aw´;* fem. of 7356; a *maiden:*— damsel.

7362. רַחְמָנִי **rachmânîy**, *rakh-maw-nee´;* from 7355; *compassionate:*— pitiful.

7363. רָחַף **râchaph**, *raw-khaf´;* a prim. root; to *brood;* by impl. to *be relaxed:*— flutter, move, shake.

7364. רָחַץ **râchats**, *raw-khats´;* a prim. root; to *lave* (the whole or a part of a thing):— bathe (self), wash (self).

7365. רְחַץ **rᵉchats** (Chald.), *rekh-ats´;* corresp. to 7364 through the accessory idea of *ministering* as a servant at the bath]; to *attend* upon:— trust.

7366. רַחַץ **rachats**, *rakh´-ats;* from 7364; a *bath:*— wash [-pot].

7367. רַחְצָה **rachtsâh**, *rakh-tsaw´;* fem. of 7366; a *bathing* place:— washing.

7368. רָחַק **râchaq**, *raw-khak´;* a prim. root; to *widen* (in any direction), i.e.

(intr.) *recede* or (tran.) *remove* (lit. or fig., of place or relation):— (a-, be, cast, drive, get, go, keep [self], put, remove, be too, [wander], withdraw) far (away, off), loose, × refrain, very, (be) a good way (off).

7369. רָחֵק **râchêq**, *raw-khake´*; from 7368; *remote*:— that are far.

רָחוֹק **râchôq**. See 7350.

7370. רָחַשׁ **râchash**, *raw-khash´*; a prim. root; to *gush*:— indite.

7371. רַחַת **rachath**, *rakh´-ath*; from 7306; a *winnowing*-fork (as *blowing* the chaff away):— shovel.

7372. רָטַב **râtab**, *raw-tab´*; a prim. root; to *be moist*:— be wet.

7373. רָטֹב **râtôb**, *raw-tobe´*; from 7372; *moist* (with sap):— green.

7374. רֶטֶט **retet**, *reh´-tet*; from an unused root mean. to *tremble*; *terror*:— fear.

7375. רֻטֲפַשׁ **rûwtăphash**, *roo-taf-ash´*; a root compounded from 7373 and 2954; to *be rejuvenated*:— be fresh.

7376. רָטַשׁ **râtash**, *raw-tash´*; a prim. root; to *dash* down:— dash (in pieces).

7377. רִי **rîy**, *ree*; from 7301; *irrigation*, i.e. a *shower*:— watering.

7378. רִיב **rîyb**, *reeb*; or

רוּב **rûwb**, *roob*; a prim. root; prop. to *toss*, i.e. *grapple*; mostly fig. to *wrangle*, i.e. *hold a controversy*; (by impl.) to *defend*:— adversary, chide, complain, contend, debate, × ever, × lay wait, plead, rebuke, strive, × thoroughly.

7379. רִיב **rîyb**, *reeb*; or

רִב **rib**, *reeb*; from 7378; a *contest* (personal or legal):— + adversary, cause, chiding, contend (-tion), controversy, multitude [from the marg.], pleading, strife, strive (-ing), suit.

7380. רִיבַי **Rîybay**, *ree-bah´-ee*; from 7378; *contentious*; *Ribai*, an Isr.:— Ribai.

7381. רֵיחַ **rêyach**, *ray´-akh*; from 7306; *odor* (as if *blown*):— savour, scent, smell.

7382. רֵיחַ **rêyach** (Chald.), *ray´-akh*; corresp. to 7381:— smell.

רֵים **rêym**. See 7214.

רֵיעַ **rêya'**. See 7453.

7383. רִיפָה **rîyphâh**, *ree-faw´*; or

רִפָה **riphâh**, *ree-faw´*; from 7322; (only plur.), *grits* (as *pounded*):— ground corn, wheat.

7384. רִיפַת **Rîyphath**, *ree-fath´*; or (prob. by orth. err.)

דִּיפַת **Dîyphath**, *dee-fath´*; of for. or.; *Riphath*, a grandson of Japheth and his desc.:— Riphath.

7385. רִיק **rîyq**, *reek*; from 7324; *emptiness*; fig. a *worthless* thing; adv. *in vain*:— empty, to no purpose, (in) vain (thing), vanity.

7386. רֵיק **rêyq**, *rake*; or (short.)

רֵק **rêq**, *rake*; from 7324; *empty*; fig. *worthless*:— emptied (-ty), vain (fellow, man).

7387. רֵיקָם **rêyqâm**, *ray-kawm´*; from

7386; *emptily*; fig. (obj.) *ineffectually*, (subj.) *undeservedly*:— without cause, empty, in vain, void.

7388. רִיר **rîyr**, *reer*; from 7325; *saliva*; by resemblance *broth*:— spittle, white [of an egg].

7389. רֵישׁ **rêysh**, *raysh*; or

רֵאשׁ **rê'sh**, *raysh*; or

רִישׁ **rîysh**, *reesh*; from 7326; *poverty*:— poverty.

7390. רַךְ **rak**, *rak*; from 7401; *tender* (lit. or fig.); by impl. *weak*:— faint [-hearted], soft, tender (l-hearted), one), weak.

7391. רֹךְ **rôk**, *roke*; from 7401; *softness* (fig.):— tenderness.

7392. רָכַב **râkab**, *raw-kab´*; a prim. root; to *ride* (on an animal or in a vehicle); caus. to *place upon* (for riding or gen.), to *despatch*:— bring (on [horse-] back), carry, get [oneself] up, on [horse-] back, put, (cause to, make to) ride (in a chariot, on, -r), set.

7393. רֶכֶב **rekeb**, *reh´-keb*; from 7392; a *vehicle*; by impl. a *team*; by extens. *cavalry*; by anal. a *rider*, i.e. the upper millstone:— chariot, (upper) millstone, multitude [from the marg.], wagon.

7394. רֵכָב **Rêkâb**, *ray-kawb´*; from 7392; *rider*; *Rekab*, the name of two Arabs and of two Isr.:— Rechab.

7395. רַכָּב **rakkâb**, *rak-kawb´*; from 7392; a *charioteer*:— chariot man, driver of a chariot, horseman.

7396. רִכְבָּה **rikbâh**, *rik-baw´*; fem. of 7393; a *chariot* (collect.):— chariots.

7397. רֵכָה **Rêkâh**, *ray-kaw´*; prob. fem. from 7401; *softness*; *Rekah*, a place in Pal.:— Rechah.

7398. רְכוּב **rekûwb**, *rek-oob´*; from pass. part. of 7392; a *vehicle* (as *ridden* on):— chariot.

7399. רְכוּשׁ **rekûwsh**, *rek-oosh´*; or

רְכֻשׁ **rekush**, *rek-oosh´*; from pass. part. of 7408; *property* (as *gathered*):— good, riches, substance.

7400. רָכִיל **râkîyl**, *raw-keel´*; from 7402 a *scandal-monger* (as *travelling* about):— slander, carry tales, talebearer.

7401. רָכַךְ **râkak**, *raw-kak´*; a prim. root; to *soften* (intr. or tran.), used fig.:— (be) faint (l-hearted), mollify, (be, make) soft (-er), be tender.

7402. רָכַל **râkal**, *raw-kal´*; a prim. root; to *travel* for trading:— (spice) merchant.

7403. רָכָל **Râkâl**, *raw-kawl´*; from 7402; *merchant*; *Rakal*, a place in Pal.:— Rachal.

7404. רְכֻלָּה **rekullâh**, *rek-ool-law´*; fem. pass. part. of 7402; *trade* (as *peddled*):— merchandise, traffic.

7405. רָכַס **râkaç**, *raw-kas´*; a prim. root; to *tie*:— bind.

7406. רֶכֶס **rekeç**, *reh´-kes*; from 7405; a mountain *ridge* (as of *tied* summits):— rough place.

7407. רֹכֶס **rôkeç**, *ro´-kes*; from 7405; a *snare* (as of *tied* meshes):— pride.

7408. רָכַשׁ **râkash**, *raw-kash´*; a prim. root; to *lay up*, i.e. *collect*:— gather, get.

7409. רֶכֶשׁ **rekesh**, *reh´-kesh*; from 7408; a *relay* of animals on a post-route (as *stored* up for that purpose); by impl. a *courser*:— dromedary, mule, swift beast.

רְכֻשׁ **rekûsh**. See 7399.

רֵם **rêm**. See 7214.

7410. רָם **Râm**, *rawm*; act. part. of 7311; *high*; *Ram*, the name of an Arabian and of an Isr.:— Ram. See also 1027.

רֻם **rûm**. See 7311.

7411. רָמָה **râmâh**, *raw-maw´*; a prim. root; to *hurl*; spec. to *shoot*; fig. to *delude* or *betray* (as if causing to fall):— beguile, betray, [bow-] man, carry, deceive, throw.

7412. רְמָה **remâh** (Chald.), *rem-aw´*; corresp. to 7411; to *throw*, *set*, (fig.) *assess*:— cast (down), impose.

7413. רָמָה **râmâh**, *raw-maw´*; fem. act. part. of 7311; a *height* (as a seat of idolatry):— high place.

7414. רָמָה **Râmâh**, *raw-maw´*; the same as 7413; *Ramah*, the name of four places in Pal.:— Ramah.

7415. רִמָּה **rimmâh**, *rim-maw´*; from 7426 in the sense of *breeding* [comp. 7311]; a *maggot* (as rapidly *bred*), lit. or fig.:— worm.

7416. רִמּוֹן **rimmôwn**, *rim-mone´*; or

רִמֹּן **rimmôn**, *rim-mone´*; from 7426; a *pomegranate*, the tree (from its *upright* growth) or the fruit (also an artificial ornament):— pomegranate.

7417. רִמּוֹן **Rimmôwn**, *rim-mone´*; or (short.)

רִמֹּן **Rimmôn**, *rim-mone´*; or

רִמּוֹנוֹ **Rimmôwnôw** (1 Chron. 6:62 [77]), *rim-mo-no´*; the same as 7416; *Rimmon*, the name of a Syrian deity, also of five places in Pal.:— Remmon, Rimmon. The addition "-methoar" (Josh. 19:13) is

הַמְּתֹאָר **ham-methô'âr**, *ham-meth-o-awr´*; pass. part. of 8388 with the art.; *the* (one) *marked off*, i.e. *which pertains*; mistaken for part of the name.

רָמוֹת **Râmôwth**. See 7418, 7433.

7418. רָמוֹת־נֶגֶב **Râmôwth-Negeb**, *raw-môth-neh´-gheb*; or

רָמַת נֶגֶב **Râmath Negeb**, *raw´-math neh´-gheb*; from the plur. or constr. form of 7413 and 5045; *heights* (or *height*) of (the) *South*; *Ramoth-Negeb* or *Ramath-Negeb*, a place in Pal.:— south Ramoth, Ramath of the south.

7419. רָמוּת **râmûwth**, *raw-mooth´*; from 7311; a *heap* (of carcases):— height.

7420. רֹמַח **rômach**, *ro´-makh*; from an unused root mean. to *hurl*; a *lance* (as *thrown*); espec. the iron *point*:— buckler, javelin, lancet, spear.

7421. רַמִּי **rammîy**, *ram-mee´*; for 761; a *Ramite*, i.e. Aramæan:— Syrian.

7422. רַמְיָה **Ramyâh**, *ram-yaw´*; from 7311 and 3050; *Jah has raised*; *Ramjah*, an Isr.:— Ramiah.

7423. רְמִיָּה **rᵉmîyâh**, *rem-ee-yaw´;* from 7411; *remissness, treachery:*— deceit (-ful, -fully), false, guile, idle, slack, slothful.

7424. רַמָּךְ **rammâk**, *ram-mawk´;* of for. or.; a brood *mare:*— dromedary.

7425. רְמַלְיָהוּ **Rᵉmalyâhûw**, *rem-al-yaw´-hoo;* from an unused root and 3050 (perh. mean. to *deck*); *Jah has bedecked; Remaljah,* an Isr.:— Remaliah.

7426. רָמַם **râmam**, *raw-mam´;* a prim. root; to *rise* (lit. or fig.):— exalt, get (oneself) up, lift up (self), mount up.

7427. רֹמֵמֻת **rômêmûth**, *ro-may-mooth´;* from the act. part. of 7426; *exaltation:*— lifting up of self.

רִמֹּן **rimmôn**. See 7416.

7428. רִמֹּן פֶּרֶץ **Rimmôn Perets**, *rim-mone´ peh´-rets;* from 7416 and 6556; *pomegranate of* (the) *breach; Rimmon-Perets,* a place in the Desert:— Rimmon-parez.

7429. רָמַס **râmaç**, *raw-mas´;* a prim. root; to *tread* upon (as a potter, in walking or abusively):— oppressor, stamp (upon), trample (under feet), tread (down, upon).

7430. רָמַשׂ **râmas**, *raw-mas´;* a prim. root; prop. to *glide* swiftly, i.e. to *crawl* or *move* with short steps; by anal. to *swarm:*— creep, move.

7431. רֶמֶשׂ **remes**, *reh´-mes;* from 7430; a *reptile* or any other rapidly moving animal:— that creepeth, creeping (moving) thing.

7432. רֶמֶת **Remeth**, *reh´-meth;* from 7411; *height; Remeth,* a place in Pal.:— Remeth.

7433. רָמֹה (or רָמוֹת **Râmôwth**) גִּלְעָד **Râmôth Gil'âd** (2 Chron. 22:5), *raw-moth´ gil-awd´;* from the plur. of 7413 and 1568; *heights of Gilad; Ramoth-Gilad,* a place E. of the Jordan:— Ramoth-gilead, Ramoth in Gilead. See also 7216.

7434. רָמַת הַמִּצְפֶּה **Râmath ham-Mitspeh**, *raw-math´ ham-mits-peh´;* from 7413 and 4707 with the art. interpolated; *height of the watch-tower; Ramath-ham-Mitspeh,* a place in Pal.:— Ramath-mizpeh.

7435. רָמָתִי **Râmâthîy**, *raw-maw-thee´;* patron. of 7414; a *Ramathite* or inhab. of Ramah:— Ramathite.

7436. רָמָתַיִם צֹפִים **Râmâthayim Tsôwphîym**, *raw-maw-thah´-yim tso-feem´;* from the dual of 7413 and the plur. of the act. part. of 6822; *double height of watchers; Ramathajim-Tsophim,* a place in Pal.:— Ramathaim-zophim.

7437. רָמַת לֶחִי **Râmath Lechîy**, *raw-math´ lekh´-ee;* from 7413 and 3895; *height of* (a) *jaw-bone; Ramath-Lechi,* a place in Pal.:— Ramath-lehi.

רָן **Rân**. See 1028.

7438. רֹן **rôn**, *rone;* from 7442; a *shout* (of deliverance):— song.

7439. רָנָה **rânâh**, *raw-naw´;* a prim. root; to *whiz:*— rattle.

7440. רִנָּה **rinnâh**, *rin-naw´;* from 7442; prop. a *creaking* (or shrill sound), i.e. *shout* (of joy or grief):— cry, gladness,

joy, proclamation, rejoicing, shouting, sing (-ing), triumph.

7441. רִנָּה **Rinnâh**, *rin-naw´;* the same as 7440; *Rinnah,* an Isr.:— Rinnah.

7442. רָנַן **rânan**, *raw-nan´;* a prim. root; prop. to *creak* (or emit a stridulous sound), i.e. to *shout* (usually for joy):— aloud for joy, cry out, be joyful (greatly, make to) rejoice, (cause to) shout (for joy), (cause to) sing (aloud, for joy, out), triumph.

7443. רֶנֶן **renen**, *reh´-nen;* from 7442; an *ostrich* (from its *wail*):— × goodly.

7444. רַנֵּן **rannên**, *ran-nane´;* intens. from 7442; *shouting* (for joy):— singing.

7445. רְנָנָה **rᵉnânâh**, *ren-aw-naw´;* from 7442; a *shout* (for joy):— joyful (voice), singing, triumphing.

7446. רִסָּה **Riççâh**, *ris-saw´;* from 7450; a *ruin* (as *dripping* to pieces); *Rissah,* a place in the Desert:— Rissah.

7447. רָסִיס **râçîyç**, *raw-sees´;* from 7450; prop. *dripping* to pieces, i.e. a *ruin;* also a *dew-drop:*— breach, drop.

7448. רֶסֶן **reçen**, *reh´-sen;* from an unused root mean. to *curb;* a *halter* (as *restraining*); by impl. the *jaw:*— bridle.

7449. רֶסֶן **Reçen**, *reh´-sen;* the same as 7448; *Resen,* a place in Ass.:— Resen.

7450. רָסַס **râçaç**, *raw-sas´;* a prim. root; to *comminute;* used only as denom. from 7447, to *moisten* (with drops):— temper.

7451. רַע **ra'**, *rah;* from 7489; *bad* or (as noun) *evil* (nat. or mor.):— adversity, affliction, bad, calamity, + displease (-ure), distress, evil (l-favouredness), man, thing), + exceedingly, × great, grief (-vous), harm, heavy, hurt (-ful), ill (favoured), + mark, mischief (-vous), misery, naught (-ty), noisome, + not please, sad (-ly), sore, sorrow, trouble, vex, wicked (-ly, -ness, one), worse (-st), wretchedness, wrong. [Incl. fem.

רָעָה **râ'âh**; *as adj. or noun.*]

7452. רֵעַ **rêa'**, *ray´-ah;* from 7321; a *crash* (of thunder), *noise* (of war), *shout* (of joy):— × aloud, noise, shouted.

7453. רֵעַ **rêa'**, *ray´-ah;* or

רֵיעַ **rêya'**, *ray´-ah;* from 7462; an *associate* (more or less close):— brother, companion, fellow, friend, husband, lover, neighbour, × (an-) other.

7454. רֵעַ **rêa'**, *ray´-ah;* from 7462; a *thought* (as *association* of ideas):— thought.

7455. רֹעַ **rôa'**, *ro´-ah;* from 7489; *badness* (as *marring*), phys. or mor.:— × be so bad, badness, (× be so) evil, naughtiness, sadness, sorrow, wickedness.

7456. רָעֵב **râ'êb**, *raw-abe´;* a prim. root; to *hunger:*— (suffer to) famish, (be, have, suffer, suffer to) hunger (-ry).

7457. רָעֵב **râ'êb**, *raw-abe´;* from 7456; *hungry* (more or less intensely):— hunger bitten, hungry.

7458. רָעָב **râ'âb**, *raw-awb´;* from 7456; *hunger* (more or less extensive):— dearth, famine, + famished, hunger.

7459. רְעָבוֹן **rᵉ'âbôwn**, *reh-aw-bone´;* from 7456; *famine:*— famine.

7460. רָעַד **râ'ad**, *raw-ad´;* a prim. root: to *shudder* (more or less violently):— tremble.

7461. רַעַד **ra'ad**, *rah´-ad;* or (fem.)

רְעָדָה **rᵉ'âdâh**, *reh-aw-daw´;* from 7460; a *shudder:*— trembling.

7462. רָעָה **râ'âh**, *raw-aw´;* a prim. root; to *tend* a flock; i.e. *pasture* it; intr. to *graze* (lit. or fig.); gen. to *rule;* by extens. to *associate* with (as a friend):— × break, companion, keep company with, devour, eat up, evil entreat, feed, use as a friend, make friendship with, herdman, keep (sheep) (-er), pastor, + shearing house, shepherd, wander, waste.

7463. רֵעֶה **rê'eh**, *ray-eh´;* from 7462; a (male) *companion:*— friend.

7464. רֵעָה **rê'âh**, *ray´-aw;* fem. of 7453; a female *associate:*— companion, fellow.

7465. רֹעָה **rô'âh**, *ro-aw´;* for 7455; *breakage:*— broken, utterly.

7466. רְעוּ **Rᵉ'ûw**, *reh-oo´;* for 7471 in the sense of 7453; *friend; Reü,* a postdiluvian patriarch:— Reu.

7467. רְעוּאֵל **Rᵉ'ûw'êl**, *reh-oo-ale´;* from the same as 7466 and 410; *friend of God; Reüel,* the name of Moses' father-in-law, also of an Edomite and an Isr.:— Raguel, Reuel.

7468. רְעוּת **rᵉ'ûwth**, *reh-ooth´;* from 7462 in the sense of 7453; a female *associate;* gen. an *additional* one:— + another, mate, neighbour.

7469. רְעוּת **rᵉ'ûwth**, *reh-ooth´;* prob. from 7462; a *feeding* upon, i.e. *grasping* after:— vexation.

7470. רְעוּת **rᵉ'ûwth** (Chald.), *reh-ooth´;* corresp. to 7469; *desire:*— pleasure, will.

7471. רְעִי **rᵉ'îy**, *reh-ee´;* from 7462; *pasture:*— pasture.

7472. רֵעִי **Rê'îy**, *ray-ee´;* from 7453; *social; Reï,* an Isr.:— Rei.

7473. רֹעִי **rô'îy**, *ro-ee´;* from act. part. of 7462; *pastoral;* as noun, a *shepherd:*— shepherd.

7474. רַעְיָה **ra'yâh**, *rah-yaw´;* fem. of 7453; a female *associate:*— fellow, love.

7475. רַעְיוֹן **ra'yôwn**, *rah-yone´;* from 7462 in the sense of 7469; *desire:*— vexation.

7476. רַעְיוֹן **ra'yôwn** (Chald.), *rah-yone´;* corresp. to 7475; a *grasp,* i.e. (fig.) mental *conception:*— cogitation, thought.

7477. רָעַל **râ'al**, *raw-al´;* a prim. root; to *reel,* i.e. (fig.) to *brandish:*— terribly shake.

7478. רַעַל **ra'al**, *rah´-al;* from 7477; a *reeling* (from intoxication):— trembling.

7479. רַעֲלָה **ra'ălâh**, *rah-al-aw´;* fem. of 7478; a long *veil* (as *fluttering*):— muffler.

7480. רְעֵלָיָה **Rᵉ'êlâyâh**, *reh-ay-law-yaw´;* from 7477 and 3050; *made to tremble* (i.e. *fearful*) *of Jah; Reëlajah,* an Isr.:— Reeliah.

7481. רָעַם **râ'am**, *raw-am´;* a prim. root; to *tumble,* i.e. be violently *agitated;* spec. to *crash* (of thunder); fig. to *irri-*

tate (with anger):— make to fret, roar, thunder, trouble.

7482. רַעַם **ra'am**, *rah'am*; from 7481; a *peal* of thunder:— thunder.

7483. רַעְמָה **ra'mâh**, *rah-maw'*; fem. of 7482; the *mane* of a horse (as *quivering* in the wind):— thunder.

7484. רַעְמָה **Ra'mâh**, *rah-maw'*; the same as 7483; *Ramah*, the name of a grandson of Ham, and of a place (perh. founded by him):— Raamah.

7485. רַעְמְיָה **Ra'amyâh**, *rah-am-yaw'*; from 7481 and 3050; *Jah has shaken*; *Raamjah*, an Isr.:— Raamiah.

7486. רַעְמְסֵס **Ra'mᵉçêç**, *rah-mes-ace'*; or

רַעְמְסֵס **Ra'amçêç**, *rah-am-sace'*; of Eg. or.; *Rameses* or *Raamses*, a place in Egypt:— Raamses, Rameses.

7487. רַעֲנַן **ra'ânan** (Chald.), *rah-aw-nan'*; corresp. to 7488; *green*, i.e. (fig.) *prosperous*:— flourishing.

7488. רַעֲנַן **ra'ânân**, *rah-an-awn'*; from an unused root mean. to *be green*; *verdant*; by anal. *new*; fig. *prosperous*:— green, flourishing.

7489. רָעַע **râ'a'**, *raw-ah'*; a prim. root; prop. to *spoil* (lit. by *breaking* to pieces); fig. to *make* (or *be*) *good for nothing*, i.e. *bad* (physically, socially or morally):— afflict, associate selves [by *mistake* for 7462], break (down, in pieces), + displease, (be, bring, do) evil (doer, entreat, man), show self friendly [by *mistake* for 7462], do harm, (do) hurt, (behave self, deal) ill, × indeed, do mischief, punish, still, vex, (do) wicked (doer, -ly), be (deal, do) worse.

7490. רְעַע **rᵉ'a'** (Chald.), *reh-ah'*; corresp. to 7489:— break, bruise.

7491. רָעַף **râ'aph**, *raw-af'*; a prim. root; to *drip*:— distil, drop (down).

7492. רָעַץ **râ'ats**, *raw-ats'*; a prim. root; to *break* in pieces; fig. *harass*:— dash in pieces, vex.

7493. רָעַשׁ **râ'ash**, *raw-ash'*; a prim. root; to *undulate* (as the earth, the sky, etc.; also a field of grain), partic. through fear; spec. to *spring* (as a locust):— make afraid, (re-) move, quake, (make to) shake, (make to) tremble.

7494. רַעַשׁ **ra'ash**, *rah'-ash*; from 7493; *vibration*, *bounding*, *uproar*:— commotion, confused noise, earthquake, fierceness, quaking, rattling, rushing, shaking.

7495. רָפָא **râphâ'**, *raw-faw'*; or

רָפָה **râphâh**, *raw-faw'*; a prim. root; prop. to *mend* (by stitching), i.e. (fig.) to *cure*:— cure, (cause to) heal, physician, repair, × thoroughly, make whole. See 7503.

7496. רָפָא **râphâ'**, *raw-faw'*; from 7495 in the sense of 7503; prop. *lax*, i.e. (fig.) a *ghost* (as *dead*; in plur. only):— dead, deceased.

7497. רָפָא **râphâ'**, *raw-faw'*; or

רָפָה **râphâh**, *raw-faw'*; from 7495 in the sense of *invigorating*; a *giant*:— giant, Rapha, Rephaim (-s). See also 1051.

7498. רָפָא **Râphâ'**, *raw-faw'*; or

רָפָה **Râphâh**, *raw-faw'*; prob. the same as 7497; *giant*; *Rapha* or *Raphah*, the name of two Isr.:— Rapha.

7499. רְפֻאָה **rᵉphû'âh**, *ref-oo-aw'*; fem. pass. part. of 7495; a *medicament*:— heal [-ed], medicine.

7500. רִפְאוּת **riph'ûwth**, *rif-ooth'*; from 7495; a *cure*:— health.

7501. רְפָאֵל **Rᵉphâ'êl**, *ref-aw-ale'*; from 7495 and 410; *God has cured*; *Rephaël*, an Isr.:— Rephael.

7502. רָפַד **râphad**, *raw-fad'*; a prim. root; to *spread* (a bed); by impl. to *refresh*:— comfort, make [a bed], spread.

7503. רָפָה **râphâh**, *raw-faw'*; a prim. root; to *slacken* (in many applications, lit. or fig.):— abate, cease, consume, draw [toward evening], fail, (be) faint, be (wax) feeble, forsake, idle, leave, let alone (go, down), (be) slack, stay, be still, be slothful, (be) weak (-en). See 7495.

7504. רָפֶה **râpheh**, *raw-feh'*; from 7503; *slack* (in body or mind):— weak.

רָפָה **râphâh**, **Râphâh**. See 7497, 7498.

רִפְאָה **riphâh**. See 7383.

7505. רָפוּא **Râphûw'**, *raw-foo'*; pass. part. of 7495; *cured*; *Raphu*, an Isr.:— Raphu.

7506. רֶפַח **Rephach**, *reh'-fakh*; from an unused root appar. mean. to *sustain*; *support*; *Rephach*, an Isr.:— Rephah.

7507. רְפִידָה **rᵉphîydâh**, *ref-ee-daw'*; from 7502; a *railing* (as *spread* along):— bottom.

7508. רְפִידִים **Rᵉphîydiym**, *ref-ee-deem'*; plur. of the masc. of the same as 7507; *ballusters*; *Rephidim*, a place in the Desert:— Rephidim.

7509. רְפָיָה **Rᵉphâyâh**, *ref-aw-yaw'*; from 7495 and 3050; *Jah has cured*; *Rephajah*, the name of five Isr.:— Rephaiah.

7510. רִפְיוֹן **riphyôwn**, *rif-yone'*; from 7503; *slackness*:— feebleness.

7511. רָפַס **râphaç**, *raw-fas'*; a prim. root; to *trample*, i.e. *prostrate*:— humble self, submit self.

7512. רְפַס **rᵉphaç** (Chald.), *ref-as'*; corresp. to 7511:— stamp.

7513. רַפְסֹדָה **raphçôdâh**, *raf-so-daw'*; from 7511; a *raft* (as *flat* on the water):— flote.

7514. רָפַק **râphaq**, *raw-fak'*; a prim. root; to *recline*:— lean.

7515. רָפַשׂ **râphas**, *raw-fas'*; a prim. root; to *trample*, i.e. *roil* water:— foul, trouble.

7516. רֶפֶשׁ **rephesh**, *reh'-fesh*; from 7515; *mud* (as *roiled*):— mire.

7517. רֶפֶת **repheth**, *reh'-feth*; prob. from 7503; a *stall* for cattle (from their *resting* there):— stall.

7518. רַץ **rats**, *rats*; contr. from 7533; a *fragment*:— piece.

7519. רָצָא **râtsâ'**, *raw-tsaw'*; a prim. root; to *run*; also to *delight* in:— accept, run.

7520. רָצַד **râtsad**, *raw-tsad'*; a prim. root; prob. to *look askant*, i.e. (fig.) be *jealous*:— leap.

same as 7497; *giant*; *Rapha* or *Raphah*, the name of two Isr.:— Rapha.

7521. רָצָה **râtsâh**, *raw-tsaw'*; a prim. root; to *be pleased with*; spec. to *satisfy* a *debt*:— (be) accept (-able), accomplish, set affection, approve, consent with, delight (self), enjoy, (be, have a) favour (-able), like, observe, pardon, (be, have, take) please (-ure), reconcile self.

7522. רָצוֹן **râtsôwn**, *raw-tsone'*; or

רָצֹן **râtsôn**, *raw-tsone'*; from 7521; *delight* (espec. as shown):— (be) acceptable (-ance, -ed), delight, desire, favour, (good) pleasure, (own, self, voluntary) will, as ... (what) would.

7523. רָצַח **râtsach**, *raw-tsakh'*; a prim. root; prop. to *dash* in pieces, i.e. *kill* (a human being), espec. to *murder*:— put to death, kill, (man-) slay (-er), murder (-er).

7524. רֶצַח **retsach**, *reh-tsakh*; from 7523; a *crushing*; spec. a *murder-cry*:— slaughter, sword.

7525. רִצְיָא **Ritsyâ'**, *rits-yaw'*; from 7521; *delight*; *Ritsjah*, an Isr.:— Rezia.

7526. רְצִין **Rᵉtsiyn**, *rets-een'*; prob. for 7522; *Retsin*, the name of a Syrian and of an Isr.:— Rezin.

7527. רָצַע **râtsa'**, *raw-tsah'*; a prim. root; to *pierce*:— bore.

7528. רָצַף **râtsaph**, *raw-tsaf'*; a denom. from 7529; to *tessellate*, i.e. embroider (as if with bright stones):— pave.

7529. רֶצֶף **retseph**, *reh'-tsef*; for 7565; a red-hot *stone* (for baking):— coal.

7530. רֶצֶף **Retseph**, *reh'-tsef*; the same as 7529; *Retseph*, a place in Ass.:— Rezeph.

7531. רִצְפָּה **ritspâh**, *rits-paw'*; fem. of 7529; a hot *stone*; also a tessellated *pavement*:— live coal, pavement.

7532. רִצְפָּה **Ritspâh**, *rits-paw'*; the same as 7531; *Ritspah*, an Israelitess:— Rizpah.

7533. רָצַץ **râtsats**, *raw-tsats'*; a prim. root; to *crack* in pieces, lit. or fig.:— break, bruise, crush, discourage, oppress, struggle together.

7534. רַק **raq**, *rak*; from 7556 in its orig. sense; *emaciated* (as if *flattened* out):— lean (I-fleshed), thin.

7535. רַק **raq**, *rak*; the same as 7534 as a noun; prop. *leanness*, i.e. (fig.) *limitation*; only adv. *merely*, or conjunc. *although*:— but, even, except, howbeit, howsoever, at the least, nevertheless, nothing but, notwithstanding, only, save, so [that], surely, yet (so), in any wise.

7536. רֹק **rôq**, *roke*; from 7556; *spittle*:— spit (-ting, -tle).

7537. רָקַב **râqab**, *raw-kab'*; a prim. root; to *decay* (as by worm-eating):— rot.

7538. רָקָב **râqâb**, *raw-kawb'*; from 7537; *decay* (by caries):— rottenness (thing).

7539. רִקָּבוֹן **riqqâbôwn**, *rik-kaw-bone'*; from 7538; *decay* (by caries):— rotten.

7540. רָקַד **râqad**, *raw-kad'*; a prim. root; prop. to *stamp*, i.e. to *spring* about (wildly or for joy):— dance, jump, leap, skip.

7541. רַקָּה **raqqâh**, *rak-kaw´;* fem. of 7534; prop. *thinness,* i.e. the *side* of the head:— temple.

7542. רַקּוֹן **Raqqôwn**, *rak-kone´;* from 7534; *thinness; Rakkon,* a place in Pal.:— Rakkon.

7543. רָקַח **râqach**, *raw-kakh´;* a prim. root; to *perfume:—* apothecary, compound, make [ointment], prepare, spice.

7544. רֶקַח **reqach**, *reh´-kakh;* from 7543; prop. *perfumery,* i.e. (by impl.) *spicery* (for flavor):— spiced.

7545. רֹקַח **rôqach**, *ro´-kakh;* from 7542; an *aromatic:—* confection, ointment.

7546. רַקָּח **raqqâch**, *rak-kawkh´;* from 7543; a male *perfumer:—* apothecary.

7547. רַקֻּחַ **raqqûach**, *rak-koo´-akh;* from 7543; a *scented* substance:— perfume.

7548. רִקֻּחָה **raqqâchâh**, *rak-kaw-khaw´;* fem. of 7547; a female *perfumer:—* confectioner.

7549. רָקִיעַ **râqîya'**, *raw-kee´-ah;* from 7554; prop. an *expanse,* i.e. the *firmament* or (appar.) visible arch of the sky:— firmament.

7550. רָקִיק **râqîyq**, *raw-keek´;* from 7556 in its orig. sense; a thin *cake:—* cake, wafer.

7551. רָקַם **râqam**, *raw-kam´;* a prim. root; to *variegate* color, i.e. *embroider;* by impl. to *fabricate:—* embroiderer, needlework, curiously work.

7552. רֶקֶם **Reqem**, *reh´-kem;* from 7551; *versi-color; Rekem,* the name of a place in Pal., also of a Midianite and an Isr.:— Rekem.

7553. רִקְמָה **riqmâh**, *rik-maw´;* from 7551; *variegation* of color; spec. *embroidery:—* broidered (work), divers colours, (raiment of) needlework (on both sides).

7554. רָקַע **râqa'**, *raw-kah´;* a prim. root; to *pound* the earth (as a sign of passion); by anal. to *expand* (by hammering); by impl. to *overlay* (with thin sheets of metal):— beat, make broad, spread abroad (forth, over, out, into plates), stamp, stretch.

7555. רִקֻּעַ **riqqûa'**, *rik-koo´-ah;* from 7554; *beaten* out, i.e. a (metallic) *plate:—* broad.

7556. רָקַק **râqaq**, *raw-kak´;* a prim. root; to *spit:—* spit.

7557. רַקַּת **Raqqath**, *rak-kath´;* from 7556 in its orig. sense of *diffusing;* a *beach* (as expanded shingle); *Rakkath,* a place in Pal.:— Rakkath.

7558. רִשְׁיוֹן **rishyôwn**, *rish-yone´;* from an unused root mean. to *have leave;* a *permit:—* grant.

7559. רָשַׁם **râsham**, *raw-sham´;* a prim. root; to *record:—* note.

7560. רְשַׁם **r e sham** (Chald.), *resh-am´;* corresp. to 7559:— sign, write.

7561. רָשַׁע **râsha'**, *raw-shah´;* a prim. root; to *be* (caus. *do* or *declare*) *wrong;* by impl. to *disturb, violate:—* condemn, make trouble, vex, be (commit, deal, depart, do) wicked (-ly, -ness).

7562. רֶשַׁע **resha'**, *reh´-shah;* from 7561;

a *wrong* (espec. moral):— iniquity, wicked (-ness).

7563. רָשָׁע **râshâ'**, *raw-shaw´;* from 7561; morally *wrong;* concr. an (actively) *bad* person:— + condemned, guilty, ungodly, wicked (man), that did wrong.

7564. רִשְׁעָה **rish'âh**, *rish-aw´;* fem. of 7562; *wrong* (espec. moral):— fault, wickedly (-ness).

7565. רֶשֶׁף **resheph**, *reh´-shef;* from 8313; a live *coal;* by anal. *lightning;* fig. an *arrow,* (as flashing through the air); spec. *fever:—* arrow, (burning) coal, burning heat, + spark, hot thunderbolt.

7566. רֶשֶׁף **Resheph**, *reh´-shef;* the same as 7565; *Resheph,* an Isr.:— Resheph.

7567. רָשַׁשׁ **râshash**, *raw-shash´;* a prim. root; to *demolish:—* impoverish.

7568. רֶשֶׁת **resheth**, *reh´-sheth;* from 3423; a *net* (as catching animals):— net [-work].

7569. רַתּוֹק **rattôwq**, *rat-toke´;* from 7576; a *chain:—* chain.

7570. רָתַח **râthach**, *raw-thakh´;* a prim. root; to *boil:—* boil.

7571. רֶתַח **rethach**, *reh´-thakh;* from 7570; a *boiling:—* × [boil] well.

7572. רַתִּיקָה **rattîyqâh**, *rat-tee-kaw´;* from 7576; a *chain:—* chain.

7573. רָתַם **râtham**, *raw-tham´;* a prim. root; to *yoke* up (to the pole of a vehicle):— bind.

7574. רֶתֶם **rethem**, *reh´-them;* or

רֹתֶם **rôthem**, *ro´-them;* from 7573; the Spanish *broom* (from its pole-like stems):— juniper (tree).

7575. רִתְמָה **Rithmâh**, *rith-maw´;* fem. of 7574; *Rithmah,* a place in the Desert:— Rithmah.

7576. רָתַק **râthaq**, *raw-thak´;* a prim. root; to *fasten:—* bind.

7577. רְתֻקָה **r e thûqâh**, *reth-oo-kaw´;* fem. pass. part. of 7576; something *fastened,* i.e. a *chain:—* chain.

7578. רְתֵת **r e thêth**, *reth-ayth´;* for 7374; *terror:—* trembling.

ש

7579. שָׁאַב **shâ'ab**, *sahw-ab´;* a prim. root; to *bale* up water:— (woman to) draw (-er, water).

7580. שָׁאַג **shâ'ag**, *shaw-ag´;* a prim. root; to *rumble* or *moan:—* × mightily, roar.

7581. שְׁאָגָה **sh e 'âgâh**, *sheh-aw-gaw´;* from 7580; a *rumbling* or *moan:—* roaring.

7582. שָׁאָה **shâ'âh**, *shaw-aw´;* a prim. root; to *rush;* by impl. to *desolate:—* be desolate, (make a) rush (-ing), (lay) waste.

7583. שָׁאָה **shâ'âh**, *shaw-aw´;* a prim. root [rather ident. with 7582 through the idea of *whirling* to giddiness]; to *stun,* i.e. (intr.) *be astonished:—* wonder.

7584. שַׁאֲוָה **sha'ăvâh**, *shah-av-aw´;* from 7582; a *tempest* (as rushing):— desolation.

7585. שְׁאוֹל **sh e 'ôwl**, *sheh-ole´;* or

שְׁאֹל **sh e 'ôl**, *sheh-ole´;* from 7592; *hades* or the world of the dead (as if a subterranean *retreat*), incl. its accessories and inmates:— grave, hell, pit.

7586. שָׁאוּל **Shâ'ûwl**, *shaw-ool´;* pass. part. of 7592; *asked; Shaül,* the name of an Edomite and two Isr.:— Saul, Shaul.

7587. שָׁאוּלִי **Shâ'ûwliy**, *shaw-oo-lee´;* patron. from 7856; a *Shaülite* or desc. of Shaul:— Shaulites.

7588. שָׁאוֹן **shâ'ôwn**, *shaw-one´;* from 7582; *uproar* (as of *rushing*); by impl. *destruction:—* × horrible, noise, pomp, rushing, tumult (×uous).

7589. שְׁאָט **sh e 'ât**, *sheh-awt´;* from an unused root mean. to *push* aside; *contempt:—* despite (-ful).

7590. שָׁאט **shâ't**, *shawt;* for act. part of 7750 [comp. 7589]; one *contemning:—* that (which) despise (-d).

7591. שְׁאִיָּה **sh e 'îyâh**, *sheh-ee-yaw´;* from 7582; *desolation:—* destruction.

7592. שָׁאַל **shâ'al**, *shaw-al´;* or

שָׁאֵל **shâ'êl**, *shaw-ale´;* a prim. root; to *inquire;* by impl. to *request;* by extens. to *demand:—* ask (counsel, on), beg, borrow, lay to charge, consult, demand, desire, × earnestly, enquire, + greet, obtain leave, lend, pray, request, require, + salute, × straitly, × surely, wish.

7593. שְׁאֵל **sh e 'êl** (Chald.), *sheh-ale´;* corresp. to 7592:— ask, demand, require.

7594. שָׁאָל **Sh e 'âl**, *sheh-awl´;* from 7592; *request; Sheäl,* an Isr.:— Sheal.

7595. שְׁאֵלָא **sh e 'êlâ'** (Chald.), *sheh-ay-law´;* from 7593; prop. a *question* (at law), i.e. judicial *decision* or mandate:— demand.

7596. שְׁאֵלָה **sh e 'êlâh**, *sheh-ay-law´;* or

שֵׁלָה **shêlâh** (1 Sam. 1:17), *shay-law´;* from 7592; a *petition;* by impl. a *loan:—* loan, petition, request.

7597. שְׁאַלְתִּיאֵל **Sh e 'altîy'êl**, *sheh-al-tee-ale´;* or

שַׁלְתִּיאֵל **Shaltîy'êl**, *shal-tee-ale´;* from 7592 and 410; *I have asked God; Sheältiël,* an Isr.:— Shalthiel, Shealtiel.

7598. שְׁאַלְתִּיאֵל **Sh e 'altîy'êl** (Chald.), *sheh-al-tee-ale´;* corresp. to 7597:— Shealtiel.

7599. שָׁאַן **shâ'an**, *shaw-an´;* a prim. root; to *loll,* i.e. *be peaceful:—* be at ease, be quiet, rest. See also 1052.

7600. שַׁאֲנָן **sha'ănân**, *shah-an-awn´;* from 7599; *secure;* in a bad sense, *haughty:—* that is at ease, quiet, tumult. Comp. 7946.

7601. שָׁאַס **shâ'aç**, *shaw-as´;* a prim. root; to *plunder:—* spoil.

7602. שָׁאַף **shâ'aph**, *shaw-af´;* a prim. root; to *inhale* eagerly; fig. to *covet;* by impl. to *be angry;* also to *hasten:—* desire (earnestly), devour, haste, pant, snuff up, swallow up.

7603. שְׂאֹר **s e 'ôr**, *seh-ore´;* from 7604; *barm* or yeast-cake (as *swelling* by fermentation):— leaven.

7604. שָׁאַר **shâ'ar**, *shaw-ar´;* a prim.

root; prop. to *swell* up, i.e. *be* (caus. *make*) *redundant*:— leave, (be) left, let, remain, remnant, reserve, the rest.

7605. שְׁאָר **sh^eâr**, *sheh-awr´*; from 7604; a *remainder*:— × other, remnant, residue, rest.

7606. שְׁאָר **sh^eâr** (Chald.), *sheh-awr´*; corresp. to 7605:— × whatsoever more, residue, rest.

7607. שְׁאֵר **sh^eêr**, *sheh-ayr´*; from 7604; *flesh* (as *swelling* out), as living or for food; gen. *food* of any kind; fig. *kindred* by blood:— body, flesh, food, (near) kin (-sman, -swoman), near (nigh) [of kin].

7608. שַׁאֲרָה **sha'ărâh**, *shah-ar-aw´*; fem. of 7607; female *kindred* by blood:— near kinswomen.

7609. שְׁאֵרָה **She'êrâh**, *sheh-er-aw´*; the same as 7608; *Sheërah*, an Israelitess:— Sherah.

7610. שְׁאָר יָשׁוּב **Sh^eâr Yâshûwb**, *sheh-awr´ yaw-shoob´*; from 7605 and 7725; a *remnant will return*; *Sheär-Jashub*, the symbol. name of one of Isaiah's sons:— Shear-jashub.

7611. שְׁאֵרִית **sh^eêrîyth**, *sheh-ay-reeth´*; from 7604; a *remainder* or residual (surviving, final) portion:— that had escaped, be left, posterity, remain (-der), remnant, residue, rest.

7612. שֵׁאת **shê'th**, *shayth*; from 7582; *devastation*:— desolation.

7613. שְׂאֵת **s^eêth**, *seh-ayth´*; from 5375; an *elevation* or leprous scab; fig. *elation* or cheerfulness; *exaltation* in rank or character:— be accepted, dignity, excellency, highness, raise up self, rising.

7614. שְׁבָא **Sh^ebâ'**, *sheb-aw´*; of for. or.; *Sheba*, the name of three early progenitors of tribes and of an Ethiopian district:— Sheba, Sabeans.

7615. שְׁבָאִי **Sh^ebâ'îy**, *sheb-aw-ee´*; patron. from 7614; a *Shebaïte* or desc. of Sheba:— Sabean.

7616. שָׁבָב **shâbâb**, *shaw-bawb´*; from an unused root mean. to *break* up; a *fragment*, i.e. *ruin*:— broken in pieces.

7617. שָׁבָה **shâbâh**, *shaw-baw´*; a prim. root; to *transport* into captivity:— (bring away, carry, carry away, lead, lead away, take) captive (-s), drive (take) away.

7618. שְׁבוּ **sh^ebûw**, *sheb-oo´*; from an unused root (prob. ident. with that of 7617 through the idea of *subdivision* into flashes or streamers [comp. 7632] mean. to *flame*; a *gem* (from its sparkle), prob. the *agate*:— agate.

7619. שְׁבוּאֵל **Sh^ebûw'êl**, *sheb-oo-ale´*; or

שׁוּבָאֵל **Shûwbâ'êl**, *shoo-baw-ale´*; from 7617 (abbrev.) or 7725 and 410; *captive* (or *returned*) *of God*; *Shebuël* or *Shubaël*, the name of two Isr.:— Shebuel, Shubael.

7620. שָׁבוּעַ **shâbûwa'**, *shaw-boo´-ah*; or

שָׁבֻעַ **shâbûa'**, *shaw-boo´-ah*; also (fem.)

שְׁבֻעָה **sh^ebû'âh**, *sheb-oo-aw´*; prop. pass. part. of 7650 as a denom. of 7651; lit. *sevened*, i.e. a *week* (spec. of years):— seven, week.

7621. שְׁבוּעָה **sh^ebûw'âh**, *sheb-oo-aw´*; fem. pass. part. of 7650; prop. something *sworn*, i.e. an *oath*:— curse, oath, × sworn.

7622. שְׁבוּת **sh^ebûwth**, *sheb-ooth´*; or

שְׁבִית **sh^ebîyth**, *sheb-eeth´*; from 7617; *exile*, concr. *prisoners*; fig. a *former state* of prosperity:— captive (-ity).

7623. שָׁבַח **shâbach**, *shaw-bakh´*; a prim. root; prop. to *address* in a loud tone, i.e. (spec.) *loud*; fig. to *pacify* (as if by words):— commend, glory, keep in, praise, still, triumph.

7624. שְׁבַח **sh^ebach** (Chald.), *sheb-akh´*; corresp. to 7623; to *adulate*, i.e. *adore*:— praise.

7625. שְׁבַט **sh^ebat** (Chald.), *sheb-at´*; corresp. to 7626; a *clan*:— tribe.

7626. שֵׁבֶט **shêbet**, *shay´-bet*; from an unused root prob. mean. to *branch* off; a *scion*, i.e. (lit.) a *stick* (for punishing, writing, fighting, ruling, walking, etc.) or (fig.) a *clan*:— × correction, dart, rod, sceptre, staff, tribe.

7627. שְׁבָט **Sh^ebât**, *sheb-awt´*; of for. or.; *Shebat*, a Jewish month:— Sebat.

7628. שְׁבִי **sh^ebîy**, *sheb-ee´*; from 7618; *exiled*; *captured*; as noun, *exile* (abstr. or concr. and collect.); by extens. *booty*:— captive (-ity), prisoners, × take away, that was taken.

7629. שֹׁבִי **Shôbîy**, *sho-bee´*; from 7617; *captor*; *Shobi*, an Ammonite:— Shobi.

7630. שֹׁבַי **Shôbay**, *sho-bah´-ee*; for 7629; *Shobai*, an Isr.:— Shobai.

7631. שְׂבִיב **s^ebîyb** (Chald.), *seb-eeb´*; corresp. to 7632:— flame.

7632. שָׁבִיב **shâbîyb**, *shaw-beeb´*; from the same as 7616; *flame* (as *split* into tongues):— spark.

7633. שִׁבְיָה **shibyâh**, *shib-yaw´*; fem. of 7628; *exile* (abstr. or concr. and collect.):— captives (-ity).

7634. שָׁבְיָה **Shobyâh**, *shob-yaw´*; fem. of the same as 7629; *captivation*; *Shobjah*, an Isr.:— Shachia [from the marg.].

7635. שָׁבִיל **shâbîyl**, *shaw-beel´*; from the same as 7640; a *track* or passageway (as if *flowing* along):— path.

7636. שָׁבִיס **shâbîyç**, *shaw-beece´*; from an unused root mean. to *interweave*; a *netting* for the hair:— caul.

7637. שְׁבִיעִי **sh^ebîy'îy**, *sheb-ee-ee´*; or

שְׁבִעִי **sh^ebî'îy**, *sheb-ee-ee´*; ord. from 7657; *seventh*:— seventh (time).

שְׁבִית **sh^ebîyth**. See 7622.

7638. שָׂבָךְ **sâbâk**, *saw-bawk´*; from an unused root mean. to *intwine*; a *netting* (ornament to the capital of a column):— net.

שַׂבְּכָא **sabb^ekâ'**. See 5443.

7639. שְׂבָכָה **s^ebâkâh**, *seb-aw-kaw´*; fem. of 7638; a *net-work*, i.e. (in hunting) a *snare*, (in arch.) a *ballustrade*; also a *reticulated* ornament to a pillar:— checker, lattice, network, snare, wreath (-enwork).

7640. שֹׁבֶל **shôbel**, *show´-bel*; from an unused root mean. to *flow*; a lady's *train* (as *trailing* after her):— leg.

7641. שִׁבֹּל **shibbôl**, *shib-bole´*; or (fem.)

שִׁבֹּלֶת **shibbôleth**, *shib-bo´-leth*; from the same as 7640; a *stream* (as *flowing*); also an *ear* of grain (as *growing* out); by anal. a *branch*:— branch, channel, ear (of corn), ([water-]) flood, Shibboleth. Comp. 5451.

7642. שַׁבְלוּל **shablûwl**, *shab-lool´*; from the same as 7640; a *snail* (as if *floating* in its own slime):— snail.

שִׁבֹּלֶת **shibbôleth**. See 7641.

7643. שְׂבָם **S^ebâm**, *seb-awm´*; or (fem.)

שִׂבְמָה **Sibmâh**, *sib-maw´*; prob. from 1313; *spice*; *Sebam* or *Sibmah*, a place in Moab:— Shebam, Shibmah, Sibmah.

7644. שֶׁבְנָא **Shebnâ'**, *sheb-naw´*; or

שֶׁבְנָה **Shebnâh**, *sheb-naw´*; from an unused root mean. to *grow*; *growth*; *Shebna* or *Shebnah*, an Isr.:— Shebna, Shebnah.

7645. שְׁבַנְיָה **Sh^ebanyâh**, *sheb-an-yaw´*; or

שְׁבַנְיָהוּ **Sh^ebanyâhûw**, *sheb-an-yaw´-hoo*; from the same as 7644 and 3050; *Jah has grown* (i.e. *prospered*); *Shebanjah*, the name of three or four Isr.:— Shebaniah.

7646. שָׂבַע **sâba'**, *saw-bah´*; or

שָׂבֵעַ **sâbêa'**, *saw-bay´-ah*; a prim. root; to *sate*, i.e. *fill* to satisfaction (lit. or fig.):— have enough, fill (full, self, with), be (to the) full (of), have plenty of, be satiate, satisfy (with), suffice, be weary of.

7647. שָׂבָע **sâbâ'**, *saw-baw´*; from 7646; *copiousness*:— abundance, plenteous (-ness, -ly).

7648. שֹׂבַע **sôba'**, *so´-bah*; from 7646; *satisfaction* (of food or [fig.] joy):— fill, full (-ness), satisfying, be satisfied.

7649. שָׂבֵעַ **sâbêa'**, *saw-bay´-ah*; from 7646; *satiated* (in a pleasant or disagreeable sense):— full (of), satisfied (with).

7650. שָׁבַע **shâba'**, *shaw-bah´*; a prim. root; prop. to *be complete*, but used only as a denom. from 7651; to *seven* oneself, i.e. *swear* (as if by repeating a declaration seven times):— adjure, charge (by an oath, with an oath), feed to the full [by mistake for 7646], take an oath, × straitly, (cause to, make to) swear.

7651. שֶׁבַע **sheba'**, *sheh-bah´*; or (masc.)

שִׁבְעָה **shib'âh**, *shib-aw´*; from 7650; a prim. cardinal number; *seven* (as the sacred *full* one); also (adv.) *seven times*; by impl. a *week*; by extens. an *indefinite* number:— (+ by) seven [-fold], -s, [-teen, teenth], -th, times). Comp. 7658.

7652. שֶׁבַע **Sheba'**, *sheh´-bah*; the same as 7651; *seven*; *Sheba*, the name of a place in Pal., and of two Isr.:— Sheba.

שָׁבַע **shâbûa'**. See 7620.

7653. שִׂבְעָה **sib'âh**, *sib-aw´*; fem. of 7647; *satiety*:— fulness.

7654. שָׂבְעָה **sob'âh**, *sob-aw´*; fem. of 7648; *satiety*:— (to have) enough, × till ... be full, [un-] satiable, satisfy, × sufficiently.

שִׁבְעָה **shib'âh**. See 7651.

Hebrew

7655. שִׁבְעָה **shib'âh** (Chald.), *shib-aw'*; corresp. to 7651:— seven (times).

7656. שִׁבְעָה **Shib'âh**, *shib-aw'*; masc. of 7651; *seven* (*-th*); *Shebah*, a well in Pal.:— Shebah.

שְׁבוּעָה **shebû'âh**. See 7620.

שְׁבִיעִי **shebîy'îy**. See 7637.

7657. שִׁבְעִים **shib'îym**, *shib-eem'*; multiple of 7651; *seventy:*— seventy, three-score and ten (+ -teen).

7658. שִׁבְעָנָה **shib'ânâh**, *shib-aw-naw'*; prol. for the masc. of 7651; *seven:*— seven.

7659. שִׁבְעָתַיִם **shib'âthayim**, *shib-aw-thah'-yim;* dual (adv.) of 7651; *seven-times:*— seven (-fold, times).

7660. שָׁבַץ **shâbats**, *shaw-bats'*; a prim. root; to *interweave* (colored) threads in squares; by impl. (of *reticulation*) to *inchase* gems in gold:— embroider, set.

7661. שָׁבָץ **shâbâts**, *shaw-bawts'*; from 7660; *intanglement*, i.e. (fig.) *perplexity:*— anguish.

7662. שְׁבַק **shebaq** (Chald.), *sheb-ak'*; corresp. to the root of 7733; to *quit*, i.e. *allow to remain:*— leave, let alone.

7663. שָׂבַר **sâbar**, *saw-bar'*; err.

שָׁבַר **shâbar** (Neh. 2:13, 15), *shaw-bar'*; a prim. root; to *scrutinize*; by impl. (of *watching*) to *expect* (with hope and patience):— hope, tarry, view, wait.

7664. שֵׂבֶר **sêber**, *say'-ber*; from 7663; *expectation:*— hope.

7665. שָׁבַר **shâbar**, *shaw-bar'*; a prim. root; to *burst* (lit. or fig.):— break (down, off, in pieces, up), broken (I-hearted]), bring to the birth, crush, destroy, hurt, quench, × quite, tear, view [by mistake for 7663].

7666. שָׁבַר **shâbar**, *shaw-bar'*; denom. from 7668; to *deal* in grain:— buy, sell.

7667. שֶׁבֶר **sheber**, *sheh'-ber*; or

שֵׁבֶר **shêber**, *shay'-ber*; from 7665; a *fracture*, fig. *ruin;* spec. a *solution* (of a dream):— affliction, breach, breaking, broken I-footed, -handed], bruise, crashing, destruction, hurt, interpretation, vexation.

7668. שֶׁבֶר **sheber**, *sheh'-ber*; the same as 7667; *grain* (as if *broken* into kernels):— corn, victuals.

7669. שֶׁבֶר **Sheber**, *sheh'-ber*; the same as 7667; *Sheber*, an Isr.:— Sheber.

7670. שִׁבְרוֹן **shibrôwn**, *shib-rone'*; from 7665; *rupture*, i.e. a *pang*; fig. *ruin:*— breaking, destruction.

7671. שְׁבָרִים **Shebârîym**, *sheb-aw-reem';* plur. of 7667; *ruins; Shebarim*, a place in Pal.:— Shebarim.

7672. שְׁבַשׁ **shebash** (Chald.), *sheb-ash'*; corresp. to 7660; to *intangle*, i.e. *perplex:*— be astonished.

7673. שָׁבַת **shâbath**, *shaw-bath'*; a prim. root; to *repose*, i.e. *desist* from exertion; used in many impl. relations (caus., fig. or spec.):— (cause to, let, make to) cease, celebrate, cause (make) to fail, keep (sabbath), suffer to be lacking, leave, put away (down), (make to) rest, rid, still, take away.

7674. שֶׁבֶת **shebeth**, *sheh'-beth*; from

7673; *rest, interruption, cessation:*— cease, sit still, loss of time.

7675. שֶׁבֶת **shebeth**, *sheh'-beth*; infin. of 3427; prop. *session*; but used also concr. an *abode* or *locality:*— place, seat. Comp. 3429.

7676. שַׁבָּת **shabbâth**, *shab-bawth';* intens. from 7673; *intermission*, i.e (spec.) the *Sabbath:*— (+ every) sabbath.

7677. שַׁבָּתוֹן **shabbâthôwn**, *shab-baw-thone';* from 7676; a *sabbatism* or special holiday:— rest, sabbath.

7678. שַׁבְּתַי **Shabbethay**, *shab-beth-ah'-ee;* from 7676; *restful; Shabbethai*, the name of three Isr.:— Shabbethai.

7679. שָׂגָא **sâgâ'**, *saw-gaw'*; a prim. root; to *grow*, i.e. (caus.) to *enlarge*, (fig.) *laud:*— increase, magnify.

7680. שְׂגָא **sega'** (Chald.), *seg-aw'*; corresp. to 7679; to *increase:*— grow, be multiplied.

7681. שָׁגֵא **Shâgê'**, *shaw-gay'*; prob. from 7686; *erring; Shage*, an Isr.:— Shage.

7682. שָׂגַב **sâgab**, *saw-gab'*; a prim. root; to *be* (caus. *make*) *lofty*, espec. *inaccessible*; by impl. *safe, strong*; used lit. and fig.— defend, exalt, be excellent, (be, set on) high, lofty, be safe, set up (on high), be too strong.

7683. שָׁגַג **shâgag**, *shaw-gag'*; a prim. root; to *stray*, i.e. (fig.) *sin* (with more or less apology):— × also for that, deceived, err, go astray, sin ignorantly.

7684. שְׁגָגָה **shegâgâh**, *sheg-aw-gaw';* from 7683; a *mistake* or inadvertent *transgression:*— error, ignorance, at unawares, unwittingly.

7685. שָׂגָה **sâgâh**, *saw-gaw'*; a prim. root; to *enlarge* (espec. upward, also fig.):— grow (up), increase.

7686. שָׁגָה **shâgâh**, *shaw-gaw'*; a prim. root; to *stray* (caus. *mislead*), usually (fig.) to *mistake*, espec. (mor.) to *transgress*; by extens. (through the idea of intoxication) to *reel*, (fig.) be *enraptured:*— (cause to) go astray, deceive, err, be ravished, sin through ignorance, (let, make to) wander.

7687. שְׂגוּב **Segûwb**, *seg-oob'*; from 7682; *aloft; Segub*, the name of two Isr.:— Segub.

7688. שָׂגַח **shâgach**, *shaw-gakh';* a prim. root; to *peep*, i.e. *glance* sharply at:— look (narrowly).

7689. שַׂגִּיא **saggîy'**, *sag-ghee';* from 7679; (superl.) *mighty:*— excellent, great.

7690. שַׂגִּיא **saggîy'** (Chald.), *sag-ghee';* corresp. to 7689; *large* (in size, quantity or number, also adv.):— exceeding, great (-ly); many, much, sore, very.

7691. שְׁגִיאָה **shegîy'âh**, *sheg-ee-aw';* from 7686; a moral *mistake:*— error.

7692. שִׁגָּיוֹן **Shiggâyôwn**, *shig-gaw-yone';* or

שִׁגָּיֹנָה **Shiggâyônâh**, *shig-gaw-yo-naw';* from 7686; prop. *aberration*, i.e. (tech.) a *dithyramb* or rambling poem:— Shiggaion, Shigionoth.

7693. שָׁגַל **shâgal**, *shaw-gal'*; a prim. root; to *copulate* with:— lie with, ravish.

7694. שֵׁגָל **shêgâl**, *shay-gawl';* from 7693; a *queen* (from cohabitation):— queen.

7695. שֵׁגָל **shêgâl** (Chald.), *shay-gawl';* corresp. to 7694; a (legitimate) *queen:*— wife.

7696. שָׁגַע **shâga'**, *shaw-gah';* a prim. root; to *rave* through insanity:— (be, play the) mad (man).

7697. שִׁגָּעוֹן **shiggâ'ôwn**, *shig-gaw-yone';* from 7696; *craziness:*— furiously, madness.

7698. שֶׁגֶר **sheger**, *sheh'-ger*; from an unused root prob. mean. to *eject*; the *fetus* (as finally *expelled*):— that cometh of, increase.

7699. שַׁד **shad**, *shad;* or

שֹׁד **shôd**, *shode;* prob. from 7736 (in its orig. sense) contr.; the *breast* of a woman or animal (as *bulging*):— breast, pap, teat.

7700. שֵׁד **shêd**, *shade;* from 7736; a *demon* (as *malignant*):— devil.

7701. שֹׁד **shôd**, *shode;* or

שׁוֹד **shôwd** (Job 5:21), *shode;* from 7736; *violence, ravage:*— desolation, destruction, oppression, robbery, spoil (-ed, -er, -ing), wasting.

7702. שָׂדַד **sâdad**, *saw-dad'*; a prim. root; to *abrade*, i.e. *harrow* a field:— break clods, harrow.

7703. שָׁדַד **shâdad**, *shaw-dad'*; a prim. root; prop. to *be burly*, i.e. (fig.) *powerful* (pass. *impregnable*); by impl. to *ravage:*— dead, destroy (-er), oppress, robber, spoil (-er), × utterly, (lay) waste.

7704. שָׂדֶה **sâdeh**, *saw-deh';* or

שָׂדַי **sâday**, *saw-dah'-ee;* from an unused root mean. to *spread* out; a *field* (as *flat*):— country, field, ground, land, soil, × wild.

7705. שִׁדָּה **shiddâh**, *shid-dah';* from 7703; a *wife* (as *mistress* of the house):— × all sorts, musical instrument.

7706. שַׁדַּי **Shadday**, *shad-dah'-ee;* from 7703; the *Almighty:*— Almighty.

7707. שְׁדֵיאוּר **Shedêy'ûwr**, *shed-ay-oor';* from the same as 7704 and 217; *spreader of light; Shedejur*, an Isr.:— Shedeur.

7708. שִׂדִּים **Siddîym**, *sid-deem';* plur. from the same as 7704; *flats; Siddim*, a valley in Pal.:— Siddim.

7709. שְׁדֵמָה **shedêmâh**, *shed-ay-maw';* appar. from 7704; a cultivated *field:*— blasted, field.

7710. שָׁדַף **shâdaph**, *shaw-daf';* a prim. root; to *scorch:*— blast.

7711. שְׁדֵפָה **shedêphâh**, *shed-ay-faw';* or

שִׁדָּפוֹן **shiddâphôwn**, *shid-daw-fone';* from 7710; *blight:*— blasted (-ing).

7712. שְׁדַר **shedar** (Chald.), *shed-ar';* a prim. root; to *endeavor:*— labour.

7713. שְׂדֵרָה **sederâh**, *sed-ay-raw';* from an unused root mean. to *regulate*; a *row*, i.e. *rank* (of soldiers), *story* (of rooms):— board, range.

7714. שַׁדְרַךְ **Shadrak**, *shad-rak';* prob. of for. or.; *Shadrak*, the Bab. name of one of Daniel's companions:— Shadrach.

7715. שַׁדְרַךְ **Shadrak** (Chald.), *shadrak*; the same as 7714:— Shadrach.

7716. שֶׂה **seh**, *seh*; or

שֵׂי **sêy**, *say*; prob. from 7582 through the idea of *pushing* out to graze; a member of a flock, i.e. a *sheep* or *goat*:— (lesser, small) cattle, ewe, goat, lamb, sheep. Comp. 2089.

7717. שָׂהֵד **sâhêd**, *saw-hade'*; from an unused root mean. to *testify*; a *witness*:— record.

7718. שֹׁהַם **shôham**, *sho'-ham*; from an unused root prob. mean to *blanch*; a gem, prob. the *beryl* (from its *pale green* color):— onyx.

7719. שֹׁהַם **Shôham**, *sho'-ham*; the same as 7718; *Shoham*, an Isr.:— Shoham.

7720. שַׂהֲרֹן **sahârôn**, *sah-har-one'*; from the same as 5469; a round *pendant* for the neck:— ornament, round tire like the moon.

שָׁו **shav**. See 7723.

7721. שׂוֹא **sôw'**, *so*; from an unused root (akin to 5375 and 7722) mean. to *rise*; a *rising*:— arise.

7722. שׁוֹא **shôw'**, *sho*; or (fem.)

שׁוֹאָה **shôw'âh**, *sho-aw'*; or

שֹׁאָה **shô'âh**, *sho-aw'*; from an unused root mean. to *rush* over; a *tempest*; by impl. *devastation*:— desolate (-ion), destroy, destruction, storm, wasteness.

7723. שָׁוְא **shâv'**, *shawv*; or

שָׁו **shav**, *shav*; from the same as 7722 in the sense of *desolating*; *evil* (as *destructive*), lit. (*ruin*) or mor. (espec. *guile*); fig. *idolatry* (as false, subj.), *uselessness* (as deceptive, obj.; also adv. in *vain*):— false (-ly), lie, lying, vain, vanity.

7724. שְׁוָא **Shevâ'**, *shev-aw'*; from the same as 7723; *false*; *Sheva*, an Isr.:— Sheva.

7725. שׁוּב **shûwb**, *shoob*; a prim. root; to *turn* back (hence, away) tran. or intr., lit. or fig. (not necessarily with the idea of *return* to the starting point); gen. to *retreat*; often adv. *again*:— ((break, build, circumcise, dig, do anything, do evil, feed, lay down, lie down, lodge, make, rejoice, send, take, weep)) × again, (cause to) answer (+ again), × in any case (wise), × at all, averse, bring (again, back, home again), call (to mind), carry again (back), cease, × certainly, come again (back), × consider, + continually, convert, deliver (again), + deny, draw back, fetch home again, × fro, get (oneself) (back) again, × give (again) go again (back, home), (go) out, hinder, let, (see) more, × needs, be past, × pay, pervert, pull in again, put (again, up again), recall, recompense, recover, refresh, relieve, render (again), requite, rescue, restore, retrieve, (cause to, make to) return, reverse, reward, + say nay, send back, set again, slide back, still, × surely, take back (off), (cause to, make to) turn (again, self again, away, back, back again, backward, from, off), withdraw.

שׁוּבָאֵל **Shûwbâ'êl**. See 7619.

7726. שׁוֹבָב **shôwbâb**, *sho-bawb'*; from 7725; *apostate*, i.e. *idolatrous*:— backsliding, frowardly, turn away (from marg.).

7727. שׁוֹבָב **Shôwbâb**, *sho-bawb'*; the same as 7726; *rebellious*; *Shobab*, the name of two Isr.:— Shobab.

7728. שׁוֹבֵב **shôwbêb**, *sho-babe'*; from 7725; *apostate*, i.e. *heathenish* or (actually) *heathen*:— backsliding.

7729. שׁוּבָה **shûwbâh**, *shoo-baw'*; from 7725; a *return*:- - returning.

7730. שׂוֹבֶךְ **sôwbek**, *so'-bek*; for 5441; a *thicket*, i.e. interlaced branches:— thick boughs.

7731. שׁוֹבָךְ **Shôwbâk**, *sho-bawk'*; perh. for 7730; *Shobak*, a Syrian:— Shobach.

7732. שׁוֹבָל **Shôwbâl**, *sho-bawl'*; from the same as 7640; *overflowing*; *Shobal*, the name of an Edomite and two Isr.:— Shobal.

7733. שׁוֹבֵק **Shôwbêq**, *sho-bake'*; act. part. from a prim. root mean. to *leave* (comp. 7662); *forsaking*; *Shobek*, an Isr.:— Shobek.

7734. שׂוּג **sûwg**, *soog*; a prim. root; to *retreat*:— turn back.

7735. שׂוּג **sûwg**, *soog*; a prim. root; to *hedge* in:— make to grow.

7736. שׁוּד **shûwd**, *shood*; a prim. root; prop. to *swell* up, i.e. fig. (by impl. of *insolence*) to *devastate*:— waste.

שׁוֹד **shôwd**. See 7699, 7701.

7737. שָׁוָה **shâvâh**, *shaw-vaw'*; a prim. root; prop. to *level*, i.e. *equalize*; fig. to *resemble*; by impl. to *adjust* (i.e. *counterbalance*, be *suitable*, *compose*, *place*, *yield*, etc.):— avail, behave, bring forth, compare, countervail, (be, make) equal, lay, be (make, a-) like, make plain, profit, reckon.

7738. שָׁוָה **shâvâh**, *shaw-vaw'*; a prim. root; to *destroy*:— × substance (from the marg.).

7739. שְׁוָה **shevâh** (Chald.), *shev-aw'*; corresp. to 7737; to *resemble*:— make like.

7740. שָׁוֵה **Shâvêh**, *shaw-vay'*; from 7737; *plain*; *Shaveh*, a place in Pal.:— Shaveh.

7741. שָׁוֵה קִרְיָתַיִם **Shâvêh Qiryâthayim**, *shaw-vay' kir-yaw-thah'-yim*; from the same as 7740 and the dual of 7151; *plain of a double city*; *Shaveh-Kirjathajim*, a place E. of the Jordan:— Shaveh Kiriathaim.

7742. שׂוּחַ **sûwach**, *soo'-akh*; a prim. root; to *muse* pensively:— meditate.

7743. שׁוּחַ **shûwach**, *shoo'-akh*; a prim. root; to *sink*, lit. or fig.:— bow down, incline, humble.

7744. שׁוּחַ **Shûwach**, *shoo'-akh*; from 7743; *dell*; *Shuäch*, a son of Abraham:— Shuah.

7745. שׁוּחָה **shûwchâh**, *shoo-khaw'*; from 7743; a *chasm*:— ditch, pit.

7746. שׁוּחָה **Shûwchâh**, *shoo-khaw'*; the same as 7745; *Shuchah*, an Isr.:— Shuah.

7747. שׁוּחִי **Shuchîy**, *shoo-khee'*; patron.

from 7744; a *Shuchite* or desc. of Shuach:— Shuhite.

7748. שׁוּחָם **Shûwchâm**, *shoo-khawm'*; from 7743; *humbly*; *Shucham*, an Isr.:— Shuham.

7749. שׁוּחָמִי **Shûwchâmîy**, *shoo-khaw-mee'*; patron. from 7748; a *Shuchamite* (collect.):— Shuhamites.

7750. שׂוּט **sûwt**, *soot*; or (by perm.)

סוּט **çûwt**, *soot*; a prim. root; to *detrude*, i.e. (intr. and fig.) *become derelict* (wrongly *practise*; namely, *idolatry*):— turn aside to.

7751. שׁוּט **shûwt**, *shoot*; a prim. root; prop. to *push* forth; (but used only fig.) to *lash*, i.e. (the sea with oars) to *row*; by impl. to *travel*:— go (about, through, to and fro), mariner, rower, run to and fro.

7752. שׁוֹט **shôwt**, *shote*; from 7751; a *lash* (lit. or fig.):— scourge, whip.

7753. שׂוּךְ **sûwk**, *sook*; a prim. root; to *entwine*, i.e. *shut* in (for formation, protection or restraint):— fence, (make an) hedge (up).

7754. שׂוֹךְ **sôwk**, *soke*; or (fem.)

שׂוֹכָה **sôwkâh**, *so-kaw'*; from 7753; a *branch* (as *interleaved*):— bough.

7755. שׂוֹכֹה **Sôwkôh**, *so-ko'*; or

שֹׂכֹה **Sôkôh**, *so-ko'*; or

שׂוֹכוֹ **Sôwkôw**, *so-ko'*; from 7753; *Sokoh* or *Soko*, the name of two places in Pal.:— Shocho, Shochoh, Sochoh, Soco, Socoh.

7756. שׂוּכָתִי **Sûwkâthîy**, *soo-kaw-thee'*; prob. patron. from a name corresp. to 7754 (fem.); a *Sukathite* or desc. of an unknown Isr. named Sukah:— Suchathite.

7757. שׁוּל **shûwl**, *shool*; from an unused root mean. to *hang* down; a *skirt*; by impl. a bottom *edge*:— hem, skirt, train.

7758. שׁוֹלָל **shôwlâl**, *sho-lawl'*; or

שֵׁילָל **shêylâl** (Mic. 1:8), *shaylawl'*; from 7997; *nude* (espec. barefoot); by impl. *captive*:— spoiled, stripped.

7759. שׁוּלַמִּית **Shûwlammîyth**, *shoo-lammeeth'*; from 7999; *peaceful* (with the art. always pref., making it a pet name); the *Shulammith*, an epithet of Solomon's queen:— Shulamite.

7760. שׂוּם **sûwm**, *soom*; or

שִׂים **sîym**, *seem*; a prim. root; to *put* (used in a great variety of applications, lit., fig., infer. and ellip.):— × any wise, appoint, bring, call (a name), care, cast in, change, charge, commit, consider, convey, determine, + disguise, dispose, do, get, give, heap up, hold, impute, lay (down, up), leave, look, make (out), mark, + name, × on, ordain, order, + paint, place, preserve, purpose, put (on), + regard, rehearse, reward, (cause to) set (on, up), shew, + stedfastly, take, × tell, + tread down, (lover-l) turn, × wholly, work.

7761. שׂוּם **sûwm** (Chald.), *soom*; corresp. to 7760:— + command, give, lay, make, + name, + regard, set.

7762. שׁוּם **shûwm**, *shoom*; from an unused root mean. to *exhale; garlic* (from its rank *odor*):— garlic.

7763. שׁוֹמֵר **Shôwmêr**, *sho-mare´*; or

שֹׁמֵר **Shômêr**, *sho-mare´*; act. part. of 8104; *keeper; Shomer*, the name of two Isr.:— Shomer.

7764. שׁוּני **Shûwnîy**, *shoo-nee´*; from an unused root mean. to *rest; quiet; Shuni*, an Isr.:— Shuni.

7765. שׁוּני **Shûwnîy**, *shoo-nee´*; patron. from 7764; a *Shunite* (collect.) or desc. of Shuni:— Shunites.

7766. שׁוּנֵם **Shûwnêm**, *shoo-name´*; prob. from the same as 7764; *quietly; Shunem*, a place in Pal:— Shunem.

7767. שׁוּנַמִּית **Shûwnammîyth**, *shoo-nam-meeth´*; patrial from 7766; a *Shunammitess*, or female inhab. of Shunem:— Shunamite.

7768. שָׁוַע **shâva´**, *shaw-vah´*; a prim. root; prop. to *be free*; but used only caus. and refl. to *halloo* (for help, i.e. *freedom* from some trouble):— cry (aloud, out), shout.

7769. שׁוּעַ **shûwa´**, *shoo´-ah*; from 7768; a *halloo:*— cry, riches.

7770. שׁוּעַ **Shûwa´**, *shoo´-ah*; the same as 7769; *Shua*, a Canaanite:— Shua, Shuah.

7771. שׁוֹעַ **shôwa´**, *sho´-ah*; from 7768 in the orig. sense of *freedom*; a *noble*, i.e. *liberal, opulent*; also (as noun in the der. sense) a *halloo:*— bountiful, crying, rich.

7772. שׁוֹעַ **Shôwa´**, *sho´-ah*; the same as 7771; *rich; Shoä*, an Oriental people:— Shoa.

7773. שֶׁוַע **sheva´**, *sheh´-vah*; from 7768; a *halloo:*— cry.

7774. שׁוּעָא **Shûwâ´**, *shoo-aw´*; from 7768; *wealth; Shuä*, an Israelitess:— Shua.

7775. שׁוּעָה **shav´âh**, *shav-aw´*; fem. of 7773; a *hallooing:*— crying.

7776. שׁוּעָל **shûw´âl**, *shoo-awl´*; or

שֻׁעָל **shû´âl**, *shoo-awl´*; from the same as 8168; a *jackal* (as a *burrower*):— fox.

7777. שׁוּעָל **Shûw´âl**, *shoo-awl´*; the same as 7776; *Shuäl*, the name of an Isr. and of a place in Pal.:— Shual.

7778. שׁוֹעֵר **shôw´êr**, *sho-are´*; or

שֹׁעֵר **shô´êr**, *sho-are´*; act. part. of 8176 (as denom. from 8179); a *janitor:*— doorkeeper, porter.

7779. שׁוּף **shûwph**, *shoof*; a prim. root; prop. to *gape*, i.e. *snap* at; fig. to *overwhelm:*— break, bruise, cover.

7780. שׁוֹפָךְ **Shôwphâk**, *sho-fawk´*; from 8210; *poured; Shophak*, a Syrian:— Shophach.

7781. שׁוּפָמִי **Shûwphâmîy**, *shoo-faw-mee´*; patron. from 8197; a *Shuphamite* (collect.) or desc. of Shephupham:— Shuphamite.

שׁוֹפָן **Shôwphân**. See 5855.

7782. שׁוֹפָר **shôwphâr**, *sho-far´*; or

שֹׁפָר **shôphâr**, *sho-far´*; from 8231 in the orig. sense of *incising*; a *cornet* (as giving a *clear* sound) or curved horn:— cornet, trumpet.

7783. שׁוּק **shûwq**, *shook*; a prim. root; to *run* after or over, i.e. *overflow:*— overflow, water.

7784. שׁוּק **shûwq**, *shook*; from 7783; a *street* (as *run* over):— street.

7785. שׁוֹק **shôwq**, *shoke*; from 7783; the (lower) *leg* (as a *runner*):— hip, leg, shoulder, thigh.

7786. שׁוּר **sûwr**, *soor*; a prim. root; prop. to *vanquish*; by impl. to *rule* (caus. *crown*):— make princes, have power, reign. See 5493.

7787. שׁוּר **sûwr**, *soor*; a prim. root [rather ident. with 7786 through the idea of *reducing* to pieces; comp. 4883]; to *saw:*— cut.

7788. שׁוּר **shûwr**, *shoor*; a prim. root; prop. to *turn*, i.e. *travel* about (as a harlot or a merchant):— go, sing. See also 7891.

7789. שׁוּר **shûwr**, *shoor*; a prim. root [rather ident. with 7788 through the idea of *going round* for inspection]; to *spy* out, i.e. (gen.) *survey*, (for evil) *lurk for*, (for good) *care for:*— behold, lay wait, look, observe, perceive, regard, see.

7790. שׁוּר **shûwr**, *shoor*; from 7889; a *foe* (as *lying in wait*):— enemy.

7791. שׁוּר **shûwr**, *shoor*; from 7788; a *wall* (as *going about*):— wall.

7792. שׁוּר **shûwr** (Chald.), *shoor*; corresp. to 7791:— wall.

7793. שׁוּר **Shûwr**, *shoor*; the same as 7791; *Shur*, a region of the Desert:— Shur.

7794. שׁוֹר **shôwr**, *shore*; from 7788; a *bullock* (as a *traveller*):— bull (-ock), cow, ox, wall [by mistake for 7791].

7795. שׁוֹרָה **sôwrâh**, *so-raw´*; from 7786 in the prim. sense of 5493; prop. a *ring*, i.e. (by anal.) a *row* (adv.):— principal.

שׁוֹרֵק **sôwrêq**. See 8321.

7796. שׂוֹרֵק **Sôwrêq**, *so-rake´*; the same as 8321; a *vine; Sorek*, a valley in Pal.:— Sorek.

7797. שׂוּשׂ **sûws**, *soos*; or

שׂישׂ **sîys**, *sece*; a prim. root; to *be bright*, i.e. *cheerful:*— be glad, × greatly, joy, make mirth, rejoice.

7798. שַׁוְשָׁא **Shavshâ´**, *shav-shaw´*; from 7797; *joyful; Shavsha*, an Isr.:— Shavsha.

7799. שׁוּשַׁן **shûwshan**, *shoo-shan´*; or

שׁוֹשָׁן **shôwshân**, *sho-shawn´*; or

שֹׁשָׁן **shôshân**, *sho-shawn´*; and (fem.)

שׁוֹשַׁנָּה **shôwshannâh**, *sho-shan-naw´*; from 7797; a *lily* (from its *whiteness*), as a flower or arch. ornament; also a (straight) *trumpet* (from the *tubular* shape):— lily, Shoshannim.

7800. שׁוּשַׁן **Shûwshan**, *shoo-shan´*; the same as 7799; *Shushan*, a place in Pers.:— Shushan.

7801. שׁוּשַׁנְכִי **Shûwshankîy** (Chald.), *shoo-shan-kee´*; of for. or.; a *Shushankite* (collect.) or inhab. of some unknown place in Ass.:— Susanchites.

7802. שׁוּשַׁן עֵדוּת **Shûwshan 'Êdûwth**,

shoo-shan´ ay-dooth´; or (plur. of former)

שׁוֹשַׁנִּים עֵדוּת **Shôwshannîym 'Êdûwth**, *sho-shan-neem´ ay-dooth´*; from 7799 and 5715; *lily* (or *trumpet*) *of assemblage; Shushan-Eduth* or *Shoshannim-Eduth*, the title of a popular song:— Shoshannim-Eduth, Shushan-eduth.

שׁוּשַׁק **Shûwshaq**. See 7895.

7803. שׁוּתֶלַח **Shûwthelach**, *shoo-theh´-lakh*; prob. from 7582 and the same as 8520; *crash of breakage; Shuthelach*, the name of two Isr.:— Shuthelah.

7804. שְׁזַב **shᵉzab** (Chald.), *shez-ab´*; corresp. to 5800; to *leave*, i.e. (caus.) *free:*— deliver.

7805. שָׁזַף **shâzaph**, *shaw-zaf´*; a prim. root; to *tan* (by sun-burning); fig. (as if by a piercing ray) to *scan:*— look up, see.

7806. שָׁזַר **shâzar**, *shaw-zar´*; a prim. root; to *twist* (a thread of straw):— twine.

7807. שַׁח **shach**, *shakh*; from 7817; *sunk*, i.e. *downcast:*— + humble.

7808. שֵׂחַ **sêach**, *say´-akh*; for 7879; *communion*, i.e. (refl.) *meditation:*— thought.

7809. שָׁחַד **shâchad**, *shaw-khad´*; a prim. root; to *donate*, i.e. *bribe:*— hire, give a reward.

7810. שַׁחַד **shachad**, *shakh´-ad*; from 7809; a *donation* (venal or redemptive):— bribe (-ry), gift, present, reward.

7811. שָׂחָה **sâchâh**, *saw-khaw´*; a prim. root; to *swim*; caus. to *inundate:*— (make to) swim.

7812. שָׁחָה **shâchâh**, *shaw-khaw´*; a prim. root; to *depress*, i.e. *prostrate* (espec. refl. in homage to royalty or God):— bow (self) down, crouch, fall down (flat), humbly beseech, do (make) obeisance, do reverence, make to stoop, worship.

7813. שָׂחוּ **sâchûw**, *saw´-khoo*; from 7811; a *pond* (for *swimming*):— to swim in.

7814. שְׂחוֹק **sᵉchôwq**, *sekh-oke´*; or

שְׂחֹק **sᵉchôq**, *sekh-oke´*; from 7832; *laughter* (in merriment or defiance):— derision, laughter (-ed to scorn, -ing), mocked, sport.

7815. שְׁחוֹר **shᵉchôwr**, *shekh-ore´*; from 7835; *dinginess*, i.e. perh. *soot:*— coal.

שְׁחוֹר **shᵉchôwr**. See 7883.

שָׁחוֹר **shâchôwr**. See 7838.

7816. שְׁחוּת **shᵉchûwth**, *shekh-ooth´*; from 7812; *pit:*— pit.

7817. שָׁחַח **shâchach**, *shaw-khakh´*; a prim. root; to *sink* or *depress* (refl. or caus.):— bend, bow (down), bring (cast) down, couch, humble self, be (bring) low, stoop.

7818. שָׂחַט **sâchaṭ**, *saw-khat´*; a prim. root; to *tread* out, i.e. *squeeze* (grapes):— press.

7819. שָׁחַט **shâchaṭ**, *shaw-khat´*; a prim. root; to *slaughter* (in sacrifice or massacre):— kill, offer, shoot out, slay, slaughter.

7820. שָׁחַט **shâchaṭ**, *shaw-khat´*; a prim. root [rather ident. with 7819 through the idea of *striking*]; to *hammer* out:— beat.

7821. שְׁחִיטָה **shᵉchîyṭâh**, *shekh-ee-taw´*; from 7819; *slaughter*:— killing.

7822. שְׁחִין **shᵉchîyn**, *shekh-een´*; from an unused root prob. mean. to *burn*; *inflammation*, i.e. an *ulcer*:— boil, botch.

7823. שָׁחִיס **shâchîyç**, *shaw-khece´*; or סָחִישׁ **çâchîysh**; *saw-kheesh´*; from an unused root appar. mean. to *sprout*; *after-growth*:— (that) which springeth of the same.

7824. שָׁחִיף **shâchîyph**, *shaw-kheef´*; from the same as 7828; a *board* (as *chipped* thin):— cieled with.

7825. שְׁחִית **shᵉchîyth**, *shekh-eeth´*; from 7812; a *pit*-fall (lit. or fig.):— destruction, pit.

7826. שַׁחַל **shachal**, *shakh´-al*; from an unused root prob. mean. to *roar*; a *lion* (from his characteristic *roar*):— (fierce) lion.

7827. שְׁחֵלֶת **shᵉchêleth**, *shekh-ay´-leth*; appar. from the same as 7826 through some obscure idea, perh. that of *peeling* off by concussion of sound; a *scale* or shell, i.e. the aromatic *mussel*:— onycha.

7828. שַׁחַף **shachaph**, *shakh´-af*; from an unused root mean. to *peel*, i.e. *emaciate*; the *gull* (as *thin*):— cuckoo.

7829. שַׁחֶפֶת **shachepheth**, *shakh-eh´-feth*; from the same as 7828; *emaciation*:— consumption.

7830. שַׁחַץ **shachats**, *shakh´-ats*; from an unused root appar. mean. to *strut*; *haughtiness* (as evinced by the attitude):— × lion, pride.

7831. שַׁחֲצוֹם **Shachatsôwm**, *shakh-ats-ome´*; from the same as 7830; *proudly*; *Shachatsom*, a place in Pal.:— Shahazimah [from the marg.].

7832. שָׂחַק **sâchaq**, *saw-khak´*; a prim. root; to *laugh* (in pleasure or detraction); by impl. to *play*:— deride, have in derision, laugh, make merry, mock (-er), play, rejoice, (laugh to) scorn, be in (make) sport.

7833. שָׁחַק **shâchaq**, *shaw-khak´*; a prim. root; to *comminate* (by trituration or attrition):— beat, wear.

7834. שַׁחַק **shachaq**, *shakh´-ak*; from 7833; a *powder* (as *beaten* small); by anal. a thin *vapor*; by extens. the *firmament*:— cloud, small dust, heaven, sky.

שְׁחֹק **sᵉchôq**. See 7814.

7835. שָׁחַר **shâchar**, *shaw-khar´*; a prim. root [rather ident. with 7836 through the idea of the *duskiness* of early dawn]; to *be dim* or dark (in color):— be black.

7836. שָׁחַר **shâchar**, *shaw-khar´*; a prim. root; prop. to *dawn*, i.e. (fig.) *be* (up) *early* at any task (with the impl. of earnestness); by extens. to *search* for (with painstaking):— [do something] betimes, enquire early, rise (seek) betimes, seek (diligently) early, in the morning.

7837. שַׁחַר **shachar**, *shakh´-ar*; from

7836; *dawn* (lit., fig. or adv.):— day (-spring), early, light, morning, whence riseth.

שִׁחֹר **Shîchôr**. See 7883.

7838. שָׁחֹר **shâchôr**, *shaw-khore´*; or שָׁחוֹר **shâchôwr**, *shaw-khore´*; from 7835; prop. *dusky*, but also (absol.) *jetty*:— black.

7839. שַׁחֲרוּת **shachărûwth**, *shakh-arooth´*; from 7836; a *dawning*, i.e. (fig.) *juvenescence*:— youth.

7840. שְׁחַרְחֹרֶת **shᵉcharchôreth**, *shekhar-kho´-reth*; from 7835; *swarthy*:— black.

7841. שְׁחַרְיָה **Shᵉcharyâh**, *shekh-ar-yaw´*; from 7836 and 3050; *Jah has sought*; *Shecharjah*, an Isr.:— Shehariah.

7842. שַׁחֲרַיִם **Shachărayim**, *shakh-arah´-yim*; dual of 7837; *double dawn*; *Shacharajim*, an Isr.:— Shaharaim.

7843. שָׁחַת **shâchath**, *shaw-khath´*; a prim. root; to *decay*, i.e. (caus.) *ruin* (lit. or fig.):— batter, cast off, corrupt (-er, thing), destroy (-er, -uction), lose, mar, perish, spill, spoiler, × utterly, waste (-r).

7844. שְׁחַת **shᵉchath** (Chald.), *shekhath´*; corresp. to 7843:— corrupt, fault.

7845. שַׁחַת **shachath**, *shakh´-ath*; from 7743; a *pit* (espec. as a trap); fig. *destruction*:— corruption, destruction, ditch, grave, pit.

7846. שֵׂט **sêṭ**, *sayte*; or שֵׂט **çêṭ**, *sayt*; from 7750; a *departure* from right, i.e. *sin*:— revolter, that turn aside.

7847. שָׂטָה **sâṭâh**, *saw-taw´*; a prim. root; to *deviate* from duty:— decline, go aside, turn.

7848. שִׁטָּה **shiṭṭâh**, *shit-taw´*; fem. of a der. [only in the plur. שִׁטִּים **shiṭṭîym**, *shit-teem´*; mean. the *sticks* of wood] from the same as 7850; the *acacia* (from its *scourging* thorns):— shittah, shittim. See also 1029.

7849. שָׁטַח **shâṭach**, *shaw-takh´*; a prim. root; to *expand*:— all abroad, enlarge, spread, stretch out.

7850. שֹׁטֵט **shôṭêṭ**, *sho-tate´*; act. part. of an otherwise unused root mean. (prop. to *pierce*; but only as a denom. from 7752) to *flog*; a *goad*:— scourge.

7851. שִׁטִּים **Shiṭṭîym**, *shit-teem´*; the same as the plur. of 7848; *acacia* trees; *Shittim*, a place E. of the Jordan:— Shittim.

7852. שָׂטַם **sâṭam**, *saw-tam´*; a prim. root; prop. to *lurk* for, i.e. *persecute*:— hate, oppose self against.

7853. שָׂטַן **sâṭan**, *saw-tan´*; a prim. root; to *attack*, (fig.) *accuse*:— (be an) adversary, resist.

7854. שָׂטָן **sâṭân**, *saw-tawn´*; from 7853; an *opponent*; espec. (with the art. pref.) *Satan*, the arch-enemy of good:— adversary, Satan, withstand.

7855. שִׂטְנָה **siṭnâh**, *sit-naw´*; from 7853; *opposition* (by letter):— accusation.

7856. שִׂטְנָה **Siṭnâh**, *sit-naw´*; the same as

7855; *Sitnah*, the name of a well in Pal.:— Sitnah.

7857. שָׁטַף **shâṭaph**, *shaw-taf´*; a prim. root; to *gush*; by impl. to *inundate*, *cleanse*; by anal. to *gallop*, *conquer*:— drown, (over-) flow (-whelm), rinse, run, rush, (throughly) wash (away).

7858. שֶׁטֶף **sheṭeph**, *sheh´-tef*; or שֵׁטֶף **shêṭeph**, *shay´-tef*; from 7857; a *deluge* (lit. or fig.):— flood, outrageous, overflowing.

7859. שְׁטַר **sᵉṭar** (Chald.), *set-ar´*; of uncert. der.; a *side*:— side.

7860. שֹׁטֵר **shôṭêr**, *sho-tare´*; act. part. of an otherwise unused root prob. mean. to *write*; prop. a *scribe*, i.e. (by anal. or impl.) an official *superintendent* or *magistrate*:— officer, overseer, ruler.

7861. שִׁטְרַי **Shiṭray**, *shit-rah´-ee*; from the same as 7860; *magisterial*; *Shitrai*, an Isr.:— Shitrai.

7862. שַׁי **shay**, *shah´-ee*; prob. from 7737; a *gift* (as *available*):— present.

7863. שִׂיא **sîy´**, *see*; from the same as 7721 by perm.; *elevation*:— excellency.

7864. שְׁיָא **Shᵉyâ´**, *sheh-yaw´*; for 7724; *Sheja*, an Isr.:— Sheva [from the marg.].

7865. שִׂיאֹן **Sîyôn**, *see-ohn´*; from 7863; *peak*; *Sion*, the summit of Mt. Hermon:— Sion.

7866. שִׁיאוֹן **Shîyôwn**, *shee-ohn´*; from the same as 7722; *ruin*; *Shijon*, a place in Pal.:— Shihon.

7867. שִׂיב **sîyb**, *seeb*; a prim. root; prop. to *become aged*, i.e. (by impl.) to *grow gray*:— (be) grayheaded.

7868. שִׂיב **sîyb** (Chald.), *seeb*; corresp. to 7867:— elder.

7869. שֵׂיב **sêyb**, *sabe*; from 7867; old *age*:— age.

7870. שִׁיבָה **shîybâh**, *shee-baw´*; by perm. from 7725; a *return* (of property):— captivity.

7871. שִׁיבָה **shîybâh**, *shee-baw´*; from 3427; *residence*:— while ... lay.

7872. שֵׂיבָה **sêybâh**, *say-baw´*; fem. of 7869; old *age*:— (be) gray (grey hoar,-y) hairs (head,-ed), old age.

7873. שִׂיג **sîyg**, *seeg*; from 7734; a *withdrawal* (into a private place):— pursuing.

7874. שִׂיד **sîyd**, *seed*; a prim. root prob. mean. to *boil* up (comp. 7736); used only as denom. from 7875; to *plaister*:— plaister.

7875. שִׂיד **sîyd**, *seed*; from 7874; *lime* (as *boiling* when slacked):— lime, plaister.

7876. שָׁיָה **shâyâh**, *shaw-yaw´*; a prim. root; to *keep* in memory:— be unmindful. [Render Deut. 32:18, "A Rock bore thee, *thou must recollect*; and (yet) thou hast forgotten," etc.]

7877. שִׁיזָא **Shîyzâ´**, *shee-zaw´*; of unknown der.; *Shiza*, an Isr.:— Shiza.

7878. שִׂיח **sîyach**, *see´-akh*; a prim. root; to *ponder*, i.e. (by impl.) *converse* (with oneself, and hence, aloud) or (tran.) *utter*:— commune, complain, declare, meditate, muse, pray, speak, talk (with).

Hebrew

7879. שִׂיחַ **sîyach**, *see´-akh;* from 7878; a *contemplation;* by impl. an *utterance:*— babbling, communication, complaint, meditation, prayer, talk.

7880. שִׂיחַ **sîyach**, *see´-akh;* from 7878; a *shoot* (as if *uttered* or put forth), i.e. (gen.) *shrubbery:*— bush, plant, shrub.

7881. שִׂיחָה **sîychâh**, *see-khaw´;* fem. of 7879; *reflection;* by extens. *devotion:*— meditation, prayer.

7882. שִׂיחָה **shîychâh**, *shee-khaw´;* for 7745; a *pit-fall:*— pit.

7883. שִׂיחוֹר **Shîychôwr**, *shee-khore´;* or

שִׁחוֹר **Shîchôwr**, *shee-khore´;* or

שִׁחֹר **Shîchôr**, *shee-khore´;* prob. from 7835; *dark,* i.e. *turbid; Shichor,* a stream of Egypt:— Shihor, Sihor.

7884. שִׁיחוֹר לִבְנָת **Shîychôwr Libnâth**, *shee-khore´ lib-nawth´;* from the same as 7883 and 3835; *darkish whiteness; Shichor-Libnath,* a stream of Pal.:— Shihor-libnath.

7885. שַׁיִט **shayiṭ**, *shay´-yit;* from 7751; an *oar;* also (comp. 7752) a *scourge°* (fig.):— oar, scourge.

7886. שִׁילֹה **Shîylôh**, *shee-lo´;* from 7951; *tranquil; Shiloh,* an epithet of the Messiah:— Shiloh.

7887. שִׁילֹה **Shîylôh**, *shee-lo´;* or

שִׁלֹה **Shîlôh**, *shee-lo´;* or

שִׁילוֹ **Shîylôw**, *shee-lo´;* or

שִׁלוֹ **Shîlôw**, *shee-lo´;* from the same as 7886; *Shiloh,* a place in Pal.:— Shiloh.

7888. שִׁילוֹנִי **Shîylôwnîy**, *shee-lo-nee´;* or

שִׁילֹנִי **Shîylônîy**, *shee-lo-nee´;* or

שִׁלֹנִי **Shîlônîy**, *shee-lo-nee´;* from 7887; a *Shilonite* or inhab. of Shiloh:— Shilonite.

שֵׁילָל **shêylâl**. See 7758.

7839. שִׁימֹן **Shîymôwn**, *shee-mone´;* appar. for 3452; *desert; Shimon,* an Isr.:— Shimon.

7890. שַׁיִן **shayin**, *shah´-yin;* from an unused root mean. to *urinate; urine:*— piss.

7891. שִׁיר **shîyr**, *sheer;* or (the orig. form)

שׁוּר **shûwr** (1 Sam. 18:6), *shoor;* a prim. root [rather ident. with 7788 through the idea of *strolling* minstrelsy]; to *sing:*— behold [by mistake for 7789], sing (-er, -ing man, -ing woman).

7892. שִׁיר **shîyr**, *sheer;* or fem.

שִׁירָה **shîyrâh**, *shee-raw´;* from 7891; a *song;* abstr. *singing:*— musical (-ick), × sing (-er, -ing), song.

שִׂיס **sîys**. See 7797.

7893. שַׁיִשׁ **shayish**, *shah´-yish;* from an unused root mean. to *bleach,* i.e. *whiten; white,* i.e. *marble:*— marble. See 8336.

7894. שִׁישָׁא **Shîyshâ'**, *shee-shaw´;* from the same as 7893; *whiteness; Shisha,* an Isr.:— Shisha.

7895. שִׁישַׁק **Shîyshaq**, *shee-shak´;* or

שׁוּשַׁק **Shûwshaq**, *shoo-shak´;* of Eg. der.; *Shishak,* an Eg. king:— Shishak.

7896. שִׁית **shîyth**, *sheeth;* a prim. root; to *place* (in a very wide application):— apply, appoint, array, bring, consider, lay (up), let alone, × look, make, mark, put (on), + regard, set, shew, be stayed, × take.

7897. שִׁית **shîyth**, *sheeth;* from 7896; a *dress* (as *put* on):— attire.

7898. שַׁיִת **shayith**, *shah´-yith;* from 7896; *scrub* or *trash,* i.e. wild *growth* of weeds or briers (as if *put* on the field):— thorns.

7899. שֵׂךְ **sêk**, *sake;* from 5526 in the sense of 7753; a *brier* (as of a hedge):— prick.

7900. שֹׂךְ **sôk**, *soke;* from 5526 in the sense of 7753; a *booth* (as *interlaced*):— tabernacle.

7901. שָׁכַב **shâkab**, *shaw-kab´;* a prim. root; to *lie* down (for rest, sexual connection, decease or any other purpose):— × at all, cast down, (Ilover-I) lay (self) (down), (make to) lie (down, down to sleep, still, with), lodge, ravish, take rest, sleep, stay.

7902. שְׁכָבָה **shᵉkâbâh**, *shek-aw-baw´;* from 7901; a *lying* down (of dew, or for the sexual act):— × carnally, copulation, × lay, seed.

7903. שְׁכֹבֶת **shᵉkôbeth**, *shek-o´-beth;* from 7901; a (sexual) *lying* with:— × lie.

7904. שָׁכָה **shâkâh**, *shaw-kaw´;* a prim. root; to *roam* (through lust):— in the morning [by mistake for 7925].

7905. שֻׂכָּה **sukkâh**, *sook-kaw´;* fem. of 7900 in the sense of 7899; a *dart* (as pointed like a *thorn*):— barbed iron.

7906. שֵׂכוּ **Sêkûw**, *say´-koo;* from an unused root appar. mean. to *surmount;* an *observatory* (with the art.); *Seku,* a place in Pal.:— Sechu.

7907. שֶׂכְוִי **sekvîy**, *sek-vee´;* from the same as 7906; *observant,* i.e. (concr.) the *mind:*— heart.

7908. שְׁכוֹל **shᵉkôwl**, *shek-ole´;* infin. of 7921; *bereavement:*— loss of children, spoiling.

7909. שַׁכּוּל **shakkuwl**, *shak-kool´;* or

שַׁכֻּל **shakkul**, *shak-kool´;* from 7921; *bereaved:*— barren, bereaved (robbed) of children (whelps).

7910. שִׁכּוֹר **shikkôwr**, *shik-kore´;* or

שִׁכֹּר **shikkôr**, *shik-kore´;* from 7937; *intoxicated,* as a state or a habit:— drunk (-ard, -en, -en man).

7911. שָׁכַח **shâkach**, *shaw-kakh´;* or

שָׁכֵחַ **shâkêach**, *shaw-kay´-akh;* a prim. root; to *mislay,* i.e. to *be oblivious of,* from want of memory or attention:— × at all, (cause to) forget.

7912. שְׁכַח **shᵉkach** (Chald.), *shek-akh´;* corresp. to 7911 through the idea of disclosure of a *covered* or *forgotten* thing; to *discover* (lit. or fig.):— find.

7913. שָׁכֵחַ **shâkêach**, *shaw-kay´-akh;* from 7911; *oblivious:*— forget.

7914. שְׂכִיָּה **sᵉkîyâh**, *sek-ee-yaw´;* fem. from the same as 7906; a *conspicuous* object:— picture.

7915. שַׂכִּין **sakkîyn**, *sak-keen´;* intens. perh. from the same as 7906 in the sense of 7753; a *knife* (as *pointed* or *edged*):— knife.

7916. שָׂכִיר **sâkîyr**, *saw-keer´;* from 7936; a man *at wages* by the day or year:— hired (man, servant), hireling.

7917. שְׂכִירָה **sᵉkîyrâh**, *sek-ee-raw´;* fem. of 7916; a *hiring:*— that is hired.

7918. שָׁכַךְ **shâkak**, *shaw-kak´;* a prim. root; to *weave* (i.e. *lay;* fig. (through the idea of *secreting*) to *allay* (passions; phys. *abate* a flood):— appease, assuage, make to cease, pacify, set.

7919. שָׂכַל **sâkal**, *saw-kal´;* a prim. root; to *be* (caus. *make* or *act*) *circumspect* and hence, *intelligent:*— consider, expert, instruct, prosper, (deal) prudent (-ly), (give) skill (-ful), have good success, teach, (have, make to) understand (-ing), wisdom, (be, behave self, consider, make) wise (-ly), guide wittingly.

7920. שְׂכַל **sᵉkal** (Chald.), *sek-al´;* corresp. to 7919:— consider.

7921. שָׁכֹל **shâkôl**, *shaw-kole´;* a prim. root; prop. to *miscarry,* i.e. *suffer abortion;* by anal. to *bereave* (lit. or fig.):— bereave (of children), barren, cast calf (fruit, young), be (make) childless, deprive, destroy, × expect, lose children, miscarry, rob of children, spoil.

7922. שֶׂכֶל **sekel**, *seh´-kel;* or

שֶׂכֶל **sêkel**, *say´-kel;* from 7919; *intelligence;* by impl. *success:*— discretion, knowledge, policy, prudence, sense, understanding, wisdom, wise.

שַׁכּוּל **shakkûl**. See 7909.

שְׂכֻלָה **siklûwth**. See 5531.

7923. שִׁכֻּלִים **shikkûlîym**, *shik-koo-leem´;* plur. from 7921; *childlessness* (by continued bereavements):— to have after loss of others.

7924. שָׂכְלְתָנוּ **soklᵉthânûw** (Chald.), *sok-leth-aw-noo´;* from 7920; *intelligence:*— understanding.

7925. שָׁכַם **shâkam**, *shaw-kam´;* a prim. root; prop. to *incline* (the shoulder to a burden); but used only as denom. from 7926; lit. to *load up* (on the back of man or beast), i.e. to *start early* in the morning:— (arise, be up, get Ioneselfl up, rise up) early (betimes), morning.

7926. שְׁכֶם **shᵉkem**, *shek-em´;* from 7925; the *neck* (between the shoulders) as the place of burdens; fig. the *spur* of a hill:— back, × consent, portion, shoulder.

7927. שְׁכֶם **Shᵉkem**, *shek-em´;* the same as 7926; *ridge; Shekem,* a place in Pal.:— Shechem.

7928. שֶׁכֶם **Shekem**, *sheh´-kem;* for 7926; *Shekem,* the name of a Hivite and two Isr.:— Shechem.

7929. שִׁכְמָה **shikmâh**, *shik-maw´;* fem. of 7926; the *shoulder*-bone:— shoulder blade.

7930. שִׁכְמִי **Shikmîy**, *shik-mee´;* patron. from 7928; a *Shikmite* (collect.), or desc. of Shekem:— Shichemites.

7931. שָׁכַן **shâkan**, *shaw-kan´;* a prim. root Iappar. akin (by transm.) to 7901 through the idea of *lodging;* comp. 5531, 7925]; to *reside* or permanently stay (lit. or fig.):— abide, continue, (cause to, make to) dwell (-er), have habitation, inhabit, lay, place, (cause to) remain, rest, set (up).

7932. שְׁכַן **sheᵉkan** (Chald.), *shek-an´;* corresp. to 7931:— cause to dwell, have habitation.

7933. שֶׁכֶן **sheken,** *sheh´-ken;* from 7931; a *residence:*— habitation.

7934. שָׁכֵן **shâkên,** *shaw-kane´;* from 7931; a *resident;* by extens. a fellow-citizen:— inhabitant, neighbour, nigh.

7935. שְׁכַנְיָה **Shᵉkanyâh,** *shek-an-yaw´;* or (prol.)

שְׁכַנְיָהוּ **Shᵉkanyâhûw,** *shek-an-yaw´-hoo;* from 7931 and 3050; *Jah has dwelt; Shekanjah,* the name of nine Isr.:— Shecaniah, Shechaniah.

7936. שָׂכַר **sâkar,** *saw-kar´;* or (by perm.)

שָׂכַר **çâkar** (Ezra 4:5), *saw-kar´;* a prim. root [appar. akin (by prosthesis) to 3739 through the idea of temporary *purchase;* comp. 7937]; to *hire:*— earn wages, hire (out self), reward, × surely.

7937. שָׁכַר **shâkar,** *shaw-kar´;* a prim. root; to *become tipsy;* in a qualified sense, to *satiate* with a stimulating drink or (fig.) influence:— (be filled with) drink (abundantly), (be, make) drunk (-en), be merry. [Superlative of 8248.]

7938. שֶׂכֶר **seker,** *seh´-ker;* from 7936; *wages:*— reward, sluices.

7939. שָׂכָר **sâkâr,** *saw-kawr´;* from 7936; *payment* of contract; concr. *salary, fare, maintenance;* by impl. *compensation, benefit:*— hire, price, reward [-ed], wages, worth.

7940. שָׂכָר **Sâkâr,** *saw-kar´;* the same as 7939; *recompense; Sakar,* the name of two Isr.:— Sacar.

7941. שֵׁכָר **shêkâr,** *shay-kawr´;* from 7937; an *intoxicant,* i.e. intensely alcoholic *liquor:*— strong drink, + drunkard, strong wine.

שִׁכֹּר **shikkôr.** See 7910.

7942. שִׁכְּרוֹן **Shikkᵉrôwn,** *shik-ker-one´;* for 7943; *drunkenness, Shikkeron,* a place in Pal.:— Shicron.

7943. שִׁכָּרוֹן **shikkârôwn,** *shik-kaw-rone´;* from 7937; *intoxication:*— (be) drunken (-ness).

7944. שַׁל **shal,** *shal;* from 7952 abbrev.; a *fault:*— error.

7945. שֶׁל **shel,** *shel;* for the rel. 834; used with prep. pref., and often followed by some pron. aff.; *on account of, what*soever, *which*soever:— cause, sake.

7946. שַׁלְאָנָן **shal'ănân,** *shal-an-awn´;* for 7600; *tranquil:*— being at ease.

7947. שָׁלַב **shâlab,** *shaw-lab´;* a prim. root; to *space off;* intens. (*evenly*) to *make equidistant:*— equally distant, set in order.

7948. שָׁלָב **shâlâb,** *shaw-lawb´;* from 7947; a *spacer* or raised *interval,* i.e. the *stile* in a frame or panel:— ledge.

7949. שָׁלַג **shâlag,** *shaw-lag´;* a prim. root; prop. mean. to *be white;* used only as denom. from 7950; to *be snow-white*

(with the linen clothing of the slain):— be as snow.

7950. שֶׁלֶג **sheleg,** *sheh´-leg;* from 7949; *snow* (prob. from its *whiteness*):— snow (-y).

7951. שָׁלָה **shâlâh,** *shaw-law´;* or

שָׁלַו **shâlav** (Job 3:26), *shaw-lav´;* a prim. root; to *be tranquil,* i.e. *secure* or *successful:*— be happy, prosper, be in safety.

7952. שָׁלָה **shâlâh,** *shaw-law´;* a prim. root [prob. rather ident. with 7953 through the idea of *educing*]; to *mislead:*— deceive, be negligent.

7953. שָׁלָה **shâlâh,** *shaw-law´;* a prim. root [rather cognate (by contr.) to the base of 5394, 7997 and their congeners through the idea of *extracting*]; to *draw* out or off, i.e. *remove* (the soul by death):— take away.

7954. שְׁלָה **sheᵉlâh** (Chald.), *shel-aw´;* corresp. to 7951; to *be secure:*— at rest.

שִׁילֹה **Shîlôh.** See 7887.

7955. שָׁלָה° **shâlâh** (Chald.), *shaw-law´;* from a root corresp. to 7952; a *wrong:*— thing amiss.

שֵׁלָה **shêlâh.** See 7596.

7956. שֵׁלָה **Shêlâh,** *shay-law´;* the same as 7596 (short.); *request; Shelah,* the name of a postdiluvian patriarch and of an Isr.:— Shelah.

7957. שַׁלְהֶבֶת **shalhebeth,** *shal-heh´-beth;* from the same as 3851 with sibilant pref.; a *flare* of fire:— (flaming) flame.

שָׁלַו **shâlav.** See 7951.

7958. שְׂלָו **sᵉlâv,** *sel-awv´;* or

שְׂלָיו **sᵉlâyv,** *sel-awv´;* by orth. var. from 7951 through the idea of *sluggishness;* the *quail* collect. (as *slow* in flight from its *weight*):— quails.

7959. שֶׁלֶו **shelev,** *sheh´-lev;* from 7951; *security:*— prosperity.

שִׁלוֹ **Shîlôw.** See 7887.

7960. שָׁלוּ **shâlûw** (Chald.), *shaw-loo´;* or

שָׁלוּת **shâlûwth** (Chald.), *shaw-looth´;* from the same as 7955; a *fault:*— error, × fail, thing amiss.

7961. שָׁלֵו **shâlêv,** *shaw-lave´;* or

שָׁלֵיו **shâlêyv,** *shaw-lave´;* fem.

שְׁלֵוָה **shᵉlêvâh,** *shel-ay-vaw´;* from 7951; *tranquil;* (in a bad sense) *careless;* abstr. *security:*— (being) at ease, peaceable, (in) prosper (-ity), quiet (-ness), wealthy.

7962. שַׁלְוָה **shalvâh,** *shal-vaw´;* from 7951; *security* (genuine or false):— abundance, peace (-ably), prosperity, quietness.

7963. שְׁלֵוָה **shᵉlêvâh** (Chald.), *shel-ay-vaw´;* corresp. to 7962; *safety:*— tranquillity. See also 7961.

7964. שִׁלּוּחַ **shillûwach,** *shil-loo´-akh;* or

שִׁלֻּחַ **shillûach,** *shil-loo´-akh;* from 7971; (only in plur.) a *dismissal,* i.e. (of a wife) *divorce* (espec. the document); also (of a daughter) *dower:*— presents, have sent back.

7965. שָׁלוֹם **shâlôwm,** *shaw-lome´;* or

שָׁלֹם **shâlôm,** *shaw-lome´;* from 7999; *safe,* i.e. (fig.) *well, happy, friendly;* also (abstr.) *welfare,* i.e. *health, prosperity, peace:*— × do, familiar, × fare, favour, + friend, × great, (good) health, (× perfect, such as be at) peace (-able, -ably), prosper (-ity, -ous), rest, safe (-ty), salute, welfare, (× all is, be) well, × wholly.

7966. שִׁלּוּם **shillûwm,** *shil-loom´;* or

שִׁלֻּם **shillûm,** *shil-loom´;* from 7999; a *requital,* i.e. (secure) *retribution,* (venal) a *fee:*— recompense, reward.

7967. שַׁלּוּם **Shallûwm,** *shal-loom´;* or (short.)

שַׁלֻּם **Shallûm,** *shal-loom´;* the same as 7966; *Shallum,* the name of fourteen Isr.:— Shallum.

שְׁלוֹמִית **Shᵉlôwmîyth.** See 8019.

7968. שַׁלּוּן **Shallûwn,** *shal-loon´;* prob. for 7967; *Shallun,* an Isr.:— Shallum.

7969. שָׁלוֹשׁ **shâlôwsh,** *shaw-loshe´;* or

שָׁלֹשׁ **shâlôsh,** *shaw-loshe´;* masc.

שְׁלוֹשָׁה **shᵉlôwshâh,** *shel-o-shaw´;* or

שְׁלֹשָׁה **shᵉlôshâh,** *shel-o-shaw´;* a prim. number; *three;* occasionally (ord.) *third,* or (multipl.) *thrice:*— + fork, + often [-times], third, thir[-teen, -teenth], three, + thrice. Comp. 7991.

7970. שְׁלוֹשִׁים **shᵉlôwshîym,** *shel-o-sheem´;* or

שְׁלֹשִׁים **shᵉlôshîym,** *shel-o-sheem´;* multiple of 7969; *thirty;* or (ord.) *thirtieth:*— thirty, thirtieth. Comp. 7991.

שָׁלוּת **shâlûwth.** See 7960.

7971. שָׁלַח **shâlach,** *shaw-lakh´;* a prim. root; to *send* away, for, or out (in a great variety of applications):— × any wise, appoint, bring (on the way), cast (away, out), conduct, × earnestly, forsake, give (up), grow long, lay, leave, let depart (down, go, loose), push away, put (away, forth, in, out), reach forth, send (away, forth, out), set, shoot (forth, out), sow, spread, stretch forth (out).

7972. שְׁלַח **sheᵉlach** (Chald.), *shel-akh´;* corresp. to 7971:— put, send.

7973. שֶׁלַח **shelach,** *sheh´-lakh;* from 7971; a *missile* of attack, i.e. *spear;* also (fig.) a *shoot* of growth; i.e. *branch:*— dart, plant, × put off, sword, weapon.

7974. שֶׁלַח **Shelach,** *sheh´-lakh;* the same as 7973; *Shelach,* a postdiluvian patriarch:— Salah, Shelah. Comp. 7975.

7975. שִׁלֹחַ **Shilôach,** *shee-lo´-akh;* or (in imitation of 7974)

שֶׁלַח **Shelach** (Neh. 3:15), *sheh´-lakh;* from 7971; *rill; Shiloäch,* a fountain of Jerusalem:— Shiloah, Siloah.

שִׁלֻּחַ **shillûach.** See 7964.

7976. שִׁלְחָה **shilluchâh,** *shil-loo-khaw´;* fem. of 7964; a *shoot:*— branch.

7977. שִׁלְחִי **Shilchîy,** *shil-khee´;* from 7973; *missive,* i.e. *armed; Shilchi,* an Isr.:— Shilhi.

7978. שִׁלְחִים **Shilchîym,** *shil-kheem´;*

plur. of 7973; *javelins* or *sprouts; Shilchim*, a place in Pal.:— Shilhim.

7979. שֻׁלְחָן **shulchân**, *shool-khawn´*; from 7971; a *table* (as *spread* out); by impl. a *meal*:— table.

7980. שָׁלַט **shâlaṭ**, *shaw-lat´*; a prim. root; to *dominate*, i.e. *govern*; by impl. to *permit*:— (bear, have) rule, have dominion, give (have) power.

7981. שְׁלֵט **sheʰlêṭ** (Chald.), *shel-ate´*; corresp. to 7980:— have the mastery, have power, bear rule, be (make) ruler.

7982. שֶׁלֶט **sheleṭ**, *sheh´-let*; from 7980; prob. a *shield* (as *controlling*, i.e. protecting the person):— shield.

7983. שִׁלְטוֹן **shilṭôwn**, *shil-tone´*; from 7980; a *potentate*:— power.

7984. שִׁלְטוֹן **shilṭôwn** (Chald.), *shiltone´*; or

שִׁלְטֹן **shilṭôn**, *shil-tone´*; corresp. to 7983:— ruler.

7985. שָׁלְטָן **sholṭân** (Chald.), *shol-tawn´*; from 7981; *empire* (abstr. or concr.):— dominion.

7986. שַׁלֶּטֶת **shalleṭeth**, *shal-leh´-teth*; fem. from 7980; a *vixen*:— imperious.

7987. שְׁלִי **sheʰliy**, *shel-ee´*; from 7951; *privacy*:— + quietly.

7988. שִׁלְיָה **shilyâh**, *shil-yaw´*; fem. from 7953; a *fetus* or *babe* (as *extruded* in birth):— young one.

שְׁלָיו **sheʰlâyv**. See 7958.

שָׁלֵיו **shalêyv**. See 7961.

7989. שַׁלִּיט **shalliyṭ**, *shal-leet´*; from 7980; *potent*; concr. a *prince* or *warrior*:— governor, mighty, that hath power, ruler.

7990. שַׁלִּיט **shalliyṭ** (Chald.), *shal-leet´*; corresp. to 7989; *mighty*; abstr. *permission*; concr. a *premier*:— captain, be lawful, rule (-r).

7991. שָׁלִישׁ **shâliysh**, *shaw-leesh´*; or

שָׁלוֹשׁ° **shâlôwsh** (1 Chron. 11:11; 12:18), *shaw-loshe´*; or

שָׁלֹשׁ° **shâlôsh** (2 Sam. 23:13), *shaw-loshe´*; from 7969; a *triple*, i.e. (as a musical instrument) a *triangle* (or perh. rather *three*-stringed lute); also (as an indef. great quantity) a *threefold* measure (perh. a *treble* ephah); also (as an officer) a general of the *third* rank (upward, i.e. the highest):— captain, instrument of musick, (great) lord, (great) measure, prince, three [from marg.].

7992. שְׁלִישִׁי **sheʰliyshiy**, *shel-ee-shee´*; ord. from 7969; *third*; fem. a *third* (part); by extens. a *third* (day, year or time); spec. a *third*-story cell):— third (part, rank, time), three (years old).

7993. שָׁלַךְ **shâlak**, *shaw-lak´*; a prim. root; to *throw* out, down or away (lit. or fig.):— adventure, cast (away, down, forth, off, out), hurl, pluck, throw.

7994. שָׁלָךְ **shâlâk**, *shaw-lawk´*; from 7993; *bird of prey*, usually thought to be the *pelican* (from *casting* itself into the sea):— cormorant.

7995. שַׁלֶּכֶת **shalleketh**, *shal-leh´-keth*; from 7993; a *felling* (of trees):— when cast.

7996. שַׁלֶּכֶת **Shalleketh**, *shal-leh´-keth*; the same as 7995; *Shalleketh*, a gate in Jerusalem:— Shalleketh.

7997. שָׁלַל **shâlal**, *shaw-lal´*; a prim. root; to *drop* or *strip*; by impl. to *plunder*:— let fall, make self a prey, × of purpose, (make a, [take]) spoil.

7998. שָׁלָל **shâlâl**, *shaw-lawl´*; from 7997; *booty*:— prey, spoil.

7999. שָׁלַם **shâlam**, *shaw-lam´*; a prim. root; to *be safe* (in mind, body or estate); fig. to *be* (caus. *make*) *completed*; by impl. to *be friendly*; by extens. to *reciprocate* (in various applications):— make amends, (make an) end, finish, full, give again, make good, (re-) pay (again), (make) (to) (be at) peace (-able), that is perfect, perform, (make) prosper (-ous), recompense, render, requite, make restitution, restore, reward, × surely.

8000. שְׁלַם **sheʰlam** (Chald.), *shel-am´*; corresp. to 7999; to *complete*, to *restore*:— deliver, finish.

8001. שְׁלָם **sheʰlâm** (Chald.), *shel-awm´*; corresp. to 7965; *prosperity*:— peace.

8002. שֶׁלֶם **shelem**, *sheh´-lem*; from 7999; prop. *requital*, i.e. a (voluntary) *sacrifice* in *thanks*:— peace offering.

8003. שָׁלֵם **shâlêm**, *shaw-lame´*; from 7999; *complete* (lit. or fig.); espec. *friendly*:— full, just, made ready, peaceable, perfect (-ed), quiet, Shalem [by mistake for a name], whole.

8004. שָׁלֵם **Shâlêm**, *shaw-lame´*; the same as 8003; *peaceful; Shalem*, an early name of Jerusalem:— Salem.

שָׁלֹם **shâlôm**. See 7965.

8005. שִׁלֵּם **shillêm**, *shil-lame´*; from 7999; *requital*:— recompense.

8006. שִׁלֵּם **Shillêm**, *shil-lame´*; the same as 8005; *Shillem*, an Isr.:— Shillem.

שִׁלֻּם **shillûm**. See 7966.

שַׁלֻּם **Shallûm**. See 7967.

8007. שַׂלְמָא **Salmâ'**, *sal-maw´*; prob. for 8008; *clothing; Salma*, the name of two Isr.:— Salma.

8008. שַׂלְמָה **salmâh**, *sal-maw´*; transp. for 8071; a *dress*:— clothes, garment, raiment.

8009. שַׂלְמָה **Salmâh**, *sal-maw´*; the same as 8008; *clothing; Salmah*, an Isr.:— Salmon. Comp. 8012.

8010. שְׁלֹמֹה **Sheʰlômôh**, *shel-o-mo´*; from 7965; *peaceful; Shelomah*, David's successor:— Solomon.

8011. שִׁלֻּמָה **shillumâh**, *shil-loo-maw´*; fem. of 7966; *retribution*:— recompense.

8012. שַׂלְמוֹן **Salmôwn**, *sal-mone´*; from 8008; *investiture; Salmon*, an Isr.:— Salmon. Comp. 8009.

8013. שְׁלֹמוֹת **Sheʰlômôwth**, *shel-o-moth´*; fem. plur. of 7965; *pacifications; Shelomoth*, the name of two Isr.:— Shelomith [from the marg.], Shelomoth. Comp. 8019.

8014. שַׂלְמַי **Salmay**, *sal-mah´-ee*; from 8008; *clothed; Salmai*, an Isr.:— Shalmai.

8015. שְׁלֹמִי **Sheʰlômîy**, *shel-o-mee´*; from

7965; *peaceable; Shelomi*, an Isr.:— Shelomi.

8016. שִׁלֵּמִי **Shillêmîy**, *shil-lay-mee´*; patron. from 8006; a *Shilemite* (collect.) or desc. of Shillem:— Shillemites.

8017. שְׁלֻמִיאֵל **Sheʰlûmîy'êl**, *shel-oo-mee-ale´*; from 7965 and 410; *peace of God; Shelumiel*, an Isr.:— Shelumiel.

8018. שֶׁלֶמְיָה **Shelemyâh**, *shel-em-yaw´*; or

שֶׁלֶמְיָהוּ **Shelemyâhuw**, *shel-em-yaw´-hoo*; from 8002 and 3050; *thank-offering of Jah; Shelemjah*, the name of nine Isr.:— Shelemiah.

8019. שְׁלֹמִית **Sheʰlômîyth**, *shel-o-meeth´*; or

שְׁלוֹמִית **Sheʰlôwmiyth** (Ezra 8:10), *shel-o-meeth´*; from 7965; *peaceableness; Shelomith*, the name of five Isr. and three Israelitesses:— Shelomith.

8020. שַׁלְמַן **Shalman**, *shal-man´*; of for. der.; *Shalman*, a king appar. of Assyria:— Shalman. Comp. 8022.

8021. שַׁלְמֹן **shalmôn**, *shal-mone´*; from 7999; a *bribe*:— reward.

8022. שַׁלְמַנְאֶסֶר **Shalman'eçer**, *shal-man-eh´-ser*; of for. der.; *Shalmaneser*, an Ass. king:— Shalmaneser. Comp 8020.

8023. שִׁלֹנִי **Shilônîy**, *shee-lo-nee´*; the same as 7888; *Shiloni*, an Isr.:— Shiloni.

8024. שֵׁלָנִי **Shêlânîy**, *shay-law-nee´*; from 7956; a *Shelanite* (collect.), or desc. of Shelah:— Shelanites.

8025. שָׁלַף **shâlaph**, *saw-laf´*; a prim. root; to *pull* out, up or off:— draw (off), grow up, pluck off.

8026. שֶׁלֶף **Sheleph**, *sheh´-lef*; from 8025; *extract; Sheleph*, a son of Jokthan:— Sheleph.

8027. שָׁלַשׁ **shâlash**, *shaw-lash´*; a prim. root perh. orig. to *intensify*, i.e. *treble*; but appar. used only as denom. from 7969, to *be* (caus. *make*) *triplicate* (by restoration, in portions, strands, days or years):— do the third time, (divide into, stay) three (days, -fold, parts, years old).

8028. שֶׁלֶשׁ **Shelesh**, *sheh´-lesh*; from 8027; *triplet; Shelesh*, an Isr.:— Shelesh.

שָׁלֹשׁ **shâlôsh**. See 7969.

8029. שִׁלֵּשׁ **shillêsh**, *shil-laysh´*; from 8027; a *desc.* of the *third* degree, i.e. *great grandchild*:— third [generation].

8030. שִׁלְשָׁה **Shilshâh**, *shil-shaw´*; fem. from the same as 8028; *triplication; Shilshah*, an Isr.:— Shilshah.

8031. שָׁלִשָׁה **Shâlishâh**, *shaw-lee-shaw´*; fem. from 8027; *trebled* land; *Shalishah*, a place in Pal.:— Shalisha.

שָׁלֹשָׁה **shâlôshâh**. See 7969.

8032. שִׁלְשׁוֹם **shilshôwm**, *shil-shome´*; or

שִׁלְשֹׁם **shilshôm**, *shil-shome´*; from the same as 8028; *trebly*, i.e. (in time) *day before yesterday*:— + before (that time, -time), excellent things [from the marg.], + heretofore, three days, + time past.

שְׁלֹשִׁים **sheʰlôshîym**. See 7970.

שְׁאַלְתִּיאֵל **Shaltiy'êl**. See 7597.

8033. שָׁם **shâm**, *shawm*; a prim. particle lrather from the rel. 834l; *there* (transferring to time) *then*; often *thither*, or *thence*:— in it, + thence, there (-in, + of, + out), + thither, + whither.

8034. שֵׁם **shêm**, *shame*; a prim. word lperh. rather from 7760 through the idea of def. and conspicuous *position*; comp. 8064l; an *appellation*, as a mark or memorial of individuality; by impl. *honor, authority, character*:— + base, lin-l fame l-ousl, named (-d), renown, report.

8035. שֵׁם **Shêm**, *shame*; the same as 8034; *name; Shem*, a son of Noah (often includ. his posterity):— Sem, Shem.

8036. שֻׁם **shum** (Chald.), *shoom*; corresp. to 8034:— name.

8037. שַׁמָּא **Shammâ'**, *sham-maw*; from 8074; *desolation; Shamma*, an Isr.:— Shamma.

8038. שְׁמְאֵבֶר **Shem'êber**, *shem-ay´-ber*; appar. from 8034 and 83; *name of pinion*, i.e. *illustrious; Shemeber*, a king of Zeboim:— Shemeber.

8039. שִׁמְאָה **Shim'âh**, *shim-aw*; perh. for 8093; *Shimah*, an Isr.:— Shimah. Comp. 8043.

8040. שְׂמֹאול **sᵉmô'wl**, *sem-ole´*; or

שְׂמֹאל **sᵉmô'l**, *sem-ole´*; a prim. word lrather perh. from the same as 8071 (by insertion of א) through the idea of *wrapping* upl; prop. *dark* (as *enveloped*), i.e. the *north*; hence (by orientation), the *left* hand:— left (hand, side).

8041. שָׂמַאל **sâma'l**, *saw-mal´*; a prim. root lrather denom. from 8040l; to use the *left* hand or pass in that direction):— (go, turn) (on the, to the) left.

8042. שְׂמָאלִי **sᵉmâ'lîy**, *sem-aw-lee´*; from 8040; situated on the *left* side:— left.

8043. שִׁמְאָם **Shim'âm**, *shim-awm´*; for 8039 lcomp. 38l; *Shimam*, an Isr.:— Shimeam.

8044. שַׁמְגַּר **Shamgar**, *sham-gar´*; of uncert. der.; *Shamgar*, an Isr. judge:— Shamgar.

8045. שָׁמַד **shâmad**, *shaw-mad´*; a prim. root; to *desolate*:— destroy (-uction), bring to nought, overthrow, perish, pluck down, × utterly.

8046. שְׁמַד **shᵉmad** (Chald.), *shem-ad´*; corresp. to 8045:— consume.

שָׁמֶה **shâmeh**. See 8064.

8047. שַׁמָּה **shammâh**, *sham-maw´*; from 8074; *ruin*; by impl. *consternation*:— astonishment, desolate (-ion), waste, wonderful thing.

8048. שַׁמָּה **Shammâh**, *sham-maw´*; the same as 8047; *Shammah*, the name of an Edomite and four Isr.:— Shammah.

8049. שַׁמְהוּת **Shamhûwth**, *sham-hooth´*; for 8048; *desolation; Shamhuth*, an Isr.:— Shamhuth.

8050. שְׁמוּאֵל **Shᵉmûw'êl**, *sehm-oo-ale´*; from the pass. part. of 8085 and 410; *heard of God; Shemuel*, the name of three Isr.:— Samuel, Shemuel.

שְׁמוֹנֶה **shᵉmôwneh**. See 8083.

שְׁמוֹנָה **shᵉmôwnâh**. See 8083.

שְׁמוֹנִים **shᵉmôwnîym**. See 8084.

8051. שַׁמּוּעַ **Shammûwa'**, *sham-moo´-ah*; from 8074; *renowned; Shammua*, the name of four Isr.:— Shammua, Shammuah.

8052. שְׁמוּעָה **shᵉmûw'âh**, *sehm-oo-aw´*; fem. pass. part. of 8074; something *heard*, i.e. an *announcement*:— bruit, doctrine, fame, mentioned, news, report, rumor, tidings.

8053. שָׁמוּר **Shâmûwr**, *shaw-moor´*; pass. part. of 8103; *observed; Shamur*, an Isr.:— Shamir lfrom the marg.l.

8054. שַׁמּוֹת **Shammôwth**, *sham-môth´*; plur. of 8047; *ruins; Shammoth*, an Isr.:— Shamoth.

8055. שָׂמַח **sâmach**, *saw-makh´*; a prim. root; prob. to *brighten* up, i.e. (fig.) be (caus. *make*) *blithe* or *gleesome*:— cheer up, be (make) glad, (have, make) joy (-ful), be (make) merry, (cause to, make to) rejoice, × very.

8056. שָׂמֵחַ **sâmêach**, *saw-may´-akh*; from 8055; *blithe* or *gleeful*:— (be) glad, joyful, (making) merry (l-heartedl, -ily), rejoice (-ing).

8057. שִׂמְחָה **simchâh**, *sim-khaw´*; from 8056; *blithesomeness* or *glee*, (relig. or festival):— × exceeding (-ly), gladness, joy (-fulness), mirth, pleasure, rejoice (-ing).

8058. שָׁמַט **shâmat**, *shaw-mat´*; a prim. root; to *fling* down; incipiently to *jostle*; fig. to *let alone, desist, remit*:— discontinue, overthrow, release, let rest, shake, stumble, throw down.

8059. שְׁמִטָּה **shᵉmittâh**, *shem-it-taw´*; from 8058; *remission* (of debt) or *suspension* of labor):— release.

8060. שַׁמַּי **Shammay**, *sham-mah´-ee*; from 8073; *destructive; Shammai*, the name of three Isr.:— Shammai.

8061. שְׁמִידָע **Shᵉmîydâ'**, *shem-ee-daw´*; appar. from 8034 and 3045; *name of knowing; Shemida*, an Isr.:— Shemida, Shemidah.

8062. שְׁמִידָעִי **Shᵉmîydâ'îy**, *shem-ee-daw-ee´*; patron. from 8061; a *Shemidaite* (collect.) or desc. of Shemida:— Shemidaites.

8063. שְׂמִיכָה **sᵉmîykâh**, *sem-ee-kaw´*; from 5564; a *rug* (as *sustaining* the Oriental sitter):— mantle.

8064. שָׁמַיִם **shâmayim**, *shaw-mah´-yim*; dual of an unused sing.

שָׁמֶה **shâmeh**, *shaw-meh´*; from an unused root mean. to *be lofty*; the *sky* (as *aloft*; the dual perh. alluding to the visible arch in which the clouds move, as well as to the higher ether where the celestial bodies revolve):— air, × astrologer, heaven (-s).

8065. שָׁמַיִן **shâmayin** (Chald.), *shaw-mah´-yin*; corresp. to 8064:— heaven.

8066. שְׁמִינִי **shᵉmîynîy**, *shem-ee-nee´*; from 8083; *eight*:— eight.

8067. שְׁמִינִית **shᵉmîynîyth**, *shem-ee-neeth´*; fem. of 8066; prob. an *eight-stringed* lyre:— Sheminith.

8068. שָׁמִיר **shâmîyr**, *shaw-meer´*; from 8104 in the orig. sense of *pricking*; a *thorn*; also (from its *keenness* for scratching) a *gem*, prob. the dia-

---

mond:— adamant (stone), brier, diamond.

8069. שָׁמִיר **Shâmîyr**, *shaw-meer´*; the same as 8068; *Shamir*, the name of two places in Pal.:— Shamir. Comp. 8053.

8070. שְׁמִירָמוֹת **Shᵉmîyrâmôwth**, *shem-ee-raw-môth´*; or

שְׁמָרִימוֹת **Shᵉmârîymôwth**, *shem-aw-ree-môth´*; prob. from 8034 and plur. of 7413; *name of heights; Shemiramoth*, the name of two Isr.:— Shemiramoth.

8071. שִׂמְלָה **simlâh**, *sim-law´*; perh. by perm. for the fem. of 5566 (through the idea of a *cover* assuming the shape of the object beneath); a *dress*, espec. a *mantle*:— apparel, cloth (-es, -ing), garment, raiment. Comp. 8008.

8072. שַׂמְלָה **Samlâh**, *sam-law´*; prob. for the same as 8071; *Samlah*, an Edomite:— Samlah.

8073. שַׂמְלַי **Shamlay**, *sham-lah´-ee*; for 8014; *Shamlai*, one of the Nethinim:— Shalmai lfrom the marg.l.

8074. שָׁמֵם **shâmêm**, *shaw-mame´*; a prim. root; to *stun* (or intr. *grow numb*), i.e. *devastate* or (fig.) *stupefy* (both usually in a pass. sense):— make amazed, be astonied, (be an) astonish (-ment), (be, bring into, unto, lay, lie, make) desolate (-ion, places), be destitute, destroy (self), (lay, lie, make) waste, wonder.

8075. שְׁמַם **shᵉmam** (Chald.), *shem-am´*; corresp. to 8074:— be astonied.

8076. שָׁמֵם **shâmêm**, *shaw-mame´*; from 8074; *ruined*:— desolate.

8077. שְׁמָמָה **shᵉmâmâh**, *shem-aw-maw´*; or

שִׁמָמָה **shîmâmâh**, *shee-mam-aw´*; fem. of 8076; *devastation*; fig. *astonishment*:— (laid, × most) desolate (-ion), waste.

8078. שִׁמָּמוֹן **shimmâmôwn**, *shim-maw-mone´*; from 8074; *stupefaction*:— astonishment.

8079. שְׂמָמִית **sᵉmâmîyth**, *sem-aw-meeth´*; prob. from 8074 (in the sense of *poisoning*); a *lizard* (from the superstition of its *noxiousness*):— spider.

8080. שָׁמַן **shâman**, *shaw-man´*; a prim. root; to *shine*, i.e. (by anal.) be (caus. *make*) *oily* or *gross*:— become (make, wax) fat.

8081. שֶׁמֶן **shemen**, *sheh´-men*; from 8080; *grease*, espec. liquid (as from the olive, often perfumed); fig. *richness*:— anointing, × fat (things), × fruitful, oil (l-edl), ointment, olive, + pine.

8082. שָׁמֵן **shâmên**, *shaw-mane´*; from 8080; *greasy*, i.e. *gross*; fig. *rich*:— fat, lusty, plenteous.

8083. שְׁמֹנֶה **shᵉmôneh**, *shem-o-neh´*; or

שְׁמוֹנֶה **shᵉmôwneh**, *shem-o-neh´*; fem.

שְׁמֹנָה **shᵉmônâh**, *shem-o-naw´*; or

שְׁמוֹנָה **shᵉmôwnâh**, *shem-o-naw´*; appar. from 8082 through the idea of *plumpness*; a cardinal number, *eight* (as if a *surplus* above the "perfect" seven); also (as ord.) *eighth*:— eight (l-een, -eenthl), eighth.

8084. שְׁמֹנִים **shᵉmônîym**, *shem-o-neem´*; or

שְׁמוֹנִים **shᵉmôwnîym**, *shem-o-neem´*; mult. from 8083; *eighty*, also *eightieth*:— eighty (-ieth), fourscore.

8085. שָׁמַע **shâma'**, *shaw-mah´*; a prim. root; to *hear* intelligently (often with impl. of attention, obedience, etc.; caus. to *tell*, etc.):— × attentively, call (gather) together, × carefully, × certainly, consent, consider, be content, declare, × diligently, discern, give ear, (cause to, let, make to) hear (-ken, tell), × indeed, listen, make (a) noise, (be) obedient, obey, perceive, (make a) proclaim (-ation), publish, regard, report, shew (forth), (make a) sound, × surely, tell, understand, whosoever [heareth], witness.

8086. שְׁמַע **shᵉma'** (Chald.), *shem-ah´*; corresp. to 8085:— hear, obey.

8087. שֶׁמַע **Shema'**, *sheh´-mah*; for the same as 8088; *Shema*, the name of a place in Pal. and of four Isr.:— Shema.

8088. שֵׁמַע **shêma'**, *shay´-mah*; from 8085; something *heard*, i.e. a *sound, rumor, announcement*; abstr. *audience*:— bruit, fame, hear (-ing), loud, report, speech, tidings.

8089. שֹׁמַע **shôma'**, *sho´-mah*; from 8085; a *report*:— fame.

8090. שְׁמָע **Shᵉmâ'**, *shem-aw´*; for 8087; *Shema*, a place in Pal.:— Shema.

8091. שָׁמָע **Shâmâ'**, *shaw-maw´*; from 8085; *obedient*; *Shama*, an Isr.:— Shama.

8092. שִׁמְעָא **Shim'â'**, *shim-aw´*; for 8093; *Shima*, the name of four Isr.:— Shimea, Shimei, Shamma.

8093. שִׁמְעָה **Shim'âh**, *shim-aw´*; fem. of 8088; *annunciation*; *Shimah*, an Isr.:— Shimeah.

8094. שְׁמָעָה **Shᵉmâ'âh**, *shem-aw-aw´*; for 8093; *Shemaah*, an Isr.:— Shemaah.

8095. שִׁמְעוֹן **Shim'ôwn**, *shim-öne´*; from 8085; *hearing*; *Shimon*, one of Jacob's sons, also the tribe desc. from him:— Simeon.

8096. שִׁמְעִי **Shim'iy**, *shim-ee´*; from 8088; *famous*; *Shimi*, the name of twenty Isr.:— Shimeah [*from the* marg.], Shimei, Shimhi, Shimi.

8097. שִׁמְעִי **Shim'iy**, *shim-ee´*; patron. from 8096; a *Shimite* (collect.) or desc. of Shimi:— of Shimi, Shimites.

8098. שְׁמַעְיָה **Shᵉma'yâh**, *shem-aw-yaw´*; or

שְׁמַעְיָהוּ **Shᵉma'yâhûw**, *shem-aw-yaw´-hoo*; from 8085 and 3050; *Jah has heard*; *Shemajah*, the name of twenty-five Isr.:— Shemaiah.

8099. שִׁמְעֹנִי **Shim'ôniy**, *shim-o-nee´*; patron. from 8095; a *Shimonite* (collect.) or desc. of Shimon:— tribe of Simeon, Simeonites.

8100. שִׁמְעָת **Shim'âth**, *shim-awth´*; fem. of 8088; *annunciation*; *Shimath*, an Ammonitess:— Shimath.

8101. שִׁמְעָתִי **Shim'âthiy**, *shim-aw-thee´*; patron. from 8093; a *Shimathite* (collect.) or desc. of Shimah:— Shimeathites.

8102. שֶׁמֶץ **shemets**, *sheh´-mets*; from an unused root mean. to *emit* a sound; an *inkling*:— a little.

8103. שִׁמְצָה **shimtsâh**, *shim-tsaw´*; fem. of 8102; scornful *whispering* (of hostile spectators):— shame.

8104. שָׁמַר **shâmar**, *shaw-mar´*; a prim. root; prop. to *hedge* about (as with thorns), i.e. *guard*; gen. to *protect, attend to*, etc.:— beware, be circumspect, take heed (to self), keep (-er, self), mark, look narrowly, observe, preserve, regard, reserve, save (self), sure, (that lay) wait (for), watch (-man).

8105. שֶׁמֶר **shemer**, *sheh´-mer*; from 8104; something *preserved*, i.e. the *settlings* (plur. only) of wine:— dregs, (wines on the) lees.

8106. שֶׁמֶר **Shemer**, *sheh´-mer*; the same as 8105; *Shemer*, the name of three Isr.:— Shamer, Shemer.

8107. שִׁמֻּר **shimmûr**, *shim-moor´*; from 8104; an *observance*:— × be (much) observed.

שֹׁמֵר **Shômêr**. See 7763.

8108. שָׁמְרָה **shomrâh**, *shom-raw´*; fem. of an unused noun from 8104 mean. a *guard; watchfulness*:— watch.

8109. שְׁמֻרָה **shᵉmûrâh**, *shem-oo-raw´*; fem. of pass. part. of 8104; something *guarded*, i.e. an *eye-lid*:— waking.

8110. שִׁמְרוֹן **Shimrôwn**, *shim-rone´*; from 8105 in its orig. sense; *guardianship*; *Shimron*, the name of an Isr. and of a place in Pal.:— Shimron.

8111. שֹׁמְרוֹן **Shômᵉrown**, *sho-mer-öne´*; from the act. part. of 8104; *watch-station*; *Shomeron*, a place in Pal.:— Samaria.

8112. שִׁמְרוֹן מְראוֹן **Shimrôwn Mᵉr'ôwn**, *shim-rone´ mer-one´*; from 8110 and a der. of 4754; *guard of lashing*; *Shimron-Meron*, a place in Pal.:— Shimron-meron.

8113. שִׁמְרִי **Shimriy**, *shim-ree´*; from 8105 in its orig. sense; *watchful*; *Shimri*, the name of four Isr.:— Shimri.

8114. שְׁמַרְיָה **Shᵉmaryâh**, *shem-ar-yaw´*; or

שְׁמַרְיָהוּ **Shᵉmaryâhûw**, *shem-ar-yaw´-hoo*; from 8104 and 3050; *Jah has guarded; Shemarjah*, the name of four Isr.:— Shamariah, Shemariah.

8070. שְׁמָרִימוֹת **Shᵉmâriymôwth**. See 8070.

8115. שָׁמְרַיִן **Shomrayin** (Chald.), *shom-rah´-yin*; corresp. to 8111; *Shomrain*, a place in Pal.:— Samaria.

8116. שִׁמְרִיה **Shimriyth**, *shim-reeth´*; fem. of 8113; *female guard; Shimrith*, a Moabitess:— Shimrith.

8117. שִׁמְרֹנִי **Shimrôniy**, *shim-ro-nee´*; patron. from 8110; a *Shimronite* (collect.) or desc. of Shimron:— Shimronites.

8118. שֹׁמְרֹנִי **Shômᵉrôniy**, *sho-mer-o-nee´*; patrial from 8111; a *Shomeronite* (collect.) or inhab. of Shomeron:— Samaritans.

8119. שִׁמְרָת **Shimrâth**, *shim-rawth´*; from 8104; *guardship; Shimrath*, an Isr.:— Shimrath.

8120. שְׁמַשׁ **shᵉmash** (Chald.), *shem-ash´*; corresp. to the root of 8121 through the idea of *activity* impl. in day-light; to *serve*:— minister.

8121. שֶׁמֶשׁ **shemesh**, *sheh´-mesh*; from an unused root mean. to *be brilliant*; the *sun*; by impl. the *east*; fig. a *ray*, i.e. (arch.) a notched *battlement*:— + east side (-ward), sun [(rising)], + west (-ward), window. See also 1053.

8122. שֶׁמֶשׁ **shemesh** (Chald.), *sheh´-mesh*; corresp. to 8121; the *sun*:— sun.

8123. שִׁמְשׁוֹן **Shimshôwn**, *shim-shone´*; from 8121; *sunlight; Shimshon*, an Isr.:— Samson.

שִׁמְשַׁי **Shimshîy**. See 1030.

8124. שִׁמְשַׁי **Shimshay** (Chald.), *shim-shah´-ee*; from 8122; *sunny; Shimshai*, a Samaritan:— Shimshai.

8125. שַׁמְשְׁרַי **Shamshᵉray**, *sham-sher-ah´-ee*; appar. from 8121; *sunlike; Shamsherai*, an Isr.:— Shamsherai.

8126. שׁוּמָתִי **Shûmâthiy**, *shoo-maw-thee´*; patron. from an unused name from 7762 prob. mean. *garlic-smell*; a *Shumathite* (collect.) or desc. of Shumah:— Shumathites.

8127. שֵׁן **shên**, *shane*; from 8150; a *tooth* (as *sharp*); spec. (for 8143) *ivory*; fig. a *cliff*:— crag, × forefront, ivory, × sharp, tooth.

8128. שֵׁן **shên** (Chald.), *shane*; corresp. to 8127; a *tooth*:— tooth.

8129. שֵׁן **Shên**, *shane*; the same as 8127; *crag; Shen*, a place in Pal.:— Shen.

8130. שָׂנֵא **sânê'**, *saw-nay´*; a prim. root; to *hate* (personally):— enemy, foe, (be) hate (-ful, -r), odious, × utterly.

8131. שְׂנֵא **sᵉnê'** (Chald.), *sen-ay´*; corresp. to 8130:— hate.

8132. שָׁנָא **shânâ'**, *shaw-naw´*; a prim. root; to *alter*:— change.

8133. שְׁנָא **shᵉnâ'** (Chald.), *shen-aw´*; corresp. to 8132:— alter, change, (be) diverse.

שֵׁנָא **shênâ'**. See 8142.

8134. שִׁנְאָב **Shin'âb**, *shin-awb´*; prob. from 8132 and 1; a *father has turned; Shinab*, a Canaanite:— Shinab.

8135. שִׂנְאָה **sin'âh**, *sin-aw´*; from 8130; *hate*:— + exceedingly, hate (-ful, -red).

8136. שִׁנְאָן **shin'ân**, *shin-awn´*; from 8132; *change*, i.e. *repetition*:— × angels.

8137. שֶׁנְאַצַּר **Shen'atstsar**, *shen-ats-tsar´*; appar. of Bab. or.; *Shenatstsar*, an Isr.:— Senazar.

8138. שָׁנָה **shânâh**, *shaw-naw´*; a prim. root; to *fold*, i.e. *duplicate* (lit. or fig.); by impl. to *transmute* (tran. or intr.):— do (speak, strike) again, alter, double, (be given to) change, disguise, (be) diverse, pervert, prefer, repeat, return, do the second time.

8139. שְׁנָה **shᵉnâh** (Chald.), *shen-aw´*; corresp. to 8142:— sleep.

8140. שְׁנָה **shᵉnâh** (Chald.), *shen-aw´*; corresp. to 8141:— year.

8141. שָׁנֶה **shâneh** (in plur. only), *shaw-neh´*; or (fem.)

שָׁנָה **shânâh**, *shaw-naw´*; from

8138; a *year* (as a *revolution* of time):— + whole age, × long, + old, year (× -ly).

8142. שֵׁנָה shênâh, *shay-naw´*; or

שֵׁנָא shênâ' (Psa. 127:2), *shay-naw´*; from 3462; *sleep:*— sleep.

8143. שֶׁנְהַבִּים shenhabbîym, *shen-hab-beem´*; from 8127 and the plur. appar. of a for. word; prob. *tooth of elephants,* i.e. *ivory tusk:*— ivory.

8144. שָׁנִי shânîy, *shaw-nee´*; of uncert. der.; *crimson,* prop. the insect or its color, also stuff dyed with it:— crimson, scarlet (thread).

8145. שֵׁנִי shênîy, *shay-nee´*; from 8138; prop. *double,* i.e. *second;* also adv. *again:*— again, either [of them], (an-) other, second (time).

8146. שָׂנִיא sânîy', *saw-nee´*; from 8130; *hated:*— hated.

8147. שְׁנַיִם shenayim, *shen-ah´-yim;* dual of 8145; fem.

שְׁתַּיִם shettayim, *shet-tah´-yim;* two; also (as ord.) *twofold:*— both, couple, double, second, twain, + twelfth, + twelve, + twenty (sixscore) thousand, twice, two.

8148. שְׁנִינָה shenîynâh, *shen-ee-naw´;* from 8150; something *pointed,* i.e. a *gibe:*— byword, taunt.

8149. שְׂנִיר Shenîyr, *shen-eer´*; or

שְׂנִיר Senîyr, *sen-eer´*; from an unused root mean. to *be pointed; peak; Shenir* or *Senir,* a summit of Lebanon:— Senir, Shenir.

8150. שָׁנַן shânan, *shaw-nan´*; a prim. root; to *point* (tran. or intr.); intens. to *pierce;* fig. to *inculcate:*— prick, sharp (-en), teach diligently, whet.

8151. שָׁנַס shânaç, *shaw-nas´*; a prim. root; to *compress* (with a belt):— gird up.

8152. שִׁנְעָר Shin`âr, *shin-awr´*; prob. of for. der.; *Shinar,* a plain in Bab.:— Shinar.

8153. שְׁנָת shenâth, *shen-awth´*; from 3462; *sleep:*— sleep.

8154. שָׁסָה shâçâh, *shaw-saw´*; or

שָׁסָה shâsâh (Isa. 10:13), *shaw-saw´*; a prim. root; to *plunder:*— destroyer, rob, spoil (-er).

8155. שָׁסַס shâçaç, *shaw-sas´*; a prim. root; to *plunder:*— rifle, spoil.

8156. שָׁסַע shâça`, *shaw-sah´*; a prim. root; to *split* or *tear;* fig. to *upbraid:*— cleave, (be) cloven (I-footed), rend, stay.

8157. שֶׁסַע sheça`, *sheh´-sah;* from 8156; a *fissure:*— cleft, clovenfooted.

8158. שָׁסַף shâçaph, *shaw-saf´*; a prim. root; to *cut* in pieces, i.e. *slaughter:*— hew in pieces.

8159. שָׁעָה shâ`âh, *shaw-aw´*; a prim. root; to *gaze* at or about (prop. for help); by impl. to *inspect, consider, compassionate,* be *nonplussed* (as looking around in amazement) or *bewildered:*— depart, be dim, be dismayed, look (away), regard, have respect, spare, turn.

8160. שָׁעָה shâ`âh (Chald.), *shaw-aw´;*

from a root corresp. to 8159; prop. a *look,* i.e. a *moment:*— hour.

שְׁעוֹר se`ôwr. See 8184.

שְׁעוֹרָה se`ôwrâh. See 8184.

8161. שַׁעֲטָה sha`ăṭâh, *shah´-at-aw;* fem. from an unused root mean. to *stamp;* a *clatter* (of hoofs):— stamping.

8162. שַׁעַטְנֵז sha`aṭnêz, *shah-at-naze´;* prob. of for. der.; *linsey-woolsey,* i.e. *cloth* of linen and wool carded and spun together:— garment of divers sorts, linen and woollen.

8163. שָׂעִיר sâ`îyr, *saw-eer´*; or

שָׂעִר sâ`îr, *saw-eer´*; from 8175; *shaggy;* as noun, a *he-goat;* by anal. a *faun:*— devil, goat, hairy, kid, rough, satyr.

8164. שָׂעִיר sâ`îyr, *saw-eer´*; formed the same as 8163; a *shower* (as *tempestuous*):— small rain.

8165. שֵׂעִיר Sê`îyr, *say-eer´*; formed like 8163; *rough; Seir,* a mountain of Idumaea and its aboriginal occupants, also one in Pal.:— Seir.

8166. שְׂעִירָה se`îyrâh, *seh-ee-raw´;* fem. of 8163; a *she-goat:*— kid.

8167. שְׂעִירָה Se`îyrâh, *seh-ee-raw´;* formed as 8166; *roughness; Seirah,* a place in Pal.:— Seirath.

8168. שֹׁעַל shô`al, *sho´-al;* from an unused root mean. to *hollow* out; the *palm;* by extens. a *handful:*— handful, hollow of the hand.

שֻׁעָל shû`âl. See 7776.

8169. שַׁעַלְבִּים Sha`albîym, *shah-al-beem´;* or

שַׁעֲלַבִּין Sha`ălabbîyn, *shah-al-ab-been´;* plur. from 7776; *fox-holes; Shaalbim* or *Shaalabbin,* a place in Pal.:— Shaalabbin, Shaalbim.

8170. שַׁעַלְבֹנִי Sha`albônîy, *shah-al-bo-nee´;* patrial from 8169; a *Shaalbonite* or inhab. of Shaalbin:— Shaalbonite.

8171. שַׁעֲלִים Sha`ălîym, *shah-al-eem´;* plur. of 7776; *foxes; Shaalim,* a place in Pal.:— Shalim.

8172. שָׁעַן shâ`an, *shaw-an´*; a prim. root; to *support* one's self:— lean, lie, rely, rest (on, self), stay.

8173. שָׁעַע shâ`a`, *shaw-ah´*; a prim. root; (in a good acceptation) to *look* upon (with complacency), i.e. *fondle, please* or *amuse* (self); (in a bad one) to *look* about (in dismay), i.e. *stare:*— cry (out) [by confusion with 7768], dandle, delight (self), play, shut.

שָׁעַף sâ`îph. See 5587.

8174. שַׁעַף Sha`aph, *shah´-af;* from 5586; *fluctuation; Shaaph,* the name of two Isr.:— Shaaph.

8175. שָׂעַר sâ`ar, *saw-ar´*; a prim. root; to *storm;* by impl. to *shiver,* i.e. *fear:*— be (horribly) afraid, fear, hurl as a storm, be tempestuous, come like (take away as with) a whirlwind.

8176. שָׁעַר shâ`ar, *shaw-ar´*; a prim. root; to *split* or *open,* i.e. (lit., but only as denom. from 8179) to *act as gatekeeper* (see 7778): (fig.) to *estimate:*— think.

8177. שְׂעַר se`ar (Chald.), *seh-ar´*; corresp. to 8181; *hair:*— hair.

8178. שַׂעַר sa`ar, *sah´-ar;* from 8175; a *tempest;* also a *terror:*— affrighted, × horribly, × sore, storm. See 8181.

8179. שַׁעַר sha`ar, *shaw´-ar;* from 8176 in its orig. sense; an *opening,* i.e. *door* or *gate:*— city, door, gate, port (× -er).

8180. שַׁעַר sha`ar, *shaw´-ar;* from 8176; a *measure* (as a *section*):— [hundred-] fold.

שָׂעִר sâ`îr. See 8163.

8181. שֵׂעָר sê`âr, *say-awr´;* or

שַׂעַר sa`ar (Isa. 7:20), *sah´-ar;* from 8175 in the sense of *dishevelling; hair* (as if *tossed* or *bristling*):— hair (-y), × rough.

שֹׂעֵר shô`êr. See 7778.

8182. שֹׂעָר shô`âr, *sho-awr´;* from 8176; *harsh* or *horrid,* i.e. *offensive:*— vile.

8183. שְׂעָרָה se`ârâh, *seh-aw-raw´;* fem. of 8178; a *hurricane:*— storm, tempest.

8184. שְׂעֹרָה se`ôrâh, *seh-o-raw´;* or

שְׂעוֹרָה se`ôwrâh, *seh-o-raw´* (fem. mean. the *plant*); and (masc. mean. the *grain*); also

שְׂעֹר se`ôr, *seh-ore´;* or

שְׂעוֹר se`ôwr, *seh-ore´;* from 8175 in the sense of *roughness; barley* (as *villose*):— barley.

8185. שַׂעֲרָה sa`ărâh, *sah-ar-aw´;* fem. of 8181; *hairiness:*— hair.

8186. שַׂעֲרוּרָה sha`ărûwrâh, *shah-ar-oo-raw´;* or

שַׂעֲרִירִיָּה sha`ărîyrîyâh, *shah-ar-ee-ree-yaw´;* or

שַׂעֲרֻרִת sha`ărûrith, *shah-ar-oo-reeth´;* fem. from 8176 in the sense of 8175; something *fearful:*— horrible thing.

8187. שְׂעַרְיָה She`aryâh, *sheh-ar-yaw´;* from 8176 and 3050; *Jah has stormed; Shearjah,* an Isr.:— Sheariah.

8188. שְׂעֹרִים Se`ôrîym, *seh-o-reem´;* masc. plur. of 8184; *barley* grains; *Seorim,* an Isr.:— Seorim.

8189. שַׁעֲרַיִם Sha`ărayim, *shah-ar-ah´-yim;* dual of 8179; *double gates; Shaarajim,* a place in Pal.:— Shaaraim.

8186 שַׂעֲרִירִיָּה sha`ărîyrîyâh. See 8186.

שַׂעֲרֻרִת sha`ărûrith. See 8186.

8190. שַׁעֲשְׁגַז Sha`ashgaz, *shah-ash-gaz´;* of Pers. der.; *Shaashgaz,* a eunuch of Xerxes:— Shaashgaz.

8191. שַׁעֲשֻׁעַ sha`shûa`, *shah-shoo´-ah;* from 8173; *enjoyment:*— delight, pleasure.

8192. שָׁפָה shâphâh, *shaw-faw´;* a prim. root; to *abrade,* i.e. *bare:*— high, stick out.

8193. שָׂפָה sâphâh, *saw-faw´;* or (in dual and plur.)

שֶׂפֶת sepheth, *sef-eth´;* prob. from 5595 or 8192 through the idea of *termination* (comp. 5490); the *lip* (as a nat. boundary); by impl. *language;* by anal. a *margin* (of a vessel, water, cloth, etc.):— band, bank, binding, border, brim, brink, edge, language, lip, prating, (lsea-l) shore, side, speech, talk, lvainl words.

8194. שְׁפָה **shâphâh**, *shaw-faw´*; from 8192 in the sense of *clarifying*; a *cheese* (as *strained* from the whey):— cheese.

8195. שְׁפוֹ **Sh⁰phôw**, *shef-o´*; or

שְׁפִי **Sh⁰phîy**, *shef-ee´*; from 8192; *baldness* [comp. 8205]; *Shepho* or *Shephi*, an Idumaean:— Shephi, Shepho.

8196. שְׁפוֹט **sh⁰phôwṭ**, *shef-ote´*; or

שְׁפוּט **sh⁰phûwṭ**, *shef-oot´*; from 8199; a judicial *sentence*, i.e. *punishment*:— judgment.

8197. שְׁפוּפָם **Sh⁰phûwphâm**, *shef-oo-fawm´*; or

שְׁפוּפָן **Sh⁰phûwphân**, *shef-oo-fawn´*; from the same as 8207; *serpent-like; Shephupham* or *Shephuphan*, an Isr.:— Shephuphan, Shupham.

8198. שִׁפְחָה **shiphchâh**, *shif-khaw´*; fem. from an unused root mean. to *spread* out (as a *family*; see 4940); a *female slave* (as a member of the *household*):— (bond-, hand-) maid (-en, -servant), wench, bondwoman, womanservant.

8199. שָׁפַט **shâphaṭ**, *shaw-fat´*; a prim. root; to *judge*, i.e. pronounce *sentence* (for or against); by impl. to *vindicate* or *punish*; by extens. to *govern*; pass. to *litigate* (lit. or fig.):— + avenge, × that condemn, contend, defend, execute (judgment), (be a) judge (-ment), × needs, plead, reason, rule.

8200. שְׁפַט **sh⁰phaṭ** (Chald.), *shef-at´*; corresp. to 8199; to *judge*:— magistrate.

8201. שֶׁפֶט **shephet**, *sheh´-fet*; from 8199; a *sentence*, i.e. *infliction*:— judgment.

8202. שָׁפָט **Shâphâṭ**, *shaw-fawt´*; from 8199; *judge; Shaphat*, the name of four Isr.:— Shaphat.

8203. שְׁפַטְיָה **Sh⁰phaṭyâh**, *shef-at-yaw´*; or

שְׁפַטְיָהוּ **Sh⁰phaṭyâhûw**, *shef-at-yaw´-hoo*; from 8199 and 3050; *Jah has judged; Shephatjah*, the name of ten Isr.:— Shephatiah.

8204. שִׁפְטָן **Shiphṭân**, *shif-tawn´*; from 8199; *judge-like; Shiphtan*, an Isr.:— Shiphtan.

8205. שְׁפִי **sh⁰phîy**, *shef-ee´*; from 8192; *bareness*; concr. a *bare* hill or plain:— high place, stick out.

8206. שֻׁפִּים **Shuppîym**, *shoop-peem´*; plur. of an unused noun from the same as 8207 and mean. the same; *serpents; Shuppim*, an Isr.:— Shuppim.

8207. שְׁפִיפֹן **sh⁰phîyphôn**, *shef-ee-fone´*; from an unused root mean. the same as 7779; a kind of *serpent* (as *snapping*), prob. the *cerastes* or horned adder:— adder.

8208. שָׁפִיר **Shâphîyr**, *shaf-eer´*; from 8231; *beautiful; Shaphir*, a place in Pal.:— Saphir.

8209. שַׁפִּיר **sappîyr** (Chald.), *shap-peer´*; intens. of a form corresp. to 8208; *beautiful:— fair*.

8210. שָׁפַךְ **shâphak**, *shaw-fak´*; a prim. root; to *spill forth* (blood, a libation,

liquid metal; or even a solid, i.e. to *mound* up); also (fig.) to *expend* (life, soul, complaint, money, etc.); intens. to *sprawl* out:— cast (up), gush out, pour (out), shed (-der, out), slip.

8211. שֶׁפֶךְ **shephek**, *sheh´-fek*; from 8210; an *emptying* place, e.g. an ash-*heap*:— are poured out.

8212. שָׁפְכָה **shophkâh**, *shof-kaw´*; fem. of a der. from 8210; a *pipe* (for *pouring* forth, e.g. wine), i.e. the *penis*:— privy member.

8213. שָׁפֵל **shâphêl**, *shaw-fale´*; a prim. root; to *depress* or *sink* (expec. fig. to *humiliate*, intr. or tran.):— abase, bring (cast, put) down, debase, humble (self), be (bring, lay, make, put) low (-er).

8214. שְׁפַל **sh⁰phal** (Chald.), *shef-al´*; corresp. to 8213:— abase, humble, put down, subdue.

8215. שְׁפַל **sh⁰phal** (Chald.), *shef-al´*; from 8214; *low*:— basest.

8216. שֵׁפֶל **shêphel**, *shay´-fel*; from 8213; an *humble* rank:— low estate (place).

8217. שָׁפָל **shâphâl**, *shaw-fawl´*; from 8213; *depressed*, lit. or fig.:— base (-st), humble, low (-er, -ly).

8218. שִׁפְלָה **shiphlâh**, *shif-law´*; fem. of 8216; *depression*:— low place.

8219. שְׁפֵלָה **sh⁰phêlâh**, *shef-ay-law´*; from 8213; *Lowland*, i.e. (with the art.) the maritime slope of Pal.:— low country, (low) plain, vale (-ley).

8220. שִׁפְלוּת **shiphlûwth**, *shif-looth´*; from 8213; *remissness*:— idleness.

8221. שְׁפָם **Sh⁰phâm**, *shef-awm´*; prob. from 8192; *bare spot; Shepham*, a place in or near Pal.:— Shepham.

8222. שָׂפָם **sâphâm**, *saw-fawm´*; from 8193; the *beard* (as a *lip-piece*):— beard, (upper) lip.

8223. שָׁפָם **Shâphâm**, *shaw-fawm´*; formed like 8221; *baldly; Shapham*, an Isr.:— Shapham.

8224. שִׂפְמוֹת **Siphmôwth**, *sif-môth´*; fem. plur. of 8221; *Siphmoth*, a place in Pal.:— Siphmoth.

8225. שִׁפְמִי **Shiphmîy**, *shif-mee´*; patrial from 8221; a *Shiphmite* or inhab. of Shepham.— Shiphmite.

8226. שָׂפַן **sâphan**, *saw-fan´*; a prim. root; to *conceal* (as a valuable):— treasure.

8227. שָׁפָן **shâphân**, *shaw-fawn´*; from 8226; a species of *rock-rabbit* (from its *hiding*), i.e. prob. the *hyrax*:— coney.

8228. שֶׁפַע **shepha'**, *sheh´-fah*; from an unused root mean. to *abound; resources*:— abundance.

8229. שִׁפְעָה **shiph'âh**, *shif-aw´*; fem. of 8228; *copiousness*:— abundance, company, multitude.

8230. שִׁפְעִי **Shiph'îy**, *shif-ee´*; from 8228; *copious; Shiphi*, an Isr.:— Shiphi.

שָׂפַק שָׂפַק **sâphaq**. See 5606.

8231. שָׁפַר **shâphar**, *shaw-far´*; a prim. root; to *glisten*, i.e. (fig.) be (caus. *make*) *fair*:— × goodly.

8232. שְׁפַר **sh⁰phar** (Chald.), *shef-ar´*; corresp. to 8231; to *be beautiful*:— be acceptable, please, + think good.

8233. שֶׁפֶר **shepher**, *sheh´-fer*; from 8231; *beauty*:— × goodly.

8234. שֶׁפֶר **Shepher**, *sheh´-fer*; the same as 8233; *Shepher*, a place in the Desert:— Shapper.

8235. שִׁפְרָה **shiphrâh**, *shif-raw´*; from 8231; *brightness*:— garnish.

8236. שִׁפְרָה **Shiphrâh**, *shif-raw´*; the same as 8235; *Shiphrah*, an Israelitess:— Shiphrah.

8237. שַׁפְרוּר° **shaphrûwr**, *shaf-roor´*; from 8231; *splendid*, i.e. a *tapestry* or *canopy*:— royal pavilion.

8238. שְׁפַרְפַר **sh⁰pharphar** (Chald.), *shef-ar-far´*; from 8231; the *dawn* (as *brilliant* with aurora):— × very early in the morning.

8239. שָׁפַת **shâphath**, *shaw-fath´*; a prim. root; to *locate*, i.e. (gen.) *hang* on or (fig.) *establish, reduce*:— bring, ordain, set on.

8240. שָׁפָת **shâphâth**, *shaw-fawth´*; from 8239; a (double) *stall* (for cattle); also a (two-pronged) *hook* (for flaying animals on):— hook, pot.

8241. שֶׁצֶף **shetseph**, *sheh´-tsef*; from 7857 (for alliteration with 7110); an *outburst* (of anger):— little.

8242. שַׂק **saq**, *sak*; from 8264; prop. a *mesh* (as allowing a liquid to *run* through), i.e. coarse loose cloth or *sacking* (used in mourning and for bagging); hence, a *bag* (for grain, etc.):— sack (-cloth, -clothes).

8243. שָׁק **shâq** (Chald.), *shawk*; corresp. to 7785; the *leg*:— leg.

8244. שָׂקַד **sâqad**, *saw-kad´*; a prim. root; to *fasten*:— bind.

8245. שָׁקַד **shâqad**, *shaw-kad´*; a prim. root; to *be alert*, i.e. *sleepless*; hence, to *be on the lookout* (whether for good or ill):— hasten, remain, wake, watch (for).

8246. שָׁקַד **shâqad**, *shaw-kad´*; a denom. from 8247; to *be* (intens. *make*) *almond-shaped*:— make like (unto, after the fashion of) almonds.

8247. שָׁקֵד **shâqêd**, *shaw-kade´*; from 8245; the *almond* (tree or nut; as being the *earliest* in bloom):— almond (tree).

8248. שָׁקָה **shâqâh**, *shaw-kaw´*; a prim. root; to *quaff*, i.e. (caus.) to *irrigate* or *furnish a potion* to:— cause to (give, give to, let, make to) drink, drown, moisten, water. See 7937, 8354.

8249. שִׁקֻּו **shiqqûv**, *shik-koov´*; from 8248; (plur. collect.) a *draught*:— drink.

8250. שִׁקּוּי **shiqqûwy**, *shik-koo-ee´*; from 8248; a *beverage; moisture*, i.e. (fig.) *refreshment*:— drink, marrow.

8251. שִׁקּוּץ **shiqqûwts**, *shik-koots´*; or

שִׁקֻּץ **shiqqûts**, *shik-koots´*; from 8262; *disgusting*, i.e. *filthy*; espec. *idolatrous* or (concr.) an *idol*:— abominable filth (idol, -ation), detestable (thing).

8252. שָׁקַט **shâqaṭ**, *shaw-kat´*; a prim. root; to *repose* (usually fig.):— appease, idleness, (at, be at, be in, give) quiet (-ness), (be at, be in, give, have, take) rest, settle, be still.

8253. שֶׁקֶט **sheqeṭ**, *sheh´-keṭ;* from 8252; *tranquillity:*— quietness.

8254. שָׁקַל **shâqal**, *shaw-kal´;* a prim. root; to *suspend* or *poise* (espec. in trade):— pay, receive (-r), spend, × throughly, weigh.

8255. שֶׁקֶל **sheqel**, *sheh´-kel;* from 8254; prob. a *weight;* used as a commercial standard:— shekel.

8256. שָׁקָם **shâqâm**, *shaw-kawm´;* or (fem.)

שִׁקְמָה **shiqmâh**, *shik-maw´;* of uncert. der.; a *sycamore* (usually the tree):— sycamore (fruit, tree).

8257. שָׁקַע **shâqa'**, *shaw-kah´;* (abb. o Am. 8:8); a prim. root; to *subside;* by impl. to *be overflowed, cease;* caus. to *abate, subdue:*— make deep, let down, drown, quench, sink.

8258. שְׁקַעֲרוּרָה **sheqa'rûwrâh**, *shek-ah-roo-raw´;* from 8257; a *depression:*— hollow strake.

8259. שָׁקַף **shâqaph**, *shaw-kaf´;* a prim. root; prop. to *lean out* (of a window), i.e. (by impl.) *peep* or *gaze* (pass. *be a spectacle*):— appear, look (down, forth, out).

8260. שֶׁקֶף **sheqeph**, *sheh´-kef;* from 8259; a *loophole* (for *looking out*), to admit light and air:— window.

8261. שָׁקוּף **shâqûph**, *shaw-koof´;* pass. part. of 8259; an *embrasure* or *opening* [comp. 8260] with a bevelled jam:— light, window.

8262. שָׁקַץ **shâqats**, *shaw-kats´;* a prim. root; to *be filthy,* i.e. (intens.) to *loathe, pollute:*— abhor, make abominable, have in abomination, detest, × utterly.

8263. שֶׁקֶץ **sheqets**, *sheh´-kets;* from 8262; *filth,* i.e. (fig. and spec.) an *idolatrous object:*— abominable (-tion).

שִׁקֻּץ **shiqquts**. See 8251.

8264. שָׁקַק **shâqaq**, *shaw-kak´;* a prim. root; to *course* (like a beast of prey); by impl. to *seek* greedily:— have appetite, justle one against another, long, range, run (to and fro).

8265. שָׂקַר **sâqar**, *saw-kar´;* a prim. root; to *ogle,* i.e. *blink* coquettishly:— wanton.

8266. שָׁקַר **shâqar**, *shaw-kar´;* a prim. root; to *cheat,* i.e. *be untrue* (usually in words):— fail, deal falsely, lie.

8267. שֶׁקֶר **sheqer**, *sheh´-ker;* from 8266; an *untruth;* by impl. a *sham* (often adv.):— without a cause, deceit (-ful), false (-hood, -ly), feignedly, liar, + lie, lying, vain (thing), wrongfully.

8268. שֹׁקֶת **shôqeth**, *sho´-keth;* from 8248; a *trough* (for *watering*):— trough.

8269. שַׂר **sar**, *sar;* from 8323; a *head* person (of any rank or class):— captain (that had rule), chief (captain), general, governor, keeper, lord, (-task-) master, prince (-ipal), ruler, steward.

8270. שֹׁר **shôr**, *shore;* from 8324; a *string* (as *twisted* [comp. 8306]), i.e. (spec.) the umbilical cord (also fig. as the centre of strength):— navel.

8271. שְׁרֵא **sherê'** (Chald.), *sher-ay´;* a root corresp. to that of 8293; to *free, separate;* fig. to *unravel, commence;* by

impl. (of unloading beasts) to *reside:*— begin, dissolve, dwell, loose.

8272. שַׁרְאֶצֶר **Shar'etser**, *shar-eh´-tser;* of for. der.; *Sharetser,* the name of an Ass. and an Isr.:— Sharezer.

8273. שְׁרָב **shârâb**, *shaw-rawb´;* from an unused root mean. to *glare;* quivering *glow* (of the air), expec. the *mirage:*— heat, parched ground.

8274. שֵׁרֵבְיָה **Shêrêbyâh**, *shay-rayb-yaw´;* from 8273 and 3050; *Jah has brought heat; Sherebjah,* the name of two Isr.:— Sherebiah.

8275. שַׁרְבִיט **sharbîyṭ**, *shar-beet´;* for 7626; a *rod* of empire:— sceptre.

8276. שָׂרַג **sârag**, *saw-rag´;* a prim. root; to *intwine:*— wrap together, wreath.

8277. שָׂרַד **sârad**, *saw-rad´;* a prim. root; prop. to *puncture* [comp. 8279], i.e. (fig. through the idea of *slipping* out) to *escape* or survive:— remain.

8278. שְׂרָד **serâd**, *ser-awd´;* from 8277; *stitching* (as *pierced* with a needle):— service.

8279. שֶׂרֶד **sered**, *seh´-red;* from 8277; a (carpenter's) *scribing-awl* (for *pricking* or scratching measurements):— line.

8280. שָׂרָה **sârâh**, *saw-raw´;* a prim. root; to *prevail:*— have power (as a prince).

8281. שָׁרָה **shârâh**, *shaw-raw´;* a prim. root; to *free:*— direct.

8282. שָׂרָה **sârâh**, *saw-raw´;* fem. of 8269; a *mistress,* i.e. *female noble:*— lady, princess, queen.

8283. שָׂרָה **Sârâh**, *saw-raw´;* the same as 8282; *Sarah,* Abraham's wife:— Sarah.

8284. שָׁרָה **shârâh**, *shaw-raw´;* prob. fem. of 7791; a *fortification* (lit. or fig.):— sing [by *mistake for* 7891], wall.

8285. שֵׁרָה **shêrâh**, *shay-raw´;* from 8324 in its orig. sense of *pressing;* a *wristband* (as *compact* or *clasping*):— bracelet.

8286. שְׂרוּג **Serûwg**, *ser-oog´;* from 8276; *tendril; Serug,* a postdiluvian patriarch:— Serug.

8287. שָׁרוּחֶן **Shârûwchen**, *shaw-roo-khen´;* prob. from 8281 (in the sense of *dwelling* [comp. 8271] and 2580; *abode of pleasure; Sharuchen,* a place in Pal.:— Sharuhen.

8288. שְׂרוֹךְ **serôwk**, *ser-oke´;* from 8308; a *thong* (as *laced* or *tied*):— (shoe-) latchet.

8289. שָׁרוֹן **Shârôwn**, *shaw-rone´;* prob. abridged from 3474; *plain; Sharon,* the name of a place in Pal.:— Lasharon, Sharon.

8290. שָׁרוֹנִי **Shârôwniy**, *shaw-ro-nee´;* patrial from 8289; a *Sharonite* or inhab. of Sharon:— Sharonite.

8291. שָׂרוּק **sarûwq**, *sar-ook´;* pass. part. from the same as 8321; a *grapevine:*— principal plant. See 8320, 8321.

8292. שְׁרוּקָה **sherûwqâh**, *sher-oo-kaw´;* or (by perm.)

שְׁרִיקָה **sherîyqâh**, *sher-ee-kaw´;* fem. pass. part. of 8319; a *whistling* (in scorn); by anal. a *piping:*— bleating, hissing.

8293. שֵׁרוּת **shêrûwth**, *shay-rooth´;* from 8281 abb.; *freedom:*— remnant.

8294. שֶׂרַח **Serach**, *seh´-rakh;* by perm. for 5629; *superfluity; Serach,* an Israelitess:— Sarah, Serah.

8295. שָׂרַט **sâraṭ**, *saw-rat´;* a prim. root; to *gash:*— cut in pieces, make [cuttings] pieces.

8296. שֶׂרֶט **sereṭ**, *seh´-ret;* and

שָׂרֶטֶת **sâreṭeth**, *saw-reh´-teth;* from 8295; an *incision:*— cutting.

8297. שָׂרַי **Sâray**, *saw-rah´-ee;* from 8269; *dominative; Sarai,* the wife of Abraham:— Sarai.

8298. שָׁרַי **Shâray**, *shaw-rah´-ee;* prob. from 8324; *hostile; Sharay,* an Isr.:— Sharai.

8299. שָׂרִיג **sârîyg**, *saw-reeg´;* from 8276; a *tendril* (as *intwining*):— branch.

8300. שָׂרִיד **sârîyd**, *saw-reed´;* from 8277; a *survivor:*— × alive, left, remain (-ing), remnant, rest.

8301. שָׂרִיד **Sârîyd**, *saw-reed´;* the same as 8300; *Sarid,* a place in Pal.:— Sarid.

8302. שִׁרְיוֹן **shiryôwn**, *shir-yone´;* or

שִׁרְיֹן **shiryôn**, *shir-yone´;* and

שִׁרְיָן **shiryân**, *shir-yawn´;* also (fem.)

שִׁרְיָה **shiryâh**, *shir-yaw´;* and

שִׁרְיוֹנָה **shiryôwnâh**, *shir-yo-naw´;* from 8281 in the orig. sense of *turning;* a *corslet* (as if *twisted*):— breastplate, coat of mail, habergeon, harness. See 5630.

8303. שִׁרְיוֹן **Shiryôwn**, *shir-yone´;* and

שִׁרְיֹן **Siryôn**, *sir-yone´;* the same as 8304 (i.e. *sheeted* with snow); *Shirjon* or *Sirjon,* a peak of the Lebanon:— Sirion.

8304. שְׂרָיָה **Serâyâh**, *ser-aw-yaw´;* or

שְׂרָיָהוּ **Serâyâhûw**, *ser-aw-yaw´-hoo;* from 8280 and 3050; *Jah has prevailed; Serajah,* the name of nine Isr.:— Seraiah.

8305. שְׂרִיקָה **serîyqâh**, *ser-ee-kaw´;* from the same as 8321 in the orig. sense of *piercing; hetchelling* (or combing flax), i.e. (concr.) *tow* (by extens. *linen* cloth):— fine.

8306. שָׂרִיר **sârîyr**, *shaw-reer´;* from 8324 in the orig. sense as in 8270 (comp. 8326); a *cord,* i.e. (by anal.) *sinew:*— navel.

8307. שְׂרִירוּת **sherîyrûwth**, *sher-ee-rooth´;* from 8324 in the sense of *twisted,* i.e. *firm; obstinacy:*— imagination, lust.

8308. שָׂרַךְ **sârak**, *saw-rak´;* a prim. root; to *interlace:*— traverse.

8309. שְׂרֵמָה **sherêmâh**, *sher-ay-maw´;* prob. by an orth. err. for 7709; a *common:*— field.

8310. שַׂרְסְכִים **Sarçekîym**, *sar-seh-keem´;* of for. der.; *Sarsekim,* a Bab. general:— Sarsechim.

8311. שָׂרַע **sâra'**, *saw-rah´;* a prim. root; to *prolong,* i.e. (reflex.) *be deformed* by excess of members:— stretch out self, (have any) superfluous thing.

8312. שְׂרָף **sar'aph**, *sar-af´*; for 5587; *cogitation:*— thought.

8313. שָׂרַף **sâraph**, *saw-raf´*; a prim. root; to *be* (caus. *set*) *on fire:*— (cause to, make a) burn (I-ingl, up) kindle, × utterly.

8314. שָׂרָף **sâraph**, *saw-rawf´*; from 8313; *burning*, i.e. (fig.) *poisonous* (serpent); spec. a *saraph* or symb. creature (from their copper color):— fiery (serpent), seraph.

8315. שָׂרָף **Sâraph**, *saw-raf´*; the same as 8314; *Saraph*, an Isr.:— Saraph.

8316. שְׂרֵפָה **serêphâh**, *ser-ay-faw´*; from 8313; *cremation:*— burning.

8317. שָׂרַץ **shârats**, *shaw-rats´*; a prim. root; to *wriggle*, i.e. (by impl.) *swarm or abound:*— breed (bring forth, increase) abundantly (in abundance), creep, move.

8318. שֶׁרֶץ **sherets**, *sheh´-rets*; from 8317; a *swarm*, i.e. active mass of minute animals:— creep (-ing thing), move (-ing creature).

8319. שָׁרַק **shâraq**, *shaw-rak´*; a prim. root; prop. to *be shrill*, i.e. to whistle or *hiss* (as a call or in scorn):— hiss.

8320. שָׂרֻק **sâruq**, *saw-rook´*; from 8319; *bright red* (as piercing to the sight), i.e. *bay:*— speckled. See 8291.

8321. שֹׂרֵק **sôrêq**, *so-rake´*; or

שׂוֹרֵק **sôwrêq**, *so-rake´*; and (fem.)

שֹׂרֵקָה **sôrêqâh**, *so-ray-kaw´*; from 8319 in the sense of *redness* (comp. 8320); a *vine* stock (prop. one yielding *purple* grapes, the richest variety):— choice (-st, noble) wine. Comp. 8291.

8322. שְׂרֵקָה **sherêqâh**, *sher-ay-kaw´*; from 8319; a *derision:*— hissing.

8323. שָׂרַר **sârar**, *saw-rar´*; a prim. root; to *have* (tran. *exercise*; refl. *get*) *dominion:*— × altogether, make self a prince, (bear) rule.

8324. שָׂרַר **shârar**, *shaw-rar´*; a prim. root; to *be hostile* (only act. part. an *opponent*):— enemy.

8325. שָׁרָר **Shârâr**, *shaw-rawr´*; from 8324; *hostile*; *Sharar*, an Isr.:— Sharar.

8326. שֹׁרֶר **shôrer**, *sho´-rer*; from 8324 in the sense of *twisting* (comp. 8270); the umbilical *cord*, i.e. (by extens.) a *bodice:*— navel.

8327. שָׁרַשׁ **shârash**, *shaw-rash´*; a prim. root; to *root*, i.e. strike into the soil, or (by impl.) to pluck from it:— (take, cause to take) root (out).

8328. שֶׁרֶשׁ **sheresh**, *sheh´-resh*; from 8327; a *root* (lit. or fig.):— bottom, deep, heel, root.

8329. שֶׁרֶשׁ **Sheresh**, *sheh´-resh*; the same as 8328; *Sheresh*, an Isr.:— Sharesh.

8330. שֹׁרֶשׁ **shôresh** (Chald.), *sho´-resh*; corresp. to 8328:— root.

8331. שַׁרְשָׁה **sharshâh**, *shar-shaw´*; from 8327; a *chain* (as rooted, i.e. *linked*):— chain. Comp. 8333.

8332. שְׁרֹשׁוּ° **sherôshûw** (Chald.), *sher-o-shoo´*; from a root corresp. to 8327; *eradication*, i.e. (fig.) *exile:*— banishment.

8333. שַׁרְשְׁרָה **sharsherâh**, *shar-sher-aw´*; from 8327 Icomp. 8331I; a *chain*; (arch.) prob. a *garland.*— chain.

8334. שָׁרַת **shârath**, *shaw-rath´*; a prim. root; to *attend* as a menial or worshipper; fig. to *contribute to:*— minister (unto), (do) serve (-ant, -ice, -itor), wait on.

8335. שָׁרֵת **shârêth**, *shaw-rayth´*; infin. of 8334; *service* (in the Temple):— minister (-ry).

8336. שֵׁשׁ **shêsh**, *shaysh*; or (for alliteration with 4897)

שְׁשִׁי **sheshiy**, *shesh-ee´*; for 7893; *bleached* stuff, i.e. *white* linen or (by anal.) *marble:*— × blue, fine (Itwinedl) linen, marble, silk.

8337. שֵׁשׁ **shêsh**, *shaysh*; masc.

שִׁשָּׁה **shishshâh**, *shish-shaw´*; a prim. number; *six* (as an overplus Isee 7797I beyond five or the fingers of the hand); as ord. *sixth:*— six (I-teen, -teenthl), sixth.

8338. שָׁוְשָׁו **shâwshâw**, *shaw-shaw´*; a prim. root; appar. to *annihilate:*— leave but the sixth part Iby confusion with 8341I.

8339. שֵׁשְׁבַּצַּר **Sheshbatstsar**, *shaysh-bats-tsar´*; of for. der.; *Sheshbatstsar*, Zerubbabel's Pers. name:— Sheshbazzar.

8340. שֵׁשְׁבַּצַּר **Sheshbatstsar** (Chald.), *shaysh-bats-tsar´*; corresp. to 8339:— Sheshbazzar.

8341. שָׁשָׁה **shâshâh**, *shaw-shaw´*; a denom. from 8337; to *sixth* or divide into *sixths:*— give the sixth part.

8342. שָׂשׂוֹן **sâsôwn**, *saw-sone´*; or

שָׂשֹׂן **sâsôn**, *saw-sone´*; from 7797; *cheerfulness*; spec. *welcome:*— gladness, joy, mirth, rejoicing.

8343. שָׁשַׁי **Shâshay**, *shaw-shah´-ee*; perh. from 8336; *whitish*; *Shashai*, an Isr.:— Shashai.

8344. שֵׁשַׁי **Shêshay**, *shay-shah´-ee*; prob. for 8343; *Sheshai*, a Canaanite:— Sheshai.

8345. שִׁשִּׁי **shishshiy**, *shish-shee´*; from 8337; *sixth*, ord. or (fem.) fractional:— sixth (part).

8346. שִׁשִּׁים **shishshiym**, *shish-sheem´*; multiple of 8337; *sixty:*— sixty, three score.

8347. שֵׁשַׁךְ **Shêshak**, *shay-shak´*; of for. der.; *Sheshak*, a symbol. name of Bab.:— Sheshach.

8348. שֵׁשָׁן **Shêshân**, *shay-shawn´*; perh. for 7799; *lily*; *Sheshan*, an Isr.:— Sheshan.

שׁוֹשָׁן **Shôshân**. See 7799.

8349. שָׁשַׁק **Shâshaq**, *shaw-shak´*; prob. from the base of 7785; *pedestrian*; *Shashak*, an Isr.:— Shashak.

8350. שָׁשַׁר **shâshar**, *shaw-shar´*; perh. from the base of 8324 in the sense of that of 8320; *red* ochre (from its *piercing* color):— vermillion.

8351. שֵׁת **shêth** (Num. 24:17), *shayth*; from 7582; *tumult:*— Sheth.

8352. שֵׁת **Shêth**, *shayth*; from 7896; *put*,

i.e. *substituted*; *Sheth*, third son of Adam:— Seth, Sheth.

8353. שֵׁת **shêth** (Chald.), *shayth*; or

שִׁת **shîth** (Chald.), *sheeth*; corresp. to 8337:— six (-th).

8354. שָׁתָה **shâthâh**, *shaw-thaw´*; a prim. root; to *imbibe* (lit. or fig.):— × assuredly, banquet, × certainly, drink (-er, -ing), drunk (× -ard), surely. IProp. *intens. of* 8248.I

8355. שְׁתָה **shethâh** (Chald.), *sheth-aw´*; corresp. to 8354:— drink.

8356. שָׁתָה **shâthâh**, *shaw-thaw´*; from 7896; a *basis*, i.e. (fig.) political or moral *support:*— foundation, purpose.

8357. שֵׁתָה **shêthâh**, *shay-thaw´*; from 7896; the *seat* (of the person):— buttock.

8358. שְׁתִי **shethiy**, *sheth-ee´*; from 8354; *intoxication:*— drunkenness.

8359. שְׁתִי **shethiy**, *sheth-ee´*; from 7896; a *fixture*, i.e. the *warp* in weaving:— warp.

8360. שְׁתִיָּה **shethiyâh**, *sheth-ee-yaw´*; fem. of 8358; *potation:*— drinking.

שְׁתִים **shettayim**. See 8147.

8361. שִׁתִּין **shittiyn** (Chald.), *shit-teen´*; corresp. to 8346 Icomp. 8353I; *sixty:*— threescore.

8362. שָׁתַל **shâthal**, *shaw-thal´*; a prim. root; to *transplant:*— plant.

8363. שְׁתִיל **shethiyl**, *sheth-eel´*; from 8362; a *sprig* (as if *transplanted*), i.e. *sucker:*— plant.

8364. שֻׁתַלְחִי **Shûthalchiy**, *shoo-thal-kee´*; patron. from 7803; a *Shuthalchite* (collect.) or desc. of Shuthelach:— Shuthalhites.

שָׁתָם **sâtham**. See 5640.

8365. שָׁתַם **shâtham**, *shaw-tham´*; a prim. root; to *unveil* (fig.):— be open.

8366. שָׁתַן **shâthan**, *shaw-than´*; a prim. root; (caus.) to *make water*, i.e. *urinate:*— piss.

8367. שָׁתַק **shâthaq**, *shaw-thak´*; a prim. root; to *subside:*— be calm, cease, be quiet.

8368. שָׂתַר **sâthar**, *saw-thar´*; a prim. root; to *break* out (as an eruption):— have in Ione'sl secret parts.

8369. שֵׁתָר **Shêthâr**, *shay-thawr´*; of for. der.; *Shethar*, a Pers. satrap:— Shethar.

8370. שְׁתַר בּוֹזְנַי **Shethar Bôwzenay**, *sheth-ar´ bo-zen-ah´-ee*; of for. der.; *Shethar-Bozenai*, a Pers. officer:— Shethar-boznai.

8371. שָׁתַת **shâthath**, *shaw-thath´*; a prim. root; to *place*, i.e. *array*; reflex. to *lie:*— be laid, set.

ת

8372. תָּא **tâ'**, *taw*; and (fem.)

תָּאָה **tâ'âh** (Ezek. 40:12), *taw-aw´*; from (the base of) 8376; a *room* (as circumscribed):— (little) chamber.

8373. תָּאַב **tâ'ab**, *taw-ab´*; a prim. root; to *desire:*— long.

8374. תָּאַב **tâ'ab**, *taw-ab´*; a prim. root Iprob. rather ident. with 8373 through the idea of *puffing* disdainfully at; comp. 3401; to *loathe* (mor.):— abhor.

8375. תַּאֲבָה **ta'âbâh**, *tah-ab-aw´*; from 8374 [comp. 15]; *desire*:— longing.

8376. תָּאָה **tâ'âh**, *taw-aw´*; a prim. root; to *mark* off, i.e. (intens.) *designate*:— point out.

8377. תְּאוֹ **t⁰ôw**, *teh-o´*; and

תּוֹא **tôw'** (the orig. form), *toh*; from 8376; a species of *antelope* (prob. from the white *stripe* on the cheek):— wild bull (ox).

8378. תַּאֲוָה **ta'ăvâh**, *tah-av-aw´*; from 183 (abb.); a *longing*; by impl. a *delight* (subj. *satisfaction*, obj. a *charm*):— dainty, desire, × exceedingly, × greedily, lust (ing), pleasant. See also 6914.

8379. תַּאֲוָה **ta'ăvâh**, *tah-av-aw´*; from 8376; a *limit*, i.e. *full extent*:— utmost bound.

8380. תְּאוֹם **tâ'ôwm**, *taw-ome´*; or

תָּאֹם **tâ'ôm**, *taw-ome´*; from 8382; a *twin* (in plur. only), lit. or fig.:— twins.

8381. תַּאֲלָה **ta'ălâh**, *tah-al-aw´*; from 422; an *imprecation*:— curse.

8382. תָּאַם **tâ'am**, *taw-am´*; a prim. root; to *be complete*; but used only as denom. from 8380, to *be* (caus. *make*) *twinned*, i.e. (fig.) *duplicate* or (arch.) *jointed*:— coupled (together), bear twins.

תָּאֹם **tâ'ôm**. See 8380.

8383. תְּאֻן **t⁰'ûn**, *teh-oon´*; from 205; *naughtiness*, i.e. *toil*:— lie.

8384. תְּאֵן **t⁰'ên**, *teh-ane´*; or (in the sing., fem.)

תְּאֵנָה **t⁰'ênâh**, *teh-ay-naw´*; perh. of for. der.; the *fig* (tree or fruit):— fig (tree).

8385. תַּאֲנָה **ta'ănâh**, *tah-an-aw´*; or

תֹּאֲנָה **tô'ănâh**, *to-an-aw´*; from 579; an *opportunity* or (subj.) *purpose*:— occasion.

8386. תַּאֲנִיָּה **ta'ănîyâh**, *tah-an-ee-yaw´*; from 578; *lamentation*:— heaviness, mourning.

8387. תַּאֲנַת שִׁלֹה **Ta'ănath Shîlôh**, *tah-an-ath´ shee-lo´*; from 8385 and 7887; *approach of Shiloh*; *Taanath-Shiloh*, a place in Pal.:— Taanath-shiloh.

8388. תָּאַר **tâ'ar**, *taw-ar´*; a prim. root; to *delineate*; reflex. to *extend*:— be drawn, mark out, [Rimmon-] methoar [by union with 7417].

8389. תֹּאַר **tô'ar**, *to´-ar*; from 8388; *outline*, i.e. *figure* or *appearance*:— + beautiful, × comely, countenance, + fair, × favoured, form, × goodly, × resemble, visage.

8390. תַּאֲרֵעַ **Ta'ărêa'**, *tah-ar-ay´-ah*; perh. from 772; *Taarea*, an Isr.:— Tarea. See 8475.

8391. תְּאַשּׁוּר **t⁰'ashshûwr**, *teh-ash-shoor´*; from 833; a species of *cedar* (from its *erectness*):— box (tree).

8392. תֵּבָה **têbâh**, *tay-baw´*; perh. of for. der.; a *box*:— ark.

8393. תְּבוּאָה **t⁰bûw'âh**, *teb-oo-aw´*; from 935; *income*, i.e. *produce* (lit. or fig.):— fruit, gain, increase, revenue.

8394. תָּבוּן **tâbûwn**, *taw-boon´*; and (fem.)

תְּבוּנָה **t⁰bûwnâh**, *teb-oo-naw´*; or

תּוֹבֻנָה **tôwbûnâh**, *to-boo-naw´*; from 995; *intelligence*; by impl. an *argument*; by extens. *caprice*:— discretion, reason, skilfulness, understanding, wisdom.

8395. תְּבוּסָה **t⁰bûwçâh**, *teb-oo-saw´*; from 947; a *treading down*, i.e. *ruin*:— destruction.

8396. תָּבוֹר **Tâbôwr**, *taw-bore´*; from a root corresp. to 8406; *broken region*; *Tabor*, a mountain in Pal., also a city adjacent:— Tabor.

8397. תֶּבֶל **tebel**, *teh´-bel*; appar. from 1101; *mixture*, i.e. *unnatural bestiality*:— confusion.

8398. תֵּבֵל **têbêl**, *tay-bale´*; from 2986; the *earth* (as *moist* and therefore inhabited); by extens. the *globe*; by impl. its *inhabitants*; spec. a partic. *land*, as Babylonia, Pal.:— habitable part, world.

תֻּבַל **Tûbal**. See 8422.

8399. תַּבְלִית **tablîyth**, *tab-leeth´*; from 1086; *consumption*:— destruction.

8400. תְּבַלֻּל **t⁰ballul**, *teb-al-lool´*; from 1101 in the orig. sense of *flowing*:— a *cataract* (in the eye):— blemish.

8401. תֶּבֶן **teben**, *teh´-ben*; prob. from 1129; prop. *material*, i.e. (spec.) refuse *haum* or stalks of grain (as *chopped* in threshing and used for fodder):— chaff, straw, stubble.

8402. תִּבְנִי **Tibnîy**, *tib-nee´*; from 8401; *strawy*; *Tibni*, an Isr.:— Tibni.

8403. תַּבְנִית **tabnîyth**, *tab-neeth´*; from 1129; *structure*; by impl. a *model*, *resemblance*:— figure, form, likeness, pattern, similitude.

8404. תַּבְעֵרָה **Tab'êrâh**, *tab-ay-raw´*; from 1197; *burning*; *Taberah*, a place in the Desert:— Taberah.

8405. תֵּבֵץ **Têbêts**, *tay-bates´*; from the same as 948; *whiteness*; *Tebets*, a place in Pal.:— Thebez.

8406. תְּבַר **t⁰bar** (Chald.), *teb-ar´*; corresp. to 7665; to *be fragile* (fig.):— broken.

8407. תִּגְלַת פִּלְאֶסֶר **Tiglath Pil'eçer**, *tig-lath´ pil-eh´-ser*; or

תִּגְלַת פְּלֶסֶר **Tiglath P⁰leçer**, *tig-lath pel-eh-ser*; or

תִּלְּגַת פִּלְנְאֶסֶר **Tilgath Piln⁰'eçer**, *til-gath´ pil-neh-eh´-ser*; or

תִּלְּגַת פִּלְנֶסֶר **Tilgath Pilneçer**, *til-gath´ pil-neh´-ser*; of for. der.; *Tiglath-Pileser* or *Tilgath-pilneser*, an Ass. king:— Tiglath-pileser, Tilgath-pilneser.

8408. תַּגְמוּל **tagmûwl**, *tag-mool´*; from 1580; a *bestowment*:— benefit.

8409. תִּגְרָה **tigrâh**, *tig-raw´*; from 1624; *strife*, i.e. *infliction*:— blow.

תֹּגַרְמָה **Tôgarmâh**. See 8425.

8410. תִּדְהָר **tidhâr**, *tid-hawr´*; appar. from 1725; *enduring*; a species of hardwood or *lasting* tree (perh. *oak*):— pine (tree).

8411. תְּדִירָא **t⁰dîyrâ'** (Chald.), *ted-ee-*

raw´; from 1753 in the orig. sense of *enduring*; *permanence*, i.e. (adv.) *constantly*:— continually.

8412. תַּדְמֹר **Tadmôr**, *tad-more´*; or

תַּמֹּר **Tammôr** (1 Kings 9:18), *tam-more´*; appar. from 8558; *palm*-city; *Tadmor*, a place near Pal.:— Tadmor.

8413. תִּדְעָל **Tid'âl**, *tid-awl´*; perh. from 1763; *fearfulness*; *Tidal*, a Canaanite:— Tidal.

8414. תֹּהוּ **tôhûw**, *to´-hoo*; from an unused root mean. to lie *waste*; a *desolation* (of surface), i.e. *desert*; fig. a *worthless* thing; adv. in *vain*:— confusion, empty place, without form, nothing, (thing of) nought, vain, vanity, waste, wilderness.

8415. תְּהוֹם **t⁰hôwm**, *teh-home´*; or

תְּהֹם **t⁰hôm**, *teh-home´*; (usually fem.) from 1949; an *abyss* (as a *surging* mass of water), espec. the *deep* (the *main* sea or the subterranean *water-supply*):— deep (place), depth.

8416. תְּהִלָּה **t⁰hillâh**, *teh-hil-law´*; from 1984; *laudation*; spec. (concr.) a *hymn*:— praise.

8417. תָּהֳלָה **tohŏlâh**, *to-hol-aw´*; fem. of an unused noun (appar. from 1984) mean. *bluster*; *braggadocio*, i.e. (by impl.) *fatuity*:— folly.

8418. תַּהֲלֻכָה **tahălûkâh**, *tah-hal-oo-kaw´*; from 1980; a *procession*:— × went.

תְּהֹם **t⁰hôm**. See 8415.

8419. תַּהְפֻּכָה **tahpûkâh**, *tah-poo-kaw´*; from 2015; a *perversity* or *fraud*:— (very) froward (-ness, thing), perverse thing.

8420. תָּו **tâv**, *tawv*; from 8427; a *mark*; by impl. a *signature*:— desire, mark.

8421. תּוּב **tûwb** (Chald.), *toob*; corresp. to 7725, to *come back*; spec. (tran. and ellip.) to *reply*:— answer, restore, return (an answer).

8422. תּוּבַל **Tûwbal**, *too-bal´*; or

תֻּבַל **Tûbal**, *too-bal´*; prob. of for. der.; *Tubal*, a postdiluvian patriarch and his posterity:— Tubal.

8423. תּוּבַל קַיִן **Tûwbal Qayin**, *too-bal´ kah´-yin*; appar. from 2986 (comp. 2981) and 7014; *offspring of Cain*; *Tubal-Kajin*, an antediluvian patriarch:— Tubal-cain.

תּוֹבֻנָה **tôwbûnâh**. See 8394.

8424. תּוּגָה **tûwgâh**, *too-gaw´*; from 3013; *depression* (of spirits); concr. a *grief*:— heaviness, sorrow.

8425. תּוֹגַרְמָה **Tôwgarmâh**, *to-gar-maw´*; or

תֹּגַרְמָה **Tôgarmâh**, *to-gar-maw´*; prob. of for. der.; *Togarmah*, a son of Gomer and his posterity:— Togarmah.

8426. תּוֹדָה **tôwdâh**, *to-daw´*; from 3034; prop. an *extension* of the hand, i.e. (by impl.) *avowal*, or (usually) *adoration*; spec. a *choir* of worshippers:— confession, (sacrifice of) praise, thanks (-giving, offering).

8427. תָּוָה **tâvâh**, *taw-vaw´*; a prim. root; to *mark* out, i.e. (prim.) *scratch* or (def.) *imprint*:— scrabble, set [a mark].

8428. תָּוָה **tâvâh**, *taw-vaw´*; a prim. root

[or perh. ident. with 8427 through a similar idea from *scraping* to pieces]; to *grieve*:— limit [by *confusion with* 8427].

8429. תְּוַהּ **tᵉvahh** (Chald.), *tev-ah´*; corresp. to 8539 or perh. to 7582 through the idea of *sweeping* to ruin [comp. 8428]; to *amaze*, i.e. (reflex. by impl.) *take alarm*:— be astonied.

8430. תּוֹחַ **Tôwach**, *to´-akh;* from an unused root mean. to *depress; humble; Toach*, an Isr.:— Toah.

8431. תּוֹחֶלֶת **tôwcheleth**, *to-kheh´-leth;* from 3176; *expectation:*— hope.

8432. תָּוֶךְ **tâvek**, *taw´-vek;* from an unused root mean. to *sever;* a *bisection*, i.e. (by impl.) the *centre:*— among (-st), × between, half, × (there-, where-) in (-to), middle, mid [-night], midst (among), × out (of), × through, × with (-in).

8433. תּוֹכֵחָה **tôwkêchâh**, *to-kay-khaw´;* and

תּוֹכַחַת **tôwkachath**, *to-kakh´-ath;* from 3198; *chastisement;* fig. (by words) *correction, refutation, proof* (even in defence):— argument, × chastened, correction, reasoning, rebuke, reproof, × be (often) reproved.

תּוּכִּי **tûwkkîy**. See 8500.

8434. תּוֹלָד **Tôwlâd**, *to-lawd´;* from 3205; *posterity; Tolad*, a place in Pal.:— Tolad. Comp. 513.

8435. תּוֹלְדָה **tôwlᵉdâh**, *to-led-aw´;* or

תֹּלְדָה **tôlᵉdâh**, *to-led-aw´;* from 3205; (plur. only) *descent*, i.e. *family;* (fig.) *history:*— birth, generations.

8436. תּוּלוֹן **Tûwlôn**, *too-lone´;* from 8524; *suspension; Tulon*, an Isr.:— Tilon [from the marg.].

8437. תּוֹלָל **tôwlâl**, *to-lawl´;* from 3213; *causing to howl*, i.e. an *oppressor:*— that wasted.

8438. תּוֹלָע **tôwlâ'**, *to-law´;* and (fem.)

תּוֹלֵעָה **tôwlê'âh**, *to-lay-aw´;* or

תּוֹלַעַת **tôwla'ath**, *to-lah´-ath;* or

תֹּלַעַת **tôla'ath**, *to-lah´-ath;* from 3216; a *maggot* (as voracious); spec. (often with ellip. of 8144) the crimson-*grub*, but used only (in this connection) of the color from it, and cloths dyed therewith:— crimson, scarlet, worm.

8439. תּוֹלָע **Tôwlâ'**, *to-law´;* the same as 8438; *worm; Tola*, the name of two Isr.:— Tola.

8440. תּוֹלָעִי **Tôwlâ'îy**, *to-law-ee´;* patron. from 8439; a *Tolaite* (collect.) or desc. of Tola:— Tolaites.

8441. תּוֹעֵבָה **tôw'êbâh**, *to-ay-baw´;* or

תֹּעֵבָה **tô'êbâh**, *to-ay-baw´;* fem. act. part. of 8581; prop. something *disgusting* (mor.), i.e. (as noun) an *abhorrence;* espec. *idolatry* or (concr.) an *idol:*— abominable (custom, thing), abomination.

8442. תּוֹעָה **tôw'âh**, *to-aw´;* fem. act. part. of 8582; *mistake*, i.e. (mor.) *impiety*, or (political) *injury:*— error, hinder.

8443. תּוֹעָפָה **tôw'âphâh**, *to-aw-faw´;*

from 3286; (only in plur. collect.) *weariness*, i.e. (by impl.) *toil* (*treasure* so obtained) or *speed:*— plenty, strength.

8444. תּוֹצָאָה **tôwtsâ'âh**, *to-tsaw-aw´;* or

תֹּצָאָה **tôtsâ'âh**, *to-tsaw-aw´;* from 3318; (only in plur. collect.) *exit*, i.e. (geographical) *boundary*, or (fig.) *deliverance*, (act.) *source:*— border (-s), going (-s) forth (out), issues, outgoings.

8445. תּוֹקַהַת **Tôwqahath**, *to-kah´-ath;* from the same as 3349; *obedience; Tokahath*, an Isr.:— Tikvath [by correction for 8616].

8446. תּוּר **tûwr**, *toor;* a prim. root; to *meander* (caus. *guide*) about, espec. for trade or reconnoitring:— chap [-man], sent to descry, be excellent, merchant [-man], search (out), seek, (e-) spy (out).

8447. תּוֹר **tôwr**, *tore;* or

תֹּר **tôr**, *tore;* from 8446; a *succession*, i.e. a *string* or (abstr.) *order:*— border, row, turn.

8448. תּוֹר **tôwr**, *tore;* prob. the same as 8447; a *manner* (as a sort of *turn*):— estate.

8449. תּוֹר **tôwr**, *tore;* or

תֹּר **tôr**, *tore;* prob. the same as 8447; a *ring*-dove, often (fig.) as a term of endearment:— (turtle) dove.

8450. תּוֹר **tôwr** (Chald.), *tore;* corresp. (by perm.) to 7794; a *bull:*— bullock, ox.

8451. תּוֹרָה **tôwrâh**, *to-raw´;* or

תֹּרָה **tôrâh**, *to-raw´;* from 3384; a *precept* or *statute*, espec. the *Decalogue* or *Pentateuch:*— law.

8452. תּוֹרָה **tôwrâh**, *to-raw´;* prob. fem. of 8448; a *custom:*— manner.

8453. תּוֹשָׁב **tôwshâb**, *to-shawb´;* or

תֹּשָׁב **tôshâb** (1 Kings 17:1), *to-shawb´;* from 3427; a *dweller* (but not outlandish [5237]); espec. (as distinguished from a native citizen [act. part. of 3427] and a temporary inmate [1616] or mere lodger [3885]) resident *alien:*— foreigner, inhabitant, sojourner, stranger.

8454. תּוּשִׁיָּה **tûwshîyâh**, *too-shee-yaw´;* or

תֻּשִׁיָּה **tûshîyâh**, *too-shee-yaw´;* from an unused root prob. mean. to *substantiate; support* or (by impl.) *ability*, i.e. (direct) *help*, (in purpose) an *undertaking*, (intellectual) *understanding:*— enterprise, that which (thing as it) is, substance, (sound) wisdom, working.

8455. תּוֹתָח **tôwthâch**, *to-thawkh´;* from an unused root mean. to *smite;* a *club:*— darts.

8456. תָּזַז **tâzaz**, *taw-zaz´;* a prim. root; to *lop* off:— cut down.

8457. תַּזְנוּת **taznûwth**, *taz-nooth´;* or

תַּזְנֻת **taznûth**, *taz-nooth´;* from 2181; *harlotry*, i.e. (fig.) *idolatry:*— fornication, whoredom.

8458. תַּחְבֻּלָה **tachbûlâh**, *takh-boo-law´;* or

תַּחְבּוּלָה **tachbûwlâh**, *takh-boo-law´;* from 2254 as denom. from 2256; (only in plur.) prop. *steerage* (as a management of ropes), i.e. (fig.) *guidance* or

(by impl.) a *plan:*— good advice, (wise) counsels.

8459. תֹּחוּ **Tôchûw**, *to´-khoo;* from an unused root mean. to *depress; abasement; Tochu*, an Isr.:— Tohu.

8460. תְּחוֹת **tᵉchôwth** (Chald.), *tekh-ôth´;* or

תְּחֹת **tᵉchôth** (Chald.), *tekh-ôth´;* corresp. to 8478; *beneath:*— under.

8461. תַּחְכְּמֹנִי **Tachkᵉmônîy**, *takh-kem-o-nee´;* prob. for 2453; *sagacious; Tachkemoni*, an Isr.:— Tachmonite.

8462. תְּחִלָּה **tᵉchillâh**, *tekh-il-law´;* from 2490 in the sense of *opening;* a *commencement;* rel. *original* (adv. *-ly*):— begin (-ning), first (time).

8463. תַּחֲלוּא **tachălûw'**, *takh-al-oo´;* or

תַּחֲלֻא **tachălû'**, *takh-al-oo´;* from 2456; a *malady:*— disease, × grievous, (that are) sick (-ness).

8464. תַּחְמָס **tachmâç**, *takh-mawce´;* from 2554; a species of unclean bird (from its *violence*), perh. an *owl:*— night hawk.

8465. תַּחַן **Tachan**, *takh´-an;* prob. from 2583; *station; Tachan*, the name of two Isr.:— Tahan.

8466. תַּחֲנָה **tachănâh**, *takh-an-aw´;* from 2583; (only plur. collect.) an *encampment:*— camp.

8467. תְּחִנָּה **tᵉchinnâh**, *tekh-in-naw´;* from 2603; *graciousness;* caus. *entreaty:*— favour, grace, supplication.

8468. תְּחִנָּה **Tᵉchinnâh**, *tekh-in-naw´;* the same as 8467; *Techinnah*, an Isr.:— Tehinnah.

8469. תַּחֲנוּן **tachănûwn**, *takh-an-oon´;* or (fem.)

תַּחֲנוּנָה **tachănûwnâh**, *takh-an-oo-naw´;* from 2603; earnest *prayer:*— intreaty, supplication.

8470. תַּחֲנִי **Tachăniy**, *takh-an-ee´;* patron. from 8465; a *Tachanite* (collect.) or desc. of Tachan:— Tahanites.

8471. תַּחְפַּנְחֵס **Tachpanchêç**, *takh-pan-khace´;* or

תְּחַפְנְחֵס **Tᵉchaphnᵉchêç** (Ezek. 30:18), *tekh-af-nekh-ace´;* or

תַּחְפְּנֵס **Tachpᵉnêç** (Jer. 2:16), *takh-pen-ace´;* of Eg. der.; *Tachpanches, Techaphneches* or *Tachpenes*, a place in Egypt:— Tahapanes, Tahpanhes, Tehaphnehes.

8472. תַּחְפְּנֵיס **Tachpᵉnêyç**, *takh-pen-ace´;* of Eg. der.; *Tachpenes*, an Eg. woman:— Tahpenes.

8473. תַּחֲרָא **tachărâ'**, *takh-ar-aw´;* from 2734 in the orig. sense of 2352 or 2353; a linen *corslet* (as *white* or *hollow*):— habergeon.

8474. תַּחֲרָה **tachărâh**, *takh-aw-raw´;* a factitious root from 2734 through the idea of the *heat* of jealousy; to *vie* with a rival:— close, contend.

8475. תַּחְרֵעַ **Tachrêa'**, *takh-ray´-ah;* for 8390; *Tachrea*, an Isr.:— Tahrea.

8476. תַּחַשׁ **tachash**, *takh´-ash;* prob. of for. der.; a (clean) animal with fur, prob. a species of *antelope:*— badger.

8477. תַּחַשׁ **Tachash**, *takh´-ash;* the

same as 8476; *Tachash*, a rel. of Abraham:— Thahash.

8478. תַּחַת **tachath**, *takh'-ath*; from the same as 8430; the *bottom* (as *depressed*); only adv. *below* (often with prep. pref. *underneath*), in *lieu of*, etc.:— as, beneath, × flat, in (-stead), (same) place (where ... is), room, for ... sake, stead of, under, × unto, × when ... was mine, whereas, [where-] fore, with.

8479. תְּחוֹת **tachath** (Chald.), *takh'-ath*; corresp. to 8478:— under.

8480. תַּחַת **Tachath**, *takh'-ath*; the same as 8478; *Tachath*, the name of a place in the Desert, also of three Isr.:— Tahath.

תְּחֹת **t°chôth**. See 8460.

8481. תַּחְתּוֹן **tachtôwn**, *takh-tone'*; or
תַּחְתֹּן **tachtôn**, *takh-tone'*; from 8478; *bottommost*:— lower (-est), nether (-most).

8482. תַּחְתִּי **tachtîy**, *takh-tee'*; from 8478; *lowermost*; as noun (fem. plur.) the *depths* (fig. a *pit*, the *womb*):— low (parts, -er, -er parts, -est), nether (part).

8483. תַּחְתִּים חָדְשִׁי **Tachtîym Chodshîy**, *takh-teem' khod-shee'*; appar. from the plur. masc. of 8482 or 8478 and 2320; *lower* (ones) *monthly*; *Tachtim-Chodshi*, a place in Pal.:— Tahtim-hodshi.

8484. תִּיכוֹן **tîykôwn**, *tee-kone'*; or
תִּיכֹן **tîykôn**, *tee-kone'*; from 8432; *central*:— middle (-most), midst.

8485. תֵּימָא **Têymâ'**, *tay-maw'*; or
תֵּמָא **Têmâ'**, *tay-maw'*; prob. of for. der.; *Tema*, a son of Ishmael, and the region settled by him:— Tema.

8486. תֵּימָן **têymân**, *tay-mawn'*; or
תֵּמָן **têmân**, *tay-mawn'*; denom. from 3225; the *south* (as being on the *right* hand of a person facing the east):— south (side, -ward, wind).

8487. תֵּימָן **Têymân**, *tay-mawn'*; or
תֵּמָן **Têmân**, *tay-mawn'*; the same as 8486; *Teman*, the name of two Edomites, and of the region and desc. of one of them:— south, Teman.

8488. תֵּימְנִי **Têym°nîy**, *tay-men-ee'*; prob. for 8489; *Temeni*, an Isr.:— Temeni.

8489. תֵּימָנִי **Têymânîy**, *tay-maw-nee'*; patron. from 8487; a *Temanite* or desc. of Teman:— Temani, Temanite.

8490. תִּימָרָה **tîymârâh**, *tee-maw-raw'*; or
תִּמָרָה **tîmârâh**, *tee-maw-raw'*; from the same as 8558; a *column*, i.e. *cloud*:— pillar.

8491. תִּיצִי **Tîytsîy**, *tee-tsee'*; patrial or patron. from an unused noun of uncert. mean.; a *Titsite* or desc. or inhab. of an unknown Tits:— Tizite.

8492. תִּירוֹשׁ **tîyrôwsh**, *tee-roshe'*; or
תִּירֹשׁ **tîyrôsh**, *tee-roshe'*; from 3423 in the sense of *expulsion*; *must* or fresh grape-juice (as just *squeezed* out); by impl. (rarely) fermented *wine*:— (new, sweet) wine.

8493. תִּירְיָא **Tîyr°yâ'**, *tee-reh-yaw'*; prob. from 3372; *fearful*, *Tirja*, an Isr.:— Tiria.

8494. תִּירָס **Tîyrâç**, *tee-rawce'*; prob. of for. der.; *Tiras*, a son of Japheth:— Tiras.

תִּירֹשׁ **tîyrôsh**. See 8492.

8495. תַּיִשׁ **tayish**, *tah'-yeesh*; from an unused root mean. to *butt*; a *buck* or he-goat (as given to *butting*):— he goat.

8496. תֹּךְ **tôk**, *toke*; or
תּוֹךְ **tôwk** (Psa. 72:14), *toke*; from the same base as 8432 (in the sense of *cutting* to pieces); *oppression*:— deceit, fraud.

8497. תָּכָה **tâkâh**, *taw-kaw'*; a prim. root; to *strew*, i.e. *encamp*:— sit down.

8498. תְּכוּנָה **t°kûwnâh**, *tek-oo-naw'*; fem. pass. part. of 8505; *adjustment*, i.e. *structure*; by impl. *equipage*:— fashion, store.

8499. תְּכוּנָה **t°kûwnâh**, *tek-oo-naw'*; from 3559; or prob. ident. with 8498; something *arranged* or *fixed*, i.e. a *place*:— seat.

8500. תֻּכִּי **tukkîy**, *took-kee'*; or
תּוּכִּי **tûwkkîy**, *took-kee'*; prob. of for. der.; some imported creature, prob. a *peacock*:— peacock.

8501. תָּכָךְ **tâkâk**, *taw-kawk'*; from an unused root mean. to *dissever*, i.e. *crush*:— deceitful.

8502. תִּכְלָה **tiklâh**, *tik-law'*; from 3615; *completeness*:— perfection.

8503. תַּכְלִית **taklîyth**, *tak-leeth'*; from 3615; *completion*; by impl. an *extremity*:— end, perfect (-ion).

8504. תְּכֵלֶת **t°kêleth**, *tek-ay'-leth*; prob. for 7827; the cerulean *mussel*, i.e. the color (*violet*) obtained therefrom or stuff dyed therewith:— blue.

8505. תָּכַן **tâkan**, *taw-kan'*; a prim. root; to *balance*, i.e. *measure out* (by weight or dimension); fig. to *arrange*, *equalize*, through the idea of *levelling* (ment. *estimate*, *test*):— bear up, direct, be ([un-]) equal, mete, ponder, tell, weigh.

8506. תֹּכֶן **tôken**, *to'-ken*; from 8505; a fixed *quantity*:— measure, tale.

8507. תֹּכֶן **Tôken**, *to'-ken*; the same as 8506; *Token*, a place in Pal.:— Tochen.

8508. תָּכְנִית **toknîyth**, *tok-neeth'*; from 8506; *admeasurement*, i.e. *consummation*:— pattern, sum.

8509. תַּכְרִיךְ **takrîyk**, *tak-reek'*; appar. from an unused root mean. to *encompass*; a *wrapper* or robe:— garment.

8510. תֵּל **têl**, *tale*; by contr. from 8524; a *mound*:— heap, × strength.

8511. תָּלָא **tâlâ'**, *taw-law'*; a prim. root; to *suspend*; fig. (through *hesitation*) to be *uncertain*; by impl. (of mental *dependence*) to *habituate*:— be bent, hang (in doubt).

8512. תֵּל אָבִיב **Têl 'Âbîyb**, *tale aw-beeb'*; from 8510 and 24; *mound of green growth*; *Tel-Abib*, a place in Chaldaea:— Tel-abib.

8513. תְּלָאָה **t°lâ'âh**, *tel-aw-aw'*; from 3811; *distress*:— travail, travel, trouble.

8514. תַּלְאוּבָה **tal'ûwbâh**, *tal-oo-baw'*; from 3851; *desiccation*:— great drought.

8515. תְּלַאשַּׂר **T°la'ssar**, *tel-as-sar'*; or

8516. תְּלַשַּׂר **T°lassar**, *tel-as-sar'*; of for. der.; *Telassar*, a region of Assyria:— Telassar.

8516. תִּלְבֹּשֶׁת **talbôsheth**, *tal-bo'-sheth*; from 3847; a *garment*:— clothing.

8517. תְּלַג **t°lag** (Chald.), *tel-ag'*; corresp. to 7950; *snow*:— snow.

תִּלְגַת **Tilgath**. See 8407.

תִּלְדָּה **tôl°dâh**. See 8435.

8518. תָּלָה **tâlâh**, *taw-law'*; a prim. root; to *suspend* (espec. to *gibbet*):— hang (up).

8519. תְּלוּנָה **t°lûwnâh**, *tel-oo-naw'*; or
תְּלֻנָּה **t°lunnâh**, *tel-oon-naw'*; from 3885 in the sense of *obstinacy*; a *grumbling*:— murmuring.

8520. תֶּלַח **Telach**, *teh'-lakh*; prob. from an unused root mean. to *dissever*; *breach*; *Telach*, an Isr.:— Telah.

8521. תֵּל חַרְשָׁא **Têl Charshâ'**, *tale khar-shaw'*; from 8510 and the fem. of 2798; *mound of workmanship*; *Tel-Charsha*, a place in Bab.:— Tel-haresha, Tel-harsha.

8522. תְּלִי **t°lîy**, *tel-ee'*; prob. from 8518; a *quiver* (as *slung*):— quiver.

8523. תְּלִיתַי **t°lîythay** (Chald.), *tel-ee-thah'-ee*; or
תַּלְתִּי **taltiy** (Chald.), *tal-tee'*; ord. from 8532; *third*:— third.

8524. תָּלַל **tâlal**, *taw-lal'*; a prim. root; to *pile* up, i.e. *elevate*:— eminent. Comp. 2048.

8525. תֶּלֶם **telem**, *teh'-lem*; from an unused root mean. to *accumulate*; a *bank* or *terrace*:— furrow, ridge.

8526. תַּלְמַי **Talmay**, *tal-mah'-ee*; from 8525; *ridged*; *Talmai*, the name of a Canaanite and a Syrian:— Talmai.

8527. תַּלְמִיד **talmîyd**, *tal-meed'*; from 3925; a *pupil*:— scholar.

8528. תֵּל מֶלַח **Têl Melach**, *tale meh'-lakh*; from 8510 and 4417; *mound of salt*; *Tel-Melach*, a place in Bab.:— Tel-melah.

תְּלֻנָּה **t°lunnâh**. See 8519.

8529. תָּלַע **tâla'**, *taw-law'*; a denom. from 8438; to *crimson*, i.e. dye that color:— × scarlet.

תּוֹלַעַת **tôla'ath**. See 8438.

8530. תַּלְפִּיָּה **talpîyâh**, *tal-pee-yaw'*; fem. from an unused root mean. to *tower*; something *tall*, i.e. (plur. collect.) *slenderness*:— armoury.

תְּלַשַּׂר **T°lassar**. See 8515.

8531. תְּלַת **t°lath** (Chald.), *tel-ath'*; from 8532; a *tertiary* rank:— third.

8532. תְּלָת **t°lâth** (Chald.), *tel-awth'*; masc.
תְּלָתָה **t°lâthâh** (Chald.), *tel-aw-thaw'*; or
תְּלָתָא **t°lâthâ'** (Chald.), *tel-aw-thaw'*; corresp. to 7969; *three* or *third*:— third, three.

תַּלְתִּי **taltiy**. See 8523.

8533. תְּלָתִין **t°lâthîyn** (Chald.), *tel-aw-theen'*; mult. of 8532; *ten times three*:— thirty.

8534. תַּלְתַּל **taltal**, *tal-tal'*; by redupl.

from 8524 through the idea of *vibration*; a trailing bough (as *pendulous*):— bushy.

8535. תָּם **tâm**, *tawm*; from 8552; *complete*; usually (mor.) *pious*; spec. *gentle*, *dear*:— coupled together, perfect, plain, undefiled, upright.

8536. תָּם **tâm** (Chald.), *tawm*; corresp. to 8033; *there*:— × thence, there, × where.

8537. תֹּם **tôm**, *tome*; from 8552; *completeness*; fig. *prosperity*; usually (mor.) *innocence*:— full, integrity, perfect (-ion), simplicity, upright (-ly, -ness), at a venture. See 8550.

תֵּמָא **Têmâ'**. See 8485.

8538. תֻּמָּה **tummâh**, *toom-maw'*; fem. of 8537; *innocence*:— integrity.

8539. תָּמַהּ **tâmahh**, *taw-mah'*; a prim. root; to *be in consternation*:— be amazed, be astonished, marvel (-lously), wonder.

8540. תְּמַהּ **tᵉmahh** (Chald.), *tem-ah'*; from a root corresp. to 8539; a *miracle*:— wonder.

8541. תִּמָּהוֹן **timmâhôwn**, *tim-maw-hone'*; from 8539; *consternation*:— astonishment.

8542. תַּמּוּז **Tammûwz**, *tam-mooz'*; of uncert. der.; *Tammuz*, a Phoenician deity:— Tammuz.

8543. תְּמוֹל **tᵉmôwl**, *tem-ole'*; or

תְּמֹל **tᵉmôl**, *tem-ole'*; prob. for 865; prop. *ago*, i.e. a (short or long) *time since*; espec. *yesterday*, or (with 8032) *day before* yesterday:— + before (-time), + these [three] days, + heretofore, + time past, yesterday.

8544. תְּמוּנָה **tᵉmûwnâh**, *tem-oo-naw'*; or

תְּמֻנָה **tᵉmûnâh**, *tem-oo-naw'*; from 4327; *something portioned* (i.e. *fashioned*) out, as a *shape*, i.e. (indef.) *phantom*, or (spec.) *embodiment*, or (fig.) *manifestation* (of favor):— image, likeness, similitude.

8545. תְּמוּרָה **tᵉmûwrâh**, *tem-oo-raw'*; from 4171; *barter*, *compensation*:— (ex-) change (-ing), recompense, restitution.

8546. תְּמוּתָה **tᵉmûwthâh**, *tem-oo-thaw'*; from 4191; *execution* (as a doom):— death, die.

8547. תֶּמַח **Temach**, *teh'-makh*; of uncert. der.; *Temach*, one of the Nethinim:— Tamah, Thamah.

8548. תָּמִיד **tâmîyd**, *taw-meed'*; from an unused root mean. to *stretch*; prop. *continuance* (as indef. *extension*); but used only (attributively as adj.) *constant* (or adv. *constantly*); ellipt. the *regular* (daily) *sacrifice*:— alway (-s), continual (employment, -ly), daily, (in-) ever (-more), perpetual.

8549. תָּמִים **tâmîym**, *taw-meem'*; from 8552; *entire* (lit., fig. or mor.); also (as noun) *integrity*, *truth*:— without blemish, complete, full, perfect, sincerely (-ity), sound, without spot, undefiled, upright (-ly), whole.

8550. תֻּמִּים **Tummîym**, *toom-meem'*; plur. of 8537; *perfections*, i.e. (tech.) one of the epithets of the objects in the high-priest's breastplate as an emblem of *complete* Truth:— Thummim.

8551. תָּמַךְ **tâmak**, *taw-mak'*; a prim. root; to *sustain*; by impl. to *obtain*, *keep fast*; fig. to *help*, *follow close*:— (take, up-) hold (up), maintain, retain, stay (up).

תְּמֹל **tᵉmôl**. See 8543.

8552. תָּמַם **tâmam**, *taw-mam'*; a prim. root; to *complete*, in a good or a bad sense, lit. or fig., tran. or intr. (as follows):— accomplish, cease, be clean [pass-] ed, consume, have done, (come to an, have an, make an) end, fail, come to the full, be all gone, × be all here, be (make) perfect, be spent, sum, be (shew self) upright, be wasted, whole.

8553. תִּמְנָה **Timnâh**, *tim-naw'*; from 4487; a *portion* assigned; *Timnah*, the name of two places in Pal.:— Timnah, Timnath, Thimnathah.

תִּמְנָה **tᵉmûnâh**. See 8544.

8554. תִּמְנִי **Timniy**, *tim-nee'*; patrial from 8553; a *Timnite* or inhab. of Timnah:— Timnite.

8555. תִּמְנָע **Timnâ'**, *tim-naw'*; from 4513; *restraint*; *Timna*, the name of two Edomites:— Timna, Timnah.

8556. תִּמְנַת חֶרֶס **Timnath Chereç**, *tim-nath kheh'-res*; or

תִּמְנַת סֶרַח **Timnath Çerach**, *tim-nath seh'-rakh*; from 8553 and 2775; *portion of* (the) *sun*; *Timnath-Cheres*, a place in Pal.:— Timnath-heres, Timnath-serah.

8557. תֶּמֶס **temeç**, *teh'-mes*; from 4529; *liquefaction*, i.e. *disappearance*:— melt.

8558. תָּמָר **tâmâr**, *taw-mawr'*; from an unused root mean. to *be erect*; a *palm tree*:— palm (tree).

8559. תָּמָר **Tâmâr**, *taw-mawr'*; the same as 8558; *Tamar*, the name of three women and a place:— Tamar.

8560. תֹּמֶר **tômer**, *to'-mer*; from the same root as 8558; a *palm trunk*:— palm tree.

8561. תִּמֹּר **timmôr** (plur. only), *tim-more'*; or (fem.)

תִּמֹּרָה **timmôrâh** (sing. and plur.), *tim-mo-raw'*; from the same root as 8558; (arch.) a *palm*-like pilaster (i.e. *umbellate*):— palm tree.

תִּמֹּר **Tammôr**. See 8412.

תִּמָרָה **timârâh**. See 8490.

8562. תַּמְרוּק **tamrûwq**, *tam-rook'*; or

תַּמְרֻק **tamrûq**, *tam-rook'*; or

תַּמְרִיק **tamrîyq**, *tam-reek'*; from 4838; prop. a *scouring*, i.e. *soap* or *perfumery* for the bath; fig. a *detergent*:— × cleanse, (thing for) purification (-fying).

8563. תַּמְרוּר **tamrûwr**, *tam-roor'*; from 4843; *bitterness* (plur. as collect.):— × most bitter (-ly).

תַּמְרוּק **tamrûq** and

תַּמְרִיק **tamrîyq**. See 8562.

8564. תַּמְרוּר **tamrûwr**, *tam-roor'*; from the same root as 8558; an *erection*, i.e.

pillar (prob. for a guide-board):— high heap.

8565. תַּן **tan**, *tan*; from an unused root prob. mean. to *elongate*; a *monster* (as preternaturally formed), i.e. a *sea-serpent* (or other huge marine animal); also a *jackal* (or other hideous land animal):— dragon, whale. Comp. 8577.

8566. תָּנָה **tânâh**, *taw-naw'*; a prim. root; to *present* (a mercenary inducement), i.e. *bargain* with (a harlot):— hire.

8567. תָּנָה **tânâh**, *taw-naw'*; a prim. root [rather ident. with 8566 through the idea of *attributing* honor]; to *ascribe* (praise), i.e. *celebrate*, *commemorate*:— lament, rehearse.

8568. תַּנָּה **tannâh**, *tan-naw'*; prob. fem. of 8565; a female *jackal*:— dragon.

8569. תְּנוּאָה **tᵉnûw'âh**, *ten-oo-aw'*; from 5106; *alienation*; by impl. *enmity*:— breach of promise, occasion.

8570. תְּנוּבָה **tᵉnûwbâh**, *ten-oo-baw'*; from 5107; *produce*:— fruit, increase.

8571. תְּנוּךְ **tᵉnûwk**, *ten-ook'*; perh. from the same as 594 through the idea of *protraction*; a *pinnacle*, i.e. *extremity*:— tip.

8572. תְּנוּמָה **tᵉnûwmâh**, *ten-oo-maw'*; from 5123; *drowsiness*, i.e. *sleep*:— slumber (-ing).

8573. תְּנוּפָה **tᵉnûwphâh**, *ten-oo-faw'*; from 5130; a *brandishing* (in threat); by impl. *tumult*; spec. the official *undulation* of sacrificial offerings:— offering, shaking, wave (offering).

8574. תַּנּוּר **tannûwr**, *tan-noor'*; from 5216; a *fire-pot*:— furnace, oven.

8575. תַּנְחוּם **tanchûwm**, *tan-khoom'*; or

תַּנְחֻם **tanchûm**, *tan-khoom'*; and (fem.)

תַּנְחוּמָה **tanchûwmâh**, *tan-khoo-maw'*; from 5162; *compassion*, *solace*:— comfort, consolation.

8576. תַּנְחֻמֶת **Tanchûmeth**, *tan-khoo'-meth*; for 8575 (fem.); *Tanchumeth*, an Isr.:— Tanhumeth.

8577. תַּנִּין **tannîyn**, *tan-neen'*; or

תַּנִּים **tannîym** (Ezek. 29:3), *tan-neem'*; intens. from the same as 8565; a marine or land *monster*, i.e. *sea-serpent* or *jackal*:— dragon, sea-monster, serpent, whale.

8578. תִּנְיָן **tinyân** (Chald.), *tin-yawn'*; corresp. to 8147; *second*:— second.

8579. תִּנְיָנוּת **tinyânûwth** (Chald.), *tin-yaw-nooth'*; from 8578; a *second time*:— again.

8580. תַּנְשֶׁמֶת **tanshemeth**, *tan-sheh'-meth*; from 5395; prop. a hard *breather*, i.e. the name of two unclean creatures, a lizard and a bird (both perh. from changing color through their *irascibility*), prob. the *tree-toad* and the *waterhen*:— mole, swan.

8581. תָּעַב **tâ'ab**, *taw-ab'*; a prim. root; to *loathe*, i.e. (mor.) *detest*:— (make to be) abhor (-red), (be, commit more, do) abominable (-y), × utterly.

תּוֹעֵבָה **tô'êbâh**. See 8441.

8582. תָּעָה **tâ'âh**, *taw-aw'*; a prim. root; to *vacillate*, i.e. *reel* or *stray* (lit. or fig.); also caus. of both:— (cause to) go astray, deceive, dissemble, (cause to, make to) err, pant, seduce, (make to) stagger, (cause to) wander, be out of the way.

8583. תֹּעוּ Tô'ûw, *to´-oo;* or

תֹּעִי Tô'îy, *to´-ee;* from 8582; *error,* Tou or Toi, a Syrian king:— Toi, Tou.

8584. תְּעוּדָה tᵉ'ûwdâh, *teh-oo-daw´;* from 5749; *attestation,* i.e. a *precept, usage:*— testimony.

8585. תְּעָלָה tᵉ'âlâh, *teh-aw-law´;* from 5927; a *channel* (into which water is *raised* for irrigation); also a *bandage* or *plaster* (as placed *upon* a wound):— conduit, cured, healing, little river, trench, watercourse.

8586. תַּעֲלוּל ta'ălûwl, *tah-al-ool´;* from 5953; *caprice* (as a fit *coming on*), i.e. *vexation;* concr. a *tyrant:*— babe, delusion.

8587. תַּעֲלֻמָּה ta'ălummâh, *tah-al-oom-maw´;* from 5956; a *secret:*— thing that is hid, secret.

8588. תַּעֲנוּג ta'ănûwg, *tah-an-oog´;* or

תַּעֲנֻג ta'ănûg, *tah-an-oog´;* and (fem.)

תַּעֲנֻגָה ta'ănûgâh, *tah-ah-oog-aw´;* from 6026; *luxury:*— delicate, delight, pleasant.

8589. תַּעֲנִית ta'ănîyth, *tah-an-eeth´;* from 6031; *affliction* (of self), i.e. *fasting:*— heaviness.

8590. תַּעֲנָךְ Ta'ănâk, *tah-an-awk´;* or

תַּעְנָךְ Ta'nâk, *tah-nawk´;* of uncert. der.; *Taanak* or *Tanak,* a place in Pal.:— Taanach, Tanach.

8591. תָּעַע tâ'a', *taw-ah´;* a prim. root; to *cheat;* by anal. to *maltreat:*— deceive, misuse.

8592. תַּעֲצֻמָה ta'àtsûmâh, *tah-ats-oo-maw´;* from 6105; *might* (plur. collect.):— power.

8593. תַּעַר ta'ar, *tah´-ar;* from 6168; a *knife* or *razor* (as *making* bare): also a *scabbard* (as *being* bare, i.e. *empty*):— [pen-] knife, rasor, scabbard, shave, sheath.

8594. תַּעֲרֻבָה ta'ărûbâh, *tah-ar-oo-baw´;* from 6148; *suretyship,* i.e. (concr.) a *pledge:*— + hostage.

8595. תַּעְתֻּעַ ta'tûa', *tah-too´-ah;* from 8591; a *fraud:*— error.

8596. תֹּף tôph, *tofe;* from 8608 contr.; a *tambourine:*— tabret, timbrel.

8597. תִּפְאָרָה tiph'ârâh, *tif-aw-raw´;* or

תִּפְאֶרֶת tiph'ereth, *tif-eh´-reth;* from 6286; *ornament* (abstr. or concr., lit. or fig.):— beauty (-iful), bravery, comely, fair, glory (-ious), honour, majesty.

8598. תַּפּוּחַ tappûwach, *tap-poo´-akh;* from 5301; an *apple* (from its *fragrance*), i.e. the fruit or the tree (prob. includ. others of the *pome* order, as the quince, the orange, etc.):— apple (tree). See also 1054.

8599. תַּפּוּחַ Tappûwach, *tap-poo´-akh;* the same as 8598; *Tappuach,* the name of two places in Pal., also of an Isr.:— Tappuah.

8600. תְּפוֹצָה tᵉphôwtsâh, *tef-o-tsaw´;* from 6327; a *dispersal:*— dispersion.

8601. תֻּפִין tûphîyn, *too-feen´;* from 644; *cookery,* i.e. (concr.) a *cake:*— baked piece.

8602. תָּפֵל tâphêl, *taw-fale´;* from an unused root mean. to *smear; plaster* (as *gummy*) or *slime;* (fig.) *frivolity:*— foolish things, unsavoury, untempered.

8603. תֹּפֶל Tôphel, *to´-fel;* from the same as 8602; *quagmire; Tophel,* a place near the Desert:— Tophel.

8604. תִּפְלָה tiphlâh, *tif-law´;* from the same as 8602; *frivolity:*— folly, foolishly.

8605. תְּפִלָּה tᵉphillâh, *tef-il-law´;* from 6419; *intercession, supplication;* by impl. a *hymn:*— prayer.

8606. תִּפְלֶצֶת tiphletseth, *tif-leh´-tseth;* from 6426; *fearfulness:*— terrible. ·

8607. תִּפְסַח Tiphsach, *tif-sakh´;* from 6452; *ford; Tiphsach,* a place in Mesopotamia:— Tipsah.

8608. תָּפַף tâphaph, *taw-faf´;* a prim. root; to *drum,* i.e. play (as) on the tambourine:— taber, play with timbrels.

8609. תָּפַר tâphar, *taw-far´;* a prim. root; to *sew:*— (women that) sew (together).

8610. תָּפַס tâphas, *taw-fas´;* a prim. root; to *manipulate,* i.e. *seize;* chiefly to *capture, wield;* spec. to *overlay;* fig. to *use* unwarrantably:— catch, handle, (lay, take) hold (on, over), stop, × surely, surprise, take.

8611. תֹּפֶת tôpheth, *to´-feth;* from the base of 8608; a *smiting,* i.e. (fig.) *contempt:*— tabret.

8612. תֹּפֶת Tôpheth, *to´-feth;* the same as 8611; *Topheth,* a place near Jerusalem:— Tophet, Topheth.

8613. תָּפְתֶּה Tophteh, *tof-teh´;* prob. a form of 8612; *Tophteh,* a place of cremation:— Tophet.

8614. תִּפְתָּי tiphtay (Chald.), *tif-tah´-ee;* perh. from 8199; *judicial,* i.e. a *lawyer:*— sheriff.

תּוֹצָאָה tôtsâ'âh. See 8444.

8615. תִּקְוָה tiqvâh, *tik-vaw´;* from 6960; lit. a *cord* (as an *attachment* [comp. 6961]); fig. *expectancy:*— expectation ([-ted]), hope, live, thing that I long for.

8616. תִּקְוָה Tiqvâh, *tik-vaw´;* the same as 8615; *Tikvah,* the name of two Isr.:— Tikvah.

8617. תְּקוּמָה tᵉqûwmâh, *tek-oo-maw´;* from 6965; *resistfulness:*— power to stand.

8618. תְּקוֹמֵם tᵉqôwmêm, *tek-o-mame´;* from 6965; an *opponent:*— rise up against.

8619. תָּקוֹעַ tâqôwa', *taw-ko´-ah;* from 8628 (in the musical sense); a *trumpet:*— trumpet.

8620. תְּקוֹעַ Tᵉqôwa', *tek-o´-ah;* a form of 8619; *Tekoa,* a place in Pal.:— Tekoa, Tekoah.

8621. תְּקוֹעִי Tᵉqô'îy, *tek-o-ee´;* or

תְּקֹעִי Tᵉqô'îy, *tek-o-ee´;* patron. from 8620; a *Tekoite* or inhab. of Tekoah:— Tekoite.

8622. תְּקוּפָה tᵉqûwphâh, *tek-oo-faw´;* or

תְּקֻפָה tᵉqûphâh, *tek-oo-faw´;* from 5362; a *revolution,* i.e. (of the sun) *course,* (of time) *lapse:*— circuit, come about, end.

8623. תַּקִּיף taqqîyph, *tak-keef´;* from 8630; *powerful:*— mightier.

8624. תַּקִּיף taqqîyph (Chald.), *tak-keef´;* corresp. to 8623:— mighty, strong.

8625. תְּקַל tᵉqal (Chald.), *tek-al´;* corresp. to 8254; to *balance:*— Tekel, be weighed.

8626. תָּקַן tâqan, *taw-kan´;* a prim. root; to *equalize,* i.e. *straighten* (intr. or tran.); fig. to *compose:*— set in order, make straight.

8627. תְּקַן tᵉqan (Chald.), *tek-an´;* corresp. to 8626; to *straighten* up, i.e. *confirm:*— establish.

8628. תָּקַע tâqa', *taw-kah´;* a prim. root; to *clatter,* i.e. *slap* (the hands together), *clang* (an instrument); by anal. to *drive* (a nail or tent-pin, a dart, etc.); by impl. to *become bondsman* (by handclasping):— blow (la trumpet]), cast, clap, fasten, pitch [tent], smite, sound, strike, × suretiship, thrust.

8629. תֶּקַע têqa', *tay-kah´;* from 8628; a *blast* of a trumpet:— sound.

תְּקֹעַ Tᵉqô'îy. See 8621.

8630. תָּקַף tâqaph, *taw-kaf´;* a prim. root; to *overpower:*— prevail (against).

8631. תְּקֵף tᵉqêph (Chald.), *tek-afe´;* corresp. to 8630; to *become* (caus. *make*) *mighty* or (fig.) *obstinate:*— make firm, harden, be (-come) strong.

8632. תְּקֹף tᵉqôph (Chald.), *tek-ofe´;* corresp. to 8633; *power:*— might, strength.

8633. תֹּקֶף tôqeph, *to´-kef;* from 8630; *might* or (fig.) *positiveness:*— authority, power, strength.

תְּקוּפָה tᵉqûwphâh. See 8622.

תּוֹר tôr. See 8447, 8449.

8634. תַּרְאֵלָה Tar'âlâh, *tar-al-aw´;* prob. for 8653; a *reeling; Taralah,* a place in Pal.:— Taralah.

8635. תַּרְבּוּת tarbûwth, *tar-booth´;* from 7235; *multiplication,* i.e. *progeny:*— increase.

8636. תַּרְבִּית tarbîyth, *tar-beeth´;* from 7235; *multiplication,* i.e. *percentage* or *bonus* in addition to principal:— increase, unjust gain.

8637. תִּרְגַּל tirgal, *teer-gal´;* a denom. from 7270; to *cause to walk:*— teach to go.

8638. תִּרְגַּם tirgam, *teer-gam´;* a denom. from 7275 in the sense of *throwing* over; to *transfer,* i.e. *translate:*— interpret.

תּוֹרָה tôrâh. See 8451.

8639. תַּרְדֵּמָה tardêmâh, *tar-day-maw´;* from 7290; a *lethargy* or (by impl.) *trance:*— deep sleep.

8640. תִּרְהָקָה Tirhâqâh, *teer-haw´-kaw;* of for. der.; *Tirhakah,* a king of Kush:— Tirhakah.

8641. תְּרוּמָה tᵉrûwmâh, *ter-oo-maw´;* or

תְּרֻמָה tᵉrûmâh (Deut. 12:11), *ter-oo-maw´;* from 7311; a *present* (as offered *up*), espec. in *sacrifice* or as tribute:— gift, heave offering (Ishoulder!), oblation, offered (-ing).

8642. תְּרוּמִיָּה **teruwmîyâh**, ter-oo-mee-yaw'; formed as 8641; a sacrificial offering:— oblation.

8643. תְּרוּעָה **terûw'âh**, ter-oo-aw'; from 7321; clamor, i.e. acclamation of joy or a battle-cry; espec. clangor of trumpets, as an alarum:— alarm, blow (-ing) (of, the) (trumpets), joy, jubile, loud noise, rejoicing, shout (-ing), (high, joyful) sound (-ing).

8644. תְּרוּפָה **terûwphâh**, ter-oo-faw'; from 7322 in the sense of its congener 7495; a remedy:— medicine.

8645. תִּרְזָה **tirzâh**, teer-zaw'; prob. from 7329; a species of tree (appar. from its slenderness), perh. the cypress:— cypress.

8646. תֶּרַח **Terach**, teh'-rakh; of uncert. der.; Terach, the father of Abraham; also a place in the Desert:— Tarah, Terah.

8647. תִּרְחֲנָה **Tirchănâh**, teer-khan-aw'; of uncert. der.; Tirchanah, an Isr.:— Tirhanah.

8648. תְּרֵין **terêyn** (Chald.), ter-ane'; fem.

תַּרְתֵּין **tartêyn**, tar-tane'; corresp. to 8147; two:— second, + twelve, two.

8649. תָּרְמָה **tormâh**, tor-maw'; and

תַּרְמוּת **tarmûwth**, tar-mooth'; or

תַּרְמִית **tarmîyth**, tar-meeth'; from 7411; fraud:— deceit (-ful), privily.

תְּרֻמָה **terûmâh**. See 8641.

8650. תֹּרֶן **tôren**, to'-ren; prob. for 766; a pole (as a mast or flag-staff):— beacon, mast.

8651. תְּרַע **tera'** (Chald.), ter-ah'; corresp. to 8179; a door; by impl. a palace:— gate mouth.

8652. תְּרָע **târâ'** (Chald.), taw-raw'; from 8651; a doorkeeper:— porter.

8653. תַּרְעֵלָה **tar'êlâh**, tar-ay-law'; from 7477; reeling:— astonishment, trembling.

8654. תִּרְעָתִי **Tir'âthîy**, teer-aw-thee'; patrial from an unused name mean. gate; a Tirathite or inhab. of an unknown Tirah:— Tirathite.

8655. תְּרָפִים **terâphîym**, ter-aw-feme'; plur. perh. from 7495; a healer; Teraphim (sing. or plur.) a family idol:— idols (-atry), images, teraphim.

8656. תִּרְצָה **Tirtsâh**, teer-tsaw'; from 7521; delightsomeness; Tirtsah, a place in Pal.; also an Israelitess:— Tirzah.

8657. תֶּרֶשׁ **Teresh**, teh'-resh; of for. der.; Teresh, a eunuch of Xerxes:— Teresh.

8658. תַּרְשִׁישׁ **tarshîysh**, tar-sheesh'; prob. of for. der. lcomp. 8659l; a gem, perh. the topaz:— beryl.

8659. תַּרְשִׁישׁ **Tarshîysh**, tar-sheesh'; prob. the same as 8658 (as the region of the stone, or the reverse); Tarshish, a place on the Mediterranean, hence, the epithet of a merchant vessel (as if for or from that port); also the name of a Pers. and of an Isr.:— Tarshish, Tharshish.

8660. תִּרְשָׁתָא **Tirshâthâ'**, teer-shaw-thaw'; of for. der.; the title of a Pers. deputy or governor:— Tirshatha.

תַּרְתֵּין **tartêyn**. See 8648.

8661. תַּרְתָּן **Tartân**, tar-tawn'; of for. der.; Tartan, an Ass.:— Tartan.

8662. תַּרְתָּק **Tartâq**, tar-tawk'; of for. der.; Tartak, a deity of the Avvites:— Tartak.

8663. תְּשֻׁאָה **teshu'âh**, tesh-oo-aw'; from 7722; a crashing or loud clamor:— crying, noise, shouting, stir.

תּוֹשָׁב **tôshâb**. See 8453.

8664. תִּשְׁבִּי **Tishbîy**, tish-bee'; patrial from an unused name mean. recourse; a Tishbite or inhab. of Tishbeh (in Gilead):— Tishbite.

8665. תַּשְׁבֵּץ **tashbêts**, tash-bates'; from 7660; checkered stuff (as reticulated):— broidered.

8666. תְּשׁוּבָה **teshûwbâh**, tesh-oo-baw'; or

תְּשֻׁבָה **teshûbâh**, tesh-oo-baw'; from 7725; a recurrence (of time or place); a reply (as returned):— answer, be expired, return.

8667. תְּשׁוּמֶת **tesûwmeth**, tes-oo-meth'; from 7760; a deposit, i.e. pledging:— + fellowship.

8668. תְּשׁוּעָה **teshûw'âh**, tesh-oo-aw'; or

תְּשֻׁעָה **teshû'âh**, tesh-oo-aw'; from 7768 in the sense of 3467; rescue (lit. or fig., pers., national or spir.):— deliverance, help, safety, salvation, victory.

8669. תְּשׁוּקָה **teshûwqâh**, tesh-oo-kaw'; from 7783 in the orig. sense of stretching out after; a longing:— desire.

8670. תְּשׁוּרָה **teshûwrâh**, tesh-oo-raw'; from 7788 in the sense of arrival; a gift:— present.

תַּשְׁחֵת **tashchêth**. See 516.

תּוּשִׁיָּה **tûshîyâh**. See 8454.

8671. תְּשִׁיעִי **teshiy'îy**, tesh-ee-ee'; ord. from 8672; ninth:— ninth.

תְּשֻׁעָה **teshû'âh**. See 8668.

8672. תֵּשַׁע **têsha'**, tay'-shah; or (masc.)

תִּשְׁעָה **tish'âh**, tish-aw'; perh. from 8159 through the idea of a turn to the next or full number ten; nine or (ord.) ninth:— nine (+ -teen, + -teenth, -th).

8673. תִּשְׁעִים **tish'îym**, tish-eem'; multiple from 8672; ninety:— ninety.

8674. תַּתְּנַי **Tattenay**, tat-ten-ah'-ee; of for. der.; Tattenai, a Pers.:— Tatnai.

New Strong's™
Concise Dictionary
of the Words in the
Greek Testament

with their Renderings in the
King James Version

Read this first!

How to Use the Greek Dictionary

For many people Strong's unique system of numbers continues to be *the* bridge between the original languages of the Bible and the English of the *King James Version* (AV). In order to enhance the strategic importance of *Strong's Greek Dictionary* for Bible students, it has been significantly improved in this brand-new, up-to-date edition. It is now completely re-typeset with modern, larger typefaces that are kind to the eye, and all known errors in the original typesetting have been corrected, bringing this pivotal work to a new level of usefulness and accuracy.

1. What the Dictionary Is

Strong's Greek Dictionary is a fully integrated companion to the main concordance. Its compact entries contain a wealth of information about the words of the Bible in their original language. You can enrich your study of the Bible enormously if you will invest the time to understand the various elements included in each entry and their significance. The example that follows identifies many of these entry elements; and the following sections on the transliteration, abbreviations, and special symbols used offer fuller explanations. While no dictionary designed for readers who do not know biblical Hebrew can explain all that a faithful student of the language would know, this *Dictionary* gives the serious student of the English Bible the basic information needed to pursue infinitely deeper and broader studies of God's Word. Vast amounts of biblical insight can be gained by using this *Concordance* alone or in conjunction with other time-proven biblical reference works, such as Thomas Nelson's *Vine's Complete Expository Dictionary of Old and New Testament Words* and *Nelson's New Illustrated Bible Dictionary*.

2. Using the Dictionary with the Main Concordance

To use this *Dictionary*, locate the number given next to the biblical reference for any particular entry in the main concordance. For example, under "EARNEST," you find *Strong's* number *728* next to the first Bible reference, "Eph. 1:14." Since Ephesians is in the New Testament (and since this numeral is set in italic type [and not regular type], you know that it refers to the *Greek Dictionary*. You may view that enlarged entry, here, or on page 13 in this *Dictionary*. The enlarged example that follows, together with the following sections of explanation, identify the kinds of information such entries provide.

3. Using the Dictionary to Do Word Studies

Careful Bible students do word studies, and *The New Strong's™ Exhaustive Concordance* with this revised, newly-typeset *Greek Dictionary*, offers unique assistance. Consider the word "love" as found the King James Bible. By skimming the main concordance, you find these numbers for Greek words that the King James Bible translates with the English word "love": *25, 5368, 26, 5360, 5362, 5363, 5361*. Now for any one Bible reference in this entry there is only one Greek word cited, and you may be interested only in establishing the precise meaning for just that word in that occurrence. If so, it will be very helpful for your to observe that same Greek word in *each* of its occurrences in the Bible. In that way, you develop an idea of its possible range of meanings, and you help clarify what it probably meant precisely in the specific Bible reference you are studying.

But don't overlook exploring each Greek word translated as "love." You may wish to take notes as you look up each occurrence of the word that goes with *25*, and then each occurrence of the word that goes with *26*, and so forth. This method gives you an excellent basis for understanding all that the New Testament signifies with the King James Version's word "love."

Now see the *Dictionary* entry *25* itself, and notice that after the symbol :— all the words and word prefixes and suffixes are listed. These show you that this one Greek word, *agapao*, is translated into a few similar words in the King James Bible: beloved, love, loved. This list tells you the range of uses of the one Greek word in the King James Bible. This information can help you distinguish between the nuances of meaning found where this and the other Greek words are translated by these same words and similar ones in the King James Bible.

These three ways of using the *Dictionary* in conjunction with the main concordance show you only a sampling of the many ways *The New Strong's™ Exhaustive Concordance* can enrich your study of the Bible. And they show you why it is important that you take the time to become familiar with each feature in the *Dictionary* as illustrated in the example on the following page.

An Example
from the
Greek New Testament Dictionary

Strong's number in *italics*, corresponding to the numbers at the ends of the context lines in the main concordance.

An unnumbered cross-reference entry.

The word as it appears in the original Greek spelling.

Where appropriate, important discussion of multiple uses and functions of the word.

The Greek word represented in English letters in **bold** type (the transliteration).

Strong's syllable-by-syllable pronunciation in *italics*, with the emphasized syllable marked by the accent.

When the Greek word relates to a Hebrew or Aramaic word from the Old Testament, the Strong's numbers is encased in square brackets [...].

Brief English definitions (shown by italics).

ἀπέπω **apĕpō**. See 550.

728. ἀῤῥαβών **arrhabōn**, *ar-hrab-ohn´;* of Heb. or. [6162]; a *pledge*, i.e. part of the purchase-money or property given in advance as *security* for the rest:— earnest.

3360. μέχρι **mĕchri** *mekh´-ree;* or

μεχρίς **mĕchris** *mekh-ris´;* from 3372; *as far as*, i.e. *up to* a certain point (as a prep. of extent [denoting the *terminus*, whereas *891* refers espec. to the *space* of time or place intervening] or a conjunc.):— till, (un-) to, until.

3361. μή **mē** *may;* a primary particle of qualified *negation* (whereas *3756* expresses an absolute denial); (adv.) *not*, (conjunc.) *lest;* also (as an interrog. implying a *neg.* answer [whereas *3756* expects an *affirmative* one]) *whether:*— any, but (that) × forbear, + God forbid, + lack, lest, neither, never, no (× wise in), none, nor, [can-] not, nothing, that not, un [-taken], without. Often used in compounds in substantially the same relations. See also *3362, 3363, 3364, 3372, 3373, 3375, 3378.*

See "Special Symbols."

Italic Strong's numbers refer to related Greek words in this Dictionary.

After the long dash (—), there is a complete, alphabetical listing of all ways this Greek word is translated in the KJV. (See also "Special Symbols").

Improved, consistent abbreviations. All abbreviations occur with their full spelling in the list of abbreviations.

Note that Greek spelling variations are conveniently indented for easy comparison.

Plan of the Greek Dictionary

1. All the original words are presented in their alphabetical order (according to Greek). They are numbered for easy matching between this Dictionary and the main part of the Concordance. Many reference books also use these same numbers which were originally created by Dr. Strong.

2. Immediately after each word, the exact equivalent of each sound (phoneme) is given in English characters, according to the transliteration system given below.

3. Next follows the precise pronunciation with the proper stress mark.

4. Then comes the etymology, root meaning, and common uses of the word, along with any other important related details.

5. In the case of proper names, the normal English spelling is given, accompanied by a few words of explanation.

6. Finally, after the colon and the dash (:—), all the different ways that the word appears in the Authorized Version (KJV) are listed in alphabetical order. When the Greek word appears in English as a phrase, the main word of the phrase is used to alphabetize it.

By looking up these words in the main concordance and by noting the passages which display the same number in the right-hand column, the reader also possesses a complete *Greek New Testament Concordance*, expressed in the words of the Authorized Version.

Transliteration and Pronunciation of the Greek

The following shows how the Greek words are transliterated into English in this Dictionary.

1. The *Alphabet* is as follows:

No.	Form upper	lower	Name	Transliteration and Pronunciation
1.	A	α	Alpha (*al´-fah*)	**a**, as in *Arm* or *mAn* [1]
2.	B	β	Bēta (*bay´-tah*)	**b**
3.	Γ	γ	Gamma (*gam´-mah*)	**g**, as in *Guard* [2]
4.	Δ	δ	Dĕlta (*del´-tah*)	**d**
5.	E	ε	Ĕpsilŏn (*ep´-see-lon*)	**ĕ**, as in *mEt*
6.	Z	ζ	Zēta (*dzay´-tah*)	**z**, as in *aDZe* [3]
7.	H	η	Ēta (*ay´-tah*)	**ē**, as in *thEy*
8.	Θ	θ	Thēta (*thay´-tah*)	**th**, as in *THin* [4]
9.	I	ι	Iota (*ee-o´-tah*)	**i**, as in *machIne* [5]
10.	K	κ	Kappa (*kap´-pah*)	**k**
11.	Λ	λ	Lambda (*lamb´-dah*)	**l**
12.	M	μ	Mu (*moo*)	**m**
13.	N	ν	Nu (*noo*)	**n**
14.	Ξ	ξ	Xi (*ksee*)	**x** = *ks*
15.	O	o	Omikrŏn (*om´-e-cron*)	**ŏ**, as in *not*
16.	Π	π	Pi (*pee or pai*)	**p**
17.	P	ρ	Rhō (*hro*)	**r**
18.	Σ	σ, final ς	Sigma (*sig´-mah*)	**s** sharp
19.	T	τ	Tau (*tŏw*)	**t**, as in *Tree* [6]
20.	Υ	υ	Upsilŏn (*u´-pse-lon*)	**u**, as in *fUll*
21.	Φ	φ	Phi (*fee or fai*)	**ph** = *f*
22.	X	χ	Chi (*khee or khai*)	German **ch** [7]
23.	Ψ	ψ	Psi (*psee or psai*)	**ps**
24.	Ω	ω	Omĕga (*o´-meg-ah*)	**ŏ**, as in *no*

---

[1] α, when *final*, or before a final ρ or followed by any *other* consonant, is sounded like *a* in *Arm*; elsewhere like *a* in *mAn*.

[2] γ, when followed by γ, κ, c, or ξ is sounded like *ng* in *kiNG*.

[3] ζ is always sounded like *dz*.

[4] θ never has the guttural sound, like *th* in *THis*.

[5] ι has the sound of *ee* when it *ends* an *accented* syllable; in other situations a more obscure sound, like *i* in *amIable* or *Imbecile*.

[6] τ never has an s-sound, like *t* in *naTion*.

[7] From the difficulty of producing the true sound of χ, it is generally sounded like *k*.

2. The mark ', placed over the *initial* vowel of a word, is called the *Rough Breathing*, and is equivalent to the English *h*, by which we have accordingly represented it. Its *absence* over an initial vowel is indicated by the mark ', called the *Smooth Breathing*, which is silent, and is therefore not represented in our method of transliteration. [8]

3. The following are the Greek *diphthongs*, properly so called: [9]

Form	Transliteration and Pronunciation
αι	**ai** (*ah´ee*) [ă + ē]
ει	**ei**, as in h*EI*ght
οι	**oi**, as in *OI*l
υι	**we**, as in s*WE*et
αυ	**ow**, as in n*OW*
ευ	**eu**, as in f*EU*d
ου	**ou**, as in thr*OU*gh

4. The *accent* (stress of voice) falls on the syllable where it is written. [10] It occurs in three forms: the *acute* (´), which is the only true accent; the *grave* (`) which is its substitute; and the *circumflex* (^), which is the union of the two. The acute may stand on any one of the last *three* syllables, and in case it occurs on the final syllable, before another word in the same sentence, it is written as a grave. The grave is understood (but never written as such) on every other syllable. The circumflex is written on any syllable (necessarily the last syllable or next to the last syllable of a word) formed by the contraction of two syllables, of which the *first* would properly have the acute accent.

5. The following *punctuation* marks are used: the comma (,), the semicolon (·), the colon or period (.), the question mark (;), and by some editors, also the exclamation mark, parentheses, and quotation marks.

Special Symbols

+ (*addition*) denotes a rendering in the A.V. of one or more Greek words in connection with the one under consideration. For example, in Rev. 17:17, No. 1106, γνώμη (**gnōmē**) is translated as a verb ("to agree"), when it is actually a noun and part of a Greek idiom that is literally translated "to do one mind."

× (*multiplication*) denotes a rendering in the A.V. that results from an idiom peculiar to the Greek. For example, in Heb. 12:21, the whole Greek phrase in which ἔντρομος, **ĕntrŏmŏs** (1790) appears is a way of expressing great anxiety. The same idiom is used about Moses in Acts 7:32.

( ) (*parentheses*), in the renderings from the A.V., denote a word or syllable which is sometimes given in connection with the principal word to which it is attached. In Mark 15:39 there are two Greek prepositions (1537 and 1727) which are used together ("over against"). One English preposition, "opposite," communicates the same idea.

[ ] (*brackets*), in the rendering from the A.V., denote the inclusion of an additional word in the Greek. For example, No. 2596 κατά (**kata**) is translated "daily" in Luke 19:47, along with No. 2250 ἡμέρα (**hēmĕra**). So, two Greek words were translated by one English word.

Italics, at the end of a rendering from the A.V., denote an explanation of the variations from the usual form.

Note

Because of some changes in the numbering system (while the original work was in progress) no Greek words are cited for 2717 or 3203-3302. These numbers were dropped altogether. This will not cause any problems in *Strong's* numbering system. **No Greek words have been left out.** Because so many other reference works use this numbering system, it has **not** been revised. If it were revised, much confusion would certainly result.

---

[8] These signs are placed over the *second* vowel of a *diphthong*. The same is true of the accents.

The *Rough* Breathing always belongs to an initial υ.

The *Rough* Breathing is always used with ρ, when it begins a word. If this letter is doubled in the middle of a word, the first ρ takes the Smooth Breathing mark and the second ρ takes the Rough Breathing mark.

Since these signs cannot conveniently be written above the first letter of a word, when it is a *capital*, they are placed *before* it in such cases. This observation applies also to the *accents*. The aspiration *always* begins the syllable.

Occasionally, in consequence of a contraction (*crasis*), the Smooth Breathing is made to stand in the middle of a word, and is then called *Coro´nis*.

[9] The above are combinations of two *short* vowels, and are pronounced like their respective elements, but in more rapid succession than otherwise. Thus, αι is midway between *i* in h*I*gh, and *ay* in s*AY*.

Besides these, there are what are called *improper* diphthongs, in which the former is a *long* vowel. In these,

ᾳ sounds like	α
ῃ "	η
ῳ "	ω
ηυ "	η + υ
ωυ "	ω + υ

the second vowel, when it is ι, is written *under* the first vowel (unless it is a capital), and is *silent*; when it is υ, it is sounded separately. When the initial vowel is a capital, the ι is placed after it, but it does not take a breathing mark or any accent.

The sign ¨ is called *diær;esis*. It is placed over the *second* of two vowels, indicating that they do *not* form a diphthong.

[10] Every word (except a few monosyllables, called *Aton´ics*) must have one accent; several small words (called *Enclit´ics*) put their accent (always as an acute) on the last syllable of the preceding word (in addition to its own accent, which still has the principal stress), where this is possible.

Abbreviations

abb. = abbreviated
   abbreviation
abstr. = abstract
   abstractly
act. = active (voice)
   actively
acc. = accusative (case) [1]
adj. = adjective
   adjectivally
adv. = adverb
   adverbial
   adverbially
aff. = affix [2]
   affixed
affin. = affinity
alt. = alternate
   alternately
anal. = analogy
appar. = apparent
   apparently
arch. = architecture
   architectural
   architecturally
art. = article [3]
artif. = artificial
   artificially
Ass. = Assyrian
A.V. = Authorized Version
   (King James Version)
Bab. = Babylon
   Babylonia
   Babylonian
caus. = causative [4]
   causatively
cerem. = ceremony
   ceremonial
   ceremonially
Chald. = Chaldee (Aramaic)
   Chaldaism
   (Aramaism)
Chr. = Christian
collat. = collateral
   collaterally
collect. = collective
   collectively
comp. = compare [5]
   comparison
   comparative
   comparatively
concr. = concrete
   concretely
conjec. = conjecture
   conjectural
   conjecturally
conjug. = conjugation [6]
   conjugational
   conjugationally
conjunc. = conjunction
   conjunctional
   conjunctionally
constr. = construct [7]
   construction
   constructive
   constructively

contr. = contracted [8]
   contraction
correl. = correlated
   correlation
   correlative
   correlatively
corresp. = corresponding
   correspondingly
dat. = dative (case) [9]
def. = definite [10]
   definitely
demonstr. = demonstrative [11]
denom. = denominative [12]
   denominatively
der. = derived
   derivation
   derivative
   derivatively
desc. = descended
   descendant
   descendants
dimin. = diminutive [13]
dir. = direct
   directly
E. = East
   Eastern
eccl. = ecclesiastical
   ecclesiastically
e.g. = for example
Eg. = Egypt
   Egyptian
   Egyptians
ellip. = ellipsis [14]
   elliptical
   elliptically
emphat. = emphatic
   emphatically
equiv. = equivalent
   equivalently
err. = error
   erroneous
   erroneously
espec. = especially
etym. = etymology [15]
   etymological
   etymologically
euphem. = euphemism [16]
   euphemistic
   euphemistically
euphon. = euphonious [17]
   euphonically
extens. = extension [18]
   extensive
extern. = external
   externally
fem. = feminine (gender)
fig. = figurative
   figuratively
for. = foreign
   foreigner
freq. = frequentative
   frequentatively
fut. = future

gen. = general
   generally
   generic
   generical
   generically
Gr. = Greek
   Graecism
gut. = guttural [19]
Heb. = Hebrew
   Hebraism
i.e. = that is
ident. = identical
   identically
immed. = immediate
   immediately
imper. = imperative [20]
   imperatively
imperf. = imperfect [21]
impers. = impersonal
   impersonally
impl. = implied
   impliedly
   implication
incept. = inceptive [22]
   inceptively
incl. = including
   inclusive
   inclusively
indef. = indefinite
   indefinitely
ind. = indicative [23]
   indicatively
indiv. = individual
   individually
infer. = inference
   inferential
   inferentially
infin. = infinitive
inhab. = inhabitant
   inhabitants
ins. = inserted
intens. = intensive
   intensively
interch. = interchangeable
intern. = internal
   internally
interj. = interjection [24]
   interjectional
   interjectionally
interrog. = interrogative [25]
   interrogatively
intr. = intransitive [26]
   intransitively
invol. = involuntary
   involuntarily
irreg. = irregular
   irregularly
Isr. = Israelite
   Israelites
   Israelitish
Lat. = Latin
Levit. = Levitical
   Levitically

lit. = literal
   literally
marg. = margin
   marginal reading
masc. = masculine (gender)
mean. = meaning
ment. = mental
   mentally
metaph. = metaphorical
   metaphorically
mid. = middle (voice) [27]
modif. = modified
   modification
mor. = moral
   morally
mult. = multiplicative [28]
nat. = natural
   naturally
neg. = negative
   negatively
neut. = neuter (gender)
obj. = object
   objective
   objectively
obs. = obsolete
ord. = ordinal [29]
or. = origin
orig. = original
   originally
orth. = orthography [30]
   orthographical
   orthographically
Pal. = Palestine
part. = participle
pass. = passive (voice)
   passively
patron. = patronymic [31]
   patronymical
   patronymically
perh. = perhaps
perm. = permutation [32] (of
   adjacent letters)
pers. = person
   personal
   personally
Pers. = Persia
   Persian
   Persians
phys. = physical
   physically
plur. = plural
poet. = poetry
   poetical
   poetically
pos. = positive
   positively
pref. = prefix
   prefixed
prep. = preposition
   prepositional
   prepositionally
prim. = primitive
prob. = probable
   probably

prol. = prolonged [33]
   prolongation
pron. = pronoun
   pronominal
   pronominally
prop. = properly
prox. = proximate
   proximately
recip. = reciprocal
   reciprocally
redupl. = reduplicated [34]
   reduplication
refl. = reflexive [35]
   reflexively
reg. = regular
rel. = relative
   relatively
relig. = religion
   religious
   religiously
Rom. = Roman
second. = secondary
   secondarily
signif. = signification
   signifying
short. = shorter
   shortened
sing. = singular
spec. = specific
   specifically
streng. = strengthening
subdiv. = subdivision
   subdivisional
   subdivisionally
subj. = subjectively
   subjective
   subject
substit. = substituted
suff. = suffix
superl. = superlative [36]
   superlatively
symb. = symbolic
   symbolical
   symbolically
tech. = technical
   technically
term. = termination
tran. = transitive [37]
   transitively
transc. = transcription
transm. = transmutation [38]
transp. = transposed [39]
   transposition
typ. = typical
   typically
uncert. = uncertain
   uncertainly
var. = various
   variation
voc. = vocative (case) [40]
vol. = voluntary
   voluntarily

---

[1] often indicating the direct object of an action verb

[2] part of a word which, when attached to the beginning of the word is called a prefix; if attaching within a word, an infix; and if at the end, a suffix

[3] "the" is the definite article; "a" and "an" are indefinite articles

[4] expressing or denoting causation

[5] the comparative of an adjective or adverb expresses a greater degree of an attribute, e.g. "higher"; "more slowly"

[6] a systematic array of various verbal forms

[7] the condition in Hebrew and Aramaic when two adjacent nouns are combined semantically as follows, e.g. "sword" + "king" = "(the) sword of (the) king" or "(the) king's sword". These languages tend to throw the stress of the entire noun phrase toward the end of the whole expression.

[8] a shortened form of a word. It is made by omitting or combining some elements or by reducing vowels or syllables, e.g. "is not" becomes "isn't".

[9] often the indirect object of an action verb

[10] the definite article ("the")

[11] demonstrative pronouns which point (show), e.g. "this," "that"

[12] derived from a noun

[13] a grammatical form which expresses smallness and/or endearment

[14] a construction which leaves out understood words

[15] the historical origin of a word

[16] the use of a pleasant, polite, or harmless-sounding word or phrase to hide harsh, rude, or infamous truths, e.g. "to pass away" = "to die"

[17] a linguistic mechanism to make pronunciation easier, e.g. "an" before "hour" instead of "a"

[18] when a general term can denote an entire class of things

[19] speech sounds which are produced deep in the throat

[20] the mood which expresses a command

[21] used of a tense which expresses a continuous but unfinished action or state

[22] used of a verbal aspect which denotes the beginning of an action

[23] used of the mood which expresses a verbal action as actually occurring (not hypothetical)

[24] an exclamation which expresses emotion

[25] indicating a question

[26] referring to verbs which do not govern direct objects

[27] reflexive

[28] capable of multiplying or tending to multiply

[29] This shows the position or the order within a series, e.g. "second"; the corresponding cardinal number is "two".

[30] the written system of spelling in a given language

[31] a name derived from that of a paternal ancestor, often created by an affix in various languages

[32] a rearrangement

[33] lengthening a pronunciation

[34] the repetition of a letter or syllable to form a new, inflected word

[35] denoting an action by the subject upon itself

[36] expressing the highest degree of comparison of the quality indicated by an adjective or an adverb, e.g. "highest"; "most timely"

[37] expressing an action directed toward a person or a thing (the direct object)

[38] the change of one grammatical element to another

[39] switching word order

[40] an inflection which is used when one is addressing a person or a thing directly, e.g. "John, come here!"

GREEK DICTIONARY OF THE NEW TESTAMENT

A

N. B.—The numbers *not in italics* refer to the words in the *Hebrew Dictionary*. Significations within quotation marks are derivative representatives of the Greek.

1. **A A**, *al´-fah;* of Heb. or.; the first letter of the alphabet; fig. only (from its use as a numeral) the *first:*— Alpha. Often used (usually ἀν **an**, before a vowel) also in composition (as a contr. from *427*) in the sense of *privation;* so in many words beginning with this letter; occasionally in the sense of *union* (as a contr. of *260*).

2. Ἀαρών **Aarōn**, *ah-ar-ohn´;* of Heb. or. [175]; *Aaron*, the brother of Moses:— Aaron.

3. Ἀβαδδών **Abaddōn**, *ab-ad-dohn´;* of Heb. or. [11]; a *destroying angel:*— Abaddon.

4. ἀβαρής **abarēs**, *ab-ar-ace´;* from *1* (as a neg. particle) and *922; weightless,* i.e. (fig.) *not burdensome:*— from being burdensome.

5. Ἀββᾶ **Abba**, *ab-bah´;* of Chald. or. [2]; *father* (as a voc.):— Abba.

6. Ἄβελ **Abĕl**, *ab´-el;* of Heb. or. [1893]; *Abel,* the son of Adam:— Abel.

7. Ἀβιά **Abia**, *ab-ee-ah´;* of Heb. or. [29]; *Abijah,* the name of two Isr.:— Abia.

8. Ἀβιάθαρ **Abiathar**, *ab-ee-ath´-ar;* of Heb. or. [54]; *Abiathar,* an Isr.:— Abiathar.

9. Ἀβιληνή **Abilēnē**, *ab-ee-lay-nay´;* of for. or. [comp. 58]; *Abilene,* a region of Syria:— Abilene.

10. Ἀβιούδ **Abiŏud**, *ab-ee-ood´;* of Heb. or. [31]; *Abihud,* an Isr.:— Abiud.

11. Ἀβραάμ **Abraam**, *ab-rah-am´;* of Heb. or. [85]; *Abraham,* the Heb. patriarch:— Abraham. [In Acts 7:16 the text should perh. read *Jacob.*]

12. ἄβυσσος **abussŏs**, *ab´-us-sos;* from *1* (as a neg. particle) and a var. of *1037; depthless,* i.e. (spec.) (infernal) "abyss":— deep, (bottomless) pit.

13. Ἄγαβος **Agabŏs**, *ag´-ab-os;* of Heb. or. [comp. 2285]; *Agabus,* an Isr.:— Agabus.

14. ἀγαθοεργέω **agathŏĕrgĕō**, *ag-ath-er-gheh´-o;* from *18* and *2041;* to *work good:*— do good.

15. ἀγαθοποιέω **agathŏpŏiĕō**, *ag-ath-op-oy-eh´-o;* from *17;* to *be a well-doer* (as a favor or a duty):— (when) do good (well).

16. ἀγαθοποιΐα **agathŏpŏiïa**, *ag-ath-op-oy-ee´-ah;* from *17; well-doing,* i.e. *virtue:*— well-doing.

17. ἀγαθοποιός **agathŏpŏiŏs**, *ag-ath-op-oy-os´;* from *18* and *4160;* a *well-doer,* i.e. *virtuous:*— them that do well.

18. ἀγαθός **agathŏs**, *ag-ath-os´;* a prim. word; "good" (in any sense, often as noun):— benefit, good (-s, things), well. Comp. *2570.*

19. ἀγαθωσύνη **agathōsunē**, *ag-ath-o-soo´-nay;* from *18; goodness,* i.e. *virtue* or *beneficence:*— goodness.

20. ἀγαλλίασις **agalliasis**, *ag-al-lee´-as-is;* from *21; exultation;* spec. *welcome:*— gladness, (exceeding) joy.

21. ἀγαλλιάω **agalliaō**, *ag-al-lee-ah´-o;* from ἄγαν **agan** (*much*) and *242;* prop. to *jump for joy,* i.e. *exult:*— be (exceeding) glad, with exceeding joy, rejoice (greatly).

22. ἄγαμος **agamŏs**, *ag´-am-os;* from *1* (as a neg. particle) and *1062; unmarried:*— unmarried.

23. ἀγανακτέω **aganaktĕō**, *ag-an-akteh´-o;* from ἄγαν **agan** (*much*) and ἄχθος **achthŏs** (*grief;* akin to the base of *43*); to *be greatly afflicted,* i.e. (fig.) *indignant:*— be much (sore) displeased, have (be moved with, with) indignation.

24. ἀγανάκτησις **aganaktēsis**, *ag-an-ak´-tay-sis;* from *23; indignation:*— indignation.

25. ἀγαπάω **agapaō**, *ag-ap-ah´-o;* perh. from ἄγαν **agan** (*much*) [or comp. 5689]; to *love* (in a social or moral sense):— (be-) love (-ed). Comp. *5368.*

26. ἀγάπη **agapē**, *ag-ah´-pay;* from *25; love,* i.e. *affection* or *benevolence;* spec. (plur.) a *love-feast:*— (feast of) charity ([-ably]), dear, love.

27. ἀγαπητός **agapētŏs**, *ag-ap-ay-tos´;* from *25; beloved:*— (dearly, well) beloved, dear.

28. Ἄγαρ **Agar**, *ag´-ar;* of Heb. or. [1904]; *Hagar,* the concubine of Abraham:— Hagar.

29. ἀγγαρεύω **aggarĕuō**, *ang-ar-yew´-o;* of for. or. [comp. 104]; prop. to *be a courier,* i.e. (by impl.) to *press into public service:*— compel (to go).

30. ἀγγεῖον **aggĕiŏn**, *ang-eye´-on;* from ἄγγος **aggŏs** (a *pail,* perh. as *bent;* comp. the base of *43*); a *receptacle:*— vessel.

31. ἀγγελία **aggĕlia**, *ang-el-ee´-ah;* from *32;* an *announcement,* i.e. (by impl.) *precept:*— message.

32. ἄγγελος **aggĕlŏs**, *ang´-el-os;* from ἀγγέλλω **aggĕllō** [prob. der. from *71;* comp. *34*] (to *bring tidings*); a *messenger;* esp. an "angel"; by impl. a *pastor:*— angel, messenger.

33. ἄγε **agĕ**, *ag´-eh;* imper. of *71;* prop. *lead,* i.e. *come on:*— go to.

34. ἀγέλη **agĕlē**, *ag-el´-ay;* from *71* [comp. *32*]; a *drove:*— herd.

35. ἀγενεαλόγητος **agĕnĕalŏgētŏs**, *ag-en-eh-al-og´-ay-tos;* from *1* (as neg. particle) and *1075; unregistered* as to *birth:*— without descent.

36. ἀγενής **agĕnēs**, *ag-en-ace´;* from *1* (as neg. particle) and *1085;* prop. *without kin,* i.e. (of unknown descent, and by impl.) *ignoble:*— base things.

37. ἁγιάζω **hagiazō**, *hag-ee-ad´-zo;* from *40;* to *make holy,* i.e. (cer.) *purify* or *consecrate;* (mentally) to *venerate:*— hallow, be holy, sanctify.

38. ἁγιασμός **hagiasmŏs**, *hag-ee-as-mos´;* from *37;* prop. *purification,* i.e. (the state) *purity;* concr. (by Heb.) a *purifier:*— holiness, sanctification.

39. ἅγιον **hagiŏn**, *hag´-ee-on;* neut. of *40;* a *sacred thing* (i.e. spot):— holiest (of all), holy place, sanctuary.

40. ἅγιος **hagiŏs**, *hag´-ee-os;* from ἄγος **hagŏs** (an *awful* thing) [comp. 53, 2282]; *sacred* (phys. *pure,* mor. *blameless* or *religious,* cer. *consecrated*):— (most) holy (one, thing), saint.

41. ἁγιότης **hagiŏtēs**, *hag-ee-ot´-ace;* from *40; sanctity* (i.e. prop. the state):— holiness.

42. ἁγιωσύνη **hagiōsunē**, *hag-ee-o-soo´-nay;* from *40; sacredness* (i.e. prop. the quality):— holiness.

43. ἀγκάλη **agkalē**, *ang-kal´-ay;* from ἄγκος **agkŏs** (a *bend,* "ache"); an *arm* (as *curved*):— arm.

44. ἄγκιστρον **agkistrŏn**, *ang´-kis-tron;* from the same as *43;* a *hook* (as *bent*):— hook.

45. ἄγκυρα **agkura**, *ang´-koo-rah;* from the same as *43;* an "anchor" (as *crooked*):— anchor.

46. ἄγναφος **agnaphŏs**, *ag´-naf-os;* from *1* (as a neg. particle) and the same as *1102;* prop. *unfulled,* i.e. (by impl.) *new* (cloth):— new.

47. ἁγνεία **hagnĕia**, *hag-ni´-ah;* from *53; cleanliness* (the quality), i.e. (spec.) *chastity:*— purity.

48. ἁγνίζω **hagnizō**, *hag-nid´-zo;* from *53;* to *make clean,* i.e. (fig.) *sanctify* (cer. or mor.):— purify (self).

49. ἁγνισμός **hagnismŏs**, *hag-nis-mos´;* from *48;* a *cleansing* (the act), i.e. (cer.) *lustration:*— purification.

50. ἀγνοέω **agnŏĕō**, *ag-no-eh´-o;* from *1* (as a neg. particle) and *3539; not to know* (through lack of information or intelligence); by impl. to *ignore* (through disinclination):— (be) ignorant (-ly), not know, not understand, unknown.

51. ἀγνόημα **agnŏēma**, *ag-no´-ay-mah;* from *50;* a thing *ignored,* i.e. *shortcoming:*— error.

52. ἄγνοια **agnŏia**, *ag´-noy-ah;* from *50; ignorance* (prop. the quality):— ignorance.

53. ἁγνός **hagnŏs**, *hag-nos´;* from the same as *40;* prop. *clean,* i.e. (fig.) *innocent, modest, perfect:*— chaste, clean, pure.

54. ἁγνότης **hagnŏtēs**, *hag-not´-ace;* from *53; cleanness* (the state), i.e. (fig.) *blamelessness:*— pureness.

55. ἁγνῶς **hagnōs**, *hag-noce´;* adv. from *53; purely,* i.e. *honestly:*— sincerely.

56. ἀγνωσία **agnōsia**, *ag-no-see´-ah;* from *1* (as neg. particle) and *1108; ignorance* (prop. the state):— ignorance, not the knowledge.

57. ἄγνωστος **agnōstŏs**, *ag´-noce-tos´;* from *1* (as neg. particle) and *1110; unknown:—* unknown.

58. ἀγορά **agŏra**, *ag-or-ah´;* from ἀγείρω **agĕirō** (to *gather;* prob. akin to *1453*); prop. the *town-square* (as a place of public resort); by impl. a *market* or *thoroughfare:—* market (-place), street.

59. ἀγοράζω **agŏrazō**, *ag-or-ad´-zo;* from *58;* prop. to *go to market,* i.e. (by impl.) to *purchase;* spec. to *redeem:—* buy, redeem.

60. ἀγοραῖος **agŏraiŏs**, *ag-or-ah´-yos;* from *58; relating to the market-place,* i.e. *forensic* (times); by impl. *vulgar:—* baser sort, low.

61. ἄγρα **agra**, *ag´-rah;* from *71;* (abstr.) a *catching* (of fish); also (concr.) a *haul* (of fish):— draught.

62. ἀγράμματος **agrammatŏs**, *ag-ram-mat-os;* from *1* (as neg. particle) and *1121; unlettered,* i.e. *illiterate:—* unlearned.

63. ἀγραυλέω **agraulĕō**, *ag-row-leh´-o;* from *68* and *832* (in the sense of *833*); to *camp out:—* abide in the field.

64. ἀγρεύω **agrĕuō**, *ag-rew´-o;* from *61;* to *hunt,* i.e. (fig.) to *entrap:—* catch.

65. ἀγριέλαιος **agriĕlaiŏs**, *ag-ree-el´-ah-yos;* from *66* and *1636;* an *oleaster:—* olive tree (which is) wild.

66. ἄγριος **agriŏs**, *ag´-ree-os;* from *68; wild* (as pertaining to the *country*), lit. (*natural*) or fig. (*fierce*):— wild, raging.

67. Ἀγρίππας **Agrippas**, *ag-rip´-pas;* appar. from *66* and *2462; wild-horse tamer; Agrippas,* one of the Herods:— Agrippa.

68. ἀγρός **agrŏs**, *ag-ros´;* from *71;* a *field* (as a *drive* for cattle); gen. the *country;* spec. a *farm,* i.e. *hamlet:—* country, farm, piece of ground, land.

69. ἀγρυπνέω **agrupnĕō**, *ag-roop-neh´-o;* ultimately from *1* (as neg. particle) and *5258;* to *be sleepless,* i.e. *keep awake:—* watch.

70. ἀγρυπνία **agrupnia**, *ag-roop-nee´-ah;* from *69; sleeplessness,* i.e. a *keeping awake:—* watch.

71. ἄγω **agō**, *ag´-o;* a prim. verb; prop. to *lead;* by impl. to *bring, drive,* (refl.) *go,* (spec.) *pass* (time), or (fig.) *induce:—* be, bring (forth), carry, (let) go, keep, lead away, be open.

72. ἀγωγή **agōgē**, *ag-o-gay´;* redupl. from *71;* a *bringing* up, i.e. *mode of living:—* manner of life.

73. ἀγών **agōn**, *ag-one´;* from *71;* prop. a place of *assembly* (as if *led*), i.e. (by impl.) a *contest* (held there); fig. an *effort* or *anxiety:—* conflict, contention, fight, race.

74. ἀγωνία **agōnia**, *ag-o-nee´-ah;* from *73;* a *struggle* (prop. the state), i.e. (fig.) *anguish:—* agony.

75. ἀγωνίζομαι **agōnizŏmai**, *ag-o-nid´-zom-ahee;* from *75;* to *struggle,* lit. (to *compete* for a prize), fig. (to *contend* with an adversary), or gen. (to *endeavor* to accomplish something):— fight, labor fervently, strive.

76. Ἀδάμ **Adam**, *ad-am´;* of Heb. or. [121]; *Adam,* the first man; typ. (of Jesus) *man* (as his representative):— Adam.

77. ἀδάπανος **adapanŏs**, *ad-ap´-an-os;* from *1* (as neg. particle) and *1160; costless,* i.e. *gratuitous:—* without expense.

78. Ἀδδί **Addi**, *ad-dee´;* prob. of Heb. or. [comp. 5716]; *Addi,* an Isr.:— Addi.

79. ἀδελφή **adĕlphē**, *ad-el-fay´;* fem of *80;* a *sister* (nat. or eccl.):— sister.

80. ἀδελφός **adĕlphŏs**, *ad-el-fos´;* from *1* (as a connective particle) and δελφύς **dĕlphus** (the *womb*); a *brother* (lit. or fig.) near or remote [much like 1]:— brother.

81. ἀδελφότης **adĕlphŏtēs**, *ad-el-fot´-ace;* from *80; brotherhood* (prop. the feeling of *brotherliness*), i.e. the (Chr.) *fraternity:—* brethren, brotherhood.

82. ἄδηλος **adēlŏs**, *ad´-ay-los;* from *1* (as a neg. particle) and *1212; hidden,* fig. *indistinct:—* appear not, uncertain.

83. ἀδηλότης **adēlŏtēs**, *ad-ay-lot´-ace;* from *82; uncertainty:—* × uncertain.

84. ἀδήλως **adēlōs**, *ad-ay´-loce;* adv. from *82; uncertainly:—* uncertainly.

85. ἀδημονέω **adēmŏnĕō**, *ad-ay-mon-eh´-o;* from a der. of ἀδέω **adeo** (to be *sated* to loathing); to *be in distress* (of mind):— be full of heaviness, be very heavy.

86. ᾅδης **haidēs**, *hah´-dace;* from *1* (as neg. particle) and *1492;* prop. *unseen,* i.e. "*Hades*" or the place (state) of departed souls:— grave, hell.

87. ἀδιάκριτος **adiakritŏs**, *ad-ee-ak´-ree-tos;* from *1* (as a neg. particle) and a der. of *1252;* prop. *undistinguished,* i.e. (act.) *impartial:—* without partiality.

88. ἀδιάλειπτος **adialĕiptŏs**, *ad-ee-al´-ipe-tos;* from *1* (as a neg. particle) and a der. of a compound of *1223* and *3007; unintermitted,* i.e. *permanent:—* without ceasing, continual.

89. ἀδιαλείπτως **adialĕiptōs**, *ad-ee-al-ipe´-toce;* adv. from *88; uninterruptedly,* i.e. *without omission* (on an appropriate occasion):— without ceasing.

90. ἀδιαφθορία **adiaphthŏria**, *ad-ee-af-thor-ee´-ah;* from a der. of a compound of *1* (as a neg. particle) and a der. of *1311; incorruptibleness,* i.e. (fig.) *purity* (of doctrine):— uncorruptness.

91. ἀδικέω **adikĕō**, *ad-ee-keh´-o;* from *94;* to *be unjust,* i.e. (act.) *do wrong* (mor., socially or phys.):— hurt, injure, be an offender, be unjust, (do, suffer, take) wrong.

92. ἀδίκημα **adikēma**, *ad-eek´-ay-mah;* from *91;* a *wrong* done:— evil doing, iniquity, matter of wrong.

93. ἀδικία **adikia**, *ad-ee-kee´-ah;* from *94;* (legal) *injustice* (prop. the quality, by impl. the act); mor. *wrongfulness* (of character, life or act):— iniquity, unjust, unrighteousness, wrong.

94. ἄδικος **adikŏs**, *ad´-ee-kos;* from *1* (as a neg. particle) and *1349; unjust;* by extens. *wicked;* by impl. *treacherous;* spec. *heathen:—* unjust, unrighteous.

95. ἀδίκως **adikōs**, *ad-ee´-koce;* adv. from *94; unjustly:—* wrongfully.

96. ἀδόκιμος **adŏkimŏs**, *ad-ok´-ee-mos;* from *1* (as a neg. particle) and *1384; unapproved,* i.e. *rejected;* by impl. *worthless* (lit. or mor.):— castaway, rejected, reprobate.

97. ἄδολος **adŏlŏs**, *ad´-ol-os;* from *1* (as a neg. particle) and *1388; undeceitful,* i.e. (fig.) *unadulterated:—* sincere.

98. Ἀδραμυττηνός **Adramuttēnŏs**, *ad-ram-oot-tay-nos´;* from Ἀδραμύττειον **Adramuttĕiŏn** (a place in Asia Minor); *Adramyttene* or belonging to Adramyttium:— of Adramyttium.

99. Ἀδρίας **Adrias**, *ad-ree´-as;* from Ἀδρία **Adria** (a place near its shore); the *Adriatic* sea (incl. the Ionian):— Adria.

100. ἁδρότης **hadrŏtēs**, *had-rot´-ace;* from ἁδρός **hadrŏs** (stout); *plumpness,* i.e. (fig.) *liberality:—* abundance.

101. ἀδυνατέω **adunatĕō**, *ad-oo-nat-eh´-o;* from *102;* to *be unable,* i.e. (pass.) *impossible:—* be impossible.

102. ἀδύνατος **adunatŏs**, *ad-oo´-nat-os;* from *1* (as a neg. particle) and *1415; unable,* i.e. *weak* (lit. or fig.); pass. *impossible:—* could not do, impossible, impotent, not possible, weak.

103. ᾄδω **aidō**, *ad´-o´* a prim. verb; to *sing:—* sing.

104. ἀεί **aĕi**, *ah-eye´;* from an obs. prim. noun (appar. mean. continued *duration*); "*ever*," by qualification *regularly;* by impl. *earnestly:—* always, ever.

105. ἀετός **aětŏs**, *ah-et-os´;* from the same as *109;* an *eagle* (from its *wind-like* flight):— eagle.

106. ἄζυμος **azumŏs**, *ad´-zoo-mos;* from *1* (as a neg. particle) and *2219; unleavened,* i.e. (fig.) *uncorrupted;* (in the neut. plur.) spec. (by impl.) the *Passover* week:— unleavened (bread).

107. Ἀζώρ **Azōr**, *ad-zore´;* of Heb. or. [comp. 5809]; *Azor,* an Isr.:— Azor.

108. Ἄζωτος **Azōtŏs**, *ad´-zo-tos;* of Heb. or. [795]; *Azotus* (i.e. Ashdod), a place in Pal.:— Azotus.

109. ἀήρ **aēr**, *ah-ayr´;* from ἄημι **aēmi** (to *breathe* unconsciously, i.e. *respire;* by anal. to *blow*); "*air*" (as naturally *circumambient*):— air. Comp. 5594.

ἀθά **atha**. See *3134.*

110. ἀθανασία **athanasia**, *ath-an-as-ee´-ah;* from a compound of *1* (as a neg. particle) and *2288; deathlessness:—* immortality.

111. ἀθέμιτος **athĕmitŏs**, *ath-em´-ee-tos;* from *1* (as a neg. particle) and a der. of θέμις **thĕmis** (*statute;* from the base of *5087*); *illegal;* by impl. *flagitious:—* abominable, unlawful thing.

112. ἄθεος **athĕŏs**, *ath´-eh-os;* from *1* (as a neg. particle) and *2316; godless:—* without God.

113. ἄθεσμος **athĕsmŏs**, *ath´-es-mos;* from *1* (as a neg. particle) and a der. of *5087* (in the sense of *enacting*); *lawless,* i.e. (by impl.) *criminal:—* wicked.

114. ἀθετέω **athĕtĕō**, *ath-et-eh´-o;* from a compound of *1* (as a neg. particle)

and a der. of *5087;* to *set aside,* i.e. (by impl.) to *disesteem, neutralize* or *violate:*— cast off, despise, disannul, frustrate, bring to nought, reject.

115. ἀθέτησις **athĕtēsis,** *ath-et´-ay-sis;* from *114; cancellation* (lit. or fig.):— disannulling, put away.

116. 'Αθῆναι **Athēnai,** *ath-ay-nahee;* plur. of 'Αθήνη **Athēnē** (the goddess of wisdom, who was reputed to have founded the city); *Athenæ,* the capitol of Greece:— Athens.

117. 'Αθηναῖος **Athēnaiŏs,** *ath-ay-nah´-yos;* from *116;* an *Athenæan* or inhab. of Athenæ:— Athenian.

118. ἀθλέω **athlĕō,** *ath-leh´-o;* from ἆθλος **athlŏs** (a *contest* in the public lists); to *contend* in the competitive games:— strive.

119. ἄθλησις **athlēsis,** *ath´-lay-sis;* from *118;* a *struggle* (fig.):— fight.

120. ἀθυμέω **athumĕō,** *ath-oo-meh´-o;* from a comp. of *1* (as a neg. particle) and *2372;* to be *spiritless,* i.e. *disheartened:*— be dismayed.

121. ἄθῶος **athŏŏs,** *ath´-o-os;* from *1* (as a neg. particle) and prob. a der. of *5087* (mean. a *penalty*); *not guilty:*— innocent.

122. αἴγειος **aigĕiŏs,** *ah´-ee-ghi-os;* from αἴξ **aix** (a *goat*); belonging to a *goat:*— goat.

123. αἰγιαλός **aigialŏs,** *ahee-ghee-al-os´;* from ἀίσσω **aïssō** (to *rush*) and *251* (in the sense of the *sea*; a *beach* (on which the *waves dash*):— shore.

124. Αἰγύπτιος **Aiguptiŏs,** *ahee-goop´-tee-os;* from *125;* an *Ægyptian* or inhab. of Ægyptus:— Egyptian.

125. Αἴγυπτος **Aiguptŏs,** *ah´-ee-goop-tos;* of uncert. der.; *Ægyptus,* the land of the Nile:— Egypt.

126. ἀΐδιος **aïdiŏs,** *ah-id´-ee-os;* from *104; everduring* (forward and backward, or forward only):— eternal, everlasting.

127. αἰδώς **aidōs,** *ahee-doce´;* perh. from *1* (as a neg. particle) and *1492* (through the idea of *downcast* eyes); *bashfulness,* i.e. (toward men), *modesty* or (toward God) *awe:*— reverence, shamefacedness.

128. Αἰθίοψ **Aithiŏps,** *ahee-thee´-ops;* from αἴθω **aithō** (to *scorch*) and ὤψ **ŏps** (the *face,* from *3700;* an *Æthiopian* (as a *blackamoor*):— Ethiopian.

129. αἶμα **haima,** *hah´-ee-mah;* of uncert. der.; *blood,* lit. (of men or animals), fig. (the *juice* of grapes) or spec. (the atoning *blood* of Christ); by impl. *bloodshed,* also *kindred:*— blood.

130. αἰματεκχυσία **haimatĕkchusia,** *ha-hee-mat-ek-khoo-see´-ah;* from *129* and a der. of *1632;* an *effusion of blood:*— shedding of blood.

131. αἱμόῤῥέω **haimŏrrhĕō,** *hahee-mor-hreh´-o;* from *129* and *4482;* to *flow blood,* i.e. *have a hemorrhage:*— diseased with an issue of blood.

132. Αἰνέας **Ainĕas,** *ahee-neh´-as;* of uncert. der.; *Æneas,* an Isr.:— Æneas.

133. αἴνεσις **ainĕsis,** *ah´-ee-nes-is;*

from *134;* a *praising* (the act), i.e. (spec.) a *thank* (-offering):— praise.

134. αἰνέω **ainĕō,** *ahee-neh´-o;* from *136;* to *praise* (God):— praise.

135. αἴνιγμα **ainigma,** *ah´-ee-nig-ma;* from a der. of *136* (in its prim. sense); an *obscure* saying ("enigma"), i.e. (abstr.) *obscureness:*— × darkly.

136. αἶνος **ainŏs,** *ah´-ee-nos;* appar. a prim. word; prop. a *story,* but used in the sense of *1868; praise* (of God):— praise.

137. Αἰνών **Ainōn,** *ahee-nohn´;* of Heb. or. la der. of 5869, *place of springsl; Ænon,* a place in Pal.:— Ænon.

138. αἱρέομαι **hairĕŏmai,** *hahee-reh´-om-ahee;* prob. akin to *142;* to *take for oneself,* i.e. to *prefer:*— choose. Some of the forms are borrowed from a cognate ἕλλομαι **hellŏmai** *hel´-lom-ahee;* which is otherwise obsolete.

139. αἵρεσις **hairĕsis,** *hah´-ee-res-is;* from *138;* prop. a *choice,* i.e. (spec.) a *party* or (abstr.) *disunion:*— heresy lwhich is the Gr. word itselfl, sect.

140. αἱρετίζω **hairĕtizō,** *hahee-ret-id´-zo;* from a der. of *138;* to *make a choice:*— choose.

141. αἱρετικός **hairĕtikŏs,** *hahee-ret-ee-kos´;* from the same as *140;* a *schismatic:*— heretic l the Gr. word itself l.

142. αἴρω **airō,** *ah´-ee-ro;* a prim. verb; to *lift;* by impl. to *take up* or *away;* fig. to *raise* (the voice), *keep in suspense* (the mind), spec. to *sail* away (i.e. *weigh* anchor); by Heb. lcomp. 5375l to *expiate* sin:— away with, bear (up), carry, lift up, loose, make to doubt, put away, remove, take (away, up).

143. αἰσθάνομαι **aisthanŏmai,** *ahee-sthan´-om-ahee;* of uncert. der.; to *apprehend* (prop. by the senses):— perceive.

144. αἴσθησις **aisthēsis,** *ah´-ee-sthay-sis;* from *143; perception,* i.e. (fig.) *discernment:*— judgment.

145. αἰσθητήριον **aisthētēriŏn,** *ahee-sthay-tay´-ree-on;* from a der. of *143;* prop. an *organ of perception,* i.e. (fig.) *judgment:*— senses.

146. αἰσχροκερδής **aischrŏkĕrdēs,** *ahee-skhrok-er-dace´;* from *150* and κέρδος **kerdos** (*gain*); *sordid:*— given to (greedy ofl filthy lucre.

147. αἰσχροκερδῶς **aischrŏkĕrdōs,** *ahee-skhrok-er-doce´;* adv. from *146; sordidly:*— for filthy lucre's sake.

148. αἰσχρολογία **aischrŏlŏgia,** *ahee-skhrol-og-ee´-ah;* from *150* and *3056; vile conversation:*— filthy communication.

149. αἰσχρόν **aischrŏn,** *ahee-skhron´;* neut. of *150;* a *shameful* thing, i.e. *indecorum:*— shame.

150. αἰσχρός **aischrŏs,** *ahee-skhros´;* from the same as *153; shameful,* i.e. *base* (spec. *venal*):— filthy.

151. αἰσχρότης **aischrŏtēs,** *ahee-skhrot´-ace;* from *150; shamefulness,* i.e. *obscenity:*— filthiness.

152. αἰσχύνη **aischunē,** *ahee-skhoo´-nay;* from *153; shame* or *disgrace* (abstr. or concr.):— dishonesty, shame.

153. αἰσχύνομαι **aischunŏmai,** *ahee-skhoo´-nom-ahee;* from αἶσχος **aischŏs** (*disfigurement,* i.e. *disgrace*); to *feel shame* (for oneself):— be ashamed.

154. αἰτέω **aitĕō,** *ahee-teh´-o;* of uncert. der.; to *ask* (in gen.):— ask, beg, call for, crave, desire, require. Comp. *4441.*

155. αἴτημα **aitēma,** *ah´-ee-tay-mah;* from *154;* a *thing asked* or (abstr.) an *asking:*— petition, request, required.

156. αἰτία **aitia,** *ahee-tee´-a;* from the same as *154;* a *cause* (as if *asked* for), i.e. (logical) *reason* (motive, matter), (legal) *crime* (alleged or proved):— accusation, case, cause, crime, fault, lwh-lerel-forel.

157. αἰτίαμα **aitiama,** *ahee-tee´-am-ah;* from a der. of *156;* a *thing charged:*— complaint.

158. αἴτιον **aitiŏn,** *ah´-ee-tee-on;* neut. of *159;* a *reason* or *crime* llike *156l:*— cause, fault.

159. αἴτιος **aitiŏs,** *ah´-ee-tee-os;* from the same as *154; causative,* i.e. (concr.) a *causer:*— author.

160. αἰφνίδιος **aiphnidiŏs,** *aheef-nid´-ee-os;* from a comp. of *1* (as a neg. particle) and *5316* lcomp. *1810l* (mean. *non-apparent*); *unexpected,* i.e. (adv.) *suddenly:*— sudden, unawares.

161. αἰχμαλωσία **aichmalōsia,** *aheekh-mal-o-see´-ah;* from *164; captivity:*— captivity.

162. αἰχμαλωτεύω **aichmalŏtĕuō,** *aheekh-mal-o-tew´-o;* from *164;* to *capture* llike *163l:*— lead captive.

163. αἰχμαλωτίζω **aichmalŏtizō,** *aheekh-mal-o-tid´-zo;* from *164;* to *make captive:*— lead away captive, bring into captivity.

164. αἰχμαλωτός **aichmalōtŏs,** *aheekh-mal-o-tos´;* from αἰχμή **aichmē** (a *spear*) and a der. of the same as *259;* prop. a *prisoner of war,* i.e. (gen.) a *captive:*— captive.

165. αἰών **aiōn,** *ahee-ohn´;* from the same as *104;* prop. an *age;* by extens. *perpetuity* (also past); by impl. the *world;* spec. (Jewish) a Messianic period (present or future):— age, course, eternal, (for) ever (-more), (n-)ever, (beginning of the, while the) world (began, without end). Comp. *5550.*

166. αἰώνιος **aiōniŏs,** *ahee-o´-nee-os;* from *165; perpetual* (also used of past time, or past and future as well):— eternal, for ever, everlasting, world (began).

167. ἀκαθαρσία **akatharsia,** *ak-ath-ar-see´-ah;* from *169; impurity* (the quality), phys. or mor.:— uncleanness.

168. ἀκαθάρτης **akathartēs,** *ak-ath-ar´-tace;* from *169; impurity* (the state), mor.:— filthiness.

169. ἀκάθαρτος **akathartŏs,** *ak-ath´-artos;* from *1* (as a neg. particle) and a presumed der. of *2508* (mean. *cleansed*); *impure* (cer., mor. llewdl or spec. ldemonicl):— foul, unclean.

170. ἀκαιρέομαι **akairĕŏmai,** *ak-ahee-reh´-om-ahee;* from a comp. of *1* (as a neg. particle) and *2540* (mean. *unseasonable*); to be *inopportune* (for one-

self), i.e. to *fail of a proper occasion*:— lack opportunity.

171. ἀκαίρως **akairōs**, *ak-ah´-ee-roce*; adv. from the same as *170; inopportunely*:— out of season.

172. ἄκακος **akakŏs**, *ak´-ak-os*; from *1* (as a neg. particle) and *2556; not bad*, i.e. (obj.) *innocent* or (subj.) *unsuspecting*:— harmless, simple.

173. ἄκανθα **akantha**, *ak´-an-thah*; prob. from the same as *188*; a *thorn*:— thorn.

174. ἀκάνθινος **akanthinŏs**, *ak-an´-thee-nos*; from *173; thorny*:— of thorns.

175. ἄκαρπος **akarpŏs**, *ak´-ar-pos*; from *1* (as a neg. particle) and *2590; barren* (lit. or fig.):— without fruit, unfruitful.

176. ἀκατάγνωστος **akatagnōstŏs**, *ak-at-ag´-noce-tos*; from *1* (as a neg. particle) and a der. of *2607; unblamable*:— that cannot be condemned.

177. ἀκατακάλυπτος **akatakaluptŏs**, *ak-at-ak-al´-oop-tos*; from *1* (as a neg. particle) and a der. of a comp. of *2596* and *2572; unveiled*:— uncovered.

178. ἀκατάκριτος **akatakritŏs**, *ak-at-ak´-ree-tos*; from *1* (as a neg. particle) and a der. of *2632; without* (legal) *trial*:— uncondemned.

179. ἀκατάλυτος **akatalutŏs**, *ak-at-al´-oo-tos*; from *1* (as a neg. particle) and a der. of *2647; indissoluble*, i.e. (fig.) *permanent*:— endless.

180. ἀκατάπαυστος **akatapaustŏs**, *ak-at-ap´-ow-stos*; from *1* (as a neg. particle) and a der. of *2664; unrefraining*:— that cannot cease.

181. ἀκαταστασία **akatastasia**, *ak-at-as-tah-see´-ah*; from *182; instability*, i.e. *disorder*:— commotion, confusion, tumult.

182. ἀκατάστατος **akatastatŏs**, *ak-at-as´-tat-os*; from *1* (as a neg. particle) and a der. of *2525; inconstant*:— unstable.

183. ἀκατάσχετος **akataschĕtŏs**, *ak-at-as´-khet-os*; from *1* (as a neg. particle) and a der. of *2722; unrestrainable*:— unruly.

184. Ἀκελδαμά **Akeldama**, *ak-el-dam-ah´*; of Chald. or. [mean. *field of blood*; corresp. to 2506 and 1818]; *Akeldama*, a place near Jerusalem:— Aceldama.

185. ἀκέραιος **akĕraiŏs**, *ak-er´-ah-yos*; from *1* (as a neg. particle) and a presumed der. of *2767; unmixed*, i.e. (fig.) *innocent*:— harmless, simple.

186. ἀκλινής **aklinēs**, *ak-lee-nace´*; from *1* (as a neg. particle) and *2827; not leaning*, i.e. (fig.) *firm*:— without wavering.

187. ἀκμάζω **akmazō**, *ak-mad´-zo*; from the same as *188; to make a point*, i.e. (fig.) *mature*:— be fully ripe.

188. ἀκμήν **akmēn**, *ak-mane´*; acc. of a noun ("*acme*") akin to ἀκή **akē** (a *point*) and mean. the same; adv. *just* now, i.e. *still*:— yet.

189. ἀκοή **akŏē**, *ak-o-ay´*; from *191; hearing* (the act, the sense or the thing heard):— audience, ear, fame, which ye heard, hearing, preached, report, rumor.

190. ἀκολουθέω **akŏlŏuthĕō**, *ak-ol-oo-theh´-o*; from *1* (as a particle of union) and κέλευθος **kĕlĕuthŏs** (a *road*); prop. to *be in the same way with*, i.e. to *accompany* (spec. as a disciple):— follow, reach.

191. ἀκούω **akŏuō**, *ak-oo´-o*; a prim. verb; to *hear* (in various senses):— give (in the) audience (of), come (to the ears), ([shall]) hear (-er, -ken), be noised, be reported, understand.

192. ἀκρασία **akrasia**, *ak-ras-ee´-a*; from *193; want of self-restraint*:— excess, incontinency.

193. ἀκράτης **akratēs**, *ak-rat´-ace*; from *1* (as a neg. particle) and *2904; powerless*, i.e. *without self-control*:— incontinent.

194. ἄκρατος **akratŏs**, *ak´-rat-os*; from *1* (as a neg. particle) and a presumed der. of *2767; undiluted*:— without mixture.

195. ἀκρίβεια **akribĕia**, *ak-ree´-bi-ah*; from the same as *196; exactness*:— perfect manner.

196. ἀκριβέστατος **akribĕstatŏs**, *ak-ree-bes´-ta-tos*; superlative of ἀκριβής **akribēs** (a der. of the same as *206*); *most exact*:— most straitest.

197. ἀκριβέστερον **akribĕstĕrŏn**, *ak-ree-bes´-ter-on*; neut. of the comparative of the same as *196*; (adv.) *more exactly*:— more perfect (-ly).

198. ἀκριβόω **akribŏō**, *ak-ree-bŏ´-o*; from the same as *196*; to *be exact*, i.e. *ascertain*:— enquire diligently.

199. ἀκριβῶς **akribōs**, *ak-ree-boce´*; adv. from the same as *196; exactly*:— circumspectly, diligently, perfect (-ly).

200. ἀκρίς **akris**, *ak-rece´*; appar. from the same as *206*; a *locust* (as *pointed*, or as *lightning* on the *top* of vegetation):— locust.

201. ἀκροατήριον **akrŏatēriŏn**, *ak-rŏ-at-ay´-ree-on*; from *202*; an *audience-room*:— place of hearing.

202. ἀκροατής **akrŏatēs**, *ak-rŏ-at-ace´*; from ἀκροάομαι **akrŏaŏmai** (to *listen*; appar. an intens. of *191*); a *hearer* (merely):— hearer.

203. ἀκροβυστία **akrŏbustia**, *ak-rob-oos-tee´-ah*; from *206* and prob. a modified form of πόσθη **pŏsthē** (the *penis* or male sexual organ); the *prepuce*; by impl. an *uncircumcised* (i.e. gentile, fig. *unregenerate*) state or person:— not circumcised, uncircumcised [with 2192], uncircumcision.

204. ἀκρογωνιαῖος **akrŏgōniaiŏs**, *ak-rog-o-nee-ah´-yos*; from *206* and *1137*; belonging to the extreme *corner*:— chief corner.

205. ἀκροθίνιον **akrŏthiniŏn**, *ak-roth-in´-ee-on*; from *206* and θίς **this** (a *heap*); prop. (in the plur.) the *top of the heap*, i.e. (by impl.) *best of the booty*:— spoils.

206. ἄκρον **akrŏn**, *ak´-ron*; neut. of an adj. prob. akin to the base of *188*; the *extremity*:— one end ... other, tip, top, uttermost part.

207. Ἀκύλας **Akulas**, *ak-oo´-las*; prob. for Lat. *aquila* (an *eagle*); *Akulas*, an Isr.:— Aquila.

208. ἀκυρόω **akurŏō**, *ak-oo-rŏ´-o*; from *1* (as a neg. particle) and *2964*; to *invalidate*:— disannul, make of none effect.

209. ἀκωλύτως **akōlutōs**, *ak-o-loo´-toce*; adv. from a compound of *1* (as a neg. particle) and a der. of *2967*; in an *unhindered manner*, i.e. *freely*:— no man forbidding him.

210. ἄκων **akōn**, *ak´-ohn*; from *1* (as a neg. particle) and *1635; unwilling*:— against the will.

211. ἀλάβαστρον **alabastrŏn**, *al-ab´-as-tron*; neut. of ἀλάβαστρος **alabastrŏs** (of uncert. der.), the name of a stone; prop. an "*alabaster*" box, i.e. (by extens.) a perfume *vase* (of any material):— (alabaster) box.

212. ἀλαζονεία **alazŏnĕia**, *al-ad-zon-i´-a*; from *213; braggadocio*, i.e. (by impl.) *self-confidence*:— boasting, pride.

213. ἀλαζών **alazōn**, *al-ad-zone´*; from ἄλη **alē** (*vagrancy*); *braggart*:— boaster.

214. ἀλαλάζω **alalazō**, *al-al-ad´-zo*; from ἀλαλή **alalē** (a shout; "*halloo*"); to *vociferate*, i.e. (by impl.) to *wail*; fig. to *clang*:— tinkle, wail.

215. ἀλάλητος **alalētŏs**, *al-al´-ay-tos*; from *1* (as a neg. particle) and a der. of *2980; unspeakable*:— unutterable, which cannot be uttered.

216. ἄλαλος **alalŏs**, *al´-al-os*; from *1* (a neg. particle) and *2980; mute*:— dumb.

217. ἅλας **halas**, *hal´-as*; from *251; salt*; fig. *prudence*:— salt.

218. ἀλείφω **alĕiphō**, *al-i´-fo*; from *1* (as particle of union) and the base of *3045*; to *oil* (with perfume):— anoint.

219. ἀλεκτοροφωνία **alektŏrŏphōnia**, *al-ek-tor-of-o-nee´-ah*; from *220* and *5456; cock-crow*, i.e. the third night-watch:— cockcrowing.

220. ἀλέκτωρ **alĕktōr**, *al-ek´-tore*; from ἀλέκω **alĕkō** (to *ward* off); a *cock* or male fowl:— cock.

221. Ἀλεξανδρεύς **Alĕxandrĕus**, *al-ex-and-reuce´*; from Ἀλεξάνδρεια (the city so called); an *Alexandreian* or inhab. of Alexandria:— of Alexandria, Alexandrian.

222. Ἀλεξανδρῖνος **Alĕxandrinŏs**, *al-ex-an-dree´-nos*; from the same as *221; Alexandrine*, or belonging to Alexandria:— of Alexandria.

223. Ἀλέξανδρος **Alĕxandrŏs**, *al-ex-an-dros*; from the same as (the first part of) *220* and *435; man-defender*; *Alexander*, the name of three Isr. and one other man:— Alexander.

224. ἄλευρον **alĕurŏn**, *al´-yoo-ron*; from ἀλέω **alĕō** (to *grind*); *flour*:— meal.

225. ἀλήθεια **alēthĕia**, *al-ay´-thi-a*; from *227; truth*:— true, × truly, truth, verity.

226. ἀληθεύω **alēthĕuō**, *al-ayth-yoo´-o*; from *227*; to *be true* (in doctrine and profession):— speak (tell) the truth.

227. ἀληθής **alēthēs**, *al-ay-thace´*; from *1* (as a neg. particle) and *2990; true* (as *not concealing*):— true, truly, truth.

228. ἀληθινός **alēthinŏs**, *al-ay-thee-nos´*; from *227; truthful*:— true.

229. ἀλήθω **alēthō**, *al-ay´-tho*; from the same as 224; to *grind*:— grind.

230. ἀληθῶς **alēthōs**, *al-ay-thoce´*; adv. from 227; *truly*:— indeed, surely, of a surety, truly, of a (in) truth, verily, very.

231. ἀλιεύς **haliĕus**, *hal-ee-yoos´*; from 251; a *sailor* (as engaged on the *salt* water), i.e. (by impl.) a *fisher*:— fisher (-man).

232. ἀλιεύω **haliĕuō**, *hal-ee-yoo´-o*; from 231; to *be a fisher*, i.e. (by impl.) to *fish*:— go a-fishing.

233. ἀλίζω **halizō**, *hal-id´-zo*; from 251; to *salt*:— salt.

234. ἀλίσγεμα **alisgĕma**, *al-is´-ghem-ah*; from ἀλισγέω **alisgĕō** (to *soil*); (cer.) *defilement*:— pollution.

235. ἀλλά **alla**, *al-lah´*; neut. plur. of 243; prop. *other* things, i.e. (adv.) *contrariwise* (in many relations):— and, but (even), howbeit, indeed, nay, nevertheless, no, notwithstanding, save, therefore, yea, yet.

236. ἀλλάσσω **allassō**, *al-las´-so*; from 243; to *make different*:— change.

237. ἀλλαχόθεν **allachŏthĕn**, *al-lakh-oth´-en*; from 243; *from elsewhere*:— some other way.

238. ἀλληγορέω **allēgŏrĕō**, *al-lay-gor-eh´-o*; from 243 and ἀγορέω **agŏrĕō** (to *harangue* [comp. 58]); to *allegorize*:— be an allegory [the Gr. word itself].

239. ἀλληλούϊα **allēlŏuïa**, *al-lay-loo´-ee-ah*; of Heb. or. [imper. of 1984 and 3050]; *praise ye Jah!*, an adoring exclamation:— alleluiah.

240. ἀλλήλων **allēlōn**, *al-lay´-lone*; Gen. plur. from 243 redupl.; *one another*:— each other, mutual, one another, (the other), (them-, your-) selves, (selves) together [sometimes with 3326 or 4314].

241. ἀλλογενής **allŏgĕnēs**, *al-log-en-ace´*; from 243 and 1085; *foreign*, i.e. not a Jew:— stranger.

242. ἅλλομαι **hallŏmai**, *hal´-lom-ahee*; mid. voice of appar. a prim. verb; to *jump*; fig. to *gush*:— leap, spring up.

243. ἄλλος **allŏs**, *al´-los*; a prim. word; "*else*," i.e. *different* (in many applications):— more, one (another), (an-, some an-) other (-s, -wise).

244. ἀλλοτριεπίσκοπος **allotriĕpiskŏpŏs**, *al-lot-ree-ep-is´-kop-os*; from 245 and 1985; *overseeing others'* affairs, i.e. a *meddler* (spec. in Gentile customs):— busybody in other men's matters.

245. ἀλλότριος **allŏtriŏs**, *al-lot´-ree-os*; from 243; *another's*, i.e. not one's own; by extens. *foreign, not akin, hostile*:— alien, (an-) other (man's, men's), strange (-r).

246. ἀλλόφυλος **allŏphulŏs**, *al-lof´-oo-los*; from 243 and 5443; *for.*, i.e. (spec.) *Gentile*:— one of another nation.

247. ἄλλως **allōs**, *al´-loce*; adv. from 243; *differently*:— otherwise.

248. ἀλοάω **alŏaō**, *al-o-ah´-o*; from the same as 257; to *tread* out grain:— thresh, tread out the corn.

249. ἄλογος **alŏgŏs**, *al´-og-os*; from 1 (as a neg. particle) and 3056; *irrational*:— brute, unreasonable.

250. ἀλόη **alŏē**, *al-o-ay´*; of for. or. [comp. 174]; *aloes* (the gum):— aloes.

251. ἅλς **hals**, *halce*; a prim. word; "*salt*":— salt.

252. ἁλυκός **halukŏs**, *hal-oo-kos´*; from 251; *briny*:— salt.

253. ἀλυπότερος **alupŏtĕrŏs**, *al-oo-pot´-er-os*; comparative of a comp. of 1 (as a neg. particle) and 3077; *more without grief*:— less sorrowful.

254. ἅλυσις **halusis**, *hal´-oo-sis*; of uncert. der.; a *fetter* or *manacle*:— bonds, chain.

255. ἀλυσιτελής **alusitĕlēs**, *al-oo-sit-el-ace´*; from 1 (as a neg. particle) and the base of 3081; *gainless*, i.e. (by impl.) *pernicious*:— unprofitable.

256. Ἀλφαῖος **Alphaiŏs**, *al-fah´-yos*; of Heb. or. [comp. 2501]; *Alphæus*, an Isr.:— Alpheus.

257. ἅλων **halōn**, *hal´-ohn*; prob. from the base of 1507; a *threshing-floor* (as *rolled* hard), i.e. (fig.) the *grain* (and chaff, as just threshed):— floor.

258. ἀλώπηξ **alōpēx**, *al-o´-pakes*; of uncert. der.; a *fox*, i.e. (fig.) a *cunning* person:— fox.

259. ἅλωσις **halōsis**, *hal´-o-sis*; from a collat. form of 138; *capture*:— be taken.

260. ἅμα **hama**, *ham´-ah*; a prim. particle; prop. *at* the "*same*" *time*, but freely used as a prep. or adv. denoting close association:— also, and, together, with (-al).

261. ἀμαθής **amathēs**, *am-ath-ace´*; from 1 (as a neg. particle) and 3129; *ignorant*:— unlearned.

262. ἀμαράντινος **amarantinŏs**, *am-ar-an´-tee-nos*; from 263; "*amaranthine*", i.e. (by impl.) *fadeless*:— that fadeth not away.

263. ἀμάραντος **amarantŏs**, *am-ar´-an-tos*; from 1 (as a neg. particle) and a presumed der. of 3133; *unfading*, i.e. (by impl.) *perpetual*:— that fadeth not away.

264. ἁμαρτάνω **hamartanō**, *ham-ar-tan´-o*; perh. from 1 (as a neg. particle) and the base of 3313; prop. to *miss the mark* (and so *not share* in the prize), i.e. (fig.) to *err*, esp. (mor.) to *sin*:— for your faults, offend, sin, trespass.

265. ἁμάρτημα **hamartēma**, *ham-ar´-tay-mah*; from 264; a *sin* (prop. concr.):— sin.

266. ἁμαρτία **hamartia**, *ham-ar-tee´-ah*; from 264; *sin* (prop. abstr.):— offence, sin (-ful).

267. ἀμάρτυρος **amarturŏs**, *am-ar´-too-ros*; from 1 (as a neg. particle) and a form of 3144; *unattested*:— without witness.

268. ἁμαρτωλός **hamartōlŏs**, *ham-ar-to-los´*; from 264; *sinful*, i.e. a *sinner*:— sinful, sinner.

269. ἄμαχος **amachŏs**, *am´-akh-os*; from 1 (as a neg. particle) and 3163; *peaceable*:— not a brawler.

270. ἀμάω **amaō**, *am-ah´-o*; from 260; prop. to *collect*, i.e. (by impl.) *reap*:— reap down.

271. ἀμέθυστος **amĕthustŏs**, *am-eth´-oos-tos*; from 1 (as a neg. particle) and a der. of 3184; the "*amethyst*" (supposed to *prevent intoxication*):— amethyst.

272. ἀμελέω **amĕlĕō**, *am-el-eh´-o*; from 1 (as a neg. particle) and 3199; to *be careless* of:— make light of, neglect, be negligent, not regard.

273. ἄμεμπτος **amĕmptŏs**, *am´-emp-tos*; from 1 (as a neg. particle) and a der. of 3201; *irreproachable*:— blameless, faultless, unblamable.

274. ἀμέμπτως **amĕmptōs**, *am-emp´-toce*; adv. from 273; *faultlessly*:— blameless, unblamably.

275. ἀμέριμνος **amĕrimnŏs**, *am-er´-im-nos*; from 1 (as a neg. particle) and 3308; *not anxious*:— without care (-fulness), secure.

276. ἀμετάθετος **amĕtathĕtŏs**, *am-et-ath´-et-os*; from 1 (as a neg. particle) and a der. of 3346; *unchangeable*, or (neut. as abstr.) *unchangeability*:— immutable (-ility).

277. ἀμετακίνητος **amĕtakinētŏs**, *am-et-ak-in´-ay-tos*; from 1 (as a neg. particle) and a der. of 3334; *immovable*:— unmovable.

278. ἀμεταμέλητος **amĕtamĕlētŏs**, *am-et-am-el´-ay-tos*; from 1 (as a neg. particle) and a presumed der. of 3338; *irrevocable*:— without repentance, not to be repented of.

279. ἀμετανόητος **amĕtanŏētŏs**, *am-et-an-o´-ay-tos*; from 1 (as a neg. particle) and a presumed der. of 3340; *unrepentant*:— impenitent.

280. ἄμετρος **amĕtrŏs**, *am´-et-ros*; from 1 (as a neg. particle) and 3358; *immoderate*:— (thing) without measure.

281. ἀμήν **amēn**, *am-ane´*; of Heb. or. [543]; prop. *firm*, i.e. (fig.) *trustworthy*; adv. *surely* (often as interj. *so be it*):— amen, verily.

282. ἀμήτωρ **amētōr**, *am-ay´-tore*; from 1 (as a neg. particle) and 3384; *motherless*, i.e. *of unknown maternity*:— without mother.

283. ἀμίαντος **amiantŏs**, *am-ee´-an-tos*; from 1 (as a neg. particle) and a der. of 3392; *unsoiled*, i.e. (fig.) *pure*:— undefiled.

284. Ἀμιναδάβ **Aminadab**, *am-ee-nad-ab´*; of Heb. or. [5992]; *Aminadab*, an Isr.:— Aminadab.

285. ἄμμος **ammŏs**, *am´-mos*; perh. from 260; *sand* (as *heaped* on the beach):— sand.

286. ἀμνός **amnŏs**, *am-nos´*; appar a prim. word; a *lamb*:— lamb.

287. ἀμοιβή **amŏibē**, *am-oy-bay´*; from ἀμείβω **amĕibō** (to *exchange*); *requital*:— requite.

288. ἄμπελος **ampĕlŏs**, *am´-pel-os*; prob. from the base of 297 and that of 257; a *vine* (as *coiling* about a support):— vine.

289. ἀμπελουργός **ampĕlŏurgŏs**, *am-pel-oor-gos´*; from 288 and 2041; a *vine-worker*, i.e. *pruner*:— vine-dresser.

290. ἀμπελών **ampĕlōn**, *am-pel-ohn´*; from 288; a *vineyard*:— vineyard.

291. Ἀμπλίας **Amplias**, *am-plee´-as;* contr. for Lat. *ampliatus* [enlarged]; *Amplias*, a Rom. Chr.:— Amplias.

292. ἀμύνομαι **amunōmai**, *am-oo´-nom-ahee;* mid. voice of a prim. verb; to *ward off* (for oneself), i.e. *protect:*— defend.

293. ἀμφίβληστρον **amphiblēstrŏn**, *am-feeb´-lace-tron;* from a comp. of the base of 297 and 906; a (fishing) *net* (as *thrown about* the fish):— net.

294. ἀμφιέννυμι **amphiĕnnumi**, *am-fee-en´-noo-mee;* from the base of 297 and ἕννυμι **hĕnnumi** (to *invest*); to *enrobe:*— clothe.

295. Ἀμφίπολις **Amphipolis**, *am-fip´-ol-is;* from the base of 297 and 4172; a *city surrounded* by a river; *Amphipolis*, a place in Macedonia:— Amphipolis.

296. ἄμφοδον **amphŏdon**, *am´-fod-on;* from the base of 297 and 3598; a *fork* in the road:— where two ways meet.

297. ἀμφότερος **amphŏtĕrŏs**, *am-fot´-er-os;* comp. of ἀμφί *amphi* (*around*); (in plur.) *both*:— both.

298. ἀμώμητος **amōmētŏs**, *am-o´-may-tos;* from *1* (as a neg. particle) and a der. of 3469; *unblameable*:— blameless.

299. ἄμωμος **amōmŏs**, *am´-o-mos;* from *1* (as a neg. particle) and 3470; *unblemished* (lit. or fig.):— without blame (blemish, fault, spot), faultless, unblameable.

300. Ἀμών **Amōn**, *am-one´;* of Heb. or. [526]; *Amon*, an Isr.:— Amon.

301. Ἀμώς **Amōs**, *am-oce´;* of Heb. or. [531]; *Amos*, an Isr.:— Amos.

302. ἄν **an**, *an;* a prim. particle, denoting a *supposition, wish, possibility* or *uncertainty*:— [what-, where-, wither-, who-] soever. Usually unexpressed except by the subjunctive or potential mood. Also contr. for *1437*.

303. ἀνά **ana**, *an-ah´;* a prim. prep. and adv.; prop. *up;* but (by extens.) used (distributively) *severally*, or (locally) *at* (etc.):— and, apiece, by, each, every (man), in, through. In compounds (as a prefix) it often means (by impl.) *repetition, intensity, reversal,* etc.

304. ἀναβαθμός **anabathmŏs**, *an-ab-ath-mos´;* from 305 [comp. 898]; a *stairway*:— stairs.

305. ἀναβαίνω **anabainō**, *an-ab-ah´-ee-no;* from 303 and the base of 939; to *go up* (lit. or fig.):— arise, ascend (up), climb (go, grow, rise, spring) up, come (up).

306. ἀναβάλλομαι **anaballŏmai**, *an-ab-al´-lom-ahee;* mid. voice from 303 and 906; to *put off* (for oneself):— defer.

307. ἀναβιβάζω **anabibazō**, *an-ab-ee-bad´-zo;* from 303 and a der. of the base of 939; to *cause to go up*, i.e. *haul* (a net):— draw.

308. ἀναβλέπω **anablĕpō**, *an-ab-lep´-o;* from 303 and 991; to *look up;* by impl. to *recover sight*:— look (up), see, receive sight.

309. ἀνάβλεψις **anablĕpsis**, *an-ab´-lep-sis;* from 308; *restoration of sight*:— recovery of sight.

310. ἀναβοάω **anabŏaō**, *an-ab-o-ah´-o;* from 303 and 994; to *halloo*:— cry (aloud, out).

311. ἀναβολή **anabŏlē**, *an-ab-ol-ay´;* from 306; a *putting off*:— delay.

312. ἀναγγέλλω **anaggĕllō**, *an-ang-el´-lo;* from 303 and the base of 32; to *announce* (in detail):— declare, rehearse, report, show, speak, tell.

313. ἀναγεννάω **anagĕnnaō**, *an-ag-en-nah´-o;* from 303 and 1080; to *beget* or (by extens.) *bear* (again):— beget, (bear) x (again).

314. ἀναγινώσκω **anaginōskō**, *an-ag-in-oce´-ko;* from 303 and 1097; to *know again*, i.e. (by extens.) to *read*:— read.

315. ἀναγκάζω **anagkazō**, *an-ang-kad´-zo;* from 318; to *necessitate*:— compel, constrain.

316. ἀναγκαῖος **anagkaiŏs**, *an-ang-kah´-yos;* from 318; *necessary;* by impl. *close* (of kin):— near, necessary, necessity, needful.

317. ἀναγκαστῶς **anagkastōs**, *an-ang-kas-toce´;* adv. from a der. of 315; *compulsorily*:— by constraint.

318. ἀνάγκη **anagkē**, *an-ang-kay´;* from 303 and the base of 43; *constraint* (lit. or fig.); by impl. *distress*:— distress, must needs, (of) necessity (-sary), needeth, needful.

319. ἀναγνωρίζομαι **anagnōrizŏmai**, *an-ag-no-rid´-zom-ahee;* mid. voice from 303 and 1107; to *make* (oneself) *known*:— be made known.

320. ἀνάγνωσις **anagnōsis**, *an-ag´-no-sis;* from 314; (the act of) *reading*:— reading.

321. ἀνάγω **anagō**, *an-ag´-o;* from 303 and 71; to *lead up;* by extens. to *bring out;* spec. to *sail away*:— bring (again, forth, up again), depart, launch (forth), lead (up), loose, offer, sail, set forth, take up.

322. ἀναδείκνυμι **anadĕiknumi**, *an-ad-ike´-noo-mee;* from 303 and 1166; to *exhibit*, i.e. (by impl.) to *indicate, appoint*:— appoint, shew.

323. ἀνάδειξις **anadĕixis**, *an-ad´-ike-sis;* from 322; (the act of) *exhibition*:— shewing.

324. ἀναδέχομαι **anadĕchŏmai**, *an-ad-ekh´-om-ahee;* from 303 and 1209; to *entertain* (as a guest):— receive.

325. ἀναδίδωμι **anadidōmi**, *an-ad-eed´-om-ee;* from 303 and 1325; to *hand over*:— deliver.

326. ἀναζάω **anazaō**, *an-ad-zah´-o* from 303 and 2198; to *recover life* (lit. or fig.):— (be a-) live again, revive.

327. ἀναζητέω **anazētĕō**, *an-ad-zay-teh´-o;* from 303 and 2212; to *search out*:— seek.

328. ἀναζώννυμι **anazōnnumi**, *an-ad-zone´-noo-mee;* from 303 and 2224; to *gird afresh*:— gird up.

329. ἀναζωπυρέω **anazōpurĕō**, *an-ad-zo-poor-eh´-o;* from 303 and a comp. of the base of 2226 and 4442; to *re-enkindle*:— stir up.

330. ἀναθάλλω **anathallō**, *an-ath-al´-lo;*

from 303 and θάλλω **thallō** (to *flourish*); to *revive*:— flourish again.

331. ἀνάθεμα **anathĕma**, *an-ath´-em-ah;* from 394; a (religious) *ban* or (concr.) *excommunicated* (thing or person):— accursed, anathema, curse, x great.

332. ἀναθεματίζω **anathĕmatizō**, *an-ath-em-at-id´-zo;* from 331; to *declare* or *vow under penalty of execration*:— (bind under a) curse, bind with an oath.

333. ἀναθεωρέω **anathĕōrĕō**, *an-ath-eh-o-reh´-o;* from 303 and 2334; to *look again* (i.e. *attentively*) at (lit. or fig.):— behold, consider.

334. ἀνάθημα **anathĕma**, *an-ath´-ay-mah;* from 394 [like 331, but in a good sense]; a *votive* offering:— gift.

335. ἀναίδεια **anaidĕia**, *an-ah´-ee-die-ah´;* from a comp. of *1* (as a neg. particle [comp. 427]) and 127; *impudence*, i.e. (by impl.) *importunity*:— importunity.

336. ἀναίρεσις **anairĕsis**, *an-ah´-ee-res-is;* from 337; (the act of) *killing*:— death.

337. ἀναιρέω **anairĕō**, *an-ahee-reh´-o;* from 303 and (the act. of) 138; to *take up*, i.e. *adopt;* by impl. to *take away* (violently), i.e. *abolish, murder*:— put to death, kill, slay, take away, take up.

338. ἀναίτιος **anaitiŏs**, *an-ah´-ee-tee-os;* from *1* (as a neg. particle) and 159 (in the sense of 156); *innocent*:— blameless, guiltless.

339. ἀνακαθίζω **anakathizō**, *an-ak-ath-id´-zo;* from 303 and 2523; prop. to *set up*, i.e. (refl.) to *sit up*:— sit up.

340. ἀνακαινίζω **anakainizō**, *an-ak-ahee-nid´-zo;* from 303 and a der. of 2537; to *restore*:— renew.

341. ἀνακαινόω **anakainŏō**, *an-ak-ahee-nŏ´-o;* from 303 and a der. of 2537; to *renovate*:— renew.

342. ἀνακαίνωσις **anakainōsis**, *an-ak-ah´-ee-no-sis;* from 341; *renovation*:— renewing.

343. ἀνακαλύπτω **anakaluptō**, *an-ak-al-oop´-to;* from 303 (in the sense of *reversal*) and 2572; to *unveil*:— open, ([un-])taken away.

344. ἀνακάμπτω **anakamptō**, *an-ak-amp´-to;* from 303 and 2578; to *turn back*:— (re-) turn.

345. ἀνάκειμαι **anakĕimai**, *an-ak-i´-mahee;* from 303 and 2749; to *recline* (as a corpse or at a meal):— guest, lean, lie, sit (down, at meat), at the table.

346. ἀνακεφαλαίομαι **anakĕphalaiŏmai**, *an-ak-ef-al-ah´-ee-om-ahee;* from 303 and 2775 (in its or. sense); to *sum up*:— briefly comprehend, gather together in one.

347. ἀνακλίνω **anaklinō**, *an-ak-lee´-no;* from 303 and 2827; to *lean back*:— lay, (make) sit down.

348. ἀνακόπτω **anakŏptō**, *an-ak-op´-to;* from 303 and 2875; to *beat back*, i.e. *check*:— hinder.

349. ἀνακράζω **anakrazō**, *an-ak-rad´-zo;* from 303 and 2896; to *scream up* (aloud):— cry out.

350. ἀνακρίνω **anakrinō**, *an-ak-ree´-no;*

from *303* and *2919;* prop. to *scrutinize,* i.e. (by impl.) *investigate, interrogate, determine:*— ask, question, discern, examine, judge, search.

351. ἀνάκρισις **anakrisis,** *an-ak´-ree-sis;* from *350;* a (judicial) *investigation:*— examination.

352. ἀνακύπτω **anakuptō,** *an-ak-oop´-to;* from *303* (in the sense of *reversal*) and *2955;* to *unbend,* i.e. *rise;* fig. be *elated:*— lift up, look up.

353. ἀναλαμβάνω **analambanō,** *an-al-am-ban´-o;* from *303* and *2983;* to *take up:*— receive up, take (in, unto, up).

354. ἀνάληψις **analēpsis,** *an-al´-aip-sis;* from *353; ascension:*— taking up.

355. ἀναλίσκω **analiskō,** *an-al-is´-ko;* from *303* and a form of the alt. of *138;* prop. to *use up,* i.e. *destroy:*—consume.

356. ἀναλογία **analŏgia,** *an-al-og-ee´-ah;* from a comp. of *303* and *3056; proportion:*— proportion.

357. ἀναλογίζομαι **analŏgizŏmai,** *an-al-og-id´-zom-ahee;* mid. voice from *356;* to *estimate,* i.e. (fig.) *contemplate:*— consider.

358. ἄναλος **analŏs,** *an´-al-os;* from *1* (as a neg. particle) and *251; saltless,* i.e. *insipid:*— × lose saltness.

359. ἀνάλυσις **analusis,** *an-al´-oo-sis;* from *360; departure:*— departure.

360. ἀναλύω **analuō,** *an-al-oo´-o;* from *303* and *3089;* to *break up,* i.e. *depart* (lit. or fig.):— depart, return.

361. ἀναμάρτητος **anamartētŏs,** *an-am-ar´-tay-tos;* from *1* (as a neg. particle) and a presumed der. of *264; sinless:*— that is without sin.

362. ἀναμένω **anamēnō,** *an-am-en´-o;* from *303* and *3306;* to *await:*— wait for.

363. ἀναμιμνήσκω **anamimnēskō,** *an-am-im-nace´-ko;* from *303* and *3403;* to *remind;* (refl.) to *recollect:*— call to mind, (bring to , call to, put in), remember (-brance).

364. ἀνάμνησις **anamnēsis,** *an-am´-nay-sis;* from *363; recollection:*— remembrance (again).

365. ἀνανεόω **ananĕŏō,** *an-an-neh-o´-o;* from *303* and a der. of *3501;* to *renovate,* i.e. *reform:*— renew.

366. ἀνανήφω **ananēphō,** *an-an-ay´-fo;* from *303* and *3525;* to become *sober again,* i.e. (fig.) *regain* (one's) *senses:*— recover self.

367. Ἀνανίας **Ananias,** *an-an-ee´-as;* of Heb. or. [2608]; *Ananias,* the name of three Isr.:— Ananias.

368. ἀναντίρρητος **anantirrhētŏs,** *an-an-tir´-hray-tos;* from *1* (as a neg. particle) and a presumed der. of a comp. of *473* and *4483; indisputable:*— cannot be spoken against.

369. ἀναντιρρήτως **anantirrhētŏs,** *an-an-tir-hray´-toce;* adv. from *368;* promptly:*— without gainsaying.

370. ἀνάξιος **anaxiŏs,** *an-ax´-ee-os;* from *1* (as a neg. particle) and *514; unfit:*— unworthy.

371. ἀναξίως **anaxiōs,** *an-ax-ee´-oce;* adv. from *370; irreverently:*— unworthily.

372. ἀνάπαυσις **anapausis,** *an-ap´-ŏw-sis;* from *373; intermission;* by impl. *recreation:*— rest.

373. ἀναπαύω **anapauō,** *an-ap-ow´-o;* from *303* and *3973;* (refl.) to *repose* (lit. or fig. *lbe exemptl, remain*); by impl. to *refresh:*— take ease, refresh, (give, take) rest.

374. ἀναπείθω **anapĕithō,** *an-ap-i´-tho;* from *303* and *3982;* to *incite:*— persuade.

375. ἀναπέμπω **anapĕmpō,** *an-ap-em´-po;* from *303* and *3992;* to *send up* or *back:*— send (again).

376. ἀνάπηρος **anapērŏs,** *an-ap´-ay-ros*); from *303* (in the sense of *intensity*) and πῆρος **pērŏs** (*maimed*); *crippled:*— maimed.

377. ἀναπίπτω **anapiptō,** *an-ap-ip´-to;* from *303* and *4098;* to *fall back,* i.e. *lie down, lean back:*— lean, sit down (to meat).

378. ἀναπληρόω **anaplērŏō,** *an-ap-lay-ró´-o;* from *303* and *4137;* to *complete;* by impl. to *occupy, supply;* fig. to *accomplish* (by coincidence or obedience):*— fill up, fulfill, occupy, supply.

379. ἀναπολόγητος **anapŏlŏgētŏs,** *an-ap-ol-og´-ay-tos;* from *1* (as a neg. particle) and a presumed der. of *626; indefensible:*— without excuse, inexcuseable.

380. ἀναπτύσσω **anaptussō,** *an-ap-toos´-so;* from *303* (in the sense of *reversal*) and *4428;* to *unroll* (a scroll or volume):*— open.

381. ἀνάπτω **anaptō,** *an-ap´-to;* from *303* and *681;* to *enkindle:*— kindle, light.

382. ἀναρίθμητος **anarithmētŏs,** *an-arith´-may-tos;* from *1* (as a neg. particle) and a der. of *705; unnumbered,* i.e. *without number:*— innumerable.

383. ἀνασείω **anasĕiō,** *an-as-i´-o;* from *303* and *4579;* fig. to *excite:*— move, stir up.

384. ἀνασκευάζω **anaskĕuazō,** *an-ask-yoo-ad´-zo;* from *303* (in the sense of *reversal*) and a der. of *4632;* prop. to *pack up* (baggage), i.e. (by impl. and fig.) to *upset:*— subvert.

385. ἀνασπάω **anaspaō,** *an-as-pah´-o;* from *303* and *4685;* to *take up* or *extricate:*— draw up, pull out.

386. ἀνάστασις **anastasis,** *an-as´-tas-is;* from *450;* a *standing up* again, i.e. (lit.) a *resurrection* from death (individual, gen. or by impl. [its author]), or (fig.) a (moral) *recovery* (of spiritual truth):*— raised to life again, resurrection, rise from the dead, that should rise, rising again.

387. ἀναστατόω **anastatŏō,** *an-as-tat-ŏ´-o;* from a der. of *450* (in the sense of *removal*); prop. to *drive out* of home, i.e. (by impl.) to *disturb* (lit. or fig.):*— trouble, turn upside down, make an uproar.

388. ἀνασταυρόω **anastaurŏō,** *an-as-tŏw-rŏ´-o;* from *303* and *4717;* to *recrucify* (fig.):— crucify afresh.

389. ἀναστενάζω **anastĕnazō,** *an-as-*

ten-ad´-zo; from *303* and *4727;* to *sigh deeply:*— sigh deeply.

390. ἀναστρέφω **anastrĕphō,** *an-astref´-o;* from *303* and *4762;* to *overturn;* also to *return;* by impl. to *busy* oneself, i.e. *remain, live:*— abide, behave self, have conversation, live, overthrow, pass, return, be used.

391. ἀναστροφή **anastrŏphē,** *an-as-trof-ay´;* from *390; behavior:*— conversation.

392. ἀνατάσσομαι **anatassŏmai,** *an-at-as´-som-ahee;* from *303* and the mid. voice of *5021;* to *arrange:*— set in order.

393. ἀνατέλλω **anatĕllō,** *an-at-el´-lo;* from *303* and the base of *5056;* to (*cause* to) *arise:*— (a-, make to) rise, at the rising of, spring (up), be up.

394. ἀνατίθεμαι **anatithĕmai,** *an-atith´-em-ahee;* from *303* and the mid. voice of *5087;* to *set forth* (for oneself), i.e. *propound:*— communicate, declare.

395. ἀνατολή **anatŏlē,** *an-at-ol-ay´;* from *393;* a *rising* of light, i.e. *dawn* (fig.); by impl. the *east* (also in plur.):— dayspring, east, rising.

396. ἀνατρέπω **anatrĕpō,** *an-at-rep´-o;* from *303* and the base of *5157;* to *overturn* (fig.):— overthrow, subvert.

397. ἀνατρέφω **anatrĕphō,** *an-at-ref´-o;* from *303* and *5142;* to *rear* (phys. or ment.):— bring up, nourish (up).

398. ἀναφαίνω **anaphainō,** *an-af-ah´-ee-no;* from *303* and *5316;* to *show,* i.e. (refl.) *appear,* or (pass.) to *have pointed out:*— (should) appear, discover.

399. ἀναφέρω **anaphĕrō,** *an-af-er´-o;* from *303* and *5342;* to *take up* (lit. or fig.):— bear, bring (carry, lead) up, offer (up).

400. ἀναφωνέω **anaphōnĕō,** *an-af-o-neh´-o;* from *303* and *5455;* to *exclaim:*— speak out.

401. ἀνάχυσις **anachusis,** *an-akh´-oo-sis;* from a comp. of *303* and χέω **chĕō** (to *pour*); prop. *effusion,* i.e. (fig.) *license:*— excess.

402. ἀναχωρέω **anachōrĕō,** *an-akh-o-reh´-o;* from *303* and *5562;* to *retire:*— depart, give place, go (turn) aside, withdraw self.

403. ἀνάψυξις **anapsuxis,** *an-aps´-ook-sis;* from *404;* prop. a *recovery of breath,* i.e. (fig.) *revival:*— revival.

404. ἀναψύχω **anapsuchō,** *an-aps-oo´-kho;* from *303* and *5594;* prop. to *cool off,* i.e. (fig.) *relieve:*— refresh.

405. ἀνδραποδιστής **andrapŏdistēs,** *an-drap-od-is-tace´;* from a der. of a comp. of *435* and *4228;* an *enslaver* (as bringing *men* to his *feet*):— menstealer.

406. Ἀνδρέας **Andrĕas,** *an-dreh´-as;* from *435; manly; Andreas,* an Isr.:— Andrew.

407. ἀνδρίζομαι **andrizŏmai,** *an-drid´-zom-ahee;* mid. voice from *435;* to *act manly:*— quit like men.

408. Ἀνδρόνικος **Andrŏnikŏs,** *an-dron´-ee-kos;* from *435* and *3534; man of victory; Andronicos,* an Isr.:— Adronicus.

409. ἀνδροφόνος **andrŏphŏnŏs,** *an-drof-*

on´-os; from 435 and 5408; a *murderer:*— manslayer.

410. ἀνέγκλητος **anĕgklētŏs,** *an-eng´-klay-tos;* from 1 (as a neg. particle) and a der. of 1458; *unaccused,* i.e. (by impl.) *irreproachable:*— blameless.

411. ἀνεκδιήγητος **anĕkdiēgētŏs,** *an-ek-dee-ay´-gay-tos;* from 1 (as a neg. particle) and a presumed der. of 1555; *not expounded* in full, i.e. *indescribable:*— unspeakable.

412. ἀνεκλάλητος **anĕklalētŏs,** *an-ek-lal´-ay-tos;* from 1 (as a neg. particle) and a presumed der. of 1583; *not spoken out,* i.e. (by impl.) *unutterable:*— unspeakable.

413. ἀνέκλειπτος **anĕklĕiptŏs,** *an-ek´-lipe-tos;* from 1 (as a neg. particle) and a presumed der. of 1587; *not left out,* i.e. (by impl.) *inexhaustible:*— that faileth not.

414. ἀνεκτότερος **anĕktŏtĕrŏs,** *an-ektot´-er-os;* comp. of a der. of 430; *more endurable:*— more tolerable.

415. ἀνελεήμων **anĕlĕēmōn,** *an-elehay´-mone;* from 1 (as a neg. particle) and 1655; *merciless:*— unmerciful.

416. ἀνεμίζω **anemizō,** *an-em-id´-zo;* from 417; to *toss with the wind:*— drive with the wind.

417. ἄνεμος **anĕmŏs,** *an´-em-os;* from the base of 109; *wind;* (plur.) by impl. (the four) *quarters* (of the earth):— wind.

418. ἀνένδεκτος **anĕndĕktŏs,** *an-en´-dek-tos;* from 1 (as a neg. particle) and a der. of the same as 1735; *unadmitted,* i.e. (by impl.) *not supposable:*— impossible.

419. ἀνεξερεύνητος **anĕxĕrĕunētŏs,** *an-ex-er-yoo´-nay-tos;* from 1 (as a neg. particle) and a presumed der. of 1830; *not searched out,* i.e. (by impl.) *inscrutable:*— unsearchable.

420. ἀνεξίκακος **anĕxikakŏs,** *an-ex-ik´-ak-os;* from 430 and 2556; *enduring of ill,* i.e. *forbearing:*— patient.

421. ἀνεξιχνίαστος **anĕxichniastŏs,** *an-ex-ikh-nee´-as-tos;* from 1 (as a neg. particle) and a presumed der. of a comp. of 1537 and a der. of 2487; *not tracked out,* i.e. (by impl.) *untraceable:*— past finding out; unsearchable.

422. ἀνεπαίσχυντος **anĕpaischuntŏs,** *an-ep-ah´-ee-skhoon-tos;* from 1 (as a neg. particle) and a presumed der. of a comp. of 1909 and 153; *not ashamed,* i.e. (by impl.) *irreprehensible:*— that needeth not to be ashamed.

423. ἀνεπίληπτος **anĕpilēptŏs,** *an-ep-eel´-ape-tos;* from 1 (as a neg. particle) and a der. of 1949; *not arrested,* i.e. (by impl.) *inculpable:*— blameless, unrebukeable.

424. ἀνέρχομαι **anĕrchōmai,** *an-erkh´-om-ahee;* from 303 and 2064; to *ascend:*— go up.

425. ἄνεσις **anĕsis,** *an´-es-is;* from 447; *relaxation* or (fig.) *relief:*— eased, liberty, rest.

426. ἀνετάζω **anĕtazō,** *an-et-ad´-zo;* from 303 and ἐτάζω **ĕtazō** (to *test*); to

investigate (judicially):— (should have) examine (-d).

427. ἄνευ **anĕu,** *an´-yoo;* a prim. particle; *without:*— without. Comp. 1.

428. ἀνεύθετος **anĕuthētŏs,** *an-yoo´-the-tos;* from 1 (as a neg. particle) and 2111; *not well set,* i.e. *inconvenient:*— not commodious.

429. ἀνευρίσκω **anĕuriskō,** *an-yoo-ris´-ko;* from 303 and 2147; to *find out:*— find.

430. ἀνέχομαι **anĕchōmai,** *an-ekh´-omahee;* mid. voice from 303 and 2192; to *hold oneself up* against, i.e. (fig.) *put up* with:— bear with, endure, forbear, suffer.

431. ἀνέψιος **anĕpsiŏs,** *an-eps´-ee-os;* from 1 (as a particle of union) and an obs. νέπος **nĕpŏs** (a *brood*); prop. *akin,* i.e. (spec.) a *cousin:*— sister's son.

432. ἄνηθον **anēthŏn,** *an´-ay-thon;* prob. of for. or.; *dill:*— anise.

433. ἀνήκω **anēkō,** *an-ay´-ko;* from 303 and 2240; to *attain* to, i.e. (fig.) be *proper:*— convenient, be fit.

434. ἀνήμερος **anēmĕrŏs,** *an-ay´-mer-os;* from 1 (as a neg. particle) and ἥμερος **hēmĕrŏs** (*lame*); *savage:*— fierce.

435. ἀνήρ **anēr,** *an-ayr´;* a prim. word [comp. 444]; a *man* (prop. as an indiv. male):— fellow, husband, man, sir.

436. ἀνθίστημι **anthistēmi,** *anth-is´-tay-mee;* from 473 and 2476; to *stand against,* i.e. *oppose:*— resist, withstand.

437. ἀνθομολογέομαι **anthŏmŏlŏgĕŏmai,** *anth-om-ol-og-eh´-om-ahee;* from 473 and the mid. voice of 3670; to *confess in turn,* i.e. *respond* in praise:— give thanks.

438. ἄνθος **anthŏs,** *anth´-os;* a prim. word; a *blossom:*— flower.

439. ἀνθρακιά **anthrakia,** *anth-rak-ee-ah´;* from 440; a bed of burning *coals:*— fire of coals.

440. ἄνθραξ **anthrax,** *anth´-rax;* of uncert. der.; a live *coal:*— coal of fire.

441. ἀνθρωπάρεσκος **anthrōparĕskŏs,** *anth-ro-par´-es-kos;* from 444 and 700; *man-courting,* i.e. *fawning:*— menpleaser.

442. ἀνθρώπινος **anthrōpinŏs,** *anth-ro´-pee-nos;* from 444; *human:*— human, common to man, man [-kind], [man-] kind, men's, after the manner of men.

443. ἀνθρωποκτόνος **anthrōpŏktŏnŏs,** *anth-ro-pok-ton´-os;* from 444 and κτείνω **ktĕinō** (to *kill*); a *manslayer:*— murderer. Comp. 5406.

444. ἄνθρωπος **anthrōpŏs,** *anth´-ro-pos;* from 435 and ὤψ **ōps** (the *countenance;* from 3700); *man-faced,* i.e. a *human being:*— certain, man.

445. ἀνθυπατεύω **anthupatĕuō,** *anthoo-pat-yoo´-o;* from 446; to *act as a proconsul:*— be the deputy.

446. ἀνθύπατος **anthupatŏs,** *anth-oo´-pat-os;* from 473 and a superl. of 5228; *instead* of the *highest* officer, i.e. (spec.) a Roman *proconsul:*— deputy.

447. ἀνίημι **aniēmi,** *an-ee´-ay-mee;* from 303 and ἵημι **hiēmi** (to *send*); to *let up,* i.e. (lit.) *slacken* or (fig.) *desert, desist* from:— forbear, leave, loose.

448. ἀνίλεως **anilĕōs,** *an-ee´-leh-oce;* from 1 (as a neg. particle) and 2436; *inexorable:*— without mercy.

449. ἄνιπτος **aniptŏs,** *an´-ip-tos;* from 1 (as a neg. particle) and a presumed der. of 3538; *without ablution:*— unwashen.

450. ἀνίστημι **anistēmi,** *an-is´-tay-mee;* from 303 and 2476; to *stand up* (lit. or fig., trans. or intr.):— arise, lift up, raise up (again), rise (again), stand up (-right).

451. Ἄννα **Anna,** *an´-nah;* of Heb. or. [2584]; *Anna,* an Israelitess:— Anna.

452. Ἄννας **Annas,** *an´-nas;* of Heb. or. [2608]; *Annas* (i.e. 367), an Isr.:— Annas.

453. ἀνόητος **anŏētŏs,** *an-o´-ay-tos;* from 1 (as a neg. particle) and a der. of 3539; *unintelligent;* by impl. *sensual:*— fool (-ish), unwise.

454. ἄνοια **anŏia,** *an´-oy-ah;* from a comp. of 1 (as a neg. particle) and 3563; *stupidity;* by impl. *rage:*— folly, madness.

455. ἀνοίγω **anŏigō,** *an-oy´-go;* from 303 and οἴγω **ŏigō** (to *open*); to *open up* (lit. or fig., in various applications):— open.

456. ἀνοικοδομέω **anŏikŏdŏmĕō,** *an-oy-kod-om-eh´-o;* from 303 and 3618; to *rebuild:*— build again.

457. ἄνοιξις **anŏixis,** *an´-oix-is;* from 455; *opening* (throat):— × open.

458. ἀνομία **anŏmia,** *an-om-ee´-ah;* from 459; *illegality,* i.e. *violation of law* or (gen.) *wickedness:*— iniquity, × transgress (-ion of) the law, unrighteousness.

459. ἄνομος **anŏmŏs,** *an´-om-os;* from 1 (as a neg. particle) and 3551; *lawless,* i.e. (neg.) *not subject* to (the Jewish) *law;* (by impl. a *Gentile*), or (pos.) *wicked:*— without law, lawless, transgressor, unlawful, wicked.

460. ἀνόμως **anŏmōs,** *an-om´-oce;* adv. from 459; *lawlessly,* i.e. (spec.) *not amenable to* (the Jewish) *law:*— without law.

461. ἀνορθόω **anŏrthŏō,** *an-orth-ŏ´-o;* from 303 and a der. of the base of 3717; to *straighten up:*— lift (set) up, make straight.

462. ἀνόσιος **anŏsiŏs,** *an-os´-ee-os;* from 1 (as a neg. particle) and 3741; *wicked:*— unholy.

463. ἀνοχή **anŏchē,** *an-okh-ay´;* from 430; *self-restraint,* i.e. *tolerance:*— forbearance.

464. ἀνταγωνίζομαι **antagōnizŏmai,** *an-tag-o-nid´-zom-ahee;* from 473 and 75; to *struggle against* (fig.) ["antagonize"]:— strive against.

465. ἀντάλλαγμα **antallagma,** *an-tal´-lag-mah;* from a comp. of 473 and 236; an *equivalent* or *ransom:*— in exchange.

466. ἀνταναπληρόω **antanaplērŏō,** *an-tan-ap-lay-rŏ´-o;* from 473 and 378; to *supplement:*— fill up.

467. ἀνταποδίδωμι **antapŏdidōmi,** *an-*

Greek

tap-od-ee´-do-mee; from 473 and 591; to *requite* (good or evil):— recompense, render, repay.

468. ἀνταπόδομα **antapŏdŏma**, *an-tap-od´-om-ah;* from 467; a *requital* (prop. the thing):— recompense.

469. ἀνταπόδοσις **antapŏdŏsis**, *an-tap-od´-os-is;* from 467; *requital* (prop. the act):— reward.

470. ἀνταποκρίνομαι **antapŏkrinŏmai**, *an-tap-ok-ree´-nom-ahee;* from 473 and 611; to *contradict* or *dispute:*— answer again, reply against.

471. ἀντέπω **antĕpō**, *an-tep´-o;* from 473 and 2036; to *refute* or *deny:*— gainsay, say against.

472. ἀντέχομαι **antĕchŏmai**, *an-tekh´-om-ahee;* from 473 and the mid. voice of 2192; to *hold* oneself *opposite* to, i.e. (by impl.) *adhere to;* by extens. to *care for:*— hold fast, hold to, support.

473. ἀντί **anti**, *an-tee´;* a prim. particle; *opposite,* i.e. *instead* or *because* of (rarely *in addition* to):— for, in the room of. Often used in composition to denote *contrast, requital, substitution, correspondence,* etc.

474. ἀντιβάλλω **antiballō**, *an-tee-bal´-lo;* from 473 and 906; to *bandy:*— have.

475. ἀντιδιατίθεμαι **antidiatithĕmai**, *an-tee-dee-at-eeth´-em-ahee;* from 473 and 1303; to *set oneself opposite,* i.e. *be disputatious:*— that oppose themselves.

476. ἀντίδικος **antidikŏs**, *an-tid´-ee-kos;* from 473 and 1349; an *opponent* (in a lawsuit); spec. *Satan* (as the arch-enemy):— adversary.

477. ἀντίθεσις **antithĕsis**, *an-tith´-es-is;* from a comp. of 473 and 5087; *opposition,* i.e. a *conflict* (of theories):— opposition.

478. ἀντικαθίστημι **antikathistĕmi**, *an-tee-kath-is´-tay-mee;* from 473 and 2525; to *set down* (troops) *against,* i.e. *withstand:*— resist.

479. ἀντικαλέω **antikalĕō**, *an-tee-kal-eh´-o;* from 473 and 2564; to *invite in return:*— bid again.

480. ἀντίκειμαι **antikĕimai**, *an-tik´-i-mahee;* from 473 and 2749; to *lie opposite,* i.e. *be adverse* (fig. *repugnant*) to:— adversary, be contrary, oppose.

481. ἀντικρύ **antikru**, *an-tee-kroo´;* prol. from 473; *opposite:*— over against.

482. ἀντιλαμβάνομαι **antilambanŏmai**, *an-tee-lam-ban´-om-ahee;* from 473 and the mid. voice of 2983; to *take* hold of *in turn,* i.e. *succor;* also to *participate:*— help, partaker, support.

483. ἀντιλέγω **antilĕgō**, *an-til´-eg-o;* from 473 and 3004; to *dispute, refuse:*— answer again, contradict, deny, gainsay (-er), speak against.

484. ἀντίληψις **antilĕpsis**, *an-til´-apesis;* from 482; *relief:*— help.

485. ἀντιλογία **antilŏgia**, *an-tee-log-ee´-ah;* from a der. of 483; *dispute, disobedience:*— contradiction, gainsaying, strife.

486. ἀντιλοιδορέω **antilŏidŏrĕō**, *an-tee-loy-dor-eh´-o;* from 473 and 3058; to *rail in reply:*— revile again.

---

487. ἀντίλυτρον **antilutrŏn**, *an-til´-ootron;* from 473 and 3083; a *redemption-price:*— ransom.

488. ἀντιμετρέω **antimĕtrĕō**, *an-tee-met-reh´-o;* from 473 and 3354; to *mete in return:*— measure again.

489. ἀντιμισθία **antimisthia**, *an-tee-mis-thee´-ah;* from a comp. of 473 and 3408; *requital, correspondence:*— recompense.

490. Ἀντιόχεια **Antiŏchĕia**, *an-tee-okh´-i-ah;* from Ἀντίοχος **Antiŏchus** (a Syrian king); *Antiochia,* a place in Syria:— Antioch.

491. Ἀντιοχεύς **Antiŏchĕus**, *an-tee-okh-yoos´;* from 490; an *Antiochian* or inhab. of Antiochia:— of Antioch.

492. ἀντιπαρέρχομαι **antiparĕrchŏmai**, *an-tee-par-er´-khom-ahee;* from 473 and 3928; to *go along opposite:*— pass by on the other side.

493. Ἀντίπας **Antipas**, *an-tee´-pas;* contr. for a comp. of 473 and a der. of 3962; *Antipas,* a Chr.:— Antipas.

494. Ἀντιπατρίς **Antipatris**, *an-tip-at-rece´;* from the same as 493; *Antipatris,* a place in Pal.:— Antipatris.

495. ἀντιπέραν **antipĕran**, *an-tee-per´-an;* from 473 and 4008; *on the opposite side:*— over against.

496. ἀντιπίπτω **antipiptō**, *an-tee-pip´-to;* from 473 and 4098 (incl. its alt.); to *oppose:*— resist.

497. ἀντιστρατεύομαι **antistratĕuŏmai**, *an-tee-strat-yoo´-om-ahee;* from 473 and 4754; (fig.) to *attack,* i.e. (by impl.) *destroy:*— war against.

498. ἀντιτάσσομαι **antitassŏmai**, *an-tee-tas´-som-ahee;* from 473 and the mid. voice of 5021; to *range oneself against,* i.e. *oppose:*— oppose themselves, resist.

499. ἀντίτυπον **antitupŏn**, *an-teet´-oopon;* neut. of a comp. of 473 and 5179; *corresponding* ["antitype"], i.e. a *representative, counterpart:*— (like) figure (whereunto).

500. ἀντίχριστος **antichristŏs**, *an-tee´-khris-tos;* from 473 and 5547; an *opponent of the Messiah:*— antichrist.

501. ἀντλέω **antlĕō**, *ant-leh-o;* from ἄντλος **antlŏs** (the *hold* of a ship); to *bale* up (prop. bilge water), i.e. *dip* water (with a bucket, pitcher, etc.):— draw (out).

502. ἄντλημα **antlēma**, *ant´-lay-mah;* from 501; a *baling-vessel:*— thing to draw with.

503. ἀντοφθαλμέω **antŏphthalmĕō**, *ant-of-thal-meh´-o;* from a compound of 473 and 3788; to *face:*— bear up into.

504. ἄνυδρος **anudrŏs**, *an´-oo-dros;* from 1 (as a neg. particle) and 5204; *waterless,* i.e. *dry:*— dry, without water.

505. ἀνυπόκριτος **anupŏkritŏs**, *an-oo-pok´-ree-tos;* from 1 (as a neg. particle) and a presumed der. of 5271; *undissembled,* i.e. *sincere:*— without dissimulation (hypocrisy), unfeigned.

506. ἀνυπότακτος **anupŏtaktŏs**, *an-oo-pot´-ak-tos;* from 1 (as a neg. particle) and a presumed der. of 5293; *unsub-*

---

dued, i.e. *insubordinate* (in fact or temper):— disobedient, that is not put under, unruly.

507. ἄνω **anō**, *an´-o;* adv. from 473; *upward* or *on the top:*— above, brim, high, up.

508. ἀνώγεον **anōgĕŏn**, *an-ogue´-eh-on* (or, ἀνάγαιον *an-ag-ahee´-on;* from 507 and 1093; *above the ground,* i.e. (prop.) the *second floor* of a building; used for a *dome* or a *balcony* on the upper story:— upper room.

509. ἄνωθεν **anōthĕn**, *an´-o-then;* from 507; *from above;* by anal. *from the first;* by impl. *anew:*— from above, again, from the beginning (very first), the top.

510. ἀνωτερικός **anōtĕrikŏs**, *an-o-ter-ee-kos´;* from 511; *superior,* i.e. (locally) *more remote:*— upper.

511. ἀνώτερος **anōtĕrŏs**, *an-o´-ter-os;* comparative degree of 507; *upper,* i.e. (neut. as adv.) to a *more conspicuous* place, in a *former* part of the book:— above, higher.

512. ἀνωφελές **anōphĕlĕs**, *an-o-fel´-ace;* from 1 (as a neg. particle) and the base of 5624; *useless* or (neut.) *inutility:*— unprofitable (-ness).

513. ἀξίνη **axinē**, *ax-ee´-nay;* prob. from ἄγνυμι **agnumi** (to *break;* comp. 4486); an *axe:*— axe.

514. ἄξιος **axiŏs**, *ax´-ee-os;* prob. from 71; *deserving, comparable* or *suitable* (as if *drawing* praise):— due reward, meet, [un-] worthy.

515. ἀξιόω **axiŏō**, *ax-ee-ŏ´-o;* from 514; to *deem entitled* or *fit:*— desire, think good, count (think) worthy.

516. ἀξίως **axiŏs**, *ax-ee´-oce;* adv. from 514; *appropriately:*— as becometh, after a godly sort, worthily (-thy).

517. ἀόρατος **aŏratŏs**, *ah-or´-at-os;* from 1 (as a neg. particle) and 3707; *invisible:*— invisible (thing).

518. ἀπαγγέλλω **apaggĕllō**, *ap-ang-el´-lo;* from 575 and the base of 32; to *announce:*— bring word (again), declare, report, shew (again), tell.

519. ἀπάγχομαι **apagchŏmai**, *ap-ang-khom-ahee* from 575 and ἄγχω **agchō** (to *choke;* akin to the base of 43); to *strangle oneself off* (i.e. to death):— hang himself.

520. ἀπάγω **apagō**, *ap-ag´-o;* from 575 and 71; to *take off* (in various senses):— bring, carry away, lead (away), put to death, take away.

521. ἀπαίδευτος **apaidĕutŏs**, *ap-ah´-ee-dyoo-tos;* from 1 (as a neg. particle) and a der. of 3811; *uninstructed,* i.e. (fig.) *stupid:*— unlearned.

522. ἀπαίρω **apairō**, *ap-ah´-ee-ro;* from 575 and 142; to *lift off,* i.e. *remove:*— take (away).

523. ἀπαιτέω **apaitĕō**, *ap-ah´-ee-teh-o;* from 575 and 154; to *demand back:*— ask again, require.

524. ἀπαλγέω **apalgĕō**, *ap-alg-eh´-o;* from 575 and ἀλγέω **algĕō** (to *smart*); to *grieve out,* i.e. *become apathetic:*— be past feeling.

525. ἀπαλλάσσω **apallassō**, *ap-al-las´-so;* from 575 and 236; to *change away,*

i.e. *release*, (refl.) *remove*:— deliver, depart.

526. ἀπαλλοτριόω **apallŏtriŏŏ**, *ap-al-lot-ree-ŏ´-o*; from 575 and a der. of 245; to *estrange away*, i.e. (pass. and fig.) to *be non-participant*:— alienate, be alien.

527. ἀπαλός **hapalŏs**, *hap-al-os´*; of uncert. der.; *soft*:— tender.

528. ἀπαντάω **apantaō**, *ap-an-tah´-o*; from 575 and a der. of 473; to *meet away*, i.e. *encounter*:— meet.

529. ἀπάντησις **apantēsis**, *ap-an´-tay-sis*; from 528; a (friendly) *encounter*:— meet.

530. ἅπαξ **hapax**, *hap´-ax*; prob. from 537; *one* (or a *single*) *time* (numerically or conclusively):— once.

531. ἀπαράβατος **aparabatŏs**, *ap-ar-ab´-at-os*; from 1 (as a neg. particle) and a der. of 3845; *not passing away*, i.e. *untransferable* (perpetual):— unchangeable.

532. ἀπαρασκεύαστος **aparaskĕuastŏs**, *ap-ar-ask-yoo´-as-tos*; from 1 (as a neg. particle) and a der. of 3903; *unready*:— unprepared.

533. ἀπαρνέομαι **aparnĕŏmai**, *ap-ar-neh´-om-ahee*; from 575 and 720; to *deny utterly*, i.e. *disown, abstain*:— deny.

534. ἀπάρτι **aparti**, *ap-ar´-tee*; from 575 and 737; *from now*, i.e. *henceforth* (already):— from henceforth.

535. ἀπαρτισμός **apartismŏs**, *ap-ar-tis-mos´*; from a der. of 534; *completion*:— finishing.

536. ἀπαρχή **aparchē**, *ap-ar-khay´*; from a compound of 575 and 756; a *beginning* of sacrifice, i.e. the (Jewish) *first-fruit* (fig.):— first-fruits.

537. ἅπας **hapas**, *hap´-as*; from 1 (as a particle of union) and 3956; *absolutely all* or (sing.) *every one*:— all (things), every (one), whole.

538. ἀπατάω **apataō**, *ap-at-ah´-o*; of uncert. der.; to *cheat*, i.e. *delude*:— deceive.

539. ἀπάτη **apatē**, *ap-at´-ay*; from 538; *delusion*:— deceit (-ful,fulness), deceivableness (-ving).

540. ἀπάτωρ **apatŏr**, *ap-at´-ore*; from 1 (as a neg. particle) and 3962; *fatherless*, i.e. *of unrecorded paternity*:— without father.

541. ἀπαύγασμα **apaugasma**, *ap-ŏw´-gas-mah*; from a compound of 575 and 826; an *off-flash*, i.e. *effulgence*:— brightness.

542. ἀπείδω **apĕidō**, *ap-i´-do*; from 575 and the same as 1492; to *see fully*:— see.

543. ἀπείθεια **apĕithĕia**, *ap-i´-thi-ah*; from 545; *disbelief* (obstinate and rebellious):— disobedience, unbelief.

544. ἀπειθέω **apĕithĕō**, *ap-i-theh´-o*; from 545; to *disbelieve* (wilfully and perversely):— not believe, disobedient, obey not, unbelieving.

545. ἀπειθής **apĕithēs**, *ap-i-thace´*; from 1 (as a neg. particle) and 3982; *unpersuadable*, i.e. *contumacious*:— disobedient.

546. ἀπειλέω **apĕilĕō**, *ap-i-leh´-o*; of uncert. der.; to *menace*; by impl. to *forbid*:— threaten.

547. ἀπειλή **apĕilē**, *ap-i-lay´*; from 546; a *menace*:— × straitly, threatening.

548. ἄπειμι **apĕimi**, *ap´-i-mee*; from 575 and 1510; to *be away*:— be absent. Comp. 549.

549. ἄπειμι **apĕimi**, *ap´-i-mee*; from 575 and εἶμι **ĕimi** (to go); to *go away*:— go. Comp. 548.

550. ἀπειπόμην **apĕipŏmēn**, *ap-i-pom´-ane*; refl. past of a compound of 575 and 2036; to *say off* for oneself, i.e. *disown*:— renounce.

551. ἀπείραστος **apĕirastŏs**, *ap-i´-ras-tos*; from 1 (as a neg. particle) and a presumed der. of 3987; *untried*, i.e. *not temptable*:— not to be tempted.

552. ἄπειρος **apĕirŏs**, *ap´-i-ros*; from 1 (as a neg. particle) and 3984; *inexperienced*, i.e. *ignorant*:— unskillful.

553. ἀπεκδέχομαι **apĕkdĕchŏmai**, *ap-ek-dekh´-om-ahee*; from 575 and 1551; to *expect fully*:— look (wait) for.

554. ἀπεκδύομαι **apĕkduŏmai**, *ap-ek-doo´-om-ahee*; mid. voice from 575 and 1562; to *divest wholly* oneself, or (for oneself) *despoil*:— put off, spoil.

555. ἀπέκδυσις **apĕkdusis**, *ap-ek´-doo-sis*; from 554; *divestment*:— putting off.

556. ἀπελαύνω **apĕlaunō**, *ap-el-ŏw´-no*; from 575 and 1643; to *dismiss*:— drive.

557. ἀπελεγμός **apĕlĕgmŏs**, *ap-el-eg-mos´*; from a compound of 575 and 1651; *refutation*, i.e. (by impl.) *contempt*:— nought.

558. ἀπελεύθερος **apĕlĕuthĕrŏs**, *ap-el-yoo´-ther-os*; from 575 and 1658; one *freed away*, i.e. a *freedman*:— freeman.

559. Ἀπελλῆς **Apĕllēs**, *ap-el-lace´*; of Lat. or.; *Apelles*, a Chr.:— Apelles.

560. ἀπελπίζω **apĕlpizō**, *ap-el-pid´-zo*; from 575 and 1679; to *hope out*, i.e. *fully expect*:— hope for again.

561. ἀπέναντι **apĕnanti**, *ap-en´-an-tee*; from 575 and 1725; *from in front*, i.e. *opposite, before* or *against*:— before, contrary, over against, in the presence of.

ἀπέπω **apĕpō**. See 550.

562. ἀπέραντος **apĕrantŏs**, *ap-er´-an-tos*; from 1 (as a neg. particle) and a second. der. of 4008; *unfinished*, i.e. (by impl.) *interminable*:— endless.

563. ἀπερισπάστως **apĕrispastōs**, *ap-er-is-pas-toce´*; adv. from a compound of 1 (as a neg. particle) and a presumed der. of 4049; *undistractedly*, i.e. *free from* (domestic) *solicitude*:— without distraction.

564. ἀπερίτμητος **apĕritmētŏs**, *ap-er-eet´-may-tos*; from 1 (as a neg. particle) and a presumed der. of 4059; *uncircumcised* (fig.):— uncircumcised.

565. ἀπέρχομαι **apĕrchŏmai**, *ap-erkh´-om-ahee*; from 575 and 2064; to *go off* (i.e. *depart*), *aside* (i.e. *apart*) or *behind* (i.e. *follow*), lit. or fig.:— come, depart, go (aside, away, back, out, ... ways), pass away, be past.

566. ἀπέχει **apĕchĕi**, *ap-ekh´-i*; third

pers. sing. pres. ind. act. of 568 used impers.; *it is sufficient*:— it is enough.

567. ἀπέχομαι **apĕchŏmai**, *ap-ekh´-om-ahee*; mid. voice (refl.) of 568; to *hold oneself off*, i.e. *refrain*:— abstain.

568. ἀπέχω **apĕchō**, *ap-ekh´-o*; from 575 and 2192; (act.) to *have out*, i.e. *receive in full*; (intr.) to *keep* (oneself) *away*, i.e. *be distant* (lit. or fig.):— be, have, receive.

569. ἀπιστέω **apistĕō**, *ap-is-teh´-o*; from 571; to *be unbelieving*, i.e. (trans.) *disbelieve*, or (by impl.) *disobey*:— believe not.

570. ἀπιστία **apistia**, *ap-is-tee´-ah*; from 571; *faithlessness*, i.e. (neg.) *disbelief* (want of Chr. faith), or (pos.) *unfaithfulness* (disobedience):— unbelief.

571. ἄπιστος **apistŏs**, *ap´-is-tos*; from 1 (as a neg. particle) and 4103; (act.) *disbelieving*, i.e. *without* Chr. faith (spec. a *heathen*); (pass.) *untrustworthy* (person), or *incredible* (thing):— that believeth not, faithless, incredible thing, infidel, unbeliever (-ing).

572. ἁπλότης **haplŏtēs**, *hap-lot´-ace*; from 573; *singleness*, i.e. (subj.) *sincerity* (without dissimulation or self-seeking), or (obj.) *generosity* (copious bestowal):— bountifulness, liberal (-ity), simplicity, singleness.

573. ἁπλοῦς **haplŏus**, *hap-looce´*; prob. from 1 (as a particle of union) and the base of 4120; prop. *folded together*, i.e. *single* (fig. *clear*):— single.

574. ἁπλῶς **haplōs**, *hap-loce´*; adv. from 573 (in the obj. sense of 572); *bountifully*:— liberally.

575. ἀπό **apŏ**, *apŏ´*; a primary particle; "*off*," i.e. *away* (from something near), in various senses (of place, time, or relation; lit. or fig.):— (× here-) after, ago, at, because of, before, by (the space of), for (-th), from, in, (out) of, off, (up-) on (-ce), since, with. In composition (as a prefix) it usually denotes *separation, departure, cessation, completion, reversal*, etc.

576. ἀποβαίνω **apŏbainō**, *ap-ob-ah´-eno*; from 575 and the base of 939; lit. to *disembark*; fig. to *eventuate*:— become, go out, turn.

577. ἀποβάλλω **apŏballō**, *ap-ob-al´-lo*; from 575 and 906; to *throw off*; fig. to *lose*:— cast away.

578. ἀποβλέπω **apŏblĕpō**, *ap-ob-lep´-o*; from 575 and 991; to *look away* from everything else, i.e. (fig.) *intently regard*:— have respect.

579. ἀπόβλητος **apŏblētŏs**, *ap-ob´-lay-tos*; from 577; *cast off*, i.e. (fig.) such as to *be rejected*:— be refused.

580. ἀποβολή **apŏbŏlē**, *ap-ob-ol-ay´*; from 577; *rejection*; fig. *loss*:— casting away, loss.

581. ἀπογενόμενος **apŏgĕnŏmĕnŏs**, *ap-og-en-om´-en-os*; past part. of a compound of 575 and 1096; *absent*, i.e. *deceased* (fig. *renounced*):— being dead.

582. ἀπογραφή **apŏgraphē**, *ap-og-raf-ay´*; from 583; an *enrollment*; by impl. an *assessment*:— taxing.

583. ἀπογράφω **apŏgraphō**, *ap-og-raf-*

Greek

o; from 575 and *1125;* to *write off* (a copy or list), i.e. *enroll.*— tax, write.

584. ἀποδείκνυμι **apŏdĕiknumi**, *ap-od-ike´-noo-mee;* from 575 and *1166;* to *show off*, i.e. *exhibit;* fig. to *demonstrate*, i.e. *accredit:*— (ap-) prove, set forth, shew.

585. ἀπόδειξις **apŏdĕixis**, *ap-od´-ike-sis;* from *584; manifestation:*— demonstration.

586. ἀποδεκατόω **apŏdĕkatŏō**, *ap-od-ek-at-ŏ´-o;* from 575 and *1183;* to *tithe* (as debtor or creditor):— (give, pay, take) tithe.

587. ἀπόδεκτος **apŏdĕktŏs**, *ap-od´-ek-tos;* from *588; accepted*, i.e. *agreeable:*— acceptable.

588. ἀποδέχομαι **apŏdĕchŏmai**, *ap-od-ekh´-om-ahee;* from 575 and *1209;* to *take fully*, i.e. *welcome* (persons), *approve* (things):— accept, receive (gladly).

589. ἀποδημέω **apŏdēmĕō**, *ap-od-ay-meh´-o;* from *590;* to *go abroad*, i.e. *visit a foreign land:*— go (travel) into a far country, journey.

590. ἀπόδημος **apŏdēmŏs**, *ap-od´-ay-mos;* from 575 and *1218; absent from* one's own *people*, i.e. a *foreign traveller:*— taking a far journey.

591. ἀποδίδωμι **apŏdidōmi**, *ap-od-eed´-o-mee;* from 575 and *1325;* to *give away*, i.e. *up, over, back*, etc. (in various applications):— deliver (again), give (again), (re-) pay (-ment be made), perform, recompense, render, requite, restore, reward, sell, yield.

592. ἀποδιορίζω **apŏdiŏrizō**, *ap-od-ee-or-id´-zo;* from 575 and a compound of *1223* and *3724;* to *disjoin* (by a boundary, fig. a party):— separate.

593. ἀποδοκιμάζω **apŏdŏkimazō**, *ap-od-ok-ee-mad´-zo;* from 575 and *1381;* to *disapprove*, i.e. (by impl.) to *repudiate:*— disallow, reject.

594. ἀποδοχή **apŏdŏchē**, *ap-od-okh-ay´;* from *588; acceptance:*— acceptation.

595. ἀπόθεσις **apŏthĕsis**, *ap-oth´-es-is;* from *659;* a *laying aside* (lit. or fig.):— putting away (off).

596. ἀποθήκη **apŏthēkē**, *ap-oth-ay´-kay;* from *659;* a *repository*, i.e. *granary:*— barn, garner.

597. ἀποθησαυρίζω **apŏthēsaurizō**, *ap-oth-ay-sŏw-rid´-zo;* from 575 and *2343;* to *treasure away:*— lay up in store.

598. ἀποθλίβω **apŏthlibō**, *ap-oth-lee´-bo;* from 575 and *2346;* to *crowd* (from every side):— press.

599. ἀποθνήσκω **apŏthnēskō**, *ap-oth-nace´-ko;* from 575 and *2348;* to *die off* (lit. or fig.):— be dead, death, die, lie a-dying, be slain (× with).

600. ἀποκαθίστημι **apŏkathistēmi**, *ap-ok-ath-is´-tay-mee;* from 575 and *2525;* to *reconstitute* (in health, home or organization):— restore (again).

601. ἀποκαλύπτω **apŏkaluptō**, *ap-ok-al-oop´-to;* from 575 and *2572;* to *take off the cover*, i.e. *disclose:*— reveal.

602. ἀποκάλυψις **apŏkalupsis**, *ap-ok-al´-oop-sis;* from *601; disclosure:*— ap-

pearing, coming, lighten, manifestation, be revealed, revelation.

603. ἀποκαραδοκία **apŏkaradŏkia**, *ap-ok-ar-ad-ok-ee´-ah;* from a compound of 575 and a comp. of κάρα **kara** (the *head*) and *1380* (in the sense of *watching*); *intense anticipation:*— earnest expectation.

604. ἀποκαταλλάσσω **apŏkatallassŏ**, *ap-ok-at-al-las´-so;* from 575 and *2644;* to *reconcile fully:*— reconcile.

605. ἀποκατάστασις **apŏkatastasis**, *ap-ok-at-as´-tas-is;* from *600; reconstitution:*— restitution.

606. ἀπόκειμαι **apŏkĕimai**, *ap-ok´-i-mahee;* from 575 and *2749;* to *be reserved;* fig. to *await:*— be appointed, (be) laid up.

607. ἀποκεφαλίζω **apŏkĕphalizō**, *ap-ok-ef-al-id´-zo;* from 575 and *2776;* to *decapitate:*— behead.

608. ἀποκλείω **apŏklĕiō**, *ap-ok-li´-o;* from 575 and *2808;* to *close fully:*— shut up.

609. ἀποκόπτω **apŏkŏptō**, *ap-ok-op´-to;* from 575 and *2875;* to *amputate;* refl. (by irony) to *mutilate* (the privy parts):— cut off. Comp. *2699.*

610. ἀπόκριμα **apŏkrima**, *ap-ok´-ree-mah;* from *611* (in its orig. sense of *judging*); a judicial *decision:*— sentence.

611. ἀποκρίνομαι **apŏkrinŏmai**, *ap-ok-ree´-nom-ahee;* from 575 and κρίνω **krinō**; to *conclude for oneself*, i.e. (by impl.) to *respond;* by Heb. [comp. 6030] to *begin to speak* (where an address is expected):— answer.

612. ἀπόκρισις **apŏkrisis**, *ap-ok´-ree-sis;* from *611;* a *response:*— answer.

613. ἀποκρύπτω **apŏkruptō**, *ap-ok-roop´-to;* from 575 and *2928;* to *conceal away* (i.e. *fully*); fig. to *keep secret:*— hide.

614. ἀπόκρυφος **apŏkruphŏs**, *ap-ok´-roo-fos;* from *613; secret;* by impl. *treasured:*— hid, kept secret.

615. ἀποκτείνω **apŏktĕinō**, *ap-ok-ti´-no;* from 575 and κτείνω **ktĕinō** (to *slay*); to *kill* outright; fig. to *destroy:*— put to death, kill, slay.

616. ἀποκυέω **apŏkuĕō**, *ap-ok-oo-eh´-o;* from 575 and the base of *2949;* to *breed forth*, i.e. (by transf.) to *generate* (fig.):— beget, bring forth.

617. ἀποκυλίω **apŏkuliō**, *ap-ok-oo-lee´-o;* from 575 and *2947;* to *roll away:*— roll away (back).

618. ἀπολαμβάνω **apŏlambanō**, *ap-ol-am-ban´-o;* from 575 and *2983;* to *receive* (spec. in *full*, or as a host); also to *take aside:*— receive, take.

619. ἀπόλαυσις **apŏlausis**, *ap-ol´-ow-sis;* from a compound of 575 and λαύω **lauō** (to *enjoy*); *full enjoyment:*— enjoy (-ment).

620. ἀπολείπω **apŏlĕipō**, *ap-ol-ipe´-o;* from 575 and *3007;* to *leave behind* (pass. *remain*); by impl. to *forsake:*— leave, remain.

621. ἀπολείχω **apŏlĕichō**, *ap-ol-i´-kho;* from 575 and λείχω **lĕichō** (to "*lick*"); to *lick* clean:— lick.

622. ἀπόλλυμι **apŏllumi**, *ap-ol´-loomee;* from 575 and the base of *3639;* to *destroy* fully (refl. to *perish*, or *lose*), lit. or fig.:— destroy, die, lose, mar, perish.

623. Ἀπολλύων **Apŏlluōn**, *ap-ol-loo´-ohn;* act. part. of *622;* a *destroyer* (i.e. *Satan*):— Apollyon.

624. Ἀπολλωνία **Apŏllōnia**, *ap-ol-lo-nee´-ah;* from the pagan deity Ἀπόλλων **Apŏllōn** (i.e. the *sun;* from 622); *Apollonia*, a place in Macedonia:— Apollonia.

625. Ἀπολλώς **Apŏllōs**, *ap-ol-loce´;* prob. from the same as *624; Apollos*, an Isr.:— Apollos.

626. ἀπολογέομαι **apŏlŏgĕŏmai**, *ap-ol-og-eh´-om-ahee;* mid. voice from a compound of 575 and *3056;* to give an *account* (legal *plea*) of oneself, i.e. *exculpate* (self):— answer (for self), make defence, excuse (self), speak for self.

627. ἀπολογία **apŏlŏgia**, *ap-ol-og-ee´-ah;* from the same as *626;* a *plea* ("apology"):— answer (for self), clearing of self, defence.

628. ἀπολούω **apŏlŏuō**, *ap-ol-oo´-o;* from 575 and *3068;* to *wash* fully, i.e. (fig.) *have remitted* (refl.):— wash (away).

629. ἀπολύτρωσις **apŏlutrōsis**, *ap-ol-oo´-tro-sis;* from a compound of 575 and *3083;* (the act) *ransom* in full, i.e. (fig.) *riddance*, or (spec.) Chr. *salvation:*— deliverance, redemption.

630. ἀπολύω **apŏluō**, *ap-ol-oo´-o;* from 575 and *3089;* to *free* fully, i.e. (lit.) *relieve, release, dismiss* (refl. *depart*), or (fig.) *let die, pardon* or (spec.) *divorce:*— (let) depart, dismiss, divorce, forgive, let go, loose, put (send) away, release, set at liberty.

631. ἀπομάσσομαι **apŏmassŏmai**, *ap-om-as´-som-ahee;* mid. voice from 575 and μάσσω **massō** (to *squeeze, knead, smear*); to *scrape away:*— wipe off.

632. ἀπονέμω **apŏnĕmō**, *ap-on-em´-o;* from 575 and the base of *3551;* to *apportion*, i.e. *bestow:*— give.

633. ἀπονίπτω **apŏniptō**, *ap-on-ip´-to;* from 575 and *3538;* to *wash off* (refl. one's own hands symb.):— wash.

634. ἀποπίπτω **apŏpiptō**, *ap-op-ip´-to;* from 575 and *4098;* to *fall off:*— fall.

635. ἀποπλανάω **apŏplanaō**, *ap-op-lan-ah´-o;* from 575 and *4105;* to *lead astray* (fig.); pass. to *stray* (from truth):— err, seduce.

636. ἀποπλέω **apŏplĕō**, *ap-op-leh´-o;* from 575 and *4126;* to *set sail:*— sail away.

637. ἀποπλύνω **apŏplunō**, *ap-op-loo´-no;* from 575 and *4150;* to *rinse off:*— wash.

638. ἀποπνίγω **apŏpnigō**, *ap-op-nee´-go;* from 575 and *4155;* to *stifle* (by drowning or overgrowth):— choke.

639. ἀπορέω **apŏrĕō**, *ap-or-eh´-o;* from a compound of *1* (as a neg. particle) and the base of *4198;* to *have no way* out, i.e. *be at a loss* (mentally):— (stand in) doubt, be perplexed.

640. ἀπορία **apŏria**, *ap-or-ee´-a;* from the same as *639;* a (state of) *quandary:*— perplexity.

641. ἀπορρίπτω **apŏrrhiptō**, ap-or-hrip´-to; from 575 and 4496; to *hurl off*, i.e. *precipitate* (oneself):— cast.

642. ἀπορφανίζω **apŏrphanizō**, ap-or-fan-id´-zo; from 575 and a der. of 3737; to *bereave wholly*, i.e. (fig.) *separate* (from intercourse):— take.

643. ἀποσκευάζω **apŏskĕuazō**, ap-osk-yoo-ad´-zo; from 575 and a der. of 4632; to *pack up* (one's) *baggage*:— take up ... carriages.

644. ἀποσκίασμα **apŏskiasma**, ap-os-kee´-as-mah; from a compound of 575 and a der. of 4639; a *shading off*, i.e. *obscuration*:— shadow.

645. ἀποσπάω **apŏspaō**, ap-os-pah´-o; from 575 and 4685; to *drag forth*, i.e. (lit.) *unsheathe* (a sword), or rel. (with a degree of force impl.) *retire* (pers. or factiously):— (with-) draw (away), after we were gotten from.

646. ἀποστασία **apŏstasia**, ap-os-tas-ee´-ah; fem. of the same as 647; *defection* from truth (prop. the state) ["apostasy"]:— falling away, forsake.

647. ἀποστάσιον **apŏstasiŏn**, ap-os-tas´-ee-on; neut. of a (presumed) adj. from a der. of 868; prop. something *separative*, i.e. (spec.) *divorce*:— (writing of) divorcement.

648. ἀποστεγάζω **apŏstĕgazō**, ap-os-teg-ad´-zo; from 575 and a der. of 4721; to *unroof*:— uncover.

649. ἀποστέλλω **apŏstĕllō**, ap-os-tel´-lo; from 575 and 4724; *set apart*, i.e. (by impl.) to *send out* (prop. on a mission) lit. or fig.:— put in, send (away, forth, out), set [at libertu].

650. ἀποστερέω **apŏstĕrĕō**, ap-os-ter-eh´-o; from 575 and στερέω **stĕrĕō** (to *deprive*); to *despoil*:— defraud, destitute, kept back by fraud.

651. ἀποστολή **apŏstŏlē**, ap-os-tol-ay´; from 649; *commission*, i.e. (spec.) *apostolate*:— apostleship.

652. ἀπόστολος **apŏstŏlŏs**, ap-os´-tol-os; from 649; a *delegate*; spec. an *ambassador* of the Gospel; officially a *commissioner* of Christ ["apostle"] (with miraculous powers):— apostle, messenger, he that is sent.

653. ἀποστοματίζω **apŏstŏmatizō**, ap-os-tom-at-id´-zo; from 575 and a (presumed) der. of 4750; to *speak off-hand* (prop. *dictate*), i.e. to *catechize* (in an invidious manner):— provoke to speak.

654. ἀποστρέφω **apŏstrĕphō**, ap-os-tref´-o; from 575 and 4762; to *turn away* or *back* (lit. or fig.):— bring again, pervert, turn away (from).

655. ἀποστυγέω **apŏstugĕō**, ap-os-toog-eh´-o; from 575 and the base of 4767; to *detest* utterly:— abhor.

656. ἀποσυνάγωγος **apŏsunagōgŏs**, ap-os-oon-ag´-o-gos; from 575 and 4864; *excommunicated*:— (put) out of the synagogue (-s).

657. ἀποτάσσομαι **apŏtassŏmai**, ap-ot-as´-som-ahee; mid. voice from 575 and 5021; lit. to *say adieu* (by departing or dismissing); fig. to *renounce*:— bid farewell, forsake, take leave, send away.

658. ἀποτελέω **apŏtĕlĕō**, ap-ot-el-eh´-o; from 575 and 5055; to *complete entirely*, i.e. *consummate*:— finish.

659. ἀποτίθημι **apŏtithēmi**, ap-ot-eeth´-ay-mee; from 575 and 5087; to *put away* (lit. or fig.):— cast off, lay apart (aside, down), put away (off).

660. ἀποτινάσσω **apŏtinassō**, ap-ot-in-as´-so; from 575 and τινάσσω **tinassō** (to *jostle*); to *brush off*:— shake off.

661. ἀποτίνω **apŏtinō**, ap-ot-ee´-no; from 575 and 5099; to *pay in full*:— repay.

662. ἀποτολμάω **apŏtŏlmaō**, ap-ot-ol-mah´-o; from 575 and 5111; to *venture* plainly:— be very bold.

663. ἀποτομία **apŏtŏmia**, ap-ot-om-ee´-ah; from the base of 664; (fig.) *decisiveness*, i.e. *rigor*:— severity.

664. ἀποτόμως **apŏtŏmōs**, ap-ot-om´-oce; adv. from a der. of a compound of 575 and τέμνω **tĕmnō** (to *cut*); *abruptly*, i.e. *peremptorily*:— sharply (-ness).

665. ἀποτρέπω **apŏtrĕpō**, ap-ot-rep´-o; from 575 and the base of 5157; to *deflect*, i.e. (refl.) *avoid*:— turn away.

666. ἀπουσία **apŏusia**, ap-oo-see´-ah; from the part. of 548; a *being away*:— absence.

667. ἀποφέρω **apŏhĕrō**, ap-of-er´-o; from 575 and 5342; to *bear off* (lit. or rel.):— bring, carry (away).

668. ἀποφεύγω **apŏhĕugō**, ap-of-yoo-go; from 575 and 5343; (fig.) to *escape*:— escape.

669. ἀποφθέγγομαι **apŏphthĕggŏmai**, ap-of-theng´-om-ahee; from 575 and 5350; to *enunciate* plainly, i.e. *declare*:— say, speak forth, utterance.

670. ἀποφορτίζομαι **apŏphŏrtizŏmai**, ap-of-or-tid´-zom-ahee; from 575 and the mid. voice of 5412; to *unload*:— unlade.

671. ἀπόχρησις **apŏchrēsis**, ap-okh´-ray-sis; from a compound of 575 and 5530; the act of *using up*, i.e. *consumption*:— using.

672. ἀποχωρέω **apŏchōrĕō**, ap-okh-o-reh´-o; from 575 and 5562; to *go away*:— depart.

673. ἀποχωρίζω **apŏchōrizō**, ap-okh-o-rid´-zo; from 575 and 5563; to *rend apart*; refl. to *separate*:— depart (asunder).

674. ἀποψύχω **apŏpsuchō**, ap-ops-oo´-kho; from 575 and 5594; to *breathe out*, i.e. *faint*:— hearts failing.

675. Ἄππιος **'Appiŏs**, ap´-pee-os; of Lat. or.; (in the gen., i.e. possessive case) of *Appius*, the name of a Rom.:— Appii.

676. ἀπρόσιτος **aprŏsitŏs**, ap-ros´-ee-tos; from 1 (as a neg. particle) and a der. of a compound of 4314 and εἶμι **ĕimi** (to *go*); *inaccessible*:— which no man can approach.

677. ἀπρόσκοπος **aprŏskŏpŏs**, ap-ros-kop-os; from 1 (as a neg. particle) and a presumed der. of 4350; act. *inoffensive*, i.e. *not leading into sin*; pass. *faultless*, i.e. *not led into sin*:— none (void of, without) offence.

678. ἀπροσωπολήπτως **aprŏsōpŏlēptŏs**,

ap-ros-o-pol-ape´-toce; adv. from a compound of 1 (as a neg. particle) and a presumed der. of a presumed comp. of 4383 and 2983 [comp. 4381]; in a way *not accepting* the *person*, i.e. *impartially*:— without respect of persons.

679. ἄπταιστος **aptaistŏs**, ap-tah´-ee-stos; from 1 (as a neg. particle) and a der. of 4417; *not stumbling*, i.e. (fig.) *without sin*:— from falling.

680. ἅπτομαι **haptŏmai**, hap´-tom-ahee; refl. of 681; prop. to *attach* oneself to, i.e. to *touch* (in many impl. relations):— touch.

681. ἅπτω **haptō**, hap´-to; a primary verb; prop. to *fasten* to, i.e. (spec.) to *set* on fire:— kindle, light.

682. Ἀπφία **Apphia**, ap-fee´-a; prob. of for. or.; *Apphia*, a woman of Collosæ:— Apphia.

683. ἀπωθέομαι **apōthĕŏmai**, ap-o-theh´-om-ahee; or ἀπώθομαι **apōthŏmai**, ap-o´-thom-ahee; from 575 and the mid. voice of ὠθέω **ōthĕō** or ὤθω **ōthō** (to *shove*); to *push off*, fig. to *reject*:— cast away, put away (from), thrust away (from).

684. ἀπώλεια **apŏlĕia**, ap-o´-li-a; from a presumed der. of 622; *ruin* or *loss* (phys. spiritual or eternal):— damnable (-nation), destruction, die, perdition, × perish, pernicious ways, waste.

685. ἀρά **ara**, ar-ah´; prob. from 142; prop. *prayer* (as *lifted* to Heaven), i.e. (by impl.) *imprecation*:— curse.

686. ἄρα **ara**, ar´-ah; prob. from 142 (through the idea of *drawing* a conclusion); a particle denoting an *inference* more or less decisive (as follows):— haply, (what) manner (of man), no doubt, perhaps, so be, then, therefore, truly, wherefore. Often used in connection with other particles, esp. 1065 or 3767 (after) or 1487 (before). Comp. also 687.

687. ἆρα **ara**, ar´-ah; a form of 686, denoting an *interrogation* to which a negative answer is presumed:— therefore.

688. Ἀραβία **Arabia**, ar-ab-ee´-ah; of Heb. or. [6152]; *Arabia*, a region of Asia:— Arabia.

ἄραγε **aragĕ**. See 686 and 1065.

689. Ἀράμ **Aram**, ar-am´; of Heb. or. [7410]; *Aram* (i.e. *Ram*), an Isr.:— Aram.

690. Ἄραψ **'Araps**, ar´-aps; from 688; an *Arab* or native of Arabia:— Arabian.

691. ἀργέω **argĕō**, arg-eh´-o; from 692; to *be idle*, i.e. (fig.) to *delay*:— linger.

692. ἀργός **argŏs**, ar-gos´; from 1 (as a neg. particle) and 2041; *inactive*, i.e. *unemployed*; (by impl.) *lazy*, *useless*:— barren, idle, slow.

693. ἀργύρεος **argurĕŏs**, ar-goo´-reh-os; from 696; made of *silver*:— (of) silver.

694. ἀργύριον **arguriŏn**, ar-goo´-ree-on; neut. of a presumed der. of 696; *silvery*, i.e. (by impl.) *cash*; spec. a *silverling* (i.e. *drachma* or *shekel*):— money, (piece of) silver (piece).

695. ἀργυροκόπος **argurŏkŏpŏs**, ar-goo-

rok-op´-os; from *696* and *2875;* a *beater* (i.e. *worker*) *of silver:*— silversmith.

696. ἄργυρος **argurŏs,** *ar´-goo-ros;* from ἀργός **argŏs** (*shining*); *silver* (the metal, in the articles or coin):— silver.

697. Ἄρειος Πάγος **Arěiŏs Pagŏs,** *ar´-i-os pag´-os;* from Ἄρης **Arēs** (the name of the Greek deity of war) and a der. of *4078; rock of Ares,* a place in Athens:— Areopagus, Mars' Hill.

698. Ἀρεοπαγίτης **Arěŏpagitēs,** *ar-eh-op-ag-ee´-tace;* from *697;* an *Areopagite* or member of the court held on Mars' Hill:— Areopagite.

699. ἀρέσκεια **arěskěia,** *ar-es´-ki-ah;* from a der. of *700; complaisance:*— pleasing.

700. ἀρέσκω **arěskō,** *ar-es´-ko;* prob. from *142* (through the idea of *exciting* emotion); to *be agreeable* (or by impl. to seek to be so):— please.

701. ἀρεστός **arěstŏs,** *ar-es-tos´;* from *700; agreeable;* by impl. *fit:*— (things that) please (-ing), reason.

702. Ἀρέτας **Arětas,** *ar-et´-as;* of for. or.; *Aretas,* an Arabian:— Aretas.

703. ἀρέτη **arětē,** *ar-et´-ay;* from the same as *730;* prop. *manliness* (*valor*), i.e. *excellence* (intrinsic or attributed):— praise, virtue.

704. ἀρήν **arēn,** *ar-ane´;* perh. the same as *730;* a *lamb* (as a *male*):— lamb.

705. ἀριθμέω **arithměō,** *ar-ith-meh´-o;* from *706;* to *enumerate* or *count:*— number.

706. ἀριθμός **arithmŏs,** *ar-ith-mos´;* from *142;* a *number* (as reckoned *up*):— number.

707. Ἀριμαθαία **Arimathaia,** *ar-ee-math-ah´-ee-ah;* of Heb. or. [7414]; *Arimathæa* (or *Ramah*), a place in Pal.:— Arimathæa.

708. Ἀρίσταρχος **Aristarchŏs,** *ar-is´-tar-khos;* from the same as *712* and *757; best ruling; Aristarchus,* a Macedonian:— Aristarchus.

709. ἀριστάω **aristaō,** *ar-is-tah´-o;* from *712;* to *take the principle meal:*— dine.

710. ἀριστερός **aristěrŏs,** *ar-is-ter-os´;* appar. a comparative of the same as *712;* the *left* hand (as *second-best*):— left [hand].

711. Ἀριστόβουλος **Aristŏbŏulŏs,** *ar-is-tob´-oo-los;* from the same as *712* and *1012; best counselling; Aristoboulus,* a Chr.:— Aristobulus.

712. ἄριστον **aristŏn,** *ar´-is-ton;* appar. neut. of a superl. from the same as *730;* the *best meal* [or *breakfast;* perh. from ἦρι **ēri** ("*early*")], i.e. *luncheon:*— dinner.

713. ἀρκετός **arkětŏs,** *ar-ket-os´;* from *714; satisfactory:*— enough, suffice (-ient).

714. ἀρκέω **arkěō,** *ar-keh´-o;* appar. a primary verb [but prob. akin to *142* through the idea of *raising* a barrier]; prop. to *ward off,* i.e. (by impl.) to *avail* (fig. *be satisfactory*):— content, be enough, suffice, be sufficient.

715. ἄρκτος **arktŏs,** *ark´-tos;* prob. from

714; a *bear* (as *obstructing* by ferocity):— bear.

716. ἅρμα **harma,** *har´-mah;* prob. from *142* [perh. with *1* (as a particle of union) prefixed]; a *chariot* (as *raised* or fitted *together* [comp. *719*]):— chariot.

717. Ἀρμαγεδδών **Armagĕddōn,** *ar-mag-ed-dohn´;* of Heb. or. [2022 and 4023]; *Armageddon* (or *Har-Meggiddon*), a symbol. name:— Armageddon.

718. ἁρμόζω **harmŏzō,** *har-mod´-zo;* from *719;* to *joint,* i.e. (fig.) to *woo* (refl. to *betroth*):— espouse.

719. ἁρμός **harmŏs,** *har-mos´;* from the same as *716;* an *articulation* (of the body):— joint.

720. ἀρνέομαι **arněŏmai,** *ar-neh´-om-ahee;* perh. from *1* (as a neg. particle) and the mid. voice of *4483;* to *contradict,* i.e. *disavow, reject, abnegate:*— deny, refuse.

721. ἀρνίον **arniŏn,** *ar-nee´-on;* dimin. from *704;* a *lambkin:*— lamb.

722. ἀροτριόω **arŏtriŏō,** *ar-ot-ree-o´-o;* from *723;* to *plough:*— plow.

723. ἄροτρον **arŏtrŏn,** *ar´-ot-ron;* from ἀρόω **arŏō** (to *till*); a *plow:*— plow.

724. ἁρπαγή **harpagē,** *har-pag-ay´;* from *726; pillage* (prop. abstr.):— extortion, ravening, spoiling.

725. ἁρπαγμός **harpagmŏs,** *har-pag-mos´;* from *726; plunder* (prop. concr.):— robbery.

726. ἁρπάζω **harpazō,** *har-pad´-zo;* from a der. of *138;* to *seize* (in various applications):— catch (away, up), pluck, pull, take (by force).

727. ἅρπαξ **harpax,** *har´-pax;* from *726; rapacious:*— extortion, ravening.

728. ἀρραβών **arrhabōn,** *ar-hrab-ohn´;* of Heb. or. [6162]; a *pledge,* i.e. part of the purchase-money or property given in advance as *security* for the rest:— earnest.

729. ἄρραφος **arrhaphŏs,** *ar´-hraf-os;* from *1* (as a neg. particle) and a presumed der. of the same as *4476; unsewed,* i.e. (by impl.) of a single piece:— without seam.

730. ἄρρην **arrhēn,** *ar´-hrane;* or

ἄρσην **arsēn,** *ar´-sane;* prob. from *142; male* (as stronger for *lifting*):— male, man.

731. ἄρρητος **arrhētŏs,** *ar´-hray-tos;* from *1* (as a neg. particle) and the same as *4490; unsaid,* i.e. (by impl.) *inexpressible:*— unspeakable.

732. ἄρρωστος **arrhŏstŏs,** *ar´-hroce-tos;* from *1* (as a neg. particle) and a presumed der. of *4517; infirm:*— sick (folk, -ly).

733. ἀρσενοκοίτης **arsěnŏkŏitēs,** *ar-sen-ok-oy´-tace;* from *730* and *2845;* a *sodomite:*— abuser of (that defile) self with mankind.

734. Ἀρτεμάς **Artěmas,** *ar-tem-as´;* contr. from a compound of *735* and *1435; gift of Artemis; Artemas* (or *Artemidorus*), a Chr.:— Artemas.

735. Ἄρτεμις **Artěmis,** *ar´-tem-is;* prob. from the same as *736; prompt; Artemis,* the name of a Grecian god-

dess borrowed by the Asiatics for one of their deities:— Diana.

736. ἀρτέμων **artěmōn,** *ar-tem´-ohn;* from a der. of *737;* prop. something *ready* [or else more remotely from *142* (comp. *740*); something *hung* up], i.e. (spec.) the *topsail* (rather *foresail* or *jib*) of a vessel:— mainsail.

737. ἄρτι **arti,** *ar´-tee;* adv. from a der. of *142* (comp. *740*) through the idea of *suspension;* just *now:*— this day (hour), hence [-forth], here [-after], hither [-to], (even) now, (this) present.

738. ἀρτιγέννητος **artigěnnētŏs,** *ar-teeg-en´-nay-tos;* from *737* and *1084; just born,* i.e. (fig.) a *young convert:*— new born.

739. ἄρτιος **artiŏs,** *ar´-tee-os;* from *737; fresh,* i.e. (by impl.) *complete:*— perfect.

740. ἄρτος **artŏs,** *ar´-tos;* from *142; bread* (as *raised*) or a *loaf:*— (shew-) bread, loaf.

741. ἀρτύω **artuō,** *ar-too´-o;* from a presumed der. of *142;* to *prepare,* i.e. *spice* (with *stimulating* condiments):— season.

742. Ἀρφαξάδ **Arphaxad,** *ar-fax-ad´;* of Heb. or. [775]; *Arphaxad,* a post-diluvian patriarch:— Arphaxad.

743. ἀρχάγγελος **archaggělŏs,** *ar-khang´-el-os;* from *757* and *32;* a *chief angel:*— archangel.

744. ἀρχαῖος **archaiŏs,** *ar-khah´-yos;* from *746; original* or *primeval:*— (them of) old (time).

745. Ἀρχέλαος **Archělaŏs,** *ar-khel´-ah-os;* from *757* and *2994; people-ruling; Archelaus,* a Jewish king:— Archelaus.

746. ἀρχή **archē,** *ar-khay´;* from *756;* (prop. abstr.) a *commencement,* or (concr.) *chief* (in various applications of order, time, place, or rank):— beginning, corner, (at the, the) first (estate), magistrate, power, principality, principle, rule.

747. ἀρχηγός **archēgŏs,** *ar-khay-gos´;* from *746* and *71;* a *chief leader:*— author, captain, prince.

748. ἀρχιερατικός **archiěratikŏs,** *ar-khee-er-at-ee-kos´;* from *746* and a der. of *2413; high-priestly:*— of the high-priest.

749. ἀρχιερεύς **archiěrěus,** *ar-khee-er-yuce´;* from *746* and *2409;* the *high-priest* (lit. of the Jews, typ. Christ); by extens. a *chief priest:*— chief (high) priest, chief of the priests.

750. ἀρχιποίμην **archipŏimēn,** *ar-khee-poy´-mane;* from *746* and *4166;* a *head shepherd:*— chief shepherd.

751. Ἄρχιππος **Archippŏs,** *ar´-khip-pos;* from *746* and *2462; horse-ruler; Archippus,* a Chr.:— Archippus.

752. ἀρχισυνάγωγος **archisunagōgŏs,** *ar-khee-soon-ag´-o-gos;* from *746* and *4864; director* of the *synagogue* services:— (chief) ruler of the synagogue.

753. ἀρχιτέκτων **architěktōn,** *ar-khee-tek´-tone;* from *746* and *5045;* a *chief constructor,* i.e. "*architect*":— master-builder.

754. ἀρχιτελώνης **architělōnēs,** *ar-khee-tel-o´-nace;* from *746* and *5057;* a

principle tax-gatherer:— chief among the publicans.

755. ἀρχιτρίκλινος **architriklinŏs**, *ar-khee-tree´-klee-nos;* from 746 and a compound of 5140 and 2827 (a *dinner-bed,* because composed of three couches); *director of the entertainment:*— governor (ruler) of the feast.

756. ἄρχομαι **archŏmai**, *ar´-khom-ahee;* mid. voice of 757 (through the impl. of *precedence*); to *commence* (in order of time):— (rehearse from the) begin (-ning).

757. ἄρχω **archō**, *ar´-kho;* a primary verb; to be *first* (in political rank or power):— reign (rule) over.

758. ἄρχων **archōn**, *ar´-khone;* pres. part. of 757; a *first* (in rank or power):— chief (ruler), magistrate, prince, ruler.

759. ἄρωμα **"arōma,"** *ar´-o-mah;* from 142 (in the sense of *sending* off scent); an *aromatic:*— (sweet) spice.

760. Ἀσά **Asa**, *as-ah´;* of Heb. or. [609]; *Asa,* an Isr.:— Asa.

761. ἀσάλευτος **asalĕutŏs**, *as-al´-yoo-tos;* from 1 (as a neg. particle) and a der. of 4531; *unshaken,* i.e. (by impl.) *immovable* (fig.):— which cannot be moved, unmovable.

762. ἄσβεστος **asbĕstŏs**, *as´-bes-tos;* from 1 (as a neg. particle) and a der. of 4570; *not extinguished,* i.e. (by impl.) *perpetual:*— not to be quenched, unquenchable.

763. ἀσέβεια **asĕbĕia**, *as-eb´-i-ah;* from 765; *impiety,* i.e. (by impl.) *wickedness:*— ungodly (-liness).

764. ἀσεβέω **asĕbĕō**, *as-eb-eh´-o;* from 765; to *be* (by impl. *act*) *impious* or *wicked:*— commit (live, that after should live) ungodly.

765. ἀσεβής **asĕbēs**, *as-eb-ace´;* from 1 (as a neg. particle) and a presumed der. of 4576; *irreverent,* i.e. (by extens.) *impious* or *wicked:*— ungodly (man).

766. ἀσέλγεια **asĕlgĕia**, *as-elg´-i-a;* from a compound of 1 (as a neg. particle) and a presumed σελγής **sĕlgēs** (of uncert. der., but appar. mean. *continent*); *licentiousness* (sometimes incl. other vices):— filthy, lasciviousness, wantonness.

767. ἄσημος **asēmŏs**, *as´-ay-mos;* from 1 (as a neg. particle) and the base of 4591; *unmarked,* i.e. (fig.) *ignoble:*— mean.

768. Ἀσήρ **Asēr**, *as-ayr´;* of Heb. or. [836]; *Aser* (i.e. *Asher*), an Isr. tribe:— Aser.

769. ἀσθένεια **asthĕnĕia**, *as-then´-i-ah;* from 772; *feebleness* (of body or mind); by impl. *malady;* mor. *frailty:*— disease, infirmity, sickness, weakness.

770. ἀσθενέω **asthĕnĕō**, *as-then-eh´-o;* from 772; to *be feeble* (in any sense):— be diseased, impotent folk (man), (be) sick, (be, be made) weak.

771. ἀσθένημα **asthĕnēma**, *as-then´-ay-mah;* from 770; a *scruple* of conscience:— infirmity.

772. ἀσθενής **asthĕnēs**, *as-then-ace´;* from 1 (as a neg. particle) and the base of 4599; *strengthless* (in various appli-

cations, lit., fig. and mor.):— more feeble, impotent, sick, without strength, weak (-er, -ness, thing).

773. Ἀσία **Asia**, *as-ee´-ah;* of uncert. der.; *Asia,* i.e. *Asia Minor,* or (usually) only its western shore:— Asia.

774. Ἀσιανός **Asianŏs**, *as-ee-an-os´;* from 773; an *Asian* (i.e. *Asiatic*) or an inhabitant of Asia:— of Asia.

775. Ἀσιάρχης **Asiarchēs**, *as-ee-ar´-khace;* from 773 and 746; an *Asiarch* or president of the public festivities in a city of Asia Minor:— chief of Asia.

776. ἀσιτία **asitia**, *as-ee-tee´-ah;* from 777; *fasting* (the state):— abstinence.

777. ἄσιτος **asitŏs**, *as´-ee-tos;* from 1 (as a neg. particle) and 4621; *without* (taking) *food:*— fasting.

778. ἀσκέω **askĕō**, *as-keh´-o;* prob. from the same as 4632; to *elaborate,* i.e. (fig.) *train* (by impl. *strive*):— exercise.

779. ἀσκός **askŏs**, *as-kos´;* from the same as 778; a *leathern* (or skin) *bag* used as a bottle:— bottle.

780. ἀσμένως **asmĕnōs**, *as-men´-oce;* adv. from a der. of the base of 2237; *with pleasure:*— gladly.

781. ἄσοφος **asŏphŏs**, *as´-of-os;* from 1 (as a neg. particle) and 4680; *unwise:*— fool.

782. ἀσπάζομαι **aspazŏmai**, *as-pad´-zom-ahee;* from 1 (as a particle of union) and a presumed form of 4685; to *enfold* in the arms, i.e. (by impl.) to *salute,* (fig.) to *welcome:*— embrace, greet, salute, take leave.

783. ἀσπασμός **aspasmŏs**, *as-pas-mos´;* from 782; a *greeting* (in person or by letter):— greeting, salutation.

784. ἄσπιλος **aspilŏs**, *as´-pee-los;* from 1 (as a neg. particle) and 4695; *unblemished* (phys. or mor.):— without spot, unspotted.

785. ἀσπίς **aspis**, *as-pece´;* of uncert. der.; a *buckler* (or *round* shield); used of a serpent (as *coiling* itself), prob. the "*asp*":— asp.

786. ἄσπονδος **aspŏndŏs**, *as´-pon-dos;* from 1 (as a neg. particle) and a der. of 4689; lit. *without libation* (which usually accompanied a treaty), i.e. (by impl.) *truceless:*— implacable, truce-breaker.

787. ἀσσάριον **assariŏn**, *as-sar´-ee-on;* of Lat. or.; an *assarius* or *as,* a Roman coin:— farthing.

788. ἆσσον **assŏn**, *as´-son;* neut. comparative of the base of 1451; *more nearly,* i.e. *very near:*— close.

789. Ἄσσος **Assŏs**, *as´-sos;* prob. of for. or.; *Assus,* a city of Asia Minor:— Assos.

790. ἀστατέω **astatĕō**, *as-tat-eh´-o;* from 1 (as a neg. particle) and a der. of 2476; to *be non-stationary,* i.e. (fig.) *homeless:*— have no certain dwelling-place.

791. ἀστεῖος **astĕiŏs**, *as-ti´-os;* from ἄστυ (a *city*); *urbane,* i.e. (by impl.) *handsome:*— fair.

792. ἀστήρ **astēr**, *as-tare´;* prob. from the base of 4766; a *star* (as *strown* over the sky), lit. or fig.:— star.

793. ἀστήρικτος **astēriktŏs**, *as-tay´-rik-tos;* from 1 (as a neg. particle) and a presumed der. of 4741; *unfixed,* i.e. (fig.) *vacillating:*— unstable.

794. ἄστοργος **astŏrgŏs**, *as´-tor-gos;* from 1 (as a neg. particle) and a presumed der. of στέργω **stērgō** (to *cherish* affectionately); *hard-hearted* toward kindred:— without natural affection.

795. ἀστοχέω **astŏchĕō**, *as-tokh-eh´-o;* from a compound of 1 (as a neg. particle) and στόιχος **stŏichŏs** (an *aim*); to *miss* the mark, i.e. (fig.) *deviate* from truth:— err, swerve.

796. ἀστραπή **astrapē**, *as-trap-ay´;* from 797; *lightning;* by anal. *glare:*— lightning, bright shining.

797. ἀστράπτω **astraptō**, *as-trap´-to;* prob. from 792; to *flash* as lightning:— lighten, shine.

798. ἄστρον **astrŏn**, *as´-tron;* neut. from 792; prop. a *constellation;* put for a single *star* (nat. or artif.):— star.

799. Ἀσύγκριτος **Asugkritŏs**, *as-oong-kree-tos;* from 1 (as a neg. particle) and a der. of 4793; *incomparable; Asyncritus,* a Chr.:— Asyncritus.

800. ἀσύμφωνος **asumphōnŏs**, *as-oom´-fo-nos;* from 1 (as a neg. particle) and 4859; *inharmonious* (fig.):— agree not.

801. ἀσύνετος **asunĕtŏs**, *as-oon´-ay-tos;* from 1 (as a neg. particle) and 4908; *unintelligent;* by impl. *wicked:*— foolish, without understanding.

802. ἀσύνθετος **asunthĕtŏs**, *as-oon´-thet-os;* from 1 (as a neg. particle) and a der. of 4934; prop. *not agreed,* i.e. *treacherous* to compacts:— covenant-breaker.

803. ἀσφάλεια **asphalĕia**, *as-fal´-i-ah;* from 804; *security* (lit. or fig.):— certainty, safety.

804. ἀσφαλής **asphalēs**, *as-fal-ace´;* from 1 (as a neg. particle) and σφάλλω **sphallō** (to "*fail*"); *secure* (lit. or fig.):— certain (-ty), safe, sure.

805. ἀσφαλίζω **asphalizō**, *as-fal-id´-zo;* from 804; to *render secure:*— make fast (sure).

806. ἀσφαλῶς **asphalōs**, *as-fal-oce´;* adv. from 804; *securely* (lit. or fig.):— assuredly, safely.

807. ἀσχημονέω **aschēmŏnĕō**, *as-kay-mon-eh´-o;* from 809; to *be* (i.e. *act*) *unbecoming:*— behave self uncomely (unseemly).

808. ἀσχημοσύνη **aschēmŏsunē**, *as-kay-mos-oo´-nay;* from 809; an *indecency;* by impl. the *pudenda:*— shame, that which is unseemly.

809. ἀσχήμων **aschēmōn**, *as-kay´-mone;* from 1 (as a neg. particle) and a presumed der. of 2192 (in the sense of its congener 4976); prop. *shapeless,* i.e. (fig.) *inelegant:*— uncomely.

810. ἀσωτία **asōtia**, *as-o-tee´-ah;* from a compound of 1 (as a neg. particle) and a presumed der. of 4982; prop. *un-savedness,* i.e. (by impl.) *profligacy:*— excess, riot.

811. ἀσώτως **asōtōs**, *as-o´-toce;* adv. from the same as 810; *dissolutely:*— riotous.

812. ἀτακτέω **ataktéō**, *at-ak-teh´-o;* from *813;* to *be* (i.e. *act*) *irregular:*— behave self disorderly.

813. ἄτακτος **ataktŏs**, *at´-ak-tos;* from *1* (as a neg. particle) and a der. of *5021; unarranged,* i.e. (by impl.) *insubordinate* (religiously):— unruly.

814. ἀτάκτως **ataktōs**, *at-ak´-toce;* adv. from *813; irregularly* (mor.):— disorderly.

815. ἄτεκνος **atĕknŏs**, *at´-ek-nos;* from *1* (as a neg. particle) and *5043; childless:*— childless, without children.

816. ἀτενίζω **atĕnizō**, *at-en-id´-zo;* from a compound of *1* (as a particle of union) and τείνω **tĕinō** (to *stretch*); to *gaze* intently:— behold earnestly (stedfastly), fasten (eyes), look (earnestly, stedfastly, up stedfastly), set eyes.

817. ἄτερ **atĕr**, *at´-er;* a particle prob. akin to *427; aloof,* i.e. *apart* from (lit. or fig.):— in the absence of, without.

818. ἀτιμάζω **atimazō**, *at-im-ad´-zo;* from *820;* to *render infamous,* i.e. (by impl.) *contemn* or *maltreat:*— despise, dishonour, suffer shame, entreat shamefully.

819. ἀτιμία **atimia**, *at-ee-mee´-ah;* from *820; infamy,* i.e. (subj.) comparative indignity, (obj.) *disgrace:*— dishonour, reproach, shame, vile.

820. ἄτιμος **atimŏs**, *at´-ee-mos;* from *1* (as a neg. particle) and *5092;* (neg.) *unhonoured* or (pos.) *dishonoured:*— despised, without honour, less honourable [comparative degree].

821. ἀτιμόω **atimŏō**, *at-ee-mŏ´-o;* from *820;* used like *818,* to *maltreat:*— handle shamefully.

822. ἀτμίς **atmis**, *at-mece´;* from the same as *109; mist:*— vapour.

823. ἄτομος **atŏmŏs**, *at´-om-os;* from *1* (as a neg. particle) and the base of *5114; uncut,* i.e. (by impl.) *indivisible* [an "*atom*" of time]:— moment.

824. ἄτοπος **atŏpŏs**, *at´-op-os;* from *1* (as a neg. particle) and *5117; out of place,* i.e. (fig.) *improper, injurious, wicked:*— amiss, harm, unreasonable.

825. Ἀττάλεια **Attalĕia**, *at-tal´-i-ah;* from Ἄτταλος **Attalŏs** (a king of Pergamus); *Attaleia,* a place in Pamphylia:— Attalia.

826. αὐγάζω **augazō**, *ŏw-gad´-zo;* from *827;* to *beam forth* (fig.):— shine.

827. αὐγή **augē**, *ŏwg´-ay;* of uncert. der.; a *ray* of light, i.e. (by impl.) *radiance, dawn:*— break of day.

828. Αὔγουστος **Augŏustŏs**, *ŏw´-goos-tos;* from Lat. ["august"]; *Augustus,* a title of the Rom. emperor:— Augustus.

829. αὐθάδης **authadēs**, *ŏw-thad´-ace;* from *846* and the base of *2237; self-pleasing,* i.e. *arrogant:*— self-willed.

830. αὐθαίρετος **authairĕtŏs**, *ŏw-thah´-ee-ret-os;* from *846* and the same as *140; self-chosen,* i.e. (by impl.) *voluntary:*— of own accord, willing of self.

831. αὐθεντέω **authĕntĕō**, *ŏw-then-teh´-o;* from a compound of *846* and an obs. ἔντης **hĕntēs** (a *worker*); to *act of one-self,* i.e. (fig.) *dominate:*— usurp authority over.

832. αὐλέω **aulĕō**, *ŏw-leh´-o;* from *836;* to play the *flute:*— pipe.

833. αὐλή **aulē**, *ŏw-lay´;* from the same as *109;* a *yard* (as open to the *wind*); by impl. a *mansion:*— court, (sheep-) fold, hall, palace.

834. αὐλητής **aulētēs**, *ŏw-lay-tace´;* from *832;* a *flute-player:*— minstrel, piper.

835. αὐλίζομαι **aulizŏmai**, *ŏw-lid´-zom-ahee;* mid. voice from *833;* to *pass the night* (prop. in the open air):— abide, lodge.

836. αὐλός **aulŏs**, *ŏw-los´;* from the same as *109;* a *flute* (as *blown*):— pipe.

837. αὐξάνω **auxanō**, *ŏwx-an´-o;* a prol. form of a primary verb; to *grow* ("*wax*"), i.e. *enlarge* (lit. or fig., act. or pass.):— grow (up), (give the) increase.

838. αὔξησις **auxēsis**, *ŏwx´-ay-sis;* from *837; growth:*— increase.

839. αὔριον **auriŏn**, *ŏw´-ree-on;* from a der. of the same as *109* (mean. a *breeze,* i.e. the *morning air*); prop. *fresh,* i.e. (adv. with ellipsis of *2250*) *to-morrow:*— (to-) morrow, next day.

840. αὐστηρός **austērŏs**, *ŏw-stay-ros´;* from a (presumed) der. of the same as *109* (mean. *blown*); *rough* (prop. as a *gale*), i.e. (fig.) *severe:*— austere.

841. αὐτάρκεια **autarkeia**, *ŏw-tar´-ki-ah;* from *842; self-satisfaction,* i.e. (abstr.) *contentedness,* or (concr.) a *competence:*— contentment, sufficiency.

842. αὐτάρκης **autarkēs**, *ŏw-tar´-kace;* from *846* and *714; self-complacent,* i.e. *contented:*— content.

843. αὐτοκατάκριτος **autŏkatakritŏs**, *ŏw-tok-at-ak´-ree-tos;* from *846* and a der. or *2632; self-condemned:*— condemned of self.

844. αὐτόματος **autŏmatŏs**, *ŏw-tom´-at-os;* from *846* and the same as *3155; self-moved* ["automatic"], i.e. *spontaneous:*— of own accord, of self.

845. αὐτόπτης **autŏptēs**, *ŏw-top´-tace;* from *846* and *3700; self-seeing,* i.e. an *eyewitness:*— eye-witness.

846. αὐτός **autŏs**, *ŏw-tos´;* from the particle αὖ **au** [perh. akin to the base of *109* through the idea of a *baffling wind*] (*backward*); the refl. pron. *self,* used (alone or in the comp. *1438*) of the third pers., and (with the proper pers. pron.) of the other persons:— her, it (-self), one, the other, (mine) own, said, ([self-], the) same, ([him-, my-, thy-]) self, [your-] selves, she, that, their (-s), them ([-selves]), there [-at, -by, -in, -into, -of, -on, -with], they, (these) things, this (man), those, together, very, which. Comp. *848.*

847. αὐτοῦ **autŏu**, *ŏw-too´;* gen. (i.e. possessive) of *846,* used as an adv. of location; prop. belonging to the *same* spot, i.e. *in this* (or *that*) *place:*— (t-) here.

848. αὑτοῦ **hautŏu**, *how-too´;* contr. for *1438; self* (in some oblique case or refl. relation):— her (own), (of) him (-self), his (own), of it, thee, their (own), them (-selves), they.

849. αὐτόχειρ **autŏchĕir**, *ŏw-tokh´-ire;* from *846* and *5495; self-handed,* i.e. doing *personally:*— with ... own hands.

850. αὐχμηρός **auchmērŏs**, *ŏwkh-may-ros´;* from αὐχμός **auchmŏs** [prob. from a base akin to that of *109*] (*dust,* as *dried* by wind); prop. *dirty,* i.e. (by impl.) *obscure:*— dark.

851. ἀφαιρέω **aphairĕō**, *af-ahee-reh´-o;* from *575* and *138;* to *remove* (lit. or fig.):— cut (smite) off, take away.

852. ἀφανής **aphanēs**, *af-an-ace´;* from *1* (as a neg. particle) and *5316; non-apparent:*— that is not manifest.

853. ἀφανίζω **aphanizō**, *af-an-id´-zo;* from *852;* to *render unapparent,* i.e. (act.) *consume* (*becloud*), or (pass.) *disappear* (*be destroyed*):— corrupt, disfigure, perish, vanish away.

854. ἀφανισμός **aphanismŏs**, *af-an-is-mos´;* from *853; disappearance,* i.e. (fig.) *abrogation:*— vanish away.

855. ἄφαντος **aphantŏs**, *af´-an-tŏs;* from *1* (as a neg. particle) and a der. of *5316; non-manifested,* i.e. *invisible:*— vanished out of sight.

856. ἀφεδρών **aphĕdrōn**, *af-ed-rone´;* from a compound of *575* and the base of *1476;* a place of *sitting apart,* i.e. a *privy:*— draught.

857. ἀφειδία **aphĕidia**, *af-i-dee´-ah;* from a compound of *1* (as a neg. particle) and *5339; unsparingness,* i.e. *austerity* (ascetism):— neglecting.

858. ἀφελότης **aphĕlŏtēs**, *af-el-ot´-ace;* from a compound of *1* (as a neg. particle) and φέλλος **phĕllŏs** (in the sense of a *stone* as *stubbing* the foot); *smoothness,* i.e. (fig.) *simplicity:*— singleness.

859. ἄφεσις **aphĕsis**, *af´-es-is;* from *863; freedom;* (fig.) *pardon:*— deliverance, forgiveness, liberty, remission.

860. ἁφή **haphē**, *haf-ay´;* from *680;* prob. a *ligament* (as *fastening*):— joint.

861. ἀφθαρσία **aphtharsia**, *af-thar-see´-ah;* from *862; incorruptibility;* gen. *unending existence;* (fig.) *genuineness:*— immortality, incorruption, sincerity.

862. ἄφθαρτος **aphthartŏs**, *af´-thar-tos;* from *1* (as a neg. particle) and a der. of *5351; undecaying* (in essence or continuance):— not (in-, un-) corruptible, immortal.

863. ἀφίημι **aphiĕmi**, *af-ee´-ay-mee;* from *575* and ἵημι **hiĕmi** (to *send;* an intens. form of εἶμι **ĕimi**, to *go*); to *send forth,* in various applications (as follow):— cry, forgive, forsake, lay aside, leave, let (alone, be, go, have), omit, put (send) away, remit, suffer, yield up.

864. ἀφικνέομαι **aphiknĕŏmai**, *af-ik-neh´-om-ahee;* from *575* and the base of *2425;* to *go* (i.e. *spread*) *forth* (by rumor):— come abroad.

865. ἀφιλάγαθος **aphilagathŏs**, *af-il-ag´-ath-os;* from *1* (as a neg. particle) and *5358; hostile to virtue:*— despiser of those that are good.

866. ἀφιλάργυρος **aphilargurŏs**, *af-il-ar´-goo-ros;* from *1* (as a neg. particle) and *5366; unavaricious:*— without covetousness, not greedy of filthy lucre.

867. ἄφιξις **aphixis**, *af´-ix-is;* from *864;*

prop. *arrival*, i.e. (by impl.) *departure*:— departing.

868. ἀφίστημι **aphistēmi**, *af-is´-tay-mee*; from 575 and 2476; to *remove*, i.e. (act.) *instigate* to revolt; usually (refl.) to *desist, desert*, etc.:— depart, draw (fall) away, refrain, withdraw self.

869. ἀφνω **aphnō**, *af´-no*; adv. from 852 (contr.); *unawares*, i.e. *unexpectedly*:— suddenly.

870. ἀφόβως **aphŏbōs**, *af-ob´-oce*; adv. from a compound of 1 (as a neg. particle) and 5401; *fearlessly*:— without fear.

871. ἀφομοιόω **aphŏmŏiŏō**, *af-om-oy-ŏ´-o*; from 575 and 3666; to *assimilate* closely:— make like.

872. ἀφοράω **aphŏraō**, *af-or-ah´-o*; from 575 and 3708; to *consider* attentively:— look.

873. ἀφορίζω **aphŏrizō**, *af-or-id´-zo*; from 575 and 3724; to *set off* by boundary, i.e. (fig.) *limit, exclude, appoint*, etc.:— divide, separate, sever.

874. ἀφορμή **aphŏrmē**, *af-or-may´*; from a compound of 575 and 3729; a *starting*-point, i.e. (fig.) an *opportunity*:— occasion.

875. ἀφρίζω **aphrizō**, *af-rid´-zo*; from 876; to *froth* at the mouth (in epilepsy):— foam.

876. ἀφρός **aphrŏs**, *af-ros´*; appar. a primary word; *froth*, i.e. *slaver*:— foaming.

877. ἀφροσύνη **aphrŏsunē**, *af-ros-oo´-nay*; from 878; *senselessness*, i.e. (euphem.) *egotism*; (mor.) *recklessness*:— folly, foolishly (-ness).

878. ἀφρων **aphrōn**, *af´-rone*; from 1 (as a neg. particle) and 5424; prop. *mindless*, i.e. *stupid*, (by impl.) *ignorant*, (spec.) *egotistic*, (practically) *rash*, or (mor.) *unbelieving*:— fool (-ish), unwise.

879. ἀφυπνόω **aphupnŏō**, *af-oop-nŏ´-o*; from a compound of 575 and 5258; prop. to *become awake*, i.e. (by impl.) to *drop* (off) in slumber:— fall asleep.

880. ἀφωνος **aphōnŏs**, *af´-o-nos*; from 1 (as a neg. particle) and 5456; *voiceless*, i.e. *mute* (by nature or choice); fig. *unmeaning*:— dumb, without signification.

881. Ἀχάζ **Achaz**, *akh-adz´*; of Heb. or. [271]; *Achaz*, an Isr.:— Achaz.

882. Ἀχαία **Achaïa**, *ach-ah-ee´-ah*; of uncert. der.; *Achaia* (i.e. *Greece*), a country of Europe:— Achaia.

883. Ἀχαϊκός **Achaïkŏs**, *ach-ah-ee-kos´*; from 882; an *Achaïan/Achaïcus*, a Chr.:— Achaicus.

884. ἀχάριστος **acharistŏs**, *ach-ar´-is-tos*; from 1 (as a neg. particle) and a presumed der. of 5483; *thankless*, i.e. *ungrateful*:— unthankful.

885. Ἀχείμ **Achĕim** or Ἀχίμ **Achim**, *akh-ime´*; prob. of Heb. or. [comp. 3137]; *Achim*, an Isr.:— Achim.

886. ἀχειροποίητος **achĕirŏpŏiētŏs**, *akh-i-rop-oy´-ay-tos*; from 1 (as a neg. particle) and 5499; *unmanufactured*, i.e. *inartificial*:— made without (not made with) hands.

887. ἀχλύς **achlus**, *akh-looce´*; of uncert. der.; *dimness* of sight, i.e. (prob.) a *cataract*:— mist.

888. ἀχρεῖος **achrĕiŏs**, *akh-ri´-os*; from 1 (as a neg. particle) and a der. of 5534 [comp. 5532]; *useless*, i.e. (euphem.) *unmeritorious*:— unprofitable.

889. ἀχρειόω **achrĕiŏō**, *akh-ri-ŏ´-o*; from 888; to *render useless*, i.e. *spoil*:— become unprofitable.

890. ἀχρηστος **achrēstŏs**, *akh´-race-tos*; from 1 (as a neg. particle) and 5543; *inefficient*, i.e. (by impl.) *detrimental*:— unprofitable.

891. ἀχρι **achri**, *akh´-ree*; or ἀχρις **achris**, *akh´-rece*; akin to 206 (through the idea of a *terminus*); (of time) *until* or (of place) *up to*:— as far as, for, in (-to), till, (even, un-) to, until, while. Comp. 3360.

892. ἀχυρον **achurŏn**, *akh´-oo-ron*; perh. remotely from χέω **chĕō** (to *shed* forth); *chaff* (as *diffusive*):— chaff.

893. ἀψευδής **apsĕudēs**, *aps-yoo-dace´*; from 1 (as a neg. particle) and 5579; *veracious*:— that cannot lie.

894. ἀψινθος **apsinthŏs**, *ap´-sin-thos*; of uncert. der.; *wormwood* (as a type of *bitterness*, i.e. [fig.] *calamity*):— wormwood.

895. ἀψυχος **apsuchŏs**, *ap´-soo-khos*; from 1 (as a neg. particle) and 5590; *lifeless*, i.e. *inanimate* (mechanical):— without life.

B

896. Βάαλ **Baal**, *bah´-al*; of Heb. or. [1168]; *Baal*, a Phœnician deity (used as a symbol of idolatry):— Baal.

897. Βαβυλών **Babulōn**, *bab-oo-lone´*; of Heb. or. [894]; *Babylon*, the capital of Chaldæa (lit. or fig. [as a type of tyranny]):— Babylon.

898. βαθμός **bathmŏs**, *bath-mos´*; from the same as 899; a *step*, i.e. (fig.) *grade* (of dignity):— degree.

899. βάθος **bathŏs**, *bath´-os*; from the same as 901; *profundity*, i.e. (by impl.) *extent*; (fig.) *mystery*:— deep (-ness), things), depth.

900. βαθύνω **bathunō**, *bath-oo´-no*; from 901; to *deepen*:— deep.

901. βαθύς **bathus**, *bath-oos´*; from the base of 939; *profound* (as *going* down), lit. or fig.:— deep, very early.

902. βαΐον **baïŏn**, *bah-ee´-on*; a diminutive of a der. prob. of the base of 939; a *palm twig* (as *going* out far):— branch.

903. Βαλαάμ **Balaam**, *bal-ah-am´*; of Heb. or. [1109]; *Balaam*, a Mesopotamian (symbolic of a false teacher):— Balaam.

904. Βαλάκ **Balak**, *bal-ak´*; of Heb. or. [1111]; *Balak*, a Moabite:— Balac.

905. βαλάντιον **balantiŏn**, *bal-an´-tee-on*; prob. remotely from 906 (as a *depository*); a *pouch* (for money):— bag, purse.

906. βάλλω **ballō**, *bal´-lo*; a primary verb; to *throw* (in various applications, more or less violent or intense):— arise, cast (out), × dung, lay, lie, pour,

put (up), send, strike, throw (down), thrust. Comp. 4496.

907. βαπτίζω **baptizō**, *bap-tid´-zo*; from a der. of 911; to *make overwhelmed* (i.e. *fully wet*); used only (in the N.T.) of ceremonial *ablution*, espec. (tech.) of the ordinance of Chr. *baptism*:— baptist, baptize, wash.

908. βάπτισμα **baptisma**, *bap´-tis-mah*; from 907; *baptism* (tech. or fig.):— baptism.

909. βαπτισμός **baptismŏs**, *bap-tis-mos´*; from 907; *ablution* (cerem. or Chr.):— baptism, washing.

910. Βαπτιστής **Baptistēs**, *bap-tis-tace´*; from 907; a *baptizer*, as an epithet of Christ's forerunner:— Baptist.

911. βάπτω **baptō**, *bap´-to*; a primary verb; to *overwhelm*, i.e. cover wholly with a fluid; in the N.T. only in a qualified or special sense, i.e. (lit.) to *moisten* (a part of one's person), or (by impl.) to *stain* (as with dye):— dip.

912. Βαραββᾶς **Barabbas**, *bar-ab-bas´*; of Chald. or. [1347 and 5]; *son of Abba*; *Bar-abbas*, an Isr.:— Barabbas.

913. Βαράκ **Barak**, *bar-ak´*; of Heb. or. [1301]; *Barak*, an Isr.:— Barak.

914. Βαραχίας **Barachias**, *bar-akh-ee´-as*; of Heb. or. [1296]; *Barachias* (i.e. *Berechijah*), an Isr.:— Barachias.

915. βάρβαρος **barbarŏs**, *bar´-bar-os*; of uncert. der.; a *foreigner* (i.e. *non-Greek*):— barbarian (-rous).

916. βαρέω **barĕō**, *bar-eh´-o*; from 926; to *weigh* down (fig.):— burden, charge, heavy, press.

917. βαρέως **barĕōs**, *bar-eh´-oce*; adv. from 926; *heavily* (fig.):— dull.

918. Βαρθολομαῖος **Barthŏlŏmaiŏs**, *bar-thol-om-ah´-yos*; of Chald. or. [1247 and 8526]; *son of Tolmai*; *Bar-tholomæus*, a Chr. apostle:— Bartholomeus.

919. Βαριησοῦς **Bariēsŏus**, *bar-ee-ay-sooce´*; of Chald. or. [1247 and 3091]; *son of Jesus* (or *Joshua*); *Bar-jesus*, an Isr.:— Barjesus.

920. Βαριωνᾶς **Bariōnas**, *bar-ee-oo-nas´*; of Chald. or. [1247 and 3124]; *son of Jonas* (or *Jonah*); *Bar-jonas*, an Isr.:— Bar-jona.

921. Βαρνάβας **Barnabas**, *bar-nab´-as*; of Chald. or. [1247 and 5029]; *son of Nabas* (i.e. *prophecy*); *Barnabas*, an Isr.:— Barnabas.

922. βάρος **barŏs**, *bar´-os*; prob. from the same as 939 (through the notion of *going* down; comp. 899); *weight*; in the N.T. only fig. a *load, abundance, authority*:— burden (-some), weight.

923. Βαρσαβᾶς **Barsabas**, *bar-sab-as´*; of Chald. or. [1247 and prob. 6634]; *son of Sabas* (or *Tsaba*); *Bar-sabas*, the name of two Isr.:— Barsabas.

924. Βαρτιμαῖος **Bartimaiŏs**, *bar-tim-ah´-yos*; of Chald. or. [1247 and 2931]; *son of Timæus* (or the *unclean*); *Bartimæus*, an Isr.:— Bartimæus.

925. βαρύνω **barunō**, *bar-oo´-no*; from 926; to *burden* (fig.):— overcharge.

926. βαρύς **barus**, *bar-ooce´*; from the same as 922; *weighty*, i.e. (fig) *burden*-

some, grave:— grievous, heavy, weightier.

927. βαρύτιμος **barutimŏs**, bar-oo´-tim-os; from 926 and 5092; highly valuable:— very precious.

928. βασανίζω **basanizō**, bas-an-id´-zo; from 931; to torture:— pain, toil, torment, toss, vex.

929. βασανισμός **basanismŏs**, bas-an-is-mos´; from 928; torture:— torment.

930. βασανιστής **basanistēs**, bas-an-is-tace´; from 928; a torturer:— tormentor.

931. βάσανος **basanŏs**, bas´-an-os; perh. remotely from the same as 939 (through the notion of going to the bottom); a touch-stone, i.e. (by anal.) torture:— torment.

932. βασιλεία **basilĕia**, bas-il-i´-ah; from 935; prop. royalty, i.e. (abstr.) rule, or (concr.) a realm (lit. or fig.):— kingdom, + reign.

933. βασίλειον **basilĕiŏn**, bas-il´-i-on; neut. of 934; a palace:— king's court.

934. βασίλειος **basilĕiŏs**, bas-il´-i-os; from 935; kingly (in nature):— royal.

935. βασιλεύς **basilĕus**, bas-il-yooce´; prob. from 939 (through the notion of a foundation of power); a sovereign (abstr., rel., or fig.):— king.

936. βασιλεύω **basilĕuō**, bas-il-yoo´-o; from 935; to rule (lit. or fig.):— king, reign.

937. βασιλικός **basilikŏs**, bas-il-ee-kos´; from 935; regal (in relation), i.e. (lit.) belonging to (or befitting) the sovereign (as land, dress, or a courtier), or (fig.) preeminent:— king's, nobleman, royal.

938. βασίλισσα **basilissa**, bas-il´-is-sah; fem. from 936; a queen:— queen.

939. βάσις **basis**, bas´-ece; from βαίνω **bainō** (to walk); a pace ("base"), i.e. (by impl.) the foot:— foot.

940. βασκαίνω **baskainō**, bas-kah´-ee-no; akin to 5335; to malign, i.e. (by extens.) to fascinate (by false representations):— bewitch.

941. βαστάζω **bastazō**, bas-tad´-zo; perh. remotely der. from the base of 939 (through the idea of removal); to lift, lit. or fig. (endure, declare, sustain, receive, etc.):— bear, carry, take up.

942. βάτος **batŏs**, bat´-os; of uncert. der.; a brier shrub:— bramble, bush.

943. βάτος **batŏs**, bat´-os; of Heb. or. [1324]; a bath, or measure for liquids:— measure.

944. βάτραχος **batrachŏs**, bat´-rakh-os; of uncert. der.; a frog:— frog.

945. βαττολογέω **battŏlŏgĕō**, bat-tol-og-eh´-o; from Βάττος **Battŏs** (a proverbial stammerer) and 3056; to stutter, i.e. (by impl.) to prate tediously:— use vain repetitions.

946. βδέλυγμα **bdĕlugma**, bdel´-oog-mah; from 948; a detestation, i.e. (spec.) idolatry:— abomination.

947. βδελυκτός **bdĕluktŏs**, bdel-ook-tos´; from 948; detestable, i.e. (spec.) idolatrous:— abominable.

948. βδελύσσω **bdĕlussō**, bdel-oos´-so; from a (presumed) der. of βδέω **bdĕō** (to

stink); to be disgusted, i.e. (by impl.) detest (esp. of idolatry):— abhor, abominable.

949. βέβαιος **bĕbaiŏs**, beb´-ah-yos; from the base of 939 (through the idea of basality); stable (lit. or fig.):— firm, of force, stedfast, sure.

950. βεβαιόω **bĕbaiŏō**, beb-ah-yŏ´-o; from 949; to stabilitate (fig.):— confirm, (e-) stablish.

951. βεβαίωσις **bĕbaiōsis**, beb-ah´-yo-sis; from 950; stabiliment:— confirmation.

952. βέβηλος **bĕbēlŏs**, beb´-ay-los; from the base of 939 and βηλός **bēlŏs** (a threshold); accessible (as by crossing the door-way), i.e. (by impl. of Jewish notions) heathenish, wicked:— profane (person).

953. βεβηλόω **bĕbēlŏō**, beb-ay-lŏ´-o; from 952; to desecrate:— profane.

954. Βεελζεβούλ **Bĕĕlzĕbŏul**, beh-el-zeb-ool´; of Chald. or. [by parody on 1176]; dung-god; Beelzebul, a name of Satan:— Beelzebub.

955. Βελίαλ **Bĕlial**, bel-ee-´-al; or Βελιάρ **Beliar**, bel-ee-´-ar of Heb. or. [1100]; worthlessness; Belial, as an epithet of Satan:— Belial

956. βέλος **bĕlŏs**, bel´-os; from 906; a missile, i.e. spear or arrow:— dart.

957. βελτίον **bĕltiŏn**, bel-tee´-on; neut. of a comparative of a der. of 906 (used for the comparative of 18); better:— very well.

958. Βενιαμίν **Bĕniamin**, ben-ee-am-een´; of Heb. or. [1144]; Benjamin, an Isr.:— Benjamin.

959. Βερνίκη **Bĕrnikē**, ber-nee´-kay; from a provincial form of 5342 and 3529; victorious; Bernicè a member of the Herodian family:— Bernice.

960. Βέροια **Bĕrŏia**, ber´-oy-ah; perh. a provincial from a der. of 4008 [Pereæa, i.e. the region beyond the coast-line]; Berœa, a place in Macedonia:— Berea.

961. Βεροιαῖος **Bĕrŏiaiŏs**, ber-oy-ah´-yos; from 960; a Berœœan or native of Berœa:— of Berea.

962. Βηθαβαρά **Bēthabara**, bay-thab-ar-ah´; of Heb. or. [1004 and 5679]; ferry-house; Bethabara (i.e. Bethabarah), a place on the Jordan:— Bethabara.

963. Βηθανία **Bēthania**, bay-than-ee´-ah; of Chald. or.; date-house; Beth-any, a place in Pal.:— Bethany.

964. Βηθεσδά **Bēthĕsda**, bay-thes-dah´; of Chald. or. [compound of 1004 and 2617]; house of kindness; Beth-esda, a pool in Jerusalem:— Bethesda.

965. Βηθλεέμ **Bēthlĕĕm**, bayth-leh-em´; of Heb. or. [1036]; Bethleem (i.e. Beth-lechem), a place in Pal.:— Bethlehem.

966. Βηθσαϊδά **Bēthsaïda**, bayth-sahee-dah´; of Chald. or. [compound of 1004 and 6719]; fishing-house; Bethsaïda, a place in Pal.:— Bethsaida.

967. Βηθφαγή **Bēthphagē**, bayth-fag-ay´; of Chald. or. [compound of 1004 and 6291]; fig-house; Beth-phagè a place in Pal.:— Bethphage.

968. βῆμα **bēma**, bay´-ma; from the

base of 939; a step, i.e. foot-breath; by impl. a rostrum, i.e. a tribunal:— judgment-seat, set [foot] on, throne.

969. βήρυλλος **bērullŏs**, bay´-rool-los; of uncert. der.; a "beryl":— beryl.

970. βία **bia**, bee´-ah; prob. akin to 979 (through the idea of vital activity); force:— violence.

971. βιάζω **biazō**, bee-ad´-zo; from 970; to force, i.e. (refl.) to crowd oneself (into), or (pass.) to be seized:— press, suffer violence.

972. βίαιος **biaiŏs**, bee´-ah-yos; from 970; violent:— mighty.

973. βιαστής **biastēs**, bee-as-tace´; from 971; a forcer, i.e. (fig.) energetic:— violent.

974. βιβλιαρίδιον **bibliaridiŏn**, bib-lee-ar-id´-ee-on; a dimin. of 975; a booklet:— little book.

975. βιβλίον **bibliŏn**, bib-lee´-on; a dimin. of 976; a roll:— bill, book, scroll, writing.

976. βίβλος **biblŏs**, bib´-los; prop. the inner bark of the papyrus plant, i.e. (by impl.) a sheet or scroll of writing:— book.

977. βιβρώσκω **bibrōskō**, bib-ro´-sko; a redupl. and prol. form of an obs. primary verb [perh. caus. of 1006]; to eat:— eat.

978. Βιθυνία **Bithunia**, bee-thoo-nee´-ah; of uncert. der.; Bithynia, a region of Asia:— Bithynia.

979. βίος **biŏs**, bee´-os; a primary word; life, i.e. (lit.) the present state of existence; by impl. the means of livelihood:— good, life, living.

980. βιόω **biŏō**, bee-ŏ´-o; from 979; to spend existence:— live.

981. βίωσις **biōsis**, bee´-o-sis; from 980; living (prop. the act, by impl. the mode):— manner of life.

982. βιωτικός **biōtikŏs**, bee-o-tee-kos´; from a der. of 980; relating to the present existence:— of (pertaining to, things that pertain to) this life.

983. βλαβερός **blabĕrŏs**, blab-er-os´; from 984; injurious:— hurtful.

984. βλάπτω **blaptō**, blap´-to; a primary verb; prop. to hinder, i.e. (by impl.) to injure:— hurt.

985. βλαστάνω **blastanō**, blas-tan´-o; from βλαστός **blastŏs** (a sprout); to germinate; by impl. to yield fruit:— bring forth, bud, spring (up).

986. Βλάστος **Blastŏs**, blas´-tos; perh. the same as the base of 985; Blastus, an officer of Herod Agrippa:— Blastus.

987. βλασφημέω **blasphēmĕō**, blas-fay-meh´-o; from 989; to vilify; spec. to speak impiously:— (speak) blaspheme (-er, -mously, my), defame, rail on, revile, speak evil.

988. βλασφημία **blasphēmia**, blas-fay-me´-ah; from 989; vilification (espec. against God):— blasphemy, evil speaking, railing.

989. βλάσφημος **blasphēmŏs**, blas´-fay-mos; from a der. of 984 and 5345; scurrilous, i.e. calumnious (against man),

or (spec.) *impious* (against God):— blasphemer (-mous), railing.

990. βλέμμα **blemma**, *blem´-mah;* from *991; vision* (prop. concr.; by impl. abstr.):— seeing.

991. βλέπω **blĕpō**, *blep´-o;* a primary verb; to *look* at (lit. or fig.):— behold, beware, lie, look (on, to), perceive, regard, see, sight, take heed. Comp. 3700.

992. βλητέος **blētĕŏs**, *blay-teh´-os;* from *906;* fit *to be cast* (i.e. *applied*):— must be put.

993. Βοανεργές **Bŏanĕrgĕs**, *bŏ-an-erg-es´;* of Chald. or. [1123 and 7266]; *sons of commotion; Boänerges,* an epithet of two of the Apostles:— Boanerges.

994. βοάω **bŏaō**, *bŏ-ah´-o;* appar. a prol. form of a primary verb; to *halloo,* i.e. *shout* (for help or in a tumultuous way):— cry.

995. βοή **bŏē**, *bŏ-ay´;* from *994;* a *halloo,* i.e. *call* (for aid, etc.):— cry.

996. βοήθεια **bŏēthĕia**, *bŏ-ay´-thi-ah;* from *998; aid;* spec. a rope or chain for *frapping* a vessel:— help.

997. βοηθέω **bŏēthĕō**, *bŏ-ay-theh´-o;* from *998;* to *aid* or *relieve:*— help, succour.

998. βοηθός **bŏēthŏs**, *bŏ-ay-thos´;* from *995* and θέω **thĕō** (to *run*); a *succorer:*— helper.

999. βόθυνος **bŏthunŏs**, *both´-oo-nos;* akin to *900;* a *hole* (in the ground); spec. a *cistern:*— ditch, pit.

1000. βολή **bŏlē**, *bol-ay´;* from *906;* a *throw* (as a measure of distance):— cast.

1001. βολίζω **bŏlizō**, *bol-id´-zo;* from *1002;* to *heave* the lead:— sound.

1002. βολίς **bŏlis**, *bol-ece´;* from *906;* a *missile,* i.e. *javelin:*— dart.

1003. Βοόζ **Bŏŏz**, *bŏ-oz´;* of Heb. or. [1162]; *Booz,* (i.e. *Boäz*), an Isr.:— Booz.

1004. βόρβορος **bŏrbŏrŏs**, *bor´-bor-os;* of uncert. der.; *mud:*— mire.

1005. βορρᾶς **borrhas**, *bor-hras´;* of uncert. der.; the *north* (prop. wind):— north.

1006. βόσκω **bŏskō**, *bos´-ko;* a prol. form of a primary verb [comp. *977, 1016*]; to *pasture;* by extens. to, *fodder;* refl. to *graze:*— feed, keep.

1007. Βοσόρ **Bŏsŏr**, *bos-or´;* of Heb. or. [1160]; *Bosor* (i.e. *Beör*), a Moabite:— Bosor.

1008. βοτάνη **bŏtanē**, *bot-an´-ay;* from *1006; herbage* (as if for *grazing*):— herb.

1009. βότρυς **bŏtrus**, *bot´-rooce;* of uncert. der.; a *bunch* (of grapes):— (vine) cluster (of the vine).

1010. βουλευτής **bŏulĕutēs**, *bool-yoo-tace´;* from *1011;* an *adviser,* i.e. (spec.) a *councillor* or member of the Jewish Sanhedrin:— counsellor.

1011. βουλεύω **bŏulĕuō**, *bool-yoo´-o;* from *1012;* to *advise,* i.e. (refl.) *deliberate,* or (by impl.) *resolve:*— consult, take counsel, determine, be minded, purpose.

1012. βουλή **bŏulē**, *boo-lay´;* from *1014;*

volition, i.e. (obj.) *advice,* or (by impl.) *purpose:*— + advise, counsel, will.

1013. βούλημα **bŏulēma**, *boo´-lay-mah;* from *1014;* a *resolve:*— purpose, will.

1014. βούλομαι **bŏulŏmai**, *boo´-lom-ahee;* mid. voice of a primary verb.; to *"will,"* i.e. (refl.) *be willing:*— be disposed, minded, intend, list, (be, of own) will (-ing). Comp. 2309.

1015. βουνός **bŏunŏs**, *boo-nos´;* prob. of for. or.; a *hillock:*— hill.

1016. βοῦς **bŏus**, *booce;* prob. from the base of *1006;* an *ox* (as *grazing*), i.e. an animal of that species ("beef"):— ox.

1017. βραβεῖον **brabĕiŏn**, *brab-i´-on;* from βραβεύς **brabĕus** (an *umpire;* of uncert. der.); an *award* (of arbitration), i.e. (spec.) a *prize* in the public games:— prize.

1018. βραβεύω **brabĕuō**, *brab-yoo´-o;* from the same as *1017;* to *arbitrate,* i.e. (gen.) to *govern* (fig. *prevail*):— rule.

1019. βραδύνω **bradunō**, *brad-oo´-no;* from *1021;* to *delay:*— be slack, tarry.

1020. βραδυπλοέω **braduplŏĕō**, *brad-oo-plŏ-eh´-o;* from *1021* and a prol. form of *4126;* to *sail slowly:*— sail slowly.

1021. βραδύς **bradus**, *brad-ooce´;* of uncert. aff.; *slow;* fig. *dull:*— slow.

1022. βραδύτης **bradutēs**, *brad-oo´-tace;* from *1021; tardiness:*— slackness.

1023. βραχίων **brachiōn**, *brakh-ee-own;* prop. comp. of *1024,* but appar. in the sense of βράσσω **brassō** (to *wield*); the *arm,* i.e. (fig.) *strength:*— arm.

1024. βραχύς **brachus**, *brakh-ooce´;* of uncert. aff.; *short* (of time, place, quantity, or number):— few words, little (space, while).

1025. βρέφος **brĕphŏs**, *bref´-os;* of uncert. affin.; an *infant* (prop. unborn) lit. or fig.:— babe, (young) child, infant.

1026. βρέχω **brĕchō**, *brekh´-o;* a primary verb; to *moisten* (espec. by a shower):— (send) rain, wash.

1027. βροντή **brŏntē**, *bron-tay´;* akin to βρέμω **brĕmō** (to *roar*); *thunder:*— thunder (-ing).

1028. βροχή **brŏchē**, *brokh-ay´;* from *1026; rain:*— rain.

1029. βρόχος **brŏchŏs**, *brokh´-os;* of uncert. der.; a *noose:*— snare.

1030. βρυγμός **brugmŏs**, *broog-mos´;* from *1031;* a *grating* (of the teeth):— gnashing.

1031. βρύχω **bruchō**, *broo´-kho;* a primary verb; to *grate* the teeth (in pain or rage):— gnash.

1032. βρύω **bruō**, *broo´-o;* a primary verb; to *swell* out, i.e. (by impl.) to *gush:*— send forth.

1033. βρῶμα **brōma**, *bro´-mah;* from the base of *977; food* (lit. or fig.), espec. (cer.) articles allowed or forbidden by the Jewish law:— meat, victuals.

1034. βρώσιμος **brōsimŏs**, *bro´-sim-os;* from *1035; eatable:*— meat.

1035. βρῶσις **brōsis**, *bro´-sis;* from the base of *977;* (abstr.) *eating* (lit. or fig.); by extens. (concr.) *food* (lit. or fig.):— eating, food, meat.

1036. βυθίζω **buthizō**, *boo-thid´-zo;* from *1037;* to *sink;* by impl. to *drown:*— begin to sink, drown.

1037. βυθός **buthŏs**, *boo-thos´;* a var. of *899; depth,* i.e. (by impl.) the *sea:*— deep.

1038. βυρσεύς **bursĕus**, *boorce-yooce´;* from βύρσα **bursa** (a *hide*); a *tanner:*— tanner.

1039. βύσσινος **bussinŏs**, *boos´-see-nos;* from *1040;* made of *linen* (neut. a linen *cloth*):— fine linen.

1040. βύσσος **bussŏs**, *boos´-sos;* of Heb. or. [948]; white *linen:*— fine linen.

1041. βῶμος **bōmŏs**, *bo´-mos;* from the base of *939;* prop. a *stand,* i.e. (spec.) an *altar:*— altar.

Γ

1042. γαββαθά **gabbatha**, *gab-bath-ah´;* of Chald. or. [comp. 1355]; *the knoll; gabbatha,* a vernacular term for the Roman tribunal in Jerusalem:— Gabbatha.

1043. Γαβριήλ **Gabriēl**, *gab-ree-ale´;* of Heb. or. [1403]; *Gabriel,* an archangel:— Gabriel.

1044. γάγγραινα **gaggraina**, *gang´-grahee-nah;* from γραίνω **grainō** (to *gnaw*); an *ulcer* ("gangrene"):— canker.

1045. Γάδ **Gad**, *gad;* of Heb. or. [1410]; *Gad,* a tribe of Isr.:— Gad.

1046. Γαδαρηνός **Gadarēnŏs**, *gad-ar-ay-nos´;* from Γαδαρά (a town E. of the Jordan); a *Gadarene* or inhab. of Gadara:— Gadarene.

1047. γάζα **gaza**, *gad´-zah;* of for. or.; a *treasure:*— treasure.

1048. Γάζα **Gaza**, *gad´-zah;* of Heb. or. [5804]; *Gazah* (i.e. *Azzah*), a place in Pal.:— Gaza.

1049. γαζοφυλάκιον **gazŏphulakiŏn**, *gad-zof-oo-lak´-ee-on;* from *1047* and *5438;* a *treasure-house,* i.e. a court in the temple for the collection-boxes:— treasury.

1050. Γάϊος **Gaïŏs**, *gah´-ee-os;* of Lat. or.; *Gaïus* (i.e. *Caius*), a Chr.:— Gaius.

1051. γάλα **gala**, *gal´-ah;* of uncert. aff.; *milk* (fig.):— milk.

1052. Γαλάτης **Galatēs**, *gal-at´-ace;* from *1053;* a *Galatian* or inhab. of Galatia:— Galatian.

1053. Γαλατία **Galatia**, *gal-at-ee´-ah;* of for. or.; *Galatia,* a region of Asia:— Galatia.

1054. Γαλατικός **Galatikŏs**, *gal-at-ee-kos´;* from *1053; Galatic* or relating to Galatia:— of Galatia.

1055. γαλήνη **galēnē**, *gal-ay´-nay;* of uncert. der.; *tranquillity:*— calm.

1056. Γαλιλαία **Galilaia**, *gal-il-ah´-yah;* of Heb. or. [1551]; *Galilæa* (i.e. the heathen *circle*), a region of Pal.:— Galilee.

1057. Γαλιλαῖος **Galilaiŏs**, *gal-ee-lah´-yos;* from *1056; Galilæan* or belonging to Galilæa:— Galilæan, of Galilee.

1058. Γαλλίων **Galliōn**, *gal-lee-own´;* of Lat. or.; *Gallion* (i.e. *Gallio*), a Roman officer:— Gallio.

1059. Γαμαλιήλ **Gamaliēl**, *gam-al-ee-*

ale´; of Heb. or. [1583]; *Gamaliel* (i.e. *Gamliel*), an Isr.:— Gamaliel.

1060. γαμέω **gamĕŏ**, *gam-eh´-o;* from 1062; to *wed* (of either sex):— marry (a wife).

1061. γαμίσκω **gamiskŏ**, *gam-is´-ko;* from 1062; to *espouse* (a daughter to a husband):— give in marriage.

1062. γάμος **gamŏs**, *gam´-os;* of uncert. aff.; *nuptials*:— marriage, wedding.

1063. γάρ **gar**, *gar;* a primary particle; prop. assigning a *reason* (used in argument, explanation or intensification; often with other particles):— and, as, because (that), but, even, for, indeed, no doubt, seeing, then, therefore, verily, what, why, yet.

1064. γαστήρ **gastĕr**, *gas-tare´;* of uncert. der.; the *stomach;* by anal. the *matrix;* fig. a *gourmand:*— belly, + with child, womb.

1065. γέ **gĕ**, *gheh;* a primary particle of *emphasis* or *qualification* (often used with other particles pref.):— and besides, doubtless, at least, yet.

1066. Γεδεών **Gĕdĕōn**, *ghed-eh-own´;* of Heb. or. [1439]; *Gedeon* (i.e. *Gidlelon*), an Isr.:— Gedeon (Gideon).

1067. γέεννα **gĕĕnna**, *gheh´-en-nah;* of Heb. or. [1516 and 2011]; *valley of* (the son of) *Hinnom; ge-henna* (or *Ge-Hinnom*), a valley of Jerusalem, used (fig.) as a name for the place (or state) of everlasting punishment:— hell.

1068. Γεθσημανή **Gĕthsĕmanē**, *gheth-say-man-ay´;* of Chald. or. [comp. 1660 and 8081]; *oil-press; Gethsemane*, a garden near Jerusalem:— Gethsemane.

1069. γείτων **gĕitōn**, *ghi´-tone;* from 1093; a *neighbour* (as adjoining one's *ground*); by impl. a *friend:*— neighbour.

1070. γελάω **gĕlaō**, *ghel-ah´-o;* of uncert. aff.; to *laugh* (as a sign of joy or satisfaction):— laugh.

1071. γέλως **gĕlōs**, *ghel´-oce;* from 1070; *laughter* (as a mark of gratification):— laughter.

1072. γεμίζω **gĕmizō**, *ghem-id´-zo;* tran. from 1073; to *fill* entirely:— fill (be) full.

1073. γέμω **gĕmō**, *ghem´-o;* a primary verb; to *swell* out, i.e. *be full:*— be full.

1074. γενεά **gĕnĕa**, *ghen-eh-ah´;* from (a presumed der. of) 1085; a *generation;* by impl. an *age* (the period or the persons):— age, generation, nation, time.

1075. γενεαλογέω **gĕnĕalŏgĕō**, *ghen-eh-al-og-eh´-o;* from 1074 and 3056; to *reckon by generations*, i.e. *trace in genealogy:*— count by descent.

1076. γενεαλογία **gĕnĕalŏgia**, *ghen-eh-al-og-ee´-ah;* from the same as 1075; *tracing by generations*, i.e. "*genealogy*":— genealogy.

1077. γενέσια **gĕnĕsia**, *ghen-es´-ee-ah;* neut. plur. of a der. of 1078; *birthday* ceremonies:— birthday.

1078. γένεσις **genesis**, *ghen´-es-is;* from the same as 1074; *nativity;* fig. *nature:*— generation, nature (-ral).

1079. γενετή **gĕnĕtē**, *ghen-et-ay;* fem.

of a presumed der. of the base of 1074; *birth:*— birth.

1080. γεννάω **gĕnnaō**, *ghen-nah´-o;* from a var. of 1085; to *procreate* (prop. of the father, but by extens. of the mother); fig. to *regenerate:*— bear, beget, be born, bring forth, conceive, be delivered of, gender, make, spring.

1081. γέννημα **gĕnnēma**, or γένημα **gĕnēma**, *ghen´-nay-mah;* from 1080; *offspring;* by anal. *produce* (lit. or fig.):— fruit, generation.

1082. Γεννησαρέτ **Gĕnnēsarĕt**, *ghen-nay-sar-et´;* of Heb. or. [comp. 3672]; *Gennesaret* (i.e. *Kinnereth*), a lake and plain in Pal.:— Gennesaret.

1083. γέννησις **gĕnnēsis**, *ghen´-nay-sis;* from 1080; *nativity:*— birth.

1084. γεννητός **gĕnnētŏs**, *ghen-naytos´;* from 1080; *born:*— they that are born.

1085. γένος **gĕnŏs**, *ghen´-os;* from 1096; "*kin*" (abstr. or concr., lit. or fig., indiv. or collect.):— born, country (-man), diversity, generation, kind (-red), nation, offspring, stock.

1086. Γεργεσηνός **Gĕrgĕsēnŏs**, *gherghes-ay-nos´;* of Heb. or. [1622]; a *Gergesene* (i.e. *Girgashite*) or one of the aborigines of Pal.:— Gergesene.

1087. γερουσία **gĕrŏusia**, *gher-oo-see´-ah;* from 1088; the *eldership*, i.e. (collect.) the Jewish *Sanhedrin:*— senate.

1088. γέρων **gĕrōn**, *gher´-own;* of uncert. aff. [comp. 1094]; *aged:*— old.

1089. γεύομαι **gĕuŏmai**, *ghyoo´-om-ahee;* a primary verb; to *taste;* by impl. to *eat;* fig. to *experience* (good or ill):— eat, taste.

1090. γεωργέω **gĕōrgĕō**, *gheh-or-gheh´-o;* from 1092; to *till* (the soil):— dress.

1091. γεώργιον **gĕōrgiŏn**, *gheh-ore-ghee-on;* neut. of a (presumed) der. of 1092; *cultivable*, i.e. a *farm:*— husbandry.

1092. γεωργός **gĕōrgŏs**, *gheh-ore-gos´;* from 1093 and the base of 2041; a *land-worker*, i.e. *farmer:*— husbandman.

1093. γῆ **gē**, *ghay;* contr. from a primary word; *soil;* by extension a *region*, or the solid part or the whole of the *terrene* globe (incl. the occupants in each application):— country, earth (-ly), ground, land, world.

1094. γῆρας **gēras**, *ghay´-ras;* akin to 1088; *senility:*— old age.

1095. γηράσκω **gēraskō**, *ghay-ras´-ko;* from 1094; to be *senescent:*— be (wax) old.

1096. γίνομαι **ginŏmai**, *ghin´-om-ahee;* a prol. and mid. voice form of a primary verb; to *cause* to be ("*gen*"-*erate*), i.e. (refl.) to *become* (*come into being*), used with great latitude (lit., fig., intens., etc.):— arise, be assembled, be (-come, -fall, -have self), be brought (to pass), (be) come (to pass), continue, be divided, draw, be ended, fall, be finished, follow, be found, be fulfilled, + God forbid, grow, happen, have, be kept, be made, be married, be ordained to be, partake, pass, be performed, be published, require, seem,

be showed, × soon as it was, sound, be taken, be turned, use, wax, will, would, be wrought.

1097. γινώσκω **ginōskō**, *ghin-oce´-ko;* a prol. form of a primary verb; to "*know*" (absolutely) in a great variety of applications and with many impl. (as follow, with others not thus clearly expressed):— allow, be aware (of), feel, (have) know (-ledge), perceive, be resolved, can speak, be sure, understand.

1098. γλεῦκος **glĕukŏs**, *glyoo´-kos;* akin to 1099; *sweet* wine, i.e. (prop.) *must* (fresh juice), but used of the more saccharine (and therefore highly inebriating) fermented *wine:*— new wine.

1099. γλυκύς **glukus**, *gloo-koos´;* of uncert. aff.; *sweet* (i.e. not bitter nor salt):— sweet, fresh.

1100. γλῶσσα **glōssa**, *gloce-sah´;* of uncert. aff.; the *tongue;* by impl. a *language* (spec., one naturally unacquired):— tongue.

1101. γλωσσόκομον **glōssŏkŏmŏn**, *gloce-sok´-om-on;* from 1100 and the base of 2889; prop. a *case* (to keep mouthpieces of wind-instruments in) i.e. (by extens.) a *casket* or (spec.) *purse:*— bag.

1102. γναφεύς **gnaphĕus**, *gnaf-yuce´;* by var. for a der. from κνάπτω **knaptō** (to *tease* cloth); a cloth-*dresser:*— fuller.

1103. γνήσιος **gnēsiŏs**, *gnay´-see-os;* from the same as 1077; *legitimate* (of birth), i.e. *genuine:*— own, sincerity, true.

1104. γνησίως **gnēsiōs**, *gnay-see´-oce;* adv. from 1103; *genuinely*, i.e. *really:*— naturally.

1105. γνόφος **gnŏphŏs**, *gnof´-os;* akin to 3509; *gloom* (as of a storm):— blackness.

1106. γνώμη **gnōmē**, *gno´-may;* from 1097; *cognition*, i.e. (subj.) *opinion*, or (obj.) *resolve* (*counsel, consent*, etc.):— advice, + agree, judgment, mind, purpose, will.

1107. γνωρίζω **gnōrizō**, *gno-rid´-zo;* from a der. of 1097; to *make known;* subj. to *know:*— certify, declare, make known, give to understand, do to wit, wot.

1108. γνῶσις **gnōsis**, *gno´-sis;* from 1097; *knowing* (the act), i.e. (by impl.) *knowledge:*— knowledge, science.

1109. γνώστης **gnōstēs**, *gnoce´-tace;* from 1097; a *knower:*— expert.

1110. γνωστός **gnōstŏs**, *gnoce-tos´;* from 1097; *well-known:*— acquaintance, (which may be) known, notable.

1111. γογγύζω **gŏgguzō**, *gong-good´-zo;* of uncert. der.; to *grumble:*— murmur.

1112. γογγυσμός **gŏggusmŏs**, *gong-goos-mos´;* from 1111; a *grumbling:*— grudging, murmuring.

1113. γογγυστής **gŏggustēs**, *gong-goos-tace´;* from 1111; a *grumbler:*— murmurer.

1114. γόης **gŏēs**, *go´-ace;* from γοάω **gŏaō** (to *wail*); prop. a *wizard* (as *muttering* spells), i.e. (by impl.) an *imposter:*— seducer.

1115. Γολγοθᾶ **Golgötha**, *gol-goth-ah´;* of Chald. or. [comp. 1538]; *the skull; Golgotha,* a knoll near Jerusalem:— Golgotha.

1116. Γόμορρα **Gömörrha**, *gom´-or-hrhah;* of Heb. or. [6017]; *Gomorrha* (i.e. `Amorah*), a place near the Dead Sea:— Gomorrha.

1117. γόμος **gömös**, *gom´-os;* from *1073; a load* (as *filling*), i.e. (spec.) a *cargo,* or (by extens.) *wares:*— burden, merchandise.

1118. γονεύς **gönĕus**, *gon-yooce´;* from the base of *1096;* a *parent:*— parent.

1119. γόνυ **gönu**, *gon-oo´;* of uncert. aff.; the "*knee*":— knee (×l).

1120. γονυπετέω **gönupĕtĕö**, *gon-oo-pet-eh´-o;* from a compound of *1119* and the alt. of *4098;* to *fall* on the *knee:*— bow the knee, kneel down.

1121. γράμμα **gramma**, *gram´-mah;* from *1125;* a *writing,* i.e. a *letter, note, epistle, book,* etc.; plur. *learning:*— bill, learning, letter, scripture, writing, written.

1122. γραμματεύς **grammatĕus**, *grammat-yooce´;* from *1121;* a *writer,* i.e. (professionally) *scribe* or *secretary:*— scribe, town-clerk.

1123. γραπτός **graptös**, *grap-tos´;* from *1125; inscribed* (fig.):— written.

1124. γραφή **graphē**, *graf-ay´;* from *1125;* a *document,* i.e. holy *Writ* (or its contents or a statement in it):— scripture.

1125. γράφω **graphö**, *graf´-o;* a primary verb; to "*grave*," espec. to *write;* fig. to *describe:*— describe, write (-ing, -ten).

1126. γραώδης **graödēs**, *grah-o´-dace;* from γραύς **graus** (an old *woman*) and *1491; crone-like,* i.e. *silly:*— old wives'.

1127. γρηγορεύω **grĕgörĕuö**, *gray-goryoo´-o;* from *1453;* to *keep awake,* i.e. *watch* (lit. or fig.):— be vigilant, wake, (be) watch (-ful).

1128. γυμνάζω **gumnazö**, *goom-nad´-zo;* from *1131;* to *practise naked* (in the games), i.e. *train* (fig.):— exercise.

1129. γυμνασία **gumnasia**, *goom-nasee´-ah;* from *1128; training,* i.e. (fig.) *asceticism:*— exercise.

1130. γυμνητεύω **gumnĕtĕuö**, *goomnayt-yoo´-o* or γυμνιτεύω **gumniteuo**, *goom-niyt-yoo´-o;* from a der. of *1131;* to *strip,* i.e. (refl.) *go poorly clad:*— be naked.

1131. γυμνός **gumnös**, *goom-nos´;* of uncert. aff.; *nude* (absol. or rel., lit. or fig.):— naked.

1132. γυμνότης **gumnötēs**, *goom-not´-ace;* from *1131; nudity* (absol. or comp.):— nakedness.

1133. γυναικάριον **gunaikariön**, *goo-nahee-kar´-ee-on;* a dimin. from *1135;* a *little* (i.e. *foolish*) *woman:*— silly woman.

1134. γυναικεῖος **gunaikĕiös**, *goo-nahee-ki´-os;* from *1135; feminine:*— wife.

1135. γυνή **gunē**, *goo-nay´;* prob. from the base of *1096;* a *woman;* spec. a *wife:*— wife, woman.

1136. Γώγ **Gög**, *gogue;* of Heb. or.

[1463]; *Gog,* a symb. name for some future Antichrist:— Gog.

1137. γωνία **gönia**, *go-nee´-ah;* prob. akin to *1119;* an *angle:*— corner, quarter.

Δ

1138. Δαβίδ **Dabid**, *dab-eed´;* of Heb. or. [1732]; *Dabid* (i.e. *David*), the Isr. king:— David.

1139. δαιμονίζομαι **daimönizömai**, *dahee-mon-id´-zom-ahee;* mid. voice from *1142;* to *be exercised by a demon:*— have a (be vexed with, be possessed with) devil (-s).

1140. δαιμόνιον **daimöniön**, *daheemon´-ee-on;* neut. of a der. of *1142;* a *demonic being;* by extens. a *deity:*— devil, god.

1141. δαιμονιώδης **daimöniödēs**, *dahee-mon-ee-o´-dace;* from *1140* and *1142; demon-like:*— devilish.

1142. δαίμων **daimön**, *dah´-ee-mown;* from δαίω **daiö** (to *distribute* fortunes); a *demon* or supernatural spirit (of a bad nature):— devil.

1143. δάκνω **daknö**, *dak´-no;* a prol. form of a primary root; to *bite,* i.e. (fig.) *thwart:*— bite.

1144. δάκρυ **dakru**, *dak´-roo;* or

δάκρυον **dakruön**, *dak´-roo-on;* of uncert. affin.; a *tear:*— tear.

1145. δακρύω **dakruö**, *dak-roo´-o;* from *1144;* to *shed tears:*— weep. Comp. 2799.

1146. δακτύλιος **daktuliös**, *dak-too´-lee-os;* from *1147;* a *finger-ring:*— ring.

1147. δάκτυλος **daktulös**, *dak´-too-los;* prob. from *1176;* a *finger:*— finger.

1148. Δαλμανουθά **Dalmanöutha**, *dalman-oo-thah´;* prob. of Chald. or.; *Dalmanŭtha,* a place in Pal.:— Dalmanutha.

1149. Δαλματία **Dalmatia**, *dal-mat-ee´-ah;* prob. of for. der.; *Dalmatia,* a region of Europe:— Dalmatia.

1150. δαμάζω **damazö**, *dam-ad´-zo;* a var. of an obs. primary of the same mean.; to *tame:*— tame.

1151. δάμαλις **damalis**, *dam´-al-is;* prob. from the base of *1150;* a *heifer* (as *tame*):— heifer.

1152. Δάμαρις **Damaris**, *dam´-ar-is;* prob. from the base of *1150;* perh. *gentle; Damaris,* an Athenian woman:— Damaris.

1153. Δαμασκηνός **Damaskēnös**, *damas-kay-nos´;* from *1154;* a *Damascene* or inhab. of Damascus:— Damascene.

1154. Δαμασκός **Damaskös**, *dam-askos´;* of Heb. or. [1834]; *Damascus,* a city of Syria:— Damascus.

1155. δανείζω **danĕizö**, *dan-ayd´-zo;* or

δανίζω **danizö**, *dan-ide´-zo* from *1156;* to *loan* on interest; refl. to *borrow:*— borrow, lend.

1156. δάνειον **danĕiön**, *dan´-i-on;* from δάνος **danös** (a *gift*); prob. akin to the base of *1325;* a *loan:*— debt.

1157. δανειστής **danĕistēs**, *dan-icetace´;* or

δανιστής **danistēs**, *dan-iys-tace´* from *1155;* a *lender:*— creditor.

1158. Δανιήλ **Daniël**, *dan-ee-ale´;* of Heb. or. [1840]; *Daniel,* an Isr.:— Daniel.

1159. δαπανάω **dapanaö**, *dap-an-ah´-o;* from *1160;* to *expend,* i.e. (in a good sense) to *incur cost,* or (in a bad one) to *waste:*— be at charges, consume, spend.

1160. δαπάνη **dapanē**, *dap-an´-ay;* from δάπτω **daptö** (to *devour*); *expense* (as *consuming*):— cost.

1161. δέ **dĕ**, *deh;* a primary particle (adversative or continuative); *but, and,* etc.:— also, and, but, moreover, now [often unexpressed in English].

1162. δέησις **dĕēsis**, *deh´-ay-sis;* from *1189;* a *petition:*— prayer, request, supplication.

1163. δεῖ **dĕi**, *die;* third pers. sing. act. present of *1210;* also δέον **dĕön**, *deh-on´;* neut. act. part. of the same; both used impers.; *it is* (*was,* etc.) *necessary* (as *binding*):— behoved, be meet, must (needs), (be) need (-ful), ought, should.

1164. δεῖγμα **dĕigma**, *digh´-mah;* from the base of *1166;* a *specimen* (as *shown*):— example.

1165. δειγματίζω **dĕigmatizö**, *dighmat-id´-zo;* from *1164;* to *exhibit:*— make a shew.

1166. δεικνύω **dĕiknuö**, *dike-noo´-o;* a prol. form of an obs. primary of the same mean.; to *show* (lit. or fig.):— shew.

1167. δειλία **dĕilia**, *di-lee´-ah;* from *1169; timidity:*— fear.

1168. δειλιάω **dĕiliaö**, *di-lee-ah´-o;* from *1167;* to *be timid:*— be afraid.

1169. δειλός **dĕilös**, *di-los´;* from δέος **dĕös** (*dread*); *timid,* i.e. (by impl.) *faithless:*— fearful.

1170. δεῖνα **dĕina**, *di´-nah;* prob. from the same as *1171* (through the idea of forgetting the name as *fearful,* i.e. *strange*); *so and so* (when the person is not specified):— such a man.

1171. δεινῶς **dĕinös**, *di-noce´;* adv. from a der. of the same as *1169; terribly,* i.e. *excessively:*— grievously, vehemently.

1172. δειπνέω **dĕipnĕö**, *dipe-neh´-o;* from *1173;* to *dine,* i.e. take the principal (or evening) meal:— sup (× -er).

1173. δεῖπνον **dĕipnön**, *dipe-non;* from the same as *1160; dinner,* i.e. the chief meal (usually in the evening):— feast, supper.

1174. δεισιδαιμονέστερος **dĕisidaimönĕstĕros**, *dice-ee-dahee-mon-es´-ter-os;* the comparative of a der. of the base of *1169* and *1142; more religious* than others:— too superstitious.

1175. δεισιδαιμονία **dĕisidaimönia**, *dice-ee-dahee-mon-ee´-ah;* from the same as *1174; relig.:*— superstition.

1176. δέκα **dĕka**, *dek´-ah;* a primary number; *ten:*— [eight-] een, ten.

1177. δεκαδύο **dĕkaduö**, *dek-ad-oo´-o;* from *1176* and *1417; two* and *ten,* i.e. *twelve:*— twelve.

1178. δεκαπέντε **dĕkapĕntĕ**, *dek-ap-*

en´-teh; from *1176* and *4002;* ten and five, i.e. *fifteen.*— fifteen.

1179. Δεκάπολις **Dĕkapŏlis,** *dek-ap´-ol-is;* from *1176* and *4172;* the *ten-city* region; the *Decapolis,* a district in Syria:— Decapolis.

1180. δεκατέσσαρες **dĕkatĕssarĕs,** *dek-at-es´-sar-es;* from *1176* and *5064;* ten and *four,* i.e. *fourteen.*— fourteen.

1181. δεκάτη **dĕkatĕ,** *dek-at´-ay;* fem. of *1182;* a *tenth,* i.e. as a percentage or (tech.) *tithe:*— tenth (part), tithe.

1182. δέκατος **dĕkatŏs,** *dek´-at-os;* ordinal from *1176;* tenth:— tenth.

1183. δεκατόω **dĕkatŏō,** *dek-at-ŏ´-o;* from *1181;* to *tithe,* i.e. to *give* or *take a tenth:*— pay (receive) tithes.

1184. δεκτός **dĕktŏs,** *dek-tos´;* from *1209; approved;* (fig.) *propitious:*— accepted (-table).

1185. δελεάζω **dĕlĕazō,** *del-eh-ad´-zo;* from the base of *1388;* to *entrap,* i.e. (fig.) *delude:*— allure, beguile, entice.

1186. δένδρον **dĕndrŏn,** *den´-dron;* prob. from δρύς *drus* (an *oak*); a *tree:*— tree.

1187. δεξιολάβος **dĕxiŏlabŏs,** *dex-ee-ol-ab´-os;* from *1188* and *2983;* a *guardsman* (as if *taking the right*) or light-armed soldier:— spearman.

1188. δεξιός **dĕxiŏs,** *dex-ee-os´;* from *1209;* the *right* side or (fem.) hand (as that which usually *takes*):— right (hand, side).

1189. δέομαι **dĕŏmai,** *deh´-om-ahee;* mid. voice of *1210;* to *beg* (as *binding oneself*), i.e. *petition:*— beseech, pray (to), make request. Comp. *4441.*

δεόν **dĕŏn.** See *1163.*

1190. Δερβαῖος **Dĕrbaiŏs,** *der-bah´-ee-os;* from *1191;* a *Derbæan* or inhab. of Derbe:— of Derbe.

1191. Δέρβη **Dĕrbē,** *der-bay´;* of for. or.; *Derbè,* a place in Asia Minor:— Derbe.

1192. δέρμα **dĕrma,** *der´-mah;* from *1194;* a *hide:*— skin.

1193. δερμάτινος **dĕrmatinŏs,** *der-mat´-ee-nos;* from *1192;* made of *hide:*— leathern, of a skin.

1194. δέρω **dĕrō,** *der´-o;* a primary verb; prop. to *flay,* i.e. (by impl.) to *scourge,* or (by anal.) to *thrash:*— beat, smite.

1195. δεσμεύω **dĕsmĕuō,** *des-myoo´-o;* from a (presumed) der. of *1196;* to *be a binder* (*captor*), i.e. to *enchain* (a prisoner), to *tie on* (a load):— bind.

1196. δεσμέω **dĕsmĕō,** *des-meh´-o;* from *1199;* to *tie,* i.e. *shackle:*— bind.

1197. δεσμή **dĕsmē,** *des-may´;* from *1196;* a *bundle:*— bundle.

1198. δέσμιος **dĕsmiŏs,** *des´-mee-os;* from *1199;* a *captive* (as *bound*):— in bonds, prisoner.

1199. δεσμόν **dĕsmŏn,** *des-mon´;* or

δεσμός **dĕsmŏs,** *des-mos´;* neut. and masc. respectively from *1210;* a *band,* i.e. *ligament* (of the body) or *shackle* (of a prisoner); fig. an *impediment* or *disability:*— band, bond, chain, string.

1200. δεσμοφύλαξ **dĕsmŏphulax,** *des-*

mof-oo´-lax; from *1199* and *5441;* a *jailer* (as *guarding* the *prisoners*):— jailor, keeper of the prison.

1201. δεσμωτήριον **dĕsmōtēriŏn,** *des-mo-tay´-ree-on;* from a der. of *1199* (equiv. to *1196*); a *place of bondage,* i.e. a *dungeon:*— prison.

1202. δεσμώτης **dĕsmōtēs,** *des-mo´-tace;* from the same as *1201;* (pass.) a *captive:*— prisoner.

1203. δεσπότης **dĕspŏtēs,** *des-pot´-ace;* perh. from *1210* and πόσις **pŏsis** (a *husband*); an absolute *ruler* ("despot"):— Lord, master.

1204. δεῦρο **dĕurŏ,** *dyoo´-ro;* of uncert. aff.; *here;* used also imperative *hither!;* and of time, *hitherto:*— come (hither), hither [-to].

1205. δεῦτε **dĕutĕ,** *dyoo´-teh;* from *1204* and an imper. form of εἶμι **ĕimi** (to *go*); *come hither!:*— come, × follow.

1206. δευτεραῖος **dĕutĕraiŏs,** *dyoo-ter-ah´-yos;* from *1208; secondary,* i.e. (spec.) on the *second* day:— next day.

1207. δευτερόπρωτος **dĕutĕrŏprōtŏs,** *dyoo-ter-op´-ro-tos;* from *1208* and *4413; second-first,* i.e. (spec.) a designation of the Sabbath immediately after the Paschal week (being the *second* after Passover day, and the *first* of the seven Sabbaths intervening before Pentecost):— second ... after the first.

1208. δεύτερος **dĕutĕrŏs,** *dyoo´-ter-os;* as the comp. of *1417;* (ordinal) *second* (in time, place, or rank; also adv.):— afterward, again, second (-arily, time).

1209. δέχομαι **dĕchŏmai,** *dekh´-om-ahee;* mid. voice of a primary verb; to *receive* (in various applications, lit. or fig.):— accept, receive, take. Comp. *2983.*

1210. δέω **dĕō,** *deh´-o;* a primary verb; to *bind* (in various applications, lit. or fig.):— bind, be in bonds, knit, tie, wind. See also *1163, 1189.*

1211. δή **dē,** *day;* prob. akin to *1161;* a particle of emphasis or explicitness; *now, then,* etc.:— also, and, doubtless, now, therefore.

1212. δῆλος **dēlŏs,** *day´-los;* of uncert. der.; *clear:*— + bewray, certain, evident, manifest.

1213. δηλόω **dēlŏō,** *day-lŏ´-o;* from *1212;* to *make plain* (by words):— declare, shew, signify.

1214. Δημᾶς **Dēmas,** *day-mas´;* prob. for *1216; Demas,* a Chr.:— Demas.

1215. δημηγορέω **dēmēgŏrĕō,** *day-may-gor-eh´-o;* from a compound of *1218* and *58;* to *be a people-gatherer,* i.e. to *address* a public assembly:— make an oration.

1216. Δημήτριος **Dēmētriŏs,** *day-may´-tree-os;* from Δημήτηρ **Dēmētēr** (*Ceres*); *Demetrius,* the name of an Ephesian and of a Chr.:— Demetrius.

1217. δημιουργός **dēmiŏurgŏs,** *day-me-oor-gos´;* from *1218* and *2041;* a *worker* for the *people,* i.e. *mechanic* (spoken of the *Creator*):— maker.

1218. δῆμος **dēmŏs,** *day´-mos;* from *1210;* the *public* (as *bound* together socially):— people.

1219. δημόσιος **dēmŏsiŏs,** *day-mos´ee-os;* from *1218; public;* (fem. sing. dat. case as adv.) *in public:*— common, openly, publickly.

1220. δηνάριον **dēnariŏn,** *day-nar´-ee-on;* of Lat. or.; a *denarius* (or *ten asses*):— pence, penny [-worth].

1221. δήποτε **dēpŏtĕ,** *day´-pot-eh;* from *1211* and *4218;* a particle of generalization; *indeed, at any time:*— (what-) soever.

1222. δήπου **dēpŏu,** *day´-poo;* from *1211* and *4225;* a particle of asseveration; *indeed doubtless:*— verily.

1223. διά **dia,** *dee-ah´;* a primary prep. denoting the *channel* of an act; *through* (in very wide applications, local, causal, or occasional):— after, always, among, at, to avoid, because of (that), briefly, by, for (cause) ... fore, from, in, by occasion of, of, by reason of, for sake, that, thereby, therefore, × though, through (-out), to, wherefore, with (-in). In composition it retains the same general import.

Δία **Dia.** See *2203.*

1224. διαβαίνω **diabainō,** *dee-ab-ah´-ee-no;* from *1223* and the base of *939;* to *cross:*— come over, pass (through).

1225. διαβάλλω **diaballō,** *dee-ab-al´-lo;* from *1223* and *906;* (fig.) to *traduce:*— accuse.

1226. διαβεβαιόομαι **diabĕbaiŏŏmai,** *dee-ab-eb-ahee-ŏ´-om-ahee;* mid. voice of a compound of *1223* and *950;* to *confirm thoroughly* (by words), i.e. *asseverate:*— affirm constantly.

1227. διαβλέπω **diablĕpō,** *dee-ab-lep´-o;* from *1223* and *991;* to *look through,* i.e. *recover* full *vision:*— see clearly.

1228. διάβολος **diabŏlŏs,** *dee-ab´-ol-os;* from *1225;* a *traducer;* spec. *Satan* [comp. 7854]:— false accuser, devil, slanderer.

1229. διαγγέλλω **diaggĕllō,** *de-ang-gel´-lo;* from *1223* and the base of *32;* to *herald thoroughly:*— declare, preach, signify.

1230. διαγίνομαι **diaginŏmai,** *dee-ag-in´-om-ahee;* from *1223* and *1096;* to *elapse meanwhile:*— × after, be past, be spent.

1231. διαγινώσκω **diaginōskō,** *dee-ag-in-o´-sko;* from *1223* and *1097;* to *know thoroughly,* i.e. *ascertain exactly:*— (would) enquire, know the uttermost.

1232. διαγνωρίζω **diagnōrizō,** *dee-ag-no-rid´-zo;* from *1223* and *1107;* to *tell abroad:*— make known.

1233. διάγνωσις **diagnōsis,** *dee-ag´-no-sis;* from *1231;* (magisterial) *examination* ("diagnosis"):— hearing.

1234. διαγογγύζω **diagŏgguzō,** *dee-ag-ong-good´-zo;* from *1223* and *1111;* to *complain throughout* a crowd:— murmur.

1235. διαγρηγορέω **diagrēgŏrĕō,** *dee-ag-ray-gor-eh´-o;* from *1223* and *1127;* to *waken thoroughly:*— be awake.

1236. διάγω **diagō,** *dee-ag´-o;* from *1223* and *71;* to *pass* time or life:— lead life, living.

1237. διαδέχομαι **diadĕchŏmai,** *dee-ad-*

ekh´-om-ahee; from 1223 and 1209; to receive in turn, i.e. (fig.) succeed to:— come after.

1238. διάδημα **diadēma**, dee-ad´-ay-mah; from a compound of 1223 and 1210; a "diadem" (as bound about the head):— crown. Comp. 4735.

1239. διαδίδωμι **diadidōmi**, dee-ad-id´-o-mee; from 1223 and 1325; to give throughout a crowd, i.e. deal out; also to deliver over (as to a successor):— (make) distribute (-ion), divide, give.

1240. διάδοχος **diadŏchŏs**, dee-ad´-okh-os; from 1237; a successor in office:— room.

1241. διαζώννυμι **diazōnnumi**, dee-az-own´-noo-mee; from 1223 and 2224; to gird tightly:— gird.

1242. διαθήκη **diathēkē**, dee-ath-ay´-kay; from 1303; prop. a disposition, i.e. (spec.) a contract (espec. a devisory will):— covenant, testament.

1243. διαίρεσις **diairĕsis**, dee-ah´-ee-res-is; from 1244; a distinction or (concr.) variety:— difference, diversity.

1244. διαιρέω **diairĕō**, dee-ahee-reh´-o; from 1223 and 138; to separate, i.e. distribute:— divide.

1245. διακαθαρίζω **diakatharizō**, dee-ak-ath-ar-id´-zo; from 1223 and 2511; to cleanse perfectly, i.e. (spec.) winnow:— thoroughly purge.

1246. διακατελέγχομαι **diakatĕlĕgchŏmai**, dee-ak-at-el-eng´-khom-ahee; mid. voice from 1223 and a compound of 2596 and 1651; to prove downright, i.e. confute:— convince.

1247. διακονέω **diakŏnĕō**, dee-ak-on-eh´-o; from 1249; to be an attendant, i.e. wait upon (menially or as a host, friend, or [fig.] teacher); techn. to act as a Chr. deacon:— (ad-) minister (unto), serve, use the office of a deacon.

1248. διακονία **diakŏnia**, dee-ak-on-ee´-ah; from 1249; attendance (as a servant, etc.); fig. (eleemosynary) aid, (official) service (espec. of the Chr. teacher, or techn. of the diaconate):— (ad-) minister (-ing, -tration, -try), office, relief, service (-ing).

1249. διάκονος **diakŏnŏs**, dee-ak´-on-os; prob. from an obs. διάκω **diakō** (to run on errands; comp. 1377); an attendant, i.e. (gen.) a waiter (at table or in other menial duties); spec. a Chr. teacher and pastor (tech. a deacon or deaconess):— deacon, minister, servant.

1250. διακόσιοι **diakŏsiŏi**, dee-ak-os´-ee-oy; from 1364 and 1540; two hundred:— two hundred.

1251. διακούομαι **diakŏuŏmai**, dee-ak-oo´-om-ahee; mid. voice from 1223 and 191; to hear throughout, i.e. patiently listen (to a prisoner's plea):— hear.

1252. διακρίνω **diakrinō**, dee-ak-ree´-no; from 1223 and 2919; to separate thoroughly, i.e. (lit. and refl.) to withdraw from, or (by impl.) oppose; fig. to discriminate (by impl. decide), or (refl.) hesitate:— contend, make (to) differ (-ence), discern, doubt, judge, be partial, stagger, waver.

1253. διάκρισις **diakrisis**, dee-ak´-ree-sis; from 1252; judicial estimation:— discern (-ing), disputation.

1254. διακωλύω **diakōluō**, dee-ak-o-loo´-o; from 1223 and 2967; to hinder altogether, i.e. utterly prohibit:— forbid.

1255. διαλαλέω **dialalĕō**, dee-al-al-eh´-o; from 1223 and 2980; to talk throughout a company, i.e. converse or (gen.) publish:— commune, noise abroad.

1256. διαλέγομαι **dialĕgŏmai**, dee-al-eg´-om-ahee; mid. voice from 1223 and 3004; to say thoroughly, i.e. discuss (in argument or exhortation):— dispute, preach (unto), reason (with), speak.

1257. διαλείπω **dialĕipō**, dee-al-i´-po; from 1223 and 3007; to leave off in the middle, i.e. intermit:— cease.

1258. διάλεκτος **dialĕktŏs**, dee-al´-ek-tos; from 1256; a (mode of) discourse, i.e. "dialect":— language, tongue.

1259. διαλλάσσω **diallassō**, dee-al-las´-so; from 1223 and 236; to change thoroughly, i.e. (ment.) to conciliate:— reconcile.

1260. διαλογίζομαι **dialŏgizŏmai**, dee-al-og-id´-zom-ahee; from 1223 and 3049; to reckon thoroughly, i.e. (gen.) to deliberate (by reflection or discussion):— cast in mind, consider, dispute, muse, reason, think.

1261. διαλογισμός **dialŏgismŏs**, dee-al-og-is-mos´; from 1260; discussion, i.e. (internal) consideration (by impl. purpose), or (external) debate:— dispute, doubtful (-ing), imagination, reasoning, thought.

1262. διαλύω **dialuō**, dee-al-oo´-o; from 1223 and 3089; to dissolve utterly:— scatter.

1263. διαμαρτύρομαι **diamarturŏmai**, dee-am-ar-too´-rom-ahee; from 1223 and 3140; to attest or protest earnestly, or (by impl.) hortatively:— charge, testify (unto), witness.

1264. διαμάχομαι **diamachŏmai**, dee-am-akh´-om-ahee; from 1223 and 3164; to fight fiercely (in altercation):— strive.

1265. διαμένω **diamĕnō**, dee-am-en´-o; from 1223 and 3306; to stay constantly (in being or relation):— continue, remain.

1266. διαμερίζω **diamĕrizō**, dee-am-er-id´-zo; from 1223 and 3307; to partition thoroughly (lit. in distribution, fig. in dissension):— cloven, divide, part.

1267. διαμερισμός **diamĕrismŏs**, dee-am-er-is-mos´; from 1266; disunion (of opinion and conduct):— division.

1268. διανέμω **dianĕmō**, dee-an-em´-o; from 1223 and the base of 3551; to distribute, i.e. (of information) to disseminate:— spread.

1269. διανεύω **dianĕuō**, dee-an-yoo´-o; from 1223 and 3506; to nod (or express by signs) across an intervening space:— beckon.

1270. διανόημα **dianŏēma**, dee-an-o´-ay-mah; from a compound of 1223 and 3539; something thought through, i.e. a sentiment:— thought.

1271. διάνοια **dianŏia**, dee-an´-oy-ah; from 1223 and 3563; deep thought, prop. the faculty (mind or its disposition), by impl. its exercise:— imagination, mind, understanding.

1272. διανοίγω **dianŏigō**, dee-an-oy´-go; from 1223 and 455; to open thoroughly, lit. (as a first-born) or fig. (to expound):— open.

1273. διανυκτερεύω **dianuktĕrĕuō**, dee-an-ook-ter-yoo´-o; from 1223 and a der. of 3571; to sit up the whole night:— continue all night.

1274. διανύω **dianuō**, dee-an-oo´-o; from 1223 and ἀνύω anuō (to effect); to accomplish thoroughly:— finish.

1275. διαπαντός **diapantŏs**, dee-ap-an-tos´; from 1223 and the genit. of 3956; through all the time, i.e. (adv.) constantly:— alway (-s), continually.

1276. διαπεράω **diapĕraō**, dee-ap-er-ah´-o; from 1223 and a der. of the base of 4008; to cross entirely:— go over, pass (over), sail over.

1277. διαπλέω **diaplĕō**, dee-ap-leh´-o; from 1223 and 4126; to sail through:— sail over.

1278. διαπονέω **diapŏnĕō**, dee-ap-on-eh´-o; from 1223 and a der. of 4192; to toil through, i.e. (pass.) be worried:— be grieved.

1279. διαπορεύομαι **diapŏrĕuŏmai**, dee-ap-or-yoo´-om-ahee; from 1223 and 4198; to travel through:— go through, journey in, pass by.

1280. διαπορέω **diapŏrĕō**, dee-ap-or-eh´-o; from 1223 and 639; to be thoroughly nonplussed:— (be in) doubt, be (much) perplexed.

1281. διαπραγματεύομαι **diapragmatĕuŏmai**, dee-ap-rag-mat-yoo´-om-ahee; from 1223 and 4231; to thoroughly occupy oneself, i.e. (tran. and by impl.) to earn in business:— gain by trading.

1282. διαπρίω **diapriō**, dee-ap-ree´-o; from 1223 and the base of 4249; to saw asunder, i.e. (fig.) to exasperate:— cut (to the heart).

1283. διαρπάζω **diarpazō**, dee-ar-pad´-zo; from 1223 and 726; to seize asunder, i.e. plunder:— spoil.

1284. διαρρήσσω **diarrhēssō**, dee-ar-hrayce´-so; from 1223 and 4486; to tear asunder:— break, rend.

1285. διασαφέω **diasaphĕō**, dee-as-af-eh´-o; from 1223 and σαφής saphēs (clear); to clear thoroughly, i.e. (fig.) declare:— tell unto.

1286. διασείω **diasĕiō**, dee-as-i´-o; from 1223 and 4579; to shake thoroughly, i.e. (fig.) to intimidate:— do violence to.

1287. διασκορπίζω **diaskŏrpizō**, dee-as-kor-pid´-zo; from 1223 and 4650; to dissipate, i.e. (gen.) to rout or separate; spec., to winnow; fig. to squander:— disperse, scatter (abroad), strew, waste.

1288. διασπάω **diaspaō**, dee-as-pah´-o; from 1223 and 4685; to draw apart, i.e. sever or dismember:— pluck asunder, pull in pieces.

1289. διασπείρω **diaspēirō**, dee-as-pi´-ro; from 1223 and 4687; to sow through-

out, i.e. (fig.) *distribute* in foreign lands:— scatter abroad.

1290. διασπορά **diaspŏra**, *dee-as-por-ah´*; from *1289*; *dispersion*, i.e. (spec. and concr.) the (converted) Isr. *resident* in Gentile countries:— (which are) scattered (abroad).

1291. διαστέλλομαι **diastĕllŏmai**, *dee-as-tel´-lom-ahee*; mid. voice from *1223* and *4724*; to *set* (oneself) *apart* (fig. *distinguish*), i.e. (by impl.) to *enjoin*:— charge, that which was (give) commanded (-ment).

1292. διάστημα **diastēma**, *dee-as´-tay-mah*; from *1339*; an *interval*:— space.

1293. διαστολή **diastŏlē**, *dee-as-tol-ay´*; from *1291*; a *variation*:— difference, distinction.

1294. διαστρέφω **diastrĕphō**, *dee-as-tref´-o*; from *1223* and *4762*; to *distort*, i.e. (fig.) *misinterpret*, or (morally) *corrupt*:— perverse (-rt), turn away.

1295. διασῴζω **diasōzō**, *dee-as-odze´-o*; from *1223* and *4982*; to *save thoroughly*, i.e. (by impl. or anal.) to *cure, preserve, rescue*, etc.:— bring safe, escape (safe), heal, make perfectly whole, save.

1296. διαταγή **diatagē**, *dee-at-ag-ay´*; from *1299*; *arrangement*, i.e. *institution*:— instrumentality.

1297. διάταγμα **diatagma**, *dee-at´-ag-mah*; from *1299*; an *arrangement*, i.e. (authoritative) *edict*:— commandment.

1298. διαταράσσω **diatarassō**, *dee-at-ar-as´-so*; from *1223* and *5015*; to *disturb wholly*, i.e. *agitate* (with alarm):— trouble.

1299. διατάσσω **diatassō**, *dee-at-as´-so*; from *1223* and *5021*; to *arrange thoroughly*, i.e. (spec.) *institute, prescribe*, etc.:— appoint, command, give, (set in) order, ordain.

1300. διατελέω **diatĕlĕō**, *dee-at-el-eh´-o*; from *1223* and *5055*; to *accomplish thoroughly*, i.e. (subj.) to *persist*:— continue.

1301. διατηρέω **diatērĕō**, *dee-at-ay-reh´-o*; from *1223* and *5083*; to *watch thoroughly*, i.e. (pos. and tran.) to *observe* strictly, or (neg. and refl.) to *avoid* wholly:— keep.

1302. διατί **diati**, *dee-at-ee´*; from *1223* and *5101*; *through what* cause?, i.e. *why?*:— wherefore, why.

1303. διατίθεμαι **diatithĕmai**, *dee-at-ith´-em-ahee*; mid. voice from *1223* and *5087*; to *put apart*, i.e. (fig.) *dispose* (by assignment, compact, or bequest):— appoint, make, testator.

1304. διατρίβω **diatribō**, *dee-at-ree´-bo*; from *1223* and the base of *5147*; to *wear through* (time), i.e. *remain*:— abide, be, continue, tarry.

1305. διατροφή **diatrŏphē**, *dee-at-rof-ay´*; from a compound of *1223* and *5142*; *nourishment*:— food.

1306. διαυγάζω **diaugazō**, *dee-ow-gad´-zo*; from *1223* and *826*; to *glimmer through*), i.e. *break* (as day):— dawn.

1307. διαφανής **diaphanēs**, *dee-af-an-ace´*; from *1223* and *5316*; *appearing through*, i.e. "*diaphanous*":— transparent.

1308. διαφέρω **diaphĕrō**, *dee-af-er´-o*; from *1223* and *5342*; to *bear through*, i.e. (lit.) *transport*; usually to *bear apart*, i.e. (obj.) to *toss about* (fig. *report*); subj. to "*differ*," or (by impl.) *surpass*:— be better, carry, differ from, drive up and down, be (more) excellent, make matter, publish, be of more value.

1309. διαφεύγω **diaphĕugō**, *dee-af-yoo´-go*; from *1223* and *5343*; to *flee through*, i.e. *escape*:— escape.

1310. διαφημίζω **diaphēmizō**, *dee-af-ay-mid´-zo*; from *1223* and a der. of *5345*; to *report thoroughly*, i.e. *divulgate*:— blaze abroad, commonly report, spread abroad, fame.

1311. διαφθείρω **diaphthĕirō**, *dee-af-thi´-ro*; from *1225* and *5351*; to *rot thoroughly*, i.e. (by impl.) to *ruin* (pass. *decay* utterly, fig. *pervert*):— corrupt, destroy, perish.

1312. διαφθορά **diaphthŏra**, *dee-af-thor-ah´*; from *1311*; *decay*:— corruption.

1313. διάφορος **diaphŏrŏs**, *dee-af´-or-os*; from *1308*; *varying*; also *surpassing*:— differing, divers, more excellent.

1314. διαφυλάσσω **diaphulassō**, *dee-af-oo-las´-so*; from *1223* and *5442*; to *guard thoroughly*, i.e. *protect*:— keep.

1315. διαχειρίζομαι **diachĕirizŏmai**, *dee-akh-i-rid´-zom-ahee*; from *1223* and a der. of *5495*; to *handle thoroughly*, i.e. *lay* violent *hands* upon:— kill, slay.

1316. διαχωρίζομαι **diachōrizŏmai**, *dee-akh-o-rid´-zom-ahee*; from *1223* and the mid. voice of *5563*; to *remove* (oneself) *wholly*, i.e. *retire*:— depart.

1317. διδακτικός **didaktikŏs**, *did-ak-tik-os´*; from *1318*; *instructive* ("didactic"):— apt to teach.

1318. διδακτός **didaktŏs**, *did-ak-tos´*; from *1321*; (subj.) *instructed*, or (obj.) *communicated* by teaching:— taught, which ... teacheth.

1319. διδασκαλία **didaskalia**, *did-as-kal-ee-ah*; from *1320*; *instruction* (the function or the information):— doctrine, learning, teaching.

1320. διδάσκαλος **didaskalŏs**, *did-as´-kal-os*; from *1321*; an *instructor* (gen. or spec.):— doctor, master, teacher.

1321. διδάσκω **didaskō**, *did-as´-ko*; a prol. (caus.) form of a primary verb δάω **daō** (to *learn*); to *teach* (in the same broad application):— teach.

1322. διδαχή **didachē**, *did-akh-ay´*; from *1321*; *instruction* (the act or the matter):— doctrine, hath been taught.

1323. δίδραχμον **didrachmŏn**, *did´-rakh-mon*; from *1364* and *1406*; a *double drachma* (*didrachm*):— tribute.

1324. Δίδυμος **Didumŏs**, *did´-oo-mos*; prol. from *1364*; *double*, i.e. *twin*; *Didymus*, a Chr.:— Didymus.

1325. δίδωμι **didōmi**, *did´-o-mee*; a prol. form of a primary verb (which is used as an altern. in most of the tenses); to *give* (used in a very wide application, prop. or by impl., lit. or fig.; greatly modified by the connection):— adven-

ture, bestow, bring forth, commit, deliver (up), give, grant, hinder, make, minister, number, offer, have power, put, receive, set, shew, smite (+ with the hand), strike (+ with the palm of the hand), suffer, take, utter, yield.

1326. διεγείρω **diĕgĕirō**, *dee-eg-i´-ro*; from *1223* and *1453*; to *wake fully*; i.e. *arouse* (lit. or fig.):— arise, awake, raise, stir up.

1327. διέξοδος **diĕxŏdŏs**, *dee-ex´-od-os*; from *1223* and *1841*; an *outlet through*, i.e. prob. an open *square* (from which roads diverge):— highway.

1328. διερμηνευτής **diĕrmēnĕutēs**, *dee-er-main-yoo-tace´*; from *1329*; an *explainer*:— interpreter.

1329. διερμηνεύω **diĕrmēnĕuō**, *dee-er-main-yoo´-o*; from *1223* and *2059*; to *explain thoroughly*, by impl. to *translate*:— expound, interpret (-ation).

1330. διέρχομαι **diĕrchŏmai**, *dee-er´-khom-ahee*; from *1223* and *2064*; to *traverse* (lit.):— come, depart, go (about, abroad, everywhere, over, through, throughout), pass (by, over, through, throughout), pierce through, travel, walk through.

1331. διερωτάω **diĕrōtaō**, *dee-er-o-tah´-o*; from *1223* and *2065*; to *question throughout*, i.e. *ascertain* by interrogation:— make enquiry for.

1332. διετής **diĕtēs**, *dee-et-ace´*; from *1364* and *2094*; of *two years* (in age):— two years old.

1333. διετία **diĕtia**, *dee-et-ee-´a*; from *1332*; a space of *two years* (*biennium*):— two years.

1334. διηγέομαι **diēgĕŏmai**, *dee-ayg-eh´-om-ahee*; from *1223* and *2233*; to *relate fully*:— declare, shew, tell.

1335. διήγεσις **diēgĕsis**, *dee-ayg´-es-is*; or διήγησις **diēgēsis** *dee-ayg´-es-is*; from *1334*; a *recital*:— declaration.

1336. διηνεκές **diēnĕkĕs**, *dee-ay-nek-es´*; neut. of a compound of *1223* and a der. of an alt. of *5342*; *carried through*, i.e. (adv. with *1519* and *3588* pref.) *perpetually*:— + continually, for ever.

1337. διθάλασσος **dithalassŏs**, *dee-thal´-as-sos*; from *1364* and *2281*; *having two seas*, i.e. a *sound* with a double outlet:— where two seas meet.

1338. διϊκνέομαι **diïknĕŏmai**, *dee-ik-neh´-om-ahee*; from *1223* and the base of *2425*; to *reach through*, i.e. *penetrate*:— pierce.

1339. διΐστημι **diïstēmi**, *dee-is´-tay-mee*; from *1223* and *2476*; to *stand apart*, i.e. (refl.) to *remove, intervene*:— go further, be parted, after the space of.

1340. διϊσχυρίζομαι **diïschurizŏmai**, *dee-is-khoo-rid´-zom-ahee*; from *1223* and a der. of *2478*; to *stout it through*, i.e. *asseverate*:— confidently (constantly) affirm.

1341. δικαιοκρισία **dikaiŏkrisia**, *dik-ah-yok-ris-ee-´ah*; from *1342* and *2920*; a *just sentence*:— righteous judgment.

1342. δίκαιος **dikaiŏs**, *dik´-ah-yos*; from *1349*; *equitable* (in character or act); by impl. *innocent, holy* (absol. or rel.):— just, meet, right (-eous).

1343. δικαιοσύνη **dikaiŏsunē**, *dik-ah-yos-oo´-nay;* from *1342; equity* (of character or act); spec. (Chr.) *justification:*— righteousness.

1344. δικαιόω **dikaiŏō**, *dik-ah-yŏ´-o;* from *1342;* to *render* (i.e. *show* or *regard* as) *just* or *innocent:*— free, justify (-ier), be righteous.

1345. δικαίωμα **dikaiōma**, *dik-ah´-yo-mah;* from *1344;* an *equitable deed;* by impl. a *statute* or *decision:*— judgment, justification, ordinance, righteousness.

1346. δικαίως **dikaiōs**, *dik-ah´-yoce;* adv. from *1342; equitably:*— justly, (to) righteously (-ness).

1347. δικαίωσις **dikaiōsis**, *dik-ah´-yo-sis;* from *1344; acquittal* (for Christ's sake):— justification.

1348. δικαστής **dikastēs**, *dik-as-tace´;* from a der. of *1349;* a *judger:*— judge.

1349. δίκη **dikē**, *dee´-kay;* prob. from *1166; right* (as self-*evident*), i.e. *justice* (the principle, a decision, or its execution):— judgment, punish, vengeance.

1350. δίκτυον **diktuŏn**, *dik´-too-on;* prob. from a primary verb δίκω **dikō** (to *cast*); a *seine* (for fishing):— net.

1351. δίλογος **dilŏgŏs**, *dil´-og-os;* from *1364* and *3056;* equivocal, i.e. telling a different story:— double-tongued.

1352. διό **diŏ**, *dee-ŏ´;* from *1223* and *3739; through which* thing, i.e. *consequently:*— for which cause, therefore, wherefore.

1353. διοδεύω **diŏdĕuō**, *dee-od-yoo´-o;* from *1223* and *3593;* to *travel through:*— go throughout, pass through.

1354. Διονύσιος **Diŏnusiŏs**, *dee-on-oo´-see-os;* from Διόνυσος **Diŏnusŏs** (*Bacchus*); *reveller; Dionysius,* an Athenian:— Dionysius.

1355. διόπερ **diŏpĕr**, *dee-op´-er;* from *1352* and *4007; on which very account:*— wherefore.

1356. διοπετής **diŏpĕtēs**, *dee-op-et´-ace;* from the alt. of *2203* and the alt. of *4098; sky-fallen* (i.e. an *aerolite*):— which fell down from Jupiter.

1357. διόρθωσις **diŏrthōsis**, *dee-or´-tho-sis;* from a compound of *1223* and a der. of *3717,* mean. to *straighten thoroughly; rectification,* i.e. (spec.) the Messianic *restoration:*— reformation.

1358. διορύσσω **diŏrussō**, *dee-or-oos´-so;* from *1223* and *3736;* to *penetrate* burglariously:— break through (up).

Διός **Diŏs**. See *2203.*

1359. Διόσκουροι **Diŏskŏurŏi**, *dee-os´-koo-roy;* from the alt. of *2203* and a form of the base of *2877; sons of Jupiter,* i.e. the twins *Dioscuri:*— Castor and Pollux.

1360. διότι **diŏti**, *dee-ot´-ee;* from *1223* and *3754; on the very account that,* or *inasmuch as:*— because (that), for, therefore.

1361. Διοτρεφής **Diŏtrĕphēs**, *dee-ot-ref-ace´;* from the alt. of *2203* and *5142;*

Jove-nourished; Diotrephes, an opponent of Christianity:— Diotrephes.

1362. διπλοῦς **diplŏus**, *dip-looce´;* or διπλόος **diplŏos**, *dip-loce´* from *1364* and (prob.) the base of *4119; two-fold:*— double, two-fold more.

1363. διπλόω **diplŏō**, *dip-lŏ´-o;* from *1362;* to *render two-fold:*— double.

1364. δίς **dis**, *dece;* adv. from *1417; twice:*— again, twice.

Δίς **Dis**. See *2203.*

1365. διστάζω **distazō**, *dis-tad´-zo;* from *1364;* prop. to *duplicate,* i.e. (ment.) to *waver* (in opinion):— doubt.

1366. δίστομος **distŏmŏs**, *dis´-tom-os;* from *1364* and *4750; double-edged:*— with two edges, two-edged.

1367. δισχίλιοι **dischilioi**, *dis-khil´-ee-oy;* from *1364* and *5507; two thousand:*— two thousand.

1368. διυλίζω **diulizō**, *dee-oo-lid´-zo;* from *1223* and ὑλίζω **hulizō**, *hoo-lid´-zo* (to *filter*); to *strain out:*— strain at [*prob. by misprint*].

1369. διχάζω **dichazō**, *dee-khad´-zo;* from a der. of *1364;* to *make apart,* i.e. *sunder* (fig. *alienate*):— set at variance.

1370. διχοστασία **dichŏstasia**, *dee-khos-tas-ee´-ah;* from a der. of *1364* and *4714; disunion,* i.e. (fig.) *dissension:*— division, sedition.

1371. διχοτομέω **dichŏtŏmĕō**, *dee-khot-om-eh´-o;* from a compound of a der. of *1364* and a der. of τέμνω **tĕmnō** (to *cut*); to *bisect,* i.e. (by extens.) to *flog* severely:— cut asunder (in sunder).

1372. διψάω **dipsaō**, *dip-sah´-o;* from a var. of *1373;* to *thirst* for (lit. or fig.):— (be, be a-) thirst (-y).

1373. δίψος **dipsŏs**, *dip´-sos;* of uncert. aff.; *thirst:*— thirst.

1374. δίψυχος **dipsuchŏs**, *dip´-soo-khos;* from *1364* and *5590; two-spirited,* i.e. *vacillating* (in opinion or purpose):— double minded.

1375. διωγμός **diōgmŏs**, *dee-ogue-mos´;* from *1377; persecution:*— persecution.

1376. διώκτης **diōktēs**, *dee-oke´-tace;* from *1377;* a *persecutor:*— persecutor.

1377. διώκω **diōkō**, *dee-o´-ko;* a prol. (and caus.) form of a primary verb δίω **diō** (to *flee;* comp. the base of *1169* and *1249*); to *pursue* (lit. or fig.); by impl. to *persecute:*— ensue, follow (after), given to, (suffer) persecute (-ion), press toward.

1378. δόγμα **dŏgma**, *dog´-mah;* from the base of *1380;* a *law* (civil, cerem. or eccl.):— decree, ordinance.

1379. δογματίζω **dŏgmatizō**, *dog-mat-id´-zo;* from *1378;* to *prescribe* by statute, i.e. (refl.) to *submit* to cer. *rule:*— be subject to ordinances.

1380. δοκέω **dŏkĕō**, *dok-eh´-o;* a prol. form of a primary verb, δόκω **dŏkō**, *dok´-o* (used only in an alt. in certain tenses; comp. the base of *1166*) of the same mean.; to *think;* by impl. to *seem* (truthfully or uncertainly):— be accounted, (of own) please (-ure), be of reputation, seem (good), suppose, think, trow.

1381. δοκιμάζω **dŏkimazō**, *dok-im-ad´-zo;* from *1384;* to *test* (lit. or fig.); by impl. to *approve:*— allow, discern, examine, × like, (ap-) prove, try.

1382. δοκιμή **dŏkimē**, *dok-ee-may´;* from the same as *1384; test* (abstr. or concr.); by impl. *trustiness:*— experience (-riment), proof, trial.

1383. δοκίμιον **dŏkimiŏn**, *dok-im´-ee-on;* neut. of a presumed der. of *1382;* a *testing;* by impl. *trustworthiness:*— trial, trying.

1384. δόκιμος **dŏkimŏs**, *dok´-ee-mos;* from *1380;* prop. *acceptable* (*current* after assayal), i.e. *approved:*— approved, tried.

1385. δοκός **dŏkŏs**, *dok-os´;* from *1209* (through the idea of *holding* up); a *stick* of timber:— beam.

δόκω **dŏkō**. See *1380.*

1386. δόλιος **dŏliŏs**, *dol´-ee-os;* from *1388; guileful:*— deceitful.

1387. δολιόω **dŏliŏō**, *dol-ee-ŏ´-o;* from *1386;* to *be guileful:*— use deceit.

1388. δόλος **dŏlŏs**, *dol´-os;* from an obs. primary verb, δέλλω **dĕllō** (prob. mean. to *decoy;* comp. *1185*); a *trick* (*bait*), i.e. (fig.) *wile:*— craft, deceit, guile, subtilty (subtlety).

1389. δολόω **dŏlŏō**, *dol-ŏ´-o;* from *1388;* to *ensnare,* i.e. (fig.) *adulterate:*— handle deceitfully.

1390. δόμα **dŏma**, *dom´-ah;* from the base of *1325;* a *present:*— gift.

1391. δόξα **dŏxa**, *dox´-ah;* from the base of *1380; glory* (as very *apparent*), in a wide application (lit. or fig., obj. or subj.):— dignity, glory (-ious), honour, praise, worship.

1392. δοξάζω **dŏxazō**, *dox-ad´-zo;* from *1391;* to *render* (or *esteem*) *glorious* (in a wide application):— (make) glorify (-ious), full of (have) glory, honour, magnify.

1393. Δορκάς **Dŏrkas**, *dor-kas´; gazelle; Dorcas,* a Chr. woman:— Dorcas.

1394. δόσις **dŏsis**, *dos´-is;* from the base of *1325;* a *giving;* by impl. (concr.) a *gift:*— gift, giving.

1395. δότης **dŏtēs**, *dot´-ace;* from the base of *1325;* a *giver:*— giver.

1396. δουλαγωγέω **dŏulagōgĕō**, *doo-lag-ogue-eh´-o;* from a presumed compound of *1401* and *71;* to *be a slave-driver,* i.e. to *enslave* (fig. *subdue*):— bring into subjection.

1397. δουλεία **dŏulĕia**, *doo-li´-ah;* from *1398; slavery* (cerem. or fig.):— bondage.

1398. δουλεύω **dŏulĕuō**, *dool-yoo´-o;* from *1401;* to *be a slave* to (lit. or fig., invol. or vol.):— be in bondage, (do) serve (-ice).

1399. δούλη **dŏulē**, *doo´-lay;* fem. of *1401;* a *female slave* (invol. or vol.):— handmaid (-en).

1400. δοῦλον **dŏulŏn**, *doo´-lon;* neut. of *1401; subservient:*— servant.

1401. δοῦλος **dŏulŏs**, *doo´-los;* from *1210;* a *slave* (lit. or fig., invol. or vol.; frequently, therefore in a qualified sense of *subjection* or *subserviency*):— bond (-man), servant.

1402. δουλόω **dŏulŏō**, *doo-lŏ´-o;* from 1401; to *enslave* (lit. or fig.):— bring into (be under) bondage, × given, become (make) servant.

1403. δοχή **dŏchē**, *dokh-ay´;* from 1209; a *reception,* i.e. convivial *entertainment:*— feast.

1404. δράκων **drakōn**, *drak´-own;* prob. from an alt. form of δέρκομαι **dĕrkŏmai** (to *look*); a fabulous kind of *serpent* (perh. as supposed to *fascinate*):— dragon.

1405. δράσσομαι **drassŏmai**, *dras´-som-ahee;* perh. akin to the base of 1404 (through the idea of *capturing*); to *grasp,* i.e. (fig.) *entrap:*— take.

1406. δραχμή **drachmē**, *drakh-may´;* from 1405; a *drachma* or (silver) coin (as *handled*):— piece (of silver).

δρέμω **drĕmō**. See 5143.

1407. δρέπανον **drĕpanŏn**, *drep´-an-on;* from δρέπω **drĕpō** (to *pluck*); a *gathering hook* (espec. for harvesting):— sickle.

1408. δρόμος **drŏmŏs**, *drom´-os;* from the alt. of 5143; a *race,* i.e. (fig.) *career:*— course.

1409. Δρούσιλλα **Drŏusilla**, *droo´-sil-lah;* a fem. dimin. of *Drusus* (a Rom. name); *Drusilla,* a member of the Herodian family:— Drusilla.

δύμι **dumi**. See 1416.

1410. δύναμαι **dunamai**, *doo´-nam-ahee;* of uncert. aff.; to *be able* or *possible:*— be able, can (do, + -not), could, may, might, be possible, be of power.

1411. δύναμις **dunamis**, *doo´-nam-is;* from 1410; *force* (lit. or fig.); spec. miraculous *power* (usually by impl. a *miracle* itself):— ability, abundance, meaning, might (-ily, -y, -y deed), (worker of) miracle (-s), power, strength, violence, mighty (wonderful) work.

1412. δυναμόω **dunamŏō**, *doo-nam-ŏ´-o;* from 1411; to *enable:*— strengthen.

1413. δυνάστης **dunastēs**, *doo-nas´-tace;* from 1410; a *ruler* or *officer:*— of great authority, mighty, potentate.

1414. δυνατέω **dunatĕō**, *doo-nat-eh´-o;* from 1415; to *be efficient* (fig.):— be mighty.

1415. δυνατός **dunatŏs**, *doo-nat-os´;* from 1410; *powerful* or *capable* (lit. or fig.); neut. *possible:*— able, could, (that is) mighty (man), possible, power, strong.

1416. δύνω **dunō**, *doo´-no;* or

δύμι **dumi**, *doo´-mee;* prol. forms of an obsolete primary δύω **duō**, *doo´-o* (to *sink*); to *go "down":*— set.

1417. δύο **duō**, *doo´-ō;* a primary numeral; *"two":*— both, twain, two.

1418. δυσ- **dus-**, *doos;* a primary inseparable particle of uncert. der.; used only in composition as a pref.; *hard,* i.e. *with difficulty:*— + hard, + grievous, etc.

1419. δυσβάστακτος **dusbastaktŏs**, *doos-bas´-tak-tos;* from 1418 and a der.

of 941; *oppressive:*— grievous to be borne.

1420. δυσεντερία **dusĕntĕria**, *doos-en-ter-ee´-ah;* from 1418 and a comp. of 1787 (mean. a *bowel*); a *"dysentery":*— bloody flux.

1421. δυσερμήνευτος **dusĕrmēnĕutŏs**, *doos-er-mane´-yoo-tos;* from 1418 and a presumed der. of 2059; *difficult of explanation:*— hard to be uttered.

1422. δύσκολος **duskŏlŏs**, *doos´-kol-os;* from 1418 and κόλον **kŏlŏn** (*food*); prop. *fastidious about eating* (peevish), i.e. (gen.) *impracticable:*— hard.

1423. δυσκόλως **duskŏlōs**, *doos-kol´-oce;* adv. from 1422; *impracticably:*— hardly.

1424. δυσμή **dusmē**, *doos-may´;* from 1416; the *sun-set,* i.e. (by impl.) the *western* region:— west.

1425. δυσνόητος **dusnŏētŏs**, *doos-no´-ay-tos;* from 1418 and a der. of 3539; *difficult of perception:*— hard to be understood.

1426. δυσφημία **dusphēmia**, *doos-fay-mee´-ah;* from a compound of 1418 and 5345; *defamation:*— evil report.

δύω **duō**. See 1416.

1427. δώδεκα **dōdĕka**, *do´-dek-ah;* from 1417 and 1176; *two* and *ten,* i.e. a *dozen:*— twelve.

1428. δωδέκατος **dōdĕkatŏs**, *do-dek´-at-os;* from 1427; *twelfth:*— twelfth.

1429. δωδεκάφυλον **dōdĕkaphulŏn**, *do-dek-af´-oo-lon;* from 1427 and 5443; the *commonwealth* of Israel:— twelve tribes.

1430. δῶμα **dōma**, *do´-mah;* from δέμω **dĕmō** (to *build*); prop. an *edifice,* i.e. (spec.) a *roof:*— housetop.

1431. δωρεά **dōrĕa**, *do-reh-ah´;* from 1435; a *gratuity:*— gift.

1432. δωρεάν **dōrĕan**, *do-reh-an´;* acc. of 1431 as adv.; *gratuitously* (lit. or fig.):— without a cause, freely, for naught, in vain.

1433. δωρέομαι **dōrĕŏmai**, *do-reh´-om-ahee;* mid. voice from 1435; to *bestow* gratuitously:— give.

1434. δώρημα **dōrēma**, *do´-ray-mah;* from 1433; a *bestowment:*— gift.

1435. δῶρον **dōrŏn**, *do´-ron;* a *present;* spec. a *sacrifice:*— gift, offering.

E

1436. ἔα **ĕa**, *eh´-ah;* appar. imper. of 1439; prop. *let it be,* i.e. (as interj.) *aha!:*— let alone.

1437. ἐάν **ĕan**, *eh-an´;* from 1487 and 302; a *conditional* particle; *in case that, provided,* etc.; often used in connection with other particles to denote *indefiniteness* or *uncertainty:*— before, but, except, (and) if, (if so, (what-, whither-) soever, though, when (-soever), whether (or), to whom, [who-] so (-ever). See 3361.

ἐάν μή **ĕan mē**. See 3361 and 3362.

1438. ἑαυτοῦ **hĕautŏu**, *heh-ow-too´* (incl. all other cases); from a refl. pron. otherwise obs. and the gen. (dat. or

acc.) of 846; *him-* (*her-, it-, them-,* also [in conjunction with the pers. pron. of the other persons] *my-, thy-, our-, your-*) *self* (*selves*), etc.:— alone, her (own, -self), (he) himself, his (own), itself, one (to) another, our (thine) own (-selves), + that she had, their (own, own selves), (of) them (-selves), they, thyself, you, your (own, own conceits, own selves, -selves).

1439. ἐάω **ĕaō**, *eh-ah´-o;* of uncert. aff.; to *let be,* i.e. *permit* or *leave* alone:— commit, leave, let (alone), suffer. See also 1436.

1440. ἑβδομήκοντα **hĕbdŏmēkŏnta**, *heb-dom-ay´-kon-tah;* from 1442 and a modified form of 1176; *seventy:*— seventy, three score and ten.

1441. ἑβδομηκοντάκις **hĕbdŏmēkŏntakis**, *heb-dom-ay-kon-tak-is;* multiple adv. from 1440; *seventy times:*— seventy times.

1442. ἕβδομος **hĕbdŏmŏs**, *heb´-dom-os;* ord. from 2033; *seventh:*— seventh.

1443. Ἑβέρ **Ĕbĕr**, *eb´-er;* of Heb. or. [5677]; *Eber,* a patriarch:— Eber.

1444. Ἑβραϊκός **Hĕbraïkŏs**, *heb-rah-ee-kos´;* from 1443; *Hebraïc* or the *Jewish* language:— Hebrew (Aramaic).

1445. Ἑβραῖος **Hĕbraiŏs**, *heb-rah´-yos;* from 1443; a *Hebræan* (i.e. Hebrew) or *Jew:*— Hebrew.

1446. Ἑβραΐς **Hĕbraïs**, *heb-rah-is´;* from 1443; the *Hebraistic* (i.e. *Hebrew*) or *Jewish* (*Chaldee*) language:— Hebrew (Aramaic).

1447. Ἑβραϊστί **Hĕbraïsti**, *heb-rah-is-tee´;* adv. from 1446; *Hebraistically* or in the Jewish (Chaldee) language:— in (the) Hebrew (tongue).

1448. ἐγγίζω **ĕggizō**, *eng-id´-zo;* from 1451; to *make near,* i.e. (refl.) *approach:*— approach, be at hand, come (draw) near, be (come, draw) nigh.

1449. ἐγγράφω **ĕggraphō**, *eng-graf´-o;* from 1722 and 1125; to *"engrave,"* i.e. *inscribe:*— write (in).

1450. ἔγγυος **ĕgguŏs**, *eng´-goo-os;* from 1722 and γυῖον **guiŏn** (a *limb*); *pledged* (as if *articulated* by a member), i.e. a *bondsman:*— surety.

1451. ἐγγύς **ĕggus**, *eng-goos´;* from a primary verb ἄγχω **agchō** (to *squeeze* or *throttle;* akin to the base of 43); *near* (lit. or fig., of place or time):— from, at hand, near, nigh (at hand, unto), ready.

1452. ἐγγύτερον **ĕggutĕrŏn**, *eng-goo´-ter-on;* neut. of the comp. of 1451; *nearer:*— nearer.

1453. ἐγείρω **ĕgeirō**, *eg-i´-ro;* prob. akin to the base of 58 (through the idea of *collecting* one's faculties); to *waken* (tran. or intr.), i.e. *rouse* (lit. from sleep, from sitting or lying, from disease, from death; or fig. from obscurity, inactivity, ruins, nonexistence):— awake, lift (up), raise (again, up), rear up, (a-) rise (again, up), stand, take up.

1454. ἔγερσις **ĕgersis**, *eg´-er-sis;* from 1453; a *resurgence* (from death):— resurrection.

1455. ἐγκάθετος **ĕgkathĕtŏs**, *eng-kath´-et-os;* from 1722 and a der. of 2524;

subinduced, i.e. surreptitiously *suborned* as a lier-in-wait:— spy.

1456. ἐγκαίνια ĕgkainia, *eng-kah'-ee-nee-ah*; neut. plur. of a presumed compound from 1722 and 2537; *innovatives*, i.e. (spec.) *renewal* (of relig. services after the Antiochian interruption):— dedication.

1457. ἐγκαινίζω ĕgkainizō, *eng-kahee-nid'-zo*; from 1456; to *renew*, i.e. *inaugurate*:— consecrate, dedicate.

1458. ἐγκαλέω ĕgkalĕō, *eng-kal-eh'-o*; from 1722 and 2564; to *call in* (as a debt or demand), i.e. *bring to account* (*charge, criminate*, etc.):— accuse, call in question, implead, lay to the charge.

1459. ἐγκαταλείπω ĕgkatalĕipō, *eng-kat-al-i'-po*; from 1722 and 2641; to *leave behind* in some place, i.e. (in a good sense) *let remain over*, or (in a bad sense) to *desert*:— forsake, leave.

1460. ἐγκατοικέω ĕgkatŏikĕō, *eng-kat-oy-keh'-o*; from 1722 and 2730; to *settle down* in a place, i.e. *reside*:— dwell among.

1461. ἐγκεντρίζω ĕgkĕntrizō, *eng-ken-trid'-zo*; from 1722 and a der. of 2759; to *prick in*, i.e. *ingraft*:— graff in (-to).

1462. ἔγκλημα ĕgklēma, *eng'-klay-mah*; from 1458; an *accusation*, i.e. *offence* alleged:— crime laid against, laid to charge.

1463. ἐγκομβόομαι ĕgkŏmbŏŏmai, *eng-kom-bŏ'-om-ahee*; mid. voice from 1722 and κομβόω kŏmbŏō (to *gird*); to *engirdle* oneself (for labor), i.e. fig. (the apron being a badge of servitude) to *wear* (in token of mutual deference):— be clothed with.

1464. ἐγκοπή ĕgkŏpē, *eng-kop-ay'*; from 1465; a *hindrance*:— × hinder.

1465. ἐγκόπτω ĕgkŏptō, *eng-kop'-to*; from 1722 and 2875; to *cut into*, i.e. (fig.) *impede, detain*:— hinder, be tedious unto.

1466. ἐγκράτεια ĕgkratĕia, *eng-krat'-i-ah*; from 1468; *self-control* (espec. *continence*):— temperance.

1467. ἐγκρατεύομαι ĕgkratĕuŏmai, *eng-krat-yoo'-om-ahee*; mid. voice from 1468; to *exercise self-restraint* (in diet and chastity):— can (l-not) contain, be temperate.

1468. ἐγκρατής ĕgkratēs, *eng-krat-ace'*; from 1722 and 2904; *strong in a thing* (*masterful*), i.e. (fig. and refl.) *self-controlled* (in appetite, etc.):— temperate.

1469. ἐγκρίνω ĕgkrinō, *eng-kree'-no*; from 1722 and 2919; to *judge in*, i.e. *count* among:— make of the number.

1470. ἐγκρύπτω ĕgkruptō, *eng-kroop'-to*; from 1722 and 2928; to *conceal in*, i.e. *incorporate with*:— hid in.

1471. ἔγκυος ĕgkuŏs, *eng'-koo-os*; from 1722 and the base of 2949; *swelling inside*, i.e. *pregnant*:— great with child.

1472. ἐγχρίω ĕgchriō, *eng-khree'-o*; from 1722 and 5548; to *rub in* (oil), i.e. *besmear*:— anoint.

1473. ἐγώ ĕgō, *eg-o'*; a primary pron. of the first pers. *I* (only expressed when emphatic):— I, me. For the other cases and the plur. see 1691, 1698, 1700, 2248, 2249, 2254, 2257, etc.

1474. ἐδαφίζω ĕdaphizō, *ed-af-id'-zo*; from 1475; to *raze*:— lay even with the ground.

1475. ἔδαφος ĕdaphŏs, *ed'-af-os*; from the base of 1476; a *basis* (*bottom*), i.e. the *soil*:— ground.

1476. ἑδραῖος hĕdraiŏs, *hed-rah'-yos*; from a der. of ἕζομαι hĕzŏmai (to *sit*); *sedentary*, i.e. (by impl.) *immovable*:— settled, stedfast.

1477. ἑδραίωμα hĕdraiōma, *hed-rah'-yo-mah*; from a der. of 1476; a *support*, i.e. (fig.) *basis*:— ground.

1478. Ἐζεκίας Ĕzĕkias, *ed-zek-ee'-as*; of Heb. or. [2396]; *Ezekias* (i.e. *Hezekiah*), an Isr.:— Ezekias.

1479. ἐθελοθρησκεία ĕthĕlŏthrēskĕia, *eth-el-oth-race-ki'-ah*; from 2309 and 2356; *voluntary* (*arbitrary* and *unwarranted*) *piety*, i.e. *sanctimony*:— will worship.

ἐθέλω ĕthĕlō. See 2309.

1480. ἐθίζω ĕthizō, *eth-id'-zo*; from 1485; to *accustom*, i.e. (neut. pass. part.) *customary*:— custom.

1481. ἐθνάρχης ĕthnarchēs, *eth-nar'-khace*; from 1484 and 746; the *governor* [not king] *of a district*:— ethnarch.

1482. ἐθνικός ĕthnikŏs, *eth-nee-kos'*; from 1484; *national* ("ethnic"), i.e. (spec.) a *Gentile*:— heathen (man).

1483. ἐθνικῶς ĕthnikōs, *eth-nee-koce'*; adv. from 1482; *as a Gentile*:— after the manner of Gentiles.

1484. ἔθνος ĕthnŏs, *eth'-nos*; prob. from 1486; a *race* (as of the same *habit*), i.e. a *tribe*; spec. a *foreign* (*non-Jewish*) one (usually by impl. *pagan*):— Gentile, heathen, nation, people.

1485. ἔθος ĕthŏs, *eth'-os*; from 1486; a *usage* (prescribed by habit or law):— custom, manner, be wont.

1486. ἔθω ĕthō, *eth'-o*; a primary verb; to *be used* (by habit or conventionality); neut. perfect part. *usage*:— be custom (manner, wont).

1487. εἰ ĕi, *i*; a primary particle of conditionality; *if, whether, that*, etc.:— forasmuch as, if, that, ((al-)though, whether. Often used in connection or composition with other particles, espec. as in 1489, 1490, 1499, 1508, 1509, 1512, 1513, 1536, 1537. See also 1437.

1488. εἶ ĕi, *i*; second pers. sing. present of 1510; thou *art*:— art, be.

1489. εἴγε ĕigĕ, *i'-gheh*; from 1487 and 1065; *if indeed, seeing that, unless*, (with neg.) *otherwise*:— if (so be that, yet).

1490. εἰ δὲ μή(γε) ĕi dĕ mē(gĕ) *i deh may'-(gheh)*; from 1487, 1161, and 3361 (sometimes with 1065 added); *but if not*:— (or) else, if (not, otherwise), otherwise.

1491. εἶδος ĕidŏs, *i'-dos*; from 1492; a *view*, i.e. *form* (lit. or fig.):— appearance, fashion, shape, sight.

1492. εἴδω ĕidō, *i'-do*; a primary verb; used only in certain past tenses, the others being borrowed from the equiv. 3700 and 3708; prop. to *see* (lit. or fig.); by impl. (in the perf. only) to *know*:— be aware, behold, × can (+ not tell), consider, (have) know (-ledge), look (on), perceive, see, be sure, tell, understand, wish, wot. Comp. 3700.

1493. εἰδωλεῖον ĕidōlĕion, *i-do-li'-on*; neut. of a presumed der. of 1497; an *image-fane*:— idol's temple.

1494. εἰδωλόθυτον ĕidōlŏthuton, *i-do-loth'-oo-ton*; neut. of a compound of 1497 and a presumed der. of 2380; an *image-sacrifice*, i.e. part of an *idolatrous offering*:— (meat, thing that is) offered (in sacrifice, sacrificed) to (unto) idols.

1495. εἰδωλολατρεία ĕidōlŏlatrĕia, *i-do-lol-at-ri'-ah*; from 1497 and 2999; *image-worship* (lit. or fig.):— idolatry.

1496. εἰδωλολάτρης ĕidōlŏlatrēs, *i-do-lol-at'-race*; from 1497 and the base of 3000; an *image-*(*servant* or) *worshipper* (lit. or fig.):— idolater.

1497. εἴδωλον ĕidōlŏn, *i'-do-lon*; from 1491; an *image* (i.e. for worship); by impl. a heathen *god*, or (plur.) the *worship* of such:— idol.

1498. εἴην ĕiēn, *i'-ane*; optative (i.e. English subjunctive) present of 1510 (incl. the other pers.); *might* (*could, would*, or *should*) *be*:— mean, + perish, should be, was, were.

1499. εἰ καί ĕi kai, *i kahee*; from 1487 and 2532; *if also* (or *even*):— if (that), though.

1500. εἰκῆ ĕikē, *i-kay'*; prob. from 1502 (through the idea of *failure*); *idly*, i.e. *without reason* (or *effect*):— without a cause, (in) vain (-ly).

1501. εἴκοσι ĕikŏsi, *i'-kos-ee*; of uncert. aff.; a *score*:— twenty.

1502. εἴκω ĕikō, *i'-ko*; appar. a primary verb; prop. to *be weak*, i.e. *yield*:— give place.

1503. εἴκω ĕikō, *i'-ko*; appar. a primary verb [perh. akin to 1502 through the idea of *faintness* as a copy]; to *resemble*:— be like.

1504. εἰκών ĕikōn, *i-kone'*; from 1503; a *likeness*, i.e. (lit.) *statue, profile*, or (fig.) *representation, resemblance*:— image.

1505. εἰλικρίνεια ĕilikrinĕia, *i-lik-ree'-ni-ah*; from 1506; *clearness*, i.e. (by impl.) *purity* (fig.):— sincerity.

1506. εἰλικρινής ĕilikrinēs, *i-lik-ree-nace'*; from εἴλη hĕilē (the sun's *ray*) and 2919; *judged by sunlight*, i.e. tested as *genuine* (fig.):— pure, sincere.

1507. εἰλίσσω ĕilissō, *hi-lis'-so*; a prol. form of a primary but defective verb εἴλω hĕilō (of the same mean.); to *coil* or *wrap*:— roll together. See also 1667.

1508. εἰ μή ĕi mē, *i may*; from 1487 and 3361; *if not*:— but, except (that), if not, more than, save (only) that, saving, till.

1509. εἰ μή τι ĕi mē ti, *i may tee*; from 1508 and the neut. of 5100; *if not somewhat*:— except.

1510. εἰμί ĕimi, *i-mee'*; the first pers. sing. present ind.; a prol. form of a primary and defective verb; *I exist* (used only when emphatic):— am, have been, × it is I, was. See also 1488, 1498, 1511,

2258, 2071, 2070, 2075, 2076, 2771, 2468, 5600, 5607.

1511. εἶναι **ĕinai**, *i´-nahee;* present infin. from 1510; to *exist:*— am, are, come, is, × lust after, × please well, there is, to be, was.

εἵνεκεν **hĕinĕkĕn**. See 1752.

1512. εἴ περ **ĕi pĕr**, *i per;* from 1487 and 4007; *if perhaps:*— if so be (that), seeing, though.

1513. εἴ πως **ĕi pōs**, *i poce;* from 1487 and 4458; *if somehow:*— if by any means.

1514. εἰρηνεύω **ĕirēnĕuō**, *i-rane-yoo´-o;* from 1515; to *be* (*act*) *peaceful:*— be at (have, live in) peace, live peaceably.

1515. εἰρήνη **ĕirēnē**, *i-ray´-nay;* prob. from a primary verb εἴρω **ĕirō** (to *join*); *peace* (lit. or fig.); by impl. *prosperity:*— one, peace, quietness, rest, + set at one again.

1516. εἰρηνικός **ĕirēnikŏs**, *i-ray-nee-kos´;* from 1515; *pacific;* by impl. *salutary:*— peaceable.

1517. εἰρηνοποιέω **ĕirēnŏpŏiĕō**, *i-ray-nop-oy-eh´-o;* from 1518; to *be a peacemaker,* i.e. (fig.) to *harmonize:*— make peace.

1518. εἰρηνοποιός **ĕirēnŏpŏiŏs**, *i-ray-nop-oy-os´;* from 1515 and 4160; *pacificatory,* i.e. (subj.) *peaceable:*— peacemaker.

εἴρω **ĕirō**. See 1515, 4483, 5346.

1519. εἰς **ĕis**, *ice;* a primary prep.; *to* or *into* (indicating the point reached or entered), of place, time, or (fig.) purpose (result, etc.); also in adv. phrases:— [abundant-] ly, against, among, as, at, [back-] ward, before, by, concerning, + continual, + far more exceeding, for [intent, purpose], fore, + forth, in (among, at, unto, -so much that,to), to the intent that, + of one mind, + never, of, (up-) on, + perish, + set at one again, (so) that, therefore (-unto), throughout, till, to (be, the end, -ward), (here-) until (-to), ... ward, [where-] fore, with. Often used in composition with the same general import, but only with verbs (etc.) expressing motion (lit. or fig.).

1520. εἷς **hĕis**, *hice;* (incl. the neut. [etc.] ἔν **hĕn**); a primary numeral; *one:*— a (-n, -ny, certain), + abundantly, man, one (another), only, other, some. See also 1527, 3367, 3391, 3762.

1521. εἰσάγω **ĕisagō**, *ice-ag´-o;* from 1519 and 71; to *introduce* (lit. or fig.):— bring in (-to), (+ was to) lead into.

1522. εἰσακούω **ĕisakŏuō**, *ice-ak-oo´-o;* from 1519 and 191; to *listen to:*— hear.

1523. εἰσδέχομαι **ĕisdĕchŏmai**, *ice-dekh´-om-ahee;* from 1519 and 1209; to *take into* one's favor:— receive.

1524. εἴσειμι **ĕisĕimi**, *ice´-i-mee;* from 1519 and εἶμι **ĕimi** (to go); to *enter:*— enter (go) into.

1525. εἰσέρχομαι **ĕisĕrchŏmai**, *ice-er´-khom-ahee;* from 1519 and 2064; to *enter* (lit. or fig.):— × arise, come (in, into), enter in (-to), go in (through).

1526. εἰσί **ĕisi**, *i-see´;* third pers. plur.

present ind. of 1510; they *are:*— agree, are, be, dure, × is, were.

1527. εἷς καθ᾽ εἷς **hĕis kath' hĕis**, *hice kath hice;* from 1520 repeated with 2596 inserted; *severally:*— one by one.

1528. εἰσκαλέω **ĕiskalĕō**, *ice-kal-eh´-o;* from 1519 and 2564; to *invite* in:— call in.

1529. εἴσοδος **ĕisŏdŏs**, *ice´-od-os;* from 1519 and 3598; an *entrance* (lit. or fig.):— coming, enter (-ing) in (to).

1530. εἰσπηδάω **ĕispēdaō**, *ice-pay-dah´-o;* from 1519 and πηδάω **pēdaō** (to *leap*); to *rush in:*— run (spring) in.

1531. εἰσπορεύομαι **ĕispŏrĕuŏmai**, *ice-por-yoo´-om-ahee;* from 1519 and 4198; to *enter* (lit. or fig.):— come (enter) in, go into.

1532. εἰστρέχω **ĕistrĕchō**, *ice-trekh´-o;* from 1519 and 5143; to *hasten inward:*— run in.

1533. εἰσφέρω **ĕisphĕrō**, *ice-fer´-o;* from 1519 and 5342; to *carry inward* (lit. or fig.):— bring (in), lead into.

1534. εἶτα **ĕita**, *i´-tah;* of uncert. aff.; a particle of *succession* (in time or logical enumeration), *then, moreover:*— after that (-ward), furthermore, then. See also 1899.

1535. εἴτε **ĕitĕ**, *i´-teh;* from 1487 and 5037; *if too:*— if, or, whether.

1536. εἴ τις **ĕi tis**, *i tis;* from 1487 and 5100; *if any:*— he that, if a (-ny) man ('s, thing, from any, ought), whether any, whosoever.

1537. ἐκ **ĕk**, *ek* or

ἐξ **ĕx**, *ex;* a primary prep. denoting *origin* (the point *whence* motion or action proceeds), *from, out* (of place, time, or cause; lit. or fig.; direct or remote):— after, among, × are, at, betwixt (-yond), by (the means of), exceedingly, (+ abundantly above), for (-th), from (among, forth, up), + grudgingly, + heartily, × heavenly, × hereby, + very highly, in, ... ly, (because, by reason) of, off (from), on, out among (from, of), over, since, × thenceforth, through, × unto, × vehemently, with (-out). Often used in composition, with the same general import; often of completion.

1538. ἕκαστος **hĕkastŏs**, *hek´-as-tos;* as if a superl. of ἕκας **hĕkas** (*afar*); *each* or *every:*— any, both, each (one), every (man, one, woman), particularly.

1539. ἑκάστοτε **hĕkastŏtĕ**, *hek-as´-tot-eh;* as if from 1538 and 5119; at *every time:*— always.

1540. ἑκατόν **hĕkatŏn**, *hek-at-on´;* of uncert. aff.; a *hundred:*— hundred.

1541. ἑκατονταέτης **hĕkatŏntaĕtēs**, *hek-at-on-tah-et´-ace;* from 1540 and 2094; *centenarian:*— hundred years old.

1542. ἑκατονταπλασίων **hĕkatŏntaplasiōn**, *hek-at-on-ta-plah-see´-own;* from 1540 and a presumed der. of 4111; *a hundred times:*— hundredfold.

1543. ἑκατοντάρχης **hĕkatŏntarchēs**, *hek-at-on-tar´-khace;* or

ἑκατόνταρχος **hĕkatŏntarchŏs**, *hek-at-on´-tar-khos;* from 1540 and

757; the *captain of one hundred men:*— centurion.

1544. ἐκβάλλω **ĕkballō**, *ek-bal´-lo;* from 1537 and 906; to *eject* (lit. or fig.):— bring forth, cast (forth, out), drive (out), expel, leave, pluck (pull, take, thrust) out, put forth (out), send away (forth, out).

1545. ἔκβασις **ĕkbasis**, *ek´-bas-is;* from a compound of 1537 and the base of 939 (mean. to *go out*); an *exit* (lit. or fig.):— end, way to escape.

1546. ἐκβολή **ĕkbŏlē**, *ek-bol-ay´;* from 1544; *ejection,* i.e. (spec.) a *throwing overboard* of the cargo:— + lighten the ship.

1547. ἐκγαμίζω **ĕkgamizō**, *ek-gam-id´-zo;* from 1537 and a form of 1061 [comp. 1548]; to *marry off* a daughter:— give in marriage.

1548. ἐκγαμίσκω **ĕkgamiskō**, *ek-gam-is´-ko;* from 1537 and 1061; the same as 1547:— give in marriage.

1549. ἔκγονον **ĕkgŏnŏn**, *ek´-gon-on;* neut. of a der. of a compound of 1537 and 1096; a *descendant,* i.e. (spec.) *grandchild:*— nephew.

1550. ἐκδαπανάω **ĕkdapanaō**, *ek-dap-an-ah´-o;* from 1537 and 1159; to *expend* (wholly), i.e. (fig.) *exhaust:*— spend.

1551. ἐκδέχομαι **ĕkdĕchŏmai**, *ek-dekh´-om-ahee;* from 1537 and 1209; to *accept from* some source, i.e. (by impl.) to *await:*— expect, look (tarry) for, wait (for).

1552. ἔκδηλος **ĕkdēlŏs**, *ek´-day-los;* from 1537 and 1212; *wholly evident:*— manifest.

1553. ἐκδημέω **ĕkdēmĕō**, *ek-day-meh´-o;* from a compound of 1537 and 1218; to *emigrate,* i.e. (fig.) *vacate* or *quit:*— be absent.

1554. ἐκδίδωμι **ĕkdidōmi**, *ek-did-o´-mee;* from 1537 and 1325; to *give forth,* i.e. (spec.) to *lease:*— let forth (out).

1555. ἐκδιηγέομαι **ĕkdiēgĕŏmai**, *ek-dee-ayg-eh´-om-ahee;* from 1537 and a compound of 1223 and 2233; to *narrate* through wholly:— declare.

1556. ἐκδικέω **ĕkdikĕō**, *ek-dik-eh´-o;* from 1558; to *vindicate, retaliate, punish:*— a (re-) venge.

1557. ἐκδίκησις **ĕkdikēsis**, *ek-dik´-ay-sis;* from 1556; *vindication, retribution:*— (a-, re-) venge (-ance), punishment.

1558. ἔκδικος **ĕkdikŏs**, *ek´-dik-os;* from 1537 and 1349; carrying *justice* out, i.e. a *punisher:*— a (re-) venger.

1559. ἐκδιώκω **ĕkdiōkō**, *ek-dee-o´-ko;* from 1537 and 1377; to *pursue out,* i.e. *expel* or *persecute* implacably:— persecute.

1560. ἔκδοτος **ĕkdŏtŏs**, *ek´-dot-os;* from 1537 and a der. of 1325; *given out* or *over,* i.e. *surrendered:*— delivered.

1561. ἐκδοχή **ĕkdŏchē**, *ek-dokh-ay´;* from 1551; *expectation:*— looking for.

1562. ἐκδύω **ĕkduō**, *ek-doo´-o;* from 1537 and the base of 1416; to *cause to sink out of,* i.e. (spec. as of clothing) to *divest:*— strip, take off from, unclothe.

1563. ἐκεῖ **ĕkĕi**, ek-i´; of uncert. aff.; *there*; by extens. *thither:*— there, thither (-ward), (to) yonder (place).

1564. ἐκεῖθεν **ĕkĕithĕn**, ek-i´-then; from 1563; *thence:*— from that place, (from) thence, there.

1565. ἐκεῖνος **ĕkĕinŏs**, ek-i´-nos; from 1563; *that* one (or [neut.] thing); often intensified by the art. prefixed:— he, it, the other (same), selfsame, that (same, very), × their, × them, they, this, those. See also 3778.

1566. ἐκεῖσε **ĕkĕisĕ**, ek-i´-seh; from 1563; *thither:*— there.

1567. ἐκζητέω **ĕkzētĕō**, ek-zay-teh´-o; from 1537 and 2212; to *search out*, i.e. (fig.) *investigate, crave, demand,* (by Heb.) *worship:*— en- (re-) quire, seek after (carefully, diligently).

1568. ἐκθαμβέω **ĕkthambĕō**, ek-tham-beh´-o; from 1569; to *astonish* utterly:— affright, greatly (sore) amaze.

1569. ἔκθαμβος **ĕkthambŏs**, ek´-tham-bos; from 1537 and 2285; *utterly astounded:*— greatly wondering.

1570. ἔκθετος **ĕkthĕtŏs**, ek´-thet-os; from 1537 and a der. of 5087; *put out,* i.e. *exposed* to perish:— cast out.

1571. ἐκκαθαίρω **ĕkkathairō**, ek-kath-ah´-ee-ro; from 1537 and 2508; to *cleanse thoroughly:*— purge (out).

1572. ἐκκαίω **ĕkkaiō**, ek-kah´-yo; from 1537 and 2545; to *inflame* deeply:— burn.

1573. ἐκκακέω **ĕkkakĕō**, ek-kak-eh´-o or ἐγκακέω **egkakĕō** eng-kak-eh´-o; from 1537 and 2556; to *be* (*bad* or) *weak*, i.e. (by impl.) to *fail* (in heart):— faint, be weary.

1574. ἐκκεντέω **ĕkkĕntĕō**, ek-ken-teh´-o; from 1537 and the base of 2759; to *transfix:*— pierce.

1575. ἐκκλάω **ĕkklaō**, ek-klah´-o; from 1537 and 2806; to *exscind:*— break off.

1576. ἐκκλείω **ĕkklĕiō**, ek-kli´-o; from 1537 and 2808; to *shut out* (lit. or fig.):— exclude.

1577. ἐκκλησία **ĕkklēsia**, ek-klay-see´-ah; from a compound of 1537 and a der. of 2564; a *calling out*, i.e. (concr.) a popular *meeting*, espec. a religious *congregation* (Jewish *synagogue*, or Chr. community of members on earth or saints in heaven or both):— assembly, church.

1578. ἐκκλίνω **ĕkklinō**, ek-klee´-no; from 1537 and 2827; to *deviate*, i.e. (absolutely) to *shun* (lit. or fig.), or (rel.) to *decline* (from piety):— avoid, eschew, go out of the way.

1579. ἐκκολυμβάω **ĕkkŏlumbaō**, ek-kol-oom-bah´-o; from 1537 and 2860; to *escape* by *swimming:*— swim out.

1580. ἐκκομίζω **ĕkkŏmizō**, ek-kom-id´-zo; from 1537 and 2865; to *bear forth* (to burial):— carry out.

1581. ἐκκόπτω **ĕkkŏptō**, ek-kop´-to; from 1537 and 2875; to *exscind*; fig. to *frustrate:*— cut down (off, out), hew down, hinder.

1582. ἐκκρέμαμαι **ĕkkrĕmamai**, ek-krem´-am-ahee; mid. voice from 1537 and 2910; to *hang upon* the lips of a speaker, i.e. *listen closely:*— be very attentive.

1583. ἐκλαλέω **ĕklalĕō**, ek-lal-eh´-o; from 1537 and 2980; to *divulge:*— tell.

1584. ἐκλάμπω **ĕklampō**, ek-lam´-po; from 1537 and 2989; to *be resplendent:*— shine forth.

1585. ἐκλανθάνομαι **ĕklanthanŏmai**, ek-lan-than´-om-ahee; mid. voice from 1537 and 2990; to *be* utterly *oblivious* of:— forget.

1586. ἐκλέγομαι **ĕklĕgŏmai**, ek-leg´-om-ahee; mid. voice from 1537 and 3004 (in its primary sense); to *select:*— make choice, choose (out), chosen.

1587. ἐκλείπω **ĕklĕipō**, ek-li´-po; from 1537 and 3007; to *omit*, i.e. (by impl.) *cease* (*die*):— fail.

1588. ἐκλεκτός **ĕklĕktŏs**, ek-lek-tos´; from 1586; *select*; by impl. *favorite:*— chosen, elect.

1589. ἐκλογή **ĕklŏgē**, ek-log-ay´; from 1586; (*divine*) *selection* (abstr. or concr.):— chosen, election.

1590. ἐκλύω **ĕkluō**, ek-loo´-o; from 1537 and 3089; to *relax* (lit. or fig.):— faint.

1591. ἐκμάσσω **ĕkmassō**, ek-mas´-so; from 1537 and the base of 3145; to *knead out*, i.e. (by anal.) to *wipe dry:*— wipe.

1592. ἐκμυκτερίζω **ĕkmuktĕrizō**, ek-mook-ter-id´-zo; from 1537 and 3456; to *sneer* outright at:— deride.

1593. ἐκνεύω **ĕknĕuō**, ek-nyoo´-o; from 1537 and 3506; (by anal.) to *slip off*, i.e. quietly *withdraw:*— convey self away.

1594. ἐκνήφω **ĕknēphō**, ek-nay´-fo; from 1537 and 3525; (fig.) to *rouse* (oneself) *out of* stupor:— awake.

1595. ἐκούσιον **hĕkousiŏn**, hek-oo´-see-on; neut. of a der. from 1635; *voluntarily:*— willingly.

1596. ἐκουσίως **hĕkŏusiōs**, hek-oo-see-oce; adv. from the same as 1595; *voluntarily:*— wilfully, willingly.

1597. ἔκπαλαι **ĕkpalai**, ek´-pal-ahee; from 1537 and 3819; *long ago, for a long while:*— of a long time, of old.

1598. ἐκπειράζω **ĕkpĕirazō**, ek-pi-rad´-zo; from 1537 and 3985; to *test thoroughly:*— tempt.

1599. ἐκπέμπω **ĕkpĕmpō**, ek-pem´-po; from 1537 and 3992; to *despatch:*— send away (forth).

ἐκπερισσοῦ **ĕkpĕrissŏu**. See 1537 and 4053.

1600. ἐκπετάννυμι **ĕkpĕtannumi**, ek-pet-an´-noo-mee; from 1537 and a form of 4072; to *fly out*, i.e. (by anal.) to *extend:*— stretch forth.

1601. ἐκπίπτω **ĕkpiptō**, ek-pip´-to; from 1537 and 4098; to *drop away*; spec., *be driven out* of one's course; fig. to *lose, become inefficient:*— be cast, fail, fall (away, off), take none effect.

1602. ἐκπλέω **ĕkplĕō**, ek-pleh´-o; from 1537 and 4126; to *depart* by ship:— sail (away, thence).

1603. ἐκπληρόω **ĕkplērŏō**, ek-play-ro´-o; from 1537 and 4137; to *accomplish* entirely:— fulfill.

1604. ἐκπλήρωσις **ĕkplērōsis**, ek-play´-ro-sis; from 1603; *completion:*— accomplishment.

1605. ἐκπλήσσω **ĕkplēssō**, ek-place´-so; from 1537 and 4141; to *strike* with astonishment:— amaze, astonish.

1606. ἐκπνέω **ĕkpnĕō**, ek-pneh´-o; from 1537 and 4154; to *expire:*— give up the ghost.

1607. ἐκπορεύομαι **ĕkpŏrĕuŏmai**, ek-por-yoo´-om-ahee; from 1537 and 4198; to *depart, be discharged, proceed, project:*— come (forth, out of), depart, go (forth, out), issue, proceed (out of).

1608. ἐκπορνεύω **ĕkpŏrnĕuō**, ek-porn-yoo´-o; from 1537 and 4203; to *be utterly unchaste:*— give self over to fornication.

1609. ἐκπτύω **ĕkptuō**, ek-ptoo´-o; from 1537 and 4429; to *spit out*, i.e. (fig.) *spurn:*— reject.

1610. ἐκριζόω **ĕkrizŏō**, ek-rid-zo´-o; from 1537 and 4492; to *uproot:*— pluck up by the root, root up.

1611. ἔκστασις **ĕkstasis**, ek´-stas-is; from 1839; a *displacement* of the mind, i.e. *bewilderment*, "*ecstasy*":— + be amazed, amazement, astonishment, trance.

1612. ἐκστρέφω **ĕkstrĕphō**, ek-stref´-o; from 1537 and 4762; to *pervert* (fig.):— subvert.

1613. ἐκταράσσω **ĕktarassō**, ek-tar-as´-so; from 1537 and 5015; to *disturb wholly:*— exceedingly trouble.

1614. ἐκτείνω **ĕktĕinō**, ek-ti´-no; from 1537 and τείνω **tĕinō** (to *stretch*); to *extend:*— cast, put forth, stretch forth (out).

1615. ἐκτελέω **ĕktĕlĕō**, ek-tel-eh´-o; from 1537 and 5055; to *complete* fully:— finish.

1616. ἐκτένεια **ĕktĕnĕia**, ek-ten-i´-ah; from 1618; *intentness:*— × instantly.

1617. ἐκτενέστερον **ĕktĕnĕstĕrŏn**, ek-ten-es´-ter-on; neut. of the comparative of 1618; *more intently:*— more earnestly.

1618. ἐκτενής **ĕktĕnēs**, ek-ten-ace´; from 1614; *intent:*— without ceasing, fervent.

1619. ἐκτενῶς **ĕktĕnōs**, ek-ten-oce´; adv. from 1618; *intently:*— fervently.

1620. ἐκτίθημι **ĕktithēmi**, ek-tith´-ay-mee; from 1537 and 5087; to *expose*; fig. to *declare:*— cast out, expound.

1621. ἐκτινάσσω **ĕktinassō**, ek-tin-as´-so; from 1537 and τινάσσω **tinassō** (to *swing*); to *shake* violently:— shake (off).

1622. ἐκτός **ĕktŏs**, ek-tos´; from 1537; the *exterior*; fig. (as a prep.) *aside from, besides:*— but, except (-ed), other than, out of, outside, unless, without.

1623. ἕκτος **hĕktŏs**, hek´-tos; ordinal from 1803; *sixth:*— sixth.

1624. ἐκτρέπω **ĕktrĕpō**, ek-trep´-o; from 1537 and the base of 5157; to *deflect*, i.e. *turn away* (lit. or fig.):— avoid, turn (aside, out of the way).

1625. ἐκτρέφω **ĕktrĕphō**, ek-tref´-o; from 1537 and 5142; to *rear up* to maturity, i.e. (gen.) to *cherish* or *train*:— bring up, nourish.

1626. ἔκτρωμα **ĕktrōma**, *ek´-tro-mah*; from a compound of *1537* and τιτρώσκω **titrōskō** (to *wound*); a *miscarriage* (*abortion*), i.e. (by anal.) *untimely birth*:— born out of due time.

1627. ἐκφέρω **ĕkphĕrō**, *ek-fer´-o*; from *1537* and *5342*; to *bear out* (lit. or fig.):— bear, bring forth, carry forth (out).

1628. ἐκφεύγω **ĕkphĕugō**, *ek-fyoo´-go*; from *1537* and *5343*; to *flee out*:— escape, flee.

1629. ἐκφοβέω **ĕkphŏbĕō**, *ek-fob-eh´-o*; from *1537* and *5399*; to *frighten utterly*:— terrify.

1630. ἔκφοβος **ĕkphŏbŏs**, *ek´-fob-os*; from *1537* and *5401*; *frightened out of* one's wits: sore afraid, exceedingly fear.

1631. ἐκφύω **ĕkphuō**, *ek-foo´-o*; from *1537* and *5453*; to *sprout up*:— put forth.

1632. ἐκχέω **ĕkchĕō**, *ek-kheh´-o*; or (by var.)

ἐκχύνω **ĕkchunō**, *ek-khoo´-no*; from *1537*; and χέω **chĕō** (to *pour*); to *pour forth*; fig. to *bestow*:— gush (pour) out, run greedily (out), shed (abroad, forth), spill.

1633. ἐκχωρέω **ĕkchōrĕō**, *ek-kho-reh´-o*; from *1537* and *5562*; to *depart*:— depart out.

1634. ἐκψύχω **ĕkpsuchō**, *ek-psoo´-kho*; from *1537* and *5594*; to *expire*:— give (yield) up the ghost.

1635. ἑκών **hĕkōn**, *hek-own´*; of uncert. aff.; *voluntary*:— willingly.

1636. ἐλαία **ĕlaia**, *el-ah´-yah*; fem. of a presumed der. from an obsolete primary; an *olive* (the tree or the fruit):— olive (berry, tree).

1637. ἔλαιον **ĕlaiŏn**, *el´-ah-yon*; neut. of the same as *1636*; olive *oil*:— oil.

1638. ἐλαιών **ĕlaiōn**, *el-ah-yone´*; from *1636*; an *olive-orchard*, i.e. (spec.) the *Mt. of Olives*:— Olivet.

1639. Ἐλαμίτης **Ĕlamitēs**, *el-am-ee´-tace*; of Heb. or. [5867]; an *Elamite* or *Persian*:— Elamite.

1640. ἐλάσσων **ĕlasson**, *el-as´-sone*; or

ἐλάττων **ĕlatton** *el-at-tone´*; comparative of the same as *1646*; *smaller* (in size, quantity, age or quality):— less, under, worse, younger.

1641. ἐλαττονέω **ĕlattŏnĕō**, *el-at-ton-eh-o*; from *1640*; to *diminish*, i.e. *fall short*:— have lack.

1642. ἐλαττόω **ĕlattŏō**, *el-at-tŏ´-o*; from *1640*; to *lessen* (in rank or influence):— decrease, make lower.

1643. ἐλαύνω **ĕlaunō**, *el-ŏw´-no*; a prol. form of a primary verb (obsolete except in certain tenses as an altern. of this) of uncert. affin; to *push* (as wind, oars or demoniacal power):— carry, drive, row.

1644. ἐλαφρία **ĕlaphria**, *el-af-ree´-ah*; from *1645*; *levity* (fig.), i.e. *fickleness*:— lightness.

1645. ἐλαφρός **ĕlaphrŏs**, *el-af-ros´*; prob. akin to *1643* and the base of *1640*; *light*, i.e. *easy*:— light.

1646. ἐλάχιστος **ĕlachistŏs**, *el-akh´-is-tos*; superl. of ἐλαχύς **ĕlachus** (*short*); used as equiv. to *3398*; *least* (in size, amount, dignity, etc.):— least, very little (small), smallest.

1647. ἐλαχιστότερος **ĕlachistŏtĕrŏs**, *el-akh-is-tot´-er-os*; comparative of *1646*; *far less*:— less than the least.

1648. Ἐλεάζαρ **Ĕlĕazar**, *el-eh-ad´-zar*; of Heb. or. [499]; *Eleazar*, an Isr.:— Eleazar.

1649. ἔλεγξις **ĕlĕgxis**, *el´-eng-xis*; from *1651*; *refutation*, i.e. *reproof*:— rebuke.

1650. ἔλεγχος **ĕlĕgchŏs**, *el´-eng-khos*; from *1651*; *proof*, *conviction*:— evidence, reproof.

1651. ἐλέγχω **ĕlĕgchō**, *el-eng´-kho*; of uncert. aff.; to *confute*, *admonish*:— convict, convince, tell a fault, rebuke, reprove.

1652. ἐλεεινός **ĕlĕĕinŏs**, *el-eh-i-nos´*; from *1656*; *pitiable*:— miserable.

1653. ἐλεέω **ĕlĕĕō**, *el-eh-eh´-o*; from *1656*; to *compassionate* (by word or deed, spec., by divine grace):— have compassion (pity on), have (obtain, receive, shew) mercy (on).

1654. ἐλεημοσύνη **ĕlĕĕmŏsunē**, *el-eh-ay-mos-oo´-nay*; from *1656*; *compassionateness*, i.e. (as exercised toward the poor) *beneficence*, or (concr.) a *benefaction*:— alms (-deeds).

1655. ἐλεήμων **ĕlĕēmōn**, *el-eh-ay´-mone*; from *1653*; *compassionate* (actively):— merciful.

1656. ἔλεος **ĕlĕŏs**, *el´-eh-os*; of uncert. aff.; *compassion* (human or divine, espec. active):— (+ tender) mercy.

1657. ἐλευθερία **ĕlĕuthĕria**, *el-yoo-ther-ee´-ah*; from *1658*; *freedom* (legitimate or licentious, chiefly mor. or cerem.):— liberty.

1658. ἐλεύθερος **ĕlĕuthĕrŏs**, *el-yoo´-ther-os*; prob. from the alt. of *2064*; *unrestrained* (to go at pleasure), i.e. (as a citizen) *not a slave* (whether *freeborn* or *manumitted*), or (gen.) *exempt* (from obligation or liability):— free (man, woman), at liberty.

1659. ἐλευθερόω **ĕlĕuthĕrŏō**, *el-yoo-ther-ŏ´-o*; from *1658*; to *liberate*, i.e. (fig.) to *exempt* (from mor., cerem. or mortal liability):— deliver, make free.

ἐλεύθω **ĕlĕuthō**. See *2064*.

1660. ἔλευσις **ĕlĕusis**, *el´-yoo-sis*; from the alt. of *2064*; an *advent*:— coming.

1661. ἐλεφάντινος **ĕlĕphantinŏs**, *el-ef-an´-tee-nos*; from ἔλεφας **ĕlĕphas** (an "*elephant*"); *elephantine*, i.e. (by impl.) composed of *ivory*:— of ivory.

1662. Ἐλιακείμ **Ĕliakĕim**, *el-ee-ak-ehm´* or Ἐλιακίμ **Ĕliakim** *el-ee-ak-ime´*; of Heb. or. [471]; *Eliakim*, an Isr.:— Eliakim.

1663. Ἐλιέζερ **Ĕliĕzĕr**, *el-ee-ed´-zer*; of Heb. or. [461]; *Eliezer*, an Isr.:— Eliezer.

1664. Ἐλιούδ **Ĕliŏud**, *el-ee-ood´*; of Heb. or. [410 and 1935]; *God of majesty*; *Eliud*, an Isr.:— Eliud.

1665. Ἐλισάβετ **Ĕlisabĕt**, *el-ee-sab´-et*; of Heb. or. [472]; *Elisabet*, an Israelitess:— Elisabeth.

1666. Ἐλισσαῖος **Ĕlissaiŏs**, *el-is-sah´-yos*; of Heb. or. [477]; *Elissæus*, an Isr.:— Elissæus.

1667. ἐλίσσω **hĕlissō**, *hel-is´-so*; a form of *1507*; to *coil* or *wrap*:— fold up.

1668. ἕλκος **hĕlkŏs**, *hel-kos*; prob. from *1670*; an *ulcer* (as if drawn together):— sore.

1669. ἑλκόω **hĕlkŏō**, *hel-kŏ´-o*; from *1668*; to *cause to ulcerate*, i.e. (pass.) *be ulcerous*:— full of sores.

1670. ἑλκύω **hĕlkuō**, *hel-koo´-o*; or

ἕλκω **hĕlkō**, *hel´-ko*; prob. akin to *138*; to *drag* (lit. or fig.):— draw. Comp. *1667*.

1671. Ἑλλάς **Hĕllas**, *hel-las´*; of uncert. aff.; *Hellas* (or *Greece*), a country of Europe:— Greece.

1672. Ἕλλην **Hĕllēn**, *hel´-lane*; from *1671*; a *Hellen* (*Grecian*) or inhab. of Hellas; by extens. a *Greek-speaking* person, espec. a *non-Jew*:— Gentile, Greek.

1673. Ἑλληνικός **Hĕllēnikŏs**, *hel-lay-nee-kos´*; from *1672*; *Hellenic*, i.e. *Grecian* (in language):— Greek.

1674. Ἑλληνίς **Hĕllēnis**, *hel-lay-nis´*; fem. of *1672*; a *Grecian* (i.e. *non-Jewish*) woman:— Greek.

1675. Ἑλληνιστής **Hĕllēnistēs**, *hel-lay-nis-tace´*; from a der. of *1672*; a *Hellenist* or Greek-speaking Jew:— Grecian.

1676. Ἑλληνιστί **Hĕllēnisti**, *hel-lay-nis-tee´*; adv. from the same as *1675*; *Hellenistically*, i.e. in the Grecian language:— Greek.

1677. ἐλλογέω **ĕllŏgĕō**, *el-log-eh´-o*; from *1722* and *3056* (in the sense of account); to *reckon in*, i.e. *attribute*:— impute, put on account.

ἔλλομαι **hĕllŏmai**. See *138*.

1678. Ἐλμωδάμ **Ĕlmōdam**, *el-mo-dam´*; of Heb. or. [perh. for 486]; *Elmodam*, an Isr.:— Elmodam.

1679. ἐλπίζω **ĕlpizō**, *el-pid´-zo*; from *1680*; to *expect* or *confide*:— (have, thing) hope (-d) (for), trust.

1680. ἐλπίς **ĕlpis**, *el-pece´*; from a primary ἔλπω **ĕlpō** (to *anticipate*, usually with pleasure); *expectation* (abstr. or concr.) or *confidence*:— faith, hope.

1681. Ἐλύμας **Ĕlumas**, *el-oo´-mas*; of for. or.; *Elymas*, a wizard:— Elymas.

1682. ἐλοΐ **ĕlŏï**, *el-o-ee´*; of Chald. or. [426 with pron. suff.] *my God*:— Eloi.

1683. ἐμαυτοῦ **ĕmautŏu**, *em-ŏw-too´*; gen. compound of *1700* and *846*; *of myself* (so likewise the dat.

ἐμαυτῷ **ĕmautŏi**, *em-ow-to´*; and acc.

ἐμαυτόν **ĕmautŏn**, *em-ow-ton´*):— me, mine own (self), myself.

1684. ἐμβαίνω **ĕmbainō**, *em-ba´-hee-no*; from *1722* and the base of *939*; to *walk on*, i.e. *embark* (aboard a vessel), *reach* (a pool):— come (get) into, enter (into), go (up) into, step in, take ship.

1685. ἐμβάλλω **ĕmballō**, *em-bal´-lo*; from *1722* and *906*; to *throw on*, i.e. (fig.)

subject to (eternal punishment):— cast into.

1686. ἐμβάπτω **ĕmbaptō**, em-bap´-to; from 1722 and 911; to whelm on, i.e. wet (a part of the person, etc.) by contact with a fluid:— dip.

1687. ἐμβατεύω **ĕmbatĕuō**, em-bat-yoo´-o; from 1722 and a presumed der. of the base of 939; equiv. to 1684; to intrude on (fig.):— intrude into.

1688. ἐμβιβάζω **ĕmbibazō**, em-bib-ad´-zo; from 1722 and βιβάζω bibazō (to mount; caus. of 1684); to place on, i.e. transfer (aboard a vessel):— put in.

1689. ἐμβλέπω **ĕmblĕpō**, em-blep´-o; from 1722 and 991; to look on, i.e. (rel.) to observe fixedly, or (absolutely) to discern clearly:— behold, gaze up, look upon, (could) see.

1690. ἐμβριμάομαι **ĕmbrimaŏmai**, em-brim-ah´-om-ahee; from 1722 and βριμάομαι brimaŏmai (to snort with anger); to have indignation on, i.e. (tran.) to blame, (intr.) to sigh with chagrin, (spec.) to sternly enjoin:— straitly charge, groan, murmur against.

1691. ἐμέ **ĕmĕ**, em-eh´; a prol. form of 3165; me:— I, me, my (-self).

1692. ἐμέω **ĕmĕō**, em-eh´-o; of uncert. aff.; to vomit:— (will) spue.

1693. ἐμμαίνομαι **ĕmmainŏmai**, em-mah´-ee-nom-ahee; from 1722 and 3105; to rave on, i.e. rage at:— be mad against.

1694. Ἐμμανουήλ **Ĕmmanŏuēl**, em-man-oo-ale´; of Heb. or. [6005]; God with us; Emmanuel, a name of Christ:— Emmanuel.

1695. Ἐμμαούς **Ĕmmaŏus**, em-mah-ooce´; prob. of Heb. or. [comp. 3222]; Emmaüs, a place in Pal.:— Emmaus.

1696. ἐμμένω **ĕmmĕnō**, em-men´-o; from 1722 and 3306; to stay in the same place, i.e. (fig.) persevere:— continue.

1697. Ἐμμόρ **Ĕmmŏr**, em-mor´; of Heb. or. [2544]; Emmor (i.e. Chamor), a Canaanite:— Emmor.

1698. ἐμοί **ĕmŏi**, em-oy´; a prol. form of 3427; to me:— I, me, mine, my.

1699. ἐμός **ĕmŏs**, em-os´; from the oblique cases of 1473 (1698, 1700, 1691); my:— of me, mine (own), my.

1700. ἐμοῦ **ĕmŏu**, em-oo´; a prol. form of 3450; of me:— me, mine, my.

1701. ἐμπαιγμός **ĕmpaigmŏs**, emp-aheeg-mos´; from 1702; derision:— mocking.

1702. ἐμπαίζω **ĕmpaizō**, emp-aheed´-zo; from 1722 and 3815; to jeer at, i.e. deride:— mock.

1703. ἐμπαίκτης **ĕmpaiktēs**, emp-aheek-tace´; from 1702; a derider, i.e. (by impl.) a false teacher:— mocker, scoffer.

1704. ἐμπεριπατέω **ĕmpĕripatĕō**, em-per-ee-pat-eh´-o; from 1722 and 4043; to perambulate on a place, i.e. (fig.) to be occupied among persons:— walk in.

1705. ἐμπίπλημι **ĕmpiplēmi**, em-pip´-lay-mee; or

ἐμπλήθω **ĕmplēthō**, em-play´-tho; from 1722 and the base of 4118; to fill in

(up), i.e. (by impl.) to satisfy (lit. or fig.):— fill.

1706. ἐμπίπτω **ĕmpiptō**, em-pip´-to; from 1722 and 4098; to fall on, i.e. (lit.) to be entrapped in, or (fig.) be overwhelmed with:— fall among (into).

1707. ἐμπλέκω **ĕmplĕkō**, em-plek´-o; from 1722 and 4120; to entwine, i.e. (fig.) involve with:— entangle (in, self with).

ἐμπλήθω **ĕmplēthō**. See 1705.

1708. ἐμπλοκή **ĕmplŏkē**, em-plok-ay´; from 1707; elaborate braiding of the hair:— plaiting.

1709. ἐμπνέω **ĕmpnĕō**, emp-neh´-o; from 1722 and 4154; to inhale, i.e. (fig.) to be animated by (bent upon):— breathe.

1710. ἐμπορεύομαι **ĕmpŏrĕuŏmai**, em-por-yoo´-om-ahee; from 1722 and 4198; to travel in (a country as a pedlar), i.e. (by impl.) to trade:— buy and sell, make merchandise.

1711. ἐμπορία **ĕmpŏria**, em-por-ee´-ah; fem. from 1713; traffic:— merchandise.

1712. ἐμπόριον **ĕmpŏriŏn**, em-por´-ee-on; neut. from 1713; a mart ("emporium"):— merchandise.

1713. ἔμπορος **ĕmpŏrŏs**, em´-por-os; from 1722 and the base of 4198; a (wholesale) tradesman:— merchant.

1714. ἐμπρήθω **ĕmprēthō**, em-pray´-tho; from 1722 and πρήθω prēthō (to blow a flame); to enkindle, i.e. set on fire:— burn up.

1715. ἔμπροσθεν **ĕmprŏsthĕn**, em´-pros-then; from 1722 and 4314; in front of (in place [lit. or fig.] or time):— against, at, before, (in presence, sight) of.

1716. ἐμπτύω **ĕmptuō**, emp-too´-o; from 1722 and 4429; to spit at or on:— spit (upon).

1717. ἐμφανής **ĕmphanēs**, em-fan-ace´; from a compound of 1722 and 5316; apparent in self:— manifest, openly.

1718. ἐμφανίζω **ĕmphanizō**, em-fan-id´-zo; from 1717; to exhibit (in person) or disclose (by words):— appear, declare (plainly), inform, (will) manifest, shew, signify.

1719. ἔμφοβος **ĕmphŏbŏs**, em´-fob-os; from 1722 and 5401; in fear, i.e. alarmed:— affrighted, afraid, tremble.

1720. ἐμφυσάω **ĕmphusaō**, em-foo-sah´-o; from 1722 and φυσάω phusaō (to puff) [comp. 5453]; to blow at or on:— breathe on.

1721. ἔμφυτος **ĕmphutŏs**, em´-foo-tos; from 1722 and a der. of 5453; implanted (fig.):— engrafted.

1722. ἐν **ĕn**, en; a primary prep. denoting (fixed) position (in place, time or state), and (by impl.) instrumentality (medially or constructively), i.e. a relation of rest (intermediate between 1519 and 1537); "in," at, (up-) on, by, etc.:— about, after, against, + almost, × altogether, among, × as, at, before, between, (here-) by (+ all means), for (...sake of), + give self wholly to, (here-) in (-to, wardly), × mightily, (because) of, (up-) on, [open-] ly, × outwardly, one, × quickly, × shortly, [speedi-] ly, × that, ×

there (-in, -on), through (-out), (un-) to (-ward), under, when, where (-with), while, with (-in). Often used in compounds, with substantially the same import; rarely with verbs of motion, and then not to indicate direction, except (elliptically) by a separate (and different) prep.

1723. ἐναγκαλίζομαι **ĕnagkalizŏmai**, en-ang-kal-id´-zom-ahee; from 1722 and a der. of 43; to take in one's arms, i.e. embrace:— take up in arms.

1724. ἐνάλιος **ĕnaliŏs**, en-al´-ee-os; from 1722 and 251; in the sea, i.e. marine:— thing in the sea.

1725. ἔναντι **ĕnanti**, en´-an-tee; from 1722 and 473; in front (i.e. fig. presence) of:— before.

1726. ἐναντίον **ĕnantiŏn**, en-an-tee´-on; neut. of 1727; (adv.) in the presence (view) of:— before, in the presence of.

1727. ἐναντίος **ĕnantiŏs**, en-an-tee´-os; from 1725; opposite; fig. antagonistic:— (over) against, contrary.

1728. ἐνάρχομαι **ĕnarchŏmai**, en-ar´-khom-ahee; from 1722 and 756; to commence on:— rule [by mistake for 757].

1729. ἐνδεής **ĕndĕēs**, en-deh-ace´; from a compound of 1722 and 1210 (in the sense of lacking); deficient in:— lacking.

1730. ἔνδειγμα **ĕndĕigma**, en´-dighe-mah; from 1731; an indication (concr.):— manifest token.

1731. ἐνδείκνυμι **ĕndĕiknumi**, en-dike´-noo-mee; from 1722 and 1166; to indicate (by word or act):— do, show (forth).

1732. ἔνδειξις **ĕndĕixis**, en´-dike-sis; from 1731; indication (abstr.):— declare, evident token, proof.

1733. ἕνδεκα **hĕndĕka**, hen´-dek-ah; from (the neut. of) 1520 and 1176; one and ten, i.e. eleven:— eleven.

1734. ἑνδέκατος **hĕndĕkatŏs**, hen-dek´-at-os; ord. from 1733; eleventh:— eleventh.

1735. ἐνδέχεται **ĕndĕchĕtai**, en-dekh´-et-ahee; third pers. sing. present of a compound of 1722 and 1209; (impers.) it is accepted in, i.e. admitted (possible):— can (+ not) be.

1736. ἐνδημέω **ĕndēmĕō**, en-day-meh´-o; from a compound of 1722 and 1218; to be in one's own country, i.e. home (fig.):— be at home (present).

1737. ἐνδιδύσκω **ĕndiduskō**, en-did-oos´-ko; a prol. form of 1746; to invest (with a garment):— clothe in, wear.

1738. ἔνδικος **ĕndikŏs**, en´-dee-kos; from 1722 and 1349; in the right, i.e. equitable:— just.

1739. ἐνδόμησις **ĕndŏmēsis**, en-dom´-ay-sis; from a compound of 1722 and a der. of the base of 1218; a housing in (residence), i.e. structure:— building.

1740. ἐνδοξάζω **ĕndŏxazō**, en-dox-ad´-zo; from 1741; to glorify:— glorify.

1741. ἔνδοξος **ĕndŏxŏs**, en´-dox-os; from 1722 and 1391; in glory, i.e. splendid, (fig.) noble:— glorious, gorgeous [-ly], honourable.

1742. ἔνδυμα **ĕnduma**, en´-doo-mah;

from *1746; apparel* (espec. the outer *robe*):— clothing, garment, raiment.

1743. ἐνδυναμόω **ĕndunamŏō**, *en-doo-nam-ó´-o;* from *1722* and *1412;* to *empower:*— enable, (increase in) strength (-en), be (make) strong.

1744. ἐνδύνω **ĕndunō**, *en-doo´-no;* from *1772* and *1416;* to *sink* (by impl. *wrap* [comp. *1746*]) *on,* i.e. (fig.) *sneak:*— creep.

1745. ἔνδυσις **ĕndusis**, *en´-doo-sis;* from *1746; investment* with clothing:— putting on.

1746. ἐνδύω **ĕnduō**, *en-doo´-o;* from *1722* and *1416* (in the sense of *sinking* into a garment); to *invest* with clothing (lit. or fig.):— array, clothe (with), endue, have (put) on.

ἐνέγκω **ĕnĕgkō**. See 5342.

1747. ἐνέδρα **ĕnĕdra**, *en-ed´-rah;* fem. from *1722* and the base of *1476;* an *ambuscade,* i.e. (fig.) *murderous purpose:*— lay wait. See also *1749.*

1748. ἐνεδρεύω **ĕnĕdrĕuō**, *en-ed-ryoo´-o;* from *1747;* to *lurk,* i.e. (fig.) *plot* assassination:— lay wait for.

1749. ἔνεδρον **ĕnĕdrŏn**, *en´-ed-ron;* neut. of the same as *1747;* an *ambush,* i.e. (fig.) *murderous design:*— lying in wait.

1750. ἐνειλέω **ĕnĕilĕō**, *en-i-leh´-o;* from *1772* and the base of *1507;* to *enwrap:*— wrap in.

1751. ἔνειμι **ĕnĕimi**, *en´-i-mee;* from *1772* and *1510;* to *be within* (neut. part. plur.):— such things as ... have. See also *1762.*

1752. ἕνεκα **hĕnĕka**, *hen´-ek-ah;* or

ἕνεκεν **hĕnĕkĕn**, *hen´-ek-en;* or

εἵνεκεν **hĕinĕkĕn**, *hi´-nek-en;* of uncert. aff.; *on account of:*— because, for (cause, sake), (where-) fore, by reason of, that.

1753. ἐνέργεια **ĕnĕrgĕia**, *en-erg´-i-ah;* from *1756; efficiency* ("energy"):— operation, strong, (effectual) working.

1754. ἐνεργέω **ĕnĕrgĕō**, *en-erg-eh´-o;* from *1756;* to *be active, efficient:*— do, (be) effectual (fervent), be mighty in, shew forth self, work (effectually in).

1755. ἐνέργημα **ĕnĕrgēma**, *en-erg´-ay-mah;* from *1754;* an *effect:*— operation, working.

1756. ἐνεργής **ĕnĕrgēs**, *en-er-gace´;* from *1722* and *2041; active, operative:*— effectual, powerful.

1757. ἐνευλογέω **ĕnĕulŏgĕō**, *en-yoo-log-eh´-o;* from *1722* and *2127;* to *confer a benefit on:*— bless.

1758. ἐνέχω **ĕnĕchō**, *en-ekh´-o;* from *1722* and *2192;* to *hold in* or *upon,* i.e. *ensnare;* by impl. to *keep a grudge:*— entangle with, have a quarrel against, urge.

1759. ἐνθάδε **ĕnthadĕ**, *en-thad´-eh;* from a prol. form of *1722;* prop. *within,* i.e. (of place) *here, hither:*— (t-) here, hither.

1760. ἐνθυμέομαι **ĕnthumĕŏmai**, *en-thoo-meh´-om-ahee;* from a compound of *1722* and *2372;* to *be inspirited,* i.e. *ponder:*— think.

1761. ἐνθύμησις **ĕnthumēsis**, *en-thoo´-may-sis;* from *1760; deliberation:*— device, thought.

1762. ἔνι **ĕni**, *en´-ee;* contr. for the third pers. sing. pres. ind. of *1751;* impers. *there is* in or among:— be, (there) is.

1763. ἐνιαυτός **ĕniautŏs**, *en-ee-ŏw-tos´;* prol. from a primary ἔνος **ĕnŏs** (a *year*); a *year:*— year.

1764. ἐνίστημι **ĕnistēmi**, *en-is´-tay-mee;* from *1722* and *2476;* to *place on* hand, i.e. (refl.) *impend,* (part.) be *instant:*— come, be at hand, present.

1765. ἐνισχύω **ĕnischuō**, *en-is-khoo´-o;* from *1722* and *2480;* to *invigorate* (tran. or refl.):— strengthen.

1766. ἔννατος **ĕnnatŏs**, *en´-nat-os;* ord. from *1767; ninth:*— ninth.

1767. ἐννέα **ĕnnĕa**, *en-neh´-ah;* a primary number; *nine:*— nine.

1768. ἐννενηκονταεννέα **ĕnnĕnēkŏntaĕnnĕa**, *en-nen-ay-kon-tah-en-neh´-ah;* from a (tenth) multiple of *1767* and *1767* itself; *ninety-nine:*— ninety and nine.

1769. ἐννεός **ĕnnĕŏs**, *en-neh-os´;* from *1770; dumb* (as *making signs*), i.e. *silent* from astonishment:— speechless.

1770. ἐννεύω **ĕnnĕuō**, *en-nyoo´-o;* from *1722* and *3506;* to *nod at,* i.e. *beckon* or *communicate by gesture:*— make signs.

1771. ἔννοια **ĕnnŏia**, *en´-noy-ah;* from a compound of *1722* and *3563; thoughtfulness,* i.e. *moral understanding:*— intent, mind.

1772. ἔννομος **ĕnnŏmŏs**, *en´-nom-os;* from *1722* and *3551;* (subj.) *legal,* or (obj.) *subject* to:— lawful, under law.

1773. ἔννυχον **ĕnnuchŏn**, *en´-noo-khon;* neut. of a compound of *1722* and *3571;* (adv.) *by night:*— before day.

1774. ἐνοικέω **ĕnŏikĕō**, *en-oy-keh´-o;* from *1722* and *3611;* to *inhabit* (fig.):— dwell in.

1775. ἐνότης **ĕnŏtēs**, *hen-ot-ace´;* from *1520; oneness,* i.e. (fig.) *unanimity:*— unity.

1776. ἐνοχλέω **ĕnŏchlĕō**, *en-okh-leh´-o;* from *1722* and *3791;* to *crowd in,* i.e. (fig.) to *annoy:*— trouble.

1777. ἔνοχος **ĕnŏchŏs**, *en´-okh-os;* from *1758; liable* to (a condition, penalty or imputation):— in danger of, guilty of, subject to.

1778. ἔνταλμα **ĕntalma**, *en´-tal-mah;* from *1781;* an *injunction,* i.e. relig. *precept:*— commandment.

1779. ἐνταφιάζω **ĕntaphiazō**, *en-taf-ee-ad´-zo;* from a compound of *1722* and *5028;* to *inswathe* with cerements for interment:— bury.

1780. ἐνταφιασμός **ĕntaphiasmŏs**, *en-taf-ee-as-mos´;* from *1779; preparation* for interment:— burying.

1781. ἐντέλλομαι **ĕntĕllŏmai**, *en-tel´-lom-ahee;* from *1722* and the base of *5056;* to *enjoin:*— (give) charge, (give) command (-ments), injoin.

1782. ἐντεῦθεν **ĕntĕuthĕn**, *ent-yoo´-then;* from the same as *1759; hence* (lit.

or fig.); (repeated) *on both sides:*— (from) hence, on either side.

1783. ἔντευξις **ĕntĕuxis**, *ent´-yook-sis;* from *1793;* an *interview,* i.e. (spec.) *supplication:*— intercession, prayer.

1784. ἔντιμος **ĕntimŏs**, *en´-tee-mos;* from *1722* and *5092; valued* (fig.):— dear, more honourable, precious, in reputation.

1785. ἐντολή **ĕntŏlē**, *en-tol-ay´;* from *1781; injunction,* i.e. an authoritative *prescription:*— commandment, precept.

1786. ἐντόπιος **ĕntŏpiŏs**, *en-top´-ee-os;* from *1722* and *5117;* a *resident:*— of that place.

1787. ἐντός **ĕntŏs**, *en-tos´;* from *1722; inside* (adverb or noun):— within.

1788. ἐντρέπω **ĕntrĕpō**, *en-trep´-o;* from *1722* and the base of *5157;* to *invert,* i.e. (fig. and refl.) in a good sense, to *respect;* or in a bad one, to *confound:*— regard, (give) reverence, shame.

1789. ἐντρέφω **ĕntrĕphō**, *en-tref´-o;* from *1722* and *5142;* (fig.) to *educate:*— nourish up in.

1790. ἔντρομος **ĕntrŏmŏs**, *en´-trom-os;* from *1722* and *5156; terrified:*— × quake, × trembled.

1791. ἐντροπή **ĕntrŏpē**, *en-trop-ay´;* from *1788; confusion:*— shame.

1792. ἐντρυφάω **ĕntruphaō**, *en-troo-fah´-o;* from *1722* and *5171;* to *revel in:*— sporting selves.

1793. ἐντυγχάνω **ĕntugchanō**, *en-toong-khan´-o;* from *1722* and *5177;* to *chance upon,* i.e. (by impl.) *confer with;* by extens. to *entreat* (in favor or against):— deal with, make intercession.

1794. ἐντυλίσσω **ĕntulissō**, *en-too-lis´-so;* from *1722* and τυλίσσω **tulissō** (to *twist;* prob. akin to *1507*); to *entwine,* i.e. *wind up in:*— wrap in (together).

1795. ἐντυπόω **ĕntupŏō**, *en-too-pŏ´-o;* from *1722* and a der. of *5179;* to *enstamp,* i.e. *engrave:*— engrave.

1796. ἐνυβρίζω **ĕnubrizō**, *en-oo-brid´-zo;* from *1722* and *5195;* to *insult:*— do despite unto.

1797. ἐνυπνιάζομαι **ĕnupniazŏmai**, *en-oop-nee-ad´-zom-ahee;* mid. voice from *1798;* to *dream:*— dream (-er).

1798. ἐνύπνιον **ĕnupniŏn**, *en-oop´-nee-on;* from *1722* and *5258; something seen in sleep,* i.e. a *dream* (*vision* in a dream):— dream.

1799. ἐνώπιον **ĕnōpiŏn**, *en-o´-pee-on;* neut. of a compound of *1722* and a der. of *3700; in the face* of (lit. or fig.):— before, in the presence (sight) of, to.

1800. Ἐνώς **Ĕnōs**, *en-oce´;* of Heb. or. [*583*]; *Enos* (i.e. *Enosh*), a patriarch:— Enos.

1801. ἐνωτίζομαι **ĕnōtizŏmai**, *en-o-tid´-zom-ahee;* mid. voice from a compound of *1722* and *3775;* to take *in one's ear,* i.e. to *listen:*— hearken.

1802. Ἐνώχ **Ĕnōch**, *en-oke´;* of Heb. or. [*2585*]; *Enoch* (i.e. *Chanok*), an antediluvian:— Enoch.

ἐξ **ĕx**. See *1537.*

1803. ἕξ hĕx, *hex*; a primary numeral; *six:*— six.

1804. ἐξαγγέλλω ĕxaggĕllō, *ex-ang-el´-lo;* from *1537* and the base of *32*; to *publish,* i.e. *celebrate:*— shew forth.

1805. ἐξαγοράζω ĕxagŏrazō, *ex-ag-or-ad´-zo;* from *1537* and *59*; to *buy up,* i.e. *ransom;* fig. to *rescue* from loss (*improve* opportunity):— redeem.

1806. ἐξάγω ĕxagō, *ex-ag´-o;* from *1537* and *71*; to *lead forth:*— bring forth (out), fetch (lead) out.

1807. ἐξαιρέω ĕxairĕō, *ex-ahee-reh´-o;* from *1537* and *138*; act. to *tear out;* mid. voice to *select;* fig. to *release:*— deliver, pluck out, rescue.

1808. ἐξαίρω ĕxairō, *ex-ah´-ee-ro;* from *1537* and *142*; to *remove:*— put (take) away.

1809. ἐξαιτέομαι ĕxaitĕŏmai, *ex-ahee-teh´-om-ahee;* mid. voice from *1537* and *154*; to *demand* (for trial):— desire.

1810. ἐξαίφνης ĕxaiphnĕs, *ex-ah´-eef-nace;* from *1537* and the base of *160*; of a *sudden* (*unexpectedly*):— suddenly. Comp. *1819.*

1811. ἐξακολουθέω ĕxakŏlŏuthĕō, *ex-ak-ol-oo-theh´-o;* from *1537* and *190*; to *follow out,* i.e. (fig.) to *imitate, obey, yield to:*— follow.

1812. ἑξακόσιοι hĕxakŏsiŏi, *hex-ak-os´-ee-oy;* plur. ordinal from *1803* and *1540; six hundred:*— six hundred.

1813. ἐξαλείφω ĕxalĕiphō, *ex-al-i´-fo;* from *1537* and *218*; to *smear out,* i.e. *obliterate* (*erase* tears, fig. *pardon* sin):— blot out, wipe away.

1814. ἐξάλλομαι ĕxallŏmai, *ex-al´-lom-ahee;* from *1537* and *242*; to *spring forth:*— leap up.

1815. ἐξανάστασις ĕxanastasis, *ex-an-as´-tas-is;* from *1817;* a *rising from* death:— resurrection.

1816. ἐξανατέλλω ĕxanatĕllō, *ex-an-at-el´-lo;* from *1537* and *393*; to *start up out* of the ground, i.e. *germinate:*— spring up.

1817. ἐξανίστημι ĕxanistēmi, *ex-an-is´-tay-mee;* from *1537* and *450;* obj. to *produce,* i.e. (fig.) *beget;* subj. to *arise,* i.e. (fig.) *object:*— raise (rise) up.

1818. ἐξαπατάω ĕxapataō, *ex-ap-at-ah´-o;* from *1537* and *538;* to *seduce wholly:*— beguile, deceive.

1819. ἐξάπινα ĕxapina, *ex-ap´-ee-nah;* from *1537* and a der. of the same as *160;* of a *sudden,* i.e. *unexpectedly:*— suddenly. Comp. *1810.*

1820. ἐξαπορέομαι ĕxapŏrĕŏmai, *ex-ap-or-eh´-om-ahee;* mid. voice from *1537* and *639;* to *be utterly at a loss,* i.e. *despond:*— (in) despair.

1821. ἐξαποστέλλω ĕxapŏstĕllō, *ex-ap-os-tel´-lo;* from *1537* and *649;* to *send away forth,* i.e. (on a mission) to *despatch,* or (peremptorily) to *dismiss:*— send (away, forth, out).

1822. ἐξαρτίζω ĕxartizō, *ex-ar-tid´-zo;* from *1537* and a der. of *739;* to *finish out* (time); fig. to *equip fully* (a teacher):— accomplish, thoroughly furnish.

1823. ἐξαστράπτω ĕxastraptō, *ex-as-*

trap´-to; from *1537* and *797;* to *lighten forth,* i.e. (fig.) to *be radiant* (of very white garments):— glistening.

1824. ἐξαύτης ĕxautēs, *ex-ow´-tace;* from *1537* and the gen. sing. fem. of *846* (*5610* being understood); *from that* hour, i.e. *instantly:*— by and by, immediately, presently, straightway.

1825. ἐξεγείρω ĕxĕgĕirō, *ex-eg-i´-ro;* from *1537* and *1453;* to *rouse fully,* i.e. (fig.) to *resuscitate* (from death), *release* (from infliction):— raise up.

1826. ἔξειμι ĕxĕimi, *ex´-i-mee;* from *1537* and εἶμι ĕimi (to go); to *issue,* i.e. *leave* (a place), *escape* (to the shore):— depart, get (to land), go out.

1827. ἐξελέγχω ĕxĕlĕgchō, *ex-el-eng´-kho;* from *1537* and *1651;* to *convict fully,* i.e. (by impl.) to *punish:*— convince.

1828. ἐξέλκω ĕxĕlkō, *ex-el´-ko;* from *1537* and *1670;* to *drag forth,* i.e. (fig.) to *entice* (to sin):— draw away.

1829. ἐξέραμα ĕxĕrama, *ex-er´-am-ah;* from a compound of *1537* and a presumed ἐράω ĕraō (to *spue*); *vomit,* i.e. *food disgorged:*— vomit.

1830. ἐξερευνάω ĕxĕrĕunaō, *ex-er-yoo-nah´-o;* from *1537* and *2045;* to *explore* (fig.):— search diligently.

1831. ἐξέρχομαι ĕxĕrchŏmai, *ex-er´-khom-ahee;* from *1537* and *2064;* to *issue* (lit. or fig.):— come (forth, out), depart (out of), escape, get out, go (abroad, away, forth, out, thence), proceed (forth), spread abroad.

1832. ἔξεστι ĕxĕsti, *ex´-es-tee* or ἔξεστιν exestin, *ex´-es-teen;* third pers. sing. pres. ind. of a compound of *1537* and *1510;* so also

    ἐξόν ĕxŏn, *ex-on´;* neut. pres. part. of the same (with or without some form of *1510* expressed); impers. *it is right* (through the fig. idea of *being out* in public):— be lawful, let, × may (-est).

1833. ἐξετάζω ĕxĕtazō, *ex-et-ad´-zo;* from *1537* and ἐτάζω ĕtazō (to *examine*); to *test thoroughly* (by questions), i.e. *ascertain* or *interrogate:*— ask, enquire, search.

1834. ἐξηγέομαι ĕxēgĕŏmai, *ex-ayg-eh´-om-ahee;* from *1537* and *2233;* to *consider out* (aloud), i.e. *rehearse, unfold:*— declare, tell.

1835. ἑξήκοντα hĕxēkŏnta, *hex-ay´-kon-tah;* the tenth multiple of *1803; sixty:*— sixty (-fold), threescore.

1836. ἑξῆς hĕxēs, *hex-ace´;* from *2192* (in the sense of *taking hold of,* i.e. *adjoining*); *successive:*— after, following, × morrow, next.

1837. ἐξηχέομαι ĕxēchĕŏmai, *ex-ay-kheh´-om-ahee;* mid. voice from *1537* and *2278;* to "*echo*" forth, i.e. *resound* (be generally *reported*):— sound forth.

1838. ἕξις hĕxis, *hex´-is;* from *2192; habit,* i.e. (by impl.) *practice:*— use.

1839. ἐξίστημι ĕxistēmi, *ex-is´-tay-mee;* from *1537* and *2476;* to *put* (*stand*) *out of wits,* i.e. *astound,* or (refl.) *become astounded, insane:*— amaze, be (make) astonished, be beside self (selves), bewitch, wonder.

1840. ἐξισχύω ĕxischuō, *ex-is-khoo´-o;* from *1537* and *2480;* to *have full strength,* i.e. *be entirely competent:*— be able.

1841. ἔξοδος ĕxŏdŏs, *ex´-od-os;* from *1537* and *3598;* an *exit,* i.e. (fig.) *death:*— decease, departing.

1842. ἐξολοθρεύω ĕxŏlŏthrĕuō, *ex-ol-oth-ryoo´-o;* from *1537* and *3645;* to *extirpate:*— destroy.

1843. ἐξομολογέω ĕxŏmŏlŏgĕō, *ex-om-ol-og-eh´-o;* from *1537* and *3670;* to *acknowledge* or (by impl. of *assent*) *agree fully:*— confess, profess, promise.

    ἐξόν ĕxŏn. See *1832.*

1844. ἐξορκίζω ĕxŏrkizō, *ex-or-kid´-zo;* from *1537* and *3726;* to *exact an oath,* i.e. *conjure:*— adjure.

1845. ἐξορκιστής ĕxŏrkistēs, *ex-or-kis-tace´;* from *1844;* one *that binds by an oath* (or *spell*), i.e. (by impl.) an "*exorcist*" (*conjurer*):— exorcist.

1846. ἐξορύσσω ĕxŏrussō, *ex-or-oos´-so;* from *1537* and *3736;* to *dig out,* i.e. (by extens.) to *extract* (an eye), *remove* (roofing):— break up, pluck out.

1847. ἐξουδενόω ĕxŏudĕnŏō, *ex-oo-den-ŏ´-o;* from *1537* and a der. of the neut. of *3762;* to *make utterly nothing of,* i.e. *despise:*— set at nought. See also *1848.*

1848. ἐξουθενέω ĕxŏuthĕnĕō, *ex-oo-then-eh´-o;* a var. of *1847* and mean. the same:— contemptible, despise, least esteemed, set at nought.

1849. ἐξουσία ĕxŏusia, *ex-oo-see´-ah;* from *1832* (in the sense of *ability*); *privilege,* i.e. (subj.) *force, capacity, competency, freedom,* or (obj.) *mastery* (concr. *magistrate, superhuman, potentate, token of control*), delegated *influence:*— authority, jurisdiction, liberty, power, right, strength.

1850. ἐξουσιάζω ĕxŏusiazō, *ex-oo-see-ad´-zo;* from *1849;* to *control:*— exercise authority upon, bring under the (have) power of.

1851. ἐξοχή ĕxŏchē, *ex-okh-ay´;* from a compound of *1537* and *2192* (mean. to *stand out*); *prominence* (fig.):— principal.

1852. ἐξυπνίζω ĕxupnizō, *ex-oop-nid´-zo;* from *1853;* to *waken:*— awake out of sleep.

1853. ἔξυπνος ĕxupnŏs, *ex´-oop-nos;* from *1537* and *5258; awake:*— × out of sleep.

1854. ἔξω ĕxō, *ex´-o;* adv. from *1537; out* (-side, of doors), lit. or fig.:— away, forth, (with-) out (of, -ward), strange.

1855. ἔξωθεν ĕxōthĕn, *ex´-o-then;* from *1854; external* (-ly):— out (-side, -ward, -wardly), (from) without.

1856. ἐξωθέω ĕxōthĕō, *ex-o-theh´-o;* or

    ἐξώθω ĕxōthō, *ex-o´-tho;* from *1537* and ὠθέω ōthĕō (to *push*); to *expel;* by impl. to *propel:*— drive out, thrust in.

1857. ἐξώτερος ĕxōtĕrŏs, *ex-o´-ter-os;* comp. of *1854; exterior:*— outer.

1858. ἑορτάζω hĕŏrtazō, *heh-or-tad´-zo;* from *1859;* to *observe a festival:*— keep the feast.

1859. ἑορτή **hĕŏrtē**, *heh-or-tay'*; of uncert. aff.; a *festival:*— feast, holyday.

1860. ἐπαγγελία **ĕpaggĕlia**, *ep-ang-el-ee'-ah*; from *1861*; an *announcement* (for information, assent or pledge; espec. a divine *assurance* of good):— message, promise.

1861. ἐπαγγέλλω **ĕpaggĕllō**, *ep-ang-el'-lo*; from *1909* and the base of *32*; to *announce upon* (refl.), i.e. (by impl.) to *engage* to do something, to *assert* something respecting oneself:— profess, (make) promise.

1862. ἐπάγγελμα **ĕpaggĕlma**, *ep-ang'-el-mah*; from *1861*; a *self-committal* (by *assurance* of conferring some good):— promise.

1863. ἐπάγω **ĕpagō**, *ep-ag'-o*; from *1909* and *71*; to *superinduce*, i.e. *inflict* (an evil), *charge* (a crime):— bring upon.

1864. ἐπαγωνίζομαι **ĕpagōnizŏmai**, *ep-ag-o-nid'-zom-ahee*; from *1909* and *75*; to *struggle for:*— earnestly contend for.

1865. ἐπαθροίζω **ĕpathrŏizō**, *ep-ath-roid'-zo*; from *1909* and ἀθροίζω **athrŏizō** (to *assemble*); to *accumulate:*— gather thick together.

1866. Ἐπαίνετος **Ĕpainĕtŏs**, *ep-a'-hee-net-os*; from *1867; praised; Epænetus*, a Chr.:— Epenetus.

1867. ἐπαινέω **ĕpainĕō**, *ep-ahee-neh'-o*; from *1909* and *134*; to *applaud:*— commend, laud, praise.

1868. ἔπαινος **ĕpainŏs**, *ep'-ahee-nos*; from *1909* and the base of *134; laudation;* concr. a *commendable* thing:— praise.

1869. ἐπαίρω **ĕpairō**, *ep-ahee'-ro*; from *1909* and *142*; to *raise up* (lit. or fig.):— exalt self, poise (lift, take) up.

1870. ἐπαισχύνομαι **ĕpaischunŏmai**, *ep-ahee-skhoo'-nom-ahee*; from *1909* and *153*; to *feel shame for* something:— be ashamed.

1871. ἐπαιτέω **ĕpaitĕō**, *ep-ahee-teh'-o*; from *1909* and *154*; to *ask for:*— beg.

1872. ἐπακολουθέω **ĕpakŏlŏuthĕō**, *ep-ak-ol-oo-theh'-o*; from *1909* and *190*; to *accompany:*— follow (after).

1873. ἐπακούω **ĕpakŏuō**, *ep-ak-oo'-o*; from *1909* and *191*; to *hearken* (favorably) *to:*— hear.

1874. ἐπακροάομαι **ĕpakrŏaŏmai**, *ep-ak-rŏ-ah'-om-ahee*; from *1909* and the base of *202*; to *listen* (intently) *to:*— hear.

1875. ἐπάν **ĕpan**, *ep-an'*; from *1909* and *302*; a particle of indef. contemporaneousness; *whenever, as soon as:*— when.

1876. ἐπάναγκες **ĕpanagkĕs**, *ep-an'-ang-kes*; neut. of a presumed compound of *1909* and *318*; (adv.) *on necessity*, i.e. *necessarily:*— necessary.

1877. ἐπανάγω **ĕpanagō**, *ep-an-ag'-o*; from *1909* and *321*; to *lead up on*, i.e. (tech.) to *put out* (to sea); (intr.) to *return:*— launch (thrust) out, return.

1878. ἐπαναμιμνήσκω **ĕpanamimnēskō**, *ep-an-ah-mim-nace'-ko*; from *1909* and *363*; to *remind of:*— put in mind.

1879. ἐπαναπαύομαι **ĕpanapauŏmai**, *ep-an-ah-pŏw'-om-ahee*; mid. voice

from *1909* and *373*; to *settle on*; lit. (*remain*) or fig. (*rely*):— rest in (upon).

1880. ἐπανέρχομαι **ĕpanĕrchŏmai**, *ep-an-er'-khom-ahee*; from *1909* and *424*; to *come up on*, i.e. *return:*— come again, return.

1881. ἐπανίσταμαι **ĕpanistamai**, *ep-an-is'-tam-ahee*; mid. voice from *1909* and *450*; to *stand up on*, i.e. (fig.) to *attack:*— rise up against.

1882. ἐπανόρθωσις **ĕpanŏrthōsis**, *ep-an-or'-tho-sis*; from a compound of *1909* and *461*; a *straightening up again*, i.e. (fig.) *rectification* (*reformation*):— correction.

1883. ἐπάνω **ĕpanō**, *ep-an'-o*; from *1909* and *507; up above*, i.e. *over* or *on* (of place, amount, rank, etc.):— above, more than, (up-) on, over.

1884. ἐπαρκέω **ĕparkĕō**, *ep-ar-keh'-o*; from *1909* and *714*; to *avail for*, i.e. *help:*— relieve.

1885. ἐπαρχία **ĕparchia**, *ep-ar-khee'-ah* or ἐπαρχεία **ĕparchĕia**, *ep-ar-khi'-ah*; from a compound of *1909* and *757* (mean. a *governor* of a district, "eparch"); a *special region of government*, i.e. a Roman *præfecture:*— province.

1886. ἔπαυλις **ĕpaulis**, *ep'-ŏw-lis*; from *1909* and an equiv. of *833*; a *hut over the head*, i.e. a *dwelling*.

1887. ἐπαύριον **ĕpauriŏn**, *ep-ow'-ree-on*; from *1909* and *839*; occurring *on the succeeding* day, i.e. (*2250* being implied) *to-morrow:*— day following, morrow, next day (after).

1888. ἐπαυτοφώρῳ **ĕpautŏphōrŏi**, *ep-ow-tof-o'-ro*; from *1909* and *846* and (the dat. sing. of) a der. of φώρ **phōr** (a *thief*); *in theft itself*, i.e. (by anal.) in *actual crime:*— in the very act.

1889. Ἐπαφρᾶς **Ĕpaphras**, *ep-af-ras'*; contr. from *1891; Epaphras*, a Chr.:— Epaphras.

1890. ἐπαφρίζω **ĕpaphrizō**, *ep-af-rid'-zo*; from *1909* and *875*; to *foam upon*, i.e. (fig.) to *exhibit* (a vile passion):— foam out.

1891. Ἐπαφρόδιτος **Ĕpaphrŏditŏs**, *ep-af-rod'-ee-tos*; from *1909* (in the sense of *devoted* to) and Ἀφροδίτη **Aphrŏditē** (*Venus*); *Epaphroditus*, a Chr.:— Epaphroditus. Comp. *1889*.

1892. ἐπεγείρω **ĕpĕgĕirō**, *ep-eg-i'-ro*; from *1909* and *1453*; to *rouse upon*, i.e. (fig.) to *excite* against:— raise, stir up.

1893. ἐπεί **ĕpĕi**, *ep-i'*; from *1909* and *1487; thereupon*, i.e. *since* (of time or cause):— because, else, for that (then, -asmuch as), otherwise, seeing that, since, when.

1894. ἐπειδή **ĕpĕidē**, *ep-i-day'*; from *1893* and *1211; since now*, i.e. (of time) *when*, or (of cause) *whereas:*— after that, because, for (that, -asmuch as), seeing, since.

1895. ἐπειδήπερ **ĕpĕidēpĕr**, *ep-i-day'-per*; from *1894* and *4007; since indeed* (of cause):— forasmuch.

1896. ἐπεῖδον **ĕpĕidŏn**, *ep-i'-don*; and other moods and persons of the same tense; from *1909* and *1492*; to *regard*

(favorably or otherwise):— behold, look upon.

1897. ἐπείπερ **ĕpĕipĕr**, *ep-i'-per*; from *1893* and *4007; since* indeed (of cause):— seeing.

1898. ἐπεισαγωγή **ĕpĕisagōgē**, *ep-ice-ag-o-gay'*; from a compound of *1909* and *1521*; a *superintroduction:*— bringing in.

1899. ἔπειτα **ĕpĕita**, *ep'-i-tah*; from *1909* and *1534; thereafter:*— after that (-ward), then.

1900. ἐπέκεινα **ĕpĕkĕina**, *ep-ek'-i-nah*; from *1909* and (the acc. plur. neut. of) *1565; upon those* parts of, i.e. *on the further side of:*— beyond.

1901. ἐπεκτείνομαι **ĕpĕktĕinŏmai**, *ep-ek-ti'-nom-ahee*; mid. voice from *1909* and *1614*; to *stretch* (oneself) forward *upon:*— reach forth.

1902. ἐπενδύομαι **ĕpĕnduŏmai**, *ep-en-doo'-om-ahee*; mid. voice from *1909* and *1746*; to *invest upon* oneself:— be clothed upon.

1903. ἐπενδύτης **ĕpĕndutēs**, *ep-en-doo'-tace*; from *1902*; a *wrapper*, i.e. outer garment:— fisher's coat.

1904. ἐπέρχομαι **ĕpĕrchŏmai**, *ep-er'-khom-ahee*; from *1909* and *2064*; to *supervene*, i.e. *arrive, occur, impend, attack*, (fig.) *influence:*— come (in, upon).

1905. ἐπερωτάω **ĕpĕrōtaō**, *ep-er-o-tah'-o*; from *1909* and *2065*; to *ask for*, i.e. *inquire, seek:*— ask (after, questions), demand, desire, question.

1906. ἐπερώτημα **ĕpĕrōtēma**, *ep-er-o'-tay-mah*; from *1905*; an *inquiry:*— answer.

1907. ἐπέχω **ĕpĕchō**, *ep-ekh'-o*; from *1909* and *2192*; to *hold upon*, i.e. (by impl.) to *retain*; (by extens.) to *detain*; (with impl. of *3563*) to *pay attention to:*— give (take) heed unto, hold forth, mark, stay.

1908. ἐπηρεάζω **ĕpērĕazō**, *ep-ay-reh-ad'-zo*; from a comp. of *1909* and (prob.) ἀρειά **arĕia** (*threats*); to *insult, slander:*— use despitefully, falsely accuse.

1909. ἐπί **ĕpi**, *ep-ee'*; a primary prep.; prop. mean. *superimposition* (of time, place, order, etc.), as a relation of *distribution* (with the gen.), i.e. *over, upon*, etc.; of *rest* (with the dat.) *at, on*, etc.; of *direction* (with the acc.) *toward, upon*, etc.:— about (the times), above, after, against, among, as long as (touching), at, beside, × have charge of, (be-, [where-])fore, in (a place, as much as, the time of, -to), (because of, (up-) on (behalf of), over, (by, for) the space of, through (-out), (un-) to (-ward), with. In compounds it retains essentially the same import, *at, upon*, etc. (lit. or fig.).

1910. ἐπιβαίνω **ĕpibainō**, *ep-ee-bah'-ee-no*; from *1909* and the base of *939*; to *walk upon*, i.e. *mount, ascend, embark, arrive:*— come (into), enter into, go abroad, sit upon, take ship.

1911. ἐπιβάλλω **ĕpiballō**, *ep-ee-bal'-lo*; from *1909* and *906*; to *throw upon* (lit. or fig., tran. or refl.); usually with more or less force; spec. (with *1438* implied) to *reflect*; impers. to *belong to:*— beat into, cast (up-) on, fall, lay (on), put (unto), stretch forth, think on.

1912. ἐπιβαρέω **ĕpibarĕō**, *ep-ee-bar-eh´-o;* from *1909* and *916;* to *be heavy upon,* i.e. (pecuniarily) to *be expensive to;* fig. to *be severe toward:*— be chargeable to, overcharge.

1913. ἐπιβιβάζω **ĕpibibazō**, *ep-ee-bee-bad´-zo;* from *1909* and a redupl. deriv. of the base of *939* [comp. *307*]; to *cause to mount* (an animal):— set on.

1914. ἐπιβλέπω **ĕpiblĕpō**, *ep-ee-blep´-o;* from *1909* and *991;* to *gaze at* (with favor, pity or partiality):— look upon, regard, have respect to.

1915. ἐπίβλημα **ĕpiblēma**, *ep-ib´-lay-mah;* from *1911;* a *patch:*— piece.

1916. ἐπιβοάω **ĕpibŏaō**, *ep-ee-bo-ah´-o;* from *1909* and *994;* to *exclaim against:*— cry.

1917. ἐπιβουλή **ĕpibŏulē**, *ep-ee-boo-lay´;* from a presumed compound of *1909* and *1014;* a *plan against* someone, i.e. a *plot:*— laying (lying) in wait.

1918. ἐπιγαμβρεύω **ĕpigambrĕuō**, *ep-ee-gam-bryoo´-o;* from *1909* and a der. of *1062;* to *form affinity with,* i.e. (spec.) in a levirate way:— marry.

1919. ἐπίγειος **ĕpigĕiŏs**, *ep-ig´-i-os;* from *1909* and *1093; worldly* (phys. or mor.):— earthly, in earth, terrestrial.

1920. ἐπιγίνομαι **ĕpiginŏmai**, *ep-ig-in´-om-ahee;* from *1909* and *1096;* to *arrive upon,* i.e. *spring up* (as a wind):— blow.

1921. ἐπιγινώσκω **ĕpiginōskō**, *ep-ig-in-oce´-ko;* from *1909* and *1097;* to *know upon* some mark, i.e. *recognize;* by impl. to *become fully acquainted with,* to *acknowledge:*— (ac-, have, take) know (-ledge, well), perceive.

1922. ἐπίγνωσις **ĕpignōsis**, *ep-ig´-no-sis;* from *1921; recognition,* i.e. (by impl.) full *discernment, acknowledgement:*— (ac-) knowledge (-ing, -ment).

1923. ἐπιγραφή **ĕpigraphē**, *ep-ig-raf-ay´;* from *1924;* an *inscription:*— superscription.

1924. ἐπιγράφω **ĕpigraphō**, *ep-ee-graf-o;* from *1909* and *1125;* to *inscribe* (phys. or ment.):— inscription, write in (over, thereon).

1925. ἐπιδείκνυμι **ĕpidĕiknumi**, *ep-ee-dike´-noo-mee;* from *1909* and *1166;* to *exhibit* (phys. or ment.):— shew.

1926. ἐπιδέχομαι **ĕpidĕchŏmai**, *ep-ee-dekh´-om-ahee;* from *1909* and *1209;* to *admit* (as a guest or [fig.] teacher):— receive.

1927. ἐπιδημέω **ĕpidēmĕō**, *ep-ee-day-meh´-o;* from a compound of *1909* and *1218;* to *make oneself at home,* i.e. (by extens.) to *reside* (in a foreign country):— [be] dwelling (which were) there, stranger.

1928. ἐπιδιατάσσομαι **ĕpidiatassŏmai**, *ep-ee-dee-ah-tas´-som-ahee;* mid. voice from *1909* and *1299;* to *appoint besides,* i.e. *supplement* (as a codicill):— add to.

1929. ἐπιδίδωμι **ĕpididōmi**, *ep-ee-did´-o-mee;* from *1909* and *1325;* to *give over* (by hand or surrender):— deliver unto, give, let (+ [her drive]), offer.

1930. ἐπιδιορθόω **ĕpidiŏrthŏō**, *ep-ee-dee-or-thŏ´-o;* from *1909* and a der. of *3717;* to *straighten further,* i.e. (fig.) *arrange additionally:*— set in order.

1931. ἐπιδύω **ĕpiduō**, *ep-ee-doo´-o;* from *1909* and *1416;* to *set fully* (as the sun):— go down.

1932. ἐπιείκεια **ĕpiĕikĕia**, *ep-ee-i´-ki-ah;* from *1933; suitableness,* i.e. (by impl.) *equity, mildness:*— clemency, gentleness.

1933. ἐπιεικής **ĕpiĕikēs**, *ep-ee-i-kace´;* from *1909* and *1503; appropriate,* i.e. (by impl.) *mild:*— gentle, moderation, patient.

1934. ἐπιζητέω **ĕpizētĕō**, *ep-eed-zay-teh´-o;* from *1909* and *2212;* to *search* (*inquire*) *for;* intens. to *demand,* to *crave:*— desire, enquire, seek (after, for).

1935. ἐπιθανάτιος **ĕpithanatiŏs**, *ep-ee-than-at´-ee-os;* from *1909* and *2288;* doomed to *death:*— appointed to death.

1936. ἐπίθεσις **ĕpithĕsis**, *ep-ith´-es-is;* from *2007;* an *imposition* (of hands officially):— laying (putting) on.

1937. ἐπιθυμέω **ĕpithumĕō**, *ep-ee-thoo-meh´-o;* from *1909* and *2372;* to *set the heart upon,* i.e. *long for* (rightfully or otherwise):— covet, desire, would fain, lust (after).

1938. ἐπιθυμητής **ĕpithumĕtēs**, *ep-ee-thoo-may-tace´;* from *1937;* a *craver:*— + lust after.

1939. ἐπιθυμία **ĕpithumia**, *ep-ee-thoo-mee´-ah;* from *1937;* a *longing* (espec. for what is forbidden):— concupiscence, desire, lust (after).

1940. ἐπικαθίζω **ĕpikathizō**, *ep-ee-kath-id´-zo;* from *1909* and *2523;* to *seat upon:*— set on.

1941. ἐπικαλέομαι **ĕpikalĕŏmai**, *ep-ee-kal-eh´-om-ahee;* mid. voice from *1909* and *2564;* to *entitle;* by impl. to *invoke* (for aid, worship, testimony, decision, etc.):— appeal (unto), call (on, upon), surname.

1942. ἐπικάλυμα **ĕpikaluma**, *ep-ee-kal´-oo-mah;* from *1943;* a *covering,* i.e. (fig.) *pretext:*— cloke.

1943. ἐπικαλύπτω **ĕpikaluptō**, *ep-ee-kal-oop´-to;* from *1909* and *2572;* to *conceal,* i.e. (fig.) *forgive:*— cover.

1944. ἐπικατάρατος **ĕpikataratŏs**, *ep-ee-kat-ar´-at-os;* from *1909* and a der. of *2672; imprecated,* i.e. *execrable:*— accursed.

1945. ἐπίκειμαι **ĕpikĕimai**, *ep-ik´-i-mahee;* from *1909* and *2749;* to *rest upon* (lit. or fig.):— impose, be instant, (be) laid (there-, up-) on, (when) lay (on), lie (on), press upon.

1946. Ἐπικούρειος **Ĕpikŏurĕiŏs**, *ep-ee-koo´-ri-os* or Ἐπικούριος **Ĕpikŏuriŏs**, *ep-ee-koo´-ree-os;* from Ἐπίκουρος **Ĕpikŏurŏs** [comp. *1947*] (a noted philosopher); an *Epicurean* or follower of Epicurus:— Epicurean.

1947. ἐπικουρία **ĕpikŏuria**, *ep-ee-koo-ree´-ah;* from a compound of *1909* and a (prol.) form of the base of *2877* (in the sense of *servant*); *assistance:*— help.

1948. ἐπικρίνω **ĕpikrinō**, *ep-ee-kree´-no;* from *1909* and *2919;* to *adjudge:*— give sentence.

1949. ἐπιλαμβάνομαι **ĕpilambanŏmai**, *ep-ee-lam-ban´-om-ahee;* mid. voice from *1909* and *2983;* to *seize* (for help, injury, attainment, or any other purpose; lit. or fig.):— catch, lay hold (up-) on, take (by, hold of, on).

1950. ἐπιλανθάνομαι **ĕpilanthanŏmai**, *ep-ee-lan-than´-om-ahee;* mid. voice from *1909* and *2990;* to *lose out of* mind; by impl. to *neglect:*— (be) forget (-ful of).

1951. ἐπιλέγομαι **ĕpilĕgŏmai**, *ep-ee-leg´-om-ahee;* mid. voice from *1909* and *3004;* to *surname, select:*— call, choose.

1952. ἐπιλείπω **ĕpilĕipō**, *ep-ee-li´-po;* from *1909* and *3007;* to *leave upon,* i.e. (fig.) to *be insufficient for:*— fail.

1953. ἐπιλησμονή **ĕpilēsmŏnē**, *ep-ee-lace-mon-ay´;* from a der. of *1950; negligence:*— × forgetful.

1954. ἐπίλοιπος **ĕpilŏipŏs**, *ep-il´-oy-pos;* from *1909* and *3062; left over,* i.e. *remaining:*— rest.

1955. ἐπίλυσις **ĕpilusis**, *ep-il´-oo-sis;* from *1956; explanation,* i.e. *application:*— interpretation.

1956. ἐπιλύω **ĕpiluō**, *ep-ee-loo´-o;* from *1909* and *3089;* to *solve further,* i.e. (fig.) to *explain, decide:*— determine, expound.

1957. ἐπιμαρτυρέω **ĕpimarturĕō**, *ep-ee-mar-too-reh´-o;* from *1909* and *3140;* to *attest further,* i.e. *corroborate:*— testify.

1958. ἐπιμέλεια **ĕpimĕlĕia**, *ep-ee-mel´-i-ah;* from *1959; carefulness,* i.e. kind *attention* (*hospitality*):— + refresh self.

1959. ἐπιμελέομαι **ĕpimĕlĕŏmai**, *ep-ee-mel-eh´-om-ahee;* mid. voice from *1909* and the same as *3199;* to *care for* (phys. or otherwise):— take care of.

1960. ἐπιμελῶς **ĕpimĕlōs**, *ep-ee-mel-oce´;* adv. from a der. of *1959; carefully:*— diligently.

1961. ἐπιμένω **ĕpimĕnō**, *ep-ee-men´-o;* from *1909* and *3306;* to *stay over,* i.e. *remain* (fig. *persevere*):— abide (in), continue (in), tarry.

1962. ἐπινεύω **ĕpinĕuō**, *ep-een-yoo´-o;* from *1909* and *3506;* to *nod at,* i.e. (by impl.) to *assent:*— consent.

1963. ἐπίνοια **ĕpinŏia**, *ep-in´-oy-ah;* from *1909* and *3563; attention* (of the mind, i.e. (by impl.) *purpose:*— thought.

1964. ἐπιορκέω **ĕpiŏrkĕō**, *ep-ee-or-keh´-o;* from *1965;* to *commit perjury:*— forswear self.

1965. ἐπίορκος **ĕpiŏrkŏs**, *ep-ee´-or-kos;* from *1909* and *3727; on oath,* i.e. (falsely) a *forswearer:*— perjured person.

1966. ἐπιοῦσα **ĕpiŏusa**, *ep-ee-oo´-sah;* fem. sing. part. of a compound of *1909* and εἰμι **ĕimi** (to *go*); *supervening,* i.e. (*2250* or *3571* being expressed or implied) the *ensuing* day or night:— following, next.

1967. ἐπιούσιος **ĕpiŏusiŏs**, *ep-ee-oo´-see-os;* perh. from the same as *1966; tomorrow's;* but more prob. from *1909* and a der. of the pres. part. fem. of

1510; *for subsistence,* i.e. *needful:*— daily.

1968. ἐπιπίπτω **ĕpipiptō,** *ep-ee-pip´-to;* from *1909* and *4098;* to *embrace* (with affection) or *seize* (with more or less violence; lit. or fig.):— fall into (on, upon) lie on, press upon.

1969. ἐπιπλήσσω **ĕpiplēssō,** *ep-ee-place´-so;* from *1909* and *4141;* to *chastise,* i.e. (with words) to *upbraid:*— rebuke.

1970. ἐπιπνίγω **ĕpipnigō,** *ep-ee-pnee´-go;* from *1909* and *4155;* to *throttle upon,* i.e. (fig.) *overgrow:*— choke.

1971. ἐπιποθέω **ĕpipŏthĕō,** *ep-ee-poth-eh´-o;* from *1909* and ποθέω pŏthĕō (to *yearn*) to *dote upon,* i.e. *intensely crave* possession (lawfully or wrongfully):— (earnestly) desire (greatly), (greatly) long (after), lust.

1972. ἐπιπόθησις **ĕpipŏthēsis,** *ep-ee-poth´-ay-sis;* from *1971;* a *longing for:*— earnest (vehement) desire.

1973. ἐπιπόθητος **ĕpipŏthētŏs,** *ep-ee-poth´-ay-tos;* from *1909* and a der. of the latter part of *1971; yearned upon,* i.e. *greatly loved:*— longed for.

1974. ἐπιποθία **ĕpipŏthia,** *ep-ee-poth-ee´-ah;* from *1971; intense longing:*— great desire.

1975. ἐπιπορεύομαι **ĕpipŏrĕuŏmai,** *ep-ee-por-yoo´-om-ahee;* from *1909* and *4198;* to *journey further,* i.e. *travel on* (reach):— come.

1976. ἐπιρράπτω **ĕpirrhaptō,** *ep-ir-hrap´-to;* from *1909* and the base of *4476;* to *stitch upon,* i.e. *fasten* with the needle:— sew on.

1977. ἐπιρρίπτω **ĕpirrhiptō,** *ep-ir-hrip´-to;* from *1909* and *4496;* to *throw upon* (lit. or fig.):— cast upon.

1978. ἐπίσημος **ĕpisēmŏs,** *ep-is´-ay-mos;* from *1909* and some form of the base of *4591; remarkable,* i.e. (fig.) *eminent:*— notable, of note.

1979. ἐπισιτισμός **ĕpisitismŏs,** *ep-ee-sit-is-mos´;* from a compound of *1909* and a der. of *4621;* a *provisioning,* i.e. (concr.) *food:*— victuals.

1980. ἐπισκέπτομαι **ĕpiskĕptŏmai,** *ep-ee-skep´-tom-ahee;* mid. voice from *1909* and the base of *4649;* to *inspect,* i.e. (by impl.) to *select;* by extens. to *go to see, relieve:*— look out, visit.

1981. ἐπισκηνόω **ĕpiskēnŏō,** *ep-ee-skay-nŏ´-o;* from *1909* and *4637;* to *tent upon,* i.e. (fig.) *abide with:*— rest upon.

1982. ἐπισκιάζω **ĕpiskiazō,** *ep-ee-skee-ad´-zo;* from *1909* and a der. of *4639;* to *cast a shade upon,* i.e. (by anal.) to *envelop* in a haze of brilliancy; fig. to *invest* with preternatural influence:— overshadow.

1983. ἐπισκοπέω **ĕpiskŏpĕō,** *ep-ee-skop-eh´-o;* from *1909* and *4648;* to *oversee;* by impl. to *beware:*— look diligently, take the oversight.

1984. ἐπισκοπή **ĕpiskŏpē,** *ep-is-kop-ay´;* from *1980; inspection* (for relief) by impl. *superintendence;* spec., the Chr. "*episcopate*":— the office of a "bishop," bishoprick, visitation.

1985. ἐπίσκοπος **ĕpiskŏpŏs,** *ep-is´-kop-*

os; from *1909* and *4649* (in the sense of *1983*); a *superintendent,* i.e. Chr. officer in general charge of a (or the) church (lit. or fig.):— bishop, overseer.

1986. ἐπισπάομαι **ĕpispaŏmai,** *ep-ee-spah´-om-ahee;* from *1909* and *4685;* to *draw over,* i.e. (with 203 impl.) *efface* the mark of *circumcision* (by recovering with the foreskin):— become uncircumcised.

1987. ἐπίσταμαι **ĕpistamai,** *ep-is´-tam-ahee;* appar. a mid. voice of *2186* (with *3563* implied); to *put* the mind *upon,* i.e. *comprehend,* or *be acquainted with:*— know, understand.

1988. ἐπιστάτης **ĕpistatēs,** *ep-is-tat´-ace;* from *1909* and a presumed der. of *2476;* an *appointee over,* i.e. *commander (teacher):*— master.

1989. ἐπιστέλλω **ĕpistēllō,** *ep-ee-stel´-lo;* from *1909* and *4724;* to *enjoin* (by writing), i.e. (gen.) to *communicate by letter* (for any purpose):— write (a letter, unto).

1990. ἐπιστήμων **ĕpistēmōn,** *ep-ee-stay´-mone;* from *1987; intelligent:*— endued with knowledge.

1991. ἐπιστηρίζω **ĕpistērizō,** *ep-ee-stay-rid´-zo;* from *1909* and *4741;* to *support further,* i.e. *reestablish:*— confirm, strengthen.

1992. ἐπιστολή **ĕpistŏlē,** *ep-is-tol-ay´;* from *1989;* a *written message:*— "epistle," letter.

1993. ἐπιστομίζω **ĕpistŏmizō,** *ep-ee-stom-id´-zo;* from *1909* and *4750;* to put something over the *mouth,* i.e. (fig.) to *silence:*— stop mouths.

1994. ἐπιστρέφω **ĕpistrĕphō,** *ep-ee-stref´-o;* from *1909* and *4762;* to *revert* (lit., fig. or mor.):— come (go) again, convert, (re-) turn (about, again).

1995. ἐπιστροφή **ĕpistrŏphē,** *ep-is-trof-ay´;* from *1994; reversion,* i.e. mor. *revolution:*— conversion.

1996. ἐπισυνάγω **ĕpisunagō,** *ep-ee-soon-ag´-o;* from *1909* and *4863;* to *collect upon* the same place:— gather (together).

1997. ἐπισυναγωγή **ĕpisunagōgē,** *ep-ee-soon-ag-o-gay´;* from *1996;* a complete *collection;* spec. a Chr. *meeting* (for worship):— assembling (gathering) together.

1998. ἐπισυντρέχω **ĕpisuntrĕchō,** *ep-ee-soon-trekh´-o;* from *1909* and *4936;* to *hasten together upon* one place (or a particular occasion):— come running together.

1999. ἐπισύστασις **ĕpisustasis,** *ep-ee-soo´-stas-is;* from the mid. voice of a compound of *1909* and *4921;* a *conspiracy,* i.e. *concourse* (riotous or friendly):— that which cometh upon, + raising up.

2000. ἐπισφαλής **ĕpisphalēs,** *ep-ee-sfal-ace´;* from a compound of *1909* and σφάλλω sphallō (to *trip*); fig. *insecure:*— dangerous.

2001. ἐπιχύω **ĕpischuō,** *ep-is-khoo´-o;* from *1909* and *2480;* to *avail further,* i.e. (fig.) *insist stoutly:*— be the more fierce.

2002. ἐπισωρεύω **ĕpisōrĕuō,** *ep-ee-so-ryoo´-o;* from *1909* and *4987;* to *accumulate further,* i.e. (fig.) *seek* additionally:— heap.

2003. ἐπιταγή **ĕpitagē,** *ep-ee-tag-ay´;* from *2004;* an *injunction* or *decree;* by impl. *authoritativeness:*— authority, commandment.

2004. ἐπιτάσσω **ĕpitassō,** *ep-ee-tas´-so;* from *1909* and *5021;* to *arrange upon,* i.e. *order:*— charge, command, injoin.

2005. ἐπιτελέω **ĕpitĕlĕō,** *ep-ee-tel-eh´-o;* from *1909* and *5055;* to *fulfill further* (or *completely*), i.e. *execute;* by impl. to *terminate, undergo:*— accomplish, do, finish, (make) (perfect), perform (× -ance).

2006. ἐπιτήδειος **ĕpitēdĕiŏs,** *ep-ee-tay´-di-os;* from ἐπιτηδές **ĕpitēdĕs** (*enough*); *serviceable,* i.e. (by impl.) *requisite:*— things which are needful.

2007. ἐπιτίθημι **ĕpitithēmi,** *ep-ee-tith´-ay-mee;* from *1909* and *5087;* to *impose* (in a friendly or hostile sense):— add unto, lade, lay upon, put (up) on, set on (up), + surname, × wound.

2008. ἐπιτιμάω **ĕpitimaō,** *ep-ee-tee-mah´-o;* from *1909* and *5091;* to *tax upon,* i.e. *censure* or *admonish;* by impl. *forbid:*— (straitly) charge, rebuke.

2009. ἐπιτιμία **ĕpitimia,** *ep-ee-tee-mee´-ah;* from a compound of *1909* and *5092;* prop. *esteem,* i.e. *citizenship;* used (in the sense of *2008*) of a *penalty:*— punishment.

2010. ἐπιτρέπω **ĕpitrĕpō,** *ep-ee-trep´-o;* from *1909* and the base of *5157;* to *turn over* (*transfer*), i.e. *allow:*— give leave (liberty, license), let, permit, suffer.

2011. ἐπιτροπή **ĕpitrŏpē,** *ep-ee-trop-ay´;* from *2010; permission,* i.e. (by impl.) full *power:*— commission.

2012. ἐπίτροπος **ĕpitrŏpŏs,** *ep-it´-rop-os;* from *1909* and *5158* (in the sense of *2011*); a *commissioner,* i.e. *domestic manager, guardian:*— steward, tutor.

2013. ἐπιτυγχάνω **ĕpitugchanō,** *ep-ee-toong-khan´-o;* from *1909* and *5177;* to *chance upon,* i.e. (by impl.) to *attain:*— obtain.

2014. ἐπιφαίνω **ĕpiphainō,** *ep-ee-fah´-ee-no;* from *1909* and *5316;* to *shine upon,* i.e. *become* (lit.) *visible* or (fig.) *known:*— appear, give light.

2015. ἐπιφάνεια **ĕpiphanĕia,** *ep-if-an´-i-ah;* from *2016;* a *manifestation,* i.e. (spec.) the *advent* of Christ (past or future):— appearing, brightness.

2016. ἐπιφανής **ĕpiphanēs,** *ep-if-an-ace´;* from *2014; conspicuous,* i.e. (fig.) *memorable:*— notable.

2017. ἐπιφαύω **ĕpiphauō,** *ep-ee-fŏw´-o;* a form of *2014;* to *illuminate* (fig.):— give light.

2018. ἐπιφέρω **ĕpiphĕrō,** *ep-ee-fer´-o;* from *1909* and *5342;* to *bear upon* (or *further*), i.e. *adduce* (pers. or judicially [*accuse, inflict*]), *superinduce:*— add, bring (against), take.

2019. ἐπιφωνέω **ĕpiphōnĕō,** *ep-ee-foneh´-o;* from *1909* and *5455;* to *call at* something, i.e. *exclaim:*— cry (against); give a shout.

2020. ἐπιφώσκω **ĕpiphōskō,** *ep-ee-foce´-ko;* a form of *2017;* to begin to *grow light:*— begin to dawn, × draw on.

2021. ἐπιχειρέω **ĕpichĕirĕō,** *ep-ee-khi-reh´-o;* from *1909* and *5495;* to put the *hand upon,* i.e. *undertake:*— go about, take in hand (upon).

2022. ἐπιχέω **ĕpichĕō,** *ep-ee-kheh´-o;* from *1909* and χέω **chĕō** (to pour);—to *pour upon:*— pour in.

2023. ἐπιχορηγέω **ĕpichŏrēgĕō,** *ep-ee-khor-ayg-eh´-o;* from *1909* and *5524;* to *furnish besides,* i.e. fully *supply,* (fig.) *aid* or *contribute:*— add, minister (nourishment, unto).

2024. ἐπιχορηγία **ĕpichŏrēgia,** *ep-ee-khor-ayg-ee´-ah;* from *2023; contribution:*— supply.

2025. ἐπιχρίω **ĕpichriō,** *ep-ee-khree´-o;* from *1909* and *5548;* to *smear over:*— anoint.

2026. ἐποικοδομέω **ĕpŏikŏdŏmĕō,** *ep-oy-kod-om-eh´-o;* from *1909* and *3618;* to *build upon,* i.e. (fig.) to *rear up:*— build thereon (thereupon, on, upon).

2027. ἐποκέλλω **ĕpŏkĕllō,** *ep-ok-el´-lo;* from *1909* and ὀκέλλω **ŏkĕllō** (to *urge*); to *drive upon* the shore, i.e. to *beach* a vessel:— run aground.

2028. ἐπονομάζω **ĕpŏnŏmazō,** *ep-on-om-ad´-zo;* from *1909* and *3687;* to *name further,* i.e. *denominate:*— call.

2029. ἐποπτεύω **ĕpŏptĕuō,** *ep-opt-yoo´-o;* from *1909* and a der. of *3700;* to *inspect,* i.e. *watch:*— behold.

2030. ἐπόπτης **ĕpŏptēs,** *ep-op´-tace;* from *1909* and a presumed der. of *3700;* a *looker-on:*— eye-witness.

2031. ἔπος **ĕpŏs,** *ep´-os;* from *2036;* a *word:*— × say.

2032. ἐπουράνιος **ĕpŏuraniŏs,** *ep-oo-ran´-ee-os;* from *1909* and *3772; above* the *sky:*— celestial, (in) heaven (-ly), high.

2033. ἑπτά **hĕpta,** *hep-tah´;* a primary number; *seven:*— seven.

2034. ἑπτάκις **hĕptakis,** *hep-tak-is´;* adv. from *2033; seven times:*— seven times.

2035. ἑπτακισχίλιοι **hĕptakischiliŏi,** *hep-tak-is-khil´-ee-oy;* from *2034* and *5507; seven times a thousand:*— seven thousand.

2036. ἔπω **ĕpō,** *ep´-o;* a primary verb (used only in the def. past tense, the others being borrowed from *2046, 4483,* and *5346*); to *speak* or *say* (by word or writing):— answer, bid, bring word, call, command, grant, say (on), speak, tell. Comp. *3004.*

2037. Ἔραστος **Ĕrastŏs,** *er´-as-tos;* from ἐράω **ĕraō** (to *love*); *beloved; Erastus,* a Chr.:— Erastus.

ἐραυνάω **ĕraunaō.** See *2045.*

2038. ἐργάζομαι **ĕrgazŏmai,** *er-gad´-zom-ahee;* mid. voice from *2041;* to *toil* (as a task, occupation, etc.), (by impl.) *effect, be engaged in* or *with,* etc.:— commit, do, labor for, minister about, trade (by), work.

2039. ἐργασία **ĕrgasia,** *er-gas-ee´-ah;* from *2040; occupation;* by impl. *profit, pains:*— craft, diligence, gain, work.

2040. ἐργάτης **ĕrgatēs,** *er-gat´-ace;* from *2041;* a *toiler;* fig. a *teacher:*— labourer, worker (-men).

2041. ἔργον **ĕrgŏn,** *er´-gon;* from a primary (but obs.) ἔργω **ĕrgō** (to *work*); *toil* (as an effort or occupation); by impl. an *act:*— deed, doing, labour, work.

2042. ἐρεθίζω **ĕrĕthizō,** *er-eth-id´-zo;* from a presumed prol. form of *2054;* to *stimulate* (espec. to anger):— provoke.

2043. ἐρείδω **ĕrĕidō,** *er-i´-do;* of obscure aff.; to *prop,* i.e. (refl.) *get fast:*— stick fast.

2044. ἐρεύγομαι **ĕrĕugŏmai,** *er-yoog´-om-ahee;* of uncert. aff.; to *belch,* i.e. (fig.) to *speak out:*— utter.

2045. ἐρευνάω **ĕrĕunaō,** *er-yoo-nah´-o* or ἐραυνάω **ĕraunaō,** *er-ouw-nah´-o;* appar. from *2046* (through the idea of *inquiry*); to *seek,* i.e. (fig.) to *investigate:*— search.

2046. ἐρέω **ĕrĕō,** *er-eh´-o;* prob. a fuller form of *4483;* an alternate for *2036* in cert. tenses; to *utter,* i.e. *speak* or *say:*— call, say, speak (of), tell.

2047. ἐρημία **ĕrēmia,** *er-ay-mee´-ah;* from *2048; solitude* (concr.):— desert, wilderness.

2048. ἔρημος **ĕrēmŏs,** *er´-ay-mos;* of uncert. aff.; *lonesome,* i.e. (by impl.) *waste* (usually as a noun, *5561* being implied):— desert, desolate, solitary, wilderness.

2049. ἐρημόω **ĕrēmŏō,** *er-ay-mŏ´-o;* from *2048;* to *lay waste* (lit. or fig.):— (bring to, make) desolate (-ion), come to nought.

2050. ἐρήμωσις **ĕrēmōsis,** *er-ay´-mo-sis;* from *2049; despoliation:*— desolation.

2051. ἐρίζω **ĕrizō,** *er-id´-zo;* from *2054;* to *wrangle:*— strive.

2052. ἐριθεία **ĕrithĕia,** *er-ith-i´-ah;* perh. as the same as *2042;* prop. *intrigue,* i.e. (by impl.) *faction:*— contention (-ious), strife.

2053. ἔριον **ĕriŏn,** *er´-ee-on;* of obscure aff.; *wool:*— wool.

2054. ἔρις **ĕris,** *er´-is;* of uncert. aff.; a *quarrel,* i.e. (by impl.) *wrangling:*— contention, debate, strife, variance.

2055. ἐρίφιον **ĕriphiŏn,** *er-if´-ee-on;* from *2056;* a *kidling,* i.e. (gen.) *goat* (symbol. *wicked* person):— goat.

2056. ἔριφος **ĕriphŏs,** *er´-if-os;* perh. from the same as *2053* (through the idea of *hairiness*); a *kid* or (gen.) *goat:*— goat, kid.

2057. Ἑρμᾶς **Hĕrmas,** *her-mas´;* prob. from *2060; Hermas,* a Chr.:— Hermas.

2058. ἑρμηνεία **hĕrmēnĕia,** *her-may-ni´-ah;* from the same as *2059; translation:*— interpretation.

2059. ἑρμηνεύω **hĕrmēnĕuō,** *her-mayn-yoo´-o;* from a presumed der. of *2060* (as the god of language); to *translate:*— interpret.

2060. Ἑρμῆς **Hĕrmēs,** *her-mace´;* perh. from *2046; Hermes,* the name of the messenger of the Gr. deities; also of a Chr.:— Hermes, Mercury.

2061. Ἑρμογένης **Hĕrmŏgĕnēs,** *her-mog-en´-ace;* from *2060* and *1096; born* of *Hermes; Hermogenes,* an apostate Chr.:— Hermogenes.

2062. ἑρπετόν **hĕrpĕtŏn,** *her-pet-on´;* neut. of a der. of ἕρπω **hĕrpō** (to *creep*); a *reptile,* i.e. (by Heb. [comp. 7431]) a small *animal:*— creeping thing, serpent.

2063. ἐρυθρός **ĕruthrŏs,** *er-oo-thros´;* of uncert. aff.; *red,* i.e. (with *2281*) the *Red* Sea:— red.

2064. ἔρχομαι **ĕrchŏmai,** *er´-khom-ahee;* mid. voice of a primary verb (used only in the present and imperfect tenses, the others being supplied by a kindred [mid. voice]

ἐλεύθομαι **ĕlĕuthŏmai,** *el-yoo´-thom-ahee;* or [act.]

ἔλθω **ĕlthō,** *el´-tho;* which do not otherwise occur); to *come* or *go* (in a great variety of applications, lit. and fig.):— accompany, appear, bring, come, enter, fall out, go, grow, × light, × next, pass, resort, be set.

2065. ἐρωτάω **ĕrōtaō,** *er-o-tah´-o;* appar. from *2046* [comp. 2045]; to *interrogate;* by impl. to *request:*— ask, beseech, desire, intreat, pray. Comp. *4441.*

2066. ἐσθής **ĕsthēs,** *es-thace´;* from ἕννυμι **hĕnnumi** (to *clothe*); *dress:*— apparel, clothing, raiment, robe.

2067. ἔσθησις **ĕsthēsis,** *es´-thay-sis;* from a der. of *2066; clothing* (concr.):— garment.

2068. ἐσθίω **ĕsthiō,** *es-thee´-o;* strengthened for a primary ἔδω **ĕdō** (to *eat*); used only in certain tenses, the rest being supplied by *5315;* to *eat* (usually lit.):— devour, eat, live.

2069. Ἐσλί **Ĕslí,** *es-lee´;* of Heb. or. [prob. for 454]; *Esli,* an Isr.:— Esli.

2070. ἐσμέν **ĕsmĕn,** *es-men´;* first pers. plur. ind. of *1510;* we *are:*— are, be, have our being, × have hope, + [the gospel] was [preached unto] us.

2071. ἔσομαι **ĕsŏmai,** *es´-om-ahee;* future of *1510; will be:*— shall (should) be (have), (shall) come (to pass), × may have, × fall, what would follow, × live long, × sojourn.

2072. ἔσοπτρον **ĕsŏptrŏn,** *es´-op-tron;* from *1519* and a presumed der. of *3700;* a *mirror* (for *looking into*):— glass. Comp. *2734.*

2073. ἑσπέρα **hĕspĕra,** *hes-per´-ah;* fem. of an adj. ἕσπερός **hĕspĕrŏs** (*evening*); the *eve* (*5610* being implied):— evening (-tide).

2074. Ἐσρώμ **Ĕsrōm,** *es-rome;* of Heb. or. [2696]; *Esrom* (i.e. *Chetsron*), an Isr.:— Esrom.

2075. ἐστέ **ĕstĕ,** *es-teh´;* second pers. plur. pres. ind. of *1510;* ye *are:*— be, have been, belong.

2076. ἐστί **ĕstí,** *es-tee´;* third pers. sing. pres. ind. of *1510;* he (she or it) *is;* also (with neut. plur.) they *are:*— are, be (-long), call, × can [-not], come, consisteth, × dure for a while, + follow, ×

Greek

have, (that) is (to say), make, meaneth, × must needs, + profit, + remaineth, + wrestle.

2077. ἔστω **ĕstō,** *es´-to;* second pers. sing. pres. imper. of *1510; be* thou; also

ἔστωσαν **ĕstōsan,** *es´-to-san;* third pers. of the same; *let* them *be:*— be.

2078. ἔσχατος **ĕschatŏs,** *es´-khat-os;* a superl. prob. from *2192* (in the sense of *contiguity*); *farthest, final* (of place or time):— ends of, last, latter end, lowest, uttermost.

2079. ἐσχάτως **ĕschatōs,** *es-khat´-oce;* adv. from *2078; finally,* i.e. (with *2192*) *at the extremity* of life:— point of death.

2080. ἔσω **ĕsō,** *es´-o;* from *1519; inside* (as prep. or adj.):— (with-) in (-ner, -to, -ward).

2081. ἔσωθεν **ĕsōthĕn,** *es´-o-then;* from *2080; from inside;* also used as equiv. to *2080* (*inside*):— inward (-ly), (from) within, without.

2082. ἐσώτερος **ĕsōtĕrŏs,** *es-o´-ter-os;* comparative of *2080; interior:*— inner, within.

2083. ἑταῖρος **hĕtairŏs,** *het-ah´-ee-ros;* from ἔτης **ĕtēs** (a *clansman*); a *comrade:*— fellow, friend.

2084. ἑτερόγλωσσος **hĕtĕrŏglōssŏs,** *het-er-og´-loce-sos;* from *2087* and *1100; other-tongued,* i.e. a *foreigner:*— man of other tongue.

2085. ἑτεροδιδασκαλέω **hĕtĕrŏdidaskalĕō,** *het-er-od-id-as-kal-eh´-o;* from *2087* and *1320; to instruct differently:*— teach other doctrine (-wise).

2086. ἑτεροζυγέω **hĕtĕrŏzugĕō,** *het-er-od-zoog-eh´-o;* from a compound of *2087* and *2218; to yoke* up *differently,* i.e. (fig.) to *associate discordantly:*— unequally yoke together with.

2087. ἕτερος **hĕtĕrŏs,** *het´-er-os;* of uncert. aff.; (an-, the) *other* or *different:*— altered, else, next (day), one, (an-) other, some, strange.

2088. ἑτέρως **hĕtĕrōs,** *het-er´-oce;* adv. from *2087; differently:*— otherwise.

2089. ἔτι **ĕti,** *et´-ee;* perh. akin to *2094; "yet," still* (of time or degree):— after that, also, ever, (any) further, (t-) henceforth (more), hereafter, (any) longer, (any) more (-one), now, still, yet.

2090. ἑτοιμάζω **hĕtŏimazō,** *het-oy-mad´-zo;* from *2092; to prepare:*— prepare, provide, make ready. Comp. *2680.*

2091. ἑτοιμασία **hĕtŏimasia,** *het-oy-mas-ee´-ah;* from *2090; preparation:*— preparation.

2092. ἕτοιμος **hĕtŏimŏs,** *het´-oy-mos;* from an old noun ἔτεος **hĕtĕŏs** (*fitness*); *adjusted,* i.e. *ready:*— prepared, (made) ready (-iness, to our hand).

2093. ἑτοίμως **hĕtŏimōs,** *het-oy´-moce;* adv. from *2092; in readiness:*— ready.

2094. ἔτος **ĕtŏs,** *et´-os;* appar. a primary word; a *year:*— year.

2095. εὖ **ĕu,** *yoo;* neut. of a primary εὖς **ĕus** (*good*); (adv.) *well:*— good, well (done).

2096. Εὖα **Ĕua,** *yoo´-ah;* of Heb. or. [2332]; *Eua* (or *Eva,* i.e. *Chavvah*), the first woman:— Eve.

2097. εὐαγγελίζω **ĕuaggĕlizō,** *yoo-ang-ghel-id´-zo;* from *2095* and *32; to announce good* news ("evangelize") espec. the gospel:— declare, bring (declare, show) glad (good) tidings, preach (the gospel).

2098. εὐαγγέλιον **ĕuaggĕliŏn,** *yoo-ang-ghel´-ee-on;* from the same as *2097;* a *good message,* i.e. the *gospel:*— gospel.

2099. εὐαγγελιστής **ĕuaggĕlistēs,** *yoo-ang-ghel-is-tace´;* from *2097;* a *preacher* of the gospel:— evangelist.

2100. εὐαρεστέω **ĕuarĕstĕō,** *yoo-ar-es-teh´-o;* from *2101; to gratify entirely:*— please (well).

2101. εὐάρεστος **ĕuarĕstŏs,** *yoo-ar´-es-tos;* from *2095* and *701; fully agreeable:*— acceptable (-ted), wellpleasing.

2102. εὐαρέστως **ĕuarĕstōs,** *yoo-ar-es´-toce;* adv. from *2101; quite agreeably:*— acceptably, + please well.

2103. Εὔβουλος **Ĕubŏulŏs,** *yoo´-boo-los;* from *2095* and *1014; good-willer; Eubulus,* a Chr.:— Eubulus.

2104. εὐγένης **ĕugĕnēs,** *yoog-en´-ace;* from *2095* and *1096; well born,* i.e. (lit.) *high* in rank, or (fig.) *generous:*— more noble, nobleman.

2105. εὐδία **ĕudia,** *yoo-dee´-ah;* fem. from *2095* and the alternate of *2203* (as the god of the weather); a *clear sky,* i.e. *fine weather:*— fair weather.

2106. εὐδοκέω **ĕudŏkĕō,** *yoo-dok-eh´-o;* from *2095* and *1380; to think well* of, i.e. *approve* (an act); spec., to *approbate* (a person or thing):— think good, (be well) please (-d), be the good (have, take) pleasure, be willing.

2107. εὐδοκία **ĕudŏkia,** *yoo-dok-ee´-ah;* from a presumed compound of *2095* and the base of *1380; satisfaction,* i.e. (subj.) *delight,* or (obj.) *kindness, wish, purpose:*— desire, good pleasure (will), × seem good.

2108. εὐεργεσία **ĕuĕrgĕsia,** *yoo-erg-es-ee´-ah;* from *2110; beneficence* (gen. or spec.):— benefit, good deed done.

2109. εὐεργετέω **ĕuĕrgĕtĕō,** *yoo-erg-et-eh´-o;* from *2110; to be philanthropic:*— do good.

2110. εὐεργέτης **ĕuĕrgĕtēs,** *yoo-erg-et´-ace;* from *2095* and the base of *2041;* a *worker* of *good,* i.e. (spec.) a *philanthropist:*— benefactor.

2111. εὔθετος **ĕuthĕtŏs,** *yoo´-thet-os;* from *2095* and a der. of *5087; well placed,* i.e. (fig.) *appropriate:*— fit, meet.

2112. εὐθέως **ĕuthĕōs,** *yoo-theh´-oce;* adv. from *2117; directly,* i.e. *at once* or *soon:*— anon, as soon as, forthwith, immediately, shortly, straightway.

2113. εὐθυδρομέω **ĕuthudrŏmĕō,** *yoo-thoo-drom-eh´-o;* from *2117* and *1408; to lay* a *straight course,* i.e. *sail direct:*— (come) with a straight course.

2114. εὐθυμέω **ĕuthumĕō,** *yoo-thoo-meh´-o;* from *2115; to cheer up,* i.e. (intr.) *be cheerful;* neut. comparative

(adv.) *more cheerfully:*— be of good cheer (merry).

2115. εὔθυμος **ĕuthumŏs,** *yoo´-thoo-mos;* from *2095* and *2372;* in *fine spirits,* i.e. *cheerful:*— of good cheer, the more cheerfully.

2116. εὐθύνω **ĕuthunŏ,** *yoo-thoo´-no;* from *2117; to straighten* (level); tech. to *steer:*— governor, make straight.

2117. εὐθύς **ĕuthus,** *yoo-thoos´;* perh. from *2095* and *5087; straight,* i.e. (lit.) *level,* or (fig.) *true;* adv. (of time) *at once:*— anon, by and by, forthwith, immediately, straightway.

2118. εὐθύτης **ĕuthutēs,** *yoo-thoo´-tace;* from *2117; rectitude:*— righteousness.

2119. εὐκαιρέω **ĕukairĕō,** *yoo-kahee-reh´-o;* from *2121; to have good time,* i.e. *opportunity* or *leisure:*— have leisure (convenient time), spend time.

2120. εὐκαιρία **ĕukairia,** *yoo-kahee-ree´-ah;* from *2121;* a *favorable occasion:*— opportunity.

2121. εὔκαιρος **ĕukairŏs,** *yoo´-kahee-ros;* from *2095* and *2540; well-timed,* i.e. *opportune:*— convenient, in time of need.

2122. εὐκαίρως **ĕukairōs,** *yoo-kah´-ee-roce;* adv. from *2121; opportunely:*— conveniently, in season.

2123. εὐκοπώτερος **ĕukŏpōtĕrŏs,** *yoo-kop-o´-ter-os;* comp. of a compound of *2095* and *2873; better for toil,* i.e. *more facile:*— easier.

2124. εὐλάβεια **ĕulabĕia,** *yoo-lab´-i-ah;* from *2126;* prop. *caution,* i.e. (religiously) *reverence* (*piety*); by impl. *dread* (concr.):— fear (-ed).

2125. εὐλαβέομαι **ĕulabĕŏmai,** *yoo-lab-eh´-om-ahee;* mid. voice from *2126;* to *be circumspect,* i.e. (by impl.) *to be apprehensive;* religiously to *reverence:*— (moved with) fear.

2126. εὐλαβής **ĕulabēs,** *yoo-lab-ace´;* from *2095* and *2983; taking well* (*carefully*), i.e. *circumspect* (religiously, *pious*):— devout.

2127. εὐλογέω **ĕulŏgĕō,** *yoo-log-eh´-o;* from a compound of *2095* and *3056; to speak well of,* i.e. (religiously) to *bless* (*thank* or *invoke* a *benediction upon, prosper*):— bless, praise.

2128. εὐλογητός **ĕulŏgētŏs,** *yoo-log-ay-tos´;* from *2127; adorable:*— blessed.

2129. εὐλογία **ĕulŏgia,** *yoo-log-ee´-ah;* from the same as *2127; fine speaking,* i.e. *elegance of language; commendation* ("*eulogy*"), i.e. (reverentially) *adoration;* religiously *benediction;* by impl. *consecration;* by extens. *benefit* or *largess:*— blessing (a matter of) bounty (× -tifully), fair speech.

2130. εὐμετάδοτος **ĕumĕtadŏtŏs,** *yoo-met-ad´-ot-os;* from *2095* and a presumed der. of *3330; good at imparting,* i.e. *liberal:*— ready to distribute.

2131. Εὐνίκη **Ĕunikē,** *yoo-nee´-kay;* from *2095* and *3529; victorious; Eunice,* a Jewess:— Eunice.

2132. εὐνοέω **ĕunŏĕō,** *yoo-no-eh´-o;* from a compound of *2095* and *3563; to be well-minded,* i.e. *reconcile:*— agree.

2133. εὔνοια **ĕunŏia,** *yoo´-noy-ah;* from

the same as *2132; kindness;* euphem. *conjugal duty:*— benevolence, good will.

2134. εὐνουχίζω **ĕunŏuchizō,** *yoo-noo-khid´-zo;* from *2135;* to *castrate* (fig. *live unmarried*):— make ... eunuch.

2135. εὐνοῦχος **ĕunŏuchŏs,** *yoo-noo´-khos;* from εὐνή **ĕunē** (a *bed*) and *2192;* a *castrated* person (such being employed in Oriental bed-chambers); by extens. an *impotent* or *unmarried* man; by impl. a *chamberlain* (*state-officer*):— eunuch.

2136. Εὐοδία **Ĕuŏdia,** *yoo-od-ee´-ah;* from the same as *2137; fine travelling; Euodia,* a Chr. woman:— Euodias.

2137. εὐοδόω **ĕuŏdŏō,** *yoo-od-ŏ´-o;* from a compound of *2095* and *3598;* to *help* on the *road,* i.e. (pass.) *succeed in reaching;* fig. to *succeed* in business affairs:— (have a) prosper (-ous journey).

2138. εὐπειθής **ĕupĕithēs,** *yoo-pi-thace´;* from *2095* and *3982; good for persuasion,* i.e. (intr.) *compliant:*— easy to be intreated.

2139. εὐπερίστατος **ĕupĕristatŏs,** *yoo-per-is´-tat-os;* from *2095* and a der. of a presumed compound of *4012* and *2476; well standing around,* i.e. (a *competitor*) *thwarting* (a racer) in every direction (fig. of sin in gen.):— which doth so easily beset.

2140. εὐποιΐα **ĕupŏïïa,** *yoo-poy-ee´-ah;* from a compound of *2095* and *4160; well-doing,* i.e. *beneficence:*— to do good.

2141. εὐπορέω **ĕupŏrĕō,** *yoo-por-eh´-o;* from a compound of *2090* and the base of *4197;* (intr.) to *be* good *for passing through,* i.e. (fig.) *have* pecuniary *means:*— ability.

2142. εὐπορία **ĕupŏria,** *yoo-por-ee´-ah;* from the same as *2141;* pecuniary *resources:*— wealth.

2143. εὐπρέπεια **ĕuprĕpĕia,** *yoo-prep´-i-ah;* from a compound of *2095* and *4241; good suitableness,* i.e. *gracefulness:*— grace.

2144. εὐπρόσδεκτος **ĕuprŏsdĕktŏs,** *yoo-pros´-dek-tos;* from *2095* and a der. of *4327; well-received,* i.e. *approved, favorable:*— acceptable (-ted).

2145. εὐπρόσεδρος **ĕuprŏsĕdrŏs,** *yoo-pros´-ed-ros;* from *2095* and the same as *4332; sitting well toward,* i.e. (fig.) *assiduous* (neut. *diligent service*):— × attend upon.

2146. εὐπροσωπέω **ĕuprŏsōpĕō,** *yoo-pros-o-peh´-o;* from a compound of *2095* and *4383;* to *be of good countenance,* i.e. (fig.) to *make a display:*— make a fair show.

2147. εὑρίσκω **hĕuriskō,** *hyoo-ris´-ko;* a prol. form of a primary

εὕρω **hĕurō,** *hyoo´-ro;* which (together with another cognate form

εὑρέω **hĕurĕō,** *hyoo-reh´-o)* is used for it in all the tenses except the present and imperfect; to *find* (lit. or fig.):— find, get, obtain, perceive, see.

2148. Εὐροκλύδων **Ĕurŏklŭdōn,** *yoo-rok-loo´-dohn;* from Εὖρος **Ĕurŏs** (the *east*

wind) and *2830;* a *storm from the East* (or *Southeast*), i.e. (in modern phrase) a *Levanter:*— Euroklydon.

2149. εὐρύχωρος **ĕuruchōrŏs,** *yoo-roo´-kho-ros;* from εὐρύς **ĕurus** (*wide*) and *5561; spacious:*— broad.

2150. εὐσέβεια **ĕusĕbĕia,** *yoo-seb´-i-ah;* from *2152; piety;* spec. the *gospel* scheme:— godliness, holiness.

2151. εὐσεβέω **ĕusĕbĕō,** *yoo-seb-eh´-o;* from *2152;* to *be pious,* i.e. (toward God) to *worship,* or (toward parents) to *respect* (*support*):— show piety, worship.

2152. εὐσεβής **ĕusĕbēs,** *yoo-seb-ace´;* from *2095* and *4576; well-reverent,* i.e. *pious:*— devout, godly.

2153. εὐσεβῶς **ĕusĕbōs,** *yoo-seb-oce´;* adv. from *2152; piously:*— godly.

2154. εὔσημος **ĕusēmŏs,** *yoo-say-mos;* from *2095* and the base of *4591; well indicated,* i.e. (fig.) *significant:*— easy to be understood.

2155. εὔσπλαγχνος **ĕusplagchnŏs,** *yoo-splangkh-nos;* from *2095* and *4698; well compassioned,* i.e. *sympathetic:*— pitiful, tender-hearted.

2156. εὐσχημόνως **ĕuschēmŏnōs,** *yoo-skhay-mon´-oce;* adv. from *2158; decorously:*— decently, honestly.

2157. εὐσχημοσύνη **ĕuschēmŏsunē,** *yoo-skhay-mos-oo´-nay;* from *2158; decorousness:*— comeliness.

2158. εὐσχήμων **ĕuschēmōn,** *yoo-skhay´-mone;* from *2095* and *4976; well-formed,* i.e. (fig.) *decorous, noble* (in rank):— comely, honourable.

2159. εὐτόνως **ĕutŏnōs,** *yoo-ton´-oce;* adv. from a compound of *2095* and a der. of τείνω **tĕinō** (to *stretch*); *in a well-strung manner,* i.e. (fig.) *intensely* (in a good sense, *cogently;* in a bad one, *fiercely*):— mightily, vehemently.

2160. εὐτραπελία **ĕutrapĕlia,** *yoo-trap-el-ee´-ah;* from a compound of *2095* and a der. of the base of *5157* (mean. *well-turned,* i.e. *ready at repartee, jocose*); *witticism,* i.e. (in a vulgar sense) *ribaldry:*— jesting.

2161. Εὔτυχος **Ĕutuchŏs,** *yoo´-too-khos;* from *2095* and a der. of *5177; well-fated,* i.e. *fortunate; Eutychus,* a young man:— Eutychus.

2162. εὐφημία **ĕuphēmia,** *yoo-fay-mee´-ah;* from *2163; good language* (*"euphemy"*), i.e. *praise* (*repute*):— good report.

2163. εὔφημος **ĕuphēmŏs,** *yoo´-fay-mos;* from *2095* and *5345; well spoken of,* i.e. *reputable:*— of good report.

2164. εὐφορέω **ĕuphŏrĕō,** *yoo-for-eh´-o;* from *2095* and *5409;* to *bear well,* i.e. *be fertile:*— bring forth abundantly.

2165. εὐφραίνω **ĕuphrainō,** *yoo-frah´-ee-no;* from *2095* and *5424;* to *put* (mid. or pass. *be*) *in a good* frame *of mind,* i.e. *rejoice:*— fare, make glad, be (make) merry, rejoice.

2166. Εὐφράτης **Ĕuphratēs,** *yoo-frat´-ace;* of for. or. [comp. 6578]; *Euphrates,* a river of Asia:— Euphrates.

2167. εὐφροσύνη **ĕuphrŏsunē,** *yoo-fros-oo´-nay;* from the same as *2165; joyfulness:*— gladness, joy.

2168. εὐχαριστέω **ĕucharistĕō,** *yoo-khar-is-teh´-o;* from *2170;* to *be grateful,* i.e. (act.) to *express gratitude* (toward); spec. to *say grace* at a meal:— (give) thank (-ful, -s).

2169. εὐχαριστία **ĕucharistia,** *yoo-khar-is-tee´-ah;* from *2170; gratitude;* act. *grateful language* (to God, as an act of worship):— thankfulness, (giving of) thanks (-giving).

2170. εὐχάριστος **ĕucharistŏs,** *yoo-khar´-is-tos;* from *2095* and a der. of *5483; well favored,* i.e. (by impl.) *grateful:*— thankful.

2171. εὐχή **ĕuchē,** *yoo-khay´;* from *2172;* prop. a *wish,* expressed as a *petition* to God, or in *votive* obligation:— prayer, vow.

2172. εὔχομαι **ĕuchŏmai,** *yoo´-khom-ahee;* mid. voice of a primary verb; to *wish;* by impl. to *pray* to God:— pray, will, wish.

2173. εὔχρηστος **ĕuchrēstŏs,** *yoo´-khrays-tos;* from *2095* and *5543; easily used,* i.e. *useful:*— profitable, meet for use.

2174. εὐψυχέω **ĕupsuchĕō,** *yoo-psoo-kheh´-o;* from a compound of *2095* and *5590;* to *be in good spirits,* i.e. *feel encouraged:*— be of good comfort.

2175. εὐωδία **ĕuōdia,** *yoo-o-dee´-ah;* from a compound of *2095* and a der. of *3605; good-scentedness,* i.e. *fragrance:*— sweet savour (smell, -smelling).

2176. εὐώνυμος **ĕuōnumŏs,** *yoo-o´-noo-mos;* from *2095* and *3686;* prop. *well-named* (*good-omened*), i.e. the *left* (which was the *lucky* side among the pagan Greeks); neut. as adv. *at the left* hand:— (on the) left.

2177. ἐφάλλομαι **ĕphallŏmai,** *ef-al´-lom-ahee;* from *1909* and *242;* to *spring upon:*— leap on.

2178. ἐφάπαξ **ĕphapax,** *ef-ap´-ax;* from *1909* and *530; upon one occasion* (only):— (at) once (for all).

2179. Ἐφεσῖνος **Ĕphĕsinŏs,** *ef-es-ee´-nos;* from *2181; Ephesine,* or situated at Ephesus:— of Ephesus.

2180. Ἐφέσιος **Ĕphĕsiŏs,** *ef-es´-ee-os;* from *2181;* an *Ephesian* or inhab. of Ephesus:— Ephesian, of Ephesus.

2181. Ἔφεσος **Ĕphĕsŏs,** *ef´-es-os;* prob. of for. or.; *Ephesus,* a city of Asia Minor:— Ephesus.

2182. ἐφευρέτης **ĕphĕurĕtēs,** *ef-yoo-ret´-ace;* from a compound of *1909* and *2147;* a *discoverer,* i.e. *contriver:*— inventor.

2183. ἐφημερία **ĕphēmĕria,** *ef-ay-mer-ee´-ah;* from *2184; diurnality,* i.e. (spec.) the *quotidian rotation* or *class* of the Jewish priests' service at the Temple, as distributed by families:— course.

2184. ἐφήμερος **ĕphēmĕrŏs,** *ef-ay´-mer-os;* from *1909* and *2250; for a day* (*"ephemeral"*), i.e. *diurnal:*— daily.

2185. ἐφικνέομαι **ĕphiknĕŏmai,** *ef-ik-neh´-om-ahee;* from *1909* and a cognate of *2240;* to *arrive upon,* i.e. *extend to:*— reach.

2186. ἐφίστημι **ĕphistēmi,** *ef-is´-tay-*

Greek

mee; from 1909 and 2476; to *stand upon*, i.e. be *present* (in various applications, friendly or otherwise, usually lit.);—assault, come (in, to, unto, upon), be at hand (instant), present, stand (before, by, over).

2187. Ἐφραίμ **Ephraïm**, *ef-rah-im´*; of Heb. or. [669 or better 6085]; *Ephraïm*, a place in Pal.:— Ephraim.

2188. ἐφφαθά **ephphatha**, *ef-fath-ah´*; of Chald. or. [6606]; *be opened!*:— Ephphatha.

2189. ἔχθρα **echthra**, *ekh´-thrah*; fem. of 2190; *hostility*; by impl. a reason for *opposition*:— enmity, hatred.

2190. ἐχθρός **echthrŏs**, *ekh-thros´*; from a primary ἔχθω echthō (to *hate*); *hateful* (pass. *odious*, or act. *hostile*); usually as a noun, an *adversary* (espec. *Satan*):— enemy, foe.

2191. ἔχιδνα **echidna**, *ekh´-id-nah*; of uncert. or.; an *adder* or other poisonous snake (lit. or fig.):— viper.

2192. ἔχω **echō**, *ekh´-o*; incl. an alt. form

σχέω **schĕō**, *skheh´-o*; used in certain tenses only); a primary verb; to *hold* (used in very various applications, lit. or fig., direct or remote; such as *possession; ability, contiguity, relation,* or *condition*):— be (able, × hold, possessed with), accompany, + begin to amend, can (+ -not), × conceive, count, diseased, do + eat, + enjoy, + fear, following, have, hold, keep, + lack, + go to law, lie, + must needs, + of necessity, + need, next, + recover, + reign, + rest, return, × sick, take for, + tremble, + uncircumcised, use.

2193. ἕως **hĕōs**, *heh´-oce*; of uncert. aff.; a conjunc., prep. and adv. of continuance, *until* (of time and place):— even (until, unto), (as) far (as), how long, (un-) til (-l), (hither-, un-, up) to, while (-s).

Z

2194. Ζαβουλών **Zabŏulon**, *dzab-oo-lone´*; of Heb. or. [2074]; *Zabulon* (i.e. *Zebulon*), a region of Pal.:— Zabulon.

2195. Ζακχαῖος **Zakchaiŏs**, *dzak-chah´-ee-yos*; of Heb. or. [comp. 2140]; *Zacchæus*, an Isr.:— Zacchæus.

2196. Ζαρά **Zara**, *dzar-ah´*; of Heb. or. [2226]; *Zara*, (i.e. *Zerach*), an Isr.:— Zara.

2197. Ζαχαρίας **Zacharias**, *dzakh-ar-ee´-as*; of Heb. or. [2148]; *Zacharias* (i.e. *Zechariah*), the name of two Isr.:— Zacharias.

2198. ζάω **zaō**, *dzah´-o*; a primary verb; to *live* (lit. or fig.):— life (-time), (a-) live (-ly), quick.

2199. Ζεβεδαῖος **Zĕbĕdaiŏs**, *dzeb-ed-ah´-yos*; of Heb. or. [comp. 2067]; *Zebedæus*, an Isr.:— Zebedee.

2200. ζεστός **zĕstŏs**, *dzes-tos´*; from 2204; *boiled*, i.e. (by impl.) *calid* (fig. *fervent*):— hot.

2201. ζεῦγος **zĕugŏs**, *dzyoo´-gos*; from the same as 2218; a *couple*, i.e. a *team* (of oxen yoked together) or *brace* (of birds tied together):— yoke, pair.

2202. ζευκτηρία **zĕuktēria**, *dzook-tay-ree´-ah*; fem. of a der. (at the second stage) from the same as 2218; a *fastening* (*tiller-rope*):— band.

2203. Ζεύς **Zĕus**, *dzyooce*; of uncert. aff.; in the oblique cases there is used instead of it a (prob. cognate) name

Δίς **Dis**, *deece*, which is otherwise obs.; *Zeus* or *Dis* (among the Latins *Jupiter* or *Jove*), the supreme deity of the Greeks:— Jupiter.

2204. ζέω **zĕō**, *dzeh´-o*; a primary verb; to *be hot* (boil, of liquids; or *glow*, of solids), i.e. (fig.) *be fervid* (*earnest*):— be fervent.

2205. ζῆλος **zēlŏs**, *dzay´-los*; from 2204; prop. *heat*, i.e. (fig.) "*zeal*" (in a favorable sense, *ardor*; in an unfavorable one, *jealousy*, as of a husband [fig. of God], or an enemy, *malice*):— emulation, envy (-ing), fervent mind, indignation, jealousy, zeal.

2206. ζηλόω **zēlŏō**, *dzay-lŏ´-o* or ζηλεύω **zēlĕuō** *dzay-loo´-o*; from 2205; to *have warmth* of feeling for or against:— affect, covet (earnestly), (have) desire, (move with) envy, be jealous over, (be) zealous (-ly affect).

2207. ζηλωτής **zēlōtēs**, *dzay-lo-tace´*; from 2206; a "*zealot*":— zealous.

2208. Ζηλωτής **Zēlōtēs**, *dzay-lo-tace´*; the same as 2208; a *Zealot*, i.e. (spec.) *partisan* for Jewish political independence:— Zelotes.

2209. ζημία **zēmia**, *dzay-mee´-ah*; prob. akin to the base of 1150 (through the idea of *violence*); *detriment*:— damage, loss.

2210. ζημιόω **zēmiŏō**, *dzay-mee-ŏ´-o*; from 2209; to *injure*, i.e. (refl. or pass.) to *experience detriment*:— be cast away, receive damage, lose, suffer loss.

2211. Ζηνᾶς **Zēnas**, *dzay-nas´*; prob. contr. from a poetic form of 2203 and 1435; *Jove-given; Zenas*, a Chr.:— Zenas.

2212. ζητέω **zētĕō**, *dzay-teh´-o*; of uncert. aff.; to *seek* (lit. or fig.); spec. (by Heb.) to *worship* (God), or (in a bad sense) to *plot* (against life):— be (go) about, desire, endeavour, enquire (for), require, (× will) seek (after, for, means). Comp. 4441.

2213. ζήτημα **zētēma**, *dzay´-tay-mah*; from 2212; a *search* (prop. concr.), i.e. (in words) a *debate*:— question.

2214. ζήτησις **zētēsis**, *dzay´-tay-sis*; from 2212; a *searching* (prop. the act), i.e. a *dispute* or its *theme*:— question.

2215. ζιζάνιον **zizaniŏn**, *dziz-an´-ee-on*; of uncert. or.; *darnel* or false *grain*:— tares.

2216. Ζοροβάβελ **Zŏrŏbabĕl**, *dzor-ob-ab´-el*; of Heb. or. [2216]; *Zorobabel* (i.e. *Zerubbabel*), an Isr.:— Zorobabel.

2217. ζόφος **zŏphŏs**, *dzof´-os*; akin to the base of 3509; *gloom* (as shrouding like a *cloud*):— blackness, darkness, mist.

2218. ζυγός **zugŏs**, *dzoo-gos´*; from the root of ζεύγνυμι **zĕugnumi** (to *join*, espec. by a "yoke"); a *coupling*, i.e. (fig.) *servitude* (a *law* or *obligation*); also

(lit.) the *beam* of the balance (as *connecting* the scales):— pair of balances, yoke.

2219. ζύμη **zumē**, *dzoo´-may*; prob. from 2204; *ferment* (as if *boiling* up):— leaven.

2220. ζυμόω **zumŏō**, *dzoo-mŏ´-o*; from 2219; to *cause to ferment*:— leaven.

2221. ζωγρέω **zōgrĕō**, *dzogue-reh´-o*; from the same as 2226 and 64; to *take alive* (*make a prisoner of war*), i.e. (fig.) to *capture* or *ensnare*:— take captive, catch.

2222. ζωή **zōē**, *dzo-ay´*; from 2198; *life* (lit. or fig.):— life (-time). Comp. 5590.

2223. ζώνη **zōnē**, *dzo´-nay*; prob. akin to the base of 2218; a *belt*; by impl. a *pocket*:— girdle, purse.

2224. ζώννυμι **zōnnumi**, *dzone´-noo-mi*; from 2223; to *bind about* (espec. with a belt):— gird.

2225. ζωογονέω **zōŏgŏnĕō**, *dzo-og-on-eh´-o*; from the same as 2226 and a der. of 1096; to *engender alive*, i.e. (by anal.) to *rescue* (pass. *be saved*) from death:— live, preserve.

2226. ζῶον **zōŏn**, *dzo´-on*; neut. of a der. of 2198; a *live* thing, i.e. an *animal*:— beast.

2227. ζωοποιέω **zōŏpŏiĕō**, *dzo-op-oy-eh´-o*; from the same as 2226 and 4160; to (re-) *vitalize* (lit. or fig.):— make alive, give life, quicken.

H

2228. ἤ **ē**, *ay*; a primary particle of distinction between two connected terms; disjunctive, *or*; comparative, *than*:— and, but (either), (n-) either, except it be, (n-) or (else), rather, save, than, that, what, yea. Often used in connection with other particles. Comp. especially 2235, 2260, 2273.

2229. ἦ **ē**, *ay*; an adv. of *confirmation*; perh. intens. of 2228; used only (in the N.T.) before 3303; *assuredly*:— surely.

ἡ **hē**. See 3588.

ἡ **hē**. See 3739.

ἦ **ēi**. See 5600.

2230. ἡγεμονεύω **hēgĕmŏnĕuō**, *hayg-em-on-yoo´-o*; from 2232; to *act as ruler*:— be governor.

2231. ἡγεμονία **hēgĕmŏnia**, *hayg-em-on-ee´-ah*; from 2232; *government*, i.e. (in time) official *term*:— reign.

2232. ἡγεμών **hēgĕmōn**, *hayg-em-ohn´*; from 2233; a *leader*, i.e. *chief* person (or fig. place) of a province:— governor, prince, ruler.

2233. ἡγέομαι **hēgĕŏmai**, *hayg-eh´-om-ahee*; mid. voice of a (presumed) strengthened form of 71; to *lead*, i.e. *command* (with official authority); fig. to *deem*, i.e. *consider*:— account, (be) chief, count, esteem, governor, judge, have the rule over, suppose, think.

2234. ἡδέως **hēdĕōs**, *hay-deh´-oce*; adv. from a der. of the base of 2237; *sweetly*, i.e. (fig.) *with pleasure*:— gladly.

2235. ἤδη **ēdē**, *ay´-day*; appar. from 2228 (or possibly 2229) and 1211; *even* *now:—* already, (even) now (already), by this time.

2236. ἥδιστα **hēdista**, *hay´-dis-tah;* neut. plur. of the superl. of the same as 2234; *with great pleasure:—* most (very) gladly.

2237. ἡδονή **hēdŏnē**, *hay-don-ay´;* from ἁνδάνω **handanō** (to *please*); sensual *delight;* by impl. *desire:—* lust, pleasure.

2238. ἡδύοσμον **hēduŏsmŏn**, *hay-doo´-os-mon;* neut. of the compound of the same as 2234 and 3744; a *sweet-scented* plant, i.e. *mint:—* mint.

2239. ἦθος **ēthŏs**, *ay´-thos;* a strengthened form of 1485; *usage,* i.e. (plur.) moral *habits:—* manners.

2240. ἥκω **hēkō**, *hay´-ko;* a primary verb; to *arrive,* i.e. *be present* (lit. or fig.):— come.

2241. ἠλί **ēli**, *ay-lee´* or ἐλοι **ĕloi** ay-lo´-ee; of Heb. or. [410 with pron. suff.]; *my God:—* Eli.

2242. Ἡλί **Hēli**, *hay-lee´;* of Heb. or. [5941]; *Heli* (i.e. *Eli*), an Isr.:— Heli.

2243. Ἡλίας **Hēlias**, *hay-lee´-as;* of Heb. or. [452]; *Helias* (i.e. *Elijah*), an Isr.:— Elias.

2244. ἡλικία **hēlikia**, *hay-lik-ee´-ah;* from the same as 2245; *maturity* (in years or size):— age, stature.

2245. ἡλίκος **hēlikŏs**, *hay-lee´-kos;* from ἧλιξ **hēlix** (a *comrade,* i.e. one of the same age); *as big as,* i.e. (interjectively) *how much:—* how (what) great.

2246. ἥλιος **hēliŏs**, *hay´-lee-os;* from ἕλη **hēlē** (a *ray;* perh. akin to the alt. of 138); the *sun;* by impl. *light:—* + east, sun.

2247. ἦλος **hēlŏs**, *hay´-los;* of uncert. aff.; a *stud,* i.e. *spike:—* nail.

2248. ἡμᾶς **hēmas**, *hay-mas´;* acc. plur. of 1473; *us:—* our, us, we.

2249. ἡμεῖς **hēmĕis**, *hay-mice´;* nom. plur. of 1473; *we* (only used when emphat.):— us, we (ourselves).

2250. ἡμέρα **hēmĕra**, *hay-mer´-ah;* fem. (with 5610 impl.) of a der. of ἧμαι **hēmai** (to *sit;* akin to the base of 1476) mean. *tame,* i.e. *gentle; day,* i.e. (lit.) the time space between dawn and dark, or the whole 24 hours (but several days were usually reckoned by the Jews as inclusive of the parts of both extremes); fig. a *period* (always defined more or less clearly by the context):— age, + alway, (mid-) day (by day, [-lyl], + for ever, judgment, (day) time, while, years.

2251. ἡμέτερος **hēmĕtĕrŏs**, *hay-met´-er-os;* from 2349; *our:—* our, your [by a *different reading*].

2252. ἤμην **ēmēn**, *ay´-mane;* a prol. form of 2358; I *was:—* be, was. [*Sometimes unexpressed*].

2253. ἡμιθανής **hēmithanēs**, *hay-mee-than-ace´;* from a presumed compound of the base of 2255 and 2348; *half dead,* i.e. *entirely exhausted:—* half dead.

2254. ἡμῖν **hēmin**, *hay-meen´;* dat. plur. of 1473; *to* (or *for, with, by) us:—* our, (for) us, we.

2255. ἥμισυ **hēmisu**, *hay´-mee-soo;*

neut. of a der. from an inseparable pref. akin to 260 (through the idea of *partition* involved in *connection*) and mean. *semi-;* (as noun) *half:—* half.

2256. ἡμιώριον **hēmiōriŏn**, *hay-mee-o´-ree-on;* from the base of 2255 and 5610; a *half-hour:—* half an hour.

2257. ἡμῶν **hēmōn**, *hay-mone´;* gen. plur. of 1473; *of* (or *from) us:—* our (company), us, we.

2258. ἦν **ēn**, *ane;* imperf. of 1510; I (*thou,* etc.) *was* (*wast* or *were*):— + agree, be, × have (+ charge of), hold, use, was (-t), were.

2259. ἡνίκα **hēnika**, *hay-nee´-kah;* of uncert. aff.; *at which time:—* when.

2260. ἤπερ **ēpĕr**, *ay´-per;* from 2228 and 4007; *than at all* (or *than perhaps, than indeed):—* than.

2261. ἤπιος **ēpiŏs**, *ay´-pee-os;* prob. from 2031; prop. *affable,* i.e. *mild* or *kind:—* gentle.

2262. Ἤρ **Ēr**, *ayr;* of Heb. or. [6147]; *Er,* an Isr.:— Er.

2263. ἤρεμος **ērĕmŏs**, *ay´-rem-os;* perh. by transposition from 2048 (through the idea of *stillness); tranquil:—* quiet.

2264. Ἡρώδης **Hērōdēs**, *hay-ro´-dace;* compound of ἥρως **hērŏs** (a "*hero*") and 1491; *heroic; Herod,* the name of four Jewish kings:— Herod.

2265. Ἡρωδιανοί **Hērōdianŏi**, *hay-ro-dee-an-oy´;* plur. of a der. of 2264; *Herodians,* i.e. partisans of Herod:— Herodians.

2266. Ἡρωδιάς **Hērōdias**, *hay-ro-dee-as´;* from 2264; *Herodias,* a woman of the Herodian family:— Herodias.

2267. Ἡρωδίων **Hērōdiōn**, *hay-ro-dee-ohn;* from 2264; *Herodion,* a Chr.:— Herodion.

2268. Ἡσαΐας **Hēsaïas**, *hay-sah-ee´-as;* of Heb. or. [3470]; *Hesaias* (i.e. *Jeshajah*), an Isr.:— Esaias.

2269. Ἠσαῦ **Ēsau**, *ay-sow´;* of Heb. or. [6215]; *Esau,* an Edomite:— Esau.

2270. ἡσυχάζω **hēsuchazō**, *hay-soo-khad´-zo;* from the same as 2272; to *keep still* (intr.), i.e. *refrain* from labor, meddlesomeness or speech:— cease, hold peace, be quiet, rest.

2271. ἡσυχία **hēsuchia**, *hay-soo-khee´-ah;* fem. of 2272; (as noun) *stillness,* i.e. desistance from bustle or language:— quietness, silence.

2272. ἡσύχιος **hēsuchiŏs**, *hay-soo´-khee-os;* a prol. form of a compound prob. of a der. of the base of 1476 and perh. 2192; prop. *keeping* one's *seat* (*sedentary*), i.e. (by impl.) *still* (*undisturbed, undisturbing*):— peaceable, quiet.

2273. ἤτοι **ētŏi**, *ay´-toy;* from 2228 and 5104; *either indeed:—* whether.

2274. ἡττάω **hēttaō**, *hayt-tah´-o;* from the same as 2276; to *make worse,* i.e. *vanquish* (lit. or fig.); by impl. to *rate lower:—* be inferior, overcome.

2275. ἥττημα **hēttēma**, *hayt´-tay-mah;* from 2274; a *deterioration,* i.e. (obj.) *failure* or (subj.) *loss:—* diminishing, fault.

2276. ἥττον **hēttŏn**, *hate´-ton;* neut. of comp. of ἥκα **hēka** (*slightly*) used for that of 2556; *worse* (as noun); by impl. *less* (as adv.):— less, worse.

2277. ἤτω **ētō**, *ay´-to;* third pers. sing. imper. of 1510; *let him* (or *it) be:—* let ... be.

2278. ἠχέω **ēchĕō**, *ay-kheh´-o;* from 2279; to *make* a loud *noise,* i.e. *reverberate:—* roar, sound.

2279. ἦχος **ēchŏs**, *ay´-khos;* of uncert. aff.; a loud or confused *noise* ("*echo*"), i.e. *roar;* fig. a *rumor:—* fame, sound.

Θ

2280. Θαδδαῖος **Thaddaiŏs**, *thad-dah´-yos;* of uncert. or.; *Thaddæus,* one of the Apostles:— Thaddæus.

2281. θάλασσα **thalassa**, *thal´-as-sah;* prob. prol. from 251; the *sea* (gen. or spec.):— sea.

2282. θάλπω **thalpō**, *thal´-po;* prob. akin to θάλλω **thallō** (to *warm*); to *brood,* i.e. (fig.) to *foster:—* cherish.

2283. Θάμαρ **Thamar**, *tham´-ar;* of Heb. or. [8559]; *Thamar* (i.e. *Tamar*), an Israelitess:— Thamar.

2284. θαμβέω **thambĕō**, *tham-beh´-o;* from 2285; to *stupefy* (with surprise), i.e. *astound:—* amaze, astonish.

2285. θάμβος **thambŏs**, *tham´-bos;* akin to an obs. τάφω **taphō** (to *dumbfound*); *stupefaction* (by surprise), i.e. *astonishment:—* × amazed, + astonished, wonder.

2286. θανάσιμος **thanasimŏs**, *than-as´-ee-mos;* from 2288; *fatal,* i.e. *poisonous:—* deadly.

2287. θανατήφορος **thanatēphŏrŏs**, *than-at-ay´-for-os;* from (the fem. form of) 2288 and 5342; *death-bearing,* i.e. *fatal:—* deadly.

2288. θάνατος **thanatŏs**, *than´-at-os;* from 2348; (prop. an adj. used as a noun) *death* (lit. or fig.):— × deadly, (be...) death.

2289. θανατόω **thanatŏō**, *than-at-ŏ´-o;* from 2288; to *kill* (lit. or fig.):— become dead, (cause to be) put to death, kill, mortify.

θάνω **thanō**. See 2348.

2290. θάπτω **thaptō**, *thap´-to;* a primary verb; to *celebrate funeral rites,* i.e. *inter:—* bury.

2291. Θάρα **Thara**, *thar´-ah;* of Heb. or. [8646]; *Thara* (i.e. *Terach*), the father of Abraham:— Thara.

2292. θαρρέω **tharrhĕō**, *thar-hreh´-o;* another form for 2293; to *exercise courage:—* be bold, × boldly, have confidence, be confident. Comp. 5111.

2293. θαρσέω **tharsĕō**, *thar-seh´-o;* from 2294; to *have courage:—* be of good cheer (comfort). Comp. 2292.

2294. θάρσος **tharsŏs**, *thar´-sos;* akin (by transp.) to θράσος **thrasŏs** (*daring*); *boldness* (subj.):— courage.

2295. θαῦμα **thauma**, *thŏu´-mah;* appar. from a form of 2300; *wonder* (prop. concr.; but by impl. abstr.):— admiration.

2296. θαυμάζω **thaumazō**, *thŏu-mad´-*

zo; from 2295; to *wonder*; by impl. to *admire*:— admire, have in admiration, marvel, wonder.

2297. θαυμάσιος **thaumasiŏs**, *thŏw-mas´-ee-os*; from 2295; *wondrous*, i.e. (neut. as noun) a *miracle*:— wonderful thing.

2298. θαυμαστός **thaumastŏs**, *thŏw-mas-tos´*; from 2296; *wondered* at, i.e. (by impl.) *wonderful*:— marvel (-lous).

2299. θεά **thĕa**, *theh-ah´*; fem. of 2316; a female *deity*:— goddess.

2300. θεάομαι **theaŏmai**, *theh-ah´-om-ahee*; a prol. form of a primary verb; to *look* closely at, i.e. (by impl.) *perceive* (lit. or fig.); by extens. to *visit*:— behold, look (upon), see. Comp. 3700.

2301. θεατρίζω **thĕatrizō**, *theh-at-rid´-zo*; from 2302; to *expose as a spectacle*:— make a gazing stock.

2302. θέατρον **thĕatrŏn**, *theh´-at-ron*; from 2300; a *place for public show* ("theatre"), i.e. general *audience-room*; by impl. a *show* itself (fig.):— spectacle, theatre.

2303. θεῖον **thĕiŏn**, *thi´-on*; prob. neut. of 2304 (in its orig. sense of *flashing*); *sulphur*:— brimstone.

2304. θεῖος **thĕiŏs**, *thi´-os*; from 2316; *godlike* (neut. as noun, *divinity*):— divine, godhead.

2305. θειότης **thĕiŏtēs**, *thi-ot´-ace*; from 2304; *divinity* (abstr.):— godhead.

2306. θειώδης **thĕiōdēs**, *thi-o´-dace*; from 2303 and 1491; *sulphur-like*, i.e. *sulphurous*:— brimstone.

θελέω **thĕlĕō**. See 2309.

2307. θέλημα **thĕlēma**, *thel´-ay-mah*; from the prol. form of 2309; a *determination* (prop. the thing), i.e. (act.) *choice* (spec. *purpose, decree*; abstr. *volition*) or (pass.) *inclination*:— desire, pleasure, will.

2308. θέλησις **thĕlēsis**, *thel´-ay-sis*; from 2309; *determination* (prop. the act), i.e. *option*:— will.

2309. θέλω **thĕlō**, *thel´-o*; or ἐθέλω **ĕthĕlō**, *eth-el´-o*; in certain tenses θελέω **thĕlĕō**, *thel-eh´-o*; and ἐθελέω **ĕthĕlĕō**, *eth-el-eh´-o*; which are otherwise obs.; appar. strengthened from the alt. form of 138; to *determine* (as an act. *option* from subj. impulse; whereas 1014 prop. denotes rather a pass. *acquiescence* in obj. considerations), i.e. *choose* or *prefer* (lit. or fig.); by impl. to *wish*, i.e. be *inclined* to (sometimes adv. *gladly*); impers. for the future tense, to be *about to*; by Heb. to *delight in*:— desire, be disposed (forward), intend, list, love, mean, please, have rather, (be) will (have, -ling, -ling [-lyl).

2310. θεμέλιος **thĕmĕliŏs**, *them-el´-ee-os*; from a der. of 5087; something *put down*, i.e. a *substruction* (of a building, etc.), (lit. or fig.):— foundation.

2311. θεμελιόω **thĕmĕliŏō**, *them-el-ee-ŏ´-o*; from 2310; to *lay a basis* for, i.e. (lit.) *erect*, or (fig.) *consolidate*:— (lay the) found (-ation), ground, settle.

2312. θεοδίδακτος **thĕŏdidaktŏs**, *theh-od-id´-ak-tos*; from 2316 and 1321; *divinely instructed*:— taught of God.

2312'. θεολόγος **thĕŏlŏgŏs**, *theh-ol-og´-os*; from 2316 and 3004; a "*theologian*":— divine.

2313. θεομαχέω **thĕŏmachĕō**, *theh-o-makh-eh´-o*; from 2314; to *resist deity*:— fight against God.

2314. θεόμαχος **thĕŏmachŏs**, *theh-om´-akh-os*; from 2316 and 3164; an *opponent of deity*:— to fight against God.

2315. θεόπνευστος **thĕŏpnĕustŏs**, *theh-op´-nyoo-stos*; from 2316 and a presumed der. of 4154; *divinely breathed in*:— given by inspiration of God.

2316. θεός **thĕŏs**, *theh´-os*; of uncert. aff.; a *deity*, espec. (with 3588) the supreme *Divinity*; fig. a *magistrate*; by Heb. *very*:— × exceeding, God, god [-ly, -wardl.

2317. θεοσέβεια **thĕŏsĕbĕia**, *theh-os-eb´-i-ah*; from 2318; *devoutness*, i.e. *piety*:— godliness.

2318. θεοσεβής **thĕŏsĕbēs**, *theh-os-eb-ace´*; from 2316 and 4576; *reverent of God*, i.e. *pious*:— worshipper of God.

2319. θεοστυγής **thĕŏstugēs**, *theh-os-too-gace´*; from 2316 and the base of 4767; *hateful to God*, i.e. *impious*:— hater of God.

2320. θεότης **thĕŏtēs**, *theh-ot´-ace*; from 2316; *divinity* (abstr.):— godhead.

2321. Θεόφιλος **Thĕŏphilŏs**, *theh-of´-il-os*; from 2316 and 5384; *friend of God*; *Theophilus*, a Chr.:— Theophilus.

2322. θεραπεία **thĕrapĕia**, *ther-ap-i´-ah*; from 2323; *attendance* (spec. medical, i.e. *cure*); fig. and collec. *domestics*:— healing, household.

2323. θεραπεύω **thĕrapĕuō**, *ther-ap-yoo´-o*; from the same as 2324; to *wait upon* menially, i.e. (fig.) to *adore* (God), or (spec.) to *relieve* (of disease):— cure, heal, worship.

2324. θεράπων **thĕrapōn**, *ther-ap´-ohn*; appar. a part. from an otherwise obs. der. of the base of 2330; a menial *attendant* (as if *cherishing*):— servant.

2325. θερίζω **thĕrizō**, *ther-id´-zo*; from 2330 (in the sense of the *crop*); to *harvest*:— reap.

2326. θερισμός **thĕrismŏs**, *ther-is-mos´*; from 2325; *reaping*, i.e. the *crop*:— harvest.

2327. θεριστής **thĕristēs**, *ther-is-tace´*; from 2325; a *harvester*:— reaper.

2328. θερμαίνω **thĕrmainō**, *ther-mah´-ee-no*; from 2329; to *heat* (oneself):— (be) warm (-ed, self).

2329. θέρμη **thĕrmē**, *ther´-may*; from the base of 2330; *warmth*:— heat.

2330. θέρος **thĕrŏs**, *ther´-os*; from a primary θέρω **thĕrō** (to *heat*); prop. *heat*, i.e. *summer*:— summer.

2331. Θεσσαλονικεύς **Thĕssalŏnikĕus**, *thes-sal-on-ik-yoos´*; from 2332; a *Thessalonican*, i.e. inhab. of Thessalonice:— Thessalonian.

2332. Θεσσαλονίκη **Thĕssalŏnikē**, *thes-sal-on-ee´-kay*; from Θεσσαλός **Thĕssalŏs** (a *Thessalian*) and 3529; *Thessalonice*, a place in Asia Minor:— Thessalonica.

2333. Θευδᾶς **Thĕudas**, *thyoo-das´*; of

uncert. or.; *Theudas*, an Isr.:— Theudas.

θέω **thĕō**. See 5087.

2334. θεωρέω **thĕōrĕō**, *theh-o-reh´-o*; from a der. of 2300 (perh. by add. of 3708); to *be a spectator* of, i.e. *discern*, (lit., fig. [*experience*] or intens. [*acknowledge*]):— behold, consider, look on, perceive, see. Comp. 3700.

2335. θεωρία **thĕōria**, *theh-o-ree´-ah*; from the same as 2334; *spectatorship*, i.e. (concr.) a *spectacle*:— sight.

2336. θήκη **thēkē**, *thay´-kay*; from 5087; a *receptacle*, i.e. *scabbard*:— sheath.

2337. θηλάζω **thēlazō**, *thay-lad´-zo*; from θηλή **thēlē** (the *nipple*); to *suckle*, (by impl.) to *suck*:— (give) suck (-ling).

2338. θῆλυς **thēlus**, *thay´-loos*; from the same as 2337; *female*:— female, woman.

2339. θήρα **thēra**, *thay´-rah*; from θήρ **thēr** (a wild *animal*, as *game*); *hunting*, i.e. (fig.) *destruction*:— trap.

2340. θηρεύω **thērĕuō**, *thay-ryoo´-o*; from 2339; to *hunt* (an animal), i.e. (fig.) to *carp at*:— catch.

2341. θηριομαχέω **thēriŏmachĕō**, *thay-ree-om-akh-eh´-o*; from a compound of 2342 and 3164; to *be a beast-fighter* (in the gladiatorial show), i.e. (fig.) to *encounter* (furious men):— fight with wild beasts.

2342. θηρίον **thēriŏn**, *thay-ree´-on*; dimin. from the same as 2339; a *dangerous animal*:— (venomous, wild) beast.

2343. θησαυρίζω **thēsaurizō**, *thay-sŏw-rid´-zo*; from 2344; to *amass* or *reserve* (lit. or fig.):— lay up (treasure), (keep) in store, (heap) treasure (together, up).

2344. θησαυρός **thēsaurŏs**, *thay-sow-ros´*; from 5087; a *deposit*, i.e. *wealth* (lit. or fig.):— treasure.

2345. θιγγάνω **thigganō**, *thing-gan´-o*; a prol. form of an obs. primary θίγω **thigō** (to *finger*); to *manipulate*, i.e. *have to do with*; by impl. to *injure*:— handle, touch.

2346. θλίβω **thlibō**, *thlee´-bo*; akin to the base of 5147; to *crowd* (lit. or fig.):— afflict, narrow, throng, suffer tribulation, trouble.

2347. θλίψις **thlipsis**, *thlip´-sis*; from 2346; *pressure* (lit. or fig.):— afflicted (-tion), anguish, burdened, persecution, tribulation, trouble.

2348. θνήσκω **thnēskō**, *thnay´-sko*; a strengthened form of a simpler primary θάνω **thanō**, *than´-o* (which is used for it only in certain tenses); to *die* (lit. or fig.):— be dead, die.

2349. θνητός **thnētŏs**, *thnay-tos´*; from 2348; *liable to die*:— mortal (-ity).

2350. θορυβέω **thŏrubĕō**, *thor-oo-beh´-o*; from 2351; to *be in tumult*, i.e. *disturb, clamor*:— make ado (a noise), trouble self, set on an uproar.

2351. θόρυβος **thŏrubŏs**, *thor´-oo-bos*; from the base of 2360; a *disturbance*:— tumult, uproar.

2352. θραύω **thrauō**, *thrŏw´-o*; a primary verb; to *crush*:— bruise. Comp. 4486.

2353. θρέμμα **thrĕmma**, *threm´-mah;* from 5142; *stock* (as *raised* on a farm):— cattle.

2354. θρηνέω **thrēnĕō**, *thray-neh´-o;* from 2355; to *bewail*:— lament, mourn.

2355. θρῆνος **thrēnŏs**, *thray´-nos;* from the base of 2360; *wailing*:— lamentation.

2356. θρησκεία **thrēskĕia**, *thrace-ki´-ah;* from a der. of 2357; ceremonial *observance*:— religion, worshipping.

2357. θρῆσκος **thrēskŏs**, *thrace´-kos;* prob. from the base of 2360; *ceremonious* in worship (as *demonstrative*), i.e. *pious*:— religious.

2358. θριαμβεύω **thriambĕuō**, *three-am-byoo´-o;* from a prol. compound of the base of 2360; and a der. of 680 (mean. a *noisy iambus,* sung in honor of Bacchus); to *make an acclamatory procession,* i.e. (fig.) to *conquer* or (by Heb.) to *give victory*:— (cause) to triumph (over).

2359. θρίξ **thrix**, *threeks;* gen. τριχός **trichŏs**, etc.; of uncert. der.; *hair*:— hair. Comp. 2864.

2360. θροέω **thrŏĕō**, *thrŏ-eh´-o;* from θρέομαι **thrĕŏmai** to *wail;* to *clamor,* i.e. (by impl.) to *frighten*:— trouble.

2361. θρόμβος **thrŏmbŏs**, *throm´-bos;* perh. from 5142 (in the sense of *thickening*); a *clot*:— great drop.

2362. θρόνος **thrŏnŏs**, *thron´-os;* from θράω **thraō** (to *sit*); a stately *seat* ("*throne*"); by impl. *power* or (concr.) a *potentate*:— seat, throne.

2363. Θυάτειρα **Thuatĕira**, *thoo-at´-i-rah;* of uncert. der.; *Thyatira,* a place in Asia Minor:— Thyatira.

2364. θυγάτηρ **thugatĕr**, *thoo-gat´-air;* appar. a primary word (comp. "*daughter*"); a *female child,* or (by Heb.) *descendant* (or *inhabitant*):— daughter.

2365. θυγάτριον **thugatriŏn**, *thoo-gat´-ree-on;* from 2364; a *daughterling*:— little (young) daughter.

2366. θύελλα **thuĕlla**, *thoo´-el-lah;* from 2380 (in the sense of *blowing*) a *storm*:— tempest.

2367. θύϊνος **thuïnŏs**, *thoo´-ee-nos;* from a der. of 2380 (in the sense of *blowing;* denoting a certain *fragrant* tree); made of *citron*-wood:— thyine.

2368. θυμίαμα **thumiama**, *thoo-mee´-am-ah;* from 2370; an *aroma,* i.e. fragrant *powder* burnt in relig. service; by impl. the *burning* itself:— incense, odour.

2369. θυμιαστήριον **thumiastĕriŏn**, *thoo-mee-as-tay´-ree-on;* or

θυμιατήριον **thumiatĕrion**, *thoo-mee-a-tay´-ree-on;* from a der. of 2370; a *place of fumigation,* i.e. the *alter of incense* (in the Temple):— censer.

2370. θυμιάω **thumiaō**, *thoo-mee-ah´-o;* from a der. of 2380 (in the sense of *smoking*); to *fumigate,* i.e. *offer* aromatic *fumes*:— burn incense.

2371. θυμομαχέω **thumŏmachĕō**, *thoo-mom-akh-eh´-o;* from a presumed compound of 2372 and 3164; to *be in a furious fight,* i.e. (fig.) to *be exasperated*:— be highly displeased.

2372. θυμός **thumŏs**, *thoo-mos´;* from 2380; *passion* (as if *breathing* hard):— fierceness, indignation, wrath. Comp. 5590.

2373. θυμόω **thumŏō**, *tho-mŏ´-o;* from 2372; to *put in a passion,* i.e. *enrage*:— be wroth.

2374. θύρα **thura**, *thoo´-rah;* appar. a primary word (comp. "door"); a *portal* or *entrance* (the opening or the closure, lit. or fig.):— door, gate.

2375. θυρεός **thurĕŏs**, *thoo-reh-os´;* from 2374; a large *shield* (as door-shaped):— shield.

2376. θυρίς **thuris**, *thoo-rece´;* from 2374; an *aperture,* i.e. *window*:— window.

2377. θυρωρός **thurōrŏs**, *thoo-ro-ros´;* from 2374 and οὖρος **ŏurŏs** (a *watcher*); a *gate-warden*:— that kept the door, porter.

2378. θυσία **thusia**, *thoo-see´-ah;* from 2380; *sacrifice* (the act or the victim, lit. or fig.):— sacrifice.

2379. θυσιαστήριον **thusiastĕriŏn**, *thoo-see-as-tay´-ree-on;* from a der. of 2378; a *place of sacrifice,* i.e. an *altar* (spec. or gen., lit. or fig.):— altar.

2380. θύω **thuō**, *thoo´-o;* a primary verb; prop. to *rush* (*breathe* hard, *blow, smoke*), i.e. (by impl.) to *sacrifice* (prop. by fire, but gen.); by extens. to *immolate* (*slaughter* for any purpose):— kill, (do) sacrifice, slay.

2381. Θωμᾶς **Thōmas**, *tho-mas´;* of Chald. or. (comp. 8380); *the twin; Thomas,* a Chr.:— Thomas.

2382. θώραξ **thōrax**, *tho´-rax;* of uncert. aff.; the *chest* ("*thorax*"), i.e. (by impl.) a *corslet*:— breast-plate.

I

2383. Ἰάειρος **Iaĕirŏs**, *ee-ah´-i-ros;* or

Ἰάϊρος **Iairŏs**, *ee-ahee´-ros;* of Heb. or. (2971); *Jaïrus* (i.e. *Jair*), an Isr.:— Jairus.

2384. Ἰακώβ **Iakōb**, *ee-ak-obe´;* of Heb. or. (3290); *Jacob* (i.e. *Ja´akob*), the progenitor of the Isr.:— also an Isr.:— Jacob.

2385. Ἰάκωβος **Iakōbŏs**, *ee-ak´-o-bos;* the same as 2384 Græcized; *Jacobus,* the name of three Isr.:— James.

2386. ἴαμα **iama**, *ee´-am-ah;* from 2390; a *cure* (the effect):— healing.

2387. Ἰαμβρῆς **Iambrēs**, *ee-am-brace´;* of Eg. or.; *Jambres,* an Eg.:— Jambres.

2388. Ἰαννά **Ianna**, *ee-an-nah´;* prob. of Heb. or. (comp. 3238); *Janna,* an Isr.:— Janna.

2389. Ἰαννῆς **Iannēs**, *ee-an-nace´;* of Eg. or.; *Jannes,* an Eg.:— Jannes.

2390. ἰάομαι **iaŏmai**, *ee-ah´-om-ahee;* mid. voice of appar. a primary verb; to *cure* (lit. or fig.):— heal, make whole.

2391. Ἰάρεδ **Iarĕd**, *ee-ar´-ed* or

Ἰάρετ **Iaret**, *ee-ar´-et;* of Heb. or. (3382); *Jared* (i.e. *Jered*), an antediluvian:— Jared.

2392. ἴασις **iasis**, *ee´-as-is;* from 2390; *curing* (the act):— cure, heal (-ing).

2393. ἴασπις **iaspis**, *ee´-as-pis;* prob. of for. or. (see 3471); "*jasper,*" a gem:— jasper.

2394. Ἰάσων **Iasōn**, *ee-as´-oan;* future act. part. masc. of 2390; *about to cure; Jason,* a Chr.:— Jason.

2395. ἰατρός **iatrŏs**, *ee-at-ros´;* from 2390; a *physician*:— physician.

2396. ἴδε **idĕ**, *id´-eh;* second pers. sing. imper. act. of 1492; used as an interj. to denote *surprise; lo!*:— behold, lo, see.

2397. ἰδέα **idĕa**, *id-eh´-ah;* from 1492; a *sight* (comp. fig. "idea"), i.e. *aspect*:— countenance.

2398. ἴδιος **idiŏs**, *id´-ee-os;* of uncert. aff.; *pertaining to self,* i.e. one's *own;* by impl. *private* or *separate*:— × his acquaintance, when they were alone, apart, aside, due, his (own, proper, several), home, (her, our, thine, your) own (business), private (-ly), proper, severally, their (own).

2399. ἰδιώτης **idiōtēs**, *id-ee-o´-tace;* from 2398; a *private* person, i.e. (by impl.) an *ignoramus* (comp. "idiot"):— ignorant, rude, unlearned.

2400. ἰδού **idŏu**, *id-oo´;* second pers. sing. imper. mid. voice of 1492; used as imper. *lo!*:—behold, lo, see.

2401. Ἰδουμαία **Idŏumaia**, *id-oo-mah´-yah;* of Heb. or. (123); *Idumæa* (i.e. *Edom*), a region E. (and S.) of Pal.:— Idumæa.

2402. ἰδρώς **hidrōs**, *hid-roce´;* a strengthened form of a primary ἴδος **idŏs** (*sweat*); *perspiration*:— sweat.

2403. Ἰεζαβήλ **Iĕzabĕl**, *ee-ed-zab-ale´;* of Heb. or. (348); *Jezebel* (i.e. *Jezebel*), a Tyrian woman (used as a synonym of a termagant or false teacher):— Jezabel.

2404. Ἱεράπολις **Hiĕrapŏlis**, *hee-er-ap´-ol-is;* from 2413 and 4172; *holy city; Hierapolis,* a place in Asia Minor:— Hierapolis.

2405. ἱερατεία **hiĕratĕia**, *hee-er-at-i´-ah;* from 2407; *priestliness,* i.e. the *sacerdotal function*:— office of the priesthood, priest's office.

2406. ἱεράτευμα **hiĕratĕuma**, *hee-er-at´-yoo-mah;* from 2407; the *priestly fraternity,* i.e. *sacerdotal order* (fig.):— priesthood.

2407. ἱερατεύω **hiĕratĕuō**, *hee-er-at-yoo´-o;* prol. from 2409; to *be a priest,* i.e. *perform his functions*:— execute the priest's office.

2408. Ἱερεμίας **Hiĕrĕmias**, *hee-er-em-ee´-as;* of Heb. or. (3414); *Hieremias* (i.e. *Jermijah*), an Isr.:— Jeremiah.

2409. ἱερεύς **hiĕrĕus**, *hee-er-yooce´;* from 2413; a *priest* (lit. or fig.):— (high) priest.

2410. Ἱεριχώ **Hiĕrichō**, *hee-er-ee-kho´;* of Heb. or. (3405); *Jericho,* a place in Pal.:— Jericho.

2411. ἱερόν **hiĕrŏn**, *hee-er-on´;* neut. of 2413; a *sacred* place, i.e. the entire precincts (whereas 3485 denotes the central *sanctuary* itself) of the *Temple* (at Jerusalem or elsewhere):— temple.

2412. ἱεροπρεπής **hiĕrŏprĕpēs**, *hee-er-op-rep-ace´;* from 2413 and the same as 4241; *reverent*:— as becometh holiness.

2413. ἱερός **hiĕrŏs**, *hee-er-os´;* of uncert. aff.; *sacred:*— holy.

2414. Ἱεροσόλυμα **Hiĕrŏsŏluma**, *hee-er-os-ol´-oo-mah;* of Heb. or. [3389]; *Hierosolyma* (i.e. *Jerushalaïm*), the capital of Pal.:— Jerusalem. Comp. *2419.*

2415. Ἱεροσολυμίτης **Hiĕrŏsŏlumitēs**, *hee-er-os-ol-oo-mee´-tace;* from *2414;* a *Hierosolymite*, i.e. inhab. of Hierosolyma:— of Jerusalem.

2416. ἱεροσυλέω **hiĕrŏsulĕō**, *hee-er-os-ool-eh´-o;* from *2417;* to *be a temple-robber* (fig.):— commit sacrilege.

2417. ἱερόσυλος **hiĕrŏsulŏs**, *hee-er-os´-oo-los;* from *2411* and *4813;* a *temple-despoiler:*— robber of churches.

2418. ἱερουργέω **hiĕrŏurgĕō**, *hee-er-oorg-eh´-o;* from a compound of *2411* and the base of *2041;* to *be a temple-worker*, i.e. *officiate as a priest* (fig.):— minister.

2419. Ἱερουσαλήμ **Hiĕrŏusalēm**, *hee-er-oo-sal-ame´;* of Heb. or. [3389]; *Hierusalem* (i.e. *Jerushalem*), the capital of Pal.:— Jerusalem. Comp. *2414.*

2420. ἱερωσύνη **hiĕrŏsunē**, *hee-er-o-soo´-nay;* from *2413; sacredness,* i.e. (by impl.) the *priestly office:*— priesthood.

2421. Ἰεσσαί **Iĕssai**, *es-es-sah´-ee;* of Heb. or. [3448]; *Jessae* (i.e. *Jishai*), an Isr.:— Jesse.

2422. Ἰεφθάε **Iĕphthaĕ**, *ee-ef-thah´-eh;* of Heb. or. [3316]; *Jephthaë* (i.e. *Jiphtach*), an Isr.:— Jephthah.

2423. Ἰεχονίας **Iĕchŏnias**, *ee-ekh-on-ee´-as;* of Heb. or. [3204]; *Jechonias* (i.e. *Jekonjah*), an Isr.:— Jechonias.

2424. Ἰησοῦς **Iēsŏus**, *ee-ay-sooce´;* of Heb. or. [3091]; *Jesus* (i.e. *Jehoshua*), the name of our Lord and two (three) other Isr.:— Jesus.

2425. ἱκανός **hikanŏs**, *hik-an-os´;* from ἵκω **hikō** [ἱκάνω **hikanō** or ἱκνέομαι **hiknĕŏmai**, akin to 2240] (to *arrive*); *competent* (as if *coming* in season), i.e. *ample* (in amount) or *fit* (in character):— able, + content, enough, good, great, large, long (while), many, meet, much, security, sore, sufficient, worthy.

2426. ἱκανότης **hikanŏtēs**, *hik-an-ot´-ace;* from *2425; ability:*— sufficiency.

2427. ἱκανόω **hikanŏō**, *hik-an-ŏ´-o;* from *2425;* to *enable,* i.e. *qualify:*— make able (meet).

2428. ἱκετηρία **hikĕtēria**, *hik-et-ay-ree´-ah;* from a der. of the base of *2425* (through the idea of *approaching* for a favor); *intreaty:*— supplication.

2429. ἱκμάς **hikmas**, *hik-mas´;* of uncert aff.; *dampness:*— moisture.

2430. Ἰκόνιον **Ikŏniŏn**, *ee-kon´-ee-on;* perh. from *1504; image-like; Iconium,* a place in Asia Minor:— Iconium.

2431. ἱλαρός **hilarŏs**, *hil-ar-os´;* from the same as *2436; propitious* or *merry* ("*hilarious*"), i.e. *prompt* or *willing:*— cheerful.

2432. ἱλαρότης **hilarŏtēs**, *hil-ar-ot´-ace;* from *2431; alacrity:*— cheerfulness.

2433. ἱλάσκομαι **hilaskŏmai**, *hil-as´-kom-ahee;* mid. voice from the same as

2436; to *conciliate,* i.e. (tran.) to *atone* for (sin), or (intr.) *be propitious:*— be merciful, make reconciliation for.

2434. ἱλασμός **hilasmŏs**, *hil-as-mos´; atonement,* i.e. (concr.) an *expiator:*— propitiation.

2435. ἱλαστήριον **hilastēriŏn**, *hil-as-tay´-ree-on;* neut. of a der. of *2433;* an *expiatory* (place or thing), i.e. (concr.) an atoning *victim*, or (spec.) the *lid* of the Ark (in the Temple):— mercyseat, propitiation.

2436. ἵλεως **hilĕōs**, *hil´-eh-oce;* perh. from the alt. form of *138; cheerful* (as *attractive*), i.e. *propitious;* adv. (by Heb.) God be *gracious!,* i.e. (in averting some calamity) *far* be it:— be it far, merciful.

2437. Ἰλλυρικόν **Illurikŏn**, *il-loo-ree-kon´;* neut. of an adj. from a name of uncert. der.: (the) *Illyrican* (shore), i.e. (as a name itself) *Illyricum,* a region of Europe:— Illyricum.

2438. ἱμάς **himas**, *hee-mas´;* perh. from the same as *260;* a *strap,* i.e. (spec.) the *tie* (of a sandal) or the *lash* (of a scourge):— latchet, thong.

2439. ἱματίζω **himatizō**, *him-at-id´-zo;* from *2440;* to *dress:*— clothe.

2440. ἱμάτιον **himatiŏn**, *him-at´-ee-on;* neut. of a presumed der. of ἕννυμι **ĕnnumi** (to *put on*); a *dress* (inner or outer):— apparel, cloke, clothes, garment, raiment, robe, vesture.

2441. ἱματισμός **himatismŏs**, *him-at-is-mos´;* from *2439; clothing:*— apparel (x -led), array, raiment, vesture.

2442. ἱμείρομαι **himĕirŏmai**, *him-i´-rom-ahee;* mid. voice from ἵμερος **himĕrŏs** (a *yearning;* of uncert. aff.); to *long for:*— be affectionately desirous.

2443. ἵνα **hina**, *hin´-ah;* prob. from the same as the former part of *1438* (through the demonstrative idea; comp. *3588*); in order *that* (denoting the *purpose* or the *result*):— albeit, because, to the intent (that), lest, so as, (so) that, (for) to. Comp. *3363.*

ἵνα μή **hina mē**. See *3363.*

2444. ἱνατί **hinati**, *hin-at-ee´;* from *2443* and *5101; for what* reason?, i.e. *why?:*— wherefore, why.

2445. Ἰόππη **Iŏppē**, *ee-op´-pay;* of Heb. or. [3305]; *Joppe* (i.e. *Japho*), a place in Pal.:— Joppa.

2446. Ἰορδάνης **Iŏrdanēs**, *ee-or-dan´-ace;* of Heb. or. [3383]; the *Jordanes* (i.e. *Jarden*), a river of Pal.:— Jordan.

2447. ἰός **iŏs**, *ee-os´;* perh. from εἷμι **ĕimi** (to *go*) or ἵημι **hiēmi** (to *send*); *rust* (as if *emitted* by metals); also *venom* (as *emitted* by serpents):— poison, rust.

2448. Ἰουδά **Iŏuda**, *ee-oo-dah´;* of Heb. or. [3063 or perh. 3194]; *Judah* (i.e. *Jehudah* or *Juttah*), a part of (or place in) Pal.:— Judah.

2449. Ἰουδαία **Iŏudaia**, *ee-oo-dah´-yah;* fem. of *2453* (with *1093* impl.); the *Judæan* land (i.e. *Judæa*), a region of Pal.:— Judæa.

2450. Ἰουδαΐζω **Iŏudaïzō**, *ee-oo-dah-id´-zo;* from *2453;* to *become a Judæan,* i.e. "*Judaize*":— live as the Jews.

2451. Ἰουδαϊκός **Iŏudaïkŏs**, *ee-oo-dah-ee-kos´;* from *2453; Judaïc,* i.e. *resembling a Judæan:*— Jewish.

2452. Ἰουδαϊκῶς **Iŏudaïkōs**, *ee-oo-dah-ee-koce´;* adv. from *2451; Judaïcally* or *in a manner resembling a Judæan:*— as do the Jews.

2453. Ἰουδαῖος **Iŏudaiŏs**, *ee-oo-dah´-yos;* from *2448* (in the sense of *2455* as a country); *Judæan,* i.e. belonging to *Jehudah:*— Jew (-ess), of Judæa.

2454. Ἰουδαϊσμός **Iŏudaismŏs**, *ee-oo-dah-is-mos´;* from *2450;* "*Judaïsm*", i.e. the *Jewish* faith and usages:— Jews' religion.

2455. Ἰουδάς **Iŏudas**, *ee-oo-das´;* of Heb. or. [3063]; *Judas* (i.e. *Jehudah*), the name of ten Isr.; also of the posterity of one of them and its region:— Juda (-h, -s); Jude.

2456. Ἰουλία **Iŏulia**, *ee-oo-lee´-ah;* fem. of the same as *2457; Julia,* a Chr. woman:— Julia.

2457. Ἰούλιος **Iŏuliŏs**, *ee-oo´-lee-os;* of Lat. or.; *Julius,* a centurion:— Julius.

2458. Ἰουνίας **Iŏunias**, *ee-oo-nee´-as;* of Lat. or.; *Junias,* a Chr.:— Junias.

2459. Ἰοῦστος **Iŏustŏs**, *ee-ooce´-tos;* of Lat. or. ("*just*"); *Justus,* the name of three Chr.:— Justus.

2460. ἱππεύς **hippĕus**, *hip-yooce´;* from *2462;* an *equestrian,* i.e. member of a *cavalry* corps.:— horseman.

2461. ἱππικόν **hippikŏn**, *hip-pee-kon´;* neut. of a der. of *2462;* the *cavalry* force:— horse (-men).

2462. ἵππος **hippŏs**, *hip´-pos;* of uncert. aff.; a *horse:*— horse.

2463. ἶρις **iris**, *ee´-ris;* perh. from *2046* (as a symbol of the female *messenger* of the pagan deities); a *rainbow* ("*iris*"):— rainbow.

2464. Ἰσαάκ **Isaak**, *ee-sah-ak´;* of Heb. or. [3327]; *Isaac* (i.e. *Jitschak*), the son of Abraham:— Isaac.

2465. ἰσάγγελος **isaggĕlŏs**, *ee-sang´-el-los;* from *2470* and *32; like an angel,* i.e. *angelic:*— equal unto the angels.

2466. Ἰσαχάρ **Isachar**, *ee-sakh-ar´;* of Heb. or. [3485]; *Isachar* (i.e. *Jissaskar*), a son of Jacob (fig. his desc.):— Issachar.

2467. ἴσημι **isēmi**, *is´-ay-mee;* assumed by some as the base of cert. irreg. forms of *1492;* to *know:*— know.

2468. ἴσθι **isthi**, *is´-thee;* second pers. imper. present of *1510; be thou:*— + agree, be, x give thyself wholly to.

2469. Ἰσκαριώτης **Iskariŏtēs**, *is-kar-ee-o´-tace;* of Heb. or. [prob. 377 and 7149]; *inhabitant of Kerioth; Iscariotes* (i.e. *Keriothite*), an epithet of Judas the traitor:— Iscariot.

2470. ἴσος **isŏs**, *ee´-sos;* prob. from *1492* (through the idea of *seeming*); *similar* (in amount and kind):— + agree, as much, equal, like.

2471. ἰσότης **isŏtēs**, *ee-sot´-ace; likeness* (in condition or proportion); by impl. *equity:*— equal (-ity).

2472. ἰσότιμος **isŏtimŏs**, *ee-sot´-ee-*

mos; from 2470 and 5092; *of equal value* or *honor*:— like precious.

2473. ἰσόψυχος **isŏpsuchŏs**, *ee-sop'-soo-khos*; from 2470 and 5590; *of similar spirit*:— likeminded.

2474. Ἰσραήλ **Israēl**, *is-rah-ale'*; of Heb. or. [3478]; *Israel* (i.e. *Jisrael*), the adopted name of Jacob, incl. his desc. (lit. or fig.):— Israel.

2475. Ἰσραηλίτης **Israēlitēs**, *is-rah-ale-ee'-tace*; from 2474; an *"Israelite"*, i.e. desc. of Israel (lit. or fig.):— Israelite.

2476. ἵστημι **histēmi**, *his'-tay-mee*; a prol. form of a primary στάω **staŏ**, *stah'-o* (of the same mean., and used for it in certain tenses); to *stand* (tran. or intr.), used in various applications (lit. or fig.):— abide, appoint, bring, continue, covenant, establish, hold up, lay, present, set (up), stanch, stand (by, forth, still, up). Comp. 5087.

2477. ἱστορέω **histŏrĕō**, *his-tor-eh'-o*; from a der. of 1492; to *be knowing* (*learned*), i.e. (by impl.) to *visit* for information (*interview*):— see.

2478. ἰσχυρός **ischurŏs**, *is-khoo-ros'*; from 2479; *forcible* (lit. or fig.):— boisterous, mighty (-ier), powerful, strong (-er, man), valiant.

2479. ἰσχύς **ischus**, *is-khoos'*; from a der. of ἴς is (*force*; comp. ἔσχον **ĕschŏn**, a form of 2192); *forcefulness* (lit. or fig.):— ability, might (I-ilyl), power, strength.

2480. ἰσχύω **ischuō**, *is-khoo'-o*; from 2479; to *have* (or *exercise*) force (lit. or fig.):— be able, avail, can do (I-notl), could, be good, might, prevail, be of strength, be whole, + much work.

2481. ἴσως **isŏs**, *ee'-soce*; adv. from 2470; *likely*, i.e. *perhaps*:— it may be.

2482. Ἰταλία **Italia**, *ee-tal-ee'-ah*; prob. of for. or.; *Italia*, a region of Europe:— Italy.

2483. Ἰταλικός **Italikŏs**, *ee-tal-ee-kos'*; from 2482; *Italic*, i.e. belonging to Italia:— Italian.

2484. Ἰτουραία **Itŏuraia**, *ee-too-rah'-yah*; of Heb. or. [3195]; *Ituræa* (i.e. *Jetur*), a region of Pal.:— Ituræa.

2485. ἰχθύδιον **ichthudiŏn**, *ikh-thoo'-dee-on*; dimin. from 2486; a *petty fish*:— little (small) fish.

2486. ἰχθύς **ichthus**, *ikh-thoos'*; of uncert. aff.; a *fish*:— fish.

2487. ἴχνος **ichnŏs**, *ikh'-nos*; from ἱκνέομαι **iknĕŏmai** (to *arrive*; comp. 2240); a *track* (fig.):— step.

2488. Ἰωάθαμ **Iŏatham**, *ee-o-ath'-am*; of Heb. or. [3147]; *Joatham* (i.e. *Jotham*), an Isr.:— Joatham.

2489. Ἰωάννα **Iŏanna**, *ee-o-an'-nah*; fem. of the same as 2491; *Joanna*, a Chr.:— Joanna.

2490. Ἰωαννᾶς **Iŏannas**, *ee-o-an-nas'*; a form of 2491; *Joannas*, an Isr.:— Joannas.

2491. Ἰωάννης **Iŏannēs**, *ee-o-an'-nace*; of Heb. or. [3110]; *Joannes* (i.e. *Jochanan*), the name of four Isr.:— John.

2492. Ἰώβ **Iŏb**, *ee-obe'*; of Heb. or. [347]; *Job* (i.e. *Ijob*), a patriarch:— Job.

2493. Ἰωήλ **Iŏēl**, *ee-o-ale'*; of Heb. or. [3100]; *Joel*, an Isr.:— Joel.

2494. Ἰωνάν **Iŏnan**, *ee-o-nan'* or Ἰωναμ **Iŏnam**, *ee-o-nam'*; prob. for 2491 or 2495; *Jonan*, an Isr.:— Jonan (Jonam).

2495. Ἰωνᾶς **Iŏnas**, *ee-o-nas'*; of Heb. or. [3124]; *Jonas* (i.e. *Jonah*), the name of two Isr.:— Jonas.

2496. Ἰωράμ **Iŏram**, *ee-o-ram'*; of Heb. or. [3141]; *Joram*, an Isr.:— Joram.

2497. Ἰωρείμ **Iŏrĕim**, *ee-o-rime'* or Ἰωρίμ **Iŏrim**, *ee-o-reem'*; perh. for 2496; *Jorim*, an Isr.:— Jorim.

2498. Ἰωσαφάτ **Iŏsaphat**, *ee-o-saf-at'*; of Heb. or. [3092]; *Josaphat* (i.e. *Jehoshaphat*), an Isr.:— Josaphat.

2499. Ἰωσή **Iŏsē**, *ee-o-say'*; gen. of 2500; *Jose*, an Isr.:— Jose.

2500. Ἰωσῆς **Iŏsēs**, *ee-o-sace'*; perh. for 2501; *Joses*, the name of two Isr.:— Joses. Comp. 2499.

2501. Ἰωσήφ **Iŏsēph**, *ee-o-safe'*; of Heb. or. [3130]; *Joseph*, the name of seven Isr.:— Joseph.

2502. Ἰωσίας **Iŏsias**, *ee-o-see'-as*; of Heb. or. [2977]; *Josias* (i.e. *Joshiah*), an Isr.:— Josias.

2503. ἰῶτα **iŏta**, *ee-o'-tah*; of Heb. or. [the tenth letter of the Heb. alphabet]; *"iota,"* the name of the eighth letter of the Greek alphabet, put (fig.) for a very small part of anything:— jot.

K

2504. κἀγώ **kagō**, *kag-o'*; from 2532 and 1473 (so also the dat.

κἀμοί **kamŏi**, *kam-oy'*; and acc.

κἀμέ **kamĕ**, *kam-eh'*; and (or *also*, *even*, etc.) *I*, (*to*) *me*:— (and, even, even so, so) I (also, in like wise), both me, me also.

2505. κατά **katha**, *kath-ah'*; from 2596 and the neut. plur. of 3739; *according to which* things, i.e. *just as*:— as.

2506. καθαίρεσις **kathairĕsis**, *kath-ah'-ee-res-is*; from 2507; *demolition*; fig. *extinction*:— destruction, pulling down.

2507. καθαιρέω **kathairĕō**, *kath-ahee-reh'-o*; from 2596 and 138 (incl. its alt.); to *lower* (or with violence) *demolish* (lit. or fig.):— cast (pull, put, take) down, destroy.

2508. καθαίρω **kathairō**, *kath-ah'-ee-ro*; from 2513; to *cleanse*, i.e. (spec.) to *prune*; fig. to *expiate*:— purge.

2509. καθάπερ **kathapĕr**, *kath-ap'-er*; from 2505 and 4007; *exactly as*:— (even, as well) as.

2510. καθάπτω **kathaptō**, *kath-ap'-to*; from 2596 and 680; to *seize upon*:— fasten on.

2511. καθαρίζω **katharizō**, *kath-ar-id'-zo*; from 2513; to *cleanse* (lit. or fig.):— (make) clean (-se), purge, purify.

2512. καθαρισμός **katharismŏs**, *kath-ar-is-mos'*; from 2511; a *washing off*, i.e. (cer.) *ablution*, (mor.) *expiation*:— cleansing, + purge, purification (-fying).

2513. καθαρός **katharŏs**, *kath-ar-os'*; of

uncert. aff.; *clean* (lit. or fig.):— clean, clear, pure.

2514. καθαρότης **katharŏtēs**, *kath-ar-ot'-ace*; from 2513; *cleanness* (cer.):— purification.

2515. καθέδρα **kathĕdra**, *kath-ed'-rah*; from 2596 and the same as 1476; a *bench* (lit. or fig.):— seat.

2516. καθέζομαι **kathĕzŏmai**, *kath-ed'-zom-ahee*; from 2596 and the base of 1476; to *sit down*:— sit.

2517. καθεξῆς **kathĕxēs**, *kath-ex-ace'*; from 2596 and 1836; thereafter, i.e. consecutively; as a noun (by ellip. of noun) a *subsequent* person or time:— after (-ward), by (in) order.

2518. καθεύδω **kathĕudō**, *kath-yoo'-do*; from 2596 and εὕδω **hĕudō** (to *sleep*); to lie *down* to *rest*, i.e. (by impl.) to *fall asleep* (lit. or fig.):— (be a-) sleep.

2519. καθηγητής **kathēgĕtēs**, *kath-ayg-ay'-tace*; from a compound of 2596 and 2233; a *guide*, i.e. (fig.) a *teacher*:— master.

2520. καθήκω **kathēkō**, *kath-ay'-ko*; from 2596 and 2240; to *reach to*, i.e. (neut. of pres. act. part., fig. as adj.) *becoming*:— convenient, fit.

2521. κάθημαι **kathēmai**, *kath'-ay-mahee*; from 2596; and ἧμαι **hēmai** (to *sit*; akin to the base of 1476); to *sit down*; fig. to *remain*, *reside*:— dwell, sit (by, down).

2522. καθημερινός **kathēmĕrinŏs**, *kath-ay-mer-ee-nos'*; from 2596 and 2250; *quotidian*:— daily.

2523. καθίζω **kathizō**, *kath-id'-zo*; another (act.) form for 2516; to *seat down*, i.e. *set* (fig. *appoint*); intr. to *sit* (down); fig. to *settle* (*hover*, *dwell*):— continue, set, sit (down), tarry.

2524. καθίημι **kathiēmi**, *kath-ee'-ay-mee*; from 2596; and ἵημι **hiēmi** (to *send*); to *lower*:— let down.

2525. καθίστημι **kathistēmi**, *kath-is'-tay-mee*; from 2596 and 2476; to *place down* (permanently), i.e. (fig.) to *designate*, *constitute*, *convoy*:— appoint, be, conduct, make, ordain, set.

2526. καθό **kathŏ**, *kath-o'*; from 2596 and 3739; *according to which* thing, i.e. *precisely as*, in proportion as:— according to that, (inasmuch) as.

2526'. καθολικός **kathŏlikŏs**, *kath-ol-ee-kos'*; from 2527; *universal*:— general.

2527. καθόλου **kathŏlŏu**, *kath-ol'-oo*; from 2596 and 3650; *on the whole*, i.e. *entirely*:— at all.

2528. καθοπλίζω **kathŏplizō**, *kath-op-lid'-zo*; from 2596; and 3695; to *equip fully* with armor:— arm.

2529. καθοράω **kathŏraō**, *kath-or-ah'-o*; from 2596 and 3708; to *behold fully*, i.e. (fig.) *distinctly apprehend*:— clearly see.

2530. καθότι **kathŏti**, *kath-ot'-ee*; from 2596; and 3739 and 5100; *according to which certain* thing, i.e. *as far* (or *inasmuch*) *as*:— (according, forasmuch) as, because (that).

2531. καθώς **kathōs**, *kath-oce'*; from 2596 and 5613; *just* (or *inasmuch*) *as*, *that:*— according to, (according, even) as, how, when.

2532. καί **kai**, *kahee;* appar. a primary particle, having a *copulative* and sometimes also a *cumulative* force; *and, also, even, so, then, too,* etc.; often used in connection (or composition) with other particles or small words:— and, also, both, but, even, for, if, indeed, likewise, moreover, or, so, that, then, therefore, when, yet.

2533. Καϊάφας **Kaïaphas**, *kah-ee-af'-as;* of Chald. or.; *the dell; Caïaphas* (i.e. *Cajepha*), an Isr.:— Caiaphas.

2534. καίγε **kaigĕ**, *kah'-ee-gheh;* from 2532 and 1065; *and at least* (or *even, indeed*):— and, at least.

2535. Κάϊν **Kaïn**, *kah'-in;* of Heb. or. [7014]; *Cain,* (i.e. *Cajin*), the son of Adam:— Cain.

2536. Καϊνάν **Kaïnan**, *kah-ee-nan'* or

Καϊνάμ **Kaïnam** *kah-ee-nam';* of Heb. or. [7018]; *Caïnan* (i.e. *Kenan*), the name of two patriarchs:— Cainan (Cainam).

2537. καινός **kainŏs**, *kahee-nos';* of uncert. aff.; *new* (espec. in *freshness;* while 3501 is prop. so with respect to *age:*— new.

2538. καινότης **kainŏtēs**, *kahee-not'-ace;* from 2537; *renewal* (fig.):— newness.

2539. καίπερ **kaipĕr**, *kah'-ee-per;* from 2532 and 4007; *and indeed,* i.e. *nevertheless* or *notwithstanding:*— and yet, although.

2540. καιρός **kairŏs**, *kahee-ros';* of uncert. aff.; an *occasion,* i.e. *set* or *proper* time:— × always, opportunity, (convenient, due) season, (due, short, while) time, a while. Comp. 5550.

2541. Καῖσαρ **Kaisar**, *kah'-ee-sar;* of Lat. or.; *Cæsar,* a title of the Rom. emperor:— Cæsar.

2542. Καισάρεια **Kaisarĕia**, *kahee-sar'-i-a;* from 2541; *Cæsaria,* the name of two places in Pal.:— Cæsarea.

2543. καίτοι **kaitŏi**, *kah'-ee-toy;* from 2532 and 5104; *and yet,* i.e. *nevertheless:*— although.

2544. καίτοιγε **kaitŏigĕ**, *kah'-ee-toyg-eh;* from 2543 and 1065; *and yet indeed,* i.e. *although really:*— nevertheless, though.

2545. καίω **kaiō**, *kah'-yo;* appar. a primary verb; *to set on fire,* i.e. *kindle* or (by impl.) *consume:*— burn, light.

2546. κἀκεῖ **kakĕi**, *kak-i';* from 2532 and 1563; *likewise in that place:*— and there, there (thither) also.

2547. κἀκεῖθεν **kakĕithĕn**, *kak-i'-then;* from 2532 and 1564; *likewise from that place* (or *time*):— and afterward (from) (thence), thence also.

2548. κἀκεῖνος **kakĕinŏs**, *kak-i'-nos;* from 2532 and 1565; *likewise that* (or *those*):— and him (other, them), even he, him also, them (also), (and) they.

2549. κακία **kakia**, *kak-ee'-ah;* from 2556; *badness,* i.e. (subj.) *depravity,* or (act.) *malignity,* or (pass.) *trouble:*— evil, malice (-iousness), naughtiness, wickedness.

2550. κακοήθεια **kakŏēthĕia**, *kak-ŏ-ay'-thi-ah;* from a compound of 2556 and 2239; *bad character,* i.e. (spec.) *mischievousness:*— malignity.

2551. κακολογέω **kakŏlŏgĕō**, *kak-ol-og-eh'-o;* from a compound of 2556 and 3056; *to revile:*— curse, speak evil of.

2552. κακοπάθεια **kakŏpathĕia**, *kak-op-ath'-i-ah;* from a compound of 2556 and 3806; *hardship:*— suffering affliction.

2553. κακοπαθέω **kakŏpathĕō**, *kak-op-ath-eh'-o;* from the same as 2552; to *undergo hardship:*— be afflicted, endure afflictions (hardness), suffer trouble.

2554. κακοποιέω **kakŏpŏiĕō**, *kak-op-oy-eh'-o;* from 2555; *to be a bad-doer,* i.e. (obj.) to *injure,* or (gen.) to *sin:*— do (ing) evil.

2555. κακοποιός **kakŏpŏiŏs**, *kak-op-oy-os';* from 2556 and 4160; a *bad-doer;* (spec.) a *criminal:*— evil-doer, malefactor.

2556. κακός **kakŏs**, *kak-os';* appar. a primary word; *worthless* (*intrinsically,* such; whereas 4190 prop. refers to *effects*), i.e. (subj.) *depraved,* or (obj.) *injurious:*— bad, evil, harm, ill, noisome, wicked.

2557. κακοῦργος **kakŏurgŏs**, *kak-oor'-gos;* from 2556 and the base of 2041; a *wrong-doer,* i.e. *criminal:*— evil-doer, malefactor.

2558. κακουχέω **kakŏuchĕō**, *kak-oo-kheh'-o;* from a presumed compound of 2556 and 2192; to *maltreat:*— which suffer adversity, torment.

2559. κακόω **kakŏō**, *kak-ŏ'-o;* from 2556; to *injure;* fig. to *exasperate:*— make evil affected, entreat evil, harm, hurt, vex.

2560. κακῶς **kakōs**, *kak-oce';* from 2556; *badly* (phys. or mor.):— amiss, diseased, evil, grievously, miserably, sick, sore.

2561. κάκωσις **kakōsis**, *kak'-o-sis;* from 2559; *maltreatment:*— affliction.

2562. καλάμη **kalamē**, *kal-am'-ay;* fem. of 2563; a *stalk* of grain, i.e. (collect.) *stubble:*— stubble.

2563. κάλαμος **kalamŏs**, *kal'-am-os;* or uncert. aff.; a *reed* (the plant or its stem, or that of a similar plant); by impl. a *pen:*— pen, reed.

2564. καλέω **kalĕō**, *kal-eh'-o;* akin to the base of 2753; to *"call"* (prop. aloud, but used in a variety of applications, dir. or otherwise):— bid, call (forth), (whose, whose sur-) name (was [called]).

2565. καλλιέλαιος **kalliĕlaiŏs**, *kal-le-el'-ah-yos;* from the base of 2566 and 1636; a *cultivated olive* tree, i.e. a *domesticated* or *improved* one:— good olive tree.

2566. κάλλιον **kalliŏn**, *kal-lee'-on;* neut. of the (irreg.) comp. of 2570; (adv.) *better* than many:— very well.

2567. καλοδιδάσκαλος **kalŏdidaskalŏs**, *kal-od-id-as'-kal-os;* from 2570 and 1320; a *teacher* of the *right:*— teacher of good things.

2568. Καλοὶ Λιμένες **Kalŏi Limĕnĕs**, *kal-oy' lee-men'-es;* plur. of 2570 and 3040; *Good Harbors,* i.e. *Fairhaven,* a bay of Crete:— fair havens.

2569. καλοποιέω **kalŏpŏiĕō**, *kal-op-oy-eh'-o;* from 2570 and 4160; to *do well,* i.e. live virtuously:— well doing.

2570. καλός **kalŏs**, *kal-os';* of uncert. aff.; prop. *beautiful,* but chiefly (fig.) *good* (lit. or mor.), i.e. *valuable* or *virtuous* (for *appearance* or *use,* and thus distinguished from 18, which is prop. *intrinsic*):— × better, fair, good (-ly), honest, meet, well, worthy.

2571. κάλυμα **kaluma**, *kal'-oo-mah;* from 2572; a *cover,* i.e. *veil:*— vail.

2572. καλύπτω **kaluptō**, *kal-oop'-to;* akin to 2813 and 2928; to *cover up* (lit. or fig.):— cover, hide.

2573. καλῶς **kalōs**, *kal-oce';* adv. from 2570; *well* (usually mor.):— (in a) good (place), honestly, + recover, (full) well.

2574. κάμηλος **kamēlŏs**, *kam'-ay-los;* of Heb. or. [1581]; a *"camel":*— camel.

2575. κάμινος **kaminŏs**, *kam'-ee-nos;* prob. from 2545; a *furnace:*— furnace.

2576. καμμύω **kammuō**, *kam-moo'-o;* from a compound of 2596 and the base of 3466; to *shut down,* i.e. *close* the eyes:— close.

2577. κάμνω **kamnō**, *kam'-no;* appar. a primary verb; prop. to *toil,* i.e. (by impl.) to *tire* (fig. *faint, sicken*):— faint, sick, be wearied.

2578. κάμπτω **kamptō**, *kamp'-to;* appar. a primary verb; to *bend:*— bow.

2579. κἄν **kan**, *kan;* from 2532 and 1437; *and* (or *even*) *if:*— and (also) if (so much as), if but, at the least, though, yet.

2580. Κανᾶ **Kana**, *kan-ah';* of Heb. or. [comp. 7071]; *Cana,* a place in Pal.:— Cana.

2581. Κανανίτης **Kananitēs**, *kan-an-ee'-tace;* of Chald. or. [comp. 7067]; *zealous; Cananitēs,* an epithet:— Canaanite [by mistake for a der. from 5477].

2582. Κανδάκη **Kandakē**, *kan-dak'-ay;* of for. or.; *Candacë,* an Eg. queen:— Candace.

2583. κανών **kanōn**, *kan-ohn';* from κάνη **kanē** (a straight *reed,* i.e. *rod*); a *rule* (*"canon"*), i.e. (fig.) a *standard* (of faith and practice); by impl. a *boundary,* i.e. (fig.) a *sphere* (of activity):— line, rule.

2584. Καπερναούμ **Kapĕrnaŏum**, *kap-er-nah-oom';* of Heb. or. [prob. 3723 and 5151]; *Capernaüm* (i.e. *Caphanachum*), a place in Pal.:— Capernaum.

2585. καπηλεύω **kapēlĕuō**, *kap-ale-yoo'-o;* from κάπηλος **kapēlŏs** (a *huckster*); to *retail,* i.e. (by impl.) to *adulterate* (fig.):— corrupt.

2586. καπνός **kapnŏs**, *kap-nos';* of uncert. aff.; *smoke:*— smoke.

2587. Καππαδοκία **Kappadŏkia**, *kap-pad-ok-ee'-ah;* of for. or.; *Cappadocia,* a region of Asia Minor:— Cappadocia.

2588. καρδία **kardia**, *kar-dee'-ah;* prol. from a primary κάρ **kar** (Lat. *cor, "heart"*); the *heart,* i.e. (fig.) the *thoughts* or *feelings* (*mind*); also (by anal.) the *middle*:— (+ broken-) heart (-ed).

2589. καρδιογνώστης **kardiŏgnōstēs**. *kar-dee-og-noce'-tace;* from 2588 and 1097; a *heart-knower:*— which knowest the hearts.

2590. καρπός **karpŏs**. *kar-pos';* prob. from the base of 726; *fruit* (as *plucked*), lit. or fig.:— fruit.

2591. Κάρπος **Karpŏs**, *kar'-pos;* perh. for 2590; *Carpus*, prob. a Chr.:— Carpus.

2592. καρποφορέω **karpŏphŏrĕō**, *kar-pof-or-eh'-o;* from 2593; to *be fertile* (lit. or fig.):— be (bear, bring forth) fruit (-ful).

2593. καρποφόρος **karpŏphŏrŏs**, *kar-pof-or'-os;* from 2590 and 5342; *fruit-bearing* (fig.):— fruitful.

2594. καρτερέω **kartĕrĕō**, *kar-ter-eh'-o;* from a der. of 2904 (transp.); to *be strong*, i.e. (fig.) *steadfast* (*patient*):— endure.

2595. κάρφος **karphŏs**, *kar'-fos;* from κάρφω **karphō** (to *wither*); a dry *twig* or *straw:*— mote.

2596. κατά **kata**, *kat-ah';* a primary particle; (prep.) *down* (in place or time), in varied relations (according to the case [gen., dat. or acc.] with which it is joined):— about, according as (to), after, against, (when they were) × alone, among, and, × apart, (even, like) as (concerning, pertaining to touching), × aside, at, before, beyond, by, to the charge of, [charita-] bly, concerning, + covered, [dai-] ly, down, every, (+ far more) exceeding, × more excellent, for, from … to, godly, in (-asmuch, divers, every, × respect of), … by, after the manner of, + by any means, beyond (out of) measure, × mightily, more, × natural, of (up-) on (× part), out (of every), over against, (+ your) × own, + particularly, so, through (-oughout, oughout every), thus, (un-) to (-gether, -ward), × uttermost, where (-by), with. In composition it retains many of these applications, and frequently denotes *opposition, distribution,* or *intensity.*

2597. καταβαίνω **katabainō**, *kat-ab-ah'-ee-no;* from 2596 and the base of 939; to *descend* (lit. or fig.):— come (get, go, step) down, descend, fall (down).

2598. καταβάλλω **kataballō**, *kat-ab-al'-lo;* from 2596 and 906; to *throw down:*— cast down, descend, fall (down), lay.

2599. καταβαρέω **katabarĕō**, *kat-ab-ar-eh'-o;* from 2596 and 916; to *impose upon:*— burden.

2600. κατάβασις **katabasis**, *kat-ab'-as-is;* from 2597; a *declivity:*— descent.

2601. καταβιβάζω **katabibazō**, *kat-ab-ib-ad'-zo;* from 2596 and a der. of the base of 939; to *cause to go down*, i.e. *precipitate:*— bring (thrust) down.

2602. καταβολή **katabŏlē**, *kat-ab-ol-ay';* from 2598; a *deposition*, i.e. *founding;* fig. *conception:*— conceive, foundation.

2603. καταβραβεύω **katabrabĕuō**, *kat-ab-rab-yoo'-o;* from 2596 and 1018 (in its orig. sense); to *award* the price

against, i.e. (fig.) to *defraud* (of salvation):— beguile of reward.

2604. καταγγελεύς **kataggĕlĕus**, *kat-ang-gel-yooce';* from 2605; a *proclaimer:*— setter forth.

2605. καταγγέλλω **kataggĕllō**, *kat-ang-gel'-lo;* from 2596 and the base of 32; to *proclaim, promulgate:*— declare, preach, shew, speak of, teach.

2606. καταγελάω **katagĕlaō**, *kat-ag-el-ah'-o;* to *laugh down*, i.e. *deride:*— laugh to scorn.

2607. καταγινώσκω **kataginōskō**, *kat-ag-in-o'-sko;* from 2596 and 1097; to *note against*, i.e. *find fault with:*— blame, condemn.

2608. κατάγνυμι **katagnumi**, *kat-ag'-noo-mee;* from 2596 and the base of 4486; to *rend in pieces*, i.e. *crack apart:*— break.

2609. κατάγω **katagō**, *kat-ag'-o;* from 2596 and 71; to *lead down;* spec. to *moor* a vessel:— bring (down, forth), (bring to) land, touch.

2610. καταγωνίζομαι **katagōnizŏmai**, *kat-ag-o-nid'-zom-ahee;* from 2596 and 75; to *struggle against*, i.e. (by impl.) to *overcome:*— subdue.

2611. καταδέω **katadĕō**, *kat-ad-eh'-o;* from 2596 and 1210; to *tie down*, i.e. *bandage* (a wound):— bind up.

2612. κατάδηλος **katadēlŏs**, *kat-ad'-ay-los;* from 2596 intens. and 1212; *manifest:*— far more evident.

2613. καταδικάζω **katadikazō**, *kat-ad-ik-ad'-zo;* from 2596 and a der. of 1349; to *adjudge against*, i.e. *pronounce guilty:*— condemn.

2614. καταδιώκω **katadiōkō**, *kat-ad-ee-o'-ko;* from 2596 and 1377; to *hunt down*, i.e. *search for:*— follow after.

2615. καταδουλόω **katadŏulŏō**, *kat-ad-oo-lŏ'-o;* from 2596 and 1402; to *enslave utterly:*— bring into bondage.

2616. καταδυναστεύω **katadunastĕuō**, *kat-ad-oo-nas-tyoo'-o;* from 2596 and a der. of 1413; to *exercise dominion against*, i.e. *oppress:*— oppress.

2617. καταισχύνω **kataischunō**, *kat-ahee-skhoo'-no;* from 2596 and 153; to *shame down*, i.e. *disgrace* or (by impl.) *put to the blush:*— confound, dishonour, (be a-, make a-) shame (-d).

2618. κατακαίω **katakaiō**, *kat-ak-ah'-ee-o;* from 2596 and 2545; to *burn down* (to the ground), i.e. *consume wholly:*— burn (up, utterly).

2619. κατακαλύπτω **katakaluptō**, *kat-ak-al-oop'-to;* from 2596 and 2572; to *cover wholly*, i.e. *veil:*— cover, hide.

2620. κατακαυχάομαι **katakauchaŏmai**, *kat-ak-ŏw-khah'-om-ahee;* from 2596 and 2744; to *exult against* (i.e. *over*):— boast (against), glory, rejoice against.

2621. κατάκειμαι **katakĕimai**, *kat-ak'-i-mahee;* from 2596 and 2749; to *lie down*, i.e. (by impl.) *be sick;* spec. to *recline* at a meal:— keep, lie, sit at meat (down).

2622. κατακλάω **kataklaō**, *kat-ak-lah'-o;* from 2596 and 2806; to *break down*, i.e. *divide:*— break.

2623. κατακλείω **katakleiō**, *kat-ak-li'-o;* from 2596 and 2808; to *shut down* (in a dungeon), i.e. *incarcerate:*— shut up.

2624. κατακληροδοτέω **kataklērŏdŏtĕō**, *kat-ak-lay-rod-ot-eh'-o;* from 2596 and a der. of a compound of 2819 and 1325; to *be a giver of lots to each*, i.e. (by impl.) to *apportion an estate:*— divide by lot.

2625. κατακλίνω **kataklinō**, *kat-ak-lee'-no;* from 2596 and 2827; to *recline down*, i.e. (spec.) to *take a place* at table:— (make) sit down (at meat).

2626. κατακλύζω **katakluzō**, *kat-ak-lood'-zo;* from 2596 and the base of 2830; to *dash* (*wash*) *down*, i.e. (by impl.) to *deluge:*— overflow.

2627. κατακλυσμός **kataklusmŏs**, *kat-ak-looce-mos';* from 2626; an *inundation:*— flood.

2628. κατακολουθέω **katakŏlŏuthĕō**, *kat-ak-ol-oo-theh'-o;* from 2596 and 190; to *accompany closely:*— follow (after).

2629. κατακόπτω **katakŏptō**, *kat-ak-op'-to;* from 2596 and 2875; to *chop down*, i.e. *mangle:*— cut.

2630. κατακρημνίζω **katakrēmnizō**, *kat-ak-rame-nid'-zo;* from 2596 and a der. of 2911; to *precipitate down:*— cast down headlong.

2631. κατάκριμα **katakrima**, *kat-ak'-ree-mah;* from 2632; an *adverse sentence* (the verdict):— condemnation.

2632. κατακρίνω **katakrinō**, *kat-ak-ree'-no;* from 2596 and 2919; to *judge against*, i.e. *sentence:*— condemn, damn.

2633. κατάκρισις **katakrisis**, *kat-ak'-ree-sis;* from 2632; *sentencing adversely* (the act):— condemn (-ation).

2634. κατακυριεύω **katakuriĕuō**, *kat-ak-oo-ree-yoo'-o;* from 2596 and 2961; to *lord against*, i.e. *control, subjugate:*— exercise dominion over (lordship), be lord over, overcome.

2635. καταλαλέω **katalalĕō**, *kat-al-al-eh'-o;* from 2637; to *be a traducer*, i.e. to *slander:*— speak against (evil of).

2636. καταλαλία **katalalia**, *kat-al-al-ee'-ah;* from 2637; *defamation:*— backbiting, evil speaking.

2637. κατάλαλος **katalalŏs**, *kat-al'-al-os;* from 2596 and the base of 2980; *talkative against*, i.e. a *slanderer:*— backbiter.

2638. καταλαμβάνω **katalambanō**, *kat-al-am-ban'-o;* from 2596 and 2983; to *take eagerly*, i.e. *seize, possess*, etc. (lit. or fig.):— apprehend, attain, come upon, comprehend, find, obtain, perceive, (over-) take.

2639. καταλέγω **katalĕgō**, *kat-al-eg'-o;* from 2596 and 3004 (in its orig. mean.); to *lay down*, i.e. (fig.) to *enrol:*— take into the number.

2640. κατάλειμμα **katalĕimma**, *kat-al'-ime-mah;* from 2641; a *remainder*, i.e. (by impl.) a *few:*— remnant.

2641. καταλείπω **katalĕipō**, *kat-al-i'-po;* from 2596 and 3007; to *leave down*, i.e. *behind;* by impl. to *abandon, have remaining:*— forsake, leave, reserve.

2642. καταλιθάζω **katalithazō**, *kat-al-ith-ad´-zo*; from 2596 and 3034; to *stone down*, i.e. *to death*:— stone.

2643. καταλλαγή **katallagē**, *kat-al-lag-ay´*; from 2644; *exchange* (fig. *adjustment*), i.e. *restoration* to (the divine) favor:— atonement, reconciliation (-ing).

2644. καταλλάσσω **katallassō**, *kat-al-las´-so*; from 2596 and 236; to *change mutually*, i.e. (fig.) to *compound* a difference:— reconcile.

2645. κατάλοιπος **kataloipos**, *kat-al´-oy-pos*; from 2596 and 3062; *left down (behind)*, i.e. *remaining* (plur. the *rest*):— residue.

2646. κατάλυμα **kataluma**, *kat-al´-oo-mah*; from 2647; prop. a *dissolution* (breaking up of a journey), i.e. (by impl.) a *lodging-place*:— guestchamber, inn.

2647. καταλύω **kataluō**, *kat-al-oo´-o*; from 2596 and 3089; to *loosen down* (*disintegrate*), i.e. (by impl.) to *demolish* (lit. or fig.); spec. [comp. 2646] to *halt* for the night:— destroy, dissolve, be guest, lodge, come to nought, overthrow, throw down.

2648. καταμανθάνω **katamanthanō**, *kat-am-an-than´-o*; from 2596 and 3129; to *learn thoroughly*, i.e. (by impl.) to *note carefully*:— consider.

2649. καταμαρτυρέω **katamartureō**, *kat-am-ar-too-reh´-o*; from 2596 and 3140; to *testify against*:— witness against.

2650. καταμένω **katamenō**, *kat-am-en´-o*; from 2596 and 3306; to *stay fully*, i.e. *reside*:— abide.

2651. καταμόνας **katamonas**, *kat-am-on´-as*; from 2596 and acc. plur. fem. of 3441 (with 5561 impl.); *according to sole places*, i.e. (adv.) *separately*:— alone.

2652. κατανάθεμα **katanathĕma**, *kat-an-ath´-em-ah*; from 2596 (intens.) and 331; an *imprecation*:— curse.

2653. καταναθεματίζω **katanathĕmatizō**, *kat-an-ath-em-at-id´-zo*; from 2596 (intens.) and 332; to *imprecate*:— curse.

2654. καταναλίσκω **katanaliskō**, *kat-an-al-is´-ko*; from 2596 and 355; to *consume utterly*:— consume.

2655. καταναρκάω **katanarkaō**, *kat-an-ar-kah´-o*; from 2596 and ναρκάω **narkaō** (to *be numb*); to *grow utterly torpid*, i.e. (by impl.) *slothful* (fig. *expensive*):— be burdensome (chargeable).

2656. κατανεύω **katanĕuō**, *kat-an-yoo´-o*; from 2596 and 3506; to *nod down (toward)*, i.e. (by anal.) to *make signs to*:— beckon.

2657. κατανοέω **katanoĕō**, *kat-an-o-eh´-o*; from 2596 and 3539; to *observe fully*:— behold, consider, discover, perceive.

2658. καταντάω **katantaō**, *kat-an-tah´-o*; from 2596 and a der. of 473; to *meet against*, i.e. *arrive* at (lit. or fig.):— attain, come.

2659. κατάνυξις **katanuxis**, *kat-an´-oox-is*; from 2660; a *prickling* (sensa-

tion, as of the limbs *asleep*), i.e. (by impl. [perh. by some confusion with 3506 or even with 3571]) *stupor* (*lethargy*):— slumber.

2660. κατανύσσω **katanussō**, *kat-an-oos´-so*; from 2596 and 3572; to *pierce thoroughly*, i.e. (fig.) to *agitate* violently ("sting to the quick"):— prick.

2661. καταξιόω **kataxiŏō**, *kat-ax-ee-ŏ´-o*; from 2596 and 515; to *deem entirely deserving*:— (ac-) count worthy.

2662. καταπατέω **katapateō**, *kat-ap-at-eh´-o*; from 2596 and 3961; to *trample down*; fig. to *reject* with disdain:— trample, tread (down, underfoot).

2663. κατάπαυσις **katapausis**, *kat-ap-ow-sis*; from 2664; *reposing down*, i.e. (by Heb.) *abode*:— rest.

2664. καταπαύω **katapauō**, *kat-ap-ow´-o*; from 2596 and 3973; to *settle down*, i.e. (lit.) to *colonize*, or (fig.) to (*cause to*) *desist*:— cease, (give) rest (-rain).

2665. καταπέτασμα **katapĕtasma**, *kat-ap-et´-as-mah*; from a compound of 2596 and a congener of 4072; something *spread thoroughly*, i.e. (spec.) the door *screen* (to the Most Holy Place) in the Jewish Temple:— vail.

2666. καταπίνω **katapinō**, *kat-ap-ee´-no*; from 2596 and 4095; to *drink down*, i.e. *gulp entire* (lit. or fig.):— devour, drown, swallow (up).

2667. καταπίπτω **katapiptō**, *kat-ap-ip´-to*; from 2596 and 4098; to *fall down*:— fall (down).

2668. καταπλέω **kataplĕō**, *kat-ap-leh´-o*; from 2596 and 4126; to *sail down* upon a place, i.e. to *land* at:— arrive.

2669. καταπονέω **kataponĕō**, *kat-ap-on-eh´-o*; from 2596 and a der. of 4192; to *labor down*, i.e. *wear with toil* (fig. *harass*):— oppress, vex.

2670. καταποντίζω **katapontizō**, *kat-ap-on-tid´-zo*; from 2596 and a der. of the same as 4195; to *plunge down*, i.e. *submerge*:— drown, sink.

2671. κατάρα **katara**, *kat-ar´-ah*; from 2596 (intens.) and 685; *imprecation, execration*:— curse (-d, ing).

2672. καταράομαι **kataraŏmai**, *kat-ar-ah´-om-ahee*; mid. voice from 2671; to *execrate*; by anal. to *doom*:— curse.

2673. καταργέω **katargeō**, *kat-arg-eh´-o*; from 2596 and 691; to *be* (*render*) *entirely idle* (*useless*), lit. or fig.:— abolish, cease, cumber, deliver, destroy, do away, become (make) of no (none, without) effect, fail, loose, bring (come) to nought, put away (down), vanish away, make void.

2674. καταριθμέω **katarithmĕō**, *kat-ar-ith-meh´-o*; from 2596 and 705; to *reckon among*:— number with.

2675. καταρτίζω **katartizō**, *kat-ar-tid´-zo*; from 2596 and a der. of 739; to *complete thoroughly*, i.e. *repair* (lit. or fig.) or *adjust*:— fit, frame, mend, (make) perfect (-ly join together), prepare, restore.

2676. κατάρτισις **katartisis**, *kat-ar´-tis-is*; from 2675; *thorough equipment* (subj.):— perfection.

2677. καταρτισμός **katartismŏs**, *kat-ar-

tis-mos´*; from 2675; *complete furnishing* (obj.):— perfecting.

2678. κατασείω **katasĕiō**, *kat-as-i´-o*; from 2596 and 4579; to *sway downward*, i.e. *make a signal*:— beckon.

2679. κατασκάπτω **kataskaptō**, *kat-as-kap´-to*; from 2596 and 4626; to *undermine*, i.e. (by impl.) *destroy*:— dig down, ruin.

2680. κατασκευάζω **kataskĕuazō**, *kat-ask-yoo-ad´-zo*; from 2596 and a der. of 4632; to *prepare thoroughly* (prop. by extern. *equipment*; whereas 2090 refers rather to intern. *fitness*); by impl. to *construct, create*:— build, make, ordain, prepare.

2681. κατασκηνόω **kataskĕnŏō**, *kat-as-kay-nŏ´-o*; from 2596 and 4637; to *camp down*, i.e. *haunt*; fig. to *remain*:— lodge, rest.

2682. κατασκήνωσις **kataskĕnōsis**, *kat-as-kay´-no-sis*; from 2681; an *encamping*, i.e. (fig.) a *perch*:— nest.

2683. κατασκιάζω **kataskiazō**, *kat-as-kee-ad´-zo*; from 2596 and a der. of 4639; to *overshade*, i.e. *cover*:— shadow.

2684. κατασκοπέω **kataskŏpĕō**, *kat-as-kop-eh´-o*; from 2685; to *be a sentinel*, i.e. to *inspect* insidiously:— spy out.

2685. κατάσκοπος **kataskŏpŏs**, *kat-as´-kop-os*; from 2596 (intens.) and 4649 (in the sense of a *watcher*); a *reconnoiterer*:— spy.

2686. κατασοφίζομαι **katasŏphizŏmai**, *kat-as-of-id´-zom-ahee*; mid. voice from 2596 and 4679; to *be crafty against*, i.e. *circumvent*:— deal subtilly (subtly) with.

2687. καταστέλλω **katastĕllō**, *kat-as-tel´-lo*; from 2596 and 4724; to *put down*, i.e. *quell*:— appease, quiet.

2688. κατάστημα **katastēma**, *kat-as´-tay-mah*; from 2525; prop. a *position* or *condition*, i.e. (subj.) *demeanor*:— behaviour.

2689. καταστολή **katastŏlē**, *kat-as-tol-ay´*; from 2687; a *deposit*, i.e. (spec.) *costume*:— apparel.

2690. καταστρέφω **katastrĕphō**, *kat-as-tref´-o*; from 2596 and 4762; to *turn upside down*, i.e. *upset*:— overthrow.

2691. καταστρηνιάω **katastrēniaō**, *kat-as-tray-nee-ah´-o*; from 2596 and 4763; to *become voluptuous against*:— begin to wax wanton against.

2692. καταστροφή **katastrŏphē**, *kat-as-trof-ay´*; from 2690; an *overturn* ("*catastrophe*"), i.e. *demolition*; fig. *apostasy*:— overthrow, subverting.

2693. καταστρώννυμι **katastrōnnumi**, *kat-as-trone´-noo-mee*; from 2596 and 4766; to *strew down*, i.e. (by impl.) to *prostrate* (*slay*):— overthrow.

2694. κατασύρω **katasurō**, *kat-as-oo´-ro*; from 2596 and 4951; to *drag down*, i.e. *arrest* judicially:— hale.

2695. κατασφάττω **katasphattō**, *kat-as-fat´-to*; from 2596 and 4969; to *kill down*, i.e. *slaughter*:— slay.

2696. κατασφραγίζω **katasphragizō**, *kat-as-frag-id´-zo*; from 2596 and 4972; to *seal closely*:— seal.

2697. κατάσχεσις **kataschĕsis**, *kat-as´-khes-is;* from 2722; a *holding down,* i.e. *occupancy:*— possession.

2698. κατατίθημι **katatithēmi**, *kat-at-ith´-ay-mee;* from 2596 and 5087; to *place down,* i.e. *deposit* (lit. or fig.):— do, lay, shew.

2699. κατατομή **katatŏmē**, *kat-at-om-ay´;* from a compound of 2596 and τέμνω **tĕmnō** (to *cut*); a *cutting down* (off), i.e. *mutilation* (ironically):— concision. Comp. 609.

2700. κατατοξεύω **katatŏxĕuō**, *kat-at-ox-yoo´-o;* from 2596 and a der. of 5115; to *shoot down* with an arrow or other missile:— thrust through.

2701. κατατρέχω **katatrĕchō**, *kat-at-rekh´-o;* from 2596 and 5143; to *run down,* i.e. *hasten* from a tower:— run down.

καταφάγω **kataphagō**. See 2719. ·

2702. καταφέρω **kataphĕrō**, *kat-af-er´-o;* from 2596 and 5342 (incl. its alt.); to *bear down,* i.e. (fig.) *overcome* (with drowsiness); spec. to *cast* a vote:— fall, give, sink down.

2703. καταφεύγω **kataphĕugō**, *kat-af-yoo´-go;* from 2596 and 5343; to *flee down* (away):— flee.

2704. καταφθείρω **kataphthĕirō**, *kat-af-thi´-ro;* from 2596 and 5351; to *spoil entirely,* i.e. (lit.) to *destroy;* or (fig.) to *deprave:*— corrupt, utterly perish.

2705. καταφιλέω **kataphilĕō**, *kat-af-ee-leh´-o;* from 2596 and 5368; to *kiss earnestly:*— kiss.

2706. καταφρονέω **kataphrŏnĕō**, *kat-af-ron-eh´-o;* from 2596 and 5426; to *think against,* i.e. *disesteem:*— despise.

2707. καταφροντής **kataphrŏntēs**, *kat-af-ron-tace´;* from 2706; a *contemner:*— despiser.

2708. καταχέω **katachĕō**, *kat-akh-eh´-o;* from 2596 and χέω **chĕō** (to *pour*); to *pour down* (out):— pour.

2709. καταχθόνιος **katachthŏniŏs**, *kat-akh-thon´-ee-os;* from 2596 and χθών **chthōn** (the *ground*); *subterranean,* i.e. *infernal* (belonging to the world of departed spirits):— under the earth.

2710. καταχράομαι **katachraŏmai**, *kat-akh-rah´-om-ahee;* from 2596 and 5530; to *overuse,* i.e. *misuse:*— abuse.

2711. καταψύχω **katapsuchō**, *kat-ap-soo´-kho;* from 2596 and 5594; to *cool down* (off), i.e. *refresh:*— cool.

2712. κατείδωλος **katĕidōlŏs**, *kat-i´-do-los;* from 2596 (intens.) and 1497; *utterly idolatrous:*— wholly given to idolatry.

κατελεύθω **katĕlĕuthō**. See 2718.

2713. κατέναντι **katĕnanti**, *kat-en´-an-tee;* from 2596 and 1725; *directly opposite:*— before, over against.

κατενέγκω **katĕnĕgkō**. See 2702.

2714. κατενώπιον **katĕnōpiŏn**, *kat-en-o´-pee-on;* from 2596 and 1799; *dir. in front of:*— before (the presence of), in the sight of.

2715. κατεξουσιάζω **katĕxŏusiazō**, *kat-ex-oo-see-ad´-zo;* from 2596 and 1850; to *have* (wield) *full privilege over:*— exercise authority.

2716. κατεργάζομαι **katĕrgazŏmai**, *kat-er-gad´-zom-ahee;* from 2596 and 2038; do *work fully,* i.e. *accomplish;* by impl. to *finish, fashion:*— cause, do (deed), perform, work (out).

2717. Because of some changes in the numbering system (while the original work was in progress) no Greek words were cited for 2717 or 3203-3302. These numbers were dropped altogether. This will not cause any problems in Strong's numbering system. No Greek words have been left out. Because so many other reference works use this numbering system, it has not been revised. If it were revised, much confusion would certainly result.

2718. κατέρχομαι **katĕrchŏmai**, *kat-er-khom-ahee;* from 2596 and 2064 (incl. its alt.); to *come* (or *go*) *down* (lit. or fig.):— come (down), depart, descend, go down, land.

2719. κατεσθίω **katĕsthiō**, *kat-es-thee-o;* from 2596 and 2068 (incl. its alt.); to *eat down,* i.e. *devour* (lit. or fig.):— devour.

2720. κατευθύνω **katĕuthunō**, *kat-yoo-thoo´-no;* from 2596 and 2116; to *straighten fully,* i.e. (fig.) *direct:*— guide, direct.

2721. κατεφίστημι **katĕphistēmi**, *kat-ef-is´-tay-mee;* from 2596 and 2186; to *stand over against,* i.e. *rush upon* (assault):— make insurrection against.

2722. κατέχω **katĕchō**, *kat-ekh´-o;* from 2596 and 2192; to *hold down* (fast), in various applications (lit. or fig.):— have, hold (fast), keep (in memory), let, × make toward, possess, retain, seize on, stay, take, withhold.

2723. κατηγορέω **katēgŏrĕō**, *kat-ay-gor-eh´-o;* from 2725; to *be a plaintiff,* i.e. to *charge* with some offence:— accuse, object.

2724. κατηγορία **katēgŏria**, *kat-ay-gor-ee´-ah;* from 2725; a *complaint* ("category"), i.e. criminal *charge:*— accusation (× -ed).

2725. κατήγορος **katēgŏrŏs**, *kat-ay-gor-os;* from 2596 and 58; *against* one in the *assembly,* i.e. a *complainant* at law; spec. *Satan:*— accuser.

2726. κατήφεια **katēphĕia**, *kat-ay-fi-ah;* from a compound of 2596 and perh. a der. of the base of 5316 (mean. *downcast* in look); *demureness,* i.e. (by impl.) *sadness:*— heaviness.

2727. κατηχέω **katēchĕō**, *kat-ay-kheh´-o;* from 2596 and 2279; to *sound down* into the ears, i.e. (by impl.) to *indoctrinate* ("catechize") or (gen.) to *apprise* of:— inform, instruct, teach.

2728. κατιόω **katiŏō**, *kat-ee-ŏ´-o;* from 2596 and a der. of 2447; to *rust down,* i.e. *corrode:*— canker.

2729. κατισχύω **katischuō**, *kat-is-khoo´-o;* from 2596 and 2480; to *overpower:*— prevail (against).

2730. κατοικέω **katŏikĕō**, *kat-oy-keh´-o;* from 2596 and 3611; to *house permanently,* i.e. *reside* (lit. or fig.):— dwell (-er), inhabitant (-ter).

2731. κατοίκησις **katŏikēsis**, *kat-oy´-kay-sis;* from 2730; *residence* (prop. the

act; but by impl. concr. the mansion):— dwelling.

2732. κατοικητήριον **katŏikētēriŏn**, *kat-oy-kay-tay´-ree-on;* from a der. of 2730; a *dwelling-place:*— habitation.

2733. κατοικία **katŏikia**, *kat-oy-kee´-ah;* *residence* (prop. the condition; but by impl. the abode itself):— habitation.

2734. κατοπτρίζομαι **katŏptrizŏmai**, *kat-op-trid´-zom-ahee;* mid. voice from a compound of 2596 and a der. of 3700 [comp. 2072]; to *mirror oneself,* i.e. to *see reflected* (fig.):— behold as in a glass.

2735. κατόρθωμα **katŏrthōma**, *kat-or´-tho-mah;* from a compound of 2596 and a der. of 3717 [comp. 1357]; something *made fully upright,* i.e. (fig.) *rectification* (spec. *good* public *administration*):— very worthy deed.

2736. κάτω **katō**, *kat´-o;* also (comparative)

κατωτέρω **katōtĕrō**, *kat-o-ter´-o;* [comp. 2737]; adv. from 2596; *downwards:*— beneath, bottom, down, under.

2737. κατώτερος **katōtĕrŏs**, *kat-o´-ter-os;* comparative from 2736; *inferior* (locally, of Hades):— lower.

2738. καῦμα **kauma**, *kŏw´-mah;* from 2545; prop. a *burn* (concr.), but used (abstr.) of a *glow:*— heat.

2739. καυματίζω **kaumatizō**, *kŏw-mat-id´-zo;* from 2738; to *burn:*— scorch.

2740. καῦσις **kausis**, *kŏw´-sis;* from 2545; *burning* (the act):— be burned.

2741. καυσόω **kausŏō**, *kŏw-sŏ´-o;* from 2740; to *set on fire:*— with fervent heat.

2742. καύσων **kausōn**, *kŏw´-sone;* from 2741; a *glare:*— (burning) heat.

2743. καυτηριάζω **kautēriazō**, *kŏw-tay-ree-ad´-zo* or

καυστηριάζω **kaustēriazō**, *kŏws-tay-ree-ad´-zo;* from a der. of 2545; to *brand* ("cauterize"), i.e. (by impl.) to *render unsensitive* (fig.):— sear with a hot iron.

2744. καυχάομαι **kauchaŏmai**, *kŏw-khah´-om-ahee;* from some (obsolete) base akin to that of αὐχέω **auchĕō** (to *boast*) and 2172; to *vaunt* (in a good or a bad sense):— (make) boast, glory, joy, rejoice.

2745. καύχημα **kauchēma**, *kŏw´-khay-mah;* from 2744; a *boast* (prop. the obj.; by impl. the act) in a good or a bad sense:— boasting, (whereof) to glory (of), glorying, rejoice (-ing).

2746. καύχησις **kauchēsis**, *kŏw´-khay-sis;* from 2744; *boasting* (prop. the act; by impl. the obj.), in a good or a bad sense:— boasting, whereof I may glory, glorying, rejoicing.

2747. Κεγχρεαί **Kĕgchrĕai**, *keng-khreh-a´-hee;* prob. from κέγχρος **kĕgchrŏs** (*millet*); *Cenchreæ,* a port of Corinth:— Cenchrea.

2748. Κεδρών **Kĕdrōn**, *ked-rone´;* of Heb. or. [6939]; *Cedron* (i.e. *Kidron*), a brook near Jerusalem:— Cedron.

2749. κεῖμαι **kĕimai**, *ki´-mahee;* mid. voice of a primary verb; to *lie out-*

stretched (lit. or fig.):— be (appointed, laid up, made, set), lay, lie. Comp. 5087.

2750. κειρία **kĕiria**, ki-ree´-ah; of uncert. aff.; a *swathe*, i.e. *winding-sheet*:— graveclothes.

2751. κείρω **kĕirō**, ki´-ro; a primary verb; to *shear*:— shear (-er).

2752. κέλευμα **kĕlĕuma**, kel´-yoo-mah or

κέλευσμα **kĕlĕusma**, kel´-yoos-mah; from 2753; a *cry* of incitement:— shout.

2753. κελεύω **kĕlĕuō**, kel-yoo´-o; from a primary κέλλω **kĕllō** (to *urge* on); "hail;" to *incite* by word, i.e. *order*:— bid, (at, give) command (-ment).

2754. κενοδοξία **kĕnŏdŏxia**, ken-od-ox-ee´-ah; from 2755; *empty glorying*, i.e. *self-conceit*:— vain-glory.

2755. κενόδοξος **kĕnŏdŏxŏs**, ken-od´-ox-os; from 2756 and 1391; *vainly glorifying*, i.e. *self-conceited*:— desirous of vain-glory.

2756. κενός **kĕnŏs**, ken-os´; appar. a primary word; *empty* (lit. or fig.):— empty, (in) vain.

2757. κενοφωνία **kĕnŏphōnia**, ken-of-o-nee´-ah; from a presumed compound of 2756 and 5456; *empty sounding*, i.e. *fruitless discussion*:— vain.

2758. κενόω **kĕnŏō**, ken-ŏ´-o; from 2756; to *make empty*, i.e. (fig.) to *abase*, *neutralize*, *falsify*:— make (of none effect, of no reputation, void), be in vain.

2759. κέντρον **kĕntrŏn**, ken´-tron; from κεντέω **kĕntĕō** (to *prick*); a *point* ("centre"), i.e. a *sting* (fig. *poison*) or *goad* (fig. divine *impulse*):— prick, sting.

2760. κεντυρίων **kĕnturiōn**, ken-too-ree´-ohn; of Lat. or.; a *centurion*, i.e. *captain* of one hundred soldiers:— centurion.

2761. κενῶς **kĕnōs**, ken-oce´; adv. from 2756; *vainly*, i.e. *to no purpose*:— in vain.

2762. κεραία **kĕraia**, ker-ah´-yah; fem. of a presumed der. of the base of 2768; something *horn-like*, i.e. (spec.) the *apex* of a Heb. letter (fig. the least *particle*):— tittle.

2763. κεραμεύς **kĕramĕus**, ker-am-yooce´; from 2766; a *potter*:— potter.

2764. κεραμικός **kĕramikŏs**, ker-am-ik-os´; from 2766; *made of clay*, i.e. *earthen*:— of a potter.

2765. κεράμιον **kĕramiŏn**, ker-am´-ee-on; neut. of a presumed der. of 2766; an *earthenware* vessel, i.e. *jar*:— pitcher.

2766. κέραμος **kĕramŏs**, ker´-am-os; prob. from the base of 2767 (through the idea of *mixing* clay and water); *earthenware*, i.e. a *tile* (by anal. a thin *roof* or *awning*):— tiling.

2767. κεράννυμι **kĕrannumi**, ker-an´-noo-mee; a prol. form of a more primary κεράω **kĕraō**, ker-ah´-o (which is used in certain tenses); to *mingle*, i.e. (by impl.) to *pour* out (for drinking):— fill, pour out. Comp. 3396.

2768. κέρας **kĕras**, ker´-as; from a primary κάρ **kar** (the *hair* of the head); a *horn* (lit. or fig.):— horn.

2769. κεράτιον **kĕratiŏn**, ker-at´-ee-on; neut. of a presumed der. of 2768; something *horned*, i.e. (spec.) the *pod* of the carob-tree:— husk.

κεράω **kĕraō**. See 2767.

2770. κερδαίνω **kĕrdainō**, ker-dah´-ee-no; from 2771; to *gain* (lit. or fig.):— (get) gain, win.

2771. κέρδος **kĕrdŏs**, ker´-dos; of uncert. aff.; *gain* (pecuniary or gen.):— gain, lucre.

2772. κέρμα **kĕrma**, ker´-mah; from 2751; a *clipping* (*bit*), i.e. (spec.) a *coin*:— money.

2773. κερματιστής **kĕrmatistēs**, ker-mat-is-tace´; from a der. of 2772; a *handler of coins*, i.e. *money-broker*:— changer of money.

2774. κεφάλαιον **kĕphalaiŏn**, kef-al´-ah-yon; neut. of a der. of 2776; a *principal* thing, i.e. *main point*; spec. an *amount* (of money):— sum.

2775. κεφαλαιόω **kĕphalaiŏō**, kef-al-ahee-ŏ´-o; from the same as 2774; (spec.) to *strike on the head*:— wound in the head.

2776. κεφαλή **kĕphalē**, kef-al-ay´; prob. from the primary κάπτω **kaptō** (in the sense of *seizing*); the *head* (as the part most readily *taken* hold of), lit. or fig.:— head.

2777. κεφαλίς **kĕphalis**, kef-al-is´; from 2776; prop. a *knob*, i.e. (by impl.) a *roll* (by extens. from the *end* of a stick on which the MS. was rolled):— volume.

2778. κῆνσος **kēnsŏs**, kane´-sos; of Lat. or.; prop. an *enrollment* ("*census*"), i.e. (by impl.) a *tax*:— tribute.

2779. κῆπος **kēpŏs**, kay´-pos; of uncert. aff.; a *garden*:— garden.

2780. κηπουρός **kēpŏurŏs**, kay-poo-ros´; from 2779 and οὖρος **ŏurŏs** (a *warden*); a *garden-keeper*, i.e. *gardener*:— gardener.

2781. κηρίον **kēriŏn**, kay-ree´-on; dimin. from κηός **kēŏs** (*wax*); a *cell* for honey, i.e. (collect.) the *comb*:— [honey-] comb.

2782. κήρυγμα **kērugma**, kay´-roog-mah; from 2784; a *proclamation* (espec. of the gospel; by impl. the *gospel* itself):— preaching.

2783. κῆρυξ **kērux**, kay´-roox; from 2784; a *herald*, i.e. of divine truth (espec. of the gospel):— preacher.

2784. κηρύσσω **kērussō**, kay-roos´-so; of uncert. aff.; to *herald* (as a public *crier*), espec. divine truth (the gospel):— preacher (-er), proclaim, publish.

2785. κῆτος **kētŏs**, kay´-tos; prob. from the base of 5490; a huge *fish* (as *gaping* for prey):— whale.

2786. Κηφᾶς **Kēphas**, kay-fas´; of Chald. or. [comp. 3710]; *the Rock*; *Cephas* (i.e. *Kepha*), a surname of Peter:— Cephas.

2787. κιβωτός **kibōtŏs**, kib-o-tos´; of uncert. der.; a *box*, i.e. the sacred *ark* and that of Noah:— ark.

2788. κιθάρα **kithara**, kith-ar´-ah; of uncert. aff.; a *lyre*:— harp.

2789. κιθαρίζω **kitharizō**, kith-ar-id´-zo; from 2788; to *play on a lyre*:— harp.

2790. κιθαρῳδός **kitharōıdŏs**, kith-ar-o´-dos; from 2788 and a der. of the same as 5603; a *lyre-singer* (-player), i.e. *harpist*:— harper.

2791. Κιλικία **Kilikia**, kil-ik-ee´-ah; prob. of for. or.; *Cilicia*, a region of Asia Minor:— Cilicia.

2792. κινάμωμον **kinamōmŏn**, kin-am´-o-mon; of for. or. [comp. 7076]; *cinnamon*:— cinnamon.

2793. κινδυνεύω **kindunĕuō**, kin-doon-yoo´-o; from 2794; to *undergo peril*:— be in danger, be (stand) in jeopardy.

2794. κίνδυνος **kindunŏs**, kin´-doo-nos; of uncert. der.; *danger*:— peril.

2795. κινέω **kinĕō**, kin-eh´-o; from κίω **kiō** (poetic for εἶμι **ĕimi**, to *go*); to *stir* (tran.), lit. or fig.:— (re-) move (-r), way.

2796. κίνησις **kinēsis**, kin´-ay-sis; from 2795; a *stirring*:— moving.

2797. Κίς **Kis**, kis; of Heb. or. [7027]; *Cis* (i.e. *Kish*), an Isr.:— Cis.

κίχρημι **kichrēmi**. See 5531.

2798. κλάδος **kladŏs**, klad´-os; from 2806; a *twig* or *bough* (as if broken off):— branch.

2799. κλαίω **klaiō**, klah´-yo; of uncert. aff.; to *sob*, i.e. *wail aloud* (whereas 1145 is rather to *cry* silently):— bewail, weep.

2800. κλάσις **klasis**, klas´-is; from 2806; *fracture* (the act):— breaking.

2801. κλάσμα **klasma**, klas´-mah; from 2806; a *piece* (*bit*):— broken, fragment.

2802. Κλαύδη **Klaudē**, klŏw´-day or

Καύδη **Kaudē**, kŏw´-day; of uncert. der.; *Claude*, an island near Crete:— Clauda (Cauda).

2803. Κλαυδία **Klaudia**, klŏw-dee´-ah; fem. of 2804; *Claudia*, a Chr. woman:— Claudia.

2804. Κλαύδιος **Klaudiŏs**, klŏw´-dee-os; of Lat. or.; *Claudius*, the name of two Romans:— Claudius.

2805. κλαυθμός **klauthmŏs**, klŏwth-mos´; from 2799; *lamentation*:— wailing, weeping, × wept.

2806. κλάω **klaō**, klah´-o; a primary verb; to *break* (spec. of bread):— break.

2807. κλείς **klĕis**, klice; from 2808; a *key* (as *shutting* a lock), lit. or fig.:— key.

2808. κλείω **klĕiō**, kli´-o; a primary verb; to *close* (lit. or fig.):— shut (up).

2809. κλέμμα **klĕmma**, klem´-mah; from 2813; *stealing* (prop. the thing stolen, but used of the act):— theft.

2810. Κλεόπας **Klĕŏpas**, kleh-op´-as; prob. contr. from Κλεόπατρος **Klĕŏpatrŏs** (compound of 2811 and 3962); *Cleopas*, a Chr.:— Cleopas.

2811. κλέος **klĕŏs**, kleh´-os; from a short. form of 2564; *renown* (as if being *called*):— glory.

2812. κλέπτης **klĕptēs**, klep´-tace; from 2813; a *stealer* (lit. or fig.):— thief. Comp. 3027.

2813. κλέπτω **klĕptō**, klep´-to; a primary verb; to *filch*:— steal.

2814. κλῆμα **klēma**, _klay´-mah;_ from 2806; a _limb_ or _shoot_ (as if _broken_ off):— branch.

2815. Κλήμης **Klēmēs**, _klay´-mace;_ of Lat. or.; _merciful; Clemes_ (i.e. _Clemens_), a Chr.:— Clement.

2816. κληρονομέω **klērŏnŏmĕō**, _klay-ron-om-eh´-o;_ from 2818; to be an _heir_ to (lit. or fig.):— be heir, (obtain by) inherit (-ance).

2817. κληρονομία **klērŏnŏmia**, _klay-ron-om-ee´-ah;_ from 2818; _heirship_, i.e. (concr.) a _patrimony_ or (gen.) a _possession_:— inheritance.

2818. κληρονόμος **klērŏnŏmŏs**, _klay-ron-om´-os;_ from 2819 and the base of 3551 (in its orig. sense of _partitioning_, i.e. [refl.] _getting_ by apportionment); a _sharer by lot_, i.e. _inheritor_ (lit. or fig.); by impl. a _possessor_:— heir.

2819. κλῆρος **klērŏs**, _klay´-ros;_ prob. from 2806 (through the idea of using _bits_ of wood, etc., for the purpose); a _die_ (for drawing chances); by impl. a _portion_ (as if so secured); by extens. an _acquisition_ (espec. a _patrimony_, fig.):— heritage, inheritance, lot, part.

2820. κληρόω **klērŏō**, _klay-rŏ´-o;_ from 2819; to _allot_, i.e. (fig.) to _assign_ (a privilege):— obtain an inheritance.

2821. κλῆσις **klēsis**, _klay´-sis;_ from a shorter form of 2564; an _invitation_ (fig.):— calling.

2822. κλητός **klētŏs**, _klay-tos´;_ from the same as 2821; _invited_, i.e. _appointed_, or (spec.) a _saint_:— called.

2823. κλίβανος **klibanŏs**, _klib´-an-os;_ of uncert. der.; an earthen _pot_ used for baking in:— oven.

2824. κλίμα **klima**, _klee´-mah;_ from 2827; a _slope_, i.e. (spec.) a "_clime_" or _tract_ of country:— part, region.

2825. κλίνη **klinē**, _klee´-nay;_ from 2827; a _couch_ (for sleep, sickness, sitting or eating):— bed, table.

2826. κλινίδιον **klinidiŏn**, _kleen-eed´-ee-on;_ neut. of a presumed der. of 2825; a _pallet_ or _little couch_:— bed.

2827. κλίνω **klinō**, _klee´-no;_ a primary verb; to _slant_ or _slope_, i.e. _incline_ or _recline_ (lit. or fig.):— bow (down), be far spent, lay, turn to flight, wear away.

2828. κλισία **klisia**, _klee-see´-ah;_ from a der. of 2827; prop. _reclination_, i.e. (concr. and spec.) a _party_ at a meal:— company.

2829. κλοπή **klŏpē**, _klop-ay´;_ from 2813; _stealing_:— theft.

2830. κλύδων **kludōn**, _kloo´-dohn;_ from κλύω **kluzō** (to _billow_ or _dash_ over); a _surge_ of the sea (lit. or fig.):— raging, wave.

2831. κλυδωνίζομαι **kludōnizŏmai**, _kloo-do-nid´-zom-ahee;_ mid. voice from 2830; to _surge_, i.e. (fig.) to _fluctuate_:— toss to and fro.

2832. Κλωπᾶς **Klōpas**, _klo-pas´;_ of Chald. or. (corresp. to 256); _Clopas_, an Isr.:— Clopas.

2833. κνήθω **knēthō**, _knay´-tho;_ from a primary κνάω knaō (to _scrape_); to _scratch_, i.e. (by impl.) to _tickle_:— × itching.

2834. Κνίδος **Knidŏs**, _knee´-dos;_ prob. of for. or.; _Cnidus_, a place in Asia Minor:— Cnidus.

2835. κοδράντης **kŏdrantēs**, _kod-ran´-tace;_ of Lat. or.; a _quadrans_, i.e. the fourth part of an as:— farthing.

2836. κοιλία **kŏilia**, _koy-lee´-ah;_ from κοῖλος **kŏilŏs** ("_hollow_"); a _cavity_, i.e. (spec.) the _abdomen_; by impl. the _matrix_; fig. the _heart_:— belly, womb.

2837. κοιμάω **kŏimaō**, _koy-mah´-o;_ from 2749; to _put to sleep_, i.e. (pass. or refl.) to _slumber_; fig. to _decease_:— (be a-, fall a-, fall on) sleep, be dead.

2838. κοίμησις **kŏimēsis**, _koy´-may-sis;_ from 2837; _sleeping_, i.e. (by impl.) _repose_:— taking of rest.

2839. κοινός **kŏinŏs**, _koy-nos´;_ prob. from 4862; _common_, i.e. (lit.) _shared_ by all or several, or (cer.) _profane_:— common, defiled, unclean, unholy.

2840. κοινόω **kŏinŏō**, _koy-nŏ´-o;_ from 2839; to _make_ (or _consider_) _profane_ (ceremon.):— call common, defile, pollute, unclean.

2841. κοινωνέω **kŏinōnĕō**, _koy-no-neh´-o;_ from 2844; to _share_ with others (obj. or subj.):— communicate, distribute, be partaker.

2842. κοινωνία **kŏinōnia**, _koy-nohn-ee´-ah;_ from 2844; _partnership_, i.e. (lit.) _participation_, or (social) _intercourse_, or (pecuniary) _benefaction_:— (to) communicate (-ation), communion, (contri-) distribution, fellowship.

2843. κοινωνικός **kŏinōnikŏs**, _koy-no-nee-kos´;_ from 2844; _communicative_, i.e. (pecuniarily) _liberal_:— willing to communicate.

2844. κοινωνός **kŏinōnŏs**, _koy-no-nos´;_ from 2839; a _sharer_, i.e. _associate_:— companion, × fellowship, partaker, partner.

2845. κοίτη **kŏitē**, _koy´-tay;_ from 2749; a _couch_; by extens. _cohabitation_; by impl. the male _sperm_:— bed, chambering, × conceive.

2846. κοιτών **kŏitōn**, _koy-tone´;_ from 2845; a _bedroom_:— + chamberlain.

2847. κόκκινος **kŏkkinŏs**, _kok´-kee-nos;_ from 2848 (from the _kernel_-shape of the insect); _crimson_-colored:— scarlet (colour, coloured).

2848. κόκκος **kŏkkŏs**, _kok´-kos;_ appar. a primary word; a _kernel_ of seed:— corn, grain.

2849. κολάζω **kŏlazō**, _kol-ad´-zo;_ from κόλος **kŏlŏs** (_dwarf_); prop. to _curtail_, i.e. (fig.) to _chastise_ (or _reserve_ for infliction):— punish.

2850. κολακεία **kŏlakĕia**, _kol-ak-i´-ah;_ from a der. of κόλαξ **kŏlax** (a _fawner_); _flattery_:— × flattering.

2851. κόλασις **kŏlasis**, _kol´-as-is;_ from 2849; penal _infliction_:— punishment, torment.

2852. κολαφίζω **kŏlaphizō**, _kol-af-id´-zo;_ from a der. of the base of 2849; to _rap_ with the fist:— buffet.

2853. κολλάω **kŏllaō**, _kol-lah´-o;_ from κόλλα **kŏlla** ("_glue_"); to _glue_, i.e. (pass. or refl.) to _stick_ (fig.):— cleave, join (self), keep company.

2854. κολλούριον **kŏllŏuriŏn**, _kol-loo´-ree-on;_ neut. of a presumed der. of κολλύρα **kŏllura** (a _cake;_ prob akin to the base of 2853); prop. a _poultice_ (as made of or in the form of _crackers_), i.e. (by anal.) a _plaster_:— eyesalve.

2855. κολλυβιστής **kŏllubistēs**, _kol-loo-bis-tace´;_ from a presumed der. of κόλλυβος **kŏllubŏs** (a small _coin;_ prob. akin to 2854); a _coin-dealer_:— (money-) changer.

2856. κολοβόω **kŏlŏbŏō**, _kol-ob-ŏ´-o;_ from a der. of the base of 2849; to _dock_, i.e. (fig.) _abridge_:— shorten.

2857. Κολοσσαί **Kŏlŏssai**, _kol-os-sah´-ee;_ appar. fem. plur. of κολοσσός **kŏlŏssŏs** ("_colossal_"); _Colossæ_, a place in Asia Minor:— Colosse.

2858. Κολοσσαεύς **Kŏlŏssaĕus**, _kol-os-sayoos´;_ from 2857; a _Colossæan_, (i.e. inhab. of Colossæ:— Colossian.

2859. κόλπος **kŏlpŏs**, _kol´-pos;_ appar. a primary word; the _bosom;_ by anal. a _bay_:— bosom, creek.

2860. κολυμβάω **kŏlumbaō**, _kol-oom-bah´-o;_ from κόλυμβος **kŏlumbŏs** (a _diver_); to _plunge_ into water:— swim.

2861. κολυμβήθρα **kŏlumbēthra**, _kol-oom-bay´-thrah;_ from 2860; a _diving-place_, i.e. _pond_ for bathing (or swimming):— pool.

2862. κολωνία **kŏlōnia**, _kol-o-nee´-ah;_ of Lat. or.; a Rom. "_colony_" for veterans:— colony.

2863. κομάω **kŏmaō**, _kom-ah´-o;_ from 2864; to _wear tresses_ of hair:— have long hair.

2864. κόμη **kŏmē**, _kom´-ay;_ appar. from the same as 2865; the _hair_ of the head (_locks_, as _ornamental_, and thus differing from 2359; which prop. denotes merely the _scalp_):— hair.

2865. κομίζω **kŏmizō**, _kom-id´-zo;_ from a primary κομέω **kŏmĕō** (to _tend_, i.e. take care of); prop. to _provide_ for, i.e. (by impl.) to _carry_ off (as if from harm; generally _obtain_):— bring, receive.

2866. κομψότερον **kŏmpsŏtĕrŏn**, _komp-sot´-er-on;_ neut. comparative of a der. of the base of 2865 (mean. prop. _well dressed_, i.e. _nice_); fig. _convalescent_:— + began to amend.

2867. κονιάω **kŏniaō**, _kon-ee-ah´-o;_ from κονία **kŏnia** (_dust;_ by anal. _lime_); to _whitewash_:— whiten.

2868. κονιορτός **kŏniŏrtŏs**, _kon-ee-or-tos´;_ from the base of 2867 and ὄρνυμι **ŏrnumi** (to "_rouse_"); _pulverulence_ (as _blown_ about):— dust.

2869. κοπάζω **kŏpazō**, _kop-ad´-zo;_ from 2873; to _tire_, i.e. (fig.) to _relax_:— cease.

2870. κοπετός **kŏpĕtŏs**, _kop-et-os´;_ from 2875; _mourning_ (prop. by _beating_ the breast):— lamentation.

2871. κοπή **kŏpē**, _kop-ay´;_ from 2875; _cutting_, i.e. _carnage_:— slaughter.

2872. κοπιάω **kŏpiaō**, _kop-ee-ah´-o;_ from a der. of 2873; to _feel fatigue;_ by impl. to _work hard_:— (bestow) labour, toil, be wearied.

2873. κόπος **kŏpŏs**, _kop´-os;_ from 2875; a _cut_, i.e. (by anal.) _toil_ (as _reducing_ the strength), lit. or fig.; by impl. *pains:*— labour, + trouble, weariness.

2874. κοπρία **kŏpria**, *kop-ree´-ah;* from κόπρος **kŏprŏs** (*ordure;* perh. akin to 2875); *manure:*— dung (-hill).

2875. κόπτω **kŏptō**, *kop´-to;* a primary verb; to "*chop;*" spec. to *beat* the breast in grief:— cut down, lament, mourn, (be-) wail. Comp. the base of 5114.

2876. κόραξ **kŏrax**, *kor´-ax;* perh. from 2880; a *crow* (from its *voracity*):— raven.

2877. κοράσιον **kŏrasiŏn**, *kor-as´-ee-on;* neut. of a presumed der. of κόρη **kŏrē** (a *maiden*); a (little) *girl:*— damsel, maid.

2878. κορβᾶν **kŏrban**, *kor-ban´;* and

κορβανᾶς **kŏrbanas**, *kor-ban-as´;* of Heb. and Chald. or. respectively [7133]; a votive *offering* and *the offering;* a *consecrated present* (to the Temple fund); by extens. (the latter term) the *Treasury* itself, i.e. the room where the contribution boxes stood:— Corban, treasury.

2879. Κορέ **Kŏrĕ**, *kor-eh´;* of Heb. or. [7141]; *Corë* (i.e. *Korach*), an Isr.:— Core.

2880. κορέννυμι **kŏrĕnnumi**, *kor-en´-noo-mee;* a primary verb; to *cram,* i.e. *glut* or *sate:*— eat enough, full.

2881. Κορίνθιος **Kŏrinthiŏs**, *kor-in´-thee-os;* from 2882; a *Corinthian,* i.e. inhab. of Corinth:— Corinthian.

2882. Κόρινθος **Kŏrinthŏs**, *kor´-in-thos;* of uncert. der.; *Corinthus,* a city of Greece:— Corinth.

2883. Κορνήλιος **Kŏrnēliŏs**, *kor-nay´-lee-os;* of Lat. or.; *Cornelius,* a Rom.:— Cornelius.

2884. κόρος **kŏrŏs**, *kor´-os;* of Heb. or. [3734]; a *cor,* i.e. a spec. measure:— measure.

2885. κοσμέω **kŏsmĕō**, *kos-meh´-o;* from 2889; to *put in* proper *order,* i.e. *decorate* (lit. or fig.); spec. to *snuff* (a wick):— adorn, garnish, trim.

2886. κοσμικός **kŏsmikŏs**, *kos-mee-kos´;* from 2889 (in its second. sense); *terrene* ("*cosmic*"), lit. (*mundane*) or fig. (*corrupt*):— worldly.

2887. κόσμιος **kŏsmiŏs**, *kos´-mee-os;* from 2889 (in its primary sense); *orderly,* i.e. *decorous:*— of good behaviour, modest.

2888. κοσμοκράτωρ **kŏsmŏkratōr**, *kos-mok-rat´-ore;* from 2889 and 2902; a *world-ruler,* an epithet of Satan:— ruler.

2889. κόσμος **kŏsmŏs**, *kos´-mos;* prob. from the base of 2865; orderly *arrangement,* i.e. *decoration;* by impl. the *world* (in a wide or narrow sense, incl. its inhab., lit. or fig. [mor.]):— adorning, world.

2890. Κόυαρτος **Kŏuartŏs**, *koo´-ar-tos;* of Lat. or. (*fourth*); *Quartus,* a Chr.:— Quartus.

2891. κοῦμι **kŏumi**, *koo´-mee* or κουμ **koum**, *koom´;* of Chald. origin [6966]; *cumi* (i.e. *rise!*):— cumi.

2892. κουστωδία **kŏustōdia**, *koos-to-*

dee´-ah; of Lat. or.; "*custody,*" i.e. a Rom. *sentry:*— watch.

2893. κουφίζω **kŏuphizō**, *koo-fid´-zo;* from κοῦφος **kŏuphŏs** (*light* in weight); to *unload:*— lighten.

2894. κόφινος **kŏphinŏs**, *kof´-ee-nos;* of uncert. der.; a (small) *basket:*— basket.

2895. κράββατος **krabbatŏs**, *krab´-bat-os;* prob. of for. or.; a *mattress:*— bed.

2896. κράζω **krazō**, *krad´-zo;* a primary verb; prop. to "*croak*" (as a raven) or *scream,* i.e. (gen.) to *call* aloud (*shriek, exclaim, intreat*):— cry (out).

2897. κραιπάλη **kraipalē**, *krahee-pal´-ay;* prob. from the same as 726; prop. a *headache* (as a *seizure* of pain) from drunkenness, i.e. (by impl.) a *debauch* (by anal. a *glut*):— surfeiting.

2898. κρανίον **kraniŏn**, *kran-ee´-on;* dimin. of a der. of the base of 2768; a *skull* ("*cranium*"):— Calvary, skull.

2899. κράσπεδον **kraspĕdŏn**, *kras´-ped-on;* of uncert. der.; a *margin,* i.e. (spec.) a *fringe* or *tassel:*— border, hem.

2900. κραταιός **krataiŏs**, *krat-ah-yos´;* from 2904; *powerful:*— mighty.

2901. κραταιόω **krataiŏō**, *krat-ah-yŏ´-o;* from 2900; to *empower,* i.e. (pass.) *increase in vigor:*— be strengthened, be (wax) strong.

2902. κρατέω **kratĕō**, *krat-eh´-o;* from 2904; to *use strength,* i.e. *seize* or *retain* (lit. or fig.):— hold (by, fast), keep, lay hand (hold) on, obtain, retain, take (by).

2903. κράτιστος **kratistŏs**, *krat´-is-tos;* superl. of a der. of 2904; *strongest,* i.e. (in dignity) *very honorable:*— most excellent (noble).

2904. κράτος **kratŏs**, *krat´-os;* perh. a primary word; *vigor* ["great"] (lit. or fig.):— dominion, might [-ily], power, strength.

2905. κραυγάζω **kraugazō**, *krŏw-gad´-zo;* from 2906; to *clamor:*— cry out.

2906. κραυγή **kraugē**, *krŏw-gay´;* from 2896; an *outcry* (in notification, tumult or grief):— clamour, cry (-ing).

2907. κρέας **krĕas**, *kreh´-as;* perh. a primary word; (butcher's) *meat:*— flesh.

2908. κρεῖσσον **krĕissŏn**, *krice´-son;* neut. of an alt. form of 2909; (as noun) *better,* i.e. *greater advantage:*— better.

2909. κρείττων **krĕittōn**, *krite´-tohn;* comparative of a der. of 2904; *stronger,* i.e. (fig.) *better,* i.e. *nobler:*— best, better.

2910. κρεμάννυμι **krĕmannumi**, *kreman´-noo-mee;* a prol. form of a primary verb; to *hang:*— hang.

2911. κρημνός **krĕmnŏs**, *krame-nos´;* from 2910; *overhanging,* i.e. a *precipice:*— steep place.

2912. Κρής **Krēs**, *krace;* from 2914; a *Cretan,* i.e. inhab. of Crete:— Crete, Cretian.

2913. Κρήσκης **Krēskēs**, *krace´-kace;* of Lat. or.; *growing; Cresces* (i.e. *Crescens*), a Chr.:— Crescens.

2914. Κρήτη **Krētē**, *kray´-tay;* of un-

cert. der.; *Cretë,* an island in the Mediterranean:— Crete.

2915. κριθή **krithē**, *kree-thay´;* of uncert. der.; *barley:*— barley.

2916. κρίθινος **krithinŏs**, *kree´-thee-nos;* from 2915; consisting of *barley:*— barley.

2917. κρίμα **krima**, *kree´-mah;* from 2919; a *decision* (the function or the effect, for or against ["*crime*"]):— avenge, condemned, condemnation, damnation, + go to law, judgment.

2918. κρίνον **krinŏn**, *kree´-non;* perh. a prim word; a *lily:*— lily.

2919. κρίνω **krinō**, *kree´-no;* prop. to distinguish, i.e. *decide* (mentally or judicially); by impl. to *try, condemn, punish:*— avenge, conclude, condemn, damn, decree, determine, esteem, judge, go to (sue at the) law, ordain, call in question, sentence to, think.

2920. κρίσις **krisis**, *kree´-sis;* decision (subj. or obj., for or against); by extens. a *tribunal;* by impl. *justice* (spec. divine *law*):— accusation, condemnation, damnation, judgment.

2921. Κρίσπος **Krispŏs**, *kris´-pos;* of Lat. or.; "*crisp*"; *Crispus,* a Corinthian:— Crispus.

2922. κριτήριον **kritēriŏn**, *kree-tay´-ree-on;* neut. of a presumed der. of 2923; a *rule* of *judging* ("*criterion*"), i.e. (by impl.) a *tribunal:*— to judge, judgment (seat).

2923. κριτής **kritēs**, *kree-tace´;* from 2919; a *judge* (gen. or spec.):— judge.

2924. κριτικός **kritikŏs**, *krit-ee-kos´;* from 2923; *decisive* ("*critical*"), i.e. *discriminative:*— discerner.

2925. κρούω **krŏuō**, *kroo´-o;* appar. a primary verb; to *rap:*— knock.

2926. κρυπτή **kruptē**, *kroop-tay´;* fem. of 2927; a *hidden* place, i.e. *cellar* ("*crypt*"):— secret.

2927. κρυπτός **kruptŏs**, *kroop-tos´;* from 2928; *concealed,* i.e. *private:*— hid (-den), inward [-ly], secret.

2928. κρύπτω **kruptō**, *kroop´-to;* a primary verb; to *conceal* (prop. by *covering*):— hide (self), keep secret, secret [-ly].

2929. κρυσταλλίζω **krustallizō**, *kroostal-lid´-zo;* from 2930; to *make* (i.e. intr. *resemble*) *ice* ("crystallize"):— be clear as crystal.

2930. κρύσταλλος **krustallŏs**, *kroos´-tallos;* from a der. of κρύος **kruos** (*frost*); *ice,* i.e. (by anal.) rock "*crystal*":— crystal.

2931. κρυφῇ **kruphē**, *kroo-fay´;* adv. from 2928; *privately:*— in secret.

2932. κτάομαι **ktaŏmai**, *ktah´-om-ahee;* a primary verb; to *get,* i.e. *acquire* (by any means; *own*):— obtain, possess, provide, purchase.

2933. κτῆμα **ktēma**, *ktay´-mah;* from 2932; an *acquirement,* i.e. *estate:*— possession.

2934. κτῆνος **ktēnŏs**, *ktay´-nos;* from 2932; *property,* i.e. (spec.) a domestic *animal:*— beast.

2935. κτήτωρ **ktētōr**, *ktay´-tore;* from 2932; an *owner:*— possessor.

2936. κτίζω **ktizō**, *ktid´-zo;* prob. akin to 2932 (through the idea of *proprietorship* of the *manufacturer*); to *fabricate,* i.e. *found* (*form* orig.):— create, Creator, make.

2937. κτίσις **ktisis**, *ktis´-is;* from 2936; orig. *formation* (prop. the act; by impl. the thing, lit. or fig.):— building, creation, creature, ordinance.

2938. κτίσμα **ktisma**, *ktis´-mah;* from 2936; an orig. *formation* (concr.), i.e. *product* (created thing):— creature.

2939. κτιστής **ktistēs**, *ktis-tace´;* from 2936; a *founder,* i.e. *God* (as author of all things):— Creator.

2940. κυβεία **kubĕia**, *koo-bi´-ah;* from κύβος **kubŏs** (a "*cube,*" i.e. *die* for playing); *gambling,* i.e. (fig.) *artifice* or *fraud:*— sleight.

2941. κυβέρνησις **kubĕrnēsis**, *koo-ber´-nay-sis;* from κυβερνάω **kubĕrnaō** (of Lat. or., to *steer*); *pilotage,* i.e. (fig.) *directorship* (in the church):— government.

2942. κυβερνήτης **kubĕrnētēs**, *koo-ber-nay´-tace;* from the same as *2941; helmsman,* i.e. (by impl.) *captain:*— (ship) master.

2943. κυκλόθεν **kuklŏthĕn**, *koo-kloth´-en;* adv. from the same as *2945; from* the *circle,* i.e. *all around:*— (round) about.

κύκλος **kuklŏs**. See 2945.

2944. κυκλόω **kuklŏō**, *koo-klŏ´-o;* from the same as *2945;* to *encircle,* i.e. *surround:*— compass (about), come (stand) round about.

2945. κύκλῳ **kuklŏi**, *koo´-klo;* as if dat. of κύκλος **kuklŏs** (a *ring,* "*cycle*"; akin to 2947); i.e. *in a circle* (by impl. of *1722*), i.e. (adv.) *all around:*— round about.

2946. κύλισμα **kulisma**, *koo´-lis-mah;* from *2947;* a *wallow* (the effect of *rolling*), i.e. *filth:*— wallowing.

2947. κυλίόω **kuliŏō**, *koo-lee-ŏ´-o;* from the base of *2949* (through the idea of *circularity;* comp. *2945, 1507*); to *roll* about:— wallow.

2948. κυλλός **kullŏs**, *kool-los´;* from the same as *2947; rocking* about, i.e. *crippled* (*maimed,* in feet or hands):— maimed.

2949. κύμα **kuma**, *koo´-mah;* from κύω **kuō** (to *swell* [with young], i.e. *bend, curve*); a *billow* (as *bursting* or *toppling*):— wave.

2950. κύμβαλον **kumbalŏn**, *koom´-bal-on;* from a der. of the base of *2949;* a "*cymbal*" (as *hollow*):— cymbal.

2951. κύμινον **kuminŏn**, *koo´-min-on;* of for. or. [comp. *3646*]; *dill* or *fennel* ("*cummin*"):— cummin.

2952. κυνάριον **kunariŏn**, *koo-nar´-ee-on;* neut. of a presumed der. of *2965;* a *puppy:*— dog.

2953. Κύπριος **Kupriŏs**, *koo´-pree-os;* from *2954;* a *Cyprian* (*Cypriot*), i.e. inhab. of Cyprus:— of Cyprus.

2954. Κύπρος **Kuprŏs**, *koo´-pros;* of un-

cert. or.; *Cyprus,* an island in the Mediterranean:— Cyprus.

2955. κύπτω **kuptō**, *koop´-to;* prob. from the base of *2949;* to *bend* forward:— stoop (down).

2956. Κυρηναῖος **Kurēnaiŏs**, *koo-ray-nah´-yos;* from *2957;* i.e. *Cyrenæan,* i.e. inhab. of Cyrene:— of Cyrene, Cyrenian.

2957. Κυρήνη **Kurēnē**, *koo-ray´-nay;* of uncert. der.; *Cyrenē,* a region of Africa:— Cyrene.

2958. Κυρήνιος **Kurēniŏs**, *koo-ray´-nee-os;* of Lat. or.; *Cyrenius* (i.e. *Quirinus*), a Rom.:— Cyrenius.

2959. Κυρία **Kuria**, *koo-ree´-ah;* fem. of *2962; Cyria,* a Chr. woman:— lady.

2960. κυριακός **kuriakŏs**, *koo-ree-ak-os´;* from *2962; belonging to* the *Lord* (Jehovah or Jesus):— Lord's.

2961. κυριεύω **kuriĕuō**, *koo-ree-yoo´-o;* from *2962;* to *rule:*— have dominion over, lord, be lord of, exercise lordship over.

2962. κύριος **kuriŏs**, *koo´-ree-os;* from κύρος **kurŏs** (*supremacy*); *supreme* in authority, i.e. (as noun) *controller;* by impl. *Mr.* (as a respectful title):— God, Lord, master, Sir.

2963. κυριότης **kuriŏtēs**, *koo-ree-ot´-ace;* from *2962; mastery,* i.e. (concr. and collect.) *rulers:*— dominion, government.

2964. κυρόω **kurŏō**, *koo-rŏ´-o;* from the same as *2962;* to *make authoritative,* i.e. *ratify:*— confirm.

2965. κύων **kuōn**, *koo´-ohn;* a primary word; a *dog* ["*hound*"] (lit. or fig.):— dog.

2966. κῶλον **kōlŏn**, *ko´-lon;* from the base of *2849;* a *limb* of the body (as if *lopped*):— carcase (carcass).

2967. κωλύω **kōluō**, *ko-loo´-o;* from the base of *2849;* to *estop,* i.e. *prevent* (by word or act):— forbid, hinder, keep from, let, not suffer, withstand.

2968. κώμη **kōmē**, *ko´-may;* from *2749;* a *hamlet* (as if *laid* down):— town, village.

2969. κωμόπολις **kōmŏpŏlis**, *ko-mop´-ol-is;* from *2968* and *4172;* an unwalled *city:*— town.

2970. κῶμος **kōmŏs**, *ko´-mos;* from *2749;* a *carousal* (as if *letting loose*):— revelling, rioting.

2971. κώνωψ **kōnōps**, *ko´-nopes;* appar. a der. of the base of *2759* and a der. of *3700;* a *mosquito* (from its *stinging* proboscis):— gnat.

2972. Κῶς **Kōs**, *koce;* of uncert. or.; *Cos,* an island in the Mediterranean:— Cos.

2973. Κωσάμ **Kōsam**, *ko-sam´;* of Heb. or. [comp. 7081]; *Cosam* (i.e. *Kosam*) an Isr.:— Cosam.

2974. κωφός **kōphŏs**, *ko-fos´;* from *2875; blunted,* i.e. (fig.) of hearing (*deaf*) or speech (*dumb*):— deaf, dumb, speechless.

Λ

2975. λαγχάνω **lagchanō**, *lang-khan´-o;*

a prol. form of a primary verb, which is only used as an alt. in certain tenses; to *lot,* i.e. *determine* (by impl. *receive*) espec. by lot:— his lot be, cast lots, obtain.

2976. Λάζαρος **Lazarŏs**, *lad´-zar-os;* prob. of Heb. or. [499]; *Lazarus* (i.e. *Elazar*), the name of two Isr. (one imaginary):— Lazarus.

2977. λάθρα **lathra**, *lath´-rah;* adv. from *2990; privately:*— privily, secretly.

2978. λαῖλαψ **lailaps**, *lah´-ee-laps;* of uncert. der.; a *whirlwind* (*squall*):— storm, tempest.

2979. λακτίζω **laktizō**, *lak-tid´-zo;* from adv. λάξ **lax** (*heelwise*); to *recalcitrate:*— kick.

2980. λαλέω **lalĕō**, *lal-eh´-o;* a prol. form of an otherwise obs. verb; to *talk,* i.e. *utter* words:— preach, say, speak (after), talk, tell, utter. Comp. *3004.*

2981. λαλιά **lalia**, *lal-ee-ah´;* from *2980; talk:*— saying, speech.

2982. λαμά **lama**, *lam-ah´;* or

λαμμᾶ **lamma**, *lam-mah´;* or

λεμά **lĕma**, *leh-mah´;* of Heb. or. [4100 with prep. pref.]; *lama* (i.e. *why*):— lama.

2983. λαμβάνω **lambanō**, *lam-ban´-o;* a prol. form of a primary verb, which is use only as an alt. in certain tenses; to *take* (in very many applications, lit. and fig. [properly obj. or act., to *get hold of;* whereas *1209* is rather subj. or pass., to *have offered* to one; while *138* is more violent, to *seize* or *remove*]):— accept, + be amazed, assay, attain, bring, × when I call, catch, come on (× unto), + forget, have, hold, obtain, receive (× after), take (away, up).

2984. Λάμεχ **Lamĕch**, *lam´-ekh;* of Heb. or. [3929]; *Lamech* (i.e. *Lemek*), a patriarch:— Lamech.

λαμμᾶ **lamma**. See 2982.

2985. λαμπάς **lampas**, *lam-pas´;* from *2989;* a "*lamp*" or *flambeau:*— lamp, light, torch.

2986. λαμπρός **lamprŏs**, *lam-pros´;* from the same as *2985; radiant;* by anal. *limpid;* fig. *magnificent* or *sumptuous* (in appearance):— bright, clear, gay, goodly, gorgeous, white.

2987. λαμπρότης **lamprŏtēs**, *lam-prot´-ace;* from *2986; brilliancy:*— brightness.

2988. λαμπρῶς **lamprōs**, *lam-proce´;* adv. from *2986; brilliantly,* i.e. fig. *luxuriously:*— sumptuously.

2989. λάμπω **lampō**, *lam´-po;* a primary verb; to *beam,* i.e. *radiate* brilliancy (lit. or fig.):— give light, shine.

2990. λανθάνω **lanthanō**, *lan-than´-o;* a prol. form of a primary verb, which is used only an alt. in certain tenses; to *lie hid* (lit. or fig.); often used adv. *unwittingly:*— be hid, be ignorate of, unawares.

2991. λαξευτός **laxĕutŏs**, *lax-yoo-tos´;* from a compound of λᾶς **las** (a *stone*) and the base of *3584* (in its orig. sense of *scraping*); *rock-quarried:*— hewn in stone.

2992. λαός **laŏs**, *lah-os´;* appar. a primary word; a *people* (in general; thus differing from *1218*, which denotes one's *own* populace):— people.

2993. Λαοδίκεια **Laŏdikĕia**, *lah-od-ik'-i-ah;* from a compound of *2992* and *1349; Laodicia,* a place in Asia Minor:— Laodicea.

2994. Λαοδικεύς **Laŏdikĕus**, *lah-od-ik-yooce';* from *2993;* a *Laodicean,* i.e. inhab. of Laodicia:— Laodicean.

2995. λάρυγξ **larugx**, *lar'-oongks;* of uncert. der.; the *throat* ("*larynx*"):— throat.

2996. Λασαία **Lasaia**, *las-ah'-yah;* of uncert. or.; *Lasæa,* a place in Crete:— Lasea.

2997. λάσχω **laschō**, *las'-kho;* a strengthened form of a primary verb, which only occurs in this and another prol. form as alt. in certain tenses; to *crack* open (from a fall):— burst asunder.

2998. λατομέω **latŏmĕō**, *lat-om-eh'-o;* from the same as the first part of *2991* and the base of *5114;* to *quarry:*— hew.

2999. λατρεία **latrĕia**, *lat-ri'-ah;* from *3000; ministration* of God, i.e. *worship:*— (divine) service.

3000. λατρεύω **latrĕuō**, *lat-ryoo'-o;* from λάτρις **latris** (a hired *menial);* to *minister* (to God), i.e. *render,* relig. *homage:*— serve, do the service, worship (-per).

3001. λάχανον **lachanŏn**, *lakh'-an-on;* from λαχαίνω **lachainō** (to *dig);* a *vegetable:*— herb.

3002. Λεββαῖος **Lĕbbaiŏs**, *leb-bah'-yos;* of uncert. or.; *Lebbæus,* a Chr.:— Lebbæus.

3003. λεγεών **lĕgĕōn**, *leg-eh-ohn'* or

    λεγιών **lĕgiōn**, *leg-ee-ohn';* of Lat. or.; a "*legion,*" i.e. Rom. *regiment* (fig.):— legion.

3004. λέγω **lĕgō**, *leg'-o;* a primary verb; prop. to "*lay*" forth, i.e. (fig.) *relate* (in words [usually of systematic or set *discourse;* whereas *2036* and *5346* generally refer to an *individual* expression or speech respectively; while *4483* is prop. to *break silence* merely, and *2980* means an *extended* or random harangue]) by impl. to *mean:*— ask, bid, boast, call, describe, give out, name, put forth, say (-ing, on), shew, speak, tell, utter.

3005. λεῖμμα **lĕimma**, *lime'-mah;* from *3007;* a *remainder:*— remnant.

3006. λεῖος **lĕiŏs**, *li'-os;* appar. a primary word; *smooth,* i.e. "*level*":— smooth.

3007. λείπω **lĕipō**, *li'-po;* a primary verb; to *leave,* i.e. (intr. or pass.) to *fail* or *be absent:*— be destitute (wanting), lack.

3008. λειτουργέω **lĕitŏurgĕō**, *li-toorg-eh'-o;* from *3011;* to be a *public servant,* i.e. (by anal.) to *perform* relig. or charitable *functions* (*worship, obey, relieve*):— minister.

3009. λειτουργία **lĕitŏurgia**, *li-toorg-ee'-ah;* from *3008; public function* (as priest ["liturgy"] or almsgiver):— ministration (-try), service.

3010. λειτουργικός **lĕitŏurgikŏs**, *li-toorg-ik-os';* from the same as *3008; functional publicly* ("liturgic"); i.e. *beneficent:*— ministering.

3011. λειτουργός **lĕitŏurgŏs**, *li-toorg-os';* from a der. of *2992* and *2041;* a *public servant,* i.e. a *functionary* in the Temple or Gospel, or (gen.) a *worshipper* (of God) or *benefactor* (of man):— minister (-ed).

3012. λέντιον **lĕntiŏn**, *len'-tee-on;* of Lat. or.; a "*linen*" cloth, i.e. *apron:*— towel.

3013. λεπίς **lĕpis**, *lep-is';* from λέπω **lĕpō** (to *peel);* a *flake:*— scale.

3014. λέπρα **lĕpra**, *lep'-rah;* from the same as *3013; scaliness,* i.e. "*leprosy*":— leprosy.

3015. λεπρός **lĕprŏs**, *lep-ros';* from the same as *3014; scaly,* i.e. *leprous* (a *leper):*— leper.

3016. λεπτόν **lĕptŏn**, *lep-ton';* neut. of a der. of the same as *3013; something scaled* (*light),* i.e. a small *coin:*— mite.

3017. Λευΐ **Lĕuï**, *lyoo-ee';* of Heb. or. [3878]; *Levi,* the name of three Isr.:— Levi. Comp. *3018.*

3018. Λευΐς **Lĕuïs**, *lyoo-is';* a form of *3017; Lewis* (i.e. *Levi),* a Chr.:— Levi.

3019. Λευΐτης **Lĕuïtēs**, *lyoo-ee'-tace;* from *3017;* a *Levite,* i.e. desc. of Levi:— Levite.

3020. Λευϊτικός **Lĕuïtikŏs**, *lyoo-it-ee-kos';* from *3019; Levitic,* i.e. relating to the Levites:— Levitical.

3021. λευκαίνω **lĕukainō**, *lyoo-kah'-ee-no;* from *3022;* to *whiten:*— make white, whiten.

3022. λευκός **lĕukŏs**, *lyoo-kos';* from λύκη **lukē**, ("*light*"); *white:*— white.

3023. λεών **lĕōn**, *leh-ohn';* a primary word; a "*lion*":— lion.

3024. λήθη **lēthē**, *lay'-thay;* from *2990; forgetfulness:*— + forget.

3025. ληνός **lēnŏs**, *lay-nos';* appar. a primary word; a *trough,* i.e. wine-*vat:*— winepress.

3026. λῆρος **lērŏs**, *lay'-ros;* appar. a primary word; *twaddle,* i.e. an *incredible* story:— idle tale.

3027. ληστής **lēistēs**, *lace-tace';* from λῄζομαι **leizomai** (to *plunder);* a *brigand:*— robber, thief.

3028. λῆμψις **lēmpsis**, *lemp'-sis;* from *2983; receipt* (the act):— receiving.

3029. λίαν **lian**, *lee'-an;* of uncert. aff.; *much* (adv.):— exceeding, great (-ly) sore, very (+ chiefest).

3030. λίβανος **libanŏs**, *lib'-an-os;* of for. or. [3828]; the *incense*-tree, i.e. (by impl.) *incense* itself:— frankincense.

3031. λιβανωτός **libanōtŏs**, *lib-an-o-tos';* from *3030; frankincense,* i.e. (by extens.) a *censer* for burning it:— censer.

3032. Λιβερτῖνος **Libĕrtinŏs**, *lib-er-tee-nos;* of Lat. or.; a Rom. *freedman:*— Libertine.

3033. Λιβύη **Libuē**, *lib-oo'-ay;* prob. from *3047; Libye,* a region of Africa:— Libya.

3034. λιθάζω **lithazō**, *lith-ad'-zo;* from *3037;* to *lapidate:*— stone.

3035. λίθινος **lithinŏs**, *lith-ee'-nos;* from *3037; stony,* i.e. made of *stone:*— of stone.

3036. λιθοβολέω **lithŏbŏlĕō**, *lith-ob-ol-eh'-o;* from a compound of *3037* and *906;* to *throw stones,* i.e. *lapidate:*— stone, cast stones.

3037. λίθος **lithŏs**, *lee'-thos;* appar. a primary word; a *stone* (lit. or fig.):— (mill-, stumbling-) stone.

3038. λιθόστρωτος **lithŏstrōtŏs**, *lith-os'-tro-tos;* from *3037* and a der. of *4766; stone-strewed,* i.e. a tessellated *mosaic* on which the Rom. tribunal was placed:— Pavement.

3039. λικμάω **likmaō**, *lik-mah'-o;* from λικμός **likmŏs**, the equiv. of λίκνον **liknŏn** (a winnowing *fan* or basket); to *winnow,* i.e. (by anal.) to *triturate:*— grind to powder.

3040. λιμήν **limēn**, *lee-mane';* appar. a primary word; a *harbor:*— haven. Comp. *2568.*

3041. λίμνη **limnē**, *lim'-nay;* prob. from *3040* (through the idea of nearness of shore); a *pond* (large or small):— lake.

3042. λιμός **limŏs**, *lee-mos';* prob. from *3007* (through the idea of *destitution);* a *scarcity* of food:— dearth, famine, hunger.

3043. λίνον **linŏn**, *lee'-non;* prob. a primary word; *flax,* i.e. (by impl.) "*linen*":— linen.

3044. Λίνος **Linŏs**, *lee'-nos;* perh. from *3043; Linus,* a Chr.:— Linus.

3045. λιπαρός **liparŏs**, *lip-ar-os';* from λίπος **lipŏs** (*grease); fat,* i.e. (fig.) *sumptuous:*— dainty.

3046. λίτρα **litra**, *lee'-trah;* of Lat. or. [*libra*]; a *pound* in weight:— pound.

3047. λίψ **lips**, *leeps;* prob. from λείβω **lĕibō** (to *pour* a "libation"); the *south* (-west) wind (as bringing rain, i.e. (by extens.) the *south* quarter):— southwest.

3048. λογία **lŏgia**, *log-ee'-ah* or

    λογεία **lŏgĕia**, *log-i'-ah;* from *3056* (in the commercial sense); a *contribution:*— collection, gathering.

3049. λογίζομαι **lŏgizŏmai**, *log-id'-zom-ahee;* mid. voice from *3056;* to *take an inventory,* i.e. *estimate* (lit. or fig.):— conclude, (ac-) count (of), + despise, esteem, impute, lay, number, reason, reckon, suppose, think (on).

3050. λογικός **lŏgikŏs**, *log-ik-os';* from *3056; rational* ("*logical*"):— reasonable, of the word.

3051. λόγιον **lŏgiŏn**, *log'-ee-on;* neut. of *3052;* an *utterance* (of God):— oracle.

3052. λόγιος **lŏgiŏs**, *log'-ee-os;* from *3056; fluent,* i.e. an *orator:*— eloquent.

3053. λογισμός **lŏgismŏs**, *log-is-mos';* from *3049; computation,* i.e. (fig.) *reasoning* (*conscience, conceit*):— imagination, thought.

3054. λογομαχέω **lŏgŏmachĕō**, *log-om-akh-eh'-o;* from a compound of *3056* and *3164;* to *be disputatious* (on trifles):— strive about words.

3055. λογομαχία **lŏgŏmachia**, *log-om-akh-ee´-ah;* from the same as *3054; disputation* about trifles ("*logomachy*"):— strife of words.

3056. λόγος **lŏgŏs**, *log´-os;* from *3004;* something *said* (incl. the *thought*); by impl. a *topic* (subject of discourse), also *reasoning* (the mental faculty) or *motive;* by extens. a *computation;* spec. (with the art. in John) the Divine *Expression* (i.e. *Christ*):— account, cause, communication, × concerning, doctrine, fame, × have to do, intent, matter, mouth, preaching, question, reason, + reckon, remove, say (-ing), shew, × speaker, speech, talk, thing, + none of these things move me, tidings, treatise, utterance, word, work.

3057. λόγχη **lŏgchē**, *long´-khay;* perh. a primary word; a "*lance*":— spear.

3058. λοιδορέω **lŏidŏrĕō**, *loy-dor-eh´-o;* from *3060;* to *reproach,* i.e. *vilify:*— revile.

3059. λοιδορία **lŏidŏria**, *loy-dor-ee´-ah;* from *3060; slander* or *vituperation:*— railing, reproach [-fully].

3060. λοίδορος **lŏidŏrŏs**, *loy´-dor-os;* from λοιδός **lŏidŏs** (*mischief*); *abusive,* i.e. a *blackguard:*— railer, reviler.

3061. λοιμός **lŏimŏs**, *loy´-mos;* of uncert. aff.; a *plague* (lit. the *disease,* or fig. a *pest*):— pestilence (-t).

3062. λοιποί **lŏipŏi**, *loy-poy´;* masc. plur. of a der. of *3007; remaining* ones:— other, which remain, remnant, residue, rest.

3063. λοιπόν **lŏipŏn**, *loy-pon´;* neut. sing. of the same as *3062;* something *remaining* (adv.):— besides, finally, furthermore, (from) henceforth, moreover, now, + it remaineth, then.

3064. λοιποῦ **lŏipŏu**, *loy-poo´;* gen. sing. of the same as *3062; remaining* time:— from henceforth.

3065. Λουκᾶς **Lŏukas**, *loo-kas´;* contr. from Lat. *Lucanus; Lucas,* a Chr.:— Lucas, Luke.

3066. Λούκιος **Lŏukiŏs**, *loo´-kee-os;* of Lat. or.; *illuminative; Lucius,* a Chr.:— Lucius.

3067. λουτρόν **lŏutrŏn**, *loo-tron´;* from *3068;* a *bath,* i.e. (fig.), *baptism:*— washing.

3068. λούω **lŏuō**, *loo´-o;* a primary verb; to *bathe* (the *whole* person; whereas *3538* means to *wet* a *part* only, and *4150* to wash, cleanse *garments* exclusively):— wash.

3069. Λύδδα **Ludda**, *lud´-dah;* of Heb. or. [3850]; *Lydda* (i.e. *Lod*), a place in Pal.:— Lydda.

3070. Λυδία **Ludia**, *loo-dee´-ah;* prop. fem. of Λύδιος **Ludiŏs** [of for. or.] (a *Lydian,* in Asia Minor); *Lydia,* a Chr. woman:— Lydia.

3071. Λυκαονία **Lukaŏnia**, *loo-kah-on-ee´-ah;* perh. remotely from *3074; Lycaonia,* a region of Asia Minor:— Lycaonia.

3072. Λυκαονιστί **Lukaŏnisti**, *loo-kah-on-is-tee´;* adv. from a der. of *3071; Lycaonistically,* i.e. in the language of the Lycaonians:— in the speech of Lycaonia.

3073. Λυκία **Lukia**, *loo-kee´-ah;* prob. remotely from *3074; Lycia,* a province of Asia Minor:— Lycia.

3074. λύκος **lukŏs**, *loo´-kos;* perh. akin to the base of *3022* (from the *whitish* hair); a *wolf:*— wolf.

3075. λυμαίνομαι **lumainŏmai**, *loo-mah´-ee-nom-ahee;* mid. voice from a prob. der. of *3089* (mean. *filth*); prop. to *soil,* i.e. (fig.) *insult* (*maltreat*):— make havock of.

3076. λυπέω **lupĕō**, *loo-peh´-o;* from *3077;* to *distress;* refl. or pass. to *be sad:*— cause grief, grieve, be in heaviness, (be) sorrow (-ful), be (make) sorry.

3077. λύπη **lupē**, *loo´-pay;* appar. a primary word; *sadness:*— grief, grievous, + grudgingly, heaviness, sorrow.

3078. Λυσανίας **Lusanias**, *loo-san-ee´-as;* from *3080* and ἀνία **ania** (*trouble*); *grief-dispelling; Lysanias,* a governor of Abilene:— Lysanias.

3079. Λυσίας **Lusias**, *loo-see´-as;* of uncert. aff.; *Lysias,* a Rom.:— Lysias.

3080. λύσις **lusis**, *loo´-sis;* from *3089;* a *loosening,* i.e. (spec.) *divorce:*— to be loosed.

3081. λυσιτελεῖ **lusitĕlĕi**, *loo-sit-el-i´;* third pers. sing. pres. ind. act. of a der. of a compound of *3080* and *5056;* impers. it *answers* the *purpose,* i.e. is *advantageous:*— it is better.

3082. Λύστρα **Lustra**, *loos´-trah;* of uncert. or.; *Lystra,* a place in Asia Minor:— Lystra.

3083. λύτρον **lutrŏn**, *loo´-tron;* from *3089;* something to *loosen* with, i.e. a redemption *price* (fig. *atonement*):— ransom.

3084. λυτρόω **lutrŏō**, *loo-trŏ´-o;* from *3083;* to *ransom* (lit. or fig.):— redeem.

3085. λύτρωσις **lutrŏsis**, *loo´-tro-sis;* from *3084;* a *ransoming* (fig.):— + redeemed, redemption.

3086. λυτρωτής **lutrŏtēs**, *loo-tro-tace´;* from *3084;* a *redeemer* (fig.):— deliverer.

3087. λυχνία **luchnia**, *lookh-nee´-ah;* from *3088;* a *lamp-stand* (lit. or fig.):— candlestick.

3088. λύχνος **luchnŏs**, *lookh´-nos;* from the base of *3022;* a portable *lamp* or other *illuminator* (lit. or fig.):— candle, light.

3089. λύω **luō**, *loo´-o;* a primary verb; to "*loosen*" (lit. or fig.):— break (up), destroy, dissolve, (un-) loose, melt, put off. Comp. *4486.*

3090. Λωΐς **Lŏis**, *lo-ece´;* of uncert. or.; *Loïs,* a Chr. woman:— Lois.

3091. Λώτ **Lōt**, *lote;* of Heb. or. [3876]; *Lot,* a patriarch:— Lot.

M

3092. Μαάθ **Maath**, *mah-ath´;* prob. of Heb. or.; *Maath,* an Isr.:— Maath.

3093. Μαγδαλά **Magdala**, *mag-dal-ah´;* of Chald. or. [comp. 4026]; *the tower; Magdala* (i.e. *Migdala*), a place in Pal.:— Magdala.

3094. Μαγδαληνή **Magdalēnē**, *mag-dal-ay-nay´;* fem. of a der. of *3093;* a female *Magdalene,* i.e. inhab. of *Magdala:*— Magdalene.

3095. μαγεία **magĕia**, *mag-i´-ah;* from *3096;* "*magic*":— sorcery.

3096. μαγεύω **magĕuō**, *mag-yoo´-o;* from *3097;* to *practice magic:*— use sorcery.

3097. μάγος **magŏs**, *mag´-os;* of for. or. [7248]; a *Magian,* i.e. Oriental *scientist;* by impl. a *magician:*— sorcerer, wise man.

3098. Μαγώγ **Magōg**, *mag-ogue´;* of Heb. or. [4031]; *Magog,* a for. nation, i.e. (fig.) an Antichristian party:— Magog.

3099. Μαδιάν **Madian**, *mad-ee-on´* or

Μαδιάμ **Madiam**, *mad-ee-on´;* of Heb. origin [4080]; *Madian* (i.e. *Midian*), a region of Arabia:— Madian.

3100. μαθητεύω **mathētĕuō**, *math-ayt-yoo´-o;* from *3101;* intr. to *become a pupil;* tran. to *disciple,* i.e. enroll as scholar:— be disciple, instruct, teach.

3101. μαθητής **mathētēs**, *math-ay-tes´;* from *3129;* a *learner,* i.e. *pupil:*— disciple.

3102. μαθήτρια **mathētria**, *math-ay´-tree-ah;* fem. from *3101;* a female *pupil:*— disciple.

3103. Μαθουσάλα **Mathŏusala**, *math-oo-sal´-ah;* of Heb. or. [4968]; *Mathusala* (i.e. *Methushelach*), an antediluvian:— Mathusala.

3104. Μαϊνάν **Maïnan**, *mahee-nan´;* prob. of Heb. or.; *Maïnan,* an Isr.:— Mainan.

3105. μαίνομαι **mainŏmai**, *mah´-ee-nom-ahee;* mid. voice from a primary μάω **maō** (to *long* for; through the idea of insensate *craving*); to *rave* as a "maniac":— be beside self (mad).

3106. μακαρίζω **makarizō**, *mak-ar-id´-zo;* from *3107;* to *beatify,* i.e. *pronounce* (or *esteem*) *fortunate:*— call blessed, count happy.

3107. μακάριος **makariŏs**, *mak-ar´-ee-os;* a prol. form of the poet. μάκαρ **makar** (mean. the same); supremely *blest;* by extens. *fortunate, well off:*— blessed, happy (× -ier).

3108. μακαρισμός **makarismŏs**, *mak-ar-is-mos´;* from *3106; beatification,* i.e. *attribution* of *good fortune:*— blessedness.

3109. Μακεδονία **Makĕdŏnia**, *mak-ed-on-ee´-ah;* from *3110; Macedonia,* a region of Greece:— Macedonia.

3110. Μακεδών **Makĕdōn**, *mak-ed´-ohn;* of uncert. der.; a *Macedon* (*Macedonian*), i.e. inhab. of *Macedonia:*— of Macedonia, Macedonian.

3111. μάκελλον **makĕllŏn**, *mak´-el-lon;* of Lat. or. [macellum]; a *butcher's stall, meat market* or *provision-shop:*— shambles.

3112. μακράν **makran**, *mak-ran´;* fem. acc. sing. of *3117* (*3598* being impl.); *at a distance* (lit. or fig.):— (a-) far (off), good (great) way off.

3113. μακρόθεν **makrŏthĕn**, *mak-roth´-*

en; adv. from 3117; *from a distance* or *afar:*— afar off, from far.

3114. μακροθυμέω **makrŏthumĕō**, *mak-roth-oo-meh´-o;* from the same as *3116;* to *be long-spirited,* i.e. (obj.) *forbearing* or (subj.) *patient:*— bear (suffer) long, be longsuffering, have (long) patience, be patient, patiently endure.

3115. μακροθυμία **makrŏthumia**, *mak-roth-oo-mee´-ah;* from the same as *3116; longanimity,* i.e. (obj.) *forbearance* or (subj.) *fortitude:*— longsuffering, patience.

3116. μακροθυμώς **makrŏthumōs**, *mak-roth-oo-moce´;* adv. of a compound of *3117* and *2372; with long (enduring) temper,* i.e. *leniently:*— patiently.

3117. μακρός **makrŏs**, *mak-ros´;* from *3372; long* (in place [*distant*] or time [neut. plur.l):— far, long.

3118. μακροχρόνιος **makrŏchrŏniŏs**, *mak-rokh-ron´-ee-os;* from *3117* and *5550; long-timed,* i.e. *long-lived:*— live long.

3119. μαλακία **malakia**, *mal-ak-ee´-ah;* from *3120; softness,* i.e. *enervation (debility):*— disease.

3120. μαλακός **malakŏs**, *mal-ak-os´;* of uncert. aff.; *soft,* i.e. *fine* (clothing); fig. a *catamite:*— effeminate, soft.

3121. Μαλελεήλ **Malĕlĕēl**, *mal-el-eh-ale´;* of Heb. or. [4111l; *Maleleël* (i.e. *Mahalalel*), an antediluvian:— Maleleel.

3122. μάλιστα **malista**, *mal´-is-tah;* neut. plur. of the superl. of an appar. primary adv. μάλα **mala** (*very*); (adv.) *most* (*in the greatest degree*) or *particularly:*— chiefly, most of all, (e-) specially.

3123. μᾶλλον **mallŏn**, *mal´-lon;* neut. of the comparative of the same as *3122;* (adv.) *more* (*in a greater degree*) or *rather:*— + better, x far, (the) more (and more), (so) much (the more), rather.

3124. Μάλχος **Malchŏs**, *mal´-khos;* of Heb. or. [4429l; *Malchus,* an Isr.:— Malchus.

3125. μάμμη **mammē**, *mam´-may;* of nat. or. ["mammy"]; a *grandmother:*— grandmother.

3126. μαμμωνᾶς **mammōnas** *mam-mo-nas´,* or

μαμωνᾶς **mamōnas** *mam-o-nas´;* of Chald. or. (*confidence,* i.e. *wealth,* personified); *mammonas,* i.e. *avarice* (deified):— mammon.

3127. Μαναήν **Manaēn**, *man-ah-ane´;* of uncert. or.; *Manaën,* a Chr.:— Manaen.

3128. Μανασσῆς **Manassēs**, *man-as-sace´;* of Heb. or. [4519l; *Mannasses* (i.e. *Menashsheh*), an Isr.:— Manasses.

3129. μανθάνω **manthanō**, *man-than´-o;* prol. from a primary verb, another form of which, μαθέω **mathĕō**, is used as an alt. in cert. tenses; to *learn* (in any way):— learn, understand.

3130. μανία **mania**, *man-ee´-ah;* from *3105; craziness:*— [+ makel × mad.

3131. μάννα **manna**, *man´-nah;* of Heb. or. [4478l; *manna* (i.e. *man*), an edible gum:— manna.

3132. μαντεύομαι **mantĕuŏmai**, *mant-yoo´-om-ahee;* from a der. of *3105* (mean. a *prophet,* as supposed to *rave* through *inspiration*); to *divine,* i.e. *utter spells* (under pretense of foretelling:— by soothsaying.

3133. μαραίνω **marainō**, *mar-ah´-ee-no;* of uncert. aff.; to *extinguish* (as fire), i.e. (fig. and pass.) to *pass away:*— fade away.

3134. μαρὰν ἀθά **maran atha**, *mar-an´ath-ah´;* of Chald. or. (mean. *our Lord has come*); *maranatha,* i.e. an exclamation of the approaching *divine judgment:*— Maran-atha.

3135. μαργαρίτης **margaritēs**, *mar-gar-ee´-tace;* from μάργαρος **margarŏs** (a pearl-*oyster*); a *pearl:*— pearl.

3136. Μάρθα **Martha**, *mar´-thah;* prob. of Chald. or. (mean. *mistress*); *Martha,* a Chr. woman:— Martha.

3137. Μαρία **Maria**, *mar-ee´-ah;* or

Μαριάμ **Mariam**, *mar-ee-am´;* of Heb. or. [4813l; *Maria* or *Mariam* (i.e. *Mirjam*), the name of six Chr. females:— Mary.

3138. Μάρκος **Markŏs**, *mar´-kos;* of Lat. or.; *Marcus,* a Chr.:— Marcus, Mark.

3139. μάρμαρος **marmarŏs**, *mar´-mar-os;* from μαρμαίρω **marmairō**, (to *glisten*); *marble* (as sparkling *white*):— marble.

μάρτυρ **martur**. See *3144.*

3140. μαρτυρέω **marturĕō**, *mar-too-reh´-o;* from *3144;* to *be a witness,* i.e. *testify* (lit. or fig.):— charge, give [evidence], bear record, have (obtain, of) good (honest) report, be well reported of, testify, give (have) testimony, (be, bear, give, obtain) witness.

3141. μαρτυρία **marturia**, *mar-too-ree´-ah;* from *3144; evidence* given (judicially or gen.):— record, report, testimony, witness.

3142. μαρτύριον **marturiŏn**, *mar-too-ree-on;* neut. of a presumed der. of *3144;* something *evidential,* i.e. (gen.) *evidence* given or (spec.) the *Decalogue* (in the sacred Tabernacle):— to be testified, testimony, witness.

3143. μαρτύρομαι **marturŏmai**, *mar-too´-rom-ahee;* mid. voice from *3144;* to *be adduced* as *a witness,* i.e. (fig.) to *obtest* (in affirmation or exhortation):— take to record, testify.

3144. μάρτυς **martus**, *mar´-toos;* of uncert. aff.; a *witness* (lit. [judicially] or fig. [gen.l); by anal. a *"martyr"*:— martyr, record, witness.

3145. μασσάομαι **massaŏmai**, *mas-sah´-om-ahee;* from a primary μάσσω **massō** (to *handle* or *squeeze*); to *chew:*— gnaw.

3146. μαστιγόω **mastigŏō**, *mas-tig-ŏ´-o;* from *3148;* to *flog* (lit. or fig.):— scourge.

3147. μαστίζω **mastizō**, *mas-tid´-zo;* from *3149;* to *whip* (lit.):— scourge.

3148. μάστιξ **mastix**, *mas´-tix;* prob. from the base of *3145* (through the idea of *contact*); a *whip* (lit. the Rom. *flagellum* for criminals; fig. a *disease*):— plague, scourging.

3149. μαστός **mastŏs**, *mas-tos´;* from

the base of *3145;* a (prop. female) *breast* (as if *kneaded* up):— pap.

3150. ματαιολογία **mataiŏlŏgia**, *mat-ah-yol-og-ee´-ah;* from *3151; random talk,* i.e. *babble:*— vain jangling.

3151. ματαιολόγος **mataiŏlŏgŏs**, *mat-ah-yol-og´-os;* from *3152* and *3004;* an *idle* (i.e. *senseless* or *mischievous*) *talker,* i.e. a *wrangler:*— vain talker.

3152. μάταιος **mataiŏs**, *mat´-ah-yos;* from the base of *3155; empty,* i.e. (lit.) *profitless,* or (spec.) an *idol:*— vain, vanity.

3153. ματαιότης **mataiŏtēs**, *mat-ah-yot´-ace;* from *3152; inutility;* fig. *transientness;* mor. *depravity:*— vanity.

3154. ματαιόω **mataiŏō**, *mat-ah-yŏ´-o;* from *3152;* to *render* (pass. *become*) *foolish,* i.e. (mor.) *wicked* or (spec.) *idolatrous:*— become vain.

3155. μάτην **matēn**, *mat´-ane;* accus. of a der. of the base of *3145* (through the idea of tentative *manipulation,* i.e. unsuccessful *search,* or else of *punishment*); *folly,* i.e. (adv.) to *no purpose:*— in vain.

3156. Ματθαῖος **Matthaiŏs**, *mat-thah´-yos;* or

Μαθθαῖος **Maththaiŏs**, *math-thah´-yos;* a short. form of *3161; Matthæus* (i.e. *Matthitjah*), an Isr. and a Chr.:— Matthew.

3157. Ματθάν **Matthan**, *mat-than´;* of Heb. or. [4977l; *Matthan* (i.e. *Mattan*), an Isr.:— Matthan.

3158. Ματθάτ **Matthat**, *mat-that´;* or

Μαθθάτ **Maththat**, *math-that´;* prob. a short. form of *3161; Matthat* (i.e. *Mattitjah*), the name of two Isr.:— Mathat.

3159. Ματθίας **Matthias** *mat-thee´-as,* or Μαθθίας **Maththias**, *math-thee´-as;* appar. a short. form of *3161; Matthias* (i.e. *Mattithjah*), an Isr.:— Matthias.

3160. Ματταθά **Mattatha**, *mat-tath-ah´;* prob. a short. form of *3161* [comp. 4992l; *Mattatha* (i.e. *Mattithjah*), an Isr.:— Mattatha.

3161. Ματταθίας **Mattathias**, *mat-tath-ee´-as;* of Heb. or. [4993l; *Mattathias* (i.e. *Mattithjah*), an Isr. and a Chr.:— Mattathias.

3162. μάχαιρα **machaira**, *makh´-ahee-rah;* prob. fem. of a presumed der. of *3163;* a *knife,* i.e. *dirk;* fig. *war,* judicial *punishment:*— sword.

3163. μάχη **machē**, *makh´-ay;* from *3164;* a *battle,* i.e. (fig.) *controversy:*— fighting, strive, striving.

3164. μάχομαι **machŏmai**, *makh´-om-ahee;* mid. voice of an appar. primary verb; to *war,* i.e. (fig.) to *quarrel, dispute:*— fight, strive.

3165. μέ **mĕ**, *meh;* a short. (and prob. orig.) form of *1691; me:*— I, me, my.

3166. μεγαλαυχέω **mĕgalauchĕō**, *meg-al-ow-kheh´-o;* from a compound of *3173* and αὐχέω **auchĕō**, (to *boast;* akin to *837* and *2744*); to *talk big,* i.e. *be grandiloquent* (*arrogant, egotistic*):— boast great things.

3167. μεγαλεῖος **mĕgalĕiŏs**, *meg-al-i´-*

os; from *3173; magnificent,* i.e. (neut, plur. as noun) a conspicuous *favor,* or (subj.) *perfection:*— great things, wonderful works.

3168. μεγαλειότης **měgalěiŏtēs,** *meg-al-i-ot´-ace;* from *3167; superbness,* i.e. *glory* or *splendor:*— magnificence, majesty, mighty power.

3169. μεγαλοπρεπής **měgalŏprěpēs,** *meg-al-op-rep-ace´;* from *3173* and *4241; befitting greatness* or *magnificence (majestic):*— excellent.

3170. μεγαλύνω **měgalunō,** *meg-al-oo´-no;* from *3173;* to make (or *declare) great,* i.e. *increase* or (fig.) *extol:*— enlarge, magnify, shew great.

3171. μεγάλως **měgalōs,** *meg-al´-oce;* adv. from *3173; much:*— greatly.

3172. μεγαλωσύνη **měgalōsunē,** *meg-al-o-soo´-nay;* from *3173; greatness,* i.e. (fig.) *divinity* (often *God* himself):— majesty.

3173. μέγας **měgas,** *meg´-as;* (incl. the prol. forms, fem.

μεγάλη **měgalē,** plur.

μεγάλοι **měgalŏi,** etc.; comp. also *3176, 3187*); *big* (lit. or fig. in a very wide application):— (+ *fear) exceedingly, great* (-est), *high, large, loud, mighty,* + (be) *sore* (afraid), *strong,* × to *years.*

3174. μέγεθος **měgěthŏs,** *meg´-eth-os;* from *3173; magnitude* (fig.):— greatness.

3175. μεγιστᾶνες **měgistaněs,** *meg-is-tan´-es;* plur. from *3176; grandees:*— great men, lords.

3176. μέγιστος **měgistŏs,** *meg´-is-tos;* superl. of *3173; greatest* or *very great:*— exceeding great.

3177. μεθερμηνεύω **měthěrměněuō,** *meth-er-mane-yoo´-o;* from *3326* and *2059;* to *explain over,* i.e. *translate:*— (by) interpret (-ation).

3178. μέθη **měthē,** *meth´-ay;* appar. a primary word; an *intoxicant,* i.e. (by impl.) *intoxication:*— drunkenness.

3179. μεθίστημι **měthistēmi,** *meth-is´-tay-mee;* or (1 Cor. 13:2)

μεθιστάνω **měthistanō,** *meth-is-tan´-o;* from *3326* and *2476;* to *transfer,* i.e. *carry away, depose* or (fig.) *exchange, seduce:*— put out, remove, translate, turn away.

3180. μεθοδεία **měthŏděia,** *meth-od-i´-ah;* from a compound of *3326* and *3593* [comp. "method"]; *travelling over,* i.e. *travesty (trickery):*— wile, lie in wait.

3181. μεθόριος **měthŏriŏs,** *meth-or´-ee-os;* from *3326* and *3725; bounded alongside,* i.e. *contiguous* (neut. plur. as noun, *frontier):*— border.

3182. μεθύσκω **měthuskō,** *meth-oos´-ko;* a prol. (tran.) form of *3184;* to *intoxicate:*— be drunk (-en).

3183. μέθυσος **měthusŏs,** *meth´-oo-sos;* from *3184; tipsy,* i.e. (as noun) a *sot:*— drunkard.

3184. μεθύω **měthuō,** *meth-oo´-o;* from another form of *3178;* to *drink* to *intoxication,* i.e. *get drunk:*— drink well, make (be) drunk (-en).

3185. μεῖζον **měizŏn,** *mide´-zon;* neut.

of *3187;* (adv.) in *greater* degree:— the more.

3186. μειζότερος **měizŏtěrŏs,** *mide-zot´-er-os;* continued comparative of *3187; still larger* (fig.):— greater.

3187. μείζων **měizōn,** *mide´-zone;* irreg. comparative of *3173; larger* (lit. or fig. spec. in age):— elder, greater (-est), more.

3188. μέλαν **mělan,** *mel´-an;* neut. of *3189* as noun; *ink:*— ink.

3189. μέλας **mělas,** *mel´-as;* appar. a primary word; *black:*— black.

3190. Μελεᾶς **Mělěas,** *mel-eh-as´;* of uncert. or.; *Meleas,* an Isr.:— Meleas.

μέλει **mělěi.** See *3199.*

3191. μελετάω **mělětaō,** *mel-et-ah´-o;* from a presumed der. of *3199;* to *take care of,* i.e. (by impl.) *revolve* in the mind:— imagine, (pre-) meditate.

3192. μέλι **měli,** *mel´-ee;* appar. a primary word; *honey:*— honey.

3193. μελίσσιος **mělissiŏs,** *mel-is´-see-os;* from *3192; relating to honey,* i.e. *bee* (comb):— honeycomb.

3194. Μελίτη **Mělitē,** *mel-ee´-tay;* of uncert. or.; *Melita,* an island in the Mediterranean:— Melita.

3195. μέλλω **měllō,** *mel´-lo;* a strengthened form of *3199* (through the idea of *expectation);* to *intend,* i.e. *be about* to be, do, or suffer something (of persons or things, espec. events; in the sense of *purpose, duty, necessity, probability, possibility,* or *hesitation):*— about, after that, be (almost), (that which is, things, + which was for) to come, intend, was to (be), mean, mind, be at the point, (be) ready, + return, shall (begin), (which, that) should (after, afterwards, hereafter) tarry, which was for, will, would, be yet.

3196. μέλος **mělŏs,** *mel´-os;* of uncert. aff.; a *limb* or *part* of the body:— member.

3197. Μελχί **Mělchi,** *mel-khee´;* of Heb. or [4428 with pron. suffix *my king*]; *Melchi* (i.e. *Malki),* the name of two Isr.:— Melchi.

3198. Μελχισεδέκ **Mělchisěděk,** *mel-khis-ed-ek´;* of Heb. or. [4442]; *Melchisedek* (i.e. *Malkitsedek),* a patriarch:— Melchisedec.

3199. μέλω **mělō,** *mel´-o;* a primary verb; to *be of interest* to, i.e. to *concern* (only third pers. sing. pres. ind. used impers. *it matters):*— (take) care.

3200. μεμβράνα **měmbrana,** *mem-bran´-ah;* of Lat. or. ("*membrane*"); a (written) sheep-*skin:*— parchment.

3201. μέμφομαι **měmphŏmai,** *mem-fom-ahee;* mid. voice of an appar. primary verb; to *blame:*— find fault.

3202. μεμψίμοιρος **měmpsimŏirŏs,** *mem-psim´-oy-ros;* from a presumed der. of *3201* and μοῖρα **mŏira,** *(fate;* akin to the base of *3313); blaming fate,* i.e. *querulous (discontented):*— complainer.

3203-3302. Because of some changes in the numbering system (while the original work was in progress) no Greek words were cited for *2717* or

3203-3302. These numbers were dropped altogether. This will not cause any problems in Strong's numbering system. No Greek words have been left out. Because so many other reference works use this numbering system, it has not been revised. If it were revised, much confusion would certainly result.

3303. μέν **měn,** *men;* a primary particle; prop. ind. of *affirmation* or *concession (in fact);* usually followed by a *contrasted* clause with *1161* (*this* one, the *former,* etc):— even, indeed, so, some, truly, verily. Often compounded with other particles in an *intens.* or *asseverative* sense.

3304. μενοῦνγε **měnŏungě,** *men-oon´-geh* or

μενοῦν **měnŏun,** *men-oon´* or

μενοῦν γε **měnŏun ge** *men-oon´geh;* from *3203* and *3767* and *1065;* so *then at least:*— nay but, yea doubtless (rather, verily).

3305. μέντοι **měntŏi,** *men´-toy;* from *3303* and *5104; indeed though,* i.e. *however:*— also, but, howbeit, nevertheless, yet.

3306. μένω **měnō,** *men´-o;* a primary verb; to *stay* (in a given place, state, relation or expectancy):— abide, continue, dwell, endure, be present, remain, stand, tarry (for), × thine own.

3307. μερίζω **měrizō,** *mer-id´-zo;* from *3313;* to *part,* i.e. (lit.) to *apportion, bestow, share,* or (fig.) to *disunite, differ:*— deal, be difference between, distribute, divide, give part.

3308. μέριμνα **měrimna,** *mer´-im-nah;* from *3307* (through the idea of *distraction*); *solicitude:*— care.

3309. μεριμνάω **měrimnaō,** *mer-im-nah´-o;* from *3308;* to *be anxious* about:— (be, have) care (-ful), take thought.

3310. μερίς **měris,** *mer-ece´;* fem. of *3313;* a *portion,* i.e. *province, share* or (abstr.) *participation:*— part (× -akers).

3311. μερισμός **měrismŏs,** *mer-is-mos´;* from *3307;* a *separation* or *distribution:*— dividing asunder, gift.

3312. μεριστής **měristēs,** *mer-is-tace´;* from *3307;* an *apportioner (administrator):*— divider.

3313. μέρος **měrŏs,** *mer´-os;* from an obs. but more primary form of μείρομαι **měirŏmai** (to *get* as a *section* or *allotment*); a *division* or *share* (lit. or fig. in a wide application):— behalf, coast, course, craft, particular (+ -ly), part (+ -ly), piece, portion, respect, side, some sort (-what).

3314. μεσημβρία **měsēmbria,** *mes-ame-bree´-ah;* from *3319* and *2250; midday;* by impl. the *south:*— noon, south.

3315. μεσιτεύω **měsitěuō,** *mes-it-yoo´-o;* from *3316;* to *interpose* (as arbiter), i.e (by impl.) to *ratify* (as surety):— confirm.

3316. μεσίτης **měsitēs,** *mes-ee´-tace;* from *3319;* a *go-between,* i.e. (simply) an *internunciator,* or (by impl.) a *reconciler (intercessor):*— mediator.

3317. μεσονύκτιον **mĕsŏnuktiŏn**, *mes-on-ook´-tee-on;* neut. of compound of *3319* and *3571; midnight* (espec. as a watch):— midnight.

3318. Μεσοποταμία **Mĕsŏpŏtamia**, *mes-op-ot-am-ee´-ah;* from *3319* and *4215; Mesopotamia* (as lying between the Euphrates and the Tigris; comp. *763*), a region of Asia:— Mesopotamia.

3319. μέσος **mĕsŏs**, *mes´-os;* from *3326; middle* (as an adj. or [neut.] noun):— among, × before them, between, + forth, mid [-day,night], midst, way.

3320. μεσότοιχον **mĕsŏtŏichŏn**, *mes-ot´-oy-khon;* from *3319* and *5109;* a *partition* (fig.):— middle wall.

3321. μεσουράνημα **mĕsŏuranēma**, *mes-oo-ran´-ay-mah;* from a presumed compound of *3319* and *3772; mid-sky:*— midst of heaven.

3322. μεσόω **mĕsŏō**, *mes-ŏ´-o;* from *3319;* to *form* the *middle*, i.e. (in point of time), to *be half-way* over:— be about the midst.

3323. Μεσσίας **Mĕssias**, *mes-see´-as;* of Heb. or. [4899]; the *Messias* (i.e. *Mashiach*), or Christ:— Messias.

3324. μεστός **mĕstŏs**, *mes-tos´;* of uncert. der.; *replete* (lit. or fig.):— full.

3325. μεστόω **mĕstŏō**, *mes-tŏ´-o;* from *3324;* to *replenish*, i.e. (by impl.) to *intoxicate:*— fill.

3326. μετά **mĕta**, *met-ah´;* a primary prep. (often used adv.); prop. denoting *accompaniment;* "*amid*" (local or causal); modif. variously according to the case (gen. *association*, or acc. *succession*) with which it is joined; occupying an intermediate position between *575* or *1537* and *1519* or *4314;* less intimate than *1722* and less close than *4862*):— after (-ward), × that he again, against, among, × and, + follow, hence, hereafter, in, of, (up-) on, + our, × and setting, since, (un-) to, + together, when, with (+ -out). Often used in composition, in substantially the same relations of *participation* or *proximity*, and *transfer* or *sequence.*

3327. μεταβαίνω **mĕtabainō**, *met-ab-ah´-ee-no;* from *3326* and the base of *939;* to *change place:*— depart, go, pass, remove.

3328. μεταβάλλω **mĕtaballō**, *met-ab-al´-lo;* from *3326* and *906;* to *throw over*, i.e. (mid. voice fig.) to *turn about* in opinion:— change mind.

3329. μετάγω **mĕtagō**, *met-ag´-o;* from *3326* and *71;* to *lead over*, i.e. *transfer* (*direct*):— turn about.

3330. μεταδίδωμι **mĕtadidōmi**, *met-ad-id´-o-mee;* from *3326* and *1325;* to *give over*, i.e. *share:*— give, impart.

3331. μετάθεσις **mĕtathĕsis**, *met-ath´-es-is;* from *3346; transp.*, i.e. *transferral* (to heaven), *disestablishment* (of a law):— change, removing, translation.

3332. μεταίρω **mĕtairō**, *met-ah´-ee-ro;* from *3326* and *142;* to *betake* oneself, i.e. *remove* (locally):— depart.

3333. μετακαλέω **mĕtakalĕō**, *met-ak-al-eh´-o;* from *3326* and *2564;* to *call elsewhere*, i.e. *summon:*— call (for, hither).

3334. μετακινέω **mĕtakinĕō**, *met-ak-ee-neh´-o;* from *3326* and *2795;* to *stir* to a place *elsewhere*, i.e. *remove* (fig.):— move away.

3335. μεταλαμβάνω **mĕtalambanō**, *met-al-am-ban´-o;* from *3326* and *2983;* to *participate;* generally to *accept* (and use):— eat, have, be partaker, receive, take.

3336. μετάλημψις **mĕtalēmpsis**, *met-al´-ampe-sis;* from *3335; participation:*— taking.

3337. μεταλλάσσω **mĕtallassō**, *met-allas´-so;* from *3326* and *236;* to *exchange:*— change.

3338. μεταμέλλομαι **mĕtamĕllŏmai**, *met-am-el´-lom-ahee;* from *3326* and the mid. voice of *3199;* to *care afterwards*, i.e. *regret:*— repent (self).

3339. μεταμορφόω **mĕtamŏrphŏō**, *met-am-or-fŏ´-o;* from *3326* and *3445;* to *transform* (lit. or fig. "metamorphose"):— change, transfigure, transform.

3340. μετανοέω **mĕtanŏĕō**, *met-an-ŏeh´-o;* from *3326* and *3539;* to *think differently* or *afterwards*, i.e. *reconsider* (mor. *feel compunction*):— repent.

3341. μετάνοια **mĕtanŏia**, *met-an´-oy-ah;* from *3340;* (subj.) *compunction* (for guilt, incl. *reformation*); by impl. *reversal* (of [another's] decision):— repentance.

3342. μεταξύ **mĕtaxu**, *met-ax-oo´;* from *3326* and a form of *4862; betwixt* (of place or pers.); (of time) as adj. *intervening*, or (by impl.) *adjoining:*— between, mean while, next.

3343. μεταπέμπω **mĕtapĕmpō**, *met-apemp´-o;* from *3326* and *3992;* to *send* from *elsewhere*, i.e. (mid. voice) to *summon* or *invite:*— call (send) for.

3344. μεταστρέφω **mĕtastrĕphō**, *met-as-tref´-o;* from *3326* and *4762;* to *turn across*, i.e. *transmute* or (fig.) *corrupt:*— pervert, turn.

3345. μετασχηματίζω **mĕtaschēmatizō**, *met-askh-ay-mat-id´-zo;* from *3326* and a der. of *4976;* to *transfigure* or *disguise;* fig. to *apply* (by accommodation):— transfer, transform (self).

3346. μετατίθημι **mĕtatithēmi**, *met-atith´-ay-mee;* from *3326* and *5087;* to *transfer*, i.e. (lit.) *transport*, (by impl.) *exchange* (refl.) *change sides*, or (fig.) *pervert:*— carry over, change, remove, translate, turn.

3347. μετέπειτα **mĕtĕpĕita**, *met-ep´-i-tah;* from *3326* and *1899; thereafter:*— afterward.

3348. μετέχω **mĕtĕchō**, *met-ekh´-o;* from *3326* and *2192;* to *share* or *participate;* by impl. *belong* to, *eat* (or *drink*):— be partaker, pertain, take part, use.

3349. μετεωρίζω **mĕtĕōrizō**, *met-eh-o-rid´-zo;* from a compound of *3326* and a collat. form of *142* or perh. rather *109* (comp. "*meteor*"); to *raise* in *mid-air*, i.e. (fig.) *suspend* (pass. *fluctuate* or *be anxious*):— be of doubtful mind.

3350. μετοικεσία **mĕtŏikĕsia**, *met-oy-kes-ee´-ah;* from a der. of a compound of *3326* and *3624;* a *change of abode*, i.e.

(spec.) *expatriation:*— × brought, carried (-ying) away (in-) to.

3351. μετοικίζω **mĕtŏikizō**, *met-oykid´-zo;* from the same as *3350;* to *transfer* as a *settler* or *captive*, i.e *colonize* or *exile:*— carry away, remove into.

3352. μετοχή **mĕtŏchē**, *met-okh-ay´;* from *3348; participation*, i.e. *intercourse:*— fellowship.

3353. μέτοχος **mĕtŏchŏs**, *met´-okh-os;* from *3348; participant*, i.e. (as noun) a *sharer;* by impl. an *associate:*— fellow, partaker, partner.

3354. μετρέω **mĕtrĕō**, *met-reh´-o;* from *3358;* to *measure* (i.e. ascertain in size by a fixed standard); by impl. to *admeasure* (i.e. allot by rule); fig. to *estimate:*— measure, mete.

3355. μετρητής **mĕtrĕtēs**, *met-ray-tace´;* from *3354;* a *measurer*, i.e. (spec.) a certain standard *measure* of capacity for liquids:— firkin.

3356. μετριοπαθέω **mĕtriŏpathĕō**, *met-ree-op-ath-eh´-o;* from a compound of the base of *3357* and *3806;* to *be moderate* in passion, i.e. *gentle* (to *treat indulgently*):— have compassion.

3357. μετρίως **mĕtriŏs**, *met-ree´-oce;* adv. from a der. of *3358; moderately*, i.e. *slightly:*— a little.

3358. μέτρον **mĕtrŏn**, *met´-ron;* an appar. primary word; a *measure* ("metre"), lit. or fig.; by impl. a limited *portion* (*degree*):— measure.

3359. μέτωπον **mĕtōpŏn**, *met´-o-pon ;* from *3326* and ὤψ **ōps** (the *face*); the *forehead* (as *opposite*, the *countenance*):— forehead.

3360. μέχρι **mĕchri** *mekh´-ree;* or

μεχρίς **mĕchris**, *mekh-ris´;* from *3372; as far as*, i.e. *up* to a certain point (as a prep. of extent [denoting the *terminus*, whereas *891* refers espec. to the *space* of time or place intervening] or a conjunc.):— till, (un-) to, until.

3361. μή **mē**, *may;* a primary particle of qualified *negation* (whereas *3756* expresses an absolute denial); (adv.) *not*, (conjunc.) *lest;* also (as an interrog. implying a *neg.* answer [whereas *3756* expects an *affirmative* one]) *whether:*— any, but (that), × forbear, + God forbid, + lack, lest, neither, never, no (× wise in), none, nor, [can-] not, nothing, that not, un [-taken], without. Often used in compounds in substantially the same relations. See also *3362, 3363, 3364, 3372, 3373, 3375, 3378.*

3362. ἐὰν μή **ĕan mē**, *eh-an´ may;* i.e. *1437* and *3361; if not*, i.e. *unless:*— × before, but, except, if, no, (if, + whosoever) not.

3363. ἵνα μή **hina mē** *hin´-ah may;* i.e. *2443* and *3361; in order* (or *so*) *that not:*— albeit not, lest, that, no (-t, [-thing]).

3364. οὐ μή **ŏu mē**, *oo may;* i.e. *3756* and *3361;* a double neg. streng. the denial; *not at all:*— any more, at all, by any (no) means, neither, never, no (at all), in no case (wise) nor, ever, not (at all, in any wise). Comp. *3378.*

3365. μηδαμῶς **mēdamŏs**, *may-dam-*

oce´; adv. from a compound of *3361* and ἀμός **amŏs** (*somebody*); *by no means:*— not so.

3366. μηδέ **mēdĕ**, *may-deh´*; from *3361* and *1161*; *but not, not even*; in a continued negation, *nor:*— neither, nor (yet), (no) not (once, so much as).

3367. μηδείς **mēdĕis**, *may-dice´*; incl. the irreg. fem. μηδεμία **mēdĕmia** *may-dem-ee´-ah*; and the neut. μηδέν **mēdĕn**, *may-den´*; from *3361* and *1520*; *not even one* (man, woman, thing):— any (man, thing), no (man), none, not (at all, any man, a whit), nothing, + without delay.

3368. μηδέποτε **mēdĕpŏtĕ**, *may-dep´-ot-eh*; from *3366* and *4218*; *not even ever:*— never.

3369. μηδέπω **mēdĕpŏ**, *may-dep´-o*; from *3366* and *4452*; *not even yet:*— not yet.

3370. Μῆδος **Mēdŏs**, *may´-dos*; of for. or. [comp. *4074*]; a *Median*, or inhab. of Media:— Mede.

3371. μηκέτι **mēkĕti**, *may-ket´-ee*; from *3361* and *2089*; *no further:*— any longer, (not) henceforth, hereafter, no henceforward (longer, more, soon), not any more.

3372. μῆκος **mēkŏs**, *may´-kos*; prob. akin to *3173*; *length* (lit. or fig.) length.

3373. μηκύνω **mēkunŏ**, *may-koo´-no*; from *3372*; to *lengthen*, i.e. (mid. voice) to *enlarge:*— grow up.

3374. μηλωτή **mēlŏtē**, *may-lo-tay´*; from μῆλον **mēlŏn**, (a *sheep*); a *sheep-skin:*— sheepskin.

3375. μήν **mēn**, *mane*; a stronger form of *3303*; a particle of affirmation (only with *2229*); *assuredly:*— + surely.

3376. μήν **mēn**, *mane*; a primary word; a *month:*— month.

3377. μηνύω **mēnuŏ**, *may-noo´-o*; prob. from the same base as *3145* and *3415* (i.e. μάω **maŏ**, to *strive*); to *disclose* (through the idea of ment. *effort* and thus calling to *mind*), i.e. *report, declare, intimate:*— shew, tell.

3378. μὴ οὐκ **mē ŏuk**, *may ook*; i.e. *3361* and *3756*; as interrog. and neg. *is it not that?:*— neither (followed by *no*), + never, not. Comp. *3364*.

3379. μήποτε **mēpŏtĕ**, *may´-pot-eh*; or

μή ποτε **mē pŏtĕ**, *may pot´-eh*; from *3361* and *4218*; *not ever*; also *if* (or *lest*) *ever* (or *perhaps*):— if peradventure, lest (at any time, haply), not at all, whether or not.

3380. μήπω **mēpŏ**, *may´-po*; from *3361* and *4452*; *not yet:*— not yet.

3381. μήπως **mēpŏs**, *may´-poce*; or

μή πως **mē pŏs**, *may poce*; from *3361* and *4458*; *lest somehow:*— lest (by any means, by some means, haply, perhaps).

3382. μηρός **mērŏs**, *may-ros´*; perh. a primary word; a *thigh:*— thigh.

3383. μήτε **mētĕ**, *may´-teh*; from *3361* and *5037*; *not too*, i.e. (in continued negation) *neither* or *nor*; also, *not even:*— neither, (n-) or, so as much.

3384. μήτηρ **mētēr**, *may´-tare*; appar. a

primary word; a *"mother"* (lit. or fig., immed. or remote):— mother.

3385. μήτι **mēti**, *may´-tee*; from *3361* and the neut. of *5100*; *whether at all:*— not [the particle usually not expressed, except by the form of the question].

3386. μήτιγε **mētigĕ**, *may´-tig-eh*; from *3385* and *1065*; *not at all then*, i.e. *not to say* (*the rather still*):— how much more.

3387. μήτις **mētis**, *may´-tis*; or

μή τις **mē tis** *may tis*; from *3361* and *5100*; *whether any:*— any [sometimes unexpressed except by the simple interrogative form of the sentence].

3388. μήτρα **mētra**, *may´-trah*; from *3384*; the *matrix:*— womb.

3389. μητραλῴας **mētralǫ̆as**, *may-tralo´-as* or

μετρολῴας **mĕtrolǫ̆as**, *may-trolo´-as*; from *3384* and the base of *257*; a *mother-thresher*, i.e. *matricide:*— murderer of mothers.

3390. μητρόπολις **mētrŏpŏlis**, *may-trop´-ol-is*; from *3384* and *4172*; a *mother city*, i.e. *"metropolis":*— chiefest city.

3391. μία **mia**, *mee´-ah*; irreg. fem. of *1520*; *one* or *first:*— a (certain), + agree, first, one, × other.

3392. μιαίνω **miainŏ**, *me-ah´-ee-no*; perh. a primary verb; to *sully* or *taint*, i.e. *contaminate* (cer. or mor.):— defile.

3393. μίασμα **miasma**, *mee´-as-mah*; from *3392* (*"miasma"*); (mor.) *foulness* (prop. the effect):— pollution.

3394. μιασμός **miasmŏs**, *mee-as-mos´*; from *3392*; (mor.) *contamination* (prop.the act):— uncleanness.

3395. μίγμα **migma**, *mig´-mah*; from *3396*; a *compound:*— mixture.

3396. μίγνυμι **mignumi**, *mig´-noo-mee*; a primary verb; to *mix:*— mingle.

3397. μικρόν **mikrŏn**, *mik-ron´*; masc. or neut. sing. of *3398* (as noun); a *small* space of *time* or *degree:*— a (little) (while).

3398. μικρός **mikrŏs**, *mik-ros´*; incl. the comp.

μικρότερος **mikrŏtĕrŏs**, *mik-rot´-er-os*; appar. a primary word; *small* (in size, quantity, number or (fig.) dignity):— least, less, little, small.

3399. Μίλητος **Milētŏs**, *mil´-ay-tos*; of uncert. or.; *Miletus*, a city of Asia Minor:— Miletus.

3400. μίλιον **miliŏn**, *mil´-ee-on*; of Lat. or.; a *thousand* paces, i.e. a *"mile":*— mile.

3401. μιμέομαι **mimĕŏmai**, *mim-eh´-om-ahee*; mid. voice from μῖμος **mimŏs** (a *"mimic"*); to *imitate:*— follow.

3402. μιμητής **mimētēs**, *mim-ay-tace´*; from *3401*; an *imitator:*— follower.

3403. μιμνήσκω **mimnēskŏ**, *mim-nace´-ko*; a prol. form of *3415* (from which some of the tenses are borrowed); to *remind*, i.e. (mid. voice) to *recall to mind:*— be mindful, remember.

3404. μισέω **misĕŏ**, *mis-eh´-o*; from a primary μῖσος **misŏs** (*hatred*); to *detest*

(espec. to *persecute*); by extens. to *love less:*— hate (-ful).

3405. μισθαποδοσία **misthapŏdŏsia**, *mis-thap-od-os-ee´-ah*; from *3406*; *requital* (good or bad):— recompence of reward.

3406. μισθαποδότης **misthapŏdŏtēs**, *mis-thap-od-ot´-ace*; from *3409* and *591*; a *renumerator:*— rewarder.

3407. μίσθιος **misthiŏs**, *mis´-thee-os*; from *3408*; a *wage-earner:*— hired servant.

3408. μισθός **misthŏs**, *mis-thos´*; appar. a primary word; *pay* for services (lit. or fig.), good or bad:— hire, reward, wages.

3409. μισθόω **misthŏŏ**, *mis-thŏ´-o*; from *3408*; to *let* out for wages, i.e. (mid. voice) to *hire:*— hire.

3410. μίσθωμα **misthŏma**, *mis´-thomah*; from *3409*; a *rented* building:— hired house.

3411. μισθωτός **misthŏtŏs**, *mis-tho-tos´*; from *3409*; a *wage-worker* (good or bad):— hired servant, hireling.

3412. Μιτυλήνη **Mitulēnē**, *mit-oo-lay´-nay*; for μυτιλήνη **mutilēnē**, (*abounding in shell-fish*); *Mitylene* (or *Mytilene*), a town on the island of Lesbos:— Mitylene.

3413. Μιχαήλ **Michaēl**, *mikh-ah-ale´*; of Heb. or. [4317]; *Michaël*, an archangel:— Michael.

3414. μνᾶ **mna**, *mnah*; of Lat. or.; a *mna* (i.e. *mina*), a certain *weight:*— pound.

3415. μνάομαι **mnaŏmai**, *mnah´-om-ahee*; mid. voice of a der. of *3306* or perh. of the base of *3145* (through the idea of *fixture* in the mind or of mental *grasp*); to *bear* in mind, i.e. *recollect*; by impl. to *reward* or *punish:*— be mindful, remember, come (have) in remembrance. Comp. *3403*.

3416. Μνάσων **Mnasŏn**, *mnah´-sohn*; of uncert. or.; *Mnason*, a Chr.:— Mnason.

3417. μνεία **mnĕia**, *mni´-ah*; from *3415* or *3403*; *recollection*; by impl. *recital:*— mention, remembrance.

3418. μνῆμα **mnēma**, *mnay´-mah*; from *3415*; a *memorial*, i.e. sepulchral *monument* (*burial-place*):— grave, sepulchre, tomb.

3419. μνημεῖον **mnēmĕiŏn**, *mnay-mi´-on*; from *3420*; a *remembrance*, i.e. *cenotaph* (*place of interment*):— grave, sepulchre, tomb.

3420. μνήμη **mnēmē**, *mnay´-may*; from *3403*; *memory:*— remembrance.

3421. μνημονεύω **mnēmŏnĕuŏ**, *mnay-mon-yoo´-o*; from a der. of *3420*; to *exercise memory*, i.e. *recollect*; by impl. to *punish*; also to *rehearse:*— make mention; be mindful, remember.

3422. μνημόσυνον **mnēmŏsunŏn**, *mnay-mos´-oo-non*; from *3421*; a *reminder* (*memorandum*), i.e. *record:*— memorial.

3423. μνηστεύω **mnēstĕuŏ**, *mnace-tyoo´-o*; from a der. of *3415*; to *give a souvenir* (engagement present), i.e. *betroth:*— espouse.

3424. μογιλάλος **mŏgilalŏs**, *mog-il-al´-*

os; from 3425 and 2980; hardly talking, i.e. dumb (tongue-tied):— having an impediment in his speech.

3425. μόγις **mōgis**, mog´-is; adv. from a primary μόγος **mōgŏs**, (toil); with difficulty:— hardly.

3426. μόδιος **mŏdiŏs**, mod´-ee-os; of Lat. or.; a modius, i.e. certain measure for things dry (the quantity or the utensil):— bushel.

3427. μοί **mŏi**, moy; the simpler form of 1698; to me:— I, me, mine, my.

3428. μοιχαλίς **mŏichalis**, moy-khal-is´; a prol. form of the fem. of 3432; an adulteress (lit. or fig.):— adulteress (-ous, -y).

3429. μοιχάω **mŏichaō**, moy-khah´-o; from 3432; (mid. voice) to commit adultery:— commit adultery.

3430. μοιχεία **mŏichĕia**, moy-khi´-ah; from 3431; adultery:— adultery.

3431. μοιχεύω **mŏichĕuō**, moy-khyoo´-o; from 3432; to commit adultery:— commit adultery.

3432. μοιχός **mŏichŏs**, moy-khos´; perh. a primary word; a (male) paramour; fig. apostate:— adulterer.

3433. μόλις **mŏlis**, mol´-is; prob. by var. for 3425; with difficulty:— hardly, scarce (-ly), + with much work.

3434. Μολόχ **Mŏlŏch**, mol-okh´; of Heb. or. [4432]; Moloch (i.e. Molek), an idol:— Moloch.

3435. μολύνω **mŏlunō**, mol-oo´-no; prob. from 3189; to soil (fig.):— defile.

3436. μολυσμός **mŏlusmŏs**, mol-oos-mos´; from 3435; a stain; i.e. (fig.) immorality:— filthiness.

3437. μομφή **mŏmphē**, mom-fay´; from 3201; blame, i.e. (by impl.) a fault:— quarrel.

3438. μονή **mŏnē**, mon-ay´; from 3306; a staying, i.e. residence (the act or the place):— abode, mansion.

3439. μονογενής **mŏnŏgĕnēs**, mon-og-en-ace´; from 3441 and 1096; only-born, i.e. sole:— only (begotten, child).

3440. μόνον **mŏnŏn**, mon´-on; neut. of 3441 as adv.; merely:— alone, but, only.

3441. μόνος **mŏnŏs**, mon´-os; prob. from 3306; remaining, i.e. sole or single; by impl. mere:— alone, only, by themselves.

3442. μονόφθαλμος **mŏnŏphthalmŏs**, mon-of´-thal-mos; from 3441 and 3788; one-eyed:— with one eye.

3443. μονόω **mŏnŏō**, mon-ŏ´-o; from 3441; to isolate, i.e. bereave:— be desolate.

3444. μορφή **mŏrphē**, mor-fay´; perh. from the base of 3313 (through the idea of adjustment of parts); shape; fig. nature:— form.

3445. μορφόω **mŏrphŏō**, mor-fŏ´-o; from the same as 3444; to fashion (fig.):— form.

3446. μόρφωσις **mŏrphōsis**, mor´-fo-sis; from 3445; formation, i.e. (by impl.) appearance (semblance or [concr.] formula):— form.

3447. μοσχοποιέω **mŏschŏpŏiĕō**, mos-

khop-oy-eh´-o; from 3448 and 4160; to fabricate the image of a bullock:— make a calf.

3448. μόσχος **mŏschŏs**, mos´-khos; prob. strengthened for ὄσχος **ŏschŏs** (a shoot); a young bullock:— calf.

3449. μόχθος **mŏchthŏs**, mokh´-thos; from the base of 3425; toil, i.e. (by impl.) sadness:— painfulness, travail.

3450. μοῦ **mŏu**, moo; the simpler form of 1700; of me:— I, me, mine (own), my.

3451. μουσικός **mŏusikŏs**, moo-sik-os´; from Μοῦσα **Mŏusa**, (a Muse); "musical", i.e. (as noun) a minstrel:— musician.

3452. μυελός **muĕlŏs**, moo-el-os´; perh. a primary word; the marrow:— marrow.

3453. μυέω **muĕō**, moo-eh´-o; from the base of 3466; to initiate, i.e. (by impl.) to teach:— instruct.

3454. μῦθος **muthŏs**, moo´-thos; perh. from the same as 3453 (through the idea of tuition); a tale, i.e. fiction ("myth"):— fable.

3455. μυκάομαι **mukaŏmai**, moo-kah´-om-ahee; from a presumed der. of μύζω **muzō** (to "moo"); to bellow (roar):— roar.

3456. μυκτηρίζω **muktērizō**, mook-tay-rid´-zo; from a der. of the base of 3455 (mean. snout, as that whence lowing proceeds); to make mouths at, i.e. ridicule:— mock.

3457. μυλικός **mulikŏs**, moo-lee-kos´; from 3458; belonging to a mill:— mill [-stone].

3458. μύλος **mulŏs**, moo´-los; prob. ultimately from the base of 3433 (through the idea of hardship); a "mill", i.e. (by impl.) a grinder (millstone):— millstone.

3459. μύλων **mulōn**, moo´-lone; from 3458; a mill-house:— mill.

3460. Μύρα **Mura**, moo´-rah; of uncert. der.; Myra, a place in Asia Minor:— Myra.

3461. μυρίας **murias**, moo-ree´-as; from 3463; a ten-thousand; by extens. a "myriad" or indef. number:— ten thousand.

3462. μυρίζω **murizō**, moo-rid´-zo; from 3464; to apply (perfumed) unguent to:— anoint.

3463. μύριοι **muriŏi**, moo´-ree-oi; plur. of an appar. primary word (prop. mean. very many); ten thousand; by extens. innumerably many:— ten thousand.

3464. μύρον **murŏn**, moo´-ron; prob. of for. or. [comp. 4753, 4666]; "myrrh", i.e. (by impl.) perfumed oil:— ointment.

3465. Μυσία **Musia**, moo-see´-ah; of uncert. or.; Mysia, a region of Asia Minor:— Mysia.

3466. μυστήριον **mustēriŏn**, moos-tay´-ree-on; from a der. of μύω **muō** (to shut the mouth); a secret or "mystery" (through the idea of silence imposed by initiation into relig. rites):— mystery.

3467. μυωπάζω **muōpazō**, moo-ope-ad´-zo; from a compound of the base of

3466 and ὤψ **ŏps** (the face; from 3700); to shut the eyes, i.e. blink (see indistinctly):— cannot see far off.

3468. μώλωψ **mōlōps**, mo´-lopes; from μώλος **mōlŏs**, ("moil;" prob. akin to the base of 3433) and prob. ὤψ **ŏps**, (the face; from 3700); a mole ("black eye") or blow-mark:— stripe.

3469. μωμάομαι **mōmaŏmai**, mo-mah´-om-ahee; from 3470; to carp at, i.e. censure (discredit):— blame.

3470. μῶμος **mōmŏs**, mo´-mos; perh. from 3201; a flaw or blot, i.e. (fig.) disgraceful person:— blemish.

3471. μωραίνω **mōrainō**, mo-rah´-ee-no; from 3474; to become insipid; fig. to make (pass. act) as a simpleton:— become fool, make foolish, lose savour.

3472. μωρία **mōria**, mo-ree´-ah; from 3474; silliness, i.e. absurdity:— foolishness.

3473. μωρολογία **mōrŏlŏgia**, mo-rol-og-ee´-ah; from a compound of 3474 and 3004; silly talk, i.e. buffoonery:— foolish talking.

3474. μωρός **mōrŏs**, mo-ros´; prob. from the base of 3466; dull or stupid (as if shut up), i.e. heedless, (mor.) blockhead, (appar.) absurd:— fool (-ish, × -ishness).

3475. Μωσεύς **Mōsĕus**, moce-yoos´; or

Μωσῆς **Mōsēs**, mo-sace´; or

Μωϋσῆς **Mōusēs**, mo-oo-sace´; of Heb. or.; [4872]; Moseus, Moses, or Moüses (i.e. Mosheh), the Heb. lawgiver:— Moses.

N

3476. Ναασσών **Naassōn**, nah-as-sone´; of Heb. or. [5177]; Naasson (i.e. Nachshon), an Isr.:— Naasson.

3477. Ναγγαί **Naggai**, nang-gah´-ee; prob. of Heb. or. [comp. 5052]; Nangæ (i.e. perh. Nogach), an Isr.:— Nagge.

3478. Ναζαρέθ **Nazarĕth**, nad-zar-eth´; or

Ναζαρέτ **Nazarĕt**, nad-zar-et´; of uncert. der.; Nazareth or Nazaret, a place in Pal.:— Nazareth.

3479. Ναζαρηνός **Nazarēnŏs**, nad-zar-ay-nos´; from 3478; a Nazarene, i.e. inhab. of Nazareth:— of Nazareth.

3480. Ναζωραῖος **Nazōraiŏs**, nad-zo-rah´-yos; from 3478; a Nazoræan, i.e. inhab. of Nazareth; by extens. a Christian:— Nazarene, of Nazareth.

3481. Ναθάν **Nathan**, nath-an´, or

Ναθάμ **Natham**, nath-am´; of Heb. or. [5416]; Nathan, an Isr.:— Nathan (Natham).

3482. Ναθαναήλ **Nathanaēl**, nath-an-ah-ale´; of Heb. or. [5417]; Nathanaël (i.e. Nathanel), an Isr. and Chr.:— Nathanael.

3483. ναί **nai**, nahee; a primary particle of strong affirmation; yes:— even so, surely, truth, verily, yea, yes.

3484. Ναΐν **Naïn**, nah-in´; prob. of Heb. or. [comp. 4999]; Naïn, a place in Pal.:— Nain.

3485. ναός **naŏs**, nah-os´; from a primary ναίω **naiŏ** (to *dwell*); a *fane, shrine, temple:*— shrine, temple. Comp 2411.

3486. Ναούμ **Naŏum,** *nah-oom´;* of Heb. or. [5151]; *Naüm* (i.e. *Nachum*), an Isr.:— Naum.

3487. νάρδος **nardŏs,** *nar´dos;* of for. or. [comp. 5373]; *"nard":*— [spike-] nard.

3488. Νάρκισσος **Narkissŏs,** *nar´-kissos;* a flower of the same name, from νάρκη **narkē** (*stupefaction,* as a "narcotic"); *Narcissus,* a Rom.:— Narcissus.

3489. ναυαγέω **nauagĕō,** *now-ag-eh´-o;* from a compound of 3491 and 71; to be *shipwrecked* (*stranded,* "navigate"), lit. or fig.:— make (suffer) shipwreck.

3490. ναύκληρος **nauklērŏs,** *now´-klay-ros;* from 3491 and 2819 ("clerk"); a *captain:*— owner of a ship.

3491. ναῦς **naus,** *nŏwce;* from νάω **naŏ** or νέω **nĕŏ** (to *float*); a *boat* (of any size):— ship.

3492. ναύτης **nautēs,** *now´-tace;* from 3491; a *boatman,* i.e. *seaman:*— sailor, shipman.

3493. Ναχώρ **Nachōr,** *nakh-ore´;* of Heb. or. [5152]; *Nachor,* the grandfather of Abraham:— Nachor.

3494. νεανίας **nĕanias,** *neh-an-ee´-as;* from a der. of 3501; a *youth* (up to about forty years):— young man.

3495. νεανίσκος **nĕaniskŏs,** *neh-an-is´-kos;* from the same as 3494; a *youth* (under forty):— young man.

3496. Νεάπολις **Nĕapŏlis,** *neh-ap´-ol-is;* from 3501 and 4172; *new town; Neápolis,* a place in Macedonia:— Neapolis.

3497. Νεεμάν **Nĕĕman,** *neh-eh-man´* or

Ναϊμάν **Naïman,** *nah-ee-man´;* of Heb. or. [5283]; *Neĕman* (i.e. *Naaman*), a Syrian:— Naaman.

3498. νεκρός **nĕkrŏs,** *nek-ros´;* from an appar. primary νέκυς **nĕkus** (a *corpse*); *dead* (lit. or fig.; also as noun):— dead.

3499. νεκρόω **nĕkrŏō,** *nek-rŏ´-o;* from 3498; to *deaden,* i.e. (fig.) to *subdue:*— be dead, mortify.

3500. νέκρωσις **nĕkrōsis,** *nek´-ro-sis;* from 3499; *decease;* fig. *impotency:*— deadness, dying.

3501. νέος **nĕŏs,** *neh´-os;* incl. the comparative νεώτερος **nĕōtĕrŏs,** *neh-o´-ter-os;* a primary word; *"new",* i.e. (of persons) *youthful,* or (of things) *fresh;* fig. *regenerate:*— new, young.

3502. νεοσσός **nĕŏssŏs,** *neh-os-sos´* or

νοσσός **nŏssŏs,** *nos-sos´;* from 3501; a *youngling* (*nestling*):— young.

3503. νεότης **nĕŏtēs,** *neh-ot´-ace;* from 3501; *newness,* i.e. *youthfulness:*— youth.

3504. νεόφυτος **nĕŏphutŏs,** *neh-of´-oo-tos;* from 3501 and of 5453; *newly planted,* i.e. (fig.) a *young convert* ("neophyte"):— novice.

3505. Νέρων **Nĕrōn,** *ner´-ohn;* of Lat. or.; *Neron* (i.e. *Nero*), a Rom. emperor:— Nero.

3506. νεύω **nĕuō,** *nyoo´-o;* appar. a primary verb; to *"nod,"* i.e. (by anal.) *signal:*— beckon.

3507. νεφέλη **nĕphĕlē,** *nef-el´-ay;* from

3509; prop. *cloudiness,* i.e. (concr.) a *cloud:*— cloud.

3508. Νεφθαλείμ **Nĕphthalĕim,** *nef-thal-ime´;* of Heb. or. [5321]; *Nephthaleim* (i.e. *Naphthali*), a tribe in Pal.:— Nephthalim.

3509. νέφος **nĕphŏs,** *nef´-os;* appar. a primary word; a *cloud:*— cloud.

3510. νεφρός **nĕphrŏs,** *nef-ros´;* of uncert. aff.; a *kidney* (plur.), i.e. (fig.) the inmost *mind:*— reins.

3511. νεωκόρος **nĕōkŏrŏs,** *neh-o-kor´-os;* from a form of 3485 and κορέω **kŏrĕō** (to *sweep*); a *temple-servant,* i.e. (by impl.) a *votary:*— worshipper.

3512. νεωτερικός **nĕōtĕrikŏs,** *neh-o-ter´-ik-os;* from the comparative of 3501; *appertaining to younger* persons, i.e. *juvenile:*— youthful.

νεώτερος **nĕōtĕrŏs.** See 3501.

3513. νή **nē,** *nay;* prob. an intens. form of 3483; a particle of attestation (accompanied by the obj. invoked or appealed to in confirmation); *as sure as:*— I protest by.

3514. νήθω **nēthō,** *nay´-tho;* from νέω **nĕŏ** (of like mean.); to *spin:*— spin.

3515. νηπιάζω **nēpiazō,** *nay-pee-ad´-zo;* from 3516; to *act* as a *babe,* i.e. (fig.) *innocently:*— be a child.

3516. νήπιος **nēpiŏs,** *nay´-pee-os;* from an obs. particle νη- **nē-** (implying *negation*) and 2031; *not speaking,* i.e. an *infant* (*minor*); fig. a *simple-minded* person, an *immature* Christian:— babe, child (+ -ish).

3517. Νηρεύς **Nērĕus,** *nare-yoos´;* appar. from a der. of the base of 3491 (mean. *wet*); *Nereus,* a Chr.:— Nereus.

3518. Νηρί **Nēri,** *nay-ree´;* of Heb. or. [5374]; *Neri* (i.e. *Nerijah*), an Isr.:— Neri.

3519. νησίον **nēsiŏn,** *nay-see´-on;* dimin. of 3520; an *islet:*— island.

3520. νῆσος **nēsŏs,** *nay´-sos;* prob. from the base of 3491; an *island:*— island, isle.

3521. νηστεία **nēstĕia,** *nace-ti´-ah;* from 3522; *abstinence* (from lack of food, or vol. and relig.); spec. the *fast* of the Day of Atonement:— fast (-ing.).

3522. νηστεύω **nēstĕuō,** *nace-tyoo´-o;* from 3523; to *abstain* from food (religiously):— fast.

3523. νῆστις **nēstis,** *nace´-tis;* from the insep. neg. particle νη- **nē-,** (*not*) and 2068; *not eating,* i.e. *abstinent* from food (relig.):— fasting.

3524. νηφάλεος **nēphalĕŏs,** *nay-fal´-eh-os;* or

νηφάλιος **nēphaliŏs,** *nay-fal´-ee-os;* from 3525; *sober,* i.e. (fig.) *circumspect:*— sober, vigilant.

3525. νήφω **nēphō,** *nay´-fo;* of uncert. aff.: to *abstain* from wine (*keep sober*), i.e. (fig.) *be discreet:*— be sober, watch.

3526. Νίγερ **Nigĕr,** *neeg´-er;* of Lat. or.; *black; Niger,* a Chr.:— Niger.

3527. Νικάνωρ **Nikanōr,** *nik-an´-ore;* prob. from 3528; *victorious; Nicanor,* a Chr.:— Nicanor.

3528. νικάω **nikaō,** *nik-ah´-o;* from

3529; to *subdue* (lit. or fig.):— conquer, overcome, prevail, get the victory.

3529. νίκη **nikē,** *nee´-kay;* appar. a primary word; *conquest* (abstr.), i.e. (fig.) the *means of success:*— victory.

3530. Νικόδημος **Nikŏdēmŏs,** *nik-od´-ay-mos;* from 3534 and 1218; *victorious* among his *people; Nicodemus,* an Isr.:— Nicodemus.

3531. Νικολαΐτης **Nikŏlaïtēs,** *nik-ol-ah-ee´-tace;* from 3532; a *Nicolaïte,* i.e. adherent of *Nicolaüs:*— Nicolaitane.

3532. Νικόλαος **Nikŏlaŏs,** *nik-ol´-ah-os;* from 3534 and 2992; *victorious* over the *people; Nicolaüs,* a heretic:— Nicolaus.

3533. Νικόπολις **Nikŏpŏlis,** *nik-op´-ol-is;* from 3534 and 4172; *victorious city; Nicopolis,* a place in Macedonia:— Nicopolis.

3534. νίκος **nikŏs,** *nee´-kos;* from 3529; a *conquest* (concr.), i.e. (by impl.) *triumph:*— victory.

3535. Νινευί **Ninĕuï,** *nin-yoo-ee´;* of Heb. or. [5210]; *Ninevi* (i.e. *Nineveh*), the capital of Assyria:— Nineve.

3536. Νινευίτης **Ninĕuïtēs,** *nin-yoo-ee´-tace;* from 3535; a *Ninevite,* i.e. inhab. of Nineveh:— of Nineve, Ninevite.

3537. νιπτήρ **niptēr,** *nip-tare´;* from 3538; a *ewer:*— bason.

3538. νίπτω **niptō,** *nip´-to;* to *cleanse* (espec. the hands or the feet or the face); cerem. to *perform ablution:*— wash. Comp. 3068.

3539. νοιέω **nŏiĕō,** *noy-eh´-o;* from 3563

νοέω **nŏĕō** *no-eh´-o;* to *exercise* the *mind,* (*observe*), i.e. (fig.) to *comprehend, heed:*— consider, perceive, think, understand.

3540. νόημα **nŏēma,** *nŏ´-ay-mah;* from 3539; a *perception,* i.e. *purpose,* or (by impl.) the *intellect, disposition,* itself:— device, mind, thought.

3541. νόθος **nŏthŏs,** *noth´-os;* of uncert. aff.; a *spurious* or *illegitimate* son:— bastard.

3542. νομή **nŏmē,** *nom-ay´;* fem. from the same as 3551; *pasture,* i.e. (the act) *feeding* (fig. *spreading* of a gangrene), or (the food) *pasturage:*— × eat, pasture.

3543. νομίζω **nŏmizō,** *nom-id´-zo;* from 3551; prop. to *do* by *law* (*usage*), i.e. to *accustom* (pass. *be usual*); by extens. to *deem* or *regard:*— suppose, thing, be wont.

3544. νομικός **nŏmikŏs,** *nom-ik-os´;* from 3551; *according* (or *pertaining*) to *law,* i.e. *legal* (cer.); as noun, an *expert* in the (Mosaic) *law:*— about the law, lawyer.

3545. νομίμως **nŏmimōs,** *nom-im´-oce;* adv. from a der. of 3551; *legitimately* (spec. agreeably to the rules of the lists):— lawfully.

3546. νόμισμα **nŏmisma,** *nom´-is-mah;* from 3543; *what is reckoned* as of value (after the Lat. *numisma*), i.e. current *coin:*— money.

3547. νομοδιδάσκαλος **nŏmŏdidaskalŏs,** *nom-od-id-as´-kal-os;* from 3551 and 1320; an *expounder* of the (Jewish) *law,* i.e. a *Rabbi*:— doctor (teacher) of the law.

3548. νομοθεσία **nŏmŏthĕsia**, *nom-oth-es-ee´-ah;* from 3550; *legislation* (spec. the *institution* of the Mosaic *code*):— giving of the law.

3549. νομοθετέω **nŏmŏthĕtĕō**, *nom-oth-et-eh´-o;* from 3550; to *legislate*, i.e. (pass.) to *have* (the Mosaic) *enactments* injoined, *be sanctioned* (by them):— establish, receive the law.

3550. νομοθέτης **nŏmŏthĕtēs**, *nom-oth-et´-ace;* from 3551 and a der. of 5087; a *legislator*:— lawgiver.

3551. νόμος **nŏmŏs**, *nom´-os;* from a primary νέμω **nĕmō**, (to *parcel* out, espec. *food* or *grazing* to animals); *law* (through the idea of prescriptive *usage*), gen. (*regulation*), spec. (of Moses [incl. the volume]; also of the Gospel), or fig. (a *principle*):— law.

3552. νοσέω **nŏsĕō**, *nos-eh´-o;* from 3554; to *be sick*, i.e. (by impl. of a diseased appetite) to *hanker* after (fig. to *harp* upon):— dote.

3553. νόσημα **nŏsēma**, *nos´-ay-ma;* from 3552; an *ailment*:— disease.

3554. νόσος **nŏsŏs**, *nos´-os;* of uncert. aff.; a *malady* (rarely fig. of mor. *disability*):— disease, infirmity, sickness.

3555. νοσσιά **nŏssia**, *nos-see-ah´;* from 3502; a *brood* (of chickens):— brood.

3556. νοσσίον **nŏssiŏn**, *nos-see´-on;* dimin. of 3502; a *birdling*:— chicken.

3557. νοσφίζομαι **nŏsphizŏmai**, *nos-fid´-zom-ahee;* mid. voice from νοσφί **nŏsphi** (*apart* or *clandestinely*); to *sequestrate*, for oneself, i.e. *embezzle*:— keep back, purloin.

3558. νότος **nŏtŏs**, *not´-os;* of uncert. aff.; the *south* (*-west*) *wind*; by extens. the *southern quarter* itself:— south (wind).

3559. νουθεσία **nŏuthĕsia**, *noo-thes-ee´-ah;* from 3563 and a der. of 5087; calling *attention* to, i.e. (by impl.) mild *rebuke* or *warning*:— admonition.

3560. νουθετέω **nŏuthĕtĕō**, *noo-thet-eh´-o;* from the same as 3559; to *put in mind*, i.e. (by impl.) to *caution* or *reprove* gently:— admonish, warn.

3561. νουμηνία **nŏumēnia**, *noo-may-nee´-ah;* fem. of a compound of 3501 and 3376 (as noun by impl. of 2250); the festival of *new moon*:— new moon.

3562. νουνεχῶς **nŏunĕchōs**, *noon-ekh-oce´;* adv. from a comp. of the acc. of 3563 and 2192; in a *mind-having* way, i.e. *prudently*:— discreetly.

3563. νοῦς **nŏus**, *nooce;* prob. from the base of 1097; the *intellect*, i.e. *mind* (divine or human; in thought, feeling, or will); by impl. *meaning*:— mind, understanding. Comp. 5590.

3564. Νυμφᾶς **Numphas**, *noom-fas´;* prob. contr. for a compound of 3565 and 1435; *nymph-given* (i.e. *-born*); *Nymphas*, a Chr.:— Nymphas.

3565. νύμφη **numphē**, *noom-fay´;* from a primary but obs. verb νύπτω **nuptō**, (to *veil* as a bride; comp. Lat. "*nupto*," to *marry*); a young *married* woman (as

veiled), incl. a *betrothed* girl; by impl. a *son's wife*:— bride, daughter in law.

3566. νυμφίος **numphiŏs**, *noom-fee´-os;* from 3565; a *bride-groom* (lit. or fig.):— bridegroom.

3567. νυμφών **numphōn**, *noom-fohn´;* from 3565; the *bridal* room:— bridechamber.

3568. νῦν **nun**, *noon;* a primary particle of present time; "*now*" (as adv. of date, a transition or emphasis); also as noun or adj. *present* or *immediate*:— henceforth, + hereafter, of late, soon, present, this (time). See also 3569, 3570.

3569. τανῦν **tanun**, *tan-oon´;* or

τὰ νῦν **ta nun** *tah noon;* from neut. plur. of 3588 and 3568; *the* things *now*, i.e. (adv.) *at present*:— (but) now.

3570. νυνί **nuni**, *noo-nee´;* a prol. form of 3568 for emphasis; *just now*:— now.

3571. νύξ **nux**, *noox;* a primary word; "*night*" (lit. or fig.):— (mid-) night.

3572. νύσσω **nussō**, *noos´-so;* appar. a primary word; to *prick* ("nudge"):— pierce.

3573. νυστάζω **nustazō**, *noos-tad´-zo;* from a presumed der. of 3506; to *nod*, i.e. (by impl.) to *fall asleep;* fig. to *delay*:— slumber.

3574. νυχθήμερον **nuchthēmĕrŏn**, *nookh-thay´-mer-on;* from 3571 and 2250; a *day*-and-*night*, i.e. full *day* of twenty-four hours:— night and day.

3575. Νῶε **Nŏĕ**, *no´-eh;* of Heb. or. [5146]; *Noë*, (i.e. *Noäch*), a patriarch:— Noe.

3576. νωθρός **nōthrŏs**, *no-thros´;* from a der. of 3541; *sluggish*, i.e. (lit.) *lazy*, or (fig.) *stupid*:— dull, slothful.

3577. νῶτος **nōtŏs**, *no´-tos;* of uncert. aff.; the *back*:— back.

Ξ

3578. ξενία **xĕnia**, *xen-ee´-ah;* from 3581; *hospitality*, i.e. (by impl.) a *place of entertainment*:— lodging.

3579. ξενίζω **xĕnizō**, *xen-id´-zo;* from 3581; to *be a host* (pass. a *guest*); by impl. *be* (*make, appear*) *strange*:— entertain, lodge, (think it) strange.

3580. ξενοδοχέω **xĕnŏdŏchĕō**, *xen-od-okh-eh´-o;* from a compound of 3581 and 1209; to *be hospitable*:— lodge strangers.

3581. ξένος **xĕnŏs**, *xen´-os;* appar. a primary word; *for.* (lit. *alien*, or fig. *novel*) by impl. a *guest* or (vice-versa) *entertainer*:— host, strange (*-r*).

3582. ξέστης **xĕstēs**, *xes´-tace;* as if from ξέω **xĕō**, (prop. to *smooth;* by impl. [of *friction*] to *boil* or *heat*); a *vessel* (as *fashioned* or for *cooking*) [or perh. by corruption from the Lat. *sextarius*, the *sixth* of a modius, i.e. about a *pint*], i.e. (spec.) a *measure* for liquids or solids, (by anal. a *pitcher*):— pot.

3583. ξηραίνω **xērainō**, *xay-rah´-ee-no;* from 3584; to *desiccate;* by impl. to *shrivel*, to *mature*:— dry up, pine away, be ripe, wither (away).

3584. ξηρός **xĕrŏs**, *xay-ros´;* from the base of 3582 (through the idea of

scorching); *arid;* by impl. *shrunken*, *earth* (as opposed to water):— dry land, withered.

3585. ξύλινος **xulinŏs**, *xoo´-lin-os;* from 3586; *wooden*:— of wood.

3586. ξύλον **xulŏn**, *xoo´-lon;* from another form of the base of 3582; *timber* (as fuel or material); by impl. a *stick, club* or *tree* or other wooden art. or substance:— staff, stocks, tree, wood.

3587. ξυράω **xuraō**, *xoo-rah´-o;* from a der. of the same as 3586 (mean. a *razor*); to *shave* or "*shear*" the hair:— shave.

Ο

3588. ὁ **hŏ**, *hŏ;* incl. the fem.

ἡ **hē**, *hay;* and the neut.

τό **tŏ**, *tŏ;* in all their inflections; the def. art.; *the* (sometimes to be supplied, at others omitted, in English idiom):— the, this, that, one, he, she, it, etc.

ὅ **hŏ**. See 3739.

3589. ὀγδοήκοντα **ŏgdŏēkŏnta**, *og-do-ay´-kon-tah;* from 3590; *ten times eight*:— fourscore.

3590. ὄγδοος **ŏgdŏŏs**, *og´-do-os;* from 3638; the *eighth*:— eighth.

3591. ὄγκος **ŏgkŏs**, *ong´-kos;* prob. from the same as 43; a *mass* (as *bending* or *bulging* by its load), i.e. *burden* (*hindrance*):— weight.

3592. ὅδε **hŏdĕ**, *hod´-eh;* incl. the fem.

ἥδε **hēdĕ**, *hay´-deh;* and the neut.

τόδε **tŏdĕ**, *tod´-e;* from 3588 and 1161; the *same*, i.e. *this* or *that* one (plur. *these* or *those*); often used as pers. pron.:— he, she, such, these, thus.

3593. ὁδεύω **hŏdĕuō**, *hod-yoo´-o;* from 3598; to *travel*:— journey.

3594. ὁδηγέω **hŏdēgĕō**, *hod-ayg-eh´-o;* from 3595; to *show the way* (lit. or fig. [*teach*]):— guide, lead.

3595. ὁδηγός **hŏdēgŏs**, *hod-ayg-os´;* from 3598 and 2233; a *conductor* (lit. or fig. [*teacher*]:— guide, leader.

3596. ὁδοιπορέω **hŏdŏipŏrĕō**, *hod-oy-por-eh´-o;* from a compound of 3598 and 4198; to *be a wayfarer*, i.e. *travel*:— go on a journey.

3597. ὁδοιπορία **hŏdŏipŏria**, *hod-oy-por-ee´-ah;* from the same as 3596; *travel*:— journey (*-ing*).

3598. ὁδός **hŏdŏs**, *hod-os´;* appar. a primary word; a *road;* by impl. a *progress* (the route, act or distance); fig. a *mode* or *means*:— journey, (high-) way.

3599. ὀδούς **ŏdŏus**, *od-ooce;* perh. from the base of 2068; a "*tooth*":— tooth.

3600. ὀδυνάω **ŏdunaō**, *od-oo-nah´-o;* from 3601; to *grieve*:— sorrow, torment.

3601. ὀδύνη **ŏdunē**, *od-oo´-nay;* from 1416; *grief* (as *dejecting*):— sorrow.

3602. ὀδυρμός **ŏdurmŏs**, *od-oor-mos´;* from a der. of the base of 1416; *moaning*, i.e. *lamentation*:— mourning.

3603. ὅ ἐστι **hŏ esti**, *hŏ es-tee´* or

ὅ ἐστιν **hŏ estin**, *hŏ es-teen´;* from

the neut. of 3739 and the third pers. sing. pres. ind. of 1510; *which is:*— called, which is (make), i.e. (to say).

3604. Ὀζίας **Ŏzias**, *od-zee´-as;* of Heb. or. [5818]; *Ozias* (i.e. *Uzzijah*), an Isr.:— Ozias.

3605. ὄζω **ŏzō**, *od´-zo;* a primary verb (in a strengthened form); to *scent* (usually an ill "odor"): stink.

3606. ὅθεν **hŏthĕn**, *hoth´-en;* from 3739 with the directive enclitic of source; *from which* place or source or cause (adv. or conjunc.):— from thence, (from) whence, where (-by, -fore, -upon).

3607. ὀθόνη **ŏthŏnē**, *oth-on´-ay;* of uncert. aff.; a *linen* cloth, i.e. (espec.) a *sail:*— sheet.

3608. ὀθόνιον **ŏthŏniŏn**, *oth-on´-ee-on;* neut. of a presumed der. of 3607; a linen *bandage:*— linen clothes.

3609. οἰκεῖος **ŏikĕiŏs**, *oy-ki´-os;* from 3624; *domestic*, i.e. (as noun), a *relative, adherent:*— (those) of the (his own) house (-hold).

3610. οἰκέτης **ŏikĕtēs**, *oy-ket´-ace;* from 3611; a fellow *resident*, i.e. menial *domestic:*— (household) servant.

3611. οἰκέω **ŏikĕō**, *oy-keh´-o;* from 3624; to *occupy a house*, i.e. *reside* (fig. *inhabit, remain, inhere*); by impl. to *cohabit:*— dwell. See also 3625.

3612. οἴκημα **ŏikēma**, *oy´-kay-mah;* from 3611; a *tenement*, i.e. (spec.) a *jail:*— prison.

3613. οἰκητήριον **ŏikētēriŏn**, *oy-kay-tay´-ree-on;* neut. of a presumed der. of 3611 (equiv. to 3612); a *residence* (lit. or fig.):— habitation, house.

3614. οἰκία **ŏikia**, *oy-kee´-ah;* from 3624; prop. *residence* (abstr.), but usually (concr.) an *abode* (lit. or fig.); by impl. a *family* (espec. *domestics*):— home, house (-hold).

3615. οἰκιακός **ŏikiakŏs**, *oy-kee-ak-os´;* from 3614; *familiar*, i.e. (as noun) *relatives:*— they (them) of (his own) household.

3616. οἰκοδεσποτέω **ŏikŏdĕspŏtĕō**, *oy-kod-es-pot-eh´-o;* from 3617; to *be the head of* (i.e. *rule*) *a family:*— guide the house.

3617. οἰκοδεσπότης **ŏikŏdĕspŏtēs**, *oy-kod-es-pot´-ace;* from 3624 and 1203; *the head of a family:*— goodman (of the house), householder, master of the house.

3618. οἰκοδομέω **ŏikŏdŏmĕō**, *oy-kod-om-eh´-o;* from the same as 3619; to *be a house-builder*, i.e. *construct* or (fig.) *confirm:*— (be in) build (-er, -ing, up), edify, embolden.

3619. οἰκοδομή **ŏikŏdŏmē**, *oy-kod-om-ay´;* fem. (abstr.) of a compound of 3624 and the base of 1430; *architecture*, i.e. (concr.) a *structure;* fig. *confirmation:*— building, edify (-ication, ing).

3620. οἰκοδομία **ŏikŏdŏmia**, *oy-kod-om-ee´-ah;* from the same as 3619; *confirmation:*— edifying.

3621. οἰκονομέω **ŏikŏnŏmĕō**, *oy-kon-om-eh´-o;* from 3623; to *manage* (a house, i.e. an estate):— be steward.

3622. οἰκονομία **ŏikŏnŏmia**, *oy-kon-om-ee´-ah;* from 3623; *administration* (of a household or estate); spec. a (relig.) *"economy":*— dispensation, stewardship.

3623. οἰκονόμος **ŏikŏnŏmŏs**, *oy-kon-om´-os;* from 3624 and the base of 3551; a *house-distributor* (i.e. *manager*), or *overseer*, i.e. an employee in that capacity; by extens. a fiscal *agent* (*treasurer*); fig. a *preacher* (of the Gospel):— chamberlain, governor, steward.

3624. οἶκος **ŏikŏs**, *oy´-kos;* of uncert. aff.; a *dwelling* (more or less extens., lit. or fig.); by impl. a *family* (more or less related, lit. or fig.):— home, house (-hold), temple.

3625. οἰκουμένη **ŏikŏumĕnē**, *oy-kou-men´-ay;* fem. part. pres. pass. of 3611 (as noun, by impl. of 1093); *land*, i.e. the (terrene part of the) *globe;* spec. the Rom. *empire:*— earth, world.

3626. οἰκουρός **ŏikŏurŏs**, *oy-koo-ros´* or

οἰκουργός **ŏikŏurgŏs**, *oy-koor-gos´;* from 3624 and οὖρος **ŏurŏs** (a *guard;* be "ware"); a *stayer at home*, i.e. *domestically inclined* (a "good housekeeper"):— keeper at home.

3627. οἰκτείρω **ŏiktĕirō**, *oyk-ti´-ro;* also (in certain tenses) prol.

οἰκτερέω **ŏiktĕrĕō**, *oyk-ter-eh´-o;* from οἶκτος **ŏiktŏs**, (*pity*); to *exercise pity:*— have compassion on.

3628. οἰκτιρμός **ŏiktirmŏs**, *oyk-tir-mos´;* from 3627; *pity:*— mercy.

3629. οἰκτίρμων **ŏiktirmōn**, *oyk-tir´-mone;* from 3627; *compassionate:*— merciful, of tender mercy.

3630. οἶμαι **ŏimai**. See 3633.

3630. οἰνοπότης **ŏinŏpŏtēs**, *oy-nop-ot´-ace;* from 3631 and a der. of the alt. of 4095; a *tippler:*— winebibber.

3631. οἶνος **ŏinŏs**, *oy´-nos;* a primary word (or perh. of Heb. origin [3196]); *"wine"* (lit. or fig.):— wine.

3632. οἰνοφλυγία **ŏinŏphlugia**, *oy-nof-loog-ee´-ah;* from 3631 and a form of the base of 5397; an *overflow* (or surplus) *of wine*, i.e. *vinolency* (*drunkenness*):— excess of wine.

3633. οἶμαι **ŏiŏmai**, *oy´-om-ahee;* or (shorter)

οἶμαι **ŏimai**, *oy´-mahee;* mid. voice appar. from 3634; to *make like* (oneself), i.e. *imagine* (be of the opinion):— suppose, think.

3634. οἶος **hŏiŏs**, *hoy´-os;* prob. akin to 3588, 3739, and 3745; *such* or *what sort* of (as a correl. or exclamation); espec. the neut. (adv.) with neg. not *so:*— so (as), such as, what (manner of), which.

3635. οἴω **ŏiō**. See 5342.

3635. ὀκνέω **ŏknĕō**, *ok-neh´-o;* from ὄκνος **ŏknŏs**, (*hesitation*); to *be slow* (fig. *loath*):— delay.

3636. ὀκνηρός **ŏknērŏs**, *ok-nay-ros´;* from 3635; *tardy*, i.e. *indolent;* (fig.) *irksome:*— grievous, slothful.

3637. ὀκταήμερος **ŏktaēmĕrŏs**, *ok-tah-ay´-mer-os;* from 3638 and 2250; an *eight-day* old person or act:— the eighth day.

3638. ὀκτώ **ŏktō**, *ok-to´;* a primary numeral; *"eight":*— eight.

3639. ὄλεθρος **ŏlĕthrŏs**, *ol´-eth-ros;* from a primary ὄλλυμι **ŏllumi** (to *destroy;* a prol. form); *ruin*, i.e. *death, punishment:*— destruction.

3640. ὀλιγόπιστος **ŏligŏpistŏs**, *ol-ig-op´-is-tos;* from 3641 and 4102; *incredulous*, i.e. *lacking confidence* (in Christ):— of little faith.

3641. ὀλίγος **ŏligŏs**, *ol-ee´-gos;* of uncert. aff.; *puny* (in extent, degree, number, duration or value); espec. neut. (adv.) *somewhat:*— + almost, brief l-lyl, few, (a) little, + long, a season, short, small, a while.

3642. ὀλιγόψυχος **ŏligŏpsuchŏs**, *ol-ig-op´-soo-khos;* from 3641 and 6590; *little-spirited*, i.e. *faint-hearted:*— feeble-minded.

3643. ὀλιγωρέω **ŏligōrĕō**, *ol-ig-o-reh´-o;* from a compound of 3641 and ὥρα **ōra** (*"care"*); to *have little regard*, for, i.e. to *disesteem:*— despise.

3644. ὀλοθρευτής **ŏlŏthrĕutēs**, *ol-oth-ryoo-tace´;* from 3645; a *ruiner*, i.e. (spec.) a venomous *serpent:*— destroyer.

3645. ὀλοθρεύω **ŏlŏthrĕuō**, *ol-oth-ryoo´-o;* from 3639; to *spoil*, i.e. *slay:*— destroy.

3646. ὁλοκαύτωμα **hŏlŏkautōma**, *hol-ok-ŏw´-to-mah;* from a der. of a compound of 3650 and a der. of 2545; a *wholly-consumed* sacrifice ("holocaust"):— (whole) burnt offering.

3647. ὁλοκληρία **hŏlŏklēria**, *hol-ok-lay-ree´-ah;* from 3648; *integrity*, i.e. phys. *wholeness:*— perfect soundness.

3648. ὁλόκληρος **hŏlŏklērŏs**, *hol´-ok´-lay-ros;* from 3650 and 2819; *complete in every part*, i.e. perfectly *sound* (in body):— entire, whole.

3649. ὀλολύζω **ŏlŏluzō**, *ol-ol-ood´-zo;* a redupl. primary verb; to *"howl"* or *"halloo"*, i.e. *shriek:*— howl.

3650. ὅλος **hŏlŏs**, *hol´-os;* a primary word; *"whole"* or *"all"*, i.e. *complete* (in extent, amount, time or degree); espec. (neut.) as noun or adv.:— all, altogether, every whit, + throughout, whole.

3651. ὁλοτελής **hŏlŏtĕlēs**, *hol-ot-el-ace´;* from 3650 and 5056; *complete to the end*, i.e. *absolutely perfect:*— wholly.

3652. Ὀλυμπᾶς **Olumpas**, *ol-oom-pas´;* prob. a contr. from Ὀλυμπιόδωρος **Olumpiŏdōrŏs**, (*Olympian-bestowed*, i.e. *heaven-descended*); *Olympas*, a Chr.:— Olympas.

3653. ὄλυνθος **ŏlunthŏs**, *ol´-oon-thos;* of uncert. der.; an *unripe* (because out of season) *fig:*— untimely fig.

3654. ὅλως **hŏlŏs**, *hol´-oce;* adv. from 3650; *completely*, i.e. *altogether;* (by anal.) *everywhere;* (neg.) not *by any means:*— at all, commonly, utterly.

3655. ὄμβρος **ŏmbrŏs**, *om´-bros;* of uncert. aff.; a thunder *storm:*— shower.

3656. ὁμιλέω **hŏmilĕō**, *hom-il-eh´-o;* from 3658; to *be in company* with, i.e.

(by impl.) to *converse:*— commune, talk.

3657. ὁμιλία **hŏmilia**, *hom-il-ee´-ah;* from 3658; *companionship* ("homily"), i.e. (by impl.) *intercourse:*— communication.

3658. ὅμιλος **hŏmilŏs**, *hom´-il-os;* from the base of 3674 and a der. of the alt. of 138 (mean. a *crowd*); *association together*, i.e. a *multitude:*— company.

3659. ὄμμα **ŏmma**, *om´-mah;* from 3700; a *sight*, i.e. (by impl.) the *eye:*— eye.

3660. ὀμνύω **ŏmnuō**, *om-noo´-o;* a prol. form of a primary but obsolete ὄμω **ŏmō**, for which another prol. form ὀμόω **ŏmŏō** *om-ŏ´-o*) is used in certain tenses; to *swear*, i.e. *take* (or *declare on*) *oath:*— swear.

3661. ὁμοθυμαδόν **hŏmŏthumadŏn**, *hom-oth-oo-mad-on´;* adv. from a compound of the base of 3674 and 2372; *unanimously:*— with one accord (mind).

3662. ὁμοιάζω **hŏmŏiazō**, *hom-oy-ad´-zo;* from 3664; to *resemble:*— agree.

3663. ὁμοιοπαθής **hŏmŏiŏpathēs**, *hom-oy-op-ath-ace´;* from 3664 and the alt. of 3958; *similarly affected:*— of (subject to) like passions.

3664. ὅμοιος **hŏmŏiŏs**, *hom´-oy-os;* from the base of 3674; *similar* (in appearance or character):— like, + manner.

3665. ὁμοιότης **hŏmŏiŏtēs**, *hom-oy-ot´-ace;* from 3664; *resemblance:*— like as, similitude.

3666. ὁμοιόω **hŏmŏiŏō**, *hom-oy-ŏ´-o;* from 3664; to *assimilate*, i.e. *compare;* pass. to *become similar:*— be (make) like, (in the) liken (-ess), resemble.

3667. ὁμοίωμα **hŏmŏiōma**, *hom-oy-o´-mah;* from 3666; a *form;* abstr. *resemblance:*— made like to, likeness, shape, similitude.

3668. ὁμοίως **hŏmŏiōs**, *hom-oy-oce;* adv. from 3664; *similarly:*— likewise, so.

3669. ὁμοίωσις **hŏmŏiōsis**, *hom-oy-o-sis;* from 3666; *assimilation*, i.e. *resemblance:*— similitude.

3670. ὁμολογέω **hŏmŏlŏgĕō**, *hom-ol-og-eh´-o;* from a compound of the base of 3674 and 3056; to *assent*, i.e. *covenant, acknowledge:*— con- (pro-) fess, confession is made, give thanks, promise.

3671. ὁμολογία **hŏmŏlŏgia**, *hom-ol-og-ee´-ah;* from the same as 3670; *acknowledgment:*— con- (pro-) fession, professed.

3672. ὁμολογουμένως **hŏmŏlŏgŏumĕnōs**, *hom-ol-og-ŏw-men´-oce;* adv. of pres. pass. part. of 3670; *confessedly:*— without controversy.

3673. ὁμότεχνος **hŏmŏtĕchnŏs**, *hom-ot´-ekh-nos;* from the base of 3674 and 5078; a *fellow-artificer:*— of the same craft.

3674. ὁμοῦ **hŏmŏu**, *hom-oo´;* gen. of ὁμός **hŏmŏs**, (the *same;* akin to 260) as adv.; *at* the *same* place or time:— together.

3675. ὁμόφρων **hŏmŏphrōn**, *hom-of´-*

rone; from the base of 3674 and 5424; *like-minded*, i.e. *harmonious:*— of one mind.

ὁμόω **ŏmŏō**. See 3660.

3676. ὅμως **hŏmōs**, *hom´-oce;* adv. from the base of 3674; *at* the *same* time, i.e. (conjunc.) *notwithstanding, yet still:*— and even, nevertheless, though but.

3677. ὄναρ **ŏnar**, *on´-ar;* of uncert. der.; a *dream:*— dream.

3678. ὀνάριον **ŏnariŏn**, *on-ar´-ee-on;* neut. of a presumed der. of 3688; a *little ass:*— young ass.

ὀνάω **ŏnaō**. See 3685.

3679. ὀνειδίζω **ŏnĕidizō**, *on-i-did´-zo;* from 3681; to *defame*, i.e. *rail at, chide, taunt:*— cast in teeth, (suffer) reproach, revile, upbraid.

3680. ὀνειδισμός **ŏnĕidismŏs**, *on-i-dis-mos´;* from 3679; *contumely:*— reproach.

3681. ὄνειδος **ŏnĕidŏs**, *on´-i-dos;* prob. akin to the base of 3686; *notoriety*, i.e. a *taunt* (*disgrace*):— reproach.

3682. Ὀνήσιμος **Ŏnēsimŏs**, *on-ay´-sim-os;* from 3685; *profitable; Onesimus*, a Chr.:— Onesimus.

3683. Ὀνησίφορος **Ŏnēsiphŏrŏs**, *on-ay-sif´-or-os;* from a der. of 3685 and 5411; *profit-bearer; Onesiphorus*, a Chr.:— Onesiphorus.

3684. ὀνικός **ŏnikŏs**, *on-ik-os´;* from 3688; *belonging to* an *ass*, i.e. *large* (so as to be turned by an ass):— millstone.

3685. ὀνίνημι **ŏninēmi**, *on-in´-ay-mee;* a prol. form of an appar. primary verb

(ὄνομαι **ŏnŏmai**, to *slur*); for which another prol. form (ὀνάω **ŏnaō**) is used as an alt. in some tenses (unless indeed it be ident. with the base of 3686 through the idea of *notoriety*); to *gratify*, i.e. (mid. voice) to *derive pleasure* or *advantage* from:— have joy.

3686. ὄνομα **ŏnŏma**, *on´-om-ah;* from a presumed der. of the base of 1097 (comp. 3685); a "*name*" (lit. or fig.) (*authority, character*):— called, (+ sur-) name (-d).

3687. ὀνομάζω **ŏnŏmazō**, *on-om-ad´-zo;* from 3686; to *name*, i.e. *assign an appellation;* by extens. to *utter, mention, profess:*— call, name.

3688. ὄνος **ŏnŏs**, *on´-os;* appar. a primary word; a *donkey:*— an ass.

3689. ὄντως **ŏntōs**, *on´-toce;* adv. of the oblique cases of 5607; *really:*— certainly, clean, indeed, of a truth, verily.

3690. ὄξος **ŏxŏs**, *ox-os;* from 3691; *vinegar*, i.e. *sour* wine:— vinegar.

3691. ὀξύς **ŏxus**, *ox-oos´;* prob. akin to the base of 188 ("*acid*"); *keen;* by anal. *rapid:*— sharp, swift.

3692. ὀπή **ŏpē**, *op-ay´;* prob. from 3700; a *hole* (as if for *light*), i.e. *cavern;* by anal. a *spring* (of water):— cave, place.

3693. ὄπισθεν **ŏpisthĕn**, *op´-is-then;* from ὄπις **ŏpis**, (*regard;* from 3700) with enclitic of source; from *the rear* (as a secure *aspect*), i.e. *at the back* (adv. and prep. of place or time):— after, backside, behind.

3694. ὀπίσω **ŏpisō**, *op-is´-o;* from the

same as 3693 with enclitic of direction; *to the back*, i.e. *aback* (as adv. or prep. of time or place; or as noun):— after, back (-ward), (+ get) behind, + follow.

3695. ὁπλίζω **hŏplizō**, *hop-lid´-zo;* from 3696; to *equip* (with weapons (mid. voice and fig.)):— arm self.

3696. ὅπλον **hŏplŏn**, *hop´-lon;* prob. from a primary ἕπω **hĕpō** (to be *busy* about); an *implement*, or *utensil* or *tool* (lit. or fig., espec. offensive for war):— armour, instrument, weapon.

3697. ὁποῖος **hŏpŏiŏs**, *hop-oy´-os;* from 3739 and 4169; of *what* kind *that*, i.e. *how* (*as*) *great* (*excellent*) (spec. as an indef. correl. to the antecedent def. 5108 of quality):— what manner (sort) of, such as whatsoever.

3698. ὁπότε **hŏpŏtĕ**, *hop-ot´-eh;* from 3739 and 4218; *what* (-ever) *then*, i.e. (of time) *as soon as:*— when.

3699. ὅπου **hŏpŏu**, *hop´-oo;* from 3739 and 4225; *what* (-ever) *where*, i.e. *at whichever* spot:— in what place, where (-as, -soever), whither (+ soever).

3700. ὀπτάνομαι **ŏptanŏmai**, *op-tan´-om-ahee;* a (mid. voice) prol. form of the primary (mid. voice)

(ὄπτομαι **ŏptŏmai**, *op´-tom-ahee;* which is used for it in certain tenses; and both as alternate of 3708; to *gaze* (i.e. with wide-open eyes, as at something remarkable; and thus differing from 991, which denotes simply *voluntary* observation; and from 1492, which expresses merely mechanical, passive or casual vision; while 2300, and still more emphatically its intensive 2334, signifies an earnest but more continued *inspection;* and 4648 a watching *from a distance*):— appear, look, see, shew self.

3701. ὀπτασία **ŏptasia**, *op-tas-ee´-ah;* from a presumed der. of 3700; *visuality*, i.e. (concr.) an *apparition:*— vision.

ὄπτομαι **ŏptŏmai**. See 3700.

3702. ὀπτός **ŏptŏs**, *op-tos´;* from an obs. verb akin to ἕπσω **hĕpsō** (to "*steep*"); *cooked*, i.e. *roasted:*— broiled.

3703. ὀπώρα **ŏpōra**, *op-o´-rah;* appar. from the base of 3796 and 5610; prop. *even-tide* of the (summer) season (*dog-days*), i.e. (by impl.) *ripe* fruit:— fruit.

3704. ὅπως **hŏpōs**, *hop´-oce;* from 3739 and 4459; *what* (-ever) *how*, i.e. *in* the *manner that* (as adv. or conjunc. of coincidence, intentional or actual):— because, how, (so) that, to, when.

3705. ὅραμα **hŏrama**, *hor´-am-ah;* from 3708; *something gazed at*, i.e. a *spectacle* (espec. *supernatural*):— sight, vision.

3706. ὅρασις **hŏrasis**, *hor´-as-is;* from 3708; the act of *gazing*, i.e. (external) an *aspect* or (intern.) an inspired *appearance:*— sight, vision.

3707. ὁρατός **hŏratŏs**, *hor-at-os´;* from 3708; *gazed at*, i.e. (by impl.) *capable of being seen:*— visible.

3708. ὁράω **hŏraō**, *hor-ah´-o;* prop. to *stare* at (comp. 3700), i.e. (by impl.) to *discern* clearly (phys. or ment.); by extens. to *attend* to; by Heb. to *experi-*

ence; pass. to *appear:*— behold, perceive, see, take heed.

3709. ὀργή **ŏrgē,** *or-gay´;* from 3713; prop. *desire* (as a *reaching* forth or *excitement* of the mind), i.e. (by anal.) violent *passion* (*ire,* or [justifiable] *abhorrence*); by impl. *punishment:*— anger, indignation, vengeance, wrath.

3710. ὀργίζω **ŏrgizō,** *or-gid´-zo;* from 3709; to *provoke* or *enrage,* i.e. (pass.) *become exasperated:*— be angry (wroth).

3711. ὀργίλος **ŏrgilŏs,** *org-ee´-los;* from 3709; *irascible:*— soon angry.

3712. ὀργυιά **ŏrguia,** *org-wee-ah´;* from 3713; a *stretch* of the arms, i.e. a *fathom:*— fathom.

3713. ὀρέγομαι **ŏrĕgŏmai,** *or-eg´-om-ahee;* mid. voice of appar. a prol. form of an obs. primary [comp. 3735]; to *stretch* oneself, i.e. *reach* out after (*long* for):— covet after, desire.

3714. ὀρεινός **ŏrĕinŏs,** *or-i-nos;* from 3735; *mountainous,* i.e. (fem. by impl. of 5561) the *Highlands* (of Judæa):— hill country.

3715. ὄρεξις **ŏrĕxis,** *or´-ex-is;* from 3713; *excitement* of the mind, i.e. *longing* after:— lust.

3716. ὀρθοποδέω **ŏrthŏpŏdĕō,** *or-thop-od-eh´-o;* from a compound of 3717 and 4228; to be *straight-footed,* i.e. (fig.) to go *directly* forward:— walk uprightly.

3717. ὀρθός **ŏrthŏs,** *or-thos;* prob. from the base of 3735; *right* (as *rising*), i.e. (perpendicularly) *erect* (fig. *honest*), or (horizontally) *level* or *direct:*— straight, upright.

3718. ὀρθοτομέω **ŏrthŏtŏmĕō,** *or-thot-om-eh´-o;* from a compound of 3717 and the base of 5114, to *make a straight cut,* i.e. (fig.) to *dissect* (*expound*) *correctly* (the divine message):— rightly divide.

3719. ὀρθρίζω **ŏrthrizō,** *or-thrid´-zo;* from 3722; to *use* the *dawn,* i.e. (by impl.) to *repair betimes:*— come early in the morning.

3720. ὀρθρινός **ŏrthrinŏs,** *or-thrin-os´;* from 3722; *relating to* the *dawn,* i.e. *matutinal* (as an epithet of Venus, espec. brilliant in the early day):— morning.

3721. ὄρθριος **ŏrthriŏs,** *or´-three-os;* from 3722; *in* the *dawn,* i.e. up *at daybreak:*— early.

3722. ὄρθρος **ŏrthrŏs,** *or´-thros;* from the same as 3735; *dawn* (as *sun-rise, rising* of light); by extens. *morn:*— early in the morning.

3723. ὀρθῶς **ŏrthōs,** *or-thoce´;* adv. from 3717; *in a straight* manner, i.e. (fig.) *correctly* (also mor.):— plain, right (-ly).

3724. ὁρίζω **hŏrizō,** *hor-id´-zo;* from 3725; to *mark out* or *bound* ("horizon"), i.e. (fig.) to *appoint, decree, specify:*— declare, determine, limit, ordain.

3725. ὅριον **hŏriŏn,** *hor´-ee-on;* neut. of a der. of an appar. primary ὅρος **hŏrŏs** (a *bound* or *limit*); a *boundary*-line, i.e. (by impl.) a *frontier* (*region*):— border, coast.

3726. ὁρκίζω **hŏrkizō,** *hor-kid´-zo;* from

3727; to *put on oath,* i.e. *make swear;* by anal. to solemnly *enjoin:*— adjure, charge.

3727. ὅρκος **hŏrkŏs,** *hor´-kos;* from ἕρκος **hĕrkŏs,** (a *fence;* perh. akin to 3725); a *limit,* i.e. (sacred) *restraint* (spec. an *oath*):— oath.

3728. ὁρκωμοσία **hŏrkōmŏsia,** *hor-ko-mos-ee´ah;* from a compound of 3727 and a der. of 3660; *asseveration on oath:*— oath.

3729. ὁρμάω **hŏrmaō,** *hor-mah´-o;* from 3730; to *start, spur* or *urge* on, i.e. (refl.) to *dash* or *plunge:*— run (violently), rush.

3730. ὁρμή **hŏrmē,** *hor-may´;* of uncert. aff.; a violent *impulse,* i.e. *onset:*— assault.

3731. ὅρμημα **hŏrmēma,** *hor´-may-mah;* from 3730; an *attack,* i.e. (abstr.) *precipitancy:*— violence.

3732. ὄρνεον **ŏrnĕŏn,** *or´-neh-on;* neut. of a presumed der. of 3733; a *birdling:*— bird, fowl.

3733. ὄρνις **ŏrnis,** *or´-nis;* prob. from a prol. form of the base of 3735; a *bird* (as *rising* in the air), i.e. (spec.) a *hen* (or female domestic fowl):— hen.

3734. ὁροθεσία **hŏrŏthĕsia,** *hor-oth-es-ee´-ah;* from a compound of the base of 3725 and a der. of 5087; a *limit-placing,* i.e. (concr.) *boundary-line:*— bound.

3735. ὄρος **ŏrŏs,** *or´-os;* prob. from an obs. ὄρω **ŏrō** (to *rise* or "*rear;*" perh. akin to 142; comp. 3733); a *mountain* (as *lifting* itself above the plain):— hill, mount (-ain).

3736. ὀρύσσω **ŏrussō,** *or-oos´-so;* appar. a primary verb; to "*burrow*" in the ground, i.e. *dig:*— dig.

3737. ὀρφανός **ŏrphanŏs,** *or-fan-os´;* of uncert. aff.; *bereaved* ("*orphan*"), i.e. *parentless:*— comfortless, fatherless.

3738. ὀρχέομαι **ŏrchĕŏmai,** *or-kheh´-om-ahee;* mid. voice from ὄρχος **ŏrchŏs** (a *row* or *ring*); to *dance,* (from the *ranklike* or *regular* motion):— dance.

3739. ὅς **hŏs,** *hos;* incl. fem.

ἥ **hē,** *hay;* and neut.

ὅ **hŏ** *hŏ;* prob. a primary word (or perh. a form of the art. 3588); the rel. (sometimes demonstr.) pron., *who, which, what, that:*— one, (an-, the) other, some, that, what, which, who (-m, -se), etc. See also 3757.

3740. ὁσάκις **hŏsakis,** *hos-ak´-is;* multiple adv. from 3739; *how* (i.e. with 302, so) *many times* as:— as oft (-en) as.

3741. ὅσιος **hŏsiŏs,** *hos´-ee-os;* of uncert. aff.; prop. *right* (by intrinsic or divine character; thus distinguished from 1342, which refers rather to *human* statutes and relations; from 2413, which denotes formal *consecration;* and from 40, which relates to *purity* from defilement), i.e. *hallowed* (*pious, sacred, sure*):— holy, mercy, shalt be.

3742. ὁσιότης **hŏsiŏtēs,** *hos-ee-ot´-ace;* from 3741; *piety:*— holiness.

3743. ὁσίως **hŏsiōs,** *hos-ee-oce´;* adv. from 3741; *piously:*— holily.

3744. ὀσμή **ŏsmē,** *os-may´;* from 3605; *fragrance* (lit. or fig.):— odour, savour.

3745. ὅσος **hŏsŏs,** *hos´-os;* by redupl. from 3739; *as* (*much, great, long,* etc.) *as:*— all (that), as (long, many, much) (as), how great (many, much), [in-] asmuch as, so many as, that (ever), the more, those things, what (great, -soever), wheresoever, wherewithsoever, which, × while, who (-soever).

3746. ὅσπερ **hŏspĕr,** *hos´-per;* from 3739 and 4007; *who especially:*— whomsoever.

3747. ὀστέον **ŏstĕŏn,** *os-teh´-on;* or contr.

ὀστοῦν **ŏstŏun,** *os-toon´;* of uncert. aff.; a *bone:*— bone.

3748. ὅστις **hŏstis,** *hos´-tis;* incl. the fem.

ἥτις **hētis,** *hay´-tis;* and the neut.

ὅ,τι **hŏ,ti,** *hot´-ee;* from 3739 and 5100; *which some,* i.e. *any that;* also (def.) *which same:*— × and (they), (such) as, (they) that, in that they, what (-soever), whereas ye, (they) which, who (-soever). Comp. 3754.

3749. ὀστράκινος **ŏstrakinŏs,** *os-tra´-kin-os;* from ὄστρακον **ŏstrakŏn,** ["oyster"] (a *tile,* i.e. *terra cotta*); *earthenware,* i.e. *clayey;* by impl. *frail:*— of earth, earthen.

3750. ὄσφρησις **ŏsphrēsis,** *os´-fray-sis;* from a der. of 3605; *smell* (the sense):— smelling.

3751. ὀσφύς **ŏsphus,** *os-foos´;* of uncert. aff.; the *loin* (extern.), i.e. the *hip;* intern. (by extens.) *procreative power:*— loin.

3752. ὅταν **hŏtan,** *hot´-an;* from 3753 and 302; *whenever* (implying *hypothesis* or more or less *uncertainty*); also caus. (conjunc.) *inasmuch as:*— as long (soon) as, that, + till, when (-soever), while.

3753. ὅτε **hŏtĕ,** *hot´-eh;* from 3739 and 5037; *at which* (thing) *too,* i.e. *when:*— after (that), as soon as, that, when, while.

ὅ, τε **hŏ, tĕ,** *hŏ,t´-eh;* also fem.

ἥ, τε **hē, tĕ,** *hay´-teh;* and neut.

τό, τε **tŏ, tĕ,** *tot´-eh;* simply the art. 3588 followed by 5037; so written (in some editions) to distinguish them from 3752 and 5119.

3754. ὅτι **hŏti,** *hot´-ee;* neut. of 3748 as conjunc.; demonst. *that* (sometimes redundant); caus. *because:*— as concerning that, as though, because (that), for (that), how (that), (in) that, though, why.

3755. ὅτου **hŏtŏu,** *hot´-oo;* for the gen. of 3748 (as adverb); *during which same* time, i.e. *whilst:*— whiles.

3756. οὐ **ŏu,** *oo;* also (before a vowel)

οὐκ **ŏuk,** *ook;* and (before an aspirate)

οὐχ **ŏuch,** *ookh;* a primary word; the absolute neg. [comp. 3361] adv.; *no* or *not:*— + long, nay, neither, never, no (× man), none, [can-] not, + nothing, + special, un (I-worthy), when, + without, + yet but. See also 3364, 3372.

3757. οὗ **hŏu**, *hoo;* gen. of 3739 as adv.; at *which* place, i.e. *where:*— where (-in), whither (l-soever).

3758. οὐά **ŏua**, *oo-ah´;* a primary exclamation of surprise; "*ah*":— ah.

3759. οὐαί **ŏuai**, *oo-ah´-ee;* a primary exclamation of grief; "*woe*":— alas, woe.

3760. οὐδαμῶς **ŏudamōs**, *oo-dam-oce´;* adv. from (the fem.) of 3762; *by no means:*— not.

3761. οὐδέ **ŏudĕ**, *oo-deh´;* from 3756 and 1161; *not however,* i.e. *neither, nor, not even:*— neither (indeed), never, no (more, nor, not), nor (yet) (also, even, then) not (even, so much as), + nothing, so much as.

3762. οὐδείς **ŏudĕis**, *oo-dice´;* incl. fem.

οὐδεμία **ŏudĕmia**, *oo-dem-ee´-ah;* and neut.

οὐδέν **ŏudĕn**, *oo-den´;* from 3761 and 1520; *not even one* (man, woman or thing), i.e. *none, nobody, nothing:*— any (man), aught, man, neither any (thing), never (man), no (man), none (+ of these things), not (any, at all, -thing), nought.

3763. οὐδέποτε **ŏudĕpŏtĕ**, *oo-dep´-ot-eh;* from 3761 and 4218; *not even at any time,* i.e. *never at all:*— neither at any time, never, nothing at any time.

3764. οὐδέπω **ŏudĕpō**, *oo-dep´-o;* from 3761 and 4452; *not even yet:*— as yet not, never before (yet), (not) yet.

3765. οὐκέτι **ŏukĕti**, *ook-et´-ee;* also (separately)

οὐκ ἔτι **ŏuk ĕti**, *ook et´-ee;* from 3756 and 2089; *not yet, no longer:*— after that (not), (not) any more, henceforth (hereafter) not, no longer (more), not as yet (now), now no more (not), yet (not).

3766. οὐκοῦν **ŏukŏun**, *ook-oon´;* from 3756 and 3767; is it *not therefore* that, i.e. (affirmatively) *hence* or *so:*— then.

3767. οὖν **ŏun**, *oon;* appar. a primary word; (adv.) *certainly,* or (conjunc.) *accordingly:*— and (so, truly), but, now (then), so (likewise then), then, therefore, verily, wherefore.

3768. οὔπω **ŏupō**, *oo´-po;* from 3756 and 4452; *not yet:*— hitherto not, (no ...) as yet, not yet.

3769. οὐρά **ŏura**, *oo-rah´;* appar. a primary word; a *tail:*— tail.

3770. οὐράνιος **ŏuraniŏs**, *oo-ran´-ee-os;* from 3772; *celestial,* i.e. *belonging to* or *coming from the sky:*— heavenly.

3771. οὐρανόθεν **ŏuranŏthĕn**, *oo-ran-oth´-en;* from 3772 and the enclitic of source; *from the sky:*— from heaven.

3772. οὐρανός **ŏuranŏs**, *oo-ran-os´;* perh. from the same as 3735 (through the idea of *elevation*); the *sky;* by extens. *heaven* (as the abode of God); by impl. *happiness, power, eternity;* spec. the *Gospel* (*Christianity*):— air, heaven (l-lyl), sky.

3773. Οὐρβανός **Ŏurbanŏs**, *oor-ban-os´;* of Lat. or.; *Urbanus* (*of the city,* "*urbane*"), a Chr.:— Urbanus.

3774. Οὐρίας **Ŏurias**, *oo-ree´-as;* of Heb.

or. [223]; *Urias* (i.e. *Urijah*), a Hittite:— Urias.

3775. οὖς **ŏus**, *ooce;* appar. a primary word; the *ear* (phys. or ment.):— ear.

3776. οὐσία **ŏusia**, *oo-see´-ah;* from the fem. of 5607; *substance,* i.e. *property* (*possessions*):— goods, substance.

3777. οὔτε **ŏutĕ**, *oo´-teh;* from 3756 and 5037; *not too,* i.e. *neither* or *nor;* by anal. *not even:*— neither, none, nor (yet) (no, yet) not, nothing.

3778. οὗτος **hŏutŏs**, *hoo´-tos;* incl. nom. masc. plur.

οὗτοι **hŏutŏi**, *hoo´-toy;* nom. fem. sing.

αὕτη **hautē**, *hŏw´-tay;* and nom. fem. plur.

αὗται **hautai**, *hŏw´-tahee;* from the art. 3588 and 846; *the he* (*she* or it), i.e. *this* or *that* (often with art. repeated):— he (it was that), hereof, it, she, such as, the same, these, they, this (man, same, woman), which, who.

3779. οὕτω **hŏutō**, *hoo´-to;* or (before a vowel)

οὕτως **hŏutŏs**, *hoo´-toce;* adv. from 3778; *in this way* (referring to what precedes or follows):— after that, after (in) this manner, as, even (so), for all that, like (-wise), no more, on this fashion (-wise), so (in like manner), thus, what.

3780. οὐχί **ŏuchi**, *oo-khee´;* intens. of 3756; *not indeed:*— nay, not.

3781. ὀφειλέτης **ŏphĕilĕtēs**, *of-i-let´-ace;* from 3784; an *ower,* i.e. person *indebted;* fig. a *delinquent;* mor. a *transgressor* (against God):— debtor, which owed, sinner.

3782. ὀφειλή **ŏphĕilē**, *of-i-lay´;* from 3784; *indebtedness,* i.e. (concr.) a *sum* owed; fig. *obligation,* i.e. (conjugal) *duty:*— debt, due.

3783. ὀφείλημα **ŏphĕilēma**, *of-i´-lay-mah;* from (the alt. of) 3784; *something owed,* i.e. (fig.) a *due;* mor. a *fault:*— debt.

3784. ὀφείλω **ŏphĕilō**, *of-i´-lo;* or (in certain tenses) its prol. form

ὀφειλέω **ŏphĕilĕō**, *of-i-leh´-o;* prob. from the base of 3786 (through the idea of *accruing*); to *owe* (pecuniarily); fig. to *be under obligation* (*ought, must, should*); mor. to *fail in duty:*— behove, be bound, (be) debt (-or), (be) due (-ty), be guilty (indebted), (must) need (-s), ought, owe, should. See also 3785.

3785. ὄφελον **ŏphĕlŏn**, *of´-el-on;* first pers. sing. of a past tense of 3784; *I ought* (*wish*), i.e. (interj.) *oh that!:*— would (to God).

3786. ὄφελος **ŏphĕlŏs**, *of´-el-os;* from ὀφέλλω **ŏphĕllō**, (to *heap up,* i.e. *accumulate* or *benefit*); *gain:*— advantageth, profit.

3787. ὀφθαλμοδουλεία **ŏphthalmŏdŏulĕia**, *of-thal-mod-oo-li´-ah;* from 3788 and 1397; *sight-labor,* i.e. that needs watching (*remissness*):— eye-service.

3788. ὀφθαλμός **ŏphthalmŏs**, *of-thal-mos´;* from 3700; the *eye* (lit. or fig.); by

impl. *vision;* fig. *envy* (from the jealous side-glance):— eye, sight.

3789. ὄφις **ŏphis**, *of´-is;* prob. from 3700 (through the idea of *sharpness* of vision); a *snake,* fig. (as a type of sly cunning) an artful *malicious* person, espec. *Satan:*— serpent.

3790. ὀφρύς **ŏphrus**, *of-roos´;* perh. from 3700 (through the idea of the *shading* or proximity to the organ of *vision*); the eye-"*brow*" or *forehead,* i.e. (fig.) the *brink* of a precipice:— brow.

3791. ὀχλέω **ŏchlĕō**, *okh-leh´-o;* from 3793; to *mob,* i.e. (by impl.) to *harass:*— vex.

3792. ὀχλοποιέω **ŏchlŏpŏiĕō**, *okh-lop-oy-eh´-o;* from 3793 and 4160; to *make a crowd,* i.e. *raise a* public *disturbance:*— gather a company.

3793. ὄχλος **ŏchlŏs**, *okh´los;* from a der. of 2192 (mean. a *vehicle*); a *throng* (as *borne* along); by impl. the *rabble;* by extens. a *class* of people; fig. a *riot:*— company, multitude, number (of people), people, press.

3794. ὀχύρωμα **ŏchurōma**, *okh-oo´-ro-mah;* from a remote der. of 2192 (mean. to *fortify,* through the idea of *holding* safely); a *castle* (fig. *argument*):— stronghold.

3795. ὀψάριον **ŏpsariŏn**, *op-sar´-ee-on;* neut. of a presumed der. of the base of 3702; a *relish* to other food (as if cooked *sauce*), i.e. (spec.) *fish* (presumably salted and dried as a condiment):— fish.

3796. ὀψέ **ŏpsĕ**, *op-seh´;* from the same as 3694 (through the idea of *backwardness*); (adv.) *late* in the day; by extens. *after the close* of the day:— (at) even, in the end.

3797. ὄψιμος **ŏpsimŏs**, *op´-sim-os;* from 3796; *later,* i.e. *vernal* (showering):— latter.

3798. ὄψιος **ŏpsiŏs**, *op´-see-os;* from 3796; *late;* fem. (as noun) *afternoon* (early eve) or *nightfall* (later eve):— even (-ing, l-tidel).

3799. ὄψις **ŏpsis**, *op´-sis;* from 3700; prop. *sight* (the act), i.e. (by impl) the *visage,* an extern. *show:*— appearance, countenance, face.

3800. ὀψώνιον **ŏpsōniŏn**, *op-so´-nee-on;* neut. of a presumed der. of the same as 3795; *rations* for a soldier, i.e. (by extens.) his *stipend* or *pay:*— wages.

3801. ὁ ὢν καί ὁ ἦν καί ὁ ἐρχόμενος **hŏ ōn kai hŏ ēn kai hŏ ĕrchŏmĕnŏs**, *hŏ own kahee hŏ ane kahee hŏ er-khom´-en-os;* a phrase combining 3588 with the pres. part. and imperf. of 1510 and the pres. part. of 2064 by means of 2532; *the one being* and *the one that was* and *the one coming,* i.e. *the Eternal,* as a divine epithet of Christ:— which art (is, was), and (which) wast (is, was), and art (is) to come (shalt be).

Π

3802. παγιδεύω **pagidĕuō**, *pag-id-yoo´-o;* from 3803; to *ensnare* (fig.):— entangle.

3803. παγίς **pagis**, *pag-ece´;* from 4078; a *trap* (as *fastened* by a noose or notch);

fig. a *trick* or *statagem* (*temptation*):— snare.

Πάγος **Pagŏs.** See *697*.

3804. πάθημα **pathēma,** *path´-ay-mah;* from a presumed der. of *3806;* something *undergone,* i.e. *hardship* or *pain;* subj. an *emotion* or *influence:*— affection, affliction, motion, suffering.

3805. παθητός **pathētŏs,** *path-ay-tos´;* from the same as *3804;* *liable* (i.e. *doomed*) to experience *pain:*— suffer.

3806. πάθος **pathŏs,** *path´-os;* from the alt. of *3958;* prop. *suffering* ("*pathos*"), i.e. (subj.) a *passion* (espec. *concupiscence*):— (inordinate) affection, lust.

πάθω **pathō.** See *3958.*

3807. παιδαγωγός **paidagōgŏs,** *pahee-dag-o-gos´;* from *3816* and a redupl. form of *71;* a *boy-leader,* i.e. a servant whose office it was to take the children to school; (by impl. [fig.] a *tutor* ["*pæda-gogue*"]):— instructor, schoolmaster.

3808. παιδάριον **paidariŏn,** *pahee-dar´-ee-on;* neut. of a presumed der. of *3816;* a *little boy:*— child, lad.

3809. παιδεία **paidĕia,** *pahee-di´-ah;* from *3811;* *tutorage,* i.e. *education* or *training;* by impl. disciplinary *correction:*— chastening, chastisement, instruction, nurture.

3810. παιδευτής **paidĕutēs,** *pahee-dyoo-tace´;* from *3811;* a *trainer,* i.e. *teacher* or (by impl.) *discipliner:*— which corrected, instructor.

3811. παιδεύω **paidĕuō,** *pahee-dyoo´-o;* from *3816;* to *train* up a child, i.e. *educate,* or (by impl.) *discipline* (by punishment):— chasten (-ise), instruct, learn, teach.

3812. παιδιόθεν **paidiŏthĕn,** *pahee-dee-oth´-en;* adv. (of *source*) from *3813;* *from infancy:*— of a child.

3813. παιδίον **paidiŏn,** *pahee-dee´-on;* neut. dimin. of *3816;* a *childling* (of either sex), i.e. (prop.) an infant, or (by extens.) a half-grown *boy* or girl; fig. an *immature* Chr.:— (little, young) child, damsel.

3814. παιδίσκη **paidiskē,** *pahee-dis´-kay;* fem. dimin. of *3816;* a *girl,* i.e. (spec.) a *female slave* or *servant:*— bondmaid (-woman), damsel, maid (-en).

3815. παίζω **paizō,** *paheed´-zo;* from *3816;* to *sport* (as a boy):— play.

3816. παῖς **pais,** *paheece;* perh. from *3817;* a *boy* (as often *beaten* with impunity), or (by anal.) a *girl,* and (gen.) a *child;* spec. a *slave* or *servant* (espec. a *minister* to a king; and by eminence to God):— child, maid (-en), (man) servant, son, young man.

3817. παίω **paiō,** *pah´-yo;* a primary verb; to *hit* (as if by a single blow and less violently than *5180*); spec. to *sting* (as a scorpion):— smite, strike.

3818. Πακατιανή **Pakatianē,** *pak-at-ee-an-ay´;* fem. of an adj. of uncert. der.; *Pacatianian,* a section of Phrygia:— Pacatiana.

3819. πάλαι **palai,** *pal´-ahee;* prob. another form for *3825* (through the idea of *retrocession*); (adv.) *formerly,* or (by

rel.) *sometime since;* (ellip. as adj.) *ancient:*— any while, a great while ago, (of) old, in time past.

3820. παλαιός **palaiŏs,** *pal-ah-yos´;* from *3819;* *antique,* i.e. *not recent, worn out:*— old.

3821. παλαιότης **palaiŏtēs,** *pal-ah-yot´-ace;* from *3820;* *antiquatedness:*— oldness.

3822. παλαιόω **palaiŏō,** *pal-ah-yŏ´-o;* from *3820;* to *make* (pass. *become*) *worn out,* or *declare obs.:*— decay, make (wax) old.

3823. πάλη **palē,** *pal´-ay;* from πάλλω **pallō,** (to *vibrate;* another form for *906*); *wrestling:*— + wrestle.

3824. παλιγγενεσία **paliggĕnĕsia,** *pal-ing-ghen-es-ee´-ah;* from *3825* and *1078;* (spiritual) *rebirth* (the state or the act), i.e. (fig.) spiritual *renovation;* spec. Messianic *restoration:*— regeneration.

3825. πάλιν **palin,** *pal´-in;* prob. from the same as *3823* (through the idea of *oscillatory* repetition); (adv.) *anew,* i.e. (of place) *back,* (of time) *once more,* or (conjunc.) *furthermore* or *on the other hand:*— again.

3826. παμπληθεί **pamplēthĕi,** *pam-play-thi´;* dat. (adv.) of a compound of *3956* and *4128;* *in full multitude,* i.e. *concertedly* or *simultaneously:*— all at once.

3827. πάμπολυς **pampŏlus,** *pam-pol-ooce;* from *3956* and *4183;* *full many,* i.e. *immense:*— very great.

3828. Παμφυλία **Pamphulia,** *pam-fool-ee´-ah;* from a compound of *3956* and *5443;* *every-tribal,* i.e. *heterogeneous* (*5561* being impl.); *Pamphylia,* a region of Asia Minor:— Pamphylia.

3829. πανδοχεῖον **pandŏchĕiŏn,** *pan-dokh-i´-on;* neut. of a presumed compound of *3956* and a der. of *1209;* *all-receptive,* i.e. a public *lodging*-place (*caravanserai* or *khan*):— inn.

3830. πανδοχεύς **pandŏchĕus,** *pan-dokh-yooce´;* from the same as *3829;* an *innkeeper* (*warden of a caravanserai*):— host.

3831. πανήγυρις **panēguris,** *pan-ay-goo-ris´;* from *3956* and a der. of *58;* a *mass-meeting,* i.e. (fig.) *universal companionship:*— gen. assembly.

3832. πανοικί **panŏiki,** *pan-oy-kee´* or

πανοικεί **panŏikei,** *pan-oy-ki´* adv. from *3956* and *3624;* *with the whole family:*— with all his house.

3833. πανοπλία **panŏplia,** *pan-op-lee´-ah;* from a compound of *3956* and *3696;* *full armor* ("*panoply*"):— all (whole) armour.

3834. πανουργία **panŏurgia,** *pan-oorg-ee´-ah;* from *3835;* *adroitness,* i.e. (in a bad sense) *trickery* or *sophistry:*— (cunning) craftiness, subtilty (subtlety).

3835. πανοῦργος **panŏurgŏs,** *pan-oor´-gos;* from *3956* and *2041;* *all-working,* i.e. *adroit* (*shrewd*):— crafty.

3836. πανταχόθεν **pantachŏthĕn,** *pan-takh-oth´-en;* adv. (of *source*) from *3837;* *from all* directions:— from every quarter.

3837. πανταχοῦ **pantachŏu,** *pan-takh-oo´;* gen. (as adv. of *place*) of a presumed der. of *3956;* *universally:*— in all places, everywhere.

3838. παντελής **pantĕlēs,** *pan-tel-ace´;* from *3956* and *5056;* *full-ended,* i.e. *entire* (neut. as noun, *completion*):— + [no] wise, uttermost.

3839. πάντη **pantē,** *pan´-tay;* adv. (of *manner*) from *3956;* *wholly:*— always.

3840. παντόθεν **pantŏthĕn,** *pan-toth´-en;* adv. (of *source*) from *3956;* *from* (i.e. *on*) *all* sides:— on every side, round about.

3841. παντοκράτωρ **pantŏkratōr,** *pan-tok-rat´-ore;* from *3956* and *2904;* the *all-ruling,* i.e. *God* (as absolute and universal *sovereign*):— Almighty, Omnipotent.

3842. πάντοτε **pantŏtĕ,** *pan´-tot-eh;* from *3956* and *3753;* *every when,* i.e. *at all* times:— alway (-s), ever (-more).

3843. πάντως **pantōs,** *pan´-toce;* adv. from *3956;* *entirely;* spec. *at all events,* (with neg. following) *in no event:*— by all means, altogether, at all, needs, no doubt, in [no] wise, surely.

3844. παρά **para,** *par-ah´;* a primary prep.; prop. *near;* i.e. (with gen.) *from beside* (lit. or fig.), (with dat.) *at* (or *in*) the *vicinity* of (object or subject), (with acc.) to the *proximity* with (local [espec. *beyond* or *opposed* to] or causal [on *account* of]:— above, against, among, at, before, by, contrary to, × friend, from, + give [such things as they], + that [she] had, × his, in, more than, nigh unto, (out) of, past, save, side ... by, in the sight of, then, [there-] fore, with. In compounds it retains the same variety of application.

3845. παραβαίνω **parabainō,** *par-ab-ah´-ee-no;* from *3844* and the base of *939;* to *go contrary* to, i.e. *violate* a command:— (by) transgress (-ion).

3846. παραβάλλω **paraballō,** *par-ab-al´-lo;* from *3844* and *906;* to *throw alongside,* i.e. (refl.) to *reach* a place, or (fig.) to *liken:*— arrive, compare.

3847. παράβασις **parabasis,** *par-ab´-as-is;* from *3845;* *violation:*— breaking, transgression.

3848. παραβάτης **parabatēs,** *par-ab-at´-ace;* from *3845;* a *violator:*— breaker, transgress (-or).

3849. παραβιάζομαι **parabiazŏmai,** *par-ab-ee-ad´-zom-ahee;* from *3844* and the mid. voice of *971;* to *force contrary* to (nature), i.e. *compel* (by entreaty):— constrain.

3850. παραβολή **parabŏlē,** *par-ab-ol-ay´;* from *3846;* a *similitude* ("*parable*"), i.e. (symbol.) *fictitious narrative* (of common life conveying a mor.), *apothegm* or *adage:*— comparison, figure, parable, proverb.

3851. παραβουλεύομαι **parabŏulĕuŏmai,** *par-ab-ool-yoo´-om-ahee* or

παραβολεύομαι **parabŏlĕuŏmai,** *par-ab-ol-yoo´-om-ahee* from *3844,* and the mid. voice of *1011;* to *misconsult,* i.e. *disregard:*— not (to) regard (-ing).

3852. παραγγελία **paraggĕlia,** *par-ang-*

Greek

gel-ee´-ah; from *3853;* a *mandate:*— charge, command.

3853. παραγγέλλω **paraggĕllō,** *par-ang-gel´-lo;* from *3844* and the base of *32;* to *transmit a message,* i.e. (by impl.) to *enjoin:*— (give in) charge, (give) command (-ment), declare.

3854. παραγίνομαι **paraginŏmai,** *par-ag-in´-om-ahee;* from *3844* and *1096;* to *become near,* i.e. *approach* (*have arrived*); by impl. to *appear* publicly:— come, go, be present.

3855. παράγω **paragō,** *par-ag´-o;* from *3844* and *71;* to *lead near,* i.e. (refl. or intr.) to *go along* or *away:*— depart, pass (away, by, forth).

3856. παραδειγματίζω **paradĕigmatizō,** *par-ad-igue-mat-id´-zo;* from *3844* and *1165;* to *show alongside* (the public), i.e. *expose* to *infamy:*— make a public example, put to an open shame.

3857. παράδεισος **paradĕisŏs,** *par-ad´-i-sos;* of Oriental or. [comp. 6508]; a *park,* i.e. (spec.) an *Eden* (place of future happiness, *"paradise"*):— paradise.

3858. παραδέχομαι **paradĕchŏmai,** *par-ad-ekh´-om-ahee;* from *3844* and *1209;* to *accept near,* i.e. *admit* or (by impl.) *delight* in:— receive.

3859. παραδιατριβή **paradiatribē,** *par-ad-ee-at-ree-bay´;* from a compound of *3844* and *1304; misemployment,* i.e. *meddlesomeness:*— perverse disputing.

3860. παραδίδωμι **paradidōmi,** *par-ad-id´-o-mee;* from *3844* and *1325;* to *surrender,* i.e *yield up, intrust, transmit:*— betray, bring forth, cast, commit, deliver (up), give (over, up), hazard, put in prison, recommend.

3861. παράδοξος **paradŏxŏs,** *par-ad´-ox-os;* from *3844* and *1391* (in the sense of *seeming*); *contrary to expectation,* i.e. *extraordinary* (*"paradox"*):— strange.

3862. παράδοσις **paradŏsis,** *par-ad´-os-is;* from *3860; transmission,* i.e. (concr.) a *precept;* spec. the Jewish *traditionary law:*— ordinance, tradition.

3863. παραζηλόω **parazēlŏō,** *par-ad-zay-lŏ´-o;* from *3844* and *2206;* to *stimulate alongside,* i.e. *excite to rivalry:*— provoke to emulation (jealousy).

3864. παραθαλάσσιος **parathalassiŏs,** *par-ath-al-as´-see-os;* from *3844* and *2281; along the sea,* i.e. *maritime* (*lacustrine*):— upon the sea coast.

3865. παραθεωρέω **parathĕōrĕō,** *par-ath-eh-o-reh´-o;* from *3844* and *2334;* to *overlook* or *disregard:*— neglect.

3866. παραθήκη **parathēkē,** *par-ath-ay´-kay;* from *3908;* a *deposit,* i.e. (fig.) *trust:*— committed unto.

3867. παραινέω **parainĕō,** *par-ahee-neh´-o;* from *3844* and *134;* to *mispraise,* i.e. *recommend* or *advise* (a different course):— admonish, exhort.

3868. παραιτέομαι **paraitĕŏmai,** *par-ahee-teh´-om-ahee;* from *3844* and the mid. voice of *154;* to *beg off,* i.e. *deprecate, decline, shun:*— avoid, (make) excuse, intreat, refuse, reject.

3869. παρακαθίζω **parakathizō,** *par-ak-ath-id´-zo;* from *3844* and *2523;* to *sit down near:*— sit.

3870. παρακαλέω **parakalĕō,** *par-ak-al-eh´-o;* from *3844* and *2564;* to *call near,* i.e. *invite, invoke* (by *imploration, hortation* or *consolation*):— beseech, call for, (be of good) comfort, desire, (give) exhort (-ation), intreat, pray.

3871. παρακαλύπτω **parakaluptō,** *par-ak-al-oop´-to;* from *3844* and *2572;* to *cover alongside,* i.e. *veil* (fig.):— hide.

3872. παρακαταθήκη **parakatathēkē,** *par-ak-at-ath-ay´-kay;* from a compound of *3844* and *2698;* something *put down alongside,* i.e. a *deposit* (sacred *trust*):— that (thing) which is committed (un-) to (trust).

3873. παράκειμαι **parakĕimai,** *par-ak´-i-mahee;* from *3844* and *2749;* to *lie near,* i.e. *be at hand* (fig. *be prompt* or *easy*):— be present.

3874. παράκλησις **paraklēsis,** *par-ak´-lay-sis;* from *3870; imploration, hortation, solace:*— comfort, consolation, exhortation, intreaty.

3875. παράκλητος **paraklētŏs,** *par-ak´-lay-tos;* an *intercessor, consoler:*— advocate, comforter.

3876. παρακοή **parakŏē,** *par-ak-ŏ-ay´;* from *3878; inattention,* i.e. (by impl.) *disobedience:*— disobedience.

3877. παρακολουθέω **parakŏlŏuthĕō,** *par-ak-ol-oo-theh´-o;* from *3844* and *190;* to *follow near,* i.e. (fig.) *attend* (as a result), *trace out, conform* to:— attain, follow, fully know, have understanding.

3878. παρακούω **parakŏuō,** *par-ak-oo´-o;* from *3844* and *191;* to *mishear,* i.e. (by impl.) to *disobey:*— neglect to hear.

3879. παρακύπτω **parakuptō,** *par-ak-oop´-to;* from *3844* and *2955;* to *bend beside,* i.e. *lean over* (so as to *peer within*):— look (into), stoop down.

3880. παραλαμβάνω **paralambanō,** *par-al-am-ban´-o;* from *3844* and *2983;* to *receive near,* i.e. *associate with* oneself (in any familiar or intimate act or relation); by anal. to *assume* an office; fig. to *learn:*— receive, take (unto, with).

3881. παραλέγομαι **paralĕgŏmai,** *par-al-eg´-om-ahee;* from *3844* and the mid. voice of *3004* (in its orig. sense); (spec.) to *lay* one's course *near,* i.e. *sail past:*— pass, sail by.

3882. παράλιος **paraliŏs,** *par-al´-ee-os;* from *3844* and *251; beside the salt* (sea), i.e. *maritime:*— sea coast.

3883. παραλλαγή **parallagē,** *par-al-lag-ay´;* from a compound of *3844* and *236; transmutation* (of phase or orbit), i.e. (fig.) *fickleness:*— variableness.

3884. παραλογίζομαι **paralŏgizŏmai,** *par-al-og-id´-zom-ahee;* from *3844* and *3049;* to *misreckon,* i.e. *delude:*— beguile, deceive.

3885. παραλυτικός **paralutikŏs,** *par-al-oo-tee-kos´;* from a der. of *3886;* as if *dissolved,* i.e. *"paralytic":*— that had (sick of) the palsy.

3886. παραλύω **paraluō,** *par-al-oo´-o;* from *3844* and *3089;* to *loosen beside,*

i.e. *relax* (perf. pass. part. *paralyzed* or *enfeebled*):— feeble, sick of the (taken with) palsy.

3887. παραμένω **paramĕnō,** *par-am-en´-o;* from *3844* and *3306;* to *stay near,* i.e. *remain* (lit. *tarry,* or fig. *be permanent, persevere*):— abide, continue.

3888. παραμυθέομαι **paramuthĕŏmai,** *par-am-oo-theh´-om-ahee;* from *3844* and the mid. voice of a der. of *3454;* to *relate near,* i.e. (by impl.) *encourage, console:*— comfort.

3889. παραμυθία **paramuthia,** *par-am-oo-thee´-ah;* from *3888; consolation* (prop. abstr.):— comfort.

3890. παραμύθιον **paramuthiŏn,** *par-am-oo´-thee-on;* neut. of *3889; consolation* (prop. concr.):— comfort.

3891. παρανομέω **paranŏmĕō,** *par-an-om-eh´-o;* from a compound of *3844* and *3551;* to *be opposed to law,* i.e. to *transgress:*— contrary to law.

3892. παρανομία **paranŏmia,** *par-an-om-ee´-ah;* from the same as *3891; transgression:*— iniquity.

3893. παραπικραίνω **parapikrainō,** *par-ap-ik-rah´-ee-no;* from *3844* and *4087;* to *embitter alongside,* i.e. (fig.) to *exasperate:*— provoke.

3894. παραπικρασμός **parapikrasmŏs,** *par-ap-ik-ras-mos´;* from *3893; irritation:*— provocation.

3895. παραπίπτω **parapiptō,** *par-ap-ip´-to;* from *3844* and *4098;* to *fall aside,* i.e. (fig.) to *apostatize:*— fall away.

3896. παραπλέω **paraplĕō,** *par-ap-leh´-o;* from *3844* and *4126;* to *sail near:*— sail by.

3897. παραπλήσιον **paraplēsiŏn,** *par-ap-lay´-see-on;* neut. of a compound of *3844* and the base of *4139* (as adv.); *close by,* i.e. (fig.) *almost:*— nigh unto.

3898. παραπλησίως **paraplēsiōs,** *par-ap-lay-see´-oce;* adv. from the same as *3897; in a manner near by,* i.e. (fig.) *similarly:*— likewise.

3899. παραπορεύομαι **parapŏrĕuŏmai,** *par-ap-or-yoo´-om-ahee;* from *3844* and *4198;* to *travel near:*— go, pass (by).

3900. παράπτωμα **paraptōma,** *par-ap´-to-mah;* from *3895;* a *side-slip* (*lapse* or *deviation*), i.e. (unintentional) *error* or (willful) *transgression:*— fall, fault, offence, sin, trespass.

3901. παραρρυέω **pararrhuĕō,** *par-ar-hroo-eh´-o;* from *3844* and the alternate of *4482;* to *flow by,* i.e. (fig.) carelessly *pass* (*miss*):— let slip.

3902. παράσημος **parasēmŏs,** *par-as´-ay-mos;* from *3844* and the base of *4591; side-marked,* i.e. *labelled* (with a *badge* [*figure-head*] of a ship):— sign.

3903. παρασκευάζω **paraskĕuazō,** *par-ask-yoo-ad´-zo;* from *3844* and a der. of *4632;* to *furnish aside,* i.e. *get ready:*— prepare self, be (make) ready.

3904. παρασκευή **paraskĕuē,** *par-ask-yoo-ay´;* as if from *3903; readiness:*— preparation.

3905. παρατείνω **paratĕinō,** *par-at-i´-no;* from *3844* and *τείνω* **tĕinō** (to stretch); to *extend along,* i.e. *prolong* (in point of time):— continue.

3906. παρατηρέω **paratērĕō**, par-at-ay-reh´-o; from 3844 and 5083; to inspect alongside, i.e. note insidiously or scrupulously:— observe, watch.

3907. παρατήρησις **paratērēsis**, par-at-ay´-ray-sis; from 3906; inspection, i.e. ocular evidence:— observation.

3908. παρατίθημι **paratithēmi**, par-at-ith´-ay-mee; from 3844 and 5087; to place alongside, i.e. present (food, truth); by impl. to deposit (as a trust or for protection):— allege, commend, commit (the keeping of), put forth, set before.

3909. παρατυγχάνω **paratugchanō**, par-at-oong-khan´-o; from 3844 and 5177; to chance near, i.e. fall in with:— meet with.

3910. παραυτίκα **parautika**, par-ŏw-tee´-kah; from 3844 and a der. of 846; at the very instant, i.e. momentary:— but for a moment.

3911. παραφέρω **paraphĕrō**, par-af-er´-o; from 3844 and 5342 (incl. its alt. forms); to bear along or aside, i.e. carry off (lit. or fig.); by impl. to avert:— remove, take away.

3912. παραφρονέω **paraphrŏnĕō**, par-af-ron-eh´-o; from 3844 and 5426; to misthink, i.e. be insane (silly):— as a fool.

3913. παραφρονία **paraphrŏnia**, par-af-ron-ee´-ah; from 3912; insanity, i.e. foolhardiness:— madness.

3914. παραχειμάζω **parachĕimazō**, par-akh-i-mad´-zo; from 3844 and 5492; to winter near, i.e. stay with over the rainy season:— winter.

3915. παραχειμασία **parachĕimasia**, par-akh-i-mas-ee´-ah; from 3914; a wintering over:— winter in.

3916. παραχρῆμα **parachrēma**, par-akh-ray´-mah; from 3844 and 5536 (in its orig. sense); at the thing itself, i.e. instantly:— forthwith, immediately, presently, straightway, soon.

3917. πάρδαλις **pardalis**, par´-dal-is; fem. of πάρδος pardŏs (a panther); a leopard:— leopard.

3918. πάρειμι **parĕimi**, par´-i-mee; from 3844 and 1510 (incl. its various forms); to be near, i.e. at hand; neut. pres. part. (sing.) time being, or (plural) property:— come, × have, be here, + lack, (be here) present.

3919. παρεισάγω **parĕisagō**, par-ice-ag´-o; from 3844 and 1521; to lead in aside, i.e. introduce surreptitiously:— privily bring in.

3920. παρείσακτος **parĕisaktŏs**, par-ice´-ak-tos; from 3919; smuggled in:— unawares brought in.

3921. παρεισδύνω **parĕisdunō**, par-ice-doo´-no; from 3844 and a compound of 1519 and 1416; to settle in alongside, i.e. lodge stealthily:— creep in unawares.

3922. παρεισέρχομαι **parĕisĕrchŏmai**, par-ice-er´-khom-ahee; from 3844 and 1525; to come in alongside, i.e. supervene additionally or stealthily:— come in privily, enter.

3923. παρεισφέρω **parĕisphĕrō**, par-ice-fer´-o; from 3844 and 1533; to bear in

alongside, i.e. introduce simultaneously:— give.

3924. παρεκτός **parĕktŏs**, par-ek-tos´; from 3844 and 1622; near outside, i.e. besides:— except, saving, without.

3925. παρεμβολή **parĕmbŏlē**, par-em-bol-ay´; from a compound of 3844 and 1685; a throwing in beside (juxtaposition), i.e. (spec.) battle-array, encampment or barracks (tower Antonia):— army, camp, castle.

3926. παρενοχλέω **parĕnŏchlĕō**, par-en-okh-leh´-o; from 3844 and 1776; to harass further, i.e. annoy:— trouble.

3927. παρεπίδημος **parepidēmŏs**, par-ep-id´-ay-mos; from 3844 and the base of 1927; an alien alongside, i.e. a resident foreigner:— pilgrim, stranger.

3928. παρέρχομαι **parĕrchŏmai**, par-er´-khom-ahee; from 3844 and 2064; to come near or aside, i.e. to approach (arrive), go by (or away), (fig.) perish or neglect, (caus.) avert:— come (forth), go, pass (away, by, over), past, transgress.

3929. πάρεσις **parēsis**, par´-es-is; from 2935; prætermission, i.e. toleration:— remission.

3930. παρέχω **parĕchō**, par-ekh´-o; from 3844 and 2192; to hold near, i.e. present, afford, exhibit, furnish occasion:— bring, do, give, keep, minister, offer, shew, + trouble.

3931. παρηγορία **parēgŏria**, par-ay-gor-ee´-ah; from a compound of 3844 and a der. of 58 (mean. to harangue an assembly); an address alongside, i.e. (spec.) consolation:— comfort.

3932. παρθενία **parthĕnia**, par-then-ee´-ah; from 3933; maidenhood:— virginity.

3933. παρθένος **parthĕnŏs**, par-then´-os; of unknown or.; a maiden; by impl. an unmarried daughter:— virgin.

3934. Πάρθος **Parthŏs**, par´-thos; prob. of for. or.; a Parthian, i.e. inhab. of Parthia:— Parthian.

3935. παρίημι **pariēmi**, par-ee´-ay-mi; from 3844 and ἵημι hiēmi, (to send); to let by, i.e. relax:— hang down.

3936. παρίστημι **paristēmi**, par-is´-tay-mee; or prol.

παριστάνω **paristanō** par-is-tan´-o; from 3844, and 2476; to stand beside, i.e. (tran.) to exhibit, proffer, (spec.) recommend, (fig.) substantiate; or (intr.) to be at hand (or ready), aid:— assist, bring before, command, commend, give presently, present, prove, provide, shew, stand (before, by, here, up, with), yield.

3937. Παρμενᾶς **Parmĕnas**, par-men-as´; prob. by contr. for Παρμενίδης Parmĕnidēs (a der. of a compound of 3844 and 3306); constant; Parmenas, a Chr.:— Parmenas.

3938. πάροδος **parŏdŏs**, par´-od-os; from 3844 and 3598; a by-road, i.e. (act.) a route:— way.

3939. παροικέω **parŏikĕō**, par-oy-keh´-o; from 3844 and 3611; to dwell near, i.e. reside as a foreigner:— sojourn in, be a stranger.

3940. παροικία **parŏikia**, par-oy-kee´-ah; from 3941; foreign residence:— sojourning, × as strangers.

3941. πάροικος **parŏikŏs**, par´-oy-kos; from 3844 and 3624; having a home near, i.e. (as noun) a by-dweller (alien resident):— foreigner, sojourn, stranger.

3942. παροιμία **parŏimia**, par-oy-mee´-ah; from a compound of 3844 and perh. a der. of 3633; appar. a state alongside of supposition, i.e. (concr.) an adage; spec. an enigmatical or fictitious illustration:— parable, proverb.

3943. πάροινος **parŏinŏs**, par´-oy-nos; from 3844 and 3631; staying near wine, i.e. tippling (a toper):— given to wine.

3944. παροίχομαι **parŏichŏmai**, par-oy´-khom-ahee; from 3844 and οἴχομαι ŏichŏmai (to depart); to escape along, i.e. be gone:— past.

3945. παρομοιάζω **parŏmŏiazō**, par-om-oy-ad´-zo; from 3946; to resemble:— be like unto.

3946. παρόμοιος **parŏmŏiŏs**, par-om´-oy-os; from 3844 and 3664; alike nearly, i.e. similar:— like.

3947. παροξύνω **parŏxunō**, par-ox-oo´-no; from 3844 and a der. of 3691; to sharpen alongside, i.e. (fig.) to exasperate:— easily provoke, stir.

3948. παροξυσμός **parŏxusmŏs**, par-ox-oos-mos´; from 3947 ("paroxysm"); incitement (to good), or dispute (in anger):— contention, provoke unto.

3949. παροργίζω **parŏrgizō**, par-org-id´-zo; from 3844 and 3710; to anger alongside, i.e. enrage:— anger, provoke to wrath.

3950. παροργισμός **parŏrgismŏs**, par-org-is-mos´; from 3949; rage:— wrath.

3951. παροτρύνω **parŏtrunō**, par-ot-roo´-no; from 3844 and ὀτρύνω ŏtrunō (to spur); to urge along, i.e. stimulate (to hostility):— stir up.

3952. παρουσία **parŏusia**, par-oo-see´-ah; from the present part. of 3918; a being near, i.e. advent (often, return; spec. of Christ to punish Jerusalem, or finally the wicked); (by impl.) phys. aspect:— coming, presence.

3953. παροψίς **parŏpsis**, par-op-sis´; from 3844 and the base of 3795; a side-dish (the receptacle):— platter.

3954. παρρησία **parrhēsia**, par-rhay-see´-ah; from 3956 and a der. of 4483; all out-spokenness, i.e. frankness, bluntness, publicity; by impl. assurance:— bold (× -ly, -ness, -ness of speech), confidence, × freely, × openly, × plainly (-ness).

3955. παρρησιάζομαι **parrhēsiazŏmai**, par-hray-see-ad´-zom-ahee; mid. voice from 3954; to be frank in utterance, or confident in spirit and demeanor:— be (wax) bold, (preach, speak) boldly.

3956. πᾶς **pas** pas; incl. all the forms of declension; appar. a primary word; all, any, every, the whole:— all (manner of, means), alway (-s), any (one), × daily, + ever, every (one, way), as many as, + (-thing), × thoroughly, whatsoever, whole, whosoever.

3957. πάσχα **pascha**, *pas´-khah;* of Chald. or. [comp. 6453]; the *Passover* (the meal, the day, the festival or the special sacrifices connected with it):— Easter, Passover.

3958. πάσχω **paschō**, *pas´-kho;* incl. the forms

πάθω (**pathō**, *path´-o*) and

πένθω (**pĕnthō**, *pen´-tho*), used only in certain tenses for it; appar. a primary verb; to *experience* a sensation or impression (usually painful):— feel, passion, suffer, vex.

3959. Πάταρα **Patara**, *pat´-ar-ah;* prob. of for. or.; *Patara*, a place in Asia Minor:— Patara.

3960. πατάσσω **patassō**, *pat-as´-so;* prob. prol. from 3817; to *knock* (gently or with a weapon or fatally):— smite, strike. Comp. 5180.

3961. πατέω **patĕō**, *pat-eh´-o;* from a der. prob. of 3817 (mean. a *"path"*); to *trample* (lit. or fig.):— tread (down, under foot).

3962. πατήρ **patĕr**, *pat-ayr´;* appar. a primary word; a *"father"* (lit. or fig., near or more remote):— father, parent.

3963. Πάτμος **Patmŏs**, *pat´-mos;* of uncert. der.; *Patmus*, an islet in the Mediterranean:— Patmos.

3964. πατραλῴας **patralōas**, *pat-ral-o´-as* πατρολῴας **patrŏlōas**, *pat-rol-o´-as;* from 3962 and the same as the latter part of 3389; a *parricide:*— murderer of fathers.

3965. πατριά **patria**, *pat-ree-ah´;* as if fem. of a der. of 3962; paternal *descent,* i.e. (concr.) a *group* of families or a whole *race* (*nation*):— family, kindred, lineage.

3966. πατριάρχης **patriarchēs**, *pat-ree-arkh´-ace;* from 3965 and 757; a *progenitor* ("patriarch"):— patriarch.

3967. πατρικός **patrikŏs**, *pat-ree-kos´;* from 3962; *paternal,* i.e. *ancestral:*— of fathers.

3968. πατρίς **patris**, *pat-rece´;* from 3962; a *father-land,* i.e. *native town;* (fig.) heavenly *home:*— (own) country.

3969. Πατρόβας **Patrŏbas**, *pat-rob´-as;* perh. contr. for Πατρόβιος **Patrŏbiŏs** (a compound of 3962 and 979); *father's life; Patrobas,* a Chr.:— Patrobas.

3970. πατροπαράδοτος **patrŏparadŏtŏs**, *pat-rop-ar-ad´-ot-os;* from 3962 and a der. of 3860 (in the sense of *handing over* or *down*); *traditionary:*— received by tradition from fathers.

3971. πατρῷος **patrōjŏs**, *pat-ro´-os;* from 3962; *paternal,* i.e. *hereditary:*— of fathers.

3972. Παῦλος **Paulŏs**, *pŏw´-los;* of Lat. or.; (*little;* but remotely from a der. of 3973, mean. the same); *Paulus,* the name of a Rom. and of an apostle:— Paul, Paulus.

3973. παύω **pauō**, *pŏw´-o;* a primary verb (*"pause"*); to *stop* (tran. or intr.), i.e. *restrain, quit, desist, come to an end:*— cease, leave, refrain.

3974. Πάφος **Paphŏs**, *paf´-os;* of uncert.

der.; *Paphus,* a place in Cyprus:— Paphos.

3975. παχύνω **pachunō**, *pakh-oo´-no;* from a der. of 4078 (mean. *thick*); to *thicken,* i.e. (by impl.) to *fatten* (fig. *stupefy* or *render callous*):— wax gross.

3976. πέδη **pĕdē**, *ped´-ay;* ultimately from 4228; a *shackle* for the feet:— fetter.

3977. πεδινός **pĕdinŏs**, *ped-ee-nos´;* from a der. of 4228 (mean. the *ground*); *level* (as easy for the *feet*):— plain.

3978. πεζεύω **pĕzĕuō**, *ped-zyoo´-o;* from the same as 3979; to *foot* a journey, i.e. *travel* by land:— go afoot.

3979. πεζῇ **pĕzĕi**, *ped-zay´;* dat. fem. of a der. of 4228 (as adv.); *foot-wise,* i.e. by *walking:*— a- (on) foot.

3980. πειθαρχέω **pĕitharchĕō**, *pi-tharkh-eh´-o;* from a compound of 3982 and 757; to *be persuaded* by a *ruler,* i.e. (gen.) to *submit* to authority; by anal. to *conform* to advice:— hearken, obey (magistrates).

3981. πειθός **pĕithŏs**, *pi-thos´;* from 3982; *persuasive:*— enticing.

3982. πείθω **pĕithō**, *pi´-tho;* a primary verb; to *convince* (by argument, true or false); by anal. to *pacify* or *conciliate* (by other fair means); refl. or pass. to *assent* (to evidence or authority), to *rely* (by inward certainty):— agree, assure, believe, have confidence, be (wax) confident, make friend, obey, persuade, trust, yield.

3983. πεινάω **pĕinaō**, *pi-nah´-o;* from the same as 3993 (through the idea of pinching *toil; "pine"*); to *famish* (absol. or comp.); fig. to *crave:*— be an hungered.

3984. πεῖρα **pĕira**, *pi´-rah;* from the base of 4008 (through the idea of *piercing*); a *test,* i.e. *attempt, experience:*— assaying, trial.

3985. πειράζω **pĕirazō**, *pi-rad´-zo;* from 3984; to *test* (obj.), i.e. *endeavor, scrutinize, entice, discipline:*— assay, examine, go about, prove, tempt (-er), try.

3986. πειρασμός **pĕirasmŏs**, *pi-rasmos´;* from 3985; a putting to *proof* (by experiment [of good], *experience* [of evil], solicitation, discipline or provocation); by impl. *adversity:*— temptation, × try.

3987. πειράω **pĕiraō**, *pi-rah´-o;* from 3984; to *test* (subj.), i.e. (refl.) to *attempt:*— assay.

3988. πεισμονή **pĕismŏnē**, *pice-monay´;* from a presumed der. of 3982; *persuadableness,* i.e. *credulity:*— persuasion.

3989. πέλαγος **pĕlagŏs**, *pel´-ag-os;* of uncert. aff.; deep or open *sea,* i.e. the *main:*— depth, sea.

3990. πελεκίζω **pĕlĕkizō**, *pel-ek-id´-zo;* from a der. of 4141 (mean. an *axe*); to *chop* off (the head), i.e. *truncate:*— behead.

3991. πέμπτος **pĕmptŏs**, *pemp´-tos;* from 4002; *fifth:*— fifth.

3992. πέμπω **pĕmpō**, *pem´-po;* appar. a primary verb; to *dispatch* (from the subj. view or point of *departure,*

whereas ἵημι **hiĕmi** [as a stronger form of εἶμι **ĕimi**] refers rather to the obj. point or *terminus ad quem,* and 4724 denotes prop. the *orderly* motion involved), espec. on a temporary errand; also to *transmit, bestow,* or *wield:*— send, thrust in.

3993. πένης **pĕnēs**, *pen´-ace;* from a primary πένω **pĕnō**, (to *toil* for daily subsistence); *starving,* i.e. *indigent:*— poor. Comp. 4434.

3994. πενθερά **pĕnthĕra**, *pen-ther-ah´;* fem. of 3995; a *wife's mother:*— mother in law, wife's mother.

3995. πενθερός **pĕnthĕrŏs**, *pen-ther-os´;* of uncert. aff.; a *wife's father:*— father in law.

3996. πενθέω **pĕnthĕō**, *pen-theh´-o;* from 3997; to *grieve* (the feeling or the act):— mourn, (be-) wail.

3997. πένθος **pĕnthŏs**, *pen´-thos;* strengthened from the alt. of 3958; *grief:*— mourning, sorrow.

3998. πενιχρός **pĕnichrŏs**, *pen-ikh-ros´;* prol. from the base of 3993; *necessitous:*— poor.

3999. πεντακίς **pĕntakis**, *pen-tak-ece´;* mult. adv. from 4002; *five times:*— five times.

4000. πεντακισχίλιοι **pĕntakischiliŏi**, *pen-tak-is-khil´-ee-oy;* from 3999 and 5507; *five times a thousand:*— five thousand.

4001. πεντακόσιοι **pĕntakŏsiŏi**, *pen-tak-os´-ee-oy;* from 4002 and 1540; *five hundred:*— five hundred.

4002. πέντε **pĕntĕ**, *pen´-teh;* a primary number; *"five":*— five.

4003. πεντεκαιδέκατος **pĕntĕkaidĕkatŏs**, *pen-tek-ahee-dek´-at-os;* from 4002 and 2532 and 1182; *five and tenth:*— fifteenth.

4004. πεντήκοντα **pĕntēkŏnta**, *pen-tay´-kon-tah;* mult. of 4002; *fifty:*— fifty.

4005. πεντηκοστή **pĕntēkŏstē**, *pen-tay-kos-tay´;* fem. of the ord. of 4004; *fiftieth* (2250 being impl.) from Passover, i.e. the festival of *"Pentecost":*— Pentecost.

4006. πεποίθησις **pĕpŏithēsis**, *pep-oy´-thay-sis;* from the perfect of the alt. of 3958; *reliance:*— confidence, trust.

4007. περ **pĕr**, *per;* from the base of 4008; an enclitic particle significant of *abundance* (thoroughness), i.e. *emphasis; much, very* or *ever:*— [whom-] soever.

4008. πέραν **pĕran**, *per´-an;* appar. acc. of an obs. der. of πείρω **pĕirō**, (to *"pierce"*); *through* (as adv. or prep.), i.e. *across:*— beyond, farther (other) side, over.

4009. πέρας **pĕras**, *per´-as;* from the same as 4008; an *extremity:*— end, ut- (ter-) most part.

4010. Πέργαμος **Pĕrgamŏs**, *per´-gam-os;* from 4444; *fortified; Pergamus,* a place in Asia Minor:— Pergamos.

4011. Πέργη **Pĕrgē**, *perg´-ay;* prob. from the same as 4010; a *tower; Perga,* a place in Asia Minor:— Perga.

4012. περί **pĕri**, *per-ee´;* from the base of 4008; prop. *through* (all over), i.e.

around; fig. *with respect* to; used in various applications, of place, cause or time (with the gen. denoting the *subject* or *occasion* or *superlative* point; with the acc. the *locality, circuit, matter, circumstance* or general *period*):— (there-) about, above, against, at, on behalf of, × and his company, which concern, (as) concerning, for, × how it will go with, ((there-, where-)) of, on, over, pertaining (to), for sake, × (e-) state, (as) touching, (where-) by (in), with. In composition it retains substantially the same meaning of circuit (*around*), excess (*beyond*), or completeness (*through*).

4013. περιάγω **pĕriagō**, *per-ee-ag´-o;* from 4012 and 71; to *take around* (as a companion); refl. to *walk around:*— compass, go (round) about, lead about.

4014. περιαιρέω **pĕriairĕō**, *per-ee-aheereh´-o;* from 4012 and 138 (incl. its alt.); to *remove* all *around,* i.e. *unveil, cast off* (anchor); fig. to *expiate:*— take away (up).

4015. περιαστράπτω **pĕriastraptō**, *per-ee-as-trap´-to;* from 4012 and 797; to *flash* all *around,* i.e. *to envelop in light:*— shine round (about).

4016. περιβάλλω **pĕriballō**, *per-ee-bal´-lo;* from 4012 and 906; to *throw* all *around,* i.e. *invest* (with a palisade or with clothing):— array, cast about, clothe (-d me), put on.

4017. περιβλέπω **pĕriblĕpō**, *per-ee-blep´-o;* from 4012 and 991; to *look* all *around:*— look (round) about (on).

4018. περιβόλαιον **pĕribŏlaiŏn**, *per-ib-ol´-ah-yon;* neut. of a presumed der. of 4016; something *thrown around* one, i.e. a *mantle, veil:*— covering, vesture.

4019. περιδέω **pĕridĕō**, *per-ee-deh´-o;* from 4012 and 1210; to *bind around* one, i.e. *enwrap:*— bind about.

περιδρέμω **pĕridrĕmō**. See 4063.

περιέλλω **pĕriĕllō**. See 4014.

περιέλθω **pĕriĕlthō**. See 4022.

4020. περιεργάζομαι **pĕriĕrgazŏmai**, *per-ee-er-gad´-zom-ahee;* from 4012 and 2038; to *work* all *around,* i.e. *bustle about* (*meddle*):— be a busybody.

4021. περίεργος **pĕriĕrgŏs**, *per-ee´-er-gos;* from 4012 and 2041; *working all around,* i.e. *officious* (*meddlesome,* neut. plur. *magic*):— busybody, curious arts.

4022. περιέρχομαι **pĕriĕrchŏmai**, *per-ee-er´-khom-ahee;* from 4012 and 2064 (incl. its alt.); to *come* all *around,* i.e. *stroll, vacillate, veer:*— fetch a compass, vagabond, wandering about.

4023. περιέχω **pĕriĕchō**, *per-ee-ekh´-o;* from 4012 and 2192; to *hold* all *around,* i.e. *include, clasp* (fig.):— + astonished, contain, after (this manner).

4024. περιζώννυμι **pĕrizŏnnumi**, *per-id-zone´-noo-mee;* from 4012 and 2224; to *gird* all *around,* i.e. (middle or passive voice) to *fasten on one's belt* (lit. or fig.):— gird (about, self).

4025. περίθεσις **pĕrithĕsis**, *per-ith´-es-is;* from 4060; a *putting* all *around,* i.e. *decorating* oneself with:— wearing.

4026. περιίστημι **pĕriistēmi**, *per-ee-is´-tay-mee;* from 4012 and 2476; to *stand* all *around,* i.e. (near) to *be a bystander,* or (aloof) to *keep away* from:— avoid, shun, stand by (round about).

4027. περικάθαρμα **pĕrikatharma**, *per-ee-kath´-ar-mah;* from a compound of 4012 and 2508; something *cleaned* off all *around,* i.e. *refuse* (fig.):— filth.

4028. περικαλύπτω **pĕrikaluptō**, *per-ee-kal-oop´-to;* from 4012 and 2572; to *cover* all *around,* i.e. *entirely* (the face, a surface):— blindfold, cover, overlay.

4029. περίκειμαι **pĕrikĕimai**, *per-ik´-i-mahee;* from 4012 and 2749; to *lie* all *around,* i.e. *enclose, encircle, hamper* (lit. or fig.):— be bound (compassed) with, hang about.

4030. περικεφαλαία **pĕrikĕphalaia**, *per-ee-kef-al-ah´-yah;* fem. of a compound of 4012 and 2776; *encirclement of the head,* i.e. a *helmet:*— helmet.

4031. περικρατής **pĕrikratēs**, *per-ee-krat-ace´;* from 4012 and 2904; *strong* all *around,* i.e. a *master* (*manager*):— + come by.

4032. περικρύπτω **pĕrikruptō**, *per-ee-kroop´-to;* from 4012 and 2928; to *conceal* all *around,* i.e. *entirely:*— hide.

4033. περικυκλόω **pĕrikuklŏō**, *per-ee-koo-klŏ´-o;* from 4012 and 2944; to *encircle* all *around,* i.e. *blockade completely:*— compass round.

4034. περιλάμπω **pĕrilampō**, *per-ee-lam´-po;* from 4012 and 2989; to *illuminate* all *around,* i.e. *invest with a halo:*— shine round about.

4035. περιλείπω **pĕrilĕipō**, *per-ee-li´-po;* from 4012 and 3007; to *leave* all *around,* i.e. (pass.) *survive:*— remain.

4036. περίλυπος **pĕrilupŏs**, *per-il´-oo-pos;* from 4012 and 3077; *grieved* all *around,* i.e. *intensely sad:*— exceeding (very) sorry (-owful).

4037. περιμένω **pĕrimĕnō**, *per-ee-men´-o;* from 4012 and 3306; to *stay around,* i.e. *await:*— wait for.

4038. πέριξ **pĕrix**, *per´-ix;* adv. from 4012; *all around,* i.e. (as an adj.) *circumjacent:*— round about.

4039. περιοικέω **pĕriŏikĕō**, *per-ee-oy-keh´-o;* from 4012 and 3611; to *reside around,* i.e. *be a neighbor:*— dwell round about.

4040. περίοικος **pĕriŏikŏs**, *per-ee´-oy-kos;* from 4012 and 3624; *housed around,* i.e. *neighboring* (ellip. used as a noun):— neighbour.

4041. περιούσιος **pĕriŏusiŏs**, *per-ee-oo´-see-os;* from the pres. part. fem. of a compound of 4012 and 1510; *being beyond* usual, i.e. *special* (one's *own*):— peculiar.

4042. περιοχή **pĕriŏchē**, *per-ee-okh-ay´;* from 4023; a *being held around,* i.e. (concr.) a *passage* (of Scripture, as *circumscribed*):— place.

4043. περιπατέω **pĕripatĕō**, *per-ee-pat-eh´-o;* from 4012 and 3961; to *tread* all *around,* i.e. *walk at large* (espec. as proof of ability); fig. to *live, deport oneself, follow* (as a companion or vo-

tary):— go, be occupied with, walk (about).

4044. περιπείρω **pĕripĕirō**, *per-ee-pi´-ro;* from 4012 and the base of 4008; to *penetrate entirely,* i.e. *transfix* (fig.):— pierce through.

4045. περιπίπτω **pĕripiptō**, *per-ee-pip´-to;* from 4012 and 4098; to *fall into* something i.e. all *around,* i.e. *light among* or *upon, be surrounded with:*— fall among (into).

4046. περιποιέομαι **pĕripŏiĕŏmai**, *per-ee-poy-eh´-om-ahee;* mid. voice from 4012 and 4160; to *make around oneself,* i.e. *acquire* (*buy*):— purchase.

4047. περιποίησις **pĕripŏiēsis**, *per-ee-poy´-ay-sis;* from 4046; *acquisition* (the act or the thing); by extens. *preservation:*— obtain (-ing), peculiar, purchased, possession, saving.

4048. περιρρήγνυμι **pĕrirrhēgnumi**, *per-ir-hrayg´-noo-mee;* from 4012 and 4486; to *tear* all *around,* i.e. *completely away:*— rend off.

4049. περισπάω **pĕrispaō**, *per-ee-spah´-o;* from 4012 and 4685; to *drag* all *around,* i.e. (fig.) to *distract* (with care):— cumber.

4050. περισσεία **pĕrissĕia**, *per-is-si´-ah;* from 4052; *surplusage,* i.e. *superabundance:*— abundance (-ant, (-ly)), superfluity.

4051. περίσσευμα **pĕrissĕuma**, *per-is´-syoo-mah;* from 4052; a *surplus,* or *superabundance:*— abundance, that was left, over and above.

4052. περισσεύω **pĕrissĕuō**, *per-is-syoo´-o;* from 4053; to *superabound* (in quantity or quality), *be in excess, be superfluous;* also (tran.) to *cause to superabound* or *excel:*— (make, more) abound, (have, have more) abundance (be more) abundant, be the better, enough and to spare, exceed, excel, increase, be left, redound, remain (over and above).

4053. περισσός **pĕrissŏs**, *per-is-sos´;* from 4012 (in the sense of *beyond*); *superabundant* (in quantity) or *superior* (in quality); by impl. *excessive;* adv. (with 1537) *violently;* neut. (as noun) *preeminence:*— exceeding abundantly above, more abundantly, advantage, exceedingly, very highly, beyond measure, more, superfluous, vehement (-ly).

4054. περισσότερον **pĕrissŏtĕron**, *per-is-sot´-er-on;* neut. of 4055 (as adv.); in a *more superabundant* way:— more abundantly, a great deal, far more.

4055. περισσότερος **pĕrissŏtĕrŏs**, *per-is-sot´-er-os;* comp. of 4053; *more superabundant* (in number, degree or character):— more abundant, greater (much) more, overmuch.

4056. περισσοτέρως **pĕrissŏtĕrōs**, *per-is-sot-er´-oce;* adv. from 4055; *more superabundantly:*— more abundant (-ly), × the more earnest, (more) exceedingly, more frequent, much more, the rather.

4057. περισσῶς **pĕrissōs**, *per-is-soce´;* adv. from 4053; *superabundantly:*— exceedingly, out of measure, the more.

Greek

4058. περιστερά **pĕristĕra**, *per-is-ter-ah´;* of uncert. der.; a *pigeon:*— dove, pigeon.

4059. περιτέμνω **pĕritĕmnō**, *per-ee-tem´-no;* from *4012* and the base of *5114;* to *cut around,* i.e. (spec.) to *circumcise:*— circumcise.

4060. περιτίθημι **pĕritithēmi**, *per-ee-tith´-ay-mee;* from *4012* and *5087;* to *place around;* by impl. to *present:*— bestow upon, hedge round about, put about (on, upon), set about.

4061. περιτομή **pĕritŏmē**, *per-it-om-ay´;* from *4059; circumcision* (the rite, the condition or the people, lit. or fig.):— × circumcised, circumcision.

4062. περιτρέπω **pĕritrĕpō**, *per-ee-trep´-o;* from *4012* and the base of *5157;* to *turn around,* i.e. (ment.) to *craze:*— + make mad.

4063. περιτρέχω **pĕritrĕchō**, *per-ee-trekh´-o;* from *4012* and *5143* (incl. its alt.); to *run around,* i.e. *traverse:*— run through.

4064. περιφέρω **pĕriphĕrō**, *per-ee-fer´-o;* from *4012* and *5342;* to *convey around,* i.e. *transport hither and thither:*— bear (carry) about.

4065. περιφρονέω **pĕriphrŏneō**, *per-ee-fron-eh´-o;* from *4012* and *5426;* to *think beyond,* i.e. *depreciate (contemn):*— despise.

4066. περίχωρος **pĕrichōrŏs**, *per-ikh´-o-ros;* from *4012* and *5561; around* the *region,* i.e. *circumjacent* (as noun, with *1093* impl. *vicinity*):— country (round) about, region (that lieth) round about.

4067. περίψωμα **pĕripsōma**, *per-ip´-so-mah* or

περίψημα **pĕripsēma**, *per-ip´-say-mah;* from a compound of *4012* and ψάω psaō (to *rub*); something *brushed all around,* i.e. *off-scrapings* (fig. *scum*):— offscouring.

4068. περπερεύομαι **pĕrpĕrĕuŏmai**, *per-per-yoo´-om-ahee;* mid. voice from πέρπερος **pĕrpĕrŏs** (*braggart;* perh. by redupl. of the base of *4008*); to *boast:*— vaunt itself.

4069. Περσίς **Pĕrsis**, *per-sece´;* a *Pers.* woman; *Persis,* a Chr. female:— Persis.

4070. πέρυσι **pĕrusi**, *per´-oo-si;* adv. from *4009;* the *by-gone,* i.e. (as noun) *last year:*— + a year ago.

πετάομαι **pĕtaŏmai**. See *4072.*

4071. πετεινόν **pĕtĕinŏn**, *pet-i-non´;* neut. of a der. of *4072;* a *flying* animal, i.e. *bird:*— bird, fowl.

4072. πέτομαι **pĕtŏmai**, *pet´-om-ahee;* or prol.

πετάομαι **pĕtaŏmai**, *pet-ah´-om-ahee;* or contr. πτάομαι **ptaŏmai**, *ptah´-om-ahee;* mid. voice of a primary verb; to *fly:*— fly (-ing).

4073. πέτρα **pĕtra**, *pet´-ra;* fem. of the same as *4074;* a (mass of) *rock* (lit. or fig.):— rock.

4074. Πέτρος **Pĕtrŏs**, *pet´-ros;* appar. a primary word; a (piece of) *rock* (larger than *3037*); as a name, *Petrus,* an apostle:— Peter, rock. Comp. *2786.*

4075. πετρώδης **pĕtrōdēs**, *pet-ro´-dace;*

from *4073* and *1491; rock-like,* i.e. *rocky:*— stony.

4076. πήγανον **pēganŏn**, *pay´-gan-on;* from *4078; rue* (from its thick or fleshy leaves):— rue.

4077. πηγή **pēgē**, *pay-gay´;* prob. from *4078* (through the idea of *gushing* plumply); a *fount* (lit. or fig.), i.e. *source* or *supply* (of water, blood, enjoyment) (not necessarily the orig. spring):— fountain, well.

4078. πήγνυμι **pēgnumi**, *payg´-noo-mee;* a prol. form of a primary verb (which in its simpler form occurs only as an alt. in certain tenses); to *fix* ("*peg*"), i.e. (spec.) to *set up* (a tent):— pitch.

4079. πηδάλιον **pēdalion**, *pay-dal´-ee-on;* neut. of a (presumed) der. of πηδόν **pēdŏn** (the *blade* of an oar; from the same as *3976*); a "*pedal*," i.e. *helm:*— rudder.

4080. πηλίκος **pēlikŏs**, *pay-lee´-kos;* a quantitative form (the fem.) of the base of *4225; how much* (as an indef.), i.e. in size or (fig.) dignity:— how great (large).

4081. πηλός **pēlos**, *pay-los´;* perh. a primary word; *clay:*— clay.

4082. πήρα **pēra**, *pay´-rah;* of uncert. aff.; a *wallet* or leather *pouch* for food:— scrip.

4083. πῆχυς **pēchus**, *pay´-khoos;* of uncert. aff.; the *fore-arm,* i.e. (as a measure) a *cubit:*— cubit.

4084. πιάζω **piazō**, *pee-ad´-zo;* prob. another form of *971;* to *squeeze,* i.e. *seize* (gently by the hand [*press*], or officially [*arrest*], or in hunting [*capture*]):— apprehend, catch, lay hand on, take. Comp. *4085.*

4085. πιέζω **piĕzō**, *pee-ed´-zo;* another form for *4084;* to *pack:*— press down.

4086. πιθανολογία **pithanŏlŏgia**, *pith-an-ol-og-ee´-ah;* from a compound of a der. of *3982* and *3056; persuasive language:*— enticing words.

4087. πικραίνω **pikrainō**, *pik-rah´-ee-no;* from *4089;* to *embitter* (lit. or fig.):— be (make) bitter.

4088. πικρία **pikria**, *pik-ree´-ah;* from *4089; acridity* (espec. *poison*), lit. or fig.:— bitterness.

4089. πικρός **pikrŏs**, *pik-ros´;* perh. from *4078* (through the idea of *piercing*); *sharp* (*pungent*), i.e. *acrid* (lit. or fig.):— bitter.

4090. πικρῶς **pikrōs**, *pik-roce´;* adv. from *4089; bitterly,* i.e. (fig.) *violently:*— bitterly.

4091. Πιλᾶτος **Pilatŏs**, *pil-at´-os;* of Lat. or.; *close-pressed,* i.e. *firm; Pilatus,* a Rom.:— Pilate.

πίμπλημι **pimplēmi**. See *4130.*

4092. πίμπρημι **pimprēmi**, *pim´-pray-mee;* a redupl. and prol. form of a primary

πρέω **prēō**, *preh´-o;* which occurs only as an alt. in certain tenses); to *fire,* i.e. *burn* (fig. and pass. *become inflamed* with fever):— be (× should have) swollen.

4093. πινακίδιον **pinakidiŏn**, *pin-ak-id´-ee-on;* dimin. of *4094;* a *tablet* (for writing on):— writing table.

4094. πίναξ **pinax**, *pin´-ax;* appar. a form of *4109;* a *plate:*— charger, platter.

4095. πίνω **pinō**, *pee´-no;* a prol. form of

πίω **piō**, *pee´-o;* which (together with another form πόω **pŏō**, *pŏ´-o;* occurs only as an alt. in certain tenses; to *imbibe* (lit. or fig.):— drink.

4096. πιότης **piŏtēs**, *pee-ot´-ace;* from πίων **piōn**, (*fat;* perh. akin to the alt. of *4095* through the idea of *repletion*); *plumpness,* i.e. (by impl.) *richness* (oiliness):— fatness.

4097. πιπράσκω **pipraskō**, *pip-ras´-ko;* a redupl. and prol. form of

πράω **praō**, *prah´-o;* (which occurs only as an alt. in certain tenses); contr. from περάω **pĕraō** (to *traverse;* from the base of *4008*); to *traffic* (by *travelling*), i.e. *dispose* of as merchandise or into slavery (lit. or fig.):— sell.

4098. πίπτω **piptō**, *pip´-to;* a redupl. and contr. form of πέτω **pĕtō**, *pet´-o;* (which occurs only as an alt. in certain tenses); prob. akin to *4072* through the idea of *alighting;* to *fall* (lit. or fig.):— fail, fall (down), light on.

4099. Πισιδία **Pisidia**, *pis-id-ee´-ah;* prob. of for. or.; *Pisidia,* a region of Asia Minor:— Pisidia.

4100. πιστεύω **pistĕuō**, *pist-yoo´-o;* from *4102;* to *have faith* (in, upon, or with respect to, a person or thing), i.e. *credit;* by impl. to *entrust* (espec. one's spiritual well-being to Christ):— believe (-r), commit (to trust), put in trust with.

4101. πιστικός **pistikŏs**, *pis-tik-os´;* from *4102; trustworthy,* i.e. *genuine* (*unadulterated*):— spike-[nard].

4102. πίστις **pistis**, *pis´-tis;* from *3982; persuasion,* i.e. *credence;* mor. *conviction* (of *relig.* truth, or the truthfulness of God or a relig. teacher); espec. *reliance* upon Christ for salvation; abstr. *constancy* in such profession; by extension, the system of religious (Gospel) *truth* itself:— assurance, belief, believe, faith, fidelity.

4103. πιστός **pistŏs**, *pis-tos´;* from *3982;* obj. *trustworthy;* subj. *trustful:*— believe (-ing, -r), faithful (-ly), sure, true.

4104. πιστόω **pistŏō**, *pis-tŏ´-o;* from *4103;* to *assure:*— assure of.

4105. πλανάω **planaō**, *plan-ah´-o;* from *4106;* to (prop. *cause* to) *roam* (from safety, truth, or virtue):— go astray, deceive, err, seduce, wander, be out of the way.

4106. πλάνη **planē**, *plan´-ay;* fem. of *4108* (as abstr.); obj. *fraudulence;* subj. a *straying* from orthodoxy or piety:— deceit, to deceive, delusion, error.

4107. πλανήτης **planētēs**, *plan-ay´-tace;* from *4108;* a *rover* ("planet"), i.e. (fig.) an *erratic* teacher:— wandering.

4108. πλάνος **planŏs**, *plan´-os;* of uncert. aff.; *roving* (as a *tramp*), i.e. (by impl.) an *impostor* or *misleader:*— deceiver, seducing.

4109. πλάξ **plax**, *plax;* from *4111;* a *moulding-board*, i.e. *flat* surface (*"plate"*, or *tablet*, lit. or fig.):— table.

4110. πλάσμα **plasma**, *plas´-mah;* from *4111;* something *moulded:*— thing formed.

4111. πλάσσω **plassō**, *plas´-so;* a primary verb; to *mould*, i.e. *shape* or *fabricate:*— form.

4112. πλαστός **plastŏs**, *plas-tos´;* from *4111; moulded*, i.e. (by impl.) *artificial* or (fig.) *fictitious* (*false*):— feigned.

4113. πλατεία **platĕia**, *plat-i´-ah;* fem. of *4116;* a *wide "plat"* or *"place"*, i.e. open *square:*— street.

4114. πλάτος **platŏs**, *plat´-os;* from *4116; width:*— breadth.

4115. πλατύνω **platunō**, *plat-oo´-no;* from *4116;* to *widen* (lit. or fig.):— make broad, enlarge.

4116. πλατύς **platus**, *plat-oos´;* from *4111;* spread out *"flat"* (*"plot"*), i.e. *broad:*— wide.

4117. πλέγμα **plĕgma**, *pleg´-mah;* from *4120;* a *plait* (of hair):— broidered hair.

πλεῖον **plĕiŏn**. See *4119*.

4118. πλεῖστος **plĕistŏs**, *plice´-tos;* irreg. superl. of *4183;* the *largest number* or *very large:*— very great, most.

4119. πλείων **plĕiŏn**, *pli-own;* neut.

πλεῖον **plĕiŏn**, *pli´-on;* or

πλέον **plĕŏn**, *pleh´-on;* comparative of *4183; more* in quantity, number, or quality; also (in plur.) the *major portion:*— × above, + exceed, more excellent, further, (very) great (-er), long (-er), (very) many, greater (more) part, + yet but.

4120. πλέκω **plĕkō**, *plek´-o;* a primary word; to *twine* or *braid:*— plait.

πλέον **plĕŏn**. See *4119*.

4121. πλεονάζω **plĕŏnazō**, *pleh-on-ad´-zo;* from *4119;* to *do, make* or *be more*, i.e. *increase* (tran. or intr.); by extens. to *superabound:*— abound, abundant, make to increase, have over.

4122. πλεονεκτέω **plĕŏnĕktĕō**, *pleh-on-ek-teh´-o;* from *4123;* to *be covetous*, i.e. (by impl.) to *over-reach:*— get an advantage, defraud, make a gain.

4123. πλεονέκτης **plĕŏnĕktēs**, *pleh-on-ek´-tace;* from *4119* and *2192; holding* (*desiring*) *more*, i.e. *eager for gain* (*avaricious*, hence, a *defrauder*):— covetous.

4124. πλεονεξία **plĕŏnĕxia**, *pleh-on-ex-ee´-ah;* from *4123; avarice*, i.e. (by impl.) *fraudulency, extortion:*— covetous (-ness) practices, greediness.

4125. πλευρά **plĕura**, *plyoo-rah´;* of uncert. aff.; a *rib*, i.e. (by extens.) *side:*— side.

4126. πλέω **plĕō**, *pleh´-o;* another form for

πλεύω **plĕuō**, *plyoo´-o;* which is used as an alt. in certain tenses; prob. a form of *4150* (through the idea of *plunging* through the water); to *pass* in a vessel:— sail. See also *4130*.

4127. πληγή **plēgē**, *play-gay´;* from *4141;* a *stroke;* by impl. a *wound;* fig. a

4128. πλῆθος **plēthŏs**, *play´-thos;* from *4130;* a *fulness*, i.e. a *large number, throng, populace:*— bundle, company, multitude.

4129. πληθύνω **plēthunō**, *play-thoo´-no;* from another form of *4128;* to *increase* (tran. or intr.):— abound, multiply.

4130. πλήθω **plēthō**, *play´-tho;* a prol. form of a primary πλέω **plĕō**, *pleh´-o* (which appears only as an alt. in certain tenses and in the redupl. form πίμπλημι **pimplēmi**); to *"fill"* (lit. or fig. *limbue, influence, supply*l); spec. to *fulfil* (time):— accomplish, full (...come), furnish.

4131. πλήκτης **plēktēs**, *plake´-tace;* from *4141;* a *smiter*, i.e. *pugnacious* (*quarrelsome*):— striker.

4132. πλημμύρα **plēmmura**, *plame-moo´-rah;* prol. from *4130; flood-tide*, i.e. (by anal.) a *freshet:*— flood.

4133. πλήν **plēn**, *plane;* from *4119; moreover* (*besides*), i.e. *albeit, save that, rather, yet:*— but (rather), except, nevertheless, notwithstanding, save, than.

4134. πλήρης **plērēs**, *play´-race;* from *4130; replete*, or *covered* over; by anal. *complete:*— full.

4135. πληροφορέω **plērŏphŏrĕō**, *play-rof-or-eh´-o;* from *4134* and *5409;* to *carry* out *fully* (in evidence), i.e. *completely assure* (or *convince*), *entirely accomplish:*— most surely believe, fully know (persuade), make full proof of.

4136. πληροφορία **plērŏphŏria**, *play-rof-or-ee´-ah;* from *4135; entire confidence:*— (full) assurance.

4137. πληρόω **plērŏō**, *play-rŏ´-o;* from *4134;* to *make replete*, i.e. (lit.) to *cram* (a net), *level* up (a hollow), or (fig.) to *furnish* (or *imbue, diffuse, influence*), *satisfy, execute* (an office), *finish* (a period or task), *verify* (or *coincide* with a prediction), etc.:— accomplish, × after, (be) complete, end, expire, fill (up), fulfil, (be, make) full (come), fully preach, perfect, supply.

4138. πλήρωμα **plērōma**, *play´-ro-mah;* from *4137; repletion* or *completion*, i.e. (subj.) what *fills* (as contents, supplement, copiousness, multitude), or (obj.) what is *filled* (as container, performance, period):— which is put in to fill up, piece that filled up, fulfilling, full, fulness.

4139. πλησίον **plēsiŏn**, *play-see´-on;* neut. of a der. of πέλας **pĕlas** (near); (adv.) *close* by; as noun, a *neighbor*, i.e. *fellow* (as man, countryman, Chr. or friend):— near, neighbour.

4140. πλησμονή **plēsmŏnē**, *place-mon-ay´;* from a presumed der. of *4130;* a *filling* up, i.e. (fig.) *gratification:*— satisfying.

4141. πλήσσω **plēssō**, *place´-so;* appar. another form of *4111* (through the idea of *flattening* out); to *pound*, i.e. (fig.) to *inflict* with (calamity):— smite. Comp. *5180*.

4142. πλοιάριον **plŏiariŏn**, *ploy-ar´-ee-*

on; neut. of a presumed der. of *4143;* a *boat:*— boat, little (small) ship.

4143. πλοῖον **plŏiŏn**, *ploy´-on;* from *4126;* a *sailer*, i.e. *vessel:*— ship (-ping).

4144. πλόος **plŏŏs**, *plŏ´-os;* from *4126;* a *sail*, i.e. *navigation:*— course, sailing, voyage.

4145. πλούσιος **plŏusiŏs**, *ploo´-see-os;* from *4149; wealthy;* fig. *abounding with:*— rich.

4146. πλουσίως **plŏusiŏs**, *ploo-see´-oce;* adv. from *4145; copiously:*— abundantly, richly.

4147. πλουτέω **plŏutĕō**, *ploo-teh´-o;* from *4148;* to *be* (or *become*) *wealthy* (lit. or fig.):— be increased with goods, (be made, wax) rich.

4148. πλουτίζω **plŏutizō**, *ploo-tid´-zo;* from *4149;* to *make wealthy* (fig.):— en-(make) rich.

4149. πλοῦτος **plŏutŏs**, *ploo´-tos;* from the base of *4130; wealth* (as *fulness*), i.e. (lit.) *money, possessions*, or (fig.) *abundance, richness*, (spec.) valuable *bestowment:*— riches.

4150. πλύνω **plunō**, *ploo´-no;* a prol. form of an obs. πλύω **pluō**, (to *"flow"*); to *"plunge,"* i.e. *launder* clothing:— wash. Comp. *3068, 3538*.

4151. πνεῦμα **pnĕuma**, *pnyoo´-mah;* from *4154;* a *current* of air, i.e. *breath* (*blast*) or a *breeze;* by anal. or fig. a *spirit*, i.e. (human) the rational *soul*, (by impl.) *vital principle*, ment. *disposition*, etc., or (superhuman) an *angel, demon*, or (divine) *God*, Christ's *spirit*, the Holy *Spirit:*— ghost, life, spirit (-ual, -ually), mind. Comp. *5590*.

4152. πνευματικός **pnĕumatikŏs**, *pnyoo-mat-ik-os´;* from *4151; non-carnal*, i.e. (humanly) *ethereal* (as opposed to gross), or (demoniacally) a *spirit* (concr.), or (divinely) *supernatural, regenerate, religious:*— spiritual. Comp. *5591*.

4153. πνευματικῶς **pnĕumatikōs**, *pnyoo-mat-ik-oce´;* adv. from *4152; non-physical*, i.e. *divinely, figuratively:*— spiritually.

4154. πνέω **pnĕō**, *pneh´-o;* a primary word; to *breathe* hard, i.e. *breeze:*— blow. Comp. *5594*.

4155. πνίγω **pnigō**, *pnee´-go;* strengthened from *4154;* to *wheeze*, i.e. (cause. by impl.) to *throttle* or *strangle* (*drown*):— choke, take by the throat.

4156. πνικτός **pniktŏs**, *pnik-tos´;* from *4155; throttled*, i.e. (neut. concr.) an animal *choked* to death (*not bled*):— strangled.

4157. πνοή **pnŏē**, *pno-ay´;* from *4154; respiration*, a *breeze:*— breath, wind.

4158. ποδήρης **pŏdērēs**, *pod-ay´-race;* from *4228* and another element of uncert. aff.; a *dress* (*2066* impl.) *reaching* the *ankles:*— garment down to the foot.

4159. πόθεν **pŏthĕn**, *poth´-en;* from the base of *4213* with enclitic adverb of origin; *from which* (as interr.) or *what* (as rel.) place, state, source or cause:— whence.

4160. ποιέω **pŏiĕō**, *poy-eh´-o;* appar. a

prol. form of an obs. primary; to *make* or *do* (in a very wide application, more or less dir.):— abide, + agree, appoint, × avenge, + band together, be, bear, + bewray, bring (forth), cast out, cause, commit, + content, continue, deal, + without any delay, (would) do (-ing), execute, exercise, fulfil, gain, give, have, hold, × journeying, keep, + lay wait, + lighten the ship, make, × mean, + none of these things move me, observe, ordain, perform, provide, + have purged, purpose, put, + raising up, × secure, shew, × shoot out, spend, take, tarry, + transgress the law, work, yield. Comp. *4238*.

4161. ποίημα **pŏiēma**, *poy´-ay-mah*; from *4160*; a *product*, i.e. *fabric* (lit. or fig.):— thing that is made, workmanship.

4162. ποίησις **pŏiēsis**, *poy´-ay-sis*; from *4160*; *action*, i.e. *performance* (of the law):— deed.

4163. ποιητής **pŏiētēs**, *poy-ay-tace´*; from *4160*; a *performer*; spec. a "*poet*":— doer, poet.

4164. ποικίλος **pŏikilos**, *poy-kee´-los*; of uncert. der.; *motley*, i.e. *various* in character:— divers, manifold.

4165. ποιμαίνω **pŏimainō**, *poy-mah´-ee-no*; from *4166*; to *tend* as a shepherd (or fig. *superviser*):— feed (cattle), rule.

4166. ποιμήν **pŏimēn**, *poy-mane´*; of uncert. aff.; a *shepherd* (lit. or fig.):— shepherd, pastor.

4167. ποίμνη **pŏimnē**, *poym´-nay*; contr. from *4165*; a *flock* (lit. or fig.):— flock, fold.

4168. ποίμνιον **pŏimniŏn**, *poym´-nee-on*; neut. of a presumed der. of *4167*; a *flock*, i.e. (fig.) *group* (of believers):— flock.

4169. ποῖος **pŏiŏs**, *poy´-os*; from the base of *4226* and *3634*; individualizing interr. (of character) *what* sort of, or (of number) *which* one:— what (manner of), which.

4170. πολεμέω **pŏlĕmĕō**, *pol-em-eh´-o*; from *4171*; to *be* (engaged) in *warfare*, i.e. to *battle* (lit. or fig.):— fight, (make) war.

4171. πόλεμος **pŏlĕmŏs**, *pol´-em-os*; from πέλομαι **pĕlŏmai**, (to *bustle*); *warfare* (lit. or fig.; a single encounter or a series):— battle, fight, war.

4172. πόλις **pŏlis**, *pol´-is*; prob. from the same as *4171*, or perh. from *4183*; a *town* (prop. with walls, of greater or less size):— city.

4173. πολιτάρχης **pŏlitarchēs**, *pol-it-ar´-khace*; from *4172* and *757*; a *town-officer*, i.e. *magistrate*:— ruler of the city.

4174. πολιτεία **pŏlitĕia**, *pol-ee-ti´-ah*; from *4177* ("*polity*"); *citizenship*; concr. a *community*:— commonwealth, freedom.

4175. πολίτευμα **pŏlitĕuma**, *pol-it´-yoo-mah*; from *4176*; a *community*, i.e. (abstr.) *citizenship* (fig.):— conversation.

4176. πολιτεύομαι **pŏlitĕuŏmai**, *pol-it-yoo´-om-ahee*; mid. voice of a der. of

4177; to *behave* as a citizen (fig.):— let conversation be, live.

4177. πολίτης **pŏlitēs**, *pol-ee´-tace*; from *4172*; a *townsman*:— citizen.

4178. πολλάκις **pŏllakis**, *pol-lak´-is*; mult. adv. from *4183*; *many times*, i.e. *frequently*:— oft (-en, -entimes, -times).

4179. πολλαπλασίων **pŏllaplasiōn**, *pol-lap-las-ee´-ohn*; from *4183* and prob. a der. of *4120*; *manifold*, i.e. (neut. as noun) *very much more*:— manifold more.

4180. πολυλογία **pŏlulŏgia**, *pol-oo-log-ee´-ah*; from a compound of *4183* and *3056*; *loquacity*, i.e. *prolixity*:— much speaking.

4181. πολυμέρως **pŏlumĕrōs**, *pol-oo-mer´-oce*; adv. from a compound of *4183* and *3313*; *in many portions*, i.e. *variously* as to time and agency (*piecemeal*):— at sundry times.

4182. πολυποίκιλος **pŏlupŏikilŏs**, *pol-oo-poy´-kil-os*; from *4183* and *4164*; *much variegated*, i.e. *multifarious*:— manifold.

4183. πολύς **pŏlus**, *pol-oos´*; incl. the forms from the alt. πολλός **pŏllŏs**; (sing.) *much* (in any respect) or (plural) *many*; neut. (sing.) as adv. *largely*; neut. (plural) as adv. or noun *often, mostly, largely*:— abundant, + altogether, common, + far (passed, spent), (+ be of a) great (age, deal, -ly, while), long, many, much, oft (-en [-times]), plenteous, sore, straitly. Comp. *4118, 4119*.

4184. πολύσπλαγχνος **pŏlusplagchnŏs**, *pol-oo´-splankh-nos*; from *4183* and *4698* (fig.); *extremely compassionate*:— very pitiful.

4185. πολυτελής **pŏlutelēs**, *pol-oo-tel-ace´*; from *4183* and *5056*; *extremely expensive*:— costly, very precious, of great price.

4186. πολύτιμος **pŏlutimŏs**, *pol-oot´-ee-mos*; from *4183* and *5092*; *extremely valuable*:— very costly, of great price.

4187. πολυτρόπως **pŏlutrŏpŏs**, *pol-oot-rop´-oce*; adv. from a compound of *4183* and *5158*; *in many ways*, i.e. *variously* as to method or form:— in divers manners.

4188. πόμα **pŏma**, *pom´-ah*; from the alt. of *4095*; a *beverage*:— drink.

4189. πονηρία **pŏnēria**, *pon-ay-ree´-ah*; from *4190*; *depravity*, i.e. (spec.) *malice*; plur. (concr.) *plots, sins*:— iniquity, wickedness.

4190. πονηρός **pŏnērŏs**, *pon-ay-ros´*; from a der. of *4192*; *hurtful*, i.e. *evil* (prop. in effect or influence, and thus differing from *2556*, which refers rather to *essential* character, as well as from *4550*, which indicates *degeneracy* from original virtue); fig. *calamitous*; also (pass.) *ill*, i.e. *diseased*; but espec. (mor.) *culpable*, i.e. *derelict, vicious, facinorous*; neut. (sing.) *mischief, malice*, or (plural) *guilt*; masc. (sing.) the *devil*, or (plural) *sinners*:— bad, evil, grievous, harm, lewd, malicious, wicked (-ness). See also *4191*.

4191. πονηρότερος **pŏnērŏtĕrŏs**, *pon-ay-rot´-er-os*; comp. of *4190*; *more evil*:— more wicked.

4192. πόνος **pŏnŏs**, *pon´-os*; from the base of *3993*; *toil*, i.e. (by impl.) *anguish*:— pain.

4193. Ποντικός **Pŏntikŏs**, *pon-tik-os´*; from *4195*; a *Pontican*, i.e. native of Pontus:— born in Pontus.

4194. Πόντος **Pŏntiŏs**, *pon´-tee-os*; of Lat. or.; appar. *bridged*; *Pontius*, a Rom.:— Pontius.

4195. Πόντος **Pŏntŏs**, *pon´-tos*; a *sea*; *Pontus*, a region of Asia Minor:— Pontus.

4196. Πόπλιος **Pŏpliŏs**, *pop´-lee-os*; of Lat. or.; appar. "*popular*"; *Poplius* (i.e. *Publius*), a Rom.:— Publius.

4197. πορεία **pŏrĕia**, *por-i´-ah*; from *4198*; *travel* (by land); fig. (plural) *proceedings*, i.e. *career*:— journey [-ing], ways.

4198. πορεύομαι **pŏrĕuŏmai**, *por-yoo´-om-ahee*; mid. voice from a der. of the same as *3984*; to *traverse*, i.e. *travel* (lit. or fig.; espec. to *remove* [fig. *die*], *live*, etc.):— depart, go (away, forth, one's way, up), (make a, take a) journey, walk.

4199. πορθέω **pŏrthĕō**, *por-theh´-o*; prol. from πέρθω **pĕrthō**, (to *sack*); to *ravage* (fig.):— destroy, waste.

4200. πορισμός **pŏrismŏs**, *por-is-mos´*; from a der. of πόρος **pŏrŏs** (a *way*, i.e. *means*); *furnishing*, (*procuring*), i.e. (by impl.) *money-getting* (*acquisition*):— gain.

4201. Πόρκιος **Pŏrkiŏs**, *por´-kee-os*; of Lat. or.; appar. *swinish*; *Porcius*, a Rom.:— Porcius.

4202. πορνεία **pŏrnĕia**, *por-ni´-ah*; from *4203*; *harlotry* (incl. *adultery* and *incest*); fig. *idolatry*:— fornication.

4203. πορνεύω **pŏrnĕuō**, *porn-yoo´-o*; from *4204*; to *act the harlot*, i.e. (lit.) *indulge* unlawful *lust* (of either sex), or (fig.) *practice idolatry*:— commit (fornication).

4204. πόρνη **pŏrnē**, *por´-nay*; fem. of *4205*; a *strumpet*; fig. an *idolater*:— harlot, whore.

4205. πόρνος **pŏrnŏs**, *por´-nos*; from πέρνημι **pĕrnēmi**, (to *sell*; akin to the base of *4097*); a (male) *prostitute* (as *venal*), i.e. (by anal.) a *debauchee* (*libertine*):— fornicator, whoremonger.

4206. πόρρω **pŏrrhō**, *por´-rho*; adv. from *4253*; *forwards*, i.e. *at a distance*:— far, a great way off. See also *4207*.

4207. πόρρωθεν **pŏrrhōthĕn**, *por´-rho-then*; from *4206* with adv. enclitic of source; *from far*, or (by impl.) *at a distance*, i.e. *distantly*:— afar off.

4208. πορρωτέρω **pŏrrhōtĕrō**, *por-rho-ter´-o*; adv. comparative of *4206*; *further*, i.e. *a greater distance*:— farther.

4209. πορφύρα **pŏrphura**, *por-foo´-rah*; of Lat. or.; the "*purple*" mussel, i.e. (by impl.) the *red-blue* color itself, and finally a garment dyed with it:— purple.

4210. πορφυροῦς **pŏrphurŏus**, *por-foo-rooce´*; from *4209*; *purpureal*, i.e. *bluish red*:— purple.

4211. πορφυρόπωλις **pŏrphurŏpŏlis**, *por-foo-rop´-o-lis*; fem. of a compound of *4209* and *4453;* a *female trader in purple* cloth:— seller of purple.

4212. ποσάκις **pŏsakis**, *pos-ak´-is;* mult. from *4214;* how many times:— how oft (-en).

4213. πόσις **pŏsis**, *pos´-is;* from the alt. of *4095;* a *drinking* (the act), i.e. (concr.) a *draught:*— drink.

4214. πόσος **pŏsŏs**, *pos´-os;* from an obs. πός **pŏs**, (*who, what*) and *3739;* interr. pron. (of amount) *how much* (*large, long* or [plural] *many*):— how great (long, many), what.

4215. ποταμός **pŏtamŏs**, *pot-am-os´;* prob. from a der. of the alt. of *4095* (comp. *4224*); a *current, brook* or *freshet* (as *drinkable*), i.e. *running water:*— flood, river, stream, water.

4216. ποταμοφόρητος **pŏtamŏphŏrētŏs**, *pot-am-of-or´-ay-tos;* from *4215* and a der. of *5409; river-borne,* i.e. *overwhelmed by a stream:*— carried away of the flood.

4217. ποταπός **pŏtapŏs**, *pot-ap-os´;* appar. from *4219* and the base of *4226;* interrog. *whatever,* i.e. of *what possible* sort:— what (manner of).

4218. ποτέ **pŏtě**, *pot-eh´;* from the base of *4225* and *5037;* indef. adv., at *some time, ever:*— afore-(any, some-) time (-s), at length (the last), (+ n-) ever, in the old time, in time past, once, when.

4219. πότε **pŏtě**, *pot´-eh;* from the base of *4226* and *5037;* interr. adv., at *what time:*— + how long, when.

4220. πότερον **pŏtěrŏn**, *pot´-er-on;* neut. of a comparative of the base of *4226;* interr. as adv., *which* (of two), i.e. *is it* this or that:— whether.

4221. ποτήριον **pŏtēriŏn**, *pot-ay´-ree-on;* neut. of a der. of the alt. of *4095;* a *drinking-vessel;* by extens. the contents thereof, i.e. a *cupful* (*draught*); fig. a *lot* or *fate:*— cup.

4222. ποτίζω **pŏtizō**, *pot-id´-zo;* from a der. of the alt. of *4095;* to *furnish drink, irrigate:*— give (make) to drink, feed, water.

4223. Ποτίολοι **Pŏtiŏlŏi**, *pot-ee´-ol-oy;* of Lat. or.; *little wells,* i.e. *mineral springs; Potioli* (i.e. *Puteoli*), a place in Italy:— Puteoli.

4224. πότος **pŏtŏs**, *pot´-os;* from the alt. of *4095;* a *drinking-bout* or *carousal:*— banqueting.

4225. πού **pŏu**, *poo;* gen. of an indef. pron. πός **pŏs** (*some*) otherwise obs. (comp. *4214*); as adv. of place, *somewhere,* i.e. *nearly:*— about, a certain place.

4226. πού **pŏu**, *poo;* gen. of an interr. pron. πός **pŏs**, (*what*) otherwise obs. (perh. the same as *4225* used with the rising slide of inquiry); as adv. of place; *at* (by impl. to) *what* locality:— where, whither.

4227. Πούδης **Pŏudēs**, *poo´-dace;* of Lat. or.; *modest; Pudes* (i.e. *Pudens*), a Chr.:— Pudens.

4228. πούς **pŏus**, *pooce;* a primary word; a "*foot*" (fig. or lit.):— foot (-stool).

4229. πρᾶγμα **pragma**, *prag´-mah;* from *4238;* a *deed;* by impl. an *affair;* by ex-

tens. an *object* (material):— business, matter, thing, work.

4230. πραγματεία **pragmatěia**, *prag-mat-i´-ah;* from *4231;* a *transaction,* i.e. *negotiation:*— affair.

4231. πραγματεύομαι **pragmatěuŏmai**, *prag-mat-yoo´-om-ahee;* from *4229;* to *busy oneself* with, i.e. to *trade:*— occupy.

4232. πραιτώριον **praitŏriŏn**, *prahee-to´-ree-on;* of Lat. or.; the *prætorium* or governor's *court-room* (sometimes incl. the whole *edifice* and *camp*):— (common, judgment) hall (of judgment), palace, prætorium.

4233. πράκτωρ **praktōr**, *prak´-tor;* from a der. of *4238;* a *practiser,* i.e. (spec.) an official *collector:*— officer.

4234. πρᾶξις **praxis**, *prax´-is;* from *4238; practice,* i.e. (concr.) an *act;* by extens. a *function.*— deed, office, work.

4235. πρᾷος **praÿŏs**, *prah´-os;* a form of *4239,* used in certain parts; *gentle,* i.e. *humble:*— meek.

4236. πραότης **praÿŏtēs**, *prah-ot´-ace;* from *4235; gentleness,* by impl. *humility:*— meekness.

4237. πρασιά **prasia**, *pras-ee-ah´;* perh. from πράσον **prasŏn** (a *leek,* and so an *onion-patch*); a *garden plot,* i.e. (by impl. of reg. *beds*) a *row* (repeated in plur. by Heb., to indicate an arrangement):— in ranks.

4238. πράσσω **prassō**, *pras´-so;* a primary verb; to "*practice*", i.e. *perform repeatedly* or *habitually* (thus differing from *4160,* which prop. refers to a *single* act); by impl. to *execute, accomplish,* etc.; spec. to *collect* (dues), *fare* (personally):— commit, deeds, do, exact, keep, require, use arts.

4239. πραΰς **praÿs**, *prah-ooce´;* appar. a primary word; *mild,* i.e. (by impl.) *humble:*— meek. See also *4235.*

4240. πραΰτης **praÿtēs**, *prah-oo-tace´;* from *4239; mildness,* i.e. (by impl.) *humility:*— meekness.

4241. πρέπω **prěpō**, *prep´-o;* appar. a primary verb; to *tower up* (be *conspicuous*), i.e. (by impl.) to *be suitable* or *proper* (third pers. sing. pres. ind., often used impers., it is *fit* or *right*):— become, comely.

4242. πρεσβεία **prěsběia**, *pres-bi´-ah;* from *4243; seniority* (*eldership*), i.e. (by impl.) an *embassy* (concr. *ambassadors*):— ambassage, message.

4243. πρεσβεύω **prěsběuō**, *pres-byoo´-o;* from the base of *4245;* to be a *senior,* i.e. (by impl.) *act as a representative* (fig. *preacher*):— be an ambassador.

4244. πρεσβυτέριον **prěsbutěriŏn**, *pres-boo-ter´-ee-on;* neut. of a presumed der. of *4245;* the *order of elders,* i.e. (spec.) Isr. *Sanhedrin* or Chr. "*presbytery*":— (estate of) elder (-s), presbytery.

4245. πρεσβύτερος **prěsbutěrŏs**, *pres-boo´-ter-os;* comparative of πρέσβυς **prěsbus** (*elderly*); *older;* as noun, a *senior;* spec. an Isr. *Sanhedrist* (also fig. member of the celestial council) or Chr. "*presbyter*":— elder (-est), old.

4246. πρεσβύτης **prěsbutēs**, *pres-boo´-tace;* from the same as *4245;* an *old man:*— aged (man), old man.

4247. πρεσβῦτις **prěsbutis**, *pres-boo´-tis;* fem. of *4246;* an *old woman:*— aged woman.

πρήθω **prēthō**. See *4092.*

4248. πρηνής **prēnēs**, *pray-nace´;* from *4253; leaning* (*falling*) *forward* ("*prone*"), i.e. *head foremost:*— headlong.

4249. πρίζω **prizō**, *prid´-zo;* a strengthened form of a primary πρίω **priō**, (to *saw*); to *saw* in two:— saw asunder.

4250. πρίν **prin**, *prin;* adv. from *4253; prior, sooner:*— before (that), ere.

4251. Πρίσκα **Priska**, *pris´-kah;* of Lat. or.; fem. of *Priscus, ancient; Priska,* a Chr. woman:— Prisca. See also *4252.*

4252. Πρίσκιλλα **Priskilla**, *pris´-kil-lah;* dimin. of *4251; Priscilla* (i.e. *little Prisca*), a Chr. woman:— Priscilla.

4253. πρό **prŏ**, *prŏ;* a primary prep.; "*fore*", i.e. *in front of, prior* (fig. *superior*) *to:*— above, ago, before, or ever. In composition it retains the same significations.

4254. προάγω **prŏagō**, *prŏ-ag´-o;* from *4253* and *71;* to *lead forward* (magisterially); intr. to *precede* (in place or time [part. *previous*]):— bring (forth, out), go before.

4255. προαιρέομαι **prŏairěŏmai**, *prŏ-ahee-reh´-om-ahee;* from *4253* and *138;* to *choose for oneself before* another thing (*prefer*), i.e. (by impl.) to *propose* (*intend*):— purpose.

4256. προαιτιάομαι **prŏaitiaŏmai**, *prŏ-ahee-tee-ah´-om-ahee;* from *4253* and a der. of *156;* to *accuse already,* i.e. *previously charge:*— prove before.

4257. προακούω **prŏakŏuō**, *prŏ-ak-oo´-o;* from *4253* and *191;* to *hear already,* i.e. *anticipate:*— hear before.

4258. προαμαρτάνω **prŏamartanō**, *prŏ-am-ar-tan´-o;* from *4253* and *264;* to *sin previously* (to conversion):— sin already, heretofore sin.

4259. προαύλιον **prŏauliŏn**, *prŏ-ŏw´-lee-on;* neut. of a presumed compound of *4253* and *833;* a *forecourt,* i.e. *vestibule* (*alley-way*):— porch.

4260. προβαίνω **prŏbainō**, *prob-ah´-ee-no;* from *4253* and the base of *939;* to *walk forward,* i.e. *advance* (lit. or in years):— + be of a great age, go farther (on), be well stricken.

4261. προβάλλω **prŏballō**, *prob-al´-lo;* from *4253* and *906;* to *throw forward,* i.e. *push to the front, germinate:*— put forward, shoot forth.

4262. προβατικός **prŏbatikŏs**, *prob-at-ik-os´;* from *4263; relating to sheep,* i.e. (a *gate*) through which they were led into Jerusalem:— sheep (market).

4263. πρόβατον **prŏbatŏn**, *prob´-at-on;* prob. neut. of a presumed der. of *4260; something that walks forward* (a *quadruped*), i.e. (spec.) a *sheep* (lit. or fig.):— sheep (l-fold]).

4264. προβιβάζω **prŏbibazō**, *prob-ib-ad´-zo;* from *4253* and a redupl. form of *971;* to *force forward,* i.e. *bring to the* *front, instigate:*— draw, before instruct.

4265. προβλέπω **prŏblĕpō**, *prob-lep´-o;* from 4253 and 991; to *look* out *beforehand,* i.e. *furnish in advance:*— provide.

4266. προγίνομαι **prŏginŏmai**, *prog-in´-om-ahee;* from 4253 and 1096; to *be already,* i.e. *have previously transpired:*— be past.

4267. προγινώσκω **prŏginōskō**, *prog-in-oce´-ko;* from 4253 and 1097; to *know beforehand,* i.e. *foresee:*— foreknow (ordain), know (before).

4268. πρόγνωσις **prŏgnōsis**, *prog´-no-sis;* from 4267; *forethought:*— foreknowledge.

4269. πρόγονος **prŏgŏnŏs**, *prog´-on-os;* from 4266; an *ancestor,* (grand-) *parent:*— forefather, parent.

4270. προγράφω **prŏgraphō**, *prog-raf´-o;* from 4253 and 1125; to *write previously;* fig. to *announce, prescribe:*— before ordain, evidently set forth, write (afore, aforetime).

4271. πρόδηλος **prŏdēlŏs**, *prod´-ay-los;* from 4253 and 1212; *plain before* all men, i.e. *obvious:*— evident, manifest (open) beforehand.

4272. προδίδωμι **prŏdidōmi**, *prod-id´-o-mee;* from 4253 and 1325; to *give before* the other party has given:— first give.

4273. προδότης **prŏdŏtēs**, *prod-ot´-ace;* from 4272 (in the sense of *giving forward* into another's [the enemy's] hands); a *surrender:*— betrayer, traitor.

προδρέμω **prŏdrĕmō**. See 4390.

4274. πρόδρομος **prŏdrŏmŏs**, *prod´-rom-os;* from the alt. of 4390; a *runner ahead,* i.e. *scout* (fig. *precursor*):— forerunner.

4275. προείδω **prŏeidō**, *pro-i´-do;* from 4253 and 1492; *foresee:*— foresee, saw before.

προειρέω **prŏĕirĕō**. See 4280.

4276. προελπίζω **prŏĕlpizō**, *prŏ-el-pid´-zo;* from 4253 and 1679; to *hope in advance* of other confirmation:— first trust.

4277. προέπω **prŏĕpō**, *prŏ-ep´-o;* from 4253 and 2036; to *say already,* to *predict:*— forewarn, say (speak, tell) before. Comp. 4280.

4278. προενάρχομαι **prŏĕnarchŏmai**, *prŏ-en-ar´-khom-ahee;* from 4253 and 1728; to *commence already:*— begin (before).

4279. προεπαγγέλλομαι **prŏĕpaggĕllŏmai**, *prŏ-ep-ang-ghel´-lom-ahee;* mid. voice from 4253 and 1861; to *promise of old:*— promise before.

4280. προερέω **prŏĕrĕō**, *prŏ-er-eh´-o;* from 4253 and 2046; used as alt. of 4277; to *say already, predict:*— foretell, say (speak, tell) before.

4281. προέρχομαι **prŏĕrchŏmai**, *prŏ-er´-khom-ahee;* from 4253 and 2064 (incl. its alt.); to *go onward, precede* (in place or time):— go before (farther, forward), outgo, pass on.

4282. προετοιμάζω **prŏĕtŏimazō**, *pro-*

et-oy-mad´-zo; from 4253 and 2090; to *fit* up *in advance* (lit. or fig.):— ordain before, prepare afore.

4283. προευαγγελίζομαι **prŏĕuaggĕlizŏmai**, *prŏ-yoo-ang-ghel-id´-zom-ahee;* mid. voice from 4253 and 2097; to *announce* glad news *in advance:*— preach before the gospel.

4284. προέχομαι **prŏĕchŏmai**, *prŏ-ekh-om-ahee;* mid. voice from 4253 and 2192; to *hold* oneself *before* others, i.e. (fig.) to *excel:*— be better.

4285. προηγέομαι **prŏēgĕŏmai**, *prŏ-ay-geh´-om-ahee;* from 4253 and 2233; to *lead the way* for others, i.e. *show deference:*— prefer.

4286. πρόθεσις **prŏthĕsis**, *proth´-es-is;* from 4388; a *setting forth,* i.e. (fig.) proposal (*intention*); spec. the *show*-bread (in the Temple) as *exposed* before God:— purpose, shew [-bread].

4287. προθέσμιος **prŏthĕsmiŏs**, *prothes´-mee-os;* from 4253 and a der. of 5087; *fixed beforehand,* i.e. (fem. with 2250 implied) a *designated* day:— time appointed.

4288. προθυμία **prŏthumia**, *proth-oo-mee´-ah;* from 4289; *predisposition,* i.e. *alacrity:*— forwardness of mind, readiness (of mind), ready (willing) mind.

4289. πρόθυμος **prŏthumŏs**, *proth´-oo-mos;* from 4253 and 2372; *forward* in *spirit,* i.e. *predisposed;* neut. (as noun) *alacrity:*— ready, willing.

4290. προθύμως **prŏthumōs**, *proth-oo´-moce;* adv. from 4289; *with alacrity:*— willingly.

4291. προΐστημι **prŏïstēmi**, *prŏ-is´-tay-mee;* from 4253 and 2476; to *stand before,* i.e. (in rank) to *preside,* or (by impl.) to *practice:*— maintain, be over, rule.

4292. προκαλέομαι **prŏkalĕŏmai**, *prok-al-eh´-om-ahee;* mid. voice from 4253 and 2564; to *call forth to oneself* (challenge), i.e. (by impl.) to *irritate:*— provoke.

4293. προκαταγγέλλω **prŏkataggĕllō**, *prok-at-ang-ghel´-lo;* from 4253 and 2605; to *announce beforehand,* i.e. *predict, promise:*— foretell, have notice, (shew) before.

4294. προκαταρτίζω **prŏkatartizō**, *prok-at-ar-tid´-zo;* from 4253 and 2675; to *prepare in advance:*— make up beforehand.

4295. πρόκειμαι **prŏkĕimai**, *prok´-i-mahee;* from 4253 and 2749; to *lie before* the view, i.e. (fig.) to *be present* (to the mind), to *stand forth* (as an example or reward):— be first, set before (forth).

4296. προκηρύσσω **prŏkērussō**, *prok-ay-rooce´-so;* from 4253 and 2784; to *herald* (i.e. *proclaim*) *in advance:*— before (first) preach.

4297. προκοπή **prŏkŏpē**, *prok-op-ay´;* from 4298; *progress,* i.e. *advancement* (subj. or obj.):— furtherance, profit.

4298. προκόπτω **prŏkŏptō**, *prok-op´-to;* from 4253 and 2875; to *drive forward* (as if by beating), i.e. (fig. and intr.) to *advance* (in amount, to *grow;* in time, to *be well along*):— increase, proceed, profit, be far spent, wax.

4299. πρόκριμα **prŏkrima**, *prok´-ree-mah;* from a compound of 4253 and 2919; a *prejudgment* (*prejudice*), i.e. *prepossession:*— prefer one before another.

4300. προκυρόω **prŏkurŏō**, *prok-oo-rŏ´-o;* from 4253 and 2964; to *ratify previously:*— confirm before.

4301. προλαμβάνω **prŏlambanō**, *prolam-ban´-o;* from 4253 and 2983; to *take in advance,* i.e. (lit.) *eat before* others have an opportunity; (fig.) to *anticipate, surprise:*— come aforehand, overtake, take before.

4302. προλέγω **prŏlĕgō**, *prol-eg´-o;* from 4253 and 3004; to *say beforehand,* i.e. *predict, forewarn:*— foretell, tell before.

4303. προμαρτύρομαι **prŏmarturŏmai**, *prom-ar-too´-rom-ahee;* from 4253 and 3143; to *be a witness in advance,* i.e. *predict:*— testify beforehand.

4304. προμελετάω **prŏmĕlĕtaō**, *prom-el-et-ah´-o;* from 4253 and 3191; to *premeditate:*— meditate before.

4305. προμεριμνάω **prŏmĕrimnaō**, *prom-er-im-nah´-o;* from 4253 and 3309; to *care* (anxiously) *in advance:*— take thought beforehand.

4306. προνοέω **prŏnŏĕō**, *pron-ŏ-eh´-o;* from 4253 and 3539; to *consider in advance,* i.e. *look* out for *beforehand* (act. by way of *maintenance* for others; mid. voice by way of *circumspection* for oneself):— provide (for).

4307. πρόνοια **prŏnŏia**, *pron´-oy-ah;* from 4306; *forethought,* i.e. *provident care* or *supply:*— providence, provision.

4308. προοράω **prŏŏraō**, *prŏ-or-ah´-o;* from 4253 and 3708; to *behold in advance,* i.e. (act.) to *notice* (another) *previously,* or (mid. voice) to *keep in* (one's own) *view:*— foresee, see before.

4309. προορίζω **prŏŏrizō**, *prŏ-or-id´-zo;* from 4253 and 3724; to *limit in advance,* i.e. (fig.) *predetermine:*— determine before, ordain, predestinate.

4310. προπάσχω **prŏpaschō**, *prop-as´-kho;* from 4253 and 3958; to *undergo hardship previously:*— suffer before.

4311. προπέμπω **prŏpĕmpō**, *prop-em´-po;* from 4253 and 3992; to *send forward,* i.e. *escort* or *aid* in travel:— accompany, bring (forward) on journey (way), conduct forth.

4312. προπετής **prŏpĕtēs**, *prop-et-ace´;* from a compound of 4253 and 4098; *falling forward,* i.e. *headlong* (fig. *precipitate*):— heady, rash [-ly].

4313. προπορεύομαι **prŏpŏrĕuŏmai**, *prop-or-yoo´-om-ahee;* from 4253 and 4198; to *precede* (as guide or herald):— go before.

4314. πρός **prŏs**, *pros;* a strengthened form of 4253; a prep. of direction; *forward to,* i.e. *toward* (with the gen. the *side* of, i.e. *pertaining to;* with the dat. *by the side of,* i.e. *near to;* usually with the acc., the place, time, occasion, or respect, which is the *destination* of the relation, i.e. *whither* or *for* which it is predicated):— about, according to, against, among, at, because of, before, between, (lwhere-l) by, for, × at thy house, in, for intent, nigh unto, of, which pertain to, that, to (the end that), + together, to (lyoul) -ward, unto, with (-in). In composition it denotes essentially the same applications, namely, motion *toward*, accession *to*, or nearness *at*.

4315. προσάββατον **prŏsabbatŏn**, *pros-ab´-bat-on*; from 4253 and 4521; a *fore-sabbath*, i.e. the *Sabbath-eve*:— day before the sabbath. Comp. 3904.

4316. προσαγορεύω **prŏsagŏrĕuŏ**, *pros-ag-or-yoo´-o*; from 4314 and a der. of 58 (mean to *harangue*); to *address*, i.e. salute by *name*:— call.

4317. προσάγω **prŏsagō**, *pros-ag´-o*; from 4314 and 71; to *lead toward*, i.e. (tran.) to *conduct near* (*summon, present*), or (intr.) to *approach*:— bring, draw near.

4318. προσαγωγή **prŏsagōgē**, *pros-ag-ogue-ay´*; from 4317 (comp. 72); *admission*:— access.

4319. προσαιτέω **prŏsaitĕō**, *pros-aheeteh´-o*; from 4314 and 154; to *ask repeatedly* (*importune*), i.e. *solicit*:— beg.

4320. προσαναβαίνω **prŏsanabainō**, *pros-an-ab-ah´-ee-no*; from 4314 and 305; to *ascend farther*, i.e. *be promoted* (*take an upper* lmore honorablel *seat*):— go up.

4321. προσαναλίσκω **prŏsanaliskō**, *pros-an-al-is´-ko*; from 4314 and 355; to *expend further*:— spend.

4322. προσαναπληρόω **prŏsanaplērŏō**, *pros-an-ap-lay-ro´-o*; from 4314 and 378; to *fill up further*, i.e. *furnish fully*:— supply.

4323. προσανατίθημι **prŏsanatithēmi**, *pros-an-at-ith´-ay-mee*; from 4314 and 394; to *lay up in addition*, i.e. (mid. voice and fig.) to *impart* or (by impl.) to *consult*:— in conference add, confer.

4324. προσαπειλέω **prŏsapĕilĕō**, *pros-ap-i-leh´-o*; from 4314 and 546; to *menace additionally*:— threaten further.

4325. προσδαπανάω **prŏsdapanaō**, *pros-dap-an-ah´-o*; from 4314 and 1159; to *expend additionally*:— spend more.

4326. προσδέομαι **prŏsdĕŏmai**, *pros-deh´-om-ahee*; from 4314 and 1189; to *require additionally*, i.e. *want further*:— need.

4327. προσδέχομαι **prŏsdĕchŏmai**, *pros-dekh´-om-ahee*; from 4314 and 1209; to *admit* (to intercourse, hospitality, credence, or lfig.l endurance); by impl. to *await* (with confidence or patience):— accept, allow, look (wait) for, take.

4328. προσδοκάω **prŏsdŏkaō**, *pros-dok-ah´-o*; from 4314 and δοκεύω **dŏkĕuŏ** (to watch); to *anticipate* (in thought, hope or fear); by impl. to *await*:— (be in) expect (-ation), look (for), when looked, tarry, wait for.

4329. προσδοκία **prŏsdŏkia**, *pros-dok-ee´-ah*; from 4328; *apprehension* (of evil); by impl. *infliction* anticipated:— expectation, looking after.

προσδρέμω **prŏsdrĕmō**. See 4370.

4330. προσεάω **prŏsĕaō**, *pros-eh-ah´-o*;

from 4314 and 1439; to *permit further progress*:— suffer.

4331. προσεγγίζω **prŏsĕggizō**, *pros-eng-ghid´-zo*; from 4314 and 1448; to *approach near*:— come nigh.

4332. προσεδρεύω **prŏsĕdrĕuō**, *pros-ed-ryoo´-o*; from a compound of 4314 and the base of 1476; to *sit near*, i.e. *attend* as a servant:— wait at.

4333. προσεργάζομαι **prŏsĕrgazŏmai**, *pros-er-gad´-zom-ahee*; from 4314 and 2038; to *work additionally*, i.e. (by impl.) *acquire besides*:— gain.

4334. προσέρχομαι **prŏsĕrchŏmai**, *pros-er´-khom-ahee*; from 4314 and 2064 (incl. its alt.); to *approach*, i.e. (lit.) *come near, visit*, or (fig.) *worship, assent to*:— (as soon as he) come (unto), come thereunto, consent, draw near, go (near, to, unto).

4335. προσευχή **prŏsĕuchē**, *pros-yookhay´*; from 4336; *prayer* (*worship*); by impl. an *oratory* (*chapel*):— × pray earnestly, prayer.

4336. προσεύχομαι **prŏsĕuchŏmai**, *pros-yoo´-khom-ahee*; from 4314 and 2172; to *pray to God*, i.e. *supplicate, worship*:— pray (× earnestly, for), make prayer.

4337. προσέχω **prŏsĕchō**, *pros-ekh´-o*; from 4314 and 2192; (fig.) to *hold the mind* (3563 impl.) *toward*, i.e. *pay attention to, be cautious about, apply oneself to, adhere to*:— (give) attend (-ance, -ance at, -ance to, unto), beware, be given to, give (take) heed (to, unto); have regard.

4338. προσηλόω **prŏsēlŏō**, *pros-ay-lŏ´-o*; from 4314 and a der. of 2247; to *peg to*, i.e. *spike fast*:— nail to.

4339. προσήλυτος **prŏsēlutŏs**, *pros-ay´-loo-tos*; from the alt. of 4334; an *arriver* from a for. region, i.e. (spec.) an *acceder* (*convert*) to Judaism ("*proselyte*"):— proselyte.

4340. πρόσκαιρος **prŏskairŏs**, *pros´-kahee-ros*; from 4314 and 2540; for the *occasion* only, i.e. *temporary*:— dur-lethl for awhile, endure for a time, for a season, temporal.

4341. προσκαλέομαι **prŏskalĕŏmai**, *pros-kal-eh´-om-ahee*; mid. voice from 4314 and 2564; to *call toward oneself*, i.e. *summon, invite*:— call (for, to, unto).

4342. προσκαρτερέω **prŏskartĕrĕō**, *pros-kar-ter-eh´-o*; from 4314 and 2594; to *be earnest toward*, i.e. (to a thing) to *persevere, be constantly diligent*, or (in a place) to *attend* assiduously all the exercises, or (to a person) to *adhere* closely to (as a servitor):— attend (give self) continually (upon), continue (in, instant in, with), wait on (continually).

4343. προσκαρτέρησις **prŏskartĕrēsis**, *pros-kar-ter´-ay-sis*; from 4342; *persistency*:— perseverance.

4344. προσκεφάλαιον **prŏskĕphalaiŏn**, *pros-kef-al´-ahee-on*; neut. of a presumed compound of 4314 and 2776; something *for the head*, i.e. a *cushion*:— pillow.

4345. προσκληρόω **prŏsklērŏō**, *pros-klay-rŏ´-o*; from 4314 and 2820; to *give a*

common *lot to*, i.e. (fig.) to *associate with*:— consort with.

4346. πρόσκλισις **prŏsklisis**, *pros´-klis-is*; from a compound of 4314 and 2827; a *leaning toward*, i.e. (fig.) *proclivity* (*favoritism*):— partiality.

4347. προσκολλάω **prŏskŏllaō**, *pros-kol-lah´-o*; from 4314 and 2853; to *glue to*, i.e. (fig.) to *adhere*:— cleave, join (self).

4348. πρόσκομμα **prŏskŏmma**, *pros´-kom-mah*; from 4350; a *stub*, i.e. (fig.) *occasion of apostasy*:— offence, stumbling (-block, l-stonel).

4349. προσκοπή **prŏskŏpē**, *pros-kop-ay´*; from 4350; a *stumbling*, i.e. (fig. and concr.) *occasion of sin*:— offence.

4350. προσκόπτω **prŏskŏptō**, *pros-kop´-to*; from 4314 and 2875; to *strike at*, i.e. *surge against* (as water); spec. to *stub on*, i.e. *trip up* (lit. or fig.):— beat upon, dash, stumble (at).

4351. προσκυλίω **prŏskuliō**, *pros-koo-lee´-o*; from 4314 and 2947; to *roll toward*, i.e. *block against*:— roll (to).

4352. προσκυνέω **prŏskunĕō**, *pros-koo-neh´-o*; from 4314 and a probable der. of 2965 (mean. to *kiss*, like a dog *licking* his master's hand); to *fawn* or *crouch to*, i.e. (lit. or fig.) *prostrate* oneself in homage (do *reverence to, adore*):— worship.

4353. προσκυνητής **prŏskunētēs**, *pros-koo-nay-tace´*; from 4352; an *adorer*:— worshipper.

4354. προσλαλέω **prŏslalĕō**, *pros-lal-eh´-o*; from 4314 and 2980; to *talk to*, i.e. *converse with*:— speak to (with).

4355. προσλαμβάνω **prŏslambanō**, *pros-lam-ban´-o*; from 4314 and 2983; to *take to* oneself, i.e. *use* (food), *lead* (aside), *admit* (to friendship or hospitality):— receive, take (unto).

4356. πρόσληψις **prŏslēpsis**, *pros´-lapesis*; from 4355; *admission*:— receiving.

4357. προσμένω **prŏsmĕnō**, *pros-men´-o*; from 4314 and 3306; to *stay further*, i.e. *remain* in a place, with a person; fig. to *adhere to, persevere in*:— abide still, be with, cleave unto, continue in (with).

4358. προσορμίζω **prŏsŏrmizō**, *pros-or-mid´-zo*; from 4314 and a der. of the same as 3730 (mean. to *tie* lanchorl or *lull*); to *moor to*, i.e. (by impl.) *land at*:— draw to the shore.

4359. προσοφείλω **prŏsŏphĕilō**, *pros-of-i´-lo*; from 4314 and 3784; to *be indebted additionally*:— over besides.

4360. προσοχθίζω **prŏsŏchthizō**, *pros-okh-thid´-zo*; from 4314 and a form of ὀχθέω **ŏchthĕō** (to *be vexed* with something irksome); to *feel indignant at*:— be grieved with.

4361. πρόσπεινος **prŏspĕinŏs**, *pros´-pinos*; from 4314 and the same as 3983; *hungering further*, i.e. *intensely hungry*:— very hungry.

4362. προσπήγνυμι **prŏspēgnumi**, *pros-payg´-noo-mee*; from 4314 and 4078; to *fasten to*, i.e. (spec.) to *impale* (on a cross):— crucify.

4363. προσπίπτω **prŏspiptō**, *pros-pip´-to*; from 4314 and 4098; to *fall toward*, i.e. (gently) *prostrate* oneself (in supplication or homage), or (violently) to *rush* upon (in storm):— beat upon, fall (down) at (before).

4364. προσποιέομαι **prŏspŏiĕōmai**, *pros-poy-eh´-om-ahee;* mid. voice from *4314* and *4160;* to *do forward for oneself,* i.e. *pretend* (as if about to do a thing):— make as though.

4365. προσπορεύομαι **prŏspŏrĕuŏmai**, *pros-por-yoo´-om-ahee;* from *4314* and *4198;* to *journey toward,* i.e. *approach* [not the same as *4313*]:— go before.

4366. προσρήγνυμι **prŏsrēgnumi**, *pros-rayg´-noo-mee;* from *4314* and *4486;* to *tear toward,* i.e. *burst upon* (as a tempest or flood):— beat vehemently against (upon).

4367. προστάσσω **prŏstassō**, *pros-tas´-so;* from *4314* and *5021;* to *arrange toward,* i.e. (fig.) *enjoin:*— bid, command.

4368. προστάτις **prŏstatis**, *pros-tat´-is;* fem. of a der. of *4291;* a *patroness,* i.e. *assistant:*— succourer.

4369. προστίθημι **prŏstithēmi**, *pros-tith´-ay-mee;* from *4314* and *5087;* to *place additionally,* i.e. *lay beside, annex, repeat:*— add, again, give more, increase, lay unto, proceed further, speak to any more.

4370. προστρέχω **prŏstrĕchō**, *pros-trekh´-o;* from *4314* and *5143* (incl. its alt.); to *run toward,* i.e. *hasten to meet* or join:— run (thither to, to).

4371. προσφάγιον **prŏsphagiŏn**, *pros-fag´-ee-on;* neut. of a presumed der. of a compound of *4314* and *5315;* something *eaten in addition* to bread, i.e. a *relish* (spec. *fish;* comp. *3795*):— meat.

4372. πρόσφατος **prŏsphatŏs**, *pros´-fat-os;* from *4253* and a der. of *4969;* previously (recently) *slain* (fresh), i.e. (fig.) *lately made:*— new.

4373. προσφάτως **prŏsphatŏs**, *pros-fat´-oce;* adv. from *4372; recently:*— lately.

4374. προσφέρω **prŏsphĕrō**, *pros-fer´-o;* from *4314* and *5342* (incl. its alt.); to *bear toward,* i.e. *lead to, tender* (espec. to God), *treat:*— bring (to, unto), deal with, do, offer (unto, up), present unto, put to.

4375. προσφιλής **prŏsphilēs**, *pros-fee-lace´;* from a presumed compound of *4314* and *5368; friendly toward,* i.e. *acceptable:*— lovely.

4376. προσφορά **prŏsphŏra**, *pros-for-ah´;* from *4374; presentation;* concr. an *oblation* (bloodless) or *sacrifice:*— offering (up).

4377. προσφωνέω **prŏsphōnĕō**, *pros-fo-neh´-o;* from *4314* and *5455;* to *sound toward,* i.e. *address, exclaim, summon:*— call unto, speak (un-) to.

4378. πρόσχυσις **prŏschusis**, *pros´-khoo-sis;* from a comp. of *4314* and χέω **chĕō** (to *pour*); a *shedding forth,* i.e. *affusion:*— sprinkling.

4379. προσψαύω **prŏspsauō**, *pros-psŏw´-o;* from *4314* and ψαύω **psauō** (to *touch*); to *impinge,* i.e. *lay a finger on* (in order to relieve):— touch.

4380. προσωπολημπτέω **prŏsōpŏlēptĕō**, *pros-o-pol-ape-teh´-o;* from *4381;* to

favor an individual, i.e. *show partiality:*— have respect to persons.

4381. προσωπολήπτης **prŏsōpŏlēptēs**, *pros-o-pol-ape´-tace;* from *4383* and *2983;* an *accepter of a face (individual),* i.e. (spec.) one *exhibiting partiality:*— respecter of persons.

4382. προσωποληψία **prŏsōpŏlēpsia**, *pros-o-pol-ape-see´-ah;* from *4381; partiality,* i.e. *favoritism:*— respect of persons.

4383. πρόσωπον **prŏsōpŏn**, *pros´-o-pon;* from *4314* and ὤψ **ōps** (the *visage,* from *3700*); the *front,* (as being *toward view*), i.e. the *countenance, aspect, appearance, surface;* by impl. *presence, person:*— (outward) appearance, × before, countenance, face, fashion, (men's) person, presence.

4384. προτάσσω **prŏtassō**, *prot-as´-so;* from *4253* and *5021;* to *pre-arrange,* i.e. *prescribe:*— before appoint.

4385. προτείνω **prŏtĕinō**, *prot-i´-no;* from *4253* and τείνω **tĕinō** (to *stretch*); to *protend,* i.e. *tie prostrate* (for scourging):— bind.

4386. πρότερον **prŏtĕrŏn**, *prot´-er-on;* neut. of *4387* as adv. (with or without the art.); *previously:*— before, (at the) first, former.

4387. πρότερος **prŏtĕrŏs**, *prot´-er-os;* comp. of *4253; prior* or *previous:*— former.

4388. προτίθεμαι **prŏtithĕmai**, *prot-ith´-em-ahee;* mid. voice from *4253* and *5087;* to *place before,* i.e. (for oneself) to *exhibit;* (to oneself) to *propose (determine):*— purpose, set forth.

4389. προτρέπομαι **prŏtrĕpŏmai**, *prot-rep´-om-ahee;* mid. voice from *4253* and the base of *5157;* to *turn forward* for oneself, i.e. *encourage:*— exhort.

4390. προτρέχω **prŏtrĕchō**, *prot-rekh´-o;* from *4253* and *5143* (incl. its alt.); to *run forward,* i.e. *outstrip, precede:*— outrun, run before.

4391. προϋπάρχω **prŏüparchō**, *prŏ-oop-ar´-kho;* from *4253* and *5225;* to *exist before,* i.e. (adv.) to *be* or *do* something *previously:*— + be before (-time).

4392. πρόφασις **prŏphasis**, *prof´-as-is;* from a compound of *4253* and *5316;* an *outward showing,* i.e. *pretext:*— cloke, colour, pretence, show.

4393. προφέρω **prŏphĕrō**, *prof-er´-o;* from *4253* and *5342;* to *bear forward,* i.e. *produce:*— bring forth.

4394. προφητεία **prŏphĕtĕia**, *prof-ay-ti´-ah;* from *4396* ("*prophecy*"); *prediction* (scriptural or other):— prophecy, prophesying.

4395. προφητεύω **prŏphĕtĕuō**, *prof-ate-yoo´-o;* from *4396;* to *foretell* events, *divine, speak* under *inspiration, exercise* the prophetic office:— prophesy.

4396. προφήτης **prŏphētēs**, *prof-ay´-tace;* from a compound of *4253* and *5346;* a *foreteller* ("*prophet*"); by anal. an *inspired speaker;* by extens. a *poet:*— prophet.

4397. προφητικός **prŏphētikŏs**, *prof-ay-tik-os´;* from *4396; pertaining to a fore-

teller ("*prophetic*"):— of prophecy, of the prophets.

4398. προφῆτις **prŏphētis**, *prof-ay´-tis;* fem. of *4396;* a *female foreteller* or an *inspired woman:*— prophetess.

4399. προφθάνω **prŏphthanō**, *prof-than´-o;* from *4253* and *5348;* to *get an earlier start of,* i.e. *anticipate:*— prevent.

4400. προχειρίζομαι **prŏchĕirizŏmai**, *prokh-i-rid´-zom-ahee;* mid. voice from *4253* and a der. of *5495;* to *handle for oneself in advance,* i.e. (fig.) to *purpose:*— choose, make.

4401. προχειροτονέω **prŏchĕirŏtŏnĕō**, *prokh-i-rot-on-eh´-o;* from *4253* and *5500;* to *elect in advance:*— choose before.

4402. Πρόχορος **Prŏchŏrŏs**, *prokh´-or-os;* from *4253* and *5525; before the dance; Prochorus,* a Chr.:— Prochorus.

4403. πρύμνα **prumna**, *proom´-nah;* fem. of πρυμνός **prumnus** (*hindmost*); the *stern* of a ship:— hinder part, stern.

4404. πρωΐ **prŏï**, *pro-ee´;* adv. from *4253;* at *dawn;* by impl. the *day-break watch:*— early (in the morning), (in the) morning.

4405. πρωΐα **prŏïa**, *pro-ee´-ah;* fem. of a der. of *4404* as noun; *day-dawn:*— early, morning.

4406. πρώϊμος **prŏïmŏs**, *pro´-ee-mos;* from *4404; dawning,* i.e. (by anal.) *autumnal* (showering, the first of the rainy season):— early.

4407. πρωϊνός **prŏïnŏs**, *pro-ee-nos´;* from *4404; pertaining to the dawn,* i.e. *matutinal:*— morning.

4408. πρῶρα **prōra**, *pro´-ra;* fem. of a presumed der. of *4253* as noun; the *prow,* i.e. *forward part of a vessel:*— forepart (-ship).

4409. πρωτεύω **prōtĕuō**, *prote-yoo´-o;* from *4413;* to *be first* (in rank or influence):— have the preeminence.

4410. πρωτοκαθεδρία **prōtŏkathĕdria**, *pro-tok-ath-ed-ree´-ah;* from *4413* and *2515;* a *sitting first* (in the front row), i.e. *preeminence in council:*— chief (highest, uppermost) seat.

4411. πρωτοκλισία **prōtŏklisia**, *pro-tok-lis-ee´-ah;* from *4413* and *2828;* a *reclining first* (in the place of honor) at the dinner-bed, i.e. *preeminence at meals:*— chief (highest, uppermost) room.

4412. πρῶτον **prōtŏn**, *pro´-ton;* neut. of *4413* as adv. (with or without *3588*); *firstly* (in time, place, order, or importance):— before, at the beginning, chiefly (at, at the) first (of all).

4413. πρῶτος **prōtŏs**, *pro´-tos;* contr. superl. of *4253; foremost* (in time, place, order or importance):— before, beginning, best, chief (-est), first (of all), former.

4414. πρωτοστάτης **prōtŏstatēs**, *pro-tos-tat´-ace;* from *4413* and *2476;* one *standing first* in the ranks, i.e. a *captain* (champion):— ringleader.

4415. πρωτοτόκια **prōtŏtŏkia**, *pro-tot-ok´-ee-ah;* from *4416; primogeniture* (as a privilege):— birthright.

4416. πρωτότοκος prōtŏtŏkŏs, *pro-tot-ok´-os*; from 4413 and the alt. of 5088; *first-born* (usually as noun, lit. or fig.):— firstbegotten (-born).

4417. πταίω ptaiō, *ptah´-yo*; a form of 4098; to *trip*, i.e. (fig.) to *err, sin, fail* (of salvation):— fall, offend, stumble.

4418. πτέρνα ptĕrna, *pter´-nah*; of uncert. der.; the *heel* (fig.):— heel.

4419. πτερύγιον ptĕrugiŏn, *pter-oog´-ee-on*; neut. of a presumed der. of 4420; a *winglet*, i.e. (fig.) *extremity* (top corner):— pinnacle.

4420. πτέρυξ ptĕrux, *pter´-oox*; from a der. of 4072 (mean. a *feather*); a *wing*:— wing.

4421. πτηνόν ptĕnŏn, *ptay-non´*; contr. for 4071; a *bird*:— bird.

4422. πτοέω ptŏĕō, *ptŏ-eh´-o*; prob. akin to the alt. of 4098 (through the idea of causing to *fall*) or to 4072 (through that of causing to *fly* away); to *scare*:— frighten.

4423. πτόησις ptŏĕsis, *ptŏ´-ay-sis*; from 4422; *alarm*:— amazement.

4424. Πτολεμαΐς Ptŏlĕmaïs, *ptol-em-ah-is´*; from Πτολεμαῖος Ptŏlĕmaïŏs (*Ptolemy*, after whom it was named); *Ptolemais*, a place in Pal.:— Ptolemais.

4425. πτύον ptuŏn, *ptoo´-on*; from 4429; a *winnowing-fork* (as *scattering* like spittle):— fan.

4426. πτύρω pturō, *ptoo´-ro*; from a presumed der. of 4429 (and thus akin to 4422); to *frighten*:— terrify.

4427. πτύσμα ptusma, *ptoos´-mah*; from 4429; *saliva*:— spittle.

4428. πτύσσω ptussō, *ptoos´-so*; prob. akin to πετάννυμι pĕtannumi, (to *spread*; and thus appar. allied to 4072 through the idea of *expansion*, and to 4429 through that of *flattening*; comp. 3961); to *fold*, i.e. *furl* a scroll:— close.

4429. πτύω ptuō, *ptoo´-o*; a primary verb (comp. 4428); to *spit*:— spit.

4430. πτῶμα ptōma, *pto´-mah*; from the alt. of 4098; a *ruin*, i.e. (spec.) lifeless *body* (*corpse, carrion*):— dead body, carcase, corpse.

4431. πτῶσις ptōsis, *pto´-sis*; from the alt. of 4098; a *crash*, i.e. *downfall* (lit. or fig.):— fall.

4432. πτωχεία ptōchĕia, *pto-khi´-ah*; from 4433; *beggary*, i.e. *indigence* (lit. or fig.):— poverty.

4433. πτωχεύω ptōchĕuō, *pto-khyoo´-o*; from 4434; to *be a beggar*, i.e. (by impl.) to *become indigent* (fig.):— become poor.

4434. πτωχός ptōchŏs, *pto-khos´*; from πτώσσω ptōssō, to *crouch*; akin to 4422 and the alt. of 4098; a *beggar* (as *cringing*), i.e. *pauper* (strictly denoting absolute or public *mendicancy*, although also used in a qualified or relative sense; whereas 3993 prop. means only *straitened* circumstances in private), lit. (often used as a noun) or fig. (*distressed*):— beggar (-ly), poor.

4435. πυγμή pugmē, *poog-may´*; from a primary πύξ pux (the *fist*, as a weapon); the clenched *hand*, i.e. (only in dat. as

adverb) *with* the *fist* (hard *scrubbing*):— oft.

4436. Πύθων Puthŏn, *poo´-thone*; from Πυθώ Puthō (the *name* of the region where Delphi, the seat of the famous *oracle*, was located); a *Python*, i.e. (by anal. with the supposed *diviner* there) *inspiration* (*soothsaying*):— divination.

4437. πυκνός puknŏs, *pook-nos´*; from the same as 4635; *clasped* (*thick*), i.e. (fig.) *frequent*; neut. plur. (as adv.) *frequently*:— often (-er).

4438. πυκτέω puktĕō, *pook-teh´-o*; from a der. of the same as 4435; to *box* (with the fist), i.e. *contend* (as a boxer) at the games (fig.):— fight.

4439. πύλη pulē, *poo´-lay*; appar. a primary word; a *gate*, i.e. the leaf or wing of a folding *entrance* (lit. or fig.):— gate.

4440. πυλών pulōn, *poo-lone´*; from 4439; a *gate-way, door-way* of a building or city; by impl. a *portal* or *vestibule*:— gate, porch.

4441. πυνθάνομαι punthanŏmai, *poon-than´-om-ahee*; mid. voice prol. from a primary πύθω puthō (which occurs only as an alt. in certain tenses); to *question*, i.e. *ascertain* by inquiry (as a matter of *information* merely; and thus differing from 2065, which prop. means a *request* as a favor; and from 154, which is strictly a *demand* for something due; as well as from 2212, which implies a *search* for something hidden; and from 1189, which involves the idea of urgent *need*); by impl. to *learn* (by casual intelligence):— ask, demand, enquire, understand.

4442. πῦρ pur, *poor*; a primary word; "*fire*" (lit. or fig., spec. *lightning*):— fiery, fire.

4443. πυρά pura, *poo-rah´*; from 4442; a *fire* (concr.):— fire.

4444. πύργος purgŏs, *poor´-gos*; appar. a primary word ("*burgh*"); a *tower* or *castle*:— tower.

4445. πυρέσσω purĕssō, *poo-res´-so*; from 4443; to *be on fire*, i.e. (spec.) to *have a fever*:— be sick of a fever.

4446. πυρετός purĕtŏs, *poo-ret-os´*; from 4445; *inflamed*, i.e. (by impl.) *feverish* (as noun, *fever*):— fever.

4447. πύρινος purinŏs, *poo´-ree-nos*; from 4443; *fiery*, i.e. (by impl.) *flaming*:— of fire.

4448. πυρόω purŏō, *poo-ro´-o*; from 4442; to *kindle*, i.e. (pass.) to *be ignited, glow* (lit.), *be refined* (by impl.), or (fig.) to *be inflamed* (with anger, grief, lust):— burn, fiery, be on fire, try.

4449. πυρράζω purrhazō, *poor-hrad´-zo*; from 4450; to *redden* (intr.):— be red.

4450. πυρρός purrhŏs, *poor-hros´*; from 4442; *fire-like*, i.e. (spec.) *flame-colored*:— red.

4451. πύρωσις purōsis, *poo´-ro-sis*; from 4448; *ignition*, i.e. (spec.) *smelting* (fig. *conflagration, calamity* as a *test*):— burning, trial.

4452. -πω -pō, *po*; another form of the base of 4458; an enclitic particle of indefiniteness; *yet, even*; used only in

composition. See 3369, 3380, 3764, 3768, 4455.

4453. πωλέω pōlĕō, *po-leh´-o*; prob. ultimately from πέλομαι pĕlŏmai (to *be busy*, to *trade*); to *barter* (as a *pedlar*), i.e. to *sell*:— sell, whatever is sold.

4454. πῶλος pōlŏs, *po´-los*; appar. a primary word; a "*foal*" or "*filly*", i.e. (spec.) a *young ass*:— colt.

4455. πώποτε pōpŏtĕ, *po´-pot-e*; from 4452 and 4218; *at any time*, i.e. (with neg. particle) *at no time*:— at any time, + never (... to any man), + yet, never man.

4456. πωρόω pōrŏō, *po-ro´-o*; appar. from πῶρος pōrŏs, (a kind of *stone*); to *petrify*, i.e. (fig.) to *indurate* (*render stupid* or *callous*):— blind, harden.

4457. πώρωσις pōrōsis, *po´-ro-sis*; from 4456; *stupidity* or *callousness*:— blindness, hardness.

4458. -πώς -pōs, *poce*; adv. from the base of 4225; an enclitic particle of indefiniteness of manner; *somehow* or *anyhow*; used only in composition:— haply, by any (some) means, perhaps. See 1513, 3381. Comp. 4459.

4459. πῶς pōs, *poce*; adv. from the base of 4226; an interr. particle of manner; *in what way*? (sometimes the question is indirect, *how*?); also as exclamation, *how* much!:— how, after (by) what manner (means), that. [*Occasionally unexpressed in English*].

P

4460. Ῥαάβ Rhaab, *hrah-ab´*; of Heb. or. [7343]; *Raab* (i.e. *Rachab*), a Canaanitess:— Rahab. See also 4477.

4461. ῥαββί rhabbi, *hrab-bee´*; of Heb. or. [7227 with pron. suff.); *my master*, i.e *Rabbi*, as an official title of honor:— Master, Rabbi.

4462. ῥαββονί rhabbŏni, *hrab-bon-ee´*; or

    ῥαββουνί rhabbŏuni, *hrab-boo-nee´*; of Chald. or.; corresp. to 4461:— Lord, Rabboni.

4463. ῥαβδίζω rhabdizō, *hrab-did´-zo*; from 4464; to *strike with a stick*, i.e. *bastinado*:— beat (with rods).

4464. ῥάβδος rhabdŏs, *hrab´-dos*; from the base of 4474; a *stick* or *wand* (as a *cudgel*, a *cane* or a *baton* of royalty):— rod, sceptre, staff.

4465. ῥαβδοῦχος rhabdŏuchŏs, *hrab-doo´-khos*; from 4464 and 2192; a *rod-* (the Lat. *fasces*) *holder*, i.e. a Rom. *lictor* (*constable* or *executioner*):— serjeant.

4466. Ῥαγαῦ Rhagau, *hrag-ŏw´*; of Heb. or. [7466]; *Ragaü* (i.e. *Reu*), a patriarch:— Ragau.

4467. ῥαδιούργημα rhadiŏurgēma, *hrad-ee-oorg´-ay-mah*; from a comp. of ῥᾴδιος rhadiŏs (*easy*, i.e. *reckless*) and 2041; *easy-going* behavior, i.e. (by extens.) a *crime*:— lewdness.

4468. ῥαδιουργία rhadiŏurgia, *hrad-ee-oorg-ee´-a*; from the same as 4467; *recklessness*, i.e. (by extens.) *malignity*:— mischief.

4469. ῥακά rhaka, *hrak-ah´*; of Chald.

or. [comp. 7386]; O *empty* one, i.e. thou *worthless* (as a term of utter vilification):— Raca.

4470. ῥάκος **rhakŏs**, *hrak´-os;* from 4486; a "*rag*," i.e. *piece* of cloth:— cloth.

4471. 'Pαμᾶ **Rhama**, *hram-ah´;* of Heb. or. [7414]; *Rama* (i.e. *Ramah*), a place in Pal.:— Rama.

4472. ῥαντίζω **rhantizō**, *hran-tid´-zo;* from a der. of ῥαίνω **rhainō** (to *sprinkle*); to *render besprinkled*, i.e. *asperse* (cerem. or fig.):— sprinkle.

4473. ῥαντισμός **rhantismŏs**, *hran-tis-mos´;* from 4472; *aspersion* (cerem. or fig.):— sprinkling.

4474. ῥαπίζω **rhapizō**, *hrap-id´-zo;* from a der. of a primary ῥέπω **rhĕpō** (to *let fall*, "*rap*"); to *slap:—* smite (with the palm of the hand). Comp. 5180.

4475. ῥάπισμα **rhapisma**, *hrap´-is-mah;* from 4474; a *slap:—* (+ strike with the) palm of the hand, smite with the hand.

4476. ῥαφίς **rhaphis**, *hraf-ece´;* from a primary ῥάπτω **rhaptō** (to *sew;* perh. rather akin to the base of 4474 through the idea of *puncturing*); a *needle:—* needle.

4477. 'Pαχάβ **Rhachab**, *hrakh-ab´;* from the same as 4460; *Rachab*, a Canaanitess:— Rachab.

4478. 'Pαχήλ **Rhachēl**, *hrakh-ale´;* of Heb. or. [7354]; *Rachel*, the wife of Jacob:— Rachel.

4479. 'Pεβέκκα **Rhĕbĕkka**, *hreb-bek´-kah;* of Heb. or. [7259]; *Rebecca* (i.e. *Ribkah*), the wife of Isaac:— Rebecca.

4480. ῥέδα **rhĕda**, *hred´-ah;* of Lat. or.; a *rheda*, i.e. *four-wheeled carriage* (*wagon* for riding):— chariot.

4481. 'Pεμφάν **Rhĕmphan**, *hrem-fan´* or

'Pαιφάν **Rhaiphan**, *hrahee-fan´;* by incorrect transliteration for a word of Heb. of [3594]; *Remphan* (i.e. *Kijun*), an Eg. idol:—Remphan.

4482. ῥέω **rhĕō**, *hreh´-o;* a primary verb; for some tenses of which a prol. form

ῥεύω **rhĕuō**, *hryoo´-o* is used; to *flow* ("*run*"; as water):— flow.

4483. ῥέω **rhĕō**, *hreh´-o;* for certain tenses of which a prol. form

ἐρέω **ĕrĕō**, *er-eh´-o;* is used; and both as alt. for 2036; perh. akin (or ident.) with 4482 (through the idea of *pouring* forth); to *utter*, i.e. *speak* or *say:—* command, make, say, speak (of). Comp. 3004.

4484. 'Pήγιον **Rhēgiŏn**, *hrayg´-ee-on;* of Lat. or.; *Rhegium*, a place in Italy:— Rhegium.

4485. ῥῆγμα **rhēgma**, *hrayg´-mah;* from 4486; something *torn*, i.e. a *fragment* (by impl. and abstr. a *fall*):— ruin.

4486. ῥήγνυμι **rhēgnumi**, *hrayg´-noo-mee;* or

ῥήσσω **rhēssō**, *hrace´-so;* both prol. forms of ῥήκω **rhēkō** (which appears only in certain forms, and is itself prob. a strengthened form of ἄγνυμι **agnumi**, [see in 2608]); to "*break*," "*wreck*" or "*crack*", i.e. (espec.) to *sunder* (by *separation* of the parts;

2608 being its intensive [with the prep. in composition], and 2352 a *shattering* to minute fragments; but not a *reduction* to the constituent particles, like 3089) or *disrupt*, *lacerate;* by impl. to *convulse* (with *spasms*); fig. to *give vent* to joyful emotions:— break (forth), burst, rend, tear.

4487. ῥῆμα **rhēma**, *hray´-mah;* from 4483; an *utterance* (indiv., collect. or spec.); by impl. a *matter* or *topic* (espec. of narration, command or dispute); with a neg. *naught* whatever:— + evil, + nothing, saying, word.

4488. 'Pησά **Rhēsa**, *hray-sah´;* prob. of Heb. or. [appar. for 7509]; *Resa* (i.e. *Rephajah*), an Isr.:— Rhesa.

4489. ῥήτωρ **rhētōr**, *hray´-tore;* from 4483; a *speaker*, i.e. (by impl.) a forensic *advocate:—* orator.

4490. ῥητῶς **rhētōs**, *hray-toce´;* adv. from a der. of 4483; *out-spokenly*, i.e. *distinctly:—* expressly.

4491. ῥίζα **rhiza**, *hrid´-zah;* appar. a primary word; a "*root*" (lit. or fig.):— root.

4492. ῥιζόω **rhizŏō**, *hrid-zŏ´-o;* from 4491; to *root* (fig. *become stable*):— root.

4493. ῥιπή **rhipē**, *hree-pay´;* from 4496; a *jerk* (of the eye, i.e. [by anal.] an *instant*):— twinkling.

4494. ῥιπίζω **rhipizō**, *hrip-id´-zo;* from a der. of 4496 (mean. a *fan* or *bellows*); to *breeze up*, i.e. (by anal.) to *agitate* (into waves):— toss.

4495. ῥιπτέω **rhiptĕō**, *hrip-teh´-o;* from a der. of 4496; to *toss* up:— cast off.

4496. ῥίπτω **rhiptō**, *hrip´-to;* a primary verb (perh. rather akin to the base of 4474, through the idea of sudden *motion*); to *fling* (prop. with a quick *toss*, thus differing from 906, which denotes a *deliberate* hurl; and from τείνω **tĕinō**, [see in 1614], which indicates an *extended* projection); by qualification, to *deposit* (as if a load); by extens. to *disperse:—* cast (down, out), scatter abroad, throw.

4497. 'Pοβοάμ **Rhŏbŏam**, *hrob-ŏ-am´;* of Heb. or. [7346]; *Roboäm* (i.e. *Rechabam*), an Isr.:— Roboam.

4498. 'Pόδη **Rhŏdē**, *hrod´-ay;* prob. for ῥοδῆ **rhŏdē**, (a *rose*); *Rodē*, a servant girl:— Rhoda.

4499. 'Pόδος **Rhŏdŏs**, *hrod´-os;* prob. from ῥόδον **rhŏdŏn**, (a *rose*); *Rhodus*, an island of the Mediterranean:— Rhodes.

4500. ῥοιζηδόν **rhŏizēdŏn**, *hroyd-zay-don´;* adv. from a der. of ῥοῖζος **rhŏizŏs** (a *whir*); *whizzingly*, i.e. *with a crash:—* with a great noise.

4501. ῥομφαία **rhŏmphaia**, *hrom-fah´-yah;* prob. of for. or.; a *sabre*, i.e. a long and broad *cutlass* (any *weapon* of the kind, lit. or fig.):— sword.

4502. 'Pουβήν **Rhŏubēn**, *hroo-bane´;* of Heb. or. [7205]; *Ruben* (i.e. *Reuben*), an Isr.:— Reuben.

4503. 'Pούθ **Rhŏuth**, *hrooth;* of Heb. or. [7327]; *Ruth*, a Moabitess:— Ruth.

4504. 'Pοῦφος **Rhŏuphŏs**, *hroo´-fos;* of Lat. or.; *red; Rufus*, a Chr.:— Rufus.

4505. ῥύμη **rhumē**, *hroo´-may;* prol. from 4506 in its orig. sense; an *alley* or *avenue* (as crowded):— lane, street.

4506. ῥύομαι **rhuŏmai**, *hroo´-om-ahee;* mid. voice of an obs. verb, akin to 4482 (through the idea of a *current;* comp. 4511); to *rush* or *draw* (for oneself), i.e. *rescue:—* deliver (-er).

4507. ῥυπαρία **rhuparia**, *hroo-par-ee´-ah;* from 4508; *dirtiness* (mor.):— turpitude.

4508. ῥυπαρός **rhuparŏs**, *hroo-par-os´;* from 4509; *dirty*, i.e. (rel.) *cheap* or *shabby;* mor. *wicked.—* vile.

4509. ῥύπος **rhupŏs**, *hroo´-pos;* of uncert. aff.; *dirt*, i.e. (mor.) *depravity:—* filth.

4510. ῥυπόω **rhupŏō**, *hroo-pŏ´-o;* from 4509; to *soil*, i.e. (intr.) to *become dirty* (mor.):— be filthy.

4511. ῥύσις **rhusis**, *hroo´-sis;* from 4506 in the sense of its congener 4482; a *flux* (of blood):— issue.

4512. ῥυτίς **rhutis**, *hroo-tece´;* from 4506; a *fold* (as *drawing* together), i.e. a *wrinkle* (espec. on the face):— wrinkle.

4513. 'Pωμαϊκός **Rhōmaïkŏs**, *hro-mah-ee-kos´;* from 4514; *Romaïc*, i.e. *Lat.:—* Latin.

4514. 'Pωμαῖος **Rhōmaïŏs**, *hro-mah´-yos;* from 4516; *Romæan*, i.e. *Roman* (as noun):— Roman, of Rome.

4515. 'Pωμαϊστί **Rhōmaïsti**, *hro-mah-is-tee´;* adv. from a presumed der. of 4516; *Romaïstically*, i.e. in the *Latin* language:— Latin.

4516. 'Pώμη **Rhōmē**, *hro´-may;* from the base of 4517; *strength; Roma*, the capital of Italy:— Rome.

4517. ῥώννυμι **rhōnnumi**, *hrone´-noo-mee;* prol. from ῥώομαι **rhŏōmai** (to *dart;* prob. akin to 4506); to *strengthen*, i.e. (impers. pass.) *have health* (as a parting exclamation, *good-bye*):— farewell.

Σ

4518. σαβαχθανί **sabachthani**, *sab-akh-than-ee´;* of Chald. or [7662 with pron. suff.]; *thou hast left me; sabachthani* (i.e. *shebakthani*), a cry of distress:— sabachthani.

4519. σαβαώθ **sabaōth**, *sab-ah-owth´;* of Heb. or. [6635 in fem. plur.]; *armies; sabaoth* (i.e. *tsebaoth*), a military epithet of God:— sabaoth.

4520. σαββατισμός **sabbatismŏs**, *sab-bat-is-mos´;* from a der. of 4521; a "*sabbatism*," i.e. (fig.) the *repose* of Christianity (as a type of heaven):— rest.

4521. σάββατον **sabbatŏn**, *sab´-bat-on;* of Heb. or. [7676]; the *Sabbath* (i.e. *Shabbath*), or day of weekly *repose* from secular avocations (also the observance or institution itself); by extens. a se'*nnight*, i.e. the interval between two Sabbaths; likewise the plural in all the above applications:— sabbath (day), week.

4522. σαγήνη **sagēnē**, *sag-ay´-nay;* from a der. of σάττω **sattō** (to *equip*) mean. *furniture*, espec. a *pack-saddle* (which in the E. is merely a bag of *netted* rope); a "*seine*" for fishing:— net.

4523. Σαδδουκαῖος **Saddŏukaiŏs**, *saddoo-kah´-yos;* prob. from 4524; a *Sadducæan* (i.e. *Tsadokian*), or follower of a certain heretical Isr.:— Sadducee.

4524. Σαδώκ **Sadōk**, *sad-oke´;* of Heb. or. [6659]; *Sadoc* (i.e. *Tsadok*), an Isr.:— Sadoc.

4525. σαίνω **sainō**, *sah´-ee-no;* akin to 4579; to *wag* (as a dog its tail fawningly), i.e. (gen.) to *shake* (fig. *disturb*):— move.

4526. σάκκος **sakkŏs**, *sak´-kos;* of Heb. or. [8242]; "*sack*"*-cloth*, i.e. *mohair* (the material or garments made of it, worn as a sign of grief):— sackcloth.

4527. Σαλά **Sala**, *sal-ah´;* of Heb. or. [7974]; *Sala* (i.e. *Shelach*), a patriarch:— Sala.

4528. Σαλαθιήλ **Salathiēl**, *sal-ath-ee-ale´;* of Heb. or. [7597]; *Salathiël* (i.e. *Sheältiël*), an Isr.:— Salathiel.

4529. Σαλαμίς **Salamis**, *sal-am-ece´;* prob. from 4535 (from the *surge* on the shore); *Salamis*, a place in Cyprus:— Salamis.

4530. Σαλείμ **Salĕim**, *sal-ime´;* prob. from the same as 4531; *Salim*, a place in Pal.:— Salim.

4531. σαλεύω **salĕuō**, *sal-yoo´-o;* from 4535; to *waver*, i.e. *agitate, rock, topple* or (by impl.) *destroy;* fig. to *disturb, incite:*— move, shake (together), which can [-not] be shaken, stir up.

4532. Σαλήμ **Salēm**, *sal-ame´;* of Heb. or. [8004]; *Salem* (i.e. *Shalem*), a place in Pal.:— Salem.

4533. Σαλμών **Salmōn**, *sal-mone´;* of Heb. or. [8012]; *Salmon*, an Isr.:— Salmon.

4534. Σαλμώνη **Salmōnē**, *sal-mo´-nay;* perh. of similar or. to 4529; *Salmone*, a place in Crete:— Salmone.

4535. σάλος **salŏs**, *sal´-os;* prob. from the base of 4525; a *vibration*, i.e. (spec.) *billow:*— wave.

4536. σάλπιγξ **salpigx**, *sal´-pinx;* perh. from 4535 (through the idea of *quavering* or *reverberation*); a *trumpet:*— trump (-et).

4537. σαλπίζω **salpizō**, *sal-pid´-zo;* from 4536; to *trumpet*, i.e. *sound a blast* (lit. or fig.):— (which are yet to) sound (a trumpet).

4538. σαλπιστής **salpistēs**, *sal-pis-tace´;* from 4537; a *trumpeter:*— trumpeter.

4539. Σαλώμη **Salōmē**, *sal-o´-may;* prob. of Heb. or. [fem. from 7965]; *Salomè* (i.e. *Shelomah*), an Israelitess:— Salome.

4540. Σαμάρεια **Samarĕia**, *sam-ar´-i-ah;* of Heb. or. [8111]; *Samaria* (i.e. *Shomeron*), a city and region of Pal.:— Samaria.

4541. Σαμαρείτης **Samarĕitēs**, *sam-ar-i´-tace* or

Σαμαρίτης **Samaritēs**, *sam-ar-ee´-tace;* from 4540; a *Samarite*, i.e. inhab. of Samaria:— Samaritan.

4542. Σαμαρεῖτις **Samarĕitis**, *sam-ar-i´-tis* or

Σαμαριτῖς **Samaritis**, *sam-ar-ee´-tis* fem. of 4541; a *Samaritess*, i.e. woman of Samaria:— of Samaria.

4543. Σαμοθρᾴκη **Samŏthraįkē**, *sam-oth-rak´-ay;* from 4544 and Θρᾴκη **Thraįkē** (*Thrace*); *Samo-thracè* (*Samos of Thrace*), an island in the Mediterranean:— Samothracia.

4544. Σάμος **Samŏs**, *sam´-os;* of uncert. aff.; *Samus*, an island of the Mediterranean:— Samos.

4545. Σαμουήλ **Samŏuēl**, *sam-oo-ale´;* of Heb. or. [8050]; *Samuel* (i.e. *Shemuel*), an Isr.:— Samuel.

4546. Σαμψών **Sampsōn**, *samp-sone´;* of Heb. or. [8123]; *Sampson* (i.e. *Shimshon*), an Isr.:— Samson.

4547. σανδάλιον **sandaliŏn**, *san-dal´-ee-on;* neut. of a der. of σάνδαλον **sandalŏn** (a "*sandal*"; of uncert. or.); a *slipper* or *sole-pad:*— sandal.

4548. σανίς **sanis**, *san-ece´;* of uncert. aff.; a *plank:*— board.

4549. Σαούλ **Saŏul**, *sah-ool´;* of Heb. or. [7586]; *Saül* (i.e. *Shaül*), the Jewish name of *Paul:*— Saul. Comp. 4569.

4550. σαπρός **saprŏs**, *sap-ros´;* from 4595; *rotten*, i.e. *worthless* (lit. or mor.):— bad, corrupt. Comp. 4190.

4551. Σαπφείρη **Sapphĕirē**, *sap-fi´-ray;* fem. of 4552; *Sapphirè*, an Israelitess:— Sapphira.

4552. σάπφειρος **sapphĕirŏs**, *sap´-fi-ros;* of Heb. or. [5601]; a "*sapphire*" or *lapis-lazuli* gem:— sapphire.

4553. σαργάνη **sarganē**, *sar-gan´-ay;* appar. of Heb. or. [8276]; a *basket* (as *interwoven* or *wicker*-work:— basket.

4554. Σάρδεις **Sardĕis**, *sar´-dice;* plur. of uncert. der.; *Sardis*, a place in Asia Minor:— Sardis.

4555. σάρδινος **sardinŏs**, *sar´-dee-nos;* from the same as 4556; *sardine* (3037 being impl.), i.e. a gem, so called:— sardine.

4556. σάρδιος **sardiŏs**, *sar´-dee-os;* prop. an adj. from an uncert. base; *sardian* (3037 being impl.), i.e. (as noun) the gem so called:— sardius.

4557. σαρδόνυξ **sardŏnux**, *sar-don´-oox;* from the base of 4556 and ὄνυξ **ŏnux** (the *nail* of a finger; hence, the "*onyx*" stone); a "*sardonyx*", i.e. the gem so called:— sardonyx.

4558. Σάρεπτα **Sarĕpta**, *sar´-ep-tah;* of Heb. or. [6886]; *Sarepta* (i.e. *Tsarephath*), a place in Pal.:— Sarepta.

4559. σαρκικός **sarkikŏs**, *sar-kee-kos´;* from 4561; *pertaining to flesh*, i.e. (by extens.) *bodily, temporal*, or (by impl.) *animal, unregenerate:*— carnal, fleshly.

4560. σάρκινος **sarkinŏs**, *sar´-kee-nos;* from 4561; *similar to flesh*, i.e. (by anal.) *soft:*— fleshly.

4561. σάρξ **sarx**, *sarx;* prob. from the base of 4563; *flesh* (as *stripped* of the skin), i.e. (strictly) the *meat* of an animal (as food), or (by extens.) the *body* (as opposed to the soul [or spirit], or as

the symbol of what is external, or as the means of kindred), or (by impl.) *human nature* (with its frailties [phys. or mor.] and passions), or (spec.) a *human being* (as such):— carnal (-ly, + -ly minded), flesh ([-ly]).

4562. Σαρούχ **Sarŏuch** *sa-rooch´*, or

Σερούχ **Sĕrŏuch**, *seh-rooch´;* of Heb. or. [8286]; *Saruch* (i.e. *Serug*), a patriarch:— Saruch.

4563. σαρόω **sarŏō**, *sar-ŏ´-o;* from a der. of σαίρω **sairō** (to *brush* off; akin to 4951); mean. a *broom;* to *sweep:*— sweep.

4564. Σάρρα **Sarrha**, *sar´-hrah;* of Heb. or. [8283]; *Sarra* (i.e. *Sarah*), the wife of Abraham:— Sara, Sarah.

4565. Σάρων **Sarōn**, *sar´-one;* of Heb. or. [8289]; *Saron* (i.e. *Sharon*), a district of Pal.:— Saron.

4566. Σατᾶν **Satan**, *sat-an´;* of Heb. or. [7854]; *Satan*, i.e. the *devil:*— Satan. Comp. 4567.

4567. Σατανᾶς **Satanas**, *sat-an-as´;* of Chald. or. corresp. to 4566 (with the def. aff.); *the accuser*, i.e. the *devil:*— Satan.

4568. σάτον **satŏn**, *sat´-on;* of Heb. or. [5429]; a certain *measure* for things dry:— measure.

4569. Σαῦλος **Saulŏs**, *sŏw´-los;* of Heb. or., the same as 4549; *Saulus* (i.e. *Shaül*), the Jewish name of *Paul:*— Saul.

σαυτοῦ **sautŏu**. etc. See 4572.

4570. σβέννυμι **sbĕnnumi**, *sben´-noo-mee;* a prol. form of an appar. primary verb; to *extinguish* (lit. or fig.):— go out, quench.

4571. σέ **sĕ**, *seh;* acc. sing. of 4771; *thee:*— thee, thou, × thy house.

4572. σεαυτοῦ **sĕautŏu**, *seh-ŏw-too´;* gen. from 4571 and 846; also dat. of the same,

σεαυτῷ **sĕautŏį**, *seh-ŏw-to´;* and acc.

σεαυτόν **sĕautŏn**, *seh-ŏw-ton´;* likewise contr.

σαυτοῦ **sautŏu**, *sŏw-too´;*

σαυτῷ **sautŏį**, *sŏw-to´;* and

σαυτόν **sautŏn**, *sŏw-ton´;* respectively; *of* (*with, to*) *thyself:*— thee, thine own self, (thou) thy (-self).

4573. σεβάζομαι **sĕbazŏmai**, *seb-ad´-zom-ᵃahee;* mid. voice from a der. of 4576; to *venerate*, i.e. *adore:*— worship.

4574. σέβασμα **sĕbasma**, *seb´-as-mah;* from 4573; something *adored*, i.e. an *object of worship* (god, altar, etc):— devotion, that is worshipped.

4575. σεβαστός **sĕbastŏs**, *seb-as-tos´;* from 4573; *venerable* (*august*), i.e. (as noun) a title of the Rom. *Emperor*, or (as adj.) *imperial:*— Augustus (-').

4576. σέβομαι **sĕbŏmai**, *seb´-om-ahee;* mid. voice of an appar. primary verb; to *revere*, i.e. *adore:*— devout, religious, worship.

4577. σειρά **sĕira**, *si-rah´;* prob. from 4951 through its congener εἴρω **ĕirō** (to *fasten;* akin to *138);* a *chain,* (as *binding* or *drawing):*— chain.

4578. σεισμός **sĕismŏs,** *sice-mos´;* from *4579;* a *commotion,* i.e. (of the air) a *gale,* (of the ground) an *earthquake:*— earthquake, tempest.

4579. σείω **sĕiō,** *si´-o;* appar. a primary verb; to *rock* (*vibrate,* prop. sideways or to and fro), i.e. (gen.) to *agitate* (in any direction; cause to *tremble*); fig. to throw into a *tremor* (of fear or concern):— move, quake, shake.

4580. Σεκοῦνδος **Sĕkŏundŏs,** *sek-oon´-dos;* of Lat. or.; *"second"; Secundus,* a Chr.:— Secundus.

4581. Σελεύκεια **Sĕlĕukĕia,** *sel-yook´-i-ah;* from Σέλευκος **Sĕlĕukŏs,** (*Seleucus,* a Syrian king); *Seleuceia,* a place in Syria:— Seleucia.

4582. σελήνη **sĕlēnē,** *sel-ay´-nay;* from σέλας **sĕlas,** (*brilliancy;* prob. akin to the alt. of *138,* through the idea of *attractiveness*); the *moon:*— moon.

4583. σεληνιάζομαι **sĕlēniazŏmai,** *sel-ay-nee-ad´-zom-ahee;* middle or passive voice from a presumed der. of *4582;* to *be moon-struck,* i.e. *crazy:*— be a lunatic.

4584. Σεμεΐ **Sĕmĕï,** *sem-eh-ee´* or

Σεμεΐν **Sĕmĕïn,** *sem-eh-een´* of Heb. or. [8096]; *Semeï* (i.e. *Shimi*), an Isr.:— Semei (Semein).

4585. σεμίδαλις **sĕmidalis,** *sem-id´-al-is;* prob. of for. origin; fine wheaten *flour:*— fine flour.

4586. σεμνός **sĕmnŏs,** *sem-nos´;* from *4576; venerable,* i.e. *honorable:*— grave, honest.

4587. σεμνότης **sĕmnŏtēs,** *sem-not´-ace;* from *4586; venerableness,* i.e. *probity:*— gravity, honesty.

4588. Σέργιος **Sĕrgiŏs,** *serg´-ee-os;* of Lat. or.; *Sergius,* a Rom.:— Sergius.

4589. Σήθ **Sēth,** *sayth;* of Heb. or. [8352]; *Seth* (i.e. *Sheth*), a patriarch:— Seth.

4590. Σήμ **Sēm,** *same;* of Heb. or. [8035]; *Sem* (i.e. *Shem*), a patriarch:— Sem.

4591. σημαίνω **sēmainō,** *say-mah´-ee-no;* from σῆμα **sēma,** (a *mark;* of uncert. der.); to *indicate:*— signify.

4592. σημεῖον **sēmĕiŏn,** *say-mi´-on;* neut. of a presumed der. of the base of *4591;* an *indication,* espec. cerem. or supernat.:— miracle, sign, token, wonder.

4593. σημειόω **sēmĕiŏō,** *say-mi-ŏ´-o;* from *4592;* to *distinguish,* i.e. *mark* (for avoidance):— note.

4594. σήμερον **sēmĕrŏn,** *say´-mer-on;* neut. (as adv.) of a presumed compound of the art. *3588* (τ changed to σ) and *2250;* on *the* (i.e. *this*) *day* (or *night* current or just passed); gen. *now* (i.e. at *present, hitherto*):— this (to-) day.

4595. σήπω **sēpō,** *say´-po;* appar. a primary verb; to *putrefy,* i.e. (fig.) *perish:*— be corrupted.

4596. σηρικός **sērikŏs,** *say-ree-kos´* or

σιρικός **sirikŏs,** *see-ree-kos´;* from Σήρ **Sēr,** (an Indian tribe from whom *silk* was procured; hence, the name of the *silk-worm*); *Seric,* i.e.

silken (neut. as noun, a *silky* fabric):— silk.

4597. σής **sēs,** *sace;* appar. of Heb. or. [5580]; a *moth:*— moth.

4598. σητόβρωτος **sētŏbrŏtŏs,** *say-tob´-ro-tos;* from *4597* and a der. of *977; moth-eaten:*— motheaten.

4599. σθενόω **sthĕnŏō,** *sthen-ŏ´-o;* from σθένος **sthĕnŏs,** (bodily *vigor;* prob. akin to the base of *2476*); to *strengthen,* i.e. (fig.) *confirm* (in spiritual knowledge and power):— strengthen.

4600. σιαγών **siagōn,** *see-ag-one´;* of uncert. der.; the *jaw*-bone, i.e. (by impl.) the *cheek* or side of the face:— cheek.

4601. σιγάω **sigaō,** *see-gah´-o;* from *4602;* to *keep silent* (tran. or intr.):— keep close (secret, silence), hold peace.

4602. σιγή **sigē,** *see-gay´;* appr. from σίζω **sizō** (to *hiss,* i.e. *hist* or *hush*); *silence:*— silence. Comp. *4623.*

4603. σιδήρεος **sidērĕŏs,** *sid-ay´-reh-os;* from *4604;* made of *iron:*— (of) iron.

4604. σίδηρος **sidērŏs,** *sid´-ay-ros;* of uncert. der.; *iron:*— iron.

4605. Σιδών **Sidōn,** *sid-one´;* of Heb. or. [6721]; *Sidon* (i.e. *Tsidon*), a place in Pal.:— Sidon.

4606. Σιδώνιος **Sidōniŏs,** *sid-o´-nee-os;* from *4605;* a *Sidonian,* i.e. inhab. of Sidon:— of Sidon.

4607. σικάριος **sikariŏs,** *sik-ar´-ee-os;* of Lat. or.; a *dagger-man* or *assassin;* a *freebooter* (Jewish *fanatic* outlawed by the Romans):— murderer. Comp. *5406.*

4608. σίκερα **sikĕra,** *sik´-er-ah;* of Heb. or. [7941]; an *intoxicant,* i.e. intensely fermented *liquor:*— strong drink.

4609. Σίλας **Silas,** *see´-las;* contr. for *4610; Silas,* a Chr.:— Silas.

4610. Σιλουανός **Silŏuanŏs,** *sil-oo-an-os´;* of Lat. or.; *"silvan;" Silvanus,* a Chr.:— Silvanus. Comp. *4609.*

4611. Σιλωάμ **Silōam,** *sil-o-am´;* of Heb. or. [7975]; *Siloäm* (i.e. *Shiloäch*), a pool of Jerusalem:— Siloam.

4612. σιμικίνθιον **simikinthiŏn,** *sim-ee-kin´-thee-on;* of Lat. or.; a *semicinctium* or *half-girding,* i.e. narrow covering (*apron*):— apron.

4613. Σίμων **Simōn,** *see´-mone;* of Heb. or. [8095]; *Simon* (i.e. *Shimon*), the name of nine Isr.:— Simon. Comp. *4826.*

4614. Σινᾶ **Sina,** *see-nah´;* of Heb. or. [5514]; *Sina* (i.e. *Sinai*), a mountain in Arabia:— Sina.

4615. σίναπι **sinapi,** *sin´-ap-ee;* perh. from σίνομαι **sinŏmai** (to *hurt,* i.e. *sting*); *mustard* (the plant):— mustard.

4616. σινδών **sindōn,** *sin-done´;* of uncert. (perh. for.) or.; *byssos* or bleached *linen* (the cloth or a garment of it):— (fine) linen (cloth).

4617. σινιάζω **siniazō,** *sin-ee-ad´-zo;* from σινίον **siniŏn,** (a *sieve*); to *riddle* (fig.):— sift.

σῖτα **sita.** See *4621.*

4618. σιτευτός **sitĕutŏs,** *sit-yoo-tos´;*

from a der. of *4621; grain-fed,* i.e. *fattened:*— fatted.

4619. σιτιστός **sitistŏs,** *sit-is-tos´;* from a der. of *4621; grained,* i.e. *fatted:*— fatling.

4620. σιτόμετρον **sitŏmĕtrŏn,** *sit-om´-et-ron;* from *4621* and *3358;* a *grain-measure,* i.e. (by impl.) *ration* (*allowance* of food):— portion of meat.

4621. σῖτος **sitŏs,** *see´-tos;* plur. irreg. neut.

σῖτα **sita,** *see´-tah;* of uncert. der.; *grain,* espec. *wheat:*— corn, wheat.

4622. Σιών **Siōn,** *see-own´;* of Heb. or. [6726]; *Sion* (i.e. *Tsijon*), a hill of Jerusalem; fig. the *Church* (militant or triumphant):— Sion.

4623. σιωπάω **siōpaō,** *see-o-pah´-o;* from σιωπή **siōpē,** (*silence,* i.e. a *hush;* prop. *muteness,* i.e. *involuntary* stillness, or *inability* to speak; and thus differing from *4602,* which is rather a voluntary *refusal* or *indisposition* to speak, although the terms are often used synonymously); to *be dumb* (but not *deaf* also, like *2974* prop.); fig. to *be calm* (as *quiet* water):— dumb, (hold) peace.

4624. σκανδαλίζω **skandalizō,** *skandal-id´-zo* ("scandalize"); *scandal-ize,* i.e. *entrap,* i.e. *trip* up (fig. *stumble* [tran.] or *entice* to sin, apostasy or displeasure):— (make to) offend.

4625. σκάνδαλον **skandalŏn,** *skan´-dal-on* ("scandal"); prob. from a der. of *2578;* a *trap-stick* (*bent sapling*), i.e. *snare* (fig. *cause* of displeasure or sin):— occasion to fall (of stumbling), offence, thing that offends, stumblingblock.

4626. σκάπτω **skaptō,** *skap´-to;* appar. a primary verb; to *dig:*— dig.

4627. σκάφη **skaphē,** *skaf´-ay;* a *"skiff"* (as if *dug* out), or *yawl* (carried aboard a large vessel for landing):— boat.

4628. σκέλος **skĕlŏs,** *skel´-os;* appar. from σκέλλω **skĕllō,** (to *parch;* through the idea of *leanness*); the *leg* (as *lank*):— leg.

4629. σκέπασμα **skĕpasma,** *skep´-as-mah;* from a der. of σκέπας **skĕpas** (a *covering;* perh. akin to the base of *4649,* through the idea of *noticeableness*); *clothing:*— raiment.

4630. Σκευᾶς **Skĕuas,** *skyoo-as´;* appar. of Lat. or.; *left-handed; Scevas* (i.e. *Scœvus*), an Isr.:— Sceva.

4631. σκευή **skĕuē,** *skyoo-ay´;* from *4632; furniture,* i.e. spare *tackle:*— tackling.

4632. σκεῦος **skĕuŏs,** *skyoo´-os;* of uncert. aff.; a *vessel, implement, equipment* or *apparatus* (lit. or fig. [spec. a *wife* as contributing to the usefulness of the husband]):— goods, sail, stuff, vessel.

4633. σκηνή **skēnē,** *skay-nay´;* appar. akin to *4632* and *4639;* a *tent* or *cloth hut* (lit. or fig.):— habitation, tabernacle.

4634. σκηνοπηγία **skēnŏpēgia,** *skay-nop-ayg-ee´-ah;* from *4636* and *4078;*

the *Festival of Tabernacles* (so called from the custom of erecting booths for temporary homes):— tabernacles.

4635. σκηνοποιός **skēnŏpŏiŏs**, *skay-nop-oy-os´*; from 4633 and 4160; a *manufacturer of tents*:— tent-maker.

4636. σκῆνος **skēnŏs**, *skay´-nos*; from 4633; a *hut* or temporary residence, i.e. (fig.) the human *body* (as the abode of the spirit):— tabernacle.

4637. σκηνόω **skēnŏō**, *skay-nŏ´-o*; from 4636; to *tent* or *encamp*, i.e. (fig.) to *occupy* (as a mansion) or (spec.) to *reside* (as God did in the Tabernacle of old, a symbol of protection and communion):— dwell.

4638. σκήνωμα **skēnōma**, *skay´-no-mah*; from 4637; an *encampment*, i.e. (fig.) the *Temple* (as God's residence), the *body* (as a tenement for the soul):— tabernacle.

4639. σκία **skia**, *skee´-ah*; appar. a primary word; *"shade"* or a shadow (lit. or fig. [darkness of *error* or an *adumbration*]):— shadow.

4640. σκιρτάω **skirtaō**, *skeer-tah´-o*; akin to σκαίρω **skairō**, (to *skip*); to *jump*, i.e. sympathetically *move* (as the *quickening* of a fetus):— leap (for joy).

4641. σκληροκαρδία **sklērŏkardia**, *sklay-rok-ar-dee´-ah*; fem. of a compound of 4642 and 2588; *hard-heartedness*, i.e. (spec.) *destitution of* (spiritual) *perception*:— hardness of heart.

4642. σκληρός **sklērŏs**, *sklay-ros´*; from the base of 4628; *dry*, i.e. *hard* or *tough* (fig. *harsh, severe*):— fierce, hard.

4643. σκληρότης **sklērŏtēs**, *sklay-rot´-ace*; from 4642; *callousness*, i.e. (fig.) *stubbornness*:— hardness.

4644. σκληροτράχηλος **sklērŏtrachēlŏs**, *sklay-rot-rakh´-ay-los*; from 4642 and 5137; *hardnaped*, i.e. (fig.) *obstinate*:— stiffnecked.

4645. σκληρύνω **sklērunō**, *sklay-roo´-no*; from 4642; to *indurate*, i.e. (fig.) *render stubborn*:— harden.

4646. σκολιός **skŏliŏs**, *skol-ee-os´*; from the base of 4628; *warped*, i.e. *winding*; fig. *perverse*:— crooked, froward, untoward.

4647. σκόλοψ **skŏlŏps**, *skol´-ops*; perh. from the base of 4628 and 3700; *withered* at the *front*, i.e. a *point* or *prickle* (fig. a bodily *annoyance* or *disability*):— thorn.

4648. σκοπέω **skŏpĕō**, *skop-eh´-o*; from 4649; to take *aim* at (spy), i.e. (fig.) *regard*:— consider, take heed, look at (on), mark. Comp. 3700.

4649. σκοπός **skŏpŏs**, *skop-os´* ("scope"); from σκέπτομαι **skěptŏmai** (to *peer* about or l"skeptic"l; perh. akin to 4626 through the idea of *concealment*; comp. 4629); a *watch* (*sentry* or *scout*), i.e. (by impl.) a *goal*:— mark.

4650. σκορπίζω **skŏrpizō**, *skor-pid´-zo*; appar. from the same as 4651 (through the idea of *penetrating*); to *dissipate*, i.e. (fig.) *put to flight, waste, be liberal*:— disperse abroad, scatter (abroad).

4651. σκορπίος **skŏrpiŏs**, *skor-pee´-os*;

prob. from an obs. σκέρπω **skěrpō** (perh. strengthened from the base of 4649, and mean. to *pierce*); a *"scorpion"* (from its *sting*):— scorpion.

4652. σκοτεινός **skŏtĕinŏs**, *skot-i-nos´*; from 4655; *opaque*, i.e. (fig.) *benighted*:— dark, full of darkness.

4653. σκοτία **skŏtia**, *skot-ee´-ah*; from 4655; *dimness, obscurity* (lit. or fig.):— dark (-ness).

4654. σκοτίζω **skŏtizō**, *skot-id-zo*; from 4655; to *obscure* (lit. or fig.):— darken.

4655. σκότος **skŏtŏs**, *skot´-os*; from the base of 4639; *shadiness*, i.e. *obscurity* (lit. or fig.):— darkness.

4656. σκοτόω **skŏtŏō**, *skot-ŏ´-o*; from 4655; to *obscure* or *blind* (lit. or fig.):— be full of darkness.

4657. σκύβαλον **skubalŏn**, *skoo´-bal-on*; neut. of a presumed der. of 1519 and 2965 and 906; what is *thrown to* the *dogs*, i.e. *refuse* (*ordure*):— dung.

4658. Σκύθης **Skuthēs**, *skoo´-thace*; prob. of for. or.; a *Scythene* or *Scythian*, i.e. (by impl.) a *savage*:— Scythian.

4659. σκυθρωπός **skuthrōpŏs**, *skoo-thro-pos´*; from σκυθρός **skuthrŏs**, (*sullen*) and a der. of 3700; *angry-visaged*, i.e. *gloomy* or affecting a *mournful* appearance:— of a sad countenance.

4660. σκύλλω **skullō**, *skool´-lo*; appar. a primary verb; to *flay*, i.e. (fig.) to *harass*:— trouble (self).

4661. σκῦλον **skulŏn**, *skoo´-lon*; neut. from 4660; something *stripped* (as a *hide*), i.e. *booty*:— spoil.

4662. σκωληκόβρωτος **skōlēkŏbrōtŏs**, *sko-lay-kob´-ro-tos*; from 4663 and a der. of 977; *worm-eaten*, i.e. *diseased with maggots*:— eaten of worms.

4663. σκώληξ **skōlēx**, *sko´-lakes*; of uncert. der.; a *grub, maggot* or *earthworm*:— worm.

4664. σμαράγδινος **smaragdinŏs**, *smar-ag´-dee-nos*; from 4665; consisting of *emerald*:— emerald.

4665. σμάραγδος **smaragdŏs**, *smar´-ag-dos*; of uncert. der.; the *emerald* or green gem so called:— emerald.

4666. σμύρνα **smurna**, *smoor´-nah*; appar. strengthened for 3464; *myrrh*:— myrrh.

4667. Σμύρνα **Smurna**, *smoor´-nah*; the same as 4666; *Smyrna*, a place in Asia Minor:— Smyrna.

4668. Σμυρναῖος **Smurnaiŏs**, *smoor-nah´-yos*; from 4667; a *Smyrnæan*:— in Smyrna.

4669. σμυρνίζω **smurnizō**, *smoor-nid´-zo*; from 4667; to *tincture with myrrh*, i.e. *embitter* (as a narcotic):— mingle with myrrh.

4670. Σόδομα **Sŏdŏma**, *sod´-om-ah*; plur. of Heb. or. [5467]; *Sodoma* (i.e. *Sedom*), a place in Pal.:— Sodom.

4671. σοί **sŏi**, *soy*; dat. of 4771; to *thee*:— thee, thine own, thou, thy.

4672. Σολομών or Σολομῶν **Sŏlŏmōn**, *sol-om-one´*; of Heb. or. [8010]; *Solomon* (i.e. *Shelomoh*), the son of David:— Solomon.

4673. σορός **sŏrŏs**, *sor-os´*; prob. akin to

the base of 4987; a *funereal receptacle* (*urn, coffin*), i.e. (by anal.) a *bier*:— bier.

4674. σός **sŏs**, *sos*; from 4771; *thine*:— thine (own), thy (friend).

4675. σοῦ **sŏu**, *soo*; gen. of 4771; *of thee, thy*:— × home, thee, thine (own), thou, thy.

4676. σουδάριον **sŏudariŏn**, *soo-dar´-ee-on*; of Lat. or.; a *sudarium* (*sweat-cloth*), i.e. *towel* (for wiping the perspiration from the face, or binding the face of a corpse):— handkerchief, napkin.

4677. Σουσάννα **Sŏusanna**, *soo-san´-nah*; of Heb. or. [7799 fem.]; *lily*; *Susannah* (i.e. *Shoshannah*), an Israelitess:— Susanna.

4678. σοφία **sŏphia**, *sof-ee´-ah*; from 4680; *wisdom* (higher or lower, worldly or spiritual):— wisdom.

4679. σοφίζω **sŏphizō**, *sof-id´-zo*; from 4680; to *render wise*; in a sinister acceptation, to *form "sophisms"*, i.e. *continue plausible error*:— cunningly devised, make wise.

4680. σοφός **sŏphŏs**, *sof-os´*; akin to σαφής **saphēs**, (*clear*); *wise* (in a most gen. application):— wise. Comp. 5429.

4681. Σπανία **Spania**, *span-ee´-ah*; prob. of for. or.; *Spania*, a region of Europe:— Spain.

4682. σπαράσσω **sparassō**, *spar-as´-so*; prol. from σπαίρω **spairō** (to *gasp*; appar. strengthened from 4685, through the idea of *spasmodic* contraction); to *mangle*, i.e. *convulse* with epilepsy:— rend, tear.

4683. σπαργανόω **sparganŏō**, *spar-gan-ŏ´-o*; from σπάργανον **sparganŏn**, (a *strip*; from a der. of the base of 4682 mean. to *strap* or *wrap* with strips); to *swathe* (an infant after the Oriental custom):— wrap in swaddling clothes.

4684. σπαταλάω **spatalaō**, *spat-al-ah´-o*; from σπατάλη **spatalē**, (*luxury*); to be *voluptuous*:— live in pleasure, be wanton.

4685. σπάω **spaō**, *spah´-o*; a primary verb; to *draw*:— draw (out).

4686. σπεῖρα **spĕira**, *spi´-rah*; of immed. Lat. or., but ultimately a der. of 138 in the sense of its cognate 1507; a *coil* (*spira*, "spire"), i.e. (fig.) a *mass* of men (a Rom. military *cohort*; also lby anal.l a *squad* of Levitical janitors):— band.

4687. σπείρω **spĕirō**, *spi´-ro*; prob. strengthened from 4685 (through the idea of *extending*); to *scatter*, i.e. *sow* (lit. or fig.):— sow (-er), receive seed.

4688. σπεκουλάτωρ **spĕkŏulatŏr**, *spek-oo-lat´-ore*; of Lat. or.; a *speculator*, i.e. military *scout* (*spy* or lby extens.l *life-guardsman*):— executioner.

4689. σπένδω **spĕndō**, *spen´-do*; appar. a primary verb; to *pour out* as a libation, i.e. (fig.) to *devote* (one's life or blood, as a sacrifice) ("*spend*"):— (be ready to) be offered.

4690. σπέρμα **spĕrma**, *sper´-mah*; from 4687; something *sown*, i.e. *seed* (incl. the male *"sperm"*); by impl. *offspring*;

Greek

spec. a *remnant* (fig. as if kept over for planting):— issue, seed.

4691. σπερμολόγος **spĕrmŏlŏgŏs**, *sper-mol-og´-os;* from *4690* and *3004;* a *seed-picker* (as the crow), i.e. (fig.) a *sponger, loafer* (spec. a *gossip* or *trifler* in talk):— babbler.

4692. σπεύδω **spĕudō**, *spyoo´-do;* prob. strengthened from *4228;* to "*speed*" ("study"), i.e. *urge* on (diligently or earnestly); by impl. to *await* eagerly:— (make, with) haste unto.

4693. σπήλαιον **spēlaiŏn**, *spay´-lah-yon;* neut. of a presumed der. of σπέος **spĕŏs** (a *grotto*); a *cavern;* by impl. a *hiding-place* or *resort:*— cave, den.

4694. σπιλάς **spilas**, *spee-las´;* of uncert. der.; a *ledge* or *reef* of rock in the sea:— spot [by confusion with *4696*].

4695. σπιλόω **spilŏō**, *spee-lŏ´-o;* from *4696;* to *stain* or *soil* (lit. or fig.):— defile, spot.

4696. σπίλος **spilŏs**, *spee´-los;* of uncert. der.: a *stain* or *blemish*, i.e. (fig.) *defect, disgrace:*— spot.

4697. σπλαγχνίζομαι **splagchnizŏmai**, *splangkh-nid´-zom-ahee;* mid. voice from *4698;* to have the *bowels* yearn, i.e. (fig.) *feel sympathy*, to *pity:*— have (be moved with) compassion.

4698. σπλάγχνον **splagchnŏn**, *splangkh´-non;* prob. strengthened from σπλήν **splēn** (the "*spleen*"); an *intestine*, (plural); fig. *pity* or *sympathy:*— bowels, inward affection, + tender mercy.

4699. σπόγγος **spŏggŏs**, *spong´-gos;* perh. of for. or.; a "*sponge*":— spunge.

4700. σποδός **spŏdŏs**, *spod-os´;* of uncert. der.; *ashes:*— ashes.

4701. σπορά **spŏra**, *spor-ah´;* from *4687;* a *sowing*, i.e. (by impl.) *parentage:*— seed.

4702. σπόριμος **spŏrimŏs**, *spor´-ee-mos;* from *4703; sown*, i.e. (neut. plur.) a planted *field:*— corn (-field).

4703. σπόρος **spŏrŏs**, *spor´-os;* from *4687;* a *scattering* (of seed), i.e. (concr.) *seed* (as sown):— seed (× sown).

4704. σπουδάζω **spŏudazō**, *spoo-dad´-zo;* from *4710;* to *use* speed, i.e. to *make effort, be prompt* or *earnest:*— do (give) diligence, be diligent (forward), endeavour, labour, study.

4705. σπουδαῖος **spŏudaiŏs**, *spoo-dah´-yos;* from *4710; prompt, energetic, earnest:*— diligent.

4706. σπουδαιότερον **spŏudaiŏtĕrŏn**, *spoo-dah-yot´-er-on;* neut. of *4707* as adv.; *more earnestly* than others, i.e. *very promptly:*— very diligently.

4707. σπουδαιότερος **spŏudaiŏtĕrŏs**, *spoo-dah-yot´-er-os;* comparative of *4705; more prompt, more earnest:*— more diligent (forward).

4708. σπουδαιοτέρως **spŏudaiŏtĕrōs**, *spoo-dah-yot-er´-oce;* adv. from *4707; more speedily*, i.e. *sooner* than otherwise:— more carefully.

4709. σπουδαίως **spŏudaiōs**, *spoo-dah´-yoce;* adv. from *4705; earnestly, promptly:*— diligently, instantly.

4710. σπουδή **spŏudē**, *spoo-day´;* from *4692;* "*speed*", i.e. (by impl.) *despatch, eagerness, earnestness:*— business, (earnest) care (-fulness), diligence, forwardness, haste.

4711. σπυρίς **spuris**, *spoo-rece´;* from *4687* (as *woven*); a *hamper* or *lunch-receptacle:*— basket.

4712. στάδιον **stadiŏn**, *stad´-ee-on;* or masc. (in plur.) στάδιος **stadiŏs**, *stad´-ee-os;* from the base of *2476*, (as *fixed*); a *stade* or certain measure of distance; by impl. a *stadium* or *race-course:*— furlong, race.

4713. στάμνος **stamnŏs**, *stam´-nos;* from the base of *2476* (as *stationary*); a *jar* or earthen *tank:*— pot.

4714. στάσις **stasis**, *stas´-is;* from the base of *2476;* a *standing* (prop. the act), i.e. (by anal.) *position* (*existence*); by impl. a popular *uprising;* fig. *controversy:*— dissension, insurrection, × standing, uproar.

4715. στατήρ **statēr**, *stat-air´;* from the base of *2746;* a *stander* (*standard* of value), i.e. (spec.) a *stater* or certain coin:— piece of money.

4716. σταυρός **staurŏs**, *stŏw-ros´;* from the base of *2476;* a *stake* or post (as set upright), i.e. (spec.) a *pole* or *cross* (as an instrument of capital punishment); fig. *exposure to death*, i.e. *self-denial;* by impl. the *atonement* of Christ:— cross.

4717. σταυρόω **staurŏō**, *stŏw-rŏ´-o;* from *4716;* to *impale* on the cross; fig. to *extinguish* (*subdue*) passion or selfishness:— crucify.

4718. σταφυλή **staphulē**, *staf-oo-lay´;* prob. from the base of *4735;* a *cluster* of grapes (as if *intertwined*):— grapes.

4719. στάχυς **stachus**, *stakh´-oos;* from the base of *2476;* a *head* of grain (as *standing* out from the stalk):— ear (of corn).

4720. Στάχυς **Stachus**, *stakh´-oos;* the same as *4719; Stachys*, a Chr.:— Stachys.

4721. στέγη **stĕgē**, *steg-ay;* strengthened from a primary τέγος **tĕgŏs** (a "*thatch*" or "*deck*" of a building); a *roof:*— roof.

4722. στέγω **stĕgō**, *steg´-o;* from *4721;* to *roof* over, i.e. (fig.) to *cover* with silence (*endure* patiently):— (for-) bear, suffer.

4723. στεῖρος **stĕirŏs**, *sti´-ros;* a contr. from *4731* (as *stiff* and *unnatural*); "*sterile*":— barren.

4724. στέλλω **stĕllō**, *stel´-lo;* prob. strengthened from the base of *2476;* prop. to *set* fast ("*stall*"), i.e. (fig.) to *repress* (refl. *abstain* from associating with):— avoid, withdraw self.

4725. στέμμα **stĕmma**, *stem´-mah;* from the base of *4735;* a *wreath* for show:— garland.

4726. στεναγμός **stĕnagmŏs**, *sten-ag-mos´;* from *4727;* a *sigh:*— groaning.

4727. στενάζω **stĕnazō**, *sten-ad´-zo;* from *4728;* to *make* (intr. *be*) *in straits*, i.e. (by impl.) to *sigh, murmur, pray* inaudibly:— with grief, groan, grudge, sigh.

4728. στενός **stĕnŏs**, *sten-os´;* prob. from the base of *2476; narrow* (from obstacles *standing* close about):— strait.

4729. στενοχωρέω **stĕnŏchōrĕō**, *sten-okh-o-reh´-o;* from the same as *4730;* to *hem* in closely, i.e. (fig.) *cramp:*— distress, straiten.

4730. στενοχωρία **stĕnŏchōria**, *sten-okh-o-ree´-ah;* from a compound of *4728* and *5561; narrowness of room*, i.e. (fig.) *calamity:*— anguish, distress.

4731. στερεός **stĕrĕŏs**, *ster-eh-os´;* from *2476; stiff*, i.e. *solid, stable* (lit. or fig.):— stedfast, strong, sure.

4732. στερεόω **stĕrĕŏō**, *ster-eh-ŏ´-o;* from *4731;* to *solidify*, i.e. *confirm* (lit. or fig.):— establish, receive strength, make strong.

4733. στερέωμα **stĕrĕōma**, *ster-eh´-o-mah;* from *4732;* something *established*, i.e. (abstr.) *confirmation* (*stability*):— stedfastness.

4734. Στεφανᾶς **Stĕphanas**, *stef-an-as´;* prob. contr. for στεφανωτός **stĕphanōtŏs** (*crowned;* from *4737*); *Stephanas*, a Chr.:— Stephanas.

4735. στέφανος **stĕphanŏs**, *stef´-an-os;* from an appar. primary στέφω **stĕphō** (to *twine* or *wreathe*); a *chaplet*, (as a badge of royalty, a prize in the public games or a symbol of honor gen.; but more conspicuous and elaborate than the simple *fillet*, *1238*), lit. or fig.:— crown.

4736. Στέφανος **Stĕphanŏs**, *stef´-an-os;* the same as *4735; Stephanus*, a Chr.:— Stephen.

4737. στεφανόω **stephanŏō**, *stef-an-ŏ´-o;* from *4735;* to *adorn with* an honorary *wreath* (lit. or fig.):— crown.

4738. στῆθος **stēthŏs**, *stay´-thos;* from *2476* (as *standing* prominently); the (entire extern.) *bosom*, i.e. *chest:*— breast.

4739. στήκω **stēkō**, *stay´-ko;* from the perfect tense of *2476;* to *be stationary*, i.e. (fig.) to *persevere:*— stand (fast).

4740. στηριγμός **stērigmŏs**, *stay-rig-mos´;* from *4741; stability* (fig.):— stedfastness.

4741. στηρίζω **stērizō**, *stay-rid´-zo;* from a presumed der. of *2476* (like *4731*); to *set fast*, i.e. (lit.) to *turn resolutely* in a certain direction, or (fig.) to *confirm:*— fix, (e-) stablish, stedfastly set, strengthen.

4742. στίγμα **stigma**, *stig´-mah;* from a primary στίζω **stizō** (to "*stick*", i.e. *prick*); a *mark* incised or punched (for recognition of ownership), i.e. (fig.) *scar* of service:— mark.

4743. στιγμή **stigmē**, *stig-may´;* fem. of *4742;* a *point* of time, i.e. an *instant:*— moment.

4744. στίλβω **stilbō**, *stil´-bo;* appar. a primary verb; to *gleam*, i.e. *flash* intensely:— shining.

4745. στοά **stŏa**, *stŏ-ah´;* prob. from *2476;* a *colonnade* or interior *piazza:*— porch.

4746. στοιβάς **stŏibas**, *stoy-bas´* or στιβάς **stibas**, *stee-bas´;* from a primary στείβω **stĕibō** (to "*step*" or "*stamp*"); a *spread* (as if *tramped* flat) of loose materials for a couch, i.e. (by impl.) a *bough* of a tree so employed:— branch.

4747. στοιχεῖον **stŏichĕiŏn**, *stoy-khi'-on*; neut. of a presumed der. of the base of *4748*; something *orderly* in arrangement, i.e. (by impl.) a *serial* (*basal, fundamental, initial*) constituent (lit.), proposition (fig.):— element, principle, rudiment.

4748. στοιχέω **stŏichĕō**, *stoy-kheh'-o*; from a der. of στείχω **stĕichō** (to *range* in regular line); to *march*, in (military) rank (*keep step*), i.e. (fig.) to *conform* to virtue and piety:— walk (orderly).

4749. στολή **stŏlē**, *stol-ay'*; from *4724*; *equipment*, i.e. (spec.) a "*stole*" or long-fitting *gown* (as a mark of dignity):— long clothing (garment), (long) robe.

4750. στόμα **stŏma**, *stom'-a*; prob. strengthened from a presumed der. of the base of *5114*; the *mouth* (as if a *gash* in the face); by impl. *language* (and its relations); fig. an *opening* (in the earth); spec. the *front* or *edge* (of a weapon):— edge, face, mouth.

4751. στόμαχος **stŏmachŏs**, *stom'-akh-os*; from *4750*; an *orifice* (the *gullet*), i.e. (spec.) the "*stomach*":— stomach.

4752. στρατεία **stratĕia**, *strat-i'-ah*; from *4754*; military *service*, i.e. (fig.) the apostolic *career* (as one of hardship and danger):— warfare.

4753. στράτευμα **stratĕuma**, *strat'-yoo-mah*; from *4754*; an *armament*, i.e. (by impl.) a body of *troops* (more or less extensive or systematic):— army, soldier, man of war.

4754. στρατεύομαι **stratĕuŏmai**, *strat-yoo'-om-ahee*; mid. voice from the base of *4756*; to *serve* in a military campaign; fig. to *execute the apostolate* (with its arduous duties and functions), to *contend* with carnal inclinations:— soldier, (go to) war (-fare).

4755. στρατηγός **stratēgŏs**, *strat-ay-gos'*; from the base of *4756* and *71* or *2233*; a *general*, i.e. (by impl. or anal.) a (military) *governor* (*prætor*), the chief (*præfect*) of the (Levitical) temple-wardens:— captain, magistrate.

4756. στρατία **stratia**, *strat-ee'-ah*; fem. of a der. of στρατός **stratŏs**, (an *army*; from the base of *4766*, as *encamped*); *camp-likeness*, i.e. an *army*, i.e. (fig.) the *angels*, the celestial *luminaries*:— host.

4757. στρατιώτης **stratiōtēs**, *strat-ee-o'-tace*; from a presumed der. of the same as *4756*; a *camper-out*, i.e. a (common) *warrior* (lit. or fig.):— soldier.

4758. στρατολογέω **stratŏlŏgĕō**, *strat-ol-og-eh'-o*; from a compound of the base of *4756* and *3004* (in its orig. sense); to *gather* (or *select*) as a *warrior*, i.e. *enlist* in the army:— choose to be a soldier.

4759. στρατοπεδάρχης **stratŏpĕdarchēs**, *strat-op-ed-ar'-khace*; from *4760* and *757*; a *ruler of an army*, i.e. (spec.) a *Prætorian præfect*:— captain of the guard.

4760. στρατόπεδον **stratŏpĕdŏn**, *strat-op'-ed-on*; from the base of *4756* and the same as *3977*; a *camping-ground*, i.e. (by impl.) a body of *troops*:— army.

4761. στρεβλόω **strĕblŏō**, *streb-lŏ'-o*; from a der. of *4762*; to *wrench*, i.e. (spec.) to *torture* (by the rack), but only fig. to *pervert*:— wrest.

4762. στρέφω **strĕphō**, *stref'-o*; strengthened from the base of *5157*; to *twist*, i.e. *turn* quite around or *reverse* (lit. or fig.):— convert, turn (again, back again, self, self about).

4763. στρηνιάω **strēniaō**, *stray-nee-ah'-o*; from a presumed der. of *4764*; to *be luxurious*:— live deliciously.

4764. στρῆνος **strēnŏs**, *stray'-nos*; akin to *4731*; a "*straining*", "*strenuousness*" or "*strength*", i.e. (fig.) *luxury* (*voluptuousness*):— delicacy.

4765. στρουθίον **strŏuthiŏn**, *stroo-thee'-on*; dimin. of στρουθός **strŏuthŏs** (a *sparrow*); a *little sparrow*:— sparrow.

4766. στρώννυμι **strōnnumi**, *strone'-noo-mee*; or simpler

στρωννύω **strōnnuō**, *strone-noo'-o*; prol. from a still simpler

στρόω **strŏō**, *strŏ'-o* (used only as an alt. in certain tenses; prob. akin to *4731* through the idea of *positing*); to "*strew*", i.e. *spread* (as a carpet or couch):— make bed, furnish, spread, strew.

4767. στυγνητός **stugnētŏs**, *stoog-nay-tos'*; from a der. of an obs. appar. primary στύγω **stugō** (to *hate*); *hated*, i.e. *odious*:— hateful.

4768. στυγνάζω **stugnazō**, *stoog-nad'-zo*; from the same as *4767*; to *render gloomy*, i.e. (by impl.) *glower* (*be overcast* with clouds, or *sombreness* of speech):— lower, be sad.

4769. στύλος **stulŏs**, *stoo'-los*; from στύω **stuō** (to *stiffen*; prob. akin to the base of *2476*); a *post* ("*style*"), i.e. (fig.) *support*:— pillar.

4770. Στωϊκός **Stōĭkŏs**, *sto-ik-os'*; from *4745*; a "*Stoic*" (as occupying a particular porch in Athens), i.e. adherent of a certain philosophy:— Stoick.

4771. σύ **su**, *soo*; the pers. pron. of the second pers. sing.; *thou*:— thou. See also *4571, 4671, 4675*; and for the plur. *5209, 5210, 5213, 5216*.

4772. συγγένεια **suggĕnĕia**, *soong-ghen'-i-ah*; from *4773*; *relationship*, i.e. (concr.) *relatives*:— kindred.

4773. συγγενής **suggĕnēs**, *soong-ghen-ace'*; from *4862* and *1085*; a *relative* (by blood); by extens. a fellow *countryman*:— cousin, kin (-sfolk, -sman).

4774. συγγνώμη **suggnōmē**, *soong-gno'-may*; from a compound of *4862* and *1097*; *fellow knowledge*, i.e. *concession*:— permission.

4775. συγκάθημαι **sugkathēmai**, *soong-kath'-ay-mahee*; from *4862* and *2521*; to *seat oneself* in company *with*:— sit with.

4776. συγκαθίζω **sugkathizō**, *soong-kath-id'-zo*; from *4862* and *2523*; to *give* (or *take*) *a seat* in company *with*:— (make) sit (down) together.

4777. συγκακοπαθέω **sugkakŏpathĕō**, *soong-kak-op-ath-eh'-o*; from *4862* and *2553*; to *suffer hardship* in company *with*:— be partaker of afflictions.

4778. συγκακουχέω **sugkakŏuchĕō**, *soong-kak-oo-kheh'-o*; from *4862* and *2558*; to *maltreat* in company *with*, i.e. (pass.) *endure persecution together*:— suffer affliction with.

4779. συγκαλέω **sugkalĕō**, *soong-kal-eh'-o*; from *4862* and *2564*; to *convoke*:— call together.

4780. συγκαλύπτω **sugkaluptō**, *soong-kal-oop'-to*; from *4862* and *2572*; to *conceal altogether*:— cover.

4781. συγκάμπτω **sugkamptō**, *soong-kamp'-to*; from *4862* and *2578*; to *bend together*, i.e. (fig.) to *afflict*:— bow down.

4782. συγκαταβαίνω **sugkatabainō**, *soong-kat-ab-ah'-ee-no*; from *4862* and *2597*; to *descend* in company *with*:— go down with.

4783. συγκατάθεσις **sugkatathĕsis**, *soong-kat-ath'-es-is*; from *4784*; a *deposition* (of sentiment) in company *with*, i.e. (fig.) *accord* with:— agreement.

4784. συγκατατίθεμαι **sugkatatithĕmai**, *soong-kat-at-ith'-em-ahee*; mid. from *4862* and *2698*; to *deposit* (one's vote or opinion) in company *with*, i.e. (fig.) to *accord* with:— consent.

4785. συγκαταψηφίζω **sugkatapsēphizō**, *soong-kat-aps-ay-fid'-zo*; from *4862* and a compound of *2596* and *5585*; to *count down* in company *with*, i.e. *enroll among*:— number with.

4786. συγκεράννυμι **sugkĕrannumi**, *soong-ker-an'-noo-mee*; from *4862* and *2767*; to *commingle*, i.e. (fig.) to *combine* or *assimilate*:— mix with, temper together.

4787. συγκινέω **sugkinĕō**, *soong-kin-eh'-o*; from *4682* and *2795*; to *move together*, i.e. (spec.) to *excite* as a mass (to sedition):— stir up.

4788. συγκλείω **sugklĕiō**, *soong-kli'-o*; from *4862* and *2808*; to *shut together*, i.e. *include* or (fig.) *embrace* in a common subjection to:— conclude, inclose, shut up.

4789. συγκληρονόμος **sugklērŏnŏmŏs**, *soong-klay-ron-om'-os*; from *4862* and *2818*; a *co-heir*, i.e. (by anal.) *participant in common*:— fellow (joint)-heir, heir together, heir with.

4790. συγκοινωνέω **sugkŏinōnĕō**, *soong-koy-no-neh'-o*; from *4862* and *2841*; to *share* in company *with*, i.e. *co-participate* in:— communicate (have fellowship) with, be partaker of.

4791. συγκοινωνός **sugkŏinōnŏs**, *soong-koy-no-nos'*; from *4862* and *2844*; a *co-participant*:— companion, partake (-r, -r with).

4792. συγκομίζω **sugkŏmizō**, *soong-kom-id'-zo*; from *4862* and *2865*; to *convey together*, i.e. *collect* or *bear* away in company *with* others:— carry.

4793. συγκρίνω **sugkrinō**, *soong-kree-no*; from *4862* and *2919*; to *judge* of one thing in connection *with* another, i.e. *combine* (spiritual ideas with appropriate expressions) or *collate* (one person with another by way of contrast or resemblance):— compare among (with).

4794. συγκύπτω **sugkuptō**, *soong-koop´-to;* from *4862* and *2955;* to *stoop altogether,* i.e. *be completely overcome* by:— bow together.

4795. συγκυρία **sugkuria**, *soong-koo-ree´-ah;* from a compound of *4862* and κυρέω **kurĕō**, (to *light* or *happen;* from the base of *2962*); *concurrence,* i.e. *accident:*— chance.

4796. συγχαίρω **sugchairō**, *soong-khah´-ee-ro;* from *4862* and *5463;* to *sympathize in gladness, congratulate:*— rejoice in (with).

4797. συγχέω **sugchĕō**, *soong-kheh´-o;* or

συγχύνω **sugchunō**, *soong-khoo´-no;* from *4862* and χέω **chĕō** (to *pour*) or its alt.; to *commingle,* promiscuously, i.e. (fig.) to *throw* (an assembly) *into disorder,* to *perplex* (the mind):— confound, confuse, stir up, be in an uproar.

4798. συγχράομαι **sugchraŏmai**, *soong-khrah´-om-ahee;* from *4862* and *5530;* to *use jointly,* i.e. (by impl.) to *hold intercourse in common:*— have dealings with.

4799. σύγχυσις **sugchusis**, *soong´-khoo-sis;* from *4797; commixture,* i.e. (fig.) riotous *disturbance:*— confusion.

4800. συζάω **suzaō**, *sood-zah´-o;* from *4862* and *2198;* to continue to *live in common with,* i.e. *co-survive* (lit. or fig.):— live with.

4801. συζεύγνυμι **suzĕugnumi**, *sood-zyoog´-noo-mee;* from *4862* and the base of *2201;* to *yoke together,* i.e. (fig.) *conjoin* (in marriage):— join together.

4802. συζητέω **suzētĕō**, *sood-zay-teh´-o;* from *4862* and *2212;* to *investigate jointly,* i.e. *discuss, controvert, cavil:*— dispute (with), enquire, question (with), reason (together).

4803. συζήτησις **suzētēsis**, *sood-zay´-tay-sis;* from *4802; mutual questioning,* i.e. *discussion:*— disputation (-ting), reasoning.

4804. συζητητής **suzētētēs**, *sood-zay-tay-tace´;* from *4802;* a *disputant,* i.e. *sophist:*— disputer.

4805. σύζυγος **suzugŏs**, *sood´-zoo-gos;* from *4801; co-yoked,* i.e. (fig.) as noun, a *colleague;* prob. rather as a proper name; *Syzygus,* a Chr.:— yokefellow.

4806. συζωοποιέω **suzōŏpŏiĕō**, *sood-zo-op-oy-eh´-o;* from *4862* and *2227;* to *re-animate conjointly* with (fig.):— quicken together with.

4807. συκάμινος **sukaminŏs**, *soo-kam-ee-nos;* of Heb. or. [8256] in imitation of *4809;* a *sycamore-fig tree:*— sycamine tree.

4808. συκῆ **sukē**, *soo-kay´;* from *4810;* a *fig-tree:*— fig tree.

4809. συκομωραία **sukŏmōraia**, *soo-kom-o-rah´-yah;* from *4810* and μόρον **mŏrŏn** (the *mulberry*); the *"sycamore-"* fig tree:— sycamore tree. Comp. *4807.*

4810. σῦκον **sukŏn**, *soo´-kon;* appar. a primary word; a *fig:*— fig.

4811. συκοφαντέω **sukŏphantĕō**, *soo-kof-an-teh´-o;* from a compound of *4810* and a der. of *5316;* to *be a fig-informer* (reporter of the law forbidding the exportation of figs from Greece), *"sycophant",* i.e. (gen. and by extens.) to *defraud* (*exact* unlawfully, *extort*):— accuse falsely, take by false accusation.

4812. συλαγωγέω **sulagōgĕō**, *soo-lag-ogue-eh´-o;* from the base of *4813* and (the redupl. form of) *71;* to *lead away as booty,* i.e. (fig.) *seduce:*— spoil.

4813. συλάω **sulaō**, *soo-lah´-o;* from a der. of σύλλω **sullō** (to *strip;* prob. akin to *138;* comp. *4661*); to *despoil:*— rob.

4814. συλλαλέω **sullalĕō**, *sool-lal-eh´-o;* from *4862* and *2980;* to *talk together,* i.e. *converse:*— commune (confer, talk) with, speak among.

4815. συλλαμβάνω **sullambanō**, *sool-lam-ban´-o;* from *4862* and *2983;* to *clasp,* i.e. *seize* (*arrest, capture*); spec. to *conceive* (lit. or fig.); by impl. to *aid:*— catch, conceive, help, take.

4816. συλλέγω **sullĕgō**, *sool-leg´-o;* from *4862* and *3004* in its orig. sense; to *collect:*— gather (together, up).

4817. συλλογίζομαι **sullŏgizŏmai**, *sool-log-id´-zom-ahee;* from *4862* and *3049;* to *reckon together* (with oneself), i.e. *deliberate:*— reason with.

4818. συλλυπέω **sullupĕō**, *sool-loop-eh´-o;* from *4862* and *3076;* to *afflict jointly,* i.e. (pass.) *sorrow at* (on account of) someone:— be grieved.

4819. συμβαίνω **sumbainō**, *soom-bah-ee-no;* from *4862* and the base of *939;* to *walk* (fig. *transpire*) *together,* i.e. *concur* (*take place*):— be (-fall), happen (unto).

4820. συμβάλλω **sumballō**, *soom-bal´-lo;* from *4862* and *906;* to *combine,* i.e. (in speaking) to *converse, consult, dispute,* (mentally) to *consider,* (by impl.) to *aid,* (personally) to *join, attack:*— confer, encounter, help, make, meet with, ponder.

4821. συμβασιλεύω **sumbasilĕuō**, *soom-bas-il-yoo´-o;* from *4862* and *936;* to *be co-regent* (fig.):— reign with.

4822. συμβιβάζω **sumbibazō**, *soom-bib-ad´-zo;* from *4862* and βιβάζω **bibazō** (to *force;* caus. [by redupl.] of the base of *939*); to *drive together,* i.e. *unite* (in association or affection), (mentally) to *infer, show, teach:*— compact, assuredly gather, intrust, knit together, prove.

4823. συμβουλεύω **sumbŏulĕuō**, *soom-bool-yoo´-o;* from *4862* and *1011;* to *give* (or *take*) *advice jointly,* i.e. *recommend, deliberate* or *determine:*— consult, (give, take) counsel (together).

4824. συμβούλιον **sumbŏuliŏn**, *soom-boo´-lee-on;* neut. of a presumed der. of *4825; advisement;* spec. a *deliberative body,* i.e. the provincial *assessors* or *lay-court:*— consultation, counsel, council.

4825. σύμβουλος **sumbŏulŏs**, *soom´-boo-los;* from *4862* and *1012;* a *consultor,* i.e. *adviser:*— counsellor.

4826. Συμεών **Sumĕōn**, *soom-eh-one´;* from the same as *4613; Symeon* (i.e.

Shimon), the name of five Isr.:— Simeon, Simon.

4827. συμμαθητής **summathētēs**, *soom-math-ay-tace´;* from a compound of *4862* and *3129;* a *co-learner* (of Christianity):— fellowdisciple.

4828. συμμαρτυρέω **summarturĕō**, *soom-mar-too-reh´-o;* from *4862* and *3140;* to *testify jointly,* i.e. *corroborate* by (concurrent) evidence:— testify unto, (also) bear witness (with).

4829. συμμερίζομαι **summĕrizŏmai**, *soom-mer-id´-zom-ahee;* mid. voice from *4862* and *3307;* to *share jointly,* i.e. *participate* in:— be partaker with.

4830. συμμέτοχος **summĕtŏchŏs**, *soom-met´-okh-os;* from *4862* and *3353;* a *co-participant:*— partaker.

4831. συμμιμητής **summimētēs**, *soom-mim-ay-tace´;* from a presumed compound of *4862* and *3401;* a *co-imitator,* i.e. *fellow votary:*— follower together.

4832. συμμορφός **summŏrphŏs**, *soom-mor-fos´;* from *4862* and *3444; jointly formed,* i.e. (fig.) *similar:*— conformed to, fashioned like unto.

4833. συμμορφόω **summŏrphŏō**, *soom-mor-fŏ´-o;* from *4832;* to *render like,* i.e. (fig.) to *assimilate:*— make conformable unto.

4834. συμπαθέω **sumpathĕō**, *soom-path-eh´-o;* from *4835;* to *feel "sympathy"* with, i.e. (by impl.) to *commiserate:*— have compassion, be touched with a feeling of.

4835. συμπαθής **sumpathēs**, *soom-path-ace´;* from *4841; having a fellow-feeling* (*"sympathetic"*), i.e. (by impl.) *mutually commiserative:*— having compassion one of another.

4836. συμπαραγίνομαι **sumparaginŏmai**, *soom-par-ag-in´-om-ahee;* from *4862* and *3854;* to *be present together,* i.e. to *convene;* by impl. to *appear in aid:*— come together, stand with.

4837. συμπαρακαλέω **sumparakalĕō**, *soom-par-ak-al-eh´-o;* from *4862* and *3870;* to *console jointly:*— comfort together.

4838. συμπαραλαμβάνω **sumparalambanō**, *soom-par-al-am-ban´-o;* from *4862* and *3880;* to *take along in company:*— take with.

4839. συμπαραμένω **sumparamĕnō**, *soom-par-am-en´-o;* from *4862* and *3887;* to *remain in company,* i.e. *still live:*— continue with.

4840. συμπάρειμι **sumparĕimi**, *soom-par´-i-mee;* from *4862* and *3918;* to *be at hand together,* i.e. *now present:*— be here present with.

4841. συμπάσχω **sumpaschō**, *soom-pas´-kho;* from *4862* and *3958* (incl. its alt.); to *experience pain jointly* or of the *same kind* (spec. *persecution;* to *"sympathize"*):— suffer with.

4842. συμπέμπω **sumpĕmpō**, *soom-pem´-po;* from *4862* and *3992;* to *dispatch in company:*— send with.

4843. συμπεριλαμβάνω **sumpĕrilambanō**, *soom-per-ee-lam-ban´-o;* from *4862* and a compound of *4012* and *2983;* to *take by enclosing altogether,* i.e. *ear-*

nestly throw the arms about one:— embrace.

4844. συμπίνω **sumpinō**, *soom-pee´-no*; from 4862 and 4095; to *partake a beverage in company:*— drink with.

4845. συμπληρόω **sumplērŏō**, *soom-play-rŏ´-o*; from 4862 and 4137; to *implenish completely*, i.e. (of space) to *swamp* (a boat), or (of time) to *accomplish* (pass. be *complete*):— (fully) come, fill up.

4846. συμπνίγω **sumpnigō**, *soom-pnee´-go*; from 4862 and 4155; to *strangle completely*, i.e. (lit.) to *drown*, or (fig.) to *crowd:*— choke, throng.

4847. συμπολίτης **sumpŏlitēs**, *soom-pol-ee´-tace*; from 4862 and 4177; a *native of the same town*, i.e. (fig.) *co-religionist* (*fellow-Christian*):— fellow-citizen.

4848. συμπορεύομαι **sumpŏrĕuŏmai**, *soom-por-yoo´-om-ahee*; from 4862 and 4198; to *journey together*; by impl. to *assemble:*— go with, resort.

4849. συμπόσιον **sumpŏsiŏn**, *soom-pos´-ee-on*; neut. of a der. of the alt. of 4844; a *drinking-party* (*"symposium"*), i.e. (by extens.) a *room of guests:*— company.

4850. συμπρεσβύτερος **sumprĕsbutĕrŏs**, *soom-pres-boo´-ter-os*; from 4862 and 4245; a *co-presbyter:*— presbyter, also an elder.

συμφάγω **sumphagō**. See 4906.

4851. συμφέρω **sumphĕrō**, *soom-fer´-o*; from 4862 and 5342 (incl. its alt.); to *bear together* (*contribute*), i.e. (lit.) to *collect*, or (fig.) to *conduce; espec.* (neut. part. as a noun) *advantage:*— be better for, bring together, be expedient (for), be good, (be) profit (-able for).

4852. σύμφημι **sumphēmi**, *soom´-faymee*; from 4862 and 5346; to *say jointly*, i.e. *assent to:*— consent unto.

4853. συμφυλέτης **sumphulĕtēs**, *soom-foo-let´-ace*; from 4862 and a der. of 5443; a *co-tribesman*, i.e. *native of the same country:*— countryman.

4854. σύμφυτος **sumphutŏs**, *soom´-footos*; from 4862 and a der. of 5453; *grown along with* (*connate*), i.e. (fig.) closely *united* to:— planted together.

4855. συμφύω **sumphuō**, *soom-foo´-o*; from 4862 and 5453; pass. to *grow jointly:*— spring up with.

4856. συμφωνέω **sumphōnĕō**, *soom-foneh´-o*; from 4859; to be *harmonious*, i.e. (fig.) to *accord* (*be suitable, concur*) or *stipulate* (by compact):— agree (together, with).

4857. συμφώνησις **sumphōnēsis**, *soom-fo´-nay-sis*; from 4856; *accordance:*— concord.

4858. συμφωνία **sumphōnia**, *soom-fonee´-ah*; from 4859; *unison* of sound (*"symphony"*), i.e. a *concert* of instruments (harmonious *note*):— music.

4859. σύμφωνος **sumphōnŏs**, *soom´-fonos*; from 4862 and 5456; *sounding together* (*alike*), i.e. (fig.) *accordant* (neut. as noun, *agreement*):— consent.

4860. συμψηφίζω **sumpsēphizō**, *soom-*

psay-fid´-zo; from 4862 and 5585; to *compute jointly:*— reckon.

4861. σύμψυχος **sumpsuchŏs**, *soom´-psoo-khos*; from 4862 and 5590; *co-spirited*, i.e. *similar in sentiment:*— like-minded.

4862. σύν **sun**, *soon*; a primary prep. denoting *union; with* or *together* (but much closer than 3326 or 3844), i.e. by association, companionship, process, resemblance, possession, instrumentality, addition, etc.:— beside, with. [In composition, it has similar applications, including *completeness*.]

4863. συνάγω **sunagō**, *soon-ag´-o*; from 4862 and 71; to *lead together*, i.e. *collect* or *convene*; spec. to *entertain* (hospitably):— + accompany, assemble (selves, together), bestow, come together, gather (selves together, up, together), lead into, resort, take in.

4864. συναγωγή **sunagōgē**, *soon-ag-o-gay´*; from (the redupl. form of) 4863; an *assemblage* of persons; spec. a Jewish *"synagogue"* (the meeting or the place); by anal. a Christian *church:*— assembly, congregation, synagogue.

4865. συναγωνίζομαι **sunagōnizŏmai**, *soon-ag-o-nid´-zom-ahee*; from 4862 and 75; to *struggle* in company *with*, i.e. (fig.) to *be a partner* (*assistant*):— strive together with.

4866. συναθλέω **sunathlĕō**, *soon-ath-leh´-o*; from 4862 and 118; to *wrestle* in company *with*, i.e. (fig.) to *seek jointly:*— labour with, strive together for.

4867. συναθροίζω **sunathrŏizō**, *soon-ath-royd´-zo*; from 4862 and ἀθροίζω athrŏizō (to *hoard*); to *convene:*— call (gather) together.

4868. συναίρω **sunairō**, *soon-ah´-ee-ro*; from 4862 and 142; to *make up together*, i.e. (fig.) to *compute* (an account):— reckon, take.

4869. συναιχμάλωτος **sunaichmalŏtŏs**, *soon-aheekh-mal´-o-tos*; from 4862 and 164; a *co-captive:*— fellowprisoner.

4870. συνακολουθέω **sunakŏlŏuthĕō**, *soon-ak-ol-oo-theh´-o*; from 4862 and 190; to *accompany:*— follow.

4871. συναλίζω **sunalizō**, *soon-al-id´-zo*; from 4862 and ἁλίζω halizō (to *throng*); to *accumulate*, i.e. *convene:*— assemble together.

4872. συναναβαίνω **sunanabainō**, *soon-an-ab-ah´-ee-no*; from 4862 and 305; to *ascend* in company *with:*— come up with.

4873. συνανάκειμαι **sunanakĕimai**, *soon-an-ak´-i-mahee*; from 4862 and 345; to *recline* in company *with* (at a meal):— sit (down, at the table, together) with (at meat).

4874. συναναμίγνυμι **sunanamignumi**, *soon-an-am-ig´-noo-mee*; from 4862 and a compound of 303 and 3396; to *mix up together*, i.e. (fig.) *associate with:*— (have, keep) company (with).

4875. συναναπαύομαι **sunanapauŏmai**, *soon-an-ap-ŏw´-om-ahee*; mid. voice from 4862 and 373; to *recruit oneself* in company *with:*— refresh with.

4876. συναντάω **sunantaō**, *soon-an-*

tah´-o; from 4862 and a der. of 473; to *meet with*; fig. to *occur:*— befall, meet.

4877. συνάντησις **sunantēsis**, *soon-an´-tay-sis*; from 4876; a *meeting with:*— meet.

4878. συναντιλαμβάνομαι **sunantilambanŏmai**, *soon-an-tee-lam-ban´-om-ahee*; from 4862 and 482; to *take hold of opposite together*, i.e. *co-operate* (*assist*):— help.

4879. συναπάγω **sunapagō**, *soon-ap-ag´-o*; from 4862 and 520; to *take off together*, i.e. *transport with* (*seduce*, pass. *yield*):— carry (lead) away with, condescend.

4880. συναποθνήσκω **sunapŏthnĕskō**, *soon-ap-oth-nace´-ko*; from 4862 and 599; to *decease* (lit.) in company *with*, or (fig.) similarly *to:*— be dead (die) with.

4881. συναπόλλυμι **sunapŏllumi**, *soon-ap-ol´-loo-mee*; from 4862 and 622; to *destroy* (middle or passive voice *be slain*) in company *with:*— perish with.

4882. συναποστέλλω **sunapŏstĕllō**, *soon-ap-os-tel´-lo*; from 4862 and 649; to *despatch* (on an errand) in company *with:*— send with.

4883. συναρμολογέω **sunarmŏlŏgĕō**, *soon-ar-mol-og-eh´-o*; from 4862 and a der. of a compound of 719 and 3004 (in its orig. sense of *laying*); to *render close-jointed together*, i.e. *organize compactly:*— be fitly framed (joined) together.

4884. συναρπάζω **sunarpazō**, *soon-ar-pad´-zo*; from 4862 and 726; to *snatch together*, i.e. *seize:*— catch.

4885. συναυξάνω **sunauxanō**, *soon-ŏwx-an´-o*; from 4862 and 837; to *increase* (*grow up*) *together:*— grow together.

4886. σύνδεσμος **sundĕsmŏs**, *soon´-des-mos*; from 4862 and 1199; a *joint tie*, i.e. *ligament*, (fig.) *uniting principle, control:*— band, bond.

4887. συνδέω **sundĕō**, *soon-deh´-o*; from 4862 and 1210; to *bind with*, i.e. (pass.) *be a fellow-prisoner* (fig.):— be bound with.

4888. συνδοξάζω **sundŏxazō**, *soon-dox-ad´-zo*; from 4862 and 1392; to *exalt* to dignity in company (i.e. *similarly*) *with:*— glorify together.

4889. σύνδουλος **sundŏulŏs**, *soon´-doolos*; from 4862 and 1401; a *co-slave*, i.e. *servitor* or *ministrant of the same master* (human or divine):— fellowservant.

συνδρέμω **sundrĕmō**. See 4936.

4890. συνδρομή **sundrŏmē**, *soon-drom-ay´*; from (the alt. of) 4936; a *running together*, i.e. (riotous) *concourse:*— run together.

4891. συνεγείρω **sunĕgĕirō**, *soon-eg-i´-ro*; from 4862 and 1453; to *rouse* (from death) in company *with*, i.e. (fig.) to *revivify* (spiritually) in resemblance *to:*— raise up together, rise with.

4892. συνέδριον **sunĕdriŏn**, *soon-ed´-ree-on*; neut. of a presumed der. of a compound of 4862 and the base of 1476; a *joint session*, i.e. (spec.) the Jewish *Sanhedrin*; by anal. a subordinate *tribunal:*— council.

Greek

4893. συνείδησις **suněidēsis**, soon-i´-day-sis; from a prol. form of 4894; co-perception, i.e. moral consciousness:— conscience.

4894. συνείδω **suněidō**, soon-i´-do; from 4862 and 1492; to see completely; used (like its primary) only in two past tenses, respectively mean. to understand or become aware, and to be conscious or (clandestinely) informed of:— consider, know, be privy, be ware of.

4895. σύνειμι **suněimi**, soon´-i-mee; from 4862 and 1510 (incl. its various inflections); to be in company with, i.e. present at the time:— be with.

4896. σύνειμι **suněimi**, soon´-i-mee; from 4862 and εἶμι **ěimi** (to go); to assemble:— gather together.

4897. συνεισέρχομαι **suněisěrchŏmai**, soon-ice-er´-khom-ahee; from 4862 and 1525; to enter in company with:— go in with, go in into.

4898. συνέκδημος **suněkdēmŏs**, soon-ek´-day-mos; from 4862 and the base of 1553; a co-absentee from home, i.e. fellow-traveller:— companion in travel, travel with.

4899. συνεκλεκτός **suněklěktŏs**, soon-ek-lek-tos´; from a compound of 4862 and 1586; chosen in company with, i.e. co-elect (fellow Christian):— elected together with.

4900. συνελαύνω **sunělaunō**, soon-el-ow´-no; from 4862 and 1643; to drive together, i.e. (fig.) exhort (to reconciliation):— + set at one again.

4901. συνεπιμαρτυρέω **suněpimarturěō**, soon-ep-ee-mar-too-reh´-o; from 4862 and 1957; to testify further jointly, i.e. unite in adding evidence:— also bear witness.

4902. συνέπομαι **suněpŏmai**, soon-ep´-om-ahee; mid. voice from 4862 and a primary ἕπω **hěpō** (to follow); to attend (travel) in company with:— accompany.

4903. συνεργέω **suněrgěō**, soon-erg-eh´-o; from 4904; to be a fellow-worker, i.e. co-operate:— help (work) with, work (-er) together.

4904. συνεργός **suněrgŏs**, soon-er-gos´; from a presumed compound of 4862 and the base of 2041; a co-laborer, i.e. coadjutor:— companion in labour, (fellow-) helper (-labourer, -worker), labourer together with, workfellow.

4905. συνέρχομαι **suněrchŏmai**, soon-er´-khom-ahee; from 4862 and 2064; to convene, depart in company with, associate with, or (spec.) cohabit (conjugally):— accompany, assemble (with), come (together), come (company, go) with, resort.

4906. συνεσθίω **suněsthiō**, soon-es-thee´-o; from 4862 and 2068 (incl. its alt.); to take food in company with:— eat with.

4907. σύνεσις **suněsis**, soon´-es-is; from 4920; a mental putting together, i.e. intelligence or (concr.) the intellect:— knowledge, understanding.

4908. συνετός **sunětŏs**, soon-et´-os; from 4920; mentally put (or putting) together, i.e. sagacious:— prudent. Comp. 5429.

4909. συνευδοκέω **suněudŏkěō**, soon-yoo-dok-eh´-o; from 4862 and 2106; to think well of in common, i.e. assent to, feel gratified with:— allow, assent, be pleased, have pleasure.

4910. συνευωχέω **suněuōchěō**, soon-yoo-o-kheh´-o; from 4862 and a der. of a presumed compound of 2095 and a der. of 2192 (mean. to be in good condition, i.e. [by impl.] to fare well, or feast); to entertain sumptuously in company with, i.e. (middle or passive voice) to revel together:— feast with.

4911. συνεφίστημι **suněphistēmi**, soon-ef-is´-tay-mee; from 4862 and 2186; to stand up together, i.e. to resist (or assault) jointly:— rise up together.

4912. συνέχω **suněchō**, soon-ekh´-o; from 4862 and 2192; to hold together, i.e. to compress (the ears, with a crowd or siege) or arrest (a prisoner); fig. to compel, perplex, afflict, preoccupy:— constrain, hold, keep in, press, lie sick of, stop, be in a strait, straiten, be taken with, throng.

4913. συνήδομαι **suněndŏmai**, soon-ay´-dom-ahee; mid. voice from 4862 and the base of 2237; to rejoice in with oneself, i.e. feel satisfaction concerning:— delight.

4914. συνήθεια **suněthěia**, soon-ay´-thi-ah; from a compound of 4862 and 2239; mutual habitation, i.e. usage:— custom.

4915. συνηλικιώτης **sunělikiōtēs**, soon-ay-lik-ee-o´-tace; from 4862 and a der. of 2244; a co-aged person, i.e. alike in years:— equal.

4916. συνθάπτω **sunthaptō**, soon-thap´-to; from 4862 and 2290; to inter in company with, i.e. (fig.) to assimilate spiritually (to Christ by a sepulture as to sin):— bury with.

4917. συνθλάω **sunthlaō**, soon-thlah´-o; from 4862 and θλάω **thlaō** (to crush); to dash together, i.e. shatter:— break.

4918. συνθλίβω **sunthlibō**, soon-thlee´-bo; from 4862 and 2346; to compress, i.e. crowd on all sides:— throng.

4919. συνθρύπτω **sunthruptō**, soon-throop´-to; from 4862 and θρύπτω **thruptō** (to crumble); to crush together, i.e. (fig.) to dispirit:— break.

4920. συνίημι **suniēmi**, soon-ee´-ay-mee; from 4862 and ἵημι **hiēmi** (to send); to put together, i.e. (mentally) to comprehend; by impl. to act piously:— consider, understand, be wise.

4921. συνιστάω **sunistaō**, soon-is-tah´-o; or (strengthened)

συνιστάνω **sunistanō**, soon-is-tan´-o; or

συνίστημι **sunistēmi**, soon-is´-tay-mee; from 4862 and 2476 (incl. its collat. forms); to set together, i.e. (by impl.) to introduce (favorably), or (fig.) to exhibit; intr. to stand near, or (fig.) to constitute:— approve, commend, consist, make, stand (with).

4922. συνοδεύω **sunŏděuō**, soon-od-yoo´-o; from 4862 and 3593; to travel in company with:— journey with.

4923. συνοδία **sunŏdia**, soon-od-ee´-ah; from a compound of 4862 and 3598 ("synod"); companionship on a journey, i.e. (by impl.) a caravan:— company.

4924. συνοικέω **sunŏikěō**, soon-oy-keh´-o; from 4862 and 3611; to reside together (as a family):— dwell together.

4925. συνοικοδομέω **sunŏikŏdŏměō**, soon-oy-kod-om-eh´-o; from 4862 and 3618; to construct, i.e. (pass.) to compose (in company with other Christians, fig.):— build together.

4926. συνομιλέω **sunŏmilěō**, soon-om-il-eh´-o; from 4862 and 3656; to converse mutually:— talk with.

4927. συνομορέω **sunŏmŏrěō**, soon-om-or-eh´-o; from 4862 and a der. of a compound of the base of 3674 and the base of 3725; to border together, i.e. adjoin:— join hard.

4928. συνοχή **sunŏchē**, soon-okh-ay´; from 4912; restraint, i.e. (fig.) anxiety:— anguish, distress.

4929. συντάσσω **suntassō**, soon-tas-so; from 4862 and 5021; to arrange jointly, i.e. (fig.) to direct:— appoint.

4930. συντέλεια **suntělěia**, soon-tel´-i-ah; from 4931; entire completion, i.e. consummation (of a dispensation):— end.

4931. συντελέω **suntělěō**, soon-tel-eh´-o; from 4862 and 5055; to complete entirely; gen. to execute (lit. or fig.):— end, finish, fulfil, make.

4932. συντέμνω **suntěmnō**, soon-tem-no; from 4862 and the base of 5114; to contract by cutting, i.e. (fig.) do concisely (speedily):— (cut) short.

4933. συντηρέω **suntērěō**, soon-tay-reh´-o; from 4862 and 5083; to keep closely together, i.e. (by impl.) to conserve (from ruin); ment. to remember (and obey):— keep, observe, preserve.

4934. συντίθεμαι **suntithěmai**, soon-tith´-em-ahee; mid. voice from 4862 and 5087; to place jointly, i.e. (fig.) to consent (bargain, stipulate), concur:— agree, assent, covenant.

4935. συντόμως **suntŏmōs**, soon-tom´-oce; adv. from a der. of 4932; concisely (briefly):— a few words.

4936. συντρέχω **suntrěchō**, soon-trekh´-o; from 4862 and 5143 (incl. its alt.); to rush together (hastily assemble) or headlong (fig.):— run (together, with).

4937. συντρίβω **suntribō**, soon-tree´-bo; from 4862 and the base of 5147; to crush completely, i.e. to shatter (lit. or fig.):— break (in pieces), broken to shivers (+ -hearted), bruise.

4938. σύντριμμα **suntrimma**, soon-trim´-mah; from 4937; concussion or utter fracture (prop. concr.), i.e. complete ruin:— destruction.

4939. σύντροφος **suntrŏphŏs**, soon-trof-os; from 4862 and 5162 (in a pass. sense); a fellow-nursling, i.e. comrade:— brought up with.

4940. συντυγχάνω **suntugchanō**, soon-toong-khan´-o; from 4862 and 5177; to chance together, i.e. meet with (reach):— come at.

4941. Συντύχη **Suntuchē**, *soon-too´-khay;* from *4940;* an *accident; Syntyche,* a Chr. female:— Syntyche.

4942. συνυποκρίνομαι **sunupŏkrinŏmai**, *soon-oo-pok-rin´-om-ahee;* from *4862* and *5271;* to *act hypocritically* in concert *with:*— dissemble with.

4943. συνυπουργέω **sunupŏurgĕō**, *soon-oop-oorg-eh´-o;* from *4862* and a der. of a compound of *5259* and the base of *2041;* to *be a co-auxiliary,* i.e. *assist:*— help together.

4944. συνωδίνω **sunōdinō**, *soon-o-dee´no;* from *4862* and *5605;* to *have* (parturition) *pangs* in company (concert, simultaneously) *with,* i.e. (fig.) to *sympathize* (in expectation of relief from suffering):— travail in pain together.

4945. συνωμοσία **sunōmŏsia**, *soon-o-mos-ee´-ah;* from a compound of *4862* and *3660;* a *swearing together,* i.e. (by impl.) a *plot:*— conspiracy.

4946. Συράκουσαι **Surakŏusai**, *soo-rak´oo-sahee;* plur. of uncert. der.; *Syracuse,* the capital of Sicily:— Syracuse.

4947. Συρία **Suria**, *soo-ree´-ah;* prob. of Heb. or. [6865]; *Syria* (i.e. *Tsyria* or *Tyre*), a region of Asia:— Syria.

4948. Σύρος **Surŏs**, *soo´-ros;* from the same as *4947;* a *Syran* (i.e. prob. *Tyrian*), a native of Syria:— Syrian.

4949. Συροφοίνισσα **Surŏphŏinissa**, *soo-rof-oy´-nis-sah;* fem. of a compound of *4948* and the same as *5403;* a *Syro-phœnician* woman, i.e. a female native of Phœnicia in Syria:— Syrophenician.

4950. σύρτις **surtis**, *soor´-tis;* from *4951;* a *shoal* (from the sand *drawn* thither by the waves), i.e. the *Syrtis* Major or great bay on the N. coast of Africa:— quicksands.

4951. σύρω **surō**, *soo´-ro;* prob. akin to *138;* to *trail:*— drag, draw, hale.

4952. συσπαράσσω **susparassŏ**, *soos-par-as´-so;* from *4862* and *4682;* to *rend completely,* i.e. (by anal.) to *convulse* violently:— throw down.

4953. σύσσημον **sussēmŏn**, *soos´-say-mon;* neut. of a compound of *4862* and the base of *4591;* a *sign in common,* i.e. preconcerted *signal:*— token.

4954. σύσσωμος **sussōmŏs**, *soos´-so-mos;* from *4862* and *4983;* of a *joint body,* i.e. (fig.) a *fellow-member* of the Chr. community:— of the same body.

4955. συστασιαστής **sustasiastēs**, *soos-tas-ee-as-tace´;* from a compound of *4862* and a der. of *4714;* a *fellow-insurgent:*— make insurrection with.

4956. συστατικός **sustatikŏs**, *soos-tat-ee-kos´;* from a der. of *4921; introductory,* i.e. *recommendatory:*— of commendation.

4957. συσταυρόω **sustaurŏō**, *soos-tow-rŏ´-o;* from *4862* and *4717;* to *impale in company with* (lit. or fig.):— crucify with.

4958. συστέλλω **sustĕllō**, *soos-tel´-lo;* from *4862* and *4724;* to *send* (draw) *together,* i.e. *enwrap* (enshroud a corpse for burial), *contract* (an interval):— short, wind up.

4959. συστενάζω **sustĕnazō**, *soos-ten-ad´-zo;* from *4862* and *4727;* to *moan jointly,* i.e. (fig.) *experience a common calamity:*— groan together.

4960. συστοιχέω **sustŏichĕō**, *soos-toy-kheh´-o;* from *4862* and *4748;* to *file together* (as soldiers in ranks), i.e. (fig.) to *correspond* to:— answer to.

4961. συστρατιώτης **sustratiōtēs**, *soos-trat-ee-o´-tace;* from *4862* and *4757;* a *co-campaigner,* i.e. (fig.) an *associate* in Chr. toil:— fellowsoldier.

4962. συστρέφω **sustrĕphō**, *soos-tref´-o;* from *4862* and *4762;* to *twist together,* i.e. *collect* (a bundle, a crowd):— gather.

4963. συστροφή **sustrŏphē**, *soos-trof-ay´;* from *4962;* a *twisting together,* i.e. (fig.) a *secret coalition,* riotous *crowd:*— + band together, concourse.

4964. συσχηματίζω **suschēmatizō**, *soos-khay-mat-id´-zo;* from *4862* and a der. of *4976;* to *fashion alike,* i.e. *conform* to the same pattern (fig.):— conform to, fashion self according to.

4965. Συχάρ **Suchar**, *soo-khar´;* of Heb. or. [7941]; *Sychar* (i.e. *Shekar*), a place in Pal.:— Sychar.

4966. Συχέμ **Suchĕm**, *soo-khem´;* of Heb. or. [7927]; *Sychem* (i.e. *Shekem*), the name of a Canaanite and of a place in Pal.:— Sychem.

4967. σφαγή **sphagē**, *sfag-ay´;* from *4969; butchery* (of animals for food or sacrifice, or [fig.] of men [destruction]):— slaughter.

4968. σφάγιον **sphagiŏn**, *sfag´-ee-on;* neut. of a der. of *4967;* a *victim* (in sacrifice):— slain beast.

4969. σφάζω **sphazō**, *sfad´-zo;* a primary verb; to *butcher* (espec. an animal for food or in sacrifice) or (gen.) to *slaughter,* or (spec.) to *maim* (violently):— kill, slay, wound.

4970. σφόδρα **sphŏdra**, *sfod´-rah;* neut. plur. of σφοδρός **sphŏdrŏs**, *(violent;* of uncert. der.) as adv.; *vehemently,* i.e. in a *high degree, much:*— exceeding (-ly), greatly, sore, very.

4971. σφοδρῶς **sphŏdrōs**, *sfod-roce´;* adv. from the same as *4970; very much:*— exceedingly.

4972. σφραγίζω **sphragizō**, *sfrag-id´-zo;* from *4973;* to *stamp* (with a signet or private mark) for security or preservation (lit. or fig.); by impl. to *keep secret,* to *attest:*— (set a, set to) seal up, stop.

4973. σφραγίς **sphragis**, *sfrag-ece´;* prob. strengthened from *5420;* a *signet* (as *fencing* in or protecting from misappropriation); by impl. the *stamp* impressed (as a mark of privacy, or genuineness), lit. or fig.:— seal.

4974. σφυρόν **sphurŏn**, *sfoo-ron´;* neut. of a presumed der. prob. of the same as σφαῖρα **sphaira** (a *ball,* "sphere;" compare the fem. σφῦρα **sphura**, a *hammer*); the *ankle* (as *globular*):— ancle bone.

4975. σχεδόν **schĕdŏn**, *skhed-on´;* neut.

of a presumed der. of the alt. of *2192* as adv.; *nigh,* i.e. *nearly:*— almost.

σχέω **schĕō**. See *2192.*

4976. σχῆμα **schēma**, *skhay´-mah;* from the alt. of *2192;* a *figure* (as a *mode* or *circumstance*), i.e. (by impl.) extern. *condition:*— fashion.

4977. σχίζω **schizō**, *skhid´-zo;* appar. a primary verb; to *split* or *sever* (lit. or fig.):— break, divide, open, rend, make a rent.

4978. σχίσμα **schisma**, *skhis´-mah;* from *4977;* a *split* or *gap* ("schism"), lit. or fig.:— division, rent, schism.

4979. σχοινίον **schŏiniŏn**, *skhoy-nee´on;* dimin. of σχοῖνος **schŏinŏs** (a *rush* or *flag-plant;* of uncert. der.); a *rushlet,* i.e. *grass-withe* or *tie* (gen.):— small cord, rope.

4980. σχολάζω **schŏlazō**, *skhol-ad´-zo;* from *4981;* to *take a holiday,* i.e. *be at leisure* for (by impl. *devote oneself* wholly to); fig. to *be vacant* (of a house):— empty, give self.

4981. σχολή **schŏlē**, *skhol-ay´;* prob. fem. of a presumed der. of the alt. of *2192;* prop. *loitering* (as a *withholding* of oneself from work) or *leisure,* i.e. (by impl.) a *"school"* (as *vacation* from phys. employment):— school.

4982. σώζω **sōzō**, *sode´-zo;* from a primary σῶς **sōs** (contr. for obs. σάος **saŏs**, *"safe"*); to *save,* i.e. *deliver* or *protect* (lit. or fig.):— heal, preserve, save (self), do well, be (make) whole.

4983. σῶμα **sōma**, *so´-mah;* from *4982;* the *body* (as a *sound* whole), used in a very wide application, lit. or fig.:— bodily, body, slave.

4984. σωματικός **sōmatikŏs**, *so-mat-ee-kos´;* from *4983; corporeal* or *physical:*— bodily.

4985. σωματικῶς **sōmatikōs**, *so-mat-ee-koce´;* adv. from *4984; corporeally* or *physically:*— bodily.

4986. Σώπατρος **Sōpatrŏs**, *so´-pat-ros;* from the base of *4982* and *3962;* of a *safe father; Sopatrus,* a Chr.:— Sopater. Comp. *4989.*

4987. σωρεύω **sōrĕuō**, *sore-yoo´-o;* from another form of *4673;* to *pile* up (lit. or fig.):— heap, load.

4988. Σωσθένης **Sōsthĕnēs**, *soce-then´ace;* from the base of *4982* and that of *4599;* of *safe strength; Sosthenes,* a Chr.:— Sosthenes.

4989. Σωσίπατρος **Sōsipatrŏs**, *so-sip´at-ros;* prol. for *4986; Sosipatrus,* a Chr.:— Sosipater.

4990. σωτήρ **sōtēr**, *so-tare´;* from *4982;* a *deliverer,* i.e. God or Christ:— saviour.

4991. σωτηρία **sōtēria**, *so-tay-ree´-ah;* fem. of a der. of *4990* as (prop. abstr.) noun; *rescue* or *safety* (phys. or mor.):— deliver, health, salvation, save, saving.

4992. σωτήριον **sōtēriŏn**, *so-tay´-ree-on;* neut. of the same as *4991* as (prop. concr.) noun; *defender* or (by impl.) *defence:*— salvation.

4993. σωφρονέω **sōphrŏnĕō**, *so-fron-eh´o;* from *4998;* to *be of sound mind,* i.e. *sane,* (fig.) *moderate:*— be in right mind, be sober (minded), soberly.

Greek

4994. σωφρονίζω **sōphrŏnizō**, *so-fron-id´-zo;* from *4998;* to *make of sound mind,* i.e. (fig.) to *discipline* or *correct:*— teach to be sober.

4995. σωφρονισμός **sōphrŏnismŏs**, *so-fron-is-mos´;* from *4994; discipline,* i.e. *self-control:*— sound mind.

4996. σωφρόνως **sōphrŏnōs**, *so-fron´-oce;* adv. from *4998; with sound mind,* i.e. *moderately:*— soberly.

4997. σωφροσύνη **sōphrŏsunē**, *so-fros-oo´-nay;* from *4998; soundness of mind,* i.e. (lit.) *sanity* or (fig.) *self-control:*— soberness, sobriety.

4998. σώφρων **sōphrŏn**, *so´-frone;* from the base of *4982* and that of *5424; safe* (*sound*) in *mind,* i.e. *self-controlled* (*moderate* as to opinion or passion):— discreet, sober, temperate.

T

τά **ta.** See *3588.*

4999. Ταβέρναι **Tabĕrnai**, *tab-er´-nahee* or

Ταβερνῶν **Tabĕrnōn**, *tab-er-non´;* plur. of Lat. or.; *huts* or *wooden-walled* buildings; *Tabernæ:*— taverns.

5000. Ταβιθά **Tabitha**, *tab-ee-thah´;* of Chald. or. [comp. 6646]; *the gazelle; Tabitha* (i.e. *Tabjetha*), a Chr. female:— Tabitha.

5001. τάγμα **tagma**, *tag´-mah;* from *5021;* something orderly in *arrangement* (a troop), i.e. (fig.) a *series* or *succession:*— order.

5002. τακτός **taktŏs**, *tak-tos´;* from *5021; arranged,* i.e. *appointed* or *stated:*— set.

5003. ταλαιπωρέω **talaipōrĕō**, *tal-ahee-po-reh´-o;* from *5005;* to *be wretched,* i.e. *realize* one's own *misery:*— be afflicted.

5004. ταλαιπωρία **talaipōria**, *tal-ahee-po-ree´-ah;* from *5005; wretchedness,* i.e. *calamity:*— misery.

5005. ταλαίπωρος **talaipōrŏs**, *tal-ah´-ee-po-ros;* from the base of *5007* and a der. of the base of *3984; enduring trial,* i.e. *miserable:*— wretched.

5006. ταλαντιαῖος **talantiaiŏs**, *tal-an-tee-ah´-yos;* from *5007; talent-like* in weight:— weight of a talent.

5007. τάλαντον **talantŏn**, *tal´-an-ton;* neut. of a presumed der. of the orig. form of τλάω **tlaō** (to *bear;* equiv. to *5342*); a *balance* (as *supporting* weights), i.e. (by impl.) a certain *weight* (and thence a *coin* or rather *sum* of money) or "*talent*":— talent.

5008. ταλιθά **talitha**, *tal-ee-thah´;* of Chald. or. [comp. 2924]; *the fresh,* i.e. *young girl; talitha* (O *maiden*):— talitha.

5009. ταμεῖον **tamĕiŏn**, *tam-i´-on;* neut. contr. of a presumed der. of ταμίας **tamias** (a *dispenser* or *distributor;* akin to τέμνω **tĕmnō**, to *cut*); a *dispensary* or *magazine,* i.e. a chamber on the ground-floor or interior of an Oriental house (gen. used for *storage* or *privacy,* a spot for retirement):— secret chamber, closet, storehouse.

τανῦν **tanun.** See *3568.*

5010. τάξις **taxis**, *tax´-is;* from *5021;* reg. *arrangement,* i.e. (in time) fixed *succession* (of rank or character), official *dignity:*— order.

5011. ταπεινός **tapĕinŏs**, *tap-i-nos´;* of uncert. der.; *depressed,* i.e. (fig.) *humiliated* (in circumstances or disposition):— base, cast down, humble, of low degree (estate), lowly.

5012. ταπεινοφροσύνη **tapĕinŏphrŏsunē**, *tap-i-nof-ros-oo´-nay;* from a compound of *5011* and the base of *5424; humiliation of mind,* i.e. *modesty:*— humbleness of mind, humility (of mind, loneliness (of mind).

5013. ταπεινόω **tapĕinŏō**, *tap-i-nŏ´-o;* from *5011;* to *depress;* fig. to *humiliate* (in condition or heart):— abase, bring low, humble (self).

5014. ταπείνωσις **tapĕinōsis**, *tap-i´-no-sis;* from *5013; depression* (in rank or feeling):— humiliation, be made low, low estate, vile.

5015. ταράσσω **tarassō**, *tar-as´-so;* of uncert. aff.; to *stir* or *agitate* (*roil* water):— trouble.

5016. ταραχή **tarachē**, *tar-akh-ay´;* fem. from *5015; disturbance,* i.e. (of water) *roiling,* or (of a mob) *sedition:*— trouble (-ing).

5017. τάραχος **tarachŏs**, *tar´-akh-os;* masc. from *5015;* a *disturbance,* i.e. (popular) *tumult:*— stir.

5018. Ταρσεύς **Tarsĕus**, *tar-syoos´;* from *5019;* a *Tarsean,* i.e. native of Tarsus:— of Tarsus.

5019. Ταρσός **Tarsŏs**, *tar-sos´;* perh. the same as ταρσός **tarsŏs** (a *flat* basket); *Tarsus,* a place in Asia Minor:— Tarsus.

5020. ταρταρόω **tartaroō**, *tar-tar-ŏ´-o;* from Τάρταρος **Tartarŏs**, (the deepest *abyss* of Hades); to *incarcerate* in eternal torment:— cast down to hell.

5021. τάσσω **tassō**, *tas´-so;* a prol. form of a primary verb (which latter appears only in certain tenses); to *arrange* in an orderly manner, i.e. *assign* or *dispose* (to a certain position or lot):— addict, appoint, determine, ordain, set.

5022. ταῦρος **taurŏs**, *tow´-ros;* appar. a primary word [comp. 8450, "*steer*"]; a *bullock:*— bull, ox.

5023. ταῦτα **tauta**, *tŏw´-tah;* nominative or acc. neut. plur. of *3778; these* things:— + afterward, follow, + hereafter, × him, the same, so, such, that, then, these, they, this, those, thus.

5024. ταὐτά **tauta**, *tŏw-tah´;* neut. plur. of *3588* and *846* as adv.; in *the same* way:— even thus, (manner) like, so.

5025. ταύταις **tautais**, *tŏw´-taheece;* and

ταύτας **tautas**, *tŏw´-tas;* dat. and acc. fem. plur. respectively of *3778;* (*to* or *with* or *by,* etc.) *these:*— hence, that, then, these, those.

5026. ταύτῃ **tautē̦**, *tŏw´-tay;* and

ταύτην **tautēn**, *tŏw´-tane;* and

ταύτης **tautēs**, *tŏw´-tace;* dat., acc., and gen. respectively of the fem. sing. of *3778;* (*toward* or *of*) *this:*— her,

+ hereof, it, that, + thereby, the (same), this (same).

5027. ταφή **taphē**, *taf-ay´;* fem. from *2290; burial* (the act):— × bury.

5028. τάφος **taphŏs**, *taf´-os;* masc. from *2290;* a *grave* (the place of interment):— sepulchre, tomb.

5029. τάχα **tacha**, *takh´-ah;* as if neut. plur. of *5036* (adv.); *shortly,* i.e. (fig.) *possibly:*— peradventure (-haps).

5030. ταχέως **tachĕōs**, *takh-eh´-oce;* adv. from *5036; briefly,* i.e. (in time) *speedily,* or (in manner) *rapidly:*— hastily, quickly, shortly, soon, suddenly.

5031. ταχινός **tachinŏs**, *takh-ee-nos´;* from *5034; curt,* i.e. *impending:*— shortly, swift.

5032. τάχιον **tachiŏn**, *takh-´ee-on;* neut. sing. of the comp. of *5036* (as adv.); *more swiftly,* i.e. (in manner) *more rapidly,* or (in time) *more speedily:*— out [runl, quickly, shortly, sooner.

5033. τάχιστα **tachista**, *takh-´is-tah;* neut. plur. of the superl. of *5036* (as adv.); *most quickly,* i.e. (with *5613* pref.) *as soon as* possible:— + with all speed.

5034. τάχος **tachŏs**, *takh´-os;* from the same as *5036;* a *brief* space (of time), i.e. (with *1722* pref.) in *haste:*— + quickly, + shortly, + speedily.

5035. ταχύ **tachu**, *takh-oo´;* neut. sing. of *5036* (as adv.); *shortly,* i.e. *without delay, soon,* or (by surprise) *suddenly,* or (by impl. of ease) *readily:*— lightly, quickly.

5036. ταχύς **tachus**, *takh-oos´;* of uncert. aff.; *fleet,* i.e. (fig.) *prompt* or *ready:*— swift.

5037. τε **tĕ**, *teh;* a primary particle (enclitic) of connection or addition; *both* or *also* (prop. as correl. of *2532*):— also, and, both, even, then, whether. Often used in comp., usually as the latter part.

5038. τεῖχος **tĕichŏs**, *ti´-khos;* akin to the base of *5088;* a *wall* (as *formative* of a house):— wall.

5039. τεκμήριον **tĕkmēriŏn**, *tek-may´-ree-on;* neut. of a presumed der. of τεκμάρ **tĕkmar** (a *goal* or fixed *limit*); a *token,* (as *defining* a fact), i.e. *criterion* of certainty:— infallible proof.

5040. τεκνίον **tĕkniŏn**, *tek-nee´-on;* dimin. of *5043;* an *infant,* i.e. (plur. fig.) *darlings* (Chr. *converts*):— little children.

5041. τεκνογονέω **tĕknŏgŏnĕō**, *tek-nog-on-eh´-o;* from a compound of *5043* and the base of *1096;* to *be a child-bearer,* i.e. *parent* (*mother*):— bear children.

5042. τεκνογονία **tĕknŏgŏnia**, *tek-nog-on-ee´-ah;* from the same as *5041; childbirth* (*parentage*), i.e. (by impl.) *maternity* (the performance of *maternal duties*):— childbearing.

5043. τέκνον **tĕknŏn**, *tek´-non;* from the base of *5098;* a *child* (as *produced*):— child, daughter, son.

5044. τεκνοτροφέω **tĕknŏtrŏphĕō**, *tek-not-rof-eh´-o;* from a compound of *5043* and *5142;* to *be a child-rearer,* i.e. *fulfil* the duties of a *female parent*:— bring up children.

5045. τέκτων **tĕktōn**, *tek´-tone;* from the base of *5098;* an *artificer* (as *producer* of fabrics), i.e. (spec.) a *craftsman* in wood:— carpenter.

5046. τέλειος **tĕlĕiŏs**, *tel´-i-os;* from *5056; complete* (in various applications of labor, growth, ment. and mor. character, etc.); neut. (as noun, with *3588*) *completeness*:— of full age, man, perfect.

5047. τελειότης **tĕlĕiŏtēs**, *tel-i-ot´-ace;* from *5046;* (the state) *completeness* (ment. or mor.):— perfection (-ness).

5048. τελειόω **tĕlĕiŏō**, *tel-i-ŏ´-o;* from *5046;* to *complete*, i.e. (lit.) *accomplish*, or (fig.) *consummate* (in character):— consecrate, finish, fulfil, make) perfect.

5049. τελείως **tĕlĕiŏs**, *tel-i´-oce;* adv. from *5046; completely*, i.e. (of hope) *without wavering*:— to the end.

5050. τελείωσις **tĕlĕiōsis**, *tel-i´-o-sis;* from *5448;* (the act) *completion*, i.e. (of prophecy) *verification*, or (of expiation) *absolution*:— perfection, performance.

5051. τελειωτής **tĕlĕiōtēs**, *tel-i-o-tace´;* from *5048;* a *completer*, i.e. *consummater:* —finisher.

5052. τελεσφορέω **tĕlĕsphŏrĕō**, *tel-es-for-eh´-o;* from a compound of *5056* and *5342;* to *be a bearer to completion* (maturity), i.e. to *ripen* fruit (fig.):— bring fruit to perfection.

5053. τελευτάω **tĕlĕutaō**, *tel-yoo-tah´-o;* from a presumed der. of *5055;* to *finish* life (by impl. of *979*), i.e. *expire* (*demise*):— be dead, decease, die.

5054. τελευτή **tĕlĕutē**, *tel-yoo-tay´;* from *5053; decease*:— death.

5055. τελέω **tĕlĕō**, *tel-eh´-o;* from *5056;* to *end*, i.e. *complete, execute, conclude, discharge* (a debt):— accomplish, make an end, expire, fill up, finish, go over, pay, perform.

5056. τέλος **tĕlŏs**, *tel´-os;* from a primary τέλλω **tĕllō**, (to *set out* for a def. point or *goal*); prop. the point aimed at as a *limit*, i.e. (by impl.) the *conclusion* of an act or state (*termination* [lit., fig. or indef.], *result* [immed., ultimate or prophetic], *purpose*); spec. an *impost* or *levy* (as *paid*):— + continual, custom, end (-ing), finally, uttermost. Comp. *5411.*

5057. τελώνης **tĕlōnēs**, *tel-o´-nace;* from *5056* and *5608;* a *tax-farmer*, i.e. *collector of* public *revenue*:— publican.

5058. τελώνιον **tĕlōniŏn**, *tel-o´-nee-on;* neut. of a presumed der. of *5057;* a *tax-gatherer's* place of business:— receipt of custom.

5059. τέρας **tĕras**, *ter´-as;* of uncert. aff.; a *prodigy* or *omen*:— wonder.

5060. Τέρτιος **Tĕrtiŏs**, *ter´-tee-os;* of Lat. or.; *third; Tertius*, a Chr.:— Tertius.

5061. Τέρτυλλος **Tĕrtullŏs**, *ter´-tool-los;* of uncert. der.; *Tertullus*, a Rom.:— Tertullus.

τέσσαρα **tĕssara**. See *5064.*

5062. τεσσαράκοντα **tĕssarakŏnta**, *tes-*

---

sar-ak´-on-tah; the decade of *5064; forty*:— forty.

5063. τεσσαρακονταετής **tĕssarakŏntaĕtēs**, *tes-sar-ak-on-tah-et-ace´;* from *5062* and *2094; of forty years* of age:— (+ full, of) forty years (old).

5064. τέσσαρες **tĕssarĕs**, *tes´-sar-es;* neut.

τέσσαρα **tĕssara**, *tes´-sar-ah;* a plur. number; *four*:— four.

5065. τεσσαρεσκαιδέκατος **tĕssarĕskaidĕkatŏs**, *tes-sar-es-kahee-dek´-at-os;* from *5064* and *2532* and *1182; fourteenth*:— fourteenth.

5066. τεταρταῖος **tĕtartaiŏs**, *tet-ar-tah´-yos;* from *5064;* pertaining to the *fourth* day:— four days.

5067. τέταρτος **tĕtartŏs**, *tet´-ar-tos;* ord. from *5064; fourth*:— four (-th).

5068. τετράγωνος **tĕtragōnŏs**, *tet-rag´-o-nos;* from *5064* and *1137; four-cornered*, i.e. *square*:— foursquare.

5069. τετράδιον **tĕtradiŏn**, *tet-rad´-ee-on;* neut. of a presumed der. of τέτρας **tĕtras** (a *tetrad;* from *5064*); a *quaternion*, or squad (picket) of four Rom. soldiers:— quaternion.

5070. τετρακισχίλιοι **tĕtrakischiliŏi**, *tet-rak-is-khil´-ee-oy;* from the mult. adv. of *5064* and *5507; four times a thousand*:— four thousand.

5071. τετρακόσιοι **tĕtrakŏsiŏi**, *tet-rak-os´-ee-oy;* neut. τετρακόσια **tĕtrakŏsia**, *tet-rak-os´-ee- ah;* plur. from *5064* and *1540; four hundred*:— four hundred.

5072. τετράμηνον **tĕtramēnŏn**, *tet-ram´-ay-non;* neut. of a compound of *5064* and *3376;* a *four months'* space:— four months.

5073. τετραπλόος **tĕtraplŏŏs**, *tet-rap-lŏ´-os;* from *5064* and a der. of the base of *4118; quadruple*:— fourfold.

5074. τετράπους **tĕtrapŏus**, *tet-rap´-ooce;* from *5064* and *4228;* a *quadruped*:— fourfooted beast.

5075. τετραρχέω **tĕtrarchĕō**, *tet-rar-kheh´-o;* from *5076;* to *be a tetrarch*:— (be) tetrarch.

5076. τετράρχης **tĕtrarchēs**, *tet-rar´-khace;* from *5064* and *757;* the *ruler of a fourth* part of a country ("*tetrarch*"):— tetrarch.

τεύχω **tĕuchō**. See *5177.*

5077. τεφρόω **tĕphrŏō**, *tef-rŏ´-o;* from τέφρα **tephra**, (*ashes*); to *incinerate*, i.e. *consume*:— turn to ashes.

5078. τέχνη **tĕchnē**, *tekh´-nay;* from the base of *5088; art* (as *productive*), i.e. (spec.) a *trade*, or (gen.) *skill*:— art, craft, occupation.

5079. τεχνίτης **tĕchnitēs**, *tekh-nee´-tace;* from *5078;* an *artisan;* fig. a *founder* (*Creator*):— builder, craftsman.

5080. τήκω **tēkō**, *tay´-ko;* appar. a primary verb; to *liquefy*:— melt.

5081. τηλαυγῶς **tēlaugōs**, *tay-lŏw-goce´;* adv. from a compound of a der. of *5056* and *827;* in a *far-shining* manner, i.e. *plainly*:— clearly.

5082. τηλικοῦτος **tēlikŏutŏs**, *tay-lik-oo´-tos;* fem.

τηλικαύτη **tēlikautē**, *tay-lik-ŏw´-tay;* from a compound of *3588* with *2245* and *3778; such as this*, i.e. (in [fig.] magnitude) *so vast*:— so great, so mighty.

5083. τηρέω **tērĕō**, *tay-reh´-o;* from τερός **tērŏs**, (a *watch;* perh. akin to *2334*); to *guard* (from *loss* or *injury*, prop. by keeping *the eye* upon; and thus differing from *5442*, which is prop. to *prevent* escaping; and from *2892*, which implies a *fortress* or full military lines of apparatus), i.e. to *note* (a prophecy; fig. to *fulfil* a command); by impl. to *detain* (in custody; fig. to *maintain*); by extens. to *withhold* (for personal ends; fig. to *keep unmarried*):— hold fast, keep (-er), (pre-, re-) serve, watch.

5084. τήρησις **tērēsis**, *tay´-ray-sis;* from *5083;* a *watching*, i.e. (fig.) *observance*, or (concr.) a *prison*:— hold.

τῇ **tēi**, τήν **tēn**, τῆς **tēs**. See *3588.*

5085. Τιβεριάς **Tibĕrias**, *tib-er-ee-as´;* from *5086; Tiberias*, the name of a town and a lake in Pal.:— Tiberias.

5086. Τιβέριος **Tibĕriŏs**, *tib-er´-ee-os;* of Lat. or.; prob. *pertaining to the* river *Tiberis* or *Tiber; Tiberius*, a Rom. emperor:— Tiberius.

5087. τίθημι **tithēmi**, *tith´-ay-mee;* a prol. form of a primary

θέω **thĕō**, *theh´-o* (which is used only as alt. in certain tenses); to *place* (in the widest application, lit. and fig.; prop. in a pass. or horizontal posture, and thus different from *2476*, which prop. denotes an upright and active position, while *2749* is prop. refl. and utterly prostrate):— + advise, appoint, bow, commit, conceive, give, × kneel down, lay (aside, down, up), make, ordain, purpose, put, set (forth), settle, sink down.

5088. τίκτω **tiktō**, *tik´-to;* a strengthened form of a primary τέκω **tekō**, *tek´-o* (which is used only as alt. in certain tenses); to *produce* (from seed, as a mother, a plant, the earth, etc.), lit. or fig.:— bear, be born, bring forth, be delivered, be in travail.

5089. τίλλω **tillō**, *til´-lo;* perh. akin to the alt. of *138*, and thus to *4951;* to *pull* off:— pluck.

5090. Τίμαιος **Timaiŏs**, *tim´-ah-yos;* prob. of Chald. or. [comp. *2931*]; *Timæus* (i.e. *Timay*), an Isr.:— Timæus.

5091. τιμάω **timaō**, *tim-ah´-o;* from *5093;* to *prize*, i.e. *fix a valuation* upon; by impl. to *revere*:— honour, value.

5092. τιμή **timē**, *tee-may´;* from *5099;* a *value*, i.e. *money paid*, or (concr. and collect.) *valuables;* by anal. *esteem* (espec. of the highest degree), or the *dignity* itself:— honour, precious, price, some.

5093. τίμιος **timiŏs**, *tim´-ee-os;* including the comparative

τιμώτερος **timiŏtĕrŏs**, *tim-ee-o´-ter-os;* and the superlative

τιμιώτατος **timiŏtatŏs**, *tim-ee-o´-tat-os;* from *5092; valuable*, i.e. (obj.) *costly*, or (subj.) *honored, esteemed*, or (fig.) *beloved*:— dear, honourable,

Greek

(more, most) precious, had in reputation.

5094. τιμιότης **timiōtēs**, *tim-ee-ot´-ace*; from *5093*; *expensiveness*, i.e. (by impl.) *magnificence*:— costliness.

5095. Τιμόθεος **Timŏthĕŏs**, *tee-moth´-eh-os*; from *5092* and *2316*; *dear to God*; *Timotheus*, a Chr.:— Timotheus, Timothy.

5096. Τίμων **Timŏn**, *tee´-mone*; from *5092*; *valuable*; *Timon*, a Chr.:— Timon.

5097. τιμωρέω **timōrĕō**, *tim-o-reh´-o*; from a comp. of *5092* and οὖρος **ŏurŏs** (a *guard*); prop. to *protect*, one's *honor*, i.e. to *avenge* (*inflict a penalty*):— punish.

5098. τιμωρία **timōria**, *tee-mo-ree´-ah*; from *5097*; *vindication*, i.e. (by impl.) a *penalty*:— punishment.

5099. τίνω **tinō**, *tee´-no*; strengthened for a primary

    τίω **tiō**, *tee´-o* (which is only used as an alt. in certain tenses); to *pay* a price, i.e. as a *penalty*:— be punished with.

5100. τὶς **tis**, *tis*; an enclit. indef. pron.; *some* or *any* person or object:— a (kind of), any (man, thing, thing at all), certain (thing), divers, he (every) man, one (× thing), ought, + partly, some (man, body, -thing, -what), (+ that no-) thing, what (-soever), × wherewith, whom (-soever), whose (-soever).

5101. τίς **tis**, *tis*; prob. emphat. of *5100*; an interrog. pron., *who, which* or *what* (in direct or indirect ∙ questions):— every man, how (much), + no (-ne, thing), what (manner, thing), where (l-by, -fore, -of, -unto, -with, -withall), whether, which, who (-m, -se), why.

5102. τίτλος **titlŏs**, *tit´-los*; of Lat. or.: a *titulus* or "*title*" (*placard*):— title.

5103. Τίτος **Titŏs**, *tee´-tos*; of Lat. or. but uncert. signif.; *Titus*, a Chr.:— Titus.

    τίω **tiō**. See *5099*.

    τό **tŏ**. See *3588*.

5104. τοί **tŏi**, *toy*; prob. for the dat. of *3588*; an enclit. particle of *asseveration* by way of contrast; *in sooth*:— [used only with other particles in comp. as *2544, 3305, 5105, 5106,* etc.].

5105. τοιγαροῦν **tŏigarŏun**, *toy-gar-oon´*; from *5104* and *1063* and *3767*; *truly for then*, i.e. *consequently*:— there-(where-) fore.

    τοίγε **tŏigĕ**. See *2544*.

5106. τοίνυν **tŏinun**, *toy´-noon*; from *5104* and *3568*; *truly now*, i.e. *accordingly*:— then, therefore.

5107. τοιόσδε **tŏiŏsdĕ**, *toy-os´-deh*; (incl. the other inflections); from a der. of *5104* and *1161*; *such-like then*, i.e. *so great*:— such.

5108. τοιοῦτος **tŏiŏutŏs**, *toy-oo´-tos*; (incl. the other inflections); from *5104* and *3778*; *truly this*, i.e. *of this sort* (to denote character or individuality):— like, such (an one).

5109. τοῖχος **tŏichŏs**, *toy´-khos*; another form of *5038*; a *wall*:— wall.

5110. τόκος **tŏkŏs**, *tok´-os*; from the base of *5088*; *interest* on money loaned (as a *produce*):— usury.

5111. τολμάω **tŏlmaō**, *tol-mah´-o*; from τόλμα **tŏlma**, (*boldness*; prob. itself from the base of *5056* through the idea of *extreme* conduct); to *venture* (obj. or in *act*; while *2292* is rather subj. or in *feeling*); by impl. to be *courageous*:— be bold, boldly, dare, durst.

5112. τολμηρότερον **tŏlmērŏtĕrŏn**, *tol-may-rot´-er-on*; neut. of the comparative of a der. of the base of *5111* (as adv.); *more daringly*, i.e. *with greater confidence* than otherwise:— the more boldly.

5113. τολμητής **tŏlmētēs**, *tol-may-tace´*; from *5111*; a *daring* (*audacious*) man:— presumptuous.

5114. τομώτερος **tŏmōtĕrŏs**, *tom-o´-ter-os*; comparative of a der. of the primary τέμνω **tĕmnō** (to *cut*; more comprehensive or decisive than *2875*, as if by a *single* stroke; whereas that implies repeated blows, like *hacking*); *more keen*:— sharper.

5115. τόξον **tŏxŏn**, *tox´-on*; from the base of *5088*; a *bow* (appar. as the simplest fabric):— bow.

5116. τοπάζιον **tŏpaziŏn**, *top-ad´-zee-on*; neut. of a presumed der. (alt.) of τόπαζος **tŏpazŏs** (a "*topaz*"; of uncert. or.); a gem, prob. the *chrysolite*:— topaz.

5117. τόπος **tŏpŏs**, *top´-os*; appar. a primary word; a *spot* (gen. in *space*, but limited by occupancy; whereas *5561* is a larger but part. *locality*), i.e. *location* (as a position, home, tract, etc.); fig. *condition, opportunity*; spec. a *scabbard*:— coast, licence, place, × plain, quarter, + rock, room, where.

5118. τοσοῦτος **tŏsŏutŏs**, *tos-oo´-tos*; from τόσος **tŏsŏs** (*so much*; appar. from *3588* and *3739*) and *3778* (including its variations); so *vast as this*, i.e. *such* (in quantity, amount, number or space):— as large, so great (long, many, much), these many.

5119. τότε **tŏtĕ**, *tot´-eh*; from (the neut. of) *3588* and *3753*; *the when*, i.e. *at the time* that (of the past or future, also in consecution):— that time, then.

5120. τοῦ **tŏu**, *too*; prop. the gen. of *3588*; sometimes used for *5127*; *of this person*:— his.

5121. τοὐναντίον **tŏunantiŏn**, *too-nan-tee´-on*; contr. for the neut. of *3588* and *1726*; *on the contrary*:— contrariwise.

5122. τοὔνομα **tŏunŏma**, *too´-no-mah*; contr. for the neut. of *3588* and *3686*; *the name* (is):— named.

5123. τουτέστι **tŏutĕsti**, *toot-es´-tee*; contr. for *5124* and *2076*; *that is*:— that is (to say).

5124. τοῦτο **tŏutŏ**, *too´-tŏ*; neut. sing. nom. or acc. of *3778*; *that* thing:— here [-unto, it, partly, self [-same], so, that (intent), the same, there [-fore, -unto], this, thus, where [-fore].

5125. τούτοις **tŏutŏis**, *too´-toice*; dat. plur. masc. or neut. of *3778*; *to* (for, in, with or by) these (persons or things):— such, them, there [-in, -with], these, this, those.

5126. τοῦτον **tŏutŏn**, *too´-ton*; acc. sing. masc. of *3778*; *this* (person, as obj. of verb or prep.):— him, the same, that, this.

5127. τούτου **tŏutŏu**, *too´-too*; gen. sing. masc. or neut. of *3778*; *of* (from or concerning) *this* (person or thing):— here [-by], him, it, + such manner of, that, thence [-forth], thereabout, this, thus.

5128. τούτους **tŏutŏus**, *too´-tooce*; acc. plur. masc. of *3778*; *these* (persons, as obj. of verb or prep.):— such, them, these, this.

5129. τούτῳ **tŏutōi**, *too´-to*; dat. sing. masc. or neut. of *3778*; *to* (in, with or by) *this* (person or thing):— here [-by, -in], him, one, the same, there [-in], this.

5130. τούτων **tŏutōn**, *too´-tone*; gen. plur. masc. or neut. of *3778*; *of* (from or concerning) *these* (persons or things):— such, their, these (things), they, this sort, those.

5131. τράγος **tragŏs**, *trag´-os*; from the base of *5176*; a *he-goat* (as a *gnawer*):— goat.

5132. τράπεζα **trapĕza**, *trap´-ed-zah*; prob. contr. from *5064* and *3979*; a *table* or *stool* (as being *four-legged*), usually for food (fig. a *meal*); also a *counter* for money (fig. a broker's *office* for loans at interest):— bank, meat, table.

5133. τραπεζίτης **trapĕzitēs**, *trap-ed-zee´-tace*; from *5132*; a *money-broker* or *banker*:— exchanger.

5134. τραῦμα **trauma**, *trŏw´-mah*; from the base of τιτρώσκω **titrŏskō**, (to *wound*; akin to the base of *2352, 5147, 5149,* etc.); a *wound*:— wound.

5135. τραυματίζω **traumatizō**, *trŏw-mat-id´-zo*; from *5134*; to *inflict a wound*:— wound.

5136. τραχηλίζω **trachēlizō**, *trakh-ay-lid´-zo*; from *5137*; to *seize by the throat* or *neck*, i.e. to *expose the gullet* of a victim for killing (gen. to *lay bare*):— opened.

5137. τράχηλος **trachēlŏs**, *trakh´-ay-los*; prob. from *5143* (through the idea of *mobility*); the *throat* (*neck*), i.e. (fig.) *life*:— neck.

5138. τραχύς **trachus**, *trakh-oos´*; perh. strengthened from the base of *4486* (as if *jagged* by rents); *uneven, rocky* (*reefy*):— rock, rough.

5139. Τραχωνῖτις **Trachōnitis**, *trakh-o-nee´-tis*; from a der. of *5138*; *rough* district; *Trachonitis*, a region of Syria:— Trachonitis.

5140. τρεῖς **trĕis**, *trice*; neut.

    τρία **tria**, *tree´-ah*; or

    τριῶν **triŏn**, *tree-on´*; a primary (plural) number; "*three*":— three.

5141. τρέμω **trĕmō**, *trem´-o*; strengthened from a primary τρέω **trĕō** (to "*dread*", "*terrify*"); to "*tremble*" or *fear*:— be afraid, trembling.

5142. τρέφω **trĕphō**, *tref´-o*; a primary verb (prop. θρέφω **thrĕphō**; but perhaps strengthened from the base of *5157* through the idea of *convolution*); prop. to *stiffen*, i.e. *fatten* (by impl. to *cherish* [with food, etc.], *pamper, rear*):— bring up, feed, nourish.

5143. τρέχω **trĕchō**, trekh´-o; appar. a primary verb (prop. θρέχω **thrĕchō**; comp. 2359); which uses δρέμω **drĕmō**, drem´-o (the base of 1408) as alt. in certain tenses; to run or walk hastily (lit. or fig.):— have course, run.

5144. τριάκοντα **triakŏnta**, tree-ak´-on-tah; the decade of 5140; thirty:— thirty.

5145. τριακόσιοι **triakŏsiŏi**, tree-ak-os´-ee-oy; plur. from 5140 and 1540; three hundred:— three hundred.

5146. τρίβολος **tribŏlŏs**, trib´-ol-os; from 5140 and 956; prop. a crow-foot (three-pronged obstruction in war), i.e. (by anal.) a thorny plant (caltrop):— brier, thistle.

5147. τρίβος **tribŏs**, tree´-bos; from τρίβω **tribō** (to "rub"; akin to τείρω **tĕirō**, τρύω **truō**, and the base of 5131, 5134); a rut, or worn track:— path.

5148. τριετία **triĕtia**, tree-et-ee´-ah; from a compound of 5140 and 2094; a three years' period (triennium):— space of three years.

5149. τρίζω **trizō**, trid´-zo; appar. a primary verb; to creak (squeak), i.e. (by anal.) to grate the teeth (in frenzy):— gnash.

5150. τρίμηνον **trimēnŏn**, trim´-ay-non; neut. of a compound of 5140 and 3376 as noun; a three months' space:— three months.

5151. τρίς **tris**, trece; adv. from 5140; three times:— three times, thrice.

5152. τρίστεγον **tristĕgŏn**, tris´-teg-on; neut. of a compound of 5140 and 4721 as noun; a third roof (story):— third loft.

5153. τρισχίλιοι **trischiliŏi**, tris-khil´-ee-oy; from 5151 and 5507; three times a thousand:— three thousand.

5154. τρίτος **tritŏs**, tree´-tos; ord. from 5140; third; neut. (as noun) a third part, or (as adv.) a (or the) third time, thirdly:— third (-ly).

τρίχες **trichĕs**, etc. See 2359.

5155. τρίχινος **trichinŏs**, trikh´-ee-nos; from 2359; hairy, i.e. made of hair (mohair):— of hair.

5156. τρόμος **trŏmŏs**, trom´-os; from 5141; a "trembling", i.e. quaking with fear:— + tremble (-ing).

5157. τροπή **trŏpē**, trop-ay´; from an appar. primary τρέπω **trĕpō**, to turn); a turn ("trope"), i.e. revolution (fig. variation):— turning.

5158. τρόπος **trŏpŏs**, trop´-os; from the same as 5157; a turn, i.e. (by impl.) mode or style (espec. with prep. or rel. pref. as adv. like); fig. deportment or character:— (even) as, conversation, l+ likel manner, (+ by any) means, way.

5159. τροποφορέω **trŏpŏphŏrĕō**, trop-of-or-eh´-o; from 5158 and 5409; to endure one's habits:— suffer the manners.

5160. τροφή **trŏphē**, trof-ay´; from 5142; nourishment (lit. or fig.); by impl. rations (wages):— food, meat.

5161. Τρόφιμος **Trŏphimŏs**, trof´-ee-mos; from 5160; nutritive; Trophimus, a Chr.:— Trophimus.

5162. τροφός **trŏphŏs**, trof-os´; from 5142; a nourisher, i.e. nurse:— nurse.

5163. τροχιά **trŏchia**, trokh-ee-ah´; from 5164; a track (as a wheel-rut), i.e. (fig.) a course of conduct:— path.

5164. τροχός **trŏchŏs**, trokh-os´; from 5143; a wheel (as a runner), i.e. (fig.) a circuit of phys. effects:— course.

5165. τρύβλιον **trubliŏn**, troob´-lee-on; neut. of a presumed der. of uncert. aff.; a bowl:— dish.

5166. τρυγάω **trugaō**, troo-gah´-o; from a der. of τρύγω **trugō** (to dry) mean. ripe fruit (as if dry); to collect the vintage:— gather.

5167. τρυγών **trugōn**, troo-gone´; from τρύζω **truzō** (to murmur; akin to 5149, but denoting a duller sound); a turtledove (as cooing):— turtle-dove.

5168. τρυμαλιά **trumalia**, troo-mal-ee-ah´; from a der. of τρύω **truō** (to wear, away; akin to the base of 5134, 5147 and 5176); an orifice, i.e. needle's eye:— eye. Comp. 5169.

5169. τρύπημα **trupēma**, troo´-pay-mah; from a der. of the base of 5168; an aperture, i.e. a needle's eye:— eye.

5170. Τρύφαινα **Truphaina**, troo´-fahee-nah; from 5172; luxurious; Tryphæna, a Chr. woman:— Tryphena.

5171. τρυφάω **truphaō**, troo-fah´-o; from 5172; to indulge in luxury:— live in pleasure.

5172. τρυφή **truphē**, troo-fay´; from θρύπτω **thruptō** (to break, up or lfig.l enfeeble, espec. the mind and body by indulgence); effeminacy, i.e. luxury or debauchery:— delicately, riot.

5173. Τρυφῶσα **Truphōsa**, troo-fo´-sah; from 5172; luxuriating; Tryphosa, a Chr. female:— Tryphosa.

5174. Τρωάς **Trōas**, tro-as´; from Τρός **Trŏs** (a Trojan); the Troad (or plain of Troy), i.e. Troas, a place in Asia Minor:— Troas.

5175. Τρωγύλλιον **Trōgulliŏn**, tro-gool´-lee-on; of uncert. der.; Trogyllium, a place in Asia Minor:— Trogyllium.

5176. τρώγω **trōgō**, tro´-go; probably strengthened from a collateral form of the base of 5134 and 5147 through the idea of corrosion or wear; or perh. rather of a base of 5167 and 5149 through the idea of a crunching sound; to gnaw or chew, i.e. (gen.) to eat:— eat.

5177. τυγχάνω **tugchanō**, toong-khan´-o; prob. for an obs. τύχω **tuchō** (for which the mid. voice of another alt. τεύχω **tĕuchō** lto make ready or bring to passl is used in certain tenses; akin to the base of 5088 through the idea of effecting; prop. to affect; or (spec.) to hit or light upon (as a mark to be reached), i.e. (tran.) to attain or secure an object or end, or (intr.) to happen (as if meeting with); but in the latter application only impers. (with 1487), i.e. perchance; or (pres. part.) as adj. usual (as if commonly met with, with 3756, extraordinary), neut. (as adv.) perhaps; or (with another verb) as adv. by accident (as it were):— be, chance, enjoy, little, obtain, × refresh ... self, + special. Comp. 5180.

5178. τυμπανίζω **tumpanizō**, toom-pan-id´-zo; from a der. of 5180 (mean. a drum, "tympanum"); to stretch on an instrument of torture resembling a drum, and thus beat to death:— torture.

5179. τύπος **tupŏs**, too´-pos; from 5180; a die (as struck), i.e. (by impl.) a stamp or scar; by anal. a shape, i.e. a statue, (fig.) style or resemblance; spec. a sampler ("type"), i.e. a model (for imitation) or instance (for warning):— en- (ex-) ample, fashion, figure, form, manner, pattern, print.

5180. τύπτω **tuptō**, toop´-to; a primary verb (in a strengthened form); to "thump", i.e. cudgel or pummel (prop. with a stick or bastinado), but in any case by repeated blows; thus differing from 3817 and 3960, which denote a lusually singlel blow with the hand or any instrument, or 4141 with the fist lor a hammerl, or 4474 with the palm; as well as from 5177, an accidental collision); by impl. to punish; fig. to offend (the conscience):— beat, smite, strike, wound.

5181. Τύραννος **Turannŏs**, too´-ran-nos; a provincial form of the der. of the base of 2962; a "tyrant"; Tyrannus, an Ephesian:— Tyrannus.

5182. τυρβάζω **turbazō**, toor-bad´-zo; from τύρβη **turbē**, (Lat. turba, a crowd; akin to 2351); to make "turbid", i.e. disturb:— trouble.

5183. Τύριος **Turiŏs**, too´-ree-os; from 5184; a Tyrian, i.e. inhab. of Tyrus:— of Tyre.

5184. Τύρος **Turŏs**, too´-ros; of Heb. or. [6865l: Tyrus (i.e. Tsor), a place in Pal.:— Tyre.

5185. τυφλός **tuphlŏs**, toof-los´; from 5187; opaque (as if smoky), i.e. (by anal.) blind (phys. or ment.):— blind.

5186. τυφλόω **tuphlŏō**, toof-lŏ´-o; from 5185; to make blind, i.e. (fig.) to obscure:— blind.

5187. τυφόω **tuphŏō**, toof-ŏ´-o; from a der. of 5188; to envelop with smoke, i.e. (fig.) to inflate with self-conceit:— high-minded, be lifted up with pride, be proud.

5188. τύφω **tuphō**, too´-fo; appar. a primary verb; to make a smoke, i.e. slowly consume without flame:— smoke.

5189. τυφωνικός **tuphōnikŏs**, too-fo-nee-kos´; from a der. of 5188; stormy (as if smoky):— tempestuous.

5190. Τυχικός **Tuchikŏs**, too-khee-kos´; from a der. of 5177; fortuitous, i.e. fortunate; Tychicus, a Chr.:— Tychicus.

Υ

5191. ὑακίνθινος **huakinthinŏs**, hoo-ak-in´-thee-nos; from 5192; "hyacinthine" or "jacinthine", i.e. deep blue:— jacinth.

5192. ὑάκινθος **huakinthŏs**, hoo-ak´-in-thos; of uncert. der.; the "hyacinth" or "jacinth", i.e. some gem of a deep blue color, prob. the zirkon:— jacinth.

5193. ὑάλινος **hualinŏs**, hoo-al´-ee-nos; from 5194; glassy, i.e. transparent:— of glass.

5194. ὕαλος **hualŏs**, hoo´-al-os; perh.

from the same as *5205* (as being transparent like *rain*); *glass:*— glass.

5195. ὑβρίζω **hubrizō**, *hoo-brid´-zo*; from *5196*; to *exercise violence*, i.e. *abuse:*— use despitefully, reproach, entreat shamefully (spitefully).

5196. ὕβρις **hubris**, *hoo´-bris*; from *5228*; *insolence* (as *over*-bearing), i.e. *insult*, *injury:*— harm, hurt, reproach.

5197. ὑβριστής **hubristēs**, *hoo-bris-tace´*; from *5195*; an *insulter*, i.e. *maltreater:*— despiteful, injurious.

5198. ὑγιαίνω **hugiainō**, *hoog-ee-ah´-ee-no*; from *5199*; to *have* sound *health*, i.e. *be well* (in body); fig. to *be uncorrupt* (*true* in doctrine):— be in health, (be safe and) sound, (be) whole (-some).

5199. ὑγιής **hugiēs**, *hoog-ee-ace´*; from the base of *837*; *healthy*, i.e. *well* (in body); fig. *true* (in doctrine):— sound, whole.

5200. ὑγρός **hugrŏs**, *hoo-gros´*; from the base of *5205*; *wet* (as if with *rain*), i.e. (by impl.) *sappy* (*fresh*):— green.

5201. ὑδρία **hudria**, *hoo-dree-ah´*; from *5204*; a *water-jar*, i.e. *receptacle* for family supply:— water-pot.

5202. ὑδροποτέω **hudrŏpŏtĕō**, *hoo-drop-ot-eh´-o*; from a compound of *5204* and a der. of *4095*; *to be a water-drinker*, i.e. to *abstain from vinous beverages:*— drink water.

5203. ὑδρωπικός **hudrōpikŏs**, *hoo-dro-pik-os´*; from a compound of *5204* and a der. of *3700* (as if *looking watery*); *to be "dropsical":*— have the dropsy.

5204. ὕδωρ **hudōr**, *hoo´-dore*; gen., ὕδατος **hudatŏs**, *hoo´-dat-os*, etc.; from the base of *5205*; *water* (as if *rainy*) lit. or fig.:— water.

5205. ὑετός **huĕtŏs**, *hoo-et-os´*; from a primary ὕω **huō**, (to *rain*); *rain*, espec. a *shower:*— rain.

5206. υἱοθεσία **huiŏthĕsia**, *hwee-oth-es-ee´-ah*; from a presumed compound of *5207* and a der. of *5087*; the *placing as a son*, i.e. *adoption* (fig. Chr. *sonship* in respect to God):— adoption (of children, of sons).

5207. υἱός **huiŏs**, *hwee-os´*; appar. a primary word; a *"son"* (sometimes of animals), used very widely of immed. remote or fig. kinship:— child, foal, son.

5208. ὕλη **hulē**, *hoo´-lay*; perh. akin to *3586*; a *forest*, i.e. (by impl.) *fuel:*— matter.

5209. ὑμᾶς **humas**, *hoo-mas´*; acc. of *5210*; *you* (as the obj. of a verb or prep.):— ye, you (+ -ward), your (+ own).

5210. ὑμεῖς **humĕis**, *hoo-mice´*; irreg. plur. of *4771*; *you* (as subj. of verb):— ye (yourselves), you.

5211. Ὑμεναῖος **Humĕnaiŏs**, *hoo-men-ah´-yos*; from Ὑμήν **Humēn**, (the god of *weddings*); *"hymenæal"*; *Hymenæus*, an opponent cf Christianity:— Hymenæus.

5212. ὑμέτερος **humĕtĕrŏs**, *hoo-met´-er-os*; from *5210*; *yours*, i.e. *pertaining to you:*— your (own).

5213. ὑμῖν **humin**, *hoo-min´*; irreg. dat. of *5210*; *to* (*with* or *by*) *you:*— ye, you, your (-selves).

5214. ὑμνέω **humnĕō**, *hoom-neh´-o*; from *5215*; to *hymn*, i.e. sing a relig. ode; by impl. to *celebrate* (God) in song:— sing a hymn (praise unto).

5215. ὕμνος **humnŏs**, *hoom´-nos*; appar. from a simpler (obs.) form of ὕδέω **hudĕō**, (to *celebrate*; prob. akin to *103*; comp. *5667*); a *"hymn"* or relig. ode (one of the Psalms):— hymn.

5216. ὑμῶν **humōn**, *hoo-mone´*; gen. of *5210*; of (*from* or *concerning*) *you:*— ye, you, your (own, -selves).

5217. ὑπάγω **hupagō**, *hoop-ag´-o*; from *5259* and *71*; to *lead* (oneself) *under*, i.e. *withdraw* or *retire* (as if *sinking* out of sight), lit. or fig.:— depart, get hence, go (a-) way.

5218. ὑπακοή **hupakŏē**, *hoop-ak-ŏ-ay´*; from *5219*; *attentive hearkening*, i.e. (by impl.) *compliance* or *submission:*— obedience, (make) obedient, obey (-ing).

5219. ὑπακούω **hupakŏuō**, *hoop-ak-oo´-o*; from *5259* and *191*; to *hear under* (as a *subordinate*), i.e. to *listen attentively*; by impl. to *heed* or *conform* to a command or authority:— hearken, be obedient to, obey.

5220. ὕπανδρος **hupandrŏs**, *hoop´-an-dros*; from *5259* and *435*; in subjection *under* a man, i.e. a *married* woman:— which hath an husband.

5221. ὑπαντάω **hupantaō**, *hoop-an-tah´-o*; from *5259* and a der. of *473*; to *go opposite* (*meet*) *under* (*quietly*), i.e. to *encounter*, *fall in with:*— (go to) meet.

5222. ὑπάντησις **hupantēsis**, *hoop-an´-tay-sis*; from *5221*; an *encounter* or *concurrence* (with *1519* for infin. in order to *fall in with*):— meeting.

5223. ὕπαρξις **huparxis**, *hoop´-arx-is*; from *5225*; *existency* or *proprietorship*, i.e. (concr.) *property*, *wealth:*— goods, substance.

5224. ὑπάρχοντα **huparchŏnta**, *hoop-ar´-khon-tah*; neut. plur. of pres. part. act. of *5225* as noun; things *extant* or *in hand*, i.e. *property* or *possessions:*— goods, that which one has, things which (one) possesseth, substance, that hast.

5225. ὑπάρχω **huparchō**, *hoop-ar´-kho*; from *5259* and *756*; to *begin under* (*quietly*), i.e. *come into existence* (*be present* or *at hand*); expletively, to *exist* (as copula or subordinate to an adj., part., adv. or prep., or as auxil. to principal verb):— after, behave, live.

5226. ὑπείκω **hupĕikō**, *hoop-i´-ko*; from *5259* and εἴκω **ĕikō** (to *yield*, be *"weak"*); to *surrender:*— submit self.

5227. ὑπεναντίος **hupĕnantiŏs**, *hoop-en-an-tee´-os*; from *5259* and *1727*; *under* (*covertly*) *contrary to*, i.e. *opposed* or (as noun) an *opponent:*— adversary, against.

5228. ὑπέρ **hupĕr**, *hoop-er´*; a primary prep.; *"over"*, i.e. (with the gen.) of place, *above*, *beyond*, *across*, or causal, *for* the sake of, *instead*, *regarding*; with the acc. *superior to*, more *than:*— (+ exceeding, abundantly) above, in (on)

behalf of, beyond, by, + very chiefest, concerning, exceeding (above, -ly), for, + very highly, more (than), of, over, on the part of, for sake of, in stead, than, to (-ward), very. [In composition, it retains many of the above applications.]

5229. ὑπεραίρομαι **hupĕrairŏmai**, *hoop-er-ah´-ee-rom-ahee*; mid. voice from *5228* and *142*; to *raise* oneself *over*, i.e. (fig.) to *become haughty:*— exalt self, be exalted above measure.

5230. ὑπέρακμος **hupĕrakmŏs**, *hoop-er´-ak-mos*; from *5228* and the base of *188*; *beyond* the *"acme"*, i.e. fig. (of a daughter) *past* the *bloom* (*prime*) of youth:— + pass the flower of (her) age.

5231. ὑπεράνω **hupĕranō**, *hoop-er-an´-o*; from *5228* and *507*; *above upward*, i.e. *greatly higher* (in place or rank):— far above, over.

5232. ὑπεραυξάνω **hupĕrauxanō**, *hoop-er-ŏwx-an´-o*; from *5228* and *837*; to *increase above* ordinary degree:— grow exceedingly.

5233. ὑπερβαίνω **hupĕrbainō**, *hoop-er-bah´-ee-no*; from *5228* and the base of *939*; to *transcend*, i.e. (fig.) to *overreach:*— go beyond.

5234. ὑπερβαλλόντως **hupĕrballŏntōs**, *hoop-er-bal-lon´-toce*; adv. from pres. part. act. of *5235*; *excessively:*— beyond measure.

5235. ὑπερβάλλω **hupĕrballō**, *hoop-er-bal´-lo*; from *5228* and *906*; to *throw beyond* the usual mark, i.e. (fig.) to *surpass* (only act. part. *supereminent*):— exceeding, excel, pass.

5236. ὑπερβολή **hupĕrbŏlē**, *hoop-er-bol-ay´*; from *5235*; a *throwing beyond* others, i.e. (fig.) *supereminence*; adv. (with *1519* or *2596*) *pre-eminently:*— abundance, (far more) exceeding, excellency, more excellent, beyond (out of) measure.

5237. ὑπερείδω **hupĕrĕidō**, *hoop-er-i´-do*; from *5228* and *1492*; to *overlook*, i.e. *not punish:*— wink at.

5238. ὑπερέκεινα **hupĕrĕkĕina**, *hoop-er-ek´-i-nah*; from *5228* and the neut. plur. of *1565*; *above those* parts, i.e. *still farther:*— beyond.

5239. ὑπερεκτείνω **hupĕrĕktĕinō**, *hoop-er-ek-ti´-no*; from *5228* and *1614*; to *extend inordinately:*— stretch beyond.

5240. ὑπερεκχύνω **hupĕrĕkchunō**, *hoop-er-ek-khoo´-no*; from *5228* and the alt. form of *1632*; to *pour out over*, i.e. (pass.) to *overflow:*— run over.

ὑπερεκπερισσοῦ **hupĕrĕkpĕrissŏu**. See *5228* and *1537* and *4053*.

5241. ὑπερεντυγχάνω **hupĕrĕntugchanō**, *hoop-er-en-toong-khan´-o*; from *5228* and *1793*; to *intercede in behalf of:*— make intercession for.

5242. ὑπερέχω **hupĕrĕchō**, *hoop-er-ekh´-o*; from *5228* and *2192*; to *hold* oneself *above*, i.e. (fig.) to *excel*; part. (as adj. or neut. as noun) *superior*, *superiority:*— better, excellency, higher, pass, supreme.

5243. ὑπερηφανία **hupĕrēphania**, *hoop-er-ay-fan-ee´-ah*; from *5244*; *haughtiness:*— pride.

5244. ὑπερήφανος **hupĕrĕphanŏs**, hoop-er-ay´-fan-os; from 5228 and 5316; appearing above others (conspicuous), i.e. (fig.) haughty:— proud.

ὑπερλίαν **hupĕrlian**. See 5228 and 3029.

5245. ὑπερνικάω **hupĕrnikaŏ**, hoop-er-nik-ah´-o; from 5228 and 3528; to vanquish beyond, i.e. gain a decisive victory:— more than conquer.

5246. ὑπέρογκος **hupĕrŏgkŏs**, hoop-er´-ong-kos; from 5228 and 3591; bulging over, i.e. (fig.) insolent:— great swelling.

5247. ὑπεροχή **hupĕrŏchē**, hoop-er-okh-ay´; from 5242; prominence, i.e. (fig.) superiority (in rank or character):— authority, excellency.

5248. ὑπερπερισσεύω **hupĕrpĕrissĕuō**, hoop-er-per-is-syoo´-o; from 5228 and 4052; to super-abound:— abound much more, exceeding.

5249. ὑπερπερισσῶς **hupĕrpĕrissŏs**, hoop-er-per-is-soce´; from 5228 and 4057; superabundantly, i.e. exceedingly:— beyond measure.

5250. ὑπερπλεονάζω **hupĕrplĕŏnazō**, hoop-er-pleh-on-ad´-zo; from 5228 and 4121; to superabound:— be exceeding abundant.

5251. ὑπερυψόω **hupĕrupsŏō**, hoop-er-oop-so´-o; from 5228 and 5312; to elevate above others, i.e. raise to the highest position:— highly exalt.

5252. ὑπερφρονέω **hupĕrphrŏnĕō**, hoop-er-fron-eh´-o; from 5228 and 5426; to esteem oneself overmuch, i.e. be vain or arrogant:— think more highly.

5253. ὑπερῷον **hupĕrōiŏn**, hoop-er-o´-on; neut. of a der. of 5228; a higher part of the house, i.e. apartment in the third story:— upper chamber (room).

5254. ὑπέχω **hupĕchō**, hoop-ekh´-o; from 5259 and 2192; to hold oneself under, i.e. endure with patience:— suffer.

5255. ὑπήκοος **hupĕkŏŏs**, hoop-ay´-kŏ-os; from 5219; attentively listening, i.e. (by impl.) submissive:— obedient.

5256. ὑπηρετέω **hupĕrĕtĕō**, hoop-ay-ret-eh´-o; from 5257; to be a subordinate, i.e. (by impl.) subserve:— minister (unto), serve.

5257. ὑπηρέτης **hupĕrĕtēs**, hoop-ay-ret´-ace; from 5259 and a der. of ἐρέσσω ĕrĕssō (to row); an under-oarsman, i.e. (gen.) subordinate (assistant, sexton, constable):— minister, officer, servant.

5258. ὕπνος **hupnŏs**, hoop´-nos; from an obs. primary (perh. akin to 5259 through the idea of subsilience); sleep, i.e. (fig.) spiritual torpor:— sleep.

5259. ὑπό **hupŏ**, hoop-o´; a primary prep.; under, i.e. (with the gen.) of place (beneath), or with verbs (the agency or means, through); (with the acc.) of place (whither lunderneathl or where lbelowl or time (when latl):— among, by, from, in, of, under, with. (In composition, it retains the same general applications, espec. of inferior position or condition, and spec. covertly or moderately.l

5260. ὑποβάλλω **hupŏballŏ**, hoop-ob-al´-lo; from 5259 and 906; to throw in stealthily, i.e. introduce by collusion:— suborn.

5261. ὑπογραμμός **hupŏgrammŏs**, hoop-og-ram-mos´; from a compound of 5259 and 1125; an underwriting, i.e. copy for imitation (fig.):— example.

5262. ὑπόδειγμα **hupŏdĕigma**, hoop-od´-igue-mah; from 5263; an exhibit for imitation or warning (fig. specimen, adumbration):— en- (ex-) ample, pattern.

5263. ὑποδείκνυμι **hupŏdĕiknumi**, hoop-od-ike´-noo-mee; from 5259 and 1166; to exhibit under the eyes, i.e. (fig.) to exemplify (instruct, admonish):— show, (fore-) warn.

5264. ὑποδέχομαι **hupŏdĕchŏmai**, hoop-od-ekh´-om-ahee; from 5259 and 1209; to admit under one's roof, i.e. entertain hospitably:— receive.

5265. ὑποδέω **hupŏdĕō**, hoop-od-eh´-o; from 5259 and 1210; to bind under one's feet, i.e. put on shoes or sandals:— bind on, (be) shod.

5266. ὑπόδημα **hupŏdēma**, hoop-od´-ay-mah; from 5265; something bound under the feet, i.e. a shoe or sandal:— shoe.

5267. ὑπόδικος **hupŏdikŏs**, hoop-od´-ee-kos; from 5259 and 1349; under sentence, i.e. (by impl.) condemned:— guilty.

5268. ὑποζύγιον **hupŏzugiŏn**, hoop-od-zoog´-ee-on; neut. of a compound of 5259 and 2218; an animal under the yoke (draught-beast), i.e. (spec.) a donkey:— ass.

5269. ὑποζώννυμι **hupŏzōnnumi**, hoop-od-zone´-noo-mee; from 5259 and 2224; to gird under, i.e. frap (a vessel with cables across the keel, sides and deck):— undergirt.

5270. ὑποκάτω **hupŏkatō**, hoop-ok-at´-o; from 5259 and 2736; down under, i.e. beneath:— under.

5271. ὑποκρίνομαι **hupŏkrinŏmai**, hoop-ok-rin´-om-ahee; mid. voice from 5259 and 2919; to decide (speak or act) under a false part, i.e. (fig.) dissemble (pretend):— feign.

5272. ὑπόκρισις **hupŏkrisis**, hoop-ok´-ree-sis; from 5271; acting under a feigned part, i.e. (fig.) deceit ("hypocrisy"):— condemnation, dissimulation, hypocrisy.

5273. ὑποκριτής **hupŏkritēs**, hoop-ok-ree-tace´; from 5271; an actor under an assumed character (stage-player), i.e. (fig.) a dissembler ("hypocrite"):— hypocrite.

5274. ὑπολαμβάνω **hupŏlambanō**, hoop-ol-am-ban´-o; from 5259 and 2983; to take from below, i.e. carry upward; fig. to take up, i.e. continue a discourse or topic; ment. to assume (presume):— answer, receive, suppose.

5275. ὑπολείπω **hupŏlĕipō**, hoop-ol-i´-po; from 5295 and 3007; to leave under (behind), i.e. (pass.) to remain (survive):— be left.

5276. ὑπολήνιον **hupŏlēniŏn**, hoop-ol-ay´-nee-on; neut. of a presumed compound of 5259 and 3025; vessel or receptacle under the press, i.e. lower winevat:— winefat.

5277. ὑπολιμπάνω **hupŏlimpanō**, hoop-ol-im-pan´-o; a prol. form for 5275; to leave behind, i.e. bequeath:— leave.

5278. ὑπομένω **hupŏmĕnō**, hoop-om-en´-o; from 5259 and 3306; to stay under (behind), i.e. remain; fig. to undergo, i.e. bear (trials), have fortitude, persevere:— abide, endure, (take) patient (-ly), suffer, tarry behind.

5279. ὑπομιμνήσκω **hupŏmimnēskō**, hoop-om-im-nace´-ko; from 5259 and 3403; to remind quietly, i.e. suggest to the (mid. voice, one's own) memory:— put in mind, remember, bring to (put in) remembrance.

5280. ὑπόμνησις **hupŏmnēsis**, hoop-om´-nay-sis; from 5279; a reminding or (refl.) recollection:— remembrance.

5281. ὑπομονή **hupŏmŏnē**, hoop-om-on-ay´; from 5278; cheerful (or hopeful) endurance, constancy:— enduring, patience, patient continuance (waiting).

5282. ὑπονοέω **hupŏnŏĕō**, hoop-on-ŏ-eh´-o; from 5259 and 3539; to think under (privately), i.e. to surmise or conjec.:— think, suppose, deem.

5283. ὑπόνοια **hupŏnŏia**, hoop-on´-oy-ah; from 5282; suspicion:— surmising.

5284. ὑποπλέω **hupŏplĕō**, hoop-op-leh´-o; from 5259 and 4126; to sail under the lee of:— sail under.

5285. ὑποπνέω **hupŏpnĕō**, hoop-op-neh´-o; from 5259 and 4154; to breathe gently, i.e. breeze:— blow softly.

5286. ὑποπόδιον **hupŏpŏdiŏn**, hoop-op-od´-ee-on; neut. of a compound of 5259 and 4228; something under the feet, i.e. a foot-rest (fig.):— footstool.

5287. ὑπόστασις **hupŏstasis**, hoop-os´-tas-is; from a compound of 5259 and 2476; a setting under (support), i.e. (fig.) concr. essence, or abstr. assurance (obj. or subj.):— confidence, confident, person, substance.

5288. ὑποστέλλω **hupŏstĕllō**, hoop-os-tel´-lo; from 5259 and 4724; to withhold under (out of sight), i.e. (refl.) to cower or shrink, (fig.) to conceal (reserve):— draw (keep) back, shun, withdraw.

5289. ὑποστολή **hupŏstŏlē**, hoop-os-tol-ay´; from 5288; shrinkage (timidity), i.e. (by impl.) apostasy:— draw back.

5290. ὑποστρέφω **hupŏstrĕphō**, hoop-os-tref´-o; from 5259 and 4762; to turn under (behind), i.e. to return (lit. or fig.):— come again, return (again, back again), turn back (again).

5291. ὑποστρώννυμι **hupŏstrōnnumi**, hoop-os-trone´-noo-mee; from 5259 and 4766; to strew underneath (the feet as a carpet):— spread.

5292. ὑποταγή **hupŏtagē**, hoop-ot-ag-ay´; from 5293; subordination:— subjection.

5293. ὑποτάσσω **hupŏtassō**, hoop-ot-as´-so; from 5259 and 5021; to subordinate; refl. to obey:— be under obedience (obedient), put under, subdue unto, (be, make) subj. (to, unto), be (put) in subjection (to, under), submit self unto.

5294. ὑποτίθημι **hupŏtithēmi**, *hoop-ot-ith´-ay-mee*; from 5259 and 5087; to *place underneath*, i.e. (fig.) to *hazard*, (refl.) to *suggest*:— lay down, put in remembrance.

5295. ὑποτρέχω **hupŏtrĕchō**, *hoop-ot-rekh´-o*; from 5259 and 5143 (incl. its alt.); to *run under*, i.e. (spec.) to *sail past*:— run under.

5296. ὑποτύπωσις **hupŏtupōsis**, *hoop-ot-oop´-o-sis*; from a compound of 5259 and a der. of 5179; *typification under* (*after*), i.e. (concr.) a *sketch* (fig.) for imitation:— form, pattern.

5297. ὑποφέρω **hupŏphĕrō**, *hoop-of-er´-o*; from 5259 and 5342; to *bear from underneath*, i.e. (fig.) to *undergo* hardship:— bear, endure.

5298. ὑποχωρέω **hupŏchōrĕō**, *hoop-okh-o-reh´-o*; from 5259 and 5562; to *vacate down*, i.e. *retire* i.e. *retire* quietly:— go aside, withdraw self.

5299. ὑπωπιάζω **hupōpiazō**, *hoop-o-pee-ad´-zo*; from a compound of 5259 and a der. of 3700; to *hit under the eye* (*buffet* or *disable* an antagonist as a pugilist), i.e. (fig.) to *tease* or *annoy* (into compliance), *subdue* (one's passions):— keep under, weary.

5300. ὗς **hus**, *hoos*; appar. a primary word; a *hog* ("*swine*"):— sow.

5301. ὕσσωπος **hussōpŏs**, *hoos´-so-pos*; of for. or. [231]; "*hyssop*":— hyssop.

5302. ὑστερέω **hustĕrĕō**, *hoos-ter-eh´-o*; from 5306; to *be later*, i.e. (by impl.) to *be inferior*; gen. to *fall short* (be *deficient*):— come behind (short), be destitute, fail, lack, suffer need, (be in) want, be the worse.

5303. ὑστέρημα **hustĕrēma**, *hoos-ter´-ay-mah*; from 5302; a *deficit*; spec. *poverty*:— that which is behind, (that which was) lack (-ing), penury, want.

5304. ὑστέρησις **hustĕrēsis**, *hoos-ter´-ay-sis* from 5302; a *falling short*, i.e. (spec.) *penury*:— want.

5305. ὕστερον **hustĕrŏn**, *hoos´-ter-on*; neut. of 5306 as adv.; *more lately*, i.e. *eventually*:— afterward, (at the) last (of all).

5306. ὕστερος **hustĕrŏs**, *hoos´-ter-os*; comparative from 5259 (in the sense of *behind*); *later*:— latter.

5307. ὑφαντός **huphantŏs**, *hoo-fan-tos´*; from ὑφαίνω **huphainō**, to *weave*; *woven*, i.e. (perh.) *knitted*:— woven.

5308. ὑψηλός **hupsēlŏs**, *hoop-say-los´*; from 5311; *lofty* (in place or character):— high (-er, -ly) (esteemed).

5309. ὑψηλοφρονέω **hupsēlŏphrŏnĕō**, *hoop-say-lo-fron-eh´-o*; from a compound of 5308 and 5424; to *be lofty in mind*, i.e. *arrogant*:— be highminded.

5310. ὕψιστος **hupsistŏs**, *hoop´-sis-tos*; superl. from the base of 5311; *highest*, i.e. (masc. sing.) the *Supreme* (God), or (neut. plur.) the *heavens*:— most high, highest.

5311. ὕψος **hupsŏs**, *hoop´-sos*; from a der. of 5228; *elevation*, i.e. (abstr.) *altitude*, (spec.) the *sky*, or (fig.) *dignity*:— be exalted, height, (on) high.

5312. ὑψόω **hupsŏō**, *hoop-sŏ´-o*; from 5311; to *elevate* (lit. or fig.):— exalt, lift up.

5313. ὕψωμα **hupsōma**, *hoop´-so-mah*; from 5312; an *elevated* place or thing, i.e. (abstr.) *altitude*, or (by impl.) a *barrier* (fig.):— height, high thing.

Φ

5314. φάγος **phagŏs**, *fag´-os*; from 5315; a *glutton*:— gluttonous.

5315. φάγω **phagō**, *fag´-o*; a primary verb (used as an alt. of 2068 in certain tenses); to *eat* (lit. or fig.):— eat, meat.

φαιλόνης **phailŏnēs**, *fahee-lohn´-ace*; an alt. spelling of 5341 which see; found only in 2 Tim. 4:13.

5316. φαίνω **phainō**, *fah´-ee-no*; prol. for the base of 5457; to *lighten* (*shine*), i.e. *show* (tran. or intr., lit. or fig.):— appear, seem, be seen, shine, × think.

5317. Φάλεκ **Phalĕk**, *fal´-ek*; of Heb. or. [6389]; *Phalek* (i.e. *Peleg*), a patriarch:— Phalec.

5318. φανερός **phanĕrŏs**, *fan-er-os´*; from 5316; *shining*, i.e. *apparent* (lit. or fig.); neut. (as adv.) *publicly*, *extern.*:— abroad, + appear, known, manifest, open [+ -ly], outward (l+ly]).

5319. φανερόω **phanĕrŏō**, *fan-er-ŏ´-o*; from 5318; to *render apparent* (lit. or fig.):— appear, manifestly declare, (make) manifest (forth), shew (self).

5320. φανερῶς **phanĕrōs**, *fan-er-oce´*; adv. from 5318; *plainly*, i.e. *clearly* or *publicly*:— evidently, openly.

5321. φανέρωσις **phanĕrōsis**, *fan-er´-o-sis*; from 5319; *exhibition*, i.e. (fig.) *expression*, (by extens.) a *bestowment*:— manifestation.

5322. φανός **phanŏs**, *fan-os´*; from 5316; a *lightener*, i.e. *light*; *lantern*:— lantern.

5323. Φανουήλ **Phanŏuēl**, *fan-oo-ale´*; of Heb. or. [6439]; *Phanuël* (i.e. *Penuël*), an Isr.:— Phanuel.

5324. φαντάζω **phantazō**, *fan-tad´-zo*; from a der. of 5316; to *make apparent* i.e. (pass.) to *appear* (neut. part. as noun, a *spectacle*):— sight.

5325. φαντασία **phantasia**, *fan-tas-ee´-ah*; from a der. of 5324; (prop. abstr.) a (vain) *show* ("fantasy"):— pomp.

5326. φάντασμα **phantasma**, *fan´-tas-mah*; from 5324; (prop. concr.) a (mere) *show* ("phantasm"), i.e. *spectre*:— spirit.

5327. φάραγξ **pharagx**, *far´-anx*; prop. streng. from the base of 4008 or rather of 4486; a *gap* or *chasm*, i.e. *ravine* (winter-torrent):— valley.

5328. Φαραώ **Pharaō**, *far-ah-o´*; of for. or. [6547]; *Pharaō* (i.e. *Pharoh*), an Eg. king:— Pharaoh.

5329. Φαρές **Pharĕs**, *far-es´*; of Heb. or. [6557]; *Phares* (i.e. *Perets*), an Isr.:— Phares.

5330. Φαρισαῖος **Pharisaiŏs**, *far-is-ah´-yos*; of Heb. or. [comp. 6567]; a *separatist*, i.e. exclusively *relig.*; a *Phariséean*, i.e. Jewish sectary:— Pharisee.

5331. φαρμακεία **pharmakĕia**, *far-mak-i´-ah*; from 5332; *medication* ("phar-

macy"), i.e. (by extens.) *magic* (lit. or fig.):— sorcery, witchcraft.

5332. φαρμακεύς **pharmakĕus**, *far-mak-yoos´*; from φάρμακον **pharmakŏn**, (a *drug*, i.e. spell-giving *potion*); a *druggist* ("pharmacist") or *poisoner*, i.e. (by extens.) a *magician*:— sorcerer.

5333. φαρμακός **pharmakŏs**, *far-mak-os´*; the same as 5332:— sorcerer.

5334. φάσις **phasis**, *fas´-is*; from 5346 (not the same as "phase", which is from 5316); a *saying*, i.e. *report*:— tidings.

5335. φάσκω **phaskō**, *fas´-ko*; prol. from the same as 5346; to *assert*:— affirm, profess, say.

5336. φάτνη **phatnē**, *fat´-nay*; from πατέομαι **patĕŏmai** (to *eat*); a *crib* (for fodder):— manger, stall.

5337. φαῦλος **phaulŏs**, *fŏw´-los*; appar. a primary word; "*foul*" or "*flawy*", i.e. (fig.) *wicked*:— evil.

5338. φέγγος **phĕggŏs**, *feng´-gos*; prob. akin to the base of 5457 [comp. 5350]; *brilliancy*:— light.

5339. φείδομαι **phĕidŏmai**, *fī´-dom-ahee*; of uncert. aff.; to *be chary* of, i.e. (subj.) to *abstain* or (obj.) to *treat leniently*:— forbear, spare.

5340. φειδομένως **phĕidŏmĕnōs**, *fī-dom-en´-oce*; adv. from part. of 5339; *abstemiously*, i.e. *stingily*:— sparingly.

5341. φελόνης **phĕlŏnēs**, *fel-on´-ace* or

φαιλόνης **phailŏnēs**, *fayl-on´-ace*; by transp. for a der. prob. of 5316 (as *showing* outside the other garments); a *mantle* (*surtout*):— cloke.

5342. φέρω **phĕrō**, *fer´-o*; a primary verb (for which other and appar. not cognate ones are used in certain tenses only; namely,

οἴω **ŏiō**, *oy´-o*; and

ἐνέγκω **ĕnĕgkō**, *en-eng´-ko*; to "*bear*" or *carry* (in a very wide application, lit. and fig. as follows):— be, bear, bring (forth), carry, come, + let her drive, be driven, endure, go on, lay, lead, move, reach, rushing, uphold.

5343. φεύγω **phĕugō**, *fyoo´-go*; appar. a primary verb; to *run away* (lit. or fig.); by impl. to *shun*; by anal. to *vanish*:— escape, flee (away).

5344. Φῆλιξ **Phēlix**, *fay´-lix*; of Lat. or.; *happy*; *Phelix* (i.e. *Felix*), a Rom.:— Felix.

5345. φήμη **phēmē**, *fay´-may*; from 5346; a *saying*, i.e. *rumor* ("fame"):— fame.

5346. φημί **phēmi**, *fay-mee´*; prop. the same as the base of 5457 and 5316; to *show* or *make known* one's thoughts, i.e. *speak* or *say*:— affirm, say. Comp. 3004.

5347. Φῆστος **Phēstŏs**, *face´-tos*; of Lat. der.; *festal*; *Phestus* (i.e. *Festus*), a Rom.:— Festus.

5348. φθάνω **phthanō**, *fthan´-o*; appar. a primary verb; to *be beforehand*, i.e. *anticipate* or *precede*; by extens. to *have arrived* at:— (already) attain, come, prevent.

5349. φθαρτός **phthartŏs**, *fthar-tos´*;

from 5351; decayed, i.e. (by impl.) per-ishable:— corruptible.

5350. φθέγγομαι phthĕggŏmai, ftheng'-gom-ahee; prob. akin to 5338 and thus to 5346; to utter a clear sound, i.e. (gen.) to proclaim:— speak.

5351. φθείρω phthĕirō, fthi'-ro; probably strengthened from φθίω phthiō (to pine or waste); prop. to shrivel, or wither, i.e. to spoil (by any process) or (gen.) to ruin (espec. fig., by mor. influences, to deprave):— corrupt (self), defile, destroy.

5352. φθινοπωρινός phthinŏpōrinŏs, fthin-op-o-ree-nos'; from der. of φθίω phthiō (to wane; akin to the base of 5351) and 3703 (mean. late autumn); autumnal (as stripped of leaves):— whose fruit withereth.

5353. φθόγγος phthŏggŏs, fthong'-gos; from 5350; utterance, i.e. a musical note (vocal or instrumental):— sound.

5354. φθονέω phthŏnĕō, fthon-eh'-o; from 5355; to be jealous of:— envy.

5355. φθόνος phthŏnŏs, fthon'-os; prob. akin to the base of 5351; ill-will (as detraction), i.e. jealousy (spite):— envy.

5356. φθορά phthŏra, fthor-ah'; from 5351; decay, i.e. ruin (spontaneous or inflicted, lit. or fig.):— corruption. destroy, perish.

5357. φιάλη phialē, fee-al'-ay; of uncert. aff.; a broad shallow cup ("phial"):— vial.

5358. φιλάγαθος philagathŏs, fil-ag'-ath-os; from 5384 and 18; fond to good, i.e. a promoter of virtue:— love of good men.

5359. Φιλαδέλφεια Philadĕlphĕia, fil-ad-el'-fee-ah; from Φιλάδελφος Philadĕlphŏs (the same as 5361), a king of Pergamos; Philadelphia, a place in Asia Minor:— Philadelphia.

5360. φιλαδελφία philadĕlphia, fil-ad-el-fee'-ah; from 5361; fraternal affection:— brotherly love (kindness), love of the brethren.

5361. φιλάδελφος philadĕlphŏs, fil-ad'-el-fos; from 5384 and 80; fond of brethren, i.e. fraternal:— love as brethren.

5362. φίλανδρος philandrŏs, fil'-an-dros; from 5384 and 435; fond of man, i.e. affectionate as a wife:— love their husbands.

5363. φιλανθρωπία philanthrŏpia, fil-an-thro-pee'-ah; from the same as 5364; fondness of mankind, i.e. benevolence ("philanthropy"):— kindness, love toward man.

5364. φιλανθρώπως philanthrŏpōs, fil-an-thro'-poce; adv. from a compound of 5384 and 444; fondly to man ("philanthropically"), i.e. humanely:— courteously.

5365. φιλαργυρία philarguria, fil-ar-goo-ree'-ah; from 5366; avarice:— love of money.

5366. φιλάργυρος philargurŏs, fil-ar'-goo-ros; from 5384 and 696; fond of silver (money), i.e. avaricious:— covetous.

5367. φίλαυτος philautŏs, fil'-ŏw-tos; from 5384 and 846; fond of self, i.e. selfish:— lover of own self.

5368. φιλέω philĕō, fil-eh'-o; from 5384; to be a friend to (fond of [an indiv. or an obj.]), i.e. have affection for (denoting personal attachment, as a matter of sentiment or feeling; while 25 is wider, embracing espec. the judgment and the deliberate assent of the will as a matter of principle, duty and propriety: the two thus stand related very much as 2309 and 1014, or as 2372 and 3563 respectively; the former being chiefly of the heart and the latter of the head; spec. to kiss (as a mark of tenderness):— kiss, love.

5369. φιλήδονος philēdŏnŏs, fil-ay'-don-os; from 5384 and 2237; fond of pleasure, i.e. voluptuous:— lover of pleasure.

5370. φίλημα philēma, fil'-ay-mah; from 5368; a kiss:— kiss.

5371. Φιλήμων Philēmōn, fil-ay'-mone; from 5368; friendly; Philemon, a Chr.:— Philemon.

5372. Φιλητός Philētŏs, fil-ay-tos'; from 5368; amiable; Philetus, an opposer of Christianity:— Philetus.

5373. φιλία philia, fil-ee'-ah; from 5384; fondness:— friendship.

5374. Φιλιππήσιος Philippēsiŏs, fil-ip-pay'-see-os; from 5375; a Philippesian (Philippian), i.e. native of Philippi:— Philippian.

5375. Φίλιπποι Philippŏi, fil'-ip-poy; plur. of 5376; Philippi, a place in Macedonia:— Philippi.

5376. Φίλιππος Philippŏs, fil'-ip-pos; from 5384 and 2462; fond of horses; Philippus, the name of four Isr.:— Philip.

5377. φιλόθεος philŏthĕŏs, fil-oth'-eh-os; from 5384 and 2316; fond of God, i.e. pious:— lover of God.

5378. Φιλόλογος Philŏlŏgŏs, fil-ol'-og-os; from 5384 and 3056; fond of words, i.e. talkative (argumentative, learned, "philological"); Philologus, a Chr.:— Philologus.

5379. φιλονεικία philŏnĕikia, fil-on-i-kee'-ah; from 5380; quarrelsomeness, i.e. a dispute:— strife.

5380. φιλόνεικος philŏnĕikŏs, fil-on'-i-kos; from 5384 and νεῖκος nĕikŏs (a quarrel; prob. akin to 3534); fond of strife, i.e. disputatious:— contentious.

5381. φιλονεξία philŏnĕxia, fil-on-ex-ee'-ah; from 5382; hospitableness:— entertain strangers, hospitality.

5382. φιλόξενος philŏxĕnŏs, fil-ox'-en-os; from 5384 and 3581; fond of guests, i.e. hospitable:— given to (lover of, use) hospitality.

5383. φιλοπρωτεύω philŏprōtĕuō, fil-op-rote-yoo'-o; from a compound of 5384 and 4413; to be fond of being first, i.e. ambitious of distinction:— love to have the preeminence.

5384. φίλος philŏs, fee'-los; prop. dear, i.e. a friend; act. fond, i.e. friendly (still as a noun, an associate, neighbor, etc.):— friend.

5385. φιλοσοφία philŏsŏphia, fil-os-of-ee'-ah; from 5386; "philosophy", i.e. (spec.) Jewish sophistry:— philosophy.

5386. φιλόσοφος philŏsŏphŏs, fil-os'-of-os; from 5384 and 4680; fond of wise things, i.e. a "philosopher":— philosopher.

5387. φιλόστοργος philŏstŏrgŏs, fil-os'-tor-gos; from 5384 and στοργή stŏrgē (cherishing one's kindred, espec. parents or children); fond of natural relatives, i.e. fraternal toward fellow Chr.:— kindly affectioned.

5388. φιλότεκνος philŏtĕknŏs, fil-ot'-ek-nos; from 5384 and 5043; fond of one's children, i.e. maternal:— love their children.

5389. φιλοτιμέομαι philŏtimĕŏmai, fil-ot-im-eh'-om-ahee; mid. voice from a compound of 5384 and 5092; to be fond of honor, i.e. emulous (eager or earnest to do something):— labour, strive, study.

5390. φιλοφρόνως philŏphrŏnōs, fil-of-ron'-oce; adv. from 5391; with friendliness of mind, i.e. kindly:— courteously.

5391. φιλόφρων philŏphrōn, fil-of'-rone; from 5384 and 5424; friendly of mind, i.e. kind:— courteous.

5392. φιμόω phimŏō, fee-mŏ'-o; from φιμός phimŏs, (a muzzle); to muzzle:— muzzle.

5393. Φλέγων Phlĕgōn, fleg'-one; act. part. of the base of 5395; blazing; Phlegon, a Chr.:— Phlegon.

5394. φλογίζω phlŏgizō, flog-id'-zo; from 5395; to cause a blaze, i.e. ignite (fig. to inflame with passion):— set on fire.

5395. φλόξ phlŏx, flox; from a primary φλέγω phlĕgō, (to "flash" or "flame"); a blaze:— flame (-ing).

5396. φλυαρέω phluarĕō, floo-ar-eh'-o; from 5397; to be a babbler or trifler, i.e. (by impl.) to berate idly or mischievously:— prate against.

5397. φλύαρος phluarŏs, floo'-ar-os; from φλύω phluō, (to bubble); a garrulous person, i.e. prater:— tattler.

5398. φοβερός phŏbĕrŏs, fob-er-os'; from 5401; frightful, i.e. (obj.) formidable:— fearful, terrible.

5399. φοβέω phŏbĕō, fob-eh'-o; from 5401; to frighten, i.e. (pass.) to be alarmed; by anal. to be in awe of, i.e. revere:— be (+ sore) afraid, fear (exceedingly), reverence.

5400. φόβητρον phŏbētrŏn, fob'-ay-tron; neut. of a der. of 5399; a frightening thing, i.e. terrific portent:— fearful sight.

5401. φόβος phŏbŏs, fob'-os; from a primary φέβομαι phĕbŏmai (to be put in fear); alarm, or fright:— be afraid, + exceedingly, fear, terror.

5402. Φοίβη Phŏibē, foy'-bay; fem. of φοῖβος phŏibŏs, (bright; prob. akin to the base of 5457); Phœbe, a Chr. woman:— Phebe.

5403. Φοινίκη Phŏinikē, foy-nee'-kay; from 5404; palm-country; Phœnice (or Phœnicia), a region of Pal.:— Phenice, Phenicia.

5404. φοῖνιξ phŏinix, foy'-nix; of uncert. der.; a palm-tree:— palm (tree).

5405. Φοῖνιξ Phŏinix, foy'-nix; prob. the

same as *5404; Phœnix*, a place in Crete:— Phenice.

5406. φονεύς **phŏnĕus**, *fon-yooce´*; from *5408*; a *murderer* (always of *criminal* lor at least *intentional*] homicide; which *443* does not necessarily imply; while *4607* is a special term for a *public* bandit):— murderer.

5407. φονεύω **phŏnĕuō**, *fon-yoo´-o*; from *5406*; to *be a murderer* (of):— kill, do murder, slay.

5408. φόνος **phŏnŏs**, *fon´-os*; from an obs. primary φένω **phĕnō** (to *slay*); *murder*:— murder, + be slain with, slaughter.

5409. φορέω **phŏrĕō**, *for-eh´-o*; from *5411*; to *have a burden*, i.e. (by anal.) to *wear* as clothing or a constant accompaniment:— bear, wear.

5410. Φόρον **Phŏrŏn**, *for´-on*; of Lat. or.; a *forum* or market-place; only in comparison with *675*; a *station* on the Appian road:— forum.

5411. φόρος **phŏrŏs**, *for´-os*; from *5342*; a *load* (as *borne*), i.e. (fig.) a *tax* (prop. an indiv. *assessment* on persons or property; whereas *5056* is usually a gen. *toll* on goods or travel):— tribute.

5412. φορτίζω **phŏrtizō**, *for-tid´-zo*; from *5414*; to *load* up (prop. as a vessel or animal), i.e. (fig.) to *overburden* with cerem. (or spiritual anxiety):— lade, be heavy laden.

5413. φορτίον **phŏrtiŏn**, *for-tee´-on*; dimin. of *5414*; an *invoice* (as part of *freight*), i.e. (fig.) a *task* or *service*:— burden.

5414. φόρτος **phŏrtŏs**, *for´-tos*; from *5342*; something *carried*, i.e. the *cargo* of a ship:— lading.

5415. Φορτουνάτος **Phŏrtŏunatŏs**, *for-too-nat´-os*; of Lat. or.; "*fortunate*," *Fortunatus*, a Chr.:— Fortunatus.

5416. φραγέλλιον **phragĕlliŏn**, *frag-el´-le-on*; neut. of a der. from the base of *5417*; a *whip*, i.e. Rom. *lash* as a public punishment:— scourge.

5417. φραγελλόω **phragĕllŏō**, *frag-el-lŏ´-o*; from a presumed equiv. of the Lat. *flagellum*; to *whip*, i.e. *lash* as a public punishment:— scourge.

5418. φραγμός **phragmŏs**, *frag-mos´*; from *5420*; a *fence*, or inclosing *barrier* (lit. or fig.):— hedge (+ round about), partition.

5419. φράζω **phrazō**, *frad´-zo*; prob. akin to *5420* through the idea of *defining*; to *indicate* (by word or act), i.e. (spec.) to *expound*:— declare.

5420. φράσσω **phrassō**, *fras´-so*; appar. a streng. form of the base of *5424*; to *fence* or *inclose*, i.e. (spec.) to *block* up (fig. to *silence*):— stop.

5421. φρέαρ **phrĕar**, *freh´-ar*; of uncert. der.; a *hole* in the ground (dug for obtaining or holding water or other purposes), i.e. a *cistern* or *well*; fig. an *abyss* (as a *prison*):— well, pit.

5422. φρεναπατάω **phrĕnapataō**, *fren-ap-at-ah´-o*; from *5423*; to *be a mind-misleader*, i.e. *delude*:— deceive.

5423. φρεναπάτης **phrĕnapatēs**, *fren-*

ap-at´-ace; from *5424* and *539*; a *mind-misleader*, i.e. *seducer*:— deceiver.

5424. φρήν **phrēn**, *frane*; prob. from an obs. φράω **phraō** (to *rein* in or *curb*; comp. *5420*); the *midrif* (as a *partition* of the body), i.e. (fig. and by impl. of sympathy) the *feelings* (or sensitive nature; by extens. [also in the plur.] the *mind* or cognitive faculties):— understanding.

5425. φρίσσω **phrissō**, *fris´-so*; appar. a primary verb; to "*bristle*" or *chill*, i.e. *shudder* (*fear*):— tremble.

5426. φρονέω **phrŏnĕō**, *fron-eh´-o*; from *5424*; to *exercise* the *mind*, i.e. *entertain* or *have* a *sentiment* or *opinion*; by impl. to be (mentally) *disposed* (more or less earnestly in a certain direction); intens. to *interest oneself* in (with concern or obedience):— set the affection on, (be) care (-ful), (be like-, + be of one, + be of the same, + let this) mind (-ed), regard, savour, think.

5427. φρόνημα **phrŏnēma**, *fron´-ay-mah*; from *5426*; (mental) *inclination* or *purpose*: —(be, + be carnally, + be spiritually) mind (-ed).

5428. φρόνησις **phrŏnēsis**, *fron´-ay-sis*; from *5426*; mental *action* or *activity*, i.e. intellectual or mor. *insight*:— prudence, wisdom.

5429. φρόνιμος **phrŏnimŏs**, *fron´-ee-mos*; from *5424*; *thoughtful*, i.e. *sagacious* or *discreet* (implying a *cautious* character; while *4680* denotes *practical* skill or acumen; and *4908* indicates rather *intelligence* or mental acquirement); in a bad sense *conceited* (also in the comparative):— wise (-r).

5430. φρονίμως **phrŏnimōs**, *fron-im´-oce*; adv. from *5429*; *prudently*:— wisely.

5431. φροντίζω **phrŏntizō**, *fron-tid´-zo*; from a der. of *5424*; to *exercise* thought, i.e. *be anxious*:— be careful.

5432. φρουρέω **phrŏurĕō**, *froo-reh´-o*; from a compound of *4253* and *3708*; to *be a watcher* in advance, i.e. to *mount guard* as a sentinel (*post* spies at gates); fig. to *hem* in, *protect*:— keep (with a garrison). Comp. *5083*.

5433. φρυάσσω **phruassō**, *froo-as´-so*; akin to *1032, 1031*; to *snort* (as a spirited horse), i.e. (fig.) to *make* a *tumult*:— rage.

5434. φρύγανον **phruganŏn**, *froo´-gan-on*; neut. of a presumed der. of φρύγω **phrugō** (to *roast* or *parch*; akin to the base of *5395*); something *desiccated*, i.e. a dry *twig*:— stick.

5435. Φρυγία **Phrugia**, *froog-ee´-ah*; prob. of for. or.; *Phrygia*, a region of Asia Minor:— Phrygia.

5436. Φύγελλος **Phugĕllŏs**, *foog´-el-los*; prob. from *5343*; *fugitive*; *Phygellus*, an apostate Chr.:— Phygellus.

5437. φυγή **phugē**, *foog-ay´*; from *5343*; a *fleeing*, i.e. *escape*:— flight.

5438. φυλακή **phulakē**, *foo-lak-ay´*; from *5442*; a *guarding* or (concr. *guard*), the act, the person; fig. the place, the condition, or (spec.) the time (as a division of day or night), lit. or

fig.:— cage, hold, (im-) prison (-ment), ward, watch.

5439. φυλακίζω **phulakizō**, *foo-lak-id´-zo*; from *5441*; to *incarcerate*:— imprison.

5440. φυλακτήριον **phulaktēriŏn**, *foo-lak-tay´-ree-on*; neut. of a der. of *5442*; a *guard-case*, i.e. "*phylactery*" for wearing slips of Scripture texts:— phylactery.

5441. φύλαξ **phulax**, *foo´-lax*; from *5442*; a *watcher* or *sentry*:— keeper.

5442. φυλάσσω **phulassō**, *foo-las´-so*; prob. from *5443* through the idea of *isolation*; to *watch*, i.e. *be on guard* (lit. or fig.); by impl. to *preserve, obey, avoid*:— beware, keep (self), observe, save. Comp. *5083*.

5443. φυλή **phulē**, *foo-lay´*; from *5453* (comp. *5444*); an *offshoot*, i.e. *race* or *clan*:— kindred, tribe.

5444. φύλλον **phullŏn**, *fool´-lon*; from the same as *5443*; a *sprout*, i.e. *leaf*:— leaf.

5445. φύραμα **phurama**, *foo´-ram-ah*; from a prol. form of φύρω **phurō** (to *mix* a liquid with a solid; perh. akin to *5453* through the idea of *swelling* in bulk), mean to *knead*; a *mass* of dough:— lump.

5446. φυσικός **phusikŏs**, *foo-see-kos´*; from *5449*; "*physical*", i.e. (by impl.) *instinctive*:— natural. Comp. *5591*.

5447. φυσικῶς **phusikōs**, *foo-see-koce´*; adv. from *5446*; "*physically*", i.e. (by impl.) *instinctively*:— naturally.

5448. φυσιόω **phusiŏō**, *foo-see-ŏ´-o*; from *5449* in the primary sense of *blowing*; to *inflate*, i.e. (fig.) *make proud* (*haughty*):— puff up.

5449. φύσις **phusis**, *foo´-sis*; from *5453*; *growth* (by *germination* or *expansion*), i.e. (by impl.) natural *production* (lineal *descent*); by extens. a *genus* or *sort*; fig. native *disposition*, *constitution* or *usage*:— (Iman-]) kind, nature (I-all).

5450. φυσίωσις **phusiōsis**, *foo-see´-o-sis*; from *5448*; *inflation*, i.e. (fig.) *haughtiness*:— swelling.

5451. φυτεία **phutĕia**, *foo-ti´-ah*; from *5452*; *trans-planting*, i.e. (concr.) a *shrub* or *vegetable*:— plant.

5452. φυτεύω **phutĕuō**, *foot-yoo´-o*; from a der. of *5453*; to *set out* in the earth, i.e. *implant*; fig. to *instil* doctrine:— plant.

5453. φύω **phuō**, *foo´-o*; a primary verb; prob. orig. to "*puff*" or *blow*, i.e. to *swell* up; but only used in the impl. sense, to *germinate* or *grow* (*sprout, produce*), lit. or fig.:— spring (up).

5454. φωλεός **phōlĕŏs**, *fo-leh-os´*; of uncert. der.; a *burrow* or *lurking-place*:— hole.

5455. φωνέω **phōnĕō**, *fo-neh´-o*; from *5456*; to emit a *sound* (animal, human or instrumental); by impl. to *address* in words or by name, also in imitation:— call (for), crow, cry.

5456. φωνή **phōnē**, *fo-nay´*; prob. akin to *5316* through the idea of *disclosure*; a *tone* (articulate, bestial or artif.); by impl. an *address* (for any purpose), *saying* or *language*:— noise, sound, voice.

5457. φῶς **phōs**, *foce;* from an obs. φάω **phaō** (to *shine*, or make *manifest*, espec. by *rays;* comp. 5316, 5346); *luminousness* (in the widest application, nat. or artif., abstr. or concr., lit. or fig.):— fire, light.

5458. φωστήρ **phōstēr**, *foce-tare´;* from 5457; an *illuminator*, i.e. (concr.) a *luminary*, or (abstr.) *brilliancy:*— light.

5459. φωσφόρος **phōsphŏrŏs**, *foce-for´-os;* from 5457 and 5342; *light-bearing* ("phosphorus"), i.e. (spec.) the *morning-star* (fig.):— day star.

5460. φωτεινός **phōtĕinŏs**, *fo-ti-nos´;* from 5457; *lustrous*, i.e. *transparent* or *well-illuminated* (fig.):— bright, full of light.

5461. φωτίζω **phōtizō**, *fo-tid´-zo;* from 5457; to *shed rays*, i.e. to *shine* or (tran.) to *brighten* up (lit. or fig.):— enlighten, illuminate, (bring to, give) light, make to see.

5462. φωτισμός **phōtismŏs**, *fo-tis-mos´;* from 5461; *illumination* (fig.):— light.

X

5463. χαίρω **chairō**, *khah´-ee-ro;* a primary verb; to be *"cheer"ful*, i.e. calmly *happy* or well-off; impers. espec. as salutation (on meeting or parting), *be well:*— farewell, be glad, God speed, greeting, hall, joy (- fully), rejoice.

5464. χάλαζα **chalaza**, *khal´-ad-zah;* prob. from 5465; *hail:*— hail.

5465. χαλάω **chalaō**, *khal-ah´-o;* from the base of 5490; to *lower* (as into a *void*):— let down, strike.

5466. Χαλδαῖος **Chaldaiŏs**, *khal-dah´-yos;* prob. of Heb. or [3778]; a *Chaldæan* (i.e. *Kasdi*), or native or the region of the lower Euphrates:— Chaldæan.

5467. χαλεπός **chalepŏs**, *khal-ep-os´;* perh. from 5465 through the idea of *reducing* the strength; *difficult*, i.e. *dangerous*, or (by impl.) *furious:*— fierce, perilous.

5468. χαλιναγωγέω **chalinagōgeō**, *khal-in-ag-ogue-eh´-o;* from a compound of 5469 and the redupl. form of 71; to *be a bit-leader*, i.e. to *curb* (fig.):— bridle.

5469. χαλινός **chalinŏs**, *khal-ee-nos´;* from 5465; a *curb* or *head-stall* (as *curbing* the spirit):— bit, bridle.

5470. χάλκεος **chalkĕŏs**, *khal´-keh-os;* from 5475; *coppery:*— brass.

5471. χαλκεύς **chalkĕus**, *khalk-yooce´;* from 5475; a *copper-worker* or *brazier:*— coppersmith.

5472. χαλκηδών **chalkēdōn**, *khal-kay-dōhn´;* from 5475 and perh. 1491; *copper-like*, i.e. *"chalcedony":*— chalcedony.

5473. χαλκίον **chalkiŏn**, *khal-kee´-on;* dimin. from 5475; a *copper dish:*— brazen vessel.

5474. χαλκολίβανον **chalkŏlibanŏn**, *khal-kol-ib´-an-on;* neut. of a compound of 5475 and 3030 (in the impl. mean of *whiteness* or *brilliancy*); *burnished copper*, an alloy of copper (or

gold) and silver having a brilliant lustre:— fine brass.

5475. χαλκός **chalkŏs**, *khal-kos´;* perh. from 5465 through the idea of *hollowing* out as a vessel (this metal being chiefly used for that purpose); *copper* (the substance, or some implement or coin made of it):— brass, money.

5476. χαμαί **chamai**, *kham-ah´-ee;* adv. perh. from the base of 5490 through the idea of a *fissure* in the soil; *earthward*, i.e. *prostrate:*— on (to) the ground.

5477. Χαναάν **Chanaan**, *khan-ah´-an;* of Heb. or. [3667]; *Chanaan* (i.e. *Kenaan*), the early name of Pal.:— Chanaan.

5478. Χαναναῖος **Chanaanaiŏs**, *khan-ah-an-ah´-yos;* from 5477; a *Chanaanæan* (i.e. *Kenaanite*), or native of Gentile Pal.:— of Canaan.

5479. χαρά **chara**, *khar-ah´;* from 5463; *cheerfulness*, i.e. calm *delight:*— gladness, × greatly, (× be exceeding) joy (-ful, -fully,fulness, -ous).

5480. χάραγμα **charagma**, *khar´-ag-mah;* from the same as 5482; a *scratch* or *etching*, i.e. *stamp* (as a *badge* of servitude), or *sculptured* figure (*statue*):— graven, mark.

5481. χαρακτήρ **charaktēr**, *khar-ak-tare´;* from the same as 5482; a *graver* (the tool or the person), i.e. (by impl.) *engraving* (["character"]), the *figure* stamped, i.e. an exact *copy* or [fig.] *representation*):— express image.

5482. χάραξ **charax**, *khar´-ax;* from χαράσσω **charassō** (to *sharpen*, to a point; akin to 1125 through the idea of *scratching*); a *stake*, i.e. (by impl.) a *palisade* or *rampart* (military *mound* for circumvallation in a siege):— trench.

5483. χαρίζομαι **charizŏmai**, *khar-id´-zom-ahee;* mid. voice from 5485; to grant as a *favor*, i.e. gratuitously, in kindness, pardon or rescue:— deliver, (frankly) forgive, (freely) give, grant.

5484. χάριν **charin**, *khar´-in;* acc. of 5485 as prep.; through *favor* of, i.e. on *account* of:— be- (for) cause of, for sake of, + ... fore, × reproachfully.

5485. χάρις **charis**, *khar´-ece;* from 5463; *graciousness* (as *gratifying*), of manner or act (abstr. or concr.; lit., fig., or spiritual; espec. the divine influence upon the heart, and its reflection in the life; incl. *gratitude*):— acceptable, benefit, favour, gift, grace (-ious), joy, liberality, pleasure, thank (-s, worthy).

5486. χάρισμα **charisma**, *khar´-is-mah;* from 5483; a (divine) *gratuity*, i.e. *deliverance* (from danger or passion); (spec.) a (spiritual) *endowment*, i.e. (subj.) relig. *qualification*, or (obj.) miraculous *faculty:*— (free) gift.

5487. χαριτόω **charitŏō**, *khar-ee-tŏ´-o;* from 5485; to *grace*, i.e. indue with special *honor:*— make accepted, be highly favoured.

5488. Χαρράν **Charrhan**, *khar-hran´;* of Heb. or. [2771]; *Charrhan* (i.e. *Charan*), a place in Mesopotamia:— Charran.

5489. χάρτης **chartēs**, *khar´-tace;* from the same as 5482; a *sheet* ("chart") of

writing-material (as to be *scribbled* over):— paper.

5490. χάσμα **chasma**, *khas´-mah;* from a form of an obs. primary χάω **chaō**, (to *"gape"* or *"yawn"*); a *"chasm"* or *vacancy* (impassable *interval*):— gulf.

5491. χεῖλος **chĕilŏs**, *khi´-los;* from a form of the same as 5490; a *lip* (as a *pouring* place); fig. a *margin* (of water):— lip, shore.

5492. χειμάζω **chĕimazō**, *khi-mad´-zo;* from the same as 5494; to *storm*, i.e. (pass.) to *labor under a gale:*— be tossed with tempest.

5493. χείμαρρος **chĕimarrhŏs**, *khi´-mar-hros;* from the base of 5494 and 4482; a *storm-runlet*, i.e. *winter-torrent:*— brook.

5494. χειμών **chĕimōn**, *khi-mone´;* from a der. of χέω **chĕō**, (to *pour;* akin to the base of 5490 through the idea of a *channel*), mean. a *storm* (as *pouring* rain); by impl. the *rainy* season, i.e. *winter:*— tempest, foul weather, winter.

5495. χείρ **chĕir**, *khire;* perh. from the base of 5494 in the sense of its congener the base of 5490 (through the idea of *hollowness* for grasping); the *hand* (lit. or fig. [power]; espec. [by Heb.] a *means* or *instrument*):— hand.

5496. χειραγωγέω **chĕiragōgeō**, *khi-rag-ogue-eh´-o;* from 5497; to be a *hand-leader*, i.e. to *guide* (a blind person):— lead by the hand.

5497. χειραγωγός **chĕiragōgŏs**, *khi-rag-o-gos´;* from 5495 and a redupl. form of 71; a *hand-leader*, i.e. personal *conductor* (of a blind person):— some to lead by the hand.

5498. χειρόγραφον **chĕirŏgraphŏn**, *khi-rog´-raf-on;* neut. of a compound of 5495 and 1125; something *hand-written* ("chirograph"), i.e. a *manuscript* (spec. a legal *document* or *bond* [fig.]):— handwriting.

5499. χειροποίητος **chĕirŏpŏiētŏs**, *khi-rop-oy´-ay-tos;* from 5495 and a der. of 4160; *manufactured*, i.e. of *human* construction:— made by (make with) hands.

5500. χειροτονέω **chĕirŏtŏneō**, *khi-rot-on-eh´-o;* from a comp. of 5495 and τείνω **tĕinō** (to *stretch*); to be a *hand-reacher*, or *voter* (by raising the hand), i.e. (gen.) to *select* or *appoint:*— choose, ordain.

5501. χείρων **chĕirōn**, *khi´-rone;* irreg. comp. of 2556; from an obs. equiv. χέρης **chĕrēs** (of uncert. der.); *more evil* or *aggravated* (phys., ment. or mor.):— sorer, worse.

5502. χερουβίμ **chĕrŏubim**, *kher-oo-beem´;* plur. of Heb. or. [3742]; *"cherubim"* (i.e. *cherubs* or *kerubim*):— cherubims.

5503. χήρα **chēra**, *khay´-rah;* fem. of a presumed der. appar. from the base of 5490 through the idea of *deficiency;* a *widow* (as *lacking* a husband), lit. or fig.:— widow.

5504. χθές **chthĕs**, *khthes;* of uncert. der.; *"yesterday"*; by extens. *in time past* or *hitherto:*— yesterday.

5505. χιλιάς **chilias**, *khil-ee-as´;* from 5507; one *thousand* (*"chiliad"*):— thousand.

5506. χιλίαρχος **chiliarchŏs**, *khil-ee´-ar-khos;* from 5507 and 757; the *commander of a thousand* soldiers (*"chiliarch"*), i.e. *colonel:*— (chief, high) captain.

5507. χίλιοι **chiliŏi**, *khil´-ee-oy;* plur. of uncert. aff.; a *thousand:*— thousand.

5508. Χίος **Chiŏs**, *khee´-os;* of uncert. der.; *Chios*, an island in the Mediterranean:— Chios.

5509. χιτών **chiton**, *khee-tone´;* of for. or. [3801]; a *tunic* or *shirt:*— clothes, coat, garment.

5510. χιών **chiŏn**, *khee-one´;* perh. akin to the base of 5490 (5465) or 5494 (as *descending* or *empty*); *snow:*— snow.

5511. χλαμύς **chlamus**, *khlam-ooce´;* of uncert. der.; a military *cloak:*— robe.

5512. χλευάζω **chlĕuazō**, *khlyoo-ad´-zo;* from a der. prob. of 5491; to *throw out the lip*, i.e. *jeer* at:— mock.

5513. χλιαρός **chliarŏs**, *khlee-ar-os´;* from χλίω **chliō**, (to *warm*); *tepid:*— lukewarm.

5514. Χλόη **Chlŏē**, *khlŏ´-ay;* fem. of appar. a primary word; *"green";* *Chlŏĕ*, a Chr. female:— Chloe.

5515. χλωρός **chlōrŏs**, *khlo-ros´;* from the same as 5514; *greenish*, i.e. *verdant, dun-colored:*— green, pale.

5516. χξς **chi xi stigma**, *khee xee stig´-ma;* the 22nd, 14th and an obs. letter (4742 as a *cross*) of the Greek alphabet (intermediate between the 5th and 6th), used as numbers; denoting respectively 600, 60 and 6; 666 as a numeral:— six hundred threescore and six.

5517. χοϊκός **chŏïkŏs**, *khŏ-ik-os´;* from 5522; *dusty* or *dirty* (*soil*-like), i.e. (by impl.) *terrene:*— earthy.

5518. χοῖνιξ **chŏinix**, *khoy´-nix;* of uncertain der.; a *chœnix* or certain dry measure:— measure.

5519. χοῖρος **chŏirŏs**, *khoy´-ros;* of uncert. der.; a *hog:*— swine.

5520. χολάω **chŏlaō**, *khol-ah´-o;* from 5521; to *be bilious*, i.e. (by impl.) *irritable* (*enraged*, *"choleric"*):— be angry.

5521. χολή **chŏlē**, *khol-ay´;* fem. of an equiv. perh. akin to the same as 5514 (from the *greenish* hue); *"gall"* or *bile*, i.e. (by anal.) *poison* or an *anodyne* (wormwood, poppy, etc.):— gall.

5522. χόος **chŏŏs**, *khŏ´-os;* from the base of 5494; a *heap* (as *poured* out), i.e. *rubbish;* loose *dirt:*— dust.

5523. Χοραζίν **Chŏrazin**, *khor-ad-zin´;* of uncert. der.; *Chorazin*, a place in Pal.:— Chorazin.

5524. χορηγέω **chŏrēgĕō**, *khor-ayg-eh´-o;* from a compound of 5525 and 71; to be a *dance-leader*, i.e. (gen.) to *furnish:*— give, minister.

5525. χορός **chŏrŏs**, *khor-os´;* of uncert. der.; a *ring*, i.e. round *dance* (*"choir"*):— dancing.

5526. χορτάζω **chŏrtazō**, *khor-tad´-zo;* from 5528; to *fodder*, i.e. (gen.) to *gorge* (*supply food* in abundance):— feed, fill, satisfy.

5527. χόρτασμα **chŏrtasma**, *khor´-tas-mah;* from 5526; *forage*, i.e. *food:*— sustenance.

5528. χόρτος **chŏrtŏs**, *khor´-tos;* appar. a primary word; a *"court"* or *"garden"*, i.e. (by impl. of *pasture*) *herbage* or *vegetation:*— blade, grass, hay.

5529. Χουζᾶς **Chŏuzas**, *khood-zas´;* of uncert. or.: *Chuzas*, an officer of Herod:— Chuza.

5530. χράομαι **chraŏmai**, *khrah´-om-ahee;* mid. voice of a primary verb (perh. rather from 5495, to *handle*); to *furnish* what is needed; (give an *oracle*, *"graze"* [touch slightly], *light* upon, etc.), i.e. (by impl.) to *employ* or (by extens.) to *act toward* one in a given manner:— entreat, use. Comp. 5531; 5534.

5531. χράω **chraō**, *khrah´-o;* prob. the same as the base of 5530; to *loan:*— lend.

5532. χρεία **chrĕia**, *khri´-ah;* from the base of 5530 or 5534; *employment*, i.e. an *affair;* also (by impl.) *occasion, demand, requirement* or *destitution:*— business, lack, necessary (-ity), need (-ful), use, want.

5533. χρεωφειλέτης **chrĕōphĕilĕtēs**, *khreh-o-fi-let´-ace;* from a der. of 5531 and 3781; a *loan-ower*, i.e. *indebted* person:— debtor.

5534. χρή **chrē**, *khray;* third pers. sing. of the same as 5530 or 5531 used impers.; it *needs* (*must* or *should*) be:— ought.

5535. χρῄζω **chrēizō**, *khrade´-zo;* from 5532; to *make* (i.e. *have*) *necessity*, i.e. *be in want* of:— (have) need.

5536. χρῆμα **chrēma**, *khray´-mah;* something *useful* or *needed*, i.e. *wealth, price:*— money, riches.

5537. χρηματίζω **chrēmatizō**, *khray-mat-id´-zo;* from 5536; to *utter an oracle* (comp. the orig. sense of 5530), i.e. *divinely intimate;* by impl. (comp. the secular sense of 5532) to constitute a *firm* for business, i.e. (gen.) *bear* as a *title:*— be called, be admonished (warned) of God, reveal, speak.

5538. χρηματισμός **chrēmatismŏs**, *khray-mat-is-mos´;* from 5537; a *divine response* or *revelation:*— answer of God.

5539. χρήσιμος **chrēsimŏs**, *khray´-see-mos;* from 5540; *serviceable:*— profit.

5540. χρῆσις **chrēsis**, *khray´-sis;* from 5530; *employment*, i.e. (spec.) sexual *intercourse* (as an *occupation* of the body):— use.

5541. χρηστεύομαι **chrēstĕuŏmai**, *khraste-yoo´-om-ahee;* mid. voice from 5543; to *show oneself useful*, i.e. *act benevolently:*— be kind.

5542. χρηστολογία **chrēstŏlŏgia**, *khrase-tol-og-ee´-ah;* from a compound of 5543 and 3004; *fair speech*, i.e. *plausibility:*— good words.

5543. χρηστός **chrēstŏs**, *khrase-tos´;* from 5530; *employed*, i.e. (by impl.) *use-*
ful (in manner or morals):— better, easy, good (-ness), gracious, kind.

5544. χρηστότης **chrēstŏtēs**, *khray-stot´-ace;* from 5543; *usefulness*, i.e. mor. *excellence* (in character or demeanor):— gentleness, good (-ness), kindness.

5545. χρῖσμα **chrisma**, *khris´-mah;* from 5548; an *unguent* or *smearing*, i.e. (fig.) the spec. *endowment* (*"chrism"*) of the Holy Spirit:— anointing, unction.

5546. Χριστιανός **Christianŏs**, *khris-tee-an-os´;* from 5547; a *Christian*, i.e. follower of Christ:— Christian.

5547. Χριστός **Christŏs**, *khris-tos´;* from 5548; *anointed*, i.e. the *Messiah*, an epithet of Jesus:— Christ.

5548. χρίω **chriō**, *khree´-o;* prob. akin to 5530 through the idea of *contact;* to *smear* or *rub* with oil, i.e. (by impl.) to *consecrate* to an office or relig. service:— anoint.

5549. χρονίζω **chrŏnizō**, *khron-id´-zo;* from 5550; to *take time*, i.e. *linger:*— delay, tarry.

5550. χρόνος **chrŏnŏs**, *khron´-os;* of uncert. der.; a space of *time* (in gen., and thus prop. distinguished from 2540, which designates a *fixed* or special occasion; and from 165, which denotes a particular *period*) or *interval;* by extens. an indiv. *opportunity;* by impl. *delay:*— + years old, season, space, (× often-) time (-s), (a) while.

5551. χρονοτριβέω **chrŏnŏtribĕō**, *khron-ot-rib-eh´-o;* from a presumed compound of 5550 and the base of 5147; to be a *time-wearer*, i.e. to *procrastinate* (*linger*):— spend time.

5552. χρύσεος **chrusĕŏs**, *khroo´-seh-os;* from 5557; made of *gold:*— of gold, golden.

5553. χρυσίον **chrusiŏn**, *khroo-see´-on;* dimin. of 5557; a *golden* article, i.e. gold plating, ornament, or coin:— gold.

5554. χρυσοδακτύλιος **chrusŏdaktuliŏs**, *khroo-sod-ak-too´-lee-os;* from 5557 and 1146; *gold-ringed*, i.e. *wearing* a golden finger-ring or similar *jewelry:*— with a gold ring.

5555. χρυσόλιθος **chrusŏlithŏs**, *khroo-sol´-ee-thos;* from 5557 and 3037; *gold-stone*, i.e. a *yellow gem* (*"chrysolite"*):— chrysolite.

5556. χρυσόπρασος **chrusŏprasŏs**, *khroo-sop´-ras-os;* from 5557 and πράσον **prasŏn** (a *leek*); a *greenish-yellow* gem (*"chrysoprase"*):— chrysoprase.

5557. χρυσός **chrusŏs**, *khroo-sos´;* perh. from the base of 5530 (through the idea of the *utility* of the metal); *gold;* by extens. a *golden* article, as an ornament or coin:— gold.

5558. χρυσόω **chrusŏō**, *khroo-sŏ´-o;* from 5557; to *gild*, i.e. *bespangle* with golden ornaments:— deck.

5559. χρώς **chrōs**, *khroce;* prob. akin to the base of 5530 through the idea of *handling;* the *body* (prop. its *surface* or *skin*):— body.

5560. χωλός **chōlŏs**, *kho-los´;* appar. a

primary word; "*halt,*" i.e. *limping:*— cripple, halt, lame.

5561. χώρα **chōra**, *kho´-rah;* fem. of a der. of the base of *5490* through the idea of *empty* expanse; *room,* i.e. a space of *territory* (more or less extens.; often incl. its inhab.):— coast, county, fields, ground, land, region. Comp. *5117.*

5562. χωρέω **chōrĕō**, *kho-reh´-o;* from *5561;* to *be* in (*give*) *space,* i.e. (intr.) to *pass, enter,* or (tran.) to *hold, admit* (lit. or fig.):— come, contain, go, have place, (can, be room to) receive.

5563. χωρίζω **chōrizō**, *kho-rid´-zo;* from *5561;* to *place room* between, i.e. *part;* refl. to *go away:*— depart, put asunder, separate.

5564. χωρίον **chōriŏn**, *kho-ree´-on;* dimin. of *5561;* a *spot* or *plot* of ground:— field, land, parcel of ground, place, possession.

5565. χωρίς **chōris**, *kho-rece´;* adv. from *5561;* at a *space,* i.e. *separately* or *apart* from (often as prep.):— beside, by itself, without.

5566. χῶρος **chōrŏs**, *kho´-ros;* of Lat. or.; the *north-west* wind:— north west.

Ψ

5567. ψάλλω **psallō**, *psal´-lo;* probably strengthened from ψάω **psaō**, (to *rub* or *touch* the surface; comp. *5597*); to *twitch* or *twang,* i.e. to *play* on a stringed instrument (*celebrate* the divine worship *with music* and accompanying odes):— make melody, sing (psalms).

5568. ψαλμός **psalmŏs**, *psal-mos´;* from *5567;* a set piece of *music,* i.e. a sacred *ode* (accompanied with the voice, harp or other instrument; a "*psalm*"); collect. the book of the *Psalms:*— psalm. Comp. *5603.*

5569. ψευδάδελφος **psĕudadĕlphŏs**, *psyoo-dad´-el-fos;* from *5571* and *80;* a *spurious brother,* i.e. *pretended associate:*— false brethren.

5570. ψευδαπόστολος **psĕudapŏstŏlŏs**, *psyoo-dap-os´-tol-os;* from *5571* and *652;* a *spurious apostle,* i.e. *pretended preacher:*— false teacher.

5571. ψευδής **psĕudēs**, *psyoo-dace´;* from *5574; untrue,* i.e. *erroneous, deceitful, wicked:*— false, liar.

5572. ψευδοδιδάσκαλος **psĕudŏdidaskalŏs**, *psyoo-dod-id-as´-kal-os;* from *5571* and *1320;* a *spurious teacher,* i.e. *propagator of erroneous* Chr. *doctrine:*— false teacher.

5573. ψευδολόγος **psĕudŏlŏgŏs**, *psyoo-dol-og´-os;* from *5571* and *3004; mendacious,* i.e. *promulgating erroneous* Chr. *doctrine:*— speaking lies.

5574. ψεύδομαι **psĕudŏmai**, *psyoo´-dom-ahee;* mid. voice of an appar. primary verb; to *utter an untruth* or attempt to *deceive* by falsehood:— falsely, lie.

5575. ψευδομάρτυρ **psĕudŏmartur**, *psyoo-dom-ar´-toor;* from *5571* and a kindred form of *3144;* a *spurious witness,* i.e. *bearer of untrue testimony:*— false witness.

5576. ψευδομαρτυρέω **psĕudŏmarturĕō**, *psyoo-dom-ar-too-reh´-o;* from *5575;* to *be an untrue testifier,* i.e. *offer falsehood in evidence:*— be a false witness.

5577. ψευδομαρτυρία **psĕudŏmarturia**, *psyoo-dom-ar-too-ree´-ah;* from *5575; untrue testimony:*— false witness.

5578. ψευδοπροφήτης **psĕudŏprŏphētēs**, *psyoo-dop-rof-ay´-tace;* from *5571* and *4396;* a *spurious prophet,* i.e. *pretended foreteller* or relig. *impostor:*— false prophet.

5579. ψεῦδος **psĕudŏs**, *psyoo´-dos;* from *5574;* a *falsehood:*— lie, lying.

5580. ψευδόχριστος **psĕudŏchristŏs**, *psyoo-dokh´-ris-tos;* from *5571* and *5547;* a *spurious Messiah:*— false Christ.

5581. ψευδώνυμος **psĕudōnumŏs**, *psyoo-do´-noo-mos;* from *5571* and *3686; untruly named:*— falsely so called.

5582. ψεῦσμα **psĕusma**, *psyoos´-mah;* from *5574;* a *fabrication,* i.e. *falsehood:*— lie.

5583. ψεύστης **psĕustēs**, *psyoos-tace´;* from *5574;* a *falsifier:*— liar.

5584. ψηλαφάω **psēlaphaō**, *psay-laf-ah´-o;* from the base of *5567* (comp. *5586*); to *manipulate,* i.e. *verify* by contact; fig. to *search* for:— feel after, handle, touch.

5585. ψηφίζω **psēphizō**, *psay-fid´-zo;* from *5586;* to *use pebbles* in enumeration, i.e. (gen.) to *compute:*— count.

5586. ψῆφος **psēphŏs**, *psay´-fos;* from the same as *5584;* a *pebble* (as worn smooth by *handling*), i.e. (by impl. of use as a *counter* or *ballot*) a *verdict* (of acquittal) or *ticket* (of admission); a *vote:*— stone, voice.

5587. ψιθυρισμός **psithurismŏs**, *psith-oo-ris-mos´;* from a der. of ψίθος **psithŏs** (a *whisper;* by impl. a *slander;* prob. akin to 5574); *whispering,* i.e. secret *detraction:*— whispering.

5588. ψιθυριστής **psithuristēs**, *psith-oo-ris-tace´;* from the same as *5587;* a secret *calumniator:*— whisperer.

5589. ψιχίον **psichiŏn**, *psikh-ee´-on;* dimin. from a der. of the base of *5567* (mean. a *crumb*); a *little bit* or *morsel:*— crumb.

5590. ψυχή **psuchē**, *psoo-khay´;* from *5594; breath,* i.e. (by impl.) *spirit,* abstr. or concr. (the *animal* sentient principle only; thus distinguished on the one hand from *4151,* which is the rational and immortal *soul;* and on the other from *2222,* which is mere *vitality,* even of plants: these terms thus exactly correspond respectively to the Heb. 5315, 7307 and 2416):— heart (+ -ily), life, mind, soul, + us, + you.

5591. ψυχικός **psuchikŏs**, *psoo-khee-kos´;* from *5590; sensitive,* i.e. *animate* (in distinction on the one hand from *4152,* which is the higher or *renovated* nature; and on the other from *5446,* which is the lower or *bestial* nature):— natural, sensual.

5592. ψῦχος **psuchŏs**, *psoo´-khos;* from *5594; coolness:*— cold.

5593. ψυχρός **psuchrŏs**, *psoo-chros´;* from *5592; chilly* (lit. or fig.):— cold.

5594. ψύχω **psuchō**, *psoo´-kho;* a primary verb; to *breathe* (*voluntarily* but *gently,* thus differing on the one hand from *4154,* which denotes prop. a *forcible* respiration; and on the other from the base of *109,* which refers prop. to an inanimate *breeze*), i.e. (by impl. of reduction of temperature by evaporation) to *chill* (fig.):— wax cold.

5595. ψωμίζω **psōmizō**, *pso-mid´-zo;* from the base of *5596;* to *supply* with *bits,* i.e. (gen.) to *nourish:*— (bestow to) feed.

5596. ψωμίον **psōmiŏn**, *pso-mee´-on;* dimin. from a der. of the base of *5597;* a *crumb* or *morsel* (as if *rubbed* off), i.e. a *mouthful:*— sop.

5597. ψώχω **psōchō**, *pso´-kho;* prol. from the same base as *5567;* to *triturate,* i.e. (by anal.) to *rub* out (kernels from husks with the fingers or hand):— rub.

Ω

5598. Ω **Ō**, i.e. ὠμεγα **ōmĕga**, *o´-meg-ah;* the last letter of the Greek alphabet, i.e. (fig.) the *finality:*— Omega.

5599. ὦ **ō**, *o;* a primary interj.; as a sign of the voc. *O;* as a note of exclamation, *oh:*— O.

5600. ὦ **ō**, *o;* incl. the oblique forms, as well as ἦς **ēs**, *ace;* ἦ **ē**, *ay;* etc.; the subjunctive of *1510;* (*may, might, can, could, would, should, must,* etc.; also with *1487* and its comp., as well as with other particles) *be:*— + appear, are, (may, might, should) be, × have, is, + pass the flower of her age, should stand, were.

5601. Ὠβήδ **Ōbēd**, *o-bade´* or Ἰωβήδ **Iōbēd**, *yo-bade´;* of Heb. or. [5744]; *Obed,* an Isr.:— Obed.

5602. ὧδε **hōdĕ**, *ho´-deh;* from an adv. form of *3592; in this* same spot, i.e. *here* or *hither:*— here, hither, (in) this place, there.

5603. ᾠδή **ōidē**, *o-day´;* from *103;* a *chant* or "*ode*" (the gen. term for any words sung; while *5215* denotes espec. a *relig.* metrical composition, and *5568* still more spec. a *Heb.* cantillation):— song.

5604. ὠδίν **ōdin**, *o-deen´;* akin to *3601;* a *pang* or *throe,* espec. of childbirth:— pain, sorrow, travail.

5605. ὠδίνω **ōdinō**, *o-dee´-no;* from *5604;* to *experience* the *pains* of parturition (lit. or fig.):— travail in (birth).

5606. ὦμος **ōmŏs**, *o´-mos;* perh. from the alt. of *5342;* the *shoulder* (as that on which burdens are *borne*):— shoulder.

5607. ὤν **ōn**, *oan;* incl. the fem.

οὖσα **ŏusa**, *oo´-sah;* and the neut.

ὄν **ŏn**, *on;* pres. part. of *1510; being:*— be, come, have.

5608. ὠνέομαι **ōnĕŏmai**, *o-neh´-om-ahee;* mid. voice from an appar. primary ὦνος **ōnŏs** (a *sum* or *price*); to *purchase,* (synonymous with the earlier *4092*):— buy.

ᾠόν ōŏn, *o-on´;* appar. a primary word; an *"egg":*— egg.

5610. ὥρα hōra, *ho´-rah;* appar. a primary word; an *"hour"* (lit. or fig.):— day, hour, instant, season, × short, [even-] tide, (high) time.

5611. ὡραῖος hōraiŏs, *ho-rah´-yos;* from 5610; belonging to the right hour or season *(timely),* i.e. (by impl.) *flourishing (beauteous* [fig.]):— beautiful.

5612. ὠρύομαι ōruŏmai, *o-roo´-om-ahee;* mid. voice of an appar. primary verb; to *"roar":*— roar.

5613. ὡς hōs, *hoce;* prob. adv. of comparison from 3739; *which how,* i.e. *in that manner* (very variously used, as follows):— about, after (that), (according) as (it had been, it were), as soon (as), even as (like), for, how (greatly), like (as, unto), since, so (that), that, to wit, unto, when ([-soever]), while, × with all speed.

5614. ὡσαννά hōsanna, *ho-san-nah´;* of Heb. or. [3467 and 4994]; *oh save!; hosanna* (i.e. *hoshia-na),* an exclamation of adoration:— hosanna.

5615. ὡσαύτως hōsautōs, *ho-sŏw´-toce;* from 5613 and an adv. from 846; as *thus,* i.e. *in the same way:*— even so, likewise, after the same (in like) manner.

5616. ὡσεί hōsĕi, *ho-si´;* from 5613 and 1487; *as if:*— about, as (it had been, it were), like (as).

5617. Ὡσηέ Hōsĕē, *ho-say-eh´;* of Heb. or. [1954]; *Hoseë* (i.e. *Hosheä),* an Isr.:— Osee.

5618. ὥσπερ hōspĕr, *hoce´-per;* from 5613 and 4007; *just as,* i.e. *exactly like:*— (even, like) as.

5619. ὡσπερεί hōspĕrĕi, *hoce-per-i´;* from 5618 and 1487; *just as if,* i.e. *as it were:*— as.

5620. ὥστε hōstĕ, *hoce´-teh;* from 5613 and 5037; *so too,* i.e. *thus therefore* (in various relations of *consecution,* as follow):— (insomuch) as, so that (then), (insomuch) that, therefore, to, wherefore.

5621. ὠτίον ōtiŏn, *o-tee´-on;* dimin. of 3775; an *earlet,* i.e. *one* of the ears, or perh. the *lobe* of the ear:— ear.

5622. ὠφέλεια ōphĕlĕia, *o-fel´-i-ah;* from a der. of the base of 5624; *usefulness,* i.e. *benefit:*— advantage, profit.

5623. ὠφελέω ōphĕlĕō, *o-fel-eh´-o;* from the same as 5622; to *be useful,* i.e. to *benefit:*— advantage, better, prevail, profit.

5624. ὠφέλιμος ōphĕlimŏs, *o-fel´-ee-mos;* from a form of 3786; *helpful* or *serviceable,* i.e. *advantageous:*— profit (-able).